sky SPORTS

FOOTBALL
YEARBOOK
2016-2017

Compiled by
John Anderson

headline

First published in 2016
by HEADLINE PUBLISHING GROUP

1

Front cover photographs:
(left) Dele Alli (Tottenham Hotspur) – *Action Images via Reuters/Paul Childs*;
(centre and background) Jamie Vardy (Leicester City) – *Action Images via Reuters/
Andrew Yates*;
(right) Dimitri Payet (West Ham United) – *Steve Paston/PA Archive/
Press Association Images*

Spine photograph:
Leicester City manager Claudio Ranieri with the Premier League trophy, May 2016 –
Nigel French/EMPICS Sport/Press Association Images

Back cover photographs:
(above) Gareth Bale (Wales) and Craig Cathcart (Northern Ireland),
UEFA European Championships 2016 Group B match – *David Klein/Sportimage/
Press Association Images*; (below) Adam Rooney (Aberdeen) and Nir Bitton (Celtic) –
Action Images via Reuters/Graham Stuart Livepic

Cataloguing in Publication Data is available from the British Library

ISBN 978 1 4722 3394 3 (Hardback)
ISBN 978 1 4722 3395 0 (Trade paperback)

Typeset by Wearset Ltd, Boldon, Tyne and Wear

Printed and bound in the UK by CPI Mackays, Chatham ME5 8TD

MIX
Paper from
responsible sources
FSC
www.fsc.org   FSC® C104740

Headline's policy is to use papers that are natural, renewable and recyclable
products and made from wood grown in sustainable forests.

HEADLINE PUBLISHING GROUP
An Hachette UK Company
Carmelite House
50 Victoria Embankment
London EC4Y 0DZ

www.headline.co.uk
www.hachette.co.uk

CONTENTS

WELCOME

Welcome to the 2016–17 edition of the *Sky Sports Football Yearbook*.

Last season was a vintage year for football – it stunned everyone. Leicester City, tipped by many for relegation, led a sensational charge to the title. Spurs showed signs of a very promising future, while Arsenal fell just short again. Chelsea and Manchester United endured frustrating seasons, and we also saw some big clubs drop out of the league in Aston Villa and Newcastle United. After a season of shocks and surprises, there are many questions to be answered during the coming season: how will Leicester fare as they defend their title? How will Pep Guardiola and Antonio Conte adapt to life in the Premier League? And will Jose Mourinho achieve success again as he moves to Old Trafford?

With unpredictability on the pitch, one of the consistencies off it is that Sky Sports remains the home of football. As we enter our 25th season covering the Premier League, we take great pride in continuing to push the boundaries of football coverage to offer only the best.

This season, we'll have even more of English football's top level – 126 live games from the Premier League, including, for the very first time, regular live football on Friday nights. Our award-winning team of experts continue to raise the bar, offering the best analysis of football to be found anywhere. Nowhere was this emphasised more clearly than when Monday Night Football secured the Royal Television Society's Best Sports Programme Award earlier this year.

The Sky Bet EFL also forms a big part of our football coverage, and last year there were some incredible stories. A captivating race for promotion from the Championship went all the way to that final day clash between Middlesbrough and Brighton, and, in League One, a remarkable rise continued for Burton Albion who will now rub shoulders with giants of the game, while Wigan Athletic started their climb back up through the leagues. League Two was arguably the site of the most captivating drama in the Football League, as Northampton Town, blighted by off-the-field problems, cruised to the title – joined by Bristol Rovers who secured a second consecutive promotion, and most amazingly of all, AFC Wimbledon, founded just 14 years ago.

With 127 games from across the Sky Bet EFL, as well as the EFL Cup, EFL Trophy and the excitement of the end-of-season play-offs again in 2016–17, another fantastic and thoroughly unpredictable season lies in store.

The EFL and its supporters are emblematic of how important local clubs and their traditions are to communities across the country. This is one of the things that inspires and motivates us at Sky Sports, and this year, with our wide portfolio given analysis by an experienced team we will endeavour again to bring football supporters into as close contact as possible with the clubs they follow.

With Sky Sports Mix launching later this year, we will also be bringing football from all these competitions to more fans across the country. We are excited to share some of the great stories of the Premier League and EFL with more people and welcome them into our football family.

We are shaped by what our viewers want. This is a feature of the way we work, and from the breadth and quality of our offering, we always look to provide the viewing experience fans want, as and where they want it. From technological innovation, such as the development of VR content and broadcasting in Ultra High Definition, to our online partnership with Whistle Sports and our award-winning digital coverage, to the variety of linear, on-demand, and mobile ways to watch, Sky Sports continues to offer the best experience of watching sport in the widest number of ways.

We can't wait to share the journey with you across another season in the beautiful game. After the unpredictability of last season, anything is possible in 2016–17.

Barney Francis

Barney Francis

FOREWORD

I've been watching football for more than 50 years and I thought I had seen the lot. Northampton Town's rise to the top division and subsequent fall; Wimbledon's FA Cup triumph; the injury-time goal by goalkeeper Jimmy Glass to keep Carlisle United in the Football League; the heart-stopping Sergio Aguero winner for Manchester City against Queens Park Rangers to snatch the Premier League crown from their neighbours, United. But I was wrong! I had never seen anything like Leicester City's joyous, bookie-bashing, pundit-perplexing title-winning campaign of 2015–16.

No one could have foreseen what was in store when Claudio Ranieri took over Leicester City last summer. But a side tipped for relegation turned the established order on its head and posed many questions about where club football is heading. Was this a one-off? Could Leicester do it again? Or perhaps another previously unconsidered team could become champions. I can't wait to see what's in store next season – anything is possible.

Leicester's story was remarkable. They achieved their title win with players who, on paper, had no right to hit the levels they did – Wes Morgan, Jamie Vardy, N'Golo Kanté and Riyad Mahrez. Led by an unlikely hero in Claudio Ranieri, it was a season in which everything clicked. They set down a new marker in the footballing world, proving money does not rule, pre-season odds do not define, and that with team spirit and hard work, anyone can achieve the seemingly impossible. They will start again in August keen to prove they can maintain a place among English football's best.

It was a remarkable season for underdogs across the country, too, with some fantastic stories. Burton Albion, playing in the Conference as recently as 2009, have completed their climb all the way into the Championship. Next year they will rub shoulders with giants of the game: the respective travelling support of Aston Villa, Newcastle United and Leeds United could all comfortably fill the Pirelli Stadium. Plus, they can look forward to a contest their fans could hardly dream about against local rivals Derby County. I'm fascinated to see how the Championship will play out next year – there are a lot of big teams in the division, but given what's happened this year, Burton and teams of their stature will feel they have every chance of playing those teams and beating them.

AFC Wimbledon will start life in League One just 14 years after they were formed by a group of fans and were competing in the Combined Counties League. Their romantic story shows no sign of ending.

Northampton Town, who were blighted by off-the-pitch problems, had a stunning season in taking the League Two title, while Bristol Rovers secured back-to-back promotions in the most thrilling fashion on the final day.

Across all four divisions, after a season like that, much is up in the air as we head into 2016–17. One thing is certain: at football's top table, the established teams will be looking to respond emphatically.

It is up to Arsenal, Manchester United, Manchester City, Chelsea, Tottenham Hotspur and Liverpool to remind the world why they have sat at football's top table for so long.

With Pep Guardiola bringing his quality to Manchester City and old adversary Jose Mourinho taking the top job at United, next year's title race will have an extra dimension. After 20 consecutive top-four finishes, there are no prizes for guessing that Arsenal will be in the mix.

Chelsea, under former Italy manager Antonio Conte, will be looking to do better than last year domestically and Spurs will be out to consolidate what they achieved last season and perhaps go one or two better. Arguably the Premier League side with the most to look forward to is Liverpool. Jurgen Klopp, so brilliant at Borussia Dortmund, is a wonderful addition to the Premier League and has already made an impact by taking the club to the Europa League final. I believe they can be top four or possibly better this season under the charismatic Klopp.

Fans of the promoted sides may have their sights set on more than a battle against relegation. After all, Watford and Bournemouth both adapted to life in the top flight nicely last season. Burnley are back up – in Sean Dyche they have an exciting manager who is set to go on to big things. They are joined back in the Premier League by Middlesbrough, their promotion reward for the unswerving backing of Chairman Steve Gibson. And Hull City, back at the first time of asking via the play-offs. The step-up for all three will be big, but they all have players capable of making an impact in the top division. Let's hope that however the promoted clubs fare, their owners stand by the managers who have brought them back to the Premier League.

In the Championship, things could be incredibly tight – there are now a number of teams in that league who will feel they have a right to be back in the Premier League: Newcastle United, Aston Villa, Derby County, Norwich City, Sheffield Wednesday and Leeds United, to name a few, along with Brighton who went agonisingly close last time. It's a mighty tough league to get out of, though, and it would be foolish to predict who will win it. So here goes – with 50,000 Geordies behind them, I think Newcastle will be promoted at the first time of asking. As for predicting the other two places, I'm not that daft!

In League One, could Sheffield United finally start the climb back up the leagues? Could Bristol Rovers replicate the work of Burton and win another promotion? Can Hartlepool United challenge at the top of League 2? How will Cheltenham Town and Grimsby Town fare on their return to the League? Who knows? All I know is these leagues always provide skill, drama, joy and heartbreak. Where else in the world would a fourth-tier club be regularly backed by 17,000 fans as Portsmouth are? I tell you, unashamedly, I love it!

When the football season returns, it's always a special feeling. I can't wait for the first *Soccer Saturday* of the season, to be joined by Merse, Tommo, Tiss, Charlie and others to share in another hectic year of football.

Whatever lies in store, Sky Sports will be the place to see the best football next season from the first kick to the last – I hope you enjoy the journey with me.

Jeff Stelling

INTRODUCTION

The 47th edition of the Yearbook is our fourteenth with sponsors Sky Sports and includes every game of the 2016 European Championship Qualifying campaign together with every game from the Finals in France. Full match line-ups and league tables are included for all of the qualifying and finals matches. Other international football at various levels is also well catered for in this edition.

The concise feature entitled Cups and Ups and Downs is again included with dates of those events affecting cup finals, plus promotion and relegation issues. In a season where yet again a record number of managerial changes were made, the Managers In and Out section is once again included, with a diary of managerial changes throughout the year. As women's football continues to grow, the Super League and Premier Leagues are included.

At European level, both the Champions League and Europa League have their usual comprehensive details included, with results, goalscorers, attendances, full line-ups and formations from the qualifying rounds onwards and also including all the league tables from the respective group stages.

The 2015–16 season will long be remembered with Leicester City becoming only the 6th different club to win the Premier League. They did so from a starting position of 5000/1, having made a great escape to avoid relegation the previous season. Claudio Ranieri was voted Manager of the Year by his peers at the League Managers Association, Jamie Vardy won the Football Writers' Footballer of the Year award and Riyad Mahrez won the PFA Player of the Year award – a remarkable season indeed for the Foxes. The Championship season ended with Burnley and Middlesbrough promoted automatically, joined by Hull City who defeated Sheffield Wednesday in the play-off final.

All of these statistics are reproduced in the pages devoted not only to the Premier League, but the three Football League competitions too, as well as all major allied cup competitions.

While transfer fees are invariably those reported at the time and rarely given as official figures, the edition reflects those listed at the time.

In the club-by-club pages that contain the line-ups of all league matches, appearances are split into starting and substitute appearances. In the Players Directory the totals show figures combined.

The Players Directory and its accompanying A to Z index enables the reader to quickly find the club of any specific player.

Throughout the book players sent off are designated with ▪, substitutes in the club pages are 12, 13 and 14. Included again in main cup competitions are the formations for each team.

In addition to competitions already mentioned there is full coverage of Scottish Premier League and Scottish League and cup competitions. There are also sections devoted to Welsh, Irish, Women's football, the Under-21s and various other UEFA youth levels, schools, reserve team, academies, referees and the leading non-league competitions as well as the work of the chaplains at clubs. The chief tournaments outside the UK at club and national level are not forgotten. The International Directory itself features Europe in some depth as well as every FIFA-affiliated country's international results for the period 5 July 2015 to 10 July 2016.

Naturally there are international appearances and goals scored by players for England, Scotland, Northern Ireland, Wales and the Republic. For easy reference, those players making appearances and scoring goals in the season covered are picked out in bold type.

The Yearbook would like to extend its appreciation to the publishers Headline for excellent support in the preparation of this edition, particularly Jonathan Taylor for photographic selection throughout the book and to Graham Green for his continued support.

ACKNOWLEDGEMENTS

In addition the Yearbook is also keen to thank the following individuals and organisations for their co-operation.

Special thanks to Barney Francis, Jeff Stelling, Thierry Henry and Peter Smith from Sky Sports for their pieces, and to Jamie Carragher for his Sky Sports Team of the Season.

Thanks are also due to Ian Nannestad for the Obituaries, Did You Know? and Fact File features in the club section. Many thanks also to John English for his conscientious proof reading and compilation of the International Directory.

The Yearbook is grateful to the Football Association, the Scottish Professional Football League, the Football League, Rev. Nigel Sands for his contribution to the Chaplain's page and Bob Bannister, Kenny Holmes and Martin Cooper for their help.

Sincere thanks to George Schley and Simon Dunnington for their excellent work on the database, and to Andy Cordiner, Geoff Turner, Brian Tait, Mick Carruthers, Robin Middlemiss and the staff at Wearset for their much appreciated efforts in the production of the book throughout the year.

EDITORIAL

Last season we witnessed something truly special. Leicester City shocked English football, but they were deserved winners. They were well-disciplined, well-organised and had the balance between skill and hard work that all successful teams must have to win major trophies. From their opening day win over Sunderland right through to the vital point at Manchester United, Leicester were relentless.

Jamie Vardy terrorised defences with his pace on the counter attack. Riyad Mahrez was both brilliant and inspirational. Wes Morgan and Robert Huth were true leaders at the back. The dynamo driving them all forward, N'Golo Kanté, was arguably the revelation of the season.

Of course it is arguable that they might have been able to achieve this success only because the regular title challengers were not good enough this season. Defending champions Chelsea suffered terribly in the first half of the campaign and the gap became insurmountable. Arsenal and Manchester City were far too inconsistent to win a league title. Although Arsenal beat Leicester twice, they lost to teams in the bottom half of the table such as West Bromwich Albion and Swansea City. In the end, it cost them dearly. City clearly struggled and were left fighting for fourth place on the last day of the season. Despite a good run in the Champions League and winning the Capital One Cup, they would now view this campaign as a disappointing season.

The only team that looked remotely like pushing Leicester for the title were Tottenham Hotspur, but they were derailed at the end of the campaign following a disappointing home draw against West Brom. In the end their title challenge faltered to the extent that Arsenal managed to pip them to second place on the last day. However, provided they keep hold of their terrific young spine including Hugo Lloris, Eric Dier, Dele Alli, Christian Eriksen and Harry Kane, Spurs will be confident they can mount a challenge again next season.

Liverpool and West Ham United are two other teams that have decent potential. Now, with Jurgen Klopp and the impressive Slaven Bilic at the helm of those clubs, don't be surprised if they are challenging for the top-four mix next year. Manchester United though should be the biggest threat with the arrival of Jose Mourinho. Whatever you say about the man, he does deliver silverware and you can be sure that United will be a much more serious proposition for title contenders.

Next season will not be the same as this one. At the top and bottom of the league, the future is uncertain. Leicester proved last year that any team with good spirit and a strong work ethic can beat any other side on their day.

While the league is unpredictable on the pitch, one of the notable consistencies off the pitch is the great support that fans provide. It never ceases to amaze me. Through thick and thin, they turn up in their tens of thousands, week in, week out to follow their teams.

This adds the extra dimension and atmosphere that makes football so great in this country. With a genuinely unpredictable season on the pitch round the corner again, I can't wait to see what's in store for the new campaign. Bring it on.

Thierry Henry

Thierry Henry

SKY SPORTS TEAM OF THE SEASON

JAMIE CARRAGHER'S SKY SPORTS
TEAM OF THE SEASON 2015–16

David De Gea
(Manchester U)

Nathaniel Clyne	Toby Alderweireld	Wes Morgan	Danny Rose
(Liverpool)	*(Tottenham H)*	*(Leicester C)*	*(Tottenham H)*

Riyad Mahrez	Dele Alli	N'Golo Kanté	Dimitri Payet
(Leicester C)	*(Tottenham H)*	*(Leicester C)*	*(West Ham U)*

Jamie Vardy   Harry Kane
(Leicester C)   *(Tottenham H)*

EUROPEAN GOLDEN SHOE

The European Golden Shoe award is presented to the leading goalscorer in European League football. However, the determination of the winner comes from a points system which depends on the status of the country involved. The goals total is multiplied by a factor of either two, one and a half, or just by one.

The top 30 places were as follows:

	Scorer	Team	Country	Goals	Factor	Points
1	Luis Suarez	Barcelona	Spain	40	2	80
2	Gonzalo Higuain	Napoli	Italy	36	2	72
3	Cristiano Ronaldo	Real Madrid	Spain	35	2	70
4	Jonas	Benfica	Portugal	32	2	64
5	Robert Lewandowski	Bayern Munich	Germany	30	2	60
6	Zlatan Ibrahimovic	Paris Saint-Germain	France	38	1.5	57
7	Islam Slimani	Sporting Lisbon	Portugal	27	2	54
8	Eran Zahavi	Maccabi Tel Aviv	Israel	35	1.5	52.5
9	Lionel Messi	Barcelona	Spain	26	2	52
10	Harry Kane	Tottenham H	England	25	2	50
11	Pierre-Emerick Aubameyang	Borussia Dortmund	Germany	25	2	50
12	Jamie Vardy	Leicester C	England	24	2	48
13	Neymar	Barcelona	Spain	24	2	48
14	Sergio Aguero	Manchester C	England	24	2	48
15	Karim Benzema	Real Madrid	Spain	24	2	48
16	Antoine Griezmann	Atletico Madrid	Spain	22	2	44
17	Nemanja Nikolic	Legia Warsaw	Poland	28	1.5	42
18	Vincent Janssen	AZ Alkmaar	Netherlands	27	1.5	40.5
19	Thomas Muller	Bayern Munich	Germany	20	2	40
20	Aritz Aduriz	Athletic Bilbao	Spain	20	2	40
21	Konstantinos Mitroglou	Benfica	Portugal	20	2	40
22	Luke De Jong	PSV Eindhoven	Netherlands	26	1.5	39
23	Mario Gomez	Besiktas	Turkey	26	1.5	39
24	Paulo Dybala	Juventus	Italy	19	2	38
25	Gareth Bale	Real Madrid	Spain	19	2	38
26	Ilija Nestorovski	Inter Zapresic	Croatia	25	1.5	37.5
27	Ruben Castro	Real Betis	Spain	18	2	36
28	Romelu Lukaku	Everton	England	18	2	36
29	Carlos Bacca	AC Milan	Italy	18	2	36
30	Lucas Perez	Deportivo La Coruna	Spain	17	2	34

FOOTBALL AWARDS 2015–16

FOOTBALLER OF THE YEAR

The Football Writers' Association Sir Stanley Matthews Trophy for the Footballer of the Year was awarded to Jamie Vardy of Leicester C and England. Riyad Mahrez (Leicester C and Algeria) was runner-up and N'Golo Kanté (Leicester C and France) came third.

Past Winners

1947–48 Stanley Matthews (Blackpool), 1948–49 Johnny Carey (Manchester U), 1949–50 Joe Mercer (Arsenal), 1950–51 Harry Johnston (Blackpool), 1951–52 Billy Wright (Wolverhampton W), 1952–53 Nat Lofthouse (Bolton W), 1953–54 Tom Finney (Preston NE), 1954–55 Don Revie (Manchester C), 1955–56 Bert Trautmann (Manchester C), 1956–57 Tom Finney (Preston NE), 1957–58 Danny Blanchflower (Tottenham H), 1958–59 Syd Owen (Luton T), 1959–60 Bill Slater (Wolverhampton W), 1960–61 Danny Blanchflower (Tottenham H), 1961–62 Jimmy Adamson (Burnley), 1962–63 Stanley Matthews (Stoke C), 1963–64 Bobby Moore (West Ham U), 1964–65 Bobby Collins (Leeds U), 1965–66 Bobby Charlton (Manchester U), 1966–67 Jackie Charlton (Leeds U), 1967–68 George Best (Manchester U), 1968–69 Dave Mackay (Derby Co) shared with Tony Book (Manchester C), 1969–70 Billy Bremner (Leeds U), 1970–71 Frank McLintock (Arsenal), 1971–72 Gordon Banks (Stoke C), 1972–73 Pat Jennings (Tottenham H), 1973–74 Ian Callaghan (Liverpool), 1974–75 Alan Mullery (Fulham), 1975–76 Kevin Keegan (Liverpool), 1976–77 Emlyn Hughes (Liverpool), 1977–78 Kenny Burns (Nottingham F), 1978–79 Kenny Dalglish (Liverpool), 1979–80 Terry McDermott (Liverpool), 1980–81 Frans Thijssen (Ipswich T), 1981–82 Steve Perryman (Tottenham H), 1982–83 Kenny Dalglish (Liverpool), 1983–84 Ian Rush (Liverpool), 1984–85 Neville Southall (Everton), 1985–86 Gary Lineker (Everton), 1986–87 Clive Allen (Tottenham H), 1987–88 John Barnes (Liverpool), 1988–89 Steve Nicol (Liverpool), 1989–90 John Barnes (Liverpool), 1990–91 Gordon Strachan (Leeds U), 1991–92 Gary Lineker (Tottenham H), 1992–93 Chris Waddle (Sheffield W), 1993–94 Alan Shearer (Blackburn R), 1994–95 Jurgen Klinsmann (Tottenham H), 1995–96 Eric Cantona (Manchester U), 1996–97 Gianfranco Zola (Chelsea), 1997–98 Dennis Bergkamp (Arsenal), 1998–99 David Ginola (Tottenham H), 1999–2000 Roy Keane (Manchester U), 2000–01 Teddy Sheringham (Manchester U), 2001–02 Robert Pires (Arsenal), 2002–03 Thierry Henry (Arsenal), 2003–04 Thierry Henry (Arsenal), 2004–05 Frank Lampard (Chelsea), 2005–06 Thierry Henry (Arsenal), 2006–07 Cristiano Ronaldo (Manchester U), 2007–08 Cristiano Ronaldo (Manchester U), 2008–09 Ryan Giggs (Manchester U), 2009–10 Wayne Rooney (Manchester U), 2010–11 Scott Parker (West Ham U), 2011–12 Robin van Persie (Arsenal), 2012–13 Gareth Bale (Tottenham H), 2013–14 Luis Suarez (Liverpool), 2014–15 Eden Hazard (Chelsea), 2015–16 Jamie Vardy (Leicester C).

THE PFA AWARDS 2016

Player of the Year: Riyad Mahrez, Leicester C and Algeria
Young Player of the Year: Dele Alli, Tottenham H and England
Women's Player of the Year: Izzy Christiansen, Manchester C and England
Women's Young Player of the Year: Beth Mead, Sunderland and England
PFA Merit Award: Ryan Giggs

PFA Premier League Team of the Year 2016
David De Gea (Manchester U); Hector Bellerin (Arsenal), Toby Alderweireld (Tottenham H), Wes Morgan (Leicester C), Danny Rose (Tottenham H); Riyad Mahrez (Leicester C), N'Golo Kanté (Leicester C), Dele Alli (Tottenham H), Dimitri Payet (West Ham U); Jamie Vardy (Leicester C), Harry Kane (Tottenham H).

PFA Championship Team of the year 2016
Tom Heaton (Burnley); Bruno Saltor (Brighton & HA), Michael Keane (Burnley), Michael Dawson (Hull C) / Daniel Ayala (Middlesbrough), George Friend (Middlesbrough); Alan Judge (Brentford), Joey Barton (Burnley), Barry Bannan (Sheffield W), Adam Clayton (Middlesbrough); Andre Gray (Burnley), Ross McCormack (Fulham).

PFA League 1 Team of the Year 2016
Jon McLaughlin (Burton Alb); Reece Wabara (Wigan Ath), John Egan (Gillingham), Craig Morgan (Wigan Ath), Rico Henry (Walsall); Bradley Dack (Gillingham), Romaine Sawyers (Walsall), Mark Duffy (Burton Alb, on loan from Birmingham C), Yanic Wildschut (Wigan Ath); Adam Armstrong (Coventry C, on loan from Newcastle U), Will Grigg (Wigan Ath).

PFA League 2 Team of the Year 2016
Adam Smith (Northampton T); George Baldock (Oxford U, on loan from Milton Keynes D), Aaron Pierre (Wycombe W), Curtis Nelson (Plymouth Arg), Joe Jacobson (Wycombe W); Kemar Roofe (Oxford U), Ricky Holmes (Northampton T), Matt Crooks (Accrington S), John-Joe O'Toole (Northampton T); Jay Simpson (Leyton Orient), Matty Taylor (Bristol R).

SCOTTISH AWARDS 2015–16

SCOTTISH PFA PLAYER OF THE YEAR AWARDS 2016

Player of the Year: Leigh Griffiths, Celtic and Scotland
Young Player of the Year: Kieran Tierney, Celtic and Scotland
Manager of the Year: Mark Warburton, Rangers
Championship Player of the Year: Lee Wallace, Rangers and Scotland
League One Player of the Year: Faissal El Bakhtaoui, Dunfermline Ath
League Two Player of the Year: Nathan Austin, East Fife (on loan from Falkirk)
Goal of the Season: Barrie McKay, Rangers v Celtic, Scottish FA Cup Semi-Final, 17 April 2016
Special Merit Award: Show Racism the Red Card

SCOTTISH FOOTBALL WRITERS' ASSOCIATION 2016

Player of the Year: Leigh Griffiths, Celtic and Scotland
Young Player of the Year: Kieran Tierney, Celtic and Scotland
Manager of the Year: Jim McIntyre, Ross Co
International Player of the Year: Matt Ritchie, Bournemouth and Scotland

PREMIER LEAGUE AWARDS 2015–16

PLAYER OF THE MONTH AWARDS 2015–16

August	Andre Ayew (Swansea C)
September	Anthony Martial (Manchester U)
October	Jamie Vardy (Leicester C)
November	Jamie Vardy (Leicester C)
December	Odion Ighalo (Watford)
January	Sergio Aguero (Manchester C)
February	Fraser Forster (Southampton)
March	Harry Kane (Tottenham H)
April	Sergio Aguero (Manchester C)

MANAGER OF THE MONTH AWARDS 2015–16

August	Manuel Pellegrini (Manchester C)
September	Mauricio Pochettino (Tottenham H)
October	Arsene Wenger (Arsenal)
November	Claudio Ranieri (Leicester C)
December	Quique Sanchez Flores (Watford)
January	Ronald Koeman (Southampton)
February	Mauricio Pochettino (Tottenham H)
March	Claudio Ranieri (Leicester C)
April	Claudio Ranieri (Leicester C)

SKY BET LEAGUE AWARDS 2015–16

SKY BET FOOTBALL LEAGUE PLAYER OF THE MONTH AWARDS 2015–16

	Sky Bet Championship	*Sky Bet League 1*	*Sky Bet League 2*
August	Kazenga LuaLua (Brighton & HA)	Adam Armstrong (Coventry C)	Dean Cox (Leyton Orient)
September	Jordan Rhodes (Blackburn R)	Peter Vincenti (Rochdale)	Michael Gash (Barnet)
October	Alan Judge (Brentford)	Aiden O'Brien (Milwall)	Shaun Miller (Morecambe)
November	Daryl Murphy (Ipswich T)	Jacob Murphy (Coventry C)	Jay Simpson (Northampton T)
December	Adam Clayton (Middlesbrough)	Andy Williams (Doncaster R)	Gareth Evans (Portsmouth)
January	Abel Hernandez (Hull C)	Sam Winnall (Barnsley)	Ricky Holmes (Northampton T
February	Aden Flint (Bristol C)	Jordan Archer (Millwall)	Bradley Fewster (York C)
March	Sam Vokes (Burnley)	Sullay Kaikai (Shrewsbury T)	Matty Taylor (Bristol R)
April	Anthony Knockaert (Brighton &HA)	Will Grigg (Wigan Ath)	Tarique Fosu (Reading)

SKY BET FOOTBALL LEAGUE MANAGER OF THE MONTH AWARDS 2015–16

	Sky Bet Championship	*Sky Bet League 1*	*Sky Bet League 2*
August	Chris Hughton (Brighton & HA)	Dean Smith (Walsall)	Ian Hendon (Leyton Orient)
September	Aitor Karanka (Middlesbrough)	Jimmy Floyd Hasselbaink (Burton Alb)	John Coleman (Accrington S)
October	Lee Carsley (Brentford)	Mark Robins (Scunthorpe U)	Derek Adams (Plymouth Arg)
November	Mick McCarthy (Ipswich T)	Graham Westley (Peterborough U)	Chris Wilder (Northampton T)
December	Aitor Karanka (Middlesbrough)	Nigel Adkins (Sheffield U)	Shaun Derry (Cambridge U)
January	Steve Bruce (Hull C)	Lee Johnson (Barnsley)	Chris Wilder (Northampton T)
February	Sean Dyce (Burnley)	Gary Caldwell (Wigan Ath)	Chris Wilder (Northampton T)
March	Neil Warnock (Rotherham U)	Paul Heckingbottom (Barnsley)	Darrell Clarke (Bristol R)
April	Chris Hughton (Brighton & HA)	Graham Alexander (Scunthorpe U)	Neal Ardley (AFC Wimbledon)

LEAGUE MANAGERS ASSOCIATION AWARDS 2015–16

LMA MANAGER OF THE YEAR SPONSORED BY BARCLAYS
Claudio Ranieri (Leicester C)

BARCLAYS PREMIER LEAGUE MANAGER OF THE YEAR
Claudio Ranieri (Leicester C)

SKY BET FOOTBALL LEAGUE CHAMPIONSHIP MANAGER OF THE YEAR
Chris Hughton (Brighton & HA)

SKY BET FOOTBALL LEAGUE 1 MANAGER OF THE YEAR
Gary Caldwell (Wigan Ath)

SKY BET FOOTBALL LEAGUE 2 MANAGER OF THE YEAR
Chris Wilder (Northampton T)

LMA SPECIAL ACHIEVEMENT AWARDS
Michael O'Neill (Northern Ireland)

LMA SERVICE TO FOOTBALL AWARD
Brian Lee MBE

OTHER AWARDS

EUROPEAN FOOTBALLER OF THE YEAR 2015
Lionel Messi, Barcelona and Argentina

EUROPEAN WOMEN'S PLAYER OF THE YEAR 2015
Celia Sasic, Frankfurt and Germany

FIFA BALLON D'OR PLAYER OF THE YEAR 2015
Lionel Messi, Barcelona and Argentina

FIFA BALLON D'OR WOMEN'S PLAYER OF THE YEAR 2015
Carli Lloyd, Houston Dash and USA

FIFA PUSKAS AWARD GOAL OF THE YEAR
Wendell Lira, Goianesia v Atletico-GO, Goias State Championship, 11 March 2015

BARCLAYS PREMIER LEAGUE 2015–16

(P) *Promoted into division at end of 2014–15 season.*

			Home				Away					Total						
		P	W	D	L	F	A	W	D	L	F	A	W	D	L	F	A	GD	Pts
1	Leicester C	38	12	6	1	35	18	11	6	2	33	18	23	12	3	68	36	32	81
2	Arsenal	38	12	4	3	31	11	8	7	4	34	25	20	11	7	65	36	29	71
3	Tottenham H	38	10	6	3	35	15	9	7	3	34	20	19	13	6	69	35	34	70
4	Manchester C	38	12	2	5	47	21	7	7	5	24	20	19	9	10	71	41	30	66
5	Manchester U	38	12	5	2	27	9	7	4	8	22	26	19	9	10	49	35	14	66
6	Southampton	38	11	3	5	39	22	7	6	6	20	19	18	9	11	59	41	18	63
7	West Ham U	38	9	7	3	34	26	7	7	5	31	25	16	14	8	65	51	14	62
8	Liverpool	38	8	8	3	33	22	8	4	7	30	28	16	12	10	63	50	13	60
9	Stoke C	38	8	4	7	22	24	6	5	8	19	31	14	9	15	41	55	–14	51
10	Chelsea	38	5	9	5	32	30	7	5	7	27	23	12	14	12	59	53	6	50
11	Everton	38	6	5	8	35	30	5	9	5	24	25	11	14	13	59	55	4	47
12	Swansea C	38	8	6	5	20	20	4	5	10	22	32	12	11	15	42	52	–10	47
13	Watford (P)	38	6	6	7	20	19	6	3	10	20	31	12	9	17	40	50	–10	45
14	WBA	38	6	5	8	20	26	4	8	7	14	22	10	13	15	34	48	–14	43
15	Crystal Palace	38	6	3	10	19	23	5	6	8	20	28	11	9	18	39	51	–12	42
16	Bournemouth (P)	38	5	5	9	23	34	6	4	9	22	33	11	9	18	45	67	–22	42
17	Sunderland	38	6	6	7	23	20	3	6	10	25	42	9	12	17	48	62	–14	39
18	Newcastle U	38	7	7	5	32	24	2	3	14	12	41	9	10	19	44	65	–21	37
19	Norwich C (P)	38	6	5	8	26	30	3	2	14	13	37	9	7	22	39	67	–28	34
20	Aston Villa	38	2	5	12	14	35	1	3	15	13	41	3	8	27	27	76	–49	17

BARCLAYS PREMIER LEAGUE LEADING GOALSCORERS 2015–16

	League	FA Cup	Capital One Cup	Other	Total
Sergio Aguero (*Manchester C*)	24	1	2	2	29
Harry Kane (*Tottenham H*)	25	1	0	2	28
Romelu Lukaku (*Everton*)	18	3	4	0	25
Jamie Vardy (*Leicester C*)	24	0	0	0	24
Olivier Giroud (*Arsenal*)	16	3	0	5	24
Riyad Mahrez (*Leicester C*)	17	0	1	0	18
Jermain Defoe (*Sunderland*)	15	0	3	0	18
Anthony Martial (*Manchester U*)	11	2	1	4	18
Odion Ighalo (*Watford*)	15	2	0	0	17
Alexis Sanchez (*Arsenal*)	13	1	0	3	17
Diego Costa (*Chelsea*)	12	2	0	2	16
Troy Deeney (*Watford*)	13	2	0	0	15
Sadio Mane (*Southampton*)	11	0	3	1	15
Graziano Pelle (*Southampton*)	11	0	1	2	14
Shane Long (*Southampton*)	10	0	2	1	13
Andre Ayew (*Swansea C*)	12	0	0	0	12
Marko Arnautovic (*Stoke C*)	11	0	1	0	12
Dimitri Payet (*West Ham U*)	9	3	0	0	12
Georginio Wijnaldum (*Newcastle U*)	11	0	0	0	11
Gylfi Sigurdsson (*Swansea C*)	11	0	0	0	11
Roberto Firmino (*Liverpool*)	10	0	0	1	11
Dele Alli (*Tottenham H*)	10	0	0	0	10
Christian Benteke (*Liverpool*)	9	0	0	1	10
Aleksandar Mitrovic (*Newcastle U*)	9	0	0	0	9
Andy Carroll (*West Ham U*)	9	0	0	0	9

Other matches consist of European games, Community Shield.

BARCLAYS PREMIER LEAGUE – RESULTS 2015-16

	Arsenal	Aston Villa	Bournemouth	Chelsea	Crystal Palace	Everton	Leicester C	Liverpool	Manchester C	Manchester U	Newcastle U	Norwich C	Southampton	Stoke C	Sunderland	Swansea C	Tottenham H	Watford	WBA	West Ham U
Arsenal	—	4-0	2-0	0-1	1-1	2-1	2-1	0-0	2-1	3-0	1-0	1-0	0-0	2-0	3-1	1-2	1-1	4-0	2-0	0-2
Aston Villa	0-2	—	1-2	0-4	1-0	1-3	1-1	0-6	0-4	0-1	0-0	2-0	2-4	0-1	2-2	1-2	0-2	2-3	0-1	1-1
Bournemouth	0-2	0-1	—	1-4	0-0	3-3	1-1	1-2	0-4	2-1	0-1	3-0	2-0	1-3	2-0	3-2	1-5	1-1	1-1	1-3
Chelsea	2-0	2-0	0-1	—	1-2	3-3	1-1	1-3	0-3	1-1	5-1	1-0	1-3	2-1	3-1	2-2	2-2	1-2	2-2	2-2
Crystal Palace	1-2	2-1	1-2	0-3	—	0-0	0-1	1-2	0-1	0-0	5-1	1-0	1-0	2-1	0-1	0-0	1-3	1-2	2-0	1-3
Everton	0-2	4-0	2-1	3-1	1-1	—	2-3	1-1	0-2	0-3	3-0	3-0	1-1	3-4	6-2	1-2	1-1	2-2	0-1	2-3
Leicester C	2-5	3-2	0-0	2-1	1-0	3-1	—	2-0	3-0	1-1	1-0	1-0	1-0	3-0	4-2	4-0	1-1	2-1	2-2	2-2
Liverpool	3-3	3-2	1-1	1-1	1-2	4-0	1-0	—	3-0	1-1	2-2	1-1	1-1	4-1	2-2	1-0	1-1	2-0	2-2	0-3
Manchester C	2-2	4-0	5-1	3-0	4-0	0-0	1-3	1-4	—	0-1	6-1	2-1	3-1	4-0	4-1	2-1	1-2	2-0	2-1	1-2
Manchester U	3-2	1-0	5-1	0-0	2-0	1-0	1-1	3-1	0-0	—	0-0	3-0	3-1	3-0	3-0	1-0	1-0	1-0	2-0	0-0
Newcastle U	0-1	1-1	1-3	2-2	1-0	0-1	0-3	2-0	1-1	3-3	—	6-2	2-2	0-0	1-1	3-0	5-1	1-2	1-0	2-1
Norwich C	1-1	2-0	3-1	1-2	1-3	1-1	1-2	4-5	0-0	0-1	3-2	—	1-0	1-1	0-3	1-0	0-3	4-2	0-1	2-2
Southampton	4-0	1-1	2-0	1-2	4-1	0-3	2-2	3-2	4-2	2-3	3-1	3-0	—	0-1	1-1	3-1	0-2	2-0	3-0	1-0
Stoke C	0-0	2-1	1-0	0-1	1-2	0-3	0-2	0-1	2-0	2-0	1-0	3-1	1-2	—	1-1	2-2	0-4	0-2	0-1	2-1
Sunderland	0-3	3-1	2-2	1-0	1-1	0-0	0-3	3-1	0-1	2-1	3-0	1-3	0-1	2-0	—	1-1	2-2	1-0	1-0	0-0
Swansea C	2-2	3-1	3-0	0-0	1-1	0-0	0-1	0-0	1-1	2-1	2-0	1-0	0-1	2-2	2-4	—	2-1	1-0	1-0	4-1
Tottenham H	0-3	3-1	3-0	0-0	1-0	1-1	0-1	3-0	4-1	3-0	1-2	3-0	1-2	2-2	4-1	2-1	—	1-0	1-1	4-1
Watford	2-1	3-2	0-0	2-3	0-1	1-1	0-1	3-0	1-2	1-2	2-1	2-0	0-0	1-2	2-2	1-0	1-2	—	0-0	2-0
WBA	2-1	0-0	1-2	2-3	3-2	2-3	2-3	1-1	0-3	1-0	1-0	0-1	0-0	2-1	1-0	1-1	1-1	0-1	—	0-3
West Ham U	3-3	2-0	3-4	2-1	2-2	1-1	1-2	2-0	2-2	3-2	2-0	2-2	2-1	0-0	1-0	1-4	1-0	3-1	1-1	—

SKY BET CHAMPIONSHIP 2015–16

(P) *Promoted into division at end of 2014–15 season.*   (R) *Relegated into division at end of 2014–15 season.*

		P	W	D	L	F	A	W	D	L	F	A	W	D	L	F	A	GD	Pts
				Home						*Away*					*Total*				
1	Burnley (R)	46	15	6	2	38	14	11	9	3	34	21	26	15	5	72	35	37	93
2	Middlesbrough	46	16	5	2	34	8	10	6	7	29	23	26	11	9	63	31	32	89
3	Brighton & HA	46	15	5	3	40	8	9	12	2	32	24	24	17	5	72	42	30	89
4	Hull C¶ (R)	46	15	7	1	47	12	9	4	10	22	23	24	11	11	69	35	34	83
5	Derby Co	46	12	7	4	37	16	9	8	6	29	27	21	15	10	66	43	23	78
6	Sheffield W	46	13	8	2	42	17	6	9	8	24	28	19	17	10	66	45	21	74
7	Ipswich T	46	9	8	6	28	24	9	7	7	25	27	18	15	13	53	51	2	69
8	Cardiff C	46	12	9	2	33	20	5	8	10	23	31	17	17	12	56	51	5	68
9	Brentford	46	10	4	9	33	30	9	4	10	39	37	19	8	19	72	67	5	65
10	Birmingham C	46	9	5	9	27	27	7	10	6	26	22	16	15	15	53	49	4	63
11	Preston NE (P)	46	7	10	6	21	21	8	7	8	24	24	15	17	14	45	45	0	62
12	QPR (R)	46	10	9	4	37	25	4	9	10	17	29	14	18	14	54	54	0	60
13	Leeds U	46	7	8	8	23	28	7	9	7	27	30	14	17	15	50	58	−8	59
14	Wolverhampton W	46	7	10	6	26	26	7	6	10	27	32	14	16	16	53	58	−5	58
15	Blackburn R	46	8	8	7	29	23	5	8	10	17	23	13	16	17	46	46	0	55
16	Nottingham F	46	7	8	8	25	26	6	8	9	18	21	13	16	17	43	47	−4	55
17	Reading	46	8	9	6	25	20	5	4	14	27	39	13	13	20	52	59	−7	52
18	Bristol C (P)	46	7	7	9	34	34	6	6	11	20	37	13	13	20	54	71	−17	52
19	Huddersfield T	46	7	6	10	33	33	6	6	11	26	37	13	12	21	59	70	−11	51
20	Fulham	46	8	5	10	36	36	4	10	9	30	43	12	15	19	66	79	−13	51
21	Rotherham U	46	8	6	9	31	34	5	4	14	22	37	13	10	23	53	71	−18	49
22	Charlton Ath	46	5	8	10	23	35	4	5	14	17	45	9	13	24	40	80	−40	40
23	Milton Keynes D (P)	46	7	3	13	21	37	2	9	12	18	32	9	12	25	39	69	−30	39
24	Bolton W	46	5	11	7	24	26	0	4	19	17	55	5	15	26	41	81	−40	30

¶*Hull C promoted via play-offs.*

SKY BET CHAMPIONSHIP LEADING GOALSCORERS 2015–16

	League	FA Cup	Capital One Cup	Play-Offs	Total
Andre Gray *(Burnley)*	25	0	0	0	25
(Includes 2 League goals for Brentford.)					
Ross McCormack *(Fulham)*	21	0	2	0	23
Abel Hernandez *(Hull C)*	20	0	1	1	22
Jonathan Kodjia *(Bristol C)*	19	1	0	0	20
Nahki Wells *(Huddersfield T)*	17	1	0	0	18
Tomer Hemed *(Brighton & HA)*	17	0	0	0	17
Jordan Rhodes *(Middlesbrough)*	16	1	0	0	17
(Includes 10 League goals and 1 FA Cup goal for Blackburn R.)					
Moussa Dembele *(Fulham)*	15	1	1	0	17
Sam Vokes *(Burnley)*	15	1	0	0	16
Fernando Forestieri *(Sheffield W)*	15	0	0	0	15
Chris Martin *(Derby Co)*	15	0	0	0	15
Lasse Vibe *(Brentford)*	14	0	0	0	14
Gary Hooper *(Sheffield W)*	13	0	0	0	13
Chris Wood *(Leeds U)*	13	0	0	0	13
Tom Ince *(Derby Co)*	12	0	0	0	12
Alan Judge *(Brentford)*	14	0	0	0	11
Clayton Donaldson *(Birmingham C)*	11	0	0	0	11
Nick Blackman *(Derby Co)*	11	0	0	0	11
Brett Pitman *(Ipswich T)*	10	0	1	0	11
Mohamed Diame *(Hull C)*	9	0	0	1	10
Johnny Russell *(Derby Co)*	9	0	0	1	10
Tjaronn Chery *(QPR)*	10	0	0	0	10
Daryl Murphy *(Ipswich T)*	10	0	0	0	10
Mirco Antenucci *(Leeds U)*	9	0	0	0	9
Anthony Pilkington *(Cardiff C)*	9	0	0	0	9

SKY BET CHAMPIONSHIP – RESULTS 2015–16

	Birmingham C	Blackburn R	Bolton W	Brentford	Brighton & HA	Bristol C	Burnley	Cardiff C	Charlton Ath	Derby Co	Fulham	Huddersfield T	Hull C	Ipswich T	Leeds U	Middlesbrough	Milton Keynes D	Nottingham F	Preston NE	QPR	Reading	Rotherham U	Sheffield W	Wolverhampton W
Birmingham C	—	0-0	0-1	0-2	2-1	1-0	1-2	1-0	0-1	1-1	1-1	0-2	1-0	3-0	1-2	2-2	1-0	0-1	2-2	2-1	2-1	0-2	1-2	0-2
Blackburn R	2-0	—	1-0	1-1	0-1	2-2	0-1	1-1	3-0	0-0	3-0	0-2	0-2	2-0	1-2	2-1	3-2	0-0	1-2	1-1	3-1	1-0	2-2	1-2
Bolton W	0-1	1-0	—	1-1	2-2	0-0	1-2	2-3	3-0	0-0	2-2	0-2	1-0	2-2	1-1	1-2	3-1	1-1	1-2	1-1	0-1	2-1	0-0	2-1
Brentford	0-2	3-1	1-1	—	2-2	2-1	1-3	2-1	1-2	1-3	3-0	4-2	0-2	2-2	1-1	0-3	2-0	2-1	2-1	4-0	1-3	2-1	1-0	3-0
Brighton & HA	2-1	1-0	3-0	2-1	—	2-1	2-2	1-1	3-2	1-1	5-0	2-1	0-2	0-1	4-0	0-3	2-1	1-0	0-0	4-0	1-0	2-1	1-0	3-0
Bristol C	0-0	0-2	6-0	2-4	0-4	—	1-2	0-2	1-1	2-3	1-4	4-0	1-0	2-1	2-2	1-0	1-1	2-0	1-2	1-1	0-2	1-1	4-1	1-0
Burnley	2-2	1-0	2-0	1-0	1-2	4-0	—	4-0	4-0	4-1	3-1	2-1	1-0	0-0	1-0	1-1	2-1	1-0	0-2	1-0	1-2	2-0	3-1	1-0
Cardiff C	1-1	1-0	2-1	1-0	1-1	0-0	2-2	—	2-1	2-1	1-1	2-0	0-2	1-0	1-0	1-0	0-0	1-1	0-2	0-0	2-0	2-0	3-1	2-0
Charlton Ath	1-1	1-0	2-2	0-3	1-3	0-3	0-0	0-0	—	0-1	1-1	1-2	2-1	0-3	0-0	2-0	0-1	1-1	0-3	2-0	3-4	1-1	3-1	0-2
Derby Co	0-3	1-0	4-1	2-0	1-3	4-0	0-0	2-1	0-1	—	2-0	1-2	4-0	0-3	1-2	2-0	0-1	1-0	0-3	2-0	1-1	1-1	1-1	0-3
Fulham	2-5	2-1	1-0	2-2	1-2	1-2	2-3	2-1	3-0	1-1	—	1-1	4-0	0-1	1-1	0-2	0-1	1-1	1-1	4-0	1-1	3-0	1-1	1-0
Huddersfield T	1-1	1-1	4-1	1-5	1-1	1-2	2-3	2-1	5-0	1-1	2-0	—	0-1	1-2	1-1	0-2	2-1	1-3	1-1	4-0	4-2	4-1	1-1	0-3
Hull C	2-0	1-1	1-0	2-0	1-1	4-0	3-0	2-0	6-0	0-2	2-1	2-0	—	3-0	3-0	3-0	2-0	1-1	2-0	1-1	2-1	5-1	0-0	1-0
Ipswich T	1-1	2-0	2-0	1-3	2-3	2-2	0-1	1-1	0-2	0-1	2-1	0-0	0-1	—	2-1	0-2	3-2	1-0	1-0	2-1	2-1	0-1	2-1	2-2
Leeds U	0-2	2-1	2-1	1-1	1-2	0-1	1-1	1-0	0-0	1-2	1-1	0-0	0-1	0-1	—	1-1	1-1	0-1	1-0	1-1	2-1	0-1	1-1	2-1
Middlesbrough	0-0	3-0	3-0	0-1	1-1	3-0	1-0	1-0	3-0	2-0	0-0	3-0	0-1	0-0	3-0	—	2-0	0-1	0-1	1-0	2-1	1-0	1-2	1-0
Milton Keynes D	0-2	3-0	1-0	1-4	1-2	0-2	0-5	1-0	4-0	1-3	1-1	0-2	0-2	0-0	3-0	1-1	—	1-2	0-1	2-0	1-0	0-4	2-1	1-2
Nottingham F	1-1	1-1	3-0	0-3	1-2	1-1	1-1	1-2	0-0	1-0	3-0	0-2	0-1	1-1	1-2	1-1	2-1	—	1-0	0-0	3-1	2-1	0-3	1-1
Preston NE	1-1	1-2	0-0	1-3	0-0	1-1	0-1	0-0	2-1	1-2	1-2	2-1	1-0	1-2	1-1	0-0	1-1	1-0	—	1-1	1-0	2-1	1-0	1-1
QPR	2-0	2-2	4-3	3-0	2-2	1-0	0-0	2-2	2-1	2-0	1-3	1-1	1-2	1-0	1-0	2-3	3-0	1-2	0-0	—	1-1	4-2	1-0	1-1
Reading	0-2	0-1	2-1	1-1	1-1	1-1	0-0	2-2	2-1	0-1	2-2	2-2	1-2	5-1	0-0	1-0	3-0	2-1	0-0	1-1	—	1-0	1-2	1-0
Rotherham U	0-0	4-0	2-1	1-1	1-1	3-0	1-2	2-1	1-4	3-3	1-3	1-1	2-0	2-5	2-0	1-4	1-0	0-0	1-2	0-3	1-1	—	1-2	1-2
Sheffield W	3-0	2-1	3-2	4-0	0-0	2-0	1-1	3-0	3-0	0-0	3-2	3-1	1-1	1-1	2-0	1-3	0-0	1-0	3-1	1-1	1-0	0-1	—	4-1
Wolverhampton W	0-0	0-0	2-2	0-2	0-0	2-1	0-0	1-3	2-1	2-1	3-2	3-0	1-1	0-0	2-3	1-3	0-0	1-1	1-2	2-3	1-0	0-0	2-1	—

SKY BET LEAGUE 1 2015–16

(P) *Promoted into division at end of 2014–15 season.*   (R) *Relegated into division at end of 2014–15 season.*

			Home					Away					Total					
		P	W	D	L	F	A	W	D	L	F	A	W	D	L	F	A	GD	Pts
1	Wigan Ath (R)	46	14	6	3	39	17	10	9	4	43	28	24	15	7	82	45	37	87
2	Burton Alb (P)	46	13	8	2	32	16	12	2	9	25	21	25	10	11	57	37	20	85
3	Walsall	46	11	6	6	31	26	13	6	4	40	23	24	12	10	71	49	22	84
4	Millwall (R)	46	13	3	7	34	22	11	6	6	39	27	24	9	13	73	49	24	81
5	Bradford C	46	14	5	4	32	16	9	6	8	23	24	23	11	12	55	40	15	80
6	Barnsley¶	46	11	4	8	35	24	11	4	8	35	30	22	8	16	70	54	16	74
7	Scunthorpe U	46	12	6	5	28	15	9	5	9	32	32	21	11	14	60	47	13	74
8	Coventry C	46	12	6	5	41	24	7	6	10	26	25	19	12	15	67	49	18	69
9	Gillingham	46	13	4	6	41	24	6	8	9	30	32	19	12	15	71	56	15	69
10	Rochdale	46	12	6	5	41	25	7	6	10	27	36	19	12	15	68	61	7	69
11	Sheffield U	46	11	4	8	37	29	7	8	8	27	30	18	12	16	64	59	5	66
12	Port Vale	46	12	7	4	35	25	6	4	13	21	33	18	11	17	56	58	-2	65
13	Peterborough U	46	9	4	10	42	37	10	2	11	40	36	19	6	21	82	73	9	63
14	Southend U (P)	46	10	5	8	30	26	6	6	11	28	38	16	11	19	58	64	-6	59
15	Swindon T	46	10	4	9	39	36	6	7	10	25	35	16	11	19	64	71	-7	59
16	Bury (P)*	46	10	8	5	36	29	6	4	13	20	44	16	12	18	56	73	-17	57
17	Oldham Ath	46	7	5	11	25	35	5	13	5	19	23	12	18	16	44	58	-14	54
18	Chesterfield	46	6	6	11	36	39	9	2	12	22	31	15	8	23	58	70	-12	53
19	Fleetwood T	46	9	8	6	33	20	3	7	13	19	36	12	15	19	52	56	-4	51
20	Shrewsbury T (P)	46	5	5	13	29	39	8	6	9	29	40	13	11	22	58	79	-21	50
21	Doncaster R	46	7	7	9	27	24	4	6	13	21	40	11	13	22	48	64	-16	46
22	Blackpool (R)	46	8	5	10	22	24	4	5	14	18	39	12	10	24	40	63	-23	46
23	Colchester U	46	4	9	10	32	43	5	4	14	25	56	9	13	24	57	99	-42	40
24	Crewe Alex	46	4	7	12	25	40	3	6	14	21	43	7	13	26	46	83	-37	34

¶*Barnsley promoted via play-offs. *Bury deducted 3 points for fielding an ineligible player.*

SKY BET LEAGUE 1 LEADING GOALSCORERS 2015–16

	League	FA Cup	Capital One Cup	J Paint Trophy	Play-Offs	Total
William Grigg (*Wigan Ath*)	25	0	1	2	0	28
Lee Gregory (*Millwall*)	18	1	0	6	2	27
Nicky Ajose (*Swindon T*)	24	1	0	0	0	25
Sam Winnall (*Barnsley*)	21	0	1	0	2	24
Paddy Madden (*Scunthorpe U*)	20	2	1	0	0	23
Billy Sharp (*Sheffield U*)	21	0	0	0	0	21
Adam Armstrong (*Coventry C*)	20	0	0	0	0	20
Tom Bradshaw (*Walsall*)	17	0	3	0	0	20
Steve Morison (*Millwall*)	15	1	1	1	1	19
Leon Clarke (*Bury*)	15	1	2	0	0	18
Andy Williams (*Doncaster R*)	12	2	2	0	0	16
Lee Novak (*Chesterfield*)	14	1	0	0	0	15
Bradley Dack (*Gillingham*)	13	0	1	1	0	15
George Moncur (*Colchester U*)	12	2	0	0	0	14
Ian Henderson (*Rochdale*)	13	0	0	0	0	13
Marcus Maddison (*Peterborough U*)	11	1	1	0	0	13
Jon Tayloz (*Peterborough U*)	11	2	0	0	0	13
James Hanson (*Bradford C*)	11	1	1	0	0	13
Aiden O'Brien (*Millwall*)	10	1	0	2	0	13
Lucas Akins (*Burton Alb*)	12	0	0	0	0	12
Jonathan Obika (*Swindon T*)	11	0	1	0	0	12
Che Adams (*Sheffield U*)	11	0	0	1	0	12
Lee Angol (*Peterborough U*)	11	0	0	0	0	11
Conor Hourihane (*Barnsley*)	10	0	1	0	0	11
Michael Jacobs (*Wigan Ath*)	10	0	0	0	0	10

SKY BET LEAGUE 1 – RESULTS 2015–16

	Barnsley	Blackpool	Bradford C	Burton Alb	Bury	Chesterfield	Colchester U	Coventry C	Crewe Alex	Doncaster R	Fleetwood T	Gillingham	Millwall	Oldham Ath	Peterborough U	Port Vale	Rochdale	Scunthorpe U	Sheffield U	Shrewsbury T	Southend U	Swindon T	Walsall	Wigan Ath
Barnsley	—	4-2	0-0	1-0	3-0	1-2	2-2	2-0	1-2	1-0	0-1	2-0	2-1	2-1	1-0	1-2	6-1	0-0	1-1	1-2	0-2	4-1	0-2	0-2
Blackpool	1-1	—	0-1	1-2	1-1	2-0	0-1	0-1	2-0	0-2	1-0	1-0	1-1	0-0	2-0	0-1	0-2	5-0	0-0	2-3	2-0	1-0	0-4	0-4
Bradford C	0-1	1-0	—	2-0	2-1	1-0	1-2	0-0	2-1	2-1	2-1	1-2	2-1	1-0	0-2	2-0	2-2	1-0	2-2	2-0	2-0	1-0	4-0	1-1
Burton Alb	0-0	1-0	3-1	—	1-1	1-0	5-1	1-2	0-0	2-1	2-1	2-1	2-1	0-0	2-1	2-0	1-0	2-1	0-0	1-2	2-0	1-0	0-0	1-1
Bury	0-0	4-3	0-1	1-0	—	1-0	5-2	2-1	0-0	1-0	3-4	0-1	1-3	1-1	3-1	3-2	0-0	1-2	1-0	2-2	3-2	2-2	2-3	2-2
Chesterfield	3-1	1-1	0-1	1-2	1-0	—	3-3	1-1	3-1	1-1	0-0	1-3	1-2	1-2	0-1	4-2	1-2	0-3	0-3	7-1	3-0	0-4	1-4	2-3
Colchester U	2-3	2-2	2-0	0-3	0-1	1-1	—	1-3	2-3	4-1	1-1	2-1	0-0	0-0	0-1	2-1	1-2	2-2	1-2	0-0	0-2	1-4	4-4	3-3
Coventry C	4-3	0-0	1-0	0-2	6-0	1-0	0-1	—	3-2	2-2	1-2	4-1	2-1	1-1	3-2	2-1	0-1	1-2	3-1	3-0	2-2	0-0	1-1	2-0
Crewe Alex	1-2	1-2	0-1	1-1	3-3	3-3	0-1	0-5	—	3-1	1-1	0-1	1-3	1-0	1-5	1-0	0-1	2-3	3-1	3-0	1-2	1-3	1-1	2-0
Doncaster R	2-1	0-1	0-1	0-0	1-1	3-0	1-1	2-0	3-2	—	2-0	2-2	2-1	1-0	1-5	1-2	2-0	0-1	1-0	0-1	0-0	1-3	1-2	3-1
Fleetwood T	0-2	0-0	1-1	4-0	2-0	0-1	4-0	0-1	2-0	0-0	—	2-1	2-1	1-1	2-0	0-2	1-1	2-1	2-2	0-0	1-1	5-1	0-1	1-3
Gillingham	2-1	2-1	3-0	0-3	3-1	1-2	4-1	0-0	3-0	1-0	5-1	—	1-2	3-3	2-1	0-2	2-0	2-1	4-0	2-3	1-1	0-0	1-2	2-0
Millwall	2-3	3-0	0-0	2-0	1-0	0-2	4-1	0-4	1-1	2-0	1-0	0-3	—	3-0	3-0	3-1	3-1	0-2	1-0	3-1	0-2	2-0	0-1	0-0
Oldham Ath	1-2	5-1	1-2	0-1	1-0	0-2	1-1	0-2	0-2	1-2	1-0	2-1	1-2	—	1-5	3-1	2-3	2-4	1-1	3-1	2-5	2-0	1-0	0-0
Peterborough U	3-2	5-1	1-1	0-1	2-3	2-1	2-1	3-1	3-0	4-0	2-1	2-1	1-2	1-2	—	2-3	1-2	0-2	1-3	1-1	0-0	1-2	1-3	2-3
Port Vale	0-1	2-0	1-1	0-4	1-0	3-2	2-0	1-1	1-1	3-0	0-0	1-1	5-3	1-2	1-1	—	4-1	1-1	2-1	2-0	3-1	1-0	0-5	3-2
Rochdale	3-0	3-0	1-3	2-1	3-0	2-3	3-1	1-0	2-2	2-0	1-0	0-0	0-1	0-0	2-0	2-1	—	2-1	2-0	3-2	4-1	2-2	1-2	0-2
Scunthorpe U	2-0	0-1	0-2	1-0	2-1	1-1	3-0	1-0	2-0	2-0	1-0	0-0	0-0	1-1	0-4	1-0	1-1	—	0-1	2-1	1-0	6-0	0-1	1-1
Sheffield U	0-0	2-0	3-1	0-1	1-3	2-0	2-3	1-0	3-2	3-1	3-0	0-0	1-2	3-0	2-3	1-0	3-2	0-2	—	2-4	2-2	1-1	2-0	0-2
Shrewsbury T	0-3	1-0	1-1	0-1	2-0	1-0	4-2	2-1	0-1	1-2	1-1	2-2	1-2	0-1	3-4	1-0	2-0	2-2	3-1	—	1-2	0-1	1-3	1-5
Southend U	2-1	1-0	0-1	3-1	4-1	0-1	3-0	3-0	2-2	0-3	2-2	1-1	0-4	0-1	2-1	1-0	2-2	2-1	3-1	0-1	—	0-1	0-2	0-0
Swindon T	0-1	3-2	4-1	0-1	0-1	1-0	1-2	2-2	4-3	1-1	1-1	1-3	0-3	1-2	2-0	2-2	2-1	2-1	0-2	3-0	4-2	—	2-1	1-4
Walsall	1-3	1-1	2-1	2-0	0-1	1-2	2-1	2-1	1-1	2-0	3-1	3-2	0-3	1-1	2-0	2-0	0-3	0-0	1-1	2-1	1-0	1-1	—	1-2
Wigan Ath	1-4	0-1	1-0	0-1	3-0	3-1	5-0	1-0	1-0	0-0	2-1	3-2	2-2	0-0	1-1	3-0	1-0	3-0	3-3	1-0	4-1	1-0	0-0	—

SKY BET LEAGUE 2 2015–16

(P) Promoted into division at end of 2014–15 season.   *(R) Relegated into division at end of 2014–15 season.*

		P	W	D	L	F	A	W	D	L	F	A	W	D	L	F	A	GD	Pts
				Home					Away					Total					
1	Northampton T	46	15	5	3	38	19	14	7	2	44	27	29	12	5	82	46	36	99
2	Oxford U	46	10	7	6	37	20	14	7	2	47	21	24	14	8	84	41	43	86
3	Bristol R (P)	46	15	2	6	41	21	11	5	7	36	25	26	7	13	77	46	31	85
4	Accrington S	46	11	9	3	43	30	13	4	6	31	18	24	13	9	74	48	26	85
5	Plymouth Arg	46	12	3	8	39	26	12	6	5	33	20	24	9	13	72	46	26	81
6	Portsmouth	46	10	7	6	38	19	11	8	4	37	25	21	15	10	75	44	31	78
7	AFC Wimbledon¶	46	11	4	8	30	25	10	8	5	34	25	21	12	13	64	50	14	75
8	Leyton Orient (R)	46	11	4	8	33	31	8	8	7	27	30	19	12	15	60	61	−1	69
9	Cambridge U	46	10	6	7	37	28	8	8	7	29	27	18	14	14	66	55	11	68
10	Carlisle U	46	10	6	7	38	35	7	10	6	29	27	17	16	13	67	62	5	67
11	Luton T	46	7	6	10	27	29	12	3	8	36	32	19	9	18	63	61	2	66
12	Mansfield T	46	7	10	6	34	26	10	3	10	27	27	17	13	16	61	53	8	64
13	Wycombe W	46	9	6	8	25	24	8	7	8	20	20	17	13	16	45	44	1	64
14	Exeter C	46	6	11	6	32	33	11	2	10	31	32	17	13	16	63	65	−2	64
15	Barnet (P)	46	13	3	7	37	27	4	8	11	30	41	17	11	18	67	68	−1	62
16	Hartlepool U	46	9	3	11	27	32	6	3	14	22	40	15	6	25	49	72	−23	51
17	Notts Co (R)	46	9	4	10	30	38	5	5	13	24	45	14	9	23	54	83	−29	51
18	Stevenage	46	6	8	9	23	32	5	7	11	29	35	11	15	20	52	67	−15	48
19	Yeovil T (R)	46	6	9	8	23	27	5	6	12	20	32	11	15	20	43	59	−16	48
20	Crawley T (R)	46	8	5	10	21	30	5	3	15	24	48	13	8	25	45	78	−33	47
21	Morecambe	46	7	3	13	36	47	5	7	11	33	44	12	10	24	69	91	−22	46
22	Newport Co	46	4	8	11	21	35	6	5	12	22	29	10	13	23	43	64	−21	43
23	Dagenham & R	46	3	5	15	17	37	5	5	13	29	44	8	10	28	46	81	−35	34
24	York C	46	6	7	10	33	41	1	6	16	18	46	7	13	26	51	87	−36	34

¶AFC Wimbledon promoted via play-offs.

SKY BET LEAGUE 2 LEADING GOALSCORERS 2015–16

	League	FA Cup	Capital One Cup	J Paint Trophy	Play-Offs	Total
Matty Taylor *(Bristol R)*	27	0	0	1	0	28
Kemar Roofe *(Oxford U)*	18	3	1	4	0	26
Jay Simpson *(Leyton Orient)*	25	0	0	0	0	25
John Akinde *(Barnet)*	23	0	1	0	0	24
Lyle Taylor *(AFC Wimbledon)*	20	0	0	1	2	23
Marc Richards *(Northampton T)*	15	1	1	1	0	18
Billy Kee *(Accrington S)*	17	0	0	0	0	17
Josh Windass *(Accrington S)*	15	1	0	0	1	17
Liam Sercombe *(Oxford U)*	14	2	1	0	0	17
Matt Green *(Mansfield T)*	16	0	0	0	0	16
Shaun Miller *(Morecambe)*	15	0	0	1	0	16
Jack Marriott *(Luton T)*	14	0	2	0	0	16
Jabo Ibehre *(Carlisle U)*	15	0	0	0	0	15
Billy Paynter *(Hartlepool U)*	14	0	1	0	0	15
Scott Boden *(Newport Co)*	13	1	1	0	0	15
Charlie Wyke *(Carlisle U)*	12	3	0	0	0	15
Danny Hylton *(Oxford U)*	12	0	1	1	0	14
Cameron McGeehan *(Luton T)*	12	0	1	1	0	14
Billy Bodin *(Bristol R)*	13	0	0	0	0	13
Luke Berry *(Cambridge U)*	12	1	0	0	0	13
Ben Williamson *(Cambridge U)*	12	0	0	0	0	12
Barry Corr *(Cambridge U)*	12	0	0	0	0	12
John-Joe O'Toole *(Northampton T)*	12	0	0	0	0	12
Jayden Stockley *(Exeter C)*	12	0	0	0	0	12
(Includes 2 league goals for Portsmouth.)						
Graham Carey *(Plymouth Arg)*	11	0	0	1	0	12

SKY BET LEAGUE 2 – RESULTS 2015–16

	AFC Wimbledon	Accrington S	Barnet	Bristol R	Cambridge U	Carlisle U	Crawley T	Dagenham & R	Exeter C	Hartlepool U	Leyton Orient	Luton T	Mansfield T	Morecambe	Newport Co	Northampton T	Notts Co	Oxford U	Plymouth Arg	Portsmouth	Stevenage	Wycombe W	Yeovil T	York C
AFC Wimbledon	—	0-0	2-0	0-0	1-2	1-0	1-0	0-1	2-1	2-0	1-0	4-1	3-1	2-5	1-0	1-1	2-1	1-2	0-2	0-1	1-2	1-1	2-3	2-1
Accrington S	3-4	—	2-2	1-0	1-1	1-1	4-1	3-1	4-2	3-1	1-0	1-1	1-0	2-2	2-2	1-1	3-2	1-3	2-1	1-3	0-0	1-1	2-1	3-0
Barnet	1-2	2-2	—	1-0	1-1	0-0	4-2	3-1	2-0	1-3	3-0	2-1	1-3	0-0	2-0	2-0	3-1	0-3	2-1	1-0	3-2	0-2	3-4	3-1
Bristol R	3-1	0-1	1-0	—	3-0	2-0	3-0	2-1	3-1	4-1	2-1	1-3	1-1	0-1	1-4	2-1	0-0	0-1	1-1	1-0	1-2	3-0	2-1	2-1
Cambridge U	1-4	2-0	3-2	1-2	—	0-0	0-3	1-0	1-0	1-1	1-1	1-2	1-1	7-0	3-0	1-4	3-1	0-0	2-2	1-3	1-0	1-0	3-0	3-1
Carlisle U	1-1	0-3	0-3	2-1	4-4	—	3-1	2-1	1-0	1-0	2-2	2-1	1-2	2-3	0-1	1-2	3-0	0-2	0-2	2-2	1-0	1-1	3-2	1-1
Crawley T	1-2	0-1	0-2	0-3	1-0	3-0	—	3-2	0-2	0-1	4-0	0-2	0-1	1-1	2-0	1-2	0-1	1-5	1-1	0-0	2-1	0-0	0-1	1-0
Dagenham & R	0-2	0-2	1-1	2-1	0-3	0-1	3-0	—	1-2	0-1	1-3	2-1	3-4	2-1	0-0	1-2	1-1	0-1	1-1	1-4	1-1	1-2	0-1	1-0
Exeter C	0-2	0-1	2-1	1-1	0-3	2-2	2-2	1-2	—	2-1	3-1	0-2	2-3	1-1	1-1	0-0	1-1	0-1	2-1	1-1	3-3	0-2	3-2	0-0
Hartlepool U	1-0	1-2	2-0	0-3	1-2	3-4	1-2	3-1	2-1	—	3-1	2-3	1-0	2-0	1-0	0-4	1-1	1-4	1-2	2-1	0-1	1-0	0-0	2-1
Leyton Orient	1-1	0-1	2-0	2-0	0-0	1-2	2-0	3-2	3-1	3-1	—	0-1	1-0	1-0	1-0	3-4	0-1	0-1	1-3	3-2	3-0	1-1	1-1	3-2
Luton T	2-0	2-3	1-1	0-1	1-1	2-3	0-1	1-0	4-1	0-0	1-1	—	1-0	1-0	1-0	2-2	5-0	2-3	1-2	1-2	2-1	0-2	1-1	1-1
Mansfield T	2-1	1-1	1-1	1-2	0-0	1-1	4-0	3-2	0-2	3-1	1-1	0-2	—	2-1	2-1	2-4	4-1	1-1	0-0	1-1	1-4	0-2	0-1	1-1
Morecambe	2-1	1-0	4-2	3-4	1-2	1-0	3-1	1-0	1-1	2-5	2-1	2-1	2-1	—	3-0	2-2	0-1	2-4	0-2	1-1	2-2	0-1	2-1	1-1
Newport Co	2-2	0-3	0-3	0-3	1-0	1-2	0-3	2-2	3-0	0-0	1-2	3-0	1-2	1-2	—	1-2	2-2	1-1	0-2	0-1	2-1	1-0	0-0	0-3
Northampton T	1-1	1-0	3-0	3-0	1-0	3-2	2-1	0-0	1-4	2-1	0-4	3-2	3-4	2-2	2-2	—	3-1	1-0	1-0	1-2	1-0	1-0	2-0	2-0
Notts Co	0-2	1-1	4-2	4-2	1-0	0-5	4-1	4-0	3-0	3-1	0-1	2-3	2-2	3-1	1-0	3-1	—	2-4	1-0	2-1	1-1	0-0	2-0	2-0
Oxford U	1-0	1-0	2-3	1-2	1-2	1-1	1-1	2-3	1-2	2-0	0-1	0-1	3-0	2-2	1-1	0-1	3-1	—	1-0	1-1	1-1	3-0	2-0	4-0
Plymouth Arg	1-2	1-0	2-1	1-1	1-2	4-1	3-0	3-0	1-2	5-0	1-1	0-0	0-0	0-0	1-0	1-2	1-0	2-2	—	1-2	3-2	0-1	1-0	3-2
Portsmouth	0-0	0-1	3-1	3-1	2-1	1-0	0-1	1-3	0-2	4-0	0-1	0-1	0-0	3-3	0-3	2-3	4-0	2-2	1-2	—	1-1	2-1	0-0	6-0
Stevenage	0-0	1-1	0-0	0-0	2-0	2-1	0-1	1-1	2-0	2-0	2-2	3-2	0-2	4-3	2-1	1-2	0-2	0-1	1-2	1-1	—	2-1	1-1	2-2
Wycombe W	1-2	0-1	1-1	1-0	1-0	1-1	2-0	2-2	0-2	2-1	1-0	0-1	1-0	0-2	0-2	1-1	2-2	1-5	2-1	1-0	2-1	—	0-0	3-0
Yeovil T	1-1	1-0	2-2	0-1	2-3	0-0	2-1	2-2	2-0	2-1	0-1	2-3	0-1	2-4	1-0	1-1	2-0	0-0	0-0	1-3	1-0	0-1	—	1-0
York C	1-3	1-5	1-1	1-4	2-2	2-2	2-2	2-2	2-0	1-2	1-1	2-3	1-2	2-1	0-1	1-2	2-1	1-2	1-2	2-1	2-1	1-1	1-0	—

FOOTBALL LEAGUE PLAY-OFFS 2015–16

SKY BET CHAMPIONSHIP SEMI-FINALS FIRST LEG

Friday, 13 May 2016

Sheffield W (1) 2 *(Wallace 45, Lee 73)*

Brighton & HA (0) 0   34,260

Sheffield W: (4411) Westwood; Hunt, Lees, Loovens, Pudil; Wallace (Marco Matias 68), Lee, Lopez (Nuhiu 63), Bannan; Forestieri; Hooper (Lucas Joao 83).
Brighton & HA: (442) Stockdale; Saltor, Goldson (Rosenior 40), Greer, Bong; Knockaert, Sidwell (Towell 50), Kayal, Skalak; Baldock, Hemed (Wilson 39).

Saturday, 14 May 2016

Derby Co (0) 0

Hull C (2) 3 *(Hernandez 30, Shackell 40 (og), Robertson 90)*   29,969

Derby Co: (433) Carson; Christie, Keogh, Shackell, Olsson; Bryson, Johnson (Butterfield 60), Hughes (Bent 87); Russell (Blackman 71), Martin, Ince.
Hull C: (4411) Jakupovic; Odubajo, Dawson, Davies, Robertson; Elmohamady, Livermore, Huddlestone, Snodgrass (Clucas 87); Diame (Bruce 90); Hernandez (Akpom 83).

SKY BET CHAMPIONSHIP SEMI-FINALS SECOND LEG

Monday, 16 May 2016

Brighton & HA (1) 1 *(Dunk 19)*

Sheffield W (1) 1 *(Wallace 28)*   27,272

Brighton & HA: (442) Stockdale; Saltor, Greer (Rosenior 77), Dunk, Bong; Knockaert, Sidwell, Kayal, Skalak; Wilson, Baldock (LuaLua 61).
Sheffield W: (4411) Westwood; Hunt, Lees, Loovens, Pudil; Wallace (Helan 66), Lee, Lopez (Hutchinson 46), Bannan; Forestieri; Hooper (Nuhiu 71).
Sheffield W won 3-1 on aggregate.

Tuesday, 17 May 2016

Hull C (0) 0

Derby Co (2) 2 *(Russell 7, Robertson 36 (og))*   20,470

Hull C: (4411) Jakupovic; Odubajo, Dawson, Davies, Robertson; Elmohamady, Huddlestone (Meyler 52), Livermore, Snodgrass (Maguire 90); Diame (Clucas 90); Hernandez.
Derby Co: (433) Carson; Christie, Keogh, Shackell, Olsson (Camara 90); Bryson, Hendrick, Hughes; Russell (Bent 83), Martin, Weimann (Ince 60).
Hull C won 3-2 on aggregate.

SKY BET CHAMPIONSHIP FINAL (at Wembley)

Saturday, 28 May 2016

Hull C (0) 1 *(Diame 72)*

Sheffield W (0) 0   70,189

Hull C: (4231) Jakupovic; Odubajo, Dawson, Davies, Robertson; Livermore, Huddlestone; Elmohamady, Diame (Maguire 89), Snodgrass (Clucas 82); Hernandez (Meyler 85).
Sheffield W: (4411) Westwood; Hunt, Lees, Loovens, Pudil (Nuhiu 76); Wallace (Helan 63), Hutchinson, Lee, Bannan; Forestieri; Hooper.
Referee: Bobby Madeley.

SKY BET LEAGUE ONE SEMI-FINALS FIRST LEG

Saturday, 14 May 2016

Barnsley (1) 3 *(Demetriou 45 (og), Winnall 54, 55)*

Walsall (0) 0   16,051

Barnsley: (442) Davies; Scowen, Roberts, Mawson, Williams G; Isgrove (Chapman 84), Brownhill, Hourihane, Hammill; Fletcher (White A 77), Winnall (Toney 67).
Walsall: (433) Etheridge; Demetriou, Downing, O'Connor, Henry; Morris M (Mantom 60), Chambers, Sawyers; Forde, Bradshaw (Hiwula 71), Lalkovic (Cook 84).

Sunday, 15 May 2016

Bradford C (1) 1 *(McMahon 13 (pen))*

Millwall (3) 3 *(Gregory 15, Morison 34, Martin J 45)* 19,241

Bradford C: (4411) Williams; Darby, McArdle, Clarke N, Meredith; McMahon (Anderson 82), Cullen, Evans, Reid; Morais (Davies 70); Proctor.
Millwall: (442) Archer; Edwards, Webster, Beevers, Martin J (Craig 71); Taylor, Abdou, Thompson, Ferguson (Williams 90); Morison, Gregory (O'Brien 66).

SKY BET LEAGUE ONE SEMI-FINALS SECOND LEG

Thursday, 19 May 2016

Walsall (0) 1 *(Cook 85)*

Barnsley (1) 3 *(Hammill 18, Fletcher 66, Brownhill 90)*   8022

Walsall: (352) Etheridge; Downing, O'Connor, Taylor (Cook 63); Demetriou, Sawyers, Chambers, Mantom, Henry; Hiwula (Lalkovic 72), Bradshaw (Forde 83).
Barnsley: (442) Davies; Scowen, Roberts, Mawson, Williams G; Isgrove, Brownhill, Hourihane, Hammill (Chapman 74); Winnall (Toney 70), Fletcher (McCourt 70).
Barnsley won 6-1 on aggregate.

City's captain, Michael Dawson, with the Championship Play-off final trophy following a 1-0 victory over Sheffield Wednesday at Wembley Stadium on 28 May. (Adam Davy/EMPICS Sport)

Lloyd Isgrove (far left) celebrates scoring Barnsley's third goal in their 3-1 defeat of Millwall in the League One Play-off final at Wembley Stadium on 29 May. (Action Images/John Sibley Livepic)

Friday, 20 May 2016

Millwall (1) 1 *(Gregory 34)*

Bradford C (1) 1 *(Proctor 44)*   16,301

Millwall: (442) Archer; Edwards, Webster (Craig 90), Beevers, Martin J; Taylor, Abdou, Thompson, Ferguson; Gregory (Williams 89), Morison.
Bradford C: (4411) Williams; Darby, McArdle, Clarke N (Davies 74), Meredith; McMahon (Anderson 67), Evans, Cullen (Thorpe 46), Reid; Clarke; Proctor.
Millwall won 4-2 on aggregate.

SKY BET LEAGUE ONE FINAL (at Wembley)
Sunday, 29 May 2016

Barnsley (2) 3 *(Fletcher 2, Hammill 19, Isgrove 74)*

Millwall (1) 1 *(Beevers 34)*   51,277

Barnsley: (442) Davies; Scowen, Roberts, Mawson, Williams G; Isgrove (Watkins 85), Brownhill, Hourihane, Hammill; Winnall, Fletcher (Toney 81).
Millwall: (442) Archer; Edwards (Williams 82), Craig, Beevers, Martin J (O'Brien 43); Taylor, Thompson (Onyedinma 76), Abdou, Ferguson; Gregory, Morison.
Referee: Stuart Attwell.

SKY BET LEAGUE TWO SEMI-FINALS FIRST LEG
Thursday, 12 May 2016

Portsmouth (1) 2 *(McNulty 3, Roberts 51 (pen))*

Plymouth Arg (2) 2 *(Matt 9, 19)*   17,622

Portsmouth: (4231) Allsop; Davies, Burgess, Barton, Stevens; Doyle, Hollands; Evans, Roberts, Bennett (Naismith 62); McNulty (McGurk 81).
Plymouth Arg: (4231) McCormick; Mellor, Nelson, Hartley, Sawyer; McHugh, Boateng (Purrington 80); Jervis, Carey, Wylde; Matt (Tanner 90).

Saturday, 14 May 2016

AFC Wimbledon (0) 1 *(Beere 90)*

Accrington S (0) 0   4870

AFC Wimbledon: (442) Roos; Fuller, Robinson, Charles, Kennedy; Rigg (Beere 86), Reeves, Bulman, Barcham; Elliott (Akinfenwa 59), Taylor (Azeez 77).

Accrington S: (4411) Etheridge; Pearson, Davies, Buxton, Hughes; Mingoia (McCartan 88), Conneely, Brown, McConville (Fosu 58); Windass; Kee (Gornell 79).

SKY BET LEAGUE TWO SEMI-FINALS SECOND LEG
Sunday, 15 May 2016

Plymouth Arg (0) 1 *(Hartley 90)*

Portsmouth (0) 0   15,011

Plymouth Arg: (4231) McCormick; Mellor, Nelson, Hartley, Sawyer; McHugh, Boateng; Jervis, Carey, Wylde (Tanner 75); Matt.
Portsmouth: (442) Allsop; Davies, Burgess, Barton, Stevens; Evans (McGurk 31), Hollands (Close 44), Doyle, Bennett (Chaplin 90); McNulty, Roberts.
Plymouth Arg won 3-2 on aggregate.

Wednesday, 18 May 2016

Accrington S (1) 2 *(Windass 39 (pen), Mingoia 59)*

AFC Wimbledon (0) 2 *(Akinfenwa 68, Taylor 104)*   4634

Accrington S: (4411) Etheridge; Pearson (Halliday 99), Davies, Hughes, Buxton; Mingoia (Gornell 106), Conneely, Brown, McCartan (Boco 90); Windass; Kee.
AFC Wimbledon: (442) Roos; Fuller, Robinson, Charles, Kennedy; Reeves, Rigg (Azeez 65), Bulman, Barcham (Beere 99); Elliott (Akinfenwa 46), Taylor.
aet; AFC Wimbledon won 3-2 on aggregate.

SKY BET LEAGUE TWO FINAL (at Wembley)
Monday, 30 May 2016

AFC Wimbledon (0) 2 *(Taylor 78, Akinfenwa 90 (pen))*

Plymouth Arg (0) 0   57,956

AFC Wimbledon: (442) Roos; Fuller, Robinson, Charles, Kennedy; Smith (Meades 69), Bulman, Reeves, Barcham; Taylor (Azeez 90), Elliott (Akinfenwa 77).
Plymouth Arg: (4231) McCormick; Mellor, Nelson, Hartley (Forster 86), Sawyer; McHugh, Boateng; Jervis (Tanner 68), Carey, Wylde (Reid 82); Matt.
Referee: Iain Williamson.

REVIEW OF THE SEASON 2015–16

Leicester City shocked the world of football with the most unexpected English league title win in history in 2015–16, lifting the Premier League trophy just 12 months after pulling off a stunning escape from the relegation zone.

Coached by the charismatic Claudio Ranieri, who had never won a top-flight title before, Leicester were 5,000/1 to win the Premier League at the start of the season but defied those odds thanks to the goal-scoring brilliance of Jamie Vardy (24 goals and a record-breaking 11-game scoring streak) and spellbinding style of Riyad Mahrez (17 goals, 11 assists).

The Foxes won the Premier League like no other champion had before, giving up possession and territory to hit their opponents with direct, lightning-quick counter attacks. When the pressure ramped up in the second half of the campaign their defence – led by skipper Wes Morgan – stood firm, while central midfielder N'Golo Kanté – widely considered the signing of the season – offered vital protection.

In the end Leicester were comfortable winners, finishing 10 points clear of runners-up Arsenal. The Gunners will no doubt look back on a season of what could have been, as injuries to key midfielders Santi Cazorla and Francis Coquelin, along with wasteful finishing in the final third, hampered their title chances.

In the stands at the Emirates there were protests about manager Arsene Wenger's methods but, for the twenty-first season in a row, the Frenchman once again steered the club to a finish above north London rivals Tottenham Hotspur, who spurned a second-place finish with a shock final-day 5-1 thrashing at already relegated Newcastle.

It was a disappointing end to what had been a hugely enjoyable season for Spurs fans, with Mauricio Pochettino leading his talented young squad into a title race few expected them to be ready for, and securing Champions League football for next season.

Jamie Vardy scores Leicester City's goal in their 1-1 draw with Manchester United at the King Power Stadium in November. (Mike Egerton/PA Archive/Press Association Images)

Harry Kane beats Petr Cech as Tottenham and Arsenal draw 1-1 at the Emirates Stadium in November.
(Tim Ireland/AP/Press Association Images)

Harry Kane and Dele Alli were their star performers, with the former silencing suggestions he'd be a one-season wonder with a Premier League-high 25 goals, while Alli scooped the young player of the year prizes and goal of the season gong for a wondrous flick-and-volley at Crystal Palace.

Manchester City grabbed fourth place on goal difference from neighbours Manchester United and also lifted the Capital One Cup by defeating Liverpool at Wembley. There was a run to the semi-finals of the Champions League, too. But, with Manuel Pellegrini to be replaced by Pep Guardiola this summer, the club and its supporters will be expecting more in 2016–17.

The same goes for United, where Louis van Gaal's 'three-year transition' project was cut short 12 months early, following a disappointing fifth-place finish.

The Dutchman did deliver an FA Cup win – the club's first major trophy success since the days of Sir Alex Ferguson – but, after United scored fewer Premier League goals than ever before, exited the Champions League at the group phase and were knocked out of the Europa League by Liverpool, the board decided to act. With Jose Mourinho named as Van Gaal's replacement, significant improvements are expected.

Southampton, meanwhile, enjoyed another impressive season under Ronald Koeman, finishing sixth, while West Ham United – who registered impressive wins over Arsenal, Manchester City and Liverpool (twice) – signed off in style from Upton Park with a thrilling 3-2 victory over Manchester United as they ended up seventh.

Brendan Rodgers' sacking made way for Jurgen Klopp's arrival at Liverpool and the charming German inspired the Reds – for the first time in 17 years playing without inspirational captain Steven Gerrard – to Capital One Cup and Europa League finals.

Mark Hughes delivered another top-10 finish for his increasingly stylish Stoke City but his old club Chelsea, who made the worst-ever Premier League title defence, only scraped into the upper half of the division under Guus Hiddink, following Mourinho's sacking in December.

There was also discontentment at Everton, where Roberto Martinez lost his job following the club's worst-ever points haul at Goodison Park, and Swansea City, who terminated Garry Monk's 11-year relationship with the club to halt a slide towards the relegation spots. Italian Francesco Guidolin stepped in to guarantee the Welsh side another season in the Premier League.

Top-flight survival wasn't enough for Watford, though, who ended Quique Sanchez Flores' tenure despite a thirteenth-place finish in their first season back in the Premier League. Odion Ighalo and Troy Deeney had formed a devastating 28-goal frontline pairing for the Hornets.

West Bromwich Albion striker Saido Berahino made headlines for different reasons as speculation about his future bubbled away for much of the season, but Tony Pulis oversaw another mid-table finish for the Baggies, while Crystal Palace slipped down the order after a strong start. They enjoyed a run to the final of the FA Cup, though, where they were edged out in extra-time by Manchester United.

Bournemouth achieved their ultimate aim of Premier League survival in their first-ever top-flight season, while Sunderland – who swapped Dick Advocaat for Sam Allardyce in October – also guaranteed another term among the elite at the expense of local rivals Newcastle United.

Rafa Benitez – who had started the season at Real Madrid – inspired an upturn at St James' Park but his replacement of much-maligned Steve McClaren came too late. After managing at the Bernabeu in 2015–16, the Spaniard will take Newcastle to Burton next season. Norwich City will also be back in the Championship in 2016–17, along with Aston Villa, who, for the first time, were relegated from the Premier League.

Villa finished rock-bottom with the third-lowest points total ever. A 19-game winless streak from August to January – a club record – left the club marooned and they never looked like producing a Leicester-style surge to survival.

West Ham's Dimitri Payet converts a direct free-kick as the Hammers draw 2-2 with Crystal Palace in one of the last games at Upton Park. (Reuters/Paul Childs Livepic)

Manchester United's Juan Mata scores an equaliser against Crystal Palace in the FA Cup final at Wembley Stadium on 21 May. United won 2-1 after extra time. (Reuters/Toby Melville Livepic)

Taking their place in the Premier League next season will be Championship winners Burnley, who make an immediate return to the top flight, Middlesbrough, who defeated Brighton on the last day to hold onto the final automatic promotion place on goal difference from their opponents, and play-off winners Hull City.

It will be League One football for Charlton Athletic, though, who endured protests and problems off the field as they slipped out of the second tier, finishing nine points behind a Rotherham United side revitalised by Neil Warnock's appointment in February. MK Dons and financially struggling Bolton Wanderers were also relegated.

Wigan make a swift return to the Championship after winning League One while Burton Albion pulled off a stunning second straight promotion by finishing as runners-up.

They'll be joined by Barnsley, who, despite being bottom of the League One table at Christmas, beat Millwall at Wembley in the play-off final – their second success of the season at the national stadium, after winning the Johnstone's Paint Trophy final against Oxford United.

At the other end, Blackpool, just five years after playing in the Premier League, were relegated to League Two, along with Colchester United and Crewe Alexandra, with Northampton Town (who defied financial problems to win the fourth-tier title with 99 points), Oxford United and Bristol Rovers (who sealed their second successive promotion in injury time on the final day) replacing them.

AFC Wimbledon will be in League One, too, as their remarkable 14-year rise through the leagues continues thanks to a play-off final triumph over Plymouth. They'll come up against MK Dons for the first time next season.

Dagenham & Redbridge and York City drop out of the Football League, though, after both finished nine points adrift of safety, with National League winners Cheltenham Town and Grimsby Town moving up.

Peter Smith

CUPS AND UPS AND DOWNS DIARY

AUGUST 2015
2   FA Community Shield: Arsenal 1 Chelsea 0.

OCTOBER 2015
4   Chelsea Champions of Women's Super League.

JANUARY 2016
23   Welsh TheWord League Cup Final: The New Saints 2 Denbigh T 0.

FEBRUARY 2016
28   Capital One Cup Final: Manchester C 1 Liverpool 1. *(aet; Manchester C won 3-1 on penalties)*

MARCH 2016
13   Scottish League Cup Presented by QTS Final: Ross Co 2 Hibernian 1.
26   Dunfermline Ath Champions of Scottish League 1 and promoted to Scottish Championship.

APRIL 2016
2   Alloa Ath relegated from Scottish Championship to Scottish League 1.
3   Johnstone's Paint Trophy Final: Barnsley 3 Oxford U 2.
5   Rangers Champions of Scottish Championship and promoted to Scottish Premiership.
9   Bolton W relegated from Football League Championship to Football League 1. Crewe Alex relegated from Football League 1 to Football League 2. Northampton T assured of automatic promotion from Football League 2 to Football League 1. East Stirlingshire finish bottom of Scottish League 2 and will enter a play-off against Edinburgh C to stay in the league. The New Saints Champions of Welsh Premier League.
10   Scottish Petrofac Training Cup Final: Rangers 4 Peterhead 0.
16   Aston Villa relegated from Premier League to Football League Championship. Dagenham & R relegated from Football League 2 to Vanarama National League. Northampton T Champions of Football League 2 and promoted to Football League 1. Cheltenham T champions of Vanarama National League and promoted to Football League 2. East Fife Champions of Scottish League 2 and promoted to Scottish League 1. Kidderminster H and Welling U relegated from Vanarama National League.
19   Charlton Ath relegated from Football League Championship to Football League 1.
23   Milton Keynes D relegated from Football League Championship to Football League 1. Colchester U relegated from Football League 1 to Football League 2. York C relegated from Football League 2 to Vanarama National League. Forfar Ath relegated from Scottish League 1 to Scottish League 2.
30   FC Halifax T relegated from Vanarama National League. Altrincham relegated from Vanarama National League.

MAY 2016
2   Leicester C Champions of Premier League. Dundee U relegated from Scottish Premiership to Scottish Championship.
3   Welsh FA Cup Final: The New Saints 2 Airbus UK Broughton 0.
7   Burnley Champions of Football League Championship and promoted to Premier League. Middlesbrough Runners-up of Football League Championship and promoted to Premier League. Oxford U Runners-up of Football League 2 and promoted to Football League 1. Bristol R third place in Football League 2 and promoted to Football League 1. Scottish League 2 Relegation Play-Off Final 1st leg: Edinburgh C 1 East Stirlingshire 1. Livingston relegated from Scottish Championship to Scottish League 1.
8   Celtic Champions of Scottish Premiership. Wigan Ath Champions of Football League 1 and promoted to Football League Championship. Burton Alb Runners-up of Football League 1 and promoted to Football League Championship. Doncaster R relegated from Football League 1 to Football League 2. Blackpool relegated from Football League 1 to Football League 2. Cowdenbeath relegated from Scottish League 1 to Scottish League 2.
10   Scottish League 1 Play-Off Final 1st leg: Clyde 1 Queen's Park 3. Newcastle U and Norwich C relegated from Premier League to Football League Championship. Scottish Championship Play-Off Final 1st leg: Stranraer 1 Ayr U 1.
14   Scottish League 1 Play-Off Final 2nd leg: Queen's Park 0, Clyde 1
(Queen's Park won 3-2 on aggregate and promoted to Scottish League 1)
Scottish League 2 Play-Off Final 2nd leg: East Stirlingshire 0, Edinburgh C 1. *(Edinburgh C won 2-1 on aggregate and promoted into Scottish League 2)*
15   Vanarama National League Play-Off Final: Grimsby T 3, Forest Green R 1. *(Grimsby T promoted to Football League 2)*. Scottish Championship Play-Off Final 2nd leg: Ayr U 0, Stranraer 0. *(1-1 on aggregate; Ayr U won 3-1 on penalties and promoted to Scottish Championship)*
18   Europa League Final: Sevilla 3, Liverpool 1.
19   Scottish Premier League Play-Off Final 1st leg: Falkirk 1, Kilmarnock 0.
21   FA Cup Final: Manchester U 2, Crystal Palace 1 *(aet)*. Scottish FA Cup Final: Hibernian 3, Rangers 2.
22   Scottish Premier League Play-Off Final 2nd leg: Kilmarnock 4, Falkirk 0. *(Kilmarnock won 4-1 on aggregate)* FA Trophy Final: Halifax T 1, Grimsby T 0. FA Vase Final: Morpeth T 4, Hereford U 1.
28   Champions League Final: Atletico Madrid 1, Real Madrid 1. *(aet; Real Madrid won 5-3 on penalties)* Football League Championship Play-Off Final: Hull C 1, Sheffield W 0. *(Hull C promoted to Premier League)*
29   Football League 1 Play-Off Final: Barnsley 3, Millwall 1. *(Barnsley promoted to Football League Championship)*
30   Football League 2 Play-Off Final: AFC Wimbledon 2, Plymouth Arg 0. *(AFC Wimbledon promoted to Football League 1)*

JULY 2016
10   Euro 2016 Final: France 0, Portugal 1 *aet*.

THE FA COMMUNITY SHIELD WINNERS 1908–2015

CHARITY SHIELD 1908–2001

Year	Match	Score
1908	Manchester U v QPR	1-1
Replay	Manchester U v QPR	4-0
1909	Newcastle U v Northampton T	2-0
1910	Brighton v Aston Villa	1-0
1911	Manchester U v Swindon T	8-4
1912	Blackburn R v QPR	2-1
1913	Professionals v Amateurs	7-2
1920	WBA v Tottenham H	2-0
1921	Tottenham H v Burnley	2-0
1922	Huddersfield T v Liverpool	1-0
1923	Professionals v Amateurs	2-0
1924	Professionals v Amateurs	3-1
1925	Amateurs v Professionals	6-1
1926	Amateurs v Professionals	6-3
1927	Cardiff C v Corinthians	2-1
1928	Everton v Blackburn R	2-1
1929	Professionals v Amateurs	3-0
1930	Arsenal v Sheffield W	2-1
1931	Arsenal v WBA	1-0
1932	Everton v Newcastle U	5-3
1933	Arsenal v Everton	3-0
1934	Arsenal v Manchester C	4-0
1935	Sheffield W v Arsenal	1-0
1936	Sunderland v Arsenal	2-1
1937	Manchester C v Sunderland	2-0
1938	Arsenal v Preston NE	2-1
1948	Arsenal v Manchester U	4-3
1949	Portsmouth v Wolverhampton W	1-1*
1950	English World Cup XI v FA Canadian Touring Team	4-2
1951	Tottenham H v Newcastle U	2-1
1952	Manchester U v Newcastle U	4-2
1953	Arsenal v Blackpool	3-1
1954	Wolverhampton W v WBA	4-4*
1955	Chelsea v Newcastle U	3-0
1956	Manchester U v Manchester C	1-0
1957	Manchester U v Aston Villa	4-0
1958	Bolton W v Wolverhampton W	4-1
1959	Wolverhampton W v Nottingham F	3-1
1960	Burnley v Wolverhampton W	2-2*
1961	Tottenham H v FA XI	3-2
1962	Tottenham H v Ipswich T	5-1
1963	Everton v Manchester U	4-0
1964	Liverpool v West Ham U	2-2*
1965	Manchester U v Liverpool	2-2*
1966	Liverpool v Everton	1-0
1967	Manchester U v Tottenham H	3-3*
1968	Manchester C v WBA	6-1
1969	Leeds U v Manchester C	2-1
1970	Everton v Chelsea	2-1
1971	Leicester C v Liverpool	1-0
1972	Manchester C v Aston Villa	1-0
1973	Burnley v Manchester C	1-0
1974	Liverpool v Leeds U	1-1
	Liverpool won 6-5 on penalties.	
1975	Derby Co v West Ham U	2-0
1976	Liverpool v Southampton	1-0
1977	Liverpool v Manchester U	0-0*
1978	Nottingham F v Ipswich T	5-0
1979	Liverpool v Arsenal	3-1
1980	Liverpool v West Ham U	1-0
1981	Aston Villa v Tottenham H	2-2*
1982	Liverpool v Tottenham H	1-0
1983	Manchester U v Liverpool	2-0
1984	Everton v Liverpool	1-0
1985	Everton v Manchester U	2-0
1986	Everton v Liverpool	1-1*
1987	Everton v Coventry C	1-0
1988	Liverpool v Wimbledon	2-1
1989	Liverpool v Arsenal	1-0
1990	Liverpool v Manchester U	1-1*
1991	Arsenal v Tottenham H	0-0*
1992	Leeds U v Liverpool	4-3
1993	Manchester U v Arsenal	1-1
	Manchester U won 5-4 on penalties.	
1994	Manchester U v Blackburn R	2-0
1995	Everton v Blackburn R	1-0
1996	Manchester U v Newcastle U	4-0
1997	Manchester U v Chelsea	1-1
	Manchester U won 4-2 on penalties.	
1998	Arsenal v Manchester U	3-0
1999	Arsenal v Manchester U	2-1
2000	Chelsea v Manchester U	2-0
2001	Liverpool v Manchester U	2-1

COMMUNITY SHIELD 2002–15

Year	Match	Score
2002	Arsenal v Liverpool	1-0
2003	Manchester U v Arsenal	1-1
	Manchester U won 4-3 on penalties.	
2004	Arsenal v Manchester U	3-1
2005	Chelsea v Arsenal	2-1
2006	Liverpool v Chelsea	2-1
2007	Manchester U v Chelsea	1-1
	Manchester U won 3-0 on penalties.	
2008	Manchester U v Portsmouth	0-0
	Manchester U won 3-1 on penalties.	
2009	Chelsea v Manchester U	2-2
	Chelsea won 4-1 on penalties.	
2010	Manchester U v Chelsea	3-1
2011	Manchester U v Manchester C	3-2
2012	Manchester C v Chelsea	3-2
2013	Manchester U v Wigan Ath	2-0
2014	Arsenal v Manchester C	3-0
2015	Arsenal v Chelsea	1-0

* Each club retained shield for six months.

THE FA COMMUNITY SHIELD 2015

Arsenal (1) 1, Chelsea (0) 0

at Wembley, Sunday 2 August 2015, attendance 85,437

Arsenal: (4-1-4-1): Cech; Bellerin, Mertesacker, Koscielny, Monreal; Coquelin; Ramsey, Cazorla, Oxlade-Chamberlain (Arteta 77), Ozil (Gibbs 81); Walcott (Giroud 65).
Scorer: Oxlade-Chamberlain 24.

Chelsea: (4-2-3-1): Courtois; Ivanovic, Cahill, Terry (Moses 82), Azpilicueta (Zouma 69); Ramires (Oscar 54), Matic; Willian, Fabregas, Hazard; Remy (Falcao 46).

Referee: Anthony Taylor.

ACCRINGTON STANLEY

FOUNDATION

Accrington Football Club, founder members of the Football League in 1888, were not connected with Accrington Stanley. In fact both clubs ran concurrently between 1891 when Stanley were formed and 1895 when Accrington FC folded. Actually Stanley Villa was the original name, those responsible for forming the club living in Stanley Street and using the Stanley Arms as their meeting place. They became Accrington Stanley in 1893. In 1894–95 they joined the Accrington & District League, playing at Moorhead Park. Subsequently they played in the North-East Lancashire Combination and the Lancashire Combination before becoming founder members of the Third Division (North) in 1921, two years after moving to Peel Park. In 1962 they resigned from the Football League, were wound up, re-formed in 1963, disbanded in 1966 only to restart as Accrington Stanley (1968), returning to the Lancashire Combination in 1970.

Wham Stadium, Livingstone Road, Accrington, Lancashire BB5 5BX.

Telephone: (0871) 434 1968. *Fax:* (01254) 356 951.

Ticket Office: (0871) 434 1968.

Website: www.accringtonstanley.co.uk

Email: info@accringtonstanley.co.uk

Ground Capacity: 5,070.

Record Attendance: 13,181 v Hull C, Division 3 (N), 28 September 1948 (at Peel Park); 4,634 v AFC Wimbledon, FL 2 Play-Offs, 18 May 2016 (at Wham Stadium).

Pitch Measurements: 101.5m × 65m (111yd × 71yd).

Chairman: Peter Marsden.

Managing Director: David Burgess.

Manager: John Coleman.

Assistant Manager: Jimmy Bell.

Physio: Ian Liversedge.

Colours: Red and white striped shirts, red shorts, red socks with white trim.

Year Formed: 1891, reformed 1968.

Turned Professional: 1919.

Club Nickname: 'The Reds', 'Stanley'.

Previous Names: 1891, Stanley Villa; 1893, Accrington Stanley.

Grounds: 1891, Moorhead Park; 1897, Bell's Ground; 1919, Peel Park; 1970, Crown Ground (renamed Interlink Express Stadium, Fraser Eagle Stadium, Store First Stadium 2013, Wham Stadium 2015).

First Football League Game: 27 August 1921, Division 3 (N), v Rochdale (a) L 3-6 – Tattersall; Newton, Baines, Crawshaw, Popplewell, Burkinshaw, Oxley, Makin, Green (1), Hosker (2), Hartles.

Record League Victory: 8–0 v New Brighton, Division 3 (N), 17 March 1934 – Maidment; Armstrong (pen), Price, Dodds, Crawshaw, McCulloch, Wyper, Lennox (2), Cheetham (4), Leedham (1), Watson.

HONOURS

League Champions: Conference – 2005–06.
Runners-up: Division 3N – 1954–55, 1957–58.
FA Cup: 4th rd – 1927, 1937, 1959, 2010.
League Cup: never past 2nd rd.

sky SPORTS FACT FILE

The original Accrington Stanley club considered applying for Football League membership back in 1906. A proposal was submitted to the club's annual general meeting that year but was rejected by 172 votes to 124.

Record Cup Victory: 7–0 v Spennymoor U, FA Cup 2nd rd, 8 December 1938 – Tootill; Armstrong, Whittaker, Latham, Curran, Lee, Parry (2), Chadwick, Jepson (3), McLoughlin (2), Barclay.

Record Defeat: 1–9 v Lincoln C, Division 3 (N), 3 March 1951.

Most League Points (2 for a win): 61, Division 3 (N), 1954–55.

Most League Points (3 for a win): 85, FL 2, 2015–16.

Most League Goals: 96, Division 3 (N), 1954–55.

Highest League Scorer in Season: George Stewart, 35, Division 3 (N), 1955–56; George Hudson, 35, Division 4, 1960–61.

Most League Goals in Total Aggregate: George Stewart, 136, 1954–58.

Most League Goals in One Match: 5, Billy Harker v Gateshead, Division 3 (N), 16 November 1935; George Stewart v Gateshead, Division 3 (N), 27 November 1954.

Most Capped Player: Romuald Boco, 19 (48), Benin.

Most League Appearances: Andy Procter, 264, 2006–12, 2014–15.

Youngest League Player: Ian Gibson, 15 years 358 days, v Norwich C, 23 March 1959.

Record Transfer Fee Received: £50,000 (rising to £250,000) from Blackpool for Brett Ormerod, March 1997.

Record Transfer Fee Paid: £85,000 (rising to £150,000) to Swansea C for Ian Craney, January 2008.

Football League Record: 1921 Original Member of Division 3 (N); 1958–60 Division 3; 1960–62 Division 4; 2006– FL 2.

LATEST SEQUENCES

Longest Sequence of League Wins: 7, 27.12.1954 – 5.2.1955.

Longest Sequence of League Defeats: 9, 8.3.1930 – 21.4.1930.

Longest Sequence of League Draws: 4, 10.9.1927 – 27.9.1927.

Longest Sequence of Unbeaten League Matches: 14, 15.3.2011 – 6.8.2011.

Longest Sequence Without a League Win: 18, 17.9.1938 – 31.12.1938.

Successive Scoring Runs: 22 from 14.11.1936.

Successive Non-scoring Runs: 5 from 15.3.1930.

MANAGERS

William Cronshaw *c.*1894
John Haworth 1897–1910
Johnson Haworth *c.*1916
Sam Pilkingson 1919–24
  (*Tommy Booth p-m 1923–24*)
Ernie Blackburn 1924–32
Amos Wade 1932–35
John Hacking 1935–49
Jimmy Porter 1949–51
Walter Crook 1951–53
Walter Galbraith 1953–58
George Eastham snr 1958–59
Harold Bodle 1959–60
James Harrower 1960–61
Harold Mather 1962–63
Jimmy Hinksman 1963–64
Terry Neville 1964–65
Ian Bryson 1965
Danny Parker 1965–66
Gerry Keenan
Gary Pierce
Dave Thornley
Phil Staley
Eric Whalley
Stan Allen 1995–96
Tony Greenwood 1996–98
Billy Rodaway 1998
Wayne Harrison 1998–99
John Coleman 1999–2012
Paul Cook 2012
Leam Richardson 2012–13
James Beattie 2013–14
John Coleman September 2014–

TEN YEAR LEAGUE RECORD

		P	W	D	L	F	A	Pts	Pos
2006-07	FL 2	46	13	11	22	70	81	50	20
2007-08	FL 2	46	16	3	27	49	83	51	17
2008-09	FL 2	46	13	11	22	42	59	50	16
2009-10	FL 2	46	18	7	21	62	74	61	15
2010-11	FL 2	46	18	19	9	73	55	73	5
2011-12	FL 2	46	14	15	17	54	66	57	14
2012-13	FL 2	46	14	12	20	51	68	54	18
2013-14	FL 2	46	14	15	17	54	56	57	15
2014-15	FL 2	46	15	11	20	58	77	56	17
2015-16	FL 2	46	24	13	9	74	48	85	4

DID YOU KNOW ?

Centre-forward Harry Howell, who made three appearances for Accrington Stanley in the 1922–23 season, was a talented cricketer who played for Warwickshire and England. He was a member of the tour party to Australia for the 1921–22 Ashes series, playing in three of the Tests.

ACCRINGTON STANLEY – FOOTBALL LEAGUE TWO 2015–16 LEAGUE RECORD

Match No.	Date	Venue	Opponents	Result	H/T Score	Lg Pos.	Goalscorers	Attendance
1	Aug 8	H	Luton T	D	1-1	0-0	10	Windass (pen) [61]	2359
2	15	A	Morecambe	L	0-1	0-1	18		1865
3	18	H	Mansfield T	W	1-0	1-0	12	McConville [33]	1073
4	22	A	Notts Co	D	1-1	0-0	13	Crooks [90]	3825
5	29	H	Northampton T	D	1-1	0-1	15	Windass (pen) [55]	1526
6	Sept 5	A	Portsmouth	D	0-0	0-0	15		15,745
7	12	A	Bristol R	W	1-0	0-0	10	Kee [68]	6351
8	19	H	Exeter C	W	4-2	2-0	6	Windass 2 [33, 34], Mingoia [61], Kee [63]	1403
9	26	A	Crawley T	W	3-0	2-0	5	Windass (pen) [45], Crooks [45], Kee [89]	1659
10	29	H	Yeovil T	W	2-1	1-1	4	Windass [8], Crooks [54]	1309
11	Oct 3	A	Oxford U	L	1-3	0-1	7	Crooks [70]	1755
12	10	A	Barnet	W	2-1	1-1	5	Togwell (og) [23], McConville [62]	2229
13	17	H	Plymouth Arg	L	0-1	0-0	6		7865
14	20	H	AFC Wimbledon	L	3-4	3-3	8	Kee 2 [5, 10], McConville [36]	1315
15	24	H	Dagenham & R	W	3-1	2-0	7	Conneely [2], Pearson [45], Windass [49]	1104
16	31	A	Leyton Orient	W	1-0	1-0	4	Windass [25]	4701
17	Nov 14	H	Newport Co	D	2-2	0-0	4	Kee [58], Crooks [77]	1552
18	21	A	Cambridge U	W	3-2	1-2	4	McConville [29], Davies [48], Windass (pen) [53]	5107
19	28	A	York C	W	5-1	2-0	4	Pearson [15], Kee 2 [33, 72], Windass (pen) [61], McCartan [88]	2825
20	Dec 19	A	Stevenage	D	1-1	0-1	6	Kee (pen) [85]	2818
21	28	A	Northampton T	L	0-1	0-0	8		5269
22	Jan 2	A	Mansfield T	W	3-2	1-1	7	Mingoia [4], Kee [72], Gornell [85]	3271
23	19	H	Hartlepool U	W	3-1	2-0	6	Buxton [23], McCartan 2 [45, 58]	1211
24	23	A	Exeter C	L	1-2	1-1	6	McCartan [3]	3669
25	30	H	Bristol R	W	1-0	0-0	5	McConville [69]	2027
26	Feb 6	A	Carlisle U	L	0-2	0-2	8		4709
27	13	H	Crawley T	W	4-1	0-1	6	Kee [48], Pearson [73], Conneely [87], Mingoia [90]	1374
28	16	H	Carlisle U	D	1-1	0-0	4	Gornell [58]	2080
29	20	A	Oxford U	W	2-1	0-1	4	Kee [46], Brown [88]	6792
30	23	H	Notts Co	W	3-2	2-0	4	Kee [14], Boco 2 [21, 51]	1215
31	27	H	Barnet	D	2-2	0-0	4	Kee [57], Crooks [74]	1416
32	Mar 1	A	Yeovil T	L	0-1	0-0	4		3207
33	5	A	AFC Wimbledon	D	0-0	0-0	4		3627
34	8	H	Portsmouth	L	1-3	0-3	6	McCartan [83]	1841
35	12	H	Plymouth Arg	W	2-1	0-1	5	Kee (pen) [85], McCartan [90]	2044
36	16	H	Wycombe W	D	1-1	1-0	5	McCartan [45]	1403
37	19	A	Dagenham & R	W	1-0	0-0	5	Kee [83]	1345
38	25	A	Leyton Orient	W	1-0	0-0	5	Brown [51]	2783
39	28	H	Newport Co	W	2-0	2-0	4	Kee [35], Windass [37]	2218
40	Apr 2	H	Cambridge U	D	1-1	0-0	5	Fosu [77]	2185
41	9	A	Luton T	W	2-0	0-0	3	Brown [47], Gornell [84]	7467
42	16	H	Morecambe	D	2-2	1-1	4	Windass 2 (1 pen) [21, 48 (p)]	2609
43	19	A	Hartlepool U	W	2-1	2-1	2	Conneely [3], Fosu [45]	3445
44	23	H	York C	W	3-0	1-0	2	Fosu [35], Windass 2 [69, 90]	2222
45	30	A	Wycombe W	W	1-0	0-0	2	Hughes [78]	4041
46	May 7	H	Stevenage	D	0-0	0-0	4		4386

Final League Position: 4

GOALSCORERS

League (74): Kee 17 (2 pens), Windass 15 (6 pens), McCartan 7, Crooks 6, McConville 5, Brown 3, Conneely 3, Fosu 3, Gornell 3, Mingoia 3, Pearson 3, Boco 2, Buxton 1, Davies 1, Hughes 1, own goal 1.
FA Cup (3): Crooks 1, McConville 1, Windass 1 (pen).
Capital One Cup (2): Crooks 1, Gornell 1.
Johnstone's Paint Trophy (1): Bruna 1.
League Two Play-Offs (2): Mingoia 1, Windass 1 (pen).

Mooney J 25+1	Pearson M 46	Winnard D 14+1	Davies T 31+1	Buxton A 25+3	Crooks M 32	Conneely S 46	Mingoia P 46	Windass J 30	McConville S 40+2	Gornell T 8+12	Kee B 39+6	Barry A 2+6	Wright J 19+1	Wakefield L 7+5	Morgan A —+2	Bruna G —+3	Procter A 1+10	McCartan S 10+17	Mohamed K —+3	Halliday B 31+1	Carver M —+2	Etheridge R 21	Boco R 6+5	Brown S 8+5	Shaw B —+4	Hughes M 15	Fosu T 4+4	Match No.
1	2	3	4	5^3	6	7	8	9	10^2	11	12	13	14															1
1	5	4	3		7	8^2	6	10	13	11^1	12	9^3		2	14													2
1	2	4	3	5		7	6	10^2	9^1		11	12				13												3
1	2	4	3	5	7	9^1	6	10^2	12	11	13	8^3		14														4
1	2	3	4	5^1	7	6^2	8	9	10	11	12	13		14														5
1	2	3	4	5	7^2	6	8	9	10	11^1	12						13											6
1	2	3	4	5	7	8^3	6	10^1	9^2	11	13									14	12							7
1	5	4	3	2	10^1	7^2	6	8	9		11	13								12								8
1	5	4^1		2	10	7	6	8	9		11		3	12														9
1	4			5	8	7	6	10	9		11		3	2														10
1	4	12		5	8	7	6	10^1	9^2 14	11		3^3	2				13											11
1	3	4		5	7	8	6^1	10^2	9	13	11		2							12								12
1	3	4			8	7	6^2	10^1	9	13	11	5	2							12								13
1	5	4^1			8	6	7	9	11^1	10	3				13	12^3 14				2								14
1	4			5^1	6	7	8	9	10		11	12^2	3						13	2								15
1	4	5			6	7	8	9^1	10		11	3					12			2								16
1	5	4^1	3		7	8	6	11	9	10	12									2								17
1	5		4	8^2	7	6	10^1	9	14	11^3	3				13	12				2								18
1	3		4	7	8	6	11^2	9	13	10^1	5						12			2								19
1	2		3	7	4	6	8^1	11	12	10	5						13			12						9^2		20
1	5		3	7	8	6^1	10	9	13	11	4						12			2^2								21
1	2		4	14	8	7	9^1	10^2	6^3	13	11	3					12			5								22
1	3		5	8	7	6	9^2	12	11^3	4			13	14	10^1			2										23
1	3		5	6	7	8	10^2	12	11	4					9^1			2	13									24
	3		5	6	7	8	10	11	4						9		2	1										25
	3		5	7^3	8	6	9	11	4	12				10^2	2^1	1	13	14										26
	3		5	8^2	7	6	9^1	11	4			13	10^4	2	1	12												27
	4^1	12	5^1	6	8	10	13	11	3		7			2	1	9^2												28
5	3^1		8	6	9	11	4^1	12	13				2	1	9^2													29
	3	5	6	7	8	10	11	13				2	1	9^2	12	4^1												30
	5	4	7	6	8	10	11					2	1	9	3													31
	5	4	14	6	7	8	9^3	11				12	2^2	13	1	10^1	3											32
12	3	4	7	8	6	9	11		2			10^1	5	1^1														33
1	4	3	7	6^3	8^1	10^2	11	2				9	5			13	12	14										34
2	4	5	8^1	7	6	9^2	11					13				10^3	12	14	3									35
2	3	5^1	6	8	10^1	11				13	7	12	1			9^2	14	4										36
	5	4	8	6	7	11				13	9^2	2	1	12	10^1	3												37
	5	3	6	8	10	11				9	2	1	7	4														38
	5	4	7	10	8^2	9^1	11				2	1	12	6		3	13											39
	2	4	14	8	6^3	10^1	9^2	11				12	3	1		5		7	13									40
	5	3	7	8	9	10^1	11					2	1	6		4	12											41
	5	4	8	6^3	10	9^2	11				12	14	2	1		7^1	3	13										42
	2	4	5	8	6	10	11					12	7	1		3	9^1											43
	2	3	5	8	6	10	11					12	7	1		4	9^1											44
	2	3	5	6	8^1	9	11					12	7	1		4	10											45
	2	3	5^2	7	6	10	14	11				13	8^1	1		12	4	9^3										46

FA Cup

First Round	York C	(h)	3-2
Second Round	Portsmouth	(a)	0-1

Capital One Cup

First Round	Hull C	(h)	2-2

(aet; Hull C won 4-3 on penalties)

Johnstone's Paint Trophy

First Round	Bury	(h)	1-2

League Two Play-Offs

Semi-Final 1st leg	AFC Wimbledon	(a)	0-1
Semi-Final 2nd leg	AFC Wimbledon	(h)	2-2

(aet; AFC Wimbledon won 3-2 on aggregate)

AFC WIMBLEDON

FOUNDATION

While the history of AFC Wimbledon is straightforward since it was a new club formed in 2002, there were in effect two clubs operating for two years with Wimbledon connections. The other club was MK Dons, of course. In August 2001, the Football League had rejected the existing Wimbledon's application to move to Milton Keynes. In May 2002, they rejected local sites and were given permission to move by an independent commission set up by the Football League. AFC Wimbledon was founded in the summer of 2002 and held its first trials on Wimbledon Common. In subsequent years, there was considerable debate over the rightful home of the trophies obtained by the former Wimbledon football club. In October 2006, an agreement was reached between Milton Keynes Dons FC, its Supporters Association, the Wimbledon Independent Supporters Association and the Football Supporters Federation to transfer such trophies and honours to the London Borough of Merton.

The Cherry Red Records Stadium, Kingsmeadow, Jack Goodchild Way, 422a Kingston Road, Kingston-upon-Thames, Surrey KT1 3PB.

Telephone: (0208) 547 3528.

Fax: (0808) 2800 816.

Website: www.afcwimbledon.co.uk

Email: info@afcwimbledon.co.uk

Ground Capacity: 5,027.

Record Attendance: 4,870 v Accrington S, FL 2 Play-Offs, 14 May 2016.

Pitch Measurements: 104m × 66m (113.5yd × 72yd).

President: Dickie Guy.

Chief Executive: Erik Samuelson.

Manager: Neal Ardley.

Assistant Coach: Neil Cox.

First-Team Coach: Simon Bassey.

Physio: Stuart Douglas.

Club Nickname: 'The Dons'.

Colours: Blue shirts with thin black stripes and yellow trim, black shorts with yellow trim, blue socks with yellow trim.

Year Formed: 2002.

Turned Professional: 2002.

HONOURS

League: Runners-up: FL 2 – (7th) 2015–16 *(promoted via play-offs)*; Conference – (2nd) 2010–11 *(promoted via play-offs)*.

FA Cup: 3rd rd – 2015.

League Cup: never past 1st rd.

sky SPORTS FACT FILE

AFC Wimbledon are the youngest team in membership of the Premier and Football Leagues, having been established only in 2002. Despite this it took the Dons only nine years to gain a place in the Football League.

Grounds: 2002, Kingsmeadow (renamed The Cherry Red Records Stadium).

First Football League Game: 6 August 2011, FL 2 v Bristol R (h) L 2–3 – Brown; Hatton, Gwillim (Bush), Porter (Minshull), Stuart (1), Johnson B, Moore L, Wellard, Jolley (Ademeno (1)), Midson, Yussuff.

Record League Victory: 4–0 v Burton Alb, FL 2, 24 March 2012 – Brown; Hatton, Gwillim, Moncur (1), Mitchel-King, Balkestein, Moore S (1), Knott (Wellard), Jolley, Midson, Moore L (1) (Harrison (1)); 4-0 v Portsmouth, FL 2, 16 November 2012 – Worner; Bennett, Fuller, Frampton (2), Kennedy, Sweeney (Moore L), Moore S (1), Porter, Pell, Smith (1), Mohamed (Francomb).

Record Cup Victory: 4–3 v York City, FA Cup 1st rd replay, 12 November 2012 – Brown; Fenlon (Osano), Mambo, Mitchel-King, Cummings, Jolley, Gregory, Johnson (Harrison (1)), Yussuff (Long), Midson (1), Strutton (2).

Record Defeat: 2–6 v Burton Alb, FL 2, 25 August 2012.

Most League Points (3 for a win): 75, FL 2, 2015–16.

Most League Goals: 64, FL 2, 2015–16.

Highest League Scorer in Season: Jack Midson, 18, 2011–12.

Most League Goals in Total Aggregate: Kevin Cooper, 107, 2002–04.

Most Capped Player: Shane Smeltz, 5 (51), New Zealand.

Most League Appearances: Sammy Moore, 139, 2011–15.

Youngest League Player: Ben Harrison, 17 years 195 days v Accrington S, 13 September 2014.

Record Transfer Fee Received: £120,000 from Coventry C for Chris Hussey, January 2010.

Record Transfer Fee Paid: £25,000 (in excess of) to Stevenage for Byron Harrison, January 2012.

Football League Record: 2011 Promoted from Conference Premier; 2011– FL 2.

MANAGERS

Terry Eames 2002–04
Nicky English *(Caretaker)* 2004
Dave Anderson 2004–07
Terry Brown 2007–12
Neal Ardley October 2012–

LATEST SEQUENCES

Longest Sequence of League Wins: 5, 2.4.2016 – 23.4.2016.

Longest Sequence of League Defeats: 6, 26.11.2011 – 2.1.2012.

Longest Sequence of League Draws: 3, 12.1.2013 – 2.2.2013.

Longest Sequence of Unbeaten League Matches: 6, 19.12.2016 – 23.1.2016.

Longest Sequence Without a League Win: 12, 15.10.2011 – 2.1.2012.

Successive Scoring Runs: 10 from 28.12.2016.

Successive Non-scoring Runs: 3 from 24.2.2015.

TEN YEAR LEAGUE RECORD

		P	W	D	L	F	A	Pts	Pos
2006-07	Isth PR	42	21	15	6	76	37	75	5
2007-08	Isth PR	42	22	9	11	81	47	75	3
2008-09	Conf S	42	26	10	6	86	36	88	1
2009-10	Conf P	44	18	10	16	61	47	64	8
2010-11	Conf P	46	27	9	10	83	47	90	2
2011-12	FL 2	46	15	9	22	62	78	54	16
2012-13	FL 2	46	14	11	21	54	76	53	20
2013-14	FL 2	46	14	14	18	49	57	53*	20
2014-15	FL 2	46	14	16	16	54	60	58	15
2015-16	FL 2	46	21	12	13	64	50	75	7

* 3 pts deducted.

DID YOU KNOW

AFC Wimbledon have appeared in the final of the Supporters Direct Cup (for supporter-owned clubs) a record six times including the first four finals. Their most recent appearance was in July 2009 when they defeated FC United of Manchester 2-0 at Kingsmeadow.

AFC WIMBLEDON – FOOTBALL LEAGUE TWO 2015–16 LEAGUE RECORD

Match No.	Date	Venue	Opponents	Result	H/T Score	Lg Pos.	Goalscorers	Attendance
1	Aug 8	H	Plymouth Arg	L	0-2	0-1	18		4805
2	15	A	Crawley T	W	2-1	0-1	11	Akinfenwa [51], Barcham [76]	2988
3	18	H	Cambridge U	L	1-2	1-0	13	Elliott [12]	4114
4	22	A	Carlisle U	D	1-1	1-0	14	Barcham [36]	5949
5	29	A	Exeter C	W	2-1	1-1	12	Francomb [28], Azeez [82]	3803
6	Sept 5	A	Mansfield T	D	1-1	1-1	13	Elliott [6]	3042
7	12	A	Yeovil T	D	1-1	0-1	13	Akinfenwa [79]	3687
8	19	H	Notts Co	W	2-1	0-1	12	Bulman [85], Akinfenwa [90]	3962
9	26	A	Luton T	L	0-2	0-0	15		8415
10	29	H	Northampton T	D	1-1	1-1	16	Azeez [24]	3525
11	Oct 3	H	Barnet	W	2-0	1-0	13	Taylor [7], Rigg [90]	4068
12	10	A	Oxford U	L	0-1	0-0	14		6301
13	17	H	Morecambe	L	2-5	1-3	16	Barcham [3], Akinfenwa [49]	3679
14	20	A	Accrington S	W	4-3	3-3	13	Bulman 2 [19, 44], Taylor 2 [25, 64]	1315
15	24	A	York C	W	3-1	1-0	12	Azeez [15], Taylor [65], Elliott [85]	3000
16	31	H	Hartlepool U	W	2-0	2-0	10	Kennedy [18], Taylor [28]	3638
17	Nov 15	A	Portsmouth	D	0-0	0-0	9		15,892
18	21	H	Wycombe W	D	1-1	0-0	8	Azeez [90]	4482
19	24	H	Dagenham & R	L	0-1	0-0	11		3557
20	28	A	Leyton Orient	D	1-1	0-1	11	Akinfenwa [80]	6024
21	Dec 12	A	Stevenage	L	1-2	1-0	13	Francomb [43]	3846
22	19	A	Newport Co	D	2-2	0-2	14	Taylor 2 [46, 79]	2798
23	26	H	Bristol R	D	0-0	0-0	13		4668
24	28	A	Exeter C	W	2-0	2-0	12	Elliott [17], Taylor [31]	5072
25	Jan 2	A	Cambridge U	W	4-1	1-1	10	Robinson [10], Taylor [64], Meades [76], Azeez [86]	5754
26	16	H	Mansfield T	W	3-1	0-1	8	Taylor [49], Meades [78], Azeez [87]	4089
27	23	A	Notts Co	W	2-0	1-0	7	Elliott [8], Barcham [83]	5301
28	30	H	Yeovil T	L	2-3	2-2	10	Fitzpatrick [9], Elliott [29]	4525
29	Feb 13	H	Luton T	W	4-1	2-0	10	Marriott (og) [23], Taylor 2 [25, 49], Rigg [47]	4439
30	20	A	Barnet	W	2-1	0-0	10	Taylor [46], Azeez [85]	3289
31	23	H	Carlisle U	W	1-0	0-0	5	Robinson [53]	3526
32	27	H	Oxford U	L	1-2	1-1	8	Barcham [33]	4628
33	Mar 1	A	Northampton T	D	1-1	0-1	8	Taylor [62]	5124
34	5	H	Accrington S	D	0-0	0-0	7		3627
35	8	A	Bristol R	L	1-3	0-2	7	Meades [52]	7778
36	12	A	Morecambe	L	1-2	0-0	9	Francomb [90]	1477
37	19	H	York C	W	2-1	0-1	9	Murphy [68], Reeves [90]	3883
38	25	A	Hartlepool U	L	0-1	0-1	9		4365
39	Apr 2	A	Wycombe W	W	2-1	1-0	9	Taylor 2 (1 pen) [12, 66 (p)]	4560
40	9	A	Plymouth Arg	W	2-1	1-0	7	Taylor [30], Akinfenwa [88]	8852
41	16	H	Crawley T	W	1-0	0-0	7	Robinson [83]	4356
42	19	H	Dagenham & R	W	2-0	1-0	7	Taylor 2 [33, 61]	2027
43	23	H	Leyton Orient	W	1-0	1-0	7	Taylor [17]	4732
44	26	H	Portsmouth	L	0-1	0-1	7		4799
45	30	A	Stevenage	D	0-0	0-0	7		4011
46	May 7	H	Newport Co	W	1-0	0-0	7	Olusanya (pen) [80]	4427

Final League Position: 7

GOALSCORERS

League (64): Taylor 20 (1 pen), Azeez 7, Akinfenwa 6, Elliott 6, Barcham 5, Bulman 3, Francomb 3, Meades 3, Robinson 3, Rigg 2, Fitzpatrick 1, Kennedy 1, Murphy 1, Olusanya 1 (1 pen), Reeves 1, own goal 1.
FA Cup (1): Kennedy 1.
Capital One Cup (0).
Johnstone's Paint Trophy (2): Azeez 1, Taylor 1.
League Two Play-Offs (5): Akinfenwa 2 (1 pen), Taylor 2, Beere 1.

Shea J 21	Fuller B 45	Robinson P 44	Osborne K 21 + 2	Francomb G 36 + 4	Reeves J 39 + 1	Bulman D 39 + 3	Barcham A 31 + 2	Taylor L 38 + 4	Akinfenwa A 20 + 18	Elliott T 25 + 14	Rigg S 18 + 21	Azeez A 9 + 33	Meades J 40 + 1	Kennedy C 10 + 9	Beere T 1 + 1	Nightingale W 3 + 1	Kaja E — + 2	Oakley G — + 1	Ajayi S 5	Wilson B 8	Toonga C 2 + 2	Fitzpatrick D 2 + 2	Roos K 17	Sweeney R 10	Smith C 7 + 3	Murphy R 6 + 1	Charles D 9	Olusanya T — + 1	Match No.
1	2	3	4	5	6	7^2	8	9^1	10^3	11	12	13	14																1
1	2	3	4	5	6	12	8	9^1	10^1	11^2	14	13	7																2
1	2	4	3	14	8	7	6	12	10	11^1	9^3	13		5^2															3
1	2	4	3	6	8	7^2	9	11^3	13	10^1			14	5	12														4
1	2	3	4	6	8			9^1	12	11^3	10^1	14	13	5		7													5
1	2	4	3^1	6	8	7		13^4	11^2	10^3	9		14	5			12												6
1	2	3			9	8	7	6^1		10	11^2	13	12	5			4												7
1	2	4	12	6	7	8	9^3		10	11^2	13	14		5				3^1											8
1	2	3	4^4	6	8	7^2	9^1		11		12	10^1		5		13	14												9
1	2	4		6^2	8	7		9	12	10^1		13	11^3	5		14		3											10
1	2	3		6^1	8	7		9	10^3	12		13	11	5^2	14			4											11
1	2	3	12		7	6	8	11^3	13	14	9	10^1	4	5^2															12
1	2	3		12	8	7		9^2	10	11	13	6^1		4			5												13
	2	3		9	8	7		10^1	11^2	12	6	13	4				5	1											14
	2	3	4	6	8	7		11^1		13	9^2	10^3	5	12			1	14											15
	2	3	4	8	7^3	6		10^1	12	13		11^1	5	9			1	14											16
	2	3	4	6	8	7		10	12		9^2	11^1	5	13			1												17
	2	3	4	9		6		10	11^1	14	8^2	12	5	13			1	7^3											18
	2	3	4	6^3	8	7		11	10^2	13	12	14	5	9^1			1												19
	2	3	4	6	8	7^1		11	10	13	9^2	12	5				1												20
		4	3	6	8	7		10	11^2	13	9^1	12	2	5			1												21
1	2	3	4^3	5		6	8	11	12	13		10^2	7								9^1	14							22
1	2	3^4	4	6	8	7	9^3	10^2	11^1	12	14		5	13															23
1	2	3	4	6	8	7	14	10^1	12	11^2	9^3	13	5																24
1	2	4	3	6	8	7	9	11^3	10^2	12	14	13	5																25
1	2	3	4		7	8	11^2	10^1	9	6	13	5	12																26
1	2	4	3		8		6	11^1	12	10^1	9^2	14	5	7											13				27
1	2	3	4	14	7		9	11^3	12	10^2		13	8	5											6^1				28
	2	5		9	4^3	6	8	10^1	13	11^2	12	14	3										1	7					29
	2	3		9^2	8	7		6	10^3	12	11	14	13	4									1	5					30
	5	4		9^1	7	14	6	11^2	12	10^3		13	2										1	3	8				31
	2	3	12	7^2	8	9^1	11	13	10^3	6		5											1	4	14				32
	2	4		6	8	7	9^2	11^1		10	13	12	5										1	3					33
	2	3		6^2	7	13	9^1	11	14	10^3	12		5										1	4	8				34
	2	3		8	7	13	10^1	14^4	11^2	9	12	5											1	4	6^3				35
	2	3		6	7	8	9^2	10		12	13	5											1	4^4		11^1			36
	2	3		6	7	8	9^1	11		12		13	5										1	4		10^2	4		37
	2			6	7	8	9^1	11^3	13	12		14	5										1	4		10^2	3		38
	2	3		6	8	7		11^2		10	13	12	5										1		9^1	4			39
	2	3		6	8	7	9^2	10^3	12	11^1	14	13	5										1			4			40
	2	4		6		7		9	10^1		14	13	5^2	12									1		8^3	11	3		41
	2	4		8^2		7	6	11		10^1	9	13	5^3	12									1		14		3		42
	2	3		6^1		7	9	11^2		10	12	13	5										1		8		4		43
	5	4		12	7	6^1	10		11^2	9^3	13	2											1		8	14	3		44
	2	3		6	7^2	8		10	14	11^1	9	13	5										1		12		4		45
1	2			7			11			13	9^1		5	12	3								8		4	6^2	10^3	14	46

FA Cup

First Round — Forest Green R — (h) — 1-2

Capital One Cup

First Round — Cardiff C — (a) — 0-1

Johnstone's Paint Trophy

First Round — Plymouth Arg — (h) — 2-3

League Two Play-Offs

Semi-Final 1st leg — Accrington S — (h) — 1-0

Semi-Final 2nd leg — Accrington S — (a) — 2-2

(aet; AFC Wimbledon won 3-2 on aggregate)

Final — Plymouth Arg — (Wembley) — 2-0

ARSENAL

FOUNDATION

Formed by workers at the Royal Arsenal, Woolwich in 1886, they began as Dial Square (name of one of the workshops), and included two former Nottingham Forest players, Fred Beardsley and Morris Bates. Beardsley wrote to his old club seeking help and they provided the new club with a full set of red jerseys and a ball. The club became known as the 'Woolwich Reds' although their official title soon after formation was Woolwich Arsenal.

Emirates Stadium, Highbury House, 75 Drayton Park, Islington, London N5 1BU.

Telephone: (020) 7619 5003.

Fax: (020) 7704 4001.

Ticket Office: (020) 7619 5000.

Website: www.arsenal.com

Email: ask@arsenal.co.uk

Ground Capacity: 60,260.

Record Attendance: 73,295 v Sunderland, Div 1, 9 March 1935 (at Highbury); 73,707 v RC Lens, UEFA Champions League, 25 November 1998 (at Wembley); 60,162 v Manchester U, FA Premier League, 3 November 2007 (at Emirates).

Pitch Measurements: 105m × 68m (114yd × 74yd).

Chairman: Sir John 'Chips' Keswick.

Chief Executive: Ivan Gazidis.

Manager: Arsène Wenger.

Assistant Manager: Steve Bould.

Head of Medical Services: Colin Lewin.

Colours: Red shirts with white sleeves, white shorts, white socks with black trim.

Year Formed: 1886.

Turned Professional: 1891.

Previous Names: 1886, Dial Square; 1886, Royal Arsenal; 1891, Woolwich Arsenal; 1914, Arsenal.

Club Nickname: 'The Gunners'.

Grounds: 1886, Plumstead Common; 1887, Sportsman Ground; 1888, Manor Ground; 1890, Invicta Ground; 1893, Manor Ground; 1913, Highbury; 2006, Emirates Stadium.

HONOURS

League Champions: FA Premier League – 1997–98, 2001–02, 2003–04; Division 1 – 1930–31, 1932–33, 1933–34, 1934–35, 1937–38, 1947–48, 1952–53, 1970–71, 1988–89, 1990–91.
Runners-up: FA Premier League – 1998–99, 1999–2000, 2000–01, 2002–03, 2004–05, 2015–16; Division 1 – 1925–26, 1931–32, 1972–73; Division 2 – 1903–04.
FA Cup Winners: 1930, 1936, 1950, 1971, 1979, 1993, 1998, 2002, 2003, 2005, 2014, 2015.
Runners-up: 1927, 1932, 1952, 1972, 1978, 1980, 2001.
League Cup Winners: 1987, 1993.
Runners-up: 1968, 1969, 1988, 2007, 2011.
Double performed: 1970–71, 1997–98, 2001–02.
European Competitions
European Cup: 1971–72 *(qf)*, 1991–92.
UEFA Champions League: 1998–99, 1999–2000, 2000–01, 2001–02, 2002–03, 2003–04, 2004–05, 2005–06 *(runners-up)*, 2006–07, 2007–08 *(qf)*, 2008–09 *(sf)*, 2009–10*(qf)*, 2010–11, 2011–12, 2012–13, 2013–14, 2014–15, 2015–16.
Fairs Cup: 1963–64, 1969–70 *(winners)*, 1970–71.
UEFA Cup: 1978–79, 1981–82, 1982–83, 1996–97, 1997–98, 1999–2000 *(runners-up)*.
European Cup-Winners' Cup: 1979–80 *(runners-up)*, 1993–94 *(winners)*, 1994–95 *(runners-up)*.
Super Cup: 1994 *(runners-up)*.

sky SPORTS FACT FILE

Arsenal were the first English team to travel by plane to play a match. In October 1932 a group of players and officials travelled from Croydon Airport to Le Bourget. The Gunners beat Racing Club de Paris 5-2 in a friendly match before returning home.

First Football League Game: 2 September 1893, Division 2, v Newcastle U (h) D 2–2 – Williams; Powell, Jeffrey; Devine, Buist, Howat; Gemmell, Henderson, Shaw (1), Elliott (1), Booth.

Record League Victory: 12–0 v Loughborough T, Division 2, 12 March 1900 – Orr; McNichol, Jackson; Moir, Dick (2), Anderson (1); Hunt, Cottrell (2), Main (2), Gaudie (3), Tennant (2).

Record Cup Victory: 11–1 v Darwen, FA Cup 3rd rd, 9 January 1932 – Moss; Parker, Hapgood; Jones, Roberts, John; Hulme (2), Jack (3), Lambert (2), James, Bastin (4).

Record Defeat: 0–8 v Loughborough T, Division 2, 12 December 1896.

Most League Points (2 for a win): 66, Division 1, 1930–31.

Most League Points (3 for a win): 90, FA Premier League, 2003–04.

Most League Goals: 127, Division 1, 1930–31.

Highest League Scorer in Season: Ted Drake, 42, 1934–35.

Most League Goals in Total Aggregate: Thierry Henry, 175, 1999–2007; 2011–12.

Most League Goals in One Match: 7, Ted Drake v Aston Villa, Division 1, 14 December 1935.

Most Capped Player: Thierry Henry, 81 (123), France.

Most League Appearances: David O'Leary, 558, 1975–93.

Youngest League Player: Jack Wilshere, 16 years 256 days v Blackburn R, 13 September 2008.

Record Transfer Fee Received: £25,400,000 (rising to £29,800,000) from Barcelona for Cesc Fabregas, August 2011.

Record Transfer Fee Paid: £42,400,000 to Real Madrid for Mesut Ozil, September 2013.

Football League Record: 1893 Elected to Division 2; 1904–13 Division 1; 1913–19 Division 2; 1919–92 Division 1; 1992– FA Premier League.

MANAGERS

Sam Hollis 1894–97
Tom Mitchell 1897–98
George Elcoat 1898–99
Harry Bradshaw 1899–1904
Phil Kelso 1904–08
George Morrell 1908–15
Leslie Knighton 1919–25
Herbert Chapman 1925–34
George Allison 1934–47
Tom Whittaker 1947–56
Jack Crayston 1956–58
George Swindin 1958–62
Billy Wright 1962–66
Bertie Mee 1966–76
Terry Neill 1976–83
Don Howe 1984–86
George Graham 1986–95
Bruce Rioch 1995–96
Arsène Wenger September 1996–

LATEST SEQUENCES

Longest Sequence of League Wins: 14, 10.2.2002 – 18.8.2002.

Longest Sequence of League Defeats: 7, 12.2.1977 – 12.3.1977.

Longest Sequence of League Draws: 6, 4.3.1961 – 1.4.1961.

Longest Sequence of Unbeaten League Matches: 49, 7.5.2003 – 24.10.2004.

Longest Sequence Without a League Win: 23, 28.9.1912 – 1.3.1913.

Successive Scoring Runs: 55 from 19.5.2001.

Successive Non-scoring Runs: 6 from 25.2.1987.

TEN YEAR LEAGUE RECORD

		P	W	D	L	F	A	Pts	Pos
2006-07	PR Lge	38	19	11	8	63	35	68	4
2007-08	PR Lge	38	24	11	3	74	31	83	3
2008-09	PR Lge	38	20	12	6	68	37	72	4
2009-10	PR Lge	38	23	6	9	83	41	75	3
2010-11	PR Lge	38	19	11	8	72	43	68	4
2011-12	PR Lge	38	21	7	10	74	49	70	3
2012-13	PR Lge	38	21	10	7	72	37	73	4
2013-14	PR Lge	38	24	7	7	68	41	79	4
2014-15	PR Lge	38	22	9	7	71	36	75	3
2015-16	PR Lge	38	20	11	7	65	36	71	2

DID YOU KNOW ?

Tom Whittaker, who was first-team trainer of Arsenal from 1927 to 1947 and then manager until his death in 1956, introduced a number of innovations in training and physiotherapy during his time at Highbury. He is credited as being the inventor of head tennis.

ARSENAL – FA PREMIER LEAGUE 2015–16 LEAGUE RECORD

Match No.	Date	Venue	Opponents	Result	H/T Score	Lg Pos.	Goalscorers	Attendance
1	Aug 9	H	West Ham U	L 0-2	0-1	20		59,996
2	16	A	Crystal Palace	W 2-1	1-1	11	Giroud [16], Delaney (og) [55]	24,732
3	24	H	Liverpool	D 0-0	0-0	9		60,080
4	29	A	Newcastle U	W 1-0	0-0	5	Coloccini (og) [52]	50,388
5	Sept 12	H	Stoke C	W 2-0	1-0	3	Walcott [31], Giroud [85]	59,963
6	19	A	Chelsea	L 0-2	0-0	5		41,584
7	26	A	Leicester C	W 5-2	2-1	4	Walcott [18], Sanchez 3 [33, 57, 81], Giroud [90]	32,047
8	Oct 4	H	Manchester U	W 3-0	3-0	2	Sanchez 2 [6, 19], Ozil [7]	60,084
9	17	A	Watford	W 3-0	0-0	2	Sanchez [62], Giroud [68], Ramsey [74]	20,721
10	24	H	Everton	W 2-1	2-1	1	Giroud [36], Koscielny [38]	59,985
11	31	A	Swansea C	W 3-0	0-0	2	Giroud [49], Koscielny [68], Campbell [73]	20,937
12	Nov 8	H	Tottenham H	D 1-1	0-1	2	Gibbs [77]	60,060
13	21	A	WBA	L 1-2	1-2	4	Giroud [28]	24,343
14	29	A	Norwich C	D 1-1	1-1	4	Ozil [30]	27,091
15	Dec 5	H	Sunderland	W 3-1	1-1	2	Campbell [33], Giroud [63], Ramsey [90]	59,937
16	13	A	Aston Villa	W 2-0	2-0	1	Giroud (pen) [8], Ramsey [38]	33,285
17	21	H	Manchester C	W 2-1	2-0	2	Walcott [33], Giroud [45]	60,053
18	26	A	Southampton	L 0-4	0-1	2		31,669
19	28	H	Bournemouth	W 2-0	1-0	1	Gabriel [27], Ozil [63]	59,983
20	Jan 2	H	Newcastle U	W 1-0	0-0	1	Koscielny [72]	59,257
21	13	A	Liverpool	D 3-3	2-2	1	Ramsey [14], Giroud 2 [25, 55]	44,109
22	17	A	Stoke C	D 0-0	0-0	1		27,683
23	24	H	Chelsea	L 0-1	0-1	3		60,072
24	Feb 2	A	Southampton	D 0-0	0-0	4		60,044
25	7	A	Bournemouth	W 2-0	2-0	3	Ozil [23], Oxlade-Chamberlain [24]	11,357
26	14	H	Leicester C	W 2-1	0-1	3	Walcott [70], Welbeck [90]	60,009
27	28	A	Manchester U	L 2-3	1-2	3	Welbeck [40], Ozil [69]	75,329
28	Mar 2	A	Swansea C	L 1-2	1-1	3	Campbell [15]	59,905
29	5	A	Tottenham H	D 2-2	1-0	3	Ramsey [39], Sanchez [76]	35,762
30	19	A	Everton	W 2-0	2-0	3	Welbeck [7], Iwobi [42]	39,270
31	Apr 2	H	Watford	W 4-0	2-0	3	Sanchez [4], Iwobi [38], Bellerin [48], Walcott [90]	59,981
32	9	A	West Ham U	D 3-3	2-2	3	Ozil [18], Sanchez [35], Koscielny [70]	34,977
33	17	H	Crystal Palace	D 1-1	1-0	4	Sanchez [45]	59,961
34	21	H	WBA	W 2-0	2-0	3	Sanchez 2 [6, 38]	59,568
35	24	A	Sunderland	D 0-0	0-0	4		45,420
36	30	H	Norwich C	W 1-0	0-0	3	Welbeck [59]	59,989
37	May 8	A	Manchester C	D 2-2	1-1	3	Giroud [10], Sanchez [68]	54,425
38	15	H	Aston Villa	W 4-0	1-0	2	Giroud 3 [5, 78, 80], Bunn (og) [90]	60,007

Final League Position: 2

GOALSCORERS

League (65): Giroud 16 (1 pen), Sanchez 13, Ozil 6, Ramsey 5, Walcott 5, Koscielny 4, Welbeck 4, Campbell 3, Iwobi 2, Bellerin 1, Gabriel 1, Gibbs 1, Oxlade-Chamberlain 1, own goals 3.
FA Cup (10): Giroud 3, Walcott 2, Campbell 1, Chambers 1, Ramsey 1, Sanchez 1, Welbeck 1.
Capital One Cup (2): Flamini 2.
UEFA Champions League (13): Giroud 5 (1 pen), Sanchez 3, Ozil 2, Walcott 2, El-Nenny 1.

Cech P 34	Debuchy M 2	Mertesacker P 24	Koscielny L 33	Monreal N 36 + 1	Ramsey A 29 + 2	Coquelin F 21 + 5	Oxlade-Chamberlain A 9 + 13	Özil M 35	Cazorla S 15	Giroud O 26 + 12	Walcott T 15 + 13	Sanchez A 28 + 2	Bellerin H 36	Arteta M — + 9	Gibbs K 3 + 12	Chambers C 2 + 10	Gabriel A 18 + 3	Flamini M 12 + 4	Campbell J 11 + 8	Iwobi A 8 + 5	Welbeck D 7 + 4	El-Nenny M 9 + 2	Ospina D 4	Wilshere J 1 + 2	Match No.
1	2^2	3	4	5	6	7^1	8	9	10	11	12	13													1
1		3	4	5	8	6^1	12	9^3	7	11		10^2	2	13	14										2
1				5	8	6^2	13	9	7	11^{11}	12	10	2			3	4								3
1			4	5	9	6	8^2		7	12	11^1	10	2	13			3								4
1			4	5	8	7	13	9^2	6	12	11^1	10^3	2	14			3								5
1			4	5	8	6^1	14	9^3	7^4	13	11	10^2	2			12	3^4								6
1		3	4	5	8^2		13	9	7	14	11^3	10	2	12							6^1				7
1		3		5	8	6	13	9^2	7	12	11^1	10^3	2		14		4								8
1		3	4	5	8	6	13	9^3	7	12	11^1	10^2	2	14											9
1			4	5		6	8^1	9	7	11		10^2	2	13			3	12							10
1		3	4	5		6		9^3	7	11^1		10	2		12	13			8^2	14					11
1	2^3	3	4	5		7		9	6^1	11		10		14	13			12	8^2						12
1		3	4	5		6^1		9	7	11		8	2	12^3	10^2			13	14						13
1		3	4^1	5	8^3		14	9	7	11		10^2	2		12	6	13								14
1		3	4	5	6		10^1	9		11^3	12		2	13	14		7	8^2							15
1		3	4	5	7		13	9^3		11	10^2		2	12	14		6	8^1							16
1		3	4	5	7		13	9^2		11	10^3		2	12	14		6	8^1							17
1		3	4	5	6		12	9		11	10^3		2		13		7^4	8^1	14						18
1		3	13	7			8^3	9		11^1	10		2	5^2	6	4		12	14						19
1		3	4	5	7		8^1	9		11^3	10^2		2	13	14		6	12							20
1		3	4	5	6		12	9^3		11	10^2		2	14	13		7	8^1							21
1		3	4	5	7		9^2			11	10^1		2		13		6	8	12						22
1	3^4		4	5	7		14	9		11^1	10^3	13	2			12	6	8^2							23
1			4	5	7	13		9		11^3	11	12	10	2			3	6^2	8^1						24
1			4	5	7	12	8^1	9		11^3	14	10^2	2	13			3	6							25
1		3	4^1	5	7	6^2	8^3	9		11	13	10	2		12				14						26
1			4	5	7	6^2		9		12	11^1	10	2			3			14	8^3	13				27
1		3		5	6	7		9		11	13	10^2	2		4		8^1		12						28
		3			8	6^4		9^3		12		10	2	5		4	13	14		11^2	7^1	1			29
			4	5		7		9^1		13		8	2	12	14	3			10^3	11^2	6	1			30
			4	5		7		9		12	13	8^3	2			3		14	10^2	11^1	6	1			31
			4	5	12	7^1		9		13	14	8	2			3			10	11^3	6^2	1			32
1			4	5	13	7		9		12	14	8	2			3			10^2	11^1	6^3				33
1		3	4	5	7	12		9^3		11	13	8^2	2					14	10^1		6				34
1		3	4	5	7			9^3		11^2	12	8	2						10^1	13	6		14		35
1		3^1	4	5	7	14		9		11		8	2			12			10^2	13	6				36
1			4	5	7^4					11	13	8	2			3			9^2	10^1	6^3		12		37
1			4	5		7		9^4	6^3	11		10	2	14		3		13			12		8^1		38

FA Cup

Third Round	Sunderland	(h)	3-1
Fourth Round	Burnley	(h)	2-1
Fifth Round	Hull C	(h)	0-0
Replay	Hull C	(a)	4-0
Sixth Round	Watford	(h)	1-2

Capital One Cup

Third Round	Tottenham H	(a)	2-1
Fourth Round	Sheffield W	(a)	0-3

UEFA Champions League

Group F	Dinamo Zagreb	(a)	1-2
Group F	Olympiacos	(h)	2-3
Group F	Bayern Munich	(h)	2-0
Group F	Bayern Munich	(a)	1-5
Group F	Dinamo Zagreb	(h)	3-0
Group F	Olympiacos	(a)	3-0
Round of 16 1st leg	Barcelona	(h)	0-2
Round of 16 2nd leg	Barcelona	(a)	1-3
(Barcelona won 5-1 on aggregate)			

ASTON VILLA

FOUNDATION

Cricketing enthusiasts of Villa Cross Wesleyan Chapel, Aston, Birmingham decided to form a football club during the winter of 1874–75. Football clubs were few and far between in the Birmingham area and in their first game against Aston Brook St Mary's rugby team they played one half rugby and the other soccer. In 1876 they were joined by Scottish soccer enthusiast George Ramsay who was immediately appointed captain and went on to lead Aston Villa from obscurity to one of the country's top clubs in a period of less than ten years.

Villa Park, Birmingham B6 6HE.
Telephone: (0121) 327 2299.
Fax: (0121) 322 2107.
Ticket Office/Consumer Sales: (0800) 612 0970.
Website: www.avfc.co.uk
Email: postmaster@avfc.co.uk
Ground Capacity: 42,660.
Record Attendance: 76,588 v Derby Co, FA Cup 6th rd, 2 March 1946.
Pitch Measurements: 105m × 68m (114yd × 74yd).
Chairman: Steve Hollis.
Chief Executive: Keith Wyness.
Manager: Roberto Di Matteo.
Assistant Manager: Steve Clarke.
Physio: Ricky Shamji.
Colours: Claret shirts, sky blue sleeves with claret trim, white shorts with claret trim, sky blue socks with claret hoops.
Year Formed: 1874.
Turned Professional: 1885.
Club Nickname: 'The Villans'.
Grounds: 1874, Wilson Road and Aston Park (also used Aston Lower Grounds for some matches); 1876, Wellington Road, Perry Barr; 1897, Villa Park.
First Football League Game: 8 September 1888, Football League, v Wolverhampton W (a) D 1–1 – Warner; Cox, Coulton; Yates, Harry Devey, Dawson; Albert Brown, Green (1), Allen, Garvey, Hodgetts.
Record League Victory: 12–2 v Accrington S, Division 1, 12 March 1892 – Warner; Evans, Cox; Harry Devey, Jimmy Cowan, Baird; Athersmith (1), Dickson (2), John Devey (4), Lewis Campbell (4), Hodgetts (1).

HONOURS

League Champions: Division 1 – 1893–94, 1895–96, 1896–97, 1898–99, 1899–1900, 1909–10, 1980–81; Division 2 – 1937–38, 1959–60; Division 3 – 1971–72.
Runners-up: FA Premier League – 1992–93; Division 1 – 1902–03, 1907–08, 1910–11, 1912–13, 1913–14, 1930–31, 1932–33, 1989–90; Football League 1888–89; Division 2 – 1974–75, 1987–88.

FA Cup Winners: 1887, 1895, 1897, 1905, 1913, 1920, 1957.
Runners-up: 1892, 1924, 2000, 2015.
League Cup Winners: 1961, 1975, 1977, 1994, 1996.
Runners-up: 1963, 1971, 2010.
Double Performed: 1896–97.
European Competitions
European Cup: 1981–82 *(winners)*, 1982–83 *(qf)*.
UEFA Cup: 1975–76, 1977–78 *(qf)*, 1983–84, 1990–91, 1993–94, 1994–95, 1996–97, 1997–98 *(qf)*, 1998–99, 2001–02, 2008–09.
Europa League: 2009–10, 2010–11.
Intertoto Cup: 2000, 2001 *(winners)*, 2002 *(sf)*, 2008 *(qualified for UEFA Cup)*.
Super Cup: 1982 *(winners)*.
World Club Championship: 1982.

sky SPORTS FACT FILE

Aston Villa's Charlie Wallace was the first player to miss a penalty in an FA Cup final. Villa were awarded a spot kick on 14 minutes of the 1913 final against Sunderland only for Wallace's 'miserable effort' to miss the target. He made up for it later on, delivering the corner from which Tommy Barber headed home the winner.

Record Cup Victory: 13–0 v Wednesbury Old Ath, FA Cup 1st rd, 30 October 1886 – Warner; Coulton, Simmonds; Yates, Robertson, Burton (2); Richard Davis (1), Albert Brown (3), Hunter (3), Loach (2), Hodgetts (2).

Record Defeat: 0–8 v Chelsea, FA Premier League, 23 December 2012.

Most League Points (2 for a win): 70, Division 3, 1971–72.

Most League Points (3 for a win): 78, Division 2, 1987–88.

Most League Goals: 128, Division 1, 1930–31.

Highest League Scorer in Season: 'Pongo' Waring, 49, Division 1, 1930–31.

Most League Goals in Total Aggregate: Harry Hampton, 215, 1904–15.

Most League Goals in One Match: 5, Harry Hampton v Sheffield W, Division 1, 5 October 1912; 5, Harold Halse v Derby Co, Division 1, 19 October 1912; 5, Len Capewell v Burnley, Division 1, 29 August 1925; 5, George Brown v Leicester C, Division 1, 2 January 1932; 5, Gerry Hitchens v Charlton Ath, Division 2, 18 November 1959.

Most Capped Player: Steve Staunton 64 (102), Republic of Ireland.

Most League Appearances: Charlie Aitken, 561, 1961–76.

Youngest League Player: Jimmy Brown, 15 years 349 days v Bolton W, 17 September 1969.

Record Transfer Fee Received: £32,500,000 from Liverpool for Christian Benteke, July 2015.

Record Transfer Fee Paid: £18,000,000 (rising to £24,000,000) to Sunderland for Darren Bent, January 2011.

Football League Record: 1888 Founder Member of the League; 1936–38 Division 2; 1938–59 Division 1; 1959–60 Division 2; 1960–67 Division 1; 1967–70 Division 2; 1970–72 Division 3; 1972–75 Division 2; 1975–87 Division 1; 1987–88 Division 2; 1988–92 Division 1; 1992–2016 FA Premier League; 2016– FL C.

MANAGERS

George Ramsay 1884–1926
 (Secretary-Manager)
W. J. Smith 1926–34
 (Secretary-Manager)
Jimmy McMullan 1934–35
Jimmy Hogan 1936–44
Alex Massie 1945–50
George Martin 1950–53
Eric Houghton 1953–58
Joe Mercer 1958–64
Dick Taylor 1964–67
Tommy Cummings 1967–68
Tommy Docherty 1968–70
Vic Crowe 1970–74
Ron Saunders 1974–82
Tony Barton 1982–84
Graham Turner 1984–86
Billy McNeill 1986–87
Graham Taylor 1987–90
Dr Jozef Venglos 1990–91
Ron Atkinson 1991–94
Brian Little 1994–98
John Gregory 1998–2002
Graham Taylor OBE 2002–03
David O'Leary 2003–06
Martin O'Neill 2006–10
Gerard Houllier 2010–11
Alex McLeish 2011–12
Paul Lambert 2012–15
Tim Sherwood 2015
Remi Garde 2015–16
Roberto Di Matteo June 2016–

LATEST SEQUENCES

Longest Sequence of League Wins: 9, 15.10.1910 – 10.12.1910.

Longest Sequence of League Defeats: 11, 14.2.2016 – 30.4.2016.

Longest Sequence of League Draws: 6, 12.9.1981 – 10.10.1981.

Longest Sequence of Unbeaten League Matches: 15, 12.3.1949 – 27.8.1949.

Longest Sequence Without a League Win: 19, 14.8.2015 – 2.1.2016.

Successive Scoring Runs: 35 from 10.11.1895.

Successive Non-scoring Runs: 6 from 26.12.2014.

TEN YEAR LEAGUE RECORD

		P	W	D	L	F	A	Pts	Pos
2006-07	PR Lge	38	11	17	10	43	41	50	11
2007-08	PR Lge	38	16	12	10	71	51	60	6
2008-09	PR Lge	38	17	11	10	54	48	62	6
2009-10	PR Lge	38	17	13	8	52	39	64	6
2010-11	PR Lge	38	12	12	14	48	59	48	9
2011-12	PR Lge	38	7	17	14	37	53	38	16
2012-13	PR Lge	38	10	11	17	47	69	41	15
2013-14	PR Lge	38	10	8	20	39	61	38	15
2014-15	PR Lge	38	10	8	20	31	57	38	17
2015-16	PR Lge	38	3	8	27	27	76	17	20

DID YOU KNOW ?

When local rivals West Bromwich Albion were struggling financially in 1905 the Aston Villa directors helped them out with a donation. A cheque for 100 guineas (£105) was sent to The Hawthorns to help ensure the Baggies' survival.

ASTON VILLA – FA PREMIER LEAGUE 2015–16 LEAGUE RECORD

Match No.	Date	Venue	Opponents	Result		H/T Score	Lg Pos.	Goalscorers	Attendance
1	Aug 8	A	Bournemouth	W	1-0	0-0	3	Gestede [72]	11,155
2	14	H	Manchester U	L	0-1	0-1	7		42,200
3	22	A	Crystal Palace	L	1-2	0-0	11	Souare (og) [77]	25,295
4	29	H	Sunderland	D	2-2	2-1	12	Sinclair 2 (1 pen) [11 (pl, 41]	35,399
5	Sept 13	A	Leicester C	L	2-3	1-0	15	Grealish [39], Gil [63]	31,733
6	19	H	WBA	L	0-1	0-1	17		36,321
7	26	A	Liverpool	L	2-3	0-1	18	Gestede 2 [66, 71]	44,228
8	Oct 3	H	Stoke C	L	0-1	0-0	18		33,189
9	17	A	Chelsea	L	0-2	0-1	18		41,596
10	24	H	Swansea C	L	1-2	0-0	19	Ayew [62]	33,324
11	Nov 2	A	Tottenham H	L	1-3	0-2	20	Ayew [79]	34,882
12	8	H	Manchester C	D	0-0	0-0	20		36,757
13	21	A	Everton	L	0-4	0-3	20		38,424
14	28	H	Watford	L	2-3	1-1	20	Richards [41], Ayew [89]	35,057
15	Dec 5	A	Southampton	D	1-1	1-0	20	Lescott [44]	29,645
16	13	H	Arsenal	L	0-2	0-2	20		33,285
17	19	A	Newcastle U	D	1-1	0-1	20	Ayew [61]	48,234
18	26	H	West Ham U	D	1-1	0-1	20	Ayew (pen) [62]	38,193
19	28	A	Norwich C	L	0-2	0-1	20		27,071
20	Jan 2	A	Sunderland	L	1-3	0-1	20	Gil [63]	41,535
21	12	H	Crystal Palace	W	1-0	0-0	20	Hennessey (og) [58]	28,245
22	16	H	Leicester C	D	1-1	0-1	20	Gestede [75]	32,763
23	23	A	WBA	D	0-0	0-0	20		26,165
24	Feb 2	A	West Ham U	L	0-2	0-0	20		34,914
25	6	H	Norwich C	W	2-0	1-0	20	Klose (og) [45], Agbonlahor [51]	32,472
26	14	H	Liverpool	L	0-6	0-2	20		35,798
27	27	A	Stoke C	L	1-2	0-0	20	Bacuna [79]	27,703
28	Mar 1	H	Everton	L	1-3	0-2	20	Gestede [79]	29,755
29	5	A	Manchester C	L	0-4	0-0	20		53,892
30	13	H	Tottenham H	L	0-2	0-1	20		32,393
31	19	A	Swansea C	L	0-1	0-0	20		20,454
32	Apr 2	H	Chelsea	L	0-4	0-2	20		31,120
33	9	H	Bournemouth	L	1-2	0-1	20	Ayew [86]	31,057
34	16	A	Manchester U	L	0-1	0-1	20		75,411
35	23	H	Southampton	L	2-4	1-2	20	Westwood 2 [45, 85]	29,729
36	30	A	Watford	L	2-3	1-1	20	Clark [28], Ayew [48]	20,653
37	May 7	H	Newcastle U	D	0-0	0-0	20		33,055
38	15	A	Arsenal	L	0-4	0-1	20		60,007

Final League Position: 20

GOALSCORERS

League (27): Ayew 7 (1 pen), Gestede 5, Gil 2, Sinclair 2 (1 pen), Westwood 2, Agbonlahor 1, Bacuna 1, Clark 1, Grealish 1, Lescott 1, Richards 1, own goals 3.
FA Cup (3): Clark 1, Gana 1, Richards 1.
Capital One Cup (7): Sinclair 4 (2 pens), Bennett 1, Gestede 1, Traore 1.

Guzan B 28	Bacuna L 27+4	Richards M 23+1	Clark C 16+2	Amavi J 9+1	Veretout J 21+4	Gana J 35	Westwood A 31+1	Ayew J 27+3	Agbonlahor G 13+2	Sinclair S 19+8	Gestede R 14+18	Sanchez C 16+4	Richardson K 8+3	Grealish J 9+7	Traore A —+10	Hutton A 26+2	Gil C 17+6	Lescott J 30	Crespo J 1	N'Zogbia C —+2	Okore J 12	Cissokho A 18	Kozak L 3+1	Bunn M 10	Lyden J 2+2	Green A —+2	Toner K 3+1	Hepburn-Murphy R —+1	Match No.
1	2	3	4	5	6[2]	7	8	9	10	11[3]	12	13	14																1
1	2	3	4	5	6[2]	7	8	9	10	11[1]	12	13																	2
1	2	3	4	5		6	8		9		10	7[1]				11	12												3
1	9[1]	3	4	5		8	6			11	10	7				2	12												4
1	2[3]	3		5			7	12	11[2]	10	13	6		9		14	8[1]	4											5
1	13	3		5	14		7		11	10[1]	12	8[3]		9		2	6[2]	4											6
1		3		5	12	8	7		9	10	6[1]	11[2]	13			2		4											7
1		3		9	6	8	7[3]	13		10[2]	11		12			5	14	4[1]	2										8
1		3		12		7	6	10[2]		11		5[1]	9	13		2	8	4											9
1	6	3			7		8	10[2]		11		5	9[1]	13		2	12	4											10
1	8		3			7[1]	12	11[2]	10	13	6	5	9[1]			2	14	4											11
1	13	3	4	5	6	8		10[3]		11[2]	14	7				2	9[1]			12									12
1		3	4		6	8[1]	7	10		13	12	5	11[3]			2	9[2]			14									13
1		3	4		6	8[2]		10		11	13	7	5		12	2	9[1]												14
1	5[2]				6	8	12	11	14	9	10[1]	7[3]	13		2		4				3								15
1	5				6	8[2]		11		9[3]	10[1]	7		13	14	2	12	4			3								16
1	5				9	8	6	11		10[1]	12	7				2		4			3								17
1	5				9[2]	8	6	11		10	7[1]			13		2	12	4			3								18
1	5[2]	3	4		9[3]	6	7	11		8[1]	13		10	14	12	2													19
1	6	3			8	7			14	10		11[1]	12[3]	2[2]	9		4					5	13						20
	2		12		6	8	7	11						9[1]		4					3	5	10	1					21
	2				6	7	8	11[2]		13	12			9[1]		4					3	5	10	1					22
	6	2			13	7	8	11		12[2]				9		4					3	5	10[1]	1					23
	6	2			8	7		10[8]	11[2]	13		12		9[1]		4					3	5		1					24
	6	2[1]	12		10	7	8		11					9		4					3	5		1					25
	6[2]	2[3]			9	8	7		11[1]	12			14	10		4					3	5		1	13				26
	9				6[2]	8	7		10	12	13			2	11[1]	4					3	5		1					27
1	7	3	5		13	8	9[2]	10	11[1]		12			2		4						6							28
1	13	2	4		8[2]	7	6	11[3]	10[1]	14	12			5		3						9							29
1					6[1]	8	7	11		13	10			2	9[2]	4				3	5					12			30
1			4		9[1]	7	6	10	13			11		2	8[2]	3				5						12			31
1	13	3			6[3]	8	11			10	7[2]		12	2[8]	9[1]	4				5		14							32
1	2		4		10	8	11		6[2]	12		9[3]	14	13		3				5		7[1]							33
1	6		4		9	7	11		8	12		10[1]		2	3					5									34
1	9	3[1]			7	6	10[2]		11	13	8[3]		14	2	4					5						12			35
	7	2			8[2]	6	10[1]		13	11	12			5	3	9[4]	1							4					36
	2	4			8	6	10		11[1]	7				5	3		1									9	12		37
	3	12			9	7	11			10		8	13		4[1]			6	1	2[2]		5							38

BARNET

The Hive Stadium, Camrose Avenue, Edgware HA8 6AG.

Telephone: (020) 831 3800.

Ticket Office: (020) 831 3800 (ext. 1028)

Website: www.barnetfc.com

Email: tellus@barnetfc.com

Ground Capacity: 5,454.

Record Attendance: 11,026 v Wycombe Wanderers, FA Amateur Cup 4th rd, 1951–52.

Pitch Measurements: 102m × 65m (111.5yd × 71yd).

Chairman: Anthony Kleanthous.

Group Finance Director: Andrew Adie.

Head Coach: Martin Allen.

Physio: Luigi Cerullo.

Colours: Black and amber hooped shirts, black shorts, black socks with amber trim.

Year Formed: 1888.

Turned Professional: 1965.

Previous Name: 1906, Barnet Alston FC; 1919, Barnet.

Club Nickname: 'The Bees'.

Grounds: 1888, Queen's Road; 1901, Totteridge Lane; 1907, Barnet Lane; 2013, The Hive.

First Football League Game: 17 August 1991, Division 4, v Crewe Alex (h) L 4–7 – Phillips; Blackford, Cooper (Murphy), Horton, Bodley (Stein), Johnson, Showler, Carter (2), Bull (2), Lowe, Evans.

Record League Victory: 7–0 v Blackpool, Division 3, 11 November 2000 – Naisbitt; Stockley, Sawyers, Niven (Brown), Heald, Arber (1), Currie (3), Doolan, Richards (2) (McGleish), Cottee (1) (Riza), Toms.

Record Cup Victory: 6–1 v Newport Co, FA Cup 1st rd, 21 November 1970 – McClelland; Lye, Jenkins, Ward, Embery, King, Powell (1), Ferry, Adams (1), Gray, George (3), (1 og).

HONOURS

League Champions: Conference – 1990–91, 2004–05, 2014–15.
Runners-up: Conference – 1986–87, 1987–88, 1989–90. Division 3 – (3rd) 1992–93 *(promoted).*
FA Cup: 4th rd – 2007, 2008.
League Cup: 3rd rd – 2006.
FA Amateur Cup Winners: 1946.

sky SPORTS FACT FILE

Barnet's first two games as a Football League club produced a total of 21 goals. A 7-4 defeat by Crewe Alexandra in a Division Four fixture was followed by a 5-5 draw at home to Brentford in the Football League Cup three days later.

Record Defeat: 1–9 v Peterborough U, Division 3,
5 September 1998.

Most League Points (3 for a win): 79, Division 3, 1992–93.

Most League Goals: 81, Division 4, 1991–92.

Highest League Scorer in Season: Dougie Freedman, 24,
Division 3, 1994–95.

Most League Goals in Total Aggregate: Sean Devine, 47,
1995–99.

Most League Goals in One Match: 4, Dougie Freedman v
Rochdale, Division 3, 13 September 1994; 4, Lee Hodges v
Rochdale, Division 3, 8 April 1996.

Most Capped Player: Ken Charlery, 4, St Lucia.

Most League Appearances: Lee Harrison, 270, 1996–2002,
2006–09.

Youngest League Player: Kieran Adams, 17 years 71 days v
Mansfield T, 31 December 1994.

Record Transfer Fee Received: £800,000 from Crystal
Palace for Dougie Freedman, September 1995.

Record Transfer Fee Paid: £130,000 to Peterborough U for
Greg Heald, August 1997.

Football League Record: 1991 Promoted to Division 4 from
Conference; 1991–92 Division 4; 1992–93 Division 3;
1993–94 Division 2; 1994–2001 Division 3; 2001–05
Conference; 2005–13 FL 2; 2013–15 Conference Premier;
2015– FL 2.

LATEST SEQUENCES

Longest Sequence of League Wins: 6, 28.8.1993 – 25.9.1999.

Longest Sequence of League Defeats: 11, 8.5.1993 –
2.10.1993.

Longest Sequence of League Draws: 4, 22.1.1994 –
12.2.1994.

Longest Sequence of Unbeaten League Matches: 12,
5.12.1992 – 2.3.1993.

Longest Sequence Without a League Win: 14, 11.12.1993 – 8.3.1994.

Successive Scoring Runs: 12 from 19.3.1995.

Successive Non-scoring Runs: 5 from 12.2.2000.

MANAGERS

Lester Finch
George Wheeler
Dexter Adams
Tommy Coleman
Gerry Ward
Gordon Ferry
Brian Kelly
Bill Meadows 1976–79
Barry Fry 1979–85
Roger Thompson 1985
Don McAllister 1985–86
Barry Fry 1986–93
Edwin Stein 1993
Gary Phillips (*Player-Manager*)
  1993–94
Ray Clemence 1994–96
Alan Mullery (*Director of
Football*) 1996–97
Terry Bullivant 1997
John Still 1997–2000
Tony Cottee 2000–01
John Still 2001–02
Peter Shreeves 2002–03
Martin Allen 2003–04
Paul Fairclough 2004–08
Ian Hendon 2008–10
Mark Stimson 2010–11
Martin Allen 2011
Lawrie Sanchez 2011–12
Mark Robson 2012
Edgar Davids 2012–14
Ulrich Landvreugd and
  Dick Schreuder 2014
Martin Allen March 2014–

TEN YEAR LEAGUE RECORD

		P	W	D	L	F	A	Pts	Pos
2006-07	FL 2	46	16	11	19	55	70	59	14
2007-08	FL 2	46	16	12	18	56	63	60	12
2008-09	FL 2	46	11	15	20	56	74	48	17
2009-10	FL 2	46	12	12	22	47	63	48	21
2010-11	FL 2	46	12	12	22	58	77	48	22
2011-12	FL 2	46	12	10	24	52	79	46	22
2012-13	FL 2	46	13	12	21	47	59	51	23
2013-14	Conf P	46	19	13	14	58	53	70	8
2014-15	Conf P	46	28	8	10	94	46	92	1
2015-16	FL 2	46	17	11	18	67	68	62	15

DID YOU KNOW ?

Barnet have gained automatic
promotion to the Football
League on a record three
occasions (1991, 2005 and
2015). Only one other club has
achieved this twice:
Cheltenham Town (1999 and
2016).

BARNET – FOOTBALL LEAGUE TWO 2015–16 LEAGUE RECORD

Match No.	Date	Venue	Opponents	Result	Score	H/T Score	Lg Pos.	Goalscorers	Attendance
1	Aug 8	A	Leyton Orient	L	0-2	0-0	18		6151
2	15	H	Wycombe W	L	0-2	0-0	23		2563
3	18	H	Northampton T	W	2-0	0-0	15	Akinde 2 (1 pen) [63 (pen), 90]	2466
4	22	A	Bristol R	L	1-3	0-1	21	Weston [85]	7107
5	29	H	Cambridge U	D	0-0	0-0	18		2406
6	Sept 5	A	Carlisle U	L	2-3	2-2	21	Dembele [29], Gash [31]	4925
7	12	A	Portsmouth	L	1-3	1-1	23	Yiadom [25]	16,217
8	19	H	Stevenage	W	3-2	0-1	21	N'Gala [48], McLean [63], Gash [78]	2480
9	26	H	Dagenham & R	W	3-1	2-0	18	Gash 2 [1, 56], Yiadom [34]	2079
10	29	A	Plymouth Arg	L	1-2	1-0	18	McLean [30]	6115
11	Oct 3	A	AFC Wimbledon	L	0-2	0-1	19		4068
12	10	H	Accrington S	L	1-2	1-1	20	Gash [34]	2229
13	17	H	York C	W	3-1	0-0	19	Akinde [59], Gash [82], Clarke [90]	1767
14	20	A	Hartlepool U	D	1-1	0-1	19	Akinde [64]	3124
15	24	A	Oxford U	W	3-2	3-2	18	Weston [26], Akinde [29], Clarke [31]	6137
16	31	H	Exeter C	W	2-0	1-0	16	Brown (og) [34], Clarke [54]	2105
17	Nov 14	A	Luton T	L	0-2	0-1	18		8497
18	21	H	Morecambe	D	0-0	0-0	17		1632
19	24	A	Notts Co	L	2-4	0-2	18	McLean [77], Gambin [90]	3098
20	28	H	Mansfield T	L	1-3	0-1	19	Akinde (pen) [77]	1775
21	Dec 12	A	Yeovil T	D	2-2	2-0	19	McLean 2 [18, 45]	3162
22	19	H	Crawley T	W	4-2	1-0	19	Dembele 2 [45, 52], Akinde (pen) [83], Young (og) [85]	1888
23	26	H	Newport Co	W	2-0	0-0	17	Akinde 2 (1 pen) [54 (pen), 89]	1831
24	28	A	Cambridge U	L	1-2	0-0	18	Akinde [60]	6003
25	Jan 2	A	Northampton T	L	0-3	0-1	18		5153
26	9	H	Bristol R	W	1-0	1-0	15	Hoyte [5]	2770
27	16	H	Carlisle U	D	0-0	0-0	17		2079
28	23	A	Stevenage	D	0-0	0-0	18		3801
29	Feb 13	A	Dagenham & R	W	2-0	1-0	17	Gambin [24], Nelson [69]	1728
30	20	A	AFC Wimbledon	L	1-2	0-0	18	Stevens [87]	3289
31	23	H	Portsmouth	W	1-0	1-0	15	Akinde (pen) [41]	2557
32	27	A	Accrington S	D	2-2	0-0	15	Gambin [79], Akinde [90]	1416
33	Mar 1	H	Plymouth Arg	W	1-0	0-0	15	Yiadom [69]	2209
34	5	A	Hartlepool U	L	1-3	1-2	15	Shomotun [11]	1734
35	8	H	Newport Co	W	3-0	2-0	15	Yiadom [9], Randall [45], Akinde [69]	2032
36	12	A	York C	D	1-1	1-1	15	Akinde [37]	2890
37	19	H	Oxford U	L	0-3	0-0	15		3264
38	25	A	Exeter C	D	1-1	1-1	15	Weston [27]	4389
39	28	H	Luton T	W	2-1	0-0	15	Gambin [49], Akinde (pen) [90]	4008
40	Apr 2	A	Morecambe	L	2-4	0-2	15	Gash 2 [70, 90]	1175
41	9	H	Leyton Orient	W	3-0	1-0	14	Akinde 2 [26, 57], Togwell [49]	3401
42	16	A	Wycombe W	D	1-1	0-0	15	Yiadom [72]	3715
43	19	H	Notts Co	W	3-1	0-1	15	Akinde (pen) [47], Randall [57], Yiadom [63]	1322
44	23	A	Mansfield T	D	1-1	1-1	15	Akinde [6]	2573
45	30	H	Yeovil T	L	3-4	1-0	15	Gash [22], Akinde 2 (1 pen) [52 (pen), 62]	2379
46	May 7	A	Crawley T	W	3-0	1-0	15	Johnson [39], Akinde 2 [78, 90]	2293

Final League Position: 15

GOALSCORERS

League (67): Akinde 23 (8 pens), Gash 9, Yiadom 6, McLean 5, Gambin 4, Clarke 3, Dembele 3, Weston 3, Randall 2, Hoyte 1, Johnson 1, N'Gala 1, Nelson 1, Shomotun 1, Stevens 1, Togwell 1, own goals 2.
FA Cup (2): Champion 1, Gash 1.
Capital One Cup (3): Akinde 1 (pen), Dembele 1, Yiadom 1.
Johnstone's Paint Trophy (0).

Stack G 7	Hoyte G 16+3	N'Gala B 39+3	Dembele B 25+1	Johnson E 41	Yiadom E 41	Weston C 36+1	Togwell S 34+5	Villhete M 8+7	Gash M 20+14	Akinde J 41+2	Muggleton S 8+15	Gambin L 30+14	Stevens M 2+8	Champion T 19+7	Tomlinson B 1+2	Batt S 4+12	Nelson M 22+5	McLean A 13+7	Stephens J 29	McKenzie-Lyle K —+1	Crocombe M 5	Lisbie K —+3	Day T —+1	Clarke J 10	Nwogu J 2+2	Bailey N 1+1	Stacey J 2	Lawlor I 5	Taylor H 4+4	Odofin H —+1	Hackett C 5	Sesay A 10+3	Randall M 8+4	Pearson J 14+1	Shomotun F 3+7	Roberts J 1+1	Kyei N 1	Fonguck W —+1	Match No.
1	2^1	3	4	5	6	7	8		9^3	10^2	11	12	13	14																									1
1	2^3	4	3	5	6	7^1	8		12	10		11^1		9	13	14																							2
1	2	4	3	5	6	7^3	8		9	11^2	14	12			10^1	13																						3
1	2^2	4	3	5		7	8		6^1	12	10	14		9			13	11^3																				4
	2^2	4	3	5	6	7	9	8^1	11^3	10		12				13		14	1																			5
		3	4	5	2	8	7^1	6^2	11^3	10	14	9		13			12	1																				6
	2	3	4	5	10	7	8	6^2	13	11^3	12	9^1							1^8	14																		7
	2	4	3	5	6	7	8^1	9^2	13	11^3		12					14	10		1																		8
13	3		5	2^2	8	7	12	11	10	14	9^1						4	6^1		1																		9
13	3		5	2	7	6	12	9^3	11		10^1		14				4	8^2		1																		10
2	4		5	6	7	8^1	9^3	12	11	14	13						3^2	10		1																		11
3	4	5	2	6^1	7	8^4	9^3	11		10			13		12			14	1																			12
	3		5	2	9^1	14		10	12		7^3		8				4	11^2	1			6	13															13
2	4	3	5	9	12	7		11	10^1		13		8^2			14		1				6^1																14
2^2	4	3	5	9	6			12	11^3	10^1	13		7				14	1				8																15
	4	3^1	6	7	9^3	13		11	10^1		12		8			5		1				2	14															16
	3		5	2	7			11	10^2	13	9^1		8^3		12	4	14	1				6																17
	3		5	2	7			11^1	10	14	9^2		8		12	4	13	1				6^3																18
3	4		5	2	7^1	8		12			13		9		11^3		14	1				10^2		6														19
	3		5		7			10^3	12	13	9				14	4	11	1				2^8		8^1	6^2													20
	3	4	5	2	7	8		13	10^1		6	12			14	11^3		1				9^2				1												21
	12	4	5	2	7^2	8		13	10		9	14			3^3	11^1		1				6				1												22
2	4	3	5	6	7^2	8		12	10^1		9					11^3			14							1	13											23
2^1	4	3	5	6	9	7^3		12	11	13		8				10^2			14							1												24
12	4	3	5	6	7^2	8		10		9		2^3	13			11^1										1	14											25
2	4	3	5	8^8	6	7		11^1		10	13	12				9^2	1																					26
2	4	3	5		7^2	8	10^3		9	13	11				1												6^1	12	14									27
2^1	4	3	5		7	8^2		6	11^3	10		1							14							9	12	13										28
	3		5		6	7		9	11	12	10^2	4		1									8^1	2^3		13	14											29
	4		5	6	8	7^2		11		9	13	12^3	3		1								10^1		14	2												30
	3			6	7	12	13		11^3	5		9^1	8		4			1								14	10^2	2										31
		9		8				11	5^1	14	13	7^2		4			1									6	3	12	2	10^3								32
	3		5	7				10	12	9^1	11^2	6		14			1									4	8^1	2		13								33
	3		5	2	9	8^2		11	13	14	12			4			1										7^3		6	10^1								34
	4^1		5	2	12	13		11		8^2	6			3			1									7	9^3	10	14									35
		5	6		7	12		11		9^2	8^1	14	3		1											4	10^3	2	13									36
	8		5	6	7	14		11	10^1	9^2		12	3		1											4^3		2	13									37
	3		5^3	6	10			14	11		12		7^2		4			1				9^1			8				2	13								38
1	12			6	7^3	8	13	11^1	10	5	9^1	14		3													4		2									39
1	4			6		8	12	13	11	5	9^1	14	7														3	10^2	2^3									40
		4	5	6	7^2	8		10^3	11	14	9^1	13				3		1										2	12									41
1	14	4	5	6		7		11^3	10^1	9^2	12			13^3	3			1								8			2									42
	4	12	5	2				13	11		9^2	8					1							6^1			14		3	7			10^1					43
	3	4	5	6		7		11	10	9^2	13					1										12			8^1	2								44
	4	5	6		7			11	10	14	9		13			3		1								8^2				2^1	12^3							45
	3	4^3	2			8		11	10		7^2					1				13		14				6^1		5							9	12		46

FA Cup
First Round   Blackpool   (h) 2-0
Second Round Newport Co   (h) 0-1

Capital One Cup
First Round   Millwall   (a) 2-1
(aet)
Second Round Wolverhampton W (a) 1-2

Johnstone's Paint Trophy
First Round   Yeovil T   (a) 0-1

BARNSLEY

FOUNDATION

Many clubs owe their inception to the Church and Barnsley are among them, for they were formed in 1887 by the Rev. T. T. Preedy, curate of Barnsley St Peter's, and went under that name until it was dropped in 1897 a year before being admitted to the Second Division of the Football League.

Oakwell Stadium, Grove Street, Barnsley, South Yorkshire S71 1ET.

Telephone: (01226) 211 211.

Fax: (01226) 211 444.

Ticket Office: (01226) 211 183.

Website: www.barnsleyfc.co.uk

Email: thereds@barnsleyfc.co.uk

Ground Capacity: 23,287.

Record Attendance: 40,255 v Stoke C, FA Cup 5th rd, 15 February 1936.

Pitch Measurements: 100.5m × 67m (110yd × 73yd).

Chairman: Maurice Watkins.

Chief Executive: Ben Mansford.

Head Coach: Paul Heckingbottom.

Assistant Head Coach: Tommy Wright.

Head Physio: Craig Sedgwick.

Colours: Red shirts with white trim, white shorts with red trim, red socks.

Year Formed: 1887.

Turned Professional: 1888.

Previous Name: 1887, Barnsley St Peter's; 1897, Barnsley.

Club Nickname: 'The Tykes', 'The Reds', 'The Colliers'.

Ground: 1887, Oakwell.

First Football League Game: 1 September 1898, Division 2, v Lincoln C (a) L 0–1 – Fawcett; McArtney, Nixon; King, Burleigh, Porteous; Davis, Lees, Murray, McCullough, McGee.

Record League Victory: 9–0 v Loughborough T, Division 2, 28 January 1899 – Greaves; McArtney, Nixon; Porteous, Burleigh, Howard; Davis (4), Hepworth (1), Lees (1), McCullough (1), Jones (2). 9–0 v Accrington S, Division 3 (N), 3 February 1934 – Ellis; Cookson, Shotton; Harper, Henderson, Whitworth; Spence (2), Smith (1), Blight (4), Andrews (1), Ashton (1).

Record Cup Victory: 6–0 v Blackpool, FA Cup 1st rd replay, 20 January 1910 – Mearns; Downs, Ness; Glendinning, Boyle (1), Utley; Bartrop, Gadsby (1), Lillycrop (2), Tufnell (2), Forman. 6–0 v Peterborough U, League Cup 1st rd 2nd leg, 15 September 1981 – Horn; Joyce, Chambers, Glavin (2), Banks, McCarthy, Evans, Parker (2), Aylott (1), McHale, Barrowclough (1).

Record Defeat: 0–9 v Notts Co, Division 2, 19 November 1927.

Most League Points (2 for a win): 67, Division 3 (N), 1938–39.

HONOURS

League Champions: Division 3N – 1933–34, 1938–39, 1954–55.
Runners-up: First Division – 1996–97; Division 3 – 1980–81; Division 3N – 1953–54; Division 4 – 1967–68.
FA Cup Winners: 1912.
Runners-up: 1910.
League Cup: quarter-final – 1982.
League Trophy Winners: 2016.

sky SPORTS FACT FILE

The record average attendance at Oakwell was 21,262 achieved in the 1947–48 season when Barnsley finished in a mid-table position in Division Two. The highest attendance that season was 33,131 for the visit of Sheffield Wednesday.

Most League Points (3 for a win): 82, Division 1, 1999–2000.

Most League Goals: 118, Division 3 (N), 1933–34.

Highest League Scorer in Season: Cecil McCormack, 33, Division 2, 1950–51.

Most League Goals in Total Aggregate: Ernest Hine, 123, 1921–26 and 1934–38.

Most League Goals in One Match: 5, Frank Eaton v South Shields, Division 3 (N), 9 April 1927; 5, Peter Cunningham v Darlington, Division 3 (N), 4 February 1933; 5, Beau Asquith v Darlington, Division 3 (N), 12 November 1938; 5, Cecil McCormack v Luton T, Division 2, 9 September 1950.

Most Capped Player: Gerry Taggart, 35 (51), Northern Ireland.

Most League Appearances: Barry Murphy, 514, 1962–78.

Youngest League Player: Reuben Noble-Lazarus, 15 years 45 days v Ipswich T, 30 September 2008.

Record Transfer Fee Received: £4,500,000 from Blackburn R for Ashley Ward, December 1998.

Record Transfer Fee Paid: £1,500,000 to Partizan Belgrade for Georgi Hristov, July 1997.

Football League Record: 1898 Elected to Division 2; 1932–34 Division 3 (N); 1934–38 Division 2; 1938–39 Division 3 (N); 1946–53 Division 2; 1953–55 Division 3 (N); 1955–59 Division 2; 1959–65 Division 3; 1965–68 Division 4; 1968–72 Division 3; 1972–79 Division 4; 1979–81 Division 3; 1981–92 Division 2; 1992–97 Division 1; 1997–98 FA Premier League; 1998–2002 Division 1; 2002–04 Division 2; 2004–06 FL 1; 2006–14 FL C; 2014– FL 1.

LATEST SEQUENCES

Longest Sequence of League Wins: 10, 5.3.1955 – 23.4.1955.

Longest Sequence of League Defeats: 9, 14.3.1953 – 25.4.1953.

Longest Sequence of League Draws: 7, 28.3.1911 – 22.4.1911.

Longest Sequence of Unbeaten League Matches: 21, 1.1.1934 – 5.5.1934.

Longest Sequence Without a League Win: 26, 13.12.1952 – 26.8.1953.

Successive Scoring Runs: 44 from 2.10.1926.

Successive Non-scoring Runs: 6 from 27.11.1971.

MANAGERS

Arthur Fairclough 1898–1901
  (*Secretary-Manager*)
John McCartney 1901–04
  (*Secretary-Manager*)
Arthur Fairclough 1904–12
John Hastie 1912–14
Percy Lewis 1914–19
Peter Sant 1919–26
John Commins 1926–29
Arthur Fairclough 1929–30
Brough Fletcher 1930–37
Angus Seed 1937–53
Tim Ward 1953–60
Johnny Steele 1960–71
  (*continued as General Manager*)
John McSeveney 1971–72
Johnny Steele (*General Manager*)
  1972–73
Jim Iley 1973–78
Allan Clarke 1978–80
Norman Hunter 1980–84
Bobby Collins 1984–85
Allan Clarke 1985–89
Mel Machin 1989–93
Viv Anderson 1993–94
Danny Wilson 1994–98
John Hendrie 1998–99
Dave Bassett 1999–2000
Nigel Spackman 2001
Steve Parkin 2001–02
Glyn Hodges 2002–03
Gudjon Thordarson 2003–04
Paul Hart 2004–05
Andy Ritchie 2005–06
Simon Davey 2007–09
  (*Caretaker from November 2006*)
Mark Robins 2009–11
Keith Hill 2011–12
David Flitcroft 2012–13
Danny Wilson 2013–15
Lee Johnson 2015–16
Paul Heckingbottom June 2016–

TEN YEAR LEAGUE RECORD

		P	W	D	L	F	A	Pts	Pos
2006-07	FL C	46	15	5	26	53	85	50	20
2007-08	FL C	46	14	13	19	52	65	55	18
2008-09	FL C	46	13	13	20	45	58	52	20
2009-10	FL C	46	14	12	20	53	69	54	18
2010-11	FL C	46	14	14	18	55	66	56	17
2011-12	FL C	46	13	9	24	49	74	48	21
2012-13	FL C	46	14	13	19	56	70	55	21
2013-14	FL C	46	9	12	25	44	77	39	23
2014-15	FL 1	46	17	11	18	62	61	62	11
2015-16	FL 1	46	22	8	16	70	54	74	6

DID YOU KNOW ?

George Donkin, who made over 200 appearances for Barnsley, was rewarded by the Royal Humane Society for rescuing a drowning child from a local canal in April 1922. Sadly he subsequently suffered a breakdown and was committed to an institution in Huddersfield where he died just five years later.

BARNSLEY – FOOTBALL LEAGUE ONE 2015–16 LEAGUE RECORD

Match No.	Date		Venue	Opponents	Result	H/T Score	Lg Pos.	Goalscorers	Attendance
1	Aug	8	A	Chesterfield	L 1-3	1-0	20	Wilkinson [4]	8117
2		15	H	Burton Alb	W 1-0	0-0	10	Hourihane (pen) [67]	8583
3		18	A	Millwall	W 3-2	1-1	7	Winnall [38], Mawson [56], Nyatanga [90]	7657
4		22	H	Bradford C	D 0-0	0-0	10		10,342
5		29	A	Rochdale	L 0-3	0-2	12		3618
6	Sept	5	H	Shrewsbury T	L 1-2	1-1	14	Winnall [38]	8630
7		12	H	Swindon T	W 4-1	2-1	11	Nyatanga [59], Watkins [22], Wabara [44], Hourihane [76]	8227
8		19	A	Blackpool	D 1-1	1-0	11	Hourihane [8]	7542
9		26	H	Gillingham	W 2-0	2-0	8	Pearson [18], Winnall [45]	8354
10	Oct	3	A	Doncaster R	L 1-2	0-1	13	Winnall [60]	9033
11		10	H	Crewe Alex	L 1-2	1-1	13	Mawson [16]	8406
12		17	A	Southend U	L 1-2	1-2	17	Scowen (pen) [24]	6572
13		20	H	Walsall	L 0-2	0-0	19		8561
14		24	H	Fleetwood T	L 0-1	0-1	21		8764
15		31	A	Scunthorpe U	L 0-2	0-2	22		4147
16	Nov	3	A	Coventry C	L 3-4	2-2	22	Mawson [48], Scowen 2 (1 pen) [54, 90 (p)]	10,954
17		14	H	Port Vale	L 1-2	0-1	23	Winnall [77]	8696
18		21	A	Oldham Ath	W 2-1	1-0	21	Hourihane [30], Long [89]	4300
19		24	A	Peterborough U	L 2-3	1-1	22	Hourihane (pen) [38], Winnall [77]	4783
20		28	H	Sheffield U	D 1-1	0-1	24	Hourihane [90]	13,571
21	Dec	12	A	Colchester U	W 3-2	2-0	21	Hourihane [18], Hammill [40], Toney [60]	3265
22		19	H	Wigan Ath	L 0-2	0-1	21		8866
23		28	H	Blackpool	W 4-2	1-0	19	Winnall 2 [3, 54], Watkins [56], Templeton [90]	9072
24	Jan	2	A	Millwall	W 2-1	1-0	17	Winnall [12], Hammill [67]	8700
25		16	A	Shrewsbury T	W 3-0	2-0	17	Winnall 2 [15, 21], Mawson [72]	5446
26		23	H	Rochdale	W 6-1	1-0	17	Mawson [8], Winnall 3 [52, 69, 89], Watkins [84], Long [90]	8823
27		26	A	Bradford C	W 1-0	1-0	13	Watkins [2]	17,470
28		30	A	Swindon T	W 1-0	0-0	12	Winnall [88]	7532
29	Feb	7	H	Bury	W 3-0	1-0	10	Watkins [20], Winnall [55], Hammill [66]	9443
30		13	A	Gillingham	L 1-2	0-1	12	Hourihane [62]	5887
31		20	H	Doncaster R	W 1-0	0-0	10	Fletcher [81]	11,638
32		23	A	Bury	D 0-0	0-0	10		3160
33		27	A	Crewe Alex	W 2-1	0-1	9	Winnall [53], Mawson [67]	4451
34	Mar	1	H	Coventry C	W 2-0	1-0	7	Roberts [10], Fletcher [60]	9344
35		5	A	Walsall	W 3-1	1-1	6	Fletcher [17], Brownhill [50], Chapman [56]	5199
36		12	H	Southend U	L 0-2	0-1	8		9903
37		19	A	Fleetwood T	W 2-0	0-0	6	Davis (og) [47], Scowen [84]	3470
38		25	H	Scunthorpe U	D 0-0	0-0	6		10,122
39		28	A	Port Vale	W 1-0	1-0	7	Hourihane [9]	4839
40	Apr	9	H	Chesterfield	L 1-2	0-0	7	Hammill [75]	10,645
41		12	H	Oldham Ath	W 2-1	1-0	7	Winnall 2 (1 pen) [45, 83 (p)]	8871
42		16	A	Burton Alb	D 0-0	0-0	7		4858
43		19	H	Peterborough U	W 1-0	0-0	7	Williams, G [90]	8886
44		23	A	Sheffield U	D 0-0	0-0	6		23,307
45		30	A	Colchester U	D 2-2	0-1	6	Fletcher 2 [57, 80]	12,021
46	May	8	A	Wigan Ath	W 4-1	2-1	6	Winnall 2 (1 pen) [33 (p), 44], Hourihane [56], Brownhill [74]	18,730

Final League Position: 6

GOALSCORERS

League (70): Winnall 21 (2 pens), Hourihane 10 (2 pens), Mawson 6, Fletcher 5, Watkins 5, Hammill 4, Scowen 4 (2 pens), Brownhill 2, Long 2, Nyatanga 2, Chapman 1, Pearson 1, Roberts 1, Templeton 1, Toney 1, Wabara 1, Wilkinson 1, Williams, G 1, own goal 1.
FA Cup (0).
Capital One Cup (4): Crowley 1, Scowen 1 (pen), Watkins 1, Winnall 1.
Johnstone's Paint Trophy (13): Hammill 3, Fletcher 2, Watkins 2, Hourihane 1, Mawson 1, Nyatanga 1, Pearson 1, Toney 1, own goal 1.
League One Play-Offs (9): Fletcher 2, Hammill 2, Winnall 2, Brownhill 1, Isgrove 1, own goal 1.

Davies A 38	Scowen J 23+11	Mawson A 45	Roberts M 27+5	Nyatanga L 19+2	Smith G 14+5	Crowley D 6+5	Pearson B 23	Hourihane C 40+1	Wilkinson C 2+6	Winnall S 36+7	Watkins M 32+2	Williams G 16+3	Rothwell J 2+2	Bree J 17+2	Wabara R 18+1	Harris K 7+4	Smith M 4+9	Townsend N 8	Williams R 1+4	Jackson S 1+8	Isgrove L 27	Digby P 1	Maris G —+1	Templeton M —+2	Hammill A 25	Toney I 10+5	Long K 11	White A 14	Brownhill J 21+1	Fletcher A 12+9	Khan O —+3	Tuton S —+7	Chapman H 3+8	Connolly C 3	McCourt J —+1	Match No.
1	2	3	4	5	6^2	7^1	8	9	10^3	11	12	13	14																							1
1	7	3	4	5	6^2	12	8	13	14	11^3	10			9^1	2																					2
1	6	3	4	5		7	9^2	8	14	10^1	11			13	2^3	12																				3
1	8	4	3	5	6	7^2	9	13		11^1	10				2																					4
1		3	4	5^2	14	12	9	8	11^1	13	6			7^3	2	10																				5
1	8	4	3	5		10^1	7	9^2		11	6			2	12	13																				6
	7	3		4	5		9	8		12	11		14	2^3	10^2		1	6^1	13																	7
	8	4		3	5	6^1	7	10^2		11	2			9	12		1	13																		8
	8	3	14	4	5	12	7^3	9		11^2	6			2	10^1	13	1																			9
	7^1	3	13	4	5^3	12	8	9		11	6			2^2	10	14	1																			10
	7	3		4	5		8	9		11	6			2	10^1	12	1																			11
1	8	3	2	4	9	7	6			12	10^2			5^3	14	11^1	13																			12
	7	3	4	5	6^1	13	9		14	11				2	12	8^2	1	10^3																		13
	7	4	3^2	12	5	9^3				11				2	10	13	1		14	6^1	8															14
	7	4	3	5	6^3		8	12		11				2	10^1	1				9^2	13	14														15
1	7	6	3	4	5		9	12		10^2				2	11^1	13	8																			16
1		3	4	5		7	8			12	10			2		13									6^2				9	11^1						17
1		3		13		7	8			12	10			2							14				9^2				6	11^1	4	5^2				18
1		3	14	5		7	8			12	10			2							13^3				9^2				6	11^1	4^1					19
1		3	4	14		7	8			10	11^1			2						12					6^2	9	13			5^3						20
1		3		4		7	8			10	6			2							9				11		5									21
1		4				7	8			10	6^1			2		12	13				9				11^{12}		3	5								22
1		4				7	8			10	11^3			2	14	12					6^1			13	9^2		3	5								23
1		4				7	8			11	10^1			12	2	13					6				9		3	5^2								24
1		4	14				7			10	11^3			2^1		13					6^2				9		3	5	8	12						25
1	13	4	14				8			11	10	5		2^2							6^1				9		3		7^3	12						26
1	13	4^1	12				7			11	6	5		2							9^3						3		8	10^1	14					27
1	12	4					7			11	8	5		2							9						3		6	10^1						28
1	13	4					8			10^1	11			2							6^2				9^3		3	5	7	12		14				29
1	13	8					4			5	6^3			2							9^2				7		3	10	11^1	12	14					30
1	14	4	3				8			11	10	12		2							6^2				9			5^1	7^1	13						31
1	8^1	4	3				7			10	11^2	5		2							6				9^4				12	13						32
1	13	4	3				7			11^1	6	5		2							9^2				8				10^3	14	12					33
1	13	4	3	14			8			11^2	6	5		2^1							9^3				7		10			12						34
1	12	3	4				8			11	5			6^3											7	10^1	13	14		9^2	2					35
1		4	3	13			8			12	11	2^2									9						7	10^1		14	6^3	5				36
1	12	4	3				8			11	5			6^1							9						7	10^2			13	2				37
1	8	4	3				9				2										10	11			5	7			12	6^1						38
1	6	4	3				8				2										9	11^1			5	7	10		12							39
1		4	3				8			11	12			2							6^2				9	13		5^1	7	10^1		14				40
1	14	4	3				7			11	9^3	12		5^2							6	10^1			2	8	13									41
1	2	3	4				7			10	5										6^2				9	11^1			8	12		13				42
1	2	4	3				8			11	5										6^2				9	10^1			7	12		13				43
1	2	4	3				8			10	5										6				9	12			7	11^1						44
1	2	4	3				8			11^2	5										6^3				9	14			7	10^1	13	12				45
1	5	3	4				7			11^1	2										9^3				6	14			8	10^2		12			13	46

FA Cup
First Round — Altrincham (a) 0-1

League One Play-Offs
Semi-Final 1st leg — Walsall (h) 3-0
Semi-Final 2nd leg — Walsall (a) 3-1
(Barnsley won 6-1 on aggregate)
Final — Millwall (Wembley) 3-1

Johnstone's Paint Trophy
First Round — Scunthorpe U (a) 2-1
Second Round — Bradford C (a) 2-1
Northern Quarter-Final — York C (h) 2-1
Northern Semi-Final — Wigan Ath (a) 2-2
(aet; Barnsley won 4-2 on penalties)
Northern Final 1st leg — Fleetwood T (h) 1-1
Northern Final 2nd leg — Fleetwood T (a) 1-1
(aet; Barnsley won 4-2 on penalties)
Final — Oxford U (Wembley) 3-2

Capital One Cup
First Round — Scunthorpe U (a) 1-1
(aet; Barnsley won 7-6 on penalties)
Second Round — Everton (aet) (h) 3-5

BIRMINGHAM CITY

FOUNDATION

In 1875, cricketing enthusiasts who were largely members of Trinity Church, Bordesley, determined to continue their sporting relationships throughout the year by forming a football club which they called Small Heath Alliance. For their earliest games played on waste land in Arthur Street, the team included three Edden brothers and two James brothers.

St Andrew's Stadium, Birmingham B9 4RL.

Telephone: (0344) 557 1875.

Fax: (0344) 557 1975.

Ticket Office: (0844) 557 1875 (then option 2).

Website: www.bcfc.com

Email: reception@bcfc.com

Ground Capacity: 29,409.

Record Attendance: 66,844 v Everton, FA Cup 5th rd, 11 February 1939.

Pitch Measurements: 100m × 66m (109.5yd × 72yd).

Directors: Pano Pavlakis, Shui Cheong Ma.

Manager: Gary Rowett.

Assistant Manager: Kevin Summerfield.

Physio: Dave Hunt.

Colours: Blue shirts with white trim and white diagonal stripe, white shorts, blue socks.

Year Formed: 1875.

Turned Professional: 1885.

Previous Names: 1875, Small Heath Alliance; 1888, dropped 'Alliance'; 1905, Birmingham; 1945, Birmingham City.

Club Nickname: 'Blues'.

Grounds: 1875, waste ground near Arthur St; 1877, Muntz St, Small Heath; 1906, St Andrew's.

First Football League Game: 3 September 1892, Division 2, v Burslem Port Vale (h) W 5–1 – Charsley; Bayley, Speller; Ollis, Jenkyns, Devey; Hallam (1), Edwards (1), Short (1), Wheldon (2), Hands.

Record League Victory: 12–0 v Walsall T Swifts, Division 2, 17 December 1892 – Charsley; Bayley, Jones; Ollis, Jenkyns, Devey; Hallam (2), Walton (3), Mobley (3), Wheldon (2), Hands (2). 12–0 v Doncaster R, Division 2, 11 April 1903 – Dorrington; Goldie, Wassell; Beer, Dougherty (1), Howard; Athersmith, Leonard (4), McRoberts (1), Wilcox (4), Field (1), (1 og).

Record Cup Victory: 9–2 v Burton W, FA Cup 1st rd, 31 October 1885 – Hedges; Jones, Evetts (1); Fred James, Felton, Arthur James (1); Davenport (2), Stanley (4), Simms, Figures, Morris (1).

Record Defeat: 1–9 v Blackburn R, Division 1, 5 January 1895; 1–9 v Sheffield W, Division 1, 13 December 1930; 0–8 v Bournemouth, FLC, 25 October 2014.

HONOURS

League Champions: Division 2 – 1892–93, 1920–21, 1947–48, 1954–55; Second Division – 1994–95. *Runners-up:* FL C – 2006–07, 2008–09; Division 2 – 1893–94, 1900–01, 1902–03; 1971–72, 1984–85; Division 3 – 1991–92.

FA Cup: Runners-up: 1931, 1956.

League Cup Winners: 1963, 2011. *Runners-up:* 2001.

League Trophy Winners: 1991, 1995.

European Competitions
Fairs Cup: 1955–58, 1958–60 *(runners-up)*, 1960–61 *(runners-up)*, 1961–62.
Europa League: 2011–12.

sky SPORTS FACT FILE

Birmingham City did not take part in the FA Cup for 1921–22. Club officials failed to submit their application for exemption from the early rounds of the competition and the directors chose to withdraw.

Most League Points (2 for a win): 59, Division 2, 1947–48.

Most League Points (3 for a win): 89, Division 2, 1994–95.

Most League Goals: 103, Division 2, 1893–94 (only 28 games).

Highest League Scorer in Season: Walter Abbott, 34, Division 2, 1898–99 (Small Heath); Joe Bradford, 29, Division 1, 1927–28 (Birmingham City).

Most League Goals in Total Aggregate: Joe Bradford, 249, 1920–35.

Most League Goals in One Match: 5, Walter Abbott v Darwen, Division 2, 26 November, 1898; 5, John McMillan v Blackpool, Division 2, 2 March 1901; 5, James Windridge v Glossop, Division 2, 23 January 1915.

Most Capped Player: Maik Taylor, 58 (including 8 on loan at Fulham) (88), Northern Ireland.

Most League Appearances: Frank Womack, 491, 1908–28.

Youngest League Player: Trevor Francis, 16 years 139 days v Cardiff C, 5 September 1970.

Record Transfer Fee Received: £6,700,000 (rising to £8,000,000) from Liverpool for Jermaine Pennant, July 2006.

Record Transfer Fee Paid: £6,000,000 to Valencia for Nikola Zigic, May 2010; £6,000,000 to Manchester U for Ben Foster, June 2010.

Football League Record: 1892 Elected to Division 2; 1894–96 Division 1; 1896–1901 Division 2; 1901–02 Division 1; 1902–03 Division 2; 1903–08 Division 1; 1908–21 Division 2; 1921–39 Division 1; 1946–48 Division 2; 1948–50 Division 1; 1950–55 Division 2; 1955–65 Division 1; 1965–72 Division 2; 1972–79 Division 1; 1979–80 Division 2; 1980–84 Division 1; 1984–85 Division 2; 1985–86 Division 1; 1986–89 Division 2; 1989–92 Division 3; 1992–94 Division 1; 1994–95 Division 2; 1995–2002 Division 1; 2002–06 FA Premier League; 2006–07 FL C; 2007–08 FA Premier League; 2008–09 FL C; 2009–11 FA Premier League; 2011– FL C.

LATEST SEQUENCES

Longest Sequence of League Wins: 13, 17.12.1892 – 16.9.1893.

Longest Sequence of League Defeats: 8, 28.9.1985 – 23.11.1985.

Longest Sequence of League Draws: 8, 18.9.1990 – 23.10.1990.

Longest Sequence of Unbeaten League Matches: 20, 3.9.1994 – 2.1.1995.

Longest Sequence Without a League Win: 17, 28.9.1985 – 18.1.1986.

Successive Scoring Runs: 24 from 24.9.1892.

Successive Non-scoring Runs: 6 from 11.2.1989.

MANAGERS

Alfred Jones 1892–1908 (*Secretary-Manager*)
Alec Watson 1908–10
Bob McRoberts 1910–15
Frank Richards 1915–23
Billy Beer 1923–27
William Harvey 1927–28
Leslie Knighton 1928–33
George Liddell 1933–39
William Camkin and Ted Goodier 1939–45
Harry Storer 1945–48
Bob Brocklebank 1949–54
Arthur Turner 1954–58
Pat Beasley 1959–60
Gil Merrick 1960–64
Joe Mallett 1964–65
Stan Cullis 1965–70
Fred Goodwin 1970–75
Willie Bell 1975–77
Sir Alf Ramsay 1977–78
Jim Smith 1978–82
Ron Saunders 1982–86
John Bond 1986–87
Garry Pendrey 1987–89
Dave Mackay 1989–91
Lou Macari 1991
Terry Cooper 1991–93
Barry Fry 1993–96
Trevor Francis 1996–2001
Steve Bruce 2001–07
Alex McLeish 2007–11
Chris Hughton 2011–12
Lee Clark 2012–14
Gary Rowett October 2014–

TEN YEAR LEAGUE RECORD

		P	W	D	L	F	A	Pts	Pos
2006-07	FL C	46	26	8	12	67	42	86	2
2007-08	PR Lge	38	8	11	19	46	62	35	19
2008-09	FL C	46	23	14	9	54	37	83	2
2009-10	PR Lge	38	13	11	14	38	47	50	9
2010-11	PR Lge	38	8	15	15	37	58	39	18
2011-12	FL C	46	20	16	10	78	51	76	4
2012-13	FL C	46	15	16	15	63	69	61	12
2013-14	FL C	46	11	11	24	58	74	44	21
2014-15	FL C	46	16	15	15	54	64	63	10
2015-16	FL C	46	16	15	15	53	49	63	10

DID YOU KNOW ?

Torrential rain fell during the first half of the First Division game between Birmingham City and Notts County at St Andrew's on 19 September 1925, forcing the referee to temporarily suspend the game for over an hour to allow conditions to improve. The visitors won 1-0 in front of a crowd of just 3,977.

BIRMINGHAM CITY – FL CHAMPIONSHIP 2015–16 LEAGUE RECORD

Match No.	Date	Venue	Opponents	Result	H/T Score	Lg Pos.	Goalscorers	Atten-dance
1	Aug 8	H	Reading	W 2-1	1-0	5	Cotterill [40], Toral [47]	19,171
2	15	A	Burnley	D 2-2	1-0	5	Toral [10], Caddis (pen) [63]	12,430
3	21	H	Derby Co	D 1-1	1-0	7	Gleeson [45]	18,134
4	29	A	Milton Keynes D	W 2-0	0-0	7	Gleeson [57], Maghoma [79]	14,626
5	Sept 12	H	Bristol C	W 4-2	3-1	4	Donaldson 3 (1 pen) [10, 20, 41 (p)], Grounds [77]	18,819
6	15	H	Nottingham F	L 0-1	0-0	7		16,604
7	18	A	Ipswich T	D 1-1	1-1	6	Cotterill [22]	18,973
8	26	H	Rotherham U	L 0-2	0-1	9		17,307
9	29	A	Brentford	W 2-0	0-0	5	Morrison [71], Donaldson [90]	9528
10	Oct 3	A	Leeds U	W 2-0	1-0	4	Gray [31], Maghoma [90]	24,601
11	17	H	QPR	W 2-1	1-1	4	Robinson [24], Caddis (pen) [63]	19,161
12	20	A	Bolton W	W 1-0	1-0	2	Robinson [20]	13,703
13	24	A	Hull C	L 0-2	0-2	6		17,436
14	31	H	Wolverhampton W	L 0-2	0-1	6		18,946
15	Nov 3	H	Blackburn R	D 0-0	0-0	6		15,701
16	7	A	Fulham	W 5-2	3-0	6	Gleeson [19], Caddis (pen) [22], Toral [31], Donaldson [82], Solomon-Otabor [90]	18,888
17	21	H	Charlton Ath	L 0-1	0-0	6		16,514
18	28	A	Brighton & HA	L 1-2	1-1	6	Toral [21]	27,242
19	Dec 5	H	Huddersfield T	L 0-2	0-1	7		15,931
20	12	A	Middlesbrough	D 0-0	0-0	9		20,929
21	15	A	Preston NE	D 1-1	0-1	8	Morrison [67]	10,668
22	18	H	Cardiff C	W 1-0	1-0	7	Caddis (pen) [45]	14,414
23	26	A	Sheffield W	L 0-3	0-2	10		28,523
24	28	H	Milton Keynes D	W 1-0	0-0	9	Maghoma [63]	19,714
25	Jan 2	H	Brentford	W 2-1	0-0	8	Maghoma [55], Kieftenbeld [89]	17,555
26	12	A	Nottingham F	D 1-1	1-1	8	Toral [24]	18,342
27	16	A	Derby Co	W 3-0	0-0	8	Robinson [59], Gleeson [74], Kieftenbeld [80]	32,895
28	23	H	Ipswich T	W 3-0	1-0	7	Buckley [23], Toral [54], Kieftenbeld [70]	18,272
29	30	A	Bristol C	D 0-0	0-0	6		15,728
30	Feb 6	H	Sheffield W	L 1-2	1-0	8	Donaldson [45]	20,302
31	13	A	Rotherham U	D 0-0	0-0	7		11,018
32	23	H	Bolton W	W 1-0	1-0	7	Donaldson [29]	15,992
33	27	A	QPR	L 0-2	0-2	8		17,110
34	Mar 3	H	Hull C	W 1-0	1-0	7	Toral [14]	18,105
35	8	A	Blackburn R	L 0-2	0-2	9		12,774
36	13	A	Wolverhampton W	D 0-0	0-0	8		21,464
37	19	H	Fulham	D 1-1	0-1	9	Morrison [56]	17,104
38	Apr 2	A	Charlton Ath	L 1-2	1-1	9	Toral [32]	15,742
39	5	H	Brighton & HA	L 1-2	1-1	9	Lafferty [16]	16,143
40	9	A	Reading	W 2-0	2-0	9	Donaldson [2], Shotton [27]	17,868
41	12	H	Leeds U	L 1-2	1-0	9	Donaldson [53]	16,081
42	16	H	Burnley	L 1-2	0-1	9	Maghoma [55]	19,151
43	19	H	Preston NE	D 2-2	1-0	9	Donaldson 2 [13, 59]	14,366
44	23	A	Huddersfield T	D 1-1	0-0	9	Cotterill [73]	13,054
45	29	H	Middlesbrough	D 2-2	1-1	9	Gleeson [33], Davis [68]	21,380
46	May 7	A	Cardiff C	D 1-1	1-1	10	Cotterill [11]	21,022

Final League Position: 10

GOALSCORERS

League (53): **Donaldson** 11 (1 pen), **Toral** 8, **Gleeson** 5, **Maghoma** 5, **Caddis** 4 (4 pens), **Cotterill** 4, **Kieftenbeld** 3, **Morrison** 3, **Robinson** 3, **Buckley** 1, **Davis** 1, **Gray** 1, **Grounds** 1, **Lafferty** 1, **Shotton** 1, **Solomon-Otabor** 1.
FA Cup (1): **Morrison** 1.
Capital One Cup (4): **Thomas** 2, **Maghoma** 1, **Shinnie** 1.

Kuszczak T 41	Caddis P 37 + 2	Morrison M 46	Spector J 22 + 3	Grounds J 45	Gleeson S 42 + 2	Kieftenbeld M 41 + 1	Cotterill D 24 + 5	Toral J 28 + 8	Gray D 22 + 2	Donaldson C 38 + 2	Davis D 23 + 12	Shinnie A 5 + 9	Robinson P 20 + 5	Maghoma J 25 + 15	Brock-Madsen N 3 + 3	Solomon-Otabor V 2 + 20	Eardley N 5	Brown R — + 1	Vaughan J 5 + 10	Halford G — + 3	Lowry S 1	Buckley W 5 + 5	Adams C 1 + 1	Fabbrini D 7 + 7	Shotton R 9	Lafferty K 4 + 2	Legzdins A 5	Match No.
1	2	3	4	5	6	7^1	8^3	9^2	10	11	12	13	14															1
1	2	4	3	5	6	7	8^3	9^1	10^2	11	12			13	14													2
1	2	3		5	6	7	8^1	9^3	10	11		12		13														3
1	2	3	4	5	7^1	6	8	9^2	10^3	11	13	14		12														4
1	2	3	4	5	6	7	8	9^2	10^1	11	13			12														5
1	2	3	4	5	6	7	8^3	9^2	12	11			10^1	13	14													6
1	12	3	4	5	7	6	8		10^2	11		9^3	14	13			2^1											7
1	2	3	4	5	6	7^1	8^3	9^2	10	11		12		13	14													8
1	2	3		5	6	7	8		10	11	9^1		4	12														9
1	2	3	13	5	6	7	8^1		10^2	11	9^3		4	12		14												10
1	2	3		5	6	7			10^1	11	9^2	12	4	8		13												11
1	2	3	12	5	6	7		14	10^3	11		9^2	4	8^1		13												12
1	2	3	7^3	5	6	8	13	14	11^2	10		12	4^1	9														13
1	2	3		5	6	9^2	12	13	10	11	8^3		4	7^1	14													14
1	2	3	4	5	6		8^1	12	10	11	7	9^2		13														15
1	2	3	4	5	6	12		9^3	8	11	7		10^1	13														16
1	2	3	4	5	6		9	8		7^1		10^2	11	13		12												17
1	2	3	4	5	6	7		9	10^2		12		8^1	11^3	14		13											18
1		3	4	5	7	6		9	11^3			8^1	14	12	10^2	13	2											19
1		3	4	5	6	7		10^3		12	9^2		8	10	13^2	2			11^1	14								20
1		3	4	5	6	7		12	10		14		9^3	8^2		2			11^1	13								21
1	12	3	4		6	7		9^3	10		13			8		2^1			11	14	5^2							22
1	2	3	4	5		7		9^1	10^3	13	6	14		8	12				11^2									23
1	2	3		5	6	7		9^2	12	11	13		4	10	8^1													24
1	2	3		5	6	7		9^2		11^3	13	14	4	10^1		8			12									25
1	2	3		5	7	8		9^2		10	6^1		4	11		13			12									26
1	2	3		5	6	7		8^2		11	9^1		4	10					13			12						27
1	2	3		5	7	6^1		9		11	10^3		4			12			13			8^2	14					28
1	2	3		5	6	7		9^3		11	10^1		4	12					14			8^2	13					29
1	2	3		5	6	7		9^3		11			4	10^2	14				13			8^1	12					30
1		3		5	6	7	14	9^1		11			4	10^3	12							8^2	13	2				31
1		3		5	6	7	13	12		11			4	10^1								8^2	9^1	2				32
1		3		5	6	7^2	8	12		11			4	10^1					13			14	9^3	2				33
1	2	3		5	6	7	8^1	9		11	12		4	10														34
1	2	3		5	6	7^3	8^2	9		11			4	10^1	14							13	12					35
1	2	3	4	5	6	9^1	8	10		11	7		12															36
1	2	3	4	5	8	7^2	9^3	11^1		10	6		12						13	14								37
1	2	3		5	7		8^3	10^1		13	6		4	12	14				11				9^2					38
1	2	3	4	5	8	7	14	10^2		9	12			6^3									13			11^1	1	39
	2	3		5	6	7	8^2			10	9			12	13								4	11^1	1			40
	2	3		5	7^1	6	8^2	12		10	9											13	4	11	1			41
	2	3		5		6	8^1	9^4		11	7			10^2								12	4	13	1			42
1	2	3		5	12	6^3	10			11	7			8								9^1	4	13				43
1	2	3		5	7		6^3			9	8	14		13								12	10^2	4	11^1			44
	2^3	3	14	5	6	7	8			11	10^2		12		13								9^1	4		1		45
	3	2	5	12	6	8				11	10^1		4		13				14				7^2	9^3	1			46

FA Cup
Third Round   Bournemouth   (h)   1-2

Capital One Cup
First Round   Bristol R   (a)   2-1
Second Round   Gillingham   (h)   2-0
Third Round   Aston Villa   (a)   0-1

BLACKBURN ROVERS

FOUNDATION

It was in 1875 that some public school old boys called a meeting at which the Blackburn Rovers club was formed and the colours blue and white adopted. The leading light was John Lewis, later to become a founder of the Lancashire FA, a famous referee who was in charge of two FA Cup finals, and a vice-president of both the FA and the Football League.

Ewood Park, Blackburn, Lancashire BB2 4JF.

Telephone: (01254) 372 001.

Fax: (01254) 671 042.

Ticket Office: (01254) 372 000.

Website: www.rovers.co.uk

Email: (via website)

Ground Capacity: 31,154.

Record Attendance: 62,522 v Bolton W, FA Cup 6th rd, 2 March 1929.

Pitch Measurements: 105m × 66m (115yd × 72yd).

Finance Director: Mike Chesterton.

Directors: Robert Coar, Gandhi Babu.

Manager: Owen Coyle.

Assistant Manager: Alan Irvine.

Physio: Neil Fitzhenry.

Colours: Blue and white halved shirts, white shorts with red trim, blue socks.

Year Formed: 1875.

Turned Professional: 1880.

Club Nickname: 'Rovers'.

HONOURS

League Champions: FA Premier League – 1994–95; Division 1 – 1911–12, 1913–14; Division 2 – 1938–39; Division 3 – 1974–75.
Runners-up: FA Premier League – 1993–94; First Division – 2000–01; Division 2 – 1957–58; Division 3 – 1979–80.
FA Cup Winners: 1884, 1885, 1886, 1890, 1891, 1928.
Runners-up: 1882, 1960.
League Cup Winners: 2002.
Full Members' Cup Winners: 1987.
European Competitions
European Cup: 1995–96.
UEFA Cup: 1994–95, 1998–99, 2002–03, 2003–04, 2006–07, 2007–08.
Intertoto Cup: 2007.

Grounds: 1875, all matches played away; 1876, Oozehead Ground; 1877, Pleasington Cricket Ground; 1878, Alexandra Meadows; 1881, Leamington Road; 1890, Ewood Park.

First Football League Game: 15 September 1888, Football League, v Accrington (h) D 5–5 – Arthur; Beverley, James Southworth; Douglas, Almond, Forrest; Beresford (1), Walton, John Southworth (1), Fecitt (1), Townley (2).

Record League Victory: 9–0 v Middlesbrough, Division 2, 6 November 1954 – Elvy; Suart, Eckersley; Clayton, Kelly, Bell; Mooney (3), Crossan (2), Briggs, Quigley (3), Langton (1).

Record Cup Victory: 11–0 v Rossendale, FA Cup 1st rd, 13 October 1884 – Arthur; Hopwood, McIntyre; Forrest, Blenkhorn, Lofthouse; Sowerbutts (2), Jimmy Brown (1), Fecitt (4), Barton (3), Birtwistle (1).

sky SPORTS FACT FILE

The highest attendance for a Football League game at Ewood Park is 52,656 against Preston North End on Boxing Day 1921. This figure has been exceeded on at least three occasions for FA Cup ties but never for a League game.

Record Defeat: 0–8 v Arsenal, Division 1, 25 February 1933; 0-8 v Lincoln C, Division 2, 29 August 1953.

Most League Points (2 for a win): 60, Division 3, 1974–75.

Most League Points (3 for a win): 91, Division 1, 2000–01.

Most League Goals: 114, Division 2, 1954–55.

Highest League Scorer in Season: Ted Harper, 43, Division 1, 1925–26.

Most League Goals in Total Aggregate: Simon Garner, 168, 1978–92.

Most League Goals in One Match: 7, Tommy Briggs v Bristol R, Division 2, 5 February 1955.

Most Capped Player: Morten Gamst Pedersen, 70 (83), Norway.

Most League Appearances: Derek Fazackerley, 596, 1970–86.

Youngest League Player: Harry Dennison, 16 years 155 days v Bristol C, 8 April 1911.

Record Transfer Fee Received: £18,000,000 from Manchester C for Roque Santa Cruz, June 2009.

Record Transfer Fee Paid: £8,000,000 to Huddersfield T for Jordan Rhodes, August 2012; £8,000,000 to Manchester U for Andy Cole, December 2001.

Football League Record: 1888 Founder Member of the League; 1936–39 Division 2; 1946–48 Division 1; 1948–58 Division 2; 1958–66 Division 1; 1966–71 Division 2; 1971–75 Division 3; 1975–79 Division 2; 1979–80 Division 3; 1980–92 Division 2; 1992–99 FA Premier League; 1999–2001 Division 1; 2001–12 FA Premier League; 2012– FL C.

LATEST SEQUENCES

Longest Sequence of League Wins: 8, 1.3.1980 – 7.4.1980.

Longest Sequence of League Defeats: 7, 12.3.1966 – 16.4.1966.

Longest Sequence of League Draws: 5, 11.10.1975 – 1.11.1975.

Longest Sequence of Unbeaten League Matches: 23, 30.9.1987 – 27.2.1988.

Longest Sequence Without a League Win: 16, 11.11.1978 – 24.3.1979.

Successive Scoring Runs: 32 from 24.4.1954.

Successive Non-scoring Runs: 4 from 14.12.2015.

MANAGERS

Thomas Mitchell 1884–96
(Secretary-Manager)
J. Walmsley 1896–1903
(Secretary-Manager)
R. B. Middleton 1903–25
Jack Carr 1922–26
(Team Manager under Middleton to 1925)
Bob Crompton 1926–31
(Hon. Team Manager)
Arthur Barritt 1931–36
(had been Secretary from 1927)
Reg Taylor 1936–38
Bob Crompton 1938–41
Eddie Hapgood 1944–47
Will Scott 1947
Jack Bruton 1947–49
Jackie Bestall 1949–53
Johnny Carey 1953–58
Dally Duncan 1958–60
Jack Marshall 1960–67
Eddie Quigley 1967–70
Johnny Carey 1970–71
Ken Furphy 1971–73
Gordon Lee 1974–75
Jim Smith 1975–78
Jim Iley 1978
John Pickering 1978–79
Howard Kendall 1979–81
Bobby Saxton 1981–86
Don Mackay 1987–91
Kenny Dalglish 1991–95
Ray Harford 1995–96
Roy Hodgson 1997–98
Brian Kidd 1998–99
Graeme Souness 2000–04
Mark Hughes 2004–08
Paul Ince 2008
Sam Allardyce 2008–10
Steve Kean 2010–12
Henning Berg 2012
Michael Appleton 2013
Gary Bowyer 2013–15
Paul Lambert 2015–16
Owen Coyle June 2016–

TEN YEAR LEAGUE RECORD

		P	W	D	L	F	A	Pts	Pos
2006-07	PR Lge	38	15	7	16	52	54	52	10
2007-08	PR Lge	38	15	13	10	50	48	58	7
2008-09	PR Lge	38	10	11	17	40	60	41	15
2009-10	PR Lge	38	13	11	14	41	55	50	10
2010-11	PR Lge	38	11	10	17	46	59	43	15
2011-12	PR Lge	38	8	7	23	48	78	31	19
2012-13	FL C	46	14	16	16	55	62	58	17
2013-14	FL C	46	18	16	12	70	62	70	8
2014-15	FL C	46	17	16	13	66	59	67	9
2015-16	FL C	46	13	16	17	46	46	55	15

DID YOU KNOW ?

Inside-forward Eddie Latheron was one of the stars of the Blackburn Rovers team in the seasons leading up to the First World War, making over 250 appearances and scoring close on 100 goals. He enlisted in the Royal Field Artillery and in March 1917 was posted to Flanders. On 14 October 1917 he was killed in action.

BLACKBURN ROVERS – FL CHAMPIONSHIP 2015–16 LEAGUE RECORD

Match No.	Date	Venue	Opponents	Result		H/T Score	Lg Pos.	Goalscorers	Attendance
1	Aug 8	H	Wolverhampton W	L	1-2	1-2	18	Conway [39]	16,159
2	15	A	Huddersfield T	D	1-1	0-1	17	Delfouneso [60]	11,338
3	18	H	Cardiff C	D	1-1	0-1	16	Hanley [88]	12,025
4	22	A	Brighton & HA	L	0-1	0-1	22		22,659
5	28	H	Bolton W	D	0-0	0-0	20		14,632
6	Sept 13	A	Fulham	L	1-2	0-2	22	Rhodes (pen) [68]	14,372
7	16	A	QPR	D	2-2	1-0	23	Duffy [14], Rhodes [60]	14,007
8	19	H	Charlton Ath	W	3-0	1-0	19	Rhodes 2 [45, 75], Lawrence [85]	12,088
9	26	A	Hull C	D	1-1	0-0	18	Rhodes [90]	16,486
10	Oct 3	H	Ipswich T	W	2-0	2-0	14	Rhodes 2 (1 pen) [12 (p), 16]	12,672
11	17	A	Milton Keynes D	L	0-3	0-1	15		11,548
12	21	H	Derby Co	D	0-0	0-0	17		12,968
13	24	H	Burnley	L	0-1	0-0	18		19,897
14	29	A	Leeds U	W	2-0	2-0	14	Conway [1], Rhodes [6]	19,666
15	Nov 3	A	Birmingham C	D	0-0	0-0	15		15,701
16	7	H	Brentford	D	1-1	1-1	16	Lawrence [37]	12,328
17	21	A	Preston NE	W	2-1	1-0	13	Pickford (og) [31], Rhodes (pen) [52]	19,852
18	28	H	Sheffield W	D	2-2	2-1	14	Akpan [5], Evans [44]	15,837
19	Dec 5	A	Bristol C	W	2-0	0-0	13	Hanley [59], Marshall (pen) [86]	15,021
20	11	A	Rotherham U	W	1-0	1-0	12	Hyam (og) [30]	13,054
21	14	H	Nottingham F	D	0-0	0-0	11		12,002
22	20	A	Reading	L	0-1	0-1	14		16,529
23	28	A	Bolton W	L	0-1	0-0	16		18,048
24	Jan 2	A	Cardiff C	L	0-1	0-0	17		14,385
25	12	H	QPR	D	1-1	0-1	18	Akpan [85]	12,285
26	16	H	Brighton & HA	L	0-1	0-1	18		12,930
27	23	A	Charlton Ath	D	1-1	1-1	18	Rhodes [45]	13,512
28	Feb 6	A	Middlesbrough	D	1-1	0-0	18	Gomez [72]	26,244
29	13	H	Hull C	L	0-2	0-0	19		13,902
30	16	H	Fulham	W	3-0	1-0	18	Marshall (pen) [15], Duffy [62], Graham [87]	12,157
31	24	A	Derby Co	L	0-1	0-1	19		27,411
32	27	A	Milton Keynes D	W	3-2	0-1	18	Gomez 2 [53, 90], Bennett [71]	12,693
33	Mar 1	H	Middlesbrough	W	2-1	0-0	16	Akpan [47], Graham [83]	16,601
34	5	A	Burnley	L	0-1	0-1	17		20,478
35	8	H	Birmingham C	W	2-0	2-0	16	Watt [20], Graham [23]	12,774
36	12	H	Leeds U	L	1-2	0-1	16	Jackson [89]	16,017
37	15	A	Ipswich T	L	0-2	0-0	16		16,488
38	19	A	Brentford	W	1-0	0-0	14	Duffy [86]	10,575
39	Apr 2	H	Preston NE	L	1-2	1-2	15	Ward [13]	21,029
40	5	A	Sheffield W	L	1-2	0-0	16	Conway [46]	21,803
41	9	A	Wolverhampton W	D	0-0	0-0	16		19,538
42	16	H	Huddersfield T	L	0-2	0-1	18		15,061
43	19	A	Nottingham F	D	1-1	1-1	17	Graham [22]	16,449
44	23	A	Bristol C	D	2-2	1-0	18	Graham 2 [17, 80]	12,752
45	30	A	Rotherham U	W	1-0	1-0	15	Duffy [6]	11,035
46	May 7	H	Reading	W	3-1	2-1	15	Bennett [8], Graham [14], Jackson [86]	13,140

Final League Position: 15

GOALSCORERS

League (46): Rhodes 10 (3 pens), Graham 7, Duffy 4, Akpan 3, Conway 3, Gomez 3, Bennett 2, Hanley 2, Jackson 2, Lawrence 2, Marshall 2 (2 pens), Delfouneso 1, Evans 1, Ward 1, Watt 1, own goals 2.
FA Cup (6): Marshall 4 (2 pens), Rhodes 1, Watt 1.
Capital One Cup (1): Delfouneso 1.

Raya D 5	Henley A 20+4	Hanley G 44	Duffy S 41	Olsson M 19+1	Marshall B 44	Guthrie D 10+6	Lowe J 9+1	Conway C 29+6	Delfouneso N 7+8	Rhodes J 25	Evans C 26+4	Koita F 8+6	Barrow M 1+3	Akpan D 29+6	Spurr T 20+3	Lawrence T 14+7	Kilgallon M 7+3	Steele J 41	Williamson L 2+8	Taylor C 6+6	O'Sullivan J —+2	Henry D —+1	Brown C 4+13	Lenihan D 18+5	Bennett E 16+5	Jackson S 3+14	Graham D 18	Ward E 6+1	Gomez J 17+2	Watt T 6+3	Grimes M 9+4	Mahoney C 2	Match No.
1	2	3	4	5	6	7^8	8	9	10^1	11	12	13																					1
1	2	3	4	5	10	8^1	7	9	14	11^{12}		12	6^3	13																			2
1	2^1	4	3		9	13	8	6	10					11^2	12	7	5																3
1		4	3		2	7		9	11					10^1	12	8	5	6^2	13														4
1	2	4	3		9^1	13	7	6	10^3	11	8^2	12	14	5																			5
	2	3	4		6	7		9^1	10^3	11	8^2		13	5	14		1																6
	2	4	3	12	6^1	7		9	13	10	8	11^2		5^3	14		1																7
	2	4	3	5	6	7^1		9		11	8^3	10^2		13		12		1	14														8
	2	4	3	5	6^1	7^2		9	13	11	8			12	14	10^3		1															9
	2	3	4	5	6			9		11	7			8		10^1		1	12														10
	2^8	3	4	5^3	6			9	13	11	8^2			7^1	14	10		1	12														11
		4	3	5	2^2			6	11	7				8^3	14	10		1	13	9^1	12												12
		4	3	5	2			9	6^1	11	7			8		10		1	12														13
		4^2	3	5	2			9	13	11	8			7		10^1	12	1		6^3	14												14
12		4	3	5	2			9		11				8		10^2		1		7	6^1												15
13		4	3	5	2			9^1	12	11	7^2			8		10		1	14	6^1													16
	2	4	3	5	6	13		9^1		11^2	7	14		8		10^3		1	12														17
	2	4^3	3	5	6^1	12		9^2		11	7			8		14		1		10	13												18
	2	4	3	5	6	13		9		11^3	7^2			8		10^1		1	12	14													19
	2	4	3	5	6^1	14		9		11^3	8			7		10^2		1		13	12												20
	2	4	3	5	6^3	7^1		9		11	12	10		8^2				1	14	13													21
	2	4	3	5	9^1	8^2		6^3		11		10		7		12		1	13				14										22
	2^1	4	3	5	9	8		6		12^{11^2}		10^3		7		13		1	14														23
		4	3	5	2			9	12	11		10^1		8		6		1	7^2				13										24
		4	3^1		2			9		11	7^3			8	5	10^2		1	14				13	12	6								25
13		3			2			9^1	10					8	5	12	4	1					11	7^2	6^3	14							26
	2	4	3					9		10	8			7^1	5			1					14	12	13	11^2							27
		4			2					7				8	5			1		6^3			6	13	12	10	3		9^1	11^2			28
		3			2			8			7				5			1					12	6	13	11^1		4	9	10^2			29
		4	3		2			12			8				5			1					10	7	6	13	11^1		9^2				30
		4	3		2						8				5			1					12	7	10		11		6		9^1		31
14		4	3		2^1						7^2				5			1					10^3	8	6	13	11		9		12		32
		4	3		2			14			8				5			1						7	13	12	11		6^3	10^2	9^1		33
		4	3		2						8^2				5			1					13	7	10		11		6	12	9^1		34
		4	3		2			6							5			1					14	7	9	13	11^3		8^2	10^1	12		35
		4	3		2			13							5			1					7^1	6	12	11		9^2	10^1	14			36
	2	4	3					6^3			7	5						1					11	12	9	10^1		14	13	8^2			37
	4^8	3			2			9^2			8	5						1					7	6		11^3	12	10^1	13	14			38
		3^8			2						8^2	5	13		1							14	7	6	12^3	10	4	9	11^1			39
5	4	3			2			9^8							12			1					13	7^3	10^2	14	11	3	6^1				40
	4	3			2	7									5	1							12	8	10	13	11^2		6	9^1			41
	4	3			2	12								14	5	1							13	6	7^3	11^1	10^2		9	8			42
	4		11		2				7					6^1	5	1							14	8	12	10^3	3	13			9^2		43
	4		9		2	12			14					8^3	7	5	1						14	13	11	3	10^2			6^1		44
	4	3	6		2	14		13							5	1							7	10^3	12	11		8^1	9^2				45
	4	3	2^2		7	14		12							5	1							6	9^1	13	10		8	11^3				46

FA Cup

Round	Opponent		Score
Third Round	Newport Co	(a)	2-1
Fourth Round	Oxford U	(a)	3-0
Fifth Round	West Ham U	(h)	1-5

Capital One Cup

Round	Opponent		Score
First Round	Shrewsbury T	(h)	1-2

BLACKPOOL

FOUNDATION

Old boys of St John's School, who had formed themselves into a football club, decided to establish a club bearing the name of their town and Blackpool FC came into being at a meeting at the Stanley Arms Hotel in the summer of 1887. In their first season playing at Raikes Hall Gardens, the club won both the Lancashire Junior Cup and the Fylde Cup.

Bloomfield Road, Seasiders Way, Blackpool, Lancashire FY1 6JJ.

Telephone: (01253) 685 000.

Fax: (01253) 405 011.

Ticket Office: (0844) 847 1953.

Website: www.blackpoolfc.co.uk

Email: secretary@blackpoolfc.co.uk

Ground Capacity: 16,476.

Record Attendance: 38,098 v Wolverhampton W, Division 1, 17 September 1955.

Pitch Measurements: 100m × 64m (109.5yd × 70yd).

Chairman: Karl Oyston.

Manager: Gary Bowyer.

First-Team Coach: Richie Kyle.

Physio: Phil Horner.

Colours: Tangerine shirts with thin white stripes, white shorts with tangerine trim, tangerine socks with white hoops.

Year Formed: 1887.

Turned Professional: 1887.

Previous Name: 'South Shore' combined with Blackpool in 1899, twelve years after the latter had been formed on the breaking up of the old 'Blackpool St John's' club.

Club Nickname: 'The Seasiders'.

Grounds: 1887, Raikes Hall Gardens; 1897, Athletic Grounds; 1899, Raikes Hall Gardens; 1899, Bloomfield Road.

First Football League Game: 5 September 1896, Division 2, v Lincoln C (a) L 1–3 – Douglas; Parr, Bowman; Stuart, Stirzaker, Norris; Clarkin, Donnelly, Robert Parkinson, Mount (1), Jack Parkinson.

Record League Victory: 7–0 v Reading, Division 2, 10 November 1928 – Mercer; Gibson, Hamilton, Watson, Wilson, Grant, Ritchie, Oxberry (2), Hampson (5), Tufnell, Neal. 7–0 v Preston NE (away), Division 1, 1 May 1948 – Robinson; Shimwell, Crosland; Buchan, Hayward, Kelly; Hobson, Munro (1), McIntosh (5), McCall, Rickett (1). 7–0 v Sunderland, Division 1, 5 October 1957 – Farm; Armfield, Garrett, Kelly J, Gratrix, Kelly H, Matthews, Taylor (2), Charnley (2), Durie (2), Perry (1).

Record Cup Victory: 7–1 v Charlton Ath, League Cup 2nd rd, 25 September 1963 – Harvey; Armfield, Martin; Crawford, Gratrix, Cranston; Lea, Ball (1), Charnley (4), Durie (1), Oates (1).

HONOURS

League Champions: Division 2 – 1929–30.
Runners-up: Division 1 – 1955–56; Division 2 – 1936–37, 1969–70; Division 4 – 1984–85.
FA Cup Winners: 1953.
Runners-up: 1948, 1951.
League Cup: semi-final – 1962.
League Trophy Winners: 2002, 2004.
Anglo-Italian Cup Winners: 1971.
Runners-up: 1972.

sky SPORTS FACT FILE

When Blackpool won at Scunthorpe United on 5 September 2015 they ended a club record sequence of 23 Football League games without a win. Their previous success had been on 31 January 2015 when they defeated Brighton & Hove Albion at Bloomfield Road.

Record Defeat: 1–10 v Small Heath, Division 2, 2 March 1901 and v Huddersfield T, Division 1, 13 December 1930.

Most League Points (2 for a win): 58, Division 2, 1929–30 and Division 2, 1967–68.

Most League Points (3 for a win): 86, Division 4, 1984–85.

Most League Goals: 98, Division 2, 1929–30.

Highest League Scorer in Season: Jimmy Hampson, 45, Division 2, 1929–30.

Most League Goals in Total Aggregate: Jimmy Hampson, 248, 1927–38.

Most League Goals in One Match: 5, Jimmy Hampson v Reading, Division 2, 10 November 1928; 5, Jimmy McIntosh v Preston NE, Division 1, 1 May 1948.

Most Capped Player: Jimmy Armfield, 43, England.

Most League Appearances: Jimmy Armfield, 568, 1952–71.

Youngest League Player: Matty Kay, 16 years 32 days v Scunthorpe U, 13 November 2005.

Record Transfer Fee Received: £6,750,000 from Liverpool for Charlie Adam, July 2011.

Record Transfer Fee Paid: £1,250,000 to Leicester C for D.J. Campbell, August 2010.

Football League Record: 1896 Elected to Division 2; 1899 Failed re-election; 1900 Re-elected; 1900–30 Division 2; 1930–33 Division 1; 1933–37 Division 2; 1937–67 Division 1; 1967–70 Division 2; 1970–71 Division 1; 1971–78 Division 2; 1978–81 Division 3; 1981–85 Division 4; 1985–90 Division 3; 1990–92 Division 4; 1992–2000 Division 2; 2000–01 Division 3; 2001–04 Division 2; 2004–07 FL 1; 2007–10 FL C; 2010–11 FA Premier League; 2011–15 FL C; 2015–16 FL 1; 2016– FL 2.

LATEST SEQUENCES

Longest Sequence of League Wins: 9, 21.11.1936 – 1.1.1937.

Longest Sequence of League Defeats: 8, 26.11.1898 – 7.1.1899.

Longest Sequence of League Draws: 5, 4.12.1976 – 1.1.1977.

Longest Sequence of Unbeaten League Matches: 17, 6.4.1968 – 21.9.1968.

Longest Sequence Without a League Win: 23, 7.2.2015 – 29.8.2015.

Successive Scoring Runs: 33 from 23.2.1929.

Successive Non-scoring Runs: 5 from 25.11.1989.

MANAGERS

Tom Barcroft 1903–33
  (*Secretary-Manager*)
John Cox 1909–11
Bill Norman 1919–23
Maj. Frank Buckley 1923–27
Sid Beaumont 1927–28
Harry Evans 1928–33
  (*Hon. Team Manager*)
Alex 'Sandy' Macfarlane 1933–35
Joe Smith 1935–58
Ronnie Suart 1958–67
Stan Mortensen 1967–69
Les Shannon 1969–70
Bob Stokoe 1970–72
Harry Potts 1972–76
Allan Brown 1976–78
Bob Stokoe 1978–79
Stan Ternent 1979–80
Alan Ball 1980–81
Allan Brown 1981–82
Sam Ellis 1982–89
Jimmy Mullen 1989–90
Graham Carr 1990
Bill Ayre 1990–94
Sam Allardyce 1994–96
Gary Megson 1996–97
Nigel Worthington 1997–99
Steve McMahon 2000–04
Colin Hendry 2004–05
Simon Grayson 2005–08
Ian Holloway 2009–12
Michael Appleton 2012–13
Paul Ince 2013–14
José Riga 2014
Lee Clark 2014–15
Neil McDonald 2015–16
Gary Bowyer June 2016–

TEN YEAR LEAGUE RECORD

		P	W	D	L	F	A	Pts	Pos
2006-07	FL 1	46	24	11	11	76	49	83	3
2007-08	FL C	46	12	18	16	59	64	54	19
2008-09	FL C	46	13	17	16	47	58	56	16
2009-10	FL C	46	19	13	14	74	58	70	6
2010-11	PR Lge	38	10	9	19	55	78	39	19
2011-12	FL C	46	20	15	11	79	59	75	5
2012-13	FL C	46	14	17	15	62	63	59	15
2013-14	FL C	46	11	13	22	38	66	46	20
2014-15	FL C	46	4	14	28	36	91	26	24
2015-16	FL 1	46	12	10	24	40	63	46	22

DID YOU KNOW ?

In the early 1950s legendary Seasiders winger Stanley Matthews became a racehorse owner when he purchased the four-year-old colt Parbleu. He adopted the racing colours of orange, red and white, a combination of the colours of Blackpool and his former club Stoke City.

BLACKPOOL – FOOTBALL LEAGUE ONE 2015–16 LEAGUE RECORD

Match No.	Date	Venue	Opponents	Result	H/T Score	Lg Pos.	Goalscorers	Attendance
1	Aug 8	A	Colchester U	D	2-2	2-1	8	Cullen 2 [18, 45]	4438
2	15	H	Rochdale	L	0-2	0-0	20		7076
3	18	H	Burton Alb	L	1-2	1-0	22	Redshaw [26]	6197
4	22	A	Sheffield U	L	0-2	0-0	24		20,199
5	29	H	Walsall	L	0-4	0-1	24		7489
6	Sept 5	A	Scunthorpe U	W	1-0	1-0	22	Potts [35]	3313
7	12	A	Gillingham	L	1-2	0-1	23	Jackson (og) [51]	6231
8	19	H	Barnsley	D	1-1	0-1	24	Redshaw [55]	7542
9	26	A	Shrewsbury T	L	0-2	0-0	24		5241
10	29	H	Chesterfield	W	2-0	1-0	23	Cullen [2], Potts [68]	5960
11	Oct 3	H	Swindon T	W	1-0	1-0	22	Cullen [38]	6704
12	17	A	Coventry C	D	0-0	0-0	22		12,094
13	20	A	Millwall	D	1-1	0-1	21	Redshaw (pen) [82]	6225
14	24	H	Crewe Alex	W	2-0	0-0	19	White [64], Redshaw (pen) [87]	6970
15	31	A	Bury	L	3-4	2-4	20	Cullen [12], Robertson [44], Redshaw (pen) [84]	5013
16	Nov 3	A	Bradford C	L	0-1	0-1	20		17,435
17	14	H	Doncaster R	L	0-2	0-2	21		6597
18	21	A	Southend U	L	0-1	0-0	23		6290
19	24	A	Port Vale	L	0-2	0-0	23		3640
20	28	H	Fleetwood T	W	1-0	0-0	22	Pond (og) [17]	7755
21	Dec 12	A	Wigan Ath	W	1-0	1-0	19	Aldred [36]	8424
22	19	H	Peterborough U	W	2-0	2-0	17	Cullen [3], Potts [31]	6204
23	28	A	Barnsley	L	2-4	0-1	18	Cullen [52], Little [90]	9072
24	Jan 2	A	Burton Alb	L	0-1	0-0	21		4339
25	9	H	Port Vale	L	0-1	0-0	21		6527
26	16	H	Scunthorpe U	W	5-0	3-0	19	Aldred [2], Potts 2 [12, 28], Norris [55], Phillискirk [82]	6004
27	23	A	Walsall	D	1-1	0-0	19	Philliskirk [90]	5022
28	26	H	Sheffield U	D	0-0	0-0	18		6296
29	30	H	Gillingham	W	1-0	1-0	18	Redshaw (pen) [45]	6828
30	Feb 13	H	Shrewsbury T	L	2-3	1-3	18	Aldred [36], Philliskirk [54]	6873
31	16	H	Oldham Ath	D	0-0	0-0	18		7197
32	20	A	Swindon T	L	2-3	1-1	18	Aldred [2], Philliskirk (pen) [65]	7412
33	27	H	Bradford C	L	0-1	0-0	20		8780
34	Mar 1	A	Chesterfield	D	1-1	0-0	21	Potts [53]	5915
35	5	A	Millwall	L	0-3	0-2	21		9753
36	12	H	Coventry C	L	0-1	0-1	21		8869
37	15	A	Oldham Ath	L	0-1	0-0	22		3715
38	19	A	Crewe Alex	W	2-1	1-0	20	Redshaw [34], Aldred [84]	4480
39	25	H	Bury	D	1-1	0-0	20	Philliskirk (pen) [74]	7645
40	28	A	Doncaster R	W	1-0	0-0	19	Cullen [87]	5575
41	Apr 2	H	Southend U	W	2-0	0-0	19	Cullen [49], Blyth [79]	6979
42	9	H	Colchester U	L	0-1	0-0	21		6242
43	16	A	Rochdale	L	0-3	0-1	21		3247
44	23	A	Fleetwood T	D	0-0	0-0	21		5123
45	30	H	Wigan Ath	L	0-4	0-0	21		9226
46	May 8	A	Peterborough U	L	1-5	1-0	22	Blyth [16]	6005

Final League Position: 22

GOALSCORERS

League (40): Cullen 9, Redshaw 7 (4 pens), Potts 6, Aldred 5, Philliskirk 5 (2 pens), Blyth 2, Little 1, Norris 1, Robertson 1, White 1, own goals 2.
FA Cup (0).
Capital One Cup (0).
Johnstone's Paint Trophy (2): Rivers 1, Robertson 1.

Doyle C 33	Boyce E 17+9	Jones L 10	Robertson D 35+3	Ferguson D 29+1	Cameron H 12+2	Potts B 45	McAlister J 43+1	Samuel B 10+13	Cullen M 37+4	Redshaw J 27+9	Cubero J 4+3	Thomas K 2+16	Letheren K 4+1	Oliver C 1+3	Dunne C 2+2	Aldred T 42	Rivers J 2+8	Herron J 5+10	Norris D 34+4	Paterson M —+17	White H 29	Lyness D 9	Little A 3+2	Lee E 3+1	Aimson W 14+1	Yeates M 8+3	Philliskirk D 22	Ikpeazu U 3+9	Higham L 11	Smith L 4+4	Blyth J 6+2	Match No.
1²	2	3	4	5	6³	7	8	9¹	10	11	12	13	14																			1
	2	4	3	5	9	7	8²	6¹	10	11		12	1	13																		2
	2	3	4	5	6	7³	9¹		11	10²		14	1	13	12																	3
	2		4	5	9³	8	6		11	10¹	12	13	14	1	7²	3																4
	2		3	5	6	7³	8	9²	10	11¹	12	13		1		4	14															5
1	2	4	13	5	6¹	7	9		11			8²		14		3		10³	12													6
1	2	4		5	10¹	9	8	14	11²		6	13				3		7²	12													7
1	2	3		5	6³	10	9		11	13	7²	12				4		8¹	14													8
1	2	4	5	14	13	8			10	9		11³				3²	7	6¹	12													9
1	2	4	3	5	14	6²	8	9		11³	10¹			13		12	7															10
1	2		3	5	6¹	7	9	12	11²	10			14			4	13	8³														11
1	2		4	5	9²	6	8	13	10	11¹	7	7²				3																12
			3	5	6³	7	9²	12	10¹	11			14			4	13	8		2												13
1	13		3	5		8	6	9²	11¹	10			14			4	12	7		2³												14
1	2		3	5³		8	9¹		10²	11			14			4	12	7	13	6												15
1	12		3		13	7	9²		10	11			14	5	4	6		8³		2¹												16
			3	2		7	9		10	11¹		12		5	4	6²		8	13	2	1											17
			3	5		7	9	6¹	10²	14		12				4		8	13	2	1	11¹										18
			9	5		8¹	4	6²	11³	13		10				3		12	7	14	2	1										19
	14		3	5		7	9	6¹	10	11²						4	13	8		2³	1		12									20
	13		3	5		8	6		11²							4	14	9	12	2	1			10¹	7³							21
	14		3	2		9	6		11²							4		7	13³	5	1		12	10¹	8							22
			3	5¹		8	9²	13	11							4	12		7	2	1	14	10³	6								23
1	14		4¹	5		8	9	6	11²							3	12	13		2	10			7³								24
1			5			7²	6	13		12						3	14	8³		2	10¹		4	9	11							25
1			5			8	6	12		10						4	13	7²		2			3	9¹	11							26
1			5			7¹	6		13	11²						3	14	8		2			4	9²	10	12						27
1		14	5			7	6³		13	10¹						3		8		2			4²	9	11	12						28
1	2	12	5			7			10¹	11²						3	14	8³		2			4	9	6	13						29
	2		5			8	12		10³	11²						4		7	14		1		3	9¹	6	13						30
		5				6	8		11¹	9³						3	13	7²	12	2	1		4		10	14						31
1		5				8	6	12	10¹	14						3	13	8	13	2			4	9²	11							32
1		5				7	6³		10¹	14						3		8	13	2			4⁸	9²	11	12						33
1	12		3	5⁸		7	6			9¹						4	13	8		2²					10	11						34
1	12		5¹			6	8		13	11						4	7²		14	2⁸			3		9	10¹						35
1	2	4				8	9	12	13	10¹						3		7²							11	14	5	6³				36
1		4				9	8³	13								3		6	14	2				12	10¹	11	5	7²				37
1	12		4			7	8		9¹	10⁸						3		6		2					11²	13	5					38
1		4				7²	9	12	11³							3		8	14	2				13	6		5		10¹			39
1		4				8	9²	12	11							3		7³	13	2					6		5	14	10¹			40
1		3				7¹	9		11²							4		8		2			13		6		5	12	10			41
1		3				8¹	9	12	11²	13						4		7		2					6³		5	14	10			42
1	2	3				8³	9		11	12						4		7¹	14						6²		5	13	10			43
1		4				9			11³	10³						3		8	12	2				14	6		5	7²	13			44
1		4				7	9		10¹	11²						3		13		2					6	14	5	8³	12			45
1		4				7	9			11						3		8		2					6		5		10			46

FA Cup
First Round   Barnet   (a)   0-2

Capital One Cup
First Round   Northampton T   (a)   0-3

Johnstone's Paint Trophy
Second Round   Port Vale   (a)   2-1
Northern Quarter-Final   Wigan Ath   (a)   0-4

BOLTON WANDERERS

FOUNDATION

In 1874 boys of Christ Church Sunday School, Blackburn Street, led by their master Thomas Ogden, established a football club which went under the name of the school and whose president was vicar of Christ Church. Membership was 6d (two and a half pence). When their president began to lay down too many rules about the use of church premises, the club broke away and formed Bolton Wanderers in 1877, holding their earliest meetings at the Gladstone Hotel.

Macron Stadium, Burnden Way, Lostock, Bolton BL6 6JW.

Telephone: (0844) 871 2932. *Fax:* (01204) 673 773.

Ticket Office: (0844) 871 2932.

Website: www.bwfc.co.uk

Email: reception@bwfc.co.uk

Ground Capacity: 28,063.

Record Attendance: 69,912 v Manchester C, FA Cup 5th rd, 18 February 1933 (at Burnden Park); 28,353 v Leicester C, FA Premier League, 23 December 2003 (at The Reebok Stadium).

Pitch Measurements: 105m × 68m (115yd × 74.5yd).

Chairman: Ken Anderson.

Chief Excutive: Dean Holdsworth.

Manager: Phil Parkinson.

Assistant Manager: Steve Parkin.

Head of Sports Science: Mark Leather.

Colours: White shirts with blue body trim, blue shorts, blue socks with white trim.

Year Formed: 1874.

Turned Professional: 1880.

Previous Name: 1874, Christ Church FC; 1877, Bolton Wanderers.

Club Nickname: 'The Trotters'.

Grounds: Park Recreation Ground and Cockle's Field before moving to Pike's Lane ground 1881; 1895, Burnden Park; 1997, Reebok Stadium (renamed Macron Stadium 2014).

First Football League Game: 8 September 1888, Football League, v Derby Co (h) L 3–6 – Harrison; Robinson, Mitchell; Roberts, Weir, Bullough, Davenport (2), Milne, Coupar, Barbour, Brogan (1).

Record League Victory: 8–0 v Barnsley, Division 2, 6 October 1934 – Jones; Smith, Finney; Goslin, Atkinson, George Taylor; George T. Taylor (2), Eastham, Milsom (1), Westwood (4), Cook, (1 og).

Record Cup Victory: 13–0 v Sheffield U, FA Cup 2nd rd, 1 February 1890 – Parkinson; Robinson (1), Jones; Bullough, Davenport, Roberts; Rushton, Brogan (3), Cassidy (5), McNee, Weir (4).

HONOURS

League Champions: First Division – 1996–97; Division 2 – 1908–09, 1977–78; Division 3 – 1972–73. *Runners-up:* Division 2 – 1899–1900, 1904–05, 1910–11, 1934–35; Second Division – 1992–93.

FA Cup Winners: 1923, 1926, 1929, 1958. *Runners-up:* 1894, 1904, 1953.

League Cup: Runners-up: 1995, 2004.

League Trophy Winners: 1989. *Runners-up:* 1986.

European Competitions *UEFA Cup:* 2005–06, 2007–08.

sky SPORTS FACT FILE

J.J. Bentley, who served Bolton Wanderers for many years as secretary and then chairman of the board, was one of the most influential figures in the early days of the Football League. He served the League as president from 1894 to 1910 and was also a well-known referee and editor of *The Athletic News*.

Record Defeat: 1–9 v Preston NE, FA Cup 2nd rd, 5 November 1887.

Most League Points (2 for a win): 61, Division 3, 1972–73.

Most League Points (3 for a win): 98, Division 1, 1996–97.

Most League Goals: 100, Division 1, 1996–97.

Highest League Scorer in Season: Joe Smith, 38, Division 1, 1920–21.

Most League Goals in Total Aggregate: Nat Lofthouse, 255, 1946–61.

Most League Goals in One Match: 5, Tony Caldwell v Walsall, Division 3, 10 September 1983.

Most Capped Player: Ricardo Gardner, 72 (112), Jamaica.

Most League Appearances: Eddie Hopkinson, 519, 1956–70.

Youngest League Player: Ray Parry, 15 years 267 days v Wolverhampton W, 13 October 1951.

Record Transfer Fee Received: £15,000,000 from Chelsea for Nicolas Anelka, January 2008.

Record Transfer Fee Paid: £8,200,000 to Toulouse for Johan Elmander, July 2008.

Football League Record: 1888 Founder Member of the League; 1899–1900 Division 2; 1900–03 Division 1; 1903–05 Division 2; 1905–08 Division 1; 1908–09 Division 2; 1909–10 Division 1; 1910–11 Division 2; 1911–33 Division 1; 1933–35 Division 2; 1935–64 Division 1; 1964–71 Division 2; 1971–73 Division 3; 1973–78 Division 2; 1978–80 Division 1; 1980–83 Division 2; 1983–87 Division 3; 1987–88 Division 4; 1988–92 Division 3; 1992–93 Division 2; 1993–95 Division 1; 1995–96 FA Premier League; 1996–97 Division 1; 1997–98 FA Premier League; 1998–2001 Division 1; 2001–12 FA Premier League; 2012–16 FL C; 2016– FL 1.

LATEST SEQUENCES

Longest Sequence of League Wins: 11, 5.11.1904 – 2.1.1905.

Longest Sequence of League Defeats: 11, 7.4.1902 – 18.10.1902.

Longest Sequence of League Draws: 6, 25.1.1913 – 8.3.1913.

Longest Sequence of Unbeaten League Matches: 23, 13.10.1990 – 9.3.1991.

Longest Sequence Without a League Win: 26, 7.4.1902 – 10.1.1903.

Successive Scoring Runs: 24 from 22.11.1996.

Successive Non-scoring Runs: 5 from 27.4.2015.

MANAGERS

Tom Rawthorne 1874–85
 (*Secretary*)
J. J. Bentley 1885–86
 (*Secretary*)
W. G. Struthers 1886–87
 (*Secretary*)
Fitzroy Norris 1887
 (*Secretary*)
J. J. Bentley 1887–95
 (*Secretary*)
Harry Downs 1895–96
 (*Secretary*)
Frank Brettell 1896–98
 (*Secretary*)
John Somerville 1898–1910
Will Settle 1910–15
Tom Mather 1915–19
Charles Foweraker 1919–44
Walter Rowley 1944–50
Bill Ridding 1951–68
Nat Lofthouse 1968–70
Jimmy McIlroy 1970
Jimmy Meadows 1971
Nat Lofthouse 1971
 (*then Admin. Manager to 1972*)
Jimmy Armfield 1971–74
Ian Greaves 1974–80
Stan Anderson 1980–81
George Mulhall 1981–82
John McGovern 1982–85
Charlie Wright 1985
Phil Neal 1985–92
Bruce Rioch 1992–95
Roy McFarland 1995–96
Colin Todd 1996–99
Roy McFarland and Colin Todd
 joint managers 1995–96
Sam Allardyce 1999–2007
Sammy Lee 2007
Gary Megson 2007–09
Owen Coyle 2010–12
Dougie Freedman 2012–14
Neil Lennon 2014–16
Phil Parkinson June 2016

TEN YEAR LEAGUE RECORD

		P	W	D	L	F	A	Pts	Pos
2006-07	PR Lge	38	16	8	14	47	52	56	7
2007-08	PR Lge	38	9	10	19	36	54	37	16
2008-09	PR Lge	38	11	8	19	41	53	41	13
2009-10	PR Lge	38	10	9	19	42	67	39	14
2010-11	PR Lge	38	12	10	16	52	56	46	14
2011-12	PR Lge	38	10	6	22	46	77	36	18
2012-13	FL C	46	18	14	14	69	61	68	7
2013-14	FL C	46	14	17	15	59	60	59	14
2014-15	FL C	46	13	12	21	54	67	51	18
2015-16	FL C	46	5	15	26	41	81	30	24

DID YOU KNOW ?

Bolton Wanderers went 36 Football League games without an away win between November 1948 and September 1950. The unfortunate sequence was ended when Willie Moir's goal earned Wanderers a 1-0 win at Villa Park.

BOLTON WANDERERS – FL CHAMPIONSHIP 2015–16 LEAGUE RECORD

Match No.	Date	Venue	Opponents	Result	H/T Score	Lg Pos.	Goalscorers	Attendance
1	Aug 8	H	Derby Co	D	0-0	0-0	14		17,162
2	15	A	Middlesbrough	L	0-3	0-3	21		23,333
3	18	A	Milton Keynes D	L	0-1	0-0	23		10,765
4	22	H	Nottingham F	D	1-1	0-0	23	Dobbie [90]	16,410
5	28	A	Blackburn R	D	0-0	0-0	22		14,632
6	Sept12	H	Wolverhampton W	W	2-1	2-0	16	Feeney [17], Clough (pen) [45]	14,698
7	15	H	Sheffield W	D	0-0	0-0	17		14,438
8	19	A	Huddersfield T	L	1-4	1-1	21	Feeney [3]	11,762
9	26	H	Brighton & HA	D	2-2	1-2	21	Danns [41], Madine [90]	13,405
10	Oct 3	A	QPR	L	3-4	2-2	22	Madine [8], Feeney [11], Silva [85]	16,026
11	17	A	Burnley	L	0-2	0-0	24		17,632
12	20	H	Birmingham C	L	0-1	0-1	24		13,703
13	24	H	Leeds U	D	1-1	1-0	24	Ameobi [32]	18,178
14	31	A	Preston NE	D	0-0	0-0	22		14,494
15	Nov 3	A	Ipswich T	L	0-2	0-1	22		17,017
16	7	H	Bristol C	D	0-0	0-0	23		14,239
17	21	A	Reading	L	1-2	0-2	24	Feeney (pen) [80]	16,420
18	30	H	Brentford	D	1-1	0-1	24	Danns [65]	12,731
19	Dec 5	H	Cardiff C	L	2-3	1-1	24	Madine [17], Dervite [71]	13,241
20	12	A	Hull C	L	0-1	0-1	24		15,739
21	15	A	Charlton Ath	D	2-2	2-2	24	Heskey [32], Vela [42]	12,294
22	19	H	Fulham	D	2-2	0-1	24	Clough 2 [61, 74]	14,543
23	26	A	Rotherham U	L	0-4	0-0	24		11,315
24	28	H	Blackburn R	W	1-0	0-0	24	Madine [77]	18,048
25	Jan 2	A	Huddersfield T	L	0-2	0-0	24		15,969
26	12	A	Sheffield W	L	2-3	1-1	24	Madine [19], Wheater [62]	20,757
27	16	A	Nottingham F	L	0-3	0-2	24		18,465
28	23	H	Milton Keynes D	W	3-1	2-0	24	Holding [7], Pratley [41], Ameobi [90]	13,932
29	Feb 2	A	Wolverhampton W	D	2-2	0-1	24	Silva [81], Dobbie [88]	17,825
30	6	H	Rotherham U	W	2-1	1-1	23	Spearing [2], Woolery [90]	14,641
31	13	A	Brighton & HA	L	2-3	1-2	24	Heskey [22], Spearing [52]	26,717
32	20	H	QPR	D	1-1	0-0	23	Clough [68]	14,085
33	23	A	Birmingham C	L	0-1	0-1	23		15,992
34	27	H	Burnley	L	1-2	0-1	23	Feeney [69]	17,484
35	Mar 5	A	Leeds U	L	1-2	0-1	24	Woolery [74]	21,070
36	8	H	Ipswich T	D	2-2	0-1	24	Wilson [73], Dobbie (pen) [90]	12,681
37	12	H	Preston NE	L	1-2	1-0	24	Trotter [22]	18,423
38	19	A	Bristol C	L	0-6	0-2	24		15,608
39	Apr 2	H	Reading	L	0-1	0-0	24		13,469
40	5	A	Brentford	L	1-3	0-3	24	Clough (pen) [70]	9062
41	9	A	Derby Co	L	1-4	0-2	24	Clough (pen) [73]	29,674
42	16	H	Middlesbrough	L	1-2	0-0	24	Vela [61]	18,196
43	19	H	Charlton Ath	D	0-0	0-0	24		12,257
44	23	A	Cardiff C	L	1-2	1-0	24	Clough [7]	24,189
45	30	H	Hull C	W	1-0	0-0	24	Dobbie [65]	14,366
46	May 7	A	Fulham	L	0-1	0-0	24		17,207

Final League Position: 24

GOALSCORERS

League (41): Clough 7 (3 pens), Feeney 5 (1 pen), Madine 5, Dobbie 4 (1 pen), Ameobi 2, Danns 2, Heskey 2, Silva 2, Spearing 2, Vela 2, Woolery 2, Dervite 1, Holding 1, Pratley 1, Trotter 1, Wheater 1, Wilson 1.
FA Cup (5): Pratley 3, Madine 1, Moxey 1.
Capital One Cup (0).

Amos B 40	Wilson L 11 + 1	Dervite D 21 + 1	Gouano P 19	Moxey D 33	Spearing J 18 + 4	Pratley D 36	Feeney L 36 + 1	Clough Z 25 + 3	Danns N 21 + 11	Madine G 22 + 10	Heskey E 14 + 15	Trotter L 8 + 5	Holding R 26	Vela J 30 + 1	Davies M 34 + 2	Walker T 3 + 4	Dobbie S 3 + 21	Silva W 14 + 8	Osede D 22 + 1	Finney A 1 + 1	Pisano F 2 + 1	Wheater D 26 + 2	Clayton M 5 + 3	Casado J 9	Woolery K 5 + 12	Ameobi S 6 + 2	Twardzik F — + 2	Rachubka P 6 + 1	Maher N 5	Samizadeh A — + 1	Threlkeld O 3	Garrett T 2 + 1	Newell G — + 2	Match No.
1	2	3	4	5	6▪	7¹	8	9²	10	11	12	13																						1
1	14	3	2	5	6³		8²	12	10	11				4¹	7	9	13																	2
1	2	3	4	5⁴			10²	9	8	11	13			6¹	7	14	13																	3
1	2	3	4	5			12	9¹	6	11	13			7	10³	14	8²																	4
1	2	3▪	4	5			8	9	6	11	12			7			10¹																	5
1	2		3	5			8	9²	7¹	11	13			12	6		10	4																6
1	2		3	5			8	9²	7	11	13			6			12	10	4															7
1	2		3	5			8		6	12	11²			7	13		9³	10¹	4▪	14														8
1			4	5	14		8		7²	11				6	13	12	10³				2	3	9¹											9
1		4	3	5	13	9¹	8		6	11				7			14			2²	12	10¹												10
1		3			6³	9	8		7²	11	13			12			14	10¹	2		4		5											11
1		3				8⁶	6		13	10	11²			7			9¹				4	12	5	14										12
1	14	3▪				8	11		7³	10²				6	9¹	13		2			4		5		12									13
1		3			6¹	8	10		13	12				7				2³		14	4	9	5	11²										14
1		3	2²		6³	8	10			11	14			7				12			4	9¹	5	13										15
1		3			6	7	10			12¹				2	8		9²				4	14	5¹		11	13								16
1		3			7¹	9	6		8	12	14			2	10²						4	13	5		11³									17
1		3				10	8		6	12				2	7²	13					4	9¹	5		11									18
1		3	9¹		7	6²			8	10	13			2							4		5▪		11³	14								19
1		3	6	12	9¹	10			8		13		5	2³	7		14				4				11²									20
1		3	5	7		8	9²	13	12	11¹				2	6¹	10	14				4													21
1		3	5	6²	7	8	9¹	12	11¹	13				2	10	14				4														22
1		3		5	6²	10	8	9	7	12	11¹			2			13				4													23
1		3	5		7	8	9		11					2	6	10					12													24
1		3	5		6	8	9		11					2¹	7	10					12													25
1		3		5	9	8	12		11		7			2	6²						10¹		4		13									26
1▪		3		5	9	7		13	11		8	2	6²			10³					4¹		14			12								27
1		4		5	13	8	7		11²		6	3	2	9			10¹									12								28
1		3		5	6	7				12	8¹	4	2	9	13 10						11²													29
1		3		5	6	8²	7			11¹ 12		4	2	9	14 10³						13													30
1		3		6³	8	7	12	14		11		4	2	9²	10¹ 5						13													31
1		3		5	6	7	10	9¹	13	12	11²		4	2							8													32
		3³		5	6¹	9	7	11	12			4	8² 10		14 13	2										1								33
				5	6²	8	10	9¹		12 11¹		3	2	7	13 14	4										1								34
				5	6	7¹	10	9²		11	12		4	2³	8	14		13								1								35
2				5	6	8²	10	11¹		12		7²	4	9	13 14	3										1								36
2²				5	7²	10	9¹	11		6		4	8		14 12	3					13					1								37
				5	8				12	10		4	7	6¹	9² 14 13³	2		3			11				1									38
1				5	9	10² 13		14	12		3▪	6			8¹	7		4			11³				2									39
1				5	8	11	13		7	10	9²			3	4³	12				6¹		2 14												40
1				5	8	9	6		12	10²		3	7¹	11		2				4		11												41
1				5	6	9			10¹ 12	3	8²	11	7			4		13			2													42
1					9	10			11¹	3	8	7		6			4				12				5	2								43
					9¹	10	7		11²	3	8			6			4				13		5▪		2 12									44
1	2				8	11¹	6		10²	3		9	12	7			4									6	5	13						45
1	2				9¹	10	8		11²			7	14	3³			4				12					6	5	13						46

FA Cup

Third Round	Eastleigh	(a)	1-1	
Replay	Eastleigh	(h)	3-2	
Fourth Round	Leeds U	(h)	1-2	

Capital One Cup

First Round	Burton Alb	(h)	0-1

AFC BOURNEMOUTH

FOUNDATION

There was a Bournemouth FC as early as 1875, but the present club arose out of the remnants of the Boscombe St John's club (formed 1890). The meeting at which Boscombe FC came into being was held at a house in Gladstone Road in 1899. They began by playing in the Boscombe and District Junior League.

Vitality Stadium, Dean Court, Kings Park, Bournemouth, Dorset BH7 7AF.

Telephone: (0344) 576 1910.

Fax: (01202) 726 373.

Ticket Office: (0344) 576 1910.

Website: www.afcb.co.uk

Email: enquiries@afcb.co.uk

Ground Capacity: 11,464.

Record Attendance: 28,799 v Manchester U, FA Cup 6th rd, 2 March 1957.

Pitch Measurements: 105m × 68m (115yd × 74.5yd).

Chairman: Jeff Mostyn.

Chief Executive: Neill Blake.

Manager: Eddie Howe.

Assistant Manager: Jason Tindall.

Physio: Steve Hard.

Colours: Red and black striped shirts, black shorts, black socks with red trim.

Year Formed: 1899.

Turned Professional: 1910.

Previous Names: 1890, Boscombe St John's; 1899, Boscombe FC; 1923, Bournemouth & Boscombe Ath FC; 1972, AFC Bournemouth.

Club Nickname: 'Cherries'.

Grounds: 1899, Castlemain Road, Pokesdown; 1910, Dean Court (renamed Fitness First Stadium 2001, Seward Stadium 2011, Goldsands Stadium 2012, Vitality Stadium 2015).

First Football League Game: 25 August 1923, Division 3 (S), v Swindon T (a) L 1–3 – Heron; Wingham, Lamb; Butt, Charles Smith, Voisey; Miller, Lister (1), Davey, Simpson, Robinson.

Record League Victory: 8–0 v Birmingham C, FL C, 25 October 2014 – Boruc; Francis, Elphick, Cook, Daniels; Ritchie (1), Arter (Gosling), Surman, Pugh (3); Pitman (1) (Rantie 2 (1 pen)), Wilson (1) (Fraser). 10–0 win v Northampton T at start of 1939–40 expunged from the records on outbreak of war.

Record Cup Victory: 11–0 v Margate, FA Cup 1st rd, 20 November 1971 – Davies; Machin (1), Kitchener, Benson, Jones, Powell, Cave (1), Boyer, MacDougall (9 incl. 1p), Miller, Scott (De Garis).

HONOURS

League Champions: FL C – 2014–15; Division 3 – 1986–87.
Runners-up: FL 1 – 2012–13; Division 3S – 1947–48; FL 2 – 2009–10; Division 4 – 1970–71.
FA Cup: 6th rd – 1957.
League Cup: quarter-final – 2015.
League Trophy Winners: 1984. *Runners-up:* 1998.

sky SPORTS FACT FILE

Although Bournemouth's official record League victory is 7-0, they have achieved a greater winning margin in a Football League match. On 2 September 1939 they defeated Northampton Town 10-0 at Dean Court in a Division Three South fixture. Unfortunately for the Cherries war was declared and the results expunged from the records.

Record Defeat: 0–9 v Lincoln C, Division 3, 18 December 1982.

Most League Points (2 for a win): 62, Division 3, 1971–72.

Most League Points (3 for a win): 97, Division 3, 1986–87.

Most League Goals: 98, FL C, 2014–15.

Highest League Scorer in Season: Ted MacDougall, 42, 1970–71.

Most League Goals in Total Aggregate: Ron Eyre, 202, 1924–33.

Most League Goals in One Match: 4, Jack Russell v Clapton Orient, Division 3 (S), 7 January 1933; 4, Jack Russell v Bristol C, Division 3 (S), 28 January 1933; 4, Harry Mardon v Southend U, Division 3 (S), 1 January 1938; 4, Jack McDonald v Torquay U, Division 3 (S), 8 November 1947; 4, Ted MacDougall v Colchester U, 18 September 1970; 4, Brian Clark v Rotherham U, 10 October 1972; 4, Luther Blissett v Hull C, 29 November 1988; 4, James Hayter v Bury, Division 2, 21 October 2000.

Most Capped Player: Tokelo Rantie, 24 (37), South Africa.

Most League Appearances: Steve Fletcher, 628, 1992–2007; 2008–13.

Youngest League Player: Jimmy White, 15 years 321 days v Brentford, 30 April 1958.

Record Transfer Fee Received: £1,000,000 from Burnley for Danny Ings, August 2011.

Record Transfer Fee Paid: £15,000,000 to Liverpool for Jordan Ibe, July 2016.

Football League Record: 1923 Elected to Division 3 (S) and remained a Third Division club for record number of years until 1970; 1970–71 Division 4; 1971–75 Division 3; 1975–82 Division 4; 1982–87 Division 3; 1987–90 Division 2; 1990–92 Division 3; 1992–2002 Division 2; 2002–03 Division 3; 2003–04 Division 2; 2004–08 FL 1; 2008–10 FL 2; 2010–13 FL 1; 2013–15 FL C; 2015– FA Premier League.

MANAGERS

Vincent Kitcher 1914–23
(Secretary-Manager)
Harry Kinghorn 1923–25
Leslie Knighton 1925–28
Frank Richards 1928–30
Billy Birrell 1930–35
Bob Crompton 1935–36
Charlie Bell 1936–39
Harry Kinghorn 1939–47
Harry Lowe 1947–50
Jack Bruton 1950–56
Fred Cox 1956–58
Don Welsh 1958–61
Bill McGarry 1961–63
Reg Flewin 1963–65
Fred Cox 1965–70
John Bond 1970–73
Trevor Hartley 1974–75
John Benson 1975–78
Alec Stock 1979–80
David Webb 1980–82
Don Megson 1983
Harry Redknapp 1983–92
Tony Pulis 1992–94
Mel Machin 1994–2000
Sean O'Driscoll 2000–06
Kevin Bond 2006–08
Jimmy Quinn 2008
Eddie Howe 2008–11
Lee Bradbury 2011–12
Paul Groves 2012
Eddie Howe October 2012–

LATEST SEQUENCES

Longest Sequence of League Wins: 8, 12.3.2013 – 20.4.2013.

Longest Sequence of League Defeats: 7, 13.8.1994 – 13.9.1994.

Longest Sequence of League Draws: 5, 25.4.2000 – 19.8.2000.

Longest Sequence of Unbeaten League Matches: 18, 6.3.1982 – 28.8.1982.

Longest Sequence Without a League Win: 14, 6.3.1974 – 27.4.1974.

Successive Scoring Runs: 31 from 28.10.2000.

Successive Non-scoring Runs: 6 from 1.2.1975.

TEN YEAR LEAGUE RECORD

		P	W	D	L	F	A	Pts	Pos
2006-07	FL 1	46	13	13	20	50	64	52	19
2007-08	FL 1	46	17	7	22	62	72	48*	21
2008-09	FL 2	46	17	12	17	59	51	46†	21
2009-10	FL 2	46	25	8	13	61	44	83	2
2010-11	FL 1	46	19	14	13	75	54	71	6
2011-12	FL 1	46	15	13	18	48	52	58	11
2012-13	FL 1	46	24	11	11	76	53	83	2
2013-14	FL C	46	18	12	16	67	66	66	10
2014-15	FL C	46	26	12	8	98	45	90	1
2015-16	PR Lge	38	11	9	18	45	67	42	16

*10 pts deducted; †17 pts deducted.

DID YOU KNOW ?

Bournemouth were elected to the Football League in 1923 when known as Boscombe. After their election they considered changing their name to Bournemouth United or Bournemouth County before eventually opting for Bournemouth & Boscombe Athletic.

AFC BOURNEMOUTH – FA PREMIER LEAGUE 2015–16 LEAGUE RECORD

Match No.	Date	Venue	Opponents	Result	H/T Score	Lg Pos.	Goalscorers	Attendance
1	Aug 8	H	Aston Villa	L	0-1	0-0	17		11,155
2	17	A	Liverpool	L	0-1	0-1	19		44,102
3	22	A	West Ham U	W	4-3	2-0	10	Wilson 3 (1 pen) [11, 28, 79 (p)], Pugh [66]	34,977
4	29	H	Leicester C	D	1-1	1-0	11	Wilson [24]	11,155
5	Sept 12	A	Norwich C	L	1-3	0-1	15	Cook [81]	27,018
6	19	H	Sunderland	W	2-0	2-0	11	Wilson [4], Ritchie [9]	11,271
7	26	A	Stoke C	L	1-2	0-1	16	Gosling [76]	27,742
8	Oct 3	H	Watford	D	1-1	1-1	15	Murray [28]	11,187
9	17	A	Manchester C	L	1-5	1-4	17	Murray [22]	54,502
10	25	H	Tottenham H	L	1-5	1-3	17	Ritchie [1]	11,332
11	Nov 1	A	Southampton	L	0-2	0-2	17		31,229
12	7	A	Newcastle U	L	0-1	0-1	18		11,155
13	21	A	Swansea C	D	2-2	2-2	18	King [10], Gosling [28]	20,878
14	28	H	Everton	D	3-3	0-2	18	Smith [80], Stanislas 2 [67, 90]	11,228
15	Dec 5	A	Chelsea	W	1-0	0-0	17	Murray [82]	41,631
16	12	H	Manchester U	W	2-1	1-1	14	Stanislas [2], King [54]	11,334
17	19	A	WBA	W	2-1	0-0	14	Smith [52], Daniels (pen) [87]	26,127
18	26	H	Crystal Palace	D	0-0	0-0	14		11,218
19	28	A	Arsenal	L	0-2	0-1	16		59,983
20	Jan 2	A	Leicester C	D	0-0	0-0	15		32,006
21	12	H	West Ham U	L	1-3	1-0	16	Arter [17]	11,071
22	16	H	Norwich C	W	3-0	1-0	15	Gosling [10], Daniels (pen) [54], Afobe [75]	11,065
23	23	A	Sunderland	D	1-1	1-1	15	Afobe [13]	41,367
24	Feb 2	A	Crystal Palace	W	2-1	1-1	15	Pugh [34], Afobe [57]	24,855
25	7	H	Arsenal	L	0-2	0-2	15		11,357
26	13	H	Stoke C	L	1-3	0-1	15	Ritchie [57]	10,863
27	27	A	Watford	D	0-0	0-0	15		20,831
28	Mar 1	A	Southampton	W	2-0	1-0	15	Cook [31], Afobe [79]	11,033
29	5	A	Newcastle U	W	3-1	1-0	14	Taylor (og) [28], King [70], Daniels [90]	52,107
30	12	H	Swansea C	W	3-2	1-1	13	Gradel [37], King [50], Cook [78]	11,179
31	20	A	Tottenham H	L	0-3	0-2	13		36,084
32	Apr 2	H	Manchester C	L	0-4	0-3	13		11,192
33	9	A	Aston Villa	W	2-1	1-0	11	Cook [45], King [74]	31,057
34	17	H	Liverpool	L	1-2	0-2	13	King [90]	11,386
35	23	H	Chelsea	L	1-4	1-2	13	Elphick [36]	11,365
36	30	A	Everton	L	1-2	1-1	14	Pugh [9]	38,345
37	May 7	H	WBA	D	1-1	0-1	16	Ritchie [82]	11,040
38	17	A	Manchester U	L	1-3	0-1	16	Smalling (og) [90]	74,363

Final League Position: 16

GOALSCORERS

League (45): King 6, Wilson 5 (1 pen), Afobe 4, Cook 4, Ritchie 4, Daniels 3 (2 pens), Gosling 3, Murray 3, Pugh 3, Stanislas 3, Smith 2, Arter 1, Elphick 1, Gradel 1, own goals 2.
FA Cup (4): King 1, Murray 1, Pugh 1, Tomlin 1 (pen).
Capital One Cup (6): Stanislas 2, Gosling 1, Kermorgant 1, MacDonald 1, Pugh 1.

Boruc A 32	Francis S 38	Elphick T 11 +1	Cook S 36	Daniels C 37	Ritchie M 33 +4	Gosling D 28 +6	Surman A 38	Pugh M 15 +11	King J 24 +7	Wilson C 9 +4	Kermorgant Y — +7	Gradel M 11 +3	O'Kane E 6 +10	Tomlin L 3 +3	Smith A 22 +9	Mings T — +1	Stanislas J 17 +4	Murray G 6 +13	Distin S 9 +3	Federici A 6	MacDonald S — +3	Arter H 21	Rantie T — +3	Allsop R — +1	Afobe B 12 +3	Iturbe J — +2	Grabban L 4 +11	Match No.
1	2	3	4	5	6	7³	8	9³	10¹	11	12	13	14															1
1	2	3	4	5	6	14	8		11¹	10		9³	7³	12	13													2
1	2	3	4	5	6³	13	8	12	11¹	10		9³	7	14														3
1	2	3	4	5¹	6		8	14		11		9³	7	10	13	12³												4
1	2	3	4		6	14	7	10²	11	13		8³		5		9¹	12											5
1	2		3	5	6³	8	7	9		11²	12	10¹	14		13		4											6
1	2		3	5	6	8	7	9³	13	11¹		10²	14		12		4											7
1	2		3	5	6	7	8	9¹	10²			13			12		11	4										8
	2		3	5	9	7	8	14	13			10¹			6³		11²	4	1	12								9
1	2		3	5	6	8	7	9³	10¹		13	12			14		11²	4										10
	3		5	6	8	7	9¹	13				14	2		12	11²	4	1		10³								11
	3		5	6	8	7	11²	12			13	2			9¹		4	1		10³	14							12
	2	3	5	6¹	8	7	11²					12			9	13	4	1	14	10³								13
	2	3²	5	6	7	8	11					12			9	14	4	1¹		10³	13							14
1	3		4	5	7	8	6	11¹				2			10	12		9										15
1	3		4	5	7	9	6	11¹			13	2			10	12		8²										16
1	3		4	5	7	8	6	12		13		2			10¹	11²		9³	14									17
1	3		4	5	7	8²	6	14		12		2			10	11²		9¹	13									18
1	3		4	5	7	8²	6	10¹	11³			13			2		12	14		9								19
1	3⁴		4	5	7	8	6	11¹				2			10	12	13	9²										20
1	3		4	5	7¹	8	6					2			10	14		9³				11²	12	13				21
1	3		4	5		8	6	10		14	12	2			7	13		11²										22
1	3		4	5	12	8	6	10¹				2			7³	14		9				11²	13					23
1	3		4	5	7²	8	6	10	12			2			14			9³				11¹	13					24
1	3		4	5	7²	8¹	6	10	13			2			12			9				11³	14					25
1	3		4	5	12	8²	6	10	13			2			7³			9				11	14					26
1	3		4	5	6³	13	8	10		12		2			9¹	14		7				11²						27
1	3		4	5	6	12	7	14	11²		9³	2			8¹			10					13					28
1	3		4	5	6³	7	8	12	11		9¹	2			14			10²					13					29
1	3		4	5	6	7¹	8	14	10		9³	12			2			11²					13					30
1	3		4	5	6		7	14	10		9³	13			2			8¹				11²	12					31
1	3	13	4	5	6	14	8	12	11¹		9³	7			2²			10										32
1	2	3	4	5	6	7	8	12	11³	14	9¹							13					10²					33
1	2	3	4	5	7³	8	6	13	11	14	10²				9¹								12					34
1	2	3	4	5	14	8	7	9	11¹	13					6³									12	10²			35
1	2	3	4	5	6		8	9¹	11²	10³					12						7				13	14		36
1	2	3		5	14		7		13	12		9²			6³						8				10¹	11		37
	2	3	4	5	6	8	7	9¹	11²	10³		12								1					13	14		38

FA Cup

Round	Opponent		Score
Third Round	Birmingham C	(a)	2-1
Fourth Round	Portsmouth	(a)	2-1
Fifth Round	Everton	(h)	0-2

Capital One Cup

Round	Opponent		Score
Second Round	Hartlepool U	(a)	4-0
Third Round	Preston NE	(a)	2-2
(aet; Bournemouth won 3-2 on penalties)			
Fourth Round	Liverpool	(a)	0-1

BRADFORD CITY

Coral Windows Stadium, Valley Parade, Bradford, West Yorkshire BD8 7DY.

Telephone: (0871) 978 1911.

Fax: (01274) 773 356.

Ticket Office: (0871) 978 8000.

Website: www.bradfordcityfc.co.uk

Email: (via website).

Ground Capacity: 25,137.

Record Attendance: 39,146 v Burnley, FA Cup 4th rd, 11 March 1911.

Pitch Measurements: 103.5m × 64m (113yd × 70yd).

Joint Chairmen: Julian Rhodes and Mark Lawn.

Chief Operating Officer: James Mason.

Manager: Stuart McCall.

Assistant Manager: Kenny Black.

Head Physio: Matt Barrass.

Colours: Claret and amber shirts, amber shorts, amber socks.

Year Formed: 1903.

Turned Professional: 1903.

Club Nickname: 'The Bantams'.

Ground: 1903, Valley Parade (renamed Bradford & Bingley Stadium 1999, Intersonic Stadium 2007, Coral Windows Stadium 2007).

First Football League Game: 1 September 1903, Division 2, v Grimsby T (a) L 0–2 – Seymour; Wilson, Halliday; Robinson, Millar, Farnall; Guy, Beckram, Forrest, McMillan, Graham.

Record League Victory: 11–1 v Rotherham U, Division 3 (N), 25 August 1928 – Sherlaw; Russell, Watson; Burkinshaw (1), Summers, Bauld; Harvey (2), Edmunds (3), White (3), Cairns, Scriven (2).

Record Cup Victory: 11–3 v Walker Celtic, FA Cup 1st rd (replay), 1 December 1937 – Parker; Rookes, McDermott; Murphy, Mackie, Moore; Bagley (1), Whittingham (1), Deakin (4 incl. 1p), Cooke (1), Bartholomew (4).

HONOURS

League Champions: Division 2 – 1907–08; Division 3 – 1984–85; Division 3N – 1928–29.
Runners-up: First Division – 1998–99; Division 4 – 1981–82.
FA Cup Winners: 1911.
League Cup: Runners-up: 2013.
European Competitions:
Intertoto Cup: 2000.

sky SPORTS FACT FILE

In January 1940 the directors of Bradford City and Bradford Park Avenue met to discuss the possibility of amalgamating the two clubs. The proposal was rejected by City as they had no wish to take on the debts of the Park Avenue club.

Record Defeat: 1–9 v Colchester U, Division 4, 30 December 1961.

Most League Points (2 for a win): 63, Division 3 (N), 1928–29.

Most League Points (3 for a win): 94, Division 3, 1984–85.

Most League Goals: 128, Division 3 (N), 1928–29.

Highest League Scorer in Season: David Layne, 34, Division 4, 1961–62.

Most League Goals in Total Aggregate: Bobby Campbell, 121, 1981–84, 1984–86.

Most League Goals in One Match: 7, Albert Whitehurst v Tranmere R, Division 3 (N), 6 March 1929.

Most Capped Player: Jamie Lawrence, 19 (24), Jamaica.

Most League Appearances: Cec Podd, 502, 1970–84.

Youngest League Player: Robert Cullingford, 16 years 141 days v Mansfield T, 22 April 1970.

Record Transfer Fee Received: £2,000,000 from Newcastle U for Des Hamilton, March 1997; £2,000,000 from Newcastle U for Andrew O'Brien, March 2001.

Record Transfer Fee Paid: £2,500,000 to Leeds U for David Hopkin, July 2000.

Football League Record: 1903 Elected to Division 2; 1908–22 Division 1; 1922–27 Division 2; 1927–29 Division 3 (N); 1929–37 Division 2; 1937–61 Division 3; 1961–69 Division 4; 1969–72 Division 3; 1972–77 Division 4; 1977–78 Division 3; 1978–82 Division 4; 1982–85 Division 3; 1985–90 Division 2; 1990–92 Division 3; 1992–96 Division 2; 1996–99 Division 1; 1999–2001 FA Premier League; 2001–04 Division 1; 2004–07 FL 1; 2007–13 FL 2; 2013– FL 1.

LATEST SEQUENCES

Longest Sequence of League Wins: 10, 26.11.1983 – 3.2.1984.

Longest Sequence of League Defeats: 8, 21.1.1933 – 11.3.1933.

Longest Sequence of League Draws: 6, 30.1.1976 – 13.3.1976.

Longest Sequence of Unbeaten League Matches: 21, 11.1.1969 – 2.5.1969.

Longest Sequence Without a League Win: 16, 28.8.1948 – 20.11.1948.

Successive Scoring Runs: 30 from 26.12.1961.

Successive Non-scoring Runs: 7 from 18.4.1925.

MANAGERS

Robert Campbell 1903–05
Peter O'Rourke 1905–21
David Menzies 1921–26
Colin Veitch 1926–28
Peter O'Rourke 1928–30
Jack Peart 1930–35
Dick Ray 1935–37
Fred Westgarth 1938–43
Bob Sharp 1943–46
Jack Barker 1946–47
John Milburn 1947–48
David Steele 1948–52
Albert Harris 1952
Ivor Powell 1952–55
Peter Jackson 1955–61
Bob Brocklebank 1961–64
Bill Harris 1965–66
Willie Watson 1966–69
Grenville Hair 1967–68
Jimmy Wheeler 1968–71
Bryan Edwards 1971–75
Bobby Kennedy 1975–78
John Napier 1978
George Mulhall 1978–81
Roy McFarland 1981–82
Trevor Cherry 1982–87
Terry Dolan 1987–89
Terry Yorath 1989–90
John Docherty 1990–91
Frank Stapleton 1991–94
Lennie Lawrence 1994–95
Chris Kamara 1995–98
Paul Jewell 1998–2000
Chris Hutchings 2000
Jim Jefferies 2000–01
Nicky Law 2001–03
Bryan Robson 2003–04
Colin Todd 2004–07
Stuart McCall 2007–10
Peter Taylor 2010–11
Peter Jackson 2011
Phil Parkinson 2011–16
Stuart McCall June 2016–

TEN YEAR LEAGUE RECORD

		P	W	D	L	F	A	Pts	Pos
2006-07	FL 1	46	11	14	21	47	65	47	22
2007-08	FL 2	46	17	11	18	63	61	62	10
2008-09	FL 2	46	18	13	15	66	55	67	9
2009-10	FL 2	46	16	14	16	59	62	62	14
2010-11	FL 2	46	15	7	24	43	68	52	18
2011-12	FL 2	46	12	14	20	54	59	50	18
2012-13	FL 2	46	18	15	13	63	52	69	7
2013-14	FL 1	46	14	17	15	57	54	59	11
2014-15	FL 1	46	17	14	15	55	55	65	7
2015-16	FL 1	46	23	11	12	55	40	80	5

DID YOU KNOW ?

Bradford City played local rivals Park Avenue 4 times in the emergency competitions in 1943–44, losing on each occasion. In the two home games City went down 6-1 and 5-1, while they also lost away by 8-0 and 1-0.

BRADFORD CITY – FOOTBALL LEAGUE ONE 2015–16 LEAGUE RECORD

Match No.	Date		Venue	Opponents	Result		H/T Score	Lg Pos.	Goalscorers	Attendance
1	Aug	8	A	Swindon T	L	1-4	1-0	23	Morris [4]	8090
2		15	H	Shrewsbury T	D	1-1	1-0	23	Clarke, B [43]	18,039
3		18	H	Gillingham	L	1-2	1-0	24	Hanson [7]	17,496
4		22	A	Barnsley	D	0-0	0-0	22		10,342
5		29	H	Port Vale	W	1-0	0-0	16	Cole [90]	17,806
6	Sept	5	A	Oldham Ath	W	2-1	1-0	11	Burke [21], Cole [63]	5619
7		12	A	Fleetwood T	D	1-1	1-1	14	Hanson [20]	4044
8		20	H	Sheffield U	D	2-2	1-0	12	Meredith [33], Cole [47]	19,317
9		26	H	Peterborough U	L	0-2	0-0	18		17,970
10		29	A	Colchester U	L	0-2	0-2	19		3334
11	Oct	3	A	Rochdale	W	3-1	1-1	16	Evans [34], Cole [59], Lancashire (og) [61]	4534
12		17	A	Doncaster R	W	1-0	1-0	15	Cole [1]	8410
13		20	H	Bury	W	2-1	1-0	11	McArdle [45], Brown (og) [51]	17,575
14		24	H	Wigan Ath	D	1-1	0-0	14	Hanson [63]	19,171
15		31	A	Millwall	D	0-0	0-0	14		9367
16	Nov	3	H	Blackpool	W	1-0	1-0	9	Hanson [45]	17,435
17		14	H	Crewe Alex	W	2-0	1-0	7	Liddle [45], Clarke, B [58]	17,546
18		21	A	Scunthorpe U	W	2-0	1-0	7	McMahon (pen) [28], Leigh [52]	4865
19		24	H	Coventry C	D	0-0	0-0	6		17,757
20		28	A	Walsall	L	1-2	0-1	9	Evans [64]	4668
21	Dec	19	A	Chesterfield	W	1-0	0-0	8	McMahon [72]	6795
22		28	A	Sheffield U	L	1-3	0-1	10	Liddle [83]	24,777
23	Jan	2	A	Gillingham	L	0-3	0-2	12		6446
24		16	H	Oldham Ath	W	1-0	0-0	10	McMahon [50]	18,522
25		23	A	Port Vale	D	1-1	0-1	10	Proctor [65]	4849
26		26	H	Barnsley	L	0-1	0-1	11		17,470
27		30	H	Fleetwood T	W	2-1	0-0	10	Hanson [67], Davies [90]	17,554
28	Feb	6	A	Burton Alb	L	1-3	0-1	11	McArdle [90]	3796
29		13	A	Peterborough U	W	4-0	1-0	11	Hanson 2 [45, 68], Reid [56], Davies [77]	5816
30		16	H	Southend U	W	2-0	1-0	8	McMahon [17], Hanson [74]	17,701
31		20	H	Rochdale	D	2-2	1-1	8	McArdle [40], Davies [62]	17,936
32		27	A	Blackpool	W	1-0	0-0	7	Reid [54]	8780
33	Mar	1	H	Colchester U	L	1-2	1-1	9	Thomas [17]	16,786
34		5	A	Bury	D	0-0	0-0	8		4036
35		8	H	Burton Alb	W	2-0	2-0	7	Reid [13], Burke [28]	17,500
36		12	H	Doncaster R	W	2-1	1-0	6	Proctor 2 [7, 49]	17,889
37		19	A	Wigan Ath	L	0-1	0-0	7		10,890
38		26	H	Millwall	W	1-0	0-0	6	Davies [79]	18,538
39		28	A	Crewe Alex	W	1-0	0-0	6	Proctor [50]	5320
40	Apr	2	H	Scunthorpe U	W	1-0	0-0	5	Davies [68]	17,873
41		9	H	Swindon T	W	1-0	1-0	3	Clarke, B [20]	18,043
42		16	A	Shrewsbury T	D	1-1	0-0	4	Proctor [71]	6247
43		19	A	Coventry C	L	0-1	0-0	5		10,241
44		23	A	Walsall	W	4-0	0-0	5	Morais [54], Hanson 3 [58, 72, 73]	19,336
45		30	A	Southend U	W	1-0	1-0	5	Evans [12]	8571
46	May	8	H	Chesterfield	W	2-0	1-0	5	Evans [7], Clarke, B [87]	20,807

Final League Position: 5

GOALSCORERS
League (55): Hanson 11, Cole 5, Davies 5, Proctor 5, Clarke, B 4, Evans 4, McMahon 4 (1 pen), McArdle 3, Reid 3, Burke 2, Liddle 2, Leigh 1, Meredith 1, Morais 1, Morris 1, Thomas 1, own goals 2.
FA Cup (6): Cole 1, Hanson 1, Leigh 1, Liddle 1, McMahon 1 (pen), Reid 1.
Capital One Cup (2): Hanson 1, Routis 1.
Johnstone's Paint Trophy (1): Knott 1.
League One Play-Offs (2): McMahon 1 (pen), Proctor 1.

Williams B 43	Darby S 46	McArdle R 35	Clarke N 19 + 6	Meredith J 39 + 3	McMahon T 39 + 1	Routis C 9 + 2	Morris J 8 + 5	Knott B 17 + 7	Hanson J 30 + 11	Clarke S 21 + 8	Davies S 7 + 18	Anderson P 5 + 6	Marshall M 8 + 23	Sheehan A 2	Liddle G 17 + 3	James L 1 + 8	Burke R 34	Evans L 34 + 1	Cole D 12 + 7	Jones B 3	Mottley-Henry D — + 1	Reid K 32 + 2	Leigh G 6	Bowery J 1 + 2	Proctor J 13 + 5	Thomas W 6 + 4	Cullen J 15	Thorpe T 2 + 1	Morais F 2 + 5	Match No.
1	2	3	4	5	6	7	8¹	9²	10	11³	12	13	14																	1
1	2	3		5		7	8³	14	11		9³	10¹	12	13	4	6														2
1	2	3			6	7²	8³	9	11		13	12	14	5	4	10¹														3
1	2	3		5			12		11		10¹	9²	6		7	13	4	8												4
1	2	3		5			12	14	11		10²	6³	9	8		4	7¹	13												5
1	2	4		5	14		8	9¹	10		13	7³		6	12	3		11²												6
1	2	4		5			9	6²	11		14	12	7¹	8		3	13	10³												7
	2	3		5				12	10		13	6	9¹		7	14	4	8²	11³	1										8
	2	3		5				13	10		12	6¹	9²	8³		4	7	11	1	14										9
	2			5	7	3		8¹	10		9²		12		13	4	6	11	1											10
1	2	3		5	6			12			10³		14	7	13	4	8	11²				9¹								11
1	2	3		5	6			12			11²		13	7		4	8	10				9¹								12
1	2	3		5	6			8	12		10³		13		14	4	7	11²				9¹								13
1	2	3		5	6			7	11		12			13	14	4	8³	10²				9¹								14
1	2	3		5	6			10	13		12		7			4	8	11²				9¹								15
1	2	3	12	5	6			7	11	14			13			4²	8³	10¹				9								16
1	2	4	3		6	14		7¹	10	11³			13	8				12				9²	5							17
1	2	3	4		6				11				13	8	12		7					9²	5	10¹						18
1	2	3	4		6			8	10²	11³			14				7¹	12				9	5	13						19
1	2	3	4²	5	6³			8	10	11			13				7	12				9¹		14						20
1	2	3		13	6			10	11²				7		4	8	12				9¹	5								21
1	2	3		12	6			13	11	10¹			7		4	8³	14				9	5²								22
1	2¹	3	12⁴	5	6			7³	10	13			14	8		4³		11				9								23
1	2	3	4	5	6	8¹	12		10	11²			14				7	13				9²								24
1	2	3		5	8	14			10	13			12	7²		4	6⁴					9³		11¹						25
1	2	3	12	5	7	8¹	9	14		10⁴	13		6			4²								11						26
1	2	3	4	5	6	8³	9²	7	11		14		10¹						13						12					27
1	2	3	4	14	7	6²	9	8	11				12										5¹		10³	13				28
1	2	4		5	6				10³		12		13			3	8					9²			14	11¹	7			29
1	2		3	5	6¹			14	11		12		13			4	7					9³				10²	8			30
1	2	3		5	6			8²	11³	13	12		14			4	7					9				10¹				31
1	2	3	13	5	6				11	14	12³					4¹	8					9				10²	7			32
1	5	4	3²	2	9				10	12			13				8					6			14	11¹	7³			33
1	2	3		5	6				10¹	13			12			4	7					9²			14	11³	8			34
1	2		4	5	8				10				12			3	7					9¹			11		6			35
1	2		3	5	6				12	11²						4	8					9			10¹	13	7			36
1	2		3	5	6				14	10¹			12			4	7					9			11²	13	8³			37
1	2		3	5	6		14		7	13	11¹	12				4						9³			10²			8		38
1	2		3	5	6	4	14		7	13	10¹	12										9²			11²			8		39
1	2	3	5	6					13	10²	12					4	7					9³			11¹		8		14	40
1	2	3	5	6					13	10¹	14					4	8					9³			11²		7		12	41
1	2	3	5	6					13	11³	12					4	8					9²			10¹		7		14	42
1	2	3³	5	6²					14	10¹	12⁴					4	8					9			11		7		13	43
1	2	3	13	5	6				11¹	14						4²	8					9			12		7		10³	44
1	2	3		5	6				11			13				4	8³					9²			12		7	14	10¹	45
1	2	3	12	5	6				11		9²					4³	7					13			10		8¹	14		46

FA Cup

First Round	Aldershot T	(a)	0-0	
Replay	Aldershot T	(h)	2-0	
Second Round	Chesham U	(h)	4-0	
Third Round	Bury	(a)	0-0	
Replay	Bury	(h)	0-0	
(aet; Bury won 4-2 on penalties)				

Johnstone's Paint Trophy

Second Round	Barnsley	(h)	1-2

Capital One Cup

First Round	York C	(a)	2-2
(aet; York C won 4-2 on penalties)			

League One Play-Offs

Semi-Final 1st leg	Millwall	(h)	1-3
Semi-Final 2nd leg	Millwall	(a)	1-1
(Millwall won 4-2 on aggregate)			

BRENTFORD

FOUNDATION

Formed as a small amateur concern in 1889 they were very successful in local circles. They won the championship of the West London Alliance in 1893 and a year later the West Middlesex Junior Cup before carrying off the Senior Cup in 1895. After winning both the London Senior Amateur Cup and the Middlesex Senior Cup in 1898 they were admitted to the Second Division of the Southern League.

Griffin Park, Braemar Road, Brentford, Middlesex TW8 0NT.

Telephone: (0845) 3456 442.

Ticket Office: (0845) 3456 442 (option 1).

Website: www.brentfordfc.co.uk

Email: enquiries@brentfordfc.co.uk

Ground Capacity: 12,802.

Record Attendance: 38,678 v Leicester C, FA Cup 6th rd, 26 February 1949.

Pitch Measurements: 99.5m × 67m (109yd × 73yd).

Chairman: Cliff Crown.

Chief Executive: Mark Devlin.

Head Coach: Dean Smith

Assistant Head Coach: Richard O'Kelly.

Physio: Daryl Martin.

Colours: Red and white striped shirts with black trim, black shorts with white trim, black socks with white trim.

Year Formed: 1889.

Turned Professional: 1899.

Club Nickname: 'The Bees'.

Grounds: 1889, Clifden Road; 1891, Benns Fields, Little Ealing; 1895, Shotters Field; 1898, Cross Road, S. Ealing; 1900, Boston Park; 1904, Griffin Park.

First Football League Game: 28 August 1920, Division 3, v Exeter C (a) L 0–3 – Young; Hodson, Rosier, Jimmy Elliott, Levitt, Amos, Smith, Thompson, Spreadbury, Morley, Henery.

Record League Victory: 9–0 v Wrexham, Division 3, 15 October 1963 – Cakebread; Coote, Jones; Slater, Scott, Higginson; Summers (1), Brooks (2), McAdams (2), Ward (2), Hales (1), (1 og).

Record Cup Victory: 7–0 v Windsor & Eton (away), FA Cup 1st rd, 20 November 1982 – Roche; Rowe, Harris (Booker), McNichol (1), Whitehead, Hurlock (2), Kamara, Joseph (1), Mahoney (3), Bowles, Roberts. *N.B.* 8–0 v Uxbridge: Frail, Jock Watson, Caie, Bellingham, Parsonage (1), Jay, Atherton, Leigh (1), Bell (2), Buchanan (2), Underwood (2), FA Cup, 3rd Qual rd, 31 October 1903.

Record Defeat: 0–7 v Swansea T, Division 3 (S), 8 November 1924; v Walsall, Division 3 (S), 19 January 1957; v Peterborough U, 24 November 2007.

HONOURS

League Champions: Division 2 – 1934–35; Division 3 – 1991–92; Division 3S – 1932–33; FL 2 – 2008–09; Third Division – 1998–99; Division 4 – 1962–63.
Runners-up: FL 1 – 2013–14; Second Division – 1994–95; Division 3S – 1929–30, 1957–58.
FA Cup: 6th rd – 1938, 1946, 1949, 1989.
League Cup: 4th rd – 1983, 2011.
League Trophy: Runners-up: 1985, 2001, 2011.

sky SPORTS FACT FILE

Many of the scenes for the 1953 film *The Great Game* were shot at Brentford FC's Griffin Park. The film, which had a football theme, starred James Hayter, Diana Dors and Thora Hird and also featured a number of the Bees' players including star centre-forward Tommy Lawton.

Most League Points (2 for a win): 62, Division 3 (S), 1932–33 and Division 4, 1962–63.

Most League Points (3 for a win): 94, FL 1, 2013–14.

Most League Goals: 98, Division 4, 1962–63.

Highest League Scorer in Season: Jack Holliday, 38, Division 3 (S), 1932–33.

Most League Goals in Total Aggregate: Jim Towers, 153, 1954–61.

Most League Goals in One Match: 5, Jack Holliday v Luton T, Division 3 (S), 28 January 1933; 5, Billy Scott v Barnsley, Division 2, 15 December 1934; 5, Peter McKennan v Bury, Division 2, 18 February 1949.

Most Capped Player: John Buttigieg, 22 (98), Malta.

Most League Appearances: Ken Coote, 514, 1949–64.

Youngest League Player: Danis Salman, 15 years 248 days v Watford, 15 November 1975.

Record Transfer Fee Received: £9,000,000 from Burnley for Andre Gray, August 2015.

Record Transfer Fee Paid: £2,100,000 to FC Twente for Andreas Bjelland, July 2015.

Football League Record: 1920 Original Member of Division 3; 1921–33 Division 3 (S); 1933–35 Division 2; 1935–47 Division 1; 1947–54 Division 2; 1954–62 Division 3 (S); 1962–63 Division 4; 1963–66 Division 3; 1966–72 Division 4; 1972–73 Division 3; 1973–78 Division 4; 1978–92 Division 3; 1992–93 Division 1; 1993–98 Division 2; 1998–99 Division 3; 1999–2004 Division 2; 2004–07 FL 1; 2007–09 FL 2; 2009–14 FL 1; 2014– FL C.

LATEST SEQUENCES

Longest Sequence of League Wins: 9, 30.4.1932 – 24.9.1932.

Longest Sequence of League Defeats: 9, 20.10.1928 – 25.12.1928.

Longest Sequence of League Draws: 5, 16.3.1957 – 6.4.1957.

Longest Sequence of Unbeaten League Matches: 26, 20.2.1999 – 16.10.1999.

Longest Sequence Without a League Win: 18, 9.9.2006 – 26.12.2006.

Successive Scoring Runs: 26 from 4.3.1963.

Successive Non-scoring Runs: 7 from 7.3.2000.

MANAGERS

Will Lewis 1900–03
  (*Secretary-Manager*)
Dick Molyneux 1902–06
W. G. Brown 1906–08
Fred Halliday 1908–12, 1915–21, 1924–26
  (*only Secretary to 1922*)
Ephraim Rhodes 1912–15
Archie Mitchell 1921–24
Harry Curtis 1926–49
Jackie Gibbons 1949–52
Jimmy Bain 1952–53
Tommy Lawton 1953
Bill Dodgin Snr 1953–57
Malcolm Macdonald 1957–65
Tommy Cavanagh 1965–66
Billy Gray 1966–67
Jimmy Sirrel 1967–69
Frank Blunstone 1969–73
Mike Everitt 1973–75
John Docherty 1975–76
Bill Dodgin Jnr 1976–80
Fred Callaghan 1980–84
Frank McLintock 1984–87
Steve Perryman 1987–90
Phil Holder 1990–93
David Webb 1993–97
Eddie May 1997
Micky Adams 1997–98
Ron Noades 1998–2000
Ray Lewington 2000–01
Steve Coppell 2001–02
Wally Downes 2002–04
Martin Allen 2004–06
Leroy Rosenior 2006
Scott Fitzgerald 2006–07
Terry Butcher 2007
Andy Scott 2007–11
Nicky Forster 2011
Uwe Rosler 2011–13
Mark Warburton 2013–15
Marinus Dijkhuizen 2015
Dean Smith December 2015–

TEN YEAR LEAGUE RECORD

		P	W	D	L	F	A	Pts	Pos
2006-07	FL 1	46	8	13	25	40	79	37	24
2007-08	FL 2	46	17	8	21	52	70	59	14
2008-09	FL 2	46	23	16	7	65	36	85	1
2009-10	FL 1	46	14	20	12	55	52	62	9
2010-11	FL 1	46	17	10	19	55	62	61	11
2011-12	FL 1	46	18	13	15	63	52	67	9
2012-13	FL 1	46	21	16	9	62	47	79	3
2013-14	FL 1	46	28	10	8	72	43	94	2
2014-15	FL C	46	23	9	14	78	59	78	5
2015-16	FL C	46	19	8	19	72	67	65	9

DID YOU KNOW ?

Brentford twice entered the FA Amateur Cup and on both occasions withdrew from the competition. In 1897–98 they were drawn against Wandsworth and scratched. The following season they defeated Wycombe Wanderers before scratching to Grimsby All Saints.

BRENTFORD – FL CHAMPIONSHIP 2015–16 LEAGUE RECORD

Match No.	Date	Venue	Opponents	Result		H/T Score	Lg Pos.	Goalscorers	Attendance
1	Aug 8	H	Ipswich T	D	2-2	0-1	8	Tarkowski [90], Gray [90]	10,789
2	15	A	Bristol C	W	4-2	2-2	3	Judge 2 [9, 42], Gray [60], Hofmann [71]	14,291
3	22	A	Burnley	L	0-1	0-1	14		14,928
4	29	H	Reading	L	1-3	0-2	18	Vibe [67]	10,206
5	Sept 12	A	Leeds U	D	1-1	1-0	18	Djuricin [29]	25,126
6	15	A	Middlesbrough	L	1-3	0-1	21	Vibe [49]	20,138
7	19	H	Preston NE	W	2-1	0-1	17	Vibe [62], Djuricin [65]	9463
8	26	A	Sheffield W	L	1-2	0-1	19	Judge [77]	9756
9	29	H	Birmingham C	L	0-2	0-0	19		9528
10	Oct 3	A	Derby Co	L	0-2	0-2	20		29,467
11	17	H	Rotherham U	W	2-1	1-0	19	Judge 2 [2, 57]	10,293
12	21	A	Wolverhampton W	W	2-0	1-0	15	Djuricin [17], Hofmann [88]	18,167
13	24	A	Charlton Ath	W	3-0	1-0	12	Swift [26], Judge [55], Vibe [86]	14,585
14	30	H	QPR	W	1-0	0-0	10	Djuricin [56]	12,037
15	Nov 3	H	Hull C	L	0-2	0-0	12		9221
16	7	A	Blackburn R	D	1-1	1-1	11	Vibe [24]	12,328
17	21	H	Nottingham F	W	2-1	0-0	11	Canos [63], Hofmann [90]	11,403
18	30	A	Bolton W	D	1-1	1-0	11	Swift [10]	12,731
19	Dec 5	H	Milton Keynes D	W	2-0	1-0	10	Vibe [20], Judge [71]	9682
20	12	A	Fulham	D	2-2	1-1	10	Judge (pen) [18], O'Connell [71]	19,411
21	15	A	Cardiff C	L	2-3	0-2	10	Bidwell [69], Swift [86]	12,729
22	19	H	Huddersfield T	W	4-2	3-0	9	Canos [5], Vibe [21], Judge 2 (1 pen) [31, 55 (p)]	10,262
23	26	H	Brighton & HA	D	0-0	0-0	9		12,202
24	28	A	Reading	W	2-1	1-0	8	Woods [17], Canos [72]	20,563
25	Jan 2	A	Birmingham C	L	1-2	0-0	10	Hofmann [77]	17,555
26	12	H	Middlesbrough	L	0-1	0-0	11		10,312
27	15	H	Burnley	L	1-3	0-3	11	Judge [57]	10,039
28	23	A	Preston NE	W	3-1	2-1	10	Bidwell [22], Judge [43], Swift [80]	11,080
29	26	H	Leeds U	D	1-1	1-0	10	Saunders [27]	10,051
30	Feb 5	A	Brighton & HA	L	0-3	0-2	10		24,096
31	13	A	Sheffield W	L	0-4	0-3	13		20,921
32	20	H	Derby Co	L	1-3	0-0	14	Judge [51]	10,627
33	23	A	Wolverhampton W	W	3-0	1-0	11	Swift 2 [38, 67], Canos [56]	8769
34	27	A	Rotherham U	L	1-2	1-1	14	Judge [43]	8534
35	Mar 5	H	Charlton Ath	L	1-2	1-1	14	Barbet [26]	10,108
36	12	A	QPR	L	0-3	0-1	17		17,894
37	19	H	Blackburn R	L	0-1	0-0	18		10,575
38	Apr 2	A	Nottingham F	W	3-0	0-0	17	Vibe [49], Yennaris [65], Canos [87]	19,444
39	5	H	Bolton W	W	3-1	3-0	14	Yennaris [17], Vibe 2 [26, 36]	9062
40	9	A	Ipswich T	W	3-1	1-0	13	Saunders [29], Vibe 2 [64, 68]	18,845
41	16	H	Bristol C	D	1-1	0-1	13	Hogan [90]	12,071
42	19	H	Cardiff C	W	2-1	0-0	13	Hogan 2 [83, 86]	8363
43	23	A	Milton Keynes D	W	4-1	1-1	10	Canos [9], Vibe [49], Woods [78], Bidwell [89]	11,564
44	26	A	Hull C	L	0-2	0-2	10		15,225
45	30	H	Fulham	W	3-0	3-0	10	Saunders [5], Hogan 2 [7, 40]	12,301
46	May 7	H	Huddersfield T	W	5-1	1-0	9	Canos [1], Hogan 2 [52, 62], Vibe [67], Swift [88]	13,397

Final League Position: 9

GOALSCORERS

League (72): Judge 14 (2 pens), Vibe 14, Canos 7, Hogan 7, Swift 7, Djuricin 4, Hofmann 4, Bidwell 3, Saunders 3, Gray 2, Woods 2, Yennaris 2, Barbet 1, O'Connell 1, Tarkowski 1.
FA Cup (0).
Capital One Cup (0).

Button D 46	McCormack A 25 + 2	Dean H 42	Tarkowski J 23	Bidwell J 45	Jota R 1 + 4	Diagouraga T 26 + 1	Kerschbaumer K 18 + 12	Gogia A 5 + 8	Judge A 38	Hofmann P 5 + 16	Gray A 1 + 1	Vibe L 29 + 12	O'Connell J 9 + 7	Colin M 20 + 1	Udumaga J — + 3	Clarke J 4 + 7	Saunders S 12 + 13	Djuricin M 17 + 5	Woods R 38 + 3	Canos S 18 + 20	Barbet Y 18	Yennaris N 28 + 3	Swift J 23 + 4	McEachran J 10 + 4	Macleod L — + 1	Rodriguez L 2	Hogan S 2 + 5	Field T 1	Match No.
1	2^1	3	4	5	6	7	8^2	9	10	11	12	13																	1
1	2	3	4^1	5		7	8^2	11	6	10		9	13	12															2
1	2^2	4	3	5		6	7	9	11	8				12	13														3
1	12	3	4	5		6^1	7^2	10^2	9	11		8			13	14													4
1	7	4	3	5		8	6		11	12^3		9		2^1				10^1	13	14									5
1	7^2	4		5		6	8		11			9	2	12				10^1	13		3								6
1	7	3		5		8	6		11			9^2	14	13	2^3			10^1		12	4								7
1	6^2	3	4^4	5		7	9^2		10			8	12		2^1		11	14	13										8
1	2	3		5		7	8^1	13	11			9	4				10	6^2	12										9
1		3	4	5	7^1			9^2	10	13		8^1					11	6	12		2	14							10
1	6	3	4	5	14			13	10	12							11^3	7	8^2		2	9^1							11
1	7^1	3	4	5		6	14		11	13							10^3	8^2	12		2	9							12
1	8^2	3	4	5		7	12		9			13					10^3	6	14		2	11^1							13
1	6^2	3	4	5		7	12		9^1	14		13					10^3	8			2	11							14
1	6	3	4	5		7^1	12			14		9^2					10	8	13		2^1	11							15
1	8	3	4	5		7	12					9			13		10^1	6^2	14		2	11^3							16
1	8	3^4	4	5		7		9^2	13			10^1	14				6	12			2	11^2							17
1	6		3	5		7	13	9^3			11	4		14			8^1	12			2	10^2							18
1			3	5	13	7	10	9	14		11^3	4					12	6^1	8^3		2								19
1			3	5	13	7	10^3	9	14		11^3	4					6	8^1			2	12							20
1			3	5	12	7^4	8^1	9	14		11^3	4					6				2	10	13						21
1		3	4	5	14	7		9			11	2				12	6^2	8^2				10^1	13						22
1	13	3	4	5	6			9	12		11^3						14	7^1	8^2		2	10							23
1		3	4	5	6			9	13		11^2	2					14	8	12			10^3	7^1						24
1		3	4	5	6		14	9	12		11^1	2					7	8^2				10^3	13						25
1		3	4	5	7			9	14		11^2	2					8^3	13	6	12		10^1							26
1		3		5	7			9			12	4	2				13	11^1	6	8^3		14	10^2						27
1		3		5			12	9			11	2					8^3		6	13	4	14	10^1	7^2					28
1		3		5			13	9			11^1	2					8^3	12	6		4	14	10^2	7					29
1		3		5				9			11^3	2					8^1	13	6	12	4		10	7^2	14				30
1		3		5		6^2		9	11			12	2				13		7	8^3	4^4	10^1		14					31
1		3		5		10^2		9			11^1	4	2				13	8	14		6	12	7^1						32
1		3		5		13		9	12		14	4					12	11^1	6	8^3		2	10	7^1					33
1		3		5		13		9	12		14	4						11^2	7	8^1		2	10	6^3					34
1		3		5				9	14		12						13	11^3	6	8^1	4	2	10	7^2					35
1	6	3		5		14		11			12						13		9	8^3	4	2	10^1	7^2					36
1	6	3		5				9			14						10^3		8^2	12	4	2		7		11^1	13		37
1	6	3		5				9			12		2^1				14	10^3	8	13	4	7				11^2			38
1	6	3		5				9			11^2		2^1				14	10^3	8	12	4	7					13		39
1	7	3		5		12	13	10^3			11		2					9^1	8	6^2	4						14		40
1	6	3		5		12		11			2		14					9^2	8^3	10^1	4	7					13		41
1	6	3		5		10^1		11			2						2	9^2	8	12	4	7					13		42
1	7	3		5		9	14				11^1		2^1				13		12	8	10^3	4	6						43
1	6	3		5^1		12		13					2				14	11	8	10^2	4	7	9^3						44
1		3		5		8	12		13				2				14	11^1	6	9	4	7					10^3	5^2	45
1		3		5		9^2		12					2				13	10	6	8^1	4	7	14				11^1		46

FA Cup
Third Round   Walsall   (h)   0-1

Capital One Cup
First Round   Oxford U   (h)   0-4

BRIGHTON & HOVE ALBION

FOUNDATION

A professional club Brighton United was formed in November 1897 at the Imperial Hotel, Queen's Road, but folded in March 1900 after less than two seasons in the Southern League at the County Ground. An amateur team Brighton & Hove Rangers was then formed by some prominent United supporters and after one season at Withdean, decided to turn semi-professional and play at the County Ground. Rangers were accepted into the Southern League but folded in June 1901. John Jackson, the former United manager, organised a meeting at the Seven Stars public house, Ship Street on 24 June 1901 at which a new third club Brighton & Hove United was formed. They took over Rangers' place in the Southern League and pitch at County Ground. The name was changed to Brighton & Hove Albion before a match was played because of objections by Hove FC.

American Express Community Stadium, Village Way, Falmer, Brighton BN1 9BL.
Telephone: (0344) 324 6282.
Fax: (01273) 878 238.
Ticket Office: (0844) 327 1901.
Website: www.seagulls.co.uk
Email: supporter.services@bhafc.co.uk
Ground Capacity: 30,303.
Record Attendance: 36,747 v Fulham, Division 2, 27 December 1958 (at Goldstone Ground); 8,691 v Leeds U, FL 1, 20 October 2007 (at Withdean); 30,292 v Derby Co, FL C, 2 May 2016 (at Amex).
Pitch Measurements: 105m × 68m (115yd × 74.5yd).
Chairman: Tony Bloom.
Chief Executive: Paul Barber.
Manager: Chris Hughton.
Assistant Manager: Colin Calderwood.
Physios: Sam Blanchard and Paul Watson.
Colours: Blue and white striped shirts with blue sleeves, blue shorts, blue socks with white trim.
Year Formed: 1901.
Turned Professional: 1901.
Club Nickname: 'The Seagulls'.
Grounds: 1901, County Ground; 1902, Goldstone Ground; 1997, groundshare at Gillingham FC; 1999, Withdean Stadium; 2011, American Express Community Stadium.
First Football League Game: 28 August 1920, Division 3, v Southend U (a) L 0–2 – Hayes; Woodhouse, Little; Hall, Comber, Bentley; Longstaff, Ritchie, Doran, Rodgerson, March.
Record League Victory: 9–1 v Newport Co, Division 3 (S), 18 April 1951 – Ball; Tennant (1p), Mansell (1p); Willard, McCoy, Wilson; Reed, McNichol (4), Garbutt, Bennett (2), Keene (1). 9–1 v Southend U, Division 3, 27 November 1965 – Powney; Magill, Baxter; Leck, Gall, Turner; Gould (1), Collins (1), Livesey (2), Smith (3), Goodchild (2).

HONOURS

League Champions: FL 1 – 2010–11; Second Division – 2001–02; Division 3S – 1957–58; Third Division – 2000–01; Division 4 – 1964–65.
Runners-up: Division 2 – 1978–79; Division 3 – 1971–72, 1976–77, 1987–88; Division 3S – 1953–54, 1955–56.
FA Cup: Runners-up: 1983.
League Cup: 5th rd – 1979.

sky SPORTS FACT FILE

Jonny Dixon spent 18 months on the books of Brighton & Hove Albion after signing in January 2008. He went on to make five first-team appearances before retiring from the game to concentrate on a career as a film director and producer. He has since worked on a number of well-known television programmes including *Come Dine With Me* and *Secret Shopper*.

Record Cup Victory: 10–1 v Wisbech, FA Cup 1st rd, 13 November 1965 – Powney; Magill, Baxter; Collins (1), Gall, Turner; Gould, Smith (2), Livesey (3), Cassidy (2), Goodchild (1), (1 og).

Record Defeat: 0–9 v Middlesbrough, Division 2, 23 August 1958.

Most League Points (2 for a win): 65, Division 3 (S), 1955–56 and Division 3, 1971–72.

Most League Points (3 for a win): 95, FL 1, 2010–11.

Most League Goals: 112, Division 3 (S), 1955–56.

Highest League Scorer in Season: Peter Ward, 32, Division 3, 1976–77.

Most League Goals in Total Aggregate: Tommy Cook, 114, 1922–29.

Most League Goals in One Match: 5, Jack Doran v Northampton T, Division 3 (S), 5 November 1921; 5, Adrian Thorne v Watford, Division 3 (S), 30 April 1958.

Most Capped Player: Steve Penney, 17, Northern Ireland.

Most League Appearances: Ernie 'Tug' Wilson, 509, 1922–36.

Youngest League Player: Ian Chapman, 16 years 259 days v Birmingham C, 14 February 1987.

Record Transfer Fee Received: £8,000,000 from Leicester C for Leonardo Ulloa, July 2014.

Record Transfer Fee Paid: £2,500,000 to Peterborough U for Craig Mackail-Smith, July 2011.

Football League Record: 1920 Original Member of Division 3; 1921–58 Division 3 (S); 1958–62 Division 2; 1962–63 Division 3; 1963–65 Division 4; 1965–72 Division 3; 1972–73 Division 2; 1973–77 Division 3; 1977–79 Division 2; 1979–83 Division 1; 1983–87 Division 2; 1987–88 Division 3; 1988–96 Division 2; 1996–2001 Division 3; 2001–02 Division 2; 2002–03 Division 1; 2003–04 Division 2; 2004–06 FL C; 2006–11 FL 1; 2011– FL C.

MANAGERS

John Jackson 1901–05
Frank Scott-Walford 1905–08
John Robson 1908–14
Charles Webb 1919–47
Tommy Cook 1947
Don Welsh 1947–51
Billy Lane 1951–61
George Curtis 1961–63
Archie Macaulay 1963–68
Fred Goodwin 1968–70
Pat Saward 1970–73
Brian Clough 1973–74
Peter Taylor 1974–76
Alan Mullery 1976–81
Mike Bailey 1981–82
Jimmy Melia 1982–83
Chris Cattlin 1983–86
Alan Mullery 1986–87
Barry Lloyd 1987–93
Liam Brady 1993–95
Jimmy Case 1995–96
Steve Gritt 1996–98
Brian Horton 1998–99
Jeff Wood 1999
Micky Adams 1999–2001
Peter Taylor 2001–02
Martin Hinshelwood 2002
Steve Coppell 2002–03
Mark McGhee 2003–06
Dean Wilkins 2006–08
Micky Adams 2008–09
Russell Slade 2009
Gus Poyet 2009–13
Óscar Garcia 2013–14
Sammi Hyypia 2014
Chris Hughton December 2014–

LATEST SEQUENCES

Longest Sequence of League Wins: 9, 2.10.1926 – 20.11.1926.

Longest Sequence of League Defeats: 12, 17.8.2002 – 26.10.2002.

Longest Sequence of League Draws: 6, 16.2.1980 – 15.3.1980.

Longest Sequence of Unbeaten League Matches: 22, 2.5.2015 – 15.12.2015.

Longest Sequence Without a League Win: 15, 21.10.1972 – 27.1.1973.

Successive Scoring Runs: 31 from 4.2.1956.

Successive Non-scoring Runs: 6 from 23.9.1970.

TEN YEAR LEAGUE RECORD

		P	W	D	L	F	A	Pts	Pos
2006-07	FL 1	46	14	11	21	49	58	53	18
2007-08	FL 1	46	19	12	15	58	50	69	7
2008-09	FL 1	46	13	13	20	55	70	52	16
2009-10	FL 1	46	15	14	17	56	60	59	13
2010-11	FL 1	46	28	11	7	85	40	95	1
2011-12	FL C	46	17	15	14	52	52	66	10
2012-13	FL C	46	19	18	9	69	43	75	4
2013-14	FL C	46	19	15	12	55	40	72	6
2014-15	FL C	46	10	17	19	44	54	47	20
2015-16	FL C	46	24	11	5	72	42	89	3

DID YOU KNOW ?

Brighton & Hove Albion clinched the 1964–65 Division Four title with a 3-1 home win over Darlington. The attendance of 31,461 was a near record for English football's fourth tier and higher that season than anything achieved in Division Three.

BRIGHTON & HOVE ALBION – FL CHAMPIONSHIP 2015–16 LEAGUE RECORD

Match No.	Date	Venue	Opponents	Result	H/T Score	Lg Pos.	Goalscorers	Attendance
1	Aug 7	H	Nottingham F	W 1-0	0-0	1	LuaLua [50]	24,623
2	15	A	Fulham	W 2-1	1-1	1	Baldock [30], Hemed (pen) [90]	19,029
3	18	A	Huddersfield T	D 1-1	1-0	2	Kayal [1]	10,168
4	22	H	Blackburn R	W 1-0	1-0	2	LuaLua [35]	22,659
5	29	A	Ipswich T	W 3-2	2-0	1	LuaLua [10], Hemed 2 [12, 67]	21,034
6	Sept 12	H	Hull C	W 1-0	1-0	1	Hemed [5]	24,815
7	15	H	Rotherham U	W 2-1	1-0	1	Hemed [27], Stephens [67]	21,397
8	19	A	Wolverhampton W	D 0-0	0-0	1		20,382
9	26	A	Bolton W	D 2-2	2-1	1	Stephens [31], Murphy [35]	13,405
10	Oct 3	H	Cardiff C	D 1-1	1-1	1	Stephens [38]	26,399
11	17	A	Leeds U	W 2-1	1-1	1	March [14], Zamora [89]	22,736
12	20	A	Bristol C	W 2-1	0-1	1	Baldock [53], Zamora [82]	23,181
13	24	H	Preston NE	D 0-0	0-0	1		24,629
14	31	A	Reading	D 1-1	0-0	1	Murphy [51]	21,244
15	Nov 3	A	Sheffield W	D 0-0	0-0	3		23,712
16	7	H	Milton Keynes D	W 2-1	2-1	2	March [5], Murphy [19]	23,661
17	22	A	Burnley	D 1-1	1-1	2	Zamora [1]	15,622
18	28	H	Birmingham C	W 2-1	1-1	1	March [17], Zamora [47]	27,242
19	Dec 5	H	Charlton Ath	W 3-2	0-2	1	Wilson [50], Zamora [83], Hemed [85]	24,587
20	12	A	Derby Co	D 2-2	1-1	1	Wilson [22], van La Parra [75]	30,537
21	15	H	QPR	D 2-2	0-0	2	Stephens [53], van La Parra [55]	15,268
22	19	H	Middlesbrough	L 0-3	0-2	3		26,445
23	26	A	Brentford	D 0-0	0-0	4		12,202
24	29	A	Ipswich T	L 0-1	0-1	4		27,689
25	Jan 1	H	Wolverhampton W	L 0-1	0-1	4		26,321
26	12	A	Rotherham U	L 0-2	0-1	6		9269
27	16	A	Blackburn R	W 1-0	1-0	5	Zamora [3]	12,930
28	23	H	Huddersfield T	W 2-1	1-1	3	Zamora [30], Wilson [66]	25,367
29	Feb 5	H	Brentford	W 3-0	2-0	3	Knockaert [27], Hemed [43], Murphy [90]	24,096
30	13	A	Bolton W	W 3-2	2-1	4	Murphy [11], Hemed [43], Kayal [58]	26,717
31	16	A	Hull C	D 0-0	0-0	3		17,321
32	20	A	Cardiff C	L 1-4	0-3	4	Stephens [55]	14,143
33	23	A	Bristol C	W 4-0	2-0	4	Murphy [8], Baldock [21], Hemed [56], Little (og) [75]	15,256
34	29	H	Leeds U	W 4-0	4-0	4	Hemed 2 (1 pen) [18 (p), 28], Cooper (og) [22], Dunk [38]	25,150
35	Mar 5	A	Preston NE	D 0-0	0-0	4		11,881
36	8	H	Sheffield W	D 0-0	0-0	3		26,128
37	15	H	Reading	W 1-0	1-0	2	Wilson [25]	23,418
38	19	A	Milton Keynes D	W 2-1	0-0	2	Hemed 2 (1 pen) [56 (p), 62]	21,345
39	Apr 2	H	Burnley	D 2-2	2-1	3	Stephens [30], Knockaert [45]	29,683
40	5	A	Birmingham C	W 2-1	1-1	3	Goldson [29], Dunk [48]	16,143
41	11	A	Nottingham F	W 2-1	1-0	3	Dunk [27], Sidwell [90]	17,642
42	15	H	Fulham	W 5-0	2-0	2	Hemed 3 (1 pen) [29 (p), 34, 79], Saltor [54], Knockaert [87]	28,505
43	19	H	QPR	W 4-0	1-0	2	Knockaert 2 [45, 84], Skalak [51], Goldson [73]	25,411
44	23	A	Charlton Ath	W 3-1	1-0	3	Baldock [8], Skalak [55], Hemed (pen) [90]	17,160
45	May 2	H	Derby Co	D 1-1	0-0	3	Wilson [90]	30,292
46	7	A	Middlesbrough	D 1-1	0-1	3	Stephens [55]	33,806

Final League Position: 3

GOALSCORERS

League (72): Hemed 17 (5 pens), Stephens 7, Zamora 7, Murphy 6, Knockaert 5, Wilson 5, Baldock 4, Dunk 3, LuaLua 3, March 3, Goldson 2, Kayal 2, Skalak 2, van La Parra 2, Saltor 1, Sidwell 1, own goals 2.
FA Cup (0).
Capital One Cup (2): Forster-Caskey 1 (pen), LuaLua 1.
Championship Play-Offs (1): Dunk 1.

Stockdale D 46	Saltor B 46	Greer G 20	Dunk L 37+1	Bong G 13+3	March S 13+3	Kayal B 43	Stephens D 45	LuaLua K 9+9	Baldock S 25+3	Hemed T 40+4	Ince R 1+11	O'Grady C —+3	Rosenior L 27+4	Hunemeier U 13+2	Forster-Caskey J —+2	Murphy J 31+6	Zamora B 10+16	Manu E —+8	Calderon I 10+7	Crofts A 5+12	Holla D —+1	Wilson J 11+14	van La Parra R 4+2	Chicksen A —+1	Goldson C 22+2	Ridgewell L 5	Knockaert A 18+1	Sidwell S 4+12	Skalak J 8+4	Match No.
1	2	3	4	5	6	7	8	9^2	10^3	11^1	12	13	14																	1
1	2	3		5	6^3	7^2		9	11^1	10	12	13	4	14																2
1	2	3		5	6^1	7	8	9	11^3	10^3	12	13	14	4																3
1	2	3		5	12	8	7	9	11^1	10^3	13	14	4			6^2														4
1	2	3	12	5		7	8	9	11^3	10^3	14	6	4^1			13														5
1	2	3		5		8	7	9	11^2	10^3	12	6	4			14	13													6
1	2	3		5	6^3	7	8		11^1	10^3	13	14	4			6														7
1	2	3	4	5		8	7	9^2		11^1		6				10	13	12												8
1	2^3	3		5	13	8	7		10^1		12	6	4			9^1	11^2	14												9
1	2	3	4	5	9	8	7		10^1	11^2		6				12	13													10
1	2	3^1	4	5	9	7	8		11	10^3				6^2	12	14				13										11
1	2		4	5	9^2	8	7		10	11^3		6^1	3			13			14	12										12
1	2		4	5	13			11	10^3	8		6^1	3			9^2	12		7	14										13
1	2^3		4			8^2	7		11	10^1	14	5	3			9	12		13	6										14
1	2		4		9	7	8		11^2	10^1		5	3			9			13	6	12									15
1	2		4		6	8	7		10^1	11^2		5	3			9^3	12	14	13											16
1	2	3	4		6	8	7		10^2			5		12		9	11^1	13												17
1	2	3	4		6	8	7		10^2	14		5^1				9	11^3		12			13								18
1	2	3	4		6	8	7		12			9^2	11				5^1					10^1	13	14						19
1	2	3	4		6^3	8	7		11^2	14		9	13			5			10^1	12										20
1	2	3	4^8			8	7		11^1					14		9^3	12		5	13		10^2	6							21
1	2	3				8	7		10^1				4^2			9^3	13		5	14		11	6		12					22
1	2	3^1	4			7	8		11^1							9	13		5	12		10^2	6		14					23
1	2		4			8^3	6		10^2							11^1	12	14	5	7		13	9		3					24
1	2		4			7	8		13							9	11^1	12	5	6^2		10			3					25
1	2	3^1	4			8	7	13	11							9^2	12			14		10^3				5	6			26
1	2		4			7	8		11							9^2	10^3		13	14		12			3	5	6^1			27
1	2		4			8	7^1	14		11		9^2				9	10^3			12		13			3	5	6			28
1	2		4			8^3	7		10^2							9	11^1			13		12			3	5	6	14		29
1	2		4			8	7	13	11							9	10^3	12							3	5^1	6^2	14		30
1	2		4			9^1	7		12	11^3						10			5	13					3		6^2	8	14	31
1	2		4			6		14	12		13					11^3			5^1	8					3		7	9^1	10	32
1	2^1		4			8	7		11^3	10^2		5				9						13			3		6	14		33
1	2		4			8^1	7		11^2	10^3		5				9						13			3		6	14	12	34
1	2		4			8	7		11^2	10^3		5				9						12			3		6^1	14	13	35
1	2		4			8	13		11^3	10^2		5				9	12					14			3		6^1	7		36
1	2		4	12		8	7	13	10^3			5				9^1						11			3		6^2	14		37
1	2		4			7	8	14	11^1	12		5				9						10^3			3			13	6^2	38
1	2^1		4	13		8	7		10^2	11^{13}		5				9						12			3		6	14		39
1	2		4			8	7	9^1		11^2		5				12						13			3		10	6		40
1	2		4			8^2	7		11			5				10^1						12			3		13	14	6	41
1	2		4			8	7	13		10^2		5				14						11^3			3		6	12	9^1	42
1	2		4			8	7		12	10^1		5				13						11^3			3		6	14	9^2	43
1	2		4	12		8	7		10^3	11		5^2				14									3		6	13	9^1	44
1	2		4^8			8	7	12	11^2	10		5				13									3		6		9^1	45
1	2	4^2				8	7^8	14	11^1	10		5				9^5						12			3		6	13		46

FA Cup
Third Round   Hull C   (a)   0-1

Capital One Cup
First Round   Southend U   (a)   1-0
Second Round   Walsall   (a)   1-2

Championship Play-Offs
Semi-Final 1st leg   Sheffield W   (a)   0-2
Semi-Final 2nd leg   Sheffield W   (h)   1-1
(Sheffield W won 3-1 on aggregate)

BRISTOL CITY

FOUNDATION

The name Bristol City came into being in 1897 when the Bristol South End club, formed three years earlier, decided to adopt professionalism and apply for admission to the Southern League after competing in the Western League. The historic meeting was held at the Albert Hall, Bedminster. Bristol City employed Sam Hollis from Woolwich Arsenal as manager and gave him £40 to buy players. In 1900 they merged with Bedminster, another leading Bristol club.

Ashton Gate Stadium, Bristol BS3 2EJ.

Telephone: (0117) 963 0600.

Fax: (0117) 963 0700.

Ticket Office: (0117) 963 0600 (option 1).

Website: www.bcfc.co.uk

Email: enquiries@bcfc.co.uk

Ground Capacity: 16,757.

Record Attendance: 43,335 v Preston NE, FA Cup 5th rd, 16 February 1935.

Pitch Measurements: 105m × 68.5m (115yd × 75yd).

Chairman: Keith Dawe.

Chief Operating Officer: Mark Ashton.

Head Coach: Lee Johnson.

First-Team Coach: John Pemberton.

Physio: Steve Allen.

Colours: Red shirts with white trim, white shorts with red trim, red socks with white trim.

Year Formed: 1894.

Turned Professional: 1897.

Previous Name: 1894, Bristol South End; 1897, Bristol City.

Club Nickname: 'Robins'.

Grounds: 1894, St John's Lane; 1904, Ashton Gate.

First Football League Game: 7 September 1901, Division 2, v Blackpool (a) W 2–0 – Moles; Tuft, Davies; Jones, McLean, Chambers; Bradbury, Connor, Boucher, O'Brien (2), Flynn.

Record League Victory: 9–0 v Aldershot, Division 3 (S), 28 December 1946 – Eddols; Morgan, Fox; Peacock, Roberts, Jones (1); Chilcott, Thomas, Clark (4 incl. 1p), Cyril Williams (1), Hargreaves (3).

Record Cup Victory: 11–0 v Chichester C, FA Cup 1st rd, 5 November 1960 – Cook; Collinson, Thresher; Connor, Alan Williams, Etheridge; Tait (1), Bobby Williams (1), Atyeo (5), Adrian Williams (3), Derrick, (1 og).

HONOURS

League Champions: Division 2 – 1905–06; FL 1 – 2014–15; Division 3S – 1922–23, 1926–27, 1954–55.
Runners-up: Division 1 – 1906–07; Division 2 – 1975–76; FL 1 – 2006–07; Second Division – 1997–98; Division 3 – 1964–65, 1989–90; Division 3S – 1937–38.

FA Cup: Runners-up: 1909.

League Cup: semi-final – 1971, 1989.

League Trophy Winners: 1986, 2003, 2015.
Runners-up: 1987, 2000.

Welsh Cup Winners: 1934.

Anglo-Scottish Cup Winners: 1978.

sky SPORTS FACT FILE

Bristol City were elected to the Football League for the 1901–02 season, finishing level top of the votes with 23, the same as Burton United. At that time the only other club in the competition south of Birmingham was Woolwich Arsenal.

Record Defeat: 0–9 v Coventry C, Division 3 (S), 28 April 1934.

Most League Points (2 for a win): 70, Division 3 (S), 1954–55.

Most League Points (3 for a win): 99, FL 1, 2014–15.

Most League Goals: 104, Division 3 (S), 1926–27.

Highest League Scorer in Season: Don Clark, 36, Division 3 (S), 1946–47.

Most League Goals in Total Aggregate: John Atyeo, 314, 1951–66.

Most League Goals in One Match: 6, Tommy 'Tot' Walsh v Gillingham, Division 3 (S), 15 January 1927.

Most Capped Player: Billy Wedlock, 26, England.

Most League Appearances: John Atyeo, 596, 1951–66.

Youngest League Player: Marvin Brown, 16 years 105 days v Bristol R, 17 October 1999.

Record Transfer Fee Received: £3,500,000 from Wolverhampton W for Ade Akinbiyi, September 1999.

Record Transfer Fee Paid: £2,250,000 to Crewe Alex for Nicky Maynard, August 2008.

Football League Record: 1901 Elected to Division 2; 1906–11 Division 1; 1911–22 Division 2; 1922–23 Division 3 (S); 1923–24 Division 2; 1924–27 Division 3 (S); 1927–32 Division 2; 1932–55 Division 3 (S); 1955–60 Division 2; 1960–65 Division 3; 1965–76 Division 2; 1976–80 Division 1; 1980–81 Division 2; 1981–82 Division 3; 1982–84 Division 4; 1984–90 Division 3; 1990–92 Division 2; 1992–95 Division 1; 1995–98 Division 2; 1998–99 Division 1; 1999–2004 Division 2; 2004–07 FL 1; 2007–13 FL C; 2013–15 FL 1; 2015– FL C.

LATEST SEQUENCES

Longest Sequence of League Wins: 14, 9.9.1905 – 2.12.1905.

Longest Sequence of League Defeats: 7, 6.10.2012 – 11.11.2012.

Longest Sequence of League Draws: 4, 6.11.1999 – 27.11.1999.

Longest Sequence of Unbeaten League Matches: 24, 9.9.1905 – 10.2.1906.

Longest Sequence Without a League Win: 21, 16.3.2013 – 22.10.2013.

Successive Scoring Runs: 25 from 26.12.1905.

Successive Non-scoring Runs: 6 from 20.12.1980.

MANAGERS

Sam Hollis 1897–99
Bob Campbell 1899–1901
Sam Hollis 1901–05
Harry Thickett 1905–10
Frank Bacon 1910–11
Sam Hollis 1911–13
George Hedley 1913–17
Jack Hamilton 1917–19
Joe Palmer 1919–21
Alex Raisbeck 1921–29
Joe Bradshaw 1929–32
Bob Hewison 1932–49
  (*under suspension 1938–39*)
Bob Wright 1949–50
Pat Beasley 1950–58
Peter Doherty 1958–60
Fred Ford 1960–67
Alan Dicks 1967–80
Bobby Houghton 1980–82
Roy Hodgson 1982
Terry Cooper 1982–88
  (*Director from 1983*)
Joe Jordan 1988–90
Jimmy Lumsden 1990–92
Denis Smith 1992–93
Russell Osman 1993–94
Joe Jordan 1994–97
John Ward 1997–98
Benny Lennartsson 1998–99
Tony Pulis 1999–2000
Tony Fawthrop 2000
Danny Wilson 2000–04
Brian Tinnion 2004–05
Gary Johnson 2005–10
Steve Coppell 2010
Keith Millen 2010–11
Derek McInnes 2011–13
Sean O'Driscoll 2013
Steve Cotterill 2013–16
Lee Johnson February 2016–

TEN YEAR LEAGUE RECORD

		P	W	D	L	F	A	Pts	Pos
2006-07	FL 1	46	25	10	11	63	39	85	2
2007-08	FL C	46	20	14	12	54	53	74	4
2008-09	FL C	46	15	16	15	54	54	61	10
2009-10	FL C	46	15	18	13	56	65	63	10
2010-11	FL C	46	17	9	20	62	65	60	15
2011-12	FL C	46	12	13	21	44	68	49	20
2012-13	FL C	46	11	8	27	59	84	41	24
2013-14	FL 1	46	13	19	14	70	67	58	12
2014-15	FL 1	46	29	12	5	96	38	99	1
2015-16	FL C	46	13	13	20	54	71	52	18

DID YOU KNOW ?

In the 1930s a number of English clubs entered the Welsh Cup. Bristol City won the trophy in 1933–34, defeating Cardiff City, New Brighton and Port Vale to reach the final where they overcame Tranmere Rovers after a replay.

BRISTOL CITY – FL CHAMPIONSHIP 2015–16 LEAGUE RECORD

Match No.	Date	Venue	Opponents	Result	H/T Score	Lg Pos.	Goalscorers	Attendance
1	Aug 8	A	Sheffield W	L 0-2	0-0	21		23,255
2	15	H	Brentford	L 2-4	2-2	23	Kodjia [2], Wilbraham [23]	14,291
3	19	H	Leeds U	D 2-2	0-1	22	Agard [89], Flint [90]	14,712
4	22	A	Middlesbrough	W 1-0	1-0	18	Bryan [8]	22,236
5	29	H	Burnley	L 1-2	0-2	20	Kodjia [90]	15,002
6	Sept 12	A	Birmingham C	L 2-4	1-3	21	Kodjia 2 [32, 66]	18,819
7	15	H	Preston NE	D 1-1	0-0	22	Wilbraham [81]	9963
8	19	H	Reading	L 0-2	0-2	23		15,385
9	26	A	Ipswich T	D 2-2	0-0	24	Freeman [53], Kodjia [56]	20,347
10	Oct 3	H	Milton Keynes D	D 1-1	1-0	24	Kodjia [6]	14,535
11	16	H	Nottingham F	W 2-0	2-0	19	Wilbraham 2 [4, 11]	15,285
12	20	A	Brighton & HA	L 1-2	1-0	21	Williams [17]	23,181
13	26	A	Cardiff C	D 0-0	0-0	20		15,287
14	31	H	Fulham	L 1-4	0-4	21	Kodjia [90]	15,752
15	Nov 3	H	Wolverhampton W	W 1-0	1-0	21	Kodjia [45]	15,517
16	7	A	Bolton W	D 0-0	0-0	20		14,239
17	21	H	Hull C	D 1-1	1-0	19	Agard [39]	14,590
18	28	A	Rotherham U	L 0-3	0-2	20		8949
19	Dec 5	H	Blackburn R	L 0-2	0-0	21		15,021
20	12	A	Huddersfield T	W 2-1	2-0	19	Kodjia [7], Flint [29]	13,255
21	15	A	Derby Co	L 0-4	0-1	21		27,781
22	19	H	QPR	D 1-1	0-0	20	Wilbraham [80]	15,754
23	26	A	Charlton Ath	D 1-1	1-0	22	Baker [45]	15,285
24	28	H	Burnley	L 0-4	0-2	22		17,234
25	Jan 2	A	Reading	L 0-1	0-0	22		19,677
26	12	H	Preston NE	L 1-2	0-0	22	Wilbraham [56]	14,586
27	16	H	Middlesbrough	W 1-0	0-0	22	Burns [90]	15,670
28	23	A	Leeds U	L 0-1	0-0	22		20,441
29	30	H	Birmingham C	D 0-0	0-0	22		15,728
30	Feb 6	A	Charlton Ath	W 1-0	1-0	20	Tomlin (pen) [21]	14,342
31	13	H	Ipswich T	W 2-1	2-0	21	Flint 2 [20, 35]	15,736
32	20	A	Milton Keynes D	W 2-0	1-0	20	Kodjia 2 [45, 60]	12,825
33	23	H	Brighton & HA	L 0-4	0-2	20		15,256
34	27	A	Nottingham F	W 2-1	1-1	19	Kodjia [41], Flint [70]	20,551
35	Mar 5	H	Cardiff C	L 0-2	0-1	20		15,758
36	8	A	Wolverhampton W	L 1-2	0-0	20	Flint [77]	17,459
37	12	A	Fulham	W 2-1	0-1	19	Pack [69], Tomlin [90]	20,316
38	19	H	Bolton W	W 6-0	2-0	19	Wilbraham [3], Tomlin [10], Odemwingie [53], Wagstaff [79], Kodjia 2 [86, 87]	15,608
39	Apr 2	A	Hull C	L 0-4	0-2	19		16,521
40	5	H	Rotherham U	D 1-1	0-1	20	Odemwingie [54]	15,248
41	9	H	Sheffield W	W 4-1	3-0	18	Palmer (og) [10], Reid [13], Tomlin (pen) [42], Kodjia (pen) [52]	15,854
42	16	A	Brentford	D 1-1	1-0	17	Tomlin [45]	12,071
43	19	H	Derby Co	L 2-3	2-1	21	Kodjia [38], Reid [44]	15,341
44	23	A	Blackburn R	D 2-2	0-1	20	Kodjia [70], Wilbraham [74]	12,752
45	30	H	Huddersfield T	W 4-0	1-0	18	Kodjia 2 [45, 67], Bryan [64], Tomlin [77]	15,791
46	May 7	A	QPR	L 0-1	0-0	18		16,679

Final League Position: 18

GOALSCORERS

League (54): Kodjia 19 (1 pen), Wilbraham 8, Flint 6, Tomlin 6 (2 pens), Agard 2, Bryan 2, Odemwingie 2, Reid 2, Baker 1, Burns 1, Freeman 1, Pack 1, Wagstaff 1, Williams 1, own goal 1.
FA Cup (2): Agard 1, Kodjia 1.
Capital One Cup (1): Robinson 1.

Fielding F 21	Fredericks R 3 + 1	Ayling L 29 + 4	Flint A 44	Williams D 21 + 3	Bryan J 34 + 5	Freeman L 36 + 5	Pack M 45	Smith K 36	Wilbraham A 25 + 18	Kodjia J 42 + 3	Burns W 2 + 12	Robinson C 1 + 5	Agard K 7 + 18	Hamer B 4	Reid B 16 + 12	Little M 10 + 13	Wagstaff S 1 + 8	Moore L 5 + 5	Baker N 36	Bennett E 15	Cox S — + 4	O'Donnell R 21	Gladwin B 1	Pearce A 3 + 4	Golbourne S 16	Tomlin L 18	Vyner Z 2 + 2	Matthews A 9	Odemwingie P 3 + 4	Dowling G — + 2	Match No.
1	2²	3	4	5	6³	7	8	9	10	11¹	12	13	14																		1
	2³	3	4	5	6	8¹	9	7	10²	11¹	14	12	13	1																	2
	2¹	3	4	5	6		9	7	10	11³	12		8²	14	1	13															3
13		3	4	5	6		7	8	10	11¹	12			1	9²	2³	14														4
		3	4	5	6¹		9	7	10	11	12	13		1	8	2²															5
1		5	3	13	9¹	8	7²	6	10	11			12		14		2²	4													6
1		5	3	12	9	8	7	6	11	10¹			14			13	2²	4³													7
1		2	4	5	6	9	7³	8	10¹	11	12		14		13		3²														8
1		3	4	6	9	7	8		10	11	12					2		5													9
1		3	4	12	6²	8¹	9		10³	11	13	14		7	2			5													10
1		2	3	8²	12	9¹	7	6	10	11					13	14			4	5¹											11
1		3¹	4	6		9	8	7	10³	11			14					12	5	2²	13										12
1		2	3	8	12	9	6	7	10	11									4¹	5											13
1		3	4	5	6³	8²	9	7	10¹	11			14	12						2	13										14
1		3	4	6		8¹	9	7	13	11			10³			12	14	5	2²												15
1		3	4	6²	12	8	9	7	13	11			10¹			14		5	2³												16
1		2	3	8		9	6	7	12	11¹			10		13			4	5²												17
1		3	4	6		8	9	7	13	11²			10³			12	5¹	2	14												18
1		3	4	6¹	14	8²		7	13	11			10²		9		12	5¹	2												19
1		3	4		6	8²	9	7	10³	11¹			12			14		5		2	13										20
1			3	9	8¹	11	7²	6	14				10		12	13	2	4	5¹												21
1		3	4		6²	12	8	9	7	10			11		13			5	2¹												22
1		3	4		6	8	9	7	10	11	12							5	2												23
1		2	3	9		7²	6	8	10	11³	13		14		12			4	5³												24
1		2	3		9	7¹	6	8	10	11³	14		13			12	4¹	5													25
		2	3		9	7¹	6	8	10³	11	13		14		12	5²		4				1									26
		2	3	5¹	10		8	9	13	11¹	6		7		14	12		4²				1									27
		2	3	5	10	6²	7	14	11	8			13					4¹				1	9³	12							28
			3			8	6	7	13	11³	12		14		9²	2		4			1				5	10¹					29
			3			8	6	7	12	11¹			14		9³	2	13	4			1				5	10²					30
			3	10¹	8	6	7	12	11²				13			2	14	4			1				5	9¹					31
			3	9	6	8	7	13	11¹				14					4²			1			12	5	10³	2				32
			3	10²	8	6	7	12	11³				14			13		4			1			4	5	9³	2¹				33
			3		8	6	7	13	11¹				14		10²	2	12	4			1				5	9³					34
	13		3		7	8	6	12	11¹				14		9²	2¹		4			1				5	10					35
			3	7	10	6		12	11³	13			14				8¹	4			1				5	9		2²			36
	14		3		8	6¹	7		10	11²	13					4					1				5	9	2³	12			37
			3		7	13	6		11³	12					9²	14		4			1				5	8¹	2	10			38
			3		7	13	6		14	11					9¹			4²			1			12	5	8	2	10³			39
			3		10	12	6		7	11	13							4			1				5¹	9	2	8²			40
			3		5	8	7	6		11³			14		9¹		12	4			1					10²	2	13			41
	14		3		10	8	7	6		11			12					4			1				5²	9¹	2³	13			42
			3		5	8³	7	6	14	11			9¹				13	4			1					10²	2	12			43
	13		3³		10	8	7	7¹	11	14					8¹			4			1					10²	2	2²			44
		2		4¹	8	14	6		11			10³		7²				4		1				3	5	9	12			13	45
		2¹			8²	13	6		10³	11			7					4		1				3	5	9	14			12	46

FA Cup
Third Round   WBA   (a)   2-2
Replay   WBA   (h)   0-1

Capital One Cup
First Round   Luton T   (a)   1-3

BRISTOL ROVERS

FOUNDATION

Bristol Rovers were formed at a meeting in Stapleton Road, Eastville, in 1883. However, they first went under the name of the Black Arabs (wearing black shirts). Changing their name to Eastville Rovers in their second season in 1888–89, they won the Gloucestershire Senior Cup. Original members of the Bristol & District League in 1892, this eventually became the Western League and Eastville Rovers adopted professionalism in 1897.

The Memorial Stadium, Filton Avenue, Horfield, Bristol BS7 0BF.
Telephone: (0117) 909 6648.
Fax: (0117) 907 4312.
Ticket Office: (0117) 909 6648 (option 1).
Website: www.bristolrovers.co.uk
Email: dave@bristolrovers.co.uk
Ground Capacity: 11,485.
Record Attendance: 38,472 v Preston NE, FA Cup 4th rd, 30 January 1960 (at Eastville); 9,464 v Liverpool, FA Cup 4th rd, 8 February 1992 (at Twerton Park); 12,011 v WBA, FA Cup 6th rd, 9 March 2008 (at Memorial Stadium).
Pitch Measurements: 100m × 64m (109.5yd × 70yd).
Chairman: Steve Hamer.
Manager: Darrell Clarke.
Assistant Manager: Marcus Stewart.
Physio: Paul Maxwell.
Colours: Blue and white quartered shirts with blue sleeves, blue shorts with white trim, white socks.
Year Formed: 1883.
Turned Professional: 1897.
Previous Names: 1883, Black Arabs; 1884, Eastville Rovers; 1897, Bristol Eastville Rovers; 1898, Bristol Rovers. *Club Nicknames:* 'The Pirates', 'The Gas'.
Grounds: 1883, Purdown; Three Acres, Ashley Hill; Rudgeway, Fishponds; 1897, Eastville; 1986, Twerton Park; 1996, The Memorial Stadium.
First Football League Game: 28 August 1920, Division 3, v Millwall (a) L 0–2 – Stansfield; Bethune, Panes; Boxley, Kenny, Steele; Chance, Bird, Sims, Bell, Palmer.
Record League Victory: 7–0 v Brighton & HA, Division 3 (S), 29 November 1952 – Hoyle; Bamford, Fox; Pitt, Warren, Sampson; McIlvenny, Roost (2), Lambden (1), Bradford (1), Petherbridge (2), (1 og). 7–0 v Swansea T, Division 2, 2 October 1954 – Radford; Bamford, Watkins; Pitt, Muir, Anderson; Petherbridge, Bradford (2), Meyer, Roost (1), Hooper (2), (2 og). 7–0 v Shrewsbury T, Division 3, 21 March 1964 – Hall; Hillard, Gwyn Jones; Oldfield, Stone (1), Mabbutt; Jarman (2), Brown (1), Biggs (1p), Hamilton, Bobby Jones (2).
Record Cup Victory: 7–1 v Dorchester, FA Cup 4th qualifying rd, 25 October 2014 – Midenhall; Locyer, Trotman (McChrystal), Parkes, Monkhouse (2), Clarke, Mansell (1) (Thomas), Brown, Gosling, Harrison (3), Taylor (1) (White).
Record Defeat: 0–12 v Luton T, Division 3 (S), 13 April 1936.

HONOURS

League Champions: Division 3 – 1989–90; Division 3S – 1952–53.
Runners-up: Division 3 – 1973–74; Conference – (2nd) 2014–15 *(promoted via play-offs).*
FA Cup: 6th rd – 1951, 1958, 2008.
League Cup: 5th rd – 1971, 1972.
League Trophy: *Runners-up:* 1990, 2007.

sky SPORTS FACT FILE

Bristol Rovers did not adopt their traditional colours of blue and white quarters until 1931. In the 1920s they played in white shirts with blue shorts and were often known as 'the Lilywhites'.

Most League Points (2 for a win): 64, Division 3 (S), 1952–53.
Most League Points (3 for a win): 93, Division 3, 1989–90.
Most League Goals: 92, Division 3 (S), 1952–53.
Highest League Scorer in Season: Geoff Bradford, 33, Division 3 (S), 1952–53.
Most League Goals in Total Aggregate: Geoff Bradford, 242, 1949–64.
Most League Goals in One Match: 4, Sidney Leigh v Exeter C, Division 3 (S), 2 May 1921; 4, Jonah Wilcox v Bournemouth, Division 3 (S), 12 December 1925; 4, Bill Culley v QPR, Division 3 (S), 5 March 1927; 4, Frank Curran v Swindon T, Division 3 (S), 25 March 1939; 4, Vic Lambden v Aldershot, Division 3 (S), 29 March 1947; 4, George Petherbridge v Torquay U, Division 3 (S), 1 December 1951; 4, Vic Lambden v Colchester U, Division 3 (S), 14 May 1952; 4, Geoff Bradford v Rotherham U, Division 2, 14 March 1959; 4, Robin Stubbs v Gillingham, Division 2, 10 October 1970; 4, Alan Warboys v Brighton & HA, Division 3, 1 December 1973; 4, Jamie Cureton v Reading, Division 2, 16 January 1999.
Most Capped Player: Vitalijs Astafjevs, 31 (167), Latvia.
Most League Appearances: Stuart Taylor, 546, 1966–80.
Youngest League Player: Ronnie Dix, 15 years 173 days v Charlton Ath, 25 February 1928.
Record Transfer Fee Received: £2,100,000 from Fulham for Barry Hayles, November 1998; £2,100,000 from WBA for Jason Roberts, July 2000.
Record Transfer Fee Paid: £375,000 to QPR for Andy Tillson, November 1992.
Football League Record: 1920 Original Member of Division 3; 1921–53 Division 3 (S); 1953–62 Division 2; 1962–74 Division 3; 1974–81 Division 2; 1981–90 Division 3; 1990–92 Division 2. 1992–93 Division 1; 1993–2001 Division 2; 2001–04 Division 3; 2004–07 FL 2; 2007–11 FL 1; 2011–14 FL 2; 2014–15 Conference Premier; 2015–16 FL 2; 2016– FL 1.

LATEST SEQUENCES

Longest Sequence of League Wins: 12, 18.10.1952 – 17.1.1953.
Longest Sequence of League Defeats: 8, 26.10.2002 – 21.12.2002.
Longest Sequence of League Draws: 5, 1.11.1975 – 22.11.1975.
Longest Sequence of Unbeaten League Matches: 32, 7.4.1973 – 27.1.1974.
Longest Sequence Without a League Win: 20, 5.4.1980 – 1.11.1980.
Successive Scoring Runs: 26 from 26.3.1927.
Successive Non-scoring Runs: 6 from 14.10.1922.

MANAGERS

Alfred Homer 1899–1920
  (*continued as Secretary to 1928*)
Ben Hall 1920–21
Andy Wilson 1921–26
Joe Palmer 1926–29
Dave McLean 1929–30
Albert Prince-Cox 1930–36
Percy Smith 1936–37
Brough Fletcher 1938–49
Bert Tann 1950–68 (*continued as General Manager to 1972*)
Fred Ford 1968–69
Bill Dodgin Snr 1969–72
Don Megson 1972–77
Bobby Campbell 1978–79
Harold Jarman 1979–80
Terry Cooper 1980–81
Bobby Gould 1981–83
David Williams 1983–85
Bobby Gould 1985–87
Gerry Francis 1987–91
Martin Dobson 1991
Dennis Rofe 1992
Malcolm Allison 1992–93
John Ward 1993–96
Ian Holloway 1996–2001
Garry Thompson 2001
Gerry Francis 2001
Garry Thompson 2001–02
Ray Graydon 2002–04
Ian Atkins 2004–05
Paul Trollope 2005–10
Dave Penney 2011
Paul Buckle 2011–12
Mark McGhee 2012
John Ward 2012–14
Darrell Clarke March 2014–

TEN YEAR LEAGUE RECORD

		P	W	D	L	F	A	Pts	Pos
2006-07	FL 2	46	20	12	14	49	42	72	6
2007-08	FL 1	46	12	17	17	45	53	53	16
2008-09	FL 1	46	17	12	17	79	61	63	11
2009-10	FL 1	46	19	5	22	59	70	62	11
2010-11	FL 1	46	11	12	23	48	82	45	22
2011-12	FL 2	46	15	12	19	60	70	57	13
2012-13	FL 2	46	16	12	18	60	69	60	14
2013-14	FL 2	46	12	14	20	43	54	50	23
2014-15	Conf P	46	25	16	5	73	34	91	2
2015-16	FL 2	46	26	7	13	77	46	85	3

DID YOU KNOW ?

Bristol Rovers gained their first-ever trophy in April 1889 when (as Eastville Rovers) they defeated Warmley 1-0 to win the Gloucestershire Cup. The goalscorer was Walter Perrin.

BRISTOL ROVERS – FOOTBALL LEAGUE TWO 2015–16 LEAGUE RECORD

Match No.	Date	Venue	Opponents	Result	H/T Score	Lg Pos.	Goalscorers	Attendance
1	Aug 8	H	Northampton T	L 0-1	0-0	17		8712
2	15	A	Yeovil T	W 1-0	0-0	10	Harrison 88	5895
3	18	A	Luton T	W 1-0	0-0	8	Sinclair 90	8061
4	22	H	Barnet	W 3-1	1-0	4	Brown 2, Easter 77, Taylor 87	7107
5	29	A	Leyton Orient	L 0-2	0-2	7		5777
6	Sept 6	H	Oxford U	L 0-1	0-0	10		7038
7	12	H	Accrington S	L 0-1	0-0	15		6351
8	19	A	Plymouth Arg	D 1-1	0-0	15	Harrison (pen) 90	10,633
9	26	H	Portsmouth	L 1-2	0-1	17	Easter 48	8555
10	29	A	Hartlepool U	W 3-0	1-0	14	Taylor 32, Bodin 64, Easter 78	3788
11	Oct 3	A	Morecambe	W 4-3	1-1	12	Mansell 26, Bodin 47, Taylor 58, Harrison (pen) 80	1712
12	17	A	Mansfield T	W 2-1	1-0	11	Easter 15, Taylor 90	4196
13	20	H	Notts Co	D 0-0	0-0	11		6743
14	24	H	Newport Co	L 1-4	1-1	13	Bodin 15	7442
15	30	A	Cambridge U	W 2-1	0-1	9	Harrison 66, Taylor 82	5115
16	Nov 14	H	Carlisle U	W 2-0	0-0	8	Taylor 2 66, 87	6423
17	21	A	Crawley T	L 1-2	0-2	12	Taylor (pen) 87	2612
18	24	H	Stevenage	L 1-2	1-1	13	Taylor 33	5819
19	28	A	Exeter C	D 1-1	0-0	12	Sinclair 83	5548
20	Dec 1	H	Wycombe W	W 3-0	0-0	10	Taylor 3 60, 62, 72	6136
21	12	H	York C	W 2-1	0-1	8	Easter 71, Taylor 90	6916
22	19	A	Dagenham & R	W 3-0	1-0	7	Brown 33, Gaffney 83, Bodin 90	1820
23	26	A	AFC Wimbledon	D 0-0	0-0	5		4668
24	28	H	Leyton Orient	W 2-1	1-1	6	Gaffney 2 31, 53	9836
25	Jan 2	H	Luton T	W 2-0	0-0	5	Gaffney 2 60, 72	9131
26	9	A	Barnet	L 0-1	0-1	5		2770
27	17	A	Oxford U	W 2-1	0-0	4	Taylor 52, Harrison (pen) 88	9492
28	23	H	Plymouth Arg	D 1-1	0-0	4	Bodin 79	10,190
29	30	A	Accrington S	L 0-1	0-0	4		2027
30	Feb 13	A	Portsmouth	L 1-3	0-2	8	Brown 90	17,808
31	20	H	Morecambe	W 2-1	0-1	6	Gaffney 68, Bodin 78	7400
32	27	A	Wycombe W	L 0-1	0-0	10		4759
33	Mar 1	H	Hartlepool U	W 4-1	3-0	6	Taylor 3 10, 38, 56, Gaffney 31	6634
34	5	A	Notts Co	W 2-0	1-0	6	Montano 43, Brown 50	5052
35	8	H	AFC Wimbledon	W 3-1	2-0	5	Easter 28, Clarke, O 38, Taylor 78	7778
36	12	H	Mansfield T	W 1-0	0-0	4	Taylor 61	7847
37	19	A	Newport Co	W 4-1	1-1	3	Clarke, O 15, Montano 55, Taylor 61, Harrison 85	3663
38	25	H	Cambridge U	W 3-0	2-0	3	Bodin 2 9, 18, Taylor 73	10,262
39	28	A	Carlisle U	L 2-3	1-1	5	Bodin 27, Taylor 57	4718
40	Apr 2	H	Crawley T	W 3-0	0-0	3	Taylor 2 53, 79, Lawrence 75	8250
41	9	A	Northampton T	D 2-2	0-1	4	Taylor 76, Harrison 88	7579
42	16	H	Yeovil T	W 2-1	1-0	3	Gaffney 42, Taylor 77	10,264
43	19	A	Stevenage	D 0-0	0-0	5		3836
44	23	H	Exeter C	W 3-1	2-0	4	Bodin 13, Brown 45, Taylor 69	10,254
45	30	A	York C	W 4-1	1-0	4	Bodin 2 19, 71, Easter 80, Mansell 88	4525
46	May 7	H	Dagenham & R	W 2-1	1-1	3	Bodin 15, Brown 90	11,130

Final League Position: 3

GOALSCORERS

League (77): Taylor 27 (1 pen), Bodin 13, Gaffney 8, Easter 7, Harrison 7 (3 pens), Brown 6, Clarke, O 2, Mansell 2, Montano 2, Sinclair 2, Lawrence 1.
FA Cup (0).
Capital One Cup (1): Harrison 1.
Johnstone's Paint Trophy (2): Easter 1, Taylor 1.

Match No.	Mildenhall S 25+1	Leadbitter D 28+5	Clarke J 36+1	Parkes T 29+2	Brown L 46	Lockyer T 42+1	Lines C 30+3	Sinclair S 30	Montano C 12+15	Taylor M 38+8	Easter J 21+22	Harrison E 10+20	Monakana J —+3	Bodin B 26+12	Chapman A 5	Clarke D 22+11	Gosling J 8+10	Lyttle T 1	Mansell L 28	Nicholls L 15	Lucas J —+1	McChrystal M 20+1	Blissett N —+2	Cowan-Hall P 2+1	Gaffney R 23+1	Puddy W 1	Lawrence L 8+4	Fallon R —+3	McBurnie O —+5	Broom R —+1
1	1	2	3	4	5	6	7	8	9	10²	11³	12	13	14																
2		5	3	4	2	6²	7	8	13	11¹	12	10	14				9³			1										
3		5	4	3	9	2	7	8	12	11	10					6				1										
4		2²	3	5	6	4	8	7	13	11	10³			14		12	9			1										
5			3	5	6	4	8	7	12	14	10³	11	13				9²			1		2¹								
6			3³	5	6	4	8	2	13	10²	11	12	14			9¹	7¹			1										
7			3	5	6	4	7	2		11¹	13	10	14	12		8²	9³			1										
8		2	4	5	3	8	7	12	10³	11²	13			14		6	9¹			1										
9		2	3¹	5	6	4	9	7	14	11¹	10	13				8¹	12			1										
10		2	13	5	3		7		10	11³	12	6²	14	9		8			1			4¹								
11		14	2		5	3	8		11¹	10²	12	6³	13	9		7			1			4								
12		2³	5	3	6	4	7²	9		10	11⁴	13				12	14		8¹	1										
13		2		5	3		8	13	11¹	12	10³	9²				6			7	1		4		14						
14		2		4	5	3	12	8	13	10	11³	14		9			6²		7¹	1										
15		2			5	3		7	12	11¹	10			9		6			8	1		4								
16		2		4	5		7¹	8	6²	10	11²			9	14	12			1		3	13								
17		7¹		4	2	13	6	11	9⁵	5	8	12	10			14			1		3³									
18		14	2¹	4	5	3	7	8	13	10	11³	12		9					1					6²						
19		5¹	2	4	9	3		8		10²	14	13		12		6			7	1				11³						
20		5¹	2	4	9	3		8		10²	14			12		7³			6	1				13	11					
21		12	2¹	4	5	3		7		10	14			9²		13			8	1				6³	11					
22	12	5²	4	3	9	2	7³			10				14		8	13		6						11		11¹			
23	1	12	3²		2	4		13	11		10³			9		7			8¹	6		5			14					
24	1	2	13	4	5	3		8	9²	12	10³			6¹	14	7									11					
25	1	2	3	5	6	4		8		10²	12	13		9		7									11¹					
26	1	5	2¹	4	9	3	12	8		11	13	10				7¹			6²						14					
27	1	6	5	3	2	4	9	8		10¹	13	14		12		7³									11²					
28	1	6	2²	4	5	3	7		9	12	10³	14	13			8¹									11					
29	1		2	4	5	3	7	12	10	14	9²					8									11¹		6³	13		
30	1	2		4	5	3	14	8	13	12	10¹			9		7²									11		6¹			
31	1	2	3¹	5	6	4	7²	9		10³	13	12		14					4						11		8			
32	1	5¹	2		9	3			13	10⁵				12		7			6			4			11		8²	14		
33	1		2	5	3		7			10²	12	13		6		14			8¹			4			11³	9				
34	1		2	5	3		8¹			12	10	11³		6		13			7			4			9²	14				
35	1	2¹	3	5	6	4		9		14	10	11²		7		8³			13										12	
36	1	2		5	3		8³		9	10²	11¹	14		6		13			7			4							12	
37	1		5		2	3	7		10³	9²		13		8		6			4						11¹		12		12	14
38	1	2	3	13	5		7		9²	10	14			6		8¹			4						11³		12			
39	1	14	3	2	5		7		9²	10	13			6		8³			4						11¹		12			
40	1	2		5	3		7	12		10²	14			6		9			4						11³		8¹	13		
41	1	2		5	3		7	13		10	14	12		6³		9			4						11¹		8²			
42	1	2		5	3		8		9¹	10²	12	13		6		7			4						11¹				14	
43	1	2¹	4	8	5	3	7			11	14	13		12		9			6¹						10³					
44	1	2		5	3		7		9²	10³	13			6		12			8¹			4			11		14			
45	1	2		5	3		8		9¹	11³	14	13		6		12			7			4			10²					
46	1	2		5	3		7		9²	10	14	13		6		12			8¹			4			11³					

FA Cup
First Round   Chesham U   (h) 0-1

Capital One Cup
First Round   Birmingham C   (h) 1-2

Johnstone's Paint Trophy
Second Round   Wycombe W   (h) 2-0
Southern Quarter-Final   Southend U   (a) 0-1

BURNLEY

FOUNDATION

On 18 May 1882 Burnley (Association) Football Club was still known as Burnley Rovers as members of that rugby club had decided on that date to play Association Football in the future. It was only a matter of days later that the members met again and decided to drop Rovers from the club's name.

Turf Moor, Harry Potts Way, Burnley, Lancashire BB10 4BX.

Telephone: (0871) 221 1882.

Fax: (01282) 700 014.

Ticket Office: (0871) 221 1914.

Website: www.burnleyfootballclub.com

Email: info@burnleyfc.com

Ground Capacity: 21,401.

Record Attendance: 54,775 v Huddersfield T, FA Cup 3rd rd, 23 February 1924.

Pitch Measurements: 103m × 65m (112.5yd × 71yd).

Chairman: Mike Garlick.

Chief Executive: Dave Baldwin.

Manager: Sean Dyche.

Assistant Manager: Ian Woan.

Head Physio: Ally Beattie.

Colours: Claret shirts with blue sleeves, blue shorts with claret trim, white socks with claret and blue trim.

Year Formed: 1882.

Turned Professional: 1883.

Previous Name: 1882, Burnley Rovers; 1882, Burnley.

Club Nickname: 'The Clarets'.

Grounds: 1882, Calder Vale; 1883, Turf Moor.

First Football League Game: 8 September 1888, Football League, v Preston NE (a) L 2–5 – Smith; Lang, Bury, Abrahams, Friel, Keenan, Brady, Tait, Poland (1), Gallocher (1), Yates.

Record League Victory: 9–0 v Darwen, Division 1, 9 January 1892 – Hillman; Walker, McFettridge, Lang, Matthews, Keenan, Nicol (3), Bowes, Espie (1), McLardie (3), Hill (2).

Record Cup Victory: 9–0 v Crystal Palace, FA Cup 2nd rd (replay), 10 February 1909 – Dawson; Barron, McLean; Cretney (2), Leake, Moffat; Morley, Ogden, Smith (3), Abbott (2), Smethams (1). 9–0 v New Brighton, FA Cup 4th rd, 26 January 1957 – Blacklaw; Angus, Winton; Seith, Adamson, Miller; Newlands (1), McIlroy (3), Lawson (3), Cheesebrough (1), Pilkington (1). 9–0 v Penrith, FA Cup 1st rd, 17 November 1984 – Hansbury; Miller, Hampton, Phelan, Overson (Kennedy), Hird (3 incl. 1p), Grewcock (1), Powell (2), Taylor (3), Biggins, Hutchison.

Record Defeat: 0–11 v Darwen, FA Cup 1st rd, 17 October 1885.

HONOURS

League Champions: Division 1 – 1920–21, 1959–60; FL C – 2015–16; Division 2 – 1897–98, 1972–73; Division 3 – 1981–82; Division 4 – 1991–92.
Runners-up: Division 1 – 1919–20, 1961–62; FL C – 2013–14; Division 2 – 1912–13, 1946–47; Second Division – 1999–2000.

FA Cup Winners: 1914.
Runners-up: 1947, 1962.

League Cup: semi-final – 1961, 1969, 1983, 2009.

League Trophy: Runners-up: 1988.

Anglo–Scottish Cup Winners: 1979.

European Competitions
European Cup: 1960–61 (*qf*).
Fairs Cup: 1966–67.

sky SPORTS FACT FILE

On 13 October 1886 Prince Albert Victor, grandson of Queen Victoria, became the first member of the Royal Family to attend a professional football match when he was present at Turf Moor for the first half of the game between Burnley and Bolton Wanderers. The visitors won the game 4-3.

Most League Points (2 for a win): 62, Division 2, 1972–73.

Most League Points (3 for a win): 93, FL C, 2013–14; FL C, 2015–16.

Most League Goals: 102, Division 1, 1960–61.

Highest League Scorer in Season: George Beel, 35, Division 1, 1927–28.

Most League Goals in Total Aggregate: George Beel, 179, 1923–32.

Most League Goals in One Match: 6, Louis Page v Birmingham C, Division 1, 10 April 1926.

Most Capped Player: Jimmy McIlroy, 51 (55), Northern Ireland.

Most League Appearances: Jerry Dawson, 522, 1907–28.

Youngest League Player: Tommy Lawton, 16 years 174 days v Doncaster R, 28 March 1936.

Record Transfer Fee Received: £7,000,000 from Southampton for Jay Rodriguez, June 2012.

Record Transfer Fee Paid: £9,000,000 to Brentford for Andre Gray, August 2015.

Football League Record: 1888 Original Member of the Football League; 1897–98 Division 2; 1898–1900 Division 1; 1900–13 Division 2; 1913–30 Division 1; 1930–47 Division 2; 1947–71 Division 1; 1971–73 Division 2; 1973–76 Division 1; 1976–80 Division 2; 1980–82 Division 3; 1982–83 Division 2; 1983–85 Division 3; 1985–92 Division 4; 1992–94 Division 2; 1994–95 Division 1; 1995–2000 Division 2; 2000–04 Division 1; 2004–09 FL C; 2009–10 FA Premier League; 2010–14 FL C; 2014–15 FA Premier League; 2015–16 FL C; 2016– FA Premier League.

LATEST SEQUENCES

Longest Sequence of League Wins: 10, 16.11.1912 – 18.1.1913.

Longest Sequence of League Defeats: 8, 2.1.1995 – 25.2.1995.

Longest Sequence of League Draws: 6, 21.2.1931 – 28.3.1931.

Longest Sequence of Unbeaten League Matches: 30, 6.9.1920 – 25.3.1921.

Longest Sequence Without a League Win: 24, 16.4.1979 – 17.11.1979.

Successive Scoring Runs: 27 from 13.2.1926.

Successive Non-scoring Runs: 6 from 21.3.2015.

MANAGERS

Harry Bradshaw 1894–99
    (*Secretary-Manager from 1897*)
Club Directors 1899–1900
J. Ernest Mangnall 1900–03
    (*Secretary-Manager*)
Spen Whittaker 1903–10
    (*Secretary-Manager*)
John Haworth 1910–24
    (*Secretary-Manager*)
Albert Pickles 1925–31
    (*Secretary-Manager*)
Tom Bromilow 1932–35
Selection Committee 1935–45
Cliff Britton 1945–48
Frank Hill 1948–54
Alan Brown 1954–57
Billy Dougall 1957–58
Harry Potts 1958–70
    (*General Manager to 1972*)
Jimmy Adamson 1970–76
Joe Brown 1976–77
Harry Potts 1977–79
Brian Miller 1979–83
John Bond 1983–84
John Benson 1984–85
Martin Buchan 1985
Tommy Cavanagh 1985–86
Brian Miller 1986–89
Frank Casper 1989–91
Jimmy Mullen 1991–96
Adrian Heath 1996–97
Chris Waddle 1997–98
Stan Ternent 1998–2004
Steve Cotterill 2004–07
Owen Coyle 2007–10
Brian Laws 2010
Eddie Howe 2011–12
Sean Dyche October 2012–

TEN YEAR LEAGUE RECORD

		P	W	D	L	F	A	Pts	Pos
2006-07	FL C	46	15	12	19	52	49	57	15
2007-08	FL C	46	16	14	16	60	67	62	13
2008-09	FL C	46	21	13	12	72	60	76	5
2009-10	PR Lge	38	8	6	24	42	82	30	18
2010-11	FL C	46	18	14	14	65	61	68	8
2011-12	FL C	46	17	11	18	61	58	62	13
2012-13	FL C	46	16	13	17	62	60	61	11
2013-14	FL C	46	26	15	5	72	37	93	2
2014-15	PR Lge	38	7	12	19	28	53	33	19
2015-16	FL C	46	26	15	5	72	35	93	1

DID YOU KNOW ?

Bob Lord, who was chairman of Burnley from 1955 to 1981, also served on the Football League Management Committee from 1967 to 1970. Notoriously opposed to television, he banned the cameras from Turf Moor for a five-year period in the mid-1960s.

BURNLEY – FL CHAMPIONSHIP 2015–16 LEAGUE RECORD

Match No.	Date	Venue	Opponents	Result	H/T Score	Lg Pos.	Goalscorers	Attendance
1	Aug 8	A	Leeds U	D 1-1	0-0	10	Vokes [86]	27,672
2	15	H	Birmingham C	D 2-2	0-1	13	Keane [51], Taylor [81]	12,430
3	18	A	Ipswich T	L 0-2	0-0	17		18,353
4	22	H	Brentford	W 1-0	1-0	13	Keane [26]	14,928
5	29	A	Bristol C	W 2-1	2-0	9	Mee [34], Keane [40]	15,002
6	Sept 12	H	Sheffield W	W 3-1	1-1	5	Jones [7], Taylor [78], Gray [90]	17,277
7	15	H	Milton Keynes D	W 2-1	1-1	3	Vokes [32], Boyd [49]	15,845
8	21	A	Derby Co	D 0-0	0-0	3		26,834
9	26	H	Reading	L 1-2	0-2	6	Darikwa [67]	15,226
10	Oct 2	A	Rotherham U	W 2-1	1-0	3	Gray [9], Vokes [81]	9752
11	17	H	Bolton W	W 2-0	0-0	5	Gray 2 [56, 68]	17,632
12	20	A	Nottingham F	D 1-1	0-0	5	Taylor [90]	17,721
13	24	A	Blackburn R	W 1-0	0-0	3	Arfield [63]	19,897
14	31	H	Huddersfield T	W 2-1	2-0	3	Gray 2 (1 pen) [12 (p), 43]	16,749
15	Nov 3	A	Fulham	W 3-1	2-0	2	Gray 2 [18, 37], Taylor [90]	15,080
16	7	A	Wolverhampton W	D 0-0	0-0	3		20,684
17	22	H	Brighton & HA	D 1-1	1-1	5	Gray (pen) [4]	15,622
18	28	A	Cardiff C	D 2-2	0-1	5	Hennings [86], Connolly (og) [90]	15,133
19	Dec 5	H	Preston NE	L 0-2	0-0	5		18,614
20	12	A	QPR	D 0-0	0-0	5		16,576
21	15	A	Middlesbrough	L 0-1	0-0	5		19,966
22	19	H	Charlton Ath	W 4-0	1-0	5	Arfield 2 [44, 53], Gray [55], Vokes [78]	15,697
23	26	A	Hull C	L 0-3	0-0	5		21,842
24	28	A	Bristol C	W 4-0	2-0	5	Gray 3 [37, 45, 78], Arfield [71]	17,234
25	Jan 2	H	Ipswich T	D 0-0	0-0	5		16,307
26	12	A	Milton Keynes D	W 5-0	1-0	4	Barton [14], Vokes [46], Gray [64], Lowton [71], Boyd [82]	10,011
27	15	A	Brentford	W 3-1	3-0	4	Arfield [12], Barton [30], Boyd [39]	10,039
28	25	H	Derby Co	W 4-1	1-1	3	Keogh (og) [29], Gray (pen) [54], Vokes (pen) [58], Arfield [66]	15,214
29	Feb 2	A	Sheffield W	D 1-1	1-0	3	Gray [3]	19,762
30	6	H	Hull C	W 1-0	0-0	3	Vokes [77]	17,667
31	13	A	Reading	D 0-0	0-0	3		16,773
32	20	H	Rotherham U	W 2-0	1-0	2	Vokes (pen) [27], Arfield [86]	15,849
33	23	H	Nottingham F	W 1-0	0-0	2	Vokes [68]	15,517
34	27	A	Bolton W	W 2-1	0-0	1	Gray 2 [74, 85]	17,484
35	Mar 5	H	Blackburn R	W 1-0	1-0	1	Gray (pen) [16]	20,478
36	8	A	Fulham	W 3-2	1-2	1	Vokes 2 (1 pen) [9, 49 (p)], Gray [61]	15,281
37	12	A	Huddersfield T	W 3-1	3-1	1	Ward [14], Vokes [30], Mee [45]	13,917
38	19	H	Wolverhampton W	D 1-1	0-0	1	Vokes [68]	17,411
39	Apr 2	A	Brighton & HA	D 2-2	1-2	1	Gray [33], Keane [90]	29,683
40	5	H	Cardiff C	D 0-0	0-0	1		15,740
41	9	H	Leeds U	W 1-0	1-0	1	Arfield [1]	18,229
42	16	A	Birmingham C	W 2-1	1-0	2	Boyd [31], Gray [77]	19,151
43	19	H	Middlesbrough	D 1-1	0-0	2	Keane [90]	20,197
44	22	A	Preston NE	W 1-0	1-0	1	Barton [6]	17,789
45	May 2	H	QPR	W 1-0	0-0	1	Vokes [61]	19,362
46	7	A	Charlton Ath	W 3-0	1-0	1	Vokes [20], Boyd [49], Gray [51]	16,199

Final League Position: 1

GOALSCORERS

League (72): Gray 23 (4 pens), Vokes 15 (3 pens), Arfield 8, Boyd 5, Keane 5, Taylor 4, Barton 3, Mee 2, Darikwa 1, Hennings 1, Jones 1, Lowton 1, Ward 1, own goals 2.
FA Cup (3): Hennings 1, Vokes 1, Ward 1.
Capital One Cup (0).

Heaton T 46	Darikwa T 21	Duff M 23 + 1	Keane M 44	Mee B 46	Boyd G 42 + 2	Jones D 39 + 2	Arfield S 46	Kightly M 12 + 6	Jutkiewicz L 3 + 2	Vossen J 3 + 1	Sordell M — + 3	Vokes S 39 + 4	Taylor M 1 + 26	Hennings R 3 + 23	Gray A 41	Long C 1 + 9	Barton J 37 + 1	Lowton M 25 + 2	Ward S 23 + 1	Marney D 7 + 5	Ulvestad F 1 + 4	Tarkowski J 2 + 2	Barnes A 1 + 7	Dyer L — + 3	Match No.
1	2	3	4	5	6	7	8	9[3]	10[3]	11[1]	12	13	14												1
1	2	3	4	5	6	7	8	9[2]	11[3]	10[1]	14	12	13												2
1	2	3	4	5	6	7[3]	8	9	13	11[2]		10[1]	14	12											3
1	2	3	4	5	6	8	7	9[1]	11[3]			14	12	13	10[2]										4
1	2	3	4	5	6	7	8	9[3]	12	13		10[2]	14		11[1]										5
1	2	3	4	5	6	7	8	9[1]				10[1]	12	13	11[3]	14									6
1	2	3	4	5	6	8	7	9[2]				10[1]	14	12	11[3]	13									7
1	2	3	4	5	6	7	8	9[1]				10	13	12	11[2]										8
1	2	3	4	5	6	7[1]	8	9[1]				10	14	11[2]		12	13								9
1	2	3	4	5	6[2]	7	9					10	12		11[1]	13	8								10
1	2	3	4	5	6[1]	7	9					10	12		11[2]	13	8								11
1	2[1]	3	4	5		7[2]	9	12				10	6	14	11[3]		8	13							12
1	2	3	4	5	6	7	9					10			11[1]	12	8								13
1	2	3	4	5	6	7	9					10			11[1]	12	8								14
1	2	3	4	5	9[1]	7	6					10	12		11[2]	13	8								15
1	2	3	4	5[3]	6[1]	7	9					10[2]	13	12	11		8		14						16
1	2	3	4	5	6	7	9					10[1]	11	12			8								17
1	2	3	4	5	6	7[2]	9[3]						12	14	11	10[1]	8			13					18
1	2[1]	3	4	5	6[2]	7	9[2]	13				10	12		11		8	14							19
1	2	3	4	5	6	7	9					10			11		8								20
1	2[1]	3	4	5	7[3]	9[2]	10	13				12		14	11		6			8					21
1		3	4	5	6[5]	9[2]	13					10	14	12	11[1]		8	2		7					22
1		3	4	5	6[2]	9[1]	12					10	14	13	11[2]		8	2		7					23
1		3	4	8	6[2]	9						10	14	12	11[1]		7[3]	2	5	13					24
1		3	4	12	8	6[1]	9[3]					10	14	13	11[2]		7	2	5	13					25
1		3	4	12	7	9	6[1]					10[3]	14	11			8[3]	2	5	13					26
1		3	4	6	7	9						10	12	11[1]			8	2	5						27
1		3	4	6	7	9						10[1]	12	11[2]			8	2	5	13					28
1		3	4	6[1]	7	9						10	12	13	11[2]		8	2	5						29
1		3	4	6	8	9						10	12	11[1]			7	2	5						30
1		3	4	6	7	9						10	12	11[1]			8	2	5						31
1		3[3]	4	6[1]	7	9						10	14	13	11[2]		8	2	5				12		32
1			4	6	7	9						10		11			8	2	5				3		33
1			4	6[1]	7[3]	9						10	12	14	11[2]		8	2	5		13	3			34
1		3	4	6	7[2]	9						10		13	11[1]		8	2	5		12				35
1		3	4	6		9						10		11			8	2	5	12	7[1]				36
1		3	4	6	7	9[2]	12					10	13	11[1]			8	2	5						37
1		3	4	6	7	9						10	12	11[1]			8	2	5						38
1		3	4	6	8[1]	9[2]						10	12	11[1]			7	2	5	13			14		39
1		3	4	6	7	9[2]						10	12	11[1]			8	2	5				13		40
1		3	4	6	7[1]	9						10[3]	14	11[1]			8	2	5	13			12		41
1		3	4	9	12	6[2]								11[3]			8[1]	2	5	7		14	10	13	42
1		3	4	6[1]		9[2]						10	14	11[3]			8	2	5	7		13	12		43
1		3	4	6	13	9						10		11[1]			8	2	5	7[2]		12			44
1		3	4	6	7	9						10		11[1]			8	2	5			12			45
1	14	3[3]	4	6		9[2]						10[5]		11			8	2	5	7		12	13[3]		46

BURTON ALBION

FOUNDATION

Once upon a time there were three Football League clubs bearing the name Burton. Then there was none. In reality it had been two. Originally Burton Swifts and Burton Wanderers competed in it until 1901 when they amalgamated to form Burton United. This club disbanded in 1910. There was no senior club representing the town until 1924 when Burton Town, formerly known as Burton All Saints, played in the Birmingham & District League, subsequently joining the Midland League in 1935–36. When the Second World War broke out the club fielded a team in a truncated version of the Birmingham & District League taking over from the club's reserves. But it was not revived in peacetime. So it was not until a further decade that a club bearing the name of Burton reappeared. Founded in 1950 Burton Albion made progress from the Birmingham & District League, too, then into the Southern League and because of its geographical situation later had spells in the Northern Premier League. In April 2009 Burton Albion restored the name of the town to the Football League competition as champions of the Blue Square Premier League.

Pirelli Stadium, Princess Way, Burton-on-Trent, Staffordshire DE13 0AR.

Telephone: (01283) 565 938.

Fax: (01283) 523 199.

Ticket Office: (01283) 565 938.

Website: www.burtonalbionfc.co.uk

Email: bafc@burtonalbionfc.co.uk

Ground Capactiy: 6,972.

Record Attendance: 5,806 v Weymouth, Southern League Cup final 2nd leg 1964 (at Eton Park); 6,192 v Oxford U, Blue Square Premier, 17 April 2009 (at Pirelli Stadium).

Pitch Measurements: 100m × 68.5m (109.5yd × 75yd).

Chairman: Ben Robinson.

Manager: Nigel Clough.

Assistant Manager: Gary Crosby.

Physio: Nick Fenton.

Colours: Yellow and black striped shirts, black shorts with yellow trim, black socks with yellow trim.

Year Formed: 1950.

Turned Professional: 1950.

Club Nickname: 'The Brewers'.

HONOURS

League Champions: FL 2 – 2014–15; Conference – 2008–09.
Runners-up: FL 1 – 2015–16.
FA Cup: 4th rd – 2011.
League Cup: 3rd rd – 2013, 2015.

sky SPORTS FACT FILE

Burton Albion will become the fourth club from the town to appear in English football's second tier in 2016–17, after Burton Swifts, Burton Wanderers and Burton United. With the exception of London, no other English town or city has hosted as many senior clubs at this level.

Grounds: 1950, Eton Park; 2005, Pirelli Stadium.

First Football League Game: 8 August 2009, FL 2, v Shrewsbury T (a) L 1–3 – Redmond; Edworthy, Boertien, Austin, Branston, McGrath, Maghoma, Penn, Phillips (Stride), Walker, Shroot (Pearson) (1).

Record League Victory: 6-1 v Aldershot T, FL 2, 12 December 2009 – Krysiak; James, Boertien, Stride, Webster, McGrath, Jackson, Penn, Kabba (2), Pearson (3) (Harrad) (1), Gilroy (Maghoma).

Record Cup Victory: 12–1 v Coalville T, Birmingham Senior Cup, 6 September 1954.

Record Defeat: 0–10 v Barnet, Southern League, 7 February 1970.

Most League Points (3 for a win): 94, FL 2, 2014–15.

Most League Goals: 71, FL 2, 2009–10; 2012–13.

Highest League Scorer in Season: Shaun Harrad, 21, 2009–10.

Most League Goals in Total Aggregate: Billy Kee, 39, 2011–15.

Most League Goals in One Match: 3, Greg Pearson v Aldershot T, FL 2, 12 December 2009; 3, Shaun Harrad v Rotherham U, FL 2, 11 September 2010; 3, Lucas Akins v Colchester U, FL 1, 23 April 2016.

Most Capped Player: Joachim Aurelien, 6 (62), Luxembourg.

Most League Appearances: Jacques Maghoma, 155, 2009–13.

Youngest League Player: Sam Austin, 17 years 310 days v Stevenage, 25 October 2014.

Record Transfer Fee Received: £200,000 from Derby Co for Adam Legzdins, June 2011.

Record Transfer Fee Paid: £500,000 to Milton Keynes D for Kyle McFadzean, July 2016.

Football League Record: 2009 Promoted from Blue Square Premier; 2009–15 FL 2; 2015–16 FL 1; 2016– FL C.

MANAGERS

Reg Weston
Sammy Crooks 1957
Eddie Shimwell 1958
Bill Townsend 1959–62
Peter Taylor 1962–65
Richie Norman
Reg Gutteridge
Harold Bodle 1974–76
Ian Storey-Moore 1978–81
Neil Warnock 1981–86
Brian Fidler 1986–88
Vic Halom 1988
Bobby Hope 1988
Chris Wright 1988–89
Ken Blair 1989–90
Steve Powell 1990–91
Brian Fidler 1991–92
Brian Kenning 1992–94
John Barton 1994–98
Nigel Clough 1998–2009
Roy McFarland 2009
Paul Peschisolido 2009–12
Gary Rowett 2012–14
Jimmy Floyd Hasselbaink 2014–15
Nigel Clough December 2015–

LATEST SEQUENCES

Longest Sequence of League Wins: 4, 24.11.2015 – 12.12.2015.

Longest Sequence of League Defeats: 8, 25.2.2012 – 24.3.2012.

Longest Sequence of League Draws: 6, 25.4.2011 – 16.8.2011.

Longest Sequence of Unbeaten League Matches: 13, 7.3.2015 – 8.8.2015.

Longest Sequence Without a League Win: 16, 31.12.2011 – 24.3.2012.

Successive Scoring Runs: 18 from 16.4.2011 – 8.10.2011.

Successive Non-scoring Runs: 5 from 25.2.2012 – 10.3.2012.

TEN YEAR LEAGUE RECORD

		P	W	D	L	F	A	Pts	Pos
2006-07	Conf	46	22	9	15	52	47	75	6
2007-08	Conf P	46	23	12	11	79	56	81	5
2008-09	Conf P	46	27	7	12	81	52	88	1
2009-10	FL 2	46	17	11	18	71	71	62	13
2010-11	FL 2	46	12	15	19	56	70	51	19
2011-12	FL 2	46	14	12	20	54	81	54	17
2012-13	FL 2	46	22	10	14	71	65	76	4
2013-14	FL 2	46	19	15	12	47	42	72	6
2014-15	FL 2	46	28	10	8	69	39	94	1
2015-16	FL 1	46	25	10	11	57	37	85	2

DID YOU KNOW ?

Burton Albion's first-ever manager was Don McPhail, who had played for the old Burton Town club before the war. McPhail was a winger who had previously played in the Football League for a number of clubs, finishing off with a spell at Swindon Town.

BURTON ALBION – FOOTBALL LEAGUE ONE 2015–16 LEAGUE RECORD

Match No.	Date	Venue	Opponents	Result		H/T Score	Lg Pos.	Goalscorers	Attendance
1	Aug 8	H	Scunthorpe U	W	2-1	0-0	6	Beavon [55], Akins (pen) [72]	4064
2	15	A	Barnsley	L	0-1	0-0	9		8583
3	18	A	Blackpool	W	2-1	0-1	6	El Khayati 2 [58, 85]	6197
4	22	H	Peterborough U	W	2-1	1-0	5	El Khayati [36], Beavon [54]	3407
5	29	A	Shrewsbury T	W	1-0	0-0	3	Duffy [90]	4780
6	Sept 6	H	Coventry C	L	1-2	1-1	5	Martin (og) [11]	4633
7	12	H	Rochdale	W	1-0	1-0	3	Beavon [24]	2787
8	19	A	Swindon T	W	1-0	1-0	1	Beavon [27]	7005
9	26	A	Chesterfield	W	2-1	0-1	1	Beavon [46], Williams [90]	6752
10	29	H	Sheffield U	D	0-0	0-0	1		5029
11	Oct 3	H	Southend U	W	1-0	0-0	1	Prosser (og) [51]	2948
12	10	A	Walsall	L	0-2	0-1	2		6812
13	17	A	Fleetwood T	L	0-4	0-1	3		2893
14	20	H	Crewe Alex	D	0-0	0-0	3		2666
15	24	H	Port Vale	W	2-0	0-0	3	Naylor [84], El Khayati [90]	4076
16	31	A	Oldham Ath	W	1-0	1-0	2	El Khayati [17]	3795
17	Nov 21	A	Bury	L	0-1	0-1	5		3788
18	24	A	Wigan Ath	W	1-0	0-0	3	El Khayati [74]	8117
19	28	H	Colchester U	W	5-1	2-1	3	El Khayati [25], Duffy [34], Naylor [51], Akins [72], Thiele [81]	2893
20	Dec 1	H	Millwall	W	2-1	2-0	1	McCrory [35], El Khayati [42]	2888
21	12	A	Gillingham	W	3-0	0-0	1	McCrory [59], Akins [90], O'Connor [90]	6230
22	19	H	Doncaster R	D	3-3	1-1	1	Butcher 2 [18, 61], Duffy [89]	4103
23	28	H	Swindon T	W	1-0	0-0	2	Akins (pen) [77]	4816
24	Jan 2	H	Blackpool	W	1-0	0-0	1	Duffy [63]	4339
25	16	A	Coventry C	W	2-0	0-0	1	Butcher [49], Beavon [72]	17,140
26	23	H	Shrewsbury T	L	1-2	1-0	2	McCrory [18]	3870
27	26	A	Peterborough U	W	1-0	1-0	1	Naylor [3]	4798
28	30	A	Rochdale	L	1-2	0-2	1	Akins [78]	2994
29	Feb 6	H	Bradford C	W	3-1	1-0	1	Bennett [17], Naylor [73], Duffy [77]	3796
30	12	H	Chesterfield	W	1-0	1-0	1	Butcher [45]	4489
31	22	A	Southend U	L	1-3	1-1	1	Beavon [44]	6503
32	27	H	Walsall	D	0-0	0-0	1		5512
33	Mar 1	A	Sheffield U	W	1-0	0-0	1	Akins [49]	17,927
34	5	A	Crewe Alex	D	1-1	1-1	1	Akins [35]	4380
35	8	A	Bradford C	L	0-2	0-2	1		17,500
36	12	H	Fleetwood T	W	2-1	1-0	1	Duffy 2 [26, 63]	4415
37	19	A	Port Vale	W	4-0	2-0	1	Akins [34], Grant (og) [45], Duffy [50], Butcher [60]	6157
38	26	H	Oldham Ath	D	0-0	0-0	1		4283
39	28	A	Millwall	L	0-2	0-2	1		8012
40	Apr 2	H	Bury	D	1-1	0-0	2	Walker [90]	3331
41	9	A	Scunthorpe U	L	0-1	0-0	2		3888
42	16	H	Barnsley	D	0-0	0-0	2		4858
43	19	H	Wigan Ath	D	1-1	1-1	2	Naylor [38]	5461
44	23	A	Colchester U	W	3-0	1-0	2	Akins 3 [45, 49, 60]	4292
45	30	H	Gillingham	W	2-1	1-0	2	Akins [44], Naylor [90]	5388
46	May 8	A	Doncaster R	D	0-0	0-0	2		9803

Final League Position: 2

GOALSCORERS

League (57): Akins 12 (2 pens), Duffy 8, El Khayati 8, Beavon 7, Naylor 6, Butcher 5, McCrory 3, Bennett 1, O'Connor 1, Thiele 1, Walker 1, Williams 1, own goals 3.
FA Cup (0).
Capital One Cup (2): Palmer 1, own goal 1.
Johnstone's Paint Trophy (0).

Matthews R 1 + 1	Edwards P 46	Mousinho J 46	Cansdell-Sherriff S 29	McCrory D 37 + 1	Akins L 31 + 13	Naylor T 35 + 6	Weir R 32 + 4	El Khayati A 23 + 1	Duffy M 44 + 1	Beavon S 41 + 2	Williams J 8 + 7	Palmer M 7 + 7	Thiele T 7 + 15	McLaughlin J 45	Butcher C 29 + 10	Joachim A — + 7	O'Connor A 12 + 9	Ismail Z — + 3	Flanagan T 13 + 5	Reilly C 4 + 10	Bennett M 6 + 10	Choudhury H 9 + 4	Harness M — + 5	Walker T 1 + 5	Match No.
1	2	3	4	5	6	7	8	9¹	10²	11¹	12	13	14												1
	2	3	5	8	6¹	4	7³	10	9	11³	12	14	13	1											2
	2	4	3	5	13	7	9	6	10¹	11²				1	8³	12	14								3
	2	3	4	5	14	7	8	9¹	6	11²	12	10¹		1		13									4
	2	3	4	5		12	8	9²	6	11³	13	10		1	7²	14									5
	2	3	4		13	8	7²	9²	6¹	10	5	12	11	1	7	14									6
12	2	3	4	5	8	13	6		9³	11	10²			1	7	14									7
	2	3	4	5	9		10	12	8³	11²	6¹	13	14	1	7										8
	2	3		5	8¹		6	10	9²	11	12	13		1	7		4								9
	2	4		5	12	13	6	8	9¹	11	10³		14	1	7²	3									10
	2	4		5	8	7	6	9³	11¹		12	13	1	14	3										11
	2	3		5	8²		6	9³	11	12	10	13		1	7¹		4	14							12
	2	3		5	6		7	10³	13	11	14	9²		1	8¹	12	4								13
	2	3	4	5	8¹	6	7	10³	9		12		11²	1		14	13								14
	2³	3	4		8²	7	6¹	10	9¹		5		11	1	14	13	12								15
	2	4	3²		6	8		10³	9	13	5		11¹	1	7	14	12								16
	2	3	4²		8¹	7		10	9	11³	5		12	1	14	13	6								17
	2	3			12	7	6	11³	9	10²		13		1	8¹		5	4	14						18
	2	3		12	13	8	6	9	7	11³	10¹		14	1			5²	4							19
	2	3		5	13	6		9¹	10	11²	8	7		1			4								20
	2	3		5	12	6	7	11²	9	10¹		14		1	8²	13	4								21
	2	3		5	12	9		10	7	11				1	8¹	6	4								22
	2	3	4	5	12	9	6³	10²	7	11		13		1	8¹	14	4								23
	2	3	4	5	6	8	7*	9¹	10	11¹		12		1			13								24
	2	3¹	4	5	12	9		10³	7	11²				1	8¹	6			13	14					25
	2	3		5	13	6		10³	7	11				1	9	4			8¹	12					26
	2	3	4	5	7	8	6		10	11²	12			1	9¹	13									27
	2	3	4	5	10	8	6¹		7	11	12			1	9²										28
	2	3	4	5	6	8	7		10²	11¹		1	12						14	13	9³				29
	2	3	4³	5	12	9	6		7	11		1	8²						13	14	10¹				30
	2	3	4	5	12	8	6		7	11		1	9¹						13	10²					31
	2	3	4	5	7	9	6			11³		1	8						14	10²	12	13			32
	2	3	4	5	7	8	6		10²	11³		1	9¹						14	13	12				33
	2	3	4	5	6	13	7		10	12		1	9³						8	11²	14				34
	2	3²	4	5	7	9	6¹		10	11³		1	8						14		13	12			35
	2	3	4	5	7¹	9	12		10	11		1	8³						14	13	6¹				36
	2	3		5²	10	8			7	11¹		1	9³						4	13	12	6	14		37
	2	3		5	10	9¹	12		7	11		1	8						4		13	6²			38
	2	3		5	10	9¹			7³	11²		1	8						4		13	6	14	12	39
	2³	3		5	9		7¹		6	10		1	14						4		11³	8¹	12	13	40
	2	3			10	8	6²	7				1	9						4	5	12		13	11¹	41
	2	3	4		10	14	6¹	7	11³	8		1	9²						5			12		13	42
	5	4	3		10	8³	13	7	11	9		1	14						2²	12		6¹			43
	2	3	4	9³	10	5		7	11²	8¹		1	12						14	6		13			44
	2	3	4	5	7	8		10²	11¹	9²		1	12	14					6			13			45
	2	3	4	5	7	8²	13		10	11¹	9	1	12						6						46

FA Cup
First Round   Peterborough U   (h)   0-3

Capital One Cup
First Round   Bolton W   (a)   1-0
Second Round   Middlesbrough   (h)   1-2
(aet)

Johnstone's Paint Trophy
First Round   Doncaster R   (a)   0-0
(aet; Doncaster R won 5-3 on penalties)

BURY

Gigg Lane, Bury, Lancashire BL9 9HR.

Telephone: (0871) 222 1885.

Fax: (0161) 764 5521.

Ticket Office: (0871) 221 1885.

Website: www.buryfc.co.uk

Email: info@buryfc.co.uk

Ground Capacity: 11,376.

Record Attendance: 35,000 v Bolton W, FA Cup 3rd rd, 9 January 1960.

Pitch Measurements: 102.5m × 67m (112yd × 73yd).

Chairman: Stewart Day.

Chief Executive: Glenn Thomas.

Manager: David Flitcroft.

Assistant Manager: Ben Futcher.

Physio: Nick Mearce.

Colours: White shirts with blue trim, blue shorts with white trim, blue socks.

Year Formed: 1885.

Turned Professional: 1885.

Club Nickname: 'The Shakers'.

Ground: 1885, Gigg Lane (renamed JD Stadium 2013); 2015 Gigg Lane.

First Football League Game: 1 September 1894, Division 2, v Manchester C (h) W 4–2 – Lowe; Gillespie, Davies; White, Clegg, Ross; Wylie, Barbour (2), Millar (1), Ostler (1), Plant.

Record League Victory: 8–0 v Tranmere R, Division 3, 10 January 1970 – Forrest; Tinney, Saile; Anderson, Turner, McDermott; Hince (1), Arrowsmith (1), Jones (4), Kerr (1), Grundy, (1 og).

Record Cup Victory: 12–1 v Stockton, FA Cup 1st rd (replay), 2 February 1897 – Montgomery; Darroch, Barbour; Hendry (1), Clegg, Ross (1); Wylie (3), Pangbourn, Millar (4), Henderson (2), Plant, (1 og).

Record Defeat: 0–10 v Blackburn R, FA Cup pr rd, 1 October 1887. 0–10 v West Ham U, Milk Cup 2nd rd 2nd leg, 25 October 1983.

Most League Points (2 for a win): 68, Division 3, 1960–61.

Most League Points (3 for a win): 85, FL 2, 2014–15.

HONOURS

League Champions: Division 2 – 1894–95; Second Division – 1996–97; Division 3 – 1960–61.
Runners-up: Division 2 – 1923–24; Division 3 – 1967–68; FL 2 – 2010–11.
FA Cup Winners: 1900, 1903.
League Cup: semi-final – 1963.

sky SPORTS FACT FILE

Bury met Stoke City seven times in less than a month during the 1954–55 season and didn't win a single game. The teams met twice over the Christmas period and then their FA Cup third round tie went to five matches before the Potters eventually triumphed 3-2 after extra time at Old Trafford.

Most League Goals: 108, Division 3, 1960–61.

Highest League Scorer in Season: Craig Madden, 35, Division 4, 1981–82.

Most League Goals in Total Aggregate: Craig Madden, 129, 1978–86.

Most League Goals in One Match: 5, Eddie Quigley v Millwall, Division 2, 15 February 1947; 5, Ray Pointer v Rotherham U, Division 2, 2 October 1965.

Most Capped Player: Bill Gorman, 11 (13), Republic of Ireland and (4), Northern Ireland.

Most League Appearances: Norman Bullock, 505, 1920–35.

Youngest League Player: Brian Williams, 16 years 133 days v Stockport Co, 18 March 1972; Callum Styles, 16 years 41 days v Southend U, 8 May 2016 (later found to be an ineligible player).

Record Transfer Fee Received: £1,100,000 from Ipswich T for David Johnson, November 1997.

Record Transfer Fee Paid: £200,000 to Ipswich T for Chris Swailes, November 1997; £200,000 to Swindon T for Darren Bullock, February 1999.

Football League Record: 1894 Elected to Division 2; 1895–1912 Division 1; 1912–24 Division 2; 1924–29 Division 1; 1929–57 Division 2; 1957–61 Division 3; 1961–67 Division 2; 1967–68 Division 3; 1968–69 Division 2; 1969–71 Division 3; 1971–74 Division 4; 1974–80 Division 3; 1980–85 Division 4; 1985–96 Division 3; 1996–97 Division 2; 1997–99 Division 1; 1999–2002 Division 2; 2002–04 Division 3; 2004–11 FL 2; 2011–13 FL 1; 2013–15 FL 2; 2015– FL 1.

LATEST SEQUENCES

Longest Sequence of League Wins: 9, 26.9.1960 – 19.11.1960.

Longest Sequence of League Defeats: 8, 18.8.2001 – 25.9.2001.

Longest Sequence of League Draws: 6, 6.3.1999 – 3.4.1999.

Longest Sequence of Unbeaten League Matches: 18, 4.2.1961 – 29.4.1961.

Longest Sequence Without a League Win: 19, 1.4.1911 – 2.12.1911.

Successive Scoring Runs: 24 from 1.9.1894.

Successive Non-scoring Runs: 6 from 11.1.1969.

MANAGERS

T. Hargreaves 1887 (*Secretary-Manager*)
H. S. Hamer 1887–1907 (*Secretary-Manager*)
Archie Montgomery 1907–15
William Cameron 1919–23
James Hunter Thompson 1923–27
Percy Smith 1927–30
Arthur Paine 1930–34
Norman Bullock 1934–38
Charlie Dean 1938–44
Jim Porter 1944–45
Norman Bullock 1945–49
John McNeil 1950–53
Dave Russell 1953–61
Bob Stokoe 1961–65
Bert Head 1965–66
Les Shannon 1966–69
Jack Marshall 1969
Colin McDonald 1970
Les Hart 1970
Tommy McAnearney 1970–72
Alan Brown 1972–73
Bobby Smith 1973–77
Bob Stokoe 1977–78
David Hatton 1978–79
Dave Connor 1979–80
Jim Iley 1980–84
Martin Dobson 1984–89
Sam Ellis 1989–90
Mike Walsh 1990–95
Stan Ternent 1995–98
Neil Warnock 1998–99
Andy Preece 1999–2003
Graham Barrow 2003–05
Chris Casper 2005–08
Alan Knill 2008–11
Richie Barker 2011–12
Kevin Blackwell 2012–13
David Flitcroft December 2013–

TEN YEAR LEAGUE RECORD

		P	W	D	L	F	A	Pts	Pos
2006-07	FL 2	46	13	11	22	46	61	50	21
2007-08	FL 2	46	16	11	19	58	61	59	13
2008-09	FL 2	46	21	15	10	63	43	78	4
2009-10	FL 2	46	19	12	15	54	59	69	9
2010-11	FL 2	46	23	12	11	82	50	81	2
2011-12	FL 1	46	15	11	20	60	79	56	14
2012-13	FL 1	46	9	14	23	45	73	41	22
2013-14	FL 2	46	13	20	13	59	51	59	12
2014-15	FL 2	46	26	7	13	60	40	85	3
2015-16	FL 1	46	16	12	18	56	73	57*	16

*3 pts deducted.

DID YOU KNOW ❓

Following promotion to the old First Division, Bury attracted a then-record gate of 33,523 for the visit of Manchester City for the opening game of 1924–25. Attendances that season were the highest in the club's history with an average of 19,333 recorded.

BURY – FOOTBALL LEAGUE ONE 2015–16 LEAGUE RECORD

Match No.	Date	Venue	Opponents	Result	H/T Score	Lg Pos.	Goalscorers	Attendance
1	Aug 8	A	Doncaster R	D 1-1	0-0	10	Clarke, L [90]	6429
2	15	H	Swindon T	D 2-2	1-0	14	Pope [4], Mayor [52]	3947
3	18	H	Fleetwood T	L 3-4	2-2	17	Clarke, L [4], Soares [19], Rose [84]	2992
4	22	A	Crewe Alex	D 3-3	2-2	16	Mayor [23], Soares [45], Rose [58]	4125
5	29	H	Oldham Ath	D 1-1	0-1	17	Pope [65]	5448
6	Sept 5	A	Walsall	W 1-0	1-0	12	Jones [6]	4829
7	12	A	Sheffield U	W 3-1	0-0	9	Pope [61], Riley [83], Clarke, L [90]	20,708
8	19	H	Port Vale	W 1-0	0-0	6	Cameron [78]	4323
9	26	H	Coventry C	W 2-1	1-0	5	Clarke, L 2 (1 pen) [19, 51 (p)]	4526
10	29	A	Peterborough U	W 3-2	1-1	4	Clarke, L [28], Cameron [64], Pope [81]	4208
11	Oct 3	A	Colchester U	W 1-0	0-0	3	Clarke, L [75]	4032
12	10	H	Wigan Ath	D 2-2	1-0	4	Cameron [6], Pope [60]	5931
13	17	H	Rochdale	D 0-0	0-0	4		6470
14	20	A	Bradford C	L 1-2	0-1	6	Rose [90]	17,575
15	24	A	Shrewsbury T	L 0-2	0-1	7		4945
16	31	H	Blackpool	W 4-3	4-2	6	Rose 2 [2, 10], Hussey [27], Soares [34]	5013
17	Nov 14	A	Gillingham	L 1-3	1-2	6	Clarke, L [4]	6063
18	21	H	Burton Alb	W 1-0	1-0	6	Dodoo [40]	3788
19	24	H	Scunthorpe U	L 1-2	0-1	9	Clarke, L [50]	2483
20	28	A	Millwall	L 0-1	0-1	10		8311
21	Dec 12	H	Chesterfield	W 1-0	0-0	7	Mayor [68]	2962
22	18	A	Southend U	L 1-4	1-2	8	Clarke, L [43]	6127
23	28	A	Port Vale	L 0-1	0-0	12		5467
24	Jan 2	A	Fleetwood T	L 0-2	0-1	14		3301
25	16	H	Walsall	L 2-3	0-3	15	Clarke, L 2 [65, 66]	3532
26	23	A	Oldham Ath	W 1-0	1-0	13	Clarke, L [10]	5537
27	26	H	Crewe Alex	D 0-0	0-0	12		2343
28	Feb 7	A	Barnsley	L 0-3	0-1	15		9443
29	13	A	Coventry C	L 0-6	0-4	16		11,024
30	16	H	Sheffield U	W 1-0	1-0	14	Jones [27]	3081
31	20	H	Colchester U	W 5-2	1-2	14	Lowe [34], Tutte 3 [51, 51, 62], Jones [56]	3428
32	23	A	Barnsley	D 0-0	0-0	14		3160
33	27	A	Wigan Ath	L 0-3	0-3	16		9490
34	Mar 1	H	Peterborough U	W 3-1	2-0	13	Clarke, L [29], Lowe [33], Tutte [80]	2180
35	5	H	Bradford C	D 0-0	0-0	14		4036
36	12	A	Rochdale	L 0-3	0-2	15		4538
37	19	A	Shrewsbury T	D 2-2	1-2	15	Soares [30], Clarke, P [65]	3248
38	25	A	Blackpool	D 1-1	0-0	16	Mayor [76]	7645
39	28	H	Gillingham	L 0-1	0-1	16		2907
40	Apr 2	A	Burton Alb	D 1-1	0-0	16	Lowe [74]	3331
41	9	H	Doncaster R	W 1-0	0-0	15	Clarke, L [77]	3233
42	16	A	Swindon T	W 1-0	0-0	15	Mayor [63]	6759
43	19	A	Scunthorpe U	L 1-2	0-1	15	Pope [61]	3188
44	23	H	Millwall	L 1-3	1-2	15	Lowe [45]	3669
45	30	A	Chesterfield	L 0-3	0-2	15		7232
46	May 8	H	Southend U	W 3-2	2-2	14	Barrett (og) [21], Lowe 2 (1 pen) [29, 90 (p)]	3575

Final League Position: 14 – revised to 16 after being deducted 3 points for fielding an ineligible player on 8/5/16.

GOALSCORERS
League (56): Clarke, L 15 (1 pen), Lowe 6 (1 pen), Pope 6, Mayor 5, Rose 5, Soares 4, Tutte 4, Cameron 3, Jones 3, Clarke, P 1, Dodoo 1, Hussey 1, Riley 1, own goal 1.
FA Cup (6): Cameron 1, Clarke, L 1, Jones 1, Mayor 1, Pope 1, Rose 1.
Capital One Cup (3): Clarke, L 2 (1 pen), Mayor 1.
Johnstone's Paint Trophy (2): Hope 1, Tutte 1.

Walton C 4	Riley J 32+1	Clarke P 44+1	Cameron N 28	Hussey C 39+2	Pugh D 28+11	Etuhu K 16+2	Mayor D 43+1	Soares T 42	Clarke L 32	Pope T 21+15	Tutte A 21+1	Mellis J 14+9	Hope H 1+5	Rose D 7+21	Sedgwick C —+1	Lainton R 10	Jones C 28+8	Lowe R 12+7	Brown R 15+13	Erwin L 1+2	McCarey A 1	Eagles C 1+3	Styles C —+1	Mohammed K —+1	Bachmann D 8	Burgess S 1+2	Ruddy J 1	Dodoo J 4	Nardiello D —+1	Dudley A 2+1	Lawlor I 12	O'Sullivan J 12+7	Miller G —+1	Clare S —+4	Gardner D 4+2	Neal C 10	Bolger C 9	Delfouneso N 3+1	Match No.
1	2	3	4	5	6¹	7	8	9	10	11²	12	13																											1
1	2	4	3	5	12	7¹	9²	8	10	11³	6	13	14																										2
1	2	4	3	5		7	9	6²	10	11¹	8	12		13																									3
1	2	3	4	5	6³		8	9²		10	7	14	13	11¹	12																								4
	2	3	4	5	8¹		9	6		10	7¹	14		11²		1	12	13																					5
	2²	4	3	5	14		10	7	11³	13	8	9¹				1	6	12																					6
	2	4	3	5	14		10	8	11	13	9¹	7³				1	6²	12																					7
	2	3	4	5	14		9	6	10	11¹	7²			13		1	12	8²																					8
	2	3	4	5	7²		10	6	11¹	9¹	14	12				1	8	13																					9
	2	3	4	5	7		10	6	11	14	9¹	12	13¹			1	8²																						10
	2	3	4	5	7		10¹	8	11	12		6²				1	9	13																					11
	2	4	3	5¹	8		6	10	12	7²						1	9	13	11¹																				12
	2	3	4		5		9	8	11	10²	12					1	6¹	7	13																				13
	2	3	4	5²			9	7	10	13	11	12³	14			1	6	8¹																					14
	2	4	3²	5			9	8	11	12	10		13	7³						1	6¹	14																	15
	2	3		5	6		9¹	8		11		7²		10³			4	12				13		1	14														16
	2	3	4	5	6²		9	8	10	11		7¹		12			13						1																17
	2	4	3	5	7	12	9	8	10¹	11²		14		13								1				6⁹													18
	2	4	3	5	9		6	11	12			8²		10¹			13					1			7														19
	2²	4	3	5	14		8	9	7	10	13			12			11¹					1			6⁹														20
	2	4	3		5		7	9	8		11²			10¹			12	14				1			6⁹	13													21
	2	3	4	5	9¹	6	10	8³	11	14		13		7²			12					1																	22
	2³	3	4	5	8²	7	9		10	11¹				13			6	12				1									14								23
		3¹	4	5	14		11		10		7²			13			2	6			12		1	8			9⁹												24
	2³		3	5			8	10	7	11	14	9²	6¹	13				4														1	12						25
		3		5	8	7	9¹	2	11	10³	6²		14				13	4														1	12						26
		4		5	7¹	8	12	2	10	11²	6						13	14	3													1	9³						27
		3	4	5	9⁹		7	8	10	11		14					12		2²													1	6¹	13					28
	3	14	4	5³	13	7²	10	9	11	6							12		2¹													1	8						29
	5	3	4		2		6	7	11	12	9						8	10¹														1							30
	2	4	3	14	5²		9	8³	10¹	12	7						6	11	13													1							31
	2	4		5			9¹	8		11	7	14		12²			6	10²	3													1	13						32
	5	3		2	12		6	7¹		11²	8			14			9	10³	4													1	13						33
		3		4	5		9²	8	10	13	7	2³					6	11¹									14					1	12						34
		4		5	8		9		11		7						2	10	3													1	6¹	12					35
		3		13	5		9	10		8				12			2	11¹	4													1	7³	14	6²				36
	2¹	4		5	13		9	8		7				14			6²	10³														12				1	3	11	37
	14	3		5	12		9	7				8²		11¹			2³	13														6				1	4	10	38
	2	4		5	8³		9²	7						13			10	14														6		12		1	3	11¹	39
	2²	4		5	9		10	8		11¹				6			14															7		12	1	3	13	40
		3		5²	14	12	9	8	10	11¹				6			13															7			2³	1	4		41
		3		5			9	6	7	11				2			13	12														10²			8¹	1	4		42
		3		5		9⁸	6	7	11	12				2				14														10²		13	8¹	1	4		43
		3		5	8		9	7		10				13			2	11²														6¹		12		1	4		44
		4		5	8		9	7		10²				6¹			2³	11	12													13				1	3		45
		3		5		7	9¹	4		8	6³	12					2	10							13							14		11²		1			46

FA Cup

First Round	Wigan Ath	(h)	4-0
Second Round	Rochdale	(a)	1-0
Third Round	Bradford C	(h)	0-0
Replay	Bradford C	(a)	0-0
(aet; Bury won 4-2 on penalties)			
Fourth Round	Hull C	(h)	1-3

Capital One Cup

First Round	Wigan Ath	(a)	2-1
Second Round	Leicester C	(h)	1-4

Johnstone's Paint Trophy

First Round	Accrington S	(a)	2-1
Second Round	Morecambe	(h)	0-1

CAMBRIDGE UNITED

FOUNDATION

The football revival in Cambridge began soon after World War II when the Abbey United club (formed 1912) decided to turn professional in 1949. In 1951 they changed their name to Cambridge United. They were competing in the United Counties League before graduating to the Eastern Counties League in 1951 and the Southern League in 1958.

The R Costings Abbey Stadium, Newmarket Road, Cambridge CB5 8LN.

Telephone: (01223) 566 500.

Ticket Office: (01223) 566 500.

Website: www.cambridge-united.co.uk

Email: info@cambridge-united.co.uk

Ground Capacity: 7,897.

Record Attendance: 14,000 v Chelsea, Friendly, 1 May 1970.

Pitch Measurements: 100.5m × 67.5m (110yd × 74yd).

Chairman: Dave Doggett.

Vice-chairman: Eddie Clarke.

Manager: Shaun Derry.

Assistant Manager: Joe Dunne.

Physio: Nick Irwin.

Colours: Amber and black striped shirts, black shorts with amber trim, amber socks with black trim.

Year Formed: 1912.

Turned Professional: 1949.

Ltd Co.: 1948.

Previous Name: 1919, Abbey United; 1951, Cambridge United.

Club Nickname: The 'U's'.

Grounds: 1932, Abbey Stadium (renamed R Costings Abbey Stadium 2009).

First Football League Game: 15 August 1970, Division 4, v Lincoln C (h) D 1–1 – Roberts; Thompson, Meldrum (1), Slack, Eades, Hardy, Leggett, Cassidy, Lindsey, McKinven, Harris.

Record League Victory: 7–0 v Morecambe, FL 2, 19 April 2016 – Norris; Roberts (1), Coulson, Clark, Dunne (Williams), Ismail (1), Berry (2 pens), Ledson (Spencer), Dunk (2), Williamson (1) (Simpson).

Record Cup Victory: 5–1 v Bristol C, FA Cup 5th rd second replay, 27 February 1990 – Vaughan; Fensome, Kimble, Bailie (O'Shea), Chapple, Daish, Cheetham (Robinson), Leadbitter (1), Dublin (2), Taylor (1), Philpott (1).

Record Defeat: 0–7 v Sunderland, League Cup 2nd rd, 1 October 2002.

HONOURS

League Champions: Division 3 – 1990–91; Division 4 – 1976–77. *Runners-up:* Division 3 – 1977–78; Fourth Division – (6th) 1989–90 *(promoted via play-offs)*, Third Division – 1998–99; Conference – (2nd) 2013–14 *(promoted via play-offs)*.

FA Cup: 6th rd – 1990, 1991.

League Cup: quarter-final – 1993.

League Trophy: Runners-up: 2002.

sky SPORTS FACT FILE

After Cambridge United defeated Oldham Athletic on 1 October 1983 they played the next 31 League games without recording a single victory, a then record for the Football League. The sequence was broken on 28 April 1984 when a Kevin Smith penalty earned the U's a surprise 1-0 home win over Newcastle United.

Most League Points (2 for a win): 65, Division 4, 1976–77.

Most League Points (3 for a win): 86, Division 3, 1990–91.

Most League Goals: 87, Division 4, 1976–77.

Highest League Scorer in Season: David Crown, 24, Division 4, 1985–86.

Most League Goals in Total Aggregate: John Taylor, 86, 1988–92; 1996–2001.

Most League Goals in One Match: 5, Steve Butler v Exeter C, Division 2, 4 April 1994.

Most Capped Player: Tom Finney, 7 (15), Northern Ireland.

Most League Appearances: Steve Spriggs, 416, 1975–87.

Youngest League Player: Andy Sinton, 16 years 228 days v Wolverhampton W, 2 November 1982.

Record Transfer Fee Received: £1,000,000 from Manchester U for Dion Dublin, August 1992; £1,000,000 from Leicester C for Trevor Benjamin, July 2000.

Record Transfer Fee Paid: £192,000 to Luton T for Steve Claridge, November 1992.

Football League Record: 1970 Elected to Division 4; 1973–74 Division 3; 1974–77 Division 4; 1977–78 Division 3; 1978–84 Division 2; 1984–85 Division 3; 1985–90 Division 4; 1990–91 Division 3; 1991–92 Division 2; 1992–93 Division 1; 1993–95 Division 2; 1995–99 Division 3; 1999–2002 Division 2; 2002–04 Division 3; 2004–05 FL2; 2005–14 Conference; 2014– FL 2.

MANAGERS

Bill Whittaker 1949–55
Gerald Williams 1955
Bert Johnson 1955–59
Bill Craig 1959–60
Alan Moore 1960–63
Roy Kirk 1964–66
Bill Leivers 1967–74
Ron Atkinson 1974–78
John Docherty 1978–83
John Ryan 1984–85
Ken Shellito 1985
Chris Turner 1985–90
John Beck 1990–92
Ian Atkins 1992–93
Gary Johnson 1993–95
Tommy Taylor 1995–96
Roy McFarland 1996–2001
John Beck 2001
John Taylor 2001–04
Claude Le Roy 2004
Herve Renard 2004
Steve Thompson 2004–05
Rob Newman 2005–06
Jimmy Quinn 2006–08
Gary Brabin 2008–09
Martin Ling 2009–11
Jez George 2011–12
Richard Money 2012–15
Shaun Derry November 2015–

LATEST SEQUENCES

Longest Sequence of League Wins: 7, 19.2.1977 – 1.4.1977.

Longest Sequence of League Defeats: 7, 8.4.1985 – 30.4.1985.

Longest Sequence of League Draws: 6, 6.9.1986 – 30.9.1986.

Longest Sequence of Unbeaten League Matches: 14, 9.9.1972 – 10.11.1972.

Longest Sequence Without a League Win: 31, 8.10.1983 – 23.4.1984.

Successive Scoring Runs: 26 from 9.4.2002.

Successive Non-scoring Runs: 5 from 29.9.1973.

TEN YEAR LEAGUE RECORD

		P	W	D	L	F	A	Pts	Pos
2006-07	Conf	46	15	10	21	57	66	55	17
2007-08	Conf P	46	25	11	10	68	41	86	2
2008-09	Conf P	46	24	14	8	65	39	86	2
2009-10	Conf P	44	15	14	15	65	53	59	10
2010-11	Conf P	46	11	17	18	53	61	50	17
2011-12	Conf P	46	19	14	13	57	41	71	9
2012-13	Conf P	46	15	14	17	68	69	59	14
2013-14	Conf P	46	23	13	10	72	35	82	2
2014-15	FL 2	46	13	12	21	61	66	51	19
2015-16	FL 2	46	18	14	14	66	55	68	9

DID YOU KNOW ?

Only 6 Football League and FA Cup games survived the severe wintry weather on 26 January 1963. As a result Anglia Television showed highlights of the Southern League game between Bedford Town and Cambridge United played on that day, a rare occasion when non-league football featured on television at the time.

CAMBRIDGE UNITED – FOOTBALL LEAGUE TWO 2015–16 LEAGUE RECORD

Match No.	Date	Venue	Opponents	Result	H/T Score	Lg Pos.	Goalscorers	Attendance
1	Aug 8	H	Newport Co	W 3-0	1-0	1	Corr 2 [24, 65], Simpson [80]	5022
2	15	A	Carlisle U	D 4-4	3-2	6	Corr 2 [11, 45], Taft [21], Berry [58]	6354
3	18	A	AFC Wimbledon	W 2-1	0-1	4	Legge [46], Corr [48]	4114
4	22	H	Crawley T	L 0-3	0-1	7		5459
5	29	A	Barnet	D 0-0	0-0	9		2406
6	Sept 5	H	Luton T	L 1-3	1-1	12	Legge [28]	6298
7	12	H	Leyton Orient	D 1-1	0-0	12	Blyth [53]	5821
8	19	A	Hartlepool U	D 0-0	0-0	13		3665
9	26	H	Stevenage	W 1-0	0-0	10	Dunk [90]	4852
10	29	A	Wycombe W	L 0-1	0-0	15		3152
11	Oct 3	A	York C	D 2-2	0-0	15	Roberts [71], Corr [81]	2987
12	10	H	Portsmouth	L 1-3	1-0	16	Simpson [6]	6607
13	17	H	Northampton T	W 2-1	1-0	14	Dunk [39], Corr [50]	5459
14	21	A	Exeter C	L 0-1	0-1	16		2883
15	24	H	Yeovil T	W 3-2	3-1	14	Gaffney 2 [4, 26], Berry [35]	3224
16	30	H	Bristol R	L 1-2	1-0	14	Corr [33]	5115
17	Nov 14	A	Oxford U	L 0-1	0-1	17		6958
18	21	H	Accrington S	L 2-3	2-1	18	Corr [13], Berry [37]	5107
19	24	A	Morecambe	W 4-2	3-1	17	Legge [12], Donaldson [34], Gayle [35], Williamson [48]	1689
20	28	H	Notts Co	W 3-1	0-1	14	Corr (pen) [50], Williamson [77], Berry [87]	4596
21	Dec 12	A	Plymouth Arg	W 2-1	1-0	12	Williamson [6], Berry [86]	7246
22	19	H	Mansfield T	D 1-1	1-1	11	Donaldson [36]	4589
23	26	A	Dagenham & R	W 3-0	0-0	11	Simpson 2 [51, 65], Corr [76]	2425
24	28	H	Barnet	W 2-1	0-0	10	Berry [71], Corr [72]	6003
25	Jan 2	H	AFC Wimbledon	L 1-4	1-1	11	Berry [26]	5754
26	9	A	Crawley T	L 0-1	0-1	12		2320
27	16	A	Luton T	D 0-0	0-0	12		9227
28	23	H	Hartlepool U	D 1-1	0-0	12	Williamson [90]	5054
29	30	A	Leyton Orient	W 3-1	1-0	11	Williamson 2 [10, 53], Spencer [63]	6526
30	Feb 6	H	Dagenham & R	W 1-0	0-0	9	Berry (pen) [82]	4494
31	13	A	Stevenage	L 0-2	0-1	11		3945
32	20	H	York C	W 3-1	2-1	11	Spencer [10], Coulson [26], Williamson [60]	4822
33	27	A	Portsmouth	L 1-2	0-1	12	Berry [90]	15,425
34	Mar 1	H	Wycombe W	W 1-0	1-0	12	Stewart (og) [27]	4141
35	5	H	Exeter C	L 0-1	0-0	13		4573
36	12	A	Northampton T	D 1-1	0-0	12	Spencer [90]	5828
37	19	H	Yeovil T	W 3-0	2-0	10	Williamson 2 [4, 45], Spencer [87]	4956
38	25	A	Bristol R	L 0-3	0-2	11		10,262
39	28	H	Oxford U	D 0-0	0-0	12		6108
40	Apr 2	A	Accrington S	D 1-1	0-0	12	Spencer [55]	2185
41	9	A	Newport Co	W 1-0	0-0	12	Dunne [68]	2330
42	16	H	Carlisle U	D 0-0	0-0	12		5806
43	19	H	Morecambe	W 7-0	5-0	9	Berry 2 (2 pens) [6, 90], Dunk 2 [17, 26], Williamson [29], Roberts [45], Ismail [59]	3941
44	23	A	Notts Co	W 2-1	1-1	8	Berry [4], Williamson [54]	4450
45	30	H	Plymouth Arg	D 2-2	0-0	8	Williamson [84], Spencer [86]	6714
46	May 7	A	Mansfield T	D 0-0	0-0	9		3548

Final League Position: 9

GOALSCORERS

League (66): Berry 12 (3 pens), Corr 12 (1 pen), Williamson 12, Spencer 6, Dunk 4, Simpson 4, Legge 3, Donaldson 2, Gaffney 2, Roberts 2, Blyth 1, Coulson 1, Dunne 1, Gayle 1, Ismail 1, Taft 1, own goal 1.
FA Cup (2): Berry 1, Hughes J 1.
Capital One Cup (0).
Johnstone's Paint Trophy (0).

Match No	Beasant S 14+1	Legge L 39	Roberts M 26+4	Coulson J 22+1	Newton C 16+6	Keane K 3+1	Hughes L 11+5	Dunk H 41+4	Donaldson R 18+12	Slew J 4+6	Corr B 19+3	Berry L 41+5	Morrissey G —+2	Simpson R 14+18	Taft G 10+1	Omozusi E 9+5	Carr D 1+3	Taylor G 12+4	Ismail Z 8+3	Dunn C 11	Blyth J 2+3	Clark M 7+2	Hughes J 7+2	Demetriou M 12+3	Chiedozie J —+2	Gaffney R 3+3	Williams D —+1	Sesay A 5	Kennedy T 2	Ledson R 27	Williamson B 27+1	Gayle C 4	Jones J 1	Page L 6	Norris W 21	Furlong D 21	Dunne J 19	Ahearne-Grant K 1+2	Spencer J 11+7	Haynes R 10	O'Neill Shane 1+1
1	1	2	3	4^2	5	6	7	8	9^1	10^3	11	12	13	14																											
2	1	2	3	6^2	7	12			9^1	11^3	10	8			4	5	13	14																							
3		2	4	3^2	14	8	12	6	10^3		11	13			7^1	9			5	1																					
4		3	2^2			7^1	6^3	12	8	9		13	10			4	5	14		1	11																				
5		3	4					8	5	6	10^3		7		11^2			12	14	2	1	13	9^1																		
6		3	4	12			8^1	9^4	6^3		10	7			11^2			14		2	1	13		5																	
7		3	2	4	7		13			10^2		6			8			8		5	11^1		1	12	9																
8		2	3	12	6		13	8^2			7				10^1	4^3	5			1	11		9	14																	
9		2	3		7^1		6	8			10				11	4^1	5^2		13	1			9	12	14																
10	12	3	2		6^2		11	8	14			7			10	4^1	5^3		13	1^*			9																		
11	1	4	3				11	8^2	6^1		10	13			2			5				7	9	12																	
12	1	3	4^4		13			9^2	6^3		10	8	14	11^1	12	2						7	5			3															
13	1			13			7	9^2	6		10	12			11^1			2				8	5		3																
14	1			14			8^2	9	6	12	11	13			10^3	4			2			7^1	5		3																
15	1						6	5	9^1	14	10	8				3^3	12		2			7	13	11^2	4																
16		4		14			6^1	5	9^2		10	8			11^2			2	1			7	12	13^3	3																
17		4	3	8^3				11		6	12	10	7		14			1		13	2^1		9^2	5																	
18		4		12				9	6^1	13	10	7						2^2	1			5		3	8	11															
19	1	3	4	6				9^1	10		13	8		12						5		7	11^2	2																	
20	1	2	3	6				9		13	8		12					12			14		4^2	7	11^3	5	10^1														
21	1	4	3	8				9^1	12		10	6						5				7	11^2	2																	
22	1	3	4	7				9	12		10	6						5				8	11	2^1																	
23	1	4	3	8				5	6^3	14	11^1	9		13			12	2^2				7	10																		
24	1	3	4	8^1				5			11	9		10	2						12		7	6																	
25	1	4	3	8^1				9			11	6		12	2								7	10																	
26		3	4	7				9			10	6		12									11^1							8					5	1	2				
27		3	4					12	14		11^3	6		10^2																8^1	9				5	1	2	7	13		
28		3	4					12	14		13	7		9^3																8^2	11				5	1	2	6	10^1		
29		3		4				10^2	8^1		9	13																		6^2	11				5	1	2	7	12		
30		3		4				9	12		6	13																		7^1	11				5	1	2	8	10^2		
31		3		4				9	6^2		10	14																		7	11				1	2	8^3	13	12	5^1	
32		3		4				9	12		6	13																		7	11				1	2	8	10^1	5		
33		3^2	14	4				9	12		6	13																		7	11				1	2		10^1	5	8^3	
34		3		4				11^1	14		6	12																		7^3	9				1	2	8	10^2	5	13	
35		3		4				9^1	13		6	14										12								7^2	11				1	2	8	10^1	5		
36		3		4				10^1			8							13				6^2								7	11				1	2	9	12	5		
37		3		4				10			9											8								6^1	11				1	2	6^1	12	5		
38		3	14	4				8			7^1	12										9^3	13							11					1	2	6	10^2	5		
39		3		4				10			9	13										12	7^4							8^1					1	2	6	11	5		
40		4		3				12			9											10^1	8							7^2	13				1	5	6	11	2		
41		4		3				5			6	12											9							8	11^1				1	2	7	10	5		
42		3^1	12	4				8			7	14										13	5							9	11				1	2	6^3	10^2			
43		3	4					10			8	13										7	5				14			9^1	11^2				1	2	6^3	12			
44		3	4					10			7											6	5							9^1	11				1	2	8	12			
45		3	4					10	12		9											8	5^2							7	11				1	2	6^1	13			
46		3	12	4^1				5	14		6^2											9	13							8	11^3				1	2	7	10			

FA Cup

First Round	Basingstoke T	(h)	1-0
Second Round	Doncaster R	(h)	1-3

Capital One Cup

First Round	Rotherham U	(a)	0-1

Johnstone's Paint Trophy

First Round	Dagenham & R	(h)	0-2

CARDIFF CITY

FOUNDATION

Credit for the establishment of a first class professional football club in such a rugby stronghold as Cardiff is due to members of the Riverside club formed in 1899 out of a cricket club of that name. Cardiff became a city in 1905 and in 1908 the South Wales and Monmouthshire FA granted Riverside permission to call themselves Cardiff City. The club turned professional under that name in 1910.

Cardiff City Stadium, Leckwith Road, Cardiff CF11 8AZ.

Telephone: (0845) 365 1115. *Fax:* (0845) 365 1116.

Ticket Office: (0845) 345 1400.

Website: www.cardiffcityfc.co.uk

Email: club@cardiffcityfc.co.uk

Ground Capacity: 33,280.

Record Attendance: 57,893 v Arsenal, Division 1, 22 April 1953 (at Ninian Park); 28,680 v Derby Co, FL C, 2 April 2016 (at Cardiff City Stadium).

Ground Record Attendance: 62,634, Wales v England, 17 October 1959 (at Ninian Park).

Pitch Measurements: 105m × 68m (115yd × 74.5yd).

Chairman: Mehmet Dalman.

Chief Executive: Ken Choo.

Manager: Paul Trollope.

Assistant Manager: Scott Young.

Physio: Edward Richmond.

Colours: Blue shirts with white trim, blue shorts with white trim, blue socks with white trim.

Year Formed: 1899.

Turned Professional: 1910.

Previous Names: 1899, Riverside; 1902, Riverside Albion; 1908, Cardiff City.

Club Nickname: 'The Bluebirds'.

Grounds: Riverside, Sophia Gardens, Old Park and Fir Gardens; 1910, Ninian Park; 2009, Cardiff City Stadium.

First Football League Game: 28 August 1920, Division 2, v Stockport Co (a) W 5–2 – Kneeshaw; Brittan, Leyton; Keenor (1), Smith, Hardy; Grimshaw (1), Gill (2), Cashmore, West, Evans (1).

Record League Victory: 9–2 v Thames, Division 3 (S), 6 February 1932 – Farquharson; Eric Morris, Roberts; Galbraith, Harris, Ronan; Emmerson (1), Keating (1), Jones (1), McCambridge (1), Robbins (5).

Record Cup Victory: 8–0 v Enfield, FA Cup 1st rd, 28 November 1931 – Farquharson; Smith, Roberts; Harris (1), Galbraith, Ronan; Emmerson (2), Keating (3); O'Neill (2), Robbins, McCambridge.

HONOURS

League Champions: FL C – 2012–13; Division 3S – 1946–47; Third Division – 1992–93.

Runners-up: Division 1 – 1923–24; Division 2 – 1920–21, 1951–52, 1959–60; Division 3 – 1975–76, 1982–83; Third Division – 2000–01; Division 4 – 1987–88.

FA Cup Winners: 1927.

Runners-up: 1925, 2008.

League Cup: Runners-up: 2012.

Welsh Cup Winners: 22 times (joint record).

European Competitions
European Cup-Winners' Cup: 1964–65 *(qf)*, 1965–66, 1967–68 *(sf)*, 1968–69, 1969–70, 1970–71 *(qf)*, 1971–72, 1973–74, 1974–75, 1976–77, 1977–78, 1988–89, 1992–93, 1993–94.

sky SPORTS FACT FILE

George Latham was Cardiff City's trainer for many years from their Southern League days and was in charge of the team that defeated Arsenal in the 1927 FA Cup final. He enlisted with the Royal Welch Fusiliers in the First World War, winning the Military Cross for gallantry in 1917.

Record Defeat: 2–11 v Sheffield U, Division 1, 1 January 1926.

Most League Points (2 for a win): 66, Division 3 (S), 1946–47.

Most League Points (3 for a win): 87, FL C, 2012–13.

Most League Goals: 95, Division 3, 2000–01.

Highest League Scorer in Season: Robert Earnshaw, 31, Division 2, 2002–03.

Most League Goals in Total Aggregate: Len Davies, 128, 1920–31.

Most League Goals in One Match: 5, Hugh Ferguson v Burnley, Division 1, 1 September 1928; 5, Walter Robbins v Thames, Division 3 (S), 6 February 1932; 5, William Henderson v Northampton T, Division 3 (S), 22 April 1933.

Most Capped Player: Aron Gunnarsson, 41 (64), Iceland.

Most League Appearances: Phil Dwyer, 471, 1972–85.

Youngest League Player: Bob Adams, 15 years 355 days v Southend U, 18 February 1933.

Record Transfer Fee Received: £8,000,000 from QPR for Steven Caulker, July 2014.

Record Transfer Fee Paid: £11,000,000 to Sevilla for Gary Medel, August 2013.

Football League Record: 1920 Elected to Division 2; 1921–29 Division 1; 1929–31 Division 2; 1931–47 Division 3 (S); 1947–52 Division 2; 1952–57 Division 1; 1957–60 Division 2; 1960–62 Division 1; 1962–75 Division 2; 1975–76 Division 3; 1976–82 Division 2; 1982–83 Division 3; 1983–85 Division 2; 1985–86 Division 3; 1986–88 Division 4; 1988–90 Division 3; 1990–92 Division 4; 1992–93 Division 3; 1993–95 Division 2; 1995–99 Division 3; 1999–2000 Division 2; 2000–01 Division 3; 2001–03 Division 2; 2003–04 Division 1; 2004–13 FL C; 2013–14 FA Premier League; 2014– FL C.

LATEST SEQUENCES

Longest Sequence of League Wins: 9, 26.10.1946 – 28.12.1946.

Longest Sequence of League Defeats: 7, 4.11.1933 – 25.12.1933.

Longest Sequence of League Draws: 6, 29.11.1980 – 17.1.1981.

Longest Sequence of Unbeaten League Matches: 21, 21.9.1946 – 1.3.1947.

Longest Sequence Without a League Win: 15, 21.11.1936 – 6.3.1937.

Successive Scoring Runs: 24 from 25.8.2012.

Successive Non-scoring Runs: 8 from 20.12.1952.

MANAGERS

Davy McDougall 1910–11
Fred Stewart 1911–33
Bartley Wilson 1933–34
B. Watts-Jones 1934–37
Bill Jennings 1937–39
Cyril Spiers 1939–46
Billy McCandless 1946–48
Cyril Spiers 1948–54
Trevor Morris 1954–58
Bill Jones 1958–62
George Swindin 1962–64
Jimmy Scoular 1964–73
Frank O'Farrell 1973–74
Jimmy Andrews 1974–78
Richie Morgan 1978–81
Graham Williams 1981–82
Len Ashurst 1982–84
Jimmy Goodfellow 1984
Alan Durban 1984–86
Frank Burrows 1986–89
Len Ashurst 1989–91
Eddie May 1991–94
Terry Yorath 1994–95
Eddie May 1995
Kenny Hibbitt (*Chief Coach*) 1995–96
Phil Neal 1996
Russell Osman 1996–97
Kenny Hibbitt 1997–98
Frank Burrows 1998–2000
Billy Ayre 2000
Bobby Gould 2000
Alan Cork 2000–02
Lennie Lawrence 2002–05
Dave Jones 2005–11
Malky Mackay 2011–13
Ole Gunnar Solskjaer 2014
Russell Slade 2014–16
Paul Trollope May 2016–

TEN YEAR LEAGUE RECORD

		P	W	D	L	F	A	Pts	Pos
2006-07	FL C	46	17	13	16	57	53	64	13
2007-08	FL C	46	16	16	14	59	55	64	12
2008-09	FL C	46	19	17	10	65	53	74	7
2009-10	FL C	46	22	10	14	73	54	76	4
2010-11	FL C	46	23	11	12	76	54	80	4
2011-12	FL C	46	19	18	9	66	53	75	6
2012-13	FL C	46	25	12	9	72	45	87	1
2013-14	PR Lge	38	7	9	22	32	74	30	20
2014-15	FL C	46	16	14	16	57	61	62	11
2015-16	FL C	46	17	17	12	56	51	68	8

DID YOU KNOW ?

Cardiff City failed to score a single goal in eight League matches between 20 December 1952 and 14 February 1953, although five of these games produced goalless draws. The Bluebirds broke the run in style with a 6-0 home win over Manchester City.

CARDIFF CITY – FL CHAMPIONSHIP 2015–16 LEAGUE RECORD

Match No.	Date	Venue	Opponents	Result	H/T Score	Lg Pos.	Goalscorers	Attendance
1	Aug 8	H	Fulham	D 1-1	0-0	10	Noone [86]	15,429
2	15	A	QPR	D 2-2	0-1	13	Morrison [63], Malone [90]	14,927
3	18	A	Blackburn R	D 1-1	1-0	13	Mason [5]	12,025
4	22	H	Wolverhampton W	W 2-0	1-0	7	Jones [44], Ameobi [60]	14,820
5	29	A	Nottingham F	W 2-1	1-0	5	Jones [23], Mason [49]	18,762
6	Sept 12	H	Huddersfield T	W 2-0	0-0	2	Pilkington [69], Mason [77]	13,715
7	15	H	Hull C	L 0-2	0-1	6		13,763
8	19	A	Rotherham U	L 1-2	1-1	8	Whittingham (pen) [45]	8935
9	26	H	Charlton Ath	W 2-1	0-0	5	Mason [53], Morrison [76]	13,980
10	Oct 3	A	Brighton & HA	D 1-1	1-1	8	Mason [5]	26,399
11	17	A	Preston NE	D 0-0	0-0	8		11,125
12	20	H	Middlesbrough	W 1-0	0-0	8	Friend (og) [86]	13,371
13	26	H	Bristol C	D 0-0	0-0	8		15,287
14	31	A	Ipswich T	D 0-0	0-0	9		17,169
15	Nov 3	A	Leeds U	L 0-1	0-0	9		17,914
16	7	A	Reading	W 2-0	1-0	7	Jones [44], Connolly [53]	15,414
17	21	A	Derby Co	L 0-2	0-0	9		29,526
18	28	H	Burnley	D 2-2	1-0	10	Gunnarsson [41], Morrison [64]	15,133
19	Dec 5	A	Bolton W	W 3-2	1-1	6	Watt [13], Malone [53], Pilkington [80]	13,241
20	12	H	Sheffield W	D 2-2	2-0	7	Noone (pen) [21], Pilkington [34]	14,526
21	15	H	Brentford	W 3-2	2-0	7	Watt [20], Jones 2 [34, 90]	12,729
22	18	A	Birmingham C	L 0-1	0-1	7		14,414
23	26	A	Milton Keynes D	L 1-2	0-0	8	Noone [81]	12,510
24	29	H	Nottingham F	D 1-1	1-1	10	Gunnarsson [13]	15,461
25	Jan 2	A	Blackburn R	W 1-0	0-0	9	Mason [58]	14,385
26	13	A	Hull C	L 0-2	0-1	9		15,549
27	16	A	Wolverhampton W	W 3-1	2-1	9	Noone 2 [28, 36], Ralls [48]	24,238
28	23	H	Rotherham U	D 2-2	1-1	9	Pilkington 2 [25, 60]	14,885
29	30	A	Huddersfield T	W 3-2	1-1	9	Whittingham 2 [37, 79], Immers [61]	11,002
30	Feb 6	H	Milton Keynes D	D 0-0	0-0	9		13,833
31	13	A	Charlton Ath	D 0-0	0-0	9		16,755
32	20	H	Brighton & HA	W 4-1	3-0	7	Whittingham 2 (1 pen) [16, 66 (p)], Pilkington [19], Immers [30]	14,143
33	23	A	Middlesbrough	L 1-3	1-1	8	Da Silva [20]	24,322
34	27	H	Preston NE	W 2-1	1-0	7	Pilkington 2 (2 pens) [44, 80]	15,566
35	Mar 5	A	Bristol C	W 2-0	1-0	7	Immers [21], O'Keefe [83]	15,758
36	8	H	Leeds U	L 0-2	0-1	7		15,273
37	12	H	Ipswich T	W 1-0	0-0	7	Ecuele Manga [18]	15,175
38	19	A	Reading	D 1-1	0-1	7	Immers [65]	17,407
39	Apr 2	H	Derby Co	W 2-1	1-0	7	Ecuele Manga [37], O'Keefe [68]	28,680
40	5	A	Burnley	D 0-0	0-0	7		15,740
41	9	A	Fulham	L 1-2	1-0	7	Immers [41]	17,149
42	16	H	QPR	D 0-0	0-0	7		27,874
43	19	A	Brentford	L 1-2	0-0	7	Zohore [89]	8363
44	23	H	Bolton W	W 2-1	0-1	7	Zohore [55], Whittingham (pen) [90]	24,189
45	30	A	Sheffield W	L 0-3	0-0	7		31,843
46	May 7	H	Birmingham C	D 1-1	1-1	8	Pilkington [26]	21,022

Final League Position: 8

GOALSCORERS

League (56): Pilkington 9 (2 pens), Mason 6, Whittingham 6 (3 pens), Immers 5, Jones 5, Noone 5 (1 pen), Morrison 3, Ecuele Manga 2, Gunnarsson 2, Malone 2, O'Keefe 2, Watt 2, Zohore 2, Ameobi 1, Connolly 1, Da Silva 1, Ralls 1, own goal 1.
FA Cup (0).
Capital One Cup (2): Noone 1, Revell 1.

Moore S 6 + 1	Peltier L 38 + 3	Morrison S 29 + 1	Connolly M 43	Malone S 36 + 5	Pilkington A 38 + 3	Whittingham P 34 + 2	Dikgacoi K 16 + 7	Ralls J 42 + 1	Mason J 21 + 2	Revell A 7 + 3	Ameobi S 8 + 28	Noone C 24 + 14	Jones K 15 + 4	Marshall D 40	Gunnarsson A 16 + 12	Da Silva F 18 + 5	Ecuele Manga B 19 + 5	John D — + 1	O'Keefe S 19 + 5	Saadi I — + 2	Kennedy M — + 1	Watt T 9	Macheda F — + 6	Immers L 14 + 1	Lawrence T 11 + 3	Zohore K 2 + 10	Harris K — + 3	Turner B 1	Match No.
1	2	3	4	5	6	7	8[2]	9	10	11[1]	12	13																	1
1	2	4	3	5	6[1]	8	7[2]	9	10	11[3]	14	13	12																2
	2	3	4	5	6	7	8[1]	9	11[2]	10[3]	14	12		1	13														3
	2	3	4		6	7	8	9	11		12		10[1]	1		5[3]	13												4
	2	3	4	13	6[3]	8	7	9	10		12	14	11[1]	1		5[2]													5
	2[1]	3	4	12	6	8	7	9	11[2]		13		10[3]	1	14	5													6
	2	3	4[1]		6[3]	8	7	9[2]	11		13	14	10	1		5	12												7
12	2	3	4		8	7	9	11[1]	14	10[3]	6[2]	13		1[3]		5													8
1		3	4	5	6[2]	8	7	9	10[3]		12	13	11	14	2														9
1	14	3	4	5[1]	6[2]	8	7	9	11		13	12	10[3]		2														10
	2	3	4	5	6[1]	8	7	9[3]	11	13	10[2]	12		1			14												11
	2	3	4	14		9	8	10[2]	11[1]	12	6			1		7[3]	5		13										12
	2	3	4		14	9	7[2]	12	10	11[3]	13	6[1]		1	8	5													13
	2	3	4	12	14	8[3]		9	11	10	6[1]	13		1	7	5[2]													14
	2	3	4	5	14	8[2]		9	10	11[2]	12	6[1]	13	1	7														15
	2	3	4	5	9[2]		8	10[3]		12	6	11[1]		1	7				14	13									16
	2	3	4	5		8[3]	7[2]	9	11[1]	12	6	10		1	13			14											17
	2	3	4	5		9		8	12		6	11[2]		1	7[3]			13						10[1]	14				18
	2[3]	3	4	5	9[1]	14	8		13	6	11			1	7	12								10[2]					19
	2	3	4	5	9[2]		8		12	6	11[1]			1	7	13								10					20
	2	3	4	13	9[2]		8	12		14	6[1]	10		1	7	5								11[3]					21
	2	3[1]	4	5	9[3]	14	8		6	13	10			1	7[2]	12								11					22
	2		4	5	9		8		6[1]	12	11			1	7	3								10					23
	2		4		9	13	8		12	6[1]	11[3]			1	7[2]	5	3							10	14				24
	2[2]		4	5	9		7	10[3]	14	6				1	8	12	3							13		11[1]			25
	2		4	5	9		8		11[2]	12	6			1	7	3								10[1]	13				26
	2		4	5	10[1]	9[2]	12	8	11[2]	14	6			1	13	3	7							11					27
	2[4]		4	5	10	9[1]	8	11[3]		13	6[2]			1	14	3	7								12				28
			4	5	10[2]	9	14	8		6				1	13	2	3		7[3]						12	11[1]			29
			4	5	10[2]	8		6		1		2	3	7				13					11	12					30
12			4	5	10	9[1]	8		6[4]		1	14	2[3]	3	7[2]				13			11							31
12			4	5	10[1]	9	8		1	13	2[3]	3	7						11[3]	6[2]	14								32
			4	5	10	9[1]	8	12		1	13	2	3	7[2]					11[2]	6	14								33
	2		4	5	10[3]		12	9		13		1	8	3	7				11[2]	6[1]	14								34
	2[1]	12	4	5	10	9[2]	14	8		13		1		3	7				11[2]	6									35
			4	5	11	9[1]	8		13	12		1	2[4]	3	7[3]				10	6[2]	14								36
1	2		4	5	10[2]	9		13	8	6	12	3	7				11												37
1	2		4	5	11		8	12	6[1]	13	3	7[2]		10	9														38
	2	3		5	10[1]	9	13	8		6[2]	1	12	4	7[3]				11	14										39
	2	3		5	10[3]		8	9		13	1	12	4	7[2]				11	6[1]	14									40
	2	3		5			9	8		6	1	7[1]	4		13				11	10[2]	12								41
	2	3	4	5	11	9[1]	8	12		6	1	14		7[3]				10[1]	13										42
	2	3	4	5	11	9	8	14		6[3]	1		7[2]				10[1]	12	13										43
	2	3	4[1]	5	10	9	8[2]	12		6	1		7				13	11[13]	14										44
	2	3[1]	4	5	10[3]	9	8[2]	12		6	1		13	7			11	14											45
	2		3	5	10	8		6		1		14	7				11[2]	9[3]	12	13	4[1]								46

CARLISLE UNITED

Brunton Park, Warwick Road, Carlisle, Cumbria CA1 1LL.

Telephone: (01228) 526 237.

Fax: (01228) 554 141.

Ticket Office: (0844) 371 1921.

Website: www.carlisleunited.co.uk

Email: enquiries@carlisleunited.co.uk

Ground Capacity: 17,902.

Record Attendance: 27,500 v Birmingham C, FA Cup 3rd rd, 5 January 1957 and v Middlesbrough, FA Cup 5th rd, 7 February 1970.

Pitch Measurements: 102.5m × 67.5m (112yd × 74yd).

Chairman: Andrew Jenkins.

Finance Director: Suzanne Kidd.

Manager: Keith Curle.

Assistant Manager: Colin West.

Physio: Neil Dalton.

HONOURS

League Champions: Division 3 – 1964–65; FL 2 – 2005–06; Third Division – 1994–95.
Runners-up: Division 3 – 1981–82; Division 4 – 1963–64; Conference – (3rd) 2004–05 *(promoted via play-offs)*.
FA Cup: 6th rd – 1975.
League Cup: semi-final – 1970.
League Trophy Winners: 1997, 2011. *Runners-up:* 1995, 2003, 2006, 2010.

Colours: Blue shirts with white and red trim, white shorts with blue and red trim, blue socks.

Year Formed: 1904. *Turned Professional:* 1921.

Previous Name: 1904, Shaddongate United; 1904, Carlisle United.

Club Nicknames: 'The Cumbrians', 'The Blues'.

Grounds: 1904, Milholme Bank; 1905, Devonshire Park; 1909, Brunton Park.

First Football League Game: 25 August 1928, Division 3 (N), v Accrington S (a) W 3–2 – Prout; Coulthard, Cook; Harrison, Ross, Pigg; Agar (1), Hutchison, McConnell (1), Ward (1), Watson.

Record League Victory: 8–0 v Hartlepool U, Division 3 (N), 1 September 1928 – Prout; Smiles, Cook; Robinson (1) Ross, Pigg; Agar (1), Hutchison (1), McConnell (4), Ward (1), Watson. 8–0 v Scunthorpe U, Division 3 (N), 25 December 1952 – MacLaren; Hill, Scott; Stokoe, Twentyman, Waters; Harrison (1), Whitehouse (5), Ashman (2), Duffett, Bond.

Record Cup Victory: 6–0 v Shepshed Dynamo, FA Cup 1st rd, 16 November 1996 – Caig; Hopper, Archdeacon (pen), Walling, Robinson, Pounewatchy, Peacock (1), Conway (1) (Jansen), Smart (McAlindon (1)), Hayward, Aspinall (Thorpe), (2 og). 6–0 v Tipton T, FA Cup 1st rd, 6 November 2010 – Collin; Simek, Murphy, Chester, Cruise, Robson (McKenna), Berrett, Taiwo (Hurst), Marshall, Zoko (Curran) (2), Madine (4).

Record Defeat: 1–11 v Hull C, Division 3 (N), 14 January 1939.

Most League Points (2 for a win): 62, Division 3 (N), 1950–51.

Most League Points (3 for a win): 91, Division 3, 1994–95.

Most League Goals: 113, Division 4, 1963–64.

Highest League Scorer in Season: Jimmy McConnell, 42, Division 3 (N), 1928–29.

Most League Goals in Total Aggregate: Jimmy McConnell, 124, 1928–32.

Most League Goals in One Match: 5, Hugh Mills v Halifax T, Division 3 (N), 11 September 1937; 5, Jim Whitehouse v Scunthorpe U, Division 3 (N), 25 December 1952.

Most Capped Player: Eric Welsh, 4, Northern Ireland.

Most League Appearances: Allan Ross, 466, 1963–79.

Youngest League Player: John Slaven, 16 years 162 days v Scunthorpe U, 16 March 2002.

Record Transfer Fee Received: £1,000,000 from Crystal Palace for Matt Jansen, February 1998.

Record Transfer Fee Paid: £140,000 to Blackburn R for Joe Garner, August 2007.

Football League Record: 1928 Elected to Division 3 (N); 1958–62 Division 4; 1962–63 Division 3; 1963–64 Division 4; 1964–65 Division 3; 1965–74 Division 2; 1974–75 Division 1; 1975–77 Division 2; 1977–82 Division 3; 1982–86 Division 2; 1986–87 Division 3; 1987–92 Division 4; 1992–95 Division 3; 1995–96 Division 2; 1996–97 Division 3; 1997–98 Division 2; 1998–2004 Division 3; 2004–05 Conference; 2005–06 FL 2; 2006–14 FL 1; 2014– FL 2.

LATEST SEQUENCES

Longest Sequence of League Wins: 7, 18.2.2006 – 8.4.2006.

Longest Sequence of League Defeats: 12, 27.9.2003 – 13.12.2003.

Longest Sequence of League Draws: 6, 11.2.1978 – 11.3.1978.

Longest Sequence of Unbeaten League Matches: 19, 1.10.1994 – 11.2.1995.

Longest Sequence Without a League Win: 15, 12.4.2014 – 20.9.2014.

Successive Scoring Runs: 26 from 23.8.1947.

Successive Non-scoring Runs: 5 from 16.8.2003.

MANAGERS

Harry Kirkbride 1904–05 (*Secretary-Manager*)
McCumiskey 1905–06 (*Secretary-Manager*)
Jack Houston 1906–08 (*Secretary-Manager*)
Bert Stansfield 1908–10
Jack Houston 1910–12
Davie Graham 1912–13
George Bristow 1913–30
Billy Hampson 1930–33
Bill Clarke 1933–35
Robert Kelly 1935–36
Fred Westgarth 1936–38
David Taylor 1938–40
Howard Harkness 1940–45
Bill Clark 1945–46 (*Secretary-Manager*)
Ivor Broadis 1946–49
Bill Shankly 1949–51
Fred Emery 1951–58
Andy Beattie 1958–60
Ivor Powell 1960–63
Alan Ashman 1963–67
Tim Ward 1967–68
Bob Stokoe 1968–70
Ian MacFarlane 1970–72
Alan Ashman 1972–75
Dick Young 1975–76
Bobby Moncur 1976–80
Martin Harvey 1980
Bob Stokoe 1980–85
Bryan 'Pop' Robson 1985
Bob Stokoe 1985–86
Harry Gregg 1986–87
Cliff Middlemass 1987–91
Aidan McCaffery 1991–92
David McCreery 1992–93
Mick Wadsworth (*Director of Coaching*) 1993–96
Mervyn Day 1996–97
David Wilkes & John Halpin (*Directors of Coaching*), and Michael Knighton 1997–99
Nigel Pearson 1998–99
Keith Mincher 1999
Martin Wilkinson 1999–2000
Ian Atkins 2000–01
Roddy Collins 2001–02; 2002–03
Paul Simpson 2003–06
Neil McDonald 2006–07
John Ward 2007–08
Greg Abbott 2008–13
Graham Kavanagh 2013–14
Keith Curle September 2014–

TEN YEAR LEAGUE RECORD

		P	W	D	L	F	A	Pts	Pos
2006-07	FL 1	46	19	11	16	54	55	68	8
2007-08	FL 1	46	23	11	12	64	46	80	4
2008-09	FL 1	46	12	14	20	56	69	50	20
2009-10	FL 1	46	15	13	18	63	66	58	14
2010-11	FL 1	46	16	11	19	60	62	59	12
2011-12	FL 1	46	18	15	13	65	66	69	8
2012-13	FL 1	46	14	13	19	56	77	55	17
2013-14	FL 1	46	11	12	23	43	76	45	22
2014-15	FL 2	46	14	8	24	56	74	50	20
2015-16	FL 2	46	17	16	13	67	62	67	10

DID YOU KNOW ?

Carlisle United captain Bob Bradley complained of feeling ill after appearing in the Division Three North game at Chester on 17 February 1934. He was taken to his lodgings on his return to Carlisle but died the following day. A verdict of natural causes was recorded.

CARLISLE UNITED – FOOTBALL LEAGUE TWO 2015–16 LEAGUE RECORD

Match No.	Date	Venue	Opponents	Result	H/T Score	Lg Pos.	Goalscorers	Attendance
1	Aug 8	A	Mansfield T	D	1-1	1-1	10	Ibohro 45	4146
2	15	H	Cambridge U	D	4-4	2-3	14	Ibehre 3 42, 44, 76, Wyke 50	6354
3	18	A	Plymouth Arg	L	1-4	0-1	20	Thompson 90	6071
4	22	H	AFC Wimbledon	D	1-1	0-1	20	Ibehre 67	5949
5	29	A	Hartlepool U	W	3-2	0-1	16	Ibehre 2 57, 84, Miller 76	4935
6	Sept 5	H	Barnet	W	3-2	2-2	11	Miller 2, Asamoah 2 19, 64	4925
7	12	H	Dagenham & R	W	2-1	1-1	9	Balanta 37, Ibehre 53	3871
8	19	A	York C	D	2-2	2-0	10	Miller 26, Archibald-Henville 42	3692
9	26	H	Newport Co	L	0-1	0-0	12		4402
10	29	A	Leyton Orient	W	2-1	0-0	8	Asamoah 62, Sweeney 72	4408
11	Oct 3	A	Stevenage	W	1-0	0-0	8	Miller 82	2999
12	10	H	Morecambe	L	2-3	1-1	9	Grainger 23, Asamoah 90	5303
13	17	H	Exeter C	W	1-0	0-0	7	Gilliead 77	4021
14	20	A	Northampton T	L	2-3	1-1	9	Gilliead 29, Wyke 90	3642
15	24	A	Wycombe W	D	1-1	0-0	9	Archibald-Henville 48	3457
16	31	H	Yeovil T	W	3-2	1-2	8	Raynes 2 31, 75, Gillesphey 55	4095
17	Nov 14	A	Bristol R	L	0-2	0-0	9		6423
18	21	H	Portsmouth	D	2-2	1-0	9	Grainger 2 (1 pen) 44 (pl) 90	5503
19	24	A	Luton T	W	4-3	1-1	7	Wyke 45, Gilliead 66, Ibehre 79, Asamoah 80	7298
20	28	H	Crawley T	W	3-1	2-1	6	Wyke 2 2, 29, Ibehre 49	4641
21	Dec 12	A	Oxford U	D	1-1	1-1	6	Dunkley (og) 45	5936
22	19	H	Notts Co	W	3-0	2-0	5	Grainger (pen) 6, Ibehre 2 45, 59	3336
23	Jan 2	H	Plymouth Arg	L	0-2	0-1	9		4415
24	16	A	Barnet	D	0-0	0-0	10		2079
25	23	H	York C	D	1-1	1-0	10	Kennedy 15	7461
26	Feb 6	H	Accrington S	W	2-0	2-0	12	Wyke 27, Gilliead 38	4709
27	13	A	Newport Co	L	0-1	0-0	12		2106
28	16	A	Accrington S	D	1-1	1-0	12	Hope 17	2080
29	20	H	Stevenage	W	1-0	0-0	12	Ibehre 59	4780
30	23	A	AFC Wimbledon	L	0-1	0-0	12		3526
31	27	A	Morecambe	W	2-1	0-1	11	Wyke (pen) 83, Asamoah 84	3070
32	Mar 1	H	Leyton Orient	D	2-2	1-0	11	Gillesphey 17, Raynes 84	3721
33	5	H	Northampton T	L	1-4	0-2	11	Hope 47	4892
34	8	A	Dagenham & R	D	0-0	0-0	11		1695
35	12	A	Exeter C	D	2-2	1-1	10	Wyke 27, Hope 85	3375
36	19	H	Wycombe W	D	1-1	1-1	11	Wyke 26	4532
37	25	A	Yeovil T	D	0-0	0-0	10		4075
38	28	H	Bristol R	W	3-2	1-1	9	Stacey 11, Wyke 49, Kennedy 85	4718
39	Apr 2	A	Portsmouth	L	0-1	0-0	11		15,416
40	5	H	Hartlepool U	W	1-0	0-0	8	Hope 55	4767
41	9	H	Mansfield T	L	1-2	0-1	10	Miller 90	4426
42	16	A	Cambridge U	D	0-0	0-0	11		5806
43	19	H	Luton T	L	1-2	0-1	14	Stacey 61	3497
44	23	A	Crawley T	W	1-0	0-0	10	Wyke 78	1940
45	30	H	Oxford U	L	0-2	0-1	12		6948
46	May 7	A	Notts Co	W	5-0	3-0	10	Gilliead 4, Grainger 28, Ibehre 2 40, 54, Wyke 80	5405

Final League Position: 10

GOALSCORERS

League (67): Ibehre 15, Wyke 12 (1 pen), Asamoah 6, Gilliead 5, Grainger 5 (2 pens), Miller 5, Hope 4, Raynes 3, Archibald-Henville 2, Gillesphey 2, Kennedy 2, Stacey 2, Balanta 1, Sweeney 1, Thompson 1, own goal 1.
FA Cup (10): Sweeney 3, Wyke 3, Grainger 2 (1 pen), Ellis 1, Hope 1.
Capital One Cup (6): Asamoah 2, Ibehre 2, Kennedy 1, Osei 1.
Johnstone's Paint Trophy (0).

Gillespie M 45	Raynes M 39 + 1	Grainger D 36	Atkinson D 23 + 1	Miller T 28 + 1	Hery B 16 + 4	Kennedy J 44	Joyce L 34 + 3	Brough P 6 + 1	Ibehre J 29 + 7	Asamoah D 13 + 30	Balanta A 4 + 3	Osei K 1 + 7	Dicker G 13 + 6	Thompson J 4 + 11	Wyke C 29 + 5	McQueen A 15 + 6	Archibald-Henville T 6 + 6	Rigg S 2 + 6	Sweeney A 11 + 8	Gilliead A 23 + 12	Gillesphey M 18 + 5	Hope H 16 + 5	Ellis M 30	Comley B 12	Hanford D 1 + 1	Smith M 1 + 1	Stacey J 7 + 2	Pedro L — + 1	Match No.
1	2	3	4	5	6²	7	8	9¹	10	11³	12	13	14																1
1	3	4		2	8³	7	6	9²	10			13	12		5¹	11	14												2
1	3	4		2	14	8	7		10	13	5²	9¹	6	12	11¹														3
1	3	5		2¹	9	7	6	13	11	10³			8¹		12	14	4												4
1	4	9		2	8³	6	7		10	12			14	13		5²	3	11¹											5
1	3	4		2	9¹	8	7	5²	11	10		14	13	6³		12													6
1	3	4		2	13	7	6		10	11²	9¹	12	8	14		5³													7
1	3	5		2		7	6		10		12	13	9				4			8¹	11²								8
1	3			8		6	9	11²	12		7³	14		5¹		13	2			10	4								9
1	4	5	13	2		6³	3		9¹			8			11	14		7²	12	10									10
1	3	5		2	14	6	9		10		8³			11¹	13		7²	12	4										11
1	3	8		2	10²	9	7³		11		14	6			5		12	13		4¹									12
1	4²	5	3	2	11	6	7		13				10¹		12	14	8³	9											13
1		9	2	5	7	6			11³			8¹	14	13		3	12		10	4²									14
1		4	2		8	6	5¹		14			12	13	10²		3		9	7³		11¹								15
1	3	5		2	14	8²	7		13			6		10¹					9²	12	11	4							16
1			3	2			9	13	11	10³		8	6¹	14	5²		12	7			4								17
1	3²	5	2	8		7	6³		11¹	13		9		12			14	10			4								18
1	3	9	2	5³	8²	6	7		13	10			11¹				14	12			4								19
1	3	5	2		7	8		10¹	12		14	13	11³			9²	6			4								20
1	3	5	2		7	8		11	12		13	10			9²	6¹			4								21
1	3	9¹	2		7		10²	12		8	14	11	13			6¹		5		4							22
1	3	5	2		8	7¹		10³	12	14	11		13	9²	6		11³	3			4					23
1	4	5	2	7²	6	8	9¹	14	10			13	12												24
1	4		2	6¹	7³	9	10	11²	8			14	12	5	13	3									25
1	3¹		2		7	11²	13	10	5	14	6²	12	9	4	8							26
1	3		2	8	12	10¹	14	11	9²	6¹	5	13	4	7⁴						27
1	4		5	7²	9	8	10⁴	13	11³	2	14	12	6³	3						28
1	3	5²		6	7¹	11	14	10	2	13	12	9²	4	8						29
1⁴	4		8	10	13	11	9²	14	7³	2	6	3	5¹	12				30
3			14	7	12	11	13	10	2²	6	5	9²	4	8¹	1			31
1	3		7	8	10	13	11¹	2²	12	6	5	9	4				32
1	3	5	2	9²	7	8¹	10	11	12	6	13	4			33
1	3	9¹	5	2	7	8	10	12	11²	13	6	4			34
1	13	9	3²	2	8	7	14	10	11²	12	5¹	6	4		35
1	3	9	5¹	2	8	7²	14	12	11	6²	10	4	13		36
1	4	5	2	6	8	12	13	9	14	11³	3	7¹	10²	37
1	4	5¹	2	7	12	13	10	6³	9	3	8	11³	14	38
1	4	3	2	8	6	14	13	10	12	11	5¹	7³	9²	39
1	3	9	2	7	10³	14	13	6³	5	12	4¹	8	11	40
1	3	9	2	7¹	10²	13	11	6	5	12	4³	8	14	41
1	3³	5	2	8	7	12	10²	14	11	13	9⁴	4⁴	6¹	42
1	5¹	3³	7	6	12	14	10	2	13	11	4	8²	9	43
1	5	7	6	11³	14	12	10	2	13	4	3	8¹	9²	44
1	4	3	6	7	9³	10	14	11¹	5	12	2	8²	13	45
1	3	9	2	8	7	10³	13	14	12	11¹	5	6²	4	46

FA Cup

First Round	Plymouth Arg	(a)	2-0
Second Round	Welling U	(a)	5-0
Third Round	Yeovil T	(h)	2-2
Replay	Yeovil T	(a)	1-1
(aet; Carlisle U won 5-4 on penalties)			
Fourth Round	Everton	(h)	0-3

Capital One Cup

First Round	Chesterfield	(h)	3-1
(aet)			
Second Round	QPR	(a)	2-1
Third Round	Liverpool	(a)	1-1
(aet; Liverpool won 3-2 on penalties)			

Johnstone's Paint Trophy

First Round	Port Vale	(a)	0-1

CHARLTON ATHLETIC

FOUNDATION

The club was formed on 9 June 1905, by a group of 14- and 15-year-old youths living in streets by the Thames in the area which now borders the Thames Barrier. The club's progress through local leagues was so rapid that after the First World War they joined the Kent League where they spent a season before turning professional and joining the Southern League in 1920. A year later they were elected to the Football League's Division 3 (South).

The Valley, Floyd Road, Charlton, London SE7 8BL.

Telephone: (020) 8333 4000.

Fax: (020) 8333 4001.

Ticket Office: (03330) 144 444.

Website: www.cafc.co.uk

Email: info@cafc.co.uk

Ground Capacity: 27,111.

Record Attendance: 75,031 v Aston Villa, FA Cup 5th rd, 12 February 1938 (at The Valley).

Pitch Measurements: 101.5m × 66m (111yd × 72yd).

Non-Executive Chairman: Richard Murray.

Head Coach: Russell Slade.

First-Team Coach: Simon Clark.

Head Physio: Erol Umut.

Colours: Red shirts with white trim, white shorts, red socks.

Year Formed: 1905.

Turned Professional: 1920.

Club Nickname: 'The Addicks'.

Grounds: 1906, Siemen's Meadow; 1907, Woolwich Common; 1909, Pound Park; 1913, Horn Lane; 1920, The Valley; 1923, Catford (The Mount); 1924, The Valley; 1985, Selhurst Park; 1991, Upton Park; 1992, The Valley.

First Football League Game: 27 August 1921, Division 3 (S), v Exeter C (h) W 1–0 – Hughes; Johnny Mitchell, Goodman; Dowling (1), Hampson, Dunn; Castle, Bailey, Halse, Green, Wilson.

Record League Victory: 8–1 v Middlesbrough, Division 1, 12 September 1953 – Bartram; Campbell, Ellis; Fenton, Ufton, Hammond; Hurst (2), O'Linn (2), Leary (1), Firmani (3), Kiernan.

Record Cup Victory: 7–0 v Burton A, FA Cup 3rd rd, 7 January 1956 – Bartram; Campbell, Townsend; Hewie, Ufton, Hammond; Hurst (1), Gauld (1), Leary (3), White, Kiernan (2).

Record Defeat: 1–11 v Aston Villa, Division 2, 14 November 1959.

Most League Points (2 for a win): 61, Division 3 (S), 1934–35.

HONOURS

League Champions: First Division – 1999–2000; FL 1 – 2011–12; Division 3S – 1928–29, 1934–35.
Runners-up: Division 1 – 1936–37; Division 2 – 1935–36, 1985–86.
FA Cup Winners: 1947.
Runners-up: 1946.
League Cup: quarter-final – 2007.
Full Members' Cup: Runners-up 1987.

sky SPORTS FACT FILE

Hans Jeppson joined Charlton Athletic as an amateur in January 1951. The Addicks were in danger of relegation from the old First Division at the time, but Jeppson scored a last-minute winner on his debut, going on to net 9 goals in 11 games including a hat-trick at Arsenal. Charlton finished the season well clear of the drop in 17th position.

Most League Points (3 for a win): 101, FL 1, 2011–12.

Most League Goals: 107, Division 2, 1957–58.

Highest League Scorer in Season: Ralph Allen, 32, Division 3 (S), 1934–35.

Most League Goals in Total Aggregate: Stuart Leary, 153, 1953–62.

Most League Goals in One Match: 5, Wilson Lennox v Exeter C, Division 3 (S), 2 February 1929; 5, Eddie Firmani v Aston Villa, Division 1, 5 February 1955; 5, John Summers v Huddersfield T, Division 2, 21 December 1957; 5, John Summers v Portsmouth, Division 2, 1 October 1960.

Most Capped Player: Jonatan Johansson, 42 (106), Finland.

Most League Appearances: Sam Bartram, 579, 1934–56.

Youngest League Player: Jonjo Shelvey, 16 years 59 days v Burnley, 26 April 2008.

Record Transfer Fee Received: £16,500,000 from Tottenham H for Darren Bent, May 2007.

Record Transfer Fee Paid: £4,750,000 to Wimbledon for Jason Euell, January 2001.

Football League Record: 1921 Elected to Division 3 (S); 1929–33 Division 2; 1933–35 Division 3 (S); 1935–36 Division 2; 1936–57 Division 1; 1957–72 Division 2; 1972–75 Division 3; 1975–80 Division 2; 1980–81 Division 3; 1981–86 Division 2; 1986–90 Division 1; 1990–92 Division 2; 1992–98 Division 1; 1998–99 FA Premier League; 1999–2000 Division 1; 2000–07 FA Premier League; 2007–09 FL C; 2009–12 FL 1; 2012–16 FL C; FL 1 2016–.

LATEST SEQUENCES

Longest Sequence of League Wins: 12, 26.12.1999 – 7.3.2000.

Longest Sequence of League Defeats: 10, 11.4.1990 – 15.9.1990.

Longest Sequence of League Draws: 6, 13.12.1992 – 16.1.1993.

Longest Sequence of Unbeaten League Matches: 15, 4.10.1980 – 20.12.1980.

Longest Sequence Without a League Win: 18, 18.10.2008 – 17.1.2009.

Successive Scoring Runs: 25 from 26.12.1935.

Successive Non-scoring Runs: 5 from 17.10.2015.

MANAGERS

Walter Rayner 1920–25
Alex Macfarlane 1925–27
Albert Lindon 1928
Alex Macfarlane 1928–32
Albert Lindon 1932–33
Jimmy Seed 1933–56
Jimmy Trotter 1956–61
Frank Hill 1961–65
Bob Stokoe 1965–67
Eddie Firmani 1967–70
Theo Foley 1970–74
Andy Nelson 1974–79
Mike Bailey 1979–81
Alan Mullery 1981–82
Ken Craggs 1982
Lennie Lawrence 1982–91
Steve Gritt/Alan Curbishley 1991–95
Alan Curbishley 1995–2006
Iain Dowie 2006
Les Reed 2006
Alan Pardew 2006–08
Phil Parkinson 2008–11
Chris Powell 2011–14
José Riga 2014
Bob Peeters 2014–15
Guy Luzon 2015
Karel Fraeye 2015–16
José Riga 2016
Russell Slade June 2016–

TEN YEAR LEAGUE RECORD

		P	W	D	L	F	A	Pts	Pos
2006-07	PR Lge	38	8	10	20	34	60	34	19
2007-08	FL C	46	17	13	16	63	58	64	11
2008-09	FL C	46	8	15	23	52	74	39	24
2009-10	FL 1	46	23	15	8	71	48	84	4
2010-11	FL 1	46	15	14	17	62	66	59	13
2011-12	FL 1	46	30	11	5	82	36	101	1
2012-13	FL C	46	17	14	15	65	59	65	9
2013-14	FL C	46	13	12	21	41	61	51	18
2014-15	FL C	46	14	18	14	54	60	60	12
2015-16	FL C	46	9	13	24	40	80	40	22

DID YOU KNOW ?

In April 1937 world champions Italy withdrew from a friendly with France just days before the game was due to take place. Charlton replaced them at short notice and beat the France international team 5-2 at the Parc des Princes.

CHARLTON ATHLETIC – FL CHAMPIONSHIP 2015–16 LEAGUE RECORD

Match No.	Date	Venue	Opponents	Result	H/T Score	Lg Pos.	Goalscorers	Attendance
1	Aug 8	H	QPR	W 2-0	0-0	2	Watt [52], Fox [72]	19,469
2	15	A	Derby Co	D 1-1	0-0	4	Watt [48]	29,045
3	18	A	Nottingham F	D 0-0	0-0	5		17,801
4	22	H	Hull C	W 2-1	0-0	3	Makienok Christoffersen [52], Gudmundsson [90]	14,844
5	29	A	Wolverhampton W	L 1-2	0-0	8	Gudmundsson [55]	19,583
6	Sept12	H	Rotherham U	D 1-1	0-1	10	Bauer [65]	15,220
7	15	H	Huddersfield T	L 1-2	1-2	12	Sarr [40]	13,873
8	19	A	Blackburn R	L 0-3	0-1	15		12,088
9	26	A	Cardiff C	L 1-2	0-0	17	Ahearne-Grant [49]	13,980
10	Oct 4	H	Fulham	D 2-2	0-1	17	Jackson [81], Cousins [90]	14,662
11	17	A	Reading	L 0-1	0-0	20		17,614
12	20	H	Preston NE	L 0-3	0-2	22		13,586
13	24	H	Brentford	L 0-3	0-1	22		14,585
14	31	A	Middlesbrough	L 0-3	0-0	23		20,943
15	Nov 3	A	Milton Keynes D	L 0-1	0-1	23		9575
16	7	H	Sheffield W	W 3-1	2-0	22	Jackson [26], Makienok Christoffersen [45], Ghoochannejhad [55]	16,267
17	21	A	Birmingham C	W 1-0	0-0	20	Jackson [61]	16,514
18	28	H	Ipswich T	L 0-3	0-2	21		15,870
19	Dec 5	A	Brighton & HA	L 2-3	2-0	22	Lookman [2], Ghoochannejhad [5]	24,587
20	12	H	Leeds U	D 0-0	0-0	21		15,867
21	15	H	Bolton W	D 2-2	2-2	22	Lookman 2 [1, 26]	12,294
22	19	A	Burnley	L 0-4	0-1	23		15,697
23	26	A	Bristol C	D 1-1	0-1	23	Lennon [90]	15,285
24	28	H	Wolverhampton W	L 0-2	0-0	23		18,059
25	Jan 2	H	Nottingham F	D 1-1	0-1	23	Makienok Christoffersen [70]	16,090
26	12	A	Huddersfield T	L 0-5	0-2	23		10,215
27	16	A	Hull C	L 0-6	0-4	23		16,430
28	23	H	Blackburn R	D 1-1	1-1	23	Lennon [30]	13,512
29	30	A	Rotherham U	W 4-1	2-1	23	Makienok Christoffersen 2 [4, 69], Vetokele [44], Lookman [90]	9227
30	Feb 6	H	Bristol C	L 0-1	0-1	24		14,342
31	13	H	Cardiff C	D 0-0	0-0	23		16,755
32	20	A	Fulham	L 0-3	0-1	24		16,565
33	23	A	Preston NE	L 1-2	1-1	24	Gudmundsson [37]	10,075
34	27	H	Reading	L 3-4	1-3	24	Sanogo 3 [6, 49, 84]	21,506
35	Mar 5	A	Brentford	W 2-1	1-1	23	Harriott 2 [1, 69]	10,108
36	8	H	Milton Keynes D	D 0-0	0-0	23		13,146
37	13	H	Middlesbrough	W 2-0	0-0	23	Teixeira [57], Harriott [80]	14,636
38	19	A	Sheffield W	L 0-3	0-0	23		29,668
39	Apr 2	H	Birmingham C	W 2-1	1-1	23	Gudmundsson [38], Teixeira [90]	15,742
40	5	A	Ipswich T	D 0-0	0-0	23		17,787
41	9	A	QPR	L 1-2	0-1	23	Cousins [62]	15,834
42	16	H	Derby Co	L 0-1	0-0	23		15,857
43	19	A	Bolton W	D 0-0	0-0	23		12,257
44	23	H	Brighton & HA	L 1-3	0-1	23	Gudmundsson [51]	17,160
45	30	A	Leeds U	W 2-1	1-0	22	Gudmundsson [39], Lookman [49]	25,458
46	May 7	H	Burnley	L 0-3	0-1	22		16,199

Final League Position: 22

GOALSCORERS

League (40): Gudmundsson 6, Lookman 5, Makienok Christoffersen 5, Harriott 3, Jackson 3, Sanogo 3, Cousins 2, Ghoochannejhad 2, Lennon 2, Teixeira 2, Watt 2, Ahearne-Grant 1, Bauer 1, Fox 1, Sarr 1, Vetokele 1.
FA Cup (1): Ghoochannejhad 1.
Capital One Cup (9): Ahearne-Grant 2 (1 pen), Bergdich 1, Ghoochannejhad 1, Kashi 1, Kennedy 1, Sarr 1, Vetokele 1, Watt 1.

Pope N 24	Solly C 33+1	Diarra A 31+1	Bauer P 19	Fox M 40+2	Gudmundsson J 39+1	Kashi A 11	Ba E 13+12	Cousins J 39	Ahearne-Grant K 7+10	Makienok Christoffersen S 22+14	Watt T 11+3	Bergdich Z 11+12	Ceballos C 3+2	Jackson J 21+8	Ghoochannejhad R 10+13	Charles R —+1	Harriott C 15+5	Vetokele I 11+5	Sarr N 9+3	McAleny C 3+5	Kennedy M 2	Moussa F 2+4	Holmes-Dennis T 5+6	Henderson S 22	Lookman A 17+7	Vaz Te R 8+3	Lennon H 16+3	Williams R 2+1	Johnson R 4	Poyet D 4+2	Umerah J —+1	Teixeira J 19	Sango Y 4+4	Motta M 9+3	Fanni R 13+1	Yun S 7+2	Match No.
1	2	3	4	5	6²	7	8¹	9	10³	11	12	13	14																								1
1	2	3	4	5	6¹	7	14	8			11³	10	12	9²	13																						2
1	2	3	4	5	6	7	8	13	10	11²	14			9¹	12³																						3
1		3	4	5	8	7	6¹	2	12	10	11²			9³	13	14																					4
1	2	3	4	5	6	7	13	8	10¹	11²				9³	14			12																			5
1	2	3	4	5	6		8	7¹	9		12	10	13					11²																			6
1	2		4	5²	6		8	7¹	9		11³	10	12					14	3	13																	7
1	2	3	4	5	6		8	7	14	11²				9³			12	13	10¹																		8
1	2		3	5	10	7²	8	12	11	9²							4	13	6¹	14																	9
1	2	3	4	5²	6	7¹	8	10	11	12				9²			14	13																			10
1	2	3	4¹	13	6¹	14	8	10	12	5							7³	9	11²																		11
1	2	3		8²	7	11¹	14	10	6³					13			4	12	9																		12
	2		3	5	6		8	14	11¹	10²				7	12		4	13	9³					1													13
	2	3	4	5	7		6²	9	10³	11¹	12			8	13				14		1																14
	2	3	4	5	6		8²	12	13	11				7	10²			9¹			1					14											15
	2³	7	3	5	9		6²		10					8	11¹		4		13	12	1	14															16
	7	3	5	9²			6	13	11¹					8	14		4			2	1	10³	12														17
12	7	3	5²	9			6		11¹					8³	14		4			2	1	10	13														18
	2	7	3¹	5	8²		13	6						9			12			14	1	10	11¹	4³													19
	2	3		8			12	6	14	13				7³	9¹					5	1	10	11²	4													20
	2	3		8²			13	6	14	12				7¹	9					5	1	10³	11	4													21
	2	6¹	3²	5			7	12	11		13			8	9			14			1		10³	4													22
	2	3¹		5			14	6²	11					7	9		12			13	1	8	10³	4													23
	2			5²			6	11	12				14	7	9²		3			13	1	10¹	8	4													24
	2			5	12		6²	7		10				8¹			9	3		13¹	1		11³	4	14												25
	2			5²	9³				14					8	13¹		11			12	1		10	4	7¹	3	6										26
	2			12	9		6							8	11	10²				1			14	5	4¹	3	7²	13									27
	2			5	6		7			11²				8	12	13	10³				1			4				3									28
	2			5	6		11²			9				8	12		10¹				1	13		4				3									29
	2			5²	6		14			11				8²	12	13					1		10¹	4				3									30
	2			5	10		12	7³		11				8²	6¹						1			4					14	3	13						31
	2			5	8		7¹			11				10²		14	9				1	12		4			6³			3		13					32
8²				6	7		12	9¹		11							1	10	5¹	4									3	14	2³	13					33
	7			9		6²			10	12				14	13					1						3			4	11³	5¹	2	8				34
1	7³		5	10²		8	13			14					6¹													12		4	11	2	3	9			35
1			5	10		7	11¹	13						6²			14						8³						4	12²	2	3	9			36
1	7		5	6¹		8		13		12	10²			11³	14													4			2	3	9			37
1	8¹		5	6	7³			13	11¹²	10	12			14													4			2¹	3	9³			38
1	8		5	6²		7	14		13	10	11			12													4			2¹	3	9³			39
1	2	7	5	6²		8	14			10¹	13			9													4	11	12²	3					40
1	2	7	5²			8	12		14	6	10			9³	13													4	11¹	3						41
1	2¹	8³	5	10		7	13	14		6	11			9²													4		12	3						42
1	13			7	11	14	6³		12	10³				9	4					3			5	2	8¹												43
1	7		5	6		8	14		10	11¹				9	13					4	12³	2³	3														44
1	3		5	10²	7	14	13			8	11³			9¹						4			2	12													45
1	3		5	10¹	7	14	8			12	6³	11		9						4			2	13													46

FA Cup
Third Round   Colchester U   (a)   1-2

Capital One Cup
First Round   Dagenham & R   (h)   4-1
Second Round   Peterborough U   (a)   4-1
Third Round   Crystal Palace   (a)   1-4

CHELSEA

Stamford Bridge, Fulham Road, London SW6 1HS.
Telephone: (0871) 984 1955. *Fax:* (020) 7381 4831.
Ticket Office: (0871) 984 1905.
Website: www.chelseafc.com
Email: enquiries@chelseafc.com
Ground Capacity: 41,663.
Record Attendance: 82,905 v Arsenal, Division 1, 12 October 1935.
Pitch Measurements: 103m × 67.5m (112yd × 74yd).
Chairman: Bruce Buck.
Chief Executive: Marina Granovskaia.
Manager: Antonio Conte.
Technical Director: Michael Emenalo.
Assistant First-Team Coach: Steve Holland.
Medical Director: Paco Biosca.
Colours: Chelse blue shirt with white trim, Chelsea blue shorts with white trim, white socks with Chelsea blue trim.
Year Formed: 1905. *Turned Professional:* 1905.
Club Nickname: 'The Blues'.
Ground: 1905, Stamford Bridge.
First Football League Game: 2 September 1905, Division 2, v Stockport Co (a) L 0–1 – Foulke; Mackie, McEwan; Key, Harris, Miller; Moran, Jack Robertson, Copeland, Windridge, Kirwan.
Record League Victory: 8–0 v Wigan Ath, FA Premier League, 9 May 2010 – Cech; Ivanovic (Belletti), Ashley Cole (1), Ballack (Matic), Terry, Alex, Kalou (1) (Joe Cole), Lampard (pen), Anelka (2), Drogba (3, 1 pen), Malouda; 8–0 v Aston Villa, FA Premier League, 23 December 2012 – Cech; Azpilicueta, Ivanovic (1), Cahill, Cole, Luiz (1), Lampard (1) (Ramirez (2)), Moses, Mata (Piazon), Hazard (1), Torres (1) (Oscar (1)).

HONOURS

League Champions: FA Premier League – 2004–05, 2005–06, 2009–10, 2014–15; Division 1 – 1954–55; Division 2 – 1983–84, 1988–89.
Runners-up: FA Premier League – 2003–04, 2006–07, 2007–08, 2010–11; Division 2 – 1906–07, 1911–12, 1929–30, 1962–63, 1976–77.
FA Cup Winners: 1970, 1997, 2000, 2007, 2009, 2010, 2012.
Runners-up: 1915, 1967, 1994, 2002.
League Cup Winners: 1965, 1998, 2005, 2007, 2015.
Runners-up: 1972, 2008.
Full Members' Cup Winners: 1986, 1990.
European Competitions
Champions League: 1999–2000, 2003–04 *(sf)*, 2004–05 *(sf)*, 2005–06, 2006–07 *(sf)*, 2007–08 *(runners-up)*, 2008–09 *(sf)*, 2009–10, 2010–11 *(qf)*, 2011–12 *(winners)*, 2012–13, 2013–14 *(sf)*, 2014–15, 2015–16.
Fairs Cup: 1958–60, 1965–66, 1968–69.
UEFA Cup: 2000–01, 2001–02, 2002–03.
Europa League: 2012–13 *(winners)*.
European Cup-Winners' Cup: 1970–71 *(winners)*, 1971–72, 1994–95 *(sf)*, 1997–98 *(winners)*, 1998–99 *(sf)*.
Super Cup: 1998 *(winners)*, 2012, 2013.
Club World Cup: 2012 *(runners-up)*.

sky SPORTS FACT FILE

Half-back Nils Middelboe signed for Chelsea towards the end of 1913 having previously appeared for Denmark in the 1908 and 1912 Olympic Games. The club's first recruit from European football, he added a further three caps for Denmark during his time at Stamford Bridge.

Record Cup Victory: 13–0 v Jeunesse Hautcharage, ECWC, 1st rd 2nd leg, 29 September 1971 – Bonetti; Boyle, Harris (1), Hollins (1p), Webb (1), Hinton, Cooke, Baldwin (3), Osgood (5), Hudson (1), Houseman (1).

Record Defeat: 1–8 v Wolverhampton W, Division 1, 26 September 1953; 0–7 v Nottingham F, Division 1, 20 April 1991.

Most League Points (2 for a win): 57, Division 2, 1906–07.

Most League Points (3 for a win): 99, Division 2, 1988–89.

Most League Goals: 103, FA Premier League, 2009–10.

Highest League Scorer in Season: Jimmy Greaves, 41, 1960–61.

Most League Goals in Total Aggregate: Bobby Tambling, 164, 1958–70.

Most League Goals in One Match: 5, George Hilsdon v Glossop, Division 2, 1 September 1906; 5, Jimmy Greaves v Wolverhampton W, Division 1, 30 August 1958; 5, Jimmy Greaves v Preston NE, Division 1, 19 December 1959; 5, Jimmy Greaves v WBA, Division 1, 3 December 1960; 5, Bobby Tambling v Aston Villa, Division 1, 17 September 1966; 5, Gordon Durie v Walsall, Division 2, 4 February 1989.

Most Capped Player: Frank Lampard, 104 (106), England.

Most League Appearances: Ron Harris, 655, 1962–80.

Youngest League Player: Ian Hamilton, 16 years 138 days v Tottenham H, 18 March 1967.

Record Transfer Fee Received: £50,000,000 from Paris Saint-Germain for David Luiz, July 2014.

Record Transfer Fee Paid: £50,000,000 to Liverpool for Fernando Torres, January 2011.

Football League Record: 1905 Elected to Division 2; 1907–10 Division 1; 1910–12 Division 2; 1912–24 Division 1; 1924–30 Division 2; 1930–62 Division 1; 1962–63 Division 2; 1963–75 Division 1; 1975–77 Division 2; 1977–79 Division 1; 1979–84 Division 2; 1984–88 Division 1; 1988–89 Division 2; 1989–92 Division 1; 1992– FA Premier League.

MANAGERS

John Tait Robertson 1905–07
David Calderhead 1907–33
Leslie Knighton 1933–39
Billy Birrell 1939–52
Ted Drake 1952–61
Tommy Docherty 1961–67
Dave Sexton 1967–74
Ron Suart 1974–75
Eddie McCreadie 1975–77
Ken Shellito 1977–78
Danny Blanchflower 1978–79
Geoff Hurst 1979–81
John Neal 1981–85 (*Director to 1986*)
John Hollins 1985–88
Bobby Campbell 1988–91
Ian Porterfield 1991–93
David Webb 1993
Glenn Hoddle 1993–96
Ruud Gullit 1996–98
Gianluca Vialli 1998–2000
Claudio Ranieri 2000–04
Jose Mourinho 2004–07
Avram Grant 2007–08
Luiz Felipe Scolari 2008–09
Guus Hiddink 2009
Carlo Ancelotti 2009–11
Andre Villas-Boas 2011–12
Roberto Di Matteo 2012
Rafael Benitez 2012–13
Jose Mourinho 2013–15
Gus Hiddink 2015–16
Antonio Conte June 2016–

LATEST SEQUENCES

Longest Sequence of League Wins: 11, 25.4.2009 – 20.9.2009.

Longest Sequence of League Defeats: 7, 1.11.1952 – 20.12.1952.

Longest Sequence of League Draws: 6, 20.8.1969 – 13.9.1969.

Longest Sequence of Unbeaten League Matches: 40, 23.10.2004 – 29.10.2005.

Longest Sequence Without a League Win: 21, 3.11.1987 – 2.4.1988.

Successive Scoring Runs: 27 from 29.10.1988.

Successive Non-scoring Runs: 9 from 14.3.1981.

TEN YEAR LEAGUE RECORD

		P	W	D	L	F	A	Pts	Pos
2006-07	PR Lge	38	24	11	3	64	24	83	2
2007-08	PR Lge	38	25	10	3	65	26	85	2
2008-09	PR Lge	38	25	8	5	68	24	83	3
2009-10	PR Lge	38	27	5	6	103	32	86	1
2010-11	PR Lge	38	21	8	9	69	33	71	2
2011-12	PR Lge	38	18	10	10	65	46	64	6
2012-13	PR Lge	38	22	9	7	75	39	75	3
2013-14	PR Lge	38	25	7	6	71	27	82	3
2014-15	PR Lge	38	26	9	3	73	32	87	1
2015-16	PR Lge	38	12	14	12	59	53	50	10

DID YOU KNOW ?

Chelsea initially shared their Stamford Bridge ground with the London Athletic Club for many years. The previous winter tenants, the Lennox rugby union club, left at the end of the 1903–04 season when the stadium was substantially redeveloped.

CHELSEA – FA PREMIER LEAGUE 2015–16 LEAGUE RECORD

Match No.	Date		Venue	Opponents	Result		H/T Score	Lg Pos.	Goalscorers	Attendance
1	Aug	8	H	Swansea C	D	2-2	2-1	5	Oscar [23], Fernandez (og) [30]	41,232
2		16	A	Manchester C	L	0-3	0-1	16		54,331
3		23	A	WBA	W	3-2	3-1	9	Pedro [20], Costa [30], Azpilicueta [42]	23,256
4		29	H	Crystal Palace	L	1-2	0-0	13	Falcao [79]	41,581
5	Sept	12	A	Everton	L	1-3	1-2	16	Matic [36]	38,311
6		19	H	Arsenal	W	2-0	0-0	13	Zouma [53], Chambers (og) [90]	41,584
7		26	A	Newcastle U	D	2-2	0-1	15	Ramires [79], Willian [86]	48,682
8	Oct	3	H	Southampton	L	1-3	1-1	16	Willian [10]	41,642
9		17	H	Aston Villa	W	2-0	1-0	11	Costa [34], Hutton (og) [54]	41,596
10		24	A	West Ham U	L	1-2	0-1	15	Cahill [56]	34,977
11		31	H	Liverpool	L	1-3	1-1	15	Ramires [4]	41,577
12	Nov	7	A	Stoke C	L	0-1	0-0	16		27,550
13		21	H	Norwich C	W	1-0	0-0	15	Costa [64]	41,582
14		29	A	Tottenham H	D	0-0	0-0	14		35,639
15	Dec	5	H	Bournemouth	L	0-1	0-0	14		41,631
16		14	A	Leicester C	L	1-2	0-1	16	Remy [77]	32,054
17		19	H	Sunderland	W	3-1	2-0	15	Ivanovic [5], Pedro [13], Oscar (pen) [50]	41,562
18		26	H	Watford	D	2-2	1-1	15	Costa 2 [32, 65]	41,630
19		28	A	Manchester U	D	0-0	0-0	14		75,275
20	Jan	3	A	Crystal Palace	W	3-0	1-0	14	Oscar [29], Willian [60], Costa [66]	24,854
21		13	A	WBA	D	2-2	1-1	14	Azpilicueta [20], McAuley (og) [73]	40,945
22		16	H	Everton	D	3-3	0-0	14	Terry [90], Costa [64], Fabregas [66]	41,633
23		24	A	Arsenal	W	1-0	1-0	13	Costa [23]	60,072
24	Feb	3	A	Watford	D	0-0	0-0	13		20,910
25		7	H	Manchester U	D	1-1	0-0	13	Costa [90]	41,434
26		13	H	Newcastle U	W	5-1	3-0	12	Costa [5], Pedro 2 [9, 59], Willian [17], Traore [83]	41,622
27		27	A	Southampton	W	2-1	0-1	11	Fabregas [75], Ivanovic [89]	31,688
28	Mar	1	A	Norwich C	W	2-1	2-0	8	Kenedy [1], Costa [45]	27,091
29		5	H	Stoke C	D	1-1	1-0	10	Traore [39]	41,381
30		19	H	West Ham U	D	2-2	1-1	10	Fabregas 2 (1 pen) [45, 89 (p)]	41,623
31	Apr	2	A	Aston Villa	W	4-0	2-0	10	Loftus-Cheek [26], Alexandre Pato (pen) [45], Pedro 2 [46, 59]	31,120
32		9	H	Swansea C	L	0-1	0-1	10		20,966
33		16	H	Manchester C	L	0-3	0-1	10		41,212
34		23	A	Bournemouth	W	4-1	2-1	9	Pedro [5], Hazard 2 [34, 90], Willian [71]	11,365
35	May	2	H	Tottenham H	D	2-2	0-2	9	Cahill [58], Hazard [83]	41,545
36		7	A	Sunderland	L	2-3	2-1	9	Costa [14], Matic [45]	47,050
37		11	A	Liverpool	D	1-1	1-0	9	Hazard [32]	43,210
38		15	H	Leicester C	D	1-1	0-0	10	Fabregas (pen) [66]	41,494

Final League Position: 10

GOALSCORERS

League (59): Costa 12, Pedro 7, Fabregas 5 (2 pens), Willian 5, Hazard 4, Oscar 3 (1 pen), Azpilicueta 2, Cahill 2, Ivanovic 2, Matic 2, Ramires 2, Traore 2, Alexandre Pato 1 (1 pen), Falcao 1, Kenedy 1, Loftus-Cheek 1, Remy 1, Terry 1, Zouma 1, own goals 4.
FA Cup (12): Oscar 3, Costa 2, Hazard 2 (1 pen), Traore 2, Cahill 1, Loftus-Cheek 1, Willian 1.
Capital One Cup (5): Remy 2, Kenedy 1, Pedro 1, Ramires 1.
UEFA Champions League (15): Willian 5, Costa 2, Oscar 2 (1 pen), Cahill 1, Fabregas 1, Mikel 1, Zouma 1, own goals 2.

Courtois T 23	Ivanovic B 33	Cahill G 21+2	Terry J 24	Azpilicueta C 36+1	Fabregas F 33+4	Matic N 28+5	Willian d 32+3	Oscar E 20+7	Hazard E 25+6	Costa D 27+1	Begovic A 15+2	Zouma K 21+2	Falcao R 1+9	Ramires 7+5	Cuadrado J —+1	Pedro R 24+5	Mikel J 19+6	Kenedy R 4+10	Loftus-Cheek R 4+9	Remy L 3+10	Baba A 11+4	Traore B 4+6	Miazga M 2	Alexandre Pato d 1+1	Clarke-Salter J —+1	Abraham T —+2	Tomori F —+1	Match No.
1¹	2	3	4	5	6²	7	8³	9¹	10	11	12	13	14															1
	2	3	4¹	5	6	7	9³		10	11	1	12	14			8²	13											2
1	2	12	4*	5	6	7	9¹		10	11²		3	13			8³	14											3
1	2	4		5¹	6	7³	9¹		10	11		3	12			8	13	14										4
	2			4	5	9³	7	14	10	11	1	3	13			8²	6¹	12										5
	2		4	5	6³	7	9¹		10	11²	1	3	12			8	14		13									6
	2		4	5	6	7²	12	9¹	10		1	3	13	14		8			11¹									7
	2	3	4	5	7	12³	8²	9	10		1		11	6¹		13												8
		4	2	7	12	8³		13	11	1	3		6			10²		9¹	14	5								9
		3	4	5¹	9¹	7*	8		10	11	1	2	13	6²		12			14									10
		3	4	5²	13		8	10	9¹	11	1	2	14	6		7²	12											11
		4	2	12	7	9	13	10	11	1	3		6³			8²		14	5¹									12
	2		4	14	6	7	8²	12	9³	11	1	3	13			10¹	5											13
	2	4		5	6	7	8¹	9	11		1	3				10²		12	13									14
1	2	4		6³	7	8	9¹	11	12		3					10			13	5²	14							15
1	2		4²	5	13	7	8	9²	10¹	11		3		6		12			14									16
1	2		4	5	6¹	7	8	9³		11²		3		14		10	12		13									17
1	2	3	4	5	6¹	7	8	9	13	11						10²	12											18
1	2		4	5		7	8¹	9²	11			3		12		10	6	13										19
1	2		4	5	6	13	8	9	10¹	11		3				12	7											20
1	2		4	5	7²	13	8	9		11		3				10¹	6	12										21
1	2		4	5	9	6¹	8	12		11³		3				10²	7	13		14								22
1	2		4	5	9	7	8	10²	13	11¹		3				6		12										23
1	2		4	5	9	7¹	8	10	12	11		3				6												24
1	2	13	4	5	9	7	8	10¹	12	11				3²		14	6											25
1	2	3	4¹	5	6	7	9³		8	11²						10		14		12	13							26
1	4	3		2	6	14	9	12	8³	11						10¹	7	13		5²								27
1	4	3		2	6	7	12	9²	10	11						13	5³			14	8¹							28
1	4	3		2	14	6³	8	9	10¹							7	12	13	5	11²								29
1	2	3	4	5	6		8	9³								12	7	10¹	14	11²	13							30
1	4			2	6		13									8³	7	10²	9	11¹	5	3	12	14				31
	4			2	7		8			1		14				10	6	12	9³	5	13	3¹	11²					32
1*	4	3		2	6		8²		11	14						10¹	7³	12	9	5	13							33
	4			2	7	6	9¹		10	11	1					8	3	12	5									34
	2	3	4	5	9	7²	8	13	12	11	1					10¹	6											35
1	2¹	3	4*	5	9	7	8²	13	10	11						6³			12	14								36
		3		2	6	7	8¹		9		1					10²	4	12	14	5	11²					13		37
1	4³	3		2	6	7	9		10							8⁴		13	5	11¹						12	14	38

FA Cup

Third Round	Scunthorpe U	(h)	2-0
Fourth Round	Milton Keynes D	(a)	5-1
Fifth Round	Manchester C	(h)	5-1
Sixth Round	Everton	(a)	0-2

Capital One Cup

Third Round	Walsall	(a)	4-1
Fourth Round	Stoke C	(a)	1-1

(aet; Stoke C won 5-4 on penalties)

UEFA Champions League

Group G	Maccabi Tel Aviv	(h)	4-0
Group G	Porto	(a)	1-2
Group G	Dynamo Kyiv	(a)	0-0
Group G	Dynamo Kyiv	(h)	2-1
Group G	Maccabi Tel Aviv	(a)	4-0
Group G	Porto	(h)	2-0
Round of 16 1st leg	Paris Saint-Germain	(a)	1-2
Round of 16 2nd leg	Paris Saint-Germain	(h)	1-2

(Paris Saint-Germain won 4-2 on aggregate)

CHELTENHAM TOWN

FOUNDATION

Although a scratch team representing Cheltenham played a match against Gloucester in 1884, the earliest recorded match for Cheltenham Town FC was a friendly against Dean Close School on 12 March 1892. The School won 4–3 and the match was played at Prestbury (half a mile from Whaddon Road). Cheltenham Town played Wednesday afternoon friendlies at a local cricket ground until entering the Mid Gloucester League. In those days the club played in deep red coloured shirts and were nicknamed 'the Rubies'. The club moved to Whaddon Lane for season 1901–02 and changed to red and white colours two years later.

World of Smile Stadium, Whaddon Road, Cheltenham, Gloucestershire GL52 5NA.

Telephone: (01242) 573 558.

Fax: (01242) 224 675.

Ticket Office: (01242) 588 117.

Website: www.ctfc.com

Email: info@ctfc.com

Ground Capacity: 7,066.

HONOURS

League Champions: Conference – 1998–99, 2015–16.
Runners-up: Conference – 1997–98.
FA Cup: 5th rd – 2002.
League Cup: never past 2nd rd.

Record Attendance: 10,389 v Blackpool, FA Cup 3rd rd, 13 January 1934 (at Cheltenham Athletic Ground); 8,326 v Reading, FA Cup 1st rd, 17 November 1956 (at Whaddon Road).

Pitch Measurements: 102.5m × 66m (112yd × 72yd)

Chairman: Paul Baker.

Vice-chairman: Colin Farmer.

Manager: Gary Johnson.

Assistant Manager: Russell Milton.

Senior Sports Therapist: Gavin Crowe.

Colours: Red and white striped shirts, black shorts, black socks.

Year Formed: 1892.

Turned Professional: 1932.

Club Nickname: 'The Robins'.

Grounds: Pre-1932, Agg-Gardner's Recreation Ground; Whaddon Lane; Carter's Lane; 1932, Whaddon Road (renamed The Abbey Business Stadium 2009, World of Smile Stadium 2015).

First Football League Game: 7 August 1999, Division 3, v Rochdale (h) L 0–2 – Book; Griffin, Victory, Banks, Freeman, Brough (Howarth), Howells, Bloomer (Devaney), Grayson, Watkins (McAuley), Yates.

Record League Victory: 5–0 v Mansfield T, FL 2, 6 May 2006 – Higgs; Gallinagh, Bell, McCann (1) (Connolly), Caines, Duff, Wilson, Bird (1p), Gillespie (1) (Spencer), Guinan (Odejayi (1)), Vincent (1).

Record Cup Victory: 12–0 v Chippenham R, FA Cup 3rd qual. rd, 2 November 1935 – Bowles; Whitehouse, Williams; Lang, Devonport (1), Partridge (2); Perkins, Hackett, Jones (4), Black (4), Griffiths (1).

sky SPORTS FACT FILE

Cheltenham Town fielded a full semi-professional team from the 1935–36 season following their election to the Southern League. The Robins also appointed a new manager in George Carr, the former Middlesbrough and Leicester City player.

Record Defeat: 1–8 v Crewe Alex, FL 2, 2 April 2011; 0–7 v Crystal Palace, League Cup 2nd rd, 2 October 2014.
N.B. 1–10 v Merthyr T, Southern League, 8 March 1952.

Most League Points (2 for a win): 60, Southern League Division 1, 1963–64.

Most League Points (3 for a win): 78, Division 3, 2001–02.

Most League Goals: 66, Division 3, 2001–02; 66, FL 2, 2011–12.

Highest League Scorer in Season: Julian Alsop, 20, Division 3, 2001–02.

Most League Goals in Total Aggregate: Julian Alsop, 39, 2000–03; 2009–10.

Most League Goals in One Match: 3, Martin Devaney v Plymouth Arg, Division 3, 23 September 2000; 3, Neil Grayson v Cardiff C, Division 3, 1 April 2001; 3, Damien Spencer v Hull C, Division 3, 23 August 2003; 3, Damien Spencer v Milton Keynes D, FL 1, 31 January 2009; 3, Michael Pook v Burton Alb, FL 2, 13 March 2010.

Most Capped Player: Grant McCann, 7 (39), Northern Ireland.

Most League Appearances: David Bird, 288, 2001–11.

Youngest League Player: Kyle Haynes, 17 years 85 days v Oldham Ath, 24 March 2009.

Record Transfer Fee Received: £400,000 from Colchester U for Steve Gillespie, July 2008.

Record Transfer Fee Paid: £60,000 to Aldershot T for Jermaine McGlashan, January 2012.

Football League Record: 1999 Promoted to Division 3; 2002 Division 2; 2003–04 Division 3; 2004–06 FL 2; 2006–09 FL 1; 2009–15 FL 2; 2015–16 National League; 2016–17 FL 2.

LATEST SEQUENCES

Longest Sequence of League Wins: 5, 29.10.2011 – 10.12.2011.

Longest Sequence of League Defeats: 7, 27.1.2009 – 28.2.2009.

Longest Sequence of League Draws: 5, 5.4.2003 – 21.4.2003.

Longest Sequence of Unbeaten League Matches: 16, 1.12.2001 – 12.3.2002.

Longest Sequence Without a League Win: 14, 20.12.2008 – 7.3.2009.

Successive Scoring Runs: 17 from 16.2.2008.

Successive Non-scoring Runs: 5 from 10.3.2012 – 30.3.2012.

MANAGERS

George Blackburn 1932–34
George Carr 1934–37
Jimmy Brain 1937–48
Cyril Dean 1948–50
George Summerbee 1950–52
William Raeside 1952–53
Arch Anderson 1953–58
Ron Lewin 1958–60
Peter Donnelly 1960–61
Tommy Cavanagh 1961
Arch Anderson 1961–65
Harold Fletcher 1965–66
Bob Etheridge 1966–73
Willie Penman 1973–74
Dennis Allen 1974–79
Terry Paine 1979
Alan Grundy 1979–82
Alan Wood 1982–83
John Murphy 1983–88
Jim Barron 1988–90
John Murphy 1990
Dave Lewis 1990–91
Ally Robertson 1991–92
Lindsay Parsons 1992–95
Chris Robinson 1995–97
Steve Cotterill 1997–2002
Graham Allner 2002–03
Bobby Gould 2003
John Ward 2003–07
Keith Downing 2007–08
Martin Allen 2008–09
Mark Yates 2009–14
Paul Buckle 2014–15
Gary Johnson March 2015–

TEN YEAR LEAGUE RECORD

		P	W	D	L	F	A	Pts	Pos
2006-07	FL 1	46	15	9	22	49	61	54	17
2007-08	FL 1	46	13	12	21	42	64	51	19
2008-09	FL 1	46	9	12	25	51	91	39	23
2009-10	FL 2	46	10	18	18	54	71	48	22
2010-11	FL 2	46	13	13	20	56	77	52	17
2011-12	FL 2	46	23	8	15	66	50	77	6
2012-13	FL 2	46	20	15	11	58	51	75	5
2013-14	FL 2	46	15	16	17	53	63	55	17
2014-15	FL 2	46	9	14	23	40	67	41	23
2015-16	NL	46	30	11	5	87	30	101	1

DID YOU KNOW ?

The first Cheltenham Town player to gain international honours was goalkeeper Frank Davis who was capped for England Amateurs against Wales in January 1934. Soon afterwards he signed professional forms for the club.

CHESTERFIELD

FOUNDATION

Chesterfield are fourth only to Stoke, Notts County and Nottingham Forest in age for they can trace their existence as far back as 1866, although it is fair to say that they were somewhat casual in the first few years of their history, playing only a few friendlies a year. However, their rules of 1871 are still in existence, showing an annual membership of 2s (10p), but it was not until 1891 that they won a trophy (the Barnes Cup) and followed this a year later by winning the Sheffield Cup, Barnes Cup and the Derbyshire Junior Cup.

The Proact Stadium, 1866 Sheffield Road, Whittington Moor, Chesterfield, Derbyshire S41 8NZ.

Telephone: (01246) 269 300.

Fax: (01246) 556 799.

Ticket Office: (01246) 269 300.

Website: www.chesterfield-fc.co.uk

Email: reception@chesterfield-fc.co.uk

Ground Capacity: 10,401.

Record Attendance: 30,968 v Newcastle U, Division 2, 7 April 1939 (at Saltergate); 10,089 v Rotherham U, FL 2, 18 March 2011 (at b2net Stadium (now called the Proact Stadium)).

Pitch Measurements: 103m × 67m (112.5yd × 73.5yd).

Chairman: Dave Allen.

Chief Executive: Chris Turner.

Manager: Danny Wilson.

First-Team Coach: Chris Morgan.

Sports Science and Medicine: Jamie Hewitt.

Colours: Blue shirts with white trim, white shorts with blue trim, blue socks with white trim.

Year Formed: 1866.

Turned Professional: 1891.

Previous Name: 1867, Chesterfield Town; 1919, Chesterfield.

Club Nicknames: 'The Blues', 'The Spireites'.

Grounds: 1867, Drill Field; 1871, Recreation Ground, Saltergate; 2010, b2net Stadium (renamed The Proact Stadium 2012).

First Football League Game: 2 September 1899, Division 2, v Sheffield W (a) L 1–5 – Hancock; Pilgrim, Fletcher; Ballantyne, Bell, Downie; Morley, Thacker, Gooing, Munday (1), Geary.

Record League Victory: 10–0 v Glossop NE, Division 2, 17 January 1903 – Clutterbuck; Thorpe, Lerper; Haig, Banner, Thacker; Tomlinson (2), Newton (1), Milward (3), Munday (2), Steel (2).

Record Cup Victory: 6–0 v Braintree T (a), FA Cup 1st rd, 8 November 2014 – Lee; Darikwa, Evatt, Raglan, Jones (Humphreys), Morsy, Ryan, O'Shea (1) (Gardner), Clucas (1), Roberts (1) (Boco), Doyle (2), own goal (1).

HONOURS

League Champions: Division 3N – 1930–31, 1935–36; FL 2 – 2010–11, 2013–14; Division 4 – 1969–70, 1984–85.
Runners-up: Division 3N – 1933–34.
FA Cup: semi-final – 1997.
League Cup: 4th rd – 1965, 2007.
League Trophy Winners: 2012.
Runners-up: 2014.
Anglo-Scottish Cup Winners: 1981.

sky SPORTS FACT FILE

Chesterfield reached the final of the FA Youth Cup in 1955–56 when they were narrowly defeated by Manchester United by 4-3 on aggregate over the two legs. A crowd of 15,838 watched the second leg of the match at the Recreation Ground.

Record Defeat: 0–10 v Gillingham, Division 3, 5 September 1987.

Most League Points (2 for a win): 64, Division 4, 1969–70.

Most League Points (3 for a win): 91, Division 4, 1984–85.

Most League Goals: 102, Division 3 (N), 1930–31.

Highest League Scorer in Season: Jimmy Cookson, 44, Division 3 (N), 1925–26.

Most League Goals in Total Aggregate: Ernie Moss, 162, 1969–76, 1979–81 and 1984–86.

Most League Goals in One Match: 4, Jimmy Cookson v Accrington S, Division 3 (N), 16 January 1926; 4, Jimmy Cookson v Ashington, Division 3 (N), 1 May 1926; 4, Jimmy Cookson v Wigan Borough, Division 3 (N), 4 September 1926; 4, Tommy Lyon v Southampton, Division 2, 3 December 1938.

Most Capped Player: Walter McMillen, 4 (7), Northern Ireland; Mark Williams, 4 (36), Northern Ireland.

Most League Appearances: Dave Blakey, 617, 1948–67.

Youngest League Player: Dennis Thompson, 16 years 160 days v Notts Co, 26 December 1950.

Record Transfer Fee Received: £1,300,000 from Hull C for Sam Clucas, July 2015.

Record Transfer Fee Paid: £250,000 to Watford for Jason Lee, August 1998.

Football League Record: 1899 Elected to Division 2; 1909 failed re-election; 1921–31 Division 3 (N); 1931–33 Division 2; 1933–36 Division 3 (N); 1936–51 Division 2; 1951–58 Division 3 (N); 1958–61 Division 3; 1961–70 Division 4; 1970–83 Division 3; 1983–85 Division 4; 1985–89 Division 3; 1989–92 Division 4; 1992–95 Division 3; 1995–2000 Division 2; 2000–01 Division 3; 2001–04 Division 2; 2004–07 FL 1; 2007–11 FL 2; 2011–12 FL 1; 2012–14 FL 2; 2014– FL 1.

LATEST SEQUENCES

Longest Sequence of League Wins: 10, 6.9.1933 – 4.11.1933.

Longest Sequence of League Defeats: 9, 22.10.1960 – 27.12.1960.

Longest Sequence of League Draws: 8, 26.11.2005 – 2.1.2006.

Longest Sequence of Unbeaten League Matches: 21, 26.12.1994 – 29.4.1995.

Longest Sequence Without a League Win: 18, 11.9.1999 – 3.1.2000.

Successive Scoring Runs: 46 from 25.12.1929.

Successive Non-scoring Runs: 7 from 23.9.1977.

MANAGERS

E. Russell Timmeus 1891–95 (*Secretary-Manager*)
Gilbert Gillies 1895–1901
E. F. Hind 1901–02
Jack Hoskin 1902–06
W. Furness 1906–07
George Swift 1907–10
G. H. Jones 1911–13
R. L. Weston 1913–17
T. Callaghan 1919
J. J. Caffrey 1920–22
Harry Hadley 1922
Harry Parkes 1922–27
Alec Campbell 1927
Ted Davison 1927–32
Bill Harvey 1932–38
Norman Bullock 1938–45
Bob Brocklebank 1945–48
Bobby Marshall 1948–52
Ted Davison 1952–58
Duggie Livingstone 1958–62
Tony McShane 1962–67
Jimmy McGuigan 1967–73
Joe Shaw 1973–76
Arthur Cox 1976–80
Frank Barlow 1980–83
John Duncan 1983–87
Kevin Randall 1987–88
Paul Hart 1988–91
Chris McMenemy 1991–93
John Duncan 1993–2000
Nicky Law 2000–01
Dave Rushbury 2002–03
Roy McFarland 2003–07
Lee Richardson 2007–09
John Sheridan 2009–12
Paul Cook 2012–15
Dean Saunders 2015
Danny Wilson December 2015–

TEN YEAR LEAGUE RECORD

		P	W	D	L	F	A	Pts	Pos
2006-07	FL 1	46	12	11	23	45	53	47	21
2007-08	FL 2	46	19	12	15	76	56	69	8
2008-09	FL 2	46	16	15	15	62	57	63	10
2009-10	FL 2	46	21	7	18	61	62	70	8
2010-11	FL 2	46	24	14	8	85	51	86	1
2011-12	FL 1	46	10	12	24	56	81	42	22
2012-13	FL 2	46	18	13	15	60	45	67	8
2013-14	FL 2	46	23	15	8	71	40	84	1
2014-15	FL 1	46	19	12	15	68	55	69	6
2015-16	FL 1	46	15	8	23	58	70	53	18

DID YOU KNOW ?

In the early 1890s Chesterfield Town, as the club was then known, wore shirts with a union flag covering the full area of the body of the shirt. The team was nicknamed 'the Union Jacks'.

CHESTERFIELD – FOOTBALL LEAGUE ONE 2015–16 LEAGUE RECORD

Match No.	Date		Venue	Opponents	Result		H/T Score	Lg Pos.	Goalscorers	Atten- dance
1	Aug	8	H	Barnsley	W	3-1	0-1	3	O'Shea [49], Ebanks-Blake [72], Morsy [73]	8117
2		15	A	Sheffield U	L	0-2	0-1	8		23,031
3		18	A	Shrewsbury T	W	2-1	0-0	5	Ebanks-Blake [49], Morsy [64]	4935
4		22	H	Rochdale	D	0-0	0-0	9		6254
5		29	A	Millwall	W	2-0	1-0	6	O'Shea 2 [17, 90]	8374
6	Sept	5	H	Wigan Ath	L	2-3	0-0	8	Gardner [62], Barnett (og) [68]	7145
7		12	H	Colchester U	D	3-3	1-1	7	Jones [22], Novak [62], Morsy [74]	5227
8		19	A	Coventry C	L	0-1	0-0	9		11,003
9		26	H	Burton Alb	L	1-2	1-0	15	Hird [2]	6752
10		29	A	Blackpool	L	0-2	0-1	17		5960
11	Oct	3	A	Crewe Alex	W	2-1	1-1	14	Gardner 2 [6, 57]	4053
12		10	H	Gillingham	L	1-3	1-1	16	Simons [35]	6026
13		17	A	Walsall	W	2-1	1-0	14	Ebanks-Blake [5], Evatt [54]	4766
14		20	H	Southend U	W	3-0	2-0	9	Novak [8], Ebanks-Blake 2 [37, 62]	5703
15		24	H	Scunthorpe U	L	0-3	0-0	13		6340
16		31	H	Fleetwood T	W	1-0	1-0	10	Ebanks-Blake [30]	3107
17	Nov	14	H	Oldham Ath	L	1-2	1-0	14	Ebanks-Blake [34]	6178
18		21	A	Port Vale	L	2-3	1-2	15	Novak [8], Simons [90]	4420
19		24	A	Doncaster R	L	0-3	0-0	15		5521
20		28	H	Swindon T	L	0-4	0-2	16		5540
21	Dec	12	A	Bury	L	0-1	0-0	17		2962
22		19	H	Bradford C	L	0-1	0-0	18		6795
23		26	A	Peterborough U	L	0-2	0-1	20		7153
24		28	H	Coventry C	D	1-1	1-0	20	Novak [38]	9057
25	Jan	2	A	Shrewsbury T	W	7-1	3-0	18	O'Shea 2 (1 pen) [28, 40 (p)], Novak 3 (1 pen) [45, 81 (p), 89], Simons 2 [73, 87]	6233
26		9	A	Rochdale	W	3-2	1-0	17	O'Shea [26], Novak [78], Ebanks-Blake [80]	2965
27		16	A	Wigan Ath	L	1-3	0-3	18	Banks [79]	9091
28		23	H	Millwall	L	1-2	1-1	18	Morsy [25]	7078
29	Feb	6	H	Peterborough U	L	0-1	0-0	19		6544
30		12	A	Burton Alb	L	0-1	0-1	19		4489
31		16	A	Colchester U	D	1-1	0-0	20	Novak (pen) [72]	6167
32		20	H	Crewe Alex	W	3-1	2-1	19	Ebanks-Blake [7], Novak [12], Dimaio [56]	6264
33		27	A	Gillingham	W	2-1	2-0	18	Ebanks-Blake [36], Novak [45]	6012
34	Mar	1	H	Blackpool	D	1-1	0-0	18	O'Shea [57]	5915
35		5	A	Southend U	W	1-0	0-0	17	Novak [89]	7518
36		12	H	Walsall	L	1-4	1-1	18	O'Connor (og) [19]	6938
37		19	A	Scunthorpe U	D	1-1	0-1	18	Campbell-Ryce [60]	3871
38		26	H	Fleetwood T	D	0-0	0-0	18		6435
39		28	A	Oldham Ath	L	0-1	0-0	18		4483
40	Apr	2	H	Port Vale	W	4-2	0-1	17	Campbell-Ryce [47], Hird [60], Ariyibi [73], O'Shea [83]	5917
41		9	A	Barnsley	W	2-1	0-0	17	Novak [57], Banks [81]	10,645
42		16	H	Sheffield U	L	0-3	0-2	17		9402
43		19	H	Doncaster R	D	1-1	1-1	18	Ariyibi [18]	6461
44		23	A	Swindon T	L	0-1	0-0	18		7015
45		30	H	Bury	W	3-0	2-0	18	O'Shea (pen) [29], Novak [45], Gardner [71]	7232
46	May	8	A	Bradford C	L	0-2	0-1	18		20,807

Final League Position: 18

GOALSCORERS

League (58): Novak 14 (2 pens), Ebanks-Blake 10, O'Shea 9 (2 pens), Gardner 4, Morsy 4, Simons 4, Ariyibi 2, Banks 2, Campbell-Ryce 2, Hird 2, Dimaio 1, Evatt 1, Jones 1, own goals 2.
FA Cup (5): Ariyibi 1, Banks 1, Morsy 1, Novak 1, Simons 1.
Capital One Cup (1): Dieseruvwe 1.
Johnstone's Paint Trophy (1): own goal 1.

Lee T 46	Talbot D 29 + 5	Hird S 39 + 1	Evatt I 23	Jones D 19	Gardner D 22 + 8	Morsy S 26	Banks O 24 + 8	Ariyibi G 27 + 11	O'Shea J 39 + 7	Ebanks-Blake S 29 + 4	Raglan C 22 + 5	Gnandullet A — + 9	Dieseruvwe E 3 + 13	Novak L 32 + 3	Martinez A 3	O'Neil L 24 + 2	Humphreys R — + 3	Fitzwater J — + 1	Harrison B — + 3	Donohue D 15 + 2	Herd C 20 + 3	Simons R 6 + 14	Wood R 4 + 1	Daley D 1	Anderson T 18	Liddle G 15	Dimaio C 9 + 2	John D 5 + 1	Slew J — + 7	Campbell-Ryce J 6 + 3	Orrell J — + 2	Match No.
1	2²	3	4	5	6	7	8	9³	10	11¹	12	13	14																			1
1	2³	3	4	5	8²	7	9¹	12	6	10	13	14		11																		2
1	6	2	4	5	3²	7		12	9	10¹		13		11	8																	3
1	2	3	4	5	7²	8	13	12	6	11¹		14		10³	9																	4
1		3	4	5	6¹	2		9²	11	10²	14	13	12			7	8															5
1		3	4	5	10	7	6	8³	9		12	13		11¹		2²	14															6
1	2⁴		3	5	10³	6	7	8¹	9		4			11²				12	13	14												7
1		3	4	5	8²	6	14	12	9	11		13⁵	10¹			7				2³												8
1	2	4	3	5	10²	6		8	9	11¹		13				7					12											9
1	13	3	4	5	8¹	7	9³		6	10	11	12				6				2²	14											10
1	13	12	4	5	9	7		6		3	14	11³				8				2¹	10²											11
1			4	5	9	8		10	11	3		12				2					7¹	6										12
1	2		4	5	8	7		10	11¹	3		12	9²								6	13										13
1	2		3	5	9¹	8		6	11³	4	13	10				12					7²	14										14
1	2	4		5⁴	9	8³	14	6	11¹	3		10				13					7²	12										15
1	5	2	4		9¹	7		13	6	10	3	12									8	11²										16
1	2		3	5	9³	7		14	6	11	13			10							8¹	12	4²									17
1		2	4	5	6¹	8	13	12	9	10				11							7³	14	3²									18
1		2	3	5	6¹	8	12	14	9	10				11²							7³	13	4									19
1			4	5²		6	7	9	8		3			12	11¹	2					13	10										20
1	5	2	3		13	6	9		12	10	4			11¹		7³				8³		14										21
1	5²	9	4		13		8	7¹	6	11	3					2¹	12			10		14										22
1		6	4		7²		9		8	11	3³			2						10		14	12	5¹								23
1		4	3¹			7	14	10	9³	11		13	12			2				8	6²		5									24
1		4			14	8		9³	6¹	10²	3			11		2			13	5	7	12										25
1		4			13	8	12	9⁴	6³	10²	3			14	11	2				5	7¹											26
1	13	4			6³	7	12		9	10¹	3			11		8				2	5²	14										27
1	2³	3			12	8		6¹	9	10²	4			14	11	7			13	5												28
1	6³	3			14			13	9¹	10²				11		2				5	7	12			4	8						29
1	8	4			12		13	7	10			14				2³				5	6¹	11²			3	9						30
1	2	4				6	8	9	11²	13		10³	12			5					14				3	7⁴	8¹					31
1	2	4				8	9	12	10¹			13	11			6²									3		7	5				32
1	2	4				8²	9	13	10¹				11	6							12				3		7	5				33
1	2	3				9	8	12	11²				10	6							4					7¹	5	13				34
1		3				8	7	12					11	2							5				4	6	9	10¹				35
1	2³	3				9	6	10²	13				11¹		14					5⁴					4	7	8	12				36
1	13	4				9²	6	10					11	2											3	8	7¹	5		12		37
1	5	3				8	9	11¹	13				10²	2						6³					4	7			14	12		38
1	5	8				9²	12	10¹	3				11	2									11¹		4	7		13	6²	14		39
1	5	2				8	12	13	4				10										11¹		3	7	6³		9²	14		40
1	5	3				8	10	7	2				11¹								13				4	9		12	6⁴			41
1	5	3				10	9	6	2				11												4	8	7¹	12				42
1	5	3				7	9	10¹	12				11							13					4	8				6²		43
1	5	4				9	8	10	2⁴				11¹							6²					3	7		13	12	9³		44
1	2	4		12		8	10²	9					11			5									3	6	13		7¹			45
1	12	3⁴		11¹		7	6	10	2					5											4²	8	14	13	9³			46

FA Cup

First Round	FC United of Manchester	(a)	4-1
Second Round	Walsall	(h)	1-1
Replay	Walsall	(a)	0-0

(aet; Walsall won 5-3 on penalties)

Capital One Cup

First Round	Carlisle U	(a)	1-3

(aet)

Johnstone's Paint Trophy

Second Round	Rochdale	(a)	1-2

COLCHESTER UNITED

*Weston Homes Community Stadium, United Way,
Colchester, Essex CO4 5UP.*

Telephone: (01206) 755 100.

Fax: (01206) 715 327.

Ticket Office: (0845) 437 9089.

Website: www.cu-fc.com

Email: media@colchesterunited.net

Ground Capacity: 10,105.

Record Attendance: 19,072 v Reading, FA Cup 1st rd,
27 November 1948 (at Layer Road); 10,064 v Norwich C, FL 1, 16 January 2010 (at Community
Stadium).

Pitch Measurements: 100.5m × 65m (110yd × 71yd).

Executive Chairman: Robbie Cowling.

Vice-chairman: Richard Cowling.

Manager: John McGreal.

Assistant Manager: Steve Ball.

Physio: Tony Flynn.

Colours: Royal blue and white striped shirts, royal blue shorts with white trim, white socks with royal
blue trim.

Year Formed: 1937.

Turned Professional: 1937.

Club Nickname: 'The U's'.

Grounds: 1937, Layer Road; 2008, Weston Homes Community Stadium.

First Football League Game: 19 August 1950, Division 3 (S), v Gillingham (a) D 0–0 – Wright; Kettle,
Allen; Bearryman, Stewart, Elder; Jones, Curry, Turner, McKim, Church.

Record League Victory: 9–1 v Bradford C, Division 4, 30 December 1961 – Ames; Millar, Fowler;
Harris, Abrey, Ron Hunt; Foster, Bobby Hunt (4), King (4), Hill (1), Wright.

Record Cup Victory: 9-1 v Leamington, FA Cup 1st rd, 5 November 2005 – Davison; Stockley
(Garcia), Duguid, Brown (1), Chilvers, Watson (1), Halford (1), Izzet (Danns) (2), Iwelumo (1)
(Williams), Cureton (2), Yeates (1).

Record Defeat: 0–8 v Leyton Orient, Division 4, 15 October 1988.

Most League Points (2 for a win): 60, Division 4, 1973–74.

Most League Points (3 for a win): 81, Division 4, 1982–83.

Most League Goals: 104, Division 4, 1961–62.

Highest League Scorer in Season: Bobby Hunt, 38, Division 4, 1961–62.

Most League Goals in Total Aggregate: Martyn King, 130, 1956–64.

Most League Goals in One Match: 4, Bobby Hunt v Bradford C, Division 4, 30 December 1961; 4, Martyn King v Bradford C, Division 4, 30 December 1961; 4, Bobby Hunt v Doncaster R, Division 4, 30 April 1962.

Most Capped Player: Bela Balogh, 2 (9), Hungary.

Most League Appearances: Micky Cook, 613, 1969–84.

Youngest League Player: Lindsay Smith, 16 years 218 days v Grimsby T, 24 April 1971.

Record Transfer Fee Received: £2,500,000 from Reading for Greg Halford, January 2007.

Record Transfer Fee Paid: £400,000 to Cheltenham T for Steve Gillespie, July 2008.

Football League Record: 1950 Elected to Division 3 (S); 1958–61 Division 3; 1961–62 Division 4; 1962–65 Division 3; 1965–66 Division 4; 1966–68 Division 3; 1968–74 Division 4; 1974–76 Division 3, 1976–77 Division 4; 1977–81 Division 3; 1981–90 Division 4; 1990–92 Conference; 1992–98 Division 3; 1998–2004 Division 2; 2004–06 FL 1; 2006–08 FL C; 2008–16 FL 1; 2016– FL 2.

MANAGERS

Ted Fenton 1946–48
Jimmy Allen 1948–53
Jack Butler 1953–55
Benny Fenton 1955–63
Neil Franklin 1963–68
Dick Graham 1968–72
Jim Smith 1972–75
Bobby Roberts 1975–82
Allan Hunter 1982–83
Cyril Lea 1983–86
Mike Walker 1986–87
Roger Brown 1987–88
Jock Wallace 1989
Mick Mills 1990
Ian Atkins 1990–91
Roy McDonough 1991–94
George Burley 1994
Steve Wignall 1995–99
Mick Wadsworth 1999
Steve Whitton 1999–2003
Phil Parkinson 2003–06
Geraint Williams 2006–08
Paul Lambert 2008–09
Aidy Boothroyd 2009–10
John Ward 2010–12
Joe Dunne 2012–14
Tony Humes 2014–15
Kevin Keen 2015–16
John McGreal May 2016–

LATEST SEQUENCES

Longest Sequence of League Wins: 7, 31.12.2005 – 7.2.2006.

Longest Sequence of League Defeats: 9, 31.10.2015 – 28.12.2015.

Longest Sequence of League Draws: 6, 21.3.1977 – 11.4.1977.

Longest Sequence of Unbeaten League Matches: 20, 22.12.1956 – 19.4.1957.

Longest Sequence Without a League Win: 20, 2.3.1968 – 31.8.1968.

Successive Scoring Runs: 24 from 15.9.1962.

Successive Non-scoring Runs: 5 from 11.2.2006.

TEN YEAR LEAGUE RECORD

		P	W	D	L	F	A	Pts	Pos
2006-07	FL C	46	20	9	17	70	56	69	10
2007-08	FL C	46	7	17	22	62	86	38	24
2008-09	FL 1	46	18	9	19	58	58	63	12
2009-10	FL 1	46	20	12	14	64	52	72	8
2010-11	FL 1	46	16	14	16	57	63	62	10
2011-12	FL 1	46	13	20	13	61	66	59	10
2012-13	FL 1	46	14	9	23	47	68	51	20
2013-14	FL 1	46	13	14	19	53	61	53	16
2014-15	FL 1	46	14	10	22	58	77	52	19
2015-16	FL 1	46	9	13	24	57	99	40	23

DID YOU KNOW ?

Colchester United went straight into the Southern League following their formation. Their first-ever game in the competition was on 28 August 1937 when they lost 3-0 away to Yeovil & Petters United.

COLCHESTER UNITED – FOOTBALL LEAGUE ONE 2015–16 LEAGUE RECORD

Match No.	Date	Venue	Opponents	Result	H/T Score	Lg Pos.	Goalscorers	Attendance
1	Aug 8	H	Blackpool	D	2-2	1-2	8	Gilbey [22], Ambrose [56]	4438
2	15	A	Peterborough U	L	1-2	1-2	17	Bonne [30]	5339
3	18	A	Oldham Ath	D	0-0	0-0	18		2917
4	22	A	Fleetwood T	L	0-4	0-2	23		2888
5	29	H	Scunthorpe U	D	2-2	1-2	20	Moncur [33], Elokobi [81]	3019
6	Sept 12	A	Chesterfield	D	3-3	1-1	22	Massey [29], Moncur [76], Raglan (og) [90]	5227
7	15	A	Sheffield U	W	3-2	2-0	19	Moncur 2 [6, 23], Sordell [82]	17,623
8	19	H	Gillingham	W	2-1	2-1	12	Massey [4], Harriott [29]	4694
9	26	A	Swindon T	W	2-1	2-1	10	Moncur [3], Harriott [42]	6687
10	29	A	Bradford C	W	2-0	2-0	8	Harriott [7], Sordell [32]	3334
11	Oct 3	H	Bury	L	0-1	0-0	10		4032
12	10	A	Shrewsbury T	L	2-4	2-0	12	Ellis (og) [36], Eastman [79]	4947
13	17	A	Wigan Ath	L	0-5	0-4	16		8048
14	20	H	Port Vale	W	2-1	1-1	12	Elokobi [25], Sordell [73]	2785
15	24	A	Walsall	D	4-4	0-2	15	Moncur [49], Sordell [52], Garvan [60], Ambrose [80]	3630
16	31	A	Doncaster R	L	0-2	0-1	16		5324
17	Nov 14	H	Coventry C	L	1-3	1-2	17	Bonne [17]	5275
18	21	A	Millwall	L	1-4	0-2	17	Porter [55]	8739
19	24	H	Crewe Alex	L	2-3	1-0	19	Harriott [40], Moncur [48]	2602
20	28	A	Burton Alb	L	1-5	1-2	20	Harriott [4]	2893
21	Dec 12	H	Barnsley	L	2-3	0-2	22	Moncur [67], Porter [70]	3265
22	19	A	Rochdale	L	1-3	1-2	24	Porter [21]	2205
23	26	H	Southend U	L	0-2	0-0	24		9222
24	28	A	Gillingham	L	0-1	0-0	24		7109
25	Jan 2	A	Oldham Ath	D	1-1	0-1	23	Porter [81]	3535
26	16	H	Sheffield U	L	1-2	0-1	23	Eastman [59]	4322
27	19	H	Fleetwood T	D	1-1	1-0	22	Gilbey [38]	2493
28	23	A	Scunthorpe U	L	0-3	0-0	22		3332
29	Feb 6	A	Southend U	L	0-3	0-0	24		10,279
30	13	H	Swindon T	L	1-4	0-1	24	Edwards [64]	3269
31	16	H	Chesterfield	D	1-1	0-0	24	Bonne [69]	6167
32	20	A	Bury	L	2-5	2-1	24	Porter [4], Massey [17]	3428
33	27	H	Shrewsbury T	D	0-0	0-0	24		3057
34	Mar 1	A	Bradford C	W	2-1	1-1	24	Ambrose 2 [23, 57]	16,786
35	5	A	Port Vale	L	0-2	0-1	24		4116
36	12	H	Wigan Ath	D	3-3	1-2	24	Gilbey [40], Lee [50], Moncur (pen) [60]	3761
37	19	A	Walsall	L	1-2	1-0	24	Gilbey [45]	5818
38	25	H	Doncaster R	W	4-1	0-1	23	Porter [62], Lee [71], Gilbey [72], Brindley [87]	3771
39	29	A	Coventry C	W	1-0	1-0	23	Massey [18]	10,027
40	Apr 2	H	Millwall	D	0-0	0-0	23		5377
41	9	A	Blackpool	W	1-0	0-0	23	Porter [60]	6242
42	16	H	Peterborough U	L	1-4	0-1	23	Moncur [76]	5965
43	19	A	Crewe Alex	D	1-1	0-0	23	Moncur (pen) [65]	3094
44	23	H	Burton Alb	L	0-3	0-1	23		4292
45	30	A	Barnsley	D	2-2	1-0	23	Moncur [42], Lapslie [90]	12,021
46	May 8	H	Rochdale	L	1-2	0-1	23	Edwards [53]	3435

Final League Position: 23

GOALSCORERS

League (57): Moncur 12 (2 pens), Porter 7, Gilbey 5, Harriott 5, Ambrose 4, Massey 4, Sordell 4, Bonne 3, Eastman 2, Edwards 2, Elokobi 2, Lee 2, Brindley 1, Garvan 1, Lapslie 1, own goals 2.
FA Cup (12): Bonne 4, Harriott 2, Moncur 2, Sordell 2, Lapslie 1, own goal 1.
Capital One Cup (0).
Johnstone's Paint Trophy (2): Bonne 2.

Parish E 25	Brindley R 17+4	Eastman T 43	Wynter A 9+3	Briggs M 25+1	Gilbey A 31+6	Edwards J 40+2	Massey G 37+5	Moncur G 40+5	Ambrose D 13+12	Porter C 26+6	Bonne M 13+20	Vincent-Young K 10+4	Sembie-Ferris D 1+7	Szmidics S 1+4	Elokobi G 15+2	Harriott C 19+1	Garvan O 28+4	Wright D 1+10	Jones J 17	Sordell M 19+2	Kent F 23+3	Olufemi T 10	Lapslie T 7+3	Kean J 3	Lee E 11+4	Shorey N 13+2	Harney J 1+3	Chambers L 5+1	Oduwa N —+2	Akinwande F 1+1	Dunne L 1+1	Bransgrove J 1	James C —+1	Match No.
1	2	3	4	5^1	6	7	8	9	10^1	11^3	12	13	14																					1
1	2	4	3	5^2	7	6^1	9	8^3	11			10	12	13	14																			2
1	2	4	3		8	7	11			9^1		10	5	12	6																			3
1	5^2	4	3		8	7^3	11	9	6^1		10	2	12	14	13																			4
1		3		5	6	7^3	8	9^1		11^2	2		14	4	10	12	13																	5
	3		5^1	8	7^2	9	12			13	2			4	11	6		1	10															6
	3		5		8	6	7^3	12		14	9		4^4	11^1	2		1	10^2	13															7
	4		5	13	6	8	9^1	12			2			10^2	7		1	11	3															8
	3		5	13	6	8	9^1	12		14				10^2	7		1	11^2	4	2														9
	4		5		6	8	9^1		12					10	7		1	11	3	2														10
	4		5	12	6^2	8	9		13					10	7		1	11	3	2^1														11
	4			13	6^2	9	8^1			12				5	10	7		1	11	3	2													12
	4		5	8	7^2		13	12	11^3			6^1			9		1	10	3	2	14													13
	3		5	6	12		9	8^2			13			4	10	7^1	1	11		2														14
	4			6	13		9^1	8			12			5	10^2	7	1	11	3	2														15
	4		5	6			7	8^2	13					3^1	10	9	1	11	12	2														16
	4^1		5	7	3	13	9			8				12	2		1	11	10		6^2													17
	3			6	2	8	9		12	7				4	10		1	11^1		5														18
	4			6	8	9		11^1	12						10		1		3	2	7													19
	2^2	4		5	6	7	8^1	9		11			13		10		1	12	3															20
	2	3		5^1	8	6^2	9^1	7		12	14	13			4	11	1	10																21
	4	5		2	6	8^1	10^2	9		11	14		12		3	7	1	13^3																22
1		3	2	5	6	7^1	14	9	8^3	11	12			4	10^2			13																23
1	2	3		5	6	8^2	9^3	7		11^1				4	12	14	13	10																24
1	2	3	13	5^2	6	7^3	9	8^1	14	10				4	12		11																	25
	2^2	4	3	5	7		6^1	9	12	11	13				8		10				1													26
	2	3	4	5	7		6^3	9		11^2	13				8	12	10^1				1	14												27
	2	3	4	5	7		6^3	13		9^2	12	11	14		8		10^1				1													28
1	5	2			12^3	7^4	6	9^2	10^1	13	11				4		8					3			14									29
1	2	4			8	6^3	7	9^1	10^2	13					12	14						3			11	5								30
1	2	3				8^2	14	13	6^3	10	9	5			4		7	12							11^1									31
1	5^3	3^4			7	6	13	9^1	11^2	10	2				8						4						14	12						32
1					6	11^1	7		10^2	13	5				8	9^3					4				12	2		3	14					33
1		4			12	6	8	9^1	10^3	11	13	5			7								2	14	3									34
1		3				6	7	10^2	8^3	9	11^1	14			2							13	5	4		12								35
1		4		5	7	2	12	9		13	11^3				6							10^2			3			8^1	14					36
1				7	2	8	9^2	13	11^1	14					6	12					4		10^3	5	3									37
1	13	3			7	2	9	8		10^3	14				6						12		11^2	5	4^1									38
1	12	4			8	2^1	6	9^2		10					7						3	13	11^1	5	14									39
1	2^1	4			7		6^3	10	13	11		12						14			3	8^2	9	5										40
1	13	4			7^2	2	8	9^1	14	11					6						3	12	10^1	5										41
1		4				2	8^1	9	12	11^3	13				6						3	7^2	10	5					14					42
1	12	4			6	2	8	9^2		11	10^1				7						3			5		13								43
1		4	12			2^4	8^2	13		11^1	10				6	14					3		7	5						9^3				44
1	4^1	12		13		2	9^2	6		11					7	14					3		8	10^3	5									45
	4	5^1		6	2^1	9	7			13	11^2										3		10	8	12							1	14	46

FA Cup

First Round	Wealdstone	(a)	6-2
Second Round	Altrincham	(h)	3-2
Third Round	Charlton Ath	(h)	2-1
Fourth Round	Tottenham H	(h)	1-4

Capital One Cup

First Round	Reading	(h)	0-1
(aet)			

Johnstone's Paint Trophy

First Round	Northampton T	(a)	2-3

COVENTRY CITY

FOUNDATION

Workers at Singers' cycle factory formed a club in 1883. The first success of Singers' FC was to win the Birmingham Junior Cup in 1891 and this led in 1894 to their election to the Birmingham & District League. Four years later they changed their name to Coventry City and joined the Southern League in 1908 at which time they were playing in blue and white quarters.

Ricoh Arena, Phoenix Way, Coventry CV6 6GE.

Telephone: (02476) 991 987.

Ticket Office: (02476) 991 987.

Website: www.ccfc.co.uk

Email: info@ccfc.co.uk

Ground Capacity: 32,604.

Record Attendance: 51,455 v Wolverhampton W, Division 2, 29 April 1967 (at Highfield Road); 31,407 v Chelsea, FA Cup 6th rd, 7 March 2009 (at Ricoh Arena).

Pitch Measurements: 100m × 68m (109.5yd × 74.5yd).

Chairman: Tim Fisher.

Managing Director: Chris Anderson.

Manager: Tony Mowbray.

First-Team Coach: Jamie Clapham.

Physio: David Hart.

Colours: Sky blue and white striped shirts, dark blue shorts, sky blue socks.

Year Formed: 1883.

Turned Professional: 1893.

Previous Name: 1883, Singers' FC; 1898, Coventry City.

Club Nickname: 'Sky Blues'.

Grounds: 1883, Binley Road; 1887, Stoke Road; 1899, Highfield Road; 2005, Ricoh Arena; 2013, Sixfields Stadium (groundshare with Northampton T); 2014, Ricoh Arena.

First Football League Game: 30 August 1919, Division 2, v Tottenham H (h) L 0–5 – Lindon; Roberts, Chaplin, Allan, Hawley, Clarke, Sheldon, Mercer, Sambrooke, Lowes, Gibson.

Record League Victory: 9–0 v Bristol C, Division 3 (S), 28 April 1934 – Pearson; Brown, Bisby; Perry, Davidson, Frith; White (2), Lauderdale, Bourton (5), Jones (2), Lake.

Record Cup Victory: 8–0 v Rushden & D, League Cup 2nd rd, 2 October 2002 – Debec; Caldwell, Quinn, Betts (1p), Konjic (Shaw), Davenport, Pipe, Safri (Stanford), Mills (2) (Bothroyd (2)), McSheffery (3), Partridge.

Record Defeat: 2–10 v Norwich C, Division 3 (S), 15 March 1930.

Most League Points (2 for a win): 60, Division 4, 1958–59 and Division 3, 1963–64.

HONOURS

League Champions: Division 2 – 1966–67; Division 3 – 1963–64; Division 3S – 1935–36.
Runners-up: Division 3S – 1933–34; Division 4 – 1958–59.
FA Cup Winners: 1987.
League Cup: semi-final – 1981, 1990.
European Competitions
Fairs Cup: 1970–71.

sky SPORTS FACT FILE

When Coventry City played their Southern League game at Mardy in December 1914, the score was reported as a 2-1 win for the home team. However, the score recorded in the league records was 1-1 and this is what was included in the season's final table.

Most League Points (3 for a win): 69, FL 1, 2015–16.

Most League Goals: 108, Division 3 (S), 1931–32.

Highest League Scorer in Season: Clarric Bourton, 49, Division 3 (S), 1931–32.

Most League Goals in Total Aggregate: Clarrie Bourton, 173, 1931–37.

Most League Goals in One Match: 5, Clarrie Bourton v Bournemouth, Division 3 (S), 17 October 1931; 5, Arthur Bacon v Gillingham, Division 3 (S), 30 December 1933.

Most Capped Player: Magnus Hedman, 44 (58), Sweden.

Most League Appearances: Steve Ogrizovic, 507, 1984–2000.

Youngest League Player: Ben Mackey, 16 years 167 days v Ipswich T, 12 April 2003.

Record Transfer Fee Received: £13,000,000 from Internazionale for Robbie Keane, July 2000.

Record Transfer Fee Paid: £6,500,000 to Norwich C for Craig Bellamy, August 2000.

Football League Record: 1919 Elected to Division 2; 1925–26 Division 3 (N); 1926–36 Division 3 (S); 1936–52 Division 2; 1952–58 Division 3 (S); 1958–59 Division 4; 1959–64 Division 3; 1964–67 Division 2; 1967–92 Division 1; 1992–2001 FA Premier League; 2001–04 Division 1; 2004–12 FL C; 2012– FL 1.

LATEST SEQUENCES

Longest Sequence of League Wins: 6, 25.4.1964 – 5.9.1964.

Longest Sequence of League Defeats: 9, 30.8.1919 – 11.10.1919.

Longest Sequence of League Draws: 6, 1.11.2003 – 29.11.2003.

Longest Sequence of Unbeaten League Matches: 25, 26.11.1966 – 13.5.1967.

Longest Sequence Without a League Win: 19, 30.8.1919 – 20.12.1919.

Successive Scoring Runs: 25 from 10.9.1966.

Successive Non-scoring Runs: 11 from 11.10.1919.

MANAGERS

H. R. Buckle 1909–10
Robert Wallace 1910–13
  (*Secretary-Manager*)
Frank Scott-Walford 1913–15
William Clayton 1917–19
H. Pollitt 1919–20
Albert Evans 1920–24
Jimmy Kerr 1924–28
James McIntyre 1928–31
Harry Storer 1931–45
Dick Bayliss 1945–47
Billy Frith 1947–48
Harry Storer 1948–53
Jack Fairbrother 1953–54
Charlie Elliott 1954–55
Jesse Carver 1955–56
George Raynor 1956
Harry Warren 1956–57
Billy Frith 1957–61
Jimmy Hill 1961–67
Noel Cantwell 1967–72
Bob Dennison 1972
Joe Mercer 1972–75
Gordon Milne 1972–81
Dave Sexton 1981–83
Bobby Gould 1983–84
Don Mackay 1985–86
George Curtis 1986–87
  (*became Managing Director*)
John Sillett 1987–90
Terry Butcher 1990–92
Don Howe 1992
Bobby Gould 1992–93
  (*with Don Howe, June 1992*)
Phil Neal 1993–95
Ron Atkinson 1995–96
  (*became Director of Football*)
Gordon Strachan 1996–2001
Roland Nilsson 2001–02
Gary McAllister 2002–04
Eric Black 2004
Peter Reid 2004–05
Micky Adams 2005–07
Iain Dowie 2007–08
Chris Coleman 2008–10
Aidy Boothroyd 2010–11
Andy Thorn 2011–12
Mark Robins 2012–13
Steven Pressley 2013–15
Tony Mowbray March 2015–

TEN YEAR LEAGUE RECORD

		P	W	D	L	F	A	Pts	Pos
2006-07	FL C	46	16	8	22	47	62	56	17
2007-08	FL C	46	14	11	21	52	64	53	21
2008-09	FL C	46	13	15	18	47	58	54	17
2009-10	FL C	46	13	15	18	47	64	54	19
2010-11	FL C	46	14	13	19	54	58	55	18
2011-12	FL C	46	9	13	24	41	65	40	23
2012-13	FL 1	46	18	11	17	66	59	55*	15
2013-14	FL 1	46	16	13	17	74	77	51*	18
2014-15	FL 1	46	13	16	17	49	60	55	17
2015-16	FL 1	46	19	12	15	67	49	69	8

* 10 pts deducted.

DID YOU KNOW ?

Coventry City's Highfield Road ground became England's first all-seater stadium for the 1981–82 season. Gates dropped and the move was so unpopular that terracing was quietly reintroduced. The scheme was abandoned altogether at the beginning of 1983.

COVENTRY CITY – FOOTBALL LEAGUE ONE 2015–16 LEAGUE RECORD

Match No.	Date	Venue	Opponents	Result	H/T Score	Lg Pos.	Goalscorers	Attendance
1	Aug 8	H	Wigan Ath	W 2-0	1-0	4	Armstrong 2 [15, 62]	13,131
2	15	A	Millwall	W 4-0	3-0	1	Armstrong 2 [6, 24], Lameiras [19], O'Brien [80]	11,197
3	18	H	Crewe Alex	W 3-2	1-1	1	Fleck [14], Armstrong [51], O'Brien [83]	11,511
4	22	A	Walsall	L 1-2	0-1	3	Murphy [56]	7176
5	31	H	Southend U	D 2-2	1-2	5	Johnson [34], Ricketts [72]	12,967
6	Sept 6	A	Burton Alb	W 2-1	1-1	2	Tudgay [20], Vincelot [56]	4633
7	12	A	Scunthorpe U	L 0-1	0-0	4		3746
8	19	H	Chesterfield	W 1-0	0-0	4	Armstrong [50]	11,003
9	26	A	Bury	L 1-2	0-1	4	Johnson [62]	4526
10	Oct 3	H	Shrewsbury T	W 3-0	2-0	5	Armstrong 2 [26, 65], Fortune (pen) [45]	11,445
11	10	H	Fleetwood T	W 1-0	0-0	5	Wood (og) [90]	3864
12	17	H	Blackpool	D 0-0	0-0	5		12,094
13	20	A	Rochdale	D 0-0	0-0	4		2495
14	24	A	Swindon T	D 2-2	0-0	4	Vincelot [66], Tudgay [81]	8309
15	31	H	Peterborough U	W 3-2	0-2	4	Vincelot [56], Armstrong 2 [80, 87]	11,853
16	Nov 3	H	Barnsley	W 4-3	2-0	4	Kent [3], Armstrong 2 [18, 52], Cole [60]	10,954
17	14	A	Colchester U	W 3-1	2-1	2	Murphy 2 [32, 40], Fortune [49]	5275
18	21	H	Gillingham	W 4-1	4-0	1	Murphy 3 [34, 41, 44], Turner [37]	15,604
19	24	A	Bradford C	D 0-0	0-0	1		17,757
20	28	H	Doncaster R	D 2-2	1-0	1	Armstrong [30], Fleck [59]	11,885
21	Dec 13	A	Sheffield U	L 0-1	0-0	2		18,074
22	19	H	Oldham Ath	D 1-1	0-0	3	Martin [49]	15,419
23	26	H	Port Vale	W 1-0	0-0	4	Maddison [80]	17,779
24	28	A	Chesterfield	D 1-1	0-1	4	Maddison [89]	9057
25	Jan 2	A	Crewe Alex	W 5-0	4-0	4	Armstrong 3 (1 pen) [11, 30 (p), 45], Murphy 2 [27, 85]	5946
26	12	H	Walsall	D 1-1	1-0	4	Stokes [34]	15,671
27	16	H	Burton Alb	L 0-2	0-0	4		17,140
28	23	A	Southend U	L 0-3	0-2	5		8767
29	30	H	Scunthorpe U	L 1-2	0-1	5	Armstrong (pen) [86]	11,138
30	Feb 7	A	Port Vale	D 1-1	1-0	5	Murphy [42]	6320
31	13	H	Bury	W 6-0	4-0	5	Stokes [4], Cargill [12], Maddison [16], Fleck [43], Armstrong 2 [68, 70]	11,024
32	27	A	Fleetwood T	L 1-2	0-0	6	Tudgay [75]	11,160
33	Mar 1	A	Barnsley	L 0-2	0-1	6		9344
34	5	H	Rochdale	L 0-1	0-0	7		9942
35	8	A	Shrewsbury T	L 1-2	1-2	8	Martin [4]	6023
36	12	A	Blackpool	W 1-0	1-0	7	Fortune [26]	8869
37	19	A	Swindon T	D 0-0	0-0	8		12,322
38	25	A	Peterborough U	L 1-3	0-1	9	Cole [65]	6021
39	29	H	Colchester U	L 0-1	0-1	9		10,027
40	Apr 2	A	Gillingham	D 0-0	0-0	11		7200
41	9	A	Wigan Ath	L 0-1	0-0	13		10,415
42	16	H	Millwall	W 2-1	0-1	12	Fleck [61], Tudgay [70]	11,632
43	19	H	Bradford C	W 1-0	0-0	11	Rose [59]	10,241
44	23	A	Doncaster R	L 0-2	0-2	12		6364
45	30	H	Sheffield U	W 3-1	2-0	9	Fortune [4], Rose [8], Lameiras [87]	13,177
46	May 8	A	Oldham Ath	W 2-0	0-0	8	Vincelot [74], Armstrong [81]	4928

Final League Position: 8

GOALSCORERS

League (67): Armstrong 20 (2 pens), Murphy 9, Fleck 4, Fortune 4 (1 pen), Tudgay 4, Vincelot 4, Maddison 3, Cole 2, Johnson 2, Lameiras 2, Martin 2, O'Brien 2, Rose 2, Stokes 2, Cargill 1, Kent 1, Ricketts 1, Turner 1, own goal 1.
FA Cup (1): Murphy 1.
Capital One Cup (1): Tudgay 1.
Johnstone's Paint Trophy (0).

Burge L 9	Willis J 4	Ricketts S 43	Johnson R 12	Stokes C 36	Lameiras R 18 + 11	Vincelot R 45	Fleck J 40	O'Brien J 20 + 6	Maddison J 14 + 9	Armstrong A 38 + 2	Phillips A 17 + 6	Morris B 1 + 5	Thomas G 2 + 5	Murphy J 29 + 11	Tudgay M 6 + 19	Martin A 29	Fortune M 14 + 11	Thomas C — + 3	Haynes R 4 + 5	Kent R 10 + 7	Charles-Cook R 37	Cole J 18 + 4	Turner B 5	Bigirimana G 9 + 4	Ramage P 3 + 1	Hunt S 5	Lorentzson M 5 + 2	Rose A 7 + 5	Stephens J 16	Cargill B 5	Henderson D — + 5	Jones J 4 + 2	Gatzhev V — + 2	Harries C 1	Kelly-Evans D — + 1	Match No.
1		2³	3	4	5	6¹	7	8	9²	10	11	12	13	14																						1
1		2	3	4	5	9³	7	8	6	10²	11¹			14	12	13																				2
1		2	3	4	5	8¹	6	7	10²	9³	11			14		12	13																			3
1		2²	4	3	5	8	6	7	10¹	9³	11		14	13			12																			4
1		3	4	5	9¹	6	7	8		11	2			10	12																					5
1		2	3	5	9²	7	6	8		10¹	11³						4	12	13	14																6
1		2	4	5	8³	6	7		11		14	10¹	9¹		3	13				12																7
1		2	4	5	13	7	6	8¹		11²		10			3	12		9																	8
1		2	3	5		6	7	8²		11		10¹	12		4	13		9																	9
		2	4	5	14	6	7¹		11		12	10²	13	3	8³		9	1																	10
		2	3	5	9²	6	7	8¹		12	10	13	4	11	14		1																	11
		2	4²	5	12	6¹	7		9	14	13	10	3	11	8¹	1																		12
		3		5		6		10	8¹	2	7	14	12	4	11¹	13	1	9²																	13
		4		5	12	6	7	8	11³	2	13	14	3	10¹	1	9²																			14
		3		5²	8¹	6	7	13	9	2	10	4	11³	14	12	1																			15
		4		5	12	6	7	10³	11	2	13	14	3	8¹	1	9²																			16
		4		5	8³	6	7	10¹		2	9	12	3	11²	14	13	1																		17
		2		5		6	7	9³	11	12	10²	3		14	8	1	4¹	13																	18
		2		5	9¹	7	12	6	10	4	11²	13	1	3	8																				19
		2		5	6	7	10	11	9	3	8	1	4																							20
		2¹		5	10²	7³	8	6¹	11	9	3	14	13	1	12	4																			21
		5		6	10	14	11	2	3	13	12	8¹	1	9²	4³	7																			22
		4		5	8³	6	13	12	11	2	10²	3	14	1	9¹	7																			23
		2		5	3	6	10	9	12	4²	13	14	11³	7	8¹	1																			24
		2		5		7	6²	14	9¹	11	3	10	4	13	1	8³	12																		25
		3		4	6	7	8¹	12	11	2	10	13	5	1	9²																				26
		4		5	8¹	6	7	9²	11	2³	10	12	1	14	13	3																			27
		2	3	13	6¹	8	12	11¹	14	5²	1	9	7	4	10																				28
		3		6¹	13	9	11	14	10	1	7³	4	8¹	2³	12																				29
		4		5	6	14	10¹	11	9²	1	12	8³	7	2	3	13																			30
		3		5	12	6	7	8¹	11	10²	1	9	13	2	4																				31
		2		5	13	6	7	9¹	11	8³	14	12	1	10³	3	2	4																		32
		3		5	8²	7	14	10	6	11¹	1	9³	12	3	2	4	13																		33
		2		5	8²	6	7	9	11	13	14	1	10³	12	3	4¹																			34
		5	2	12	8²	7	14	11	6¹	4	10	1	9³	3	13																				35
		2		5	6	7	8²	9	10¹	14	4	11³	1	13	12	3																			36
		5		6	7	12	9	13	3	11²	1	10¹	2³	8	4	14																			37
		5		3	6	9	14	4	11²	1	10	7³	2	8¹	13	12																			38
		5	13	6	7	14	10²	12	3	11¹	1	9	2³	4	8																				39
		2		9	7	12	5	10	11	3	1	6	4	8¹																					40
		2		9³	8	10	5	14	11³	3	13	1	12	7²	4	6																			41
		5²	10³	6¹	7	12	11	2	13	3	1	9	14	8	4																				42
		5	8¹	6	7	9³	11	2	14	3	1	10²	13	12	4																				43
		2	7³	6	14	11	5	10²	13	4	1	9	3	8¹	12																				44
		14	2	7	11	13	10³	3	8²	1	6	5	9¹	4	12																				45
		11²	2	6	10	9	14	3	8²	1	8	5¹	7³	3	13	4	12																			46

FA Cup
First Round   Northampton T   (h)   1-2

Capital One Cup
First Round   Rochdale   (a)   1-1
(aet; Rochdale won 5-3 on penalties)

Johnstone's Paint Trophy
Second Round   Yeovil T   (a)   0-0
(aet; Yeovil won 4-3 on penalties)

CRAWLEY TOWN

FOUNDATION

Formed in 1896, Crawley Town initially entered the West Sussex League before switching to the mid-Sussex League in 1901, winning the Second Division in its second season. The club remained at such level until 1951 when it became members of the Sussex County League and five years later moved to the Metropolitan League while remaining as an amateur club. It was not until 1962 that the club turned semi-professional and a year later, joined the Southern League. Many honours came the club's way, but the most successful run was achieved in 2010–11 when they reached the fifth round of the FA Cup and played before a crowd of 74,778 spectators at Old Trafford against Manchester United. Crawley Town spent 48 years at the Town Mead ground before a new site was occupied at Broadfield in 1997, ideally suited to access from the neighbouring motorway. History was also made on 9 April when the team won promotion to the Football League after beating Tamworth 3-0 to stretch their unbeaten League record to 26 games. They finished the season with a Conference record points total of 105 and at the same time, established another milestone for the longest unbeaten run, having extended it to 30 matches by the end of the season.

Checkatrade.com Stadium, Winfield Way, Crawley, West Sussex RH11 9RX.

Telephone: (01293) 410 000.

Fax: (01293) 410 002.

Ticket Office: (01293) 410 005.

Website: www.crawleytownfc.com

Email: feedback@crawleytownfc.com

Ground Capacity: 5,748.

Record Attendance: 5,880 v Reading, FA Cup 3rd rd, 5 January 2013.

Pitch Measurements: 103.5m × 66m (113yd × 72yd).

Chairman: Ziya Eren.

Operations Director: Kelly Derham.

Manager: Dermont Drummy.

Assistant Manager: Matt Gray.

Physio: Paul Wilson.

Colours: Red and black shirts, red shorts with black trim, red socks with black trim.

Year Formed: 1896. *Turned Professional:* 1962.

Club Nickname: 'The Red Devils'.

Grounds: Up to 1997, Town Mead; 1997 Broadfield Stadium (renamed Checkatrade.com Stadium 2013).

First Football League Game: 6 August 2011, FL 2 v Port Vale (a) D 2-2 – Shearer; Hunt, Howell, Bulman, McFadzean (1), Dempster (Thomas), Simpson, Torres, Tubbs (Neilson), Barnett (1) (Wassmer), Smith.

HONOURS

League Champions: Conference – 2010–11.
FL 2 – (3rd) 2011–12 *(promoted)*.
FA Cup: 5th rd – 2011, 2012.
League Cup: 3rd rd – 2013.

sky SPORTS FACT FILE

Fred Cook was appointed as the first full-time manager of Crawley Town from January 1962 having previously held the post on a part-time basis from July 1961. At the time the club were members of the Metropolitan League but had ambitions of gaining a place in the Southern League.

Record League Victory: 5–1 v Barnsley, FL 1, 14 February 2015 – Price; Dickson, Bradley (1), Ward, Fowler (Smith); Young, Elliott (1), Edwards, Wordsworth (Morgan), Pogba (Tomlin); McLeod (3).

Record League Defeat: 6-0 v Morecambe, FL 2, 10 September 2011.

Most League Points (3 for a win): 84, FL 2, 2011–12.

Most League Goals: 76, FL 2, 2011–12.

Highest League Scorer in Season: Izale McLeod, 19, 2014–15.

Most League Goals in Total Aggregate: Billy Clarke, 20, 2011–14; Matt Tubbs, 20, 2011–12, 2013–14.

Most League Goals in One Match: 3, Izale McLeod v Barnsley, FL 1, 14 February 2015.

Most Capped Player: Dean Morgan, 1 (3), Montserrat.

Most League Appearances: Josh Simpson, 122, 2011–15.

Youngest League Player: Hiram Boateng, 18 years 55 days v Stevenage, 4 March 2014.

Record Transfer Fee Received: £1,100,000 from Peterborough U for Tyrone Barnett, July 2012.

Record Transfer Fee Paid: £100,000 to Peterborough U for Sergio Raul Torres, July 2010; £100,000 to Peterborough U for Emile Sinclair, August 2013.

Football League Record: 2011 Promoted from Conference Premier; 2011–12 FL 2; 2012–15 FL 1; 2015– FL 2.

MANAGERS

John Maggs 1978–90
Brian Sparrow 1990–92
Steve Wicks 1992–93
Ted Shepherd 1993–95
Colin Pates 1995–96
Billy Smith 1997–99
Cliff Cant 1999–2000
Billy Smith 2000–03
Francis Vines 2003–05
John Hollins 2005–06
David Woozley, Ben Judge, John Yems 2006–07
Steve Evans 2007–12
Sean O'Driscoll 2012
Richie Barker 2012–13
John Gregory 2013–14
Dean Saunders 2014–15
Mark Yates 2015–16
Dermot Drummy April 2016–

LATEST SEQUENCES

Longest Sequence of League Wins: 7, 17.9.2011 – 25.10.2011.

Longest Sequence of League Defeats: 8, 28.3.2016 – 7.5.2016.

Longest Sequence of League Draws: 5, 25.10.2014 – 29.11.2014.

Longest Sequence of Unbeaten League Matches: 13, 17.9.2011 – 17.12.2011.

Longest Sequence Without a League Win: 13, 25.10.2014 – 27.1.2015.

Successive Scoring Runs: 16 from 17.9.2011.

Successive Non-scoring Runs: 4 from 22.10.2013.

TEN YEAR LEAGUE RECORD

		P	W	D	L	F	A	Pts	Pos
2006-07	Conf	46	17	12	17	52	52	53	18
2007-08	Conf P	46	19	9	18	73	67	60	15
2008-09	Conf P	46	19	14	13	77	55	70	9
2009-10	Conf P	44	19	9	16	50	57	66	7
2010-11	Conf P	46	31	12	3	93	50	105	1
2011-12	FL 2	46	23	15	8	76	54	84	3
2012-13	FL 1	46	18	14	14	59	58	68	10
2013-14	FL 1	46	14	15	17	48	54	57	14
2014-15	FL 1	46	13	11	22	53	79	50	22
2015-16	FL 2	46	13	8	25	45	78	47	20

DID YOU KNOW ?

Crawley Town competed in the Brighton & District League in the early post-war period before moving up to the Sussex County League for 1951–52. Player-coach at the time was Tom Jarvie who had made over 200 appearances for Hamilton Academical between 1936 and 1944.

CRAWLEY TOWN – FOOTBALL LEAGUE TWO 2015–16 LEAGUE RECORD

Match No.	Date	Venue	Opponents		Result	H/T Score	Lg Pos.	Goalscorers	Attendance
1	Aug 8	A	Oxford U	D	1-1	0-0	10	Edwards [56]	6349
2	15	H	AFC Wimbledon	L	1-2	1-0	17	Edwards [34]	2988
3	18	H	Portsmouth	D	0-0	0-0	19		4003
4	22	A	Cambridge U	W	3-0	1-0	11	Deacon 2 [39, 47], Edwards [87]	5459
5	29	H	Wycombe W	D	0-0	0-0	14		2466
6	Sept 12	A	Mansfield T	L	0-4	0-1	19		2524
7	19	H	Yeovil T	L	0-1	0-1	22		2112
8	22	A	Notts Co	L	1-4	1-2	23	Murphy [24]	3267
9	26	H	Accrington S	L	0-3	0-2	23		1659
10	29	A	Newport Co	W	3-0	2-0	21	Edwards 2 [36, 42], Harrold [61]	2137
11	Oct 3	A	Plymouth Arg	L	1-2	0-1	21	Deacon [85]	7173
12	10	H	Leyton Orient	W	3-2	3-1	18	Deacon [27], Hancox [37], Walton (pen) [45]	2575
13	17	H	Luton T	W	2-1	0-1	18	Murphy [67], Harrold [81]	3335
14	20	A	Morecambe	L	1-3	0-1	18	Murphy [84]	1098
15	24	A	Hartlepool U	W	2-1	0-0	17	Walton (pen) [66], Murphy [76]	3262
16	31	H	York C	W	1-0	0-0	15	Walton (pen) [86]	1950
17	Nov 14	A	Exeter C	D	2-2	1-2	16	Bradley [28], Rooney [90]	3664
18	21	H	Bristol R	W	2-1	2-0	14	Murphy 2 [9, 10]	2612
19	24	H	Northampton T	L	1-2	0-2	15	Walton (pen) [61]	2325
20	28	A	Carlisle U	L	1-3	1-2	16	Murphy [34]	4641
21	Dec 12	A	Dagenham & R	W	3-2	2-0	15	Harrold [40], Murphy 2 [45, 82]	1543
22	19	A	Barnet	L	2-4	0-1	16	Hancox [76], Smith, J [79]	1888
23	26	H	Stevenage	W	2-1	0-0	12	Edwards [68], Deacon [90]	2289
24	28	A	Wycombe W	L	0-2	0-1	13		4153
25	Jan 2	A	Portsmouth	L	0-3	0-2	14		16,606
26	9	H	Cambridge U	W	1-0	1-0	13	Harrold [36]	2320
27	16	H	Notts Co	L	0-1	0-0	15		2074
28	23	A	Yeovil T	L	1-2	0-0	16	Barnard [83]	3423
29	30	H	Mansfield T	L	0-1	0-0	17		1981
30	Feb 6	A	Stevenage	W	1-0	1-0	15	Harrold [44]	2639
31	13	A	Accrington S	L	1-4	1-0	15	Edwards [21]	1374
32	20	H	Plymouth Arg	D	1-1	0-0	16	Fenelon [83]	3522
33	27	A	Leyton Orient	L	0-2	0-1	17		4610
34	Mar 1	H	Newport Co	W	2-0	1-0	16	Boden (og) [36], Fenelon [53]	2003
35	5	H	Morecambe	D	1-1	0-0	16	Harrold [54]	1697
36	12	A	Luton T	W	1-0	1-0	16	Harrold [12]	8264
37	19	H	Hartlepool U	D	0-0	0-0	16		1883
38	25	A	York C	D	2-2	1-1	16	Harrold [5], McAlinden [48]	2942
39	28	H	Exeter C	L	0-2	0-1	16		2416
40	Apr 2	A	Bristol R	L	0-3	0-0	16		8250
41	9	H	Oxford U	L	1-5	1-1	17	McNerney [28]	3340
42	16	A	AFC Wimbledon	L	0-1	0-0	18		4356
43	19	A	Northampton T	L	1-2	0-0	18	Edwards [85]	5327
44	23	H	Carlisle U	L	0-1	0-0	18		1940
45	30	A	Dagenham & R	L	0-3	0-0	20		1643
46	May 7	H	Barnet	L	0-3	0-1	20		2293

Final League Position: 20

GOALSCORERS

League (45): Murphy 9, Edwards 8, Harrold 8, Deacon 5, Walton 4 (4 pens), Fenelon 2, Hancox 2, Barnard 1, Bradley 1, McAlinden 1, McNerney 1, Rooney 1, Smith, J 1, own goal 1.
FA Cup (1): Harrold 1.
Capital One Cup (0).
Johnstone's Paint Trophy (0).

Woodman F 11	Donnelly L 9+1	McNerney J 10+1	Ashton J 26+4	Bradley S 46	Walton S 31+6	Smith J 29+2	Rooney L 9+10	Edwards G 40+2	Barnard L 14+14	Deacon R 21+16	Henderson C 2+1	Young L 29+9	Harrold M 33+4	Van Den Bogaert B 1	Bawling B 7+8	Scales C 7+1	Jenkins R 7+7	Murphy R 15	Fenelon S 9+21	Yorwerth J 23+1	Hancox M 15	Preston C 9	Tomlin G 11+5	Flahavan D 13	Emmanuel J 1+1	Smith G 4	Atkinson C 5+2	Jones P 8	Dallison T 1	Bond A 11+1	Della Verde L 10+2	Oyebanjo L 7	Dunne C 12	Sutherland F 10+1	McAlinden L 5+1	Rose J 5	Match No.
1	2	3	4	5	6^2	7	8	9	10^3	11^1	12	13	14																								1
1	4		5	3	7^2	8	6	9	12	10^1		13	11	2																							2
1	2	3	4	5	9	7	8^1	6	11^2			10	12					13																			3
1	5^1	3	2	4	8	14		7	13	11^2		6^1	10^1					12	9																		4
1	2^1		4	3	8	7	12	9	10			6	11					5																			5
1	2^1	3	4	7	8	13	6^4	12	11			9^1	10^2					14	5																		6
1	2		3	4	8^1	7	6		10	11^3	9^2	12				13	5	14																			7
1	14		3	4	13	6	9^3		12	8		10				2^1	5^2	7	11																		8
1	2	3^1	4	7	9	6^4		14	12			10^2				5	8	11^3	13																		9
1	2			3	14			8^2		6^3		13				9	11	12	5	7		10^1	4														10
1	2		4	13	7		9	12	6^1	11						8^2	10^3	14	3	5																	11
	2^1	12	3	6	7		8		10^2			5	11					9^3	14		4	1	13														12
			5	2	3	12	7		8^1			4	6^2					13	9		10	11		1													13
			3	8	7	13	9		6^1			2	10^2					11	12	4	5		1														14
			4	7³	8		9		14			2	10					12 13	11^1	6^2	3	5		1													15
			4	8	7		6		13	12		2	10^2					11	9^1	3	5		1														16
		4^2	3	7	8		12		9 14	6		2	11^3					10^1	13		5		1														17
		14	4	7	8	12	9¹	13	6			2	10^2					11^3		3	5		1														18
			4	7^2	8	13	6	14	9			2	10^1					11^3	12	3	5		1														19
			3	8	7^1	13	9	14				2	6^1					11 12	4	5		1	2^3														20
			4	7	8^1	6	14	9^3				2	10^2					13 11 12		3	5		1														21
			4	7	8	6^2	9	13				2	10^1					11 12		3	5		1														22
			4	5	7	8	6	12	13			2	11^2					10^1	3	9	1																23
			4	5^2	7	8	6	10	11^1			2	12					13 3	5	9	1																24
		12	4	7	8^2	9^3	10	6				2	11					3^1	5	14	1	13															25
		3	4	7		13	6	10^2				2	11	12		8						9^1	1		5												26
		4	3	8		6	10^2 14	2	11				7^1	13								9^3	1		5 12												27
		2	4	6		9	13	10^3	5^1			11^1	14				3		1 12			8 7															28
			4	7		9	10^3 12	2^1 11	6			8^1	14	3		1						5 13															29
		3	4	8		12 6	5	11	7	13		2				10^1		9^2	1																		30
		2^2	4	5^1	10	14	9	11^3	6	12		13	3			7^1		8	1																		31
		3	9	11	10	5		12		2	6		8^1			1		4	7																		32
		3	4	10	11^1	9	12	5^3	13	2		7^2				6	1					8 14															33
		4	3	6^3 14	12	11	13	9^1	1	10		8	2^1			5	7																				34
		4	3	7	12	10	9	1	8			11^1				2	5 6																				35
		3	4	12	6	13	10	13	1			7	9^1			2	5		8	11^2																	36
		4	3	12	6	10		13				14	1			8^2	9^3		2	5	7	11^1															37
		4	3	8	6^1	12	11^2	13	1	14		2	9^3			5	7	10																			38
	14	4^3	3	8^1	12	13	9	11	1	6^2		2	5				7	10																			39
		3	13	6	14	8^1	9	11^3	12	5	1	2	10				4	7^2																			40
		3		5	7^1	13	6	11^2	12	4			10				14	9	2	8^3		1															41
		3	4	10	7^2	6	11^1	14	13	12		8	9^3			2	5		1																		42
		3	13	4	6	10	11	12	14	8^2			7^4			2^1	5	9^3	1																		43
		3	4^2	5	7	8	6	10	12	14		13	11^1			9^3	2	1																			44
		3^2	4	7	10	2	12	8	14	1		9^3	6			5	13	11^1																			45
		3	7	12	11^3	5	8	6^1	4	10^2	14		2			9	13	1																			46

FA Cup
First Round   Luton T   (h) 1-2

Capital One Cup
First Round   Peterborough U   (a) 0-2

Johnstone's Paint Trophy
Second Round   Southend U   (h) 0-3

CREWE ALEXANDRA

The Alexandra Stadium, Gresty Road, Crewe, Cheshire CW2 6EB.

Telephone: (01270) 213 014.

Fax: (01270) 216 320.

Ticket Office: (01270) 252 610.

Website: www.crewealex.net

Email: info@crewealex.net

Ground Capacity: 10,109.

Record Attendance: 20,000 v Tottenham H, FA Cup 4th rd, 30 January 1960.

Pitch Measurements: 100.5m × 67m (110yd × 73yd).

Chairman: John Bowler MBE.

Vice-chairman: David Rowlinson.

Director of Football: Dario Gradi MBE.

Manager: Steve Davis.

First-Team Coach: James Collins.

Head Physio: Rob Sharp.

Colours: Red shirts with white trim, white shorts with red trim, red socks with white trim.

Year Formed: 1877. *Turned Professional:* 1893. *Club Nickname:* 'The Railwaymen'.

Ground: 1898, Gresty Road.

First Football League Game: 3 September 1892, Division 2, v Burton Swifts (a) L 1–7 – Hickton; Moore, Cope; Linnell, Johnson, Osborne; Bennett, Pearson (1), Bailey, Barnett, Roberts.

Record League Victory: 8–0 v Rotherham U, Division 3 (N), 1 October 1932 – Foster; Pringle, Dawson; Ward, Keenor (1), Turner (1); Gillespie, Swindells (1), McConnell (2), Deacon (2), Weale (1).

Record Cup Victory: 8–0 v Hartlepool U, Auto Windscreens Shield 1st rd, 17 October 1995 – Gayle; Collins (1), Booty, Westwood (Unsworth), Macauley (1), Whalley (1), Garvey (1), Murphy (1), Savage (1) (Rivers (1p)), Lennon, Edwards, (1 og). 8–0 v Doncaster R, LDV Vans Trophy 3rd rd, 10 November 2002 – Bankole; Wright, Walker, Foster, Tierney; Lunt (1), Brammer, Sorvel, Vaughan (1) (Bell); Ashton (3) (Miles), Jack (2) (Jones (1)).

HONOURS
League: Runners-up: Second Division – 2002–03.
FA Cup: semi-final – 1888.
League Cup: never past 3rd rd.
League Trophy Winners: 2013.
Welsh Cup Winners: 1936, 1937.

Record Defeat: 2–13 v Tottenham H, FA Cup 4th rd replay, 3 February 1960.

Most League Points (2 for a win): 59, Division 4, 1962–63.

Most League Points (3 for a win): 86, Division 2, 2002–03.

Most League Goals: 95, Division 3 (N), 1931–32.

Highest League Scorer in Season: Terry Harkin, 35, Division 4, 1964–65.

Most League Goals in Total Aggregate: Bert Swindells, 126, 1928–37.

Most League Goals in One Match: 5, Tony Naylor v Colchester U, Division 3, 24 April 1993.

Most Capped Player: Clayton Ince, 38 (79), Trinidad & Tobago.

Most League Appearances: Tommy Lowry, 436, 1966–78.

Youngest League Player: Steve Walters, 16 years 119 days v Peterborough U, 6 May 1988.

Record Transfer Fee Received: £3,000,000 (rising to £6,000,000) from Manchester U for Nick Powell, June 2012.

Record Transfer Fee Paid: £650,000 to Torquay U for Rodney Jack, June 1998.

Football League Record: 1892 Original Member of Division 2; 1896 Failed re-election; 1921 Re-entered Division (N); 1958–63 Division 4; 1963–64 Division 3; 1964–68 Division 4; 1968–69 Division 3; 1969–89 Division 4; 1989–91 Division 3; 1991–92 Division 4; 1992–94 Division 3; 1994–97 Division 2; 1997–2002 Division 1; 2002–03 Division 2; 2003–04 Division 1; 2004–06 FL C; 2006–09 FL 1; 2009–12 FL 2; 2012–16 FL 1; 2016– FL 2.

LATEST SEQUENCES

Longest Sequence of League Wins: 7, 30.4.1994 – 3.9.1994.

Longest Sequence of League Defeats: 10, 16.4.1979 – 22.8.1979.

Longest Sequence of League Draws: 5, 18.9.2010 – 9.10.2010.

Longest Sequence of Unbeaten League Matches: 17, 25.3.1995 – 16.9.1995.

Longest Sequence Without a League Win: 30, 22.9.1956 – 6.4.1957.

Successive Scoring Runs: 26 from 7.4.1934.

Successive Non-scoring Runs: 9 from 6.11.1974.

MANAGERS

W. C. McNeill 1892–94
(*Secretary-Manager*)
J. G. Hall 1895–96
(*Secretary-Manager*)
R. Roberts (*1st team Secretary-Manager*) 1897
J. B. Blomerley 1898–1911
(*Secretary-Manager, continued as Hon. Secretary to 1925*)
Tom Bailey (*Secretary only*) 1925–38
George Lillycrop (*Trainer*) 1938–44
Frank Hill 1944–48
Arthur Turner 1948–51
Harry Catterick 1951–53
Ralph Ward 1953–55
Maurice Lindley 1956–57
Willie Cook 1957–58
Harry Ware 1958–60
Jimmy McGuigan 1960–64
Ernie Tagg 1964–71
(*continued as Secretary to 1972*)
Dennis Viollet 1971
Jimmy Melia 1972–74
Ernie Tagg 1974
Harry Gregg 1975–78
Warwick Rimmer 1978–79
Tony Waddington 1979–81
Arfon Griffiths 1981–82
Peter Morris 1982–83
Dario Gradi 1983–2007
Steve Holland 2007–08
Gudjon Thordarson 2008–09
Dario Gradi 2009–11
Steve Davis October 2011–

TEN YEAR LEAGUE RECORD

		P	W	D	L	F	A	Pts	Pos
2006-07	FL 1	46	17	9	20	66	72	60	13
2007-08	FL 1	46	12	14	20	47	65	50	20
2008-09	FL 1	46	12	10	24	59	82	46	22
2009-10	FL 2	46	15	10	21	68	73	55	18
2010-11	FL 2	46	18	11	17	87	65	65	10
2011-12	FL 2	46	20	12	14	67	59	72	7
2012-13	FL 1	46	18	10	18	54	62	64	13
2013-14	FL 1	46	13	12	21	54	80	51	19
2014-15	FL 1	46	14	10	22	43	75	52	20
2015-16	FL 1	46	7	13	26	46	83	34	24

DID YOU KNOW

Crewe Alexandra were one of the pioneering clubs to play under the early floodlighting systems of the 1870s. On 16 November 1878 Alexandra drew 0-0 with Nantwich in a game played under Grammes Lights. Both teams had a goal disallowed.

CREWE ALEXANDRA – FOOTBALL LEAGUE ONE 2015–16 LEAGUE RECORD

Match No.	Date	Venue	Opponents	Result		H/T Score	Lg Pos.	Goalscorers	Attendance
1	Aug 8	H	Port Vale	D	0-0	0-0	16		6751
2	15	A	Scunthorpe U	L	0-2	0-1	22		3188
3	18	A	Coventry C	L	2-3	1-1	23	Inman 31, Haber 53	11,511
4	22	H	Bury	D	3-3	2-2	20	King 3, Colclough 37, Inman 80	4125
5	29	A	Wigan Ath	L	0-1	0-1	23		8647
6	Sept 5	H	Swindon T	L	1-3	0-0	24	King 61	4400
7	12	H	Millwall	L	1-3	1-1	24	Dalla Valle 36	4293
8	19	A	Shrewsbury T	W	1-0	1-0	23	King 2	5481
9	26	A	Walsall	D	1-1	1-1	23	Nugent 18	4229
10	29	H	Southend U	L	1-2	0-0	24	Inman 49	3404
11	Oct 3	H	Chesterfield	L	1-2	1-1	24	Fox 36	4053
12	10	A	Barnsley	W	2-1	1-1	24	Colclough 14, Dalla Valle 79	8406
13	17	H	Gillingham	L	0-1	0-0	24		3924
14	20	A	Burton Alb	D	0-0	0-0	24		2666
15	24	H	Blackpool	L	0-2	0-0	24		6970
16	31	H	Sheffield U	W	1-0	0-0	24	Colclough 71	5227
17	Nov 14	A	Bradford C	L	0-2	0-1	24		17,546
18	21	H	Peterborough U	L	1-5	0-1	24	Colclough 64	4094
19	24	A	Colchester U	W	3-2	0-1	24	Colclough 61, Haber 80, Lowe 90	2602
20	28	H	Oldham Ath	W	1-0	1-0	23	King 21	3969
21	Dec 12	A	Doncaster R	L	2-3	1-1	24	Haber 26, Saunders 90	5342
22	19	H	Fleetwood T	D	1-1	1-1	23	Lowe 5	3749
23	28	H	Shrewsbury T	L	1-2	1-1	23	Colclough 26	5506
24	Jan 2	A	Coventry C	L	0-5	0-4	24		5946
25	16	A	Swindon T	L	3-4	3-1	24	Inman 2 20, 40, Colclough 26	6888
26	23	H	Wigan Ath	D	1-1	1-1	24	Inman 43	6010
27	26	A	Bury	D	0-0	0-0	23		2343
28	30	A	Millwall	D	1-1	0-0	23	Inman (pen) 59	9044
29	Feb 6	H	Rochdale	W	2-0	2-0	22	Haber 31, Inman 45	4130
30	13	H	Walsall	D	1-1	0-1	22	Inman 49	5123
31	16	A	Rochdale	D	2-2	2-2	22	Haber 24, Seager 27	1985
32	20	A	Chesterfield	L	1-3	1-2	23	Bakayogo 27	6264
33	27	H	Barnsley	L	1-2	1-0	23	Guthrie 32	4451
34	Mar 1	A	Southend U	D	1-1	0-0	23	Cooper 86	5444
35	5	H	Burton Alb	D	1-1	1-1	23	Haber 14	4380
36	12	A	Gillingham	L	0-3	0-1	23		5656
37	19	H	Blackpool	L	1-2	0-1	23	Haber 83	4480
38	25	A	Sheffield U	L	2-3	0-1	24	Fox 68, Davis 82	18,539
39	28	H	Bradford C	L	0-1	0-0	24		5320
40	Apr 2	A	Peterborough U	L	0-3	0-2	24		4881
41	9	A	Port Vale	L	0-3	0-1	24		5771
42	16	H	Scunthorpe U	L	2-3	1-1	24	Turton 15, Haber 79	3852
43	19	H	Colchester U	D	1-1	0-0	24	Saunders 90	3094
44	23	A	Oldham Ath	L	0-1	0-0	24		4571
45	30	H	Doncaster R	W	3-1	1-1	24	Ainley 43, Haber 57, Inman 89	4403
46	May 8	A	Fleetwood T	L	0-2	0-2	24		3302

Final League Position: 24

GOALSCORERS

League (46): Inman 10 (1 pen), Haber 9, Colclough 7, King 4, Dalla Valle 2, Fox 2, Lowe 2, Saunders 2, Ainley 1, Bakayogo 1, Cooper 1, Davis 1, Guthrie 1, Nugent 1, Seager 1, Turton 1.
FA Cup (0).
Capital One Cup (1): King 1.
Johnstone's Paint Trophy (2): Colclough 1, Haber 1.

Garratt B 46	Turton O 46	Ray G 19 + 3	Nugent B 39	Guthrie J 38 + 1	Bingham B 17 + 4	Fox D 39	King A 22 + 2	Haber M 36 + 4	Dalla Valle L 10 + 4	Colclough R 23 + 4	Inman B 33 + 6	Cooper G 13 + 14	Atkinson C 7 + 8	Saunders C 6 + 12	Baillie J 1 + 2	Kingsley S 9 + 3	Davis H 10 + 1	Ainley C 6 + 10	Wilson H 3 + 4	Jones J 29 + 2	Wintle R — + 3	Lowe R 5 + 1	Ajayi S 13	Ng P 1 + 5	Bakayogo Z 16 + 6	Howell J — + 2	Seager R 3 + 1	Kirk C 9 + 5	Hitchcock T 6 + 1	Udoh D 1 + 5	Match No.
1	2	3	4	5	6	7	8³	9¹	10	11²	12	13	14																		1
1	2	3	4	5	8	7¹	6	10⁵	9²	11	12	13	14																		2
1	2	3	4	5	8	7	6³	10²	12	9	11¹	13	14																		3
1	2	3²	4	5	8	6	7¹	9		11	10	13			12																4
1	2	3	4		8³	6	7	11¹	13	10	5	14	12			9²															5
1	2		4			6	8	10¹	9	11	12	7²				5	3	13													6
1	2		4			6¹	8	10²	9	11	13	7				5	3	12													7
1	2	13	4³	12	9	6	14	8¹	7²	10	5					11	3														8
1	2	12	4		9	6	14	8¹	7	10	5³					11	3²	13													9
1	2	5	7		6¹	4		11²	9	8	10	14					3	12	13												10
1	2	3	4			6	7	11	9	8	10¹	12				5															11
1	5	3	4			8		10		11	6	9				7	2														12
1	2	4	3			7	8	13	10²	11	9	12	14			5³	6¹														13
1	2	3	4	5		7	8	10¹		11	13	6²	14						9³	12											14
1	2	3	4	5	6¹	7³		10		11	12	14	13						9²	8											15
1	2	3	4	5	6		14	10		11³	8¹	13							9²	12	7										16
1	2	3	4	5³	6¹	7²	9	10		11	12	13										8	14								17
1	2	3	4	8	6¹		9³	10²		11	12					5						13	7	14							18
1	2	3²	4	5	6		10	11			8	13										9¹	7	12							19
1	2		4	5	6²	7	11	9³		12		8						13		10¹			3	14							20
1	2	3		5	6³	7	11	9¹		13		8						12		10²			4	14							21
1	2		4	5		7	8²	9¹		11	13	12					3			10		6									22
1	2		4	5		7	8¹	9		11	12						3			10		6									23
1	2		4	5		7²	8	9¹		11	12	13					3			10		6									24
1	2		4	5		7	8²	9		11¹	10	12					3					6	13								25
1	5	3	2				8	9¹		11	10									7		6	12		4						26
1	2	3		5	6		8	9¹		11	10²									7			13		4	12					27
1	2	3		5	6²	7	8	9¹		11	10												13		4		12				28
1	2	3		5	6²	7	8	9³		11¹	10												13		4	14	12				29
1	2	3		5	6	7	8	9¹		11²	10												13		4		12				30
1	2		4	5	6	7	8	9		11	12²									10¹			13		3						31
1	2		4	5	6	7	8	9²		11	10¹												13		3		12				32
1	2		4	5	6	7	8¹	9			10						13						13		3		12	11²			33
1	2	3	4		6¹	7³		9			10						13			8			14				5	11²	12		34
1	8	3¹	4		6	7		9			10					13							2				5	11²	12		35
1	2		4		6	7²				3³	13		14							8			9					12	11¹?	10¹	36
1	2	13	4		6	7	8³	9¹		3	10²		14			5												11²	12		37
1	5	3¹	4		6	7		9		2	10		14			8³												7	11²	12	38
1	2	3	4		6²		8				10					5				7			13					11¹	9	12	39
1	5	3	4		6		8³			2	10¹		14							7			13					9	12	11²	40
1	2	3	4		6	7¹		9			13		14			5³				8								11	12	10²	41
1	2	3	4	5	6	7	8	9²			10¹		14										13					11¹	12		42
1	2	3	4	5	6	7	8¹	9			10²		14															11³	12	13	43
1	2	3	4		6	7²	8				10												13					9	12	11¹	44
1	2	14	4	5	6	7	8	9²			10²														3				12	13	45
1	2	3	4	5	6	7		9			10³		14															8¹	12	13	46

FA Cup
First Round   Eastleigh   (h)   0-1

Capital One Cup
First Round   Preston NE   (h)   1-3

Johnstone's Paint Trophy
Second Round   Wigan Ath   (h)   2-3

CRYSTAL PALACE

FOUNDATION

There was a Crystal Palace club as early as 1861 but the present organisation was born in 1905 after the formation of a club by the company that controlled the Crystal Palace (building) had been rejected by the FA, who did not like the idea of the Cup Final hosts running their own club. A separate company had to be formed and they had their home on the old Cup Final ground until 1915.

Selhurst Park Stadium, Whitehorse Lane, London SE25 6PU.

Telephone: (020) 8768 6000.

Fax: (020) 8771 5311.

Ticket Office: (0871) 200 0071.

Website: www.cpfc.co.uk

Email: info@cpfc.co.uk

Ground Capacity: 25,073.

Record Attendance: 51,482 v Burnley, Division 2, 11 May 1979 (at Selhurst Park).

Pitch Measurements: 101m × 68m (109yd × 75yd).

Chairman: Steve Parish.

Chief Executive: Phil Alexander.

Manager: Alan Pardew.

Assistant Manager: Keith Millen.

Physio: Alex Manos.

HONOURS

League Champions: First Division – 1993–94; Division 2 – 1978–79; Division 3S – 1920–21.
Runners-up: Division 2 – 1968–69; Division 3 – 1963–64; Division 3S – 1928–29, 1930–31, 1938–39; Division 4 – 1960–61.
FA Cup: Runners-up: 1990, 2016.
League Cup: semi-final – 1993, 1995, 2001, 2012.
Full Members' Cup Winners: 1991.
European Competition
Intertoto Cup: 1998.

Colours: Red and blue striped shirts, blue shorts with red trim, blue socks with red trim.

Year Formed: 1905.

Turned Professional: 1905.

Club Nickname: 'The Eagles'.

Grounds: 1905, Crystal Palace; 1915, Herne Hill; 1918, The Nest; 1924, Selhurst Park.

First Football League Game: 28 August 1920, Division 3, v Merthyr T (a) L 1–2 – Alderson; Little, Rhodes; McCracken, Jones, Feebury; Bateman, Conner, Smith, Milligan (1), Whibley.

Record League Victory: 9–0 v Barrow, Division 4, 10 October 1959 – Rouse; Long, Noakes; Truett, Evans, McNichol; Gavin (1), Summersby (4 incl. 1p), Sexton, Byrne (2), Colfar (2).

Record Cup Victory: 8–0 v Southend U, Rumbelows League Cup 2nd rd (1st leg), 25 September 1990 – Martyn; Humphrey (Thompson (1)), Shaw, Pardew, Young, Thorn, McGoldrick, Thomas, Bright (3), Wright (3), Barber (Hodges (1)).

Record Defeat: 0–9 v Burnley, FA Cup 2nd rd replay, 10 February 1909; 0–9 v Liverpool, Division 1, 12 September 1990.

sky SPORTS FACT FILE

The Admiralty took over the old Crystal Palace ground soon after the First World War broke out and in January 1915 the club were informed that they could no longer play at the ground. At short notice they relocated to the nearby Herne Hill track, which was better known as a cycling venue.

Most League Points (2 for a win): 64, Division 4, 1960–61.

Most League Points (3 for a win): 90, Division 1, 1993–94.

Most League Goals: 110, Division 4, 1960–61.

Highest League Scorer in Season: Peter Simpson, 46, Division 3 (S), 1930–31.

Most League Goals in Total Aggregate: Peter Simpson, 153, 1930–36.

Most League Goals in One Match: 6, Peter Simpson v Exeter C, Division 3 (S), 4 October 1930.

Most Capped Player: Miles Jedinak, 38 (64), Australia.

Most League Appearances: Jim Cannon, 571, 1973–88.

Youngest League Player: John Bostock, 15 years 287 days v Watford, 29 October 2007.

Record Transfer Fee Received: £15,000,000 from Manchester U for Wilfried Zaha, January 2013.

Record Transfer Fee Paid: £13,000,000 to Newcastle U for Andros Townsend, July 2016.

Football League Record: 1920 Original Members of Division 3; 1921–25 Division 2; 1925–58 Division 3 (S); 1958–61 Division 4; 1961–64 Division 3; 1964–69 Division 2; 1969–73 Division 1; 1973–74 Division 2; 1974–77 Division 3; 1977–79 Division 2; 1979–81 Division 1; 1981–89 Division 2; 1989–92 Division 1; 1992–93 FA Premier League; 1993–94 Division 1; 1994–95 FA Premier League; 1995–97 Division 1; 1997–98 FA Premier League; 1998–2004 Division 1; 2004–05 FA Premier League; 2005–13 FL C; 2013– FA Premier League.

LATEST SEQUENCES

Longest Sequence of League Wins: 8, 9.2.1921 – 26.3.1921.

Longest Sequence of League Defeats: 8, 10.1.1998 – 14.3.1998.

Longest Sequence of League Draws: 5, 21.9.2002 – 19.10.2002.

Longest Sequence of Unbeaten League Matches: 18, 22.2.1969 – 13.8.1969.

Longest Sequence Without a League Win: 20, 3.3.1962 – 8.9.1962.

Successive Scoring Runs: 24 from 27.4.1929.

Successive Non-scoring Runs: 9 from 19.11.1994.

MANAGERS

John T. Robson 1905–07
Edmund Goodman 1907–25
  (*Secretary 1905–33*)
Alex Maley 1925–27
Fred Mavin 1927–30
Jack Tresadern 1930–35
Tom Bromilow 1935–36
R. S. Moyes 1936
Tom Bromilow 1936–39
George Irwin 1939–47
Jack Butler 1947–49
Ronnie Rooke 1949–50
Charlie Slade and Fred Dawes
  (*Joint Managers*) 1950–51
Laurie Scott 1951–54
Cyril Spiers 1954–58
George Smith 1958–60
Arthur Rowe 1960–62
Dick Graham 1962–66
Bert Head 1966–72 (*continued as General Manager to 1973*)
Malcolm Allison 1973–76
Terry Venables 1976–80
Ernie Walley 1980
Malcolm Allison 1980–81
Dario Gradi 1981
Steve Kember 1981–82
Alan Mullery 1982–84
Steve Coppell 1984–93
Alan Smith 1993–95
Steve Coppell (*Technical Director*) 1995–96
Dave Bassett 1996–97
Steve Coppell 1997–98
Attilio Lombardo 1998
Terry Venables (*Head Coach*) 1998–99
Steve Coppell 1999–2000
Alan Smith 2000–01
Steve Bruce 2001
Trevor Francis 2001–03
Steve Kember 2003
Iain Dowie 2003–06
Peter Taylor 2006–07
Neil Warnock 2007–10
Paul Hart 2010
George Burley 2010–11
Dougie Freedman 2011–12
Ian Holloway 2012–13
Tony Pulis 2013–14
Neil Warnock 2014
Alan Pardew January 2015–

TEN YEAR LEAGUE RECORD

		P	W	D	L	F	A	Pts	Pos
2006-07	FL C	46	18	11	17	59	51	65	12
2007-08	FL C	46	18	17	11	58	42	71	5
2008-09	FL C	46	15	12	19	52	55	57	15
2009-10	FL C	46	14	17	15	50	53	49*	21
2010-11	FL C	46	12	12	22	44	69	48	20
2011-12	FL C	46	13	17	16	46	51	56	17
2012-13	FL C	46	19	15	12	73	62	72	5
2013-14	PR Lge	38	13	6	19	33	48	45	11
2014-15	PR Lge	38	13	9	16	47	51	48	10
2015-16	PR Lge	38	11	9	18	39	51	42	15

* 10 pts deducted.

DID YOU KNOW ?

Crystal Palace played their first-ever game on 1 September 1905. They won 3-0 away at New Brompton (now Gillingham) in a United League fixture. Palace also entered and won the Southern League Division Two title in their inaugural season, losing just once.

CRYSTAL PALACE – FA PREMIER LEAGUE 2015–16 LEAGUE RECORD

Match No.	Date		Venue	Opponents		Result	H/T Score	Lg Pos.	Goalscorers	Attendance
1	Aug	8	A	Norwich C	W	3-1	1-0	2	Zaha [39], Delaney [49], Cabaye [90]	27,036
2		16	H	Arsenal	L	1-2	1-1	6	Ward [28]	24,732
3		22	H	Aston Villa	W	2-1	0-0	4	Dann [71], Sako [87]	25,295
4		29	A	Chelsea	W	2-1	0-0	2	Sako [65], Ward [81]	41,581
5	Sept	12	H	Manchester C	L	0-1	0-0	4		25,167
6		20	A	Tottenham H	L	0-1	0-0	8		35,723
7		27	A	Watford	W	1-0	0-0	6	Cabaye (pen) [71]	20,168
8	Oct	3	H	WBA	W	2-0	0-0	3	Bolasie [68], Cabaye (pen) [89]	24,033
9		17	H	West Ham U	L	1-3	1-1	6	Cabaye (pen) [25]	24,812
10		24	A	Leicester C	L	0-1	0-0	6		31,752
11		31	H	Manchester U	D	0-0	0-0	8		24,854
12	Nov	8	A	Liverpool	W	2-1	1-1	8	Bolasie [21], Dann [82]	44,115
13		23	H	Sunderland	L	0-1	0-0	10		24,361
14		28	H	Newcastle U	W	5-1	3-1	6	McArthur 2 [14, 90], Bolasie 2 [17, 47], Zaha [41]	24,833
15	Dec	7	A	Everton	D	1-1	0-0	6	Dann [76]	35,736
16		12	H	Southampton	W	1-0	0-0	6	Cabaye [38]	24,914
17		19	A	Stoke C	W	2-1	1-0	6	Wickham (pen) [45], Lee [88]	27,500
18		26	A	Bournemouth	D	0-0	0-0	5		11,218
19		28	H	Swansea C	D	0-0	0-0	5		23,714
20	Jan	3	H	Chelsea	L	0-3	0-1	7		24,854
21		12	A	Aston Villa	L	0-1	0-0	7		28,245
22		16	A	Manchester C	L	0-4	0-2	8		53,983
23		23	H	Tottenham H	L	1-3	1-0	11	Vertonghen (og) [30]	24,867
24	Feb	2	H	Bournemouth	L	1-2	1-1	11	Dann [27]	24,855
25		6	A	Swansea C	D	1-1	0-1	12	Dann [47]	20,492
26		13	H	Watford	L	1-2	1-1	13	Adebayor [45]	24,564
27		27	A	WBA	L	2-3	0-3	14	Wickham 2 [48, 60]	24,806
28	Mar	1	A	Sunderland	D	2-2	0-1	14	Wickham 2 [61, 67]	39,795
29		6	H	Liverpool	L	1-2	0-0	15	Ledley [48]	24,709
30		19	H	Leicester C	L	0-1	0-1	16		25,041
31	Apr	2	A	West Ham U	D	2-2	1-2	16	Delaney [15], Gayle [75]	34,857
32		9	A	Norwich C	W	1-0	0-0	16	Puncheon [68]	24,960
33		13	H	Everton	D	0-0	0-0	16		23,528
34		17	A	Arsenal	D	1-1	0-1	16	Bolasie [81]	59,961
35		20	A	Manchester U	L	0-2	0-1	16		75,277
36		30	A	Newcastle U	L	0-1	0-0	16		52,107
37	May	7	H	Stoke C	W	2-1	0-1	14	Gayle 2 [47, 68]	23,990
38		15	A	Southampton	L	1-4	0-1	15	Puncheon [64]	31,313

Final League Position: 15

GOALSCORERS

League (39): Bolasie 5, Cabaye 5 (3 pens), Dann 5, Wickham 5 (1 pen), Gayle 3, Delaney 2, McArthur 2, Puncheon 2, Sako 2, Ward 2, Zaha 2, Adebayor 1, Ledley 1, Lee 1, own goal 1.
FA Cup (9): Zaha 2, Bolasie 1, Cabaye 1 (pen), Campbell 1, Kelly 1, Puncheon 1, Ward 1, Wickham 1.
Capital One Cup (9): Gayle 4 (3 pens), Campbell 1, Delaney 1, Lee 1, Murray 1 (pen), Zaha 1.

McCarthy A 7	Ward J 30	Dann S 35	Delaney D 32	Souare P 34	Zaha W 30+4	Cabaye Y 32+1	McArthur J 26+2	Puncheon J 31	Mutch J 7+13	Murray G 2	Jedinek M 16+11	Bolasie Y 23+3	Wickham C 15+6	Lee C 4+9	Bamford P —+6	Sako B 11+9	Gayle D 8+8	Ledley J 11+8	Kelly M 11+2	Hangeland B 7	Campbell F 4+7	Hennessey W 29	Mariappa A 3	Chamakh M 1+9	Williams Jon —+1	Adebayor E 7+5	Boateng H —+1	Speroni J 2	Kaikai S —+1	Match No.
1	2	3	4	5	6^1	7	8	9	10^2	11^3	12	13	14																	1
1	2	3	4	5	6^2	8	9^3	7	12		10^1	11	13	14																2
1	2	3	4	5	8^2	7^3	6	9	13	11^1	14					10	12													3
1	2	3	4	5	10^1	7^2	6	8			12	11	14			9^3	13													4
1		3		5	10	6	7	9^3				13	11^2	14			8^1	12		2	4									5
1			4	5	8^1	6	7^2	9	13			11		14	10^3					2	3	12								6
		3		5	12	6^2	13	8				10				9^1	11^3	7		2	4	14	1							7
		3		5	8^2	6	7	9				10					11^1	13	2	4	12	1								8
		3		5	8^1	6^3	7^2	9			13	10				12	11^*	14	2	4		1								9
		3			13	6	7	9^2			14	10			12	8		5	4	11^1	1	2^3								10
5		3	4		8	6^1	7	9			12	10					11		2			1								11
		3	4	5	8	6^3	7	9^2	14		10	12					11^1	13	2			1								12
	2	3	4	5	10	6	7	9^1				8	11^2			13	12^3				1			14						13
	2	3	4	5	10^1	6^3	7	9			12	8	11^3	13	14					1										14
	2	3	4	5		8^2	6	11	13			7	9	10^1			12				1									15
	2	3	4	5	6	7	8	9^1	12			10	11^2							1			13							16
	2	3	4	5	6^3		8	9^2	13			11	10^1	14		7				1			12							17
	2	3	4	5	8	12	7	10	9^1	14						6^3			11^2	1			13							18
	2	3		5	8	9	7^3	10^2	14		6		13	12			4			11^1			1							19
	2	3	4	5	9		6	8			7^2		10^3					11^1	1		12	14								20
	2	3	4	5	11	7	8^3	9	14		12					10^2	6^1			1			13							21
	2	3	4	5	11^3	7	8^2	9	13			10^1	14			6				1			12							22
	2	3	4	5	6	7^2	10^1	9			12	11				8		13	1											23
	2	3	4	5	8		7^1	9	12	6			10^3				11^2	1		14			13							24
	2	3	4	5	8	9^3		6	7			10^1				14	1			12			11^3	13						25
	2	3	4	5^1	6	7		9^2	8			10^1	12			13	1			11										26
5		3	4		6	7^2		9	14	12	11			13	8^3	2		1			10^1									27
	2	3	4		8	6^1		9	7	10^2	11^3		13	12	5			1			14									28
1	2	3	4	5	8	6^1		12	6	10		13	14	7^3				1			11^2									29
	2	3	4	5^2	6	7		8	10		13	14	9^3	12			1			11^1										30
	2	3	4	5	8^1		10		6	9	11	12	7^2	13	1															31
	2	3	4	5	12	6	9^2		7	8	14	10^1	11^3	13			1													32
	2	3	4	5	9^3	6	8		7	11^2	12	14	10^1	1			13													33
	2	3	4	5	14	6	8^3		7^1	9	11^2	12	10	1			13													34
		4	5	8	6^2	13	12	7	14	9^1	10	2	3	11^3	1															35
	2	3	4	5	7	8^1	10^2	6	9	11^3	12	13	1			14														36
	2	3	4	5	8^1	7	6	13	9	11	14	10^2	12^3	1																37
	2^5		4	5	7^2	8	9^1	6	13	10	14	3	11	1	12															38

DAGENHAM & REDBRIDGE

FOUNDATION

The roots of Dagenham & Redbridge lie firmly in the Essex side of the Greater London area. Though formed only in 1992 their complex origins date back to the 19th century involving Ilford (founded 1881) and Leytonstone (1886) who merged in 1979 to form Leytonstone-Ilford. They and Walthamstow Avenue (1900) joined together in 1988 to become Redbridge Forest who in turn merged with Dagenham FC (1949) in 1992. Victoria Road has existed as a football ground since 1917. Initially used by Sterling Works, in the summer of 1955 Briggs Sports vacated the premises and Dagenham FC moved in and the pitch was enclosed.

The London Borough of Barking and Dagenham Stadium, Victoria Road, Dagenham, Essex RM10 7XL.

Telephone: (020) 8592 1549.

Fax: (020) 8593 7227.

Ticket Office: (020) 8592 1549 (extension 21).

Website: www.daggers.co.uk

Email: info@daggers.co.uk

Ground Capacity: 6,077.

Record Attendance: 5,949 v Ipswich T, FA Cup 3rd rd, 5 January 2002.

Pitch Measurements: 100.5m × 64m (110yd × 70yd).

Chairman: David Bennett.

Managing Director: Stephen Thompson MBE.

Manager: John Still.

First-Team Coaches: Darren Currie and Ian Culverhouse.

Physio: John Gowens.

Colours: Red shirts with blue stripes, blue shorts with red trim, blue socks.

Year Formed: 1992.

Turned Professional: 1992.

Club Nickname: 'The Daggers'.

Ground: 1992, Victoria Road (renamed The London Borough of Barking and Dagenham Stadium 2009).

First Football League Game: 11 August 2007, FL 2 v Stockport Co (a) L 0–1 – Roberts; Foster, Griffiths, Rainford, Uddin, Boardman, Saunders (Strevens), Southam, Benson (Moore), Nurse, Sloma (Huke).

HONOURS

League Champions: Conference – 2006–07.
Runners-up: Conference – 2001–02.
FA Cup: 3rd rd – 2008, 2012, 2016.
League Cup: never past 1st rd.

sky SPORTS FACT FILE

Dagenham & Redbridge's first competitive match following their formation in 1992 saw them win 2-0 at Merthyr Tydfil in what was then the GM Vauxhall Conference. The Daggers finished the season in third place behind the champions Wycombe Wanderers and runners-up Bromsgrove Rovers.

Record League Victory: 6–0 v Chester C, FL 2, 9 August 2008 – Roberts; Okuonghae, Griffiths, Arber, Uddin, Taiwo, Saunders (2), Green (1) (Southam), Benson (1) (Nurse), Strevens (1p) (Nwokeji (1)), Gain.

Record Cup Victory: 6–1 v Stowmarket T, FA Cup 2nd qual rd, 28 September 1992; 6–1 v Wealdstone (a), FA Cup 3rd qual rd, 12 October 1992.

Record Defeat: 0–9 v Hereford U, Conference, 27 February 2004.

Most League Points (3 for a win): 72, FL 2, 2009–10.

Most League Goals: 77, FL 2, 2008–09.

Highest League Scorer in Season: Paul Benson, 28, Conference, 2006–07.

Most League Goals in Total Aggregate: 40, Paul Benson, 2007–11.

Most League Goals in One Match: 4, Paul Benson v Shrewsbury T, FL 2, 18 August 2009.

Most Capped Player: Andre Boucaud, 22 (39), Trinidad & Tobago.

Most League Appearances: Scott Doe, 243, 2009–15.

Youngest League Player: Jodi Jones, 17 years 111 days v Portsmouth, 10 February 2015.

Record Transfer Fee Received: £700,000 from Peterborough U for Dwight Gayle, January 2013.

Record Transfer Fee Paid: £20,000 to Plymouth Arg for Damien McCrory, February 2010.

Football League Record: 2006–07 Promoted from Conference; 2007–10 FL 2; 2010–11 FL 1; 2011–16 FL 2; 2016– NL.

MANAGERS
John Still 1992–94
Dave Cusack 1994–95
Graham Carr 1995–96
Ted Hardy 1996–99
Garry Hill 1999–2004
John Still 2004–13
Wayne Burnett 2013–15
John Still December 2015–

LATEST SEQUENCES

Longest Sequence of League Wins: 5, 12.2.2008 – 1.3.2008.

Longest Sequence of League Defeats: 9, 8.10.2011 – 10.12.2011.

Longest Sequence of League Draws: 3, 21.9.2010 – 28.9.2010.

Longest Sequence of Unbeaten League Matches: 8, 1.3.2014 – 5.4.2014.

Longest Sequence Without a League Win: 11, 12.9.2015 – 21.11.2015.

Successive Scoring Runs: 16 from 12.4.2008.

Successive Non-scoring Runs: 4 from 13.12.2014.

TEN YEAR LEAGUE RECORD

		P	W	D	L	F	A	Pts	Pos
2006-07	Conf	46	28	11	7	93	48	95	1
2007-08	FL 2	46	13	10	23	49	70	49	20
2008-09	FL 2	46	19	11	16	77	53	68	8
2009-10	FL 2	46	20	12	14	69	58	72	7
2010-11	FL 1	46	12	11	23	52	70	47	21
2011-12	FL 2	46	14	8	24	50	72	50	19
2012-13	FL 2	46	13	12	21	55	62	51	22
2013-14	FL 2	46	15	15	16	53	59	60	9
2014-15	FL 2	46	17	8	21	58	59	59	14
2015-16	FL 2	46	8	10	28	46	81	34	23

DID YOU KNOW ?

The Daggers clinched promotion to the Football League in April 2007 when they defeated Aldershot at the Victoria Ground to become Conference champions with five games still to play. The match attracted an attendance of 4,044 which is the club's highest home crowd for a match in the Conference.

DAGENHAM & REDBRIDGE – FOOTBALL LEAGUE TWO 2015–16 LEAGUE RECORD

Match No.	Date	Venue	Opponents	Result		H/T Score	Lg Pos.	Goalscorers	Attendance
1	Aug 8	A	Portsmouth	L	0-3	0-0	22		16,948
2	15	H	Leyton Orient	L	1-3	0-2	24	Cureton [90]	3336
3	18	H	Exeter C	L	1-2	0-1	24	Jones [86]	1567
4	22	A	Wycombe W	D	1-1	1-0	24	McClure [7]	3343
5	29	H	Stevenage	D	1-1	1-0	23	Hemmings [29]	1653
6	Sept 5	A	Northampton T	W	2-1	2-1	20	McClure 2 [28, 39]	4032
7	12	A	Carlisle U	L	1-2	1-1	21	Doidge [11]	3871
8	19	H	Newport Co	D	0-0	0-0	23		1654
9	26	A	Barnet	L	1-3	0-2	22	Jones [66]	2079
10	29	H	Notts Co	D	1-1	0-1	23	Jones [72]	1327
11	Oct 3	H	Mansfield T	L	3-4	3-2	23	McClure [9], Chambers 2 [30, 32]	1597
12	10	A	Yeovil T	D	2-2	2-0	23	Ferdinand [18], Raymond [44]	3204
13	17	H	Hartlepool U	L	0-1	0-1	23		1771
14	20	A	York C	D	2-2	1-1	22	Hemmings [31], Cureton [56]	2559
15	24	A	Accrington S	L	1-3	0-2	24	Nosworthy [62]	1104
16	Nov 1	H	Luton T	L	0-2	0-1	24		2723
17	21	H	Oxford U	L	0-1	0-0	24		1980
18	24	A	AFC Wimbledon	W	1-0	0-0	22	Cureton [80]	3557
19	28	H	Plymouth Arg	D	1-1	0-0	22	Labadie [59]	2344
20	Dec 1	A	Morecambe	L	0-1	0-1	22		1027
21	12	A	Crawley T	L	2-3	0-2	22	Doidge [64], Cureton [85]	1543
22	19	H	Bristol R	L	0-3	0-1	24		1820
23	26	H	Cambridge U	L	0-3	0-0	24		2425
24	28	A	Stevenage	W	3-1	3-1	23	Chambers [18], Labadie [19], Doidge [37]	3152
25	Jan 2	A	Exeter C	W	2-1	1-1	22	Labadie [11], Chambers [74]	3451
26	16	H	Northampton T	L	1-2	0-0	22	Doidge [62]	2379
27	23	A	Newport Co	D	2-2	2-0	23	Doidge [1], Worrall [6]	2323
28	Feb 6	A	Cambridge U	L	0-1	0-0	23		4494
29	9	H	Wycombe W	L	1-2	0-1	23	Guttridge [72]	1446
30	13	H	Barnet	L	0-2	0-1	24		1728
31	20	A	Mansfield T	L	2-3	1-0	24	Hawkins [42], Cureton [86]	2822
32	27	L	Yeovil T	L	0-1	0-0	24		2942
33	Mar 1	A	Notts Co	D	0-0	0-0	24		3147
34	5	H	York C	W	1-0	0-0	24	Passley [78]	1767
35	8	H	Carlisle U	D	0-0	0-0	24		1695
36	12	A	Hartlepool U	L	1-3	1-2	24	Cash [33]	3947
37	15	A	Oxford U	L	0-4	0-1	24		5319
38	19	H	Accrington S	L	0-1	0-0	24		1345
39	Apr 5	H	Morecambe	W	2-1	2-0	24	Labadie [8], Cureton [30]	1233
40	9	H	Portsmouth	L	1-4	1-0	24	Hemmings [34]	3122
41	12	A	Luton T	L	0-1	0-1	24		6997
42	16	A	Leyton Orient	L	2-3	0-2	24	Cureton [59], Dikamona [60]	5696
43	19	H	AFC Wimbledon	L	0-2	0-1	24		2027
44	23	A	Plymouth Arg	W	3-2	3-0	24	Dikamona [13], Cash [24], Doidge [41]	9211
45	30	H	Crawley T	W	3-0	0-0	24	Doidge 2 [51, 53], Hemmings [80]	1643
46	May 7	A	Bristol R	L	1-2	1-1	23	Cash [12]	11,130

Final League Position: 23

GOALSCORERS

League (46): Doidge 8, Cureton 7, Chambers 4, Hemmings 4, Labadie 4, McClure 4, Cash 3, Jones 3, Dikamona 2, Ferdinand 1, Guttridge 1, Hawkins 1, Nosworthy 1, Passley 1, Raymond 1, Worrall 1.
FA Cup (8): Vassell 3 (1 pen), Cureton 1, Dunne 1, Labadie 1, Obileye 1, Passley 1.
Capital One Cup (1): Doidge 1.
Johnstone's Paint Trophy (4): Chambers 1, Cureton 1, Hemmings 1, McClure 1.

Cousins M 22+1	Passley J 36+2	Nosworthy N 16+1	Partridge M 2	Widdowson J 31	Jones J 12+15	Boucaud A 21+4	Richards M 9+1	Hemmings A 37+2	Cureton J 21+17	McClure M 11+9	Ferdinand K 14+1	Dikamona C 23+4	Chambers A 22+9	Doidge C 29+6	O'Brien L 24	Obileye A 15+1	Connors J 7+2	Hines Z 1+5	Hamalainen N 1	Hoyte J 22+3	Raymond F 8+2	Mulraney J 3+3	Yusuff A —+1	Sutherland F 2+2	Pask J 5	Labadie J 26+2	Dunne J 9	Vassell K 4+4	Worrall J 14	Muldoon O 18	Hawkins O 4+14	Guttridge L 2+1	Hyam D 16	Cash M 12	Taylor Q 1+1	Pennell L 4+1	Shepherd J 2	Match No.
1	2	3	4	5	6	7	8	9	10	11^1	12																											1
1	2	3		5	12	7		9	11		8	4	6^1	10																								2
1	2	3	4	5	6	7^2		9^3	12	11	13	8	14	10^1																								3
	2	3		5	9^1	8		6^2		10^1	7	12	11		1		4	13																				4
	2	3^1		5	6^2	8		9	10		7	12	11		1		4	13																				5
	2	3		5			7	9		10^1	8	13	6^2	11	1		4	12																				6
	2	3		5	13	7		9^2	14	10^1	8		6^1	11	1		4	12																				7
	2	4		5	13	8		9	12	10^1	7		11^1		1	3		6^1																				8
	2	3		5	13	8		6^1	10		9		11		1	4		12						7^2														9
				5	6^3	8		9	13	10^2	7	4	12	11^1	1	3	2	14																				10
				5	6^1	8		9	12	10^2	7	4	11	13	1	3	2																					11
	2	4				6^1		5	10		7		11		1					3	8	9		12^2	13													12
	2	3			12			10	11	13	7		9^3		1					5	6^1	8^2		14	4													13
13	2	3				8^2		9	10^1	12	7		11		1^3					5				6	4	14												14
	2	3			12	7^1		10	11		8		9		1					5				6^2	4	13												15
					6^2			9	11	13			10^1		1	4	5			2	12			3	8	7												16
	2	3		5	14			9^1	10^3	13		4	6^2		1						12					7	8	11										17
1	2	3^3			14			9	12	11^1		4		13	5						6^2					7	8	10										18
1	2					8^1	9	10	11		4	12			3	5										7	6											19
	2				13	8		10^3	11		4	6^2			1	3	5					14				7^1	9	12									20
1	2	4		5	9			11			3		12							10						8	7	6^1										21
1	6	12			9^2	8			13		4	11	10^3		3^1	5				2						7	14											22
	6			5	13			9^2	11		14		12	1	3					2						4^1	7	8	10^3									23
1	6			5	13			9^2	10^1		3				2	11										8	7	12										24
1	2				12			6	14		3	11^3	10^1	5		4	9									7^2	8	13										25
1	2				14	7^1		6	13		5	10^3	11^2		4					8									3	9	12							26
1	5					7^2	9				2	11	10^1		3					6								4	8	12	13							27
1	2			5	14			9	13		6^2	11^3			7													3	8^2	12	10^1	4						28
1	2^1			5	6^1			9^3			11				12	14				7								3	8^2	13	10	4						29
1				5	12	7^2		11^1			13	14			2	6				9								3	8^3	10	4							30
	5^2				9	14		12			13	10^1			2	8				1						6		3	7^1	11	4							31
	2				6	12		8^1			13	11^2			14	1				4						7		3	9	10^3	5							32
	2			5				8	11		9	10	1		12					6						3	7^1	4										33
	2			5			7	11			12	9^1	10^3	1		14				6						3	8	13	4^3									34
	6			5			7		9	13		4	11^2	1		2										3	8	12	10^1									35
	6			5			7^1		9^2	14		3	13	11^3	1		2									4	8	12	10									36
	6^2			5	14				13		11^1	12		1		2				8						4	7	9^3	3	10^3								37
	6^2			5				9^1	12		13	11		1		2				8						3	7	14	4	10^3								38
1	12			5				9	11^1		10					2				7						3	8		4	6								39
1	6^2			5	13			9^2	11		3	11				2				7						8^1	14	4	10^3									40
1				5			7^2	11	12		3	14	10^3			2				6						8^1	13	4	9									41
1				5			7	9	11	14	4	10				2^1				8						3^3	6^2	12	13									42
1				5		12	8^2	9	11		3	10^3				13				7^1						14		6	2	4								43
1	5^2			9				13		11^1	2	12	10^3			8										6	14	3	7		4							44
1	12							9	11^1	13	2	10				8										6^2	14	3	7	4	5^2							45
1						6^1		9	13		3^3	11^3	10		12					8						14	4	7	2	5								46

FA Cup

First Round	Morecambe	(h)	0-0
Replay	Morecambe	(a)	4-2
Second Round	Whitehawk	(h)	1-1
Replay	Whitehawk	(a)	3-2
(aet)			
Third Round	Everton	(a)	0-2

Capital One Cup

First Round	Charlton Ath	(a)	1-4

Johnstone's Paint Trophy

First Round	Cambridge U	(a)	2-0
Second Round	Stevenage	(a)	2-1
Southern Quarter-Final	Oxford U	(h)	0-2

DERBY COUNTY

Derby County was formed by members of the Derbyshire County Cricket Club in 1884, when football was booming in the area and the cricketers thought that a football club would help boost finances for the summer game. To begin with, they sported the cricket club's colours of amber, chocolate and pale blue, and went into the game at the top immediately entering the FA Cup.

The iPro Stadium, Pride Park, Derby DE24 8XL.

Telephone: (0871) 472 1884.

Fax: (01332) 667 519.

Ticket Office: (0871) 472 1884 (option 1).

Website: www.dcfc.co.uk

Email: derby.county@dcfc.co.uk

Ground Capacity: 33,055.

Record Attendance: 41,826 v Tottenham H, Division 1, 20 September 1969 (at Baseball Ground); 33,378 v Liverpool, FA Premier League, 18 March 2000 (at Pride Park).

Stadium Record Attendance: 33,597, England v Mexico, 25 May 2001 (at Pride Park).

Pitch Measurements: 100.5m × 66m (110yd × 72yd).

Chairman: Mel Morris.

Chief Operating Officer: John Vicars.

Head Coach: Nigel Pearson.

First-Team Coach: Chris Powell.

Physio: Neil Sullivan.

HONOURS

League Champions: Division 1 – 1971–72, 1974–75; Division 2 – 1911–12, 1914–15, 1968–69, 1986–87; Division 3N – 1956–57.
Runners-up: Division 1 – 1895–96, 1929–30, 1935–36; First Division – 1995–96; Division 2 – 1925–26; Division 3N – 1955–56.
FA Cup Winners: 1946.
Runners-up: 1898, 1899, 1903.
League Cup: semi-final – 1968, 2009.
Texaco Cup Winners: 1972.
Anglo-Italian Cup: Runners-up: 1993–94, 1994–95.

European Competitions
European Cup: 1972–73 (sf), 1975–76.
UEFA Cup: 1974–75, 1976–77.

Colours: White shirts with black trim, black shorts, black socks with white trim.

Year Formed: 1884.

Turned Professional: 1884.

Club Nickname: 'The Rams'.

Grounds: 1884, Racecourse Ground; 1895, Baseball Ground; 1997, Pride Park (renamed The iPro Stadium 2013).

First Football League Game: 8 September 1888, Football League, v Bolton W (a) W 6–3 – Marshall; Latham, Ferguson, Williamson; Monks, Walter Roulstone; Bakewell (2), Cooper (2), Higgins, Harry Plackett, Lol Plackett (2).

Record League Victory: 9–0 v Wolverhampton W, Division 1, 10 January 1891 – Bunyan; Archie Goodall, Roberts; Walker, Chalmers, Walter Roulstone (1); Bakewell, McLachlan, Johnny Goodall (1), Holmes (2), McMillan (5). 9–0 v Sheffield W, Division 1, 21 January 1899 – Fryer; Methven, Staley; Cox, Archie Goodall, May; Oakden (1), Bloomer (6), Boag, McDonald (1), Allen, (1 og).

sky SPORTS FACT FILE

Derby County's first-ever competitive game at their Pride Park stadium was staged against Wimbledon in August 1997 when the match was abandoned after 56 minutes due to floodlight failure. County's first goal at the new ground was scored by Ashley Ward who also scored their last Premier League goal at the Baseball Ground.

Record Cup Victory: 12–0 v Finn Harps, UEFA Cup 1st rd 1st leg, 15 September 1976 – Moseley; Thomas, Nish, Rioch (1), McFarland, Todd (King), Macken, Gemmill, Hector (5), George (3), James (3).

Record Defeat: 2–11 v Everton, FA Cup 1st rd, 1889–90.

Most League Points (2 for a win): 63, Division 2, 1968–69 and Division 3 (N), 1955–56 and 1956–57.

Most League Points (3 for a win): 85, FL C, 2013–14.

Most League Goals: 111, Division 3 (N), 1956–57.

Highest League Scorer in Season: Jack Bowers, 37, Division 1, 1930–31; Ray Straw, 37 Division 3 (N), 1956–57.

Most League Goals in Total Aggregate: Steve Bloomer, 292, 1892–1906 and 1910–14.

Most League Goals in One Match: 6, Steve Bloomer v Sheffield W, Division 1, 2 January 1899.

Most Capped Player: Deon Burton, 42 (59), Jamaica.

Most League Appearances: Kevin Hector, 486, 1966–78 and 1980–82.

Youngest League Player: Mason Bennett, 15 years 99 days v Middlesbrough 22 October 2011.

Record Transfer Fee Received: £7,000,000 from Leeds U for Seth Johnson, October 2001.

Record Transfer Fee Paid: £4,750,000 to Hull C for Tom Ince, July 2015.

Football League Record: 1888 Founder Member of the Football League; 1907–12 Division 2; 1912–14 Division 1; 1914–15 Division 2; 1915–21 Division 1; 1921–26 Division 2; 1926–53 Division 1; 1953–55 Division 2; 1955–57 Division 3 (N); 1957–69 Division 2; 1969–80 Division 1; 1980–84 Division 2; 1984–86 Division 3; 1986–87 Division 2; 1987–91 Division 1; 1991–92 Division 2; 1992–96 Division 1; 1996–2002 FA Premier League; 2002–04 Division 1; 2004–07 FL C; 2007–08 FA Premier League; 2008– FL C.

MANAGERS

W. D. Clark 1896–1900
Harry Newbould 1900–06
Jimmy Methven 1906–22
Cecil Potter 1922–25
George Jobey 1925–41
Ted Magner 1944–46
Stuart McMillan 1946–53
Jack Barker 1953–55
Harry Storer 1955–62
Tim Ward 1962–67
Brian Clough 1967–73
Dave Mackay 1973–76
Colin Murphy 1977
Tommy Docherty 1977–79
Colin Addison 1979–82
Johnny Newman 1982
Peter Taylor 1982–84
Roy McFarland 1984
Arthur Cox 1984–93
Roy McFarland 1993–95
Jim Smith 1995–2001
Colin Todd 2001–02
John Gregory 2002–03
George Burley 2003–05
Phil Brown 2005–06
Billy Davies 2006–07
Paul Jewell 2007–08
Nigel Clough 2009–13
Steve McClaren 2013–15
Paul Clement 2015–16
Darren Wassall 2016
Nigel Pearson May 2016–

LATEST SEQUENCES

Longest Sequence of League Wins: 9, 15.3.1969 – 19.4.1969.

Longest Sequence of League Defeats: 8, 12.12.1987 – 10.2.1988.

Longest Sequence of League Draws: 6, 26.3.1927 – 18.4.1927.

Longest Sequence of Unbeaten League Matches: 22, 8.3.1969 – 20.9.1969.

Longest Sequence Without a League Win: 36, 22.9.2007 – 30.8.2008.

Successive Scoring Runs: 29 from 3.12.1960.

Successive Non-scoring Runs: 8 from 30.10.1920.

TEN YEAR LEAGUE RECORD

		P	W	D	L	F	A	Pts	Pos
2006-07	FL C	46	25	9	12	62	46	84	3
2007-08	PR Lge	38	1	8	29	20	89	11	20
2008-09	FL C	46	14	12	20	55	67	54	18
2009-10	FL C	46	15	11	20	53	63	56	14
2010-11	FL C	46	13	10	23	58	71	49	19
2011-12	FL C	46	18	10	18	50	58	64	12
2012-13	FL C	46	16	13	17	65	62	61	10
2013-14	FL C	46	25	10	11	84	52	85	3
2014-15	FL C	46	21	14	11	85	56	77	8
2015-16	FL C	46	21	15	10	66	43	78	5

DID YOU KNOW ?

Roy McFarland was voted as Derby County's first Player of the Year when the award was inaugurated in the 1968–69 season. The winner receives the Jack Stamps Trophy named in honour of the centre-forward who scored two goals in the Rams' 1946 FA Cup final victory over Charlton Athletic.

DERBY COUNTY – FL CHAMPIONSHIP 2015–16 LEAGUE RECORD

Match No.	Date	Venue	Opponents	Result	H/T Score	Lg Pos.	Goalscorers	Attendance
1	Aug 8	A	Bolton W	D 0-0	0-0	14		17,162
2	15	H	Charlton Ath	D 1-1	0-0	15	Martin 68	29,045
3	18	H	Middlesbrough	D 1-1	0-1	14	Russell 88	30,855
4	21	A	Birmingham C	D 1-1	0-1	12	Russell 61	18,134
5	29	H	Leeds U	L 1-2	0-1	19	Martin 48	29,386
6	Sept 12	A	Preston NE	W 2-1	2-0	13	Martin 2 23, 36	14,552
7	15	A	Reading	W 1-0	0-0	10	Ince 69	15,697
8	21	H	Burnley	D 0-0	0-0	11		26,834
9	26	A	Milton Keynes D	W 3-1	0-0	8	Johnson 53, Bent 89, Ince 90	13,554
10	Oct 3	H	Brentford	W 2-0	2-0	7	Martin 20, Ince 44	29,467
11	18	H	Wolverhampton W	W 4-2	3-1	6	Martin 2 3, 28, Johnson 45, Russell 57	20,063
12	21	A	Blackburn R	D 0-0	0-0	7		12,968
13	24	A	Huddersfield T	W 2-1	1-1	5	Martin 15, Thorne 48	15,371
14	31	H	Rotherham U	W 3-0	2-0	5	Weimann 7, Butterfield 45, Keogh 76	30,172
15	Nov 3	H	QPR	W 1-0	0-0	5	Weimann 51	28,502
16	6	A	Nottingham F	L 0-1	0-1	5		25,114
17	21	H	Cardiff C	W 2-0	0-0	4	Thorne 55, Weimann 76	29,526
18	27	A	Hull C	W 2-0	2-0	1	Butterfield 2 16, 34	17,410
19	Dec 6	A	Sheffield W	D 0-0	0-0	3		19,252
20	12	H	Brighton & HA	D 2-2	1-1	4	Johnson 41, Martin (pen) 88	30,537
21	15	H	Bristol C	W 4-0	1-0	3	Ince 3 42, 63, 71, Russell 76	27,781
22	19	A	Ipswich T	W 1-0	1-0	2	Ince 40	20,161
23	26	H	Fulham	W 2-0	0-0	1	Hyndman (og) 52, Butterfield 84	32,134
24	29	A	Leeds U	D 2-2	1-1	2	Hendrick 13, Ince 78	23,027
25	Jan 2	A	Middlesbrough	L 0-2	0-0	2		32,870
26	12	H	Reading	D 1-1	1-1	2	Shackell 11	28,175
27	16	H	Birmingham C	L 0-3	0-0	3		32,895
28	25	A	Burnley	L 1-4	1-1	5	Butterfield 30	15,214
29	Feb 2	A	Preston NE	D 0-0	0-0	4		27,252
30	6	A	Fulham	D 1-1	1-1	5	Bryson 44	18,472
31	13	H	Milton Keynes D	L 0-1	0-0	6		30,075
32	20	A	Brentford	W 3-1	0-0	5	Hendrick 80, Christie 83, Martin 90	10,627
33	24	H	Blackburn R	W 1-0	1-0	5	Butterfield 8	27,411
34	27	A	Wolverhampton W	L 1-2	1-1	5	Martin 44	19,389
35	Mar 5	H	Huddersfield T	W 2-0	1-0	5	Martin 31, Russell 73	29,698
36	8	A	QPR	L 0-2	0-1	5		14,049
37	12	A	Rotherham U	D 3-3	0-0	5	Ince 2 55, 65, Martin 63	11,163
38	19	H	Nottingham F	W 1-0	0-0	5	Olsson 79	33,010
39	Apr 2	A	Cardiff C	L 1-2	0-1	6	Martin 49	28,680
40	5	H	Hull C	W 4-0	2-0	6	Johnson 2 29, 38, Martin 84, Bryson 90	29,078
41	9	H	Bolton W	W 4-1	2-0	5	Russell 2 13, 77, Ince 38, Butterfield 69	29,674
42	16	A	Charlton Ath	W 1-0	0-0	5	Russell 60	15,857
43	19	A	Bristol C	W 3-2	1-2	5	Russell 37, Bryson 52, Ince 57	15,341
44	23	H	Sheffield W	D 1-1	0-0	5	Bent 62	31,825
45	May 2	A	Brighton & HA	D 1-1	0-0	5	Weimann 71	30,292
46	7	H	Ipswich T	L 0-1	0-1	5		29,854

Final League Position: 5

GOALSCORERS

League (66): Martin 15 (1 pen), Ince 12, Russell 9, Butterfield 7, Johnson 5, Weimann 4, Bryson 3, Bent 2, Hendrick 2, Thorne 2, Christie 1, Keogh 1, Olsson 1, Shackell 1, own goal 1.
FA Cup (3): Bent 1, Butterfield 1, Thorne 1.
Capital One Cup (1): Shackell 1.
Championship Play-Offs (2): Russell 1, own goal 1.

Carson S 36	Baird C 8+6	Keogh R 46	Shackell J 46	Warnock S 19+1	Thorne G 32+2	Bryson C 14+7	Hughes W 4+2	Ince T 37+5	Russell J 35+10	Martin C 42+3	Hendrick J 21+11	Shotton R —+6	Weimann A 12+18	Forsyth C 10+2	Hanson J 10+8	Christie C 40+2	Bent D 4+17	Grant L 10	Johnson B 30+1	Butterfield J 29+8	Blackman N 5+9	Camara A —+4	Olsson M 16	Buxton J —+3	Match No.
1	2	3	4	5	6	7[1]	8[2]	9	10[3]	11	12	13	14												1
1	2	3	4		7			9	11[2]	10	6		12	5	8[1]	13									2
1	2	3	4	5	7			9	13	10	8[2]	12	11[3]		6[1]		14								3
1	7	3	4		8			6	9	10		13	12	5		2[1]	11[2]								4
1	2	3	4		7[3]			9	11[2]	10	8	14	12	5		6[1]	13								5
	7	3	4	5[3]				9[3]	11	10	12		13	14		2		1	6	8[1]					6
1		3	4					9[3]	11	10	6[2]		14	5	13	2	12		7	8[1]					7
1		3	4		7[1]			9	10	12			11	5	13	2			6	8[2]					8
1	7[2]	3	4	5				9	11	10[3]	13		12			2	14		8	6[1]					9
1		3	4[3]		7[2]			9	11	10	6	12	14	5	13	2			8[1]						10
1	13	3	4		7			9	11	10[3]	6[2]			5		2[1]	14		8	12					11
1		3	4	5[1]	7			9	11	10[3]			14	12		2	13		8	6[2]					12
1		3	4		7			9[3]	11[2]	10[1]			12	5	13	2	14		8	6					13
1		3	4		7[1]	14			9	10[3]	12		11	5		2	13		8	6[2]					14
1	13	3	4	12[2]				9	10	6[1]			11	5[2]	14	2			7	8					15
1		3	4	5	7			12	9[1]	10	6[2]		11[3]			2	14		8	13					16
1	14	3	4	5	7	13		9[3]	12	10			11			2[1]			6	8[2]					17
1		3	4	5	7	12		9	13	10	6		11[1]			2				8[2]					18
1	13	3	4	5[1]	7			9[3]	12	10			11[2]			2	14	1	8	6					19
		3	4	5	7[1]			9	12	10	13		11[2]			2	14	1	8	6[3]					20
	14	3	4	5[3]	12			9	10		6[1]		8[2]			2	11	1	7	13					21
	14	3	4	5	7			9[3]	11[1]	10	13		12			2		1	8	6[2]					22
		3	4	5	7[1]			9	11[3]	10	13		12			2	14	1	8	6					23
		3	4[1]	5				14	9	13	6	12	11[2]			2	10[3]	1	7	8					24
		3	4	5	7[1]			9	11	10	12		13			2		1	8	6[2]					25
		3	4	5				9	10[1]	11	12					2		1	7[2]	6	8	13			26
		3	4	5	7[1]			9[3]	11[2]	14	6					2		1	8	12	10	13			27
1		3	4	5	7	14		9[1]	13	10						2			8[2]	6	11[3]	12			28
1		3	4	5	7	13		9[1]	14	10	6[2]					2			8	11[3]	12				29
1	7[2]	3	4		8[3]			9	10	6	11[1]					2			13	12	14		5		30
1		3	4		8[1]			6	11[2]	10	7[3]	14				2			13	9	12		5		31
1		3	4		14			9[1]	12	6	7[2]					2	10[3]		11	8	13		5		32
1		3	4		13			12	9[2]	10	6					7[1]	2		11	8[3]	14		5		33
1		3	4		7[2]			12	9[3]	10	6	13				2			11[1]	8	14		5		34
1		3	4		14	13		11	12	10	8					7[2]	2		6[1]	9[3]			5		35
1		3	4		6[1]			11	9[3]	10	12					7	2		13	8[2]	14		5		36
1		3	4		7[1]	8		9		10[2]	6					2	12		11		13		5		37
1		3	4[1]		7	6		9	12	10	8			2[3]	14		11[2]						5	13	38
1		3	4		7[2]	8		9	12	10				2			11		6[1]		13		5		39
1		3	4		7	6		11	9[3]	10			14	13		2			8[1]	12			5[2]		40
1		3	4		7	6	12	11[1]	9	10		13				2			9[2]				5		41
1		3	4		7	6	12	11	9	10	5					2			8[1]						42
1		3	4		7	6		11	9[1]	10	12					2			8				5		43
1		3	4		6	7[3]		11[1]	9	10	12			2	13				8[2]	14			5		44
1		3	4		7	6[2]	8[2]	9[1]	11	10	12			2		14							5	13	45
1		3[2]	4		7	6	8[3]	11	9	10[1]				2	13		14						5	12	46

FA Cup
Third Round	Hartlepool U	(a)	2-1
Fourth Round	Manchester U	(h)	1-3

Capital One Cup
First Round	Portsmouth	(a)	1-2

Championship Play-Offs
Semi-Final 1st leg	Hull C	(h)	0-3
Semi-Final 2nd leg	Hull C	(a)	2-0

(Hull C won 3-2 on aggregate)

DONCASTER ROVERS

FOUNDATION

In 1879, Mr Albert Jenkins assembled a team to play a match against the Yorkshire Institution for the Deaf. The players remained together as Doncaster Rovers, joining the Midland Alliance in 1889 and the Midland Counties League in 1891.

Keepmoat Stadium, Stadium Way, Lakeside, Doncaster, South Yorkshire DN4 5JW.

Telephone: (01302) 764 664.

Fax: (01302) 363 525.

Ticket Office: (01302) 762 576.

Website: www.doncasterroversfc.co.uk

Email: info@doncasterroversfc.co.uk

Ground Capacity: 15,125.

Record Attendance: 37,149 v Hull C, Division 3 (N), 2 October 1948 (at Belle Vue); 15,001 v Leeds U, FL 1, 1 April 2008 (at Keepmoat Stadium).

Pitch Measurements: 100m × 66m (109.5yd × 72yd).

Chairman: David Blunt.

Chief Executive: Gavin Baldwin.

Manager: Darren Ferguson.

First-Team Coach: Paul Butler.

Physio: Alex Dalton.

Colours: Red and white hooped shirts, white shorts with red trim, white socks with red trim.

Year Formed: 1879.

Turned Professional: 1885.

Club Nickname: 'Rovers', 'Donny'.

Grounds: 1880–1916, Intake Ground; 1920, Benetthorpe Ground; 1922, Low Pasture, Belle Vue; 2007, Keepmoat Stadium.

First Football League Game: 7 September 1901, Division 2, v Burslem Port Vale (h) D 3–3 – Eggett; Simpson, Layton; Longden, Jones, Wright, Langham, Murphy, Price, Goodson (2), Bailey (1).

Record League Victory: 10–0 v Darlington, Division 4, 25 January 1964 – Potter; Raine, Meadows, Windross (1), White, Ripley (2), Robinson, Book (2), Hale (4), Jeffrey, Broadbent (1).

Record Cup Victory: 7–0 v Blyth Spartans, FA Cup 1st rd, 27 November 1937 – Imrie; Shaw, Rodgers, McFarlane, Bycroft, Cyril Smith, Burton (1), Killourhy (4), Morgan (2), Malam, Dutton.

Record Defeat: 0–12 v Small Heath, Division 2, 11 April 1903.

Most League Points (2 for a win): 72, Division 3 (N), 1946–47.

HONOURS

League Champions: FL 1 – 2012–13; Division 3N – 1934–35, 1946–47, 1949–50; Third Division – 2003–04; Division 4 – 1965–66, 1968–69. *Runners-up:* Division 3N – 1937–38, 1938–39; Division 4 – 1983–84; Conference – (3rd) 2002–03 *(promoted via play-offs (and golden goal)).*

FA Cup: 5th rd – 1952, 1954, 1955, 1956.

League Cup: 5th rd – 1976, 2006.

League Trophy Winners: 2007.

sky SPORTS FACT FILE

Doncaster Rovers' first round Northern Section Cup tie against Stockport in 1945–46 proved a real marathon. They drew at Belle Vue in the first leg and were level again at Stockport after 90 minutes. The game went into sudden death but was finally abandoned due to poor light with seven minutes left of the fourth period of extra-time. The replay saw Doncaster win 4-0 to go into the next round.

Most League Points (3 for a win): 92, Division 3, 2003–04.

Most League Goals: 123, Division 3 (N), 1946–47.

Highest League Scorer in Season: Clarrie Jordan, 42, Division 3 (N), 1946–47.

Most League Goals in Total Aggregate: Tom Keetley, 180, 1923–29.

Most League Goals in One Match: 6, Tom Keetley v Ashington, Division 3 (N), 16 February 1929.

Most Capped Player: Len Graham, 14, Northern Ireland.

Most League Appearances: Fred Emery, 417, 1925–36.

Youngest League Player: Alick Jeffrey, 15 years 229 days v Fulham, 15 September 1954.

Record Transfer Fee Received: £2,000,000 from Reading for Matthew Mills, July 2009.

Record Transfer Fee Paid: £1,150,000 to Sheffield U for Billy Sharp, August 2010.

Football League Record: 1901 Elected to Division 2; 1903 Failed re-election; 1904 Re-elected; 1905 Failed re-election; 1923 Re-elected to Division 3 (N); 1935–37 Division 2; 1937–47 Division 3 (N); 1947–48 Division 2; 1948–50 Division 3 (N); 1950–58 Division 2; 1958–59 Division 3; 1959–66 Division 4; 1966–67 Division 3; 1967–69 Division 4; 1969–71 Division 3; 1971–81 Division 4; 1981–83 Division 3; 1983–84 Division 4; 1984–88 Division 3; 1988–92 Division 4; 1992–98 Division 3; 1998–2003 Conference; 2003–04 Division 3; 2004–08 FL 1; 2008–12 FL C; 2012–13 FL 1; 2013–14 FL C; 2014–16 FL 1; 2016– FL 2.

LATEST SEQUENCES

Longest Sequence of League Wins: 10, 22.1.1947 – 4.4.1947.

Longest Sequence of League Defeats: 9, 14.1.1905 – 1.4.1905.

Longest Sequence of League Draws: 4, 19.9.2009 – 3.10.2009.

Longest Sequence of Unbeaten League Matches: 20, 26.12.1968 – 12.4.1969.

Longest Sequence Without a League Win: 20, 9.8.1997 – 29.11.1997.

Successive Scoring Runs: 27 from 10.11.1934.

Successive Non-scoring Runs: 7 from 27.9.1947.

MANAGERS

Arthur Porter 1920–21
Harry Tufnell 1921–22
Arthur Porter 1922–23
Dick Ray 1923–27
David Menzies 1928–36
Fred Emery 1936–40
Bill Marsden 1944–46
Jackie Bestall 1946–49
Peter Doherty 1949–58
Jack Hodgson and Sid Bycroft
  (*Joint Managers*) 1958
Jack Crayston 1958–59
  (*continued as Secretary-Manager to 1961*)
Jackie Bestall (*TM*) 1959–60
Norman Curtis 1960–61
Danny Malloy 1961–62
Oscar Hold 1962–64
Bill Leivers 1964–66
Keith Kettleborough 1966–67
George Raynor 1967–68
Lawrie McMenemy 1968–71
Maurice Setters 1971–74
Stan Anderson 1975–78
Billy Bremner 1978–85
Dave Cusack 1985–87
Dave Mackay 1987–89
Billy Bremner 1989–91
Steve Beaglehole 1991–93
Ian Atkins 1994
Sammy Chung 1994–96
Kerry Dixon (*Player-Manager*)
  1996–97
Dave Cowling 1997
Mark Weaver 1997–98
Ian Snodin 1998–99
Steve Wignall 1999–2001
Dave Penney 2002–06
Sean O'Driscoll 2006–11
Dean Saunders 2011–13
Brian Flynn 2013
Paul Dickov 2013–15
Darren Ferguson October 2015–

TEN YEAR LEAGUE RECORD

		P	W	D	L	F	A	Pts	Pos
2006-07	FL 1	46	16	15	15	52	47	63	11
2007-08	FL 1	46	23	11	12	65	41	80	3
2008-09	FL C	46	17	7	22	42	53	58	14
2009-10	FL C	46	15	15	16	59	58	60	12
2010-11	FL C	46	11	15	20	55	81	48	21
2011-12	FL C	46	8	12	26	43	80	36	24
2012-13	FL 1	46	25	9	12	62	44	84	1
2013-14	FL C	46	11	11	24	39	70	44	22
2014-15	FL 1	46	16	13	17	58	62	61	13
2015-16	FL 1	46	11	13	22	48	64	46	21

DID YOU KNOW

James Coppinger set a new all-time appearance record for Rovers in the FA Cup first round tie against Stalybridge Celtic in November 2015 when he played his 469th game for the club. James was made captain for the day as Rovers overcame their Conference North opponents 2-0 to progress into the second round draw.

DONCASTER ROVERS – FOOTBALL LEAGUE ONE 2015–16 LEAGUE RECORD

Match No.	Date	Venue	Opponents	Result		H/T Score	Lg Pos.	Goalscorers	Attendance
1	Aug 8	H	Bury	D	1-1	0-0	10	Forrester [90]	6429
2	16	A	Wigan Ath	D	0-0	0-0	15		8813
3	19	H	Southend U	D	0-0	0-0	14		5164
4	22	A	Port Vale	L	0-3	0-1	17		4775
5	29	H	Fleetwood T	W	2-0	2-0	14	Coppinger [17], Main [24]	4876
6	Sept 5	A	Gillingham	L	0-1	0-0	17		5685
7	12	A	Walsall	L	0-2	0-0	21		4127
8	19	H	Oldham Ath	D	1-1	1-1	22	Butler [26]	5647
9	26	A	Sheffield U	L	1-3	1-2	22	Stewart [25]	20,869
10	29	A	Swindon T	D	2-2	0-0	22	Anderson [73], Williams (pen) [80]	4693
11	Oct 3	H	Barnsley	W	2-1	1-0	21	Anderson [35], Chaplow [90]	9033
12	17	H	Bradford C	L	0-1	0-1	23		8410
13	20	A	Shrewsbury T	W	2-1	1-1	20	Coppinger [14], Anderson [87]	4735
14	24	A	Peterborough U	L	0-4	0-2	22		6092
15	27	A	Millwall	L	0-2	0-2	22		8294
16	31	H	Colchester U	W	2-0	1-0	18	Grant [41], Williams [64]	5324
17	Nov 14	A	Blackpool	W	2-0	2-0	16	Williams [5], Taylor-Sinclair [40]	6597
18	21	H	Rochdale	L	0-2	0-0	16		6125
19	24	H	Chesterfield	W	3-0	0-0	16	Tyson [62], Williams [70], Stewart [90]	5521
20	28	A	Coventry C	D	2-2	0-1	15	Tyson 2 [52, 72]	11,885
21	Dec 12	H	Crewe Alex	W	3-2	1-1	15	Grant [32], Williams [90], Stewart [90]	5342
22	19	A	Burton Alb	D	3-3	1-1	15	Williams [4], Keegan [70], Tyson (pen) [83]	4103
23	26	H	Scunthorpe U	L	0-1	0-1	16		8744
24	28	A	Oldham Ath	W	2-1	2-0	15	Williams 2 [12, 45]	4432
25	Jan 2	A	Southend U	W	3-0	1-0	11	Williams [44], Taylor-Sinclair [54], Tyson (pen) [58]	7134
26	16	H	Gillingham	D	2-2	0-1	12	Stewart [75], Williams [88]	6077
27	23	A	Fleetwood T	D	0-0	0-0	12		3508
28	26	H	Port Vale	L	1-2	0-1	14	Evina [88]	4799
29	Feb 2	H	Walsall	L	1-2	0-0	16	Mandeville [80]	5056
30	13	H	Sheffield U	L	0-1	0-1	17		10,168
31	20	A	Barnsley	L	0-1	0-0	17		11,638
32	27	H	Millwall	D	1-1	1-1	17	Chaplow [37]	6810
33	Mar 1	A	Swindon T	L	0-2	0-1	19		6556
34	5	H	Shrewsbury T	L	0-1	0-0	20		5878
35	8	A	Scunthorpe U	L	0-2	0-1	20		4887
36	12	A	Bradford C	L	1-2	0-1	20	Tyson [90]	17,889
37	19	H	Peterborough U	L	1-2	1-1	21	Coppinger [5]	7884
38	25	A	Colchester U	L	1-4	1-0	22	McSheffrey [21]	3771
39	28	H	Blackpool	L	0-1	0-0	22		5575
40	Apr 2	A	Rochdale	D	2-2	0-1	22	Lund [57], Butler [68]	2727
41	9	A	Bury	L	0-1	0-0	22		3233
42	16	H	Wigan Ath	W	3-1	0-1	22	Butler 2 [50, 54], Williams (pen) [88]	6987
43	19	A	Chesterfield	D	1-1	1-1	22	Rowe [6]	6461
44	23	H	Coventry C	W	2-0	0-0	22	Rowe [21], Williams [32]	6364
45	30	A	Crewe Alex	L	1-3	1-1	22	Rowe [28]	4403
46	May 8	H	Burton Alb	D	0-0	0-0	21		9803

Final League Position: 21

GOALSCORERS

League (48): Williams 12 (2 pens), Tyson 6 (2 pens), Butler 4, Stewart 4, Anderson 3, Coppinger 3, Rowe 3, Chaplow 2, Grant 2, Taylor-Sinclair 2, Evina 1, Forrester 1, Keegan 1, Lund 1, Main 1, Mandeville 1, McSheffrey 1.
FA Cup (6): Grant 2, Williams 2, Lund 1, Tyson 1.
Capital One Cup (2): Williams 2 (1 pen).
Johnstone's Paint Trophy (0).

Stuckmann T 35+1	McCullough L 28+4	Jones R 2	Butler A 40	Taylor-Sinclair A 38+5	Coppinger J 38+1	Chaplow R 20+7	Wellens R 11+1	Forrester H 3+4	Main C 6+4	Williams A 41+5	Tyson N 22+10	Evina C 38+4	Middleton H 24+10	MacKenzie B 11+4	Whitehouse B —+2	Lund M 25+5	Stewart C 11+15	Gobern O 4+1	N'Guessan D 1+7	Keegan P 11+4	Anderson K 5+2	Mandeville L 2+6	Grant C 18+1	Horsfield J 2	Felipe Mattioni R 5	Alcock C 24+3	Gooch L 7+3	Marosi M —+1	Lecygne E —+1	Neal C 2	Calder R 7+5	Rowe T 9+1	Matthews R 9	McSheffrey G 7	Longbottom W —+1	Match No.
1	2	3	4	5	6	7¹	8	9	10²	11¹	12	13	14																							1
1	2		3	5	10		8		6	12	11¹	9	7	4																						2
1	2		4	5	10	12	8		6²	13	11	9¹	7²	3	14																					3
1	2		4	5	10		8	7	12	11	6¹	9²		3	13																					4
1			4	5	6		8			11¹	10	9	7	3		2	12																			5
1			3	5	6		8			10²	11	9¹		4		2	12	7	13																	6
1			3	5	6		8¹			10	11²	12		4		2	9¹	7	14	13																7
1			4	5	2		13			10	11²	6		3		9	8¹	12	7																	8
1			4	3	2	12	8²	13		10		5	11⁸			9⁵	14		7¹	6																9
1	3¹		4	12	9	7	6	14		10		5	8³							13	11²	2														10
1			3	4	13	6²	8	7		9		5	12							10³	11	2	14													11
1	2		4²	12	9³	6¹	7			10	13	5	14		3		8				11															12
1	13		3	6	8³	7	14			10¹	5	12	4²			2	9				11															13
1			3	4	12	6	9¹	7²	14	10³	11	5	13			2	8																			14
1			3	4	5	7		8¹	12	14	11	6	9			2²	10⁵		13																	15
1	12		4	3	6				13	10³	11	5¹	7			2	9²			14						8										16
1			3	4	8					11	10²	9	7			2¹	14			13					6	5³	12									17
1			3	4	6					10	11¹	9	8			14			13	12³					7	5²	2									18
1			3	4	6					10	11¹	9	8			12									7	5	2									19
1	12		3	4	6					10²	11	9	8			13									7	5¹	2									20
1			3	4	6					10	11	9	7			5¹	12								8		2									21
1	13		3	4	7²	14				10	11	9³	6			5¹									8		2									22
1			3	4	6					10	11	9	7³			5²	13	14	12						8		2									23
1			3	4	10¹	14				11²	13	9	6			12			7						8	5³	2									24
1	2		4	5	7²					11	10	6¹	13			12									8	9	3									25
1	3		4¹	5	7					11²	10	6				14	12³			8			13		9	2										26
1	3			5	7	12				11		6				4¹				8			9²		2	10										27
1¹	4			5	7³	8				10		6				3²				14	9		2	11	12	13										28
	3			4	7¹	9³				11		5	8			14	13			6			12		2²	10					1					29
	2	3³	4			14				11	8	9	6				5¹			7			13		12	10²			1							30
1	2			4	12					10	11	9	8			3	5²			7³			6		13	14										31
1	3			4			6			10¹	11	9	12			5				7¹			8		2	13										32
1	2			4		7⁴				10³	11	9	8¹	14		5²	13						6		3	12										33
1	7		4	5¹						12	11	13				2	14						10³	8	3	6					9²					34
1	2		3	4		6				12	11	9				5²			7						13	10					8¹					35
1	3		4	5		6³				10	11	2	12	14		13				7²			9								8¹					36
1	6		3	4	7					11	10	5	8²			9¹							2								13	12				37
			4	5	6¹					13	10	2³	7	12		9³				3								1			14	8	1		11	38
			4	5	6					10	12		7			2	13			9³			3			5¹		1			8	9	1		11²	39
	8		4	3	7	12				11	14		13			2³										5⁹		1			6²	9	1		10¹	40
12	3		4	5	6³	7¹				11	13			8	14	2												1²				9	1²	10		41
	6		4	5²	7¹	8				10	14	12				2							3					1			13	9	1		11³	42
	6		4		7	9¹				10²	12	5				2							3					1			13	8	1		11	43
	9		4	6						11	12	5	13			2							3					1			8²	7	1		10¹	44
	6	3	12	7						10	11¹	5				2²	14			13			4					1			9³	8	1			45
	6		4	5	8³					11	12		7²			2				10¹			3					1			13	9	1		14	46

FA Cup

First Round	Stalybridge Celtic	(h)	2-0
Second Round	Cambridge U	(a)	3-1
Third Round	Stoke C	(h)	1-2

Capital One Cup

| First Round | Leeds U | (h) | 1-1 |

(aet; Doncaster R won 4-2 on penalties)

| Second Round | Ipswich T | (h) | 1-4 |

(aet)

Johnstone's Paint Trophy

| First Round | Burton Alb | (h) | 0-0 |

(aet; Doncaster R won 5-3 on penalties)

| Second Round | York C | (a) | 0-2 |

EVERTON

FOUNDATION

St Domingo Church Sunday School formed a football club in 1878 which played at Stanley Park. Enthusiasm was so great that in November 1879 they decided to expand membership and changed the name to Everton, playing in black shirts with a scarlet sash and nicknamed the 'Black Watch'. After wearing several other colours, royal blue was adopted in 1901.

Goodison Park, Goodison Road, Liverpool L4 4EL.

Telephone: (0151) 556 1878.

Fax: (0151) 281 1046.

Ticket Office: (0151) 556 1878.

Website: www.evertonfc.com

Email: everton@evertonfc.com

Ground Capacity: 39,571.

Record Attendance: 78,299 v Liverpool, Division 1, 18 September 1948.

Pitch Measurements: 100.48m × 68m (109yd × 74yd).

Chairman: Bill Kenwright CBE.

Chief Executive: Robert Elstone.

Manager: Ronald Koeman.

Assistant Manager: Erwin Koeman.

Physio: Matt Connery.

Colours: Blue shirts with white trim, white shorts with blue trim, white socks with blue trim.

Year Formed: 1878.

Turned Professional: 1885.

Previous Name: 1878, St Domingo FC; 1879, Everton.

Club Nickname: 'The Toffees'.

Grounds: 1878, Stanley Park; 1882, Priory Road; 1884, Anfield Road; 1892, Goodison Park.

HONOURS

League Champions: Division 1 – 1914–15, 1927–28, 1931–32, 1938–39, 1962–63, 1969–70, 1984–85, 1986–87; Football League 1890–91; Division 2 – 1930–31.
Runners-up: Division 1 – 1894–95, 1901–02, 1904–05, 1908–09, 1911–12, 1985–86; Football League 1889–90; Division 2 – 1953–54.
FA Cup Winners: 1906, 1933, 1966, 1984, 1995.
Runners-up: 1893, 1897, 1907, 1968, 1985, 1986, 1989, 2009.
League Cup: Runners-up: 1977, 1984.
League Super Cup: Runners-up: 1986.
Full Members' Cup: Runners-up: 1989, 1991.
European Competitions
European Cup: 1963–64, 1970–71 *(qf)*.
Champions League: 2005–06.
Fairs Cup: 1962–63, 1964–65, 1965–66.
UEFA Cup: 1975–76, 1978–79, 1979–80, 2005–06, 2007–08, 2008–09.
Europa League: 2009–10, 2014–15.
European Cup-Winners' Cup: 1966–67, 1984–85 *(winners)*, 1995–96.

First Football League Game: 8 September 1888, Football League, v Accrington (h) W 2–1 – Smalley; Dick, Ross; Holt, Jones, Dobson; Fleming (2), Waugh, Lewis, Edgar Chadwick, Farmer.

Record League Victory: 9–1 v Manchester C, Division 1, 3 September 1906 – Scott; Balmer, Crelley; Booth, Taylor (1), Abbott (1); Sharp, Bolton (1), Young (4), Settle (2), George Wilson. 9–1 v Plymouth Arg, Division 2, 27 December 1930 – Coggins; Williams, Cresswell; McPherson, Griffiths, Thomson; Critchley, Dunn, Dean (4), Johnson (1), Stein (4).

sky SPORTS FACT FILE

David Moyes, who managed Everton between 2002 and 2013, had the distinction of winning the League Managers' Association Manager of the Year Award in his first season in charge of the club. He went on to win the title twice more with successes in the 2004–05 and 2008–09 seasons.

Record Cup Victory: 11–2 v Derby Co, FA Cup 1st rd, 18 January 1890 – Smalley; Hannah, Doyle (1); Kirkwood, Holt (1), Parry; Latta, Brady (3), Geary (3), Edgar Chadwick, Millward (3).

Record Defeat: 4–10 v Tottenham H, Division 1, 11 October 1958.

Most League Points (2 for a win): 66, Division 1, 1969–70.

Most League Points (3 for a win): 90, Division 1, 1984–85.

Most League Goals: 121, Division 2, 1930–31.

Highest League Scorer in Season: William Ralph 'Dixie' Dean, 60, Division 1, 1927–28 (All-time League record).

Most League Goals in Total Aggregate: William Ralph 'Dixie' Dean, 349, 1925–37.

Most League Goals in One Match: 6, Jack Southworth v WBA, Division 1, 30 December 1893.

Most Capped Player: Neville Southall, 92 (1 on loan at Port Vale), Wales; Tim Howard, 92 (109), USA.

Most League Appearances: Neville Southall, 578, 1981–98.

Youngest League Player: Jose Baxter, 16 years 191 days v Blackburn R, 16 August 2008.

Record Transfer Fee Received: £25,000,000 (rising to £29,000,000) from Manchester U for Wayne Rooney, August 2004.

Record Transfer Fee Paid: £28,000,000 to Chelsea for Romelu Lukaku, July 2014.

Football League Record: 1888 Founder Member of the Football League; 1930–31 Division 2; 1931–51 Division 1; 1951–54 Division 2; 1954–92 Division 1; 1992– FA Premier League.

MANAGERS

W. E. Barclay 1888–89
(Secretary-Manager)
Dick Molyneux 1889–1901
(Secretary-Manager)
William C. Cuff 1901–18
(Secretary-Manager)
W. J. Sawyer 1918–19
(Secretary-Manager)
Thomas H. McIntosh 1919–35
(Secretary-Manager)
Theo Kelly 1936–48
Cliff Britton 1948–56
Ian Buchan 1956–58
Johnny Carey 1958–61
Harry Catterick 1961–73
Billy Bingham 1973–77
Gordon Lee 1977–81
Howard Kendall 1981–87
Colin Harvey 1987–90
Howard Kendall 1990–93
Mike Walker 1994
Joe Royle 1994–97
Howard Kendall 1997–98
Walter Smith 1998–2002
David Moyes 2002–13
Roberto Martinez 2013–16
Ronald Koeman June 2016–

LATEST SEQUENCES

Longest Sequence of League Wins: 12, 24.3.1894 – 13.10.1894.

Longest Sequence of League Defeats: 6, 27.8.2005– 15.10.2005.

Longest Sequence of League Draws: 5, 4.5.1977 – 16.5.1977.

Longest Sequence of Unbeaten League Matches: 20, 29.4.1978 – 16.12.1978.

Longest Sequence Without a League Win: 14, 6.3.1937 – 4.9.1937.

Successive Scoring Runs: 40 from 15.3.1930.

Successive Non-scoring Runs: 6 from 27.8.2005.

TEN YEAR LEAGUE RECORD

		P	W	D	L	F	A	Pts	Pos
2006-07	PR Lge	38	15	13	10	52	36	58	6
2007-08	PR Lge	38	19	8	11	55	33	65	5
2008-09	PR Lge	38	17	12	9	55	37	63	5
2009-10	PR Lge	38	16	13	9	60	49	61	8
2010-11	PR Lge	38	13	15	10	51	45	54	7
2011-12	PR Lge	38	15	11	12	50	40	56	7
2012-13	PR Lge	38	16	15	7	55	40	63	6
2013-14	PR Lge	38	21	9	8	61	39	72	5
2014-15	PR Lge	38	12	11	15	48	50	47	11
2015-16	PR Lge	38	11	14	13	59	55	47	11

DID YOU KNOW ?

Everton's Goodison Park stadium hosted five matches in the 1966 World Cup finals including the semi-final tie between West Germany and the Soviet Union. The Germans triumphed 2-1 in front of a crowd of 39,840.

EVERTON – FA PREMIER LEAGUE 2015–16 LEAGUE RECORD

Match No.	Date	Venue	Opponents	Result	H/T Score	Lg Pos.	Goalscorers	Attendance
1	Aug 8	H	Watford	D	2-2	0-1	5	Barkley 76, Kone 86	39,063
2	15	A	Southampton	W	3-0	2-0	3	Lukaku 2 22, 45, Barkley 84	30,966
3	23	H	Manchester C	L	0-2	0-0	7		38,523
4	29	A	Tottenham H	D	0-0	0-0	9		35,865
5	Sept 12	H	Chelsea	W	3-1	2-1	5	Naismith 3 17, 22, 82	38,311
6	19	A	Swansea C	D	0-0	0-0	6		20,805
7	28	H	WBA	W	3-2	0-1	5	Lukaku 2 55, 84, Kone 75	24,240
8	Oct 4	H	Liverpool	D	1-1	1-1	7	Lukaku 45	39,598
9	17	H	Manchester U	L	0-3	0-2	9		39,553
10	24	A	Arsenal	L	1-2	1-2	10	Barkley 44	59,985
11	Nov 1	H	Sunderland	W	6-2	2-1	9	Deulofeu 19, Kone 3 31, 62, 76, Coates (og) 55, Lukaku 60	36,617
12	7	A	West Ham U	D	1-1	1-1	8	Lukaku 43	34,977
13	21	H	Aston Villa	W	4-0	3-0	7	Barkley 2 17, 42, Lukaku 2 28, 59	38,424
14	28	A	Bournemouth	D	3-3	2-0	7	Funes Mori 25, Lukaku 36, Barkley 90	11,228
15	Dec 7	H	Crystal Palace	D	1-1	0-0	9	Lukaku 81	35,736
16	12	H	Norwich C	D	1-1	1-0	9	Lukaku 15	27,027
17	19	H	Leicester C	L	2-3	1-1	10	Lukaku 32, Mirallas 89	39,570
18	26	A	Newcastle U	W	1-0	0-0	9	Cleverley 90	51,682
19	28	H	Stoke C	L	3-4	1-2	11	Lukaku 2 22, 64, Deulofeu 71	39,340
20	Jan 3	H	Tottenham H	D	1-1	1-1	11	Lennon 22	38,482
21	13	A	Manchester C	D	0-0	0-0	11		53,796
22	16	A	Chelsea	D	3-3	0-0	11	Terry (og) 50, Mirallas 56, Funes Mori 90	41,633
23	24	H	Swansea C	L	1-2	1-2	12	Cork (og) 26	36,908
24	Feb 3	H	Newcastle U	W	3-0	1-0	11	Lennon 23, Barkley 2 (2 pens) 88, 90	36,061
25	6	A	Stoke C	W	3-0	3-0	8	Lukaku (pen) 11, Coleman 28, Lennon 42	27,733
26	13	H	WBA	L	0-1	0-1	10		38,103
27	Mar 1	A	Aston Villa	W	3-1	2-0	10	Funes Mori 5, Lennon 30, Lukaku 60	29,755
28	5	H	West Ham U	L	2-3	1-0	11	Lukaku 13, Lennon 56	39,000
29	19	H	Arsenal	L	0-2	0-2	12		39,270
30	Apr 3	A	Manchester U	L	0-1	0-0	12		75,341
31	9	A	Watford	D	1-1	1-1	14	McCarthy 45	20,663
32	13	A	Crystal Palace	D	0-0	0-0	12		23,528
33	16	H	Southampton	D	1-1	0-0	11	Funes Mori 68	36,761
34	20	A	Liverpool	L	0-4	0-2	11		43,854
35	30	H	Bournemouth	W	2-1	1-1	11	Cleverley 7, Baines 64	38,345
36	May 7	A	Leicester C	L	1-3	0-2	12	Mirallas 88	32,140
37	11	A	Sunderland	L	0-3	0-2	12		46,454
38	15	H	Norwich C	W	3-0	2-0	11	McCarthy 19, Baines (pen) 44, Mirallas 48	36,691

Final League Position: 11

GOALSCORERS

League (59): Lukaku 18 (1 pen), Barkley 8 (2 pens), Kone 5, Lennon 5, Funes Mori 4, Mirallas 4, Naismith 3, Baines 2 (1 pen), Cleverley 2, Deulofeu 2, McCarthy 2, Coleman 1, own goals 3.
FA Cup (10): Lukaku 3, Barkley 2, Kone 2, Lennon 1, Mirallas 1 (pen), own goal 1.
Capital One Cup (13): Lukaku 4, Barkley 2, Deulofeu 2, Funes Mori 1, Mirallas 1, Naismith 1, Osman 1, own goal 1.

Howard T 25	Coleman S 27+1	Stones J 31+2	Jagielka P 21	Galloway B 14+1	McCarthy J 29	Barry G 32+1	Mirallas K 10+13	Barkley R 36+2	Cleverley T 17+5	Lukaku R 36+1	Kone A 16+9	Oviedo B 12+2	Naismith S 4+6	Browning T 3+2	Deulofeu G 16+10	Besic M 7+5	Lennon A 17+8	Funes Mori R 24+4	Gibson D 2+5	Osman L 2+7	Baines L 16+2	Pienaar S —+4	Robles J 13	Niasse O 2+3	Connolly C —+1	Davies T 1+1	Pennington M 4	Hibbert T —+1	Dowell K 1+1	Kenny J —+1	Match No.
1	2	3	4	5^1	6	7	8^2	9	10	11^3	12	13	14																		1
1	2	3	4	5^2	6	7		9	10	11^3	8^1	12	13	14																	2
1	2	3	4	5^1	6	7		9	10^3	11	8^2	13	12	14																	3
1	2	3	4		6	7	12	9	10^1	11^2	8^3	5	13		14																4
1	2^3	3	4	5	6	7		9		11	10^2		12				8^1	13	14												5
1		3	4	5	6	7	13■	9■		11	8^1		10	2	12																6
		3		5	6	7		9		11^3	12		10^2	2^1	8		14	4	13												7
		3		5	6	7		9		11		13	10^2	2	8^1			12	4												8
1	2	3	4	5	6	7		9		11		12	10^1		13			8^2													9
1	2^3	3	4^1	5	6	7■	13	9		11		14			8			10^2	12												10
1	2	3	12		6	7	13	9		11^3	10	5^1			8^2			4		14											11
1	2	3		5	6	7	12	9		11	10^1				8^2			4													12
1	2	3		5	6^3	7	12	9^1		11	10				8^2			4	14	13											13
1	2	3		5	6^1	7		9	12	11	10^3				8^2		13	4	14												14
1	2	3		5^1		7		9	6	11	10				8			4			12										15
1	2	3				7	12	9■	6	11	10				8^1		4	13			5										16
1	2	3				7	13	9	6	11	10^1				8^2		12				5										17
1	2	3				7	11^3	6	8	10					13	12	9^2	4		14	5										18
1	2	3		5	8^1	7		6		8	10	11		13	9			4													19
1	2	3				7		6	8	10	11^1				13	12	9^2	4			5										20
	2	3				7		9		11	12				8^1	6		4		10^2	5	13									21
	3	4			6	10		9^1		11			2^1		13	7	8^2	12			5	14									22
1	14	3			6	10^2	9	12	11			2^3		8	7^1		4				5	13									23
	2		3			6	7		9	10	11^1	12	5			8	4						1								24
	2		3		6^3	7	13	9^2	10	11^1	12	5				8	4	14				1									25
	2		3		6^3	7		9	10^1	11	12	5		13		8^2	4	14				1									26
	2^1	12	3		6	7	10^3	9		11		5^2				8	4		13			1	14								27
5	2^1	3		6	14	11■	7		10^3		8			12	9^2	4					1	13									28
2	12	3		6			9^2	10	11		13	7^1	8		4		5		1												29
2	3	4		6		12	7^2	8	10			9^1		11		5	1	13													30
2	3	4^3		6		7	13	9	12	11			8^2		10	14		5	1												31
2	3		6■	7	14	9^1		11	8^1	13			12	10^2	4			5	1												32
2^1	3			11	13		10	5	9^2	6		4	7^3	8		1		12	14												33
3^3		6	7^1	8	9^3	13	11		2			12	10	4■			5	14	1												34
1	3		6		9^3	10	13			2^1	8		7	5			11^2			4	12	14									35
	3	8		12	7^3	9^1	11	2			6	13	14	5	1	10^2			4												36
	3	7	6	10	9^1	8^2	11			12	4		13	5	1			2													37
1	3	4	6^2	7	10	14		11			13			5				9	2^1			8^3	12								38

FA Cup

Third Round	Dagenham & R	(h)	2-0
Fourth Round	Carlisle U	(a)	3-0
Fifth Round	Bournemouth	(a)	2-0
Sixth Round	Chelsea	(h)	2-0
Semi-Final	Manchester U	(Wembley)	1-2

Capital One Cup

Second Round	Barnsley	(a)	5-3
(aet)			
Third Round	Reading	(a)	2-1
Fourth Round	Norwich C	(h)	1-1
(aet; Everton won 4-3 on penalties)			
Quarter-Final	Middlesbrough	(a)	2-0
Semi-Final 1st leg	Manchester C	(h)	2-1
Semi-Final 2nd leg	Manchester C	(a)	1-3
(Manchester C won 4-3 on aggregate)			

EXETER CITY

FOUNDATION

Exeter City was formed in 1904 by the amalgamation of St Sidwell's United and Exeter United. The club first played in the East Devon League and then the Plymouth & District League. After an exhibition match between West Bromwich Albion and Woolwich Arsenal, which was held to test interest as Exeter was then a rugby stronghold, it was decided to form Exeter City. At a meeting at the Red Lion Hotel in 1908, the club turned professional.

St James Park, Stadium Way, Exeter, Devon EX4 6PX.

Telephone: (01392) 411 243.

Fax: (01392) 413 959.

Ticket Office: (01392) 411 243.

Website: www.exetercityfc.co.uk

Email: reception@exetercityfc.co.uk

Ground Capacity: 8,714.

Record Attendance: 20,984 v Sunderland, FA Cup 6th rd (replay), 4 March 1931.

Pitch Measurements: 104m × 64m (113.5yd × 70yd).

Vice Chairman: Julian Tagg.

Manager: Paul Tisdale.

Director of Football: Steve Perryman.

Physio: Ade Saunderson.

Colours: Red and white striped shirts with red sleeves, black shorts with red trim, white socks with black hoops.

Year Formed: 1904.

Turned Professional: 1908.

Club Nickname: 'The Grecians'.

Ground: 1904, St James Park.

HONOURS

League Champions: Division 4 – 1989–90.
Runners-up: Division 3S – 1932–33; FL 2 – 2008–09; Division 4 – 1976–77; Conference – (4th) 2007–08 *(promoted via play-offs).*
FA Cup: 6th rd replay – 1931; 6th rd – 1981.
League Cup: never past 4th rd.

First Football League Game: 28 August 1920, Division 3, v Brentford (h) W 3–0 – Pym; Coleburne, Feebury (1p); Crawshaw, Carrick, Mitton; Appleton, Makin, Wright (1), Vowles (1), Dockray.

Record League Victory: 8–1 v Coventry C, Division 3 (S), 4 December 1926 – Bailey; Pollard, Charlton; Pullen, Pool, Garrett; Purcell (2), McDevitt, Blackmore (2), Dent (2), Compton (2). 8–1 v Aldershot, Division 3 (S), 4 May 1935 – Chesters; Gray, Miller; Risdon, Webb, Angus; Jack Scott (1), Wrightson (1), Poulter (3), McArthur (1), Dryden (1), (1 og).

Record Cup Victory: 14–0 v Weymouth, FA Cup 1st qual rd, 3 October 1908 – Fletcher; Craig, Bulcock; Ambler, Chadwick, Wake; Parnell (1), Watson (1), McGuigan (4), Bell (6), Copestake (2).

Record Defeat: 0–9 v Notts Co, Division 3 (S), 16 October 1948. 0–9 v Northampton T, Division 3 (S), 12 April 1958.

sky SPORTS FACT FILE

In May 2004 Exeter City marked their centenary with a fixture against a Brazil Masters XI at St James Park. The opposition, which included former World Cup winner Dunga, triumphed 1-0 in a game which also celebrated the 90th anniversary of the Grecians' visit to South America back in 1914, when they provided the first-ever opponents for the Brazil national team.

Most League Points (2 for a win): 62, Division 4, 1976–77.

Most League Points (3 for a win): 89, Division 4, 1989–90.

Most League Goals: 88, Division 3 (S), 1932–33.

Highest League Scorer in Season: Fred Whitlow, 33, Division 3 (S), 1932–33.

Most League Goals in Total Aggregate: Tony Kellow, 129, 1976–78, 1980–83, 1985–88.

Most League Goals in One Match: 4, Harold 'Jazzo' Kirk v Portsmouth, Division 3 (S), 3 March 1923; 4, Fred Dent v Bristol R, Division 3 (S), 5 November 1927; 4, Fred Whitlow v Watford, Division 3 (S), 29 October 1932.

Most Capped Player: Joel Grant, 2 (14), Jamaica.

Most League Appearances: Arnold Mitchell, 495, 1952–66.

Youngest League Player: Cliff Bastin, 16 years 31 days v Coventry C, 14 April 1928.

Record Transfer Fee Received: £500,000 from Manchester C for Martin Phillips, November 1995.

Record Transfer Fee Paid: £65,000 to Blackpool for Tony Kellow, March 1980.

Football League Record: 1920 Elected to Division 3; 1921–58 Division 3 (S); 1958–64 Division 4; 1964–66 Division 3; 1966–77 Division 4; 1977–84 Division 3; 1984–90 Division 4; 1990–92 Division 3; 1992–94 Division 2; 1994–2003 Division 3; 2003–08 Conference; 2008–09 FL 2; 2009–12 FL 1; 2012– FL 2.

LATEST SEQUENCES

Longest Sequence of League Wins: 7, 23.4.1977 – 20.8.1977.

Longest Sequence of League Defeats: 7, 14.1.1984 – 25.2.1984.

Longest Sequence of League Draws: 6, 13.9.1986 – 4.10.1986.

Longest Sequence of Unbeaten League Matches: 13, 23.8.1986 – 25.10.1986.

Longest Sequence Without a League Win: 18, 21.2.1995 – 19.8.1995.

Successive Scoring Runs: 22 from 15.9.1958.

Successive Non-scoring Runs: 6 from 17.1.1986.

MANAGERS

Arthur Chadwick 1910–22
Fred Mavin 1923–27
Dave Wilson 1928–29
Billy McDevitt 1929–35
Jack English 1935–39
George Roughton 1945–52
Norman Kirkman 1952–53
Norman Dodgin 1953–57
Bill Thompson 1957–58
Frank Broome 1958–60
Glen Wilson 1960–62
Cyril Spiers 1962–63
Jack Edwards 1963–65
Ellis Stuttard 1965–66
Jock Basford 1966–67
Frank Broome 1967–69
Johnny Newman 1969–76
Bobby Saxton 1977–79
Brian Godfrey 1979–83
Gerry Francis 1983–84
Jim Iley 1984–85
Colin Appleton 1985–87
Terry Cooper 1988–91
Alan Ball 1991–94
Terry Cooper 1994–95
Peter Fox 1995–2000
Noel Blake 2000–01
John Cornforth 2001–02
Neil McNab 2002–03
Gary Peters 2003
Eamonn Dolan 2003–04
Alex Inglethorpe 2004–06
Paul Tisdale June 2006–

TEN YEAR LEAGUE RECORD

		P	W	D	L	F	A	Pts	Pos
2006-07	Conf	46	22	12	12	67	48	78	5
2007-08	Conf P	46	22	17	7	83	58	83	4
2008-09	FL 2	46	22	13	11	65	50	79	2
2009-10	FL 1	46	11	18	17	48	60	51	18
2010-11	FL 1	46	20	10	16	66	73	70	8
2011-12	FL 1	46	10	12	24	46	75	42	23
2012-13	FL 2	46	18	10	18	63	62	64	10
2013-14	FL 2	46	14	13	19	54	57	55	16
2014-15	FL 2	46	17	13	16	61	65	64	10
2015-16	FL 2	46	17	13	16	63	65	64	14

DID YOU KNOW ?

Jack Banks became the first professional player taken on by Exeter City when he signed in December 1907. Jack, a wing-half who appeared in the 1895 FA Cup final for West Bromwich Albion, combined his playing duties with the role of club trainer.

EXETER CITY – FOOTBALL LEAGUE TWO 2015–16 LEAGUE RECORD

Match No.	Date	Venue	Opponents	Result		H/T Score	Lg Pos.	Goalscorers	Attendance
1	Aug 8	H	Yeovil T	W	3-2	2-0	8	Nichols (pen) [31], Wheeler [41], Hoskins [84]	5659
2	15	A	Northampton T	L	0-3	0-2	13		4313
3	18	A	Dagenham & R	W	2-1	1-0	9	Harley [36], Brown [62]	1567
4	22	H	York C	D	0-0	0-0	8		3139
5	29	A	AFC Wimbledon	L	1-2	1-1	13	Harley [33]	3803
6	Sept 5	H	Leyton Orient	W	4-0	2-0	6	Nichols 2 (2 pens) [5, 56], Nicholls [37], Wheeler [77]	3648
7	12	H	Hartlepool U	W	1-0	0-0	6	Ribeiro [90]	3135
8	19	A	Accrington S	L	2-4	0-2	9	Holmes [75], Grant [90]	1403
9	26	H	Wycombe W	L	0-2	0-0	14		3639
10	29	A	Portsmouth	W	2-1	1-0	9	Wheeler [20], Davies [56]	15,822
11	Oct 3	A	Newport Co	D	1-1	0-0	11	Grant [61]	2870
12	11	H	Stevenage	D	3-3	2-2	11	Wheeler 2 [4, 80], Morrison [15]	3235
13	17	A	Carlisle U	L	0-1	0-0	13		4021
14	21	H	Cambridge U	W	1-0	1-0	11	Nichols [9]	2883
15	24	H	Notts Co	D	1-1	1-1	11	Nichols [20]	3429
16	31	A	Barnet	L	0-2	0-1	13		2105
17	Nov 14	H	Crawley T	D	2-2	2-1	14	Nicholls [8], Nichols [45]	3664
18	21	A	Plymouth Arg	W	2-1	2-0	13	Harley 2 (1 pen) [30 (p), 39]	14,008
19	24	A	Mansfield T	W	2-0	2-0	10	Grant [6], Holmes [41]	2435
20	28	A	Bristol R	D	1-1	0-0	10	Reid [90]	5548
21	Dec 19	H	Luton T	L	2-3	0-2	12	Nichols [71], Nicholls [82]	3777
22	26	A	Oxford U	L	0-3	0-0	14		9683
23	28	H	AFC Wimbledon	L	0-2	0-2	16		5072
24	Jan 2	H	Dagenham & R	L	1-2	1-1	16	Nichols [43]	3451
25	12	A	Morecambe	D	1-1	0-0	15	Stockley [54]	1040
26	16	A	Leyton Orient	W	3-1	3-1	14	Stockley 2 [14, 32], Nichols [23]	5758
27	23	H	Accrington S	W	2-1	1-1	13	Nichols [5], Ribeiro [79]	3669
28	30	A	Hartlepool U	W	2-0	1-0	12	Nicholls [36], Grant [85]	3678
29	Feb 13	A	Wycombe W	L	0-1	0-0	13		3358
30	16	A	York C	L	0-2	0-1	13		2920
31	20	H	Newport Co	D	1-1	0-0	14	Tillson [51]	3924
32	23	H	Oxford U	L	1-4	0-2	14	Nicholls [77]	3089
33	27	A	Stevenage	W	2-0	0-0	14	Stockley 2 [84, 90]	2812
34	Mar 1	H	Portsmouth	D	1-1	0-1	14	Watkins [90]	3855
35	5	A	Cambridge U	W	1-0	0-0	14	Watkins [76]	4573
36	12	H	Carlisle U	D	2-2	1-1	14	Stockley [7], Wheeler [79]	3375
37	19	A	Notts Co	W	4-1	1-1	14	Stockley [8], Taylor [68], Ribeiro [71], Watkins [78]	3813
38	25	H	Barnet	D	1-1	1-1	13	Stockley [20]	4389
39	28	A	Crawley T	W	2-0	1-0	11	Taylor [28], Watkins [74]	2416
40	Apr 2	H	Plymouth Arg	W	2-1	0-0	10	Watkins 2 [80, 90]	7177
41	9	A	Yeovil T	W	2-0	1-0	9	Watkins [16], Taylor [69]	5394
42	16	H	Northampton T	D	0-0	0-0	9		5077
43	19	H	Mansfield T	L	2-3	0-1	10	Watkins [64], Ribeiro [79]	3407
44	23	A	Bristol R	L	1-3	0-2	12	Taylor [48]	10,254
45	30	H	Morecambe	D	1-1	0-0	11	Stockley (pen) [89]	3936
46	May 7	A	Luton T	L	1-4	0-3	14	Stockley [47]	8427

Final League Position: 14

GOALSCORERS

League (63): Nichols 10 (3 pens), Stockley 10 (1 pen), Watkins 8, Wheeler 6, Nicholls 5, Grant 4, Harley 4 (1 pen), Ribeiro 4, Taylor 4, Holmes 2, Brown 1, Davies 1, Hoskins 1, Morrison 1, Reid 1, Tillson 1.
FA Cup (7): Nichols 2, Holmes 1, Morrison 1, Nicholls 1, Tillson 1, Watkins 1.
Capital One Cup (5): Wheeler 2, McCready 1, Nicholls 1, Oyeleke 1.
Johnstone's Paint Trophy (2): Harley 1 (pen), Nicholls 1.

Olejnik R 45	Davies A 18 + 10	Ribeiro C 31 + 4	Brown T 39 + 1	McAllister J 25 + 3	Wheeler D 26 + 5	Harley R 26 + 2	Oakley M 24 + 5	Noble D 24 + 6	Nicholls A 26 + 9	Nichols T 19 + 4	Hoskins W 2 + 7	Morrison C 4 + 16	Oyeleke E 4 + 4	Tillson J 22 + 4	Holmes L 30 + 7	Woodman C 22 + 3	Butterfield D 8 + 2	McCready T 8 + 2	Grant J 19 + 7	Moore-Taylor J 32	Watkins O 15 + 5	Reid J 8 + 5	Stockley J 21 + 1	Taylor J 7 + 9	Hamon J 1	Match No.
1	2	3	4	5	6	7	8	9¹	10³	11²	12	13	14													1
1	6	2	4	5¹	8	7			11³	10	13			3²	12	14										2
1	14	2	4	5		7	13	8²	6¹	11	12		9	3	10³											3
1	8	2¹	3	5		9	4		10²	11³	13	14	7	12	6											4
1	2³		3	5	9	6	8	7²			10¹	14	13	4	11		12									5
1		2	4	5¹	11¹	7	6	9²	8	10				14	3		12		13							6
1		2	3	5	6	7	8²	9	10³	11¹		12		4	13			14								7
1		2	3		11³		6¹	7	8²	10		13	12	4	9	5		14								8
1		2	3		6		8	7	13	14	11²	12		9	5¹			10³	4							9
1	8	2	4		10		6³			14		7¹	3	11		12	13	9²	5							10
1	14	5	2		6³		8	9	12	13		11²		3	7¹			10	4							11
1	13	2	3	5¹	9		7²	8		12		10³		14	6			11	4							12
1	6	2	4	5¹	9			10¹		14	12			13	7	8		11²	3							13
1		2		5	10		8	12	11					4	9¹		7		6	3						14
1	12	2		5	9³	14		7	6	10		13		4²			8		11¹	3						15
1	12	4	3	5	10²	9		7		11¹		13					8	2³	6		14					16
1	2		3	5	12	7		8	9	10		11¹						6	4							17
1	2	12	3	5¹	8	9	13	6						7¹				4	10	11						18
1	2	3	4		12	8	13	6	7	11¹				9³	14			10²	5							19
1	2		3		6	8		7¹	9	14		10⁵		13	12	5²			6	4	11					20
1	2						7¹		8	10		13		3	9	5			6	4	12	11²				21
1	6				13		7¹		8	11		14		5	12	3			2³	4	9	10²				22
1	2³	14					7²		8	10¹		12		4	6	5			9	3	13	11				23
1	2³		3¹				13	12	7	10		14		8	9	5			6	4		11²				24
1			7	2			6	12	13	11³	14			8		5			4²	9¹	3		10			25
1	13	2	3	14			12	7³	6	10					9²	5¹	8		4			11				26
1	13	12	3	5			7		9	11³				8			2	6²	4¹		14	10				27
1	12	4	3	5			9		8²					7	6¹			2	10³			14	11	13		28
1		4	2	3	7²	13		9						12		5	6	8³			11¹		10	14		29
1		3³	4	13		7¹	8²	14			12			9	6		2		5			11	10			30
1	2		3	5	10¹	9		7						8	6				4		13	11²	12			31
1	2		3		10	8		7			13			4	6³			9¹	5	14		11²	12			32
1		3	13		11	9	7	8³	6					12	5	2¹			4		10²	14				33
1		2¹	3²		9		8	13	7				14	6	5			12	4	10		11³				34
1		2	3		7¹	9	8							6	5				4	10		11	12			35
1		2	3		6	7	8							9	5				4	11		10				36
1		2	3		6²	9	8	13						10¹	5			14	4	7		11³	12			37
1		2¹	3		10²	7	8		13					9	5				4	6		11	12			38
1	6		3	11	4	12	7							9	5			13		8²		10	2¹			39
1	12	4	3	2¹	10³	8	7¹	14						9	5				6			11	13			40
1	13		3	2		7		6	12					9	5				4	8²		10	11¹			41
1		3	2	13	7		8	6							5				4	11²	12	10¹	9			42
1	13	3	2²		8	7	12							6¹	5				4	10		11	9			43
1	2	4²	12		8	7	13							6¹	5⁵			14	3	9		11	10			44
1	2	3		12										7	6²	5¹		8	14	4	10³	13	11	9		45
	2	3	5				7	11				6²	4	14		8			13		9¹	10¹	12		1	46

FA Cup

First Round	Didcot T	(a)	3-0
Second Round	Port Vale	(h)	2-0
Third Round	Liverpool	(h)	2-2
Replay	Liverpool	(a)	0-3

Capital One Cup

First Round	Swindon T	(a)	2-1
Second Round	Sunderland	(a)	3-6

Johnstone's Paint Trophy

First Round	Portsmouth	(h)	2-0
Second Round	Plymouth Arg	(a)	0-2

FLEETWOOD TOWN

FOUNDATION

Originally formed in 1908 as Fleetwood FC, it was liquidated in 1976. Re-formed as Fleetwood Town in 1977, it folded again in 1996. Once again, it was re-formed a year later as Fleetwood Wanderers, but a sponsorship deal saw the club's name immediately changed to Fleetwood Freeport through the local retail outlet centre. This sponsorship ended in 2002, but since then local energy businessman Andy Pilley took charge and the club has risen through the non-league pyramid until finally achieving Football League status in 2012 as Fleetwood Town.

Highbury Stadium, Park Avenue, Fleetwood, Lancashire FY7 6TX.

Telephone: (01253) 775 080.

Ticket Office: (01253) 775 080

Website: www.fleetwoodtownfc.com

Email: info@fleetwoodtownfc.com

Ground Capacity: 5,133.

Record Attendance: (Before 1997) 6,150 v Rochdale, FA Cup 1st rd, 13 November 1965; (Since 1997) 5,194 v York C, FL 2 Play-Off semi-final 2nd leg, 16 May 2014.

Pitch Measurements: 100.5m × 65m (110yd × 71yd).

Chairman: Andy Pilley.

Chief Executive: Steve Curwood.

Manager: Steven Pressley.

Assistant Managers: Chris Lucketti and Neil MacFarlane.

Physio: Luke Bussey.

Colours: Red shirts with white sleeves and trim, white shorts with red trim, red socks with white trim.

Year Formed: 1908 (re-formed 1997).

Previous Names: 1908, Fleetwood FC; 1977, Fleetwood Town; 1978, Fleetwood Wanderers; 2002 Fleetwood Town.

Club Nicknames: 'The Trawlermen', 'The Cod Army'.

Grounds: 1908, North Euston Hotel; 1934, Memorial Park (now Highbury Stadium).

HONOURS

League Champions: Conference – 2011–12.
FA Cup: 3rd rd – 2012.
League Cup: never past 1st rd.

sky SPORTS FACT FILE

Fleetwood Town were established as Fleetwood Wanderers in 1997 and the club's official ownership is still held with Fleetwood Wanderers Limited, with Fleetwood Town as a trading name. They actually played a couple of games under this name before adopting the title Fleetwood Freeport following a sponsorship deal.

First Football League Game: 18 August 2012, FL 2, v Torquay U (h) D 0–0 – Davies; Beeley, Mawene, McNulty, Howell, Nicolson, Johnson, McGuire, Ball, Parkin, Mangan.

Record League Victory: 13–0 v Oldham T, North West Counties Div 2, 5 December 1998.

Record Defeat: 0–7 v Billingham T, FA Cup 1st qual rd, 15 September 2001.

Most League Points (3 for a win): 76, FL 2, 2013–14

Most League Goals: 66, FL 2, 2013–14.

Most League Goals in Total Aggregate: David Ball, 23, 2012–15.

Most League Goals in One Match: 3, Steven Schumacher v Newport Co, FL 2, 2 November 2013.

Most Capped Player: Conor McLaughlin, 10, Northern Ireland.

Most League Appearances: David Ball, 96, 2012–15.

Youngest League Player: Jamie Allen, 17 years 227 days v Northampton T, 5 January 2013.

Record Transfer Fee Received: £1,000,000 from Leicester C for Jamie Vardy, May 2012.

Record Transfer Fee Paid: £300,000 to Kidderminster H for Jamille Matt, January 2013.

Football League Record: 2012 Promoted from Conference Premier; 2012–14 FL 2; 2014– FL 1.

MANAGER
Alan Tinsley 1997
Mark Hughes 1998
Brian Wilson 1998–99
Mick Hoyle 1999–2001
Les Attwood 2001
Mark Hughes 2001
Alan Tinsley 2001–02
Mick Hoyle 2002–03
Tony Greenwood 2003–08
Micky Mellon 2008–12
Graham Alexander 2012–15
Steven Pressley October 2015–

LATEST SEQUENCES

Longest Sequence of League Wins: 4, 1.1.2014 – 27.1.2014.

Longest Sequence of League Defeats: 5, 19.9.2015 – 10.10.2015.

Longest Sequence of League Draws: 3, 27.10.2012 – 10.11.2012.

Longest Sequence of Unbeaten League Matches: 7, 25.3.2014 – 26.4.2014.

Longest Sequence Without a League Win: 8, 29.8.2015 – 10.10.2015.

Successive Scoring Runs: 9 from 25.3.2014.

Successive Non-scoring Runs: 4 from 22.2.2014.

TEN YEAR LEAGUE RECORD

		P	W	D	L	F	A	Pts	Pos
2006-07	Uni Pr	42	19	10	13	71	60	67	8
2007-08	Uni Pr	40	28	7	5	81	39	91	1
2008-09	Conf N	42	17	11	14	70	66	62	8
2009-10	Conf N	42	26	7	7	86	44	85	2
2010-11	Conf P	46	22	12	12	68	42	78	5
2011-12	Conf P	46	31	10	5	102	48	103	1
2012-13	FL 2	46	15	15	16	55	57	60	13
2013-14	FL 2	46	22	10	14	66	52	76	4
2014-15	FL 1	46	17	12	17	49	52	63	10
2015-16	FL 1	46	12	15	19	52	56	51	19

DID YOU KNOW ?

Fleetwood Town had to wait until their third Football League game before they registered a goal in the competition. Full-back Dean Howell was the scorer at Burton Albion and it proved enough to give the club their first-ever League victory. Coincidentally, Howell was born in Burton-on-Trent.

FLEETWOOD TOWN – FOOTBALL LEAGUE ONE 2015–16 LEAGUE RECORD

Match No.	Date	Venue	Opponents	Result	H/T Score	Lg Pos.	Goalscorers	Attendance
1	Aug 8	H	Southend U	D	1-1	1-0	10	McManus [33]	3228
2	15	A	Oldham Ath	L	0-1	0-1	19		4139
3	18	A	Bury	W	4-3	2-2	11	McLaughlin [17], Hornby-Forbes [29], Proctor [69], Sarcevic (pen) [82]	2992
4	22	H	Colchester U	W	4-0	2-0	7	Ryan [24], Ball [26], Proctor [49], Matt [86]	2888
5	29	A	Doncaster R	L	0-2	0-2	9		4876
6	Sept 5	H	Rochdale	D	1-1	0-0	10	Matt [87]	3511
7	12	H	Bradford C	D	1-1	1-1	13	Ryan [3]	4044
8	19	A	Wigan Ath	L	1-2	0-1	14	Hornby-Forbes [61]	8603
9	26	H	Port Vale	L	1-2	1-0	19	Grant, R [14]	3560
10	29	A	Gillingham	L	1-5	1-4	20	Grant, R [12]	5231
11	Oct 3	A	Scunthorpe U	L	0-1	0-0	23		3095
12	10	H	Coventry C	L	0-1	0-0	23		3864
13	17	H	Burton Alb	W	4-0	1-0	19	Proctor [42], Grant, R 2 [58, 71], Hunter [80]	2893
14	20	A	Sheffield U	L	0-3	0-1	22		17,879
15	24	A	Barnsley	W	1-0	1-0	20	Proctor [29]	8764
16	31	H	Chesterfield	L	0-1	0-1	21		3107
17	Nov 14	A	Peterborough U	L	1-2	0-0	22	Ball [66]	5462
18	21	H	Swindon T	W	5-1	1-0	19	El-Abd (og) [34], Sarcevic (pen) [55], Henen [64], Fosu [69], Grant, R [84]	2880
19	24	H	Millwall	W	2-1	0-0	17	Jonsson [65], Grant, R [89]	3326
20	28	A	Blackpool	L	0-1	0-1	18		7755
21	Dec 19	A	Crewe Alex	D	1-1	1-1	19	Ball [10]	3749
22	26	H	Shrewsbury T	D	1-1	0-1	18	Hunter [86]	5749
23	28	H	Wigan Ath	L	1-3	0-1	21	Sarcevic (pen) [69]	4232
24	Jan 2	H	Bury	W	2-0	0-0	19	Hunter [49], Grant, R [76]	3301
25	19	A	Colchester U	D	1-1	0-1	20	Jonsson [60]	2493
26	23	H	Doncaster R	D	0-0	0-0	21		3508
27	30	A	Bradford C	L	1-2	0-0	21	Matt [59]	17,554
28	Feb 7	H	Shrewsbury T	D	0-0	0-0	21		2539
29	13	A	Port Vale	D	0-0	0-0	20		4194
30	20	H	Scunthorpe U	W	2-1	2-0	20	Hunter [16], Grant, R [29]	3098
31	23	A	Rochdale	L	0-1	0-1	20		1767
32	27	A	Coventry C	W	2-1	0-0	19	Burns [56], Ball [83]	11,160
33	Mar 1	H	Gillingham	W	2-1	2-1	17	Burns [3], Ameobi [9]	2133
34	5	A	Sheffield U	D	2-2	1-1	18	Nilsson [60], Hunter [31]	3479
35	12	A	Burton Alb	L	1-2	0-1	19	Burns [47]	4415
36	15	H	Walsall	L	0-1	0-0	19		2569
37	19	H	Barnsley	L	0-2	0-0	19		3470
38	26	A	Chesterfield	D	0-0	0-0	19		6435
39	Apr 2	A	Swindon T	D	1-1	1-0	20	Burns [6]	6311
40	5	H	Peterborough U	W	2-0	1-0	19	Burns [38], Jonsson [68]	2134
41	9	A	Southend U	D	2-2	0-0	19	Grant, R [53], McLaughlin [90]	6644
42	16	A	Oldham Ath	D	1-1	0-0	19	Scougall [67]	3889
43	19	A	Millwall	L	0-1	0-0	19		7865
44	23	H	Blackpool	D	0-0	0-0	20		5123
45	May 2	A	Walsall	L	1-3	0-2	20	Cole [84]	6628
46	8	H	Crewe Alex	W	2-0	2-0	19	Grant, R [21], Cole [24]	3302

Final League Position: 19

GOALSCORERS
League (52): Grant, R 10, Burns 5, Hunter 5, Ball 4, Proctor 4, Jonsson 3, Matt 3, Sarcevic 3 (3 pens), Cole 2, Hornby-Forbes 2, McLaughlin 2, Ryan 2, Ameobi 1, Fosu 1, Henen 1, McManus 1, Nilsson 1, Scougall 1, own goal 1.
FA Cup (0).
Capital One Cup (0).
Johnstone's Paint Trophy (6): Hunter 2, Ball 1, Grant, R 1, Ryan 1, own goal 1.

Maxwell C 46	McLaughlin C 37	Jordan S 20+1	Jonsson E 36+3	Andrew D 8+1	Bell A 44	Ryan J 43	Sarcevic A 37+2	Grant R 25+13	Matt J 7+10	McManus D 3+4	Proctor J 13+10	Della Verde L 6+1	Sanogo V —+1	Ball D 26+11	Pond N 20+1	Hornby-Forbes T 11+5	Sowerby J 3+5	Nirennold V 11+6	Haughton N 7+11	Wood R 6	Dionatan T 8	Davis J 17+2	Hunter A 12+12	Henen D 9+2	Fosu T 4+2	Cole D 3+11	Kiwomya A 2+2	Nilsson M 11+2	Ameobi S 7+3	Burns W 11+3	Harris R 1	Grant T 3	Scougall S 9+1	Deacon K —+1	Match No.
1	2	3	4	5	6	7	8	9[2]	10[3]	11[1]	12	13	14																						1
1	5	3	2	4	9	8	6	7[1]	10[2]	11[3]	13			12	14																				2
1	3	2			4	8	7	6			12			10	9			11[1]											5						3
1	2	3			4	9	6	8[1]			12			10				5	13																4
1	2	3[2]			4	9	8	7	13	12	14	10	6		11[1]			5[1]																	5
		2	4	9	6	7[1]	14	12			11[3]	8		10[2]			5		3	13															6
1	2		4	9	7	6		12	10		11[2]	8[1]		5	13	3																			7
1	2	3[3]	9	5	8	7	10[2]	14	11[1]	13	6		4	12																					8
1	5	14			7	6	8	11[3]	13	12		10[2]		2[1]	3	9	4																		9
1	3	4[1]	12	5	2	7	6	10	11[2]		14	8		13	9[1]																				10
1	2				5	8	14	7	12	10[2]		11[3]		9[1]		6	13	3	4																11
1		12			5	8	6	13			11			14		7[2]	9[1]	3	4	2	10[3]														12
1	2		7		5	6	8[3]	9[1]	13		10			12		14		11[2]	3	4		12													13
1	2		8		5	9	7	10[3]	13		11[2]			12				14	3	4		6[1]													14
1	2		7		5	8	6	9[2]	12		10			11[1]					3	4		13													15
1	2[3]		8			6	9		12	10				11[1]	3		7[2]		14		4	13													16
1			7[1]		5	8	6	14						12	4	9[2]		11[3]			3	2		10	13										17
1	2		7		5	6	8	13			12			11[1]	3	14					4		10[2]	9[3]											18
1	2[2]		7		5	6	8	14				13		9[3]	3	12					4		10	11[1]											19
1	2		7[3]		5	6	8	12			13			10[1]	3			14			4		9	11[2]											20
1	2		8		5	7	6	9[2]				13		10[1]	3			12			4		11												21
1	2		6[1]		5	7	8	9[3]			13			10[2]	3						4	14	11	12											22
1	2		7[3]		5	8	6	14			13			10[1]	3			9[2]			4	12		11											23
1	2		7		5	8	6	9[1]			10				3	12	13		4			11[2]													24
1	2		7		5	6	8	11	12		9[2]				3			13			4	10[1]													25
1	2		7		5	6	8	9							3			11[2]			4		10[1]		12	13									26
1	2		7		5	6	8	12	10						3			13			4	11[1]			9[2]										27
1	7	3			5			14						8	4[1]	2	6					10[3]	12	11	9[2]	13									28
1	2	7	3		5			8	6[1]					9[2]				13				12		11[3]	14	4	10								29
1	2[2]	4	7		5	6	8	10[3]								12		14				9[1]			3	11	13								30
1		5[1]	4			7	8	11[3]								2[2]		14			12	9			3	10	13	6							31
1		7			5	8	6[1]							9			13	2			4	11[2]			12	3	14	10[1]							32
1		7			5	8	6[1]	13						9[2]				2			4	12			14	3	10	11[3]							33
1		7			5	6			14					8			12[3]	2	13[4]		4[1]	9[2]				3	10	11							34
1	2	6			5	7		13[4]						9[3]				8[1]			4	10			14	3	11[2]	12							35
1	2	8[3]	6		5	6								10[2]				14			4	11[1]			12	3	9	7							36
1	2	7[2]			5	6	13							9[3]				4				12			3	10[1]	11	8	14						37
1		3	14		5	7								10	2						9	11[2]	12	4					6[1]	8[1]	13				38
1	2	3	7		5	8		10[3]						9[1]							12	14	13	4		11[2]				6					39
1	2	4	7		5	6	9	11[2]						12	3	13		14									10[1]		8[3]						40
1	2	4	7[3]		5	6	9	11[1]						12	3			13			14						10		8[2]						41
1	2	4	7		5	8	11	9						12	3												10		6[1]						42
1	2	4	6[2]		5	9	10	8[2]						13	3			14				12					11		7[1]						43
1	2	4	7		5	6	11[3]	9[2]						12	3			13							14	10	8[1]								44
1	2	3[2]	6[1]		5	7[3]	8							10	4			14	11						13	12	9								45
1	2	4	6	12	5	7		8[1]						9[2]	3			13				14					11[3]		10						46

FA Cup

First Round	Walsall	(a)	0-2

Capital One Cup

First Round	Hartlepool U	(h)	0-1

Johnstone's Paint Trophy

Second Round	Shrewsbury T	(h)	2-1
Northern Quarter-Final	Sheffield U	(h)	0-0

(aet; Fleetwood T won 4-1 on penalties)

Northern Semi-Final	Morecambe	(h)	2-0
Northern Final 1st leg	Barnsley	(a)	1-1
Northern Final 2nd leg	Barnsley	(h)	1-1

(aet; Barnsley won 4-2 on penalties)

FULHAM

FOUNDATION

Churchgoers were responsible for the foundation of Fulham, which first saw the light of day as Fulham St Andrew's Church Sunday School FC in 1879. They won the West London Amateur Cup in 1887 and the championship of the West London League in its initial season of 1892–93. The name Fulham had been adopted in 1888.

Craven Cottage, Stevenage Road, London SW6 6HH.

Telephone: (0843) 208 1222.

Fax: (0870) 442 0236 (Motspur Park).

Ticket Line: (0843) 208 1234.

Website: www.fulhamfc.co.uk

Email: enquiries@fulhamfc.com

Ground Capacity: 25,700.

Record Attendance: 49,335 v Millwall, Division 2, 8 October 1938.

Pitch Measurements: 100m × 65m (109.5yd × 71yd).

Chairman: Shadid Khan.

Chief Executive: Alistair Mackintosh.

Head Coach: Slavisa Jokanovic.

Assistant Head Coach: Javier Pereira.

Director of Sports Medicine and Exercise Science: Mark Taylor.

HONOURS

League Champions: First Division – 2000–01; Division 2 – 1948–49; Second Division – 1998–99; Division 3S – 1931–32.
Runners-up: Division 2 – 1958–59; Division 3 – 1970–71; Third Division – 1996–97.

FA Cup: Runners-up: 1975.

League Cup: quarter-final – 1968, 1971, 2000, 2005.

European Competitions
UEFA Cup: 2002–03.
Europa League: 2009–10 *(runners-up)*, 2011–12.
Intertoto Cup: 2002 *(winners)*.

Colours: White shirts with black trim, black shorts with white trim, white socks with black hoops.

Year Formed: 1879.

Turned Professional: 1898.

Reformed: 1987.

Previous Name: 1879, Fulham St Andrew's; 1888, Fulham.

Club Nickname: 'The Cottagers'.

Grounds: 1879, Star Road, Fulham; c.1883, Eel Brook Common, 1884, Lillie Road; 1885, Putney Lower Common; 1886, Ranelagh House, Fulham; 1888, Barn Elms, Castelnau; 1889, Purser's Cross (Roskell's Field), Parsons Green Lane; 1891, Eel Brook Common; 1891, Half Moon, Putney; 1895, Captain James Field, West Brompton; 1896, Craven Cottage.

First Football League Game: 3 September 1907, Division 2, v Hull C (h) L 0–1 – Skene; Ross, Lindsay; Collins, Morrison, Goldie; Dalrymple, Freeman, Bevan, Hubbard, Threlfall.

Record League Victory: 10–1 v Ipswich T, Division 1, 26 December 1963 – Macedo; Cohen, Langley; Mullery (1), Keetch, Robson (1); Key, Cook (1), Leggat (4), Haynes, Howfield (3).

Record Cup Victory: 7–0 v Swansea C, FA Cup 1st rd, 11 November 1995 – Lange; Jupp (1), Herrera, Barkus (Brooker (1)), Moore, Angus, Thomas (1), Morgan, Brazil (Hamill), Conroy (3) (Bolt), Cusack (1).

Record Defeat: 0–10 v Liverpool, League Cup 2nd rd 1st leg, 23 September 1986.

sky SPORTS FACT FILE

Fulham, under manager Malcolm Macdonald, were denied back-to-back promotions when they lost by a single goal to Derby County in the final game of the 1982–83 season. A victory for the Cottagers would have given them third place in the Division Two table which would have been enough to see them promoted into top-flight football.

Most League Points (2 for a win): 60, Division 2, 1958–59 and Division 3, 1970–71.

Most League Points (3 for a win): 101, Division 2, 1998–99. 101, Division 1, 2000–01.

Most League Goals: 111, Division 3 (S), 1931–32.

Highest League Scorer in Season: Frank Newton, 43, Division 3 (S), 1931–32.

Most League Goals in Total Aggregate: Gordon Davies, 159, 1978–84, 1986–91.

Most League Goals in One Match: 5, Fred Harrison v Stockport Co, Division 2, 5 September 1908; 5, Bedford Jezzard v Hull C, Division 2, 8 October 1955; 5, Jimmy Hill v Doncaster R, Division 2, 15 March 1958; 5, Steve Earle v Halifax T, Division 3, 16 September 1969.

Most Capped Player: Johnny Haynes, 56, England.

Most League Appearances: Johnny Haynes, 594, 1952–70.

Youngest League Player: Matthew Briggs, 16 years 65 days v Middlesbrough, 13 May 2007.

Record Transfer Fee Received: £15,000,000 from Tottenham H for Moussa Dembele, August 2012.

Record Transfer Fee Paid: £12,400,00 to Olympiacos for Konstantinos Mitroglou, January 2014.

Football League Record: 1907 Elected to Division 2; 1928–32 Division 3 (S); 1932–49 Division 2; 1949–52 Division 1; 1952–59 Division 2; 1959–68 Division 1; 1968–69 Division 2; 1969–71 Division 3; 1971–80 Division 2; 1980–82 Division 3; 1982–86 Division 2; 1986–92 Division 3; 1992–94 Division 2; 1994–97 Division 3; 1997–99 Division 2; 1999–2001 Division 1; 2001–14 FA Premier League; 2014– FL C.

LATEST SEQUENCES

Longest Sequence of League Wins: 12, 7.5.2000 – 18.10.2000.

Longest Sequence of League Defeats: 11, 2.12.1961 – 24.2.1962.

Longest Sequence of League Draws: 6, 23.12.2006 – 20.1.2007.

Longest Sequence of Unbeaten League Matches: 15, 26.1.1999 – 13.4.1999.

Longest Sequence Without a League Win: 15, 25.2.1950 – 23.8.1950.

Successive Scoring Runs: 26 from 28.3.1931.

Successive Non-scoring Runs: 6 from 21.8.1971.

MANAGERS

Harry Bradshaw 1904–09
Phil Kelso 1909–24
Andy Ducat 1924–26
Joe Bradshaw 1926–29
Ned Liddell 1929–31
Jim McIntyre 1931–34
Jimmy Hogan 1934–35
Jack Peart 1935–48
Frank Osborne 1948–64
 (was Secretary-Manager or General Manager for most of this period and Team Manager 1953–56)
Bill Dodgin Snr 1949–53
Duggie Livingstone 1956–58
Bedford Jezzard 1958–64
 (General Manager for last two months)
Vic Buckingham 1965–68
Bobby Robson 1968
Bill Dodgin Jnr 1968–72
Alec Stock 1972–76
Bobby Campbell 1976–80
Malcolm Macdonald 1980–84
Ray Harford 1984–96
Ray Lewington 1986–90
Alan Dicks 1990–91
Don Mackay 1991–94
Ian Branfoot 1994–96
 (continued as General Manager)
Micky Adams 1996–97
Ray Wilkins 1997–98
Kevin Keegan 1998–99
 (Chief Operating Officer)
Paul Bracewell 1999–2000
Jean Tigana 2000–03
Chris Coleman 2003–07
Lawrie Sanchez 2007
Roy Hodgson 2007–10
Mark Hughes 2010–11
Martin Jol 2011–13
Rene Muelensteen 2013–14
Felix Magath 2014
Kit Symons 2014–15
Slavisa Jokanovic December 2015–

TEN YEAR LEAGUE RECORD

		P	W	D	L	F	A	Pts	Pos
2006-07	PR Lge	38	8	15	15	38	60	39	16
2007-08	PR Lge	38	8	12	18	38	60	36	17
2008-09	PR Lge	38	14	11	13	39	34	53	7
2009-10	PR Lge	38	12	10	16	39	46	46	12
2010-11	PR Lge	38	11	16	11	49	43	49	8
2011-12	PR Lge	38	14	10	14	48	51	52	9
2012-13	PR Lge	38	11	10	17	50	60	43	12
2013-14	PR Lge	38	9	5	24	40	85	32	19
2014-15	FL C	46	14	10	22	62	83	52	17
2015-16	FL C	46	12	15	19	66	79	51	20

DID YOU KNOW ?

Frank Osborne became the first Fulham player to win an England cap when he appeared for his country in a 2-0 win against Ireland in October 1922. Frank, who went on to win a second cap against France the following year, subsequently managed Fulham for a period in the 1950s.

FULHAM – FL CHAMPIONSHIP 2015–16 LEAGUE RECORD

Match No.	Date	Venue	Opponents	Result	H/T Score	Lg Pos.	Goalscorers	Attendance
1	Aug 8	A	Cardiff C	D	1-1	0-0	10	Smith 47	15,429
2	15	H	Brighton & HA	L	1-2	1-1	17	Cairney 43	19,029
3	19	A	Hull C	L	1-2	0-1	21	Cairney 69	16,579
4	22	H	Huddersfield T	D	1-1	0-0	21	Woodrow 90	14,283
5	29	A	Rotherham U	W	3-1	2-0	14	Pringle 7, McCormack (pen) 16, Woodrow 90	8839
6	Sept 13	H	Blackburn R	W	2-1	2-0	11	McCormack 4, Dembele 30	14,372
7	19	A	Sheffield W	L	2-3	1-2	16	O'Hara 31, Cairney 67	18,706
8	25	H	QPR	W	4-0	3-0	11	Dembele 2, Pringle 19, McCormack 2 31, 63	19,784
9	29	H	Wolverhampton W	L	0-3	0-0	14		14,838
10	Oct 4	A	Charlton Ath	D	2-2	1-0	13	Tunnicliffe 32, McCormack 59	14,662
11	17	A	Middlesbrough	D	0-0	0-0	13		22,498
12	21	H	Leeds U	D	1-1	1-0	13	Dembele 23	19,969
13	24	H	Reading	W	4-2	0-1	11	McCormack 50, Dembele 2 54, 74, Kacaniklic 56	18,618
14	31	A	Bristol C	W	4-1	4-0	10	Dembele 2 2, 18, McCormack 33, Tunnicliffe 36	15,752
15	Nov 3	A	Burnley	L	1-3	0-2	11	McCormack 51	15,080
16	7	H	Birmingham C	L	2-5	0-3	12	Kacaniklic 66, McCormack 90	18,888
17	21	A	Milton Keynes D	D	1-1	1-1	12	Dembele 44	14,508
18	28	H	Preston NE	D	1-1	0-1	13	McCormack 77	17,362
19	Dec 5	A	Nottingham F	L	0-3	0-1	16		18,377
20	12	H	Brentford	D	2-2	1-1	17	Tarkowski (og) 40, Dembele 64	19,411
21	15	H	Ipswich T	L	1-2	1-1	17	McCormack 14	15,245
22	19	A	Bolton W	D	2-2	1-0	18	Garbutt 28, McCormack 85	14,543
23	26	A	Derby Co	L	0-2	0-0	18		32,134
24	29	H	Rotherham U	W	4-1	2-1	18	Woodrow 2 6, 45, Kacaniklic 59, McCormack 69	16,333
25	Jan 2	A	Sheffield W	L	0-1	0-1	19		19,263
26	12	A	Wolverhampton W	L	2-3	1-2	19	Christensen 24, McCormack 74	17,387
27	16	A	Huddersfield T	D	1-1	1-1	19	McCormack 2	12,039
28	23	H	Hull C	L	0-1	0-0	19		16,935
29	Feb 6	H	Derby Co	D	1-1	1-1	19	Olsson (og) 17	18,472
30	13	A	QPR	W	3-1	3-0	18	McCormack 35, Dembele 40, Cairney 45	17,335
31	16	A	Blackburn R	L	0-3	0-1	19		12,157
32	20	A	Charlton Ath	W	3-0	1-0	18	Cairney 2 32, 78, Madl 59	16,565
33	23	A	Leeds U	D	1-1	1-1	18	Cairney 17	17,103
34	27	H	Middlesbrough	L	0-2	0-2	20		18,862
35	Mar 5	A	Reading	D	2-2	1-2	19	Dembele 8, McCormack (pen) 52	17,859
36	8	H	Burnley	L	2-3	2-1	19	McCormack 17, Dembele 22	15,281
37	12	H	Bristol C	L	1-2	1-0	20	McCormack 3	20,316
38	19	A	Birmingham C	D	1-1	1-0	21	Ince 38	17,104
39	Apr 2	H	Milton Keynes D	W	2-1	0-0	21	McCormack 54, Dembele 75	17,588
40	5	A	Preston NE	W	2-1	1-0	19	McCormack 5, Dembele 74	10,358
41	9	H	Cardiff C	W	2-1	0-1	17	Parker 46, Hyndman 90	17,149
42	15	A	Brighton & HA	L	0-5	0-2	17		28,505
43	19	A	Ipswich T	D	1-1	0-0	19	Dembele 66	16,953
44	23	H	Nottingham F	L	1-3	0-2	21	Smith 62	18,253
45	30	A	Brentford	L	0-3	0-3	21		12,301
46	May 7	H	Bolton W	W	1-0	0-0	20	Cairney 77	17,207

Final League Position: 20

GOALSCORERS

League (66): McCormack 21 (2 pens), Dembele 15, Cairney 8, Woodrow 4, Kacaniklic 3, Pringle 2, Smith 2, Tunnicliffe 2, Christensen 1, Garbutt 1, Hyndman 1, Ince 1, Madl 1, O'Hara 1, Parker 1, own goals 2.
FA Cup (1): Dembele 1.
Capital One Cup (4): McCormack 2 (1 pen), Dembele 1, Kacaniklic 1.

Lonergan A 28+1	Richards A 21+1	Hutchinson S 8+1	Burn D 28+4	Voser K 4+3	Cairney T 37+2	Christensen L 17+10	Pringle B 12+3	O'Hara J 32+5	McCormack R 45	Smith M 5+15	Dembele M 37+6	Bettinelli M 11	Bodurov N 2+1	Kacaniklic A 10+13	Woodrow C 1+13	Ream T 27+2	Husband J 12	Tunnicliffe R 23+4	Stearman R 27+2	Fredericks R 23+9	Mattila S 2+4	Garbutt L 19+6	Lewis J 7+1	Kavanagh S 2	Parker S 20+4	Hyndman E 9+7	Williams G —+1	Amorebieta F 14	Ince R 8+2	Madl M 12+1	Labyad Z —+2	Baird C 3+4	Match No.
1	2	3	4	5	6	7	8	9	10	11[1]	12																						1
	2	3		5	6	7	9[1]	8	10	11[2]	13	1	4	12																			2
13	2	3		5	6	7	9[1]	8	10	11[2]	12	1[3]	4	14																			3
1	2	3[2]	4	5	6	7		8	10		11			12	9[1]	13																	4
1	2		4		6	13	9[3]	8	10[2]		11[1]					14	12	3	5	7													5
1	2	13			6		9[1]	8	10		11							3	5[2]	7	4	12											6
1	2	12			6	13	9[3]	8	11		10[1]			14		4		5[2]	7	3													7
1			14		6	12	9	8[2]	10		11[1]					13		4	5	7	3	2[3]											8
1			13		6[4]	12	9[1]	8	10		11					4	5	7	3	2[2]	14												9
1	2				6		9[2]	8[3]	10		11[1]					13	4	5	7	3		14	12										10
1[1]	2		4		6		9[2]	8	10		11						7	3	13			5	12										11
	2		4		6[1]	9[2]	8	10		11[3]			13	14			7	3	12			5	1										12
	2[1]				7	9		10		11			12		4	5	8	3	6				1										13
1		3			6	12		7	11	13	10[1]				4	9[2]	8	2	5[3]			14											14
		3			6	13		7	10	14	11				4[2]	9	8	2	5[3]			1											15
		4			8	9[2]		7	10	13	11[3]			12		2	5[2]	6[1]	3			14	1										16
		4	12	9			6	10		11					7[1]	3	2[3]	13	5	1	8												17
	12			6			14	7	10	13	11				4	5[1]	3	2		1	9[3]	8[2]											18
				6		9[2]	7	11	10[3]			13	12	4	5	3	2			8[1]	14												19
1	2			9[1]			8	11	14	10		13	12	4		3	6[3]	5		7[2]													20
1	5	3		7[1]			8[2]	11	13	10		6[3]	14	4		2		9			12												21
1	2	4			13	14	10		11[2]			6	12	5		3		9[1]		8[2]	7												22
1		4	13	14			7[3]	10	12	11		6[2]		5		3	2	9			8[1]												23
1		4	6[2]		12	14	10	13		9[3]	11	5		3	2			7[1]	8														24
1	2	4			8[1]	10		11	6[2]	14	5			3		7[3]	13	12	9														25
1	2[2]	3	4		7	9[3]		8	10	14	11	6[1]				13		5		12													26
1	2	3	4		9	6		8[2]	11		13	10[1]						14	5		12	7[3]											27
1	2		3		10	9[1]		8	14	11	6[2]	4						5		7[3]	13	12											28
1	2		3		6	9[3]		8	10	13	11[2]	12						5		14		4	7[1]										29
1			4		7	6[3]		9	10		11[2]					2		12		8[1]	14		5	13	3								30
1			4		7			8	10		11		12	13				2	9[1]	6[2]				5[3]		3	14						31
		3			6[1]			8	10		11		9[3]			14		2		5		7		4		12			13				32
1	14				9			8[1]	10		11		13			12		2[3]		6[3]				5[3]		3		7					33
1			4		7			14	10		12					11[3]	3[4]	2[2]		6		8				5	13	9[1]					34
1	2				10[1]			8[2]	9		11		13			12		6[3]		5		14		4		3	7						35
1		3[1]			8			10	12	11						6		5		9		7[2]		4	13	2							36
1		3			6			13	10		11[2]			14	12	8		5		9[3]		7[1]		4		2							37
			4		6			10	13	11[1]	1				5		2	12		7	9[2]			8	3							38
		14			9[3]			11[1]	13	10	1				5		8	2[2]	12		7			4	6	3							39
		14			7[3]			13	11	10	1				5[2]		9	12	2		6			4	8	3[1]							40
				13				10		11	1				7[1]		2	12		5		6[3]	9	4	8	3[2]			14				41
				12			8[1]	10		11	1		14	5		7	3	2			6[2]	9	4[3]			13							42
	3	4	13	9[3]			11[2]	10	1					5		7	2	12			6[1]			8		14							43
			7[1]	12			10	13	11	1				5		14	2				6[2]	9[3]	4	8	3							44
2[2]			8	7[1]			11	12	1					5		10	3	13			6	14	4	9[1]									45
	3	4	6	9[3]			10	11	1					5[1]		8	12	2[2]		14		7	13										46

FA Cup
Third Round   Sheffield W   (a)   1-2

Capital One Cup
First Round   Wycombe W   (a)   1-0
Second Round   Sheffield U   (h)   3-0
Third Round   Stoke C   (h)   0-1

GILLINGHAM

FOUNDATION

The success of the pioneering Royal Engineers of Chatham excited the interest of the residents of the Medway Towns and led to the formation of many clubs including Excelsior. After winning the Kent Junior Cup and the Chatham District League in 1893, Excelsior decided to go for bigger things and it was at a meeting in the Napier Arms, Brompton, in 1893 that New Brompton FC came into being, buying and developing the ground which is now Priestfield Stadium. They changed their name to Gillingham in 1913, when they also changed their strip from black and white stripes to predominantly blue.

MEMS Priestfield Stadium, Redfern Avenue, Gillingham, Kent ME7 4DD.

Telephone: (01634) 300 000.

Fax: (01634) 850 986.

Ticket Office: (01634) 300 000 (option 1).

Website: www.gillinghamfootballclub.com

Email: info@priestfield.com

Ground Capacity: 11,440.

Record Attendance: 23,002 v QPR, FA Cup 3rd rd, 10 January 1948.

Pitch Measurements: 100.5m × 64m (110yd × 70yd).

Chairman: Paul D. P. Scally.

Vice-chairman: Michael Anderson.

Manager: Justin Edinburgh.

Assistant Manager: David Kerslake.

Physio: Gary Hemens.

Colours: Blue shirts with white stripe, blue shorts with white trim, white socks with blue trim.

Year Formed: 1893.

Turned Professional: 1894.

Previous Name: 1893, New Brompton; 1913, Gillingham.

Club Nickname: 'The Gills'.

Ground: 1893, Priestfield Stadium (renamed KRBS Priestfield Stadium 2009, MEMS Priestfield Stadium 2011).

First Football League Game: 28 August 1920, Division 3, v Southampton (h) D 1–1 – Branfield; Robertson, Sissons; Battiste, Baxter, Wigmore; Holt, Hall, Gilbey (1), Roe, Gore.

Record League Victory: 10–0 v Chesterfield, Division 3, 5 September 1987 – Kite; Haylock, Pearce, Shipley (2) (Lillis), West, Greenall (1), Pritchard (2), Shearer (2), Lovell, Elsey (2), David Smith (1).

Record Cup Victory: 10–1 v Gorleston, FA Cup 1st rd, 16 November 1957 – Brodie; Parry, Hannaway; Riggs, Boswell, Laing; Payne, Fletcher (2), Saunders (5), Morgan (1), Clark (2).

HONOURS

League Champions: FL 2 – 2012–13; Division 4 – 1963–64.
Runners-up: Third Division – 1995–96; Division 4 – 1973–74.
FA Cup: 6th rd – 2000.
League Cup: 4th rd – 1964, 1997.

sky SPORTS FACT FILE

New Brompton changed their name to Gillingham for the 1912–13 season, although the formal change of the company name was not ratified until later. The first Southern League match under the name Gillingham resulted in a 2-1 defeat at Northampton Town.

Record Defeat: 2–9 v Nottingham F, Division 3 (S), 18 November 1950.

Most League Points (2 for a win): 62, Division 4, 1973–74.

Most League Points (3 for a win): 85, Division 2, 1999–2000.

Most League Goals: 90, Division 4, 1973–74.

Highest League Scorer in Season: Ernie Morgan, 31, Division 3 (S), 1954–55; Brian Yeo, 31, Division 4, 1973–74.

Most League Goals in Total Aggregate: Brian Yeo, 135, 1963–75.

Most League Goals in One Match: 6, Fred Cheesmur v Merthyr T, Division 3 (S), 26 April 1930.

Most Capped Player: Andrew Crofts, 13 (includes 1 on loan from Brighton & HA) (28), Wales.

Most League Appearances: John Simpson, 571, 1957–72.

Youngest League Player: Luke Freeman, 15 years 247 days v Hartlepool U, 24 November 2007.

Record Transfer Fee Received: £1,500,000 from Manchester C for Robert Taylor, November 1999.

Record Transfer Fee Paid: £600,000 to Reading for Carl Asaba, August 1998.

Football League Record: 1920 Original Member of Division 3; 1921 Division 3 (S); 1938 Failed re-election; Southern League 1938–44; Kent League 1944–46; Southern League 1946–50; 1950 Re-elected to Division 3 (S); 1958–64 Division 4; 1964–71 Division 3; 1971–74 Division 4; 1974–89 Division 3; 1989–92 Division 4; 1992–96; Division 3; 1996–2000 Division 2; 2000–04 Division 1; 2004–05 FL C; 2005–08 FL 1; 2008–09 FL 2; 2009–10 FL 1; 2010–13 FL 2; 2013– FL 1.

LATEST SEQUENCES

Longest Sequence of League Wins: 7, 18.12.1954 – 29.1.1955.

Longest Sequence of League Defeats: 10, 20.9.1988 – 5.11.1988.

Longest Sequence of League Draws: 5, 28.8.1993 – 18.9.1993.

Longest Sequence of Unbeaten League Matches: 20, 13.10.1973 – 10.2.1974.

Longest Sequence Without a League Win: 15, 1.4.1972 – 2.9.1972.

Successive Scoring Runs: 20 from 31.10.1959.

Successive Non-scoring Runs: 6 from 11.2.1961.

MANAGERS

W. Ironside Groombridge
  1896–1906 *(Secretary-Manager)*
  (previously Financial Secretary)
Steve Smith 1906–08
W. I. Groombridge 1908–19
  (Secretary-Manager)
George Collins 1919–20
John McMillan 1920–23
Harry Curtis 1923–26
Albert Hoskins 1926–29
Dick Hendrie 1929–31
Fred Mavin 1932–37
Alan Ure 1937–38
Bill Harvey 1938–39
Archie Clark 1939–58
Harry Barratt 1958–62
Freddie Cox 1962–65
Basil Hayward 1966–71
Andy Nelson 1971–74
Len Ashurst 1974–75
Gerry Summers 1975–81
Keith Peacock 1981–87
Paul Taylor 1988
Keith Burkinshaw 1988–89
Damien Richardson 1989–92
Glenn Roeder 1992–93
Mike Flanagan 1993–95
Neil Smillie 1995
Tony Pulis 1995–99
Peter Taylor 1999–2000
Andy Hessenthaler 2000–04
Stan Ternent 2004–05
Neale Cooper 2005
Ronnie Jepson 2005–07
Mark Stimson 2007–10
Andy Hessenthaler 2010–12
Martin Allen 2012–13
Peter Taylor 2013–14
Justin Edinburgh February 2015–

TEN YEAR LEAGUE RECORD

		P	W	D	L	F	A	Pts	Pos
2006-07	FL 1	46	17	8	21	56	77	59	16
2007-08	FL 1	46	11	13	22	44	73	46	22
2008-09	FL 2	46	21	12	13	58	55	75	5
2009-10	FL 1	46	12	14	20	48	64	50	21
2010-11	FL 2	46	17	17	12	67	57	68	8
2011-12	FL 2	46	20	10	16	79	62	70	8
2012-13	FL 2	46	23	14	9	66	39	83	1
2013-14	FL 1	46	15	8	23	60	79	53	17
2014-15	FL 1	46	16	14	16	65	66	62	12
2015-16	FL 1	46	19	12	15	71	56	69	9

DID YOU KNOW ?

After losing at home to Barrow on 12 April 1963, Gillingham went almost two years without suffering a home defeat in a League or Cup game. The run, which comprised 52 games, was ended by Exeter City on 10 April 1965.

GILLINGHAM – FOOTBALL LEAGUE ONE 2015–16 LEAGUE RECORD

Match No.	Date	Venue	Opponents	Result	H/T Score	Lg Pos.	Goalscorers	Attendance
1	Aug 8	H	Sheffield U	W 4-0	2-0	1	Norris [8], Oshilaja [43], Egan [82], Dack [90]	7511
2	15	A	Port Vale	D 1-1	1-1	3	Dack [17]	5067
3	18	A	Bradford C	W 2-1	0-1	2	Hanson (og) [71], Norris [51]	17,496
4	22	H	Wigan Ath	W 2-0	1-0	1	Dack 2 (1 pen) [37, 82 (p)]	5692
5	29	A	Peterborough U	D 1-1	0-0	4	Oshilaja [85]	5083
6	Sept 5	H	Doncaster R	W 1-0	0-0	1	Hessenthaler [66]	5685
7	12	H	Blackpool	W 2-1	1-0	1	Loft [17], Dack [81]	6231
8	19	A	Colchester U	L 1-2	1-2	3	Norris [7]	4694
9	26	A	Barnsley	L 0-2	0-2	3		8354
10	29	H	Fleetwood T	W 5-1	4-1	3	Donnelly 2 [18, 34], Houghton [28], Egan [31], McDonald [87]	5231
11	Oct 3	H	Oldham Ath	D 3-3	2-2	3	Donnelly 2 [8, 33], Hessenthaler [57]	6157
12	10	A	Chesterfield	W 3-1	1-1	3	Egan [26], Donnelly [54], Lennon [72]	6026
13	17	A	Crewe Alex	W 1-0	0-0	1	Donnelly [90]	3924
14	20	H	Scunthorpe U	W 2-1	0-0	1	Dickenson [59], Lennon [90]	4823
15	24	H	Southend U	D 1-1	0-1	1	Loft [89]	6981
16	31	A	Walsall	L 2-3	2-2	3	McDonald [12], Dack (pen) [32]	6663
17	Nov 14	H	Bury	W 3-1	2-1	1	Samuel [6], Egan [10], Osaoabe [87]	6063
18	21	A	Coventry C	L 1-4	0-4	2	Dack [63]	15,604
19	24	H	Rochdale	W 2-0	1-0	2	Dack [7], Oshilaja [80]	5088
20	28	A	Shrewsbury T	D 2-2	1-1	2	McDonald [37], Jackson [59]	4959
21	Dec 12	H	Burton Alb	L 0-3	0-0	4		6230
22	19	A	Millwall	W 3-0	2-0	2	Samuel 2 [20, 89], Dack (pen) [28]	12,032
23	26	A	Swindon T	W 3-1	2-1	3	Dack [19], Hessenthaler [35], Jackson [69]	9228
24	28	H	Colchester U	W 1-0	0-0	3	Samuel [70]	7109
25	Jan 2	H	Bradford C	W 3-0	2-0	2	Dack [4], Donnelly [11], Loft [89]	6446
26	7	A	Wigan Ath	L 2-3	1-0	2	Samuel [24], Donnelly [53]	7923
27	16	A	Doncaster R	D 2-2	1-0	3	Donnelly 2 [9, 47]	6077
28	23	H	Peterborough U	W 2-1	0-1	1	Norris [49], Dack [65]	6449
29	30	A	Blackpool	L 0-1	0-1	2		6828
30	Feb 6	H	Swindon T	D 0-0	0-0	4		6398
31	13	H	Barnsley	L 1-2	1-0	2	Samuel [25], Dack [63]	5887
32	20	A	Oldham Ath	L 1-2	1-0	3	Loft [16]	3874
33	27	H	Chesterfield	L 1-2	0-2	3	Osaoabe [80]	6012
34	Mar 1	A	Fleetwood T	L 1-2	1-2	4	Norris [36]	2133
35	5	A	Scunthorpe U	D 0-0	0-0	3		3355
36	12	H	Crewe Alex	W 3-0	1-0	2	Samuel [12], Guthrie (og) [61], Wright [90]	5656
37	19	A	Southend U	D 1-1	0-1	4	Norris [53]	9135
38	28	A	Bury	W 1-0	1-0	4	Norris [27]	2907
39	Apr 2	H	Coventry C	D 0-0	0-0	4		7200
40	9	A	Sheffield U	D 0-0	0-0	5		18,152
41	12	H	Walsall	L 1-2	0-0	6	Norris [90]	6246
42	16	H	Port Vale	L 0-2	0-2	6		5887
43	19	A	Rochdale	D 1-1	0-1	6	Egan [77]	2385
44	23	A	Shrewsbury T	L 2-3	1-1	7	McDonald [45], Hessenthaler [61]	6906
45	30	A	Burton Alb	L 1-2	0-1	8	McDonald [49]	5388
46	May 8	H	Millwall	L 1-2	0-0	9	Egan [90]	9375

Final League Position: 9

GOALSCORERS

League (71): Dack 13 (3 pens), Donnelly 10, Norris 8, Samuel 7, Egan 6, McDonald 5, Hessenthaler 4, Loft 4, Oshilaja 3, Jackson 2, Lennon 2, Osaoabe 2, Dickenson 1, Houghton 1, Wright 1, own goals 2.
FA Cup (0).
Capital One Cup (2): Dack 1, Hessenthaler 1.
Johnstone's Paint Trophy (3): Dack 1, Ehmer 1, Garmston 1.

Nelson S 46	Jackson R 34 + 3	Egan J 35 + 1	Oshilaja A 21 + 1	Dickenson B 21 + 12	Houghton J 10 + 1	Morris A 31 + 4	Williamson B 4 + 5	Dack B 39 + 1	Osaoabe E 10 + 8	Norris L 25 + 8	Hessenthaler J 26 + 12	Wright J 40 + 1	Garmston B 23 + 10	Donnelly R 24 + 14	McGlashan J 6 + 11	Loft D 16 + 10	McDonald C 13 + 9	Ehmer M 30	Lennon H 6	Samuel D 24 + 1	List E — + 6	Chicksen A 5 + 1	Williams G 3 + 7	El-Abd A 8	Crofts A 6	Match No.
1	2	3	4	5	6	7¹	8	9	10²	11	12	13														1
1	2	4	3	6	8¹	11³	7		10	12	9		5²	13	14											2
1	2	3	4	5	7		12	9		10¹	8	6		11												3
1	2	3	4	5	7		12	8		10²	9	6		11¹	13											4
1	2	3	4	5		7²		8	12	10	9³	6		11¹		13	14									5
1	2			4¹			13	8	7	11²	12	6	5	14			9	10³	3							6
1	2	3		5			13	9	12	11³	6	7		14			8²	10¹		4						7
1	2	3		5¹	7			11	13	6³	12	14		8	10²					4						8
1	2	3		5		11³	9	8¹	10²	14	6		13		7	12				4						9
1	2³	3		5²	7	12		9		10		6	13	11¹		8	14			4						10
1		3		5	7	2		9	14	10²	12	6¹		11		8³	13			4						11
1		2		9²		12		7	14	11	6	8	13	10	5¹			3³		4						12
1	13	3		14		2		7		10³	8	6¹	5²	11	9		12			4						13
1		3		12	14	2	11³	9	7²		8¹	6¹	5	10	13					4						14
1	2³	3		10	6¹	7		9	14			5²	11	8	13	12				4						15
1	2³	3		5²		6	14	9		13		12	10	7¹	8	11				4						16
1	2	3³	14		12		9	7		8	6²	5	10			13	4	11¹								17
1	2	3	4	13		14		9	8²		7	6¹	5		12	10³				11						18
1	2	3	4	12		6¹		9	7²		8		5	10	13					11						19
1	2	4	3			7		8		6		5		9	10					11						20
1	2	3	4	12		7		9			7	5¹	13	14	8⁴	10²				11						21
1	2¹	3	4			7		9	13	14	8	6	5	12			10³			11²						22
1	2	3	4			8		9		12	7	6	5	10²						11¹	13					23
1	2	3				7		9²		12	8	6¹	5	11¹³	14	13				4	10					24
1	2	3				7		9		12³	8	6¹	5	11²		13				4	10	14				25
1	5	4				6²		9	13		8¹	7³	2	11	14	12				3	10					26
1	2	3				6		8		9²	7¹	5	11	12	13					4	10					27
1	2	3		12		7		9		11²	8³	6	5¹		13					4	10	14				28
1	2	3		13		7		9		10¹		6		12		8				4	11³	14	5²			29
1	2	3		12		7		9		13		6		11³		8				4	10²	14	5¹			30
1		3				7		10	8¹			11	2²	9	13	5				4	6	12				31
1						2		8	6¹	13	12	7	5	11		9²				3	10³		4	14		32
1	2					7		9¹	8	14		6	13	11						4	10⁵	5²	12	3		33
1	2			8		7			11³		6	14	10²							4	13	12	5¹	9	3	34
1			5	2				11³	7		6	14	13	12	8		3			10²		9¹	4			35
1			5	2				10¹	13	7	12	14	6	8²		3	11					9	4³			36
1	13		4	9				11	6²	7			5¹			3				10		12		8		37
1	5¹		4	9		8		11³	14	6	12	13				2²				10			3	7		38
1	2³		5	11		9¹		7		6	14	12				3				10²		13	4	8		39
1	5		4	9				14	11	6²	8		10¹			13	2					12³	3	7		40
1	5	12	4¹	14				9³	11	13	6	8		10		3						2²	7			41
1	2¹	3	5²	12		6		13	7		10	14		11		4							8³			42
1	2⁴	4	5			9³		11	14	10	7¹	8	6			12	13	3					13			43
1		2	4	12		6²		7		11	8	5	9³	14		10¹	3						13			44
1		3	2	12		8¹		9			7	6	5²	14		13	10	4		11³						45
1	12	3	2	5				8		14	9²	6		7¹		10	4			11³		13				46

FA Cup

First Round	Stevenage	(a)	0-3

Capital One Cup

First Round	Plymouth Arg	(a)	2-1
Second Round	Birmingham C	(a)	0-2

Johnstone's Paint Trophy

Second Round	Luton T	(h)	2-1
Southern Quarter-Final	Yeovil T	(h)	1-1

(aet; Yeovil T won 5-4 on penalties)

GRIMSBY TOWN

FOUNDATION

Grimsby Pelham FC, as they were first known, came into being at a meeting held at the Wellington Arms in September 1878. Pelham is the family name of big landowners in the area, the Earls of Yarborough. The receipts for their first game amounted to 6s. 9d. (approx. 39p). After a year, the club name was changed to Grimsby Town.

Blundell Park, Cleethorpes, North East Lincolnshire DN35 7PY.

Telephone: (01472) 605 050.

Fax: (01472) 693 665.

Ticket Office: (01472) 605 050 (option 4).

Website: www.grimsby-townfc.co.uk

Email: webmaster@gtfc.co.uk

Ground Capacity: 9,106.

Record Attendance: 31,657 v Wolverhampton W, FA Cup 5th rd, 20 February 1937.

Pitch Measurements: 111yd × 75yd.

Chairman: John Fenty.

Chief Executive: Ian Fleming.

Manager: Paul Hurst.

Assistant Manager: Chris Doig.

Physio: Dave Moore.

HONOURS

League Champions: Division 2 – 1900–01, 1933–34; Division 3 – 1979–80; Division 3N – 1925–26, 1955–56; Division 4 – 1971–72. *Runners-up:* Division 2 – 1928–29; Division 3 – 1961–62; Division 3N – 1951–52; Division 4 – 1978–79, 1989–90. Conference – (4th) 2015–16 *(promoted via play-offs).*

FA Cup: semi-final – 1936, 1939.

League Cup: 5th rd – 1980, 1985.

League Trophy Winners: 1998. *Runners-up:* 2008.

Colours: Black and white striped shirts with red trim, black shorts with red and white trim, red socks with white trim.

Year Formed. 1878. *Turned Professional:* 1890. *Ltd Co.:* 1890.

Previous Name: 1878, Grimsby Pelham; 1879, Grimsby Town.

Club Nickname: 'The Mariners'.

Grounds: 1880, Clee Park; 1889, Abbey Park; 1899, Blundell Park.

First Football League Game: 3 September 1892, Division 2, v Northwich Victoria (h) W 2–1 – Whitehouse; Lundie, T. Frith; C. Frith, Walker, Murrell; Higgins, Henderson, Brayshaw, Riddoch (2), Ackroyd.

Record League Victory: 9–2 v Darwen, Division 2, 15 April 1899 – Bagshaw; Lockie, Nidd; Griffiths, Bell (1), Nelmes; Jenkinson (3), Richards (1), Cockshutt (3), Robinson, Chadburn (1).

Record Cup Victory: 8–0 v Darlington, FA Cup 2nd rd, 21 November 1885 – G. Atkinson; J. H. Taylor, H. Taylor; Hall, Kimpson, Hopewell; H. Atkinson (1), Garnham, Seal (3), Sharman, Monument (4).

Record Defeat: 1–9 v Arsenal, Division 1, 28 January 1931.

Most League Points (2 for a win): 68, Division 3 (N), 1955–56.

sky SPORTS FACT FILE

In August 1971 Grimsby Town played the Japan national team in a pre-season friendly, winning 7-2 with striker Mike Hickman scoring a hat-trick. The Mariners subsequently went on to win the Fourth Division championship that season, ending the campaign three points ahead of runners-up Southend United.

Most League Points (3 for a win): 83, Division 3, 1990–91.

Most League Goals: 103, Division 2, 1933–34.

Highest League Scorer in Season: Pat Glover, 42, Division 2, 1933–34.

Most League Goals in Total Aggregate: Pat Glover, 180, 1930–39.

Most League Goals in One Match: 6, Tommy McCairns v Leicester Fosse, Division 2, 11 April 1896.

Most Capped Player: Pat Glover, 7, Wales.

Most League Appearances: John McDermott, 647, 1987–2007.

Youngest League Player: Tony Ford, 16 years 143 days v Walsall, 4 October 1975.

Record Transfer Fee Received: £1,500,000 from Everton for John Oster, July 1997.

Record Transfer Fee Paid: £500,000 to Preston NE for Lee Ashcroft, August 1998.

Football League Record: 1892 Original Member of Division 2; 1901–03 Division 1; 1903 Division 2; 1910 Failed re-election; 1911 re-elected Division 2; 1920–21 Division 3; 1921–26 Division 3 (N); 1926–29 Division 2; 1929–32 Division 1; 1932–34 Division 2; 1934–48 Division 1; 1948–51 Division 2; 1951–56 Division 3 (N); 1956–59 Division 2; 1959–62 Division 3; 1962–64 Division 2; 1964–68 Division 3; 1968–72 Division 4; 1972–77 Division 3; 1977–79 Division 4; 1979–80 Division 3; 1980–87 Division 2; 1987–88 Division 3; 1988–90 Division 4; 1990–91 Division 3; 1991–92 Division 2; 1992–97 Division 1; 1997–98 Division 2; 1998–2003 Division 1; 2003–04 Division 2; 2004–10 FL 2; 2010–16 Conferencc/National League; 2016– FL 2.

LATEST SEQUENCES

Longest Sequence of League Wins: 11, 19.1.1952 – 29.3.1952.

Longest Sequence of League Defeats: 9, 30.11.1907 – 18.1.1908.

Longest Sequence of League Draws: 5, 6.2.1965 – 6.3.1965.

Longest Sequence of Unbeaten League Matches: 19, 16.2.1980 – 30.8.1980.

Longest Sequence Without a League Win: 22, 24.3.2008 – 1.11.2008.

Successive Scoring Runs: 33 from 6.10.1928.

Successive Non-scoring Runs: 6 from 11.3.2000.

MANAGERS

H. N. Hickson 1902–20
(Secretary-Manager)
Haydn Price 1920
George Fraser 1921–24
Wilf Gillow 1924–32
Frank Womack 1932–36
Charles Spencer 1937–51
Bill Shankly 1951–53
Billy Walsh 1954–55
Allenby Chilton 1955–59
Tim Ward 1960–62
Tom Johnston 1962–64
Jimmy McGuigan 1964–67
Don McEvoy 1967–68
Bill Harvey 1968–69
Bobby Kennedy 1969–71
Lawrie McMenemy 1971–73
Ron Ashman 1973–75
Tom Casey 1975–76
Johnny Newman 1976–79
George Kerr 1979–82
David Booth 1982–85
Mike Lyons 1985–87
Bobby Roberts 1987–88
Alan Buckley 1988–94
Brian Laws 1994–96
Kenny Swain 1997
Alan Buckley 1997–2000
Lennie Lawrence 2000–01
Paul Groves 2001–04
Nicky Law 2004
Russell Slade 2004–06
Graham Rodger 2006
Alan Buckley 2006–08
Mike Newell 2008–09
Neil Woods 2009–11
Rob Scott and Paul Hurst (joint) 2011–13
Paul Hurst September 2013–

TEN YEAR LEAGUE RECORD

		P	W	D	L	F	A	Pts	Pos
2006-07	FL 2	46	17	8	21	57	73	59	15
2007-08	FL 2	46	15	10	21	55	66	55	16
2008-09	FL 2	46	9	14	23	51	69	41	22
2009-10	FL 2	46	9	17	20	45	71	44	23
2010-11	Conf	46	15	17	14	72	62	62	11
2011-12	Conf	46	19	13	14	79	60	70	11
2012-13	Conf	46	23	14	9	70	38	83	4
2013-14	Conf	46	22	12	12	65	46	78	4
2014-15	Conf	46	25	11	10	74	40	86	3
2015-16	NL	46	22	14	10	82	45	80	4

DID YOU KNOW ?

Centre-forward Jimmy Carmichael finished as the Football League's leading scorer in the 1921–22 season after notching 37 goals for Grimsby Town. He twice scored four goals in a game as the Mariners missed out on promotion after finishing third in Division Three North.

HARTLEPOOL UNITED

FOUNDATION

The inspiration for the launching of Hartlepool United was the West Hartlepool club which won the FA Amateur Cup in 1904–05. They had been in existence since 1881 and their cup success led in 1908 to the formation of the new professional concern which first joined the North-Eastern League. In those days they were Hartlepools United and won the Durham Senior Cup in their first two seasons.

Victoria Park, Clarence Road, Hartlepool TS24 8BZ.

Telephone: (01429) 272 584.

Fax: (01429) 863 007.

Ticket Office: (01429) 272 584 (option 2).

Website: www.hartlepoolunited.co.uk

Email: enquires@hartlepoolunited.co.uk

Ground Capacity: 7,856.

Record Attendance: 17,426 v Manchester U, FA Cup 3rd rd, 5 January 1957.

Pitch Measurements: 100.5m × 67.5m (110yd × 74yd).

Chairman: Gary Coxall.

Chief Executive: Russ Green.

Manager: Craig Hignett.

First-Team Coach: Curtis Fleming.

Physio: Ian Gallagher.

Colours: Blue shirts with white diagonal stripe, blue shorts, white socks.

Year Formed: 1908.

Turned Professional: 1908.

Previous Names: 1908, Hartlepools United; 1968, Hartlepool; 1977, Hartlepool United.

Club Nickname: 'The Pool', 'Monkey Hangers'.

Ground: 1908, Victoria Park.

First Football League Game: 27 August 1921, Division 3 (N), v Wrexham (a) W 2–0 – Gill; Thomas, Crilly; Dougherty, Hopkins, Short; Kessler, Mulholland (1), Lister (1), Robertson, Donald.

Record League Victory: 10–1 v Barrow, Division 4, 4 April 1959 – Oakley; Cameron, Waugh; Johnson, Moore, Anderson; Scott (1), Langland (1), Smith (3), Clark (2), Luke (2), (1 og).

Record Cup Victory: 6–0 v North Shields, FA Cup 1st rd, 30 November 1946 – Heywood; Brown, Gregory; Spelman, Lambert, Jones; Price, Scott (2), Sloan (4), Moses, McMahon; 6–0 v Gainsborough Trinity (a), FA Cup 1st rd, 10 November 2007 – Budtz; McCunnie, Humphreys, Liddle (1) (Antwi), Nelson, Clark, Moore (1), Sweeney, Barker (2) (Monkhouse), Mackay (Porter 1), Brown (1).

Record Defeat: 1–10 v Wrexham, Division 4, 3 March 1962.

HONOURS

League: Runners-up: Division 3N – 1956–57; FL 2 – 2006–07; Third Division – 2002–03.

FA Cup: 4th rd – 1955, 1978, 1989, 1993, 2005, 2009.

League Cup: 4th rd – 1975.

sky SPORTS FACT FILE

John McGovern became Pool's youngest first-team player when he was given his debut by manager Brian Clough on the final day of the 1965–66 season aged 16 years and 205 days. John made over 80 first-team appearances for United before Clough signed him for Derby County. He later followed Clough to Leeds United and Nottingham Forest, appearing for the Reds in their two European Cup final winning teams.

Most League Points (2 for a win): 60, Division 4, 1967–68.

Most League Points (3 for a win): 88, FL 2, 2006–07.

Most League Goals: 90, Division 3 (N), 1956–57.

Highest League Scorer in Season: William Robinson, 28, Division 3 (N), 1927–28; Joe Allon, 28, Division 4, 1990–91.

Most League Goals in Total Aggregate: Ken Johnson, 98, 1949–64.

Most League Goals in One Match: 5, Harry Simmons v Wigan Borough, Division 3 (N), 1 January 1931; 5, Bobby Folland v Oldham Ath, Division 3 (N), 15 April 1961.

Most Capped Player: Ambrose Fogarty, 1 (11), Republic of Ireland.

Most League Appearances: Richie Humphreys, 481, 2001–13.

Youngest League Player: David Foley, 16 years 105 days v Port Vale, 25 August 2003.

Record Transfer Fee Received: £750,000 from Ipswich T for Tommy Miller, July 2001.

Record Transfer Fee Paid: £80,000 to Mansfield T for Darrell Clarke, July 2001.

Football League Record: 1921 Original Member of Division 3 (N); 1958–68 Division 4; 1968–69 Division 3; 1969–91 Division 4; 1991–92 Division 3; 1992–94 Division 2; 1994–2003 Division 3; 2003–04 Division 2; 2004–06 FL 1; 2006–07 FL 2; 2007–13 FL 1; 2013– FL 2.

LATEST SEQUENCES

Longest Sequence of League Wins: 9, 18.11.2006 – 1.1.2007.

Longest Sequence of League Defeats: 8, 27.1.1993 – 27.2.1993.

Longest Sequence of League Draws: 6, 30.4.2011 – 20.8.2011.

Longest Sequence of Unbeaten League Matches: 23, 18.11.2006 – 30.3.2007.

Longest Sequence Without a League Win: 20, 8.9.2012 – 26.12.2012.

Successive Scoring Runs: 27 from 18.11.2006.

Successive Non-scoring Runs: 11 from 9.1.1993.

MANAGERS

Alfred Priest 1908–12
Percy Humphreys 1912–13
Jack Manners 1913–20
Cecil Potter 1920–22
David Gordon 1922–24
Jack Manners 1924–27
Bill Norman 1927–31
Jack Carr 1932–35
 (had been Player-Coach from 1931)
Jimmy Hamilton 1935–43
Fred Westgarth 1943–57
Ray Middleton 1957–59
Bill Robinson 1959–62
Allenby Chilton 1962–63
Bob Gurney 1963–64
Alvan Williams 1964–65
Geoff Twentyman 1965
Brian Clough 1965–67
Angus McLean 1967–70
John Simpson 1970–71
Len Ashurst 1971–74
Ken Hale 1974–76
Billy Horner 1976–83
Johnny Duncan 1983
Mike Docherty 1983
Billy Horner 1984–86
John Bird 1986–88
Bobby Moncur 1988–89
Cyril Knowles 1989–91
Alan Murray 1991–93
Viv Busby 1993
John MacPhail 1993–94
David McCreery 1994–95
Keith Houchen 1995–96
Mick Tait 1996–99
Chris Turner 1999–2002
Mike Newell 2002–03
Neale Cooper 2003–05
Martin Scott 2005–06
Danny Wilson 2006–08
Chris Turner 2008–10
Mick Wadsworth 2010–11
Neale Cooper 2011–12
John Hughes 2012–13
Colin Cooper 2013–14
Paul Murray 2014
Ronnie Moore 2014–16
Craig Hignett February 2016–

TEN YEAR LEAGUE RECORD

		P	W	D	L	F	A	Pts	Pos
2006-07	FL 2	46	26	10	10	65	40	88	2
2007-08	FL 1	46	15	9	22	63	66	54	15
2008-09	FL 1	46	13	11	22	66	79	50	19
2009-10	FL 1	46	14	11	21	59	67	50*	20
2010-11	FL 1	46	15	12	19	47	65	57	16
2011-12	FL 1	46	14	14	18	50	55	56	13
2012-13	FL 1	46	9	14	23	39	67	41	23
2013-14	FL 2	46	14	11	21	50	56	53	19
2014-15	FL 2	46	12	9	25	39	70	45	22
2015-16	FL 2	46	15	6	25	49	72	51	16

*3 pts deducted.

DID YOU KNOW ?

Goalkeeper Fred Mearns was Hartlepool United's first professional signing after the club was established in 1908. Fred was a near ever-present in Pool's inaugural season, playing in the North Eastern League before moving to Barnsley with whom he gained an FA Cup winners' medal in 1910.

HARTLEPOOL UNITED – FOOTBALL LEAGUE TWO 2015–16 LEAGUE RECORD

Match No.	Date	Venue	Opponents	Result		H/T Score	Lg Pos.	Goalscorers	Attendance
1	Aug 8	H	Morecambe	W	2-0	1-0	4	Paynter [25], Bingham [65]	4289
2	15	A	York C	W	2-1	0-0	5	Paynter [71], Woods [81]	4890
3	18	H	Newport Co	W	1-0	0-0	3	Fenwick [51]	3739
4	22	A	Stevenage	L	0-2	0-1	5		2639
5	29	H	Carlisle U	L	2-3	1-0	6	Harrison, S [6], Paynter (pen) [70]	4935
6	Sept 5	A	Wycombe W	L	1-2	1-1	10	Magnay [43]	3468
7	12	A	Exeter C	L	0-1	0-0	13		3135
8	19	H	Cambridge U	D	0-0	0-0	14		3665
9	26	A	Yeovil T	W	2-1	1-1	11	Fenwick [32], Walker [83]	3078
10	29	H	Bristol R	L	0-3	0-1	17		3788
11	Oct 3	H	Luton T	L	1-4	1-1	17	Paynter [44]	3876
12	10	A	Northampton T	L	1-2	1-2	17	Bingham [31]	4477
13	17	A	Dagenham & R	W	1-0	1-0	17	Paynter [34]	1771
14	20	H	Barnet	D	1-1	1-0	17	Oates [7]	3124
15	24	A	Crawley T	L	1-2	0-0	19	Paynter [80]	3262
16	31	A	AFC Wimbledon	L	0-2	0-2	19		3638
17	Nov 15	H	Leyton Orient	W	3-1	1-1	19	Oyenuga (pen) [20], Gray 2 [70, 85]	4081
18	21	A	Mansfield T	L	1-3	1-1	19	Pearce (og) [37]	3031
19	28	A	Oxford U	L	0-1	0-0	20		3622
20	Dec 12	A	Portsmouth	L	0-4	0-2	20		15,610
21	19	H	Plymouth Arg	L	1-2	0-0	21	Fenwick (pen) [84]	3534
22	Jan 16	H	Wycombe W	W	1-0	1-0	21	Fenwick [33]	3721
23	19	A	Accrington S	L	1-3	0-2	21	Bingham [77]	1211
24	23	A	Cambridge U	D	1-1	0-0	21	Gray [71]	5054
25	30	H	Exeter C	L	0-2	0-1	21		3678
26	Feb 9	H	Stevenage	L	1-2	0-1	22	Paynter [68]	3308
27	13	H	Yeovil T	W	2-1	0-0	21	Paynter (pen) [58], Jackson [71]	3923
28	16	A	Notts Co	L	2-3	0-2	21	Gray [62], Paynter [66]	3433
29	20	A	Luton T	L	1-2	0-0	21	Jackson [65]	7880
30	27	H	Northampton T	D	0-0	0-0	22		4012
31	Mar 1	A	Bristol R	L	1-4	0-3	22	Paynter [52]	6634
32	5	A	Barnet	W	3-1	2-1	22	Hawkins 2 [34, 40], Thomas [62]	1734
33	12	H	Dagenham & R	W	3-1	2-1	22	Paynter (pen) [4], Carroll [14], Gray [53]	3947
34	15	A	Newport Co	D	0-0	0-0	21		2394
35	19	A	Crawley T	D	0-0	0-0	21		1883
36	25	H	AFC Wimbledon	W	1-0	1-0	21	Jackson [22]	4365
37	28	A	Leyton Orient	W	2-0	0-0	17	Paynter [49], Thomas [69]	5543
38	Apr 2	H	Mansfield T	W	2-1	1-0	17	Paynter 2 (2 pens) [24, 85]	3893
39	5	A	Carlisle U	L	0-1	0-0	17		4767
40	9	A	Morecambe	W	5-2	2-1	16	Woods [4], Thomas 2 [6, 50], James (pen) [76], Oates [89]	2005
41	12	A	Notts Co	L	0-1	0-0	16		3597
42	16	H	York C	W	2-1	1-1	16	Thomas [24], Woods [72]	4781
43	19	H	Accrington S	L	1-2	1-2	16	Bingham [25]	3445
44	23	A	Oxford U	L	0-2	0-1	16		7955
45	30	H	Portsmouth	L	0-2	0-0	16		5046
46	May 7	A	Plymouth Arg	L	0-5	0-2	16		10,019

Final League Position: 16

GOALSCORERS

League (49): Paynter 14 (5 pens), Gray 5, Thomas 5, Bingham 4, Fenwick 4 (1 pen), Jackson 3, Woods 3, Hawkins 2, Oates 2, Carroll 1, Harrison, S 1, James 1 (1 pen), Magnay 1, Oyenuga 1 (1 pen), Walker 1, own goal 1.
FA Cup (5): Fenwick 1, Gray 1, Mandron 1, Oates 1 (pen), Oyenuga 1.
Capital One Cup (1): Paynter 1.
Johnstone's Paint Trophy (1): Fenwick 1.

Bartlett A 12	Duckworth M 11 + 2	Harrison S 21 + 1	Worley H 3	Carroll J 41	Featherstone N 40 + 4	Magnay C 30 + 3	Woods M 26 + 7	Paynter B 31 + 1	Fenwick S 11 + 12	Bingham R 18 + 13	Smith C 2 + 3	Oates R 21 + 17	Bates M 30 + 2	Walker B 8 + 15	Boyce A 7 + 1	Nelson-Addy E — + 2	Jones D 10 + 1	Oyenuga K 2 + 6	Halliday B 6	Carson T 34	Hendrie L 3	Okuonghae M 4	Banton J — + 4	Jackson A 28 + 1	Naismith K 4	Gray J 26 + 3	Mandron M 3 + 2	Richards J 8 + 3	Thomas N 21 + 1	Hawkins L 18 + 5	Harrison E 2	James L 19 + 1	Laurent J 1 + 2	Jones R 5 + 2	Blackford J — + 1	Match No.
1	2	3	4	5	6	7	8	9	10²	11¹	12	13																								1
1	2	3	4⁵	5	8	6	7²	10	9¹	11		13	12	14																						2
1	2	3		5	6	7	8¹	10	9²	11		12	4	13																						3
1	7	3		5	6	2	8³	9	11²	10		13	4¹		12	14																				4
1	2	3		5	7	8²	6	10	13	9		11¹					4	12																		5
1	4	3		9	8	2⁴	7	11²	12	10	14	6¹				5³	13																			6
1	4	11		8		6					12	10¹	9	7		3	5	2																		7
1	4			5		8		6²	10	12		9¹	11	7	13	3		12	2																	8
1	4			5		6		8²		10		9¹		14	11¹	7	13	3	12	2																9
1		3		5	8	13			10	11		9	7¹	6²	4		12	2																		10
1		3		5	13	8	7²	10¹	12	11	6	9			4			2																		11
1		3		5	8		7²	11¹	14	10	6	9¹			13	4		2																		12
		3		9	8		13	10		11³		6²	14	7		5¹				1	2	4	12													13
		3		9¹	8		12	10		11		6		7²		5				1	2	4	13													14
14		3⁴		9¹	7		13	10		11		6		8³		5²				1	2	4	12													15
9				5	6		7	11¹	13	10³		8		3			4	12				2³	14													16
	2³	13		5	14	7		10¹				12	3					9²		1				4		6	8	11								17
	2			5		8		13	11			12	3					9¹		1				4		6	7	10²								18
	2			5	7	6¹			14			9²	3	12		13				1				4		11	8¹	10								19
	5			2	7	8¹			11²	10		9	3	13						1				4		6	12									20
	2			5	7		8			10	12	11²	3							1				4		9	6¹	13								21
	3			5	6		7			11	13	10								1				4		8¹			2	9²	12					22
	3			5	7		8²			11¹	13	6								1				4		14			2	9³	12	10				23
				5	8		7			12		9²				13				1				4		10			2	6		11¹				24
	3			5	9³	14		7²		13		11		10¹						1				4		6			2	12	8					25
				5		8			10	12	13					3				1				4		7¹		9³	2	6²		11	14			26
				6²	12	8	10¹	14	13							3			5	1				4		9		7³	2		11					27
				13	7¹	8²	10	14					3				5			1				4		6		2¹	11	12	9					28
				5	6	2	11					12	3	9						1				4		8		10¹	7							29
				5	6	2	10					13	3	7²						1				4		8		11¹	12	9						30
	4			5	8³	2	10¹	12				14	7							1				3		9		6²	13	11						31
				5	8	2	12	11				13	4	14						1						7²	10³	9¹	6			3				32
				5	9²	2		11	14			4	13							1	12					8³	10	7	6			3¹				33
				5	7	2		11				12	3							1				4		6		6¹	8	10						34
				5	7	2		10					3	12						1				4		6		11	8¹	9						35
				5	7	2	12	10				13	3							1				4		6¹	14	11¹	8	9						36
				5	7	2	13	10				14	4	13						1				4		6¹		11	8³	9²						37
				5	7	2	13	10				14	3							1				4		6²		9¹	8	11³	12					38
				5	8	2		11²	12			10	3	13						1				4		7¹			9	6						39
				5	7	2	6²					13	14							1				3		11³		9¹	8	10	12	4				40
5					7	2	6		12			9¹	13							1				3		11²			10	8		4				41
9²				5⁵	6	2	8					12	3							1				4				13	10¹	7	11			14		42
				5	12		8			10¹		14	3	7³						1				4		9²		2	11		13	6				43
14				5	7	2	8¹			13		12	3							1				4		9³		11	6	10²						44
				6	2	8¹	10²			13	3⁰					5				1				4		14		9	7	11	12					45
				7	2⁴	8	10						14				5			1				4		12		13	11³	6	9		3¹			46

FA Cup

First Round	Cheltenham T	(h)	1-0
Second Round	Salford C	(a)	1-1
Replay	Salford C	(h)	2-0
(aet)			
Third Round	Derby Co	(h)	1-2

Capital One Cup

First Round	Fleetwood T	(a)	1-0
Second Round	Bournemouth	(h)	0-4

Johnstone's Paint Trophy

First Round	Sheffield U	(h)	1-1

(aet; Sheffield U won 4-3 on penalties)

HUDDERSFIELD TOWN

FOUNDATION

A meeting, attended largely by members of the Huddersfield &
District FA, was held at the Imperial Hotel in 1906 to discuss the
feasibility of establishing a football club in this rugby stronghold.
However, it was not until a man with both the enthusiasm and the
money to back the scheme came on the scene that real progress
was made. This benefactor was Mr Hilton Crowther and it was at a
meeting at the Albert Hotel in 1908 that the club formally came
into existence with an investment of £2,000 and joined the
North-Eastern League.

*John Smith's Stadium, Stadium Way, Leeds Road,
Huddersfield, West Yorkshire HD1 6PX.*
Telephone: (01484) 484 112.
Fax: (01484) 484 101.
Ticket Office: (01484) 484 123.
Website: www.htafc.com
Email: info@htafc.com
Ground Capacity: 24,590.
Record Attendance: 67,037 v Arsenal, FA Cup 6th rd,
27 February 1932 (at Leeds Road); 23,678 v Liverpool,
FA Cup 3rd rd, 12 December 1999 (at Alfred McAlpine
Stadium).
Pitch Measurements: 105m × 69.5m (115yd × 76yd).
Chairman: Dean Hoyle.
Operations Director: Ann Hough.
Head Coach: David Wagner.
Assistant Head Coach: Christoph Buehler.
Physio: Ian Kirkpatrick.
Colours: Blue and white striped shirts with black trim, white shorts with black trim, white socks with
black trim.
Year Formed: 1908.
Turned Professional: 1908.
Club Nickname: 'The Terriers'.
Grounds: 1908, Leeds Road; 1994, The Alfred McAlpine Stadium (renamed the Galpharm Stadium
2004, John Smith's Stadium 2012).
First Football League Game: 3 September 1910, Division 2, v Bradford PA (a) W 1–0 – Mutch;
Taylor, Morris; Beaton, Hall, Bartlett; Blackburn, Wood, Hamilton (1), McCubbin, Jee.
Record League Victory: 10–1 v Blackpool, Division 1, 13 December 1930 – Turner; Goodall, Spencer;
Redfern, Wilson, Campbell; Bob Kelly (1), McLean (4), Robson (3), Davies (1), Smailes (1).
Record Cup Victory: 7–0 v Lincoln U, FA Cup 1st rd, 16 November 1991 – Clarke; Trevitt, Charlton,
Donovan (2), Mitchell, Doherty, O'Regan (1), Stapleton (1) (Wright), Roberts (2), Onuora (1), Barnett
(Ireland). *N.B.* 11–0 v Heckmondwike (a), FA Cup pr rd, 18 September 1909 – Doggart; Roberts,
Ewing; Hooton, Stevenson, Randall; Kenworthy (2), McCreadie (1), Foster (4), Stacey (4), Jee.

HONOURS

League Champions: Division 1 –
1923–24, 1924–25, 1925–26; Division 2
– 1969–70; Division 4 – 1979–80.
Runners-up: Division 1 – 1926–27,
1927–28, 1933–34; Division 2 –
1919–20, 1952–53.
FA Cup Winners: 1922.
Runners-up: 1920, 1928, 1930, 1938.
League Cup: semi-final – 1968.
League Trophy: Runners-up: 1994.

sky SPORTS FACT FILE

Huddersfield Town's 4,000-seater grandstand was destroyed by fire in
April 1950 forcing the Terriers to switch their home games 16 miles away
to Leeds United. A crowd of more than 30,000 saw them defeat Derby
County at Elland Road but after one further home fixture on the ground
of their local rivals they were able to move back to Leeds Road.

Record Defeat: 1–10 v Manchester C, Division 2, 7 November 1987.

Most League Points (2 for a win): 66, Division 4, 1979–80.

Most League Points (3 for a win): 87, FL 1, 2010–11.

Most League Goals: 101, Division 4, 1979–80.

Highest League Scorer in Season: Sam Taylor, 35, Division 2, 1919–20; George Brown, 35, Division 1, 1925–26; Jordan Rhodes, 35, 2011–12.

Most League Goals in Total Aggregate: George Brown, 142, 1921–29; Jimmy Glazzard, 142, 1946–56.

Most League Goals in One Match: 5, Dave Mangnall v Derby Co, Division 1, 21 November 1931; 5, Alf Lythgoe v Blackburn R, Division 1, 13 April 1935; 5, Jordan Rhodes v Wycombe W, FL 1, 6 January 2012.

Most Capped Player: Jimmy Nicholson, 31 (41), Northern Ireland.

Most League Appearances: Billy Smith, 521, 1914–34.

Youngest League Player: Denis Law, 16 years 303 days v Notts Co, 24 December 1956.

Record Transfer Fee Received: £8,000,000 from Blackburn R for Jordan Rhodes, August 2012.

Record Transfer Fee Paid: £1,800,000 to TSV 1860 Munich for Christopher Schindler, June 2016.

Football League Record: 1910 Elected to Division 2; 1920–52 Division 1; 1952–53 Division 2; 1953–56 Division 1; 1956–70 Division 2; 1970–72 Division 1; 1972–73 Division 2; 1973–75 Division 3; 1975–80 Division 4; 1980–83 Division 3; 1983–88 Division 2; 1988–92 Division 3; 1992–95 Division 2; 1995–2001 Division 1; 2001–03 Division 2; 2003–04 Division 3; 2004–12 FL 1; 2012– FL C.

LATEST SEQUENCES

Longest Sequence of League Wins: 11, 5.4.1920 – 4.9.1920.

Longest Sequence of League Defeats: 7, 8.10.1955 – 19.11.1955.

Longest Sequence of League Draws: 6, 3.3.1987 – 3.4.1987.

Longest Sequence of Unbeaten League Matches: 43, 1.1.2011 – 19.11.2011.

Longest Sequence Without a League Win: 22, 4.12.1971 – 29.4.1972.

Successive Scoring Runs: 27 from 12.3.2005.

Successive Non-scoring Runs: 7 from 14.10.2000.

MANAGERS

Fred Walker 1908–10
Richard Pudan 1910–12
Arthur Fairclough 1912–19
Ambrose Langley 1919–21
Herbert Chapman 1921–25
Cecil Potter 1925–26
Jack Chaplin 1926–29
Clem Stephenson 1929–42
Ted Magner 1942–43
David Steele 1943–47
George Stephenson 1947–52
Andy Beattie 1952–56
Bill Shankly 1956–59
Eddie Boot 1960–64
Tom Johnston 1964–68
Ian Greaves 1968–74
Bobby Collins 1974
Tom Johnston 1975–78
 (had been General Manager since 1975)
Mike Buxton 1978–86
Steve Smith 1986–87
Malcolm Macdonald 1987–88
Eoin Hand 1988–92
Ian Ross 1992–93
Neil Warnock 1993–95
Brian Horton 1995–97
Peter Jackson 1997–99
Steve Bruce 1999–2000
Lou Macari 2000–02
Mick Wadsworth 2002–03
Peter Jackson 2003–07
Andy Ritchie 2007–08
Stan Ternent 2008
Lee Clark 2008–12
Simon Grayson 2012–13
Mark Robins 2013–14
Chris Powell 2014–15
David Wagner November 2015–

TEN YEAR LEAGUE RECORD

		P	W	D	L	F	A	Pts	Pos
2006-07	FL 1	46	14	17	15	60	69	59	15
2007-08	FL 1	46	20	6	20	50	62	66	10
2008-09	FL 1	46	18	14	14	62	65	68	9
2009-10	FL 1	46	23	11	12	82	56	80	6
2010-11	FL 1	46	25	12	9	77	48	87	3
2011-12	FL 1	46	21	18	7	79	47	81	4
2012-13	FL C	46	15	13	18	53	73	58	19
2013-14	FL C	46	14	11	21	58	65	53	17
2014-15	FL C	46	13	16	17	58	75	55	16
2015-16	FL C	46	13	12	21	59	70	51	19

DID YOU KNOW ?

In 1914 Huddersfield Town introduced military drill instruction for their players following the commencement of the First World War with trainer William Norman, a former army drill instructor, giving out the orders. The club also planned a rifle range at their home ground for the use of players and season ticket holders.

HUDDERSFIELD TOWN – FL CHAMPIONSHIP 2015–16 LEAGUE RECORD

Match No.	Date	Venue	Opponents	Result	H/T Score	Lg Pos.	Goalscorers	Attendance
1	Aug 8	A	Hull C	L	0-2	0-1	21		19,361
2	15	H	Blackburn R	D	1-1	1-0	20	Wells [10]	11,338
3	18	H	Brighton & HA	D	1-1	0-1	18	Butterfield [54]	10,168
4	22	A	Fulham	D	1-1	0-0	20	Wells [63]	14,283
5	29	H	QPR	L	0-1	0-0	22		11,189
6	Sept 12	A	Cardiff C	L	0-2	0-0	23		13,715
7	15	A	Charlton Ath	W	2-1	2-1	20	Bunn [11], Huws [34]	13,873
8	19	H	Bolton W	W	4-1	1-1	13	Huws 2 [45, 74], Carayol [51], Lynch [83]	11,762
9	24	H	Nottingham F	D	1-1	0-1	13	Huws [84]	11,299
10	Oct 3	A	Wolverhampton W	L	0-3	0-1	17		18,166
11	17	A	Ipswich T	D	0-0	0-0	17		17,937
12	20	H	Milton Keynes D	W	2-0	0-0	13	Wells [58], Paterson [90]	11,471
13	24	H	Derby Co	L	1-2	1-1	15	Bunn [31]	15,371
14	31	A	Burnley	L	1-2	0-2	16	Duff (og) [88]	16,749
15	Nov 3	A	Reading	D	2-2	2-1	18	Paterson [2], Wells [26]	14,379
16	7	H	Leeds U	L	0-3	0-2	19		17,118
17	21	A	Sheffield W	L	1-3	0-0	21	Scannell [53]	21,191
18	28	H	Middlesbrough	L	0-2	0-1	22		15,434
19	Dec 5	H	Birmingham C	W	2-0	1-0	19	Lolley [1], Wells [81]	15,931
20	12	A	Bristol C	L	1-2	0-2	20	Bunn [84]	13,255
21	15	H	Rotherham U	W	2-0	1-0	19	Carayol [31], Miller [73]	12,763
22	19	A	Brentford	L	2-4	0-3	19	Lolley [46], Dempsey [90]	10,262
23	26	H	Preston NE	W	3-1	1-0	19	Wells 2 [38, 55], Huws [76]	14,697
24	28	A	QPR	D	1-1	0-0	18	Wells [86]	16,662
25	Jan 2	A	Bolton W	W	2-0	0-0	18	Lolley [61], Carayol [87]	15,969
26	12	H	Charlton Ath	W	5-0	2-0	16	Hudson [17], Wells [44], Paterson [75], Holmes [79], Davidson [90]	10,215
27	16	H	Fulham	D	1-1	1-1	16	Hudson [19]	12,039
28	23	A	Brighton & HA	L	1-2	1-1	17	Bunn [45]	25,367
29	30	H	Cardiff C	L	2-3	1-1	17	Wells [40], Bunn [90]	11,002
30	Feb 6	A	Preston NE	L	1-2	0-0	17	Wells [80]	12,653
31	13	A	Nottingham F	W	2-0	1-0	17	Mills (og) [14], Billing [84]	19,984
32	20	H	Wolverhampton W	W	1-0	0-0	15	Wells [78]	12,714
33	23	A	Milton Keynes D	D	1-1	0-1	16	Wells [86]	9402
34	27	H	Ipswich T	L	0-1	0-1	16		12,644
35	Mar 5	A	Derby Co	L	0-2	0-1	18		29,698
36	8	H	Reading	W	3-1	0-0	18	Wells [51], Paterson [61], Bajaj [87]	10,167
37	12	H	Burnley	L	1-3	1-3	18	Lolley [44]	13,917
38	19	A	Leeds U	W	4-1	1-1	16	Hudson [41], Bunn [69], Matmour [73], Wells [77]	29,311
39	Apr 2	H	Sheffield W	L	0-1	0-0	18		15,469
40	5	A	Middlesbrough	L	0-3	0-2	18		24,669
41	9	H	Hull C	D	2-2	1-0	19	Paterson [40], Maguire (og) [90]	12,883
42	16	A	Blackburn R	W	2-0	1-0	16	Wells [35], Kilgallon (og) [54]	15,061
43	19	A	Rotherham U	D	1-1	1-1	16	Wells [22]	10,292
44	23	H	Birmingham C	D	1-1	0-0	16	Lynch [82]	13,054
45	30	A	Bristol C	L	0-4	0-1	19		15,791
46	May 7	H	Brentford	L	1-5	0-1	19	Paterson [50]	13,397

Final League Position: 19

GOALSCORERS

League (59): Wells 17, Bunn 6, Paterson 6, Huws 5, Lolley 4, Carayol 3, Hudson 3, Lynch 2, Bajaj 1, Billing 1, Butterfield 1, Davidson 1, Dempsey 1, Holmes 1, Matmour 1, Miller 1, Scannell 1, own goals 4.
FA Cup (4): Paterson 2, Smith 1, Wells 1 (pen).
Capital One Cup (1): Wallace 1.

Smithies A 1	Cranie M 28 + 9	Hudson M 39	Lynch J 34 + 3	Smith T 33 + 3	Hogg J 19 + 3	Whitehead D 31 + 3	Butterfield J 5	Davidson J 26 + 1	Wells N 39 + 5	Bunn H 34 + 8	Miller I 12 + 6	Hammill A — + 1	Dempsey K 10 + 11	Murphy J 7	Scannell S 20 + 9	Vaughan J — + 4	Lolley J 25 + 7	Carayol M 9 + 6	Steer J 38	Ward E 5	Paterson J 22 + 12	Huws E 27 + 3	Billing P 8 + 5	Bajaj F — + 8	Wallace M 1 + 1	Holmes D 2 + 4	Chilwell B 7 + 1	Husband J 10 + 1	Matmour K 7 + 9	Manu E — + 5	Boyle W — + 1	van La Parra R 7 + 1	Allinson L — + 1	Match No.
1	2	3	4	5^2	6^3	7^1	8	9	10	11	12	13	14																					1
	3	4	2	8	7	6		9	10	12	11^1			1	5																			2
	3	4	2	8	7	6	5	9	11	10^1				1		12																		3
14	3	4	2	8	7	6^2	5		10^1	11	12		13	1	9^3																			4
12	3^2	4	2	6	7	8	5		11^1		10			1	9^3		13	14																5
	2	4	5	7^2	8			11		9^1	14				6		13		1		3	10^3	12											6
	2	4	14	7			5		11	10		13			6^1				1		9^2	3	8^3	12										7
	2	4	12	7			5		14	10	11^2				6				1		9^1	3	8^3	13										8
	2	4	13	7			5		12	10	11				6^1				1		9^2	3	8											9
	2	4	13	7			5		12	10^1	11				6				1		9^2	3	8^3	14										10
	2	3	4	7			5		10	9	11^1				6^2	13			1		12	8												11
	2	3	4	13			7		10^1	9	11^3				6^2				1		12	8	14											12
	2	3	4				7		5	10	9^2		11^3		6^1				1		12	8	14											13
	2	3	4				7^1		5	12	9		11^2	13					1		6^2	10	8	14										14
	2	3	4	14					5	10^3	11				6^2				1		9^1	8	7											15
	2	3					7		5	10^3	11				6	1	13	9^1	1		12	8^2		4	14									16
	4	3		2	12	6^1			11	9			5	1	8^2		13	10^3	1		7			14										17
	4	3		2		6			11				12		8^2		10^1		1		9^3	7	14		13	5								18
	4	3		2	6^1				11^2		14		13		8		10^2	12	1		9^3	7				5								19
	4	3		2	6				11^1	14	13		12		8		10	1	1		9^3	7^2				5								20
	3	4	2	6					11^1	9	12				8^3		13	10	1		14					7^2	5							21
6	3	4	2						13		11^2		12		14		8	10^1	1		9					7^2	5							22
13	3	4	2	6^2					11	12			9^1		8		10		1		14	7^1					5							23
	4	3		2	6			5^1	11	8				1	14	13	10^3		1		9^1	7					12							24
14	3	4	2	6					11	9^2					8^3		10	13	1		12	7^1					5							25
14	3^1	4	2	6				5	11	8			13				10^1		1		9	7^2					12							26
4	3	13	2	6					11^3	8^2							10^1		1		9^3	7	14		12		5							27
6	3	4	2^1		13			5^1	11	8					10				1		9^3	7^1	14					12						28
3		4	2	6	12			5	11	10			2^2				1		1		9^1	7^1	13					8						29
3		4	2	6					11	8^3					10^2				1		9^1		7					5	12	13	14			30
13	3	4	2	7^2	12				11	8^3			14		10				1			6^1						5	9					31
14	3	4	2	6					11^3	8					10^1				1		9^2	7					5	12	13					32
4	3	14	2	6					11	9^1					10^3				1		7	12^4					5^2	8	13					33
12	3	4^1	2	7	6				11	10			9^2						1		13							8^3	14					34
4	3		2		7				11	10^2			6		8^1				1		9^3		14					5	12	13				35
4	3		2		6			14	11^2	10^3			7		12		8		1		9		13					5^1						36
4	3		2		7			5^1	11	12					8^3		10		1		13	6						14	9^1					37
	3	4	2	6					11	12					8				1		9^1	14	7^3					5	13		10^2			38
13	3^3	4	2	6					11	10^2					14		8		1		12	7						5	9^1					39
	3	4	2	6^2				5	11^1	10					14		8^3		1		9	7	13								12			40
4^3	3	14	2	6				11	13				12		8^2		9		1		7					5				10^1				41
	3	4	2	6^2				5	11	9^3		13			8^1				1		7	14					12	10						42
	3	4	2	6				5	11	9^1					14		8^2		1		12	7					13	10^3						43
	3	4		6				5	11	12		2			14		8^3		1		9^2	7					13	10^1						44
	3	4		6				5^1	11^1	9		2			14		8^3		1		12^2	7					13	10^2						45
5	3	4	2		6				14						8^1		13		1^2		11^3	7					10				9	12	46

HULL CITY

The KC Stadium, West Park, Hull, East Yorkshire HU3 6HU.

Telephone: (01482) 504 600.

Fax: (01482) 304 882.

Ticket Office: (01482) 505 600.

Website: www.hullcitytigers.com

Email: info@hulltigers.com

Ground Capacity: 24,983.

Record Attendance: 55,019 v Manchester U, FA Cup 6th rd, 26 February 1949 (at Boothferry Park); 25,512 v Sunderland, FL C, 28 October 2007 (at KC Stadium).

Pitch Measurements: 105m × 68m (115yd × 74.5yd).

Chairman: Dr Assem Allam.

Vice-chairman: Ehab Allam.

Manager: Steve Bruce.

Assistant Manager: Mike Phelan.

Physio: Stuart Leake.

Colours: Amber shirts with thin black stripes and black sleeves, black shorts, amber socks with black trim.

Year Formed: 1904.

Turned Professional: 1905.

Club Nickname: 'The Tigers'.

Grounds: 1904, Boulevard Ground (Hull RFC); 1905, Anlaby Road (Hull CC); 1944, Boulevard Ground; 1946, Boothferry Park; 2002, Kingston Communications Stadium.

First Football League Game: 2 September 1905, Division 2, v Barnsley (h) W 4–1 – Spendiff; Langley, Jones; Martin, Robinson, Gordon (2); Rushton, Spence (1), Wilson (1), Howe, Raisbeck.

Record League Victory: 11–1 v Carlisle U, Division 3 (N), 14 January 1939 – Ellis; Woodhead, Dowen; Robinson (1), Blyth, Hardy; Hubbard (2), Richardson (2), Dickinson (2), Davies (2), Cunliffe (2).

Record Cup Victory: 8–2 v Stalybridge Celtic (a), FA Cup 1st rd, 26 November 1932 – Maddison; Goldsmith, Woodhead; Gardner, Hill (1), Denby; Forward (1), Duncan, McNaughton (1), Wainscoat (4), Sargeant (1).

sky SPORTS FACT FILE

In 1948–49 the Tigers won through five rounds to reach the quarter-finals of the FA Cup. They met the Cup holders Manchester United at Boothferry Park for the chance of making history by becoming the first Division Three North team to reach the last four of the competition, only to lose out to a goal 15 minutes from time. The game attracted a crowd of 55,000.

Record Defeat: 0–8 v Wolverhampton W, Division 2, 4 November 1911.

Most League Points (2 for a win): 69, Division 3, 1965–66.

Most League Points (3 for a win): 90, Division 4, 1982–83.

Most League Goals: 109, Division 3, 1965–66.

Highest League Scorer in Season: Bill McNaughton, 39, Division 3 (N), 1932–33.

Most League Goals in Total Aggregate: Chris Chilton, 193, 1960–71.

Most League Goals in One Match: 5, Ken McDonald v Bristol C, Division 2, 17 November 1928; 5, Simon 'Slim' Raleigh v Halifax T, Division 3 (N), 26 December 1930.

Most Capped Player: Theo Whitmore, 28 (105), Jamaica.

Most League Appearances: Andy Davidson, 520, 1952–67.

Youngest League Player: Matthew Edeson, 16 years 63 days v Fulham, 10 October 1992.

Record Transfer Fee Received: £12,000,000 from Southampton for Shane Long, August 2014.

Record Transfer Fee Paid: £10,000,000 to Palermo for Abel Hernandez, September 2014.

Football League Record: 1905 Elected to Division 2; 1930–33 Division 3 (N); 1933–36 Division 2; 1936–49 Division 3 (N); 1949–56 Division 2; 1956–58 Division 3 (N); 1958–59 Division 3; 1959–60 Division 2; 1960–66 Division 3; 1966–78 Division 2; 1978–81 Division 3; 1981–83 Division 4; 1983–85 Division 3; 1985–91 Division 2; 1991–92 Division 3; 1992–96 Division 2; 1996–2004 Division 3; 2004–05 FL 1; 2005–08 FL C; 2008–10 FA Premier League; 2010–13 FL C; 2013–15 FA Premier League; 2015–16 FL C; 2016– FA Premier League.

LATEST SEQUENCES

Longest Sequence of League Wins: 10, 23.2.1966 – 20.4.1966.

Longest Sequence of League Defeats: 8, 7.4.1934 – 8.9.1934.

Longest Sequence of League Draws: 5, 14.2.2012 – 10.3.2012.

Longest Sequence of Unbeaten League Matches: 19, 13.3.2001 – 22.9.2001.

Longest Sequence Without a League Win: 27, 27.3.1989 – 4.11.1989.

Successive Scoring Runs: 26 from 10.4.1990.

Successive Non-scoring Runs: 6 from 13.11.1920.

MANAGERS

James Ramster 1904–05
  (Secretary-Manager)
Ambrose Langley 1905–13
Harry Chapman 1913–14
Fred Stringer 1914–16
David Menzies 1916–21
Percy Lewis 1921–23
Bill McCracken 1923–31
Haydn Green 1931–34
John Hill 1934–36
David Menzies 1936
Ernest Blackburn 1936–46
Major Frank Buckley 1946–48
Raich Carter 1948–51
Bob Jackson 1952–55
Bob Brocklebank 1955–61
Cliff Britton 1961–70
  (continued as General Manager to 1971)
Terry Neill 1970–74
John Kaye 1974–77
Bobby Collins 1977–78
Ken Houghton 1978–79
Mike Smith 1979–82
Bobby Brown 1982
Colin Appleton 1982–84
Brian Horton 1984–88
Eddie Gray 1988–89
Colin Appleton 1989
Stan Ternent 1989–91
Terry Dolan 1991–97
Mark Hateley 1997–98
Warren Joyce 1998–2000
Brian Little 2000–02
Jan Molby 2002
Peter Taylor 2002–06
Phil Parkinson 2006
Phil Brown *(after caretaker role December 2006)* 2007–10
Ian Dowie *(consultant)* 2010
Nigel Pearson 2010–11
Nick Barmby 2011–12
Steve Bruce June 2012–

TEN YEAR LEAGUE RECORD

		P	W	D	L	F	A	Pts	Pos
2006-07	FL C	46	13	10	23	51	67	49	21
2007-08	FL C	46	21	12	13	65	47	75	3
2008-09	PR Lge	38	8	11	19	39	64	35	17
2009-10	PR Lge	38	6	12	20	34	75	30	19
2010-11	FL C	46	16	17	13	52	51	65	11
2011-12	FL C	46	19	11	16	47	44	68	8
2012-13	FL C	46	24	7	15	61	52	79	2
2013-14	PR Lge	38	10	7	21	38	53	37	16
2014-15	PR Lge	38	8	11	19	33	51	35	18
2015-16	FL C	46	24	11	11	69	35	83	4

DID YOU KNOW

Hull City were unsuccessful with their bid to be elected to the Football League at the annual meeting in May 1905, losing out to Leeds City, Burslem Port Vale and Chelsea. Later in the meeting a resolution was agreed to increase League membership from 36 to 40 and the Tigers were one of the extra clubs voted into the Second Division.

HULL CITY – FL CHAMPIONSHIP 2015–16 LEAGUE RECORD

Match No.	Date	Venue	Opponents	Result	H/T Score	Lg Pos.	Goalscorers	Attendance
1	Aug 8	H	Huddersfield T	W 2-0	1-0	2	Clucas [39], Akpom [71]	19,361
2	16	A	Wolverhampton W	D 1-1	1-0	4	Jelavic (pen) [22]	20,062
3	19	H	Fulham	W 2-1	1-0	2	Elmohamady [34], Aluko [86]	16,579
4	22	A	Charlton Ath	L 1-2	0-0	5	Hernandez [89]	14,844
5	29	H	Preston NE	W 2-0	1-0	2	Hernandez [37], Davies [82]	16,949
6	Sept 12	A	Brighton & HA	L 0-1	0-1	6		24,815
7	15	A	Cardiff C	W 2-0	1-0	4	Diame [8], Hernandez [80]	13,763
8	19	H	QPR	D 1-1	1-1	3	Dawson [38]	16,651
9	26	H	Blackburn R	D 1-1	0-0	4	Hernandez [73]	16,486
10	Oct 3	A	Nottingham F	W 1-0	1-0	5	Hernandez [41]	20,985
11	17	A	Sheffield W	D 1-1	0-1	6	Hernandez [51]	20,389
12	20	H	Ipswich T	W 3-0	2-0	4	Bruce [36], Akpom [43], Meyler [58]	15,942
13	24	H	Birmingham C	W 2-0	2-0	2	Meyler [36], Hernandez [38]	17,436
14	31	A	Milton Keynes D	W 2-0	1-0	2	Elmohamady [19], Diame [90]	15,360
15	Nov 3	A	Brentford	W 2-0	0-0	1	Robertson [67], Clucas [86]	9221
16	7	H	Middlesbrough	W 3-0	1-0	1	Diame [44], Clucas [67], Huddlestone [83]	20,352
17	21	A	Bristol C	D 1-1	0-1	1	Maloney [73]	14,590
18	27	H	Derby Co	L 0-2	0-2	2		17,410
19	Dec 5	A	Leeds U	L 1-2	0-2	4	Elmohamady [51]	24,962
20	12	H	Bolton W	W 1-0	1-0	3	Akpom [19]	15,739
21	16	H	Reading	W 2-1	0-1	4	Hernandez [62], Livermore [90]	15,139
22	19	A	Rotherham U	L 0-2	0-1	4		10,355
23	26	H	Burnley	W 3-0	0-0	3	Livermore [57], Hernandez [66], Clucas [90]	21,842
24	28	A	Preston NE	L 0-1	0-0	3		13,891
25	Jan 1	A	QPR	W 2-1	0-0	3	Hernandez [61], Diomande [90]	16,205
26	13	H	Cardiff C	W 2-0	1-0	2	Hernandez (pen) [40], Clucas [51]	15,549
27	16	H	Charlton Ath	W 6-0	4-0	2	Hernandez 3 [9, 16, 39], Snodgrass [33], Diame [58], Hayden [80]	16,430
28	23	A	Fulham	W 1-0	0-0	1	Hernandez (pen) [80]	16,935
29	Feb 6	A	Burnley	L 0-1	0-0	1		17,667
30	13	A	Blackburn R	W 2-0	0-0	1	Hernandez [53], Diame [63]	13,902
31	16	H	Brighton & HA	D 0-0	0-0	1		17,321
32	23	A	Ipswich T	W 1-0	0-0	1	Diame [48]	17,630
33	26	H	Sheffield W	D 0-0	0-0	1		17,884
34	Mar 3	A	Birmingham C	L 0-1	0-1	2		18,105
35	12	H	Milton Keynes D	D 1-1	0-0	3	Clucas [53]	16,183
36	15	H	Nottingham F	D 1-1	0-1	4	Aluko [73]	15,663
37	18	A	Middlesbrough	L 0-1	0-0	4		26,791
38	Apr 2	H	Bristol C	W 4-0	2-0	4	Davies [14], Snodgrass [39], Diame [71], Aluko [80]	16,521
39	5	A	Derby Co	L 0-4	0-2	4		29,078
40	9	A	Huddersfield T	D 2-2	0-1	4	Hernandez [76], Diomande [90]	12,883
41	15	H	Wolverhampton W	W 2-1	1-1	4	Diomande [5], Snodgrass [90]	15,504
42	19	A	Reading	W 2-1	1-1	4	Hernandez [18], Robertson [79]	12,949
43	23	H	Leeds U	D 2-2	2-1	4	Huddlestone [45], Hernandez [45]	20,732
44	26	H	Brentford	W 2-0	2-0	4	Dean (og) [31], Diame [45]	15,225
45	30	A	Bolton W	L 0-1	0-0	4		14,366
46	May 7	H	Rotherham U	W 5-1	4-1	4	Snodgrass [25], Hernandez [27], Livermore 2 [40, 59], Diame [42]	18,670

Final League Position: 4

GOALSCORERS

League (69): Hernandez 20 (2 pens), Diame 9, Clucas 6, Livermore 4, Snodgrass 4, Akpom 3, Aluko 3, Diomande 3, Elmohamady 3, Davies 2, Huddlestone 2, Meyler 2, Robertson 2, Bruce 1, Dawson 1, Hayden 1, Jelavic 1 (1 pen), Maloney 1, own goal 1.
FA Cup (4): Akpom 3 (1 pen), Snodgrass 1 (pen).
Capital One Cup (6): Luer 2, Akpom 1, Hernandez 1, Meyler 1, Robertson 1.
Championship Play-Offs (4): Diame 1, Hernandez 1, Robertson 1, own goal 1.

McGregor A 44	Taylor R 1 + 3	Dawson M 32	Davies C 37 + 2	Robertson A 41 + 1	Elmohamady A 31 + 10	Hayden I 9 + 9	Huddlestone T 24 + 13	Clucas S 39 + 5	Akpom C 19 + 16	Jelavic N 3 + 1	Aluko S 8 + 17	Meyler D 20 + 6	Luer G — + 2	Odubajo M 42	Jahraldo-Martin C — + 1	Hernandez A 34 + 5	Diame M 31 + 7	Maloney S 8 + 12	Bruce A 9 + 2	Livermore J 33 + 1	Maguire H 17 + 5	Snodgrass R 18 + 6	Diomande A 3 + 8	Powell N — + 3	Jakupovic E 2	Lenihan B 1	Match No.
1	2^1	3	4	5	6	7	8	9	10^2	11^3	12	13	14														1
1		3	4	5	6^2	7^1	8	9^3	10	11	13	12		2	14												2
1		3	4	5	6	14	8^2	12	10^3	13	9	7		2		11^1											3
1		3	4	5^1	6	12	8^1	14	11^3	10	9	7		2		13											4
1		3	4	5	6	14		9	11^3		12	7		2		10^2	8^1	13									5
1		3	4			9	8^3	12		5	10^1	13	6^2	2	14	11	7										6
1		2	4	8^2	12		6	7	13		10^3	14		5		11^1	9		3								7
1		2	4	8	14		6	7	12		10^2			5		11	9^1	13	3^3								8
1		3	4	5^1	6		7	9	10			14		2		11^2	8^3	12	13								9
1		3	4		2		7^1	9	13		12	14		5		10^2	8^3	11			6						10
1		3	4	13	2		7	9	12			14		5		10	8^2	11^3			6^1						11
1	3^1		4^3	5	6			9	10		13	8		2		11^2				12	7	14					12
1	3		5	6				9	10^3			8		2		11^2	14	13	4^1	7	12						13
1	3		5	6				9	11^1			8		2		10^2	12	13	4	7	12						14
1	3		5	6	14			9	10^1			8		2		11^2		13	4^3	7	12						15
1	3		5	6	14	13		9	12			8^1		2		11^3	10^2			7	4						16
1	3^2	12	5	6		7		9	11^1			14		2^3		10	13			8	4						17
1	4^1			2	14		6	8	13		12			5^2		10	9^1	11		7	3						18
1		12	5	6			8	9	13			11^2		2		10			4^3	7	3^1	14					19
1	3^3	4	5	6				9	11^1			8		2		10^2				7	14	12	13				20
1		4	5	6				9	11^2			8		2		10^1	12			7	3	13	14				21
1		4	5	6	14				10			8^2		2^1			11^1	12	9	7	3	13					22
1		4	5	6	14	12		9				8		2		11^3	10^1			7^2	3	13					23
1		4	5	2			12	9	11^1			7^2				13	14			10^3	6	3	8				24
1		4	5	6^1			13	9				8		2		11^3	10^2			7	3	12	14				25
1		4	5	6			13	9	12			8	14	2		11^1	10^2			7^3	3						26
1	14	4	5^1				8	9	12			13		2		11^3	10			7^2	3	6					27
1		4	5	13			8^1	9	12							11^2	10		14	7	3	6^3					28
1		3	4	5	8	14		9	13		12			2		11^2	10^1			7^3	6						29
1		3	4	5			13	8	9		12		14	2		11^3	10^2			7	6^1						30
1		3	4	5	14	12	8^1	9	13					2		11	10^3			7	6^1						31
1		3	4	5	14			9	12			8^1		2		11^2	10^3			7	6		13				32
1		3	4	5	14			9	13			8^1				11	10^3			7	6^2	12					33
1		3	4	5	14		8^3	9						2^2		11	10^1			7		6	12	13			34
1		3	4	5	6	7^3	13	8	11		12			2^2		10	9^1					14					35
1		3	4	5^1	6	7	8		13		12			2^2		11	10					9					36
1		3	4	5		7	13		10			11^2		2		12	9				6	8^1					37
1		3	4	5			12	8	9			11^3		2		14	10^1			7	6^1						38
1		3	4	5^3			13	8	9			11^3		2^1		12	10^1		14	7	6						39
1	2^3	9	5	8			14									10	7^1	12	3	6	4	11^2	13				40
1			4	5	6			9^2	13		14			2^3		8	11		3		7	12		10^1			41
1			4	5	12	14		8	13			7^1				11		9^3			3	6	14				42
1			4	5				8	13		10^1			2		11^2	9^3	12		7	3	6	14				43
	14		5^1		6			8	9		13			2		10^3		12	4	7	3	11^1			1		44
	14	3			6	7	8^2		5		11^1	12				13	10^3				4		9		1	2	45
1		3	4	5	6			8	13				14	2		11^2	10^3			7		12	9^1				46

FA Cup

Third Round	Brighton & HA	(h)	1-0
Fourth Round	Bury	(a)	3-1
Fifth Round	Arsenal	(a)	0-0
Replay	Arsenal	(h)	0-4

Championship Play-Offs

Semi-Final 1st leg	Derby Co	(a)	3-0
Semi-Final 2nd leg	Derby Co	(h)	0-2
(Hull C won 3-2 on aggregate)			
Final	Sheffield W	(Wembley)	1-0

Capital One Cup

First Round	Accrington S	(a)	2-2
(aet; Hull C won 4-3 on penalties)			
Second Round	Rochdale	(h)	1-0
Third Round	Swansea C	(h)	1-0
Fourth Round	Leicester C	(h)	1-1
(aet; Hull C won 5-4 on penalties)			
Quarter-Final	Manchester C	(a)	1-4

IPSWICH TOWN

FOUNDATION

Considering that Ipswich Town only reached the Football League in 1938, many people outside of East Anglia may be surprised to learn that this club was formed at a meeting held in the Town Hall as far back as 1878 when Mr T. C. Cobbold, MP, was voted president. Originally it was the Ipswich Association FC to distinguish it from the older Ipswich Football Club which played rugby. These two amalgamated in 1888 and the handling game was dropped in 1893.

Portman Road, Ipswich, Suffolk IP1 2DA.

Telephone: (01473) 400 500.

Fax: (01473) 400 040.

Ticket Office: (03330) 050 503

Website: www.itfc.co.uk

Email: customerservices@itfc.co.uk

Ground Capacity: 30,311.

Record Attendance: 38,010 v Leeds U, FA Cup 6th rd, 8 March 1975.

Pitch Measurements: 102.5m × 66m (112yd × 72.5yd).

Managing Directors: Ian Milne, Jonathan Symonds.

Manager: Mick McCarthy.

Assistant Manager: Terry Connor.

Physios: Matt Byard, Alex Chapman.

Colours: Blue shirts with thin white stripes, white shorts with blue trim, blue socks with white trim.

Year Formed: 1878.

Turned Professional: 1936.

HONOURS

League Champions: Division 1 – 1961–62; Division 2 – 1960–61, 1967–68, 1991–92; Division 3S – 1953–54, 1956–57.
Runners-up: Division 1 – 1980–81, 1981–82.
FA Cup Winners: 1978.
League Cup: semi-final – 1982, 1985, 2001, 2011.
Texaco Cup Winners: 1973.
European Competitions
European Cup: 1962–63.
UEFA Cup: 1973–74, 1974–75, 1975–76, 1977–78, 1979–80, 1980–81 *(winners)*, 1981–82, 1982–83, 2001–02, 2002–03.
European Cup-Winners' Cup: 1978–79 *(qf)*.

Previous Name: 1878, Ipswich Association FC; 1888, Ipswich Town.

Club Nicknames: 'The Blues', 'Town', 'The Tractor Boys'.

Grounds: 1878, Broom Hill and Brook's Hall; 1884, Portman Road.

First Football League Game: 27 August 1938, Division 3 (S), v Southend U (h) W 4–2 – Burns; Dale, Parry; Perrett, Fillingham, McLuckie; Williams, Davies (1), Jones (2), Alsop (1), Little.

Record League Victory: 7–0 v Portsmouth, Division 2, 7 November 1964 – Thorburn; Smith, McNeil; Baxter, Bolton, Thompson; Broadfoot (1), Hegan (2), Baker (1), Leadbetter, Brogan (3). 7–0 v Southampton, Division 1, 2 February 1974 – Sivell; Burley, Mills (1), Morris, Hunter, Beattie (1), Hamilton (2), Viljoen, Johnson, Whymark (2), Lambert (1) (Woods). 7–0 v WBA, Division 1, 6 November 1976 – Sivell; Burley, Mills, Talbot, Hunter, Beattie (1), Osborne, Wark (1), Mariner (1) (Bertschin), Whymark (4), Woods.

sky SPORTS FACT FILE

Ipswich Town's debut in the European Cup in the 1962–63 competition saw them drawn against Floriana of Malta in the preliminary round. Town won 4-1 in the first leg away from home, with Ray Crawford netting twice. The return game at Portman Road saw Town 6-0 ahead at half-time and they eventually hit double figures with a 10-0 victory, including five from Crawford.

Record Cup Victory: 10–0 v Floriana, European Cup prel. rd, 25 September 1962 – Bailey; Malcolm, Compton; Baxter, Laurel, Elsworthy (1); Stephenson, Moran (2), Crawford (5), Phillips (2), Blackwood.

Record Defeat: 1–10 v Fulham, Division 1, 26 December 1963.

Most League Points (2 for a win): 64, Division 3 (S), 1953–54 and 1955–56.

Most League Points (3 for a win): 87, Division 1, 1999–2000.

Most League Goals: 106, Division 3 (S), 1955–56.

Highest League Scorer in Season: Ted Phillips, 41, Division 3 (S), 1956–57.

Most League Goals in Total Aggregate: Ray Crawford, 204, 1958–63 and 1966–69.

Most League Goals in One Match: 5, Alan Brazil v Southampton, Division 1, 16 February 1981.

Most Capped Player: Allan Hunter, 47 (53), Northern Ireland.

Most League Appearances: Mick Mills, 591, 1966–82.

Youngest League Player: Jason Dozzell, 16 years 56 days v Coventry C, 4 February 1984.

Record Transfer Fee Received: £8,000,000 from Sunderland for Connor Wickham, June 2011; £8,000,000 from AFC Bournemouth for Tyrone Mings, June 2015.

Record Transfer Fee Paid: £5,000,000 to Sampdoria for Matteo Sereni, August 2001.

Football League Record: 1938 Elected to Division 3 (S); 1954–55 Division 2; 1955–57 Division 3 (S); 1957–61 Division 2; 1961–64 Division 1; 1964–68 Division 2; 1968–86 Division 1; 1986–92 Division 2; 1992–95 FA Premier League; 1995–2000 Division 1; 2000–02 FA Premier League; 2002–04 Division 1; 2004– FL C.

MANAGERS

Mick O'Brien 1936–37
Scott Duncan 1937–55
  (continued as Secretary)
Alf Ramsey 1955–63
Jackie Milburn 1963–64
Bill McGarry 1964–68
Bobby Robson 1969–82
Bobby Ferguson 1982–87
Johnny Duncan 1987–90
John Lyall 1990–94
George Burley 1994–2002
Joe Royle 2002–06
Jim Magilton 2006–09
Roy Keane 2009–11
Paul Jewell 2011–12
Mick McCarthy November 2012–

LATEST SEQUENCES

Longest Sequence of League Wins: 8, 23.9.1953 – 31.10.1953.
Longest Sequence of League Defeats: 10, 4.9.1954 – 16.10.1954.
Longest Sequence of League Draws: 7, 10.11.1990 – 21.12.1990.
Longest Sequence of Unbeaten League Matches: 23, 8.12.1979 – 26.4.1980.
Longest Sequence Without a League Win: 21, 28.8.1963 – 14.12.1963.
Successive Scoring Runs: 31 from 7.3.2004.
Successive Non-scoring Runs: 7 from 28.2.1995.

TEN YEAR LEAGUE RECORD

		P	W	D	L	F	A	Pts	Pos
2006-07	FL C	46	18	8	20	64	59	62	14
2007-08	FL C	46	18	15	13	65	56	69	8
2008-09	FL C	46	17	15	14	62	53	66	9
2009-10	FL C	46	12	20	14	50	61	56	15
2010-11	FL C	46	18	8	20	62	68	62	13
2011-12	FL C	46	17	10	19	69	77	61	15
2012-13	FL C	46	16	12	18	48	61	60	14
2013-14	FL C	46	18	14	14	60	54	68	9
2014-15	FL C	46	22	12	12	72	54	78	6
2015-16	FL C	46	18	15	13	53	51	69	7

DID YOU KNOW

In June 1936 the Irish international centre-half Mick O'Brien was appointed the first manager of Ipswich Town following the club's decision to turn professional. They won the Southern League in his first season but he then departed and was later secretary-manager of Cork Celtic. He passed away in 1940 at the age of 47.

IPSWICH TOWN – FL CHAMPIONSHIP 2015–16 LEAGUE RECORD

Match No.	Date	Venue	Opponents	Result	H/T Score	Lg Pos.	Goalscorers	Attendance
1	Aug 8	A	Brentford	D	2-2	1-0	8	Bru [45], Fraser [50]	10,789
2	15	H	Sheffield W	W	2-1	1-1	5	Sears [21], Smith [53]	20,081
3	18	H	Burnley	W	2-0	0-0	1	Sears [66], McGoldrick [71]	18,353
4	22	A	Preston NE	W	2-1	1-1	1	Pitman [24], Fraser [65]	12,330
5	29	H	Brighton & HA	L	2-3	0-2	3	Sears [54], McGoldrick (pen) [65]	21,034
6	Sept 11	A	Reading	L	1-5	1-2	4	Sears [11]	16,809
7	15	A	Leeds U	W	1-0	1-0	5	Smith [32]	21,312
8	18	H	Birmingham C	D	1-1	1-1	4	Pitman (pen) [32]	18,973
9	26	H	Bristol C	D	2-2	0-0	7	Chambers [46], Fraser [86]	20,347
10	Oct 3	A	Blackburn R	L	0-2	0-2	12		12,672
11	17	H	Huddersfield T	D	0-0	0-0	10		17,937
12	20	A	Hull C	L	0-3	0-2	11		15,942
13	24	A	Nottingham F	D	1-1	0-0	13	Parr [74]	19,616
14	31	H	Cardiff C	D	0-0	0-0	14		17,169
15	Nov 3	H	Bolton W	W	2-0	1-0	10	Maitland-Niles [13], Pitman [70]	17,017
16	7	A	Rotherham U	W	5-2	3-0	10	Pitman [8], Douglas [22], Murphy 3 [43, 48, 72]	9162
17	21	A	Wolverhampton W	D	2-2	1-1	10	Douglas [16], Murphy [54]	19,227
18	28	A	Charlton Ath	W	3-0	2-0	7	Murphy 2 [28, 68], Sears [45]	15,870
19	Dec 4	H	Middlesbrough	L	0-2	0-0	8		17,662
20	12	A	Milton Keynes D	W	1-0	1-0	6	Pitman [10]	13,520
21	15	A	Fulham	W	2-1	1-1	6	Sears [1], Pitman [57]	15,245
22	19	H	Derby Co	L	0-1	0-1	6		20,161
23	26	H	QPR	W	2-1	0-1	6	Douglas [77], Chambers [90]	23,615
24	29	A	Brighton & HA	W	1-0	1-0	6	Murphy [32]	27,689
25	Jan 2	A	Burnley	D	0-0	0-0	6		16,307
26	12	H	Leeds U	W	2-1	0-1	5	Chambers [50], Pitman [90]	19,146
27	16	H	Preston NE	D	1-1	1-1	7	Murphy [38]	21,108
28	23	A	Birmingham C	L	0-3	0-1	8		18,272
29	Feb 2	A	Reading	W	2-1	0-0	6	Fraser [57], Pitman [89]	16,616
30	6	A	QPR	L	0-1	0-0	7		17,044
31	13	A	Bristol C	L	1-2	0-2	8	Pitman [61]	15,736
32	23	H	Hull C	L	0-1	0-0	10		17,630
33	27	A	Huddersfield T	W	1-0	1-0	9	Pringle [19]	12,644
34	Mar 5	H	Nottingham F	W	1-0	0-0	9	Pringle [63]	20,658
35	8	A	Bolton W	D	2-2	1-0	8	Bru [24], Berra [72]	12,681
36	12	A	Cardiff C	L	0-1	0-1	8		15,175
37	15	H	Blackburn R	W	2-0	0-0	8	Murphy 2 (1 pen) [67 (p), 87]	16,488
38	19	H	Rotherham U	L	0-1	0-1	8		20,318
39	Apr 2	A	Wolverhampton W	D	0-0	0-0	8		20,225
40	5	H	Charlton Ath	D	0-0	0-0	8		17,787
41	9	H	Brentford	L	1-3	0-1	8	Feeney [88]	18,845
42	16	A	Sheffield W	D	1-1	0-1	8	Dozzell [71]	25,082
43	19	H	Fulham	D	1-1	0-0	8	Knudsen [90]	16,953
44	23	A	Middlesbrough	D	0-0	0-0	8		30,505
45	30	H	Milton Keynes D	W	3-2	1-1	8	McGoldrick [16], Pitman [68], Varney [90]	19,631
46	May 7	A	Derby Co	W	1-0	1-0	7	McGoldrick (pen) [34]	29,854

Final League Position: 7

GOALSCORERS

League (53): Murphy 10 (1 pen), Pitman 10 (1 pen), Sears 6, Fraser 4, McGoldrick 4 (2 pens), Chambers 3, Douglas 3, Bru 2, Pringle 2, Smith 2, Berra 1, Dozzell 1, Feeney 1, Knudsen 1, Maitland-Niles 1, Parr 1, Varney 1.
FA Cup (3): Fraser 1, Maitland-Niles 1, Oar 1.
Capital One Cup (6): Alabi 1, Fraser 1, McGoldrick 1, Pitman 1, Tabb 1, Yorwerth 1.

Bialkowski B 20	Emmanuel J 3+1	Chambers L 45	Smith T 45	Knudsen J 42	Maitland-Niles A 21+9	Skuse C 39	Bru K 20+8	Fraser R 15+3	Sears F 44+1	Murphy D 30+4	Coke G 1+9	Douglas J 32+6	McGoldrick D 9+15	Berra C 43	Pitman B 24+18	Gerken D 26	Toure L 3+4	Malarczyk P —+3	Oar T 1+5	Parr J 3+6	Varney L 2+16	Hyam L 9+6	Foley K 6+2	Pringle B 9+1	Digby P 1+3	Feeney L 7+2	Bishop T 2+2	Dozzell A 1+1	Kenlock M 2	McDonnell A 1	Match No.
1	2	3	4	5	6²	7	8¹	9²	10	11	12	13	14																		1
1	2	3		5	6²	7		9³	10	11	14	8¹	12	4	13																2
1	2	3		5	6¹	7		9¹	11	10²	14	8	12	4	13																3
14	2	3		5	12	6		10¹	8³	7		9²	4	11		1	13														4
2²	3	4	5	6¹	7³		9	11		14	8	12	10	1		13															5
	2	3	5	13	7		9²	6	12		8	10	4	11¹	1																6
	2	3	5	6²	7³		9¹		10	13	8	11	4	14	1		12														7
	2	3	5	9³	7		14	11	12		8	13	4	10¹	1	6²															8
	2²	3	5	6¹	8		9	10	11³		7	12	4	13	1		14														9
	2	3		6³	8			10	11²		7	12	4	13	1	9¹		5	14												10
	2	3	5	6²	7			10	13		8	12	4	11¹	1	14			9¹												11
	2	3	5	13		9		12	10	7¹	8		4	14	1	11³			6²												12
	2	3	5¹	6	7²	8		9³	11		13	10	4		1		14	12													13
	2	3		6²	7	8		9	11¹		10		4	13	1		5	12													14
	2	3	5	6¹	7	8		9	10		12	13	4	11²	1																15
	2	3	5	12	7	6²		9¹	10³	13	8		4	11	1		14														16
	2	3	5	12	7	6¹		11	10				4	9	1																17
	2	3	5	6¹	7			11²	10	12	8		4	9	1		13														18
	2	3	5	6²	7			11	10	12	8	13	4	9¹	1																19
	2	3	5	6¹	7			9²	10		8	13	4	11	1	12															20
	2	3	5	6²	7³	12		11	10		8		4	9¹	1	13	14														21
	2	3	5	6³	7	13	12	11	9		8²		4	10¹	1	14															22
	2	3	5	6²	7		12	11	10¹		8		4	9³	1	13	14														23
	2	3	5		7	8¹	11³	9	10³		6		4	13	1	14	12														24
	2	3	5		8	7²	11³	9	10¹				4	13	1	12	14	6													25
	2	3	5		7	6²	9	10	11¹	8			4	12	1		13														26
	2	3	5		6	9²	10	8	11¹	7³			4	12	1	14	13														27
	2	3	5		6	9²	10	8¹	11³	7⁴			4	14	1	13	12														28
1	2	3	5	6¹	7	12	9	10	11³				4	13			14	8¹													29
1	2	3	5		7³	6	8¹	11	12	13			4	9		14		10²													30
1	2	4	5	9¹		7		11	10				3	12		14		13		6²	8¹										31
1	2	3	5			12		9	10	6			4	11				13	7¹		8²										32
1	2	3	5	13		12		11¹	10	6			4	9							7³	8¹	14								33
1	2	3	5	12		7²		9					4	11³			13	10	6	8¹	14										34
1	2	3	5	14		6¹		10		7			4	11			12	13	8²	9¹											35
1	2	3¹	5	14	7	6²		10	11				4	12			13	8		9³											36
1	2	3	5	7¹			9	10		8			4	11²			12³	6	13		14										37
1	2	3	5		7	14		11	10	6²			4	9³				8¹		13		12									38
1	2	3	5		7	12		11		8	14		4	11²			13			6¹		9¹									39
1	2	3	5		8			9		7	13		4	11²			12			10³		6¹	14								40
1		3		5	6²	8			10			13	12	4			11¹	7⁴	2	9³		14									41
1	2	3	5			6¹		10				7	11	4	13					8²			9	12							42
1	2	3	5		7	12		9		8²	13		4	11							6		10¹								43
1		2	4	5²		7	6¹	11		14	10						8³	13			3	9	12								44
	2	3			7	8	11		10		4	12	1			13								9²	6¹		5				45
1		2	3		7³		11		13	10	4	14					12							9	6²		5	8¹			46

FA Cup
Third Round Portsmouth (h) 2-2
Replay Portsmouth (a) 1-2

Capital One Cup
First Round Stevenage (h) 2-1
Second Round Doncaster R (a) 4-1
(aet)
Third Round Manchester U (a) 0-3

LEEDS UNITED

FOUNDATION

Immediately the Leeds City club (founded in 1904) was wound up by the FA in October 1919, following allegations of illegal payments to players, a meeting was called by a Leeds solicitor, Mr Alf Masser, at which Leeds United was formed. They joined the Midland League, playing their first game in that competition in November 1919. It was in this same month that the new club had discussions with the directors of a virtually bankrupt Huddersfield Town who wanted to move to Leeds in an amalgamation. But Huddersfield survived even that crisis.

Elland Road, Leeds, West Yorkshire LS11 0ES.

Telephone: (0871) 334 1919.

Fax: (0113) 367 6050.

Ticket Office: (0871) 334 1992.

Website: www.leedsunited.com

Email: reception@leedsunited.com

Ground Capacity: 37,890.

Record Attendance: 57,892 v Sunderland, FA Cup 5th rd (replay), 15 March 1967.

Pitch Measurements: 96m × 58.5m (105yd × 64yd).

Chairman: Massimo Cellino.

Head Coach: Garry Monk.

Assistant Head Coach: Pep Clotet.

Physio: Steve Megson.

Colours: White shirts with blue trim, white shorts, white socks with blue trim.

Year Formed: 1919, as Leeds United after disbandment (by FA order) of Leeds City (formed in 1904).

Turned Professional: 1920.

Club Nickname: 'The Whites'.

Ground: 1919, Elland Road.

HONOURS

League Champions: Division 1 – 1968–69, 1973–74, 1991–92; Division 2 – 1923–24, 1963–64, 1989–90. *Runners-up:* Division 1 – 1964–65, 1965–66, 1969–70, 1970–71, 1971–72; Division 2 – 1927–28, 1931–32, 1955–56; FL 1 – 2009–10.
FA Cup Winners: 1972. *Runners-up:* 1965, 1970, 1973.
League Cup Winners: 1968. *Runners-up:* 1996.
European Competitions
European Cup: 1969–70 *(sf)*, 1974–75 *(runners-up)*.
Champions League: 1992–93, 2000–01 *(sf)*.
Fairs Cup: 1965–66 *(sf)*, 1966–67 *(runners-up)*, 1967–68 *(winners)*, 1968–69 *(qf)*, 1970–71 *(winners)*.
UEFA Cup: 1971–72, 1973–74, 1979–80, 1995–96, 1998–99, 1999–2000 *(sf)*, 2001–02, 2002–03.
European Cup-Winners' Cup: 1972–73 *(runners-up)*.

First Football League Game: 28 August 1920, Division 2, v Port Vale (a) L 0–2 – Down; Duffield, Tillotson; Musgrove, Baker, Walton; Mason, Goldthorpe, Thompson, Lyon, Best.

Record League Victory: 8–0 v Leicester C, Division 1, 7 April 1934 – Moore; George Milburn, Jack Milburn; Edwards, Hart, Copping; Mahon (2), Firth (2), Duggan (2), Furness (2), Cochrane.

sky SPORTS FACT FILE

Centre-forward Albert Wakefield joined Leeds United as an amateur in 1940, turning professional two years later. After enlisting in the Royal Engineers he was posted to serve in Italy where he became a prolific scorer in Army football, also turning out for the Serie B club Pro Gorizia before returning to Elland Road for the 1947–48 season.

Record Cup Victory: 10–0 v Lyn (Oslo), European Cup 1st rd 1st leg, 17 September 1969 – Sprake; Reaney, Cooper, Bremner (2), Charlton, Hunter, Madeley, Clarke (2), Jones (3), Giles (2) (Bates), O'Grady (1).

Record Defeat: 1–8 v Stoke C, Division 1, 27 August 1934.

Most League Points (2 for a win): 67, Division 1, 1968–69.

Most League Points (3 for a win): 86, FL 1, 2009–10.

Most League Goals: 98, Division 2, 1927–28.

Highest League Scorer in Season: John Charles, 42, Division 2, 1953–54.

Most League Goals in Total Aggregate: Peter Lorimer, 168, 1965–79 and 1983–86.

Most League Goals in One Match: 5, Gordon Hodgson v Leicester C, Division 1, 1 October 1938.

Most Capped Player: Lucas Radebe, 58 (70), South Africa.

Most League Appearances: Jack Charlton, 629, 1953–73.

Youngest League Player: Peter Lorimer, 15 years 289 days v Southampton, 29 September 1962.

Record Transfer Fee Received: £30,800,000 from Manchester U for Rio Ferdinand, July 2002.

Record Transfer Fee Paid: £18,000,000 to West Ham U for Rio Ferdinand, November 2000.

Football League Record: 1920 Elected to Division 2; 1924–27 Division 1; 1927–28 Division 2; 1928–31 Division 1; 1931–32 Division 2; 1932–47 Division 1; 1947–56 Division 2; 1956–60 Division 1; 1960–64 Division 2; 1964–82 Division 1; 1982–90 Division 2; 1990–92 Division 1; 1992–2004 FA Premier League; 2004–07 FL C; 2007–10 FL 1; 2010– FL C.

LATEST SEQUENCES

Longest Sequence of League Wins: 9, 18.4.2009 – 5.9.2009.

Longest Sequence of League Defeats: 6, 28.12.2003 – 7.2.2004.

Longest Sequence of League Draws: 5, 2.5.2015 – 22.8.2015.

Longest Sequence of Unbeaten League Matches: 34, 26.10.1968 – 26.8.1969.

Longest Sequence Without a League Win: 17, 1.2.1947 – 26.5.1947.

Successive Scoring Runs: 30 from 27.8.1927.

Successive Non-scoring Runs: 6 from 30.1.1982.

MANAGERS

Dick Ray 1919–20
Arthur Fairclough 1920–27
Dick Ray 1927–35
Bill Hampson 1935–47
Willis Edwards 1947–48
Major Frank Buckley 1948–53
Raich Carter 1953–58
Bill Lambton 1958–59
Jack Taylor 1959–61
Don Revie OBE 1961–74
Brian Clough 1974
Jimmy Armfield 1974–78
Jock Stein CBE 1978
Jimmy Adamson 1978–80
Allan Clarke 1980–82
Eddie Gray MBE 1982–85
Billy Bremner 1985–88
Howard Wilkinson 1988–96
George Graham 1996–98
David O'Leary 1998–2002
Terry Venables 2002–03
Peter Reid 2003
Eddie Gray *(Caretaker)* 2003–04
Kevin Blackwell 2004–06
Dennis Wise 2006–08
Gary McAllister 2008
Simon Grayson 2008–12
Neil Warnock 2012–13
Brian McDermott 2013–14
Dave Hockaday 2014
Darko Milanic 2014
Neil Redfearn 2014–15
Uwe Rosler 2015
Steve Evans 2015–16
Garry Monk April 2016–

TEN YEAR LEAGUE RECORD

		P	W	D	L	F	A	Pts	Pos
2006-07	FL C	46	13	7	26	46	72	36*	24
2007-08	FL 1	46	27	10	9	72	38	76†	5
2008-09	FL 1	46	26	6	14	77	49	84	4
2009-10	FL 1	46	25	11	10	77	44	86	2
2010-11	FL C	46	19	15	12	81	70	72	7
2011-12	FL C	46	17	10	19	65	68	61	14
2012-13	FL C	46	17	10	19	57	66	61	13
2013-14	FL C	46	16	9	21	59	67	57	15
2014-15	FL C	46	15	11	20	50	61	56	15
2015-16	FL C	46	14	17	15	50	58	59	13

*10 pts deducted; †15 pts deducted.

DID YOU KNOW ?

Leeds United played their first game under floodlights against Hibernian on 9 November 1953. The match was a great success, attracting an attendance of 31,500 with United, who included manager Raich Carter in their line-up, winning 4-1 with two goals apiece from Carter and John Charles.

LEEDS UNITED – FL CHAMPIONSHIP 2015–16 LEAGUE RECORD

Match No.	Date	Venue	Opponents		Result	H/T Score	Lg Pos.	Goalscorers	Attendance
1	Aug 8	H	Burnley	D	1-1	0-0	10	Antenucci [83]	27,672
2	16	A	Reading	D	0-0	0-0	15		21,581
3	19	A	Bristol C	D	2-2	1-0	15	Antenucci (pen) [39], Wood [52]	14,712
4	22	H	Sheffield W	D	1-1	0-1	15	Wood [61]	22,597
5	29	A	Derby Co	W	2-1	1-0	10	Adeyemi [43], Wood [88]	29,386
6	Sept 12	H	Brentford	D	1-1	0-1	11	Antenucci [76]	25,126
7	15	H	Ipswich T	L	0-1	0-1	14		21,312
8	19	A	Milton Keynes D	W	2-1	2-0	10	Wood (pen) [31], Taylor [43]	19,284
9	27	A	Middlesbrough	L	0-3	0-2	14		27,694
10	Oct 3	H	Birmingham C	L	0-2	0-2	16		24,601
11	17	H	Brighton & HA	L	1-2	1-1	18	Cooper [22]	22,736
12	21	A	Fulham	D	1-1	0-1	18	Wood (pen) [64]	19,969
13	24	A	Bolton W	D	1-1	0-1	17	Antenucci (pen) [71]	18,178
14	29	H	Blackburn R	L	0-2	0-2	18		19,666
15	Nov 3	H	Cardiff C	W	1-0	0-0	17	Mowatt [63]	17,914
16	7	A	Huddersfield T	W	3-0	2-0	15	Antenucci [45], Wood [45], Mowatt [54]	17,118
17	21	H	Rotherham U	L	0-1	0-0	16		25,802
18	28	A	QPR	L	0-1	0-0	17		18,031
19	Dec 5	H	Hull C	W	2-1	2-0	17	Wood [30], Adeyemi [45]	24,962
20	12	A	Charlton Ath	D	0-0	0-0	18		15,867
21	17	A	Wolverhampton W	W	3-2	1-1	14	Byram 2 [44, 60], Dallas [51]	19,592
22	20	H	Preston NE	W	1-0	0-0	13	Browne (og) [46]	22,641
23	27	A	Nottingham F	D	1-1	0-1	12	Byram [80]	27,551
24	29	H	Derby Co	D	2-2	1-1	12	Bamba [42], Wood [71]	23,027
25	Jan 2	H	Milton Keynes D	D	1-1	0-1	13	Kay (og) [87]	24,356
26	12	A	Ipswich T	L	1-2	1-0	15	Doukara [1]	19,146
27	16	A	Sheffield W	L	0-2	0-0	17		23,909
28	23	H	Bristol C	W	1-0	0-0	16	Doukara [59]	20,441
29	26	A	Brentford	D	1-1	0-1	14	Carayol [84]	10,051
30	Feb 6	H	Nottingham F	L	0-1	0-0	16		24,079
31	15	H	Middlesbrough	D	0-0	0-0	16		20,424
32	23	H	Fulham	D	1-1	1-1	17	Cook [38]	17,103
33	29	A	Brighton & HA	L	0-4	0-4	17		25,150
34	Mar 5	H	Bolton W	W	2-1	1-0	16	Antenucci 2 [39, 62]	21,070
35	8	A	Cardiff C	W	2-0	1-0	15	Doukara [37], Antenucci [90]	15,273
36	12	A	Blackburn R	W	2-1	1-0	12	Bamba [34], Antenucci [69]	16,017
37	19	H	Huddersfield T	L	1-4	1-1	13	Dallas [22]	29,311
38	Apr 2	A	Rotherham U	L	1-2	0-1	14	Murphy [79]	11,418
39	5	H	QPR	D	1-1	0-0	15	Wood [70]	17,388
40	9	A	Burnley	L	0-1	0-1	15		18,229
41	12	A	Birmingham C	W	2-1	1-0	15	Dallas 2 [11, 50]	16,081
42	16	H	Reading	W	3-2	0-1	12	Diagouraga [48], Wood 2 [69, 85]	20,881
43	19	H	Wolverhampton W	W	2-1	0-0	11	Bamba [60], Diagouraga [64]	17,694
44	23	A	Hull C	D	2-2	1-2	12	Wood [15], Dallas [88]	20,732
45	30	H	Charlton Ath	L	1-2	0-1	12	Bamba [71]	25,458
46	May 7	A	Preston NE	D	1-1	0-0	13	Wood (pen) [78]	18,473

Final League Position: 13

GOALSCORERS

League (50): Wood 13 (3 pens), Antenucci 9 (2 pens), Dallas 5, Bamba 4, Byram 3, Doukara 3, Adeyemi 2, Diagouraga 2, Mowatt 2, Carayol 1, Cook 1, Cooper 1, Murphy 1, Taylor 1, own goals 2.
FA Cup (4): Doukara 2, Carayol 1, Diagouraga 1.
Capital One Cup (1): Cook 1.

Silvestri M 45	Berardi G 25+3	Bellusci G 25+2	Bamba S 28+2	Taylor C 39	Cook L 41+2	Adeyemi T 17+6	Mowatt A 22+12	Byram S 16+6	Wood C 33+3	Dallas S 38+7	Antenucci M 21+18	Doukara S 13+10	Wootton S 21+2	Cooper L 39	Philips K 3+7	Murphy L 25+11	Botaka J 3+10	Buckley W 1+3	Erwin L 2+9	Bridcutt L 23+1	Coyle L 6+5	Carayol M 6+6	Diagouraga T 13+4	Peacock-Farrell B 1	Vieira R —+1	Match No.
1	2	3	4	5	6^1	7	8^2	9	10	11^3	12	13	14													1
1	2		3	5		7	8^2	9	10	11	13			4	6^1	12										2
1	13	4	3	5		6	12	8^2	11	10	9^1		2	7												3
1	2		3	5		6	12	8^2	11	10^1	9	14		4		7^2	13									4
1	2		3	5	6	7	8^1	9^2	10	11	13			4		12										5
1	2		3	5	6	7^1	8^2	9	10	11	12			4		13										6
1	2		3	5	8	7^1	13	12	10	11^2	9			4		6										7
1		14	3	5	6	12	8^1	9^2	10	11^3	13		2	4		7										8
1	2	3	4	5	6	7	8			11	10	12			13	9^2										9
1	2^3		3	5	6		8^2	14	10	11	13			4		7	12		9^1							10
1	5		3		6	7	8^2	14	10	11^1	13		2	4				9^3	12							11
1	5		3		9	7		2	11^3	6^1	10		4	14	8^2	12	13									12
1	5		3		9^3	8	12	2	11	6^2	10		4	14	7^1		13									13
1	5		3		9^1	7^2	14	2	11^3	6	10	13		4		8	12									14
1	5	3			8		9^3	12	11	6^1	10^2	14	2	4	13	7										15
1	5	3	12		8	13	9		11	6^2	10		2^1	4^3		7	14									16
1	5^1	3			7^1	12	9		10	6^2	11		2	4		8^3	13	14								17
1		3		5	8		6^1		11	9	10^2		2	4		12				13	7					18
1		3		5	8	9	7^3	12	11^2	10^1		14	2	4	13					6						19
1	12^3	3		5	8	9	10^2	14	11	7			2^1	4		13				6						20
1		3		5	9	8^1	14	7	11^3	10^1	13	12		2	4					6						21
1		3		5	8		7	11^3	10^1	13	12		2	4	14	9^2				6						22
1		3		5	8^3		7^2	11	10^1	13	12		2	4		9				6	14					23
1		3	5	12	10^1		6^2	11^2	9		13	2	4	14	8					7						24
1		3	5	8		7		10^2	12	11^1	2	4		9^2		13	6	14								25
1		3		5	6^1		9^3	8		13	14	11	2	4	12		7				10^2					26
1		3		5	9		12		8	13	11	2	4	6^1		7					10^2					27
1		3		5	9	14		12	8	13	11^2	2	4	7^1		6					10^3					28
1		3		5	9		11^2	6^1	12	10	2	4	7^2		8			14	13							29
1		3		5	9	14		8	11	10	2^2	4		13	7		12	6^3								30
1		3		5	9	12		8	11^1	10	2	4	14		13	6		7^3								31
1			3	5	9	7^1	10^3		13	11^2	8	4			14	12	2		6							32
1			3	5	9	10			11^3	2^2	4	14		13	6	8	12	7^1								33
1	12	3	13	5	8		14	10	11	4^1				7	2^3	9^2	6									34
1	2	4	3	5	9	8^1		13	10	11^3		7		14	6^2	12										35
1	2	4	3	5	9	8^1	13	12	10	11^3		14		6	7^2											36
1	2	4	3	5	12	9	13	6^3	10	11^1		7^2		8	14											37
1^*	2^3	3	4	5	7^1	9^2	10	13	11	14	8	12	6													38
	2	3		5	9	14	11	8^2		4	7^1			6	13	10^3	12	1								39
1	2		3	5	9	13	14	11	8^1	12	4	7				10^3	6^2									40
1	2	14	3	5	9	12^*	11	6^2	10^3	4	7^1		13	8												41
1	2	3		5	8		11	10^1	9^3	4	12	7		13	14		6^2									42
1	2		3	5	9		11	12		4	7^2	13	10^1	14	8^3	6										43
1	2^3		3	5	9		11	8		4	13	12	10^1	6	14	7^2										44
1		3	5	9	12		11	10^1	13	4	7^2	8		6^3	2	14										45
1		3	5	9	10^3		11	8^1	13	12	4^2	7		2	6	14										46

FA Cup

Third Round	Rotherham U	(h)	2-0
Fourth Round	Bolton W	(a)	2-1
Fifth Round	Watford	(a)	0-1

Capital One Cup

First Round　　Doncaster R　　(a)　1-1
(aet; Doncaster R won 4-2 on penalties)

LEICESTER CITY

FOUNDATION

In 1884 a number of young footballers, who were mostly old boys of Wyggeston School, held a meeting at a house on the Roman Fosse Way and formed Leicester Fosse FC. They collected 9d (less than 4p) towards the cost of a ball, plus the same amount for membership. Their first professional, Harry Webb from Stafford Rangers, was signed in 1888 for 2s 6d (12p) per week, plus travelling expenses.

King Power Stadium, Filbert Way, Leicester LE2 7FL.
Telephone: (0344) 815 5000.
Fax: (0116) 291 5278.
Ticket Office: (0344) 815 5000.
Website: www.lcfc.co.uk
Email: sales@lcfc.co.uk
Ground Capacity: 32,312.
Record Attendance: 47,298 v Tottenham H, FA Cup 5th rd, 18 February 1928 (at Filbert Street); 32,242 v Sunderland, FA Premier League, 8 August 2016 (at King Power Stadium).
Pitch Measurements: 105m × 68m (115yd × 75yd).
Chairman: Khun Vichai Srivaddhanaprabha.
Chief Executive: Susan Whelan.
Manager: Claudio Ranieri.
Assistant Managers: Craig Shakespeare, Steve Walsh, Paolo Benetti.
Physio: Dave Rennie.
Colours: Blue shirts with yellow trim, blue shorts with yellow trim, blue socks with yellow trim.
Year Formed: 1884.
Turned Professional: 1888.
Previous Name: 1884, Leicester Fosse; 1919, Leicester City.
Club Nickname: 'The Foxes'.
Grounds: 1884, Victoria Park; 1887, Belgrave Road; 1888, Victoria Park; 1891, Filbert Street; 2002, Walkers Stadium (now known as King Power Stadium from 2011).
First Football League Game: 1 September 1894, Division 2, v Grimsby T (a) L 3–4 – Thraves; Smith, Bailey; Seymour, Brown, Henrys; Hill, Hughes, McArthur (1), Skea (2), Priestman.
Record League Victory: 10–0 v Portsmouth, Division 1, 20 October 1928 – McLaren; Black, Brown; Findlay, Carr, Watson; Adcock, Hine (3), Chandler (6), Lochhead, Barry (1).
Record Cup Victory: 8–1 v Coventry C (a), League Cup 5th rd, 1 December 1964 – Banks; Sjoberg, Norman (2); Roberts, King, McDerment; Hodgson (2), Cross, Goodfellow, Gibson (1), Stringfellow (2), (1 og).
Record Defeat: 0–12 (as Leicester Fosse) v Nottingham F, Division 1, 21 April 1909.

HONOURS

League Champions: FA Premier League – 2015–16; FL C – 2013–14; Division 2 – 1924–25, 1936–37, 1953–54, 1956–57, 1970–71, 1979–80; FL 1 – 2008–09.
Runners-up: Division 1 – 1928–29; First Division – 2002–03; Division 2 – 1907–08.
FA Cup: Runners-up: 1949, 1961, 1963, 1969.
League Cup Winners: 1964, 1997, 2000.
Runners-up: 1965, 1999.

European Competitions
UEFA Cup: 1997–98, 2000–01.
European Cup-Winners' Cup: 1961–62.

sky SPORTS FACT FILE

Although the first Sunday Football League games were played in January 1974, it was a decade before Leicester City's Filbert Street hosted a game on a Sunday. On 23 December 1984 Leicester defeated Coventry City 5-1, scoring their 5,000th League goal in the process.

Most League Points (2 for a win): 61, Division 2, 1956–57.

Most League Points (3 for a win): 102, FL C, 2013–14.

Most League Goals: 109, Division 2, 1956–57.

Highest League Scorer in Season: Arthur Rowley, 44, Division 2, 1956–57.

Most League Goals in Total Aggregate: Arthur Chandler, 259, 1923–35.

Most League Goals in One Match: 6, John Duncan v Port Vale, Division 2, 25 December 1924; 6, Arthur Chandler v Portsmouth, Division 1, 20 October 1928.

Most Capped Player: John O'Neill, 39, Northern Ireland.

Most League Appearances: Adam Black, 528, 1920–35.

Youngest League Player: Dave Buchanan, 16 years 192 days v Oldham Ath, 1 January 1979.

Record Transfer Fee Received: £30,000,000 from Chelsea for N'Golo Kanté, July 2016.

Record Transfer Fee Paid: £16,600,000 to CSKA Moscow for Ahmed Musa, July 2016.

Football League Record: 1894 Elected to Division 2; 1908–09 Division 1; 1909–25 Division 2; 1925–35 Division 1; 1935–37 Division 2; 1937–39 Division 1; 1946–54 Division 2; 1954–55 Division 1; 1955–57 Division 2; 1957–69 Division 1; 1969–71 Division 2; 1971–78 Division 1; 1978–80 Division 2; 1980–81 Division 1; 1981–83 Division 2; 1983–87 Division 1; 1987–92 Division 2; 1992–94 Division 1; 1994–95 FA Premier League; 1995–96 Division 1; 1996–2002 FA Premier League; 2002–03 Division 1; 2003–04 FA Premier League; 2004–08 FL C; 2008–09 FL 1; 2009–14 FL C; 2014– FA Premier League.

LATEST SEQUENCES

Longest Sequence of League Wins: 9, 21.12.2013 – 1.2.2014.

Longest Sequence of League Defeats: 8, 17.3.2001 – 28.4.2001.

Longest Sequence of League Draws: 6, 2.10.2004 – 2.11.2004.

Longest Sequence of Unbeaten League Matches: 23, 1.11.2008 – 7.3.2009.

Longest Sequence Without a League Win: 18, 12.4.1975 – 1.11.1975.

Successive Scoring Runs: 32 from 23.11.2013.

Successive Non-scoring Runs: 7 from 21.11.1987.

MANAGERS

Frank Gardner 1884–92
Ernest Marson 1892–94
J. Lee 1894–95
Henry Jackson 1895–97
William Clark 1897–98
George Johnson 1898–1912
Jack Bartlett 1912–14
Louis Ford 1914–15
Harry Linney 1915–19
Peter Hodge 1919–26
Willie Orr 1926–32
Peter Hodge 1932–34
Arthur Lochhead 1934–36
Frank Womack 1936–39
Tom Bromilow 1939–45
Tom Mather 1945–46
John Duncan 1946–49
Norman Bullock 1949–55
David Halliday 1955–58
Matt Gillies 1958–68
Frank O'Farrell 1968–71
Jimmy Bloomfield 1971–77
Frank McLintock 1977–78
Jock Wallace 1978–82
Gordon Milne 1982–86
Bryan Hamilton 1986–87
David Pleat 1987–91
Gordon Lee 1991
Brian Little 1991–94
Mark McGhee 1994–95
Martin O'Neill 1995–2000
Peter Taylor 2000–01
Dave Bassett 2001–02
Micky Adams 2002–04
Craig Levein 2004–06
Robert Kelly 2006–07
Martin Allen 2007
Gary Megson 2007
Ian Holloway 2007–08
Nigel Pearson 2008–10
Paulo Sousa 2010
Sven-Göran Eriksson 2010–11
Nigel Pearson 2011–15
Claudio Ranieri July 2015–

TEN YEAR LEAGUE RECORD

		P	W	D	L	F	A	Pts	Pos
2006-07	FL C	46	13	14	19	49	64	53	19
2007-08	FL C	46	12	16	18	42	45	52	22
2008-09	FL 1	46	27	15	4	84	39	96	1
2009-10	FL C	46	21	13	12	61	45	76	5
2010-11	FL C	46	19	10	17	76	71	67	10
2011-12	FL C	46	18	12	16	66	55	66	9
2012-13	FL C	46	19	11	16	71	48	68	6
2013-14	FL C	46	31	9	6	83	43	102	1
2014-15	PR Lge	38	11	8	19	46	55	41	14
2015-16	PR Lge	38	23	12	3	68	36	81	1

DID YOU KNOW

Right-half John Duncan was a near ever-present for Leicester City in the 1929–30 season. However, over the summer of 1930 he became the licensee of the Turk's Head public house in Welford Road and the club immediately cancelled his contract.

LEICESTER CITY – FA PREMIER LEAGUE 2015–16 LEAGUE RECORD

Match No.	Date	Venue	Opponents	Result	H/T Score	Lg Pos.	Goalscorers	Attendance
1	Aug 8	H	Sunderland	W 4-2	3-0	1	Vardy [11], Mahrez 2 (1 pen) [18, 25 (p)], Albrighton [66]	32,242
2	15	A	West Ham U	W 2-1	2-0	1	Okazaki [27], Mahrez [38]	34,857
3	22	H	Tottenham H	D 1-1	0-0	1	Mahrez [82]	31,971
4	29	A	Bournemouth	D 1-1	0-1	3	Vardy (pen) [86]	11,155
5	Sept 13	H	Aston Villa	W 3-2	0-1	2	De Laet [72], Vardy [82], Dyer [89]	31,733
6	19	A	Stoke C	D 2-2	0-2	3	Mahrez (pen) [51], Vardy [69]	27,642
7	26	H	Arsenal	L 2-5	1-2	6	Vardy 2 [13, 89]	32,047
8	Oct 3	A	Norwich C	W 2-1	1-0	4	Vardy (pen) [28], Schlupp [47]	27,067
9	17	A	Southampton	D 2-2	0-2	5	Vardy 2 [66, 90]	31,559
10	24	H	Crystal Palace	W 1-0	0-0	5	Vardy [59]	31,752
11	31	A	WBA	W 3-2	0-1	3	Mahrez 2 [57, 64], Vardy [77]	24,150
12	Nov 7	H	Watford	W 2-1	0-0	3	Kante [52], Vardy (pen) [65]	32,029
13	21	A	Newcastle U	W 3-0	1-0	1	Vardy [45], Ulloa [62], Okazaki [83]	50,151
14	28	H	Manchester U	D 1-1	1-1	2	Vardy [24]	32,115
15	Dec 5	A	Swansea C	W 3-0	2-0	1	Mahrez 3 [5, 22, 67]	20,836
16	14	H	Chelsea	W 2-1	1-0	1	Vardy [34], Mahrez [48]	32,054
17	19	A	Everton	W 3-2	1-1	1	Mahrez 2 (2 pens) [27, 65], Okazaki [69]	39,570
18	26	H	Liverpool	L 0-1	0-0	1		44,123
19	29	H	Manchester C	D 0-0	0-0	2		32,072
20	Jan 2	H	Bournemouth	D 0-0	0-0	2		32,006
21	13	A	Tottenham H	W 1-0	0-0	2	Huth [83]	35,850
22	16	A	Aston Villa	D 1-1	1-0	1	Okazaki [28]	32,763
23	23	H	Stoke C	W 3-0	1-0	1	Drinkwater [42], Vardy [66], Ulloa [87]	32,018
24	Feb 2	A	Liverpool	W 2-0	0-0	1	Vardy 2 [60, 71]	32,121
25	6	A	Manchester C	W 3-1	1-0	1	Huth 2 [3, 60], Mahrez [48]	54,693
26	14	A	Arsenal	L 1-2	1-0	1	Vardy (pen) [45]	60,009
27	27	H	Norwich C	W 1-0	0-0	1	Ulloa [89]	32,114
28	Mar 1	H	WBA	D 2-2	2-1	1	Olsson (og) [30], King [45]	32,018
29	5	A	Watford	W 1-0	0-0	1	Mahrez [56]	20,884
30	14	H	Newcastle U	W 1-0	1-0	1	Okazaki [25]	31,824
31	19	A	Crystal Palace	W 1-0	1-0	1	Mahrez [34]	25,041
32	Apr 3	H	Southampton	W 1-0	1-0	1	Morgan [38]	32,071
33	10	A	Sunderland	W 2-0	0-0	1	Vardy 2 [66, 90]	46,531
34	17	H	West Ham U	D 2-2	1-0	1	Vardy [18], Ulloa (pen) [90]	32,104
35	24	H	Swansea C	W 4-0	2-0	1	Mahrez [10], Ulloa 2 [30, 60], Albrighton [85]	31,962
36	May 1	A	Manchester U	D 1-1	1-1	1	Morgan [17]	75,275
37	7	H	Everton	W 3-1	2-0	1	Vardy 2 (1 pen) [5, 65 (p)], King [33]	32,140
38	15	A	Chelsea	D 1-1	0-0	1	Drinkwater [82]	41,494

Final League Position: 1

GOALSCORERS

League (68): Vardy 24 (5 pens), Mahrez 17 (4 pens), Ulloa 6 (1 pen), Okazaki 5, Huth 3, Albrighton 2, Drinkwater 2, King 2, Morgan 2, De Laet 1, Dyer 1, Kante 1, Schlupp 1, own goal 1.
FA Cup (2): Okazaki 1, Wasilewski 1.
Capital One Cup (7): Dodoo 4, King 1, Kramaric 1, Mahrez 1.

Schmeichel K 38	De Laet R 7 + 5	Huth R 35	Morgan W 38	Schlupp J 14 + 10	Albrighton M 34 + 4	King A 9 + 16	Drinkwater D 35	Mahrez R 36 + 1	Okazaki S 28 + 8	Vardy J 36	Benalouane Y — + 4	Fuchs C 30 + 2	Kante N 33 + 4	Inler G 3 + 2	Ulloa J 7 + 22	Dodoo J — + 1	Dyer N — + 12	Kramaric A — + 2	Simpson D 30	Wasilewski M 3 + 1	Gray D 1 + 11	Amartey D 1 + 4	Match No.
1	2^1	3	4	5	6	7	8	9^2	10	11^3	12	13	14										1
1	2^2	3	4	5	9	7	8	6^3	11^1	10	13	14	12										2
1	2	3	4	5	9^1	7	8^2	6^3	10	11		12	13	14									3
1	2^3	3	4	5	10^2	7	6	8^1	12	11	14		9		13								4
1	2	3	4	5	9^3		8	6	10^1	11		14			7^2	13	12						5
1	2	3	4	5	12	14	7	6	10^2	11		9^3			8^1	13							6
1	2	3	4	5	9^2	12	8^3	6	10^1	11		7			13		14						7
1		3	4	9^1	6	14	7		11^2	10	12	5	8		13				2^1				8
1		4	3	9^1	6		7	13	11^2	10		5	8			12			2				9
1		4	3	9	6^1		7	10^2	12	11		5	8			13			2				10
1		4	3	5	9^2	12	7^3	6	14	11		8		10^1		13			2				11
1		4	3	9^1	6	14	8^3	10^2	12	11		5	7			13			2				12
1		4	3		9	13	8	6^3	12	11^2		5	7		10^1	14			2				13
1	14	4	3	13	9^2		8	6	10^1	11		5	7		12				2^3				14
1		4	3	13	9	12	7	6^2		11		5	8		10^1				2				15
1		4	3		9	12	7^1	6^4	14	11^3		5	8	13	10				2				16
1	13		4		9^1	7		6^2	11	10^3		5	8		14		12		2	3			17
1		4	3		9	7		6^3	10^1	11^2		5	8		13		12	14	2				18
1	14	4	3		10^3	13	7^2	6		11		5	9	8^1	12				2				19
1	14	4	3		9^2		7	6	13	11		5	8		10^1		12		2^3				20
1		4	3		9	13	8	6^3	10^2	11^1		5	7		12		14		2				21
1	12	4	3		9^3		8	6^2	10^1	11		5	7		13				2		14		22
1		4	3		9^2		8	6	10^1	11		5	7		12				2		13		23
1		4	3		9^1	13	8	6^3	10^2	11		5	7		14				2		12		24
1		4	3		9^3		7	6^1	10^2	11		5	8		13		14		2		12		25
1		4	3		9^3	14	7	6^1	10^2	11		5	8						2^4	12	13		26
1		4	3	12	9	13	8	6	10^2	11		5	8^2		14				2			2^3	27
1		4	3	13	9^1	7	8	6	10^2	11		5^1			12				2		14		28
1		4	3	13	9^2	12		6^1	11	10		5	8						2		14		29
1		4	3	12	9^2		8	6	10^1	11		5	7		13				2				30
1		4	3	13	9		8	6^2	10^1	11^3		5	7		12				2		14		31
1		4	3		9^3		7	6^2	11^1	10		5	8		12		14		2		13		32
1		4	3		9^3		7	6^2	10^1	11		5	8		12				2		13	14	33
1		4	3	12	9^1		7	6^2	10^2	11^4		5	8		13				2			14	34
1		4	3	9^2	14	13	8	6	11^1			5	7		10^2				2		12		35
1		4	3	9^2	13	14	8^4	6^2	10^1			5	7		11				2		12		36
1		4	13	9^2	8			6^3	10^1	11		5	7		12				2	3	14		37
1		4	12	14		9	6	8^1	13	11		5	7						2	3	10^2		38

FA Cup

Third Round	Tottenham H	(a)	2-2
Replay	Tottenham H	(h)	0-2

Capital One Cup

Second Round	Bury	(a)	4-1
Third Round	West Ham U	(h)	2-1
(aet)			
Fourth Round	Hull C	(a)	1-1
(aet; Hull C won 5-4 on penalties)			

LEYTON ORIENT

FOUNDATION

There is some doubt about the foundation of Leyton Orient, and, indeed, some confusion with clubs like Leyton and Clapton over their early history. As regards the foundation, the most favoured version is that Leyton Orient was formed originally by members of Homerton Theological College who established Glyn Cricket Club in 1881 and then carried on through the following winter playing football. Eventually many employees of the Orient Shipping Line became involved and so the name Orient was chosen in 1888.

Matchroom Stadium, Brisbane Road, Leyton, London E10 5NF.

Telephone: (0871) 310 1881.

Fax: (0871) 310 1882.

Ticket Office: (0871) 310 1883.

Website: www.leytonorient.com

Email: info@leytonorient.net

Ground Capacity: 9,136.

Record Attendance: 34,345 v West Ham U, FA Cup 4th rd, 25 January 1964.

Pitch Measurements: 100.5m × 65m (110yd × 71yd).

Chairman: Francesco Becchetti.

Chief Executive: Alessandro Angelieri.

Manager: Andy Hessenthaler.

Assistant Manager: Andy Edwards.

Physio: Peter Webb.

Colours: Red shirts with white trim, red shorts, red socks.

Year Formed: 1881.

Turned Professional: 1903.

Previous Names: 1881, Glyn Cricket and Football Club; 1886, Eagle Football Club; 1888, Orient Football Club; 1898, Clapton Orient; 1946, Leyton Orient; 1966, Orient; 1987, Leyton Orient.

Club Nickname: 'The O's'.

Grounds: 1884, Glyn Road; 1896, Whittles Athletic Ground; 1900, Millfields Road; 1930, Lea Bridge Road; 1937, Brisbane Road (renamed Matchroom Stadium).

First Football League Game: 2 September 1905, Division 2, v Leicester Fosse (a) L 1–2 – Butler; Holmes, Codling; Lamberton, Boden, Boyle; Kingaby (1), Wootten, Leigh, Evenson, Bourne.

Record League Victory: 8–0 v Crystal Palace, Division 3 (S), 12 November 1955 – Welton; Lee, Earl; Blizzard, Aldous, McKnight; White (1), Facey (3), Burgess (2), Heckman, Hartburn (2). 8–0 v Rochdale, Division 4, 20 October 1987 – Wells; Howard, Dickenson (1), Smalley (1), Day, Hull, Hales (2), Castle (Sussex), Shinners (2), Godfrey (Harvey), Comfort (2). 8–0 v Colchester U, Division 4, 15 October 1988 – Wells; Howard, Dickenson, Hales (1p), Day (1), Sitton (1), Baker (1), Ward, Hull (3), Juryeff, Comfort (1). 8–0 v Doncaster R, Division 3, 28 December 1997 – Hyde; Channing, Naylor, Smith (1p), Hicks, Clark, Ling, Roger Joseph, Griffiths (3) (Harris), Richards (2) (Baker (1)), Inglethorpe (1) (Simpson).

HONOURS

League Champions: Division 3 – 1969–70; Division 3S – 1955–56. *Runners-up:* Division 2 – 1961–62; Division 3S – 1954–55.

FA Cup: semi-final – 1978.

League Cup: 5th rd – 1963.

sky SPORTS FACT FILE

Leyton Orient suffered their worst-ever run of results in the 1962–63 season, their only season of top-flight football. The O's established a club record sequence of 23 Football League games without a victory, before they eventually won 1-0 at Bolton on 15 April 1963. Ironically during this time they played eight Cup games, winning five including a best-ever 9-2 League Cup defeat of Chester.

Record Cup Victory: 9–2 v Chester, League Cup 3rd rd, 15 October 1962 – Robertson; Charlton, Taylor; Gibbs, Bishop, Lea; Deeley (1), Waites (3), Dunmore (2), Graham (3), Wedge.

Record Defeat: 0–8 v Aston Villa, FA Cup 4th rd, 30 January 1929.

Most League Points (2 for a win): 66, Division 3 (S), 1955–56.

Most League Points (3 for a win): 86, FL 1, 2013–14.

Most League Goals: 106, Division 3 (S), 1955–56.

Highest League Scorer in Season: Tom Johnston, 35, Division 2, 1957–58.

Most League Goals in Total Aggregate: Tom Johnston, 121, 1956–58, 1959–61.

Most League Goals in One Match: 4, Wally Leigh v Bradford C, Division 2, 13 April 1906; 4, Albert Pape v Oldham Ath, Division 2, 1 September 1924; 4, Peter Kitchen v Millwall, Division 3, 21 April 1984.

Most Capped Players: Jobi McAnuff, 23 (30), Jamaica.

Most League Appearances: Peter Allen, 432, 1965–78.

Youngest League Player: Paul Went, 15 years 327 days v Preston NE, 4 September 1965.

Record Transfer Fee Received: £1,000,000 from Fulham for Gabriel Zakuani, July 2006; £1,000,000 from Brentford for Moses Odubajo, June 2014.

Record Transfer Fee Paid: £175,000 to Wigan Ath for Paul Beesley, October 1989.

Football League Record: 1905 Elected to Division 2; 1929–56 Division 3 (S); 1956–62 Division 2; 1962–63 Division 1; 1963–66 Division 2; 1966–70 Division 3; 1970–82 Division 2; 1982–85 Division 3; 1985–89 Division 4; 1989–92 Division 3; 1992–95 Division 2; 1995–2004 Division 3; 2004–06 FL 2; 2006–15 FL 1; 2015– FL 2.

LATEST SEQUENCES

Longest Sequence of League Wins: 10, 21.1.1956 – 30.3.1956.

Longest Sequence of League Defeats: 9, 1.4.1995 – 6.5.1995.

Longest Sequence of League Draws: 6, 30.11.1974 – 28.12.1974.

Longest Sequence of Unbeaten League Matches: 15, 13.4.2013 – 19.10.2013.

Longest Sequence Without a League Win: 23, 6.10.1962 – 13.4.1963.

Successive Scoring Runs: 22 from 12.3.1927.

Successive Non-scoring Runs: 8 from 19.11.1994.

MANAGERS

Sam Omerod 1905–06
Ike Ivenson 1906
Billy Holmes 1907–22
Peter Proudfoot 1922–29
Arthur Grimsdell 1929–30
Peter Proudfoot 1930–31
Jimmy Seed 1931–33
David Pratt 1933–34
Peter Proudfoot 1935–39
Tom Halsey 1939
Bill Wright 1939–45
Willie Hall 1945
Bill Wright 1945–46
Charlie Hewitt 1946–48
Neil McBain 1948–49
Alec Stock 1949–59
Les Gore 1959–61
Johnny Carey 1961–63
Benny Fenton 1963–64
Dave Sexton 1965
Dick Graham 1966–68
Jimmy Bloomfield 1968–71
George Petchey 1971–77
Jimmy Bloomfield 1977–81
Paul Went 1981
Ken Knighton 1981–83
Frank Clark 1983–91
(Managing Director)
Peter Eustace 1991–94
Chris Turner/John Sitton 1994–95
Pat Holland 1995–96
Tommy Taylor 1996–2001
Paul Brush 2001–03
Martin Ling 2003–09
Geraint Williams 2009–10
Russell Slade 2010–14
Kevin Nugent 2014
Mauro Milanese 2014
Fabio Liverani 2014–15
Ian Hendon 2015–16
Kevin Nolan 2016
Andy Hessenthaler April 2016–

TEN YEAR LEAGUE RECORD

		P	W	D	L	F	A	Pts	Pos
2006-07	FL 1	46	12	15	19	61	77	51	20
2007-08	FL 1	46	16	12	18	49	63	60	14
2008-09	FL 1	46	15	11	20	45	57	56	14
2009-10	FL 1	46	13	12	21	53	63	51	17
2010-11	FL 1	46	19	13	14	71	62	70	7
2011-12	FL 1	46	13	11	22	48	75	50	20
2012-13	FL 1	46	21	8	17	55	48	71	7
2013-14	FL 1	46	25	11	10	85	45	86	3
2014-15	FL 1	46	12	13	21	59	69	49	23
2015-16	FL 2	46	19	12	15	60	61	69	8

DID YOU KNOW

After Orient experienced financial difficulties in March 1931, control of the club was transferred to a receiver. It was not until the following February that the directors were permitted to take charge once again. A new manager, Jimmy Seed, was appointed by the receiver during his period in charge.

LEYTON ORIENT – FOOTBALL LEAGUE TWO 2015–16 LEAGUE RECORD

Match No.	Date		Venue	Opponents	Result		H/T Score	Lg Pos.	Goalscorers	Attendance
1	Aug	8	H	Barnet	W	2-0	0-0	4	Simpson [74], McCallum [75]	6151
2		15	A	Dagenham & R	W	3-1	2-0	2	McCallum [19], James (pen) [28], Cox [56]	3336
3		18	H	Stevenage	W	3-0	0-0	1	Simpson [74], Turgott [84], Palmer [90]	4949
4		22	A	Newport Co	W	3-2	2-2	1	McCallum [4], Simpson [7], Cox [59]	2779
5		29	H	Bristol R	W	2-0	2-0	1	James (pen) [23], Simpson [45]	5777
6	Sept	5	A	Exeter C	L	0-4	0-2	1		3648
7		12	A	Cambridge U	D	1-1	0-0	1	Simpson [72]	5821
8		19	H	Wycombe W	D	1-1	0-1	1	Simpson [66]	5946
9		26	A	Northampton T	D	1-1	0-0	3	Cox [90]	5061
10		29	H	Carlisle U	L	1-2	0-0	5	Baudry [64]	4408
11	Oct	3	H	Notts Co	W	3-1	1-0	3	Moore 2 [16, 84], Simpson [79]	5193
12		10	A	Crawley T	L	2-3	1-3	7	Simpson 2 [8, 82]	2575
13		17	A	Oxford U	D	2-2	0-2	5	Simpson [64], Kashket [90]	6296
14		20	A	Luton T	D	1-1	0-1	6	Simpson [47]	8022
15		24	H	Morecambe	W	1-0	0-0	6	Payne [28]	2105
16		31	A	Accrington S	L	0-1	0-1	7		4701
17	Nov	15	A	Hartlepool U	L	1-3	1-1	7	Pritchard [13]	4081
18		21	H	York C	W	3-2	2-1	7	Baudry [21], Simpson 2 [45, 64]	4897
19		24	A	Plymouth Arg	D	1-1	1-0	6	Simpson [4]	6469
20		28	H	AFC Wimbledon	D	1-1	0-0	8	Simpson [10]	6024
21	Dec	12	H	Mansfield T	D	1-1	1-1	9	Simpson [12]	2935
22		19	H	Yeovil T	D	1-1	0-1	10	McAnuff [74]	4686
23		26	H	Portsmouth	W	3-2	2-1	9	Simpson (pen) [23], Palmer 2 [45, 52]	5848
24		28	A	Bristol R	L	1-2	1-1	9	Simpson [45]	9836
25	Jan	2	A	Stevenage	D	2-2	0-0	8	Simpson 2 (1 pen) [60 (p), 90]	4022
26		16	A	Exeter C	L	1-3	1-3	11	Palmer [1]	5758
27		23	A	Wycombe W	W	2-0	0-0	8	Simpson [64], Jahraldo-Martin [89]	4432
28		26	H	Newport Co	W	1-0	0-0	6	Simpson (pen) [85]	4209
29		30	H	Cambridge U	L	1-3	0-1	9	Gnanduillet [57]	6526
30	Feb	6	A	Portsmouth	W	1-0	0-0	6	McAnuff [53]	15,643
31		13	H	Northampton T	L	0-4	0-0	9		6131
32		20	A	Notts Co	W	1-0	0-0	9	Brisley [76]	4878
33		27	H	Crawley T	W	2-0	1-0	7	Gnanduillet 2 [42, 71]	4610
34	Mar	1	A	Carlisle U	D	2-2	0-1	7	Simpson [50], Palmer [72]	3721
35		5	H	Luton T	L	0-1	0-1	8		5684
36		12	A	Oxford U	W	1-0	0-0	7	McAnuff [74]	7102
37		19	H	Morecambe	W	1-0	0-0	7	Edwards (og) [80]	4442
38		25	A	Accrington S	L	0-1	0-0	8		2783
39		28	H	Hartlepool U	L	0-2	0-0	8		5543
40	Apr	2	A	York C	D	1-1	0-1	8	James [75]	3234
41		9	A	Barnet	L	0-3	0-1	11		3401
42		16	H	Dagenham & R	W	3-2	2-0	10	Simpson 2 [3, 45], Gnanduillet [65]	5696
43		19	H	Plymouth Arg	L	1-3	0-1	11	James (pen) [82]	4908
44		23	A	AFC Wimbledon	L	0-1	0-1	14		4732
45		30	H	Mansfield T	W	1-0	0-0	9	Palmer [48]	4257
46	May	7	A	Yeovil T	W	1-0	0-0	8	Palmer [87]	4163

Final League Position: 8

GOALSCORERS

League (60): Simpson 25 (3 pens), Palmer 7, Gnanduillet 4, James 4 (3 pens), Cox 3, McAnuff 3, McCallum 3, Baudry 2, Moore 2, Brisley 1, Jahraldo-Martin 1, Kashket 1, Payne 1, Pritchard 1, Turgott 1, own goal 1.
FA Cup (6): Cox 2, Palmer 2, Clohessy 1, Marquis 1.
Capital One Cup (1): own goal 1.
Johnstone's Paint Trophy (1): James 1 (pen).

Cisak A 43	Clohessy S 41 + 1	Essam C 23 + 1	Baudry M 33 + 1	Shaw F 20 + 5	James L 17 + 8	Moore S 27 + 3	Cox D 12 + 2	Simpson J 45	McCallum P 8 + 2	Pritchard B 24 + 5	Dunne A 3 + 5	Turgott B 10 + 21	Palmer O 25 + 20	Kashket S 1 + 14	Grainger C 2	Payne J 26 + 3	Chicksen A 6	Marquis J 9 + 4	Mvoto J 8	Kpekawa C 8 + 1	McAnuff J 14 + 3	Adeboyejo V — + 1	Jahraldo-Martin C 8 + 7	Atangana N 16	Gnanduillet A 8 + 9	Nolan K 12 + 2	Hunt N 16	Brisley S 16	Williams J 12 + 1	Ramage P 8	Koroma J — + 3	Semedo S 2 + 1	Pollock A 2	Sargeant S 1	Match No.
1	2	3	4	5	6	7[3]	8	9[1]	10[2]	11	12	13	14																						1
1	2	3	4[3]	5	7	8	11	10[2]	9[1]	6	13	14	12																						2
1	2	3	4	5	6[2]	8	9[3]	10	11[1]	7	14	12	13																						3
1	2	3	4	5	7[2]	8	9[1]	10[3]	11	6		13	12	14																					4
1	2	4	5[1]	3	7	9	6	11[2]	10	8[1]	12	14	13																						5
	2	3	4	8	7[1]	9	11	10[2]	6	5[3]	12	14	13		1																				6
1	2	4	3	5	7[1]	9		11	10[2]	6		12	13			8																			7
1	2	4	3	5	7[2]	6	9	10	11[1]		13	12				8																			8
1	2	4	3	5		8[1]	9	11	13[3]	7		12	10[2]	14		6																			9
1	2	3	4	5[1]		8[2]	6	11		9		12	10			7																			10
1	2	4	3			8	9	11[1]		7	13	12	10			6[2]	5																		11
1	2	4			7	9[1]	11	6		3[1]	13	10[3]	14			8[2]	5	12																	12
1	2	4	3		7	9[3]	11	8		6[2]	13	14				12	5	10[1]																	13
1	2	4	3		13	8	12	7		11[1]						6	5	8[3]																	14
1	2	4	3		12	7		10[1]								6	5	9[2]																	15
1	2	4[1]	3		13	7[2]	12	10		8		11	14			6	5	9[1]					·												16
	2		3	5	7			9		8[2]	4[1]	13	10	12	1	6		11																	17
1	2		3[2]	5		8		9[3]		14	10					7		11[1]	4	12	13														18
1	2		5	12[2]	8			11[1]		7			10	13		6		9	4	3															19
1	2	12	5	14	7[1]			9[2]	8			13	10[3]			6		11[1]	4	3															20
1	2	3		8				11[1]	13			6[2]	12	14		7		10[2]	4	5	9														21
1		2	5	7				11		6		9[1]	12	10[1]		8[2]			3	4	13	14													22
1	6	3	2[1]	12				11[1]		7		14	10[2]			7			13	4	5	8[3]													23
1	2	4		12				11		7		6	10[1]	14		8		13	3[3]	5	9[2]														24
1	2	3		5				10		7		9[1]	11			4		13		8	6[2]		12												25
1	2	3		13				11		8[2]		6[1]	10	14		7			4[1]	5	9		12												26
1	2	3	4	5				11		12			10[2]			7			9		6		8[1]	13											27
1	2	4	3	5				9[2]	14				11[3]			7			10		8[1]	6	12	13											28
1	2	3	4	5				11				13	10[2]			6[3]			9		8[1]	7	12	14											29
1	13		4	5		9[1]		11[2]	12				6						10		7		14	8[3]	2	3									30
1			3	5		7[1]	11	13				14				6[1]			10		9[2]		12	8	2	4									31
1			3			9[2]	10						12			14			6		13	8	11[3]	7[1]	2	4	5								32
1	6		3			9[1]	11						13						12		7	10[2]	8	2	4	5									33
1	6[2]		3			12	11						13						10[1]		7	9	8	2	4	5									34
1	6		3			9[3]	10						11[2]						12		14	7	13	8	2	4	5								35
1	6	14	3[8]			10[2]	13						11						9[1]		7	12[3]	8	2	4	5									36
	6[3]			13	12	10							14						9			7[2]	11	8[1]	2	4	5	3							37
	6[1]		14			9[3]	11					13	12						12			7	10[2]	8	2	4	5	3							38
	2		12	14		10						13	11			6[1]						7	9[2]	8[3]	3	5	4								39
	6[1]		13			11							10[2]						9			12	7[3]	14	8	2	4	5	3						40
1			7			11[2]							10						8		6	13	9[1]	2	3	5	4	12							41
	6	4	7			10						9	12			13						8[1]	11[2]	2	3	5									42
1	6[2]	3	7			11						9[1]	12	13					14		8	10[3]	2	4	5										43
1	6[2]	3		7	8			9[1]	11	12			10											2	4	5				5		13			44
1	2			8	12	10		6	9				7[1]						4	13	5[1]	14	11[2]	3											45
	6			7	8	11[1]	14					12	10										2	4[2]	5	13	9	3[3]	1						46

FA Cup

First Round	Staines T	(h)	6-1
Second Round	Scunthorpe U	(h)	0-0
Replay	Scunthorpe U	(a)	0-3

Capital One Cup

First Round	Milton Keynes D	(a)	1-2

Johnstone's Paint Trophy

First Round	Luton T	(a)	1-2

LIVERPOOL

FOUNDATION

But for a dispute between Everton FC and their landlord at Anfield in 1892, there may never have been a Liverpool club. This dispute persuaded the majority of Evertonians to quit Anfield for Goodison Park, leaving the landlord, Mr John Houlding, to form a new club. He originally tried to retain the name 'Everton' but when this failed, he founded Liverpool Association FC on 15 March 1892.

Anfield Stadium, Anfield Road, Anfield, Liverpool L4 0TH.

Telephone: (0151) 263 2361.

Fax: (0151) 260 8813.

Ticket Office: (0843) 170 5555.

Website: www.liverpoolfc.com

Email: customerservices@liverpoolfc.com

Ground Capacity: 44,742.

Record Attendance: 61,905 v Wolverhampton W, FA Cup 4th rd, 2 February 1952.

Pitch Measurements: 101m × 68m (110yd × 74yd).

Chairman: Tom Werner.

Managing Director: Ian Ayre.

Manager: Jürgen Klopp.

Assistant Coach: Zeljko Buvac.

Physio: Chris Morgan.

Colours: Red shirts, red shorts, red socks.

Year Formed: 1892.

Turned Professional: 1892.

Club Nicknames: 'The Reds', 'Pool'.

Ground: 1892, Anfield.

First Football League Game: 2 September 1893, Division 2, v Middlesbrough Ironopolis (a) W 2–0 – McOwen; Hannah, McLean; Henderson, McQue (1), McBride; Gordon, McVean (1), Matt McQueen, Stott, Hugh McQueen.

HONOURS

League Champions: Division 1 – 1900–01, 1905–06, 1921–22, 1922–23, 1946–47, 1963–64, 1965–66, 1972–73, 1975–76, 1976–77, 1978–79, 1979–80, 1981–82, 1982–83, 1983–84, 1985–86, 1987–88, 1989–90; Division 2 – 1893–94, 1895–96, 1904–05, 1961–62.
Runners-up: FA Premier League – 2001–02, 2008–09, 2013–14; Division 1 – 1898–99, 1909–10, 1968–69, 1973–74, 1974–75, 1977–78, 1984–85, 1986–87, 1988–89, 1990–91.
FA Cup Winners: 1965, 1974, 1986, 1989, 1992, 2001, 2006.
Runners-up: 1914, 1950, 1971, 1977, 1988, 1996, 2012.
League Cup Winners: 1981, 1982, 1983, 1984, 1995, 2001, 2003, 2012.
Runners-up: 1978, 1987, 2005, 2016.
League Super Cup Winners: 1986.

European Competitions
European Cup: 1964–65 *(sf)*, 1966–67, 1973–74, 1976–77 *(winners)*, 1977–78 *(winners)*, 1978–79, 1979–80, 1980–81 *(winners)*, 1981–82 *(qf)*, 1982–83 *(qf)*, 1983–84 *(winners)*, 1984–85 *(runners-up)*.
Champions League: 2001–02 *(qf)*, 2002–03, 2004–05 *(winners)*, 2005–06, 2006–07 *(runners-up)*, 2007–08 *(sf)*, 2008–09 *(qf)*, 2009–10, 2014–15.
Fairs Cup: 1967–68, 1968–69, 1969–70, 1970–71 *(sf)*.
UEFA Cup: 1972–73 *(winners)*, 1975–76 *(winners)*, 1991–92 *(qf)*, 1995–96, 1997–98, 1998–99, 2000–01 *(winners)*, 2002–03 *(qf)*, 2003–04.
Europa League: 2009–10 *(sf)*, 2010–11, 2012–13, 2014–15, 2015–16 *(runners-up)*.
European Cup-Winners' Cup: 1965–66 *(runners-up)*, 1971–72, 1974–75, 1992–93, 1996–97 *(sf)*.
Super Cup: 1977 *(winners)*, 1978, 1984, 2001 *(winners)*, 2005 *(winners)*.
World Club Championship: 1981, 1984.
FIFA Club World Cup: 2005.

Record League Victory: 10–1 v Rotherham T, Division 2, 18 February 1896 – Storer; Goldie, Wilkie; McCartney, McQue, Holmes; McVean (3), Ross (2), Allan (4), Becton (1), Bradshaw.

Record Cup Victory: 11–0 v Stromsgodset Drammen, ECWC 1st rd 1st leg, 17 September 1974 – Clemence; Smith (1), Lindsay (1p), Thompson (2), Cormack (1), Hughes (1), Boersma (2), Hall, Heighway (1), Kennedy (1), Callaghan (1).

Record Defeat: 1–9 v Birmingham C, Division 2, 11 December 1954.

Most League Points (2 for a win): 68, Division 1, 1978–79.

Most League Points (3 for a win): 90, Division 1, 1987–88.

Most League Goals: 106, Division 2, 1895–96.

Highest League Scorer in Season: Roger Hunt, 41, Division 2, 1961–62.

Most League Goals in Total Aggregate: Roger Hunt, 245, 1959–69.

Most League Goals in One Match: 5, Andy McGuigan v Stoke C, Division 1, 4 January 1902; 5, John Evans v Bristol R, Division 2, 15 September 1954; 5, Ian Rush v Luton T, Division 1, 29 October 1983.

Most Capped Player: Steven Gerrard, 114, England.

Most League Appearances: Ian Callaghan, 640, 1960–78.

Youngest League Player: Jack Robinson, 16 years 250 days v Hull C, 9 May 2010.

Record Transfer Fee Received: £75,000,000 from Barcelona for Luis Suarez, July 2014.

Record Transfer Fee Paid: £35,000,000 to Newcastle U for Andy Carroll, January 2011.

Football League Record: 1893 Elected to Division 2; 1894–95 Division 1; 1895–96 Division 2; 1896–1904 Division 1; 1904–05 Division 2; 1905–54 Division 1; 1954–62 Division 2; 1962–92 Division 1; 1992– FA Premier League.

MANAGERS

W. E. Barclay 1892–96
Tom Watson 1896–1915
David Ashworth 1920–23
Matt McQueen 1923–28
George Patterson 1928–36
   (continued as Secretary)
George Kay 1936–51
Don Welsh 1951–56
Phil Taylor 1956–59
Bill Shankly 1959–74
Bob Paisley 1974–83
Joe Fagan 1983–85
Kenny Dalglish 1985–91
Graeme Souness 1991–94
Roy Evans 1994–98
   (then Joint Manager)
Gerard Houllier 1998–2004
Rafael Benitez 2004–10
Roy Hodgson 2010–11
Kenny Dalglish 2011–12
Brendan Rodgers 2012–15
Jürgen Klopp October 2015–

LATEST SEQUENCES

Longest Sequence of League Wins: 12, 21.4.1990 – 6.10.1990.

Longest Sequence of League Defeats: 9, 29.4.1899 – 14.10.1899.

Longest Sequence of League Draws: 6, 19.2.1975 – 19.3.1975.

Longest Sequence of Unbeaten League Matches: 31, 4.5.1987 – 16.3.1988.

Longest Sequence Without a League Win: 14, 12.12.1953 – 20.3.1954.

Successive Scoring Runs: 29 from 27.4.1957.

Successive Non-scoring Runs: 5 from 21.4.2000.

TEN YEAR LEAGUE RECORD

		P	W	D	L	F	A	Pts	Pos
2006-07	PR Lge	38	20	8	10	57	27	68	3
2007-08	PR Lge	38	21	13	4	67	28	76	4
2008-09	PR Lge	38	25	11	2	77	27	86	2
2009-10	PR Lge	38	18	9	11	61	35	63	7
2010-11	PR Lge	38	17	7	14	59	44	58	6
2011-12	PR Lge	38	14	10	14	47	40	52	8
2012-13	PR Lge	38	16	13	9	71	43	61	7
2013-14	PR Lge	38	26	6	6	101	50	84	2
2014-15	PR Lge	38	18	8	12	52	48	62	6
2015-16	PR Lge	38	16	12	10	63	50	60	8

DID YOU KNOW ?

Liverpool were the first British club to travel to Germany to entertain the troops after the Second World War ended. The Reds won 7-0 against an RAF XI at Celle on 28 July 1945 then drew 3-3 with a British Land Army XI at Hanover the following day.

LIVERPOOL – FA PREMIER LEAGUE 2015–16 LEAGUE RECORD

Match No.	Date	Venue	Opponents	Result	H/T Score	Lg Pos.	Goalscorers	Attendance
1	Aug 9	A	Stoke C	W 1-0	0-0	4	Coutinho [86]	27,654
2	17	H	Bournemouth	W 1-0	1-0	3	Benteke [26]	44,102
3	24	A	Arsenal	D 0-0	0-0	3		60,080
4	29	A	West Ham U	L 0-3	0-2	6		43,680
5	Sept 12	A	Manchester U	L 1-3	0-0	9	Benteke [84]	75,347
6	20	H	Norwich C	D 1-1	0-0	13	Ings [48]	44,072
7	26	H	Aston Villa	W 3-2	1-0	7	Milner [2], Sturridge 2 [59, 67]	44,228
8	Oct 4	A	Everton	D 1-1	1-1	10	Ings [41]	39,598
9	17	A	Tottenham H	D 0-0	0-0	10		35,926
10	25	H	Southampton	D 1-1	0-0	9	Benteke [77]	44,171
11	31	A	Chelsea	W 3-1	1-1	7	Coutinho 2 [45, 74], Benteke [83]	41,577
12	Nov 8	H	Crystal Palace	L 1-2	1-1	10	Coutinho [42]	44,115
13	21	A	Manchester C	W 4-1	3-1	9	Mangala (og) [7], Coutinho [23], Firmino [32], Skrtel [81]	54,444
14	29	H	Swansea C	W 1-0	0-0	6	Milner (pen) [62]	43,905
15	Dec 6	A	Newcastle U	L 0-2	0-0	7		51,273
16	13	H	WBA	D 2-2	1-1	9	Henderson [21], Origi [90]	44,147
17	20	A	Watford	L 0-3	0-2	9		20,707
18	26	H	Leicester C	W 1-0	0-0	8	Benteke [63]	44,123
19	30	A	Sunderland	W 1-0	0-0	7	Benteke [46]	45,765
20	Jan 2	A	West Ham U	L 0-2	0-1	8		34,977
21	13	H	Arsenal	D 3-3	2-2	9	Firmino 2 [10, 19], Allen [90]	44,109
22	17	H	Manchester U	L 0-1	0-0	9		43,865
23	23	A	Norwich C	W 5-4	1-2	7	Firmino 2 [18, 63], Henderson [55], Milner [75], Lallana [90]	27,108
24	Feb 2	A	Leicester C	L 0-2	0-0	8		32,121
25	6	H	Sunderland	D 2-2	0-0	9	Firmino [59], Lallana [70]	44,179
26	14	A	Aston Villa	W 6-0	2-0	8	Sturridge [16], Milner [25], Can [58], Origi [63], Clyne [65], Toure [71]	35,798
27	Mar 2	H	Manchester C	W 3-0	2-0	8	Lallana [34], Milner [41], Firmino [57]	43,597
28	6	A	Crystal Palace	W 2-1	0-0	7	Firmino [72], Benteke (pen) [90]	24,709
29	20	A	Southampton	L 2-3	2-0	9	Coutinho [17], Sturridge [22]	31,596
30	Apr 2	H	Tottenham H	D 1-1	0-0	9	Coutinho [51]	44,062
31	10	H	Stoke C	W 4-1	2-1	8	Moreno [8], Sturridge [32], Origi 2 [50, 65]	43,688
32	17	A	Bournemouth	W 2-1	2-0	8	Firmino [41], Sturridge [45]	11,386
33	20	H	Everton	W 4-0	2-0	7	Origi [43], Sakho [45], Sturridge [61], Coutinho [76]	43,854
34	23	H	Newcastle U	D 2-2	2-0	9	Sturridge [2], Lallana [30]	43,837
35	May 1	A	Swansea C	L 1-3	0-2	8	Benteke [65]	20,972
36	8	H	Watford	W 2-0	1-0	8	Allen [35], Firmino [76]	43,341
37	11	H	Chelsea	D 1-1	0-1	8	Benteke [90]	43,210
38	15	A	WBA	D 1-1	1-1	8	Ibe [23]	26,196

Final League Position: 8

GOALSCORERS

League (63): Firmino 10, Benteke 9 (1 pen), Coutinho 8, Sturridge 8, Milner 5 (1 pen), Origi 5, Lallana 4, Allen 2, Henderson 2, Ings 2, Can 1, Clyne 1, Ibe 1, Moreno 1, Sakho 1, Skrtel 1, Toure 1, own goal 1.
FA Cup (6): Allen 1, Coutinho 1, Ojo 1, Sinclair 1, Smith 1, Teixeira 1.
Capital One Cup (10): Origi 3, Ibe 2, Sturridge 2, Clyne 1, Coutinho 1, Ings 1.
UEFA Europa League (19): Lallana 3, Sturridge 3 (1 pen), Coutinho 2, Milner 2 (2 pens), Origi 2, Benteke 1, Can 1, Firmino 1, Ibe 1, Lovren 1, Sakho 1, own goal 1.

Mignolet S 34	Clyne N 33	Skrtel M 21 + 1	Lovren D 22 + 2	Gomez J 5	Milner J 28	Henderson J 15 + 2	Ibe J 12 + 15	Coutinho P 24 + 2	Lallana A 23 + 7	Benteke C 14 + 15	Can E 28 + 2	Firmino R 24 + 7	Moreno A 28 + 4	Lucas 21 + 6	Rossiter J — +1	Ings D 3 + 3	Origi D 7 + 9	Sakho M 21 + 1	Sturridge D 11 + 3	Allen J 8 + 11	Toure K 9 + 5	Bogdan A 2	Smith B 3 + 1	Caulker S — + 3	Teixeira J — + 1	Stewart K 6 + 1	Flanagan J 5	Ojo S 5 + 3	Ward D 2	Randall C 2 + 1	Chirivella P 1	Brannagan C 1 + 2	Canos S — + 1	Match No.
1	2	3	4	5	6	7	8²	9	10¹	11	12	13																						1
1	2	3	4	5	6	7¹	10²	8³	9	11	12	13	14																					2
1	2	3	4	5	6		12	11³		10	8	9¹	14	7²	13																			3
1	2	3	4	5¹	8		14	11¹		10	6¹	9²	12	7		13																		4
1	2	3	4	5	6		12			10	8	9¹	14	7¹		11²	13																	5
1	5	3			6			9	13	11¹	2	14	8	7¹	12			4	10²															6
1	5	3			6			9			2		8	7	10			4	11¹	12														7
1	5	3			6			9	12		2		8	7²	11¹			4	10	13														8
1	2	3			8	13	10²	9¹		7		5	6					11	4	12														9
1	2	3			6	14	10³	9²	12	8	13	5	7					11¹	4															10
1	2	3	14		6¹	13	10	9³	12	8	11²	5	7						4															11
1	2	3	12			8³	10	9	11	6²	13	5	7					14	4³															12
1	2	3	4		6	12	11¹	9³	13	8	10²	5	7																					13
1	2	3	4		6	12	9³		8	10²	7	11¹	5					13	14															14
1	2	3	4		10		8³		12	11¹		9²	5	6		14		13	7															15
1	2	3	4²		8	6	12	11¹		9³	10	7	14	5				13																16
	2	3¹			6	14	11		9²	13	8	10³	5	7				12	4				1											17
1	2		3			6		10³	8²	12	7	9	5	13				11¹	4		14													18
1	2		3			6¹	13	10²	8	11	7	9³	5	12				4			14													19
1	2		3			8	10	13	11	6		9¹	5²	7				4³		14			12											20
1	2				8¹	6	9		11³	12	7²	10	5					4		13	3			14										21
1	2		3			6		9³		12		11¹	13	8	10	5	7			4			3²		14									22
1	2		3			9	6²	11¹		12	13	8	11	7	9³	5	12			4			3		14									23
1	2		3			10	8¹		9	12	6²	11³	5	7				4		13				14										24
1	2		3¹			9	6³	13	11		7	10	5	14				4		8¹²	12													25
1	2				6	7		9²		14	8	11³	5			12	4	10¹		3				13										26
1	5		4		6³	7	14		9	12	8	10²		11¹					13	3			2											27
			3		6⁴	7		12	9	13	8	10³	5			11²	4			14			2¹											28
1	5	12	3¹				9	6	13	7		10	4	11²	8³								2	14										29
1	2		3		8³	6	14	10	9²		7		5	12		4	11¹	13																30
1	2	3			7			13			10²	5	14			12		11	9³	4			8		6¹									31
						9³	14			10²		4					13	12	11	8	3¹	5		7		6	1	2						32
1	2		3		7³	14	9	6		10²	5	8				11¹	4	12	13															33
1			3		7			12	9³		10	5	13			11	8²	4						6		14		2¹						34
	2	3	4			9³	10²		12			13					11						5⁸		8		6	1		7¹	14			35
1		3				9	10¹		11		12	5³	4				6									7	2	8²		14	13			36
1	2		3		7¹			9	6²	12	8	10	5				11	13	4³											14				37
	3				12	9¹			10			4		13				8²		1	5			7	2	11³						6	14	38

FA Cup

Third Round	Exeter C	(a)	2-2	
Replay	Exeter C	(h)	3-0	
Fourth Round	West Ham U	(h)	0-0	
Replay	West Ham U	(a)	1-2	
(aet)				

Capital One Cup

Third Round	Carlisle U	(h)	1-1
(aet; Liverpool won 3-2 on penalties)			
Fourth Round	Bournemouth	(h)	1-0
Quarter-Final	Southampton	(a)	6-1
Semi-Final 1st leg	Stoke C	(a)	1-0
Semi-Final 2nd leg	Stoke C	(h)	0-1
(aet)			
Final	Manchester C	(Wembley)	1-1
(aet; Manchester C won 3-1 on penalties)			

UEFA Europa League

Group B	Bordeaux	(a)	1-1
Group B	FC Sion	(h)	1-1
Group B	Rubin Kazan	(h)	1-1
Group B	Rubin Kazan	(a)	1-0
Group B	Bordeaux	(h)	2-1
Group B	FC Sion	(a)	0-0
Round of 32 1st leg	Augsburg	(a)	0-0
Round of 32 2nd leg	Augsburg	(h)	1-0
(Liverpool won 1-0 on aggregate)			
Round of 16 1st leg	Manchester U	(h)	2-0
Round of 16 2nd leg	Manchester U	(a)	1-1
(Liverpool won 3-1 on aggregate)			
Quarter-Final 1st leg	Borussia Dortmund	(a)	1-1
Quarter-Final 2nd leg	Borussia Dortmund	(h)	4-3
(Liverpool won 5-4 on aggregate)			
Semi-Final 1st leg	Villarreal	(a)	0-1
Semi-Final 2nd leg	Villarreal	(h)	3-0
(Liverpool won 3-1 on aggregate)			
Final	Sevilla	(Basel)	1-3

LUTON TOWN

Kenilworth Road Stadium, 1 Maple Road, Luton, Bedfordshire LU4 8AW.

Telephone: (01582) 411 622.

Fax: (01582) 405 070.

Ticket Office: (01582) 416 976.

Website: www.lutontown.co.uk

Email: info@lutontown.co.uk

Ground Capacity: 10,413.

Record Attendance: 30,069 v Blackpool, FA Cup 6th rd replay, 4 March 1959.

Pitch Measurements: 101m × 66m (110yd × 72yd).

Chairman: Nick Owen.

Chief Executive: Gary Sweet.

Manager: Nathan Jones.

Assistant Manager: Paul Hart.

Physio: Simon Parsell.

Colours: Orange shirts with navy trim, navy blue shorts with white trim, white socks with orange trim.

Year Formed: 1885.

Turned Professional: 1890.

Ltd Co.: 1897.

Club Nickname: 'The Hatters'.

Grounds: 1885, Excelsior, Dallow Lane; 1897, Dunstable Road; 1905, Kenilworth Road.

First Football League Game: 4 September 1897, Division 2, v Leicester Fosse (a) D 1–1 – Williams; McCartney, McEwen; Davies, Stewart, Docherty; Gallacher, Coupar, Birch, McInnes, Ekins (1).

Record League Victory: 12–0 v Bristol R, Division 3 (S), 13 April 1936 – Dolman; Mackey, Smith; Finlayson, Nelson, Godfrey; Rich, Martin (1), Payne (10), Roberts (1), Stephenson.

Record Cup Victory: 9–0 v Clapton, FA Cup 1st rd (replay after abandoned game), 30 November 1927 – Abbott; Kingham, Graham; Black, Rennie, Fraser; Pointon, Yardley (4), Reid (2), Woods (1), Dennis (2).

Record Defeat: 0–9 v Small Heath, Division 2, 12 November 1898.

HONOURS

League Champions: Division 2 – 1981–82; FL 1 – 2004–05; Division 3S – 1936–37; Division 4 – 1967–68; Conference – 2013–14. *Runners-up:* Division 2 – 1954–55, 1973–74; Division 3 – 1969–70; Division 3S – 1935–36; Third Division – 2001–02.

FA Cup: Runners-up: 1959.

League Cup Winners: 1988. *Runners-up:* 1989.

League Trophy Winners: 2009.

Full Members' Cup: Runners-up: 1988.

Most League Points (2 for a win): 66, Division 4, 1967–68.

Most League Points (3 for a win): 98, FL 1 2004–05.

Most League Goals: 103, Division 3 (S), 1936–37.

Highest League Scorer in Season: Joe Payne, 55, Division 3 (S), 1936–37.

Most League Goals in Total Aggregate: Gordon Turner, 243, 1949–64. .

Most League Goals in One Match: 10, Joe Payne v Bristol R, Division 3 (S), 13 April 1936.

Most Capped Player: Mal Donaghy, 58 (91), Northern Ireland.

Most League Appearances: Bob Morton, 495, 1948–64.

Youngest League Player: Mike O'Hara, 16 years 32 days v Stoke C, 1 October 1960.

Record Transfer Fee Received: £3,000,000 from WBA for Curtis Davies, August 2005; £3,000,000 from Birmingham C for Rowan Vine, January 2007.

Record Transfer Fee Paid: £850,000 to Odense for Lars Elstrup, August 1989.

Football League Record: 1897 Elected to Division 2; 1900 Failed re-election; 1920 Division 3; 1921–37 Division 3 (S); 1937–55 Division 2; 1955–60 Division 1; 1960–63 Division 2; 1963–65 Division 3; 1965–68 Division 4; 1968–70 Division 3; 1970–74 Division 2; 1974–75 Division 1; 1975–82 Division 2; 1982–96 Division 1; 1996–2001 Division 2; 2001–02 Division 3; 2002–04 Division 2; 2004–05 FL 1; 2005–07 FL C; 2007–08 FL 1; 2008–09 FL 2; 2009–14 Conference Premier; 2014– FL 2.

LATEST SEQUENCES

Longest Sequence of League Wins: 12, 19.2.2002 – 6.4.2002.

Longest Sequence of League Defeats: 8, 11.11.1899 – 6.1.1900.

Longest Sequence of League Draws: 5, 28.8.1971 – 18.9.1971.

Longest Sequence of Unbeaten League Matches: 19, 8.4.1969 – 7.10.1969.

Longest Sequence Without a League Win: 16, 9.9.1964 – 6.11.1964.

Successive Scoring Runs: 25 from 24.10.1931.

Successive Non-scoring Runs: 5 from 10.4.1973.

MANAGERS

Charlie Green 1901–28
(Secretary-Manager)
George Thomson 1925
John McCartney 1927–29
George Kay 1929–31
Harold Wightman 1931–35
Ted Liddell 1936–38
Neil McBain 1938–39
George Martin 1939–47
Dally Duncan 1947–58
Syd Owen 1959–60
Sam Bartram 1960–62
Bill Harvey 1962–64
George Martin 1965–66
Allan Brown 1966–68
Alec Stock 1968–72
Harry Haslam 1972–78
David Pleat 1978–86
John Moore 1986–87
Ray Harford 1987–89
Jim Ryan 1990–91
David Pleat 1991–95
Terry Westley 1995
Lennie Lawrence 1995–2000
Ricky Hill 2000
Lil Fuccillo 2000
Joe Kinnear 2001–03
Mike Newell 2003–07
Kevin Blackwell 2007–08
Mick Harford 2008–09
Richard Money 2009–11
Gary Brabin 2011–12
Paul Buckle 2012–13
John Still 2013–15
Nathan Jones January 2016–

TEN YEAR LEAGUE RECORD

		P	W	D	L	F	A	Pts	Pos
2006-07	FL C	46	10	10	26	53	81	40	23
2007-08	FL 1	46	11	10	25	43	63	33*	24
2008-09	FL 2	46	13	17	16	58	65	26†	24
2009-10	Conf P	44	26	10	8	84	40	88	2
2010-11	Conf P	46	23	15	8	85	37	84	3
2011-12	Conf P	46	22	15	9	78	42	81	5
2012-13	Conf P	46	18	13	15	70	62	67	7
2013-14	Conf P	46	30	11	5	102	35	101	1
2014-15	FL 2	46	19	11	16	54	44	68	8
2015-16	FL 2	46	19	9	18	63	61	66	11

10 pts deducted; †30 points deducted.

DID YOU KNOW

Luton Town's visit to play Thames in a Division Three South game on 6 December 1930 attracted the lowest recorded attendance at a Football League game. Just 469 fans turned out at Thames's Custom House ground – a stadium with a capacity of 120,000!

LUTON TOWN – FOOTBALL LEAGUE TWO 2015–16 LEAGUE RECORD

Match No.	Date	Venue	Opponents	Result	H/T Score	Lg Pos.	Goalscorers	Attendance
1	Aug 8	A	Accrington S	D	1-1	0-0	10	Smith [90]	2359
2	15	H	Oxford U	D	2-2	1-0	15	Wilkinson [42], McGeehan [69]	8877
3	18	H	Bristol R	L	0-1	0-0	18		8061
4	22	A	Yeovil T	L	2-3	2-1	22	Mackail-Smith [4], Benson [19]	3830
5	29	H	Portsmouth	L	1-2	1-1	22	Mackail-Smith (pen) [15]	9083
6	Sept 5	A	Cambridge U	W	3-1	1-1	19	Guttridge [21], Wilkinson [66], Green [84]	6298
7	12	A	Notts Co	L	2-3	0-1	20	McGeehan [71], Smith [76]	5820
8	19	H	Mansfield T	W	1-0	0-0	18	Mackail-Smith (pen) [59]	7939
9	26	H	AFC Wimbledon	W	2-0	0-0	16	Marriott 2 [79, 90]	8415
10	29	A	Morecambe	W	3-1	2-1	11	Wilkinson [13], McGeehan [27], Smith [88]	1388
11	Oct 3	A	Hartlepool U	W	4-1	1-1	10	Smith [17], Marriott 2 [53, 57], Lee [90]	3876
12	10	H	York C	D	1-1	0-1	10	McGeehan (pen) [63]	8618
13	17	A	Crawley T	L	1-2	1-0	12	McGeehan [31]	3335
14	20	H	Leyton Orient	D	1-1	1-0	12	Marriott [33]	8022
15	24	H	Plymouth Arg	L	1-2	0-1	15	McQuoid [76]	8703
16	Nov 1	A	Dagenham & R	W	2-0	1-0	13	Guttridge [41], Lawless [65]	2723
17	14	H	Barnet	W	2-0	1-0	10	Green [25], McGeehan [67]	8497
18	21	A	Stevenage	D	0-0	0-0	10		4782
19	24	H	Carlisle U	L	3-4	1-1	12	Marriott [4], McQuoid [46], Green [57]	7298
20	28	A	Newport Co	L	0-3	0-0	13		2551
21	Dec 12	H	Northampton T	L	3-4	1-3	17	Benson 2 [9, 52], Green (pen) [66]	8792
22	19	A	Exeter C	W	3-2	2-0	13	McGeehan (pen) [30], Green [34], Benson [90]	3777
23	26	H	Wycombe W	L	0-2	0-0	15		9676
24	28	A	Portsmouth	D	0-0	0-0	14		17,668
25	Jan 2	A	Bristol R	L	0-2	0-0	15		9131
26	16	H	Cambridge U	D	0-0	0-0	18		9227
27	23	A	Mansfield T	W	2-0	1-0	16	McCourt [7], Ruddock [54]	4245
28	30	H	Notts Co	L	0-2	0-0	16		8147
29	Feb 2	A	Yeovil T	D	1-1	0-0	16	Sheehan [84]	7538
30	6	A	Wycombe W	W	1-0	1-0	14	McGeehan [40]	4597
31	13	A	AFC Wimbledon	L	1-4	0-2	14	Marriott [59]	4439
32	20	H	Hartlepool U	W	2-1	0-0	13	McGeehan (pen) [60], Mackail-Smith [86]	7880
33	27	A	York C	W	3-2	0-0	13	McGeehan [52], Marriott [74], Lee [90]	3628
34	Mar 1	H	Morecambe	W	1-0	0-0	13	Marriott [76]	7153
35	5	A	Leyton Orient	W	1-0	1-0	12	Marriott [27]	5684
36	12	H	Crawley T	L	0-1	0-1	13		8264
37	19	A	Plymouth Arg	W	1-0	1-0	12	Marriott [27]	7973
38	28	A	Barnet	L	1-2	0-0	14	McGeehan [85]	4008
39	Apr 2	H	Stevenage	L	0-1	0-0	14		8502
40	9	H	Accrington S	L	0-2	0-0	15		7467
41	12	H	Dagenham & R	W	1-0	1-0	14	Ruddock [37]	6997
42	16	A	Oxford U	W	3-2	2-1	14	Pigott 2 [44, 58], Lee [45]	8838
43	19	A	Carlisle U	W	2-1	1-0	13	Pigott [23], McQuoid [51]	3497
44	23	H	Newport Co	D	1-1	0-0	13	Marriott [81]	7606
45	30	A	Northampton T	L	0-2	0-2	14		7664
46	May 7	H	Exeter C	W	4-1	3-0	11	McGeehan [27], Marriott 2 [33, 63], Pigott [34]	8427

Final League Position: 11

GOALSCORERS

League (63): Marriott 14, McGeehan 12 (3 pens), Green 5 (1 pen), Benson 4, Mackail-Smith 4 (2 pens), Pigott 4, Smith 4, Lee 3, McQuoid 3, Wilkinson 3, Guttridge 2, Ruddock 2, Lawless 1, McCourt 1, Sheehan 1.
FA Cup (2): McQuoid 2.
Capital One Cup (4): Marriott 2, Benson 1, McGeehan 1.
Johnstone's Paint Trophy (3): Green 1, McGeehan 1, O'Donnell 1.

Justham E 14 + 1	Cuthbert S 36	McNulty S 9 + 1	Wilkinson L 20	Griffiths S 17 + 1	Green D 19 + 6	Doyle N 6 + 5	Smith J 33 + 4	McCourt P 15 + 9	Mackail-Smith C 27 + 6	McQuoid J 20 + 9	Ruddock P 12 + 9	Benson P 13 + 7	Marriott J 21 + 19	Tyler M 27	O'Donnell S 30	McGeehan C 35 + 6	Hall R 5 + 5	O'Brien M 2 + 4	Lawless A 21 + 7	Lee O 31 + 3	Guttridge L 6 + 2	Potts D 14	Long S 7 + 2	Okuonghae M 7 + 4	Howells J 14 + 3	Sheehan A 20	Musonda F — + 3	Pigott J 10 + 5	Mitchell J 5	Rea G 10	Banton Z — + 4	Bakinson T — + 1	Justin J — + 1	Match No.
	2	3	4	5	6^2	7	8	9^1	10	11^3	12	13	14																					1
	2	3	4	9		6	14	8^2	10^3		12	11	13	1	5^1	7																		2
	2	3	4	9		8^2	12	7	11^1		13	10	14	1	5	6^2																		3
	3	4^2	2	5	9^1		7	14	11			10		1		6^3	12	13																4
1	3		4	5			7	10^2	11	14		13		2	9	6^3	8^1		12															5
	3		4	5	8		6	11	10					1	2				7	9														6
	3^1	14	5	4	7^2		6	10	11					1	2	13	12^3		8	9^1														7
	3	4	5	12			7	10^3	11	6^2				1	2	8^1		13	14	9														8
	3	4	5^2				8	10	11	6^1		13		1	2^3	7	14		12	9														9
	2^1	4	3	5	12	6	9^2	11^3	10			14		1		8			13	7														10
	2	4	3	5	13	6	11^1	10^2			12			1		8			7	9														11
	2	3	4		14	7^1	11^3	6			12			1	10		13	9	8^2	5														12
	7	9		10	5	12	11	13			4^1			1	3				6^2		2	8												13
	3	4		12	7		9^1	10^3	14		11			1	6				8^2	13	5	2												14
	3	4		8	7			14	6^3		11			1	9	13^4		12		10	5^1	2^2												15
	4	3	5		7	9		12	10			11^1		1		6^2		8		2														16
	3	4	5	6^3		7	14		11^1		10^2	12		1	9		13	2	8															17
	3	4	5	6^2		7			10		11^{14}	12		1	9^3	14	2	6^1		13														18
	3			5	6		7	13	12	10		11^1		1	9^2		4	2	8															19
	3		4	5	6	12	8	14	13	11^1		10		1		7^3			2	9^2														20
		3	5	6		8		11			10	12		1		13			7^2	9			2^1	4										21
	3		12	10^1			8^2	13		11	14			1	9				7	6			2	4	5^3									22
	4			9^2			11	12		10^1	14			1	7				6^3	8	13		2	3	5									23
	3			6			$13^{}$	8^2		11	10^3		1	2	12	9			7^1				14	4	5									24
	3			7	12		11^2	13		10^1	14		1	2	8	9			6				4	5^3										25
12	3			6^1		8			13		10^1	11	$12^{}$	2		9			7				4	5										26
1	3				6		9^2	11^3		8^1		13		2	10				7	12				5	4	14								27
1	3				6^1	10	11^2		8	14				2	9^3				7	12				5	4		13							28
1	3				13	10^5		6^3	14	12				2	9				8	7				5	4		11^1							29
1	3				14	10		13	12	9^3				2	7^1				6	8				5	4		11^2							30
1	4				13	8^1	11^3		10	9				2	6				7^2				12	5	3		14							31
	3			9				13		14		11	1	2^3	7	12			6^1	8				5	4		10^2							32
	4			6		12		13			11	1	2	8				7^3	9				14	5	3^2		10^1							33
	3					7	9^1	10		12		11		2	6				8					5	4									34
	4		13		3	6^2	11		12		9^3		2	7		10			5^1	14			8			1								35
	3		13		7^2		9	10^3		14	11^1		2	6		8			5				4		12	1								36
	4		13		6		10^5	11		12	9		2	8					5^3			14	3			1		7						37
	3		14		7^2	12		8	10^3	11			2	9					4				5		13	1		6^1						38
	4^3		12		8	7^1	13	14		10			2	9		6								5		11^2	1	3						39
1					7^2		10	6	12	11^3			2	9			8		5^1					4	14			3	13					40
1				6^1	7^2		11	9		10^3			2			13	8		5					4		12		3	14					41
1				9^2			10^2	6		2	12		7	8^1		5			14	4			11			3								42
1				9^2			10^6	6^1		14		2	12	7	8		5			13	4		11			3								43
1				6^2			10^1	8		14		2	12	7	$9^{}$	5							4			11		3	13					44
1				10^1		6		12		9^3		13		2	8				7^2				5		14	4		11	3					45
1							7^3	10						2^1	8				6				5				9^2	4	14	11	3	12	13	46

FA Cup

First Round	Crawley T	(a)	2-1
Second Round	Peterborough U	(a)	0-2

Capital One Cup

First Round	Bristol C	(h)	3-1
Second Round	Stoke C	(h)	1-1

(aet; Stoke C won 8-7 on penalties)

Johnstone's Paint Trophy

First Round	Leyton Orient	(h)	2-1
Second Round	Gillingham	(a)	1-2

MANCHESTER CITY

FOUNDATION

Manchester City was formed as a limited company in 1894 after their predecessors Ardwick had been forced into bankruptcy. However, many historians like to trace the club's lineage as far back as 1880 when St Mark's Church, West Gorton added a football section to their cricket club. They amalgamated with Belle Vue for one season before splitting again under the name Gorton Association FC in 1884–85. In 1887 Gorton AFC turned professional and moved ground to Hyde Road under the new name Ardwick AFC.

Etihad Stadium, Etihad Campus, Manchester M11 3FF.
Telephone: (0161) 444 1894.
Fax: (0161) 438 7999.
Ticket Office: (0161) 444 1894.
Website: www.mcfc.co.uk
Email: mcfc@mcfc.co.uk
Ground Capacity: 55,097.
Record Attendance: 84,569 v Stoke C, FA Cup 6th rd, 3 March 1934 (at Maine Road; British record for any game outside London or Glasgow); 54,693 v Leicester C, FA Premier League, 6 February 2016 (at Etihad Stadium).
Pitch Measurements: 105m × 68m (114yd × 74yd).
Chairman: Khaldoon Al Mubarak.
Chief Executive: Ferran Soriano.
Manager: Pep Guardiola.
Assistant Managers: Ruben Cousillas Fuse, Brian Kidd.
Fitness Coach: Jose Cabello.
Colours: Field blue shirts with white trim, white shorts with field blue trim, field blue socks with white trim.
Year Formed: 1887 as Ardwick FC; 1894 as Manchester City.
Turned Professional: 1887 as Ardwick FC.
Previous Names: 1880, St Mark's Church, West Gorton; 1884, Gorton; 1887, Ardwick; 1894, Manchester City.
Club Nicknames: 'The Blues', 'The Citizens'.
Grounds: 1880, Clowes Street; 1881, Kirkmanshulme Cricket Ground; 1882, Queens Road; 1884, Pink Bank Lane; 1887, Hyde Road (1894–1923 as City); 1923, Maine Road; 2003, City of Manchester Stadium (renamed Etihad Stadium 2011).

HONOURS

League Champions: FA Premier League – 2011–12, 2013–14; Division 1 – 1936–37, 1967–68; First Division – 2001–02; Division 2 – 1898–99, 1902–03, 1909–10, 1927–28, 1946–47, 1965–66.
Runners-up: FA Premier League – 2012–13, 2014–15; Division 1 – 1903–04, 1920–21, 1976–77; First Division – 1999–2000; Division 2 – 1895–96, 1950–51, 1988–89.
FA Cup Winners: 1904, 1934, 1956, 1969, 2011.
Runners-up: 1926, 1933, 1955, 1981, 2013.
League Cup Winners: 1970, 1976, 2014, 2016.
Runners-up: 1974.
Full Members Cup: Runners-up: 1986.
European Competitions
European Cup: 1968–69.
Champions League: 2011–12, 2012–13, 2013–14, 2014–15, 2015–16 *(sf)*.
UEFA Cup: 1972–73, 1976–77, 1977–78, 1978–79 *(qf)*, 2003–04, 2008–09 *(qf)*.
Europa League: 2010–11, 2011–12.
European Cup-Winners' Cup: 1969–70 *(winners)*, 1970–71 *(sf)*.

First Football League Game: 3 September 1892, Division 2, v Bootle (h) W 7–0 – Douglas; McVickers, Robson; Middleton, Russell, Hopkins; Davies (3), Morris (2), Angus (1), Weir (1), Milarvie.
Record League Victory: 10–1 v Huddersfield T, Division 2, 7 November 1987 – Nixon; Gidman, Hinchcliffe, Clements, Lake, Redmond, White (3), Stewart (3), Adcock (3), McNab (1), Simpson.
Record Cup Victory: 10–1 v Swindon T, FA Cup 4th rd, 29 January 1930 – Barber; Felton, McCloy; Barrass, Cowan, Heinemann; Toseland, Marshall (5), Tait (3), Johnson (1), Brook (1).

sky SPORTS FACT FILE

Max Woosnam, who made 93 appearances for Manchester City between 1919 and 1924, was a multi-talented sportsman who also excelled at lawn tennis. He captained the Great Britain Davis Cup team, won gold (men's doubles) and silver (mixed doubles) at the 1920 Olympic Games as well as winning the men's doubles at Wimbledon in 1921.

Record Defeat: 1–9 v Everton, Division 1, 3 September 1906.

Most League Points (2 for a win): 62, Division 2, 1946–47.

Most League Points (3 for a win): 99, Division 1, 2001–02.

Most League Goals: 108, Division 2, 1926–27, 108, Division 1, 2001–02.

Highest League Scorer in Season: Tommy Johnson, 38, Division 1, 1928–29.

Most League Goals in Total Aggregate: Tommy Johnson, 158, 1919–30.

Most League Goals in One Match: 5, Fred Williams v Darwen, Division 2, 18 February 1899; 5, Tom Browell v Burnley, Division 2, 24 October 1925; 5, Tom Johnson v Everton, Division 1, 15 September 1928; 5, George Smith v Newport Co, Division 2, 14 June 1947; 5, Sergio Aguero v Newcastle U, FA Premier League, 3 October 2015.

Most Capped Player: David Silva, 65 (103), Spain.

Most League Appearances: Alan Oakes, 564, 1959–76.

Youngest League Player: Glyn Pardoe, 15 years 314 days v Birmingham C, 11 April 1962.

Record Transfer Fee Received: £21,000,000 from Chelsea for Shaun Wright-Phillips, July 2005.

Record Transfer Fee Paid: £55,000,000 to Wolfsburg for Kevin De Bruyne, August 2015.

Football League Record: 1892 Ardwick elected founder member of Division 2; 1894 Newly-formed Manchester C elected to Division 2; Division 1 1899–1902, 1903–09, 1910–26, 1928–38, 1947–50, 1951–63, 1966–83, 1985–87, 1989–92; Division 2 1902–03, 1909–10, 1926–28, 1938–47, 1950–51, 1963–66, 1983–85, 1987–89; 1992–96 FA League; 1996–98 Division 1; 1998–99 Division 2; 1999–2000 Division 1; 2000–01 FA Premier League; 2001–02 Division 1; 2002– FA Premier League.

LATEST SEQUENCES

Longest Sequence of League Wins: 11, 19.4.2015 – 12.9.2015.

Longest Sequence of League Defeats: 8, 23.8.1995 – 14.10.1995.

Longest Sequence of League Draws: 7, 5.10.2009 – 28.11.2009.

Longest Sequence of Unbeaten League Matches: 22, 16.11.1946 – 19.4.1947.

Longest Sequence Without a League Win: 17, 26.12.1979 – 7.4.1980.

Successive Scoring Runs: 44 from 3.10.1936.

Successive Non-scoring Runs: 6 from 30.1.1971.

MANAGERS

Joshua Parlby 1893–95
(Secretary-Manager)
Sam Omerod 1895–1902
Tom Maley 1902–06
Harry Newbould 1906–12
Ernest Magnall 1912–24
David Ashworth 1924–25
Peter Hodge 1926–32
Wilf Wild 1932–46
(continued as Secretary to 1950)
Sam Cowan 1946–47
John 'Jock' Thomson 1947–50
Leslie McDowall 1950–63
George Poyser 1963–65
Joe Mercer 1965–71
(continued as General Manager to 1972)
Malcolm Allison 1972–73
Johnny Hart 1973
Ron Saunders 1973–74
Tony Book 1974–79
Malcolm Allison 1979–80
John Bond 1980–83
John Benson 1983
Billy McNeill 1983–86
Jimmy Frizzell 1986–87
(continued as General Manager)
Mel Machin 1987–89
Howard Kendall 1989–90
Peter Reid 1990–93
Brian Horton 1993–95
Alan Ball 1995–96
Steve Coppell 1996
Frank Clark 1996–98
Joe Royle 1998–2001
Kevin Keegan 2001–05
Stuart Pearce 2005–07
Sven-Göran Eriksson 2007–08
Mark Hughes 2008–09
Roberto Mancini 2009–13
Manuel Pellegrini 2013–16
Pep Guardiola June 2016–

TEN YEAR LEAGUE RECORD

		P	W	D	L	F	A	Pts	Pos
2006-07	PR Lge	38	11	9	18	29	44	42	14
2007-08	PR Lge	38	15	10	13	45	53	55	9
2008-09	PR Lge	38	15	5	18	58	50	50	10
2009-10	PR Lge	38	18	13	7	73	45	67	5
2010-11	PR Lge	38	21	8	9	60	33	71	3
2011-12	PR Lge	38	28	5	5	93	29	89	1
2012-13	PR Lge	38	23	9	6	66	34	78	2
2013-14	PR Lge	38	27	5	6	102	37	86	1
2014-15	PR Lge	38	24	7	7	83	38	79	2
2015-16	PR Lge	38	19	9	10	71	41	66	4

DID YOU KNOW

Manchester City leased their former ground at Hyde Road from the Manchester Tramways Committee. The lease was due to expire in 1923 and City sought a 20-year extension which was refused, forcing them to look elsewhere. They subsequently purchased land for a new ground which became Maine Road, their home until 2003.

MANCHESTER CITY – FA PREMIER LEAGUE 2015–16 LEAGUE RECORD

Match No.	Date	Venue	Opponents	Result	H/T Score	Lg Pos.	Goalscorers	Attendance
1	Aug 10	A	WBA	W 3-0	2-0	1	Silva [9], Toure [24], Kompany [59]	24,564
2	16	H	Chelsea	W 3-0	1-0	1	Aguero [31], Kompany [79], Fernandinho [85]	54,331
3	23	A	Everton	W 2-0	0-0	1	Kolarov [60], Nasri [88]	38,523
4	29	H	Watford	W 2-0	0-0	1	Sterling [47], Fernandinho [56]	53,218
5	Sept 12	A	Crystal Palace	W 1-0	0-0	1	Iheanacho [90]	25,167
6	19	H	West Ham U	L 1-2	1-2	1	De Bruyne [45]	53,545
7	26	A	Tottenham H	L 1-4	1-1	2	De Bruyne [25]	35,867
8	Oct 3	H	Newcastle U	W 6-1	1-1	1	Aguero 5 [42, 49, 50, 60, 62], De Bruyne [53]	53,850
9	17	H	Bournemouth	W 5-1	4-1	1	Sterling 3 [7, 29, 45], Bony 2 [11, 89]	54,502
10	25	A	Manchester U	D 0-0	0-0	1		75,329
11	31	H	Norwich C	W 2-1	0-0	1	Otamendi [67], Toure (pen) [89]	53,418
12	Nov 8	A	Aston Villa	D 0-0	0-0	1		36,757
13	21	H	Liverpool	L 1-4	1-3	3	Aguero [44]	54,444
14	28	H	Southampton	W 3-1	2-0	1	De Bruyne [9], Delph [20], Kolarov [69]	54,102
15	Dec 5	A	Stoke C	L 0-2	0-2	3		27,264
16	12	H	Swansea C	W 2-1	1-0	1	Bony [26], Iheanacho [90]	53,052
17	21	A	Arsenal	L 1-2	0-2	3	Toure [82]	60,053
18	26	H	Sunderland	W 4-1	3-0	3	Sterling [12], Toure [17], Bony [22], De Bruyne [54]	54,523
19	29	A	Leicester C	D 0-0	0-0	3		32,072
20	Jan 2	A	Watford	W 2-1	0-0	3	Toure [82], Aguero [84]	20,676
21	13	H	Everton	D 0-0	0-0	3		53,796
22	16	H	Crystal Palace	W 4-0	2-0	2	Delph [22], Aguero 2 [41, 68], Silva [84]	53,983
23	23	A	West Ham U	D 2-2	1-1	2	Aguero 2 (1 pen) [9 (p), 81]	34,977
24	Feb 2	H	Sunderland	W 1-0	1-0	2	Aguero [16]	38,852
25	6	H	Leicester C	L 1-3	0-1	3	Aguero [87]	54,693
26	14	H	Tottenham H	L 1-2	0-0	4	Iheanacho [74]	54,551
27	Mar 2	A	Liverpool	L 0-3	0-2	4		43,597
28	5	H	Aston Villa	W 4-0	0-0	4	Toure [48], Aguero 2 [50, 60], Sterling [66]	53,892
29	12	A	Norwich C	D 0-0	0-0	4		26,323
30	20	H	Manchester U	L 0-1	0-1	4		54,557
31	Apr 2	A	Bournemouth	W 4-0	3-0	4	Fernando [7], De Bruyne [12], Aguero [19], Kolarov [90]	11,192
32	9	H	WBA	W 2-1	1-1	4	Aguero (pen) [19], Nasri [66]	53,920
33	16	A	Chelsea	W 3-0	1-0	3	Aguero 3 (1 pen) [33, 54, 80 (p)]	41,212
34	19	A	Newcastle U	D 1-1	1-1	3	Aguero [14]	46,424
35	23	H	Stoke C	W 4-0	2-0	3	Fernando [35], Aguero (pen) [43], Iheanacho 2 [64, 74]	53,974
36	May 1	A	Southampton	L 2-4	1-2	4	Iheanacho 2 [44, 78]	31,472
37	8	H	Arsenal	D 2-2	1-1	4	Aguero [8], De Bruyne [51]	54,425
38	15	A	Swansea C	D 1-1	1-1	4	Iheanacho [5]	20,934

Final League Position: 4

GOALSCORERS

League (71): Aguero 24 (4 pens), Iheanacho 8, De Bruyne 7, Sterling 6, Toure 6 (1 pen), Bony 4, Kolarov 3, Delph 2, Fernandinho 2, Fernando 2, Kompany 2, Nasri 2, Silva 2, Otamendi 1.
FA Cup (8): Iheanacho 4 (1 pen), Aguero 1, De Bruyne 1, Faupala 1, Sterling 1.
Capital One Cup (18): De Bruyne 5, Aguero 2 (1 pen), Bony 2, Fernandinho 2, Iheanacho 2, Garcia 1, Jesus Navas 1, Sterling 1, Toure 1 (pen), own goal 1.
UEFA Champions League (18): De Bruyne 3, Sterling 3, Aguero 2 (1 pen), Bony 2, Fernandinho 2, Silva 2, Otamendi 1, Toure 1, own goals 2.

Hart J 35	Sagna B 27+1	Kompany V 13+1	Mangala E 23	Kolarov A 25+4	Toure Y 28+4	Fernandinho L 31+2	Jesus Navas G 24+10	Silva D 22+2	Sterling R 23+8	Bony W 13+13	Aguero S 29+1	Nasri S 4+8	Demichelis M 10+10	Delph F 8+9	Iheanacho K 7+19	De Bruyne K 22+3	Otamendi N 30	Caballero W 3+1	Fernando F 17+7	Roberts P —+1	Zabaleta P 12+1	Clichy G 12+2	Celina B —+1	Garcia M —+1	Match No.
1	2	3	4	5	6³	7	8	9	10²	11¹	12	13	14												1
1	2	3	4	5	6	7	8¹	9	10²	14	11³	12	13												2
1	2	3	4	5	7	6	8	9¹	10¹	13	11²	12²	12		14										3
1	2	3	4	5	6	7	8¹	9²	10³	11	12		13	14											4
1	2	3	4	5	8	7	6		10²	11¹	9³	14		13	12										5
1	2		4¹	5³	6	7	8		10²	13	11		12	14	9	3									6
	2			5	9¹	7²	12		10		11³	13	3		8	4	1	6	14						7
1		4	5		7	12	8³	10¹	13	11²			14	9	3		6		2						8
1	5		4	6¹	7	8		9³	11		13			14	10⁵	3		12	2						9
1	2	3		5	9²	7	12	10¹	11³		13			14	8	4		6							10
1	2	3		5	6³	7	8	12	11		14		9¹	10⁷	4		13								11
1	2	3		5	9²	6	12	10³	11¹		13	14	8	4	7										12
1	2		4	5	6²	12	8¹	10	11³		3	13	14	9				7							13
	2		5	9	6	14	10³	12	11¹		3	7²		8	4	1	13								14
1	2		5		7¹	14	9³	10	11²		3	12	13	8	4		6								15
1	2	4		6	7	8	9²	10¹	11¹				12	14	13	3					5				16
1	2	4	5	7	8	14	10¹	12	13	11²				9¹		6	3								17
1	2	13³	4	5	7²	6		9	10	11			14	12		8	3¹								18
1	2		4	5	6	7	13	9²	10³	12	11¹			14	8	3									19
1	2		4²	5	7	6	12	9	10¹	13	11³		14			8	3								20
1	2				7		6	12	10		11		4			9¹	3		8			5			21
1				5¹	13		14	9			11³		4	8	10²	7	3		6		2	12			22
1	2				6		8¹	9³	12		11		4	7²	13	10	3		14			5			23
1	2		14	8³	7	6²	9	13		11			4	7²	12		3		12			5			24
1			5	9¹	6		8³	10		11			4	7²	12		3		13	2		14			25
1	3			13	9	7		8	10		11			12		4			6¹	2	5²				26
1	3		14		7²	8	9	10¹	12	11				13		4			6	2	5³				27
1	2	3		7³	8	6	9²	12	10¹	11				13		4					5		14		28
1	2³	3		7	6²	9	12	10¹	11				13			4		8		14	5				29
1²	2		4	6	7	8	9	10¹	14	11			3³					13	12		5				30
			4	12	7	8	9²		11³	13			14	10¹	3	1	6			2	5				31
1		4	5	13		6			10¹	11³	9		8²		12	3			7		2	14			32
1	12		4	5	6	7	8		11³	10²	13	14		9	3				2¹						33
1	3		4	5	6²	13	8³		12	14	11		10¹	9				7		2					34
1			4	5	8		6	9¹		13	11²	14	12	10	3				7³		2				35
1			4	5		7¹	13		9	11	6	12	8²	10	3						2				36
1	2		4		14	7	6²		12	13	11			10¹	9	3			8³		5				37
1	2		4		13	8	6			11²	12			10¹	9	3			7		5				38

FA Cup

Third Round	Norwich C	(a)	3-0	
Fourth Round	Aston Villa	(a)	4-0	
Fifth Round	Chelsea	(a)	1-5	

Capital One Cup

Third Round	Sunderland	(a)	4-1	
Fourth Round	Crystal Palace	(h)	5-1	
Quarter-Final	Hull C	(h)	4-1	
Semi-Final 1st leg	Everton	(a)	1-2	
Semi-Final 2nd leg	Everton	(h)	3-1	
(Manchester C won 4-3 on aggregate)				
Final	Liverpool	(Wembley)	1-1	
(aet; Manchester C won 3-1 on penalties)				

UEFA Champions League

Group D	Juventus	(h)	1-2
Group D	Borussia M'gladbach	(a)	2-1
Group D	Sevilla	(h)	2-1
Group D	Sevilla	(a)	3-1
Group D	Juventus	(a)	0-1
Group D	Borussia M'gladbach	(h)	4-2
Round of 16 1st leg	Dynamo Kyiv	(a)	3-1
Round of 16 2nd leg	Dynamo Kyiv	(h)	0-0
(Manchester C won 3-1 on aggregate)			
Quarter-Final 1st leg	Paris Saint-Germain	(a)	2-2
Quarter-Final 2nd leg	Paris Saint-Germain	(h)	1-0
(Manchester C won 3-2 on aggregate)			
Semi-Final 1st leg	Real Madrid	(h)	0-0
Semi-Final 2nd leg	Real Madrid	(a)	0-1
(Real Madrid won 1-0 on aggregate)			

MANCHESTER UNITED

FOUNDATION

Manchester United was formed as comparatively recently as 1902 after their predecessors, Newton Heath, went bankrupt. However, it is usual to give the date of the club's foundation as 1878 when the dining room committee of the carriage and waggon works of the Lancashire and Yorkshire Railway Company formed Newton Heath L and YR Cricket and Football Club. They won the Manchester Cup in 1886 and as Newton Heath FC were admitted to the Second Division in 1892.

Old Trafford, Sir Matt Busby Way, Manchester M16 0RA.

Telephone: (0161) 868 8000.

Fax: (0161) 868 8804.

Ticket Office: (0161) 868 8000 (option 1).

Website: www.manutd.com

Email: enquiries@manutd.co.uk

Ground Capacity: 75,653.

Record Attendance: 76,098 v Blackburn R, FA Premier League, 31 March 2007.

Ground Record Attendance: 76,962 Wolverhampton W v Grimsby T, FA Cup semi-final, 25 March 1939.

Pitch Measurements: 105m × 68m (114yd × 74yd).

Co-Chairmen: Joel and Avram Glazer.

Chief Executive: Edward Woodward.

Manager: Jose Mourinho.

Assistant Manager: Rui Faria.

Physio: Neil Hough.

Colours: Red shirts with white trim, white shorts with red trim, black socks with red trim.

Year Formed: 1878 as Newton Heath LYR; 1902, Manchester United.

Turned Professional: 1885.

Previous Name: 1880, Newton Heath; 1902, Manchester United.

Club Nickname: 'Red Devils'.

Grounds: 1880, North Road, Monsall Road; 1893, Bank Street; 1910, Old Trafford (played at Maine Road 1941–49).

HONOURS

League Champions: FA Premier League – 1992–93, 1993–94, 1995–96, 1996–97, 1998–99, 1999–2000, 2000–01, 2002–03, 2006–07, 2007–08, 2008–09, 2010–11, 2012–13; Division 1 – 1907–08, 1910–11, 1951–52, 1955–56, 1956–57, 1964–65, 1966–67; Division 2 – 1935–36, 1974–75.
Runners-up: FA Premier League – 1994–95, 1997–98, 2005–06, 2009–10, 2011–12; Division 1 – 1946–47, 1947–48, 1948–49, 1950–51, 1958–59, 1963–64, 1967–68, 1979–80, 1987–88, 1991–92; Division 2 – 1896–97, 1905–06, 1924–25, 1937–38.
FA Cup Winners: 1909, 1948, 1963, 1977, 1983, 1985, 1990, 1994, 1996, 1999, 2004, 2016.
Runners-up: 1957, 1958, 1976, 1979, 1995, 2005, 2007.

League Cup Winners: 1992, 2006, 2009, 2010.
Runners-up: 1983, 1991, 1994, 2003.

European Competitions
European Cup: 1956–57 (sf), 1957–58 (sf), 1965–66 (sf), 1967–68 (winners), 1968–69 (sf).
Champions League: 1993–94, 1994–95, 1996–97 (sf), 1997–98 (qf), 1998–99 (winners), 1999–2000 (qf), 2000–01 (qf), 2001–02 (sf), 2002–03 (qf), 2003–04, 2004–05, 2005–06, 2006–07 (sf), 2007–08 (winners), 2008–09 (runners-up), 2009–10 (qf), 2010–11 (runners-up), 2011–12, 2012–13, 2013–14 (qf), 2015–16.
Fairs Cup: 1964–65.
UEFA Cup: 1976–77, 1980–81, 1982–83, 1984–85 (qf), 1992–93, 1995–96.
Europa League: 2011–12, 2015–16.
European Cup-Winners' Cup: 1963–64 (qf), 1977–78, 1983–84 (sf), 1990–91 (winners). 1991–92. *Super Cup:* 1991 (winners), 1999, 2008. *World Club Championship:* 1968, 1999 (winners), 2000.
FIFA Club World Cup: 2008 (winners).
NB: In 1958–59 FA refused permission to compete in European Cup.

sky SPORTS FACT FILE

Old Trafford was closed for the opening two matches of the 1971–72 season due to crowd troubles. The opening 'home' game with Arsenal was played at Anfield, while the fixture with West Bromwich Albion was played at Stoke's Victoria Ground. Although United won both games attendances were below 30,000, well down on the club's normal 50,000-plus gates at that time.

First Football League Game: 3 September 1892, Division 1, v Blackburn R (a) L 3–4 – Warner; Clements, Brown; Perrins, Stewart, Erentz; Farman (1), Coupar (1), Donaldson (1), Carson, Mathieson.

Record League Victory (as Newton Heath): 10–1 v Wolverhampton W, Division 1, 15 October 1892 – Warner; Mitchell, Clements; Perrins, Stewart (3), Erentz; Farman (1), Hood (1), Donaldson (3), Carson (1), Hendry (1).

Record League Victory (as Manchester U): 9–0 v Ipswich T, FA Premier League, 4 March 1995 – Schmeichel; Keane (1) (Sharpe), Irwin, Bruce (Butt), Kanchelskis, Pallister, Cole (5), Ince (1), McClair, Hughes (2), Giggs.

Record Cup Victory: 10–0 v RSC Anderlecht, European Cup prel. rd 2nd leg, 26 September 1956 – Wood; Foulkes, Byrne; Colman, Jones, Edwards; Berry (1), Whelan (2), Taylor (3), Viollet (4), Pegg.

Record Defeat: 0–7 v Blackburn R, Division 1, 10 April 1926; 0–7 v Aston Villa, Division 1, 27 December 1930; 0–7 v Wolverhampton W, Division 2, 26 December 1931.

Most League Points (2 for a win): 64, Division 1, 1956–57.

Most League Points (3 for a win): 92, FA Premier League, 1993–94.

Most League Goals: 103, Division 1, 1956–57 and 1958–59.

Highest League Scorer in Season: Dennis Viollet, 32, 1959–60.

Most League Goals in Total Aggregate: Bobby Charlton, 199, 1956–73.

Most League Goals in One Match: 5, Andy Cole v Ipswich T, FA Premier League, 3 March 1995; 5, Dimitar Berbatov v Blackburn R, FA Premier League, 27 November 2010.

Most Capped Player: Bobby Charlton, 106, England.

Most League Appearances: Ryan Giggs, 672, 1991–2014.

Youngest League Player: Jeff Whitefoot, 16 years 105 days v Portsmouth, 15 April 1950.

Record Transfer Fee Received: £80,000,000 from Real Madrid for Cristiano Ronaldo, July 2009.

Record Transfer Fee Paid: £59,700,000 to Real Madrid for Angel Di Maria, August 2014.

Football League Record: 1892 Newton Heath elected to Division 1; 1894–1906 Division 2; 1906–22 Division 1; 1922–25 Division 2; 1925–31 Division 1; 1931–36 Division 2; 1936–37 Division 1; 1937–38 Division 2; 1938–74 Division 1; 1974–75 Division 2; 1975–92 Division 1; 1992– FA Premier League.

MANAGERS

J. Ernest Mangnall 1903–12
John Bentley 1912–14
John Robson 1914–21
  (Secretary-Manager from 1916)
John Chapman 1921–26
Clarence Hilditch 1926–27
Herbert Bamlett 1927–31
Walter Crickmer 1931–32
Scott Duncan 1932–37
Walter Crickmer 1937–45
  (Secretary-Manager)
Matt Busby 1945–69
  (continued as General Manager then Director)
Wilf McGuinness 1969–70
Sir Matt Busby 1970–71
Frank O'Farrell 1971–72
Tommy Docherty 1972–77
Dave Sexton 1977–81
Ron Atkinson 1981–86
Sir Alex Ferguson 1986–2013
David Moyes 2013–14
Louis van Gaal 2014–16
Jose Mourinho June 2016–

LATEST SEQUENCES

Longest Sequence of League Wins: 14, 15.10.1904 – 3.1.1905.
Longest Sequence of League Defeats: 14, 26.4.1930 – 25.10.1930.
Longest Sequence of League Draws: 6, 30.10.1988 – 27.11.1988.
Longest Sequence of Unbeaten League Matches: 29, 11.4.2010 – 1.2.2011.
Longest Sequence Without a League Win: 16, 19.4.1930 – 25.10.1930.
Successive Scoring Runs: 36 from 3.12.2007.
Successive Non-scoring Runs: 5 from 7.2.1981.

TEN YEAR LEAGUE RECORD

		P	W	D	L	F	A	Pts	Pos
2006-07	PR Lge	38	28	5	5	83	27	89	1
2007-08	PR Lge	38	27	6	5	80	22	87	1
2008-09	PR Lge	38	28	6	4	68	24	90	1
2009-10	PR Lge	38	27	4	7	86	28	85	2
2010-11	PR Lge	38	23	11	4	78	37	80	1
2011-12	PR Lge	38	28	5	5	89	33	89	2
2012-13	PR Lge	38	28	5	5	86	43	89	1
2013-14	PR Lge	38	19	7	12	64	43	64	7
2014-15	PR Lge	38	20	10	8	62	37	70	4
2015-16	PR Lge	38	19	9	10	49	35	66	5

DID YOU KNOW ?

Manchester United's trip to Hamburg in March 1946 to play a British Forces' team was anything but easy. The players only reached the ground two hours before kick-off then had to return by train and boat due to adverse weather conditions which prevented them from flying. United lost the game 2-1.

MANCHESTER UNITED – FA PREMIER LEAGUE 2015–16 LEAGUE RECORD

Match No.	Date	Venue	Opponents	Result	H/T Score	Lg Pos.	Goalscorers	Attendance
1	Aug 8	H	Tottenham H	W 1-0	1-0	3	Walker (og) [22]	75,261
2	14	A	Aston Villa	W 1-0	1-0	1	Januzaj [29]	42,200
3	22	H	Newcastle U	D 0-0	0-0	2		75,354
4	30	A	Swansea C	L 1-2	0-0	5	Mata [48]	20,828
5	Sept 12	H	Liverpool	W 3-1	0-0	2	Blind [49], Ander Herrera (pen) [70], Martial [86]	75,347
6	20	A	Southampton	W 3-2	1-1	2	Martial 2 [34, 50], Mata [68]	31,588
7	26	H	Sunderland	W 3-0	1-0	1	Depay [45], Rooney [46], Mata [90]	75,328
8	Oct 4	A	Arsenal	L 0-3	0-3	3		60,084
9	17	A	Everton	W 3-0	2-0	3	Schneiderlin [18], Ander Herrera [22], Rooney [62]	39,553
10	25	H	Manchester C	D 0-0	0-0	4		75,329
11	31	A	Crystal Palace	D 0-0	0-0	4		24,854
12	Nov 7	A	WBA	W 2-0	0-0	4	Lingard [52], Mata (pen) [90]	75,410
13	21	A	Watford	W 2-1	1-0	2	Depay [11], Deeney (og) [90]	20,702
14	28	A	Leicester C	D 1-1	1-1	3	Schweinsteiger [45]	32,115
15	Dec 5	H	West Ham U	D 0-0	0-0	4		75,350
16	12	A	Bournemouth	L 1-2	1-0	4	Fellaini [24]	11,334
17	19	H	Norwich C	L 1-2	0-1	5	Martial [66]	75,320
18	26	A	Stoke C	L 0-2	0-2	6		27,426
19	28	H	Chelsea	D 0-0	0-0	6		75,275
20	Jan 2	A	Swansea C	W 2-1	0-0	5	Martial [47], Rooney [77]	75,415
21	12	A	Newcastle U	D 3-3	2-1	6	Rooney 2 (1 pen) [9 (p), 79], Lingard [38]	49,673
22	17	A	Liverpool	W 1-0	0-0	5	Rooney [78]	43,865
23	23	H	Southampton	L 0-1	0-0	5		75,408
24	Feb 2	H	Stoke C	W 3-0	2-0	5	Lingard [14], Martial [23], Rooney [53]	75,234
25	7	A	Chelsea	D 1-1	0-0	5	Lingard [61]	41,434
26	13	A	Sunderland	L 1-2	1-1	5	Martial [39]	41,687
27	28	H	Arsenal	W 3-2	2-1	5	Rashford 2 [29, 32], Ander Herrera [65]	75,329
28	Mar 2	H	Watford	W 1-0	0-0	5	Mata [83]	75,272
29	6	A	WBA	L 0-1	0-0	6		24,878
30	20	A	Manchester C	W 1-0	1-0	6	Rashford [16]	54,557
31	Apr 3	H	Everton	W 1-0	0-0	5	Martial [54]	75,341
32	10	A	Tottenham H	L 0-3	0-0	5		35,761
33	16	H	Aston Villa	W 1-0	1-0	5	Rashford [32]	75,411
34	20	H	Crystal Palace	W 2-0	1-0	5	Delaney (og) [4], Darmian [55]	75,277
35	May 1	H	Leicester C	D 1-1	1-1	5	Martial [8]	75,275
36	7	A	Norwich C	W 1-0	0-0	5	Mata [72]	27,132
37	10	A	West Ham U	L 2-3	0-1	5	Martial 2 [51, 72]	34,602
38	17	H	Bournemouth	W 3-1	1-0	5	Rooney [43], Rashford [74], Young [87]	74,363

Final League Position: 5

GOALSCORERS

League (49): Martial 11, Rooney 8 (1 pen), Mata 6 (1 pen), Rashford 5, Lingard 4, Ander Herrera 3 (1 pen), Depay 2, Blind 1, Darmian 1, Fellaini 1, Januzaj 1, Schneiderlin 1, Schweinsteiger 1, Young 1, own goals 3.
FA Cup (14): Mata 3, Fellaini 2, Lingard 2, Martial 2, Rooney 2 (1 pen), Blind 1, Rashford 1, Smalling 1.
Capital One Cup (3): Andreas Pereira 1, Martial 1, Rooney 1.
UEFA Champions League (20): Hernandez 5 (1 pen), Rooney 4, Depay 3, Martial 3, Ander Herrera 1, Fellaini 1, Mata 1 (pen), Smalling 1, own goal 1.
UEFA Europa League (7): Depay 2, Rashford 2, Ander Herrera 1 (pen), Martial 1 (pen), own goal 1.

Romero S 4	Darmian M 24 + 4	Smalling C 35	Blind D 35	Shaw L 5	Carrick M 22 + 6	Schneiderlin M 25 + 4	Mata J 34 + 4	Depay M 16 + 13	Young A 11 + 7	Rooney W 27 + 1	Schweinsteiger B 13 + 5	Ander Herrera A 17 + 10	Valencia A 8 + 6	Januzaj A 2 + 3	Hernandez J — + 1	Fellaini M 12 + 6	De Gea D 34	Martial A 29 + 2	Rojo M 15 + 1	McNair P 3 + 5	Jones P 6 + 4	Wilson J — + 1	Lingard J 19 + 6	Borthwick-Jackson C 6 + 4	Pereira A — + 4	Varela G 3 + 1	Powell N — + 1	Love D — + 1	Keane W — + 1	Rashford M 11	Fosu-Mensah T 2 + 6	Weir J — + 1	Match No.
1	2^3	3	4	5	6^1	7	8	9^2	10	11	12	13	14																				1
1	2	3	4	5	6^2	7	8	10^3	14	11	12	13		9^1																			2
1	2^3	3	4	5	12	6	8	10	11	7^1			14	9^2		13																	3
1	2	3	4	5	13	6^2	8^1	10	12	11	7	9^3					14																4
	2	3	4	5	6^3	14	8^2	10^1	12	7	9					11	1	13															5
	2^1	3	4		6^2	7	8	10		9	13	12					1	11	5^3	14													6
		3	4^2	5	6^1	7	8	10^3	14	9	12		2				1	11			13												7
	2^2	3	4		6		8^3	10^1	5	9	7	12				13	1	11					14										8
	2		4		13	6	8^1			11		7^2	9^1			14	1	10	5	3	12												9
	14		4			6	8^1			11		7^2	9	2^3		13	1	10	5	3	12												10
	2^1	3	4			6	8^3	12		11		7^2	9			13	1	10	5	14													11
		3	4			6	8					2^1	9^2		7		1	11	5^2	12			10	13									12
		4	5			6	8^3	11	2	7	9^1						1	12	13	3^2		10		14									13
	5	3	4			6		9	12	8	11^1	7					1	10	2														14
	5	3	4		12	6	8	14			7^3					9	1	11	2^2				10			13							15
		4				6		9	10							7^2	1	11	3^1	14			8^1	5	12	2	13						16
		4	5			6		9	10	2		11				12		7^1	1	8	3												17
		4	5			6	8	10^1	2			12				7^2	9	1	11	3			13										18
	5^1	4^3			6	8^2	13	2	11	7	9						1	10		14			12										19
	12	4^5	5		14	6	8	2^2	11	7	9^3						1	10		13	3^1												20
	5	3	4			6	13	12	2	11		9^2				7	1	8					10^1										21
	5	3	4			6	13	14	2^1	11		9^1				7	1	8					8^2	12									22
	2^2	3	4			6	12					11	9	14		7^1	1	10	13				5	8^3									23
	2	3	4		7		9^2	12		11		13				6^2	1	10^1					8	5	14								24
	2	3	4		7	12	9^3	13		11		14				6^1	1	10					8^2	5									25
	2^1	3	4		7	6^2	9	13		11						1	10						8^2	5					12	14			26
		4			3	6	9	10				8^3		13		1		5^1		7				2					11^2	12	14		27
	12		4			7	9^3	10				6^2				1	8	5^1	14	13			2						11	3			28
	2^3	3	4		6	12	8^1	13				9^1				1	10	5^1		7									11^2	14			29
	2^3	3	4		6	9	7^2			13		12				1	10	5^1		8									11	14			30
	2	3	4^3		6^2	9	7			13	14					1	10	5^1		8									11	12			31
	13	3	4		7	6	8^3	14	12			9^1				1	10	5		9									11^1	2^2			32
		3	4		6	7^3	10		9^1		2					8	1	13	5		12									11^2	14		33
	5	3	4		6	8	12		9^3	13	2					14	1	10					7^2						11^1			34
		3	4		6		12	14	9	13	2					8^2	1	10	5				7^1						11^3			35
	5^1	3			6^3	13	7	10		11	8	2				1		4					9^2	12					14			36
		3	4		12	6^1	7		9			8^2	2^3	14		1	10	5					13							11			37
		3	4		6		8^1	13	14	9	12		2			1	10^3						7	5						11^2			38

FA Cup

Third Round	Sheffield U	(h)	1-0
Fourth Round	Derby Co	(a)	3-1
Fifth Round	Shrewsbury T	(a)	3-0
Sixth Round	West Ham U	(h)	1-1
Replay	West Ham U	(a)	2-1
Semi-Final	Everton	(Wembley)	2-1
Final	Crystal Palace	(Wembley)	2-1
(aet)			

Capital One Cup

Third Round	Ipswich T	(h)	3-0
Fourth Round	Middlesbrough	(h)	0-0
(aet; Middlesbrough won 3-1 on penalties)			

UEFA Champions League

Play-Off 1st leg	Club Brugge	(h)	3-1
Play-Off 2nd leg	Club Brugge	(a)	4-0
(Manchester U won 7-1 on aggregate)			
Group B	PSV Eindhoven	(a)	1-2
Group B	Wolfsburg	(h)	2-1
Group B	CSKA Moscow	(a)	1-1
Group B	CSKA Moscow	(h)	1-0
Group B	PSV Eindhoven	(h)	0-0
Group B	Wolfsburg	(a)	2-3

UEFA Europa League

Round of 32 1st leg	Midtjylland	(a)	1-2
Round of 32 2nd leg	Midtjylland	(h)	5-1
(Manchester U won 6-3 on aggregate)			
Round of 16 1st leg	Liverpool	(a)	0-2
Round of 16 2nd leg	Liverpool	(h)	1-1
(Liverpool won 3-1 on aggregate)			

MANSFIELD TOWN

FOUNDATION

The club was formed as Mansfield Wesleyans in 1897, and changed their name to Mansfield Wesley in 1906 and Mansfield Town in 1910. This was after the Mansfield Wesleyan Chapel trustees had requested that the club change its name as 'it has no longer had any connection with either the chapel or school'. The new club participated in the Notts and Derby District League, but in the following season 1911–12 joined the Central Alliance.

One Call Stadium, Quarry Lane, Mansfield, Nottinghamshire NG18 5DA.

Telephone: (01623) 482 482.

Fax: (01623) 482 495.

Ticket Office: (01623) 482 482.

Website: www.mansfieldtown.net

Email: info@mansfieldtown.net

Ground Capacity: 9,186.

Record Attendance: 24,467 v Nottingham F, FA Cup 3rd rd, 10 January 1953.

Pitch Measurements: 100.5m × 64m (110yd × 70yd).

Chairman: John Radford.

Chief Executive: Carolyn Radford.

Manager: Adam Murray.

First-Team Coach: Richard Cooper.

Physio: Dan Kent.

Colours: Yellow shirts with blue stripe and trim, blue shorts, blue socks.

Year Formed: 1897.

Turned Professional: 1906.

Ltd Co.: 1922.

Previous Name: 1897, Mansfield Wesleyans; 1906, Mansfield Wesley; 1910, Mansfield Town.

Grounds: 1897–99, Westfield Lane; 1899–1901, Ratcliffe Gate; 1901–12, Newgate Lane; 1912–16, Ratcliffe Gate; 1916, Field Mill (renamed One Call Stadium 2012).

Club Nickname: 'The Stags'.

First Football League Game: 29 August 1931, Division 3 (S), v Swindon T (h) W 3–2 – Wilson; Clifford, England; Wake, Davis, Blackburn; Gilhespy, Readman (1), Johnson, Broom (2), Baxter.

Record League Victory: 9–2 v Rotherham U, Division 3 (N), 27 December 1932 – Wilson; Anthony, England; Davies, S. Robinson, Slack; Prior, Broom, Readman (3), Hoyland (3), Bowater (3).

Record Cup Victory: 8–0 v Scarborough (a), FA Cup 1st rd, 22 November 1952 – Bramley; Chessell, Bradley; Field, Plummer, Lewis; Scott, Fox (3), Marron (2), Sid Watson (1), Adam (2).

Record Defeat: 1–8 v Walsall, Division 3 (N), 19 January 1933.

HONOURS

League Champions: Division 3 – 1976–77; Division 4 – 1974–75; Conference – 2012–13.
Runners-up: Division 3N – 1950–51, Third Division – (3rd) 2001–02 *(promoted to Second Division).*
FA Cup: 6th rd – 1969.
League Cup: 5th rd – 1976.
League Trophy Winners: 1987.

sky SPORTS FACT FILE

Mansfield Wesley opted for a change of name at their annual general meeting in June 1910. Two new names were suggested and Mansfield Town was selected in preference to Mansfield United. The first competitive game under the new title produced a 2-2 draw away to Sutton Junction in a Notts & Derbyshire League match.

Most League Points (2 for a win): 68, Division 4, 1974–75.

Most League Points (3 for a win): 81, Division 4, 1985–86.

Most League Goals: 108, Division 4, 1962–63.

Highest League Scorer in Season: Ted Harston, 55, Division 3 (N), 1936–37.

Most League Goals in Total Aggregate: Harry Johnson, 104, 1931–36.

Most League Goals in One Match: 7, Ted Harston v Hartlepools U, Division 3N, 23 January 1937.

Most Capped Player: John McClelland, 6 (53), Northern Ireland; Reggie Lambe, 6 (21), Bermuda.

Most League Appearances: Rod Arnold, 440, 1970–83.

Youngest League Player: Cyril Poole, 15 years 351 days v New Brighton, 27 February 1937.

Record Transfer Fee Received: £175,000 from Sunderland for Liam Lawrence, June 2004.

Record Transfer Fee Paid: £150,000 to Carlisle U for Lee Peacock, October 1997.

Football League Record: 1931 Elected to Division 3 (S); 1932–37 Division 3 (N); 1937–47 Division 3 (S); 1947–58 Division 3 (N); 1958–60 Division 3; 1960–63 Division 4; 1963–72 Division 3; 1972–75 Division 4; 1975–77 Division 3; 1977–78 Division 2; 1978–80 Division 3; 1980–86 Division 4; 1986–91 Division 3; 1991–92 Division 4; 1992–93 Division 2; 1993–2002 Division 3; 2002–03 Division 2; 2003–04 Division 3; 2004–08 FL 2; 2008–13 Conference Premier; 2013– FL 2.

LATEST SEQUENCES

Longest Sequence of League Wins: 7, 13.9.1991 – 26.10.1991.

Longest Sequence of League Defeats: 7, 18.1.1947 – 15.3.1947.

Longest Sequence of League Draws: 5, 18.10.1986 – 22.11.1986.

Longest Sequence of Unbeaten League Matches: 20, 14.2.1976 – 21.8.1976.

Longest Sequence Without a League Win: 14, 25.3.2000 – 2.9.2000.

Successive Scoring Runs: 27 from 1.10.1962.

Successive Non-scoring Runs: 8 from 25.3.2000.

MANAGERS

John Baynes 1922–25
Ted Davison 1926–28
Jack Hickling 1928–33
Henry Martin 1933–35
Charlie Bell 1935
Harold Wightman 1936
Harold Parkes 1936–38
Jack Poole 1938–44
Lloyd Barke 1944–45
Roy Goodall 1945–49
Freddie Steele 1949–51
George Jobey 1952–53
Stan Mercer 1953–55
Charlie Mitten 1956–58
Sam Weaver 1958–60
Raich Carter 1960–63
Tommy Cummings 1963–67
Tommy Eggleston 1967–70
Jock Basford 1970–71
Danny Williams 1971–74
Dave Smith 1974–76
Peter Morris 1976–78
Billy Bingham 1978–79
Mick Jones 1979–81
Stuart Boam 1981–83
Ian Greaves 1983–89
George Foster 1989–93
Andy King 1993–96
Steve Parkin 1996–99
Billy Dearden 1999–2002
Stuart Watkiss 2002
Keith Curle 2002–04
Carlton Palmer 2004–05
Peter Shirtliff 2005–06
Billy Dearden 2006–08
Paul Holland 2008
Billy McEwan 2008
David Holdsworth 2008–10
Duncan Russell 2010–11
Paul Cox 2011–14
Adam Murray December 2014–

TEN YEAR LEAGUE RECORD

		P	W	D	L	F	A	Pts	Pos
2006-07	FL 2	46	14	12	20	58	63	54	17
2007-08	FL 2	46	11	9	26	48	68	42	23
2008-09	Conf P	46	19	9	18	57	55	62	12
2009-10	Conf P	44	17	11	16	69	60	62	9
2010-11	Conf P	46	17	10	19	73	75	61	13
2011-12	Conf P	46	25	14	7	87	48	89	3
2012-13	Conf P	46	30	5	11	92	52	95	1
2013-14	FL 2	46	15	15	16	49	58	60	11
2014-15	FL 2	46	13	9	24	38	62	48	21
2015-16	FL 2	46	17	13	16	61	53	64	12

DID YOU KNOW ?

Inside-forward Ian Hall made 145 Football League appearances for Mansfield Town between 1962 and 1968. He was also a talented cricketer who played in 270 First Class matches for Derbyshire (1959–72), scoring over 1,000 runs in a season on five occasions.

MANSFIELD TOWN – FOOTBALL LEAGUE TWO 2015–16 LEAGUE RECORD

Match No.	Date	Venue	Opponents	Result		H/T Score	Lg Pos.	Goalscorers	Atten- dance
1	Aug 8	H	Carlisle U	D	1-1	1-1	10	Benning [29]	4146
2	14	A	Notts Co	W	2-0	1-0	1	Clements [36], Tafazolli [80]	10,074
3	18	A	Accrington S	L	0-1	0-1	11		1073
4	22	H	Oxford U	D	1-1	1-0	12	Westcarr [3]	3112
5	29	A	York C	W	2-1	2-1	8	Green 2 [13, 30]	3215
6	Sept 5	H	AFC Wimbledon	D	1-1	1-1	8	Clements [15]	3042
7	12	H	Crawley T	W	4-0	1-0	7	Thomas, N [44], Rose [47], Green [71], Westcarr [72]	2524
8	19	A	Luton T	L	0-1	0-0	11		7939
9	26	H	Plymouth Arg	D	0-0	0-0	9		3185
10	29	A	Stevenage	W	2-0	0-0	7	Tafazolli [47], Thomas, J [51]	2509
11	Oct 3	A	Dagenham & R	W	4-3	2-3	6	Benning [6], Green (pen) [37], Pearce [81], Yussuf [85]	1597
12	10	H	Newport Co	W	3-0	0-0	4	Westcarr [50], Benning [70], Yussuf [90]	3278
13	17	H	Bristol R	L	1-2	0-1	4	Tafazolli [81]	4196
14	20	A	Yeovil T	W	1-0	0-0	4	Lambe [90]	2954
15	24	A	Portsmouth	D	0-0	0-0	5		16,210
16	31	H	Wycombe W	L	0-2	0-1	6		3165
17	Nov 14	A	Northampton T	L	0-1	0-1	6		5454
18	21	H	Hartlepool U	W	3-1	1-1	6	Green 2 [24, 81], Yussuf [57]	3031
19	24	H	Exeter C	L	0-2	0-2	8		2435
20	28	A	Barnet	W	3-1	1-0	7	Lambe [31], Green [60], Gambin (og) [88]	1775
21	Dec 12	H	Leyton Orient	D	1-1	1-1	7	Lambe [40]	2935
22	19	A	Cambridge U	D	1-1	1-1	8	Chapman [23]	4589
23	28	H	York C	D	1-1	1-1	11	Pearce [31]	3958
24	Jan 2	H	Accrington S	L	2-3	1-1	12	Green [27], Clements [88]	3271
25	9	H	Stevenage	W	2-1	1-0	8	Clements [42], Baxendale [65]	3126
26	16	A	AFC Wimbledon	L	1-3	1-0	9	Green [11]	4089
27	23	H	Luton T	L	0-2	0-1	11		4245
28	26	A	Morecambe	W	2-1	0-0	9	Clements [86], Yussuf [90]	1047
29	30	A	Crawley T	W	1-0	0-0	7	Beardsley [60]	1981
30	Feb 6	H	Morecambe	W	2-1	2-1	5	Blair [15], Pearce [24]	3090
31	9	A	Oxford U	D	2-2	1-1	4	Green [22], Thomas, J [89]	5346
32	13	A	Plymouth Arg	L	0-3	0-2	7		7494
33	20	H	Dagenham & R	W	3-2	0-1	5	Blair [53], Yussuf [67], Green [84]	2822
34	27	A	Newport Co	L	0-1	0-0	9		2361
35	Mar 5	H	Yeovil T	L	0-1	0-0	10		2713
36	12	A	Bristol R	L	0-1	0-0	11		7847
37	19	H	Portsmouth	D	1-1	1-1	13	Green [26]	3980
38	25	A	Wycombe W	L	0-1	0-0	14		5003
39	28	H	Northampton T	D	2-2	2-0	13	Green 2 [12, 16]	4367
40	Apr 2	A	Hartlepool U	L	1-2	0-1	13	Daniel [76]	3893
41	9	A	Carlisle U	W	2-1	1-0	13	Daniel [21], Lambe [62]	4426
42	16	H	Notts Co	W	5-0	1-0	13	Green 2 [6, 60], Chapman [57], Lambe [67], Rose [83]	6357
43	19	A	Exeter C	W	3-2	1-0	12	Tafazolli 2 [11, 82], Benning [56]	3407
44	23	H	Barnet	D	1-1	1-1	11	Dieseruvwe [30]	2573
45	30	A	Leyton Orient	L	0-1	0-0	13		4257
46	May 7	H	Cambridge U	D	0-0	0-0	12		3548

Final League Position: 12

GOALSCORERS

League (61): Green 16 (1 pen), Clements 5, Lambe 5, Tafazolli 5, Yussuf 5, Benning 4, Pearce 3, Westcarr 3, Blair 2, Chapman 2, Daniel 2, Rose 2, Thomas, J 2, Baxendale 1, Beardsley 1, Dieseruvwe 1, Thomas, N 1, own goal 1.
FA Cup (0).
Capital One Cup (1): Tafazolli 1.
Johnstone's Paint Trophy (1): Westcarr 1 (pen).

Shearer S 21	Hunt N 19	Pearce K 36 + 2	Tafazolli R 44	Benning M 30 + 1	Rose M 26 + 8	Clements C 32 + 6	Chapman A 36 + 1	Lambe R 30 + 7	Green M 44	Thomas N 9 + 8	Yussuf A — + 26	Westcarr C 21 + 3	Thomas J 15 + 18	Jensen B 25	Beardsley C 6 + 8	McGuire J 15 + 5	Collins L 29 + 6	Blair M 20 + 12	Adams B 13	Baxendale J 11 + 4	Kavanagh S 2 + 5	Alfei D 8 + 4	Daniel C 5 + 4	Dieseruvwe E 9 + 1	Hakeem Z — + 1	Match No.
1	2	3	4	5	6²	7	8	9¹	10	11³	12	13	14													1
	2	3	4	5	9³	8	6	10	11¹	7²			12		13	14										2
	2	3	4	5	6	8	7²	9¹		10¹	12	14	13	1	11											3
2²		3	4	5	8³	6	7	11¹	10	13		9	12	1		14										4
	2	3	4	5	6³	8	7	9²	10			11¹	12	1	14	13										5
	2	3	4	5	8²	6	7	9	10	12		11¹	14	1	13											6
	2	4	3¹	5	6²	8	7	12	10	9	14	11³		1		13										7
	2	4	3	5	6²	8¹	7	13	11	9¹	14	10	12	1												8
		4	3	5	6		7	13	10	9²	12	11³	8¹	1		2	14									9
		4	3	5	2		6	7	10¹	11²	8		1	13	9	12										10
	2	4	3	5	8	9	11³	13	12	6¹	10²		1	7	14											11
	2	3	4	5	12	13	8	9³	10¹		14	11	7²	1	6											12
2ª	3ª	4	5		13	7	11²	10	14	12	9	8³	1	6¹												13
		4		2	14	7²	11	10		13	9¹	8³	1	6	3	12	5									14
7		4		2	6	8	11²	10³	13	14	9¹		1	3	12	5										15
2		4		13	6	10¹	11	14	12	9		1	7³	3	8²	5										16
2	14	4	6¹	7	8	9³	11	13	10²		1	3	12	5												17
	3	4	2	7	6	10¹	11	9²	12	8³		1	13	14	5											18
	3	4	2	13	6	8¹	11	10¹	12	9		1	7²	14	5											19
	3	4	6¹	7ª	8	9	11³	10²		1	14	13	2	12	5											20
	3	4	6	7	9	10	11¹		1	8	2	12	5													21
	4	3	6	9	8	10	11	12	13		1	2	7²	5												22
	3		2	7	6	10	11	12	13	9¹		1	4	8²	5											23
	4		5	7	6	8	11²	10³	14	13	9		1	3	12	2										24
2	3	4		13	6	7	12	11		8¹	9²	1			14	5	10³									25
2	3	4		12	7	6²	9	11		10³	14	1	13		5	8¹										26
1	2	4	3	10²	7	6³	8¹	11		13	14	12		9	5											27
1	2	3	4		7		11	12		14	10²	8³	5	6¹	9	13										28
1		3	2	5²	13	8	11ª		12	10¹	6	4	9	7ª	14											29
1		3	4	5	7	13		8¹	12	10²	11	2	6	9												30
1		3	4	5	7	11¹	10		14	12	8	2	6²	9³		13										31
1		3	4	5	8		11	13	14	10¹	6	2	9²	7³	12											32
1		2ª	4	9	7	6	13	10¹	12	11²	3	8	5													33
1		4	5	13	8	10	12	7	3	6¹	11²	14	2	9³												34
1		4	5	6	7²	11	10	12	14	3	9³	13	2	8¹												35
1		4	5	6	7²	8	9¹	10	14	13	6	12	2	11¹												36
1		3	4	5	7²	8	10¹	13	6	12	9³	2	14	11												37
1		4	3	5²	7³	8	11	14	6	9¹	13	2	12	10												38
1		4	3¹	5	14	8	13	11	7	2ª	6	9²	12	10³												39
1		3ª	4		6¹	7	11	9	14	2	8	12²	13	10²												40
1		4	12	13	7	6	11	8³	14	3	9	2	5²	10¹												41
1		4	2	12	7	11	3	10¹	5	8	13	9	6¹													42
1		4	5	8²	6	10	11¹	9³	13	3	7	12	2	14												43
1	12	3	5	7	13	10	8	4	9	6³	2²	11¹														44
1	3	4	5	7³	12	8	6¹	10	14	2	9	13	11²													45
1	3	4³	5	6	8	7	11¹	14	2	9	12	10²	13													46

FA Cup
First Round — Oldham Ath — (h) — 0-0
Replay — Oldham Ath — (a) — 0-2

Capital One Cup
First Round — Sheffield W — (a) — 1-4

Johnstone's Paint Trophy
First Round — Notts Co — (a) — 1-3

MIDDLESBROUGH

FOUNDATION

A previous belief that Middlesbrough Football Club was founded at a tripe supper at the Corporation Hotel has proved to be erroneous. In fact, members of Middlesbrough Cricket Club were responsible for forming it at a meeting in the gymnasium of the Albert Park Hotel in 1875.

Riverside Stadium, Middlesbrough TS3 6RS.

Telephone: (0844) 499 6789.

Fax: (01642) 757 697.

Ticket Office: (0844) 499 1234.

Website: www.mfc.co.uk

Email: enquiries@mfc.co.uk

Ground Capacity: 34,773.

Record Attendance: 53,536 v Newcastle U, Division 1, 27 December 1949 (at Ayresome Park); 34,814 v Newcastle U, FA Premier League, 5 March 2003 (at Riverside Stadium); 35,000, England v Slovakia, Euro 2004 qualifier, 11 June 2003.

Pitch Measurements: 105m × 68m (115yd × 74.5yd).

Chairman: Steve Gibson.

Chief Executive: Neil Bausor.

Head Coach: Aitor Karanka.

Assistant Head Coach: Steve Agnew.

Physio: Chris Moseley.

HONOURS

League Champions: First Division – 1994–95; Division 2 – 1926–27, 1928–29, 1973–74.
Runners-up: FL C – 2015–16; First Division – 1997–98; Division 2 – 1901–02, 1991–92; Division 3 – 1966–67, 1986–87.

FA Cup: Runners-up: 1997.

League Cup Winners: 2004.
Runners-up: 1997, 1998.

Amateur Cup Winners: 1895, 1898.

Anglo-Scottish Cup Winners: 1976.

Full Members' Cup: Runners-up: 1990.

European Competitions
UEFA Cup: 2004–05, 2005–06 *(runners-up).*

Colours: Red shirts with white trim, red shorts with white trim, red socks with white trim.

Year Formed: 1876; re-formed 1986.

Turned Professional: 1889; became amateur 1892, and professional again, 1899.

Club Nickname: 'Boro'.

Grounds: 1877, Old Archery Ground, Albert Park; 1879, Breckon Hill; 1882, Linthorpe Road Ground; 1903, Ayresome Park; 1995, Riverside Stadium.

First Football League Game: 2 September 1899, Division 2, v Lincoln C (a) L 0–3 – Smith; Shaw, Ramsey; Allport, McNally, McCracken; Wanless, Longstaffe, Gettins, Page, Pugh.

Record League Victory: 9–0 v Brighton & HA, Division 2, 23 August 1958 – Taylor; Bilcliff, Robinson; Harris (2p), Phillips, Walley; Day, McLean, Clough (5), Peacock (2), Holliday.

Record Cup Victory: 7–0 v Hereford U, Coca-Cola Cup 2nd rd, 1st leg, 18 September 1996 – Miller; Fleming (1), Branco (1), Whyte, Vickers, Whelan, Emerson (1), Mustoe, Stamp, Juninho, Ravanelli (4).

sky SPORTS FACT FILE

After a poor performance against Stockton in March 1893, the Middlesbrough directors proposed a cut in wages for the players. The players responded by calling a strike and the Boro line-up for the following game against Royal Arsenal included six amateurs. Shortly afterwards the club decided to revert to amateur status.

Record Defeat: 0–9 v Blackburn R, Division 2, 6 November 1954.

Most League Points (2 for a win): 65, Division 2, 1973–74.

Most League Points (3 for a win): 94, Division 3, 1986–87.

Most League Goals: 122, Division 2, 1926–27.

Highest League Scorer in Season: George Camsell, 59, Division 2, 1926–27 (Second Division record).

Most League Goals in Total Aggregate: George Camsell, 325, 1925–39.

Most League Goals in One Match: 5, John Wilkie v Gainsborough T, Division 2, 2 March 1901; 5, Andy Wilson v Nottingham F, Division 1, 6 October 1923; 5, George Camsell v Manchester C, Division 2, 25 December 1926; 5, George Camsell v Aston Villa, Division 1, 9 September 1935; 5, Brian Clough v Brighton & HA, Division 2, 22 August 1958.

Most Capped Player: Mark Schwarzer, 52, Australia.

Most League Appearances: Tim Williamson, 563, 1902–23.

Youngest League Player: Luke Williams, 16 years 200 days v Barnsley, 18 December 2009.

Record Transfer Fee Received: £12,000,000 from Atletico Madrid for Juninho, July 1997; £12,000,000 from Aston Villa for Stewart Downing, July 2009.

Record Transfer Fee Paid: £12,000,000 to Heerenveen for Afonso Alves, January 2008; £12,000,000 to Atalanta for Marten de Roon, July 2106.

Football League Record: 1899 Elected to Division 2; 1902–24 Division 1; 1924–27 Division 2; 1927–28 Division 1; 1928–29 Division 2; 1929–54 Division 1; 1954–66 Division 2; 1966–67 Division 3; 1967–74 Division 2; 1974–82 Division 1; 1982–86 Division 2; 1986–87 Division 3; 1987–88 Division 2; 1988–89 Division 1; 1989–92 Division 2; 1992–93 FA Premier League; 1993–95 Division 1; 1995–97 FA Premier League; 1997–98 Division 1; 1998–2009 FA Premier League; 2009–16 FL C; 2016– FA Premier League.

MANAGERS

John Robson 1899–1905
Alex Mackie 1905–06
Andy Aitken 1906–09
J. Gunter 1908–10
  (Secretary-Manager)
Andy Walker 1910–11
Tom McIntosh 1911–19
Jimmy Howie 1920–23
Herbert Bamlett 1923–26
Peter McWilliam 1927–34
Wilf Gillow 1934–44
David Jack 1944–52
Walter Rowley 1952–54
Bob Dennison 1954–63
Raich Carter 1963–66
Stan Anderson 1966–73
Jack Charlton 1973–77
John Neal 1977–81
Bobby Murdoch 1981–82
Malcolm Allison 1982–84
Willie Maddren 1984–86
Bruce Rioch 1986–90
Colin Todd 1990–91
Lennie Lawrence 1991–94
Bryan Robson 1994–2001
Steve McClaren 2001–06
Gareth Southgate 2006–09
Gordon Strachan 2009–10
Tony Mowbray 2010–13
Aitor Karanka November 2013–

LATEST SEQUENCES

Longest Sequence of League Wins: 9, 16.2.1974 – 6.4.1974.

Longest Sequence of League Defeats: 8, 26.12.1995 – 17.2.1996.

Longest Sequence of League Draws: 8, 3.4.1971 – 1.5.1971.

Longest Sequence of Unbeaten League Matches: 24, 8.9.1973 – 19.1.1974.

Longest Sequence Without a League Win: 19, 3.10.1981 – 6.3.1982.

Successive Scoring Runs: 26 from 21.9.1946.

Successive Non-scoring Runs: 7, 25.1.2014 – 1.3.2014.

TEN YEAR LEAGUE RECORD

		P	W	D	L	F	A	Pts	Pos
2006-07	PR Lge	38	12	10	16	44	49	46	12
2007-08	PR Lge	38	10	12	16	43	53	42	13
2008-09	PR Lge	38	7	11	20	28	57	32	19
2009-10	FL C	46	16	14	16	58	50	62	11
2010-11	FL C	46	17	11	18	68	68	62	12
2011-12	FL C	46	18	16	12	52	51	70	7
2012-13	FL C	46	18	5	23	61	70	59	16
2013-14	FL C	46	16	16	14	62	50	64	12
2014-15	FL C	46	25	10	11	68	37	85	4
2015-16	FL C	46	26	11	9	63	31	89	2

DID YOU KNOW ?

In 1997 Middlesbrough became the first English football club to launch its own dedicated television channel. Boro TV was launched through NTL cable television and continued broadcasting until the summer of 2005. The service was available at homes in the Teesside and Darlington areas.

MIDDLESBROUGH – FL CHAMPIONSHIP 2015–16 LEAGUE RECORD

Match No.	Date	Venue	Opponents		Result	H/T Score	Lg Pos.	Goalscorers	Attendance
1	Aug 9	A	Preston NE	D	0-0	0-0	14		15,974
2	15	H	Bolton W	W	3-0	3-0	2	Fabbrini [7], Garcia 2 [17, 32]	23,333
3	18	A	Derby Co	D	1-1	1-0	4	Garcia [16]	30,855
4	22	H	Bristol C	L	0-1	0-1	8		22,236
5	29	A	Sheffield W	W	3-1	1-0	6	Reach [42], Fabbrini [67], Stuani [86]	20,976
6	Sept 12	H	Milton Keynes D	W	2-0	0-0	3	Downing [70], Nugent [81]	21,448
7	15	H	Brentford	W	3-1	1-0	2	Stuani 2 [35, 69], Adomah [77]	20,138
8	19	A	Nottingham F	W	2-1	2-1	2	Nugent [3], Ayala [32]	20,993
9	27	H	Leeds U	W	3-0	2-0	2	Nugent [3], Bellusci (og) [32], Fabbrini [81]	27,694
10	Oct 3	A	Reading	L	0-2	0-1	2		19,516
11	17	H	Fulham	D	0-0	0-0	2		22,498
12	20	A	Cardiff C	L	0-1	0-0	6		13,371
13	24	A	Wolverhampton W	W	3-1	0-1	4	Fabbrini [71], Leadbitter (pen) [82], Downing [90]	22,006
14	31	H	Charlton Ath	W	3-0	0-0	4	Nugent [60], Adomah [66], Ayala [78]	20,943
15	Nov 3	H	Rotherham U	W	1-0	1-0	4	Downing [16]	21,144
16	7	A	Hull C	L	0-3	0-1	4		20,352
17	20	H	QPR	W	1-0	0-0	3	Leadbitter (pen) [90]	20,299
18	28	A	Huddersfield T	W	2-0	1-0	2	Clayton [9], Nsue [84]	15,434
19	Dec 4	A	Ipswich T	W	2-0	0-0	1	Stuani [54], Nugent [74]	17,662
20	12	H	Birmingham C	D	0-0	0-0	2		20,929
21	15	H	Burnley	W	1-0	0-0	1	Nsue [54]	19,966
22	19	A	Brighton & HA	W	3-0	2-0	1	Garcia [4], Adomah [44], Stuani [62]	26,445
23	28	H	Sheffield W	W	1-0	1-0	1	Stuani [1]	29,363
24	Jan 2	H	Derby Co	W	2-0	0-0	1	Adomah [83], Friend [84]	32,870
25	12	A	Brentford	W	1-0	0-0	1	Ayala [59]	10,312
26	16	A	Bristol C	L	0-1	0-0	1		15,670
27	23	H	Nottingham F	L	0-1	0-0	2		24,975
28	Feb 6	H	Blackburn R	D	1-1	0-0	2	Nugent [79]	26,244
29	9	A	Milton Keynes D	D	1-1	0-1	1	Rhodes [90]	11,256
30	15	A	Leeds U	D	0-0	0-0	2		20,424
31	23	H	Cardiff C	W	3-1	1-1	3	Connolly (og) [25], Ramirez [63], Nugent [83]	24,322
32	27	A	Fulham	W	2-0	2-0	3	Adomah [3], Leadbitter (pen) [20]	18,862
33	Mar 1	A	Blackburn R	L	1-2	0-0	3	Forshaw [90]	16,601
34	4	H	Wolverhampton W	W	2-1	1-0	1	Ramirez 2 [24, 56]	22,110
35	8	A	Rotherham U	L	0-1	0-0	2		10,783
36	13	A	Charlton Ath	L	0-2	0-0	2		14,636
37	18	H	Hull C	W	1-0	0-0	2	Nugent [90]	26,791
38	Apr 1	A	QPR	W	3-2	1-1	2	Rhodes [18], Ramirez [51], Gibson [57]	16,058
39	5	H	Huddersfield T	W	3-0	2-0	2	Leadbitter (pen) [32], Ramirez 2 [33, 77]	24,669
40	9	H	Preston NE	W	1-0	1-0	2	Adomah [32]	26,390
41	12	A	Reading	W	2-1	1-0	1	Nsue [10], Forshaw [90]	23,746
42	16	A	Bolton W	W	2-1	0-0	1	Rhodes 2 [73, 90]	18,196
43	19	A	Burnley	D	1-1	0-0	1	Rhodes [70]	20,197
44	23	H	Ipswich T	W	0-0	0-0	2		30,505
45	29	A	Birmingham C	D	2-2	1-1	1	Rhodes [40], Ramirez [57]	21,380
46	May 7	H	Brighton & HA	D	1-1	1-0	2	Stuani [19]	33,806

Final League Position: 2

GOALSCORERS

League (63): Nugent 8, Ramirez 7, Stuani 7, Adomah 6, Rhodes 6, Fabbrini 4, Garcia 4, Leadbitter 4 (4 pens), Ayala 3, Downing 3, Nsue 3, Forshaw 2, Clayton 1, Friend 1, Gibson 1, Reach 1, own goals 2.
FA Cup (1): Fabbrini 1.
Capital One Cup (8): Stuani 4, Adomah 2, Fabbrini 1, Wildschut 1.

Konstantopoulos D 46	Kalas T 19 + 7	Ayala D 34 + 1	Fry D 7	Friend G 39 + 1	Clayton A 41 + 2	Leadbitter G 39 + 2	Adomah A 36 + 7	Downing S 40 + 5	Reach A 3 + 1	Garcia E 10 + 9	Fabbrini D 14 + 8	Stuani C 20 + 16	Forshaw A 9 + 20	Nsue E 37 + 3	Nugent D 24 + 14	Gibson B 32 + 1	Wildschut Y 1	Amorebieta F 11 + 2	De Pena C 3 + 3	Zuculini B 3 + 2	Stephens J — + 1	De Laet R 9 + 1	Kike Sola C 1 + 1	Rhodes J 13 + 5	Ramirez G 15 + 3	De Sart J — + 2	Match No.
1	2	3	4	5	6	7^1	8	9	10^2	11^3	12	13	14														1
1	3	4		5	6	7	8^3	10		11^1	9^2	12	13	2	14												2
1	2	3		5	6	7	8	10^3	12	11^1	9^2	13	14			4											3
1	4	3		5	6	7	13	9		14	12	8^2		2^5		10^1											4
1		3		5	6	7		8^3	10	11^1	9^2	13	14	2	12	4											5
1	2	3		5	6	7		8	10^2		9^3	13	14	11	4^1		12										6
1		3		5	6	7	12	10		14	9^2	8^1	13	2	11^1	4											7
1		3		5	6	7	8^1	10		13	12	9^1	14	2	11^3	4											8
1	2	3		5	6	7	10^3	9			12	8^2	14	13	11	4											9
1	2^2	3		5	6	7	14	10		11	9^5	8		13		4	12										10
1	2	3		5	6	7	12	8		13	9^2			11	4		10^1										11
1	2	3		5	6	7^1	8^2	10		14	9^9		12	13	11	4											12
1	2^1	3		5	6	7	13^3	12		9		8	11	14		4	10^2										13
1		3^1			6		8	10^3		14	9^2		2	11	4	5	13	7	12								14
1	3			5	6	7^2	8	9		13			2	11	4	10^1	12										15
1	2	3		5	6^1	13	8	10		12	9		11^2	4	7												16
1		3		5	6	7	8^2	10		13	9^1	12	2	11	4												17
1		3		5	6		8^1	10			9^2	13	12	2	11	4	7										18
1		3		5	6	7	10	9			8^1	12	2	11	4												19
1		3		5	6	7	10^1	9		13	8^2	12	2	11^4	4												20
1	2	3		5	6	12	14	10		11^1	9^2	13	7^3	8	4												21
1	13	3		5	6^3	7	10	9		11^2	12	8		2^1	4			14									22
1	13	3		5	6	7	10^1	9		11^2	12	8		2^2	4	14											23
1		3		5	6	7	10	9		11^1		8		2	12	4											24
1		3		5	6	7	10^1	9			8	12	2	11	4												25
1		3		5	6^1	7	10	9		11^2		8	13	2	12	4											26
1	12	3		5^3	6	7	10	9^2		14		8	13	2	11	4											27
1	12	3^1			6	7	8^2	10			13		2	11	4						5	9^3	14				28
1	3				7		10				8^1	6^3	2	11	4		12				5	14	13	9^2			29
1	14	3			6	7	12	10			8^3		2	13	4^1						5		11^2	9^1			30
1	3		4	5		7^2	8	10			13	6	2	12									11^1	9^3	14		31
1		3	14			7	8	10^3			12	6	2	11^1	4						5		13	9^2			32
1		3	5	12		7^1	8	10^3			14	6		9^2	4						2		11	13			33
1	3			5	6		10				8	7	2		4								11	9^1	12		34
1		3	5	7			10	12			8^1	6	2	11^2	4								13	9			35
1		3	5	6	7	8	10^2				13		2	12	4								11^1	9			36
1	3			5	6	7	10	12			8^1	14	2	13	4								11^2	9^1			37
1	3	14		5	6	7	8	10^1				12	2	13	4								11^2	9^3			38
1	3			5	6^2	7	8	10			14	12	2	13	4								11^1	9^3			39
1		3		5	13	7	10	12			8^1	6	2	11	4									9^1			40
1		3		5	6	7^2	10	9			12	8^1	14	4									2	11^3	13		41
1	14	3		5	6		10	9^2			7	8^1	13	4									2	11^3	12		42
1	14	3		5^2	6	7	8	10^1			13	2		4									12	11	9^3		43
1		3			6	7	8	10^2			12		2	13	4								5	11	9^1		44
1		3			6	7	8	10^2			12		2	13	4								5	11^1	9		45
1		3		5	6	7	10	12			8		2	11^1	4									13	9^2		46

FA Cup

Third Round	Burnley	(h)	1-2

Capital One Cup

First Round	Oldham Ath	(a)	3-1
Second Round *(aet)*	Burton Alb	(a)	2-1
Third Round	Wolverhampton W	(h)	3-0
Fourth Round *(aet; Middlesbrough won 3-1 on penalties)*	Manchester U	(a)	0-0
Quarter-Final	Everton	(h)	0-2

MILLWALL

FOUNDATION

Formed in 1885 as Millwall Rovers by employees of Morton & Co, a jam and marmalade factory in West Ferry Road. The founders were predominantly Scotsmen. Their first headquarters was The Islanders pub in Tooke Street, Millwall. Their first trophy was the East End Cup in 1887.

The Den, Zampa Road, London SE16 3LN.
Telephone: (020) 7232 1222. *Fax:* (020) 7231 3663.
Ticket Office: (0844) 826 2004.
Website: www.millwallfc.co.uk
Email: questions@millwallplc.com
Ground Capacity: 19,734.
Record Attendance: 48,672 v Derby Co, FA Cup 5th rd, 20 February 1937 (at The Den, Cold Blow Lane); 20,093 v Arsenal, FA Cup 3rd rd, 10 January 1994 (at The Den, Bermondsey).
Pitch Measurements: 106m × 68m (116yd × 74.5yd).
Chairman: John G. Berylson.
Chief Executive: Andy Ambler.
Manager: Neil Harris.
Assistant Manager: Dave Livermore.
Physio: Bobby Bacic.
Colours: Blue shirts with white sleeves, white shorts with blue trim, blue socks with white hoops.
Year Formed: 1885.
Turned Professional: 1893.
Previous Names: 1885, Millwall Rovers; 1889, Millwall Athletic; 1899, Millwall; 1985, Millwall Football & Athletic Company.
Club Nickname: 'The Lions'.
Grounds: 1885, Glengall Road, Millwall; 1886, Back of 'Lord Nelson'; 1890, East Ferry Road; 1901, North Greenwich; 1910, The Den, Cold Blow Lane; 1993, The Den, Bermondsey.
First Football League Game: 28 August 1920, Division 3, v Bristol R (h) W 2–0 – Lansdale; Fort, Hodge; Voisey (1), Riddell, McAlpine; Waterall, Travers, Broad (1), Sutherland, Dempsey.
Record League Victory: 9–1 v Torquay U, Division 3 (S), 29 August 1927 – Lansdale, Tilling, Hill, Amos, Bryant (3), Graham, Chance, Hawkins (3), Landells (1), Phillips (2), Black. 9–1 v Coventry C, Division 3 (S), 19 November 1927 – Lansdale, Fort, Hill, Amos, Collins (1), Graham, Chance, Landells (4), Cock (2), Phillips (2), Black.
Record Cup Victory: 7–0 v Gateshead, FA Cup 2nd rd, 12 December 1936 – Yuill; Ted Smith, Inns; Brolly, Hancock, Forsyth; Thomas (1), Mangnall (1), Ken Burditt (2), McCartney (2), Thorogood (1).
Record Defeat: 1–9 v Aston Villa, FA Cup 4th rd, 28 January 1946.
Most League Points (2 for a win): 65, Division 3 (S), 1927–28 and Division 3, 1965–66.
Most League Points (3 for a win): 93, Division 2, 2000–01.

HONOURS

League Champions: Division 2 – 1987–88; Second Division – 2000–01; Division 3S – 1927–28, 1937–38; Division 4 – 1961–62.
Runners-up: Division 3 – 1965–66, 1984–85; Division 3S – 1952–53; Division 4 – 1964–65.
FA Cup: Runners-up: 2004.
League Cup: 5th rd – 1974, 1977, 1995.
League Trophy: Runners-up: 1999.
European Competitions
UEFA Cup: 2004–05.

sky **SPORTS** FACT FILE

Bob Hunter was one of the key figures in the early history of Millwall. Previously trainer of Montrose, he joined Millwall as trainer around 1897 and then served as manager from 1919 until his death in March 1933. As trainer he helped the team reach two FA Cup semi-finals, while as manager he won the Division Three South title in 1927–28.

Most League Goals: 127, Division 3 (S), 1927–28.

Highest League Scorer in Season: Richard Parker, 37, Division 3 (S), 1926–27.

Most League Goals in Total Aggregate: Neil Harris, 124, 1995–2004; 2006–11.

Most League Goals in One Match: 5, Richard Parker v Norwich C, Division 3 (S), 28 August 1926.

Most Capped Player: David Forde, 24, Republic of Ireland.

Most League Appearances: Barry Kitchener, 523, 1967–82.

Youngest League Player: Moses Ashikodi, 15 years 240 days v Brighton & HA, 22 February 2003.

Record Transfer Fee Received: £2,800,000 from Norwich C for Steve Morison, June 2011.

Record Transfer Fee Paid: £800,000 to Derby Co for Paul Goddard, December 1989.

Football League Record: 1920 Original Members of Division 3; 1921 Division 3 (S); 1928–34 Division 2; 1934–38 Division 3 (S); 1938–48 Division 2; 1948–58 Division 3 (S); 1958–62 Division 4; 1962–64 Division 3; 1964–65 Division 4; 1965–66 Division 3; 1966–75 Division 2; 1975–76 Division 3; 1976–79 Division 2; 1979–85 Division 3; 1985–88 Division 2; 1988–90 Division 1; 1990–92 Division 2; 1992–96 Division 1; 1996–2001 Division 2; 2001–04 Division 1; 2004–06 FL C; 2006–10 FL 1; 2010–15 FL C; 2015– FL 1.

LATEST SEQUENCES

Longest Sequence of League Wins: 10, 10.3.1928 – 25.4.1928.

Longest Sequence of League Defeats: 11, 10.4.1929 – 16.9.1929.

Longest Sequence of League Draws: 5, 22.12.1973 – 12.1.1974.

Longest Sequence of Unbeaten League Matches: 19, 22.8.1959 – 31.10.1959.

Longest Sequence Without a League Win: 20, 26.12.1989 – 5.5.1990.

Successive Scoring Runs: 22 from 27.11.1954.

Successive Non-scoring Runs: 6 from 27.4.2013.

MANAGERS

F. B. Kidd 1894–99
(Hon. Treasurer/Manager)
E. R. Stopher 1899–1900
(Hon. Treasurer/Manager)
George Saunders 1900–11
(Hon. Treasurer/Manager)
Herbert Lipsham 1911–19
Robert Hunter 1919–33
Bill McCracken 1933–36
Charlie Hewitt 1936–40
Bill Voisey 1940–44
Jack Cock 1944–48
Charlie Hewitt 1948–56
Ron Gray 1956–57
Jimmy Seed 1958–59
Reg Smith 1959–61
Ron Gray 1961–63
Billy Gray 1963–66
Benny Fenton 1966–74
Gordon Jago 1974–77
George Petchey 1978–80
Peter Anderson 1980–82
George Graham 1982–86
John Docherty 1986–90
Bob Pearson 1990
Bruce Rioch 1990–92
Mick McCarthy 1992–96
Jimmy Nicholl 1996–97
John Docherty 1997
Billy Bonds 1997–98
Keith Stevens 1998–2000
(then Joint Manager)
(*plus* **Alan McLeary** 1999–2000)
Mark McGhee 2000–03
Dennis Wise 2003–05
Steve Claridge 2005
Colin Lee 2005
David Tuttle 2005–06
Nigel Spackman 2006
Willie Donachie 2006–07
Kenny Jackett 2007–13
Steve Lomas 2013
Ian Holloway 2014–15
Neil Harris March 2015–

TEN YEAR LEAGUE RECORD

		P	W	D	L	F	A	Pts	Pos
2006-07	FL 1	46	19	9	18	59	62	66	10
2007-08	FL 1	46	14	10	22	45	60	52	17
2008-09	FL 1	46	25	7	14	63	53	82	5
2009-10	FL 1	46	24	13	9	76	44	85	3
2010-11	FL C	46	18	13	15	62	48	67	9
2011-12	FL C	46	15	12	19	55	57	57	16
2012-13	FL C	46	15	11	20	51	62	56	20
2013-14	FL C	46	11	15	20	46	74	48	19
2014-15	FL C	46	9	14	23	42	76	41	22
2015-16	FL 1	46	24	9	13	73	49	81	4

DID YOU KNOW ?

Alf Moule, who made over 200 appearances for Millwall as a centre-forward in the 1920s, was also a useful cricketer who played in the County Championship for Essex and in the Minor Counties for Devon. He claimed to have batted alongside the legendary W.G. Grace as a youngster.

MILLWALL – FOOTBALL LEAGUE ONE 2015–16 LEAGUE RECORD

Match No.	Date		Venue	Opponents	Result	H/T Score	Lg Pos.	Goalscorers	Atten-dance
1	Aug	8	A	Shrewsbury T	W 2-1	0-0	6	Morison [59], Gregory (pen) [67]	6671
2		15	H	Coventry C	L 0-4	0-3	13		11,197
3		18	H	Barnsley	L 2-3	1-1	15	Onyedinma 2 [26, 82]	7657
4		22	A	Scunthorpe U	D 0-0	0-0	15		3382
5		29	H	Chesterfield	L 0-2	0-1	19		8374
6	Sept	12	A	Crewe Alex	W 3-1	1-1	18	O'Brien 3 [21, 64, 74]	4293
7		15	A	Port Vale	W 2-0	0-0	12	Beevers [58], Gregory (pen) [90]	4477
8		19	H	Southend U	L 0-2	0-1	13		10,228
9		26	H	Rochdale	W 3-1	2-1	11	Abdou [4], Williams [45], Morison [60]	8023
10		29	A	Wigan Ath	D 2-2	0-0	12	Onyedinma [69], Beevers [74]	7991
11	Oct	3	A	Peterborough U	L 3-5	0-2	15	Webster [52], Craig [55], Beevers [74]	6402
12		17	H	Swindon T	W 2-0	2-0	13	Gregory [19], O'Brien [26]	8524
13		20	A	Blackpool	D 1-1	1-0	14	Beevers [35]	6225
14		24	A	Sheffield U	W 2-1	1-0	10	O'Brien 2 [30, 80]	19,617
15		27	H	Doncaster R	W 2-0	2-0	8	Morison 2 [5, 8]	8294
16		31	H	Bradford C	D 0-0	0-0	7		9367
17	Nov	21	H	Colchester U	W 4-1	2-0	8	Gregory [13], Ferguson 2 [38, 62], Webster [81]	8739
18		24	A	Fleetwood T	L 1-2	0-0	11	Webster [90]	3326
19		28	H	Bury	W 1-0	1-0	7	Williams [14]	8311
20	Dec	1	A	Burton Alb	L 1-2	0-2	7	Martin, J [75]	2888
21		19	H	Gillingham	L 0-3	0-2	11		12,032
22		26	H	Walsall	L 0-1	0-1	11		8364
23		28	A	Southend U	W 4-0	3-0	9	Martin, J [27], Cummings [35], Onyedinma [45], O'Brien [70]	10,099
24	Jan	2	A	Barnsley	L 1-2	0-1	10	Morison [61]	8700
25		9	A	Oldham Ath	W 2-1	1-0	7	Gregory [2], Morison [85]	3558
26		17	H	Port Vale	W 3-1	3-0	8	Gregory 2 (1 pen) [14, 34 (p)], Morison [44]	7773
27		23	A	Chesterfield	W 2-1	1-1	6	O'Brien [27], Gregory [47]	7078
28		30	A	Crewe Alex	D 1-1	0-0	6	Gregory (pen) [64]	9044
29	Feb	6	A	Walsall	W 3-0	0-0	6	Gregory 2 [61, 77], Romeo [70]	4843
30		13	A	Rochdale	W 1-0	0-0	6	Gregory [54]	2882
31		16	H	Scunthorpe U	L 0-2	0-1	6		8036
32		20	H	Peterborough U	W 3-0	1-0	5	Morison 2 [30, 62], Gregory [49]	8722
33		27	A	Doncaster R	D 1-1	1-1	5	Morison [6]	6810
34	Mar	1	H	Wigan Ath	D 0-0	0-0	5		7981
35		5	H	Blackpool	W 3-0	2-0	5	Gregory [8], Wallace [24], Morison (pen) [84]	9753
36		12	A	Swindon T	D 2-2	2-0	5	Gregory [6], Morison [11]	8623
37		19	A	Sheffield U	W 1-0	1-0	5	Taylor [2]	11,175
38		26	A	Bradford C	L 0-1	0-0	5		18,538
39		28	H	Burton Alb	W 2-0	2-0	5	O'Brien [12], Gregory [18]	8012
40	Apr	2	A	Colchester U	D 0-0	0-0	6		5377
41		9	H	Shrewsbury T	W 3-1	0-1	4	Thompson [57], Morison [61], Gregory (pen) [90]	9583
42		16	A	Coventry C	L 1-2	1-0	5	Webster [19]	11,632
43		19	H	Fleetwood T	W 1-0	0-0	4	Morison [52]	7865
44		23	A	Bury	W 3-1	2-1	5	Taylor 2 [4, 83], Morison [33]	3669
45		30	H	Oldham Ath	W 3-0	2-0	3	Webster 2 [5, 54], Ferguson [40]	12,419
46	May	8	A	Gillingham	W 2-1	0-0	4	O'Brien [55], Gregory (pen) [90]	9375

Final League Position: 4

GOALSCORERS

League (73): Gregory 18 (6 pens), Morison 15 (1 pen), O'Brien 10, Webster 6, Beevers 4, Onyedinma 4, Ferguson 3, Taylor 3, Martin, J 2, Williams 2, Abdou 1, Craig 1, Cummings 1, Romeo 1, Thompson 1, Wallace 1.
FA Cup (4): Gregory 1, Morison 1, O'Brien 1, Thompson 1.
Capital One Cup (1): Morison 1.
Johnstone's Paint Trophy (11): Gregory 6 (1 pen), O'Brien 2, Williams 1, Morison 1.
League One Play-Offs (5): Gregory 2, Beevers 1, Martin J 1, Morison 1.

Forde D 7 + 1	Cummings S 15 + 1	Webster B 35 + 5	Craig T 16 + 2	Beevers M 42	Onyedinma F 18 + 16	Williams S 32 + 1	Upson E 16 + 16	Martin L 2 + 6	Morison S 44 + 2	Gregory L 32 + 9	Ferguson S 28 + 11	Marquis J — + 10	Thompson B 19 + 9	Cowan-Hall P — + 3	Nelson S 9	Abdou N 27 + 2	O'Brien A 31 + 12	Archer J 39	Powell J 1	Edwards C 15	Martin J 27 + 2	Saville G 12	Pavey A — + 4	Chesmain N — + 1	Wallace J 12	Romeo M 18	Philpot J — + 6	Taylor C 9 + 1	Match No.
1	2	3	4	5	6	7	8	9^1	10	11^2	12	13																	1
1	2	3	4	5^1	6	8	7^2	9^3	11	10	13				12	14													2
1	2		4		6	8^3	9^1	14	11	10	5^2		12			3	7	13											3
	2	12	3	5	6	7			10	11^1			8			4^2	9	13	1										4
2^3		5	3	6					11	10^1		14	9	13		4	7	12	1	8^2									5
	12	5	4	7^3	6	10			9	14	13					3^1	8	11^2	1		2								6
		4	5	7	6^3	3	8		10^1	12	13	14					9	11^2	1		2								7
		3	5	4^1	8	9^2			11	12	14	13					7	10	1		2								8
		3	5	4	6^1	7	12	14	10	9^3	13						8	11^2	1		2								9
		3	5	4	12	7	6^1		13	10	9^2	14					8	11^3	1		2								10
		3	5	4	9	7	6^1		10	14	13	12^3					8^2	11	1		2								11
		3		4	12	7		13	11^2	10^1	9^3					6		1		2	5	8	14						12
	14	3	4	13	8^1			10	11^3	9^2	12					6		1		2^4	5	7							13
	2	14	3	4	6^1		13	10	11^2	12		7				9^3		1			5	8							14
		14	3	4	12		13	11	10^1	9^2	8					6^3		1		2	5	7							15
		12	3^1	4	13	7		11	10^3	9^2						6		1		2	5	8	14						16
	2	3		4	12	8	13	14	11	10^1	9^2					6^3		1			5	7							17
	2	4		3	13	7	12		10	11	9^1					6		1			5	8^2							18
	2	4		3	6^2	8	9^3		12	11	5^1	13				10		1				7		14					19
	2^2			4^1	6	7	14		10	12	9^1	13		3		11		1			5	8							20
12		3		4^3	14	7	9^1		11	10	13					6	1^1			2	5^3	8							21
1				4	6^2	8	12		11		9				3	7	10			2	5^1	13							22
1	2	3		4	9^3	8	6		11^2		13	12				10^1					5	7	14						23
1		4			6^1	7	9^2		11	12	13			14	10					2^3	5	8							24
1	2	4		3	13	7			10^3	11^1	9	14				8	12				5					6^2			25
	2	3		4	13	8	12		10	11^2	5	14				7	9^3	1								6^1			26
	2	3		4	14	8	13		11	10^2	5^3					7	9^1	1			12					6			27
	2	4		3		8			10	11	5					7	9	1								6			28
		3				8	6		11^1	10^2	2	13			4	7	14	1			12					9^3	5		29
		4				8	9		11	10^1		12			3	7		1			5					6	2		30
		4				8^2			10	11	5	13	12		3	7^1	9	1			5					6	2		31
		4	3	7	14				11^1	10^3	9^2	12	8			6	13	1			5					4	2		32
		4	3	13					10	11	9^1	7				8	12	1			5					6^2	2		33
		4	3		12				10	11	9	7^2				8	13	1			5^1					6	2		34
		4	3			12			11^2	10^1	6	9				7	13	1		5^1						8	2	14	35
		3	4			13			11	10^1	9	8				7	12	1		5^2						6	2		36
	2	4				13			10	11^2	9^1	8				7	12	1			5					6	3		37
		3	4	6^2	8	9^1			11	13		7				10^3		1			5					2	14	12	38
		3	4	14	8	12			11^3	10^2		7				9^1		1			5					2	13	6	39
		3	4		8				11	10	12	7				9^1		1			5					2		6	40
		4	3		7	13			10	10^1	9	8				12		1			5^2					2		6	41
		4	3		7^4	13			10	14	9^3	8				12	11^1	1			5					2		6^2	42
		3	4	13					10^2	11^3		7				8	9^1	1			5					2	12	6	43
	3	14	4	6^3		12			10^2			7				8	11^1	1			5					2	13	9	44
		3	4	12					10			9^1	8			7	11	1			5					2	13	6^2	45
	3	14	4		12				10^2	13	9^3	8				7	11^1	1			5					2^4		6	46

FA Cup

First Round		AFC Fylde	(h)	3-1
Second Round		Wycombe W	(h)	1-2

Capital One Cup

First Round		Barnet	(h)	1-2

(aet)

Johnstone's Paint Trophy

First Round		Peterborough U	(h)	1-0
Second Round		Northampton T	(h)	2-0
Southern Quarter-Final		Plymouth Arg	(a)	5-3
Southern Semi-Final		Southend U	(a)	2-0
Southern Final 1st leg		Oxford U	(h)	0-2
Southern Final 2nd leg		Oxford U	(a)	1-0

(Oxford U won 2-1 on aggregate)

League One Play-Offs

Semi-Final 1st leg		Bradford C	(a)	3-1
Semi-Final 2nd leg		Bradford C	(h)	1-1

(Millwall won 4-2 on aggregate)

Final		Barnsley	(Wembley)	1-3

MILTON KEYNES DONS

FOUNDATION

In July 2004 Wimbledon became MK Dons and relocated to Milton Keynes. In 2007 it recognised itself as a new club with no connection to the old Wimbledon FC. In August of that year the replica trophies and other Wimbledon FC memorabilia were returned to the London Borough of Merton.

Stadiummk, Stadium Way West, Milton Keynes, Buckinghamshire MK1 1ST.

Telephone: (01908)) 622 922.

Fax: (01908) 622 933.

Ticket Office: (0333) 200 5343.

Website: www.mkdons.com

Email: info@mkdons.com

Ground Capacity: 30,582.

Record Attendance: 28,127 v Chelsea, FA Cup 4th rd, 31 January 2016.

Pitch Measurements: 104m × 67.5m (114yd × 74yd).

Chairman: Pete Winkelman.

Executive Director: Andrew Cullen.

Manager: Karl Robinson.

Head of Coaching: Richie Barker.

Head of Sports Medicine: Simon Crampton.

Colours: White shirts with red and black trim, white shorts with red and black trim, white socks with red and black trim.

Year Formed: 2004.

Turned Professional: 2004.

Club Nickname: 'The Dons'.

Grounds: 2004, The National Hockey Stadium; 2007, Stadiummk.

First Football League Game: 7 August 2004, FL 1, v Barnsley (h) D 1–1 – Rachubka; Palmer, Lewington, Harding, Williams, Oyedele, Kamara, Smith, Smart (Herve), McLeod (1) (Hornuss), Small.

Record League Victory: 7–0 v Oldham Ath, FL 1, 20 December 2014 – Martin; Spence, McFadzean, Kay (Baldock), Lewington; Potter (1), Alli (1); Baker C (1), Carruthers (Green), Bowditch (1) (Afobe (1)); Grigg (2).

Record Cup Victory: 6–0 v Nantwich T, FA Cup 1st rd, 12 November 2011 – Martin; Chicksen, Baldock G, Doumbe (1), Flanagan, Williams S, Powell (1) (O'Shea (1), Chadwick (Galloway), Bowditch (2), MacDonald (Williams G (1)), Balanta.

HONOURS

League Champions: FL 2 – 2007–08.
Runners-up: FL 1 – 2014–15.
FA Cup: 5th rd – 2013.
League Cup: 4th rd – 2015.
League Trophy Winners: 2008.

sky SPORTS FACT FILE

Milton Keynes Dons established three new attendance records in 2015–16. A new ground record of 28,127 attended the FA Cup tie with Chelsea and a new ground Football League record of 21,345 was present for the game with Brighton & Hove Albion in March. To add to this the average league attendance at stadium:mk was 13,157, another new club record.

Record Defeat: 0–6 v Southampton, Capital One Cup 3rd rd, 23 September 2015.

Most League Points (3 for a win): 97, FL 2, 2007–08.

Most League Goals: 101, FL 1, 2014–15.

Highest League Scorer in Season: Izale McLeod, 21, 2006–07.

Most League Goals in Total Aggregate: Izale McLeod, 62, 2004–07; 2012–14.

Most Capped Player: Lee Hodson, 7 (16), Northern Ireland.

MANAGERS

Stuart Murdock 2004
Danny Wilson 2004–06
Martin Allen 2006–07
Paul Ince 2007–08
Roberto Di Matteo 2008–09
Paul Ince 2009–10
Karl Robinson May 2010–

Most League Goals in One Match: 3, Clive Platt v Barnet, FL 2, 20 January 2007; 3, Mark Wright v Bury, FL 2, 2 February 2008; 3, Aaron Wilbraham v Cheltenham T, FL 1, 31 January 2009; 3, Sam Baldock v Colchester U, FL 1, 12 March 2011; 3, Sam Baldock v Chesterfield, FL 1, 20 August 2012; 3, Dean Bowditch v Bury, FL 1, 22 September 2012; 3, Dele Alli v Notts Co, FL 1, 11 March 2014; 3, Dele Alli v Crewe Alex, FL 1, 20 September 2014; 3, Benik Afobe v Colchester U, FL 1, 29 November 2014; 3, Robert Hall v Leyton Orient, FL 1, 18 April 2015.

Most League Appearances: Dean Lewington, 469, 2004–15.

Youngest League Player: Brendon Galloway, 16 years 42 days v Rochdale, 28 April 2012.

Record Transfer Fee Received: £5,000,000 from Tottenham H for Dele Alli, February 2015.

Record Transfer Fee Paid: £100,000 to Plymouth Arg for Scott Taylor, January 2006.

Football League Record: 2004–06 FL 1; 2006–08 FL 2; 2008–15 FL 1; 2015–16 FL C; 2016– FL 1.

LATEST SEQUENCES

Longest Sequence of League Wins: 8, 7.9.2007 – 20.10.2007.

Longest Sequence of League Defeats: 4, 29.8.2015 – 26.9.2015.

Longest Sequence of League Draws: 4, 12.2.2013 – 2.3.2013.

Longest Sequence of Unbeaten League Matches: 18, 29.1.2008 – 3.5.2008.

Longest Sequence Without a League Win: 11, 8.3.2016 – 7.5.2016.

Successive Scoring Runs: 18 from 7.4.2007.

Successive Non-scoring Runs: 4, 17.12.2005.

TEN YEAR LEAGUE RECORD

		P	W	D	L	F	A	Pts	Pos
2006-07	FL 2	46	25	9	12	76	58	84	4
2007-08	FL 2	46	29	10	7	82	37	97	1
2008-09	FL 1	46	26	9	11	83	47	87	3
2009-10	FL 1	46	17	9	20	60	68	60	12
2010-11	FL 1	46	23	8	15	67	60	77	5
2011-12	FL 1	46	22	14	10	84	47	80	5
2012-13	FL 1	46	19	13	14	62	45	70	8
2013-14	FL 1	46	17	9	20	63	65	60	10
2014-15	FL 1	46	27	10	9	101	44	91	2
2015-16	FL C	46	9	12	25	39	69	39	23

DID YOU KNOW ?

Milton Keynes Dons narrowly avoided relegation from League One in 2004–05, their first season as a Football League club. On the final day of the season they defeated Tranmere Rovers 2-1, while rivals Torquay United lost 2-1 at Colchester United ensuring the Dons stayed up on goal difference.

MILTON KEYNES DONS FC – FL CHAMPIONSHIP 2015–16 LEAGUE RECORD

Match No.	Date	Venue	Opponents	Result	H/T Score	Lg Pos.	Goalscorers	Attendance
1	Aug 8	A	Rotherham U	W 4-1	3-1	1	Hall [5], Collins (og) [28], Bowditch [35], Baker [75]	9869
2	15	H	Preston NE	L 0-1	0-1	8		11,035
3	18	H	Bolton W	W 1-0	0-0	3	Powell [60]	10,765
4	22	A	Reading	D 0-0	0-0	4		16,547
5	29	H	Birmingham C	L 0-2	0-0	11		14,626
6	Sept 12	A	Middlesbrough	L 0-2	0-0	14		21,448
7	15	A	Burnley	L 1-2	1-1	16	Baker [45]	15,845
8	19	H	Leeds U	L 1-2	0-2	20	Church [74]	19,284
9	26	H	Derby Co	L 1-3	0-0	23	Murphy [60]	13,554
10	Oct 3	A	Bristol C	D 1-1	0-1	19	Powell [90]	14,535
11	17	H	Blackburn R	W 3-0	1-0	16	Reeves 2 (1 pen) [11 (p), 89], Church [71]	11,548
12	20	A	Huddersfield T	L 0-2	0-0	18		11,471
13	24	A	QPR	L 0-3	0-0	20		15,567
14	31	H	Hull C	L 0-2	0-1	20		15,360
15	Nov 3	H	Charlton Ath	W 1-0	1-0	20	Bowditch [29]	9575
16	7	A	Brighton & HA	L 1-2	1-2	21	Maynard [23]	23,661
17	21	H	Fulham	D 1-1	1-1	22	Bowditch [30]	14,508
18	28	A	Wolverhampton W	D 0-0	0-0	19		19,814
19	Dec 5	A	Brentford	L 0-2	0-1	20		9682
20	12	H	Ipswich T	L 0-1	0-1	20		13,520
21	15	H	Sheffield W	W 2-1	1-0	20	Baker [25], Maynard [50]	11,422
22	19	A	Nottingham F	L 1-2	0-2	21	Murphy [81]	19,975
23	26	H	Cardiff C	W 2-1	0-0	20	Maynard [49], Murphy [90]	12,510
24	28	A	Birmingham C	L 0-1	0-0	20		19,714
25	Jan 2	A	Leeds U	D 1-1	1-0	20	Hall [30]	24,356
26	12	H	Burnley	L 0-5	0-1	21		10,011
27	16	H	Reading	W 1-0	0-0	20	Walsh [78]	13,062
28	23	A	Bolton W	L 1-3	0-2	20	Murphy [89]	13,932
29	Feb 6	A	Cardiff C	D 0-0	0-0	21		13,833
30	9	H	Middlesbrough	D 1-1	1-0	20	Bowditch [9]	11,256
31	13	A	Derby Co	W 1-0	0-0	20	Forster-Caskey [82]	30,075
32	20	H	Bristol C	L 0-2	0-1	21		12,825
33	23	H	Huddersfield T	D 1-1	1-0	21	Revell [28]	9402
34	27	A	Blackburn R	L 2-3	1-0	21	Carruthers [36], Revell [86]	12,693
35	Mar 5	H	QPR	W 2-0	0-0	21	Lewington [49], Reeves (pen) [90]	14,796
36	8	A	Charlton Ath	D 0-0	0-0	21		13,146
37	12	H	Hull C	D 1-1	0-0	21	Kay [51]	16,183
38	19	H	Brighton & HA	L 1-2	0-0	22	Kay [70]	21,345
39	Apr 2	A	Fulham	L 1-2	0-0	22	Murphy [63]	17,588
40	5	H	Wolverhampton W	L 1-2	1-0	22	Maynard [6]	12,131
41	9	H	Rotherham U	L 0-4	0-2	22		13,048
42	16	A	Preston NE	D 1-1	0-1	22	Maynard [54]	10,457
43	19	A	Sheffield W	D 0-0	0-0	22		20,220
44	23	H	Brentford	L 1-4	1-1	22	Maynard [6]	11,564
45	30	A	Ipswich T	L 2-3	1-1	23	Revell 2 (1 pen) [45 (p), 74]	19,631
46	May 7	H	Nottingham F	L 1-2	1-1	23	Maynard [19]	15,486

Final League Position: 23

GOALSCORERS

League (39): Maynard 7, Murphy 5, Bowditch 4, Revell 4 (1 pen), Baker 3, Reeves 3 (2 pens), Church 2, Hall 2, Kay 2, Powell 2, Carruthers 1, Forster-Caskey 1, Lewington 1, Walsh 1, own goal 1.
FA Cup (6): Church 1 (pen), Maynard 1, Murphy 1, Potter 1, Reeves 1 (pen), own goal 1.
Capital One Cup (4): Baker 2, Murphy 1, own goal 1.

Martin D 35	Spence J 31 + 2	McFadzean K 39	Kay A 33 + 1	Lewington D 46	Potter D 36 + 1	Carruthers S 33 + 6	Hall R 18 + 9	Reeves B 9 + 9	Bowditch D 26 + 11	Gallagher S 6 + 7	Baker C 18 + 16	Powell D 7 + 15	Church S 9 + 10	Benavente C 1 + 1	Jennings D — + 1	Upson M 1 + 2	Poyet D 17 + 1	Hodson L — + 3	Murphy J 33 + 9	Forster-Caskey J 19 + 1	Maynard N 23 + 12	Walsh J 17 + 1	Williams J 11 + 2	Rasulo G — + 1	Baldock G 15	Emmanuel-Thomas J 2 + 2	Revell A 8 + 9	Cropper C 8 + 1	Burns C 3 + 1	Long K 2	Furlong C — + 1	Jackson O — + 1	Match No.
1	2	3	4	5	6	7	8³	9	10²	11¹	12	13	14																				1
1	2	3	4	5	6	7³		9	10¹	11			8²	14	12	13																	2
1	2	3	4	5	7	6			10²	13	8	12	11¹	9³		14																	3
1	2	3	4	5	6	9¹	8³		10	13	14	12	11²				7																4
	2³	3	4	5	7	9³	8		10¹	11	13						6		12	14													5
1	2	3	4	5		7³	14	9	11¹	13	10²	12					6		8														6
1	2	3	4	5		6	8³	9¹	13	10	14	11²					7		12														7
1	2³	3	4	5		7⁴	9¹	12	14	11³	8		13				6		10														8
1	2	3	4	5			13	9¹	14		8²		11³				6		10	7	12												9
1	2¹	3	4	5			12	9			8	14	11³				6		10²	7	13												10
1	2	3	4	5		14	8³	9	12			11²					7		10¹	6	13												11
1	2	3	4	5		7²			12		8¹	13	14				6		10	9	11²												12
1	2	3	4	5		12	8²	9³				13	11				6¹		10	7	14												13
1	2	3	4	5		7³	14		9¹		8	13	11²				6		10	12													14
1	2	3		5	7	9			10¹	13	14			4³	6	12	8		11²														15
1	2	3		5	6	8²		12	9¹	10³	14				7				13	J1													16
1	2	3	4	5	6	8³	12	9¹	13	14					7				10¹		11²												17
1	2	3	4	5	6	8		9³	14	12	13				7				10¹		11²												18
1	2	3	4	5	6	14		9²	13	8	12				7¹				10³		11												19
1	2³	3	4	5	6	7	14	12	9²		8¹	13							10		11												20
1	2	3	4	5	7	6¹	9³	12			8	13				14			10²		11												21
1	2³	3	4	5	7	6	8	9²	10¹	14	13								12		11												22
1	2	3	4	5	6	7	8¹	9²	14	13	12								10		11²												23
1	2	3		5		7		14	9	11²	8	10³					6		12		13	4¹											24
1	2	3	4	5	6	7	9³		12		8¹		13						10		11²	14											25
1	2	3	4⁴	5	6	7	8³	9²				12	14						10	13	11¹												26
1	2	3		5	6	9¹	8³		14								12		13	10²	7	11	4										27
1	2		3	5	6	8¹			13			14	11³				10	7			4	9²	12										28
1		3		5	6	9	8³		14								13		7	11²	4	10¹			2	12							29
1	14		3	5	12	6			8³								10	7	13	4					2	9²	11¹						30
1		3		5	6	9¹	8		13								10	7	11²	4					2	9²	13						31
1		3		5	6		8⁹	14	12								10¹	7	11	4					2	9²	13						32
		3		5	6		12		8								10²	7	13	4	9¹				2	11	1						33
		3		5	6	10¹	14		8								12	7	11³	4	9²				2	13	1						34
1		3	4	5	6	12	13	14	10								8²	7¹			9¹				2	11							35
1		3	4	5	6	7	12	13	8¹								10		11²		9³				2	14							36
1²		3	4	5	6	7	9¹		13					10³			8					14			2	11	12						37
	14	3⁴	4	5	6		9¹					13	8³				10		11		7²				2	12	1						38
		3		5	7				8³		12	14					10	6²	13	4	9¹				2	11	1						39
		3		5	6				8¹	10²							12	7	11³	4					2	14	13	1					40
		3³		5	7	13			8¹		12						10	6	14	4	9²				2	11	1						41
	2³	3		5	7	9			8			14					10	6¹	11²	4	12					13	1¹						42
	2	3		5	6	7²			10¹		8	13					12		14	4	9³					11		1					43
		3	12	5	6				8								10	7	11	4¹	9³				2	14	12	13					44
				5	6	7³		9¹			12	8					10		13	4					2	11²		1	3	14			45
	2²			5	6	7³		12	9	8							10		11¹	4						13		1	3		14		46

FA Cup

Third Round	Northampton T	(a)	2-2
Replay	Northampton T	(h)	3-0
Fourth Round	Chelsea	(h)	1-5

Capital One Cup

First Round	Leyton Orient	(h)	2-1
Second Round	Cardiff C	(h)	2-1
(aet)			
Third Round	Southampton	(h)	0-6

MORECAMBE

FOUNDATION

Several attempts to start a senior football club in a rugby stronghold finally succeeded on 7 May 1920 at the West View Hotel, Morecambe and a team competed in the Lancashire Combination for 1920–21. The club shared with a local cricket club at Woodhill Lane for the first season and a crowd of 3,000 watched the first game. The club moved to Roseberry Park, the name of which was changed to Christie Park after J.B. Christie who as President had purchased the ground.

Globe Arena, Christie Way, Westgate, Morecambe, Lancashire LA4 4TB,

Telephone: (01524) 411 797.

Fax: (01524) 832 230.

Ticket Office: (01524) 411 797.

Website: www.morecambefc.com

Email: office@morecambefc.com

Ground Capacity: 6,241.

HONOURS

League: Runners-up: Conference – (3rd) 2006–07 *(promoted via play-offs)*.

FA Cup: 3rd rd – 1962, 2001, 2003.

League Cup: 3rd rd – 2008.

Record Attendance: 9,383 v Weymouth, FA Cup 3rd rd, 6 January 1962 (at Christie Park). 5,375 v Newcastle U, League Cup, 28 August 2013 (at Globe Arena).

Pitch Measurements: 101m × 66m (110.5yd × 72yd).

Chairman: Peter McGuigan.

Manager: Jim Bentley.

Assistant Manager: Ken McKenna.

Physio: Simon Farnworth.

Colours: Red and black striped shirts, black shorts with red trim, black socks with red trim.

Year Formed: 1920.

Turned Professional: 1920.

Club Nickname: 'The Shrimps'.

Grounds: 1920, Woodhill Lane; 1921, Christie Park; 2010, Globe Arena.

First Football League game: 11 August 2007, FL 2, v Barnet (h) D 0–0 – Lewis; Yates, Adams, Artell, Bentley, Stanley, Baker (Burns), Sorvel, Twiss (Newby), Curtis, Hunter (Thompson).

sky SPORTS FACT FILE

Morecambe joined the Lancashire Combination for their first season of competitive football in 1920–21. Their first major success came in 1924–25 when they won the Lancashire Combination and lost out to Chorley in the Combination Cup final. For good measure the Shrimps' reserve team also won the North Lancashire League that season.

Record League Victory: 6–0 v Crawley T, FL 2, 10 September 2011 – Roche; Reid, Wilson (pen), McCready, Haining (Parrish), Fenton (1), Drummond, McDonald, Price (Jevons), Carlton (3) (Alessandra), Ellison (1).

Record Cup Victory: 6–2 v Nelson (a), Lancashire Trophy, 27 January 2004.

Record Defeat: 0–7 v Cambridge U, FL 2, 19 April 2016

Most League Points (3 for a win): 73, FL 2, 2009–10.

Most League Goals: 73, FL 2, 2009–10.

Highest League Scorer in Season: Phil Jevons, 18, 2009–10.

Most League Goals in Total Aggregate: Kevin Ellison, 47, 2011–15.

Most League Goals in One Match: 3, Jon Newby v Rotherham U, FL 2, 29 March 2008.

Most League Appearances: Stuart Drummond, 277, 2007–15.

Youngest League Player: Aaron McGowan, 16 years 263 days, 20 April 2013.

Record Transfer Fee Received: £225,000 from Stockport Co for Carl Baker, July 2008.

Record Transfer Fee Paid: £50,000 to Southport for Carl Baker, July 2007.

Football League Record: 2006–07 Promoted from Conference; 2007– FL 2.

MANAGERS

Jimmy Milne 1947–48
Albert Dainty 1955–56
Ken Horton 1956–61
Joe Dunn 1961–64
Geoff Twentyman 1964–65
Ken Waterhouse 1965–69
Ronnie Clayton 1969–70
Gerry Irving/Ronnie Mitchell 1970
Ken Waterhouse 1970–72
Dave Roberts 1972–75
Alan Spavin 1975–76
Johnny Johnson 1976–77
Tommy Ferber 1977–78
Mick Hogarth 1978–79
Don Curbage 1979–81
Jim Thompson 1981
Les Rigby 1981–84
Sean Gallagher 1984–85
Joe Wojciechowicz 1985–88
Eric Whalley 1988
Billy Wright 1988–89
Lawrie Milligan 1989
Bryan Griffiths 1989–93
Leighton James 1994
Jim Harvey 1994–2006
Sammy McIlroy 2006–11
Jim Bentley May 2011–

LATEST SEQUENCES

Longest Sequence of League Wins: 7, 31.10.2009 – 12.12.2009.

Longest Sequence of League Defeats: 4, 6.2.2016 – 1.3.2016.

Longest Sequence of League Draws: 5, 3.1.2015 – 31.1.2015.

Longest Sequence of Unbeaten League Matches: 12, 31.1.2009 – 21.3.2009.

Longest Sequence Without a League Win: 10, 29.12.2013 – 1.3.2014.

Successive Scoring Runs: 17 from 13.8.2011.

Successive Non-scoring Runs: 3 from 24.10.2015.

TEN YEAR LEAGUE RECORD

		P	W	D	L	F	A	Pts	Pos
2006-07	Conf	46	23	12	11	64	46	81	3
2007-08	FL 2	46	16	12	18	59	63	60	11
2008-09	FL 2	46	15	18	13	53	56	63	11
2009-10	FL 2	46	20	13	13	73	64	73	4
2010-11	FL 2	46	13	12	21	54	73	51	20
2011-12	FL 2	46	14	14	18	63	57	56	15
2012-13	FL 2	46	15	13	18	55	61	58	16
2013-14	FL 2	46	13	15	18	52	64	54	18
2014-15	FL 2	46	17	12	17	53	52	63	11
2015-16	FL 2	46	12	10	24	69	91	46	21

DID YOU KNOW ?

Morecambe goalkeeper Charles Clarke was injured playing in a Lancashire Combination game on 7 January 1933. The injury exacerbated an existing kidney problem and he was detained in hospital for several months. He passed away at the end of June that year having failed to recover health.

MORECAMBE – FOOTBALL LEAGUE TWO 2015–16 LEAGUE RECORD

Match No.	Date	Venue	Opponents	Result	H/T Score	Lg Pos.	Goalscorers	Attendance
1	Aug 8	A	Hartlepool U	L	0-2	0-1	18		4289
2	15	H	Accrington S	W	1-0	1-0	12	Wildig [13]	1865
3	18	H	Wycombe W	L	0-1	0-0	16		1395
4	22	A	Portsmouth	D	3-3	3-1	14	Barkhuizen [11], Goodall [25], Fleming [38]	16,052
5	29	H	Notts Co	W	4-1	1-1	10	Goodall [20], Mullin [65], Kenyon [88], Devitt [90]	1621
6	Sept 5	A	Yeovil T	W	4-2	0-2	5	Wildig [64], Fleming [71], Molyneux [84], Ellison [90]	3024
7	12	A	Newport Co	W	2-1	1-0	5	Goodall [34], Mullin (pen) [90]	2068
8	19	H	Northampton T	L	2-4	0-2	7	Byrom (og) [86], Barkhuizen [67]	1778
9	26	A	Oxford U	D	0-0	0-0	7		5273
10	29	H	Luton T	L	1-3	1-2	12	Barkhuizen [25]	1388
11	Oct 3	H	Bristol R	L	3-4	1-1	14	Miller [43], Barkhuizen [60], Mullin (pen) [87]	1712
12	10	A	Carlisle U	W	3-2	1-1	11	Miller 2 [35, 74], Barkhuizen [63]	5303
13	17	A	AFC Wimbledon	W	5-2	3-1	10	Miller 2 (1 pen) [8 (p), 13], Goodall [45], Barkhuizen [80], Mullin [90]	3679
14	20	H	Crawley T	W	3-1	1-0	7	Ellison [41], Miller [65], Mullin (pen) [90]	1098
15	24	H	Leyton Orient	L	0-1	0-1	8		2105
16	31	H	Plymouth Arg	L	0-2	0-2	11		7574
17	Nov 21	A	Barnet	D	0-0	0-0	15		1632
18	24	H	Cambridge U	L	2-4	1-3	16	Molyneux [21], Murphy [67]	1689
19	28	A	Stevenage	L	3-4	1-2	17	Ellison 2 [13, 90], Mullin (pen) [82]	2415
20	Dec 1	H	Dagenham & R	W	1-0	1-0	13	Mullin [31]	1027
21	19	A	York C	L	1-2	0-1	17	Devitt [54]	2769
22	28	A	Notts Co	D	2-2	2-1	17	Miller [8], Ellison [23]	4556
23	Jan 2	A	Wycombe W	W	2-0	0-0	13	Miller [54], Devitt (pen) [84]	3555
24	12	H	Exeter C	D	1-1	0-0	14	Miller (pen) [49]	1040
25	16	H	Yeovil T	W	2-1	0-0	13	Ellison [74], Miller [80]	1340
26	23	A	Northampton T	L	1-3	0-2	14	Mullin [72]	4652
27	26	H	Mansfield T	L	1-2	0-0	14	Mullin (pen) [71]	1047
28	30	H	Newport Co	L	1-2	0-1	15	Miller [60]	1342
29	Feb 2	H	Portsmouth	D	1-1	0-1	14	Roche [90]	1399
30	6	A	Mansfield T	L	1-2	1-2	16	Ellison [1]	3090
31	13	H	Oxford U	L	2-4	1-1	16	Molyneux [23], Barkhuizen [90]	1749
32	20	A	Bristol R	L	1-2	1-0	17	Devitt (pen) [12]	7400
33	27	H	Carlisle U	L	1-2	1-0	18	Ellison [27]	3070
34	Mar 1	A	Luton T	L	0-1	0-0	18		7153
35	5	A	Crawley T	D	1-1	0-0	18	Miller [83]	1697
36	12	H	AFC Wimbledon	W	2-1	0-0	17	Fleming [76], Devitt (pen) [80]	1477
37	19	A	Leyton Orient	L	0-1	0-0	18		4442
38	25	H	Plymouth Arg	L	0-2	0-1	18		2081
39	Apr 2	H	Barnet	W	4-2	2-0	18	Miller 2 (1 pen) [1, 8 (p)], Kenyon [48], Stockton [88]	1175
40	5	A	Dagenham & R	L	1-2	0-2	18	Barkhuizen [76]	1233
41	9	H	Hartlepool U	L	2-5	1-2	19	Kenyon [25], Barkhuizen [87]	2005
42	16	A	Accrington S	D	2-2	1-1	19	Miller [12], Barkhuizen [79]	2609
43	19	A	Cambridge U	L	0-7	0-5	20		3941
44	23	H	Stevenage	L	1-4	1-2	21	Stockton [20]	1129
45	30	A	Exeter C	D	1-1	0-0	21	Ellison [86]	3936
46	May 7	H	York C	D	1-1	0-1	21	Devitt [51]	1620

Final League Position: 21

GOALSCORERS

League (69): Miller 15 (3 pens), Barkhuizen 10, Ellison 9, Mullin 9 (5 pens), Devitt 6 (3 pens), Goodall 4, Fleming 3, Kenyon 3, Molyneux 3, Stockton 2, Wildig 2, Murphy 1, Roche 1, own goal 1.
FA Cup (2): Barkhuizen 1, Wildig 1.
Capital One Cup (0).
Johnstone's Paint Trophy (4): Barkhuizen 1, Devitt 1, Miller 1, Mullin 1.

Roche B 42	Beeley S 39	Edwards R 35 + 2	Parrish A 31 + 1	Wilson L 15 + 3	Murphy P 5 + 2	Wildig A 22 + 10	Devitt J 34 + 5	Molyneux L 18 + 16	Ellison K 36 + 8	Mullin P 11 + 29	Kenyon A 21 + 8	Miller S 32 + 5	Ryan J — + 3	Goodall A 32 + 5	Fleming A 29 + 4	Barkhuizen T 36 + 4	Dugdale A 24	McGowan A 14 + 7	Kelleher J — + 1	Forrester A 1 + 2	Thompson T — + 1	O'Hara K 4 + 1	Conlan L 14 + 2	Doyle C 8	Oliver C 1 + 4	Stockton C 2 + 5	Match No.
1	2	3	4	5	6^1	7	8	9^2	10	11^3	12	13	14														1
1	2	3	4	5		7	8^2	9^1	10	11^1	14			12	6	13											2
1	2	4	3	5	6		8		10	13	11^1			7	9^2	12											3
1	2		4	5		9	6	13			12	10^1		7^2	8	11^3	3	14									4
1	2^2		3			7^1	10	14		13	12	11		6	9	8^3	4	5									5
1		4		5		7	10	12	14	13				11^3				6^1	9	8	3	2^2					6
1		4				9	10^2	5	13	14	12	11^1		6	7	8^3	3	2									7
1	2	3		5^2		9	8^1	13	11	12				6^2	7	10	4	14									8
1	2	4		5^1		9	14	8^2	11	13				6	7	10^3	3	12									9
1	5	3^1	2			7	13	9	12	10^1	8^2	14		6	11	4											10
1	5	3	2			9^3	10^2	13	14	12	11		7^1	6	8	4											11
1	5	4	2			6^3	13	9^2	12	7	10	14	8	11^1			3										12
1	5	4	2		12	9^2		6	13	8	10^1		7	11			3										13
1	2	4	3		12	6^2		9	13	7^1	11^1		8	14	10		5										14
1	2	4	3		12	9	13	10	11^3	6^2			7^1	7	8		5	14									15
1	2	3	4		7	9^1	14	10	13		11^2		6^3	12	8		5										16
1	2	3	4	12		9^2	10	11^3	14	13		7	6	8		5^1											17
1	2	4	3	5	12	14		6	9	13	8^2	10^3		7^1	11												18
1	2	3	4	5	13	8		7	9	12		10^2		11^3	6			14									19
1^2	5	3	2	14	8	11		7	10			13			9	4		6^3	12								20
1	2	4			6	8	10	9^3	13	14	7^1	11^2			3	5		12									21
1	2	4		5	6	12	9^1		10^2	13		11^1		14	7	8	3										22
1	2		4	5	6^3	13	9^1		10	14		11^2		12	7	8	3										23
1	5^2		4	2		13	9^1	14	8	12		11^3		7	6	10	3										24
1		4	2	5		9^1	8^1		10	12	6	11		13^2	7		3										25
	2		4	5		9^3	12	10	13	7	11^2			6	8^1	3				1	14						26
1	5	2^1	4	8		12	9^2	11	10	7^3				14	6	13	3	3									27
1	2		4			9			10	12		11		7^1	6	8	3						5				28
1	2		3			9^1	13	10^2	12		11			7	6	8	4						5				29
1		4	2			14	9	12	10	13		11^3		7^1	6	8^2	3						5				30
1	2	13	4			9^1	10		12			11^1		6	7	8	3						5^1				31
1	2	4	5	13		14	6^3		9	11^2	12			7	8^1	10	3^1										32
1	8	2				7	9^2	13	11	10^1	6			3		5		12							4		33
1	8^2	2				7	9	13	10	11	6			3^1		5							12	4			34
1	5	3				10^2	6^1		8	13	7	11		2									9	4			35
1	2	3	13			9		10	14	6	11^1			7^3	12	8							5	4^2			36
1^1	2	3				14	9^3		8		6	11^1		4	7	10		13			12		5^2				37
	2	3				9^2	10^1	12		7^1	11^3			6	8					1	5		4	13	14		38
1	2	3	4			12	9^3	10	13	8	11^2			7	6^1						5					14	39
1	2	3	6			11		13	9^1		14			4	8^1	12							5		7^2	10	40
1^1	2	4	3					9^1	10		6	11^3		7		8		12					5^2		14	13	41
	2	3	4			9^1	14	12	10^2		6^1	11			7	8	5			1					13		42
		3				9	10	13	14	6	11^1			12	7	8		2^1		1		5^2	4				43
1	2^1					8^3	7	14	11					6		3	12						5^2	4	13	10	44
1		3				8	9	12	11	14	7	10^3			6^1		4	2					5^2			13	45
1	12					9	8	5	10	13		11^2		6^1	7		3^3	2							4	14	46

FA Cup
First Round — Dagenham & R — (a) — 0-0
Replay — Dagenham & R — (h) — 2-4

Capital One Cup
First Round — Sheffield U — (h) — 0-1

Johnstone's Paint Trophy
First Round — Walsall — (h) — 2-0
Second Round — Bury — (a) — 1-0
Northern Quarter-Final — Rochdale — (a) — 1-0
Northern Semi-Final — Fleetwood T — (a) — 0-2

NEWCASTLE UNITED

St James' Park, Newcastle-upon-Tyne NE1 4ST.
Telephone: (0844) 372 1892.
Fax: (0191) 201 8600.
Ticket Office: (0844) 372 1892 (option 1).
Website: www.nufc.co.uk
Email: admin@nufc.co.uk
Ground Capacity: 52,338.
Record Attendance: 68,386 v Chelsea, Division 1, 3 September 1930.
Pitch Measurements: 105m × 68m (114yd × 74yd).
Managing Director: Lee Charnley.
Manager: Rafael Benitez.
First-Team Coaches: Mikel Antia, Antonio Gomez Perez, Ian Cathro.
Head of Physiotherapy: Derek Wright.
Colours: Black and white striped shirts, black shorts, black socks.
Year Formed: 1881.
Turned Professional: 1889.
Previous Names: 1881, Stanley; 1882, Newcastle East End; 1892, Newcastle United.
Club Nickname: 'The Magpies', 'The Toon'.
Grounds: 1881, South Byker; 1886, Chillingham Road, Heaton; 1892, St James' Park.
First Football League Game: 2 September 1893, Division 2, v Royal Arsenal (a) D 2–2 – Ramsay; Jeffery, Miller; Crielly, Graham, McKane; Bowman, Crate (1), Thompson, Sorley (1), Wallace. Graham not Crate scored according to some reports.

HONOURS

League Champions: Division 1 – 1904–05, 1906–07, 1908–09, 1926–27; FL C – 2009–10; First Division – 1992–93; Division 2 – 1964–65.
Runners-up: FA Premier League – 1995–96, 1996–97; Division 2 – 1897–98, 1947–48.
FA Cup Winners: 1910, 1924, 1932, 1951, 1952, 1955.
Runners-up: 1905, 1906, 1908, 1911, 1974, 1998, 1999.
League Cup: Runners-up: 1976.
Texaco Cup Winners: 1974, 1975.
Anglo-Italian Cup Winners: 1972–73.
European Competitions
Champions League: 1997–98, 2002–03, 2003–04.
Fairs Cup: 1968–69 *(winners)*, 1969–70 *(qf)*, 1970–71.
UEFA Cup: 1977–78, 1994–95, 1996–97 *(qf)*, 1999–2000, 2003–04 *(sf)*, 2004–05 *(qf)*, 2006–07.
Europa League: 2012–13 *(qf)*.
European Cup Winners' Cup: 1998–99.
Intertoto Cup: 2001 *(runners-up)*, 2005, 2006 *(winners)*.

Record League Victory: 13–0 v Newport Co, Division 2, 5 October 1946 – Garbutt; Cowell, Graham; Harvey, Brennan, Wright; Milburn (2), Bentley (1), Wayman (4), Shackleton (6), Pearson.

Record Cup Victory: 9–0 v Southport (at Hillsborough), FA Cup 4th rd, 1 February 1932 – McInroy; Nelson, Fairhurst; McKenzie, Davidson, Weaver (1); Boyd (1), Jimmy Richardson (3), Cape (2), McMenemy (1), Lang (1).

Record Defeat: 0–9 v Burton Wanderers, Division 2, 15 April 1895.

Most League Points (2 for a win): 57, Division 2, 1964–65.

Most League Points (3 for a win): 102, FL C, 2009–10.

Most League Goals: 98, Division 1, 1951–52.

Highest League Scorer in Season: Hughie Gallacher, 36, Division 1, 1926–27.

Most League Goals in Total Aggregate: Jackie Milburn, 177, 1946–57.

Most League Goals in One Match: 6, Len Shackleton v Newport Co, Division 2, 5 October 1946.

Most Capped Player: Shay Given, 82 (134), Republic of Ireland.

Most League Appearances: Jim Lawrence, 432, 1904–22.

Youngest League Player: Steve Watson, 16 years 223 days v Wolverhampton W, 10 November 1990.

Record Transfer Fee Received: £35,000,000 from Liverpool for Andy Carroll, January 2011.

Record Transfer Fee Paid: £16,000,000 to Real Madrid for Michael Owen, September 2005.

Football League Record: 1893 Elected to Division 2; 1898–1934 Division 1; 1934–48 Division 2; 1948–61 Division 1; 1961–65 Division 2; 1965–78 Division 1; 1978–84 Division 2; 1984–89 Division 1; 1989–92 Division 2; 1992–93 Division 1; 1993–2009 FA Premier League; 2009–10 FL C; 2010–16 FA Premier League; 2016– FL C.

LATEST SEQUENCES

Longest Sequence of League Wins: 13, 25.4.1992 – 18.10.1992.

Longest Sequence of League Defeats: 10, 23.8.1977 – 15.10.1977.

Longest Sequence of League Draws: 4, 15.11.2008 – 6.12.2008.

Longest Sequence of Unbeaten League Matches: 17, 13.2.2010 – 2.5.2010.

Longest Sequence Without a League Win: 21, 14.1.1978 – 23.8.1978.

Successive Scoring Runs: 25 from 15.4.1939.

Successive Non-scoring Runs: 6 from 29.10.1988.

MANAGERS

Frank Watt 1895–32
  (Secretary-Manager)
Andy Cunningham 1930–35
Tom Mather 1935–39
Stan Seymour 1939–47
  (Hon. Manager)
George Martin 1947–50
Stan Seymour 1950–54
  (Hon. Manager)
Duggie Livingstone 1954–56
Stan Seymour 1956–58
  (Hon. Manager)
Charlie Mitten 1958–61
Norman Smith 1961–62
Joe Harvey 1962–75
Gordon Lee 1975–77
Richard Dinnis 1977
Bill McGarry 1977–80
Arthur Cox 1980–84
Jack Charlton 1984
Willie McFaul 1985–88
Jim Smith 1988–91
Ossie Ardiles 1991–92
Kevin Keegan 1992–97
Kenny Dalglish 1997–98
Ruud Gullit 1998–99
Sir Bobby Robson 1999–2004
Graeme Souness 2004–06
Glenn Roeder 2006–07
Sam Allardyce 2007–08
Kevin Keegan 2008
Joe Kinnear 2008–09
Alan Shearer 2009
Chris Hughton 2009–10
Alan Pardew 2010–15
John Carver 2015
Steve McClaren 2015–16
Rafael Benitez March 2016–

TEN YEAR LEAGUE RECORD

		P	W	D	L	F	A	Pts	Pos
2006-07	PR Lge	38	11	10	17	38	47	43	13
2007-08	PR Lge	38	11	10	17	45	65	43	12
2008-09	PR Lge	38	7	13	18	40	59	34	18
2009-10	FL C	46	30	12	4	90	35	102	1
2010-11	PR Lge	38	11	13	14	56	57	46	12
2011-12	PR Lge	38	19	8	11	56	51	65	5
2012-13	PR Lge	38	11	8	19	45	68	41	16
2013-14	PR Lge	38	15	4	19	43	59	49	10
2014-15	PR Lge	38	10	9	19	40	63	39	15
2015-16	PR Lge	38	9	10	19	44	65	37	18

DID YOU KNOW ?

In the post-Great War era clubs often employed silver or brass bands to entertain the fans before kick-off. Newcastle United were one of the first clubs to install a loudspeaker system and from 1930 fans were entertained by 'canned' (recorded) music rather than live bands.

NEWCASTLE UNITED – FA PREMIER LEAGUE 2015–16 LEAGUE RECORD

Match No.	Date	Venue	Opponents	Result	H/T Score	Lg Pos.	Goalscorers	Atten-dance
1	Aug 9	H	Southampton	D	2-2	1-1	7	Cisse [42], Wijnaldum [48]	49,019
2	15	A	Swansea C	L	0-2	0-1	15		20,678
3	22	A	Manchester U	D	0-0	0-0	16		75,354
4	29	H	Arsenal	L	0-1	0-0	18		50,388
5	Sept 14	A	West Ham U	L	0-2	0-1	20		34,907
6	19	H	Watford	L	1-2	0-2	19	Janmaat [62]	47,806
7	26	H	Chelsea	D	2-2	1-0	19	Perez [42], Wijnaldum [60]	48,682
8	Oct 3	A	Manchester C	L	1-6	1-1	20	Mitrovic [18]	53,850
9	18	H	Norwich C	W	6-2	3-2	18	Wijnaldum 4 [14, 26, 66, 85], Perez [33], Mitrovic [64]	47,006
10	25	A	Sunderland	L	0-3	0-1	19		47,653
11	31	H	Stoke C	D	0-0	0-0	18		47,139
12	Nov 7	A	Bournemouth	W	1-0	1-0	17	Perez [27]	11,155
13	21	H	Leicester C	L	0-3	0-1	17		50,151
14	28	A	Crystal Palace	L	1-5	1-3	19	Cisse [10]	24,833
15	Dec 6	H	Liverpool	W	2-0	0-0	18	Skrtel (og) [69], Wijnaldum [90]	51,273
16	13	A	Tottenham H	W	2-1	0-1	15	Mitrovic [74], Perez [90]	35,768
17	19	H	Aston Villa	D	1-1	1-0	17	Coloccini [38]	48,234
18	26	H	Everton	L	0-1	0-0	18		51,682
19	28	A	WBA	L	0-1	0-0	18		26,313
20	Jan 2	A	Arsenal	L	0-1	0-0	18		59,257
21	12	H	Manchester U	D	3-3	1-2	18	Wijnaldum [42], Mitrovic (pen) [67], Dummett [90]	49,673
22	16	H	West Ham U	W	2-1	2-0	17	Perez [6], Wijnaldum [15]	50,031
23	23	A	Watford	L	1-2	0-0	18	Lascelles [71]	20,611
24	Feb 3	A	Everton	L	0-3	0-1	18		36,061
25	6	H	WBA	W	1-0	1-0	17	Mitrovic [32]	50,152
26	13	A	Chelsea	L	1-5	0-3	18	Townsend [90]	41,622
27	Mar 2	A	Stoke C	L	0-1	0-0	18		27,331
28	5	H	Bournemouth	L	1-3	0-1	19	Perez [80]	52,107
29	14	A	Leicester C	L	0-1	0-1	19		31,824
30	20	H	Sunderland	D	1-1	0-1	19	Mitrovic [83]	52,311
31	Apr 2	A	Norwich C	L	2-3	0-1	19	Mitrovic 2 (1 pen) [71, 86 (p)]	27,137
32	9	A	Southampton	L	1-3	0-2	19	Townsend [65]	31,542
33	16	H	Swansea C	W	3-0	1-0	19	Lascelles [40], Sissoko [82], Townsend [89]	48,949
34	19	H	Manchester C	D	1-1	1-1	19	Anita [31]	46,424
35	23	A	Liverpool	D	2-2	0-2	19	Cisse [48], Colback [66]	43,837
36	30	H	Crystal Palace	W	1-0	0-0	17	Townsend [58]	52,107
37	May 7	A	Aston Villa	D	0-0	0-0	18		33,055
38	15	H	Tottenham H	W	5-1	2-0	18	Wijnaldum 2 (1 pen) [18, 73 (p)], Mitrovic [39], Aarons [85], Janmaat [86]	52,183

Final League Position: 18

GOALSCORERS

League (44): Wijnaldum 11 (1 pen), Mitrovic 9 (2 pens), Perez 6, Townsend 4, Cisse 3, Janmaat 2, Lascelles 2, Aarons 1, Anita 1, Colback 1, Coloccini 1, Dummett 1, Sissoko 1, own goal 1.
FA Cup (0).
Capital One Cup (4): De Jong 1, Janmaat 1, Thauvin 1, Williamson 1.

Krul T 8	Janmaat D 32	Mbemba C 33	Coloccini F 26	Haidara M 6 + 1	Anita V 24 + 4	Colback J 28 + 1	Sissoko M 37	Wijnaldum G 36 + 2	Obertan G 3 + 2	Cisse P 14 + 7	Mitrovic A 22 + 12	De Jong S 3 + 15	Taylor S 9 + 1	Aarons R 3 + 7	Perez A 22 + 12	Thauvin F 3 + 10	Mbabu K 2 + 1	Toney I — + 2	Gouffran Y 2 + 6	Lascelles J 10 + 8	Elliot R 21	Dummett P 23	Darlow K 9	Shelvey J 11 + 4	Saivet H 2 + 2	Riviere E 1 + 2	Townsend A 12 + 1	Doumbia S — + 3	Sterry J — + 1	Match No.
1	2	3	4	5	6[1]	7	8	9[3]	10	11[12]	12	13	14																	1
1	2[a]	3	4	5	6	7	8[1]	9	10[3]	11[12]	14		12	13																2
1	2		4	5	6	7		9	10[1]	14	13	11[3]	3		8[2]	12														3
1	2	3	4	5	6[1]	7	8[2]	9		13	11[4]	14			12	10[3]														4
1	2	3	4	5	6[1]	7	8	9[3]		11		13	14		12	10[2]														5
1	2	3	4	5[2]		7	9	6		14	11[1]	12	13		10	8[3]														6
1	2	3	4		8	7[1]	6[3]	9	12		11[2]	14			10				5	13										7
1	2	3	4			7	6[2]	9		13	10	11	14	5[1]	8[3]	12														8
	2	3	4	13	12	8	6	9		14	7[1]	11[3]			10						1	5[2]								9
	2	3	4[a]	13	8[2]	6	9			7[1]	11				10	14			12		1	5[3]								10
	2[2]	3	4		7	6	9			8[1]	10	12			11				13		1	5								11
	2	3	4		8[3]	6	9			12	7	10[1]			11[2]	13	14				1	5								12
	2	3	4		7	6	9			13	8[1]	10[2]	14		11[3]	12					1	5								13
	2	3	4		7	6[2]	8	10[3]		11		13			9[1]				14	12	1	5								14
	2	4	3		8	7[2]	6	9		11[3]		10[1]			12	14				13	1	5								15
	2	3	4		7[3]	8	6	9		11[2]		13	10[1]		12					14	1	5								16
	2	3	4		7[3]	8	6	9		11[1]		12	10[2]		13	14					1	5								17
	2	3	4		7	8	6	9		11		10[1]	12								1	5								18
	2	3	4		7[1]	6[3]	8	10		12	11	13			9[2]	14					5	1								19
	2	3	4		8[1]	6	9			7[2]	11	13			10	12					1	5								20
	2	3	4		6[1]	8	9			7[2]	11	14			10[3]						1	5								21
	2	3	4		6	8	9			11[3]		10[2]			13	14				5[1]	1		7	12						22
5	4	3[3]			9	10		11			8[1]	12			13	2	1						6	7[3]	14					23
2	3[1]	4			8	9		14		13	11	12[a]	1	5[2]					7	6[1]		10								24
2		4			8	9		7	11	3	5	12		13	1				6[2]	13		10[1]								25
2		4			12	8	9[1]			7[2]	11[3]	3	5			13	1		6			10	14							26
2					7[2]	8	9			11[3]		3			13	10[1]	4	1	5	6		12		14						27
2			12		7	8[3]	10			13		3	14	9			4	1	5[1]	6		11[2]								28
2			6[1]		5	10	9			11	13	3		8[2]			4	1	7[3]			12	14							29
2[2]	3		13		5[1]	10	7			14		11	12	9			4	1	6			8[3]								30
2	3		5[2]			10	9			11	7[1]	13	4		12			1	6			8								31
2[1]	4		5		6	9		14		11	12	3[2]	10[3]		13			1	7			8								32
	3		2	7	9	10[2]	11[3]	6[1]	14		13		4		5	1	12	8												33
	3		2	7	9	13	11[1]	6	12	14	10[3]		4		5	1	8[2]													34
	3		2	7	9	12	11[2]	6[3]	13	10[1]			4		5	1	14	8												35
	3		2[3]	7	9	10[2]	11[1]	6	12	13			4		5	1	14	8												36
	3		2	7[3]	9	10	11[1]	6[2]	12	14		13	4		5	1	8													37
	2	4		7	9[3]	8[2]	6[1]	11[a]	3	13		5	1	12	10	14														38

FA Cup

Third Round	Watford	(a)	0-1

Capital One Cup

Second Round	Northampton T	(h)	4-1
Third Round	Sheffield W	(h)	0-1

NEWPORT COUNTY

FOUNDATION

In 1912 Newport County were formed following a meeting at The Tredegar Arms Hotel. A professional football club had existed in the town called Newport FC, but they ceased to exist in 1907. The first season as Newport County was in the second division of the Southern League. They started life playing at Somerton Park where they remained through their League years. They were elected to the Football League for the beginning of the 1920–21 season as founder members of Division 3. At the end of the 1987–88 season, they were relegated from the Football League and replaced by Lincoln City. On February 27 1989, Newport County went out of business and from the ashes Newport AFC was born. Starting down the pyramid in the Hellenic League, they eventually gained promotion to the Conference in 2011 and were promoted to the Football League after a play-off with Wrexham in 2013.

Rodney Parade, Newport, South Wales NP19 0UU.

Telephone: (01633) 670 690.

Ticket Office: (01633) 674 990.

Website: www.newport-county.co.uk

Email: office@newport-county.co.uk

Ground Capacity: 8,381.

Record Attendance: 24,268 v Cardiff C, Division 3 (S), 16 October 1937 (Somerton Park); 4,660 v Swansea C, FA Cup 1st rd, 11 November 2006 (Newport Stadium); 6,615 v Grimsby T, Conference National Play-off semi-final, 28 April 2013 (Rodney Parade).

Pitch Measurements: 100.5m × 64m (110yd × 70yd).

Chairman: Tony Pring (interim).

Manager: Warren Feeney.

First-Team Coach: Sean McCarthy.

Colours: Amber shirts with black trim, black shorts with amber trim, amber socks with black hoops.

Year Formed: 1912.

Turned Professional: 1912.

Previous Names: Newport County, 1912; Newport AFC, 1989; Newport County, 1999.

Club Nicknames: 'The Exiles', 'The Ironsides', 'The Port', 'The County'.

Grounds: 1912–89, 1990–92, Somerton Park; 1992–94, Meadow Park Stadium; 1994, Newport Stadium; 2012, Rodney Parade.

First Football League Game: 28 August 1920, Division 3, v Reading (h) L 0–1.

HONOURS

League Champions: Division 3S – 1938–39.
Runners-up: Conference – (3rd) 2012–13 *(promoted via play-offs).*
FA Cup: 5th rd – 1949.
League Cup: never past 3rd rd.
Welsh Cup Winners: 1980.
Runners-up: 1963, 1987.
European Competitions
European Cup Winners' Cup: 1980–81 *(qf).*

sky SPORTS FACT FILE

The reformed Newport County have made two appearances at Wembley Stadium in their relatively short history. In 2012 they lost out to York City in the FA Trophy final in front of a crowd of 19,844 while 12 months later they defeated Wrexham in an all-Wales Conference play-off final before 16,346 fans.

Record League Victory: 10-0 v Merthyr T, Division 3(S), 10 April 1930 – Martin (5), Gittins (2), Thomas (1), Bagley (1), Lawson (1).

Record Cup Victory: 7-0 v Working, FA Cup 1st rd, 24 November 1928 – Young (3), Pugh (2) Gittins (1), Reid (1).

Record Defeat: 0–13 v Newcastle U, Division 2, 5 October 1946.

Most League Points (2 for a win): 61, Division 4, 1979–80.

Most League Points (3 for a win): 78, Division 3, 1982–83.

Most League Goals: 85, Division 4, 1964–65.

Highest League Scorer in Season: Tudor Martin, 34, Division 3 (S), 1929–30.

Most League Goals in Total Aggregate: Reg Parker, 99, 1948–54.

Most League Goals in One Match: 5, Tudor Martin v Merthyr T, Dvision 3 (S), 10 April 1930.

Most Capped Player: Nigel Vaughan, 3 (10), Wales.

Most League Appearances: Len Weare, 527, 1955–70.

Youngest League Player: Regan Poole, 16 years 94 days v Shrewsbury T, 20 September 2014.

Record Transfer Fee Received: £500,000 from Peterborough U for Conor Washington, January 2014.

Record Transfer Fee Paid: £80,000 to Swansea C for Alan Waddle, January 1981.

Football League Record: 1920 Original member of Division 3; 1921–31 Divsion 3 (S) – dropped out of Football League; 1932 Re-elected to Division 3 (S); 1932–39 Division 3 (S); 1946–47 Division 2; 1947–58 Division 3 (S); 1958–62 Division 3; 1962–80 Division 4; 1980–87 Division 3; 1987–88 Division 4 (relegated from Football League); 2011 Promoted to Conference; 2011–13 Conference Premier; 2013– FL 2.

LATEST SEQUENCES

Longest Sequence of League Wins: 4, 26.12.2014 – 10.1.2015.

Longest Sequence of League Defeats: 6, 19.3.2016 – 16.4.2016.

Longest Sequence of League Draws: 4, 31.10.2015 – 24.11.2015.

Longest Sequence of Unbeaten League Matches: 9, 10.11.2014 – 13.12.2014

Longest Sequence Without a League Win: 11, 15.3.2016 – 7.5.2016.

Successive Scoring Runs: 9 from 11.10.2014.

Successive Non-scoring Runs: 4 from 17.1.2015.

MANAGERS

Davy McDougle 1912–13
(Player-Manager)
Sam Hollis 1913–17
Harry Parkes 1919–22
Jimmy Hindmarsh 1922–35
Louis Page 1935–36
Tom Bromilow 1936–37
Billy McCandless 1937–45
Tom Bromilow 1945–50
Fred Stansfield 1950–53
Billy Lucas 1953–61
Bobby Evans 1961–62
Billy Lucas 1962–67
Leslie Graham 1967–69
Bobby Ferguson 1969–70
(Player-Manager)
Billy Lucas 1970–74
Brian Harris 1974–75
Dave Elliott 1975–76
(Player-Manager)
Jimmy Scoular 1976–77
Colin Addison 1977–78
Len Ashurst 1978–82
Colin Addison 1982–85
Bobby Smith 1985–86
John Relish 1986
Jimmy Mullen 1986–87
John Lewis 1987
Brian Eastick 1987–88
David Williams 1988
Eddie May 1988
John Mahoney 1988–89
John Relish 1989–93
Graham Rogers 1993–96
Chris Price 1997
Tim Harris 1997–2002
Peter Nicholas 2002–04
John Cornforth 2004–05
Peter Beadle 2005–08
Dean Holdsworth 2008–11
Anthony Hudson 2011
Justin Edinburgh 2011–15
Jimmy Dack 2015
Terry Butcher 2015
John Sheridan 2015–16
Warren Feeney January 2016–

TEN YEAR LEAGUE RECORD

		P	W	D	L	F	A	Pts	Pos
2006-07	Conf S	42	21	7	14	83	57	70	6
2007-08	Conf S	42	18	12	12	64	49	66	9
2008-09	Conf S	42	16	11	15	50	51	59	10
2009-10	Conf S	42	32	7	3	93	26	103	1
2010-11	Conf P	46	18	15	13	78	60	69	9
2011-12	Conf P	46	11	14	21	53	65	47	19
2012-13	Conf P	46	25	10	11	85	60	85	3
2013-14	FL 2	46	14	16	16	56	59	58	14
2014-15	FL 2	46	18	11	17	51	54	65	9
2015-16	FL 2	46	10	13	23	43	64	43	22

DID YOU KNOW ?

Newport County's first game on entering the Football League for the 2012–13 season was at home to Accrington Stanley, both clubs having previously been members before folding and reforming. County won the match 4-1 with goals from Harry Worley, Chris Zebroski (2) and Christian Jolley.

NEWPORT COUNTY – FOOTBALL LEAGUE TWO 2015–16 LEAGUE RECORD

Match No.	Date	Venue	Opponents	Result	H/T Score	Lg Pos.	Goalscorers	Attendance
1	Aug 8	A	Cambridge U	L	0-3	0-1	22		5022
2	15	H	Stevenage	D	2-2	0-1	20	Collins [58], Boden [79]	2521
3	18	A	Hartlepool U	L	0-1	0-0	21		3739
4	22	H	Leyton Orient	L	2-3	2-2	23	Boden [41], Byrne [42]	2779
5	29	A	Plymouth Arg	L	0-1	0-1	24		7811
6	Sept 5	H	York C	L	0-3	0-1	24		2459
7	12	H	Morecambe	L	1-2	0-1	24	Barrow [67]	2068
8	19	A	Dagenham & R	D	0-0	0-0	24		1654
9	26	A	Carlisle U	W	1-0	0-0	24	Blackwood [68]	4402
10	29	H	Crawley T	L	0-3	0-2	24		2137
11	Oct 3	H	Exeter C	D	1-1	0-0	24	John-Lewis [73]	2870
12	10	A	Mansfield T	L	0-3	0-0	24		3278
13	17	H	Portsmouth	L	0-1	0-1	24		3298
14	20	A	Wycombe W	W	2-0	0-0	24	Bean (og) [62], Boden [89]	2940
15	24	A	Bristol R	W	4-1	1-1	22	Parkes (og) [13], Ansah 2 [52, 57], O'Sullivan [75]	7442
16	31	H	Northampton T	D	2-2	2-2	21	Barrow [31], John-Lewis [38]	2424
17	Nov 14	A	Accrington S	D	2-2	0-0	21	Klukowski [54], Boden [66]	1552
18	21	H	Yeovil T	D	0-0	0-0	21		3084
19	24	A	Oxford U	D	1-1	1-0	21	John-Lewis [43]	5479
20	28	H	Luton T	W	3-0	0-0	21	McBurnie 3 [63, 79, 86]	2551
21	Dec 12	A	Notts Co	L	3-4	2-2	21	Byrne [5], Rodman [10], Boden [83]	4105
22	19	H	AFC Wimbledon	D	2-2	2-0	20	Rodman [14], Robinson (og) [30]	2798
23	26	A	Barnet	L	0-2	0-0	20		1831
24	28	H	Plymouth Arg	L	1-2	1-0	20	Boden [24]	4314
25	Jan 16	A	York C	W	1-0	1-0	20	Collins [8]	2923
26	23	H	Dagenham & R	D	2-2	0-2	20	Ayina [83], Wilkinson [88]	2323
27	26	A	Leyton Orient	L	0-1	0-0	20		4209
28	30	A	Morecambe	W	2-1	1-0	20	Boden 2 [1, 69]	1342
29	Feb 13	H	Carlisle U	W	1-0	0-0	20	Boden [56]	2106
30	20	A	Exeter C	D	1-1	0-0	20	Boden [84]	3924
31	27	H	Mansfield T	W	1-0	0-0	19	Boden [86]	2361
32	Mar 1	A	Crawley T	L	0-2	0-1	19		2003
33	5	H	Wycombe W	W	1-0	1-0	19	Boden [25]	2325
34	8	H	Barnet	L	0-3	0-2	19		2032
35	12	A	Portsmouth	W	3-0	1-0	18	Jones [34], Boden [69], Morgan [87]	16,245
36	15	H	Hartlepool U	D	0-0	0-0	17		2394
37	19	H	Bristol R	L	1-4	1-1	17	Rodman [2]	3663
38	25	A	Northampton T	L	0-1	0-1	17		5630
39	28	H	Accrington S	L	0-2	0-2	18		2218
40	Apr 2	A	Yeovil T	L	0-1	0-1	21		4063
41	9	H	Cambridge U	L	0-1	0-0	21		2330
42	16	A	Stevenage	L	1-2	0-2	22	Rodman [87]	2673
43	19	H	Oxford U	D	1-1	1-1	22	Elito [14]	2847
44	23	A	Luton T	D	1-1	1-0	22	Coulibaly [88]	7606
45	30	H	Notts Co	L	0-1	0-1	22		4903
46	May 7	A	AFC Wimbledon	L	0-1	0-0	22		4427

Final League Position: 22

GOALSCORERS

League (43): Boden 13, Rodman 4, John-Lewis 3, McBurnie 3, Ansah 2, Barrow 2, Byrne 2, Collins 2, Ayina 1, Blackwood 1, Coulibaly 1, Elito 1, Jones 1, Klukowski 1, Morgan 1, O'Sullivan 1, Wilkinson 1, own goals 3.
FA Cup (8): John-Lewis 2 (1 pen), Bennett 1, Boden 1, Byrne 1, Klukowski 1, Rodman 1, own goal 1.
Capital One Cup (1): Boden 1.
Johnstone's Paint Trophy (1): Collins 1.

Day J 41	Holmes D 33 + 2	Barrow S 27 + 7	Hayden A 4 + 1	Byrne M 45 + 1	Feely K 3	Elito M 36 + 2	Klukowski Y 17 + 11	Boden S 30 + 15	John-Lewis L 26 + 2	Rodman A 25 + 4	Collins A 8 + 10	Owen-Evans T 6 + 9	Poole R 3 + 1	Parselle K 7	Nana Ofori-Twumasi S 9 + 1	Ansah Z 9 + 4	Coulibaly S 2 + 4	Laurent J — + 3	Partridge M 19 + 1	Bamford L — + 1	Donacien J 24 + 5	Blackwood T 1 + 2	Taylor R 1	Taylor M 2 + 2	Bennett S 12	Barnum-Bobb J 11 + 1	O'Sullivan T 14 + 6	Hughes A 24 + 1	McBurnie O 2 + 1	Beeney M 4	Davies B 16 + 3	Dymond C 1	Smalley D 3	Wilkinson C 10 + 2	Ayina J 10 + 4	Jones D 17	Morgan D 2 + 7	Gosling J 2 + 4	Meechan T — + 3	Match No.
1	2	3	4	5	6^2	7	8	9	10^3	11^1	12	13	14																											1
1	2	5^2	12	7		6	8	10^1		11	13				4	3	9																							2
1	2	5		7		6	8^1	11		10	12				4	3	9																							3
1	2	5		7	3	6	8^3	11^2		12	14				4		9	10^1	13																					4
1	2^3	5	3	7	4	6	8^1	11^2	10		12						9	14	13																					5
1	2^4	5	3	8			7^2	11^1	10		6	12					9	13		4																				6
1		9	2	7		13		6^1	11		10^2	8		3	5	12			4																					7
1	2	5		7		9^2			10^1	11	8		4	6	12^3	13	3	14																						8
1	2^3	3		7				12	6		11^2	10		5	4			9		8^1	13	14																		9
1		9		7		14		8^2	10^1	12	13	6		4^3	5			3		2	11																			10
1	2	5		8		6	9^1	7^3	11	14	10^2	12						4	13	3																				11
1	2^3	5		8		9		7^1	14	10^2	13						12	11		3		4	6																	12
1	9^1		6	8				12	11^1	14	13								10^0	4	2				3	5	7													13
1	9		8	6		13		12	11										10^1	3	2				4	5	7^2													14
1	14	6^2		7		9		12	13	11									10^0	2	4				3	5	8^1													15
1	9		6	7		13		12	11^1		14								10^2	4	2				3	5	8^3													16
1	9		7	8		12		13	11	6									10^0	2	4^1				3	5														17
1	9^1		7	8		14		12	10	6^3									11^2	2					3	5	13	4												18
1	12		8	5		9^2		14	11	10	13									2					3^1	7	6^3	4												19
1			7	9		8^3		14	10^1	6	13								11^3	3					4	2	12	5	13											20
1	12		7	9				14	10^1	6	13									3	2				5^0	8^3	4	11											21
1			7	6				12	10	8										3	13				4	2	9^0	5	11^1											22
1	2	13		7		9^4		11	10	6^2	14									3					4	12^3	8^1	5												23
1		5^1	8					10	11	12									4	3					9	2	6	7												24
	2	13	8			9		12	10^2		11								3^1	5	14					6		1	4	7^3										25
	2	14	7			8^2	11		9	13									4^3							5		1	3	6^1	10	12								26
	2		7	10		9^1	13	6											4									1	5	8	11^2	12	3							27
	2	12	7	8		10		6											4									1	5	9^2	11^1	13	3							28
1	2	5^1	8			7^3	13	11^2	6										12									4		10	9	3	14							29
1	2		8			8	14	10	6^3										4^1							12		5		11	9^2	3	13							30
1	2	6^2	8			7	12	10											4									5		11	9	3	13							31
1	2		8	6^4		7^2	11												13									4		5^1	10	9^0	3	12	14					32
1	2		7	8		11^2	6												4									5		13	10	9	3	12						33
1	2^1		7	8^2		10	6			13									4^3									5		14	11	9	3	12						34
1	2		7	9^2		10^1	6												4									8	5		12	11^3	3	14	13					35
1	2	13	7	8		10	9												4									11^3	5^1		14		3	6^2	12					36
1	2^1		7	8		13	11	6											4									12	5		14	10^3	9	3^2						37
1	2	12		6		8	13	11	7										3									4^2	5		10^1			9						38
1	5	9		7			6^3	10	8	12								13	3^1									4^2			2			11	14				39
1	2		8	9			10	12	6										11^2									4^1		7	5			3		13			40
1	2^1	9^2	7	8			11^3	10	6										14									13		5	4		12	3					41
1	2	5		6		13	10^1	11											14									12		7^2	4		3^3	9	8				42
1	5	9		7		8	6^1	10	11										13									12	2		4			3					43
1	2	9^2	7	8		11^1	10^2	6											13									14	4		5			3	12				44
1	9	5	12	8		13	14		7^1	2					10	4^3	3											6								11^2			45
	2	9^2	7				11	10^3	6	8^1						12	3						1				13	4		5							14	46

FA Cup

First Round	Brackley T	(a)	2-2
Replay	Brackley T	(h)	4-1
Second Round	Barnet	(a)	1-0
Third Round	Blackburn R	(h)	1-2

Capital One Cup

First Round	Wolverhampton W	(a)	1-2

Johnstone's Paint Trophy

First Round	Swindon T	(h)	1-1

(*aet; Swindon T won 7-6 on penalties*)

NORTHAMPTON TOWN

FOUNDATION

Formed in 1897 by schoolteachers connected with the Northampton & District Elementary Schools' Association, they survived a financial crisis at the end of their first year when they were £675 in the red and became members of the Midland League – a fast move indeed for a new club. They achieved Southern League membership in 1901.

Sixfields Stadium, Upton Way, Northampton NN5 5QA.

Telephone: (01604) 683 700.

Fax: (01604) 751 613.

Ticket Office: (01604) 683 777.

Website: www.ntfc.co.uk

Email: gareth.willsher@ntfc.tv

Ground Capacity: 5,869.

Record Attendance: 24,523 v Fulham, Division 1, 23 April 1966 (at County Ground); 7,664 v Luton T, FL 2, 30 April 2016 (at Sixfields Stadium).

Pitch Measurements: 106m × 66m (116yd × 72yd).

Chairman: Kelvin Thomas.

Manager: Rob Page.

Assistant Manager: Paul Wilkinson.

Physio: Anders Braastad.

Colours: Claret shirts with white trim, white shorts with claret trim, claret socks with white trim.

Year Formed: 1897.

Turned Professional: 1901.

Grounds: 1897, County Ground; 1994, Sixfields Stadium.

Club Nickname: 'The Cobblers'.

First Football League Game: 28 August 1920, Division 3, v Grimsby T (a) L 0–2 – Thorpe; Sproston, Hewison; Jobey, Tomkins, Pease; Whitworth, Lockett, Thomas, Freeman, MacKechnie.

Record League Victory: 10–0 v Walsall, Division 3 (S), 5 November 1927 – Hammond; Watson, Jeffs; Allen, Brett, Odell; Daley, Smith (3), Loasby (3), Hoten (1), Wells (3).

Record Cup Victory: 10–0 v Sutton T, FA Cup prel rd, 7 December 1907 – Cooch; Drennan, Lloyd Davies, Tirrell (1), McCartney, Hickleton, Badenock (3), Platt (3), Lowe (1), Chapman (2), McDiarmid.

Record Defeat: 0–11 v Southampton, Southern League, 28 December 1901.

HONOURS

League Champions: Division 3 – 1962–63; FL 2 – 2015–16; Division 4 – 1986–87.
Runners-up: Division 2 – 1964–65; Division 3S – 1927–28, 1949–50; FL 2 – 2005–06; Division 4 – 1975–76.
FA Cup: 5th rd – 1934, 1950, 1970.
League Cup: 5th rd – 1965, 1967.

sky SPORTS FACT FILE

Jimmy McGuire, who made 70 appearances for Northampton Town between 1932 and 1936, later emigrated to the United States where he had previously played for Brooklyn Wanderers. He became a leading administrator of the game, serving the USSFA as president on two occasions and as a member of the FIFA Organizing Committee for the 1974 World Cup finals in West Germany.

Most League Points (2 for a win): 68, Division 4, 1975–76.

Most League Points (3 for a win): 99, Division 4, 1986–87; FL 2, 2015–16.

Most League Goals: 109, Division 3, 1962–63 and Division 3 (S), 1952–53.

Highest League Scorer in Season: Cliff Holton, 36, Division 3, 1961–62.

Most League Goals in Total Aggregate: Jack English, 135, 1947–60.

Most League Goals in One Match: 5, Ralph Hoten v Crystal Palace, Division 3 (S), 27 October 1928.

Most Capped Player: Edwin Lloyd Davies, 12 (16), Wales.

Most League Appearances: Tommy Fowler, 521, 1946–61.

Youngest League Player: Adrian Mann, 16 years 297 days v Bury, 5 May 1984.

Record Transfer Fee Received: £470,000 from Blackburn R for Mark Bunn, September 2008.

Record Transfer Fee Paid: £165,000 to Oldham Ath for Josh Low, July 2003.

Football League Record: 1920 Original Member of Division 3 (S); 1921 Division 3 (S); 1958–61 Division 4; 1961–63 Division 3; 1963–65 Division 2; 1965–66 Division 1; 1966–67 Division 2; 1967–69 Division 3; 1969–76 Division 4; 1976–77 Division 3; 1977–87 Division 4; 1987–90 Division 3; 1990–92 Division 4; 1992–97 Division 3; 1997–99 Division 2; 1999–2000 Division 3; 2000–03 Division 2; 2003–04 Division 3; 2004–06 FL 2; 2006–09 FL 1; 2009–16 FL 2; 2016– FL 1.

LATEST SEQUENCES

Longest Sequence of League Wins: 10, 28.12.2015 – 23.2.2016.

Longest Sequence of League Defeats: 8, 26.10.1935 – 21.12.1935.

Longest Sequence of League Draws: 6, 5.2.2011 – 26.2.2011.

Longest Sequence of Unbeaten League Matches: 24, 28.12.2015 – 7.5.2016.

Longest Sequence Without a League Win: 18, 5.2.2011 – 25.4.2011.

Successive Scoring Runs: 28 from 29.8.2015.

Successive Non-scoring Runs: 7 from 7.4.1939.

MANAGERS

Arthur Jones 1897–1907
(Secretary-Manager)
Herbert Chapman 1907–12
Walter Bull 1912–13
Fred Lessons 1913–19
Bob Hewison 1920–25
Jack Tresadern 1925–30
Jack English 1931–35
Syd Puddefoot 1935–37
Warney Cresswell 1937–39
Tom Smith 1939–49
Bob Dennison 1949–54
Dave Smith 1954–59
David Bowen 1959–67
Tony Marchi 1967–68
Ron Flowers 1968–69
Dave Bowen 1969–72
(continued as General Manager and Secretary 1972–85 when joined the board)
Billy Baxter 1972–73
Bill Dodgin Jnr 1973–76
Pat Crerand 1976–77
By committee 1977
Bill Dodgin Jnr 1977
John Petts 1977–78
Mike Keen 1978–79
Clive Walker 1979–80
Bill Dodgin Jnr 1980–82
Clive Walker 1982–84
Tony Barton 1984–85
Graham Carr 1985–90
Theo Foley 1990–92
Phil Chard 1992–93
John Barnwell 1993–94
Ian Atkins 1995–99
Kevin Wilson 1999–2001
Kevan Broadhurst 2001–03
Terry Fenwick 2003
Martin Wilkinson 2003
Colin Calderwood 2003–06
John Gorman 2006
Stuart Gray 2007–09
Ian Sampson 2009–11
Gary Johnson 2011
Aidy Boothroyd 2011–13
Chris Wilder 2014–16
Rob Page May 2016–

TEN YEAR LEAGUE RECORD

		P	W	D	L	F	A	Pts	Pos
2006-07	FL 1	46	15	14	17	48	51	59	14
2007-08	FL 1	46	17	15	14	60	55	66	9
2008-09	FL 1	46	12	13	21	61	65	49	21
2009-10	FL 2	46	18	13	15	62	53	67	11
2010-11	FL 2	46	11	19	16	63	71	52	16
2011-12	FL 2	46	12	12	22	56	79	48	20
2012-13	FL 2	46	21	10	15	64	55	73	6
2013-14	FL 2	46	13	14	19	42	57	53	21
2014-15	FL 2	46	18	7	21	67	62	61	12
2015-16	FL 2	46	29	12	5	82	46	99	1

DID YOU KNOW

Northampton Town were run by a committee elected by the membership of the club until 1922 when it was resolved to establish a limited company. The Northampton Town Football Club Limited was then formed with share capital of £8,000.

NORTHAMPTON TOWN – FOOTBALL LEAGUE TWO 2015–16 LEAGUE RECORD

Match No.	Date	Venue	Opponents	Result	H/T Score	Lg Pos.	Goalscorers	Attendance
1	Aug 8	A	Bristol R	W 1-0	0-0	9	O'Toole [49]	8712
2	15	H	Exeter C	W 3-0	2-0	4	Taylor [25], Cresswell [38], Richards [89]	4313
3	18	A	Barnet	L 0-2	0-0	7		2466
4	22	H	Plymouth Arg	L 0-2	0-1	10		4505
5	29	A	Accrington S	D 1-1	1-0	11	Richards [39]	1526
6	Sept 5	H	Dagenham & R	L 1-2	1-2	16	Richards [23]	4032
7	12	H	Oxford U	W 1-0	1-0	11	Hoskins [23]	4838
8	19	A	Morecambe	W 4-2	2-0	8	D'Ath [31], Hoskins [34], Byrom [48], Calvert-Lewin [69]	1778
9	26	H	Leyton Orient	D 1-1	0-0	8	Calvert-Lewin [90]	5061
10	29	A	AFC Wimbledon	D 1-1	1-1	10	O'Toole [35]	3525
11	Oct 3	A	Wycombe W	W 3-2	1-1	9	Richards [35], D'Ath [47], Brisley [51]	4227
12	10	H	Hartlepool U	W 2-1	2-1	8	Richards [4], Adams [21]	4477
13	17	A	Cambridge U	L 1-2	0-1	9	Richards (pen) [59]	5459
14	20	H	Carlisle U	W 3-2	1-1	5	Calvert-Lewin 2 [45, 63], Hoskins [47]	3642
15	24	H	Stevenage	W 2-1	0-1	4	Calvert-Lewin [49], Potter [62]	4492
16	31	A	Newport Co	D 2-2	2-2	5	Hoskins [10], Richards [30]	2424
17	Nov 14	H	Mansfield T	W 1-0	1-0	3	Richards [4]	5454
18	21	A	Notts Co	W 2-1	1-0	3	McDonald [31], Moloney [76]	5513
19	24	A	Crawley T	W 2-1	2-0	3	Byrom [6], O'Toole [20]	2325
20	28	H	Yeovil T	W 2-0	1-0	3	D'Ath [35], Richards [57]	4989
21	Dec 12	A	Luton T	W 4-3	3-1	1	O'Toole [18], D'Ath [30], Richards [42], Holmes [69]	8792
22	19	H	Portsmouth	L 1-2	1-1	2	Cresswell [17]	5859
23	28	H	Accrington S	W 1-0	0-0	2	Richards [63]	5269
24	Jan 2	A	Barnet	W 3-0	1-0	2	Hoskins [5], Holmes [52], Richards [60]	5153
25	12	A	Plymouth Arg	W 2-1	1-0	2	Collins [38], Richards [58]	9241
26	16	A	Dagenham & R	W 2-1	0-0	2	O'Toole [70], Holmes [79]	2379
27	23	H	Morecambe	W 3-1	2-0	1	Collins [30], O'Toole [40], McDonald [51]	4652
28	Feb 6	H	York C	W 2-0	1-0	1	O'Toole [21], Richards [54]	5342
29	13	A	Leyton Orient	W 4-0	0-0	1	McDonald [54], Holmes [64], Collins 2 [84, 90]	6131
30	16	A	Oxford U	W 1-0	0-0	1	Richards (pen) [59]	9559
31	20	H	Wycombe W	W 1-0	0-0	1	Rose [63]	5755
32	23	A	York C	W 2-1	1-0	1	Collins [40], Marquis [51]	2887
33	27	A	Hartlepool U	D 0-0	0-0	1		4012
34	Mar 1	H	AFC Wimbledon	D 1-1	1-0	1	O'Toole [45]	5124
35	5	A	Carlisle U	W 4-1	2-0	1	Marquis [16], O'Toole 2 [33, 59], Collins [74]	4892
36	12	H	Cambridge U	D 1-1	1-0	1	Marquis [71]	5828
37	19	A	Stevenage	W 3-2	1-2	1	Collins [41], O'Toole [51], Holmes [90]	3902
38	25	H	Newport Co	W 1-0	1-0	1	Marquis [22]	5630
39	28	A	Mansfield T	D 2-2	0-2	1	Holmes (pen) [64], Marquis [68]	4367
40	Apr 2	H	Notts Co	D 2-2	1-1	1	Holmes 2 (1 pen) [32, 76 (p)]	6428
41	9	A	Bristol R	D 2-2	1-0	1	Adams [23], Hoskins [49]	7579
42	16	A	Exeter C	D 0-0	0-0	1		5077
43	19	H	Crawley T	W 2-1	0-0	1	Holmes (pen) [48], O'Toole [80]	5327
44	23	A	Yeovil T	D 1-1	1-1	1	Adams [35]	4008
45	30	H	Luton T	W 2-0	1-0	1	Diamond [4], Marquis [36]	7664
46	May 7	A	Portsmouth	W 2-1	1-0	1	Whatmough (og) [14], Collins [81]	18,746

Final League Position: 1

GOALSCORERS

League (82): Richards 15 (2 pens), O'Toole 12, Holmes 9 (3 pens), Collins 8, Hoskins 6, Marquis 6, Calvert-Lewin 5, D'Ath 4, Adams 3, McDonald 3, Byrom 2, Cresswell 2, Brisley 1, Diamond 1, Moloney 1, Potter 1, Rose 1, Taylor 1, own goal 1.
FA Cup (7): Holmes 2, Calvert-Lewin 1, Diamond 1, Hoskins 1, Richards 1, Taylor 1.
Capital One Cup (4): Calvert-Lewin 1, Hackett 1, Hoskins 1, Richards 1 (pen).
Johnstone's Paint Trophy (3): Calvert-Lewin 1, Richards 1, Watson 1.

Smith A 46	Lelan J 10+1	Cresswell R 18+6	Diamond Z 37+2	Buchanan D 46	Potter A 12+9	Adams N 34+5	O'Toole J 36+2	Taylor J 8+22	Byron J 33+2	Richards M 28+3	Holmes R 20+8	Hoskins S 16+18	Corry P —+3	D'Ath L 25+14	McDonald R 21+2	Calvert-Lewin D 7+13	Hackett C 2+4	Watson R 4+7	Yates A 1	Furlong D 10	Brisley S 9	Moloney B 25	Collins J 16+5	Martin L 9+1	Rose D 13+2	Marquis J 13+2	Prosser L 7+1	Match No.
1	2	3	4	5	6^1	7^3	8^2	9	10	11	12	13	14															1
1	2	4	3^3	5	6		8^2	7	9	11	13	14		10^1	12													2
1		4	3	5			12	2^4		7	13	10^2																3
1	2^4	4	3	5	6^3	9^2		8^1	11		13	14	10		12		7											4
1		4		5	8^1	9		7^1	6	11			12	10^3	3		13	14	2									5
1	2^1	3		5	8^3	6			9	11		13		10^2	4	14	12	7										6
1		3		5	14	10^1	6^4	7^2	11		9^1	13	8			12				2	4							7
1		4		5	12	9	13		6			7^2		8^1	11	10				2	3							8
1		4	5^2	13	10	12		7	14		9^3		8^1	11		6				2	3							9
1	13	4	5		6	7		8	10		12		9^1	11^3	14					2	3^2							10
1		3	14	4	9^3	7		8	10		11^2		6^1	12	13					2	5							11
1		3		5	9^3	7	14	8	10		11^1		12	13	6^2					2	4							12
1		3		5	10	7		6	11		9^1		8^4	12	13					2^4	4							13
1	3^3	12		5	13	8	7	14	6	11			10^2		9^1					2	4							14
1		3	5	13	8	7		6	11		10^2		12	9^3	14					2	4^1							15
1		4	5	12	8	7	13	9^2	10		11^1		3	6^3	14					2								16
1	14	4	5	10^2	8^3	6	13	7	11		9^1	3	12										2					17
1		3	5	9	10^3	7	13	6	11^1		8^2	4	12		14								2					18
1	12	4	3	5	10^3	9^2	7	14	6	11^1		8	13										2^4					19
1	2	4	3	5	10^1	9	7^2	13	6	11^3		8	12		14								2					20
1		4	3	5	8^1	10^2	9^3	13	7	11	12		6		14								2					21
1		4	3^1	5	10^2	9^1	7		6	11	13	14	8		12								2					22
1		4	3	5	9^3	10^1	6	14	7	11^2	13		8		12								2					23
1		4	3	5	12	7	14	6	11^1	10^2	9^3		8		13								2					24
1	14	4	5	12	6	13	7	11^1	8^2		10^3	3											2	9				25
1		3	4		7^3	6	14	9	12	13	10^3			5									2	11	8^1			26
1		3	5	13	8	12	7	11^1	6	14			4										2	10^2	9^3			27
1	12	3^1	5	13	7	14	8	11^2	6^3				4										2	10	9			28
1	14	3	5		8	13		11^3	6^2	12	4												2	10	9^1	7		29
1		3	4		8	14		10^1	6^2	13	7	5											2	11^1	12	9		30
1		3	5		9^1	6	13		8^2	14	12	4											2	11	10^1	7		31
1		3	5		6^3		8	14		13	12	9^1	4										2	10		7	11^2	32
1		3	5		8	14		6			4^2												2	10	9^1	7	11^3 12	33
1		3	5		10^1	7		6		9			8										2	11		12	4	34
1		3	5		8	14	7		6^2	13		12											2	10	9^1	11^3	4	35
1		3	5		8		7		6			12											2	10^1	9^2 13	11	4	36
1		3	5		9^3	8	14	7		6^2 12	13												2	4		11^1 10		37
1		3	5		7		8^3		6	13		12											2	10^2	9^1 13	11	4	38
1		3	5		7	6^1		9^2 13	14	12	4											2	11		8	10^2	39
1		3	5		9^1	7		10^3	6	14	12	4											2	11^2		8	13	40
1		3	5		10^3	6	14		8	9^1	12	4											2	13		7	11^2	41
1		3	5		10^1	6	14		8	12	9^2	4											2	13		7	11^1	42
1	2	14	3	5	12	10^1	6		8^2	9	13	4														7	11^2	43
1	2		3	5	12	6^1	7		9	10^3	14	4											13			8	11^1	44
1	2		3	5	9^1	7	14		6	10^1	12	13	8										13			11^3	4	45
1	2		3	5	12	9^1	6		10	14		8^1											13			7	11^2 4	46

FA Cup

First Round	Coventry C	(a)	2-1
Second Round	Northwich Vic	(h)	3-2
Third Round	Milton Keynes D	(h)	2-2
Replay	Milton Keynes D	(a)	0-3

Capital One Cup

First Round	Blackpool	(h)	3-0
Second Round	Newcastle U	(a)	1-4

Johnstone's Paint Trophy

First Round	Colchester U	(h)	3-2
Second Round	Millwall	(a)	0-2

NORWICH CITY

FOUNDATION

Formed in 1902, largely through the initiative of two local schoolmasters who called a meeting at the Criterion Cafe, they were shocked by an FA Commission which in 1904 declared the club professional and ejected them from the FA Amateur Cup. However, this only served to strengthen their determination. New officials were appointed and a professional club established at a meeting in the Agricultural Hall in March 1905.

Carrow Road, Norwich, Norfolk NR1 1JE.

Telephone: (01603) 760 760.

Fax: (01603) 613 886.

Ticket Office: (0870) 444 1902.

Website: www.canaries.co.uk

Email: reception@ncfc-canaries.co.uk

Ground Capacity: 27,010.

Record Attendance: 25,037 v Sheffield W, FA Cup 5th rd, 16 February 1935 (at The Nest); 43,984 v Leicester C, FA Cup 6th rd, 30 March 1963 (at Carrow Road).

Pitch Measurements: 105m × 68m (114yd × 74yd).

Chairman: Ed Balls.

Joint Majority Shareholders: Delia Smith and Michael Wynn-Jones.

Chief Executive: David McNally.

Manager: Alex Neil.

First-Team Coaches: Frank McAvoy and Gary Holt.

Physio: Stuart Wardle.

Colours: Yellow shirts and green halved shirts, green shorts with yellow trim, yellow socks with green trim.

Year Formed: 1902.

Turned Professional: 1905.

Club Nickname: 'The Canaries'.

Grounds: 1902, Newmarket Road; 1908, The Nest, Rosary Road; 1935, Carrow Road.

First Football League Game: 28 August 1920, Division 3, v Plymouth Arg (a) D 1–1 – Skermer; Gray, Gadsden; Wilkinson, Addy, Martin; Laxton, Kidger, Parker, Whitham (1), Dobson.

Record League Victory: 10–2 v Coventry C, Division 3 (S), 15 March 1930 – Jarvie; Hannah, Graham; Brown, O'Brien, Lochhead (1); Porter (1), Anderson, Hunt (5), Scott (2), Slicer (1).

Record Cup Victory: 8–0 v Sutton U, FA Cup 4th rd, 28 January 1989 – Gunn; Culverhouse, Bowen, Butterworth, Linighan, Townsend (Crook), Gordon, Fleck (3), Allen (4), Phelan, Putney (1).

Record Defeat: 2–10 v Swindon T, Southern League, 5 September 1908.

HONOURS

League Champions: First Division – 2003–04; Division 2 – 1971–72, 1985–86; FL 1 – 2009–10; Division 3S – 1933–34.
Runners-up: FL C – 2010–11; Division 3 – 1959–60; Division 3S – 1950–51.

FA Cup: semi-final – 1959, 1989, 1992.

League Cup Winners: 1962, 1985.
Runners-up: 1973, 1975.

European Competitions
UEFA Cup: 1993–94.

sky SPORTS FACT FILE

Norwich City reached the quarter-finals of the FA Amateur Cup in 1903–04, defeating Harwich & Parkeston, Leiston, Kirkley, Lowestoft Town and Ilford before falling to Ealing in a replay. They then received a bye to the first round proper the following season but the FA decided they were a professional club and barred them from taking part.

Most League Points (2 for a win): 64, Division 3 (S), 1950–51.

Most League Points (3 for a win): 95, FL 1, 2009–10.

Most League Goals: 99, Division 3 (S), 1952–53.

Highest League Scorer in Season: Ralph Hunt, 31, Division 3 (S), 1955–56.

Most League Goals in Total Aggregate: Johnny Gavin, 122, 1945–54, 1955–58.

Most League Goals in One Match: 5, Tommy Hunt v Coventry C, Division 3 (S), 15 March 1930; 5, Roy Hollis v Walsall, Division 3 (S), 29 December 1951.

Most Capped Player: Mark Bowen, 35 (41), Wales.

Most League Appearances: Ron Ashman, 592, 1947–64.

Youngest League Player: Ryan Jarvis, 16 years 282 days v Walsall, 19 April 2003.

Record Transfer Fee Received: £8,000,000 from QPR for Leroy Fer, August 2014.

Record Transfer Fee Paid: £8,500,000 to Sporting Lisbon for Ricky van Wolfswinkel, July 2013.

Football League Record: 1920 Original Member of Division 3; 1921 Division 3 (S): 1934–39 Division 2; 1946–58 Division 3 (S); 1958–60 Division 3; 1960–72 Division 2; 1972–74 Division 1; 1974–75 Division 2; 1975–81 Division 1; 1981–82 Division 2; 1982–85 Division 1; 1985–86 Division 2; 1986–92 Division 1; 1992–95 FA Premier League; 1995–2004 Division 1; 2004–05 FA Premier League; 2005–09 FL C; 2009–10 FL 1; 2010–11 FL C; 2011–14 FA Premier League; 2014–15 FL C; 2015–16 FA Premier League; 2016– FL C.

LATEST SEQUENCES

Longest Sequence of League Wins: 10, 23.11.1985 – 25.1.1986.

Longest Sequence of League Defeats: 7, 1.4.1995 – 6.5.1995.

Longest Sequence of League Draws: 7, 15.1.1994 – 26.2.1994.

Longest Sequence of Unbeaten League Matches: 20, 31.8.1950 – 30.12.1950.

Longest Sequence Without a League Win: 25, 22.9.1956 – 23.2.1957.

Successive Scoring Runs: 25 from 14.9.2009.

Successive Non-scoring Runs: 5 from 18.9.2007.

MANAGERS

John Bowman 1905–07
James McEwen 1907–08
Arthur Turner 1909–10
Bert Stansfield 1910–15
Major Frank Buckley 1919–20
Charles O'Hagan 1920–21
Albert Gosnell 1921–26
Bert Stansfield 1926
Cecil Potter 1926–29
James Kerr 1929–33
Tom Parker 1933–37
Bob Young 1937–39
Jimmy Jewell 1939
Bob Young 1939–45
Duggie Lochhead 1945–46
Cyril Spiers 1946–47
Duggie Lochhead 1947–50
Norman Low 1950–55
Tom Parker 1955–57
Archie Macaulay 1957–61
Willie Reid 1961–62
George Swindin 1962
Ron Ashman 1962–66
Lol Morgan 1966–69
Ron Saunders 1969–73
John Bond 1973–80
Ken Brown 1980–87
Dave Stringer 1987–92
Mike Walker 1992–94
John Deehan 1994–95
Martin O'Neill 1995
Gary Megson 1995–96
Mike Walker 1996–98
Bruce Rioch 1998–2000
Bryan Hamilton 2000
Nigel Worthington 2000–06
Peter Grant 2006–07
Glenn Roeder 2007–09
Bryan Gunn 2009
Paul Lambert 2009–12
Chris Hughton 2012–14
Neil Adams 2014–15
Alex Neil January 2015–

TEN YEAR LEAGUE RECORD

		P	W	D	L	F	A	Pts	Pos
2006-07	FL C	46	16	9	21	56	71	57	16
2007-08	FL C	46	15	10	21	49	59	55	17
2008-09	FL C	46	12	10	24	57	70	46	22
2009-10	FL 1	46	29	8	9	89	47	95	1
2010-11	FL C	46	23	15	8	83	58	84	2
2011-12	PR Lge	38	12	11	15	52	66	47	12
2012-13	PR Lge	38	10	14	14	41	58	44	11
2013-14	PR Lge	38	8	9	21	28	62	33	18
2014-15	FL C	46	25	11	10	88	48	86	3
2015-16	PR Lge	38	9	7	22	39	67	34	19

DID YOU KNOW ?

The Norwich City Player of the Season Award was introduced in 1966–67. The winner receives the Barry Butler Memorial Trophy named after the former club captain killed in a car accident in April 1966. The first winner was long-serving player Terry Allcock.

NORWICH CITY – FA PREMIER LEAGUE 2015–16 LEAGUE RECORD

Match No.	Date		Venue	Opponents	Result		H/T Score	Lg Pos.	Goalscorers	Attendance
1	Aug	8	H	Crystal Palace	L	1-3	0-1	20	Redmond [69]	27,036
2		15	A	Sunderland	W	3-1	2-0	9	Martin [26], Whittaker [37], Redmond [57]	41,379
3		22	A	Stoke C	D	1-1	1-1	8	Martin [28]	26,771
4		30	A	Southampton	L	0-3	0-1	14		29,573
5	Sept	12	H	Bournemouth	W	3-1	1-0	8	Jerome [35], Hoolahan [52], Jarvis [67]	27,018
6		20	A	Liverpool	D	1-1	0-0	11	Martin [61]	44,072
7		26	A	West Ham U	D	2-2	1-1	13	Brady [9], Redmond [83]	34,857
8	Oct	3	H	Leicester C	L	1-2	0-1	13	Mbokani [68]	27,067
9		18	A	Newcastle U	L	2-6	2-3	16	Mbokani [20], Redmond [34]	47,006
10		24	H	WBA	L	0-1	0-0	16		26,983
11		31	A	Manchester C	L	1-2	0-0	16	Jerome [83]	53,418
12	Nov	7	H	Swansea C	W	1-0	0-0	15	Howson [70]	27,029
13		21	A	Chelsea	L	0-1	0-0	16		41,582
14		29	H	Arsenal	D	1-1	1-1	16	Grabban [43]	27,091
15	Dec	5	A	Watford	L	0-2	0-1	16		20,422
16		12	H	Everton	D	1-1	0-1	17	Hoolahan [47]	27,027
17		19	A	Manchester U	W	2-1	1-0	16	Jerome [38], Tettey [54]	75,320
18		26	A	Tottenham H	L	0-3	0-2	17		35,198
19		28	H	Aston Villa	W	2-0	1-0	15	Howson [24], Mbokani [87]	27,071
20	Jan	2	A	Southampton	W	1-0	0-0	14	Tettey [76]	27,022
21		13	A	Stoke C	L	1-3	0-0	15	Howson [55]	27,274
22		16	A	Bournemouth	L	0-3	0-1	16		11,065
23		23	H	Liverpool	L	4-5	2-1	16	Mbokani [29], Naismith [41], Hoolahan (pen) [54], Bassong [90]	27,108
24	Feb	2	H	Tottenham H	L	0-3	0-2	17		27,067
25		6	A	Aston Villa	L	0-2	0-1	18		32,472
26		13	H	West Ham U	D	2-2	0-0	17	Brady [54], Hoolahan [65]	27,101
27		27	A	Leicester C	L	0-1	0-0	17		32,114
28	Mar	1	A	Chelsea	L	1-2	0-2	18	Redmond [68]	27,091
29		5	A	Swansea C	L	0-1	0-0	18		20,929
30		12	H	Manchester C	D	0-0	0-0	18		26,323
31		19	A	WBA	W	1-0	0-0	17	Brady [50]	25,039
32	Apr	2	H	Newcastle U	W	3-2	1-0	17	Klose [45], Mbokani [74], Olsson [90]	27,137
33		9	A	Crystal Palace	L	0-1	0-0	17		24,960
34		16	H	Sunderland	L	0-3	0-1	17		27,117
35		30	A	Arsenal	L	0-1	0-0	19		59,989
36	May	7	H	Manchester U	L	0-1	0-0	19		27,132
37		11	H	Watford	W	4-2	3-1	18	Redmond [15], Mbokani 2 [18, 57], Cathcart (og) [37]	26,279
38		15	A	Everton	L	0-3	0-2	19		36,691

Final League Position: 19

GOALSCORERS

League (39): Mbokani 7, Redmond 6, Hoolahan 4 (1 pen), Brady 3, Howson 3, Jerome 3, Martin 3, Tettey 2, Bassong 1, Grabban 1, Jarvis 1, Klose 1, Naismith 1, Olsson 1, Whittaker 1, own goal 1.
FA Cup (0).
Capital One Cup (6): Bassong 1, Howson 1, Jarvis 1, Lafferty 1, van Wolfswinkel 1, own goal 1.

Ruddy J 27	Whittaker S 8	Martin R 30	Bassong S 30 + 2	Brady R 24 + 2	Howson J 33 + 3	Dorrans G 14 + 7	Hoolahan W 25 + 5	Tettey A 23	Johnson B 1 + 3	Grabban L 3 + 3	Redmond N 24 + 11	Jerome C 19 + 15	Hooper G — + 2	O'Neil G 19 + 8	Wisdom A 9 + 1	Jarvis M 13 + 6	Olsson M 20 + 4	Mbokani D 15 + 14	Lafferty K — + 1	Bennett R 20 + 2	Mulumbu Y 5 + 2	Odjidja-Ofoe V 3 + 7	Rudd D 11	Ivo Pinto D 9 + 1	Naismith S 11 + 2	Klose T 10	Bamford P 2 + 5	Match No.
1	2	3	4	5	6	7^3	8	9^2	10	11^1	12	13	14															1
1	2	3	4	5	10	6	9^1	7	12	13	8^3	11^2		14														2
1	2	3	4	5	9^2	7	10^1	8	12		6	11		13														3
1	2^4	3	4	5	9	7	10^1	8	13		6	11^3		14	12													4
1		3	4	5	7	12	10^1	8			6	11^3			2	9^2	13	14										5
1	2	3	4	5	9	8^2	6		12	7	11^1	13		10														6
1	2	3	4	10	8	6^2	9^3	7			13	11^1		14		5	12											7
1	2	3	4	5	6	8^1	10	7			12	11^3			9^2		13	14										8
1	2	3	4	10	9	6^2	12	7^1			8	13		14			5^3	11										9
1		2	4	5	8		10^1	7			6	12			9			11		3								10
1		4^4	5	2	7			8			14	12	11^3		13	10^1	6			3	9^2							11
1			4	9	6		10^2	7				11^1		8	2		5	12		3	13							12
1			4	9	6^1	13	12				10	14		7	2		5	11^2		3	8^3							13
1			4	10	8^1	7	9^2				11^3	12	14	6	2		5			3		13						14
			4	10	9^3	7		8			11^2	6^1	13		2		5	12		3		14	1					15
		3	4	10	13		9^2	6			8	11		7	2^1		5			12			1					16
		2	4	10	12		9^1	7			8	11^3		6^2			5	14		3	13		1					17
		2	4	10^3	12	13		7			8	11					5	14		3	6^2	9^1	1					18
		2	4	5	6	8^1	10^3	7			9	14		12				11^2		3		13	1					19
		2	4	5	10		9^3	7			6^1	13		8			14	11^2		3		12	1					20
		2	4	5	9		10^2	7			12	14		8^4		13		11^3		3		6^1	1					21
		2	4	5	8	14	10^3	7			12	13				9^1		11		3		6^2	1					22
		3	4	5	7	6	10^1				8^2	14			12	13	11							1	2	9^3		23
			4		6			7				12			9^1	5	11			8	13	1		2	10^2	3		24
		2	4	5	6		9^2				12			7		14		11			8^1		1		10^3	3	13	25
1		2	4	5	8	14	10^3				6	11^2		7		12	13								9^1	3		26
1		4		6	9			8			7	11^3			12		14	3						2	10^1	5^2	13	27
1		4		6	9		10	8^1			7	11		12			13	3^2						2	5			28
1		3		5^1	8		10				6	11^3		7			14	12		3				2	9^2	4	13	29
1		2			8	12	10^2				6^1	13		7		9	5	14		3						4	11^3	30
1		2	4	9^2	8			7			6	5	11			6^3?						13		14	12	3	10^1	31
1			9	7		13					12	14		8	2	6^1	5	11^3		3					10^2	4		32
1		12	9	8							14			7	2	6^2	5	11		3					10^2	4^1	13	33
1		4	9^1	8		13					12	14		7	2	6^2	5	11		3					10^3			34
1		3	4^3	9^2	8		10^1				6	11		7		14	5	12						2	13			35
1		3	4	9^1	8^3	13	10				6	11^2		7		5	12							2			14	36
1		4		12		7	10^1				8^2			6	13	5	11			3		14		2	9^3			37
1		3	13	12			8	14			6	11		7		9^3	5^1			4^2				2	10			38

FA Cup
Third Round   Manchester C   (h)   0-3

Capital One Cup
Second Round   Rotherham U   (a)   2-1
Third Round   WBA   (h)   3-0
Fourth Round   Everton   (a)   1-1
(aet; Everton won 4-3 on penalties)

NOTTINGHAM FOREST

FOUNDATION

One of the oldest football clubs in the world, Nottingham Forest was formed at a meeting in the Clinton Arms in 1865. Known originally as the Forest Football Club, the game which first drew the founders together was 'shinney', a form of hockey. When they determined to change to football in 1865, one of their first moves was to buy a set of red caps to wear on the field.

The City Ground, Pavilion Road, Nottingham NG2 5FJ.
Telephone: (0115) 982 4444.
Fax: (0115) 982 4455.
Ticket Office: (0115) 982 4388
Website: www.nottinghamforest.co.uk
Email: info@nottinghamforest.co.uk
Ground Capacity: 30,445.
Record Attendance: 49,946 v Manchester U, Division 1, 28 October 1967.
Pitch Measurements: 102.5m × 67.5m (112yd × 74yd).
Chairman: Fawaz Mubarak Al-Hasawi.
Head Coach: Philippe Montanier.
First-Team Assistant: Serge Romano.
Physio: Steve Devine.
Colours: Red shirt with gold trim, white shorts with gold trim, red socks with gold trim.
Year Formed: 1865.
Turned Professional: 1889.
Previous Name: Forest Football Club.
Club Nickname: 'The Reds'.
Grounds: 1865, Forest Racecourse; 1879, The Meadows; 1880, Trent Bridge Cricket Ground; 1882, Parkside, Lenton; 1885, Gregory, Lenton; 1890, Town Ground; 1898, City Ground.

HONOURS

League Champions: Division 1 – 1977–78; First Division – 1997–98; Division 2 – 1906–07, 1921–22; Division 3S – 1950–51.
Runners-up: Division 1 – 1966–67, 1978–79; First Division – 1993–94; Division 2 – 1956–57; FL 1 – 2007–08.
FA Cup Winners: 1898, 1959.
Runners-up: 1991.
League Cup Winners: 1978, 1979, 1989, 1990.
Runners-up: 1980, 1992.
Anglo-Scottish Cup Winners: 1977.
Full Members' Cup Winners: 1989, 1992.
European Competitions
European Cup: 1978–79 *(winners)*, 1979–81 *(winners)*, 1980–81.
Fairs Cup: 1961–62, 1967–68.
UEFA Cup: 1983–84 *(sf)*, 1984–85, 1995–96 *(qf)*.
Super Cup: 1979 *(winners)*, 1980.
World Club Championship: 1980.

First Football League Game: 3 September 1892, Division 1, v Everton (a) D 2–2 – Brown; Earp, Scott; Hamilton, Albert Smith, McCracken; McCallum, 'Tich' Smith, Higgins (2), Pike, McInnes.
Record League Victory: 12–0 v Leicester Fosse, Division 1, 12 April 1909 – Iremonger; Dudley, Maltby; Hughes (1), Needham, Armstrong; Hooper (3), Marrison, West (3), Morris (2), Spouncer (3 incl. 1p).
Record Cup Victory: 14–0 v Clapton (away), FA Cup 1st rd, 17 January 1891 – Brown; Earp, Scott; Albert Smith, Russell, Jeacock; McCallum (2), 'Tich' Smith (1), Higgins (5), Lindley (4), Shaw (2).
Record Defeat: 1–9 v Blackburn R, Division 2, 10 April 1937.
Most League Points (2 for a win): 70, Division 3 (S), 1950–51.
Most League Points (3 for a win): 94, Division 1, 1997–98.
Most League Goals: 110, Division 3 (S), 1950–51.

sky SPORTS FACT FILE

Nottingham Forest players made a significant contribution in the First World War. A total of 11 out of 16 of the men who played in 1914–15 joined the Forces. Goalkeeper Bill Fiske was killed in action, captain Joe Mercer spent 18 months as a prisoner of war, while both Mercer and Edwin Neve died prematurely due to the effects of being gassed.

Highest League Scorer in Season: Wally Ardron, 36, Division 3 (S), 1950–51.

Most League Goals in Total Aggregate: Grenville Morris, 199, 1898–1913.

Most League Goals in One Match: 4, Enoch West v Sunderland, Division 1, 9 November 1907; 4, Tommy Gibson v Burnley, Division 2, 25 January 1913; 4, Tom Peacock v Port Vale, Division 2, 23 December 1933; 4, Tom Peacock v Barnsley, Division 2, 9 November 1935; 4, Tom Peacock v Port Vale, Division 2, 23 November 1935; 4, Tom Peacock v Doncaster R, Division 2, 26 December 1935; 4, Tommy Capel v Gillingham, Division 3 (S), 18 November 1950; 4, Wally Ardron v Hull C, Division 2, 26 December 1952; 4, Tommy Wilson v Barnsley, Division 2, 9 February 1957; 4, Peter Withe v Ipswich T, Division 1, 4 October 1977; 4, Marlon Harewood v Stoke C, Division 1, 22 February 2003; Gareth McCleary v Leeds U, FL C, 20 March 2012.

Most Capped Player: Stuart Pearce, 76 (78), England.

Most League Appearances: Bob McKinlay, 614, 1951–70.

Youngest League Player: Craig Westcarr, 16 years 257 days v Burnley, 13 October 2001.

Record Transfer Fee Received: £8,500,000 from Liverpool for Stan Collymore, June 1995.

Record Transfer Fee Paid: £5,500,000 to Peterborough U for Britt Assombalonga, August 2014.

Football League Record: 1892 Elected to Division 1; 1906–07 Division 2; 1907–11 Division 1; 1911–22 Division 2; 1922–25 Division 1; 1925–49 Division 2; 1949–51 Division 3 (S); 1951–57 Division 2; 1957–72 Division 1; 1972–77 Division 2; 1977–92 Division 1; 1992–93 FA Premier League; 1993–94 Division 1; 1994–97 FA Premier League; 1997–98 Division 1; 1998–99 FA Premier League; 1999–2004 Division 1; 2004–05 FL C; 2005–08 FL 1; 2008– FL C.

LATEST SEQUENCES

Longest Sequence of League Wins: 7, 9.5.1979 – 1.9.1979.
Longest Sequence of League Defeats: 14, 21.3.1913 – 27.9.1913.
Longest Sequence of League Draws: 7, 29.4.1978 – 2.9.1978.
Longest Sequence of Unbeaten League Matches: 42, 26.11.1977 – 25.11.1978.
Longest Sequence Without a League Win: 19, 8.9.1998 – 16.1.1999.
Successive Scoring Runs: 22 from 28.3.1931.
Successive Non-scoring Runs: 7 from 26.11.2011.

MANAGERS

Harry Radford 1889–97
  (Secretary-Manager)
Harry Haslam 1897–1909
  (Secretary-Manager)
Fred Earp 1909–12
Bob Masters 1912–25
John Baynes 1925–29
Stan Hardy 1930–31
Noel Watson 1931–36
Harold Wightman 1936–39
Billy Walker 1939–60
Andy Beattie 1960–63
Johnny Carey 1963–68
Matt Gillies 1969–72
Dave Mackay 1972
Allan Brown 1973–75
Brian Clough 1975–93
Frank Clark 1993–96
Stuart Pearce 1996–97
Dave Bassett 1997–99
  (previously General Manager)
Ron Atkinson 1999
David Platt 1999–2001
Paul Hart 2001–04
Joe Kinnear 2004
Gary Megson 2005–06
Colin Calderwood 2006–08
Billy Davies 2009–11
Steve McClaren 2011
Steve Cotterill 2011–12
Sean O'Driscoll 2012
Alex McLeish 2012–13
Billy Davies 2013–14
Stuart Pearce 2014–15
Dougie Freedman 2015–16
Philippe Montanier June 2016–

TEN YEAR LEAGUE RECORD

		P	W	D	L	F	A	Pts	Pos
2006-07	FL 1	46	23	13	10	65	41	82	4
2007-08	FL 1	46	22	16	8	64	32	82	2
2008-09	FL C	46	13	14	19	50	65	53	19
2009-10	FL C	46	22	13	11	65	40	79	3
2010-11	FL C	46	20	15	11	69	50	75	6
2011-12	FL C	46	14	8	24	48	63	50	19
2012-13	FL C	46	17	16	13	63	59	67	8
2013-14	FL C	46	16	17	13	67	64	65	11
2014-15	FL C	46	15	14	17	71	69	59	14
2015-16	FL C	46	13	16	17	43	47	55	16

DID YOU KNOW ?

Ernest Jardine, who made three FA Cup appearances for Nottingham Forest in the 1870s, became a leading industrialist in Nottingham. He was also prominent in politics, serving as MP for East Somerset from 1910 to 1918 before being appointed a baronet in 1919. In later life he held the post of club president.

NOTTINGHAM FOREST – FL CHAMPIONSHIP 2015–16 LEAGUE RECORD

Match No.	Date	Venue	Opponents	Result	H/T Score	Lg Pos.	Goalscorers	Attendance
1	Aug 7	A	Brighton & HA	L	0-1	0-0	24		24,623
2	15	H	Rotherham U	W	2-1	1-1	12	Mills [45], Antonio [61]	19,885
3	18	H	Charlton Ath	D	0-0	0-0	11		17,801
4	22	A	Bolton W	D	1-1	0-0	11	Vaughan [81]	16,410
5	29	H	Cardiff C	L	1-2	0-1	16	Antonio [86]	18,762
6	Sept 12	A	QPR	W	2-1	0-0	12	Lansbury (pen) [75], Nelson Oliveira [82]	15,424
7	15	A	Birmingham C	W	1-0	0-0	8	Blackstock [54]	16,604
8	19	H	Middlesbrough	L	1-2	1-2	11	Mills [7]	20,993
9	24	A	Huddersfield T	D	1-1	1-0	10	Mendes [23]	11,299
10	Oct 3	H	Hull C	L	0-1	0-1	13		20,985
11	16	A	Bristol C	L	0-2	0-2	14		15,285
12	20	H	Burnley	D	1-1	0-0	15	Lichaj [73]	17,721
13	24	H	Ipswich T	D	1-1	0-0	16	Trotter [90]	19,616
14	31	A	Sheffield W	L	0-1	0-0	17		22,465
15	Nov 3	A	Preston NE	L	0-1	0-1	19		10,216
16	6	H	Derby Co	W	1-0	1-0	15	Nelson Oliveira [5]	25,114
17	21	A	Brentford	L	1-2	0-0	18	Lansbury [74]	11,403
18	28	H	Reading	W	3-1	2-1	16	O'Grady [20], Nelson Oliveira 2 [31, 49]	18,128
19	Dec 5	H	Fulham	W	3-0	1-0	15	Mills 2 [45, 78], O'Grady [52]	18,377
20	11	A	Wolverhampton W	D	1-1	0-1	15	Blackstock [80]	20,000
21	14	A	Blackburn R	D	0-0	0-0	15		12,002
22	19	H	Milton Keynes D	W	2-1	2-0	13	Nelson Oliveira [2], Mendes [16]	19,975
23	27	H	Leeds U	D	1-1	1-0	13	Nelson Oliveira [17]	27,551
24	29	A	Cardiff C	D	1-1	1-1	14	Burke, O [9]	15,461
25	Jan 2	A	Charlton Ath	D	1-1	1-0	14	Osborn [44]	16,090
26	12	H	Birmingham C	D	1-1	1-1	14	Mills [30]	18,342
27	16	H	Bolton W	W	3-0	2-0	12	Nelson Oliveira (pen) [12], Burke, O [16], Ward [83]	18,465
28	23	A	Middlesbrough	W	1-0	0-0	11	Ward [70]	24,975
29	26	H	QPR	D	0-0	0-0	11		17,030
30	Feb 6	A	Leeds U	W	1-0	0-0	10	Nelson Oliveira [60]	24,079
31	13	H	Huddersfield T	L	0-2	0-1	10		19,984
32	23	H	Burnley	L	0-1	0-0	12		15,517
33	27	H	Bristol C	L	1-2	1-1	15	Osborn [30]	20,551
34	Mar 5	A	Ipswich T	L	0-1	0-0	15		20,658
35	8	H	Preston NE	W	1-0	1-0	13	Nelson Oliveira [37]	16,747
36	12	H	Sheffield W	L	0-3	0-1	14		20,690
37	15	A	Hull C	D	1-1	1-0	14	Gardner [28]	15,663
38	19	A	Derby Co	L	0-1	0-0	15		33,010
39	Apr 2	H	Brentford	L	0-3	0-0	16		19,444
40	5	A	Reading	L	1-2	1-0	17	Osborn [41]	15,678
41	11	H	Brighton & HA	L	1-2	0-1	20	Blackstock [50]	17,642
42	16	A	Rotherham U	D	0-0	0-0	19		11,503
43	19	H	Blackburn R	D	1-1	1-1	18	Blackstock [15]	16,449
44	23	A	Fulham	W	3-1	2-0	17	Tesche [23], Lansbury 2 (1 pen) [43 (pl), 70]	18,253
45	30	H	Wolverhampton W	D	1-1	0-0	17	Gardner [68]	22,291
46	May 7	A	Milton Keynes D	W	2-1	1-1	16	Cohen [8], Assombalonga [74]	15,486

Final League Position: 16

GOALSCORERS
League (43): Nelson Oliveira 9 (1 pen), Mills 5, Blackstock 4, Lansbury 4 (2 pens), Osborn 3, Antonio 2, Burke, O 2, Gardner 2, Mendes 2, O'Grady 2, Ward 2, Assombalonga 1, Cohen 1, Lichaj 1, Tesche 1, Trotter 1, Vaughan 1.
FA Cup (1): Ward 1.
Capital One Cup (3): Antonio 2, Walker 1.

De Vries D 45	Lichaj E 43	Mills M 42	Hobbs J 18 + 2	Fox D 8 + 2	Tesche R 17 + 7	Lansbury H 26 + 2	Mancienne M 29 + 2	Ward J 20 + 11	Blackstock D 12 + 17	Antonio M 4	Vaughan D 31 + 4	Walker T 5 + 9	Paterson J — + 1	Wilson K 11 + 3	Burke C 7 + 2	Burke O 6 + 12	Grant J 2 + 8	Pinillos D 19	Ebecilio K 3 + 2	Osborn B 32 + 4	McDonagh G — + 1	Mendes R 26 + 6	O'Grady C 15 + 6	Nelson Oliveira M 24 + 4	Williams J 4 + 6	Trotter L 5 + 4	Evtimov D 1	Cohen C 11 + 4	Jokic B 19 + 1	Gardner G 18 + 2	Petravicius D — + 1	Macheda F 3	Assombalonga B — + 4	Match No.
1	2	3	4	5^1	6^2	7	8	9^3	10	11	12	13	14																					1
1	5	3			7	2	10^2	12	6	8	11^1			4	9	13																		2
1	2	3			7	5	10^1	11^2			8	12		4	9	6	13																	3
1	2	3	4	14		9	7				8	13		11^1		12		5		6^2	10^3													4
1	2	3	4			6		13	10		9	11^2		7^1				5		8^3	12	14												5
1	2	3			6	7^1	12				8	9^2		4				5	13^3			10	11	14										6
1	2	4				7		11^2	10^1		14			3	9			5	8^3	6		13	12											7
1	2	3^3	12			7		13			8			4				5		9^1		11	6	10^2	14									8
1	2		4			8	6	7^2	13		9	13		3	12			5				11	10^1											9
1	2	3^1	4			6	7^2	13			8	14						5	12^3			10	11^1	9										10
1		3^1	2			7		13	14		8			4	6^3			5				10	9	11^2	12									11
1	2		3			7^1		6^1	12		8	9^2		4		13	5			14	11	10^2												12
1	2		3^1					9^3	13		8			4		12	5			14	11	10	6^3	7										13
	2	3^2						10^3	11		7			4	8^1		5			12		14		9	13	6	1							14
1	2	3	4					6^1	14			13				8^3	5			9		10^2	11	12	7									15
1	2	3	4			7		8^2	14		6						5			12		10	11^3	9^1	13									16
1	2	3	4			7		6	13		9	14										10^3	11^1	12	8^2									17
1	2	3	4^4			8	13				7			12				5		9		11^3	6^2	10^1		14								18
1	2	3			14	8	4				7					12	5			9^1		11	6^3	10^2		13								19
1	2	3			7	4	12	14			8						5			9^1		11^3	6^2	10	13									20
1	2	3			7	6	4	8	11^1								5			10		13		12	9^2									21
1	2	3	12			7	4	13			8						5^2			9		10	6^1	11^3		14								22
1	2	3	4			13	7	5	12		8^3					14				9		11^1	6^2	10										23
1	2	3	4		6	14	5	10	11^2							8^1				12		13	9^3	7										24
1	2	3	4^1		12	6	5		13		7			8^3						10		9^2	11			14								25
1	2	3			7	4	12				8^4					14				9		11^3	6^2	10^1				5	13					26
1	2	3^1				8^3	4	10				12				6^1				9		14	11^2				13	5	7					27
1	2	3	4			9	6	11^1			14			7^2						10		13	12					5	8^1					28
1	2	3	4			8		7	12	14		13								9		10^3	6^2	11^1				5						29
1	2	3			8		4	7^1	13	9						12				10			11^2					5	6					30
1	2	3			6^3		4	9^2	14	8						12	13			11			10					5	7^1					31
1	2	3			6^2		4	9	12	8^3						14				11^1			10				13	5	7					32
1	2	3			7^3		4	10^1	8^2	12						9				14		11					6	5	13					33
1	2	3				4		11	8^2	12						14				9		6^3	10^2			12	5^1	7	13				34
1	2	3			8	4			14											9		10	6^2	11^3				5^1	12	7				35
1	2	3			13	4		8	14							12	10^1			9		11	6					5^2		7^3				36
1	2	3			13	4	14	7				12								10		6^1						9^2	5	8	11^3			37
1	2	3			4	12	14	7				13								11		9^2						8^3	5	6	10^1			38
1	2^8	3			13	4^1		7				12	14							11		9^2						8	5	6	10^9			39
1		3	12	14	8^1			13	11	9				4^3	6^2					10								7	5	2				40
1	2	3			4	14	9		11^2	12		7^3								8		13						10	5	6^1				41
1	2	3			4	7	9		11^1											10		12	8					5	6					42
1	2	3			4	6^1	9		11			12								10		8^2						5	7		13		43
1	2	3			4	7	10		11^1							9						6	5	8	12						12		44
1	2	3			4	7	9		11^1			12				8						10^2	5	6							13		45
1	2	3			4^6	6^3	12					9^2				11						10^1	14	8	5	7					13		46

FA Cup
Third Round   QPR   (h)   1-0
Fourth Round   Watford   (h)   0-1

Capital One Cup
First Round   Walsall   (h)   3-4

NOTTS COUNTY

FOUNDATION

According to the official history of Notts County 'the true date of Notts' foundation has to be the meeting at the George Hotel on 7 December 1864'. However, there is documented evidence of continuous play from 1862, when club members played organised matches amongst themselves in The Park in Nottingham. They are the world's oldest professional football club.

Meadow Lane Stadium, Meadow Lane, Nottingham NG2 3HJ.

Telephone: (0115) 952 9000.

Fax: (0115) 955 3994.

Ticket Office: (0115) 955 7210.

Website: www.nottscountyfc.co.uk

Email: office@nottscountyfc.co.uk

Ground Capacity: 19,841.

Record Attendance: 47,310 v York C, FA Cup 6th rd, 12 March 1955.

Pitch Measurements: 103.5m × 64m (113yd × 70yd).

Director: Aileen Trew.

Chief Executive: Jason Turner.

Manager: John Sheridan.

Assistant Manager: Mark Crossley.

Head of Sports Science and Medicine: John Wilson.

HONOURS

League Champions: Division 2 – 1896–97, 1913–14, 1922–23; Division 3S – 1930–31, 1949–50; FL 2 – 2009–10; Third Division – 1997–98; Division 4 – 1970–71.
Runners-up: Division 2 – 1894–95, 1980–81; Division 3 – 1972–73; Division 3S – 1936–37; Division 4 – 1959–60.
FA Cup Winners: 1894.
Runners-up: 1891.
League Cup: 5th rd – 1964, 1973, 1976.
Anglo-Italian Cup Winners: 1995.
Runners-up: 1994.

Colours: Black and white striped shirts, black shorts with yellow trim, black socks with white trim.

Year Formed: 1862* (*see Foundation*). *Turned Professional:* 1885.

Club Nickname: 'The Magpies'.

Grounds: 1862, The Park; 1864, The Meadows; 1877, Beeston Cricket Ground; 1880, Castle Ground; 1883, Trent Bridge; 1910, Meadow Lane.

First Football League Game: 15 September 1888, Football League, v Everton (a) L 1–2 – Holland; Guttridge, McLean; Brown, Warburton, Shelton; Hodder, Harker, Jardine, Albert Moore (1), Wardle.

Record League Victory: 11–1 v Newport Co, Division 3 (S), 15 January 1949 – Smith; Southwell, Purvis; Gannon, Baxter, Adamson; Houghton (1), Sewell (4), Lawton (4), Pimbley, Johnston (2).

Record Cup Victory: 15–0 v Rotherham T (at Trent Bridge), FA Cup 1st rd, 24 October 1885 – Sherwin; Snook, Henry Thomas Moore; Dobson (1), Emmett (1), Chapman; Gunn (1), Albert Moore (2), Jackson (3), Daft (2), Cursham (4), (1 og).

Record Defeat: 1–9 v Blackburn R, Division 1, 16 November 1889. 1–9 v Aston Villa, Division 1, 29 September 1888. 1–9 v Portsmouth, Division 2, 9 April 1927.

Most League Points (2 for a win): 69, Division 4, 1970–71.

sky SPORTS FACT FILE

As the Football League's oldest club, Notts County were the first to celebrate their centenary. They did so with a game against an England XI preparing for the 1962 World Cup finals. County lost 3-1 in front of a crowd of 11,022, with Tony Hateley scoring their only goal.

Most League Points (3 for a win): 99, Division 3, 1997–98.

Most League Goals: 107, Division 4, 1959–60.

Highest League Scorer in Season: Tom Keetley, 39, Division 3 (S), 1930–31.

Most League Goals in Total Aggregate: Les Bradd, 125, 1967–78.

Most League Goals in One Match: 5, Robert Jardine v Burnley, Division 1, 27 October 1888; 5, Daniel Bruce v Port Vale, Division 2, 26 February 1895; 5, Bertie Mills v Barnsley, Division 2, 19 November 1927.

Most Capped Player: Kevin Wilson, 15 (42), Northern Ireland.

Most League Appearances: Albert Iremonger, 564, 1904–26.

Youngest League Player: Tony Bircumshaw, 16 years 54 days v Brentford, 3 April 1961.

Record Transfer Fee Received: £2,500,000 from Derby Co for Craig Short, September 1992.

Record Transfer Fee Paid: £800,000 to Manchester C for Kasper Schmeichel, July 2009.

Football League Record: 1888 Founder Member of the Football League; 1893–97 Division 2; 1897–1913 Division 1; 1913–14 Division 2; 1914–20 Division 1; 1920–23 Division 2; 1923–26 Division 1; 1926–30 Division 2; 1930–31 Division 3 (S); 1931–35 Division 2; 1935–50 Division 3 (S); 1950–58 Division 2; 1958–59 Division 3; 1959–60 Division 4; 1960–64 Division 3; 1964–71 Division 4; 1971–73 Division 3; 1973–81 Division 2; 1981–84 Division 1; 1984–85 Division 2; 1985–90 Division 3; 1990–91 Division 2; 1991–95 Division 1; 1995–97 Division 2; 1997–98 Division 3; 1998–2004 Division 2; 2004–10 FL 2; 2010–15 FL 1; 2015– FL 2.

LATEST SEQUENCES

Longest Sequence of League Wins: 10, 3.12.1997 – 31.1.1998.

Longest Sequence of League Defeats: 9, 15.3.2011 – 16.4.2011.

Longest Sequence of League Draws: 6, 16.8.2008 – 20.9.2008.

Longest Sequence of Unbeaten League Matches: 19, 26.4.1930 – 6.12.1930.

Longest Sequence Without a League Win: 20, 3.12.1996 – 31.3.1997.

Successive Scoring Runs: 35 from 10.10.1959.

Successive Non-scoring Runs: 5 from 15.3.2011.

MANAGERS

Edwin Browne 1883–93; **Tom Featherstone** 1893; **Tom Harris** 1893–1913; **Albert Fisher** 1913–27; **Horace Henshall** 1927–34; **Charlie Jones** 1934; **David Pratt** 1935; **Percy Smith** 1935–36; **Jimmy McMullan** 1936–37; **Harry Parkes** 1938–39; **Tony Towers** 1939–42; **Frank Womack** 1942–43; **Major Frank Buckley** 1944–46; **Arthur Stollery** 1946–49; **Eric Houghton** 1949–53; **George Poyser** 1953–57; **Tommy Lawton** 1957–58; **Frank Hill** 1958–61; **Tim Coleman** 1961–63; **Eddie Lowe** 1963–65; **Tim Coleman** 1965–66; **Jack Burkitt** 1966–67; **Andy Beattie** (*General Manager*) 1967; **Billy Gray** 1967–68; **Jack Wheeler** (*Caretaker Manager*) 1968–69; **Jimmy Sirrel** 1969–75; **Ron Fenton** 1975–77; **Jimmy Sirrel** 1978–82 (*continued as General Manager to 1984*); **Howard Wilkinson** 1982–83; **Larry Lloyd** 1983–84; **Richie Barker** 1984–85; **Jimmy Sirrel** 1985–87; **John Barnwell** 1987–88; **Neil Warnock** 1989–93; **Mick Walker** 1993–94; **Russell Slade** 1994–95; **Howard Kendall** 1995; **Colin Murphy** 1995–96 (*General Manager*); **Steve Thompson** 1995–96; **Sam Allardyce** 1997–99; **Gary Brazil** 1999–2000; **Jocky Scott** 2000–01; **Gary Brazil** 2001–02; **Billy Dearden** 2002–04; **Gary Mills** 2004; **Ian Richardson** 2004–05; **Gudjon Thordarson** 2005–06; **Steve Thompson** 2006–07; **Ian McParland** 2007–09; **Hans Backe** 2009; **Sven-Göran Eriksson** 2009–10 (*Director of Football*); **Steve Cotterill** 2010; **Craig Short** 2010; **Paul Ince** 2010–11; **Martin Allen** 2011–12; **Keith Curle** 2012–13; **Chris Kiwomya** 2013; **Shaun Derry** 2013–15; **Ricardo Moniz** 2015; **Jamie Fullarton** 2016; **Mark Cooper** 2016; **John Sheridan** May 2016–

TEN YEAR LEAGUE RECORD

		P	W	D	L	F	A	Pts	Pos
2006-07	FL 2	46	16	14	16	55	53	62	13
2007-08	FL 2	46	10	18	18	37	53	48	21
2008-09	FL 2	46	11	14	21	49	69	47	19
2009-10	FL 2	46	27	12	7	96	31	93	1
2010-11	FL 1	46	14	8	24	46	60	50	19
2011-12	FL 1	46	21	10	15	75	63	73	7
2012-13	FL 1	46	16	17	13	61	49	65	12
2013-14	FL 1	46	15	5	26	64	77	50	20
2014-15	FL 1	46	12	14	20	45	63	50	21
2015-16	FL 2	46	14	9	23	54	83	51	17

DID YOU KNOW ?

Jimmy Logan is one of only three players to score a hat-trick in an FA Cup final, achieving the feat for Notts County in the 4-1 win over Bolton Wanderers in 1894. Logan rarely enjoyed the best of health and died from pneumonia just two years later at the age of 25.

NOTTS COUNTY – FOOTBALL LEAGUE TWO 2015–16 LEAGUE RECORD

Match No.	Date	Venue	Opponents	Result	H/T Score	Lg Pos.	Goalscorers	Attendance
1	Aug 8	A	Stevenage	W 2-0	1-0	4	Thompson [35], Amevor [88]	3652
2	14	H	Mansfield T	L 0-2	0-1	10		10,074
3	18	A	Oxford U	L 1-3	1-1	13	Audel [21]	5774
4	22	H	Accrington S	D 1-1	0-0	14	Burke [76]	3825
5	29	A	Morecambe	L 1-4	1-1	20	Snijders [41]	1621
6	Sept 12	H	Luton T	W 3-2	1-0	18	McLeod 2 [32, 48], Noble [90]	5820
7	19	A	AFC Wimbledon	L 1-2	1-0	19	Hollis [16]	3962
8	22	H	Crawley T	W 4-1	2-1	16	Edwards 2 [31, 77], Noble 2 (1 pen) [32, 49 (p)]	3267
9	26	H	York C	W 1-0	1-0	13	McLeod [12]	5159
10	29	A	Dagenham & R	D 1-1	1-0	13	Campbell [34]	1327
11	Oct 3	A	Leyton Orient	L 1-2	0-1	16	Stead [46]	5193
12	11	H	Plymouth Arg	L 0-2	0-1	16		5266
13	17	H	Yeovil T	W 2-0	0-0	15	Aborah [55], McLeod [61]	4030
14	20	A	Bristol R	D 0-0	0-0	15		6743
15	24	H	Exeter C	D 1-1	1-1	16	Noble [31]	3429
16	31	H	Portsmouth	W 2-1	1-1	13	Burke [22], Sheehan [77]	6917
17	Nov 21	A	Northampton T	L 1-2	0-1	16	Stead [52]	5513
18	24	H	Barnet	W 4-2	2-0	14	Edwards 2 [6, 78], Stead [9], Sheehan [73]	3098
19	28	A	Cambridge U	L 1-3	1-0	15	Campbell [24]	4596
20	Dec 12	H	Newport Co	W 4-3	2-2	14	Noble 2 [34, 90], McLeod 2 [41, 71]	4105
21	15	A	Wycombe W	D 2-2	1-1	13	Stead (pen) [8], Campbell [47]	2886
22	19	A	Carlisle U	L 0-3	0-2	15		3336
23	28	H	Morecambe	D 2-2	1-2	15	McLeod 2 [45, 63]	4556
24	Jan 2	H	Oxford U	L 2-4	0-1	17	Stead [61], Thompson [76]	5877
25	16	A	Crawley T	W 1-0	0-0	16	Valencic [63]	2074
26	23	H	AFC Wimbledon	L 0-2	0-1	17		5301
27	30	A	Luton T	W 2-0	0-0	14	Sheehan (og) [58], Stead [70]	8147
28	Feb 13	A	York C	L 1-2	0-2	18	Satka (og) [63]	3811
29	16	H	Hartlepool U	W 3-2	2-0	14	Stead 2 [4, 80], Noble [14]	3433
30	20	H	Leyton Orient	L 0-1	0-0	15		4878
31	23	A	Accrington S	L 2-3	0-2	16	Murray [72], Campbell [81]	1215
32	27	A	Plymouth Arg	L 0-1	0-0	16		7642
33	Mar 1	A	Dagenham & R	D 0-0	0-0	17		3147
34	5	H	Bristol R	L 0-2	0-1	17		5052
35	12	A	Yeovil T	L 0-1	0-0	19		3588
36	19	H	Exeter C	L 1-4	1-1	19	McLeod [35]	3813
37	25	A	Portsmouth	L 0-4	0-1	19		16,670
38	28	H	Wycombe W	D 0-0	0-0	19		4452
39	Apr 2	A	Northampton T	D 2-2	1-1	20	Audel [36], Stead (pen) [72]	6428
40	9	H	Stevenage	W 1-0	0-0	18	Noble [80]	4172
41	12	H	Hartlepool U	W 1-0	0-0	17	Stead [55]	3597
42	16	A	Mansfield T	L- 0-5	0-1	17		6357
43	19	A	Barnet	L 1-3	1-0	17	Stead (pen) [6]	1322
44	23	H	Cambridge U	L 1-2	1-1	17	Hollis [39]	4450
45	30	A	Newport Co	W 1-0	1-0	17	Snijders [39]	4903
46	May 7	H	Carlisle U	L 0-5	0-3	17		5405

Final League Position: 17

GOALSCORERS

League (54): Stead 11 (3 pens), McLeod 9, Noble 8 (1 pen), Campbell 4, Edwards 4, Audel 2, Burke 2, Hollis 2, Sheehan 2, Snijders 2, Thompson 2, Aborah 1, Amevor 1, Murray 1, Valencic 1, own goals 2.
FA Cup (0).
Capital One Cup (5): Noble 2, Burke 1, Snijders 1, Stead 1 (pen).
Johnstone's Paint Trophy (4): Stead 2, Edwards 1, McLeod 1.

Carroll R 32	Amevor M 6+5	Audel T 25+3	Sprocket C 5	Thompson C 23+3	Jenner J 4+7	De Silva K 2+2	Swerts G 12	Noble L 31+6	Aborah S 25+1	Stead J 40+3	Bennett S 5+1	Snijders G 8+6	Adams B 15	Spencer J 1+6	Burke G 21+10	Hollis H 27+2	Campbell A 29+15	Valencic F 7+2	Hewitt E 35+3	Sharpe R —+5	McLeod I 30+7	Edwards M 21+1	Smith A 25+3	Sheehan A 14	Barmby J 3+2	Loach S 14	Murray R 3+13	Bishop C —+1	Milsom R 12+2	Atkinson W 15+2	MacKenzie G 4	Banton J 9	Boyce A 3	Gibson M —+4	Sarpong L —+1	Match No.
1	2^a	3	4^1	5	6	7^2	8	9	10	11	12	13																								1
1		4	3^1	8^2	7	10^3		9	6	11	2		5		12	13	14																			2
1		4		10			2	7	6	9	3^3	13	5			8^2		11^1	12	14																3
1	3	4		12			2	7^4	8	11		6				9^1		10^2	5	13																4
1	8	3^1	4	12	6			10		5			7	2	9^2	13	11																			5
1	2^3	5		12		3	13	7	10	8^2					9	4	6^1		11	14																6
1	2	5		13		3	12	7	10	6^3		14	8^1	4	9^2		11																			7
1				12			2	10	8	13					9^1	4	6	5	11^2	3	7															8
1			13					10^1	8						9^2	4	6	2	11	3	7	5	12													9
1				14				9	7	13					6^1	4	10^2	2	11^3	3	8	5	12													10
	4	3	8	9^1	2				6				10^2		12		14		13	7	5^3	11	1													11
			13	14		4	10	8	12						9^2		6^1	2^3	11	3	7	5	1													12
1	5							8	6	10		12			13		9^1	2	11^2	3	7	4														13
1	13	3^1		7^2				6	9	10					12		11	4	8	5																14
1								9	7	8			13	12	10^1	2	11^2	3	6	4	5															15
1			14		13			8^1	7	9					11^1		12	2	10	3	6^2	4	5													16
1	5		8^3		6	9		11				7^1		14	10^2		13	2		3		4					12									17
1	5							12	8^1	10^2		14			9^2		6	2	11	3	7	4					13									18
1	5							7						6^2			10	9	2	11^3	3	8	4				12	13								19
1	13	5	3^3	7				8		10					9^1		6	2^2	11			4			14	12										20
1	14	3^1		7			2	8^a		10^2					13	12^3	6		11		9	4				5										21
1				7			2		12	11					9^1		6		10	3	8^2	4				13	5									22
1	4							7	10					12	9^1		6		11	3	8					5										23
1		13						8	10					14	9^1	4	6		11^3		7^2					12	5	3								24
1		8							11	3					4	6	9	2			12					10^1		7	5							25
1		7						12	10	3^2		5			4	9		2	11^1							13		8	6							26
1		8						9^1	10^3	7^2		5			4	6		3	14	11	12					13			2							27
1		8						9	10			5			3	12		2	11^1		7					13					4	6				28
1		7						6^2	10			2			3	12		5	11^1		8					13			14	4	9^3					29
1		6						8^1	10			5			4	12		2	11		7								3		9					30
1		7						6^2	10			5		14	3	12		2	11^1		8					13				4	9^2					31
1	13	7						12	11			5^3			3	9		2				14				10	8^2		4	6^1						32
		7						12	11			5		14	4	6		3	13					1	10^3	8^2	2		9^1						33
	4	7							10			5^7		13		6^3		3	14	11^1				1	12	8^2	2		9							34
	5	7						8	11						13	3	9	2						1	12	6^2				10^1	4					35
	4	8						9	11			5^7			13	3	12	2	10		7			1		12			6^1	3						36
		8						9	5^3	11					13	4	14	2	10		7^2					6	12			3^1						37
	5	8						9	6	11^1		14			10^2	4	7^3		13	3				1	12		2									38
	5	6^2						8	7^1	11		14			4	10^3		12	13	3				1	9	2										39
	5							6	7	11					4	8^2	10^1	2	13	12	3			1		5										40
14	5							7^3	8	10^1					4	12	9^2	2	11	3				1		6								13		41
14	7							5	8	6^2					2	12	4	3	9^3	10^1				1		11								13		42
	5							9	8^1	10					12	3	14	7^2	2	11^3	4	6		1		5								13		43
3								9^a	7					5^1	10^3	4	8		2	13				1	11^2					6				14	12	44
1	12							11				10^1	2^3		8^2	4	13	9	5		14	3	6							7						45
1	12							11				7	5		10^2	4	14	9	2		13	3^3	6^1							8						46

FA Cup
First Round — Salford C — (a) — 0-2

Capital One Cup
First Round — Huddersfield T — (a) — 2-1
Second Round — Aston Villa — (a) — 3-5
(aet)

Johnstone's Paint Trophy
First Round — Mansfield T — (h) — 3-1
Second Round — Sheffield U — (a) — 1-5

OLDHAM ATHLETIC

SportsDirect.com Park, Furtherwood Road, Oldham, Lancashire OL1 2PB.

Telephone: (0161) 624 4972.

Fax: (0161) 627 5915.

Ticket Office: (0161) 785 5150.

Website: www.oldhamathletic.co.uk

Email: enquiries@oldhamathletic.co.uk

Ground Capacity: 10,904.

Record Attendance: 46,471 v Sheffield W, FA Cup 4th rd, 25 January 1930.

Pitch Measurements: 100.5m × 68.5m (110yd × 75yd).

Chairman: Simon Corney.

Chief Executive: Neil Joy.

Manager: Stephen Robinson.

Assistant Manager: Ian Baraclough.

Physio: Stuart Irwin.

Colours: Blue shirts with red trim, blue shorts with red trim, blue socks with red trim.

Year Formed: 1895.

Turned Professional: 1899.

Previous Name: 1895, Pine Villa; 1899, Oldham Athletic.

Club Nickname: 'The Latics'.

Grounds: 1895, Sheepfoot Lane; 1900, Hudson Field; 1906, Sheepfoot Lane; 1907, Boundary Park (renamed SportsDirect.com Park 2014).

First Football League Game: 9 September 1907, Division 2, v Stoke (a) W 3–1 – Hewitson; Hodson, Hamilton; Fay, Walders, Wilson; Ward, Billy Dodds (1), Newton (1), Hancock, Swarbrick (1).

Record League Victory: 11–0 v Southport, Division 4, 26 December 1962 – Bollands; Branagan, Marshall; McCall, Williams, Scott; Ledger (1), Johnstone, Lister (6), Colquhoun (1), Whitaker (3).

Record Cup Victory: 10–1 v Lytham, FA Cup 1st rd, 28 November 1925 – Gray; Wynne, Grundy; Adlam, Heaton, Naylor (1), Douglas, Pynegar (2), Ormston (2), Barnes (3), Watson (2).

HONOURS

League Champions: Division 2 – 1990–91; Division 3 – 1973–74; Division 3N – 1952–53;.
Runners-up: Division 1 – 1914–15; Division 2 – 1909–10; Division 4 – 1962–63.
FA Cup: semi-final – 1913, 1990, 1994.
League Cup: Runners-up: 1990.

sky SPORTS FACT FILE

The first Oldham Athletic player to be capped by England was outside-left George 'Lady' Woodger who appeared against Derby County in February 1911. Woodger's nickname derived from his delicate ball-playing skills rather than his looks (he was bald headed).

Record Defeat: 4–13 v Tranmere R, Division 3 (N), 26 December 1935.

Most League Points (2 for a win): 62, Division 3, 1973–74.

Most League Points (3 for a win): 88, Division 2, 1990–91.

Most League Goals: 95, Division 4, 1962–63.

Highest League Scorer in Season: Tom Davis, 33, Division 3 (N), 1936–37.

Most League Goals in Total Aggregate: Roger Palmer, 141, 1980–94.

Most League Goals in One Match: 7, Eric Gemmell v Chester, Division 3 (N), 19 January 1952.

Most Capped Player: Gunnar Halle, 24 (64), Norway.

Most League Appearances: Ian Wood, 525, 1966–80.

Youngest League Player: Wayne Harrison, 16 years 347 days v Notts Co, 27 October 1984.

Record Transfer Fee Received: £1,700,000 from Aston Villa for Earl Barrett, February 1992.

Record Transfer Fee Paid: £750,000 to Aston Villa for Ian Olney, June 1992.

Football League Record: 1907 Elected to Division 2; 1910–23 Division 1; 1923–35 Division 2; 1935–53 Division 3 (N); 1953–54 Division 2; 1954–58 Division 3 (N); 1958–63 Division 4; 1963–69 Division 3; 1969–71 Division 4; 1971–74 Division 3; 1974–91 Division 2; 1991–92 Division 1; 1992–94 FA Premier League; 1994–97 Division 1; 1997–2004 Division 2; 2004– FL 1.

LATEST SEQUENCES

Longest Sequence of League Wins: 10, 12.1.1974 – 12.3.1974.

Longest Sequence of League Defeats: 8, 15.12.1934 – 2.2.1935.

Longest Sequence of League Draws: 5, 26.12.1982 – 15.1.1983.

Longest Sequence of Unbeaten League Matches: 20, 1.5.1990 – 10.11.1990.

Longest Sequence Without a League Win: 17, 4.9.1920 – 18.12.1920.

Successive Scoring Runs: 25 from 25.8.1962.

Successive Non-scoring Runs: 6 from 12.2.2011.

MANAGERS

David Ashworth 1906–14
Herbert Bamlett 1914–21
Charlie Roberts 1921–22
David Ashworth 1923–24
Bob Mellor 1924–27
Andy Wilson 1927–32
Bob Mellor 1932–33
Jimmy McMullan 1933–34
Bob Mellor 1934–45
  (continued as Secretary to 1953)
Frank Womack 1945–47
Billy Wootton 1947–50
George Hardwick 1950–56
Ted Goodier 1956–58
Norman Dodgin 1958–60
Danny McLennan 1960
Jack Rowley 1960–63
Les McDowall 1963–65
Gordon Hurst 1965–66
Jimmy McIlroy 1966–68
Jack Rowley 1968–69
Jimmy Frizzell 1970–82
Joe Royle 1982–94
Graeme Sharp 1994–97
Neil Warnock 1997–98
Andy Ritchie 1998–2001
Mick Wadsworth 2001–02
Iain Dowie 2002–03
Brian Talbot 2004–05
Ronnie Moore 2005–06
John Sheridan 2006–09
Joe Royle 2009
Dave Penney 2009–10
Paul Dickov 2010–13
Lee Johnson 2013–15
Dean Holden 2015
Darren Kelly 2015
David Dunn 2015–16
John Sheridan 2016
Stephen Robinson July 2016–

TEN YEAR LEAGUE RECORD

		P	W	D	L	F	A	Pts	Pos
2006-07	FL 1	46	21	12	13	69	47	75	6
2007-08	FL 1	46	18	13	15	58	46	67	8
2008-09	FL 1	46	16	17	13	66	65	65	10
2009-10	FL 1	46	13	13	20	39	57	52	16
2010-11	FL 1	46	13	17	16	53	60	56	17
2011-12	FL 1	46	14	12	20	50	66	54	16
2012-13	FL 1	46	14	9	23	46	59	51	19
2013-14	FL 1	46	14	14	18	50	59	56	15
2014-15	FL 1	46	14	15	17	54	67	57	15
2015-16	FL 1	46	12	18	16	44	58	54	17

DID YOU KNOW ?

Oldham Athletic gained their first significant trophy in April 1903 when they won the Manchester Junior Cup. The Latics defeated fellow Manchester & District League side Berry's 1-0 with a goal from Pepper to win the prize.

OLDHAM ATHLETIC – FOOTBALL LEAGUE ONE 2015–16 LEAGUE RECORD

Match No.	Date		Venue	Opponents	Result		H/T Score	Lg Pos.	Goalscorers	Attendance
1	Aug	8	A	Walsall	D	1-1	0-1	10	Forte [83]	5009
2		15	H	Fleetwood T	W	1-0	1-0	6	Philliskirk [36]	4139
3		18	A	Colchester U	D	0-0	0-0	10		2917
4		22	H	Shrewsbury T	D	1-1	0-0	12	Kelly (pen) [52]	3963
5		29	A	Bury	D	1-1	1-0	10	Croft [24]	5448
6	Sept	5	H	Bradford C	L	1-2	0-1	13	Mills [81]	5619
7		12	H	Peterborough U	L	1-5	0-2	19	Murphy [48]	3566
8		19	A	Doncaster R	D	1-1	1-1	21	Burn [34]	5647
9		26	H	Wigan Ath	D	1-1	0-1	20	Poleon [74]	5482
10		29	A	Port Vale	D	1-1	1-0	18	Higdon [35]	4065
11	Oct	3	A	Gillingham	D	3-3	2-2	18	Higdon 2 [28, 55], Poleon [36]	6157
12		10	H	Scunthorpe U	L	2-4	2-2	21	Kelly [25], Poleon [27]	4002
13		17	H	Sheffield U	D	1-1	1-1	21	Philliskirk [10]	5743
14		20	A	Swindon T	W	2-1	1-0	17	Jones [34], Philliskirk [87]	6430
15		24	A	Rochdale	D	0-0	0-0	18		5690
16		31	H	Burton Alb	L	0-1	0-1	19		3795
17	Nov	14	A	Chesterfield	W	2-1	0-1	18	Poleon [72], Philliskirk [87]	6178
18		21	H	Barnsley	L	1-2	0-1	18	Yeates [78]	4300
19		24	A	Southend U	L	2-5	0-2	21	Higdon 2 [56, 77]	3301
20		28	A	Crewe Alex	L	0-1	0-1	21		3969
21	Dec	19	A	Coventry C	D	1-1	0-0	22	Philliskirk [90]	15,419
22		28	H	Doncaster R	L	1-2	0-2	22	Murphy [74]	4432
23	Jan	2	A	Colchester U	D	1-1	1-0	22	Murphy [5]	3535
24		9	H	Millwall	L	1-2	0-1	22	Jones [59]	3558
25		16	A	Bradford C	L	0-1	0-0	22		18,522
26		23	H	Bury	L	0-1	0-1	23		5537
27		26	A	Shrewsbury T	W	1-0	1-0	22	Winchester [23]	4057
28	Feb	13	A	Wigan Ath	D	0-0	0-0	23		9817
29		16	A	Blackpool	D	0-0	0-0	23		7197
30		20	H	Gillingham	W	2-1	0-1	22	Dieng [57], Forte [73]	3874
31		23	A	Peterborough U	W	2-1	1-1	22	Dummigan [2], Kelly (pen) [73]	3544
32		27	A	Scunthorpe U	D	1-1	0-0	22	Lafferty [78]	4180
33	Mar	1	H	Port Vale	D	1-1	0-0	22	Kelly [68]	3507
34		12	A	Sheffield U	L	0-3	0-2	22		18,334
35		15	H	Blackpool	W	1-0	0-0	21	Palmer [53]	3715
36		19	H	Rochdale	L	2-3	1-1	22	Amadi-Holloway 2 [29, 71]	6117
37		26	A	Burton Alb	D	0-0	0-0	21		4283
38		28	H	Chesterfield	W	1-0	0-0	21	Jones [78]	4483
39	Apr	5	H	Swindon T	W	2-0	1-0	21	Kelly [10], Main [82]	3730
40		9	H	Walsall	W	1-0	0-0	18	Main [63]	4396
41		12	A	Barnsley	L	1-2	0-1	18	Main [68]	8871
42		16	A	Fleetwood T	D	1-1	0-0	18	Kelly [77]	3889
43		19	A	Southend U	W	1-0	0-0	17	Main [66]	6508
44		23	A	Crewe Alex	W	1-0	0-0	17	Forte [59]	4571
45		30	A	Millwall	L	0-3	0-2	17		12,419
46	May	8	H	Coventry C	L	0-2	0-0	17		4928

Final League Position: 17

GOALSCORERS

League (44): Kelly 6 (2 pens), Higdon 5, Philliskirk 5, Main 4, Poleon 4, Forte 3, Jones 3, Murphy 3, Amadi-Holloway 2, Burn 1, Croft 1, Dieng 1, Dummigan 1, Lafferty 1, Mills 1, Palmer 1, Winchester 1, Yeates 1.
FA Cup (2): Philliskirk 1, Poleon 1.
Capital One Cup (1): Philliskirk 1.
Johnstone's Paint Trophy (0).

Coleman J 32	Wilson B 22 + 4	Wilson J 42 + 1	Burn J 12	Mills J 14 + 1	Kelly L 41	Croft L 13 + 8	Winchester C 22 + 9	Jones M 29 + 6	Turner R 2 + 4	Cassidy J 8 + 13	Forte J 20 + 6	Dunn D 4 + 4	Philliskirk D 21 + 2	Brown C 10 + 3	Poleon D 14 + 11	Green G — + 3	Dieng T 34 + 4	Yeates M 8 + 8	Stankevicius S 1 + 3	O'Connell E 2	Murphy R 7 + 6	Cornell D 14	Fulton J 9 + 2	Higdon M 9 + 2	Edmundson S 2	Lafferty D 15	Dunnigan C 25 + 1	Fuller R 1 + 4	Eckersley R 3 + 1	Rasulo G 1 + 2	Wellens R 2 + 1	Palmer M 14	Gerrard A 18	Amadi-Holloway A 9 + 1	Main C 16 + 2	Thiele T — + 4	Holmes-Dennis T 10	Tuohy J — + 1	Match No.
1	2	3	4	5	6	7¹	8²	9	10¹	11	12	13	14																										1
1		4	3	5	6	8		9	12³	11¹	13	14	7		2	10²																							2
1		3	4	5	9¹	6		7	11²		10	12	8³		2		13	14																					3
1		4	3		6	9¹	12	7¹	14		10		8²	11	2		13	5																					4
1		3	4³	5		8		7	14		10²		9¹	11	2		6	12	13																				5
1		3	4²	5		14	8	12	11¹				9¹	6			7³	10			2	13																	6
1		3		5		6		14			8	7	2³	13		12	9¹	11²	4	10																			7
13		3	4¹			6	9	7					8	5	11³	14	2	10²		1	12																		8
		3	4	6²		8		9					10¹	5	12		2	13		1			7	11															9
		3	7		4	6²		8					13	5	10		2	12	14	1			9³	11¹															10
		4	3		6	12		9					10	8						1			7¹	11		2	5												11
		3	4		7	6³	14	9³					13	8¹	2	10		12		1			11	5															12
14		3	4		7		6	9²					10		11³		12			1			8¹	5		2	13												13
	3³	4			6			8	9				10		13		12	14		1			7¹	11²		5	2												14
	4	3			6¹	12	8	9					10			14				1			7²	11		5³	2	13											15
		3	4	5	6	13	9				8		11				10²			1			7¹				2	12											16
1	2	4		5	6		7²						9		8		3	10				13	11¹				12					12							17
1	3	4		5	7								6	11			8¹	9				12	13			2						10²							18
	4	3		5	7								6	11²			9					1	8	10		12	2¹	13											19
	3	4		5	7			12					6	2¹	14		9					1	8³	10				11²		13									20
	4	3			6		9	7	11¹				10		12		2²	13		1			14				5	8¹											21
	2	3¹	14	7		8²	9		11				6				4	13			10	1					12	5³											22
	3			5	7			9			10		6		12		4				11¹	1					8												23
1	4²	13			7		8	9	11	12				6³			3				10					5¹	2	14											24
1	4	2			7		8¹	6	11	13				12²	14		3				10³					9	5¹												25
1	2²	4			7	14	8	9	12	11				10³			3				13					5						6¹							26
1		2			7	13	8³	9	14	11¹				10²			3				12					5						6	4						27
1		5			7	13	10			6							4				11²					2	9					8	3¹	12					28
1		2			7		6	13			9						4				11²					5	2					8		10¹	12				29
1		2			8		12				9						4				13					5	6¹					7	3	10²	11				30
1		2			8		9				13	12					3									5	6					7	4	10²	11¹				31
1		5	9²	7		11	13	12									3						14			2	6³					8	4		10¹				32
1		2			7		13	9	12								3						14			5	6³					8	4	10¹	11²				33
1	13	2		5			10	8¹			9						4						7³									6	3	11²	12	14			34
1	5	2			7		13	6			9²						4															8	3	10¹	11	12			35
1		2			7	14		6¹			9³			12			4²										7					8	3	10	11	13	5		36
1	2	3			6		8	9	12								4						7											11¹	10		5		37
1	3	2			7			12		14	10¹						6															9	4	11²	8	13³	5		38
1		3			7	14	13	10¹		12	11²						6						2									9³	4		8		5		39
1		3			7			9			12	10¹					8						2									6	4		11		5		40
1	12³	3			8		6²	9¹			11	13					7						5										4		10		2	14	41
1	2	3¹			7	9³					13	10²					8		12	14												8	4		11		5		42
1	2				8	10					12	9¹					7															6	4		11		5		43
1	4				6	8¹	12				10²						13						7									5	3		11		9		44
1	4	2			7	11³	12	14			9						13						8²						3			6			3	10¹	5		45
1	5	3			7	14	6³	12			13	9					10²						8¹						2			2			4	11			46

FA Cup

First Round	Mansfield T	(a)	0-0	
Replay	Mansfield T	(h)	2-0	
Second Round	Sheffield U	(a)	0-1	

Capital One Cup

First Round	Middlesbrough	(h)	1-3	

Johnstone's Paint Trophy

First Round	Shrewsbury T	(a)	0-2	

OXFORD UNITED

The Kassam Stadium, Grenoble Road, Oxford OX4 4XP.

Telephone: (01865) 337 500.

Fax: (01865) 337 501.

Ticket Office: (01865) 337 533.

Website: www.oufc.co.uk

Email: admin@oufc.co.uk

Ground Capacity: 12,573.

Record Attendance: 22,730 v Preston NE, FA Cup 6th rd, 29 February 1964 (at Manor Ground); 12,243 v Leyton Orient, FL 2, 6 May 2006 (at The Kassam Stadium).

Pitch Measurements: 100.5m × 64m (110yd × 70yd).

Executive Chairman: Darryl Eales.

Head Coach: Michael Appleton.

Assistant Head Coaches: Derek Fazackerley and Chris Allen.

Physio: Andrew Procter.

Colours: Yellow shirts with blue trim, blue shorts with yellow trim, blue socks with yellow trim.

Year Formed: 1893.

Turned Professional: 1949.

Previous Names: 1893, Headington; 1894, Headington United; 1960, Oxford United.

Club Nickname: 'The U's'.

Grounds: 1893, Headington Quarry; 1894, Wootten's Fields; 1898, Sandy Lane Ground; 1902, Britannia Field; 1909, Sandy Lane; 1910, Quarry Recreation Ground; 1914, Sandy Lane; 1922, The Paddock Manor Road; 1925, Manor Ground; 2001, The Kassam Stadium.

First Football League Game: 18 August 1962, Division 4, v Barrow (a) L 2–3 – Medlock; Beavon, Quartermain; Ron Atkinson, Kyle, Jones; Knight, Graham Atkinson (1), Houghton (1), Cornwell, Colfar.

Record League Victory: 7–0 v Barrow, Division 4, 19 December 1964 – Fearnley; Beavon, Quartermain; Ron Atkinson (1), Kyle, Jones; Morris, Booth (3), Willey (1), Graham Atkinson (1), Harrington (1).

Record Cup Victory: 9–1 v Dorchester T, FA Cup 1st rd, 11 November 1995 – Whitehead; Wood (2), Mike Ford (1), Smith, Elliott, Gilchrist, Rush (1), Massey (Murphy), Moody (3), Bobby Ford (1), Angel (Beauchamp (1)).

Record Defeat: 0–7 v Sunderland, Division 1, 19 September 1998.

HONOURS

League Champions: Division 2 – 1984–85; Division 3 – 1967–68, 1983–84.
Runners-up: Second Division – 1995–96; FL 2 – 2015–16; Conference – (3rd) 2009–10 *(promoted via play-offs)*.
FA Cup: 6th rd – 1964.
League Cup Winners: 1986.
League Trophy: Runners-up: 2016.

Most League Points (2 for a win): 61, Division 4, 1964–65.

Most League Points (3 for a win): 95, Division 3, 1983–84.

Most League Goals: 91, Division 3, 1983–84.

Highest League Scorer in Season: John Aldridge, 30, Division 2, 1984–85.

Most League Goals in Total Aggregate: Graham Atkinson, 77, 1962–73.

Most League Goals in One Match: 4, Tony Jones v Newport Co, Division 4, 22 September 1962; 4, Arthur Longbottom v Darlington, Division 4, 26 October 1963; 4, Richard Hill v Walsall, Division 2, 26 December 1988; 4, John Durnin v Luton T, 14 November 1992; 4, Tom Craddock v Accrington S, FL 2, 20 October 2011.

Most Capped Player: Jim Magilton, 18 (52), Northern Ireland.

Most League Appearances: John Shuker, 478, 1962–77.

Youngest League Player: Jason Seacole, 16 years 149 days v Mansfield T, 7 September 1976.

Record Transfer Fee Received: £1,600,000 from Leicester C for Matt Elliott, January 1997.

Record Transfer Fee Paid: £475,000 to Aberdeen for Dean Windass, August 1998.

Football League Record: 1962 Elected to Division 4; 1965–68 Division 3; 1968–76 Division 2; 1976–84 Division 3; 1984–85 Division 2; 1985–88 Division 1; 1988–92 Division 2; 1992–94 Division 1; 1994–96 Division 2; 1996–99 Division 1; 1999–2001 Division 2; 2001–04 Division 3; 2004–06 FL 2; 2006–10 Conference; 2010–16 FL 2; 2016– FL 1.

LATEST SEQUENCES

Longest Sequence of League Wins: 6, 13.4.2013 – 17.8.2013.

Longest Sequence of League Defeats: 8, 18.4.2014 – 23.8.2014.

Longest Sequence of League Draws: 5, 7.10.1978 – 28.10.1978.

Longest Sequence of Unbeaten League Matches: 20, 17.3.1984 – 29.9.1984.

Longest Sequence Without a League Win: 27, 14.11.1987 – 27.8.1988.

Successive Scoring Runs: 17 from 22.4.2006.

Successive Non-scoring Runs: 6 from 26.3.1988.

MANAGERS

Harry Thompson 1949–58
 (Player-Manager) 1949-51
Arthur Turner 1959–69
 (continued as General Manager to 1972)
Ron Saunders 1969
Gerry Summers 1969–75
Mick Brown 1975–79
Bill Asprey 1979–80
Ian Greaves 1980–82
Jim Smith 1982–85
Maurice Evans 1985–88
Mark Lawrenson 1988
Brian Horton 1988–93
Denis Smith 1993–97
Malcolm Crosby 1997–98
Malcolm Shotton 1998–99
Micky Lewis 1999–2000
Denis Smith 2000
David Kemp 2000–01
Mark Wright 2001
Ian Atkins 2001–04
Graham Rix 2004
Ramon Diaz 2004–05
Brian Talbot 2005–06
Darren Patterson 2006
Jim Smith 2006–07
Darren Patterson 2007–08
Chris Wilder 2008–14
Gary Waddock 2014
Michael Appleton July 2014–

TEN YEAR LEAGUE RECORD

		P	W	D	L	F	A	Pts	Pos
2006-07	Conf	46	22	15	9	66	33	81	2
2007-08	Conf P	46	20	11	15	56	48	71	9
2008-09	Conf P	46	24	10	12	72	51	77*	7
2009-10	Conf P	44	25	11	8	64	31	86	3
2010-11	FL 2	46	17	12	17	58	60	63	12
2011-12	FL 2	46	17	17	12	59	48	68	9
2012-13	FL 2	46	19	8	19	60	61	65	9
2013-14	FL 2	46	16	14	16	53	50	62	8
2014-15	FL 2	46	15	16	15	50	49	61	13
2015-16	FL 2	46	24	14	8	84	41	86	2

*5 pts deducted.

DID YOU KNOW ?

Headington United were a relatively junior club until 1949 when they applied to join the proposed Second Division of the Southern League. Although this was shelved, the competition agreed to expand by two clubs and Headington finished one point ahead of Llanelly to gain election.

OXFORD UNITED – FOOTBALL LEAGUE TWO 2015–16 LEAGUE RECORD

Match No.	Date	Venue	Opponents	Result	H/T Score	Lg Pos.	Goalscorers	Attendance
1	Aug 8	H	Crawley T	D	1-1	0-0	10	Hylton 65	6349
2	15	A	Luton T	D	2-2	0-1	15	Roofe 82, Hoban 90	8877
3	18	A	Notts Co	W	3-1	1-1	10	O'Dowda 36, Roofe 49, Hylton 79	5774
4	22	A	Mansfield T	D	1-1	0-1	9	Roofe (pen) 58	3112
5	29	H	Yeovil T	W	2-0	1-0	5	Hylton 14, O'Dowda 75	6018
6	Sept 6	A	Bristol R	W	1-0	0-0	4	Roofe 62	7038
7	12	A	Northampton T	L	0-1	0-1	8		4838
8	19	H	Portsmouth	D	1-1	1-0	5	Sercombe 33	9093
9	26	H	Morecambe	D	0-0	0-0	6		5273
10	29	A	York C	W	2-1	1-1	6	Hylton 9, Roofe 71	2791
11	Oct 3	A	Accrington S	W	3-1	1-0	5	O'Dowda 21, Sercombe 2 (1 pen) 79, 87 (p)	1755
12	10	H	AFC Wimbledon	W	1-0	0-0	3	Baldock 80	6301
13	17	A	Leyton Orient	D	2-2	2-0	3	Roofe 16, Lundstram 33	6296
14	20	H	Plymouth Arg	W	1-0	1-0	3	Sercombe 32	7007
15	24	H	Barnet	L	2-3	2-3	3	Sercombe 2 14, 40	6137
16	31	A	Stevenage	W	5-1	2-1	2	Taylor 2 13, 72, Sercombe (pen) 27, MacDonald 66, Roofe 75	3412
17	Nov 14	H	Cambridge U	W	1-0	1-0	2	Taylor 32	6958
18	21	A	Dagenham & R	W	1-0	0-0	2	Roofe 85	1980
19	24	A	Newport Co	D	1-1	0-1	2	Hoban 72	5479
20	28	A	Hartlepool U	W	1-0	0-0	1	Hylton 70	3622
21	Dec 12	H	Carlisle U	D	1-1	1-1	2	MacDonald 34	5936
22	19	A	Wycombe W	L	1-2	0-0	3	Sercombe 65	5742
23	26	H	Exeter C	W	3-0	0-0	2	Lundstram 48, Baldock 67, Sercombe 90	9683
24	28	A	Yeovil T	D	0-0	0-0	3		4661
25	Jan 2	A	Notts Co	W	4-2	1-0	3	Sercombe (pen) 45, MacDonald 79, Roofe 90, O'Dowda 90	5877
26	17	H	Bristol R	L	1-2	0-0	3	Roofe 46	9492
27	23	H	Portsmouth	W	1-0	0-0	3	Bowery 76	17,840
28	Feb 9	H	Mansfield T	D	2-2	1-1	3	Hylton 2 30, 69	5346
29	13	A	Morecambe	W	4-2	1-1	3	Roofe 9, Lundstram 71, Hylton 74, Bowery 80	1749
30	16	H	Northampton T	L	0-1	0-0	3		9559
31	20	H	Accrington S	L	1-2	1-0	3	Roofe 29	6792
32	23	A	Exeter C	W	4-1	2-0	3	Dunkley 8, Bowery 2 41, 59, MacDonald 62	3089
33	27	A	AFC Wimbledon	W	2-1	1-1	3	Hylton 5, Bowery 59	4628
34	Mar 1	H	York C	W	4-0	1-0	2	Bowery 16, Dunkley 72, Hylton 79, Roofe 85	5654
35	5	A	Plymouth Arg	D	2-2	2-1	2	Hartley (og) 12, Roofe 35	10,091
36	12	A	Leyton Orient	L	0-1	0-0	2		7102
37	15	H	Dagenham & R	W	4-0	1-0	2	Roofe 3 15, 50, 85, MacDonald 79	5319
38	19	A	Barnet	W	3-0	0-0	2	O'Dowda 2 49, 61, Hylton 85	3264
39	25	H	Stevenage	D	1-1	0-0	2	Sercombe 58	7980
40	28	A	Cambridge U	D	0-0	0-0	2		6108
41	Apr 9	A	Crawley T	W	5-1	1-1	2	Maguire 2 (1 pen) 39, 72 (p), O'Dowda 47, Sercombe 54, Waring 86	3340
42	16	H	Luton T	L	2-3	1-2	2	Hylton 2, Dunkley 51	8838
43	19	A	Newport Co	D	1-1	1-1	3	Bowery 13	2847
44	23	H	Hartlepool U	W	2-0	1-0	3	Roofe 7, Sercombe 90	7955
45	30	A	Carlisle U	W	2-0	1-0	3	Maguire (pen) 4, Sercombe 74	6948
46	May 7	H	Wycombe W	W	3-0	0-0	2	Dunkley 54, Maguire (pen) 72, O'Dowda 90	11,815

Final League Position: 2

GOALSCORERS

League (84): Roofe 18 (1 pen), Sercombe 14 (3 pens), Hylton 12, O'Dowda 8, Bowery 7, MacDonald 5, Dunkley 4, Maguire 4 (3 pens), Lundstram 3, Taylor 3, Baldock 2, Hoban 2, Waring 1, own goal 1.
FA Cup (8): Roofe 3, Hoban 2 (1 pen), Sercombe 2 (1 pen), Taylor 1.
Capital One Cup (4): Hylton 1, Mullins 1, Roofe 1, Sercombe 1.
Johnstone's Paint Trophy (11): Roofe 4, O'Dowda 2, Evans 1, Hoban 1, Hylton 1, MacDonald 1, Maguire 1.

Slocombe S 23	Baldock G 27	Mullins J 39 + 1	Wright J 29	Skarz J 41	Roofe K 39 + 1	Rose D 11 + 2	Sercombe L 45	MacDonald A 35 + 5	Hylton D 34 + 7	Taylor R 15 + 7	Hoban P 2 + 21	O'Dowda C 18 + 20	Ruffels J 8 + 8	Lundstram J 33 + 4	Dunkley C 26 + 3	George A — + 2	Graham J 3 + 2	Buchel B 23	Maguire C 21	Evans J 4 + 5	Bowery J 9 + 8	Kenny J 17	Ismail Z — + 5	Waring G 3 + 11	Ashby J — + 3	Long S — + 1	Roberts J 1 + 3	Match No.
1	2	3	4	5	6	7^1	8	9^2	10	11^3	12	13	14															1
1	2	3	4	5	6	8	7	9^2	10	11^1	12	13																2
1	2	3	4	5	6^2	8	7	9	10^1	13	11^3	12		14														3
1	2	4	3	5	11	8	7	6^2	10^1	12	14	9^2	13															4
1	2	3	4	5	6^3	8	7	9	11^1	12	14	10^2	13															5
1	2		4	5	7^1	6	9^4	8	10^2	11^3	12		14	13		3												6
1	2		4	5^2			7	9	10	11	12	6			8	3	13											7
1	2	3	4	5	11^2	8^3	7	12	10	14		9^1	13		6													8
1	2	3	4	5	11	6^2	7		10^1	13	12	9			8													9
1	2	3	4	5	11^2	9	7		10	13		6			8^1		12											10
1	2	3	4	5	10^1	6^3	8	14	11	13		9^2			7		12											11
1	2	3	4	5	6^2		7	12	10^1	11		13			8		9											12
1	2	3	4	5	6		7	13	11^1	12		10^2			8		9^8											13
1	2	3	4	5	6^2	14	8	9^1	11	10^3	13	12	7															14
1	2	3	4^2	5	10		7	9^1	11^3	14		13			8	12	6											15
1	2	3		5	8^2		7	9^1	11	10^1		13	12	14	6	4												16
	2		4	5	6		7	9	10	11					8	3		1										17
	2	3		5	9		7	6^2	11^1	10		13	12		8		4	1										18
	2	3		5	6		8	9	10^1	11^2	12	13			7		4	1										19
	2	3		5	9	14	7	6^3	12	10^1		13			8		4	1	11^2									20
	2		4	5	11		8	9^1	12			6^2			7	3		1	10		13							21
	2	3		5^1	9		7	6^2	10^3	14		13			8		4	1	11		12							22
1	2	12	4	5	6		7	9	10^3	14		13			8	3^1			11^2									23
1	2	3^1	4	5	10		7	6	11	13		9^2			8		12											24
1	2	3	4	5	6		7	10	11^2	13		12			8				9^1									25
1	2	3	4	5	6		7	9	14	10^2	12	13			8				11^3									26
1	2	3	4	5	9		8	11^2	10^1	14		6^3			7		13		12									27
1		3	4	5	11^1		8	6^2	10			13			7				9^3		14	2		12				28
		4	3	5	11^2		7	6^2	10	14					8			1	9^1		12	2	13					29
		3	4^2	5	6		7	10^3		12					8		13	1	9^1		11	2		14				30
			4	5	10^2		7	6^1		13	12				8	3		1	9		11^3	2		14				31
			4	5^1			7	6^3	9						8	3		1	10	12	11^2	2	13	14				32
		3		5			7	6^2	11			9			8		4	1	10^1		12	2	13					33
			4	5^2	12		7	6^1	10			9			8	3		1		14	11^3	2	13					34
1			4		6^1		7		10	12					8	3			9^2	5	11	2	13					35
			4	5	11		8	14	10^3	12					7	3		1	9^1	6^2		2	13					36
			4	5	10		7^1	6	12			9	14		8^2	3		1		2				11^3	13			37
			4	5	10		7	6		13		9^2			8	3		1		12		2		11^1				38
		4	3	5	9		8	6^2	10			12			7^1			1	2		11^1		13					39
	2^1	3		5	10		7	6		13					8		4	1	9^2		11^1		14	12				40
	2						7	6	11^1			9^2			8^3		4	1	10	5	3		12	14	13			41
			4		6		8	10							7	3		1	9^1	5	12	2		11^2	13			42
			4				7	10		12					8^1	3		1	9	5^1	6^2	2		14	13	11		43
		3		5^1	10^2		7	6^1	11	12					8	13	4	1	9			2		14				44
		3		5^2			7	6^1	10^3	11					8	12	4	1	9			2	13	14				45
		3			10^3		7	6^2	11^1	12				5	8		4	1	9			2	13	14				46

FA Cup

First Round	Braintree T	(a)	1-1
Replay	Braintree T	(h)	3-1
Second Round	Forest Green R	(h)	1-0
Third Round	Swansea C	(h)	3-2
Fourth Round	Blackburn R	(h)	0-3

Capital One Cup

First Round	Brentford	(a)	4-0
Second Round	Sheffield W	(a)	0-1

Johnstone's Paint Trophy

Second Round	Swindon T	(h)	2-0
Southern Quarter-Final	Dagenham & R	(a)	2-0
Southern Semi-Final	Yeovil T	(h)	3-2
Southern Final 1st leg	Millwall	(a)	2-0
Southern Final 2nd leg	Millwall	(h)	0-1

(Oxford U won 2-1 on aggregate)

Final	Barnsley	(Wembley)	2-3

PETERBOROUGH UNITED

FOUNDATION

The old Peterborough & Fletton club, founded in 1923, was suspended by the FA during season 1932–33 and disbanded. Local enthusiasts determined to carry on and in 1934 a new professional club, Peterborough United, was formed and entered the Midland League the following year. Peterborough's first success came in 1939–40, but from 1955–56 to 1959–60 they won five successive titles. During the 1958–59 season they were undefeated in the Midland League. They reached the third round of the FA Cup, won the Northamptonshire Senior Cup, the Maunsell Cup and were runners-up in the East Anglian Cup.

ABAX Stadium, London Road, Peterborough PE2 8AL.
Telephone: (01733) 563 947. *Fax:* (01733) 344 140.
Ticket Office: (0844) 847 1934.
Website: www.theposh.com
Email: info@theposh.com
Ground Capacity: 14,084.
Record Attendance: 30,096 v Swansea T, FA Cup 5th rd, 20 February 1965.
Pitch Measurements: 102.5m × 64m (112yd × 70yd).
Chairman: Darragh MacAnthony.
Chief Executive: Bob Symns.
Manager: Grant McCann.
Head of Coaching: Dave Farrell.
Physio: Jonathan Chatfield.
Colours: Blue shirts with white trim, blue shorts with white trim, white socks.
Year Formed: 1934.
Turned Professional: 1934.
Club Nickname: 'The Posh'.
Ground: 1934, London Road Stadium (renamed ABAX Stadium 2014).

HONOURS

League Champions: Division 4 – 1960–61, 1973–74.
Runners-up: FL 1 – 2008–09; FL 2 – 2007–08.
FA Cup: 6th rd – 1965.
League Cup: semi-final – 1966.
League Trophy Winners: 2014.

First Football League Game: 20 August 1960, Division 4, v Wrexham (h) W 3–0 – Walls; Stafford, Walker; Rayner, Rigby, Norris; Hails, Emery (1), Bly (1), Smith, McNamee (1).
Record League Victory: 9–1 v Barnet (a) Division 3, 5 September 1998 – Griemink; Hooper (1), Drury (Farell), Gill, Bodley, Edwards, Davies, Payne, Grazioli (5), Quinn (2) (Rowe), Houghton (Etherington) (1).
Record Cup Victory: 9–1 v Rushden T, FA Cup 1st qual rd, 6 October 1945 – Hilliard; Bryan, Parrott, Warner, Hobbs, Woods, Polhill (1), Fairchild, Laxton (6), Tasker (1), Rodgers (1); 9–1 v Kingstonian, FA Cup 1st rd, 25 November 1992. Match ordered to be replayed by FA. Peterborough won replay 1–0.
Record Defeat: 1–8 v Northampton T, FA Cup 2nd rd (2nd replay), 18 December 1946.

sky SPORTS FACT FILE

Peterborough United enjoyed a tremendous run in the 1981–82 season and with seven games remaining they were in second place in the old Division Four. Unfortunately they lost six and drew one of their remaining fixtures and slipped to fifth position, six points adrift of a promotion slot.

Most League Points (2 for a win): 66, Division 4, 1960–61.

Most League Points (3 for a win): 92, FL 2, 2007–08.

Most League Goals: 134, Division 4, 1960–61.

Highest League Scorer in Season: Terry Bly, 52, Division 4, 1960–61.

Most League Goals in Total Aggregate: Jim Hall, 122, 1967–75.

Most League Goals in One Match: 5, Guiliano Grazioli v Barnet, Division 3, 5 September 1998.

Most Capped Player: Gabriel Zakuani, 22, DR Congo.

Most League Appearances: Tommy Robson, 482, 1968–81.

Youngest League Player: Matthew Etherington, 15 years 262 days v Brentford, 3 May 1997.

Record Transfer Fee Received: £5,500,000 from Nottingham F for Britt Assombalonga, August 2014.

Record Transfer Fee Paid: £1,250,000 to Watford for Britt Assombalonga, July 2013.

Football League Record: 1960 Elected to Division 4; 1961–68 Division 3, when they were demoted for financial irregularities; 1968–74 Division 4; 1974–79 Division 3; 1979–91 Division 4; 1991–92 Division 3; 1992–94 Division 1; 1994–97 Division 2; 1997–2000 Division 3; 2000–04 Division 2; 2004–05 FL 1; 2005–08 FL 2; 2008–09 FL 1; 2009–10 FL C; 2010–11 FL 1; 2011–13 FL C; 2013– FL 1.

LATEST SEQUENCES

Longest Sequence of League Wins: 9, 1.2.1992 – 14.3.1992.

Longest Sequence of League Defeats: 8, 16.12.2006 – 27.1.2007.

Longest Sequence of League Draws: 8, 18.12.1971 – 12.2.1972.

Longest Sequence of Unbeaten League Matches: 17, 15.1.2008 – 5.4.2008.

Longest Sequence Without a League Win: 17, 23.9.1978 – 30.12.1978.

Successive Scoring Runs: 33 from 20.9.1960.

Successive Non-scoring Runs: 6 from 13.8.2002.

MANAGERS

Jock Porter 1934–36
Fred Taylor 1936–37
Vic Poulter 1937–38
Sam Haden 1938–48
Jack Blood 1948–50
Bob Gurney 1950–52
Jack Fairbrother 1952–54
George Swindin 1954–58
Jimmy Hagan 1958–62
Jack Fairbrother 1962–64
Gordon Clark 1964–67
Norman Rigby 1967–69
Jim Iley 1969–72
Noel Cantwell 1972–77
John Barnwell 1977–78
Billy Hails 1978–79
Peter Morris 1979–82
Martin Wilkinson 1982–83
John Wile 1983–86
Noel Cantwell 1986–88 *(continued as General Manager)*
Mick Jones 1988–89
Mark Lawrenson 1989–90
Dave Booth 1990–91
Chris Turner 1991–92
Lil Fuccillo 1992–93
Chris Turner 1993–94
John Still 1994–95
Mick Halsall 1995–96
Barry Fry 1996–2005
Mark Wright 2005–06
Steve Bleasdale 2006
Keith Alexander 2006–07
Darren Ferguson 2007–09
Mark Cooper 2009–10
Jim Gannon 2010
Gary Johnson 2010–11
Darren Ferguson 2011–15
Dave Robertson 2015
Graham Westley 2015–16
Grant McCann April 2016–

TEN YEAR LEAGUE RECORD

		P	W	D	L	F	A	Pts	Pos
2006-07	FL 2	46	18	11	17	70	61	65	10
2007-08	FL 2	46	28	8	10	84	43	92	2
2008-09	FL 1	46	26	11	9	78	54	89	2
2009-10	FL C	46	8	10	28	46	80	34	24
2010-11	FL 1	46	23	10	13	106	75	79	4
2011-12	FL C	46	13	11	22	67	77	50	18
2012-13	FL C	46	15	9	22	66	75	54	22
2013-14	FL 1	46	23	5	18	72	58	74	6
2014-15	FL 1	46	18	9	19	53	56	63	9
2015-16	FL 1	46	19	6	21	82	73	63	13

DID YOU KNOW

When Peterborough United were formed in 1934 the club adopted colours of green shirts with a white 'V' and white shorts, the kit being donated by a local store. It was not until 1937 that they switched to what has become their traditional colours of blue and white.

PETERBOROUGH UNITED – FOOTBALL LEAGUE ONE 2015–16 LEAGUE RECORD

Match No.	Date	Venue	Opponents	Result	H/T Score	Lg Pos.	Goalscorers	Atten- dance
1	Aug 8	A	Rochdale	L	0-2	0-1	21		3319
2	15	H	Colchester U	W	2-1	2-1	10	Maddison 2 [31, 34]	5339
3	18	H	Sheffield U	L	1-3	0-1	14	Coulibaly [59]	6526
4	22	A	Burton Alb	L	1-2	0-1	18	Maddison [67]	3407
5	29	H	Gillingham	D	1-1	0-0	18	Taylor [90]	5083
6	Sept 5	A	Southend U	L	1-2	0-1	20	Maddison [90]	5748
7	12	A	Oldham Ath	W	5-1	2-0	17	Angol 2 [14, 78], Oztumer [38], Coulibaly 2 [62, 65]	3566
8	19	H	Walsall	D	1-1	0-0	18	Bostwick (pen) [87]	5859
9	26	A	Bradford C	W	2-0	0-0	14	Angol [56], Forrester [57]	17,970
10	29	H	Bury	L	2-3	1-1	15	Zakuani 2 [43, 49]	4208
11	Oct 3	H	Millwall	W	5-3	2-0	12	Angol [15], Taylor 2 [19, 81], Forrester [69], Washington [72]	6402
12	10	A	Swindon T	W	2-1	1-0	8	Taylor [38], Angol [52]	7025
13	17	A	Port Vale	D	1-1	0-1	9	Bostwick (pen) [56]	4864
14	20	H	Wigan Ath	L	2-3	0-2	13	Oztumer [61], Coulibaly [81]	4765
15	24	H	Doncaster R	W	4-0	2-0	9	Zakuani [9], Oztumer [36], Elder [46], Washington [73]	6092
16	31	A	Coventry C	L	2-3	2-0	12	Anderson, J [15], Oztumer [36]	11,853
17	Nov 14	H	Fleetwood T	W	2-1	0-0	10	Coulibaly [57], Anderson, J [77]	5462
18	21	A	Crewe Alex	W	5-1	1-0	9	Taylor [6], Washington [46], Anderson, J 2 [47, 82], Angol [54]	4094
19	24	H	Barnsley	W	3-2	1-1	7	Angol [24], Addison [62], Maddison [73]	4783
20	28	A	Scunthorpe U	W	4-0	1-0	6	Washington 3 [4, 82, 90], Bostwick (pen) [49]	3790
21	Dec 12	H	Shrewsbury T	D	1-1	0-0	5	Washington [56]	5568
22	19	A	Blackpool	L	0-2	0-2	6		6204
23	26	H	Chesterfield	W	2-0	1-0	5	Washington 2 [45, 76]	7153
24	28	H	Walsall	L	0-2	0-0	6		6142
25	Jan 2	A	Sheffield U	W	3-2	1-1	6	Washington [18], Oztumer [48], Samuelsen [84]	22,302
26	16	H	Southend U	D	0-0	0-0	6		7057
27	23	A	Gillingham	L	1-2	1-0	7	Oztumer [25]	6449
28	26	H	Burton Alb	L	0-1	0-1	8		4798
29	Feb 6	A	Chesterfield	W	1-0	0-0	8	Nichols [55]	6544
30	13	H	Bradford C	L	0-4	0-1	10		5816
31	20	A	Millwall	L	0-3	0-1	12		8722
32	23	A	Oldham Ath	L	1-2	1-1	12	Maddison [39]	3544
33	27	H	Swindon T	L	1-2	1-0	15	Maddison (pen) [12]	5124
34	Mar 1	A	Bury	L	1-3	0-2	16	Maddison [52]	2180
35	5	A	Wigan Ath	D	1-1	0-0	16	Maddison [80]	8877
36	12	H	Port Vale	L	2-3	2-0	16	Taylor [2], Williams [41]	4942
37	19	A	Doncaster R	W	2-1	1-1	16	Williams [44], Santos [90]	7884
38	25	H	Coventry C	W	3-1	1-0	14	Bostwick [45], Angol [61], Beautyman [69]	6021
39	Apr 2	H	Crewe Alex	W	3-0	2-0	14	Beautyman 2 [14, 40], Angol [67]	4881
40	5	A	Fleetwood T	L	0-2	0-1	14		2134
41	9	H	Rochdale	L	1-2	1-2	14	Smith [34]	4785
42	16	A	Colchester U	W	4-1	1-0	14	Taylor [2], Fox [67], Coulthirst [69], Maddison [90]	5965
43	19	A	Barnsley	L	0-1	0-0	14		8886
44	23	H	Scunthorpe U	L	0-2	0-0	14		5065
45	30	A	Shrewsbury T	W	4-3	1-0	13	Baldwin [42], Angol 2 [46, 69], Taylor [90]	6019
46	May 8	H	Blackpool	W	5-1	0-1	13	Maddison (pen) [48], Taylor 3 [74, 84, 86], Coulthirst [76]	6005

Final League Position: 13

GOALSCORERS

League (82): Angol 11, Maddison 11 (2 pens), Taylor 11, Washington 10, Oztumer 6, Coulibaly 5, Anderson, J 4, Bostwick 4 (3 pens), Beautyman 3, Zakuani 3, Coulthirst 2, Forrester 2, Williams 2, Addison 1, Baldwin 1, Elder 1, Fox 1, Nichols 1, Samuelsen 1, Santos 1, Smith 1.

FA Cup (10): Washington 4, Taylor 2, Anderson, J 1, Coulthirst 1, Maddison 1, Samuelsen 1.

Capital One Cup (3): Anderson, J 1, Maddison 1, Washington 1.

Johnstone's Paint Trophy (0).

Alnwick B 39	Adebayo-Rowling T 3+1	Zakuani G 22+2	Davey A 6+1	Ntihe K 6+1	Taylor J 32+12	Bostwick M 35+1	Anderson J 13+1	Maddison M 31+8	Washington C 21+4	Gormley J 4	Chettle C —+5	Anderson H 3+2	Gillett S 3+2	Collison J 2+8	Coulibaly S 13+14	Santos R 33+4	Brisley S —+2	Payne J 1+1	Tyler M 3	Elder C 18	Vassell K 1+4	Smith M 37+1	Forrester C 33+2	Oztumer E 28+2	Angol L 24+9	Da Silva Lopes L 4+4	Henry D —+1	Fox A 9+9	Beautyman H 19+3	Addison M 2+1	Samuelsen M 7+10	Baldwin J 17+1	Wilson L 1+1	Toffolo H 6+1	Coulthirst S 11+8	Nabi A 4+2	Nichols T 5+2	Nicholson J —+2	Williams A 6+4	Moore S 4	Match No.
1	2	3	4	5	6^{2}	7	8^{3}	9^{1}	10	11	12	13	14																												1
1	2^{3}	3	4	5	6^{2}	7^{1}	8	9	10	11	12	13	14																												2
1	2^{1}	3	4	5^{2}	6	7	8	9	10^{3}	11	12	13	14																												3
1	2^{1}	3	4^{4}	5	6^{2}	7	8	9	10	11^{3}	12	13	14																												4
1	2	3	4	5	6	7^{1}	8	9	10	11^{2}	12	13																													5
1	2	3	4^{3}	5	6	7	8	9	10^{1}	11^{2}	12	13	14																												6
1	2	3	4	5	6	7^{3}	8^{1}	9^{2}	10	11	12	13	14																												7
1	2	3	4	5	6	7^{4}	8^{2}	9^{1}	10	11^{3}	12	13	14																												8
1	2	3	4	5	6	7^{1}	8^{3}	9	10	11^{2}	12	13	14																												9
1	2	3	4	5	6	7^{1}	8	9^{2}	10^{3}	11^{1}	12	13	14																												10
1^{3}	2	3	4	5	6	7	8^{2}	9	10	11^{1}	12	13	14																												11
1	2	3	4	5	6	7	8	9^{2}	10	11^{1}	12	13																													12
1	2	3	4	5	6	7^{1}	8	9	10^{2}	11^{3}	12	13	14																												13
1	2^{3}	3	4^{1}	5	6	7	8	9^{2}	10	11	12	13	14																												14
1	2	3	4^{1}	5	6	7^{3}	8	9^{2}	10	11	12		14								13																				15
1	2	3	4	5	6^{3}	7	8^{1}	9	10	11^{2}	12		14		13																										16
1		3			6	4		9	10^{3}		12	13	14			5						2	7	8^{2}	11^{1}																17
1		3			6	4		9	10^{3}		12	13	14			5						2	7^{1}	8^{2}	11																18
1		3			6	4		9	10^{2}		12	13	14			5						2	7^{1}	8^{3}	11																19
1		3			6	4		9	10^{3}		12	13	14			5						2	7^{2}	8^{1}	11																20
1		3			6	4		9^{2}	10		12	13	14			5						2	7^{1}	8	11^{3}																21
1		3			6^{2}	4		9	10		12	13	14			5						2^{3}	7	8	11^{1}																22
1^{1}		3			6^{1}	4		9	10		12	13	14			5						2	7^{3}	8	11^{2}																23
1					6	4^{3}		9	10^{2}		12	13	14			5						2	7	8^{3}	11																24
1		3			6^{2}	4		9	10		12	13	14			5^{1}						2	7	8	11^{2}																25
1		3			6	4		9	10		12	13	14			5^{1}						2	7	8^{3}	11^{2}																26
1		3			6	4		9^{2}	10^{1}		12	13	14			5						2	7	8	11^{2}																27
1		3			6^{1}	4		9	10		12	13	14			5^{2}						2	7	8^{3}	11																28
1					6	4		9^{1}	10^{2}		12	13	14			5				2^{4}		3^{4}	7	8^{3}	11																29
1					6	4		9	10		14	13				5^{3}						2	7	8^{2}	11		12	3													30
1					5	7		9	11^{3}			14										2	6^{2}	8				3^{1}	12				10		13						31
1		3			7^{1}	5		9	11^{1}													2	6	8^{3}	10^{3}				12	4			13					14			32
1		3			9	7		8	10^{1}							5^{3}						2	6			13			12	11		14								1	33
		2			9^{2}	10^{3}	7	8	4^{4}		14					5							6^{1}					13	3		12	11								1	34
		3^{1}			9	4	11	7^{2}			14				8	2										12	6^{3}		5		10							13		1	35
					6	4	9	8			14				8	2							7^{3}	12		3		5		13	10^{2}	14	11^{1}							1	36
1		3^{1}			8^{3}	4	11								2	5					6	9^{2}			12	7	14		13						10						37
1					6^{3}	3	9				14				4							8	10^{2}	13		5	7^{1}		2		12			11						38
1					13	2	5				14		12			4						8^{2}		9			7^{3}	6		3			11			10					39
1		3			5	12	4	8					7^{1}			2							9^{3}				6		13			10			14		11^{2}				40
1					8^{2}	4	10									2	7	13	11			5^{1}	9^{3}	12	3			14		6											41
1					6	3	10									5^{2}	7	9^{3}	14		12	8		4			13						11					11^{1}			42
1	13				6	3	7^{2}									4^{3}		11^{4}	9^{1}	12	14	5	8		2			10													43
					6^{2}		9		13			3		1			7^{1}	10^{3}	8	5	2			4			14	11				12									44
		3			12		9		13					1		2	6^{2}	11	7			4			5	10^{1}	8^{3}		14												45
		3^{1}			13		9		14			12		1		2	6^{3}	11	7	5		4			10	8^{2}															46

FA Cup

First Round	Burton Alb	(a)	3-0
Second Round	Luton T	(h)	2-0
Third Round	Preston NE	(h)	2-0
Fourth Round	WBA	(a)	2-2
Replay	WBA	(h)	1-1

(aet; WBA won 4-3 on penalties)

Capital One Cup

First Round	Crawley T	(h)	2-0
Second Round	Charlton Ath	(h)	1-4

Johnstone's Paint Trophy

First Round	Millwall	(a)	0-1

PLYMOUTH ARGYLE

FOUNDATION

The club was formed in September 1886 as the Argyle Athletic Club by former public and private school pupils who wanted to continue playing the game. The meeting was held in a room above the Borough Arms (a coffee house), Bedford Street, Plymouth. It was common then to choose a local street/terrace as a club name and Argyle or Argyll was a fashionable name throughout the land due to Queen Victoria's great interest in Scotland.

Home Park, Plymouth, Devon PL2 3DQ.

Telephone: (01752) 562 561.

Fax: (01752) 606 167.

Ticket Office: (0845) 872 3335.

Website: www.pafc.co.uk

Email: argyle@pafc.co.uk

Ground Capacity: 16,388.

Record Attendance: 43,596 v Aston Villa, Division 2, 10 October 1936.

Pitch Measurements: 105m × 68.5m (115yd × 75yd).

Chairman: James Brent.

Chief Executive: Martyn Starnes.

Manager: Derek Adams.

Assistant Manager: Craig Brewster.

Physio: Paul Atkinson.

Colours: Dark green and white striped shirts, dark green shorts, white socks with dark green trim.

Year Formed: 1886.

Turned Professional: 1903.

Previous Name: 1886, Argyle Athletic Club; 1903, Plymouth Argyle.

Club Nickname: 'The Pilgrims'.

Ground: 1886, Home Park.

First Football League Game: 28 August 1920, Division 3, v Norwich C (h) D 1–1 – Craig; Russell, Atterbury; Logan, Dickinson, Forbes; Kirkpatrick, Jack, Bowler, Heeps (1), Dixon.

Record League Victory: 8–1 v Millwall, Division 2, 16 January 1932 – Harper; Roberts, Titmuss; Mackay, Pullan, Reed; Grozier, Bowden (2), Vidler (3), Leslie (1), Black (1), (1 og). 8–1 v Hartlepool U (a), Division 2, 7 May 1994 – Nicholls; Patterson (Naylor), Hill, Burrows, Comyn, McCall (1), Barlow, Castle (1), Landon (3), Marshall (1), Dalton (2).

Record Cup Victory: 6–0 v Corby T, FA Cup 3rd rd, 22 January 1966 – Leiper; Book, Baird; Williams, Nelson, Newman; Jones (1), Jackson (1), Bickle (3), Piper (1), Jennings.

HONOURS

League Champions: Second Division – 2003–04; Division 3 – 1958–59; Division 3S – 1929–30, 1951–52; Third Division – 2001–02.
Runners-up: Division 3 – 1974–75, 1985–86; Division 3S – 1921–22, 1922–23, 1923–24, 1924–25, 1925–26, 1926–27.
FA Cup: semi-final – 1984.
League Cup: semi-final – 1965, 1974.

sky SPORTS FACT FILE

Plymouth Argyle winger John Demellweek spent four seasons as a professional with the club in the 1930s after leaving the Royal Navy. He re-enlisted when war broke out in 1939 and took part in the famous raid on the French port of St Nazaire in 1942. Following the raid he was taken as a prisoner of war and remained so until hostilities ceased.

Record Defeat: 0–9 v Stoke C, Division 2, 17 December 1960.

Most League Points (2 for a win): 68, Division 3 (S), 1929–30.

Most League Points (3 for a win): 102, Division 3, 2001–02.

Most League Goals: 107, Division 3 (S), 1925–26 and 1951–52.

Highest League Scorer in Season: Jack Cock, 32, Division 3 (S), 1926–27.

Most League Goals in Total Aggregate: Sammy Black, 174, 1924–38.

Most League Goals in One Match: 5, Wilf Carter v Charlton Ath, Division 2, 27 December 1960.

Most Capped Player: Moses Russell, 20 (23), Wales.

Most League Appearances: Kevin Hodges, 530, 1978–92.

Youngest League Player: Lee Phillips, 16 years 43 days v Gillingham, 29 October 1996.

Record Transfer Fee Received: £2,000,000 from Hull C for Peter Halmosi, July 2008.

Record Transfer Fee Paid: £500,000 to Cardiff C for Steve MacLean, January 2008.

Football League Record: 1920 Original Member of Division 3; 1921–30 Division 3 (S); 1930–50 Division 2; 1950–52 Division 3 (S); 1952–56 Division 2; 1956–58 Division 3 (S); 1958–59 Division 3; 1959–68 Division 2; 1968–75 Division 3; 1975–77 Division 2; 1977–86 Division 3; 1986–95 Division 2; 1995–96 Division 3; 1996–98 Division 2; 1998–2002 Division 3; 2002–04 Division 2; 2004–10 FL C; 2010–11 FL 1; 2011– FL 2.

LATEST SEQUENCES

Longest Sequence of League Wins: 9, 8.3.1986 – 12.4.1986.

Longest Sequence of League Defeats: 9, 12.10.1963 – 7.12.1963.

Longest Sequence of League Draws: 5, 26.2.2000 – 14.3.2000.

Longest Sequence of Unbeaten League Matches: 22, 20.4.1929 – 21.12.1929.

Longest Sequence Without a League Win: 13, 13.4.2009 – 27.9.2009.

Successive Scoring Runs: 39 from 15.4.1939.

Successive Non-scoring Runs: 5 from 21.11.2009.

MANAGERS

Frank Brettell 1903–05
Bob Jack 1905–06
Bill Fullerton 1906–07
Bob Jack 1910–38
Jack Tresadern 1938–47
Jimmy Rae 1948–55
Jack Rowley 1955–60
Neil Dougall 1961
Ellis Stuttard 1961–63
Andy Beattie 1963–64
Malcolm Allison 1964–65
Derek Ufton 1965–68
Billy Bingham 1968–70
Ellis Stuttard 1970–72
Tony Waiters 1972–77
Mike Kelly 1977–78
Malcolm Allison 1978–79
Bobby Saxton 1979–81
Bobby Moncur 1981–83
Johnny Hore 1983–84
Dave Smith 1984–88
Ken Brown 1988–90
David Kemp 1990–92
Peter Shilton 1992–95
Steve McCall 1995
Neil Warnock 1995–97
Mick Jones 1997–98
Kevin Hodges 1998–2000
Paul Sturrock 2000–04
Bobby Williamson 2004–05
Tony Pulis 2005–06
Ian Holloway 2006–07
Paul Sturrock 2007–09
Paul Mariner 2009–10
Peter Reid 2010–11
Carl Fletcher 2011–13
John Sheridan 2013–15
Derek Adams June 2015–

TEN YEAR LEAGUE RECORD

		P	W	D	L	F	A	Pts	Pos
2006-07	FL C	46	17	16	13	63	62	67	11
2007-08	FL C	46	17	13	16	60	50	64	10
2008-09	FL C	46	13	12	21	44	57	51	21
2009-10	FL C	46	11	8	27	43	68	41	23
2010-11	FL 1	46	15	7	24	51	74	42*	23
2011-12	FL 2	46	10	16	20	47	64	46	21
2012-13	FL 2	46	13	13	20	46	55	52	21
2013-14	FL 2	46	16	12	18	51	58	60	10
2014-15	FL 2	46	20	11	15	55	37	71	7
2015-16	FL 2	46	24	9	13	72	46	81	5

* 10 pts deducted.

DID YOU KNOW ?

Jack Fitchett, who made 46 appearances for Plymouth Argyle in the 1903–04 season, later toured the country with Fred Karno's troupe, appearing alongside Charlie Chaplin. He subsequently worked for many years as a theatre manager, returning to Plymouth in 1925 to take charge of the Palace Theatre until 1939.

PLYMOUTH ARGYLE – FOOTBALL LEAGUE TWO 2015–16 LEAGUE RECORD

Match No.	Date	Venue	Opponents	Result		H/T Score	Lg Pos.	Goalscorers	Attendance
1	Aug 8	A	AFC Wimbledon	W	2-0	1-0	4	Wylde [40], Carey [49]	4805
2	15	H	Portsmouth	L	1-2	0-1	8	Wylde [89]	11,476
3	18	H	Carlisle U	W	4-1	1-0	6	Jervis 2 [43, 65], Reid [53], Carey [56]	6071
4	22	A	Northampton T	W	2-0	1-0	3	Carey [39], Jervis [71]	4505
5	29	H	Newport Co	W	1-0	1-0	2	Carey [43]	7811
6	Sept 5	A	Stevenage	L	1-2	0-2	3	Tanner [54]	3560
7	12	A	Wycombe W	W	2-1	2-1	2	Reid [4], Jervis [32]	4223
8	19	H	Bristol R	D	1-1	0-0	2	Jervis [85]	10,633
9	26	A	Mansfield T	D	0-0	0-0	4		3185
10	29	H	Barnet	W	2-1	0-1	2	Carey [53], Jervis [60]	6115
11	Oct 3	H	Crawley T	W	2-1	1-0	1	Reid [43], Boateng [89]	7173
12	11	A	Notts Co	W	2-0	1-0	1	Reid 2 [18, 86]	5266
13	17	H	Accrington S	W	1-0	0-0	1	Reid [64]	7865
14	20	A	Oxford U	L	0-1	0-1	1		7007
15	24	A	Luton T	W	2-1	1-0	1	McHugh [17], Brunt [90]	8703
16	31	H	Morecambe	W	2-0	2-0	1	Carey [3], Tanner [12]	7574
17	Nov 14	A	York C	W	2-1	2-0	1	Jervis [19], Carey [44]	3654
18	21	H	Exeter C	L	1-2	0-2	1	Threlkeld [61]	14,008
19	24	H	Leyton Orient	D	1-1	0-1	1	Nelson [81]	6469
20	28	A	Dagenham & R	W	1-0	0-0	2	Brunt [90]	2344
21	Dec 12	H	Cambridge U	L	1-2	0-1	3	Wylde [73]	7246
22	19	A	Hartlepool U	W	2-1	0-0	1	McHugh [76], Mellor [90]	3534
23	26	H	Yeovil T	W	1-0	0-0	1	Brunt [59]	12,821
24	28	A	Newport Co	W	2-1	0-1	1	Jervis [48], Brunt [70]	4314
25	Jan 2	A	Carlisle U	W	2-0	1-0	1	Brunt 2 [26, 90]	4415
26	12	H	Northampton T	L	1-2	0-1	1	Wylde [83]	9241
27	16	H	Stevenage	W	3-2	3-1	1	McHugh [3], Wylde [17], Tanner [40]	9546
28	23	A	Bristol R	D	1-1	0-0	2	Simpson [88]	10,190
29	30	H	Wycombe W	L	0-1	0-1	2		8458
30	Feb 13	H	Mansfield T	W	3-0	2-0	2	Wylde [33], Brunt 2 (1 pen) [36 (p), 84]	7494
31	20	A	Crawley T	D	1-1	0-0	2	Brunt [57]	3522
32	23	A	Yeovil T	D	0-0	0-0	2		5788
33	27	H	Notts Co	W	1-0	0-0	2	Carey [47]	7642
34	Mar 1	A	Barnet	L	0-1	0-0	3		2209
35	5	H	Oxford U	D	2-2	1-2	3	Nelson [15], Tanner [75]	10,091
36	12	A	Accrington S	L	1-2	1-0	3	Jervis [23]	2044
37	19	A	Luton T	L	0-1	0-1	4		7973
38	25	A	Morecambe	W	2-0	1-0	4	Houghton [14], Matt [47]	2081
39	28	H	York C	W	3-2	3-0	3	Matt [21], Reid (pen) [31], Boyle (og) [42]	8571
40	Apr 2	A	Exeter C	L	1-2	0-0	4	Matt [57]	7177
41	9	H	AFC Wimbledon	L	1-2	0-1	5	Carey [61]	8852
42	16	H	Portsmouth	W	2-1	0-1	5	Matt [86], Wylde [86]	18,423
43	19	A	Leyton Orient	W	3-1	1-0	4	Hartley [45], Jervis 2 [78, 90]	4908
44	23	H	Dagenham & R	L	2-3	0-3	5	Hartley [65], Carey [85]	9211
45	30	A	Cambridge U	D	2-2	0-0	6	Matt [71], Carey [90]	6714
46	May 7	H	Hartlepool U	W	5-0	2-0	5	Harvey, T 2 [6, 25], Rooney 2 [58, 63], Nelson [61]	10,019

Final League Position: 5

GOALSCORERS

League (72): Carey 11, Jervis 11, Brunt 9 (1 pen), Reid 7 (1 pen), Wylde 7, Matt 5, Tanner 4, McHugh 3, Nelson 3, Hartley 2, Harvey, T 2, Rooney 2, Boateng 1, Houghton 1, Mellor 1, Simpson 1, Threlkeld 1, own goal 1.
FA Cup (0).
Capital One Cup (1): Tanner 1.
Johnstone's Paint Trophy (8): Jervis 3, Boateng 1, Brunt 1, Carey 1, McHugh 1, Tanner 1.
League Two Play-Offs (3): Matt 2, Hartley 1.

McCormick L 40	Mellor K 37 + 4	Nelson C 46	Hartley P 42	Sawyer G 43	Reid R 22 + 7	McHugh C 34 + 3	Carey G 34 + 5	Boateng H 22 + 2	Jervis J 38 + 4	Wylde G 33 + 10	Purrington B 6 + 7	Tanner C 22 + 20	Brunt R 17 + 17	Simpson J 14 + 10	Threlkeld O 18 + 7	Harvey T 1 + 5	Cox L — + 4	Bittner J	Walton C 4	Croll L 3	Smalley D — + 1	Nardiello D — + 4	Forster J 8 + 4	Houghton J 10	Matt J 9 + 2	Dorel V 1	Rooney L 1	Bentley J — + 1	Match No.
1	2	3	4	5	6^3	7	8^1	9	10	11^2	12	13	14																1
1	2	3^1	4	5	11	7	9	6		10		8	12																2
1	2	3	4	5	11	6	9	7^1	8	10^2		14	13	12															3
1	2	3	4	5	11^1	6	9	7^3	8	10^2		14	12	13															4
1	2	3	4	5		6	9	7	8	12		10^1	11																5
1	2^2	4	8	5		3	7	6^3	10	9		12	11^1	13	14														6
1	2	3	4	5	11^3	6	8	7	9^1	10^2		12	13		14														7
1	2	3	4	5	11^3	6^1	9	7	8	13		10^2	14		12														8
1	2	4	3	5	11^1		9^2	7	6^3	13		12	10	8	14														9
1	2	3	4	5	11^3		9^2	7	8	10^1		12	14	6	13														10
1	2	3	4	5	11	6	9	7	8^1	10^2		13	12																11
1	2	3	4	5	11	12	13	7^3	8	10^2		9^1	14	6															12
1	2	3	4	5	11^1	12	13	7^2	8	10		9^3	14	6															13
1	2	4	5	3		9	11	8	10^1	7^2		12	13	6															14
1	2	3	4^2	5		6	9	7^3		10^1		8	11	12	14		13												15
1	2	3	4	5^2		6	9	7^1	8		14	10^2	11	12	13														16
	2	3	4	5		8^1	7		11	10^3		6^2	13	12	9	14	1												17
	2	3		5		9		11	10^1		8^2	12	6	7	13		1		4										18
	2	3		5		7	9		11	10^2		8	13	12	6^1		1		4										19
	2	3		5		6	9^2		11	10^3	13	8	12	7^1		14	1		4										20
	2	3	4	5		7		8	10		9	11	6				1												21
1	2	3	4	5		6		8^1	10^3	13	9	11^2		7	12							14							22
1	2	3	4	5	13	7		8	10^2	14	9^3	11^1	12	6															23
1	2	3	4	5		6		10	7^3	13	9^2	11	12	8															24
1	2	3	4	5		6		11^1	7		12	10	9	8															25
1	2	3	4	5	10^2	8		9	13		12	11	7	6^1															26
1	2	3	4	5	11^1	7		8	10		9^3	13	6	12															27
1	2	3	4	5	10^1	7	14		6^2	9^1		12	11	8	13														28
1	2	3	4	5	11	7	12		8^1	10		9^3	13		6^3							14							29
1		3	4	5	14	7	9		12	10^1	13	8^2	11^3		6									2					30
1		4	3	5	12	7	9		13	10		8^1	11^1		6									2					31
1	12	4	3	5	13	6	8		10	9^1		11	7											2^2					32
1	2^1	3	4	5	13		9		10^3			8^1	11	6	7									14	12				33
1	12	4	3	5	10		9		6^3			13	11^1	7	8									14	2^2				34
1	2	3	4^1	5	11^2		9		8	10	7	12		6										13					35
1	2^3	4	5	11^3		9		8^2	10^1		14		12	7												6	13		36
	3	4	5	13	14	9		12	10^3	7	8		2												6^1	11^2		37
	3	4	5	10	8^1	9^3	14	6	13		12		2											7	11^2			38
	3	4	5	10^1	8	9^2	12	6	14		13		2	7^3	11													39
	3	4	5	10	8	9^2		6			13		2^1	7	11													40
1	13	3	4	5		6	10	9^2	7	12		14		2^1	8^3	11													41
1	2	3	4		13	7	10	8	5^2	12	9^1		6	11															42
1	2	3	4		10^1	6^2	9	7	12	14	5			13	8	11^3													43
1	2^2	3	4		9	7^3	8	10	5^1	12		14		13	6	11													44
1	2	3	4^3	5		6^1	10	8	7^2	14	13		12	9	11														45
	2	3^1		5		13	8^1		9^2	7	6	10		4		14	1	11	12										46

FA Cup

First Round	Carlisle U	(h)	0-2

Capital One Cup

First Round	Gillingham	(h)	1-2

Johnstone's Paint Trophy

First Round	AFC Wimbledon	(a)	3-2
Second Round	Exeter C	(h)	2-0
Southern Quarter-Final	Millwall	(h)	3-5

League Two Play-Offs

Semi-Final 1st leg	Portsmouth	(a)	2-2
Semi-Final 2nd leg	Portsmouth	(h)	1-0

(Plymouth Arg won 3-2 on aggregate)

Final	AFC Wimbledon (Wembley)	0-2

PORT VALE

Vale Park, Hamil Road, Burslem, Stoke-on-Trent, Staffordshire ST6 1AW.

Telephone: (01782) 655 823.

Ticket Office: (01782) 655 821.

Website: www.port-vale.co.uk

Email: enquiries@port-vale.co.uk

Ground Capacity: 19,148.

Record Attendance: 22,993 v Stoke C, Division 2, 6 March 1920 (at Recreation Ground); 49,768 v Aston Villa, FA Cup 5th rd, 20 February 1960 (at Vale Park).

Pitch Measurements: 104m × 69.5m (114yd × 76yd).

Chairman: Norman Smurthwaite.

Manager: Bruno Ribeiro.

Assistant Manager: Michael Brown.

Physio: James Rowland.

Colours: White shirts with orange and black trim, black shorts with orange trim, black socks with white hoops.

Year Formed: 1876.

Turned Professional: 1885.

Previous Names: 1876, Port Vale; 1884, Burslem Port Vale; 1909, Port Vale.

Club Nickname: 'Valiants'.

Grounds: 1876, Limekin Lane, Longport; 1881, Westport; 1884, Moorland Road, Burslem; 1886, Athletic Ground, Cobridge; 1913, Recreation Ground, Hanley; 1950, Vale Park.

First Football League Game: 3 September 1892, Division 2, v Small Heath (a) L 1–5 – Frail; Clutton, Elson; Farrington, McCrindle, Delves; Walker, Scarratt, Bliss (1), Jones. (Only 10 men).

Record League Victory: 9–1 v Chesterfield, Division 2, 24 September 1932 – Leckie; Shenton, Poyser; Sherlock, Round, Jones; McGrath, Mills, Littlewood (6), Kirkham (2), Morton (1).

Record Cup Victory: 7–1 v Irthlingborough, FA Cup 1st rd, 12 January 1907 – Matthews; Dunn, Hamilton; Eardley, Baddeley, Holyhead; Carter, Dodds (2), Beats, Mountford (2), Coxon (3).

HONOURS

League Champions: Division 3N – 1929–30, 1953–54; Division 4 – 1958–59.
Runners-up: Second Division – 1993–94; Division 3N – 1952–53.
FA Cup: semi-final – 1954.
League Cup: 4th rd – 2007.
League Trophy Winners: 1993, 2001.
Anglo-Italian Cup: Runners-up: 1996.

sky SPORTS FACT FILE

Port Vale striker Theo Robinson's 37th-minute goal against Rochdale on 23 April 2016 was only his second for the club after signing in the January transfer window. It also provided the landmark 6,000th Football League goal for Vale, who went on to win the match 4-1.

Record Defeat: 0–10 v Sheffield U, Division 2, 10 December 1892. 0–10 v Notts Co, Division 2, 26 February 1895.

Most League Points (2 for a win): 69, Division 3 (N), 1953–54.

Most League Points (3 for a win): 89, Division 2, 1992–93.

Most League Goals: 110, Division 4, 1958–59.

Highest League Scorer in Season: Wilf Kirkham 38, Division 2, 1926–27.

Most League Goals in Total Aggregate: Wilf Kirkham, 153, 1923–29, 1931–33.

Most League Goals in One Match: 6, Stewart Littlewood v Chesterfield, Division 2, 24 September 1922.

Most Capped Player: Chris Birchall, 24 (43), Trinidad & Tobago.

Most League Appearances: Roy Sproson, 760, 1950–72.

Youngest League Player: Malcolm McKenzie, 15 years 347 days v Newport Co, 12 April 1966.

Record Transfer Fee Received: £2,000,000 from Wimbledon for Gareth Ainsworth, October 1998.

Record Transfer Fee Paid: £500,000 to Lincoln C for Gareth Ainsworth, September 1997.

Football League Record: 1892 Original Member of Division 2. Failed re-election in 1896; Re-elected 1898; Resigned 1907; Returned in Oct, 1919, when they took over the fixtures of Leeds City; 1929–30 Division 3 (N); 1930–36 Division 2; 1936–38 Division 3 (N); 1938–52 Division 3 (S); 1952–54 Division 3 (N); 1954–57 Division 2; 1957–58 Division 3 (S); 1958–59 Division 4; 1959–65 Division 3; 1965–70 Division 4; 1970–78 Division 3; 1978–83 Division 4; 1983–84 Division 3; 1984–86 Division 4; 1986–89 Division 3; 1989–94 Division 2; 1994–2000 Division 1; 2000–04 Division 2; 2004–08 FL 1; 2008–13 FL 2; 2013– FL 1.

LATEST SEQUENCES

Longest Sequence of League Wins: 8, 8.4.1893 – 30.9.1893.

Longest Sequence of League Defeats: 9, 9.3.1957 – 20.4.1957.

Longest Sequence of League Draws: 6, 26.4.1981 – 12.9.1981.

Longest Sequence of Unbeaten League Matches: 19, 5.5.1969 – 8.11.1969.

Longest Sequence Without a League Win: 17, 7.12.1991 – 21.3.1992.

Successive Scoring Runs: 22 from 12.9.1992.

Successive Non-scoring Runs: 4 from 7.4.2009.

MANAGERS

Sam Gleaves 1896–1905
(Secretary-Manager)
Tom Clare 1905–11
A. S. Walker 1911–12
H. Myatt 1912–14
Tom Holford 1919–24
(continued as Trainer)
Joe Schofield 1924–30
Tom Morgan 1930–32
Tom Holford 1932–35
Warney Cresswell 1936–37
Tom Morgan 1937–38
Billy Frith 1945–46
Gordon Hodgson 1946–51
Ivor Powell 1951
Freddie Steele 1951–57
Norman Low 1957–62
Freddie Steele 1962–65
Jackie Mudie 1965–67
Sir Stanley Matthews
(General Manager) 1965–68
Gordon Lee 1968–74
Roy Sproson 1974–77
Colin Harper 1977
Bobby Smith 1977–78
Dennis Butler 1978–79
Alan Bloor 1979
John McGrath 1980–83
John Rudge 1983–99
Brian Horton 1999–2004
Martin Foyle 2004–07
Lee Sinnott 2007–08
Dean Glover 2008–09
Micky Adams 2009–10
Jim Gannon 2011
Micky Adams 2011–14
Robert Page 2014–16
Bruno Ribeiro June 2016–

TEN YEAR LEAGUE RECORD

		P	W	D	L	F	A	Pts	Pos
2006-07	FL 1	46	18	6	22	64	65	60	12
2007-08	FL 1	46	9	11	26	47	81	38	23
2008-09	FL 2	46	13	9	24	44	66	48	18
2009-10	FL 2	46	17	17	12	61	50	68	10
2010-11	FL 2	46	17	14	15	54	49	65	11
2011-12	FL 2	46	20	9	17	68	60	59*	12
2012-13	FL 2	46	21	15	10	87	52	78	3
2013-14	FL 1	46	18	7	21	59	73	61	9
2014-15	FL 1	46	15	9	22	55	65	54	18
2015-16	FL 1	46	18	11	17	56	58	65	12

*10 pts deducted.

DID YOU KNOW ?

Two prominent Port Vale players of the 1930s, Harry Griffiths and Jack Roberts, also excelled at baseball. Both won international honours for the English Baseball Union before switching to the rival National Baseball Association, signing for the Everton club in 1939.

PORT VALE – FOOTBALL LEAGUE ONE 2015–16 LEAGUE RECORD

Match No.	Date	Venue	Opponents	Result	H/T Score	Lg Pos.	Goalscorers	Attendance
1	Aug 8	A	Crewe Alex	D	0-0	0-0	16		6751
2	15	H	Gillingham	D	1-1	1-1	15	Dodds [35]	5067
3	18	A	Swindon T	D	2-2	1-1	13	Ikpeazu [21], Foley (pen) [90]	7026
4	22	H	Doncaster R	W	3-0	1-0	11	Foley [35], Ikpeazu [46], Moore [88]	4775
5	29	A	Bradford C	L	0-1	0-0	13		17,806
6	Sept 12	H	Wigan Ath	W	3-2	1-0	12	Grant [34], Dodds [64], Ikpeazu [90]	5953
7	15	H	Millwall	L	0-2	0-0	14		4477
8	19	A	Bury	L	0-1	0-0	15		4323
9	26	A	Fleetwood T	W	2-1	0-1	12	Daniel [56], Foley (pen) [65]	3560
10	29	H	Oldham Ath	D	1-1	0-1	13	Ikpeazu [70]	4065
11	Oct 3	H	Sheffield U	W	2-1	2-0	8	Moore [17], Ikpeazu [45]	6822
12	10	A	Southend U	L	0-1	0-0	11		6543
13	17	H	Peterborough U	D	1-1	1-0	11	Andoh [40]	4864
14	20	A	Colchester U	L	1-2	1-1	15	Daniel [45]	2785
15	24	A	Burton Alb	L	0-2	0-0	17		4076
16	31	H	Shrewsbury T	W	2-0	0-0	15	Dodds [52], O'Connor (pen) [80]	4880
17	Nov 14	A	Barnsley	W	2-1	1-0	13	Leitch-Smith [40], Foley [47]	8696
18	21	H	Chesterfield	W	3-2	2-1	12	Kelly [6], Leitch-Smith [10], Dodds [48]	4420
19	24	H	Blackpool	W	2-0	0-0	10	Leitch-Smith [82], Birchall [86]	3640
20	28	A	Rochdale	L	1-2	1-1	11	Birchall [13]	2510
21	Dec 12	H	Scunthorpe U	D	1-1	1-1	11	Leitch-Smith [45]	3983
22	20	A	Walsall	L	0-2	0-0	13		4436
23	26	A	Coventry C	L	0-1	0-0	13		17,779
24	28	H	Bury	W	1-0	0-0	11	Kelly [57]	5467
25	Jan 9	A	Blackpool	W	1-0	0-0	10	Leitch-Smith [49]	6527
26	17	A	Millwall	L	1-3	0-3	11	Hooper [61]	7773
27	23	H	Bradford C	D	1-1	1-0	11	Leitch-Smith [2]	4849
28	26	A	Doncaster R	W	2-1	1-0	10	Leitch-Smith 2 [6, 65]	4799
29	30	A	Wigan Ath	L	0-3	0-2	11		9627
30	Feb 2	H	Swindon T	W	1-0	1-0	8	Dickinson [6]	3256
31	7	H	Coventry C	D	1-1	0-1	9	Kelly [84]	6320
32	13	H	Fleetwood T	D	0-0	0-0	9		4194
33	20	A	Sheffield U	L	0-1	0-0	11		18,276
34	26	A	Southend U	W	3-1	3-0	10	Dickinson [18], O'Connor [38], Coker (og) [40]	3957
35	Mar 1	A	Oldham Ath	D	1-1	0-0	10	Foley [60]	3507
36	5	H	Colchester U	W	2-0	1-0	9	Robinson [9], Foley [73]	4116
37	12	A	Peterborough U	W	3-2	0-2	9	Moore [49], Hooper [86], Dodds [89]	4942
38	19	H	Burton Alb	L	0-4	0-2	10		6157
39	25	A	Shrewsbury T	D	1-1	0-0	10	Dodds [60]	7019
40	28	H	Barnsley	L	0-1	0-1	11		4839
41	Apr 2	A	Chesterfield	L	2-4	1-0	13	Leitch-Smith [36], Hooper [70]	5917
42	9	H	Crewe Alex	W	3-0	1-0	12	Dodds 2 [3, 83], Hooper [90]	5771
43	16	A	Gillingham	W	2-0	2-0	11	Leitch-Smith [19], Dickinson [21]	5887
44	23	H	Rochdale	W	4-1	2-0	11	Robinson [37], O'Connor 2 (2 pens) [45, 76], Hooper [46]	4380
45	30	A	Scunthorpe U	L	0-1	0-0	12		7275
46	May 8	H	Walsall	L	0-5	0-3	12		8595

Final League Position: 12

GOALSCORERS

League (56): Leitch-Smith 10, Dodds 8, Foley 6 (2 pens), Hooper 5, Ikpeazu 5, O'Connor 4 (3 pens), Dickinson 3, Kelly 3, Moore 3, Birchall 2, Daniel 2, Robinson 2, Andoh 1, Grant 1, own goal 1.
FA Cup (4): Leitch-Smith 2, Moore 1, O'Connor 1.
Capital One Cup (1): Moore 1.
Johnstone's Paint Trophy (2): Grant 1 (pen), Ikpeazu 1.

Ainwick J 41	Purkiss B 39	Streete R 12 + 1	Duffy R 45	Dickinson C 44	Moore B 27 + 9	Grant A 38	Dodds L 31 + 6	Kelly S 9 + 19	Ikpeazu U 14 + 7	Foley S 42 + 3	Andoh E 11 + 1	Brown M 7 + 6	Leitch-Smith A 27 + 10	Inniss R 12 + 3	Daniel C 11 + 9	Lloyd R — + 5	Birchall C 4 + 7	McCourt J — + 2	McGivern R 26 + 2	O'Connor M 25 + 1	Hooper J 9 + 19	Yates A 10 + 1	Neal C 5 + 1	Kennedy M 9 + 3	Robinson T 8 + 6	Turner D — + 1	Match No.
1	2	3	4	5	6	7	8	9^2	10^3	11^1	12	13	14														1
1	2		4	5	6		8	10	12	11^2	7^3	13		3	14												2
1	2		4	5	6		8	10^2	9^1	11^3	7		12	3	14	13											3
1	2		4	5	6	7	10		11^1	8	9^2		13	3	12												4
1	2	3		5	6^3	8	10	12	11^2	7	9^1		14	4			13										5
1	2	4	3	5	6	7	11		10^1	8^2	9				13			12									6
1	2	3^2	4	5	6	7	8^1		10	11^3	9	13	12					14									7
1	2		4	5	6	7	11^2		10^1	8	9^3		12	3	13	14											8
1	2	12	3	5	9	7	6		11^2	8		10^1	4^3	13		14											9
1	2	4	3	5	6	8			12	7	9	11^1	10														10
1	2	4	3	5	6	7	12		11^2	8	9	13	10^1														11
1	2		3	5	12	8	13		11^1	7	9		10		6^2		4										12
1	2	4	3	5	6^2		13		11	8	9		10^1	14	12					7^3							13
1	2	3		5		7	13		10	8	9^2		14	11^3	12	6^1	4										14
1	2		4	5		9	6		11^1	8^2			14	10^1	13		3		7^3	12							15
1	2		3	5	6	8	10			11	9		11				4	7									16
1		3	5	6	8	10			12	9^2			11^1	13			4	7		2							17
1^2		3	5	6	7	10	9^1			8			11	13			4			2	12						18
1		3	5	6^3	8	10^1	13	14	9^2				11		12		4	7		2							19
1		4	5^1		8	11^1	12	13	9				10^3		6^2		3	7	14	2							20
1	2	3	4		7	10^1	9	12	13				11^3		6^2		4	8	14	5							21
1	2	3		8^3	7	9^2	10^1	12	13				11				3	6	14	5							22
1	2	4	5	6^2	8			14	9^1				11^3	10		12	3	7	13								23
1	2	3	5	6^2			12		10	8	11^1		9^3		14		4	7	13								24
1	2	4	5	6			13		10	8	11^1		9^2				3	7	12								25
1	2	3	5	6^3		13	12		10^2	8	11		9^1				4	7	14								26
1		3	5	13	7	6^2	9		8^1	14	11		12				4		10^3	2							27
1		4	5		8	6			12		11	14					3	7^1	10^2	2				9^3	13		28
1		3	5		7	6	13		8				10^3	12			4^1		11^2	2				9^1	14		29
1	2	3	5	14	7	6^3	13		8				11	4					12					9^1	10^2		30
1	2	3	5	6^2	7		14		8				11	4^3			12		13					9	10^1		31
1	2	3	5	6^2	7		13		8^1				10				4	14	12					9	11^3		32
	2	3	5	6^2	7	14	13		8				10^1				4		12	1		9		11^3		33
	2	3	5		7	11	13		8				10^2				4	6	12	1		9^1				34
	2	4	5		8	10			7				11^2				3	6	12	1		9^1	13			35
	2	4	5	12	7	10			9			3						8	13	1		6^2	11^1				36
	2	3	5	6^3	8	10	14		9			4^1					12	7	13	1			11^2				37
1	2	3	5	6^3	7	10^1	12		9^2								4	8	11			14	13				38
1	2	3	5	13		10	6^1		9^2	7	4						8	11^1			12	14					39
1	2		4	5	7	6	14		9	13	11	3^2					8^3	10^1			12						40
1	2	3	4	5	6^3	7	10	9	8^2			14	11^1					12			13						41
1	2	3	4	5	12	7	10	6^2	9			14	11^1					8^3	13								42
1	5	2	4	9	14	7	10^2			8^3			11^1			12	3	6	13								43
1	6	2	3	9			12		8^1	5							4	7	10					11^2	13		44
1	5		3	9	14		13		8	7	12						4	6^1	11	2^2				10^3			45
1	5	2^3	3	9	14		12		7	8	11						4^2	6^1	10	13							46

FA Cup

First Round	Maidenhead U	(h)	1-1	
Replay	Maidenhead U	(a)	3-1	
Second Round	Exeter C	(a)	0-2	

Johnstone's Paint Trophy

First Round	Carlisle U	(h)	1-0
Second Round	Blackpool	(h)	1-2

Capital One Cup

First Round	Burnley	(h)	1-0
Second Round	WBA	(a)	0-0
(aet; WBA won 5-3 on penalties)			

PORTSMOUTH

Fratton Park, Frogmore Road, Portsmouth, Hampshire PO4 8RA.

Telephone: (02392) 731 204.

Fax: (02392) 734 129.

Ticket Office: (02392) 778 559.

Website: www.portsmouthfc.co.uk

Email: info@pompeyfc.co.uk

Ground Capacity: 18,524.

Record Attendance: 51,385 v Derby Co, FA Cup 6th rd, 26 February 1949.

Pitch Measurements: 100m × 66m (109.5yd × 72yd).

Chairman: Iain McInnes.

Chief Executive: Mark Catlin.

Manager: Paul Cook.

Assistant Manager: Leam Richardson.

Colours: Blue shirts with red and white trim, white shorts with blue trim, red socks.

Year Formed: 1898.

Turned Professional: 1898.

Club Nickname: 'Pompey'.

Ground: 1898, Fratton Park.

First Football League Game: 28 August 1920, Division 3, v Swansea T (h) W 3–0 – Robson; Probert, Potts; Abbott, Harwood, Turner; Thompson, Stringfellow (1), Reid (1), James (1), Beedie.

Record League Victory: 9–1 v Notts Co, Division 2, 9 April 1927 – McPhail; Clifford, Ted Smith; Reg Davies (1), Foxall, Moffat; Forward (1), Mackie (2), Haines (3), Watson, Cook (2).

Record Cup Victory: 7–0 v Stockport Co, FA Cup 3rd rd, 8 January 1949 – Butler; Rookes, Ferrier; Scoular, Flewin, Dickinson; Harris (3), Barlow, Clarke (2), Phillips (2), Froggatt.

Record Defeat: 0–10 v Leicester C, Division 1, 20 October 1928.

Most League Points (2 for a win): 65, Division 3, 1961–62.

HONOURS

League Champions: Division 1 – 1948–49, 1949–50; First Division – 2002–03; Division 3 – 1961–62, 1982–83; Division 3S – 1923–24. *Runners-up:* Division 2 – 1926–27, 1986–87.
FA Cup Winners: 1939, 2008. *Runners-up:* 1929, 1934, 2010.
League Cup: 5th rd – 1961, 1986, 1994, 2010.
European Competitions
UEFA Cup: 2008–09.

sky SPORTS FACT FILE

After relegation to the Southern League Second Division at the end of 1910–11 Portsmouth bounced back in style. They won their first game of the season 11-0 at home to Chesham and went on to finish runners-up to Merthyr Town on goal average. Pompey dropped just a single point in 13 home games, scoring 47 goals in the process.

Most League Points (3 for a win): 98, Division 1, 2002–03.

Most League Goals: 97, Division 1, 2002–03.

Highest League Scorer in Season: Guy Whittingham, 42, Division 1, 1992–93.

Most League Goals in Total Aggregate: Peter Harris, 194, 1946–60.

Most League Goals in One Match: 5, Alf Strange v Gillingham, Division 3, 27 January 1923; 5, Peter Harris v Aston Villa, Division 1, 3 September 1958.

Most Capped Player: Jimmy Dickinson, 48, England.

Most League Appearances: Jimmy Dickinson, 764, 1946–65.

Youngest League Player: Clive Green, 16 years 259 days v Wrexham, 21 August 1976.

Record Transfer Fee Received: £20,000,000 from Real Madrid for Lassana Diarra, January 2009.

Record Transfer Fee Paid: £9,000,000 (rising to £11,000,000) to Liverpool for Peter Crouch, July 2008.

Football League Record: 1920 Original Member of Division 3; 1921 Division 3 (S); 1924–27 Division 2; 1927–59 Division 1; 1959–61 Division 2; 1961–62 Division 3; 1962–76 Division 2; 1976–78 Division 3; 1978–80 Division 4; 1980–83 Division 3; 1983–87 Division 2; 1987–88 Division 1; 1988–92 Division 2; 1992–2003 Division 1; 2003–10 FA Premier League; 2010–12 FL C; 2012–13 FL 1; 2013– FL 2.

LATEST SEQUENCES

Longest Sequence of League Wins: 7, 17.8.2002 – 17.9.2002.

Longest Sequence of League Defeats: 9, 26.12.2012 – 9.2.2013.

Longest Sequence of League Draws: 5, 16.12.2000 – 13.1.2001.

Longest Sequence of Unbeaten League Matches: 15, 18.4.1924 – 18.10.1924.

Longest Sequence Without a League Win: 25, 29.11.1958 – 22.8.1959.

Successive Scoring Runs: 23 from 30.8.1930.

Successive Non-scoring Runs: 6 from 27.12.1993.

MANAGERS

Frank Brettell 1898–1901
Bob Blyth 1901–04
Richard Bonney 1905–08
Bob Brown 1911–20
John McCartney 1920–27
Jack Tinn 1927–47
Bob Jackson 1947–52
Eddie Lever 1952–58
Freddie Cox 1958–61
George Smith 1961–70
Ron Tindall 1970–73
 (General Manager to 1974)
John Mortimore 1973–74
Ian St John 1974–77
Jimmy Dickinson 1977–79
Frank Burrows 1979–82
Bobby Campbell 1982–84
Alan Ball 1984–89
John Gregory 1989–90
Frank Burrows 1990–91
Jim Smith 1991–95
Terry Fenwick 1995–98
Alan Ball 1998–99
Tony Pulis 2000
Steve Claridge 2000–01
Graham Rix 2001–02
Harry Redknapp 2002–04
Velimir Zajec 2004–05
Alain Perrin 2005
Harry Redknapp 2005–08
Tony Adams 2008–09
Paul Hart 2009
Avram Grant 2009–10
Steve Cotterill 2010–11
Michael Appleton 2011–12
Guy Whittingham 2012–13
Richie Barker 2013–14
Andy Awford 2014–15
Paul Cook May 2015–

TEN YEAR LEAGUE RECORD

		P	W	D	L	F	A	Pts	Pos
2006-07	PR Lge	38	14	12	12	45	42	54	9
2007-08	PR Lge	38	16	9	13	48	40	57	8
2008-09	PR Lge	38	10	11	17	38	57	41	14
2009-10	PR Lge	38	7	7	24	34	66	19*	20
2010-11	FL C	46	15	13	18	53	60	58	16
2011-12	FL C	46	13	11	22	50	59	40†	22
2012-13	FL 1	46	10	12	24	51	69	32‡	24
2013-14	FL 2	46	14	17	15	56	66	59	13
2014-15	FL 2	46	14	15	17	52	54	57	16
2015-16	FL 2	46	21	15	10	75	44	78	6

*9 pts deducted; †10 pts deducted; ‡10 pts deducted.

DID YOU KNOW ❓

Fratton Park hosted the first-ever Football League game played under floodlights. On a bitterly cold evening on Wednesday 22 February 1956, Pompey went down 2-0 at home to Newcastle United in front of an attendance of 15,831. This proved to be the club's second lowest home gate of the season.

PORTSMOUTH – FOOTBALL LEAGUE TWO 2015–16 LEAGUE RECORD

Match No.	Date	Venue	Opponents	Result		H/T Score	Lg Pos.	Goalscorers	Attendance
1	Aug 8	H	Dagenham & R	W	3-0	0-0	1	Evans [51], Bennett 2 [63, 74]	16,948
2	15	A	Plymouth Arg	W	2-1	1-0	2	Tubbs (pen) [45], Roberts (pen) [86]	11,476
3	18	A	Crawley T	D	0-0	0-0	5		4003
4	22	H	Morecambe	D	3-3	1-3	6	Roberts 2 [42, 65], Stockley [90]	16,052
5	29	A	Luton T	W	2-1	1-1	4	Evans [8], Tubbs [90]	9083
6	Sept 5	H	Accrington S	D	0-0	0-0	4		15,745
7	12	H	Barnet	W	3-1	1-1	2	Chaplin 2 [37, 90], McGurk [54]	16,217
8	19	A	Oxford U	D	1-1	0-1	2	McGurk [61]	9093
9	26	A	Bristol R	W	2-1	1-0	1	Evans [29], Stockley [71]	8555
10	29	H	Exeter C	L	1-2	0-1	3	Roberts [90]	15,822
11	Oct 3	H	Yeovil T	D	0-0	0-0	4		17,309
12	10	A	Cambridge U	W	3-1	0-1	1	Legge (og) [67], Tubbs 2 [69, 87]	6607
13	17	A	Newport Co	W	1-0	1-0	2	Tubbs [45]	3298
14	20	H	Stevenage	D	1-1	0-0	2	Chaplin [77]	14,900
15	24	H	Mansfield T	D	0-0	0-0	2		16,210
16	31	A	Notts Co	L	1-2	1-1	3	Lavery [19]	6917
17	Nov 15	H	AFC Wimbledon	D	0-0	0-0	4		15,892
18	21	A	Carlisle U	D	2-2	0-1	5	Lavery [66], McNulty [68]	5503
19	24	H	York C	W	6-0	0-0	4	Davies [50], McNulty 3 [52, 60, 71], Tollitt [80], Chaplin [84]	13,616
20	28	A	Wycombe W	D	2-2	1-2	5	Lavery [45], Webster [56]	5816
21	Dec 12	H	Hartlepool U	W	4-0	2-0	4	Lavery [32], Jackson (og) [37], Evans [61], McNulty [90]	15,610
22	19	H	Northampton T	W	2-1	1-1	4	Evans [33], Chaplin [85]	5859
23	26	A	Leyton Orient	L	2-3	1-2	4	Essam (og) [4], Evans [66]	5848
24	28	H	Luton T	D	0-0	0-0	4		17,668
25	Jan 2	A	Crawley T	W	3-0	2-0	4	Clarke [13], McNulty [26], Roberts [83]	16,606
26	23	H	Oxford U	L	0-1	0-0	5		17,840
27	Feb 2	A	Morecambe	D	1-1	1-0	5	Evans [40]	1399
28	6	H	Leyton Orient	L	0-1	0-0	7		15,643
29	13	A	Bristol R	W	3-1	2-0	5	Evans [19], Smith [45], McNulty [77]	17,808
30	20	A	Yeovil T	D	1-1	0-0	7	Roberts [84]	6051
31	23	A	Barnet	L	0-1	0-1	8		2557
32	27	A	Cambridge U	W	2-1	1-0	5	McNulty [41], Webster [62]	15,425
33	Mar 1	A	Exeter C	D	1-1	1-0	5	Chaplin [31]	3855
34	5	A	Stevenage	W	2-0	1-0	5	McNulty [22], Naismith [82]	4092
35	8	A	Accrington S	W	3-1	3-0	4	Bennett [22], Pearson (og) [36], Doyle [43]	1841
36	12	H	Newport Co	L	0-3	0-1	6		16,245
37	19	A	Mansfield T	D	1-1	1-1	6	Tafazolli (og) [43]	3980
38	25	H	Notts Co	W	4-0	1-0	6	Bennett 2 [44, 49], Burgess [81], McNulty [90]	16,670
39	Apr 2	H	Carlisle U	W	1-0	0-0	6	Smith [57]	15,416
40	9	A	Dagenham & R	W	4-1	0-1	6	Doyle [59], Burgess [68], Evans [85], Bennett [88]	3122
41	16	H	Plymouth Arg	L	1-2	1-0	6	Smith [37]	18,423
42	19	A	York C	L	1-3	0-2	6	Evans [55]	3214
43	23	H	Wycombe W	W	2-1	1-0	6	Roberts [37], Chaplin [67]	16,187
44	26	A	AFC Wimbledon	W	1-0	1-0	6	Smith [35]	4799
45	30	A	Hartlepool U	W	2-0	0-0	5	Naismith [57], Chaplin [84]	5046
46	May 7	H	Northampton T	L	1-2	0-1	6	Naismith [48]	18,746

Final League Position: 6

GOALSCORERS

League (75): Evans 10, McNulty 10, Chaplin 8, Roberts 7 (1 pen), Bennett 6, Tubbs 5 (1 pen), Lavery 4, Smith 4, Naismith 3, Burgess 2, Doyle 2, McGurk 2, Stockley 2, Webster 2, Clarke 1, Davies 1, Tollitt 1, own goals 5.
FA Cup (8): McGurk 3, Roberts 2 (1 pen), Bennett 1, Chaplin 1, McNulty 1.
Capital One Cup (3): Chaplin 2, McGurk 1.
Johnstone's Paint Trophy (0).
League Two Play-Offs (2): McNulty 1, Roberts 1 (pen).

Murphy B 20 + 1	Davies B 43	Burgess C 37	Clarke M 26 + 3	Stevens E 45	Doyle M 43 + 1	Atangana N 8 + 5	Evans G 32 + 8	Roberts G 27 + 6	Bennett K 40 + 2	Tubbs M 8 + 8	Hollands D 27 + 5	Stockley J 4 + 5	Chaplin C 6 + 24	McGurk A 12 + 15	Webster A 24 + 3	Jones P 8 + 1	Barton A 11 + 5	McCarey A 6	Naismith K 10 + 9	Boco R 2 + 2	Lavery C 11 + 2	Tollitt B —+ 12	McNulty M 19 + 8	Fulton R 12	Close B 6 + 1	Smith M 13 + 3	Freeman K 4 + 3	Whatmough J 1 + 1	Haunstrup B 1	May A —+ 1	Wilkinson C —+ 1	Match No.
1	2	3	4	5	6	7^1	8	9	10^2	11^3	12	13	14																			1
1	2	3	4	5	6	7^1	8	9^3	10	11^2	13	12		14																		2
1	2^1	3	4	5	8	7	6	9	10^3	11^2			13	14	12																	3
1	2^2	3	4	5^1	7	6	8^1	9	10	11^3			12		13	14																4
1	2	3	4	5	6	7	8	9^3	10^2	12			11^1	13	14																	5
1^1	2	3	4	5	6	7	8	10	9^3	13			11^3	14		12																6
1	2	3	4^2	5	8	7	13	6^3	9	14			10	11^1	12																	7
	2	3	4	5	7^1	6^1	8		10^2	12	14		9^3	11		1	13															8
	2	3	4	5		6	12	10^2	14	7	11^3	8^1		9		1	13															9
	2	3	4	5	14		8^1	13	10	12	7^2	11	9^3		6	1																10
	2	4	3	5	7		6^3	10	9	11^1	13	12	14		8^2	1																11
	2	3	4^1	5	6	14	8^1	10	9^1	11			12	7^3	1	13																12
	2	3		5	7		8	9	11^1	13			4	10^2	1	6^3	12	14														13
	2	4		5	6	14		9	10	11^2			13	3	7^1	1		8^2	12													14
1	2	3		5	7	12			10	14	6		13		4			9^3	8^1	11^2												15
1	2	3		5	6		8		10^1	14	7		12	9^1	4				11^2	13												16
1	2	3	12	5	8	14	6^1		13		7		9^2	4					10^3		11											17
1	2	4		5	6	14	8^2		10		7		9^1	3					11	13	12^3											18
1	2^2	4		5	7		6		9^3		8		13	3					12	11	14	10^1										19
1	2	3		5	6		13		10^2		7^1		8^3	4		12			11	14	9											20
1	5	4^3	14	2	7		8		10^1		6		13	3					9^3	12	11											21
1	2		4	5	7		8		10^3		6		14	13	3				11^1	12	9^2											22
1	2		3	5	7		8	13	10^3		6^1		14	4^4					11		9^2												23
1	2		4	5	7		8	12	10^1		6		14	13					3		11^2	9^3											24
1	2		4	5	6		8^3	13	10		7		14		3				11^2	12	9^1											25
	2		3	5	6		8	9^3	10				14	13	4		7^2				11^1	1	12									26
	2			5	7		8	13	12				14	3					10^3		9^2	1	6	11^3								27
		3	4	5	7		12	6	9^3				14	13							11^1	1	8	10^2	2							28
	2	3		5	6		9	8^1	10^3				14	13	4				12		1	7	11^2									29
	2	3^1		5	6		9^3	8	10^2				14	4					12	13	1	7	11^1									30
	2		4	5	8			11^1	7				14	6	3				12		10^3	1	9^2	13								31
	2	3	13	5	7		12		6^3		8		10^2	4					9^1		14	11	1									32
	2	3		5	8		12		9^2		7		10^1	4	13				6		11	1										33
	2	3		5	6		8	9^1	10^2		7			4					12		11^3	1			13	14						34
	2	3		5	7		8	9^3	10^3		6			4					13		12	1			11^2	14						35
	2	4		5	7		8^2	9^4	10^3		6		14	3					13		11^1	1			12							36
	2	3		5	6				10^3		7		14	13	4				8^2		12^2	11^1	1		9							37
	2	3	4	5	7			9^1	10		6		13	8^3		1			12			14			11^2							38
	2	5	7	3	8		14	11^3	9^2		4			6^1		1			12			13			10							39
	2	3	4	5	6		12	10^1	8^2		7			9^3		1			12			14			11							40
	2^2	3	4	5	6		12	9^3	10		7		14	8^1		1						13			11							41
	2		4	5	6		8		10^3		7		14		3^2	1	12					13	9^1		11							42
	2^1	3	4	5	8		6	10			7		13	14		1			9^3			11^2				12						43
12		4		2	6		10^3	9			7					11	3	8					11^3	5								44
1		3^3		2	6		10	9			7		13	12			4	8^2							11^1	5	14					45
1	2				8		9				11				4		10		14			6^1			7^4	3^3	5^2	12	13			46

FA Cup

First Round	Macclesfield T	(h)	2-1
Second Round	Accrington S	(h)	1-0
Third Round	Ipswich T	(a)	2-2
Replay	Ipswich T	(h)	2-1
Fourth Round	Bournemouth	(h)	1-2

Capital One Cup

First Round	Derby Co	(h)	2-1
Second Round	Reading	(h)	1-2

Johnstone's Paint Trophy

First Round	Exeter C	(a)	0-2

League Two Play-Offs

Semi-Final 1st leg	Plymouth Arg	(h)	2-2
Semi-Final 2nd leg	Plymouth Arg	(a)	0-1

(Plymouth Arg won 3-2 on aggregate)

PRESTON NORTH END

FOUNDATION

North End Cricket and Rugby Club, which was formed in 1863, indulged in most sports before taking up soccer in about 1879. In 1881 they decided to stick to football to the exclusion of other sports and even a 16–0 drubbing by Blackburn Rovers in an invitation game at Deepdale, a few weeks after taking this decision, did not deter them for they immediately became affiliated to the Lancashire FA.

Deepdale Stadium, Sir Tom Finney Way, Deepdale, Preston, Lancashire PR1 6RU.

Telephone: (0344) 856 1964.

Fax: (01772) 693 366.

Ticket Office: (0344) 856 1966.

Website: www.pne.co.uk

Email: enquiries@pne.co.uk

Ground Capacity: 23,404.

Record Attendance: 42,684 v Arsenal, Division 1, 23 April 1938.

Pitch Measurements: 100m × 67m (109.5yd × 73.5yd).

Chief Executive: John Kay.

Manager: Simon Grayson.

Assistant Manager: Glynn Snodin.

Head Physio: Matthew Jackson.

Colours: White shirts, blue shorts, white socks with blue hoops.

Year Formed: 1880.

Turned Professional: 1885.

Club Nicknames: 'The Lilywhites', 'North End'.

Ground: 1881, Deepdale.

HONOURS

League Champions: Football League 1888–89, 1889–90; Division 2 – 1903–04, 1912–13, 1950–51; Second Division – 1999–2000; Division 3 – 1970–71; Third Division – 1995–96.
Runners-up: Football League 1890–91, 1891–92; Division 1 – 1892–93, 1905–06, 1952–53, 1957–58; Division 2 – 1914–15, 1933–34; Division 4 – 1986–87.
FA Cup Winners: 1889, 1938.
Runners-up: 1888, 1922, 1937, 1954, 1964.
League Cup: 4th rd – 1963, 1966, 1972, 1981, 2003.
Double Performed: 1888–89.

First Football League Game: 8 September 1888, Football League, v Burnley (h) W 5–2 – Trainer; Howarth, Holmes; Robertson, William Graham, Johnny Graham; Gordon (1), Jimmy Ross (2), Goodall, Dewhurst (2), Drummond.

Record League Victory: 10–0 v Stoke, Division 1, 14 September 1889 – Trainer; Howarth, Holmes; Kelso, Russell (1), Johnny Graham; Gordon, Jimmy Ross (2), Nick Ross (3), Thomson (2), Drummond (2).

Record Cup Victory: 26–0 v Hyde, FA Cup 1st rd, 15 October 1887 – Addision; Howarth, Nick Ross; Russell (1), Thomson (5), Johnny Graham (1); Gordon (5), Jimmy Ross (8), John Goodall (1), Dewhurst (3), Drummond (2).

Record Defeat: 0–7 v Nottingham F, Division 2, 9 April 1927; 0–7 v Blackpool, Division 1, 1 May 1948.

Most League Points (2 for a win): 61, Division 3, 1970–71.

Most League Points (3 for a win): 95, Division 2, 1999–2000.

Most League Goals: 100, Division 2, 1927–28 and Division 1, 1957–58.

sky SPORTS FACT FILE

Preston North End have shown remarkable stability throughout their history. They have remained at their Deepdale ground since 1875 (when they had yet to play association football), they have had unbroken membership of the Football League since 1888 and, apart from occasional minor deviations, have played in a white and navy blue strip for over 125 years.

Highest League Scorer in Season: Ted Harper, 37, Division 2, 1932–33.

Most League Goals in Total Aggregate: Tom Finney, 187, 1946–60.

Most League Goals in One Match: 4, Jimmy Ross v Stoke, Division 1, 6 October 1888; 4, Nick Ross v Derby Co, Division 1, 11 January 1890; 4, George Drummond v Notts Co, Division 1, 12 December 1891; 4, Frank Becton v Notts Co, Division 1, 31 March 1893; 4, George Harrison v Grimsby T, Division 2, 3 November 1928; 4, Alex Reid v Port Vale, Division 2, 23 February 1929; 4, James McClelland v Reading, Division 2, 6 September 1930; 4, Dick Rowley v Notts Co, Division 2, 16 April 1932; 4, Ted Harper v Burnley, Division 2, 29 August 1932; 4, Ted Harper v Lincoln C, Division 2, 11 March 1933; 4, Charlie Wayman v QPR, Division 2, 25 December 1950; 4, Alex Bruce v Colchester U, Division 3, 28 February 1978; 4, Joe Garner v Crewe Alex, FL 1, 14 March 2015.

Most Capped Player: Tom Finney, 76, England.

Most League Appearances: Alan Kelly, 447, 1961–75.

Youngest League Player: Steve Doyle, 16 years 166 days v Tranmere R, 15 November 1974.

Record Transfer Fee Received: £6,000,000 from Portsmouth for David Nugent, August 2007.

Record Transfer Fee Paid: £1,500,000 to Manchester U for David Healy, December 2000.

Football League Record: 1888 Founder Member of League; 1901–04 Division 2; 1904–12 Division 1; 1912–13 Division 2; 1913–14 Division 1; 1914–15 Division 2; 1919–25 Division 1; 1925–34 Division 2; 1934–49 Division 1; 1949–51 Division 2; 1951–61 Division 1; 1961–70 Division 2; 1970–71 Division 3; 1971–74 Division 2; 1974–78 Division 3; 1978–81 Division 3; 1981–85 Division 3; 1985–87 Division 4; 1987–92 Division 3; 1992–93 Division 2; 1993–96 Division 3; 1996–2000 Division 2; 2000–04 Division 1; 2004–11 FL C; 2011–15 FL 1; 2015– FL C.

LATEST SEQUENCES

Longest Sequence of League Wins: 14, 25.12.1950 – 27.3.1951.

Longest Sequence of League Defeats: 8, 22.9.1984 – 27.10.1984.

Longest Sequence of League Draws: 6, 24.2.1979 – 20.3.1979.

Longest Sequence of Unbeaten League Matches: 23, 8.9.1888 – 14.9.1889.

Longest Sequence Without a League Win: 15, 14.4.1923 – 20.10.1923.

Successive Scoring Runs: 30 from 15.11.1952.

Successive Non-scoring Runs: 6 from 19.11.1960.

MANAGERS

Charlie Parker 1906–15
Vincent Hayes 1919–23
Jim Lawrence 1923–25
Frank Richards 1925–27
Alex Gibson 1927–31
Lincoln Hayes 1931–32
Run by committee 1932–36
Tommy Muirhead 1936–37
Run by committee 1937–49
Will Scott 1949–53
Scot Symon 1953–54
Frank Hill 1954–56
Cliff Britton 1956–61
Jimmy Milne 1961–68
Bobby Seith 1968–70
Alan Ball Snr 1970–73
Bobby Charlton 1973–75
Harry Catterick 1975–77
Nobby Stiles 1977–81
Tommy Docherty 1981
Gordon Lee 1981–83
Alan Kelly 1983–85
Tommy Booth 1985–86
Brian Kidd 1986
John McGrath 1986–90
Les Chapman 1990–92
Sam Allardyce 1992 (*Caretaker*)
John Beck 1992–94
Gary Peters 1994–98
David Moyes 1998–2002
Kelham O'Hanlon 2002 (*Caretaker*)
Craig Brown 2002–04
Billy Davies 2004–06
Paul Simpson 2006–07
Alan Irvine 2007–09
Darren Ferguson 2010
Phil Brown 2011
Graham Westley 2012–13
Simon Grayson February 2013–

TEN YEAR LEAGUE RECORD

		P	W	D	L	F	A	Pts	Pos
2006-07	FL C	46	22	8	16	64	53	74	7
2007-08	FL C	46	15	11	20	50	56	56	15
2008-09	FL C	46	21	11	14	66	54	74	6
2009-10	FL C	46	13	15	18	58	73	54	17
2010-11	FL C	46	10	12	24	54	79	42	22
2011-12	FL 1	46	13	15	18	54	68	54	15
2012-13	FL 1	46	14	17	15	54	49	59	14
2013-14	FL 1	46	23	16	7	72	46	85	5
2014-15	FL 1	46	25	14	7	79	40	89	3
2015-16	FL C	46	15	17	14	45	45	62	11

DID YOU KNOW

Preston North End have appeared in the play-offs at all three levels. The club created a new record in 2014–15 by reaching the play-offs on ten occasions. Their 4-0 victory over Swindon Town in the Wembley final earned them promotion after nine unsuccessful attempts.

PRESTON NORTH END – FL CHAMPIONSHIP 2015–16 LEAGUE RECORD

Match No.	Date	Venue	Opponents	Result	H/T Score	Lg Pos.	Goalscorers	Attendance
1	Aug 9	H	Middlesbrough	D	0-0	0-0	14		15,974
2	15	A	Milton Keynes D	W	1-0	1-0	7	Gallagher [28]	11,035
3	18	A	Rotherham U	D	0-0	0-0	6		9078
4	22	H	Ipswich T	L	1-2	1-1	12	Johnson [37]	12,330
5	29	A	Hull C	L	0-2	0-1	17		16,949
6	Sept 12	H	Derby Co	L	1-2	0-2	20	Johnson [90]	14,552
7	15	H	Bristol C	D	1-1	0-0	19	Kilkenny [50]	9963
8	19	A	Brentford	L	1-2	1-0	22	Johnson [1]	9463
9	26	H	Wolverhampton W	D	1-1	1-0	22	Johnson [10]	13,049
10	Oct 3	A	Sheffield W	L	1-3	0-1	23	Browne [76]	20,383
11	17	H	Cardiff C	D	0-0	0-0	22		11,125
12	20	A	Charlton Ath	W	3-0	2-0	17	Gallagher 2 [2, 36], Johnson [62]	13,586
13	24	A	Brighton & HA	D	0-0	0-0	19		24,629
14	31	H	Bolton W	D	0-0	0-0	18		14,494
15	Nov 3	H	Nottingham F	W	1-0	1-0	16	Doyle [2]	10,216
16	7	A	QPR	D	0-0	0-0	17		15,190
17	21	H	Blackburn R	L	1-2	0-1	17	Garner [67]	19,852
18	28	A	Fulham	D	1-1	1-0	18	Garner [11]	17,362
19	Dec 5	A	Burnley	W	2-0	0-0	18	Keane [63], Johnson [86]	18,614
20	12	H	Reading	W	1-0	0-0	16	Garner (pen) [52]	10,649
21	15	H	Birmingham C	D	1-1	1-0	16	Reach [19]	10,668
22	20	A	Leeds U	L	0-1	0-0	16		22,641
23	26	A	Huddersfield T	L	1-3	0-1	17	Reach [90]	14,697
24	28	H	Hull C	W	1-0	0-0	17	Gallagher [66]	13,891
25	Jan 2	H	Rotherham U	W	2-1	0-1	15	Doyle [64], Clarke-Harris (og) [90]	12,027
26	12	A	Bristol C	W	2-1	0-0	13	Baker (og) [53], Cunningham [80]	14,586
27	16	A	Ipswich T	D	1-1	1-1	13	Johnson [7]	21,108
28	23	H	Brentford	L	1-3	1-2	15	Reach [24]	11,080
29	Feb 2	A	Derby Co	D	0-0	0-0	14		27,252
30	6	H	Huddersfield T	W	2-1	0-0	14	Lynch (og) [83], Browne [90]	12,653
31	13	A	Wolverhampton W	W	2-1	1-0	11	Gallagher [17], Reach [53]	21,204
32	20	H	Sheffield W	W	1-0	0-0	12	Garner [73]	16,923
33	23	H	Charlton Ath	W	2-1	1-1	9	Garner [35], Robinson [52]	10,075
34	27	A	Cardiff C	L	1-2	0-1	10	Robinson [87]	15,566
35	Mar 5	H	Brighton & HA	D	0-0	0-0	10		11,881
36	8	A	Nottingham F	L	0-1	0-1	10		16,747
37	12	A	Bolton W	W	2-1	0-1	10	Hugill [57], Doyle [86]	18,423
38	19	H	QPR	D	1-1	0-1	10	Doyle [90]	11,322
39	Apr 2	A	Blackburn R	W	2-1	2-1	10	Garner (pen) [25], Hugill [43]	21,029
40	5	H	Fulham	L	1-2	0-1	10	Vermijl [63]	10,358
41	9	A	Middlesbrough	L	0-1	0-1	10		26,390
42	16	H	Milton Keynes D	D	1-1	1-0	10	Beckford [6]	10,457
43	19	A	Birmingham C	D	2-2	0-1	10	Browne [73], Cunningham [89]	14,366
44	22	H	Burnley	L	0-1	0-1	10		17,789
45	30	A	Reading	W	2-1	0-0	11	Beckford [56], Johnson [90]	15,834
46	May 7	H	Leeds U	D	1-1	0-0	11	Hugill [90]	18,473

Final League Position: 11

GOALSCORERS

League (45): Johnson 8, Garner 6 (2 pens), Gallagher 5, Doyle 4, Reach 4, Browne 3, Hugill 3, Beckford 2, Cunningham 2, Robinson 2, Keane 1, Kilkenny 1, Vermijl 1, own goals 3.
FA Cup (0).
Capital One Cup (6): Hugill 2 (1 pen), Brownhill 1, Johnson 1 (pen), Keane 1, Vermijl 1.

Pickford J 24	Vermiji M 20+8	Clarke T 34+1	Huntington P 30+8	Wright B 38	Cunningham G 43	Johnson D 40+3	Welsh J 13+11	Gallagher P 41	Garner J 39+2	Keane W 12+8	Humphrey C 5+5	Hugill J 8+21	Browne A 27+9	Woods C 28+4	Kilkenny N 6+7	Beckford J 4+6	Reid K —+1	May S 4+3	Doyle E 15+13	Brownhill J —+3	Reach A 35	McCarthy P 1	Hudson M —+1	Johnstone S 4	Pearson B 13+2	Robinson C 4+10	Lindegaard A 14	Kirkland C 4+1	Match No.
1	2²	3	4	5	6	7	8	9	10	11³	12	13																	1
1		3	4	2	5	9	8	7³	11	10²	6¹	13¹	12	14															2
1	12	2	4	3	9	8	7¹	6	10	11³	5²	14		13															3
1		2	3	4	8²	9	7	10³	11		5			12	6¹	13	14												4
1	14	2	3	4		9	6¹	10	11	13	5³		12	8²	7														5
1	5²	2	4	3		9	8	7³	11	10¹	14				6				12	13									6
1		3	5	4	6	9	8	11	14	2³		13			7¹				10²	12	6								7
1	2	3	4	5	8		10	13	12					6²	7¹				11³	9	14								8
1		3	4⁴	5	6²	7		11⁴	10¹		13	12	8	2					9										9
1		3		5	6	8		10²	12	13	7	2		11¹	14				9	4²									10
1	14	3¹		4	5	9	8²	7	12	11		13	2						10³		6								11
1	2¹	12	4	5	9	8³	14	10	7	3			13						11²		6								12
1	2¹	13	4	5	9	8	12	11	7	3									10²		6								13
1	2²	13	4	5	9	8	10	12	7¹	3	14								11³		6								14
1	2¹	13	4	5	9	12	8	10	7³	3	14								11²		6								15
1	2		5	4	9¹	8	11³	12	13	7	3	14							10²		6								16
1	12		4	3¹	5	9³	8	11	14	7	2²							13	10¹		6								17
1	2	3	4	5	6	12	7³	10	13	8								14	11¹		9²								18
1	2	3	4	5	6¹	13	8	11	10²	12	7								9										19
1	2	3	4	5	6	12	8¹	10	11	7									9										20
1	2	3	4	5	7	13	6²	10	11¹	12	8²	14							9										21
1¹	2	3	4	5	7¹	6	11	10²	8³	13		14		9					12										22
1	2¹	3	4	5	8	6	11¹²	10	13	7³	14	12		9															23
1	2¹	4	3	5	8	7	6³	11¹²	10	14	13	12		9															24
	2	3	12	4¹	5	7	8³	6	11	14		13		10²					9			1							25
	14	3	4	5	6	7		8	10	13		2²		11³							9¹			1		12			26
		4	3	5	6	9		11¹	12	7		2		10²							9			1		8	13		27
	14	4	3	5	6	11		12	2¹	10³		9									7²			1		13			28
		3	4	5	6	9		7²	11	13	12								13		10¹				8		1		29
		3		4	5	13	12	8	11	10²		7							14		9³				6¹		1		30
		3	4	5	6	9	12	8¹	10²	7		2							13		11						1		31
		2	3	4	9	7		8²	11¹	13		6	5						10						12		1		32
		3	4	5¹	6	7	13	9²	10¹	14		8		2					11						12		1		33
		3	4³	5	6	9²		8¹	11	13		7	2						10						14	12	1		34
		3	4	5	6¹	9²		8	10³	14		7	2					13	11						12		1		35
		3	4	5²	6	7		9¹	11³	12		2						14	10						8	13	1		36
	12	3		4	5	9¹	14	8³				10²		2				13	6						7	11	1		37
		3	4	5	8	13	6		10			2	14					12	9¹						7²	11³	1		38
		3	13	4	5	12		6	10¹	11		8	2					14	9³						7²		1		39
	13	3¹	12	4	5	7		11	10³	9		2¹	14						8						6	1	1		40
	2	4	3	5	8	12	7	11	13			10						13	6¹						9²	1			41
	2	4	3	5	8	9	12		13			10²		11					7¹						6³	14	1		42
	2¹	3	12	4	5	7		10	8	14		11²							9						6		13³	13	43
		3	4	5	12	7		10¹	13	8³	2		11						9						6²	14		1	44
	12	4	3	5³	7	8		10²	14	9		2	11¹					13	6									1	45
	2	4	5		9	8	11¹	14	7³	3		10²	12						6						13			1	46

FA Cup

Third Round — Peterborough U — (a) — 0-2

Capital One Cup

First Round — Crewe Alex — (a) — 3-1
Second Round — Watford — (h) — 1-0
Third Round — Bournemouth — (h) — 2-2
(aet; Bournemouth won 3-2 on penalties)

QUEENS PARK RANGERS

FOUNDATION

There is an element of doubt about the date of the foundation of this club, but it is believed that in either 1885 or 1886 it was formed through the amalgamation of Christchurch Rangers and St Jude's Institute FC. The leading light was George Wodehouse, whose family maintained a connection with the club until comparatively recent times. Most of the players came from the Queen's Park district so this name was adopted after a year as St Jude's Institute.

Loftus Road Stadium, South Africa Road, Shepherds Bush, London W12 7PJ.

Telephone: (020) 8743 0262.

Fax: (020) 8749 0994.

Ticket Office: (08444) 777 007.

Website: www.qpr.co.uk

Email: customerservices@qpr.co.uk

Ground Capacity: 18,150.

Record Attendance: 41,097 v Leeds U, FA Cup 3rd rd, 9 January 1932 (at White City); 35,353 v Leeds U, Division 1, 27 April 1974 (at Loftus Road).

Pitch Measurements: 100.5m × 66m (110yd × 72yd).

Co-Chairmen: Tony Fernandes and Ruben Gnanalingham.

Chief Executive: Lee Hoos.

Manager: Jimmy Floyd Hasselbaink.

Assistant Manager: David Oldfield.

Physio: Nigel Cox.

Colours: Blue and white hooped shirts, white shorts, white socks.

Year Formed: 1885* (*see Foundation*).

Turned Professional: 1898.

Previous Name: 1885, St Jude's; 1887, Queens Park Rangers. *Club Nicknames:* 'Rangers', 'The Hoops', 'R's'.

Grounds: 1885* (*see Foundation*), Welford's Fields; 1888–99, London Scottish Ground, Brondesbury, Home Farm, Kensal Rise Green, Gun Club Wormwood Scrubs, Kilburn Cricket Ground; 1899, Kensal Rise Athletic Ground; 1901, Latimer Road, Notting Hill; 1904, Agricultural Society, Park Royal; 1907, Park Royal Ground; 1917, Loftus Road; 1931, White City; 1933, Loftus Road; 1962, White City; 1963, Loftus Road.

First Football League Game: 28 August 1920, Division 3, v Watford (h) L 1–2 – Price; Blackman; Wingrove; McGovern, Grant, O'Brien; Faulkner, Birch (1), Smith, Gregory, Middlemiss.

Record League Victory: 9–2 v Tranmere R, Division 3, 3 December 1960 – Drinkwater; Woods, Ingham; Keen, Rutter, Angell; Lazarus (2), Bedford (2), Evans (2), Andrews (1), Clark (2).

Record Cup Victory: 8–1 v Bristol R (a), FA Cup 1st rd, 27 November 1937 – Gilfillan; Smith, Jefferson; Lowe, James, March; Cape, Mallett, Cheetham (3), Fitzgerald (3) Bott (2). 8–1 v Crewe Alex, Milk Cup 1st rd, 3 October 1983 – Hucker; Neill, Dawes, Waddock (1), McDonald (1), Fenwick, Micklewhite (1), Stewart (1), Allen (1), Stainrod (3), Gregory.

HONOURS

League Champions: FL C – 2010–11; Division 2 – 1982–83; Division 3 – 1966–67; Division 3S – 1947–48.
Runners-up: Division 1 – 1975–76; Division 2 – 1967–68, 1972–73; Second Division – 2003–04; Division 3S – 1946–47.

FA Cup: Runners-up: 1982.

League Cup Winners: 1967.
Runners-up: 1986.

European Competitions
UEFA Cup: 1976–77 (*qf*), 1984–85.

sky SPORTS FACT FILE

Queens Park Rangers goalkeeper Reg Allen joined the Forces soon after war broke out in 1939 and was allocated to the Commandos. In August 1941 he was captured while taking part in a daring raid on Benghazi and he remained a prisoner of war until May 1945. He later helped Rangers win the Division Three South title in 1947–48.

Record Defeat: 1–8 v Mansfield T, Division 3, 15 March 1965. 1–8 v Manchester U, Division 1, 19 March 1969.

Most League Points (2 for a win): 67, Division 3, 1966–67.

Most League Points (3 for a win): 88, FL C, 2010–11.

Most League Goals: 111, Division 3, 1961–62.

Highest League Scorer in Season: George Goddard, 37, Division 3 (S), 1929–30.

Most League Goals in Total Aggregate: George Goddard, 174, 1926–34.

Most League Goals in One Match: 4, George Goddard v Merthyr T, Division 3 (S), 9 March 1929; 4, George Goddard v Swindon T, Division 3 (S), 12 April 1930; 4, George Goddard v Exeter C, Division 3 (S), 20 December 1930; 4, George Goddard v Watford, Division 3 (S), 19 September 1931; 4, Tom Cheetham v Aldershot, Division 3 (S), 14 September 1935; 4, Tom Cheetham v Aldershot, Division 3 (S), 12 November 1938.

Most Capped Player: Alan McDonald, 52, Northern Ireland.

Most League Appearances: Tony Ingham, 514, 1950–63.

Youngest League Player: Frank Sibley, 16 years 97 days v Bristol C, 10 March 1964.

Record Transfer Fee Received: £12,000,000 from Anzhi Makhachkala for Chris Samba, July 2013.

Record Transfer Fee Paid: £12,500,000 to Anzhi Makhachkala for Chris Samba, January 2013.

Football League Record: 1920 Original Members of Division 3; 1921–48 Division 3 (S); 1948–52 Division 2; 1952–58 Division 3 (S); 1958–67 Division 3; 1967–68 Division 2; 1968–69 Division 1; 1969–73 Division 2; 1973–79 Division 1; 1979–83 Division 2; 1983–92 Division 1; 1992–96 FA Premier League; 1996–2001 Division 1; 2001–04 Division 2; 2004–11 FL C; 2011–13 FA Premier League; 2013–14 FL C; 2014–15 FA Premier League; 2015– FL C.

LATEST SEQUENCES

Longest Sequence of League Wins: 8, 7.11.1931 – 28.12.1931.

Longest Sequence of League Defeats: 9, 25.2.1969 – 5.4.1969.

Longest Sequence of League Draws: 6, 29.1.2000 – 5.3.2000.

Longest Sequence of Unbeaten League Matches: 20, 11.3.1972 – 23.9.1972.

Longest Sequence Without a League Win: 20, 7.12.1968 – 7.4.1969.

Successive Scoring Runs: 33 from 9.12.1961.

Successive Non-scoring Runs: 6 from 18.3.1939.

MANAGERS

James Cowan 1906–13
Jimmy Howie 1913–20
Ned Liddell 1920–24
Will Wood 1924–25
  (had been Secretary since 1903)
Bob Hewison 1925–31
John Bowman 1931
Archie Mitchell 1931–33
Mick O'Brien 1933–35
Billy Birrell 1935–39
Ted Vizard 1939–44
Dave Mangnall 1944–52
Jack Taylor 1952–59
Alec Stock 1959–65
  (General Manager to 1968)
Bill Dodgin Jnr 1968
Tommy Docherty 1968
Les Allen 1968–71
Gordon Jago 1971–74
Dave Sexton 1974–77
Frank Sibley 1977–78
Steve Burtenshaw 1978–79
Tommy Docherty 1979–80
Terry Venables 1980–84
Gordon Jago 1984
Alan Mullery 1984
Frank Sibley 1984–85
Jim Smith 1985–88
Trevor Francis 1988–89
Don Howe 1989–91
Gerry Francis 1991–94
Ray Wilkins 1994–96
Stewart Houston 1996–97
Ray Harford 1997–98
Gerry Francis 1998–2001
Ian Holloway 2001–06
Gary Waddock 2006
John Gregory 2006–07
Luigi Di Canio 2007–08
Iain Dowie 2008
Paulo Sousa 2008–09
Jim Magilton 2009
Paul Hart 2009–10
Neil Warnock 2010–12
Mark Hughes 2012
Harry Redknapp 2012–15
Chris Ramsey 2015
Jimmy Floyd Hasselbaink
  December 2015–

TEN YEAR LEAGUE RECORD

		P	W	D	L	F	A	Pts	Pos
2006-07	FL C	46	14	11	21	54	68	53	18
2007-08	FL C	46	14	16	16	60	66	58	14
2008-09	FL C	46	15	16	15	42	44	61	11
2009-10	FL C	46	14	15	17	58	65	57	13
2010-11	FL C	46	24	16	6	71	32	88	1
2011-12	PR Lge	38	10	7	21	43	66	37	17
2012-13	PR Lge	38	4	13	21	30	60	25	20
2013-14	FL C	46	23	11	12	60	44	80	4
2014-15	PR Lge	38	8	6	24	42	73	30	20
2015-16	FL C	46	14	18	14	54	54	60	12

DID YOU KNOW ?

Loftus Road became the first English football ground to adopt an artificial surface in 1981 when an Omniturf system was installed. As this was not permitted by UEFA, Queens Park Rangers' UEFA Cup ties in 1984–85 were played at Highbury. Grass was reinstalled at the ground in 1988.

QUEENS PARK RANGERS – FL CHAMPIONSHIP 2015–16 LEAGUE RECORD

Match No.	Date	Venue	Opponents	Result	H/T Score	Lg Pos.	Goalscorers	Attendance
1	Aug 8	A	Charlton Ath	L	0-2	0-0	21		19,469
2	15	H	Cardiff C	D	2-2	1-0	19	Hill [33], Austin [56]	14,927
3	19	A	Wolverhampton W	W	3-2	1-2	13	Austin [38], Phillips 2 [52, 72]	21,032
4	22	H	Rotherham U	W	4-2	1-0	6	Chery 2 [42, 50], Austin 2 (1 pen) [63, 90 (p)]	15,009
5	29	A	Huddersfield T	W	1-0	0-0	4	Chery [84]	11,189
6	Sept12	H	Nottingham F	L	1-2	0-0	7	Austin [65]	15,424
7	16	H	Blackburn R	D	2-2	0-1	8	Austin [46], Onuoha [79]	14,007
8	19	A	Hull C	D	1-1	1-1	9	Austin [26]	16,651
9	25	A	Fulham	L	0-4	0-3	10		19,784
10	Oct 3	H	Bolton W	W	4-3	2-2	11	Emmanuel-Thomas 2 [13, 90], Fer [44], Chery [62]	16,026
11	17	A	Birmingham C	L	1-2	1-1	12	Phillips [17]	19,161
12	20	H	Sheffield W	D	0-0	0-0	10		15,471
13	24	H	Milton Keynes D	W	3-0	0-0	10	Emmanuel-Thomas [70], Phillips [78], Hoilett [88]	15,567
14	30	A	Brentford	L	0-1	0-0	11		12,037
15	Nov 3	A	Derby Co	L	0-1	0-0	13		28,502
16	7	H	Preston NE	D	0-0	0-0	13		15,190
17	20	A	Middlesbrough	L	0-1	0-0	13		20,299
18	28	H	Leeds U	W	1-0	0-0	12	Austin [58]	18,031
19	Dec 3	A	Reading	W	1-0	0-0	11	Onuoha [90]	16,365
20	12	A	Burnley	D	0-0	0-0	13		16,576
21	15	H	Brighton & HA	D	2-2	0-0	12	Austin 2 [65, 88]	15,268
22	19	A	Bristol C	D	1-1	0-0	11	Hoilett [56]	15,754
23	26	A	Ipswich T	L	1-2	1-0	12	Hoilett [45]	23,615
24	28	H	Huddersfield T	D	1-1	0-0	13	Polter [80]	16,662
25	Jan 1	H	Hull C	L	1-2	0-0	15	Polter [86]	16,205
26	12	A	Blackburn R	D	1-1	1-0	17	Fer [24]	12,285
27	16	A	Rotherham U	W	3-0	0-0	15	Hoilett [52], Phillips [54], Polter [90]	9594
28	23	H	Wolverhampton W	D	1-1	1-0	14	Polter [2]	15,266
29	26	A	Nottingham F	D	0-0	0-0	13		17,030
30	Feb 6	H	Ipswich T	W	1-0	0-0	13	Phillips [88]	17,044
31	13	H	Fulham	L	1-3	0-3	14	Chery [90]	17,335
32	20	A	Bolton W	D	1-1	0-0	12	Phillips [90]	14,085
33	23	A	Sheffield W	D	1-1	0-0	13	Tozser [57]	19,233
34	27	H	Birmingham C	W	2-0	2-0	11	Chery [35], Hoilett (pen) [39]	17,110
35	Mar 5	A	Milton Keynes D	L	0-2	0-0	12		14,796
36	8	H	Derby Co	W	2-0	1-0	11	Chery [24], Angella [86]	14,049
37	12	H	Brentford	W	3-0	1-0	11	Hoilett [38], Polter [66], Chery [71]	17,894
38	19	A	Preston NE	D	1-1	1-0	11	Polter [5]	11,322
39	Apr 1	H	Middlesbrough	L	2-3	1-1	11	Mackie [31], Chery [86]	16,058
40	5	A	Leeds U	D	1-1	0-0	11	Chery (pen) [87]	17,388
41	9	A	Charlton Ath	W	2-1	1-0	11	Phillips [45], El Khayati [90]	15,834
42	16	A	Cardiff C	D	0-0	0-0	11		27,874
43	19	A	Brighton & HA	L	0-4	0-1	12		25,411
44	23	H	Reading	D	1-1	1-1	13	Hall [35]	16,225
45	May 2	A	Burnley	L	0-1	0-0	13		19,362
46	7	H	Bristol C	W	1-0	0-0	12	Henry [63]	16,679

Final League Position: 12

GOALSCORERS

League (54): Austin 10 (1 pen), Chery 10 (1 pen), Phillips 8, Hoilett 6 (1 pen), Polter 6, Emmanuel-Thomas 3, Fer 2, Onuoha 2, Angella 1, El Khayati 1, Hall 1, Henry 1, Hill 1, Mackie 1, Tozser 1.
FA Cup (0).
Capital One Cup (4): Emmanuel-Thomas 2, Onuoha 1, Polter 1.

Green R 24	Perch J 34 + 1	Onuoha N 46	Hill C 13	Konchesky P 33 + 1	Luongo M 26 + 4	Henry K 36 + 2	Chery T 25 + 14	Phillips M 43 + 1	Austin C 12 + 4	Mackie J 6 + 9	Faurlin A 28 + 2	Emmanuel-Thomas J 5 + 7	Polter S 18 + 13	Gladwin B 3 + 4	Doughty M 1 + 4	Hall G 37 + 2	Kpekawa C 3 + 2	Angella G 16 + 1	Tozser D 11 + 5	Smithies A 17 + 1	Fer L 14 + 5	Sandro 9 + 2	Hoilett J 24 + 5	Yun S 3	Blackwood T — + 1	Petrasso M 3 + 5	Lumley J 1	Washington C 7 + 8	El Khayati A 3 + 13	Robinson J 1	Ingram M 4	Match No.
1	2	3	4	5	6	7^2	8^1	9	10^3	11	12	13	14																			1
1	2	3	4	5	6	7	9^2	8	11^3			14	13	10^1	12																	2
1	2	3		5	9	6	10^2	8	11			7^1		13	12	4																3
1	2	3		5	9^1	6	10^2	8	11			7^3		13	12	4	14															4
1	2	3		5	9		10	8	11			7			6	4																5
1^*	2	3		5	9^3	6	10	8	11			14		12		4^2	7^1	13														6
	2	3		5	9	6	10^1	8	11	12						4^1	7	1														7
1	2	3		5	9^2	7	10^1	8	11^1	12^3	6			13		4																8
1	2	3		5	9	6	10^2	8	11^1	12^3	7					4	14		13													9
1		2		5		6	10	8			11					4	3	7		9^1	12											10
1	2	3		5	12	7	10	8			11^1	14				4		13		9^2	6^3											11
1		2	4	5	9		10	8				11^1				3		7		12^1	6											12
	2	4	5	9^3	6^1	10^2	8				14^1	11				3		7		12		13										13
1	14	2	4^3	5	9^1	6	10^2	8	12			11^1				3		7					13									14
1	2^*	3		5		6^1		9	10			8^3				4		7^2		13		12	11^3	14								15
1		3		5		2	13	8	11		7	12				4				9	6^2	10^1										16
1	2	3		5		6	11				8^2	13				4		12		10^*	7^1		9^3	14								17
1	2	3		5		14	12	11	13	7						4				6	9^3	10^1		8^2								18
1	2	3		5			13	11	12	7						4				10	6	9^2		8^1								19
1	2	4		5		6^1		11	12	7	13					4				9	8	10^2										20
1	2^1	3		5		13		8	11	7		14				4	12			9^2	6^3	10										21
1		2		5		6	13	8		7	12	11^2				4		3		9		10^1										22
1		2		5		6	13	8^1		7		11				4		3		9^2	12	10										23
1		2	4	5		8	13	11^1		14	12					3			7	9^2	6^3	10										24
1		2		5	14	6^1	9^2	8	13	7		11				4		3		12		10^3										25
	2	3		5		6	13	8^1		7		11				4				9		10^2			12^1	1					26
	2	3		5	7	6	12	8^1	13			11				4			1	9		10^2										27
	2	3		5	7	6^2	12	8				11				4			1	10		9^1				13						28
	2	3		5	6		13	8^2		7		11				4			1	10		9^1				12						29
	2	3		5	7		6		13	8^2		11				4		12	1			9^1				10^3	14					30
	2	3		5	7		14	6^1	10			11^2				4		8	1			9^3				12	13					31
	2	3		5	8	7^2	14	9		6^1		13				4			1			10^3				11	12					32
5	2				6	7		9	13			12		3	4	8	1					10^2	11^1									33
5	2				6	7	9^2	8^1				11			3	4	12	1				10^3				13	14					34
5	2	12			9	6	8^1	13				14		3^3		4	7^2	1				11	10									35
5	2	4			7	10^2	6	12	8			11				3			1			9^1	13									36
5	2	4			12	7^1	9^2	8	14	6		11^3				3			1			10	13									37
5	2	4			12	6	9^3	8^1		7		11	13			3			1			10^2	14									38
5	2				7	10	9^1	6^2	8^3			11				3	4		1			12					14	13				39
5	2				6	13	8	9^3	7			12				3	4		1			10^2					11^1	14				40
2^2	3				7	6	9	8^3				11	13			4^1	12		1			10^1					14	5				41
	2	4	5	6	8	9^2	10^1		7			11^3	12			3			1			14	13						1			42
5	2	4^2			9	6	13	8		7			12			3			1			10^3				11^1	14				43
	2	3			6		9^2	10^1		7		11	8^3		4	5						13				14^1	12		1		44
	2	4			6		10			7		11^1	14			3	5			9^3		8^2				12^1	13		1		45
	2	4			6		9^1			7		14	8^1			3	5					12				13	11^2	10	1		46

FA Cup
Third Round   Nottingham F   (a)   0-1

Capital One Cup
First Round   Yeovil T   (a)   3-0
Second Round   Carlisle U   (h)   1-2

READING

FOUNDATION

Reading was formed as far back as 1871 at a public meeting held at the Bridge Street Rooms. They first entered the FA Cup as early as 1877 when they amalgamated with the Reading Hornets. The club was further strengthened in 1889 when Earley FC joined them. They were the first winners of the Berks & Bucks Cup in 1878–79.

Madejski Stadium, Junction 11, M4, Reading, Berkshire RG2 0FL.

Telephone: (0118) 968 1100.

Fax: (0870) 999 1001.

Ticket Office: (0118) 968 1313.

Website: www.readingfc.co.uk

Email: customerservice@readingfc.co.uk

Ground Capacity: 24,182.

Record Attendance: 33,042 v Brentford, FA Cup 5th rd, 19 February 1927 (at Elm Park); 24,184 v Everton, FA Premier League, 17 November 2012 (at Madejski Stadium).

Pitch Measurements: 105m × 68m (115yd × 74.5yd).

Co-Chairman: Sir John Madejski.

Co-Chairwoman: Khunying Sasima Srivikorn.

Chief Executive: Nigel Howe.

Manager: Jaap Stam.

Assistant Managers: Andries Ulderink and Said Bakkati.

Head Physio: Jonathan Unwin.

Colours: Blue and white hooped shirts, blue shorts, white socks with blue trim.

Year Formed: 1871.

Turned Professional: 1895.

Club Nickname: 'The Royals'.

Grounds: 1871, Reading Recreation; Reading Cricket Ground; 1882, Coley Park; 1889, Caversham Cricket Ground; 1896, Elm Park; 1998, Madejski Stadium.

First Football League Game: 28 August 1920, Division 3, v Newport Co (a) W 1–0 – Crawford; Smith, Horler; Christie, Mavin, Getgood; Spence, Weston, Yarnell, Bailey (1), Andrews.

Record League Victory: 10–2 v Crystal Palace, Division 3 (S), 4 September 1946 – Groves; Glidden, Gulliver; McKenna, Ratcliffe, Young; Chitty, Maurice Edelston (3), McPhee (4), Barney (1), Deverell (2).

Record Cup Victory: 6–0 v Leyton, FA Cup 2nd rd, 12 December 1925 – Duckworth; Eggo, McConnell; Wilson, Messer, Evans; Smith (2), Braithwaite (1), Davey (1), Tinsley, Robson (2).

HONOURS

League Champions: FL C – 2005–06, 2011–12; Second Division – 1993–94; Division 3 – 1985–86; Division 3S – 1925–26; Division 4 – 1978–79.
Runners-up: First Division – 1994–95; Second Division – 2001–02; Division 3S – 1931–32, 1934–35, 1948–49, 1951–52.
FA Cup: semi-final – 1927, 2015.
League Cup: 5th rd – 1996, 1998.
Full Members' Cup Winners: 1988.

sky SPORTS FACT FILE

In May 1913, Reading, then members of the Southern League, defeated both Genoa and Milan in the opening two games of their five-match tour of Italy. They went on to play Pro Vercelli, the Italian champions for the three previous seasons, and inflicted a 6-0 defeat on their opponents.

Record Defeat: 0–18 v Preston NE, FA Cup 1st rd, 1893–94.

Most League Points (2 for a win): 65, Division 4, 1978–79.

Most League Points (3 for a win): 106, Championship, 2005–06 (Football League Record).

Most League Goals: 112, Division 3 (S), 1951–52.

Highest League Scorer in Season: Ronnie Blackman, 39, Division 3 (S), 1951–52.

Most League Goals in Total Aggregate: Ronnie Blackman, 158, 1947–54.

Most League Goals in One Match: 6, Arthur Bacon v Stoke C, Division 2, 3 April 1931.

Most Capped Player: Wales; Chris Gunter, 36 (73) Wales.

Most League Appearances: Martin Hicks, 500, 1978–91.

Youngest League Player: Peter Castle, 16 years 49 days v Watford, 30 April 2003.

Record Transfer Fee Received: £7,000,000 from TSG 1899 Hoffenheim for Gylfi Sigurdsson, August 2010.

Record Transfer Fee Paid: £2,500,000 to Nantes for Emerse Fae, August 2007.

Football League Record: 1920 Original Member of Division 3; 1921–26 Division 3 (S); 1926–31 Division 2; 1931–58 Division 3 (S); 1958–71 Division 3; 1971–76 Division 4; 1976–77 Division 3; 1977–79 Division 4; 1979–83 Division 3; 1983–84 Division 4; 1984–86 Division 3; 1986–88 Division 2; 1988–92 Division 3; 1992–94 Division 2; 1994–98 Division 1; 1998–2002 Division 2; 2002–04 Division 1; 2004–06 FL C; 2006–08 FA Premier League; 2008–12 FL C; 2012–13 FA Premier League; 2013– FL C.

LATEST SEQUENCES

Longest Sequence of League Wins: 13, 17.8.1985 – 19.10.1985.

Longest Sequence of League Defeats: 8, 29.12.2007 – 24.2.2008.

Longest Sequence of League Draws: 6, 23.3.2002 – 20.4.2002.

Longest Sequence of Unbeaten League Matches: 33, 9.8.2005 – 14.2.2006.

Longest Sequence Without a League Win: 14, 30.4.1927 – 29.10.1927.

Successive Scoring Runs: 32 from 1.10.1932.

Successive Non-scoring Runs: 6 from 29.3.2008.

MANAGERS

Thomas Sefton 1897–1901
(Secretary-Manager)
James Sharp 1901–02
Harry Matthews 1902–20
Harry Marshall 1920–22
Arthur Chadwick 1923–25
H. S. Bray 1925–26
(Secretary only since 1922 and 1926–35)
Andrew Wylie 1926–31
Joe Smith 1931–35
Billy Butler 1935–39
John Cochrane 1939
Joe Edelston 1939–47
Ted Drake 1947–52
Jack Smith 1952–55
Harry Johnston 1955–63
Roy Bentley 1963–69
Jack Mansell 1969–71
Charlie Hurley 1972–77
Maurice Evans 1977–84
Ian Branfoot 1984–89
Ian Porterfield 1989–91
Mark McGhee 1991–94
Jimmy Quinn/Mick Gooding 1994–97
Terry Bullivant 1997–98
Tommy Burns 1998–99
Alan Pardew 1999–2003
Steve Coppell 2003–09
Brendan Rodgers 2009
Brian McDermott 2009–13
Nigel Adkins 2013–14
Steve Clarke 2014–15
Brian McDermott 2015–16
Jaap Stam June 2016–

TEN YEAR LEAGUE RECORD

		P	W	D	L	F	A	Pts	Pos
2006-07	PR Lge	38	16	7	15	52	47	55	8
2007-08	PR Lge	38	10	6	22	41	66	36	18
2008-09	FL C	46	21	14	11	72	40	77	4
2009-10	FL C	46	17	12	17	68	63	63	9
2010-11	FL C	46	20	17	9	77	51	77	5
2011-12	FL C	46	27	8	11	69	41	89	1
2012-13	PR Lge	38	6	10	22	43	73	28	19
2013-14	FL C	46	19	14	13	70	56	71	7
2014-15	FL C	46	13	11	22	48	69	50	19
2015-16	FL C	46	13	13	20	52	59	52	17

DID YOU KNOW ?

Reading competed in the London Cup during the 1940–41 season. They finished top of their group ahead of Tottenham Hotspur, West Ham United and Arsenal before defeating Crystal Palace in the semi-final and Brentford in the final which was played at Stamford Bridge.

READING – FL CHAMPIONSHIP 2015–16 LEAGUE RECORD

Match No.	Date	Venue	Opponents	Result	H/T Score	Lg Pos.	Goalscorers	Attendance
1	Aug 8	A	Birmingham C	L 1-2	0-1	18	Blackman [58]	19,171
2	16	H	Leeds U	D 0-0	0-0	19		21,581
3	19	A	Sheffield W	D 1-1	0-0	18	Williams [49]	20,247
4	22	H	Milton Keynes D	D 0-0	0-0	19		16,547
5	29	A	Brentford	W 3-1	2-0	13	Orlando Sa [17], Blackman 2 (1 pen) [32, 90 (p)]	10,206
6	Sept 11	H	Ipswich T	W 5-1	2-1	5	Orlando Sa 3 [7, 14, 63], Blackman [49], Norwood [87]	16,809
7	15	H	Derby Co	L 0-1	0-0	11		15,697
8	19	A	Bristol C	W 2-0	2-0	6	Blackman [9], McCleary [13]	15,385
9	26	A	Burnley	W 2-1	2-0	3	Blackman [5], Piazon [9]	15,226
10	Oct 3	H	Middlesbrough	W 2-0	1-0	3	Williams [1], Blackman (pen) [88]	19,516
11	17	H	Charlton Ath	W 1-0	0-0	2	Blackman [76]	17,614
12	20	A	Rotherham U	D 1-1	1-0	3	Blackman [26]	9071
13	24	A	Fulham	L 2-4	1-0	7	Piazon [13], Orlando Sa [49]	18,618
14	31	H	Brighton & HA	D 1-1	0-0	7	Vydra [78]	21,244
15	Nov 3	H	Huddersfield T	D 2-2	1-2	7	Norwood [15], John [84]	14,379
16	7	A	Cardiff C	L 0-2	0-1	8		15,414
17	21	H	Bolton W	W 2-1	2-0	7	Piazon [28], Williams [34]	16,420
18	28	A	Nottingham F	L 1-3	1-2	9	Vydra [14]	18,128
19	Dec 3	H	QPR	L 0-1	0-0	9		16,365
20	12	A	Preston NE	L 0-1	0-0	12		10,649
21	16	A	Hull C	L 1-2	1-0	13	Blackman [29]	15,139
22	20	H	Blackburn R	W 1-0	1-0	11	Williams [11]	16,529
23	26	A	Wolverhampton W	L 0-1	0-1	11		21,147
24	28	H	Brentford	L 1-2	0-1	12	McCleary [58]	20,563
25	Jan 2	H	Bristol C	W 1-0	0-0	12	Blackman [90]	19,677
26	12	A	Derby Co	D 1-1	1-1	12	Williams [38]	28,175
27	16	A	Milton Keynes D	L 0-1	0-0	14		13,062
28	23	H	Sheffield W	D 1-1	0-1	13	Cooper [74]	18,972
29	Feb 2	A	Ipswich T	L 1-2	0-0	16	McCleary (pen) [69]	16,616
30	6	H	Wolverhampton W	D 0-0	0-0	15		17,771
31	13	H	Burnley	D 0-0	0-0	15		16,773
32	23	H	Rotherham U	W 1-0	0-0	14	Robson-Kanu [66]	13,504
33	27	A	Charlton Ath	W 4-3	3-1	12	Kermorgant 2 [4, 35], John [42], Rakels [90]	21,506
34	Mar 5	H	Fulham	D 2-2	2-1	11	Robson-Kanu 2 (1 pen) [24 (p), 41]	17,859
35	8	A	Huddersfield T	L 1-3	0-0	14	John [90]	10,167
36	15	A	Brighton & HA	L 0-1	0-1	15		23,418
37	19	H	Cardiff C	D 1-1	1-0	17	McCleary [37]	17,407
38	Apr 2	A	Bolton W	W 1-0	0-0	13	John [90]	13,469
39	5	H	Nottingham F	W 2-1	0-1	13	Vydra [68], Norwood [81]	15,678
40	9	H	Birmingham C	L 0-2	0-2	14		17,868
41	12	A	Middlesbrough	L 1-2	0-1	14	Cox [54]	23,746
42	16	A	Leeds U	L 2-3	1-0	15	Hector [39], Rakels [81]	20,881
43	19	H	Hull C	L 1-2	1-1	15	Cooper [4]	12,949
44	23	A	QPR	D 1-1	1-1	15	Rakels [41]	16,225
45	30	H	Preston NE	L 1-2	0-0	16	Quinn [86]	15,834
46	May 7	A	Blackburn R	L 1-3	1-2	17	Kermorgant [31]	13,140

Final League Position: 17

GOALSCORERS

League (52): Blackman 11 (2 pens), Orlando Sa 5, Williams 5, John 4, McCleary 4 (1 pen), Kermorgant 3, Norwood 3, Piazon 3, Rakels 3, Robson-Kanu 3 (1 pen), Vydra 3, Cooper 2, Cox 1, Hector 1, Quinn 1.
FA Cup (14): Vydra 6, Piazon 2, Robson-Kanu 2, Alex 1, Hector 1, McShane 1, Williams 1.
Capital One Cup (4): Blackman 2, Gunter 1, McCleary 1.

Bond J 14	Gunter C 43 + 1	McShane P 35	Hector M 26 + 4	Obita J 24 + 2	Blackman N 23 + 2	Tshibola A 6 + 6	Norwood O 43	Quinn S 27	Williams D 35 + 4	Orlando Sa C 16 + 3	Robson-Kanu H 21 + 7	Cox S 6 + 7	Samuel D — + 1	Ferdinand A 18 + 1	Taylor A 17 + 2	Alex F 2 + 6	McCleary G 20 + 14	Vydra M 24 + 7	Piazon L 19 + 4	John O 8 + 20	Hurtado P — + 5	Cooper J 21 + 3	Al Habsi A 32	Liburd R — + 3	Evans G 5 + 1	Kermorgant Y 15 + 2	Rakels D 5 + 7	Barrett J 1 + 2	Dickie R — + 1	Match No.
1	2	3	4	5	6¹	7³	8	9³	10	11	12	13	14																	1
1	2	3	14	5	10²	12	6¹	9³	8	11	7	13		4																2
1	2	3	13	12	14	8	7	11	6	10¹	9³			4																3
1	2	3		5	13	7³	6	9¹	8	11	10²	12		4	14															4
1	2	3	14	5	9	13	7³	8	6	10¹	11²			4			12													5
1	2	3		5	9¹		6	7	8		10¹		14	4			11³	12	13											6
1	2	4	3				8		7					14	11³		9²			6¹			1							7
1	2	4	3	5	10	14	7	8²	6								9²	11¹	12	13			1							8
1	2	4	3	5	10	14	7	8²	6								9³	11¹	12	13			1							9
	2	4	3	5	9	13	7		6	10	11²						8¹	12				1								10
	2	4	3	5	8	7³	6	13	11						14	12	9¹	10²				1								11
	2	4	3	9		7		6	11			5				8²	12	10¹	13			1								12
	2	4	3	5	8	12	7¹		6³	11					14		9	10²	13			1								13
	2	4	3	10		7		6	11²			5				8¹	9	12	13			1								14
	2	3	5	11		6		8²	13		4				12	7¹	10	9³	14			11								15
	2		3		8		7	13	11		4	6	5¹			9³	10²	14		1	12									16
	2	4	3	12	9¹		7		6	11	5				8³	14	10²			13	1									17
	2	4¹	3		8		7		6	11³	5					9	10²	13	12		1	14								18
	2		4	10²		6		9	14	12	3	5	7³	8	11¹			13			1									19
1	2	3		9		6		7		10¹	4	5	13	8²	11		12													20
1	2	3	7	11		8		6		14	4³	5²	12	9¹	10			13												21
1	2	3	4		8		6	5	7		11					10²	9¹	12	13											22
1	2	3	4		8		6	5²	7	14	11				12	10³	9¹		13											23
1	2	3	4²		8		7	5	6		11²					13	12	9¹	10³						14					24
	2	3²			8		7	10	6	11¹	14			12	5²		13	9				4	1							25
	2						7		6		10			3	5		8	11	9			4	1							26
	2						7		6		10²	13		3	5		8	11	9¹	12		4	1							27
	2		5				7		8	6		11		3				10	9²	13		4	1			6¹	12			28
	2		5				7	8¹	6		9			3			12	11				4	1			10				29
	2	3		5			7		6		10				8¹	9²	12					4	1			11	13			30
	2	3	7	5			6²	10			8						12	9¹				4	1			11	13			31
	2	3	7	5			8¹	6			9						13		11²			4	1			10	12			32
	2	3	7	5			6¹	9¹	12		8						13		10²			4	1			11	14			33
	2		7	5			6	9¹			8²			3			12		10			4	1			11	13			34
	2³		3					7			13			5		6	9	12	4	1					8²	11	10¹	14		35
	2	3	6	5				7	8		11			4		12	9¹	10²				4	1			11	13			36
	2	3	7				9¹	6	8³	14				5		12	13	10				4	1			11²				37
	2	3		5			7	10	6		13				9	8²	12					4	1			11				38
	2	3		5			6	8	7		10¹				12	9²	13					4	1			11				39
	2²	3		5			6	8	7		11¹				13	12	9³	14				4	1			10				40
	2²	3		5²			6	10	7		11			13		12	9	8¹	14			4	1			11				41
		3					8	9			11			5	2	10	6²	13		4	1			7¹			12			42
		6					7	9			8²			3	5	2	10¹		13	4	1					12	11			43
13		12					6	8¹			9			3	5²	2	14			4	1			7	11³	10			44
5	3						6	8	9						2					4	1			7¹	10	11	12			45
5	3						8	9¹	7	13					2					4	1			14	10²	11	6¹	12		46

FA Cup

Third Round	Huddersfield T	(a)	2-2
Replay	Huddersfield T	(h)	5-2
Fourth Round	Walsall	(h)	4-0
Fifth Round	WBA	(h)	3-1
Sixth Round	Crystal Palace	(h)	0-2

Capital One Cup

First Round	Colchester U	(a)	1-0
(aet)			
Second Round	Portsmouth	(a)	2-1
Third Round	Everton	(h)	1-2

ROCHDALE

FOUNDATION

Considering the love of rugby in their area, it is not surprising that Rochdale had difficulty in establishing an Association Football club. The earlier Rochdale Town club formed in 1900 went out of existence in 1907 when the present club was immediately established and joined the Manchester League, before graduating to the Lancashire Combination in 1908.

Spotland Stadium, Willbutts Lane, Rochdale, Lancashire OL11 5DS.

Telephone: (0844) 826 1907.

Fax: (01706) 648 466.

Ticket Office: (0844) 826 1907 (option 8).

Website: www.rochdaleafc.co.uk

Email: admin@rochdaleafc.co.uk

Ground Capacity: 10,003.

Record Attendance: 24,231 v Notts Co, FA Cup 2nd rd, 10 December 1949.

Pitch Measurements: 104m × 69.5m (114yd × 76yd).

Chairman: Chris Dunphy.

Chief Executive: Colin Garlick.

Manager: Keith Hill.

Assistant Manager: Chris Beech.

Physio: Andy Thorpe.

Colours: Blue shirts with white trim, blue shorts with white trim, blue socks with white hoops.

Year Formed: 1907.

Turned Professional: 1907.

Club Nickname: 'The Dale'.

Ground: 1907, St Clements Playing Fields (original name Spotland).

First Football League Game: 27 August 1921, Division 3 (N), v Accrington Stanley (h) W 6–3 – Crabtree; Nuttall, Sheehan; Hill, Farrer, Yarwood; Hoad, Sandiford, Dennison (2), Owens (3), Carney (1).

Record League Victory: 8–1 v Chesterfield, Division 3 (N), 18 December 1926 – Hill; Brown, Ward; Hillhouse, Parkes, Braidwood; Hughes, Bertram, Whitehurst (5), Schofield (2), Martin (1).

Record Cup Victory: 8–2 v Crook T, FA Cup 1st rd, 26 November 1927 – Moody; Hopkins, Ward; Braidwood, Parkes, Barker; Tompkinson, Clennell (3) Whitehurst (4), Hall, Martin (1).

Record Defeat: 1–9 v Tranmere R, Division 3 (N), 25 December 1931.

Most League Points (2 for a win): 62, Division 3 (N), 1923–24.

HONOURS

League: Runners-up: Division 3N – 1923–24, 1926–27.

FA Cup: 5th rd – 1990, 2003.

League Cup: Runners-up: 1962.

sky SPORTS FACT FILE

Jimmy Wynn, who signed for Rochdale from Rotherham United in October 1936, set a club record in his first season at Spotland by scoring in nine consecutive games. He continued to find the net regularly for Dale up to the outbreak of the Second World War, ending up with a career total of 64 goals from his 86 Football League appearances.

Most League Points (3 for a win): 82, FL 2, 2009–10.

Most League Goals: 105, Division 3 (N), 1926–27.

Highest League Scorer in Season: Albert Whitehurst, 44, Division 3 (N), 1926–27.

Most League Goals in Total Aggregate: Reg Jenkins, 119, 1964–73.

Most League Goals in One Match: 6, Tommy Tippett v Hartlepools U, Division 3 (N), 21 April 1930.

Most Capped Player: Leo Bertos, 6 (56), New Zealand.

Most League Appearances: Gary Jones, 470, 1998–2001; 2003–12.

Youngest League Player: Zac Hughes, 16 years 105 days v Exeter C, 19 September 1987.

Record Transfer Fee Received: £750,000 from Brentford for Scott Hogan, July 2014.

Record Transfer Fee Paid: £150,000 to Stoke C for Paul Connor, March 2001.

Football League Record: 1921 Elected to Division 3 (N); 1958–59 Division 3; 1959–69 Division 4; 1969–74 Division 3; 1974–92 Division 4; 1992–2004 Division 3; 2004–10 FL 2; 2010–12 FL 1; 2012–14 FL 2; 2014– FL 1.

LATEST SEQUENCES

Longest Sequence of League Wins: 8, 29.9.1969 – 3.11.1969.

Longest Sequence of League Defeats: 17, 14.11.1931 – 12.3.1932.

Longest Sequence of League Draws: 6, 17.8.1968 – 14.9.1968.

Longest Sequence of Unbeaten League Matches: 20, 15.9.1923 – 19.1.1924.

Longest Sequence Without a League Win: 28, 14.11.1931 – 29.8.1932.

Successive Scoring Runs: 29 from 10.10.2008.

Successive Non-scoring Runs: 9 from 14.3.1980.

MANAGERS

Billy Bradshaw 1920
Run by committee 1920–22
Tom Wilson 1922–23
Jack Peart 1923–30
Will Cameron 1930–31
Herbert Hopkinson 1932–34
Billy Smith 1934–35
Ernest Nixon 1935–37
Sam Jennings 1937–38
Ted Goodier 1938–52
Jack Warner 1952–53
Harry Catterick 1953–58
Jack Marshall 1958–60
Tony Collins 1960–68
Bob Stokoe 1967–68
Len Richley 1968–70
Dick Conner 1970–73
Walter Joyce 1973–76
Brian Green 1976–77
Mike Ferguson 1977–78
Doug Collins 1979
Bob Stokoe 1979–80
Peter Madden 1980–83
Jimmy Greenhoff 1983–84
Vic Halom 1984–86
Eddie Gray 1986–88
Danny Bergara 1988–89
Terry Dolan 1989–91
Dave Sutton 1991–94
Mick Docherty 1994–96
Graham Barrow 1996–99
Steve Parkin 1999–2001
John Hollins 2001–02
Paul Simpson 2002–03
Alan Buckley 2003
Steve Parkin 2003–06
Keith Hill 2007–11
  (Caretaker from December 2006)
Steve Eyre 2011
John Coleman 2012–13
Keith Hill January 2013–

TEN YEAR LEAGUE RECORD

		P	W	D	L	F	A	Pts	Pos
2006-07	FL 2	46	18	12	16	70	50	66	9
2007-08	FL 2	46	23	11	12	77	54	80	5
2008-09	FL 2	46	19	13	14	70	59	70	6
2009-10	FL 2	46	25	7	14	82	48	82	3
2010-11	FL 1	46	18	14	14	63	55	68	9
2011-12	FL 1	46	8	14	24	47	81	38	24
2012-13	FL 2	46	16	13	17	68	70	61	12
2013-14	FL 2	46	24	9	13	69	48	81	3
2014-15	FL 1	46	19	6	21	72	66	63	8
2015-16	FL 1	46	19	12	15	68	61	69	10

DID YOU KNOW ?

In October 2013 Rochdale's Spotland ground hosted a Rugby League World Cup finals Group A game between Fiji and Ireland. Fiji won the match 32-14 in front of a sold-out attendance of 8,872. Spotland was selected because Rochdale has the largest Fijian community in the United Kingdom outside of London.

ROCHDALE – FOOTBALL LEAGUE ONE 2015–16 LEAGUE RECORD

Match No.	Date	Venue	Opponents	Result	H/T Score	Lg Pos.	Goalscorers	Attendance
1	Aug 8	H	Peterborough U	W 2-0	1-0	4	Camps [18], Noble-Lazarus [69]	3319
2	15	A	Blackpool	W 2-0	0-0	2	McDermott [58], Henderson [87]	7076
3	18	H	Walsall	L 1-2	0-0	4	Andrew [80]	2381
4	22	A	Chesterfield	D 0-0	0-0	8		6254
5	29	H	Barnsley	W 3-0	2-0	5	Andrew [8], Vincenti [36], Henderson [63]	3618
6	Sept 5	A	Fleetwood T	D 1-1	0-0	5	Vincenti [55]	3511
7	12	A	Burton Alb	L 0-1	0-1	6		2787
8	19	H	Scunthorpe U	W 2-1	0-0	5	Bunney [67], Vincenti [85]	2958
9	26	A	Millwall	L 1-3	1-2	7	Vincenti [43]	8023
10	29	H	Shrewsbury T	W 3-2	3-2	5	Vincenti [4], Henderson (pen) [12], Allen [15]	2190
11	Oct 3	H	Bradford C	L 1-3	1-1	6	Vincenti [41]	4534
12	10	A	Sheffield U	L 2-3	1-2	9	Vincenti (pen) [37], Alessandra [72]	19,039
13	17	A	Bury	D 0-0	0-0	10		6470
14	20	H	Coventry C	D 0-0	0-0	10		2495
15	24	H	Oldham Ath	D 0-0	0-0	11		5690
16	31	A	Southend U	D 2-2	0-2	13	Bunney [63], Rose [79]	6111
17	Nov 14	H	Wigan Ath	L 0-2	0-1	15		3835
18	21	A	Doncaster R	W 2-0	0-0	13	Henderson 2 [84, 90]	6125
19	24	A	Gillingham	L 0-2	0-1	14		5088
20	28	H	Port Vale	W 2-1	1-1	13	Henderson (pen) [40], Mendez-Laing [78]	2510
21	Dec 12	A	Swindon T	L 1-2	0-2	13	Lancashire [60]	7149
22	19	H	Colchester U	W 3-1	2-1	13	Henderson (pen) [30], McDermott [34], Lancashire [64]	2205
23	28	A	Scunthorpe U	D 1-1	1-1	13	Henderson [22]	3860
24	Jan 2	A	Walsall	W 3-0	1-0	9	Henderson [3], Andrew 2 [58, 77]	4857
25	9	H	Chesterfield	L 2-3	0-1	11	Henderson [58], Bennett [90]	2965
26	23	A	Barnsley	L 1-6	0-1	16	Mendez-Laing [65]	8823
27	30	H	Burton Alb	W 2-1	2-0	14	Camps [8], Henderson (pen) [24]	2994
28	Feb 6	A	Crewe Alex	L 0-2	0-2	14		4130
29	13	H	Millwall	L 0-1	0-0	15		2882
30	16	H	Crewe Alex	D 2-2	2-2	16	Bennett [2], Bunney [6]	1985
31	20	A	Bradford C	D 2-2	1-1	16	Bunney 2 [12, 51]	17,936
32	23	H	Fleetwood T	W 1-0	1-0	16	Bunney [12]	1767
33	27	H	Sheffield U	W 2-0	0-0	13	Vincenti [67], Holt [81]	4210
34	Mar 1	A	Shrewsbury T	L 0-2	0-2	15		4221
35	5	A	Coventry C	W 1-0	0-0	13	Henderson (pen) [89]	9942
36	12	H	Bury	W 3-0	2-0	12	Mendez-Laing 2 [11, 17], Eastham [53]	4538
37	19	A	Oldham Ath	W 3-2	1-1	11	Henderson (pen) [37], Gerrard (og) [49], Camps [55]	6117
38	25	H	Southend U	W 4-1	1-1	8	Holt [41], Rafferty [49], Allen [61], Bunney [90]	3018
39	28	A	Wigan Ath	L 0-1	0-0	8		10,407
40	Apr 2	H	Doncaster R	D 2-2	1-0	9	Camps [43], Canavan [90]	2727
41	9	A	Peterborough U	W 2-1	2-1	8	Bunney [8], Mendez-Laing [23]	4785
42	16	H	Blackpool	W 3-0	1-0	8	Eastham [45], Bunney [50], Mendez-Laing [60]	3247
43	19	H	Gillingham	D 1-1	1-0	8	Camps [45]	2385
44	23	A	Port Vale	L 1-4	0-2	10	Andrew [50]	4380
45	30	H	Swindon T	D 2-2	1-2	11	Allen [45], Lund [67]	2806
46	May 8	A	Colchester U	W 2-1	1-0	10	Mendez-Laing [18], Andrew [69]	3435

Final League Position: 10

GOALSCORERS

League (68): Henderson 13 (6 pens), Bunney 9, Vincenti 8 (1 pen), Mendez-Laing 7, Andrew 6, Camps 5, Allen 3, Bennett 2, Eastham 2, Holt 2, Lancashire 2, McDermott 2, Alessandra 1, Canavan 1, Lund 1, Noble-Lazarus 1, Rafferty 1, Rose 1, own goal 1.
FA Cup (3): Mendez-Laing 3 (1 pen).
Capital One Cup (1): McDermott 1.
Johnstone's Paint Trophy (2): Alessandra 1, Tanser 1.

Lillis J 40	Kennedy T 17 + 1	McNulty J 46	Lancashire O 34	Cannon A 22 + 3	Allen J 35 + 3	Camps C 28 + 4	Vincenti P 26 + 12	McDermott D 32 + 5	Bunney J 19 + 13	Henderson I 36 + 3	Andrew C 14 + 16	Noble-Lazarus R 2 + 8	Rose M 23 + 7	Rafferty J 29 + 2	Bennett R 7 + 9	Eastham A 19 + 1	Lund M 25 + 4	Mendez-Laing N 18 + 15	Alessandra L 3 + 5	Tanser S 6 + 1	Castro J 6	Hooper J 1 + 1	O'Sullivan J 2	Barry-Murphy B —+ 1	Syers D 2 + 4	Canavan N 11	Holt G 3 + 11	Match No.
1	2	3	4	5	6	7[2]	8	9[3]	10[1]	11	12	13	14															1
1	5[3]	3	4		7	10[2]	8	6[1]	9	11			14	12	2	13												2
1	5	3	4		9	10[2]	7[1]	8	13	11	14		12	2[3]	6													3
1	5	3	4[1]		8	7[2]	6	9	10[3]	11	12			2	14	13												4
1	5	4	3	10	6		7[2]	9[1]	12	8	11	13		2														5
1	5	4	3	2	7[2]		8	10[1]	13	9	11	12		6														6
1	5	3	4		7[1]		8	10[3]		9	11	12		2			6[2]	13	14									7
1	5	4	3	2[2]	8		7	9[1]	13	11	12	10[2]	14		6													8
1	5	4	3	2	9		7	14	10[1]	11[3]	12		6[2]				8	13										9
1	5	4	3	2	9[1]		7	8[2]	12	10	11			6			13											10
1	5	4	3	2	6[2]	10[1]	8	9[2]		11				7			12	14	13									11
1	5[1]	3	4	2[3]	12		10	8[2]			13			6			7	11	9	14								12
1		3	4	2	6		7	14		13	12			9[1]			8	10[2]	11[3]	5								13
1		4	3	2	6	8[1]		11[3]	12	9	10[2]						7	14	13	5								14
1		4	3	2	8[1]	6		9[3]	14								7	13	10[2]	5								15
1	2[1]	4	3		8[2]	6	9[3]		10	11	13		12				7	14		5								16
1		4		2[1]		9	8	14	11	13	12		7[2]		6	3	10[3]			5								17
1	5	3	4	2		7[3]	11[1]	6	10[2]	9	12		14		8		13				1							18
1	5[1]	3	4	2		7		9[2]		11	10		14	6[3]	8		12			1		13						19
1		4	3			7		12	8[2]	9	11			14	2		13			5	1	10[3]	6[1]					20
1		3	4			7[3]	8[1]	9[2]		11	13		5		2		6	14			1		10[8]	12				21
1		3	4	5		7	9	8		11	10		2				6				1							22
1		4	3	5		6[1]	9	8[2]		11	10		2		13		7	12			1							23
1		4	3	5	13	6[2]	9[3]	8[1]		11	10		2				7	14										24
1	12	4	3	2	6[1]		9	8[2]		10	11		5[2]		13		7	14										25
1		4	3	2[1]	13	6	7	9[2]	12	10	11[3]		5				8	14										26
1	5	4	3		8	6[1]	9			10	12			2	13		7							11[2]				27
1	5[2]	4	3		8	6	9[3]		13	10	12			2			7	14						11[1]				28
1		5	3	2[1]	9	8	12		7[3]	11	10[2]			6		4		14	13									29
1		5	3			14		9[1]	10		12	8	2	6[3]	4	7	11[2]					13						30
1		5			8			11[1]	10[2]				6	2	14	3	7	9[3]							13	4	12	31
1		5			8		14	11[3]	10		9[1]	6		2		3	7[2]							13	4	12		32
1		5			8		12	9[3]	10			7		2	14	4	6[2]	11[1]							3	13		33
1		5			7	14	9[3]		12	11		13	8[2]	2[1]		3	6								4	10		34
1		5			6	12		9[1]		10			8	2		3	7	11[2]							4	13		35
1		5			9	12		10[2]	13	11			7	2	14	3	6[1]	8[1]							4			36
1		5		14	10	6[1]	12	8[2]		9[8]			7	2		3		11[3]							4	13		37
1		5		14	7	6[1]	12	9[3]	13				8	2		3		11[2]							4	10		38
1		2			8	9[1]	12	6[2]	14	10[8]			7	5		4		11[1]							3	13		39
1		5			6	9	12	8	13				7[3]	2[1]		3	14	10[2]							4	11		40
1		5	4			12		9[3]	11[1]	8			2	3		7	10[8]							14		13		41
1		5	4	14		6	9	12	8[2]	11[1]			7	2		3	10[3]									13		42
1		5	4		6	7	12	9[2]	10[1]		14		8	2		3	11[3]									13		43
1		5	3		8	7[3]		11[2]	10[1]	12	13		6	2		4	9									14		44
1		5		2	7	6[3]		8	9[2]	10			12			3	13	11								4[1]	14	45
1		5	3	2	6	13	14	8[3]	11[1]	10	12					4	7	9[2]										46

FA Cup

First Round	Swindon T	(h)	3-1
Second Round	Bury	(h)	0-1

Capital One Cup

First Round	Coventry C	(h)	1-1
(aet; Rochdale won 5-3 on penalties)			
Second Round	Hull C	(a)	0-1

Johnstone's Paint Trophy

Second Round	Chesterfield	(h)	2-1
Northern Quarter-Final	Morecambe	(h)	0-1

ROTHERHAM UNITED

FOUNDATION

Rotherham were formed in 1870 before becoming Town in the late 1880s. Thornhill United were founded in 1877 and changed their name to Rotherham County in 1905. The Town amalgamated with Rotherham County to form Rotherham United in 1925.

The AESSEAL New York Stadium, New York Way, Rotherham, South Yorkshire S60 1AH.

Telephone: (0844) 4140 733.

Fax: (0844) 4140 744.

Ticket Office: (0844) 4140 754.

Website: www.themillers.co.uk

Email: office@rotherhamunited.net

Ground Capacity: 12,053.

Record Attendance: 25,170 v Sheffield U, Division 2, 13 December 1952 (at Millmoor); 7,082 v Aldershot T, FL 2 Play-offs semi-final 2nd leg, 19 May 2010 (at Don Valley); 11,758 v Sheffield U, FL 1, 7 September 2013 (at New York Stadium).

Pitch Measurements: 102m × 66m (111.5yd × 72yd).

Chairman: Tony Stewart.

Chief Operating Officer: Paul Douglas.

Manager: Alan Stubbs.

Assistant Manager: John Doolan.

Head of Medical: Mike Preston.

Colours: Red shirts with white trim, white shorts with red trim, red socks with white trim.

Year Formed: 1870. *Turned Professional:* 1905. *Club Nickname:* 'The Millers'.

Previous Names: 1877, Thornhill United; 1905, Rotherham County; 1925, amalgamated with Rotherham Town under Rotherham United.

Grounds: 1870, Red House Ground; 1907, Millmoor; 2008, Don Valley Stadium; 2012, New York Stadium (renamed The AESSEAL New York Stadium 2014).

First Football League Game: 2 September 1893, Division 2, Rotherham T v Lincoln C (a) D 1–1 – McKay; Thickett, Watson; Barr, Brown, Broadhead; Longden, Cutts, Leatherbarrow, McCormick, Pickering, (1 og). 30 August 1919, Division 2, Rotherham Co v Nottingham F (h) W 2–0 – Branston; Alton, Baines; Bailey, Coe, Stanton; Lee (1), Cawley (1), Glennon, Lees, Lamb.

Record League Victory: 8–0 v Oldham Ath, Division 3 (N), 26 May 1947 – Warnes; Selkirk, Ibbotson; Edwards, Horace Williams, Danny Williams; Wilson (2), Shaw (1), Ardron (3), Guest (1), Hainsworth (1).

Record Cup Victory: 6–0 v Spennymoor U, FA Cup 2nd rd, 17 December 1977 – McAlister; Forrest, Breckin, Womble, Stancliffe, Green, Finney, Phillips (3), Gwyther (2) (Smith), Goodfellow, Crawford (1). 6–0 v Wolverhampton W, FA Cup 1st rd, 16 November 1985 – O'Hanlon; Forrest, Dungworth, Gooding (1), Smith (1), Pickering, Birch (2), Emerson, Tynan (1), Simmons (1), Pugh. 6–0 v Kings Lynn, FA Cup 2nd rd, 6 December 1997 – Mimms; Clark, Hurst (Goodwin), Garner (1) (Hudson) (1), Warner (Bass), Richardson (1), Berry (1), Thompson, Druce (1), Glover (1), Roscoe.

Record Defeat: 1–11 v Bradford C, Division 3 (N), 25 August 1928.

HONOURS

League Champions: Division 3 – 1980–81; Division 3N – 1950–51; Division 4 – 1988–89.
Runners-up: Second Division – 2000–01; Division 3N – 1946–47, 1947–48, 1948–49; FL 2 – 2012–13; Third Division – 1999–2000; Division 4 – 1991–92.
FA Cup: 5th rd – 1953, 1968.
League Cup: Runners-up: 1961.
League Trophy Winners: 1996.

sky SPORTS FACT FILE

In the 1952–53 FA Cup competition Rotherham United pulled off a shock victory at First Division Newcastle United who were looking to win the trophy for a third consecutive season. The Millers went a goal behind in the second half of their fourth round tie but winger Jack Grainger, who only passed a fitness test on the morning of the game, went on to score twice and set up another as Rotherham won 3-1.

Most League Points (2 for a win): 71, Division 3 (N), 1950–51.

Most League Points (3 for a win): 91, Division 2, 2000–01.

Most League Goals: 114, Division 3 (N), 1946–47.

Highest League Scorer in Season: Wally Ardron, 38, Division 3 (N), 1946–47.

Most League Goals in Total Aggregate: Gladstone Guest, 130, 1946–56.

Most League Goals in One Match: 4, Roland Bastow v York C, Division 3 (N), 9 November 1935; 4, Roland Bastow v Rochdale, Division 3 (N), 7 March 1936; 4, Wally Ardron v Crewe Alex, Division 3 (N), 5 October 1946; 4, Wally Ardron v Carlisle U, Division 3 (N), 13 September 1947; 4, Wally Ardron v Hartlepools U, Division 3 (N), 13 October 1948; 4, Ian Wilson v Liverpool, Division 2, 2 May 1955; 4, Carl Gilbert v Swansea C, Division 3, 28 September 1971; 4, Carl Airey v Chester, Division 3, 31 August 1987; 4, Shaun Goater v Hartlepool U, Division 3, 9 April 1994; 4, Lee Glover v Hull C, Division 3, 28 December 1997; 4, Darren Byfield v Millwall, Division 1, 10 August 2002; 4, Adam Le Fondre v Cheltenham T, FL 2, 21 August 2010.

Most Capped Player: Kari Arnason, 20 (52), Iceland.

Most League Appearances: Danny Williams, 461, 1946–62.

Youngest League Player: Kevin Eley, 16 years 72 days v Scunthorpe U, 15 May 1984.

Record Transfer Fee Received: £900,000 from Bristol C for Kieran Agard, August 2014.

Record Transfer Fee Paid: £400,000 to Oldham Ath for Jonson Clarke-Harris, September 2014.

Football League Record: 1893 Rotherham Town elected to Division 2; 1896 Failed re-election; 1919 Rotherham County elected to Division 2; 1923–51 Division 3 (N); 1951–68 Division 2; 1968–73 Division 3; 1973–75 Division 4; 1975–81 Division 3; 1981–83 Division 2; 1983–88 Division 3; 1988–89 Division 4; 1989–91 Division 3; 1991–92 Division 4; 1992–97 Division 2; 1997–2000 Division 3; 2000–01 Division 2; 2001–04 Division 1; 2004–05 FL C; 2005–07 FL 1; 2007–13 FL 2; 2013–14 FL 1; 2014– FL C.

MANAGERS

Billy Heald 1925–29 *(Secretary only for several years)*
Stanley Davies 1929–30
Billy Heald 1930–33
Reg Freeman 1934–52
Andy Smailes 1952–58
Tom Johnston 1958–62
Danny Williams 1962–65
Jack Mansell 1965–67
Tommy Docherty 1967–68
Jimmy McAnearney 1968–73
Jimmy McGuigan 1973–79
Ian Porterfield 1979–81
Emlyn Hughes 1981–83
George Kerr 1983–85
Norman Hunter 1985–87
Dave Cusack 1987–88
Billy McEwan 1988–91
Phil Henson 1991–94
Archie Gemmill/John McGovern 1994–96
Danny Bergara 1996–97
Ronnie Moore 1997–2005
Mick Harford 2005
Alan Knill 2005–07
Mark Robins 2007–09
Ronnie Moore 2009–11
Andy Scott 2011–12
Steve Evans 2012–15
Neil Redfearn 2015–16
Neil Warnock 2016
Alan Stubbs June 2016–

LATEST SEQUENCES

Longest Sequence of League Wins: 9, 2.2.1982 – 6.3.1982.

Longest Sequence of League Defeats: 8, 7.4.1956 – 18.8.1956.

Longest Sequence of League Draws: 6, 13.10.1969 – 22.11.1969.

Longest Sequence of Unbeaten League Matches: 18, 13.10.1969 – 7.2.1970.

Longest Sequence Without a League Win: 21, 9.5.2004 – 20.11.2004.

Successive Scoring Runs: 30 from 3.4.1954.

Successive Non-scoring Runs: 6 from 21.8.2004.

TEN YEAR LEAGUE RECORD

		P	W	D	L	F	A	Pts	Pos
2006-07	FL 1	46	13	9	24	58	75	38	23
2007-08	FL 2	46	21	11	14	62	58	64*	9
2008-09	FL 2	46	21	12	13	60	46	58†	14
2009-10	FL 2	46	21	10	15	55	52	73	5
2010-11	FL 2	46	17	15	14	75	60	66	9
2011-12	FL 2	46	18	13	15	67	63	67	10
2012-13	FL 2	46	24	7	15	74	59	79	2
2013-14	FL 1	46	24	14	8	86	58	86	4
2014-15	FL C	46	11	16	19	46	67	46‡	21
2015-16	FL C	46	13	10	23	53	71	49	21

*10 pts deducted; †17 pts deducted; ‡3 pts deducted.

DID YOU KNOW ?

Daniel Nardiello has the distinction of being the first player to score a Football League goal at Rotherham United's New York Stadium. Daniel netted the opener from the penalty spot in the Millers' 3-0 victory over Burton Albion in August 2012.

ROTHERHAM UNITED – FL CHAMPIONSHIP 2015–16 LEAGUE RECORD

Match No.	Date	Venue	Opponents	Result	H/T Score	Lg Pos.	Goalscorers	Attendance
1	Aug 8	H	Milton Keynes D	L	1-4	1-3	24	Derbyshire [13]	9869
2	15	A	Nottingham F	L	1-2	1-1	23	Collins [13]	19,885
3	18	H	Preston NE	D	0-0	0-0	22		9078
4	22	A	QPR	L	2-4	0-1	24	Clarke-Harris [72], Thorpe [88]	15,009
5	29	H	Fulham	L	1-3	0-2	24	Clarke-Harris [72]	8839
6	Sept 12	A	Charlton Ath	D	1-1	1-0	24	Rawson [38]	15,220
7	15	A	Brighton & HA	L	1-2	0-1	24	Clarke-Harris [71]	21,397
8	19	H	Cardiff C	W	2-1	1-1	23	Odjidja-Ofoe (pen) [43], Connolly (og) [90]	8935
9	26	A	Birmingham C	W	2-0	1-0	20	Derbyshire [32], Andreu [64]	17,307
10	Oct 2	H	Burnley	L	1-2	0-1	21	Ward, G [75]	9752
11	17	A	Brentford	L	1-2	0-1	23	Mattock [46]	10,293
12	20	H	Reading	D	1-1	0-1	23	Collins [48]	9071
13	23	H	Sheffield W	L	1-2	0-0	23	Thorpe [90]	11,658
14	31	A	Derby Co	L	0-3	0-2	24		30,172
15	Nov 3	A	Middlesbrough	L	0-1	0-1	24		21,144
16	7	H	Ipswich T	L	2-5	0-3	24	Barker [56], Derbyshire [59]	9162
17	21	A	Leeds U	W	1-0	0-0	23	Newell [54]	25,802
18	28	H	Bristol C	W	3-0	2-0	23	Clarke-Harris 2 (1 pen) [9, 27 (p)], Frecklington [75]	8949
19	Dec 5	A	Wolverhampton W	L	1-2	1-2	23	Newell [18]	9759
20	11	A	Blackburn R	L	0-1	0-1	23		13,054
21	15	A	Huddersfield T	L	0-2	0-1	23		12,763
22	19	H	Hull C	W	2-0	1-0	22	Frecklington (pen) [28], Newell [57]	10,355
23	26	H	Bolton W	W	4-0	0-0	21	Ward, G [56], Ward, D [74], Newell [80], Clarke-Harris [86]	11,315
24	29	A	Fulham	L	1-4	1-2	21	Rawson [20]	16,333
25	Jan 2	A	Preston NE	L	1-2	1-0	21	Andreu [35]	12,027
26	12	H	Brighton & HA	W	2-0	1-0	20	Ward, D [45], Derbyshire [86]	9269
27	16	H	QPR	L	0-3	0-0	21		9594
28	23	A	Cardiff C	D	2-2	1-1	21	Pilkington (og) [49], Newell [44]	14,885
29	30	H	Charlton Ath	L	1-4	1-2	21	Burke [11]	9227
30	Feb 6	A	Bolton W	L	1-2	1-1	22	Burke [43]	14,641
31	13	H	Birmingham C	D	0-0	0-0	22		11,018
32	20	A	Burnley	L	0-2	0-1	22		15,849
33	23	A	Reading	L	0-1	0-0	22		13,504
34	27	H	Brentford	W	2-1	1-1	22	Derbyshire [29], Ward, D [71]	8534
35	Mar 5	A	Sheffield W	W	1-0	1-0	22	Derbyshire [21]	28,912
36	8	H	Middlesbrough	W	1-0	0-0	22	Frecklington [88]	10,783
37	12	A	Derby Co	D	3-3	0-0	22	Ward, D [83], Best 2 [85, 90]	11,163
38	19	A	Ipswich T	W	1-0	1-0	20	Best [44]	20,318
39	Apr 2	H	Leeds U	W	2-1	1-0	20	Frecklington [27], Halford (pen) [90]	11,418
40	5	A	Bristol C	D	1-1	1-0	21	Derbyshire [12]	15,248
41	9	A	Milton Keynes D	W	4-0	2-0	21	Derbyshire [1], Best (pen) [17], Broadfoot [54], Smallwood [79]	13,048
42	16	H	Nottingham F	D	0-0	0-0	21		11,503
43	19	H	Huddersfield T	D	1-1	1-1	20	Halford [10]	10,292
44	23	A	Wolverhampton W	D	0-0	0-0	19		18,757
45	30	H	Blackburn R	L	0-1	0-1	20		11,035
46	May 7	A	Hull C	L	1-5	1-4	21	Frecklington [16]	18,670

Final League Position: 21

GOALSCORERS

League (53): Derbyshire 8, Clarke-Harris 6 (1 pen), Frecklington 5 (1 pen), Newell 5, Best 4 (1 pen), Ward, D 4, Andreu 2, Burke 2, Collins 2, Halford 2 (1 pen), Rawson 2, Thorpe 2, Ward, G 2, Barker 1, Broadfoot 1, Mattock 1, Odjidja-Ofoe 1 (1 pen), Smallwood 1, own goals 2.
FA Cup (0).
Capital One Cup (2): Bowery 1, Green 1.

Roos K 4	Halford G 19 + 2	Thorpe T 5 + 2	Collins D 21 + 3	Newell J 28 + 7	Maguire C 6 + 8	Smallwood R 42 + 1	Ward G 33 + 7	White A 3 + 5	Ward D 22 + 12	Derbyshire M 28 + 7	Green P 14 + 10	Frecklington L 26 + 1	Bowery J 2 + 5	Buxton L 18 + 2	Mattock J 35	Clarke-Harris J 19 + 16	Ledesma E 1 + 4	Collin A 1	Richardson F 13 + 4	Camp L 41	Rawson F 15 + 1	Odjidja-Ofoe V 4	Bailey-King D — + 1	Andreu T 10 + 1	Broadfoot K 31 + 1	Toffolo H 6 + 1	Barker B 1 + 3	Kelly S 13 + 2	Best L 10 + 6	Hyam L 2 + 3	Facey S 5	Belaid A 3	Burke C 5	Becchio L — + 2	Shinnie A 1 + 2	Wood R 13	Doyley L 3	Thomas J 3 + 3	Match No.
1	2	3	4	5	6^2	7	8^1	9^3	10	11	12	13	14																										1
1	4	14	3	9	6^1	8^3			12	13	10			7	11^2	2	5																						2
1	3		4	9	7^3	6			12		11	14	8	10^1	2	5^2	13																						3
1	3	12	4	5	14	7^1	8^3	13		11		6			2	10	9^2																						4
	3		4	9^1	6^2	8	13	12		11	7			2		10	14	1	5^1																				5
			4	9	12	8			14	13	7^3			2	5	11^2				1	3	6		10^1															6
	14		4	8	6	7^2		9^1	12	11^3				2	5	13				1	3	10																	7
			4	8	13	7			10^2					2	5	11	12			1	3	6		9^1															8
			4	8	14	6	13		12	10^2				2	5	11^1				1	3	7		9^3															9
			4	8^1	12	6	7		13	11				2	5	10				1	3^1			9^2	14														10
			4		6^1	8	12	9^2	10	7		13		2	5^3	11	14			1	3																		11
	6		4		13	7			10^1	8		12	2		11					1	3			9^2		5													12
	6		4		12	7			10	8^2		13	2		11					1	3			9^1		5													13
			4	7^2		6	9	13	8		12			2	5	11				1					3	10^1													14
	6		4	12	14	7			10^3	8		13			11^2				2	1	3			9^1		5													15
	6^2		4			12	7		11	10	8^3			14		2	1	3			5^1	9																	16
		14		9^2		8	6	13				7		2	5^3	11^1				1					4	12		3	10^1										17
		5		9^3		8	6	10				7^2		2		11				1	12				4		14	3^1	13										18
			4	9^1		8	6^2	10^1	12			7		2		11				1					3	5	14		13										19
			4	10^2		6	8		12			9		2	5	11				1					3		13		7^1										20
			4	9^1		8^2	6	10	13			7		2	5	11				1					3				12										21
				9		7	6	11^1				10^2		12	5	13				1	3		14		4			2^3	8										22
				9^2		7	6	11^1	13	8					5	12			2	1	3		10		4														23
				9		8	6	11^3	14	13	7				5	12			2^2	1	3		10^1		4														24
		14		9		8	6	11			12	7^2			5	13				1	3^1		10^3		4					2									25
				9		8	6	11^1	10	7					5	12	13			1					3						2^2	4							26
				9		8	6	10^2	11^1	7					5	12	13			1					3						2	4							27
		14		10^3		7	9	11^1		6					5	13				1					3						2	4^2	8	12					28
				10^2		7	9	11		6^1					5	13				1	3				4						2		8^3	12	14				29
	13			9		7	8	11^3	14	12					5	13				2	1				3							6^2		10^3	4				30
	13			9^2		8	14	11	10^3	7					5^1	12				2	1				3							6^1			4^1				31
2				9		8	12	10^2		7					11					5	1				4			14				6^1		13		3^3			32
6^2				9		8	10		14	7^1					5^1	11^3				2	1				3			13						4		12			33
6				8	13			12	11	14		7^1			5					2	1				3			10^2						4		9^3			34
6			12	9		7^3		11^2	10^1		8				5					2	1				3			14	13					4		9^2			35
6^1				8				13	11	7					5^1	14				2^1	1				3			12	10^3					4					36
		4	14	8	12			10	9^1	6^2	7				5	13					1				3			2	13									11^3	37
6			12	9		7		10^2		8					5	13					1				4			2	11^1								3		38
6			13	8^3	7^1			12	$10^■$	9					5					14	1				3			2	11^2								4		39
6				9	7			12	10^1	8					5						1				3			2	11					4					40
6			12	9	7			13	10^3	8^1					5						1				3			2	11^2					4		14			41
6			13	9	7			12	10^1	8^2					5						1				3			2	11					4					42
6				9	7			11	10^1	8					5						1				3			2	12					4					43
6				9	7			10		8					5^2	13				12	1				3			2	11^1					4					44
6				9	7			14	10^1	8^3					5^2					12	1				3			2	11					4		13			45
6				9	7			10^2	14	8^1					11^3				5	1		13			3			2	12					4					46

FA Cup
Third Round — Leeds U — (a) — 0-2

Capital One Cup
First Round — Cambridge U — (h) — 1-0
Second Round — Norwich C — (h) — 1-2

SCUNTHORPE UNITED

FOUNDATION

The year of foundation for Scunthorpe United has often been quoted as 1910, but the club can trace its history back to 1899 when Brumby Hall FC, who played on the Old Showground, consolidated their position by amalgamating with some other clubs and changing their name to Scunthorpe United. The year 1910 was when that club amalgamated with North Lindsey United as Scunthorpe and Lindsey United. The link is Mr W. T. Lockwood whose chairmanship covers both years.

Glanford Park, Jack Brownsword Way, Scunthorpe, North Lincolnshire DN15 8TD.

Telephone: (01724) 840 139.

Fax: (01724) 857 986.

Ticket Office: (01724) 747 670.

Website: www.scunthorpe-united.co.uk

Email: receptionist@scunthorpe-united.co.uk

Ground Capacity: 9,144.

Record Attendance: 23,935 v Portsmouth, FA Cup 4th rd, 30 January 1954 (at Old Showground); 9,077 v Manchester U, League Cup 3rd rd, 22 September 2010 (at Glanford Park).

Pitch Measurements: 102.5m × 66m (112yd × 72yd).

Chairman: Peter Swann.

Chief Executive: James Rodwell.

Manager: Graham Alexander.

Assistant Manager: Nick Daws.

Physio: Joe Sharp.

Colours: Claret and light blue striped shirts, claret shorts, light blue socks with claret trim.

Year Formed: 1899.

Turned Professional: 1912.

Previous Names: Amalgamated first with Brumby Hall then North Lindsey United to become Scunthorpe and Lindsey United, 1910; 1958, Scunthorpe United.

Club Nickname: 'The Iron'.

Grounds: 1899, Old Showground; 1988, Glanford Park.

First Football League Game: 19 August 1950, Division 3 (N), v Shrewsbury T (h) D 0–0 – Thompson; Barker, Brownsword; Allen, Taylor, McCormick; Mosby, Payne, Gorin, Rees, Boyes.

Record League Victory: 8–1 v Luton T, Division 3, 24 April 1965 – Sidebottom; Horstead, Hemstead; Smith, Neale, Lindsey; Bramley (1), Scott, Thomas (5), Mahy (1), Wilson (1). 8–1 v Torquay U (a), Division 3, 28 October 1995 – Samways; Housham, Wilson, Ford (1), Knill (1), Hope (Nicholson), Thornber, Bullimore (Walsh), McFarlane (4) (Young), Eyre (2), Paterson.

HONOURS

League Champions: FL 1 – 2006–07; Division 3N – 1957–58. *Runners-up:* FL 2 – 2004–05, 2013–14.

FA Cup: 5th rd – 1958, 1970.

League Cup: 4th rd – 2010.

League Trophy: Runners-up: 2009.

sky SPORTS FACT FILE

Scunthorpe United won the Midland League title for the first time in 1926–27, setting a new league record by finishing 11 points ahead of their nearest challengers. During the season United achieved a club record victory when they defeated Sutton Town 10-0 with centre-forward and club captain Ernest Simms netting six goals.

Record Cup Victory: 9–0 v Boston U, FA Cup 1st rd, 21 November 1953 – Malan; Hubbard, Brownsword; Sharpe, White, Bushby; Mosby (1), Haigh (3), Whitfield (2), Gregory (1), Mervyn Jones (2).

Record Defeat: 0–8 v Carlisle U, Division 3 (N), 25 December 1952.

Most League Points (2 for a win): 66, Division 3 (N), 1956–57, 1957–58.

Most League Points (3 for a win): 91, FL 1, 2006–07.

Most League Goals: 88, Division 3 (N), 1957–58.

Highest League Scorer in Season: Barrie Thomas, 31, Division 2, 1961–62.

Most League Goals in Total Aggregate: Steve Cammack, 110, 1979–81, 1981–86.

Most League Goals in One Match: 5, Barrie Thomas v Luton T, Division 3, 24 April 1965.

Most Capped Player: Grant McCann, 11 (39), Northern Ireland.

Most League Appearances: Jack Brownsword, 597, 1950–65.

Youngest League Player: Hakeeb Adelakun, 16 years 201 days Tranmere R, 29 December 2012.

Record Transfer Fee Received: £2,500,000 from Celtic for Gary Hooper, August 2010.

Record Transfer Fee Paid: £700,000 to Hibernian for Rob Jones, July 2009.

Football League Record: 1950 Elected to Division 3 (N); 1958–64 Division 2; 1964–68 Division 3; 1968–72 Division 4; 1972–73 Division 3; 1973–83 Division 4; 1983–84 Division 3; 1984–92 Division 4; 1992–99 Division 3; 1999–2000 Division 2; 2000–04 Division 3; 2004–05 FL 2; 2005–07 FL 1; 2007–08 FL C; 2008–09 FL 1; 2009–11 FL C; 2011–13 FL 1; 2013–14 FL 2; 2014– FL 1.

MANAGERS

Harry Allcock 1915–53
(Secretary-Manager)
Tom Crilly 1936–37
Bernard Harper 1946–48
Leslie Jones 1950–51
Bill Corkhill 1952–56
Ron Suart 1956–58
Tony McShane 1959
Bill Lambton 1959
Frank Soo 1959–60
Dick Duckworth 1960–64
Fred Goodwin 1964–66
Ron Ashman 1967–73
Ron Bradley 1973–74
Dick Rooks 1974–76
Ron Ashman 1976–81
John Duncan 1981–83
Allan Clarke 1983–84
Frank Barlow 1984–87
Mick Buxton 1987–91
Bill Green 1991–93
Richard Money 1993–94
David Moore 1994–96
Mick Buxton 1996–97
Brian Laws 1997–2004; 2004–06
Nigel Adkins 2006–10
Ian Baraclough 2010–11
Alan Knill 2011–12
Brian Laws 2012–13
Russ Wilcox 2013–14
Mark Robins 2014–16
Nick Daws 2016
Graham Alexander March 2016–

LATEST SEQUENCES

Longest Sequence of League Wins: 7, 27.1.2007 – 3.3.2007.
Longest Sequence of League Defeats: 8, 29.11.1997 – 20.1.1998.
Longest Sequence of League Draws: 6, 2.1.1984 – 25.2.1984.
Longest Sequence of Unbeaten League Matches: 28, 23.11.2013 – 21.4.2014.
Longest Sequence Without a League Win: 14, 22.3.1975 – 6.9.1975.
Successive Scoring Runs: 24 from 13.1.2007.
Successive Non-scoring Runs: 7 from 19.4.1975.

TEN YEAR LEAGUE RECORD

		P	W	D	L	F	A	Pts	Pos
2006-07	FL 1	46	26	13	7	73	35	91	1
2007-08	FL C	46	11	13	22	46	69	46	23
2008-09	FL 1	46	22	10	14	82	63	76	6
2009-10	FL C	46	14	10	22	62	84	52	20
2010-11	FL C	46	12	6	28	43	87	42	24
2011-12	FL 1	46	10	22	14	55	59	52	18
2012-13	FL 1	46	13	9	24	49	73	48	21
2013-14	FL 2	46	20	21	5	68	44	81	2
2014-15	FL 1	46	14	14	18	62	75	56	16
2015-16	FL 1	46	21	11	14	60	47	74	7

DID YOU KNOW ?

Scunthorpe United was the first Football League club to have a cantilever stand. The East Side at their former home the Old Show Ground had 2,350 seats and was designed and built in 1958 by a local steel construction company.

SCUNTHORPE UNITED – FOOTBALL LEAGUE ONE 2015–16 LEAGUE RECORD

Match No.	Date		Venue	Opponents	Result		H/T Score	Lg Pos.	Goalscorers	Attendance
1	Aug	8	A	Burton Alb	L	1-2	0-0	18	Goode [90]	4064
2		15	H	Crewe Alex	W	2-0	1-0	7	Madden 2 [10, 65]	3188
3		19	A	Wigan Ath	L	0-3	0-2	15		7794
4		22	H	Millwall	D	0-0	0-0	14		3382
5		29	A	Colchester U	D	2-2	2-1	15	van Veen [7], Madden [18]	3019
6	Sept	5	H	Blackpool	L	0-1	0-1	19		3313
7		12	H	Coventry C	W	1-0	0-0	16	Madden [79]	3746
8		19	H	Rochdale	L	1-2	0-0	20	Wallace [76]	2958
9		26	A	Southend U	L	1-2	1-1	21	McSheffrey [8]	5708
10		29	H	Walsall	L	0-1	0-1	21		2596
11	Oct	3	H	Fleetwood T	W	1-0	0-0	20	Madden [68]	3095
12		10	A	Oldham Ath	W	4-2	2-2	15	McSheffrey [10], Rowe [35], Madden [69], van Veen [84]	4002
13		17	H	Shrewsbury T	W	2-1	0-1	12	Laird [58], Madden (pen) [74]	3558
14		20	A	Gillingham	L	1-2	0-0	16	Laird [53]	4823
15		24	A	Chesterfield	W	3-0	0-0	12	Madden 2 (1 pen) [56 (p), 78], McSheffrey [63]	6340
16		31	H	Barnsley	W	2-0	2-0	9	Hopper [6], McSheffrey [41]	4147
17	Nov	14	A	Swindon T	L	1-2	0-0	12	Clarke [73]	6957
18		21	H	Bradford C	L	0-2	0-1	14		4865
19		24	A	Bury	W	2-1	1-0	13	Madden (pen) [12], Williams [86]	2483
20		28	H	Peterborough U	L	0-4	0-1	14		3790
21	Dec	12	A	Port Vale	D	1-1	1-1	14	King [36]	3983
22		19	H	Sheffield U	L	0-1	0-0	16		5150
23		26	A	Doncaster R	W	1-0	1-0	14	Madden [20]	8744
24		28	H	Rochdale	D	1-1	1-1	14	Mirfin [33]	3860
25	Jan	2	A	Wigan Ath	D	1-1	1-1	15	Williams [20]	4102
26		16	A	Blackpool	L	0-5	0-3	16		6004
27		23	H	Colchester U	W	3-0	0-0	15	Hopper [60], Madden 2 [62, 68]	3332
28		30	A	Coventry C	W	2-1	1-0	13	Hopper [9], Wallace [62]	11,138
29	Feb	13	A	Southend U	W	1-0	1-0	13	Madden [11]	3550
30		16	A	Millwall	W	2-0	1-0	12	McSheffrey [17], O'Brien [90]	8036
31		20	A	Fleetwood T	L	1-2	0-2	13	Madden (pen) [70]	3098
32		27	H	Oldham Ath	D	1-1	0-0	14	Wootton [88]	4180
33	Mar	1	A	Walsall	D	0-0	0-0	14		3868
34		5	H	Gillingham	D	0-0	0-0	15		3355
35		8	H	Doncaster R	W	2-0	1-0	11	Hopper [7], Mirfin [58]	4887
36		12	A	Shrewsbury T	D	2-2	0-1	13	Wootton [69], Madden [78]	5028
37		19	H	Chesterfield	D	1-1	1-0	13	Madden [18]	3871
38		25	A	Barnsley	D	0-0	0-0	13		10,122
39		28	H	Swindon T	W	6-0	2-0	10	Townsend [27], Clarke [44], Adelakun [48], Hopper 2 [52, 76], Madden [62]	3534
40	Apr	2	A	Bradford C	L	0-1	0-0	12		17,873
41		9	H	Burton Alb	W	1-0	0-0	9	Bishop [60]	3888
42		16	A	Crewe Alex	W	3-2	1-1	10	Williams 2 [43, 75], Adelakun [64]	3852
43		19	H	Bury	W	2-1	1-0	10	Williams [19], Wootton [53]	3188
44		23	A	Peterborough U	W	2-0	0-0	8	Santos (og) [51], Hopper [76]	5065
45		30	H	Port Vale	W	1-0	0-0	7	Madden [61]	7275
46	May	8	A	Sheffield U	W	2-0	1-0	7	Hopper [39], Madden [64]	21,445

Final League Position: 7

GOALSCORERS

League (60): Madden 20 (4 pens), Hopper 8, McSheffrey 5, Williams 5, Wootton 3, Adelakun 2, Clarke 2, Laird 2, Mirfin 2, van Veen 2, Wallace 2, Bishop 1, Goode 1, King 1, O'Brien 1, Rowe 1, Townsend 1, own goal 1.
FA Cup (5): Madden 2, Adelakun 1, King 1, own goal 1.
Capital One Cup (1): Madden 1 (pen).
Johnstone's Paint Trophy (1): Goode 1.

Daniels L 39	Clarke J 29+4	King J 25+11	Canavan N 10	Wiseman S 21+3	Bishop N 42	Williams L 21+7	Dawson S 22+1	Laird S 25+7	Madden P 46	Hopper T 29+5	McSheffrey G 15+11	Goode C 6+4	Anyon J 7+1	Mirfin D 35	McAllister S 5+6	van Veen K 10+10	Henderson D 5+8	Adelakun H 9+12	Ness J 24+3	Wootton K 3+17	Wallace M 33	Syers D —+3	Lolley J 3+3	Rowe T 14	Townsend C 20	O'Brien J 7+2	Luer G 1+3	Vose D —+2	Sutton L —+1	Match No.
1^1	2	3	4^1	5	6	7^2	8	9	10	11^3	12	13	14																	1
	2		4	5^1	8			9	11	10^1	7^2			1	3	6	12	13	14											2
	2		4	5^2	8	6^1		9	10	11				1	3	14	12	7^3												3
	2		4		8			5	9	13	12			3	1	7	11^2	10^3	6^1	14										4
	5	3		7				8	11	14				4^3	1	6	9^1	10^2	12	2	13									5
1		3		5^2	8			9	10	11^2	13	2		6	7^3	14	12		4											6
1	2	3			6			5	8	11^3	10			12	9^2	13	7^1			14	4									7
1	2	3			6			5	8	11^2	10			9^3	12	13	7^1			14	4									8
1	2	3			6			5	9	11^3	10^1			12	14	7	13		4		8^2									9
1	4	2		7				5	11	10	12			6^2	14	8^1	13	3		9^3										10
1	7	2		8				5	11	13	9			4	12	3^1	10^2	6												11
1	7	2		6				5	11	8^1	9^2			3	12	13	4	10												12
1	8	2		6				5	9	10^2	11^1			3	14	13	4	12	7^3											13
1	8	2		6	12			5	9^1	10^2	11^3			3	13		4	14	7											14
1	12	7	2^1	6	13			5	9	11^3	10^1			3			4	14	8											15
1	7	2		6	13			5	9	10^1	11^2			3		12	4	8												16
	2	7	4	5		13			10	9				1	3	6^2	11^3	12	14		8^1									17
1	7		2^2		6	12		5	9	11^3				3	13	10^1	14		8		4									18
1	13	7	3	2	6	9		5^1	8	12				4^2	11	10														19
1	2	7	4		6	9		5	8	12				3^1	13	14	11^2		10^3											20
1	6		4	2	7	9^2		5	10					3		11^1	13	12			8									21
1	7^1		4	2	6^1	9		5	8					3		13	12	14	11^2		10									22
1	2^1	8	4	14	6	9	7^2	5	10	13				3^3					12		11									23
1	7	3	2		6	8^1	9^1	5	11					4		13	12				10									24
1	5	3			6	10	7	2	8					4		11^1			9		12									25
1	2^2	13		9	11	8	5	7						3		10^1			6		12		4							26
1	13		2		8	11^2	6		9	10^3				3			14		7^1		12		4		5					27
1	14	13	2		6	9^2	7^3		10	11				12			3		8		4				5					28
1	12		2^2		6	9^2	8	14	11	10				13			3		7		4				5^1					29
1	2			7	6		9^3		11^2	10^1				3			8	14			4				5	12	13			30
1	2	12			6		9^2	8	11^1	10^3				3			7				4				5	13	14			31
1	2				6		9^3	11	8^2	12				3			7	14			4				5	10^1	13			32
1	2^1	14		7	6		9		12	13				3			8				4				5	11^2	10^3			33
1	2				6		9^1	11	8^2	13				3			7	12			4				5	10^3	14			34
1	2	12			6	7^3		11	8^2	14				3			9	13			4				5	10^1				35
1	2	9^1		7	13			11	10^2					3		6	12				4				5	8				36
1	2	6^3		13	9			11	8^2	14				3			7^1	12			4				5	10				37
1	2	13		6^2	9	14	11	8						3			12	7^2			4				5	10^1				38
1	2	12		9	6^1			11	8^1					3			10	7^2	13		4				5			14		39
1	2			8	6^1		14	10	11^2					4^3			9	7	12		3				5	13				40
	2^2	13		7		9	12	14	10	11^1				1	3	6	8^3				4				5					41
	2	13		7		9	8^2	14	11	10^3				1	3	6^1	12				4				5					42
1	2	12		7		9	8		11					3		6	10^1				4				5					43
1	2	13		7		9^2	8	14	11	12				3		6^3	10^1				4				5					44
1	2	12				9^1	7	14	11	10^2				3		6^3	8	13			4				5					45
1	2				6		7		11	10	12			3^1		9	8				4				5					46

FA Cup

First Round	Southend U	(h)	2-1
Second Round	Leyton Orient	(a)	0-0
Replay	Leyton Orient	(h)	3-0
Third Round	Chelsea	(a)	0-2

Capital One Cup

First Round	Barnsley	(h)	1-1
(aet; Barnsley won 7-6 on penalties)			

Johnstone's Paint Trophy

First Round	Barnsley	(h)	1-2

SHEFFIELD UNITED

Bramall Lane Ground, Cherry Street, Bramall Lane, Sheffield, South Yorkshire S2 4SU.

Telephone: (01142) 537 200.

Fax: (0871) 663 2430.

Ticket Office: (01142) 537 200.

Website: www.sufc.co.uk

Email: info@sufc.co.uk

Ground Capacity: 32,275.

Record Attendance: 68,287 v Leeds U, FA Cup 5th rd, 15 February 1936.

Pitch Measurements: 100.5m × 67m (110yd × 73yd).

Co-Chairmen: Kevin McCabe, James Phipps.

Manager: Chris Wilder.

Assistant Manager: Alan Knill.

Physio: Ed Owen.

Colours: Red shirts with thin white stripes, red shorts with white trim, red socks with white trim.

Year Formed: 1889.

Turned Professional: 1889.

Club Nickname: 'The Blades'.

Ground: 1889, Bramall Lane.

HONOURS

League Champions: Division 1 – 1897–98; Division 2 – 1952–53; Division 4 – 1981–82.
Runners-up: Division 1 – 1896–97, 1899–1900; FL C – 2005–06; Division 2 – 1892–93, 1938–39, 1960–61, 1970–71, 1989–90; Division 3 – 1988–89.
FA Cup Winners: 1899, 1902, 1915, 1925.
Runners-up: 1901, 1936.
League Cup: semi-final – 2003, 2015.

First Football League Game: 3 September 1892, Division 2, v Lincoln C (h) W 4–2 – Lilley; Witham, Cain; Howell, Hendry, Needham (1); Wallace, Dobson, Hammond (3), Davies, Drummond.

Record League Victory: 10–0 v Burslem Port Vale (a), Division 2, 10 December 1892 – Howlett; Witham, Lilley; Howell, Hendry, Needham; Drummond (1), Wallace (1), Hammond (4), Davies (2), Watson (2). 10-0 v Burnley, Division 1 (h), 19 January 1929.

Record Cup Victory: 6–1 v Scarborough (a), FA Cup 1st qualifying rd, 5 October 1889 – Howlett; Stringer, Gilmartin, Mack, Hobson, Hudson, Galbraith (2), Robertson (1), Fraser (2), Duncan, Mosforth (1). 6–1 v Loughborough, FA Cup 4th qualifying rd, 6 December 1890. 6–1 v Lincoln C, League Cup, 22 August 2000 – Tracey; Uhlenbeek, Weber, Woodhouse (Ford), Murphy, Sandford, Devlin (pen), Ribeiro (Santos), Bent (3), Kelly (1) (Thompson), Jagielka, og (1).

Record Defeat: 0–13 v Bolton W, FA Cup 2nd rd, 1 February 1890.

Most League Points (2 for a win): 60, Division 2, 1952–53.

Most League Points (3 for a win): 96, Division 4, 1981–82.

Most League Goals: 102, Division 1, 1925–26.

Highest League Scorer in Season: Jimmy Dunne, 41, Division 1, 1930–31.

Most League Goals in Total Aggregate: Harry Johnson, 201, 1919–30.

Most League Goals in One Match: 5, Harry Hammond v Bootle, Division 2, 26 November 1892; 5, Harry Johnson v West Ham U, Division 1, 26 December 1927.

Most Capped Player: Billy Gillespie, 25, Northern Ireland.

Most League Appearances: Joe Shaw, 632, 1948–66.

Youngest League Player: Louis Reed, 16 years 257 days v Rotherham U, 8 April 2014.

Record Transfer Fee Received: £4,000,000 from Everton for Phil Jagielka, July 2007; £4,000,000 from Tottenham H for Kyle Naughton, July 2009; £4,000,000 from Tottenham H for Kyle Walker, July 2009.

Record Transfer Fee Paid: £4,000,000 to Everton for James Beattie, August 2007.

Football League Record: 1892 Elected to Division 2; 1893–1934 Division 1; 1934–39 Division 2; 1946–49 Division 1; 1949–53 Division 2; 1953–56 Division 1; 1956–61 Division 2; 1961–68 Division 1; 1968–71 Division 2; 1971–76 Division 1; 1976–79 Division 2; 1979–81 Division 3; 1981–82 Division 4; 1982–84 Division 3; 1984–88 Division 2; 1988–89 Division 3; 1989–90 Division 2; 1990–92 Division 1; 1992–94 FA Premier League; 1994–2004 Division 1; 2004–06 FL C; 2006–07 FA Premier League; 2007–11 FL C; 2011– FL 1.

LATEST SEQUENCES

Longest Sequence of League Wins: 8, 20.8.2005 – 27.9.2005.

Longest Sequence of League Defeats: 7, 19.8.1975 – 20.9.1975.

Longest Sequence of League Draws: 6, 6.5.2001 – 8.9.2001.

Longest Sequence of Unbeaten League Matches: 22, 2.9.1899 – 13.1.1900.

Longest Sequence Without a League Win: 19, 27.9.1975 – 7.2.1976.

Successive Scoring Runs: 34 from 30.3.1956.

Successive Non-scoring Runs: 6 from 4.12.1993.

MANAGERS

J. B. Wostinholm 1889–99
  (Secretary-Manager)
John Nicholson 1899–1932
Ted Davison 1932–52
Reg Freeman 1952–55
Joe Mercer 1955–58
Johnny Harris 1959–68
  (continued as General Manager to 1970)
Arthur Rowley 1968–69
Johnny Harris *(General Manager resumed Team Manager duties)* 1969–73
Ken Furphy 1973–75
Jimmy Sirrel 1975–77
Harry Haslam 1978–81
Martin Peters 1981
Ian Porterfield 1981–86
Billy McEwan 1986–88
Dave Bassett 1988–95
Howard Kendall 1995–97
Nigel Spackman 1997–98
Steve Bruce 1998–99
Adrian Heath 1999
Neil Warnock 1999–2007
Bryan Robson 2007–08
Kevin Blackwell 2008–10
Gary Speed 2010
Micky Adams 2010–11
Danny Wilson 2011–13
David Weir 2013
Nigel Clough 2013–15
Nigel Adkins 2015–16
Chris Wilder May 2016–

TEN YEAR LEAGUE RECORD

		P	W	D	L	F	A	Pts	Pos
2006-07	PR Lge	38	10	8	20	32	55	38	18
2007-08	FL C	46	17	15	14	56	51	66	9
2008-09	FL C	46	22	14	10	64	39	80	3
2009-10	FL C	46	17	14	15	62	55	65	8
2010-11	FL C	46	11	9	26	44	79	42	23
2011-12	FL 1	46	27	9	10	92	51	90	3
2012-13	FL 1	46	19	18	9	56	42	75	5
2013-14	FL 1	46	18	13	15	48	46	67	7
2014-15	FL 1	46	19	14	13	66	53	71	5
2015-16	FL 1	46	18	12	16	64	59	66	11

DID YOU KNOW

Sheffield United's Bramall Lane ground was also used as a venue for Yorkshire County Cricket matches until 1973 and was used for a Test match in July 1902 when England lost to the Australians by 143 runs. The ground has also staged five England international football matches.

SHEFFIELD UNITED – FOOTBALL LEAGUE ONE 2015–16 LEAGUE RECORD

Match No.	Date	Venue	Opponents	Result	H/T Score	Lg Pos.	Goalscorers	Attendance
1	Aug 8	A	Gillingham	L	0-4	0-2	24		7511
2	15	H	Chesterfield	W	2-0	1-0	12	Adams 2 [3, 46]	23,031
3	18	A	Peterborough U	W	3-1	1-0	7	Sammon 2 [15, 72], Baxter [85]	6526
4	22	H	Blackpool	W	2-0	0-0	4	Sharp [60], McNulty [72]	20,199
5	29	A	Swindon T	W	2-0	0-0	2	Collins [70], Sharp [75]	8614
6	Sept 12	H	Bury	L	1-3	0-0	5	Sharp (pen) [72]	20,708
7	15	H	Colchester U	L	2-3	0-2	5	Sharp (pen) [51], Woolford [61]	17,623
8	20	A	Bradford C	D	2-2	0-1	7	Meredith (og) [65], Sharp [70]	19,317
9	26	H	Doncaster R	W	3-1	2-1	6	Basham [17], Sammon [35], Sharp [79]	20,869
10	29	A	Burton Alb	D	0-0	0-0	6		5029
11	Oct 3	A	Port Vale	L	1-2	0-2	7	Done [90]	6822
12	10	H	Rochdale	W	3-2	2-1	6	Adams 2 [29, 40], Collins [74]	19,039
13	17	A	Oldham Ath	D	1-1	1-1	6	Done [30]	5743
14	20	H	Fleetwood T	W	3-0	1-0	5	Adams 2 [1, 64], Sharp [72]	17,879
15	24	H	Millwall	L	1-2	0-1	6	Baxter [70]	19,617
16	31	A	Crewe Alex	L	0-1	0-0	8		5227
17	Nov 14	H	Southend U	D	2-2	2-2	8	Baxter [36], Collins [45]	19,007
18	21	A	Walsall	D	1-1	0-0	11	Baxter [66]	5780
19	24	H	Shrewsbury T	L	2-4	1-3	12	Sammon [17], Hammond [65]	17,843
20	28	A	Barnsley	D	1-1	1-0	12	Basham [16]	13,571
21	Dec 13	H	Coventry C	W	1-0	0-0	11	Sharp [79]	18,074
22	19	A	Scunthorpe U	W	1-0	0-0	9	Sharp [50]	5150
23	28	H	Bradford C	W	3-1	1-0	8	Sharp [11], Sammon [59], Edgar [63]	24,777
24	Jan 2	H	Peterborough U	L	2-3	1-1	8	Sharp (pen) [32], Baldwin (og) [84]	22,302
25	12	A	Wigan Ath	D	3-3	0-2	7	Done 2 [68, 89], Sharp [75]	10,113
26	16	A	Colchester U	W	2-1	1-0	7	Sharp [20], Edgar [90]	4322
27	23	H	Swindon T	D	1-1	1-0	8	Sharp (pen) [8]	19,012
28	26	A	Blackpool	D	0-0	0-0	7		6296
29	Feb 6	H	Wigan Ath	L	0-2	0-0	10		20,304
30	13	A	Doncaster R	W	1-0	1-0	8	Adams [42]	10,168
31	16	A	Bury	L	0-1	0-1	9		3081
32	20	H	Port Vale	W	1-0	0-0	7	Sharp [50]	18,276
33	27	A	Rochdale	L	0-2	0-0	10		4210
34	Mar 1	H	Burton Alb	L	0-1	0-0	12		17,927
35	5	A	Fleetwood T	D	2-2	1-1	11	Nilsson (og) [29], Adams (pen) [90]	3479
36	12	H	Oldham Ath	W	3-0	2-0	11	Brayford [10], Flynn [21], Sharp [77]	18,334
37	19	A	Millwall	L	0-1	0-1	12		11,175
38	25	H	Crewe Alex	W	3-2	1-0	11	Adams [18], Flynn [61], Sharp [87]	18,539
39	30	A	Southend U	L	1-3	1-1	13	Hammond [34]	7004
40	Apr 2	A	Walsall	W	2-0	2-0	8	Basham [31], Sharp [36]	19,214
41	9	H	Gillingham	D	0-0	0-0	10		18,152
42	16	A	Chesterfield	W	3-0	2-0	9	Baptiste [4], Adams [35], Sharp [59]	9402
43	19	A	Shrewsbury T	W	2-1	1-0	8	Sharp [19], Adams [66]	5064
44	23	H	Barnsley	D	0-0	0-0	9		23,307
45	30	A	Coventry C	L	1-3	0-2	10	Sharp (pen) [58]	13,177
46	May 8	H	Scunthorpe U	L	0-2	0-1	11		21,445

Final League Position: 11

GOALSCORERS

League (64): Sharp 21 (5 pens), Adams 11 (1 pen), Sammon 5, Baxter 4, Done 4, Basham 3, Collins 3, Edgar 2, Flynn 2, Hammond 2, Baptiste 1, Brayford 1, McNulty 1, Woolford 1, own goals 3.
FA Cup (4): Baxter 1 (pen), Done 1, Freeman 1, Sammon 1.
Capital One Cup (1): Collins 1.
Johnstone's Paint Trophy (6): Baxter 2 (2 pens), Adams 1 (pen), Done 1, Flynn 1, Scougall 1.

Long G 31	Freeman K 17 + 2	Collins N 30	McEveley J 33 + 3	McFadzean C 1	Murphy J 1	Baxter J 18 + 6	Basham C 43 + 1	Woolford M 13 + 15	Sharp B 42 + 2	Adams C 29 + 7	Sammon C 15 + 12	Reed L 9 + 10	Scougall S 4 + 7	Howard M 15	Edgar D 35 + 1	Wallace J — + 4	Campbell-Ryce J 13 + 5	Wallace K 7 + 4	McNulty M 1 + 4	Alcock C 1 + 2	Higdon M — + 2	Flynn R 18 + 9	Coutts P 26 + 6	Kennedy T — + 1	Done M 25 + 6	McGahey H 5 + 2	Hammond D 30	Harris R 5	Brayford J 19	Calvert-Lewin D 3 + 6	Cuvelier F 4 + 5	Whiteman B 3 + 3	Baptiste A 10 + 1	Kelly G — + 1	Match No.
1	2	3	4	5	6	7^2	8	9^1	10	11^1	12	13	14																						1
	2	3	4			8^1	7	13	10	9^2	11	14	6^3		1	5	12																		2
	2	3^2	4			8	7		10^3	9	11		6^1		1	5	14	12	13																3
	2		4			7	8	13	10	9^3	11^1			1	3	14	6^2	5	12																4
	2	3	5			6	12	10	9	11^2	7		1	4		8^1				13	14														5
	2	4	5			7	9^1	10		11	8^3		1	3	6^2	12	14			13															6
	2	3	5			8	7	9^1	10	11^3	13		1	4	6^2	12	14																		7
	2	4	5^3			13	7	9^2	10	14	8		1	3	6^1	11	12																		8
12	4					8^2	7		10	14	11	13		1	3		5		2^1		9	6^3													9
	2	3				7	13	10^2		11		8	12	1	4		5	14			9^3	6^1													10
	2	4				7	6		10	12	11			1	3^3						8^1	9^2	13	14											11
	2	4	5^2			10	3		11	6		14	8^3	1			12					7^1			9	13									12
	2	3				9	6		11	8	12		7^2	1		13	5								10^1	4									13
	2	4				13	7	14	10	9				1							6^1	5			12		11^3	3	8^2						14
	2^3	4				12	7		10	11	13			1							6^1	5			14		9^2	3	8						15
		4				6	3		10	11	12		13	1							2	8^2			9^1		7	5							16
1	2	4				10	3		11	9						12	6					8^1					7	5							17
1	2	4				6	3		11^2	10	12		13									9^1			7		8	5							18
1	2	4^2	12			7^1	3		11	9	10	6^3		13								14			8	5									19
1	13	3	14			7	12	10						4^1	9^3							6	11^2		8	5	2								20
1		4	5			8	9^1	13		11^3		12		3							14	6	10^2		7		2								21
1		4	5^1			7^2	9	11			12	13		3			14					6	10^3		8		2								22
1		4	5			7	9^3	11^1		12				3		14					13	6	10^2		8		2								23
1		4	5^2			12	7	9	11	13	10^1			3								6			8		2								24
1	3	5^1				9	7	13	10	12				4		14					6^3		11		8^2		2								25
1	3	5				12	7	6	11^1		14			4							13	9^3	10^2		8		2								26
1	4	5				13	7^2	9	11			14		3							12	6^1	10		8^3		2								27
1	3	5				7^1		13	10^2	12^1	11			3							14	6^3			8		2								28
1	4	5				9^1	8^3		11	12	10^2			3		14						6	13		7		2								29
1	3	5				8	13	14		11		6^3		4			7^2					12			9		2	10^1							30
1		5				9	3		12	11		6^2		4			8^1					13			14		7	2	10^3						31
1		5				4	9	11	10^1		7			3							6^2	14	13		8^3		2		12						32
1		3				5	2^2	10	11		7	13		4							9^3	14	12				6		8^1						33
1	4	5^1				7		11	9					3								6^2	10				2	13	8^3	12	14				34
1						3		11	13					2							8	12	9		7		5	10^1	6^2		4				35
1		5						11	9^2		13			4							6	14	10		7^1		2	12		8^3	3				36
1		12						5	10	14	11^1			4							6	13	9		7		2	8^2			3^3				37
1		4				2		11	10^1		14										8	6^2	9	3	7^3		5	13		12					38
1		4				2	14	11	10	13											5	8^3	9	3	7^1			12		6^2					39
1		4				6	13	11	10^1					3							8	5	9^3	12	7			14			2		2^2		40
1		4				6	10	11						3							8	5	9	7							2				41
1		4				6	14	10	11^1					3							8^3	7	9^2		5			13	12		2				42
1		3				5	13	11	10^1					4							8^2	6	7		9				12		2				43
1		4^3				6	13	10	11	14				3							8	5	9^2		7^1				12		2				44
1		4				5	12	10	11					3							8^2	6	9^3							7^1	2	14		—	45
1		4				6	8^3	11	10			14		3							5^2	9	7^1							13	12	2			46

FA Cup

First Round	Worcester C	(h)	3-0
Second Round	Oldham Ath	(h)	1-0
Third Round	Manchester U	(a)	0-1

Capital One Cup

First Round	Morecambe	(a)	1-0
Second Round	Fulham	(a)	0-3

Johnstone's Paint Trophy

First Round	Hartlepool U	(a)	1-1
(aet; Sheffield U won 4-3 on penalties)			
Second Round	Notts Co	(h)	5-1
Northern Quarter-Final	Fleetwood T	(a)	0-0
(aet; Fleetwood T won 4-1 on penalties)			

SHEFFIELD WEDNESDAY

FOUNDATION

Sheffield being one of the principal centres of early Association Football, this club was formed as long ago as 1867 by the Sheffield Wednesday Cricket Club (formed 1825) and their colours from the start were blue and white. The inaugural meeting was held at the Adelphi Hotel and the original committee included Charles Stokes who was subsequently a founder member of Sheffield United.

Hillsborough Stadium, Sheffield, South Yorkshire S6 1SW.

Telephone: (0871) 995 1867.

Fax: (0114) 221 2122.

Ticket Office: (0871) 900 1867.

Website: www.swfc.co.uk

Email: footballenquiries@swfc.co.uk

Ground Capacity: 38,702.

Record Attendance: 72,841 v Manchester C, FA Cup 5th rd, 17 February 1934.

Pitch Measurements: 105m × 66m (115yd × 72yd).

Chairman: Dejphon Chansiri.

Vice-Chairman: Paul Aldridge.

Head Coach: Carlos Carvalhal.

Coaches: Lee Bullen, Joao Mario Oliveria, Bruno Lage, Jhony Conceicao.

Head Physio: Paul Smith.

Colours: Blue and white striped shirts, black shorts with white trim, white socks.

Year Formed: 1867 (fifth oldest League club).

Turned Professional: 1887.

Previous Name: The Wednesday until 1929.

Club Nickname: 'The Owls'.

Grounds: 1867, Highfield; 1869, Myrtle Road; 1877, Sheaf House; 1887, Olive Grove; 1899, Owlerton (since 1912 known as Hillsborough). Some games were played at Endcliffe in the 1880s. Until 1895 Bramall Lane was used for some games.

First Football League Game: 3 September 1892, Division 1, v Notts Co (a) W 1–0 – Allan; Tom Brandon (1), Mumford; Hall, Betts, Harry Brandon; Spiksley, Brady, Davis, Bob Brown, Dunlop.

Record League Victory: 9–1 v Birmingham, Division 1, 13 December 1930 – Brown; Walker, Blenkinsop; Strange, Leach, Wilson; Hooper (3), Seed (2), Ball (2), Burgess (1), Rimmer (1).

Record Cup Victory: 12–0 v Halliwell, FA Cup 1st rd, 17 January 1891 – Smith; Thompson, Brayshaw; Harry Brandon (1), Betts, Cawley (2); Winterbottom, Mumford (2), Bob Brandon (1), Woolhouse (5), Ingram (1).

HONOURS

League Champions: Division 1 – 1902–03, 1903–04, 1928–29, 1929–30; Division 2 – 1899–1900, 1925–26, 1951–52, 1955–56, 1958–59. *Runners-up:* Division 1 – 1960–61; Division 2 – 1949–50, 1983–84; FL 1 – 2011–12.

FA Cup Winners: 1896, 1907, 1935. *Runners-up:* 1890, 1966, 1993.

League Cup Winners: 1991. *Runners-up:* 1993.

European Competitions
Fairs Cup: 1961–62 (*qf*), 1963–64.
UEFA Cup: 1992–93.
Intertoto Cup: 1995.

sky SPORTS FACT FILE

Sheffield Wednesday set a club record in 1983–84 when they began the season with a 15-match unbeaten run in the old Division Two. The Owls won 11 and drew four of their opening games before eventually going down to defeat at Crystal Palace in November. They finished the campaign as runners-up to the champions Chelsea on goal difference.

Record Defeat: 0–10 v Aston Villa, Division 1, 5 October 1912.

Most League Points (2 for a win): 62, Division 2, 1958–59.

Most League Points (3 for a win): 93, FL 1, 2011–12.

Most League Goals: 106, Division 2, 1958–59.

Highest League Scorer in Season: Derek Dooley, 46, Division 2, 1951–52.

Most League Goals in Total Aggregate: Andrew Wilson, 199, 1900–20.

Most League Goals in One Match: 6, Doug Hunt v Norwich C, Division 2, 19 November 1938.

Most Capped Player: Nigel Worthington, 50 (66), Northern Ireland.

Most League Appearances: Andrew Wilson, 501, 1900–20.

Youngest League Player: Peter Fox, 15 years 269 days v Orient, 31 March 1973.

Record Transfer Fee Received: £3,000,000 from WBA for Chris Brunt, August 2007.

Record Transfer Fee Paid: £4,500,000 to Celtic for Paolo Di Canio, August 1997.

Football League Record: 1892 Elected to Division 1; 1899–1900 Division 2; 1900–20 Division 1; 1920–26 Division 2; 1926–37 Division 1; 1937–50 Division 2; 1950–51 Division 1; 1951–52 Division 2; 1952–55 Division 1; 1955–56 Division 2; 1956–58 Division 1; 1958–59 Division 2; 1959–70 Division 1; 1970–75 Division 2; 1975–80 Division 3; 1980–84 Division 2; 1984–90 Division 1; 1990–91 Division 2; 1991–92 Division 1; 1992–2000 FA Premier League; 2000–03 Division 1; 2003–04 Division 2; 2004–05 FL 1; 2005–10 FL C; 2010–12 FL 1; 2012– FL C.

LATEST SEQUENCES

Longest Sequence of League Wins: 9, 23.4.1904 – 15.10.1904.

Longest Sequence of League Defeats: 8, 9.9.2000 – 17.10.2000.

Longest Sequence of League Draws: 7, 15.3.2008 – 14.4.2008.

Longest Sequence of Unbeaten League Matches: 19, 10.12.1960 – 8.4.1961.

Longest Sequence Without a League Win: 20, 11.1.1975 – 30.8.1975.

Successive Scoring Runs: 40 from 14.11.1959.

Successive Non-scoring Runs: 8 from 8.3.1975.

MANAGERS

Arthur Dickinson 1891–1920
(Secretary-Manager)
Robert Brown 1920–33
Billy Walker 1933–37
Jimmy McMullan 1937–42
Eric Taylor 1942–58
(continued as General Manager to 1974)
Harry Catterick 1958–61
Vic Buckingham 1961–64
Alan Brown 1964–68
Jack Marshall 1968–69
Danny Williams 1969–71
Derek Dooley 1971–73
Steve Burtenshaw 1974–75
Len Ashurst 1975–77
Jackie Charlton 1977–83
Howard Wilkinson 1983–88
Peter Eustace 1988–89
Ron Atkinson 1989–91
Trevor Francis 1991–95
David Pleat 1995–97
Ron Atkinson 1997–98
Danny Wilson 1998–2000
Peter Shreeves *(Acting)* 2000
Paul Jewell 2000–01
Peter Shreeves 2001
Terry Yorath 2001–02
Chris Turner 2002–04
Paul Sturrock 2004–06
Brian Laws 2006–09
Alan Irvine 2010–11
Gary Megson 2011–12
Dave Jones 2012–13
Stuart Gray 2013–15
Carlos Carvalhal June 2015–

TEN YEAR LEAGUE RECORD

		P	W	D	L	F	A	Pts	Pos
2006-07	FL C	46	20	11	15	70	66	71	9
2007-08	FL C	46	14	13	19	54	55	55	16
2008-09	FL C	46	16	13	17	51	58	61	12
2009-10	FL C	46	11	14	21	49	69	47	22
2010-11	FL 1	46	16	10	20	67	67	58	15
2011-12	FL 1	46	28	9	9	81	48	93	2
2012-13	FL C	46	16	10	20	53	61	58	18
2013-14	FL C	46	13	14	19	63	65	53	16
2014-15	FL C	46	14	18	14	43	49	60	13
2015-16	FL C	46	19	17	10	66	45	74	6

DID YOU KNOW ?

Sheffield Wednesday hosted a World Cup qualifying tie in September 1973 when Northern Ireland played out a goalless draw against Bulgaria. The fixture, which was moved because of The Troubles, attracted an attendance of just 6,292 to Hillsborough.

SHEFFIELD WEDNESDAY – FL CHAMPIONSHIP 2015–16 LEAGUE RECORD

Match No.	Date	Venue	Opponents	Result	H/T Score	Lg Pos.	Goalscorers	Attendance
1	Aug 8	H	Bristol C	W 2-0	0-0	2	Lees [60], McGugan [71]	23,255
2	15	A	Ipswich T	L 1-2	1-1	10	Wallace [19]	20,081
3	19	H	Reading	D 1-1	0-0	9	Sougou [90]	20,247
4	22	A	Leeds U	D 1-1	1-0	9	Marco Matias [37]	22,597
5	29	H	Middlesbrough	L 1-3	0-1	15	Marco Matias [64]	20,976
6	Sept 12	A	Burnley	L 1-3	1-1	19	Nuhiu [20]	17,277
7	15	A	Bolton W	D 0-0	0-0	18		14,438
8	19	H	Fulham	W 3-2	2-1	14	Forestieri [13], Lees [37], Turner [50]	18,706
9	26	A	Brentford	W 2-1	1-0	11	Nuhiu (pen) [37], Lucas Joao [90]	9756
10	Oct 3	H	Preston NE	W 3-1	1-0	10	Lee [45], Pudil [55], McGugan [90]	20,383
11	17	H	Hull C	D 1-1	1-0	9	Forestieri [28]	20,389
12	20	A	QPR	D 0-0	0-0	9		15,471
13	23	A	Rotherham U	W 2-1	0-0	9	Lucas Joao [46], Forestieri [50]	11,658
14	31	H	Nottingham F	W 1-0	0-0	8	Forestieri [68]	22,465
15	Nov 3	H	Brighton & HA	D 0-0	0-0	8		23,712
16	7	A	Charlton Ath	L 1-3	0-2	9	Forestieri [73]	16,267
17	21	H	Huddersfield T	W 3-1	0-0	8	Lucas Joao 2 [78, 90], Lee [83]	21,191
18	28	A	Blackburn R	D 2-2	1-2	8	Sougou [39], Lucas Joao [84]	15,837
19	Dec 6	H	Derby Co	D 0-0	0-0	7		19,252
20	12	A	Cardiff C	D 2-2	0-2	8	Forestieri [61], Bannan [76]	14,526
21	15	A	Milton Keynes D	L 1-2	0-1	9	Hooper [77]	11,422
22	20	H	Wolverhampton W	W 4-1	2-1	7	Forestieri 2 (1 pen) [20 (p), 25], Pudil [59], Hooper [90]	19,529
23	26	H	Birmingham C	W 3-0	2-0	7	Forestieri 2 [37, 48], Lee [39]	28,523
24	28	A	Middlesbrough	L 0-1	0-1	7		29,363
25	Jan 2	A	Fulham	W 1-0	1-0	7	Wallace [29]	19,263
26	12	H	Bolton W	W 3-2	1-1	7	Forestieri [14], Hooper 2 [52, 77]	20,757
27	16	H	Leeds U	W 2-0	0-0	6	Hooper 2 [47, 50]	23,909
28	23	A	Reading	D 1-1	1-0	6	Hooper [10]	18,972
29	Feb 2	H	Burnley	D 1-1	0-1	7	Lee [48]	19,762
30	6	A	Birmingham C	W 2-1	0-1	6	Hooper 2 [77, 79]	20,302
31	13	H	Brentford	W 4-0	3-0	5	Forestieri [12], Hooper [30], Lee [45], Lucas Joao [89]	20,921
32	20	A	Preston NE	L 0-1	0-0	6		16,923
33	23	H	QPR	D 1-1	0-0	5	Nuhiu [63]	19,233
34	26	A	Hull C	D 0-0	0-0	6		17,884
35	Mar 5	H	Rotherham U	L 0-1	0-1	6		28,912
36	8	A	Brighton & HA	D 0-0	0-0	6		26,128
37	12	A	Nottingham F	W 3-0	1-0	6	McGeady [30], Hooper [62], Marco Matias [85]	20,690
38	19	H	Charlton Ath	W 3-0	0-0	6	Lees [64], Forestieri [70], Ba (og) [77]	29,668
39	Apr 2	A	Huddersfield T	W 1-0	0-0	5	Forestieri [83]	15,469
40	5	H	Blackburn R	W 2-1	0-0	5	Henley (og) [51], Wallace [62]	21,803
41	9	H	Bristol C	L 1-4	0-3	6	Wallace [61]	15,854
42	16	H	Ipswich T	D 1-1	1-0	6	Forestieri [42]	25,082
43	19	H	Milton Keynes D	D 0-0	0-0	6		20,220
44	23	A	Derby Co	D 1-1	0-0	6	Bannan [69]	31,825
45	30	H	Cardiff C	W 3-0	0-0	6	Hooper 2 [64, 90], Peltier (og) [75]	31,843
46	May 7	A	Wolverhampton W	L 1-2	0-2	6	McGugan (pen) [90]	25,488

Final League Position: 6

GOALSCORERS

League (66): Forestieri 15 (1 pen), Hooper 13, Lucas Joao 6, Lee 5, Wallace 4, Lees 3, Marco Matias 3, McGugan 3 (1 pen), Nuhiu 3 (1 pen), Bannan 2, Pudil 2, Sougou 2, McGeady 1, Turner 1, own goals 3.
FA Cup (4): McGugan 2, Bannan 1, Nuhiu 1.
Capital One Cup (9): Lucas Joao 2, Hutchinson 1, Lee 1, McGugan 1, Nuhiu 1, Semedo 1, Sougou 1, Wallace 1.
Championship Play-Offs (3): Wallace 2, Lee 1.

Westwood K 34	Hunt J 33+1	Lees T 34	Loovens G 31	Helan J 6+14	Lopez A 14+8	Hutchinson S 25	Wallace R 34+6	McGugan L 5+8	Marco Matias A 9+8	Nuhiu A 22+19	Lucas Joao E 15+25	Lee K 40+3	Palmer L 13+2	Wildsmith J 8+1	Price L 4+1	Wiggins R 5+1	Sasso V 11+3	Sougou M 5+4	Bus S —+2	Semedo J 7+3	Pudil D 35+1	Forestieri F 35+1	Bannan B 35	Turner M 11	Hooper G 22+7	McGeady A 10+3	Bennett J 3	Stobbs J —+1	Match No.
	2³	3	4	5	6	7	8¹	9	10	11²	12	13	14																1
1¹	2	3	4	5	6	7²	8	9³	10	13	11	14			12														2
	2	3	4²		6	7	8	9³	10¹		11				1	5	12	13	14										3
12		3		13	14	6			10²	11			9	2	1	5	4	8¹		7³									4
	2	3			7³	6¹	8²		10	13	11		9		1	5	4	14			12								5
		3	4			7	8²		12	11	13	6	2	1							5	9	10¹						6
	2	3		14			8¹	6²	11³	13		7		1			12				5	10	9	4					7
1	2	3	13	8		6				11¹	12	7									5	10¹	9	4					8
1	2	3	12⁴	7		8			9²	11³	13	6									5¹		10	4					9
1	2	3	14			6	8²	12		11¹	13	7									5	9¹	10	4					10
1	2	3	13			8	6¹			12	11²	7									5	10	9	4					11
1		2	3			12	6²			11	13	14	5				8			10³	4	9¹	7						12
	2	3	4			8³	6			12	11²	7						13	14	5	10¹	9							13
	2	3	4	13		6				11¹	12	8								7²	5	10³	9	14					14
	2	3	4	13		7	6²			12	11¹	8								5	10	9							15
	2	3	4¹			8³	6	14		13		7					12			5	10	9		11²					16
	2	3	4	9³		6	13		11¹	12	7								8²	5	10			14					17
		3	4	9³		14			11¹	12	7	2					6²		8	5	10		13					18
			4	8	3	6			11¹	7	2								5	10	9	12							19
			4	12	8¹	6		14	11¹	7²	2								5	10	9	3	13						20
1	2		4		6²	12			11¹	13	7								8³	5	9	10	3	14					21
	2		4	12	3	6			13	10²	7								5	9¹	8		11					22
	2		4	12	3¹	6²	13		10	7		1	14						5	9¹	8	11							23
			4	10²	3¹		14	11	8	2	1	5	7			6³	13	12	9									24
			4	14		6³	11¹	13	8	2	1		3	12	5	9²	7	10											25
	2³		4	13		6	10¹	12	7	14	1	3	5	9¹	8	11													26
	2		4	13	8	6¹	12	7	1	3	14	5	10¹	9	11²														27
	2		4	13	6	8²	14	12	7	3	5	9²	10	11¹															28
	2		4	3	6²	11¹	12	7	5	9	8	10	13																29
1³	2	3	7²	6	13	14	12	4	5	10	8	11	9¹																30
	2	3	6³	13	11²	14	7	4	5	9	8	10¹	12																31
	2³	3	6	13	14	11²	12	7¹	4	5	9⁸	8	10																32
1		3	6	11	12	7	4	5	8	10	9¹																		33
1		3	13	8¹	12	14	7	2	10⁸	9	4	11²	6¹	5															34
1	2²	3	6	13	10	12	7	5	8	4	11	9¹																	35
		3	4	7	13	9¹	12	11²	6	2	8	10	5																36
		3	4	12	6²	13	14	7	2	5	10	8⁸	11³	9¹															37
1	2	3	4	13	8²	6¹	14	12	7	5	10	11	9³																38
1	2	3	4	8	6	14	12	13	7	10³	11¹	9²	5																39
1	2	3	4³	8	6¹	14	9	7	12	5	11²	10	13																40
		3	7²	12	14	11³	13	6	2	1	5	10	8	4	9¹														41
1	2	3	4	8¹	6	13	11²	7	5	10	9	12																	42
1	2	3	4	8²	6⁸	12	13	7	5	10	9	11¹																	43
1	2	3	4	14	8	12	13	7	5	10¹	9	11²	6³																44
1	2	3	4	13	7	14	12	10²	6	5¹	11³	8	9																45
			5	8	9	11¹	10	2	1	3	7	4	6	12															46

FA Cup

Third Round	Fulham	(h)	2-1
Fourth Round	Shrewsbury T	(a)	2-3
Fourth Round	Arsenal	(h)	3-0
Quarter-Final	Stoke C	(a)	0-2

Capital One Cup

First Round	Mansfield T	(h)	4-1
Second Round	Oxford U	(h)	1-0
Third Round	Newcastle U	(a)	1-0

Championship Play-Offs

Semi-Final 1st leg	Brighton & HA	(h)	2-0
Semi-Final 2nd leg	Brighton & HA	(a)	1-1
(Sheffield W won 3-1 on aggregate)			
Final	Hull C	(Wembley)	0-1

SHREWSBURY TOWN

FOUNDATION

Shrewsbury School having provided a number of the early
England and Wales international players it is not surprising that
there was a Town club as early as 1876 which won the Birmingham
Senior Cup in 1879. However, the present Shrewsbury Town club
was formed in 1886 and won the Welsh FA Cup as early as 1891.

Greenhous Meadow, Oteley Road, Shrewsbury,
Shropshire SY2 6ST.

Telephone: (01743) 289 177.

Fax: (01743) 246 942.

Ticket Office: (01743) 273 943.

Website: www.shrewsburytown.com

Email: info@shrewsburytown.co.uk

Ground Capacity: 9,875.

Record Attendance: 18,917 v Walsall, Division 3,
26 April 1961 (at Gay Meadow); 10,210 v Chelsea, League
Cup 4th rd, 28 October 2014 (at Greenhous Meadow).

Pitch Measurements: 105m × 68.5m (115yd × 75yd).

Chairman: Roland Wycherley.

Manager: Micky Mellon.

Chief Executive: Brian Caldwell.

Assistant Manager: Mike Jackson.

Physio: Chris Skitt.

HONOURS

League Champions: Division 3 –
1978–79; Third Division – 1993–94.
Runners-up: FL 2 – 2011–12, 2014–15;
Division 4 – 1974–75; Conference –
(3rd) 2003–04 *(promoted via play-offs).*

FA Cup: 6th rd – 1979, 1982.

League Cup: semi-final – 1961.

League Trophy: *Runners-up:* 1996.

Welsh Cup Winners: 1891, 1938, 1977,
1979, 1984, 1985.
Runners-up: 1931, 1948, 1980.

Colours: Blue and yellow striped shirts, blue shorts with yellow trim, blue socks with yellow trim.

Year Formed: 1886.

Turned Professional: 1896.

Club Nicknames: 'Town', 'Blues', 'Salop'. The name 'Salop' is a colloquialism for the county of Shropshire.
Since Shrewsbury is the only club in Shropshire, cries of 'Come on Salop' are frequently used!

Grounds: 1886, Old Racecourse Ground; 1889, Ambler's Field; 1893, Sutton Lane; 1895, Barracks
Ground; 1910, Gay Meadow; 2007, New Meadow (re-named ProStar Stadium 2008;
Greenhous Meadow 2010).

First Football League Game: 19 August 1950, Division 3 (N), v Scunthorpe U (a) D 0–0 – Egglestone;
Fisher, Lewis; Wheatley, Depear, Robinson; Griffin, Hope, Jackson, Brown, Barker.

Record League Victory: 7–0 v Swindon T, Division 3 (S), 6 May 1955 – McBride; Bannister, Skeech;
Wallace, Maloney, Candlin; Price, O'Donnell (1), Weigh (4), Russell, McCue (2); 7-0 v Gillingham, FL 2,
13 September 2008 – Daniels; Herd, Tierney, Davies (2), Jackson (1) (Langmead), Coughlan (1),
Cansdell-Sherriff (1), Thornton, Hibbert (1) (Hindmarch), Holt (pen), McIntyre (Ashton).

Record Cup Victory: 11–2 v Marine, FA Cup 1st rd, 11 November 1995 – Edwards; Seabury (Dempsey
(1)), Withe (1), Evans (1), Whiston (2), Scott (1), Woods, Stevens (1), Spink (3) (Anthrobus), Walton,
Berkley, (1 og).

sky SPORTS FACT FILE

In 2003–04 Shrewsbury Town won their place back in the Football League thanks
to their success from the penalty spot. The Shrews finished third in the
Conference and reached the play-off final by beating Barnet 5-3 on penalties
after the teams were level 2-2 over two legs. Shrewsbury drew 1-1 with Aldershot
Town in the final but again triumphed in the penalty shoot-out, going through 3-0.

Record Defeat: 1–8 v Norwich C, Division 3 (S), 13 September 1952; 1–8 v Coventry C, Division 3, 22 October 1963.

Most League Points (2 for a win): 62, Division 4, 1974–75.

Most League Points (3 for a win): 89, FL 2, 2014–15.

Most League Goals: 101, Division 4, 1958–59.

Highest League Scorer in Season: Arthur Rowley, 38, Division 4, 1958–59.

Most League Goals in Total Aggregate: Arthur Rowley, 152, 1958–65 (thus completing his League record of 434 goals).

Most League Goals in One Match: 5, Alf Wood v Blackburn R, Division 3, 2 October 1971.

Most Capped Player: Jimmy McLaughlin, 5 (12), Northern Ireland; Bernard McNally, 5, Northern Ireland.

Most League Appearances: Mickey Brown, 418, 1986–91; 1992–94; 1996–2001.

Youngest League Player: Graham French, 16 years 177 days v Reading, 30 September 1961.

Record Transfer Fee Received: £600,000 (rising to £1,500,000) from Manchester C for Joe Hart, May 2006.

Record Transfer Fee Paid: £170,000 to Nottingham F for Grant Holt, June 2008.

Football League Record: 1950 Elected to Division 3 (N); 1951–58 Division 3 (S); 1958–59 Division 4; 1959–74 Division 3; 1974–75 Division 4; 1975–79 Division 3; 1979–89 Division 2; 1989–94 Division 3; 1994–97 Division 2; 1997–2003 Division 3; 2003–04 Conference; 2004–12 FL 2; 2012–14 FL 1; 2014–15 FL 2; 2015– FL 1.

LATEST SEQUENCES

Longest Sequence of League Wins: 7, 28.10.1995 – 16.12.1995.

Longest Sequence of League Defeats: 11, 9.4.2003 – 14.8.2004. (Spread over 2 periods in Football League. 2003–04 season in Conference.)

Longest Sequence of League Draws: 6, 30.10.1963 – 14.12.1963.

Longest Sequence of Unbeaten League Matches: 16, 30.10.1993 – 26.2.1994. (Spread over 2 periods in Football League. 2003–04 season in Conference.)

Longest Sequence Without a League Win: 18, 8.3.2003 – 14.8.2004.

Successive Scoring Runs: 28 from 7.9.1960.

Successive Non-scoring Runs: 6 from 1.1.1991.

MANAGERS

W. Adams 1905–12
(Secretary-Manager)
A. Weston 1912–34
(Secretary-Manager)
Jack Roscamp 1934–35
Sam Ramsey 1935–36
Ted Bousted 1936–40
Leslie Knighton 1945–49
Harry Chapman 1949–50
Sammy Crooks 1950–54
Walter Rowley 1955–57
Harry Potts 1957–58
Johnny Spuhler 1958
Arthur Rowley 1958–68
Harry Gregg 1968–72
Maurice Evans 1972–73
Alan Durban 1974–78
Richie Barker 1978
Graham Turner 1978–84
Chic Bates 1984–87
Ian McNeill 1987–90
Asa Hartford 1990–91
John Bond 1991–93
Fred Davies 1994–97
(previously Caretaker-Manager 1993–94)
Jake King 1997–99
Kevin Ratcliffe 1999–2003
Jimmy Quinn 2003–04
Gary Peters 2004–08
Paul Simpson 2008–10
Graham Turner 2010–14
Mike Jackson 2014
Micky Mellon May 2014–

TEN YEAR LEAGUE RECORD

		P	W	D	L	F	A	Pts	Pos
2006-07	FL 2	46	18	17	11	68	46	71	7
2007-08	FL 2	46	12	14	20	56	65	50	18
2008-09	FL 2	46	17	18	11	61	44	69	7
2009-10	FL 2	46	17	12	17	55	54	63	12
2010-11	FL 2	46	22	13	11	72	49	79	4
2011-12	FL 2	46	26	10	10	66	41	88	2
2012-13	FL 1	46	13	16	17	54	60	55	16
2013-14	FL 1	46	9	15	22	44	65	42	23
2014-15	FL 2	46	27	8	11	67	31	89	2
2015-16	FL 1	46	13	11	22	58	79	50	20

DID YOU KNOW

Shrewsbury Town's first floodlights were officially switched on in November 1959 when the Shrews met Stoke City, then a Second Division club, in a friendly at Gay Meadow. The first use of the lights was four days earlier during a Third Division match against Queens Park Rangers.

SHREWSBURY TOWN – FOOTBALL LEAGUE ONE 2015–16 LEAGUE RECORD

Match No.	Date	Venue	Opponents	Result	H/T Score	Lg Pos.	Goalscorers	Attendance
1	Aug 8	H	Millwall	L	1-2	0-0	18	Collins [55]	6671
2	15	A	Bradford C	D	1-1	0-1	18	Barnett [46]	18,039
3	18	H	Chesterfield	L	1-2	0-0	19	Sadler [88]	4935
4	22	A	Oldham Ath	D	1-1	0-0	19	Collins [70]	3963
5	29	H	Burton Alb	L	0-1	0-0	21		4780
6	Sept 5	A	Barnsley	W	2-1	1-1	18	Ellis [6], Clark [90]	8630
7	12	A	Southend U	W	1-0	0-0	15	Knight-Percival [56]	5212
8	19	H	Crewe Alex	L	0-1	0-1	19		5481
9	26	H	Blackpool	W	2-0	0-0	16	Akpa Akpro 2 [73, 76]	5241
10	29	A	Rochdale	L	2-3	2-3	16	Knight-Percival [35], Collins (pen) [41]	2190
11	Oct 3	A	Coventry C	L	0-3	0-2	19		11,445
12	10	H	Colchester U	W	4-2	0-2	14	Barnett 2 [46, 59], KaiKai 2 [72, 81]	4947
13	17	A	Scunthorpe U	L	1-2	1-0	18	KaiKai [15]	3558
14	20	H	Doncaster R	L	1-2	1-1	18	Knight-Percival [27]	4735
15	24	H	Bury	W	2-0	1-0	16	KaiKai [28], Ogogo [73]	4945
16	31	A	Port Vale	L	0-2	0-0	17		4880
17	Nov 21	A	Wigan Ath	L	0-1	0-1	20		8803
18	24	A	Sheffield U	W	4-2	3-1	18	KaiKai [25], Black [26], Vernon [35], Collins [48]	17,843
19	28	H	Gillingham	D	2-2	1-1	19	Oshilaja (og) [31], Collins [70]	4959
20	Dec 1	H	Walsall	L	1-3	1-1	19	Cole [41]	6078
21	12	A	Peterborough U	D	1-1	0-0	18	Barnett [79]	5568
22	19	H	Swindon T	L	0-1	0-1	20		5115
23	26	H	Fleetwood T	D	1-1	1-0	19	Clark [6]	5749
24	28	A	Crewe Alex	W	2-1	1-1	17	Cole [11], Whalley [90]	5506
25	Jan 2	A	Chesterfield	L	1-7	0-3	20	Whitbread [66]	6233
26	16	H	Barnsley	L	0-3	0-2	21		5446
27	23	A	Burton Alb	W	2-1	0-1	20	Mangan [52], Whalley [90]	3870
28	26	A	Oldham Ath	L	0-1	0-1	20		4057
29	Feb 2	H	Southend U	L	1-2	0-1	20	Mangan [47]	4602
30	7	A	Fleetwood T	D	0-0	0-0	20		2539
31	13	A	Blackpool	W	3-2	3-1	19	Knight-Percival [5], Whalley [7], Mangan [29]	6873
32	27	A	Colchester U	D	0-0	0-0	21		3057
33	Mar 1	H	Rochdale	W	2-0	2-0	20	Whalley [12], Knight-Percival [45]	4221
34	5	A	Doncaster R	W	1-0	0-0	19	Whalley [62]	5878
35	8	H	Coventry C	W	2-1	2-1	17	KaiKai [9], Whalley [39]	6023
36	12	H	Scunthorpe U	D	2-2	1-0	17	KaiKai [21], Akpa Akpro [90]	5028
37	19	A	Bury	D	2-2	2-1	17	KaiKai 2 [16, 33]	3248
38	25	H	Port Vale	D	1-1	0-0	17	KaiKai [73]	7019
39	Apr 2	H	Wigan Ath	L	1-5	1-1	18	KaiKai [28]	7010
40	9	A	Millwall	L	1-3	1-0	20	Cole [5]	9583
41	16	H	Bradford C	D	1-1	0-0	20	Akpa Akpro [84]	6247
42	19	H	Sheffield U	L	1-2	0-1	20	Ogogo [54]	5064
43	23	A	Gillingham	W	3-2	1-1	19	KaiKai [16], Mangan [56], Akpa Akpro [81]	6906
44	26	A	Walsall	L	1-2	0-2	19	Sadler [60]	5339
45	30	H	Peterborough U	L	3-4	0-1	19	Akpa Akpro [74], Mangan [85], Grimmer [89]	6019
46	May 8	A	Swindon T	L	0-3	0-1	20		8012

Final League Position: 20

GOALSCORERS

League (58): KaiKai 12, Akpa Akpro 6, Whalley 6, Collins 5 (1 pen), Knight-Percival 5, Mangan 5, Barnett 4, Cole 3, Clark 2, Ogogo 2, Sadler 2, Black 1, Ellis 1, Grimmer 1, Vernon 1, Whitbread 1, own goal 1.
FA Cup (6): Akpa Akpro 1, Collins 1, Grimmer 1, Mangan 1, Ogogo 1, Whalley 1.
Capital One Cup (3): Barnett 1, Collins 1, Tootle 1.
Johnstone's Paint Trophy (3): Barnett 1, Brown 1, McAlinden 1.

Leutwiler J 29	Tootle M 16	Grandison J 19	Goldson C 2	Sadler M 19 + 5	Barnett T 11 + 10	Woods R 5	Woods M 4	Akpa Akpro J 16 + 22	Collins J 18 + 5	Ogogo A 42	Brown J 29 + 2	Whalley S 13 + 11	McAlinden L 2 + 6	Lawrence L 10 + 8	Ellis M 9	Clark J 13 + 7	Knight-Percival N 33 + 2	Wesolowski J 5	Cole L 24 + 5	KaiKai S 23 + 3	Halstead M 16	Smith D 17 + 4	Black L 26 + 4	Whitbread Z 21 + 1	Gerrard A 10 + 1	Vernon S 9 + 4	Grimmer J 21	Mangan A 15 + 4	Wallace J 3 + 4	Wellens R 7 + 5	Vassell K 11 + 2	Hendry J 6	Demetriou M 1	Burton C 1	Jones E — + 1	Match No.
1	2	3	4	5	6	7	8^2	9	10^3	11	12	13	14																							1
1	2	3	4	5	11	6	7	12	10^1	9		13	8^2																							2
1	2	3		5	11^2/7			9^3	13	10	8	12		14	6^1	4																				3
1	2^2	3		5	10^1	7	8		13	9	6^3		14	11		4	12																			4
1	5	3	4	12		7		10^2	11^1	8	9				13	6	2																			5
1	5	2		13	10^3			14			8	9^1			6	3	11	4	7^2	12																6
1	5	2		9	11^1			12	13	7				6	3	10	4		8^2																	7
1	5	3		9^3	10^2			12	14	11^1				7	2	8	4		6	13																8
	2			5	10^1			11	12	9				13	4	6^2	3		7	8	1															9
	2			5	13			10	11^1	6		12			3	9^2	4		8	7	1															10
	2	3		5	12			11	10^1	8			7			4	6	9	1																	11
1	2			12				11	7	9		14	3^1	10^3	5		6	13			4	8^2														12
1	2			11^2				13	10	8	5	14			3		7^3	9			4	6^1	12													13
1	2			13				10^2		8	5			6		12	4		11	9		3	7^1													14
1	5^3			10				12	14	7	9			6		4			8^2	11^1		2		3	13											15
1	2			11				8	12	7	6			9^1		13	5^2	10^1			3	14	4													16
1		2		5	14			11^3	6	10^2		13				9	7		8^1	4	3	12														17
1		2		13				12	10^3	8	5	14				9^2	6		7^1	3	4	11														18
1		2		13				10	7	5				4		9	6		8	3	11															19
1		2		12				10	8	5			13			4	6^1	9		7^*	3	11^{12}														20
	2			13				10^2	8	5		14	12			6^1	4		9	1		7^3	3	11												21
				13				10^1	7	5	14	12				8^2	4		9^2	1	2	6	3	11												22
		12						13	11	7	5^3		9^1	14		8^2	4			1	2	6	3	10												23
				13				12	10^3	8	5	6^1				14	9		1	2	7	3	4	11^2												24
	2							10	6^2	5^*	7		13			14	8		1	12	9	4	3^1	11^3												25
								9								6^3	2		7	1		8^1	3	4	11^2	5	10	12	13	14						26
1								14				5	13			12	4		9^3			6^1	3			2	11	7	8	10^2						27
1								13				5	12				4		6^2			7	3		14	2	11	9	8^1	10^3						28
1								11				9	12			4						2	6	3^1		13	5	10	8^2	7						29
1	3	13						11		8	9	7				4						2	6^1					5^2	10		12					30
1	2							11		7	9	6^2				4						12	8	3				5^1	10^2		13	14				31
1								11^3		7	8	9^1				14	4		12			2^6	6	3		13	5	10								32
1								12		8	5	6				9	4					7	3			2	10^1			11					33
1									7	5	10					6	4		13			12	8^2	3^1			2	9^1		14	11					34
		12						13		7	2^2	10				14	3		6^3	9^1	1	4	8			5					11					35
		5						12		7		6^2				10	4		8	9^1	1	3				2	13				11					36
								12		7	5	6				13	3		9^1	1	4					2	11^2			8	10					37
	2							12		7	5	6^2				4^*	14		9	1		13				3	11^3			8	10^1					38
	4	12						14		9	5^2	8					10^1	1	13	6	3^*					2				7^3	11					39
1		4^3						14		7						9	10	1^*	3	6^1					5	13		12	11^2	2	8					40
1		8						11		7		13				9^2	10		4	6^3	3					5	12	14			2^1					41
1		8						10		7		13					4	6		9			3			5	12			11^1	2^2					42
1		8						10		7							4	6		9		12	3			5	11^1				2					43
1		5						11^3		6		13				2	7^2	14	9			12	3			8	10			4^1						44
		5						13		7^2		8				4			9^1	10	1		6^3	3		2	11	12								45
		9						10		6							8	13				2^3	4			5	11^1	12	7^3	3			1	14	46

FA Cup

First Round	Gainsborough Trinity	(a)	1-0
Second Round	Grimsby T	(a)	0-0
Replay	Grimsby T	(h)	1-0
Third Round	Cardiff C	(a)	1-0
Fourth Round	Sheffield W	(h)	3-2
Fifth Round	Manchester U	(h)	0-3

Capital One Cup

First Round	Blackburn R	(a)	2-1
Second Round	Crystal Palace	(a)	1-4
(aet)			

Johnstone's Paint Trophy

First Round	Oldham Ath	(h)	2-0
Second Round	Fleetwood T	(a)	1-2

SOUTHAMPTON

FOUNDATION

The club was formed by members of the St Mary's Church of England Young Men's Association at a meeting of the Y.M.A. in November 1885 and it was named as such. For the sake of brevity this was usually shortened to St Mary's Y.M.A. The rector Canon Albert Basil Orme Wilberforce was elected president. The name was changed to plain St Mary's during 1887–88 and did not become Southampton St Mary's until 1894, the inaugural season in the Southern League.

St Mary's Stadium, Britannia Road, Southampton, Hampshire SO14 5FP.

Telephone: (0845) 688 9448.

Fax: (02380) 727 727.

Ticket Office: (0845) 688 9288.

Website: www.saintsfc.co.uk

Email: sfc@saintsfc.co.uk

Ground Capacity: 32,505.

Record Attendance: 31,044 v Manchester U, Division 1, 8 October 1969 (at The Dell); 32,363 v Coventry C, FL C, 28 April 2012 (at St Mary's).

Pitch Measurements: 105m × 68m (114yd × 74yd).

Chairman: Ralph Krueger.

Chief Executive: Gareth Rogers.

Manager: Claude Puel.

Assistant Manager: Eric Black.

Physios: Tom Sturdy and Steve Wright.

Colours: Red and white striped shirts, black shorts, red socks with black hoops.

Year Formed: 1885.

Turned Professional: 1894.

Previous Names: 1885, St Mary's Young Men's Association; 1887–88, St Mary's; 1894–95 Southampton St Mary's; 1897, Southampton.

Club Nickname: 'Saints'.

Grounds: 1885, 'The Common' (from 1887 also used the County Cricket Ground and Antelope Cricket Ground); 1889, Antelope Cricket Ground; 1896 The County Cricket Ground; 1898, The Dell; 2001, St Mary's.

First Football League Game: 28 August 1920, Division 3, v Gillingham (a) D 1–1 – Allen; Parker, Titmuss; Shelley, Campbell, Turner; Barratt, Dominy (1), Rawlings, Moore, Foxall.

Record League Victory: 8–0 v Sunderland, FA Premier League, 18 October 2014 – Forster; Clyne, Fonte, Alderweireld, Bertrand; Davis S (Mane), Schneiderlin, Cork (1); Long (Wanyama (1)), Pelle (2) (Mayuka), Tadic (1) (plus 3 Sunderland own goals).

HONOURS

League Champions: Division 3 – 1959–60; Division 3S – 1921–22.
Runners-up: Division 1 – 1983–84; FL C – 2011–12; Division 2 – 1965–66, 1977–78; FL 1 – 2010–11; Division 3 – 1920–21.

FA Cup Winners: 1976.
Runners-up: 1900, 1902, 2003.

League Cup: Runners-up: 1979.

League Trophy Winners: 2010.

Full Members' Cup: Runners-up: 1992.

European Competitions
Fairs Cup: 1969–70.
UEFA Cup: 1971–72, 1981–82, 1982–83, 1984–85, 2003–04.
Europa League: 2015–16.
European Cup-Winners' Cup: 1976–77 *(qf)*.

sky SPORTS FACT FILE

Southampton players Bill Rawlings and Fred Titmuss both made their debut for England against Wales at Anfield in March 1922. At the time the Saints were in Division Three South and the match is the only occasion England has included two players from the third tier of the Football League in their line-up in the same game.

Record Cup Victory: 7–1 v Ipswich T, FA Cup 3rd rd, 7 January 1961 – Reynolds; Davies, Traynor, Conner, Page, Huxford, Paine (1), O'Brien (3 incl. 1p), Reeves, Mulgrew (2), Penk (1).

Record Defeat: 0–8 v Tottenham H, Division 2, 28 March 1936; 0–8 v Everton, Division 1, 20 November 1971.

Most League Points (2 for a win): 61, Division 3 (S), 1921–22 and Division 3, 1959–60.

Most League Points (3 for a win): 92, FL 1, 2010–11.

Most League Goals: 112, Division 3 (S), 1957–58.

Highest League Scorer in Season: Derek Reeves, 39, Division 3, 1959–60.

Most League Goals in Total Aggregate: Mike Channon, 185, 1966–77, 1979–82.

Most League Goals in One Match: 5, Charlie Wayman v Leicester C, Division 2, 23 October 1948.

Most Capped Player: Peter Shilton, 49 (125), England.

Most League Appearances: Terry Paine, 713, 1956–74.

Youngest League Player: Theo Walcott, 16 years 143 days v Wolverhampton W, 6 August 2005.

Record Transfer Fee Received: £34,000,000 from Liverpool for Sadio Mané, June 2016.

Record Transfer Fee Paid: £12,800,000 (rising to £18,000,000) to AS Roma for Pablo Daniel Osvaldo, August 2013.

Football League Record: 1920 Original Member of Division 3; 1921–22 Division 3 (S); 1922–53 Division 2; 1953–58 Division 3 (S); 1958–60 Division 3; 1960–66 Division 2; 1966–74 Division 1; 1974–78 Division 2; 1978–92 Division 1; 1992–2005 FA Premier League; 2005–09 FL C; 2009–11 FL 1; 2011–12 FL C; 2012– FA Premier League.

LATEST SEQUENCES

Longest Sequence of League Wins: 10, 16.4.2011 – 20.8.2011.

Longest Sequence of League Defeats: 5, 16.8.1998 – 12.9.1998.

Longest Sequence of League Draws: 8, 29.8.2005 – 15.10.2005.

Longest Sequence of Unbeaten League Matches: 19, 5.9.1921 – 31.12.1921.

Longest Sequence Without a League Win: 20, 30.8.1969 – 27.12.1969.

Successive Scoring Runs: 28 from 10.2.2008.

Successive Non-scoring Runs: 5 from 2.4.2001.

MANAGERS

Cecil Knight 1894–95
 (Secretary-Manager)
Charles Robson 1895–97
Er Arnfield 1897–1911
 (Secretary-Manager)
 (continued as Secretary)
George Swift 1911–12
Er Arnfield 1912–19
Jimmy McIntyre 1919–24
Arthur Chadwick 1925–31
George Kay 1931–36
George Gross 1936–37
Tom Parker 1937–43
J. R. Sarjantson stepped down
 from the board to act as
 Secretary-Manager 1943–47 with
 the next two listed being Team
 Managers during this period
Arthur Dominy 1943–46
Bill Dodgin Snr 1946–49
Sid Cann 1949–51
George Roughton 1952–55
Ted Bates 1955–73
Lawrie McMenemy 1973–85
Chris Nicholl 1985–91
Ian Branfoot 1991–94
Alan Ball 1994–95
Dave Merrington 1995–96
Graeme Souness 1996–97
Dave Jones 1997–2000
Glenn Hoddle 2000–01
Stuart Gray 2001
Gordon Strachan 2001–04
Paul Sturrock 2004
Steve Wigley 2004
Harry Redknapp 2004–05
George Burley 2005–08
Nigel Pearson 2008
Jan Poortvliet 2008–09
Mark Wotte 2009
Alan Pardew 2009–10
Nigel Adkins 2010–13
Mauricio Pochettino 2013–14
Ronald Koeman 2014–16
Claude Puel June 2016–

TEN YEAR LEAGUE RECORD

		P	W	D	L	F	A	Pts	Pos
2006-07	FL C	46	21	12	13	77	53	75	6
2007-08	FL C	46	13	15	18	56	72	54	20
2008-09	FL C	46	10	15	21	46	69	45	23
2009-10	FL 1	46	23	14	9	85	47	73*	7
2010-11	FL 1	46	28	8	10	86	38	92	2
2011-12	FL C	46	26	10	10	85	46	88	2
2012-13	PR Lge	38	9	14	15	49	60	41	14
2013-14	PR Lge	38	15	11	12	54	46	56	8
2014-15	PR Lge	38	18	6	14	54	33	60	7
2015-16	PR Lge	38	18	9	11	59	41	63	6

*10 pts deducted.

DID YOU KNOW ?

When full-back Ray Wallace made his Southampton debut against Sheffield Wednesday in October 1988 he appeared alongside his twin Rodney and their older brother Danny. The three brothers made a combined total of over 500 first-team appearances for the Saints during their careers.

SOUTHAMPTON – FA PREMIER LEAGUE 2015–16 LEAGUE RECORD

Match No.	Date	Venue	Opponents		Result	H/T Score	Lg Pos.	Goalscorers	Attendance
1	Aug 9	A	Newcastle U	D	2-2	1-1	7	Pelle [24], Long [79]	49,019
2	15	H	Everton	L	0-3	0-2	16		30,966
3	23	A	Watford	D	0-0	0-0	18		20,166
4	30	A	Norwich C	W	3-0	1-0	10	Pelle [45], Tadic 2 [64, 67]	29,573
5	Sept 12	A	WBA	D	0-0	0-0	11		24,265
6	20	H	Manchester U	L	2-3	1-1	16	Pelle 2 [13, 86]	31,588
7	26	H	Swansea C	W	3-1	1-0	9	van Dijk [11], Ki (og) [54], Mane [61]	30,704
8	Oct 3	A	Chelsea	W	3-1	1-1	9	Davis, S [43], Mane [60], Pelle [72]	41,642
9	17	H	Leicester C	D	2-2	2-0	8	Fonte [21], van Dijk [37]	31,559
10	25	A	Liverpool	D	1-1	0-0	8	Mane [86]	44,171
11	Nov 1	H	Bournemouth	W	2-0	0-0	7	Davis, S [31], Pelle [36]	31,229
12	7	A	Sunderland	W	1-0	0-0	7	Tadic (pen) [69]	41,781
13	21	H	Stoke C	L	0-1	0-1	8		30,039
14	28	A	Manchester C	L	1-3	0-2	9	Long [49]	54,102
15	Dec 5	H	Aston Villa	D	1-1	0-1	12	Romeu [73]	29,645
16	12	H	Crystal Palace	L	0-1	0-1	12		24,914
17	19	H	Tottenham H	L	0-2	0-2	12		31,636
18	26	H	Arsenal	W	4-0	1-0	12	Martina [19], Long 2 [55, 90], Fonte [69]	31,669
19	28	A	West Ham U	L	1-2	1-0	12	Jenkinson (og) [13]	34,977
20	Jan 2	A	Norwich C	L	0-1	0-0	13		27,022
21	13	H	Watford	W	2-0	1-0	12	Long [17], Tadic [73]	28,399
22	16	H	WBA	W	3-0	2-0	10	Ward-Prowse 2 (1 pen) [5, 35 (p)], Tadic [72]	29,622
23	23	A	Manchester U	W	1-0	0-0	8	Austin [87]	75,408
24	Feb 2	A	Arsenal	D	0-0	0-0	7		60,044
25	6	H	West Ham U	W	1-0	1-0	7	Yoshida [9]	29,161
26	13	A	Swansea C	W	1-0	0-0	6	Long [69]	20,890
27	27	H	Chelsea	L	1-2	1-0	7	Long [42]	31,688
28	Mar 1	A	Bournemouth	L	0-2	0-1	7		11,033
29	5	H	Sunderland	D	1-1	0-0	8	van Dijk [90]	31,458
30	12	A	Stoke C	W	2-1	2-0	7	Pelle 2 [11, 30]	27,833
31	20	H	Liverpool	W	3-2	0-2	7	Mane 2 [64, 86], Pelle [83]	31,596
32	Apr 3	A	Leicester C	L	0-1	0-1	7		32,071
33	9	H	Newcastle U	W	3-1	2-0	7	Long [4], Pelle [38], Wanyama [55]	31,542
34	16	A	Everton	D	1-1	0-0	7	Mane [76]	36,761
35	23	A	Aston Villa	W	4-2	2-1	8	Long [15], Tadic 2 [39, 71], Mane [90]	29,729
36	May 1	H	Manchester C	W	4-2	2-1	7	Long [25], Mane 3 [28, 57, 68]	31,472
37	8	A	Tottenham H	W	2-1	1-1	6	Davis, S 2 [31, 72]	35,748
38	15	H	Crystal Palace	W	4-1	1-0	5	Mane [43], Pelle [61], Bertrand (pen) [75], Davis, S [87]	31,313

Final League Position – Manchester U finished season in 5th position, their final match v Bournemouth was played after the official end of the season as the original game scheduled for 15/5/16 was postponed due to a security alert.

GOALSCORERS

League (59): Mane 11, Pelle 11, Long 10, Tadic 7 (1 pen), Davis, S 5, van Dijk 3, Fonte 2, Ward-Prowse 2 (1 pen), Austin 1, Bertrand 1 (1 pen), Martina 1, Romeu 1, Wanyama 1, Yoshida 1, own goals 2.
FA Cup (1): Romeu 1.
Capital One Cup (9): Mane 3, Long 2, Rodriguez 2 (1 pen), Pelle 1, Yoshida 1.
UEFA Europa League (6): Pelle 2, Long 1, Mane 1, Rodriguez 1 (pen), Tadic 1 (pen).

Stekelenburg M 17	Cedric Soares R 23 + 1	Fonte J 37	Yoshida M 10 + 10	Targett M 13 + 1	Davis S 31 + 3	Wanyama V 29 + 1	Tadic D 27 + 7	Mane S 30 + 7	Rodriguez J 3 + 9	Pelle G 23 + 7	Martina C 11 + 4	Long S 23 + 5	Romeu O 17 + 12	Ward-Prowse J 14 + 19	Caulker S 1 + 2	Juanmi J — + 12	van Dijk V 34	Bertrand R 32	Davis K 1	Clasie J 20 + 2	Ramirez G — + 3	Gazzaniga P 2	Reed H — + 1	Forster F 18	Austin C 2 + 5	Match No.
1	2¹	3	4	5	6	7	8	9	10²	11	12	13														1
1	2	3	4	5	6³	7	8¹	9	13	11		10²	12	14												2
1	5	3	4	9	8²	7		11¹	14	10³		12	6	13	2											3
1	2²	3	4	5	9¹		10	8²	12	11	13		6	7		14										4
1	2²	3	13	5	7	6	8	12	10¹	11			9				4									5
1		3	2	5¹	13	6	10	8		11	12	14	7²	9¹			4									6
1	2	3			9¹	7	10²	8¹	13	11			12	6		14	4	5								7
1	2	3	14		9	7	10²	8¹	13	11			6¹	12			4	5								8
	2²	3	13		6¹	7	10³	8	14	11			9				4	5	1	12						9
1	2	3			8³	7	10¹	9⁴		11			12			13	4	5		6²	14					10
1	2	3¹	12		8	6⁴	10³	9		11			13	14			4	5		7¹						11
1		3	2		6		10³	8²		11			12	9	14	13	4	5		7¹						12
1	2²	3			9²	6	10	12		11		8		13		14	4	5		7¹						13
1		3¹	2		10	6	13	8		11		7²	9³	12	14		4	5								14
1	2	3			9	6¹	10²	8³		11		14	12	7	13		4	5								15
	5	3	4²		10¹	6	13	9		12		11	7³	14			2	8					1			16
	2	3			9¹	6	10²	8		11		12		14			13	4	5	7³			1			17
1		3			10	6	13	9³		2	11	12	8²				14	4	5	7¹						18
1		3	12		10	6	8²	9³		2¹	11	7					13	4	5			14				19
1		3			9	6⁴	10²	12		2	11		8³				4	5		7¹	14	13				20
	2³	4	14	10	8²		12	9¹	13		11	6					3	5		7				1		21
	2³	4		10	8²	7	12	9¹	14	11	13	6					3	5						1		22
	2	4		10		6	8²	9¹		11	12	13					3	5		7¹				1	14	23
	2	3	14		8	11¹	9³		12		10	7	6²	13			4	5						1		24
	5	3	4		7⁴		9¹	10²		11	12	14					2	8		6²				1	13	25
	12	3	14	9²	5			11²		10	8¹	6					2	4		7				1	13	26
	2	4	10³	9			13		12		8¹	7	14				3	5		6				1	11²	27
	5	3	4¹	12		14	9	13		10¹	7	6					2	8						1	11²	28
		3¹	14		8²	10	9³	11	2		6	13		12			4	5		7¹				1		29
		14	5³	9		10²	13⁴	11	2	8	6	12					3	4		7¹				1		30
	3			6	12	9²	13	10	2	11	7³	14					4	5		8¹				1		31
	2	4	10¹	8²	6	12	9	11				14					3	5		7²				1	13	32
	3			7	10³	8	14	11	2	9¹	13	12					4	5		6²				1		33
	3¹	12		13	6²	8	10	14	11²	2	9						4	5		7				1		34
	2	3		8	7¹	10	13	9²		11	6						4	5		12				1		35
	3			9²	6	10³	8	14		2	11	12	13				4	5		7¹				1		36
	3			9	6	10³	8²	13	2	11	12	14					4	5		7¹				1		37
	3			9	6	10²	8	12	2	11¹	7¹	13					4	5						1	14	38

FA Cup

Third Round	Crystal Palace	(h)	1-2	

Capital One Cup

Third Round	Milton Keynes D	(a)	6-0	
Fourth Round	Aston Villa	(h)	2-1	
Quarter-Final	Liverpool	(h)	1-6	

UEFA Europa League

Third Qualifying 1st leg	Vitesse	(h)	3-0
Third Qualifying 2nd leg	Vitesse	(a)	2-0
(Southampton won 5-0 on aggregate)			
Play-Off 1st leg	Midtjylland	(h)	1-1
Play-Off 2nd leg	Midtjylland	(a)	0-1
(Midtjylland won 2-1 on aggregate)			

SOUTHEND UNITED

FOUNDATION

The leading club in Southend around the turn of the 20th century was Southend Athletic, but they were an amateur concern. Southend United was a more ambitious professional club when they were founded in 1906, employing Bob Jack as secretary-manager and immediately joining the Second Division of the Southern League.

Roots Hall Stadium, Victoria Avenue, Southend-on-Sea, Essex SS2 6NQ.

Telephone: (01702) 304 050.

Fax: (01702) 304 124.

Ticket Office: (08444) 770 077.

Website: www.southendunited.co.uk

Email: info@southend-united.co.uk

Ground Capacity: 12,110.

Record Attendance: 22,862 v Tottenham H, FA Cup 3rd rd replay, 11 January 1936 (at Southend Stadium); 31,090 v Liverpool, FA Cup 3rd rd, 10 January 1979 (at Roots Hall).

Pitch Measurements: 100.5m × 67.5m (110yd × 74yd).

Chairman: Ronald Martin.

Chief Executive: Steve Kavanagh.

Manager: Phil Brown.

Assistant Manager: Graham Coughlan.

Physio: Ben Clarkson.

Colours: Navy blue shirts with thin white stripes, navy blue shorts, white socks.

Year Formed: 1906.

Turned Professional: 1906.

Club Nicknames: 'The Blues', 'The Shrimpers'.

Grounds: 1906, Roots Hall, Prittlewell; 1920, Kursaal; 1934, Southend Stadium; 1955, Roots Hall Football Ground.

First Football League Game: 28 August 1920, Division 3, v Brighton & HA (a) W 2–0 – Capper; Reid, Newton; Wileman, Henderson, Martin; Nicholls, Nuttall, Fairclough (2), Myers, Dorsett.

Record League Victory: 9–2 v Newport Co, Division 3 (S), 5 September 1936 – McKenzie; Nelson, Everest (1); Deacon, Turner, Carr; Bolan, Lane (1), Goddard (4), Dickinson (2), Oswald (1).

Record Cup Victory: 10–1 v Golders Green, FA Cup 1st rd, 24 November 1934 – Moore; Morfitt, Kelly; Mackay, Joe Wilson, Carr (1); Lane (1), Johnson (5), Cheesmuir (2), Deacon (1), Oswald. 10–1 v Brentwood, FA Cup 2nd rd, 7 December 1968 – Roberts; Bentley, Birks; McMillan (1) Beesley, Kurila; Clayton, Chisnall, Moore (4), Best (5), Hamilton. 10–1 v Aldershot, Leyland DAF Cup Prel rd, 6 November 1990 – Sansome; Austin, Powell, Cornwell, Prior (1), Tilson (3), Cawley, Butler, Ansah (1), Benjamin (1), Angell (4).

HONOURS

League Champions: FL 1 – 2005–06; Division 4 – 1980–81.
Runners-up: Division 3 – 1990–91; Division 4 – 1971–72, 1977–78.
FA Cup: 3rd rd – 1921; 5th rd – 1926, 1952, 1976, 1993.
League Cup: quarter-final – 2007.
League Trophy: Runners-up: 2004, 2005, 2013.

sky SPORTS FACT FILE

On New Year's Day 1992 Southend United defeated Newcastle United 4-0 at Roots Hall to go top of the old Second Division for the only time in their history. Brett Angell scored twice with Andy Ansah and Keith Jones also finding the net in the fixture which had an early kick-off. Results later in the day meant that United lost their position and they later dropped out of the promotion race in the second half of the season, finishing the campaign in 12th position.

Record Defeat: 1–9 v Brighton & HA, Division 3, 27 November 1965; 0–8 v Crystal Palace, League Cup 2nd rd (1st leg), 25 September 1990.

Most League Points (2 for a win): 67, Division 4, 1980–81.

Most League Points (3 for a win): 85, Division 3, 1990–91.

Most League Goals: 92, Division 3 (S), 1950–51.

Highest League Scorer in Season: Jim Shankly, 31, 1928–29; Sammy McCrory, 1957–58, both in Division 3 (S).

Most League Goals in Total Aggregate: Roy Hollis, 122, 1953–60.

Most League Goals in One Match: 5, Jim Shankly v Merthyr T, Division 3 (S), 1 March 1930.

Most Capped Player: George McKenzie, 9, Republic of Ireland.

Most League Appearances: Sandy Anderson, 452, 1950–63.

Youngest League Player: Phil O'Connor, 16 years 76 days v Lincoln C, 26 December 1969.

Record Transfer Fee Received: £2,000,000 (rising to £2,750,000) from Nottingham F for Stan Collymore, June 1993.

Record Transfer Fee Paid: £80,000 to Crystal Palace for Stan Collymore, November 1992.

Football League Record: 1920 Original Member of Division 3; 1921–58 Division 3 (S); 1958–66 Division 3; 1966–72 Division 4; 1972–76 Division 3; 1976–78 Division 4; 1978–80 Division 3; 1980–81 Division 4; 1981–84 Division 3; 1984–87 Division 4; 1987–89 Division 3; 1989–90 Division 4; 1990–91 Division 3; 1991–92 Division 2; 1992–97 Division 1; 1997–98 Division 2; 1998–2004 Division 3; 2004–05 FL 2; 2005–06 FL 1; 2006–07 FL C; 2007–10 FL 1; 2010–15 FL 2; 2015– FL 1.

LATEST SEQUENCES

Longest Sequence of League Wins: 8, 29.8.2005 – 9.10.2005.

Longest Sequence of League Defeats: 6, 14.4.2007 – 18.8.2007.

Longest Sequence of League Draws: 6, 30.1.1982 – 19.2.1982.

Longest Sequence of Unbeaten League Matches: 16, 20.2.1932 – 29.8.1932.

Longest Sequence Without a League Win: 17, 26.8.2006 – 2.12.2006.

Successive Scoring Runs: 24 from 23.3.1929.

Successive Non-scoring Runs: 6 from 6.4.1979.

MANAGERS

Bob Jack 1906–10
George Molyneux 1910–11
O. M. Howard 1911–12
Joe Bradshaw 1912–19
Ned Liddell 1919–20
Tom Mather 1920–21
Ted Birnie 1921–34
David Jack 1934–40
Harry Warren 1946–56
Eddie Perry 1956–60
Frank Broome 1960
Ted Fenton 1961–65
Alvan Williams 1965–67
Ernie Shepherd 1967–69
Geoff Hudson 1969–70
Arthur Rowley 1970–76
Dave Smith 1976–83
Peter Morris 1983–84
Bobby Moore 1984–86
Dave Webb 1986–87
Dick Bate 1987
Paul Clark 1987–88
Dave Webb *(General Manager)* 1988–92
Colin Murphy 1992–93
Barry Fry 1993
Peter Taylor 1993–95
Steve Thompson 1995
Ronnie Whelan 1995–97
Alvin Martin 1997–99
Alan Little 1999–2000
David Webb 2000–01
Rob Newman 2001–03
Steve Wignall 2003
Steve Tilson 2003–10
Paul Sturrock 2010–13
Phil Brown March 2013–

TEN YEAR LEAGUE RECORD

		P	W	D	L	F	A	Pts	Pos
2006-07	FL C	46	10	12	24	47	80	42	22
2007-08	FL 1	46	22	10	14	70	55	76	6
2008-09	FL 1	46	21	8	17	58	61	71	8
2009-10	FL 1	46	10	13	23	51	72	43	23
2010-11	FL 2	46	16	13	17	62	56	61	13
2011-12	FL 2	46	25	8	13	77	48	83	4
2012-13	FL 2	46	16	13	17	61	55	61	11
2013-14	FL 2	46	19	15	12	56	39	72	5
2014-15	FL 2	46	24	12	10	54	38	84	5
2015-16	FL 1	46	16	11	19	58	64	59	14

DID YOU KNOW ?

Southend United had the distinction of playing a Division Three South fixture at Wembley in December 1930 when their opponents Clapton Orient had a difficulty with their home stadium and were given permission to switch two games. Orient defeated Southend 3-1 in front of an attendance of just 2,500.

SOUTHEND UNITED – FOOTBALL LEAGUE ONE 2015–16 LEAGUE RECORD

Match No.	Date	Venue	Opponents	Result	H/T Score	Lg Pos.	Goalscorers	Atten- dance
1	Aug 8	A	Fleetwood T	D	1-1	0-1	10	Worrall [84]	3228
2	15	H	Walsall	L	0-2	0-1	21		6149
3	19	A	Doncaster R	D	0-0	0-0	20		5164
4	22	H	Swindon T	L	0-1	0-0	21		5839
5	31	A	Coventry C	D	2-2	2-1	20	Hunt [36], Mooney (pen) [41]	12,967
6	Sept 5	H	Peterborough U	W	2-1	1-0	16	Barrett [32], Hunt [70]	5748
7	12	H	Shrewsbury T	L	0-1	0-0	20		5212
8	19	A	Millwall	W	2-0	1-0	16	Mooney [37], Barrett [49]	10,228
9	26	H	Scunthorpe U	W	2-1	1-1	13	Timlin [36], Coker [75]	5708
10	29	A	Crewe Alex	W	2-1	0-0	10	Pigott 2 [47, 53]	3404
11	Oct 3	A	Burton Alb	L	0-1	0-0	11		2948
12	10	H	Port Vale	W	1-0	0-0	7	Pigott [63]	6543
13	17	H	Barnsley	W	2-1	2-1	7	Wordsworth [36], Prosser [43]	6572
14	20	A	Chesterfield	L	0-3	0-2	8		5703
15	24	A	Gillingham	D	1-1	1-0	8	McLaughlin [11]	6981
16	31	H	Rochdale	D	2-2	2-0	11	Mooney (pen) [39], Leonard [41]	6111
17	Nov 14	A	Sheffield U	D	2-2	2-2	11	Leonard [29], Payne [31]	19,007
18	21	H	Blackpool	W	1-0	0-0	10	Thompson [76]	6290
19	24	A	Oldham Ath	W	5-2	2-0	8	Payne [5], Mooney [43], Worrall [48], Atkinson [78], Prosser [82]	3301
20	28	A	Wigan Ath	D	0-0	0-0	8		7117
21	Dec 18	H	Bury	W	4-1	2-1	7	Hunt 2 [22, 31], Mooney (pen) [74], Payne [78]	6127
22	26	A	Colchester U	W	2-0	0-0	7	White [49], Mooney [73]	9222
23	28	H	Millwall	L	0-4	0-3	7		10,099
24	Jan 2	A	Doncaster R	L	0-3	0-1	7		7134
25	9	A	Swindon T	L	2-4	2-2	8	Barnett [5], Thompson [13]	7162
26	16	A	Peterborough U	D	0-0	0-0	8		7057
27	23	H	Coventry C	W	3-0	2-0	9	Payne [24], Barnett 2 (1 pen) [31, 68 (p)]	8767
28	Feb 2	A	Shrewsbury T	W	2-1	1-0	7	Atkinson [24], Hendrie [79]	4602
29	6	H	Colchester U	W	3-0	0-0	7	Wordsworth [82], Barrett [88], McQueen [90]	10,279
30	13	A	Scunthorpe U	L	0-1	0-1	7		3550
31	16	A	Bradford C	L	0-2	0-1	7		17,701
32	22	H	Burton Alb	W	3-1	1-1	7	Wordsworth [7], Barnett [63], Moonoy [90]	0503
33	26	A	Port Vale	L	1-3	0-3	7	McQueen [90]	3957
34	Mar 1	H	Crewe Alex	D	1-1	0-0	8	Payne (pen) [90]	5444
35	5	H	Chesterfield	L	0-1	0-0	10		7518
36	12	A	Barnsley	W	2-0	1-0	10	Payne [4], Timlin [90]	9903
37	19	H	Gillingham	D	1-1	1-0	9	Wordsworth [21]	9135
38	25	A	Rochdale	L	1-4	1-1	12	Payne [28]	3018
39	30	H	Sheffield U	W	3-1	1-1	8	Barnett [28], Worrall [60], Payne [90]	7004
40	Apr 2	A	Blackpool	L	0-2	0-0	10		6979
41	9	H	Fleetwood T	D	2-2	0-0	11	Barrett [71], Payne [82]	6644
42	16	A	Walsall	L	0-1	0-0	13		5732
43	19	H	Oldham Ath	L	0-1	0-0	13		6508
44	23	A	Wigan Ath	L	1-4	0-3	13	Morgan (og) [74]	10,021
45	30	H	Bradford C	L	0-1	0-0	14		8571
46	May 8	A	Bury	L	2-3	2-2	15	Moussa [8], Mooney [23]	3575

Final League Position: 15, revised to 14 after Bury deducted 3 points for fielding an ineligible player.

GOALSCORERS

League (58): Payne 9 (1 pen), Mooney 8 (3 pens), Barnett 5 (1 pen), Barrett 4, Hunt 4, Wordsworth 4, Pigott 3, Worrall 3, Atkinson 2, Leonard 2, McQueen 2, Prosser 2, Thompson 2, Timlin 2, Coker 1, Hendrie 1, McLaughlin 1, Moussa 1, White 1, own goal 1.
FA Cup (1): Leonard 1.
Capital One Cup (0).
Johnstone's Paint Trophy (4): Pigott 2, Weston 1, White 1.

Bentley D 43	White J 27 + 2	Bolger C 22	Barrett A 37	Coker B 40	Leonard R 35 + 2	Wordsworth A 15 + 6	Atkinson W 29 + 7	Hurst K 9 + 5	Mooney D 27 + 6	Weston M 6 + 11	Hunt N 13 + 8	Worrall D 24 + 11	Pigott J 10 + 13	Deegan G 23 + 2	Payne J 25 + 7	Timlin M 17 + 4	Prosser L 11 + 2	Rea G 5 + 9	McLaughlin S 9 + 8	O'Neill L 13 + 1	Williams J — + 2	Thompson A 24 + 1	Barnett T 20	Hendrie S 5	McQueen S 4 + 14	Loza J 1 + 9	Kamara G 5 + 1	Smith T 3	Malarczyk P 2	Bridge J 1 + 1	Moussa F 1	Match No.
1	2	3	4	5	6	7	8^1	9^3	10^2	11	12	13	14																			1
1	2	3	4	5	6		8	14	11^1	9^3		13	10		7^2	12																2
1	2	3^1	4	5	7	8	6^1	11^3	12			10	14		9	13																3
1	2		4^3	5	7	13	9^1		12	11		6	14		10	8^2	3	9	13													4
1	2		4	5	8	14	6^3		10^2	12	11		9^1		7			3	13													5
1	2		4	5	7	8		11^2		10^3	6^1	12		9				3	13	14												6
1	2		4	5^1	7	8		11		10^3	6	14		13	9^2			3	12													7
1		3	4^2		7				10^3	13		6	11^1	8		9	5	12		2	14											8
1		3		5	6			11^3	13	12		9^2	10^1	7		8	4	14		2												9
1		3		5	7	14		10^2	13	12		6^1	11^1	8		9	4			2												10
1		3		5	6	13		11	12			9^1	10	7^3	14	8^2	4			2												11
1	2	3		5	6	12	13	11^3	9			14	10	7^1		8^2	4															12
1	2	3		5	6	8^2	13	10^1	11^3			9			7		4	12	14													13
1	2	3		5	6	7^2		13	9^3	11		10^1			12	8	4							14								14
1	2	3		5	6	7	12		11^2	14		10		8^1			4	13	9^1													15
1	2^2	3		5	6		13	11				14	10	7^1		8	4	12	9^1													16
1	2		4	5	7		9	8^2	11^3	13		6	12		10^1	14						3										17
1	2		4	5	7		8	9^2	11^1			6	12		10			13				3										18
1	2		4	5	8		7	9	11^2			6^3	13		10^1	14	12					3										19
1	2		4	5	7		6^1	9	10				12		11		8					3										20
1	2		4	5	7		8	12	11^2			10^3	6^1	14	9			13				3										21
1	2	3		5	8		7		11^1			10^3	6	13	9^2			14	12			4										22
1	2		4	5^2	7		8		10			11^2	6^1	14	12	9			13			3										23
1	2		4	5	6		8^3		11^2		10	12	14	13	9	7^1			3													24
1				5	7	14	12	13		10^1	6		8^2		9^3	4			2			3	11									25
1	3	4		6	9		13		12			8	10^1						2			7	11^2	5								26
1	2	3		8	6^3			13				7^8	10^1	12					5			4	11^2	9	14							27
1	4	3		8	6		11^3	10^1					7^2	$12^?$					2			5		9	14	13						28
1	2	3			7^2	13	6^1			14			10						5			4^3	11	9	8		12					29
1	3	4			13	7			14				10						2			5	11^2	6	8^3	12	9^1					30
1	3	4	5		7	6^1			11	14		9^2			8				10^3	2					12	13						31
1	3	4	5		7	6		13	10^2	14				9^1	8					2			11^3		12							32
1		4	3	5	8^1	6		14	10^2	12				9^1	7^3					2			11		13							33
1		3	4	5	8^2	6^3		10^1				12		7	14					2			11		9^3	13						34
1	2	3	4	5	8	6^3		14			12	9^1		7	10								11^2		13							35
1	2		4	5		8^1	13	9^3				6	7	14		12						3	11			10^2						36
1	2		4	5		9		6^2				7	11									3	10		13	$12^?$	8^1					37
1	2^2		4	5		8		6^1				14	7	10								3	11		12	13	9^3					38
1	13		4	5	14		7			9^2		2^3	8	10				6^1				3	11		12							39
1			4	5	14		7	12		2		2	8^2	6				9^3				3	10		13	11^1						40
1	14		3	4	6		8^2	12				5^3	7	10				9^1				2	11		13							41
1			3	4	8		6^3	13				5		7	10			9^1				2	11^2		12	14						42
1	2		4	5	7							6		8	11			9^1				3^2	10		13	12						43
	5		4	2	8		9		12			6		7^1	13			14				3	11^2		10^3				1			44
	2		4	5	7		6^1	11^2	12					9						10					14		8^3	1	3	13		45
			4	5	8		7		10			2			12							13	11		14			1	3^3	9^1	6^2	46

FA Cup
First Round	Scunthorpe U		(a)	1-2

Capital One Cup
First Round	Brighton & HA		(h)	0-1

Johnstone's Paint Trophy
Second Round	Crawley T	(a)	3-0
Southern Quarter-Final	Bristol R	(h)	1-0
Southern Semi-Final	Millwall	(h)	0-2

STEVENAGE

FOUNDATION

There have been several clubs associated with the town of Stevenage. Stevenage Town was formed in 1884. They absorbed Stevenage Rangers in 1955 and later played at Broadhall Way. The club went into liquidation in 1968 and Stevenage Athletic was formed, but they, too, followed a similar path in 1976. Then Stevenage Borough was founded. The Broadhall Way pitch was dug up and remained unused for three years. Thus the new club started its life in the modest surrounds of the King George V playing fields with a roped-off ground in the Chiltern League. A change of competition followed to the Wallspan Southern Combination and by 1980 the club returned to the council-owned Broadhall Way when "Borough" was added to the name. Entry into the United Counties League was so successful the league and cup were won in the first season. On to the Isthmian League Division Two and the climb up the pyramid continued. In 1995–96 Stevenage Borough won the Conference but was denied a place in the Football League as the ground did not measure up to the competition's standards. Subsequent improvements changed this and the 7,100 capacity venue became one of the best appointed grounds in non-league football. After winning elevation to the Football League the club dropped Borough from its title.

Lamex Stadium, Broadhall Way, Stevenage, Hertfordshire SG2 8RH.

Telephone: (01438) 223 223.

Fax: (01438) 743 666.

Ticket Office: (01438) 223 223.

Website: stevenagefc.com

Email: info@stevenagefc.com

Ground Capacity: 6,772.

Record Attendance: 8,040 v Newcastle U, FA Cup 4th rd, 25 January 1998.

Pitch Measurements: 104.5m × 64.5m (114.5yd × 70.5yd).

Chairman: Phil Wallace.

Manager: Darren Sarll.

Managerial Advisor: Glenn Roeder.

Physio: Paul Dando.

Colours: White shirts with red stripes, red shorts with black and white trim, white socks.

Nickname: 'The Boro'.

HONOURS

League Champions: Conference – 1995–96, 2009–10.

FA Cup: 5th rd – 2012.

League Cup: 2nd rd – 2012.

sky SPORTS FACT FILE

Stevenage won every home league game in 1990–91 when they were champions of Division Two North of the Isthmian League. Borough finished 25 points clear of second-placed Vauxhall Motors and the following season were champions of the league's Division One.

Previous Name: 1976, Stevenage Borough; 2010, Stevenage.

Grounds: 1976, King George V playing fields; 1980, Broadhall Way (renamed Lamex Stadium 2009).

First Football League Game: 7 August 2010, FL 2, v Macclesfield T (h) D 2–2 – Day; Henry, Laird, Bostwick, Roberts, Foster, Wilson (Sinclair), Byrom, Griffin (1), Winn (Odubade), Vincenti (1) (Beardsley).

Year Formed: 1976.

Turned Professional: 1976.

Record League Victory: 6–0 v Yeovil T, FL 2, 14 April 2012 – Day; Lascelles (1), Laird, Roberts (1), Ashton (1), Shroot (Mousinho), Wilson (Myrie-Williams), Long, Agyemang (1), Reid (Slew), Freeman (2).

Record Victory: 11–1 v British Timken Ath 1980–81.

Record Defeat: 0–7 v Southwick 1987–88.

Most League Points (3 for a win): 73, FL 1, 2011–12.

Most League Goals: 69, FL 1, 2011–12.

Highest League Scorer in Season: Francois Zoko, 14, 2013–14.

Most Goals in Total Aggregate: Luke Freeman, 15, 2011–14.

Most League Goals in One Match: 3, Chris Holroyd v Hereford U, FL 2, 28 September 2010; 3, Dani Lopez v Sheffield U, FL 1, 16 March 2013; 3, Chris Whelpdale v Morecambe, FL 2, 28 November 2015.

Most Capped Player: Marcus Haber, 5 (including 3 on loan at Notts Co) (23), Canada.

Most League Appearances: Chris Day, 189, 2010–15.

Youngest League Player: Ryan Johnson, 17 years 213 days v Brentford, 3 May 2014.

Record Transfer Fee Received: £260,000 from Peterborough U for George Boyd, January 2007.

Record Transfer Fee Paid: £75,000 (rising to £150,000) to Exeter C for James Dunne, May 2012.

Football League Record: 2011 Promoted from Conference Premier; 2010–11 FL 2; 2011–14 FL 1; 2014– FL 2.

MANAGERS

Derek Montgomery 1976–83
Frank Cornwell 1983–87
John Bailey 1987–88
Brian Wilcox 1988–90
Paul Fairclough 1990–98
Richard Hill 1998–2000
Steve Wignall 2000
Paul Fairclough 2000–02
Wayne Turner 2002–03
Graham Westley 2003–06
Mark Stimson 2006–07
Peter Taylor 2007–08
Graham Westley 2008–12
Gary Smith 2012–13
Graham Westley 2013–15
Teddy Sheringham 2015–16
Darren Sarll February 2016–

LATEST SEQUENCES

Longest Sequence of League Wins: 6, 12.3.2011 – 2.4.2011.

Longest Sequence of League Defeats: 6, 13.4.2013 – 17.8.2013.

Longest Sequence of League Draws: 5, 17.3.2012 – 31.3.2012.

Longest Sequence of Unbeaten League Matches: 17, 9.4.2012 – 6.10.2012.

Longest Sequence Without a League Win: 10, 11.3.2014 – 21.4.2014.

Successive Scoring Runs: 17 from 9.4.2012.

Successive Non-scoring Runs: 4 from 20.2.2016.

TEN YEAR LEAGUE RECORD

		P	W	D	L	F	A	Pts	Pos
2006-07	Conf	46	20	10	16	76	66	70	8
2007-08	Conf P	46	24	7	15	82	55	79	6
2008-09	Conf P	46	23	12	11	73	54	81	5
2009-10	Conf P	44	30	9	5	79	24	99	1
2010-11	FL 2	46	18	15	13	62	45	69	6
2011-12	FL 1	46	18	19	9	69	44	73	6
2012-13	FL 1	46	15	9	22	47	64	54	18
2013-14	FL 1	46	11	9	26	46	72	42	24
2014-15	FL 2	46	20	12	14	62	54	72	6
2015-16	FL 2	46	11	15	20	52	67	48	18

DID YOU KNOW ?

Stevenage reached the first round of the FA Cup for the first time in their history in 1995–96 after winning through four qualifying rounds. They were drawn away to Hereford United and went out of the competition to the Bulls after losing 2-1 at Edgar Street.

STEVENAGE – FOOTBALL LEAGUE TWO 2015–16 LEAGUE RECORD

Match No.	Date	Venue	Opponents	Result		H/T Score	Lg Pos.	Goalscorers	Attendance
1	Aug 8	H	Notts Co	L	0-2	0-1	18		3652
2	15	A	Newport Co	D	2-2	1-0	19	Akinyemi [39], Hughes [90]	2521
3	18	A	Leyton Orient	L	0-3	0-0	22		4949
4	22	H	Hartlepool U	W	2-0	1-0	17	Franks [45], Williams [88]	2639
5	29	A	Dagenham & R	D	1-1	0-1	17	Hitchcock [74]	1653
6	Sept 5	H	Plymouth Arg	W	2-1	2-0	14	Ogilvie [6], Whelpdale [38]	3560
7	12	H	York C	D	2-2	0-1	16	Whelpdale [52], Lee [55]	3319
8	19	A	Barnet	L	2-3	1-0	17	Franks [11], Hitchcock [50]	2480
9	26	A	Cambridge U	L	0-1	0-0	20		4852
10	29	H	Mansfield T	L	0-2	0-0	20		2509
11	Oct 3	H	Carlisle U	L	0-1	0-0	20		2999
12	11	A	Exeter C	D	3-3	2-2	20	Parrett [39], Kennedy [45], Whelpdale [90]	3235
13	17	H	Wycombe W	W	2-1	1-0	20	Joronen [10], Gnanduillet [60]	3292
14	20	A	Portsmouth	D	1-1	0-0	20	Williams [90]	14,900
15	24	A	Northampton T	L	1-2	1-0	20	Schumacher [24]	4492
16	31	H	Oxford U	L	1-5	1-2	20	Whelpdale [17]	3412
17	Nov 14	A	Yeovil T	D	2-2	0-0	20	Wells [55], Pett [88]	3220
18	21	H	Luton T	D	0-0	0-0	20		4782
19	24	A	Bristol R	W	2-1	1-1	20	Schumacher [4], Whelpdale [60]	5819
20	28	H	Morecambe	W	4-3	2-1	18	Wells [7], Whelpdale 3 [20, 49, 61]	2415
21	Dec 12	A	AFC Wimbledon	W	2-1	0-1	18	Matt [57], Okimo [76]	3846
22	19	H	Accrington S	D	1-1	1-0	18	Gnanduillet [1]	2818
23	26	A	Crawley T	L	1-2	0-0	19	Tonge (pen) [87]	2289
24	28	A	Dagenham & R	L	1-3	1-3	19	Franks [32]	3152
25	Jan 2	H	Leyton Orient	D	2-2	0-0	19	Gnanduillet 2 [75, 79]	4022
26	9	A	Mansfield T	L	1-2	0-1	19	Gnanduillet [90]	3126
27	16	A	Plymouth Arg	L	2-3	1-3	19	Lee 2 [6, 49]	9546
28	23	H	Barnet	D	0-0	0-0	19		3801
29	30	A	York C	L	1-2	0-1	19	Keane [78]	2951
30	Feb 6	H	Crawley T	L	0-1	0-1	19		2639
31	9	A	Hartlepool U	W	2-1	1-0	19	Conlon 2 [45, 52]	3308
32	13	H	Cambridge U	W	2-0	1-0	19	Harrison 2 [18, 63]	3945
33	20	A	Carlisle U	L	0-1	0-0	19		4780
34	27	H	Exeter C	L	0-2	0-0	20		2812
35	Mar 5	H	Portsmouth	L	0-2	0-1	21		4092
36	12	A	Wycombe W	L	0-1	0-0	21		3715
37	19	H	Northampton T	L	2-3	2-1	22	Wilkinson 2 [11, 30]	3902
38	25	A	Oxford U	D	1-1	0-0	22	Harrison [69]	7980
39	Apr 2	A	Luton T	W	1-0	0-0	22	Tonge (pen) [85]	8502
40	5	H	Yeovil T	D	0-0	0-0	22		2748
41	9	A	Notts Co	L	0-1	0-0	22		4172
42	16	H	Newport Co	W	2-1	2-0	21	Mulraney [9], O'Connor [33]	2673
43	19	H	Bristol R	D	0-0	0-0	21		3836
44	23	A	Morecambe	W	4-1	2-1	19	Goodall (og) [38], Parrett 2 [45, 71], Kennedy [86]	1129
45	30	H	AFC Wimbledon	D	0-0	0-0	19		4011
46	May 7	A	Accrington S	D	0-0	0-0	18		4386

Final League Position: 18

GOALSCORERS

League (52): Whelpdale 8, Gnanduillet 5, Franks 3, Harrison 3, Lee 3, Parrett 3, Conlon 2, Hitchcock 2, Kennedy 2, Schumacher 2, Tonge 2 (2 pens), Wells 2, Wilkinson 2, Williams 2, Akinyemi 1, Hughes 1, Joronen 1, Keane 1, Matt 1, Mulraney 1, O'Connor 1, Ogilvie 1, Okimo 1, Pett 1, own goal 1.
FA Cup (3): Gnanduillet 1, Schumacher 1, Whelpdale 1.
Capital One Cup (1): own goal 1.
Johnstone's Paint Trophy (1): Kennedy 1 (pen).

Jones J 17	Day C 19	Franks F 37 + 1	Petravicius D 1	Hughes M 19 + 1	Wells D 28	Okimo J 13	Lee C 21 + 9	Schumacher S 15	Hoban P 1	Parrett D 22 + 5	Conlon T 15 + 17	Akinyemi D 6 + 8	Williams B 7 + 8	Hedges R 5 + 1	Hitchcock T 5 + 5	Harrison B 6 + 3	McAllister D — + 1	Pett T 34 + 6	Gorman D 6 + 7	Storer J — + 1	Ogilvie C 21	Luer G 9 + 1	Gordan R 3 + 1	Whelpdale C 18 + 3	Pritchard B 4	Joronen J 10	Smith C 3 + 1	Mulraney J 5 + 1	Jebb J 3 + 2	Henry R 30 + 1	McCombe J 13 + 1	Johnson R 4 + 3	McEvoy K — + 1	Kennedy B 13 + 9	Loza J 1	Ghanduillet A 9 + 5	Adams C — + 2	Tonge M 29	Marriott A 1 + 5	Matt J 6 + 2	Cox L 9 + 3	McFadzean C 6	Keane K 5 + 1	O'Connor A 9 + 4	Wilkinson L 17 + 2	Zanzala O 1 + 1	Match No.
	1	2	3	4	5	6	7¹	8	9³	10²	11	12²	13	14																																	1
	1	2	3	4	5	8³	6²	7	13	11¹	10	12						9	14																												2
	1	2	3	4	5	9²	6	8	12	10	11¹	13						7³	14																												3
	1	2	3	4		7³	8			11²	10	14						13	9			5	6¹	12																							4
		2	4	3		9	6			12	10³	11	14					13	7¹			5		8²	1																						5
	1	2	3	4		11³				7	14		13	10				9				8	6²		5¹	12																					6
		2	3	4		10¹					14	13	12	11²				6			5	9	1	7	8³																					7
		2	3	4	5	10³	7	12			13	14	11²					9				6	1	8¹																						8
	14	4				10	7				12		11²					9³				6	1		8	2	3	5¹	13																	9
		3				7				9¹	14	10	11					6³	1	12	8²	2	4	5	13																					10
		3	4			7	8¹	6	13	11³								5			12	1		2	14			10	9²																	11
	1	2	3	4		7	6	9¹		12								13			5	10		8²				11																		12
		2	4		5	7	8	9		13								12			6²	1		3				11¹	10																	13
		2	4		5	13		14	8		10³	12	14					9				1		3				6¹	7																	14
		2	4		5	14	8			10³	12	13						9			6²	1		3				11¹	7																	15
		2	3		5		8²	9¹	14			11						6¹	1			12	4⁴		13				10	7¹																	16
	1	3		4		7	8²	11¹		13								6			5	9		2				10	12																	17
	1	3		4	8¹	7	13			9								5	6²		2			10	11			12																		18
	1	3		4	12	6²				9	13							8¹			2			10³	14	7	11																			19
	1	4²	12	3	13					9								5	6¹		2			10			8	11	7																	20
	1		3	5						10								6			2	4		12	8		11	7	9¹																	21
	1	4	5							8	12							11			2	3		10	7		6	9¹																		22
	1	3				14				10					12	6¹					2	4	5	11²	7			13	9	8³																23
	1	5	4³		9					13					10						2	3		14	12	7		11	6¹	8²																24
	1	4				7				6					5	10¹					2	3		12	13	8		11	9²																	25
	1	4				10				13					7						5	6¹		2	3			12	8	11	9²															26
	1	4				9		12	10³	13					8			5			14	2	3		6						7²	11¹														27
	1	5				10¹		12			7				3						6			4				8	9	2	11															28
	1	2	6²	4	11	13				9					5									7¹					12	8	10	3														29
		4			6	10²	8	12	14						5		9	7³			2			11¹						3	13															30
		4			7	6²	12	9²			11¹	14						5			3								13	8	10	2														31
	1	4			7			11¹	6		10²	9³						5			2			14				8			12	13	3													32
	1	4			6¹	8		9²	8²		10³	11						5			2			7	14		6				12	13	3													33
	1	3				9³		8²	10¹	11								5			2			13				7	14	6		12	4													34
	1	4				14	8	11³	10	9¹								5			2			12			6	13	7²				3													35
	1	3	4	5		7	10			13	6²				14			2¹			11			8			9³						12													36
	1	4⁴		5		2	13			11			6					10²						12			9¹		8	7			3													37
	1	4¹	5		2	13			11	12	6			10					9²			14			8³			7				3														38
	1	5	4		6³					13		10¹			8					9²			2		11			12	7			14	3													39
	1	5	4		7¹	14			13			10²		12	9			6²	2			11			8								3													40
	1	5	4			10				13	9			6¹	8²			2			14	12	7					11³	3																	41
	1	5	4	13	6					9	14	11²			8¹			2			12		7					10³	3																	42
	1	5	4	13	8					6		11¹			9²			2			12		7					10	3																	43
	1	5	4	13	7²	12				6	14				2						9		8					11¹	3																	44
	1	5	4	13	8	14				6		10²		9¹	2						11²		7	12					3																	45
	1	5	3	6	14	8				9¹		11²			13			2			4³			7	10				12																	46

FA Cup

First Round	Gillingham	(h)	3-0	
Second Round	Yeovil T	(a)	0-1	

Capital One Cup

First Round	Ipswich T	(a)	1-2

Johnstone's Paint Trophy

Second Round	Dagenham & R	(h)	1-2

STOKE CITY

FOUNDATION

The date of the formation of this club has long been in doubt. The year 1863 was claimed, but more recent research by local club historian Wade Martin has uncovered nothing earlier than 1868, when a couple of Old Carthusians, who were apprentices at the local works of the old North Staffordshire Railway Company, met with some others from that works, to form Stoke Ramblers. It should also be noted that the old Stoke club went bankrupt in 1908 when a new club was formed.

Britannia Stadium, Stanley Matthews Way, Stoke-on-Trent, Staffordshire ST4 4EG.

Telephone: (01782) 367 598.

Fax: (01782) 592 221.

Ticket Office: (01782) 367 599.

Website: www.stokecityfc.com

Email: info@stokecityfc.com

Ground Capacity: 27,740.

Record Attendance: 51,380 v Arsenal, Division 1, 29 March 1937 (at Victoria Ground); 28,218 v Everton, FA Cup 3rd rd, 5 January 2002 (at Britannia Stadium).

Pitch Measurements: 105m × 68m (115yd × 75yd).

Chairman: Peter Coates.

Chief Executive: Tony Scholes.

Manager: Mark Hughes.

Assistant Manager: Mark Bowen.

Physio: Chris Banks.

Colours: Red and white striped shirts, white shorts with red trim, red socks with white trim.

Year Formed: 1863* (*see Foundation*).

Turned Professional: 1885.

Previous Names: 1868, Stoke Ramblers; 1870, Stoke; 1925, Stoke City.

Club Nickname: 'The Potters'.

Grounds: 1875, Sweeting's Field; 1878, Victoria Ground (previously known as the Athletic Club Ground); 1997, Britannia Stadium.

First Football League Game: 8 September 1888, Football League, v WBA (h) L 0–2 – Rowley; Clare, Underwood; Ramsey, Shutt, Smith; Sayer, McSkimming, Staton, Edge, Tunnicliffe.

Record League Victory: 10–3 v WBA, Division 1, 4 February 1937 – Doug Westland; Brigham, Harbot; Tutin, Turner (1p), Kirton; Matthews, Antonio (2), Freddie Steele (5), Jimmy Westland, Johnson (2).

Record Cup Victory: 7–1 v Burnley, FA Cup 2nd rd (replay), 20 February 1896 – Clawley; Clare, Eccles; Turner, Grewe, Robertson; Willie Maxwell, Dickson, Alan Maxwell (3), Hyslop (4), Schofield.

Record Defeat: 0–10 v Preston NE, Division 1, 14 September 1889.

HONOURS

League Champions: Division 2 – 1932–33, 1962–63; Second Division – 1992–93; Division 3N – 1926–27. *Runners-up:* FL C – 2007–08; Division 2 – 1921–22.

FA Cup: Runners-up: 2011.

League Cup Winners: 1972. *Runners-up:* 1964.

League Trophy Winners: 1992, 2000.

European Competitions **UEFA Cup:** 1972–73, 1974–75. *Europa League:* 2011–12.

sky SPORTS FACT FILE

In the summer of 1967 Stoke City played in the USA, competing in the United Soccer Association as Cleveland Stokers. City finished as runners-up in the Eastern Division and had Peter Dobing, George Eastham and Roy Vernon all selected for the USA All-Star team.

Most League Points (2 for a win): 63, Division 3 (N), 1926–27.

Most League Points (3 for a win): 93, Division 2, 1992–93.

Most League Goals: 92, Division 3 (N), 1926–27.

Highest League Scorer in Season: Freddie Steele, 33, Division 1, 1936–37.

Most League Goals in Total Aggregate: Freddie Steele, 142, 1934–49.

Most League Goals in One Match: 7, Neville Coleman v Lincoln C, Division 2, 23 February 1957.

Most Capped Player: Glenn Whelan, 73, Republic of Ireland.

Most League Appearances: Eric Skeels, 507, 1958–76.

Youngest League Player: Peter Bullock, 16 years 163 days v Swansea C, 19 April 1958.

Record Transfer Fee Received: £8,000,000 from Chelsea for Asmir Begovic, July 2015.

Record Transfer Fee Paid: £18,300,000 to Porto for Gianelli Imbula, February 2016.

Football League Record: 1888 Founder Member of Football League; 1890 Not re-elected; 1891 Re-elected; relegated in 1907, and after one year in Division 2, resigned for financial reasons; 1919 re-elected to Division 2; 1922–23 Division 1; 1923–26 Division 2; 1926–27 Division 3 (N); 1927–33 Division 2; 1933–53 Division 1; 1953–63 Division 2; 1963–77 Division 1; 1977–79 Division 2; 1979–85 Division 1; 1985–90 Division 2; 1990–92 Division 3; 1992–93 Division 2; 1993–98 Division 1; 1998–2002 Division 2; 2002–04 Division 1; 2004–08 FL C; 2008– FA Premier League.

LATEST SEQUENCES

Longest Sequence of League Wins: 8, 30.3.1895 – 21.9.1895.

Longest Sequence of League Defeats: 11, 6.4.1985 – 17.8.1985.

Longest Sequence of League Draws: 5, 13.5.2012 – 15.9.2012.

Longest Sequence of Unbeaten League Matches: 25, 5.9.1992 – 20.2.1993.

Longest Sequence Without a League Win: 17, 22.4.1989 – 14.10.1989.

Successive Scoring Runs: 21 from 24.12.1921.

Successive Non-scoring Runs: 8 from 29.12.1984.

MANAGERS

Tom Slaney 1874–83
(Secretary-Manager)
Walter Cox 1883–84
(Secretary-Manager)
Harry Lockett 1884–90
Joseph Bradshaw 1890–92
Arthur Reeves 1892–95
William Rowley 1895–97
H. D. Austerberry 1897–1908
A. J. Barker 1908–14
Peter Hodge 1914–15
Joe Schofield 1915–19
Arthur Shallcross 1919–23
John 'Jock' Rutherford 1923
Tom Mather 1923–35
Bob McGrory 1935–52
Frank Taylor 1952–60
Tony Waddington 1960–77
George Eastham 1977–78
Alan A'Court 1978
Alan Durban 1978–81
Richie Barker 1981–83
Bill Asprey 1984–85
Mick Mills 1985–89
Alan Ball 1989–91
Lou Macari 1991–93
Joe Jordan 1993–94
Lou Macari 1994–97
Chic Bates 1997–98
Chris Kamara 1998
Brian Little 1998–99
Gary Megson 1999
Gudjon Thordarson 1999–2002
Steve Cotterill 2002
Tony Pulis 2002–05
Johan Boskamp 2005–06
Tony Pulis 2006–13
Mark Hughes May 2013–

TEN YEAR LEAGUE RECORD

		P	W	D	L	F	A	Pts	Pos
2006-07	FL C	46	19	16	11	62	41	73	8
2007-08	FL C	46	21	16	9	69	55	79	2
2008-09	PR Lge	38	12	9	17	38	55	45	12
2009-10	PR Lge	38	11	14	13	34	48	47	11
2010-11	PR Lge	38	13	7	18	46	48	46	13
2011-12	PR Lge	38	11	12	15	36	53	45	14
2012-13	PR Lge	38	9	15	14	34	45	42	13
2013-14	PR Lge	38	13	11	14	45	52	50	9
2014-15	PR Lge	38	15	9	14	48	45	54	9
2015-16	PR Lge	38	14	9	15	41	55	51	9

DID YOU KNOW ?

Stanley Matthews' first Football League goal came in March 1933 when he netted for Stoke City in their 3-1 victory at local rivals Port Vale. The result put City two points clear at the top of Division Two and they went on to finish the season as champions.

STOKE CITY – FA PREMIER LEAGUE 2015–16 LEAGUE RECORD

Match No.	Date	Venue	Opponents	Result		H/T Score	Lg Pos.	Goalscorers	Attendance
1	Aug 9	H	Liverpool	L	0-1	0-0	15		27,654
2	15	A	Tottenham H	D	2-2	0-2	13	Arnautovic (pen) [78], Diouf [83]	36,004
3	22	A	Norwich C	D	1-1	1-1	14	Diouf [11]	26,771
4	29	H	WBA	L	0-1	0-1	17		26,747
5	Sept 12	A	Arsenal	L	0-2	0-1	20		59,963
6	19	H	Leicester C	D	2-2	2-0	18	Bojan [13], Walters [20]	27,642
7	26	H	Bournemouth	W	2-1	1-0	17	Walters [32], Diouf [83]	27,742
8	Oct 3	A	Aston Villa	W	1-0	0-0	14	Arnautovic [55]	33,189
9	19	A	Swansea C	W	1-0	1-0	11	Bojan (pen) [4]	20,044
10	24	H	Watford	L	0-2	0-1	14		27,587
11	31	A	Newcastle U	D	0-0	0-0	14		47,139
12	Nov 7	H	Chelsea	W	1-0	0-0	12	Arnautovic [53]	27,550
13	21	A	Southampton	W	1-0	1-0	11	Bojan [10]	30,039
14	28	A	Sunderland	L	0-2	0-0	12		41,516
15	Dec 5	H	Manchester C	W	2-0	2-0	10	Arnautovic 2 [7, 15]	27,264
16	12	A	West Ham U	D	0-0	0-0	11		34,857
17	19	H	Crystal Palace	L	1-2	0-1	11	Bojan (pen) [76]	27,500
18	26	H	Manchester U	W	2-0	2-0	11	Bojan [19], Arnautovic [26]	27,426
19	28	A	Everton	W	4-3	2-1	9	Shaqiri 2 [16, 45], Joselu [80], Arnautovic (pen) [90]	39,340
20	Jan 2	A	WBA	L	1-2	0-0	10	Walters [81]	23,218
21	13	H	Norwich C	W	3-1	0-0	7	Walters [49], Joselu [67], Bennett, R (og) [78]	27,274
22	17	H	Arsenal	D	0-0	0-0	7		27,683
23	23	A	Leicester C	L	0-3	0-1	9		32,018
24	Feb 2	A	Manchester U	L	0-3	0-2	9		75,234
25	6	H	Everton	L	0-3	0-3	11		27,733
26	13	A	Bournemouth	W	3-1	1-0	9	Imbula [9], Afellay [52], Joselu [55]	10,863
27	27	H	Aston Villa	W	2-1	0-0	8	Arnautovic 2 (1 pen) [51 (p), 56]	27,703
28	Mar 2	H	Newcastle U	W	1-0	0-0	7	Shaqiri [80]	27,331
29	5	A	Chelsea	D	1-1	0-1	7	Diouf [85]	41,381
30	12	H	Southampton	L	1-2	0-2	9	Arnautovic [52]	27,833
31	19	A	Watford	W	2-1	1-0	7	Walters [18], Joselu [51]	20,759
32	Apr 2	H	Swansea C	D	2-2	1-0	8	Afellay [13], Bojan [53]	27,649
33	10	A	Liverpool	L	1-4	1-2	9	Bojan [22]	43,688
34	18	H	Tottenham H	L	0-4	0-1	9		27,442
35	23	A	Manchester C	L	0-4	0-2	10		53,974
36	30	H	Sunderland	D	1-1	0-0	9	Arnautovic [50]	27,667
37	May 7	A	Crystal Palace	L	1-2	1-0	10	Adam [26]	23,990
38	15	H	West Ham U	W	2-1	0-1	9	Imbula [55], Diouf [88]	27,721

Final League Position: 9

GOALSCORERS

League (41): Arnautovic 11 (3 pens), Bojan 7 (2 pens), Diouf 5, Walters 5, Joselu 4, Shaqiri 3, Afellay 2, Imbula 2, Adam 1, own goal 1.
FA Cup (2): Crouch 1, Walters 1.
Capital One Cup (6): Walters 2, Afellay 1, Arnautovic 1, Bardsley 1, Crouch 1.

Butland J 31	Johnson G 25	Cameron G 27+3	Muniesa M 12+3	Pieters E 35	van Ginkel M 8+9	Whelan G 37	Walters J 18+9	Adam C 12+10	Afellay I 24+7	Diouf M 12+14	Wollscheid P 30+1	Odemwingie P —+5	Sidwell S —+1	Arnautovic M 33+1	Joselu M 10+12	Ireland S —+13	Shaqiri X 27	Wilson M 1+3	Bardsley P 9+2	Bojan K 22+5	Crouch P 4+7	Shawcross R 20	Imbula G 14	Dionatan T —+1	Haugaard J 4+1	Given S 3	Match No.
1	2	3	4	5^1	6	7	8	9^3	10^2	11	12	13	14														1
1	2	3	4	5	6^1	7	8^2	14	9	11				10^3	12	13											2
1	2	3	4	5	6^3	7		14	9^1	11				10^4	12	13	8										3
1	2^1	3	4	5	7	6		9^5	10^5	11^3				13		14	8^2	12									4
1		3	4	5	6	7		9^2						10	11^1	12	8		2	13							5
1	2	3		5	7^2	6	11		10^1				14		13	8	4			9^2	12						6
1	2	3		5	14	6	11	7^3	12	13	4			10			8^1			9^2							7
1	2	3		5	13	7	8	6	12	11^3	4			10^4	14					9^1							8
1	2	3		5	12	7		6^1	13		4			10^2	11	14	8			9^3							9
1	2	3^1		5		7	13	6			4			10	11^3		8^2	12		9	14						10
1	2			5	13	7	11	6	12		4			10^2			8^3			9^1	14	3					11
1	2	12		5		6	11	7^2	13	14	4			10			8^3			9^1		3					12
1	2	13		5		6	11^3	7	12	14	4			10			8^1			9^2		3					13
1	2	12		5		6	11	7^2	14	13	4			10			8^2			9^1		3^4					14
1	2	6		5	13	7	14		9^3		4			10	12		8^2			11^1		3					15
1	2	6^1		5	9^1	7	13	14	8^2	12	4			10						11		3					16
1	2			5	6^2	7	12	13	9		4			10			8			11		3					17
1	2	6^2		5	12	7^1		14	9	13	4			10			8^2			11		3					18
1	2	6^2		5	14	7	13		9		4			10	12		8^3			11^1		3					19
1	2	6^4		5		7^2	13	14	9		4			10	12		8^3			11^1		3					20
1	2			5	13	6	8		7		4	12		10^2	11^3					9^1	14	3					21
1	2			5	14	6	8	13	7^3	12	4			10^2	11					9^1		3					22
1	2			5		6	8		7	10^2	4	13								9^3	12		14	3^1			23
1	2		4	5		6	8		7			3^1		10		13			12	9^2	11						24
1	2		4	5		7			9^1	11		3	12	10^3	14	13	8^2					6					25
1	2^2		4^1	5		6	11		9^3	10		3			13	14	8					7	12				26
1		3		5		6	11^2		9^1	14	4			10^2	12		8		2	13		7					27
1		3	12	5		7	11^2		9^3	14	4			10			8		2^1		13	6					28
1		2	4	5		6^1			9	11^2	3			10^3	13	14	8			12		7					29
1		2		5^1		6^2	14		9	11	4			10			8^1			12	13	3	7				30
1		3	5			6	8		9^1	12	4			10^2	11	13			2			7					31
		3		5		6^2		8	12	4				10	11	13			2	9^1		7				1	32
		6	14	5^2				10	12	4				13			8^1		2	9^2	11	3	7		1		33
		2	5			6^2		13	9		4			10	12		8^1			11		3	7			1	34
		6	5			7		13		8	4			10^2	11				2			3	9	12	1^1		35
		4	14	5		6	12	9^1		13				10^1			8^2		2	11		3	7			1	36
		4		5		6^2	12	9^2						10			13	8^1	2	14	11	3	7			1	37
		2^2		5		6	8	13		12	4			10	11^1				14	9^2		3	7			1	38

FA Cup

Third Round	Doncaster R	(a)	2-1	
Fourth Round	Crystal Palace	(a)	0-1	

Capital One Cup

Second Round	Luton T	(a)	1-1
(aet; Stoke C won 8-7 on penalties)			
Third Round	Fulham	(a)	1-0
Fourth Round	Chelsea	(h)	1-1
(aet; Stoke C won 5-4 on penalties)			
Quarter-Final	Sheffield W	(h)	2-0
Semi-Final 1st leg	Liverpool	(h)	0-1
Semi-Final 2nd leg	Liverpool	(a)	1-0
(aet; Liverpool won 6-5 on penalties)			

SUNDERLAND

FOUNDATION

A Scottish schoolmaster named James Allan, working at Hendon Board School, took the initiative in the foundation of Sunderland in 1879 when they were formed as The Sunderland and District Teachers' Association FC at a meeting in the Adults School, Norfolk Street. Due to financial difficulties, they quickly allowed members from outside the teaching profession and so became Sunderland AFC in October 1880.

Stadium of Light, Sunderland, Tyne and Wear SR5 1SU.

Telephone: (0871) 911 1200.

Fax: (0191) 551 5123.

Ticket Office: (0871) 911 1973.

Website: www.safc.com

Email: enquiries@safc.com

Ground Capacity: 48,707.

Record Attendance: 75,118 v Derby Co, FA Cup 6th rd replay, 8 March 1933 (at Roker Park); 48,353 v Liverpool, FA Premier League, 13 April 2002 (at Stadium of Light) (FA Premier League figure 46,062).

Pitch Measurements: 105m × 68m (114yd × 74yd).

Chairman: Ellis Short.

Chief Executive: Martin Bain.

Head Coach: Sam Allardyce.

Assistant Head Coach: Paul Bracewell.

Physio: Peter Brand.

Colours: Red and white striped shirts, black shorts with red trim, black socks with red trim.

Year Formed: 1879.

Turned Professional: 1886.

Previous Names: 1879, Sunderland and District Teachers AFC; 1880, Sunderland.

Club Nickname: 'The Black Cats'.

Grounds: 1879, Blue House Field, Hendon; 1882, Groves Field, Ashbrooke; 1883, Horatio Street; 1884, Abbs Field, Fulwell; 1886, Newcastle Road; 1898, Roker Park; 1997, Stadium of Light.

First Football League Game: 13 September 1890, Football League, v Burnley (h) L 2–3 – Kirtley; Porteous, Oliver; Wilson, Auld, Gibson; Spence (1), Miller, Campbell (1), Scott, Davy Hannah.

Record League Victory: 9–1 v Newcastle U (a), Division 1, 5 December 1908 – Roose; Forster, Melton; Daykin, Thomson, Low; Mordue (1), Hogg (3), Brown, Holley (3), Bridgett (2).

Record Cup Victory: 11–1 v Fairfield, FA Cup 1st rd, 2 February 1895 – Doig; McNeill, Johnston; Dunlop, McCreadie (1), Wilson; Gillespie (1), Millar (5), Campbell, Jimmy Hannah (3), Scott (1).

HONOURS

League Champions: Division 1 – 1892–93, 1894–95, 1901–02, 1912–13, 1935–36; Football League 1891–92; FL C – 2004–05, 2006–07; First Division – 1995–96, 1998–99; Division 2 – 1975–76; Division 3 – 1987–88. *Runners-up:* Division 1 – 1893–94, 1897–98, 1900–01, 1922–23, 1934–35; Division 2 – 1963–64, 1979–80.

FA Cup Winners: 1937, 1973. *Runners-up:* 1913, 1992.

League Cup: Runners-up: 1985, 2014.

European Competitions
European Cup-Winners' Cup: 1973–74.

sky SPORTS FACT FILE

When Sunderland won the Football League championship in 1892–93 they finished 11 points ahead of runners-up Preston North End and set a record by becoming the first team to score 100 league goals in a season. The 100th goal was scored by Scotland international Hughie Wilson who netted the third in a 3-2 win at Burnley in the Black Cats' final game of the season.

Record Defeat: 0–8 v Sheff Wed, Division 1, 26 December 1911; 0–8 v West Ham U, Division 1, 19 October 1968; 0–8 v Watford, Division 1, 25 September 1982; 0–8 v Southampton, FA Premier League, 18 October 2014.

Most League Points (2 for a win): 61, Division 2, 1963–64.

Most League Points (3 for a win): 105, Division 1, 1998–99.

Most League Goals: 109, Division 1, 1935–36.

Highest League Scorer in Season: Dave Halliday, 43, Division 1, 1928–29.

Most League Goals in Total Aggregate: Charlie Buchan, 209, 1911–25.

Most League Goals in One Match: 5, Charlie Buchan v Liverpool, Division 1, 7 December 1919; 5, Bobby Gurney v Bolton W, Division 1, 7 December 1935; 5, Dominic Sharkey v Norwich C, Division 2, 20 February 1962.

Most Capped Player: Seb Larsson, 54 (87), Sweden.

Most League Appearances: Jim Montgomery, 537, 1962–77.

Youngest League Player: Derek Forster, 15 years 184 days v Leicester C, 22 August 1964.

Record Transfer Fee Received: £18,000,000 (rising to £24,000,000) from Aston Villa for Darren Bent, January 2011.

Record Transfer Fee Paid: £12,000,000 (rising to £14,000,000) to Wolverhampton W for Steven Fletcher, August 2012.

Football League Record: 1890 Elected to Division 1; 1958–64 Division 2; 1964–70 Division 1; 1970–76 Division 2; 1976–77 Division 1; 1977–80 Division 2; 1980–85 Division 1; 1985–87 Division 2; 1987–88 Division 3; 1988–90 Division 2; 1990–91 Division 1; 1991–92 Division 2; 1992–96 Division 1; 1996–97 FA Premier League; 1997–99 Division 1; 1999–2003 FA Premier League; 2003–04 Division 1; 2004–05 FL C; 2005–06 FA Premier League; 2006–07 FL C; 2007– FA Premier League.

MANAGERS

Tom Watson 1888–96
Bob Campbell 1896–99
Alex Mackie 1899–1905
Bob Kyle 1905–28
Johnny Cochrane 1928–39
Bill Murray 1939–57
Alan Brown 1957–64
George Hardwick 1964–65
Ian McColl 1965–68
Alan Brown 1968–72
Bob Stokoe 1972–76
Jimmy Adamson 1976–78
Ken Knighton 1979–81
Alan Durban 1981–84
Len Ashurst 1984–85
Lawrie McMenemy 1985–87
Denis Smith 1987–91
Malcolm Crosby 1991–93
Terry Butcher 1993
Mick Buxton 1993–95
Peter Reid 1995–2002
Howard Wilkinson 2002–03
Mick McCarthy 2003–06
Niall Quinn 2006
Roy Keane 2006–08
Ricky Sbragia 2008–09
Steve Bruce 2009–11
Martin O'Neill 2011–13
Paolo Di Canio 2013
Gus Poyet 2013–15
Dick Advocaat 2015
Sam Allardyce October 2015–

LATEST SEQUENCES

Longest Sequence of League Wins: 13, 14.11.1891 – 2.4.1892.

Longest Sequence of League Defeats: 17, 18.1.2003 – 16.8.2003.

Longest Sequence of League Draws: 6, 26.3.1949 – 19.4.1949.

Longest Sequence of Unbeaten League Matches: 19, 3.5.1998 – 14.11.1998.

Longest Sequence Without a League Win: 22, 21.12.2002 – 16.8.2003.

Successive Scoring Runs: 29 from 8.11.1997.

Successive Non-scoring Runs: 10 from 27.11.1976.

TEN YEAR LEAGUE RECORD

		P	W	D	L	F	A	Pts	Pos
2006-07	FL C	46	27	7	12	76	47	88	1
2007-08	PR Lge	38	11	6	21	36	59	39	15
2008-09	PR Lge	38	9	9	20	34	54	36	16
2009-10	PR Lge	38	11	11	16	48	56	44	13
2010-11	PR Lge	38	12	11	15	45	56	47	10
2011-12	PR Lge	38	11	12	15	45	46	45	13
2012-13	PR Lge	38	9	12	17	41	54	39	17
2013-14	PR Lge	38	10	8	20	41	60	38	14
2014-15	PR Lge	38	7	17	14	31	53	38	16
2015-16	PR Lge	38	9	12	17	48	62	39	17

DID YOU KNOW ?

Willie Watson, who spent eight years with Sunderland, is one of the few men to have played for England at both football and cricket. Willie played four times for the England football team, including one against Wales at Roker Park in November 1950. He also played in 23 Test matches for the England cricket team.

SUNDERLAND – FA PREMIER LEAGUE 2015–16 LEAGUE RECORD

Match No.	Date	Venue	Opponents	Result	H/T Score	Lg Pos.	Goalscorers	Attendance
1	Aug 8	A	Leicester C	L	2-4	0-3	19	Defoe [60], Fletcher [71]	32,242
2	15	H	Norwich C	L	1-3	0-2	20	Watmore [88]	41,379
3	22	H	Swansea C	D	1-1	0-1	20	Defoe [62]	39,198
4	29	A	Aston Villa	D	2-2	1-2	20	M'Vila [8], Lens [52]	35,399
5	Sept 13	H	Tottenham H	L	0-1	0-0	20		40,303
6	19	A	Bournemouth	L	0-2	0-2	20		11,271
7	26	A	Manchester U	L	0-3	0-1	20		75,328
8	Oct 3	H	West Ham U	D	2-2	2-1	19	Fletcher [10], Lens [22]	42,932
9	17	A	WBA	L	0-1	0-0	19		24,225
10	25	H	Newcastle U	W	3-0	1-0	18	Johnson (pen) [45], Jones [65], Fletcher [86]	47,653
11	Nov 1	A	Everton	L	2-6	1-2	19	Defoe [45], Fletcher [50]	36,617
12	7	A	Southampton	L	0-1	0-0	19		41,781
13	23	A	Crystal Palace	W	1-0	0-0	18	Defoe [80]	24,361
14	28	H	Stoke C	W	2-0	0-0	17	Van Aanholt [82], Watmore [84]	41,516
15	Dec 5	A	Arsenal	L	1-3	1-1	18	Giroud (og) [45]	59,937
16	12	H	Watford	L	0-1	0-1	19		43,989
17	19	A	Chelsea	L	1-3	0-2	19	Borini [52]	41,562
18	26	A	Manchester C	L	1-4	0-3	19	Borini [59]	54,523
19	30	H	Liverpool	L	0-1	0-0	19		45,765
20	Jan 2	H	Aston Villa	W	3-1	0-0	19	Richards (og) [30], Defoe 2 [72, 90]	41,535
21	13	A	Swansea C	W	4-2	1-2	18	Defoe 3 [3, 61, 85], Fernandez (og) [49]	20,140
22	16	A	Tottenham H	L	1-4	1-1	19	Van Aanholt [40]	35,854
23	23	H	Bournemouth	D	1-1	1-1	19	Van Aanholt [45]	41,367
24	Feb 2	H	Manchester C	L	0-1	0-1	19		38,852
25	6	A	Liverpool	D	2-2	0-0	19	Johnson [82], Defoe [89]	44,179
26	13	H	Manchester U	W	2-1	1-1	19	Khazri [3], De Gea (og) [82]	41,687
27	27	A	West Ham U	L	0-1	0-1	19		34,946
28	Mar 1	H	Crystal Palace	D	2-2	1-0	17	N'Doye [36], Borini [90]	39,795
29	5	A	Southampton	D	1-1	0-0	17	Defoe [85]	31,458
30	20	A	Newcastle U	D	1-1	1-0	18	Defoe [44]	52,311
31	Apr 2	H	WBA	D	0-0	0-0	18		45,144
32	10	A	Leicester C	L	0-2	0-0	18		46,531
33	16	A	Norwich C	W	3-0	1-0	18	Borini (pen) [41], Defoe [53], Watmore [90]	27,117
34	24	H	Arsenal	D	0-0	0-0	17		45,420
35	30	A	Stoke C	D	1-1	0-0	18	Defoe (pen) [90]	27,667
36	May 7	H	Chelsea	W	3-2	1-2	17	Khazri [41], Borini [67], Defoe [70]	47,050
37	11	H	Everton	W	3-0	2-0	17	Van Aanholt [38], Kone 2 [42, 55]	46,454
38	15	A	Watford	D	2-2	1-0	17	Rodwell [39], Lens [51]	21,012

Final League Position: 17

GOALSCORERS

League (48): Defoe 15 (1 pen), Borini 5 (1 pen), Fletcher 4, Van Aanholt 4, Lens 3, Watmore 3, Johnson 2 (1 pen), Khazri 2, Kone 2, Jones 1, M'Vila 1, N'Doye 1, Rodwell 1, own goals 4.
FA Cup (1): Lens 1.
Capital One Cup (7): Defoe 3, Rodwell 2, Toivonen 1, Watmore 1.

Pantilimon C 17	Jones B 23+1	Coates S 14+2	Kaboul Y 22+1	Van Aanholt P 33	Cattermole L 27+4	Johnson A 11+8	Larsson S 6+12	Rodwell J 9+13	Lens J 14+6	Defoe J 28+5	Fletcher S 11+5	Matthews A —+1	M'Vila Y 36+1	Graham D 4+6	Watmore D 7+16	O'Shea J 23+5	Toivonen O 9+3	Gomez J 5+1	Borini F 22+4	Yedlin D 2+2	Brown W 6	Mannone V 19	Pickford J 2	Kirchhoff J 14+1	Kone L 15	Khazri W 13+1	N'Doye D 5+6	Robson T 1	Greenwood R 1	Honeyman G —+1	Match No.
1	2²	3	4	5	6¹	7	8	9	10	11	12	13																			1
1	2	3	4	5	7		6¹		9	11	10²		8	12	13																2
1	2	3		5	6		14	9	7³	10²	12		8	11¹	13	4															3
1	2		4	5	7²		14	8	9³	11	12		6	10¹		3	13														4
1	2		4	5	12			14	8	11			6		13	3	9³	7¹	10²												5
1	2	4	5		14			12	8	11²	13		6			9	7¹	10³													6
1	2		4	5	6		7¹	13		10		12	8			3	9²	11													7
1	5	3			7			12	13	8*		11²	6³			4	9¹	14	10	2											8
1	5		4		6	12	8¹			13	11³		7	14		3			9²	10	2										9
1	5	13	4		6		8	14		10³	12	11	7			3²	9¹			2											10
1	4	2		8	6¹	9	13	12		10	11³		7		14				5²	3											11
1	5	3	4		8		13			14	11²		6		10		9¹	7²	12	2											12
1	5	2	4	9	8		6²		12	11³	10¹		7	14	13	3															13
1		2	4	9	8	14	6²		13	11¹	10		7		12	3³		5													14
1		2	4	8		13		12	14		10³		6	11	3	7¹		9²	5												15
1	5	3		6			13		12		14	11³	9	10	4	8			7²	2¹											16
1	2	3¹	5	6		12		9		11			8	14	10³	4	7²		13												17
	2	3		5	12	6		13		10²			7¹	9³	14	4		8	11			1									18
	2	3³		5	6	9²		8¹	13	10			7	12		11	14	4				1									19
	2	14		5	6	9³				11			7	12	8¹	3	13	10²	4			1									20
	2			5	6¹	8		12		9³	11		7	13	14	3		10²	4			1									21
	2			5	6¹	8		12		9³	11		7	10²	14	3			4			1	1	13							22
	2			5	6	8		13		9³	11		7	12		3		10¹	4			1									23
	2			5	9²		13			7¹	11		8			4		10³					1		6	3	12	14			24
	2³			5	8	13				11			9		7¹	4		14					1		6²	3	10	12			25
				5	8³			12		11²			9			4	14	13	2				1		6¹	3	10	7			26
				5	8¹			12		11			9			4			2				1		6	3	10	7			27
	12		5	13³				9		11			8			4¹			7	2			1		6²	3	10	7			28
		4	5				13	9		12			8			14			7	2			1		6³	3	10²	11¹			29
	4¹	5	14				9			11			8			12			7	2			1		6³	3	10¹	13			30
		4	5	8						11			9			7³			2				1		6	3	10¹	12			31
		4	5	8		13	14	11					9²			7³			2				1		6	3	10¹	12			32
		4	5	8	13			11					9²	12	14	7			2				1		6²	3	10¹				33
		4	5	9	13			11					8	12		7¹			2				1		6²	3	10				34
		4	5	9	14			11					8	13		7¹			2				1		6³	3	10²	12			35
		4	5	8³	14			11					9	13	12	7			2				1		6²	3¹	10				36
		4	5	8²	12			11					9	14	13	7			2				1		6¹	3	10³				37
	14				6²	7	9						13	8	4				2³				1			3	11	5	10¹	12	38

FA Cup
Third Round   Arsenal   (a)   1-3

Capital One Cup
Second Round   Exeter C   (h)   6-3
Third Round   Manchester C   (h)   1-4

SWANSEA CITY

FOUNDATION

The earliest Association Football in Wales was played in the northern part of the country and no international took place in the south until 1894, when a local paper still thought it necessary to publish an outline of the rules and an illustration of the pitch markings. There had been an earlier Swansea club, but this has no connection with Swansea Town (now City) formed at a public meeting in June 1912.

Liberty Stadium, Morfa, Landore, Swansea SA1 2FA.
Telephone: (01792) 616 600.
Fax: (01792) 616 606.
Ticket Office: (0844) 815 6665.
Website: www.swanseacity.net
Email: info@swanseacityfc.co.uk
Ground Capacity: 20,909.
Record Attendance: 32,796 v Arsenal, FA Cup 4th rd, 17 February 1968 (at Vetch Field); 20,972 v Liverpool, FA Premier League, 1 May 2016 (at Liberty Stadium).
Pitch Measurements: 105m × 68m (114yd × 74yd).
Chairman: Huw Jenkins.
Vice-chairman: Leigh Dineen.
Manager: Francesco Guidolin.
First-Team Coach: Alan Curtis.
Head Physio: Kate Rees.

HONOURS

League Champions: FL 1 – 2007–08; Division 3S – 1924–25, 1948–49; Third Division – 1999–2000.
FA Cup: semi-final – 1926, 1964.
League Cup Winners: 2013.
League Trophy Winners: 1994, 2006.
Welsh Cup Winners: 11 times; *Runners-up:* 8 times.
European Competitions
Europa League: 2013–14.
European Cup-Winners' Cup: 1961–62, 1966–67, 1981–82, 1982–83, 1983–84, 1989–90, 1991–92.

Colours: White shirts with copper trim, white shorts with copper trim, white socks with copper trim.
Year Formed: 1912.
Turned Professional: 1912.
Previous Name: 1912, Swansea Town; 1970, Swansea City.
Club Nicknames: 'The Swans', 'The Jacks'.
Grounds: 1912, Vetch Field; 2005, Liberty Stadium.
First Football League Game: 28 August 1920, Division 3, v Portsmouth (a) L 0–3 – Crumley; Robson, Evans; Smith, Holdsworth, Williams; Hole, Ivor Jones, Edmundson, Rigsby, Spottiswood.
Record League Victory: 8–0 v Hartlepool U, Division 4, 1 April 1978 – Barber; Evans, Bartley, Lally (1) (Morris), May, Bruton, Kevin Moore, Robbie James (3 incl. 1p), Curtis (3), Toshack (1), Chappell.
Record Cup Victory: 12–0 v Sliema W (Malta), ECWC 1st rd 1st leg, 15 September 1982 – Davies; Marustik, Hadziabdic (1), Irwin (1), Kennedy, Rajkovic (1), Loveridge (2) (Leighton James), Robbie James, Charles (2), Stevenson (1), Latchford (1) (Walsh (3)).
Record Defeat: 0–8 v Liverpool, FA Cup 3rd rd, 9 January 1990; 0–8 v Monaco, ECWC, 1st rd 2nd leg, 1 October 1991.
Most League Points (2 for a win): 62, Division 3 (S), 1948–49.

sky SPORTS FACT FILE

In the summer of 1927 Swansea began a tour of Spain by losing to Motherwell in Madrid in a game played for a trophy donated by the King of Spain. The Swans also lost to a Spanish Army team and in a second fixture against Motherwell but defeated both Bilbao and Catalonia Athletic. The tour continued with games in Portugal and France before the team arrived home in June.

Most League Points (3 for a win): 92, FL 1, 2007–08.

Most League Goals: 90, Division 2, 1956–57.

Highest League Scorer in Season: Cyril Pearce, 35, Division 2, 1931–32.

Most League Goals in Total Aggregate: Ivor Allchurch, 166, 1949–58, 1965–68.

Most League Goals in One Match: 5, Jack Fowler v Charlton Ath, Division 3S, 27 December 1924.

Most Capped Player: Ashley Williams, 64 (65), Wales.

Most League Appearances: Wilfred Milne, 587, 1919–37.

Youngest League Player: Nigel Dalling, 15 years 289 days v Southport, 6 December 1974.

Record Transfer Fee Received: £25,000,000 (rising to £28,000,000) from Manchester C for Wilfried Bony, January 2015.

Record Transfer Fee Paid: £12,000,000 to Vitesse Arnhem for Wilfried Bony, July 2013.

Football League Record: 1920 Original Member of Division 3; 1921–25 Division 3 (S); 1925–47 Division 2; 1947–49 Division 3 (S); 1949–65 Division 2; 1965–67 Division 3; 1967–70 Division 4; 1970–73 Division 3; 1973–78 Division 4; 1978–79 Division 3; 1979–81 Division 2; 1981–83 Division 1; 1983–84 Division 2; 1984–86 Division 3; 1986–88 Division 4; 1988–92 Division 3; 1992–96 Division 2; 1996–2000 Division 3; 2000–01 Division 2; 2001–04 Division 3; 2004–05 FL 2; 2005–08 FL 1; 2008–11 FL C; 2011– FA Premier League.

LATEST SEQUENCES

Longest Sequence of League Wins: 9, 27.11.1999 – 22.01.2000.

Longest Sequence of League Defeats: 9, 26.1.1991 – 19.3.1991.

Longest Sequence of League Draws: 8, 25.11.2008 – 28.12.2008.

Longest Sequence of Unbeaten League Matches: 19, 19.10.1970 – 9.3.1971.

Longest Sequence Without a League Win: 15, 25.3.1989 – 2.9.1989.

Successive Scoring Runs: 27 from 28.8.1947.

Successive Non-scoring Runs: 6 from 6.2.1996.

MANAGERS

Walter Whittaker 1912–14
William Bartlett 1914–15
Joe Bradshaw 1919–26
Jimmy Thomson 1927–31
Neil Harris 1934–39
Haydn Green 1939–47
Bill McCandless 1947–55
Ron Burgess 1955–58
Trevor Morris 1958–65
Glyn Davies 1965–66
Billy Lucas 1967–69
Roy Bentley 1969–72
Harry Gregg 1972–75
Harry Griffiths 1975–77
John Toshack 1978–83
  (resigned October re-appointed in December) 1983–84
Colin Appleton 1984
John Bond 1984–85
Tommy Hutchison 1985–86
Terry Yorath 1986–89
Ian Evans 1989–90
Terry Yorath 1990–91
Frank Burrows 1991–95
Bobby Smith 1995
Kevin Cullis 1996
Jan Molby 1996–97
Micky Adams 1997
Alan Cork 1997–98
John Hollins 1998–2001
Colin Addison 2001–02
Nick Cusack 2002
Brian Flynn 2002–04
Kenny Jackett 2004–07
Roberto Martinez 2007–09
Paulo Sousa 2009–10
Brendan Rodgers 2010–12
Michael Laudrup 2012–14
Garry Monk 2014–15
Francesco Guidolin January 2016–

TEN YEAR LEAGUE RECORD

		P	W	D	L	F	A	Pts	Pos
2006-07	FL 1	46	20	12	14	69	53	72	7
2007-08	FL 1	46	27	11	8	82	42	92	1
2008-09	FL C	46	16	20	10	63	50	68	8
2009-10	FL C	46	17	18	11	40	37	69	7
2010-11	FL C	46	24	8	14	69	42	80	3
2011-12	PR Lge	38	12	11	15	44	51	47	11
2012-13	PR Lge	38	11	13	14	47	51	46	9
2013-14	PR Lge	38	11	9	18	54	54	42	12
2014-15	PR Lge	38	16	8	14	46	49	56	8
2015-16	PR Lge	38	12	11	15	42	52	47	12

DID YOU KNOW

Billy Ball had the distinction of scoring Swansea's first goal in competitive football when he netted in the 1-1 draw against Cardiff City in a Southern League match in September 1912. He was also the first player to score a hat-trick for the club and the first to be sent off.

SWANSEA CITY – FA PREMIER LEAGUE 2015–16 LEAGUE RECORD

Match No.	Date	Venue	Opponents	Result		H/T Score	Lg Pos.	Goalscorers	Attendance
1	Aug 8	A	Chelsea	D	2-2	1-2	5	Ayew [29], Gomis (pen) [55]	41,232
2	15	H	Newcastle U	W	2-0	1-0	4	Gomis [9], Ayew [52]	20,678
3	22	A	Sunderland	D	1-1	1-0	6	Gomis [45]	39,198
4	30	H	Manchester U	W	2-1	0-0	4	Ayew [61], Gomis [66]	20,828
5	Sept 12	A	Watford	L	0-1	0-0	7		20,057
6	19	H	Everton	D	0-0	0-0	8		20,805
7	26	A	Southampton	L	1-3	0-1	11	Sigurdsson (pen) [83]	30,704
8	Oct 4	H	Tottenham H	D	2-2	2-1	11	Ayew [16], Kane (og) [31]	20,845
9	19	H	Stoke C	L	0-1	0-1	14		20,044
10	24	A	Aston Villa	W	2-1	0-0	11	Sigurdsson [68], Ayew [87]	33,324
11	31	H	Arsenal	L	0-3	0-0	13		20,937
12	Nov 7	A	Norwich C	L	0-1	0-0	14		27,029
13	21	H	Bournemouth	D	2-2	2-2	14	Ayew [28], Shelvey (pen) [39]	20,878
14	29	A	Liverpool	L	0-1	0-0	15		43,905
15	Dec 5	H	Leicester C	L	0-3	0-2	15		20,836
16	12	A	Manchester C	L	1-2	0-1	16	Gomis [90]	53,052
17	20	A	West Ham U	D	0-0	0-0	18		20,661
18	26	H	WBA	W	1-0	1-0	16	Ki [9]	20,789
19	28	A	Crystal Palace	D	0-0	0-0	17		23,714
20	Jan 2	A	Manchester U	L	1-2	0-0	17	Sigurdsson [70]	75,415
21	13	H	Sunderland	L	2-4	2-1	17	Sigurdsson (pen) [21], Ayew [40]	20,140
22	18	H	Watford	W	1-0	1-0	17	Williams [27]	20,430
23	24	A	Everton	W	2-1	2-1	15	Sigurdsson (pen) [17], Ayew [34]	36,908
24	Feb 2	A	WBA	D	1-1	0-0	16	Sigurdsson [64]	22,062
25	6	A	Crystal Palace	D	1-1	1-0	16	Sigurdsson [13]	20,492
26	13	H	Southampton	L	0-1	0-0	16		20,890
27	28	A	Tottenham H	L	1-2	1-0	16	Paloschi [19]	35,922
28	Mar 2	A	Arsenal	W	2-1	1-1	16	Routledge [32], Williams [74]	59,905
29	5	H	Norwich C	W	1-0	0-0	16	Sigurdsson [61]	20,929
30	12	H	Bournemouth	L	2-3	1-1	16	Barrow [39], Sigurdsson [62]	11,179
31	19	H	Aston Villa	W	1-0	0-0	15	Fernandez [53]	20,454
32	Apr 2	A	Stoke C	D	2-2	0-1	15	Sigurdsson [68], Paloschi [79]	27,649
33	9	H	Chelsea	W	1-0	1-0	16	Sigurdsson [25]	20,966
34	16	A	Newcastle U	L	0-3	0-1	15		48,949
35	24	A	Leicester C	L	0-4	0-2	15		31,962
36	May 1	H	Liverpool	W	3-1	2-0	13	Ayew 2 [20, 67], Cork [33]	20,972
37	7	A	West Ham U	W	4-1	2-0	11	Routledge [25], Ayew [31], Ki [51], Gomis [90]	34,907
38	15	H	Manchester C	D	1-1	1-1	12	Ayew [45]	20,934

Final League Position: 12

GOALSCORERS

League (42): Ayew 12, Sigurdsson 11 (3 pens), Gomis 6 (1 pen), Ki 2, Paloschi 2, Routledge 2, Williams 2, Barrow 1, Cork 1, Fernandez 1, Shelvey 1 (1 pen), own goal 1.
FA Cup (2): Gomis 1, Montero 1.
Capital One Cup (3): Dyer 1, Emnes 1, Grimes 1.

Fabianski L 37	Naughton K 19 + 8	Fernandez F 32	Williams A 36	Taylor N 33 + 1	Shelvey J 14 + 2	Ki S 21 + 7	Ayew A 34	Sigurdsson G 32 + 4	Montero J 14 + 9	Gomis B 18 + 15	Cork J 28 + 7	Routledge W 22 + 6	Eder A 2 + 11	Dyer N — + 1	Britton L 19 + 6	Bartley K 3 + 2	Barrow M 6 + 16	Rangel A 20 + 3	Amat J 5 + 3	Grimes M 1	Emnes M 1 + 1	Paloschi A 7 + 3	Fer L 9 + 2	Kingsley S 4	Fulton J — + 2	Nordfeldt K 1	Match No.
1	2	3	4	5	6	7¹	8	9	10²	11³	12	13	14														1
1	2	3	4	5		7	8¹	9¹	10²	11	6	13		12	14												2
1	2	3	4	5	7		8	9	10	11¹	6		12														3
1	2	3	4	5	7³	12	8	9		11²	6	10¹	13			14											4
1	2	3	4	5	7	13	8	9²	12	11	6²	10¹	14														5
1	2	3	4	5	7	12	8³	9	10	11²	6		13			14											6
1	2	3	4	5	8³	6	9	10	13	11²	7¹		12	14													7
1		3	4	5	7²	6	8	9	10	11	13						12	2									8
1		3	4	5	6	12	9³	13	10	11	7²		14				8¹	2									9
1	2	3	4	5	7²	6	8	9	10¹	11³	13		14				12										10
1	2	3	4	5	6	7²	8	9	10¹	11³			13	14			12										11
1	2	3	4	5	7³	6	8	9²	10¹	11			12	14	13												12
1	2		4	5	9	7	10	12	13	14			8¹	11³	6²	3											13
1	2		4	5	7	10	9	14	13	12			8¹	11²	6¹	3											14
1	2		4	5	7³	10	9	12	11	14			8¹		6²	3	13										15
1		3	4	5			8	9³	10	12	14	6	11²		7¹	13		2									16
1	12	3	4	5	13		8	10²	9		11	7²			6	14		2¹									17
1		3	4	5	14	7	11	9	10¹		12	8²			6³	13		2¹									18
1	2		4	5	6¹	12		13			10	7			14	11	3³	8	9²								19
1		3	4	5	8		10³	11	14	13	6	9²			7¹		12	2									20
1	2¹	3	4	5	7		11³	9	13	14		10²			6¹		8	12									21
1	2	3	4	5	8¹		10²	9	13	7		11¹			6		12	14									22
1	14	3	4	5	8		11²	9		6		10¹	13		7		2³	12									23
1	13	3	4	5²	8¹		9³	10		6		11			7		2	14				12					24
1	13	3	4	5	8		9	14		6		11¹			7		2²					10²					25
1	13	3	4	5	6		10	14		7		9¹			8³		2²					11					26
1		3	4	5	8²		10	9	13	6		7¹			14		2					11³	12				27
1	2		4		8¹		9¹	12		11	7	10				14	3					6²		5	13		28
1		3	4	5	8³		9	14		6		10			7²		12	2				11¹	13				29
1		3	4	5	14		9		12	6		10¹					8²	2			13	11	7³				30
1	13		4	3	7¹		10			11		6	14	12			8²	2					9	5³			31
1	5³	3	4		14		9	12	10²	6		11			7¹		2					13	8				32
1	14	3	4	5	8¹		9	10³	13	6		12						2				11²	7				33
1		3	4	5	8²		9	10	13	6		14					12	2				11³	7¹				34
1		3	4	5	14		7	11³	12	8		10²			6			2				13	9¹				35
1	12		4	5			11	9	10¹	6		8			7²		2	3					13				36
1	2	3			8			10³		13		7	11²		14		9¹	12	4				6	5			37
		3					10		11²	13		6	9¹		7		12	2	4				8	5		1	38

FA Cup
Third Round   Oxford U   (a)   2-3

Capital One Cup
Second Round   York C   (h)   3-0
Third Round   Hull C   (a)   0-1

SWINDON TOWN

FOUNDATION

It is generally accepted that Swindon Town came into being in 1881, although there is no firm evidence that the club's founder, Rev. William Pitt, captain of the Spartans (an offshoot of a cricket club), changed his club's name to Swindon Town before 1883, when the Spartans amalgamated with St Mark's Young Men's Friendly Society.

The County Ground, County Road, Swindon, Wiltshire SN1 2ED.

Telephone: (0871) 876 1879.

Fax: (0844) 880 1112.

Ticket Office: (0871) 876 1993.

Website: www.swindontownfc.co.uk

Email: enquiries@swindontownfc.co.uk

Ground Capacity: 15,547.

Record Attendance: 32,000 v Arsenal, FA Cup 3rd rd, 15 January 1972.

Pitch Measurements: 100.5m × 67m (110yd × 73.5yd).

Chairman: Lee Power.

General Manager: Steve Anderson.

Manager: Luke Williams.

First-Team Coach: Ross Embleton.

Physio: Paul Godfrey.

Colours: Red shirts with white trim, white shorts with red trim, red socks with white trim.

Year Formed: 1881* (*see Foundation*).

Turned Professional: 1894.

Club Nickname: 'The Robins'.

Grounds: 1881, The Croft; 1896, County Ground.

First Football League Game: 28 August 1920, Division 3, v Luton T (h) W 9–1 – Nash; Kay, Macconachie; Langford, Hawley, Wareing; Jefferson (1), Fleming (4), Rogers, Batty (2), Davies (1), (1 og).

Record League Victory: 9–1 v Luton T, Division 3 (S), 28 August 1920 – Nash; Kay, Macconachie; Langford, Hawley, Wareing; Jefferson (1), Fleming (4), Rogers, Batty (2), Davies (1), (1 og).

Record Cup Victory: 10–1 v Farnham U Breweries (away), FA Cup 1st rd (replay), 28 November 1925 – Nash; Dickenson, Weston, Archer, Bew, Adey; Denyer (2), Wall (1), Richardson (4), Johnson (3), Davies.

HONOURS

League Champions: Second Division – 1995–96; FL 2 – 2011–12; Division 4 – 1985–86.
Runners-up: Division 3 – 1962–63, 1968–69.
FA Cup: semi-final – 1910, 1912.
League Cup Winners: 1969.
League Trophy: Runners-up: 2012.
Anglo-Italian Cup Winners: 1970.

sky SPORTS FACT FILE

Winger Titus Okere toured England with the Nigerian team in 1949, then returned early in 1953, signing for Swindon Town. Believed to be the first black player on the club's books, he played in the reserve and A teams before being released to join Western League club Chippenham United for the 1953–54 season.

Record Defeat: 1–10 v Manchester C, FA Cup 4th rd (replay), 25 January 1930.

Most League Points (2 for a win): 64, Division 3, 1968–69.

Most League Points (3 for a win): 102, Division 4, 1985–86.

Most League Goals: 100, Division 3 (S), 1926–27.

Highest League Scorer in Season: Harry Morris, 47, Division 3 (S), 1926–27.

Most League Goals in Total Aggregate: Harry Morris, 216, 1926–33.

Most League Goals in One Match: 5, Harry Morris v QPR, Division 3 (S), 18 December 1926; 5, Harry Morris v Norwich C, Division 3 (S), 26 April 1930; 5, Keith East v Mansfield T, Division 3, 20 November 1965.

Most Capped Player: Rod Thomas, 30 (50), Wales.

Most League Appearances: John Trollope, 770, 1960–80.

Youngest League Player: Paul Rideout, 16 years 107 days v Hull C, 29 November 1980.

Record Transfer Fee Received: £1,500,000 (rising to £1,900,000) from WBA for Simon Cox, July 2009.

Record Transfer Fee Paid: £800,000 to West Ham U for Joey Beauchamp, August 1994.

Football League Record: 1920 Original Member of Division 3; 1921–58 Division 3 (S); 1958–63 Division 3; 1963–65 Division 2; 1965–69 Division 3; 1969–74 Division 2; 1974–82 Division 3; 1982–86 Division 4; 1986–87 Division 3; 1987–92 Division 2; 1992–93 Division 1; 1993–94 FA Premier League; 1994–95 Division 1; 1995–96 Division 2; 1996–2000 Division 1; 2000–04 Division 2; 2004–06 FL 1; 2006–07 FL 2; 2007–11 FL 1; 2011–12 FL 2; 2012– FL 1.

LATEST SEQUENCES

Longest Sequence of League Wins: 10, 31.12.2011 – 28.2.2012

Longest Sequence of League Defeats: 8, 29.8.2005 – 8.10.2005.

Longest Sequence of League Draws: 6, 22.11.1991 – 28.12.1991.

Longest Sequence of Unbeaten League Matches: 22, 12.1.1986 – 23.8.1986.

Longest Sequence Without a League Win: 19, 30.10.1999 – 4.3.2000.

Successive Scoring Runs: 31 from 17.4.1926.

Successive Non-scoring Runs: 5 from 5.4.1997.

MANAGERS

Sam Allen 1902–33
Ted Vizard 1933–39
Neil Harris 1939–41
Louis Page 1945–53
Maurice Lindley 1953–55
Bert Head 1956–65
Danny Williams 1965–69
Fred Ford 1969–71
Dave Mackay 1971–72
Les Allen 1972–74
Danny Williams 1974–78
Bobby Smith 1978–80
John Trollope 1980–83
Ken Beamish 1983–84
Lou Macari 1984–89
Ossie Ardiles 1989–91
Glenn Hoddle 1991–93
John Gorman 1993–94
Steve McMahon 1994–98
Jimmy Quinn 1998–2000
Colin Todd 2000
Andy King 2000–01
Roy Evans 2001
Andy King 2001–05
Iffy Onuora 2005–06
Dennis Wise 2006
Paul Sturrock 2006–07
Maurice Malpas 2008
Danny Wilson 2008–11
Paul Hart 2011
Paolo Di Canio 2011–13
Kevin MacDonald 2013
Mark Cooper 2013–15
Martin Ling 2015
Luke Williams December 2015–

TEN YEAR LEAGUE RECORD

		P	W	D	L	F	A	Pts	Pos
2006-07	FL 2	46	25	10	11	58	38	85	3
2007-08	FL 1	46	16	13	17	63	56	61	13
2008-09	FL 1	46	12	17	17	68	71	53	15
2009-10	FL 1	46	22	16	8	73	57	82	5
2010-11	FL 1	46	9	14	23	50	72	41	24
2011-12	FL 2	46	29	6	11	75	32	93	1
2012-13	FL 1	46	20	14	12	72	39	74	6
2013-14	FL 1	46	19	9	18	63	59	66	8
2014-15	FL 1	46	23	10	13	76	57	79	4
2015-16	FL 1	46	16	11	19	64	71	59	15

DID YOU KNOW

Harold Fleming, who won 11 caps between 1909 and 1914, remains the only Swindon Town player to gain full international honours for England. Fleming was a religious man who throughout his career refused to play on Christmas Day and Good Friday.

SWINDON TOWN – FOOTBALL LEAGUE ONE 2015–16 LEAGUE RECORD

Match No.	Date	Venue	Opponents	Result		H/T Score	Lg Pos.	Goalscorers	Attendance
1	Aug 8	H	Bradford C	W	4-1	0-1	2	Byrne 3 [52, 61, 68], Obika [70]	8090
2	15	A	Bury	D	2-2	0-1	4	Robert [74], Rodgers [83]	3947
3	18	H	Port Vale	D	2-2	1-1	9	Robert [12], Rodgers [66]	7026
4	22	A	Southend U	W	1-0	0-0	6	Robert [62]	5839
5	29	H	Sheffield U	L	0-2	0-0	8		8614
6	Sept 5	A	Crewe Alex	W	3-1	0-0	6	Smith, T [63], Thomas [82], Ajose [90]	4400
7	12	A	Barnsley	L	1-4	1-2	8	Nyatanga (og) [20]	8227
8	19	H	Burton Alb	L	0-1	0-1	10		7005
9	26	H	Colchester U	L	1-2	1-2	17	Thomas [22]	6687
10	29	A	Doncaster R	D	2-2	0-0	14	Ajose [47], Obika [90]	4693
11	Oct 3	A	Blackpool	L	0-1	0-1	17		6704
12	10	H	Peterborough U	L	1-2	0-1	19	Bostwick (og) [73]	7025
13	17	A	Millwall	L	0-2	0-2	20		8524
14	20	H	Oldham Ath	L	1-2	0-1	23	Ajose [85]	6430
15	24	H	Coventry C	D	2-2	0-0	23	Gladwin [85], Ajose (pen) [90]	8309
16	31	A	Wigan Ath	L	0-1	0-0	23		8466
17	Nov 14	H	Scunthorpe U	W	2-1	0-0	20	Branco [55], Ajose [59]	6957
18	21	A	Fleetwood T	L	1-5	0-1	22	Ajose [78]	2880
19	24	H	Walsall	W	2-1	1-0	20	Obika [17], Thompson, L [90]	6385
20	28	A	Chesterfield	W	4-0	2-0	17	Ajose 2 [3, 80], Thompson, L [14], Obika [48]	5540
21	Dec 12	H	Rochdale	W	2-1	2-0	16	Robert [33], Gladwin [34]	7149
22	19	A	Shrewsbury T	W	1-0	1-0	14	Ajose [34]	5115
23	26	H	Gillingham	L	1-3	1-2	15	Obika [18]	9228
24	28	A	Burton Alb	L	0-1	0-0	16		4816
25	Jan 9	A	Southend U	W	4-2	2-2	16	Ajose 2 [42, 90], Obika 2 [45, 78]	7162
26	16	H	Crewe Alex	W	4-3	1-3	14	Ajose 2 [14, 90], Obika [47], Nugent (og) [52]	6888
27	23	A	Sheffield U	D	1-1	0-1	14	Ormonde-Ottewill [79]	19,012
28	30	H	Barnsley	L	0-1	0-0	17		7532
29	Feb 2	A	Port Vale	L	0-1	0-1	17		3256
30	6	A	Gillingham	D	0-0	0-0	17		6398
31	13	A	Colchester U	W	4-1	1-0	14	Ajose 2 [36, 56], Doughty 2 [58, 72]	3269
32	20	H	Blackpool	W	3-2	1-1	15	Ajose 3 [17, 61, 88]	7412
33	27	A	Peterborough U	W	2-1	0-1	12	Ajose [49], Doughty [82]	5124
34	Mar 1	H	Doncaster R	W	2-0	1-0	11	Obika 2 [45, 66]	6556
35	12	H	Millwall	D	2-2	0-2	14	Ajose (pen) [63], Doughty [90]	8623
36	19	A	Coventry C	D	0-0	0-0	14		12,322
37	25	H	Wigan Ath	L	1-4	0-1	15	Ajose [79]	9240
38	28	A	Scunthorpe U	L	0-6	0-2	15		3534
39	Apr 2	H	Fleetwood T	D	1-1	0-1	15	Ajose [68]	6311
40	5	A	Oldham Ath	L	0-2	0-1	15		3730
41	9	A	Bradford C	L	0-1	0-1	16		18,043
42	16	H	Bury	L	0-1	0-0	16		6759
43	19	A	Walsall	D	1-1	0-0	16	Doughty [59]	5095
44	23	A	Chesterfield	W	1-0	0-0	16	Kasim [77]	7015
45	30	A	Rochdale	D	2-2	2-1	16	Obika [2], Thompson, N [45]	2806
46	May 8	H	Shrewsbury T	W	3-0	1-0	16	Ajose 2 (1 pen) [45, 48], Young [86]	8012

Final League Position: 16 – revised to 15 after Bury deducted 3 points for fielding an ineligible player.

GOALSCORERS

League (64): Ajose 24 (3 pens), Obika 11, Doughty 5, Robert 4, Byrne 3, Gladwin 2, Rodgers 2, Thomas 2, Thompson, L 2, Branco 1, Kasim 1, Ormonde-Ottewill 1, Smith, T 1, Thompson, N 1, Young 1, own goals 3.
FA Cup (1): Ajose 1 (pen).
Capital One Cup (1): Obika 1.
Johnstone's Paint Trophy (1): Rodgers 1.

Vigouroux L 33	Thompson N 21 + 2	Turnbull J 42	Branco R 36	Ormonde-Ottewill B 28	Kasim Y 24 + 3	Evans J — + 1	Williams J 9	Stewart K 3 + 2	Hylton J 8 + 8	Obika J 27 + 5	Byrne N 5	Robert F 23 + 12	Rodgers A 29 + 7	Randall W — + 4	Smith M 4 + 1	Traore D 15 + 9	Storey M — + 2	Barry B 35	Brophy J 16 + 12	Ajose N 38	Thomas W 5 + 1	Smith T — + 1	Ojamaa H 7 + 2	Thompson L 23 + 5	Belford T 8	Balmy J 1 + 11	El-Abd A 13	Gladwin B 13	Iandolo E 6 + 6	Bangoura M 1	Stewart J — + 1	Doughty M 20	Young J — + 3	Marshall L — + 2	Sendles-White J 8 + 2	Cooke J — + 2	Kean J 3	Henry W 2	Match No.
1	2	3	4	5	6^1	7	8	9^1	10	11^3	12	13	14																										1
1	3	4	2	9	8	6	7^2			11^1	5	12	13		10																								2
1	2	4	3	5	7	6	13			9		11^2	8^1		10	12																							3
1	2^2	4	3	5	7	6	13		11	9		8^3	10^1		12	14																							4
1		3	2		7	4	9			5	10	6				11^1	8	12																					5
1		4	3	5^2						11^1	6	13			8			2	7	9	10	12																	6
1		4	3			7^1	5			11^2	6				8			2		10	9		12	13															7
1	2	5	3		13	4			12			14	8^2		6				11^3	10		9^1	7																8
	4	2			6^3	3	12			9^1			8					13	10	11^2		5	7	1	14														9
	4	2		7	3	13	12			10^2			6^1					5	9		11	8	1																10
1		3	4	6		12	10			8^1								2	5	11	9^2	7	13																11
1		3	5^1			8^2				6	13		7^1			10	11	14	2			4	9	12															12
1		3	5								13		6			10^1	11	2	9^2			12	4	8		7^3	14												13
1		3	5	9						7			6			2	8^1	11				12	4	10															14
1	5	3		7			12			13	6					2	10^2	11	8^1			4	9																15
1	5	3	6			12				14		7^2				2	11^3	9^1			8	13	4	10															16
1	4	2	9						10^1		13	6		7		5			11	12			3	8^2															17
1	4	2	9^2	6						12		13	7^3			5	14	10	11^1				3	8															18
1	4	2	9	6						10		12	13			5		11					3	7^1															19
1	4	5^1				7				10		6^2	7			2	13	11				8^3	14	3	9	12													20
1	5	3		7			12	10		9^2	13					2		11^3				6	14	4	8^1														21
1	5	3				14	11^1			8^3	6			12		2	13	10				7^2		4	9														22
1	5	3^1		12						11		9^1	6^4			14		2	13	10			7			4^3	8												23
1	4		5	7						13		10^2	9			6		2	12	11				7^2			3	9											24
1	4	3	5	7						13		10^2	9		6			8^1	2		11		12																25
1	12	4	3	5	8							10	9		7			6^2	2^1					13															26
1	13	4	3	5	7					11		8	9^1		12	2^3				10					14					6^2									27
1	3	4	2	9	6					10		8^1		14		5^3	12	11^2						13					7										28
1	3			5	8			10^1	11	7		6				2								9^2								4	12	13					29
1	3	4		5	8^3					11		7^1	6^2			2	14	10								12						9	13						30
1	3	4	2							14	10			8^1		13		5	9	11^2				12					6^3			7							31
1	2	4		9						10		6^1				7²		5		11				12					13			8		3					32
1	2	4		9						11		8^3	13			12		5		10				6^1	14				7					3^2					33
1	3^3	4		9						10		12	14			6		5		11				13					7^1			8^2		2					34
1	3	4	2^3	9^2						11		8^1	12			5		13	10					6					7					14					35
	3	4		9^1						11		12	8^2			5		13	10					6	7	1								2					36
	3^4	4		9						11^2		14	6^3		12	5		13	10					8	1							7		2^1					37
		4	3							11^2		2^1				9		5	6	10					8	1			12			7					13		38
		4	3	9						10^3			6^1		13	5			11					8	1				12			7		2					39
		2	4	9						10^3			6			5^2	14			7	1							11^1	8	12				3	13				40
	3	4	2							11^1			12	8		5		9						7	1				10			6							41
	3	4	2	12						10						5		9	11					8					6^1			7						1	42
	3	4	2	6						10						5		9	11					8								7						1	43
	3	4	2	6						11						5		9	10					8								7						1	44
	3	4	2	9^4						11			7^1			5		10	8^*					6								12						1	45
	2	4		7	13					11			6			5		10	9^1					8^*					9^1			8	12		3^2			1	46

FA Cup
First Round   Rochdale   (a) 1-3

Capital One Cup
First Round   Exeter C   (h) 1-2

Johnstone's Paint Trophy
First Round   Newport Co   (a) 1-1
(aet; Swindon T won 7-6 on penalties)
Second Round   Oxford U   (a) 0-2

TOTTENHAM HOTSPUR

FOUNDATION

The Hotspur Football Club was formed from an older cricket club in 1882. Most of the founders were old boys of St John's Presbyterian School and Tottenham Grammar School. The Casey brothers were well to the fore as the family provided the club's first goalposts (painted blue and white) and their first ball. They soon adopted the local YMCA as their meeting place, but after a couple of moves settled at the Red House, which is still their headquarters, although now known simply as 748 High Road.

White Hart Lane, Bill Nicholson Way, 748 High Road, Tottenham, London N17 0AP.

Telephone: (0844) 499 5000.

Fax: (020) 3544 8563.

Ticket Office: (0844) 499 5000.

Website: www.tottenhamhotspur.com

Email: email@tottenhamhotspur.com

Ground Capacity: 36,284.

Record Attendance: 75,038 v Sunderland, FA Cup 6th rd, 5 March 1938.

Pitch Measurements: 100m × 67m (109yd × 73yd).

Chairman: Daniel Levy.

Head Coach: Mauricio Pochettino.

Assistant Head Coach: Jesus Perez.

Head Physio: Geoff Scott.

Colours: White shirts, navy blue shorts, white socks with navy blue trim.

Year Formed: 1882. *Turned Professional:* 1895.

Previous Name: 1882, Hotspur Football Club; 1884, Tottenham Hotspur.

Club Nickname: 'Spurs'.

Grounds: 1882, Tottenham Marshes; 1888, Northumberland Park; 1899, White Hart Lane.

First Football League Game: 1 September 1908, Division 2, v Wolverhampton W (h) W 3–0 – Hewitson; Coquet, Burton; Morris (1), Danny Steel, Darnell; Walton, Woodward (2), Macfarlane, Bobby Steel, Middlemiss.

HONOURS

League Champions: Division 1 – 1950–51, 1960–61; Division 2 – 1919–20, 1949–50.
Runners-up: Division 1 – 1921–22, 1951–52, 1956–57, 1962–63; Division 2 – 1908–09, 1932–33.

FA Cup Winners: 1901 (as non-league club), 1921, 1961, 1962, 1967, 1981, 1982, 1991.
Runners-up: 1987.

League Cup Winners: 1971, 1973, 1999, 2008.
Runners-up: 1982, 2002, 2009, 2015.

European Competitions
European Cup: 1961–62 *(sf)*.
Champions League: 2010–11 *(qf)*.
UEFA Cup: 1971–72 *(winners)*, 1972–73 *(sf)*, 1973–74 *(runners-up)*, 1983–84 *(winners)*, 1984–85 *(qf)*, 1999–2000, 2006–07 *(qf)*, 2007–08, 2008–09.
Europa League: 2011–12, 2012–13 *(qf)*, 2013–14, 2014–15, 2015–16.
European Cup-Winners' Cup: 1962–63 *(winners)*, 1963–64, 1967–68, 1981–82 *(sf)*, 1982–83, 1991–92 *(qf)*.
Intertoto Cup: 1995.

Record League Victory: 9–0 v Bristol R, Division 2, 22 October 1977 – Daines; Naylor, Holmes, Hoddle (1), McAllister, Perryman, Pratt, McNab, Moores (3), Lee (4), Taylor (1).

Record Cup Victory: 13–2 v Crewe Alex, FA Cup 4th rd (replay), 3 February 1960 – Brown; Hills, Henry; Blanchflower, Norman, Mackay; White, Harmer (1), Smith (4), Allen (5), Jones (3 incl. 1p).

sky SPORTS FACT FILE

Tottenham Hotspur's White Hart Lane ground was requisitioned by the government in September 1916. Spurs played their home matches at Arsenal's Highbury stadium until peacetime football resumed. The favour was returned during the Second World War when Arsenal played their home games at Tottenham after Highbury was requisitioned.

Record Defeat: 0–8 v Cologne, UEFA Intertoto Cup, 22 July 1995.

Most League Points (2 for a win): 70, Division 2, 1919–20.

Most League Points (3 for a win): 77, Division 1, 1984–85.

Most League Goals: 115, Division 1, 1960–61.

Highest League Scorer in Season: Jimmy Greaves, 37, Division 1, 1962–63.

Most League Goals in Total Aggregate: Jimmy Greaves, 220, 1961–70.

Most League Goals in One Match: 5, Ted Harper v Reading, Division 2, 30 August 1930; 5, Alf Stokes v Birmingham C, Division 1, 18 September 1957; 5, Bobby Smith v Aston Villa, Division 1, 29 March 1958; 5, Jermain Defoe v Wigan Ath, FA Premier League, 22 November 2009.

Most Capped Player: Pat Jennings, 74 (119), Northern Ireland.

Most League Appearances: Steve Perryman, 655, 1969–86.

Youngest League Player: Ally Dick, 16 years 301 days v Manchester C, 20 February 1982.

Record Transfer Fee Received: £85,300,000 from Real Madrid for Gareth Bale, September 2013.

Record Transfer Fee Paid: £30,000,000 to AS Roma for Erik Lamela, August 2013.

Football League Record: 1908 Elected to Division 2; 1909–15 Division 1; 1919–20 Division 2; 1920–28 Division 1; 1928–33 Division 2; 1933–35 Division 1; 1935–50 Division 2; 1950–77 Division 1; 1977–78 Division 2; 1978–92 Division 1; 1992– FA Premier League.

LATEST SEQUENCES

Longest Sequence of League Wins: 13, 23.4.1960 – 1.10.1960.

Longest Sequence of League Defeats: 7, 1.1.1994 – 27.2.1994.

Longest Sequence of League Draws: 6, 9.1.1999 – 27.2.1999.

Longest Sequence of Unbeaten League Matches: 22, 31.8.1949 – 31.12.1949.

Longest Sequence Without a League Win: 16, 29.12.1934 – 13.4.1935.

Successive Scoring Runs: 32 from 24.2.1962.

Successive Non-scoring Runs: 6 from 28.12.1985.

MANAGERS

Frank Brettell 1898–99
John Cameron 1899–1906
Fred Kirkham 1907–08
Peter McWilliam 1912–27
Billy Minter 1927–29
Percy Smith 1930–35
Jack Tresadern 1935–38
Peter McWilliam 1938–42
Arthur Turner 1942–46
Joe Hulme 1946–49
Arthur Rowe 1949–55
Jimmy Anderson 1955–58
Bill Nicholson 1958–74
Terry Neill 1974–76
Keith Burkinshaw 1976–84
Peter Shreeves 1984–86
David Pleat 1986–87
Terry Venables 1987–91
Peter Shreeves 1991–92
Doug Livermore 1992–93
Ossie Ardiles 1993–94
Gerry Francis 1994–97
Christian Gross *(Head Coach)* 1997–98
George Graham 1998–2001
Glenn Hoddle 2001–03
David Pleat *(Caretaker)* 2003–04
Jacques Santini 2004
Martin Jol 2004–07
Juande Ramos 2007–08
Harry Redknapp 2008–12
Andre Villas-Boas 2012–13
Tim Sherwood 2013–14
Mauricio Pochettino May 2014–

TEN YEAR LEAGUE RECORD

		P	W	D	L	F	A	Pts	Pos
2006-07	PR Lge	38	17	9	12	57	54	60	5
2007-08	PR Lge	38	11	13	14	66	61	46	11
2008-09	PR Lge	38	14	9	15	45	45	51	8
2009-10	PR Lge	38	21	7	10	67	41	70	4
2010-11	PR Lge	38	16	14	8	55	46	62	5
2011-12	PR Lge	38	20	9	9	66	41	69	4
2012-13	PR Lge	38	21	9	8	66	46	72	5
2013-14	PR Lge	38	21	6	11	55	51	69	6
2014-15	PR Lge	38	19	7	12	58	53	64	5
2015-16	PR Lge	38	19	13	6	69	35	70	3

DID YOU KNOW

Erik Thorstvedt became the first goalkeeper to come off the bench as a substitute in the Premier League. He came on to replace Ian Walker at half-time in the home game with Coventry City on 19 August 1992. Tottenham were 2-0 down at the time and there were no further goals in the match.

TOTTENHAM HOTSPUR – FA PREMIER LEAGUE 2015–16 LEAGUE RECORD

Match No.	Date	Venue	Opponents	Result	H/T Score	Lg Pos.	Goalscorers	Attendance
1	Aug 8	A	Manchester U	L	0-1	0-1	17		75,261
2	15	H	Stoke C	D	2-2	2-0	13	Dier [19], Chadli [45]	36,004
3	22	A	Leicester C	D	1-1	0-0	14	Alli [81]	31,971
4	29	H	Everton	D	0-0	0-0	15		35,865
5	Sept 13	A	Sunderland	W	1-0	0-0	12	Mason [82]	40,303
6	20	H	Crystal Palace	W	1-0	0-0	9	Son [68]	35,723
7	26	H	Manchester C	W	4-1	1-1	5	Dier [45], Alderweireld [50], Kane [61], Lamela [79]	35,867
8	Oct 4	A	Swansea C	D	2-2	1-2	8	Eriksen 2 [27, 65]	20,845
9	17	H	Liverpool	D	0-0	0-0	7		35,926
10	25	A	Bournemouth	W	5-1	3-1	6	Kane 3 (1 pen) [9 (p), 56, 63], Dembele [17], Lamela [29]	11,332
11	Nov 2	H	Aston Villa	W	3-1	2-0	5	Dembele [3], Alli [45], Kane [90]	34,882
12	8	A	Arsenal	D	1-1	1-0	5	Kane [32]	60,060
13	22	H	West Ham U	W	4-1	2-0	5	Kane 2 [23, 50], Alderweireld [33], Walker [83]	35,968
14	29	H	Chelsea	D	0-0	0-0	5		35,639
15	Dec 5	A	WBA	D	1-1	1-1	5	Alli [15]	23,602
16	13	H	Newcastle U	L	1-2	1-0	5	Dier [39]	35,768
17	19	A	Southampton	W	2-0	2-0	4	Kane [40], Alli [43]	31,636
18	26	H	Norwich C	W	3-0	2-0	4	Kane 2 (1 pen) [26 (p), 42], Carroll [80]	35,198
19	28	A	Watford	W	2-1	1-1	3	Lamela [17], Son [89]	20,730
20	Jan 3	A	Everton	D	1-1	1-1	4	Alli [45]	38,482
21	13	H	Leicester C	L	0-1	0-0	4		35,850
22	16	H	Sunderland	W	4-1	1-1	4	Eriksen 2 [42, 67], Dembele [59], Kane (pen) [79]	35,854
23	23	A	Crystal Palace	W	3-1	0-1	4	Kane [63], Alli [84], Chadli [90]	24,867
24	Feb 2	A	Norwich C	W	3-0	2-0	3	Alli [2], Kane 2 (1 pen) [30 (p), 90]	27,067
25	6	H	Watford	W	1-0	0-0	2	Trippier [64]	35,997
26	14	A	Manchester C	W	2-1	0-0	2	Kane (pen) [53], Eriksen [83]	54,551
27	28	H	Swansea C	W	2-1	0-1	2	Chadli [70], Rose [77]	35,922
28	Mar 2	A	West Ham U	L	0-1	0-1	2		34,977
29	5	H	Arsenal	D	2-2	0-1	2	Alderweireld [60], Kane [62]	35,762
30	13	A	Aston Villa	W	2-0	1-0	2	Kane 2 [45, 48]	32,393
31	20	H	Bournemouth	W	3-0	2-0	2	Kane 2 [1, 16], Eriksen [52]	36,084
32	Apr 2	A	Liverpool	D	1-1	0-0	2	Kane [63]	44,062
33	10	H	Manchester U	W	3-0	0-0	2	Alli [70], Alderweireld [74], Lamela [76]	35,761
34	18	A	Stoke C	W	4-0	1-0	2	Kane 2 [9, 71], Alli 2 [67, 82]	27,442
35	25	H	WBA	D	1-1	1-0	2	Dawson (og) [33]	35,923
36	May 2	A	Chelsea	D	2-2	2-0	2	Kane [35], Son [44]	41,545
37	8	H	Southampton	L	1-2	1-1	2	Son [16]	35,748
38	15	A	Newcastle U	L	1-5	0-2	3	Lamela [60]	52,183

Final League Position: 3

GOALSCORERS

League (69): Kane 25 (5 pens), Alli 10, Eriksen 6, Lamela 5, Alderweireld 4, Son 4, Chadli 3, Dembele 3, Dier 3, Carroll 1, Mason 1, Rose 1, Trippier 1, Walker 1, own goal 1.
FA Cup (8): Chadli 3, Carroll 1, Dier 1, Eriksen 1, Kane 1 (pen), Son 1.
Capital One Cup (1): own goal 1.
UEFA Europa League (17): Lamela 6, Son 3, Kane 2, Carroll 1, Chadli 1 (pen), Dembele 1, Eriksen 1, Mason 1, own goal 1.

Vorm M 1	Walker K 33	Alderweireld T 38	Vertonghen J 29	Davies B 14 + 3	Dier E 37	Bentaleb N 2 + 3	Dembele M 27 + 2	Eriksen C 33 + 2	Chadli N 10 + 19	Kane H 38	Mason R 8 + 14	Lamela E 28 + 6	Alli B 28 + 5	Lloris H 37	Carroll T 4 + 15	Rose D 24	Pritchard A — + 1	Son H 13 + 15	Townsend A — + 3	N'Jie C — + 8	Trippier K 5 + 1	Onomah J — + 8	Wimmer K 9 + 1	Match No.
1	2	3	4	5	6³	7¹	8²	9	10	11	12	13	14											1
	2	3	4	5	6	13	8	10	9	11¹	7²	12		1										2
	2	3	4	5	6	14	8²		10	11	7³	9¹	12	1		13								3
	2	3	4		6	7	8¹		10	11	9²		12	1	5	13								4
	2	3	4	5	6				10	11	7³	13	9²	1	14			8¹	12					5
	2	3	4	5	6		12	10¹	11			8³	7	1	14			9²		13				6
	2	3	4	5	6		10¹	12	11			8³	7	1	14			9²		13				7
	2	3	4	5	6	14		9	10²	11³		8¹	7	1				12	13					8
	2	3	4		6		9	10¹	11		8²	7	1		5			13	12					9
	2²	3	4		6		9¹	10		11³	12	8	7	1		5		14	13					10
	2	3	4	13	6		9¹	10		11	12	8	7³	1		5²				14				11
	2	3	4		6		9	10³		11	13	8¹	7²	1		5	12			14				12
	2	3	4		6		7	10		11³	12	9¹	1	14	5		8²		13					13
	2	3	4		7		8	9		11	6¹	12	1		5		10²	13						14
	2	3	4		6		7	10		11		8¹	9²	1		5	12	13						15
	2	3	4		6			10	13	11		8²	9	1	7¹	5		12						16
	2	3	4	5	6		7	10²	13	11³		8	9¹	1	12			14						17
	2	3	4	5	6		7³	8¹	14	11		10	9²	1	12			13						18
		2	4		3		7¹	12	14	11		9	10³	1	6²	8		13		5				19
	2	3	4	5	6			8¹	13	11		10³	9²	1	7		12			14				20
	2	3	4	5	6³		12	9¹		11		8	10	1	7²		13			14				21
		3	4		6		7²	10		11³		8¹	9	1	13	5	14		2	12				22
		3	4²		7¹	14	6	9³	12	11			10	1		5	8		2	13				23
	2	3			7		6	9¹	12	11		14	10¹	1	13		8²			4				24
		3		5	6		7	9¹	10¹	11		8²	12	1	14		13		2	4				25
	2	3			6		7	9	14	11³		13	10²	1	12	5	8¹			4				26
	2	3			6			9	12	11³	13	10¹	7	1		5	8²		14	4				27
		3		5	6			9	8¹	11	7	10²	12	1	14		13		2	4³				28
	2	3		13	6		7³	10		11	12	8¹	9	1		5²	14			4				29
	2	3			6		7	9¹	14	11	13	8¹	10²	1	12	5				4				30
	2	3			7³		6	9	14	11	13	8¹	10²	1	12	5				4				31
	2	3			6		7	10	12	11	13		9²	1		5	8¹			4				32
	2	3	4		6		7	10	12	11²	14	8¹	9³	1		5	13							33
	2	3	4		6		7²	10	12	11	13	8³	9¹	1		5	14							34
	2	3	4		6¹		7	10	14	11	12	8²	9³	1		5	13							35
	2	3³	4	13	6		7	9	14	11	12	10		1		5²	8¹							36
	2	3	4		6			9	13	11	7²	10		1		5	8¹	12						37
	2³	3	4	5	6			9	14	11	7²	8		1	12		10¹			13				38

FA Cup

Third Round	Leicester C	(h)	2-2
Replay	Leicester C	(a)	2-0
Fourth Round	Colchester U	(a)	4-1
Fifth Round	Crystal Palace	(h)	0-1

Capital One Cup

Third Round	Arsenal	(h)	1-2

UEFA Europa League

Group J	Qarabag	(h)	3-1
Group J	Monaco	(a)	1-1
Group J	Anderlecht	(a)	1-2
Group J	Anderlecht	(h)	2-1
Group J	Qarabag	(a)	1-0
Group J	Monaco	(h)	4-1
Round of 32 1st leg	Fiorentina	(a)	1-1
Round of 32 2nd leg	Fiorentina	(h)	3-0

(Tottenham H won 4-1 on aggregate)

Round of 16 1st leg	Borussia Dortmund	(a)	0-3
Round of 16 2nd leg	Borussia Dortmund	(h)	1-2

(Borussia Dortmund won 5-1 on aggregate)

WALSALL

FOUNDATION

Two of the leading clubs around Walsall in the 1880s were Walsall Swifts (formed 1877) and Walsall Town (formed 1879). The Swifts were winners of the Birmingham Senior Cup in 1881, while the Town reached the 4th round (5th round modern equivalent) of the FA Cup in 1883. These clubs amalgamated as Walsall Town Swifts in 1888, becoming simply Walsall in 1895.

Banks's Stadium, Bescot Crescent, Walsall WS1 4SA.
Telephone: (01922) 622 791. *Fax:* (01922) 613 202.
Ticket Office: (01922) 651 414/416.
Website: www.saddlers.co.uk
Email: info@walsallfc.co.uk
Ground Capacity: 10,910.
Record Attendance: 25,453 v Newcastle U, Division 2, 29 August 1961 (at Fellows Park); 11,049 v Rotherham U, Division 1, 9 May 2004 (at Bescot Stadium).
Pitch Measurements: 100.5m × 67m (110yd × 73yd).
Chairman: Jeff Bonser.
Chief Executive: Stefan Gamble.
Manager: Jon Whitney.
First-Team Coach: Dean Holden.
Physio: Jon Whitney.
Colours: Red shirts with black and white trim, white shorts with red and black trim, red socks with black and white trim.
Year Formed: 1888.
Turned Professional: 1888.
Previous Names: Walsall Swifts (founded 1877) and Walsall Town (founded 1879) amalgamated in 1888 as Walsall Town Swifts; 1895, Walsall.
Club Nickname: 'The Saddlers'.
Grounds: 1888, Fellows Park; 1990, Bescot Stadium (renamed Banks's Stadium 2007).
First Football League Game: 3 September 1892, Division 2, v Darwen (h) L 1–2 – Hawkins; Withington, Pinches; Robinson, Whitrick, Forsyth, Marshall, Holmes, Turner, Gray (1), Pangbourn.
Record League Victory: 10–0 v Darwen, Division 2, 4 March 1899 – Tennent; Ted Peers (1), Davies; Hickinbotham, Jenkyns, Taggart; Dean (3), Vail (2), Aston (4), Martin, Griffin.
Record Cup Victory: 7–0 v Macclesfield T (a), FA Cup 2nd rd, 6 December 1997 – Walker; Evans, Marsh, Viveash (1), Ryder, Peron, Boli (2 incl. 1p) (Ricketts), Porter (2), Keates, Watson (Platt), Hodge (2 incl. 1p).
Record Defeat: 0–12 v Small Heath, 17 December 1892; 0–12 v Darwen, 26 December 1896, both Division 2.
Most League Points (2 for a win): 65, Division 4, 1959–60.
Most League Points (3 for a win): 89, FL 2, 2006–07.
Most League Goals: 102, Division 4, 1959–60.

HONOURS

League Champions: FL 2 – 2006–07; Division 4 – 1959–60.
Runners-up: Second Division – 1998–99; Division 3 – 1960–61; Third Division – 1994–95; Division 4 – 1979–80.
FA Cup: last 16 – 1889; 5th rd – 1939, 1975, 1978, 1987, 2002, 2003.
League Cup: semi-final – 1984.
League Trophy: Runners-up: 2015.

sky SPORTS FACT FILE

Goalkeeper Bert Williams was one of the finest players developed by Walsall. He made his first-team debut for the Saddlers at the age of 17. He made 28 peacetime appearances and over 100 during the war before signing for Wolverhampton Wanderers in September 1945. Bert went on to win 24 caps for England.

Highest League Scorer in Season: Gilbert Alsop, 40, Division 3 (N), 1933–34 and 1934–35.

Most League Goals in Total Aggregate: Tony Richards, 184, 1954–63; Colin Taylor, 184, 1958–63, 1964–68, 1969–73.

Most League Goals in One Match: 5, Gilbert Alsop v Carlisle U, Division 3 (N), 2 February 1935; 5, Bill Evans v Mansfield T, Division 3 (N), 5 October 1935; 5, Johnny Devlin v Torquay U, Division 3 (S), 1 September 1949.

Most Capped Player: Mick Kearns, 15 (18), Republic of Ireland.

Most League Appearances: Colin Harrison, 473, 1964–82.

Youngest League Player: Geoff Morris, 16 years 218 days v Scunthorpe U, 14 September 1965.

Record Transfer Fee Received: £1,000,000 from Coventry C for Scott Dann, January 2008.

Record Transfer Fee Paid: £175,000 to Birmingham C for Alan Buckley, June 1979.

Football League Record: 1892 Elected to Division 2; 1895 Failed re-election; 1896–1901 Division 2; 1901 Failed re-election; 1921 Original Member of Division 3 (N); 1927–31 Division 3 (S); 1931–36 Division 3 (N); 1936–58 Division 3 (S); 1958–60 Division 4; 1960–61 Division 3; 1961–63 Division 2; 1963–79 Division 3; 1979–80 Division 4; 1980–88 Division 3; 1988–89 Division 2; 1989–90 Division 3; 1990–92 Division 4; 1992–95 Division 3; 1995–99 Division 2; 1999–2000 Division 1; 2000–01 Division 2; 2001–04 Division 1; 2004–06 FL 1; 2006–07 FL 2; 2007– FL 1.

LATEST SEQUENCES

Longest Sequence of League Wins: 7, 9.4.2005 – 9.8.2005.

Longest Sequence of League Defeats: 15, 29.10.1988 – 4.2.1989.

Longest Sequence of League Draws: 5, 7.5.1988 – 17.9.1988.

Longest Sequence of Unbeaten League Matches: 21, 6.11.1979 – 22.3.1980.

Longest Sequence Without a League Win: 18, 15.10.1988 – 4.2.1989.

Successive Scoring Runs: 27 from 6.11.1979.

Successive Non-scoring Runs: 5 from 10.4.2004.

MANAGERS

H. Smallwood 1888–91 *(Secretary-Manager)*
A. G. Burton 1891–93
J. H. Robinson 1893–95
C. H. Ailso 1895–96 *(Secretary-Manager)*
A. E. Parsloe 1896–97 *(Secretary-Manager)*
L. Ford 1897–98 *(Secretary-Manager)*
G. Hughes 1898–99 *(Secretary-Manager)*
L. Ford 1899–1901 *(Secretary-Manager)*
J. E. Shutt 1908–13 *(Secretary-Manager)*
Haydn Price 1914–20
Joe Burchell 1920–26
David Ashworth 1926–27
Jack Torrance 1927–28
James Kerr 1928–29
Sid Scholey 1929–30
Peter O'Rourke 1930–32
Bill Slade 1932–34
Andy Wilson 1934–37
Tommy Lowes 1937–44
Harry Hibbs 1944–51
Tony McPhee 1951
Brough Fletcher 1952–53
Major Frank Buckley 1953–55
John Love 1955–57
Billy Moore 1957–64
Alf Wood 1964
Reg Shaw 1964–68
Dick Graham 1968
Ron Lewin 1968–69
Billy Moore 1969–72
John Smith 1972–73
Ronnie Allen 1973
Doug Fraser 1973–77
Dave Mackay 1977–78
Alan Ashman 1978
Frank Sibley 1979
Alan Buckley 1979–86
Neil Martin *(Joint Manager with Buckley)* 1981–82
Tommy Coakley 1986–88
John Barnwell 1989–90
Kenny Hibbitt 1990–94
Chris Nicholl 1994–97
Jan Sorensen 1997–98
Ray Graydon 1998–2002
Colin Lee 2002–04
Paul Merson 2004–06
Kevin Broadhurst 2006
Richard Money 2006–08
Jimmy Mullen 2008–09
Chris Hutchings 2009–11
Dean Smith 2011–15
Sean O'Driscoll 2015–16
Jon Whitney March 2016–

TEN YEAR LEAGUE RECORD

		P	W	D	L	F	A	Pts	Pos
2006-07	FL 2	46	25	14	7	66	34	89	1
2007-08	FL 1	46	16	16	14	52	46	64	12
2008-09	FL 1	46	17	10	19	61	66	61	13
2009-10	FL 1	46	16	14	16	60	63	62	10
2010-11	FL 1	46	12	12	22	56	75	48	20
2011-12	FL 1	46	10	20	16	51	57	50	19
2012-13	FL 1	46	17	17	12	65	58	68	9
2013-14	FL 1	46	14	16	16	49	49	58	13
2014-15	FL 1	46	14	17	15	50	54	59	14
2015-16	FL 1	46	24	12	10	71	49	84	3

DID YOU KNOW ?

John Mackenzie, who had featured at left-back for Walsall in the early 1920s, joined the Home Guard when war broke out in 1939. He returned to his house after night shift duty in October 1940 and collapsed and died from a heart attack. He was 55 years old.

WALSALL – FOOTBALL LEAGUE ONE 2015–16 LEAGUE RECORD

Match No.	Date	Venue	Opponents	Result		H/T Score	Lg Pos.	Goalscorers	Atten- dance
1	Aug 8	H	Oldham Ath	D	1-1	1-0	10	Sawyers [8]	5009
2	15	A	Southend U	W	2-0	1-0	5	Bradshaw [8], Mantom [48]	6149
3	18	A	Rochdale	W	2-1	0-0	3	Taylor [65], Mantom [71]	2381
4	22	H	Coventry C	W	2-1	1-0	2	Forde [40], Bradshaw [52]	7176
5	29	A	Blackpool	W	4-0	1-0	1	Sawyers 2 [25, 74], Robertson (og) [57], Mantom [67]	7489
6	Sept 5	H	Bury	L	0-1	0-1	2		4829
7	12	H	Doncaster R	W	2-0	0-0	2	Bradshaw 2 [85, 90]	4127
8	19	A	Peterborough U	D	1-1	0-0	2	Sawyers [53]	5859
9	26	H	Crewe Alex	D	1-1	1-1	2	Bradshaw [3]	4229
10	29	A	Scunthorpe U	W	1-0	1-0	2	Henry [27]	2596
11	Oct 3	A	Wigan Ath	D	0-0	0-0	2		8636
12	10	H	Burton Alb	W	2-0	1-0	1	Kinsella [36], Bradshaw (pen) [90]	6812
13	17	H	Chesterfield	L	1-2	0-1	2	Preston [90]	4766
14	20	A	Barnsley	W	2-0	0-0	2	Evans [62], Lalkovic [70]	8561
15	24	A	Colchester U	D	4-4	2-0	2	Sawyers [11], Lalkovic [30], Evans [57], O'Connor [90]	3630
16	31	H	Gillingham	W	3-2	2-2	1	Morris, K [37], Lalkovic [38], Demetriou [90]	6663
17	Nov 21	A	Sheffield U	D	1-1	0-0	3	Bradshaw [51]	5780
18	24	A	Swindon T	L	1-2	0-1	4	Bradshaw [61]	6385
19	28	H	Bradford C	W	2-1	1-0	4	Bradshaw [11], Lalkovic [73]	4668
20	Dec 1	A	Shrewsbury T	W	3-1	1-1	3	Lalkovic [45], Downing [80], Cook [90]	6078
21	20	A	Port Vale	W	2-0	0-0	2	Cook 2 [64, 83]	4436
22	26	A	Millwall	W	1-0	1-0	1	Lalkovic [29]	8364
23	28	H	Peterborough U	W	2-0	0-0	1	Demetriou [80], Evans [89]	6142
24	Jan 2	H	Rochdale	L	0-3	0-1	3		4857
25	12	A	Coventry C	D	1-1	0-1	3	Bradshaw [81]	15,671
26	16	A	Bury	W	3-2	3-0	2	Hussey (og) [16], Bradshaw [30], Forde [42]	3532
27	23	H	Blackpool	D	1-1	0-0	3	Demetriou [66]	5022
28	Feb 2	A	Doncaster R	W	2-1	0-0	2	Mantom [61], Taylor [65]	5056
29	6	H	Millwall	L	0-3	0-0	2		4843
30	13	A	Crewe Alex	D	1-1	1-0	3	Bradshaw (pen) [32]	5123
31	20	H	Wigan Ath	L	1-2	0-1	4	Mantom [68]	6740
32	27	A	Burton Alb	D	0-0	0-0	4		5512
33	Mar 1	H	Scunthorpe U	D	0-0	0-0	3		3868
34	5	H	Barnsley	L	1-3	1-1	4	Bradshaw [28]	5199
35	12	A	Chesterfield	W	4-1	1-1	4	Anderson (og) [35], Mantom 2 [57, 75], Hiwula [71]	6938
36	15	A	Fleetwood T	W	1-0	0-0	3	Bradshaw [49]	2569
37	19	H	Colchester U	W	2-1	0-1	3	Bradshaw [89], Preston [90]	5818
38	Apr 2	A	Sheffield U	L	0-2	0-2	3		19,214
39	9	A	Oldham Ath	L	0-1	0-0	6		4396
40	12	A	Gillingham	W	2-1	0-0	3	Lalkovic [68], Hiwula [77]	6246
41	16	H	Southend U	W	1-0	0-0	3	Hiwula [88]	5732
42	19	H	Swindon T	D	1-1	0-0	3	Morris, K [71]	5095
43	23	A	Bradford C	L	0-4	0-0	4		19,336
44	26	H	Shrewsbury T	W	2-1	2-0	3	Morris, K [11], Henry [44]	5339
45	May 2	H	Fleetwood T	W	3-1	2-0	3	Bradshaw [2], Downing [18], Sawyers [58]	6628
46	8	A	Port Vale	W	5-0	3-0	3	Downing [23], Bradshaw [26], Forde 2 [38, 67], Mantom [71]	8595

Final League Position: 3

GOALSCORERS

League (71): Bradshaw 17 (2 pens), Mantom 8, Lalkovic 7, Sawyers 6, Forde 4, Cook 3, Demetriou 3, Downing 3, Evans 3, Hiwula 3, Morris, K 3, Henry 2, Preston 2, Taylor 2, Kinsella 1, O'Connor 1, own goals 3.
FA Cup (4): Demetriou 1, Evans 1, Forde 1, Mantom 1.
Capital One Cup (7): Bradshaw 3 (1 pen), Henry 1, Lalkovic 1, O'Connor 1, Sawyers 1.
Johnstone's Paint Trophy (0).
League One Play-Offs (1): Cook 1.

Etheridge N 40	Downing P 46	O'Connor J 37	Taylor A 33 + 1	Demetriou J 42 + 1	Mantom S 33 + 4	Chambers A 45	Cook J 5 + 29	Henry R 30 + 5	Bradshaw T 38 + 3	Sawyers R 45 + 1	Lalkovic M 27 + 13	Forde A 26 + 15	Flanagan R 8 + 6	Baxendale J — + 3	Morris K 12 + 21	MacGillivray C 5	Kinsella L 4 + 3	Preston M 4 + 6	Evans G 12	Roberts L 1	Hiwula J 8 + 5	Morris B — + 1	Pennington M 5	Match No.
1	2	3	4	5	6	7	8^1	9^2	10	11	12	13												1
1	4	3	2	5	7	6	14		9	11^2	10		13		8^1	12								2
1	4	3	5^3	2	8	6		14	11	13	10^2	12	9^1		7									3
1	3	4	5	2	8	6	13		11	9	7^1	10^2	12											4
1	2	3	4	5	7	6	13	9^3	10^2	11		12			8^1	14								5
	3	2	4		7	6^3	12	5	10	9	14	11	8^2		13	1								6
1	2	3	4	5	7	6	13	9^1	11	10	8^2				12									7
1	4	3	2^3	7	9	5	13	6	11^2	10	12	14	8^1											8
1	3	4	5	2	7	6	12		11	9	10^1	8^2			13									9
1	3	4	9	5	7	6	8^1	2	11	10				12										10
1	4	3	5	2	8	6	13		11	9	10^2	12			7^1									11
	3	2^1	4		6	7	12	9^1	11	10		13	8^1			1	5	14						12
1	3		4^1	5	7^2	6	12	9	11	10	13		8^3		14			2						13
	3		2			7	13	6	9	10	11^1	8^1	14		12	1		5	4^3					14
	3	8	5	2		7	12		10	11	9^1	6^1	14		13	1			4^2					15
1	4	3	14	2	7	12		5^2	11	10	9^3		13		6			8^1						16
1	2	3		5		7	13	4	11	10	9^2	12			6^1			8						17
1	3	4		2		6	9^2	5	11	10	13	8	12					7^1						18
1	2	3		5		7	13	4	11	10	9^2	12			6^1			8						19
1	4	3		2		7	12	5	11^2	10	9^1	13	14		6^3			8						20
1	3	4	5	2	13	6	12		9	11	10				8^2			7^1						21
1	4	3	5^1	2		6	13		9	11^3	10				8^2		12	14	7					22
1	3^2	4	5	2	6^3	8	10^1		9	11	13				14			12	7					23
1	3	4	5^1	2		7		9^2	14	13	10	11^3	6		12			8						24
1	3	2		12	6	7	14	5	10	9	11^2	13					8^3		4^1					25
1	4	3	5	2	7	6		9^2	11^1	10			8		12			13						26
1	2	3	4	5	6	7		9^3	11^1	10^2	12	8			13			14						27
1	4	3	5	2	7	6		12	11	9	10^1	8				1								28
1	4	3	2^3	5	8	7^2	12	6	11^1	10	14	9			13				1					29
1	4		5	2	8	6		12	11	9	7^2	10^1			13			3						30
1	4		2	5	8	6	12		11	7	10	9						3^1						31
1	4	3	5	2	7	8			11	10	9	6^1			12									32
1	3	4	5	2	8	6		12	9	11	10^1	7^2			13									33
1	3	4	5	2	8	7	14		11^3	10^2	12	6			9^1						13			34
1	4	3	2^3	9	7^2	8		5	10^1	6	13	12									11	14		35
1	2	3	4	5	7	8^2		9	10^3	8	14	12					13				11^1			36
1	2	3^2	4	5	8			9^1	10	6	13				14		7^1	12			11			37
1	2		4^1	5	8^2	7		9	11	10	14	13	6^3								12	3		38
1	4		5	2	7^1	6	13		10^3	8	12	9^2			14						11	3		39
1	4		2	7	6	13	5		8^2	10^3	9^1	14			12						11	3		40
1	4		2	7^1	6	13	5		9	10^2	8	14			11						11	3		41
1	4		2^2	7	6		5	13	9	10^3	8^1	14			12						11	3		42
1	3	4	5		7^2	8	14	9^{12}	12	10		6			13		2				11^3			43
1	4	3		2	12	6	13	5	11^2	9	10^3	7			8^1						14			44
1	4	3		2	12	7	14	5	11	10^3	9^1	6			8^2						13			45
1	4	3		2	12	6	14	5	11^3	9	7^2	10			8^1						13			46

FA Cup

First Round		Fleetwood T	(h)	2-0
Second Round		Chesterfield	(a)	1-1
Replay		Chesterfield	(h)	0-0
(aet; Walsall won 5-3 on penalties)				
Third Round		Brentford	(a)	1-0
Fourth Round		Reading	(a)	0-4

Johnstone's Paint Trophy

First Round		Morecambe	(a)	0-2

Capital One Cup

First Round		Nottingham F	(a)	4-3
Second Round		Brighton & HA	(h)	2-1
Third Round		Chelsea	(h)	1-4

League One Play-Offs

Semi-Final 1st leg		Barnsley	(a)	0-3
Semi-Final 2nd leg		Barnsley	(h)	1-3
(Barnsley won 6-1 on aggregate)				

WATFORD

FOUNDATION

The club was formed as Watford Rovers in 1881. The name was changed to West Herts in 1893 and then the name Watford was adopted after rival club Watford St Mary's was absorbed in 1898.

Vicarage Road Stadium, Vicarage Road, Watford, Hertfordshire WD18 0ER.

Telephone: (01923) 496 000.

Fax: (01923) 496 001.

Ticket Office: (01923) 223 023.

Website: www.watfordfc.com

Email: yourvoice@watfordfc.com

Ground Capacity: 21,500.

Record Attendance: 34,099 v Manchester U, FA Cup 4th rd (replay), 3 February 1969.

Pitch Measurements: 105m × 68m (115yd × 74.5yd).

Executive Chairman: Raffaele Riva.

Chief Executive: Scott Duxbury.

Head Coach: Walter Mazzarri.

Head of Medical: Richard Collinge.

Colours: Yellow shirts with black trim, black shorts with yellow trim, black socks with yellow trim.

Year Formed: 1881.

Turned Professional: 1897.

Previous Names: 1881, Watford Rovers; 1893, West Herts; 1898, Watford.

Club Nickname: 'The Hornets'.

Grounds: 1883, Vicarage Meadow, Rose and Crown Meadow; 1889, Colney Butts; 1890, Cassio Road; 1922, Vicarage Road.

First Football League Game: 28 August 1920, Division 3, v QPR (a) W 2–1 – Williams; Horseman, Fred Gregory; Bacon, Toone, Wilkinson; Bassett, Ronald (1), Hoddinott, White (1), Waterall.

Record League Victory: 8–0 v Sunderland, Division 1, 25 September 1982 – Sherwood; Rice, Rostron, Taylor, Terry, Bolton, Callaghan (2), Blissett (4), Jenkins (2), Jackett, Barnes.

Record Cup Victory: 10–1 v Lowestoft T, FA Cup 1st rd, 27 November 1926 – Yates; Prior, Fletcher (1); Frank Smith, Bert Smith, Strain; Stephenson, Warner (3), Edmonds (3), Swan (1), Daniels (1), (1 og).

Record Defeat: 0–10 v Wolverhampton W, FA Cup 1st rd (replay), 24 January 1912.

Most League Points (2 for a win): 71, Division 4, 1977–78.

HONOURS

League Champions: Second Division – 1997–98; Division 3 – 1968–69; Division 4 – 1977–78.
Runners-up: Division 1 – 1982–83; FL C – 2014–15; Division 2 – 1981–82; Division 3 – 1978–79.

FA Cup: Runners-up: 1984.

League Cup: semi-final – 1979, 2005.

European Competitions
UEFA Cup: 1983–84.

sky SPORTS FACT FILE

Former England international Frank Barson signed for Watford in May 1928. After making just 10 appearances for the Hornets, he was sent off playing against Fulham on 29 September. The FA subsequently banned him for the remainder of the season. A number of petitions were submitted urging leniency, including one with 15,000 signatures, but the ban remained.

Gomes H 38	Nyom A 29 + 3	Prodl S 19 + 2	Cathcart C 34 + 1	Holebas J 11	Anya I 17 + 11	Capoue E 33	Behrami V 14 + 7	Layun M 2 + 1	Jurado J 27	Deeney T 36 + 2	Paredes J 7 + 10	Ighalo O 36 + 1	Watson B 31 + 4	Abdi A 25 + 7	Berghuis S — + 9	Diamanti A — + 3	Ake N 20 + 4	Guedioura A 3 + 15	Ibarbo V — + 4	Brítos M 24	Arlauskis G — + 1	Oulare O — + 2	Amrabat N 4 + 8	Mario Suarez M 8 + 7	Match No.
1	2	3	4	5	6	7	8^3	9^1	10^2	11	12	13	14												1
1	2	3	4		5	6	7	8^1	10^2	11		9			12	13									2
1	2	3	4	5^1	8	6	7^2		10	11		9	13				12								3
1	2	3	4	5	12	6^3	7	13	9	11		10^2	14	8^1											4
1	2	3	4		5	6	7^1		10	9^1		11^2	12	8^1	13	14									5
1	2	3	4		5	6			10^2	9		11	7^3	8^1	12		13	14							6
1	2^2	3	4		5	7			9	10		11	8^3	6^1	12		13		14						7
1	2^1	3	4		6^2	7			10	13	11	8	9^3				5	14	12						8
1	2^1	3	4		6^3	7			11	14	10	8	9^2	12			5	13							9
1	2		3			8^1	7	13		9	12	11^3	6	10^2			5	14		4					10
1	2		3			8^1	7	13		9	12	11^3	6	10^2			5	14		4					11
1	2^2		3			6	7^1			10	12	11	8	9		13	5			4					12
1	2^2		3			5	6			10^1	9	13	11	7	8		12			4					13
1^1	2		3			13	6			9	8^2	11	7	10^3			5	14		4		12			14
1	2		3			6^1	8			9^2	11	12	10^3	7	13		5	14		4					15
1	2		3			13	6			10^2	9	11	7	8^1			5	12		4					16
1	2		3			12	8	13		9^1	11	10^3	7	6^2			5	14		4					17
1	2		3	5		13	7	12		9^2	11^3	10	8	6^1				14		4					18
1	14	13	3		2	8		12		9^3	11	10	7	6^1	5		4^2								19
1	2		3	5		7				9^1	11	10	8	6		12				4					20
1	2^2		3	14	5	12	7			9	11	10	8	6^1					13	4^3					21
1	2^1		3			6	7^2			9	11	12	10	8			5			4		13			22
1	13		3			7	6			9^1	10^3	2^2	11	8	12		5			4			14		23
1	13		3	4	5	6^3	8			9^1	10	2^2	11	7	12									14	24
1	2	14	3			9	13			10	12	11	7	8^1			5			4^3				6^2	25
1	2	3	4			6^2	8				11	10	7	12			5						9^3	13	26
1		3				8^1	6			10	2	11	7	13			5			4			9^2	12	27
1	2	3	5	14		9	7^3			10	11^2	8		6^1						4		13	12		28
1	2^2	3	5	13		9^3				10	11			8	12			4				14	6	7^1	29
1	2	3		14		9	7^2	6^1		10	11						5^3	12		4			13	8	30
1	2	3	4	12		9^1				10	11^2		7	6^2			5	14					13	8	31
1		3	5			7^3	6^1			9^2	10	2	11	8			12			4			13	14	32
1	2	3				7	13			9^2	11	10	8				5	6^1		4			12		33
1		3	4	5	13		7			10^1	14	2		9^3	12			6^2				11		8	34
1		3		5						9^2	10	2^1	11	8	6		12			4		13	7		35
1	3	2		5						9^6	11	10	8	6	13		12			4		14	7^1		36
1	2^1	3		5						9^2	11	10	8^3	6			12	14		4			7		37
1	3	2^1								9^3	11	12	10	8	6^2		5	7		4			14	13	38

FA Cup

Third Round	Newcastle U	(h)	1-0
Fourth Round	Nottingham F	(a)	1-0
Fifth Round	Leeds U	(h)	1-0
Sixth Round	Arsenal	(a)	2-1
Semi-Final	Crystal Palace	(Wembley)	1-2

Capital One Cup

Second Round	Preston NE	(a)	0-1

WEST BROMWICH ALBION

FOUNDATION

There is a well known story that when employees of Salter's Spring Works in West Bromwich decided to form a football club, they had to send someone to the nearby Association Football stronghold of Wednesbury to purchase a football. A weekly subscription of 2d (less than 1p) was imposed and the name of the new club was West Bromwich Strollers.

The Hawthorns, West Bromwich, West Midlands B71 4LF.

Telephone: (0871) 271 1100.

Fax: (0871) 271 9851.

Ticket Office: (0121) 227 2227.

Website: www.wba.co.uk

Email: enquiries@wbafc.co.uk

Ground Capacity: 26,850.

Record Attendance: 64,815 v Arsenal, FA Cup 6th rd, 6 March 1937.

Pitch Measurements: 105m × 68m (114yd × 74yd).

Chairman: Jeremy Peace.

Chief Executive: Mark Jenkins.

Head Coach: Tony Pulis.

Assistant Head Coaches: David Kemp and Mark O'Connor.

Physio: Richie Rawlins.

League Champions: Division 1 – 1919–20; FL C – 2007–08; Division 2 – 1901–02, 1910–11.
Runners-up: Division 1 – 1924–25, 1953–54; FL C – 2009–10; First Division – 2001–02, 2003–04; Division 2 – 1930–31, 1948–49.
FA Cup Winners: 1888, 1892, 1931, 1954, 1968.
Runners-up: 1886, 1887, 1895, 1912, 1935.
League Cup Winners: 1966.
Runners-up: 1967, 1970.
European Competitions
Fairs Cup: 1966–67.
UEFA Cup: 1978–79 *(qf)*, 1979–80, 1981–82.
European Cup-Winners' Cup: 1968–69 *(qf)*

Colours: Navy blue and white striped shirts, white shorts with white trim, white socks with navy blue hoops.

Year Formed: 1878.

Turned Professional: 1885.

Previous Name: 1878, West Bromwich Strollers; 1881, West Bromwich Albion.

Club Nicknames: 'The Throstles', 'The Baggies', 'Albion'.

Grounds: 1878, Coopers Hill; 1879, Dartmouth Park; 1881, Bunns Field, Walsall Street; 1882, Four Acres (Dartmouth Cricket Club); 1885, Stoney Lane; 1900, The Hawthorns.

First Football League Game: 8 September 1888, Football League, v Stoke (a) W 2–0 – Roberts; Jack Horton, Green; Ezra Horton, Perry, Bayliss; Bassett, Woodhall (1), Hendry, Pearson, Wilson (1).

Record League Victory: 12–0 v Darwen, Division 1, 4 April 1892 – Reader; Jack Horton, McCulloch; Reynolds (2), Perry, Groves; Bassett (3), McLeod, Nicholls (1), Pearson (4), Geddes (1), (1 og).

Record Cup Victory: 10–1 v Chatham (away), FA Cup 3rd rd, 2 March 1889 – Roberts; Jack Horton, Green; Timmins (1), Charles Perry, Ezra Horton; Bassett (2), Walter Perry (1), Bayliss (2), Pearson, Wilson (3), (1 og).

sky SPORTS FACT FILE

Goalkeeper Hubert Pearson made over 350 first-team appearances for West Bromwich Albion between 1907 and 1925, also gaining representative honours for the Football League. He scored two goals during his career. Both came from the penalty spot during the 1911–12 season during holiday matches. He netted against Bury on Boxing Day and then against Middlesbrough on Easter Monday.

Record Defeat: 3–10 v Stoke C, Division 1, 4 February 1937.

Most League Points (2 for a win): 60, Division 1, 1919–20.

Most League Points (3 for a win): 91, FL C, 2009–10.

Most League Goals: 105, Division 2, 1929–30.

Highest League Scorer in Season: William 'Ginger' Richardson, 39, Division 1, 1935–36.

Most League Goals in Total Aggregate: Tony Brown, 218, 1963–79.

Most League Goals in One Match: 6, Jimmy Cookson v Blackpool, Division 2, 17 September 1927.

Most Capped Player: James Morrison, 39, Scotland.

Most League Appearances: Tony Brown, 574, 1963–80.

Youngest League Player: Charlie Wilson, 16 years 73 days v Oldham Ath, 1 October 1921.

Record Transfer Fee Received: £8,000,000 from Aston Villa for Curtis Davies, July 2008.

Record Transfer Fee Paid: £12,000,000 to Zenit St Petersburg for Salomon Rondon, August 2015.

Football League Record: 1888 Founder Member of Football League; 1901–02 Division 2; 1902–04 Division 1; 1904–11 Division 2; 1911–27 Division 1; 1927–31 Division 2; 1931–38 Division 1; 1938–49 Division 2; 1949–73 Division 1; 1973–76 Division 2; 1976–86 Division 1; 1986–91 Division 2; 1991–92 Division 3; 1992–93 Division 2; 1993–2002 Division 1; 2002–03 FA Premier League; 2003–04 Division 1; 2004–06 FA Premier League; 2006–08 FL C; 2008–09 FA Premier League; 2009–10 FL C; 2010– FA Premier League.

LATEST SEQUENCES

Longest Sequence of League Wins: 11, 5.4.1930 – 8.9.1930.

Longest Sequence of League Defeats: 11, 28.10.1995 – 26.12.1995.

Longest Sequence of League Draws: 5, 30.8.1999 – 3.10.1999.

Longest Sequence of Unbeaten League Matches: 17, 7.9.1957 – 7.12.1957.

Longest Sequence Without a League Win: 15, 16.10.2004 – 16.1.2005.

Successive Scoring Runs: 36 from 26.4.1958.

Successive Non-scoring Runs: 4 from 1.3.2003.

MANAGERS

Louis Ford 1890–92
(Secretary-Manager)
Henry Jackson 1892–94
(Secretary-Manager)
Edward Stephenson 1894–95
(Secretary-Manager)
Clement Keys 1895–96
(Secretary-Manager)
Frank Heaven 1896–1902
(Secretary-Manager)
Fred Everiss 1902–48
Jack Smith 1948–52
Jesse Carver 1952
Vic Buckingham 1953–59
Gordon Clark 1959–61
Archie Macaulay 1961–63
Jimmy Hagan 1963–67
Alan Ashman 1967–71
Don Howe 1971–75
Johnny Giles 1975–77
Ronnie Allen 1977
Ron Atkinson 1978–81
Ronnie Allen 1981–82
Ron Wylie 1982–84
Johnny Giles 1984–85
Nobby Stiles 1985–86
Ron Saunders 1986–87
Ron Atkinson 1987–88
Brian Talbot 1988–91
Bobby Gould 1991–92
Ossie Ardiles 1992–93
Keith Burkinshaw 1993–94
Alan Buckley 1994–97
Ray Harford 1997
Denis Smith 1997–1999
Brian Little 1999–2000
Gary Megson 2000–04
Bryan Robson 2004–06
Tony Mowbray 2006–09
Roberto Di Matteo 2009–11
Roy Hodgson 2011–12
Steve Clarke 2012–13
Pepe Mel 2014
Alan Irvine 2014
Tony Pulis January 2015–

TEN YEAR LEAGUE RECORD

		P	W	D	L	F	A	Pts	Pos
2006-07	FL C	46	22	10	14	81	55	76	4
2007-08	FL C	46	23	12	11	88	55	81	1
2008-09	PR Lge	38	8	8	22	36	67	32	20
2009-10	FL C	46	26	13	7	89	48	91	2
2010-11	PR Lge	38	12	11	15	56	71	47	11
2011-12	PR Lge	38	13	8	17	45	52	47	10
2012-13	PR Lge	38	14	7	17	53	57	49	8
2013-14	PR Lge	38	7	15	16	43	59	36	17
2014-15	PR Lge	38	11	11	16	38	51	44	13
2015-16	PR Lge	38	10	13	15	34	48	43	14

DID YOU KNOW ❓

West Bromwich Albion's 6-1 defeat by Manchester City in the FA Charity Shield match in August 1968 equalled the biggest losing margin for the fixture. Albion had a number of key players missing while goalkeeper John Osborne badly dislocated a finger early on before eventually having to leave the field.

WEST BROMWICH ALBION – FA PREMIER LEAGUE 2015–16 LEAGUE RECORD

Match No.	Date	Venue	Opponents	Result	H/T Score	Lg Pos.	Goalscorers	Attendance
1	Aug 10	H	Manchester C	L 0-3	0-2	20		24,564
2	15	A	Watford	D 0-0	0-0	17		20,011
3	23	H	Chelsea	L 2-3	1-3	20	Morrison 2 [35, 59]	23,256
4	29	A	Stoke C	W 1-0	1-0	14	Rondon [45]	26,747
5	Sept 12	H	Southampton	D 0-0	0-0	13		24,265
6	19	A	Aston Villa	W 1-0	1-0	10	Berahino [39]	36,321
7	28	H	Everton	L 2-3	1-0	15	Berahino [41], Dawson [54]	24,240
8	Oct 3	A	Crystal Palace	L 0-2	0-0	17		24,033
9	17	H	Sunderland	W 1-0	0-0	12	Berahino [54]	24,225
10	24	A	Norwich C	W 1-0	0-0	8	Rondon [46]	26,983
11	31	H	Leicester C	L 2-3	1-0	11	Rondon [30], Lambert (pen) [84]	24,150
12	Nov 7	A	Manchester U	L 0-2	0-0	13		75,410
13	21	H	Arsenal	W 2-1	2-1	12	Morrison [35], Arteta (og) [40]	24,343
14	29	A	West Ham U	D 1-1	0-1	13	Reid (og) [50]	34,914
15	Dec 5	H	Tottenham H	D 1-1	1-1	13	McClean [39]	23,602
16	13	A	Liverpool	D 2-2	1-1	13	Dawson [30], Olsson [73]	44,147
17	19	H	Bournemouth	L 1-2	0-0	13	McAuley [79]	26,127
18	26	A	Swansea C	L 0-1	0-1	13		20,789
19	28	H	Newcastle U	W 1-0	0-0	13	Fletcher [78]	26,313
20	Jan 2	H	Stoke C	W 2-1	0-0	12	Sessegnon [60], Evans [90]	23,218
21	13	A	Chelsea	D 2-2	1-1	13	Gardner [33], McClean [86]	40,945
22	16	A	Southampton	L 0-3	0-2	13		29,622
23	23	H	Aston Villa	D 0-0	0-0	13		26,165
24	Feb 2	H	Swansea C	D 1-1	0-0	13	Rondon [90]	22,062
25	6	A	Newcastle U	L 0-1	0-1	14		50,152
26	13	A	Everton	W 1-0	1-0	14	Rondon [14]	38,103
27	27	H	Crystal Palace	W 3-2	3-0	13	Gardner [12], Dawson [20], Berahino [31]	24,806
28	Mar 1	A	Leicester C	D 2-2	1-2	13	Rondon [11], Gardner [50]	32,018
29	6	H	Manchester U	W 1-0	0-0	11	Rondon [66]	24,878
30	19	H	Norwich C	L 0-1	0-0	11		25,039
31	Apr 2	A	Sunderland	D 0-0	0-0	11		45,144
32	9	A	Manchester C	L 1-2	1-1	13	Sessegnon [6]	53,920
33	16	H	Watford	L 0-1	0-1	14		25,515
34	21	A	Arsenal	L 0-2	0-2	15		59,568
35	25	A	Tottenham H	D 1-1	0-1	13	Dawson [73]	35,923
36	30	H	West Ham U	L 0-3	0-2	13		25,031
37	May 7	A	Bournemouth	D 1-1	1-0	15	Rondon [16]	11,040
38	15	H	Liverpool	D 1-1	1-1	14	Rondon [13]	26,196

Final League Position: 14

GOALSCORERS

League (34): Rondon 9, Berahino 4, Dawson 4, Gardner 3, Morrison 3, McClean 2, Sessegnon 2, Evans 1, Fletcher 1, Lambert 1 (1 pen), McAuley 1, Olsson 1, own goals 2.
FA Cup (7): Berahino 3, Fletcher 2, Morrison 1, Rondon 1.
Capital One Cup (0).

Myhill B 23	Chester J 9 + 4	Dawson C 38	Lescott J 2	Brunt C 20 + 2	Gardner C 20 + 14	Fletcher D 38	Morrison J 17 + 1	McClean J 28 + 7	Lambert R 5 + 14	Berahino S 17 + 14	Yacob C 33 + 1	Anichebe V 3 + 7	McManaman C 2 + 10	McAuley G 34	Olsson J 25 + 3	Rondon J 30 + 4	Gnabry S — + 1	Gamboa C — + 1	Evans J 30	Sessegnon S 21 + 4	Foster B 15	Sandro 5 + 7	Pritchard A — + 2	Pocognoli S — + 1	Leko J 3 + 2	Roberts T — + 1	Field S — + 1	Match No.
1	2	3	4	5	6	7	8	9^{1}	10^{2}	11^{3}	12	13	14															1
1	2			5	9^{1}	7	6	13	10^{2}	11^{3}	8			14	3	4	12											2
1	2			5	14	9	8^{3}	10^{1}	12		6			7^{2}	3	4	11	13										3
1	2	5		6^{2}	7	9	10^{3}	12		8^{1}			13	3	4	11		14										4
1	2			5	9	7		13	10^{1}	12	8		6^{2}	3	14	11			4^{3}									5
1	2			5	12	7	9	6^{2}	13	10^{1}	8			3	14	11^{3}			4									6
1	12	2		5	13	6	8	9	14	11	7^{3}			4^{1}	10^{2}				3									7
1	12	2		5	13	6	8^{3}	9	11^{2}	7		14	3		10				4^{1}									8
1	2			5	13	7		9	12	11^{2}	8			3		10^{1}			4	6								9
1	2			5	13	7		9	12	11^{2}	8			3		10^{1}			4	6								10
1	2			5^{2}		8	13	9	12	10^{1}	7^{2}		14	3		11			4	6								11
1	2			5^{2}		7	9^{1}	6	12	13	8		14	3^{1}		11^{2}			4	10								12
1	2			5	12	6	8^{3}	10	14	13	7				4	11^{2}			3	9^{1}								13
1	2					7	10	9	12		8			3	4	11			5	6^{1}								14
1	2			5	12	9	7	10						3	4	11			8	6^{1}								15
1	2			5	7	8	9	10	12					3	4	11^{1}			6									16
1	2			5^{2}	7	8^{3}	9^{1}	10^{1}	13	14				3	4	$11^{▪}$			6	12								17
1	2			5	7^{1}	8	10		11	13	9^{3}		14	3	4^{2}				6	12								18
1	2			8	12	6	10^{2}		14	13	7	11^{3}		2	3^{1}				4	9								19
1	2			5	10^{2}	6	9		11	12	7^{1}		13	3					4	8								20
1	2			7	12	8	9^{1}	10		13	6^{2}			3	4	11^{3}			5	14								21
1	2		13	10	7^{1}		9		14	8	11			3	4^{2}	12			5	6^{1}								22
	2			10^{1}	8		9		13	7	12	14		3	4	11^{2}			5	6^{3}	1							23
	2			12	9		10		13	6	14			3	4	11			5^{1}	8^{2}	1	7^{3}						24
5	2			8^{1}	9		10		13	6	11^{3}			3	4	14				1	7^{2}		12					25
5	2	12		7			9^{1}		10^{1}	8	13			4	11^{2}				3	6	1	14						26
12	2	5^{1}	8	6		13		11	7				3	4	10^{3}			9^{2}	1	14								27
5	2		9^{1}	7	12		11	8	13			3	4	10^{3}					6^{3}	1	14							28
5	2^{1}		9	8	13		11^{3}	7				3	4	10					6^{2}	1	14	12						29
	2	10^{2}	7	12	14	9	6				3	4^{1}	11	5	8^{3}	1		13										30
5	2	8^{1}	9	12	10^{2}	7	14			3	11^{3}	4		1	6		13											31
5	2	12	7	10	9		11^{1}	4	8^{1}		3			1	6		13											32
5^{2}	2	14	7	9	11	8^{3}	13	12	3	10^{1}	4	6	1															33
5^{2}	2	14	6	11^{3}	10	7	3	13	12	4	9	1	8^{1}															34
1	2	9	7	10	6	3	4	11	5	8^{1}	12																	35
	2	9^{3}	6	10^{1}	12	7^{2}	3	4	11	5	14	1	13	8														36
	2	9^{1}	7	10	12	6	3	4	11	5	1	13	8^{2}															37
12	2	9	6	10^{3}	7	3	4^{1}	11	5	1	8^{2}	13	14															38

FA Cup

Third Round	Bristol C	(h)	2-2
Replay	Bristol C	(a)	1-0
Fourth Round	Peterborough U	(h)	2-2
Replay	Peterborough U	(a)	1-1
(aet; WBA won 4-3 on penalties)			
Fifth Round	Reading	(a)	1-3

Capital One Cup

Second Round	Port Vale	(h)	0-0
(aet; WBA won 5-3 on penalties)			
Third Round	Norwich C	(a)	0-3

WEST HAM UNITED

FOUNDATION

Thames Ironworks FC was formed by employees of this famous shipbuilding company in 1895 and entered the FA Cup in their initial season at Chatham and the London League in their second. The committee wanted to introduce professional players, so Thames Ironworks was wound up in June 1900 and relaunched a month later as West Ham United.

The Boleyn Ground, Upton Park, Green Street, London E13 9AZ. (Moving to Olympic Stadium, Stratford, London from the start of 2016–17 season.)

Telephone: (020) 8548 2748.

Fax: (020) 8548 2758.

Ticket Office: (0871) 529 1966.

Website: www.whufc.com

Email: customerservices@westhamunited.co.uk

Ground Capacity: 35,345.

Record Attendance: 42,322 v Tottenham H, Division 1, 17 October 1970.

Pitch Measurements: 100.58m × 66m (109yd × 72yd).

Joint Chairmen: David Sullivan and David Gold.

Vice-chairman: Baroness Karren Brady CBE.

Chief Operating Officer: Ben Illingworth.

Manager: Slaven Bilic.

Assistant Manager: Nikola Jurcevic.

Physio: Dominic Rogan.

Colours: Claret shirts with sky blue trim, white shorts with sky blue trim, claret socks with sky blue trim.

Year Formed: 1895.

Turned Professional: 1900.

Previous Name: 1895, Thames Ironworks FC; 1900, West Ham United.

Club Nicknames: 'The Hammers', 'The Irons'.

Grounds: 1895, Memorial Recreation Ground, Canning Town; 1904, Boleyn Ground; 2016, Olympic Stadium.

First Football League Game: 30 August 1919, Division 2, v Lincoln C (h) D 1–1 – Hufton; Cope, Lee; Lane, Fenwick, McCrae; David Smith, Moyes (1), Puddefoot, Morris, Bradshaw.

Record League Victory: 8–0 v Rotherham U, Division 2, 8 March 1958 – Gregory; Bond, Wright; Malcolm, Brown, Lansdowne; Grice, Smith (2), Keeble (2), Dick (4), Musgrove. 8–0 v Sunderland, Division 1, 19 October 1968 – Ferguson; Bonds, Charles; Peters, Stephenson, Moore (1); Redknapp, Boyce, Brooking (1), Hurst (6), Sissons.

HONOURS

League Champions: Division 2 – 1957–58, 1980–81.
Runners-up: First Division – 1992–93; Division 2 – 1922–23, 1990–91.
FA Cup Winners: 1964, 1975, 1980. *Runners-up:* 1923, 2006.
League Cup: Runners-up: 1966, 1981.
European Competitions
UEFA Cup: 1999–2000; 2006–07.
Europa League: 2015–16.
European Cup-Winners' Cup: 1964–65 *(winners)*, 1965–66 *(sf)*, 1975–76 *(runners-up)*, 1980–81 *(qf)*.
Intertoto Cup: 1999 *(winners)*.

sky SPORTS FACT FILE

West Ham United won the Evening Standard five-a-side championships at Wembley Pool on three occasions: 1967, 1970 and 1984. Their first title was achieved with a 4-0 win over Arsenal in the final with Geoff Hurst scoring a hat-trick to match his feat of scoring three in a rather more important final 12 months earlier.

Record Cup Victory: 10–0 v Bury, League Cup 2nd rd (2nd leg), 25 October 1983 – Parkes; Stewart (1), Walford, Bonds (Orr), Martin (1), Devonshire (2), Allen, Cottee (4), Swindlehurst, Brooking (2), Pike.

Record Defeat: 2–8 v Blackburn R, Division 1, 26 December 1963; 0–6 v Oldham Ath, League Cup semi-final (1st leg), 14 February 1990.

Most League Points (2 for a win): 66, Division 2, 1980–81.

Most League Points (3 for a win): 88, Division 1, 1992–93.

Most League Goals: 101, Division 2, 1957–58.

Highest League Scorer in Season: Vic Watson, 42, Division 1, 1929–30.

Most League Goals in Total Aggregate: Vic Watson, 298, 1920–35.

Most League Goals in One Match: 6, Vic Watson v Leeds U, Division 1, 9 February 1929; 6, Geoff Hurst v Sunderland, Division 1, 19 October 1968.

Most Capped Player: Bobby Moore, 108, England.

Most League Appearances: Billy Bonds, 663, 1967–88.

Youngest League Player: Billy Williams, 16 years 221 days v Blackpool, 6 May 1922.

Record Transfer Fee Received: £18,000,000 from Leeds U for Rio Ferdinand, November 2000.

Record Transfer Fee Paid: £15,000,000 to Liverpool for Andy Carroll, July 2013.

Football League Record: 1919 Elected to Division 2; 1923–32 Division 1; 1932–58 Division 2; 1958–78 Division 1; 1978–81 Division 2; 1981–89 Division 1; 1989–91 Division 2; 1991–93 Division 1; 1993–2003 FA Premier League; 2003–04 Division 1; 2004–05 FL C; 2005–11 FA Premier League; 2011–12 FL C; 2012– FA Premier League.

MANAGERS

Syd King 1902–32
Charlie Paynter 1932–50
Ted Fenton 1950–61
Ron Greenwood 1961–74
 (continued as General Manager to 1977)
John Lyall 1974–89
Lou Macari 1989–90
Billy Bonds 1990–94
Harry Redknapp 1994–2001
Glenn Roeder 2001–03
Alan Pardew 2003–06
Alan Curbishley 2006–08
Gianfranco Zola 2008–10
Avram Grant 2010–11
Sam Allardyce 2011–15
Slaven Bilic June 2015–

LATEST SEQUENCES

Longest Sequence of League Wins: 9, 19.10.1985 – 14.12.1985.

Longest Sequence of League Defeats: 9, 28.3.1932 – 29.8.1932.

Longest Sequence of League Draws: 5, 29.11.2015 – 26.12.2015.

Longest Sequence of Unbeaten League Matches: 27, 27.12.1980 – 10.10.1981.

Longest Sequence Without a League Win: 17, 31.1.1976 – 21.8.1976.

Successive Scoring Runs: 27 from 5.10.1957.

Successive Non-scoring Runs: 5 from 17.9.2006.

TEN YEAR LEAGUE RECORD

		P	W	D	L	F	A	Pts	Pos
2006-07	PR Lge	38	12	5	21	35	59	41	15
2007-08	PR Lge	38	13	10	15	42	50	49	10
2008-09	PR Lge	38	14	9	15	42	45	51	9
2009-10	PR Lge	38	8	11	19	47	66	35	17
2010-11	PR Lge	38	7	12	19	43	70	33	20
2011-12	FL C	46	24	14	8	81	48	86	3
2012-13	PR Lge	38	12	10	16	45	53	46	10
2013-14	PR Lge	38	11	7	20	40	51	40	13
2014-15	PR Lge	38	12	11	15	44	47	47	12
2015-16	PR Lge	38	16	14	8	65	51	62	7

DID YOU KNOW ?

Full-back Alfred Earl made his debut for West Ham United against Aston Villa on Christmas Day 1925. He went on to appear in 206 League and Cup games for the Hammers, but never scored a goal and he holds the record of the most appearances for the club without finding the net.

WEST HAM UNITED – FA PREMIER LEAGUE 2015–16 LEAGUE RECORD

Match No.	Date	Venue	Opponents	Result	H/T Score	Lg Pos.	Goalscorers	Attendance
1	Aug 9	A	Arsenal	W 2-0	1-0	3	Kouyate [43], Zarate [57]	59,996
2	15	H	Leicester C	L 1-2	0-2	7	Payet [55]	34,857
3	22	H	Bournemouth	L 3-4	0-2	9	Noble (pen) [48], Kouyate [53], Maiga [82]	34,977
4	29	A	Liverpool	W 3-0	2-0	7	Lanzini [3], Noble [29], Sakho [90]	43,680
5	Sept 14	H	Newcastle U	W 2-0	1-0	5	Payet 2 [9, 48]	34,907
6	19	A	Manchester C	W 2-1	2-1	2	Moses [6], Sakho [31]	53,545
7	26	H	Norwich C	D 2-2	1-1	3	Sakho [33], Kouyate [90]	34,857
8	Oct 3	A	Sunderland	D 2-2	1-2	5	Jenkinson [45], Payet [60]	42,932
9	17	A	Crystal Palace	W 3-1	1-1	4	Jenkinson [22], Lanzini [88], Payet [90]	24,812
10	24	H	Chelsea	W 2-1	1-0	3	Zarate [17], Carroll [79]	34,977
11	31	A	Watford	L 0-2	0-1	5		20,598
12	Nov 7	H	Everton	D 1-1	1-1	5	Lanzini [30]	34,977
13	22	A	Tottenham H	L 1-4	0-2	6	Lanzini [87]	35,968
14	29	H	WBA	D 1-1	1-0	8	Zarate [17]	34,914
15	Dec 5	A	Manchester U	D 0-0	0-0	6		75,350
16	12	H	Stoke C	D 0-0	0-0	8		34,857
17	20	A	Swansea C	D 0-0	0-0	8		20,661
18	26	A	Aston Villa	D 1-1	1-0	10	Cresswell [45]	38,193
19	28	H	Southampton	W 2-1	0-1	7	Antonio [69], Carroll [79]	34,977
20	Jan 2	H	Liverpool	W 2-0	1-0	6	Antonio [10], Carroll [55]	34,977
21	12	A	Bournemouth	W 3-1	0-1	5	Payet [67], Valencia 2 [74, 84]	11,071
22	16	A	Newcastle U	L 1-2	0-2	5	Jelavic [49]	50,031
23	23	H	Manchester C	D 2-2	1-1	6	Valencia 2 [1, 56]	34,977
24	Feb 2	H	Aston Villa	W 2-0	0-0	6	Antonio [58], Kouyate [85]	34,914
25	6	A	Southampton	L 0-1	0-1	6		29,161
26	13	A	Norwich C	D 2-2	0-0	7	Payet [74], Noble [76]	27,101
27	27	H	Sunderland	W 1-0	1-0	6	Antonio [30]	34,946
28	Mar 2	H	Tottenham H	W 1-0	1-0	6	Antonio [7]	34,977
29	5	A	Everton	W 3-2	0-1	5	Antonio [78], Sakho [81], Payet [90]	39,000
30	19	A	Chelsea	D 2-2	1-1	5	Lanzini [17], Carroll [61]	41,623
31	Apr 2	H	Crystal Palace	D 2-2	2-1	5	Lanzini [18], Payet [41]	34,857
32	9	H	Arsenal	D 3-3	2-2	6	Carroll 3 [44, 45, 52]	34,977
33	17	A	Leicester C	D 2-2	0-1	6	Carroll (pen) [84], Cresswell [86]	32,104
34	20	H	Watford	W 3-1	2-0	6	Carroll [11], Noble 2 (2 pens) [45, 53]	34,857
35	30	A	WBA	W 3-0	2-0	5	Kouyate [34], Noble 2 [45, 79]	25,031
36	May 7	H	Swansea C	L 1-4	0-2	6	Kingsley (og) [68]	34,907
37	10	H	Manchester U	W 3-2	1-0	6	Sakho [10], Antonio [76], Reid [80]	34,602
38	15	A	Stoke C	L 1-2	1-0	7	Antonio [23]	27,721

Final League Position: 7

GOALSCORERS

League (65): Carroll 9 (1 pen), Payet 9, Antonio 8, Noble 7 (3 pens), Lanzini 6, Kouyate 5, Sakho 5, Valencia 4, Zarate 3, Cresswell 2, Jenkinson 2, Jelavic 1, Maiga 1, Moses 1, Reid 1, own goal 1.
FA Cup (10): Payet 3, Emenike 2, Antonio 1, Jelavic 1, Moses 1, Ogbonna 1, Tomkins 1.
Capital One Cup (1): Zarate 1.
UEFA Europa League (8): Sakho 2, Tomkins 2, Lanzini 1, Lee 1, Valencia 1, Zarate 1.

Adrian 32	Tomkins J 23+2	Reid W 24	Oghonna A 27+1	Cresswell A 37	Oxford R 3+4	Kouyate C 34	Noble M 37	Payet D 29+1	Zarate M 9+6	Sakho D 18+3	Jarvis M —+3	Nolan K 1+1	Maiga M —+3	Jenkinson C 13+7	Obiang P 11+13	Lanzini M 23+3	Randolph D 6	Cullen J —+1	Moses V 13+8	Carroll A 13+14	Antonio M 23+3	Jelavic N 1+12	Collins J 16+3	Valencia E 10+9	Song A 8+4	Byram S 2+2	Emenike E 5+8	Match No.
1	2	3	4	5	6^2	7	8	9	10^1	11^3	12	13	14															1
1*		3	4	5	6^1	8^2	7	9	10^3	11			14	2	12	13												2
12		3	4^1	5		8	6	9		11^3	13	10^2	14	2^4	7		1											3
	2	3	4	5	12	6	8^4	11^2		10^3	13			7	9	1		14										4
	2	3	4^1	5		7	6	9		11				12	13	8^2	1		10^3	14								5
1		3	4	5		6	9	11						2^3	7	8^2			10^1	12	13	14						6
1		3	4	5		6^3	9	14	11					2	12	8^2			10^1	13								7
1		3	4^2	5		6	7^3	9	14	11				2	8				10^1	12	13							8
1		3		5		6	7^1	10	13	11^3				2	9	8^2			12	14	4							9
1		3	14	5		7	6^3	9	10^1	11				2	13	8^2			12	4								10
1		3		5		6	7^3	9	12					2		8^2			10^1	11	14	4*^{4}	13					11
1		3	4	5		6	7^3		12	8				2		9			10^1	11^2	14	13						12
1		3	4	5		6	7^3		12	8				2		9			10^1	11^2	13		14					13
		3	4	5		8			10^3	11^2				2	6^1	9			7	12	14	13						14
1	2	3	4	5		8		9		10^3				14	13				7^1	11	12			6^2				15
1	2		4	5		9	8		7										11	10^2	13	3	12	6^1				16
1	2		4	5		8	9		10^1					14	13				7^3	11	3	12	6^2					17
1	2^1		4	5^5	14	7	9		10^3					12	6				8		3	11	13					18
1	2		4	5		7	9		10^1					5	14	12			13	8	3	11^3	6^2					19
1	2		4	5		7	8	13						14	12	9^1			10	6^3	3	11^2						20
1	2^2		4	5			6	9^3						13	7				11^1	10	12	3	8	14				21
1	2^3		4	5		7	6	11						14	8^1		13		9^2	12	3	10						22
1		4		5		6	8	11						2^1			13		9^2	14	3	10^3	7	12				23
1	2	4		5		6^3	8	11						14			12		9^2	10^1	3	11	7					24
1	2^2	4		5			6	9									10^1	13	8^3		3	11	7	12	14			25
1		4	5				6	11						8			12	13	9^3		3	10^1	7^2	2	14			26
1		4	5			6	7^3	11						14	8^2		13	12	9		3			2	10^1			27
1		4	5	12		2	6	11					14	7	8^3		13	9	3^1						10^2			28
1		4	8	3^1		2	6	10					13	7^3	9		12	5					14		11^2			29
1	3	4	5			6	7	10		11^1				14	9^3			12	2		8^2		13					30
1	3	4	5			6*^{1}	7^3	10		11^2				14	9			12	2		13		8^1					31
1	2^1	3	4	8		6	7	10							9			11	5			12						32
1	3	4	5			6	8^2	11						7^1	13			9^3	12	2			14		10			33
1	3	4	5			7	6	11^3		9^1					8			12	10^3	2	14		13					34
1	3	4	5	14		7	8	9^2		10^1					6^3			13	11	2			12					35
	3	4	5			6^2	7	10		12					8^1	11	2				14		13					36
13	3	4	5			7	8	9^3		10^2				12	6^1	1			11	2			14					37
	2^3	3	4	5		8	7			10^1					9	1	14	11^2	6				13		12			38

FA Cup

Third Round	Wolverhampton W	(h)	1-0
Fourth Round	Liverpool	(a)	0-0
Replay	Liverpool	(h)	2-1
(aet)			
Fifth Round	Blackburn R	(a)	5-1
Sixth Round	Manchester U	(a)	1-1
Replay	Manchester U	(h)	1-2

Capital One Cup

Third Round	Leicester C	(a)	1-2
(aet)			

UEFA Europa League

First Qualifying 1st leg	Lusitanos	(h)	3-0
First Qualifying 2nd leg	Lusitanos	(a)	1-0
Second Qualifying 1st leg	Birkirkara	(h)	1-0
Second Qualifying 2nd leg	Birkirkara	(a)	0-1
(aet; West Ham U won 5-3 on penalties)			
Third Qualifying 1st leg	Astra Giurgiu	(h)	2-2
Third Qualifying 2nd leg	Astra Giurgiu	(a)	1-2
(Astra Giurgiu won 4-3 on aggregate)			

WIGAN ATHLETIC

*The DW Stadium, Loire Drive, Wigan, Lancashire
WN5 0UZ.*

Telephone: (01942) 774 000.

Fax: (01942) 770 444.

Ticket Office: (0871) 663 3552.

Website: www.wiganlatics.co.uk

Email: feedback@wiganathletic.com

Ground Capacity: 25,133.

Record Attendance: 27,526 v Hereford U, 12 December
1953 (at Springfield Park); 25,133 v Manchester U, FA
Premier League, 11 May 2008 (at DW Stadium).

Pitch Measurements: 105m × 68m (115yd × 74.5yd).

Chairman: David Sharpe.

Chief Executive: Jonathan Jackson.

Manager: Gary Caldwell.

Assistant Manager: Graham Barrow.

Head Physio: Russell Hitchin.

Colours: Blue and white striped shirts with blue sleeves, blue shorts with white trim, white socks.

Year Formed: 1932.

Turned Professional: 1932.

Club Nickname: 'The Latics'.

Grounds: 1932, Springfield Park; 1999, JJB Stadium (renamed the DW Stadium in 2009).

First Football League Game: 19 August 1978, Division 4, v Hereford U (a) D 0–0 – Brown; Hinnigan,
Gore, Gillibrand, Ward, Davids, Corrigan, Purdie, Houghton, Wilkie, Wright.

Record League Victory: 7–1 v Scarborough, Division 3, 11 March 1997 – Lee Butler; John Butler,
Sharp (Morgan), Greenall, McGibbon (Biggins (1)), Martinez (1), Diaz (2), Jones (Lancashire (1)),
Lowe (2), Rogers, Kilford.

Record Cup Victory: 6–0 v Carlisle U (a), FA Cup 1st rd, 24 November 1934 – Caunce; Robinson,
Talbot; Paterson, Watson, Tufnell; Armes (2), Robson (1), Roberts (2), Felton, Scott (1).

Record Defeat: 1–9 v Tottenham H, FA Premier League, 22 November 2009; 0–8 v Chelsea, FA
Premier League, 9 May 2010.

HONOURS

League Champions: FL 1 – 2015–16;
Second Division – 2002–03; Third
Division – 1996–97.
Runners-up: FL C – 2004–05.
FA Cup Winners: 2013.
League Cup: Runners-up: 2006.
League Trophy Winners: 1985, 1999.
European Competitions
Europa League: 2013–14.

Most League Points (2 for a win): 55, Division 4, 1978–79 and 1979–80.

Most League Points (3 for a win): 100, Division 2, 2002–03.

Most League Goals: 84, Division 3, 1996–97.

Highest League Scorer in Season: Graeme Jones, 31, Division 3, 1996–97.

Most League Goals in Total Aggregate: Andy Liddell, 70, 1998–2004.

Most League Goals in One Match: Not more than three goals by one player.

Most Capped Players: Kevin Kilbane, 22 (110), Republic of Ireland; Henri Camara, 22 (99), Senegal.

Most League Appearances: Kevin Langley, 317, 1981–86, 1990–94.

Youngest League Player: Steve Nugent, 16 years 132 days v Leyton Orient, 16 September 1989.

Record Transfer Fee Received: £15,250,000 from Manchester U for Antonio Valencia, June 2009.

Record Transfer Fee Paid: £6,500,000 to Estudiantes for Mauro Boselli, August 2010.

Football League Record: 1978 Elected to Division 4; 1982–92 Division 3; 1992–93 Division 2; 1993–97 Division 3; 1997–2003 Division 2; 2003–04 Division 1; 2004–05 FL C; 2005–13 FA Premier League; 2013–15 FL C; 2015–16 FL 1; 2016– FL C.

LATEST SEQUENCES

Longest Sequence of League Wins: 11, 2.11.2002 – 18.1.2003.

Longest Sequence of League Defeats: 8, 10.9.2011 – 6.11.2011.

Longest Sequence of League Draws: 6, 11.12.2001 – 5.1.2002.

Longest Sequence of Unbeaten League Matches: 25, 8.5.1999 – 3.1.2000.

Longest Sequence Without a League Win: 14, 9.5.1989 – 17.10.1989.

Successive Scoring Runs: 24 from 27.4.1996.

Successive Non-scoring Runs: 4 from 25.4.2015.

MANAGERS

Charlie Spencer 1932–37
Jimmy Milne 1946–47
Bob Pryde 1949–52
Ted Goodier 1952–54
Walter Crook 1954–55
Ron Suart 1955–56
Billy Cooke 1956
Sam Barkas 1957
Trevor Hitchen 1957–58
Malcolm Barrass 1958–59
Jimmy Shirley 1959
Pat Murphy 1959–60
Allenby Chilton 1960
Johnny Ball 1961–63
Allan Brown 1963–66
Alf Craig 1966–67
Harry Leyland 1967–68
Alan Saunders 1968
Ian McNeill 1968–70
Gordon Milne 1970–72
Les Rigby 1972–74
Brian Tiler 1974–76
Ian McNeill 1976–81
Larry Lloyd 1981–83
Harry McNally 1983–85
Bryan Hamilton 1985–86
Ray Mathias 1986–89
Bryan Hamilton 1989–93
Dave Philpotts 1993
Kenny Swain 1993–94
Graham Barrow 1994–95
John Deehan 1995–98
Ray Mathias 1998–99
John Benson 1999–2000
Bruce Rioch 2000–01
Steve Bruce 2001
Paul Jewell 2001–07
Chris Hutchings 2007
Steve Bruce 2007–09
Roberto Martinez 2009–13
Owen Coyle 2013
Uwe Rosler 2013–14
Malky Mackay 2014–15
Gary Caldwell April 2015–

TEN YEAR LEAGUE RECORD

		P	W	D	L	F	A	Pts	Pos
2006-07	PR Lge	38	10	8	20	37	59	38	17
2007-08	PR Lge	38	10	10	18	34	51	40	14
2008-09	PR Lge	38	12	9	17	34	45	45	11
2009-10	PR Lge	38	9	9	20	37	79	36	16
2010-11	PR Lge	38	9	15	14	40	61	42	16
2011-12	PR Lge	38	11	10	17	42	62	43	15
2012-13	PR Lge	38	9	9	20	47	73	36	18
2013-14	FL C	46	21	10	15	61	48	73	5
2014-15	FL C	46	9	12	25	39	64	39	23
2015-16	FL 1	46	24	15	7	82	45	87	1

DID YOU KNOW ?

The FA Cup second round tie between Wigan Athletic and Hereford United attracted an attendance of 27,526 to Springfield Park. This remains a record attendance for a game between two non-league clubs apart from games at Wembley. Wigan won the tie 4-1.

WIGAN ATHLETIC – FOOTBALL LEAGUE ONE 2015–16 LEAGUE RECORD

Match No.	Date	Venue	Opponents	Result	H/T Score	Lg Pos.	Goalscorers	Attendance
1	Aug 8	A	Coventry C	L	0-2	0-1	21		13,131
2	16	H	Doncaster R	D	0-0	0-0	22		8813
3	19	H	Scunthorpe U	W	3-0	2-0	11	Grigg (pen) [3], Daniels [27], Davies [70]	7794
4	22	A	Gillingham	L	0-2	0-1	13		5692
5	29	H	Crewe Alex	W	1-0	1-0	11	Jacobs [12]	8647
6	Sept 5	A	Chesterfield	W	3-2	0-0	9	Barnett [81], Davies (pen) [87], Hiwula [90]	7145
7	12	A	Port Vale	L	2-3	0-1	10	McCann [66], Duffy (og) [83]	5953
8	19	H	Fleetwood T	W	2-1	1-0	7	Flores [39], Jacobs [47]	8603
9	26	A	Oldham Ath	D	1-1	1-0	9	Power [34]	5482
10	29	H	Millwall	D	2-2	0-0	9	Jacobs [54], Grigg [90]	7991
11	Oct 3	H	Walsall	D	0-0	0-0	9		8636
12	10	A	Bury	D	2-2	0-1	10	Cameron (og) [85], Morgan [90]	5931
13	17	H	Colchester U	W	5-0	4-0	8	Daniels 2 [5, 14], Power [11], Grigg 2 [33, 87]	8048
14	20	A	Peterborough U	W	3-2	2-0	7	Wildschut [11], Grigg [15], Power [82]	4765
15	24	A	Bradford C	D	1-1	0-0	5	Jacobs [52]	19,171
16	31	H	Swindon T	W	1-0	0-0	5	Junior [90]	8466
17	Nov 14	A	Rochdale	W	2-0	1-0	5	Pearce [16], Jacobs [61]	3835
18	21	H	Shrewsbury T	W	1-0	1-0	4	Revell [36]	8803
19	24	H	Burton Alb	L	0-1	0-0	5		8117
20	28	A	Southend U	D	0-0	0-0	5		7117
21	Dec 12	H	Blackpool	L	0-1	0-1	6		8424
22	19	A	Barnsley	W	2-0	1-0	5	Kellett [18], Wildschut [86]	8866
23	28	A	Fleetwood T	W	3-1	1-0	5	Kellett [39], Hiwula [83], Jacobs [90]	4232
24	Jan 2	A	Scunthorpe U	D	1-1	1-1	5	Jacobs [34]	4102
25	7	H	Gillingham	W	3-2	0-1	5	Grigg [64], Power [67], Morgan [90]	7923
26	12	H	Sheffield U	D	3-3	2-0	5	Grigg [16], Vuckic [43], McCann [66]	10,113
27	16	H	Chesterfield	W	3-1	3-0	5	Power [6], James [38], Jacobs [39]	9091
28	23	A	Crewe Alex	D	1-1	1-1	4	Wabara [16]	6010
29	30	H	Port Vale	W	3-0	2-0	4	Grigg 3 (1 pen) [7, 41 (p), 69]	9627
30	Feb 6	A	Sheffield U	W	2-0	0-0	3	Grigg (pen) [52], McAleny [55]	20,304
31	13	H	Oldham Ath	D	0-0	0-0	4		9817
32	20	A	Walsall	W	2-1	1-0	2	McAleny [39], Wildschut [90]	6740
33	27	H	Bury	W	3-0	3-0	2	Grigg 2 (1 pen) [7, 21 (p)], Colclough [9]	9490
34	Mar 1	A	Millwall	D	0-0	0-0	2		7981
35	5	H	Peterborough U	D	1-1	0-0	2	Grigg [71]	8877
36	12	A	Colchester U	D	3-3	2-1	2	Wildschut [36], Colclough [44], Grigg [90]	3761
37	19	H	Bradford C	W	1-0	0-0	2	Vuckic [80]	10,890
38	25	A	Swindon T	W	4-1	1-0	2	Grigg 2 [15, 50], Power [47], Morsy [51]	9240
39	28	H	Rochdale	W	1-0	0-0	2	McAleny [67]	10,407
40	Apr 2	A	Shrewsbury T	W	5-1	1-1	1	McAleny [33], Wildschut [57], Pearce [61], Grigg 2 (1 pen) [66 (p), 90]	7010
41	9	H	Coventry C	W	1-0	0-0	1	Grigg [57]	10,415
42	16	A	Doncaster R	L	1-3	1-0	1	Grigg [41]	6987
43	19	A	Burton Alb	D	1-1	1-1	1	Jacobs [8]	5461
44	23	H	Southend U	W	4-1	3-0	1	McCann [9], Grigg 2 [17, 36], Jacobs [50]	10,021
45	30	A	Blackpool	W	4-0	0-0	1	McCann [60], Wildschut 2 [70, 72], Grigg [85]	9226
46	May 8	H	Barnsley	L	1-4	1-2	1	Grigg [10]	18,730

Final League Position: 1

GOALSCORERS

League (82): Grigg 25 (5 pens), Jacobs 10, Wildschut 7, Power 6, McAleny 4, McCann 4, Daniels 3, Colclough 2, Davies 2 (1 pen), Hiwula 2, Kellett 2, Morgan 2, Pearce 2, Vuckic 2, Barnett 1, Flores 1, James 1, Junior 1, Morsy 1, Revell 1, Wabara 1, own goals 2.
FA Cup (0).
Capital One Cup (1): Grigg 1 (pen).
Johnstone's Paint Trophy (9): Hiwula 4 (1 pen), Grigg 2, Wildschut 2, Murray 1.

O'Donnell R 10	Kenny J 6+1	Daniels D 40+2	Morgan C 36	James R 25+1	Perkins D 44+1	Power M 43+1	Junior F 5+5	McCann C 31+7	Jacobs M 30+5	Grigg W 35+5	McNaughton K 1+1	Davies C 7+19	Murray S 2+5	Barnett L 16+4	Coulthirst S —+2	McKay B —+1	Pearce J 29+2	Flores J 2+1	Hiwula J 7+7	Vuckic H 5+10	Kellett A 4+5	Chow T 3+8	Odelusi S —+3	Jaaskelainen J 35	Wildschut Y 25+9	Love D 4+3	Holt G —+4	Cowie D 2+3	Revell A 4+2	Wabara R 14+5	Colclough R 7+3	Morsy S 13+3	McAleny C 9+4	Nicholls L 1+1	Warnock S 11	Match No.
1	2^1	3^3	4	5	6	7	8^2	9	10	11	12	13	14																							1
1	5	3	2	8	6	10^1	7^2	9	11			12		4	13																					2
1	2	4	3	5	7	14	6^1	8	9^3	10		11^2		13	12																					3
1	12	2	3	9^2	8		6^1	4	7	11	5^3	10		13			14																			4
1	5	3	4	2^1	7	8		9	10^2			11^1	12				6	13	14																	5
1		2^1		8	6	5		12	9			11	7^3	4		3		13	10^2	14																6
1	6	2^1		9^2	5			8	7			14		10		4^4	3			12	11^3	13														7
1	2	4			6	5	7^1		8	9							3		10^3	11^2		12	13	14												8
1		5			6	4	7^1		8	9							3		2^2	10^4	11^1		14	13	12											9
1		2		5^2	6	7^3	12	4	10	13					8^1		3			11		9	14													10
		2	3^9	9	6	5^1		7	8	11^1							4			10^2		14		1	12	13										11
		2	3	6	9	7	13	5	8								4			11^2				1	10	12										12
		5^1	3	9	6	7	12	4	8^3	11							2							1	10^2	14	13									13
		5	3	8	6	7		4	9^1	10^2		14					2					13		1	11^3		12									14
		5^1	3	9	8	6		2	7	11^3		14					4							1	10^2	12	13									15
		2	3	9	6	7^1	12	4	8^1	10		14												1	11^3	5		13								16
		2	3	5^1	8	7^2		12	9						11^1		4					14		1	6			13		10						17
		2	3	9	6	7		4	8^2	12		13								14				1	11					10^3						18
		2	3^3	9	6	7	14	4	8^2	13		12												1	11					10^1						19
		2		6	12	7	8^1	5^2	13	10^3							3							1					9	11	14					20
		12		9	7	8		13	6	10^1		3					4							1	11	5^2		2^3	14							21
		3	5	7	9	8		10	11^1								4			6^3	13			1	14	2^2		12								22
		2	3	9^1	6	7		12	11	10							4		14	8^2				1	13	5^1										23
		2	3		7	6		8	9	10							4		12	5^1				1	11											24
		6	4	2^1	9	8		13	10^3	11		14			5		3		12	7^2				1												25
		2	5	14	8^3	9		6	10	11					4^2		3		7^1					1	12		13									26
		5	3	9^3	7	6		11				12					2		10^1	8^2	14			1	13				4							27
		6	4	8	9		2	10^1	13			14					3		11^2	12^3				1	7				5							28
		5	3		7	6^1	9		10^2								4		14	8^3				1	11				2	12	13					29
		2	3		7	6		5	10^1	13							4							1	9				12		8	11^2				30
		3^2	2		6^9	7		5	14	11							4							1	10				9	13	12	8^1				31
		5^3	4		9	8		2	11	14							3							1	12				13	10^2	6	7^1				32
		4		6	7		2	10^1	13								3			14				1	9^3				5	11^2	8	12				33
		4		9	8		2	11^1	13	12							3							1	14				5	10^2	6^1	7^3				34
		3	4		7	6	13		11								14			2^3				1^2	10				5	8		9^1	12			35
		4^1	3		8	7			10	13							4					14	12	1	11				2	9^3	6^2				5	36
		2^3	3		8	6			10	14		13					12							1	11				5	9^2	7^1				4	37
		3	4		8	7^2		6	10^1	13							14			12				1	11^3				2	9					5	38
			4		6	7		14	10								3^3		13					1	9				5	11^1	8^1	12			2	39
		3			7	6		13	14	10							12			4				1	11^2				2^1	8	9^3				5	40
		2			8	6			13	10^3							3			4				1	11^1				12	7	9^3				5	41
		5^1			6^4	8			12	10		13					4			3				1	9				14		7^1	11^3			2	42
		14	3			8			10	9^1	11						4					13		1	12					5^1	7	6^2			2	43
		5	4		7	8^2		6	11^3	10^1							3							1	9						14	12			2	44
		3	4		8	6		9	11^1	10							14							1	12				2^1		7^3	13			5	45
		5^1	4		7	8		6^4	11^1	10							3							14				9^3		12	13		1	2	46

FA Cup
First Round Bury (a) 0-4

Capital One Cup
First Round Bury (h) 1-2

Johnstone's Paint Trophy
Second Round Crewe Alex (a) 3-2
Northern Quarter-Final Blackpool (h) 4-0
Northern Semi-Final Barnsley (h) 2-2
(aet; Barnsley won 4-2 on penalties)

WOLVERHAMPTON WANDERERS

FOUNDATION

Enthusiasts of the game at St Luke's School, Blakenhall formed a club in 1877. In the same neighbourhood a cricket club called Blakenhall Wanderers had a football section. Several St Luke's footballers played cricket for them and shortly before the start of the 1879–80 season the two amalgamated and Wolverhampton Wanderers FC was brought into being.

Molineux Stadium, Waterloo Road, Wolverhampton WV1 4QR.

Telephone: (0871) 222 2220.

Fax: (01902) 687 006.

Ticket Office: (0871) 222 1877.

Website: wolves.co.uk

Email: info@wolves.co.uk

Ground Capacity: 30,852.

Record Attendance: 61,315 v Liverpool, FA Cup 5th rd, 11 February 1939.

Pitch Measurements: 103.5m × 68m (115yd × 74.5yd).

Chief Executive: Jez Moxey.

Head Coach: Kenny Jackett.

Assistant Head Coach: Joe Gallen.

Physio: Jazz Sodhi.

Colours: Gold shirts with black trim, black shorts with gold trim, gold socks with black trim.

Year Formed: 1877* (*see Foundation*).

Turned Professional: 1888.

Previous Names: 1879, St Luke's combined with Wanderers Cricket Club to become Wolverhampton Wanderers (1923) Ltd. New limited companies followed in 1982 and 1986 (current).

Club Nickname: 'Wolves'.

HONOURS

League Champions: Division 1 – 1953–54, 1957–58, 1958–59; FL C – 2008–09; Division 2 – 1931–32, 1976–77; FL 1 – 2013–14; Division 3 – 1988–89; Division 3N – 1923–24; Division 4 – 1987–88.
Runners-up: Division 1 – 1937–38, 1938–39, 1949–50, 1954–55, 1959–60; Division 2 – 1966–67, 1982–83.
FA Cup Winners: 1893, 1908, 1949, 1960.
Runners-up: 1889, 1896, 1921, 1939.
League Cup Winners: 1974, 1980.
League Trophy Winners: 1988.
Texaco Cup Winners: 1971.

European Competitions
European Cup: 1958–59, 1959–60 (*qf*).
UEFA Cup: 1971–72 (*runners-up*), 1973–74, 1974–75, 1980–81.
European Cup-Winners' Cup: 1960–61 (*sf*).

Grounds: 1877, Windmill Field; 1879, John Harper's Field; 1881, Dudley Road; 1889, Molineux.

First Football League Game: 8 September 1888, Football League, v Aston Villa (h) D 1–1 – Baynton; Baugh, Mason; Fletcher, Allen, Lowder; Hunter, Cooper, Anderson, White, Cannon, (1 og).

Record League Victory: 10–1 v Leicester C, Division 1, 15 April 1938 – Sidlow; Morris, Dowen; Galley, Cullis, Gardiner; Maguire (1), Horace Wright, Westcott (4), Jones (1), Dorsett (4).

Record Cup Victory: 14–0 v Crosswell's Brewery, FA Cup 2nd rd, 13 November 1886 – Ike Griffiths; Baugh, Mason; Pearson, Allen (1), Lowder; Hunter (4), Knight (2), Brodie (4), Bernie Griffiths (2), Wood. Plus one goal 'scrambled through'.

sky SPORTS FACT FILE

Peter Knowles was one of the stars of the Wolverhampton Wanderers team of the 1960s. In September 1969 he announced he was giving up football to take up work as a Jehovah's Witness. He never played a competitive game again, but the club kept him on the books for a further 12 years before ending his contract.

Record Defeat: 1–10 v Newton Heath, Division 1, 15 October 1892.

Most League Points (2 for a win): 64, Division 1, 1957–58.

Most League Points (3 for a win): 103, FL 1, 2013–14.

Most League Goals: 115, Division 2, 1931–32.

Highest League Scorer in Season: Dennis Westcott, 38, Division 1, 1946–47.

Most League Goals in Total Aggregate: Steve Bull, 250, 1986–99.

Most League Goals in One Match: 5, Joe Butcher v Accrington, Division 1, 19 November 1892; 5, Tom Phillipson v Barnsley, Division 2, 26 April 1926; 5, Tom Phillipson v Bradford C, Division 2, 25 December 1926; 5, Billy Hartill v Notts Co, Division 2, 12 October 1929; 5, Billy Hartill v Aston Villa, Division 1, 3 September 1934.

Most Capped Player: Billy Wright, 105, England (70 consecutive).

Most League Appearances: Derek Parkin, 501, 1967–82.

Youngest League Player: Jimmy Mullen, 16 years 43 days v Leeds U, 18 February 1939.

Record Transfer Fee Received: £12,000,000 (rising to £14,000,000) from Sunderland for Steven Fletcher, August 2012.

Record Transfer Fee Paid: £6,500,000 to Reading for Kevin Doyle, June 2009; £6,500,000 to Burnley for Steven Fletcher, June 2010.

Football League Record: 1888 Founder Member of Football League: 1906–23 Division 2; 1923–24 Division 3 (N); 1924–32 Division 2; 1932–65 Division 1; 1965–67 Division 2; 1967–76 Division 1; 1976–77 Division 2; 1977–82 Division 1; 1982–83 Division 2; 1983–84 Division 1; 1984–85 Division 2; 1985–86 Division 3; 1986–88 Division 4; 1988–89 Division 3; 1989–92 Division 2; 1992–2003 Division 1; 2003–04 FA Premier League; 2004–09 FL C; 2009–12 FA Premier League; 2012–13 FL C; 2013–14 FL 1; 2014– FL C.

MANAGERS

George Worrall 1877–85
  (Secretary-Manager)
John Addenbrooke 1885–1922
George Jobey 1922–24
Albert Hoskins 1924–26
  (had been Secretary since 1922)
Fred Scotchbrook 1926–27
Major Frank Buckley 1927–44
Ted Vizard 1944–48
Stan Cullis 1948–64
Andy Beattie 1964–65
Ronnie Allen 1966–68
Bill McGarry 1968–76
Sammy Chung 1976–78
John Barnwell 1978–81
Ian Greaves 1982
Graham Hawkins 1982–84
Tommy Docherty 1984–85
Bill McGarry 1985
Sammy Chapman 1985–86
Brian Little 1986
Graham Turner 1986–94
Graham Taylor 1994–95
Mark McGhee 1995–98
Colin Lee 1998–2000
Dave Jones 2001–04
Glenn Hoddle 2004–06
Mick McCarthy 2006–12
Stale Solbakken 2012–13
Dean Saunders 2013
Kenny Jackett May 2013–

LATEST SEQUENCES

Longest Sequence of League Wins: 9, 11.1.2014 – 11.3.2014.

Longest Sequence of League Defeats: 8, 5.12.1981 – 13.2.1982.

Longest Sequence of League Draws: 6, 22.4.1995 – 20.8.1995.

Longest Sequence of Unbeaten League Matches: 21, 15.1.2005 – 13.8.2005.

Longest Sequence Without a League Win: 19, 1.12.1984 – 6.4.1985.

Successive Scoring Runs: 41 from 20.12.1958.

Successive Non-scoring Runs: 7 from 2.2.1985.

TEN YEAR LEAGUE RECORD

		P	W	D	L	F	A	Pts	Pos
2006-07	FL C	46	22	10	14	59	56	76	5
2007-08	FL C	46	18	16	12	53	48	70	7
2008-09	FL C	46	27	9	10	80	52	90	1
2009-10	PR Lge	38	9	11	18	32	56	38	15
2010-11	PR Lge	38	11	7	20	46	66	40	17
2011-12	PR Lge	38	5	10	23	40	82	25	20
2012-13	FL C	46	14	9	23	55	69	51	23
2013-14	FL 1	46	31	10	5	89	31	103	1
2014-15	FL C	46	22	12	12	70	56	78	7
2015-16	FL C	46	14	16	16	53	58	58	14

DID YOU KNOW ?

For many years Wolverhampton Wanderers had a nursery set-up in south Yorkshire. Run by former player Mark Crook, the club took over junior outfit Brampton Welfare which later became Wath Wanderers. By the late 1950s they were still running teams in the Northern Intermediate and Barnsley Youth Leagues.

WOLVERHAMPTON WANDERERS – FL CHAMPIONSHIP 2015–16 LEAGUE RECORD

Match No.	Date	Venue	Opponents	Result	H/T Score	Lg Pos.	Goalscorers	Attendance
1	Aug 8	A	Blackburn R	W 2-1	2-1	5	Afobe [29], Edwards [45]	16,159
2	16	H	Hull C	D 1-1	0-1	8	Henry [58]	20,062
3	19	H	QPR	L 2-3	2-1	11	Afobe [17], McDonald [24]	21,032
4	22	A	Cardiff C	L 0-2	0-1	17		14,820
5	29	H	Charlton Ath	W 2-1	0-0	12	Edwards [65], Le Fondre [85]	19,583
6	Sept 12	A	Bolton W	L 1-2	0-2	15	Afobe (pen) [68]	14,698
7	19	H	Brighton & HA	D 0-0	0-0	18		20,382
8	26	A	Preston NE	D 1-1	0-1	16	McDonald [90]	13,049
9	29	A	Fulham	W 3-0	0-0	10	Le Fondre [56], Ojo [59], Henry [78]	14,838
10	Oct 3	H	Huddersfield T	W 3-0	1-0	9	McDonald [23], Afobe 2 [66, 88]	18,166
11	18	A	Derby Co	L 2-4	1-3	11	Afobe [19], Le Fondre [64]	29,063
12	21	A	Brentford	L 0-2	0-1	12		18,167
13	24	H	Middlesbrough	L 1-3	1-0	14	Edwards [22]	22,006
14	31	A	Birmingham C	W 2-0	1-0	13	Edwards [11], Ojo [84]	18,946
15	Nov 3	A	Bristol C	L 0-1	0-1	14		15,517
16	7	H	Burnley	D 0-0	0-0	14		20,684
17	21	A	Ipswich T	D 2-2	1-1	14	Henry [38], Afobe [75]	19,227
18	28	H	Milton Keynes D	D 0-0	0-0	15		19,814
19	Dec 5	A	Rotherham U	W 2-1	2-1	14	Henry [5], Batth [44]	9759
20	11	H	Nottingham F	D 1-1	1-0	14	Ebanks-Landell [15]	20,000
21	17	H	Leeds U	L 2-3	1-1	17	Afobe [10], Byrne [81]	19,592
22	20	A	Sheffield W	L 1-4	1-2	17	Afobe (pen) [16]	19,529
23	26	H	Reading	W 1-0	1-0	16	Henry [18]	21,147
24	28	A	Charlton Ath	W 2-0	0-0	11	Graham [52], Lennon (og) [83]	18,059
25	Jan 1	A	Brighton & HA	W 1-0	1-0	11	Goldson (og) [32]	26,321
26	12	H	Fulham	W 3-2	2-1	10	Zyro 2 [6, 13], Doherty [48]	17,387
27	16	H	Cardiff C	L 1-3	1-2	10	Zyro [40]	24,238
28	23	A	QPR	D 1-1	0-1	12	Henry [48]	15,266
29	Feb 2	H	Bolton W	D 2-2	1-0	12	Mason [3], Henry [77]	17,825
30	6	A	Reading	D 0-0	0-0	11		17,771
31	13	H	Preston NE	L 1-2	0-1	12	Mason [66]	21,204
32	20	A	Huddersfield T	L 0-1	0-0	13		12,714
33	23	A	Brentford	L 0-3	0-1	15		8769
34	27	H	Derby Co	W 2-1	1-1	13	Saville 2 [14, 86]	19,389
35	Mar 4	A	Middlesbrough	L 1-2	0-1	14	Gibson (og) [89]	22,110
36	8	H	Bristol C	W 2-1	0-0	12	Byrne [47], Doherty [90]	17,459
37	13	H	Birmingham C	D 0-0	0-0	12		21,464
38	19	A	Burnley	D 1-1	0-0	12	Batth [90]	17,411
39	Apr 2	A	Ipswich T	D 0-0	0-0	12		20,225
40	5	A	Milton Keynes D	W 2-1	0-1	12	Saville [62], Price [66]	12,131
41	9	H	Blackburn R	D 0-0	0-0	12		19,538
42	15	A	Hull C	L 1-2	1-1	12	Edwards [19]	15,504
43	19	A	Leeds U	L 1-2	0-0	14	Saville [77]	17,694
44	23	H	Rotherham U	D 0-0	0-0	14		18,757
45	30	A	Nottingham F	D 1-1	0-0	14	Mason [58]	22,291
46	May 7	H	Sheffield W	W 2-1	2-0	14	Turner (og) [7], Saville [35]	25,488

Final League Position: 14

GOALSCORERS

League (53): Afobe 9 (2 pens), Henry 7, Edwards 5, Saville 5, Le Fondre 3, Mason 3, McDonald 3, Zyro 3, Batth 2, Byrne 2, Doherty 2, Ojo 2, Ebanks-Landell 1, Graham 1, Price 1, own goals 4.
FA Cup (0).
Capital One Cup (4): Afobe 1 (pen), Dicko 1, Enobakhare 1, Ojo 1.

Ikeme C 33+1	Iorfa D 42	Stearman R 4	Hause K 23+2	Golbourne S 20	Henry J 33+6	Coady C 33+4	McDonald K 32+1	Edwards D 26+3	Dicko N 4+1	Afobe B 23+2	Ojo S 5+12	Doherty M 28+6	Le Fondre A 10+16	Martinez D 13	van La Parra R 11+2	Ebanks-Landell E 21	Wallace J 6+3	Byrne N 10+14	Batth D 38	Price J 20+4	Enobakhare B 1+6	Williamson M 5	Holt G —+4	Graham J 11	Sigurdarson B 11+3	Zyro M 5+2	Saville G 16+3	Mason J 9+7	Rowe T 2+1	Helan J 8	Hunte C —+2	Deslandes S 3	Match No.
1	2	3	4	5	6^2	7	8	9	10^1	11^3	12	13	14																				1
	2	3	4	5	6^1	8	7	9	11^2	10	12			13	1																		2
	2	3	4	5	6^2	7	8	9		11^1	12	10			1	13																	3
1	2		4	5	13	7	6^2	9	12	11		10^1					8	3															4
1			4	5	9	7	8^2	6		11^3	10^1	13	12		2	3	14																5
			4	5	8	7		6		9	12	2	11		1	3	10^1																6
	2		4	5	8^2	6^1	12	7		11	10^1	14	9^3		1	3	13																7
	2		4	5	10^2		6			11	14		12	1	8^3		9^1	13	3	7													8
	2		4	5	9^1		7			10	12		11^3	1			14	6^2	3	8	13												9
	2		4	5	8^1		6	13		9	10^3	14	11^2	1					12	3	7												10
	2		4	5	8^1		7	6		9	12		11^3	1			10^2		3	7^1	14												11
	2^2		4	5	8^1	7	6			9	10^3	14	11	1	13				3	12													12
			4^3	5	13	7	6	9		11	14		2	1		10^2			8^1	3	12												13
	2			5	8^3	7	6	9			11	12	14	1					10^2	3			4	13									14
	2			5	8	7^2	6	9			11^1		14	12	1				10^2	3			4	13									15
12	2			5	8		6	9			11	10^1			1^2				13	3	7		4										16
1	2			5	8		6	9^1			11	13			12				3	7			4				10^2						17
1	2			5	8		6	9^2			11	13			12				3	7			4				10^1						18
1	2			5	8	13	7^3	9			12				11^2	4			14	3	6						10^1						19
1	2			5	8		7	9			12				11^1	4			3	6							10^1						20
1	2			5	8^3	14	7	9^1			11				12	4			13	3	6^2						10^1						21
1	2				9		6				11		5			4			8^1	3	7				12	10^1							22
1	2				8^2	7	6	9			11^1		5			4			12	3					13	10^1							23
1	2				8^2	7	6	9			11	13	5			4			12	3						10^1							24
1	2				8^1	7	6	9			11^2		5	14		4			13	3						10^3	12						25
1	2				12	6	7	8					5	14	10^2	4			13	3						9^3		11^1					26
1	2				12	6^4	7	8					5		10	4			3		13					9^1		11					27
1	2				10	6	7	9^1					5	11	8	4			3							12							28
1	2				12	6	7						5		8	4			3	14						11^1		13	9^3	10^2			29
1	2				11	8	7						5		9^1	4			12	3						10		6					30
1	2				11^1	6							5		9^3	4			12	3	7					10		8^2	13	14			31
1	2					6							5		8	4			12	3						11		7	9^1	10^1			32
1		5				7	8						2	13	6^2	4			9^1	3						11		12	10				33
1	2					8	6						5			4			7^1	3						11		9	12	10			34
1	2	12				6	7^3						5		4^2				9^1	3	14					10		8	13	11			35
1	2		4			8	6^2						5						7^1	3	14				12	9	11^3		10	13			36
1	2		4			6							5						9^2	3	7			10	12	8	13	11					37
1	2		4			8							5		9^3	14	3	7						12	10^1	6	13	11^2					38
1	2		4			12	8						5	14			3	7						9^3	10^1	6	13	11^2					39
1	2		4^2			9	6		13				5	12			3	7							11^2	8	10^1						40
1	2		4			6	7						5	11^2			3	8^1	12					14	9^3	10^1				13			41
1	3		4			8	12			9			2					6	13					11	7^1			10			5^2		42
1	2		4			8			9				5	12			3	6						11^1		7	13	10^2					43
1	3					10	6		9				2			12		4		8^1						7	11					5	44
1	3	12				10	7		8				2			6		4								9	11					5^1	45
1	2		4			10	8		13				5	12			6^1			3	7					9	11^2						46

FA Cup
Third Round   West Ham U   (a)   0-1

Capital One Cup
First Round   Newport Co   (h)   2-1
Second Round   Barnet   (h)   2-1
Third Round   Middlesbrough   (a)   0-3

WYCOMBE WANDERERS

FOUNDATION

In 1887 a group of young furniture trade workers called a meeting at the Steam Engine public house with the aim of forming a football club and entering junior football. It is thought that they were named after the famous FA Cup winners, The Wanderers, who had visited the town in 1877 for a tie with the original High Wycombe club. It is also possible that they played informally before their formation, although there is no proof of this.

Adams Park, Hillbottom Road, High Wycombe, Buckinghamshire HP12 4HJ.

Telephone: (01494) 472 100. *Fax:* (01494) 527 633.

Ticket Office: (01494) 441 118.

Website: www.wycombewanderers.co.uk.com

Email: wwfc@wwfc.com

Ground Capacity: 10,081.

Record Attendance: 15,850 v St Albans C, FA Amateur Cup 4th rd, 25 February 1950 (at Loakes Park); 9,921 v Fulham, FA Cup 3rd rd, 9 January 2002 (at Adams Park).

Pitch Measurements: 100.5m × 64m (110yd × 70yd).

Chairman: Andrew Woodward.

Manager: Gareth Ainsworth.

Assistant Manager: Richard Dobson.

Physio: Cian O'Doherty.

Colours: Light blue and dark blue quartered shirts, dark blue shorts with light blue trim, dark blue socks.

Year Formed: 1887. *Turned Professional:* 1974.

Club Nicknames: 'The Chairboys' (after High Wycombe's tradition of furniture making), 'The Blues'.

Grounds: 1887, The Rye; 1893, Spring Meadow; 1895, Loakes Park; 1899, Daws Hill Park; 1901, Loakes Park; 1990, Adams Park.

First Football League Game: 14 August 1993, Division 3 v Carlisle U (a) D 2–2: Hyde; Cousins, Horton (Langford), Kerr, Crossley, Ryan, Carroll, Stapleton, Thompson, Scott, Guppy (1) (Hutchinson), (1 og).

Record League Victory: 5–0 v Burnley, Division 2, 15 April 1997 – Parkin; Cousins, Bell, Kavanagh, McCarthy, Forsyth, Carroll (2p) (Simpson), Scott (Farrell), Stallard (1), McGavin (1) (Read (1)), Brown. 5–0 v Northampton T, Division 2, 4 January 2003 – Talia; Senda, Ryan, Thomson, McCarthy, Johnson, Bulman, Simpson (1), Faulconbridge (Harris), Dixon (1) (Roberts 3), Brown (Currie); 5–0 v Hartlepool U, FL 1, 25 February 2012 – Bull; McCoy, Basey, Eastmond (Bloomfield), Laing, Doherty (1), Hackett, Lewis, Bevon (2) (Strevons), Hayes (2) (McClure), McNamee.

Record Cup Victory: 5–0 v Hitchin T (a), FA Cup 2nd rd, 3 December 1994 – Hyde; Cousins, Brown, Crossley, Evans, Ryan (1), Carroll, Bell (1), Thompson, Garner (3) (Hemmings), Stapleton (Langford).

HONOURS

League Champions: Conference – 1992–93.
Runners-up: FL 2 – (3rd) 2008–09, 2010–11 *(promoted to FL 1)*; Conference – 1991–92.
FA Cup: semi-final – 2001.
League Cup: semi-final – 2007.
FA Amateur Cup Winners: 1931.

sky SPORTS FACT FILE

The first full-time coach appointed by Wycombe Wanderers was Jimmy McCormick who was in post for the 1951–52 season. McCormick had enjoyed a solid career in the Football League followed by recent experience coaching Sliema Wanderers of Malta and the Turkey national team. His main achievement at Wycombe was to take the team to the quarter-finals of the FA Amateur Cup.

Record Defeat: 0–7 v Shrewsbury T, Johnstone's Paint Trophy, 7 October 2008.

Most League Points (3 for a win): 84, FL 2, 2014–15.

Most League Goals: 72, FL 2, 2005–06.

Highest League Goalscorer in Season: Scott McGleish, 25, 2007–08.

Most League Goals in Total Aggregate: Nathan Tyson, 42, 2004–06.

Most League Goals in One Match: 3, Miquel Desouza v Bradford C, Division 2, 2 September 1995; 3, John Williams v Stockport Co, Division 2, 24 February 1996; 3, Mark Stallard v Walsall, Division 2, 21 October 1997; 3, Sean Devine v Reading, Division 2, 2 October 1999; 3, Sean Divine v Bury, Division 2, 26 February 2000; 3, Stuart Roberts v Northampton T, Division 2, 4 January 2003; 3, Nathan Tyson v Lincoln C, FL 2, 5 March 2005; 3, Nathan Tyson v Kidderminster H, FL 2, 2 April 2005; 3, Nathan Tyson v Stockport Co, FL 2, 10 September 2005; 3, Kevin Betsy v Mansfield T, FL 2, 24 September 2005; 3, Scott McGleish v Mansfield T, FL 2, 8 January 2008; 3, Stuart Beavon v Bury, FL 1, 17 March 2012.

Most Capped Player: Mark Rogers, 7, Canada; Marvin McCoy, 7 (8), Antigua and Barbuda.

Most League Appearances: Steve Brown, 371, 1994–2004.

Youngest League Player: Jordon Ibe, 15 years 311 days v Hartlepool U, 15 October 2011.

Record Transfer Fee Received: £675,000 from Nottingham F for Nathan Tyson, January 2006.

Record Transfer Fee Paid: £200,000 to Barnet for Sean Devine, 15 April 1999.

Football League Record: 1993 Promoted to Division 3 from Conference; 1993–94 Division 3; 1994–2004 Division 2; 2004–09 FL 2; 2009–10 FL 1; 2010–11 FL 2; 2011–12 FL 1; 2012– FL 2.

MANAGERS

First coach appointed 1951. *Prior to Brian Lee's appointment in 1969 the team was selected by a Match Committee which met every Monday evening.*

James McCormack 1951–52
Sid Cann 1952–61
Graham Adams 1961–62
Don Welsh 1962–64
Barry Darvill 1964–68
Brian Lee 1969–76
Ted Powell 1976–77
John Reardon 1977–78
Andy Williams 1978–80
Mike Keen 1980–84
Paul Bence 1984–86
Alan Gane 1986–87
Peter Suddaby 1987–88
Jim Kelman 1988–90
Martin O'Neill 1990–95
Alan Smith 1995–96
John Gregory 1996–98
Neil Smillie 1998–99
Lawrie Sanchez 1999–2003
Tony Adams 2003–04
John Gorman 2004–06
Paul Lambert 2006–08
Peter Taylor 2008–09
Gary Waddock 2009–12
Gareth Ainsworth November 2012–

LATEST SEQUENCES

Longest Sequence of League Wins: 6, 19.8.2006 – 16.9.2006.

Longest Sequence of League Defeats: 6, 18.3.2006 – 17.4.2006.

Longest Sequence of League Draws: 5, 24.1.2004 – 21.2.2004.

Longest Sequence of Unbeaten League Matches: 21, 6.8.2005 – 10.12.2005.

Longest Sequence Without a League Win: 13, 10.1.2004 – 20.3.2004.

Successive Scoring Runs: 16 from 13.9.2014.

Successive Non-scoring Runs: 5 from 15.10.1996.

TEN YEAR LEAGUE RECORD

		P	W	D	L	F	A	Pts	Pos
2006-07	FL 2	46	16	14	16	52	47	62	12
2007-08	FL 2	46	22	12	12	56	42	78	7
2008-09	FL 2	46	20	18	8	54	33	78	3
2009-10	FL 1	46	10	15	21	56	76	45	22
2010-11	FL 2	46	22	14	10	69	50	80	3
2011-12	FL 1	46	11	10	25	65	88	43	21
2012-13	FL 2	46	17	9	20	50	60	60	15
2013-14	FL 2	46	12	14	20	46	54	50	22
2014-15	FL 2	46	23	15	8	67	45	84	4
2015-16	FL 2	46	17	13	16	45	44	64	13

DID YOU KNOW ?

Wycombe Wanderers reached the FA Cup first round proper for the first time in 1932–33 after defeating Gradwell Sports, Maidenhead United, Park Royal, Slough and Camberley & Yorktown. The Chairboys were drawn away to Gillingham where they achieved a creditable 1-1 draw before going down 4-2 in the replay.

WYCOMBE WANDERERS – FOOTBALL LEAGUE TWO 2015–16 LEAGUE RECORD

Match No.	Date	Venue	Opponents	Result		H/T Score	Lg Pos.	Goalscorers	Attendance
1	Aug 8	H	York C	W	3-0	2-0	1	Stewart [7], Amadi-Holloway [28], Zubar (og) [58]	3688
2	15	A	Barnet	W	2-0	0-0	1	Thompson 2 (1 pen) [53, 90 (p)]	2563
3	18	A	Morecambe	W	1-0	0-0	2	Pierre [74]	1395
4	22	H	Dagenham & R	D	1-1	0-1	2	Pierre [90]	3343
5	29	A	Crawley T	D	0-0	0-0	3		2466
6	Sept 5	H	Hartlepool U	W	2-1	1-1	2	Harriman 2 [26, 56]	3468
7	12	H	Plymouth Arg	L	1-2	1-2	4	Banton [12]	4223
8	19	A	Leyton Orient	D	1-1	1-0	4	Ugwu [40]	5946
9	26	A	Exeter C	W	2-0	0-0	2	Jacobson [50], Thompson [57]	3639
10	29	H	Cambridge U	W	1-0	0-0	1	Harriman [70]	3152
11	Oct 3	H	Northampton T	L	2-3	1-1	2	O'Nien [2], Rowe [82]	4227
12	17	A	Stevenage	L	1-2	0-1	8	Kretzschmar [79]	3292
13	20	H	Newport Co	L	0-2	0-0	10		2940
14	24	H	Carlisle U	D	1-1	0-0	10	Hayes [90]	3457
15	31	A	Mansfield T	W	2-0	1-0	9	O'Nien [8], Amadi-Holloway [90]	3165
16	Nov 21	A	AFC Wimbledon	D	1-1	0-0	11	McCarthy [51]	4482
17	24	A	Yeovil T	W	1-0	0-0	9	O'Nien [70]	2963
18	28	H	Portsmouth	D	2-2	2-1	9	Harriman [28], Thompson [30]	5816
19	Dec 1	A	Bristol R	L	0-3	0-0	9		6136
20	15	H	Notts Co	D	2-2	1-1	10	Harriman [44], Amadi-Holloway [62]	2886
21	19	H	Oxford U	W	2-1	0-0	9	Thompson [50], McCarthy [76]	5742
22	26	A	Luton T	W	2-0	0-0	6	Thompson [51], Hayes [66]	9676
23	28	H	Crawley T	W	2-0	1-0	5	Kretzschmar [7], Wood [90]	4153
24	Jan 2	A	Morecambe	L	0-2	0-0	6		3555
25	16	A	Hartlepool U	L	0-1	0-1	6		3721
26	23	H	Leyton Orient	L	0-2	0-0	9		4432
27	30	A	Plymouth Arg	W	1-0	1-0	8	Ugwu [3]	8458
28	Feb 6	H	Luton T	L	0-1	0-1	10		4597
29	9	A	Dagenham & R	W	2-1	1-0	6	Hayes [45], Cowan-Hall [75]	1446
30	13	H	Exeter C	W	1-0	0-0	4	McGinn [53]	3358
31	20	A	Northampton T	L	0-1	0-0	8		5755
32	27	H	Bristol R	W	1-0	0-0	6	O'Nien [85]	4759
33	Mar 1	A	Cambridge U	L	0-1	0-1	9		4141
34	5	A	Newport Co	L	0-1	0-1	9		2325
35	12	H	Stevenage	W	1-0	0-0	8	O'Nien [70]	3715
36	16	H	Accrington S	D	1-1	0-1	7	Thompson [62]	1403
37	19	A	Carlisle U	D	1-1	1-1	8	Wood [12]	4532
38	25	H	Mansfield T	W	1-0	0-0	7	Harriman [68]	5003
39	28	A	Notts Co	D	0-0	0-0	7		4452
40	Apr 2	H	AFC Wimbledon	L	1-2	0-1	7	Harriman [58]	4560
41	9	A	York C	D	1-1	0-1	8	Bloomfield [88]	2864
42	16	H	Barnet	D	1-1	0-0	8	Hayes [58]	3715
43	19	H	Yeovil T	D	0-0	0-0	8		2812
44	23	A	Portsmouth	L	1-2	0-1	9	Jombati [73]	16,187
45	30	H	Accrington S	L	0-1	0-0	10		4041
46	May 7	A	Oxford U	L	0-3	0-0	13		11,815

Final League Position: 13

GOALSCORERS

League (45): Harriman 7, Thompson 7 (1 pen), O'Nien 5, Hayes 4, Amadi-Holloway 3, Kretzschmar 2, McCarthy 2, Pierre 2, Ugwu 2, Wood 2, Banton 1, Bloomfield 1, Cowan-Hall 1, Jacobson 1, Jombati 1, McGinn 1, Rowe 1, Stewart 1, own goal 1.
FA Cup (7): Amadi-Holloway 1, Harriman 1, Hayes 1, Jacobson 1 (pen), Jombati 1, Kretzschmar 1, Thompson 1.
Capital One Cup (0).
Johnstone's Paint Trophy (0).

Ingram M 24	Jombati S 32 + 2	Stewart A 27	Pierre A 40	Jacobson J 34	O'Nien L 33 + 2	Bean M 27 + 3	Wood S 25 + 3	Thompson G 35 + 8	Amadi-Holloway A 8 + 15	Hayes P 34 + 3	Sellers R — + 15	Harriman M 42 + 3	Rowe D 8 + 4	Banton J 3 + 2	McGinn S 21 + 5	Donacien J 2	Kretzschmar M 8 + 14	Ugwu C 13 + 16	Bloomfield M 20 + 7	McCarthy J 35	Lynch A 3	Utumaga J — + 4	Cowan-Hall P 4 + 1	Richardson B — + 1	Allsop R 18	Liburd R 4 + 6	Sellars J 5 + 3	Siegrist B 1	Match No.
1	2	3	4	5	6^2	7	8	9^1	10	11	12	13																	1
1	3		4	5	8	7	9	11	12	10^2		6	2^1	13															2
1	3		4	5		7	9	6	11^1	10	12	2			8														3
1	2		4	5		7	9^3	10	12	11^1	14	6			13	8	3^2												4
1	3		4	5		7	8	11	10			2			6	9													5
1	2			5	8	7		10		11^1	13	6	4	9^2			3	12											6
1	2	3		5	9	7		10	12			13	6	4^2	8^1			11											7
1	4	3		5	9	7		10^1	12			2			8		13	11	6^2										8
1	3		4	5	9^1	6		10			13^3	2	14		8		12	11	7^2										9
1	3		4	5	8	7		9	11^1			2^2	13		6			10	12										10
1	3		4	5	8^2	7	13	9	11^3			2			6^1		14	10	12										11
1	2	3		5	8	7^1		11	12		14	13						9	10^3	6^2	4								12
1	3			5	8	7^1	13	9	10	12		2			14			6^3	11^2	4									13
	2	3		5	8	7		9^2	11^3	12	10	14	6					13		4^1	1								14
1	5	3			9	7	6	8^2	11^3	12	10^1	2						13	14	4									15
1	2	3	4		8	6		9^1	12		11^2	5						13	10	7									16
1	5	4	3			7		9	10^2	12	11^1	6						13	8	2									17
1	4	3	5			8		9	11	12	10^1	2^2						13	7	6									18
1	2		4			8		9^1	11^2	12	10^3	14	6	5				13	7	3									19
1		3	4	5	6^1			9	13	11^2	10	8			12				7	2									20
1		3	4	5				9	10^1	13	11^3	6	14		12				7^2	2									21
1		3	4	5	7			9	10	11^1		6			13		12		8^2	2									22
1	5	3	4		8			9	13	10^1	12^3	6			7		11^2			2		14							23
1^1		3	4	5	8			9^1	10^3	14		6					11^2	13	7	2			12						24
1		3	4	5	8			9	10^3	13	14	6					11	7^1	2^2				12						25
	2	3	4	5	8			9	10^3			11^1			6^2				13	7	1	14	12						26
	2		4	5	13	7			14			10^1			6			11^2	8	3	1^3	9	12						27
	2		4	5	14	7			12	13		10^1			6			11^1	8	3		9^2	1						28
	5		3		7	13		9^3	10^*		11^2	2			14			12	8^1	4		6		1					29
			4	5	9		7	10		11		2			6^1			12	3			8		1					30
2	4			5	10	8^3	9^1		11	14	6^2	7			13		12			2					1				31
	3			5	8	6^2	12		10			2			11^1		13	9	4						1				32
	4			5	9		8^2	12	10	14		2			6		11^3	13	7^1	3					1				33
2^3		3	5	8				9^1	12			10^2			6			7	14	13	4				1	11			34
	3	4	5	7	13			9				10			6				12	8^1	2				1	11^2			35
	3	4	5	8	13			11^1				10			7				12	6	2				1	9^2			36
	3	4	5	8	7^1			9^1	11^2				13		6				10^3	14	2				1	12			37
	3	4	5	7				9^1	10^3	11^2	12	6			8		14			2					1	13			38
14	3	4	5					11^2	10			6			7		8^1	9^3		2					1	12	13		39
13	3	4	5^2					11^1	10^1	12^6	6				7			2							1	14	9		40
5	3	4			6			12	8	13	9	7^2							14	2					1	10^1	11^3		41
5	3	4			7			11^3	10^2			6			8		9^1	13		2					1	14	12		42
5	3	4			7			11^1	10^2			6	13		8^3		14	12		2					1		9		43
5	3	4			8			12	10^2			6^3	7		13			9		2					1	14	11^1		44
5	3	4			7			11^1	10	13		6^3	8				14	12		2					1		9^2	1	45
5	4	3			6			11^1	10^1			9	7		8^2		13	12		2					1		14		46

FA Cup

First Round	FC Halifax T	(a)	4-0
Second Round	Millwall	(a)	2-1
Third Round	Aston Villa	(h)	1-1
Replay	Aston Villa	(a)	0-2

Capital One Cup

First Round	Fulham	(h)	0-1

Johnstone's Paint Trophy

Second Round	Bristol R	(a)	0-2

YEOVIL TOWN

Huish Park, Lufton Way, Yeovil, Somerset BA22 8YF.

Telephone: (01935) 423 662.

Fax: (01935) 847 886.

Ticket Office: (01935) 847 888.

Website: www.ytfc.net

Email: info@ytfc.net

Ground Capacity: 9,565.

HONOURS

League Champions: FL 2 – 2004–05; Conference – 2002–03.
Runners-up: Conference – 2000–01.
FA Cup: 5th rd – 1949.
League Cup: never past 2nd rd.

Record Attendance: 16,318 v Sunderland, FA Cup 4th rd, 29 January 1949 (at Huish); 9,527 v Leeds U, FL 1, 25 April 2008 (at Huish Park).

Pitch Measurements: 108m × 67m (118yd × 73yd).

Chairman: John R. Fry.

Manager: Darren Way.

Assistant Manager: Terry Skiverton.

Physio: Mike Micciche.

Colours: Green and white hooped shirts, white shorts with green trim, green socks.

Year Formed: 1895.

Turned Professional: 1921.

Previous Names: 1895, Yeovil Casuals; 1907, Yeovil Town; 1915, Yeovil & Petters United; 1946, Yeovil Town.

Club Nickname: 'The Glovers'.

Grounds: 1895, Pen Mill Ground; 1921, Huish; 1990, Huish Park.

First Football League Game: 9 August 2003, Division 3 v Rochdale (a) W 3-1: Weale; Williams (Lindegaard), Crittenden, Lockwood, O'Brien, Pluck (Rodrigues), Gosling (El Kholti), Way, Jackson, Gall (2), Johnson (1).

Record League Victory: 6–1 v Oxford U, FL 2, 18 September 2004 – Weale; Rose, O'Brien, Way, Skiverton, Fontaine, Caceres (Tarachulski), Johnson, Jevons (3), Stoicers (2) (Mirza), Terry (Gall 1).

Record Cup Victory: 12–1 v Westbury United, FA Cup 1st qual rd, 1923–24.

Record Defeat: 0–8 v Manchester United, FA Cup 5th rd, 12 February 1949.

Most League Points (3 for a win): 83, FL 2, 2004–05.

Most League Goals: 90, FL 2, 2004–05.

Highest League Goalscorer in Season: Phil Jevons, 27, 2004–05.

Most League Goals in Total Aggregate: Phil Jevons, 42, 2004–06.

Most League Goals in One Match: 3, Phil Jevons v Oxford U, FL 2, 18 September 2004; 3, Phil Jevons v Chester C, FL 2, 30 October 2004; 3, Phil Jevons v Bristol R, FL 2, 12 February 2005; 3, Arron Davies v Chesterfield, FL 1, 4 March 2006; 3, Jack Compton v AFC Wimbledon, FL 2, 30 January 2016.

Most Capped Players: Joel Grant, 12 (14), Jamaica.

Most League Appearances: Terry Skiverton, 195, 2003–09.

Youngest League Player: Ollie Bassett, 17 years 197 days v Crawley T, 19 September 2015.

Record Transfer Fee Received: £1,000,000 from Nottingham F for Arron Davies and Chris Cohen, July 2007.

Record Transfer Fee Paid: £250,000 to Quilmes for Pablo Bastianini, August 2005.

Football League Record: 2003 Promoted to Division 3 from Conference; 2003–04 Division 3; 2004–05 FL 2; 2005–13 FL 1; 2013–14 FL C; 2014–15 FL 1; 2015– FL 2.

LATEST SEQUENCES

Longest Sequence of League Wins: 8, 29.12.2012 – 16.2.2013.

Longest Sequence of League Defeats: 6, 10.3.2015 – 6.4.2015.

Longest Sequence of League Draws: 3, 18.3.2014 – 25.3.2014.

Longest Sequence of Unbeaten League Matches: 9, 29.12.2012 – 23.2.2013.

Longest Sequence Without a League Win: 16, 26.9.2015 – 28.12.2015.

Successive Scoring Runs: 22 from 30.10.2004.

Successive Non-scoring Runs: 4 from 21.10.2014.

MANAGERS

Jack Gregory 1922–28
Tommy Lawes 1928–29
Dave Pratt 1929–33
Louis Page 1933–35
Dave Halliday 1935–38
Billy Kingdon 1938–46
Alec Stock 1946–49
George Patterson 1949–51
Harry Lowe 1951–53
Ike Clarke 1953–57
Norman Dodgin 1957
Jimmy Baldwin 1957–60
Basil Hayward 1960–64
Glyn Davies 1964–65
Joe McDonald 1965–67
Ron Saunders 1967–69
Mike Hughes 1969–72
Cecil Irwin 1972–75
Stan Harland 1975–81
Barry Lloyd 1978–81
Malcolm Allison 1981
Jimmy Giles 1981–83
Trevor Finnigan/Mike Hughes 1983
Steve Coles 1983–84
Ian McFarlane 1984
Gerry Gow 1984–87
Brian Hall 1987–90
Clive Whitehead 1990–91
Steve Rutter 1991–93
Brian Hall 1994–95
Graham Roberts 1995–98
Colin Lippiatt 1998–99
Steve Thompson 1999–2000
Dave Webb 2000
Gary Johnson 2001–05
Steve Thompson 2005–06
Russell Slade 2006–09
Terry Skiverton 2009–12
Gary Johnson 2012–15
Terry Skiverton 2015
Paul Sturrock 2015
Darren Way December 2015–

TEN YEAR LEAGUE RECORD

		P	W	D	L	F	A	Pts	Pos
2006-07	FL 1	46	23	10	13	55	39	79	5
2007-08	FL 1	46	14	10	22	38	59	52	18
2008-09	FL 1	46	12	15	19	41	66	51	17
2009-10	FL 1	46	13	14	19	55	59	53	15
2010-11	FL 1	46	16	11	19	56	66	59	14
2011-12	FL 1	46	14	12	20	59	80	54	17
2012-13	FL 1	46	23	8	15	71	56	77	4
2013-14	FL C	46	8	13	25	44	75	37	24
2014-15	FL 1	46	10	10	26	36	75	40	24
2015-16	FL 2	46	11	15	20	43	59	48	19

DID YOU KNOW

In April 1950 Yeovil Town entertained Scottish League side Celtic in a friendly match at Huish. A crowd of 5,000 turned out to see the home team win 2-0 with the goals coming from Bobby Hamilton and Cliff Mansley.

YEOVIL TOWN – FOOTBALL LEAGUE TWO 2015–16 LEAGUE RECORD

Match No.	Date	Venue	Opponents	Result	H/T Score	Lg Pos.	Goalscorers	Atten-dance
1	Aug 8	A	Exeter C	L	2-3	0-2	16	Cornick [46], Dolan (pen) [63]	5659
2	15	H	Bristol R	L	0-1	0-0	21		5895
3	18	A	York C	L	0-1	0-0	23		2849
4	22	H	Luton T	W	3-2	1-2	19	Arthurworrey [38], Bird 2 [62, 73]	3830
5	29	A	Oxford U	L	0-2	0-1	21		6018
6	Sept 5	H	Morecambe	L	2-4	2-0	23	Cornick [2], Sowunmi [30]	3024
7	12	H	AFC Wimbledon	D	1-1	1-0	22	Bird [26]	3687
8	19	A	Crawley T	W	1-0	1-0	19	Cornick [28]	2112
9	26	H	Hartlepool U	L	1-2	1-1	21	Bird [37]	3078
10	29	A	Accrington S	L	1-2	1-1	22	Sheehan [35]	1309
11	Oct 3	A	Portsmouth	D	0-0	0-0	22		17,309
12	10	H	Dagenham & R	D	2-2	0-2	21	Bird [69], Sokolik [76]	3204
13	17	A	Notts Co	L	0-2	0-0	22		4030
14	20	H	Mansfield T	L	0-1	0-0	23		2954
15	24	H	Cambridge U	L	2-3	1-3	23	Bird [44], Sheehan [79]	3224
16	31	A	Carlisle U	L	2-3	2-1	23	Bird [5], Cornick [8]	4095
17	Nov 14	H	Stevenage	D	2-2	0-0	23	Cornick [52], Jeffers [58]	3220
18	21	A	Newport Co	D	0-0	0-0	23		3084
19	24	H	Wycombe W	L	0-1	0-0	24		2963
20	28	A	Northampton T	L	0-2	0-1	24		4989
21	Dec 12	H	Barnet	D	2-2	0-2	23	Zoko 2 [80, 86]	3162
22	19	A	Leyton Orient	D	1-1	1-0	23	Zoko [45]	4686
23	26	A	Plymouth Arg	L	0-1	0-0	23		12,821
24	28	H	Oxford U	D	0-0	0-0	24		4661
25	Jan 2	H	York C	W	1-0	1-0	23	Dolan (pen) [40]	3866
26	16	A	Morecambe	L	1-2	0-0	23	Ward [69]	1340
27	23	H	Crawley T	W	2-1	0-0	22	Bird [59], Campbell [77]	3423
28	30	A	AFC Wimbledon	W	3-2	2-2	22	Compton 3 (1 pen) [12, 35, 63 (p)]	4525
29	Feb 2	A	Luton T	D	1-1	0-0	21	Walsh [70]	7538
30	13	A	Hartlepool U	L	1-2	0-0	22	Zoko [90]	3923
31	20	H	Portsmouth	D	1-1	0-0	23	Zoko [73]	6051
32	23	H	Plymouth Arg	D	0-0	0-0	22		5788
33	27	A	Dagenham & R	W	1-0	0-0	21	Goodship [50]	2942
34	Mar 1	H	Accrington S	W	1-0	0-0	21	Dickson [64]	3207
35	5	A	Mansfield T	W	1-0	0-0	20	Dickson [90]	2713
36	12	H	Notts Co	W	1-0	0-0	20	Zoko [50]	3588
37	19	A	Cambridge U	L	0-3	0-2	20		4956
38	25	H	Carlisle U	D	0-0	0-0	20		4075
39	Apr 2	H	Newport Co	W	1-0	1-0	19	Compton (pen) [15]	4063
40	5	A	Stevenage	D	0-0	0-0	19		2748
41	9	H	Exeter C	L	0-2	0-1	20		5394
42	16	A	Bristol R	L	1-2	0-1	20	Lita [73]	10,264
43	19	A	Wycombe W	D	0-0	0-0	19		2812
44	23	H	Northampton T	D	1-1	1-1	20	Cornick [6]	4008
45	30	A	Barnet	W	4-3	0-1	18	Dolan [55], Smith [63], Zoko [76], Cornick [90]	2379
46	May 7	H	Leyton Orient	L	0-1	0-0	19		4163

Final League Position: 19

GOALSCORERS

League (43): Bird 8, Cornick 7, Zoko 7, Compton 4 (2 pens), Dolan 3 (2 pens), Dickson 2, Sheehan 2, Arthurworrey 1, Campbell 1, Goodship 1, Jeffers 1, Lita 1, Smith 1, Sokolik 1, Sowunmi 1, Walsh 1, Ward 1.
FA Cup (5): Compton 1, Fogden 1, Jeffers 1, Tozer 1, Zoko 1.
Capital One Cup (0).
Johnstone's Paint Trophy (4): Cornick 1, Fogden 1, Jeffers 1, own goal 1.

No.	Weale C 8+1	Roberts C 45	Arthurworrey S 14	Lacey A 16+4	Smith N 38+2	Fogden W 13	Laird M 14+6	Dolan M 38+1	Dickson R 34+3	Beck M 3+5	Jeffers S 13+12	Cornick H 28+8	Sokolik J 32+2	Bird R 19+17	Krysiak A 38	Burrows J —+1	Wakefield J 5	Compton J 14+6	Allen I 2+10	Sowunmi O 3+2	Norris D —+1	Gibbons J 1+2	Howells J 5+1	Bassett O 2	Sheehan J 13	Thomas G 3+2	Ward D 18	Tozer B 22+4	Zoko F 22+3	Campbell T 8+9	Walsh L 15	Dawson K 4+6	Gillett S —+6	Goodship B 6+4	Lita L 4+4	Shephard L 6	Match No.
1	1	2	3	4^1	5	6^2	7	8	9^9	10	11	12	13	14																							1
2		2		4	7	5	9	8^8			11^2	12	6^1	3	10	1	13																				2
3		5	3	2	9	7			10^2		11^3	4	6^1	1		8	12	13	14																		3
4		2	3	7	5		8		10^9	9	4	12	1		6	11^1	13																				4
5		2	3	8^3	5		7	14	13	9	4	10^1	1		6	11^2		12																			5
6		6	4	3	5		7	14	10^4	2		13	1		9^1	12^3	11^2	8																			6
7		2	4		5		7		12		6	3	10	1	8		11^2	13	9^1																		7
8		2	3		5		8			6	4	11	1	7			12	9	10^1																		8
9		2	4		5		8	13		6	3	10	1		12			9^1	11^2	7																	9
10		2	3		5	10		7			12	6	4	11	1			9^1	8																		10
11		2	3		5	7	13	9	10		14	6^3	4^1	11	1			12	8^2																		11
12		2	4		3	8	6	7^1	5		12	11	13	10	1			9^2																			12
13		2	3		5	6	14	8^1	10^2		12	7	4	11^3			13		9																		13
14		2	4^2	13	5		7		9		11^1	6	3	10	1		12	8																			14
15		2	3		5	7		9			6	4	10	1			8	11																			15
16		2	3		5^1	7		12	9	14	13	6	4^3	10	1		8	11^2																			16
17	1	2		4	5	6		8^1	13		12	9		10			11^2									3	7										17
18	1	8		4	5	7		6	13		14	11^1		10^3											12	3	2	9^2									18
19	1	2		4	5	6		8^3	12		14	9		10^2											13	3	7	11^1									19
20	1	2		4	5	6^3			9		14	11^2		13											8^1	10^1	3	7	12								20
21	1	2		9^1		7	5		10^6	6	4	14						13							8^2		3	12	11								21
22	1	2		14	5		7	6	10		4	13					9^1								8^2		3	12	11^1								22
23	1	2		9		7	5^1		11^1		4	13		14		6^2									8		3	12	10								23
24		2	13	12		8	5^1		10		4^2		1		9^1	14									7		3	6	11								24
25		2			13	6	5		11^2		3		1		9^1	14									7^2		4	8	10	12							25
26		2				8	5		10^1		3	14	1		9^2	12											4	7	11	13	6^3						26
27		2	3			7	5		9^1		4	13	1		11^1												6	10	12	8^2	14						27
28		2	4			8	5		11^2		3		1		9^3												6	10	14	7^1	12	13					28
29	13	2		4		8	5		11^3	3			1^2		9^1												7	10			6	12	14				29
30		2		4^6		8^3	5		12	3	10^1		1		9^2												7	11	13	6		14					30
31		2				7	5		10^1	4	14		1		3			6									3	6	11^1	9^3	8		13	12			31
32		2				7	5		13	3	12		1		4			6									4	6	11	9^1	8^3		14	10^2			32
33		2			6^1	8	5		12		4	10	1		3			7									3	7		11	13		9^2				33
34		2	13			8	7	5			11^1	3^2	1		4			6									4	6	12	10		14	9^2				34
35		2		4		6	8^3	5			11^1		12		1			3									3	7	10^2	13	8	9		14			35
36		2		4		7^2	5				10^1		1		3			6									3	6	11^1	13	8	9	12	14			36
37		2		4	8		5				11^1	12	1		3			13									3	7		6^4	9^2		10^3	14			37
38		12	2	3		8	7	5	13			2	9	1				10^3									4^2	6					11^1	14			38
39		2		4		7	6^3	5	9^2		3	13	1		10^1												14	11		12					8		39
40		2		4	8^3	6	5				13	3	1		9^2												7	14	11		12		10^1				40
41		2		3			6	5			13	4	14	1	12												6^2	11	10^3	7	9				8^1		41
42		2		4		14	8^3	5				3	13	1				11^1										10		6				9^2	12	7	42
43		2	4	3	13	8^3	5				12		14	1													7	11	9^1	6				10^2			43
44		2	3	4	12	6^2	5				9^1		1		13			11									14	7					10^3	8		44
45		2	3	4	7	9	5^1		13				1		11			12									8						10^2	6		45
46		2	4	3	7^2	6	5		10^3				1		13	14											11^1	8		12				9			46

FA Cup

First Round	Maidstone U		(a)	1-0
Second Round	Stevenage		(h)	1-0
Third Round	Carlisle U		(a)	2-2
Replay	Carlisle U		(h)	1-1

(aet; Carlisle U won 5-4 on penalties)

Capital One Cup

First Round	QPR	(h)	0-3

Johnstone's Paint Trophy

First Round	Barnet	(h)	1-0
Second Round	Coventry C	(h)	0-0

(aet; Yeovil won 4-3 on penalties)

Southern Quarter-Final	Gillingham	(a)	1-1

(aet; Yeovil T won 5-4 on penalties)

Southern Semi-Final	Oxford U	(a)	2-3

YORK CITY

FOUNDATION

Although there was a York City club formed in 1903 by a soccer enthusiast from Darlington, this has no connection with the modern club because it went out of existence during World War I. Unlike many others of that period who restarted in 1919, York City did not re-form until 1922 and the tendency now is to ignore the modern club's pre-1922 existence.

Bootham Crescent, York YO30 7AQ.

Telephone: (01904) 624 447.

Fax: (01904) 631 457.

Ticket Office: (01904) 624 447 (ext 1).

Website: www.yorkcityfootballclub.co.uk

Email: enquiries@yorkcityfootballclub.co.uk

Ground Capacity: 7,192.

Record Attendance: 28,123 v Huddersfield T, FA Cup 6th rd, 5 March 1938.

Pitch Measurements: 104m × 64m (113.5yd × 70yd).

Chairman: Jason McGill.

Manager: Jackie McNamara.

Assistant Manager: Simon Donnelly.

Physio: Jeff Miller.

Colours: Red shirts with navy blue diagonal stripe, red shorts, red socks.

Year Formed: 1922.

Turned Professional: 1922.

Ltd Co.: 1922.

Club Nickname: 'Minstermen'.

Previous Grounds: 1922, Fulfordgate; 1932, Bootham Crescent.

First Football League Game: 31 August 1929, Division 3 (N), v Wigan Borough (a) W 2–0 – Farmery; Archibald, Johnson; Beck, Davis, Thompson; Evans, Gardner, Cowie (1), Smailes, Stockill (1).

Record League Victory: 9–1 v Southport, Division 3 (N), 2 February 1957 – Forgan; Phillips, Howe; Brown (1), Cairney, Mollatt; Hill, Bottom (4 incl. 1p), Wilkinson (2), Wragg (1), Fenton (1).

Record Cup Victory: 6–0 v South Shields (a), FA Cup 1st rd, 16 November 1968 – Widdowson; Baker (1p), Richardson; Carr, Jackson, Burrows; Taylor, Ross (3), MacDougall (2), Hodgson, Boyer.

Record Defeat: 0–12 v Chester, Division 3 (N), 1 February 1936.

Most League Points (2 for a win): 62, Division 4, 1964–65.

HONOURS

League Champions: Division 4 – 1983–84.
Runners-up: Division 3 – (3rd) 1973–74 *(promoted)*; Third Division – (4th) 1992–93 *(promoted via play-offs)*; Conference – (4th) 2011–12 *(promoted via play-offs)*.
FA Cup: semi-final – 1955.
League Cup: 5th rd – 1962.

sky SPORTS FACT FILE

Winger Joe Hulme, who went on to become one of the stars of the great Arsenal team of the 1930s, began his senior career with York City in their Midland League days. Signed by the Minstermen in October 1922, he made 31 appearances before moving on to Blackburn and then the Gunners. Joe also won nine caps for the England team.

Most League Points (3 for a win): 101, Division 4, 1983–84.

Most League Goals: 96, Division 4, 1983–84.

Highest League Scorer in Season: Bill Fenton, 31, Division 3 (N), 1951–52; Arthur Bottom, 31, Division 3 (N), 1954–55 and 1955–56.

Most League Goals in Total Aggregate: Norman Wilkinson, 127, 1954–66.

Most League Goals in One Match: 5, Alf Patrick v Rotherham U, Division 3N, 20 November 1948.

Most Capped Player: Peter Scott, 7 (10), Northern Ireland.

Most League Appearances: Barry Jackson, 482, 1958–70.

Youngest League Player: Reg Stockill, 15 years 281 days v Wigan Borough, 31 August 1929.

Record Transfer Fee Received: £950,000 from Sheffield W for Richard Cresswell, March 1999.

Record Transfer Fee Paid: £140,000 to Burnley for Adrian Randall, December 1995.

Football League Record: 1929 Elected to Division 3 (N); 1958–59 Division 4; 1959–60 Division 3; 1960–65 Division 4; 1965–66 Division 3; 1966–71 Division 4; 1971–74 Division 3; 1974–76 Division 2; 1976–77 Division 3; 1977–84 Division 4; 1984–88 Division 3; 1988–92 Division 4; 1992–93 Division 3; 1993–99 Division 2; 1999–04 Division 3; 2004–07 Conference; 2007–12 Conference Premier; 2012–16 FL 2; 2016– National League.

LATEST SEQUENCES

Longest Sequence of League Wins: 7, 31.10.1964 – 26.12.1964.

Longest Sequence of League Defeats: 8, 14.11.1966 – 31.12.1966.

Longest Sequence of League Draws: 6, 3.5.2014 – 30.8.2014.

Longest Sequence of Unbeaten League Matches: 21, 10.9.1973 – 12.1.1974.

Longest Sequence Without a League Win: 23, 1.2.2014 – 6.9.2014.

Successive Scoring Runs: 24 from 3.3.1984.

Successive Non-scoring Runs: 7 from 28.8.1972.

MANAGERS

Bill Sherrington 1924–60 *(was Secretary for most of this time but virtually Secretary-Manager for a long pre-war spell)*
John Collier 1929–36
Tom Mitchell 1936–50
Dick Duckworth 1950–52
Charlie Spencer 1952–53
Jimmy McCormick 1953–54
Sam Bartram 1956–60
Tom Lockie 1960–67
Joe Shaw 1967–68
Tom Johnston 1968–75
Wilf McGuinness 1975–77
Charlie Wright 1977–80
Barry Lyons 1980–81
Denis Smith 1982–87
Bobby Saxton 1987–88
John Bird 1988–91
John Ward 1991–93
Alan Little 1993–99
Neil Thompson 1999–2000
Terry Dolan 2000–03
Chris Brass 2003–04
Billy McEwan 2005–07
Colin Walker 2007–08
Martin Foyle 2008–10
Gary Mills 2010–13
Nigel Worthington 2013–14
Russ Wilcox 2014–15
Jackie McNamara November 2015–

TEN YEAR LEAGUE RECORD

		P	W	D	L	F	A	Pts	Pos
2006-07	Conf	46	23	11	12	65	45	80	4
2007-08	Conf P	46	17	11	18	71	74	62	14
2008-09	Conf P	46	11	19	16	47	51	52	17
2009-10	Conf P	44	22	12	10	62	35	78	5
2010-11	Conf P	46	19	14	13	55	50	71	8
2011-12	Conf P	46	23	14	9	81	45	83	4
2012-13	FL 2	46	12	19	15	50	60	55	17
2013-14	FL 2	46	18	17	11	52	41	71	7
2014-15	FL 2	46	11	19	16	46	51	52	18
2015-16	FL 2	46	7	13	26	51	87	34	24

DID YOU KNOW ?

York City's home game with Barnsley in March 1934 was played in bitterly cold conditions. After the match was finished, the officials returned to their dressing room where all three collapsed. The referee was in a critical state before eventually recovering over an hour later. None of the players was affected in a similar way.

YORK CITY – FOOTBALL LEAGUE TWO 2015–16 LEAGUE RECORD

Match No.	Date	Venue	Opponents	Result		H/T Score	Lg Pos.	Goalscorers	Attendance
1	Aug 8	A	Wycombe W	L	0-3	0-2	22		3688
2	15	H	Hartlepool U	L	1-2	0-0	22	Thompson [57]	4890
3	18	H	Yeovil T	W	1-0	0-0	17	Berrett [63]	2849
4	22	A	Exeter C	D	0-0	0-0	18		3139
5	29	H	Mansfield T	L	1-2	1-2	18	Thompson [6]	3215
6	Sept 5	A	Newport Co	W	3-0	1-0	16	Berrett [38], Thompson [55], Oliver [59]	2459
7	12	A	Stevenage	D	2-2	1-0	17	Nolan [39], Summerfield [74]	3319
8	19	H	Carlisle U	D	2-2	0-2	16	Summerfield (pen) [72], Carson [74]	3692
9	26	A	Notts Co	L	0-1	0-1	19		5159
10	29	H	Oxford U	L	1-2	1-1	19	Turner [38]	2791
11	Oct 3	H	Cambridge U	D	2-2	0-0	18	Coulson [50], McCombe [54]	2987
12	10	A	Luton T	D	1-1	1-0	19	Lowe [38]	8618
13	17	A	Barnet	L	1-3	0-0	21	Coulson [80]	1767
14	20	H	Dagenham & R	D	2-2	1-1	21	Oliver [14], Coulson [79]	2559
15	24	H	AFC Wimbledon	L	1-3	0-1	21	Oliver [60]	3000
16	31	A	Crawley T	L	0-1	0-0	22		1950
17	Nov 14	H	Plymouth Arg	L	1-2	0-2	22	Godfrey [90]	3654
18	21	A	Leyton Orient	L	2-3	1-2	22	Oliver 2 [45, 86]	4897
19	24	A	Portsmouth	L	0-6	0-0	23		13,616
20	28	H	Accrington S	L	1-5	0-2	23	Fewster [75]	2825
21	Dec 12	A	Bristol R	L	1-2	1-0	24	Oliver [41]	6916
22	19	H	Morecambe	W	2-1	1-0	22	Winfield [38], Berrett [52]	2769
23	28	A	Mansfield T	D	1-1	1-1	22	Winfield [10]	3958
24	Jan 2	A	Yeovil T	L	0-1	0-1	24		3866
25	16	H	Newport Co	L	0-1	0-1	24		2923
26	23	A	Carlisle U	D	1-1	0-1	24	Summerfield [87]	7461
27	30	H	Stevenage	W	2-1	1-0	24	McEvoy [15], Galbraith [90]	2951
28	Feb 6	A	Northampton T	L	0-2	0-1	24		5342
29	13	H	Notts Co	W	2-1	2-0	23	Coulson [24], Fewster [39]	3811
30	16	H	Exeter C	W	2-0	1-0	22	Fewster 2 [35, 64]	2920
31	20	A	Cambridge U	L	1-3	1-2	22	Berrett [33]	4822
32	23	H	Northampton T	L	1-2	0-1	23	Penn [90]	2887
33	27	H	Luton T	L	2-3	0-0	23	Fewster 2 [62, 82]	3628
34	Mar 1	A	Oxford U	L	0-4	0-1	23		5654
35	5	A	Dagenham & R	L	0-1	0-0	23		1767
36	12	H	Barnet	D	1-1	1-1	23	Alessandra [20]	2890
37	19	A	AFC Wimbledon	L	1-2	1-0	23	Penn [38]	3883
38	25	H	Crawley T	D	2-2	1-1	23	Summerfield (pen) [30], Coulson [69]	2942
39	28	A	Plymouth Arg	L	2-3	0-3	23	Penn [52], Summerfield (pen) [86]	8571
40	Apr 2	H	Leyton Orient	D	1-1	1-0	23	Fewster [17]	3234
41	9	H	Wycombe W	D	1-1	1-0	23	Oliver [35]	2864
42	16	A	Hartlepool U	L	1-2	1-1	23	Cameron [45]	4781
43	19	H	Portsmouth	W	3-1	2-0	23	Fewster [30], Alessandra [34], Summerfield [48]	3214
44	23	A	Accrington S	L	0-3	0-1	23		2222
45	30	H	Bristol R	L	1-4	0-1	24	McEvoy [81]	4525
46	May 7	A	Morecambe	D	1-1	1-0	24	Summerfield [45]	1620

Final League Position: 24

GOALSCORERS

League (51): Fewster 8, Oliver 7, Summerfield 7 (3 pens), Coulson 5, Berrett 4, Penn 3, Thompson 3, Alessandra 2, McEvoy 2, Winfield 2, Cameron 1, Carson 1, Galbraith 1, Godfrey 1, Lowe 1, McCombe 1, Nolan 1, Turner 1.
FA Cup (2): Coulson 1, Oliver 1.
Capital One Cup (2): Berrett 1, Summerfield 1 (pen).
Johnstone's Paint Trophy (3): Oliver 2, Coulson 1.

Flinders S 43	Lowe K 15+1	Winfield D 36+1	Zubar S 4	McCoy M 14 / Riordan D 1+2	Summerfield L 33+1	Penn R 32+2	Berrett J 33+3	Tutonda D 7+5	Oliver V 31+6	Thompson R 9+4	Nolan E 11+4	Hyde J 4+7	Straker A 6+5	Godfrey B 5+7	Ilesanmi F 35+2	Sinclair E 3+9	Carson J 6+16	Rzonca C —+1	Turner R 5+4	McCombe J 5 / Ingham M 3	Collins M 7	Coulson M 20+2	Morris B 3	Swann G 3+1 / Bennett S 11	Greening J 2+1	Boyle W 12	Lussey J 1	O'Connor S 4 / Alessandra L 11	Kitching M 1	Galbraith D 14+7	McEvoy K 10+9	Fewster B 18+6	Hendrie L 18	Cameron K 18	Massanka N 1+2	Dixon M 6+1	Satka L 5+1	Match No.
1	2	3	4	5[1]	6	7[3]	8	9[2]	10	11	12	13	14																									1
1	2	3	4	5	6	7	8	9	10	11[1]		12																										2
1	2	3	4	5		7	8	9	10	11[2]	12	13		6[1]																								3
1	2	3	4[1]	5	7[2]	6	8	9	11		13	10[3]			12	14																						4
1	3	2		5[2]	6[1]	7	8	9	10	11[3]				12	4	13	14																					5
1	2	3		5	6		8	9[1]	10[3]	11[2]	7				4	12	13	14																				6
1	3	6		2[2]	7	12	8	11[3]	10	9[1]	4				5	13	14																					7
1	3	4			8	7[1]	6	14	10■	9[3]	2				5[2]	12	13		11																			8
1	3	4			7[3]	6	8	13		10	2		14	12	5	9[2]	11[1]																					9
1	2	3		5		6	8	13		11[1]			12	7	4		9[2]		10																			10
1	4			2		7	8						11[2]	12	5	13	14		10[3]	3	6	9[1]																11
1	4			2		7	8		10				11		5				12	3	6	9[1]																12
1	3			2		7[2]	8		10[1]				11		5	12			13	4	6	9																13
1		4		2			7		10		6[2]		11[1]		5		13		12	3	8	9																14
1	4			2[3]					10		8[2]		9[1]	12	5	14	13		11	3	7	6																15
1	8			2			3		11		7				5	10[1]			12		9	4	6															16
1	14	4[3]					7	13	10		2			8	5				9[1]		6[2]	11		3	12													17
1							10	12	11		2		14	6[3]	5	13						9[2]	8	3	7[1]	4												18
1							9		11[2]		2	13	10	12	5	6[1]							8	4	7■	3												19
1							6		10					8[3]	4		13					7		14			2[1]	3	5	9[2]	11	12						20
1		4			8[3]	6	7		10				12	14	5											3		2		13	9[1]	11[2]						21
1		3			6	7	8		10		12				5		14									4		2[2]		11[3]	13	9[1]						22
1		3			6	7	9		11		2				5		12									4				8		10[1]						23
1		3			8	7	9[1]		11					12	5		14									4		2[2]		6	13	10[3]						24
1		4			6[3]	7	8		10						5							13								11[2]	9[1]	14	2	3	12			25
1		3			7	8[3]			10						5							6[2]								14	12	13	2	4	11[1]	9		26
1		4			6[2]	7			10						5							11								13	9[1]		2	3	12	8		27
1		4			6	7	13		10						5							11									9[1]		2■	3		8[2]	12	28
1		4			6[2]	7				14		13			5							10								9	8[3]	11[1]		3		12	2	29
1		4		13	12	8	7					10[2]			5		14					9[3]									6[1]	11		3			2	30
1		4			6	7[1]	9			13		12			5		14					10									8[2]	11[3]		3			2	31
1		3			7	14			13			10[3]					9[2]					6									12	11	2	5		8[1]	4	32
		3		11[3]	8	7			10	14					9[1]					1						4				6[2]	13	12	2	5				33
		3			8	7	9[1]		12						6[2]					1		11				2				13		10	4	5				34
1		3			7[1]	8■	12		10			14			5		13													9	6[2]	11[3]	2	4				35
1		3			8				14			10[1]			5							6[3]		7				11		9[2]	13	12	2	4				36
1		3			6	7			11						5									8		4		9		10[1]		12					2	37
1		3			8	6			11[1]	14					5							13		7[2]		4		10		9[3]	12		2					38
1		3		13	7	6[1]	14		12						5							9		8[3]		4		10				11[2]	2					39
1		3			8		6		13						5[2]							9[1]		7		4■		10		12		11	2					40
1		3			8		6		10[1]								13							4				9		12		11	2	5[2]		7		41
1		3■			6	8			9[1]						12									4				11		13		10	2	5		7[2]		42
1					6	7	8										5							3				11		9[1]	12	10	2	4				43
1		12			7	6	8										5							3				10		11[1]		9	2	4				44
1		3			8	7[1]	6										13							4				9		11[2]	12	10	2	5				45
		4			7		8		12								6			1				3				11			9	10[1]	2	5				46

FA Cup

First Round	Accrington S	(a)	2-3

Capital One Cup

First Round	Bradford C	(h)	2-2
(aet; York C won 4-2 on penalties)			
Second Round	Swansea C	(a)	0-3

Johnstone's Paint Trophy

Second Round	Doncaster R	(h)	2-0
Northern Quarter-Final	Barnsley	(a)	1-2

ENGLISH LEAGUE PLAYERS DIRECTORY

Players listed represent those with their clubs during the 2015–16 season.

Players are listed alphabetically on pages 539–545.

The number alongside each player corresponds to the team number heading. (Aarons, Rolando 55 = team 55 (Newcastle U)). Club names in italic indicate loans.

ACCRINGTON S (1)

BARRY, Anthony (M) 140 1
H: 5 7 W: 10 00 b.Liverpool 29-5-86
From Accrington S
2004–05	Coventry C	0	0		
2005–06	Yeovil T	4	0		
2006–07	Yeovil T	24	0		
2007–08	Yeovil T	36	0	64	0
2008–09	Chester C	43	1	43	1
2012–13	Fleetwood T	12	0	12	0

On loan from Forest Green R.
| 2014–15 | Accrington S | 13 | 0 | | |
| 2015–16 | Accrington S | 8 | 0 | 21 | 0 |

BOCO, Romuald (F) 168 17
H: 5 10 W: 10 13 b.Bernay 8-7-85
Internationals: Benin Full caps.
2006–07	Accrington S	32	3		
2007–08	Accrington S	11	0		
2008–09	Accrington S	0	0		
2009–10	Burton Alb	8	0	8	0

From Sligo
2012–13	Accrington S	42	10		
2013–14	Plymouth Arg	27	1	27	1
2014–15	Chesterfield	13	1	13	1
2014 15	Bharat FC	20	0	20	0
2015–16	Portsmouth	4	0	4	0
2015–16	Accrington S	11	2	96	15

BROWN, Scott (M) 151 12
H: 5 9 W: 10 02 b.Runcorn 8-5-85
Internationals: England U17, U18, U19.
2001–02	Everton	0	0		
2002–03	Everton	0	0		
2003–04	Everton	0	0		
2004–05	Bristol C	19	0		
2005–06	Bristol C	29	1		
2006–07	Bristol C	15	4	63	5
2006–07	Cheltenham T	4	0		
2007–08	Cheltenham T	20	0		
2008–09	Port Vale	18	1	18	1
2009–10	Cheltenham T	1	0	25	0
2010–11	Morecambe	32	3	32	3

From Fleetwood T, York C, Macclesfield T, Chester FC, Southport, Grimsby T.
| 2015–16 | Accrington S | 13 | 3 | 13 | 3 |

BRUNA, Gerardo (M) 11 0
H: 5 8 W: 10 02 b.Mendoza 29-1-91
Internationals: Spain U17.
2007–08	Liverpool	0	0		
2008–09	Liverpool	0	0		
2009–10	Liverpool	0	0		
2010–11	Liverpool	0	0		
2011–12	Blackpool	1	0		
2012–13	Blackpool	1	0		
2013–14	Blackpool	0	0	2	0
2014–15	Tranmere R	0	0		
2014–15	Accrington S	6	0		
2015–16	Accrington S	3	0	9	0

BUXTON, Adam (D) 56 2
H: 6 1 W: 12 10 b.Liverpool 12-5-92
2010–11	Wigan Ath	0	0		
2011–12	Wigan Ath	0	0		
2012–13	Wigan Ath	0	0		
2013–14	Wigan Ath	0	0		
2013–14	*Burton Alb*	0	0		
2014–15	Accrington S	11	0		
2015–16	Accrington S	28	1	56	2

CARVER, Marcus (F) 38 4
H: 5 11 W: 11 11 b.Blackburn 22-10-93
2011–12	Accrington S	2	0		
2012–13	Accrington S	11	0		
2013–14	Accrington S	6	0		
2014–15	Accrington S	17	1		
2015–16	Accrington S	2	0	38	4

CONNEELY, Seamus (D) 148 8
H: 5 9 W: 10 10 b.Galway 9-7-88
Internationals: Republic of Ireland U21, U23.
| 2008 | Galway U | 20 | 0 | | |
| 2009 | Galway U | 34 | 2 | | |

2010	Galway U	32	0	86	2
2010–11	Sheffield U	0	0		
2011–12	Sheffield U	0	0		
2014–15	Accrington S	16	3		
2015–16	Accrington S	46	3	62	6

CROOKS, Matt (M) 52 6
H: 6 0 W: 11 05 b.Leeds 20-1-94
2011–12	Huddersfield T	0	0		
2012–13	Huddersfield T	0	0		
2013–14	Huddersfield T	0	0		
2014–15	Huddersfield T	1	0	1	0
2014–15	*Hartlepool U*	3	0	3	0
2014–15	Accrington S	16	0		
2015–16	Accrington S	32	6	48	6

DAVIES, Tom (D) 32 1
H: 5 11 W: 11 00 b.Warrington 18-4-92
| 2014–15 | Fleetwood T | 0 | 0 | | |
| 2015–16 | Accrington S | 32 | 1 | 32 | 1 |

ETHERIDGE, Ross (G) 21 0
b. 4-9-94
2013–14	Derby Co	0	0		
2014–15	Derby Co	0	0		
2014–15	*Crewe Alex*	0	0		
2015–16	Accrington S	21	0	21	0

GORNELL, Terry (F) 257 47
H: 5 11 W: 12 04 b.Liverpool 16-12-89
2008–09	Tranmere R	10	1		
2008–09	*Accrington S*	11	4		
2009–10	Tranmere R	27	2		
2010–11	Tranmere R	3	0	40	3
2010–11	Accrington S	40	13		
2011–12	Shrewsbury T	41	9		
2012–13	Shrewsbury T	12	0	53	9
2012–13	*Rochdale*	19	5	19	5
2013–14	Cheltenham T	34	3		
2014–15	Cheltenham T	25	3	59	6
2014–15	Accrington S	15	4		
2015–16	Accrington S	20	3	86	24

GOULDING, Liam (D) 0 0
H: 6 1 W: 12 08 b. 28-4-96
| 2014–15 | Accrington S | 0 | 0 | | |
| 2015–16 | Accrington S | 0 | 0 | | |

HAZELDINE, Max (M) 1 0
H: 5 10 W: 11 11 b. 13-2-97
2013–14	Accrington S	0	0		
2014–15	Accrington S	1	0		
2015–16	Accrington S	0	0	1	0

HUGHES, Mark (D) 329 20
H: 6 1 W: 13 03 b.Liverpool 9-12-86
2004–05	Everton	0	0		
2005–06	Everton	0	0		
2005–06	*Stockport Co*	3	1	3	1
2006–07	Everton	1	0	1	0
2006–07	Northampton T	17	2		
2007–08	Northampton T	35	1		
2008–09	Northampton T	41	1	93	4
2009–10	Walsall	26	1	26	1
2010–11	N Queensland F	30	4	30	4
2011–12	Bury	25	0		
2012–13	Bury	27	0	52	0
2012–13	*Accrington S*	5	0		
2013–14	Morecambe	44	5		
2014–15	Morecambe	40	3	84	8
2015–16	Stevenage	20	1	20	1
2015–16	Accrington S	15	1	20	1

KEE, Billy (F) 250 76
H: 5 9 W: 11 04 b.Loughborough 1-12-90
Internationals: Northern Ireland U19, U21.
2009–10	Leicester C	0	0		
2009–10	*Accrington S*	37	9		
2010–11	Torquay U	40	9		
2011–12	Torquay U	4	0	44	9
2011–12	Burton Alb	20	12		
2012–13	Burton Alb	40	13		
2013–14	Burton Alb	37	12		
2014–15	Burton Alb	2	2	99	39
2014–15	Scunthorpe U	12	0	12	0
2014–15	*Mansfield T*	13	2	13	2
2015–16	Accrington S	45	17	82	26

McCARTAN, Shay (M) 77 14
H: 5 10 W: 11 09 b.Newry 18-5-94
Internationals: Northern Ireland U17, U19, U21.
2011–12	Burnley	1	0		
2012–13	Burnley	0	0	1	0
2013–14	Accrington S	18	1		
2014–15	Accrington S	31	6		
2015–16	Accrington S	27	7	76	14

McCONVILLE, Sean (M) 122 19
H: 5 8 W: 11 07 b.Liverpool 6-3-89
2008–09	Accrington S	5	0		
2009–10	Accrington S	28	1		
2010–11	Accrington S	0	0		
2011–12	Rochdale	4	0	4	0

From Barrow, Stalybridge Celtic, Chester.
| 2015–16 | Accrington S | 42 | 5 | 118 | 19 |

MINGOIA, Piero (M) 131 13
H: 5 6 W: 10 12 b.Enfield 20-10-91
2010–11	Watford	5	0		
2011–12	Watford	0	0		
2011–12	*Brentford*	0	0		
2012–13	Watford	0	0		
2012–13	*Accrington S*	7	1		
2013–14	Watford	0	0	5	0
2013–14	Accrington S	37	1		
2014–15	Accrington S	36	8		
2015–16	Accrington S	46	3	126	13

MOHAMED, Kaid (F) 260 55
H: 5 11 W: 12 06 b.Cardiff 23-7-84
2003–04	Cwmbran T	29	3		
2004–05	Cwmbran T	15	2		
2004–05	Llanelli	3	1		
2005–06	Carmarthen T	14	4		
2005–06	Cwmbran T	11	7	55	12
2006–07	Llanelli	5	0	8	1
2006–07	Carmarthen T	30	15	44	19
2007–08	Swindon T	11	0	11	0

From Forest Green R, Bath C, AFC Wimbledon.
2011–12	Cheltenham T	45	11		
2012–13	Cheltenham T	39	4	84	15
2013–14	Port Vale	6	0		
2013–14	*AFC Wimbledon*	5	0	5	0
2013–14	*Bristol R*	21	4	21	4
2014–15	Port Vale	0	0	6	0
2014–15	*Northampton T*	23	4	23	4

From Port Talbot T.
| 2015–16 | Accrington S | 3 | 0 | 3 | 0 |

MOONEY, Jason (G) 34 0
H: 6 9 W: 14 00 b.Belfast 26-2-89
2011–12	Wycombe W	0	0		
2012–13	Tranmere R	1	0		
2013–14	Tranmere R	3	0	4	0
2014–15	York C	4	0	4	0
2015–16	Accrington S	26	0	26	0

MORGAN, Adam (F) 26 1
H: 5 10 W: 10 03 b.Liverpool 21-4-94
Internationals: England U17, U19.
2011–12	Liverpool	0	0		
2012–13	Liverpool	0	0		
2012–13	*Rotherham U*	1	0	1	0
2013–14	Liverpool	0	0		
2013–14	Yeovil T	12	0		
2014–15	Yeovil T	6	1	18	1
2014–15	*St Johnstone*	5	0	5	0
2015–16	Accrington S	2	0	2	0

PEARSON, Matthew (D) 55 3
H: 6 3 W: 11 05 b.Keighley 3-8-93
Internationals: England C, U18.
2012–13	Rochdale	9	0		
2013–14	Rochdale	0	0	9	0
2015–16	Accrington S	46	3	46	3

PHILLIPS, Jack (M) 0 0
b.Liverpool 15-10-93
2012–13	Wigan Ath	0	0		
2013–14	Wigan Ath	0	0		
2014–15	Wigan Ath	0	0		
2015–16	Accrington S	0	0		

PROCTER, Andy (M)   341 31
H: 6 0 W: 12 04 b.Blackburn 13-3-83
Internationals: England C.

2006-07	Accrington S	43	3		
2007-08	Accrington S	43	10		
2008-09	Accrington S	37	3		
2009-10	Accrington S	44	5		
2010-11	Accrington S	43	6		
2011-12	Accrington S	25	2		
2011-12	Preston NE	19	0		
2012-13	Preston NE	15	0	34	0
2013-14	Bury	32	2	32	2
2014-15	Accrington S	29	0		
2015-16	Accrington S	11	0	275	29

QUANSAH, Keenan (D)   0 0
b. 25-5-97

2015-16	Accrington S	0	0

SHAW, Brayden (F)   4 0
b. 25-2-97

2014-15	Bury	0	0		
2015-16	Bury	0	0		
2015-16	Accrington S	4	0	4	0

STEENSON, Kealan (M)   0 0
b. 6-11-96

2014-15	Accrington S	0	0
2015-16	Accrington S	0	0

WAKEFIELD, Liam (D)   21 0
H: 6 0 W: 11 00 b.Doncaster 9-4-94

2012-13	Doncaster R	4	0		
2013-14	Doncaster R	4	0		
2014-15	Doncaster R	5	0	9	0
2015-16	Accrington S	12	0	12	0

WINDASS, Josh (M)   75 21
H: 5 9 W: 10 10 b.Hull 9-1-93

2013-14	Accrington S	10	0		
2014-15	Accrington S	35	6		
2015-16	Accrington S	30	15	75	21

WINNARD, Dean (D)   250 5
H: 5 9 W: 10 04 b.Wigan 20-8-89

2006-07	Blackburn R	0	0		
2007-08	Blackburn R	0	0		
2008-09	Blackburn R	0	0		
2009-10	Accrington S	44	0		
2010-11	Accrington S	45	1		
2011-12	Accrington S	30	1		
2012-13	Accrington S	40	1		
2013-14	Accrington S	39	2		
2014-15	Accrington S	37	0		
2015-16	Accrington S	15	0	250	5

Scholars
Blackburn, Harry; Dass, Reuben; Evans, Christian Paul; Gunner, Callum Richard Peter; Hartley, Jack Kennedy; Hickey, Roman Wes; Jones, Isaac Samuel; Little, Jack David; Moran, Luke; Ogle, Reagan; Rathbone, Joseph Arnold; Roberts, John Joseph; Scarth, Tyler Brian; Smith, Dylan Liam; Sykes, Ross James; Webb, Nathan James; Wolfenden, James Harry.

AFC WIMBLEDON (2)

AKINFENWA, Adebayo (F)   468 148
H: 5 11 W: 13 07 b.Nigeria 10-5-82

2001	Atlantas	19	4		
2002	Atlantas	4	1	23	5
From Barry T					
2003-04	Boston U	3	0	3	0
2003-04	Leyton Orient	1	0	1	0
2003-04	Rushden & D	0	0		
2003-04	Doncaster R	9	4	9	4
2004-05	Torquay U	37	14	37	14
2005-06	Swansea C	34	9		
2006-07	Swansea C	25	5		
2007-08	Swansea C	0	0	59	14
2007-08	Millwall	7	0	7	0
2007-08	Northampton T	15	7		
2008-09	Northampton T	33	13		
2009-10	Northampton T	40	17		
2010-11	Gillingham	44	11		
2011-12	Northampton T	39	18		
2012-13	Northampton T	41	16	168	71
2013-14	Gillingham	34	10	78	21
2014-15	AFC Wimbledon	45	13		
2015-16	AFC Wimbledon	38	6	83	19

AZEEZ, Adebayo (F)   114 17
H: 6 0 W: 12 07 b.Orpington 8-1-94
Internationals: England U19.

2012-13	Charlton Ath	0	0		
2012-13	Wycombe W	4	0	4	0
2012-13	Leyton Orient	1	0	1	0
2013-14	Charlton Ath	0	0		
2013-14	Torquay U	9	2	9	2
2013-14	Dagenham & R	15	3	15	3
2014-15	AFC Wimbledon	43	5		
2015-16	AFC Wimbledon	42	7	85	12

BARCHAM, Andy (F)   277 38
H: 5 8 W: 11 10 b.Basildon 16-12-86
Internationals: England U16.

2005-06	Tottenham H	0	0		
2006-07	Tottenham H	0	0		
2007-08	Tottenham H	0	0		
2007-08	Leyton Orient	25	1	25	1
2008-09	Tottenham H	0	0		
2008-09	Gillingham	33	6		
2009-10	Gillingham	42	7		
2010-11	Gillingham	24	6	99	19
2011-12	Scunthorpe U	41	9		
2012-13	Scunthorpe U	34	0	75	9
2013-14	Portsmouth	26	3		
2014-15	Portsmouth	19	1	45	4
2015-16	AFC Wimbledon	33	5	33	5

BEERE, Tom (F)   20 0
H: 5 11 W: 11 09 b.Southwark 27-1-95

2012-13	AFC Wimbledon	0	0		
2013-14	AFC Wimbledon	0	0		
2014-15	AFC Wimbledon	18	0		
2015-16	AFC Wimbledon	2	0	20	0

BULMAN, Dannie (M)   406 22
H: 5 9 W: 11 12 b.Ashford 24-1-79

1998-99	Wycombe W	11	1		
1999-2000	Wycombe W	29	1		
2000-01	Wycombe W	36	4		
2001-02	Wycombe W	46	5		
2002-03	Wycombe W	42	3		
2003-04	Wycombe W	38	0	202	14
From Stevenage, Crawley T.					
2010-11	Oxford U	5	0	5	0
2011-12	Crawley T	41	3		
2012-13	Crawley T	36	1		
2013-14	Crawley T	39	0	116	4
2014-15	AFC Wimbledon	41	1		
2015-16	AFC Wimbledon	42	3	83	4

ELLIOTT, Tom (F)   149 22
H: 6 3 W: 12 00 b.Hunslet 9-11-90
Internationals: England U16, U18.

2006-07	Leeds U	3	0		
2007-08	Leeds U	0	0		
2008-09	Leeds U	0	0		
2008-09	Macclesfield T	6	0	6	0
2009-10	Leeds U	0	0		
2009-10	Bury	16	1	16	1
2010-11	Leeds U	0	0	3	0
2010-11	Rotherham U	6	0	6	0
2011-12	Hamilton A	7	0	7	0
2011-12	Stockport Co	42	7	42	7
2014-15	Cambridge U	30	8	30	8
2015-16	AFC Wimbledon	39	6	39	6

FITZPATRICK, David (M)   7 1
b.Surbiton 10-2-95

2011-12	QPR	0	0		
2012-13	QPR	0	0		
2013-14	QPR	0	0		
2014-15	AFC Wimbledon	3	0		
2015-16	AFC Wimbledon	4	1	7	1

FRANCOMB, George (D)   154 9
H: 5 11 W: 11 07 b.Hackney 8-9-91

2009-10	Norwich C	2	0		
2010-11	Norwich C	0	0		
2010-11	Barnet	13	0	13	0
2011-12	Norwich C	0	0		
2011-12	Hibernian	14	0	14	0
2012-13	Norwich C	0	0	2	0
2013-14	AFC Wimbledon	15	0		
2013-14	AFC Wimbledon	33	3		
2014-15	AFC Wimbledon	37	3		
2015-16	AFC Wimbledon	40	3	125	9

FULLER, Barry (D)   323 2
H: 5 10 W: 11 10 b.Ashford 25-9-84
Internationals: England C.

2004-05	Charlton Ath	0	0		
2005-06	Charlton Ath	0	0		
2005-06	Barnet	15	1		
From Stevenage B.					
2007-08	Gillingham	10	0		
2008-09	Gillingham	37	0		
2009-10	Gillingham	36	0		
2010-11	Gillingham	42	0		
2011-12	Gillingham	9	0		
2012-13	Gillingham	0	0	134	0
2012-13	Barnet	39	0	54	1
2013-14	AFC Wimbledon	45	0		
2014-15	AFC Wimbledon	45	1		
2015-16	AFC Wimbledon	40	0	135	1

GALLAGHER, Dan (M)   1 0
b. 20-6-97

2014-15	AFC Wimbledon	1	0		
2015-16	AFC Wimbledon	0	0	1	0

HARRISON, Ben (M)   7 0
b. 2-3-97

2014-15	AFC Wimbledon	7	0		
2015-16	AFC Wimbledon	0	0	7	0

KAJA, Egli (M)   2 0
H: 5 10 W: 12 04 b. 26-7-97

2015-16	AFC Wimbledon	2	0	2	0

KENNEDY, Callum (D)   125 2
H: 6 1 W: 12 10 b.Chertsey 9-11-89

2007-08	Swindon T	0	0		
2008-09	Swindon T	4	0		
2009-10	Swindon T	8	0		
2010-11	Swindon T	3	0		
2010-11	Gillingham	3	0	3	0
2010-11	Rotherham U	5	0	5	0
2011-12	Swindon T	18	1	33	1
2012-13	Scunthorpe U	17	0	17	0
2013-14	AFC Wimbledon	22	0		
2014-15	AFC Wimbledon	26	0		
2015-16	AFC Wimbledon	19	1	67	1

McDONNELL, Joe (G)   4 0
H: 5 10 W: 9 13 b.Basingstoke 19-5-94

2014-15	AFC Wimbledon	4	0		
2015-16	AFC Wimbledon	0	0	4	0

MEADES, Jonathan (M)   74 4
H: 6 1 W: 13 00 b.Cardiff 2-3-92
Internationals: Wales U17, U21.

2010-11	Cardiff C	0	0		
2011-12	Cardiff C	0	0		
2012-13	Bournemouth	0	0		
2012-13	AFC Wimbledon	26	1		
2013-14	Oxford U	0	0		
2014-15	Oxford U	7	0	7	0
2015-16	AFC Wimbledon	41	3	67	4

NIGHTINGALE, Will (M)   8 0
H: 6 1 W: 13 03 b.Wandsworth 2-7-95

2013-14	AFC Wimbledon	0	0		
2014-15	AFC Wimbledon	4	0		
2015-16	AFC Wimbledon	4	0	8	0

OAKLEY, George (F)   7 0
H: 6 2 W: 13 08 b.Wandsworth 18-11-95

2013-14	AFC Wimbledon	0	0		
2014-15	AFC Wimbledon	6	0		
2015-16	AFC Wimbledon	1	0	7	0

OLUSANYA, Toyosi (M)   1 1
b. 1-2-98

2015-16	AFC Wimbledon	1	1	1	1

PILBEAM, George (D)   0 0
b. 27-9-95

2014-15	AFC Wimbledon	0	0
2015-16	AFC Wimbledon	0	0

REEVES, Jake (M)   113 4
H: 5 8 W: 11 11 b.Lewisham 30-6-93

2010-11	Brentford	1	0		
2011-12	Brentford	8	0		
2012-13	Brentford	6	0		
2012-13	AFC Wimbledon	5	0		
2013-14	Brentford	20	0	35	0
2014-15	Swindon T	10	1	10	1
2014-15	AFC Wimbledon	23	2		
2015-16	AFC Wimbledon	40	1	68	3

RIGG, Sean (F)   305 32
H: 5 9 W: 12 01 b.Bristol 1-10-88

2006-07	Bristol R	18	1		
2007-08	Bristol R	31	1		
2008-09	Bristol R	8	0		
2009-10	Bristol R	0	0	57	2
2009-10	Port Vale	26	3		
2010-11	Port Vale	25	3		
2011-12	Port Vale	42	10	93	16
2012-13	Oxford U	44	5		
2013-14	Oxford U	28	2	72	7
2014-15	AFC Wimbledon	44	5		
2015-16	AFC Wimbledon	39	2	83	7

ROBINSON, Paul (D)   393 21
H: 6 1 W: 11 09 b.Barnet 7-1-82

2000-01	Millwall	0	0		
2001-02	Millwall	0	0		
2002-03	Millwall	14	0		
2003-04	Millwall	9	0		
2004-05	Millwall	0	0		
2004-05	Torquay U	12	0	12	0
2005-06	Millwall	32	0		
2006-07	Millwall	38	3		
2007-08	Millwall	45	3		

2008–09	Millwall	26	2		
2009–10	Millwall	34	4		
2010–11	Millwall	37	3		
2011–12	Millwall	41	1		
2012–13	Millwall	3	0		
2013–14	Millwall	25	0	304	16
2014–15	Portsmouth	33	2	33	2
2015–16	AFC Wimbledon	44	3	44	3

SHEA, James (G) 60 0
H: 5 11 W: 12 00 b.Islington 16-6-91
2009–10	Arsenal	0	0		
2010–11	Arsenal	0	0		
2011–12	Arsenal	0	0		
2011–12	*Dagenham & R*	1	0	1	0
2012–13	Arsenal	0	0		
2013–14	Arsenal	0	0		
2014–15	AFC Wimbledon	38	0		
2015–16	AFC Wimbledon	21	0	59	0

SMITH, Connor (M) 32 0
H: 5 11 W: 11 06 b.London 18-2-93
Internationals: Republic of Ireland U19, U21.
2012–13	Watford	7	0		
2013–14	Watford	1	0		
2013–14	*Gillingham*	10	0	10	0
2014–15	Watford	0	0		
2015–16	Watford	0	0	8	0
2015–16	*Stevenage*	4	0	4	0
2015–16	AFC Wimbledon	10	0	10	0

SWEENEY, Ryan (D) 13 0
b.Kingston upon Thames 15-4-97
Internationals: Republic of Ireland U18.
2014–15	AFC Wimbledon	3	0		
2015–16	AFC Wimbledon	10	0	13	0

TAYLOR, Lyle (F) 152 37
H: 6 2 W: 12 00 b.Greenwich 29-3-90
Internationals: Montserrat Full caps.
2007–08	Millwall	0	0		
2008–09	Millwall	0	0		
From Concord R					
2010–11	Bournemouth	11	0		
2011–12	Bournemouth	18	0	29	0
2011–12	*Hereford U*	8	2	8	2
2013–14	Sheffield U	20	2	20	2
2013–14	*Partick Thistle*	20	7		
2014–15	Scunthorpe U	18	3	18	3
2014–15	*Partick Thistle*	15	3	35	10
2015–16	AFC Wimbledon	42	20	42	20

TOONGA, Christian (M) 4 0
b. 20-11-97
2015–16	AFC Wimbledon	4	0	4	0

Players retained with offer of contract
Bellikli, Neset Can; Egan, Alfie Patrick.

Scholars
Ano, Joshua Daniel Kwadjo; Antwi-Nyame, Jayden; Batchelor, Reece Oluwatosin Oluwaseun; Bongo, Dominique Munansi; Chapman, Judah David; Mannion, William John; Marchant, George Robert; Mbiya-Kalambayi, Paul Mbwebwe; McKillop, Seanan Bernard James; Sibbick, Toby Peter; Stanton-Cockle, Louie Joe; Stripp, Jason Oliver; Walker Barth, Antonio; Williams-Bowers, Reece Ian Seton; Wingate, Jack Steven; Wood, Nathan Laurence.

ARSENAL (3)

AKPOM, Chuba (F) 56 3
H: 6 0 W: 12 02 b.London 9-10-95
Internationals: England U16, U17, U19, U20, U21.
2012–13	Arsenal	0	0		
2013–14	Arsenal	1	0		
2013–14	*Brentford*	4	0	4	0
2013–14	*Coventry C*	6	0	6	0
2014–15	Arsenal	3	0		
2014–15	*Nottingham F*	7	0	7	0
2015–16	Arsenal	0	0	4	0
2015–16	*Hull C*	35	3	35	3

ARTETA, Mikel (M) 421 59
H: 5 9 W: 10 08 b.San Sebastian 26-3-82
Internationals: Spain U16, U17, U18, U21.
1999–2000	Barcelona B	26	1		
2000–01	Barcelona B	16	2	42	3
2000–01	Paris St Germain	6	1		
2001–02	Paris St Germain	25	1	31	2
2002–03	Rangers	27	4		
2003–04	Rangers	23	8	50	12
2004–05	Real Sociedad	14	1	14	1
2004–05	Everton	12	1		
2005–06	Everton	29	1		

2006–07	Everton	35	9		
2007–08	Everton	28	1		
2008–09	Everton	26	5		
2009–10	Everton	13	6		
2010–11	Everton	29	3		
2011–12	Everton	2	1	174	27
2011–12	Arsenal	29	6		
2012–13	Arsenal	34	6		
2013–14	Arsenal	31	2		
2014–15	Arsenal	7	0		
2015–16	Arsenal	9	0	110	14

BELLERIN, Hector (D) 64 3
H: 5 10 W: 11 09 b.Barcelona 19-3-95
Internationals: Spain U16, U17, U19, U21, Full caps.
2012–13	Arsenal	0	0		
2013–14	Arsenal	0	0		
2013–14	*Watford*	8	0	8	0
2014–15	Arsenal	20	2		
2015–16	Arsenal	36	1	56	3

BENNACER, Ismael (M) 6 0
H: 5 9 W: 11 00 b.Arles 1-12-97
Internationals: France U18, U19.
2014–15	*Arles*	6	0	6	0
2015–16	Arsenal	0	0		

BIELIK, Krystian (M) 5 0
H: 5 10 W: 11 00 b.Vrinnevi 4-1-98
Internationals: Poland U16, U17, U18.
2014–15	*Legia Warsaw*	5	0	5	0
2014–15	Arsenal	0	0		
2015–16	Arsenal	0	0		

CAMPBELL, Joel (F) 132 17
H: 5 10 W: 12 00 b.Costa Rica 26-6-92
Internationals: Costa Rica U17, U20, Full caps.
2009–10	Saprissa	1	0		
2010–11	Saprissa	2	0	3	0
2010–11	*Puntarenas*	5	0	5	0
2011–12	Arsenal	0	0		
2011–12	*Lorient*	25	3	25	3
2012–13	Arsenal	0	0		
2012–13	*Real Betis*	28	2	28	2
2013–14	Arsenal	0	0		
2013–14	*Olympiacos*	32	8	32	8
2014–15	Arsenal	4	0		
2014–15	*Villarreal*	16	1	16	1
2015–16	Arsenal	19	3	23	3

CAZORLA, Santi (M) 373 62
H: 5 5 W: 10 07 b.Lugo De Llanera 13-12-84
Internationals: Spain U21, Full caps.
2003–04	Villarreal	2	0		
2004–05	Villarreal	28	2		
2005–06	Villarreal	23	0		
2006–07	*Recreativo Huelva*	34	5	34	5
2007–08	Villarreal	36	5		
2008–09	Villarreal	30	8		
2009–10	Villarreal	15	0		
2010–11	Villarreal	37	5	180	25
2011–12	Malaga	38	9		
2012–13	Malaga	0	0	38	9
2012–13	Arsenal	38	12		
2013–14	Arsenal	31	4		
2014–15	Arsenal	37	7		
2015–16	Arsenal	15	0	121	23

CECH, Petr (G) 495 0
H: 6 5 W: 14 07 b.Plzen 20-5-82
Internationals: Czech Republic U15, U16, U17, U18, U20, U21, Full caps.
1998–99	Viktoria Plzen	0	0		
1999–2000	Chmel	1	0		
2000–01	Chmel	26	0	27	0
2001–02	Sparta Prague	26	0	26	0
2002–03	Rennes	37	0		
2003–04	Rennes	38	0	75	0
2004–05	Chelsea	35	0		
2005–06	Chelsea	34	0		
2006–07	Chelsea	20	0		
2007–08	Chelsea	35	0		
2008–09	Chelsea	35	0		
2009–10	Chelsea	34	0		
2010–11	Chelsea	38	0		
2011–12	Chelsea	36	0		
2012–13	Chelsea	36	0		
2013–14	Chelsea	34	0		
2014–15	Chelsea	7	0	333	0
2015–16	Arsenal	34	0	34	0

CHAMBERS, Calum (M) 57 1
H: 6 0 W: 10 05 b.Petersfield 20-1-95
Internationals: England U17, U19, U21, Full caps.
2011–12	Southampton	0	0		
2012–13	Southampton	0	0		

2013–14	Southampton	22	0	22	0
2014–15	Arsenal	23	1		
2015–16	Arsenal	12	0	35	1

COQUELIN, Francis (M) 114 1
H: 5 10 W: 11 08 b.Laval 13-5-91
Internationals: France U17, U18, U19, U20, U21.
2008–09	Arsenal	0	0		
2009–10	Arsenal	0	0		
2010–11	Arsenal	0	0		
2010–11	*Lorient*	24	1	24	1
2011–12	Arsenal	10	0		
2012–13	Arsenal	11	0		
2013–14	Arsenal	0	0		
2013–14	*SC Freiburg*	16	0	16	0
2014–15	Arsenal	22	0		
2014–15	*Charlton Ath*	5	0	5	0
2015–16	Arsenal	26	0	69	0

CROWLEY, Daniel (M) 11 0
H: 5 9 W: 10 10 b.Coventry 3-8-97
Internationals: Republic of Ireland U16, U17. England U16, U17, U19.
2015–16	Arsenal	0	0		
2015–16	*Barnsley*	11	0	11	0

DEBUCHY, Mathieu (D) 293 18
H: 5 10 W: 12 02 b.Fretin 28-7-85
Internationals: France U21, Full caps.
2003–04	Lille	6	0		
2004–05	Lille	16	3		
2005–06	Lille	26	4		
2006–07	Lille	22	1		
2007–08	Lille	16	0		
2008–09	Lille	30	0		
2009–10	Lille	31	1		
2010–11	Lille	35	2		
2011–12	Lille	32	5		
2012–13	Lille	15	0	229	16
2012–13	Newcastle U	14	0		
2013–14	Newcastle U	29	1	43	1
2014–15	Arsenal	10	1		
2015–16	Arsenal	2	0	12	1
2015–16	*Bordeaux*	9	0	9	0

EL-NENNY, Mohamed (M) 137 7
H: 5 11 W: 11 00 b.Al-Mahalla Al-Kubra 11-7-92
Internationals: Egypt U20, U23, Full caps.
2010–11	El Mokawloon	21	2		
2011–12	El Mokawloon	14	0	35	2
2012–13	Basel	15	0		
2013–14	Basel	32	1		
2014–15	Basel	28	2	75	3
2015–16	Basle	16	2	16	2
2015–16	Arsenal	11	0	11	0

FLAMINI, Mathieu (M) 274 17
H: 5 10 W: 10 07 b.Marseille 7-3-84
Internationals: France U21, Full caps.
2003–04	Marseille	14	0	14	0
2004–05	Arsenal	21	1		
2005–06	Arsenal	31	0		
2006–07	Arsenal	20	3		
2007–08	Arsenal	30	3		
2008–09	AC Milan	28	0		
2009–10	AC Milan	23	0		
2010–11	AC Milan	23	0		
2011–12	AC Milan	2	1		
2012–13	AC Milan	17	4	92	7
2013–14	Arsenal	27	2		
2014–15	Arsenal	23	1		
2015–16	Arsenal	16	0	168	10

GABRIEL, Armando (D) 141 2
H: 6 2 W: 13 05 b.Sao Paulo 26-11-90
2010	Vitoria	11	0		
2011	Vitoria	17	0		
2012	Vitoria	35	0		
2013	Vitoria	14	1	77	1
2013–14	*Villareal*	18	0	18	0
2014–15	Villarreal	19	0	19	0
2014–15	Arsenal	6	0		
2015–16	Arsenal	21	1	27	1

GIBBS, Kieran (M) 133 2
H: 5 10 W: 10 02 b.Lambeth 26-9-89
Internationals: England U19, U20, U21, Full caps
2007–08	Arsenal	0	0		
2007–08	*Norwich C*	7	0	7	0
2008–09	Arsenal	8	0		
2009–10	Arsenal	3	0		
2010–11	Arsenal	7	0		
2011–12	Arsenal	16	1		
2012–13	Arsenal	27	0		
2013–14	Arsenal	28	0		
2014–15	Arsenal	22	0		
2015–16	Arsenal	15	1	126	2

GIROUD, Olivier (F) 287 121
H: 6 3   W: 13 11   b.Chambery 30-9-86
Internationals: France Full caps.

Season	Club				
2005–06	Grenoble	3	0		
2006–07	Grenoble	15	2	18	2
2008–09	Tours	23	8		
2009–10	Tours	38	21	61	29
2010–11	Montpellier	37	12		
2011–12	Montpellier	36	21	73	33
2012–13	Arsenal	34	11		
2013–14	Arsenal	36	16		
2014–15	Arsenal	27	14		
2015–16	Arsenal	38	16	135	57

GNABRY, Serge (M) 11 1
H: 5 9   W: 11 06   b.Stuttgart 14-7-95
Internationals: Germany U16, U17, U18, U19, U21.

Season	Club				
2012–13	Arsenal	1	0		
2013–14	Arsenal	9	1		
2014–15	Arsenal	0	0		
2015–16	Arsenal	0	0	10	1
2015–16	*WBA*	1	0	1	0

HAYDEN, Isaac (D) 18 1
H: 6 2   W: 12 06   b.Chelmsford 22-3-95
Internationals: England U16, U17, U18, U19, U20.

Season	Club				
2011–12	Arsenal	0	0		
2012–13	Arsenal	0	0		
2013–14	Arsenal	0	0		
2014–15	Arsenal	0	0		
2015–16	Arsenal	0	0		
2015–16	*Hull C*	18	1	18	1

HUDDART, Ryan (G) 0 0
H: 6 5   b.Margate 6-3-97
Internationals: England U17.

Season	Club		
2013–14	Arsenal	0	0
2014–15	Arsenal	0	0
2015–16	Arsenal	0	0

ILIEV, Dejan (G) 0 0
H: 6 5   b.Strumica 25-2-95
Internationals: Macedonia U17, U19, U21.

Season	Club		
2012–13	Arsenal	0	0
2013–14	Arsenal	0	0
2014–15	Arsenal	0	0
2015–16	Arsenal	0	0

IWOBI, Alex (M) 13 2
H: 5 11   W: 11 11   b.Lagos 3-5-96
Internationals: England U16, U17, U18. Nigeria Full caps.

Season	Club				
2012–13	Arsenal	0	0		
2013–14	Arsenal	0	0		
2014–15	Arsenal	0	0		
2015–16	Arsenal	13	2	13	2

JENKINSON, Carl (D) 97 3
H: 6 1   W: 12 02   b.Harlow 8-2-92
Internationals: Finland U19, U21. England U17, U21, Full caps.

Season	Club				
2010–11	Charlton Ath	8	0	8	0
2010–11	Arsenal	0	0		
2011–12	Arsenal	9	0		
2012–13	Arsenal	14	0		
2013–14	Arsenal	14	1		
2014–15	Arsenal	0	0		
2014–15	*West Ham U*	32	0		
2015–16	Arsenal	0	0	37	1
2015–16	*West Ham U*	20	2	52	2

KAMARA, Glen (F) 6 0
H: 5 10   W: 13 00   b.Tampere 28-10-95
Internationals: Finland U19, U20, U21.

Season	Club				
2012–13	Arsenal	0	0		
2014–15	Arsenal	0	0		
2015–16	Arsenal	0	0		
2015–16	*Southend U*	6	0	6	0

KOSCIELNY, Laurent (D) 323 24
H: 6 1   W: 11 11   b.Tulle 10-9-85
Internationals: France Full caps.

Season	Club				
2004–05	Guingamp	11	0		
2005–06	Guingamp	9	0		
2006–07	Guingamp	21	0	41	0
2007–08	Tours	33	1		
2008–09	Tours	34	5	67	6
2009–10	Lorient	35	3	35	3
2010–11	Arsenal	30	2		
2011–12	Arsenal	33	2		
2012–13	Arsenal	25	2		
2013–14	Arsenal	32	2		
2014–15	Arsenal	27	3		
2015–16	Arsenal	33	4	180	15

MACEY, Matt (G) 4 0
H: 6 6   b.Bristol 9-9-94

Season	Club		
2011–12	Bristol R	0	0
2012–13	Bristol R	0	0
2013–14	Arsenal	0	0
2014–15	Arsenal	0	0
2014–15	*Accrington S*	4	0	4	0
2015–16	Arsenal	0	0

MAITLAND-NILES, Ainsley (F) 31 1
b.Goodmayes 29-8-97
Internationals: England U17, U18, U19.

Season	Club				
2014–15	Arsenal	1	0		
2015–16	Arsenal	0	0	1	0
2015–16	*Ipswich T*	30	1	30	1

MARTINEZ, Damian (G) 37 0
H: 6 3   W: 13 05   b.Mar del Plata 2-9-92
Internationals: Argentina U17, U20.

Season	Club				
2010–11	Arsenal	0	0		
2011–12	Arsenal	0	0		
2011–12	*Oxford U*	1	0	1	0
2012–13	Arsenal	0	0		
2013–14	Arsenal	0	0		
2013–14	*Sheffield W*	11	0	11	0
2014–15	Arsenal	4	0		
2014–15	*Rotherham U*	8	0	8	0
2015–16	Arsenal	0	0	4	0
2015–16	*Wolverhampton W*	13	0	13	0

MERTESACKER, Per (D) 369 24
H: 6 6   W: 14 -02   b.Hannover 29-9-84
Internationals: Germany U20, U21, Full caps.

Season	Club				
2003–04	Hannover	13	0		
2004–05	Hannover	31	2		
2005–06	Hannover	30	5	74	7
2006–07	Werder Bremen	25	2		
2007–08	Werder Bremen	32	1		
2008–09	Werder Bremen	23	2		
2009–10	Werder Bremen	33	5		
2010–11	Werder Bremen	29	2		
2011–12	Werder Bremen	4	0	146	12
2011–12	Arsenal	21	0		
2012–13	Arsenal	34	3		
2013–14	Arsenal	35	2		
2014–15	Arsenal	35	0		
2015–16	Arsenal	24	0	149	5

MONREAL, Nacho (D) 271 4
H: 5 10   W: 11 04   b.Pamplona 26-2-86
Internationals: Spain U19, U21, Full caps.

Season	Club				
2006–07	Osasuna	11	0		
2007–08	Osasuna	27	0		
2008–09	Osasuna	28	0		
2009–10	Osasuna	31	1		
2010–11	Osasuna	31	1	128	2
2011–12	Malaga	31	0		
2012–13	Malaga	14	1	45	1
2012–13	Arsenal	10	1		
2013–14	Arsenal	23	0		
2014–15	Arsenal	28	0		
2015–16	Arsenal	37	0	98	1

MOORE, Tafari (D) 0 0
H: 5 8   b.London 5-7-97
Internationals: England U16, U17, U18, U19.

Season	Club		
2015–16	Arsenal	0	0

O'CONNOR, Stefan (D) 4 0
b.Croydon 23-1-97
Internationals: England U17.

Season	Club				
2014–15	Arsenal	0	0		
2015–16	Arsenal	0	0		
2015–16	*York C*	4	0	4	0

OSPINA, David (G) 308 0
H: 6 0   W: 12 00   b.Medellin 31-8-88
Internationals: Colombia U20, Full caps.

Season	Club				
2006	Atletico Nacional	34	0		
2007	Atletico Nacional	47	0		
2008	Atletico Nacional	16	0	97	0
2008–09	Nice	25	0		
2009–10	Nice	37	0		
2010–11	Nice	35	0		
2011–12	Nice	26	0		
2012–13	Nice	30	0		
2013–14	Nice	29	0	189	0
2014–15	Arsenal	18	0		
2015–16	Arsenal	4	0	22	0

OXLADE-CHAMBERLAIN, Alex (M) 136 16
H: 5 11   W: 11 00   b.Portsmouth 15-8-93
Internationals: England U18, U19, U21, Full caps.

Season	Club				
2009–10	Southampton	2	0		
2010–11	Southampton	34	9	36	9
2011–12	Arsenal	16	2		
2012–13	Arsenal	25	1		
2013–14	Arsenal	14	2		
2014–15	Arsenal	23	1		
2015–16	Arsenal	22	1	100	7

OZIL, Mesut (M) 288 47
H: 5 11   W: 11 06   b.Gelsenkirchen 15-10-88
Internationals: Germany U19, U21, Full caps.

Season	Club				
2005–06	Schalke 04	0	0		
2006–07	Schalke 04	19	0		
2007–08	Schalke 04	11	0	30	0
2007–08	Werder Bremen	12	1		
2008–09	Werder Bremen	27	3		
2009–10	Werder Bremen	31	9		
2010–11	Werder Bremen	0	0	70	13
2010–11	Real Madrid	36	6		
2011–12	Real Madrid	35	4		
2012–13	Real Madrid	32	9		
2013–14	Real Madrid	2	0	105	19
2013–14	Arsenal	26	5		
2014–15	Arsenal	22	4		
2015–16	Arsenal	35	6	83	15

RAMSEY, Aaron (M) 214 30
H: 5 9   W: 10 07   b.Caerphilly 26-12-90
Internationals: Wales U17, U21, Full caps. Great Britain.

Season	Club				
2006–07	Cardiff C	1	0		
2007–08	Cardiff C	15	1		
2008–09	Arsenal	9	0		
2009–10	Arsenal	18	3		
2010–11	Arsenal	7	1		
2010–11	*Nottingham F*	5	0	5	0
2010–11	*Cardiff C*	6	1	22	2
2011–12	Arsenal	34	2		
2012–13	Arsenal	36	1		
2013–14	Arsenal	23	10		
2014–15	Arsenal	29	6		
2015–16	Arsenal	31	5	187	28

REINE-ADELAIDE, Jeff (M) 0 0
H: 6 0   W: 11 11   b.Champigny-sur-Marne 17-1-98
Internationals: France U16, U17, U18.

Season	Club		
2014–15	Lens	0	0
2015–16	Arsenal	0	0

ROSICKY, Tomas (M) 360 46
H: 5 10   W: 10 10   b.Prague 4-10-80
Internationals: Czech Republic U15, U16, U17, U18, U21, Full caps.

Season	Club				
1998–99	Sparta Prague	3	0		
1999–2000	Sparta Prague	24	5		
2000–01	Sparta Prague	14	3	41	8
2000–01	Borussia Dortmund	15	0		
2001–02	Borussia Dortmund	30	5		
2002–03	Borussia Dortmund	30	3		
2003–04	Borussia Dortmund	19	2		
2004–05	Borussia Dortmund	27	4		
2005–06	Borussia Dortmund	28	5	149	19
2006–07	Arsenal	26	3		
2007–08	Arsenal	18	6		
2008–09	Arsenal	0	0		
2009–10	Arsenal	25	3		
2010–11	Arsenal	21	0		
2011–12	Arsenal	28	1		
2012–13	Arsenal	10	2		
2013–14	Arsenal	27	2		
2014–15	Arsenal	15	2		
2015–16	Arsenal	0	0	170	19

SANCHEZ, Alexis (F) 350 105
H: 5 6   W: 11 09   b.Tocopilla 19-12-88
Internationals: Chile U20, Full caps.

Season	Club				
2005	Cobreloa	35	3		
2006	Cobreloa	12	6	47	9
2006–07	Udinese	0	0		
2006–07	*Colo Colo*	32	5	32	5
2007–08	*River Plate*	23	4	23	4
2008–09	Udinese	32	3		
2009–10	Udinese	32	5		
2010–11	Udinese	31	12	95	20
2011–12	Barcelona	25	11		
2012–13	Barcelona	29	8		
2013–14	Barcelona	34	19	88	38
2014–15	Arsenal	35	16		
2015–16	Arsenal	30	13	65	29

SANOGO, Yaya (F) 52 13
H: 6 3   W: 11 08   b.Massy 27-1-93
Internationals: France U16, U17, U18, U19, U20, U21.

Season	Club				
2009–10	Auxerre	0	0		
2010–11	Auxerre	0	0		
2011–12	Auxerre	7	1		
2012–13	Auxerre	13	9	20	10
2013–14	Arsenal	8	0		
2014–15	Arsenal	3	0		
2014–15	*Crystal Palace*	10	0	10	0
2015–16	Arsenal	0	0	11	0
2015–16	*Ajax*	3	0	3	0
2015–16	*Charlton Ath*	8	3	8	3

SHEAF, Ben (M)   0   0
b.Dartford 5-2-98
Internationals: England U18.

| 2015–16 | Arsenal | 0 | 0 | | |

SILVA, Wellington (M)   109   8
H: 5 6   W: 10 00   b.Rio de Janeiro 6-1-93
Internationals: Brazil U17, U21.

2010–11	Arsenal	0	0		
2010–11	*Levante*	2	0	2	0
2011–12	Arsenal	0	0		
2011–12	*Alcoyano*	16	3	16	3
2012–13	Arsenal	0	0		
2013–14	Arsenal	0	0		
2013–14	*Murcia*	38	3	38	3
2014–15	Arsenal	0	0		
2014–15	*Almeria*	31	0	31	0
2015–16	Arsenal	0	0		
2015–16	*Bolton W*	22	2	22	2

SZCZESNY, Wojciech (G)   194   0
H: 5 10   W: 11 11   b.Warsaw 18-4-90
Internationals: Poland U20, U21, Full caps.

2007–08	Arsenal	0	0		
2008–09	Arsenal	0	0		
2009–10	Arsenal	0	0		
2009–10	*Brentford*	28	0	28	0
2010–11	Arsenal	15	0		
2011–12	Arsenal	38	0		
2012–13	Arsenal	25	0		
2013–14	Arsenal	37	0		
2014–15	Arsenal	17	0		
2015–16	Arsenal	0	0	132	0
2015–16	*Roma*	34	0	34	0

TORAL, Jon (M)   70   14
H: 6 0   W: 12 07   b.Reus 5-2-95

2013–14	Arsenal	0	0		
2014–15	*Arsenal*	0	0		
2014–15	*Brentford*	34	6	34	6
2015–16	Arsenal	0	0		
2015–16	*Birmingham C*	36	8	36	8

WALCOTT, Theo (F)   257   59
H: 5 9   W: 11 01   b.Stanmore 16-3-89
Internationals: England U16, U17, U19, U21, Full caps.

2005–06	Southampton	21	4	21	4
2005–06	Arsenal	0	0		
2006–07	Arsenal	16	0		
2007–08	Arsenal	25	4		
2008–09	Arsenal	22	2		
2009–10	Arsenal	23	3		
2010–11	Arsenal	28	9		
2011–12	Arsenal	35	8		
2012–13	Arsenal	32	14		
2013–14	Arsenal	13	5		
2014–15	Arsenal	14	5		
2015–16	Arsenal	28	5	236	55

WELBECK, Danny (F)   162   36
H: 6 1   W: 11 07   b.Manchester 26-11-90
Internationals: England U17, U18, U19, U21, Full caps.

2007–08	Manchester U	0	0		
2008–09	Manchester U	3	1		
2009–10	Manchester U	1	0		
2009–10	*Preston NE*	8	2	8	2
2010–11	Manchester U	0	0		
2010–11	*Sunderland*	26	6	26	6
2011–12	Manchester U	30	9		
2012–13	Manchester U	27	1		
2013–14	Manchester U	25	9		
2014–15	Manchester U	0	0	92	20
2014–15	Arsenal	25	4		
2015–16	Arsenal	11	4	36	8

WILLOCK, Chris (M)   0   0
b.London 31-1-98
Internationals: England U16, U17, U18.

| 2015–16 | Arsenal | 0 | 0 | | |

WILSHERE, Jack (M)   117   7
H: 5 7   W: 11 03   b.Stevenage 1-1-92
Internationals: England U16, U17, U19, U21, Full caps.

2008–09	Arsenal	1	0		
2009–10	Arsenal	1	0		
2009–10	*Bolton W*	14	1	14	1
2010–11	Arsenal	35	1		
2011–12	Arsenal	0	0		
2012–13	Arsenal	25	0		
2013–14	Arsenal	24	3		
2014–15	Arsenal	14	2		
2015–16	Arsenal	3	0	103	6

ZELALEM, Gedion (M)   21   0
H: 5 10   b.Berlin 26-1-97
Internationals: Germany U16, U17. USA U20, U23.

2013–14	Arsenal	0	0		
2014–15	Arsenal	0	0		
2015–16	Arsenal	0	0		
2015–16	*Rangers*	21	0	21	0

Players retained or with offer of contract
Bola, Marc Joel; Bola, Tolaji; Da Graca, Kristopher Santos; Dasilva, Pelenda Joshua Tunga; Dragomir, Vlad-Mihai; Eyoma, Aaron Jordan; Fortune, Yassin Enzo; Hinds, Kaylen Miles; Johnson, Chiori; Keto, Hugo Oliver; Malen, Donyell; Mavididi, Stephy Alvaro; McGuane, Marcus; Mourgos, Savvas; Osei-Tutu, Jordi; Pleguezuelo, Julio Jose.

Scholars
Gilmour, Charlie Ian; Nketiah, Edward; Pileas, Kostas; Tella, Nathan; Willock, Joseph George.

ASTON VILLA (4)

AGBONLAHOR, Gabriel (F)   332   73
H: 5 11   W: 12 05   b.Birmingham 13-10-86
Internationals: England U21, Full caps.

2005–06	Aston Villa	9	1		
2005–06	*Watford*	2	0	2	0
2005–06	*Sheffield W*	8	0	8	0
2006–07	Aston Villa	38	9		
2007–08	Aston Villa	37	11		
2008–09	Aston Villa	36	11		
2009–10	Aston Villa	36	13		
2010–11	Aston Villa	26	3		
2011–12	Aston Villa	33	5		
2012–13	Aston Villa	28	9		
2013–14	Aston Villa	30	4		
2014–15	Aston Villa	34	6		
2015–16	Aston Villa	15	1	322	73

AMAVI, Jordan (D)   65   4
H: 5 9   W: 11 00   b.Toulon 9-3-94
Internationals: France U18, U20, U21.

2013–14	Nice	19	0		
2014–15	Nice	36	4	55	4
2015–16	Aston Villa	10	0	10	0

AYEW, Jordan (F)   189   38
H: 6 0   W: 12 11   b.Marseille 11-9-91
Internationals: Ghana U20, Full caps.

2009–10	Marseille	4	1		
2010–11	Marseille	22	2		
2011–12	Marseille	34	3		
2012–13	Marseille	35	7		
2013–14	Marseille	16	1	111	14
2013–14	*Sochaux*	17	5	17	5
2014–15	Lorient	31	12	31	12
2015–16	Aston Villa	30	7	30	7

BACUNA, Leandro (M)   138   13
H: 6 2   W: 12 00   b.Groningen 21-8-91
Internationals: Netherlands U19, U21. Curaçao Full caps.

2009–10	FC Groningen	20	2		
2012–13	FC Groningen	33	5	53	7
2013–14	Aston Villa	35	5		
2014–15	Aston Villa	19	0		
2015–16	Aston Villa	31	1	85	6

BAKER, Nathan (D)   139   1
H: 6 2   W: 11 11   b.Worcester 23-4-91
Internationals: England U19, U20, U21.

2008–09	Aston Villa	0	0		
2009–10	Aston Villa	0	0		
2009–10	*Lincoln C*	18	0	18	0
2010–11	Aston Villa	4	0		
2011–12	Aston Villa	8	0		
2011–12	*Millwall*	6	0	6	0
2012–13	Aston Villa	26	0		
2013–14	Aston Villa	30	0		
2014–15	Aston Villa	11	0		
2015–16	Aston Villa	0	0	79	0
2015–16	*Bristol C*	36	1	36	1

BENNETT, Joe (D)   159   2
H: 5 10   W: 10 04   b.Rochdale 28-3-90
Internationals: England U19, U20, U21.

2008–09	Middlesbrough	1	0		
2009–10	Middlesbrough	12	0		
2010–11	Middlesbrough	31	0		
2011–12	Middlesbrough	41	1		
2012–13	Middlesbrough	0	0	85	1
2012–13	Aston Villa	25	0		
2013–14	Aston Villa	5	0		
2014–15	*Brighton & HA*	41	1	41	1
2015–16	Aston Villa	0	0	30	0

| 2015–16 | *Bournemouth* | 0 | 0 | | |
| 2015–16 | *Sheffield W* | 3 | 0 | 3 | 0 |

BUNN, Mark (G)   164   0
H: 6 0   W: 12 02   b.Southgate 16-11-84

2004–05	Northampton T	0	0		
2005–06	Northampton T	0	0		
2006–07	Northampton T	42	0		
2007–08	Northampton T	45	0		
2008–09	Northampton T	3	0	90	0
2008–09	*Blackburn R*	0	0		
2008–09	*Leicester C*	3	0	3	0
2009–10	Blackburn R	0	0		
2009–10	*Sheffield U*	32	0	32	0
2010–11	Blackburn R	3	0		
2011–12	Blackburn R	3	0		
2012–13	Blackburn R	0	0	6	0
2012–13	Norwich C	23	0		
2013–14	Norwich C	0	0		
2014–15	Norwich C	0	0	23	0
2015–16	Aston Villa	10	0	10	0

CALDER, Ricardo (M)   23   0
H: 6 0   W: 12 06   b.Birmingham 26-1-96
Internationals: England U17.

2013–14	Aston Villa	0	0		
2014–15	Aston Villa	0	0		
2015–16	Aston Villa	0	0		
2015–16	*Dundee*	11	0	11	0
2015–16	*Doncaster R*	12	0	12	0

CISSOKHO, Aly (D)   227   3
H: 5 11   W: 11 10   b.Blois 15-9-87
Internationals: France Full caps.

2006–07	Gueugnon	1	0		
2007–08	Gueugnon	21	0	22	0
2008–09	Vitoria Setubal	13	0	13	0
2008–09	Porto	15	0	15	0
2009–10	Lyon	30	0		
2010–11	Lyon	29	1		
2011–12	Lyon	31	0		
2012–13	Lyon	2	0	92	1
2012–13	Valencia	25	2		
2013–14	Valencia	0	0	25	2
2013–14	*Liverpool*	15	0	15	0
2014–15	Aston Villa	25	0		
2015–16	Aston Villa	18	0	43	0
2015–16	*FC Porto*	2	0	2	0

CLARK, Ciaran (D)   134   7
H: 6 2   W: 12 00   b.Harrow 26-9-89
Internationals: England U17, U18, U19, U20. Republic of Ireland Full caps.

2008–09	Aston Villa	0	0		
2009–10	Aston Villa	1	0		
2010–11	Aston Villa	19	3		
2011–12	Aston Villa	15	1		
2012–13	Aston Villa	29	1		
2013–14	Aston Villa	27	0		
2014–15	Aston Villa	25	1		
2015–16	Aston Villa	18	1	134	7

CRESPO, Jose Angel (D)   149   2
H: 6 0   W: 11 05   b.Sevilla 9-2-87
Internationals: Spain U19, U20, U21.

2005–06	Sevilla	3	0		
2006–07	Sevilla	0	0		
2007–08	Sevilla	13	0		
2008–09	Sevilla	9	0		
2009–10	Sevilla	0	0	25	0
2009–10	*Racing Santander*	13	0	13	0
2010–11	*Padova*	43	1	43	1
2011–12	Bologna	7	0		
2012–13	Bologna	0	0		
2012–13	*Hellas Verona*	14	0	14	0
2013–14	Bologna	10	1		
2014–15	Bologna	0	0	17	1
2014–15	*Cordoba*	27	0	27	0
2015–16	Aston Villa	1	0	1	0
2015–16	*Rayo Vallecano*	9	0	9	0

DAVIS, Keinan (M)   0   0
H: 5 6   W: 10 10   b. 13-2-98

| 2015–16 | Aston Villa | 0 | 0 | | |

DONACIEN, Janoi (D)   62   0
H: 6 0   W: 11 11   b.St Lucia 3-11-93
Internationals: St Lucia Full caps.

2011–12	Aston Villa	0	0		
2012–13	Aston Villa	0	0		
2013–14	Aston Villa	0	0		
2014–15	Aston Villa	0	0		
2014–15	*Tranmere R*	31	0	31	0
2015–16	Aston Villa	0	0		
2015–16	*Wycombe W*	2	0	2	0
2015–16	*Newport Co*	29	0	29	0

GANA, Idrissa (M)   169   5
H: 5 9   W: 11 05   b.Dakar 26-9-89
Internationals: Senegal Full caps.

Season	Club				
2010–11	Lille	11	0		
2011–12	Lille	25	0		
2012–13	Lille	29	0		
2013–14	Lille	37	1		
2014–15	Lille	32	4	134	5
2015–16	Aston Villa	35	0	35	0

GARDNER, Gary (M)   78   9
H: 6 2   W: 12 13   b.Solihull 29-6-92
Internationals: England U17, U19, U20, U21.

Season	Club				
2009–10	Aston Villa	0	0		
2010–11	Aston Villa	0	0		
2011–12	Aston Villa	14	0		
2011–12	Coventry C	4	1	4	1
2012–13	Aston Villa	2	0		
2013–14	Aston Villa	0	0		
2013–14	Sheffield W	3	0	3	0
2014–15	Aston Villa	0	0		
2014–15	Brighton & HA	17	2	17	2
2014–15	Nottingham F	18	4		
2015–16	Aston Villa	0	0	16	0
2015–16	Nottingham F	20	2	38	6

GESTEDE, Rudy (F)   194   53
H: 6 4   W: 13 07   b.Nancy 10-10-88
Internationals: France U19. Benin Full caps.

Season	Club				
2008–09	Metz	2	0		
2009–10	Cannes	22	4	22	4
2010–11	Metz	11	3	16	3
2010–11	Metz B	3	1	3	1
2011–12	Cardiff C	25	2		
2012–13	Cardiff C	27	5		
2013–14	Cardiff C	3	0	55	7
2013–14	Blackburn R	27	13		
2014–15	Blackburn R	39	20	66	33
2015–16	Aston Villa	32	5	32	5

GIL, Carles (M)   100   8
H: 5 7   W: 10 03   b.Valencia 2-11-92
Internationals: Spain U21.

Season	Club				
2012–13	Elche	31	4		
2013–14	Elche	33	1	64	5
2014–15	Valencia	8	1	8	1
2014–15	Aston Villa	5	0		
2015–16	Aston Villa	23	2	28	2

GREALISH, Jack (M)   71   6
H: 5 9   W: 10 10   b.Birmingham 10-9-95
Internationals: Republic of Ireland U17, U18, U21. England U21.

Season	Club				
2012–13	Aston Villa	0	0		
2013–14	Aston Villa	0	0		
2013–14	Notts Co	37	5	37	5
2014–15	Aston Villa	17	0		
2015–16	Aston Villa	16	1	34	1

GREEN, Andre (F)   2   0
H: 5 11   W: 11 03   b.Solihull 2-5-98
Internationals: England U17.

Season	Club				
2014–15	Aston Villa	0	0		
2015–16	Aston Villa	2	0	2	0

GUZAN, Brad (G)   239   0
H: 6 4   W: 14 11   b.Chicago 9-9-84
Internationals: USA U23, Full caps.

Season	Club				
2005	Chivas USA	24	0		
2006	Chivas USA	13	0		
2007	Chivas USA	27	0		
2008	Chivas USA	15	0	79	0
2008–09	Aston Villa	1	0		
2009–10	Aston Villa	0	0		
2010–11	Aston Villa	0	0		
2010–11	Hull C	16	0	16	0
2011–12	Aston Villa	7	0		
2012–13	Aston Villa	36	0		
2013–14	Aston Villa	34	0		
2014–15	Aston Villa	34	0		
2015–16	Aston Villa	33	0	144	0

HEPBURN-MURPHY, Rushian (F)   2   0
H: 5 8   W: 9 04   b.Birmingham 19-9-98
Internationals: England U16, U17.

Season	Club				
2014–15	Aston Villa	1	0		
2015–16	Aston Villa	1	0	2	0

HUTTON, Alan (D)   266   4
H: 6 1   W: 11 05   b.Glasgow 30-11-84
Internationals: Scotland U21, Full caps.

Season	Club				
2004–05	Rangers	10	0		
2005–06	Rangers	19	0		
2006–07	Rangers	33	1		
2007–08	Rangers	20	0	82	1
2007–08	Tottenham H	14	0		
2008–09	Tottenham H	8	0		
2009–10	Tottenham H	8	0		
2009–10	Sunderland	11	0	11	0
2010–11	Tottenham H	21	2		

KOZAK, Libor (F)   100   18
H: 6 4   W: 12 11   b.Brumov-Bylnice 30-5-89
Internationals: Czech Republic U19, U21, Full caps.

Season	Club				
2008–09	Lazio	3	0		
2009–10	Brescia	25	4	25	4
2010–11	Lazio	19	6		
2011–12	Lazio	16	4		
2012–13	Lazio	19	0	57	10
2013–14	Aston Villa	14	4		
2014–15	Aston Villa	0	0		
2015–16	Aston Villa	4	0	18	4

LESCOTT, Joleon (D)   498   36
H: 6 2   W: 13 00   b.Birmingham 16-8-82
Internationals: England U17, U18, U20, U21, B, Full caps.

Season	Club				
1999–2000	Wolverhampton W	0	0		
2000–01	Wolverhampton W	37	2		
2001–02	Wolverhampton W	44	5		
2002–03	Wolverhampton W	44	1		
2003–04	Wolverhampton W	0	0		
2004–05	Wolverhampton W	41	4		
2005–06	Wolverhampton W	46	1	212	13
2006–07	Everton	38	2		
2007–08	Everton	38	8		
2008–09	Everton	36	4		
2009–10	Everton	1	0	113	14
2009–10	Manchester C	18	1		
2010–11	Manchester C	22	3		
2011–12	Manchester C	31	2		
2012–13	Manchester C	26	1		
2013–14	Manchester C	10	0	107	7
2014–15	WBA	34	1		
2015–16	WBA	2	0	36	1
2015–16	Aston Villa	30	1	30	1

LYDEN, Jordan (M)   4   0
H: 5 10   W: 11 00   b.Perth 30-1-96
Internationals: Australia U20.

Season	Club				
2015–16	Aston Villa	4	0	4	0

MASON, Niall (M)   0   0
b. 10-1-97

Season	Club				
2015–16	Aston Villa	0	0		

N'ZOGBIA, Charles (M)   280   28
H: 5 9   W: 11 00   b.Le Havre 28-5-86
Internationals: France U21, Full caps.

Season	Club				
2004–05	Newcastle U	14	0		
2005–06	Newcastle U	32	5		
2006–07	Newcastle U	22	0		
2007–08	Newcastle U	31	3		
2008–09	Newcastle U	18	1	117	9
2008–09	Wigan Ath	13	1		
2009–10	Wigan Ath	36	5		
2010–11	Wigan Ath	34	9	83	15
2011–12	Aston Villa	30	2		
2012–13	Aston Villa	21	2		
2013–14	Aston Villa	0	0		
2014–15	Aston Villa	27	0		
2015–16	Aston Villa	2	0	80	4

OKORE, Jores (D)   103   6
H: 6 0   W: 12 07   b.Abidjan 11-8-92
Internationals: Denmark U21, Full caps.

Season	Club				
2010–11	Nordsjaelland	11	0		
2011–12	Nordsjaelland	25	1		
2012–13	Nordsjaelland	29	4	65	5
2013–14	Aston Villa	3	0		
2014–15	Aston Villa	23	1		
2015–16	Aston Villa	12	0	38	1

RICHARDS, Micah (D)   213   8
H: 5 11   W: 13 00   b.Birmingham 24-6-88
Internationals: England U16, U19, U21, Full caps. Great Britain.

Season	Club				
2005–06	Manchester C	13	0		
2006–07	Manchester C	28	1		
2007–08	Manchester C	25	0		
2008–09	Manchester C	30	0		
2009–10	Manchester C	23	3		
2010–11	Manchester C	18	1		
2011–12	Manchester C	29	1		
2012–13	Manchester C	7	0		
2013–14	Manchester C	2	0		
2014–15	Manchester C	0	0	179	7
2014–15	Fiorentina	10	0	10	0
2015–16	Aston Villa	24	1	24	1

RICHARDSON, Kieran (M)   265   24
H: 5 9   W: 11 13   b.Greenwich 21-10-84
Internationals: England U18, U21, Full caps.

Season	Club				
2002–03	Manchester U	2	0		
2003–04	Manchester U	2	0		
2004–05	Manchester U	0	0		
2004–05	WBA	12	3	12	3
2005–06	Manchester U	22	1		
2006–07	Manchester U	15	1	41	2
2007–08	Sunderland	17	3		
2008–09	Sunderland	32	4		
2009–10	Sunderland	29	1		
2010–11	Sunderland	26	4		
2011–12	Sunderland	29	2		
2012–13	Sunderland	1	0	134	14
2012–13	Fulham	14	1		
2013–14	Fulham	31	4	45	5
2014–15	Aston Villa	22	0		
2015–16	Aston Villa	11	0	33	0

ROBINSON, Callum (F)   49   6
H: 5 10   W: 11 11   b.Birmingham 2-2-95
Internationals: England U16, U17, U19, U20.

Season	Club				
2013–14	Aston Villa	4	0		
2014–15	Aston Villa	0	0		
2014–15	Preston NE	25	4		
2015–16	Aston Villa	0	0	4	0
2015–16	Bristol C	6	0	6	0
2015–16	Preston NE	14	2	39	6

SANCHEZ, Carlos (M)   293   13
H: 6 0   W: 12 08   b.Quidbo 6-2-86
Internationals: Colombia Full caps.

Season	Club				
2005–06	River Plate	14	0		
2006–07	River Plate	26	1	40	1
2007–08	Valenciennes	34	0		
2008–09	Valenciennes	37	1		
2009–10	Valenciennes	28	5		
2010–11	Valenciennes	28	2		
2011–12	Valenciennes	21	1		
2012–13	Valenciennes	27	2	175	11
2013–14	Elche	30	0	30	0
2014–15	Aston Villa	28	1		
2015–16	Aston Villa	20	0	48	1

SARKIC, Matija (G)   0   0
b. 23-6-97
Internationals: Montenegro U19.

Season	Club				
2014–15	Anderlecht	0	0		
2015–16	Aston Villa	0	0		

SENDEROS, Philippe (D)   193   9
H: 6 1   W: 13 10   b.Geneva 14-2-85
Internationals: Switzerland U20, U21, Full caps.

Season	Club				
2001–02	Servette	3	0		
2002–03	Servette	23	3	26	3
2003–04	Arsenal	0	0		
2004–05	Arsenal	13	0		
2005–06	Arsenal	20	2		
2006–07	Arsenal	14	0		
2007–08	Arsenal	17	2		
2008–09	Arsenal	0	0		
2008–09	AC Milan	14	0	14	0
2009–10	Arsenal	0	0	64	4
2009–10	Everton	2	0	2	0
2010–11	Fulham	3	0		
2011–12	Fulham	21	1		
2012–13	Fulham	21	0		
2013–14	Fulham	12	1	57	2
2013–14	Valencia	8	0	8	0
2014–15	Aston Villa	8	0		
2015–16	Aston Villa	0	0	8	0
2015–16	Grasshoppers	14	0	14	0

SIEGRIST, Benjamin (G)   1   0
H: 6 4   W: 13 05   b.Basle 31-1-92
Internationals: Switzerland U17, U18, U19, U21.

Season	Club				
2008–09	Aston Villa	0	0		
2009–10	Aston Villa	0	0		
2010–11	Aston Villa	0	0		
2011–12	Aston Villa	0	0		
2012–13	Aston Villa	0	0		
2013–14	Aston Villa	0	0		
2013–14	Burton Alb	0	0		
2014–15	Aston Villa	0	0		
2014–15	Cambridge U	0	0		
2015–16	Aston Villa	0	0		
2015–16	Wycombe W	1	0	1	0

SINCLAIR, Scott (F)   211   37
H: 5 10   W: 10 00   b.Bath 26-3-89
Internationals: England U17, U18, U19, U20, U21. Great Britain.

Season	Club				
2004–05	Bristol R	2	0	2	0
2005–06	Chelsea	0	0		
2006–07	Chelsea	2	0		
2006–07	Plymouth Arg	15	2	15	2

TOTTENHAM H (top of column 2)

Season	Club				
2011–12	Tottenham H	0	0	51	2
2011–12	Aston Villa	31	0		
2012–13	Aston Villa	0	0		
2012–13	Nottingham F	7	0	7	0
2012–13	Mallorca	17	0	17	0
2013–14	Aston Villa	0	0		
2013–14	Bolton W	9	0	9	0
2014–15	Aston Villa	30	1		
2015–16	Aston Villa	28	0	89	1

2007–08	Chelsea	1	0		
2007–08	*QPR*	9	1	**9**	**1**
2007–08	*Charlton Ath*	3	0	**3**	**0**
2007–08	*Crystal Palace*	6	2	**6**	**2**
2008–09	Chelsea	2	0		
2008–09	*Birmingham C*	14	0	**14**	**0**
2009–10	Chelsea	0	0	**5**	**0**
2009–10	*Wigan Ath*	18	1	**18**	**1**
2010–11	Swansea C	43	19		
2011–12	Swansea C	38	8		
2012–13	Swansea C	1	1	**82**	**28**
2012–13	Manchester C	11	0		
2013–14	Manchester C	0	0		
2013–14	WBA	8	0	**8**	**0**
2014–15	Manchester C	2	0	**13**	**0**
2014–15	*Aston Villa*	9	1		
2015–16	Aston Villa	27	2	**36**	**3**

STEER, Jed (G)   **76 0**
H: 6 2   W: 14 00   b.Norwich 23-9-92
Internationals: England U16, U17, U19.

2009–10	Norwich C	0	0
2010–11	Norwich C	0	0
2011–12	Norwich C	0	0
2011–12	*Yeovil T*	12	0
2012–13	Cambridge U	0	0
2012–13	Norwich C	0	0
2013–14	Aston Villa	1	0
2014–15	Aston Villa	1	0
2014–15	*Doncaster R*	13	0	**13**	**0**
2014–15	*Yeovil T*	12	0	**24**	**0**
2015–16	Aston Villa	0	0	**1**	**0**
2015–16	*Huddersfield T*	38	0	**38**	**0**

SULIMAN, Easah (D)   **0 0**
b. 26-1-98
Internationals: England U16, U17, U18.

2015–16	Aston Villa	0	0

TAYLOR, Corey (F)   **0 0**
b. 23-9-97
Internationals: England U17.

2015–16	Aston Villa	0	0

TONER, Kevin (D)   **4 0**
b. 18-7-96
Internationals: Republic of Ireland U19.

2015–16	Aston Villa	4	0	**4**	**0**

TRAORE, Adama (F)   **11 0**
H: 5 10   W: 12 00   b.L'Hospitalet de
Llobregat 25-1-96
Internationals: Spain U16, U17, U19.

2013–14	Barcelona	1	0		
2014–15	Barcelona	0	0	**1**	**0**
2015–16	Aston Villa	10	0	**10**	**0**

VERETOUT, Jordan (M)   **155 14**
H: 5 9   W: 10 06   b.Ancenis 1-3-93
Internationals: France U18, U19, U20, U21.

2010–11	Nantes	0	0		
2011–12	Nantes	35	6		
2012–13	Nantes	31	0		
2013–14	Nantes	27	1		
2014–15	Nantes	36	7	**130**	**14**
2015–16	Aston Villa	25	0	**25**	**0**

WESTWOOD, Ashley (M)   **252 19**
H: 5 10   W: 11 00   b.Nantwich 1-4-90

2008–09	Crewe Alex	2	0		
2009–10	Crewe Alex	36	6		
2010–11	Crewe Alex	46	5		
2011–12	Crewe Alex	41	3		
2012–13	Crewe Alex	3	0	**128**	**14**
2012–13	Aston Villa	30	0		
2013–14	Aston Villa	35	3		
2014–15	Aston Villa	27	0		
2015–16	Aston Villa	32	2	**124**	**5**

Players retained or with offer of contract
Abdo, Khalid; Abdoul, Johan; Blackett-
Taylor, Corey; Borg, Oscar Francis; Cowans,
Henry Gordon Mander; Hale, Rory Danny;
Johansson, Viktor Tobias; Leggett, Thomas
Jacob; McKirdy, Harry; O'Hare, Callum;
Omerovic, Anes; Sellars, Jerell; Sundman,
Joonas Sebastian; Swift, Benjamin George;
Watkins, Bradley.

Scholars
Clark, Mitchell; Clarke, Jack Aidan; Coates,
Jack Lewis; Cox, Jordan Raymond; Doyle
Hayes, Jake Billy; Finnerty, James John; Hall,
Louis Aiden; Humphries, Jake Raymond;
Idem, Emmanuel Okokon; Knibbs, Harvey;
Linley, Joseph; Mooney, Kelsey; Pastorek,
Jozef; Prosser, Alexander.

BARNET (5)

AKINDE, John (F)   **148 35**
H: 6 2   W: 10 01   b.Camberwell 8-7-89

2008–09	Bristol C	7	1		
2008–09	*Wycombe W*	11	7		
2009–10	Bristol C	7	0		
2009–10	*Wycombe W*	6	1	**17**	**8**
2009–10	*Brentford*	2	0	**2**	**0**
2010–11	Bristol C	2	0	**16**	**1**
2010–11	*Bristol R*	14	0	**14**	**0**
2010–11	*Dagenham & R*	9	2		
2011–12	Crawley T	25	1		
2011–12	*Dagenham & R*	5	0	**14**	**2**
2012–13	Crawley T	6	0	**31**	**1**
2012–13	Portsmouth	11	0		
2013–14	Portsmouth	0	0	**11**	**0**
2015–16	Barnet	43	23	**43**	**23**

BAILEY, Nicky (M)   **358 51**
H: 5 10   W: 12 06   b.Hammersmith 10-6-84
Internationals: England C.

2005–06	Barnet	45	7		
2006–07	Barnet	44	5		
2007–08	Southend U	44	9		
2008–09	Southend U	1	0	**45**	**9**
2008–09	Charlton Ath	43	13		
2009–10	Charlton Ath	44	12	**87**	**25**
2010–11	Middlesbrough	34	0		
2011–12	Middlesbrough	37	2		
2012–13	Middlesbrough	28	2	**99**	**4**
2013–14	Millwall	28	1		
2014–15	Millwall	8	0	**36**	**1**
2015–16	Barnet	2	0	**91**	**12**

BATT, Shaun (M)   **169 15**
H: 6 3   W: 12 08   b.Harlow 22-2-87

2008–09	Peterborough U	30	2		
2009–10	Peterborough U	20	2	**50**	**4**
2009–10	*Millwall*	16	3		
2010–11	Millwall	0	0		
2011–12	Millwall	4	0		
2011–12	*Crawley T*	5	0	**5**	**0**
2012–13	Millwall	16	1		
2012–13	Leyton Orient	11	2		
2013–14	Millwall	35	4	**36**	**4**
2013–14	Leyton Orient	16	1	**62**	**7**
2015–16	Barnet	16	0	**16**	**0**

CHAMPION, Tom (M)   **64 0**
b.London 15-5-86

2014–15	Cambridge U	38	0	**38**	**0**
2015–16	Barnet	26	0	**26**	**0**

COJOCAREL, Shane (M)   **0 0**
b. 20-3-97

2015–16	Barnet	0	0

CONSTABLE, Raven (G)   **0 0**
b. 1-9-94

2015–16	Barnet	0	0

DAY, Thomas (D)   **1 0**
b. 24-10-97

2015–16	Barnet	1	0	**1**	**0**

DEMBELE, Bira (D)   **108 7**
H: 6 2   W: 11 10   b. 22-3-88
Internationals: France U21.

2007–08	Rennes	7	0		
2008–09	Rennes	2	0		
2009–10	Rennes	0	0		
2009–10	*Boulogne*	23	1	**23**	**1**
2010–11	Rennes	0	0	**9**	**0**
2011–12	Sedan	1	0		
2011–12	*Red Star 93*	9	0	**9**	**0**
2012–13	Sedan	0	0	**1**	**0**
2013–14	Stevenage	13	1		
2014–15	Stevenage	27	2	**40**	**3**
2015–16	Barnet	26	3	**26**	**3**

FONGUCK, Wesley (M)   **1 0**
b. 16-7-97

2015–16	Barnet	1	0	**1**	**0**

GAMBIN, Luke (M)   **55 6**
H: 5 6   W: 11 00   b.Surrey 16-3-93
Internationals: Malta Full caps.

2011–12	Barnet	1	0		
2012–13	Barnet	10	2		
2015–16	Barnet	44	4	**55**	**6**

GASH, Michael (F)   **34 9**
H: 5 10   W: 12 02   b.Cambridge 3-9-86
From Cambridge C, Cambridge U,
Ebbsfleet U, York C, Kidderminster H.

2015–16	Barnet	34	9	**34**	**9**

GONDOH, Ryan (F)   **0 0**
b. 6-6-97

2015–16	Barnet	0	0

HOYTE, Gavin (D)   **158 1**
H: 5 11   W: 11 00   b.Waltham Forest 6-6-90
Internationals: England U17, U18, U19, U20.
Trinidad & Tobago Full caps.

2007–08	Arsenal	0	0		
2008–09	Arsenal	1	0		
2008–09	*Watford*	7	0	**7**	**0**
2009–10	Arsenal	0	0		
2009–10	*Brighton & HA*	18	0	**18**	**0**
2010–11	Arsenal	0	0		
2010–11	*Lincoln C*	12	0	**12**	**0**
2011–12	Arsenal	0	0	**1**	**0**
2011–12	*AFC Wimbledon*	3	0	**3**	**0**
2012–13	Dagenham & R	26	0		
2013–14	Dagenham & R	42	0	**68**	**0**
2014–15	Gillingham	30	0	**30**	**0**
2015–16	Barnet	19	1	**19**	**1**

JOHNSON, Elliot (D)   **67 2**
H: 5 10   W: 12 02   b.Edgeware 17-8-94

2012–13	Barnet	26	1		
2015–16	Barnet	41	1	**67**	**2**

KYEI, Nana (M)   **1 0**
b. 10-1-98

2015–16	Barnet	1	0	**1**	**0**

LISBIE, Kevin (F)   **440 108**
H: 5 10   W: 11 06   b.Hackney 17-10-78
Internationals: England Youth. Jamaica Full
caps.

1996–97	Charlton Ath	25	1		
1997–98	Charlton Ath	17	1		
1998–99	Charlton Ath	1	0		
1998–99	*Gillingham*	7	4	**7**	**4**
1999–2000	Charlton Ath	0	0		
1999–2000	*Reading*	2	0	**2**	**0**
2000–01	Charlton Ath	18	0		
2000–01	*QPR*	2	0	**2**	**0**
2001–02	Charlton Ath	22	5		
2002–03	Charlton Ath	32	4		
2003–04	Charlton Ath	9	4		
2004–05	Charlton Ath	17	1		
2005–06	Charlton Ath	6	0		
2005–06	*Norwich C*	6	1	**6**	**1**
2005–06	*Derby Co*	7	1	**7**	**1**
2006–07	Charlton Ath	8	0	**155**	**16**
2007–08	Colchester U	42	17		
2008–09	Ipswich T	41	6		
2009–10	Ipswich T	0	0		
2009–10	*Colchester U*	41	13	**83**	**30**
2010–11	Ipswich T	0	0	**41**	**6**
2010–11	Millwall	20	4	**20**	**4**
2011–12	Leyton Orient	37	12		
2012–13	Leyton Orient	28	16		
2013–14	Leyton Orient	39	16		
2014–15	Leyton Orient	7	2	**111**	**46**
2014–15	*Stevenage*	3	0	**3**	**0**
2015–16	Barnet	3	0	**3**	**0**

McKENZIE-LYLE, Kai (G)   **1 0**
H: 6 5   W: 13 08   b. 30-11-97

2015–16	Barnet	1	0	**1**	**0**

McLEAN, Aaron (F)   **359 95**
H: 5 9   W: 10 10   b.Hammersmith 25-5-83
Internationals: England C.

1999–2000	Leyton Orient	3	0		
2000–01	Leyton Orient	2	1		
2001–02	Leyton Orient	27	1		
2002–03	Leyton Orient	8	0	**40**	**2**
	From Aldershot T, Grays Ath.				
2006–07	Peterborough U	16	7		
2007–08	Peterborough U	45	29		
2008–09	Peterborough U	42	18		
2009–10	Peterborough U	35	7		
2010–11	Peterborough U	19	10		
2010–11	Hull C	23	3		
2011–12	Hull C	39	5		
2012–13	Hull C	14	1		
2012–13	*Ipswich T*	7	1	**7**	**1**
2013–14	Hull C	1	0	**77**	**9**
2013–14	*Birmingham C*	7	0	**7**	**0**
2013–14	Bradford C	20	4		
2014–15	Bradford C	13	2	**33**	**6**
2014–15	*Peterborough U*	18	1	**175**	**72**
2015–16	Barnet	20	5	**20**	**5**

MUGGLETON, Sam (D)   **25 0**
H: 5 11   W: 11 03   b.Melton Mowbray
17-11-95

2012–13	Gillingham	1	0		
2013–14	Gillingham	1	0	**2**	**0**
2015–16	Barnet	23	0	**23**	**0**

N'GALA, Bondz (D) 171 7
H: 6 0 W: 12 03 b.Forest Gate 13-9-89

2007–08	West Ham U	0	0	
2008–09	West Ham U	0	0	
2008–09	Milton Keynes D	3	0	3 0
2009–10	West Ham U	0	0	
2009–10	Scunthorpe U	2	0	2 0
2009–10	Plymouth Arg	9	0	
2010–11	Plymouth Arg	26	1	35 1
2011–12	Yeovil T	31	2	31 2
2012–13	Stevenage	25	0	25 0
2012–13	Barnet	6	0	
2013–14	Portsmouth	27	3	27 3
2015–16	Barnet	42	1	48 1

NELSON, Michael (D) 545 36
H: 6 2 W: 13 03 b.Gateshead 15-3-82

2000–01	Bury	2	1	
2001–02	Bury	31	2	
2002–03	Bury	39	5	72 8
2003–04	Hartlepool U	40	3	
2004–05	Hartlepool U	43	1	
2005–06	Hartlepool U	43	2	
2006–07	Hartlepool U	42	1	
2007–08	Hartlepool U	45	2	
2008–09	Hartlepool U	46	5	259 14
2009–10	Norwich C	31	3	
2010–11	Norwich C	8	2	39 5
2010–11	Scunthorpe U	20	0	
2011–12	Scunthorpe U	10	1	30 1
2011–12	Kilmarnock	15	1	
2012–13	Kilmarnock	21	1	36 2
2012–13	Bradford C	13	0	13 0
2013–14	Hibernian	34	2	
2014–15	Hibernian	2	0	36 2
2014–15	Cambridge U	33	3	33 3
2015–16	Barnet	27	1	27 1

NURSE, Jon (M) 205 30
H: 5 9 W: 12 04 b.Barbados 1-3-81
Internationals: Barbados Full caps.

2007–08	Dagenham & R	30	1	
2008–09	Dagenham & R	34	4	
2009–10	Dagenham & R	38	7	
2010–11	Dagenham & R	38	10	
2011–12	Dagenham & R	39	5	179 27
2012–13	Barnet	26	3	
2015–16	Barnet	0	0	26 3

NWOGU, Justin (M) 4 0
b. 17-10-96

2015–16	Barnet	4	0	4 0

PEARSON, James (D) 18 0
H: 6 1 W: 11 11 b.Sheffield 19-1-93

2013–14	Leicester C	0	0	
2013–14	Carlisle U	3	0	3 0
2014–15	Leicester C	0	0	
2014–15	Peterborough U	0	0	
2015–16	Barnet	15	0	15 0

RANDALL, Mark (M) 108 5
H: 6 0 W: 12 12 b.Milton Keynes 28-9-89
Internationals: England U17, U18.

2006–07	Arsenal	0	0	
2007–08	Arsenal	1	0	
2007–08	Burnley	10	0	10 0
2008–09	Arsenal	1	0	
2009–10	Arsenal	0	0	
2009–10	Milton Keynes D	16	0	
2010–11	Arsenal	0	0	2 0
2010–11	Rotherham U	10	1	10 1
2011–12	Chesterfield	16	1	
2012–13	Chesterfield	29	1	
2013–14	Chesterfield	0	0	45 2
2013–14	Milton Keynes D	4	0	
2014–15	Milton Keynes D	9	0	
2015–16	Milton Keynes D	0	0	29 0
2015–16	Barnet	12	2	12 2

SESAY, Alie (D) 21 0
b. 25-7-93
Internationals: Sierra Leone Full caps.

2013–14	Leicester C	0	0	
2013–14	Colchester U	3	0	
2014–15	Colchester U	0	0	3 0
2015–16	Leicester C	0	0	
2015–16	Cambridge U	5	0	5 0
2015–16	Barnet	13	0	13 0

SHOMOTUN, Fumnaya (M) 10 1
b. 29-5-97

2015–16	Barnet	10	1	10 1

STACK, Graham (G) 151 0
H: 6 2 W: 12 06 b.Hampstead 26-9-81
Internationals: Republic of Ireland U21.

2004–05	Arsenal	0	0	
2004–05	Millwall	26	0	26 0
2005–06	Reading	1	0	
2006–07	Reading	0	0	
2006–07	Leeds U	12	0	12 0
2007–08	Reading	0	0	1 0
2007–08	Wolverhampton W	2	0	2 0
2008–09	Plymouth Arg	5	0	5 0
2009–10	Hibernian	20	0	
2010–11	Hibernian	6	0	
2011–12	Hibernian	30	0	56 0
2012–13	Barnet	42	0	
2015–16	Barnet	7	0	49 0

STEPHENS, Jamie (G) 51 0
b.Wotton 24-8-93

2012–13	Liverpool	0	0	
2012–13	Airbus UK	13	0	13 0
2013–14	Newport Co	2	0	
2014–15	Newport Co	7	0	9 0
2015–16	Barnet	29	0	29 0

STEVENS, Mathew (F) 10 1
H: 5 11 W: 11 09 b. 12-2-98

2015–16	Barnet	10	1	10 1

TAYLOR, Harry (D) 8 0
H: 6 2 b. 4-5-97

2015–16	Barnet	8	0	8 0

TOGWELL, Sam (M) 360 13
H: 5 11 W: 12 04 b.Beaconsfield 14-10-84

2002–03	Crystal Palace	1	0	
2003–04	Crystal Palace	0	0	
2004–05	Crystal Palace	0	0	
2004–05	Oxford U	4	0	4 0
2004–05	Northampton T	8	0	8 0
2005–06	Crystal Palace	0	0	
2005–06	Port Vale	27	2	27 2
2006–07	Barnsley	44	1	
2007–08	Barnsley	22	1	66 2
2008–09	Scunthorpe U	40	2	
2009–10	Scunthorpe U	41	2	
2010–11	Scunthorpe U	36	0	
2011–12	Scunthorpe U	39	1	156 5
2012–13	Chesterfield	45	3	
2013–14	Chesterfield	10	0	55 3
2013–14	Wycombe W	4	0	4 0
2015–16	Barnet	39	1	39 1

TOMLINSON, Ben (F) 28 6
H: 5 8 W: 11 11 b.Dinnington 11-9-90
From Worksop T.

2011–12	Macclesfield T	25	6	25 6

From Alfreton T, Lincoln C.

2015–16	Barnet	3	0	3 0

VILHETE, Mauro (M) 45 0
H: 5 8 W: 11 09 b.Sintra 10-5-93

2009–10	Barnet	2	0	
2010–11	Barnet	20	0	
2011–12	Barnet	3	0	
2012–13	Barnet	5	0	
2015–16	Barnet	15	0	45 0

WESTON, Curtis (M) 258 20
H: 5 11 W: 11 09 b.Greenwich 24-1-87

2003–04	Millwall	1	0	
2004–05	Millwall	3	0	
2005–06	Millwall	0	0	4 0
2006–07	Swindon T	27	1	27 1
2007–08	Leeds U	7	1	
2007–08	Scunthorpe U	7	0	7 0
2008–09	Leeds U	0	0	7 1
2008–09	Gillingham	45	5	
2009–10	Gillingham	39	6	
2010–11	Gillingham	33	4	
2011–12	Gillingham	30	0	147 15
2012–13	Barnet	29	0	
2015–16	Barnet	37	3	66 3

YIADOM, Andy (M) 86 10
H: 5 11 W: 11 11 b.Camden 9-12-91
Internationals: England C.

2011–12	Barnet	7	0	
2012–13	Barnet	39	3	
2015–16	Barnet	40	6	86 10

Players retained or with offer of contract
Taylor, Harry William.

Scholars
Booker, George Charles; Cheema, Daniel Singh; Lawton, Carlito; Leong, Louie; Mason-Clark, Ephron Jardell; McKenzie-Lyle, Kai; Ocran, Brendan; Payne, Joseph William; Smith, Darnell Tyrick; Stevens, Matthew.

BARNSLEY (6)

ABBOTT, Brad (M) 5 0
H: 5 11 W: 12 04 b. 24-12-94

2013–14	Barnsley	0	0	
2014–15	Barnsley	5	0	
2015–16	Barnsley	0	0	5 0

BREE, James (D) 31 0
H: 5 10 W: 11 09 b.Wakefield 11-10-97

2013–14	Barnsley	1	0	
2014–15	Barnsley	11	0	
2015–16	Barnsley	19	0	31 0

BROWN, Jacob (M) 0 0

2014–15	Barnsley	0	0	
2015–16	Barnsley	0	0	

COWGILL, Jack (D) 2 0
H: 6 1 W: 13 05 b.Wakefield 8-1-97

2013–14	Barnsley	0	0	
2014–15	Barnsley	2	0	
2015–16	Barnsley	0	0	2 0

DAVIES, Adam (G) 61 0
H: 6 1 W: 11 11 b.Rinteln 17-7-92

2009–10	Everton	0	0	
2010–11	Everton	0	0	
2011–12	Everton	0	0	
2013–14	Sheffield W	0	0	
2014–15	Barnsley	23	0	
2015–16	Barnsley	38	0	61 0

DIGBY, Paul (M) 25 0
H: 5 9 W: 10 00 b.Sheffield 2-2-95
Internationals: England U19, U20.

2011–12	Barnsley	4	0	
2012–13	Barnsley	0	0	
2013–14	Barnsley	5	0	
2014–15	Barnsley	11	0	
2015–16	Barnsley	1	0	21 0
2015–16	Ipswich T	4	0	4 0

DRENNAN, Ben (M) 0 0
H: 5 7 W: 10 06 b.Sunderland 14-1-97
Internationals: England U17.

2015–16	Barnsley	0	0	

EVANS, Callum (D) 0 0
b. 11-10-95
From Manchester U.

2015–16	Barnsley	0	0	

HAMMILL, Adam (M) 276 25
H: 5 11 W: 11 07 b.Liverpool 25-1-88
Internationals: England U19, U21.

2005–06	Liverpool	0	0	
2006–07	Liverpool	0	0	
2006–07	Dunfermline Ath	13	1	13 1
2007–08	Liverpool	0	0	
2007–08	Southampton	25	0	25 0
2008–09	Liverpool	0	0	
2008–09	Blackpool	22	1	22 1
2008–09	Barnsley	14	1	
2009–10	Barnsley	39	4	
2010–11	Barnsley	25	8	
2010–11	Wolverhampton W	10	0	
2011–12	Wolverhampton W	9	0	
2011–12	Middlesbrough	10	0	10 0
2012–13	Wolverhampton W	4	0	23 0
2012–13	Huddersfield T	16	2	
2013–14	Huddersfield T	44	4	
2014–15	Huddersfield T	5	0	
2014–15	Rotherham U	14	0	14 0
2015–16	Huddersfield T	1	0	66 6
2015–16	Barnsley	25	4	103 17

HARRIS, Charlie (M) 0 0
b. 30-1-96

2014–15	Brighton & HA	0	0	
2015–16	Brighton & HA	0	0	
2015–16	Barnsley	0	0	

HOURIHANE, Conor (M) 212 38
H: 5 11 W: 9 11 b.Cork 2-2-91
Internationals: Republic of Ireland U19, U21.

2008–09	Sunderland	0	0	
2009–10	Sunderland	0	0	
2010–11	Ipswich T	0	0	
2011–12	Plymouth Arg	38	2	
2012–13	Plymouth Arg	42	5	
2013–14	Plymouth Arg	45	8	125 15
2014–15	Barnsley	46	13	
2015–16	Barnsley	41	10	87 23

KAY, Josh (M) 0 0
From AFC Fylde.

2015–16	Barnsley	0	0	

KHAN, Otis (M) 5 0
H: 5 9 W: 11 03 b.Ashton-under-Lyme 5-9-95

2013–14	Sheffield U	2	0	
2014–15	Sheffield U	0	0	
2015–16	Sheffield U	0	0	2 0
2015–16	Barnsley	3	0	3 0

MARIS, George (F) 3 0
b.Sheffield 6-3-96
2014–15 Barnsley 2 0
2015–16 Barnsley 1 0 **3 0**

MAWSON, Alfie (D) 90 12
H: 5 8 W: 12 11 b.Hillingdon 19-1-94
2012–13 Brentford 0 0
2013–14 Brentford 0 0
2014–15 Brentford 0 0
2014–15 *Wycombe W* 45 6 **45 6**
2015–16 Barnsley 45 6 **45 6**

McCOURT, Jak (M) 14 0
H: 5 10 W: 10 10 b.Leicester 6-7-95
2013–14 Leicester C 0 0
2013–14 *Torquay U* 11 0 **11 0**
2014–15 Leicester C 0 0
2015–16 Leicester C 0 0
2015–16 *Port Vale* 2 0 **2 0**
2015–16 Barnsley 1 0 **1 0**

NYATANGA, Lewin (D) 311 17
H: 6 2 W: 12 08 b.Burton 18-8-88
Internationals: Wales U17, U21, Full caps.
2005–06 Derby Co 24 1
2006–07 Derby Co 7 1
2006–07 *Sunderland* 11 0 **11 0**
2006–07 *Barnsley* 10 1
2007–08 Derby Co 2 1
2007–08 *Barnsley* 41 1
2008–09 Derby Co 30 1 **63 4**
2009–10 Bristol C 37 1
2010–11 Bristol C 20 1
2010–11 *Peterborough U* 3 0 **3 0**
2011–12 Bristol C 29 0
2012–13 Bristol C 19 2 **105 4**
2013–14 Barnsley 12 0
2014–15 Barnsley 45 5
2015–16 Barnsley 21 2 **129 9**

PAYNE, Stefan (F) 29 1
H: 5 10 W: 11 07 b.Lambeth 10-8-91
2009–10 Fulham 0 0
2010–11 Gillingham 16 0
2011–12 Gillingham 12 1 **28 1**
2011–12 *Aldershot T* 1 0 **1 0**
From Sutton U, Macclesfield T, Ebbsfleet U, AFC Hornchurch, Dover Ath.
2015–16 Barnsley 0 0

ROBERTS, Marc (D) 32 1
H: 6 0 W: 12 11 b.Wakefield 26-7-90
2014–15 Barnsley 0 0
2015–16 Barnsley 32 1 **32 1**

SCOWEN, Josh (M) 146 11
H: 5 10 W: 11 09 b.Cheshunt 28-3-93
2010–11 Wycombe W 2 0
2011–12 Wycombe W 0 0
2012–13 Wycombe W 34 1
2013–14 Wycombe W 37 1
2014–15 Wycombe W 18 1 **91 3**
2014–15 Barnsley 21 4
2015–16 Barnsley 34 4 **55 8**

SMITH, George (D) 41 0
H: 6 0 W: 12 02 b.Barnsley 14-8-96
2014–15 Barnsley 18 0
2015–16 Barnsley 19 0 **37 0**
2015–16 *Crawley T* 4 0 **4 0**

TEMPLETON, Matthew (D) 2 1
H: 5 9 W: 10 06 b.Bassetlaw 28-10-96
2015–16 Barnsley 2 1 **2 1**

TOWNSEND, Nick (G) 8 0
H: 5 11 W: 13 11 b.Solihull 1-11-94
2012–13 Birmingham C 0 0
2013–14 Birmingham C 0 0
2014–15 Birmingham C 0 0
2015–16 Barnsley 8 0 **8 0**

TUTON, Shaun (F) 7 0
b.Sheffield 3-12-91
From Belper T, Matlock T, Buxton, FC Halifax T.
2015–16 Barnsley 7 0 **7 0**

WALTON, Jack (G) 0 0
H: 6 0 W: 12 02 b.Bury 23-4-98
2014–15 Barnsley 0 0
2015–16 Barnsley 0 0

WATKINS, Marley (M) 119 14
H: 5 10 W: 10 03 b.London 17-10-90
2008–09 Cheltenham T 12 0
2009–10 Cheltenham T 13 1
2010–11 Cheltenham T 1 0 **26 1**
From Bath C, Hereford U
2013–14 Inverness CT 26 1
2014–15 Inverness CT 33 7 **59 8**
2015–16 Barnsley 34 5 **34 5**

WHITE, Aidan (D) 139 5
H: 5 7 W: 10 00 b.Otley 10-10-91
Internationals: England U19. Republic of Ireland U21.
2008–09 Leeds U 5 0
2009–10 Leeds U 8 0
2010–11 Leeds U 2 0
2010–11 *Oldham Ath* 24 4 **24 4**
2011–12 Leeds U 36 0
2012–13 Leeds U 24 1
2013–14 Leeds U 9 0
2013–14 *Sheffield U* 8 0 **8 0**
2014–15 Leeds U 1 0 **85 1**
2015–16 Rotherham U 8 0 **8 0**
2015–16 Barnsley 14 0 **14 0**

WILLIAMS, George (D) 25 1
H: 5 9 W: 11 00 b.Hillingdon 14-4-93
2011–12 Milton Keynes D 2 0 **2 0**
From Worcester C.
2014–15 Barnsley 4 0
2015–16 Barnsley 19 1 **23 1**

WILLIAMS, Ryan (F) 52 7
H: 5 11 W: 12 00 b.Perth 28-10-93
Internationals: Australia U20, U23.
2011–12 Portsmouth 4 0 **4 0**
2011–12 Fulham 0 0
2012–13 Fulham 0 0
2013–14 Fulham 0 0
2013–14 *Oxford U* 36 7 **36 7**
2014–15 Fulham 2 0 **2 0**
2014–15 *Barnsley* 5 0
2015–16 Barnsley 5 0 **10 0**

WINNALL, Sam (F) 153 62
H: 5 9 W: 11 04 b.Wolverhampton 19-1-91
2009–10 Wolverhampton W 0 0
2010–11 Wolverhampton W 0 0
2010–11 *Burton Alb* 19 7 **19 7**
2011–12 Wolverhampton W 0 0
2011–12 *Hereford U* 8 2 **8 2**
2011–12 *Inverness CT* 2 0 **2 0**
2012–13 Wolverhampton W 0 0
2012–13 *Shrewsbury T* 4 0 **4 0**
2013–14 Scunthorpe U 45 23 **45 23**
2014–15 Barnsley 32 9
2015–16 Barnsley 43 21 **75 30**

Players retained or with offer of contract
Ash, Bradley Luke; McGowan, Jeffrey James; White, Harry John; Zezere Neves Carnerio, Pedro.

Scholars
Alton, Jack James; Bertie, Shamaul Daris Theo; Brown, Jacob Samuel; Gooda, Bailey Roy; Hanna, Sam James; Jeffs, Logan Liam; Lund, Adam John; Murphy, Arron James; Ottley, Samuel David; Palmer, Romal Jordan; Peters, Philroy Clifton; Proctor, George Miles; Reilly, Liam Joseph; Rowe, Louis Kofi; Saeed, Mohamed Stephen Tahar; Smith, William Owen; Wardle, Louis Aaron.

BIRMINGHAM C (7)

ADAMS, Charlee (M) 2 0
H: 5 11 W: 12 01 b.Redbridge 16-2-95
2013–14 Birmingham C 0 0
2014–15 Birmingham C 0 0
2015–16 Birmingham C 2 0 **2 0**

ARTHUR, Koby (M) 19 3
H: 5 6 W: 10 09 b.Kumasi 3-1-96
2012–13 Birmingham C 2 0
2013–14 Birmingham C 1 0
2014–15 Birmingham C 9 0
2014–15 *Cheltenham T* 7 3 **7 3**
2015–16 Birmingham C 0 0 **12 0**

BABA, Noe (D) 0 0
b. 8-8-96
Internationals: Republic of Ireland U16, U17, U19, U21.
From Fulham.
2015–16 Birmingham C 0 0

BROCK-MADSEN, Nicolai (F) 96 16
H: 6 4 W: 13 12 b. 9-1-93
Internationals: Denmark U18, U19, U20, U21.
2010–11 Randers 0 0
2011–12 Randers 14 2
2012–13 Randers 28 5
2013–14 Randers 27 4
2014–15 Randers 17 4
2015–16 Randers 4 1 **90 16**
2015–16 Birmingham C 6 0 **6 0**

BROWN, Reece (M) 11 0
H: 5 9 W: 12 04 b.Dudley 3-3-96
Internationals: England U16, U17, U18, U20.
2013–14 Birmingham C 6 0
2014–15 Birmingham C 1 0
2014–15 *Notts Co* 3 0 **3 0**
2015–16 Birmingham C 1 0 **8 0**

CADDIS, Paul (D) 254 20
H: 5 7 W: 10 07 b.Irvine 19-4-88
Internationals: Scotland U19, U21.
2007–08 Celtic 2 0
2008–09 Celtic 5 0
2008–09 *Dundee U* 11 0 **11 0**
2009–10 Celtic 10 0 **17 0**
2010–11 Swindon T 38 1
2011–12 Swindon T 39 4
2012–13 Swindon T 0 0
2012–13 *Birmingham C* 27 0
2013–14 Swindon T 0 0 **77 5**
2013–14 Birmingham C 38 5
2014–15 Birmingham C 45 6
2015–16 Birmingham C 39 4 **149 15**

COTTERILL, David (F) 350 48
H: 5 9 W: 11 02 b.Cardiff 4-12-87
Internationals: Wales U19, U21, Full caps.
2004–05 Bristol C 12 0
2005–06 Bristol C 45 7
2006–07 Bristol C 5 1 **62 8**
2006–07 Wigan Ath 16 1
2007–08 Wigan Ath 2 0 **18 1**
2007–08 *Sheffield U* 16 0
2008–09 Sheffield U 24 4
2009–10 Sheffield U 14 2 **54 6**
2009–10 Swansea C 21 3
2010–11 Swansea C 14 1
2010–11 *Portsmouth* 15 1 **15 1**
2011–12 Swansea C 0 0 **35 4**
2011–12 Barnsley 11 1 **11 1**
2012–13 Doncaster R 44 10
2013–14 Doncaster R 40 4 **84 14**
2014–15 Birmingham C 42 9
2015–16 Birmingham C 29 4 **71 13**

DAVIS, David (M) 170 6
H: 5 8 W: 12 03 b.Smethwick 20-2-91
2009–10 Wolverhampton W 0 0
2009–10 *Darlington* 5 0 **5 0**
2010–11 Wolverhampton W 0 0
2010–11 *Walsall* 7 0 **7 0**
2010–11 *Shrewsbury T* 19 2 **19 2**
2011–12 Wolverhampton W 7 0
2011–12 *Chesterfield* 9 0 **9 0**
2012–13 Wolverhampton W 28 0
2013–14 Wolverhampton W 18 0 **53 0**
2014–15 Birmingham C 42 3
2015–16 Birmingham C 35 1 **77 4**

DONALDSON, Clayton (F) 358 124
H: 6 1 W: 11 07 b.Bradford 7-2-84
Internationals: England C. Jamaica Full caps.
2002–03 Hull C 2 0
2003–04 Hull C 0 0
2004–05 Hull C 0 0 **2 0**
From York C
2007–08 Hibernian 17 5 **17 5**
2008–09 Crewe Alex 37 6
2009–10 Crewe Alex 37 13
2010–11 Crewe Alex 43 28 **117 47**
2011–12 Brentford 46 11
2012–13 Brentford 44 18
2013–14 Brentford 46 17 **136 46**
2014–15 Birmingham C 46 15
2015–16 Birmingham C 40 11 **86 26**

DUFFY, Mark (M) 256 23
H: 5 9 W: 11 05 b.Liverpool 7-10-85
2008–09 Morecambe 9 1
2009–10 Morecambe 35 4
2010–11 Morecambe 22 0 **66 5**
2010–11 Scunthorpe U 22 1
2011–12 Scunthorpe U 37 2
2012–13 Scunthorpe U 43 5 **102 8**
2013–14 Doncaster R 36 2 **36 2**
2014–15 Birmingham C 4 0
2014–15 *Chesterfield* 3 0 **3 0**
2015–16 Birmingham C 0 0 **4 0**
2015–16 *Burton Alb* 45 8 **45 8**

EARDLEY, Neal (M) 232 12
H: 5 11 W: 11 10 b.Llandudno 6-11-88
Internationals: Wales U17, U19, U21, Full caps.
2005–06 Oldham Ath 1 0
2006–07 Oldham Ath 36 2
2007–08 Oldham Ath 42 6

2008–09	Oldham Ath	34	2		
2009–10	Oldham Ath	0	0	**113**	**10**
2009–10	Blackpool	24	0		
2010–11	Blackpool	31	1		
2011–12	Blackpool	26	1		
2012–13	Blackpool	23	0	**104**	**2**
2013–14	Birmingham C	5	0		
2014–15	Birmingham C	4	0		
2014–15	*Leyton Orient*	1	0	**1**	**0**
2015–16	Birmingham C	5	0	**14**	**0**

EDGAR, David (D) 187 10
H: 6 2 W: 12 13 b.Ontario 19-5-87
Internationals: Canada U17, U20, Full caps.

2005–06	Newcastle U	0	0		
2006–07	Newcastle U	3	1		
2007–08	Newcastle U	5	0		
2008–09	Newcastle U	11	1	**19**	**2**
2009–10	Burnley	4	0		
2009–10	*Swansea C*	5	1	**5**	**1**
2010–11	Burnley	7	0		
2011–12	Burnley	44	2		
2012–13	Burnley	27	2		
2013–14	Burnley	17	0	**99**	**4**
2014–15	Birmingham C	16	1		
2014–15	*Huddersfield T*	12	0	**12**	**0**
2015–16	Birmingham C	0	0	**16**	**1**
2015–16	*Sheffield U*	36	2	**36**	**2**

FABBRINI, Diego (F) 169 13
H: 5 11 W: 11 12 b.San Giuliano Terme 31-7-90
Internationals: Italy U21, Full caps.

2009–10	Empoli	29	1		
2010–11	Empoli	26	2	**55**	**3**
2011–12	Udinese	14	2		
2012–13	Udinese	6	0	**20**	**2**
2012–13	*Palermo*	8	1	**8**	**1**
2013–14	Watford	21	1		
2013–14	*Siena*	10	1	**10**	**1**
2014–15	Watford	2	0		
2014–15	*Millwall*	12	1	**12**	**1**
2014–15	*Birmingham C*	5	0		
2015–16	Watford	0	0	**23**	**1**
2015–16	*Middlesbrough*	22	4	**22**	**4**
2015–16	Birmingham C	14	0	**19**	**0**

GLEESON, Stephen (M) 305 25
H: 6 2 W: 11 00 b.Dublin 3-8-88
Internationals: Republic of Ireland U21, Full caps.

2006–07	Wolverhampton W	3	0		
2006–07	*Stockport Co*	14	2		
2007–08	Wolverhampton W	0	0		
2007–08	*Hereford U*	4	0	**4**	**0**
2007–08	*Stockport Co*	6	0		
2008–09	Wolverhampton W	0	0	**3**	**0**
2008–09	*Stockport Co*	21	2	**41**	**4**
2008–09	*Milton Keynes D*	5	0		
2009–10	Milton Keynes D	29	0		
2010–11	Milton Keynes D	36	2		
2011–12	Milton Keynes D	39	5		
2012–13	Milton Keynes D	30	6		
2013–14	Milton Keynes D	35	3	**174**	**16**
2014–15	Birmingham C	39	0		
2015–16	Birmingham C	44	5	**83**	**5**

GROUNDS, Jonathan (D) 255 9
H: 6 1 W: 13 10 b.Thornaby 2-2-88

2007–08	Middlesbrough	5	0		
2008–09	Middlesbrough	2	0		
2008–09	*Norwich C*	16	3	**16**	**3**
2009–10	Middlesbrough	20	0		
2010–11	Middlesbrough	6	1		
2011–12	Middlesbrough	0	0	**33**	**1**
2011–12	*Chesterfield*	13	0	**13**	**0**
2011–12	*Yeovil T*	14	0	**14**	**0**
2012–13	Oldham Ath	44	1		
2013–14	Oldham Ath	45	2	**89**	**3**
2014–15	Birmingham C	45	1		
2015–16	Birmingham C	45	1	**90**	**2**

HANCOX, Mitch (D) 48 2
H: 5 10 W: 11 03 b.Solihull 9-11-93

2011–12	Birmingham C	0	0		
2012–13	Birmingham C	19	0		
2013–14	Birmingham C	14	0		
2014–15	Birmingham C	0	0		
2015–16	Birmingham C	0	0	**33**	**0**
2015–16	*Crawley T*	15	2	**15**	**2**

JOHNSTONE, Denny (F) 12 2
H: 6 2 W: 13 01 b. 9-1-95
Internationals: Scotland U16, U17, U18, U19.

2013–14	Celtic	0	0		
2014–15	Birmingham C	2	0		
2014–15	*Cheltenham T*	5	1	**5**	**1**
2014–15	*Burton Alb*	5	1	**5**	**1**
2015–16	Birmingham C	0	0	**2**	**0**

JONES, Alex (F) 0 0
b. 28-9-94
From WBA.

2015–16	Birmingham C	0	0		

KIEFTENBELD, Maikel (M) 257 8
H: 5 10 W: 11 11 b.Lemelerveld 26-6-90
Internationals: Netherlands U21.

2008–09	Go Ahead Eagles	30	1		
2009–10	Go Ahead Eagles	33	2	**63**	**3**
2010–11	Groningen	33	0		
2011–12	Groningen	26	1		
2012–13	Groningen	29	1		
2013–14	Groningen	31	0		
2014–15	Groningen	33	0	**152**	**2**
2015–16	Birmingham C	42	3	**42**	**3**

KUSZCZAK, Tomasz (G) 214 0
H: 6 3 W: 13 03 b.Krosno Odrzansia 20-3-82
Internationals: Poland U16, U18, U21, Full caps.

2001–02	Hertha Berlin	0	0		
2002–03	Hertha Berlin	0	0		
2003–04	Hertha Berlin	0	0		
2004–05	WBA	3	0		
2005–06	WBA	28	0		
2006–07	WBA	0	0	**31**	**0**
2006–07	*Manchester U*	6	0		
2007–08	Manchester U	9	0		
2008–09	Manchester U	4	0		
2009–10	Manchester U	8	0		
2010–11	Manchester U	5	0		
2011–12	Manchester U	0	0	**32**	**0**
2011–12	*Watford*	13	0	**13**	**0**
2012–13	Brighton & HA	43	0		
2013–14	Brighton & HA	41	0	**84**	**0**
2014–15	Wolverhampton W	13	0	**13**	**0**
2015–16	Birmingham C	41	0	**41**	**0**

LEGZDINS, Adam (G) 104 0
H: 6 1 W: 14 02 b.Penkridge 28-11-86

2006–07	Birmingham C	0	0		
2007–08	Birmingham C	0	0		
2008–09	Crewe Alex	0	0		
2009–10	Crewe Alex	6	0	**6**	**0**
2010–11	Burton Alb	46	0		
2011–12	Derby Co	4	0		
2011–12	*Burton Alb*	1	0	**47**	**0**
2012–13	Derby Co	31	0		
2013–14	Derby Co	0	0	**35**	**0**
2014–15	Leyton Orient	11	0	**11**	**0**
2015–16	Birmingham C	5	0	**5**	**0**

LOWRY, Shane (D) 171 3
H: 6 1 W: 13 01 b.Perth 12-6-89
Internationals: Republic of Ireland U17, U21.

2007–08	Aston Villa	0	0		
2008–09	Aston Villa	0	0		
2009–10	Aston Villa	0	0		
2009–10	*Plymouth Arg*	13	0	**13**	**0**
2009–10	*Leeds U*	11	0	**11**	**0**
2010–11	Aston Villa	0	0		
2010–11	*Sheffield U*	17	0	**17**	**0**
2011–12	Aston Villa	0	0		
2011–12	Millwall	22	1		
2012–13	Millwall	39	1		
2013–14	Millwall	22	0	**83**	**2**
2014–15	Leyton Orient	34	0		
2015–16	Leyton Orient	0	0	**34**	**0**
2015–16	Birmingham C	1	0	**1**	**0**
2015–16	Perth Glory	12	1	**12**	**1**

MAGHOMA, Jacques (M) 252 33
H: 5 9 W: 11 06 b.Lubumbashi 23-10-87
Internationals: DR Congo Full caps.

2005–06	Tottenham H	0	0		
2006–07	Tottenham H	0	0		
2007–08	Tottenham H	0	0		
2008–09	Tottenham H	0	0		
2009–10	Burton Alb	35	3		
2010–11	Burton Alb	41	4		
2011–12	Burton Alb	36	4		
2012–13	Burton Alb	43	15	**155**	**26**
2013–14	Sheffield W	25	2		
2014–15	Sheffield W	32	0	**57**	**2**
2015–16	Birmingham C	40	5	**40**	**5**

MARTIN, Josh (D) 0 0
b.Birmingham 21-10-98

2014–15	Birmingham C	0	0		
2015–16	Birmingham C	0	0		

MAXWELL, Luke (M) 0 0
b. 6-7-97

2015–16	Birmingham C	0	0		

MBENDE, Emmanuel (D) 0 0
b. 3-3-96

2014–15	Borussia Dortmund	0	0		
2015–16	Birmingham C	0	0		

MORRISON, Michael (D) 292 14
H: 6 0 W: 12 00 b.Bury St Edmunds 3-3-88
Internationals: England C.

2008–09	Leicester C	35	3		
2009–10	Leicester C	31	2		
2010–11	Leicester C	11	0	**77**	**5**
2010–11	Sheffield W	12	0	**12**	**0**
2011–12	Charlton Ath	45	4		
2012–13	Charlton Ath	44	1		
2013–14	Charlton Ath	45	1		
2014–15	Charlton Ath	2	0	**136**	**6**
2014–15	Birmingham C	21	0		
2015–16	Birmingham C	46	3	**67**	**3**

NOVAK, Lee (F) 238 58
H: 6 0 W: 12 04 b.Newcastle 28-9-88

2008–09	Huddersfield T	0	0		
2009–10	Huddersfield T	37	12		
2010–11	Huddersfield T	31	5		
2011–12	Huddersfield T	41	13		
2012–13	Huddersfield T	35	4	**144**	**34**
2013–14	Birmingham C	38	9		
2014–15	Birmingham C	21	1		
2015–16	Birmingham C	0	0	**59**	**10**
2015–16	*Chesterfield*	35	14	**35**	**14**

ROBINSON, Paul (D) 654 15
H: 5 9 W: 11 12 b.Watford 14-12-78
Internationals: England U21.

1996–97	Watford	12	0		
1997–98	Watford	22	2		
1998–99	Watford	29	0		
1999–2000	Watford	32	0		
2000–01	Watford	39	0		
2001–02	Watford	38	3		
2002–03	Watford	37	3		
2003–04	Watford	10	0	**219**	**8**
2003–04	WBA	31	0		
2004–05	WBA	30	1		
2005–06	WBA	33	0		
2006–07	WBA	42	2		
2007–08	WBA	43	1		
2008–09	WBA	35	0		
2009–10	WBA	0	0	**214**	**4**
2009–10	*Bolton W*	25	0		
2010–11	Bolton W	35	0		
2011–12	Bolton W	17	0	**77**	**0**
2011–12	*Leeds U*	10	0	**10**	**0**
2012–13	Birmingham C	35	0		
2013–14	Birmingham C	40	0		
2014–15	Birmingham C	34	0		
2015–16	Birmingham C	25	3	**134**	**3**

SHINNIE, Andrew (M) 129 23
H: 5 11 W: 10 13 b.Aberdeen 17-7-89
Internationals: Scotland U19, U21, Full caps.

2005–06	Rangers	0	0		
2006–07	Rangers	2	0		
2007–08	Rangers	0	0		
2008–09	Rangers	0	0		
2009–10	Rangers	0	0		
2010–11	Rangers	0	0	**2**	**0**
2011–12	Inverness CT	19	7		
2012–13	Inverness CT	38	12	**57**	**19**
2013–14	Birmingham C	26	2		
2014–15	Birmingham C	27	2		
2015–16	Birmingham C	14	0	**67**	**4**
2015–16	*Rotherham U*	3	0	**3**	**0**

SOLOMON-OTABOR, Viv (M) 22 1
H: 5 9 W: 12 02 b. 2-1-96
From Crystal Palace.

2015–16	Birmingham C	22	1	**22**	**1**

SPECTOR, Jonathan (D) 255 1
H: 6 0 W: 12 08 b.Chicago 1-3-86
Internationals: USA U17, U20, Full caps.

2003–04	Manchester U	0	0		
2004–05	Manchester U	3	0		
2005–06	Manchester U	0	0	**3**	**0**
2005–06	*Charlton Ath*	20	0	**20**	**0**
2006–07	West Ham U	25	0		
2007–08	West Ham U	26	0		
2008–09	West Ham U	9	0		
2009–10	West Ham U	27	0		
2010–11	West Ham U	14	1	**101**	**1**
2011–12	Birmingham C	31	0		
2012–13	Birmingham C	29	0		
2013–14	Birmingham C	22	0		
2014–15	Birmingham C	24	0		
2015–16	Birmingham C	25	0	**131**	**0**

THOMAS, Wesley (F) 215 54
H: 5 10 W: 11 00 b.Barking 23-1-87

2008–09	Dagenham & R	5	0		
2009–10	Dagenham & R	23	3	**28**	**3**
2010–11	Cheltenham T	41	18	**41**	**18**
2011–12	Crawley T	6	1	**6**	**1**
2011–12	Bournemouth	36	11		

Season	Club	A	G	A	G
2012–13	Bournemouth	6	0		
2012–13	*Portsmouth*	6	3	6	3
2012–13	*Blackpool*	9	3	9	3
2012–13	Birmingham C	11	3		
2013–14	Bournemouth	10	0	52	11
2013–14	Rotherham U	13	5	13	5
2014–15	Birmingham C	33	4		
2015–16	Birmingham C	0	0	44	7
2015–16	*Swindon T*	6	2	6	2
2015–16	*Bradford C*	10	1	10	1

TRUEMAN, Connal (G) 0 0
H: 6 1　W: 11 10　b.Birmingham 26-3-96

Season	Club	A	G	A	G
2014–15	Birmingham C	0	0		
2014–15	*Oldham Ath*	0	0		
2015–16	Birmingham C	0	0		

Players retained or with offer of contract
Bernard, Dominic Archie; Chapman Hale, Ronan Aiden Connolly Shea; Cooper, Charlie Terrence; Dacres-Cogley, Joshua Jacob; Harding, Wesley Hylton; McDonald, Wesley Nurettin; McFarlane, Raewkon Kyle; O'Neill, George Connor; Storer, Jack Frederick Wendell; Weaver, Jacob William Robert.

Scholars
Bailey-Nicholls, Khaellem-Bryce Khiyah; Beardmore, Max; Challis, Jack; Ebbutt, Cameron; Iyamu, Noskhare Michael; Lakin, Charlie; Lubala, Beryly Logos; Mbunga, Edjidja; Mulders, Oliver; O'Keeffe, Corey James John; Popa, David; Potter, Jordan William; Seddon, Steven Jeffrey; Smith, Leighton Robert Allen; Tibbetts, Joshua Joseph; Timms, Matthew; Yuill, Louis George William.

BLACKBURN R (8)

AKPAN, Hope (M) 142 9
H: 6 0　W: 10 08　b.Liverpool 14-8-91
Internationals: Nigeria Full caps.

Season	Club	A	G	A	G
2007–08	Everton	0	0		
2008–09	Everton	0	0		
2009–10	Everton	0	0		
2010–11	Everton	0	0		
2010–11	Hull C	2	0	2	0
2011–12	Crawley T	26	1		
2012–13	Crawley T	21	4	47	5
2012–13	Reading	9	0		
2013–14	Reading	29	1		
2014–15	Reading	20	0	58	1
2015–16	Blackburn R	35	3	35	3

BENNETT, Elliott (M) 274 22
H: 5 9　W: 10 11　b.Telford 18-12-88

Season	Club	A	G	A	G
2006–07	Wolverhampton W	0	0		
2007–08	Wolverhampton W	0	0		
2007–08	*Crewe Alex*	9	1	9	1
2007–08	*Bury*	19	1		
2008–09	Wolverhampton W	0	0		
2008–09	*Bury*	46	3	65	4
2009–10	Wolverhampton W	0	0		
2009–10	Brighton & HA	43	7		
2010–11	Brighton & HA	46	6		
2011–12	Norwich C	33	1		
2012–13	Norwich C	24	1		
2013–14	Norwich C	2	0		
2014–15	Norwich C	9	0		
2014–15	Brighton & HA	7	0	96	13
2015–16	Norwich C	0	0	68	2
2015–16	*Bristol C*	15	0	15	0
2015–16	*Blackburn R*	21	2	21	2

BROWN, Chris (F) 349 58
H: 6 3　W: 13 01　b.Doncaster 11-12-84

Season	Club	A	G	A	G
2002–03	Sunderland	0	0		
2003–04	Sunderland	0	0		
2003–04	*Doncaster R*	22	10		
2004–05	Sunderland	37	5		
2005–06	Sunderland	13	1		
2005–06	*Hull C*	13	1	13	1
2006–07	Sunderland	16	3	66	9
2006–07	Norwich C	4	0		
2007–08	Norwich C	14	1	18	1
2007–08	Preston NE	17	5		
2008–09	Preston NE	30	6		
2009–10	Preston NE	43	6		
2010–11	Preston NE	16	1	106	18
2011–12	Doncaster R	11	2		
2012–13	Doncaster R	36	8		
2013–14	Doncaster R	40	9	109	29
2014–15	Blackburn R	20	0		
2015–16	Blackburn R	17	0	37	0

CONWAY, Craig (M) 359 36
H: 5 7　W: 10 07　b.Irvine 2-5-85
Internationals: Scotland Full caps.

Season	Club	A	G	A	G
2002–03	Ayr U	1	0		
2003–04	Ayr U	6	0		
2004–05	Ayr U	23	3		
2005–06	Ayr U	31	4	61	7
2006–07	Dundee U	30	0		
2007–08	Dundee U	15	1		
2008–09	Dundee U	36	5		
2009–10	Dundee U	33	4		
2010–11	Dundee U	22	3	136	13
2011–12	Cardiff C	31	3		
2012–13	Cardiff C	27	2		
2013–14	Cardiff C	0	0	58	5
2013–14	*Brighton & HA*	13	1	13	1
2013–14	Blackburn R	18	4		
2014–15	Blackburn R	38	3		
2015–16	Blackburn R	35	3	91	10

DELFOUNESO, Nathan (F) 168 16
H: 6 1　W: 12 04　b.Birmingham 2-2-91
Internationals: England U16, U17, U19, U21.

Season	Club	A	G	A	G
2007–08	Aston Villa	0	0		
2008–09	Aston Villa	4	0		
2009–10	Aston Villa	9	1		
2010–11	Aston Villa	11	1		
2010–11	*Burnley*	11	1	11	1
2011–12	Aston Villa	6	0		
2011–12	*Leicester C*	4	0	4	0
2012–13	Aston Villa	1	0		
2012–13	*Blackpool*	40	6		
2013–14	Aston Villa	0	0	31	2
2013–14	*Blackpool*	11	0		
2013–14	*Coventry C*	14	3	14	3
2014–15	Blackpool	38	3	89	9
2015–16	Blackburn R	15	1	15	1
2015–16	*Bury*	4	0	4	0

DOYLE, Jack (D) 0 0
b. 2-2-97

Season	Club	A	G	A	G
2015–16	Blackburn R	0	0		

DUFFY, Shane (D) 121 8
H: 6 4　W: 12 00　b.Derry 1-1-92
Internationals: Northern Ireland U16, U17, U19, U21, B. Republic of Ireland U19, U21, Full caps.

Season	Club	A	G	A	G
2008–09	Everton	0	0		
2009–10	Everton	0	0		
2010–11	Everton	0	0		
2010–11	*Burnley*	1	0	1	0
2011–12	Everton	4	0		
2011–12	*Scunthorpe U*	18	2	18	2
2012–13	Everton	1	0		
2013–14	Everton	0	0		
2013–14	*Yeovil T*	37	1	37	1
2014–15	Everton	0	0	5	0
2014–15	Blackburn R	19	1		
2015–16	Blackburn R	41	4	60	5

EASTWOOD, Simon (G) 63 0
H: 6 2　W: 10 13　b.Huddersfield 26-6-89
Internationals: England U16, U19.

Season	Club	A	G	A	G
2005–06	Huddersfield T	0	0		
2006–07	Huddersfield T	0	0		
2007–08	Huddersfield T	0	0		
2008–09	Huddersfield T	1	0		
2009–10	Huddersfield T	0	0	1	0
2009–10	*Bradford C*	22	0	22	0
2012–13	Portsmouth	27	0	27	0
2013–14	Blackburn R	7	0		
2014–15	Blackburn R	6	0		
2015–16	Blackburn R	0	0	13	0

EVANS, Corry (M) 183 9
H: 5 8　W: 10 12　b.Belfast 30-7-90
Internationals: Northern Ireland U16, U17, U19, U21, B, Full caps.

Season	Club	A	G	A	G
2007–08	Manchester U	0	0		
2008–09	Manchester U	0	0		
2009–10	Manchester U	0	0		
2010–11	Manchester U	0	0		
2010–11	*Carlisle U*	1	0	1	0
2010–11	*Hull C*	18	3		
2011–12	Hull C	43	2		
2012–13	Hull C	32	1		
2013–14	Hull C	0	0	93	6
2013–14	Blackburn R	21	1		
2014–15	Blackburn R	38	1		
2015–16	Blackburn R	30	1	89	3

FORRESTER, Anton (F) 31 6
H: 6 0　W: 12 00　b.Liverpool 11-2-94

Season	Club	A	G	A	G
2010–11	Everton	0	0		
2011–12	Everton	0	0		
2012–13	Blackburn R	0	0		
2013–14	Blackburn R	0	0		
2013–14	*Bury*	28	6	28	6

Season	Club	A	G	A	G
2014–15	Blackburn R	0	0		
2015–16	Blackburn R	0	0		
2015–16	*Morecambe*	3	0	3	0

GUTHRIE, Danny (M) 214 12
H: 5 9　W: 11 06　b.Shrewsbury 18-4-87
Internationals: England U16.

Season	Club	A	G	A	G
2004–05	Liverpool	0	0		
2005–06	Liverpool	0	0		
2006–07	Liverpool	3	0		
2006–07	*Southampton*	10	0	10	0
2007–08	Liverpool	0	0	3	0
2007–08	*Bolton W*	25	0	25	0
2008–09	Newcastle U	24	2		
2009–10	Newcastle U	38	4		
2010–11	Newcastle U	14	0		
2011–12	Newcastle U	16	1	92	7
2012–13	Reading	21	1		
2013–14	Reading	32	4		
2014–15	Reading	9	0	62	5
2014–15	*Fulham*	6	0	6	0
2015–16	Blackburn R	16	0	16	0

HANLEY, Grant (D) 183 7
H: 6 2　W: 12 00　b.Dumfries 20-11-91
Internationals: Scotland U19, U21, Full caps.

Season	Club	A	G	A	G
2008–09	Blackburn R	0	0		
2009–10	Blackburn R	1	0		
2010–11	Blackburn R	7	0		
2011–12	Blackburn R	23	1		
2012–13	Blackburn R	39	2		
2013–14	Blackburn R	38	1		
2014–15	Blackburn R	31	1		
2015–16	Blackburn R	44	2	183	7

HENLEY, Adam (D) 78 1
H: 5 10　W: 12 02　b.Knoxville 14-6-94
Internationals: Wales U19, U21, Full caps.

Season	Club	A	G	A	G
2011–12	Blackburn R	7	0		
2012–13	Blackburn R	15	0		
2013–14	Blackburn R	14	0		
2014–15	Blackburn R	18	1		
2015–16	Blackburn R	24	0	78	1

JACKSON, Simeon (M) 268 64
H: 5 10　W: 10 12　b.Kingston, Jamaica 28-3-87
Internationals: Canada U20, Full caps.

Season	Club	A	G	A	G
2004–05	Rushden & D	0	0		
2005–06	Rushden & D	14	5		
2006–07	Rushden & D	0	0		
2007–08	Rushden & D	0	0	17	5
2007–08	Gillingham	18	4		
2008–09	Gillingham	41	17		
2009–10	Gillingham	42	14	101	35
2010–11	Norwich C	38	13		
2011–12	Norwich C	22	3		
2012–13	Norwich C	13	1	73	17
2013–14	*E Braunschweig*	9	0	9	0
2013–14	*Millwall*	14	2	14	2
2014–15	*Coventry C*	28	3	28	3
2015–16	*Barnsley*	9	2	9	2
2015–16	*Blackburn R*	17	2	17	2

KILGALLON, Matthew (D) 284 9
H: 6 1　W: 12 10　b.York 8-1-84
Internationals: England U20, U21.

Season	Club	A	G	A	G
2000–01	Leeds U	0	0		
2001–02	Leeds U	0	0		
2002–03	Leeds U	2	0		
2003–04	Leeds U	8	2		
2003–04	*West Ham U*	3	0	3	0
2004–05	Leeds U	26	0		
2005–06	Leeds U	25	1		
2006–07	Leeds U	19	0	80	3
2006–07	Sheffield U	6	0		
2007–08	Sheffield U	40	2		
2008–09	Sheffield U	40	1		
2009–10	Sheffield U	21	1	107	4
2009–10	Sunderland	7	0		
2010–11	Sunderland	0	0		
2010–11	*Middlesbrough*	2	0	2	0
2010–11	*Doncaster R*	12	0	12	0
2011–12	Sunderland	10	0		
2012–13	Sunderland	6	0	23	0
2013–14	Blackburn R	25	1		
2014–15	Blackburn R	22	1		
2015–16	Blackburn R	10	0	57	2

KOITA, Fode (F) 132 13
H: 6 1　W: 13 08　b.Paris 21-10-90
Internationals: France U21.

Season	Club	A	G	A	G
2008–09	Montpellier	1	0		
2009–10	Montpellier	5	0		
2010–11	Montpellier	0	0		
2011–12	Montpellier	4	0		
2011–12	*Lens*	17	3	17	3
2012–13	Montpellier	0	0		
2012–13	*Le Havre*	22	3	22	3

2013–14	Montpellier	0	0	**16**	**0**
2013–14	Caen	30	4		
2014–15	Caen	29	3	**59**	**7**
2015–16	Blackburn R	14	0	**14**	**0**
2015–16	*Kasimpasa*	4	0	**4**	**0**

LENIHAN, Darragh (M) 43 1
H: 5 10 W: 12 00 b.Dublin 16-3-94
Internationals: Republic of Ireland U17, U19, U21.

2011–12	Blackburn R	0	0		
2012–13	Blackburn R	0	0		
2013–14	Blackburn R	0	0		
2014–15	Blackburn R	3	0		
2014–15	*Burton Alb*	17	1	**17**	**1**
2015–16	Blackburn R	23	0	**26**	**0**

LOWE, Jason (M) 137 3
H: 6 0 W: 12 08 b.Wigan 2-9-91
Internationals: England U20, U21.

2009–10	Blackburn R	0	0		
2010–11	Blackburn R	1	0		
2010–11	*Oldham Ath*	7	2	**7**	**2**
2011–12	Blackburn R	32	0		
2012–13	Blackburn R	36	0		
2013–14	Blackburn R	39	1		
2014–15	Blackburn R	12	0		
2015–16	Blackburn R	10	0	**130**	**1**

MAHONEY, Connor (M) 6 0
H: 5 9 W: 10 08 b.Blackburn 12-2-97
Internationals: England U17, U18.

2013–14	Accrington S	4	0	**4**	**0**
2013–14	Blackburn R	0	0		
2014–15	Blackburn R	0	0		
2015–16	Blackburn R	2	0	**2**	**0**

MARSHALL, Ben (F) 256 32
H: 5 11 W: 11 13 b.Salford 29-3-91
Internationals: England U21.

2009–10	Stoke C	0	0		
2009–10	*Northampton T*	15	2	**15**	**2**
2009–10	*Cheltenham T*	6	2	**6**	**2**
2009–10	*Carlisle U*	20	3		
2010–11	Stoke C	0	0		
2010–11	*Carlisle U*	33	3	**53**	**6**
2011–12	Stoke C	0	0		
2011–12	*Sheffield W*	22	5	**22**	**5**
2011–12	Leicester C	16	3		
2012–13	Leicester C	40	4		
2013–14	Leicester C	0	0	**56**	**7**
2013–14	Blackburn R	18	2		
2014–15	Blackburn R	42	6		
2015–16	Blackburn R	44	2	**104**	**10**

NYAMBE, Ryan (D) 0 0
b. 4-12-97

2014–15	Blackburn R	0	0		
2015–16	Blackburn R	0	0		

O'SULLIVAN, John (M) 47 4
H: 5 11 W: 13 01 b.Birmingham 18-9-93
Internationals: Republic of Ireland U19, U21.

2011–12	Blackburn R	0	0		
2012–13	Blackburn R	1	0		
2013–14	Blackburn R	0	0		
2014–15	Blackburn R	2	0		
2014–15	*Accrington S*	13	4	**13**	**4**
2014–15	*Barnsley*	8	0	**8**	**0**
2015–16	Blackburn R	2	0	**5**	**0**
2015–16	*Rochdale*	2	0	**2**	**0**
2015–16	*Bury*	19	0	**19**	**0**

PRESTON, Jordan (F) 48 18
b. 26-11-95
Internationals: Scotland U19.

2014–15	Blackburn R	0	0		
2014–15	*Ayr U*	14	5		
2015–16	Blackburn R	0	0		
2015–16	*Ayr U*	34	13	**48**	**18**

RAYA, David (G) 7 0
H: 6 0 W: 12 08 b.Barcelona 15-9-95

2013–14	Blackburn R	0	0		
2014–15	Blackburn R	2	0		
2015–16	Blackburn R	5	0	**7**	**0**

RITTENBERG, Dean (F) 0 0
b. 13-5-96
Internationals: England U18.

2013–14	Blackburn R	0	0		
2014–15	Blackburn R	0	0		
2015–16	Blackburn R	0	0		

SPURR, Tommy (D) 335 9
H: 6 1 W: 11 05 b.Leeds 13-9-87

2005–06	Sheffield W	2	0		
2006–07	Sheffield W	36	0		
2007–08	Sheffield W	41	2		
2008–09	Sheffield W	41	2		
2009–10	Sheffield W	46	1		
2010–11	Sheffield W	26	0	**192**	**5**
2011–12	Doncaster R	19	0		
2012–13	Doncaster R	46	1		
2013–14	Doncaster R	0	0	**65**	**1**
2013–14	Blackburn R	43	3		
2014–15	Blackburn R	12	0		
2015–16	Blackburn R	23	0	**78**	**3**

STEELE, Jason (G) 216 0
H: 6 2 W: 12 07 b.Newton Aycliffe 18-8-90
Internationals: England U16, U17, U19, U21. Great Britain.

2007–08	Middlesbrough	0	0		
2008–09	Middlesbrough	0	0		
2009–10	Middlesbrough	0	0		
2009–10	*Northampton T*	13	0	**13**	**0**
2010–11	Middlesbrough	35	0		
2011–12	Middlesbrough	34	0		
2012–13	Middlesbrough	46	0		
2013–14	Middlesbrough	16	0		
2014–15	Middlesbrough	0	0	**131**	**0**
2014–15	*Blackburn R*	31	0		
2015–16	Blackburn R	41	0	**72**	**0**

TAYLOR, Chris (M) 348 40
H: 5 11 W: 11 00 b.Oldham 20-12-86

2005–06	Oldham Ath	14	0		
2006–07	Oldham Ath	44	4		
2007–08	Oldham Ath	42	5		
2008–09	Oldham Ath	42	10		
2009–10	Oldham Ath	32	1		
2010–11	Oldham Ath	42	11		
2011–12	Oldham Ath	38	2	**254**	**33**
2012–13	Millwall	22	3		
2013–14	Blackburn R	34	0		
2014–15	Blackburn R	16	1		
2015–16	Blackburn R	12	0	**62**	**1**
2015–16	*Millwall*	10	3	**32**	**6**

THOMSON, Connor (D) 0 0
H: 6 3 b. 14-2-96

2013–14	Carlisle U	0	0		
2014–15	Carlisle U	0	0		
2014–15	Blackburn R	0	0		
2015–16	Blackburn R	0	0		

TOMLINSON, Willem (M) 0 0
b. 27-1-98

2015–16	Blackburn R	0	0		

WARD, Elliot (D) 280 21
H: 6 2 W: 13 00 b.Harrow 19-1-85

2001–02	West Ham U	0	0		
2002–03	West Ham U	0	0		
2003–04	West Ham U	0	0		
2004–05	West Ham U	11	0		
2004–05	*Bristol R*	3	0	**3**	**0**
2005–06	West Ham U	4	0	**15**	**0**
2005–06	*Plymouth Arg*	16	1	**16**	**1**
2006–07	Coventry C	39	3		
2007–08	Coventry C	37	6		
2008–09	Coventry C	33	5		
2009–10	Coventry C	8	0	**117**	**14**
2009–10	*Doncaster R*	6	1	**6**	**1**
2009–10	*Preston NE*	4	0	**4**	**0**
2010–11	Norwich C	39	1		
2011–12	Norwich C	12	0		
2012–13	Norwich C	0	0	**51**	**1**
2012–13	*Nottingham F*	31	3	**31**	**3**
2013–14	Bournemouth	23	0		
2014–15	Bournemouth	2	0		
2015–16	Bournemouth	0	0	**25**	**0**
2015–16	*Huddersfield T*	5	0	**5**	**0**
2015–16	Blackburn R	7	1	**7**	**1**

WHARTON, Scott (D) 0 0
b. 3-10-97

2015–16	Blackburn R	0	0		

WILLIAMSON, Lee (M) 490 36
H: 5 10 W: 10 04 b.Derby 7-6-82
Internationals: Jamaica Full caps.

1999–2000	Mansfield T	4	0		
2000–01	Mansfield T	15	0		
2001–02	Mansfield T	46	3		
2002–03	Mansfield T	40	0		
2003–04	Mansfield T	35	0		
2004–05	Mansfield T	4	0	**144**	**3**
2004–05	Northampton T	37	0	**37**	**0**
2005–06	Rotherham U	37	4		
2006–07	Rotherham U	19	5	**56**	**9**
2006–07	Watford	5	0		
2007–08	Watford	32	2		
2008–09	Watford	34	2	**71**	**4**
2008–09	*Preston NE*	5	1	**5**	**1**
2009–10	Sheffield U	20	3		
2010–11	Sheffield U	16	3		
2011–12	Sheffield U	40	13		
2012–13	Sheffield U	0	0	**76**	**19**
2012–13	Portsmouth	22	0	**22**	**0**
2012–13	Blackburn R	9	0		
2013–14	Blackburn R	32	0		
2014–15	Blackburn R	28	0		
2015–16	Blackburn R	10	0	**79**	**0**

Players retained or with offer of contract
Fisher, Andrew Lee; Hardcastle, Lewis James; Mansell, Lewis David; Platt, Matthew James.

Scholars
Ascroft, Ben Paul; Askew, Joshua George Michael Peter; Callaway, Stuart Peter; Curran, Alex Samuel; Doyle, Charley Ian; Fawns, Mason Matthew; Grayson, Joseph Nicholas; Hendry, Callum David; Howarth, Ramirez; Magloire, Tyler Jordan; Makinson, Matthew Harry; Mols, Stefan Edouard; Pemberton, Tre Kingsley; Pirretas Glasmacher, Jan; Rankin-Costello, Joseph Scott; Steer, Joel Samuel Anthony; Tanner, Hyuga; Travis, Lewis; Wall, Luke Sky; Williams, Benjamin Joseph.

BLACKPOOL (9)

AIMSON, Will (D) 17 0
H: 5 10 W: 11 00 b.Christchurch 1-1-94

2013–14	Hull C	0	0		
2014–15	Hull C	0	0		
2014–15	*Tranmere R*	2	0	**2**	**0**
2015–16	Hull C	0	0		
2015–16	Blackpool	15	0	**15**	**0**

ALDRED, Tom (D) 144 8
H: 6 2 W: 13 02 b.Bolton 11-9-90
Internationals: Scotland U19.

2008–09	Carlisle U	0	0		
2009–10	Carlisle U	5	0	**5**	**0**
2010–11	Watford	0	0		
2010–11	*Stockport Co*	7	0	**7**	**0**
2011–12	Watford	0	0		
2011–12	Colchester U	0	0		
2011–12	*Torquay U*	0	0		
2012–13	Colchester U	0	0		
2012–13	Accrington S	13	0		
2013–14	Accrington S	46	2		
2014–15	Accrington S	25	1	**84**	**3**
2014–15	*Blackpool*	6	0		
2015–16	Blackpool	42	5	**48**	**5**

BONEY, Miles (G) 0 0
H: 5 11 W: 11 09 b.Blackpool 1-2-98

2014–15	Blackpool	0	0		
2015–16	Blackpool	0	0		

BOYCE, Emmerson (D) 544 23
H: 6 0 W: 12 03 b.Aylesbury 24-9-79
Internationals: Barbados Full caps.

1997–98	Luton T	0	0		
1998–99	Luton T	1	0		
1999–2000	Luton T	30	1		
2000–01	Luton T	42	3		
2001–02	Luton T	37	0		
2002–03	Luton T	34	0		
2003–04	Luton T	42	4	**186**	**8**
2004–05	Crystal Palace	27	0		
2005–06	Crystal Palace	42	2	**69**	**2**
2006–07	Wigan Ath	34	0		
2007–08	Wigan Ath	25	0		
2008–09	Wigan Ath	27	1		
2009–10	Wigan Ath	24	3		
2010–11	Wigan Ath	22	0		
2011–12	Wigan Ath	26	3		
2012–13	Wigan Ath	36	4		
2013–14	Wigan Ath	42	2		
2014–15	Wigan Ath	27	0	**263**	**13**
2015–16	Blackpool	26	0	**26**	**0**

CAMERON, Henry (M) 25 1
H: 5 10 W: 11 00 b. 28-6-97
Internationals: New Zealand Full caps.

2013–14	Blackpool	0	0		
2014–15	Blackpool	11	1		
2015–16	Blackpool	14	0	**25**	**1**

CATO, Anthony (F) 0 0

2015–16	Blackpool	0	0		

CUBERO, Jose (M) 204 17
H: 5 10 W: 11 00 b.San Jose 14-2-87
Internationals: Costa Rica Full caps.

2009–10	Herediano	14	2		
2009–10	*Puntarenas*	17	0	**17**	**0**
2010–11	Herediano	34	3		
2011–12	Herediano	40	4		
2012–13	Herediano	19	4		
2013–14	Herediano	42	3	**149**	**16**
2014–15	Blackpool	12	0		

2015–16	Blackpool	7	0	**19**	**0**
2015–16	CS Herediano	19	1	**19**	**1**

CULLEN, Mark (F) **125 24**
H: 5 9 W: 11 11 b.Ashington 21-4-92

2009–10	Hull C	3	1		
2010–11	Hull C	17	0		
2010–11	Bradford C	4	0	**4**	**0**
2011–12	Hull C	4	0		
2011–12	Bury	4	0		
2012–13	Hull C	0	0		
2012–13	Hull C	0	0	**24**	**1**
2012–13	Bury	10	1	**14**	**1**
2014–15	Luton T	42	13	**42**	**13**
2015–16	Blackpool	41	9	**41**	**9**

DOYLE, Colin (G) **81 0**
H: 6 5 W: 14 05 b.Cork 12-8-85
Internationals: Republic of Ireland U21, B, Full caps.

2004–05	Birmingham C	0	0		
2004–05	Chester C	0	0		
2004–05	Nottingham F	3	0	**3**	**0**
2005–06	Birmingham C	0	0		
2005–06	Millwall	14	0	**14**	**0**
2006–07	Birmingham C	19	0		
2007–08	Birmingham C	3	0		
2008–09	Birmingham C	2	0		
2009–10	Birmingham C	0	0		
2010–11	Birmingham C	1	0		
2011–12	Birmingham C	5	0		
2012–13	Birmingham C	0	0		
2013–14	Birmingham C	0	0		
2014–15	Birmingham C	1	0	**31**	**0**
2015–16	Blackpool	33	0	**33**	**0**

DUNNE, Charles (F) **88 0**
H: 5 9 W: 11 09 b.Lambeth 13-2-93
Internationals: Republic of Ireland U21.

2011–12	Wycombe W	3	0		
2012–13	Wycombe W	38	0		
2013–14	Blackpool	0	0		
2013–14	Wycombe W	9	0	**50**	**0**
2014–15	Blackpool	22	0		
2015–16	Blackpool	4	0	**26**	**0**
2015–16	Crawley T	12	0	**12**	**0**

FERGUSON, David (D) **40 1**
H: 5 10 W: 12 00 b.Sunderland 7-6-94

2012–13	Sunderland	0	0		
2013–14	Sunderland	0	0		
2014–15	Sunderland	0	0		
2014–15	Blackpool	10	1		
2015–16	Blackpool	30	0	**40**	**1**

HERRON, John (M) **22 0**
H: 6 0 W: 11 07 b.Coatbridge 1-2-94
Internationals: Scotland U16, U17, U18, U19, U20, U21.

2012–13	Celtic	1	0		
2013–14	Celtic	1	0		
2014–15	Celtic	0	0	**2**	**0**
2014–15	Cowdenbeath	5	0	**5**	**0**
2015–16	Blackpool	15	0	**15**	**0**

HIGHAM, Luke (M) **11 0**
H: 6 1 W: 12 02 b.Blackpool 21-10-96

2014–15	Blackpool	0	0		
2015–16	Blackpool	11	0	**11**	**0**

LETHEREN, Kyle (G) **66 0**
H: 6 2 W: 13 00 b.Swansea 26-12-87
Internationals: Wales U21.

2010–11	Kilmarnock	0	0		
2011–12	Kilmarnock	2	0		
2012–13	Kilmarnock	9	0	**11**	**0**
2013–14	Dundee	35	0		
2014–15	Dundee	15	0	**50**	**0**
2015–16	Blackpool	5	0	**5**	**0**

McALISTER, Jim (M) **240 11**
H: 5 10 W: 13 00 b.Rothesay 2-11-85

2009–10	Greenock Morton	30	1	**30**	**1**
2010–11	Hamilton A	19	0		
2011–12	Hamilton A	36	1	**55**	**1**
2012–13	Dundee	38	3		
2013–14	Dundee	36	4		
2014–15	Dundee	37	2	**111**	**9**
2015–16	Blackpool	44	0	**44**	**0**

MILTON, Daniel (G) **0 0**
H: 6 0 W: 12 04 b.Ajax, Ontario 26-11-96
Internationals: Canada U17.

2014–15	Blackpool	0	0		
2015–16	Blackpool	0	0		

NORRIS, David (M) **455 53**
H: 5 7 W: 11 06 b.Stamford 22-2-81

1999–2000	Bolton W	0	0		
2000–01	Bolton W	0	0		
2001–02	Bolton W	0	0		
2001–02	Hull C	6	1	**6**	**1**
2002–03	Bolton W	0	0		
2002–03	Plymouth Arg	33	6		
2003–04	Plymouth Arg	45	5		
2004–05	Plymouth Arg	35	3		
2005–06	Plymouth Arg	45	2		
2006–07	Plymouth Arg	41	6		
2007–08	Plymouth Arg	27	5	**226**	**27**
2007–08	Ipswich T	9	1		
2008–09	Ipswich T	37	3		
2009–10	Ipswich T	24	1		
2010–11	Ipswich T	36	8	**106**	**13**
2011–12	Portsmouth	40	8	**40**	**8**
2012–13	Leeds U	30	3		
2013–14	Leeds U	3	0		
2014–15	Leeds U	0	0	**30**	**3**
2014–15	Peterborough U	8	0	**8**	**0**
2015–16	Yeovil T	1	0	**1**	**0**
2015–16	Blackpool	38	1	**38**	**1**

OLIVER, Connor (D) **18 0**
H: 5 10 W: 12 00 b.Newcastle upon Tyne 17-1-94

2013–14	Sunderland	0	0		
2013–14	Hartlepool U	3	0	**3**	**0**
2014–15	Blackpool	6	0		
2015–16	Blackpool	4	0	**10**	**0**
2015–16	Morecambe	5	0	**5**	**0**

ORLANDI, Andrea (M) **244 22**
H: 6 0 W: 12 01 b.Barcelona 3-8-84

2005–06	Alaves	0	0		
2005–06	Barcelona	1	0	**1**	**0**
2005–06	Barcelona B	32	4		
2006–07	Barcelona B	35	1	**67**	**5**
2007–08	Swansea C	8	0		
2008–09	Swansea C	11	1		
2009–10	Swansea C	30	1		
2010–11	Swansea C	20	0		
2011–12	Swansea C	3	1		
2012–13	Swansea C	0	0	**72**	**3**
2012–13	Brighton & HA	35	6		
2013–14	Brighton & HA	14	0	**49**	**6**
2014–15	Blackpool	28	4		
2015–16	Blackpool	0	0	**28**	**4**
2015–16	An Famagusta	27	4	**27**	**4**

PATERSON, Martin (F) **256 55**
H: 5 9 W: 10 11 b.Tunstall 13-5-87
Internationals: Northern Ireland U21, Full caps.

2004–05	Stoke C	3	0		
2005–06	Stoke C	3	0		
2006–07	Stoke C	9	1	**15**	**1**
2006–07	Grimsby T	15	6	**15**	**6**
2007–08	Scunthorpe U	40	13	**40**	**13**
2008–09	Burnley	43	12		
2009–10	Burnley	23	4		
2010–11	Burnley	11	2		
2011–12	Burnley	14	3		
2012–13	Burnley	39	8	**130**	**29**
2013–14	Huddersfield T	22	5		
2013–14	Bristol C	8	1	**8**	**1**
2014–15	Huddersfield T	3	0	**25**	**5**
2014–15	Fleetwood T	3	0	**3**	**0**
2015	Orlando C	3	0	**3**	**0**
2015–16	Blackpool	17	0	**17**	**0**

PHILLISKIRK, Daniel (M) **136 18**
H: 5 10 W: 11 05 b.Oldham 10-4-91
Internationals: England U17.

2008–09	Chelsea	0	0		
2009–10	Chelsea	0	0		
2010–11	Chelsea	0	0		
2010–11	Oxford U	1	0		
2010–11	Sheffield U	3	0		
2011–12	Sheffield U	0	0		
2012–13	Oxford U	4	0	**5**	**0**
2012–13	Sheffield U	1	0	**4**	**0**
2012–13	Coventry C	1	0		
2013–14	Coventry C	0	0	**1**	**0**
2013–14	Oldham Ath	38	4		
2014–15	Oldham Ath	43	4		
2015–16	Oldham Ath	23	5	**104**	**13**
2015–16	Blackpool	22	5	**22**	**5**

POTTS, Brad (M) **148 15**
H: 6 2 W: 12 09 b.Carlisle 3-7-94
Internationals: England U19.

2012–13	Carlisle U	27	0		
2013–14	Carlisle U	37	2		
2014–15	Carlisle U	39	7	**103**	**9**
2015–16	Blackpool	45	6	**45**	**6**

RANGER, Nile (F) **101 14**
H: 6 2 W: 13 03 b.Wood Green 11-4-91
Internationals: England U19.

2008–09	Newcastle U	0	0		
2009–10	Newcastle U	25	2		
2010–11	Newcastle U	24	0		
2011–12	Newcastle U	0	0		
2011–12	Barnsley	5	0	**5**	**0**
2011–12	Sheffield W	8	2	**8**	**2**
2012–13	Newcastle U	2	0	**51**	**2**
2013–14	Swindon T	23	8	**23**	**8**
2014–15	Blackpool	14	2		
2015–16	Blackpool	0	0	**14**	**2**

REDSHAW, Jack (F) **158 43**
H: 5 6 W: 10 00 b.Salford 20-11-90

2009–10	Manchester C	0	0		
2010–11	Rochdale	2	0	**2**	**0**

From Salford C, Altrincham

2011–12	Morecambe	11	2		
2012–13	Morecambe	40	15		
2013–14	Morecambe	29	8		
2014–15	Morecambe	40	11	**120**	**36**
2015–16	Blackpool	36	7	**36**	**7**

RIVERS, Jarrett (M) **10 0**
H: 5 6 W: 12 00 b.Spennymoor 10-9-93
From Whitley Bay, Blyth Spartans.

2015–16	Blackpool	10	0	**10**	**0**

ROBERTSON, Clark (D) **95 1**
H: 6 2 W: 12 00 b.Aberdeen 5-9-93
Internationals: Scotland U19, U21.

2009–10	Aberdeen	3	0		
2010–11	Aberdeen	13	0		
2011–12	Aberdeen	9	0		
2012–13	Aberdeen	23	0		
2013–14	Aberdeen	8	0		
2014–15	Aberdeen	1	0	**57**	**0**
2015–16	Blackpool	38	1	**38**	**1**

SAMUEL, Bright (F) **29 0**
H: 5 9 W: 11 05 b. 1-2-97

2014–15	Blackpool	6	0		
2015–16	Blackpool	23	0	**29**	**0**

TELFORD, Dominic (F) **14 1**
H: 5 9 W: 11 05 b.Burnley 5-12-96

2014–15	Blackpool	14	1		
2015–16	Blackpool	0	0	**14**	**1**

WADDINGTON, Mark (M) **3 0**
H: 6 0 W: 10 06 b.Wigan 11-10-96

2013–14	Blackpool	0	0		
2014–15	Blackpool	3	0		
2015–16	Blackpool	0	0	**3**	**0**

WILSON, Macauley (M) **0 0**
H: 5 9 W: 11 00 b. 2-9-97

2015–16	Blackpool	0	0		

YEATES, Mark (F) **379 47**
H: 5 8 W: 13 03 b.Dublin 11-1-85
Internationals: Republic of Ireland U21, B.

2002–03	Tottenham H	1	0		
2003–04	Tottenham H	0	0		
2003–04	Brighton & HA	9	0	**9**	**0**
2004–05	Tottenham H	0	0		
2004–05	Swindon T	4	0	**4**	**0**
2005–06	Tottenham H	0	0		
2005–06	Colchester U	44	5		
2006–07	Tottenham H	0	0	**3**	**0**
2006–07	Hull C	5	0	**5**	**0**
2006–07	Leicester C	9	1	**9**	**1**
2007–08	Colchester U	29	8		
2008–09	Colchester U	43	12	**116**	**25**
2009–10	Middlesbrough	19	1	**19**	**1**
2009–10	Sheffield U	20	2		
2010–11	Sheffield U	35	5	**55**	**7**
2011–12	Watford	33	3		
2012–13	Watford	29	4	**62**	**7**
2013–14	Bradford C	29	2		
2014–15	Bradford C	41	3	**70**	**5**
2015–16	Oldham Ath	16	1	**16**	**1**
2015–16	Blackpool	11	0	**11**	**0**

Scholars
Agyeman-Badu, Benjamin; Boney, Myles Laurence; Cato, Anthony Robert; Chea, Raph; Doyle, James Andrew; Gregory, Kit William; N'Guessan, Christian Dashiell Ruhemann; Njie, Alieu; Pond, Elliot Daniel Lloyd; Richards, Caleb Joel; Robinson, Liam Anthony; Roscoe Byrne, Samuel Alexander; Rufus, Tyler Olushola; Sims, Jack Stephen John; Steele, Jack; Williams, Denzel Owusu.

BOLTON W (10)

AMOS, Ben (G) **93 0**
H: 6 1 W: 13 00 b.Macclesfield 10-4-90
Internationals: England U16, U17, U18, U19, U20, U21.

2007–08	Manchester U	0	0		
2008–09	Manchester U	0	0		

2009–10	Manchester U	0	0		
2009–10	*Peterborough U*	1	0	**1**	**0**
2010–11	Manchester U	0	0		
2010–11	*Oldham Ath*	16	0	**16**	**0**
2011–12	Manchester U	1	0		
2012–13	Manchester U	0	0		
2012–13	*Hull C*	17	0	**17**	**0**
2013–14	Manchester U	0	0		
2013–14	*Carlisle U*	9	0	**9**	**0**
2014–15	Manchester U	0	0	**1**	**0**
2014–15	*Bolton W*	9	0		
2015–16	Bolton W	40	0	**49**	**0**

CASADO, Jose Manuel (D) 163 1

H: 5 8 W: 11 11 b.Seville 9-8-86

2007–08	Sevilla	2	0		
2008–09	Sevilla	0	0		
2008–09	*Recreativo Huelva*	19	0	**19**	**0**
2009–10	Sevilla	0	0	**2**	**0**
2009–10	*Xerex*	27	0	**27**	**0**
2010–11	Rayo Vallecano	36	1		
2011–12	Rayo Vallecano	32	0		
2012–13	Rayo Vallecano	28	0	**96**	**1**
2013–14	Malaga	2	0		
2014–15	Malaga	0	0	**2**	**0**
2014–15	Almeria	8	0	**8**	**0**
2015–16	Bolton W	9	0	**9**	**0**

CLAYTON, Max (F) 91 10

H: 5 9 W: 11 00 b.Crewe 9-8-94

Internationals: England U16, U17, U18, U19.

2010–11	Crewe Alex	2	0		
2011–12	Crewe Alex	24	3		
2012–13	Crewe Alex	35	4		
2013–14	Crewe Alex	13	2	**74**	**9**
2014–15	Bolton W	9	1		
2015–16	Bolton W	8	0	**17**	**1**

CLOUGH, Zach (F) 36 12

b.Manchester 8-3-95

2013–14	Bolton W	0	0		
2014–15	Bolton W	8	5		
2015–16	Bolton W	28	7	**36**	**12**

DANNS, Neil (M) 393 61

H: 5 10 W: 10 12 b.Liverpool 23-11-82

Internationals: Guyana Full caps.

2000–01	Blackburn R	0	0		
2001–02	Blackburn R	0	0		
2002–03	Blackburn R	2	0		
2003–04	Blackpool	12	2	**12**	**2**
2003–04	Blackburn R	1	0		
2003–04	*Hartlepool U*	9	1	**9**	**1**
2004–05	Blackburn R	0	0	**3**	**0**
2004–05	Colchester U	32	11		
2005–06	Colchester U	41	8	**73**	**19**
2006–07	Birmingham C	29	3		
2007–08	Birmingham C	2	0	**31**	**3**
2007–08	Crystal Palace	4	0		
2008–09	Crystal Palace	20	2		
2009–10	Crystal Palace	42	8		
2010–11	Crystal Palace	37	8	**103**	**18**
2011–12	Leicester C	29	5		
2012–13	Leicester C	1	0		
2012–13	*Bristol C*	9	2	**9**	**2**
2012–13	*Huddersfield T*	17	2	**17**	**2**
2013–14	Leicester C	0	0	**30**	**5**
2013–14	Bolton W	33	6		
2014–15	Bolton W	41	1		
2015–16	Bolton W	32	2	**106**	**9**

DAVIES, Mark (M) 213 16

H: 5 11 W: 11 08 b.Willenhall 18-2-88

Internationals: England U16, U17, U19.

2004–05	Wolverhampton W	0	0		
2005–06	Wolverhampton W	20	1		
2006–07	Wolverhampton W	7	0		
2007–08	Wolverhampton W	0	0		
2008–09	Wolverhampton W	0	0	**27**	**1**
2008–09	*Leicester C*	7	1	**7**	**1**
2008–09	Bolton W	10	0		
2009–10	Bolton W	17	0		
2010–11	Bolton W	24	1		
2011–12	Bolton W	35	4		
2012–13	Bolton W	24	6		
2013–14	Bolton W	18	1		
2014–15	Bolton W	15	2		
2015–16	Bolton W	36	0	**179**	**14**

DERVITE, Dorian (D) 158 6

H: 6 3 W: 13 06 b.Lille 25-7-88

Internationals: France U16, U17, U18, U19, U21.

2008–09	Southend U	18	0	**18**	**0**
2010–11	Villarreal B	9	0		
2011–12	Villarreal B	2	0	**11**	**0**
2012–13	Villarreal	0	0		
2012–13	Charlton Ath	30	3		
2013–14	Charlton Ath	40	2	**70**	**5**
2014–15	Bolton W	37	0		
2015–16	Bolton W	22	1	**59**	**1**

DOBBIE, Stephen (F) 353 102

H: 5 10 W: 11 00 b.Glasgow 5-12-82

2002–03	Rangers	0	0		
2002–03	*Northern Spirit*	3	3	**3**	**3**
2003–04	Hibernian	28	2		
2004–05	Hibernian	7	0	**35**	**2**
2004–05	*St Johnstone*	8	2		
2005–06	St Johnstone	20	1	**28**	**3**
2006–07	*Dumbarton*	17	10	**17**	**10**
2006–07	Queen of the South	15	10		
2007–08	Queen of the South	36	16		
2008–09	Queen of the South	32	23	**83**	**49**
2009–10	Swansea C	6	0		
2009–10	*Blackpool*	16	4		
2010–11	Swansea C	41	9		
2011–12	Swansea C	8	0	**55**	**9**
2011–12	*Blackpool*	7	5		
2012–13	Brighton & HA	15	2	**15**	**2**
2012–13	*Crystal Palace*	15	3		
2013–14	Crystal Palace	1	0		
2013–14	*Blackpool*	27	4	**50**	**13**
2014–15	Crystal Palace	0	0	**16**	**3**
2014–15	*Fleetwood T*	27	4	**27**	**4**
2015–16	Bolton W	24	4	**24**	**4**

EAVES, Tom (M) 92 16

H: 6 3 W: 13 07 b.Liverpool 14-1-92

2009–10	Oldham Ath	15	0		
2010–11	Bolton W	0	0		
2010–11	*Oldham Ath*	0	0	**15**	**0**
2011–12	Bolton W	0	0		
2012–13	Bolton W	3	0		
2012–13	*Bristol R*	16	7	**16**	**7**
2012–13	*Shrewsbury T*	10	6		
2013–14	Bolton W	0	0		
2013–14	*Rotherham U*	8	0	**8**	**0**
2013–14	*Shrewsbury T*	25	2	**35**	**8**
2014–15	Bolton W	1	0		
2014–15	*Yeovil T*	5	0	**5**	**0**
2014–15	*Bury*	9	1	**9**	**1**
2015–16	Bolton W	0	0	**4**	**0**

FEENEY, Liam (M) 280 26

H: 5 10 W: 12 02 b.Hammersmith 21-1-87

2008–09	Southend U	1	0	**1**	**0**
2008–09	Bournemouth	14	3		
2009–10	Bournemouth	44	5		
2010–11	Bournemouth	46	4		
2011–12	Bournemouth	5	0	**109**	**12**
2011–12	Millwall	34	4		
2012–13	Millwall	22	1		
2013–14	Millwall	17	0	**73**	**5**
2013–14	*Bolton W*	4	0		
2013–14	*Blackburn R*	6	0	**6**	**0**
2014–15	Bolton W	41	3		
2015–16	Bolton W	37	5	**82**	**8**
2015–16	*Ipswich T*	9	1	**9**	**1**

FINNEY, Alex (D) 2 0

b. 6-6-96

2013–14	Leyton Orient	0	0		
2014–15	Leyton Orient	0	0		
2015–16	Bolton W	2	0	**2**	**0**

GARRETT, Tyler (D) 3 0

b. 26-10-96

2015–16	Bolton W	3	0	**3**	**0**

GOUANO, Prince-Desire (D) 81 0

H: 6 2 W: 11 11 b.Paris 24-12-93

Internationals: France U18, U19, U20.

2010–11	Le Havre	1	0	**1**	**0**
2011–12	Juventus	0	0		
2012–13	Juventus	0	0		
2012–13	*Virtus Lanciano*	1	0	**1**	**0**
2012–13	*Vicenza*	1	0	**1**	**0**
2013–14	Atalanta	0	0		
2013–14	*RKC Waalwijk*	20	0	**20**	**0**
2014–15	Atalanta	0	0		
2014–15	*Rio Ave*	27	0	**27**	**0**
2015–16	Atalanta	0	0		

On loan from Atalanta.

2015–16	Bolton W	19	0	**19**	**0**
2015–16	*Gaziantepspor*	12	0	**12**	**0**

HALL, Robert (F) 98 11

H: 6 2 W: 10 05 b.Aylesbury 20-10-93

Internationals: England U16, U17, U18, U19.

2010–11	West Ham U	0	0		
2011–12	West Ham U	3	0		
2011–12	*Oxford U*	13	5	**13**	**5**
2011–12	*Milton Keynes D*	2	0		
2012–13	West Ham U	1	0	**4**	**0**
2012–13	*Birmingham C*	13	0	**13**	**0**
2012–13	*Bolton W*	1	0		
2013–14	Bolton W	22	1		
2014–15	Bolton W	9	0		
2014–15	*Milton Keynes D*	7	3		
2015–16	Bolton W	0	0	**32**	**1**
2015–16	*Milton Keynes D*	27	2	**36**	**5**

HESKEY, Emile (F) 633 130

H: 6 2 W: 13 12 b.Leicester 11-1-78

Internationals: England Youth, U21, B, Full caps.

1994–95	Leicester C	1	0		
1995–96	Leicester C	30	7		
1996–97	Leicester C	35	10		
1997–98	Leicester C	35	10		
1998–99	Leicester C	30	6		
1999–2000	Leicester C	23	7	**154**	**40**
1999–2000	Liverpool	12	3		
2000–01	Liverpool	36	14		
2001–02	Liverpool	35	9		
2002–03	Liverpool	32	6		
2003–04	Liverpool	35	7	**150**	**39**
2004–05	Birmingham C	34	10		
2005–06	Birmingham C	34	4	**68**	**14**
2006–07	Wigan Ath	34	8		
2007–08	Wigan Ath	28	4		
2008–09	Wigan Ath	20	3	**82**	**15**
2008–09	Aston Villa	14	2		
2009–10	Aston Villa	31	3		
2010–11	Aston Villa	19	3		
2011–12	Aston Villa	28	1	**92**	**9**
2012–13	Newcastle Jets	23	9		
2013–14	Newcastle Jets	19	1	**42**	**10**
2014–15	Bolton W	16	1		
2015–16	Bolton W	29	2	**45**	**3**

HOLDEN, Stuart (M) 121 17

H: 5 10 W: 11 07 b.Aberdeen 1-8-85

Internationals: USA Full caps.

2005–06	Sunderland	0	0		
2006	Houston D	13	1		
2007	Houston D	21	5		
2008	Houston D	27	3		
2009	Houston D	26	6	**87**	**15**
2009–10	Bolton W	2	0		
2010–11	Bolton W	26	2		
2011–12	Bolton W	0	0		
2012–13	Bolton W	2	0		
2012–13	*Sheffield W*	4	0	**4**	**0**
2013–14	Bolton W	0	0		
2014–15	Bolton W	0	0		
2015–16	Bolton W	0	0	**30**	**2**

HOLDING, Rob (D) 27 1

b.Tameside 20-9-95

Internationals: England U21.

2014–15	Bolton W	0	0		
2014–15	*Bury*	1	0	**1**	**0**
2015–16	Bolton W	26	1	**26**	**1**

HUGHES, Andy (M) 544 39

H: 5 11 W: 12 01 b.Stockport 2-1-78

1995–96	Oldham Ath	15	1		
1996–97	Oldham Ath	8	0		
1997–98	Oldham Ath	10	0	**33**	**1**
1997–98	Notts Co	15	2		
1998–99	Notts Co	30	3		
1999–2000	Notts Co	35	7		
2000–01	Notts Co	30	5	**110**	**17**
2001–02	Reading	39	6		
2002–03	Reading	43	9		
2003–04	Reading	43	3		
2004–05	Reading	41	0	**166**	**18**
2005–06	Norwich C	36	2		
2006–07	Norwich C	36	0	**72**	**2**
2007–08	Leeds U	40	1		
2008–09	Leeds U	27	0		
2009–10	Leeds U	39	0		
2010–11	Leeds U	10	0	**116**	**1**
2010–11	Scunthorpe U	19	0	**19**	**0**
2011–12	Charlton Ath	15	0		
2012–13	Charlton Ath	6	0		
2013–14	Charlton Ath	7	0	**28**	**0**
2014–15	Bolton W	0	0		
2015–16	Bolton W	0	0		

JAASKELAINEN, William (G) 0 0

b. 25-7-98

Internationals: Finland U17, U18.

2015–16	Bolton W	0	0		

KNIGHT, Aaron (F) 0 0

b.Manchester 14-3-96

2014–15	Bolton W	0	0		
2015–16	Bolton W	0	0		

LUSSEY, Jordan (M) 1 0

b.Ormskirk 2-11-94

Internationals: England U18.

2011–12	Liverpool	0	0		
2012–13	Liverpool	0	0		
2013–14	Liverpool	0	0		
2014–15	*Bolton W*	0	0		

Season	Club	Apps	Gls	Tot Apps	Tot Gls
2015–16	Bolton W	0	0		
2015–16	York C	1	0	1	0

MADINE, Gary (F) 246 52
H: 6 1 W: 12 00 b.Gateshead 24-8-90

Season	Club	Apps	Gls	Tot Apps	Tot Gls
2007–08	Carlisle U	11	0		
2008–09	Carlisle U	14	1		
2008–09	Rochdale	3	0	3	0
2009–10	Carlisle U	20	4		
2009–10	Coventry C	9	0		
2009–10	Chesterfield	4	0	4	0
2010–11	Carlisle U	21	8		
2010–11	Sheffield W	22	5		
2011–12	Sheffield W	38	18		
2012–13	Sheffield W	30	3		
2013–14	Sheffield W	1	0		
2013–14	Carlisle U	5	2	71	15
2014–15	Sheffield W	10	0	101	26
2014–15	Coventry C	11	3	20	3
2014–15	Blackpool	15	3	15	3
2015–16	Bolton W	32	5	32	5

MAHER, Niall (D) 15 0
b.Manchester 31-7-95

Season	Club	Apps	Gls	Tot Apps	Tot Gls
2014–15	Bolton W	0	0		
2014–15	Blackpool	10	0	10	0
2015–16	Bolton W	5	0	5	0

MOXEY, Dean (D) 239 8
H: 6 2 W: 11 00 b.Exeter 14-1-86
Internationals: England C.

Season	Club	Apps	Gls	Tot Apps	Tot Gls
2008–09	Exeter C	43	4	43	4
2009–10	Derby Co	30	0		
2010–11	Derby Co	22	2	52	2
2010–11	Crystal Palace	17	1		
2011–12	Crystal Palace	24	0		
2012–13	Crystal Palace	30	0		
2013–14	Crystal Palace	20	0	91	1
2014–15	Bolton W	20	1		
2015–16	Bolton W	33	0	53	1

NEWELL, George (F) 2 0
b. 27-1-97
From Everton.

Season	Club	Apps	Gls	Tot Apps	Tot Gls
2015–16	Bolton W	2	0	2	0

OSEDE, Derik (D) 23 0
b. 21-2-93
Internationals: Spain U16, U17, U18, U19, U20, U21.

Season	Club	Apps	Gls	Tot Apps	Tot Gls
2014–15	Real Madrid	0	0		
2015–16	Bolton W	23	0	23	0

PISANO, Francesco (D) 233 1
H: 5 11 W: 11 07 b.Cagliari 24-9-86
Internationals: Italy U21.

Season	Club	Apps	Gls	Tot Apps	Tot Gls
2005–06	Cagliari	23	0		
2006–07	Cagliari	23	0		
2007–08	Cagliari	17	0		
2008–09	Cagliari	29	0		
2009–10	Cagliari	9	0		
2010–11	Cagliari	18	0		
2011–12	Cagliari	34	0		
2012–13	Cagliari	28	1		
2013–14	Cagliari	23	0		
2014–15	Cagliari	13	0	217	1
2015–16	Bolton W	3	0	3	0
2015–16	Avellino	13	0	13	0

PRATLEY, Darren (M) 358 41
H: 6 1 W: 10 12 b.Barking 22-4-85

Season	Club	Apps	Gls	Tot Apps	Tot Gls
2001–02	Fulham	0	0		
2002–03	Fulham	0	0		
2003–04	Fulham	1	0		
2004–05	Fulham	0	0		
2004–05	Brentford	14	1		
2005–06	Fulham	0	0	1	0
2005–06	Brentford	32	4	46	5
2006–07	Swansea C	28	1		
2007–08	Swansea C	42	5		
2008–09	Swansea C	37	4		
2009–10	Swansea C	36	7		
2010–11	Swansea C	34	9	177	26
2011–12	Bolton W	25	1		
2012–13	Bolton W	31	2		
2013–14	Bolton W	20	2		
2014–15	Bolton W	22	4		
2015–16	Bolton W	36	1	134	10

RACHUBKA, Paul (G) 328 0
H: 6 1 W: 13 05 b.San Luis Opispo 21-5-81
Internationals: England U16, U18, U20.

Season	Club	Apps	Gls	Tot Apps	Tot Gls
1999–2000	Manchester U	0	0		
2000–01	Manchester U	1	0		
2001–02	Manchester U	0	0	1	0
2001–02	Oldham Ath	16	0		
2001–02	Charlton Ath	0	0		
2002–03	Charlton Ath	0	0		
2003–04	Charlton Ath	0	0		
2003–04	Huddersfield T	13	0		
2004–05	Charlton Ath	0	0		
2004–05	Milton Keynes D	4	0	4	0
2004–05	Northampton T	10	0	10	0
2004–05	Huddersfield T	29	0		
2005–06	Huddersfield T	34	0		
2006–07	Huddersfield T	0	0	76	0
2006–07	Peterborough U	4	0	4	0
2006–07	Blackpool	8	0		
2007–08	Blackpool	46	0		
2008–09	Blackpool	42	0		
2009–10	Blackpool	20	0		
2010–11	Blackpool	2	0	118	0
2011–12	Leeds U	6	0		
2011–12	Tranmere R	10	0	10	0
2011–12	Leyton Orient	8	0	8	0
2012–13	Leeds U	0	0	6	0
2012–13	Accrington S	21	0	21	0
2013–14	Oldham Ath	10	0		
2014–15	Oldham Ath	22	0	48	0
2014–15	Crewe Alex	15	0	15	0
2015–16	Bolton W	7	0	7	0

SAMIZADEH, Alex (F) 1 0
b. 10-11-98

Season	Club	Apps	Gls	Tot Apps	Tot Gls
2015–16	Bolton W	1	0	1	0

SPEARING, Jay (M) 177 9
H: 5 6 W: 11 01 b.Wallasey 25-11-88

Season	Club	Apps	Gls	Tot Apps	Tot Gls
2006–07	Liverpool	0	0		
2007–08	Liverpool	0	0		
2008–09	Liverpool	0	0		
2009–10	Liverpool	3	0		
2009–10	Leicester C	7	1	7	1
2010–11	Liverpool	11	0		
2011–12	Liverpool	16	0		
2012–13	Liverpool	0	0		
2012–13	Bolton W	37	2		
2013–14	Liverpool	0	0	30	0
2013–14	Bolton W	45	2		
2014–15	Bolton W	21	1		
2014–15	Blackburn R	15	1	15	1
2015–16	Bolton W	22	2	125	7

TAYLOR, Quade (M) 3 0
H: 6 3 W: 11 00 b.Tooting 11-12-93

Season	Club	Apps	Gls	Tot Apps	Tot Gls
2010–11	Crystal Palace	0	0		
2011–12	Crystal Palace	0	0		
2012–13	Crystal Palace	0	0		
2013–14	Crystal Palace	0	0		
2014–15	Bolton W	1	0		
2015–16	Bolton W	0	0	1	0
2015–16	Dagenham & R	2	0	2	0

THOMAS, Jamie (F) 0 0
b. 10-1-97
Internationals: Wales U19.

Season	Club	Apps	Gls	Tot Apps	Tot Gls
2015–16	Bolton W	0	0		

THRELKELD, Oscar (D) 34 1
b.Bolton 15-12-94

Season	Club	Apps	Gls	Tot Apps	Tot Gls
2013–14	Bolton W	2	0		
2014–15	Bolton W	4	0		
2015–16	Bolton W	3	0	9	0
2015–16	Plymouth Arg	25	1	25	1

TROTTER, Liam (M) 249 33
H: 6 2 W: 12 02 b.Ipswich 24-8-88

Season	Club	Apps	Gls	Tot Apps	Tot Gls
2005–06	Ipswich T	1	0		
2006–07	Ipswich T	0	0		
2006–07	Millwall	2	0		
2007–08	Ipswich T	7	1		
2008–09	Ipswich T	3	1		
2008–09	Grimsby T	15	2	15	2
2008–09	Scunthorpe U	12	1	12	1
2009–10	Ipswich T	12	0	23	2
2009–10	Millwall	20	1		
2010–11	Millwall	35	7		
2011–12	Millwall	35	7		
2012–13	Millwall	36	6		
2013–14	Millwall	19	3	147	24
2013–14	Bolton W	16	1		
2014–15	Bolton W	14	1		
2015–16	Bolton W	13	1	43	3
2015–16	Nottingham F	9	1	9	1

TWARDZIK, Filip (M) 10 1
H: 5 11 W: 10 01 b.Trinec 10-2-93
Internationals: Czech Republic U17, U19.

Season	Club	Apps	Gls	Tot Apps	Tot Gls
2011–12	Celtic	1	0		
2012–13	Celtic	2	0		
2013–14	Celtic	1	0		
2014–15	Celtic	1	0	5	0
2014–15	Bolton W	3	1		
2015–16	Bolton W	2	0	5	1

VELA, Joshua (M) 74 2
H: 5 11 W: 11 07 b.Salford 14-12-93

Season	Club	Apps	Gls	Tot Apps	Tot Gls
2010–11	Bolton W	0	0		
2011–12	Bolton W	3	0		
2012–13	Bolton W	4	0		
2013–14	Bolton W	0	0		
2013–14	Notts Co	7	0	7	0
2014–15	Bolton W	29	0		
2015–16	Bolton W	31	2	67	2

WALKER, Tom (M) 18 1
b.Salford 12-12-95

Season	Club	Apps	Gls	Tot Apps	Tot Gls
2014–15	Bolton W	11	1		
2015–16	Bolton W	7	0	18	1

WHEATER, David (D) 266 17
H: 6 5 W: 12 12 b.Redcar 14-2-87
Internationals: England U16, U17, U18, U19, U21.

Season	Club	Apps	Gls	Tot Apps	Tot Gls
2004–05	Middlesbrough	0	0		
2005–06	Middlesbrough	0	0		
2005–06	Doncaster R	7	1	7	1
2006–07	Middlesbrough	2	1		
2006–07	Wolverhampton W	1	0	1	0
2006–07	Darlington	15	2	15	2
2007–08	Middlesbrough	34	3		
2008–09	Middlesbrough	32	1		
2009–10	Middlesbrough	42	1		
2010–11	Middlesbrough	24	3	140	9
2010–11	Bolton W	7	0		
2011–12	Bolton W	24	2		
2012–13	Bolton W	4	0		
2013–14	Bolton W	23	1		
2014–15	Bolton W	17	1		
2015–16	Bolton W	28	1	103	5

WHITE, Hayden (D) 47 1
H: 6 1 W: 10 10 b.Greenwich 15-4-95

Season	Club	Apps	Gls	Tot Apps	Tot Gls
2013–14	Bolton W	2	0		
2014–15	Bolton W	3	0		
2014–15	Carlisle U	8	0	8	0
2014–15	Bury	2	0	2	0
2014–15	Notts Co	3	0	3	0
2015–16	Bolton W	0	0	5	0
2015–16	Blackpool	29	1	29	1

WILKINSON, Conor (F) 45 5
H: 6 1 W: 12 02 b.Croydon 23-1-95
Internationals: Republic of Ireland U17, U19, U21.

Season	Club	Apps	Gls	Tot Apps	Tot Gls
2012–13	Millwall	0	0		
2013–14	Bolton W	0	0		
2013–14	Torquay U	3	0	3	0
2014–15	Bolton W	4	0		
2014–15	Oldham Ath	17	3	17	3
2015–16	Bolton W	0	0	4	0
2015–16	Barnsley	8	1	8	1
2015–16	Newport Co	12	1	12	1
2015–16	Portsmouth	1	0	1	0

WILSON, Lawrie (D) 201 15
H: 5 11 W: 11 06 b.London 11-9-87

Season	Club	Apps	Gls	Tot Apps	Tot Gls
2006–07	Colchester U	0	0		
2010–11	Stevenage	42	5		
2011–12	Stevenage	46	5	88	10
2012–13	Charlton Ath	30	2		
2013–14	Charlton Ath	42	2		
2014–15	Charlton Ath	24	0	96	4
2014–15	Rotherham U	3	0	3	0
2015–16	Bolton W	12	1	12	1
2015–16	Peterborough U	2	0	2	0

WOOLERY, Kaiyne (F) 23 2
H: 5 10 W: 11 07 b.Hackney 11-1-95

Season	Club	Apps	Gls	Tot Apps	Tot Gls
2014–15	Bolton W	1	0		
2014–15	Notts Co	5	0	5	0
2015–16	Bolton W	17	2	18	2

Scholars
Abdo, Anas; Allen, Max Patrick; Brockbank, Harry William; Cvetko, Christopher Brian; Earing, Jack James; Everest, Jack William; Garratt, Tyler John; Grant, Jordan Lee; Griffiths, Luke Duncan; Grivosti, Tom; Honeyball, Alexander Robert; Kenyi, Francis; Likoy Elumba, Enock; Lonsdale, Cole Stephen; Marsh, Matthew Calum; McKenna, Daniel Joseph; Palmer, Tyrell Robert; Pearson, Ronaldo Steve; Perry, Alexander Anthony; Samizadeh, Alexander; Spooner, Callum Michael; Thomas, Jamie Carl; Turner, Jake Edward; White, Ryan.

BOURNEMOUTH (11)

ADAMONIS, Marius (G) 0 0
b. 13-5-97
Internationals: Lithuania U17, U18, U19.

Season	Club	Apps	Gls
2015–16	FK Atlantas	0	0

On loan from FK Altantas.

Season	Club	Apps	Gls
2015–16	Bournemouth	0	0

AFOBE, Benik (F) 151 45
H: 5 10 W: 11 00 b.Leyton 12-2-93
Internationals: England U16, U17, U19, U21.

2009–10	Arsenal	0	0		
2010–11	Arsenal	0	0		
2010–11	Huddersfield T	28	5	28	5
2011–12	Arsenal	0	0		
2011–12	Reading	3	0	3	0
2012–13	Arsenal	0	0		
2012–13	Bolton W	20	2	20	2
2012–13	Millwall	5	0	5	0
2013–14	Arsenal	0	0		
2013–14	Sheffield W	12	2	12	2
2014–15	Arsenal	0	0		
2014–15	Milton Keynes D	22	10	22	10
2014–15	Wolverhampton W	21	13		
2015–16	Wolverhampton W	25	9	46	22
2015–16	Bournemouth	15	4	15	4

ARTER, Harry (M) 189 27
H: 5 9 W: 11 07 b.Sidcup 28-12-89
Internationals: Republic of Ireland U17, U19,
Full caps.

2007–08	Charlton Ath	0	0		
2008–09	Charlton Ath	0	0		
From Woking.					
2010–11	Bournemouth	18	0		
2010–11	Carlisle U	5	1	5	1
2011–12	Bournemouth	34	5		
2012–13	Bournemouth	37	8		
2013–14	Bournemouth	31	3		
2014–15	Bournemouth	43	9		
2015–16	Bournemouth	21	1	184	26

BORUC, Artur (G) 342 0
H: 6 4 W: 13 08 b.Siedlce 20-2-80
Internationals: Poland Full caps.

2005–06	Celtic	34	0		
2006–07	Celtic	36	0		
2007–08	Celtic	30	0		
2008–09	Celtic	34	0		
2009–10	Celtic	28	0	162	0
2010–11	Fiorentina	26	0		
2011–12	Fiorentina	36	0	62	0
2012–13	Southampton	20	0		
2013–14	Southampton	29	0		
2014–15	Southampton	0	0	49	0
2014–15	Bournemouth	37	0		
2015–16	Bournemouth	32	0	69	0

BUCKLEY, Callum (D) 0 0
b. 12-1-96

2014–15	Bournemouth	0	0		
2015–16	Bournemouth	0	0		

BUTCHER, Matt (M) 0 0
b. 14-5-97
From Poole T.

2015–16	Bournemouth	0	0		

CARGILL, Baily (D) 10 1
H: 6 2 W: 13 10 b.Winchester 13-10-95
Internationals: England U20.

2012–13	Bournemouth	0	0		
2013–14	Bournemouth	0	0		
2013–14	Torquay U	5	0	5	0
2014–15	Bournemouth	0	0		
2015–16	Bournemouth	0	0		
2015–16	Coventry C	5	1	5	1

COOK, Steve (D) 182 13
H: 6 1 W: 12 13 b.Hastings 19-4-91

2008–09	Brighton & HA	2	0		
2009–10	Brighton & HA	0	0		
2010–11	Brighton & HA	0	0		
2011–12	Brighton & HA	1	0	3	0
2011–12	Bournemouth	26	0		
2012–13	Bournemouth	33	1		
2013–14	Bournemouth	38	3		
2014–15	Bournemouth	46	5		
2015–16	Bournemouth	36	4	179	13

CORNICK, Harry (F) 36 7
b. 6-3-95

2013–14	Bournemouth	0	0		
2014–15	Bournemouth	0	0		
2014–15	Havant and W	0	0		
2015–16	Bournemouth	0	0		
2015–16	Yeovil T	36	7	36	7

COSTA, Filippo (D) 32 4
H: 5 9 W: 11 05 b.Noventa 21-5-95
Internationals: Italy U16, U17, U18, U19,
U20.

2012–13	Chievo	0	0		
2013–14	Chievo	0	0		
2014–15	Chievo	0	0		
2014–15	Pisa	26	4	26	4
2015–16	Chievo	6	0	6	0
On loan from Chievo.					
2015–16	Bournemouth	0	0		

DANIELS, Charlie (M) 312 15
H: 6 1 W: 12 12 b.Harlow 7-9-86

2005–06	Tottenham H	0	0		
2006–07	Tottenham H	0	0		
2006–07	Chesterfield	2	0	2	0
2007–08	Tottenham H	0	0		
2007–08	Leyton Orient	31	2		
2008–09	Tottenham H	0	0		
2008–09	Gillingham	5	1	5	1
2008–09	Leyton Orient	21	2		
2009–10	Leyton Orient	41	0		
2010–11	Leyton Orient	42	0		
2011–12	Leyton Orient	13	0	148	4
2011–12	Bournemouth	21	2		
2012–13	Bournemouth	34	4		
2013–14	Bournemouth	23	0		
2014–15	Bournemouth	42	1		
2015–16	Bournemouth	37	3	157	10

DISTIN, Sylvain (D) 556 11
H: 6 3 W: 14 06 b.Bagnolet 16-12-77

1998–99	Tours	26	3	26	3
1999–2000	Gueugnon	33	1	33	1
2000–01	Paris St Germain	28	0	28	0
2001–02	Newcastle U	28	0	28	0
2002–03	Manchester C	34	0		
2003–04	Manchester C	38	2		
2004–05	Manchester C	38	1		
2005–06	Manchester C	31	0		
2006–07	Manchester C	37	2	178	5
2007–08	Portsmouth	36	0		
2008–09	Portsmouth	38	0		
2009–10	Portsmouth	3	0	77	0
2009–10	Everton	29	0		
2010–11	Everton	38	2		
2011–12	Everton	27	0		
2012–13	Everton	34	0		
2013–14	Everton	33	0		
2014–15	Everton	13	0	174	2
2015–16	Bournemouth	12	0	12	0

ELPHICK, Tommy (M) 283 12
H: 5 11 W: 11 07 b.Brighton 7-9-87

2005–06	Brighton & HA	1	0		
2006–07	Brighton & HA	3	0		
2007–08	Brighton & HA	39	2		
2008–09	Brighton & HA	39	1		
2009–10	Brighton & HA	44	3		
2010–11	Brighton & HA	27	1		
2011–12	Brighton & HA	0	0	153	7
2012–13	Bournemouth	34	2		
2013–14	Bournemouth	38	1		
2014–15	Bournemouth	46	1		
2015–16	Bournemouth	12	1	130	5

FEDERICI, Adam (G) 225 1
H: 6 2 W: 14 02 b.Nowra 31-1-85
Internationals: Australia U20, U23, Full caps.

2005–06	Reading	0	0		
2006–07	Reading	2	0		
2007–08	Reading	0	0		
2008–09	Reading	15	1		
2008–09	Southend U	10	0	10	0
2009–10	Reading	46	0		
2010–11	Reading	34	0		
2011–12	Reading	46	0		
2012–13	Reading	21	0		
2013–14	Reading	2	0		
2014–15	Reading	43	0	209	1
2015–16	Bournemouth	6	0	6	0

FRANCIS, Simon (D) 477 9
H: 6 0 W: 12 06 b.Nottingham 16-2-85

2002–03	Bradford C	25	1		
2003–04	Bradford C	30	0	55	1
2003–04	Sheffield U	5	0		
2004–05	Sheffield U	6	0		
2005–06	Sheffield U	1	0	12	0
2005–06	Grimsby T	5	0	5	0
2005–06	Tranmere R	17	1	17	1
2006–07	Southend U	40	1		
2007–08	Southend U	27	2		
2008–09	Southend U	45	0		
2009–10	Southend U	45	1	157	4
2010–11	Charlton Ath	34	0		
2011–12	Charlton Ath	0	0	34	0
2011–12	Bournemouth	29	0		
2012–13	Bournemouth	42	1		
2013–14	Bournemouth	46	1		
2014–15	Bournemouth	42	1		
2015–16	Bournemouth	38	0	197	3

FRASER, Ryan (M) 102 8
H: 5 4 W: 10 13 b.Aberdeen 24-2-94
Internationals: Scotland U19, U21.

2010–11	Aberdeen	2	0		
2011–12	Aberdeen	3	0		
2012–13	Aberdeen	16	0	21	0

GOODSHIP, Brandon (F) 10 1
b. 1-1-86

2013–14	Bournemouth	0	0		
2014–15	Bournemouth	0	0		
2015–16	Bournemouth	0	0		
2015–16	Yeovil T	10	1	10	1

GOSLING, Dan (M) 134 12
H: 6 0 W: 11 00 b.Brixham 2-2-90
Internationals: England U17, U18, U19, U21.

2006–07	Plymouth Arg	12	2		
2007–08	Plymouth Arg	10	0	22	2
2007–08	Everton	0	0		
2008–09	Everton	11	2		
2009–10	Everton	11	2	22	4
2010–11	Newcastle U	1	0		
2011–12	Newcastle U	12	1		
2012–13	Newcastle U	3	0		
2013–14	Newcastle U	8	0	24	1
2013–14	Blackpool	14	2	14	2
2014–15	Bournemouth	18	0		
2015–16	Bournemouth	34	3	52	3

GRABBAN, Lewis (F) 295 83
H: 6 0 W: 11 03 b.Croydon 12-1-88

2005–06	Crystal Palace	0	0		
2006–07	Crystal Palace	8	1		
2006–07	Oldham Ath	9	0	9	0
2007–08	Crystal Palace	2	0	10	1
2007–08	Motherwell	6	0	6	0
2007–08	Millwall	13	3		
2008–09	Millwall	31	6		
2009–10	Millwall	11	0		
2009–10	Brentford	7	2		
2010–11	Millwall	1	0	56	9
2010–11	Brentford	22	5	29	7
2011–12	Rotherham U	43	18	43	18
2012–13	Bournemouth	42	13		
2013–14	Bournemouth	44	22		
2014–15	Norwich C	35	12		
2015–16	Norwich C	6	1	41	13
2015–16	Bournemouth	15	0	101	35

GRADEL, Max (M) 253 67
H: 5 10 W: 11 00 b.Abidjan 30-11-87
Internationals: Ivory Coast Full caps.

2005–06	Leicester C	0	0		
2006–07	Leicester C	0	0		
2007–08	Leicester C	0	0		
2007–08	Bournemouth	34	9		
2008–09	Leicester C	27	1		
2009–10	Leicester C	0	0	27	1
2009–10	Leeds U	32	6		
2010–11	Leeds U	41	18		
2011–12	Leeds U	4	1	77	25
2011–12	St Etienne	29	6		
2012–13	St Etienne	23	3		
2013–14	St Etienne	18	5		
2014–15	St Etienne	31	17	101	31
2015–16	Bournemouth	14	1	48	10

GREEN, Jordan (F)
b. 22-2-95

2015–16	Bournemouth	0	0		

HOLMES, Jordan (G) 0 0
b. 8-5-97

2015–16	Bournemouth	0	0		

ITURBE, Juan (F) 119 17
H: 5 7 W: 9 11 b.Buenos Aires 4-6-93
Internationals: Paraguay U17, U20, Full caps.
Argentina U20.

2009	Cerro Porteno	4	0		
2010	Cerro Porteno	3	0		
2011	Cerro Porteno	15	3	22	3
2011–12	Porto	4	0		
2012–13	Porto	0	0		
2012–13	River Plate	17	3	17	3
2013–14	Porto	1	0	6	0
2013–14	Verona	33	8	33	8
2014–15	Roma	27	2		
2015–16	Roma	12	1	39	3
On loan from Roma.					
2015–16	Bournemouth	2	0	2	0

JORDAN, Corey (D) 0 0
b. 4-3-97

2015–16	Bournemouth	0	0		

KING, Josh (F) 123 12
H: 5 11 W: 11 09 b.Oslo 15-1-92
Internationals: Norway U15, U16, U18, U19,
U21, Full caps.

2008–09	Manchester U	0	0		

2009–10	Manchester U	0	0		
2010–11	Manchester U	0	0		
2010–11	*Preston NE*	8	0	8	0
2011–12	Manchester U	0	0		
2011–12	*Moenchengladbach*	2	0	2	0
2011–12	*Hull C*	18	1	18	1
2012–13	Manchester U	0	0		
2012–13	Blackburn R	16	2		
2013–14	Blackburn R	32	2		
2014–15	Blackburn R	16	1	64	5
2015–16	Bournemouth	31	6	31	6

LEE, Jordan (D)   0   0
b. 31-12-96

2015–16	Bournemouth	0	0		

MACDONALD, Shaun (M)   169   10
H: 6 1   W: 11 04   b.Swansea 17-6-88
Internationals: Wales U19, U21, Full caps.

2005–06	Swansea C	7	0		
2006–07	Swansea C	8	0		
2007–08	Swansea C	1	0		
2008–09	Swansea C	5	0		
2008–09	*Yeovil T*	4	2		
2009–10	Swansea C	3	0		
2009–10	*Yeovil T*	31	3		
2010–11	Swansea C	0	0		
2010–11	*Yeovil T*	26	4	61	9
2011–12	Swansea C	0	0	24	0
2011–12	Bournemouth	25	1		
2012–13	Bournemouth	28	0		
2013–14	Bournemouth	23	0		
2014–15	Bournemouth	5	0		
2015–16	Bournemouth	3	0	84	1

MATTHEWS, Sam (M)   0   0
b. 1-3-97

2013–14	Bournemouth	0	0		
2014–15	Bournemouth	0	0		
2015–16	Bournemouth	0	0		

McCARTHY, Jake (D)   0   0
H: 5 8   W: 11 00   b. 2-4-96

2013–14	Bournemouth	0	0		
2014–15	Bournemouth	0	0		
2015–16	Bournemouth	0	0		

MINGS, Tyrone (D)   58   1
H: 6 3   W: 12 00   b.Bath 19-3-93

2012–13	Ipswich T	1	0		
2013–14	Ipswich T	16	0		
2014–15	Ipswich T	40	1	57	1
2015–16	Bournemouth	1	0	1	0

MURRAY, Glenn (F)   360   140
H: 6 1   W: 12 12   b.Maryport 25-9-83

2005–06	Carlisle U	26	3		
2006–07	Carlisle U	1	0	27	3
2006–07	*Stockport Co*	11	3	11	3
2006–07	Rochdale	31	16		
2007–08	Rochdale	23	9	54	25
2007–08	Brighton & HA	21	9		
2008–09	Brighton & HA	23	11		
2009–10	Brighton & HA	32	12		
2010–11	Brighton & HA	42	22	118	54
2011–12	Crystal Palace	38	6		
2012–13	Crystal Palace	42	30		
2013–14	Crystal Palace	14	1		
2014–15	Crystal Palace	17	7		
2014–15	*Reading*	18	8	18	8
2015–16	Crystal Palace	2	0	113	44
2015–16	Bournemouth	19	3	19	3

O'HANLON, Josh (F)   25   7
H: 6 0   W: 12 00   b. 25-9-95

2013	*Longford T*	22	7	22	7
2013–14	Bournemouth	0	0		
2014–15	Bournemouth	0	0		
2014–15	*York C*	3	0	3	0
2015–16	Bournemouth	0	0		

PUGH, Marc (M)   371   65
H: 5 11   W: 11 04   b.Bacup 2-4-87

2005–06	Burnley	0	0		

2005–06	Bury	6	1		
2006–07	Bury	35	3	41	4
2007–08	Shrewsbury T	37	4		
2008–09	Shrewsbury T	7	0	44	4
2008–09	*Luton T*	4	0	4	0
2008–09	Hereford U	9	1		
2009–10	Hereford U	40	13	49	14
2010–11	Bournemouth	41	11		
2011–12	Bournemouth	42	8		
2012–13	Bournemouth	40	6		
2013–14	Bournemouth	42	5		
2014–15	Bournemouth	42	9		
2015–16	Bournemouth	26	3	233	43

RANTIE, Tokelo (F)   96   22
H: 5 8   W: 11 03   b.Parys 8-9-90
Internationals: South Africa Full caps.

2011–12	Orlando Pirates	20	7	20	7
2012	Malmo FF	11	3		
2013	Malmo FF	21	7	32	10
2013–14	Bournemouth	29	3		
2014–15	Bournemouth	12	2		
2015–16	Bournemouth	3	0	44	5

RITCHIE, Matt (M)   297   71
H: 5 8   W: 11 00   b.Gosport 10-9-89
Internationals: Scotland Full caps.

2008–09	Portsmouth	0	0		
2008–09	*Dagenham & R*	37	11	37	11
2009–10	Portsmouth	2	0		
2009–10	*Notts Co*	16	3	16	3
2009–10	*Swindon T*	4	0		
2010–11	Portsmouth	5	0	7	0
2010–11	Swindon T	36	7		
2011–12	Swindon T	40	10		
2012–13	Swindon T	27	9	107	26
2012–13	Bournemouth	17	3		
2013–14	Bournemouth	30	9		
2014–15	Bournemouth	46	15		
2015–16	Bournemouth	37	4	130	31

SIMPSON, Jack (D)   0   0
b. 8-1-97

2015–16	Bournemouth	0	0		

SMITH, Adam (D)   176   6
H: 5 8   W: 10 07   b.Leytonstone 29-4-91
Internationals: England U16, U17, U19, U20, U21.

2007–08	Tottenham H	0	0		
2008–09	Tottenham H	0	0		
2009–10	Tottenham H	0	0		
2009–10	*Wycombe W*	3	0	3	0
2009–10	*Torquay U*	16	0	16	0
2010–11	Tottenham H	0	0		
2010–11	*Bournemouth*	38	1		
2011–12	Tottenham H	1	0		
2011–12	*Milton Keynes D*	17	2	17	2
2011–12	*Leeds U*	3	0	3	0
2012–13	Tottenham H	0	0		
2012–13	*Millwall*	25	1	25	1
2013–14	Tottenham H	0	0	1	0
2013–14	*Derby Co*	8	0	8	0
2013–14	Bournemouth	5	0		
2014–15	Bournemouth	29	0		
2015–16	Bournemouth	31	2	103	3

STANISLAS, Junior (M)   175   18
H: 6 0   W: 12 00   b.Kidbrooke 26-11-89
Internationals: England U20, U21.

2007–08	West Ham U	0	0		
2008–09	West Ham U	9	2		
2008–09	*Southend U*	6	1	6	1
2009–10	West Ham U	26	3		
2010–11	West Ham U	6	1		
2011–12	West Ham U	1	0	42	6
2011–12	Burnley	31	0		
2012–13	Burnley	35	5		
2013–14	Burnley	27	2	93	7
2014–15	Bournemouth	13	1		
2015–16	Bournemouth	21	3	34	4

STOCKLEY, Jayden (F)   99   22
H: 6 2   W: 12 07   b.Poole 10-10-93

2009–10	Bournemouth	2	0		
2010–11	Bournemouth	4	0		
2011–12	Bournemouth	10	0		
2011–12	*Accrington S*	9	3	9	3
2012–13	Bournemouth	0	0		
2013–14	Bournemouth	0	0		
2013–14	*Leyton Orient*	8	1	8	1
2013–14	*Torquay U*	19	1	19	1
2014–15	Bournemouth	0	0		
2014–15	*Cambridge U*	3	2	3	2
2014–15	*Luton T*	13	3	13	3
2015–16	Bournemouth	0	0	16	0
2015–16	*Portsmouth*	9	2	9	2
2015–16	*Exeter C*	22	10	22	10

SURMAN, Andrew (M)   344   33
H: 5 10   W: 11 06   b.Johannesburg 20-8-86
Internationals: England U21.

2003–04	Southampton	0	0		
2004–05	Southampton	0	0		
2004–05	*Walsall*	14	2	14	2
2005–06	Southampton	12	2		
2005–06	*Bournemouth*	24	6		
2006–07	Southampton	37	4		
2007–08	Southampton	40	2		
2008–09	Southampton	44	7		
2009–10	Southampton	0	0	133	15
2009–10	Wolverhampton W	7	0	7	0
2010–11	Norwich C	22	3		
2011–12	Norwich C	25	4		
2012–13	Norwich C	4	0		
2013–14	Norwich C	0	0		
2013–14	*Bournemouth*	35	0		
2014–15	Norwich C	1	0	52	7
2014–15	Bournemouth	41	3		
2015–16	Bournemouth	38	0	138	9

SURRIDGE, Sam (F)   0   0
b.Wimborne 28-7-98

2015–16	Bournemouth	0	0		

TOMLIN, Lee (F)   215   49
H: 5 11   W: 11 09   b.Leicester 12-1-89
Internationals: England C.

2010–11	Peterborough U	37	8		
2011–12	Peterborough U	37	8		
2012–13	Peterborough U	42	11		
2013–14	Peterborough U	19	5	135	32
2013–14	Middlesbrough	14	4		
2014–15	Middlesbrough	42	7	56	11
2015–16	Bournemouth	6	0	6	0
2015–16	*Bristol C*	18	6	18	6

WAKEFIELD, Josh (M)   8   0
H: 5 11   W: 11 05   b.Frimley 6-11-93

2011–12	Bournemouth	2	0		
2012–13	Bournemouth	1	0		
2012–13	*Dagenham & R*	0	0		
2013–14	Bournemouth	0	0		
2014–15	Bournemouth	0	0		
2015–16	Bournemouth	0	0	3	0
2015–16	*Yeovil T*	5	0	5	0
2015–16	*Walsall*	0	0		

WALSH, Mason (M)   0   0
b. 22-11-95
Internationals: England U18.

2014–15	Bournemouth	0	0		
2015–16	Bournemouth	0	0		

WHITFIELD, Ben (M)   0   0
H: 5 5   W: 9 11   b. 28-2-96

2013–14	Bournemouth	0	0		
2014–15	Bournemouth	0	0		
2015–16	Bournemouth	0	0		

WIGGINS, Rhoys (D)   198   3
H: 5 8   W: 11 05   b.Uxbridge 4-11-87
Internationals: Wales U17, U19, U21.

2006–07	Crystal Palace	0	0		
2007–08	Crystal Palace	0	0		
2008–09	Crystal Palace	1	0	1	0
2008–09	*Bournemouth*	13	0		
2009–10	Norwich C	0	0		
2009–10	*Bournemouth*	19	0		
2010–11	Bournemouth	35	2		
2011–12	Charlton Ath	45	1		
2012–13	Charlton Ath	20	0		
2013–14	Charlton Ath	38	0		
2014–15	Charlton Ath	21	0	124	1
2015–16	Sheffield W	6	0	6	0
2015–16	Bournemouth	0	0	67	2

WILSON, Callum (M)   107   47
H: 5 11   W: 10 06   b.Coventry 27-2-92
Internationals: England U21.

2009–10	Coventry C	0	0		
2010–11	Coventry C	1	0		
2011–12	Coventry C	0	0		
2012–13	Coventry C	11	1		
2013–14	Coventry C	37	21	49	22
2014–15	Bournemouth	45	20		
2015–16	Bournemouth	13	5	58	25

ZUBAR, Stephane (D)   149   5
H: 6 1   W: 12 11   b.Guadeloupe 9-10-86
Internationals: Guadeloupe Full caps.

2006–07	Caen	0	0		
2006–07	Pau	10	0	10	0
2007–08	Caen	0	0		
2007–08	*FC Brussels*	11	0	11	0
2008–09	Vaslui	0	0		
2009–10	Vaslui	26	1	36	1
2010–11	Plymouth Arg	29	2		
2011–12	Plymouth Arg	4	0	33	2

2011–12 Bournemouth 22 0
2012–13 Bournemouth 2 0
2012–13 *Bury* 6 0 **6 0**
2013–14 Bournemouth 0 0
2014–15 Bournemouth 0 0
2014–15 *Port Vale* 2 0 **2 0**
2014–15 York C 23 2
2015–16 Bournemouth 0 0 **24 0**
2015–16 *York C* 4 0 **27 2**

Players retained or with offer of contract
Allsop, Ryan; O'Flaherty, Patrick; Quigley, Joseph Richard.

Scholars
Cooper, Ben Harry Alec; Cordner, Tyler Jack; Harfield, Oliver John; Kendall, Charlie; Neale, Matthew Alexander; O'Connell, Keelan; Stanton, Callum James Frank; Stedman, Mitchell; Surridge, Samuel William; Taylor, Kyle Frazer; Worthington, Matthew Luke; York, Connor Daniel; Young, Curtis.

BRADFORD C (12)

ANDERSON, Paul (M) 253 25
H: 5 9 W: 10 04 b.Leicester 23-7-88
Internationals: England U19.
2005–06 Hull C 0 0
2005–06 Liverpool 0 0
2006–07 Liverpool 0 0
2007–08 Liverpool 0 0
2007–08 Swansea C 31 7 **31 7**
2008–09 Liverpool 0 0
2008–09 Nottingham F 26 2
2009–10 Nottingham F 37 4
2010–11 Nottingham F 36 3
2011–12 Nottingham F 17 0
2012–13 Nottingham F 0 0 **116 9**
2012–13 Bristol C 29 3 **29 3**
2013–14 Ipswich T 31 5
2014–15 Ipswich T 35 1 **66 6**
2015–16 Bradford C 11 0 **11 0**

CLARKE, Billy (F) 275 60
H: 5 7 W: 10 01 b.Cork 13-12-87
Internationals: Republic of Ireland U17, U19, U21.
2004–05 Ipswich T 0 0
2005–06 Ipswich T 2 0
2005–06 Colchester U 6 0 **6 0**
2006–07 Ipswich T 27 3
2007–08 Ipswich T 20 0
2007–08 Falkirk 8 1 **8 1**
2008–09 Ipswich T 9 3
2008–09 Darlington 20 8 **20 8**
2008–09 Northampton T 5 3 **5 3**
2008–09 Brentford 8 6 **8 6**
2009–10 Blackpool 18 1
2010–11 Blackpool 0 0
2011–12 Blackpool 9 0 **27 1**
2011–12 Sheffield U 5 1 **5 1**
2011–12 Crawley T 17 3
2012–13 Crawley T 36 10
2013–14 Crawley T 29 7 **82 20**
2014–15 Bradford C 36 13
2015–16 Bradford C 29 4 **65 17**

CLARKE, Nathan (D) 447 11
H: 6 2 W: 12 00 b.Halifax 30-11-83
2001–02 Huddersfield T 36 1
2002–03 Huddersfield T 3 0
2003–04 Huddersfield T 26 1
2004–05 Huddersfield T 37 0
2005–06 Huddersfield T 46 0
2006–07 Huddersfield T 16 0
2007–08 Huddersfield T 44 2
2008–09 Huddersfield T 38 3
2009–10 Huddersfield T 17 1
2010–11 Huddersfield T 1 0
2010–11 Colchester U 18 0 **18 0**
2011–12 Huddersfield T 0 0 **264 8**
2011–12 Oldham Ath 16 1 **16 1**
2011–12 Bury 11 0 **11 0**
2012–13 Leyton Orient 34 0
2013–14 Leyton Orient 46 2
2014–15 Leyton Orient 33 0 **113 2**
2015–16 Bradford C 25 0 **25 0**

CRACKNELL, Joe (G) 0 0
H: 6 0 W: 11 02 b. 5-6-94
2012–13 Hull C 0 0
2013–14 Hull C 0 0
2015–16 Bradford C 0 0

DARBY, Stephen (D) 243 0
H: 5 9 W: 10 00 b.Liverpool 6-10-88
Internationals: England U19.
2006–07 Liverpool 0 0

2007–08 Liverpool 0 0
2008–09 Liverpool 0 0
2009–10 Liverpool 1 0
2009–10 *Swindon T* 12 0 **12 0**
2010–11 Liverpool 0 0
2010–11 *Notts Co* 23 0 **23 0**
2011–12 Liverpool 0 0 **1 0**
2011–12 *Rochdale* 35 0 **35 0**
2012–13 Bradford C 35 0
2013–14 Bradford C 46 0
2014–15 Bradford C 45 0
2015–16 Bradford C 46 0 **172 0**

DAVIES, Steve (F) 263 53
H: 6 0 W: 12 00 b.Liverpool 29-12-87
2005–06 Tranmere R 22 2
2006–07 Tranmere R 28 1
2007–08 Tranmere R 10 2 **60 5**
2008–09 Derby Co 19 3
2009–10 Derby Co 18 1
2010–11 Derby Co 20 5
2011–12 Derby Co 26 11
2012–13 Derby Co 0 0 **83 20**
2012–13 Bristol C 37 13 **37 13**
2013–14 Blackpool 28 3
2014–15 Blackpool 17 5 **45 8**
2014–15 *Sheffield U* 13 2 **13 2**
2015–16 Bradford C 25 5 **25 5**

DEVINE, Daniel (M) 0 0
Internationals: Northern Ireland U21.
2015–16 Bradford C 0 0

HALLWOOD, Chandler (G) 0 0
b.Huddersfield 18-9-97
2014–15 Bradford C 0 0
2015–16 Bradford C 0 0

HANSON, James (F) 266 73
H: 6 4 W: 12 04 b.Bradford 9-11-87
2009–10 Bradford C 34 12
2010–11 Bradford C 36 6
2011–12 Bradford C 39 13
2012–13 Bradford C 43 10
2013–14 Bradford C 35 12
2014–15 Bradford C 38 9
2015–16 Bradford C 41 11 **266 73**

JONES, Brad (G) 131 0
H: 6 3 W: 12 01 b.Armidale 19-3-82
Internationals: Australia U20, U23, Full caps.
1998–99 Middlesbrough 0 0
1999–2000 Middlesbrough 0 0
2000–01 Middlesbrough 0 0
2001–02 Middlesbrough 0 0
2002 Shelbourne 2 0 **2 0**
2002–03 Middlesbrough 0 0
2002–03 Stockport Co 1 0 **1 0**
2003–04 Middlesbrough 1 0
2003–04 *Blackpool* 5 0
2003–04 *Rotherham U* 1 0
2004–05 Middlesbrough 5 0
2004–05 Blackpool 12 0 **17 0**
2005–06 Middlesbrough 9 0
2006–07 Middlesbrough 2 0
2006–07 *Sheffield W* 15 0 **15 0**
2007–08 Middlesbrough 1 0
2008–09 Middlesbrough 16 0
2009–10 Middlesbrough 24 0 **58 0**
2010–11 Liverpool 0 0
2010–11 *Derby Co* 7 0 **7 0**
2011–12 Liverpool 1 0
2012–13 Liverpool 7 0
2013–14 Liverpool 0 0
2014–15 Liverpool 3 0 **11 0**
2015–16 Bradford C 3 0 **3 0**
2015–16 *NEC* 17 0 **17 0**

KING, James (D) 0 0
H: 5 10 W: 11 07 b. 27-12-96
2014–15 Bradford C 0 0
2015–16 Bradford C 0 0

KNOTT, Billy (M) 120 9
H: 5 8 W: 11 02 b.Canvey Island 28-11-92
Internationals: England U16, U17, U20.
2010–11 Sunderland 0 0
2011–12 Sunderland 0 0
2011–12 *AFC Wimbledon* 20 3 **20 3**
2012–13 Sunderland 1 0
2013–14 Sunderland 0 0 **1 0**
2013–14 *Wycombe W* 17 1 **17 1**
2013–14 *Port Vale* 18 2 **18 2**
2014–15 Bradford C 40 3
2015–16 Bradford C 24 0 **64 3**

LEIGH, Greg (D) 44 2
H: 5 11 b.Manchester 30-9-94
Internationals: England U19.
2013–14 Manchester C 0 0

2014–15 Manchester C 0 0
2014–15 *Crewe Alex* 38 1 **38 1**
2015–16 Bradford C 6 1 **6 1**

MARSHALL, Mark (M) 189 14
H: 5 7 W: 10 07 b.Jamaica 9-5-86
2008–09 Swindon T 12 0
2009–10 Swindon T 7 0 **19 0**
2009–10 *Hereford U* 8 0 **8 0**
2010–11 Barnet 24 6
2011–12 Barnet 25 1 **71 7**
2013–14 Coventry C 14 0 **14 0**
2014–15 Port Vale 46 7 **46 7**
2015–16 Bradford C 31 0 **31 0**

McARDLE, Rory (D) 361 19
H: 6 1 W: 11 04 b.Doncaster 1-5-87
Internationals: Northern Ireland U21, Full caps.
2005–06 Sheffield W 0 0
2005–06 *Rochdale* 19 1
2006–07 Sheffield W 1 0 **1 0**
2006–07 Rochdale 25 0
2007–08 Rochdale 43 3
2008–09 Rochdale 41 2
2009–10 Rochdale 20 0 **148 6**
2010–11 Aberdeen 28 2
2011–12 Aberdeen 25 0 **53 2**
2012–13 Bradford C 40 2
2013–14 Bradford C 41 3
2014–15 Bradford C 43 3
2015–16 Bradford C 35 3 **159 11**

McMAHON, Tony (D) 295 12
H: 5 10 W: 11 04 b.Bishop Auckland 24-3-86
Internationals: England U16, U17, U19.
2003–04 Middlesbrough 0 0
2004–05 Middlesbrough 13 0
2005–06 Middlesbrough 3 0
2006–07 Middlesbrough 0 0
2007–08 Middlesbrough 1 0
2007–08 *Blackpool* 2 0
2008–09 Middlesbrough 13 0
2008–09 *Sheffield W* 15 1 **15 1**
2009–10 Middlesbrough 21 0
2010–11 Middlesbrough 34 2
2011–12 Middlesbrough 34 1 **119 3**
2012–13 Sheffield U 38 2
2013–14 Sheffield U 23 0 **61 2**
2013–14 Blackpool 18 0
2014–15 Blackpool 32 1 **52 1**
2014–15 *Bradford C* 8 1
2015–16 Bradford C 40 4 **48 5**

MELLOR, Luca (D) 0 0
b. 18-9-97
2015–16 Bradford C 0 0

MEREDITH, James (D) 144 2
H: 6 1 W: 11 06 b.Albury, Australia 4-4-88
Internationals: Australia Full caps.
2006–07 Derby Co 0 0
2006–07 *Chesterfield* 1 0 **1 0**
2007–08 *Shrewsbury T* 3 0 **3 0**
From York C
2012–13 Bradford C 32 1
2013–14 Bradford C 26 0
2014–15 Bradford C 40 0
2015–16 Bradford C 42 1 **140 2**

MORAIS, Filipe (M) 261 27
H: 5 9 W: 11 10 b.Lisbon 21-11-85
Internationals: Portugal U21.
2003–04 Chelsea 0 0
2004–05 Chelsea 0 0
2005–06 Chelsea 0 0
2005–06 *Milton Keynes D* 13 0 **13 0**
2006–07 Millwall 12 1 **12 1**
2006–07 *St Johnstone* 13 1
2007–08 Hibernian 28 1
2008–09 Hibernian 2 0 **30 1**
2008–09 *Inverness CT* 3 2 **13 3**
2009–10 St Johnstone 30 2 **43 3**
2010–11 Oldham Ath 23 3
2011–12 Oldham Ath 36 5
2012–13 Oldham Ath 0 0 **59 8**
2012–13 Stevenage 28 3
2013–14 Stevenage 27 4 **55 7**
2014–15 Stevenage 30 3
2015–16 Bradford C 7 1 **37 4**

MORRIS, Josh (M) 108 11
H: 5 9 W: 10 00 b.Preston 30-9-91
Internationals: England U20.
2010–11 Blackburn R 4 0
2011–12 Blackburn R 2 0
2011–12 *Yeovil T* 5 0 **5 0**
2012–13 Blackburn R 10 0
2012–13 *Rotherham U* 5 0 **5 0**

2013–14	Blackburn R	4	0		
2013–14	Carlisle U	6	0	6	0
2013–14	Fleetwood T	14	2		
2014–15	Blackburn R	0	0	20	0
2014–15	Fleetwood T	45	8	59	10
2015–16	Bradford C	13	1	13	1

MOTTLEY-HENRY, Dylan (F)   2   0
b. 2-8-97

| 2014–15 | Bradford C | 1 | 0 | | |
| 2015–16 | Bradford C | 1 | 0 | 2 | 0 |

POLLARD, James (D)   0   0
H: 5 11   W: 11 00   b. 5-5-97

2013–14	Bradford C	0	0		
2014–15	Bradford C	0	0		
2015–16	Bradford C	0	0		

PROCTOR, Jamie (F)   190   34
H: 6 2   W: 12 03   b.Preston 25-3-92

2009–10	Preston NE	1	0		
2010–11	Preston NE	5	1		
2010–11	Stockport Co	7	0	7	0
2011–12	Preston NE	31	3	37	4
2012–13	Swansea C	0	0		
2012–13	Shrewsbury T	2	0	2	0
2012–13	Crawley T	18	7		
2013–14	Crawley T	44	6	62	13
2014–15	Fleetwood T	41	8		
2015–16	Fleetwood T	23	4	64	12
2015–16	Bradford C	18	5	18	5

ROUTIS, Christopher (D)   116   7
H: 6 1   W: 13 03   b.Genf 3-3-90

2010–11	Servette	12	1		
2011–12	Servette	31	3		
2012–13	Servette	22	0		
2013–14	Servette	22	1	87	5
2014–15	Bradford C	18	2		
2015–16	Bradford C	11	0	29	2

SHEEHAN, Alan (D)   283   19
H: 5 11   W: 11 02   b.Athlone 14-9-86
Internationals: Republic of Ireland U21.

2004–05	Leicester C	1	0		
2005–06	Leicester C	2	0		
2006–07	Leicester C	0	0		
2006–07	Mansfield T	10	0	10	0
2007–08	Leicester C	20	1	23	1
2007–08	Leeds U	10	1		
2008–09	Leeds U	11	1		
2008–09	Crewe Alex	3	0	3	0
2009–10	Leeds U	0	0	21	2
2009–10	Oldham Ath	8	1	8	1
2009–10	Swindon T	22	1		
2010–11	Swindon T	21	1	43	2
2011–12	Notts Co	39	2		
2012–13	Notts Co	33	0		
2013–14	Notts Co	42	7		
2014–15	Bradford C	23	1		
2014–15	Peterborough U	2	0	2	0
2015–16	Bradford C	2	0	25	1
2015–16	Notts Co	14	2	128	11
2015–16	Luton T	20	1	20	1

WEBB-FOSTER, Reece (F)   1   0
b. 7-3-97

| 2014–15 | Bradford C | 1 | 0 | | |
| 2015–16 | Bradford C | 0 | 0 | 1 | 0 |

WILLIAMS, Ben (G)   352   0
H: 6 0   W: 13 01   b.Manchester 27-8-82

2001–02	Manchester U	0	0		
2002–03	Manchester U	0	0		
2002–03	Coventry C	0	0		
2002–03	Chesterfield	14	0	14	0
2003–04	Manchester U	0	0		
2003–04	Crewe Alex	10	0		
2004–05	Crewe Alex	23	0		
2005–06	Crewe Alex	17	0		
2006–07	Crewe Alex	39	0		
2007–08	Crewe Alex	46	0	135	0
2008–09	Carlisle U	31	0	31	0
2009–10	Colchester U	46	0		
2010–11	Colchester U	33	0		
2011–12	Colchester U	36	0	115	0
2014–15	Bradford C	14	0		
2015–16	Bradford C	43	0	57	0

Scholars
Boateng, Kwame Owusu; Cissa, Sumaili; Devine, Daniel Steven; Hallwood, Chandler Benjamin Taylor; Hudson, Ellis Luke; Kershaw, Ross David Thomas; Landu, Giovanni; McBurnie, Alexander Cameron; Mellor, Luca Daniel; Moilanen, Ville Veikko Johannes; Omolokun, Kesi Olufemi Adrian; Payne, Niah Ashante Lewis; Peters, Curtis Andrew; Waters, Jack Donald; Windle, Thomas Jack.

BRENTFORD (13)

BARBET, Yoann (D)   51   3
b.Talence 10-5-93
Internationals: France U18.

| 2014–15 | Chamois Niortais | 33 | 2 | 33 | 2 |
| 2015–16 | Brentford | 18 | 1 | 18 | 1 |

BIDWELL, Jake (D)   190   3
H: 6 0   W: 11 00   b.Southport 21-3-93
Internationals: England U16, U17, U18, U19.

2009–10	Everton	0	0		
2010–11	Everton	0	0		
2011–12	Everton	0	0		
2011–12	Brentford	24	0		
2012–13	Everton	0	0		
2012–13	Brentford	40	0		
2013–14	Brentford	38	0		
2014–15	Brentford	43	0		
2015–16	Brentford	45	3	190	3

BJELLAND, Andreas (D)   178   7
H: 6 2   W: 13 05   b. 11-7-88
Internationals: Denmark U16, U18, U19, U21, Full caps.

2007–08	Lyngby	11	0		
2008–09	Lyngby	22	1		
2009–10	Lyngby	4	0	37	1
2009–10	Nordsjaelland	22	1		
2010–11	Nordsjaelland	24	1		
2011–12	Nordsjaelland	26	1	72	3
2012–13	FC Twente	10	0		
2013–14	FC Twente	33	0		
2014–15	FC Twente	26	3	69	3
2015–16	Brentford	0	0		

BONHAM, Jack (G)   2   0
H: 6 4   W: 14 13   b.Stevenage 14-9-93
Internationals: Republic of Ireland U17.

2010–11	Watford	0	0		
2011–12	Watford	0	0		
2012–13	Watford	1	0	1	0
2013–14	Brentford	1	0		
2014–15	Brentford	0	0		
2015–16	Brentford	0	0	1	0

BUTTON, David (G)   229   0
H: 6 3   W: 13 00   b.Stevenage 27-2-89
Internationals: England U16, U17, U19, U20.

2005–06	Tottenham H	0	0		
2006–07	Tottenham H	0	0		
2007–08	Rochdale	0	0		
2007–08	Tottenham H	0	0		
2008–09	Tottenham H	0	0		
2008–09	Bournemouth	4	0	4	0
2008–09	Luton T	0	0		
2008–09	Dagenham & R	3	0	3	0
2009–10	Tottenham H	0	0		
2009–10	Crewe Alex	10	0	10	0
2009–10	Shrewsbury T	26	0	26	0
2010–11	Tottenham H	0	0		
2010–11	Plymouth Arg	30	0	30	0
2011–12	Tottenham H	0	0		
2011–12	Leyton Orient	1	0	1	0
2011–12	Doncaster R	7	0	7	0
2011–12	Barnsley	9	0	9	0
2012–13	Tottenham H	0	0		
2012–13	Charlton Ath	5	0	5	0
2013–14	Brentford	42	0		
2014–15	Brentford	46	0		
2015–16	Brentford	46	0	134	0

CALVET, Raphael (D)   1   0
H: 6 0   W: 10 13   b.Paris 7-2-94
Internationals: France U16, U18, U20.

2012–13	Auxerre	1	0	1	0
2013–14	Brentford	0	0		
2014–15	Brentford	0	0		
2015–16	Brentford	0	0		

CLARKE, Josh (M)   23   3
H: 5 8   W: 11 00   b.Waltham Forest 5-7-95

2012–13	Brentford	0	0		
2013–14	Brentford	1	0		
2014–15	Brentford	0	0		
2014–15	Dagenham & R	0	0		
2014–15	Stevenage	1	0	1	0
2015–16	Brentford	11	0	12	0
2015–16	Barnet	10	3	10	3

COLE, Reece (M)   0   0
b. 17-2-98

| 2015–16 | Brentford | 0 | 0 | | |

COLIN, Maxime (D)   147   1
H: 5 11   W: 12 00   b.Arras 15-11-91
Internationals: France U20.

2010–11	Boulogne	26	0		
2011–12	Boulogne	23	0		
2012–13	Boulogne	4	0	53	0
2012–13	Troyes	18	0		
2013–14	Troyes	35	0		
2014–15	Troyes	2	0	55	0
2014–15	Anderlecht	17	1		
2015–16	Anderlecht	1	0	18	1
2015–16	Brentford	21	0	21	0

DEAN, Harlee (M)   180   5
H: 6 0   W: 11 10   b.Basingstoke 26-7-91

2008–09	Dagenham & R	0	0		
2009–10	Dagenham & R	1	0	1	0
2010–11	Southampton	0	0		
2011–12	Southampton	0	0		
2011–12	Brentford	26	1		
2012–13	Brentford	44	3		
2013–14	Brentford	32	0		
2014–15	Brentford	35	1		
2015–16	Brentford	42	0	179	5

DJURICIN, Marco (F)   101   29
H: 5 11   W: 11 05   b.Vienna 12-12-92
Internationals: Austria U17, U18, U19, U21, Full caps.

2010–11	Hertha Berlin	9	3		
2011–12	Hertha Berlin	2	0		
2012–13	Hertha Berlin	0	0	11	3
2012–13	Jahn Regensburg	16	3	16	3
2013–14	Sturm Graz	18	6		
2014–15	Sturm Graz	18	11	36	17
2014–15	Red Bull Salzburg	13	2		
2015–16	Red Bull Salzburg	3	0	16	2

On loan from Red Bull Salzburg.

| 2015–16 | Brentford | 22 | 4 | 22 | 4 |

FERRY, James (M)   0   0
b. 20-4-97

| 2015–16 | Brentford | 0 | 0 | | |
| 2015–16 | Wycombe W | 0 | 0 | | |

FIELD, Tom (D)   1   0
H: 5 10   W: 10 13   b.Kingston upon Thames 2-8-85
Internationals: Republic of Ireland U16.

2013–14	Brentford	0	0		
2014–15	Brentford	0	0		
2015–16	Brentford	1	0	1	0

FOX, Nathan (D)   0   0
b. 8-9-96

| 2015–16 | Brentford | 0 | 0 | | |

GOGIA, Akaki (M)   119   20
H: 5 10   W: 11 07   b.Rustavi 18-1-92
Internationals: Germany U18, U19.

2010–11	Wolfsburg	0	0		
2011–12	Wolfsburg	0	0		
2011–12	Augsburg	12	0	12	0
2012–13	Wolfsburg	0	0		
2012–13	St Pauli	23	1	23	1
2013–14	Hallescher	36	8		
2014–15	Hallescher	35	11	71	19
2015–16	Brentford	13	0	13	0

HOFMANN, Philipp (F)   113   25
H: 6 4   W: 13 10   b.Arnsberg 30-3-93
Internationals: Germany U18, U19, U20, U21.

2012–13	Schalke 04	0	0		
2012–13	Paderborn	31	7	31	7
2013–14	Schalke 04	0	0		
2013–14	Ingolstadt 04	31	8	31	8
2014–15	Kaiserslautern	30	6	30	6
2015–16	Brentford	21	4	21	4

HOGAN, Scott (F)   41   24
H: 5 11   W: 10 01   b. 13-4-92

2009–10	Rochdale	0	0		
2013–14	Rochdale	33	17	33	17
2014–15	Brentford	1	0		
2015–16	Brentford	7	7	8	7

JOTA, Ramallo (M)   94   22
H: 5 11   W: 10 08   b.A Coruna 16-6-91

2010–11	Celta Vigo	4	0		
2011–12	Celta Vigo	0	0		
2012–13	Celta Vigo	0	0		
2013–14	Celta Vigo	0	0	4	0
2013–14	Eibar	35	11		
2014–15	Brentford	42	11		
2015–16	Brentford	5	0	47	11
2015–16	Eibar	8	0	43	11

JUDGE, Alan (F)   263   47
H: 5 6   W: 11 03   b.Dublin 11-11-88
Internationals: Republic of Ireland U17, U8, U19, U21, U23, Full caps.

2006–07	Blackburn R	0	0		
2007–08	Blackburn R	0	0		
2008–09	Blackburn R	0	0		
2008–09	Plymouth Arg	17	2		
2009–10	Blackburn R	0	0		

2009–10	Plymouth Arg	37	5	54	7
2010–11	Blackburn R	0	0		
2010–11	Notts Co	19	1		
2011–12	Notts Co	43	7		
2012–13	Notts Co	39	8	101	16
2013–14	Blackburn R	11	0	11	0
2013–14	Brentford	22	7		
2014–15	Brentford	37	3		
2015–16	Brentford	38	14	97	24

KERSCHBAUMER, Konstantin (M) 164 21
b. 1-7-92
Internationals: Austria, U16, U17, U18, U19.

2011–12	Vienna	32	5	32	5
2012–13	St Polten	33	6		
2013–14	St Polten	33	7		
2014–15	St Polten	20	2	86	15
2014–15	Admira Wacker	16	1	16	1
2015–16	Brentford	30	0	30	0

MACLEOD, Lewis (M) 53 11
b.Law 16-6-94
Internationals: Scotland U16, U17, U18, U19, U21.

2012–13	Rangers	21	3		
2013–14	Rangers	18	5		
2014–15	Rangers	13	3	52	11
2014–15	Brentford	0	0		
2015–16	Brentford	1	0	1	0

McCORMACK, Alan (M) 383 25
H: 5 8 W: 11 00 b.Dublin 10-1-84
Internationals: Republic of Ireland U19.

2002–03	Preston NE	0	0		
2003–04	Preston NE	5	0		
2003–04	Leyton Orient	10	0	10	0
2004–05	Preston NE	3	0		
2004–05	Southend U	7	2		
2005–06	Preston NE	0	0		
2005–06	Motherwell	24	2	24	2
2006–07	Preston NE	3	0	11	0
2006–07	Southend U	22	3		
2007–08	Southend U	42	8		
2008–09	Southend U	34	2		
2009–10	Southend U	41	3	146	18
2010–11	Charlton Ath	24	1	24	1
2011–12	Swindon T	40	2		
2012–13	Swindon T	40	0	80	2
2013–14	Brentford	43	1		
2014–15	Brentford	18	1		
2015–16	Brentford	27	0	88	2

McEACHRAN, Josh (M) 101 0
H: 5 10 W: 10 03 b.Oxford 1-3-93
Internationals: England U16, U17, U19, U20, U21.

2010–11	Chelsea	9	0		
2011–12	Chelsea	2	0		
2011–12	Swansea C	4	0	4	0
2012–13	Chelsea	0	0		
2012–13	Middlesbrough	38	0	38	0
2013–14	Chelsea	0	0		
2013–14	Watford	7	0	7	0
2013–14	Wigan Ath	8	0	8	0
2014–15	Chelsea	0	0	11	0
2014–15	Vitesse	19	0	19	0
2015–16	Brentford	14	0	14	0

MOORE, Montell (F) 0 0
b. 23-12-95

2014–15	Brentford	0	0		
2015–16	Brentford	0	0		

O'CONNELL, Jack (D) 104 6
H: 6 3 W: 13 05 b.Liverpool 29-3-94
Internationals: England U18, U19.

2012–13	Blackburn R	0	0		
2012–13	Rotherham U	3	0	3	0
2012–13	York C	18	0	18	0
2013–14	Blackburn R	0	0		
2013–14	Rochdale	38	0		
2014–15	Blackburn R	0	0		
2014–15	Rochdale	29	5	67	5
2014–15	Brentford	0	0		
2015–16	Brentford	16	1	16	1

OWENS, Seth (D) 0 0

2015–16	Brentford	0	0		

SAUNDERS, Sam (M) 235 42
H: 5 6 W: 11 04 b.Erith 29-8-83

2007–08	Dagenham & R	2	0		
2008–09	Dagenham & R	40	14	62	14
2009–10	Brentford	26	1		
2010–11	Brentford	21	2		
2011–12	Brentford	37	10		
2012–13	Brentford	31	3		
2013–14	Brentford	17	5		
2014–15	Brentford	5	2		
2014–15	Wycombe W	11	2	11	2
2015–16	Brentford	25	3	162	26

SENIOR, Courtney (F) 1 0
b. 30-6-97

2014–15	Wycombe W	1	0	1	0
2015–16	Brentford	0	0		

UDUMAGA, Jermaine (M) 7 0
b.Wandsworth Hill 22-6-95

2013–14	Crystal Palace	0	0		
2014–15	Crystal Palace	0	0		
2014–15	Brentford	0	0		
2015–16	Brentford	3	0	3	0
2015–16	Wycombe W	4	0	4	0

VIBE, Lasse (F) 231 96
H: 5 11 W: 11 07 b. 22-2-87
Internationals: Denmark Full caps.

2006–07	AGF	1	0		
2007–08	AGF	0	0	1	0
2008–09	Fyn	13	7		
2009–10	Fyn	30	7	43	14
2010–11	Vestsjaelland	29	12		
2011–12	Vestsjaelland	14	6	43	18
2011–12	SonderjyskE	14	6		
2012–13	SonderjyskE	33	13	47	19
2013	Gothenburg	14	2		
2014	Gothenburg	26	23		
2015	Gothenburg	16	6	56	31
2015–16	Brentford	41	14	41	14

WOODS, Ryan (M) 132 3
H: 5 8 b.Norton Canes 13-12-93

2012–13	Shrewsbury T	2	0		
2013–14	Shrewsbury T	41	1		
2014–15	Shrewsbury T	43	0		
2015–16	Shrewsbury T	5	0	91	1
2015–16	Brentford	41	2	41	2

YENNARIS, Nico (D) 57 3
H: 5 7 W: 10 03 b.Leytonstone 23-5-93
Internationals: England U17, U18, U19.

2010–11	Arsenal	0	0		
2011–12	Arsenal	1	0		
2011–12	Notts Co	2	0	2	0
2012–13	Arsenal	0	0		
2013–14	Arsenal	0	0	1	0
2013–14	Bournemouth	24	1		
2013–14	Brentford	8	0		
2014–15	Brentford	1	0		
2014–15	Wycombe W	14	1	14	1
2015–16	Brentford	31	2	40	2

Players retained or with offer of contract
Clayton, Bradley Luca Brand; Holldack, Jan; Jatta, Seika; Onariase, Osaore Emmanuel; Parish, Daniel David; Ramallo, Jose Ignacio Peleteiro; Rodrigues Alves, Herson Domingos; Westbrooke, Zain Sam.

Scholars
Austin, Courtney Cephas; Birse, Zachary Robert; Bohui, Joshua Raymond; Cole, Reece George; Dunn, Luke Christopher Arthur; Fenn-Evans, Julius Louis; Gonzalez Velasco, Juan Pablo; Greaves, Cameron Edward; Guppy, Anthony Adam William; Harmes, George Thomas; Kamanzi, Jerry Rawlings; Marsh-Brown, Kyjuon Jaeger; Massala, Joao Augusto; McGregor, Giovanni Donald; Mepham, Christopher James; Owens, Seth; Pennant, Romayn James.

BRIGHTON & HA (14)

BALDOCK, Sam (F) 254 79
H: 5 7 W: 10 07 b.Buckingham 15-3-89
Internationals: England U20.

2005–06	Milton Keynes D	0	0		
2006–07	Milton Keynes D	1	0		
2007–08	Milton Keynes D	5	0		
2008–09	Milton Keynes D	40	12		
2009–10	Milton Keynes D	20	5		
2010–11	Milton Keynes D	30	12		
2011–12	Milton Keynes D	4	4	100	33
2011–12	West Ham U	23	5		
2012–13	West Ham U	0	0	23	5
2012–13	Bristol C	34	10		
2013–14	Bristol C	45	24		
2014–15	Bristol C	4	0	83	34
2014–15	Brighton & HA	30	3		
2015–16	Brighton & HA	28	4	48	7

BJORDAL, Henrik Rorvik (M) 54 1
H: 5 9 W: 12 08 b. 4-2-97
Internationals: Norway U21.

2013	Aalesund	2	0		
2014	Aalesund	22	0		
2015	Aalesund	30	1	54	1
2015–16	Brighton & HA	0	0		

BONG, Gaetan (D) 208 3
H: 6 0 W: 11 09 b.Sakbayeme 25-4-88
Internationals: France U21. Cameroon Full caps.

2005–06	Metz	3	0		
2006–07	Metz	2	0		
2007–08	Metz	11	0		
2008–09	Metz	0	0	16	0
2008–09	Tours	34	0	34	0
2009–10	Valenciennes	29	2		
2010–11	Valenciennes	22	1		
2011–12	Valenciennes	28	0		
2012–13	Valenciennes	29	0		
2013–14	Valenciennes	1	0	109	3
2013–14	Olympiacos	19	0	19	0
2014–15	Wigan Ath	14	0	14	0
2015–16	Brighton & HA	16	0	16	0

CALDERON, Inigo (D) 403 26
H: 5 10 W: 12 02 b.Vitoria 4-1-82

2002–03	Alaves B	35	1		
2003–04	Alaves B	33	0	68	1
2004–05	Alicante	25	0		
2005–06	Alicante	31	4		
2006–07	Alaves	28	1	84	5
2007–08	Alaves	20	0		
2008–09	Alaves	33	2	53	2
2009–10	Brighton & HA	19	1		
2010–11	Brighton & HA	44	7		
2011–12	Brighton & HA	32	4		
2012–13	Brighton & HA	28	0		
2013–14	Brighton & HA	23	2		
2014–15	Brighton & HA	35	4		
2015–16	Brighton & HA	17	0	198	18

CHICKSEN, Adam (D) 111 2
H: 5 8 W: 11 09 b.Milton Keynes 27-9-91

2008–09	Milton Keynes D	1	0		
2009–10	Milton Keynes D	6	0		
2010–11	Milton Keynes D	14	0		
2011–12	Milton Keynes D	20	0		
2011–12	Leyton Orient	3	0		
2012–13	Milton Keynes D	32	2		
2013–14	Milton Keynes D	0	0	73	2
2013–14	Brighton & HA	1	0		
2014–15	Brighton & HA	5	0		
2014–15	Gillingham	3	0		
2014–15	Fleetwood T	13	0	13	0
2015–16	Brighton & HA	1	0	7	0
2015–16	Leyton Orient	6	0	9	0
2015–16	Gillingham	6	0	9	0

CROFTS, Andrew (D) 372 35
H: 5 10 W: 12 09 b.Chatham 29-5-84
Internationals: Wales U19, U21, Full caps.

2000–01	Gillingham	0	0		
2001–02	Gillingham	0	0		
2002–03	Gillingham	0	0		
2003–04	Gillingham	8	0		
2004–05	Gillingham	27	2		
2005–06	Gillingham	45	2		
2006–07	Gillingham	43	8		
2007–08	Gillingham	41	5		
2008–09	Gillingham	9	0		
2008–09	Peterborough U	9	0	9	0
2009–10	Brighton & HA	44	5		
2010–11	Norwich C	44	8		
2011–12	Norwich C	24	0		
2012–13	Norwich C	0	0	68	8
2012–13	Brighton & HA	24	0		
2013–14	Brighton & HA	23	5		
2014–15	Brighton & HA	7	0		
2015–16	Brighton & HA	17	0	115	10
2015–16	Gillingham	6	0	180	17

DALLISON, Tom (M) 1 0
H: 5 10 W: 14 01 b. 2-2-96

2012–13	Arsenal	0	0		
2013–14	Brighton & HA	0	0		
2014–15	Brighton & HA	0	0		
2015–16	Brighton & HA	0	0		
2015–16	Crawley T	1	0	1	0

DUNK, Lewis (D) 129 8
H: 6 3 W: 12 02 b.Brighton 1-12-91

2009–10	Brighton & HA	1	0		
2010–11	Brighton & HA	5	0		
2011–12	Brighton & HA	31	0		
2012–13	Brighton & HA	8	0		
2013–14	Brighton & HA	6	0		
2013–14	Bristol C	2	0	2	0
2014–15	Brighton & HA	38	5		
2015–16	Brighton & HA	38	3	127	8

FORSTER-CASKEY, Jake (M) 103 9
H: 5 10 W: 10 00 b.Southend 25-4-94
Internationals: England U16, U17, U18, U20, U21.

2009–10	Brighton & HA	1	0		

2010–11 Brighton & HA 0 0
2011–12 Brighton & HA 4 1
2012–13 Brighton & HA 3 0
2012–13 *Oxford U* 16 3 **16 3**
2013–14 Brighton & HA 28 3
2014–15 Brighton & HA 29 1
2015–16 Brighton & HA 2 0 **67 5**
2015–16 *Milton Keynes D* 20 1 **20 1**

GOLDSON, Connor (D)   **134 10**
H: 6 3 W: 13 05 b.York 18-12-92
2010–11 Shrewsbury T 3 0
2011–12 Shrewsbury T 4 0
2012–13 Shrewsbury T 17 1
2013–14 Shrewsbury T 36 0
2013–14 *Cheltenham T* 4 0 **4 0**
2014–15 Shrewsbury T 44 7
2015–16 Shrewsbury T 2 0 **106 8**
2015–16 Brighton & HA 24 2 **24 2**

GREER, Gordon (D)   **426 12**
H: 6 2 W: 12 05 b.Glasgow 14-12-80
Internationals: Scotland B, Full caps.
2000–01 Clyde 30 0 **30 0**
2000–01 Blackburn R 0 0
2001–02 Blackburn R 0 0
2002–03 Blackburn R 0 0
2002–03 *Stockport Co* 5 1 **5 1**
2003–04 Kilmarnock 25 0
2004–05 Kilmarnock 22 1
2005–06 Kilmarnock 27 2
2006–07 Kilmarnock 33 0 **107 3**
2007–08 Doncaster R 11 1
2008–09 Doncaster R 1 0 **12 1**
2008–09 *Swindon T* 19 1
2009–10 Swindon T 44 1 **63 2**
2010–11 Brighton & HA 32 0
2011–12 Brighton & HA 42 1
2012–13 Brighton & HA 38 1
2013–14 Brighton & HA 40 1
2014–15 Brighton & HA 37 2
2015–16 Brighton & HA 20 0 **209 5**

HAMBO, Vahid (F)   **11 5**
b.3-2-95
Internationals: Finland U21.
2014 Ilves 5 1 **5 1**
2015 Inter Turku 6 4 **6 4**
2015–16 Brighton & HA 0 0

HARPER, Jack (F)   **0 0**
b.Malaga 28-2-96
Internationals: Scotland U17, U19.
2014–15 Real Madrid 0 0
2015–16 Brighton & HA 0 0

HEMED, Tomer (F)   **296 74**
H: 6 0 W: 12 04 b.Haifa 2-5-87
Internationals: Israel U17, U18, U19, U21, Full caps.
2005–06 Maccabi Haifa 3 1
2006–07 Maccabi Haifa 8 2
2007–08 Maccabi Haifa 7 0
2007–08 *Maccabi Herzliya* 17 3 **17 3**
2008–09 Maccabi Haifa 0 0
2008–09 *Bnei Yehuda* 28 1 **28 1**
2009–10 Maccabi Haifa 0 0
2009–10 *Maccabi Ahi Nazareth* 33 9 **33 9**
2010–11 Maccabi Haifa 31 13 **49 16**
2011–12 Mallorca 29 7
2012–13 Mallorca 37 11
2013–14 Mallorca 24 2 **90 20**
2014–15 Almeria 35 8 **35 8**
2015–16 Brighton & HA 44 17 **44 17**

HOLLA, Danny (M)   **221 35**
H: 5 10 W: 11 09 b.Almere 31-12-87
2006–07 Groningen 6 0
2007–08 *Zwolle* 23 8 **23 8**
2007–08 Groningen 6 0
2008–09 Groningen 34 6
2009–10 Groningen 22 2
2010–11 Groningen 22 2
2011–12 Groningen 13 0 **103 10**
2011–12 *VVV* 16 2 **16 2**
2012–13 Den Haag 28 11
2013–14 Den Haag 26 3 **54 14**
2014–15 Brighton & HA 24 1
2015–16 Brighton & HA 1 0 **25 1**

HUNEMEIER, Uwe (D)   **161 13**
H: 6 1 W: 12 06 b.Rietberg 9-1-86
Internationals: Germany U17.
2005–06 Borussia Dortmund 2 0
2006–07 Borussia Dortmund 0 0
2007–08 Borussia Dortmund 0 0
2008–09 Borussia Dortmund 1 0
2009–10 Borussia Dortmund 0 0 **3 0**
2010–11 Energie Cottbus 30 9
2011–12 Energie Cottbus 23 0

2012–13 Energie Cottbus 23 0 **76 9**
2013–14 Paderborn 33 2
2014–15 Paderborn 32 2
2015–16 Paderborn 2 0 **67 4**
2015–16 Brighton & HA 15 0 **15 0**

HUNT, Robert (M)   **0 0**
b. 7-7-95
2013–14 Brighton & HA 0 0
2014–15 Brighton & HA 0 0
2015–16 Brighton & HA 0 0

INCE, Rohan (D)   **84 2**
H: 6 3 W: 12 08 b.Whitechapel 8-11-92
2010–11 Chelsea 0 0
2011–12 Chelsea 0 0
2012–13 Chelsea 0 0
2012–13 *Yeovil T* 2 0 **2 0**
2013–14 Brighton & HA 28 0
2014–15 Brighton & HA 32 1
2015–16 Brighton & HA 12 0 **72 1**
2015–16 *Fulham* 10 1 **10 1**

KAYAL, Beram (M)   **204 7**
H: 5 10 W: 11 09 b.Jadeidi 2-5-88
Internationals: Israel U17, U18, U19, U21, Full caps.
2008–09 Maccabi Haifa 30 1
2009–10 Maccabi Haifa 27 1 **57 2**
2010–11 Celtic 21 2
2011–12 Celtic 19 0
2012–13 Celtic 27 0
2013–14 Celtic 13 0
2014–15 Celtic 6 0 **86 2**
2014–15 Brighton & HA 18 1
2015–16 Brighton & HA 43 2 **61 3**

KNOCKAERT, Anthony (M)   **166 33**
H: 5 8 W: 10 11 b.Lille 20-11-91
Internationals: France U20, U21.
2011–12 Guingamp 34 10 **34 10**
2012–13 Leicester C 42 8
2013–14 Leicester C 42 5
2014–15 Leicester C 9 0 **93 13**
2015–16 Standard Liege 20 5 **20 5**
2015–16 Brighton & HA 19 5 **19 5**

LUALUA, Kazenga (F)   **167 17**
H: 5 11 W: 12 00 b.Kinshasa 10-12-90
2007–08 Newcastle U 2 0
2008–09 Newcastle U 3 0
2008–09 *Doncaster R* 4 0 **4 0**
2009–10 Newcastle U 1 0
2009–10 *Brighton & HA* 11 0
2010–11 Newcastle U 2 0
2010–11 *Brighton & HA* 11 4
2011–12 Newcastle U 0 0 **8 0**
2011–12 Brighton & HA 27 1
2012–13 Brighton & HA 22 5
2013–14 Brighton & HA 32 1
2014–15 Brighton & HA 34 3
2015–16 Brighton & HA 18 3 **155 17**

MAENPAA, Niki (G)   **186 0**
H: 6 3 W: 13 05 b.Espoo 23-1-85
Internationals: Finland U18, U19, U21, Full caps.
2006–07 Den Bosch 27 0
2007–08 Den Bosch 33 0
2008–09 Den Bosch 7 0 **67 0**
2009–10 Willem II 6 0
2010–11 Willem II 12 0 **18 0**
2011–12 AZ Alkmaar 0 0
2012–13 VVV-Venlo 33 0
2013–14 VVV-Venlo 33 0
2014–15 VVV-Venlo 35 0 **101 0**
2015–16 Brighton & HA 0 0

MANU, Elvis (F)   **81 21**
H: 5 8 W: 10 01 b.Rotterdam 13-8-93
Internationals: Netherlands U16, U17, U19, U20, U21.
2010–11 Feyenoord 0 0
2011–12 Feyenoord 4 1
2012–13 Feyenoord 0 0
2013–14 *Excelsior* 20 8 **20 8**
2013–14 Feyenoord 4 0
2013–14 *Cambuur* 15 5 **15 5**
2014–15 Feyenoord 27 7
2015–16 Feyenoord 1 0 **33 8**
2015–16 Brighton & HA 8 0 **8 0**
2015–16 *Huddersfield T* 5 0 **5 0**

MARCH, Solly (M)   **50 4**
b.Lewes 26-7-94
Internationals: England U20, U21.
2012–13 Brighton & HA 0 0
2013–14 Brighton & HA 23 0
2014–15 Brighton & HA 11 1
2015–16 Brighton & HA 16 3 **50 4**

MONAKANA, Jeffrey (M)   **76 5**
H: 5 10 W: 10 08 b.Enfield 5-11-93
2012–13 Preston NE 38 4
2013–14 Preston NE 2 0 **40 4**
2013–14 *Colchester U* 9 1 **9 1**
2013–14 Brighton & HA 0 0
2013–14 *Crawley T* 4 0 **4 0**
2014–15 Brighton & HA 0 0
2014–15 *Aberdeen* 10 0 **10 0**
2014–15 *Mansfield T* 6 0 **6 0**
2014–15 *Carlisle U* 1 0 **1 0**
2015–16 Brighton & HA 0 0
2015–16 *Bristol R* 3 0 **3 0**
2015–16 *Voluntari* 3 0 **3 0**

MURPHY, Jamie (F)   **308 57**
H: 6 0 W: 12 00 b.Glasgow 28-8-89
Internationals: Scotland U19, U21.
2006–07 Motherwell 2 0
2007–08 Motherwell 16 1
2008–09 Motherwell 30 2
2009–10 Motherwell 35 6
2010–11 Motherwell 35 6
2011–12 Motherwell 36 9
2012–13 Motherwell 22 10 **176 34**
2012–13 Sheffield U 17 2
2013–14 Sheffield U 34 4
2014–15 Sheffield U 43 11
2015–16 Sheffield U 1 0 **95 17**
2015–16 Brighton & HA 37 6 **37 6**

O'GRADY, Chris (F)   **400 84**
H: 6 3 W: 12 04 b.Nottingham 25-1-86
2002–03 Leicester C 1 0
2003–04 Leicester C 0 0
2004–05 Leicester C 0 0
2004–05 *Notts Co* 9 0 **9 0**
2005–06 Leicester C 13 1
2005–06 *Rushden & D* 22 4 **22 4**
2006–07 Leicester C 0 0 **24 1**
2006–07 *Rotherham U* 13 4
2007–08 Rotherham U 38 9 **51 13**
2008–09 Oldham Ath 13 0 **13 0**
2008–09 *Bury* 6 0 **6 0**
2008–09 *Bradford C* 2 0 **2 0**
2008–09 *Stockport Co* 18 2 **18 2**
2009–10 Rochdale 43 22
2010–11 Rochdale 46 9
2011–12 Rochdale 1 0 **90 31**
2011–12 Sheffield W 32 5
2012–13 Sheffield W 21 4 **53 9**
2012–13 *Barnsley* 16 5
2013–14 Barnsley 40 15 **56 20**
2014–15 Brighton & HA 28 1
2014–15 *Sheffield U* 4 1 **4 1**
2015–16 Brighton & HA 3 0 **31 1**
2015–16 *Nottingham F* 21 2 **21 2**

REA, Glen (D)   **24 0**
b.3-9-94
Internationals: Republic of Ireland U21.
2013–14 Brighton & HA 0 0
2014–15 Brighton & HA 0 0
2015–16 Brighton & HA 0 0
2015–16 *Southend U* 14 0 **14 0**
2015–16 *Luton T* 10 0 **10 0**

RIDGEWELL, Liam (D)   **375 20**
H: 5 10 W: 10 03 b.Bexley 21-7-84
Internationals: England U19, U20, U21.
2001–02 Aston Villa 0 0
2002–03 Aston Villa 0 0
2002–03 *Bournemouth* 5 0 **5 0**
2003–04 Aston Villa 11 0
2004–05 Aston Villa 15 0
2005–06 Aston Villa 32 5
2006–07 Aston Villa 21 1 **79 6**
2007–08 Birmingham C 35 1
2008–09 Birmingham C 36 1
2009–10 Birmingham C 31 3
2010–11 Birmingham C 36 4
2011–12 Birmingham C 14 0 **152 9**
2011–12 WBA 13 1
2012–13 WBA 30 0
2013–14 WBA 33 1 **76 2**
2014 Portland Timbers 15 2
2014–15 *Wigan Ath* 6 0 **6 0**
2015 Portland Timbers 37 1 **52 3**
On loan from Portland Timbers.
2015–16 Brighton & HA 5 0 **5 0**

ROSENIOR, Liam (D)   **379 4**
H: 5 10 W: 11 05 b.Wandsworth 9-7-84
Internationals: England U20, U21.
2001–02 Bristol C 1 0
2002–03 Bristol C 21 2
2003–04 Bristol C 0 0 **22 2**
2003–04 Fulham 0 0
2003–04 *Torquay U* 10 0 **10 0**

Season	Club				
2004–05	Fulham	17	0		
2005–06	Fulham	24	0		
2006–07	Fulham	38	0		
2007–08	Fulham	0	0	79	0
2007–08	Reading	17	0		
2008–09	Reading	42	0		
2009–10	Reading	5	0		
2009–10	Ipswich T	29	1	29	1
2010–11	Reading	0	0	64	0
2010–11	Hull C	26	0		
2011–12	Hull C	44	0		
2012–13	Hull C	32	0		
2013–14	Hull C	29	1		
2014–15	Hull C	13	0	144	1
2015–16	Brighton & HA	31	0	31	0

SALTOR, Bruno (D)   346   7
H: 5 10   W: 11 10   b.Masnou (Barca) 1-10-80

Season	Club				
2001–02	Espanyol	1	0	1	0
2001–02	Gimnastic	12	0	12	0
2004–05	Lleida	1	1		
2005–06	Lleida	38	0	39	1
2006–07	Almeria	23	0		
2007–08	Almeria	34	0		
2008–09	Almeria	34	0	91	0
2009–10	Valencia	26	0		
2010–11	Valencia	19	0		
2011–12	Valencia	14	0	59	0
2012–13	Brighton & HA	30	1		
2013–14	Brighton & HA	33	1		
2014–15	Brighton & HA	35	3		
2015–16	Brighton & HA	46	1	144	6

SKALAK, Jiri (F)   122   20
b. 12-3-92
Internationals: Czech Republic U16, U17, U18, U19, U20, U21, Full caps.

Season	Club				
2010–11	Sparta Prague	0	0		
2011–12	Sparta Prague	0	0		
2011–12	MFA Ruzomberok	27	3	27	3
2012–13	Sparta Prague	7	0		
2012–13	1.FC Slovacko	9	0	9	0
2013–14	Sparta Prague	3	0		
2013–14	Zbrojovka Brno	24	3	24	3
2014–15	Sparta Prague	0	0	10	0
2014–15	Mlada Boleslav	24	6		
2015–16	Mlada Boleslav	16	6	40	12
2015–16	Brighton & HA	12	2	12	2

STEPHENS, Dale (M)   240   34
H: 5 7   W: 11 04   b.Bolton 12-6-89

Season	Club				
2006–07	Bury	3	0		
2007–08	Bury	6	1	9	1
2008–09	Oldham Ath	0	0		
2009–10	Oldham Ath	26	2		
2009–10	Rochdale	6	1	6	1
2010–11	Oldham Ath	34	9	60	11
2010–11	Southampton	6	0	6	0
2011–12	Charlton Ath	30	5		
2012–13	Charlton Ath	28	2		
2013–14	Charlton Ath	26	3	84	10
2013–14	Brighton & HA	14	2		
2014–15	Brighton & HA	35	2		
2015–16	Brighton & HA	45	7	75	11

STOCKDALE, David (G)   254   0
H: 6 3   W: 13 04   b.Leeds 20-9-85
Internationals: England C.

Season	Club				
2002–03	York C	1	0		
2003–04	York C	0	0	1	0
2006–07	Darlington	6	0		
2007–08	Darlington	41	0	47	0
2008–09	Fulham	0	0		
2008–09	Rotherham U	8	0	8	0
2008–09	Leicester C	8	0	8	0
2009–10	Fulham	1	0		
2009–10	Plymouth Arg	21	0	21	0
2010–11	Fulham	7	0		
2011–12	Fulham	8	0		
2011–12	Ipswich T	18	0	18	0
2012–13	Fulham	2	0		
2012–13	Hull C	24	0	24	0
2013–14	Fulham	21	0	39	0
2014–15	Brighton & HA	42	0		
2015–16	Brighton & HA	46	0	88	0

TILLEY, James (F)   1   0
b. 13-6-98

Season	Club				
2014–15	Brighton & HA	1	0		
2015–16	Brighton & HA	0	0	1	0

TOWELL, Richie (D)   127   44
b. 17-7-91
Internationals: Republic of Ireland U17, U19, U21.

Season	Club				
2010–11	Celtic	1	0		
2011–12	Celtic	0	0		
2011–12	Hibernian	16	0		
2012–13	Celtic	0	0	1	0
2012–13	Hibernian	14	1	30	1
2013	Dundalk	31	7		
2014	Dundalk	33	11		
2015	Dundalk	32	25	96	43
2015–16	Brighton & HA	0	0		

WALTON, Christian (G)   11   0
b. 9-11-95
Internationals: England U19, U20.

Season	Club				
2011–12	Plymouth Arg	0	0		
2012–13	Plymouth Arg	0	0		
2013–14	Brighton & HA	0	0		
2014–15	Brighton & HA	3	0		
2015–16	Brighton & HA	0	0	3	0
2015–16	Bury	4	0	4	0
2015–16	Plymouth Arg	4	0	4	0

WARD, Joe (M)   0   0
b. 9-4-95

Season	Club				
2015–16	Brighton & HA	0	0		

ZAMORA, Bobby (F)   475   145
H: 6 1   W: 11 11   b.Barking 16-1-81
Internationals: England U21, Full caps.

Season	Club				
1999–2000	Bristol R	4	0	4	0
1999–2000	Brighton & HA	6	4		
2000–01	Brighton & HA	43	28		
2001–02	Brighton & HA	41	28		
2002–03	Brighton & HA	35	14		
2003–04	Tottenham H	16	0	16	0
2003–04	West Ham U	17	5		
2004–05	West Ham U	34	7		
2005–06	West Ham U	34	6		
2006–07	West Ham U	32	11		
2007–08	West Ham U	13	1	130	30
2008–09	Fulham	35	2		
2009–10	Fulham	27	8		
2010–11	Fulham	14	5		
2011–12	Fulham	15	5	91	20
2011–12	QPR	14	2		
2012–13	QPR	21	4		
2013–14	QPR	17	3		
2014–15	QPR	31	3	83	12
2015–16	Brighton & HA	26	7	151	83

Players retained or with offer of contract
Ayunga, Jonah Ananias Paul; Barclay, Benjamin Philip; Barnett, Dylan Mark; Collar, William Guy; Davis, Jason Mytton; Hutchinson, Desmond John; Lynch Sanchez, Robert; Maenpaa, Niki Emil Antonio; Starkey, Jesse Aaron; Tighe, Connor Jay; White, Benjamin William.

Scholars
Ajiboye, David Ibukun; Barker, Danny Ryan; Byrne, Thomas Justin; Cadman, Thomas Patrick; Cox, George Frederick; Davies, Archie Daniel; Garcia Martinez, Luis; Golan, Samuel Benjamin; Hobbs, George Charles; Maguire-Drew, Jordan Luke; Mandroiu, Daniel Jordan; Meyers, Remi Christopher; Molumby, Jayson Patrick; Moore, Owen James; Myles Meekums, Kyle Christopher; O'Sullivan, Rian Michael; Sanders, Max Harrison; Vose, Bailey Jack.

BRISTOL C (15)

AGARD, Kieran (F)   180   49
H: 6 1   W: 10 10   b.Newham 10-10-89

Season	Club				
2006–07	Everton	0	0		
2007–08	Everton	0	0		
2008–09	Everton	0	0		
2009–10	Everton	1	0		
2010–11	Everton	0	0	1	0
2010–11	Kilmarnock	8	1	8	1
2010–11	Peterborough U	0	0		
2011–12	Yeovil T	9	6	29	6
2012–13	Rotherham U	30	6		
2013–14	Rotherham U	46	21		
2014–15	Rotherham U	2	0	78	27
2014–15	Bristol C	39	13		
2015–16	Bristol C	25	2	64	15

AYLING, Luke (D)   245   6
H: 5 11   W: 10 08   b.Lambeth 25-8-91

Season	Club				
2009–10	Arsenal	0	0		
2009–10	Yeovil T	4	0		
2010–11	Yeovil T	37	0		
2011–12	Yeovil T	44	0		
2012–13	Yeovil T	39	0		
2013–14	Yeovil T	42	2	166	2
2014–15	Bristol C	46	4		
2015–16	Bristol C	33	0	79	4

BATTEN, Jack (M)   0   0
H: 6 3   W: 13 05   b.Bristol 22-12-95

Season	Club				
2012–13	Bristol C	0	0		
2013–14	Bristol C	0	0		
2014–15	Bristol C	0	0		
2015–16	Bristol C	0	0		

BRYAN, Joe (D)   125   11
H: 5 7   W: 11 05   b.Bristol 17-9-93

Season	Club				
2011–12	Bristol C	1	0		
2012–13	Bristol C	13	0		
2012–13	Plymouth Arg	10	1	10	1
2013–14	Bristol C	21	2		
2014–15	Bristol C	41	6		
2015–16	Bristol C	39	2	115	10

BURNS, Wes (F)   80   13
H: 5 8   W: 10 10   b.Cardiff 28-12-95
Internationals: Wales U21.

Season	Club				
2012–13	Bristol C	6	0		
2013–14	Bristol C	20	1		
2014–15	Bristol C	3	1		
2014–15	Oxford U	9	1	9	1
2014–15	Cheltenham T	14	4	14	4
2015–16	Bristol C	14	1	43	3
2015–16	Fleetwood T	14	5	14	5

DOWLING, George (M)   2   0
b. 1-8-98

Season	Club				
2015–16	Bristol C	2	0	2	0

EL-ABD, Adam (D)   361   6
H: 5 10   W: 13 05   b.Brighton 11-9-84
Internationals: Egypt Full caps.

Season	Club				
2003–04	Brighton & HA	11	0		
2004–05	Brighton & HA	16	0		
2005–06	Brighton & HA	29	0		
2006–07	Brighton & HA	42	1		
2007–08	Brighton & HA	35	1		
2008–09	Brighton & HA	31	0		
2009–10	Brighton & HA	35	1		
2010–11	Brighton & HA	37	1		
2011–12	Brighton & HA	23	0		
2012–13	Brighton & HA	32	1		
2013–14	Brighton & HA	9	0	300	5
2013–14	Bristol C	14	0		
2014–15	Bristol C	2	0		
2014–15	Bury	24	1	24	1
2015–16	Bristol C	0	0	16	0
2015–16	Swindon T	13	0	13	0
2015–16	Gillingham	8	0	8	0

ELLIOTT, Wade (M)   615   63
H: 5 10   W: 10 03   b.Eastleigh 14-12-78

Season	Club				
1999–2000	Bournemouth	12	3		
2000–01	Bournemouth	36	9		
2001–02	Bournemouth	46	8		
2002–03	Bournemouth	44	4		
2003–04	Bournemouth	39	3		
2004–05	Bournemouth	43	4	220	31
2005–06	Burnley	36	3		
2006–07	Burnley	42	4		
2007–08	Burnley	46	2		
2008–09	Burnley	42	4		
2009–10	Burnley	38	4		
2010–11	Burnley	44	2		
2011–12	Burnley	4	0	252	19
2011–12	Birmingham C	29	2		
2012–13	Birmingham C	44	6		
2013–14	Birmingham C	15	0	88	8
2013–14	Bristol C	19	3		
2014–15	Bristol C	36	2		
2015–16	Bristol C	0	0	55	5

FIELDING, Frank (G)   248   0
H: 5 11   W: 12 00   b.Blackburn 4-4-88
Internationals: England U19, U21.

Season	Club				
2006–07	Blackburn R	0	0		
2007–08	Blackburn R	0	0		
2007–08	Wycombe W	36	0	36	0
2008–09	Blackburn R	0	0		
2008–09	Northampton T	12	0	12	0
2008–09	Rochdale	23	0		
2009–10	Blackburn R	0	0		
2009–10	Rochdale	18	0	41	0
2010–11	Blackburn R	0	0		
2010–11	Derby Co	16	0		
2011–12	Derby Co	44	0		
2012–13	Derby Co	16	0	76	0
2013–14	Bristol C	16	0		
2014–15	Bristol C	46	0		
2015–16	Bristol C	21	0	83	0

FLINT, Aiden (D)   188   27
H: 6 2   W: 12 00   b.Pinxton 11-7-89
Internationals: England C.

Season	Club				
2010–11	Swindon T	3	0		
2011–12	Swindon T	32	2		
2012–13	Swindon T	29	2	64	4

2013–14	Bristol C	34	3		
2014–15	Bristol C	46	14		
2015–16	Bristol C	44	6	124	23

FREEMAN, Luke (F) 211 25
H: 6 0　W: 10 00　b.Dartford 22-3-92
Internationals: England U16, U17.

2007–08	Gillingham	1	0	1	0
2008–09	Arsenal	0	0		
2009–10	Arsenal	0	0		
2010–11	Arsenal	0	0		
2010–11	*Yeovil T*	13	2	13	2
2011–12	Arsenal	0	0		
2011–12	Stevenage	26	7		
2012–13	Stevenage	39	2		
2013–14	Stevenage	45	6	110	15
2014–15	Bristol C	46	7		
2015–16	Bristol C	41	1	87	8

GARITA, Paul Arnold (M) 29 5
H: 5 10　W: 12 02　b.Douala 18-6-95

2012–13	Chateauroux	3	0		
2013–14	Chateauroux	8	3		
2014–15	Chateauroux	13	1		
2015–16	Chateauroux	5	1	29	5
2015–16	Bristol C	0	0		

GILABERT, Luis (M) 0 0
b. 23-10-95

2014–15	Bristol C	0	0
2015–16	Bristol C	0	0

GOLBOURNE, Scott (M) 317 6
H: 5 8　W: 11 08　b.Bristol 29-2-88
Internationals: England U17, U19

2004–05	Bristol C	9	0		
2005–06	Bristol C	5	0		
2005–06	Reading	1	0		
2006–07	Reading	0	0		
2006–07	*Wycombe W*	34	1	34	1
2007–08	Reading	1	0		
2007–08	*Bournemouth*	5	0	5	0
2008–09	Reading	0	0	2	0
2008–09	*Oldham Ath*	8	0	8	0
2009–10	Exeter C	34	0		
2010–11	Exeter C	44	2		
2011–12	Exeter C	26	0	104	2
2011–12	Barnsley	12	1		
2012–13	Barnsley	31	1		
2013–14	Barnsley	4	0	47	2
2013–14	Wolverhampton W	40	1		
2014–15	Wolverhampton W	27	0		
2015–16	Wolverhampton W	20	0	87	1
2015–16	Bristol C	16	0	30	0

IVES, Levi (D) 0 0
b.Belfast 28-7-97
Internationals: Northern Ireland U17, U19.

2015–16	Bristol C	0	0

KODJIA, Jonathan (F) 159 52
H: 6 2　W: 12 02　b. 22-10-89
Internationals: Ivory Coast Full caps.

2008–09	Reims	2	0		
2009–10	Reims	0	0		
2010–11	Reims	5	0		
2011–12	Reims	2	0		
2011–12	*Cherbourg*	16	4	16	4
2012–13	Reims	0	0		
2012–13	*Amiens SC*	34	9	34	9
2013–14	Reims	0	0	9	0
2013–14	Caen	27	5	27	5
2014–15	Angers SCO	28	15	28	15
2015–16	Bristol C	45	19	45	19

LEMONHEIGH-EVANS, Connor (F) 0 0
b.24-1-97
Internationals: Wales U17.

2013–14	Bristol C	0	0
2014–15	Bristol C	0	0
2015–16	Bristol C	0	0

LITTLE, Mark (D) 282 4
H: 6 1　W: 12 10　b.Worcester 20-8-88
Internationals: England U19.

2005–06	Wolverhampton W	0	0		
2006–07	Wolverhampton W	26	0		
2007–08	Wolverhampton W	1	0		
2007–08	*Northampton T*	17	0		
2008–09	Wolverhampton W	0	0		
2008–09	*Northampton T*	9	0	26	0
2009–10	Wolverhampton W	0	0	27	0
2009–10	*Chesterfield*	12	0	12	0
2009–10	*Peterborough U*	9	0		
2010–11	Peterborough U	35	0		
2011–12	Peterborough U	35	1		
2012–13	Peterborough U	40	1		
2013–14	Peterborough U	38	1	157	3
2014–15	Bristol C	37	1		
2015–16	Bristol C	23	0	60	1

MORRELL, Joe (M) 0 0
H: 5 3　W: 11 04　b.Ipswich 3-1-97
Internationals: Wales U17, U19.

2013–14	Bristol C	0	0
2014–15	Bristol C	0	0
2015–16	Bristol C	0	0

O'DONNELL, Richard (G) 165 0
H: 6 2　W: 13 05　b.Sheffield 12-9-88

2007–08	Sheffield W	0	0		
2007–08	*Rotherham U*	0	0		
2007–08	*Oldham Ath*	4	0	4	0
2008–09	Sheffield W	0	0		
2009–10	Sheffield W	0	0		
2010–11	Sheffield W	9	0		
2011–12	Sheffield W	6	0	15	0
2011–12	*Macclesfield T*	11	0	11	0
2012–13	Chesterfield	14	0	14	0
2013–14	Walsall	46	0		
2014–15	Walsall	44	0	90	0
2015–16	Wigan Ath	10	0	10	0
2015–16	Bristol C	21	0	21	0

O'LEARY, Max (G) 0 0
H: 6 1　W: 12 03　b. 10-10-96

2013–14	Bristol C	0	0
2014–15	Bristol C	0	0
2015–16	Bristol C	0	0

OSBORNE, Karleigh (D) 230 8
H: 6 2　W: 12 04　b.Southall 19-3-88

2004–05	Brentford	1	0		
2005–06	Brentford	1	0		
2006–07	Brentford	21	0		
2007–08	Brentford	29	1		
2008–09	Brentford	23	4		
2009–10	Brentford	19	0		
2010–11	Brentford	42	1		
2011–12	Brentford	25	0	161	6
2012–13	Millwall	13	1		
2013–14	Millwall	1	0	14	1
2013–14	Brentford	27	1		
2014–15	Bristol C	0	0		
2014–15	*Colchester U*	4	0	4	0
2015–16	Bristol C	0	0	28	1
2015–16	*AFC Wimbledon*	23	0	23	0

PACK, Marlon (M) 272 19
H: 6 2　W: 11 09　b.Portsmouth 25-3-91

2008–09	Portsmouth	0	0		
2009–10	Portsmouth	0	0		
2009–10	*Wycombe W*	8	0	8	0
2009–10	*Dagenham & R*	17	1	17	1
2010–11	Portsmouth	1	0	1	0
2010–11	Cheltenham T	38	2		
2011–12	Cheltenham T	43	5		
2012–13	Cheltenham T	43	7		
2013–14	Cheltenham T	0	0	124	14
2013–14	Bristol C	43	0		
2014–15	Bristol C	34	3		
2015–16	Bristol C	45	1	122	4

REID, Bobby (M) 100 7
H: 5 7　W: 10 10　b.Bristol 1-3-93

2010–11	Bristol C	1	0		
2011–12	Bristol C	0	0		
2011–12	*Cheltenham T*	1	0	1	0
2012–13	Bristol C	4	1		
2012–13	*Oldham Ath*	7	0	7	0
2013–14	Bristol C	24	1		
2014–15	Bristol C	2	0		
2014–15	*Plymouth Arg*	33	3	33	3
2015–16	Bristol C	28	2	59	4

SMITH, Korey (M) 228 5
H: 5 9　W: 11 01　b.Hatfield 31-1-91

2008–09	Norwich C	0	0		
2009–10	Norwich C	37	4		
2010–11	Norwich C	28	0		
2011–12	Norwich C	0	0		
2011–12	*Barnsley*	12	0	12	0
2012–13	Norwich C	0	0	67	4
2012–13	*Yeovil T*	17	0	17	0
2012–13	*Oldham Ath*	10	0		
2013–14	Oldham Ath	42	1	52	1
2014–15	Bristol C	44	0		
2015–16	Bristol C	36	0	80	0

VYNER, Zak (D) 4 0
b. 14-5-97

2015–16	Bristol C	4	0	4	0

WAGSTAFF, Scott (M) 201 25
H: 5 10　W: 10 03　b.Maidstone 31-3-90

2007–08	Charlton Ath	2	0		
2008–09	Charlton Ath	2	0		
2008–09	*Bournemouth*	5	0	5	0
2009–10	Charlton Ath	30	4		
2010–11	Charlton Ath	40	8		
2011–12	Charlton Ath	44	5		

WILBRAHAM, Aaron (F) 504 117
H: 6 3　W: 12 04　b.Knutsford 21-10-79

2012–13	Charlton Ath	9	1	117	17
2012–13	*Leyton Orient*	7	0	7	0
2013–14	Bristol C	37	5		
2014–15	Bristol C	26	2		
2015–16	Bristol C	9	1	72	8
1997–98	Stockport Co	7	1		
1998–99	Stockport Co	26	0		
1999–2000	Stockport Co	26	4		
2000–01	Stockport Co	36	12		
2001–02	Stockport Co	21	3		
2002–03	Stockport Co	15	7		
2003–04	Stockport Co	41	8	172	35
2004–05	Hull C	19	2	19	2
2004–05	*Oldham Ath*	4	2	4	2
2005–06	Milton Keynes D	31	4		
2005–06	*Bradford C*	5	1	5	1
2006–07	Milton Keynes D	32	7		
2007–08	Milton Keynes D	35	10		
2008–09	Milton Keynes D	33	16		
2009–10	Milton Keynes D	35	10		
2010–11	Milton Keynes D	10	2	176	49
2010–11	Norwich C	12	1		
2011–12	Norwich C	11	1	23	2
2012–13	Crystal Palace	21	0		
2013–14	Crystal Palace	4	0	25	0
2014–15	Bristol C	37	18		
2015–16	Bristol C	43	8	80	26

WILLIAMS, Derrick (D) 112 4
H: 5 11　W: 11 11　b.Waterford 17-1-93
Internationals: Republic of Ireland U19, U21.

2009–10	Aston Villa	0	0		
2010–11	Aston Villa	0	0		
2011–12	Aston Villa	0	0		
2012–13	Aston Villa	1	0	1	0
2013–14	Bristol C	43	1		
2014–15	Bristol C	44	2		
2015–16	Bristol C	24	1	111	4

WOLLACOTT, Jojo (G) 0 0
b. 8-9-96

2015–16	Bristol C	0	0

Players retained or with offer of contract
Baldwin, Aden; Kelly, Lloyd Casius;
McCoulsky, Shawn Fitzgerald Joseph;
McNulty, Joseph Michael; Moir-Pring,
Cameron Lewis.

Non-Contract
Elliott, Wade Patrick.

Scholars
Akpobire, God'S Will Kelechi Onome;
Andrews, Jake; Barry, Owen William;
Chilekwa, Elijah; Difford, James Mark;
Edwards, Opanin Osafo-Adjei; Harper,
Ashley Stephen; Harris, Charlie; Kellow,
George Rogan; Morton, James Samuel; Moss,
Harvey; Nurse, George Damien; Parsons,
Aaron Mathew; Reeves, Harrison Jack;
Richards, Tom James; Selman, Joseph
Andrew; Smith, Harvey George Charles;
Spalding, Henry Lee.

BRISTOL R (16)

BLISSETT, Nathan (F) 2 0
H: 6 4　W: 12 04　b.West Bromwich 29-6-90
From Kidderminster H.

2015–16	Bristol R	2	0	2	0

BODIN, Billy (M) 153 27
H: 5 11　W: 11 00　b.Swindon 24-3-92
Internationals: Wales U17, U19, U21.

2009–10	Swindon T	0	0		
2010–11	Swindon T	5	0		
2011–12	Swindon T	11	3	16	3
2011–12	Torquay U	17	5		
2011–12	*Crewe Alex*	8	0	8	0
2012–13	Torquay U	43	5		
2013–14	Torquay U	27	1	87	11
2014–15	Northampton T	4	0	4	0
2015–16	Bristol R	38	13	38	13

BROOM, Ryan (M) 1 0
b. 4-9-96

2015–16	Bristol R	1	0	1	0

BROWN, Lee (M) 169 18
H: 6 0　W: 12 06　b.Bromley 10-8-90
Internationals: England C.

2008–09	QPR	0	0		
2009–10	QPR	1	0		
2010–11	QPR	0	0	1	0
2011–12	Bristol R	42	7		
2012–13	Bristol R	39	3		

Season	Club				
2013–14	Bristol R	41	2		
2015–16	Bristol R	46	6	**168**	**18**

CLARKE, James (D)   **37 0**
H: 6 0   W: 13 03   b.Aylesbury 17-11-89
From Watford, Oxford U, Oxford C, Salisbury C, Woking.

2015–16	Bristol R	37	0	**37**	**0**

CLARKE, Ollie (M)   **71 4**
H: 5 11   W: 11 11   b.Bristol 29-6-92

2009–10	Bristol R	0	0		
2010–11	Bristol R	1	0		
2011–12	Bristol R	0	0		
2012–13	Bristol R	5	0		
2013–14	Bristol R	32	2		
2015–16	Bristol R	33	2	**71**	**4**

EASTER, Jermaine (F)   **391 85**
H: 5 9   W: 12 02   b.Cardiff 15-1-82
Internationals: Wales Full caps.

2000–01	Wolverhampton W	0	0		
2000–01	Hartlepool U	4	0		
2001–02	Hartlepool U	12	2		
2002–03	Hartlepool U	8	0		
2003–04	Hartlepool U	3	0	**27**	**2**
2003–04	*Cambridge U*	15	2		
2004–05	*Cambridge U*	24	6	**39**	**8**
2004–05	Boston U	9	3	**9**	**3**
2005–06	Stockport Co	19	8	**19**	**8**
2005–06	Wycombe W	15	2		
2006–07	Wycombe W	38	17		
2007–08	Wycombe W	6	2	**59**	**21**
2007–08	Plymouth Arg	32	6		
2008–09	Plymouth Arg	4	0	**36**	**6**
2008–09	*Millwall*	5	1		
2008–09	*Colchester U*	5	2	**5**	**2**
2009–10	Milton Keynes D	36	14		
2010–11	Milton Keynes D	14	0	**50**	**14**
2010–11	*Swansea C*	6	1	**6**	**1**
2010–11	Crystal Palace	14	1		
2011–12	Crystal Palace	33	5		
2012–13	Crystal Palace	8	1	**55**	**7**
2012–13	*Millwall*	9	1		
2013–14	Millwall	20	3		
2014–15	Millwall	9	1	**43**	**6**
2015–16	Bristol R	43	7	**43**	**7**

FALLON, Rory (F)   **405 75**
H: 6 2   W: 11 09   b.Gisbourne 20-3-82
Internationals: England Youth. New Zealand Full caps.

1998–99	Barnsley	0	0		
1999–2000	Barnsley	0	0		
2000–01	Barnsley	1	0		
2001–02	Barnsley	9	0		
2001–02	*Shrewsbury T*	11	0	**11**	**0**
2002–03	Barnsley	26	7		
2003–04	Barnsley	16	4	**52**	**11**
2003–04	Swindon T	19	6		
2004–05	Swindon T	31	3		
2004–05	*Yeovil T*	6	1		
2005–06	Swindon T	25	12	**75**	**21**
2005–06	Swansea C	17	4		
2006–07	Swansea C	24	8	**41**	**12**
2006–07	Plymouth Arg	15	1		
2007–08	Plymouth Arg	29	7		
2008–09	Plymouth Arg	44	5		
2009–10	Plymouth Arg	33	5		
2010–11	Plymouth Arg	28	4	**149**	**22**
2010–11	*Ipswich T*	6	1	**6**	**1**
2011–12	*Yeovil T*	5	0	**11**	**1**
2011–12	Aberdeen	22	2		
2012–13	Aberdeen	15	1	**37**	**3**
2013–14	St Johnstone	8	1	**8**	**1**
2013–14	Crawley T	8	0	**8**	**0**
2014–15	Scunthorpe U	4	3	**4**	**3**
2015–16	Bristol R	3	0	**3**	**0**

GOSLING, Jake (M)   **39 1**
H: 5 9   W: 10 10   b.Newquay 11-8-93
Internationals: Gibraltar Full caps.

2011–12	Exeter C	0	0		
2012–13	Exeter C	12	1		
2013–14	Exeter C	3	0	**15**	**1**
2014–15	Bristol R	0	0		
2015–16	Bristol R	18	0	**18**	**0**
2015–16	*Newport Co*	6	0	**6**	**0**

GREENSLADE, Danny (D)   **0 0**
b. 23-9-96

2015–16	Bristol R	0	0		

HARRISON, Ellis (F)   **71 11**
H: 5 11   W: 12 06   b.Newport 1-2-94
Internationals: Wales U21.

2010–11	Bristol R	1	0		
2011–12	Bristol R	0	0		
2012–13	Bristol R	13	3		
2013–14	Bristol R	25	1		
2015–16	Bristol R	30	7	**69**	**11**
2015–16	*Hartlepool U*	2	0	**2**	**0**

KILGOUR, Alfie (D)   **0 0**
b. 18-5-98

2015–16	Bristol R	0	0		

LAWRENCE, Liam (M)   **490 85**
H: 5 11   W: 12 06   b.Retford 14-12-81
Internationals: Republic of Ireland Full caps.

1999–2000	Mansfield T	2	0		
2000–01	Mansfield T	18	4		
2001–02	Mansfield T	32	2		
2002–03	Mansfield T	43	10		
2003–04	Mansfield T	41	18	**136**	**34**
2004–05	Sunderland	32	7		
2005–06	Sunderland	29	3		
2006–07	Sunderland	12	0	**73**	**10**
2006–07	Stoke C	27	5		
2007–08	Stoke C	41	14		
2008–09	Stoke C	20	3		
2009–10	Stoke C	25	1		
2010–11	Stoke C	0	0	**113**	**23**
2010–11	Portsmouth	31	7		
2011–12	Portsmouth	23	0	**54**	**7**
2011–12	*Cardiff C*	13	1	**13**	**1**
2012–13	PAOK Salonika	22	3		
2013–14	PAOK Salonika	2	0	**24**	**3**
2013–14	Barnsley	14	1	**14**	**1**
2014–15	Shrewsbury T	33	5		
2015–16	Shrewsbury T	18	0	**51**	**5**
2015–16	Bristol R	12	1	**12**	**1**

LEADBITTER, Daniel (D)   **48 0**
H: 6 0   W: 11 00   b.Newcastle 17-10-90

2011–12	Torquay U	2	0		
2012–13	Torquay U	13	0	**15**	**0**
2013–14	Bristol R	33	0	**33**	**0**

LINES, Chris (M)   **325 26**
H: 6 2   W: 12 00   b.Bristol 30-11-88

2005–06	Bristol R	4	0		
2006–07	Bristol R	7	0		
2007–08	Bristol R	27	3		
2008–09	Bristol R	45	4		
2009–10	Bristol R	42	10		
2010–11	Bristol R	42	3		
2011–12	Bristol R	1	0		
2011–12	Sheffield W	41	3		
2012–13	Sheffield W	6	0	**47**	**3**
2012–13	*Milton Keynes D*	16	0	**16**	**0**
2013–14	Port Vale	34	1		
2014–15	Port Vale	27	2	**61**	**3**
2015–16	Bristol R	33	0	**201**	**20**

LOCKYER, Tom (D)   **88 1**
H: 6 0   W: 11 05   b.Bristol 30-12-94
Internationals: Wales U21.

2012–13	Bristol R	4	0		
2013–14	Bristol R	41	1		
2015–16	Bristol R	43	0	**88**	**1**

LUCAS, Jamie (F)   **2 0**
H: 6 2   W: 13 01   b.Pontypridd 6-12-95

2013–14	Bristol R	1	0		
2015–16	Bristol R	1	0	**2**	**0**

LYTTLE, Tyler (D)   **1 0**
b. 12-11-96
From Wolverhampton W.

2015–16	Bristol R	1	0	**1**	**0**

MALPAS, Jay (M)   **0 0**
b.23-5-97

2015–16	Bristol R	0	0		

MANSELL, Lee (D)   **378 33**
H: 5 10   W: 11 10   b.Gloucester 28-10-82

2000–01	Luton T	18	5		
2001–02	Luton T	11	1		
2002–03	Luton T	1	0		
2003–04	Luton T	16	2		
2004–05	Luton T	1	0	**47**	**8**
2005–06	Oxford U	44	1	**44**	**1**
2006–07	Torquay U	45	4		
2009–10	Torquay U	39	2		
2010–11	Torquay U	45	0		
2011–12	Torquay U	45	12		
2012–13	Torquay U	42	2		
2013–14	Torquay U	43	2	**259**	**22**
2015–16	Bristol R	28	2	**28**	**2**

McCHRYSTAL, Mark (D)   **195 3**
H: 6 1   W: 13 07   b.Derry 26-6-84
Internationals: Northern Ireland U18, U21.

2001–02	Wolverhampton W	0	0		
2003	Derry C	5	0		
2003	*Institute*	6	0	**6**	**0**
2004	Derry C	9	1		
2005	Derry C	9	0		
2006–07	Partick Thistle	15	1	**15**	**1**
2007	Derry C	3	0		
2008	Derry C	11	0		
2009	Derry C	13	0	**50**	**1**
2009–10	Lisburn Distillery	3	0	**3**	**0**
2010–11	Tranmere R	23	0		
2011–12	Tranmere R	18	1		
2012–13	Tranmere R	0	0	**41**	**1**
2012–13	*Scunthorpe U*	3	0	**3**	**0**
2013–14	Bristol R	21	0		
2013–14	Bristol R	35	0		
2015–16	Bristol R	21	0	**77**	**0**

MILDENHALL, Steve (G)   **427 1**
H: 6 4   W: 14 01   b.Swindon 13-5-78

1996–97	Swindon T	1	0		
1997–98	Swindon T	4	0		
1998–99	Swindon T	0	0		
1999–2000	Swindon T	5	0		
2000–01	Swindon T	23	0	**33**	**0**
2001–02	Notts Co	26	0		
2002–03	Notts Co	21	0		
2003–04	Notts Co	28	0		
2004–05	Notts Co	1	0	**76**	**0**
2004–05	Oldham Ath	6	0	**6**	**0**
2005–06	Grimsby T	46	1	**46**	**1**
2006–07	Yeovil T	46	0		
2007–08	Yeovil T	29	0	**75**	**0**
2008–09	Southend U	34	0		
2009–10	Southend U	44	0		
2010–11	Southend U	0	0	**78**	**0**
2010–11	Millwall	10	0		
2011–12	Millwall	10	0		
2012–13	Millwall	0	0	**10**	**0**
2012–13	*Scunthorpe U*	9	0	**9**	**0**
2012–13	Bristol R	22	0		
2013–14	Bristol R	46	0		
2015–16	Bristol R	26	0	**94**	**0**

MONTANO, Cristian (F)   **105 15**
H: 5 11   W: 12 00   b.Cali 11-12-91

2010–11	West Ham U	0	0		
2011–12	West Ham U	0	0		
2011–12	*Notts Co*	15	4	**15**	**4**
2011–12	*Swindon T*	4	1	**4**	**1**
2011–12	*Dagenham & R*	10	3	**10**	**3**
2011–12	*Oxford U*	9	2	**9**	**2**
2012–13	Oldham Ath	30	1		
2013–14	Oldham Ath	10	2	**40**	**3**
2015–16	Bristol R	27	2	**27**	**2**

PARKES, Tom (D)   **161 3**
H: 6 3   W: 12 05   b.Sutton-in-Ashfield 15-1-92
Internationals: England U17. England C.

2008–09	Leicester C	0	0		
2009–10	Leicester C	0	0		
2009–10	*Burton Alb*	22	1		
2010–11	Leicester C	0	0		
2010–11	*Yeovil T*	1	0	**1**	**0**
2010–11	*Burton Alb*	5	0		
2011–12	Leicester C	0	0		
2011–12	*Burton Alb*	4	0	**31**	**1**
2011–12	*Bristol R*	14	0		
2012–13	Leicester C	0	0		
2012–13	Bristol R	40	1		
2013–14	Bristol R	44	1		
2015–16	Bristol R	31	0	**129**	**2**

PRESTON, Kieran (G)   **0 0**
b.Glasgow 4-10-96
Internationals: Scotland U19.
From Derby Co, Nottingham F.

2015–16	Bristol R	0	0		

PUDDY, Will (G)   **2 0**
H: 6 1   W: 13 00   b.Salisbury 4-10-87

2005–06	Cheltenham T	0	0		
2006–07	Cheltenham T	0	0		
2007–08	Cheltenham T	0	0		
2008–09	Cheltenham T	1	0		
2009–10	Cheltenham T	0	0	**1**	**0**

From Swindon Supermarine, Chippenham T, Salisbury C.

2015–16	Bristol R	1	0	**1**	**0**

SINCLAIR, Stuart (M)   **30 2**
H: 5 7   W: 10 08   b.Houghton Conquest 9-11-87
From Luton T, Cambridge C, Bedford T, Dunstable T, Arlesey T, Salisbury C.

2015–16	Bristol R	30	2	**30**	**2**

TAYLOR, Matty (F)   **46 27**
H: 5 9   W: 11 05   b.30-3-90
Internationals: England C.
From Oxford U, North Leigh, Forest Green R.

2015–16	Bristol R	46	27	**46**	**27**

THOMAS, Dominic (M) 0 0
H: 6 1 W: 11 00 b.London 23-11-95
2013–14	Bristol R	0	0
2015–16	Bristol R	0	0

TROTMAN, Neal (D) 191 8
H: 6 3 W: 13 08 b.Manchester 11-3-87
2006–07	Oldham Ath	1	0		
2007–08	Oldham Ath	17	1		
2007–08	Preston NE	3	0		
2008–09	Preston NE	0	0		
2008–09	Colchester U	6	0	6	0
2009–10	Preston NE	0	0		
2009–10	Southampton	18	2	18	2
2009–10	Huddersfield T	21	2	21	2
2010–11	Preston NE	0	0	3	0
2010–11	Oldham Ath	18	0	36	1
2011–12	Rochdale	12	0	12	0
2011–12	Chesterfield	23	1		
2012–13	Chesterfield	31	0	54	1
2013–14	Plymouth Arg	41	2	41	2
2014–15	Bristol R	0	0		
2015–16	Bristol R	0	0		

Players retained or with offer of contract
Gaffney, Rory Nicholas.

Scholars
Blake, Samuel Joseph; Confrey, Bradley Jesse; Corp, George Philip; Davies, Blake Alan; Ellington, Lewis Owen; Fry, Thomas simon; Green, Elliot Harvey James; Hedges, Sam William; Hodges, Kieran Michael; Iles, Samuel John; Jones, Connor Stephen Malcom; Lammiman, Daniel; Leigh-Gilchrist, Lewis Gordon; Mehew, Oliver David William; Rennie, Toby James; Russe, Luke Cameron; Tucker-Dixon, Tyrone Devante Junior

BURNLEY (17)

AGYEI, Daniel (F) 0 0
b. 1-6-97
2014–15	AFC Wimbledon	0	0
2015–16	Burnley	0	0

ANDERSON, Thomas (M) 26 0
H: 6 4 W: 13 01 b.Burnley 2-9-93
2012–13	Burnley	0	0		
2013–14	Burnley	0	0		
2014–15	Burnley	0	0		
2014–15	Carlisle U	8	0	8	0
2015–16	Burnley	0	0		
2015–16	Chesterfield	18	0	18	0

ARFIELD, Scott (M) 332 38
H: 5 10 W: 10 01 b.Livingston 1-11-88
Internationals: Scotland U19, U21, B. Canada Full caps.
2007–08	Falkirk	35	3		
2008–09	Falkirk	37	7		
2009–10	Falkirk	36	3	108	13
2010–11	Huddersfield T	40	4		
2011–12	Huddersfield T	35	2		
2012–13	Huddersfield T	21	1	96	7
2013–14	Burnley	45	8		
2014–15	Burnley	37	2		
2015–16	Burnley	46	8	128	18

BARNES, Ashley (F) 241 56
H: 6 0 W: 12 00 b.Bath 30-10-89
Internationals: Austria U20.
2006–07	Plymouth Arg	0	0		
2007–08	Plymouth Arg	0	0		
2008–09	Plymouth Arg	15	1		
2009–10	Plymouth Arg	7	1	22	2
2009–10	Torquay U	6	0	6	0
2009–10	Brighton & HA	8	4		
2010–11	Brighton & HA	42	18		
2011–12	Brighton & HA	43	11		
2012–13	Brighton & HA	34	8		
2013–14	Brighton & HA	22	5	149	46
2013–14	Burnley	21	3		
2014–15	Burnley	35	5		
2015–16	Burnley	8	0	64	8

BARTON, Joey (M) 367 32
H: 5 11 W: 12 05 b.Huyton 2-9-82
Internationals: England U21, Full caps.
2001–02	Manchester C	0	0		
2002–03	Manchester C	7	1		
2003–04	Manchester C	28	1		
2004–05	Manchester C	31	1		
2005–06	Manchester C	31	6		
2006–07	Manchester C	33	6	130	15
2007–08	Newcastle U	23	1		
2008–09	Newcastle U	9	1		
2009–10	Newcastle U	15	1		
2010–11	Newcastle U	32	4		
2011–12	Newcastle U	2	0	81	7
2011–12	QPR	31	3		
2012–13	QPR	0	0		
2012–13	Marseille	25	0	25	0
2013–14	QPR	34	3		
2014–15	QPR	28	1	93	7
2015–16	Burnley	38	3	38	3

BIRCH, Arlen (D) 0 0
b. 12-9-96
Internationals: England U16, U18.
2014–15	Everton	0	0
2015–16	Burnley	0	0

BOYD, George (M) 391 81
H: 5 10 W: 11 07 b.Chatham 2-10-85
Internationals: Scotland B, Full caps.
2006–07	Peterborough U	20	6		
2007–08	Peterborough U	46	12		
2008–09	Peterborough U	46	9		
2009–10	Peterborough U	32	9		
2009–10	Nottingham F	6	1	6	1
2010–11	Peterborough U	43	15		
2011–12	Peterborough U	45	7		
2012–13	Peterborough U	31	6	263	64
2012–13	Hull C	13	4		
2013–14	Hull C	29	2		
2014–15	Hull C	1	0	43	6
2014–15	Burnley	35	5		
2015–16	Burnley	44	5	79	10

CONLAN, Luke (D) 19 0
H: 5 11 W: 11 05 b.Portaferry 31-10-94
Internationals: Northern Ireland U16, U17, U19, U21.
2011–12	Burnley	0	0		
2012–13	Burnley	0	0		
2013–14	Burnley	0	0		
2014–15	Burnley	0	0		
2015–16	Burnley	0	0		
2015–16	St Mirren	3	0	3	0
2015–16	Morecambe	16	0	16	0

DARIKWA, Tendayi (M) 146 10
H: 6 2 W: 12 02 b.Nottingham 13-12-91
2010–11	Chesterfield	2	0		
2011–12	Chesterfield	2	0		
2012–13	Chesterfield	36	5		
2013–14	Chesterfield	41	3		
2014–15	Chesterfield	46	1	125	9
2015–16	Burnley	21	1	21	1

DUFF, Michael (D) 543 19
H: 6 1 W: 11 08 b.Belfast 11-1-78
Internationals: Northern Ireland B, Full caps.
1999–2000	Cheltenham T	31	2		
2000–01	Cheltenham T	39	5		
2001–02	Cheltenham T	45	3		
2002–03	Cheltenham T	44	2		
2003–04	Cheltenham T	42	0	201	12
2004–05	Burnley	42	0		
2005–06	Burnley	41	0		
2006–07	Burnley	44	2		
2007–08	Burnley	8	1		
2008–09	Burnley	27	1		
2009–10	Burnley	11	0		
2010–11	Burnley	28	1		
2011–12	Burnley	31	0		
2012–13	Burnley	24	1		
2013–14	Burnley	41	1		
2014–15	Burnley	21	0		
2015–16	Burnley	24	0	342	7

DUMMIGAN, Cameron (D) 26 1
H: 5 11 W: 11 00 b. 2-6-96
Internationals: Northern Ireland U17, U19, U21.
2013–14	Burnley	0	0		
2014–15	Burnley	0	0		
2015–16	Burnley	0	0		
2015–16	Oldham Ath	26	1	26	1

DYER, Lloyd (M) 406 51
H: 5 8 W: 10 03 b.Birmingham 13-9-82
2001–02	WBA	0	0		
2002–03	WBA	0	0		
2003–04	WBA	0	0		
2003–04	Kidderminster H	7	1	7	1
2004–05	WBA	4	0		
2004–05	Coventry C	6	0	6	0
2005–06	WBA	0	0	21	2
2005–06	QPR	15	0	15	0
2005–06	Millwall	6	0	6	0
2006–07	Milton Keynes D	41	5		
2007–08	Milton Keynes D	45	11	86	16
2008–09	Leicester C	44	10		
2009–10	Leicester C	33	3		
2010–11	Leicester C	35	3		
2011–12	Leicester C	36	4		
2012–13	Leicester C	42	3		
2013–14	Leicester C	40	7	230	30
2014–15	Watford	14	1		
2014–15	Birmingham C	18	1	18	1
2015–16	Watford	0	0	14	1
2015–16	Burnley	3	0	3	0

FROST, Jamie (F) 0 0
b. 6-10-96
Internationals: Scotland U18.
2013–14	Burnley	0	0
2015–16	Burnley	0	0

GILKS, Matthew (G) 362 0
H: 6 3 W: 13 12 b.Rochdale 4-6-82
Internationals: Scotland Full caps.
2000–01	Rochdale	3	0		
2001–02	Rochdale	19	0		
2002–03	Rochdale	20	0		
2003–04	Rochdale	12	0		
2004–05	Rochdale	30	0		
2005–06	Rochdale	46	0		
2006–07	Rochdale	46	0	176	0
2007–08	Norwich C	0	0		
2008–09	Blackpool	5	0		
2008–09	Shrewsbury T	4	0	4	0
2009–10	Blackpool	26	0		
2010–11	Blackpool	18	0		
2011–12	Blackpool	42	0		
2012–13	Blackpool	45	0		
2013–14	Blackpool	46	0	182	0
2014–15	Burnley	0	0		
2015–16	Burnley	0	0		

GINNELLY, Josh (M) 3 0
b.Coventry 24-3-97
2013–14	Shrewsbury T	0	0		
2014–15	Shrewsbury T	3	0	3	0
2015–16	Burnley	0	0		

GRAY, Andre (F) 92 41
H: 5 10 W: 12 06 b.Shrewsbury 26-6-91
Internationals: England C.
From Hinckley U, Luton T.
2009–10	Shrewsbury T	4	0	4	0
2014–15	Brentford	45	16		
2015–16	Brentford	2	2	47	18
2015–16	Burnley	41	23	41	23

GREEN, George (M) 9 1
b.Dewsbury 2-1-96
Internationals: England U16, U17, U18.
2013–14	Everton	0	0		
2014–15	Everton	0	0		
2014–15	Tranmere R	6	1	6	1
2015–16	Oldham Ath	3	0	3	0
2015–16	Burnley	0	0		

HEATON, Tom (G) 265 0
H: 6 1 W: 13 12 b.Chester 15-4-86
Internationals: England 16, U17, U18, U19, U21, Full caps.
2003–04	Manchester U	0	0		
2004–05	Manchester U	0	0		
2005–06	Manchester U	0	0		
2005–06	Swindon T	14	0	14	0
2006–07	Manchester U	0	0		
2007–08	Manchester U	0	0		
2008–09	Manchester U	0	0		
2008–09	Cardiff C	21	0		
2009–10	Manchester U	0	0		
2009–10	Rochdale	12	0	12	0
2010–11	Cardiff C	27	0		
2011–12	Cardiff C	2	0	50	0
2012–13	Bristol C	43	0	43	0
2013–14	Burnley	46	0		
2014–15	Burnley	38	0		
2015–16	Burnley	46	0	130	0

HENDRIE, Luke (M) 21 0
b. 27-8-94
Internationals: England U16, U17.
2013–14	Derby Co	0	0		
2014–15	Derby Co	0	0		
2015–16	Burnley	0	0		
2015–16	Hartlepool U	3	0	3	0
2015–16	York C	18	0	18	0

HENNINGS, Rouwen (F) 240 55
H: 5 11 W: 12 08 b. 28-8-87
Internationals: Germany U19, U20, U21.
2005–06	Hamburg	0	0
2006–07	Hamburg	0	0
2007–08	Hamburg	0	0
2007–08	Osnabruck	29	1
2008–09	Hamburg	0	0
2008–09	St Pauli	21	2
2009–10	St Pauli	29	9
2010–11	St Pauli	16	1

2011–12	St Pauli	7	0	73	12
2011–12	*Osnabruck*	17	5	46	6
2012–13	Karlsruhe	35	9		
2013–14	Karlsruhe	31	10		
2014–15	Karlsruhe	27	17		
2015–16	Karlsruhe	2	0	95	36
2015–16	Burnley	26	1	26	1

HEWITT, Steven (M)   2 0
H: 5 7   W: 11 00   b.Manchester 5-12-93

2011–12	Burnley	1	0		
2012–13	Burnley	0	0		
2013–14	Burnley	1	0		
2014–15	Burnley	0	0		
2015–16	Burnley	0	0	2	0

JACKSON, Brad (M)   0 0
b. 20-10-96

2015–16	Burnley	0	0		

JONES, David (M)   313 26
H: 5 11   W: 10 10   b.Southport 4-11-84
Internationals: England U21.

2003–04	Manchester U	0	0		
2004–05	Manchester U	0	0		
2005–06	Manchester U	0	0		
2005–06	*Preston NE*	24	3	24	3
2005–06	*NEC Nijmegen*	17	6	17	6
2006–07	Manchester U	0	0		
2006–07	Derby Co	28	6		
2007–08	Derby Co	14	1	42	7
2008–09	Wolverhampton W	34	4		
2009–10	Wolverhampton W	20	1		
2010–11	Wolverhampton W	12	1	66	6
2011–12	Wigan Ath	16	0		
2012–13	Wigan Ath	13	0	29	0
2012–13	*Blackburn R*	12	2	12	2
2013–14	Burnley	46	1		
2014–15	Burnley	36	0		
2015–16	Burnley	41	1	123	2

JUTKIEWICZ, Lucas (F)   264 53
H: 6 1   W: 12 11   b.Southampton 20-3-89

2005–06	Swindon T	5	0		
2006–07	Swindon T	33	5	38	5
2006–07	Everton	0	0		
2007–08	Everton	0	0		
2007–08	*Plymouth Arg*	3	0	3	0
2008–09	Everton	1	0		
2008–09	*Huddersfield T*	7	0	7	0
2009–10	Everton	0	0	1	0
2009–10	*Motherwell*	33	12	33	12
2010–11	Coventry C	42	9		
2011–12	Coventry C	25	9	67	18
2011–12	Middlesbrough	19	2		
2012–13	Middlesbrough	24	8		
2013–14	Middlesbrough	22	1	65	11
2013–14	*Bolton W*	20	7	20	7
2014–15	Burnley	25	0		
2015–16	Burnley	5	0	30	0

KEANE, Michael (D)   108 10
H: 5 7   W: 12 13   b.Stockport 11-1-93
Internationals: Republic of Ireland U17.
England U19, U20, U21.

2011–12	Manchester U	0	0		
2012–13	Manchester U	0	0		
2012–13	*Leicester C*	22	2	22	2
2013–14	Manchester U	0	0		
2013–14	*Derby Co*	7	0	7	0
2013–14	*Blackburn R*	13	3	13	3
2014–15	Manchester U	1	0	1	0
2014–15	Burnley	21	0		
2015–16	Burnley	44	5	65	5

KIGHTLY, Michael (M)   232 35
H: 5 10   W: 10 10   b.Basildon 24-1-86
Internationals: England U21.

2002–03	Southend U	1	0		
2003–04	Southend U	11	0		
2004–05	Southend U	0	0	13	0
From Grays Ath.					
2006–07	Wolverhampton W	24	8		
2007–08	Wolverhampton W	21	4		
2008–09	Wolverhampton W	38	8		
2009–10	Wolverhampton W	9	0		
2010–11	Wolverhampton W	4	0		
2011–12	Wolverhampton W	18	3		
2011–12	*Watford*	12	3	12	3
2012–13	Wolverhampton W	0	0	114	23
2012–13	Stoke C	22	3		
2013–14	Stoke C	0	0	22	3
2013–14	*Burnley*	36	5		
2014–15	Burnley	17	1		
2015–16	Burnley	18	0	71	6

LAFFERTY, Danny (D)   126 9
H: 6 0   W: 12 08   b.Derry 1-4-89
Internationals: Northern Ireland U17, U19,
U21, B, Full caps.

2009–10	Celtic	0	0		
2009–10	Ayr U	14	1	14	1
2010	Derry C	12	0		
2011	Derry C	34	7	46	7
2011–12	Burnley	5	0		
2012–13	Burnley	24	0		
2013–14	Burnley	10	0		
2014–15	Burnley	1	0		
2014–15	*Rotherham U*	11	0	11	0
2015–16	Burnley	0	0	40	0
2015–16	*Oldham Ath*	15	1	15	1

LONG, Chris (F)   24 5
H: 5 7   W: 12 02   b.Huyton 25-2-95
Internationals: England U16, U17, U18, U19,
U20.

2013–14	Everton	0	0		
2013–14	*Milton Keynes D*	4	1	4	1
2014–15	Everton	0	0		
2014–15	*Brentford*	10	4	10	4
2015–16	Burnley	10	0	10	0

LONG, Kevin (D)   111 6
H: 6 3   W: 13 01   b.Cork 18-8-90

2009	Cork C	16	0	16	0
2009–10	Burnley	0	0		
2010–11	Burnley	0	0		
2010–11	*Accrington S*	15	0		
2011–12	Burnley	0	0		
2011–12	*Accrington S*	24	4	39	4
2011–12	*Rochdale*	16	0	16	0
2012–13	Burnley	14	0		
2012–13	*Portsmouth*	5	0	5	0
2013–14	Burnley	7	0		
2014–15	Burnley	1	0		
2015–16	Burnley	0	0	22	0
2015–16	*Barnsley*	11	2	11	2
2015–16	*Milton Keynes D*	2	0	2	0

LOWTON, Matt (M)   182 13
H: 5 11   W: 12 04   b.Chesterfield 9-6-89

2008–09	Sheffield U	0	0		
2009–10	Sheffield U	2	0		
2009–10	*Ferencvaros*	5	0	5	0
2010–11	Sheffield U	32	4		
2011–12	Sheffield U	44	6	78	10
2012–13	Aston Villa	37	2		
2013–14	Aston Villa	23	0		
2014–15	Aston Villa	12	0	72	2
2015–16	Burnley	27	1	27	1

MARNEY, Dean (M)   341 19
H: 5 10   W: 11 09   b.Barking 31-1-84
Internationals: England U21.

2002–03	Tottenham H	0	0		
2002–03	*Swindon T*	9	0	9	0
2003–04	Tottenham H	3	0		
2003–04	*QPR*	2	0	2	0
2004–05	Tottenham H	5	2		
2004–05	*Gillingham*	3	0	3	0
2005–06	Tottenham H	0	0	8	2
2005–06	*Norwich C*	13	0	13	0
2006–07	Hull C	37	2		
2007–08	Hull C	41	6		
2008–09	Hull C	31	0		
2009–10	Hull C	16	1	125	9
2009–10	Burnley	0	0		
2010–11	Burnley	36	3		
2011–12	Burnley	37	0		
2012–13	Burnley	38	2		
2013–14	Burnley	38	3		
2014–15	Burnley	20	0		
2015–16	Burnley	12	0	181	8

MASSANKA, Ntumba (F)   3 0
b. 30-11-96

2015–16	Burnley	0	0		
2015–16	*York C*	3	0	3	0

MEE, Ben (D)   182 5
H: 5 11   W: 11 09   b.Sale 21-9-89
Internationals: England U19, U20, U21.

2007–08	Manchester C	0	0		
2008–09	Manchester C	0	0		
2009–10	Manchester C	0	0		
2010–11	Manchester C	0	0		
2010–11	*Leicester C*	15	0	15	0
2011–12	Manchester C	0	0		
2011–12	*Burnley*	31	0		
2012–13	Burnley	19	1		
2012–13	Burnley	38	0		
2013–14	Burnley	33	2		
2015–16	Burnley	46	2	167	5

MITCHELL, Conor (G)   0 0
b. 9-5-96
Internationals: Northern Ireland U17, U19,
U21.

2015–16	Burnley	0	0		

NIZIC, Daniel (G)   0 0
b. 15-3-95
Internationals: Australia U20.

2015–16	Burnley	0	0		
2015–16	*Crewe Alex*	0	0		

ROBINSON, Paul (G)   421 1
H: 6 1   W: 14 07   b.Beverley 15-10-79
Internationals: England U21, Full caps.

1996–97	Leeds U	0	0		
1997–98	Leeds U	0	0		
1998–99	Leeds U	5	0		
1999–2000	Leeds U	0	0		
2000–01	Leeds U	16	0		
2001–02	Leeds U	0	0		
2002–03	Leeds U	38	0		
2003–04	Leeds U	36	0	95	0
2003–04	Tottenham H	0	0		
2004–05	Tottenham H	36	0		
2005–06	Tottenham H	38	0		
2006–07	Tottenham H	38	1		
2007–08	Tottenham H	25	0	137	1
2008–09	Blackburn R	35	0		
2009–10	Blackburn R	35	0		
2010–11	Blackburn R	36	0		
2011–12	Blackburn R	34	0		
2012–13	Blackburn R	21	0		
2013–14	Blackburn R	21	0		
2014–15	Blackburn R	7	0	189	0
2015–16	Burnley	0	0		

TARKOWSKI, James (D)   146 9
H: 6 1   W: 12 10   b.Manchester 19-11-92

2010–11	Oldham Ath	9	0		
2011–12	Oldham Ath	16	1		
2012–13	Oldham Ath	21	2		
2013–14	Oldham Ath	26	2	72	5
2013–14	Brentford	13	2		
2014–15	Brentford	34	1		
2015–16	Brentford	23	1	70	4
2015–16	Burnley	4	0	4	0

TAYLOR, Matthew (D)   544 68
H: 5 11   W: 12 03   b.Oxford 27-11-81
Internationals: England U21, B.

1998–99	Luton T	0	0		
1999–2000	Luton T	41	4		
2000–01	Luton T	45	1		
2001–02	Luton T	43	11	129	16
2002–03	Portsmouth	35	7		
2003–04	Portsmouth	30	0		
2004–05	Portsmouth	32	1		
2005–06	Portsmouth	34	6		
2006–07	Portsmouth	35	8		
2007–08	Portsmouth	13	1	179	23
2007–08	Bolton W	16	3		
2008–09	Bolton W	34	10		
2009–10	Bolton W	37	8		
2010–11	Bolton W	36	2	123	23
2011–12	West Ham U	28	1		
2012–13	West Ham U	28	1		
2013–14	West Ham U	20	0	76	2
2014–15	Burnley	10	0		
2015–16	Burnley	27	4	37	4

ULVESTAD, Fredrik (M)   113 14
H: 6 0   W: 12 06   b.Alesund 19-5-92
Internationals: Norway U20, U21, U23, Full
caps.

2010	Aalesund	1	0		
2011	Aalesund	24	2		
2012	Aalesund	25	2		
2013	Aalesund	27	7		
2014	Aalesund	29	3	106	14
2014–15	Burnley	2	0		
2015–16	Burnley	5	0	7	0

VOKES, Sam (F)   286 69
H: 6 1   W: 13 10   b.Lymington 21-10-89
Internationals: Wales U21, Full caps.

2006–07	Bournemouth	13	4		
2007–08	Bournemouth	41	12	54	16
2008–09	Wolverhampton W	36	6		
2009–10	Wolverhampton W	5	0		
2009–10	*Leeds U*	8	1	8	1
2010–11	Wolverhampton W	2	0		
2010–11	*Bristol C*	1	0	1	0
2010–11	*Sheffield U*	6	1	6	1
2010–11	*Norwich C*	4	1	4	1
2011–12	Wolverhampton W	9	2		
2011–12	*Burnley*	0	0		
2011–12	*Brighton & HA*	14	3	14	3
2012–13	Wolverhampton W	0	0	47	6

2012–13	Burnley	46	4		
2013–14	Burnley	39	20		
2014–15	Burnley	15	0		
2015–16	Burnley	43	15	152	41

VOSSEN, Jelle (F)   277 104
H: 5 11   W: 11 00   b.Bilzen 22-3-89
Internationals: Belgium U16, U17, U18, U19, U20, U21, Full caps.

2006–07	Genk	8	1		
2007–08	Genk	17	3		
2008–09	Genk	20	4		
2009–10	Genk	3	0		
2009–10	*Cercle Brugge*	17	6	17	6
2010–11	Genk	37	20		
2011–12	Genk	36	20		
2012–13	Genk	32	17		
2013–14	Genk	38	12		
2014–15	Genk	2	0	193	77
2014–15	*Middlesbrough*	33	7	33	7
2015–16	Burnley	4	0	4	0
2015–16	*Club Brugge*	30	14	30	14

WARD, Stephen (D)   371 25
H: 5 11   W: 12 02   b.Dublin 20-8-85
Internationals: Republic of Ireland U20, U21, B, Full caps.

2003	Bohemians	6	0		
2004	Bohemians	16	2		
2005	Bohemians	29	7		
2006	Bohemians	21	2	72	11
2006–07	Wolverhampton W	18	3		
2007–08	Wolverhampton W	29	0		
2008–09	Wolverhampton W	42	0		
2009–10	Wolverhampton W	22	0		
2010–11	Wolverhampton W	34	1		
2011–12	Wolverhampton W	38	3		
2012–13	Wolverhampton W	39	2		
2013–14	Wolverhampton W	0	0	222	9
2013–14	*Brighton & HA*	44	4	44	4
2014–15	Burnley	9	0		
2015–16	Burnley	24	1	33	1

Players retained or with offer of contract
Hill, Christian Stephen; O'Neill, Aiden Connor; Olomowewe, Taofiq Aderibigbe Akanni; Smith, Renny Piers; Whitmore, Alexander James; Yao, Abodje Freddy Bruce.

Scholars
Aghayere, Nosakhare Tony; Bayode, Olatunde Tobias; Chakwana, Tinashe; Crawford, Jamal; Dixon, Vashiko Tanaka; Dolling, Joshua Jordan; El-Fitouri, Hamam Abdel Hakim; Fenton, Miles Andrew; Grogan, Billy Richard; Hobson, Shaun Jermaine; Howarth, Mark David; King, Connor Lewis; Metz, Khius; Norvock, Lewis; Nugent, Andrew; Shrimpton, Tyler Edward Dean; Wilson, Brandon James; Wood, Tommy Paul.

BURTON ALB (18)

AKINS, Lucas (F)   258 42
H: 5 10   W: 11 07   b.Huddersfield 25-2-89

2006–07	Huddersfield T	2	0		
2007–08	Huddersfield T	3	0	5	0
2008–09	Hamilton A	11	0		
2008–09	*Partick Thistle*	9	1	9	1
2009–10	Hamilton A	0	0	11	0
2010–11	Tranmere R	33	2		
2011–12	Tranmere R	44	5	77	7
2012–13	Stevenage	46	10		
2013–14	Stevenage	31	3	77	13
2014–15	Burton Alb	35	9		
2015–16	Burton Alb	44	12	79	21

AUSTIN, Sam (M)   1 0
H: 6 0   W: 11 00   b.19-12-96

2014–15	Burton Alb	1	0		
2015–16	Burton Alb	0	0	1	0

BEAVON, Stuart (F)   260 50
H: 5 7   W: 10 10   b.Reading 5-5-84

2008–09	Wycombe W	8	0		
2009–10	Wycombe W	25	3		
2010–11	Wycombe W	37	3		
2011–12	Wycombe W	43	21		
2012–13	Wycombe W	2	1	115	28
2012–13	Preston NE	31	6		
2013–14	Preston NE	27	3	58	9
2014–15	Burton Alb	44	6		
2015–16	Burton Alb	43	7	87	13

BUTCHER, Calum (D)   63 6
H: 6 1   W: 13 01   b.Rochford 26-2-91

2007–08	Tottenham H	0	0		
2008–09	Tottenham H	0	0		
2009–10	Tottenham H	0	0		
2009–10	*Barnet*	3	0	3	0

From Hayes & Yeading.

2013–14	Dundee U	6	0		
2014–15	Dundee U	15	1	21	1
2015–16	Burton Alb	39	5	39	5

BYWATER, Steve (G)   327 0
H: 6 2   W: 12 10   b.Manchester 7-6-81
Internationals: England U20, U21.

1997–98	Rochdale	0	0		
1998–99	West Ham U	0	0		
1999–2000	West Ham U	4	0		
1999–2000	*Wycombe W*	2	0	2	0
1999–2000	*Hull C*	4	0	4	0
2000–01	West Ham U	1	0		
2001–02	West Ham U	0	0		
2001–02	*Wolverhampton W*	0	0		
2001–02	*Cardiff C*	0	0		
2002–03	West Ham U	0	0		
2003–04	West Ham U	17	0		
2004–05	West Ham U	36	0		
2005–06	West Ham U	1	0	59	0
2005–06	*Coventry C*	14	0	14	0
2006–07	Derby Co	37	0		
2007–08	Derby Co	18	0		
2007–08	*Ipswich T*	17	0	17	0
2008–09	Derby Co	31	0		
2009–10	Derby Co	42	0		
2010–11	Derby Co	22	0	150	0
2010–11	*Cardiff C*	8	0	8	0
2011–12	Sheffield W	32	0		
2012–13	Sheffield W	0	0	32	0
2013–14	Millwall	7	0		
2014–15	Millwall	0	0	7	0
2014–15	*Gillingham*	13	0	13	0
2014–15	*Doncaster R*	21	0	21	0
2015–16	Burton Alb	0	0		

CANSDELL-SHERRIFF, Shane (D)   452 25
H: 5 11   W: 11 08   b.Sydney 10-11-82
Internationals: Australia U17, U23.

1999–2000	Leeds U	0	0		
2000–01	Leeds U	0	0		
2001–02	Leeds U	0	0		
2002–03	Leeds U	0	0		
2002–03	Rochdale	3	0		
2003–04	Aarhus	29	4		
2004–05	Aarhus	26	2		
2005–06	Aarhus	27	1	82	7
2006–07	Tranmere R	44	3		
2007–08	Tranmere R	44	3	87	6
2008–09	Shrewsbury T	31	2		
2009–10	Shrewsbury T	41	1		
2010–11	Shrewsbury T	41	2		
2011–12	Shrewsbury T	37	4	150	9
2012–13	Preston NE	15	1		
2012–13	*Rochdale*	17	0	20	0
2013–14	Preston NE	0	0	15	1
2013–14	*Burton Alb*	32	0		
2014–15	Burton Alb	37	2		
2015–16	Burton Alb	29	0	98	2

CHARLES, Darius (M)   190 14
H: 6 1   W: 13 05   b.Ealing 10-12-87
Internationals: England C.

2004–05	Brentford	1	0		
2005–06	Brentford	2	0		
2006–07	Brentford	17	1		
2007–08	Brentford	17	0	37	1

From Ebbsfleet U.

2010–11	Stevenage	28	2		
2011–12	Stevenage	28	4		
2012–13	Stevenage	37	1		
2013–14	Stevenage	22	4		
2014–15	Stevenage	29	2	144	13
2015–16	Burton Alb	0	0		
2015–16	*AFC Wimbledon*	9	0	9	0

EDWARDS, Phil (D)   401 31
H: 5 8   W: 11 03   b.Bootle 8-11-85

2005–06	Wigan Ath	0	0		
2006–07	Accrington S	33	1		
2007–08	Accrington S	31	1		
2008–09	Accrington S	46	0		
2009–10	Accrington S	46	8		
2010–11	Accrington S	44	13	200	23
2011–12	Stevenage	22	0	22	0
2011–12	*Rochdale*	3	0		
2012–13	Rochdale	44	0	47	0
2013–14	Rochdale	41	2		
2014–15	Burton Alb	45	6		
2015–16	Burton Alb	46	0	132	8

FLANAGAN, Tom (D)   83 4
H: 6 2   W: 11 05   b.Hammersmith 21-10-91
Internationals: Northern Ireland U21.

2009–10	Milton Keynes D	1	0		
2010–11	Milton Keynes D	2	0		
2011–12	Milton Keynes D	21	3		
2012–13	Milton Keynes D	0	0		
2012–13	*Gillingham*	13	1	13	1
2012–13	*Barnet*	9	0	9	0
2013–14	Milton Keynes D	7	0		
2013–14	*Stevenage*	2	0	2	0
2014–15	Milton Keynes D	6	0	37	3
2014–15	*Plymouth Arg*	4	0	4	0
2015–16	Burton Alb	18	0	18	0

HARNESS, Marcus (M)   26 0
H: 6 0   W: 11 00   b. 1-8-94

2013–14	Burton Alb	3	0		
2014–15	Burton Alb	18	0		
2015–16	Burton Alb	5	0	26	0

HORNBY, Sam (G)   0 0
b. 14-2-95

2015–16	Burton Alb	0	0		

JOACHIM, Aurelien (F)   222 73
H: 6 0   W: 12 08   b. 10-8-86
Internationals: Luxembourg Full caps.

2004–05	R.E. Virton	32	1	32	1
2005–06	Bochum	0	0		
2006–07	Bochum	0	0		
2007–08	Differdange 03	11	6	11	6
2008–09	Differdange 03	24	6		
2009–10	Differdange 03	23	8		
2010–11	Differdange 03	23	16	70	30
2011–12	F91 Dudelange	23	19		
2012–13	F91 Dudelange	2	0	25	19
2012–13	Willem II	25	6	25	6
2013–14	RKC Waalwijk	32	6	32	6
2014–15	CSKA Sofia	20	5	20	5
2015–16	Burton Alb	7	0	7	0

LYNESS, Dean (G)   46 0
H: 6 3   W: 11 12   b.Birmingham 20-7-91
Internationals: England U17.

2012–13	Burton Alb	15	0		
2013–14	Burton Alb	21	0		
2014–15	Burton Alb	1	0		
2015–16	Burton Alb	0	0	37	0
2015–16	*Blackpool*	9	0	9	0

McCRORY, Damien (M)   257 11
H: 6 2   W: 12 10   b.Limerick 22-2-90
Internationals: Republic of Ireland U18, U19.

2008–09	Plymouth Arg	0	0		
2008–09	*Port Vale*	12	0		
2009–10	Plymouth Arg	0	0		
2009–10	*Port Vale*	5	0	17	0
2009–10	*Grimsby T*	10	0	10	0
2010–11	Dagenham & R	20	0		
2010–11	Dagenham & R	23	0		
2011–12	Dagenham & R	33	1	76	1
2012–13	Burton Alb	42	1		
2013–14	Burton Alb	40	1		
2014–15	Burton Alb	34	5		
2015–16	Burton Alb	38	3	154	10

McLAUGHLIN, Jon (G)   215 0
H: 6 2   W: 13 00   b.Edinburgh 9-9-87

2008–09	Bradford C	1	0		
2009–10	Bradford C	7	0		
2010–11	Bradford C	25	0		
2011–12	Bradford C	23	0		
2012–13	Bradford C	23	0		
2013–14	Bradford C	46	0	125	0
2014–15	Burton Alb	45	0		
2015–16	Burton Alb	45	0	90	0

MOUSINHO, John (M)   328 20
H: 6 1   W: 12 07   b.Hounslow 30-4-86

2005–06	Brentford	7	0		
2006–07	Brentford	34	0		
2007–08	Brentford	23	2	64	2
2008–09	Wycombe W	34	2		
2009–10	Wycombe W	39	1	73	3
2010–11	Stevenage	38	7		
2011–12	Stevenage	19	3		
2012–13	Preston NE	24	1		
2013–14	Preston NE	0	0	26	1
2013–14	*Gillingham*	4	1	4	1
2013–14	*Stevenage*	16	1	73	11
2014–15	Burton Alb	42	2		
2015–16	Burton Alb	46	0	88	2

NAYLOR, Tom (D)   112 7
H: 5 11   W: 11 05   b.Sutton-in-Ashfield 28-6-91

2011–12	Derby Co	8	0		
2012–13	Derby Co	0	0		
2012–13	*Bradford C*	5	0	5	0
2013–14	Derby Co	0	0		
2013–14	*Newport Co*	33	1	33	1
2014–15	Derby Co	0	0	8	0
2014–15	*Cambridge U*	8	0	8	0

Season	Club	Apps	Gls	Tot	TGls
2014–15	Burton Alb	17	0		
2015–16	Burton Alb	41	6	58	6

O'CONNOR, Anthony (D) 138 4
H: 6 2 W: 12 06 b.Cork 25-10-92
Internationals: Republic of Ireland U17, U19, U21.

Season	Club	Apps	Gls	Tot	TGls
2010–11	Blackburn R	0	0		
2011–12	Blackburn R	0	0		
2012–13	Blackburn R	0	0		
2012–13	Burton Alb	46	0		
2013–14	Blackburn R	0	0		
2013–14	Torquay U	31	0	31	0
2014–15	Plymouth Arg	40	3	40	3
2015–16	Burton Alb	21	1	67	1

PALMER, Matthew (M) 103 5
H: 5 10 W: 12 06 b.Derby 1-8-93

Season	Club	Apps	Gls	Tot	TGls
2012–13	Burton Alb	2	0		
2013–14	Burton Alb	40	0		
2014–15	Burton Alb	33	4		
2015–16	Burton Alb	14	0	89	4
2015–16	Oldham Ath	14	1	14	1

REILLY, Callum (M) 76 2
H: 6 1 W: 12 03 b.Warrington 3-10-93
Internationals: Republic of Ireland U21.

Season	Club	Apps	Gls	Tot	TGls
2012–13	Birmingham C	18	1		
2013–14	Birmingham C	25	0		
2014–15	Birmingham C	17	1	60	2
2014–15	Burton Alb	2	0		
2015–16	Burton Alb	14	0	16	0

SLADE, Liam (D) 6 0
H: 6 3 W: 12 08 b. 14-5-95

Season	Club	Apps	Gls	Tot	TGls
2014–15	Burton Alb	0	0		
2014–15	Burton Alb	6	0		
2015–16	Burton Alb	0	0	6	0

TAFT, George (D) 44 2
H: 5 9 W: 11 09 b.Leicester 29-7-93
Internationals: England U18, U19.

Season	Club	Apps	Gls	Tot	TGls
2010–11	Leicester C	0	0		
2011–12	Leicester C	0	0		
2012–13	Leicester C	0	0		
2013–14	Leicester C	0	0		
2013–14	York C	3	0	3	0
2014–15	Burton Alb	30	1		
2015–16	Burton Alb	0	0	30	1
2015–16	Cambridge U	11	1	11	1

THIELE, Timmy (F) 65 6
H: 6 3 W: 11 11 b.Berlin 31-7-91

Season	Club	Apps	Gls	Tot	TGls
2012–13	Alemannia Aachen	29	5	29	5
2013–14	Borussia Dortmund	0	0		
2014–15	Borussia Dortmund	0	0		
2014–15	Wiedenbruck	10	0	10	0
2015–16	Burton Alb	22	1	22	1
2015–16	Oldham Ath	4	0	4	0

WEIR, Robbie (M) 217 10
H: 5 9 W: 11 07 b.Belfast 9-12-88
Internationals: Northern Ireland U18, U19, U21, B.

Season	Club	Apps	Gls	Tot	TGls
2007–08	Sunderland	0	0		
2008–09	Sunderland	0	0		
2009–10	Sunderland	0	0		
2010–11	Sunderland	0	0		
2010–11	Tranmere R	18	0		
2011–12	Tranmere R	39	3	57	3
2012–13	Burton Alb	42	5		
2013–14	Burton Alb	41	2		
2014–15	Burton Alb	41	0		
2015–16	Burton Alb	36	0	160	7

Players retained or with offer of contract
Fenton, Nicholas Leonard; Ferguson, Nathan James Decalvia.

Scholars
Cotterill, Jayden Michael; Dinanga Nyambu, Marcus; Fox, Benjamin Jake; Garnett, Dylan Gabriel; Gatter, Charlie Anthony; Hallahan, Jack Patrick Daniel; Hammerton, Thomas James; Hornby, Charles Benjamin; Hunt, Joseph James; O'Brien, Jack Christopher; Pearson, Michael Thomas; Sbarra, Joseph Christopher; Sejdic, Mirza; Shaw, Cameron George; Smith, Brad; Troke, Lewis Andrew Harry; Walker, Lewis Joseph Paul.

BURY (19)

BOURNE, Robert (M) 1 0

Season	Club	Apps	Gls	Tot	TGls
2015–16	Bury	1	0	1	0

BROWN, Reece (D) 82 0
H: 6 2 W: 13 02 b.Manchester 1-11-91
Internationals: England U19, U20.

Season	Club	Apps	Gls	Tot	TGls
2010–11	Manchester U	0	0		
2010–11	Bradford C	3	0	3	0
2011–12	Manchester U	0	0		
2011–12	Doncaster R	3	0	3	0
2011–12	Oldham Ath	15	0	15	0
2012–13	Manchester U	0	0		
2012–13	Coventry C	6	0	6	0
2012–13	Ipswich T	1	0	1	0
2013–14	Watford	1	0	1	0
2013–14	Carlisle U	12	0	12	0
2014–15	Barnsley	13	0	13	0
2015–16	Bury	28	0	28	0

BURGESS, Scott (M) 4 0
H: 5 10 W: 11 00 b.Warrington 27-6-96

Season	Club	Apps	Gls	Tot	TGls
2013–14	Bury	1	0		
2014–15	Bury	0	0		
2015–16	Bury	3	0	4	0

CAMERON, Nathan (D) 152 9
H: 6 2 W: 12 04 b.Birmingham 21-11-91
Internationals: England U20.

Season	Club	Apps	Gls	Tot	TGls
2009–10	Coventry C	0	0		
2010–11	Coventry C	25	0		
2011–12	Coventry C	14	0		
2012–13	Coventry C	9	0	48	0
2012–13	Northampton T	3	0	3	0
2013–14	Bury	27	4		
2014–15	Bury	46	2		
2015–16	Bury	28	3	101	9

CLARKE, Leon (F) 355 106
H: 6 2 W: 14 02 b.Birmingham 10-2-85

Season	Club	Apps	Gls	Tot	TGls
2003–04	Wolverhampton W	0	0		
2003–04	Kidderminster H	4	0	4	0
2004–05	Wolverhampton W	28	7		
2005–06	Wolverhampton W	24	1		
2005–06	QPR	1	0		
2005–06	Plymouth Arg	5	0	5	0
2006–07	Wolverhampton W	22	5		
2006–07	Sheffield W	10	1		
2006–07	Oldham Ath	5	3	5	3
2007–08	Sheffield W	8	3		
2007–08	Southend U	16	8	16	8
2008–09	Sheffield W	29	8		
2009–10	Sheffield W	36	6	83	18
2010–11	QPR	13	0	14	0
2010–11	Preston NE	6	1	6	1
2011–12	Swindon T	2	0	2	0
2011–12	Chesterfield	14	9	14	9
2011–12	Charlton Ath	7	0		
2012–13	Charlton Ath	0	0	7	0
2012–13	Crawley T	4	1	4	1
2012–13	Scunthorpe U	15	11	15	11
2012–13	Coventry C	12	8		
2013–14	Coventry C	23	15	35	23
2013–14	Wolverhampton W	13	1		
2014–15	Wolverhampton W	16	2	103	16
2014–15	Wigan Ath	10	1	10	1
2015–16	Bury	32	15	32	15

CLARKE, Peter (D) 529 37
H: 6 0 W: 12 00 b.Southport 3-1-82
Internationals: England U21.

Season	Club	Apps	Gls	Tot	TGls
1998–99	Everton	0	0		
1999–2000	Everton	0	0		
2000–01	Everton	1	0		
2001–02	Everton	7	0		
2002–03	Everton	0	0		
2002–03	Blackpool	16	3		
2002–03	Port Vale	13	1	13	1
2003–04	Everton	1	0		
2003–04	Coventry C	5	0	5	0
2004–05	Everton	0	0	9	0
2004–05	Blackpool	38	5		
2005–06	Blackpool	46	6		
2006–07	Southend U	38	2		
2007–08	Southend U	45	4		
2008–09	Southend U	43	4	126	10
2009–10	Huddersfield T	46	5		
2010–11	Huddersfield T	46	4		
2011–12	Huddersfield T	31	0		
2012–13	Huddersfield T	43	0		
2013–14	Huddersfield T	26	0	192	9
2014–15	Blackpool	39	2	139	16
2015–16	Bury	45	1	45	1

DUDLEY, Anthony (F) 6 0
H: 5 10 W: 11 00 b.Manchester 3-1-96

Season	Club	Apps	Gls	Tot	TGls
2013–14	Bury	2	0		
2014–15	Bury	1	0		
2015–16	Bury	3	0	6	0

EAGLES, Chris (M) 315 50
H: 5 10 W: 11 07 b.Hemel Hempstead 19-11-85
Internationals: England Youth.

Season	Club	Apps	Gls	Tot	TGls
2003–04	Manchester U	0	0		
2004–05	Manchester U	0	0		
2004–05	Watford	13	1		
2005–06	Manchester U	0	0		
2005–06	Sheffield W	25	3	25	3
2005–06	Watford	17	3	30	4
2006–07	Manchester U	2	1		
2006–07	NEC Nijmegen	15	1	15	1
2007–08	Manchester U	4	0	6	1
2008–09	Burnley	43	8		
2009–10	Burnley	34	2		
2010–11	Burnley	43	11	120	21
2011–12	Bolton W	34	4		
2012–13	Bolton W	43	12		
2013–14	Bolton W	16	1	93	17
2014–15	Blackpool	7	1	7	1
2014–15	Charlton Ath	15	2	15	2
2015–16	Bury	4	0	4	0

ETUHU, Kelvin (F) 154 6
H: 5 11 W: 11 02 b.Kano 30-5-88

Season	Club	Apps	Gls	Tot	TGls
2005–06	Manchester C	0	0		
2006–07	Manchester C	0	0		
2006–07	Rochdale	4	2	4	2
2007–08	Manchester C	6	1		
2007–08	Leicester C	4	0	4	0
2008–09	Manchester C	4	0		
2009–10	Manchester C	0	0		
2009–10	Cardiff C	16	0	16	0
2010–11	Manchester C	0	0	10	1
2011–12	Kavala	0	0		
2011–12	Portsmouth	13	1		
2012–13	Portsmouth	0	0	13	1
2012–13	Barnsley	26	0		
2013–14	Barnsley	20	0	46	0
2014–15	Bury	43	2		
2015–16	Bury	18	0	61	2

HARKER, Rob (M) 0 0
H: 6-3-00

Season	Club	Apps	Gls	Tot	TGls
2015–16	Bury	0	0		

HOPE, Hallam (F) 61 10
H: 5 10 W: 12 00 b.Manchester 17-3-94
Internationals: England U16, U17, U18, U19.

Season	Club	Apps	Gls	Tot	TGls
2010–11	Everton	0	0		
2011–12	Everton	0	0		
2013–14	Everton	0	0		
2013–14	Northampton T	3	1	3	1
2013–14	Bury	8	5		
2014–15	Everton	0	0		
2014–15	Sheffield W	4	0	4	0
2014–15	Bury	19	0		
2015–16	Bury	6	0	33	5
2015–16	Carlisle U	21	4	21	4

HUSSEY, Chris (D) 194 4
H: 5 10 W: 10 03 b.Hammersmith 2-1-89

Season	Club	Apps	Gls	Tot	TGls
2009–10	Coventry C	8	0		
2010–11	Coventry C	11	0		
2010–11	Crewe Alex	0	0		
2011–12	Coventry C	29	0		
2012–13	Coventry C	10	0	58	0
2012–13	AFC Wimbledon	19	0		
2013–14	AFC Wimbledon	0	0	19	0
2013–14	Burton Alb	27	1	27	1
2013–14	Bury	11	2		
2014–15	Bury	38	0		
2015–16	Bury	41	1	90	3

JONES, Craig (M) 247 34
H: 5 7 W: 11 03 b.Chester 20-3-87

Season	Club	Apps	Gls	Tot	TGls
2004–05	Airbus UK	2	2		
2005–06	Airbus UK	7	6	9	8
2007–08	Rhyl	27	8		
2008–09	Rhyl	14	2	41	10
2008–09	Connah's Quay	12	0	12	0
2009–10	New Saints FC	26	7	26	7
2010–11	Port Talbot	14	1		
2011–12	Port Talbot	7	0	21	1
2012–13	Bury	25	1		
2013–14	Bury	37	1		
2014–15	Bury	40	3		
2015–16	Bury	36	3	138	8

LAINTON, Robert (G) 45 0
H: 6 2 W: 12 06 b.Ashton-under-Lyne 12-10-89

Season	Club	Apps	Gls	Tot	TGls
2009–10	Bolton W	0	0		
2010–11	Bolton W	0	0		
2011–12	Bolton W	0	0		
2012–13	Bolton W	0	0		
2013–14	Bury	4	0		
2013–14	Burton Alb	14	0	14	0
2014–15	Bury	17	0		
2015–16	Bury	10	0	31	0

LOWE, Ryan (F) 552 169
H: 5 10 W: 12 08 b.Liverpool 18-9-78

Season	Club	Apps	Gls	Tot	TGls
2000–01	Shrewsbury T	30	4		
2001–02	Shrewsbury T	38	7		
2002–03	Shrewsbury T	39	9		
2003–04	Shrewsbury T	0	0		

Season	Club				
2004–05	Shrewsbury T	30	3	137	23
2004–05	Chester C	8	4		
2005–06	Chester C	32	10		
2005–06	Crewe Alex	0	0		
2006–07	Crewe Alex	37	8		
2007–08	Crewe Alex	27	4		
2007–08	*Stockport Co*	4	0	4	0
2008–09	Chester C	45	16	85	30
2009–10	Bury	39	18		
2010–11	Bury	46	27		
2011–12	Bury	5	4		
2011–12	Sheffield W	26	8		
2012–13	Sheffield W	0	0	26	8
2012–13	Milton Keynes D	42	11	42	11
2013–14	Tranmere R	45	19	45	19
2013–14	Bury	34	9		
2014–15	Bury	34	9		
2015–16	Bury	19	6	143	64
2015–16	*Crewe Alex*	6	2	70	14

MAYOR, Danny (M)   207 20
H: 6 0 W: 11 12 b.Leyland 18-10-90

Season	Club				
2008–09	Preston NE	0	0		
2008–09	*Tranmere R*	3	0	3	0
2009–10	Preston NE	7	0		
2010–11	Preston NE	21	0		
2011–12	Preston NE	36	2		
2012–13	Preston NE	0	0	64	2
2012–13	Sheffield W	8	0		
2012–13	*Southend U*	5	0	5	0
2013–14	Sheffield W	0	0	8	0
2013–14	Bury	39	5		
2014–15	Bury	44	8		
2015–16	Bury	44	5	127	18

MELLIS, Jacob (M)   136 10
H: 5 11 W: 10 11 b.Nottingham 8-1-91
Internationals: England U16, U17, U19.

Season	Club				
2009–10	Chelsea	0	0		
2009–10	*Southampton*	12	0	12	0
2010–11	Chelsea	0	0		
2010–11	*Barnsley*	15	2		
2012–13	Barnsley	36	6		
2013–14	Barnsley	30	2	81	10
2014–15	Blackpool	13	0	13	0
2014–15	*Oldham Ath*	7	0	7	0
2015–16	Bury	23	0	23	0

MILLER, George (F)   1 0
b.Bolton

Season	Club				
2015–16	Bury	1	0	1	0

MOHAMMED, Khalid (M)   1 0
H: 5 9 W: 11 00 b.Manchester 1-2-99

Season	Club				
2015–16	Bury	1	0	1	0

NARDIELLO, Daniel (F)   333 101
H: 5 11 W: 11 04 b.Coventry 22-10-82
Internationals: Wales Full caps.

Season	Club				
1999–2000	Manchester U	0	0		
2000–01	Manchester U	0	0		
2001–02	Manchester U	0	0		
2002–03	Manchester U	0	0		
2003–04	Manchester U	0	0		
2003–04	*Swansea C*	4	0	4	0
2003–04	*Barnsley*	16	7		
2004–05	Manchester U	0	0		
2004–05	Barnsley	28	7		
2005–06	Barnsley	34	5		
2006–07	Barnsley	30	9		
2007–08	QPR	8	0	8	0
2007–08	*Barnsley*	11	2	119	30
2008–09	Blackpool	2	0		
2008–09	*Hartlepool U*	12	3	12	3
2009–10	Blackpool	5	0	7	0
2009–10	*Bury*	6	4		
2009–10	*Oldham Ath*	2	0	2	0
2010–11	Exeter C	30	10		
2011–12	Exeter C	36	9	66	19
2012–13	Rotherham U	36	19		
2013–14	Rotherham U	9	5	45	24
2013–14	Bury	27	11		
2014–15	Bury	32	10		
2015–16	Bury	1	0	66	25
2015–16	*Plymouth Arg*	4	0	4	0

POPE, Tom (F)   321 86
H: 6 3 W: 11 03 b.Stoke 27-8-85

Season	Club				
2005–06	Crewe Alex	0	0		
2006–07	Crewe Alex	0	0		
2007–08	Crewe Alex	26	7		
2008–09	Crewe Alex	26	10	56	17
2009–10	Rotherham U	35	3		
2010–11	Rotherham U	18	1	53	4
2010–11	Port Vale	13	3		
2011–12	Port Vale	41	5		
2012–13	Port Vale	46	31		
2013–14	Port Vale	43	12		
2014–15	Port Vale	33	8	176	59
2015–16	Bury	36	6	36	6

PUGH, Danny (M)   293 15
H: 6 0 W: 12 10 b.Cheadle Hulme 19-10-82

Season	Club				
2000–01	Manchester U	0	0		
2001–02	Manchester U	0	0		
2002–03	Manchester U	1	0		
2003–04	Manchester U	0	0	1	0
2004–05	Leeds U	38	5		
2005–06	Leeds U	12	0		
2006–07	Preston NE	45	4		
2007–08	Preston NE	7	0		
2007–08	Stoke C	30	0		
2008–09	Stoke C	17	0		
2009–10	Stoke C	7	1		
2010–11	Stoke C	10	0		
2010–11	*Preston NE*	5	0	57	4
2011–12	Stoke C	3	0	67	1
2011–12	Leeds U	34	2		
2012–13	Leeds U	4	0		
2012–13	*Sheffield W*	16	1	16	1
2013–14	Leeds U	20	2	108	9
2014–15	Coventry U	5	0	5	0
2015–16	Bury	39	0	39	0

RILEY, Joe (D)   75 2
H: 6 0 W: 11 02 b.Salford 13-10-91

Season	Club				
2011–12	Bolton W	0	0		
2012–13	Bolton W	0	0		
2013–14	Bolton W	0	0		
2014–15	Bolton W	0	0	3	0
2014–15	*Oxford U*	22	0	22	0
2014–15	Bury	17	1		
2015–16	Bury	33	1	50	2

ROSE, Danny (F)   86 19
H: 5 8 W: 9 00 b.Barnsley 10-12-93

Season	Club				
2010–11	Barnsley	1	0		
2011–12	Barnsley	4	0		
2012–13	Barnsley	8	1		
2013–14	Barnsley	3	0		
2013–14	*Bury*	6	3		
2014–15	Barnsley	1	0	17	1
2014–15	*Bury*	35	10		
2015–16	Bury	28	5	69	18

RUDDY, Jack (G)   1 0
H: 6 1 W: 13 01 b.Glasgow 18-5-97

Season	Club				
2014–15	Bury	0	0		
2015–16	Bury	1	0	1	0

SEDGWICK, Chris (M)   577 36
H: 5 11 W: 11 10 b.Sheffield 28-4-80

Season	Club				
1997–98	Rotherham U	4	0		
1998–99	Rotherham U	33	4		
1999–2000	Rotherham U	38	5		
2000–01	Rotherham U	21	2		
2001–02	Rotherham U	44	1		
2002–03	Rotherham U	43	1		
2003–04	Rotherham U	40	2		
2004–05	Rotherham U	20	2	243	17
2004–05	Preston NE	24	3		
2005–06	Preston NE	46	4		
2006–07	Preston NE	43	1		
2007–08	Preston NE	42	2		
2008–09	Preston NE	40	1		
2009–10	Preston NE	34	1	229	12
2010–11	Sheffield W	33	4		
2011–12	Sheffield W	10	1	43	5
2012–13	Scunthorpe U	4	0	4	0
2013–14	Bury	37	2		
2014–15	Bury	20	0		
2015–16	Bury	1	0	58	2

SOARES, Tom (M)   340 36
H: 6 0 W: 11 04 b.Reading 10-7-86
Internationals: England U20, U21.

Season	Club				
2003–04	Crystal Palace	3	0		
2004–05	Crystal Palace	22	0		
2005–06	Crystal Palace	44	1		
2006–07	Crystal Palace	37	3		
2007–08	Crystal Palace	39	6		
2008–09	Crystal Palace	4	1	149	11
2008–09	Stoke C	7	0		
2008–09	*Charlton Ath*	11	1	11	1
2009–10	Stoke C	0	0		
2009–10	*Sheffield W*	25	2	25	2
2010–11	Stoke C	0	0		
2011–12	Stoke C	0	0	7	0
2011–12	*Hibernian*	10	2	10	2
2012–13	Bury	23	2		
2013–14	Bury	30	6		
2014–15	Bury	43	8		
2015–16	Bury	42	4	138	20

STYLES, Callum (F)   1 0
b. 28-3-00

Season	Club				
2015–16	Bury	1	0	1	0

TUTTE, Andrew (M)   195 20
H: 5 9 W: 10 10 b.Huyton 21-9-90
Internationals: England U19, U20.

Season	Club				
2007–08	Manchester C	0	0		
2008–09	Manchester C	0	0		
2009–10	Manchester C	0	0		
2010–11	Manchester C	0	0		
2010–11	*Rochdale*	7	0		
2010–11	*Shrewsbury T*	2	0	2	0
2010–11	*Yeovil T*	15	2	15	2
2011–12	Rochdale	40	1		
2012–13	Rochdale	37	7		
2013–14	Rochdale	11	2	95	10
2013–14	Bury	19	1		
2014–15	Bury	42	3		
2015–16	Bury	22	4	83	8

WILLIAMS, Liam (D)   0 0

Season	Club				
2015–16	Bury	0	0		

Scholars
Arizie, Jesse Kerem; Best, Ciaran; Bourne, Robert; Crosdale, Raquarn Malique; Durham, Jake Robert; Gibson, Samuel James; Kimmins, Rowan Michael David; McCarthy, Jamie Paul; Miller, George; Mohamed, Khalid Abdi; Osgathorpe, William Alex; Turner, Nathan Les; Williams, Liam Shaun.

CAMBRIDGE U (20)

AKINTUNDE, James (M)   1 0
b. 29-3-96

Season	Club				
2014–15	Cambridge U	1	0		
2015–16	Cambridge U	0	0	1	0

BEASANT, Sam (G)   23 0
H: 6 5 W: 12 13 b.Denham 8-4-88

Season	Club				
2014–15	Stevenage	8	0	8	0
2015–16	Cambridge U	15	0	15	0

BERRY, Luke (D)   77 13
H: 5 10 W: 11 05 b.Bassingbourn 12-7-92

Season	Club				
2014–15	Barnsley	31	1	31	1
2015–16	Cambridge U	46	12	46	12

BURNS, Daniel (M)   0 0
b. 1-7-97

Season	Club				
2015–16	Cambridge U	0	0		

CARR, Daniel (F)   20 2
H: 5 11 W: 11 13 b. 30-11-93

Season	Club				
2013–14	Huddersfield T	2	0		
2013–14	*Fleetwood T*	4	1	4	1
2014–15	Huddersfield T	0	0	2	0
2014–15	*Mansfield T*	4	1	4	1
2014–15	*Dagenham & R*	6	0	6	0
2015–16	Cambridge U	4	0	4	0

CHIEDOZIE, Jordan (M)   8 0
H: 5 11 W: 11 06 b.Owerri 5-5-90

Season	Club				
2012–13	Bournemouth	0	0		
2013–14	Bournemouth	0	0		
2014–15	Cambridge U	6	0		
2015–16	Cambridge U	2	0	8	0

CORR, Barry (F)   267 75
H: 6 3 W: 12 07 b.Co Wicklow 2-4-85

Season	Club				
2001–02	Leeds U	0	0		
2002–03	Leeds U	0	0		
2003–04	Leeds U	0	0		
2004–05	Leeds U	0	0		
2005–06	Sheffield W	16	0		
2006–07	Sheffield W	1	0	17	0
2006–07	*Bristol C*	3	0	3	0
2006–07	*Swindon T*	8	3		
2007–08	Swindon T	17	5		
2008–09	Swindon T	11	2	36	10
2009–10	Exeter C	34	3	34	3
2010–11	Southend U	41	18		
2011–12	Southend U	0	0		
2012–13	Southend U	32	6		
2013–14	Southend U	43	12		
2014–15	Southend U	39	14	155	50
2015–16	Cambridge U	22	12	22	12

COULSON, Josh (D)   69 2
H: 6 3 W: 11 11 b.Cambridge 28-1-89

Season	Club				
2014–15	Cambridge U	46	1		
2015–16	Cambridge U	23	1	69	2

DAVIES, Leon (D)   0 0

Season	Club				
2015–16	Cambridge U	0	0		

DONALDSON, Ryan (M)   83 7
H: 5 9 W: 11 00 b.Newcastle 1-5-91
Internationals: England U17, U19.

Season	Club				
2008–09	Newcastle U	0	0		
2009–10	Newcastle U	0	0		

2010–11	Newcastle U	0	0	
2010–11	*Hartlepool U*	12	0	12 0
2011–12	Newcastle U	0	0	2 0
2011–12	*Tranmere R*	1	0	1 0
2014–15	Cambridge U	38	5	
2015–16	Cambridge U	30	2	68 7

DUNK, Harrison (M) 77 6
b. 25-10-90

2014–15	Cambridge U	32	2	
2015–16	Cambridge U	45	4	77 6

DUNN, Chris (G) 163 0
H: 6 5 W: 13 11 b.Brentwood 23-10-87

2006–07	Northampton T	0	0	
2007–08	Northampton T	0	0	
2008–09	Northampton T	29	0	
2009–10	Northampton T	29	0	
2010–11	Northampton T	39	0	98 0
2011–12	Coventry C	2	0	
2012–13	Coventry C	1	0	
2013–14	Coventry C	0	0	3 0
2013–14	*Yeovil T*	8	0	8 0
2014–15	Cambridge U	43	0	
2015–16	Cambridge U	11	0	54 0

DUNNE, James (M) 242 13
H: 5 11 W: 10 12 b.Bromley 18-9-89

2007–08	Arsenal	0	0	
2008–09	Arsenal	0	0	
2008–09	*Nottingham F*	0	0	
2009–10	Exeter C	23	3	
2010–11	Exeter C	42	1	
2011–12	Exeter C	45	2	110 6
2012–13	Stevenage	42	4	
2013–14	Stevenage	13	1	55 5
2013–14	*St Johnstone*	13	0	13 0
2014–15	Portsmouth	36	1	
2015–16	Portsmouth	0	0	36 1
2015–16	*Dagenham & R*	9	0	9 0
2015–16	Cambridge U	19	1	19 1

FOY, Matt (F) 0 0

2014–15	Cambridge U	0	0	
2015–16	Cambridge U	0	0	

GAFFNEY, Rory (M) 30 10
H: 6 0 W: 12 04 b. 23-10-89

2014–15	Cambridge U	0	0	
2015–16	Cambridge U	6	2	6 2
2015–16	*Bristol R*	24	8	24 8

HORNE, Ryan (M) 0 0
b. 2-11-95

2014–15	Cambridge U	0	0	
2015–16	Cambridge U	0	0	

HUGHES, Jeff (D) 404 62
H: 6 1 W: 11 00 b.Larne 29-5-85
Internationals: Northern Ireland U21, Full caps.

2003–04	Larne	21	1	
2004–05	Larne	29	0	50 1
2005–06	Lincoln C	22	2	
2006–07	Lincoln C	41	6	63 8
2007–08	Crystal Palace	10	0	10 0
2007–08	*Peterborough U*	1	1	7 1
2008–09	Bristol R	43	6	
2009–10	Bristol R	44	12	
2010–11	Bristol R	42	10	129 28
2011–12	Notts Co	45	13	
2012–13	Notts Co	44	7	89 20
2013–14	Fleetwood T	25	3	
2014–15	Fleetwood T	22	1	47 4
2015–16	Cambridge U	9	0	9 0

HUGHES, Liam (F) 56 3
H: 6 4 W: 13 08 b.Rotherham 10-8-92

2014–15	Cambridge U	10	3	
2015–16	Cambridge U	16	0	46 3
2015–16	*Inverness CT*	10	0	10 0

KEANE, Keith (M) 222 8
H: 5 9 W: 11 01 b.Luton 20-11-86
Internationals: Republic of Ireland U19, U21.

2003–04	Luton T	15	1	
2004–05	Luton T	17	0	
2005–06	Luton T	10	1	
2006–07	Luton T	19	1	
2007–08	Luton T	28	1	
2008–09	Luton T	40	0	129 4
2012–13	Preston NE	26	1	
2013–14	Preston NE	38	2	
2014–15	Preston NE	0	0	64 3
2014–15	*Crawley T*	12	0	12 0
2014–15	*Stevenage*	7	0	
2015–16	Cambridge U	4	0	4 0
2015–16	*Stevenage*	6	1	13 1

LEGGE, Leon (D) 214 20
H: 6 1 W: 11 02 b.Bexhill 1-7-85

2009–10	Brentford	29	2	
2010–11	Brentford	30	3	
2011–12	Brentford	28	4	
2012–13	Brentford	7	0	94 9
2012–13	Gillingham	22	2	
2013–14	Gillingham	37	2	
2014–15	Gillingham	22	4	81 8
2015–16	Cambridge U	39	3	39 3

LOWE, Matt (M) 0 0
b. 11-3-96

2014–15	Cambridge U	0	0	
2015–16	Cambridge U	0	0	

MORRISSEY, Gearoid (M) 10 0
H: 5 11 W: 12 11 b.Cork 17-11-91
Internationals: Republic of Ireland U17, U19.

2014–15	Cambridge U	8	0	
2015–16	Cambridge U	2	0	10 0

NEWTON, Conor (M) 51 2
H: 5 11 W: 11 00 b.Whickham 17-10-91

2010–11	Newcastle U	0	0	
2011–12	Newcastle U	0	0	
2012–13	Newcastle U	0	0	
2012–13	*St Mirren*	16	2	16 2
2013–14	Rotherham U	13	0	13 0
2015–16	Cambridge U	22	0	22 0

NORRIS, Will (G) 24 0
H: 6 5 W: 11 09 b.Royston 12-7-93

2014–15	Cambridge U	3	0	
2015–16	Cambridge U	21	0	24 0

O'NEILL, Shane (D) 54 1
b. 2-9-93
Internationals: USA U20, U23.

2012	Colorado Rapids	1	0	
2013	Colorado Rapids	26	0	
2014	Colorado Rapids	21	1	
2015	Colorado Rapids	4	0	52 1
2015–16	Apollon Limasoll	0	0	

On loan from Apollon Limasoll.

2015–16	Cambridge U	2	0	2 0

OMOZUSI, Elliot (D) 172 0
H: 5 11 W: 12 09 b.Hackney 15-12-88
Internationals: England U16, U17, U18, U19.

2005–06	Fulham	0	0	
2006–07	Fulham	0	0	
2007–08	Fulham	8	0	
2008–09	Fulham	0	0	
2008–09	Norwich C	21	0	21 0
2009–10	Fulham	0	0	8 0
2009–10	*Charlton Ath*	9	0	9 0
2010–11	Leyton Orient	40	0	
2011–12	Leyton Orient	10	0	
2012–13	Leyton Orient	6	0	
2013–14	Leyton Orient	39	0	
2014–15	Leyton Orient	25	0	120 0
2015–16	Cambridge U	14	0	14 0

ROBERTS, Mark (D) 263 22
H: 6 1 W: 12 00 b.Northwich 16-10-83

2002–03	Crewe Alex	0	0	
2003–04	Crewe Alex	0	0	
2004–05	Crewe Alex	6	0	
2005–06	Crewe Alex	0	0	
2005–06	*Chester C*	1	0	1 0
2006–07	Crewe Alex	0	0	6 0
2007–08	Accrington S	34	0	34 0

From Northwich Vic.

2010–11	Stevenage	42	6	
2011–12	Stevenage	46	6	
2012–13	Stevenage	44	2	132 14
2013–14	Fleetwood T	33	3	
2014–15	Fleetwood T	27	3	60 6
2015–16	Cambridge U	30	2	30 2

SIMPSON, Robbie (F) 248 28
H: 6 1 W: 11 11 b.Poole 15-3-85

2007–08	Coventry C	28	1	
2008–09	Coventry C	33	3	61 4
2009–10	Huddersfield T	13	0	
2010–11	Huddersfield T	0	0	
2010–11	*Brentford*	27	4	27 4
2011–12	Huddersfield T	0	0	13 0
2011–12	Oldham Ath	29	6	
2012–13	Oldham Ath	37	2	
2013–14	Oldham Ath	0	0	66 8
2013–14	*Leyton Orient*	14	0	14 0
2014–15	Cambridge U	35	8	
2015–16	Cambridge U	32	4	67 12

SPENCER, James (F) 136 31
H: 6 1 W: 13 00 b.Leeds 13-12-91

2008–09	Huddersfield T	0	0	
2009–10	Huddersfield T	0	0	
2010–11	Huddersfield T	0	0	
2010–11	*Morecambe*	32	8	32 8
2011–12	Huddersfield T	0	0	
2011–12	*Cheltenham T*	41	10	41 10
2011–12	Huddersfield T	1	0	
2012–13	*Brentford*	2	0	2 0
2013–14	Huddersfield T	0	0	1 0
2013–14	*Scunthorpe U*	13	1	13 1
2014–15	Notts Co	13	5	
2014–15	Notts Co	9	1	
2015–16	Notts Co	7	0	29 6
2015–16	Cambridge U	18	6	18 6

TAYLOR, Greg (D) 59 0
b.Bedford 15-1-90
Internationals: England C.

2008–09	Northampton T	0	0	
2014–15	Cambridge U	43	0	
2015–16	Cambridge U	16	0	59 0

WILLIAMS, Dylan (D) 1 0

2015–16	Cambridge U	1	0	1 0

Players retained or with offer of contract
Williamson, Benjamin Marc.

Scholars
Bell-Toxtle, Fernando Luis; Boddey, Owen; Brown, Jordan, Burniston, Joshua Joseph; Chambers-Shaw, Jake; Darling, Harry Jack; Emmins, Joshua Matthew; Foy, Matthew Ian; Jonas, Romario Darnell; Jones, Francis Douglas; Lea, Harry James; Leavers, Justin; Mason, Dominic; Williams, Dylan; Williams, Jordan.

CARDIFF C (21)

ADEYEMI, Tom (M) 189 13
H: 6 1 W: 12 04 b.Milton Keynes 24-10-91

2008–09	Norwich C	0	0	
2009–10	Norwich C	11	0	
2010–11	Norwich C	0	0	
2010–11	*Bradford C*	34	5	34 5
2011–12	Norwich C	0	0	
2011–12	*Oldham Ath*	36	2	36 2
2012–13	Norwich C	0	0	11 0
2012–13	*Brentford*	30	2	30 2
2013–14	Birmingham C	35	1	35 1
2014–15	Cardiff C	20	1	
2015–16	Cardiff C	0	0	20 1
2015–16	*Leeds U*	23	2	23 2

AJAYI, Semi (D) 18 0
H: 6 4 W: 13 00 b.Croydon 9-11-93
Internationals: Nigeria U20.

2012–13	Charlton Ath	0	0	
2013–14	Charlton Ath	0	0	
2014–15	Arsenal	0	0	
2014–15	*Cardiff C*	0	0	
2015–16	Cardiff C	0	0	
2015–16	*AFC Wimbledon*	5	0	5 0
2015–16	*Crewe Alex*	13	0	13 0

BARNUM-BOBB, Jazzi (D) 12 0
b.Enfield 15-9-95

2014–15	Cardiff C	0	0	
2015–16	Cardiff C	0	0	
2015–16	*Newport Co*	12	0	12 0

CONNOLLY, Matthew (D) 254 12
H: 6 1 W: 11 03 b.Barnet 24-9-87

2005–06	Arsenal	0	0	
2006–07	Arsenal	0	0	
2006–07	*Bournemouth*	5	1	5 1
2007–08	Arsenal	0	0	
2007–08	*Colchester U*	16	2	16 2
2007–08	QPR	20	0	
2008–09	QPR	35	0	
2009–10	QPR	19	2	
2010–11	QPR	36	0	
2011–12	QPR	6	0	
2011–12	*Reading*	6	0	6 0
2012–13	QPR	0	0	116 2
2012–13	Cardiff C	36	5	
2013–14	Cardiff C	3	0	
2014–15	Cardiff C	23	0	
2014–15	*Watford*	6	1	6 1
2015–16	Cardiff C	43	1	105 6

DA SILVA, Fabio (M) 107 2
H: 5 8 W: 10 03 b.Rio de Janeiro 9-7-90
Internationals: Brazil U17, Full caps.

2008–09	Manchester U	0	0	
2009–10	Manchester U	5	0	
2010–11	Manchester U	11	1	
2011–12	Manchester U	5	0	
2012–13	*QPR*	21	0	21 0

2013–14	Manchester U	1	0	22	1
2013–14	Cardiff C	13	0		
2014–15	Cardiff C	28	0		
2015–16	Cardiff C	23	1	64	1

DIKGACOI, Kagisho (M) 233 15
H: 5 11 W: 12 10 b.Brandfort 24-11-84
Internationals: South Africa Full caps.

2004–05	Bloemfontein YT	10	0	10	0
2005–06	Lamontville GA	9	0		
2006–07	Lamontville GA	25	0		
2007–08	Lamontville GA	23	4		
2008–09	Lamontville GA	23	4	80	8
2009–10	Fulham	12	0		
2010–11	Fulham	1	0	13	0
2010–11	*Crystal Palace*	13	1		
2011–12	*Crystal Palace*	27	2		
2012–13	*Crystal Palace*	39	4		
2013–14	*Crystal Palace*	26	0	105	7
2014–15	Cardiff C	2	0		
2015–16	Cardiff C	23	0	25	0

DOYLE, Eoin (F) 246 81
H: 6 0 b. 12-3-88

2009	Sligo	15	3		
2010	Sligo	35	6		
2011	Sligo	34	20	84	29
2011–12	Hibernian	13	1		
2012–13	Hibernian	36	10	49	11
2013–14	Chesterfield	43	11		
2014–15	Chesterfield	26	21	69	32
2014–15	Cardiff C	16	5		
2015–16	Cardiff C	0	0	16	5
2015–16	*Preston NE*	28	4	28	4

ECUELE MANGA, Bruno (D) 228 13
H: 6 2 W: 11 11 b.Libreville 16-7-88
Internationals: Gabon Full caps.

2008–09	Angers	29	1		
2009–10	Angers	28	3	57	4
2010–11	Lorient	31	1		
2011–12	Lorient	32	2		
2012–13	Lorient	17	0		
2013–14	Lorient	35	1		
2014–15	Lorient	3	0	118	4
2014–15	Cardiff C	29	3		
2015–16	Cardiff C	24	2	53	5

GUNNARSSON, Aron (M) 306 26
H: 5 9 W: 11 00 b.Akureyri 22-9-89
Internationals: Iceland U17, U19, U21, Full caps.

2007–08	AZ	1	0	1	0
2008–09	Coventry C	40	1		
2009–10	Coventry C	40	1		
2010–11	Coventry C	42	4	122	6
2011–12	Cardiff C	45	8		
2012–13	Cardiff C	45	8		
2013–14	Cardiff C	23	1		
2014–15	Cardiff C	45	4		
2015–16	Cardiff C	28	2	183	20

HARRIS, Kedeem (M) 57 2
H: 5 9 W: 10 08 b.Westminster 8-6-93

2009–10	Wycombe W	0	0		
2010–11	Wycombe W	0	0		
2011–12	Wycombe W	17	0	19	0
2011–12	Cardiff C	0	0		
2012–13	Cardiff C	0	0		
2013–14	Cardiff C	0	0		
2013–14	*Brentford*	10	1	10	1
2014–15	Cardiff C	14	1		
2015–16	Cardiff C	3	0	17	1
2015–16	*Barnsley*	11	0	11	0

HEALEY, Rhys (M) 29 5
H: 5 8 W: 10 10 b.Manchester 6-12-94

2012–13	Cardiff C	0	0		
2013–14	Cardiff C	1	0		
2014–15	Cardiff C	0	0		
2014–15	*Colchester U*	21	4	21	4
2015–16	Cardiff C	0	0	1	0
2015–16	*Dundee*	7	1	7	1

IMMERS, Lex (M) 261 61
H: 6 2 W: 12 04 b.Den Haag 8-6-86

2007–08	Den Haag	31	6		
2008–09	Den Haag	27	3		
2009–10	Den Haag	26	1		
2010–11	Den Haag	30	7		
2011–12	Den Haag	31	8	145	25
2012–13	Feyenoord	32	12		
2013–14	Feyenoord	33	12		
2014–15	Feyenoord	30	7		
2015–16	Feyenoord	6	0	101	31

On loan from Feyenoord.

2015–16	Cardiff C	15	5	15	5

JAMES, Tom (D) 1 0
b.Leamington Spa 19-11-88
Internationals: Wales U19.

2013–14	Cardiff C	1	0		
2014–15	Cardiff C	0	0		
2015–16	Cardiff C	0	0	1	0

JOHN, Declan (M) 48 0
H: 5 10 W: 11 10 b.Merthyr Tydfil 30-6-95
Internationals: Wales U17, U19, Full caps.

2010–11	Llanelli	1	0	1	0
2011–12	Afan Lido	5	0	5	0
2012–13	Cardiff C	0	0		
2013–14	Cardiff C	20	0		
2014–15	Cardiff C	6	0		
2014–15	*Barnsley*	9	0	9	0
2015–16	Cardiff C	1	0	27	0
2015–16	*Chesterfield*	6	0	6	0

JONES, Kenwyne (F) 354 89
H: 6 2 W: 13 06 b.Trinidad & Tobago 5-10-84
Internationals: Trinidad & Tobago Youth, U23, Full caps.

2004–05	Southampton	2	0		
2004–05	*Sheffield W*	7	7	7	7
2004–05	*Stoke C*	13	3		
2005–06	Southampton	34	4		
2006–07	Southampton	34	14		
2007–08	Southampton	1	1	71	19
2007–08	Sunderland	33	7		
2008–09	Sunderland	29	10		
2009–10	Sunderland	32	9	94	26
2010–11	Stoke C	34	9		
2011–12	Stoke C	21	1		
2012–13	Stoke C	26	3		
2013–14	Stoke C	7	0	101	16
2013–14	Cardiff C	11	1		
2014–15	Cardiff C	34	11		
2014–15	*Bournemouth*	6	1	6	1
2015–16	Cardiff C	19	5	64	17
2015–16	*Al-Jazira*	11	3	11	3

KENNEDY, Matthew (M) 69 1
H: 5 9 W: 10 02 b.Irvine 1-11-94
Internationals: Scotland U16, U17, U18, U19, U21.

2011–12	Kilmarnock	11	0		
2012–13	Kilmarnock	3	0	14	0
2012–13	Everton	0	0		
2013–14	Everton	0	0		
2013–14	*Tranmere R*	8	0	8	0
2013–14	*Milton Keynes D*	7	1	7	1
2014–15	Everton	0	0		
2014–15	*Hibernian*	13	0	13	0
2014–15	Cardiff C	14	0		
2015–16	Cardiff C	1	0	15	0
2015–16	*Port Vale*	12	0	12	0

LEWIS, Joe (G) 234 0
H: 6 5 W: 12 10 b.Bungay 6-10-87
Internationals: England U16, U17, U19, U21.

2004–05	Norwich C	0	0		
2005–06	Norwich C	0	0		
2006–07	Norwich C	0	0		
2006–07	*Stockport Co*	5	0	5	0
2007–08	Norwich C	0	0		
2007–08	*Morecambe*	19	0	19	0
2007–08	Peterborough U	22	0		
2008–09	Peterborough U	46	0		
2009–10	Peterborough U	43	0		
2010–11	Peterborough U	45	0		
2011–12	Peterborough U	11	0	167	0
2012–13	Cardiff C	0	0		
2013–14	Cardiff C	1	0		
2014–15	Cardiff C	0	0		
2014–15	*Blackpool*	34	0	34	0
2015–16	Cardiff C	0	0	1	0
2015–16	*Fulham*	8	0	8	0

MACHEDA, Federico (F) 113 23
H: 6 0 W: 11 13 b.Rome 22-8-91
Internationals: Italy U16, U17, U19, U21.

2008–09	Manchester U	4	2		
2009–10	Manchester U	7	1		
2010–11	Manchester U	7	1		
2010–11	*Sampdoria*	14	0	14	0
2011–12	Manchester U	3	0		
2011–12	*QPR*	3	0	3	0
2012–13	Manchester U	0	0		
2012–13	*Stuttgart*	14	0	14	0
2013–14	Manchester U	0	0	19	4
2013–14	*Doncaster R*	15	3	15	3
2013–14	*Birmingham C*	18	10	18	10
2014–15	Cardiff C	21	6		
2015–16	Cardiff C	6	0	27	6
2015–16	*Nottingham F*	3	0	3	0

MALONE, Scott (D) 200 14
H: 6 2 W: 11 11 b.Rowley Regis 25-3-91
Internationals: England U19.

2008–09	Wolverhampton W	0	0		
2008–09	*Ujpest*	7	1	7	1
2009–10	Wolverhampton W	0	0		
2009–10	*Southend U*	17	0	17	0
2010–11	Wolverhampton W	0	0		
2010–11	*Burton Alb*	22	1	22	1
2011–12	Wolverhampton W	0	0		
2011–12	*Bournemouth*	32	5	32	5
2012–13	Millwall	15	1		
2013–14	Millwall	33	3		
2014–15	Millwall	20	1	68	5
2014–15	Cardiff C	13	0		
2015–16	Cardiff C	41	2	54	2

MARSHALL, David (G) 389 0
H: 6 3 W: 13 04 b.Glasgow 5-3-85
Internationals: Scotland Youth, U21, B, Full caps.

2003–04	Celtic	11	0		
2004–05	Celtic	18	0		
2005–06	Celtic	4	0		
2006–07	Celtic	2	0	35	0
2006–07	Norwich C	2	0		
2007–08	Norwich C	46	0		
2008–09	Norwich C	46	0	94	0
2008–09	Cardiff C	0	0		
2009–10	Cardiff C	43	0		
2010–11	Cardiff C	11	0		
2011–12	Cardiff C	45	0		
2012–13	Cardiff C	46	0		
2013–14	Cardiff C	37	0		
2014–15	Cardiff C	38	0		
2015–16	Cardiff C	40	0	260	0

MOORE, Simon (G) 92 0
H: 6 3 W: 12 02 b.Sandown 19-5-90
Internationals: Isle of Wight Full caps.

2009–10	Brentford	1	0		
2010–11	Brentford	10	0		
2011–12	Brentford	10	0		
2012–13	Brentford	43	0	64	0
2013–14	Cardiff C	0	0		
2013–14	*Bristol C*	11	0	11	0
2014–15	Cardiff C	10	0		
2015–16	Cardiff C	7	0	17	0

MORRISON, Sean (D) 186 20
H: 6 4 W: 14 00 b.Plymouth 8-1-91

2007–08	Swindon T	2	0		
2008–09	Swindon T	20	1		
2009–10	Swindon T	9	1		
2009–10	*Southend U*	8	0	8	0
2010–11	Swindon T	19	4	50	6
2010–11	Reading	0	0		
2010–11	*Huddersfield T*	0	0		
2011–12	Reading	0	0		
2011–12	*Huddersfield T*	19	1	19	1
2012–13	Reading	16	2		
2013–14	Reading	21	1		
2014–15	Reading	1	1	38	4
2014–15	Cardiff C	41	6		
2015–16	Cardiff C	30	3	71	9

NOONE, Craig (M) 245 25
H: 6 3 W: 12 07 b.Kirkby 17-11-87

2008–09	Plymouth Arg	21	1		
2009–10	Plymouth Arg	17	1		
2009–10	*Exeter C*	7	2	7	2
2010–11	Plymouth Arg	17	3	55	5
2010–11	Brighton & HA	23	2		
2011–12	Brighton & HA	33	2		
2012–13	Brighton & HA	3	0	59	4
2012–13	Cardiff C	32	7		
2013–14	Cardiff C	17	1		
2014–15	Cardiff C	37	1		
2015–16	Cardiff C	38	5	124	14

O'KEEFE, Stuart (M) 80 3
H: 5 8 W: 10 00 b.Eye 4-3-91

2008–09	Southend U	3	0		
2009–10	Southend U	7	0		
2010–11	Southend U	0	0	10	0
2010–11	Crystal Palace	4	0		
2011–12	Crystal Palace	13	0		
2012–13	Crystal Palace	5	0		
2013–14	Crystal Palace	12	1		
2014–15	Crystal Palace	2	0	36	1
2014–15	*Blackpool*	4	0	4	0
2014–15	Cardiff C	6	0		
2015–16	Cardiff C	24	2	30	2

O'SULLIVAN, Tommy (M) 25 1
H: 5 9 W: 11 04 b.Mountain Ash 18-1-95
Internationals: Wales U17, U19, U21.

2012–13	Cardiff C	0	0		
2013–14	Cardiff C	0	0		

2014–15	Cardiff C	0	0		
2014–15	*Port Vale*	5	0	5	0
2015–16	Cardiff C	0	0		
2015–16	*Newport Co*	20	1	20	1

OSHILAJA, Adedeji (D)   55   4
H: 5 11   W: 11 10   b.Bermondsey 16-7-93

2012–13	Cardiff C	0	0		
2013–14	Cardiff C	0	0		
2013–14	*Newport Co*	8	0	8	0
2013–14	*Sheffield W*	2	0	2	0
2014–15	Cardiff C	0	0		
2014–15	*AFC Wimbledon*	23	1	23	1
2015–16	Cardiff C	0	0		
2015–16	*Gillingham*	22	3	22	3

PELTIER, Lee (D)   336   5
H: 5 10   W: 12 00   b.Liverpool 11-12-86
Internationals: England U18.

2004–05	Liverpool	0	0		
2005–06	Liverpool	0	0		
2006–07	Liverpool	0	0		
2006–07	*Hull C*	7	0	7	0
2007–08	Liverpool	0	0		
2007–08	*Yeovil T*	34	0		
2008–09	Yeovil T	35	1	69	1
2009–10	Huddersfield T	42	0		
2010–11	Huddersfield T	38	1		
2011–12	Leicester C	40	2		
2012–13	Leicester C	0	0	40	2
2012–13	Leeds U	41	0		
2013–14	Leeds U	25	1	66	1
2013–14	*Nottingham F*	7	0	7	0
2014–15	Huddersfield T	11	0	91	1
2014–15	Cardiff C	15	0		
2015–16	Cardiff C	41	0	56	0

PILKINGTON, Anthony (M)   303   59
H: 5 11   W: 12 00   b.Blackburn 3-11-87
Internationals: Republic of Ireland U21, Full caps.

2006–07	Stockport Co	24	5		
2007–08	Stockport Co	29	6		
2008–09	Stockport Co	24	5	77	16
2008–09	Huddersfield T	16	2		
2009–10	Huddersfield T	43	7		
2010–11	Huddersfield T	31	10	90	19
2011–12	Norwich C	30	8		
2012–13	Norwich C	30	5		
2013–14	Norwich C	15	1	75	14
2014–15	Cardiff C	20	1		
2015–16	Cardiff C	41	9	61	10

RALLS, Joe (M)   122   7
H: 5 10   W: 11 00   b.Farnborough 13-10-93
Internationals: England U19.

2011–12	Cardiff C	10	1		
2012–13	Cardiff C	4	0		
2013–14	Cardiff C	0	0		
2013–14	*Yeovil T*	37	3	37	3
2014–15	Cardiff C	28	2		
2015–16	Cardiff C	43	1	85	4

SAADI, Idriss (F)   101   26
H: 5 10   W: 11 11   b.Valence 8-2-92
Internationals: France U17, U17, U18, U19.

2010–11	St Etienne	9	0		
2011–12	St Etienne	7	0		
2011–12	*Reims*	10	1	10	1
2012–13	St Etienne	1	0		
2012–13	*Ajaccio*	32	7	32	7
2013–14	St Etienne	1	0	18	0
2013–14	Clermont Foot	18	7		
2014–15	Clermont Foot	21	11	39	18
2015–16	Cardiff C	2	0	2	0

SOUTHAM, Macauley (M)   0   0
b. 2-2-96

2014–15	Cardiff C	0	0
2015–16	Cardiff C	0	0

TAMAS, Gabriel (D)   305   12
H: 6 2   W: 12 02   b.Brasov 9-11-83
Internationals: Romania U16, U19, U21, Full caps.

1998–99	Brasov	1	0		
1999–2000	Brasov	0	0	1	0
2000–01	Tractorul	15	1		
2001–02	Tractorul	19	2	34	3
2002–03	Din Bucharest	19	4		
2003–04	Galatasaray	6	0	6	0
2004	Spartak Moscow	14	0		
2004–05	Din Bucharest	13	0		
2005–06	Din Bucharest	14	1		
2006	Spartak Moscow	3	0	17	0
2006–07	Celta Vigo	29	0	29	0
2007–08	Auxerre	27	0	27	0
2008–09	Din Bucharest	22	0		
2009–10	Din Bucharest	12	2	80	7
2009–10	WBA	23	2		

2010–11	WBA	26	0		
2011–12	WBA	8	0		
2012–13	WBA	11	0		
2013–14	WBA	0	0	68	2
2013–14	*Doncaster R*	14	0	14	0
2014–15	*Watford*	7	0	7	0
2014–15	Steau Bucharest	10	0		
2015–16	Steau Bucharest	12	0	22	0
2015–16	Cardiff C	0	0		

TURNER, Ben (D)   197   8
H: 6 4   W: 14 04   b.Birmingham 21-1-88
Internationals: England U19.

2005–06	Coventry C	1	0		
2006–07	Coventry C	1	0		
2006–07	*Peterborough U*	8	0	8	0
2006–07	*Oldham Ath*	1	0	1	0
2007–08	Coventry C	19	0		
2008–09	Coventry C	24	0		
2009–10	Coventry C	13	0		
2010–11	Coventry C	14	4		
2011–12	Cardiff C	37	2		
2012–13	Cardiff C	31	1		
2013–14	Cardiff C	31	0		
2014–15	Cardiff C	11	0		
2015–16	Cardiff C	1	0	111	3
2015–16	*Coventry C*	5	1	77	5

TUTONDA, David (D)   24   2
b. 11-10-95

2013–14	Cardiff C	0	0		
2014–15	*Newport Co*	12	2	12	2
2015–16	Cardiff C	0	0		
2015–16	*York C*	12	0	12	0

VELIKONJA, Etien (F)   202   82
H: 5 10   W: 11 04   b.Sempeter Pri Gorici 26-12-88
Internationals: Slovenia U19, U21, Full caps.

2006–07	Gorica	0	0		
2007–08	Gorica	31	5		
2008–09	Gorica	32	17		
2009–10	Gorica	16	5		
2010–11	Gorica	18	4	104	32
2010–11	Maribor	16	6		
2011–12	Maribor	30	15		
2012–13	Maribor	2	0	48	21
2012–13	Cardiff C	3	0		
2013–14	Cardiff C	0	0		
2014–15	*Rio Ave*	7	1	7	1
2014–15	Cardiff C	0	0		
2014–15	*Lierse*	11	4		
2015–16	Cardiff C	0	0	3	0
2015–16	*Lierse*	29	24	40	28

WHARTON, Theo (M)   0   0
b.Cwmbran 15-11-94
Internationals: Wales U17, U19, U21.

2011–12	Cardiff C	0	0
2012–13	Cardiff C	0	0
2013–14	Cardiff C	0	0
2014–15	Cardiff C	0	0
2015–16	Cardiff C	0	0

WHITTINGHAM, Peter (M)   450   79
H: 5 10   W: 9 13   b.Nuneaton 8-9-84
Internationals: England U19, U20, U21.

2002–03	Aston Villa	1	0		
2003–04	Aston Villa	32	0		
2004–05	Aston Villa	13	1		
2004–05	*Burnley*	7	0	7	0
2005–06	Aston Villa	4	0		
2005–06	*Derby Co*	11	0	11	0
2006–07	Aston Villa	3	0	56	1
2006–07	Cardiff C	19	4		
2007–08	Cardiff C	41	5		
2008–09	Cardiff C	33	3		
2009–10	Cardiff C	41	20		
2010–11	Cardiff C	45	11		
2011–12	Cardiff C	46	12		
2012–13	Cardiff C	40	8		
2013–14	Cardiff C	32	3		
2014–15	Cardiff C	43	6		
2015–16	Cardiff C	36	6	376	78

WILSON, Ben (G)   8   0
H: 6 1   W: 11 09   b.Stanley 9-8-92

2010–11	Sunderland	0	0		
2011–12	Sunderland	0	0		
2013–14	Accrington S	0	0		
2013–14	Cardiff C	0	0		
2014–15	Cardiff C	0	0		
2015–16	Cardiff C	0	0		
2015–16	*AFC Wimbledon*	8	0	8	0

ZOHORE, Kenneth (F)   80   17
H: 6 4   W: 12 06   b.Copenaghen 31-1-94
Internationals: Denmark U17, U18, U19, U21.

2009–10	Copenhagen	0	0
2010–11	Copenhagen	15	1

2011–12	Copenhagen	0	0	16	1
2011–12	Fiorentina	0	0		
2012–13	Fiorentina	0	0		
2013–14	Fiorentina	0	0		
2013–14	*Brondby*	25	5	25	5
2014–15	Fiorentina	0	0		
2014–15	*Gothenburg*	11	2	11	2
2015–16	*Odense BK*	16	7	16	7
2015–16	KV Kortrijk	0	0		

On loan from KV Kortrijk.

2015–16	Cardiff C	12	2	12	2

Players retained or with offer of contract
Abbruzzese, Rhys; Baker, Ashley Thomas; Bird, Jamie Eric Jason; Blaise, Jordan Louis Joseph; Evitt-Healey, Rhys; Humphries, Lloyd; Le Fondre, Adam James; O'Reilly, Luke Patrick; Patten, Robbie; Phipps, Elijah; Rees, Dylan Patrick James; Veale, Jamie Lawrence; Weymans, Marco.

Scholars
Baldwin, Lewis Elland; Chappell-Smith, Aidan Paul; Coughlan, Scott James; Coxe, Cameron Terry; Harris, Mark; Kelly, Isaac Benjamin; Menayese, Elvis; Menayese, Rollin; Parry, Shane Thomas; So Sani, Ibraim; Waite, James Tyler; Wakeman, Luke Oliver; Welch, Jarrad Neil; Williams, Samuel Jack Piotr; Young, Connor.

CARLISLE U (22)

ARCHIBALD-HENVILLE, Troy (D)   174   6
H: 6 2   W: 13 03   b.Newham 4-11-88

2007–08	Tottenham H	0	0		
2008–09	Tottenham H	0	0		
2008–09	Norwich C	0	0		
2008–09	Exeter C	19	0		
2009–10	Tottenham H	0	0		
2009–10	Exeter C	15	0		
2010–11	Exeter C	36	1		
2011–12	Exeter C	45	2	115	3
2012–13	Swindon T	5	0		
2013–14	Carlisle U	4	0		
2013–14	Swindon T	14	0	19	0
2014–15	Carlisle U	24	1		
2015–16	Carlisle U	12	2	40	3

ASAMOAH, Derek (F)   433   75
H: 5 6   W: 10 04   b.Ghana 1-5-81
Internationals: Ghana Full caps.

2001–02	Northampton T	40	3		
2002–03	Northampton T	42	4		
2003–04	Northampton T	31	3	113	10
2004–05	Mansfield T	30	5	30	5
2004–05	Lincoln C	10	0		
2005–06	Lincoln C	25	2	35	2
2005–06	*Chester C*	17	8	17	8
2006–07	Shrewsbury T	39	10	39	10
2007–08	Nice	0	0		
2008–09	Hamilton A	3	0	3	0
2009–10	Lokomotiv Sofia	2	0		
2010–11	Lokomotiv Sofia	14	7	36	13
2011	Pohang Steelers	27	7		
2012	Pohang Steelers	30	6		
2013	Pohang Steelers	0	0	57	13
2013	Daegu	33	4	33	4
2014–15	Carlisle U	27	4		
2015–16	Carlisle U	43	6	70	10

ATKINSON, David (D)   31   0
b.Shildon 27-4-93

2010–11	Middlesbrough	0	0		
2011–12	Middlesbrough	0	0		
2012–13	Middlesbrough	0	0		
2013–14	Middlesbrough	0	0		
2014–15	Middlesbrough	0	0		
2014–15	*Hartlepool U*	0	0		
2014–15	Carlisle U	7	0		
2015–16	Carlisle U	24	0	31	0

BACON, Morgan (G)   0   0

2015–16	Carlisle U	0	0

BALANTA, Angelo (F)   99   17
H: 5 10   W: 11 11   b.Colombia 1-7-90

2007–08	QPR	11	1		
2008–09	QPR	10	1		
2008–09	*Wycombe W*	11	3	11	3
2009–10	QPR	4	0		
2010–11	QPR	0	0		
2010–11	*Milton Keynes D*	18	6		
2011–12	*Milton Keynes D*	20	4		
2012–13	QPR	0	0		
2012–13	*Milton Keynes D*	12	1	50	11
2012–13	*Yeovil T*	6	0	6	0
2013–14	QPR	0	0	25	2

2014–15 Bristol R 0 0
2015–16 Carlisle U 7 1 7 1

BROUGH, Patrick (M) 39 0
H: 5 8 b.Carlisle 20-2-96
2013–14 Carlisle U 3 0
2014–15 Carlisle U 29 0
2015–16 Carlisle U 7 0 39 0

DICKER, Gary (M) 335 13
H: 6 0 W: 12 00 b.Dublin 31-7-86
Internationals: Republic of Ireland U19, U21.
2004 UCD 9 1
2005 UCD 31 2
2006 UCD 28 2 68 5
2006–07 Birmingham C 0 0
2007–08 Stockport Co 30 0
2008–09 Stockport Co 25 0 55 0
2008–09 *Brighton & HA* 9 1
2009–10 Brighton & HA 42 2
2010–11 Brighton & HA 46 3
2011–12 Brighton & HA 18 0
2012–13 Brighton & HA 23 0
2013–14 Brighton & HA 0 0 138 6
2013–14 Rochdale 12 1 12 1
2013–14 Crawley T 11 0 11 0
2014–15 Carlisle U 20 1
2015–16 Carlisle U 19 0 39 1
2015–16 Kilmarnock 12 0 12 0

DOUGLAS, Matt (D) 0 0
b. 17-1-98
2014–15 Carlisle U 0 0
2015–16 Carlisle U 0 0 0 0

ELLIS, Mark (D) 241 17
H: 6 2 W: 12 04 b.Kingsbridge 30-9-88
2007–08 Bolton W 0 0
2009–10 Torquay U 27 3
2010–11 Torquay U 27 2
2011–12 Torquay U 35 3 89 8
2012–13 Crewe Alex 44 5
2013–14 Crewe Alex 37 1 81 6
2014–15 Shrewsbury T 32 2
2015–16 Shrewsbury T 9 1 41 3
2015–16 Carlisle U 30 0 30 0

GILLESPIE, Mark (G) 115 0
H: 6 3 W: 13 07 b.Newcastle 27-3-92
2009–10 Carlisle U 1 0
2010–11 Carlisle U 0 0
2011–12 Carlisle U 0 0
2012–13 Carlisle U 35 0
2013–14 Carlisle U 15 0
2014–15 Carlisle U 19 0
2015–16 Carlisle U 45 0 115 0

GRAINGER, Danny (D) 219 15
H: 5 10 W: 10 10 b.Kettering 28-7-86
2008–09 Dundee U 9 0 9 0
2009–10 St Johnstone 36 1
2010–11 St Johnstone 33 2 69 3
2011–12 Hearts 27 0
2012–13 Hearts 13 2 40 2
2013–14 St Mirren 13 0 13 0
2013–14 Dunfermline Ath 11 2 11 2
2014–15 Carlisle U 41 3
2015–16 Carlisle U 36 5 77 8

HAMMELL, Connor (F) 3 0
b. 14-2-96
2014–15 Carlisle U 3 0
2015–16 Carlisle U 0 0 3 0

HANFORD, Dan (G) 55 0
H: 6 2 W: 12 04 b. 6-3-91
2013–14 Floriana 28 0 28 0
2014–15 Carlisle U 25 0
2015–16 Carlisle U 2 0 27 0

HERY, Bastien (M) 53 2
b.Brou sur Chantereine 23-3-92
Internationals: France U18.
2012–13 Sheffield W 0 0
2013–14 Rochdale 12 1
2014–15 Rochdale 21 1 33 2
2015–16 Carlisle U 20 0 20 0

IBEHRE, Jabo (F) 494 98
H: 6 2 W: 13 13 b.Islington 28-1-83
1999–2000 Leyton Orient 3 0
2000–01 Leyton Orient 5 2
2001–02 Leyton Orient 28 4
2002–03 Leyton Orient 25 5
2003–04 Leyton Orient 35 4
2004–05 Leyton Orient 19 2
2005–06 Leyton Orient 33 8
2006–07 Leyton Orient 30 4
2007–08 Leyton Orient 31 7 209 36
2008–09 Walsall 39 10 39 10
2009–10 Milton Keynes D 10 1

2009–10 *Southend U* 4 0 4 0
2009–10 *Stockport Co* 20 5 20 5
2010–11 Milton Keynes D 42 3
2011–12 Milton Keynes D 39 8
2012–13 Milton Keynes D 13 0 94 12
2012–13 Colchester U 30 8
2013–14 Colchester U 37 8
2014–15 Colchester U 5 0 72 16
2014–15 *Oldham Ath* 11 2 11 2
2014–15 *Barnsley* 9 2 9 2
2015–16 Carlisle U 36 15 36 15

JOYCE, Luke (M) 309 10
H: 5 11 W: 12 03 b.Bolton 9-7-87
2005–06 Wigan Ath 0 0
2005–06 Carlisle U 0 0
2006–07 Carlisle U 16 1
2007–08 Carlisle U 3 1
2008–09 Carlisle U 7 0
2009–10 Accrington S 41 1
2010–11 Accrington S 27 1
2011–12 Accrington S 43 2
2012–13 Accrington S 44 0
2013–14 Accrington S 46 1
2014–15 Accrington S 45 3 246 8
2015–16 Carlisle U 37 0 63 2

KENNEDY, Jason (M) 373 30
H: 6 1 W: 13 02 b.Stockton 11-9-86
2004–05 Middlesbrough 1 0
2005–06 Middlesbrough 3 0
2006–07 Middlesbrough 0 0
2006–07 Boston U 13 1 13 1
2006–07 Bury 12 0 12 0
2007–08 Middlesbrough 0 0 4 0
2007–08 Livingston 18 2 18 2
2007–08 Darlington 13 2
2008–09 Darlington 46 5 59 7
2009–10 Rochdale 42 0
2010–11 Rochdale 45 4
2011–12 Rochdale 44 4
2012–13 Rochdale 46 4
2013–14 Bradford C 8 1
2013–14 *Rochdale* 7 0 184 12
2014–15 Bradford C 20 3
2014–15 *Carlisle U* 11 3
2015–16 Carlisle U 44 2 55 5

McQUEEN, Alexander (D) 21 0
b. 24-3-95
From Tottenham H.
2015–16 Carlisle U 21 0 21 0

MEPPEN-WALTER, Courtney (D) 39 2
H: 6 0 W: 12 00 b.Bury 2-8-94
Internationals: England U17, U18.
2012–13 Manchester C 0 0
2013–14 Carlisle U 20 1
2014–15 Carlisle U 19 1
2015–16 Carlisle U 0 0 39 2

MILLER, Tom (D) 29 5
H: 5 11 W: 11 07 b.Ely 29-6-90
From Rangers, Dundalk, Newport Co, Lincoln C.
2015–16 Carlisle U 29 5 29 5

OSEI, Kevin (M) 11 0
H: 5 9 W: 11 03 b.Marseille 26-3-91
2009–10 Marseille 0 0
2010–11 Marseille 0 0
2011–12 Marseille 0 0
2011–12 *Aviron Bayonnais* 3 0 3 0
2012–13 Marseille 0 0
2013–14 Marseille 0 0
2014–15 Beveren 0 0
2015–16 Carlisle U 8 0 8 0
Released by mutual consent December 2015.

PEDRO, Luis (F) 157 36
H: 6 0 W: 11 03 b. 27-4-90
Internationals: Netherlands U18, U19.
2008–09 Feyenoord 9 0
2009–10 Feyenoord 0 0 9 0
2009–10 Excelsior 17 10 17 10
2010–11 Go Ahead Eagles 27 14 27 14
2011–12 Heracles 16 1
2012–13 Botev Polvdiv 11 3 11 3
2012–13 Heracles 13 1 29 2
2013–14 Botev Plovdiv 23 3 23 3
2014–15 Levski Sofia 23 3 23 3
2015–16 Targu Mures 17 1 17 1
2015–16 Carlisle U 1 0 1 0

RAYNES, Michael (D) 326 9
H: 6 4 W: 12 00 b.Wythenshawe 15-10-87
2004–05 Stockport Co 19 0
2005–06 Stockport Co 25 1
2006–07 Stockport Co 9 0
2007–08 Stockport Co 27 0

2008–09 Stockport Co 35 3
2009–10 Stockport Co 25 1 140 5
2009–10 Scunthorpe U 12 0
2010–11 Scunthorpe U 22 0 34 0
2011–12 Rotherham U 33 0 33 0
2012–13 Oxford U 38 1
2013–14 Oxford U 27 0
2014–15 Oxford U 4 0 69 1
2014–15 Mansfield U 10 0 10 0
2015–16 Carlisle U 40 3 40 3

RIGG, Steven (M) 36 6
b.Keswick 30-6-92
2014–15 Carlisle U 28 6
2015–16 Carlisle U 8 0 36 6

SWEENEY, Anthony (M) 433 54
H: 6 0 W: 11 07 b.Stockton 5-9-83
2001–02 Hartlepool U 2 0
2002–03 Hartlepool U 4 0
2003–04 Hartlepool U 11 1
2004–05 Hartlepool U 44 13
2005–06 Hartlepool U 35 5
2006–07 Hartlepool U 35 4
2007–08 Hartlepool U 36 4
2008–09 Hartlepool U 44 5
2009–10 Hartlepool U 42 2
2010–11 Hartlepool U 40 9
2011–12 Hartlepool U 39 8
2012–13 Hartlepool U 34 1
2013–14 Hartlepool U 19 0 385 52
2014–15 Carlisle U 29 1
2015–16 Carlisle U 19 1 48 2

TAYLOR, Carl (M) 1 0
2014–15 Carlisle U 1 0
2015–16 Carlisle U 0 0 1 0

THOMPSON, Joe (M) 188 19
H: 6 0 W: 9 07 b.Rochdale 5-3-89
2005–06 Rochdale 1 0
2006–07 Rochdale 13 0
2007–08 Rochdale 11 1
2008–09 Rochdale 30 5
2009–10 Rochdale 36 6
2010–11 Rochdale 32 2
2011–12 Rochdale 17 1
2012–13 Tranmere R 19 1
2012–13 *Rochdale* 7 0 147 15
2013–14 Tranmere R 6 2 25 3
2014–15 Bury 1 0 1 0
2015–16 Carlisle U 15 1 15 1

WYKE, Charlie (F) 106 26
b.Middlesbrough 6-12-92
2011–12 Middlesbrough 0 0
2012–13 Middlesbrough 0 0
2012–13 *Hartlepool U* 25 2
2013–14 Middlesbrough 0 0
2013–14 *AFC Wimbledon* 17 2 17 2
2014–15 Middlesbrough 0 0
2014–15 *Hartlepool U* 13 4 38 6
2014–15 Carlisle U 17 6
2015–16 Carlisle U 34 12 51 18

Scholars
Bacon, Morgan Jonathan Anthony; Bradbury, Arron Andrew; Breen, Joe; Brown, Max William; Douglas, Matthew; Egan, Jack James; Groves, Rhys Alexander; Hall, Kieran James Robert; Holt, Jordan; Hurley, Cuan francis; Pearson, Ellis James; Quigley, Michael Thomas; Robson, Joe Leigh; Rudd, Karlton Thomas; Salkeld, Cameron John; Taylor, Carl; Williams, Rhys Frederick.

CHARLTON ATH (23)

AHEARNE-GRANT, Karlan (F) 25 1
b. 19-12-97
Internationals: England U17, U18, U19.
2014–15 Charlton Ath 5 0
2015–16 Charlton Ath 17 1 22 1
2015–16 *Cambridge U* 3 0 3 0

ANSAH, Zak (F) 21 3
H: 5 10 W: 11 00 b.Sidcup 4-5-94
Internationals: England U16, U17. Ghana U20.
2010–11 Arsenal 0 0
2011–12 Arsenal 0 0
2012–13 Arsenal 0 0
2013–14 Arsenal 0 0
2014–15 Charlton Ath 0 0
2014–15 *Plymouth Arg* 8 1 8 1
2015–16 Charlton Ath 0 0
2015–16 *Newport Co* 13 2 13 2

ARIBO, Joe (M)   0 0
b. 21-7-96
From Staines T.
2015–16 Charlton Ath 0 0

BA, El-Hadji (M)   46 1
H: 6 0   W: 11 08   b.Paris 5-3-93
Internationals: France U18, U19, U20.
2011–12 Le Havre 1 0
2012–13 Le Havre 12 1 13 1
2013–14 Sunderland 1 0
2014–15 Sunderland 0 0 1 0
2014–15 Bastia 7 0 7 0
2015–16 Charlton Ath 25 0 25 0

BAUER, Patrick (D)   64 3
H: 6 4   W: 13 08   b.Backnang 28-10-92
Internationals: Germany U17, U18, U20.
2010–11 Stuttgart 0 0
2011–12 Stuttgart 0 0
2012–13 Stuttgart 0 0
2013–14 Maritimo 16 0
2014–15 Maritimo 29 2 45 2
2015–16 Charlton Ath 19 1 19 1

BEENEY, Jordan (G)   0 0
b. 12-5-98
2014–15 Charlton Ath 0 0
2015–16 Charlton Ath 0 0

BERGDICH, Zakarya (D)   124 6
H: 5 9   W: 10 10   b.Compiegne 7-1-89
Internationals: Morocco U23, Full caps.
2010–11 Lens 2 0
2011–12 Lens 25 0
2012–13 Lens 24 1 51 1
2013–14 Real Valladolid 22 0 22 0
2014–15 Real Valladolid 17 5 17 5
2014–15 *Genoa* 11 0 11 0
2015–16 Charlton Ath 23 0 23 0

CEBALLOS, Cristian (M)   23 1
H: 5 8   W: 10 08   b.Barcelona 3-12-92
2011–12 Tottenham H 0 0
2012–13 Tottenham H 0 0
2013–14 Tottenham H 0 0
2013–14 Arouca 18 1 18 1
2014–15 Tottenham H 0 0
2015–16 Charlton Ath 5 0 5 0

CHARLES, Regan (M)   1 0
b. 1-3-97
From Arsenal.
2015–16 Charlton Ath 1 0 1 0

COUSINS, Jordan (D)   125 7
H: 5 10   W: 11 05   b.Greenwich 6-3-94
Internationals: England U16, U17, U18, U20.
2011–12 Charlton Ath 0 0
2012–13 Charlton Ath 0 0
2013–14 Charlton Ath 42 2
2014–15 Charlton Ath 44 3
2015–16 Charlton Ath 39 2 125 7

DIARRA, Alou (M)   367 23
H: 6 3   W: 12 05   b.Villepinte 15-7-81
Internationals: France U20, U21, Full caps.
2002–03 Liverpool 0 0
2002–03 *Le Havre* 25 0 25 0
2003–04 Liverpool 0 0
2003–04 *Bastia* 35 4 35 4
2004–05 Liverpool 0 0
2004–05 Lens 34 2
2005–06 Lens 30 2 64 4
2006–07 Lyon 15 1 15 1
2007–08 Bordeaux 36 4
2008–09 Bordeaux 35 2
2009–10 Bordeaux 30 1
2010–11 Bordeaux 32 4 133 11
2011–12 Marseille 33 2
2012–13 Marseille 0 0 33 2
2012–13 *Rennes* 12 0 12 0
2013–14 West Ham U 3 0
2013–14 West Ham U 3 0 6 0
2014–15 Charlton Ath 12 1
2015–16 Charlton Ath 32 0 44 1

EDWARDS, Archie (D)   0 0
b. 10-7-97
Internationals: England U16, U17.
2014–15 Charlton Ath 0 0
2015–16 Charlton Ath 0 0

FANNI, Rod (D)   461 11
H: 6 1   W: 12 04   b.Martigues 6-12-81
Internationals: France Full caps.
1999–2000 Martigues 5 1
2000–01 Martigues 31 1
2001–02 Martigues 30 0 66 2
2002–03 Lens 12 0
2003–04 Lens 21 0

2004–05 Lens 0 0 33 0
2004–05 *Chateauroux* 33 1 33 1
2005–06 Nice 21 0
2006–07 Nice 36 0 57 0
2007–08 Rennes 28 0
2008–09 Rennes 37 2
2009–10 Rennes 38 0
2010–11 Rennes 11 0 114 2
2010–11 Marseille 19 0
2011–12 Marseille 29 1
2012–13 Marseille 33 2
2013–14 Marseille 22 0
2014–15 Marseille 27 2 130 5
2015–16 Al Arabi 14 1 14 1
2015–16 Charlton Ath 14 0 14 0

FOX, Morgan (D)   86 2
H: 6 1   W: 12 03   b.Chelmsford 21-9-93
Internationals: Wales U21.
2012–13 Charlton Ath 0 0
2013–14 Charlton Ath 6 0
2013–14 *Notts Co* 7 1 7 1
2014–15 Charlton Ath 31 0
2015–16 Charlton Ath 42 1 79 1

GHOOCHANNEJHAD, Reza (F)   172 63
H: 5 11   W: 11 12   b.Mashdad 20-9-87
Internationals: Netherlands U16, U17, U18, U19. Iran Full caps.
2005–06 Heerenveen 1 0
2006–07 Heerenveen 0 0
2006–07 *Go Ahead Eagles* 13 4
2007–08 Heerenveen 0 0
2008–09 Heerenveen 1 0 2 0
2008–09 *Emmen* 11 1 11 1
2009–10 Go Ahead Eagles 10 6 23 10
2009–10 Cambuur 13 2
2010–11 Cambuur 24 13 37 15
2011–12 St. Truidense 10 6
2012–13 St. Truidense 10 6 32 17
2012–13 Standard Liege 9 3
2013–14 Standard Liege 1 1 10 4
2013–14 Charlton Ath 15 1
2014–15 Charlton Ath 0 0
2014–15 *Al-Kuwait SC* 10 11 10 11
2014–15 *Al Wakra* 9 2 9 2
2015–16 Charlton Ath 23 2 38 3

GUDMUNDSSON, Johann Berg (M)   200 25
H: 6 1   W: 12 06   b.Reykjavik 27-10-90
Internationals: Iceland U19, U21, Full caps.
2009–10 AZ 0 0
2010–11 AZ 23 1
2011–12 AZ 30 3
2012–13 AZ 31 2
2013–14 AZ 35 3 119 9
2014–15 Charlton Ath 41 10
2015–16 Charlton Ath 40 6 81 16

HARRIOTT, Callum (M)   106 16
H: 5 5   W: 10 05   b.Norbury 4-3-94
Internationals: England U19.
2010–11 Charlton Ath 3 0
2011–12 Charlton Ath 0 0
2012–13 Charlton Ath 14 2
2013–14 Charlton Ath 28 5
2014–15 Charlton Ath 21 1
2015–16 Charlton Ath 20 3 86 11
2015–16 *Colchester U* 20 5 20 5

HENDERSON, Stephen (G)   150 0
H: 6 3   W: 11 00   b.Dublin 2-5-88
Internationals: Republic of Ireland U16, U17, U19, U21.
2005–06 Aston Villa 0 0
2006–07 Aston Villa 0 0
2007–08 Bristol C 1 0
2008–09 Bristol C 1 0
2009–10 Bristol C 3 0
2009–10 *Aldershot T* 8 0 8 0
2010–11 Bristol C 0 0 5 0
2010–11 *Yeovil T* 33 0 33 0
2011–12 *Portsmouth* 25 0 25 0
2011–12 West Ham U 0 0
2012–13 West Ham U 0 0
2012–13 *Ipswich T* 24 0 24 0
2013–14 West Ham U 0 0
2013–14 *Bournemouth* 2 0 2 0
2014–15 Charlton Ath 31 0
2015–16 Charlton Ath 22 0 53 0

HOLMES-DENNIS, Tareiq (M)   52 1
H: 5 9   W: 11 11   b.Farnborough 31-10-95
Internationals: England U18.
2012–13 Charlton Ath 0 0
2013–14 Charlton Ath 0 0
2014–15 Charlton Ath 20 0
2014–15 *Oxford U* 14 0 14 0
2014–15 *Plymouth Arg* 17 1 17 1

2015–16 Charlton Ath 11 0 11 0
2015–16 *Oldham Ath* 10 0 10 0

JACKSON, Johnnie (M)   404 66
H: 6 1   W: 12 00   b.Camden 15-8-82
Internationals: England U17, U18, U20.
1999–2000 Tottenham H 0 0
2000–01 Tottenham H 0 0
2001–02 Tottenham H 0 0
2002–03 Tottenham H 0 0
2002–03 *Swindon T* 13 1 13 1
2002–03 *Colchester U* 8 0
2003–04 Tottenham H 11 1
2003–04 *Coventry C* 5 2 5 2
2004–05 Tottenham H 8 0
2004–05 *Watford* 15 0 15 0
2005–06 Tottenham H 1 0 20 1
2005–06 *Derby Co* 6 0 6 0
2006–07 Colchester U 32 2
2007–08 Colchester U 46 7
2008–09 Colchester U 29 4
2009–10 Colchester U 0 0 115 13
2009–10 *Notts Co* 24 2 24 2
2009–10 *Charlton Ath* 0 0
2010–11 Charlton Ath 30 13
2011–12 Charlton Ath 36 12
2012–13 Charlton Ath 43 12
2013–14 Charlton Ath 38 5
2014–15 Charlton Ath 26 2
2015–16 Charlton Ath 29 3 206 47

JOHNSON, Roger (D)   471 35
H: 6 3   W: 11 00   b.Ashford (Middlesex) 28-4-83
1999–2000 Wycombe W 1 0
2000–01 Wycombe W 1 0
2001–02 Wycombe W 7 1
2002–03 Wycombe W 33 3
2003–04 Wycombe W 28 2
2004–05 Wycombe W 42 6
2005–06 Wycombe W 45 7 157 19
2006–07 Cardiff C 32 2
2007–08 Cardiff C 42 5
2008–09 Cardiff C 45 5 119 12
2009–10 Birmingham C 38 0
2010–11 Birmingham C 38 2 76 2
2011–12 Wolverhampton W 27 0
2012–13 Wolverhampton W 42 2
2013–14 Wolverhampton W 0 0
2013–14 *Sheffield W* 17 0 17 0
2013–14 *West Ham U* 4 0 4 0
2014–15 Wolverhampton W 0 0 69 2
2014–15 Charlton Ath 14 0
2015 *Pune C* 11 0 11 0
2015–16 Charlton Ath 4 0 18 0

KASHI, Ahmed (M)   173 5
H: 5 10   W: 12 00   b.Aubervilliers 18-11-88
Internationals: Algeria Full caps.
2008–09 Chateauroux 21 2
2009–10 Chateauroux 23 1
2010–11 Chateauroux 17 1
2011–12 Chateauroux 24 0 85 4
2012–13 Metz 25 0
2013–14 Metz 33 0
2014–15 Metz 19 1 77 1
2015–16 Charlton Ath 11 0 11 0

KENNEDY, Mikhail (D)   2 0
b. 18-8-96
Internationals: Northern Ireland U17, U19, U21.
2014–15 Charlton Ath 0 0
2015–16 Charlton Ath 2 0 2 0

KONSA, Ezri (D)   0 0
b. 23-10-97
2015–16 Charlton Ath 0 0

LENNON, Harry (M)   31 4
H: 6 3   W: 11 11   b.Barking 16-12-94
2013–14 Charlton Ath 2 0
2013–14 Charlton Ath 2 0
2014–15 Charlton Ath 2 0
2014–15 *Cambridge U* 2 0 2 0
2015–16 Charlton Ath 19 2 21 2
2015–16 *Gillingham* 6 2 8 2

LOOKMAN, Ademola (F)   24 5
b. 18-7-98
2015–16 Charlton Ath 24 5 24 5

MAKIENOK CHRISTOFFERSEN, Simon (F)   174 62
H: 6 7   W: 14 11   b.Naestved 21-11-90
Internationals: Denmark U19, U20, U21, Full caps.
2008–09 Herfolge 4 0 4 0
2009–10 HB Koge 11 1
2010–11 HB Koge 28 16

2011–12	HB Koge	17	5	56	22
2011–12	Brondby	14	5		
2012–13	Brondby	31	15		
2013–14	Brondby	24	12		
2014–15	Brondby	5	3	74	35
2014–15	Palermo	4	0		
2015–16	Palermo	0	0	4	0

On loan from Palermo.

2015–16	Charlton Ath	36	5	36	5

MITOV, Dimitar (G)   0   0
b. 22-1-97
Internationals: Bulgaria U17, U19.

2014–15	Charlton Ath	0	0
2015–16	Charlton Ath	0	0

MOTTA, Marco (D)   198   3
H: 5 11 W: 12 02 b.Bergamo 14-5-86
Internationals: Italy U16, U17, U18, U19, U20, U21, U23, Full caps.

2004–05	Atalanta	19	0	19	0
2005–06	Udinese	6	1		
2006–07	Udinese	16	0		
2007–08	Udinese	0	0		
2007–08	Torino	24	1	24	1
2008–09	Udinese	14	0	36	1
2008–09	Roma	13	0		
2009–10	Roma	16	0	29	0
2010–11	Juventus	22	0		
2011–12	Juventus	0	0		
2011–12	Catania	13	0	13	0
2012–13	Juventus	0	0		
2012–13	Bologna	19	1	19	1
2013–14	Juventus	2	0		
2013–14	Genoa	13	0	13	0
2014–15	Juventus	0	0	24	0
2014–15	Watford	9	0	9	0
2015–16	Charlton Ath	12	0	12	0

MULDOON, Oliver (M)   21   0
b. 3-9-94

2014–15	Charlton Ath	0	0		
2014–15	Gillingham	3	0	3	0
2015–16	Charlton Ath	0	0		
2015–16	Dagenham & R	18	0	18	0

OBILEYE, Ayo (D)   42   2
b.Hackney 2-9-94

2011–12	Sheffield W	0	0		
2012–13	Sheffield W	0	0		
2013–14	Sheffield W	0	0		
2014–15	Charlton Ath	0	0		
2014–15	Dagenham & R	26	2		
2015–16	Charlton Ath	0	0		
2015–16	Dagenham & R	16	0	42	2

PHILLIPS, Dillon (M)   0   0
H: 6 2 W: 11 11 b. 11-6-95

2012–13	Charlton Ath	0	0
2013–14	Charlton Ath	0	0
2014–15	Charlton Ath	0	0
2015–16	Charlton Ath	0	0

PIGOTT, Joe (F)   87   17
H: 6 0 W: 9 05 b.London 24-11-93

2012–13	Charlton Ath	0	0		
2013–14	Charlton Ath	11	0		
2013–14	Gillingham	7	1	7	1
2014–15	Charlton Ath	1	0		
2014–15	Newport Co	10	3	10	3
2014–15	Southend U	20	6		
2015–16	Charlton Ath	0	0	12	0
2015–16	Southend U	23	3	43	9
2015–16	Luton T	15	4	15	4

POPE, Nick (G)   77   0
H: 6 3 W: 11 13 b.Cambridge 19-4-92

2011–12	Charlton Ath	1	0		
2012–13	Charlton Ath	0	0		
2013–14	Charlton Ath	0	0		
2013–14	York C	22	0	22	0
2014–15	Charlton Ath	8	0		
2014–15	Bury	22	0	22	0
2015–16	Charlton Ath	24	0	33	0

SARR, Naby (D)   22   1
H: 6 5 W: 14 11 b.Marseille 13-8-93
Internationals: France U20, U21.

2012–13	Lyon	0	0		
2013–14	Lyon	2	0	2	0
2014–15	Sporting Lisbon	8	0	8	0
2015–16	Charlton Ath	12	1	12	1

SHO-SILVA, Oluwatobi (M)   5   0
b. 27-3-95
Internationals: England U18.

2012–13	Charlton Ath	0	0		
2013–14	Charlton Ath	0	0		
2014–15	Charlton Ath	0	0		
2015–16	Charlton Ath	0	0		
2015–16	Inverness CT	5	0	5	0

SOLLY, Chris (D)   197   2
H: 5 8 W: 10 07 b.Rochester 20-1-91
Internationals: England U16, U17.

2008–09	Charlton Ath	1	0		
2009–10	Charlton Ath	9	0		
2010–11	Charlton Ath	14	1		
2011–12	Charlton Ath	44	0		
2012–13	Charlton Ath	45	1		
2013–14	Charlton Ath	12	0		
2014–15	Charlton Ath	38	0		
2015–16	Charlton Ath	34	0	197	2

TEIXEIRA, Jorge (D)   172   13
b. 27-8-86

2009–10	Maccabi Haifa	24	0	24	0
2010–11	Zurich	26	4		
2011–12	Zurich	29	0		
2012–13	Zurich	12	2		
2012–13	Siena	9	0	9	0
2013–14	Zurich	25	2	92	8
2014–15	Standard Liege	12	2		
2015–16	Standard Liege	16	1	28	3
2015–16	Charlton Ath	19	2	19	2

THOMAS, Terell (D)   0   0
b. 13-10-97

2014–15	Charlton Ath	0	0
2015–16	Charlton Ath	0	0

UMERAH, Josh (F)   1   0
b. 1-4-98

2015–16	Charlton Ath	1	0	1	0

VAZ TE, Ricardo (F)   193   36
H: 6 2 W: 12 07 b.Lisbon 1-10-86
Internationals: Portugal U17, U19, U20, U21, U23.

2003–04	Bolton W	1	0		
2004–05	Bolton W	7	0		
2005–06	Bolton W	22	3		
2006–07	Bolton W	25	0		
2006–07	Hull C	6	0	6	0
2007–08	Bolton W	1	0		
2008–09	Bolton W	2	0		
2009–10	Bolton W	0	0	58	3
2010–11	Panionios	7	1	7	1
2010–11	Hibernian	10	1	10	1
2011–12	Barnsley	22	10	22	10
2011–12	West Ham U	15	10		
2012–13	West Ham U	24	3		
2013–14	West Ham U	8	2		
2014–15	West Ham U	4	0	51	15
2014–15	Akhisar Belediye	14	5		
2015–16	Charlton Ath	11	0	11	0
2015–16	Akhisar Belediye	14	1	28	6

VETOKELE, Igor (F)   139   37
H: 5 8 W: 11 00 b.Ostend 23-3-92
Internationals: Belgium U17, U18, U19, U20, U21. Angola Full caps.

2010–11	Gent	0	0		
2011–12	Cercle Brugge	34	8		
2012–13	Cercle Brugge	4	1	38	9
2012–13	Copenhagen	15	3		
2013–14	Copenhagen	29	13	44	16
2014–15	Charlton Ath	41	11		
2015–16	Charlton Ath	11	1	57	12

WATT, Tony (F)   125   30
H: 5 8 W: 12 00 b.Bellshill 29-3-93
Internationals: Scotland U19, U20, U21, Full caps.

2009–10	Airdrieonians	1	0		
2010–11	Airdrieonians	15	3	16	3
2011–12	Celtic	3	2		
2012–13	Celtic	20	5		
2013–14	Celtic	2	0	25	7
2013–14	Lierse	17	8	17	8
2014–15	Standard Liege	13	2	13	2
2014–15	Charlton Ath	22	5		
2015–16	Charlton Ath	14	2	36	7
2015–16	Cardiff C	9	2	9	2
2015–16	Blackburn R	9	1	9	1

Players retained or with offer of contract
Assiana, Elan Lumir; Barnes, Aaron Christopher; Dijksteel, Anfernee Jamal; Dmitrovic, Marko; Hanlan, Brandon Alex Graham; Lapslie, George Robert; Tucudean, George-Marius; Yao, Kenneth William.

Scholars
Bah, Sulaiman; Bangura-Williams, Mustapha Mohamed; Bone, Samuel George; Hall-Anderson, Terrique Dominic; Maloney, Taylor Peter; Maynard-Brewer, Ashley; Millar, Christopher James; Prall, Aiden Noyes; Simpson, Romarno Arnelle; Thomas, Callum.

CHELSEA (24)

ABRAHAM, Tammy (F)   2   0
b. 2-10-97
Internationals: England U18, U19.

2015–16	Chelsea	2	0	2	0

AINA, Ola (D)   0   0
H: 5 9 W: 10 03 b.London 8-10-96
Internationals: England U16, U17, U18, U19, U20.

2015–16	Chelsea	0	0

AKE, Nathan (M)   34   1
H: 5 11 W: 11 01 b.Den Haag 18-2-95
Internationals: Netherlands U15, U16, U17, U19, U21.

2012–13	Chelsea	3	0		
2013–14	Chelsea	1	0		
2014–15	Chelsea	1	0		
2014–15	Reading	5	0	5	0
2015–16	Chelsea	0	0	5	0
2015–16	Watford	24	1	24	1

ALEXANDRE PATO, da Silva (F)   220   86
H: 5 11 W: 11 03 b.Pato Branco 2-9-89
Internationals: Brazil U20, U23, Full caps.

2006	Internacional	1	1		
2006–07	Internacional	9	5	10	6
2007–08	AC Milan	18	9		
2008–09	AC Milan	36	15		
2009–10	AC Milan	23	12		
2010–11	AC Milan	25	14		
2011–12	AC Milan	11	1		
2012–13	AC Milan	4	0	117	51
2013	Corinthians	30	9		
2014	Corinthians	0	0		
2014	Sao Paulo	28	9		
2015	Corinthians	0	0	30	9
2015	Sao Paulo	33	10	61	19

On loan from Corinthians.

2015–16	Chelsea	2	1	2	1

AMELIA, Marco (G)   273   0
H: 6 2 W: 12 04 b.Frascati 2-4-82
Internationals: Italy U16, U18, U21, Full caps.

1999–2000	Roma	0	0		
2000–01	Roma	0	0		
2001–02	Livorno	1	0		
2002–03	Livorno	35	0		
2003–04	Livorno	0	0		
2003–04	Lecce	13	0	13	0
2003–04	Parma	0	0		
2004–05	Livorno	31	0		
2005–06	Livorno	36	0		
2006–07	Livorno	30	0		
2007–08	Livorno	33	0	166	0
2008–09	Palermo	34	0	34	0
2009–10	Genoa	30	0	30	0
2010–11	AC Milan	4	0		
2011–12	AC Milan	9	0		
2012–13	AC Milan	11	0		
2013–14	AC Milan	5	0	29	0
2014–15	Perugia	1	0	1	0
2015–16	Chelsea	0	0		

ATSU, Christian (F)   87   14
H: 5 8 W: 10 09 b.Ada Foah 10-1-92
Internationals: Ghana Full caps.

2010–11	Porto	0	0		
2011–12	Porto	0	0		
2011–12	Rio Ave	27	6	27	6
2012–13	Porto	17	1	17	1
2013–14	Chelsea	0	0		
2013–14	Vitesse	26	5	26	5
2014–15	Chelsea	0	0		
2014–15	Everton	5	0	5	0
2015–16	Chelsea	0	0		
2015–16	Bournemouth	0	0		
2015–16	Malaga	12	2	12	2

AZPILICUETA, Cesar (D)   268   3
H: 5 10 W: 10 13 b.Pamplona 28-8-89
Internationals: Spain U16, U17, U19, U20, U21, U23, Full caps.

2006–07	Osasuna	1	0		
2007–08	Osasuna	29	0		
2008–09	Osasuna	36	0		
2009–10	Osasuna	33	0	99	0
2010–11	Marseille	15	0		
2011–12	Marseille	30	1		
2012–13	Marseille	2	0	47	1
2012–13	Chelsea	27	0		
2013–14	Chelsea	29	0		
2014–15	Chelsea	29	0		
2015–16	Chelsea	37	2	122	2

BABA, Abdul Rahman (D) **115** **2**
H: 5 10 W: 12 00 b.Tamale 2-7-94
Internationals: Ghana U20, Full caps.

2011–12	Asante Kotoko	25	0	**25**	**0**
2012–13	Greuther Furth	20	0		
2013–14	Greuther Furth	22	0		
2014–15	Greuther Furth	2	2	**44**	**2**
2014–15	Augsburg	31	0	**31**	**0**
2015–16	Chelsea	15	0	**15**	**0**

BAKER, Lewis (M) **47** **8**
b.Luton 25-4-95
Internationals: England U17, U19, U20, U21.

2012–13	Chelsea	0	0		
2013–14	Chelsea	0	0		
2014–15	Chelsea	0	0		
2014–15	*Sheffield W*	4	0	**4**	**0**
2014–15	*Milton Keynes D*	12	3	**12**	**3**
2015–16	Chelsea	0	0		
2015–16	*Vitesse*	31	5	**31**	**5**

BAMFORD, Patrick (F) **111** **43**
H: 6 1 W: 11 02 b.Newark 5-9-93
Internationals: Republic of Ireland U18. England U18, U19, U21.

2010–11	Nottingham F	0	0		
2011–12	Nottingham F	2	0	**2**	**0**
2011–12	Chelsea	0	0		
2012–13	Chelsea	0	0		
2012–13	*Milton Keynes D*	14	4		
2013–14	Chelsea	0	0		
2013–14	*Milton Keynes D*	23	14	**37**	**18**
2013–14	*Derby Co*	21	8	**21**	**8**
2014–15	Chelsea	0	0		
2014–15	*Middlesbrough*	38	17	**38**	**17**
2015–16	Chelsea	0	0		
2015–16	*Crystal Palace*	6	0	**6**	**0**
2015–16	*Norwich C*	7	0	**7**	**0**

BEENEY, Mitchell (G) **4** **0**
H: 6 0 W: 12 04 b.Leeds 3-10-95
Internationals: England U19.

2014–15	Chelsea	0	0		
2015–16	Chelsea	0	0		
2015–16	*Newport Co*	4	0	**4**	**0**

BEGOVIC, Asmir (G) **221** **1**
H: 6 5 W: 13 01 b.Trebinje 20-6-87
Internationals: Canada U20. Bosnia & Herzogovina Full caps.

2006–07	Portsmouth	0	0		
2006–07	*Macclesfield T*	3	0	**3**	**0**
2007–08	Portsmouth	0	0		
2007–08	*Bournemouth*	8	0	**8**	**0**
2007–08	*Yeovil T*	2	0		
2008–09	Portsmouth	2	0		
2008–09	*Yeovil T*	14	0	**16**	**0**
2009–10	Portsmouth	9	0	**11**	**0**
2009–10	*Ipswich T*	6	0	**6**	**0**
2009–10	Stoke C	4	0		
2010–11	Stoke C	28	0		
2011–12	Stoke C	23	0		
2012–13	Stoke C	38	0		
2013–14	Stoke C	32	1		
2014–15	Stoke C	35	0	**160**	**1**
2015–16	Chelsea	17	0	**17**	**0**

BLACKMAN, Jamal (G) **12** **0**
H: 6 6 W: 14 09 b.Croydon 27-10-93
Internationals: England U16, U17, U18, U19.

2011–12	Chelsea	0	0		
2012–13	Chelsea	0	0		
2013–14	Chelsea	0	0		
2014–15	Chelsea	0	0		
2014–15	*Middlesbrough*	0	0		
2015–16	Chelsea	0	0		
2015–16	*Ostersunds FK*	12	0	**12**	**0**

BOGA, Jeremie (F) **27** **2**
H: 5 8 W: 10 10 b.Marseille 3-1-97
Internationals: France U16, U19.

2014–15	Chelsea	0	0		
2015–16	Chelsea	0	0		
2015–16	*Rennes*	27	2	**27**	**2**

BROWN, Isaiah (M) **24** **1**
H: 6 0 W: 10 13 b.Peterborough 7-1-97
Internationals: England U16, U17, U19.

2012–13	WBA	1	0	**1**	**0**
2013–14	Chelsea	0	0		
2014–15	Chelsea	1	0		
2015–16	Chelsea	0	0	**1**	**0**
2015–16	*Vitesse*	22	1	**22**	**1**

CAHILL, Gary (D) **326** **24**
H: 6 2 W: 12 06 b.Dronfield 19-12-85
Internationals: England U20, U21, Full caps.

2003–04	Aston Villa	0	0		
2004–05	Aston Villa	0	0		
2004–05	*Burnley*	27	1	**27**	**1**
2005–06	Aston Villa	7	1		
2006–07	Aston Villa	20	0		
2007–08	Aston Villa	1	0	**28**	**1**
2007–08	*Sheffield U*	16	2	**16**	**2**
2007–08	Bolton W	13	0		
2008–09	Bolton W	33	3		
2009–10	Bolton W	29	5		
2010–11	Bolton W	36	3		
2011–12	Bolton W	19	2	**130**	**13**
2011–12	Chelsea	10	1		
2012–13	Chelsea	26	2		
2013–14	Chelsea	30	1		
2014–15	Chelsea	36	1		
2015–16	Chelsea	23	2	**125**	**7**

CHALOBAH, Nathaniel (D) **93** **9**
H: 6 1 W: 11 11 b.Sierra Leone 12-12-94
Internationals: England U16, U17, U19, U20, U21.

2010–11	Chelsea	0	0		
2011–12	Chelsea	0	0		
2012–13	Chelsea	0	0		
2012–13	*Watford*	38	5	**38**	**5**
2013–14	Chelsea	0	0		
2013–14	*Nottingham F*	12	2	**12**	**2**
2013–14	*Middlesbrough*	19	1	**19**	**1**
2014–15	Chelsea	0	0		
2014–15	*Burnley*	4	0	**4**	**0**
2014–15	*Reading*	15	1	**15**	**1**
2015–16	Chelsea	0	0		
2015–16	*Napoli*	5	0	**5**	**0**

CHRISTENSEN, Andreas (D) **32** **3**
H: 6 2 W: 11 09 b.Allerod 10-4-96
Internationals: Denmark U16, U17, U19, U21, Full caps.

2012–13	Chelsea	0	0		
2013–14	Chelsea	0	0		
2014–15	Chelsea	1	0		
2015–16	Chelsea	0	0	**1**	**0**
2015–16	*Borussia M'gladbach*	31	3	**31**	**3**

CLARKE-SALTER, Jake (D) **1** **0**
H: 6 2 W: 11 00 b.Carshalton 22-9-97
Internationals: England U18, U19.

2015–16	Chelsea	1	0	**1**	**0**

COLKETT, Charlie (M) **0** **0**
b. 4-9-96
Internationals: England U16, U17, U18, U19, U20.

2015–16	Chelsea	0	0		

COSTA, Diego (F) **283** **113**
H: 6 1 W: 12 04 b.Lagarto 7-10-88
Internationals: Brazil Full caps. Spain Full caps.

2006–07	Penafiel	13	5	**13**	**5**
2006–07	Sporting Braga	7	0	**7**	**0**
2007–08	Celta Vigo	30	6	**30**	**6**
2008–09	Albacete	35	9	**35**	**9**
2009–10	Valladolid	34	8	**34**	**8**
2010–11	Atletico Madrid	28	6		
2011–12	Atletico Madrid	0	0		
2011–12	*Rayo Vallecano*	16	10	**16**	**10**
2012–13	Atletico Madrid	31	10		
2013–14	Atletico Madrid	35	27	**94**	**43**
2014–15	Chelsea	26	20		
2015–16	Chelsea	28	12	**54**	**32**

COURTOIS, Thibaut (G) **207** **0**
H: 6 6 W: 14 02 b.Bree 11-5-92
Internationals: Belgium U18, Full caps.

2008–09	Genk	1	0		
2009–10	Genk	0	0		
2010–11	Genk	40	0	**41**	**0**
2011–12	Chelsea	0	0		
2011–12	*Atletico Madrid*	37	0		
2012–13	Chelsea	0	0		
2012–13	*Atletico Madrid*	37	0		
2013–14	Chelsea	0	0		
2013–14	*Atletico Madrid*	37	0	**111**	**0**
2014–15	Chelsea	32	0		
2015–16	Chelsea	23	0	**55**	**0**

CUADRADO, Juan Guillermo (M) **209** **29**
H: 5 10 W: 10 06 b.Necodi 26-5-88
Internationals: Colombia Full caps.

2008	Medellin	21	2		
2009	Medellin	9	0	**30**	**2**
2009–10	Udinese	11	0		
2010–11	Udinese	9	0		
2011–12	Udinese	0	0	**20**	**0**
2011–12	*Lecce*	33	3	**33**	**3**
2012–13	Fiorentina	36	5		
2013–14	Fiorentina	32	11		
2014–15	Fiorentina	17	4	**85**	**20**
2014–15	Chelsea	12	0		
2015–16	Chelsea	1	0	**13**	**0**
2015–16	*Juventus*	28	4	**28**	**4**

DAVEY, Alex (D) **25** **0**
b.Luton 24-11-94
Internationals: Scotland U19.

2012–13	Chelsea	0	0		
2013–14	Chelsea	0	0		
2014–15	Chelsea	0	0		
2014–15	*Scunthorpe U*	13	0	**13**	**0**
2015–16	Chelsea	0	0		
2015–16	*Peterborough U*	7	0	**7**	**0**
2015–16	*Stabaek*	5	0	**5**	**0**

DJILOBODJI, Papy (D) **192** **12**
H: 6 4 W: 12 13 b.Kaolack 1-12-88
Internationals: Senegal Full caps.

2009–10	Senart-Moissy	7	1	**7**	**1**
2009–10	Nantes	13	0		
2010–11	Nantes	27	2		
2011–12	Nantes	36	4		
2012–13	Nantes	36	0		
2013–14	Nantes	28	3		
2014–15	Nantes	31	0	**171**	**9**
2015–16	Chelsea	0	0		
2015–16	*Werder Bremen*	14	2	**14**	**2**

FABREGAS, Francesc (M) **379** **71**
H: 5 11 W: 11 01 b.Arenys de Mar 4-5-87
Internationals: Spain Youth, U21, Full caps.

2003–04	Arsenal	0	0		
2004–05	Arsenal	33	2		
2005–06	Arsenal	35	3		
2006–07	Arsenal	38	2		
2007–08	Arsenal	32	7		
2008–09	Arsenal	22	3		
2009–10	Arsenal	27	15		
2010–11	Arsenal	25	3	**212**	**35**
2011–12	Barcelona	28	9		
2012–13	Barcelona	32	11		
2013–14	Barcelona	36	8	**96**	**28**
2014–15	Chelsea	34	3		
2015–16	Chelsea	37	5	**71**	**8**

FALCAO, Radamel (F) **265** **143**
H: 5 10 W: 11 11 b.Santa Marta 10-2-86
Internationals: Colombia U20, Full caps.

2005–06	River Plate	11	7		
2006–07	River Plate	20	3		
2007–08	River Plate	27	11		
2008–09	River Plate	32	13	**90**	**34**
2009–10	Porto	28	25		
2010–11	Porto	22	16		
2011–12	Porto	1	0	**51**	**41**
2011–12	Atletico Madrid	34	24		
2012–13	Atletico Madrid	34	28	**68**	**52**
2013–14	Monaco	17	9		
2014–15	Monaco	3	2		
2014–15	*Manchester U*	26	4	**26**	**4**
2015–16	Monaco	0	0	**20**	**11**

On loan from Monaco.

2015–16	Chelsea	10	1	**10**	**1**

FERUZ, Islam (F) **9** **0**
H: 5 4 W: 8 07 b.Somalia 10-9-95
Internationals: Scotland U16, U17, U19, U20, U21.

2011–12	Chelsea	0	0		
2013–14	Chelsea	0	0		
2014–15	Chelsea	0	0		
2014–15	*OFI Crete*	1	0	**1**	**0**
2014–15	*Blackpool*	2	0	**2**	**0**
2015–16	Chelsea	0	0		
2015–16	*Hibernian*	6	0	**6**	**0**

HAZARD, Eden (M) **284** **77**
H: 5 7 W: 8 11 b.La Louviere 7-1-91
Internationals: Belgium U15, U16, U17, U19, Full caps.

2007–08	Lille	3	0		
2008–09	Lille	30	4		
2009–10	Lille	37	5		
2010–11	Lille	38	7		
2011–12	Lille	38	20	**146**	**36**
2012–13	Chelsea	34	9		
2013–14	Chelsea	35	14		
2014–15	Chelsea	38	14		
2015–16	Chelsea	31	4	**138**	**41**

HECTOR, Michael (D) **172** **11**
H: 6 4 W: 12 13 b.Newham 19-7-92
Internationals: Jamaica Full caps.

2009–10	Reading	0	0		
2010–11	Reading	0	0		
2011	*Dundalk*	11	2	**11**	**2**
2011–12	Reading	0	0		
2011–12	*Barnet*	27	2	**27**	**2**
2012–13	Reading	0	0		
2012–13	*Shrewsbury T*	8	0	**8**	**0**
2012–13	*Aldershot T*	8	1	**8**	**1**
2012–13	Cheltenham T	18	1	**18**	**1**
2013–14	Reading	9	0		

2013–14	Aberdeen	20	1	20	1
2014–15	Reading	41	3		
2015–16	Chelsea	0	0		
2015–16	*Reading*	30	1	80	4

HOUGHTON, Jordan (M) 21 2
b. 9-11-95
Internationals: England U16, U17, U20.

2015–16	Chelsea	0	0		
2015–16	*Gillingham*	11	1	11	1
2015–16	*Plymouth Arg*	10	1	10	1

IVANOVIC, Branislav (M) 376 34
H: 6 0 W: 12 04 b.Sremska Mitreovica 22-2-84
Internationals: Serbia U21, Full caps.

2002–03	Sremska	19	2	19	2
2003–04	OFK Belgrade	13	0		
2004–05	OFK Belgrade	27	2		
2005–06	OFK Belgrade	15	3	55	5
2006	Loko Moscow	28	2		
2007	Loko Moscow	26	3	54	5
2007–08	Chelsea	16	0		
2008–09	Chelsea	16	0		
2009–10	Chelsea	28	1		
2010–11	Chelsea	34	4		
2011–12	Chelsea	29	3		
2012–13	Chelsea	34	5		
2013–14	Chelsea	36	3		
2014–15	Chelsea	38	4		
2015–16	Chelsea	33	2	248	22

KALAS, Tomas (D) 84 1
H: 6 0 W: 12 00 b.Olomouc 15-5-93
Internationals: Czech Republic U17, U18, U19, U21, Full caps.

2009–10	Sigma Olomouc	1	0		
2010–11	Chelsea	0	0		
2010–11	*Sigma Olomouc*	4	0	5	0
2011–12	Chelsea	0	0		
2012–13	Chelsea	0	0		
2012–13	*Vitesse*	34	1	34	1
2013–14	Chelsea	2	0		
2014–15	Chelsea	0	0		
2014–15	*Cologne*	0	0		
2014–15	*Middlesbrough*	17	0		
2015–16	Chelsea	0	0	2	0
2015–16	*Middlesbrough*	26	0	43	0

KANE, Todd (D) 88 4
H: 5 11 W: 11 00 b.Huntingdon 17-9-93
Internationals: England U19.

2011–12	Chelsea	0	0		
2012–13	Chelsea	0	0		
2012–13	*Preston NE*	3	0	3	0
2012–13	*Blackburn R*	14	0		
2013–14	Chelsea	0	0		
2013–14	*Blackburn R*	27	2	41	2
2014–15	Chelsea	0	0		
2014–15	*Bristol C*	5	0	5	0
2014–15	*Nottingham F*	8	1	8	1
2015–16	Chelsea	0	0		
2015–16	*NEC*	31	1	31	1

KENEDY, Robert (F) 44 3
H: 6 0 W: 12 08 b.Santa Rita do Sapucai 8-2-96
Internationals: Brazil U17, U20.

2013	Fluminense	9	0		
2014	Fluminense	20	2		
2015	Fluminense	1	0	30	2
2015–16	Chelsea	14	1	14	1

KIWOMYA, Alex (M) 9 0
H: 5 10 W: 10 08 b.Sheffield 20-5-96
Internationals: England U16, U17, U18, U19.

2014–15	Chelsea	0	0		
2014–15	*Barnsley*	5	0	5	0
2015–16	Chelsea	0	0		
2015–16	*Fleetwood T*	4	0	4	0

LOFTUS-CHEEK, Ruben (M) 16 1
H: 6 4 W: 11 03 b.Lewisham 23-1-96
Internationals: England U16, U17, U19, U21.

2012–13	Chelsea	0	0		
2013–14	Chelsea	0	0		
2014–15	Chelsea	3	0		
2015–16	Chelsea	13	1	16	1

MARIN, Marko (M) 202 19
H: 5 7 W: 9 12 b.Gradiska 13-3-89
Internationals: Germany U16, U17, U18, U21, Full caps.

2006–07	Moenchengladbach	3	0		
2007–08	Moenchengladbach	33	4		
2008–09	Moenchengladbach	33	4	61	8
2009–10	Werder Bremen	32	4		
2010–11	Werder Bremen	34	3		
2011–12	Werder Bremen	21	1	87	8
2012–13	Chelsea	6	1		

2013–14	Chelsea	0	0		
2013–14	*Sevilla*	18	0	18	0
2014–15	Chelsea	0	0		
2014–15	*Fiorentina*	0	0		
2014–15	*Anderlecht*	6	0	6	0
2015–16	Chelsea	0	0	6	1
2015–16	*Trabzonspor*	24	2	24	2

MATIC, Nemanja (M) 254 15
H: 6 4 W: 13 02 b.Sabac 1-8-88
Internationals: Serbia U21, Full caps.

2005–06	Jedinstvo	7	0		
2006–07	Jedinstvo	9	0	16	0
2006–07	Kosice	13	1		
2007–08	Kosice	25	1		
2008–09	Kosice	29	2	67	4
2009–10	Chelsea	2	0		
2010–11	Chelsea	0	0		
2010–11	*Vitesse*	27	2	27	2
2011–12	Benfica	16	1		
2012–13	Benfica	26	3		
2013–14	Benfica	14	2	56	6
2013–14	Chelsea	17	0		
2014–15	Chelsea	36	1		
2015–16	Chelsea	33	2	88	3

MIAZGA, Matt (D) 36 1
H: 6 4 W: 12 08 b.Clifton, NJ 19-7-95
Internationals: Poland U18. USA U18, U20, U23, Full caps.

2013	New York Red Bulls	1	0		
2014	New York Red Bulls	7	0		
2015	New York Red Bulls	26	1	34	1
2015–16	Chelsea	2	0	2	0

MIKEL, John Obi (M) 255 2
H: 6 0 W: 13 05 b.Plateau State 22-4-87
Internationals: Nigeria Youth, Full caps.

2005	Lyn	6	1	6	1
2006–07	Chelsea	22	0		
2007–08	Chelsea	29	0		
2008–09	Chelsea	34	0		
2009–10	Chelsea	25	0		
2010–11	Chelsea	28	0		
2011–12	Chelsea	22	0		
2012–13	Chelsea	22	0		
2013–14	Chelsea	24	1		
2014–15	Chelsea	18	0		
2015–16	Chelsea	25	0	249	1

MOSES, Victor (M) 214 25
H: 5 10 W: 11 07 b.Lagos 12-12-90
Internationals: England U16, U17, U19, U21. Nigeria Full caps.

2007–08	Crystal Palace	13	3		
2008–09	Crystal Palace	27	2		
2009–10	Crystal Palace	18	6	58	11
2009–10	Wigan Ath	14	1		
2010–11	Wigan Ath	21	1		
2011–12	Wigan Ath	38	6		
2012–13	Wigan Ath	1	0	74	8
2012–13	Chelsea	23	1		
2013–14	Chelsea	0	0		
2013–14	*Liverpool*	19	1	19	1
2014–15	Chelsea	0	0		
2014–15	*Stoke C*	19	3	19	3
2015–16	Chelsea	0	0	23	1
2015–16	*West Ham U*	21	1	21	1

NATHAN, de Souza (M) 29 2
b.Blumenau 13-3-96
Internationals: Brazil U17, U20.

2013	Atletico Paranaense	11	0		
2014	Atletico Paranaense	0	0		
2015	Atletico Paranaense	0	0	11	0
2015–16	Chelsea	0	0		
2015–16	*Vitesse*	18	2	18	2

OMERUO, Kenneth (D) 85 0
H: 6 1 W: 12 00 b.Nigeria 17-10-93
Internationals: Nigeria U17, U20, Full caps

2011–12	Chelsea	0	0		
2012–13	Chelsea	0	0		
2012–13	*Den Haag*	27	0	27	0
2013–14	Chelsea	0	0		
2013–14	*Middlesbrough*	14	0		
2014–15	Chelsea	0	0		
2014–15	*Middlesbrough*	19	0	33	0
2015–16	Chelsea	0	0		
2015–16	*Kasimpasa*	25	0	25	0

OSCAR, Emboaba (M) 160 31
H: 5 11 W: 10 04 b.Americana 9-9-91
Internationals: Brazil U20, U23, Full caps.

2008–09	Sao Paulo	1	0		
2009–10	Sao Paulo	3	0	4	0
2010–11	Internacional	7	2		
2011–12	Internacional	27	8	34	10
2012–13	Chelsea	34	4		
2013–14	Chelsea	33	8		

2014–15	Chelsea	28	6		
2015–16	Chelsea	27	3	122	21

PALMER, Kasey (M) 0 0
b. 9-11-96
Internationals: England U17, U18, U20, U21.

2015–16	Chelsea	0	0		

PANTIC, Danilo (M) 24 2
b.Ruma 26-10-96
Internationals: Serbia, U17, U19.

2012–13	Partizan Belgrade	1	0		
2013–14	Partizan Belgrade	10	1		
2014–15	Partizan Belgrade	7	1	18	2
2015–16	Chelsea	0	0		
2015–16	*Vitesse*	6	0	6	0

PASALIC, Mario (M) 79 17
H: 6 1 W: 12 04 b.Mainz 9-2-95
Internationals: Croatia U16, U17, U19, U21, Full caps.

2012–13	Hajduk Split	1	0		
2013–14	Hajduk Split	30	11	32	11
2014–15	Chelsea	0	0		
2014–15	*Elche*	31	3	31	3
2015–16	Chelsea	0	0		
2015–16	*Monaco*	16	3	16	3

PEDRO, Rodriguez (F) 233 65
H: 5 7 W: 10 01 b.Santa Cruz de Tenerife 28-7-87
Internationals: Spain U21, Full caps.

2007–08	Barcelona	2	0		
2008–09	Barcelona	6	0		
2009–10	Barcelona	34	12		
2010–11	Barcelona	33	13		
2011–12	Barcelona	29	5		
2012–13	Barcelona	28	7		
2013–14	Barcelona	37	15		
2014–15	Barcelona	35	6	204	58
2015–16	Chelsea	29	7	29	7

PERICA, Stipe (F) 45 14
H: 6 3 b.Zadar 7-7-95
Internationals: Croatia U19, U20, U21.

2012–13	Zadar	20	8	20	8
2013–14	Chelsea	0	0		
2013–14	*NAC Breda*	25	6	25	6
2014–15	*NAC*	0	0		
2014–15	*Udinese*	0	0		
2015–16	Chelsea	0	0		

PIAZON, Lucas (M) 64 14
H: 6 0 W: 11 11 b.Curitiba 20-1-94
Internationals: Brazil U15, U17, U20, U23.

2011–12	Chelsea	0	0		
2012–13	Chelsea	1	0		
2012–13	*Malaga*	11	0	11	0
2013–14	Chelsea	0	0		
2013–14	*Vitesse*	29	11		
2014–15	Chelsea	0	0		
2014–15	*Vitesse*	0	0	29	11
2014–15	*Eintracht Frankfurt*	0	0		
2015–16	Chelsea	0	0	1	0
2015–16	*Reading*	23	3	23	3

RAMIRES (M) 273 37
H: 5 11 W: 10 03 b.Rio de Janeiro 24-3-87
Internationals: Brazil U23, Full caps.

2006	Joinville	14	3	14	3
2007	Cruzeiro	32	3		
2008	Cruzeiro	25	6		
2009	Cruzeiro	4	1	61	10
2009–10	Benfica	26	4	26	4
2010–11	Chelsea	29	2		
2011–12	Chelsea	30	5		
2012–13	Chelsea	35	5		
2013–14	Chelsea	30	1		
2014–15	Chelsea	23	2		
2015–16	Chelsea	12	2	159	17
2015–16	*Jiangsu Suning*	13	3	13	3

REMY, Loic (F) 238 83
H: 6 0 W: 10 04 b.Lyon 2-1-87
Internationals: France U20, U21, Full caps.

2006–07	Lyon	6	0		
2007–08	Lyon	6	0	12	0
2007–08	*Lens*	10	3	10	3
2008–09	Nice	32	10		
2009–10	Nice	34	14		
2010–11	Nice	2	1	68	25
2010–11	Marseille	31	15		
2011–12	Marseille	29	11		
2012–13	Marseille	14	1	74	27
2012–13	QPR	14	6		
2013–14	QPR	14	6		
2013–14	*Newcastle U*	26	14	26	14
2014–15	QPR	2	0	16	6
2014–15	Chelsea	19	7		
2015–16	Chelsea	13	1	32	8

RODRIGUEZ, Joao (F) 10 0
b.Cali 12-5-96
Internationals: Colombia U17, U20.

2014–15	Univ Autonoma	0	0	
2014–15	Bastia	0	0	
2014–15	Chelsea	0	0	
2015–16	Chelsea	0	0	
2015–16	*St. Truidense*	10	0	10 0

SALAH, Mohamed (M) 141 39
H: 5 9 W: 11 04 b.Basion 15-6-92
Internationals: Egypt U20, U23, Full caps

2010–11	Al-Mokawloon	21	4	
2011–12	Al-Mokawloon	15	7	36 11
2012–13	Basle	29	5	
2013–14	Basle	18	4	47 9
2013–14	Chelsea	10	2	
2014–15	Chelsea	3	0	
2014–15	*Fiorentina*	16	6	16 6
2015–16	Chelsea	0	0	13 2
2015–16	*Roma*	29	11	29 11

SOLANKE, Dominic (F) 25 7
H: 6 1 W: 11 11 b.Reading 14-9-97
Internationals: England U16, U17, U18, U19, U21.

2014–15	Chelsea	0	0	
2015–16	Chelsea	0	0	
2015–16	*Vitesse*	25	7	25 7

SWIFT, John (M) 49 9
H: 6 0 W: 11 07 b.Portsmouth 23-6-95
Internationals: England U16, U17, U18, U19, U20, U21.

2013–14	Chelsea	1	0	
2014–15	Chelsea	0	0	
2014–15	*Rotherham U*	3	0	3 0
2014–15	*Swindon T*	18	2	18 2
2015–16	Chelsea	0	0	1 0
2015–16	*Brentford*	27	7	27 7

TERRY, John (D) 489 40
H: 6 1 W: 14 02 b.Barking 7-12-80
Internationals: England U21, Full caps.

1997–98	Chelsea	0	0	
1998–99	Chelsea	2	0	
1999–2000	Chelsea	4	0	
1999–2000	*Nottingham F*	6	0	6 0
2000–01	Chelsea	22	1	
2001–02	Chelsea	33	1	
2002–03	Chelsea	20	3	
2003–04	Chelsea	33	2	
2004–05	Chelsea	36	3	
2005–06	Chelsea	36	4	
2006–07	Chelsea	28	1	
2007–08	Chelsea	23	1	
2008–09	Chelsea	35	1	
2009–10	Chelsea	37	2	
2010–11	Chelsea	33	3	
2011–12	Chelsea	31	6	
2012–13	Chelsea	14	4	
2013–14	Chelsea	34	2	
2014–15	Chelsea	38	5	
2015–16	Chelsea	24	1	483 40

TOMORI, Fikayo (D) 1 0
b. 19-12-97
Internationals: England U19. Canada U20.

2015–16	Chelsea	1	0	1 0

TRAORE, Bertrand (M) 58 19
H: 5 10 W: 12 00 b.Bob-Dioulasso 6-9-95
Internationals: Burkina Faso U20, Full caps

2013–14	Chelsea	0	0	
2013–14	*Vitesse*	15	3	
2014–15	Chelsea	0	0	
2014–15	*Vitesse*	33	14	48 17
2015–16	Chelsea	10	2	10 2

VAN GINKEL, Marco (M) 145 27
H: 6 1 W: 12 11 b.Amersfoort 1-12-92
Internationals: Netherlands U15, U19, U21, Full caps

2009–10	Vitesse	3	0	
2010–11	Vitesse	26	5	
2011–12	Vitesse	34	5	
2012–13	Vitesse	33	8	96 18
2013–14	Chelsea	2	0	
2014–15	Chelsea	0	0	
2014–15	*AC Milan*	17	1	17 1
2015–16	Chelsea	0	0	2 0
2015–16	*Stoke C*	17	0	17 0
2015–16	*PSV*	13	8	13 8

WILLIAN, da Silva (M) 232 32
H: 5 9 W: 11 10 b.Ribeirao 9-8-88
Internationals: Brazil U20, Full caps.

2006	Corinthians	5	0	
2007	Corinthians	0	0	5 0
2008–09	Shakhtar Donetsk	29	5	
2009–10	Shakhtar Donetsk	22	5	
2010–11	Shakhtar Donetsk	28	3	
2011–12	Shakhtar Donetsk	27	5	
2012–13	Shakhtar Donetsk	14	2	120 20
2012–13	Anzhi Makhachkala	7	1	
2013–14	Anzhi Makhachkala	4	0	11 1
2013–14	Chelsea	25	4	
2014–15	Chelsea	36	2	
2015–16	Chelsea	35	5	96 11

ZOUMA, Kurt (D) 99 4
H: 6 2 W: 13 04 b.Lyon 27-10-94
Internationals: France U16, U17, U19, U20, U21, Full caps.

2011–12	St Etienne	20	1	
2012–13	St Etienne	18	2	
2013–14	St Etienne	0	0	
2013–14	*St Etienne*	23	0	61 3
2014–15	Chelsea	15	0	
2015–16	Chelsea	23	1	38 1

Players retained or with point of contract
Ali, Mukhtar Abdullahi; Angban, Bekanty Victorien; Christie-Davies, Isaac David; Collins, Bradley Ray; Conroy, Dion John; Cuevas Jara, Cristian Alejandro; Dabo, Sheik Mohamed Fankaty; Dasilva, Jay Rhys; Delac, Matej; Grant, Joshua; Maddox, Jacob; Mitchell, Reece Steven; Mount, Mason; Muheim, Miro Max Maria; Musonda, Charles; Oliveira Dos Santos, Wallace; Quintero Quintero, Josimar Aldair; Rodriguez Ledesma, Pedro Eliezer; Sammut, Ruben; Scott, Kyle; Suljic, Ali; Thompson, Jared; Ugbo, Ike; Wakefield, Charlie Mark.

Scholars
Baxter, Nathan; Chalobah, Trevoh Tom; Colley, Joseph; Dasilva, Cole Perry; Hinckson-Mars, Malakai Daylan; McCormick, Luke; Nartey, Richard Nicos Tettey; St Clair, Harvey.

CHESTERFIELD (25)

ARIYIBI, Gboly (M) 59 3
H: 6 0 W: 11 05 b.West Virginia 18-1-95
Internationals: USA U20, U23.

2013–14	Leeds U	2	0	2 0
2013–14	*Tranmere R*	2	0	2 0
2014–15	Chesterfield	17	1	
2015–16	Chesterfield	38	2	55 3

BANKS, Oliver (D) 85 10
H: 6 3 W: 11 11 b.Rotherham 21-9-92

2010–11	Rotherham U	1	1	
2011–12	Rotherham U	0	0	1 1
2013–14	Chesterfield	25	7	
2014–15	Chesterfield	24	0	
2014–15	*Northampton T*	3	0	3 0
2015–16	Chesterfield	32	2	81 9

BEESLEY, Jake (F) 0 0
H: 6 1 W: 10 08 b.Sheffield 2-12-96

2013–14	Chesterfield	0	0
2014–15	Chesterfield	0	0
2015–16	Chesterfield	0	0

CHAPMAN, Aaron (G) 8 0
H: 6 8 W: 14 07 b.Rotherham 29-5-90

2013–14	Chesterfield	0	0	
2014–15	Chesterfield	0	0	
2014–15	*Accrington S*	3	0	3 0
2015–16	Chesterfield	0	0	
2015–16	*Bristol R*	5	0	5 0

DALEY, Derek (M) 1 0
b.Limerick 25-8-97

2015–16	Chesterfield	1	0	1 0

DENNIS, Kristian (F) 4 1
H: 5 11 W: 11 00 b.Macclesfield 12-3-90

2007–08	Macclesfield T	1	0	
2008–09	Macclesfield T	3	1	
2009–10	Macclesfield T	0	0	4 1

From Woodley Sports, Mossley, Curzon Ashton, Stockport Co.

2015–16	Chesterfield	0	0

DIESERUWVE, Emmanuel (F) 39 1
H: 6 5 W: 11 05 b.Leeds 5-1-94

2013–14	Sheffield W	0	0	
2013–14	*Fleetwood T*	4	0	4 0
2014–15	Sheffield W	0	0	
2014–15	*Chesterfield*	9	0	
2015–16	Chesterfield	16	0	25 0
2015–16	*Mansfield T*	10	1	10 1

DIMAIO, Connor (D) 14 1
H: 5 10 W: 11 05 b.Chesterfield 28-1-96
Internationals: Republic of Ireland U16, U17, U19.

2013–14	Sheffield U	3	0	
2014–15	Sheffield U	0	0	
2015–16	Sheffield U	0	0	3 0
2015–16	Chesterfield	11	1	11 1

DONOHUE, Dion (D) 17 0
H: 5 11 W: 10 06 b.Bodedern 26-8-93

2015–16	Chesterfield	17	0	17 0

EBANKS-BLAKE, Sylvan (F) 294 93
H: 5 10 W: 13 04 b.Cambridge 29-3-86
Internationals: England U21.

2004–05	Manchester U	0	0	
2005–06	Manchester U	0	0	
2006–07	Plymouth Arg	41	10	
2007–08	Plymouth Arg	25	11	66 21
2007–08	Wolverhampton W	20	12	
2008–09	Wolverhampton W	41	25	
2009–10	Wolverhampton W	23	2	
2010–11	Wolverhampton W	30	7	
2011–12	Wolverhampton W	23	1	
2012–13	Wolverhampton W	40	14	177 61
2013–14	Ipswich T	9	0	9 0
2014–15	Preston NE	9	1	9 1
2015–16	Chesterfield	33	10	33 10

EVATT, Ian (D) 483 21
H: 6 3 W: 13 12 b.Coventry 19-11-81

1998–99	Derby Co	0	0	
1999–2000	Derby Co	0	0	
2000–01	Derby Co	1	0	
2001–02	*Northampton T*	11	0	11 0
2001–02	Derby Co	3	0	
2002–03	Derby Co	30	0	34 0
2003–04	Chesterfield	43	5	
2004–05	Chesterfield	41	4	
2005–06	QPR	27	0	
2006–07	QPR	0	0	27 0
2006–07	Blackpool	44	0	
2007–08	Blackpool	29	0	
2008–09	Blackpool	33	1	
2009–10	Blackpool	36	4	
2010–11	Blackpool	38	1	
2011–12	Blackpool	39	3	
2012–13	Blackpool	11	0	230 9
2013–14	Chesterfield	35	1	
2014–15	Chesterfield	39	1	
2015–16	Chesterfield	23	0	181 12

GARDNER, Dan (M) 75 10
H: 6 1 W: 12 05 b.Manchester 5-4-90

2009–10	Crewe Alex	2	0	2 0

From Droylsden, FC Halifax T

2013–14	Chesterfield	16	3	
2014–15	Chesterfield	17	1	
2014–15	*Tranmere R*	4	2	4 2
2015–16	Chesterfield	30	4	63 8
2015–16	*Bury*	6	0	6 0

HARRISON, Byron (F) 188 42
H: 6 3 W: 13 02 b.Wandsworth 15-6-87

2010–11	Stevenage	20	8	
2011–12	Stevenage	18	2	
2011–12	AFC Wimbledon	3	0	
2012–13	AFC Wimbledon	21	8	40 10
2012–13	Cheltenham T	17	1	
2013–14	Cheltenham T	46	13	
2014–15	Cheltenham T	23	4	86 18
2014–15	Chesterfield	12	1	
2015–16	Chesterfield	3	0	15 1
2015–16	*Stevenage*	9	3	47 13

HERD, Chris (M) 99 7
H: 5 9 W: 11 04 b.Perth 4-4-89
Internationals: Australia U20, Full caps.

2007–08	Aston Villa	0	0	
2007–08	*Port Vale*	11	2	11 2
2007–08	*Wycombe W*	4	0	4 0
2008–09	Aston Villa	0	0	
2009–10	Aston Villa	0	0	
2009–10	*Lincoln C*	20	4	20 4
2010–11	Aston Villa	6	0	
2011–12	Aston Villa	19	1	
2012–13	Aston Villa	9	0	
2013–14	Aston Villa	2	0	
2014–15	Aston Villa	0	0	36 1
2014–15	*Bolton W*	2	0	2 0
2014–15	*Wigan Ath*	3	0	3 0
2015–16	Chesterfield	23	0	23 0

HIRD, Samuel (D) 306 10
H: 5 7 W: 10 12 b.Askern 7-9-87

2005–06	Leeds U	0	0
2006–07	Leeds U	0	0
2006–07	*Doncaster R*	5	0

2007–08 Doncaster R 4 0
2007–08 *Grimsby T* 17 0 17 0
2008–09 Doncaster R 37 1
2009–10 Doncaster R 36 0
2010–11 Doncaster R 32 0
2011–12 Doncaster R 31 0 145 1
2012–13 Chesterfield 41 2
2013–14 Chesterfield 35 2
2014–15 Chesterfield 28 3
2015–16 Chesterfield 40 2 144 9

HUMPHREYS, Richie (M) 641 47
H: 5 11 W: 12 07 b.Sheffield 30-11-77
Internationals: England U20, U21.
1995–96 Sheffield W 5 0
1996–97 Sheffield W 29 3
1997–98 Sheffield W 7 0
1998–99 Sheffield W 19 1
1999–2000 Sheffield W
1999–2000 *Scunthorpe U* 6 2 6 2
1999–2000 *Cardiff C* 9 2 9 2
2000–01 Sheffield W 7 0 67 4
2000–01 Cambridge U 7 3 7 3
2001–02 Hartlepool U 46 5
2002–03 Hartlepool U 46 11
2003–04 Hartlepool U 46 3
2004–05 Hartlepool U 46 3
2005–06 Hartlepool U 46 2
2006–07 Hartlepool U 38 3
2006–07 Port Vale 7 0 7 0
2007–08 Hartlepool U 45 3
2008–09 Hartlepool U 45 0
2009–10 Hartlepool U 38 0
2010–11 Hartlepool U 25 2
2011–12 Hartlepool U 29 1
2012–13 Hartlepool U 31 1 481 34
2013–14 Chesterfield 42 2
2014–15 Chesterfield 19 0
2015–16 Chesterfield 3 0 64 2

JONES, Daniel (D) 215 6
H: 6 2 W: 13 00 b.Rowley Regis 14-7-86
2005–06 Wolverhampton W 1 0
2006–07 Wolverhampton W 8 0
2007–08 Wolverhampton W 0 0
2007–08 *Northampton T* 33 3 33 3
2008–09 Wolverhampton W 0 0
2008–09 *Oldham Ath* 23 1 23 1
2009–10 Wolverhampton W 0 0 10 0
2009–10 *Notts Co* 7 0 7 0
2009–10 *Bristol R* 17 0 17 0
2010–11 Sheffield W 25 0
2011–12 Sheffield W 3 0
2012–13 Sheffield W 9 0 37 0
2012–13 Port Vale 16 1
2013–14 Port Vale 20 0 36 1
2014–15 Chesterfield 33 0
2015–16 Chesterfield 19 1 52 1

LEE, Tommy (G) 395 0
H: 6 2 W: 12 00 b.Keighley 3-1-86
2005–06 Manchester U 0 0
2005–06 *Macclesfield T* 11 0
2006–07 Macclesfield T 34 0
2007–08 Macclesfield T 18 0 63 0
2007–08 *Rochdale* 11 0 11 0
2008–09 Chesterfield 28 0
2009–10 Chesterfield 42 0
2010–11 Chesterfield 46 0
2011–12 Chesterfield 35 0
2012–13 Chesterfield 32 0
2013–14 Chesterfield 46 0
2014–15 Chesterfield 46 0
2015–16 Chesterfield 46 0 321 0

LIDDLE, Gary (D) 401 25
H: 6 1 W: 12 06 b.Middlesbrough 15-6-86
2003–04 Middlesbrough 0 0
2004–05 Middlesbrough 0 0
2005–06 Middlesbrough 0 0
2006–07 Hartlepool U 42 3
2007–08 Hartlepool U 41 2
2008–09 Hartlepool U 43 0
2009–10 Hartlepool U 40 3
2010–11 Hartlepool U 42 6
2011–12 Hartlepool U 39 4 247 18
2012–13 Notts Co 46 0
2013–14 Notts Co 32 4 78 4
2014–15 Bradford C 41 1
2015–16 Bradford C 20 2 61 3
2015–16 Chesterfield 15 0 15 0

MAGUIRE, Laurence (D) 0 0
H: 5 10 W: 11 00 b.Sheffield 8-2-97
2013–14 Chesterfield 0 0
2014–15 Chesterfield 0 0
2015–16 Chesterfield 0 0

MARTINEZ, Angel (M) 209 10
H: 5 9 W: 11 13 b.Girona 31-1-86
Internationals: Spain U19, U21.
2006–07 Espanyol B 27 5 27 5
2006–07 Espanyol 7 0
2007–08 Espanyol 28 2
2008–09 Espanyol 15 0 50 2
2009–10 Rayo Vallecano 27 2 27 2
2010–11 Girona 36 0 36 0
2011–12 Blackpool 15 1
2012–13 Blackpool 21 0
2013–14 Blackpool 26 0 62 1
2014–15 Millwall 4 0 4 0
2015–16 Chesterfield 3 0 3 0

O'NEIL, Liam (D) 65 2
H: 6 0 W: 12 06 b.Cambridge 31-7-93
2011–12 WBA 0 0
2011–12 *VPS* 14 0 14 0
2012–13 WBA 0 0
2013–14 WBA 3 0
2014–15 WBA 0 0 3 0
2014–15 *Scunthorpe U* 22 2 22 2
2015–16 Chesterfield 26 0 26 0

O'SHEA, Jay (M) 280 54
H: 5 9 W: 12 00 b.Dun Laoghaire 10-8-88
Internationals: Republic of Ireland U19, U21, U23.
2007 Bray Wanderers 27 4 27 4
2008 Galway U 29 8
2009 Galway U 19 3 48 11
2009–10 Birmingham C 1 0
2009–10 *Middlesbrough* 2 0 2 0
2010–11 Birmingham C 0 0 1 0
2010–11 *Stevenage* 5 0 5 0
2010–11 *Port Vale* 5 1 5 1
2011–12 Milton Keynes D 28 5
2012–13 Milton Keynes D 11 1 39 6
2012–13 *Chesterfield* 26 7
2013–14 Chesterfield 40 9
2014–15 Chesterfield 41 7
2015–16 Chesterfield 46 9 153 32

ONOVWIGUN, Michael (M) 2 0
H: 6 2 W: 13 01 b.Clapham 9-4-96
2014–15 Chesterfield 0 0
2015–16 Chesterfield 0 0 2 0

ORRELL, Jake (F) 2 0
H: 5 4 W: 9 00 b.Sunderland 17-7-97
From Gateshead.
2015–16 Chesterfield 2 0 2 0

RAGLAN, Charlie (D) 45 1
H: 6 0 W: 11 13 b.Wythenshawe 28-4-93
2011–12 Port Vale 0 0
2012–13 Port Vale 0 0
2013–14 Port Vale 0 0
2014–15 Chesterfield 18 1
2015–16 Chesterfield 27 0 45 1

SIMONS, Rai (F) 20 4
H: 6 0 W: 11 05 b. 11-1-96
Internationals: Bermuda U17, U20, Full caps.
From Newcastle T, Ilkeston.
2015–16 Chesterfield 20 4 20 4

SLEW, Jordan (F) 90 7
H: 6 3 W: 12 11 b.Sheffield 7-9-92
Internationals: England U19.
2010–11 Sheffield U 7 2
2011–12 Sheffield U 4 1 11 3
2011–12 Blackburn R 1 0
2011–12 *Stevenage* 9 0 9 0
2012–13 Blackburn R 0 0
2012–13 *Oldham Ath* 3 0 3 0
2012–13 *Rotherham U* 7 0 7 0
2013–14 Blackburn R 0 0
2013–14 *Ross Co* 20 1 20 1
2014–15 Blackburn R 0 0 1 0
2014–15 *Port Vale* 9 2 9 2
2014–15 Cambridge 13 1
2015–16 Cambridge U 10 0 23 1
2015–16 Chesterfield 7 0 7 0

TALBOT, Drew (F) 334 23
H: 5 10 W: 11 00 b.Barnsley 19-7-86
2003–04 Sheffield W 0 0
2004–05 Sheffield W 21 4
2005–06 Sheffield W 0 0
2006–07 Sheffield W 8 0 29 4
2006–07 *Scunthorpe U* 3 1 3 1
2006–07 Luton T 15 3
2007–08 Luton T 27 0
2008–09 Luton T 7 0 49 3
2008–09 *Chesterfield* 17 2
2009–10 Chesterfield 30 6
2010–11 Chesterfield 44 3

2011–12 Chesterfield 43 2
2012–13 Chesterfield 42 2
2013–14 Chesterfield 25 0
2014–15 Chesterfield 9 0
2014–15 *Plymouth Arg* 9 0 9 0
2015–16 Chesterfield 34 0 244 15

WRIGHT, Myles (G) 1 0
b. 14-9-96
2014–15 Chesterfield 1 0
2015–16 Chesterfield 0 0 1 0

Players retained or with offer of contract
Graham, Liam Matthew.

Scholars
Brownell, Jack Thomas; Daly, Derek Kevin; Darwent, Owen; Daswell, Martell Jordan; German, Ricardo de niro; Holmes, Brad Geoff; Hudson, Jake Bevan; Jarrald, Thomas Lewis; Lynam, George David; Marshall, Thomas Francis; Milner, George Edward; Morrison, Curtis Lloyd; Parkin, Dylan Thomas; Randle, Luke; Rowley, Joe; Smith, Jay Alexander; Taylor, Harry; Thistlethwaite, Daniel.

COLCHESTER U (26)

AKINWANDE, Femi (F) 2 0
b. 1-5-96
2015–16 Colchester U 2 0 2 0

AMBROSE, Darren (M) 347 65
H: 6 0 W: 11 00 b.Harlow 29-2-84
Internationals: England U21.
2001–02 Ipswich T 1 0
2002–03 Ipswich T 29 8
2002–03 Newcastle U 1 0
2003–04 Newcastle U 24 2
2004–05 Newcastle U 12 3 37 5
2005–06 Charlton Ath 28 3
2006–07 Charlton Ath 26 3
2007–08 Charlton Ath 37 7
2008–09 Charlton Ath 21 0 112 13
2008–09 *Ipswich T* 9 0
2009–10 Crystal Palace 46 15
2010–11 Crystal Palace 28 7
2011–12 Crystal Palace 36 7 110 29
2012–13 Birmingham C 1 0
2013–14 Birmingham C 1 0 7 0
2013–14 *Apollon Smyrni* 11 6 11 6
2014–15 Ipswich T 6 0 45 8
2015–16 Colchester U 25 4 25 4

BARNES, Dillon (G) 0 0
H: 6 4 W: 11 11 b. 8-4-96
From Bedford T.
2015–16 Colchester U 0 0

BONNE, Macauley (F) 57 6
H: 5 11 W: 12 00 b.Ipswich 26-10-95
Internationals: Zimbabwe U23.
2013–14 Colchester U 14 2
2014–15 Colchester U 10 1
2015–16 Colchester U 33 3 57 6

BRANSGROVE, James (G) 1 0
H: 6 4 W: 12 04 b. 12-5-95
2013–14 Colchester U 0 0
2014–15 Colchester U 0 0
2015–16 Colchester U 1 0 1 0

BRIGGS, Matthew (D) 82 1
H: 6 1 W: 11 12 b.Wandsworth 6-3-91
Internationals: England U16, U17, U19, U20, U21. Guyana Full caps.
2006–07 Fulham 1 0
2007–08 Fulham 0 0
2008–09 Fulham 0 0
2009–10 Fulham 0 0
2009–10 *Leyton Orient* 1 0 1 0
2010–11 Fulham 3 0
2011–12 Fulham 2 0
2011–12 *Peterborough U* 5 0 5 0
2012–13 Fulham 5 0
2012–13 *Bristol C* 4 0 4 0
2012–13 *Watford* 7 1 7 1
2013–14 Fulham 2 0 13 0
2014–15 Millwall 8 0 8 0
2014–15 *Colchester U* 18 0
2015–16 Colchester U 26 0 44 0

BRINDLEY, Richard (D) 65 1
H: 5 10 W: 11 09 b.Coventry 30-11-87
2012–13 Chesterfield 12 0 12 0
2013–14 Rotherham U 16 0
2014–15 Rotherham U 0 0 18 0
2014–15 *Scunthorpe U* 3 0 3 0

2014–15	Oxford U	3	0	3	0
2014–15	Colchester U	8	0		
2015–16	Colchester U	21	1	29	1

CURTIS, Jack (M) 0 0
H: 5 7 W: 11 00 b. 11-9-95

2013–14	Colchester U	0	0		
2014–15	Colchester U	0	0		
2015–16	Colchester U	0	0		

DUNNE, Louis (M) 2 0
b.Waltham Forest 7-9-98

2015–16	Colchester U	2	0	2	0

EASTMAN, Tom (D) 195 8
H: 6 3 W: 13 12 b.Clacton 21-10-91

2009–10	Ipswich T	1	0		
2010–11	Ipswich T	9	0	10	0
2011–12	Colchester U	25	3		
2011–12	Crawley T	6	0	6	0
2012–13	Colchester U	29	2		
2013–14	Colchester U	36	0		
2014–15	Colchester U	46	1		
2015–16	Colchester U	43	2	179	8

EDWARDS, Joe (D) 165 6
H: 5 8 W: 11 07 b.Gloucester 31-10-90

2009–10	Bristol C	0	0		
2010–11	Bristol C	2	0		
2011–12	Bristol C	2	0		
2011–12	Yeovil T	4	1		
2012–13	Bristol C	0	0	4	0
2012–13	Yeovil T	35	2		
2013–14	Yeovil T	46	1		
2014–15	Yeovil T	34	0	119	4
2015–16	Colchester U	42	2	42	2

ELOKOBI, George (D) 183 9
H: 5 10 W: 13 02 b.Cameroon 31-1-86

2004–05	Colchester U	0	0		
2004–05	Chester C	5	0	5	0
2005–06	Colchester U	12	1		
2006–07	Colchester U	10	0		
2007–08	Colchester U	17	1		
2007–08	Wolverhampton W	15	0		
2008–09	Wolverhampton W	4	0		
2009–10	Wolverhampton W	22	0		
2010–11	Wolverhampton W	27	2		
2011–12	Wolverhampton W	9	0		
2011–12	Nottingham F	12	0	12	0
2012–13	Wolverhampton W	2	0		
2012–13	Bristol C	1	0	1	0
2013–14	Wolverhampton W	6	0	85	2
2014–15	Oldham Ath	24	3	24	3
2015–16	Colchester U	17	2	56	4

GARVAN, Owen (M) 289 24
H: 6 0 W: 10 07 b.Dublin 29-1-88
Internationals: Republic of Ireland U21.

2005–06	Ipswich T	32	3		
2006–07	Ipswich T	27	1		
2007–08	Ipswich T	43	2		
2008–09	Ipswich T	37	7		
2009–10	Ipswich T	25	0	164	13
2010–11	Crystal Palace	26	3		
2011–12	Crystal Palace	22	3		
2012–13	Crystal Palace	27	4		
2013–14	Crystal Palace	2	0		
2013–14	Millwall	13	0	13	0
2014–15	Crystal Palace	0	0	77	10
2014–15	Bolton W	3	0	3	0
2015–16	Colchester U	32	1	32	1

GILBEY, Alex (M) 110 7
H: 6 0 W: 11 07 b.Dagenham 9-12-94

2011–12	Colchester U	0	0		
2012–13	Colchester U	3	0		
2013–14	Colchester U	36	1		
2014–15	Colchester U	34	1		
2015–16	Colchester U	37	5	110	7

HARNEY, Jamie (D) 5 0
b. 4-3-96
Internationals: Northern Ireland U16, U17, U19, U20, U21.

2014–15	Colchester U	1	0		
2015–16	Colchester U	4	0	5	0

HARRISON, Callum (D) 0 0
b. 19-3-97

2015–16	Colchester U	0	0		

JAMES, Cameron (D) 1 0
H: 6 0 W: 12 00 b.Chelmsford 11-2-98

2015–16	Colchester U	1	0	1	0

KENT, Frankie (D) 37 0
H: 6 2 W: 12 00 b.Romford 21-11-95

2013–14	Colchester U	1	0		
2014–15	Colchester U	10	0		
2015–16	Colchester U	26	0	37	0

LAPSLIE, Tom (M) 21 2
H: 5 6 W: 10 12 b. 5-5-95

2013–14	Colchester U	0	0		
2014–15	Colchester U	11	1		
2015–16	Colchester U	10	1	21	2

MASSEY, Gavin (F) 189 23
H: 5 11 W: 11 06 b.Watford 14-10-92

2009–10	Watford	1	0		
2010–11	Watford	3	0		
2011–12	Watford	3	0		
2011–12	Yeovil T	16	3	16	3
2011–12	Colchester U	8	0		
2012–13	Watford	0	0	7	0
2012–13	Colchester U	40	6		
2013–14	Colchester U	30	3		
2014–15	Colchester U	46	7		
2015–16	Colchester U	42	4	166	20

MONCUR, George (M) 108 23
H: 5 9 W: 10 00 b.Swindon 18-8-93
Internationals: England U18.

2010–11	West Ham U	0	0		
2011–12	West Ham U	0	0		
2011–12	AFC Wimbledon	20	2	20	2
2012–13	West Ham U	0	0		
2013–14	West Ham U	0	0		
2013–14	*Partick Thistle*	2	1	2	1
2014–15	Colchester U	41	8		
2015–16	Colchester U	45	12	86	20

O'DONOGHUE, Michael (D) 1 0
H: 5 11 W: 11 00 b.Islington 18-1-96

2013–14	Colchester U	0	0		
2014–15	Colchester U	1	0		
2015–16	Colchester U	0	0	1	0

OLUFEMI, Tosin (M) 24 0
H: 5 8 W: 10 13 b.Hackney 13-5-94

2012–13	Colchester U	1	0		
2013–14	Colchester U	13	0		
2014–15	Colchester U	0	0		
2015–16	Colchester U	10	0	24	0

PARISH, Elliot (G) 75 0
H: 6 2 W: 13 00 b.Towcester 20-5-90
Internationals: England U20.

2008–09	Aston Villa	0	0		
2009–10	Aston Villa	0	0		
2010–11	Aston Villa	0	0		
2010–11	Lincoln C	9	0	9	0
2011–12	Aston Villa	0	0		
2011–12	Cardiff C	0	0		
2012–13	Wycombe W	2	0	2	0
2012–13	Cardiff C	0	0		
2013–14	Bristol C	19	0	19	0
2013–14	Newport Co	7	0	7	0
2014–15	Blackpool	13	0	13	0
2015–16	Colchester U	25	0	25	0

PORTER, Chris (F) 389 109
H: 6 1 W: 12 09 b.Wigan 12-12-83

2002–03	Bury	0	0		
2003–04	Bury	37	9		
2004–05	Bury	32	9	71	18
2005–06	Oldham Ath	31	7		
2006–07	Oldham Ath	35	21	66	28
2007–08	Motherwell	37	14		
2008–09	Motherwell	22	9	59	23
2008–09	Derby Co	5	3		
2009–10	Derby Co	21	4		
2010–11	Derby Co	18	2	44	9
2011–12	Sheffield U	34	5		
2012–13	Sheffield U	21	4		
2012–13	Shrewsbury T	5	1	5	1
2013–14	Sheffield U	32	7		
2013–14	Chesterfield	3	0	3	0
2014–15	Sheffield U	1	0	88	16
2014–15	Colchester U	21	7		
2015–16	Colchester U	32	7	53	14

SEMBIE-FERRIS, Dion (F) 18 0
H: 5 8 W: 11 00 b.Peterborough 23-5-96

2013–14	Colchester U	0	0		
2014–15	Colchester U	10	0		
2015–16	Colchester U	8	0	18	0

SHOREY, Nicky (D) 464 12
H: 5 9 W: 10 08 b.Romford 19-2-81
Internationals: England B, Full caps.

1999–2000	Leyton Orient	7	0		
2000–01	Leyton Orient	8	0	15	0
2000–01	Reading	0	0		
2001–02	Reading	32	0		
2002–03	Reading	43	2		
2003–04	Reading	35	2		
2004–05	Reading	44	3		
2005–06	Reading	40	2		
2006–07	Reading	37	1		
2007–08	Reading	36	2		
2008–09	Aston Villa	21	0		
2009–10	Aston Villa	3	0	24	0
2009–10	Nottingham F	9	0	9	0
2009–10	Fulham	9	0	9	0
2011–12	WBA	28	0		
2011–12	WBA	25	0	53	0
2012–13	Reading	17	0	284	12
2013–14	Bristol C	14	0	14	0
2013–14	Portsmouth	21	0		
2014–15	Portsmouth	20	0	41	0
2015–16	Colchester U	15	0	15	0

SORDELL, Marvin (F) 177 37
H: 5 9 W: 12 06 b.Pinner 17-2-91
Internationals: England U20, U21. Great Britain.

2009–10	Watford	6	1		
2009–10	Tranmere R	8	1	8	1
2010–11	Watford	43	12		
2011–12	Watford	26	8	75	21
2011–12	Bolton W	3	0		
2012–13	Bolton W	22	4		
2013–14	Bolton W	0	0	25	4
2013–14	Charlton Ath	31	7	31	7
2014–15	Burnley	14	0		
2015–16	Burnley	3	0	17	0
2015–16	Colchester U	21	4	21	4

SZMIDICS, Sammie (M) 43 4
H: 5 6 W: 10 01 b.Colchester 24-9-95

2013–14	Colchester U	7	0		
2014–15	Colchester U	31	4		
2015–16	Colchester U	5	0	43	4

VINCENT-YOUNG, Kane (D) 14 0
H: 5 11 W: 11 00 b.Camden Town 15-3-96

2014–15	Colchester U	0	0		
2015–16	Colchester U	14	0	14	0

WALKER, Sam (G) 169 0
H: 6 5 W: 14 00 b.Gravesend 2-10-91

2009–10	Chelsea	0	0		
2010–11	Chelsea	0	0		
2010–11	Barnet	7	0	7	0
2011–12	Chelsea	0	0		
2011–12	Northampton T	21	0	21	0
2011–12	Yeovil T	20	0	20	0
2012–13	Chelsea	0	0		
2012–13	Bristol R	11	0	11	0
2012–13	Colchester U	19	0		
2013–14	Colchester U	46	0		
2014–15	Colchester U	45	0		
2015–16	Colchester U	0	0	110	0

WRIGHT, Drey (M) 48 3
H: 5 9 W: 10 11 b.Greenwich 30-4-94

2012–13	Colchester U	21	3		
2013–14	Colchester U	11	0		
2014–15	Colchester U	5	0		
2015–16	Colchester U	11	0	48	3

WYNTER, Alex (M) 46 1
H: 6 0 W: 13 04 b.Camberwell 15-9-93

2009–10	Crystal Palace	0	0		
2010–11	Crystal Palace	0	0		
2011–12	Crystal Palace	0	0		
2012–13	Crystal Palace	0	0		
2013–14	Crystal Palace	0	0		
2013–14	Colchester U	6	1		
2014–15	Crystal Palace	0	0		
2014–15	Portsmouth	10	0	10	0
2015–16	Colchester U	18	0		
2015–16	Colchester U	12	0	36	1

Players retained or with offer of contract
Edge, Charley Joseph; Issa, Tariq Ahmed; James, Cameron Lewis; Regis, Christopher; Wyatt, Ben.

Scholars
Boness, Danny Michael; Brown, George Alan; Clampin, Ryan; Cosgrave, Aaron Haruna Omar Martin; Debrick, Ross Francis Okorie; Moore, Joshua Alexander; Mulryne, Jake; Ogbodu-Wilson, Osase Junior John; Partridge, Jacob Joseph; Pollard, Joshua Kelly; Robinson, Callum; Sheriff, De-Carrey Deavon; Stephens, Jamie Jack; Syrett, Josce; Tennent, Joe Stephen; Wright, Diaz Ray.

COVENTRY C (27)

ADDAI, Corey (G) 0 0
b. 10-10-97

Season	Club				
2015–16	Coventry C	0	0		

BURGE, Lee (G) 27 0
H: 5 11 W: 11 00 b.Hereford 9-1-93

2011–12	Coventry C	0	0		
2012–13	Coventry C	0	0		
2013–14	Coventry C	0	0		
2014–15	Coventry C	18	0		
2015–16	Coventry C	9	0	27	0

CHARLES-COOK, Reice (G) 39 0
H: 6 1 W: 12 08 b.London 8-4-94

2013–14	Bury	2	0	2	0
2014–15	Coventry C	0	0		
2015–16	Coventry C	37	0	37	0

COLE, Joe (M) 431 52
H: 5 9 W: 11 09 b.Camden 8-11-81
Internationals: England U16, U18, U21, B, Full caps.

1998–99	West Ham U	8	0		
1999–2000	West Ham U	22	1		
2000–01	West Ham U	30	5		
2001–02	West Ham U	30	0		
2002–03	West Ham U	36	4		
2003–04	Chelsea	35	1		
2004–05	Chelsea	28	8		
2005–06	Chelsea	34	7		
2006–07	Chelsea	13	0		
2007–08	Chelsea	33	7		
2008–09	Chelsea	14	2		
2009–10	Chelsea	26	2	183	27
2010–11	Liverpool	20	2		
2011–12	Liverpool	0	0		
2011–12	Lille	31	4	31	4
2012–13	Liverpool	6	1	26	3
2012–13	West Ham U	11	2		
2013–14	West Ham U	20	3	157	15
2014–15	Aston Villa	12	1		
2015–16	Aston Villa	0	0	12	1
2015–16	Coventry C	22	2	22	2

ELFORD-ALLIYU, Lateef (F) 80 23
H: 5 8 W: 10 12 b.Ibadan 1-6-92
Internationals: England U17.

2009–10	WBA	0	0		
2009–10	Hereford U	1	0	1	0
2010–11	WBA	0	0		
2010–11	Tranmere R	16	5		
2011–12	WBA	0	0		
2011–12	Tranmere R	4	0	20	5
2011–12	Bury	13	2		
2012–13	Bury	5	0	18	2
2012–13	Crawley T	6	0	6	0
2013–14	Valletta	9	3		
2014–15	Valletta	26	13	35	16
2015–16	Coventry C	0	0		

FINCH, Jack (M) 16 0
H: 6 1 W: 12 02 b.Southam 6-8-96

2013–14	Coventry C	0	0		
2014–15	Coventry C	16	0		
2015–16	Coventry C	0	0	16	0

FLECK, John (M) 210 10
H: 5 9 W: 11 05 b.Glasgow 24-8-91
Internationals: Scotland U17, U19, U21.

2007–08	Rangers	1	0		
2008–09	Rangers	8	1		
2009–10	Rangers	15	1		
2010–11	Rangers	13	0		
2011–12	Rangers	4	0	41	2
2011–12	Blackpool	7	0	7	0
2012–13	Coventry C	35	3		
2013–14	Coventry C	43	1		
2014–15	Coventry C	44	0		
2015–16	Coventry C	40	4	162	8

FORTUNE, Marc-Antoine (F) 475 85
H: 6 0 W: 11 13 b.Cayenne 2-7-81

2000–01	Angouleme	18	3		
2001–02	Angouleme	36	12	54	15
2002–03	Nancy	19	1		
2002–03	Lille	0	0	15	0
2003–04	Rouen	34	10	34	10
2004–05	Brest	33	10	33	10
2005–06	Utrecht	31	6		
2006–07	Utrecht	22	5	53	11
2006–07	Nancy	15	5		
2007–08	Nancy	37	6		
2008–09	Nancy	19	1	90	13
2009–10	Celtic	30	10		
2010–11	Celtic	2	0	32	10
2010–11	WBA	25	2		
2011–12	WBA	17	2		
2011–12	Doncaster R	5	1	5	1
2012–13	WBA	21	2	63	6
2013–14	Wigan Ath	36	4		
2014–15	Wigan Ath	35	1	71	5
2015–16	Coventry C	25	4	25	4

GADZHEV, Vladimir (M) 213 27
H: 5 10 W: 12 00 b. 18-7-87
Internationals: Bulgaria U21, Full caps.

2005–06	Panathinaikos	0	0		
2006–07	Panathinaikos	0	0		
2006–07	Levadiakos	26	5	26	5
2007–08	Panathinaikos	0	0		
2007–08	OFI Crete	19	0	19	0
2008–09	Panathinaikos	0	0		
2008–09	Levski Sofia	23	1		
2009–10	Levski Sofia	10	1		
2010–11	Levski Sofia	23	2		
2011–12	Levski Sofia	27	6		
2012–13	Levski Sofia	22	1		
2013–14	Levski Sofia	32	5		
2014–15	Levski Sofia	22	5		
2015–16	Levski Sofia	7	1	166	22
2015–16	Coventry C	2	0	2	0

HARRIES, Cian (D) 1 0
b. 1-4-97
Internationals: Wales U17, U19.

2015–16	Coventry C	1	0	1	0

HAYNES, Ryan (D) 48 1
H: 5 7 W: 10 10 b.Northampton 27-9-95

2012–13	Coventry C	1	0		
2013–14	Coventry C	2	0		
2014–15	Coventry C	26	1		
2015–16	Coventry C	9	0	38	1
2015–16	Cambridge U	10	0	10	0

HENDERSON, Darius (F) 437 116
H: 6 3 W: 14 03 b.Sutton 7-9-81

1999–2000	Reading	4	0		
2000–01	Reading	4	0		
2001–02	Reading	38	7		
2002–03	Reading	22	4		
2003–04	Reading	1	0	71	11
2003–04	Brighton & HA	10	2	10	2
2003–04	Gillingham	4	0		
2004–05	Gillingham	32	9	36	9
2004–05	Swindon T	6	5	6	5
2005–06	Watford	30	14		
2006–07	Watford	35	3		
2007–08	Watford	40	12	105	29
2008–09	Sheffield U	32	6		
2009–10	Sheffield U	32	12		
2010–11	Sheffield U	8	2	72	20
2011–12	Millwall	31	15		
2012–13	Millwall	20	7	51	22
2012–13	Nottingham F	11	2		
2013–14	Nottingham F	34	8	45	10
2014–15	Leyton Orient	23	8	23	8
2015–16	Scunthorpe U	13	0	13	0
2015–16	Coventry C	5	0	5	0

HUNT, Steve (M) 423 55
H: 5 9 W: 10 10 b.Port Laoise 1-8-80
Internationals: Republic of Ireland U21, B, Full caps.

1999–2000	Crystal Palace	3	0		
2000–01	Crystal Palace	0	0	3	0
2001–02	Brentford	35	4		
2002–03	Brentford	42	7		
2003–04	Brentford	40	11		
2004–05	Brentford	19	3	136	25
2005–06	Reading	38	2		
2006–07	Reading	35	4		
2007–08	Reading	37	5		
2008–09	Reading	46	6		
2009–10	Reading	0	0	156	17
2009–10	Hull C	27	6	27	6
2010–11	Wolverhampton W	20	3		
2011–12	Wolverhampton W	24	3		
2012–13	Wolverhampton W	12	1	56	7
2013–14	Ipswich T	23	0		
2014–15	Ipswich T	17	0		
2015–16	Ipswich T	0	0	40	0
2015–16	Coventry C	5	0	5	0

JOHNSON, Reda (D) 164 27
H: 6 2 W: 13 10 b.Marseille 21-3-88
Internationals: Benin Full caps.

2005–06	Gueugnon	0	0		
2006–07	Gueugnon	0	0		
2007–08	Amiens	8	0		
2008–09	Amiens	7	0	15	0
2009–10	Plymouth Arg	25	0		
2010–11	Plymouth Arg	17	2	42	2
2010–11	Sheffield W	16	3		
2011–12	Sheffield W	24	7		
2012–13	Sheffield W	16	6		
2013–14	Sheffield W	19	2	75	18
2014–15	Coventry C	20	5		
2015–16	Coventry C	12	2	32	7

JONES, Jodi (F) 41 4
b. 22-10-97

2014–15	Dagenham & R	8	1		
2014–15	Dagenham & R	27	3	35	4
2015–16	Coventry C	6	0	6	0

KELLY-EVANS, Dion (D) 1 0
H: 5 10 W: 12 06 b.Coventry 21-9-96

2014–15	Coventry C	0	0		
2015–16	Coventry C	1	0	1	0

LAMEIRAS, Ruben (M) 40 2
H: 5 9 W: 11 00 b.Lisbon 22-12-94

2014–15	Tottenham H	0	0		
2015	Atvidabergs	11	0	11	0
2015–16	Coventry C	29	2	29	2

LAWTON, Ivor (M) 0 0
b.Coventry 5-9-95

2013–14	Coventry C	0	0		
2014–15	Coventry C	0	0		
2015–16	Coventry C	0	0		

LORENTZSON, Martin (D) 248 18
H: 5 10 W: 11 00 b.Osteralje 21-7-84
Internationals: Sweden Full caps.

2006	Sleipner	20	2	20	2
2007	Assyriska F	21	0		
2008	Assyriska F	29	4		
2009	Assyriska F	27	1	77	5
2010	AIK Solna	14	0		
2011	AIK Solna	14	0		
2012	AIK Solna	29	4		
2013	AIK Solna	27	3		
2014	AIK Solna	28	3	127	11
2015	Atvidabergs	17	0	17	0
2015–16	Coventry C	7	0	7	0

MARTIN, Aaron (D) 112 6
H: 6 3 W: 11 13 b.Newport (IW) 29-9-89

2009–10	Southampton	2	0		
2010–11	Southampton	8	0		
2011–12	Southampton	10	1		
2012–13	Southampton	0	0		
2012–13	Crystal Palace	4	0	4	0
2012–13	Coventry C	12	0		
2013–14	Southampton	0	0	20	1
2013–14	Birmingham C	8	0	8	0
2014–15	Yeovil T	12	3	12	3
2014–15	Coventry C	27	0		
2015–16	Coventry C	29	2	68	2

O'BRIEN, Jim (F) 290 21
H: 6 0 W: 11 11 b.Alexandria 28-9-87
Internationals: Republic of Ireland U19, U21.

2006–07	Celtic	0	0		
2006–07	Dunfermline Ath	13	1	13	1
2007–08	Celtic	1	0	1	0
2007–08	Dundee U	10	0	10	0
2008–09	Motherwell	29	1		
2009–10	Motherwell	35	3	64	4
2010–11	Barnsley	33	1		
2011–12	Barnsley	31	2		
2012–13	Barnsley	30	2		
2013–14	Barnsley	29	2	123	7
2014–15	Coventry C	44	6		
2015–16	Coventry C	26	2	70	8
2015–16	Scunthorpe U	9	1	9	1

PHILLIPS, Aaron (D) 53 1
H: 5 7 W: 11 00 b.Warwick 20-11-93

2012–13	Coventry C	0	0		
2013–14	Coventry C	11	1		
2014–15	Coventry C	19	0		
2015–16	Coventry C	23	0	53	1

RAMAGE, Peter (D) 245 9
H: 6 3 W: 11 02 b.Whitley Bay 22-11-83

2003–04	Newcastle U	0	0		
2004–05	Newcastle U	4	0		
2005–06	Newcastle U	23	0		
2006–07	Newcastle U	21	0		
2007–08	Newcastle U	3	0	51	0
2008–09	QPR	31	0		
2009–10	QPR	33	2		
2010–11	QPR	4	0		
2011–12	QPR	0	0	68	2
2011–12	Crystal Palace	29	0		
2011–12	Birmingham C	14	0	14	0
2012–13	Crystal Palace	40	4		
2013–14	Crystal Palace	0	0		
2013–14	Barnsley	24	0		
2014–15	Crystal Palace	0	0	57	4
2014–15	Barnsley	19	3	43	3
2015–16	Coventry C	8	0	8	0
2015–16	Leyton Orient	8	0	8	0

RICHARDS, Jake (G)   0   0
H: 6 1   W: 11 05   b. 30-12-96
2014-15	Coventry C	0	0	
2015-16	Coventry C	0	0	

RICKETTS, Sam (D)   440   7
H: 6 1   W: 12 01   b.Aylesbury 11-10-81
Internationals: England C. Wales Full caps.
1999-2000	Oxford U	0	0		
2000-01	Oxford U	14	0		
2001-02	Oxford U	29	1		
2002-03	Oxford U	2	0	45	1
From Telford U					
2004-05	Swansea C	42	0		
2005-06	Swansea C	44	1	86	1
2006-07	Hull C	40	1		
2007-08	Hull C	44	0		
2008-09	Hull C	29	0		
2009-10	Hull C	0	0	113	1
2009-10	Bolton W	27	0		
2010-11	Bolton W	17	0		
2011-12	Bolton W	20	1		
2012-13	Bolton W	32	0	96	1
2013-14	Wolverhampton W	44	2		
2014-15	Wolverhampton W	4	0	48	2
2014-15	Swindon T	9	0	9	0
2015-16	Coventry C	43	1	43	1

ROSE, Andy (M)   103   7
H: 6 2   W: 12 02   b.Melbourne 13-2-90
2012	Seattle Sounders	25	1		
2013	Seattle Sounders	19	1		
2014	Seattle Sounders	18	3		
2015	Seattle Sounders	29	0	91	5
2015-16	Coventry C	12	2	12	2

SAMBOU, Bassala (F)   0   0
H: 6 1   W: 11 11   b. 15-10-97
2015-16	Coventry C	0	0

SAYOUD, Bilal (M)   0   0
b. 5-5-97
2015-16	Coventry C	0	0

SPENCE, Kyle (F)   0   0
H: 5 5   W: 11 03   b.Croydon 14-1-97
Internationals: Scotland U16.
2014-15	Coventry C	0	0
2015-16	Coventry C	0	0

STEVENSON, Ben (M)   0   0
H: 6 0   W: 10 08   b.Leicester 23-3-97
2015-16	Coventry C	0	0

STOKES, Chris (M)   54   3
H: 5 7   W: 10 04   b.Trowbridge 8-3-91
Internationals: England C, U17.
2009-10	Crewe Alex	2	0	2	0
From Forest Green R.					
2014-15	Coventry C	16	1		
2015-16	Coventry C	36	2	52	3

THOMAS, Conor (M)   100   1
H: 6 1   W: 11 05   b.Coventry 29-10-93
Internationals: England U17, U18.
2010-11	*Liverpool*	0	0		
2010-11	Coventry C	0	0		
2011-12	Coventry C	27	1		
2012-13	Coventry C	11	0		
2013-14	Coventry C	43	0		
2014-15	Coventry C	16	0		
2015-16	Coventry C	3	0	100	1

THOMAS, George (M)   19   0
H: 5 8   W: 12 00   b.Leicester 24-3-97
Internationals: Wales U17, U19.
2013-14	Coventry C	1	0		
2014-15	Coventry C	6	0		
2015-16	Coventry C	7	0	14	0
2015-16	*Yeovil T*	5	0	5	0

TUDGAY, Marcus (F)   411   91
H: 5 10   W: 12 04   b.Shoreham 3-2-83
2002-03	Derby Co	5	0		
2003-04	Derby Co	29	6		
2004-05	Derby Co	34	9		
2005-06	Derby Co	21	2	92	17
2005-06	Sheffield W	18	5		
2006-07	Sheffield W	40	11		
2007-08	Sheffield W	35	7		
2008-09	Sheffield W	42	14		
2009-10	Sheffield W	43	10		
2010-11	Sheffield W	17	2	195	49
2011-12	Nottingham F	22	7		
2012-13	Nottingham F	34	5		
2012-13	Nottingham F	3	0		
2012-13	Barnsley	9	3		
2013-14	Nottingham F	2	1	61	13
2013-14	Barnsley	5	1	14	4
2013-14	*Charlton Ath*	2	0	2	0

2014-15	Coventry C	22	4		
2015-16	Coventry C	25	4	47	8

VINCELOT, Romain (M)   271   23
H: 5 9   W: 11 02   b.Poitiers 29-10-85
2004-05	Chamois Niortais	3	0	3	0
2005-06	Chamois Niortais	28	1		
2006-07	Chamois Niortais	9	0		
2007-08	Chamois Niortais	6	0	43	1
2008-09	Gueugnon	20	0	20	0
2009-10	Dagenham & R	9	1		
2010-11	Dagenham & R	46	12	55	13
2011-12	Brighton & HA	15	1		
2012-13	Brighton & HA	0	0	15	1
2012-13	*Gillingham*	9	1	9	1
2012-13	Leyton Orient	15	1		
2013-14	Leyton Orient	39	0		
2014-15	Leyton Orient	27	2	81	3
2015-16	Coventry C	45	4	45	4

WILLIS, Jordan (D)   70   0
H: 5 11   W: 11 00   b.Coventry 24-8-94
Internationals: England U18, U19.
2011-12	Coventry C	3	0		
2012-13	Coventry C	1	0		
2013-14	Coventry C	28	0		
2014-15	Coventry C	34	0		
2015-16	Coventry C	4	0	70	0

Players retained or with offer of contract
Kelly-Evans, Devon Jerome.

Scholars
Addai, Corey Kofi Cheremeh; Albini, Jason Antonio; Bayliss, Thomas David; Camwell, Christopher Paul; Finn, Kyle Patrick; Ford, Reece Colin; Hendricks, Ronee Deshaun Anthony; Hickman, Jak Anthony; Leahy, Darragh John; Matsounga, Dagry Joph Paul; Maycock, Callum; Sambou, Bassala; Shipley, Jordan Mark Edward james; Skuza, Konrad Michal; Smith, Daniel Rhys; Thompson, Jordon; Whitmore, Jacob James.

CRAWLEY T (28)

ASHTON, Jon (D)   284   3
H: 6 2   W: 13 12   b.Nuneaton 4-10-82
Internationals: England C.
2000-01	Leicester C	0	0		
2001-02	Leicester C	7	0		
2002-03	*Notts Co*	4	0	4	0
2003-04	Leicester C	0	0	7	0
2003-04	Oxford U	34	0		
2004-05	Oxford U	30	0		
2005-06	Oxford U	33	1	97	1
From Rushden & D, Grays Ath.					
2010-11	Stevenage	38	1		
2011-12	Stevenage	43	1		
2012-13	Stevenage	8	0		
2013-14	Stevenage	40	0		
2014-15	Stevenage	17	0	146	2
2015-16	Crawley T	30	0	30	0

BARNARD, Lee (F)   251   74
H: 5 10   W: 10 10   b.Romford 18-7-84
2002-03	Tottenham H	0	0		
2002-03	*Exeter C*	3	0	3	0
2003-04	Tottenham H	0	0		
2004-05	Tottenham H	0	0		
2004-05	Leyton Orient	8	0	8	0
2004-05	Northampton T	5	0	5	0
2005-06	Tottenham H	3	0		
2006-07	Tottenham H	0	0		
2007-08	Tottenham H	0	0	3	0
2007-08	Crewe Alex	10	3	10	3
2007-08	Southend U	15	9		
2008-09	Southend U	35	11		
2009-10	Southend U	25	15		
2009-10	Southampton	20	9		
2010-11	Southampton	36	14		
2011-12	Southampton	6	0		
2012-13	Southampton	0	0		
2012-13	Bournemouth	15	4	15	4
2012-13	*Oldham Ath*	14	3	14	3
2013-14	Southampton	0	0		
2013-14	*Southend U*	13	1		
2014-15	Southampton	0	0	62	23
2014-15	*Southend U*	9	1	97	37
2014-15	Stevenage	6	3	6	3
2015-16	Crawley T	28	1	28	1

BAWLING, Bobson (M)   43   0
b.London 21-9-95
2013-14	Watford	0	0		
2014-15	Crawley T	28	0		
2015-16	Crawley T	15	0	43	0

BOLDEWIJN, Enzio (F)   135   17
H: 6 1   W: 12 06   b.Almere 17-11-92
2010-11	Utrecht	0	0		
2011-12	Utrecht	11	0	11	0
2012-13	Den Bosch	31	1	31	1
2013-14	Almere City	27	2		
2014-15	Almere City	31	7		
2015-16	Almere City	35	7	93	16
2015-16	Crawley T	0	0		

BOND, Andy (M)   159   11
H: 5 10   W: 11 07   b.Wigan 16-3-86
Internationals: England C.
2010-11	Colchester U	43	7		
2011-12	Colchester U	40	3		
2012-13	Colchester U	27	0		
2012-13	*Crewe Alex*	4	0	4	0
2013-14	Colchester U	8	1	118	11
2013-14	*Bristol R*	5	0	5	0
2014-15	Stevenage	20	0	20	0
From Chorley.					
2015-16	Crawley T	12	0	12	0

BRADLEY, Sonny (D)   163   5
H: 6 0   W: 11 05   b.Hedon 14-6-92
2011-12	Hull C	2	0		
2011-12	*Aldershot T*	14	0		
2012-13	Hull C	0	0	2	0
2012-13	*Aldershot T*	42	1	56	1
2013-14	Portsmouth	33	2	33	2
2014-15	Crawley T	26	1		
2015-16	Crawley T	46	1	72	2

DEACON, Roarie (M)   85   6
H: 5 7   W: 10 10   b.London 12-10-91
Internationals: England U19.
2012-13	Stevenage	1	0		
2013-14	Stevenage	23	0		
2014-15	Stevenage	24	1	48	1
2015-16	Crawley T	37	5	37	5

DELLA VERDE, Lyle (M)   19   0
H: 5 9   W: 11 07   b.Leeds 9-1-95
2014-15	Fulham	0	0		
2015-16	Fleetwood T	7	0	7	0
2015-16	Crawley T	12	0	12	0

EDWARDS, Gwion (M)   104   14
H: 5 9   W: 12 00   b.Carmarthen 1-3-93
Internationals: Wales U19, U21
2011-12	Swansea C	0	0		
2012-13	Swansea C	0	0		
2012-13	*St Johnstone*	6	0		
2013-14	Swansea C	0	0		
2013-14	*St Johnstone*	13	0	19	0
2013-14	Crawley T	6	2		
2014-15	Crawley T	37	4		
2015-16	Crawley T	42	8	85	14

FENELON, Shamir (M)   62   5
H: 6 1   W: 12 08   b.Brighton 3-8-94
Internationals: Republic of Ireland U21.
2011-12	Brighton & HA	0	0		
2013-14	Brighton & HA	0	0		
2013-14	*Torquay U*	12	1	12	1
2014-15	Brighton & HA	2	0	2	0
2014-15	*Rochdale*	4	0	4	0
2014-15	*Tranmere R*	10	2	10	2
2014-15	*Dagenham & R*	4	0	4	0
2015-16	Crawley T	30	2	30	2

FLAHAVAN, Darryl (G)   370   0
H: 5 11   W: 12 05   b.Southampton 9-9-77
From Woking.
2000-01	Southend U	29	0		
2001-02	Southend U	41	0		
2002-03	Southend U	41	0		
2003-04	Southend U	37	0		
2004-05	Southend U	28	0		
2005-06	Southend U	43	0		
2006-07	Southend U	46	0		
2007-08	Southend U	26	0	291	0
2008-09	Crystal Palace	1	0		
2008-09	*Leeds U*	0	0		
2009-10	Crystal Palace	1	0		
2009-10	*Oldham Ath*	18	0	18	0
2010-11	Crystal Palace	0	0	2	0
2011-12	Bournemouth	44	0		
2012-13	Bournemouth	0	0		
2013-14	Bournemouth	1	0		
2014-15	Bournemouth	1	0		
2014-15	Bournemouth	1	0	46	0
2015-16	Crawley T	13	0	13	0

HARROLD, Matt (F)   391   75
H: 6 1   W: 11 10   b.Leyton 25-7-84
2003-04	Brentford	13	2		
2004-05	Brentford	19	0	32	2
2004-05	Grimsby T	6	2	6	2
2005-06	Yeovil T	42	9		
2006-07	Yeovil T	5	0	47	9

2006–07	Southend U	36	3		
2007–08	Southend U	16	0		
2008–09	Southend U	0	0	**52**	**3**
2008–09	Wycombe W	37	9		
2009–10	Wycombe W	36	8	**73**	**17**
2010–11	Shrewsbury T	41	8	**41**	**8**
2011–12	Bristol R	40	16		
2012–13	Bristol R	6	2		
2013–14	Bristol R	30	6	**76**	**24**
2014–15	Crawley T	20	1		
2014–15	*Cambridge U*	7	1	**7**	**1**
2015–16	Crawley T	37	8	**57**	**9**

HENDERSON, Conor (M) 25 2
H: 6 1 W: 11 13 b.Sidcup 8-9-91
Internationals: England U17. Republic of Ireland U19, U21.

2008–09	Arsenal	0	0		
2009–10	Arsenal	0	0		
2010–11	Arsenal	0	0		
2011–12	Arsenal	0	0		
2012–13	Arsenal	0	0		
2012–13	*Coventry C*	2	0	**2**	**0**
2013–14	Hull C	0	0		
2013–14	*Stevenage*	3	0	**3**	**0**
2014–15	Crawley T	17	2		
2015–16	Crawley T	3	0	**20**	**2**

JENKINS, Ross (M) 102 4
H: 5 11 W: 12 06 b.Watford 9-11-90
Internationals: England U20.

2008–09	Watford	29	1		
2009–10	Watford	24	0		
2010–11	Watford	19	1		
2011–12	Watford	9	0		
2012–13	Watford	0	0		
2012–13	*Plymouth Arg*	2	1	**2**	**1**
2012–13	*Barnet*	5	1	**5**	**1**
2013–14	Watford	0	0		
2014–15	Watford	0	0	**81**	**2**
2015–16	Crawley T	14	0	**14**	**0**

LITTLE, Andy (G) 0 0
H: 6 3 W: 13 10 b.London 3-10-74
From Woking.

2015–16	Crawley T	0	0		

McNERNEY, Joe (D) 11 1
b. 24-1-89
From Woking.

2015–16	Crawley T	11	1	**11**	**1**

OYEBANJO, Lanre (D) 109 0
H: 6 1 W: 11 04 b.Hackney 24-4-90
Internationals: Republic of Ireland U19, U21.

2012–13	York C	30	0		
2013–14	York C	41	0	**71**	**0**
2014–15	Crawley T	31	0		
2015–16	Crawley T	7	0	**38**	**0**

PRESTON, Callum (G) 9 0
b.Stafford 7-1-95
Internationals: Wales U19.

2014–15	Birmingham C	0	0		
2015–16	Crawley T	9	0	**9**	**0**

ROONEY, Luke (M) 124 12
H: 5 8 W: 11 07 b.Southwark 28-12-90

2009–10	Gillingham	13	2		
2010–11	Gillingham	23	1		
2011–12	Gillingham	17	3	**53**	**6**
2011–12	Swindon T	20	2		
2012–13	Swindon T	11	0		
2012–13	*Burton Alb*	3	0	**3**	**0**
2012–13	*Rotherham U*	3	0	**3**	**0**
2013–14	Swindon T	0	0	**31**	**2**
2013–14	*Crawley T*	4	0		
2014–15	Luton T	11	3	**11**	**3**
2015–16	Crawley T	19	1	**23**	**1**

SMITH, Jimmy (M) 320 29
H: 6 0 W: 10 03 b.Newham 7-1-87
Internationals: England U16, U17, U19.

2004–05	Chelsea	0	0		
2005–06	Chelsea	1	0		
2006–07	Chelsea	0	0		
2006–07	*QPR*	29	6	**29**	**6**
2007–08	Chelsea	0	0		
2007–08	*Norwich C*	9	0	**9**	**0**
2008–09	Chelsea	0	0	**1**	**0**
2008–09	*Sheffield W*	12	0	**12**	**0**
2008–09	*Leyton Orient*	16	0		
2009–10	Leyton Orient	40	2		
2010–11	Leyton Orient	31	7		
2011–12	Leyton Orient	38	6		
2012–13	Leyton Orient	35	3		
2013–14	Leyton Orient	0	0	**160**	**18**
2013–14	Stevenage	42	3	**42**	**3**
2014–15	Crawley T	36	1		
2015–16	Crawley T	31	1	**67**	**2**

TOMLIN, Gavin (F) 255 47
H: 6 0 W: 12 02 b.Gillingham 13-1-83

2006–07	Brentford	12	0		
2007–08	Brentford	0	0	**12**	**0**

From Fisher Ath.

2008–09	Yeovil T	42	7		
2009–10	Yeovil T	35	7	**77**	**14**
2010–11	Dagenham & R	19	2		
2010–11	*Torquay U*	12	4	**12**	**4**
2011–12	Dagenham & R	17	0	**36**	**2**
2011–12	*Gillingham*	10	6	**10**	**6**
2012–13	Southend U	33	13		
2013–14	Southend U	0	0	**33**	**13**
2013–14	Port Vale	24	5	**24**	**5**
2014–15	Crawley T	35	3		
2015–16	Crawley T	16	0	**51**	**3**

VAN DEN BOGAERT, Bryan (D) 83 0
b. 14-12-91

2010–11	Cappellen	18	0		
2011–12	Cappellen	0	0		
2012–13	Cappellen	28	0	**46**	**0**
2013–14	Heist	24	0	**24**	**0**
2014–15	Antwerp	12	0	**12**	**0**
2015–16	Crawley T	1	0	**1**	**0**

WALTON, Simon (M) 306 29
H: 6 1 W: 13 05 b.Sherburn-in-Elmet 13-9-87
Internationals: England U16, U17, U19.

2004–05	Leeds U	30	3		
2005–06	Leeds U	4	0	**34**	**3**
2006–07	Charlton Ath	0	0		
2006–07	*Ipswich T*	19	3	**19**	**3**
2006–07	*Cardiff C*	6	0	**6**	**0**
2007–08	QPR	5	0	**5**	**0**
2007–08	*Hull C*	10	0	**10**	**0**
2008–09	Plymouth Arg	13	0		
2008–09	*Blackpool*	1	0	**1**	**0**
2009–10	Plymouth Arg	0	0		
2009–10	*Crewe Alex*	31	1	**31**	**1**
2010–11	Plymouth Arg	7	1		
2010–11	*Sheffield U*	0	0		
2011–12	Plymouth Arg	41	8	**61**	**9**
2012–13	Hartlepool U	34	1		
2013–14	Hartlepool U	39	3	**73**	**4**
2014–15	Stevenage	29	5	**29**	**5**
2015–16	Crawley T	37	4	**37**	**4**

YOUNG, Lewis (M) 151 0
H: 5 10 W: 11 02 b.Stevenage 27-9-89

2008–09	Watford	1	0		
2009–10	Watford	0	0	**1**	**0**
2009–10	*Hereford U*	6	0	**6**	**0**
2010–11	Burton Alb	19	0	**19**	**0**
2011–12	Northampton T	30	0	**30**	**0**
2012–13	Yeovil T	15	0		
2013–14	Yeovil T	0	0	**15**	**0**
2013–14	Bury	4	0	**4**	**0**
2014–15	Crawley T	38	0		
2015–16	Crawley T	38	0	**76**	**0**

CREWE ALEX (29)

AINLEY, Callum (M) 16 1
H: 5 8 W: 10 01 b.Middlewich 2-11-97

2015–16	Crewe Alex	16	1	**16**	**1**

ATKINSON, Chris (M) 92 8
H: 6 1 W: 11 13 b.Huddersfield 13-2-92

2010–11	Huddersfield T	2	0		
2011–12	Huddersfield T	1	0		
2012–13	Huddersfield T	7	1		
2012–13	*Chesterfield*	15	5	**15**	**5**
2013–14	Huddersfield T	0	0	**10**	**1**
2013–14	*Tranmere R*	22	2	**22**	**2**
2013–14	*Bradford C*	4	0	**4**	**0**
2014–15	Crewe Alex	19	0		
2015–16	Crewe Alex	15	0	**34**	**0**
2015–16	*Crawley T*	7	0	**7**	**0**

BAILLIE, James (D) 16 0
H: 5 11 W: 11 07 b.Warrington 27-3-96

2014–15	Crewe Alex	13	0		
2015–16	Crewe Alex	3	0	**16**	**0**

BAKAYOGO, Zaoumana (D) 166 6
H: 5 9 W: 10 08 b.Paris 11-8-86
Internationals: Ivory Coast U23.

2006–07	Millwall	5	0		
2007–08	Millwall	10	0	**15**	**0**

From Alfortville.

2009–10	Tranmere R	29	0		
2010–11	Tranmere R	27	1		
2011–12	Tranmere R	26	0		
2012–13	Tranmere R	46	4	**128**	**5**
2013–14	Leicester C	0	0		
2013–14	*Yeovil T*	1	0	**1**	**0**
2015–16	Crewe Alex	22	1	**22**	**1**

BINGHAM, Billy (D) 138 8
H: 5 11 W: 11 02 b.Welling 15-7-90

2008–09	Dagenham & R	0	0		
2009–10	Dagenham & R	2	0		
2010–11	Dagenham & R	6	0		
2011–12	Dagenham & R	27	2		
2012–13	Dagenham & R	18	2		
2013–14	Dagenham & R	30	0		
2014–15	Dagenham & R	34	4	**117**	**8**
2015–16	Crewe Alex	21	0	**21**	**0**

COOPER, George (M) 49 4
H: 5 9 W: 11 05 b.Warrington 2-11-96

2014–15	Crewe Alex	22	3		
2015–16	Crewe Alex	27	1	**49**	**4**

DALLA VALLE, Lauri (F) 74 16
H: 5 9 W: 11 03 b.Joensuu 14-9-91
Internationals: Finland U16, U17, U19, U21.

2007	JIPPO	8	0	**8**	**0**
2008–09	Liverpool	0	0		
2009–10	Liverpool	0	0		
2010–11	Fulham	0	0		
2010–11	*Bournemouth*	8	2	**8**	**2**
2011–12	Fulham	0	0		
2011–12	*Dundee U*	12	3	**12**	**3**
2011–12	*Exeter C*	5	0	**5**	**0**
2012–13	Fulham	0	0		
2012–13	*Crewe Alex*	10	5		
2014–15	Crewe Alex	17	4		
2015–16	Crewe Alex	14	2	**41**	**11**

DAVIS, Harry (D) 159 11
H: 6 2 W: 12 04 b.Burnley 24-9-91

2009–10	Crewe Alex	1	0		
2010–11	Crewe Alex	1	0		
2011–12	Crewe Alex	41	5		
2012–13	Crewe Alex	42	1		
2013–14	Crewe Alex	32	3		
2014–15	Crewe Alex	31	1		
2015–16	Crewe Alex	11	1	**159**	**11**

FINNEY, Oliver (M) 0 0
b.Stoke-on-Trent 15-12-97

2015–16	Crewe Alex	0	0		

FOX, David (M) 254 15
H: 5 9 W: 11 08 b.Leek 13-12-83
Internationals: England U16, U17, U19, U20.

2000–01	Manchester U	0	0		
2001–02	Manchester U	0	0		
2002–03	Manchester U	0	0		
2003–04	Manchester U	0	0		
2004–05	Manchester U	0	0		
2004–05	*Shrewsbury T*	4	1	**4**	**1**
2005–06	Manchester U	0	0		
2005–06	Blackpool	7	1		
2006–07	Blackpool	37	4		
2007–08	Blackpool	28	1		
2008–09	Blackpool	22	0	**94**	**6**
2009–10	Colchester U	18	3		
2010–11	Norwich C	32	1		
2011–12	Norwich C	28	0		
2012–13	Norwich C	2	0		
2013–14	Norwich C	0	0	**62**	**1**
2013–14	*Barnsley*	7	0	**7**	**0**
2014–15	Colchester U	30	2	**48**	**5**
2015–16	Crewe Alex	39	2	**39**	**2**

GARRATT, Ben (G) 103 0
H: 6 1 W: 10 06 b.Market Drayton 25-4-94
Internationals: England U17, U18, U19.

2011–12	Crewe Alex	0	0		
2012–13	Crewe Alex	1	0		
2013–14	Crewe Alex	26	0		
2014–15	Crewe Alex	30	0		
2015–16	Crewe Alex	46	0	**103**	**0**

GUTHRIE, Jon (D) 89 1
H: 5 10 W: 11 00 b.Devizes 1-2-93

2011–12	Crewe Alex	0	0		
2012–13	Crewe Alex	2	0		
2013–14	Crewe Alex	23	0		
2014–15	Crewe Alex	25	0		
2015–16	Crewe Alex	39	1	**89**	**1**

HABER, Marcus (F) 179 28
H: 6 3 W: 13 04 b.Vancouver 11-1-89
Internationals: Canada U16, U17, U20, U23 U23, Full caps.

2009–10	WBA	0	0		
2009–10	*Exeter C*	5	0	**5**	**0**
2010–11	WBA	0	0		
2010–11	*St Johnstone*	11	1		
2011–12	St Johnstone	31	2	**42**	**3**
2012–13	Stevenage	42	7		
2013–14	Stevenage	3	0	**45**	**7**
2013–14	*Notts Co*	11	2	**11**	**2**

2014–15	Crewe Alex	36	7		
2015–16	Crewe Alex	40	9	76	16

HARRISON, Keiron (G) 0 0
b.Stoke-on-Trent

2015–16	Crewe Alex	0	0		

HOWELL, Joe (M) 2 0
H: 5 6 W: 10 01 b.Chester 1-1-95

2015–16	Crewe Alex	2	0	2	0

INMAN, Bradden (M) 117 20
H: 5 9 W: 11 03 b.Adelaide 12-12-91
Internationals: Scotland U19, U21.

2009–10	Newcastle U	0	0		
2010–11	Newcastle U	0	0		
2011–12	Newcastle U	0	0		
2012–13	Newcastle U	0	0		
2012–13	*Crewe Alex*	21	5		
2013–14	Newcastle U	0	0		
2013–14	Crewe Alex	36	4		
2014–15	Crewe Alex	21	1		
2015–16	Crewe Alex	39	10	117	20

JONES, James (M) 55 1
H: 5 9 W: 10 10 b.Winsford 1-2-96
Internationals: Scotland U19.

2014–15	Crewe Alex	24	1		
2015–16	Crewe Alex	31	0	55	1

KEARNS, Joe (D) 0 0
b.Liverpool 1-1-96

2015–16	Crewe Alex	0	0		

KIRK, Charlie (M) 14 0
H: 5 7 W: 11 00 b.Winsford 24-12-97

2015–16	Crewe Alex	14	0	14	0

MULLARKEY, Toby (M) 0 0
H: 5 8 W: 10 01 b.Warrington 4-11-96

2015–16	Crewe Alex	0	0		

NG, Perry (D) 6 0
H: 5 11 W: 12 02 b.Liverpool 24-6-94

2014–15	Crewe Alex	0	0		
2015–16	Crewe Alex	6	0	6	0

NUGENT, Ben (D) 85 3
H: 6 1 W: 13 00 b.Street 28-11-93

2012–13	Cardiff C	12	1		
2013–14	Cardiff C	0	0		
2013–14	*Brentford*	0	0		
2013–14	*Peterborough U*	11	0	11	0
2014–15	Cardiff C	0	0	12	1
2014–15	*Yeovil T*	23	1	23	1
2015–16	Crewe Alex	39	1	39	1

RAY, George (D) 70 2
H: 5 10 W: 11 03 b.Warrington 13-10-93
Internationals: Wales U21.

2011–12	Crewe Alex	0	0		
2012–13	Crewe Alex	4	0		
2013–14	Crewe Alex	9	0		
2014–15	Crewe Alex	35	2		
2015–16	Crewe Alex	22	0	70	2

RICHARDS, Dave (G) 0 0
H: 5 11 W: 11 11 b.Abergavenny 31-12-93

2013–14	Cardiff C	0	0		
2013–14	Bristol C	0	0		
2014–15	Bristol C	0	0		
2015–16	Crewe Alex	0	0		

SAUNDERS, Callum (F) 22 2
H: 5 10 W: 11 11 b.Istanbul 26-9-95
Internationals: Wales U19, U21.

2014–15	Crewe Alex	4	0		
2015–16	Crewe Alex	18	2	22	2

TURTON, Oliver (D) 125 3
H: 5 11 W: 11 11 b.Manchester 6-12-92

2010–11	Crewe Alex	1	0		
2011–12	Crewe Alex	2	0		
2012–13	Crewe Alex	20	0		
2013–14	Crewe Alex	12	1		
2014–15	Crewe Alex	44	1		
2015–16	Crewe Alex	46	1	125	3

UDOH, Daniel (F) 6 0
b.30-8-96
Internationals: Nigeria U17.

2015–16	Crewe Alex	6	0	6	0

WINTLE, Ryan (M) 3 0
H: 5 5 W: 10 01 b.Newcastle-under-Lyme 13-6-97

2015–16	Crewe Alex	3	0	3	0

Players retained or with offer of contract
Dale, Owen; Pickering, Harry Leslie.

Non-Contract
Bakayogo, Zoumana.

Scholars
Culpeper, Arturo; Dowsett, Aaron Joseph Llewellyn; Harrison, Kieran James; Higham, Jonathan Mark; Hilton, Jake; Jones, Morgan Wyn; Lowery, Thomas Richard; Lundstram, Joshua; Morgan, Jamie Lee; Neal, Matthew Saul Andrew; Quinn, Thomas Evander; Reilly, Lewis Colin; Walley, Luke Antony; Wardley, Scott Graham; Wilkinson, Jamie Paul; Woodcock, Ross Callum.

CRYSTAL PALACE (30)

ADEBAYOR, Emmanuel (F) 378 135
H: 6 4 W: 11 08 b.Lome 26-2-84
Internationals: Togo Full caps.

2001–02	Metz	10	2		
2002–03	Metz	34	13	44	15
2003–04	Monaco	31	8		
2004–05	Monaco	34	9		
2005–06	Monaco	13	1	78	18
2005–06	Arsenal	13	4		
2006–07	Arsenal	29	8		
2007–08	Arsenal	36	24		
2008–09	Arsenal	26	10	104	46
2009–10	Manchester C	26	14		
2010–11	Manchester C	8	1		
2010–11	*Real Madrid*	14	5	14	5
2011–12	Manchester C	0	0		
2011–12	*Tottenham H*	33	17		
2012–13	Manchester C	0	0	34	15
2012–13	Tottenham H	25	5		
2013–14	Tottenham H	21	11		
2014–15	Tottenham H	13	2		
2015–16	Tottenham H	0	0	92	35
2015–16	Crystal Palace	12	1	12	1

ANDERSON, Keshi (F) 7 3
H: 5 9 W: 10 10 b.Luton 15-11-95

2014–15	Crystal Palace	0	0		
2015–16	*Doncaster R*	7	3	7	3

APPIAH, Kwesi (F) 52 10
H: 5 11 W: 12 08 b.Thamesmead 12-8-90
Internationals: Ghana Full caps.

2008–09	Peterborough U	0	0		

From Brackley T, Thurrock, Margate.

2011–12	Crystal Palace	4	0		
2012–13	Crystal Palace	2	0		
2012–13	*Aldershot T*	2	0	2	0
2012–13	*Yeovil T*	5	0	5	0
2013–14	Crystal Palace	0	0		
2013–14	*Notts Co*	7	0	7	0
2013–14	*AFC Wimbledon*	7	3	7	3
2014–15	Crystal Palace	0	0		
2014–15	*Cambridge U*	19	6	19	6
2014–15	*Reading*	6	1	6	1
2015–16	Crystal Palace	0	0	6	0

BOATENG, Hiram (M) 26 1
H: 5 7 W: 11 00 b.Wandsworth 8-1-96

2012–13	Crystal Palace	0	0		
2013–14	Crystal Palace	0	0		
2013–14	*Crawley T*	1	0	1	0
2014–15	Crystal Palace	0	0		
2015–16	Crystal Palace	1	0	1	0
2015–16	*Plymouth Arg*	24	1	24	1

BOLASIE, Yannick (M) 248 26
H: 6 2 W: 13 02 b.DR Congo 24-5-89
Internationals: DR Congo Full caps.

2008–09	Plymouth Arg	0	0		
2008–09	Barnet	20	3		
2009–10	Plymouth Arg	16	1		
2009–10	Barnet	22	2	42	5
2010–11	Plymouth Arg	35	7	51	8
2011–12	Bristol C	23	1		
2012–13	Bristol C	0	0	23	1
2012–13	Crystal Palace	43	3		
2013–14	Crystal Palace	29	0		
2014–15	Crystal Palace	34	4		
2015–16	Crystal Palace	26	5	132	12

CABAYE, Yohan (M) 303 53
H: 5 9 W: 11 05 b.Tourcoing 14-1-86
Internationals: France U16, U18, U19, U20, U21, Full caps.

2004–05	Lille	6	0		
2005–06	Lille	27	1		
2006–07	Lille	22	3		
2007–08	Lille	36	7		
2008–09	Lille	32	5		
2009–10	Lille	32	13		
2010–11	Lille	36	2	191	31
2011–12	Newcastle U	34	4		
2012–13	Newcastle U	26	0		

2013–14	Newcastle U	19	7	79	17
2015–16	Crystal Palace	33	5	33	5

CAMPBELL, Frazier (F) 184 39
H: 5 11 W: 12 04 b.Huddersfield 13-9-87
Internationals: England U16, U17, U18, U21, Full caps.

2005–06	Manchester U	0	0		
2006–07	Manchester U	0	0		
2007–08	Manchester U	1	0		
2007–08	*Hull C*	34	15	34	15
2008–09	Manchester U	1	0		
2008–09	*Tottenham H*	10	1	10	1
2009–10	Manchester U	0	0	2	0
2009–10	Sunderland	31	4		
2010–11	Sunderland	3	0		
2011–12	Sunderland	12	1		
2012–13	Sunderland	12	1	58	6
2012–13	Cardiff C	12	7		
2013–14	Cardiff C	37	6	49	13
2014–15	Crystal Palace	20	4		
2015–16	Crystal Palace	11	0	31	4

CHAMAKH, Marouane (F) 333 71
H: 6 1 W: 11 00 b.Tonneins 10-1-84
Internationals: France U19. Morocco Full caps.

2002–03	Bordeaux	10	1		
2003–04	Bordeaux	25	6		
2004–05	Bordeaux	33	10		
2005–06	Bordeaux	29	7		
2006–07	Bordeaux	29	5		
2007–08	Bordeaux	32	4		
2008–09	Bordeaux	34	13		
2009–10	Bordeaux	38	10	230	56
2010–11	Arsenal	29	7		
2011–12	Arsenal	11	1		
2012–13	Arsenal	0	0		
2012–13	*West Ham U*	3	0	3	0
2013–14	Arsenal	0	0	40	8
2013–14	Crystal Palace	32	5		
2014–15	Crystal Palace	18	2		
2015–16	Crystal Palace	10	0	60	7

CROLL, Luke (D) 3 0
b. 10-1-95

2014–15	Crystal Palace	0	0		
2015–16	Crystal Palace	0	0		
2015–16	*Plymouth Arg*	3	0	3	0

DANN, Scott (D) 337 25
H: 6 2 W: 12 00 b.Liverpool 14-2-87
Internationals: England U21.

2004–05	Walsall	1	0		
2005–06	Walsall	0	0		
2006–07	Walsall	30	4		
2007–08	Walsall	28	3	59	7
2007–08	Coventry C	16	0		
2008–09	Coventry C	31	3	47	3
2009–10	Birmingham C	30	0		
2010–11	Birmingham C	20	2		
2011–12	Birmingham C	0	0	50	2
2011–12	Blackburn R	27	1		
2012–13	Blackburn R	46	4		
2013–14	Blackburn R	25	0	98	5
2013–14	Crystal Palace	14	1		
2014–15	Crystal Palace	34	2		
2015–16	Crystal Palace	35	5	83	8

DELANEY, Damien (D) 543 16
H: 6 3 W: 14 00 b.Cork 20-7-81
Internationals: Republic of Ireland Full caps.

2000–01	Leicester C	5	0		
2001–02	Leicester C	3	0		
2001–02	*Stockport Co*	12	1	12	1
2001–02	*Huddersfield T*	2	0	2	0
2002–03	Leicester C	0	0	8	0
2002–03	*Mansfield T*	7	0	7	0
2002–03	Hull C	30	1		
2003–04	Hull C	46	2		
2004–05	Hull C	43	1		
2005–06	Hull C	46	0		
2006–07	Hull C	37	1		
2007–08	Hull C	22	0	224	5
2008–09	QPR	17	1		
2008–09	QPR	37	1		
2009–10	QPR	0	0	54	2
2009–10	Ipswich T	36	0		
2010–11	Ipswich T	32	2		
2011–12	Ipswich T	29	0		
2012–13	Ipswich T	1	0	98	2
2012–13	Crystal Palace	40	3		
2013–14	Crystal Palace	37	1		
2014–15	Crystal Palace	29	0		
2015–16	Crystal Palace	32	2	138	6

DREHER, Luke (M) 0 0
b. 27-11-98

2015–16	Crystal Palace	0	0		

DYMOND, Connor (M) **1 0**
b. 12-9-94

2013–14	Crystal Palace	0	0		
2014–15	Crystal Palace	0	0		
2015–16	Crystal Palace	0	0		
2015–16	*Newport Co*	1	0	**1**	**0**

FRYERS, Zeki (D) **30 0**
H: 6 0 W: 12 00 b.Manchester 9-9-92
Internationals: England U16, U17, U19.

2011–12	Manchester U	2	0	**2**	**0**
2012–13	Standard Liege	7	0	**7**	**0**
2012–13	Tottenham H	0	0		
2013–14	Tottenham H	7	0	**7**	**0**
2014–15	Crystal Palace	1	0		
2014–15	*Rotherham U*	10	0	**10**	**0**
2014–15	*Ipswich T*	3	0	**3**	**0**
2015–16	Crystal Palace	0	0	**1**	**0**

GAYLE, Dwight (F) **111 35**
H: 5 10 W: 11 07 b.Walthamstow 20-10-89

2011–12	Dagenham & R	0	0		
2012–13	Dagenham & R	18	7	**18**	**7**
2012–13	Peterborough U	29	13	**29**	**13**
2013–14	Crystal Palace	23	7		
2014–15	Crystal Palace	25	5		
2015–16	Crystal Palace	16	3	**64**	**15**

GRAY, Jake (F) **33 5**
H: 5 11 W: 11 00 b.Aylesbury 25-12-95

2014–15	Crystal Palace	0	0		
2014–15	*Cheltenham T*	4	0	**4**	**0**
2015–16	Crystal Palace	0	0		
2015–16	*Hartlepool U*	29	5	**29**	**5**

HANGELAND, Brede (D) **415 19**
H: 6 4 W: 13 05 b.Houston 20-6-81
Internationals: Norway U21, Full caps.

2000	Vidar	0	0		
2001	Viking	22	0		
2002	Viking	26	2		
2003	Viking	26	1		
2004	Viking	14	3		
2005	Viking	26	0	**114**	**6**
2005–06	FC Copenhagen	13	1		
2006–07	FC Copenhagen	32	0		
2007–08	FC Copenhagen	18	2	**63**	**3**
2007–08	Fulham	15	0		
2008–09	Fulham	37	1		
2009–10	Fulham	32	1		
2010–11	Fulham	37	6		
2011–12	Fulham	38	0		
2012–13	Fulham	35	0		
2013–14	Fulham	23	0	**217**	**8**
2014–15	Crystal Palace	14	2		
2015–16	Crystal Palace	7	0	**21**	**2**

HENNESSEY, Wayne (G) **212 0**
H: 6 0 W: 11 06 b.Anglesey 24-1-87
Internationals: Wales U17, U19, U21, Full caps.

2004–05	Wolverhampton W	0	0		
2005–06	Wolverhampton W	0	0		
2006–07	Wolverhampton W	0	0		
2006–07	*Bristol C*	0	0		
2006–07	*Stockport Co*	15	0	**15**	**0**
2007–08	Wolverhampton W	46	0		
2008–09	Wolverhampton W	35	0		
2009–10	Wolverhampton W	13	0		
2010–11	Wolverhampton W	24	0		
2011–12	Wolverhampton W	34	0		
2012–13	Wolverhampton W	0	0		
2013–14	Wolverhampton W	0	0	**152**	**0**
2013–14	*Yeovil T*	12	0	**12**	**0**
2013–14	Crystal Palace	1	0		
2014–15	Crystal Palace	3	0		
2015–16	Crystal Palace	29	0	**33**	**0**

INNISS, Ryan (D) **31 0**
H: 6 5 W: 13 02 b.Kent 5-6-95
Internationals: England U16, U17.

2012–13	Crystal Palace	0	0		
2013–14	Crystal Palace	0	0		
2013–14	*Cheltenham T*	2	0	**2**	**0**
2013–14	*Gillingham*	3	0	**3**	**0**
2014–15	Crystal Palace	0	0		
2014–15	*Yeovil T*	6	0	**6**	**0**
2014–15	*Port Vale*	5	0		
2015–16	Crystal Palace	0	0		
2015–16	*Port Vale*	15	0	**20**	**0**

JEDINAK, Mile (M) **354 39**
H: 6 2 W: 13 12 b.Sydney 3-8-84
Internationals: Australia U20, Full caps.

2000–01	Sydney U	3	0		
2001–02	Sydney U	7	1		
2002–03	Sydney U	18	2		
2003–04	Varteks	0	0		
2004–05	Sydney U	24	3		
2005–06	Sydney U	30	6	**82**	**12**
2006–07	Central Coast M	8	0		
2007–08	Central Coast M	22	2		
2008–09	Central Coast M	15	6	**45**	**8**
2008–09	Genclerbirligi	15	1		
2009–10	Genclerbirligi	2	0		
2009–10	Antalya	28	5	**28**	**5**
2010–11	Genclerbirligi	21	3	**38**	**4**
2011–12	Crystal Palace	31	1		
2012–13	Crystal Palace	41	3		
2013–14	Crystal Palace	38	1		
2014–15	Crystal Palace	24	5		
2015–16	Crystal Palace	27	0	**161**	**10**

KAIKAI, Sullay (F) **57 17**
H: 6 0 W: 11 07 b.London 26-8-95

2013–14	Crystal Palace	0	0		
2013–14	*Crawley T*	5	0	**5**	**0**
2014–15	Crystal Palace	0	0		
2014–15	*Cambridge U*	25	5	**25**	**5**
2015–16	Crystal Palace	1	0	**1**	**0**
2015–16	*Shrewsbury T*	26	12	**26**	**12**

KELLY, Martin (D) **84 1**
H: 6 3 W: 12 02 b.Bolton 27-4-90
Internationals: England U19, U20, U21, Full caps.

2007–08	Liverpool	0	0		
2008–09	Liverpool	0	0		
2008–09	*Huddersfield T*	7	1	**7**	**1**
2009–10	Liverpool	1	0		
2010–11	Liverpool	11	0		
2011–12	Liverpool	12	0		
2012–13	Liverpool	4	0		
2013–14	Liverpool	5	0	**33**	**0**
2014–15	Crystal Palace	31	0		
2015–16	Crystal Palace	13	0	**44**	**0**

LADAPO, Freddie (F) **6 0**
H: 6 0 W: 12 06 b.Romford 1-2-93

2011–12	Colchester U	0	0		
2012–13	Colchester U	4	0		
2013–14	Colchester U	2	0	**6**	**0**
2015–16	Crystal Palace	0	0		

LEDLEY, Joe (M) **397 50**
H: 6 0 W: 11 06 b.Cardiff 23-1-87
Internationals: Wales U17, U19, U21, Full caps.

2004–05	Cardiff C	28	3		
2005–06	Cardiff C	42	3		
2006–07	Cardiff C	46	2		
2007–08	Cardiff C	41	10		
2008–09	Cardiff C	40	4		
2009–10	Cardiff C	29	3	**226**	**25**
2010–11	Celtic	29	2		
2011–12	Celtic	32	7		
2012–13	Celtic	25	7		
2013–14	Celtic	20	4	**106**	**20**
2013–14	Crystal Palace	14	2		
2014–15	Crystal Palace	32	2		
2015–16	Crystal Palace	19	1	**65**	**5**

LEE, Chung Yong (M) **243 28**
H: 5 11 W: 10 09 b.Seoul 2-7-88
Internationals: South Korea U19, U20, Full caps.

2006	FC Seoul	2	0		
2007	FC Seoul	15	3		
2008	FC Seoul	20	5		
2009	FC Seoul	14	2	**51**	**10**
2009–10	Bolton W	34	4		
2010–11	Bolton W	31	3		
2011–12	Bolton W	2	0		
2012–13	Bolton W	41	4		
2013–14	Bolton W	45	3		
2014–15	Bolton W	23	3	**176**	**17**
2014–15	Crystal Palace	3	0		
2015–16	Crystal Palace	13	1	**16**	**1**

LOKILO, Jason (M) **0 0**
H: 5 9 b.Brussel 17-9-98

2014–15	Anderlecht	0	0		
2015–16	Crystal Palace	0	0		

MARIAPPA, Adrian (D) **284 6**
H: 5 10 W: 11 12 b.Harrow 3-10-86
Internationals: Jamaica Full caps.

2005–06	Watford	3	0		
2006–07	Watford	19	0		
2007–08	Watford	25	0		
2008–09	Watford	39	1		
2009–10	Watford	46	1		
2010–11	Watford	45	1		
2011–12	Watford	39	1	**216**	**4**
2012–13	Reading	29	1		
2013–14	Reading	0	0	**29**	**1**
2013–14	Crystal Palace	24	1		
2014–15	Crystal Palace	12	0		
2015–16	Crystal Palace	3	0	**39**	**1**

McARTHUR, James (M) **357 24**
H: 5 6 W: 9 13 b.Glasgow 7-10-87
Internationals: Scotland U21, Full caps.

2004–05	Hamilton A	6	0		
2005–06	Hamilton A	20	1		
2006–07	Hamilton A	36	1		
2007–08	Hamilton A	34	4		
2008–09	Hamilton A	37	2		
2009–10	Hamilton A	35	1	**168**	**9**
2010–11	Wigan Ath	18	0		
2011–12	Wigan Ath	31	3		
2012–13	Wigan Ath	34	3		
2013–14	Wigan Ath	41	4		
2014–15	Wigan Ath	5	1	**129**	**11**
2014–15	Crystal Palace	32	2		
2015–16	Crystal Palace	28	2	**60**	**4**

McCARTHY, Alex (G) **147 0**
H: 6 4 W: 11 12 b.Guildford 3-12-89
Internationals: England U21.

2008–09	Reading	0	0		
2008–09	*Aldershot T*	4	0	**4**	**0**
2009–10	Reading	0	0		
2009–10	*Yeovil T*	44	0	**44**	**0**
2010–11	Reading	13	0		
2010–11	*Brentford*	3	0	**3**	**0**
2011–12	Reading	0	0		
2011–12	*Leeds U*	6	0	**6**	**0**
2011–12	*Ipswich T*	10	0	**10**	**0**
2012–13	Reading	13	0		
2013–14	Reading	44	0	**70**	**0**
2014–15	QPR	3	0	**3**	**0**
2015–16	Crystal Palace	7	0	**7**	**0**

McCARTHY, Patrick (D) **270 12**
H: 6 2 W: 13 07 b.Dublin 31-5-83
Internationals: Republic of Ireland U17, U21, B.

2000–01	Manchester C	0	0		
2001–02	Manchester C	0	0		
2002–03	Manchester C	0	0		
2002–03	*Boston U*	12	0	**12**	**0**
2002–03	*Notts Co*	6	0	**6**	**0**
2003–04	Manchester C	0	0		
2004–05	Manchester C	0	0		
2004–05	Leicester C	12	0		
2005–06	Leicester C	38	2		
2006–07	Leicester C	22	1	**72**	**3**
2007–08	Charlton Ath	29	2	**29**	**2**
2008–09	Crystal Palace	27	3		
2009–10	Crystal Palace	20	0		
2010–11	Crystal Palace	43	1		
2011–12	Crystal Palace	43	2		
2012–13	Crystal Palace	0	0		
2013–14	Crystal Palace	1	0		
2014–15	Crystal Palace	0	0		
2014–15	*Sheffield U*	11	1	**11**	**1**
2014–15	*Bolton W*	5	0	**5**	**0**
2015–16	Crystal Palace	0	0	**134**	**6**
2015–16	*Preston NE*	1	0	**1**	**0**

MUTCH, Jordon (M) **160 16**
H: 5 9 W: 10 03 b.Derby 2-12-91
Internationals: England U17, U19, U20, U21.

2007–08	Birmingham C	0	0		
2008–09	Birmingham C	0	0		
2009–10	Birmingham C	0	0		
2009–10	*Hereford U*	3	0	**3**	**0**
2009–10	*Doncaster R*	17	2	**17**	**2**
2010–11	Birmingham C	3	0		
2010–11	*Watford*	23	5	**23**	**5**
2011–12	Birmingham C	21	2	**24**	**2**
2012–13	Cardiff C	22	0		
2013–14	Cardiff C	35	7	**57**	**7**
2014–15	QPR	9	0	**9**	**0**
2014–15	Crystal Palace	7	0		
2015–16	Crystal Palace	20	0	**27**	**0**

PUNCHEON, Jason (M) **365 59**
H: 5 9 W: 12 05 b.Croydon 26-6-86

2003–04	Wimbledon	8	0	**8**	**0**
2004–05	Milton Keynes D	25	1		
2005–06	Milton Keynes D	1	0		
2006–07	Barnet	37	5		
2007–08	Barnet	41	10	**78**	**15**
2008–09	Plymouth Arg	6	0		
2008–09	*Milton Keynes D*	27	4		
2009–10	Plymouth Arg	0	0	**6**	**0**
2009–10	*Milton Keynes D*	24	7	**77**	**12**
2009–10	Southampton	19	3		
2010–11	Southampton	15	0		
2010–11	*Millwall*	7	5	**7**	**5**
2010–11	*Blackpool*	11	3	**11**	**3**
2011–12	Southampton	8	0		
2011–12	*QPR*	2	0	**2**	**0**
2012–13	Southampton	32	6		
2013–14	Southampton	0	0	**74**	**9**
2013–14	Crystal Palace	34	7		

| 2014–15 | Crystal Palace | 37 | 6 | | |
| 2015–16 | Crystal Palace | 31 | 2 | 102 | 15 |

SAKO, Bakary (M)   308 61
H: 5 11 W: 11 12 b.Ivry Sur Seine 26-4-88
Internationals: France U21. Mali U17, Full caps.

2006–07	Chateauroux	17	0		
2007–08	Chateauroux	12	1		
2008–09	Chateauroux	35	9	64	10
2009–10	St Etienne	30	1		
2010–11	St Etienne	38	7		
2011–12	St Etienne	36	5		
2012–13	St Etienne	2	0	106	13
2012–13	Wolverhampton W	37	9		
2013–14	Wolverhampton W	40	12		
2014–15	Wolverhampton W	41	15	118	36
2015–16	Crystal Palace	20	2	20	2

SCALES, Christian (D)   8 0
b. 3-12-96
From Norwich C.

| 2015–16 | Crystal Palace | 0 | 0 | | |
| 2015–16 | Crawley T | 8 | 0 | 8 | 0 |

SOUARE, Pape (D)   122 3
H: 5 10 W: 10 10 b.Mbao 6-6-90
Internationals: Senegal U23, Full caps.

2010–11	Lille	4	0		
2011–12	Lille	7	0		
2012–13	Lille	0	0		
2012–13	Reims	23	0	23	0
2013–14	Lille	33	3		
2014–15	Lille	12	0	56	3
2014–15	Crystal Palace	9	0		
2015–16	Crystal Palace	34	0	43	0

SPERONI, Julian (G)   453 0
H: 6 0 W: 11 00 b.Buenos Aires 18-5-79
Internationals: Argentina U20, U21.

1999–2000	Platense	2	0		
2000–01	Platense	0	0	2	0
2001–02	Dundee	17	0		
2002–03	Dundee	38	0		
2003–04	Dundee	37	0	92	0
2004–05	Crystal Palace	6	0		
2005–06	Crystal Palace	4	0		
2006–07	Crystal Palace	5	0		
2007–08	Crystal Palace	46	0		
2008–09	Crystal Palace	45	0		
2009–10	Crystal Palace	45	0		
2010–11	Crystal Palace	45	0		
2011–12	Crystal Palace	42	0		
2012–13	Crystal Palace	46	0		
2013–14	Crystal Palace	37	0		
2014–15	Crystal Palace	36	0		
2015–16	Crystal Palace	2	0	359	0

WARD, Joel (D)   238 10
H: 6 2 W: 11 13 b.Emsworth 29-10-89

2008–09	Portsmouth	0	0		
2008–09	Bournemouth	21	1	21	1
2009–10	Portsmouth	3	0		
2010–11	Portsmouth	42	3		
2011–12	Portsmouth	44	3	89	6
2012–13	Crystal Palace	25	0		
2013–14	Crystal Palace	36	0		
2014–15	Crystal Palace	37	1		
2015–16	Crystal Palace	30	2	128	3

WICKHAM, Connor (F)   187 38
H: 6 0 W: 14 01 b.Hereford 31-3-93
Internationals: England U16, U17, U19, U21.

2008–09	Ipswich T	2	0		
2009–10	Ipswich T	26	4		
2010–11	Ipswich T	37	9	65	13
2011–12	Sunderland	16	1		
2012–13	Sunderland	10	0		
2012–13	Sheffield W	6	1		
2013–14	Sunderland	15	5		
2013–14	Sheffield W	11	8	17	9
2013–14	Leeds U	5	0	5	0
2014–15	Sunderland	36	5	79	11
2015–16	Crystal Palace	21	5	21	5

WILLIAMS, Jerome (D)   49 1
H: 5 11 W: 12 02 b.Croydon 7-3-95
Internationals: England U18, U19.

2013–14	Crystal Palace	0	0		
2014–15	Crystal Palace	0	0		
2014–15	Southend U	21	0	21	0
2015–16	Crystal Palace	0	0		
2015–16	Burton Alb	15	1	15	1
2015–16	Leyton Orient	13	0	13	0

WILLIAMS, Jon (M)   98 2
H: 5 6 W: 10 00 b.Tunbridge Wells 9-10-93
Internationals: Wales U17, U19, U21, Full caps.

2010–11	Crystal Palace	0	0		
2011–12	Crystal Palace	14	0		
2012–13	Crystal Palace	29	0		
2013–14	Crystal Palace	9	0		
2013–14	Ipswich T	13	1		
2014–15	Crystal Palace	2	0		
2014–15	Ipswich T	7	1	20	2
2015–16	Crystal Palace	1	0	55	0
2015–16	Nottingham F	10	0	10	0
2015–16	Milton Keynes D	13	0	13	0

ZAHA, Wilfried (F)   205 19
H: 5 11 W: 10 05 b.Ivory Coast 10-11-92
Internationals: England U19, U21, Full caps.

2009–10	Crystal Palace	1	0		
2010–11	Crystal Palace	41	1		
2011–12	Crystal Palace	41	6		
2012–13	Crystal Palace	43	6		
2012–13	Manchester U	0	0		
2013–14	Manchester U	2	0	2	0
2013–14	Cardiff C	12	0	12	0
2014–15	Crystal Palace	31	4		
2015–16	Crystal Palace	34	2	191	19

Players retained or with offer of contract
Andrews, Corie Anthony; Berkeley-Agyepong, Jacob Kwame; Lumeka, Levi Jeremiah; O'Dwyer, Oliver; Perntreou, Kleton; Phillips, Michael; Wan-Bissaka, Aaron; Williams, Randell.

Scholars
Akiotu, Jason; Coker, Andre Jordan Coleridge; Flanagan, Kian; Fundi, Victor; Hosannah, Bryce Joseph; Jones, Jalen; King-Elliott, Ryan; Linton, Nathan Dominic; McAdden, Colm Anthony; Omrore, Emmanuel Ikudehinbu; Sturgess, Callum Harry; Woods, Samuel John; Wynter, Ben Douglas; Yeboah, Emmanuel.

DAGENHAM & R (31)

BOUCAUD, Andre (M)   183 3
H: 5 8 W: 11 01 b.Enfield 10-10-84
Internationals: Trinidad & Tobago Full caps.

2002–03	Reading	0	0		
2002–03	Peterborough U	6	0		
2003–04	Reading	0	0		
2003–04	Peterborough U	8	1		
2004–05	Peterborough U	22	1		
2005–06	Peterborough U	3	0	39	2
From Kettering T					
2007–08	Wycombe W	10	0	10	0
From Kettering T, York C, Luton T					
2012–13	Notts Co	39	1		
2013–14	Notts Co	29	0	68	1
2014–15	Dagenham & R	41	0		
2015–16	Dagenham & R	25	0	66	0

CHAMBERS, Ashley (F)   128 16
H: 5 10 W: 11 06 b.Leicester 1-3-90
Internationals: England C, U16, U17, U18, U19.

2005–06	Leicester C	0	0		
2006–07	Leicester C	0	0		
2007–08	Leicester C	5	0		
2008–09	Leicester C	1	0		
2009–10	Leicester C	0	0	6	0
2009–10	Wycombe W	0	0		
2009–10	Grimsby T	0	0		
2012–13	York C	38	10		
2013–14	York C	15	0	53	10
2013–14	Dagenham & R	6	0		
2014–15	Dagenham & R	32	2		
2015–16	Dagenham & R	31	4	69	6

CONNORS, Jack (D)   49 0
H: 5 8 W: 9 06 b.Brent 24-10-94
Internationals: Republic of Ireland U21.

2013–14	Dagenham & R	23	0		
2014–15	Dagenham & R	17	0		
2015–16	Dagenham & R	9	0	49	0

COUSINS, Mark (G)   118 0
H: 6 2 W: 12 02 b.Chelmsford 9-1-87

2005–06	Colchester U	0	0		
2006–07	Colchester U	0	0		
2007–08	Colchester U	2	0		
2008–09	Colchester U	9	0		
2009–10	Colchester U	0	0		
2010–11	Colchester U	14	0		
2011–12	Colchester U	10	0		
2012–13	Colchester U	23	0		
2013–14	Colchester U	0	0	58	0
2014–15	Dagenham & R	37	0		
2015–16	Dagenham & R	23	0	60	0

CURETON, Jamie (F)   755 263
H: 5 8 W: 10 07 b.Bristol 28-8-75
Internationals: England U18.

1992–93	Norwich C	0	0		
1993–94	Norwich C	0	0		
1994–95	Norwich C	17	4		
1995–96	Norwich C	12	2		
1995–96	Bournemouth	5	0	5	0
1996–97	Bristol R	38	11		
1997–98	Bristol R	43	13		
1998–99	Bristol R	46	25		
1999–2000	Bristol R	46	22		
2000–01	Bristol R	1	1	174	72
2000–01	Reading	43	26		
2001–02	Reading	38	15		
2002–03	Reading	27	9	108	50
From Busan Icons.					
2003–04	QPR	13	2		
2004–05	QPR	30	4	43	6
2005–06	Swindon T	30	7	30	7
2005–06	Colchester U	8	4		
2006–07	Colchester U	44	23	52	27
2007–08	Norwich C	41	12		
2008–09	Norwich C	22	2		
2008–09	Barnsley	8	2	8	2
2009–10	Norwich C	6	2	98	22
2009–10	Shrewsbury T	12	0	12	0
2010–11	Exeter C	41	17		
2011–12	Leyton Orient	19	1	19	1
2011–12	Exeter C	7	1		
2012–13	Exeter C	40	21	88	39
2013–14	Cheltenham T	35	11	35	11
2014–15	Dagenham & R	45	19		
2015–16	Dagenham & R	38	7	83	26

DIKAMONA, Clevid (D)   88 6
H: 6 2 W: 13 05 b.Caen 23-6-90
Internationals: France U19. Congo Full caps.

2010–11	Le Havre	7	0		
2011–12	Le Havre	2	0		
2012–13	Le Havre	0	0	9	0
2012–13	Frejus St Raphael	18	0	18	0
2013–14	Sedan	19	3	19	3
2014–15	Le Poire SV	15	1	15	1
2015–16	Dagenham & R	27	2	27	2

DOIDGE, Christian (F)   46 10
H: 6 1 W: 12 02 b.Newport 25-8-92

| 2014–15 | Dagenham & R | 11 | 2 | | |
| 2015–16 | Dagenham & R | 35 | 8 | 46 | 10 |

FERDINAND, Kane (D)   142 12
H: 6 1 W: 13 07 b.Newham 7-10-92
Internationals: Republic of Ireland U18, U19, U21.

2010–11	Southend U	22	2		
2011–12	Southend U	36	7		
2012–13	Southend U	3	1	61	10
2012–13	Peterborough U	32	1		
2013–14	Peterborough U	2	0		
2013–14	Northampton T	4	0	4	0
2014–15	Peterborough U	12	0	46	1
2014–15	Cheltenham T	16	0	16	0
2015–16	Dagenham & R	15	1	15	1

GUTTRIDGE, Luke (M)   435 51
H: 5 6 W: 9 07 b.Barnstaple 27-3-82

1999–2000	Torquay U	1	0		
2000–01	Torquay U	0	0	1	0
2000–01	Cambridge U	1	1		
2001–02	Cambridge U	29	2		
2002–03	Cambridge U	43	3		
2003–04	Cambridge U	46	11		
2004–05	Cambridge U	17	0	136	17
2004–05	Southend U	5	0		
2005–06	Southend U	41	5		
2006–07	Southend U	17	0	63	5
2006–07	Leyton Orient	17	1	17	1
2007–08	Colchester U	14	0	14	0
2008–09	Northampton T	25	2		
2009–10	Northampton T	31	4		
2010–11	Aldershot T	41	8		
2011–12	Aldershot T	25	4	66	12
2011–12	Northampton T	19	3		
2012–13	Northampton T	25	1		
2013–14	Northampton T	0	0	100	10
2014–15	Luton T	27	3		
2015–16	Dagenham & R	8	2	35	5

HAWKINS, Oliver (F)   18 1
b. 8-4-92
From North Greenford U, Hillingdon Bor, Nothwood, Hemel Hemstead T.

| 2015–16 | Dagenham & R | 18 | 1 | 18 | 1 |

HEATHER, Kai (M)   0 0
b. 20-4-98

| 2015–16 | Dagenham & R | 0 | 0 | | |

HEMMINGS, Ashley (M) 175 14
H: 5 8 W: 11 06 b.Lewisham 3-3-91
Internationals: England U17.

2008–09	Wolverhampton W	2	0	
2008–09	Cheltenham T	1	0	1 0
2009–10	Wolverhampton W	0	0	
2010–11	Wolverhampton W	0	0	
2010–11	Torquay U	9	0	9 0
2011–12	Wolverhampton W	0	0	2 0
2011–12	Plymouth Arg	23	2	23 2
2012–13	Walsall	28	1	
2013–14	Walsall	27	2	55 3
2013–14	Burton Alb	5	0	5 0
2014–15	Dagenham & R	41	5	
2015–16	Dagenham & R	39	4	80 9

HINES, Zavon (F) 115 11
H: 5 10 W: 10 07 b.Jamaica 27-12-88
Internationals: England U21.

2007–08	West Ham U	0	0	
2007–08	Coventry C	7	1	7 1
2008–09	West Ham U	0	0	
2009–10	West Ham U	13	1	
2010–11	West Ham U	9	0	22 1
2011–12	Burnley	13	0	13 0
2011–12	Bournemouth	8	1	8 1
2012–13	Bradford C	32	2	
2013–14	Bradford C	0	0	32 2
2013–14	Dagenham & R	27	6	
2014–15	Dagenham & R	0	0	
2015–16	Dagenham & R	6	0	33 6

HOYTE, Justin (D) 235 4
H: 5 11 W: 11 00 b.Waltham Forest 20-11-84
Internationals: England U16, U19, U20, U21. Trinidad and Tobago Full caps.

2002–03	Arsenal	1	0	
2003–04	Arsenal	1	0	
2004–05	Arsenal	5	0	
2005–06	Arsenal	0	0	
2005–06	Sunderland	27	1	27 1
2006–07	Arsenal	22	1	
2007–08	Arsenal	5	0	34 1
2008–09	Middlesbrough	22	0	
2009–10	Middlesbrough	30	1	
2010–11	Middlesbrough	17	0	
2011–12	Middlesbrough	39	0	
2012–13	Middlesbrough	31	1	
2013–14	Middlesbrough	3	0	142 2
2013–14	Millwall	5	0	
2014–15	Millwall	2	0	7 0
2015–16	Dagenham & R	25	0	25 0

HYDE, Tyrique (M) 0 0
b. 5-7-97

2015–16	Dagenham & R	0	0

LABADIE, Joss (M) 203 29
H: 5 7 W: 11 02 b.Croydon 31-8-90

2008–09	WBA	0	0	
2008–09	Shrewsbury T	1	0	
2009–10	WBA	0	0	
2009–10	Shrewsbury T	13	5	14 5
2009–10	Cheltenham T	11	0	11 0
2009–10	Tranmere R	9	3	
2010–11	Tranmere R	34	2	
2011–12	Tranmere R	27	5	70 10
2012–13	Notts Co	24	2	
2012–13	Torquay U	7	4	
2013–14	Notts Co	15	1	39 3
2013–14	Torquay U	10	1	17 5
2014–15	Dagenham & R	24	2	
2015–16	Dagenham & R	28	4	52 6

McCLURE, Matt (F) 130 28
H: 5 10 W: 11 00 b.Slough 17-11-91
Internationals: Northern Ireland U19, U21.

2010–11	Wycombe W	8	0	
2011–12	Wycombe W	12	1	
2012–13	Wycombe W	27	11	
2013–14	Wycombe W	36	7	
2014–15	Wycombe W	27	5	110 24
2015–16	Dagenham & R	20	4	20 4

MITCHELL, Scott (M) 0 0
b. 1-9-98

2015–16	Dagenham & R	0	0

MOORE, Lewis (G) 0 0
b. 28-8-96

2014–15	Dagenham & R	0	0
2015–16	Dagenham & R	0	0

NOSWORTHY, Nyron (D) 434 9
H: 6 0 W: 12 08 b.Brixton 11-10-80
Internationals: Jamaica Full caps.

1998–99	Gillingham	3	0
1999–2000	Gillingham	29	1
2000–01	Gillingham	10	0
2001–02	Gillingham	29	0
2002–03	Gillingham	39	2
2003–04	Gillingham	27	2
2004–05	Gillingham	37	0	174 5
2005–06	Sunderland	30	0
2006–07	Sunderland	29	0
2007–08	Sunderland	29	0
2008–09	Sunderland	16	0
2009–10	Sunderland	10	0
2009–10	Sheffield U	19	0
2010–11	Sunderland	0	0	114 0
2010–11	Sheffield U	32	0	51 0
2011–12	Watford	32	2
2012–13	Watford	19	0
2013–14	Watford	5	0	56 2
2013–14	Bristol C	10	1	10 1
2014–15	Blackpool	5	0	5 0
2014–15	Portsmouth	7	0	7 0
2015–16	Dagenham & R	17	1	17 1

O'BRIEN, Liam (G) 55 0
H: 6 1 W: 12 06 b.Ruislip 30-11-91
Internationals: England U19.

2008–09	Portsmouth	0	0	
2009–10	Portsmouth	0	0	
2010–11	Barnet	8	0	
2011–12	Barnet	10	0	
2012–13	Barnet	3	0	21 0
2013–14	Brentford	0	0	
2014–15	Dagenham & R	10	0	
2015–16	Dagenham & R	24	0	34 0

PASSLEY, Josh (D) 56 1
H: 6 0 W: 12 06 b.Chelsea 21-9-93

2013–14	Fulham	0	0	
2014–15	Fulham	0	0	
2014–15	Shrewsbury T	6	0	6 0
2014–15	Portsmouth	12	0	12 0
2015–16	Dagenham & R	38	1	38 1

PENNELL, Luke (D) 5 0
b. 26-1-96
From Banbury U, Wolverton T, Dunstable T.

2015–16	Dagenham & R	5	0	5 0

RAYMOND, Frankie (M) 12 2
H: 5 10 W: 11 09 b.Chislehurst 18-11-92

2010–11	Reading	0	0	
2011–12	Reading	0	0	

From Eastleigh, Eastbourne Bor.

2014–15	Dagenham & R	2	1	
2015–16	Dagenham & R	10	1	12 2

RICHARDS, Matt (D) 472 41
H: 5 8 W: 11 00 b.Harlow 26-12-84
Internationals: England U16, U17, U18, U21.

2001–02	Ipswich T	0	0	
2002–03	Ipswich T	13	0	
2003–04	Ipswich T	44	1	
2004–05	Ipswich T	24	1	
2005–06	Ipswich T	38	4	
2006–07	Ipswich T	28	2	
2007–08	Ipswich T	5	0	
2007–08	Brighton & HA	28	0	
2008–09	Brighton & HA	23	1	51 1
2008–09	Wycombe W	0	0	
2008–09	Notts Co	1	0	1 0
2008–09	Ipswich T	1	0	148 8
2009–10	Walsall	40	4	
2010–11	Walsall	46	8	86 12
2011–12	Shrewsbury T	42	5	
2012–13	Shrewsbury T	43	7	85 12
2013–14	Cheltenham T	46	6	
2014–15	Cheltenham T	45	2	91 8
2015–16	Dagenham & R	10	0	10 0

SHEPHERD, Jimmy (D) 2 0
b. 23-12-97

2015–16	Dagenham & R	2	0	2 0

WIDDOWSON, Joe (D) 252 1
H: 6 0 W: 12 00 b.Forest Gate 28-3-89

2007–08	West Ham U	0	0	
2007–08	Rotherham U	3	0	3 0
2008–09	West Ham U	0	0	
2008–09	Grimsby T	20	1	
2009–10	Grimsby T	38	0	58 1
2010–11	Rochdale	34	0	
2011–12	Rochdale	32	0	66 0
2012–13	Northampton T	39	0	
2013–14	Northampton T	25	0	64 0
2014–15	Bury	1	0	1 0
2014–15	Morecambe	8	0	8 0
2014–15	Dagenham & R	21	0	
2015–16	Dagenham & R	31	0	52 0

YUSUFF, Ade (F) 19 2
H: 5 7 W: 10 06 b.Lewisham 25-5-94

2014–15	Dagenham & R	18	2	
2015–16	Dagenham & R	1	0	19 2

Scholars
Brown, Harvey Joseph; Burnett, Henry; Carter, Joseph Matthew; Foxley, Darren Stepan Stanley; Hackett-Fairchild, Reeco Lee; Heather, Kai Joseph; Holmes, Charles Stephen; Hyde-Skerritt, Tyrique Micah; Mitchell, Scott Mark; Mongoy, Jordy Bonyolo; Nicol-Wilson, David Ronald Adrian Ayodeje; Nottage, James Lloyd Thomas; Shepherd, James Frederick Alan; Symes, Paul George; White, Joseph Frederick.

DERBY CO (32)

ALBENTOSA, Raul (D) 151 12
H: 6 4 W: 14 00 b.Alzira 7-9-88

2011–12	San Rocque	31	3	31 3
2012–13	Cadiz	33	3	33 3
2013–14	Eibar	33	2	
2014–15	Eibar	17	2	50 4
2014–15	Derby Co	8	0	
2015–16	Derby Co	0	0	8 0
2015–16	Malaga	29	2	29 2

BAIRD, Chris (D) 269 7
H: 5 10 W: 11 11 b.Ballymoney 25-2-82
Internationals: Northern Ireland U18, U21, Full caps.

2000–01	Southampton	0	0	
2001–02	Southampton	0	0	
2002–03	Southampton	3	0	
2003–04	Southampton	4	0	
2003–04	Walsall	10	0	10 0
2003–04	Watford	8	0	8 0
2004–05	Southampton	0	0	
2005–06	Southampton	17	0	
2006–07	Southampton	44	3	68 3
2007–08	Fulham	18	0	
2008–09	Fulham	10	0	
2009–10	Fulham	32	0	
2010–11	Fulham	29	2	
2011–12	Fulham	19	0	
2012–13	Fulham	19	2	
2013–14	Reading	9	0	9 0
2013–14	Burnley	7	0	7 0
2014–15	WBA	19	0	19 0
2015–16	Derby Co	14	0	14 0
2015–16	Fulham	7	0	134 4

BENNETT, Mason (F) 62 3
H: 5 10 W: 10 02 b.Shirebrook 15-7-96
Internationals: England U16, U17, U19.

2011–12	Derby Co	9	0	
2012–13	Derby Co	6	0	
2013–14	Derby Co	13	1	
2013–14	Chesterfield	5	0	5 0
2014–15	Derby Co	2	0	
2015–16	Bradford C	11	1	11 1
2015–16	Derby Co	0	0	30 1
2015–16	Burton Alb	16	1	16 1

BENT, Darren (F) 434 168
H: 5 11 W: 12 07 b.Wandsworth 6-2-84
Internationals: England U15, U16, U17, U19, U21, Full caps.

2001–02	Ipswich T	5	1	
2002–03	Ipswich T	35	12	
2003–04	Ipswich T	37	16	
2004–05	Ipswich T	45	20	122 49
2005–06	Charlton Ath	36	18	
2006–07	Charlton Ath	32	13	68 31
2007–08	Tottenham H	27	6	
2008–09	Tottenham H	33	12	
2009–10	Tottenham H	0	0	60 18
2009–10	Sunderland	38	24	
2010–11	Sunderland	20	8	58 32
2010–11	Aston Villa	16	9	
2011–12	Aston Villa	22	9	
2012–13	Aston Villa	16	3	
2013–14	Aston Villa	0	0	
2013–14	Fulham	24	3	24 3
2014–15	Aston Villa	7	0	61 21
2014–15	Brighton & HA	5	2	5 2
2014–15	Derby Co	15	10	
2015–16	Derby Co	21	2	36 12

BLACKMAN, Nick (F) 208 44
H: 6 2 W: 11 08 b.Whitefield 11-11-89

2006–07	Macclesfield T	1	0	
2007–08	Macclesfield T	11	1	
2008–09	Macclesfield T	0	0	12 1
2008–09	Blackburn R	0	0	
2008–09	Blackpool	5	1	5 1
2009–10	Blackburn R	0	0	
2009–10	Oldham Ath	12	1	12 1
2010–11	Blackburn R	0	0	
2010–11	Motherwell	18	10	18 10

2010–11	Aberdeen	15	2	15	2
2011–12	Blackburn R	1	0		
2012–13	Blackburn R	0	0	1	0
2012–13	Sheffield U	28	11	28	11
2012–13	Reading	11	0		
2013–14	Reading	30	4		
2014–15	Reading	37	3		
2015–16	Reading	25	11	103	18
2015–16	Derby Co	14	0	14	0

BRYSON, Craig (M) 398 54
H: 5 7 W: 10 00 b.Rutherglen 6-11-86
Internationals: Scotland U21, Full caps.

2003–04	Clyde	0	0		
2004–05	Clyde	28	3		
2005–06	Clyde	33	2		
2006–07	Clyde	34	3	95	8
2007–08	Kilmarnock	19	4		
2008–09	Kilmarnock	33	2		
2009–10	Kilmarnock	33	4		
2010–11	Kilmarnock	33	2	118	12
2011–12	Derby Co	44	6		
2012–13	Derby Co	37	5		
2013–14	Derby Co	45	16		
2014–15	Derby Co	38	4		
2015–16	Derby Co	21	3	185	34

BUTTERFIELD, Jacob (D) 225 25
H: 5 10 W: 11 00 b.Bradford 10-6-90
Internationals: England U21.

2007–08	Barnsley	3	0		
2008–09	Barnsley	3	0		
2009–10	Barnsley	20	1		
2010–11	Barnsley	40	2		
2011–12	Barnsley	24	5	90	8
2012–13	Norwich C	0	0		
2012–13	Bolton W	8	0	8	0
2012–13	Crystal Palace	9	0	9	0
2013–14	Norwich C	0	0		
2013–14	Middlesbrough	31	3	31	3
2014–15	Huddersfield T	45	6		
2015–16	Huddersfield T	5	1	50	7
2015–16	Derby Co	37	7	37	7

BUXTON, Jake (D) 290 16
H: 6 1 W: 13 05 b.Sutton-in-Ashfield 4-3-85

2002–03	Mansfield T	0	0		
2003–04	Mansfield T	9	1		
2004–05	Mansfield T	30	1		
2005–06	Mansfield T	39	0		
2006–07	Mansfield T	30	1		
2007–08	Mansfield T	40	2		
2008–09	Mansfield T	0	0	151	5

From Burton Alb.

2008–09	Derby Co	0	0		
2009–10	Derby Co	19	1		
2010–11	Derby Co	1	0		
2011–12	Derby Co	21	2		
2012–13	Derby Co	31	3		
2013–14	Derby Co	45	2		
2014–15	Derby Co	19	3		
2015–16	Derby Co	3	0	139	11

CAMARA, Abdoul (F) 178 15
H: 5 9 W: 10 12 b.Mamar 20-2-90
Internationals: France U17, U18, U21. Ghana Full caps.

2008–09	Rennes	1	0		
2009–10	Rennes	0	0		
2009–10	Vannes	37	4	37	4
2010–11	Rennes	24	0		
2011–12	Rennes	2	0	27	0
2011–12	Sochaux	21	1		
2012–13	Sochaux	15	0		
2012–13	PAOK	13	2	13	2
2013–14	Sochaux	11	0	47	1
2013–14	Mallorca	6	0	6	0
2014–15	Angers	27	6		
2015–16	Angers	17	2	44	8
2015–16	Derby Co	4	0	4	0

CARSON, Scott (G) 346 0
H: 6 0 W: 13 06 b.Whitehaven 3-9-85
Internationals: England U18, U21, B, Full caps.

2002–03	Leeds U	0	0		
2003–04	Leeds U	3	0		
2004–05	Leeds U	0	0	3	0
2004–05	Liverpool	0	0		
2005–06	Liverpool	0	0		
2005–06	Sheffield W	9	0	9	0
2006–07	Liverpool	0	0		
2006–07	Charlton Ath	36	0	36	0
2007–08	Liverpool	0	0	4	0
2007–08	Aston Villa	35	0	35	0
2008–09	WBA	35	0		
2009–10	WBA	43	0		
2010–11	WBA	32	0	110	0

2011–12	Bursaspor	34	0		
2012–13	Bursaspor	29	0	63	0
2013–14	Wigan Ath	16	0		
2014–15	Wigan Ath	34	0	50	0
2015–16	Derby Co	36	0	36	0

CHRISTIE, Cyrus (D) 182 3
H: 6 2 W: 12 03 b.Coventry 30-9-92
Internationals: Republic of Ireland Full caps.

2011–12	Coventry C	37	0		
2012–13	Coventry C	31	2		
2013–14	Coventry C	34	0	102	2
2014–15	Derby Co	38	0		
2015–16	Derby Co	42	1	80	1

DAWKINS, Simon (F) 141 22
H: 5 10 W: 11 01 b.Edgware 1-12-87
Internationals: Jamaica Full caps.

2005–06	Tottenham H	0	0		
2006–07	Tottenham H	0	0		
2007–08	Tottenham H	0	0		
2008–09	Tottenham H	0	0		
2008–09	Leyton Orient	11	0	11	0
2009–10	Tottenham H	0	0		
2010–11	Tottenham H	0	0		
2011	San Jose Earthquakes	26	6		
2011–12	Tottenham H	0	0		
2012	San Jose Earthquakes	29	8	55	14
2012–13	Tottenham H	0	0		
2012–13	Aston Villa	4	0	4	0
2013–14	Tottenham H	0	0		
2013–14	Derby Co	26	4		
2014–15	Derby Co	34	3		
2015–16	Derby Co	0	0	60	7
2015–16	San Jose Earthquakes	11	1	11	1

ELSNIK, Timi (M) 0 0
b. 29-4-98
Internationals: Slovenia U16, U17, U19.

2015–16	Derby Co	0	0		

FORSYTH, Craig (M) 235 18
H: 6 0 W: 12 00 b.Carnoustie 24-2-89
Internationals: Scotland Full caps.

2006–07	Dundee	1	0		
2007–08	Dundee	0	0		
2007–08	Montrose	9	0	9	0
2008–09	Dundee	1	0		
2008–09	Arbroath	26	2	26	2
2009–10	Dundee	24	2		
2010–11	Dundee	33	8	59	10
2011–12	Watford	20	3		
2012–13	Watford	2	0	22	3
2012–13	Bradford C	7	0	7	0
2012–13	Derby Co	10	0		
2013–14	Derby Co	46	2		
2014–15	Derby Co	44	1		
2015–16	Derby Co	12	0	112	3

GRANT, Lee (G) 437 0
H: 6 3 W: 13 01 b.Hemel Hempstead 27-1-83
Internationals: England U16, U17, U18, U19, U21.

2000–01	Derby Co	0	0		
2001–02	Derby Co	0	0		
2002–03	Derby Co	29	0		
2003–04	Derby Co	36	0		
2004–05	Derby Co	2	0		
2005–06	Derby Co	0	0		
2005–06	Burnley	1	0		
2005–06	Oldham Ath	16	0	16	0
2006–07	Derby Co	7	0		
2007–08	Sheffield W	44	0		
2008–09	Sheffield W	46	0		
2009–10	Sheffield W	46	0	136	0
2010–11	Burnley	25	0		
2011–12	Burnley	43	0		
2012–13	Burnley	46	0	115	0
2013–14	Derby Co	46	0		
2014–15	Derby Co	40	0		
2015–16	Derby Co	10	0	170	0

GUY, Callum (M) 0 0
b. 25-11-96

2015–16	Derby Co	0	0		

HANSON, Jamie (F) 20 1
H: 6 3 W: 12 06 b.Burton-upon-Trent 10-11-95
Internationals: England U20.

2012–13	Derby Co	0	0		
2013–14	Derby Co	0	0		
2014–15	Derby Co	2	1		
2015–16	Derby Co	18	0	20	1

HENDRICK, Jeff (M) 194 22
H: 6 1 W: 11 11 b.Dublin 31-1-92
Internationals: Republic of Ireland U17, U19, U21, Full caps.

2010–11	Derby Co	4	0		
2011–12	Derby Co	42	3		
2012–13	Derby Co	45	6		
2013–14	Derby Co	30	4		
2014–15	Derby Co	41	7		
2015–16	Derby Co	32	2	194	22

HUGHES, Will (M) 127 7
H: 6 1 W: 11 08 b.Weybridge 7-4-95
Internationals: England U17, U21.

2011–12	Derby Co	3	0		
2012–13	Derby Co	35	2		
2013–14	Derby Co	41	3		
2014–15	Derby Co	42	2		
2015–16	Derby Co	6	0	127	7

INCE, Tom (M) 148 49
H: 5 10 W: 10 06 b.Stockport 30-1-92
Internationals: England U17, U19, U21.

2011–12	Blackpool	0	0		
2012–13	Blackpool	44	18		
2013–14	Blackpool	23	7	67	25
2013–14	Crystal Palace	8	1	8	1
2014–15	Hull C	7	0	7	0
2014–15	Nottingham F	6	0	6	0
2014–15	Derby Co	18	11		
2015–16	Derby Co	42	12	60	23

JOHNSON, Brad (M) 354 53
H: 6 0 W: 12 10 b.Hackney 28-4-87

2004–05	Cambridge U	1	0	1	0
2005–06	Northampton T	3	0		
2006–07	Northampton T	27	5		
2007–08	Northampton T	23	2	53	7
2007–08	Leeds U	21	3		
2008–09	Leeds U	15	1		
2008–09	Brighton & HA	10	4	10	4
2009–10	Leeds U	36	7		
2010–11	Leeds U	45	5	117	16
2011–12	Norwich C	28	2		
2012–13	Norwich C	37	1		
2013–14	Norwich C	32	3		
2014–15	Norwich C	41	15		
2015–16	Norwich C	4	0	142	21
2015–16	Derby Co	31	5	31	5

KEOGH, Richard (D) 411 15
H: 6 0 W: 11 02 b.Harlow 11-8-86
Internationals: Republic of Ireland U21, Full caps.

2004–05	Stoke C	0	0		
2005–06	Bristol C	9	1		
2005–06	Wycombe W	3	0	3	0
2006–07	Bristol C	31	2		
2007–08	Bristol C	0	0	40	3
2007–08	Huddersfield T	9	1	9	1
2007–08	Carlisle U	7	0		
2007–08	Cheltenham T	10	0	10	0
2008–09	Carlisle U	32	1		
2009–10	Carlisle U	41	3	80	4
2010–11	Coventry C	46	1		
2011–12	Coventry C	45	0	91	1
2012–13	Derby Co	46	4		
2013–14	Derby Co	41	1		
2014–15	Derby Co	45	0		
2015–16	Derby Co	46	1	178	6

LOWE, Max (D) 0 0
b. 11-5-97
Internationals: England U16, U17, U18.

2013–14	Derby Co	0	0		
2014–15	Derby Co	0	0		
2015–16	Derby Co	0	0		

MACKAY, Devlin (G) 0 0
b. 23-1-97
Internationals: Scotland U17, U19.

2015–16	Kilmarnock	0	0		

On loan from Kilmarnock.

2015–16	Derby Co	0	0		

MARTIN, Chris (F) 317 99
H: 6 2 W: 12 06 b.Beccles 4-11-88
Internationals: England U19. Scotland Full caps.

2006–07	Norwich C	18	4		
2007–08	Norwich C	7	0		
2008–09	Norwich C	0	0		
2008–09	Luton T	40	11	40	11
2009–10	Norwich C	42	17		
2010–11	Norwich C	30	4		
2011–12	Norwich C	0	0		
2011–12	Crystal Palace	26	7	26	7
2012–13	Norwich C	1	0	102	25
2012–13	Swindon T	12	1	12	1

Season	Club	Apps	Gls	Tot A	Tot G
2012–13	*Derby Co*	13	2		
2013–14	Derby Co	44	20		
2014–15	Derby Co	35	18		
2015–16	Derby Co	45	15	137	55

MITCHELL, Jonathan (G)   5   0
H: 5 11 W: 13 08 b. 24-11-94

Season	Club	Apps	Gls	Tot A	Tot G
2014–15	Derby Co	0	0		
2015–16	Derby Co	0	0		
2015–16	*Luton T*	5	0	5	0

OLSSON, Marcus (M)   220   14
H: 5 11 W: 10 10 b.Gavle 17-5-88
Internationals: Sweden U21, Full caps.

Season	Club	Apps	Gls	Tot A	Tot G
2008	Halmstad	21	2		
2009	Halmstad	20	4		
2010	Halmstad	30	4		
2011	Halmstad	29	2	100	12
2011–12	Blackburn R	12	0		
2012–13	Blackburn R	23	1		
2013–14	Blackburn R	8	0		
2014–15	Blackburn R	41	0		
2015–16	Blackburn R	20	0	104	1
2015–16	Derby Co	16	1	16	1

PEARCE, Alex (D)   265   17
H: 6 0 W: 11 10 b.Wallingford 9-11-88
Internationals: Scotland U19, U21, Full caps.

Season	Club	Apps	Gls	Tot A	Tot G
2006–07	Reading	0	0		
2006–07	*Northampton T*	15	1	15	1
2007–08	Reading	0	0		
2007–08	*Bournemouth*	11	0	11	0
2007–08	*Norwich C*	11	0	11	0
2008–09	Reading	16	1		
2008–09	*Southampton*	9	2	9	2
2009–10	Reading	25	4		
2010–11	Reading	21	1		
2011–12	Reading	46	5		
2012–13	Reading	19	0		
2013–14	Reading	45	3		
2014–15	Reading	40	0	212	14
2015–16	Derby Co	0	0		
2015–16	*Bristol C*	7	0	7	0

RAWSON, Farrend (D)   20   2
b. 11-7-96

Season	Club	Apps	Gls	Tot A	Tot G
2013–14	Derby Co	0	0		
2014–15	*Rotherham U*	4	0		
2015–16	Derby Co	0	0		
2015–16	*Rotherham U*	16	2	20	2

ROOS, Kelle (G)   21   0
H: 6 4 W: 14 02 b. 31-5-92

Season	Club	Apps	Gls	Tot A	Tot G
2013–14	Derby Co	0	0		
2014–15	Derby Co	0	0		
2014–15	Derby Co	0	0		
2015–16	*Rotherham U*	4	0	4	0
2015–16	*AFC Wimbledon*	17	0	17	0

RUSSELL, Johnny (F)   225   55
H: 5 10 W: 12 03 b.Glasgow 8-4-90
Internationals: Scotland U19, U21, Full caps.

Season	Club	Apps	Gls	Tot A	Tot G
2006–07	Dundee U	1	0		
2007–08	Dundee U	2	0		
2008–09	Dundee U	0	0		
2009–10	Dundee U	0	0		
2010–11	Dundee U	30	9		
2011–12	Dundee U	37	9		
2012–13	Dundee U	32	13	102	31
2013–14	Derby Co	39	9		
2014–15	Derby Co	39	6		
2015–16	Derby Co	45	9	123	24

SAMMON, Conor (F)   326   53
H: 5 10 W: 11 11 b.Dublin 13-4-87
Internationals: Republic of Ireland U21, U23, Full caps.

Season	Club	Apps	Gls	Tot A	Tot G
2005	UCD	7	0		
2006	UCD	31	7		
2007	UCD	31	6	69	13
2008	Derry C	16	3	16	3
2008–09	Kilmarnock	17	1		
2009–10	Kilmarnock	25	1		
2010–11	Kilmarnock	23	15	65	17
2010–11	Wigan Ath	7	1		
2011–12	Wigan Ath	25	0	32	1
2012–13	Derby Co	45	8		
2013–14	Derby Co	37	2		
2014–15	Derby Co	1	0		
2014–15	*Ipswich T*	19	1	19	1
2014–15	*Rotherham U*	15	3	15	3
2015–16	Derby Co	0	0	83	10
2015–16	*Sheffield U*	27	5	27	5

SANTOS, Alefe (M)   27   1
H: 5 10 W: 10 06 b.Sao Paulo 28-1-95

Season	Club	Apps	Gls	Tot A	Tot G
2012–13	Bristol R	1	0		
2013	Ponte Preta	0	0		
2013–14	Bristol R	23	1	24	1
2014–15	Derby Co	0	0		

Season	Club	Apps	Gls	Tot A	Tot G
2014–15	*Notts Co*	3	0	3	0
2015–16	Derby Co	0	0		

SHACKELL, Jason (D)   430   13
H: 6 4 W: 13 06 b.Stevenage 27-9-83

Season	Club	Apps	Gls	Tot A	Tot G
2002–03	Norwich C	2	0		
2003–04	Norwich C	6	0		
2004–05	Norwich C	11	0		
2005–06	Norwich C	17	0		
2006–07	Norwich C	43	3		
2007–08	Norwich C	39	0		
2008–09	Norwich C	15	0	133	3
2008–09	Wolverhampton W	12	0		
2009–10	Wolverhampton W	0	0	12	0
2009–10	*Doncaster R*	21	1	21	1
2010–11	Barnsley	44	3		
2011–12	Barnsley	0	0	44	3
2011–12	Derby Co	44	1		
2012–13	Burnley	44	2		
2013–14	Burnley	46	2		
2014–15	Burnley	38	0	128	4
2015–16	Derby Co	46	1	92	2

SHOTTON, Ryan (D)   160   10
H: 6 3 W: 13 05 b.Stoke 30-9-88

Season	Club	Apps	Gls	Tot A	Tot G
2006–07	Stoke C	0	0		
2007–08	Stoke C	0	0		
2008–09	Stoke C	0	0		
2008–09	*Tranmere R*	33	5	33	5
2009–10	Stoke C	0	0		
2009–10	*Barnsley*	30	0	30	0
2010–11	Stoke C	2	0		
2011–12	Stoke C	23	1		
2012–13	Stoke C	23	0		
2013–14	Stoke C	0	0	48	1
2013–14	*Wigan Ath*	9	1	9	1
2014–15	Derby Co	25	2		
2015–16	Derby Co	6	0	31	2
2015–16	*Birmingham C*	9	1	9	1

THOMAS, Kwame (F)   27   0
H: 5 10 W: 12 00 b.Nottingham 28-9-95
Internationals: England U16, U17, U20.

Season	Club	Apps	Gls	Tot A	Tot G
2011–12	Derby Co	0	0		
2012–13	Derby Co	0	0		
2013–14	Derby Co	0	0		
2014–15	Derby Co	4	0		
2014–15	*Notts Co*	5	0	5	0
2015–16	Derby Co	0	0	4	0
2015–16	*Blackpool*	18	0	18	0

THOMAS, Luke (F)   0   0

Season	Club	Apps	Gls	Tot A	Tot G
2015–16	Derby Co	0	0		

THORNE, George (M)   85   4
H: 6 2 W: 13 01 b.Chatham 4-1-93
Internationals: England U16, U17, U18, U19.

Season	Club	Apps	Gls	Tot A	Tot G
2009–10	WBA	1	0		
2010–11	WBA	1	0		
2011–12	WBA	3	0		
2011–12	*Portsmouth*	14	0	14	0
2012–13	WBA	5	0		
2012–13	*Peterborough U*	7	1	7	1
2013–14	WBA	0	0	10	0
2013–14	*Watford*	8	0	8	0
2013–14	*Derby Co*	9	1		
2014–15	Derby Co	3	0		
2015–16	Derby Co	34	2	46	3

TUITE, Jack (D)   0   0
b. 27-1-97
Internationals: Republic of Ireland U16, U18, U19.

Season	Club	Apps	Gls	Tot A	Tot G
2014–15	Chesterfield	0	0		
2015–16	Derby Co	0	0		

WALKER, Lewis (F)   0   0

Season	Club	Apps	Gls	Tot A	Tot G
2015–16	Derby Co	0	0		

WARNOCK, Stephen (D)   385   15
H: 5 7 W: 11 09 b.Ormskirk 12-12-81
Internationals: England Full caps.

Season	Club	Apps	Gls	Tot A	Tot G
1998–99	Liverpool	0	0		
1999-2000	Liverpool	0	0		
2000–01	Liverpool	0	0		
2001–02	Liverpool	0	0		
2002–03	Liverpool	0	0		
2002–03	*Bradford C*	12	1	12	1
2003–04	Liverpool	0	0		
2003–04	*Coventry C*	44	3	44	3
2004–05	Liverpool	19	0		
2005–06	Liverpool	20	1		
2006–07	Liverpool	1	0	40	1
2006–07	Blackburn R	13	1		
2007–08	Blackburn R	37	1		
2008–09	Blackburn R	37	3		
2009–10	Blackburn R	1	0	88	5
2009–10	Aston Villa	30	0		
2010–11	Aston Villa	19	0		
2011–12	Aston Villa	35	2		
2012–13	Aston Villa	0	0	84	2
2012–13	*Bolton W*	15	0	15	0
2012–13	Leeds U	16	1		
2013–14	Leeds U	27	1		
2014–15	Leeds U	21	1	64	3
2014–15	Derby Co	7	0		
2015–16	Derby Co	20	0	27	0
2015–16	*Wigan Ath*	11	0	11	0

WEIMANN, Andreas (F)   164   25
H: 5 9 W: 11 09 b.Vienna 5-8-91
Internationals: Austria U17, U19, U20, U21, Full caps.

Season	Club	Apps	Gls	Tot A	Tot G
2008–09	Aston Villa	0	0		
2009–10	Aston Villa	0	0		
2010–11	Aston Villa	1	0		
2010–11	*Watford*	18	4		
2011 12	Aston Villa	14	2		
2011–12	*Watford*	3	0	21	4
2012–13	Aston Villa	30	7		
2013–14	Aston Villa	37	5		
2014–15	Aston Villa	31	3	113	17
2015–16	Derby Co	30	4	30	4

YATES, Matthew (G)   0   0
Internationals: England U17.

Season	Club	Apps	Gls	Tot A	Tot G
2015–16	Derby Co	0	0		

ZANZALA, Offrande (F)   2   0
b. 13-12-97

Season	Club	Apps	Gls	Tot A	Tot G
2015–16	Derby Co	0	0		
2015–16	*Stevenage*	2	0	2	0

Players retained or with offer of contract
Babos, Alexander Jon; Barnes, Joshua Edwin; Cover, Alexander Robert; Gordon, Kellan Sheene; Jakobsen, Emil Riis; Macdonald, Calum Ross; Mellors, Thomas James; Ravas, Henrich; Stabana, Kyron Thomas; Vernam, Charles Terence Priestley; Wassall, Ethan Luca.

Scholars
Bateman, Joseph Joshua; Bird, Jared; Carvell, James Shaun; Davidson-Miller, Jahvan O'Mahr; Edwards, Micah Elijah; Goode, Harry Samuel; Magno, Giann Michael; Yates, Matthew Dean.

DONCASTER R (33)

ALCOCK, Craig (D)   257   3
H: 5 8 W: 11 00 b.Cornwall 8-12-87

Season	Club	Apps	Gls	Tot A	Tot G
2006–07	Yeovil T	1	0		
2007–08	Yeovil T	8	0		
2008–09	Yeovil T	30	1		
2009–10	Yeovil T	42	1		
2010–11	Yeovil T	26	1	107	3
2011–12	Peterborough U	41	0		
2012–13	Peterborough U	27	0		
2013–14	Peterborough U	28	0	96	0
2014–15	Sheffield U	24	0		
2015–16	Sheffield U	3	0	27	0
2015–16	Doncaster R	27	0	27	0

ASKINS, Ben (M)   0   0
H: 5 11 W: 11 05 b.Middlesbrough 2-1-96

Season	Club	Apps	Gls	Tot A	Tot G
2014–15	Doncaster R	0	0		
2015–16	Doncaster R	0	0		

BROWN, Scott (M)   0   0
b.Doncaster 16-7-96

Season	Club	Apps	Gls	Tot A	Tot G
2014–15	Doncaster R	0	0		
2015–16	Doncaster R	0	0		

BUTLER, Andy (D)   438   41
H: 6 0 W: 13 00 b.Doncaster 4-11-83

Season	Club	Apps	Gls	Tot A	Tot G
2003–04	Scunthorpe U	35	2		
2004–05	Scunthorpe U	37	10		
2005–06	Scunthorpe U	16	1		
2006–07	Scunthorpe U	11	1		
2006–07	*Grimsby T*	4	0	4	0
2007–08	Scunthorpe U	36	2	135	16
2008–09	Huddersfield T	42	4		
2009–10	Huddersfield T	11	0	53	4
2009–10	*Blackpool*	7	0	7	0
2010–11	Walsall	31	4		
2011–12	Walsall	42	5		
2012–13	Walsall	41	3		
2013–14	Walsall	45	2		
2014–15	Sheffield U	0	0		
2014–15	*Walsall*	7	0	166	14
2014–15	Doncaster R	33	3		
2015–16	Doncaster R	40	4	73	7

CARBERRY, Michael (D)   0   0
H: 5 7 W: 9 13 b.Liverpool 5-3-98

Season	Club	Apps	Gls	Tot A	Tot G
2015–16	Doncaster R	0	0		

CHAPLOW, Richard (M)   312   28
H: 5 9   W: 9 03   b.Accrington 2-2-85
Internationals: England U19, U20, U21.

2002–03	Burnley	5	0		
2003–04	Burnley	39	5		
2004–05	Burnley	21	2	65	7
2004–05	WBA	4	0		
2005–06	WBA	7	0		
2005–06	*Southampton*	11	1		
2006–07	WBA	28	1		
2007–08	WBA	5	0	44	1
2007–08	Preston NE	12	3		
2008–09	Preston NE	25	3		
2009–10	Preston NE	31	2		
2010–11	Preston NE	0	0	68	8
2010–11	Southampton	33	4		
2011–12	Southampton	25	3		
2012–13	Southampton	3	0	72	8
2012–13	*Millwall*	4	0		
2013–14	Millwall	19	1		
2014–15	Millwall	7	0	30	1
2014–15	*Ipswich T*	6	1	6	1
2015–16	Doncaster R	27	2	27	2

COPPINGER, James (F)   507   53
H: 5 7   W: 10 03   b.Middlesbrough 10-1-81
Internationals: England U16.

1997–98	Newcastle U	0	0		
1998–99	Newcastle U	0	0		
1999–2000	Newcastle U	0	0		
1999–2000	*Hartlepool U*	10	3		
2000–01	Newcastle U	1	0		
2001–02	Newcastle U	0	0	1	0
2001–02	*Hartlepool U*	14	2	24	5
2002–03	Exeter C	43	5	43	5
2004–05	Doncaster R	31	0		
2005–06	Doncaster R	36	5		
2006–07	Doncaster R	39	4		
2007–08	Doncaster R	39	3		
2008–09	Doncaster R	32	5		
2009–10	Doncaster R	39	4		
2010–11	Doncaster R	40	7		
2011–12	Doncaster R	38	2		
2012–13	Doncaster R	25	2		
2012–13	*Nottingham F*	6	0	6	0
2013–14	Doncaster R	41	4		
2014–15	Doncaster R	34	4		
2015–16	Doncaster R	39	3	433	43

DAVIES, Matthew (D)   0   0
H: 5 11   W: 10 10   b.Worksop 19-9-96

2015–16	Doncaster R	0	0	

EVINA, Cedric (D)   111   3
H: 5 11   W: 12 08   b.Cameroon 16-11-91

2009–10	Arsenal	0	0		
2010–11	Arsenal	0	0		
2010–11	Oldham Ath	27	2	27	2
2011–12	Charlton Ath	3	0		
2012–13	Charlton Ath	12	0		
2013–14	Charlton Ath	8	0	23	0
2014–15	Doncaster R	19	0		
2015–16	Doncaster R	42	1	61	1

FORRESTER, Harry (F)   126   20
H: 5 9   W: 11 03   b.Milton Keynes 2-1-91
Internationals: England U16, U17.

2007–08	Aston Villa	0	0		
2008–09	Aston Villa	0	0		
2009–10	Aston Villa	0	0		
2010–11	*Kilmarnock*	7	0	7	0
2011–12	Brentford	19	0		
2012–13	Brentford	36	8	55	8
2013–14	Doncaster R	7	0		
2014–15	Doncaster R	40	7		
2015–16	Doncaster R	7	1	54	8
2015–16	Rangers	10	4	10	4

JONES, Lewis (G)   0   0

2015–16	Doncaster R	0	0	

KEEGAN, Paul (M)   279   14
H: 5 11   W: 11 05   b.Dublin 5-7-84
Internationals: Republic of Ireland U16, U21, U23.

2000–01	Leeds U	0	0		
2001–02	Leeds U	0	0		
2002–03	Leeds U	0	0		
2003–04	Leeds U	0	0		
2003–04	*Scunthorpe U*	2	0	2	0
2004–05	Leeds U	0	0		
2005	Drogheda	11	0		
2006	Drogheda	25	4		
2007	Drogheda	30	1		
2008	Drogheda	27	1	93	6
2009	Bohemians	34	2		
2010	Bohemians	32	4	66	6
2010–11	Doncaster R	10	0		

2011–12	Doncaster R	2	0		
2012–13	Doncaster R	25	1		
2013–14	Doncaster R	34	0		
2014–15	Doncaster R	32	0		
2015–16	Doncaster R	15	1	118	2

LINELY, Jordan (M)   0   0
H: 5 7   W: 9 13   b.Doncaster 23-1-97

2015–16	Doncaster R	0	0	

LONGBOTTOM, William (F)   1   0

2015–16	Doncaster R	1	0	1	0

LUND, Mitchell (D)   34   1
H: 6 1   W: 11 11   b.Leeds 27-8-96

2014–15	Doncaster R	4	0		
2015–16	Doncaster R	30	1	34	1

MACKENZIE, Gary (D)   241   9
H: 6 3   W: 13 01   b.Lanark 15-10-85

2003–04	Rangers	2	0		
2004–05	Rangers	0	0		
2005–06	Rangers	0	0	2	0
2006–07	Dundee	21	0		
2007–08	Dundee	33	1		
2008–09	Dundee	19	0		
2009–10	Dundee	25	1	98	2
2010–11	Milton Keynes D	26	2		
2011–12	Milton Keynes D	26	1		
2012–13	Milton Keynes D	11	0	63	3
2012–13	*Blackpool*	12	2		
2013–14	Blackpool	35	1		
2014–15	Blackpool	0	0	47	3
2014–15	*Bradford C*	12	1	12	1
2015–16	Doncaster R	15	0	15	0
2015–16	*Notts Co*	4	0	4	0

MAIN, Curtis (F)   164   24
H: 5 9   W: 12 02   b.South Shields 20-6-92

2007–08	Darlington	1	0		
2008–09	Darlington	18	2		
2009–10	Darlington	26	3		
2010–11	Darlington	0	0	45	5
2011–12	Middlesbrough	12	2		
2012–13	Middlesbrough	13	3		
2013–14	Middlesbrough	23	1	48	6
2013–14	*Shrewsbury T*	5	0	5	0
2014–15	Doncaster R	38	8		
2015–16	Doncaster R	10	1	48	9
2015–16	*Oldham Ath*	18	4	18	4

MANDEVILLE, Liam (F)   11   1
H: 5 11   W: 12 02   b.Lincoln 17-2-97

2014–15	Doncaster R	3	0		
2015–16	Doncaster R	8	1	11	1

MAROSI, Marko (G)   4   0
H: 6 3   W: 12 08   b. 23-10-93
Internationals: Slovakia U21.

2013–14	Wigan Ath	0	0		
2014–15	Doncaster R	3	0		
2015–16	Doncaster R	1	0	4	0

MBUTI, Kevin (D)   0   0
H: 6 0   W: 10 10   b. 31-12-97

McCULLOUGH, Luke (D)   80   0
H: 6 2   W: 12 11   b.Portadown 15-2-94
Internationals: Northern Ireland U16, U17, U19, U20, U21, Full caps.

2012–13	Manchester U	0	0		
2012–13	*Cheltenham T*	1	0	1	0
2013–14	Doncaster R	14	0		
2014–15	Doncaster R	33	0		
2015–16	Doncaster R	32	0	79	0

McLAREN, Jack (G)   0   0

2014–15	Doncaster R	0	0	
2015–16	Doncaster R	0	0	

MIDDLETON, Harry (M)   38   0
H: 5 11   W: 11 00   b.Doncaster 12-4-95

2012–13	Doncaster R	0	0		
2013–14	Doncaster R	0	0		
2014–15	Doncaster R	4	0		
2015–16	Doncaster R	34	0	38	0

N'GUESSAN, Dany (M)   234   40
H: 6 0   W: 12 13   b.Paris 11-8-87

2006–07	Boston U	23	5	23	5
2006–07	Lincoln C	9	0		
2007–08	Lincoln C	37	7		
2008–09	Lincoln C	45	8	91	15
2009–10	Leicester C	27	3		
2010–11	Leicester C	5	0	32	3
2010–11	*Scunthorpe U*	3	1	3	1
2010–11	*Southampton*	6	0	6	0
2011–12	Millwall	15	1		
2011–12	*Charlton Ath*	7	4	7	4
2012–13	Millwall	13	1		
2013–14	Millwall	1	0	29	2

2013–14	Swindon T	24	8	24	8
2014–15	Port Vale	11	2	11	2
2015–16	Doncaster R	8	0	8	0

PUGH, Joseph (F)   0   0
b. 10-10-97

2015–16	Doncaster R	0	0	

STUCKMANN, Thorsten (G)   374   0
H: 6 6   W: 14 11   b.Gutersloh 17-3-81
Internationals: Germany U20, U21.

2000–01	Pr Munster	25	0		
2001–02	Pr Munster	19	0		
2002–03	Pr Munster	30	0	74	0
2003–04	E Braunschweig	21	0		
2004–05	E Braunschweig	36	0		
2005–06	E Braunschweig	34	0		
2006–07	E Braunschweig	34	0	125	0
2007–08	A Aachen	16	0		
2008–09	A Aachen	34	0		
2009–10	A Aachen	31	0		
2010–11	A Aachen	1	0	82	0
2011–12	Preston NE	28	0		
2012–13	Preston NE	22	0		
2013–14	Preston NE	0	0		
2014–15	Preston NE	7	0	57	0
2015–16	Doncaster R	36	0	36	0

TAYLOR-SINCLAIR, Aaron (D)   203   11
H: 6 1   W: 11 07   b.Aberdeen 8-4-91

2008–09	Montrose	1	0		
2009–10	Montrose	30	2		
2010–11	Montrose	35	3	66	5
2011–12	Partick Thistle	30	1		
2012–13	Partick Thistle	28	1		
2013–14	Partick Thistle	36	2	94	4
2014–15	Wigan Ath	0	0		
2015–16	Doncaster R	43	2	43	2

TYSON, Nathan (F)   452   102
H: 5 10   W: 10 02   b.Reading 4-5-82
Internationals: England U20.

1999–2000	Reading	1	0		
2000–01	Reading	0	0		
2001–02	Reading	0	0		
2001–02	*Swansea C*	11	1	11	1
2001–02	*Cheltenham T*	8	1	8	1
2002–03	Reading	23	1		
2003–04	Reading	8	0	33	1
2003–04	Wycombe W	21	9		
2004–05	Wycombe W	42	22		
2005–06	Wycombe W	15	11	78	42
2005–06	Nottingham F	28	10		
2006–07	Nottingham F	24	7		
2007–08	Nottingham F	34	9		
2008–09	Nottingham F	35	5		
2009–10	Nottingham F	33	2		
2010–11	Nottingham F	30	2	184	35
2011–12	Derby Co	23	0		
2012–13	Derby Co	16	4		
2012–13	*Millwall*	4	0	4	0
2013–14	Derby Co	0	0	39	4
2013–14	*Blackpool*	10	0	10	0
2013–14	*Fleetwood T*	4	0	4	0
2013–14	*Notts Co*	10	0	10	0
2014–15	Doncaster R	39	12		
2015–16	Doncaster R	32	6	71	18

WHITEHOUSE, Billy (M)   6   0
H: 5 11   W: 11 05   b.Rotherham 13-6-96

2014–15	Doncaster R	4	0		
2015–16	Doncaster R	2	0	6	0

WILLIAMS, Andy (F)   371   84
H: 5 11   W: 11 09   b.Hereford 14-8-86

2006–07	Hereford U	14	8		
2007–08	Bristol R	41	4		
2008–09	Bristol R	4	1		
2008–09	*Hereford U*	26	2	67	10
2009–10	Bristol R	43	3	88	8
2010–11	Yeovil T	37	6		
2011–12	Yeovil T	35	11		
2012–13	Swindon T	40	11		
2013–14	Swindon T	3	0		
2013–14	*Yeovil T*	9	0	81	22
2014–15	Swindon T	46	21	89	32
2015–16	Doncaster R	46	12	46	12

Scholars
Barker, Joshua Ryan; Carberry, Michael
George; Fielding, Reece Thomas; Gains,
Matthew Anthony George; Henderson, Lloyd
John; Iveson, Johnathan; Jones, Louis; Linley,
Jordan Alex; Longbottom, William Radley;
Mbuti, Sala Kevin; McCormick, Joseph
David; Parkin, Matthew David; Pugh, Joseph
James; Walker, Tyler; Wanless, Ryan
Norman; Williamson, Conner Reece.

EVERTON (34)

BAINES, Leighton (D)   425   29
H: 5 8   W: 11 00   b.Liverpool 11-12-84
Internationals: England U21, Full caps.

2002–03	Wigan Ath	6	0		
2003–04	Wigan Ath	26	0		
2004–05	Wigan Ath	41	1		
2005–06	Wigan Ath	37	0		
2006–07	Wigan Ath	35	3		
2007–08	Wigan Ath	0	0	145	4
2007–08	Everton	22	0		
2008–09	Everton	31	1		
2009–10	Everton	37	1		
2010–11	Everton	38	5		
2011–12	Everton	33	4		
2012–13	Everton	38	5		
2013–14	Everton	32	5		
2014–15	Everton	31	2		
2015–16	Everton	18	2	280	25

BARKLEY, Ross (M)   131   20
H: 6 2   W: 12 00   b.Liverpool 5-12-93
Internationals: England U16, U17, U19, U20, U21, Full caps.

2010–11	Everton	0	0		
2011–12	Everton	6	0		
2012–13	Everton	7	0		
2012–13	Sheffield W	13	4	13	4
2012–13	Leeds U	4	0	4	0
2013–14	Everton	34	6		
2014–15	Everton	29	2		
2015–16	Everton	38	8	114	16

BARRY, Gareth (M)   595   50
H: 5 11   W: 12 06   b.Hastings 23-2-81
Internationals: England B, U21, Full caps.

1997–98	Aston Villa	2	0		
1998–99	Aston Villa	32	2		
1999–2000	Aston Villa	30	1		
2000–01	Aston Villa	30	0		
2001–02	Aston Villa	20	0		
2002–03	Aston Villa	35	3		
2003–04	Aston Villa	36	3		
2004–05	Aston Villa	34	7		
2005–06	Aston Villa	36	3		
2006–07	Aston Villa	35	8		
2007–08	Aston Villa	37	9		
2008–09	Aston Villa	38	5	365	41
2009–10	Manchester C	34	2		
2010–11	Manchester C	33	2		
2011–12	Manchester C	34	1		
2012–13	Manchester C	31	1		
2013–14	Manchester C	0	0	132	6
2013–14	Everton	32	3		
2014–15	Everton	33	0		
2015–16	Everton	33	0	98	3

BESIC, Muhamed (M)   85   1
H: 5 10   W: 11 11   b.Berlin 10-9-92
Internationals: Bosnia-Herzegovina U21, Full caps.

2010–11	Hamburg	3	0		
2011–12	Hamburg	0	0		
2012–13	Hamburg	0	0	3	0
2012–13	Ferencvaros	22	1		
2013–14	Ferencvaros	25	0	47	1
2014–15	Everton	23	0		
2015–16	Everton	12	0	35	0

BROWNING, Tyias (D)   9   0
H: 5 11   W: 12 00   b.Liverpool 27-5-94
Internationals: England U17, U19, U20.

2011–12	Everton	0	0		
2012–13	Everton	0	0		
2013–14	Everton	0	0		
2013–14	Wigan Ath	2	0	2	0
2014–15	Everton	2	0		
2015–16	Everton	5	0	7	0

CLEVERLEY, Tom (M)   181   24
H: 5 9   W: 10 07   b.Basingstoke 12-8-89
Internationals: England U20, U21, Full caps. Great Britain.

2007–08	Manchester U	0	0		
2008–09	Manchester U	0	0		
2008–09	Leicester C	15	2	15	2
2009–10	Manchester U	0	0		
2009–10	Watford	33	11	33	11
2010–11	Manchester U	0	0		
2010–11	Wigan Ath	25	3	25	3
2011–12	Manchester U	10	0		
2012–13	Manchester U	22	2		
2013–14	Manchester U	22	1		
2014–15	Manchester U	1	0	55	3
2014–15	Aston Villa	31	3	31	3
2015–16	Everton	22	2	22	2

COLEMAN, Seamus (D)   189   15
H: 6 4   W: 10 07   b.Donegal 11-10-88
Internationals: Republic of Ireland U21, U23, Full caps.

2008–09	Everton	0	0		
2009–10	Everton	3	0		
2009–10	Blackpool	9	1	9	1
2010–11	Everton	34	4		
2011–12	Everton	18	0		
2012–13	Everton	26	0		
2013–14	Everton	36	6		
2014–15	Everton	35	3		
2015–16	Everton	28	1	180	14

CONNOLLY, Callum (D)   4   0
b.Liverpool 23-9-97
Internationals: England U17, U18, U19.

2015–16	Everton	1	0	1	0
2015–16	Barnsley	3	0	3	0

DAVIES, Tom (M)   2   0
b.Liverpool 30-6-98
Internationals: England U16, U17.

2015–16	Everton	2	0	2	0

DEULOFEU, Gerard (F)   53   5
H: 5 10   W: 11 01   b.Riudarenes 13-3-94
Internationals: Spain U16, U17, U19, U20, U21, Full caps.

2010–11	Barcelona	1	0		
2011–12	Barcelona	1	0		
2012–13	Barcelona	1	0		
2013–14	Barcelona	0	0	2	0
2013–14	Everton	25	3		
2015–16	Everton	26	2	51	5

DOWELL, Kieran (F)   2   0
H: 5 9   W: 9 04   b.Ormskirk 10-10-97
Internationals: England U16, U17, U18.

2014–15	Everton	0	0		
2015–16	Everton	2	0	2	0

DUFFUS, Courtney (F)   3   0
H: 5 7   W: 12 00   b.Cheltenham 24-10-95

2013–14	Everton	0	0		
2014–15	Everton	0	0		
2014–15	Bury	3	0	3	0
2015–16	Everton	0	0		

DYSON, Calum (F)   0   0
b. 19-9-96

2015–16	Everton	0	0		

FELIPE MATTIONI, Roude (D)   52   1
H: 5 10   W: 10 12   b.Natural de Ijui 15-10-88

2007–08	Gremio	13	0		
2008–09	Gremio	0	0		
2008–09	AC Milan	1	0	1	0
2009–10	Gremio	0	0	13	0
2009–10	Mallorca	20	1	20	1
2010–11	Espanyol	0	0		
2011–12	Espanyol	0	0		
2012–13	Espanyol	6	0		
2013–14	Espanyol	2	0		
2014–15	Espanyol	5	0	13	0
2015–16	Everton	0	0		
2015–16	Doncaster R	5	0	5	0

FOULDS, Matthew (D)   0   0
b.Bradford 1-2-98

2015–16	Bury	0	0		
2015–16	Everton	0	0		

FUNES MORI, Ramiro (D)   104   11
H: 6 3   W: 13 12   b.Mendoza 5-3-91
Internationals: Argentina Full caps.

2010–11	River Plate	0	0		
2011–12	River Plate	19	2		
2012–13	River Plate	10	0		
2013–14	River Plate	19	1		
2014	River Plate	17	2		
2015	River Plate	11	2	76	7
2015–16	Everton	28	4	28	4

GALLOWAY, Brendon (M)   27   0
H: 6 2   W: 13 10   b.Zimbabwe 17-3-96
Internationals: England U17, U18, U19.

2011–12	Milton Keynes D	1	0		
2012–13	Milton Keynes D	1	0		
2013–14	Milton Keynes D	8	0	10	0
2014–15	Everton	2	0		
2015–16	Everton	15	0	17	0

GARBUTT, Luke (D)   83   5
H: 5 10   W: 11 07   b.Harrogate 21-5-93
Internationals: England U16, U17, U18, U19, U20, U21.

2010–11	Everton	0	0		
2011–12	Everton	0	0		
2011–12	Cheltenham T	34	2	34	2
2012–13	Everton	0	0		

GIBSON, Darron (M)   103   6
H: 6 0   W: 12 04   b.Derry 25-10-87
Internationals: Republic of Ireland U21, B, Full caps.

2005–06	Manchester U	0	0		
2006–07	Manchester U	0	0		
2007–08	Manchester U	0	0		
2007–08	Wolverhampton W	21	1	21	1
2008–09	Manchester U	3	1		
2009–10	Manchester U	15	2		
2010–11	Manchester U	12	0		
2011–12	Manchester U	1	0	31	3
2011–12	Everton	11	1		
2012–13	Everton	23	1		
2013–14	Everton	1	0		
2014–15	Everton	9	0		
2015–16	Everton	7	0	51	2

GRANT, Conor (M)   30   3
H: 5 9   W: 12 08   b.Fazakerley 18-4-95

2013–14	Everton	0	0		
2014–15	Everton	0	0		
2014–15	Motherwell	11	1	11	1
2015–16	Everton	0	0		
2015–16	Doncaster R	19	2	19	2

GRIFFITHS, Russell (G)   0   0
b.Gravesend 13-4-96
Internationals: England U19, U20.

2014–15	Everton	0	0		
2015–16	Everton	0	0		

HENEN, David (F)   11   1
b. 19-4-96
Internationals: Belgium U16, U17, U18, U19.

2013–14	Anderlecht	0	0		
2014–15	Olympiacos	0	0		
2014–15	Everton	0	0		
2015–16	Fleetwood T	11	1	11	1

HIBBERT, Tony (D)   265   0
H: 5 9   W: 11 05   b.Liverpool 20-2-81

1998–99	Everton	0	0		
1999–2000	Everton	0	0		
2000–01	Everton	3	0		
2001–02	Everton	10	0		
2002–03	Everton	24	0		
2003–04	Everton	25	0		
2004–05	Everton	36	0		
2005–06	Everton	29	0		
2006–07	Everton	13	0		
2007–08	Everton	24	0		
2008–09	Everton	17	0		
2009–10	Everton	20	0		
2010–11	Everton	20	0		
2011–12	Everton	32	0		
2012–13	Everton	6	0		
2013–14	Everton	1	0		
2014–15	Everton	4	0		
2015–16	Everton	1	0	265	0

HOLGATE, Mason (D)   20   1
H: 5 11   W: 11 11   b.Doncaster 22-10-96
Internationals: England U20.

2014–15	Barnsley	20	1	20	1
2015–16	Everton	0	0		

HOWARD, Tim (G)   484   1
H: 6 3   W: 14 12   b.North Brunswick 6-3-79
Internationals: USA U21, U23, Full caps.

1998	NY/NJ MetroStars	1	0		
1999	NY/NJ MetroStars	9	0		
2000	NY/NJ MetroStars	9	0		
2001	NY/NJ MetroStars	26	0		
2002	NY/NJ MetroStars	27	0		
2003	NY/NJ MetroStars	13	0	85	0
2003–04	Manchester U	32	0		
2004–05	Manchester U	12	0		
2005–06	Manchester U	1	0		
2006–07	Manchester U	0	0	45	0
2006–07	Everton	36	0		
2007–08	Everton	36	0		
2008–09	Everton	38	0		
2009–10	Everton	38	0		
2010–11	Everton	38	0		
2011–12	Everton	38	1		
2012–13	Everton	36	0		
2013–14	Everton	37	0		
2014–15	Everton	32	0		
2015–16	Everton	25	0	354	0

JAGIELKA, Phil (D)   517 28
H: 6 0   W: 13 01   b.Manchester 17-8-82
Internationals: England U20, U21, B, Full caps.

Season	Club	Apps	Gls	Tot A	Tot G
1999-2000	Sheffield U	1	0		
2000-01	Sheffield U	15	0		
2001-02	Sheffield U	23	3		
2002-03	Sheffield U	42	0		
2003-04	Sheffield U	43	3		
2004-05	Sheffield U	46	0		
2005-06	Sheffield U	46	8		
2006-07	Sheffield U	38	4	254	18
2007-08	Everton	34	1		
2008-09	Everton	34	0		
2009-10	Everton	12	0		
2010-11	Everton	33	1		
2011-12	Everton	30	2		
2012-13	Everton	36	2		
2013-14	Everton	26	0		
2014-15	Everton	37	4		
2015-16	Everton	21	0	263	10

JONES, Gethin (D)   6 0
H: 5 10   W: 11 09   b.Perth 13-10-95
Internationals: Wales U17, U19, U21.

Season	Club	Apps	Gls	Tot A	Tot G
2014-15	Everton	0	0		
2014-15	Plymouth Arg	6	0	6	0
2015-16	Everton	0	0		

JUNIOR, Francisco (M)   34 3
H: 5 4   W: 10 02   b.Bissau 18-1-92
Internationals: Portugal U19, U21.

Season	Club	Apps	Gls	Tot A	Tot G
2012-13	Everton	0	0		
2013-14	Everton	0	0		
2013-14	Vitesse	2	0	2	0
2014	Stromsgodset	12	1		
2014-15	Everton	0	0		
2014-15	Port Vale	1	0	1	0
2015-16	Everton	0	0		
2015-16	Wigan Ath	10	1	10	1
2016	Stromsgodset	9	1	21	2

KENNY, Jonjoe (D)   25 0
H: 5 9   W: 10 08   b.Kirkdale 15-3-97
Internationals: England U16, U17, U18, U19.

Season	Club	Apps	Gls	Tot A	Tot G
2014-15	Everton	0	0		
2015-16	Everton	1	0	1	0
2015-16	Wigan Ath	7	0	7	0
2015-16	Oxford U	17	0	17	0

KONE, Arouna (F)   293 93
H: 6 0   W: 11 08   b.Anyama 11-11-83
Internationals: Ivory Coast Full caps.

Season	Club	Apps	Gls	Tot A	Tot G
2002-03	Lierse	21	11	21	11
2003-04	Roda JC	28	11		
2004-05	Roda JC	32	14		
2005-06	Roda JC	1	1	61	26
2005-06	PSV Eindhoven	21	11		
2006-07	PSV Eindhoven	31	10		
2007-08	PSV Eindhoven	1	0	53	21
2007-08	Sevilla	21	1		
2008-09	Sevilla	6	0		
2009-10	Sevilla	12	0		
2009-10	Hannover 96	8	2	8	2
2010-11	Sevilla	1	0	40	1
2011-12	Levante	34	15	34	15
2012-13	Wigan Ath	34	11	34	11
2013-14	Everton	5	0		
2014-15	Everton	12	1		
2015-16	Everton	25	5	42	6

LEDSON, Ryan (M)   27 0
H: 5 9   W: 10 12   b.Liverpool 19-8-97
Internationals: England U16, U17, U18, U19.

Season	Club	Apps	Gls	Tot A	Tot G
2013-14	Everton	0	0		
2014-15	Everton	0	0		
2015-16	Everton	0	0		
2015-16	Cambridge U	27	0	27	0

LENNON, Aaron (M)   343 34
H: 5 6   W: 10 03   b.Leeds 16-4-87
Internationals: England U17, U19, U21, B, Full caps.

Season	Club	Apps	Gls	Tot A	Tot G
2003-04	Leeds U	11	0		
2004-05	Leeds U	27	1	38	1
2005-06	Tottenham H	27	2		
2006-07	Tottenham H	26	3		
2007-08	Tottenham H	29	2		
2008-09	Tottenham H	35	5		
2009-10	Tottenham H	22	3		
2010-11	Tottenham H	34	3		
2011-12	Tottenham H	23	3		
2012-13	Tottenham H	34	4		
2013-14	Tottenham H	27	1		
2014-15	Tottenham H	9	0		
2014-15	Everton	14	2		
2015-16	Tottenham H	0	0	266	26
2015-16	Everton	25	5	39	7

LUKAKU, Romelu (F)   222 93
H: 6 3   W: 13 00   b.Antwerp 13-5-93
Internationals: Belgium U15, U18, U21, Full caps.

Season	Club	Apps	Gls	Tot A	Tot G
2008-09	Anderlecht	1	0		
2009-10	Anderlecht	33	15		
2010-11	Anderlecht	37	16		
2011-12	Anderlecht	2	2	73	33
2011-12	Chelsea	8	0		
2012-13	Chelsea	0	0		
2012-13	WBA	35	17	35	17
2013-14	Chelsea	2	0	10	0
2013-14	Everton	31	15		
2014-15	Everton	36	10		
2015-16	Everton	37	18	104	43

McALENY, Conor (F)   38 6
H: 5 10   W: 12 05   b.Liverpool 12-8-92

Season	Club	Apps	Gls	Tot A	Tot G
2009-10	Everton	0	0		
2010-11	Everton	0	0		
2011-12	Everton	2	0		
2011-12	Scunthorpe U	3	0	3	0
2012-13	Everton	0	0		
2013-14	Everton	0	0		
2013-14	Brentford	4	0	4	0
2014-15	Everton	0	0		
2014-15	Cardiff C	8	2	8	2
2015-16	Everton	0	0	2	0
2015-16	Charlton Ath	8	0	8	0
2015-16	Wigan Ath	13	4	13	4

McCARTHY, James (M)   306 26
H: 5 11   W: 11 05   b.Glasgow 12-11-90
Internationals: Republic of Ireland U17, U18, U19, U21, Full caps.

Season	Club	Apps	Gls	Tot A	Tot G
2006-07	Hamilton A	23	1		
2007-08	Hamilton A	35	7		
2008-09	Hamilton A	37	6	95	14
2009-10	Wigan Ath	20	1		
2010-11	Wigan Ath	24	3		
2011-12	Wigan Ath	33	0		
2012-13	Wigan Ath	38	3		
2013-14	Wigan Ath	5	0	120	7
2013-14	Everton	34	1		
2014-15	Everton	28	2		
2015-16	Everton	29	2	91	5

McGEADY, Aiden (M)   302 44
H: 5 10   W: 11 03   b.Glasgow 4-4-86
Internationals: Republic of Ireland Full caps.

Season	Club	Apps	Gls	Tot A	Tot G
2003-04	Celtic	4	1		
2004-05	Celtic	27	4		
2005-06	Celtic	20	4		
2006-07	Celtic	34	5		
2007-08	Celtic	36	7		
2008-09	Celtic	29	3		
2009-10	Celtic	35	7	185	31
2010-11	Spartak Moscow	11	2		
2011-12	Spartak Moscow	31	3		
2012-13	Spartak Moscow	17	5		
2013-14	Spartak Moscow	13	1	72	11
2013-14	Everton	16	0		
2014-15	Everton	16	1		
2015-16	Everton	0	0	32	1
2015-16	Sheffield W	13	1	13	1

MIRALLAS, Kevin (F)   288 72
H: 6 0   W: 11 10   b.Leige 5-10-87
Internationals: Belgium U16, U17, U18, U19, U21, Full caps.

Season	Club	Apps	Gls	Tot A	Tot G
2004-05	Lille	1	1		
2005-06	Lille	15	1		
2006-07	Lille	23	2		
2007-08	Lille	35	6	74	10
2008-09	St Etienne	30	3		
2009-10	St Etienne	23	0	53	3
2010-11	Olympiacos	26	14		
2011-12	Olympiacos	24	20		
2012-13	Olympiacos	0	0	50	34
2012-13	Everton	27	6		
2013-14	Everton	32	8		
2014-15	Everton	29	7		
2015-16	Everton	23	4	111	25

NIASSE, Oumar (F)   67 24
H: 6 0   b.Ouakam 18-4-90
Internationals: Senegal U23, Full caps.

Season	Club	Apps	Gls	Tot A	Tot G
2013-14	Akhisar Belediyespor	12	4	34	12
2014-15	Lokomotiv Moscow	13	4		
2015-16	Lokomotiv Moscow	18	8	28	12
2015-16	Everton	5	0	5	0

OSMAN, Leon (F)   381 48
H: 5 8   W: 10 09   b.Billinge 17-5-81
Internationals: England U16, Full caps.

Season	Club	Apps	Gls	Tot A	Tot G
1998-99	Everton	0	0		
1999-2000	Everton	0	0		
2000-01	Everton	0	0		
2001-02	Everton	0	0		
2002-03	Everton	2	0		
2002-03	Carlisle U	12	1	12	1
2003-04	Everton	4	1		
2003-04	Derby Co	17	3	17	3
2004-05	Everton	29	6		
2005-06	Everton	35	3		
2006-07	Everton	34	3		
2007-08	Everton	28	4		
2008-09	Everton	34	6		
2009-10	Everton	26	2		
2010-11	Everton	26	4		
2011-12	Everton	30	5		
2012-13	Everton	36	5		
2013-14	Everton	38	3		
2014-15	Everton	21	2		
2015-16	Everton	9	0	352	44

OVIEDO, Bryan (M)   88 4
H: 5 8   W: 10 13   b.Alajuela 18-2-90
Internationals: Costa Rica U20, Full caps.

Season	Club	Apps	Gls	Tot A	Tot G
2009-10	FC Copenhagen	3	0		
2010-11	FC Copenhagen	1	0		
2010-11	Nordsjaelland	14	0	14	0
2011-12	FC Copenhagen	22	2		
2012-13	FC Copenhagen	4	0	30	2
2012-13	Everton	15	0		
2013-14	Everton	9	2		
2014-15	Everton	6	0		
2015-16	Everton	14	0	44	2

PENNINGTON, Matthew (D)   50 2
H: 6 1   W: 12 02   b.Warrington 6-10-94
Internationals: England U19.

Season	Club	Apps	Gls	Tot A	Tot G
2013-14	Everton	0	0		
2013-14	Tranmere R	17	2	17	2
2014-15	Everton	0	0		
2014-15	Coventry C	24	0	24	0
2015-16	Everton	4	0	4	0
2015-16	Walsall	5	0	5	0

PIENAAR, Steven (M)   318 35
H: 5 10   W: 10 06   b.Westbury 17-3-82
Internationals: South Africa Full caps.

Season	Club	Apps	Gls	Tot A	Tot G
2001-02	Ajax	8	1		
2002-03	Ajax	31	5		
2003-04	Ajax	16	3		
2004-05	Ajax	24	4		
2005-06	Ajax	15	2	94	15
2006-07	Bor Dortmund	25	0	25	0
2007-08	Everton	28	2		
2008-09	Everton	28	2		
2009-10	Everton	30	4		
2010-11	Everton	18	1		
2010-11	Tottenham H	8	0		
2011-12	Tottenham H	2	0		
2011-12	Everton	14	4		
2012-13	Tottenham H	0	0	10	0
2012-13	Everton	35	6		
2013-14	Everton	23	1		
2014-15	Everton	9	0		
2015-16	Everton	4	0	189	20

ROBINSON, Antonee (D)   0 0
H: 6 0   W: 11 07   b.Milton Keynes 8-8-97
Internationals: USA U18.

Season	Club	Apps	Gls	Tot A	Tot G
2015-16	Everton	0	0		

ROBLES, Joel (G)   46 0
H: 6 5   W: 13 04   b.Leganes 17-6-90
Internationals: Spain U16, U17, U21, U23.

Season	Club	Apps	Gls	Tot A	Tot G
2009-10	Atletico Madrid	2	0		
2011-12	Rayo Vallecano	13	0	13	0
2012-13	Atletico Madrid	0	0	2	0
2012-13	Wigan Ath	9	0	9	0
2013-14	Everton	2	0		
2014-15	Everton	7	0		
2015-16	Everton	13	0	22	0

RODRIGUEZ, Leandro (F)   73 19
H: 5 10   W: 11 07   b.Montevideo 19-11-92

Season	Club	Apps	Gls	Tot A	Tot G
2012-13	Atletico River Plate	23	7		
2013-14	Atletico River Plate	23	7		
2014-15	Atletico River Plate	23	9		
2015-16	Atletico River Plate	1	0	71	19
2015-16	Everton	0	0		
2015-16	Brentford	2	0	2	0

STONES, John (D)   101 1
H: 6 2   W: 11 00   b.Barnsley 28-5-94
Internationals: England U19, U20, U21, Full caps

Season	Club	Apps	Gls	Tot A	Tot G
2011-12	Barnsley	2	0		
2012-13	Barnsley	22	0	24	0
2012-13	Everton	0	0		
2013-14	Everton	21	0		
2014-15	Everton	23	1		
2015-16	Everton	33	0	77	1

TARASHAJ, Shani (F) 52 12
b. 7-2-95
Internationals: Switzerland U17, U18, U19, U21, Full caps.
2014–15 Grasshoppers 19 1
2015–16 Grasshoppers 18 8 52 12
2015–16 Everton 0 0
2015–16 *Grasshoppers* 15 3

WALSH, Liam (M) 15 1
b. 15-9-97
Internationals: England U16, U18.
2015–16 Everton 0 0
2015–16 Yeovil T 15 1 15 1

WILLIAMS, Joe (M) 0 0
H: 5 10 W: 10 06 b.Liverpool 8-12-96
Internationals: England U20.
2014–15 Everton 0 0
2015–16 Everton 0 0

Players retained or with offer of contract
Bainbridge, Jack; Brewster, Delial Edmund; Broadhead, Nathan Paul; Byrne, Sam John; Charsley, Henry William James; Donohue, Michael John; Evans, Antony Kenneth; Feeney, Morgan; Gray, Louis; Hewelt, Mateusz Tomasz; Holland, Nathan Elliot; Hunt, Connor Charles; Kinsella, Steven; Yarney, Josef Charles; Yates, James John.

Scholars
Baningime, Beni; Bramall, Daniel Luke; Harrington, Ryan; Johnson, Matthew; Jones, Aaron William; Kiersey, Jack Alexander; Lavery, Shayne Francis; Lees, Callum Jordan; Morris, Liam George; Pierce, Benjamin Alan; Virtanen, Miko Aarne; Withe, George Peter.

EXETER C (35)

BROWN, Troy (D) 192 12
H: 6 1 W: 12 01 b.Croydon 17-9-90
Internationals: Wales U17, U19, U21.
2009–10 Ipswich T 1 0
2010–11 Ipswich T 12 0 13 0
2011–12 Rotherham U 6 1 6 1
2011–12 *Aldershot T* 17 2
2012–13 Aldershot T 34 3 51 5
2013–14 Cheltenham T 39 4
2014–15 Cheltenham T 43 1 82 5
2015–16 Exeter C 40 1 40 1

BUTTERFIELD, Danny (D) 488 9
H: 5 10 W: 11 06 b.Boston 21-11-79
1997–98 Grimsby T 7 0
1998–99 Grimsby T 12 0
1999–2000 Grimsby T 29 0
2000–01 Grimsby T 30 1
2001–02 Grimsby T 46 2 124 3
2002–03 Crystal Palace 46 1
2003–04 Crystal Palace 45 4
2004–05 Crystal Palace 7 0
2005–06 Crystal Palace 13 0
2006–07 Crystal Palace 28 0
2007–08 Crystal Palace 30 0
2008–09 Crystal Palace 26 1
2008–09 *Charlton Ath* 12 0 12 0
2009–10 Crystal Palace 37 0 232 6
2010–11 Southampton 34 0
2011–12 Southampton 10 0
2012–13 Southampton 0 0
2012–13 *Bolton W* 6 0 6 0
2013–14 Southampton 0 0 44 0
2013–14 Carlisle U 1 0 1 0
2013–14 Exeter C 29 0
2014–15 Exeter C 30 0
2015–16 Exeter C 10 0 69 0

BYRNE, Alex (M) 0 0
H: 5 9 W: 11 07 b.Barnstaple 15-6-96
2014–15 Exeter C 0 0
2015–16 Exeter C 0 0

DAVIES, Arron (M) 327 38
H: 5 9 W: 11 00 b.Cardiff 22-6-84
Internationals: Wales U19, U21, Full caps.
2002–03 Southampton 0 0
2003–04 Southampton 0 0
2003–04 *Barnsley* 4 0 4 0
2004–05 Southampton 0 0
2004–05 Yeovil T 23 8
2005–06 Yeovil T 39 8
2006–07 Yeovil T 39 6
2007–08 Nottingham F 19 1
2008–09 Nottingham F 13 0
2009–10 Nottingham F 0 0 32 1
2009–10 *Brighton & HA* 7 0 7 0
2009–10 Yeovil T 10 0 111 22

2010–11 Peterborough U 22 1 22 1
2011–12 Northampton T 15 4 15 4
2012–13 Exeter C 37 3
2013–14 Exeter C 32 2
2014–15 Exeter C 39 4
2015–16 Exeter C 28 1 136 10

EGAN, Kyle (D) 0 0
2015–16 Exeter C 0 0

GILL, Cameron (F) 0 0
b. 5-8-97
2015–16 Exeter C 0 0

GRANT, Joel (F) 255 40
H: 6 0 W: 12 01 b.Acton 26-8-87
Internationals: Jamaica U20, Full caps.
2005–06 Watford 7 0
2006–07 Watford 0 0 7 0
From Aldershot T.
2008–09 Crewe Alex 28 2
2009–10 Crewe Alex 43 9
2010–11 Crewe Alex 25 5 96 16
2011–12 Wycombe W 30 4
2012–13 Wycombe W 41 10 71 14
2013–14 Yeovil T 34 3
2014–15 Yeovil T 21 3 55 6
2015–16 Exeter C 26 4 26 4

HAMON, James (G) 22 0
H: 6 1 W: 11 00 b. 1-7-95
2013–14 Exeter C 0 0
2014–15 Exeter C 21 0
2015–16 Exeter C 1 0 22 0

HARLEY, Ryan (M) 219 35
H: 5 11 W: 11 00 b.Bristol 22-1-85
2004–05 Bristol C 2 0
2005–06 Bristol C 0 0 2 0
2008–09 Exeter C 31 4
2009–10 Exeter C 44 10
2010–11 Exeter C 21 6
2010–11 Swansea C 0 0
2010–11 *Exeter C* 21 4
2011–12 Swansea C 0 0
2011–12 Brighton & HA 16 2
2012–13 Brighton & HA 2 0 18 2
2012–13 *Milton Keynes D* 8 0 8 0
2013–14 Swindon T 21 1
2014–15 Swindon T 0 0 21 1
2014–15 Exeter C 25 4
2015–16 Exeter C 28 4 170 32

HOLMES, Lee (M) 252 19
H: 5 8 W: 10 06 b.Mansfield 2-4-87
Internationals: England U16, U17, U19.
2002–03 Derby Co 2 0
2003–04 Derby Co 23 2
2004–05 Derby Co 3 0
2004–05 *Swindon T* 15 1
2005–06 Derby Co 18 0
2005–06 Derby Co 0 0
2006–07 *Bradford C* 16 0 16 0
2007–08 Derby Co 0 0 46 2
2007–08 *Walsall* 19 4 19 4
2008–09 Southampton 11 0
2009–10 Southampton 5 0
2010–11 Southampton 7 0
2011–12 Southampton 6 1 29 1
2011–12 *Oxford U* 7 2 7 2
2011–12 *Swindon T* 10 1 25 2
2012–13 Preston NE 28 3
2013–14 Preston NE 32 3
2014–15 Preston NE 0 0 60 6
2014–15 *Portsmouth* 5 0 5 0
2014–15 Exeter C 8 0
2015–16 Exeter C 37 2 45 2

HOSKINS, Will (F) 231 53
H: 5 11 W: 11 02 b.Nottingham 6-5-86
Internationals: England U18, U19, U20
2003–04 Rotherham U 4 2
2004–05 Rotherham U 22 2
2005–06 Rotherham U 23 4
2006–07 Rotherham U 24 15
2006–07 Watford 9 0
2007–08 Watford 1 0
2007–08 *Millwall* 10 2 10 2
2007–08 *Nottingham F* 2 0 2 0
2008–09 Watford 32 4
2009–10 Watford 18 3 60 7
2010–11 Bristol R 43 17 43 17
2011–12 Brighton & HA 7 1
2011–12 *Sheffield U* 12 2 12 2
2011–12 *Rotherham U* 0 0 73 23
2012–13 Brighton & HA 11 0
2013–14 Brighton & HA 0 0 18 1
2013–14 Oxford U 4 0 4 0
2015–16 Exeter C 9 1 9 1

JAY, Matt (D) 5 0
H: 5 10 W: 10 12 b.Torbay 27-2-96
2013–14 Exeter C 2 0
2014–15 Exeter C 3 0
2015–16 Exeter C 0 0 5 0

KEADELL, Kavanagh (G) 0 0
b. 6-5-98
2014–15 Exeter C 0 0
2015–16 Exeter C 0 0

KEOHANE, Jimmy (M) 80 9
H: 5 11 W: 11 05 b.Wexford 22-1-91
Internationals: Republic of Ireland U19.
2010–11 Bristol C 0 0
2011–12 Bristol C 2 0
2011–12 Exeter C 4 0
2012–13 Exeter C 33 3
2013–14 Exeter C 20 3
2014–15 Exeter C 23 3
2015–16 Exeter C 0 0 80 9

McALLISTER, Jamie (D) 558 4
H: 5 10 W: 11 00 b.Glasgow 26-4-78
Internationals: Scotland Full caps.
1995–96 Queen of the South 2 0
1996–97 Queen of the South 6 0
1997–98 Queen of the South 15 0
1998–99 Queen of the South 27 0 50 0
1999–2000 Aberdeen 34 0
2000–01 Aberdeen 25 0
2001–02 Aberdeen 29 0
2002–03 Aberdeen 29 0 117 0
2003–04 Livingston 34 1 34 1
2004–05 Hearts 30 0
2005–06 Hearts 17 0 47 0
2006–07 Bristol C 31 1
2007–08 Bristol C 41 0
2008–09 Bristol C 35 1
2009–10 Bristol C 33 0
2010–11 Bristol C 34 1
2011–12 Bristol C 12 0 186 3
2011–12 *Preston NE* 4 0 4 0
2012–13 Yeovil T 34 0
2013–14 Yeovil T 38 0 72 0
2014–15 Kerala Blasters 6 0 6 0
2014–15 Exeter C 14 0
2015–16 Exeter C 28 0 42 0

McCREADY, Tom (M) 20 0
H: 6 0 W: 11 11 b.Chester 7-6-91
2014–15 Morecambe 7 0 7 0
2014–15 Exeter C 3 0
2015–16 Exeter C 10 0 13 0

MOORE-TAYLOR, Jordan (D) 94 3
H: 5 10 W: 13 01 b.Exeter 21-1-94
2012–13 Exeter C 7 0
2013–14 Exeter C 29 1
2014–15 Exeter C 26 2
2015–16 Exeter C 32 0 94 3

MORRISON, Clinton (F) 662 153
H: 6 0 W: 12 00 b.Tooting 14-5-79
Internationals: Republic of Ireland U21, Full caps.
1996–97 Crystal Palace 0 0
1997–98 Crystal Palace 1 1
1998–99 Crystal Palace 37 12
1999–2000 Crystal Palace 29 13
2000–01 Crystal Palace 45 14
2001–02 Crystal Palace 45 22
2002–03 Birmingham C 28 6
2003–04 Birmingham C 32 4
2004–05 Birmingham C 26 4
2005–06 Birmingham C 1 0 87 14
2005–06 Crystal Palace 40 13
2006–07 Crystal Palace 41 12
2007–08 Crystal Palace 43 16 281 103
2008–09 Coventry C 45 10
2009–10 Coventry C 46 11 91 21
2010–11 Sheffield W 35 6
2011–12 Sheffield W 19 1 54 7
2011–12 *Milton Keynes D* 6 3 6 3
2011–12 *Brentford* 8 0 8 0
2012–13 Colchester U 32 2
2013–14 Colchester U 33 2 65 4
2014–15 Exeter C 25 0
2015–16 Exeter C 45 1 70 1

NICHOLLS, Alex (M) 279 42
H: 5 10 W: 11 00 b.Stourbridge 9-12-87
2005–06 Walsall 8 0
2006–07 Walsall 10 0
2007–08 Walsall 19 2
2008–09 Walsall 45 6
2009–10 Walsall 37 4
2010–11 Walsall 37 5
2011–12 Walsall 45 7 191 24

2012–13	Northampton T	15	7		
2013–14	Northampton T	0	0		
2014–15	Northampton T	6	1	21	8
2014–15	*Exeter C*	32	5		
2015–16	Exeter C	35	5	67	10

NOBLE, David (M)   338 18
H: 6 0   W: 12 04   b.Hitchin 2-2-82
Internationals: Scotland B.

2000–01	Arsenal	0	0
2001–02	Arsenal	0	0
2001–02	*Watford*	15	1	15	1
2002–03	Arsenal	0	0
2002–03	West Ham U	0	0
2003–04	West Ham U	3	0	3	0
2003–04	Boston U	14	2
2004–05	Boston U	32	3
2005–06	Boston U	11	0	57	5
2005–06	Bristol C	24	1
2006–07	Bristol C	26	3
2007–08	Bristol C	26	2
2008–09	Bristol C	9	1	85	7
2008–09	*Yeovil T*	2	0	2	0
2009–10	Exeter C	0	0
2010–11	Exeter C	36	0
2011–12	Exeter C	42	2
2012–13	Rotherham U	22	3
2013–14	Rotherham U	0	0	22	3
2013–14	*Cheltenham T*	29	0	29	0
2014–15	Oldham Ath	2	0	2	0
2014–15	Exeter C	15	0
2015–16	Exeter C	30	0	123	2

OAKLEY, Matthew (M)   595 33
H: 5 10   W: 12 06   b.Peterborough 17-8-77
Internationals: England U21.

1994–95	Southampton	1	0
1995–96	Southampton	10	0
1996–97	Southampton	28	3
1997–98	Southampton	33	1
1998–99	Southampton	22	2
1999–2000	Southampton	31	3
2000–01	Southampton	35	1
2001–02	Southampton	27	1
2002–03	Southampton	31	0
2003–04	Southampton	7	0
2004–05	Southampton	7	1
2005–06	Southampton	29	2	261	14
2006–07	Derby Co	37	6
2007–08	Derby Co	19	3	56	9
2007–08	Leicester C	20	0
2008–09	Leicester C	45	8
2009–10	Leicester C	38	0
2010–11	Leicester C	34	2
2011–12	Leicester C	0	0	137	10
2011–12	*Exeter C*	7	0
2012–13	Exeter C	36	0
2013–14	Exeter C	24	0
2014–15	Exeter C	45	0
2015–16	Exeter C	29	0	141	0

OLEJNIK, Robert (G)   310
H: 6 0   W: 15 06   b.Vienna 26-11-86
Internationals: Austria U21.

2004–05	Aston Villa	0	0
2005–06	Aston Villa	0	0
2006–07	Aston Villa	0	0
2006–07	*Lincoln C*	0	0
2007–08	Falkirk	13	0
2008–09	Falkirk	15	0
2009–10	Falkirk	38	0
2010–11	Falkirk	36	0	102	0
2011–12	Torquay U	46	0	46	0
2012–13	Peterborough U	46	0
2013–14	Peterborough U	42	0
2014–15	Peterborough U	0	0	88	0
2014–15	*Scunthorpe U*	13	0	13	0
2014–15	*York C*	16	0	16	0
2015–16	Exeter C	45	0	45	0

OYELEKE, Emmanuel (M)   11 0
H: 5 9   W: 11 11   b.Wandsworth 24-12-92

2011–12	Brentford	1	0
2012–13	Brentford	0	0
2012–13	*Northampton T*	2	0	2	0
2013–14	Brentford	0	0
2014–15	Brentford	0	0	1	0
2014–15	Exeter C	0	0
2015–16	Exeter C	8	0	8	0

POPE, Jason (M)   0 0
H: 5 8   W: 10 01   b. 20-9-95

2014–15	Exeter C	0	0
2015–16	Exeter C	0	0

PYM, Christy (G)   34 0
H: 6 0   W: 11 09   b.Exeter 24-4-95
Internationals: England U20.

2012–13	Exeter C	0	0

2013–14	Exeter C	9	0		
2014–15	Exeter C	25	0		
2015–16	Exeter C	0	0	34	0

READ, Josh (D)   0 0
b. 13-10-97

2015–16	Exeter C	0	0

REID, Jamie (F)   23 3
H: 5 11   W: 11 09   b.Torquay 15-7-94
Internationals: Northern Ireland U21.

2012–13	Exeter C	4	2
2013–14	Exeter C	6	0
2014–15	Exeter C	0	0
2015–16	Exeter C	13	1	23	3

RIBEIRO, Christian (D)   159 8
H: 5 11   W: 12 02   b.Neath 14-12-89
Internationals: Wales U17, U19, U21, Full caps.

2006–07	Bristol C	0	0
2007–08	Bristol C	0	0
2008–09	Bristol C	0	0
2009–10	Bristol C	5	0
2009–10	*Stockport Co*	7	0	7	0
2009–10	*Colchester U*	2	0	2	0
2010–11	Bristol C	9	0
2011–12	Bristol C	0	0	14	0
2011–12	*Carlisle U*	5	0	5	0
2011–12	*Scunthorpe U*	10	0
2012–13	Scunthorpe U	28	2
2013–14	Scunthorpe U	21	0	59	2
2014–15	Exeter C	37	2
2015–16	Exeter C	35	4	72	6

RILEY-LOWE, Conor (D)   3 0
b. 10-1-96

2014–15	Exeter C	3	0
2015–16	Exeter C	0	0	3	0

TAYLOR, Jake (M)   102 10
H: 5 10   W: 12 01   b.Ascot 1-12-91
Internationals: Wales U17, U19, U21, Full caps.

2010–11	Reading	1	0
2011–12	Reading	0	0
2011–12	*Aldershot T*	3	0	3	0
2011–12	*Exeter C*	30	3
2012–13	Reading	0	0
2012–13	*Cheltenham T*	8	1	8	1
2012–13	*Crawley T*	4	0	4	0
2013–14	Reading	8	0
2014–15	Reading	22	2
2014–15	*Leyton Orient*	3	0	3	0
2015–16	Reading	0	0	31	2
2015–16	*Motherwell*	7	0	7	0
2015–16	Exeter C	16	4	46	7

TILLSON, Jordan (D)   30 1
b.Bath 5-3-93

2012–13	Exeter C	0	0
2013–14	Exeter C	1	0
2014–15	Exeter C	3	0
2015–16	Exeter C	26	1	30	1

WATKINS, Ollie (F)   23 8
b.Torbay 30-12-95

2013–14	Exeter C	1	0
2014–15	Exeter C	2	0
2015–16	Exeter C	20	8	23	8

WHEELER, David (M)   111 16
b.Brighton 4-10-90
Internationals: England U18.

2013–14	Exeter C	35	3
2014–15	Exeter C	45	7
2015–16	Exeter C	31	6	111	16

WOODMAN, Craig (D)   442 7
H: 5 9   W: 10 11   b.Tiverton 22-12-82

1999–2000	Bristol C	0	0
2000–01	Bristol C	2	0
2001–02	Bristol C	6	0
2002–03	Bristol C	10	0
2003–04	Bristol C	21	0
2004–05	Bristol C	3	0
2004–05	*Mansfield T*	8	1	8	1
2004–05	*Torquay U*	22	1
2005–06	Bristol C	37	1
2005–06	*Torquay U*	2	0	24	1
2006–07	Bristol C	11	0	90	1
2007–08	Wycombe W	29	0
2008–09	Wycombe W	46	1
2009–10	Wycombe W	44	1	119	0
2010–11	Brentford	41	1
2011–12	Brentford	18	0	59	1
2012–13	Exeter C	44	0
2013–14	Exeter C	41	1
2014–15	Exeter C	32	0
2015–16	Exeter C	25	0	142	1

Players retained or with offer of contract
Charles, Joseph Paul; Storey, Jordan.

Non-Contract
Tisdale, Paul Robert.

Scholars
Collins, Archie Finn; Down, Toby Alan; Egan, Kyle Daren; Gillard, Max Christian James; Green, Brandon Joseph Paul; Hargreaves, Cameron; Harkness, Jamie Scott; Keadell, Kavanagh Billie; Merritt, Scott Michael; Rehemi, Mustafa; Richards, William Lee; Rogers, Steven Christopher John; Seymour, Benjamin Mark; Smallcombe, Max Frederick; Williams, Lewis Benjamin.

FLEETWOOD T (36)

AMEOBI, Shola (F)   340 56
H: 6 3   W: 11 13   b.Zaria 12-10-81
Internationals: England U21. Nigeria Full caps.

1998–99	Newcastle U	0	0
1999–2000	Newcastle U	0	0
2000–01	Newcastle U	20	2
2001–02	Newcastle U	15	0
2002–03	Newcastle U	28	5
2003–04	Newcastle U	26	7
2004–05	Newcastle U	31	2
2005–06	Newcastle U	30	9
2006–07	Newcastle U	12	3
2007–08	Newcastle U	6	0
2007–08	*Stoke C*	6	0	6	0
2008–09	Newcastle U	22	4
2009–10	Newcastle U	18	10
2010–11	Newcastle U	28	6
2011–12	Newcastle U	27	2
2012–13	Newcastle U	23	1
2013–14	Newcastle U	26	2	312	53
2014–15	Crystal Palace	4	0	4	0
2015–16	Bolton W	8	2	8	2
2015–16	Fleetwood T	10	1	10	1

ANDREW, Danny (D)   82 4
H: 5 11   W: 11 06   b.Holbeach 23-12-90

2009–10	Peterborough U	2	0	2	0
2009–10	*Cheltenham T*	10	0
2010–11	Cheltenham T	43	4
2011–12	Cheltenham T	10	0
2012–13	Cheltenham T	1	0	64	4
From Gloucester C, Macclesfield T.			
2014–15	Fleetwood T	7	0
2015–16	Fleetwood T	9	0	16	0

ARESTIDOU, Andreas (G)   33 0
H: 6 2   W: 13 00   b.Lambeth 6-12-89

2007–08	Blackburn R	0	0
2008–09	Blackburn R	0	0
2009–10	Shrewsbury T	2	0	2	0
2010–11	Preston NE	0	0
2011–12	Preston NE	7	0	7	0
2012–13	Morecambe	6	0
2013–14	Morecambe	1	0
2014–15	Morecambe	17	0	24	0
2015–16	Fleetwood T	0	0

BALL, David (F)   206 41
H: 6 0   W: 11 08   b.Whitefield 14-12-89

2007–08	Manchester C	0	0
2008–09	Manchester C	0	0
2009–10	Manchester C	0	0
2010–11	Manchester C	0	0
2010–11	*Swindon T*	18	2	18	2
2010–11	Peterborough U	19	5
2011–12	Peterborough U	22	4
2011–12	*Rochdale*	14	3	14	3
2012–13	Peterborough U	0	0	41	9
2012–13	Fleetwood T	34	7
2013–14	Fleetwood T	30	8
2014–15	Fleetwood T	32	8
2015–16	Fleetwood T	37	4	133	27

BELL, Amari (D)   62 0
H: 5 11   W: 12 00   b.Burton-upon-Trent 5-5-94

2012–13	Birmingham C	0	0
2013–14	Birmingham C	1	0
2014–15	Birmingham C	0	0	1	0
2014–15	*Swindon T*	10	0	10	0
2014–15	*Gillingham*	7	0	7	0
2015–16	Fleetwood T	44	0	44	0

CARTRIGHT, Max (D)   0 0
H: 6 0   W: 10 12   b. 18-11-95

2013–14	Fleetwood T	0	0
2014–15	Fleetwood T	0	0
2015–16	Fleetwood T	0	0

COLE, Devante (F) 67 15
H: 6 1 W: 11 06 b.Alderley Edge 10-5-95
Internationals: England U16, U17, U18, U19.

Season	Club				
2013–14	Manchester C	0	0		
2014–15	Manchester C	0	0		
2014–15	*Barnsley*	19	5	19	5
2014–15	*Milton Keynes D*	15	3	15	3
2015–16	Bradford C	19	5	19	5
2015–16	Fleetwood T	14	2	14	2

DAVIS, Joe (D) 46 0
H: 6 0 W: 11 07 b.Burnley 10-11-93

Season	Club				
2010–11	Port Vale	1	0		
2011–12	Port Vale	8	0		
2012–13	Port Vale	7	0		
2013–14	Port Vale	11	0	27	0
2014–15	Leicester C	0	0		
2015–16	Leicester C	0	0		
2015–16	Fleetwood T	19	0	19	0

DEACON, Keano (M) 1 0
b. 4-4-96

Season	Club				
2013–14	Fleetwood T	0	0		
2014–15	Fleetwood T	0	0		
2015–16	Fleetwood T	1	0	1	0

DSANE, Eddie (F) 0 0
b. 5-2-97

Season	Club		
2015–16	Fleetwood T	0	0

DUNBAR, Kieran (M) 0 0
b. 14-9-96

Season	Club		
2015–16	Fleetwood T	0	0

GOGIC, Aleks (G) 0 0
b. 2-3-96

Season	Club		
2014–15	Reading	0	0
2015–16	Fleetwood T	0	0

GRANT, Robert (M) 252 58
H: 5 11 W: 12 00 b.Liverpool 1-7-90

Season	Club				
2006–07	Accrington S	1	0		
2007–08	Accrington S	7	0		
2008–09	Accrington S	15	1		
2009–10	Accrington S	42	14		
2010–11	Scunthorpe U	27	0		
2010–11	Rochdale	6	2		
2011–12	Scunthorpe U	29	7		
2011–12	*Accrington S*	8	3	73	18
2012–13	Scunthorpe U	3	0	59	7
2012–13	Rochdale	36	15	42	17
2013–14	Blackpool	6	0		
2013–14	*Fleetwood T*	1	0		
2014–15	Blackpool	0	0	6	0
2014–15	*Shrewsbury T*	33	6	33	6
2015–16	Fleetwood T	38	10	39	10

GRANT, Thomas (M) 42 3
H: 5 8 W: 9 12 b.Aberdeen 31-5-95
Internationals: Scotland U19.

Season	Club				
2012–13	Falkirk	23	1		
2013–14	Falkirk	4	0		
2014–15	Falkirk	1	0		
2014–15	*Arbroath*	11	2	11	2
2015–16	Falkirk	0	0	28	1
2015–16	Fleetwood T	3	0	3	0

HAUGHTON, Nick (M) 40 1
b. 20-9-94

Season	Club				
2013–14	Fleetwood T	0	0		
2014–15	Fleetwood T	22	1		
2015–16	Fleetwood T	18	0	40	1

HORNBY-FORBES, Tyler (M) 33 2
b. 8-3-96

Season	Club				
2014–15	Fleetwood T	17	0		
2015–16	Fleetwood T	16	2	33	2

HUNTER, Ashley (F) 36 6
H: 5 10 W: 10 08 b.Derby 29-9-93

Season	Club				
2014–15	Fleetwood T	12	1		
2015–16	Fleetwood T	24	5	36	6

JONSSON, Eggert (D) 201 16
H: 6 2 W: 11 05 b.Reykjavik 18-8-88
Internationals: Iceland Youth, U21, Full caps.

Season	Club				
2005	Fjaroabyggo	22	5	22	5
2005–06	Hearts	0	0		
2006–07	Hearts	3	0		
2007–08	Hearts	28	1		
2008–09	Hearts	30	3		
2009–10	Hearts	28	3		
2010–11	Hearts	29	0		
2011–12	Hearts	16	1	134	8
2011–12	Wolverhampton W	3	0		
2012–13	Wolverhampton W	1	0	4	0
2012–13	*Charlton Ath*	2	0	2	0
2013–14	Belenenses	0	0		
2015–16	Fleetwood T	39	3	39	3

JORDAN, Stephen (D) 250 1
H: 6 1 W: 13 00 b.Warrington 6-3-82

Season	Club				
1998–99	Manchester C	0	0		
1999–2000	Manchester C	0	0		
2000–01	Manchester C	0	0		
2001–02	Manchester C	0	0		
2002–03	Manchester C	1	0		
2002–03	*Cambridge U*	11	0	11	0
2003–04	Manchester C	2	0		
2004–05	Manchester C	19	0		
2005–06	Manchester C	18	0		
2006–07	Manchester C	13	0	53	0
2007–08	Burnley	21	0		
2008–09	Burnley	27	0		
2009–10	Burnley	25	0		
2010–11	Burnley	0	0	73	0
2010–11	Sheffield U	15	0	15	0
2010–11	*Huddersfield T*	6	0	6	0
2011–12	Rochdale	19	0	19	0
2013–14	Fleetwood T	10	0		
2014–15	Fleetwood T	42	1		
2015–16	Fleetwood T	21	0	73	1

LAVERY, Gary (F) 0 0
b. 4-5-97

Season	Club		
2015–16	Fleetwood T	0	0

LUCAS, David (G) 308 0
H: 6 1 W: 13 07 b.Preston 23-11-77
Internationals: England U18, U20.

Season	Club				
1995–96	Preston NE	1	0		
1995–96	*Darlington*	6	0		
1996–97	Preston NE	2	0		
1996–97	*Darlington*	7	0	13	0
1996–97	*Scunthorpe U*	6	0	6	0
1997–98	Preston NE	6	0		
1998–99	Preston NE	30	0		
1999–2000	Preston NE	6	0		
2000–01	Preston NE	29	0		
2001–02	Preston NE	24	0		
2002–03	Preston NE	21	0		
2003–04	Preston NE	2	0	121	0
2003–04	Sheffield W	17	0		
2004–05	Sheffield W	34	0		
2005–06	Sheffield W	18	0		
2006–07	Sheffield W	0	0	69	0
2006–07	Barnsley	3	0		
2007–08	Barnsley	0	0	3	0
2007–08	Leeds U	3	0		
2008–09	Leeds U	13	0	16	0
2009–10	Swindon T	41	0		
2010–11	Swindon T	21	0	62	0
2011–12	Rochdale	16	0	16	0
2012–13	Fleetwood T	2	0		
2013–14	Fleetwood T	0	0		
2014–15	Fleetwood T	0	0		
2015–16	Fleetwood T	0	0	2	0

MATT, Jamille (F) 75 20
H: 6 1 W: 11 11 b.Walsall 20-10-89

Season	Club				
2012–13	Fleetwood T	14	3		
2013–14	Fleetwood T	25	8		
2014–15	Fleetwood T	0	0		
2015–16	Fleetwood T	17	3	56	14
2015–16	*Stevenage*	8	1	8	1
2015–16	*Plymouth Arg*	11	5	11	5

MAXWELL, Chris (G) 110 0
H: 6 0 W: 11 07 b.Wrexham 30-7-90
Internationals: Wales U17, U19, U21, U23.

Season	Club				
2012–13	Fleetwood T	0	0		
2013–14	Fleetwood T	18	0		
2014–15	Fleetwood T	46	0		
2015–16	Fleetwood T	46	0	110	0

McLAUGHLIN, Conor (D) 158 3
H: 6 0 W: 11 02 b.Belfast 26-7-91
Internationals: Northern Ireland U21, Full caps.

Season	Club				
2009–10	Preston NE	0	0		
2010–11	Preston NE	7	0		
2011–12	Preston NE	17	0	24	0
2011–12	*Shrewsbury T*	4	0	4	0
2012–13	Fleetwood T	19	0		
2013–14	Fleetwood T	35	0		
2014–15	Fleetwood T	39	1		
2015–16	Fleetwood T	37	2	130	3

McMANUS, Declan (F) 86 26
H: 5 11 W: 11 11 b.Aberdeen 3-8-94
Internationals: Scotland U18, U19, U21.

Season	Club				
2011–12	Aberdeen	2	0		
2012–13	Aberdeen	7	0		
2013–14	Aberdeen	3	0		
2013–14	*Alloa Ath*	18	1	18	1
2014–15	Aberdeen	0	0	12	0
2014–15	*Greenock Morton*	32	20		
2015–16	Fleetwood T	7	1	7	1
2015–16	*Greenock Morton*	17	4	49	24

MOORE, Brendan (G) 0 0
b. 16-4-92

Season	Club		
2014–15	Fleetwood T	0	0
2015–16	Fleetwood T	0	0

NADESAN, Ashley (F) 0 0

Season	Club		
2015–16	Fleetwood T	0	0

NILSSON, Marcus (D) 148 4
H: 6 4 W: 12 13 b. 26-2-88
Internationals: Sweden U17, U19, U21, Full caps.

Season	Club				
2007	Helsingborgs	2	0		
2008	Helsingborgs	12	0		
2009	Helsingborgs	13	0		
2010	Helsingborgs	28	2	55	2
2011	Helsinborgs	16	0	16	0
2011–12	Utrecht	13	0		
2012–13	Utrecht	3	0		
2013–14	Utrecht	0	0	16	0
2014	Kalmar	25	1		
2015	Kalmar	23	0	48	1
2015–16	Fleetwood T	13	1	13	1

NIRENNOLD, Victor (D) 17 0
b. 5-4-91
From Miami City.

Season	Club				
2015–16	Fleetwood T	17	0	17	0

POND, Nathan (M) 101 2
H: 6 3 W: 11 00 b.Preston 5-1-85

Season	Club				
2012–13	Fleetwood T	12	0		
2013–14	Fleetwood T	41	1		
2014–15	Fleetwood T	27	1		
2015–16	Fleetwood T	21	0	101	2

RYAN, James (M) 328 34
H: 5 8 W: 11 08 b.Maghull 6-9-88
Internationals: Republic of Ireland U21.

Season	Club				
2006–07	Liverpool	0	0		
2007–08	Liverpool	0	0		
2007–08	*Shrewsbury T*	4	0	4	0
2008–09	Accrington S	44	10		
2009–10	Accrington S	39	3		
2010–11	Accrington S	46	9	129	22
2011–12	Scunthorpe U	24	2		
2012–13	Scunthorpe U	45	2	69	4
2013–14	Chesterfield	39	2		
2014–15	Chesterfield	44	4	83	6
2015–16	Fleetwood T	43	2	43	2

SANOGO, Vamara (F) 1 0
b. 22-4-95

Season	Club				
2014–15	Metz	0	0		
2015–16	Fleetwood T	1	0	1	0

SARCEVIC, Antoni (M) 130 19
H: 5 10 W: 11 00 b.Manchester 13-3-92
Internationals: England C.

Season	Club				
2009–10	Crewe Alex	0	0		
2010–11	Crewe Alex	6	1		
2011–12	Crewe Alex	6	0	12	1
2013–14	Fleetwood T	42	13		
2014–15	Fleetwood T	37	2		
2015–16	Fleetwood T	39	3	118	18

SOUTHERN, Keith (M) 377 27
H: 5 10 W: 12 06 b.Gateshead 24-4-81

Season	Club				
1998–99	Everton	0	0		
1999–2000	Everton	0	0		
2000–01	Everton	0	0		
2001–02	Everton	0	0		
2002–03	Everton	0	0		
2002–03	Blackpool	38	1		
2003–04	Blackpool	28	2		
2004–05	Blackpool	27	6		
2005–06	Blackpool	42	2		
2006–07	Blackpool	39	5		
2007–08	Blackpool	30	3		
2008–09	Blackpool	35	3		
2009–10	Blackpool	45	2		
2010–11	Blackpool	21	0		
2011–12	Blackpool	25	1	330	25
2012–13	Huddersfield T	29	1		
2013–14	Huddersfield T	10	1	39	2
2014–15	Fleetwood T	0	0		
2014–15	*Shrewsbury T*	6	0	6	0
2015–16	Fleetwood T	0	0	2	0

SOWERBY, Jack (F) 8 0
b. 23-3-95

Season	Club				
2014–15	Fleetwood T	0	0		
2015–16	Fleetwood T	8	0	8	0

TAYLOR, Joe (M) 0 0
b. 25-6-96

Season	Club		
2014–15	Fleetwood T	0	0
2015–16	Fleetwood T	0	0

WILLIAMS, Matthew (D)   0   0
b. 25-1-97

2015–16	Fleetwood T	0	0	

WRIGHT, Akil (M)   0   0
b. 13-5-96

2014–15	Fleetwood T	0	0	
2015–16	Fleetwood T	0	0	

Non-Contract
Grant, Thomas.

Scholars
Abubakar, Malki Soloman; Baines, Lewis
Robert George; Coulson, Thomas Matthew;
Djabi, Mamadou; Fisher, Luke; Garner,
Gerard; Hancox, Jordan Peter; Johnstone,
Max Oliver; McKenzie, Tyrell; Mooney,
Daniel John; Myers, Louis Christopher;
Nelson, Wesley James; Sheron, Nathan;
Shorrock, Lewis Allan James; Smith, Andrew
James; Sterling, Tre; Tetteh, Michael
Djangmatey; Wood, Liam Wayne; Wynne,
Elliot.

FULHAM (37)

AMOREBIETA, Fernando (D)   256   5
H: 6 3   W: 12 00   b.Iurreta 29-3-85
Internationals: Spain U19. Venezuela Full
caps.

2004–05	Athletic Bilbao	0	0		
2005–06	Athletic Bilbao	15	0		
2006–07	Athletic Bilbao	27	0		
2007–08	Athletic Bilbao	34	0		
2008–09	Athletic Bilbao	29	0		
2009–10	Athletic Bilbao	34	0		
2010–11	Athletic Bilbao	17	0		
2011–12	Athletic Bilbao	28	3		
2012–13	Athletic Bilbao	10	0	195	3
2013–14	Fulham	23	1		
2014–15	Fulham	7	1		
2014–15	*Middlesbrough*	4	0		
2015–16	Fulham	14	0	44	2
2015–16	*Middlesbrough*	13	0	17	0

ARTHURWORREY, Stephen (D)   60   3
H: 6 4   W: 13 12   b.Hackney 15-10-94

2011–12	Fulham	0	0		
2012–13	Fulham	0	0		
2013–14	Fulham	0	0		
2013–14	*Tranmere R*	17	0	17	0
2014–15	Fulham	0	0		
2014–15	*Yeovil T*	29	2		
2015–16	Fulham	0	0		
2015–16	*Yeovil T*	14	1	43	3

BETTINELLI, Marcus (G)   89   0
H: 6 4   W: 12 13   b.Camberwell 24-5-92
Internationals: England U21.

2010–11	Fulham	0	0		
2011–12	Fulham	0	0		
2012–13	Fulham	0	0		
2013–14	Fulham	0	0		
2013–14	*Accrington S*	39	0	39	0
2014–15	Fulham	39	0		
2015–16	Fulham	11	0	50	0

BODUROV, Nikolay (D)   246   8
H: 5 11   W: 12 04   b.30-5-86
Internationals: Bulgaria Full caps.

2005–06	Pirin Blagoevgrad	13	0		
2006–07	Pirin Blagoevgrad	19	0		
2007–08	Pirin Blagoevgrad	27	1		
2008–09	Pirin Blagoevgrad	22	0	81	0
2009–10	Litex Lovech	18	0		
2010–11	Litex Lovech	25	2		
2011–12	Litex Lovech	19	3		
2012–13	Litex Lovech	18	0		
2013–14	Litex Lovech	27	1		
2014–15	Litex Lovech	2	0	109	6
2014–15	Fulham	38	1		
2015–16	Fulham	3	0	41	1
2015–16	*FC Midtjylland*	15	0	15	0

BURGESS, Cameron (D)   4   0
H: 6 4   W: 12 11   b.Aberdeen 21-10-95
Internationals: Scotland U19. Australia U20,
U23.

2014–15	Fulham	4	0		
2014–15	*Ross Co*	0	0		
2015–16	Fulham	0	0	4	0

BURN, Dan (D)   123   3
H: 6 6   W: 13 00   b.Blyth 1-5-92

2009–10	Darlington	4	0	4	0
2010–11	Fulham	0	0		
2011–12	Fulham	0	0		
2012–13	Fulham	0	0		

2012–13	*Yeovil T*	34	2	34	2
2013–14	Fulham	9	0		
2013–14	Birmingham C	24	0	24	0
2014–15	Fulham	20	1		
2015–16	Fulham	32	0	61	1

CAIRNEY, Tom (M)   185   18
H: 6 0   W: 11 05   b.Nottingham 20-1-91
Internationals: Scotland U19, U21.

2009–10	Hull C	11	1		
2010–11	Hull C	22	1		
2011–12	Hull C	27	0		
2012–13	Hull C	10	0		
2013–14	Hull C	0	0	70	2
2013–14	Blackburn R	37	5		
2014–15	Blackburn R	39	3	76	8
2015–16	Fulham	39	8	39	8

CHRISTENSEN, Lasse Vigen (M)   52   6
H: 5 10   W: 10 04   b.Esbjerg 15-8-94
Internationals: Denmark U16, U17, U18, U19,
U21.

2012–13	Fulham	0	0		
2013–14	Fulham	0	0		
2014–15	Fulham	25	5		
2015–16	Fulham	27	1	52	6

COLE, Larnell (M)   33   3
H: 5 4   W: 12 04   b.Manchester 9-3-93
Internationals: England U19, U20.

2011–12	Manchester U	0	0		
2012–13	Manchester U	0	0		
2013–14	Manchester U	0	0		
2013–14	Fulham	1	0		
2013–14	*Milton Keynes D*	3	0	3	0
2014–15	Fulham	0	0		
2015–16	Fulham	0	0	1	0
2015–16	*Shrewsbury T*	29	3	29	3

DAWBER, Andrew (G)   5   0
b.Wigan 20-11-94

2012–13	*Accrington S*	2	0		
2013–14	*Accrington S*	3	0		
2014–15	*Accrington S*	0	0	5	0
2015–16	Fulham	0	0		

DEMBELE, Moussa (F)   56   15
H: 6 0   W: 11 08   b.Pontoise 12-7-96
Internationals: France U16, U17, U18, U19,
U20.

2013–14	Fulham	2	0		
2014–15	Fulham	11	0		
2015–16	Fulham	43	15	56	15

DONNELLY, Liam (D)   10   0
b.Dungannon 7-3-96
Internationals: Northern Ireland U16, U17,
U21, Full caps

2013–14	Fulham	0	0		
2014–15	Fulham	0	0		
2015–16	Fulham	0	0		
2015–16	*Crawley T*	10	0	10	0

EVANS, Jordan (D)   9   0
b. 23-9-95
Internationals: Wales U21.

2015–16	Fulham	0	0		
2015–16	*Oxford U*	9	0	9	0

FREDERICKS, Ryan (M)   71   1
H: 5 8   W: 11 10   b.Potters Bar 10-10-92
Internationals: England U19.

2010–11	Tottenham H	0	0		
2011–12	Tottenham H	0	0		
2012–13	Tottenham H	0	0		
2012–13	*Brentford*	4	0	4	0
2013–14	Tottenham H	0	0		
2013–14	*Millwall*	14	1	14	1
2014–15	Tottenham H	0	0		
2014–15	*Middlesbrough*	17	0	17	0
2014–15	*Bristol C*	4	0	4	0
2015–16	Fulham	32	0	32	0

GRIMMER, Jack (M)   57   2
H: 6 0   W: 12 06   b.Aberdeen 25-1-94
Internationals: Scotland U15, U16, U17, U18,
U19, U21.

2009–10	Aberdeen	2	0		
2010–11	Aberdeen	2	0		
2011–12	Aberdeen	0	0	4	0
2011–12	Fulham	0	0		
2012–13	Fulham	0	0		
2013–14	Fulham	0	0		
2013–14	*Port Vale*	13	1	13	1
2014–15	Fulham	13	0		
2014–15	*Shrewsbury T*	6	0		
2015–16	Fulham	0	0	13	0
2015–16	*Shrewsbury T*	21	1	27	1

HUTCHINSON, Shaun (D)   155   9
H: 6 1   W: 12 04   b.Newcastle-Upon-Tyne
23-11-90

2008–09	Motherwell	1	0		
2009–10	Motherwell	5	3		
2010–11	Motherwell	19	1		
2011–12	Motherwell	30	1		
2012–13	Motherwell	31	1		
2013–14	Motherwell	35	1	121	7
2014–15	Fulham	25	2		
2015–16	Fulham	9	0	34	2

HYNDMAN, Emerson (M)   25   1
H: 5 7   W: 9 08   b.Dallas 9-4-96
Internationals: USA U17, U20, U23, Full
caps.

2013–14	Fulham	0	0		
2014–15	Fulham	9	0		
2015–16	Fulham	16	1	25	1

JORONEN, Jesse (G)   36   1
H: 6 6   W: 14 00   b.Rautjarvi 21-3-93
Internationals: Finland U17, U19, U21, Full
caps.

2013–14	Fulham	0	0		
2013–14	*FC Lahti*	18	0	18	0
2014–15	Fulham	4	0		
2014–15	*Accrington S*	4	0	4	0
2015–16	Fulham	0	0	4	0
2015–16	*Stevenage*	10	1	10	1

KACANIKLIC, Alex (M)   109   13
H: 5 11   W: 10 05   b.Helsingborg 13-8-91
Internationals: Sweden U17, U19, Full caps.

2008–09	Liverpool	0	0		
2009–10	Liverpool	0	0		
2010–11	Fulham	4	0		
2011–12	Fulham	0	0		
2011–12	*Watford*	12	1	12	1
2012–13	Fulham	20	4		
2012–13	*Burnley*	6	0	6	0
2013–14	Fulham	23	1		
2014–15	Fulham	14	2		
2014–15	*FC Copenhagen*	7	2	7	2
2015–16	Fulham	23	3	84	10

KAVANAGH, Sean (D)   28   1
H: 5 8   W: 9 11   b. 24-1-94
Internationals: Republic of Ireland U21.

2014–15	Fulham	19	1		
2015–16	Fulham	2	0	21	1
2015–16	*Mansfield T*	7	0	7	0

LABYAD, Zakaria (M)   110   20
H: 5 7   W: 10 03   b.Utrecht 9-3-93
Internationals: Netherlands U17. Morocco
U23, Full caps.

2009–10	PSV Eindhoven	6	2		
2010–11	PSV Eindhoven	7	0		
2011–12	PSV Eindhoven	32	6	45	8
2012–13	Sporting Lisbon	19	2		
2013–14	Sporting Lisbon	0	0		
2013–14	*Vitesse Arnhem*	15	2		
2014–15	Sporting Lisbon	0	0		
2014–15	*Vitesse Arnhem*	29	8	44	10
2015–16	Sporting Lisbon	0	0	19	2

On loan from Sporting Lisbon.

2015–16	Fulham	2	0	2	0

LONERGAN, Andrew (G)   328   1
H: 6 4   W: 13 02   b.Preston 19-10-83
Internationals: Republic of Ireland U16.
England U20.

2000–01	Preston NE	1	0		
2001–02	Preston NE	0	0		
2002–03	Preston NE	0	0		
2002–03	*Darlington*	2	0	2	0
2003–04	Preston NE	8	0		
2004–05	Preston NE	23	1		
2005–06	Preston NE	0	0		
2005–06	*Wycombe W*	2	0	2	0
2006–07	Preston NE	13	0		
2006–07	*Swindon T*	1	0	1	0
2007–08	Preston NE	43	0		
2008–09	Preston NE	46	0		
2009–10	Preston NE	29	0		
2010–11	Preston NE	29	0	208	1
2011–12	Leeds U	35	0	35	0
2012–13	Bolton W	5	0		
2013–14	Bolton W	17	0		
2014–15	Bolton W	29	0	51	0
2015–16	Fulham	29	0	29	0

MADL, Michael (D)   222   10
b. 21-3-88
Internationals: Austria U21.

2006–07	Austria Vienna	5	0		
2007–08	Austria Vienna	0	0		
2007–08	*Wacker Innsbruck*	21	2	21	2

Season	Club				
2008–09	Austria Vienna	17	0		
2009–10	Austria Vienna	1	0	23	0
2010–11	Wiener Neustadt	23	0		
2011–12	Wiener Neustadt	31	3	54	3
2012–13	Sturm Graz	33	1		
2013–14	Sturm Graz	28	1		
2014–15	Sturm Graz	32	1		
2015–16	Sturm Graz	18	1	111	4

On loan from Sturm Graz.

2015–16	Fulham	13	1	13	1

MATTILA, Sakari (M) 159 24
H: 6 2 W: 12 04 b.Helsinki 14-7-89
Internationals: Finland U17, U19, U21, Full caps.

2007	Klubi 04	13	4	13	4
2008	HJK Helsinki	19	4		
2008–09	Udinese	0	0		
2009–10	Udinese	0	0		
2009–10	Ascoli	11	0	11	0
2010–11	Udinese	0	0		
2010–11	Bellinzona	25	1		
2011–12	Bellinzona	17	2	42	3
2012	HJK Helsinki	11	0		
2013	HJK Helsinki	20	5	50	9
2014	Aalesund	25	6		
2015	Aalesund	12	2	37	8
2015–16	Fulham	6	0	6	0

McCORMACK, Ross (F) 385 133
H: 5 9 W: 11 00 b.Glasgow 18-8-86
Internationals: Scotland U21, B, Full caps.

2003–04	Rangers	2	1		
2004–05	Rangers	1	0		
2005–06	Rangers	8	1	11	2
2005–06	Doncaster R	19	4	19	4
2006–07	Motherwell	12	2		
2007–08	Motherwell	36	9	48	11
2008–09	Cardiff C	38	21		
2009–10	Cardiff C	34	4		
2010–11	Cardiff C	2	0	74	25
2010–11	Leeds U	21	2		
2011–12	Leeds U	45	18		
2012–13	Leeds U	32	5		
2013–14	Leeds U	46	28	144	53
2014–15	Fulham	44	17		
2015–16	Fulham	45	21	89	38

O'HARA, Jamie (M) 212 19
H: 5 11 W: 12 04 b.Dartford 25-9-86
Internationals: England U21.

2004–05	Tottenham H	0	0		
2005–06	Tottenham H	0	0		
2005–06	Chesterfield	19	5	19	5
2006–07	Tottenham H	0	0		
2007–08	Tottenham H	17	1		
2007–08	Millwall	14	2	14	2
2008–09	Tottenham H	15	1		
2009–10	Tottenham H	2	0		
2009–10	Portsmouth	26	2	26	2
2010–11	Tottenham H	0	0	34	2
2010–11	Wolverhampton W	14	3		
2011–12	Wolverhampton W	19	2		
2012–13	Wolverhampton W	20	0		
2013–14	Wolverhampton W	2	0		
2014–15	Wolverhampton W	0	0	55	5
2014–15	Blackpool	27	2	27	2
2015–16	Fulham	37	1	37	1

PARKER, Scott (M) 457 31
H: 5 9 W: 11 10 b.Lambeth 13-10-80
Internationals: England U16, U18, U21, Full caps.

1997–98	Charlton Ath	3	0		
1998–99	Charlton Ath	4	0		
1999–2000	Charlton Ath	15	1		
2000–01	Charlton Ath	20	1		
2000–01	Norwich C	6	1	6	1
2001–02	Charlton Ath	38	1		
2002–03	Charlton Ath	28	4		
2003–04	Charlton Ath	20	2	128	9
2003–04	Chelsea	11	1		
2004–05	Chelsea	4	0	15	1
2005–06	Newcastle U	26	1		
2006–07	Newcastle U	29	3	55	4
2007–08	West Ham U	18	1		
2008–09	West Ham U	28	1		
2009–10	West Ham U	31	2		
2010–11	West Ham U	32	5		
2011–12	West Ham U	4	1	113	10
2011–12	Tottenham H	29	0		
2012–13	Tottenham H	21	0		
2013–14	Tottenham H	0	0	50	0
2013–14	Fulham	29	2		
2014–15	Fulham	37	3		
2015–16	Fulham	24	1	90	6

PRINGLE, Ben (M) 197 23
H: 5 8 W: 11 10 b.Whitley Bay 25-7-88

2009–10	Derby Co	5	0		
2010–11	Derby Co	15	0	20	0
2010–11	Torquay U	5	0	5	0
2011–12	Rotherham U	21	4		
2012–13	Rotherham U	41	7		
2013–14	Rotherham U	45	5		
2014–15	Rotherham U	40	3	147	19
2015–16	Fulham	15	2	15	2
2015–16	Ipswich T	10	2	10	2

REAM, Tim (D) 302 7
H: 6 1 W: 11 05 b.St Louis 5-10-87
Internationals: USA Full caps.

2006	St Louis Billikens	19	0		
2007	St Louis Billikens	19	0		
2008	St Louis Billikens	22	0		
2008	Chicago Fire	12	0		
2009	Chicago Fire	7	0	19	0
2009	St Louis Billikens	22	6	82	6
2010	New York RB	30	1		
2011	New York RB	28	0	58	1
2011–12	Bolton W	13	0		
2012–13	Bolton W	15	0		
2013–14	Bolton W	42	0		
2014–15	Bolton W	44	0	114	0
2015–16	Fulham	29	0	29	0

RICHARDS, Ashley (M) 95 0
H: 6 1 W: 12 04 b.Swansea 12-4-91
Internationals: Wales U17, U19, U21, Full caps.

2009–10	Swansea C	15	0		
2010–11	Swansea C	8	0		
2011–12	Swansea C	8	0		
2012–13	Swansea C	3	0		
2012–13	Crystal Palace	11	0	11	0
2013–14	Swansea C	0	0		
2013–14	Huddersfield T	9	0	9	0
2014–15	Swansea C	10	0	39	0
2014–15	Fulham	14	0		
2015–16	Fulham	22	0	36	0

RODAK, Marek (G) 0 0
H: 6 2 W: 10 12 b. 13-12-96
Internationals: Slovakia U16, U17, U21.

2014–15	Fulham	0	0		
2015–16	Fulham	0	0		

SMITH, Matt (F) 161 36
H: 6 6 W: 14 00 b.Birmingham 7-6-89

2011–12	Oldham Ath	28	3		
2011–12	Macclesfield T	8	1	8	1
2012–13	Oldham Ath	34	6	62	9
2013–14	Leeds U	39	12		
2014–15	Leeds U	3	0	42	12
2014–15	Fulham	15	5		
2015–16	Bristol C	14	7	14	7
2015–16	Fulham	20	2	35	7

STEARMAN, Richard (D) 372 12
H: 6 2 W: 10 08 b.Wolverhampton 19-8-87
Internationals: England U16, U17, U19, U21.

2004–05	Leicester C	8	1		
2005–06	Leicester C	34	3		
2006–07	Leicester C	35	1		
2007–08	Leicester C	39	2	116	7
2008–09	Wolverhampton W	37	1		
2009–10	Wolverhampton W	16	1		
2010–11	Wolverhampton W	31	0		
2011–12	Wolverhampton W	30	0		
2012–13	Wolverhampton W	12	1		
2012–13	Ipswich T	15	0	15	0
2013–14	Wolverhampton W	40	2		
2014–15	Wolverhampton W	42	0		
2015–16	Wolverhampton W	4	0	212	5
2015–16	Fulham	29	0	29	0

STEKELENBURG, Maarten (G) 274 0
H: 6 6 W: 14 05 b.Haarlem 22-9-82
Internationals: Netherlands U21, Full caps.

2001–02	Ajax	0	0		
2002–03	Ajax	9	0		
2003–04	Ajax	10	0		
2004–05	Ajax	11	0		
2005–06	Ajax	27	0		
2006–07	Ajax	32	0		
2007–08	Ajax	31	0		
2008–09	Ajax	12	0		
2009–10	Ajax	33	0		
2010–11	Ajax	26	0	191	0
2011–12	Roma	30	0		
2012–13	Roma	18	0	47	0
2013–14	Fulham	19	0		
2014–15	Fulham	0	0		
2014–15	Monaco	0	0		
2015–16	Fulham	0	0	19	0
2015–16	Southampton	17	0	17	0

TUNNICLIFFE, Ryan (M) 130 3
H: 6 0 W: 14 02 b.Bury 30-12-92
Internationals: England U16, U17.

2009–10	Manchester U	0	0		
2010–11	Manchester U	0	0		
2011–12	Manchester U	0	0		
2011–12	Peterborough U	27	0	27	0
2012–13	Manchester U	0	0		
2012–13	Barnsley	2	0	2	0
2013–14	Manchester U	0	0		
2013–14	Ipswich T	27	0	27	0
2013–14	Fulham	3	0		
2013–14	Wigan Ath	5	0	5	0
2014–15	Fulham	22	0		
2014–15	Blackburn R	17	1	17	1
2015–16	Fulham	27	2	52	2

VOSER, Kay (D) 136 1
H: 5 8 W: 10 12 b. 4-1-87
Internationals: Switzerland U16, U17, U20, U21.

2008–09	Grasshopper	31	0		
2009–10	Grasshopper	30	0		
2010–11	Grasshopper	13	0	74	0
2011–12	Basle	6	0		
2012–13	Basle	13	0		
2013–14	Basle	29	1	48	1
2014–15	Fulham	3	0		
2015–16	Fulham	7	0	10	0
2015–16	Sion	4	0	4	0

WILLIAMS, George (F) 29 0
H: 5 10 W: 12 04 b.Milton Keynes 7-9-95
Internationals: Wales U17, U19, U21, Full caps.

2012–13	Fulham	0	0		
2013–14	Fulham	0	0		
2014–15	Fulham	14	0		
2014–15	Milton Keynes D	4	0	4	0
2015–16	Fulham	1	0	15	0
2015–16	Gillingham	10	0	10	0

WOODROW, Cauley (F) 68 10
H: 6 0 W: 12 04 b.Hemel Hempstead 2-12-94
Internationals: England U17, U20, U21.

2011–12	Fulham	0	0		
2012–13	Fulham	0	0		
2013–14	Fulham	6	1		
2013–14	Southend U	19	2	19	2
2014–15	Fulham	29	3		
2015–16	Fulham	14	4	49	8

Players retained or with offer of contract
Adebayo, Elijah Anuoluwapo; Davies, Aron Paul; De La Torre, Lucas Daniel; Dolan, Anthony; Edun, Adetayo Oluwatosin; Humphrys, Stephen Peter; Kait, Mattias; Mitroglou, Konstantinos; Nabay, Foday; Norman, Magnus; Sheckleford, Ryheem Cole; Smile, Joshua Clifford; Walker, Joshua James.

Scholars
Adeniran, Dennis Emmanuel Abiodun; Ashby-Hammond, Taye; Fossey, Marlon Joseph; Jenz, Moritz; Kwietniewski, Mikolaj; Lukwata, Joshua Benon; Opoku, Jerome; Paton, Harrison Theodore; Pearce, Isaac Richard Kai; Shamsi, Ravin; Soutter, Jake Keith; Thomas, Cassian Diogo David; Thorsteinsson, Jon Dagur.

GILLINGHAM (38)

CUNDLE, Gregory (F) 0 0
b. 20-3-97

2015–16	Gillingham	0	0		

DACK, Bradley (M) 126 26
b.Greenwich 31-12-93

2012–13	Gillingham	16	1		
2013–14	Gillingham	28	3		
2014–15	Gillingham	42	9		
2015–16	Gillingham	40	13	126	26

DAVIES, Callum (D) 29 0
H: 6 1 W: 11 11 b.Sittingbourne 8-2-93

2010–11	Gillingham	1	0		
2011–12	Gillingham	2	0		
2012–13	Gillingham	14	0		
2013–14	Gillingham	7	0		
2014–15	Gillingham	5	0		
2015–16	Gillingham	0	0	29	0

DICKENSON, Brennan (F) 98 6
H: 6 0 W: 12 07 b.Ferndown 26-2-93

2012–13	Brighton & HA	0	0		
2012–13	Chesterfield	11	1	11	1

2012–13	*AFC Wimbledon*	7	2	**7**	**2**
2013–14	Brighton & HA	0	0		
2013–14	*Northampton T*	13	1	**13**	**1**
2014–15	Gillingham	34	1		
2015–16	Gillingham	33	1	**67**	**2**

DICKENSON, Mitchell (D) **0** **0**

b. 14-9-96

2015–16	Gillingham	0	0		

DONNELLY, Rory (F) **107** **35**

H: 6 2 W: 12 10 b.Belfast 18-2-92

Internationals: Northern Ireland U21.

2010–11	Cliftonville	31	7		
2011–12	Cliftonville	18	13	**49**	**20**
2011–12	Swansea C	0	0		
2012–13	Swansea C	0	0		
2013–14	Swansea C	0	0		
2013–14	*Coventry C*	0	0		
2014–15	Swansea C	0	0		
2014–15	*Tranmere R*	20	5	**20**	**5**
2015–16	Gillingham	38	10	**38**	**10**

EGAN, John (D) **100** **11**

H: 6 1 W: 11 11 b.Cork 20-10-92

Internationals: Republic of Ireland U17, U19, U21.

2009–10	Sunderland	0	0		
2010–11	Sunderland	0	0		
2011–12	Sunderland	0	0		
2011–12	*Crystal Palace*	1	0	**1**	**0**
2011–12	*Sheffield U*	1	0	**1**	**0**
2012–13	Sunderland	0	0		
2012–13	*Bradford C*	4	0	**4**	**0**
2013–14	Sunderland	0	0		
2013–14	*Southend U*	13	1	**13**	**1**
2014–15	Gillingham	45	4		
2015–16	Gillingham	36	6	**81**	**10**

EHMER, Max (M) **136** **3**

H: 6 2 W: 11 00 b.Frankfurt 3-2-92

2009–10	QPR	0	0		
2010–11	QPR	0	0		
2010–11	*Yeovil T*	27	0		
2011–12	QPR	0	0		
2011–12	*Yeovil T*	24	0	**51**	**0**
2011–12	*Preston NE*	9	0	**9**	**0**
2012–13	QPR	0	0		
2012–13	*Stevenage*	6	1	**6**	**1**
2013–14	QPR	1	0		
2013–14	*Carlisle U*	12	1	**12**	**1**
2014–15	QPR	0	0	**1**	**0**
2014–15	*Gillingham*	27	1		
2015–16	Gillingham	30	0	**57**	**1**

FREITER, Michael (M) **1** **0**

b. 15-1-96

2012–13	Gillingham	0	0		
2013–14	Gillingham	0	0		
2014–15	Gillingham	1	0		
2015–16	Gillingham	0	0	**1**	**0**

GARMSTON, Bradley (D) **54** **1**

H: 5 9 W: 10 12 b.Greenwich 18-1-94

Internationals: Republic of Ireland U17, U9, U21.

2012–13	WBA	0	0		
2012–13	*Colchester U*	13	0	**13**	**0**
2013–14	WBA	0	0		
2014–15	WBA	0	0		
2014–15	*Gillingham*	8	1		
2015–16	Gillingham	33	0	**41**	**1**

HADDLER, Tom (G) **0** **0**

b. 30-7-96

2014–15	Gillingham	0	0		
2015–16	Gillingham	0	0		

HARE, Josh (D) **2** **0**

H: 6 0 W: 12 04 b.Cantebury 12-8-94

2012–13	Gillingham	0	0		
2013–14	Gillingham	0	0		
2014–15	Gillingham	2	0		
2015–16	Gillingham	0	0	**2**	**0**

HESSENTHALER, Jake (M) **94** **6**

b.Gravesend 20-4-94

2012–13	Gillingham	0	0		
2013–14	Gillingham	19	1		
2014–15	Gillingham	37	1		
2015–16	Gillingham	38	4	**94**	**6**

JACKSON, Ryan (M) **107** **2**

H: 5 9 W: 10 03 b.Streatham 31-7-90

Internationals: England C.

2011–12	AFC Wimbledon	7	0	**7**	**0**
2013–14	Newport Co	29	0		
2014–15	Newport Co	34	0	**63**	**0**
2015–16	Gillingham	37	2	**37**	**2**

LIST, Elliott (M) **6** **0**

b. 12-5-97

From Crystal Palace.

2015–16	Gillingham	6	0	**6**	**0**

LOFT, Doug (M) **286** **25**

H: 6 0 W: 12 01 b.Maidstone 25-12-86

2005–06	Brighton & HA	3	1		
2006–07	Brighton & HA	11	1		
2007–08	Brighton & HA	13	0		
2008–09	Brighton & HA	12	0	**39**	**2**
2008–09	*Dagenham & R*	11	0	**11**	**0**
2009–10	Port Vale	32	3		
2010–11	Port Vale	29	1		
2011–12	Port Vale	44	4		
2012–13	Port Vale	32	1		
2013–14	Port Vale	37	9	**174**	**18**
2014–15	Gillingham	36	1		
2015–16	Gillingham	26	4	**62**	**5**

M'BO, Noel (F) **0** **0**

2015–16	Gillingham	0	0		

McDONALD, Cody (F) **224** **78**

H: 5 10 W: 11 03 b.Witham 30-5-86

2008–09	Norwich C	7	1		
2009–10	Norwich C	17	3		
2010–11	Norwich C	0	0		
2010–11	*Gillingham*	41	25		
2011–12	Norwich C	0	0	**24**	**4**
2011–12	Coventry C	23	4		
2012–13	Coventry C	20	3	**43**	**7**
2012–13	*Gillingham*	7	4		
2013–14	Gillingham	44	17		
2014–15	Gillingham	43	16		
2015–16	Gillingham	22	5	**157**	**67**

McGLASHAN, Jermaine (M) **222** **22**

H: 5 7 W: 10 00 b.Croydon 14-4-88

2010–11	Aldershot T	38	1		
2011–12	Aldershot T	23	4	**61**	**5**
2011–12	Cheltenham T	16	2		
2012–13	Cheltenham T	45	4		
2013–14	Cheltenham T	43	6	**104**	**12**
2014–15	Gillingham	40	5		
2015–16	Gillingham	17	0	**57**	**5**

MILLBANK, Aaron (F) **1** **0**

H: 6 0 W: 11 09 b.Ramsgate 4-2-95

2013–14	Gillingham	1	0		
2014–15	Gillingham	0	0		
2015–16	Gillingham	0	0	**1**	**0**

MORRIS, Aaron (D) **174** **2**

H: 6 1 W: 12 05 b.Cardiff 30-12-89

Internationals: Wales U21.

2008–09	Cardiff C	0	0		
2009–10	Cardiff C	1	0	**1**	**0**
2010–11	Aldershot T	22	0		
2011–12	Aldershot T	39	2		
2012–13	Aldershot T	37	0	**98**	**2**
2013–14	AFC Wimbledon	17	0	**17**	**0**
2014–15	Gillingham	23	0		
2015–16	Gillingham	35	0	**58**	**0**

MORRIS, Glenn (G) **193** **0**

H: 6 0 W: 12 03 b.Woolwich 20-12-83

2001–02	Leyton Orient	2	0		
2002–03	Leyton Orient	23	0		
2003–04	Leyton Orient	27	0		
2004–05	Leyton Orient	12	0		
2005–06	Leyton Orient	4	0		
2006–07	Leyton Orient	3	0		
2007–08	Leyton Orient	16	0		
2008–09	Leyton Orient	26	0		
2009–10	Leyton Orient	11	0	**124**	**0**
2010–11	Southend U	33	0		
2011–12	Southend U	24	0		
2012–13	Southend U	0	0	**57**	**0**
2012–13	Aldershot T	2	0	**2**	**0**
2014–15	Gillingham	10	0		
2015–16	Gillingham	0	0	**10**	**0**

NELSON, Stuart (G) **386** **0**

H: 6 1 W: 12 12 b.Stroud 17-9-81

2003–04	Brentford	9	0		
2004–05	Brentford	43	0		
2005–06	Brentford	45	0		
2006–07	Brentford	19	0	**116**	**0**
2007–08	Leyton Orient	30	0	**30**	**0**
2008–09	Norwich C	0	0		
2010–11	Notts Co	33	0		
2011–12	Notts Co	46	0	**79**	**0**
2012–13	Gillingham	45	0		
2013–14	Gillingham	46	0		
2014–15	Gillingham	24	0		
2015–16	Gillingham	46	0	**161**	**0**

NORRIS, Luke (F) **101** **22**

H: 6 1 W: 13 05 b.Stevenage 3-6-93

2011–12	Brentford	1	0		
2012–13	Brentford	0	0		
2013–14	Brentford	1	0	**2**	**0**
2013–14	*Northampton T*	10	4	**10**	**4**
2013–14	*Dagenham & R*	19	4	**19**	**4**
2014–15	Gillingham	37	6		
2015–16	Gillingham	33	8	**70**	**14**

OLDAKER, Darren (M) **0** **0**

b. 4-1-99

2015–16	Gillingham	0	0		

OSAOABE, Emmanuel (M) **18** **2**

b. 1-10-96

2015–16	Gillingham	18	2	**18**	**2**

PRITCHARD, Josh (M) **25** **0**

H: 5 9 W: 11 02 b.Stockport 23-9-92

Internationals: Wales U21.

2011–12	Fulham	0	0		
2012–13	Fulham	0	0		
2013–14	Fulham	0	0		
2014–15	Gillingham	25	0		
2015–16	Gillingham	0	0	**25**	**0**

WILLIAMSON, Ben (F) **202** **41**

H: 5 11 W: 11 13 b.Lambeth 25-12-88

2010–11	Jerez Industrial	12	8	**12**	**8**
2010–11	Bournemouth	4	0		
2011–12	Bournemouth	0	0	**4**	**0**
2011–12	Port Vale	35	3		
2012–13	Port Vale	33	8		
2013–14	Port Vale	38	4		
2014–15	Port Vale	43	6	**149**	**21**
2015–16	Gillingham	9	0	**9**	**0**
2015–16	*Cambridge U*	28	12	**28**	**12**

WRIGHT, Josh (M) **237** **5**

H: 6 1 W: 11 07 b.Bethnal Green 6-11-89

Internationals: England U16, U17, U18, U19.

2007–08	Charlton Ath	0	0		
2007–08	*Barnet*	32	1	**32**	**1**
2008–09	Charlton Ath	2	0	**2**	**0**
2008–09	*Brentford*	5	0	**5**	**0**
2008–09	*Gillingham*	5	0		
2009–10	Scunthorpe U	35	0		
2010–11	Scunthorpe U	36	0	**71**	**0**
2011–12	Millwall	18	1		
2012–13	Millwall	24	0		
2013–14	Millwall	3	0		
2013–14	*Leyton Orient*	2	0		
2014–15	Millwall	1	0	**46**	**1**
2014–15	*Crawley T*	4	0	**4**	**0**
2014–15	Leyton Orient	29	2	**31**	**2**
2015–16	Gillingham	41	1	**46**	**1**

Scholars

Adams, Daniel Raymond; Bowyer-O'Brien, Jake; Chapman, Benjamin Scott; Crandley, Ryan; Lawford, Samuel Dean; Mbo, Noel; Newcombe, Henry John; Nougbele, Joseph; O'Mara, Finn George; Oldaker, Darren Joseph Norman; Simpson, Aaron Michael; Stannard, Harry; Stevenson, Bradley; Stewart, Sam Ryan; Sykes, William Peter Barry; Thompson, Ricardo Dante Nathaniel; Welch, Mitchell Krane.

HARTLEPOOL U (39)

AUSTIN, Neil (D) **433** **15**

H: 5 10 W: 11 09 b.Barnsley 26-4-83

Internationals: England U16, U17.

1999–2000	Barnsley	0	0		
2000–01	Barnsley	0	0		
2001–02	Barnsley	0	0		
2002–03	Barnsley	34	0		
2003–04	Barnsley	37	0		
2004–05	Barnsley	15	0		
2005–06	Barnsley	38	0		
2006–07	Barnsley	24	0	**148**	**0**
2007–08	Darlington	29	2		
2008–09	Darlington	33	3	**62**	**5**
2009–10	Hartlepool U	39	3		
2010–11	Hartlepool U	24	2		
2011–12	Hartlepool U	46	1		
2012–13	Hartlepool U	39	2		
2013–14	Hartlepool U	29	0		
2014–15	Hartlepool U	46	2		
2015–16	Hartlepool U	0	0	**223**	**10**

BARBER, Jonathan (G) **0** **0**

b. 1-10-96

2014–15	Hartlepool U	0	0		
2015–16	Hartlepool U	0	0		

BARTLETT, Adam (G)   12   0
H: 6 0   W: 11 11   b.Newcastle-Upon-Tyne 27-2-86
Internationals: England C.
From Blyth Spartans, Kidderminster H, Hereford U, Gateshead.
2015–16   Hartlepool U   12   0   12   0

BATES, Matthew (D)   205   7
H: 5 10   W: 12 03   b.Stockton 10-12-86
Internationals: England U18, U19.
2003–04   Middlesbrough   0   0
2004–05   Middlesbrough   2   0
2004–05   *Darlington*   4   0   4   0
2005–06   Middlesbrough   16   0
2006–07   Middlesbrough   1   0
2006–07   *Ipswich T*   2   0   2   0
2007–08   Middlesbrough   0   0
2007–08   *Norwich C*   3   0   3   0
2008–09   Middlesbrough   17   1
2009–10   Middlesbrough   0   0
2010–11   Middlesbrough   31   3
2011–12   Middlesbrough   37   2   104   6
2012–13   Bristol C   13   0
2013–14   Bristol C   0   0   13   0
2013–14   Bradford C   22   0   22   0
2014–15   Hartlepool U   25   1
2015–16   Hartlepool U   32   0   57   1

BINGHAM, Rakish (F)   64   11
H: 6 0   W: 12 00   b.Newham 25-10-93
2011–12   Wigan Ath   0   0
2012–13   Wigan Ath   0   0
2013–14   Wigan Ath   0   0
2014–15   Mansfield T   28   6   28   6
2014–15   *Hartlepool U*   5   1
2015–16   Hartlepool U   31   4   36   5

BLACKFORD, Jack (M)   1   0
b.13-5-98
2015–16   Hartlepool U   1   0   1   0

CAIG, Tony (G)   310   0
H: 6 0   W: 13 02   b.Whitehaven 11-4-74
1992–93   Carlisle U   1   0
1993–94   Carlisle U   20   0
1994–95   Carlisle U   40   0
1995–96   Carlisle U   33   0
1996–97   Carlisle U   46   0
1997–98   Carlisle U   46   0
1998–99   Carlisle U   37   0
1998–99   Blackpool   10   0
1999–2000   Blackpool   33   0
2000–01   Blackpool   6   0   49   0
2000–01   Charlton Ath   1   0   1   0
2001–02   Hibernian   8   0
2002–03   Hibernian   5   0   13   0
2003–04   Newcastle U   0   0
2003–04   *Barnsley*   3   0   3   0
2007–08   Gretna   7   0   7   0
2007–08   Houston D   6   0
2008–09   Houston D   8   0   14   0
2012–13   Carlisle U   0   0
2013–14   Carlisle U   0   0
2014–15   Carlisle U   0   0
2015–16   Carlisle U   0   0   223   0
2015–16   Hartlepool U   0   0

CARROLL, Jake (D)   96   3
H: 6 0   W: 12 03   b.Dublin 11-1-91
Internationals: Republic of Ireland U18.
2011   St Patricks   7   0
2012   St Patricks   19   1
2013   St Patricks   7   0   33   1
2013–14   Huddersfield T   4   0
2013–14   *Bury*   6   1   6   1
2014–15   Huddersfield T   2   0   6   0
2014–15   *Partick Thistle*   10   0   10   0
2015–16   Hartlepool U   41   1   41   1

CARSON, Trevor (G)   212   0
H: 6 0   W: 14 11   b.Downpatrick 5-3-88
Internationals: Northern Ireland U17, U18, U19, U20, U21, B.
2004–05   Sunderland   0   0
2005–06   Sunderland   0   0
2006–07   Sunderland   0   0
2007–08   Sunderland   0   0
2008–09   Sunderland   0   0
2008–09   *Chesterfield*   18   0   18   0
2009–10   Sunderland   0   0
2010–11   Sunderland   0   0
2010–11   *Lincoln C*   16   0   16   0
2010–11   *Brentford*   1   0   1   0
2011–12   Sunderland   0   0
2011–12   *Hull C*   0   0
2011–12   Bury   17   0
2012–13   Bury   39   0
2013–14   Bury   5   0   61   0

2013–14   *Portsmouth*   36   0   36   0
2014–15   Cheltenham T   46   0   46   0
2015–16   Hartlepool U   34   0   34   0

DENTON, Peter (G)   0   0
b.22-12-96
2015–16   Hartlepool U   0   0

DUCKWORTH, Michael (M)   80   3
b.28-6-92
2013–14   Hartlepool U   30   0
2014–15   Hartlepool U   37   3
2015–16   Hartlepool U   13   0   80   3

FEATHERSTONE, Nicky (M)   206   1
H: 5 7   W: 11 02   b.Ferriby 22-9-88
2006–07   Hull C   2   0
2007–08   Hull C   6   0
2008–09   Hull C   0   0
2009–10   Hull C   0   0   8   0
2009–10   *Grimsby T*   8   0   8   0
2010–11   Hereford U   27   1
2011–12   Hereford U   38   0   65   1
2012–13   Walsall   31   0
2013–14   Walsall   25   0   56   0
2014–15   Scunthorpe U   0   0
2014–15   *Hartlepool U*   25   0
2015–16   Hartlepool U   44   0   69   0

FENWICK, Scott (F)   42   10
b.9-4-90
2014–15   Hartlepool U   19   6
2015–16   Hartlepool U   23   4   42   10

GREEN, Kieran (M)   1   0
b.30-6-97
2014–15   Hartlepool U   1   0
2015–16   Hartlepool U   0   0   1   0

HARRISON, Scott (D)   65   2
b.Middlesbrough 3-9-93
2012–13   Sunderland   0   0
2013–14   Sunderland   0   0
2013–14   *Bury*   1   0   1   0
2013–14   *Hartlepool U*   6   0
2014–15   Sunderland   0   0
2014–15   *Hartlepool U*   36   1
2015–16   Hartlepool U   22   1   64   2

HAWKINS, Lewis (M)   42   2
H: 5 10   W: 12 04   b.Middlesbrough 15-6-93
2011–12   Hartlepool U   1   0
2012–13   Hartlepool U   1   0
2013–14   Hartlepool U   5   0
2014–15   Hartlepool U   12   0
2015–16   Hartlepool U   23   2   42   2

JONES, Dan (D)   37   0
H: 6 0   W: 12 05   b.14-12-94
2013–14   Hartlepool U   1   0
2014–15   Hartlepool U   25   0
2015–16   Hartlepool U   11   0   37   0

JONES, Rob (D)   331   32
H: 6 7   W: 12 02   b.Stockton 30-11-79
2002–03   Stockport Co   0   0
2003–04   Stockport Co   16   2   16   2
2003–04   *Macclesfield T*   1   0   1   0
2004–05   Grimsby T   20   1
2005–06   Grimsby T   40   4   60   5
2006–07   Hibernian   34   4
2007–08   Hibernian   30   0
2008–09   Hibernian   32   4   96   8
2009–10   Scunthorpe U   28   1
2010–11   Scunthorpe U   14   1   42   2
2010–11   *Sheffield W*   8   1
2011–12   Sheffield W   33   4   41   5
2012–13   Doncaster R   44   7
2013–14   Doncaster R   12   1
2014–15   Doncaster R   10   2
2015–16   Doncaster R   2   0   68   10
2015–16   Hartlepool U   7   0   7   0

LAURENT, Josh (M)   6   0
b.6-5-95
2013–14   QPR   0   0
2014–15   QPR   0   0
2015–16   Brentford   0   0
2015–16   *Newport Co*   3   0   3   0
2015–16   *Hartlepool U*   3   0   3   0

MAGNAY, Carl (D)   37   1
H: 6 0   W: 12 00   b.Gateshead 20-1-89
Internationals: Northern Ireland U21.
2006–07   Chelsea   0   0
2007–08   Chelsea   0   0
2008–09   Chelsea   0   0
2008–09   *Milton Keynes D*   2   0   2   0
2008–09   *Northampton T*   2   0   2   0
2009–10   Chelsea   0   0
2010–11   Chelsea   0   0

From Gateshead, Grimsby T.
2015–16   Hartlepool U   33   1   33   1

NEARNEY, Josh (D)   0   0
b.7-9-95
2014–15   Hartlepool U   0   0
2015–16   Hartlepool U   0   0

NELSON-ADDY, Ebby (M)   4   0
b.13-9-92
From Brackley T, Worcester C
2014–15   Hartlepool U   2   0
2015–16   Hartlepool U   2   0   4   0

OATES, Rhys (D)   47   2
H: 6 0   W: 11 09   b.Pontefract 4-12-94
2012–13   Barnsley   0   0
2013–14   Barnsley   0   0
2014–15   Barnsley   9   0   9   0
2015–16   Hartlepool U   38   2   38   2

OYENUGA, Kudus (F)   10   1
H: 5 9   W: 11 00   b.Walthamstow 18-3-93
2010–11   Tottenham H   0   0
2011–12   Tottenham H   0   0
2011–12   *Bury*   1   0   1   0
2011–12   *St Johnstone*   1   0   1   0
2015–16   Hartlepool U   8   1   8   1

PAYNTER, Billy (F)   456   113
H: 6 1   W: 14 01   b.Liverpool 13-7-84
2000–01   Port Vale   1   0
2001–02   Port Vale   7   0
2002–03   Port Vale   31   5
2003–04   Port Vale   44   13
2004–05   Port Vale   45   10
2005–06   Port Vale   16   2   144   30
2005–06   Hull C   22   3   22   3
2006–07   Southend U   9   0
2006–07   *Bradford C*   15   4   15   4
2007–08   Southend U   0   0   9   0
2007–08   Swindon T   36   8
2008–09   Swindon T   42   11
2009–10   Swindon T   42   26   120   45
2010–11   Leeds U   30   2
2011–12   Leeds U   5   2
2011–12   *Brighton & HA*   10   0   10   0
2012–13   Leeds U   0   0   27   3
2012–13   Doncaster R   37   13
2013–14   Doncaster R   9   0   46   13
2013–14   *Sheffield U*   13   0   13   0
2014–15   Carlisle U   18   1   18   1
2015–16   Hartlepool U   32   14   32   14

RICHARDS, Jordan (M)   52   0
H: 5 9   W: 11 05   b.Sunderland 25-4-93
2011–12   Hartlepool U   2   0
2012–13   Hartlepool U   11   0
2013–14   Hartlepool U   19   0
2014–15   Hartlepool U   9   0
2015–16   Hartlepool U   11   0   52   0

SMITH, Connor (M)   14   0
b.14-10-96
2013–14   Hartlepool U   1   0
2014–15   Hartlepool U   8   0
2015–16   Hartlepool U   5   0   14   0

THOMAS, Nathan (F)   60   7
H: 5 10   W: 12 08   b.Barwick 27-9-94
2013–14   Plymouth Arg   10   0
2014–15   Plymouth Arg   9   1   19   1
2014–15   *Motherwell*   2   0   2   0
2015–16   Mansfield T   17   1   17   1
2015–16   Hartlepool U   22   5   22   5

WALKER, Brad (M)   87   9
H: 6 1   W: 12 08   b.25-4-95
2012–13   Hartlepool U   0   0
2013–14   Hartlepool U   36   3
2014–15   Hartlepool U   28   5
2015–16   Hartlepool U   23   1   87   9

WOODS, Michael (M)   61   6
H: 6 0   W: 12 07   b.Pocklington 6-4-90
Internationals: England U16, U17, U19.
2006–07   Chelsea   0   0
2007–08   Chelsea   0   0
2008–09   Chelsea   0   0
2009–10   Chelsea   0   0
2010–11   Chelsea   0   0
2010–11   *Notts Co*   0   0
2011–12   Chelsea   0   0
2011–12   *Yeovil T*   5   1   5   1
2012–13   Doncaster R   0   0
2014–15   Hartlepool U   23   1
2015–16   Hartlepool U   33   3   56   4

WORLEY, Harry (D)   138   7
H: 6 3   W: 13 00   b.Warrington 25-11-88
2005–06   Chelsea   0   0

Season	Club				
2006–07	Chelsea	0	0		
2006–07	Doncaster R	10	0	10	0
2007–08	Chelsea	0	0		
2007–08	Carlisle U	1	0	1	0
2007–08	Leicester C	2	0		
2008–09	Leicester C	0	0		
2008–09	Luton T	8	0	8	0
2009–10	Leicester C	0	0	2	0
2009–10	Crewe Alex	23	1	23	1
2010–11	Oxford U	43	1		
2011–12	Oxford U	10	0		
2012–13	Oxford U	9	1		
2013–14	Oxford U	0	0	62	2
2013–14	Newport Co	26	4	26	4
2014–15	Stevenage	3	0	3	0
2015–16	Hartlepool U	3	0	3	0

Scholars
Briggs, Frazer Wilkinson; Catterick, Ryan James; Cunningham, Aaron Ross; Dawson, James Edward; Elliott, Dylan Michael; Fielding, Jordan; Hawkes, Joshua Stuart; Howes, Scott Anthony; Jewson, Jordan Lewis; Male, Adam; Richardson, Kenton Terry; Skidmore, Nathaniel; Travers, Liam William Edward; Turnbull, Jack Thomas; Varga, Bradley Brian Miklos; Wood, Ethan.

HUDDERSFIELD T (40)

ALLINSON, Lloyd (G)   1 0
H: 6 2 W: 13 00 b.Rothwell 7-9-93

Season	Club				
2010–11	Huddersfield T	0	0		
2011–12	Huddersfield T	0	0		
2012–13	Huddersfield T	0	0		
2013–14	Huddersfield T	0	0		
2014–15	Huddersfield T	0	0		
2015–16	Huddersfield T	1	0	1	0

BAJAJ, Florent (M)   8 1
b. 13-4-96
Internationals: Albania U17.

Season	Club				
2013–14	Huddersfield T	0	0		
2015–16	Huddersfield T	8	1	8	1

BILLING, Phillip (M)   14 1
H: 6 4 W: 12 08 b. 11-6-96
Internationals: Denmark U19.

Season	Club				
2013–14	Huddersfield T	1	0		
2014–15	Huddersfield T	0	0		
2015–16	Huddersfield T	13	1	14	1

BOOTY, Regan (M)   0 0
b. 3-4-98

Season	Club		
2015–16	Huddersfield T	0	0

BOYLE, William (D)   14 0
H: 6 2 W: 11 00 b.Garforth 1-9-95

Season	Club				
2014–15	Huddersfield T	1	0		
2015–16	Huddersfield T	1	0	2	0
2015–16	York C	12	0	12	0

BUNN, Harry (F)   99 16
H: 5 9 W: 11 10 b.Oldham 25-11-92

Season	Club				
2010–11	Manchester C	0	0		
2011–12	Manchester C	0	0		
2011–12	Rochdale	6	0	6	0
2011–12	Preston NE	1	1	1	1
2011–12	Oldham Ath	11	0	11	0
2012–13	Manchester C	0	0		
2012–13	Crewe Alex	4	0	4	0
2013–14	Manchester C	0	0		
2013–14	Sheffield U	2	0	2	0
2013–14	Huddersfield T	3	0		
2014–15	Manchester C	0	0		
2014–15	Huddersfield T	30	9		
2015–16	Huddersfield T	42	6	75	15

CHARLES, Jake (M)   1 0
H: 6 0 W: 10 10 b.Leeds 28-2-96
Internationals: Wales U16, U17, U19, U21.

Season	Club				
2013–14	Huddersfield T	0	0		
2014–15	Huddersfield T	1	0		
2015–16	Huddersfield T	1	0	1	0

COUGHLAN, Ronan (F)   0 0
H: 5 10 W: 11 11 b. 2-10-95

Season	Club		
2015–16	Huddersfield T	0	0

CRANIE, Martin (D)   319 2
H: 6 1 W: 12 09 b.Yeovil 23-9-86
Internationals: England U17, U18, U19, U20, U21.

Season	Club				
2003–04	Southampton	1	0		
2004–05	Southampton	3	0		
2004–05	Bournemouth	3	0	3	0
2005–06	Southampton	11	0		
2006–07	Southampton	10	0	16	0
2006–07	Yeovil T	12	0	12	0
2007–08	Portsmouth	2	0		
2007–08	QPR	6	0	6	0
2008–09	Portsmouth	0	0		
2008–09	Charlton Ath	19	0	19	0
2009–10	Portsmouth	0	0	2	0
2009–10	Coventry C	40	1		
2010–11	Coventry C	36	0		
2011–12	Coventry C	38	0	114	0
2012–13	Barnsley	36	0		
2013–14	Barnsley	35	0		
2014–15	Barnsley	39	1	110	1
2015–16	Huddersfield T	37	0	37	0

DAVIDSON, Jason (D)   112 5
H: 5 11 W: 11 05 b.Melbourne 29-6-91
Internationals: Australia U20, Full caps.

Season	Club				
2009	Hume City	16	2	16	2
2009–10	Pacos de Ferreira	5	0		
2010–11	Pacos de Ferreira	0	0	5	0
2010–11	Sporting Covilha	14	0	14	0
2011–12	Heracles	6	0		
2012–13	Heracles	10	0		
2013–14	Heracles	32	2	48	2
2014–15	WBA	2	0	2	0
2015–16	Huddersfield T	27	1	27	1

DEMPSEY, Kyle (M)   68 11
b.Whitehaven 17-9-95

Season	Club				
2013–14	Carlisle U	4	0		
2014–15	Carlisle U	43	10	47	10
2015–16	Huddersfield T	21	1	21	1

HANSON, Jacob (D)   0 0
b. 30-11-97

Season	Club		
2015–16	Huddersfield T	0	0

HIWULA, Jordy (F)   54 14
H: 5 10 W: 11 12 b.Manchester 24-9-94
Internationals: England U18, U19.

Season	Club				
2013–14	Manchester C	0	0		
2014–15	Manchester C	0	0		
2014–15	Yeovil T	8	0	8	0
2014–15	Walsall	19	9		
2015–16	Huddersfield T	0	0		
2015–16	Wigan Ath	14	2	14	2
2015–16	Walsall	13	3	32	12

HOGG, Jonathan (M)   189 1
H: 5 7 W: 10 05 b.Middlesbrough 6-12-88

Season	Club				
2007–08	Aston Villa	0	0		
2008–09	Aston Villa	0	0		
2009–10	Aston Villa	0	0		
2009–10	Darlington	5	1	5	1
2010–11	Aston Villa	5	0		
2010–11	Portsmouth	19	0	19	0
2011–12	Aston Villa	0	0	5	0
2011–12	Watford	40	0		
2012–13	Watford	38	0	78	0
2013–14	Huddersfield T	34	0		
2014–15	Huddersfield T	26	0		
2015–16	Huddersfield T	22	0	82	0

HOLMES, Duane (M)   33 1
H: 5 8 W: 10 03 b.Wakefield 6-11-94

Season	Club				
2012–13	Huddersfield T	0	0		
2013–14	Huddersfield T	16	0		
2013–14	Yeovil T	5	0	5	0
2014–15	Huddersfield T	0	0		
2014–15	Bury	6	0	6	0
2015–16	Huddersfield T	6	1	22	1

HORSFALL, Fraser (D)   0 0
H: 6 3 W: 12 13 b. 12-11-96

Season	Club		
2015–16	Huddersfield T	0	0

HUDSON, Mark (D)   402 26
H: 6 1 W: 12 01 b.Guildford 30-3-82

Season	Club				
1998–99	Fulham	0	0		
1999–2000	Fulham	0	0		
2000–01	Fulham	0	0		
2001–02	Fulham	0	0		
2002–03	Fulham	0	0		
2003–04	Fulham	0	0		
2003–04	Oldham Ath	15	0	15	0
2003–04	Crystal Palace	14	0		
2004–05	Crystal Palace	7	1		
2005–06	Crystal Palace	15	0		
2006–07	Crystal Palace	39	4		
2007–08	Crystal Palace	45	2	120	7
2008–09	Charlton Ath	43	3	43	3
2009–10	Cardiff C	27	2		
2010–11	Cardiff C	40	0		
2011–12	Cardiff C	39	5		
2012–13	Cardiff C	33	4		
2013–14	Cardiff C	2	0		
2014–15	Cardiff C	3	0	144	11
2014–15	Huddersfield T	41	2		
2015–16	Huddersfield T	39	3	80	5

KANE, Danny (D)   0 0
H: 6 2 W: 11 07 b. 23-4-97
Internationals: Republic of Ireland U16, U17, U19.

Season	Club		
2015–16	Huddersfield T	0	0

LOLLEY, Joe (F)   61 7
H: 5 10 W: 11 05 b. 25-8-92
Internationals: England C.

Season	Club				
2013–14	Huddersfield T	6	1		
2014–15	Huddersfield T	17	2		
2015–16	Huddersfield T	32	4	55	7
2015–16	Scunthorpe U	6	0	6	0

LYNCH, Joel (D)   281 13
H: 6 1 W: 12 10 b.Eastbourne 3-10-87
Internationals: England Youth. Wales Full caps.

Season	Club				
2005–06	Brighton & HA	16	1		
2006–07	Brighton & HA	39	0		
2007–08	Brighton & HA	22	1		
2008–09	Brighton & HA	2	0	79	2
2008–09	Nottingham F	23	0		
2009–10	Nottingham F	10	0		
2010–11	Nottingham F	12	0		
2011–12	Nottingham F	35	3	80	3
2012–13	Huddersfield T	22	1		
2013–14	Huddersfield T	29	2		
2014–15	Huddersfield T	34	3		
2015–16	Huddersfield T	37	2	122	8

MATMOUR, Karim (F)   282 29
H: 5 11 W: 10 08 b.Strasbourg 25-6-85
Internationals: Algeria Full caps.

Season	Club				
2005–06	Freiburg	16	2		
2006–07	Freiburg	31	3		
2007–08	Freiburg	32	5	79	10
2008–09	B M'gladbach	34	3		
2009–10	B M'gladbach	25	1		
2010–11	B M'gladbach	18	0	77	4
2011–12	Eintracht Frankfurt	28	6		
2012–13	Eintracht Frankfurt	24	1	52	7
2013–14	Kaiserslautern	32	3		
2014–15	Kaiserslautern	24	2	56	5
2015	Al-Arabi	2	2	2	2
2015–16	Huddersfield T	16	1	16	1

MILLER, Ishmael (F)   224 39
H: 6 3 W: 14 00 b.Manchester 5-3-87

Season	Club				
2005–06	Manchester C	1	0		
2006–07	Manchester C	16	0		
2007–08	Manchester C	0	0	17	0
2007–08	WBA	34	9		
2008–09	WBA	15	3		
2009–10	WBA	15	2		
2010–11	WBA	6	0	70	14
2010–11	QPR	12	1	12	1
2011–12	Nottingham F	21	3		
2012–13	Nottingham F	0	0		
2012–13	Middlesbrough	25	5	25	5
2013–14	Nottingham F	4	0	25	3
2013–14	Yeovil T	19	10	19	10
2014–15	Blackpool	22	2	22	2
2014–15	Huddersfield T	16	3		
2015–16	Huddersfield T	18	1	34	4

MURPHY, Joe (G)   454 0
H: 6 2 W: 13 06 b.Dublin 21-8-81
Internationals: Republic of Ireland Youth, U21, Full caps.

Season	Club				
1999–2000	Tranmere R	21	0		
2000–01	Tranmere R	20	0		
2001–02	Tranmere R	22	0	63	0
2002–03	WBA	2	0		
2003–04	WBA	3	0		
2004–05	WBA	0	0	5	0
2004–05	Walsall	25	0		
2005–06	Sunderland	0	0		
2005–06	Walsall	14	0	39	0
2006–07	Scunthorpe U	45	0		
2007–08	Scunthorpe U	45	0		
2008–09	Scunthorpe U	42	0		
2009–10	Scunthorpe U	40	0		
2010–11	Scunthorpe U	29	0	201	0
2011–12	Coventry C	46	0		
2012–13	Coventry C	45	0		
2013–14	Coventry C	46	0	137	0
2014–15	Huddersfield T	2	0		
2014–15	Chesterfield	0	0		
2015–16	Huddersfield T	7	0	9	0

RYAN, Tadhg (G)   0 0
H: 6 0 W: 11 09 b. 3-1-97

Season	Club		
2015–16	Huddersfield T	0	0

SCANNELL, Sean (F)   273 20
H: 5 9   W: 11 07   b.Croydon 19-9-90
Internationals: Republic of Ireland U17, U18, U19, U21, B.

2007–08	Crystal Palace	23	2		
2008–09	Crystal Palace	25	2		
2009–10	Crystal Palace	26	2		
2010–11	Crystal Palace	19	2		
2011–12	Crystal Palace	37	4	130	12
2012–13	Huddersfield T	34	2		
2013–14	Huddersfield T	38	1		
2014–15	Huddersfield T	42	4		
2015–16	Huddersfield T	29	1	143	8

SENIOR, Jack (D)   0 0
H: 5 8   W: 9 13   b. 13-1-97

2015–16	Huddersfield T	0	0		

SMITH, Tommy (D)   101 0
b.Warrington 14-4-92

2012–13	Huddersfield T	0	0		
2013–14	Huddersfield T	24	0		
2014–15	Huddersfield T	41	0		
2015–16	Huddersfield T	36	0	101	0

VAN LA PARRA, Rajiv (M)   169 18
H: 5 11   W: 11 05   b.Rotterdam 4-6-91
Internationals: Netherlands, U17, U19, U21.

2008–09	Caan	2	0		
2009–10	Caan	8	1		
2010–11	Caan	6	0	16	1
2011–12	Heerenveen	23	4		
2012–13	Heerenveen	31	5		
2013–14	Heerenveen	32	5	86	14
2014–15	Wolverhampton W	40	1		
2015–16	Wolverhampton W	13	0	53	1
2015–16	*Brighton & HA*	6	2	6	2
2015–16	Huddersfield T	8	0	8	0

VAUGHAN, James (F)   185 47
H: 5 11   W: 13 00   b.Birmingham 14-7-88
Internationals: England U17, U19, U21.

2004–05	Everton	2	1		
2005–06	Everton	1	0		
2006–07	Everton	14	4		
2007–08	Everton	8	1		
2008–09	Everton	13	0		
2009–10	Everton	8	1		
2009–10	*Derby Co*	2	0	2	0
2010–11	Everton	1	0	47	7
2010–11	*Crystal Palace*	30	9	30	9
2011–12	Norwich C	5	0		
2012–13	Norwich C	0	0	5	0
2012–13	*Huddersfield T*	33	14		
2013–14	Huddersfield T	23	10		
2014–15	Huddersfield T	26	7		
2015–16	Huddersfield T	4	0	86	31
2015–16	*Birmingham C*	15	0	15	0

WALLACE, Murray (D)   103 7
H: 6 2   W: 11 07   b.Glasgow 10-1-93
Internationals: Scotland U20, U21.

2011–12	Falkirk	19	2	19	2
2011–12	Huddersfield T	0	0		
2012–13	Huddersfield T	6	1		
2013–14	Huddersfield T	17	0		
2014–15	Huddersfield T	26	2		
2015–16	Huddersfield T	2	0	51	3
2015–16	*Scunthorpe U*	33	2	33	2

WELLS, Nahki (F)   195 77
H: 5 7   W: 11 00   b.Bermuda 1-6-90
Internationals: Bermuda Full caps.

2010–11	Carlisle U	3	0	3	0
2011–12	Bradford C	33	10		
2012–13	Bradford C	39	18		
2013–14	Bradford C	19	14	91	42
2013–14	Huddersfield T	22	7		
2014–15	Huddersfield T	35	11		
2015–16	Huddersfield T	44	17	101	35

WHITEHEAD, Dean (M)   528 26
H: 5 11   W: 12 06   b.Abingdon 12-1-82

1999–2000	Oxford U	0	0		
2000–01	Oxford U	20	0		
2001–02	Oxford U	40	1		
2002–03	Oxford U	18	1		
2003–04	Oxford U	44	7	122	9
2004–05	Sunderland	42	5		
2005–06	Sunderland	37	3		
2006–07	Sunderland	45	4		
2007–08	Sunderland	27	1		
2008–09	Sunderland	34	0		
2009–10	Sunderland	0	0	185	13
2009–10	Stoke C	36	0		
2010–11	Stoke C	37	2		
2011–12	Stoke C	33	0		
2012–13	Stoke C	26	1	132	3
2013–14	Middlesbrough	37	1		

2014–15	Middlesbrough	18	0	55	1
2015–16	Huddersfield T	34	0	34	0

WRIGHT, Joe (D)   20 0
H: 6 4   W: 12 06   b. 26-2-95
Internationals: Wales U21.

2013–14	Huddersfield T	0	0		
2014–15	Huddersfield T	0	0		
2015–16	Huddersfield T	0	0		
2015–16	*Accrington S*	20	0	20	0

Players retained or with offer of contract
Bojaj, Florent; Boyle, Jack Alfie Andrew; Edmonds-Green, Rarmani River Miguel Joseph; Horsfall, Fraser Matthew; Pyke, Rekiel Leshaun.

Scholars
Brooke, Owen Harvey; Clibbens, Harry; Cogill, Dylan Joseph; Colville, Luca Robert; Elliott, Callum Keith; O'Brien, Lewis John; Porritt, Adam Thomas; Raw, Alfie; Scott, Cedwyn; Spencer, Jamie William; Warde, Sam.

HULL C (41)

ALUKO, Sone (M)   214 35
H: 5 8   W: 9 10   b.Birmingham 19-2-89
Internationals: England U16, U17, U18, U19. Nigeria U20, Full caps.

2005–06	Birmingham C	0	0		
2006–07	Birmingham C	0	0		
2007–08	Birmingham C	0	0		
2007–08	*Aberdeen*	20	3		
2008–09	Birmingham C	0	0		
2008–09	*Blackpool*	1	0	1	0
2008–09	Aberdeen	32	2		
2009–10	Aberdeen	22	3		
2010–11	Aberdeen	28	2	102	10
2011–12	Rangers	21	12	21	12
2012–13	Hull C	23	8		
2013–14	Hull C	17	1		
2014–15	Hull C	25	1		
2015–16	Hull C	25	3	90	13

BOWEN, Jarrod (F)   0 0
b.Leominster 1-1-96

2014–15	Hull C	0	0		
2015–16	Hull C	0	0		

BRUCE, Alex (D)   270 4
H: 6 0   W: 11 06   b.Norwich 28-9-84
Internationals: Republic of Ireland B, U21, Full caps. Northern Ireland Full caps.

2002–03	Blackburn R	0	0		
2003–04	Blackburn R	0	0		
2004–05	Blackburn R	0	0		
2004–05	*Oldham Ath*	12	0	12	0
2004–05	Birmingham C	0	0		
2004–05	*Sheffield W*	6	0	6	0
2005–06	Birmingham C	6	0	6	0
2005–06	*Tranmere R*	11	0	11	0
2006–07	Ipswich T	41	0		
2007–08	Ipswich T	36	0		
2008–09	Ipswich T	25	1		
2009–10	Ipswich T	13	1		
2009–10	*Leicester C*	3	0	3	0
2010–11	Ipswich T	0	0	115	2
2010–11	Leeds U	21	1		
2011–12	Leeds U	8	0	29	1
2011–12	*Huddersfield T*	3	0	3	0
2012–13	Hull C	32	0		
2013–14	Hull C	20	0		
2014–15	Hull C	22	0		
2015–16	Hull C	11	1	85	1

CLARK, Max (D)   9 0
b. 19-1-96
Internationals: England U16, U17.

2015–16	Hull C	0	0		
2015–16	*Cambridge U*	9	0	9	0

CLUCAS, Sam (M)   145 23
H: 5 10   W: 11 08   b.Lincoln 25-9-90
Internationals: England C

2009–10	Lincoln C	0	0		
2011–12	Hereford U	17	0	17	0
2013–14	Mansfield T	38	8		
2014–15	Mansfield T	5	0	43	8
2014–15	Chesterfield	41	9	41	9
2015–16	Hull C	44	6	44	6

DAVIES, Curtis (D)   368 22
H: 6 2   W: 11 13   b.Waltham Forest 15-3-85
Internationals: England U21.

2003–04	Luton T	6	0		
2004–05	Luton T	44	1		
2005–06	Luton T	6	1	56	2

2005–06	WBA	33	2		
2006–07	WBA	32	0		
2007–08	WBA	0	0	65	2
2007–08	*Aston Villa*	12	1		
2008–09	Aston Villa	35	1		
2009–10	Aston Villa	2	1		
2010–11	Aston Villa	0	0	49	3
2010–11	*Leicester C*	12	0	12	0
2010–11	Birmingham C	6	0		
2011–12	Birmingham C	42	5		
2012–13	Birmingham C	41	6	89	11
2013–14	Hull C	37	2		
2014–15	Hull C	21	0		
2015–16	Hull C	39	2	97	4

DAWSON, Michael (D)   379 16
H: 6 2   W: 12 02   b.Leyburn 18-11-83
Internationals: England U21, B, Full caps.

2000–01	Nottingham F	0	0		
2001–02	Nottingham F	1	0		
2002–03	Nottingham F	38	5		
2003–04	Nottingham F	30	1		
2004–05	Nottingham F	14	1	83	7
2004–05	Tottenham H	5	0		
2005–06	Tottenham H	32	0		
2006–07	Tottenham H	37	1		
2007–08	Tottenham H	27	1		
2008–09	Tottenham H	16	1		
2009–10	Tottenham H	29	2		
2010–11	Tottenham H	24	1		
2011–12	Tottenham H	7	0		
2012–13	Tottenham H	27	1		
2013–14	Tottenham H	32	0	236	7
2014–15	Hull C	28	1		
2015–16	Hull C	32	1	60	2

DIAME, Mohamed (M)   283 28
H: 6 1   W: 11 02   b.Creteil 14-6-87
Internationals: Senegal U23, Full caps.

2006–07	Lens	0	0		
2007–08	Linares	31	1	31	1
2008–09	Rayo Vallecano	35	2	35	2
2009–10	Wigan Ath	34	1		
2010–11	Wigan Ath	36	1		
2011–12	Wigan Ath	26	3	96	5
2012–13	West Ham U	33	3		
2013–14	West Ham U	35	4		
2014–15	West Ham U	3	0	71	7
2014–15	Hull C	12	4		
2015–16	Hull C	38	9	50	13

DIOMANDE, Adama (F)   154 64
b.Oslo 14-2-90
Internationals: Norway U23, Full caps.

2008	Lyn	2	0		
2009	Lyn	1	0	3	0
2010	Skeid	12	8	12	8
2010	Hodd	10	4		
2011	Hodd	28	14	38	18
2012	Stromsgodset	21	7		
2013	Stromsgodset	25	8	46	15
2014–15	Dynamo Minsk	23	3	23	3
2015	Stabaek	21	17	21	17
2015–16	Hull C	11	3	11	3

ELMOHAMADY, Ahmed (M)   289 25
H: 5 11   W: 12 10   b.El Mahalla El-Kubra 9-9-87
Internationals: Egypt Full caps.

2003–04	Ghazi Al-Mehalla	0	0		
2004–05	Ghazi Al-Mehalla	14	4		
2005–06	Ghazi Al-Mehalla	3	0	17	4
2006–07	ENPPI	12	2		
2007–08	ENPPI	6	1		
2008–09	ENPPI	28	6		
2009–10	ENPPI	12	1	58	10
2010–11	Sunderland	36	0		
2011–12	Sunderland	18	1		
2012–13	Sunderland	2	0	56	1
2012–13	*Hull C*	41	3		
2013–14	Hull C	38	2		
2014–15	Hull C	38	2		
2015–16	Hull C	41	3	158	10

HERNANDEZ, Abel (F)   213 67
H: 6 1   W: 11 00   b.Pando Canelones 8-8-90
Internationals: Uruguay U20, U23, Full caps.

2006–07	Central Espanol	6	0		
2007–08	Central Espanol	24	9	30	9
2008–09	Penarol	8	3	8	3
2009–10	Palermo	6	0		
2010–11	Palermo	21	7		
2011–12	Palermo	22	3		
2012–13	Palermo	14	1		
2013–14	Palermo	28	14	111	31
2014–15	Hull C	25	4		
2015–16	Hull C	39	20	64	24

HUDDLESTONE, Tom (M) 349 14
H: 6 2 W: 11 02 b.Nottingham 28-12-86
Internationals: England U16, U17, U19, U20, U21, Full caps.

Season	Club				
2003–04	Derby Co	43	0		
2004–05	Derby Co	45	0	88	0
2005–06	Tottenham H	4	0		
2005–06	Wolverhampton W	13	1	13	1
2006–07	Tottenham H	21	1		
2007–08	Tottenham H	28	3		
2008–09	Tottenham H	22	0		
2009–10	Tottenham H	33	2		
2010–11	Tottenham H	14	2		
2011–12	Tottenham H	2	0		
2012–13	Tottenham H	20	0		
2013–14	Tottenham H	0	0	144	8
2013–14	Hull C	36	3		
2014–15	Hull C	31	0		
2015–16	Hull C	37	2	104	5

JAHRALDO-MARTIN, Calaum (F) 18 1
b.St Johns 27-4-93
Internationals: Antigua and Barbuda U20, Full caps.

Season	Club				
2013–14	Hull C	0	0		
2014–15	Hull C	0	0		
2014–15	Tranmere R	2	0	2	0
2015–16	Hull C	1	0	1	0
2015–16	Leyton Orient	15	1	15	1

JAKUPOVIC, Eldin (G) 137 1
H: 6 3 W: 13 00 b.Kozarac 2-10-84
Internationals: Bosnia & Herzegovina U21, Switzerland U21, Full caps.

Season	Club				
2004–05	Grasshoppers	8	0		
2005–06	FC Thun	23	0	23	0
2007–08	Grasshoppers	23	1		
2008–09	Grasshoppers	32	0	63	1
2010–11	Olympiacos Volou	26	0	26	0
2011–12	Aris Salonika	1	0	1	0
2012–13	Hull C	5	0		
2013–14	Hull C	1	0		
2013–14	Leyton Orient	13	0	13	0
2014–15	Hull C	3	0		
2015–16	Hull C	2	0	11	0

KUCIAK, Dusan (G) 308 0
H: 6 2 W: 12 06 b.Zilina 21-5-85
Internationals: Slovakia Full caps.

Season	Club				
2001–02	Trencin	1	0	1	0
2002–03	MSK Zilina	0	0		
2003–04	MSK Zilina	0	0		
2004–05	MSK Zilina	0	0		
2004–05	West Ham U	0	0		
2005–06	MSK Zilina	21	0		
2006–07	MSK Zilina	35	0		
2007–08	MSK Zilina	33	0	89	0
2008–09	Vaslui	34	0		
2009–10	Vaslui	23	0		
2010–11	Vaslui	30	0	87	0
2011–12	Legia Warsaw	27	0		
2012–13	Legia Warsaw	30	0		
2013–14	Legia Warsaw	25	0		
2014–15	Legia Warsaw	31	0		
2015–16	Legia Warsaw	18	0	131	0
2015–16	Hull C	0	0		

LENIHAN, Brian (D) 30 0
H: 5 10 W: 12 00 b.Cork 8-6-94
Internationals: Republic of Ireland U21.

Season	Club				
2012	Cork C	3	0		
2013	Cork C	3	0		
2014	Cork C	21	0	27	0
2014–15	Hull C	0	0		
2014–15	Blackpool	2	0	2	0
2015–16	Hull C	1	0	1	0

LIVERMORE, Jake (M) 188 10
H: 5 9 W: 12 08 b.Enfield 14-11-89
Internationals: England Full caps.

Season	Club				
2006–07	Tottenham H	0	0		
2007–08	Tottenham H	0	0		
2007–08	Milton Keynes D	5	0	5	0
2008–09	Tottenham H	0	0		
2008–09	Crewe Alex	0	0		
2009–10	Tottenham H	1	0		
2009–10	Derby Co	16	1	16	1
2009–10	Peterborough U	9	1	9	1
2010–11	Tottenham H	0	0		
2010–11	Ipswich T	12	0	12	0
2010–11	Leeds U	5	0	5	0
2011–12	Tottenham H	24	0		
2012–13	Tottenham H	11	0		
2013–14	Tottenham H	0	0	36	0
2013–14	Hull C	36	3		
2014–15	Hull C	35	1		
2015–16	Hull C	34	4	105	8

LUER, Greg (F) 18 0
H: 5 11 W: 11 07 b.Brighton 6-12-94

Season	Club				
2014–15	Hull C	0	0		
2014–15	Port Vale	2	0	2	0
2015–16	Hull C	2	0	2	0
2015–16	Scunthorpe U	4	0	4	0
2015–16	Stevenage	10	0	10	0

MAGUIRE, Harry (D) 175 10
H: 6 2 W: 12 06 b.Mosborough 5-3-93
Internationals: England U21.

Season	Club				
2010–11	Sheffield U	5	0		
2011–12	Sheffield U	44	1		
2012–13	Sheffield U	44	3		
2013–14	Sheffield U	41	5	134	9
2014–15	Hull C	3	0		
2014–15	Wigan Ath	16	1	16	1
2015–16	Hull C	22	0	25	0

MALONEY, Shaun (M) 302 62
H: 5 7 W: 10 01 b.Miri 24-1-83
Internationals: Scotland U20, U21, B, Full caps.

Season	Club				
1999–2000	Celtic	0	0		
2000–01	Celtic	4	0		
2001–02	Celtic	16	5		
2002–03	Celtic	20	3		
2003–04	Celtic	17	5		
2004–05	Celtic	2	0		
2005–06	Celtic	36	13		
2006–07	Celtic	9	0		
2006–07	Aston Villa	8	1		
2007–08	Aston Villa	22	4	30	5
2008–09	Celtic	21	4		
2009–10	Celtic	10	4		
2010–11	Celtic	21	5		
2011–12	Celtic	3	0	159	39
2011–12	Wigan Ath	13	3		
2012–13	Wigan Ath	36	6		
2013–14	Wigan Ath	10	3		
2014–15	Wigan Ath	20	2	79	14
2015	Chicago Fire	14	3	14	3
2015–16	Hull C	20	1	20	1

McGREGOR, Allan (G) 354 0
H: 6 0 W: 11 08 b.Edinburgh 31-1-82
Internationals: Scotland U21, B, Full caps.

Season	Club				
1998–99	Rangers	0	0		
1999–2000	Rangers	0	0		
2000–01	Rangers	0	0		
2001–02	Rangers	2	0		
2002–03	Rangers	4	0		
2003–04	Rangers	2	0		
2005–06	Rangers	0	0		
2005–06	Dunfermline Ath	26	0	26	0
2006–07	Rangers	31	0		
2007–08	Rangers	31	0		
2008–09	Rangers	27	0		
2009–10	Rangers	34	0		
2010–11	Rangers	37	0		
2011–12	Rangers	37	0	205	0
2011–12	Besiktas	27	0	27	0
2013–14	Hull C	26	0		
2014–15	Hull C	26	0		
2015–16	Hull C	44	0	96	0

MEYLER, David (M) 139 10
H: 6 1 W: 11 00 b.Cork 29-5-89
Internationals: Republic of Ireland U21, Full caps.

Season	Club				
2008	Cork C	2	0	2	0
2008–09	Sunderland	0	0		
2009–10	Sunderland	10	0		
2010–11	Sunderland	5	0		
2011–12	Sunderland	7	0		
2012–13	Sunderland	3	0	25	0
2012–13	Hull C	28	5		
2013–14	Hull C	30	2		
2014–15	Hull C	28	1		
2015–16	Hull C	26	2	112	10

ODUBAJO, Moses (M) 180 16
H: 5 9 W: 11 05 b.Greenwich 28-7-93
Internationals: England U20.

Season	Club				
2011–12	Leyton Orient	3	1		
2012–13	Leyton Orient	44	2		
2013–14	Leyton Orient	46	10	93	13
2014–15	Brentford	45	3	45	3
2015–16	Hull C	42	0	42	0

ROBERTSON, Andrew (D) 136 7
H: 5 10 W: 10 00 b.Glasgow 11-3-94
Internationals: Scotland U21, Full caps.

Season	Club				
2012–13	Queen's Park	34	2	34	2
2013–14	Dundee U	36	3	36	3
2014–15	Hull C	24	0		
2015–16	Hull C	42	2	66	2

SNODGRASS, Robert (M) 351 71
H: 6 0 W: 12 02 b.Glasgow 7-9-87
Internationals: Scotland U20, U21, Full caps.

Season	Club				
2003–04	Livingston	0	0		
2004–05	Livingston	17	2		
2005–06	Livingston	27	4		
2006–07	Livingston	6	0		
2006–07	Stirling Alb	12	5	12	5
2007–08	Livingston	31	9	81	15
2008–09	Leeds U	42	9		
2009–10	Leeds U	44	7		
2010–11	Leeds U	37	6		
2011–12	Leeds U	43	13	166	35
2012–13	Norwich C	37	6		
2013–14	Norwich C	30	6	67	12
2014–15	Hull C	1	0		
2015–16	Hull C	24	4	25	4

TAYLOR, Ryan (M) 250 26
H: 5 8 W: 10 04 b.Liverpool 19-8-84
Internationals: England U21.

Season	Club				
2001–02	Tranmere R	0	0		
2002–03	Tranmere R	25	1		
2003–04	Tranmere R	30	5		
2004–05	Tranmere R	43	8	98	14
2005–06	Wigan Ath	11	0		
2006–07	Wigan Ath	16	1		
2007–08	Wigan Ath	17	3		
2008–09	Wigan Ath	12	2	56	6
2008–09	Newcastle U	10	0		
2009–10	Newcastle U	31	4		
2010–11	Newcastle U	5	0		
2011–12	Newcastle U	31	2		
2012–13	Newcastle U	1	0		
2013–14	Newcastle U	0	0		
2014–15	Newcastle U	14	0	92	6
2015–16	Hull C	4	0	4	0

TYMON, Josh (D) 0 0
b. 22-5-99
Internationals: England U17.

Season	Club				
2015–16	Hull C	0	0		

WATSON, Rory (G) 0 0
b. 5-2-96

Season	Club				
2014–15	Hull C	0	0		
2015–16	Hull C	0	0		
2015–16	Scunthorpe U	0	0		

Players retained or with offer of contract
Annan, William John; Clackstone, Joshua Philip; Curry, Adam; McKenzie, Robbie; Olley, Greg Thomas; Rodgers, Harvey James; Ter Horst, Johan.

Scholars
Akbas, Stephen Adam; Barkworth, Ellis; Batty, Daniel Thomas; Dunkerley, Charlie; Duxbury, Bradley Sinclair; Hamilton, Tyler Lee; Hinchliffe, Benjamin Jack; Hinchliffe, Matthew James; Kelledy, Marc Thomas Michael; Langton, Mitchell Jay; Lofts, Luke; Ritson, Lewis Barry Ryan; Saltmer, Jonathan David; Tymon, Joshua Lewis.

IPSWICH T (42)

BENYU, Kundai (M) 0 0
b. 12-12-97

Season	Club				
2014–15	Ipswich T	0	0		
2015–16	Ipswich T	0	0		

BERRA, Christophe (D) 394 16
H: 6 1 W: 12 10 b.Edinburgh 31-1-85
Internationals: Scotland U21, B, Full caps.

Season	Club				
2003–04	Hearts	6	0		
2004–05	Hearts	12	0		
2005–06	Hearts	12	1		
2006–07	Hearts	35	1		
2007–08	Hearts	35	2		
2008–09	Hearts	23	0	123	4
2008–09	Wolverhampton W	15	0		
2009–10	Wolverhampton W	32	0		
2010–11	Wolverhampton W	32	0		
2011–12	Wolverhampton W	32	0		
2012–13	Wolverhampton W	30	0	141	0
2013–14	Ipswich T	42	5		
2014–15	Ipswich T	45	6		
2015–16	Ipswich T	43	1	130	12

BIALKOWSKI, Bartosz (G) 166 0
H: 6 3 W: 12 10 b.Braniewo 6-7-87
Internationals: Poland U20, U21.

Season	Club				
2004–05	Gornik Zabrze	7	0	7	0
2005–06	Southampton	5	0		
2006–07	Southampton	8	0		
2007–08	Southampton	1	0		
2008–09	Southampton	0	0		
2009–10	Southampton	7	0		

Season	Club	App	Gls	Tot App	Tot Gls
2009–10	Barnsley	2	0	2	0
2010–11	Southampton	0	0		
2011–12	Southampton	1	0	22	0
2012–13	Notts Co	40	0		
2013–14	Notts Co	44	0	84	0
2014–15	Ipswich T	31	0		
2015–16	Ipswich T	20	0	51	0

BISHOP, Teddy (M) 37 1
H: 5 11 W: 10 03 b. 15-7-96

Season	Club	App	Gls	Tot App	Tot Gls
2013–14	Ipswich T	0	0		
2014–15	Ipswich T	33	1		
2015–16	Ipswich T	4	0	37	1

BRU, Kevin (M) 200 12
H: 6 0 W: 11 05 b. 12-12-88
Internationals: France U19. Mauritius Full caps.

Season	Club	App	Gls	Tot App	Tot Gls
2006–07	Rennes	2	0	2	0
2007–08	Chataeroux	10	0	10	0
2008–09	Clermont Foot Avergne	25	2	25	2
2009–10	Dijon	14	2		
2010–11	Dijon	11	0	25	2
2010–11	Bologne	9	0		
2011–12	Bologne	19	2	28	2
2012–13	Istres	31	2	31	2
2013–14	Levski Sofia	20	1	20	1
2014–15	Istres	31	1		
2015–16	Ipswich T	28	2	59	3

CHAMBERS, Luke (D) 509 28
H: 6 1 W: 11 13 b.Kettering 29-8-85

Season	Club	App	Gls	Tot App	Tot Gls
2002–03	Northampton T	1	0		
2003–04	Northampton T	24	0		
2004–05	Northampton T	27	0		
2005–06	Northampton T	43	0		
2006–07	Northampton T	29	1	124	1
2006–07	Nottingham F	14	0		
2007–08	Nottingham F	42	6		
2008–09	Nottingham F	39	2		
2009–10	Nottingham F	23	3		
2010–11	Nottingham F	44	6		
2011–12	Nottingham F	43	0	205	17
2012–13	Ipswich T	44	3		
2013–14	Ipswich T	46	3		
2014–15	Ipswich T	45	1		
2015–16	Ipswich T	45	3	180	10

CLARKE, Matthew (M) 33 1
H: 5 11 W: 11 00 b.Ipswich 22-9-96

Season	Club	App	Gls	Tot App	Tot Gls
2013–14	Ipswich T	0	0		
2014–15	Ipswich T	4	0		
2015–16	Ipswich T	0	0	4	0
2015–16	Portsmouth	29	1	29	1

COKE, Giles (M) 286 26
H: 6 0 W: 11 11 b.Westminster 3-6-86

Season	Club	App	Gls	Tot App	Tot Gls
2004–05	Mansfield T	9	0		
2005–06	Mansfield T	40	4		
2006–07	Mansfield T	21	1	70	5
2007–08	Northampton T	20	1		
2008–09	Northampton T	32	2	52	7
2009–10	Motherwell	32	2	32	2
2010–11	Sheffield W	27	4		
2011–12	Sheffield W	0	0		
2011–12	Bury	30	6	30	6
2012–13	Sheffield W	16	0		
2012–13	Swindon T	4	0	4	0
2013–14	Sheffield W	28	1		
2014–15	Sheffield W	13	1	84	6
2014–15	Bolton W	4	0	4	0
2015–16	Ipswich T	10	0	10	0

CROWE, Michael (G) 0 0
H: 6 2 W: 11 11 b.London 13-11-95
Internationals: Wales U19.

Season	Club	App	Gls	Tot App	Tot Gls
2013–14	Ipswich T	0	0		
2014–15	Ipswich T	0	0		
2014–15	Woking	0	0		
2015–16	Ipswich T	0	0		
2015–16	Stevenage	0	0		

DOUGLAS, Jonathan (M) 480 36
H: 5 11 W: 11 11 b.Monaghan 22-11-81
Internationals: Republic of Ireland Full caps.

Season	Club	App	Gls	Tot App	Tot Gls
1999–2000	Blackburn R	0	0		
2000–01	Blackburn R	0	0		
2001–02	Blackburn R	0	0		
2002–03	Blackburn R	1	0		
2002–03	Chesterfield	7	1	7	1
2003–04	Blackpool	16	3	16	3
2003–04	Blackburn R	14	1		
2004–05	Blackburn R	1	0		
2004–05	Gillingham	10	0	10	0
2005–06	Blackburn R	0	0		
2005–06	Leeds U	40	5		
2006–07	Blackburn R	0	0	16	1
2006–07	Leeds U	35	1		
2007–08	Leeds U	24	3		
2008–09	Leeds U	43	1	142	10
2009–10	Swindon T	43	0		
2010–11	Swindon T	39	1	82	1
2011–12	Brentford	46	2		
2012–13	Brentford	44	4		
2013–14	Brentford	35	3		
2014–15	Brentford	44	8	169	17
2015–16	Ipswich T	38	3	38	3

DOZZELL, Andre (M) 2 1
b. 2-5-99
Internationals: England U17.

Season	Club	App	Gls	Tot App	Tot Gls
2015–16	Ipswich T	2	1	2	1

EMMANUEL, Josh (D) 6 0
b. 18-8-97

Season	Club	App	Gls	Tot App	Tot Gls
2015–16	Ipswich T	4	0	4	0
2015–16	Crawley T	2	0	2	0

FOLEY, Kevin (D) 366 2
H: 5 11 W: 11 05 b.Luton 1-11-84
Internationals: Republic of Ireland U21, B, Full caps.

Season	Club	App	Gls	Tot App	Tot Gls
2002–03	Luton T	2	0		
2003–04	Luton T	33	1		
2004–05	Luton T	39	2		
2005–06	Luton T	38	0		
2006–07	Luton T	39	0	151	3
2007–08	Wolverhampton W	44	1		
2008–09	Wolverhampton W	45	1		
2009–10	Wolverhampton W	25	0		
2010–11	Wolverhampton W	33	2		
2011–12	Wolverhampton W	16	0		
2012–13	Wolverhampton W	26	0		
2013–14	Wolverhampton W	5	1		
2013–14	Blackpool	5	0	194	5
2014–15	Wolverhampton W	0	0		
2014–15	Blackpool	4	0	9	0
2014–15	FC Copenhagen	4	0	4	0
2015–16	Ipswich T	8	0	8	0

GERKEN, Dean (G) 252 0
H: 6 3 W: 12 08 b.Southend 22-5-85

Season	Club	App	Gls	Tot App	Tot Gls
2003–04	Colchester U	1	0		
2004–05	Colchester U	13	0		
2005–06	Colchester U	7	0		
2006–07	Colchester U	27	0		
2007–08	Colchester U	40	0		
2008–09	Colchester U	21	0	109	0
2008–09	Darlington	7	0	7	0
2009–10	Bristol C	39	0		
2010–11	Bristol C	1	0		
2011–12	Bristol C	10	0		
2012–13	Bristol C	3	0	53	0
2013–14	Ipswich T	41	0		
2014–15	Ipswich T	16	0		
2015–16	Ipswich T	26	0	83	0

HYAM, Luke (M) 119 3
H: 5 10 W: 11 05 b.Ipswich 24-10-91

Season	Club	App	Gls	Tot App	Tot Gls
2010–11	Ipswich T	10	0		
2011–12	Ipswich T	8	0		
2012–13	Ipswich T	30	1		
2013–14	Ipswich T	35	1		
2014–15	Ipswich T	16	1		
2015–16	Ipswich T	15	0	114	3
2015–16	Rotherham U	5	0	5	0

KENLOCK, Myles (D) 2 0
b. 29-11-96

Season	Club	App	Gls	Tot App	Tot Gls
2015–16	Ipswich T	2	0	2	0

KNUDSEN, Jonas (D) 147 5
H: 6 1 W: 11 05 b.Esbjerg 16-9-92
Internationals: Denmark U18, U19, U20, U21, Full caps.

Season	Club	App	Gls	Tot App	Tot Gls
2009–10	Esberg	7	0		
2010–11	Esberg	5	0	5	0
2011–12	Esberg	0	0		
2012–13	Esberg	32	1		
2013–14	Esberg	31	1		
2014–15	Esberg	28	2		
2015–16	Esbjerg	2	0	100	4
2015–16	Ipswich T	42	1	42	1

MALARCZYK, Piotr (D) 130 8
b. 1-8-91
Internationals: Poland U19, U20, U21.

Season	Club	App	Gls	Tot App	Tot Gls
2009–10	Korona Kielce	6	0		
2010–11	Korona Kielce	11	0		
2011–12	Korona Kielce	16	1		
2012–13	Korona Kielce	25	2		
2013–14	Korona Kielce	27	3		
2014–15	Korona Kielce	35	2		
2015–16	Korona Kielce	5	0	125	8
2015–16	Ipswich T	3	0	3	0
2015–16	Southend U	2	0	2	0

McDONNELL, Adam (M) 1 0
b. 14-5-97
Internationals: Republic of Ireland U16, U17, U18, U19.
From Shelbourne.

Season	Club	App	Gls	Tot App	Tot Gls
2014–15	Ipswich T	0	0		
2015–16	Ipswich T	1	0	1	0

McGOLDRICK, David (F) 286 74
H: 6 1 W: 11 10 b.Nottingham 29-11-87
Internationals: Republic of Ireland Full caps.

Season	Club	App	Gls	Tot App	Tot Gls
2003–04	Notts Co	4	0		
2004–05	Notts Co	0	0		
2005–06	Southampton	1	0		
2005–06	Notts Co	6	0	10	0
2006–07	Southampton	9	0		
2006–07	Bournemouth	12	6	12	6
2007–08	Southampton	8	0		
2007–08	Port Vale	17	2	17	2
2008–09	Southampton	46	12	64	12
2009–10	Nottingham F	33	3		
2010–11	Nottingham F	21	5		
2011–12	Nottingham F	9	0		
2011–12	Sheffield W	4	1	4	1
2012–13	Nottingham F	0	0	63	8
2012–13	Coventry C	22	16	22	16
2012–13	Ipswich T	13	4		
2013–14	Ipswich T	31	14		
2014–15	Ipswich T	26	7		
2015–16	Ipswich T	24	4	94	29

McLOUGHLIN, Shane (D) 0 0
b. 1-3-97
Internationals: Republic of Ireland U18.

Season	Club	App	Gls	Tot App	Tot Gls
2014–15	Ipswich T	0	0		
2015–16	Ipswich T	0	0		

MURPHY, Daryl (F) 346 84
H: 6 2 W: 13 12 b.Waterford 15-3-83
Internationals: Republic of Ireland U21, Full caps.

Season	Club	App	Gls	Tot App	Tot Gls
2000–01	Luton T	0	0		
2001–02	Luton T	0	0		
2005–06	Sunderland	18	1		
2005–06	Sheffield W	4	0	4	0
2006–07	Sunderland	38	10		
2007–08	Sunderland	28	3		
2008–09	Sunderland	23	0		
2009–10	Sunderland	3	0	110	14
2009–10	Ipswich T	18	6		
2010–11	Celtic	18	3		
2011–12	Ipswich T	33	4		
2012–13	Celtic	1	0	19	3
2012–13	Ipswich T	39	7		
2013–14	Ipswich T	45	13		
2014–15	Ipswich T	44	27		
2015–16	Ipswich T	34	10	213	67

OAR, Tommy (M) 139 6
H: 5 7 W: 10 01 b.Southport 10-12-91
Internationals: Australia U20, Full caps.

Season	Club	App	Gls	Tot App	Tot Gls
2008–09	Brisbane Roar	5	1		
2009–10	Brisbane Roar	18	1		
2010–11	Utrecht	7	0		
2011–12	Utrecht	18	2		
2012–13	Utrecht	31	1		
2013–14	Utrecht	31	1		
2014–15	Utrecht	18	0	105	4
2015–16	Utrecht	6	0	6	0
2015–16	Brisbane Roar	5	0	28	2

PARR, Jonathan (M) 264 14
H: 6 0 W: 11 11 b.Oslo 21-10-88
Internationals: Norway U17, U19, U21, Full caps.

Season	Club	App	Gls	Tot App	Tot Gls
2006	Lyn	11	0	11	0
2007	Aalesund	19	1		
2008	Aalesund	24	4		
2009	Aalesund	27	2		
2010	Aalesund	25	0		
2011	Aalesund	15	1	110	8
2011–12	Crystal Palace	39	2		
2012–13	Crystal Palace	38	0		
2013–14	Crystal Palace	15	0	92	2
2014–15	Ipswich T	31	2		
2015–16	Ipswich T	9	1	40	3
2015–16	Stromsgodset	11	1	11	1

PITMAN, Brett (F) 387 125
H: 6 0 W: 11 00 b.Jersey 31-1-88

Season	Club	App	Gls	Tot App	Tot Gls
2005–06	Bournemouth	19	1		
2006–07	Bournemouth	29	5		
2007–08	Bournemouth	39	6		
2008–09	Bournemouth	39	17		
2009–10	Bournemouth	46	26		
2010–11	Bournemouth	2	3		
2010–11	Bristol C	39	13		
2011–12	Bristol C	35	7		
2012–13	Bristol C	3	0	77	20

2012–13	Bournemouth	26	19		
2013–14	Bournemouth	34	5		
2014–15	Bournemouth	34	13	268	95
2015–16	Ipswich T	42	10	42	10

SEARS, Freddie (F) 251 48
H: 5 8 W: 10 01 b.Hornchurch 27-11-89
Internationals: England U19, U20, U21.

2007–08	West Ham U	7	1		
2008–09	West Ham U	17	0		
2009–10	West Ham U	1	0		
2009–10	*Crystal Palace*	18	0	18	0
2009–10	*Coventry C*	10	0	10	0
2010–11	West Ham U	11	1		
2010–11	*Scunthorpe U*	9	0	9	0
2011–12	West Ham U	10	0	46	2
2011–12	Colchester U	11	2		
2012–13	Colchester U	35	7		
2013–14	Colchester U	32	12		
2014–15	Colchester U	24	10	102	31
2014–15	Ipswich T	21	9		
2015–16	Ipswich T	45	6	66	15

SKUSE, Cole (M) 401 10
H: 6 1 W: 11 05 b.Bristol 29-3-86

2004–05	Bristol C	7	0		
2005–06	Bristol C	38	2		
2006–07	Bristol C	42	0		
2007–08	Bristol C	25	0		
2008–09	Bristol C	33	2		
2009–10	Bristol C	43	2		
2010–11	Bristol C	30	1		
2011–12	Bristol C	36	2		
2012–13	Bristol C	25	0	279	9
2013–14	Ipswich T	43	0		
2014–15	Ipswich T	40	1		
2015–16	Ipswich T	39	0	122	1

SMITH, Tommy (D) 248 21
H: 6 2 W: 12 02 b.Macclesfield 31-3-90
Internationals: England U17, U18. New Zealand Full caps.

2007–08	Ipswich T	0	0		
2008–09	Ipswich T	2	0		
2009–10	Ipswich T	14	0		
2009–10	*Brentford*	8	0	8	0
2010–11	Ipswich T	22	3		
2010–11	*Colchester U*	6	0	6	0
2011–12	Ipswich T	26	3		
2012–13	Ipswich T	38	3		
2013–14	Ipswich T	45	6		
2014–15	Ipswich T	42	4		
2015–16	Ipswich T	45	2	234	21

STEWART, Cameron (M) 127 8
H: 5 8 W: 11 05 b.Manchester 8-4-91
Internationals: England U17, U19, U20.

2009–10	Manchester U	0	0		
2010–11	Manchester U	0	0		
2010–11	*Yeovil T*	5	0	5	0
2010–11	Hull C	14	0		
2011–12	Hull C	31	1		
2012–13	Hull C	2	0		
2012–13	*Burnley*	9	0	9	0
2012–13	*Blackburn R*	7	0	7	0
2013–14	Hull C	0	0	47	1
2013–14	*Charlton Ath*	18	3	18	3
2014–15	Ipswich T	0	0		
2014–15	*Barnsley*	4	0	4	0
2015–16	Ipswich T	0	0		
2015–16	*Doncaster R*	26	4	26	4

TABB, Jay (M) 388 35
H: 5 7 W: 10 00 b.Tooting 21-2-84
Internationals: Republic of Ireland U21.

2000–01	Brentford	2	0		
2001–02	Brentford	3	0		
2002–03	Brentford	5	0		
2003–04	Brentford	36	9		
2004–05	Brentford	40	5		
2005–06	Brentford	42	6	128	20
2006–07	Coventry C	31	3		
2007–08	Coventry C	42	5		
2008–09	Coventry C	22	3	95	11
2008–09	Reading	9	0		
2009–10	Reading	28	0		
2010–11	Reading	21	0		
2011–12	Reading	19	0		
2012–13	Reading	12	0	89	0
2012–13	*Ipswich T*	9	1		
2013–14	Ipswich T	27	1		
2014–15	Ipswich T	40	2		
2015–16	Ipswich T	0	0	76	4

TOURE, Larsen (F) 184 26
H: 6 1 W: 11 11 b. 20-7-84
Internationals: Guinea Full caps.

2005–06	Lille	2	0		
2006–07	Lille	0	0		
2006–07	*Gueugnon*	28	5	28	5
2007–08	Lille	9	0		
2007–08	Grenoble	14	3		
2008–09	Lille	3	0		
2008–09	*Grenoble*	12	1	26	4
2009–10	Lille	14	1	28	1
2010–11	Brest	22	4		
2011–12	Brest	11	1		
2012–13	Brest	19	2	52	7
2013–14	Levski Sofia	19	4	19	4
2014–15	Arles	24	5	24	5
2015–16	Ipswich T	7	0	7	0

VARNEY, Luke (F) 363 68
H: 5 11 W: 11 00 b.Leicester 28-9-82

2002–03	Crewe Alex	0	0		
2003–04	Crewe Alex	8	1		
2004–05	Crewe Alex	26	4		
2005–06	Crewe Alex	27	5		
2006–07	Crewe Alex	34	17	95	27
2007–08	Charlton Ath	39	8		
2008–09	Charlton Ath	18	2	57	10
2008–09	*Sheffield W*	4	2		
2008–09	Derby Co	10	1		
2009–10	Derby Co	1	0		
2009–10	*Sheffield W*	39	9	43	11
2010–11	Derby Co	1	0	12	1
2010–11	Blackpool	30	5	30	5
2011–12	Portsmouth	30	6	30	6
2012–13	Leeds U	34	4		
2013–14	Leeds U	11	2	45	6
2013–14	*Blackburn R*	12	0		
2014–15	Blackburn R	11	0	23	0
2015–16	*Ipswich T*	10	1		
2015–16	Ipswich T	18	1	28	2

YORWERTH, Josh (D) 24 0
b. 1-1-95
Internationals: Wales U17, U19, U21.

2014–15	Cardiff C	0	0		
2015–16	Ipswich T	0	0		
2015–16	*Crawley T*	24	0	24	0

Players retained or with offer of contract
Hayes, Nicholas Michael; Robinson, Joe Alan; Wright, Harry Edward.

Scholars
Blanchflower, James Elliott; Cathline, Kieron Raymond Kobina; Cole, Travis Sol; Daly, Harry David; Downes, Flynn; Fowler, George Ryan; Fullwood, Callum Leigh; Ingram, Nicholas Evan Terry; Jones, Ronaldo Patrick; Marsden, Jacob Anthony; McKendry, Conor; McLoughlin, Shane Daniel; Meldrum, Ross Alexander; Morris, Benjamin James; Muamba, Daniel; Patterson, Monty Mark; Ramadan, Cemal; Saladueen, Kolade Abdulahi Olamide; Smith, Chris; Woolfenden, Luke Matthew.

LEEDS U (43)

ANTENUCCI, Mirco (F) 286 86
H: 5 5 W: 9 06 b.Termoli 8-9-84

2008–09	Catania	4	0		
2008–09	*Pisa*	20	1	20	1
2009–10	Ascoli	40	24	40	24
2010–11	Catania	13	1		
2010–11	Torino	19	6		
2011–12	Torino	41	10	60	16
2012–13	Catania	1	0	18	1
2012–13	Spezia	33	6	33	6
2013–14	Ternana	40	19	40	19
2014–15	Leeds U	36	10		
2015–16	Leeds U	39	9	75	19

BAMBA, Souleymane (D) 244 12
H: 6 3 W: 14 02 b.Ivry-sur-Seine 13-1-85
Internationals: Ivory Coast Full caps.

2004–05	Paris St Germain	1	0		
2005–06	Paris St Germain	0	0	1	0
2006–07	Dunfermline Ath	23	0		
2007–08	Dunfermline Ath	15	0		
2008–09	Dunfermline Ath	1	0	39	0
2008–09	Hibernian	29	0		
2009–10	Hibernian	30	2		
2010–11	Hibernian	16	2	75	4
2010–11	Leicester C	16	2		
2011–12	Leicester C	36	1	52	3
2012–13	Trabzonspor	18	0		
2013–14	Trabzonspor	9	0	27	0
2014–15	*Palermo*	1	0	1	0
2014–15	Leeds U	19	1		
2015–16	Leeds U	30	4	49	5

BELLUSCI, Giuseppe (D) 191 3
H: 6 1 W: 11 07 b.Trebisacce 21-8-89
Internationals: Italy U21.

2006–07	Ascoli	3	0		
2007–08	Ascoli	2	0		
2008–09	Ascoli	30	1	35	1
2009–10	Catania	12	0		
2010–11	Catania	9	0		
2011–12	Catania	32	0		
2012–13	Catania	26	0		
2013–14	Catania	20	0	99	0
2014–15	Leeds U	30	2		
2015–16	Leeds U	27	0	57	2

BERARDI, Gaetano (D) 190 0
H: 5 10 W: 11 00 b.Sorengo 21-8-88
Internationals: Switzerland U20, U21, Full caps.

2006–07	Brescia	1	0		
2007–08	Brescia	9	0		
2008–09	Brescia	26	0		
2009–10	Brescia	29	0		
2010–11	Brescia	27	0		
2011–12	Brescia	13	0	105	0
2011–12	Sampdoria	9	0		
2012–13	Sampdoria	21	0		
2013–14	Sampdoria	5	0	35	0
2014–15	Leeds U	22	0		
2015–16	Leeds U	28	0	50	0

BIANCHI, Tommaso (M) 218 15
H: 6 0 W: 10 10 b.Piombino 1-11-88
Internationals: Italy U19, U20, U21.

2008–09	Piacenza	21	2		
2009–10	Piacenza	18	2		
2010–11	Piacenza	39	4	78	8
2011–12	Sassuolo	29	0		
2012–13	Sassuolo	30	4		
2013–14	Sassuolo	0	0	59	4
2013–14	Modena	41	3	41	3
2014–15	Leeds U	24	0		
2015–16	Leeds U	0	0	24	0
2015–16	*Ascoli*	16	0	16	0

BOTAKA, Jordan (M) 87 11
H: 6 0 W: 11 07 b.Kinshasa 24-6-93
Internationals: Netherlands U19. DR Congo Full caps.

2012–13	Club Brugge	0	0		
2012–13	*Belenenses*	1	0	1	0
2013–14	Excelsior	36	10		
2014–15	Excelsior	33	1		
2015–16	Excelsior	4	0	73	11
2015–16	Leeds U	13	0	13	0

COOK, Lewis (M) 80 1
b. 3-2-97
Internationals: England U16, U17, U18, U19.

2014–15	Leeds U	37	0		
2015–16	Leeds U	43	1	80	1

COOPER, Liam (D) 160 8
H: 6 2 W: 13 07 b.Hull 30-8-91
Internationals: Scotland U19, U21.

2008–09	Hull C	0	0		
2009–10	Hull C	2	0		
2010–11	Hull C	2	0		
2010–11	*Carlisle U*	6	1	6	1
2011–12	Hull C	7	0		
2011–12	*Huddersfield T*	4	0	4	0
2012–13	Hull C	0	0	11	0
2012–13	Chesterfield	29	2		
2013–14	Chesterfield	41	3		
2014–15	Chesterfield	1	0	71	5
2014–15	Leeds U	29	1		
2015–16	Leeds U	39	1	68	2

COYLE, Lewie (M) 11 0
b. 15-10-95

2015–16	Leeds U	11	0	11	0

DALLAS, Stuart (M) 141 40
H: 6 0 W: 12 09 b.Cookstown 19-4-91
Internationals: Northern Ireland U21, U23, Full caps.

2010–11	Crusaders	13	16		
2011–12	Crusaders	8	8	21	24
2012–13	Brentford	7	0		
2013–14	Brentford	18	2		
2013–14	*Northampton T*	12	3	12	3
2014–15	Brentford	38	6	63	8
2015–16	Leeds U	45	5	45	5

DIAGOURAGA, Toumani (M) 356 12
H: 6 2 W: 11 05 b.Paris 10-6-87

2004–05	Watford	0	0		
2005–06	Watford	1	0		
2005–06	*Swindon T*	8	0	8	0
2006–07	Watford	0	0		
2006–07	*Rotherham U*	7	0	7	0

2007–08	Watford	0	0	1 0
2007–08	*Hereford U*	41	2	
2008–09	Hereford U	45	2	86 4
2009–10	Peterborough U	19	0	19 0
2009–10	*Brentford*	20	0	
2010–11	Brentford	32	1	
2011–12	Brentford	35	4	
2012–13	Brentford	39	1	
2013–14	Brentford	19	0	
2013–14	*Portsmouth*	8	0	8 0
2014–15	Brentford	38	0	
2015–16	Brentford	27	0	210 6
2015–16	Leeds U	17	2	17 2

DOUKARA, Souleymane (F) 82 14
H: 6 4   W: 13 08   b.Meudon 29-9-91

2012–13	Catania	12	0	
2013–14	Catania	1	0	13 0
2013–14	*Juve Stabia*	21	6	21 6
2014–15	Leeds U	25	5	
2015–16	Leeds U	23	3	48 8

ERWIN, Lee (F) 59 13
H: 6 2   W: 12 07   b.Bellshill 19-3-94
Internationals: Scotland U17, U18, U19.

2012–13	Motherwell	0	0	
2013–14	Motherwell	0	0	
2013–14	*Arbroath*	11	8	11 8
2014–15	Motherwell	34	5	34 5
2015–16	Leeds U	11	0	11 0
2015–16	*Bury*	3	0	3 0

McKAY, Jack (F) 4 0
b.Glasgow 19-11-96

2014–15	Doncaster R	4	0	
2015–16	Doncaster R	0	0	4 0
2015–16	Leeds U	0	0	

McKAY, Paul (M) 0 0
H: 6 3   W: 12 13   b.Glasgow 19-11-96

2014–15	Doncaster R	0	0	
2015–16	Doncaster R	0	0	
2015–16	Leeds U	0	0	

MOWATT, Alex (D) 101 12
b. 13-2-95
Internationals: England U19, U20.

2013–14	Leeds U	29	1	
2014–15	Leeds U	38	9	
2015–16	Leeds U	34	2	101 12

MURPHY, Luke (M) 264 28
H: 6 1   W: 11 05   b.Alsager 21-10-89

2008–09	Crewe Alex	9	1	
2009–10	Crewe Alex	32	3	
2010–11	Crewe Alex	39	3	
2011–12	Crewe Alex	42	8	
2012–13	Crewe Alex	39	6	161 21
2013–14	Leeds U	37	3	
2014–15	Leeds U	30	3	
2015–16	Leeds U	36	1	103 7

PARKIN, Luke (F) 0 0
b. 15-8-95

2013–14	Leeds U	0	0	
2014–15	Leeds U	0	0	
2015–16	Leeds U	0	0	

PEACOCK-FARRELL, Bailey (G) 1 0
b. 29-10-96

2015–16	Leeds U	1	0	1 0

PHILIPS, Kalvin (M) 12 1
b. 2-12-95

2014–15	Leeds U	2	1	
2015–16	Leeds U	10	0	12 1

SILVESTRI, Marco (G) 143 0
H: 6 3   W: 12 08   b.Castelnuovo ne Monti 2-3-91
Internationals: Italy U20, U21.

2011–12	Chievo	0	0	
2011–12	*Reggiana*	27	0	27 0
2012–13	Chievo	0	0	
2012–13	*Padova*	25	0	25 0
2013–14	Chievo	0	0	
2013–14	*Cagliari*	3	0	3 0
2014–15	Leeds U	43	0	
2015–16	Leeds U	45	0	88 0

SLOTH, Casper (M) 137 9
H: 5 11   b.Aarhus 26-3-92
Internationals: Denmark U17, U18, U19, U20, U21, Full caps.

2009–10	Aarhus	14	2	
2010–11	Aarhus	19	0	
2011–12	Aarhus	26	1	
2012–13	Aarhus	29	1	
2013–14	Aarhus	32	5	
2014–15	Aarhus	4	0	124 9
2014–15	Leeds U	13	0	
2015–16	Leeds U	0	0	13 0

TAYLOR, Charlie (D) 110 3
H: 5 9   W: 11 00   b.York 18-9-93
Internationals: England U19.

2011–12	Leeds U	2	0	
2011–12	*Bradford C*	3	0	3 0
2012–13	Leeds U	0	0	
2012–13	*York C*	4	0	4 0
2012–13	*Inverness CT*	7	0	7 0
2013–14	Leeds U	0	0	
2013–14	*Fleetwood T*	32	0	32 0
2014–15	Leeds U	23	2	
2015–16	Leeds U	39	1	64 3

TURNBULL, Ross (G) 148 0
H: 6 4   W: 15 00   b.Bishop Auckland 4-1-85
Internationals: England U16, U17, U18, U19.

2002–03	Middlesbrough	0	0	
2003–04	Middlesbrough	0	0	
2003–04	*Darlington*	1	0	1 0
2003–04	*Barnsley*	3	0	
2004–05	Middlesbrough	0	0	
2004–05	*Bradford C*	2	0	2 0
2004–05	*Barnsley*	23	0	
2005–06	Middlesbrough	2	0	
2005–06	*Crewe Alex*	29	0	29 0
2006–07	Middlesbrough	0	0	
2007–08	Middlesbrough	3	0	
2007–08	*Cardiff C*	6	0	6 0
2008–09	Middlesbrough	22	0	
2009–10	Middlesbrough	0	0	27 0
2009–10	Chelsea	2	0	
2010–11	Chelsea	0	0	
2011–12	Chelsea	2	0	
2012–13	Chelsea	3	0	7 0
2013–14	Doncaster R	28	0	28 0
2014–15	Barnsley	22	0	48 0
2015–16	Leeds U	0	0	

VIEIRA, Ronaldo (M) 1 0
b. 10-8-98

2015–16	Leeds U	1	0	1 0

WOOD, Chris (F) 215 59
H: 6 3   W: 12 10   b.Auckland 7-12-91
Internationals: New Zealand U17, U23, Full caps.

2008–09	WBA	2	0	
2009–10	WBA	18	1	
2010–11	WBA	1	0	
2010–11	*Barnsley*	7	0	7 0
2010–11	*Brighton & HA*	29	8	29 8
2011–12	WBA	0	0	
2011–12	*Birmingham C*	23	9	23 9
2011–12	*Bristol C*	19	3	19 3
2012–13	WBA	0	0	21 1
2012–13	*Millwall*	19	11	19 11
2012–13	Leicester C	20	9	
2013–14	Leicester C	26	4	
2014–15	Leicester C	7	1	53 14
2014–15	*Ipswich T*	8	0	
2015–16	Leeds U	36	13	36 13

WOOTTON, Scott (D) 106 2
H: 6 2   W: 13 00   b.Birkenhead 12-9-91
Internationals: England U17.

2009–10	Manchester U	0	0	
2010–11	Manchester U	0	0	
2010–11	*Tranmere R*	7	1	7 1
2011–12	Manchester U	0	0	
2011–12	*Peterborough U*	11	0	
2011–12	*Nottingham F*	13	0	13 0
2012–13	Manchester U	0	0	
2012–13	*Peterborough U*	2	1	13 1
2013–14	Manchester U	0	0	
2013–14	Leeds U	20	0	
2014–15	Leeds U	23	0	
2014–15	*Rotherham U*	7	0	7 0
2015–16	Leeds U	23	0	66 0

Players retained or with offer of contract
Denton, Tyler Jake; Mulhern, Euan Francis Peter; Purver, Alex William; Stokes, Eoghan.

Scholars
Bell, Tyla George Moses; Croft, Jake Spencer; Downing, Matthew Christopher; Ferguson, Ryan Alexander; Godden, Thomas Mackenzie; Hill, Maxwell Connor; Huffer, William Matthew Scobie; Knight, Lewis Andrew; Oduor, Clarke Sydney Omondi; Pearce, Tom Mark; Richardson, Theo Huw; Rollinson, Henry James; Sterling, Jovanni Sherma; Taylor, Michael James; Turnbull, Jack Matthew William; Vann, Jack; Vieira Nan, Ronaldo Augusto; Wilks, Mallik Rashaun Coley.

LEICESTER C (44)

ALBRIGHTON, Marc (M) 146 11
H: 6 2   W: 12 06   b.Tamworth 18-11-89
Internationals: England U20, U21.

2008–09	Aston Villa	0	0	
2009–10	Aston Villa	3	0	
2010–11	Aston Villa	29	5	
2011–12	Aston Villa	26	2	
2012–13	Aston Villa	9	0	
2013–14	Aston Villa	19	0	86 7
2013–14	*Wigan Ath*	4	0	4 0
2014–15	Leicester C	18	2	
2015–16	Leicester C	38	2	56 4

AMARTEY, Daniel (M) 83 3
H: 6 0   W: 12 04   b. 1-12-94
Internationals: Ghana U20, Full caps.

2013	Djurgardens	23	0	
2014	Djurgardens	11	0	34 0
2014–15	Copenhagen	29	3	
2015–16	Copenhagen	15	0	44 3
2015–16	Leicester C	5	0	5 0

BARMBY, Jack (M) 33 6
H: 5 10   W: 11 09   b. 14-11-94
Internationals: England U16, U18, U19, U20.

2013–14	Manchester U	0	0	
2013–14	*Hartlepool U*	17	5	17 5
2014–15	Leicester C	0	0	
2014–15	*Rotherham U*	2	0	2 0
2015–16	Leicester C	0	0	
2015–16	*Notts Co*	5	0	5 0
2015–16	*Portland Timbers*	9	1	9 1

BENALOUANE, Yohan (D) 164 5
H: 6 1   W: 12 06   b.Bagnois-sur-Ceze 28-3-87
Internationals: France U21.

2007–08	St Etienne	6	1	
2008–09	St Etienne	29	1	
2009–10	St Etienne	29	1	
2010–11	St Etienne	1	0	65 3
2010–11	Cesena	15	0	
2011–12	Cesena	11	0	
2012–13	Cesena	0	0	26 0
2012–13	*Parma*	21	1	
2013–14	Parma	4	0	25 1
2013–14	*Atalanta*	17	0	
2014–15	Atalanta	27	1	44 1
2015–16	Leicester C	4	0	4 0
2015–16	*Fiorentina*	0	0	

BLYTH, Jacob (F) 52 11
H: 6 3   W: 12 02   b.Nuneaton 14-8-92

2012–13	Leicester C	0	0	
2012–13	*Burton Alb*	2	0	
2012–13	*Notts Co*	4	0	4 0
2013–14	Leicester C	0	0	
2013–14	*Northampton T*	11	3	11 3
2014–15	Leicester C	0	0	
2014–15	*Burton Alb*	22	5	24 5
2015–16	Leicester C	0	0	
2015–16	*Cambridge U*	5	1	5 1
2015–16	*Blackpool*	8	2	8 2

CAIN, Michael (M) 34 2
H: 6 0   W: 10 08   b.Luton 18-2-94

2011–12	Leicester C	0	0	
2012–13	Leicester C	0	0	
2013–14	Leicester C	0	0	
2013–14	*Mansfield T*	2	0	2 0
2014–15	Leicester C	0	0	
2014–15	*Walsall*	32	2	32 2
2015–16	Leicester C	0	0	

CHILWELL, Ben (D) 8 0
H: 5 10   W: 11 03   b.Milton Keynes 21-12-96
Internationals: England U18, U19, U20, U21.

2015–16	Leicester C	0	0	
2015–16	*Huddersfield T*	8	0	8 0

CHOUDHURY, Hamza (M) 13 0
H: 5 10   W: 10 01   b. 1-10-97

2015–16	Leicester C	0	0	
2015–16	*Burton Alb*	13	0	13 0

DE LAET, Ritchie (D) 167 5
H: 6 1   W: 12 02   b.Antwerp 28-11-88
Internationals: Belgium U21, Full caps.

2007–08	Stoke C	0	0	
2008–09	Stoke C	0	0	
2008–09	Manchester U	1	0	
2009–10	Manchester U	2	0	
2010–11	Manchester U	0	0	
2010–11	*Sheffield U*	6	0	6 0
2010–11	*Preston NE*	5	0	5 0
2010–11	*Portsmouth*	22	0	22 0
2011–12	Manchester U	0	0	3 0

2011–12	*Norwich C*	6	1	**6**	**1**
2012–13	Leicester C	41	1		
2013–14	Leicester C	36	2		
2014–15	Leicester C	26	0		
2015–16	Leicester C	12	1	**115**	**4**
2015–16	*Middlesbrough*	10	0	**10**	**0**

DODOO, Joseph (F) **5 1**
H: 6 0 W: 12 08 b.Nottingham 6-1-95
Internationals: England U18.

2013–14	Leicester C	0	0		
2014–15	Leicester C	0	0		
2015–16	Leicester C	1	0	**1**	**0**
2015–16	*Bury*	4	1	**4**	**1**

DRINKWATER, Daniel (M) **235 15**
H: 5 10 W: 11 00 b.Manchester 5-3-90
Internationals: England U18, U19, Full caps.

2008–09	Manchester U	0	0		
2009–10	Manchester U	0	0		
2009–10	*Huddersfield T*	33	2	**33**	**2**
2010–11	Manchester U	0	0		
2010–11	*Cardiff C*	9	0	**9**	**0**
2010–11	*Watford*	12	0	**12**	**0**
2011–12	Manchester U	0	0		
2011–12	*Barnsley*	17	1	**17**	**1**
2011–12	Leicester C	19	2		
2012–13	Leicester C	42	1		
2013–14	Leicester C	45	7		
2014–15	Leicester C	23	0		
2015–16	Leicester C	35	2	**164**	**12**

ELDER, Callum (D) **39 1**
H: 5 11 W: 10 08 b.Sydney 27-1-95
Internationals: Australia U20.

2013–14	Leicester C	0	0		
2014–15	Leicester C	0	0		
2014–15	*Mansfield T*	21	0	**21**	**0**
2015–16	Leicester C	0	0		
2015–16	*Peterborough U*	18	1	**18**	**1**

FUCHS, Christian (D) **367 22**
H: 6 1 W: 12 08 b.Pitten 7-4-86
Internationals: Austria U17, U19, U21, Full caps.

2002–03	Wiener Neustadt	12	0	**12**	**0**
2003–04	Mattersburg	13	0		
2004–05	Mattersburg	24	2		
2005–06	Mattersburg	35	1		
2006–07	Mattersburg	35	6		
2007–08	Mattersburg	33	3	**140**	**12**
2008–09	Bochum	22	2		
2009–10	Bochum	31	4		
2010–11	Bochum	0	0	**53**	**6**
2010–11	*Mainz 05*	31	0	**31**	**0**
2011–12	Schalke	29	2		
2012–13	Schalke	29	0		
2013–14	Schalke	16	0		
2014–15	Schalke	25	2	**99**	**4**
2015–16	Leicester C	32	0	**32**	**0**

GRAY, Demarai (M) **84 8**
H: 5 10 W: 10 04 b.Birmingham 28-6-96
Internationals: England U18, U19, U20, U21.

2013–14	Birmingham C	7	1		
2014–15	Birmingham C	41	6		
2015–16	Birmingham C	24	1	**72**	**8**
2015–16	Leicester C	12	0	**12**	**0**

HAMER, Ben (G) **219 0**
H: 5 11 W: 12 04 b.Chard 20-11-87

2006–07	Reading	0	0		
2007–08	Reading	0	0		
2007–08	*Brentford*	20	0		
2008–09	Reading	0	0		
2008–09	*Brentford*	45	0		
2009–10	Reading	0	0		
2010–11	Reading	0	0		
2010–11	*Brentford*	10	0	**75**	**0**
2010–11	*Exeter C*	18	0	**18**	**0**
2011–12	Charlton Ath	41	0		
2012–13	Charlton Ath	41	0		
2013–14	Charlton Ath	32	0	**114**	**0**
2014–15	Leicester C	8	0		
2015–16	Leicester C	0	0	**8**	**0**
2015–16	*Bristol C*	4	0	**4**	**0**

HAMMOND, Dean (M) **432 41**
H: 6 0 W: 11 09 b.Hastings 7-3-83

2002–03	Brighton & HA	4	0		
2003–04	Brighton & HA	0	0		
2003–04	*Leyton Orient*	8	0	**8**	**0**
2004–05	Brighton & HA	30	4		
2005–06	Brighton & HA	41	4		
2006–07	Brighton & HA	37	8		
2007–08	Brighton & HA	24	5		
2007–08	Colchester U	13	0		
2008–09	Colchester U	41	5		
2009–10	Colchester U	2	0	**56**	**5**
2009–10	Southampton	40	5		
2010–11	Southampton	41	4		
2011–12	Southampton	43	1		
2012–13	Southampton	0	0	**124**	**10**
2012–13	*Brighton & HA*	37	2	**173**	**23**
2013–14	Leicester C	29	1		
2014–15	Leicester C	12	0		
2015–16	Leicester C	0	0	**41**	**1**
2015–16	*Sheffield U*	30	2	**30**	**2**

HUTH, Robert (D) **293 19**
H: 6 3 W: 14 07 b.Berlin 18-8-84
Internationals: Germany U21, Full caps.

2001–02	Chelsea	1	0		
2002–03	Chelsea	2	0		
2003–04	Chelsea	16	0		
2004–05	Chelsea	10	0		
2005–06	Chelsea	13	0	**42**	**0**
2006–07	Middlesbrough	12	1		
2007–08	Middlesbrough	13	1		
2008–09	Middlesbrough	24	0		
2009–10	Middlesbrough	4	0	**53**	**2**
2009–10	Stoke C	32	3		
2010–11	Stoke C	35	6		
2011–12	Stoke C	34	3		
2012–13	Stoke C	35	1		
2013–14	Stoke C	12	0		
2014–15	Stoke C	1	0	**149**	**13**
2014–15	Leicester C	14	1		
2015–16	Leicester C	35	3	**49**	**4**

INLER, Gokhan (M) **341 21**
H: 6 0 W: 12 02 b.Olten 27-6-84
Internationals: Turkey U21. Switzerland U21, Full caps.

2004–05	Basel	0	0		
2004–05	Aarau	14	3		
2005–06	Aarau	11	0	**25**	**3**
2005–06	Zurich	17	2		
2006–07	Zurich	35	1	**52**	**3**
2007–08	Udinese	37	2		
2008–09	Udinese	36	1		
2009–10	Udinese	33	0		
2010–11	Udinese	35	3	**141**	**6**
2011–12	Napoli	36	0		
2012–13	Napoli	31	6		
2013–14	Napoli	32	2		
2014–15	Napoli	19	1	**118**	**9**
2015–16	Leicester C	5	0	**5**	**0**

IVERSEN, Daniel (G) **0 0**
b. 19-7-97
Internationals: Denmark U16, U17, U18, U19, U20.

2014–15	Esbjerg	0	0		
2015–16	Esbjerg	0	0		
2015–16	Leicester C	0	0		

JAMES, Matthew (M) **114 6**
H: 6 0 W: 11 12 b.Bacup 22-7-91
Internationals: England U16, U17, U19, U20.

2007–08	Manchester U	0	0		
2008–09	Manchester U	0	0		
2009–10	Manchester U	0	0		
2009–10	*Preston NE*	18	2		
2010–11	Manchester U	0	0		
2010–11	*Preston NE*	10	0	**28**	**2**
2011–12	Manchester U	0	0		
2012–13	Leicester C	24	3		
2013–14	Leicester C	35	1		
2014–15	Leicester C	27	0		
2015–16	Leicester C	0	0	**86**	**4**

KANTE, Ngolo (M) **150 8**
H: 5 7 W: 11 00 b.Paris 29-3-91
Internationals: France Full caps.

2011–12	Boulogne	1	0		
2012–13	Boulogne	37	3	**38**	**3**
2013–14	Caen	38	2		
2014–15	Caen	37	2	**75**	**4**
2015–16	Leicester C	37	1	**37**	**1**

KING, Andy (M) **295 53**
H: 6 0 W: 11 10 b.Barnstaple 29-10-88
Internationals: Wales U19, U21, Full caps.

2007–08	Leicester C	11	1		
2008–09	Leicester C	45	9		
2009–10	Leicester C	43	9		
2010–11	Leicester C	45	15		
2011–12	Leicester C	30	4		
2012–13	Leicester C	42	7		
2013–14	Leicester C	30	4		
2014–15	Leicester C	24	2		
2015–16	Leicester C	25	2	**295**	**53**

KONCHESKY, Paul (D) **519 14**
H: 5 10 W: 11 07 b.Barking 15-5-81
Internationals: England U18, U20, U21, Full caps.

1997–98	Charlton Ath	3	0		
1998–99	Charlton Ath	2	0		
1999–2000	Charlton Ath	8	0		
2000–01	Charlton Ath	23	0		
2001–02	Charlton Ath	34	1		
2002–03	Charlton Ath	30	3		
2003–04	Charlton Ath	21	0		
2003–04	*Tottenham H*	12	0	**12**	**0**
2004–05	Charlton Ath	28	1	**149**	**5**
2005–06	West Ham U	37	1		
2006–07	West Ham U	22	0	**59**	**1**
2007–08	Fulham	33	0		
2008–09	Fulham	36	1		
2009–10	Fulham	27	1		
2010–11	Fulham	1	0	**97**	**2**
2010–11	Liverpool	15	0	**15**	**0**
2010–11	*Nottingham F*	15	1	**15**	**1**
2011–12	Leicester C	42	2		
2012–13	Leicester C	39	1		
2013–14	Leicester C	31	1		
2014–15	Leicester C	26	1		
2015–16	Leicester C	0	0	**138**	**5**
2015–16	*QPR*	34	0	**34**	**0**

KRAMARIC, Andrej (F) **156 74**
H: 5 10 W: 11 00 b.Zagreb 19-6-91
Internationals: Croatia U16, U17, U18, U19, U20, U21, Full caps.

2008–09	Dinamo Zagreb	1	0		
2009–10	Dinamo Zagreb	24	7		
2010–11	Dinamo Zagreb	12	1		
2011–12	Dinamo Zagreb	1	0		
2011–12	*Lokomotiv Zagreb*	13	5		
2012–13	Dinamo Zagreb	0	0		
2012–13	*Lokomotiv Zagreb*	32	15	**45**	**20**
2013–14	Dinamo Zagreb	4	2	**42**	**10**
2013–14	Rijeka	24	16		
2014–15	Rijeka	18	21	**42**	**37**
2014–15	Leicester C	13	2		
2015–16	Leicester C	2	0	**15**	**2**
2015–16	*TSG Hoffenheim*	12	5	**12**	**5**

LAWRENCE, Tom (F) **73 8**
H: 5 9 W: 11 11 b.Wrexham 13-1-94
Internationals: Wales U17, U19, U21, Full caps.

2012–13	Manchester U	0	0		
2013–14	Manchester U	1	0	**1**	**0**
2013–14	*Carlisle U*	9	3	**9**	**3**
2013–14	*Yeovil T*	19	2	**19**	**2**
2014–15	Leicester C	3	0		
2014–15	*Rotherham U*	6	1	**6**	**1**
2015–16	Leicester C	0	0	**3**	**0**
2015–16	*Blackburn R*	21	2	**21**	**2**
2015–16	*Cardiff C*	14	0	**14**	**0**

MAHREZ, Riyad (M) **144 30**
H: 5 10 W: 9 10 b.Sarcelles 21-2-91
Internationals: Algeria Full caps.

2011–12	Le Havre	9	0		
2012–13	Le Havre	32	4		
2013–14	Le Havre	17	2	**58**	**6**
2013–14	Leicester C	19	3		
2014–15	Leicester C	30	4		
2015–16	Leicester C	37	17	**86**	**24**

MOORE, Liam (D) **96 1**
H: 6 1 W: 13 08 b.Loughborough 31-1-93
Internationals: England U17, U20, U21.

2011–12	Leicester C	2	0		
2011–12	*Bradford C*	17	0	**17**	**0**
2012–13	Leicester C	16	0		
2012–13	*Brentford*	7	0		
2013–14	Leicester C	30	1		
2014–15	Leicester C	11	0		
2014–15	*Brentford*	3	0	**10**	**0**
2015–16	Leicester C	0	0	**59**	**1**
2015–16	*Bristol C*	10	0	**10**	**0**

MORGAN, Wes (D) **539 20**
H: 6 2 W: 14 00 b.Nottingham 21-1-84
Internationals: Jamaica Full caps.

2002–03	Nottingham F	0	0		
2002–03	*Kidderminster H*	5	1	**5**	**1**
2003–04	Nottingham F	32	2		
2004–05	Nottingham F	43	1		
2005–06	Nottingham F	43	2		
2006–07	Nottingham F	38	0		
2007–08	Nottingham F	42	1		
2008–09	Nottingham F	42	1		
2009–10	Nottingham F	44	3		
2010–11	Nottingham F	46	1		
2011–12	Nottingham F	22	1	**352**	**12**
2011–12	Leicester C	17	0		
2012–13	Leicester C	45	1		
2013–14	Leicester C	45	2		
2014–15	Leicester C	37	2		
2015–16	Leicester C	38	2	**182**	**7**

OKAZAKI, Shinji (F)   285 84
H: 5 9   W: 11 00   b.Hyogo 16-4-86
Internationals: Japan U23, Full caps.

Season	Club				
2005	Shimizu S-Pulse	1	0		
2006	Shimizu S-Pulse	7	0		
2007	Shimizu S-Pulse	21	5		
2008	Shimizu S-Pulse	27	10		
2009	Shimizu S-Pulse	34	14		
2010	Shimizu S-Pulse	31	13	121	42
2010-11	Stuttgart	12	2		
2011-12	Stuttgart	26	7		
2012-13	Stuttgart	25	1	63	10
2013-14	Mainz 05	33	15		
2014-15	Mainz 05	32	12	65	27
2015-16	Leicester C	36	5	36	5

SCHLUPP, Jeffrey (M)   131 6
H: 5 8   W: 11 00   b.Hamburg 23-12-92
Internationals: Ghana Full caps.

Season	Club				
2010-11	Leicester C	0	0		
2010-11	Brentford	9	6	9	6
2011-12	Leicester C	21	2		
2012-13	Leicester C	19	3		
2013-14	Leicester C	26	1		
2014-15	Leicester C	32	3		
2015-16	Leicester C	24	1	122	0

SCHMEICHEL, Kasper (G)   359 0
H: 6 1   W: 13 00   b.Copenhagen 5-11-86
Internationals: Denmark U19, U20, U21, Full caps.

Season	Club				
2003-04	Manchester C	0	0		
2004-05	Manchester C	0	0		
2005-06	Manchester C	0	0		
2005-06	Darlington	4	0	4	0
2005-06	Bury	15	0		
2006-07	Manchester C	0	0		
2006-07	Falkirk	15	0	15	0
2006-07	Bury	14	0	29	0
2007-08	Manchester C	7	0		
2007-08	Cardiff C	14	0	14	0
2007-08	Coventry C	9	0	9	0
2008-09	Manchester C	1	0		
2009-10	Manchester C	0	0	8	0
2009-10	Notts Co	43	0	43	0
2010-11	Leeds U	37	0	37	0
2011-12	Leicester C	46	0		
2012-13	Leicester C	46	0		
2013-14	Leicester C	46	0		
2014-15	Leicester C	24	0		
2015-16	Leicester C	38	0	200	0

SCHWARZER, Mark (G)   626 0
H: 6 4   W: 14 07   b.Sydney 6-10-72
Internationals: Australia U17, U20, U23, Full caps.

Season	Club				
1990-91	Marconi Stallions	1	0		
1991-92	Marconi Stallions	9	0		
1992-93	Marconi Stallions	23	0		
1993-94	Marconi Stallions	25	0	58	0
1994-95	Dynamo Dresden	2	0	2	0
1995-96	Kaiserslautern	4	0		
1996-97	Kaiserslautern	0	0	4	0
1996-97	Bradford C	13	0	13	0
1996-97	Middlesbrough	7	0		
1997-98	Middlesbrough	35	0		
1998-99	Middlesbrough	34	0		
1999-2000	Middlesbrough	37	0		
2000-01	Middlesbrough	31	0		
2001-02	Middlesbrough	21	0		
2002-03	Middlesbrough	38	0		
2003-04	Middlesbrough	36	0		
2004-05	Middlesbrough	31	0		
2005-06	Middlesbrough	27	0		
2006-07	Middlesbrough	36	0		
2007-08	Middlesbrough	34	0	367	0
2008-09	Fulham	38	0		
2009-10	Fulham	37	0		
2010-11	Fulham	31	0		
2011-12	Fulham	30	0		
2012-13	Fulham	36	0	172	0
2013-14	Chelsea	4	0		
2014-15	Chelsea	0	0	4	0
2014-15	Leicester C	0	0		
2015-16	Leicester C	0	0	6	0

SCOTT, Kris (M)   0 0
H: 5 10   W: 12 02   b.Brsitol 23-5-95
Internationals: USA U20.

Season	Club		
2013-14	Swansea C	0	0
2014-15	Leicester C	0	0
2015-16	Leicester C	0	0

SIMPSON, Danny (D)   238 1
H: 5 9   W: 11 05   b.Eccles 4-1-87

Season	Club				
2005-06	Manchester U	0	0		
2006-07	Manchester U	0	0		
2006-07	Sunderland	14	0	14	0
2007-08	Manchester U	3	0		
2007-08	Ipswich T	8	0	8	0
2008-09	Manchester U	0	0		
2008-09	Blackburn R	12	0	12	0
2009-10	Manchester U	0	0	3	0
2009-10	Newcastle U	39	1		
2010-11	Newcastle U	30	0		
2011-12	Newcastle U	35	0		
2012-13	Newcastle U	19	0	123	1
2013-14	QPR	33	0		
2014-15	QPR	1	0	34	0
2014-15	Leicester C	14	0		
2015-16	Leicester C	30	0	44	0

STANKEVICIUS, Simonas (F)   4 0
b. 3-10-95
Internationals: Lithuania Full caps.

Season	Club				
2014-15	Leicester C	0	0		
2015-16	Leicester C	0	0		
2015-16	*Oldham Ath*	4	0	4	0

ULLOA, Jose (F)   293 115
H: 6 1   W: 11 10   b.General Roca 26-7-86

Season	Club				
2004-05	San Lorenzo	0	0		
2005-06	San Lorenzo	22	3		
2006-07	San Lorenzo	6	0	25	3
2007-08	Arsenal Sarandi	6	1	6	1
2007-08	Olimpo	8	1	8	1
2008-09	Castellon	33	17		
2009-10	Castellon	32	14		
2010-11	Castellon	1	0	66	31
2010-11	Almeria	34	7		
2011-12	Almeria	28	29		
2012-13	Almeria	10	3	72	39
2012-13	Brighton & HA	17	9		
2013-14	Brighton & HA	33	14	50	23
2014-15	Leicester C	37	11		
2015-16	Leicester C	29	6	66	17

VARDY, Jamie (F)   133 49
H: 5 10   W: 11 12   b.Sheffield 11-1-87
Internationals: England Full caps.

Season	Club				
2012-13	Leicester C	26	4		
2013-14	Leicester C	37	16		
2014-15	Leicester C	34	5		
2015-16	Leicester C	36	24	133	49

WASILEWSKI, Marcin (D)   301 33
H: 6 1   W: 13 11   b.Krakow 9-6-80
Internationals: Poland Full caps.

Season	Club				
2002-03	Wisla Plock	24	1		
2003-04	Wisla Plock	21	1		
2004-05	Wisla Plock	15	1	60	3
2005-06	Amica Wronki	24	4	24	4
2006-07	Lech Poznan	14	5	14	5
2006-07	Anderlecht	14	2		
2007-08	Anderlecht	26	3		
2008-09	Anderlecht	30	8		
2009-10	Anderlecht	6	1		
2010-11	Anderlecht	17	3		
2011-12	Anderlecht	30	3		
2012-13	Anderlecht	20	0	143	20
2013-14	Leicester C	31	0		
2014-15	Leicester C	25	1		
2015-16	Leicester C	4	0	60	1

WATSON, Ryan (M)   16 0
H: 6 1   W: 11 07   b.Crewe 7-7-93

Season	Club				
2011-12	Wigan Ath	0	0		
2012-13	Wigan Ath	0	0		
2012-13	Accrington S	0	0		
2013-14	Leicester C	0	0		
2014-15	Leicester C	0	0		
2014-15	*Northampton T*	5	0		
2015-16	Leicester C	0	0		
2015-16	*Northampton T*	11	0	16	0

Players retained or with offer of contract
Barnes, Harvey Lewis; Felix-Eppiah, Joshua; Fox, Brandon Levi; Kipre, Cedric; Miles, Matthew Richard; Moore, Elliott Jordan; Ndukwu, Layton Julius; Rowe, Daniel Isaiah.

Scholars
Bolkiah, Naji Jefri; Bramley, Max; Dewsbury-Hall, Kiernan; Gruno, Kyle; Harrison, Adam; Hodby, Ethan Edward; Johnson, Darnell Tobias Jack; Knight, Joshua Michael; Muskwe, Kairo Ellis; Muskwe, Admiral Dalindlela; Pascanu, Alexandru Stefan; Sherif, Lamine Kaba; Templeton, Cal Alexander; Webber, Elliot Bradley; Yates, Cameron James.

LEYTON ORIENT (45)

ADEBOYEJO, Victor (F)   2 0
b. 12-1-98

Season	Club				
2014-15	Leyton Orient	1	0		
2015-16	Leyton Orient	1	0	2	0

AGYEMANG, Montel (M)   1 0
H: 5 9   W: 10 08   b. 11-1-97

Season	Club				
2014-15	Leyton Orient	1	0		
2015-16	Leyton Orient	0	0	1	0

ATANGANA, Nigel (M)   59 1
b.Corbeil-Essonnes 9-9-89

Season	Club				
2014-15	Portsmouth	30	1		
2015-16	Portsmouth	13	0	43	1
2015-16	Leyton Orient	16	0	16	0

BAUDRY, Mathieu (D)   175 10
H: 6 2   W: 12 08   b.Le Havre 24-2-88

Season	Club				
2007-08	Troyes	2	1		
2008-09	Troyes	17	0		
2009-10	Troyes	7	0	26	1
2010-11	Bournemouth	3	1		
2011-12	Bournemouth	7	0	10	1
2011-12	Dagenham & R	11	0	11	0
2012-13	Leyton Orient	24	3		
2013-14	Leyton Orient	39	2		
2014-15	Leyton Orient	31	1		
2015-16	Leyton Orient	34	2	128	8

CISAK, Aleksander (G)   143 0
H: 6 3   W: 14 11   b.Krakow 19-5-89
Internationals: Australia U20.

Season	Club				
2006-07	Leicester C	0	0		
2007-08	Leicester C	0	0		
2008-09	Leicester C	0	0		
2009-10	Leicester C	0	0		
2009-10	Accrington S	21	0	21	0
2011-12	Oldham Ath	38	0		
2012-13	Oldham Ath	10	0	48	0
2012-13	*Portsmouth*	1	0	1	0
2013-14	Burnley	1	0		
2014-15	Burnley	0	0	1	0
2014-15	York C	10	0	10	0
2014-15	*Leyton Orient*	19	0		
2015-16	Leyton Orient	43	0	62	0

CLOHESSY, Sean (D)   278 7
H: 5 11   W: 12 07   b.Croydon 12-12-86

Season	Club				
2005-06	Gillingham	20	1		
2006-07	Gillingham	6	0		
2007-08	Gillingham	17	0	43	1

From Salisbury C.

Season	Club				
2010-11	Southend U	46	1		
2011-12	Southend U	45	0		
2012-13	Southend U	46	3	137	4
2013-14	Kilmarnock	24	2	24	2
2014-15	Colchester U	32	0	32	0
2015-16	Leyton Orient	42	0	42	0

COX, Dean (M)   369 59
H: 5 4   W: 9 08   b.Cuckfield 12-8-87

Season	Club				
2005-06	Brighton & HA	1	0		
2006-07	Brighton & HA	42	6		
2007-08	Brighton & HA	42	6		
2008-09	Brighton & HA	40	4		
2009-10	Brighton & HA	21	0	146	16
2010-11	Leyton Orient	45	11		
2011-12	Leyton Orient	38	7		
2012-13	Leyton Orient	44	4		
2013-14	Leyton Orient	45	12		
2014-15	Leyton Orient	37	6		
2015-16	Leyton Orient	14	3	223	43

DOSSENA, Andrea (D)   317 10
H: 5 11   W: 11 08   b.Lodi 11-9-81
Internationals: Italy U20, Full caps.

Season	Club				
2001-02	Verona	2	0		
2002-03	Verona	21	1		
2003-04	Verona	37	1		
2004-05	Verona	39	1	99	3
2005-06	Treviso	21	0	21	0
2006-07	Udinese	21	0		
2007-08	Udinese	35	2	63	2
2008-09	Liverpool	16	1		
2009-10	Liverpool	2	0	18	1
2009-10	Napoli	10	0		
2010-11	Napoli	33	1		
2011-12	Napoli	33	2		
2012-13	Napoli	7	0	83	3
2012-13	*Palermo*	11	0	11	0
2013-14	Sunderland	7	0	7	0
2014-15	Leyton Orient	15	1		
2015-16	Leyton Orient	0	0	15	1

DUNNE, Alan (D)   349 17
H: 5 10   W: 10 13   b.Dublin 3-8-82

Season	Club		
1999-2000	Millwall	0	0
2000-01	Millwall	0	0
2001-02	Millwall	1	0
2002-03	Millwall	4	0
2003-04	Millwall	8	0
2004-05	Millwall	19	3
2005-06	Millwall	40	0
2006-07	Millwall	32	6

2007–08	Millwall	19	3		
2008–09	Millwall	24	0		
2009–10	Millwall	32	2		
2010–11	Millwall	39	0		
2011–12	Millwall	30	0		
2012–13	Millwall	25	1		
2013–14	Millwall	29	0		
2014–15	Millwall	39	2	**341**	**17**
2015–16	Leyton Orient	8	0	**8**	**0**

ESSAM, Connor (D) **53** **1**
H: 6 0 W: 12 00 b.Sheerness 9-7-92

2010–11	Gillingham	0	0		
2011–12	Gillingham	18	0		
2012–13	Gillingham	0	0	**18**	**0**
2012–13	Crawley T	9	1		
2013–14	Crawley T	2	0		
2014–15	Crawley T	0	0	**11**	**1**
2014–15	Dover	0	0		
2015–16	Leyton Orient	24	0	**24**	**0**

GNANDUILLET, Armand (F) **121** **21**
H: 6 4 W: 13 12 b.Angers 13-2-92
Internationals: Ivory Coast U20.

2012–13	Chesterfield	13	3		
2013–14	Chesterfield	34	5		
2014–15	Chesterfield	26	2		
2014–15	*Tranmere R*	4	2	**4**	**2**
2014–15	*Oxford U*	4	0	**4**	**0**
2015–16	Chesterfield	9	0	**82**	**10**
2015–16	*Stevenage*	14	5	**14**	**5**
2015–16	Leyton Orient	17	4	**17**	**4**

GRAINGER, Charlie (G) **2** **0**
b. 31-7-96
Internationals: England U18.

2012–13	Leyton Orient	0	0		
2013–14	Leyton Orient	0	0		
2014–15	Leyton Orient	0	0		
2015–16	Leyton Orient	2	0	**2**	**0**

HUNT, Nicky (D) **305** **2**
H: 6 1 W: 13 07 b.Westhoughton 3-9-83
Internationals: England U21.

2000–01	Bolton W	1	0		
2001–02	Bolton W	0	0		
2002–03	Bolton W	0	0		
2003–04	Bolton W	31	1		
2004–05	Bolton W	29	0		
2005–06	Bolton W	20	0		
2006–07	Bolton W	33	0		
2007–08	Bolton W	14	0		
2008–09	Bolton W	0	0		
2008–09	*Birmingham C*	11	0	**11**	**0**
2009–10	Bolton W	0	0	**128**	**1**
2009–10	*Derby Co*	21	0	**21**	**0**
2010–11	Bristol C	7	0		
2011–12	Bristol C	0	0	**7**	**0**
2011–12	Preston NE	17	1	**17**	**1**
2012–13	Rotherham U	9	0	**9**	**0**
2012–13	Accrington S	11	0		
2013–14	Accrington S	37	0		
2014–15	Accrington S	29	0	**77**	**0**
2015–16	Mansfield T	19	0	**19**	**0**
2015–16	Leyton Orient	16	0	**16**	**0**

JAMES, Lloyd (M) **236** **11**
H: 5 11 W: 11 01 b.Bristol 16-2-88
Internationals: Wales U17, U19, U21.

2005–06	Southampton	0	0		
2006–07	Southampton	0	0		
2007–08	Southampton	0	0		
2008–09	Southampton	41	0		
2009–10	Southampton	30	2	**71**	**2**
2010–11	Colchester U	28	0		
2011–12	Colchester U	23	1	**51**	**1**
2011–12	*Crawley T*	6	0	**6**	**0**
2012–13	Leyton Orient	28	0		
2013–14	Leyton Orient	42	3		
2014–15	Leyton Orient	13	1		
2015–16	Leyton Orient	25	4	**108**	**8**

JUDD, Myles (D) **0** **0**
b. 26-8-99

2015–16	Leyton Orient	0	0		

KASHKET, Scott (M) **16** **1**
H: 5 9 W: 10 06 b.London 6-7-95

2014–15	Leyton Orient	1	0		
2015–16	Leyton Orient	15	1	**16**	**1**

KOROMA, Josh (F) **3** **0**
b. 8-11-98

2015–16	Leyton Orient	3	0	**3**	**0**

LEE, Harry (M) **3** **0**
H: 6 0 W: 11 09 b.Hackney 20-3-95

2012–13	Leyton Orient	1	0		
2013–14	Leyton Orient	0	0		
2014–15	Leyton Orient	2	0		
2015–16	Leyton Orient	0	0	**3**	**0**

McANUFF, Jobi (M) **549** **54**
H: 5 11 W: 11 05 b.Edmonton 9-11-81
Internationals: Jamaica Full caps.

2000–01	Wimbledon	0	0		
2001–02	Wimbledon	38	4		
2002–03	Wimbledon	31	4		
2003–04	Wimbledon	27	5	**96**	**13**
2003–04	West Ham U	12	1		
2004–05	West Ham U	1	0	**13**	**1**
2004–05	Cardiff C	43	2	**43**	**2**
2005–06	Crystal Palace	41	8		
2006–07	Crystal Palace	34	5	**75**	**13**
2007–08	Watford	39	2		
2008–09	Watford	40	3		
2009–10	Watford	3	0	**82**	**5**
2009–10	Reading	36	3		
2010–11	Reading	40	4		
2011–12	Reading	40	5		
2012–13	Reading	38	0		
2013–14	Reading	35	2	**189**	**14**
2014–15	Leyton Orient	34	3		
2015–16	Leyton Orient	17	3	**51**	**6**

McCALLUM, Paul (F) **46** **13**
H: 6 3 W: 12 00 b.Streatham 28-7-93

2010–11	West Ham U	0	0		
2011–12	West Ham U	0	0		
2011–12	*Rochdale*	0	0		
2012–13	West Ham U	0	0		
2012–13	*AFC Wimbledon*	9	4	**9**	**4**
2012–13	*Aldershot T*	9	3	**9**	**3**
2013–14	West Ham U	0	0		
2013–14	*Torquay U*	5	3	**5**	**3**
2013–14	*Hearts*	6	0	**6**	**0**
2014–15	West Ham U	0	0		
2014–15	*Portsmouth*	7	0	**7**	**0**
2015–16	Leyton Orient	10	3	**10**	**3**

MONCUR, Freddy (M) **0** **0**
b. 8-9-96

2015–16	Leyton Orient	0	0		

MOORE, Sammy (M) **190** **16**
H: 5 8 W: 9 00 b.Dover 7-9-87

2006–07	Ipswich T	1	0		
2007–08	Ipswich T	0	0		
2007–08	*Brentford*	20	2	**20**	**2**
2008–09	Ipswich T	0	0	**1**	**0**
2011–12	AFC Wimbledon	41	6		
2012–13	AFC Wimbledon	28	2		
2013–14	AFC Wimbledon	40	4		
2014–15	AFC Wimbledon	30	0	**139**	**12**
2015–16	Leyton Orient	30	2	**30**	**2**

MVOTO, Jean Yves (D) **51** **2**
H: 6 4 W: 14 07 b.Paris 6-9-88

2009–10	*Southend U*	0	0		
2010–11	Oldham Ath	0	0		
2012–13	Oldham Ath	0	0		
2013–14	Barnsley	28	2		
2014–15	Barnsley	15	0	**43**	**2**
2015–16	Leyton Orient	8	0	**8**	**0**

NOLAN, Kevin (M) **536** **99**
H: 6 0 W: 14 00 b.Liverpool 24-6-82
Internationals: England U20, U21.

1999–2000	Bolton W	4	0		
2000–01	Bolton W	31	1		
2001–02	Bolton W	35	8		
2002–03	Bolton W	33	1		
2003–04	Bolton W	37	9		
2004–05	Bolton W	36	4		
2005–06	Bolton W	36	9		
2006–07	Bolton W	31	3		
2007–08	Bolton W	33	5		
2008–09	Bolton W	20	0	**296**	**40**
2008–09	Newcastle U	11	0		
2009–10	Newcastle U	44	17		
2010–11	Newcastle U	30	12	**85**	**29**
2011–12	West Ham U	42	12		
2012–13	West Ham U	35	10		
2013–14	West Ham U	33	7		
2014–15	West Ham U	29	1		
2015–16	West Ham U	2	0	**141**	**30**
2015–16	Leyton Orient	14	0	**14**	**0**

PALMER, Oliver (F) **99** **12**
b.London 21-1-92

2013–14	Mansfield T	38	4		
2014–15	Mansfield T	16	1	**54**	**5**
2015–16	Leyton Orient	45	7	**45**	**7**

PLASMATI, Gianvito (F) **140** **23**
H: 6 6 W: 13 05 b.Matera 28-1-83

2006–07	Catania	1	0		
2007–08	Catania	0	0		
2007–08	Foggia	15	2	**15**	**2**
2008–09	Catania	13	2		
2008–09	*Atalanta*	12	3	**12**	**3**
2009–10	Catania	13	0		
2010–11	Catania	0	0	**27**	**2**
2011–12	Nocerina	15	3	**15**	**3**
2011–12	*Varese*	9	2	**9**	**2**
2012–13	Vicenza	16	2	**16**	**2**
2012–13	Lanciano	14	4		
2013–14	Lanciano	16	3	**30**	**7**
2013–14	Siena	2	0	**2**	**0**
2014–15	Leyton Orient	14	2		
2015–16	Leyton Orient	0	0	**14**	**2**

POLLOCK, Aron (D) **2** **0**
b. 23-3-98

2015–16	Leyton Orient	2	0	**2**	**0**

PRITCHARD, Bradley (M) **143** **4**
H: 6 1 W: 14 02 b.Zimbabwe 19-12-85

2011–12	Charlton Ath	20	0		
2012–13	Charlton Ath	42	3		
2013–14	Charlton Ath	17	0	**79**	**3**
2014–15	Leyton Orient	31	0		
2015–16	Leyton Orient	29	1	**60**	**1**
2015–16	*Stevenage*	4	0	**4**	**0**

SARGEANT, Sam (G) **1** **0**
b. 23-9-97

2014–15	Leyton Orient	0	0		
2015–16	Leyton Orient	1	0	**1**	**0**

SEMEDO, Sandro (F) **3** **0**
b. 3-12-96

2015–16	Leyton Orient	3	0	**3**	**0**

SHAW, Frazer (D) **25** **0**
b. 23-12-94
Internationals: England C.

2013–14	West Ham U	0	0		

From Billericay T, Dulwich Hamlet.

2015–16	Leyton Orient	25	0	**25**	**0**

SIMPSON, Jay (F) **281** **66**
H: 5 11 W: 13 04 b.Enfield 1-12-88
Internationals: England U17.

2007–08	Arsenal	0	0		
2007–08	*Millwall*	41	6		
2008–09	Arsenal	0	0		
2008–09	*WBA*	13	1	**13**	**1**
2009–10	Arsenal	0	0		
2009–10	*QPR*	39	12	**39**	**12**
2010–11	Hull C	32	6		
2011–12	Hull C	3	0		
2011–12	*Millwall*	16	4	**57**	**10**
2012–13	Hull C	43	6		
2013–14	Hull C	0	0	**78**	**12**
2014–15	Buriram United	21	1	**21**	**1**
2014–15	Leyton Orient	28	5		
2015–16	Leyton Orient	45	25	**73**	**30**

TURGOTT, Blair (M) **48** **3**
H: 6 0 W: 10 03 b.Bromley 22-5-94
Internationals: England U16, U17, U18, U19.

2011–12	West Ham U	0	0		
2012–13	*Bradford C*	4	0	**4**	**0**
2013–14	West Ham U	0	0		
2013–14	*Colchester U*	4	1	**4**	**1**
2013–14	*Rotherham U*	1	0	**1**	**0**
2013–14	*Dagenham & R*	5	0	**5**	**0**
2014–15	West Ham U	0	0		
2014–15	Coventry C	3	1	**3**	**1**
2015–16	Leyton Orient	31	1	**31**	**1**

WOODS, Gary (G) **102** **0**
H: 6 1 W: 11 00 b.Kettering 1-10-90
Internationals: England U18.

2008–09	Doncaster R	1	0		
2009–10	Doncaster R	0	0		
2010–11	Doncaster R	16	0		
2011–12	Doncaster R	14	0		
2012–13	Doncaster R	42	0		
2013–14	Doncaster R	0	0	**73**	**0**
2013–14	Watford	0	0		
2014–15	Leyton Orient	17	0		
2015–16	Leyton Orient	0	0	**17**	**0**
2015–16	*Ross Co*	12	0	**12**	**0**

Scholars
Abrahams, Tristan; Adamson, Patrick James; Adeboyejo, Ayomide Victor; Agyemang, Montel Kofi Owusu; Alderson, Sam Edmund; Alzate, Steven; Barker, Charley Samuel; Clark, Michael Albert; Happe, Daniel Keith; Humphrey, Jack Peter; Judd, Myles Mark; Koroma, Joshua; Ling, Samuel Jack; McLean, Rian Tyrone; Moncur, Freddy Daniel; Ochieng, Henry Oliver; Owusu-Agyeman, Christian; Roach, Sam David.

LIVERPOOL (46)

ALBERTO, Luis (M)   **60 8**
H: 6 0 b.San Jose Del Valle 28-9-92
Internationals: Spain U18, U19, U21.

Season	Club				
2009–10	Sevilla	0	0		
2010–11	Sevilla	2	0		
2011–12	Sevilla	5	0		
2012–13	Sevilla	0	0	7	0
2013–14	Liverpool	9	0		
2014–15	Liverpool	0	0		
2014–15	*Malaga*	15	2	15	2
2015–16	Liverpool	0	0	9	0
2015–16	*La Coruna*	29	6	29	6

ALLEN, Joe (M)   **218 11**
H: 5 6 W: 9 10 b.Carmarthen 14-3-90
Internationals: Wales U17, U19, U21, Full caps. Great Britain.

Season	Club				
2006–07	Swansea C	1	0		
2007–08	Swansea C	6	0		
2008–09	Swansea C	23	1		
2009–10	Swansea C	21	0		
2010–11	Swansea C	40	2		
2011–12	Swansea C	36	4		
2012–13	Swansea C	0	0	127	7
2012–13	Liverpool	27	0		
2013–14	Liverpool	24	1		
2014–15	Liverpool	21	1		
2015–16	Liverpool	19	2	91	4

BALOTELLI, Mario (F)   **194 68**
H: 6 2 W: 13 08 b.Palermo 12-8-90
Internationals: Italy U21, Full caps.

Season	Club				
2005–06	Lumezzane	2	0	2	0
2006–07	Internazionale	0	0		
2007–08	Internazionale	11	3		
2008–09	Internazionale	22	8		
2009–10	Internazionale	26	9	59	20
2010–11	Manchester C	17	6		
2011–12	Manchester C	23	13		
2012–13	Manchester C	14	1	54	20
2012–13	AC Milan	13	12		
2013–14	AC Milan	30	14		
2014–15	Liverpool	16	1		
2015–16	Liverpool	0	0	16	1
2015–16	*AC Milan*	20	1	63	27

BENTEKE, Christian (F)   **222 87**
H: 6 3 W: 13 00 b.Kinshasa 3-12-90
Internationals: Belgium U17, U18, U19, U21, Full caps.

Season	Club				
2007–08	Genk	7	0		
2008–09	Genk	3	0		
2008–09	Standard Liege	9	3		
2009–10	*KV Kortrijk*	24	9	24	9
2010–11	Standard Liege	5	0		
2010–11	*KV Mechelen*	15	5	15	5
2011–12	Standard Liege	4	0	18	3
2011–12	Genk	32	16		
2012–13	Genk	5	3	47	19
2012–13	Aston Villa	34	19		
2013–14	Aston Villa	26	10		
2014–15	Aston Villa	29	13	89	42
2015–16	Liverpool	29	9	29	9

BOGDAN, Adam (G)   **107 0**
H: 6 4 W: 14 02 b.Budapest 27-9-87
Internationals: Hungary U21, Full caps.

Season	Club				
2007–08	Bolton W	0	0		
2008–09	Bolton W	0	0		
2009–10	Bolton W	0	0		
2009–10	*Crewe Alex*	1	0	1	0
2010–11	Bolton W	4	0		
2011–12	Bolton W	20	0		
2012–13	Bolton W	41	0		
2013–14	Bolton W	29	0		
2014–15	Bolton W	10	0	104	0
2015–16	Liverpool	2	0	2	0

BRANNAGAN, Cameron (M)   **3 0**
H: 5 11 W: 11 03 b.Manchester 9-5-96
Internationals: England U18, U20.

Season	Club				
2013–14	Liverpool	0	0		
2014–15	Liverpool	0	0		
2015–16	Liverpool	3	0	3	0

CAN, Emre (M)   **90 6**
H: 6 1 W: 11 09 b.Frankfurt 12-1-94
Internationals: Germany U16, U17, U19, U21, Full caps.

Season	Club				
2011–12	Bayern Munich	0	0		
2012–13	Bayern Munich	4	1	4	1
2013–14	Bayer Leverkusen	29	3	29	3
2014–15	Liverpool	29	1		
2015–16	Liverpool	30	1	57	2

CANOS, Sergi (M)   **39 7**
b. 2-2-97
Internationals: Spain U16, U17, U19.

Season	Club				
2015–16	Liverpool	1	0	1	0
2015–16	*Brentford*	38	7	38	7

CHIRIVELLA, Pedro (M)   **1 0**
b. 23-5-97
Internationals: Spain U17.

Season	Club				
2014–15	Valencia	0	0		
2015–16	Liverpool	1	0	1	0

CLYNE, Nathaniel (D)   **249 5**
H: 5 9 W: 10 07 b.Stockwell 5-4-91
Internationals: England U19, U21, Full caps.

Season	Club				
2008–09	Crystal Palace	26	0		
2009–10	Crystal Palace	22	1		
2010–11	Crystal Palace	46	0		
2011–12	Crystal Palace	28	0	122	1
2012–13	Southampton	34	1		
2013–14	Southampton	25	0		
2014–15	Southampton	35	2	94	3
2015–16	Liverpool	33	1	33	1

COUTINHO, Phillippe (M)   **157 30**
H: 5 7 W: 10 09 b.Rio de Janeiro 12-6-92
Internationals: Brazil U17, U20, Full caps.

Season	Club				
2009–10	Vasco da Gama	7	1	7	1
2010–11	Inter Milan	12	1		
2011–12	Inter Milan	5	1		
2011–12	*Espanyol*	16	5	16	5
2012–13	Inter Milan	10	1	27	3
2012–13	Liverpool	13	3		
2013–14	Liverpool	33	5		
2014–15	Liverpool	35	5		
2015–16	Liverpool	26	8	107	21

DUNN, Jack (F)   **0 0**
H: 5 8 W: 10 08 b.Liverpool 19-11-94
Internationals: England U17, U18, U19.

Season	Club		
2015–16	Liverpool	0	0

FIRMINO, Roberto (M)   **209 56**
H: 5 11 W: 12 00 b.Maceio 2-10-91
Internationals: Brazil Full caps.

Season	Club				
2009	Figueirense	2	0		
2010	Figueirense	36	8	38	8
2010–11	Hoffenheim	11	3		
2011–12	Hoffenheim	30	7		
2012–13	Hoffenheim	33	5		
2013–14	Hoffenheim	33	16		
2014–15	Hoffenheim	33	7	140	38
2015–16	Liverpool	31	10	31	10

FLANAGAN, John (D)   **40 1**
H: 5 11 W: 12 06 b.Liverpool 1-1-93
Internationals: England U19, U20, U21, Full caps.

Season	Club				
2010–11	Liverpool	7	0		
2011–12	Liverpool	5	0		
2012–13	Liverpool	0	0		
2013–14	Liverpool	23	1		
2014–15	Liverpool	0	0		
2015–16	Liverpool	5	0	40	1

FULTON, Ryan (G)   **12 0**
b.Burnley 23-5-96
Internationals: Scotland U16, U19.

Season	Club				
2015–16	Liverpool	0	0		
2015–16	*Portsmouth*	12	0	12	0

GOMEZ, Joseph (D)   **26 0**
H: 6 2 W: 14 00 b.Catford 23-5-97
Internationals: England U16, U17, U19, U21.

Season	Club				
2014–15	Charlton Ath	21	0	21	0
2015–16	Liverpool	5	0	5	0

HENDERSON, Jordan (M)   **237 24**
H: 6 0 W: 10 07 b.Sunderland 17-6-90
Internationals: England U19, U20, U21, Full caps.

Season	Club				
2008–09	Sunderland	1	0		
2008–09	*Coventry C*	10	1	10	1
2009–10	Sunderland	33	1		
2010–11	Sunderland	37	3	71	4
2011–12	Liverpool	37	2		
2012–13	Liverpool	30	5		
2013–14	Liverpool	35	4		
2014–15	Liverpool	37	6		
2015–16	Liverpool	17	2	156	19

IBE, Jordan (F)   **79 8**
H: 5 9 W: 11 00 b.Southwark 8-12-95
Internationals: England U18, U19, U20, U21.

Season	Club				
2011–12	Wycombe W	7	1	7	1
2011–12	Liverpool	0	0		
2012–13	Liverpool	1	0		
2013–14	Liverpool	0	0		
2013–14	*Birmingham C*	11	1	11	1
2014–15	Liverpool	12	0		
2014–15	*Derby Co*	20	5	20	5
2015–16	Liverpool	27	1	41	1

INGS, Danny (F)   **155 47**
H: 5 10 W: 11 07 b.Winchester 16-3-92
Internationals: England U21, Full caps.

Season	Club				
2009–10	Bournemouth	0	0		
2010–11	Bournemouth	26	7		
2011–12	Bournemouth	1	0	27	7
2011–12	Burnley	15	3		
2012–13	Burnley	32	3		
2013–14	Burnley	40	21		
2014–15	Burnley	35	11	122	38
2015–16	Liverpool	6	2	6	2

JONES, Lloyd (D)   **27 1**
H: 6 3 W: 11 11 b.Plymouth 7-10-95
Internationals: Wales U17, U18. England U19, U20.

Season	Club				
2012–13	Liverpool	0	0		
2013–14	Liverpool	0	0		
2014–15	Liverpool	0	0		
2014–15	*Cheltenham T*	6	0	6	0
2014–15	*Accrington S*	11	1	11	1
2015–16	Liverpool	0	0		
2015–16	*Blackpool*	10	0	10	0

JOSE ENRIQUE (D)   **251 4**
H: 6 0 W: 12 00 b.Valencia 23-1-86
Internationals: Spain U16, U20, U21.

Season	Club				
2004–05	Levante	19	1	19	1
2005–06	Valencia	0	0		
2005–06	Celta Vigo	14	0	14	0
2006–07	Villarreal	23	0	23	0
2007–08	Newcastle U	23	0		
2008–09	Newcastle U	26	0		
2009–10	Newcastle U	34	1		
2010–11	Newcastle U	36	0	119	1
2011–12	Liverpool	35	0		
2012–13	Liverpool	29	2		
2013–14	Liverpool	8	0		
2014–15	Liverpool	4	0		
2015–16	Liverpool	0	0	76	2

KENT, Ryan (M)   **17 1**
b.Oldham 11-11-96
Internationals: England U18, U20.

Season	Club				
2015–16	Liverpool	0	0		
2015–16	*Coventry C*	17	1	17	1

LALLANA, Adam (M)   **295 57**
H: 5 8 W: 11 06 b.St Albans 10-5-88
Internationals: England U18, U19, U21, Full caps.

Season	Club				
2005–06	Southampton	0	0		
2006–07	Southampton	1	0		
2007–08	Southampton	5	1		
2007–08	*Bournemouth*	3	0	3	0
2008–09	Southampton	40	1		
2009–10	Southampton	44	15		
2010–11	Southampton	36	8		
2011–12	Southampton	41	11		
2012–13	Southampton	30	3		
2013–14	Southampton	38	9	235	48
2014–15	Liverpool	27	5		
2015–16	Liverpool	30	4	57	9

LOVREN, Dejan (D)   **240 6**
H: 6 2 W: 13 02 b.Karlovac 5-7-89
Internationals: Croatia U17, U18, U19, U20, U21, Full caps.

Season	Club				
2005–06	Dinamo Zagreb	1	0		
2006–07	Dinamo Zagreb	0	0		
2006–07	Inter Zapresic	21	0		
2007–08	Dinamo Zagreb	0	0		
2007–08	Inter Zapresic	29	1	50	1
2008–09	Dinamo Zagreb	22	1		
2008–09	Dinamo Zagreb	14	0	37	1
2009–10	Lyon	8	0		
2010–11	Lyon	28	0		
2011–12	Lyon	18	1		
2012–13	Lyon	18	1	72	2
2013–14	Southampton	31	2	31	2
2014–15	Liverpool	26	0		
2015–16	Liverpool	24	0	50	0

LUCAS (M)   **256 5**
H: 5 10 W: 11 09 b.Dourados 9-1-87
Internationals: Brazil U20, U23, Full caps.

Season	Club				
2005	Gremio	3	0		
2006	Gremio	30	4	33	4
2007–08	Liverpool	18	0		
2008–09	Liverpool	25	1		
2009–10	Liverpool	35	0		
2010–11	Liverpool	33	0		
2011–12	Liverpool	12	0		
2012–13	Liverpool	26	0		
2013–14	Liverpool	27	0		
2014–15	Liverpool	20	0		
2015–16	Liverpool	27	0	223	1

MAGUIRE, Joe (D)   0   0
H: 5 10   W: 11 00   b.Manchester 18-1-96

Season	Club				
2015–16	Liverpool	0	0		
2015–16	*Leyton Orient*	0	0		

MARKOVIC, Lazar (F)   105   20
H: 5 9   W: 10 03   b.Cacak 2-3-94
Internationals: Serbia U17, U21, Full caps.

Season	Club				
2010–11	Partizan Belgrade	1	0		
2011–12	Partizan Belgrade	26	6		
2012–13	Partizan Belgrade	19	7	46	13
2013–14	Benfica	26	5	26	5
2014–15	Liverpool	19	2		
2015–16	Liverpool	0	0	19	2
2015–16	*Fenerbahce*	14	0	14	0

MASTERSON, Conor (D)   0   0
b.Dublin 8-9-98
Internationals: Republic of Ireland U16, U17, U18, U19.

Season	Club				
2015–16	Liverpool	0	0		

McLAUGHLIN, Ryan (D)   13   0
H: 5 9   W: 10 12   b.Belfast 30-9-94
Internationals: Northern Ireland U16, U17, U19, U21, Full caps.

Season	Club				
2011–12	Liverpool	0	0		
2013–14	Liverpool	0	0		
2013–14	*Barnsley*	9	0	9	0
2014–15	Liverpool	0	0		
2015–16	Liverpool	0	0		
2015–16	*Aberdeen*	4	0	4	0

MIGNOLET, Simon (G)   320   1
H: 6 4   W: 13 10   b.St Truiden 6-3-88
Internationals: Belgium U16, U17, U18, U19, U20, U21, Full caps.

Season	Club				
2006–07	St Truiden	2	0		
2007–08	St Truiden	25	0		
2008–09	St Truiden	35	1		
2009–10	St Truiden	37	0		
2010–11	St Truiden	23	0	122	1
2010–11	Sunderland	23	0		
2011–12	Sunderland	29	0		
2012–13	Sunderland	38	0	90	0
2013–14	Liverpool	38	0		
2014–15	Liverpool	36	0		
2015–16	Liverpool	34	0	108	0

MILNER, James (M)   423   43
H: 5 9   W: 11 00   b.Leeds 4-1-86
Internationals: England U16, U17, U19, U20, U21, Full caps.

Season	Club				
2002–03	Leeds U	18	2		
2003–04	Leeds U	30	3	48	5
2003–04	Swindon T	6	2	6	2
2004–05	Newcastle U	25	1		
2005–06	Newcastle U	3	0		
2005–06	Aston Villa	27	1		
2006–07	Newcastle U	35	3		
2007–08	Newcastle U	29	2		
2008–09	Newcastle U	2	0	94	6
2008–09	Aston Villa	36	7		
2009–10	Aston Villa	36	7		
2010–11	Aston Villa	1	1	100	12
2010–11	Manchester C	32	0		
2011–12	Manchester C	26	3		
2012–13	Manchester C	26	4		
2013–14	Manchester C	3	0		
2014–15	Manchester C	32	5	147	13
2015–16	Liverpool	28	5	28	5

MORENO, Alberto (D)   115   6
H: 5 7   W: 10 01   b.Seville 5-7-92
Internationals: Spain U21, Full caps.

Season	Club				
2011–12	Sevilla	11	0		
2012–13	Sevilla	15	0		
2013–14	Sevilla	29	3	55	3
2014–15	Liverpool	28	2		
2015–16	Liverpool	32	1	60	3

OJO, Sheyi (M)   36   2
H: 5 9   W: 10 01   b.Hemel Hempstead 19-6-97
Internationals: England U16, U17, U18, U19.

Season	Club				
2014–15	Liverpool	0	0		
2014–15	*Wigan Ath*	11	0	11	0
2015–16	Liverpool	8	0	8	0
2015–16	*Wolverhampton W*	17	2	17	2

ORIGI, Divock (F)   89   19
H: 6 1   W: 11 11   b.Oostende 18-4-95
Internationals: Belgium U16, U17, U19, U21, Full caps.

Season	Club				
2012–13	Lille	10	1		
2013–14	Lille	30	5		
2014–15	Lille	33	8	73	14
2015–16	Liverpool	16	5	16	5

PHILLIPS, Adam (M)   0   0
b.Garstang 15-1-98
Internationals: England U16, U17.

Season	Club				
2014–15	Liverpool	0	0		
2015–16	Liverpool	0	0		

RANDALL, Connor (D)   4   0
H: 5 11   W: 12 00   b.Liverpool 21-10-95
Internationals: England U17.

Season	Club				
2014–15	Liverpool	0	0		
2014–15	*Shrewsbury T*	1	0	1	0
2015–16	Liverpool	3	0	3	0

ROSSITER, Jordan (M)   1   0
H: 5 8   W: 10 10   b.Liverpool 24-3-97
Internationals: England U16, U17, U18, U19.

Season	Club				
2013–14	Liverpool	0	0		
2014–15	Liverpool	0	0		
2015–16	Liverpool	1	0	1	0

SAKHO, Mamadou (D)   207   9
H: 6 2   W: 12 07   b.Paris 13-2-90
Internationals: France U16, U17, U18, U19, U21, Full caps.

Season	Club				
2006–07	Paris St Germain	0	0		
2007–08	Paris St Germain	12	0		
2008–09	Paris St Germain	23	1		
2009–10	Paris St Germain	32	0		
2010–11	Paris St Germain	35	4		
2011–12	Paris St Germain	22	0		
2012–13	Paris St Germain	27	2	151	7
2013–14	Liverpool	18	1		
2014–15	Liverpool	16	0		
2015–16	Liverpool	22	1	56	2

SINCLAIR, Jerome (F)   3   0
H: 5 8   W: 12 06   b.Birmingham 20-9-96
Internationals: England U16, U17.

Season	Club				
2012–13	Liverpool	1	0		
2013–14	Liverpool	0	0		
2014–15	Liverpool	2	0		
2014–15	*Wigan Ath*	1	0	1	0
2015–16	Liverpool	0	0	2	0

SKRTEL, Martin (D)   351   19
H: 6 3   W: 12 10   b.Handlova 15-12-84
Internationals: Slovakia Full caps.

Season	Club				
2002–03	Trencin	1	0		
2003–04	Trencin	34	0	35	0
2004	Zenit	7	0		
2005	Zenit	18	1		
2006	Zenit	26	1		
2007	Zenit	23	1	74	3
2007–08	Liverpool	14	0		
2008–09	Liverpool	21	0		
2009–10	Liverpool	19	1		
2010–11	Liverpool	38	2		
2011–12	Liverpool	34	2		
2012–13	Liverpool	25	2		
2013–14	Liverpool	36	7		
2014–15	Liverpool	33	1		
2015–16	Liverpool	22	1	242	16

SMITH, Bradley (D)   12   0
H: 5 10   W: 11 00   b.New South Wales 9-4-94
Internationals: England U17, U19, U20. Australia U23, Full caps.

Season	Club				
2011–12	Liverpool	0	0		
2012–13	Liverpool	0	0		
2013–14	Liverpool	1	0		
2014–15	Liverpool	0	0		
2014–15	*Swindon T*	7	0	7	0
2015–16	Liverpool	4	0	5	0

STEWART, Kevin (M)   27   3
H: 5 7   W: 11 06   b.Enfield 7-9-93

Season	Club				
2012–13	Tottenham H	0	0		
2012–13	*Crewe Alex*	4	0		
2013–14	*Crewe Alex*	0	0	4	0
2014–15	Liverpool	0	0		
2014–15	*Cheltenham T*	4	1	4	1
2014–15	*Burton Alb*	7	2	7	2
2015–16	Liverpool	7	0	7	0
2015–16	*Swindon T*	5	0	5	0

STURRIDGE, Daniel (F)   165   69
H: 6 2   W: 12 00   b.Birmingham 1-9-89
Internationals: England U16, U17, U18, U19, U20, U21, Full caps. Great Britain.

Season	Club				
2006–07	Manchester C	0	0		
2007–08	Manchester C	3	1		
2008–09	Manchester C	16	4		
2009–10	Manchester C	0	0	21	5
2009–10	Chelsea	13	1		
2010–11	Chelsea	13	0		
2010–11	Bolton W	12	8	12	8
2011–12	Chelsea	30	11		
2012–13	Chelsea	7	1	63	13
2012–13	Liverpool	14	10		
2013–14	Liverpool	29	21		
2014–15	Liverpool	12	4		
2015–16	Liverpool	14	8	69	43

TEIXEIRA, Joao Carlos (M)   36   6
H: 5 9   W: 11 05   b.Braga 18-1-93
Internationals: Portugal U16, U17, U18, U19, U20, U21.

Season	Club				
2011–12	Liverpool	0	0		
2012–13	Liverpool	0	0		
2013–14	Liverpool	1	0		
2013–14	*Brentford*	2	0	2	0
2014–15	Liverpool	0	0		
2014–15	*Brighton & HA*	6	4	32	6
2015–16	Liverpool	1	0	2	0

TIAGO ILORI, Almeida (D)   21   1
H: 6 3   W: 12 07   b.London 26-2-93
Internationals: Portugal U18, U19, U20, U21, U23.

Season	Club				
2011–12	Sporting Lisbon	1	0		
2012–13	Sporting Lisbon	11	1	12	1
2013–14	Liverpool	0	0		
2013–14	*Granada*	9	0	9	0
2014–15	Liverpool	0	0		
2014–15	*Bordeaux*	0	0		
2015–16	Liverpool	0	0		
2015–16	*Aston Villa*	0	0		

TOURE, Kolo (D)   353   12
H: 5 10   W: 13 08   b.Sokuora Bouake 19-3-81
Internationals: Ivory Coast Full caps.

Season	Club				
2001–02	Arsenal	0	0		
2002–03	Arsenal	26	2		
2003–04	Arsenal	37	1		
2004–05	Arsenal	35	0		
2005–06	Arsenal	33	0		
2006–07	Arsenal	35	3		
2007–08	Arsenal	30	2		
2008–09	Arsenal	29	1		
2009–10	Manchester C	0	0	225	9
2009–10	Manchester C	31	1		
2010–11	Manchester C	22	1		
2011–12	Manchester C	14	0		
2012–13	Manchester C	15	0	82	2
2013–14	Liverpool	20	0		
2014–15	Liverpool	12	0		
2015–16	Liverpool	14	1	46	1

WARD, Danny (G)   28   0
H: 5 11   W: 13 12   b.Wrexham 22-6-93
Internationals: Wales U17, U19, U21, Full caps.

Season	Club				
2011–12	Liverpool	0	0		
2012–13	Liverpool	0	0		
2013–14	Liverpool	0	0		
2014–15	Liverpool	0	0		
2014–15	*Morecambe*	5	0	5	0
2015–16	Liverpool	2	0	2	0
2015–16	*Aberdeen*	21	0	21	0

WILLIAMS, Jordan (M)   17   0
H: 6 0   W: 12 02   b.Bangor 6-11-95
Internationals: Wales U21.

Season	Club				
2014–15	Liverpool	0	0		
2014–15	*Notts Co*	8	0	8	0
2015–16	Liverpool	0	0		
2015–16	*Swindon T*	9	0	9	0

WILSON, Harry (M)   7   0
H: 5 8   W: 11 00   b.Wrexham 22-3-97
Internationals: Wales U17, U19, U21, Full caps.

Season	Club				
2015–16	Liverpool	0	0		
2015–16	*Crewe Alex*	7	0	7	0

WISDOM, Andre (D)   82   0
H: 6 1   W: 12 04   b.Leeds 9-5-93
Internationals: England U16, U17, U19, U21.

Season	Club				
2009–10	Liverpool	0	0		
2010–11	Liverpool	0	0		
2011–12	Liverpool	0	0		
2012–13	Liverpool	12	0		
2013–14	Liverpool	2	0		
2013–14	*Derby Co*	34	0	34	0
2014–15	Liverpool	0	0		
2014–15	*WBA*	24	0	24	0
2015–16	Liverpool	0	0	14	0
2015–16	*Norwich C*	10	0	10	0

Players retained or with offer of contract
Alexander Arnold, Trent; Brimmer, Jake; Dhanda, Yan; Ejaria, Oviemuno; George, Shamal; Gomes Aju, Madger Antonio; Grabara, Kamil; Grujic, Marko; Hart, Samuel James; Kane, Herbie; Lennon, Brooks; Rodrigues De Souza, Allan; Vigouroux, Lawrence; Virtue Thick, Matthew Joseph; Whelan, Corey.

Scholars
Adekanye, Omobolaji Habeeb; Correia Gomes, Toni; Kelleher, Caoimhin; Naeem, Suleman Joseph; Owens, Kris; Parker, Mich'El; Whyte, Harvey.

LUTON T (47)

BAKINSON, Tyreeq (M)   1 0
b. 8-1-98
2015–16 Luton T   1 0   1 0

BANTON, Zane (F)   4 0
b. 6-6-96
2014–15 Luton T   0 0
2015–16 Luton T   4 0   4 0

BENSON, Paul (F)   231 73
H: 6 1 W: 11 01 b.Southend 12-10-79
Internationals: England C.
2007–08 Dagenham & R 22 6
2008–09 Dagenham & R 33 17
2009–10 Dagenham & R 45 17
2010–11 Dagenham & R 3 0   103 40
2010–11 Charlton Ath 32 10
2011–12 Charlton Ath 1 0   33 10
2011–12 Swindon T 22 11
2012–13 Swindon T 9 1
2012–13 Portsmouth 7 2   7 2
2012–13 Cheltenham T 16 4   16 4
2013–14 Swindon T 0 0   31 12
2014–15 Luton T 21 1
2015–16 Luton T 20 4   41 5

CUTHBERT, Scott (D)   282 13
H: 6 2 W: 14 00 b.Alexandria 15-6-87
Internationals: Scotland U19, U20, U21, B.
2004–05 Celtic 0 0
2005–06 Celtic 0 0
2006–07 Celtic 0 0
2006–07 Livingston 4 1   4 1
2007–08 Celtic 0 0
2008–09 Celtic 0 0
2008–09 St Mirren 29 0   29 0
2009–10 Swindon T 39 3
2010–11 Swindon T 41 2   80 5
2011–12 Leyton Orient 33 1
2012–13 Leyton Orient 18 0
2013–14 Leyton Orient 44 4
2014–15 Leyton Orient 38 2   133 7
2015–16 Luton T 36 0   36 0

DOYLE, Nathan (M)   270 4
H: 5 11 W: 12 06 b.Derby 12-1-87
Internationals: England U16, U17, U18, U19.
2003–04 Derby Co 2 0
2004–05 Derby Co 3 0
2005–06 Derby Co 4 0
2005–06 Notts Co 12 0   12 0
2006–07 Derby Co 0 0   9 0
2006–07 Bradford C 28 0
2006–07 Hull C 1 0
2007–08 Hull C 1 0
2008–09 Hull C 3 0
2009–10 Hull C 0 0   5 0
2009–10 Barnsley 34 0
2010–11 Barnsley 43 2
2011–12 Barnsley 21 0   98 2
2011–12 Preston NE 5 0   5 0
2012–13 Bradford C 37 2
2013–14 Bradford C 38 0   103 2
2014–15 Luton T 27 0
2015–16 Luton T 11 0   38 0

GOOCH, Liam (G)   0 0
b. 25-11-97
2014–15 Luton T 0 0
2015–16 Luton T 0 0

GREEN, Danny (M)   193 34
H: 5 11 W: 12 00 b.Harlow 9-7-88
2006–07 Northampton T 0 0
2007–08 Nottingham F 0 0
From Bishop's Stortford.
2009–10 Dagenham & R 46 13
2010–11 Dagenham & R 41 11   87 24
2011–12 Charlton Ath 32 3
2012–13 Charlton Ath 17 1
2013–14 Charlton Ath 13 0   62 4
2013–14 Milton Keynes D 5 0
2014–15 Milton Keynes D 14 1   19 1
2015–16 Luton T 25 5   25 5

GRIFFITHS, Scott (D)   221 5
H: 5 9 W: 11 08 b.Westminster 27-11-85
Internationals: England C.
2007–08 Dagenham & R 41 0
2008–09 Dagenham & R 44 0
2009–10 Dagenham & R 13 1   98 1

2009–10 Peterborough U 20 0
2010–11 Peterborough U 0 0
2010–11 Chesterfield 29 0
2011–12 Peterborough U 0 0
2011–12 Crawley T 6 0   6 0
2011–12 Chesterfield 3 0   32 0
2011–12 Rotherham U 8 0   8 0
2012–13 Peterborough U 0 0   20 0
2012–13 Plymouth Arg 4 0   4 0
2014–15 Luton T 35 2
2015–16 Luton T 18 0   53 2

HALL, Ryan (M)   142 23
H: 5 10 W: 10 04 b.Dulwich 4-1-88
Internationals: England C.
2005–06 Crystal Palace 0 0
2006–07 Crystal Palace 0 0
2007–08 Crystal Palace 1 0   1 0
2007–08 Dagenham & R 8 2   8 2
From Bromley.
2011–12 Southend U 41 9
2011–12 Southend U 43 10
2012–13 Southend U 2 0   86 19
2012–13 Leeds U 8 0
2013–14 Leeds U 0 0   8 0
2013–14 Sheffield U 4 0   4 0
2013–14 Milton Keynes D 11 1   11 1
2014–15 Rotherham U 3 1   3 1
2014–15 Notts Co 4 0   4 0
2014–15 Luton T 7 0
2015–16 Luton T 10 0   17 0

HOWELLS, Jake (D)   59 4
H: 5 9 W: 11 09 b.Hemel Hempstead 18-4-91
Internationals: England C. Wales U21.
2014–15 Luton T 36 4
2015–16 Luton T 17 0   53 4
2015–16 Yeovil T 6 0   6 0

JUSTHAM, Elliot (G)   30 0
H: 6 3 W: 12 06 b. 18-7-90
2014–15 Luton T 15 0
2015–16 Luton T 15 0   30 0

JUSTIN, James (F)   1 0
b. 11-7-97
2015–16 Luton T 1 0   1 0

KING, Craig (G)   0 0
b. 1-7-97
2014–15 Luton T 0 0
2015–16 Luton T 0 0

LAWLESS, Alex (M)   57 4
H: 5 11 W: 10 08 b.Llwynupion 5-2-83
Internationals: Wales U19, U21.
2003–04 Fulham 0 0
2004–05 Fulham 0 0
2005–06 Torquay U 14 0   14 0
From Forest Green R, York C.
2014–15 Luton T 15 3
2015–16 Luton T 28 1   43 4

LEE, Oliver (M)   105 9
H: 5 11 W: 12 07 b.Hornchurch 11-7-91
2010–11 West Ham U 0 0
2010–11 West Ham U 0 0
2010–11 Dagenham & R 5 0
2011–12 West Ham U 0 0
2011–12 Dagenham & R 16 3   21 3
2011–12 Gillingham 8 0   8 0
2012–13 Barnet 11 0   11 0
2013–14 Birmingham C 16 1
2014–15 Birmingham C 0 0
2014–15 Birmingham C 0 0   16 1
2014–15 Plymouth Arg 15 2   15 2
2015–16 Luton T 34 3   34 3

MACKAIL-SMITH, Craig (F)   330 105
H: 6 3 W: 12 04 b.Watford 25-2-84
Internationals: England C. Scotland Full caps.
2006–07 Peterborough U 15 8
2007–08 Peterborough U 36 12
2008–09 Peterborough U 46 23
2009–10 Peterborough U 43 10
2010–11 Peterborough U 45 27
2011–12 Brighton & HA 45 9
2012–13 Brighton & HA 29 11
2013–14 Brighton & HA 6 5
2014–15 Brighton & HA 30 1   109 21
2014–15 Peterborough U 3 0   188 80
2015–16 Luton T 33 4   33 4

MARRIOTT, Jack (F)   52 15
H: 5 8 W: 11 03 b.Beverley 9-9-94
2012–13 Ipswich T 1 0
2013–14 Ipswich T 1 0
2013–14 Gillingham 0 0   1 0
2014–15 Ipswich T 0 0   2 0
2014–15 Carlisle U 4 0   4 0

2014–15 *Colchester U* 5 1   5 1
2015–16 Luton T 40 14   40 14

McCOURT, Paddy (M)   293 34
H: 5 10 W: 10 13 b.Londonderry 16-12-83
Internationals: Northern Ireland U21, B, Full caps.
2001–02 Rochdale 23 4
2002–03 Rochdale 26 3
2003–04 Rochdale 24 2
2004–05 Rochdale 6 0   79 9
2005 Shamrock R 17 7   17 7
2005 Derry C 15 1
2006 Derry C 22 2
2007 Derry C 17 2
2008 Derry C 8 0   62 5
2008–09 Celtic 4 0
2009–10 Celtic 9 2
2010–11 Celtic 25 7
2011–12 Celtic 13 0
2012–13 Celtic 15 0   66 9
2013–14 Barnsley 23 2   23 2
2014–15 Brighton & HA 10 0   10 0
2014–15 *Notts Co* 12 1   12 1
2015–16 Luton T 24 1   24 1

McGEEHAN, Cameron (M)   60 18
H: 5 11 W: 11 03 b.Kingston upon Thames 6-4-95
Internationals: Northern Ireland U17, U19, U21.
2013–14 Norwich C 0 0
2014–15 Norwich C 0 0
2014–15 *Luton T* 3 3
2014–15 *Cambridge U* 4 3   4 3
2015–16 Luton T 41 12   56 15

McNULTY, Steve (D)   67 2
H: 6 1 W: 13 11 b.Liverpool 26-9-83
2012–13 Fleetwood T 16 2   16 2
2013–14 Luton T 41 0
2015–16 Luton T 10 0   51 0

McQUOID, Josh (F)   194 22
H: 5 9 W: 10 10 b.Southampton 15-12-89
Internationals: Northern Ireland U19, U21, B, Full caps.
2006–07 Bournemouth 2 0
2007–08 Bournemouth 5 0
2008–09 Bournemouth 16 0
2009–10 Bournemouth 29 1
2010–11 Bournemouth 17 9
2010–11 Millwall 11 1
2011–12 Millwall 5 0   16 1
2011–12 *Burnley* 17 1   17 1
2012–13 Bournemouth 34 3
2013–14 Bournemouth 1 0
2013–14 *Peterborough U* 14 1   14 1
2014–15 Bournemouth 0 0   104 13
2014–15 *Coventry C* 14 3   14 3
2015–16 Luton T 29 3   29 3

MUSONDA, Frankie (D)   3 0
b. 12-12-97
2015–16 Luton T 3 0   3 0

O'BRIEN, Mark (D)   57 0
H: 5 11 W: 12 02 b.Dublin 20-11-92
Internationals: Republic of Ireland U17, U19, U21.
2008–09 Derby Co 1 0
2009–10 Derby Co 0 0
2010–11 Derby Co 2 0
2011–12 Derby Co 20 0
2012–13 Derby Co 9 0
2013–14 Derby Co 0 0   32 0
2014–15 Motherwell 19 0   19 0
2015–16 Luton T 6 0   6 0

O'DONNELL, Stephen (D)   151 9
H: 6 0 W: 11 10 b.Bellshill 11-5-92
Internationals: Scotland U21.
2011–12 Partick Thistle 31 2
2012–13 Partick Thistle 29 2
2013–14 Partick Thistle 27 0
2014–15 Partick Thistle 34 5   121 9
2015–16 Luton T 30 0   30 0

OKUONGHAE, Magnus (D)   288 11
H: 6 3 W: 13 04 b.Nigeria 16-2-86
Internationals: England C.
2003–04 Rushden & D 1 0
2004–05 Rushden & D 0 0
2005–06 Rushden & D 21 1
2006–07 Rushden & D 0 0   22 1
2007–08 Dagenham & R 10 0
2008–09 Dagenham & R 45 2   55 2
2009–10 Colchester U 44 0
2010–11 Colchester U 14 2
2011–12 Colchester U 42 0

2012–13 Colchester U 43 3
2013–14 Colchester U 44 2
2014–15 Colchester U 9 1 **196 8**
2015–16 Luton T 11 0 **11 0**
2015–16 *Hartlepool U* 4 0 **4 0**

PARRY, Andy (D) **0 0**
H: 5 10 W: 11 07 b.Liverpool 13-9-91
2014–15 Luton T 0 0
2015–16 Luton T 0 0

POTTS, Danny (D) **29 0**
H: 5 8 W: 11 00 b.Barking 13-4-94
Internationals: USA U20. England U18, U19, U20.
2011–12 West Ham U 3 0
2012–13 West Ham U 2 0
2012–13 *Colchester U* 5 0 **5 0**
2013–14 West Ham U 0 0
2013–14 *Portsmouth* 5 0 **5 0**
2014–15 West Ham U 0 0 **5 0**
2015–16 Luton T 14 0 **14 0**

ROBINSON, Matt (M) **9 0**
H: 6 2 W: 12 08 b. 1-6-94
2014–15 Luton T 9 0
2015–16 Luton T 0 0 **9 0**

RUDDOCK, Pelly (M) **37 3**
H: 5 9 W: 9 13 b.Hendon 17-7-93
2011–12 West Ham U 0 0
2013–14 West Ham U 0 0
2014–15 Luton T 16 1
2015–16 Luton T 21 2 **37 3**

SMITH, Jonathan (M) **122 9**
H: 6 3 W: 11 02 b.Preston 17-10-86
2011–12 Swindon T 38 3 **38 3**
2012–13 York C 12 0 **12 0**
2014–15 Luton T 35 2
2015–16 Luton T 37 4 **72 6**

TYLER, Mark (G) **485 0**
H: 6 0 W: 12 09 b.Norwich 2-4-77
Internationals: England U18.
1994–95 Peterborough U 5 0
1995–96 Peterborough U 5 0
1996–97 Peterborough U 3 0
1997–98 Peterborough U 46 0
1998–99 Peterborough U 27 0
1999–2000 Peterborough U 32 0
2000–01 Peterborough U 40 0
2001–02 Peterborough U 44 0
2002–03 Peterborough U 29 0
2003–04 Peterborough U 43 0
2004–05 Peterborough U 46 0
2005–06 Peterborough U 40 0
2006–07 Peterborough U 41 0
2007–08 Peterborough U 17 0
2008–09 Peterborough U 0 0
2008–09 *Bury* 11 0 **11 0**
2014–15 Luton T 31 0
2015–16 Luton T 27 0 **58 0**
2015–16 *Peterborough U* 3 0 **416 0**

WILLIAMS, Curtley (D) **3 0**
H: 6 0 W: 11 11 b.Ipswich 19-3-90
2014–15 Luton T 3 0
2015–16 Luton T 0 0 **3 0**

Scholars
Atkinson, Alexander James; Bean, Harry George; Brown, Joshua James; Cotter, Kavan John; Craig, Geo Luca; Famewo, Akinlolu Richard Olamide; Gooch, Liam Reece; Hinds, Fredrick Peter; McGhan-George, Kyran Devante; McJannet, Cameron Allan; Murray, George William; Snelus, Jack Simon Bez; Verney, James Albert.

MANCHESTER C (48)

ADARABIOYO, Tosin (D) **0 0**
H: 6 3 b.24-9-97
Internationals: England U16, U17, U18, U19.
2014–15 Manchester C 0 0
2015–16 Manchester C 0 0

AGUERO, Sergio (F) **379 199**
H: 5 8 W: 11 09 b.Buenos Aires 2-6-88
Internationals: Argentina U17, U20, U23, Full caps.
2002–03 Independiente 1 0
2003–04 Independiente 5 0
2004–05 Independiente 12 5
2005–06 Independiente 36 18 **54 23**
2006–07 Atletico Madrid 38 6
2007–08 Atletico Madrid 37 19
2008–09 Atletico Madrid 37 17
2009–10 Atletico Madrid 31 12
2010–11 Atletico Madrid 32 20 **175 74**
2011–12 Manchester C 34 23
2012–13 Manchester C 30 12
2013–14 Manchester C 23 17
2014–15 Manchester C 33 26
2015–16 Manchester C 30 24 **150 102**

AMBROSE, Thierry (F) **0 0**
H: 5 10 W: 11 00 b.Sens 28-3-97
Internationals: France U16, U17, U18.
2014–15 Manchester C 0 0
2015–16 Manchester C 0 0

BARKER, Brandon (M) **4 1**
H: 5 9 W: 10 10 b.Manchester 4-10-96
Internationals: England U18, U19, U20.
2014–15 0 0
2015–16 Manchester C 0 0
2015–16 *Rotherham U* 4 1 **4 1**

BONY, Wilfried (F) **213 99**
H: 6 0 W: 13 11 b.Bingerville 10-12-88
Internationals: Ivory Coast Full caps.
2008–09 Sparta Prague 16 3
2009–10 Sparta Prague 29 9
2010–11 Sparta Prague 13 10 **58 22**
2010–11 Vitesse 7 3
2011–12 Vitesse 28 12
2012–13 Vitesse 30 31 **65 46**
2013–14 Swansea C 34 16
2014–15 Swansea C 20 9 **54 25**
2014–15 Manchester C 10 2
2015–16 Manchester C 26 4 **36 6**

BOSSAERTS, Mathias (D) **0 0**
H: 6 0 W: 11 12 b.Gooreind 10-7-96
Internationals: Belgium U16, U17, U19.
2013–14 Manchester C 0 0
2014–15 Manchester C 0 0
2015–16 Manchester C 0 0

BRATTAN, Luke (M) **91 4**
H: 5 9 W: 10 03 b.Hull 8-3-90
Internationals: Australia U20.
2009–10 Brisbane Roar 1 0
2010–11 Brisbane Roar 6 0
2011–12 Brisbane Roar 15 0
2012–13 Brisbane Roar 17 1
2013–14 Brisbane Roar 28 3
2014–15 Brisbane Roar 24 0 **91 4**
2015–16 Manchester C 0 0
2015–16 *Bolton W* 0 0

CABALLERO, Willy (G) **304 0**
H: 6 1 W: 12 08 b.Santa Elena 28-9-81
Internationals: Argentina U21.
2001–04 Boca Juniors 15 0 **15 0**
2004–08 Elche 67 0
2008–09 Elche 38 0
2009–10 Elche 39 0
2010–11 Malaga 22 0 **166 0**
2010–11 Malaga 15 0
2011–12 Malaga 28 0
2012–13 Malaga 36 0
2013–14 Malaga 38 0 **117 0**
2014–15 Manchester C 2 0
2015–16 Manchester C 4 0 **6 0**

CACERES, Anthony (M) **73 4**
b. 29-9-92
2012–13 Central Coast M 3 0
2013–14 Central Coast M 21 2
2014–15 Central Coast M 26 1
2015–16 Central Coast M 12 0 **62 3**
2015–16 Manchester C 0 0
2015–16 *Melbourne C* 11 1 **11 1**

CELINA, Bersant (F) **1 0**
H: 5 4 W: 9 06 b.Prizren 9-9-96
Internationals: Norway U16, U17. Kosovo Full caps.
2014–15 Manchester C 0 0
2015–16 Manchester C 1 0 **1 0**

CLICHY, Gael (D) **300 2**
H: 5 9 W: 10 04 b.Toulouse 26-7-85
Internationals: France U15, U17, U18, U19, 21, B, Full caps.
2003–04 Arsenal 12 0
2004–05 Arsenal 15 0
2005–06 Arsenal 7 0
2006–07 Arsenal 27 0
2007–08 Arsenal 38 0
2008–09 Arsenal 31 1
2009–10 Arsenal 24 0
2010–11 Arsenal 33 0 **187 1**
2011–12 Manchester C 28 0
2012–13 Manchester C 28 0
2013–14 Manchester C 20 0
2014–15 Manchester C 23 1
2015–16 Manchester C 14 0 **113 1**

DE BRUYNE, Kevin (M) **176 41**
H: 5 11 W: 12 00 b.Ghent 28-6-91
Internationals: Belgium U18, U19, U21, Full caps.
2008–09 Genk 2 0
2009–10 Genk 30 3
2010–11 Genk 32 5
2011–12 Genk 15 6 **79 14**
2011–12 Chelsea 0 0
2012–13 Chelsea 0 0
2012–13 *Werder Bremen* 33 10 **33 10**
2013–14 Chelsea 3 0 **3 0**
2014–15 Wolfsburg 34 10
2015–16 Wolfsburg 2 0 **36 10**
2015–16 Manchester C 25 7 **25 7**

DELPH, Fabian (D) **178 11**
H: 5 8 W: 11 00 b.Bradford 21-11-89
Internationals: England U19, U21, Full caps.
2006–07 Leeds U 1 0
2007–08 Leeds U 1 0
2008–09 Leeds U 42 6
2009–10 Aston Villa 8 0
2010–11 Aston Villa 7 0
2011–12 Aston Villa 11 0
2011–12 *Leeds U* 5 0 **49 6**
2012–13 Aston Villa 24 0
2013–14 Aston Villa 34 3
2014–15 Aston Villa 28 0 **112 3**
2015–16 Manchester C 17 2 **17 2**

DEMICHELIS, Martin (D) **387 25**
H: 6 0 W: 12 03 b.Cordoba 20-12-80
Internationals: Argentina Full caps.
2001 River Plate 0 0
2002 River Plate 17 0
2003 River Plate 35 1 **52 1**
2003–04 Bayern Munich 14 2
2004–05 Bayern Munich 23 0
2005–06 Bayern Munich 27 1
2006–07 Bayern Munich 26 3
2007–08 Bayern Munich 28 1
2008–09 Bayern Munich 29 4
2009–10 Bayern Munich 21 1
2010–11 Bayern Munich 6 1 **174 13**
2010–11 Malaga 17 1
2011–12 Malaga 35 3
2012–13 Malaga 31 4 **83 8**
2013–14 Atletico Madrid 0 0
2013–14 Manchester C 27 2
2014–15 Manchester C 31 1
2015–16 Manchester C 20 0 **78 3**

DENAYER, Jason (D) **46 5**
H: 6 0 b.Brussels 28-6-95
Internationals: Belgium U19, U21, Full caps.
2013–14 Manchester C 0 0
2014–15 Manchester C 0 0
2014–15 *Celtic* 29 5 **29 5**
2015–16 Manchester C 0 0
2015–16 *Galatasaray* 17 0 **17 0**

DZEKO, Edin (F) **343 147**
H: 6 3 W: 12 08 b.Doboj 17-3-86
Internationals: Bosnia & Herzegovina U19, U21, Full caps.
2004–05 Zeljeznicar 13 1 **13 1**
2005–06 Usti nad Labem 15 6 **15 6**
2005–06 Teplice 13 3
2006–07 Teplice 30 13 **43 16**
2007–08 Wolfsburg 28 8
2008–09 Wolfsburg 32 26
2009–10 Wolfsburg 34 22
2010–11 Wolfsburg 17 10 **111 66**
2010–11 Manchester C 15 2
2011–12 Manchester C 30 14
2012–13 Manchester C 32 14
2013–14 Manchester C 31 16
2014–15 Manchester C 22 4
2015–16 Manchester C 0 0 **130 50**
2015–16 *Roma* 31 8 **31 8**

FACEY, Shay (D) **27 0**
H: 5 10 W: 10 00 b.Manchester 7-1-95
Internationals: England U16, U17, U19, U20.
2013–14 Manchester C 0 0
2014–15 Manchester C 0 0
2014–15 New York City 0 0
2015–16 Manchester C 0 0
2015–16 New York City 22 0 **22 0**
2015–16 *Rotherham U* 5 0 **5 0**

FAUPALA, David (F) **0 0**
H: 6 1 b.Bully les Mines 11-2-97
Internationals: France U16, U17, U18.
2014–15 Lens 0 0
2015–16 Manchester C 0 0

FERNANDINHO, Luis (M)   325   44
H: 5 10   W: 10 09   b.Londrina 4-5-85
Internationals: Brazil Full caps.

2003	Paranaense	29	5		
2004	Paranaense	41	9		
2005	Paranaense	2	0	72	14
2005–06	Shakhtar Donetsk	22	1		
2006–07	Shakhtar Donetsk	25	1		
2008–09	Shakhtar Donetsk	21	5		
2009–10	Shakhtar Donetsk	24	4		
2010–11	Shakhtar Donetsk	15	3		
2011–12	Shakhtar Donetsk	24	4		
2012–13	Shakhtar Donetsk	23	2	154	20
2013–14	Manchester C	33	5		
2014–15	Manchester C	33	3		
2015–16	Manchester C	33	2	99	10

FERNANDO, Francisco (M)   217   7
H: 6 1   W: 11 00   b.Brasilia 25-7-87
Internationals: Brazil U20.

2007–08	Porto	0	0		
2007–08	*Estrella Amadora*	26	1	26	1
2008–09	Porto	25	0		
2009–10	Porto	25	0		
2010–11	Porto	21	0		
2011–12	Porto	22	1		
2012–13	Porto	24	1		
2013–14	Porto	25	0	142	2
2014–15	Manchester C	25	2		
2015–16	Manchester C	24	2	49	4

GARCIA, Aleix (D)   1   0
H: 5 8   W: 9 08   b.Ulldecona 28-6-97
Internationals: Spain U16, U17, U18, U19.

2014–15	*Villareal*	1	0	1	0
2015–16	Manchester C	0	0		

GARCIA, Manu (M)   1   0
H: 5 7   b.Oviedo 2-2-98
Internationals: Spain U16.

2014–15	Manchester C	0	0		
2015–16	Manchester C	1	0	1	0

GLENDON, George (M)   0   0
H: 5 10   W: 11 00   b.Manchester 3-5-95
Internationals: England U16, U17.

2013–14	Manchester C	0	0
2014–15	Manchester C	0	0
2015–16	Manchester C	0	0

GUNN, Angus (G)   0   0
H: 6 0   W: 12 02   b.Norwich 22-1-96
Internationals: England U16, U17, U18, U19, U21.

2013–14	Manchester C	0	0
2014–15	Manchester C	0	0
2015–16	Manchester C	0	0

HART, Joe (G)   365   0
H: 6 3   W: 13 03   b.Shrewsbury 19-4-87
Internationals: England U19, U21, Full caps.

2004–05	Shrewsbury T	6	0		
2005–06	Shrewsbury T	46	0	52	0
2006–07	Manchester C	1	0		
2006–07	*Tranmere R*	6	0	6	0
2006–07	*Blackpool*	5	0	5	0
2007–08	Manchester C	26	0		
2008–09	Manchester C	23	0		
2009–10	Manchester C	0	0		
2009–10	*Birmingham C*	36	0	36	0
2010–11	Manchester C	38	0		
2011–12	Manchester C	38	0		
2012–13	Manchester C	38	0		
2013–14	Manchester C	31	0		
2014–15	Manchester C	36	0		
2015–16	Manchester C	35	0	266	0

HORSFIELD, James (M)   2   0
H: 5 10   W: 11 00   b.Hazel Grove 21-9-95

2015–16	Manchester C	0	0		
2015–16	*Doncaster R*	2	0	2	0

HUMPHREYS, Cameron (D)   0   0
H: 6 2   b.Manchester 22-7-98
Internationals: England U16, U17, U18.

2015–16	Manchester C	0	0

IHEANACHO, Kelechi (M)   26   8
H: 6 2   W: 13 08   b.Imo 3-10-96
Internationals: Nigeria U17, U20, Full caps.

2014–15	Manchester C	0	0		
2015–16	Manchester C	26	8	26	8

JESUS NAVAS, Gonzalez (M)   384   27
H: 5 7   W: 9 05   b.Los Palacios 21-11-85
Internationals: Spain U21, Full caps.

2003–04	Sevilla	5	0
2004–05	Sevilla	23	2
2005–06	Sevilla	34	2
2006–07	Sevilla	29	1
2007–08	Sevilla	36	4
2008–09	Sevilla	35	4
2009–10	Sevilla	34	4
2010–11	Sevilla	15	1
2011–12	Sevilla	37	5
2012–13	Sevilla	37	0	285	23
2013–14	Manchester C	30	4
2014–15	Manchester C	35	0
2015–16	Manchester C	34	0	99	4

JOVETIC, Stevan (F)   221   61
H: 6 0   W: 12 05   b.Podgorica 2-11-89

2005–06	Partizan Belgrade	2	0		
2006–07	Partizan Belgrade	22	1		
2007–08	Partizan Belgrade	27	12	51	13
2008–09	Fiorentina	29	2		
2009–10	Fiorentina	27	5		
2010–11	Fiorentina	0	0		
2011–12	Fiorentina	27	14		
2012–13	Fiorentina	31	13	114	34
2013–14	Manchester C	17	5		
2014–15	Manchester C	17	5		
2015–16	Manchester C	0	0	30	8
2015–16	*Inter Milan*	26	6	26	6

KOLAROV, Aleksandar (D)   300   23
H: 6 2   W: 13 05   b.Belgrade 10-11-85
Internationals: Serbia U21, Full caps.

2004–05	Cukaricki	27	2		
2005–06	Cukaricki	17	0	44	2
2005–06	OFK Belgrade	27	4		
2006–07	OFK Belgrade	27	4	38	5
2007–08	Lazio	24	1		
2008–09	Lazio	25	2		
2009–10	Lazio	33	3	82	6
2010–11	Manchester C	24	1		
2011–12	Manchester C	22	0		
2012–13	Manchester C	20	1		
2013–14	Manchester C	30	1		
2014–15	Manchester C	21	2		
2015–16	Manchester C	29	3	136	10

KOMPANY, Vincent (D)   310   18
H: 6 3   W: 13 05   b.Brussels 10-4-86
Internationals: Belgium U16, U17, Full caps.

2004–05	Anderlecht	29	2		
2005–06	Anderlecht	32	2	61	4
2006–07	Hamburg	6	0		
2007–08	Hamburg	22	1		
2008–09	Hamburg	1	0	29	1
2008–09	Manchester C	34	1		
2009–10	Manchester C	25	2		
2010–11	Manchester C	37	0		
2011–12	Manchester C	31	3		
2012–13	Manchester C	26	1		
2013–14	Manchester C	28	4		
2014–15	Manchester C	25	0		
2015–16	Manchester C	14	2	220	13

LAWLOR, Ian (G)   17   0
H: 6 4   W: 12 08   b.Dublin 27-10-94
Internationals: Republic of Ireland U17, U19, U21.

2011–12	Manchester C	0	0		
2012–13	Manchester C	0	0		
2013–14	Manchester C	0	0		
2014–15	Manchester C	0	0		
2015–16	Manchester C	0	0		
2015–16	*Barnet*	5	0	5	0
2015–16	*Bury*	12	0	12	0

MAFFEO, Pablo (D)   2   0
b. 12-6-97
Internationals: Spain U16, U17.
From Espanyol.

2015–16	Manchester C	0	0		
2015–16	*Girona*	2	0	2	0

MANGALA, Eliaquim (D)   176   8
H: 6 2   W: 11 09   b.Colombes 13-2-91
Internationals: France U21, Full caps.

2008–09	Standard Liege	11	0		
2009–10	Standard Liege	31	1		
2010–11	Standard Liege	35	1	77	2
2011–12	Porto	7	0		
2012–13	Porto	29	0		
2013–14	Porto	21	2	51	6
2014–15	Manchester C	25	0		
2015–16	Manchester C	23	0	48	0

NASRI, Samir (M)   335   47
H: 5 9   W: 11 11   b.Marseille 26-6-87
Internationals: France U16, U17, U18, U19, U21, Full caps.

2004–05	Marseille	24	1		
2005–06	Marseille	30	1		
2006–07	Marseille	37	3		
2007–08	Marseille	30	6	121	11
2008–09	Arsenal	26	2		
2009–10	Arsenal	26	2		
2010–11	Arsenal	30	10		
2011–12	Arsenal	1	0	86	18
2011–12	Manchester C	30	5		
2012–13	Manchester C	28	2		
2013–14	Manchester C	34	7		
2014–15	Manchester C	24	2		
2015–16	Manchester C	12	2	128	18

NEGREDO, Alvaro (F)   271   115
H: 6 1   W: 12 11   b.Madrid 20-8-85
Internationals: Spain U21, Full caps.

2007–08	Almeria	36	13		
2008–09	Almeria	34	18	70	31
2009–10	Sevilla	35	11		
2010–11	Sevilla	38	20		
2011–12	Sevilla	30	14		
2012–13	Sevilla	36	25	139	70
2013–14	Manchester C	32	9		
2014–15	Manchester C	0	0		
2014–15	*Valencia*	30	5	30	5
2015–16	Manchester C	0	0	32	9

OTAMENDI, Nicolas (D)   187   15
H: 5 10   W: 11 09   b.Buenos Aires 12-2-88
Internationals: Argentina Full caps.

2007–08	Velez Sarsfield	1	0		
2008–09	Velez Sarsfield	18	0		
2009–10	Velez Sarsfield	19	1		
2010–11	Velez Sarsfield	2	0	40	1
2010–11	Porto	15	5		
2011–12	Porto	20	1		
2012–13	Porto	29	1		
2013–14	Porto	13	0	77	7
2013–14	*Atletico Mineiro*	5	0	5	0
2014–15	Valencia	35	6	35	6
2015–16	Manchester C	30	1	30	1

PLUMMER, Ellis (D)   9   0
H: 5 11   W: 11 00   b.Denton 2-9-94
Internationals: England U16, U17.

2011–12	Manchester C	0	0		
2012–13	Manchester C	0	0		
2013–14	Manchester C	0	0		
2013–14	*Oldham Ath*	3	0	3	0
2014–15	Manchester C	0	0		
2014–15	*St Mirren*	6	0	6	0
2015–16	Manchester C	0	0		

ROBERTS, Patrick (M)   31   6
H: 5 6   W: 10 06   b.Kingston upon Thames 5-2-97
Internationals: England U16, U17, U18, U19.

2013–14	Fulham	2	0		
2014–15	Fulham	17	0	19	0
2015–16	Manchester C	1	0	1	0
2015–16	*Celtic*	11	6	11	6

SAGNA, Bakari (D)   337   4
H: 5 10   W: 11 05   b.Sens 14-2-83
Internationals: France U21, Full caps.

2003–04	Auxerre	1	0		
2004–05	Auxerre	26	0		
2005–06	Auxerre	23	0		
2006–07	Auxerre	38	0	87	0
2007–08	Arsenal	29	1		
2008–09	Arsenal	35	0		
2009–10	Arsenal	35	0		
2010–11	Arsenal	33	1		
2011–12	Arsenal	21	1		
2012–13	Arsenal	25	0		
2013–14	Arsenal	35	1	213	4
2014–15	Manchester C	9	0		
2015–16	Manchester C	28	0	37	0

SILVA, David (F)   388   65
H: 5 7   W: 10 07   b.Arguineguin 8-1-86
Internationals: Spain U16, U17, U19, U20, U21, Full caps.

2003–04	Mestalla	14	1	14	1
2004–05	Eibar	35	5	35	5
2005–06	Celta Vigo	34	3	34	3
2006–07	Valencia	36	5		
2007–08	Valencia	34	4		
2008–09	Valencia	19	4		
2009–10	Valencia	30	8	119	21
2010–11	Manchester C	35	4		
2011–12	Manchester C	36	6		
2012–13	Manchester C	32	4		
2013–14	Manchester C	27	7		
2014–15	Manchester C	32	12		
2015–16	Manchester C	24	2	186	35

STERLING, Raheem (F)   126   24
H: 5 7   W: 10 00   b.Kingston 8-12-94
Internationals: England U16, U17, U19, U21, Full caps.

2011–12	Liverpool	3	0		
2012–13	Liverpool	24	2		
2013–14	Liverpool	33	9		
2014–15	Liverpool	35	7	95	18
2015–16	Manchester C	31	6	31	6

TASENDE, Jose (D)   0   0
H: 5 7   W: 10 10   b.Coristanco 4-1-97
Internationals: Spain U17.

2014–15	Manchester C	0	0		
2015–16	Manchester C	0	0		

TOURE, Yaya (M)   419   75
H: 6 3   W: 14 02   b.Sokoura Bouake 13-5-83
Internationals: Ivory Coast Full caps.

2001–02	Beveren	28	0		
2002–03	Beveren	30	3		
2003–04	Beveren	12	0	70	3
2003–04	Metalurgs Donetsk	11	1		
2004–05	Metalurgs Donetsk	22	2	33	3
2005–06	Olympiacos	20	3	20	3
2006–07	Monaco	27	5	27	5
2007–08	Barcelona	26	1		
2008–09	Barcelona	25	2		
2009–10	Barcelona	23	1	74	4
2010–11	Manchester C	35	8		
2011–12	Manchester C	32	6		
2012–13	Manchester C	32	7		
2013–14	Manchester C	35	20		
2014–15	Manchester C	29	10		
2015–16	Manchester C	32	6	195	57

UNAL, Enes (F)   58   13
b. 10-5-97
Internationals: Turkey U16, U17, U19, U21,
Full caps.

2013–14	Bursaspor	16	3		
2014–15	Bursaspor	19	1	35	4
2015–16	Manchester C	0	0		
2015–16	*Genk*	12	1	12	1
2015–16	*NAC*	11	8	11	8

WRIGHT, Richard (G)   380   0
H: 6 2   W: 14 04   b.Ipswich 5-11-77
Internationals: England U18, U21, Full caps.

1994–95	Ipswich T	3	0		
1995–96	Ipswich T	23	0		
1996–97	Ipswich T	40	0		
1997–98	Ipswich T	46	0		
1998–99	Ipswich T	46	0		
1999–2000	Ipswich T	46	0		
2000–01	Ipswich T	36	0		
2001–02	Arsenal	12	0	12	0
2002–03	Everton	33	0		
2003–04	Everton	4	0		
2004–05	Everton	7	0		
2005–06	Everton	15	0		
2006–07	Everton	1	0	60	0
2007–08	West Ham U	0	0		
2007–08	*Southampton*	7	0	7	0
2008–09	Ipswich T	46	0		
2009–10	Ipswich T	12	0		
2010–11	Ipswich T	0	0		
2010–11	Sheffield U	2	0	2	0
2011–12	Ipswich T	1	0	299	0
2012–13	Manchester C	0	0		
2013–14	Manchester C	0	0		
2014–15	Manchester C	0	0		
2015–16	Manchester C	0	0		

ZABALETA, Pablo (D)   356   19
H: 5 8   W: 10 12   b.Buenos Aires 16-1-85
Internationals: Argentina U20, U23, Full caps.

2002–03	San Lorenzo	11	0		
2003–04	San Lorenzo	27	3		
2004–05	San Lorenzo	28	5	66	8
2005–06	Espanyol	27	2		
2006–07	Espanyol	21	0		
2007–08	Espanyol	32	1	80	3
2008–09	Manchester C	29	1		
2009–10	Manchester C	27	0		
2010–11	Manchester C	26	2		
2011–12	Manchester C	21	1		
2012–13	Manchester C	30	2		
2013–14	Manchester C	35	1		
2014–15	Manchester C	29	1		
2015–16	Manchester C	13	0	210	8

ZUCULINI, Bruno (M)   8   0
H: 5 10   W: 11 05   b. 2-4-93
Internationals: Argentina U20.

2014–15	Racing Club	0	0		
2014–15	Manchester C	0	0		
2014–15	Valencia	0	0		
2014–15	Cordoba	0	0		
2015–16	Manchester C	0	0		
2015–16	*Middlesbrough*	5	0	5	0
2015–16	*AEK Athens*	3	0	3	0

Players retained or with offer of contract
Adjei-Boateng, Bismark; Aygepong, Thomas;
Boadu-Adjei, Denzeil; Bryan, Kean Shay;
Byrne, Jack; Bytyqi, Sinan; Denayer, Jason;
Diallo, Sadou; Dilrosun, Javairo Joreno
Faustino; Faour, Zackarias; Fernandes

Cantin, Paolo; Fofana, Seko Mohamed;
Haug, Christian Kjetil; Kongolo, Rodney;
Lejeune, Florian Gregoire Claude; Muric,
Arijanet Anan; Naah, Divine Yelsarmba;
Nemane, Aaron Evans; Ntcham, Jules
Olivier; Nwakali, Chidiebere Chikioke;
O'Brien, Billy Thomas; Oliver, Charles
William Corrigan; Sarmiento Martinez, Erik;
Smith-Brown, Ashley; Sobrino Pozuelo,
Ruben; Tanor, Collins; Yeboah, Yaw.

Scholars
Abdelkader Diaz, Brahim; Beerman, Myles;
Blackshaw, Lewis Robert; Buckley-ricketts,
Isaac; Bullock, Callum; Coveney, Joseph
Charles; Davenport, Jacob Alexander;
Duhaney, Demeaco; Grimshaw, Daniel
James; Hardy, Joseph Keith; Kigbu,
Ahogrenashinme; Nmecha, Lukas;
O'Driscoll, Aaron; Patching, William Luke.

MANCHESTER U (49)

ANDER HERRERA, Aguera (M)   213   21
H: 6 0   W: 10 10   b.Bilbao 14-8-89
Internationals: Spain U20, U21, U23.

2008–09	Real Zaragoza	17	2		
2009–10	Real Zaragoza	30	2		
2010–11	Real Zaragoza	19	1	66	5
2011–12	Athletic Bilbao	32	1		
2012–13	Althetic Bilbao	29	1	29	1
2013–14	Athletic Bilbao	33	5	65	6
2014–15	Manchester U	26	6		
2015–16	Manchester U	27	3	53	9

BLACKETT, Tyler (D)   27   0
H: 6 1   W: 11 12   b.Manchester 2-4-94
Internationals: England U16, U17, U18, U19,
U21.

2012–13	Manchester U	0	0		
2013–14	Manchester U	0	0		
2013–14	*Blackpool*	5	0	5	0
2013–14	*Birmingham C*	8	0	8	0
2014–15	Manchester U	11	0		
2015–16	Manchester U	0	0	11	0
2015–16	*Celtic*	3	0	3	0

BLIND, Daley (M)   179   6
H: 5 11   W: 10 10   b.Amsterdam 9-3-90
Internationals: Netherlands U16, U17, U19,
U21, Full caps.

2008–09	Ajax	5	0		
2009–10	Ajax	0	0		
2009–10	Groningen	17	0	17	0
2010–11	Ajax	10	0		
2011–12	Ajax	21	0		
2012–13	Ajax	34	2		
2013–14	Ajax	29	1		
2014–15	Ajax	3	0	102	3
2014–15	Manchester U	25	2		
2015–16	Manchester U	35	1	60	3

**BORTHWICK-JACKSON,
Cameron (D)**   10   0
H: 6 3   W: 13 10   b.Manchester 2-2-97
Internationals: England U16, U17, U19.

2015–16	Manchester U	10	0	10	0

CARRICK, Michael (M)   499   27
H: 6 1   W: 11 10   b.Wallsend 28-7-81
Internationals: England U18, U21, B, Full
caps.

1998–99	West Ham U	0	0		
1999–2000	West Ham U	8	1		
1999–2000	Swindon T	6	2	6	2
1999–2000	Birmingham C	2	0	2	0
2000–01	West Ham U	33	1		
2001–02	West Ham U	30	2		
2002–03	West Ham U	30	1		
2003–04	West Ham U	35	1		
2004–05	West Ham U	0	0	136	6
2004–05	Tottenham H	29	0		
2005–06	Tottenham H	35	2	64	2
2006–07	Manchester U	33	3		
2007–08	Manchester U	31	2		
2008–09	Manchester U	28	4		
2009–10	Manchester U	30	3		
2010–11	Manchester U	28	0		
2011–12	Manchester U	30	2		
2012–13	Manchester U	36	1		
2013–14	Manchester U	29	1		
2014–15	Manchester U	18	1		
2015–16	Manchester U	28	0	291	17

CASTRO, Joel (G)   6   0
H: 6 2   W: 12 13   b. 28-6-96
Internationals: Switzerland U16, U17.
Portugal U17, U18, U19.

2015–16	Manchester U	0	0		
2015–16	*Rochdale*	6	0	6	0

DARMIAN, Matteo (D)   198   5
H: 6 0   W: 11 00   b.Legnano 2-12-89
Internationals: Italy U17, U18, U19, U20,
U21, Full caps.

2006–07	AC Milan	1	0		
2007–08	AC Milan	0	0		
2008–09	AC Milan	3	0		
2009–10	AC Milan	0	0	4	0
2009–10	Padova	22	1	22	1
2010–11	Palermo	11	0	11	0
2011–12	Torino	33	1		
2012–13	Torino	30	0		
2013–14	Torino	37	0		
2014–15	Torino	33	2	133	3
2015–16	Manchester U	28	1	28	1

DE GEA, David (G)   222   0
H: 6 3   W: 12 13   b.Madrid 7-11-90
Internationals: Spain U15, U17, U19, U20,
U21, U23, Full caps.

2009–10	Atletico Madrid	19	0		
2010–11	Atletico Madrid	38	0	57	0
2011–12	Manchester U	29	0		
2012–13	Manchester U	28	0		
2013–14	Manchester U	37	0		
2014–15	Manchester U	37	0		
2015–16	Manchester U	34	0	165	0

DEPAY, Memphis (F)   119   41
H: 5 10   W: 12 04   b.Moordrecht 13-2-94
Internationals: Netherlands U16, U17, U19,
U21, Full caps.

2011–12	PSV Eindhoven	8	3		
2012–13	PSV Eindhoven	20	2		
2013–14	PSV Eindhoven	32	12		
2014–15	PSV Eindhoven	30	22	90	39
2015–16	Manchester U	29	2	29	2

FELLAINI, Marouane (M)   264   38
H: 6 4   W: 13 05   b.Brussels 22-11-87
Internationals: Belgium U18, U19, U21, Full
caps.

2006–07	Standard Liege	29	0		
2007–08	Standard Liege	30	6		
2008–09	Standard Liege	3	0	62	6
2008–09	Everton	30	8		
2009–10	Everton	23	2		
2010–11	Everton	20	1		
2011–12	Everton	34	3		
2012–13	Everton	31	11		
2013–14	Manchester U	16	0	141	25
2014–15	Manchester U	27	6		
2015–16	Manchester U	18	1	61	7

FLETCHER, Ashley (F)   21   5
H: 5 11   W: 11 05   b.Keighley 12-10-95
Internationals: England U20.

2015–16	Manchester U	0	0		
2015–16	Barnsley	21	5	21	5

FOSU-MENSAH, Timothy (D)   8   0
H: 5 10   W: 10 10   b.Amsterdam 3-1-98
Internationals: Netherlands U16, U17, U19.

2015–16	Manchester U	8	0	8	0

GOSS, Sean (M)   0   0
H: 5 10   W: 11 03   b.Wegberg 1-10-95
Internationals: Germany U16.

2015–16	Manchester U	0	0		

HENDERSON, Dean (G)   0   0
H: 6 3   W: 12 13   b.Whitehaven 12-3-97
Internationals: England U16, U17.

2015–16	Manchester U	0	0		

HERNANDEZ, Javier (F)   261   98
H: 5 8   W: 9 11   b.Guadalajara 1-6-88
Internationals: Mexico U20, Full caps.

2005–06	Tapatio	11	0		
2006–07	Tapatio	12	3		
2006–07	Guadalajara	7	1		
2007–08	Guadalajara	5	0		
2007–08	Tapatio	15	6		
2008–09	Tapatio	7	2	45	11
2008–09	Guadalajara	22	4		
2009–10	Guadalajara	28	21	62	26
2010–11	Manchester U	27	13		
2011–12	Manchester U	28	10		
2012–13	Manchester U	22	10		
2013–14	Manchester U	24	4		
2014–15	Manchester U	1	0		
2014–15	*Real Madrid*	23	7	23	7
2015–16	Manchester U	1	0	103	37
2015–16	Bayer Leverkusen	28	17	28	17

JANUZAJ, Adrian (M) **56 5**
H: 5 11 W: 11 11 b.Brussels 5-2-95
Internationals: Belgium Full caps.

2011–12	Manchester U	0	0		
2012–13	Manchester U	0	0		
2013–14	Manchester U	27	4		
2014–15	Manchester U	18	0		
2015–16	Manchester U	5	1	**50**	**5**
2015–16	*Borussia Dortmund*	6	0	**6**	**0**

JOHNSTONE, Samuel (G) **74 0**
H: 6 0 W: 12 10 b.Preston 25-3-93
Internationals: England U16, U17, U19, U20.

2009–10	Manchester U	0	0		
2010–11	Manchester U	0	0		
2011–12	Manchester U	0	0		
2011–12	*Scunthorpe U*	12	0	**12**	**0**
2012–13	Manchester U	0	0		
2012–13	*Walsall*	7	0	**7**	**0**
2013–14	Manchester U	0	0		
2013–14	*Yeovil T*	1	0	**1**	**0**
2013–14	*Doncaster R*	18	0		
2014–15	Manchester U	0	0		
2014–15	*Doncaster R*	10	0	**28**	**0**
2014–15	*Preston NE*	22	0		
2015–16	Manchester U	0	0		
2015–16	*Preston NE*	4	0	**26**	**0**

JONES, Phil (D) **139 2**
H: 5 11 W: 11 02 b.Preston 21-2-92
Internationals: England U19, U21, Full caps.

2009–10	Blackburn R	9	0		
2010–11	Blackburn R	26	0	**35**	**0**
2011–12	Manchester U	29	1		
2012–13	Manchester U	17	0		
2013–14	Manchester U	26	1		
2014–15	Manchester U	22	0		
2015–16	Manchester U	10	0	**104**	**2**

KEANE, Will (F) **49 4**
H: 6 2 W: 11 05 b.Stockport 11-1-93
Internationals: England U16, U17, U19, U20, U21.

2009–10	Manchester U	0	0		
2010–11	Manchester U	0	0		
2011–12	Manchester U	1	0		
2012–13	Manchester U	0	0		
2013–14	Manchester U	0	0		
2013–14	*Wigan Ath*	4	0	**4**	**0**
2013–14	*QPR*	10	0	**10**	**0**
2014–15	Manchester U	0	0		
2014–15	*Sheffield W*	13	3	**13**	**3**
2015–16	Manchester U	1	0	**2**	**0**
2015–16	*Preston NE*	20	1	**20**	**1**

LINGARD, Jesse (M) **73 15**
H: 5 3 W: 11 11 b.Warrington 15-12-92
Internationals: England U17, U21.

2011–12	Manchester U	0	0		
2012–13	Manchester U	0	0		
2012–13	*Leicester C*	5	0	**5**	**0**
2013–14	Manchester U	0	0		
2013–14	*Birmingham C*	13	6	**13**	**6**
2013–14	*Brighton & HA*	15	3	**15**	**3**
2014–15	Manchester U	1	0		
2014–15	*Derby Co*	14	2	**14**	**2**
2015–16	Manchester U	25	4	**26**	**4**

LOVE, Donald (D) **8 0**
H: 5 10 W: 11 05 b.Rochdale 2-12-94
Internationals: Scotland U17, U19, U21.

2015–16	Manchester U	1	0	**1**	**0**
2015–16	*Wigan Ath*	7	0	**7**	**0**

MARTIAL, Anthony (F) **83 22**
H: 5 11 W: 12 08 b.Massy 5-12-95
Internationals: France U16, U17, U18, U19, U21, Full caps.

2012–13	Lyon	3	0	**3**	**0**
2013–14	Monaco	11	2		
2014–15	Monaco	35	9		
2015–16	Monaco	3	0	**49**	**11**
2015–16	Manchester U	31	11	**31**	**11**

MATA, Juan (M) **336 82**
H: 5 7 W: 11 00 b.Ocon de Villafranca 28-4-88
Internationals: Spain U16, U17, U19, U20, U21, U23, Full caps.

2006–07	Real Madrid B	39	10	**39**	**10**
2007–08	Valencia	24	5		
2008–09	Valencia	37	11		
2009–10	Valencia	35	9		
2010–11	Valencia	33	8	**129**	**33**
2011–12	Chelsea	34	6		
2012–13	Chelsea	35	12		
2013–14	Chelsea	13	0	**82**	**18**
2013–14	Manchester U	15	6		
2014–15	Manchester U	33	9		
2015–16	Manchester U	38	6	**86**	**21**

McNAIR, Paddy (D) **24 0**
H: 5 8 W: 11 05 b.Ballyclare 27-4-95
Internationals: Northern Ireland U16, U17, U19, U21, Full caps.

2011–12	Manchester U	0	0		
2012–13	Manchester U	0	0		
2013–14	Manchester U	0	0		
2014–15	Manchester U	16	0		
2015–16	Manchester U	8	0	**24**	**0**

O'HARA, Kieran (G) **5 0**
b. 22-4-96

2015–16	Manchester U	0	0		
2015–16	*Morecambe*	5	0	**5**	**0**

PEREIRA, Andreas (M) **5 0**
H: 5 10 W: 10 06 b.Duffel 1-1-96
Internationals: Belgium U16, U17. Brazil U17, U20, U23.

2014–15	Manchester U	1	0		
2015–16	Manchester U	4	0	**5**	**0**

POOLE, Regan (D) **15 0**
b.Cardiff 18-6-98
Internationals: Wales U17.

2014–15	Newport Co	11	0		
2015–16	Newport Co	4	0	**15**	**0**
2015–16	Manchester U	0	0		

POWELL, Nick (F) **95 22**
H: 6 0 W: 10 05 b.Crewe 23-3-94
Internationals: England U16, U17, U18, U19, U21.

2010–11	Crewe Alex	17	0		
2011–12	Crewe Alex	38	14	**55**	**14**
2012–13	Manchester U	2	1		
2013–14	Manchester U	0	0		
2013–14	*Wigan Ath*	31	7	**31**	**7**
2014–15	Manchester U	0	0		
2014–15	*Leicester C*	3	0	**3**	**0**
2015–16	Manchester U	1	0	**3**	**1**
2015–16	*Hull C*	3	0	**3**	**0**

RASHFORD, Marcus (F) **11 5**
H: 5 11 W: 11 00 b.Manchester 31-10-97
Internationals: England U16, U18, U20, Full caps.

2015–16	Manchester U	11	5	**11**	**5**

ROJO, Marcos (D) **138 8**
H: 6 2 W: 12 06 b.La Plata 20-3-90
Internationals: Argentina Full caps.

2008–09	Estudiantes	6	1		
2009–10	Estudiantes	18	0		
2010–11	Estudiantes	19	2	**43**	**3**
2011–12	Spartak Moscow	8	0	**8**	**0**
2012–13	Sporting Lisbon	24	1		
2013–14	Sporting Lisbon	25	4	**49**	**5**
2014–15	Manchester U	22	0		
2015–16	Manchester U	16	0	**38**	**0**

ROMERO, Sergio (G) **173 0**
H: 6 4 W: 13 01 b.Yrigoyen 22-2-87
Internationals: Argentina U20, Full caps.

2006–07	Racing Club	5	0	**5**	**0**
2007–08	AZ Alkmaar	12	0		
2008–09	AZ Alkmaar	28	0		
2009–10	AZ Alkmaar	27	0		
2010–11	AZ Alkmaar	23	0		
2011–12	AZ Alkmaar	0	0	**90**	**0**
2011–12	Sampdoria	29	0		
2012–13	Sampdoria	32	0		
2013–14	Sampdoria	0	0		
2013–14	*Monaco*	3	0	**3**	**0**
2014–15	Sampdoria	10	0	**71**	**0**
2015–16	Manchester U	4	0	**4**	**0**

ROONEY, Wayne (F) **435 193**
H: 5 10 W: 12 13 b.Liverpool 24-10-85
Internationals: England U15, U16, U19, Full caps.

2002–03	Everton	33	6		
2003–04	Everton	34	9	**67**	**15**
2004–05	Manchester U	29	11		
2005–06	Manchester U	36	16		
2006–07	Manchester U	35	14		
2007–08	Manchester U	27	12		
2008–09	Manchester U	30	12		
2009–10	Manchester U	32	26		
2010–11	Manchester U	28	11		
2011–12	Manchester U	34	27		
2012–13	Manchester U	27	12		
2013–14	Manchester U	29	17		
2014–15	Manchester U	33	12		
2015–16	Manchester U	28	8	**368**	**178**

ROTHWELL, Joe (M) **7 0**
H: 6 1 W: 12 02 b.Manchester 11-1-95
Internationals: England U16, U17, U19, U20.

2014–15	Manchester U	0	0		
2014–15	*Blackpool*	3	0	**3**	**0**
2015–16	Manchester U	0	0		
2015–16	*Barnsley*	4	0	**4**	**0**

SCHNEIDERLIN, Morgan (M) **265 15**
H: 5 11 W: 11 11 b.Obernai 8-11-89
Internationals: France U16, U17, U18, U19, U20, U21, Full caps.

2007–08	Strasbourg	5	0	**5**	**0**
2008–09	Southampton	30	0		
2009–10	Southampton	37	1		
2010–11	Southampton	27	0		
2011–12	Southampton	42	2		
2012–13	Southampton	36	5		
2013–14	Southampton	33	2		
2014–15	Southampton	26	4	**231**	**14**
2015–16	Manchester U	29	1	**29**	**1**

SCHWEINSTEIGER, Bastian (M) **360 46**
H: 6 0 W: 12 06 b.Kolbermoor 1-8-84
Internationals: Germany U16, U18, U19, U21, Full caps.

2002–03	Bayern Munich	14	0		
2003–04	Bayern Munich	26	4		
2004–05	Bayern Munich	26	3		
2005–06	Bayern Munich	30	3		
2006–07	Bayern Munich	27	4		
2007–08	Bayern Munich	30	1		
2008–09	Bayern Munich	31	5		
2009–10	Bayern Munich	33	2		
2010–11	Bayern Munich	32	4		
2011–12	Bayern Munich	22	3		
2012–13	Bayern Munich	28	7		
2013–14	Bayern Munich	23	4		
2014–15	Bayern Munich	20	5	**342**	**45**
2015–16	Manchester U	18	1	**18**	**1**

SHAW, Luke (D) **81 0**
H: 6 1 W: 11 11 b.Kingston 12-7-95
Internationals: England U16, U17, U21, Full caps.

2011–12	Southampton	0	0		
2012–13	Southampton	25	0		
2013–14	Southampton	35	0	**60**	**0**
2014–15	Manchester U	16	0		
2015–16	Manchester U	5	0	**21**	**0**

SMALLING, Chris (D) **148 6**
H: 6 4 W: 14 02 b.Greenwich 22-11-89
Internationals: England U18, U20, U21, Full caps.

2008–09	Fulham	1	0		
2009–10	Fulham	12	0	**13**	**0**
2010–11	Manchester U	16	0		
2011–12	Manchester U	19	1		
2012–13	Manchester U	15	0		
2013–14	Manchester U	25	1		
2014–15	Manchester U	25	4		
2015–16	Manchester U	35	0	**135**	**6**

TUANZEBE, Axel (D) **0 0**
H: 6 0 W: 11 11 b.Bunia 14-11-97

2015–16	Manchester U	0	0		

VALDES, Victor (G) **394 0**
H: 6 2 W: 12 04 b.L'Hospitalet de Llobregat 14-1-82
Internationals: Spain U18, U19, U20, U21, Full caps.

2002–03	Barcelona	14	0		
2003–04	Barcelona	33	0		
2004–05	Barcelona	35	0		
2005–06	Barcelona	35	0		
2006–07	Barcelona	38	0		
2007–08	Barcelona	35	0		
2008–09	Barcelona	35	0		
2009–10	Barcelona	38	0		
2010–11	Barcelona	32	0		
2011–12	Barcelona	35	0		
2012–13	Barcelona	31	0		
2013–14	Barcelona	26	0	**387**	**0**
2014–15	Manchester U	2	0		
2015–16	Manchester U	0	0	**2**	**0**
2015–16	*Standard Liege*	5	0	**5**	**0**

VALENCIA, Antonio (M) **349 31**
H: 5 10 W: 12 04 b.Lago Agrio 5-8-85
Internationals: Ecuador U20, 21, U23, Full caps.

2002	El Nacional	1	0		
2003	El Nacional	26	2		
2004	El Nacional	42	5		
2005	El Nacional	14	4	**83**	**11**
2005–06	Villarreal	2	0	**2**	**0**
2005–06	*Recreativo*	4	0	**4**	**0**
2006–07	Wigan Ath	22	1		
2007–08	Wigan Ath	31	3		
2008–09	Wigan Ath	31	3	**84**	**7**
2009–10	Manchester U	34	5		
2010–11	Manchester U	10	1		

2011–12	Manchester U	27	4		
2012–13	Manchester U	30	1		
2013–14	Manchester U	29	2		
2014–15	Manchester U	32	0		
2015–16	Manchester U	14	0	176	13

VARELA, Guillermo (D)   4 0
H: 5 7 W: 10 11 b.Montevideo 24-3-93
Internationals: Uruguay U17, U20.

2013–14	Manchester U	0	0		
2014–15	Manchester U	0	0		
2015–16	Manchester U	4	0	4	0

WEIR, James (M)   1 0
H: 5 10 W: 11 03 b.Preston 4-8-95
Internationals: England U18, U19.

2014–15	Manchester U	0	0		
2015–16	Manchester U	1	0	1	0

WILLIAMS, Ro-Shaun (M)   0 0
b. 9-3-98
Internationals: England U17, U18.

2015–16	Manchester U	0	0		

WILSON, James (F)   40 8
H: 6 0 W: 12 04 b.Biddulph 1-12-95
Internationals: England U16, U19, U20, U21.

2013–14	Manchester U	1	2		
2014–15	Manchester U	13	1		
2015–16	Manchester U	1	0	15	3
2015–16	Brighton & HA	25	5	25	5

YOUNG, Ashley (M)   363 60
H: 5 10 W: 10 03 b.Stevenage 9-7-85
Internationals: England U21, Full caps.

2002–03	Watford	0	0		
2003–04	Watford	5	3		
2004–05	Watford	34	0		
2005–06	Watford	39	13		
2006–07	Watford	20	3	98	19
2006–07	Aston Villa	13	2		
2007–08	Aston Villa	37	9		
2008–09	Aston Villa	36	7		
2009–10	Aston Villa	36	5		
2010–11	Aston Villa	34	7	157	30
2011–12	Manchester U	25	6		
2012–13	Manchester U	19	0		
2013–14	Manchester U	20	2		
2014–15	Manchester U	26	2		
2015–16	Manchester U	18	1	108	11

Players retained or with offer of contract
Dearnley, Zachary Harry; Doughty, Joshua
Anders; El-Fitouri, Sadik; Gribbin, Callum
Anthony; Hamilton, Ethan Billy; Harrop,
Joshua Andrew; Herrera Aguera, Ander;
McIntosh-Buffonge, Darren Raekwon;
Mctominay, Scott; Mitchell, Demetri Karim;
Olosunde, Matthew Olawale; Reid, Tyler;
Riley, Joe; Warren, Tyrell Nathaniel; Willock,
Matthew.

Scholars
Boonen, Indy Zeb Pepe; Diedrick-Roberts,
Kayne Leevi; Dunne, James Gerard;
Kehinde, Tosin Samuel; Kenyon, Jake Barry;
Makela, Faustin; Moutha-Sebtaoui, Ilias;
Redmond, Devonte Vincent; Scott, Charlie
Thomas; Whelan, Callum Tyler.

MANSFIELD T (50)

BAXENDALE, James (M)   121 8
H: 5 8 W: 10 03 b.Thorne 16-9-92

2011–12	Doncaster R	2	0		
2011–12	Hereford U	1	0	1	0
2012–13	Doncaster R	0	0	2	0
2012–13	Walsall	32	4		
2013–14	Walsall	40	2		
2014–15	Walsall	28	1		
2015–16	Walsall	3	0	103	7
2015–16	Mansfield T	15	1	15	1

BEARDSLEY, Chris (F)   202 21
H: 6 0 W: 12 12 b.Derby 28-2-84

2002–03	Mansfield T	5	0		
2003–04	Mansfield T	15	1		
2004–05	Doncaster R	4	0	4	0
2004–05	Kidderminster H	25	5	25	5
2005–06	Mansfield T	3	0		
2006–07	Mansfield T	10	0		

From Rushden & D, York C, Kettering T.

2010–11	Stevenage	23	1		
2011–12	Stevenage	31	7		
2012–13	Preston NE	19	1		
2013–14	Preston NE	0	0	19	1
2013–14	Bristol R	24	1	24	1
2014–15	Stevenage	29	4	83	12
2015–16	Mansfield T	14	1	47	2

BENNING, Malvind (D)   86 6
H: 5 10 W: 12 00 b.Sandwell 2-11-93

2012–13	Walsall	10	0		
2013–14	Walsall	16	2		
2014–15	Walsall	20	0	46	2
2014–15	York C	9	0	9	0
2015–16	Mansfield T	31	4	31	4

BISHOP, Adam (G)   0 0
b. 12-6-98

2014–15	Mansfield T	0	0		
2015–16	Mansfield T	0	0		

BLAIR, Matty (M)   116 12
H: 5 10 W: 11 09 b.Coventry 30-11-87
Internationals: England C.

2012–13	York C	44	6	44	6
2013–14	Fleetwood T	24	3		
2013–14	Northampton T	3	1	3	1
2014–15	Fleetwood T	8	0	32	3
2014–15	Cambridge U	2	0	2	0
2014–15	Mansfield T	3	0		
2015–16	Mansfield T	32	2	35	2

CHAPMAN, Adam (M)   152 8
H: 5 10 W: 11 00 b.Doncaster 29-11-89
Internationals: Northern Ireland U21.

2008–09	Sheffield U	0	0		
2009–10	Sheffield U	0	0		
2010–11	Oxford U	0	0		
2011–12	Oxford U	14	1		
2012–13	Oxford U	26	1	40	2
2013–14	Mansfield T	0	0		
2013–14	Newport Co	39	1		
2014–15	Newport Co	36	3	75	4
2015–16	Mansfield T	37	2	37	2

CLEMENTS, Chris (M)   110 8
H: 5 9 W: 10 04 b.Birmingham 6-2-90

2008–09	Crewe Alex	0	0		
2009	IBV	15	1	15	1
2009–10	Crewe Alex	0	0		
2010–11	Crewe Alex	0	0		
2013–14	Mansfield T	23	1		
2014–15	Mansfield T	34	1		
2015–16	Mansfield T	38	5	95	7

COLLINS, Lee (D)   282 5
H: 6 1 W: 11 10 b.Telford 23-9-83

2006–07	Wolverhampton W	0	0		
2007–08	Wolverhampton W	0	0		
2007–08	Hereford U	16	0	16	0
2008–09	Wolverhampton W	0	0		
2008–09	Port Vale	39	1		
2009–10	Port Vale	45	1		
2010–11	Port Vale	42	2		
2011–12	Port Vale	16	0	142	4
2011–12	Barnsley	7	0		
2012–13	Barnsley	0	0	7	0
2012–13	Shrewsbury T	8	0	8	0
2012–13	Northampton T	15	0		
2013–14	Northampton T	22	1		
2014–15	Northampton T	37	0	74	1
2015–16	Mansfield T	35	0	35	0

FITZPATRICK, Joe (M)   3 0
b. 20-8-97

2014–15	Mansfield T	3	0		
2015–16	Mansfield T	0	0	3	0

FLETCHER, Dan (F)   1 0
b. 4-3-97

2014–15	Mansfield T	1	0		
2015–16	Mansfield T	0	0	1	0

GREEN, Matt (F)   100 17
H: 6 0 W: 12 09 b.Bath 2-1-87

2006–07	Cardiff C	6	0		
2007–08	Cardiff C	0	0		
2007–08	Darlington	4	0	4	0

From Torquay U

2010–11	Oxford U	17	0	17	0
2010–11	Cheltenham T	19	0	19	0

From Mansfield T

2013–14	Birmingham C	10	1		
2014–15	Birmingham C	0	0	10	1
2015–16	Mansfield T	44	16	44	16

HAKEEM, Zayn (M)   1 0
b. 15-2-99

2015–16	Mansfield T	1	0	1	0

JENSEN, Brian (G)   399 0
H: 6 1 W: 12 10 b.Copenhagen 8-6-75

1997–98	AZ	0	0		
1998–99	AZ	1	0	1	0
1999–2000	WBA	12	0		
2000–01	WBA	33	0		
2001–02	WBA	1	0		
2002–03	WBA	0	0	46	0
2003–04	Burnley	46	0		
2004–05	Burnley	27	0		
2005–06	Burnley	39	0		
2006–07	Burnley	31	0		
2007–08	Burnley	19	0		
2008–09	Burnley	45	0		
2009–10	Burnley	38	0		
2010–11	Burnley	21	0		
2011–12	Burnley	4	0		
2012–13	Burnley	1	0	271	0
2013–14	Bury	36	0	36	0
2014–15	Crawley T	20	0	20	0
2015–16	Mansfield T	25	0	25	0

JONES, Luke (D)   48 0
H: 6 0 W: 13 04 b.Darwen 10-4-87

2005–06	Blackburn R	0	0		
2005–06	Cercle Brugge	8	0	8	0
2006–07	Shrewsbury T	7	0		
2007–08	Shrewsbury T	7	0	14	0

From Kidderminster H, Mansfield T, Forest
Green R

2013–14	Stevenage	26	0	26	0
2014–15	Mansfield T	0	0		
2015–16	Mansfield T	0	0		

LAMBE, Reggie (M)   141 13
H: 5 7 W: 10 09 b.Bermuda 4-2-91
Internationals: Bermuda Full caps.

2009–10	Ipswich T	0	0		
2010–11	Ipswich T	2	0	2	0
2010–11	Bristol R	7	0	7	0
2012	Toronto	27	2		
2013	Toronto	27	0	54	2
2014	Nykoping	11	1	11	1
2014–15	Mansfield T	30	5		
2015–16	Mansfield T	37	5	67	10

LAW, Jason (F)   0 0

2015–16	Mansfield T	0	0		

MARSDEN, Liam (D)   12 0
b.Creswell 21-11-94

2013–14	Mansfield T	2	0		
2014–15	Mansfield T	10	0		
2015–16	Mansfield T	0	0	12	0

McGUIRE, Jamie (M)   113 4
H: 5 7 W: 10 13 b.Birkenhead 13-11-83

2001–02	Tranmere R	0	0		
2002–03	Tranmere R	0	0		
2003–04	Tranmere R	0	0		

From Northwich Vic (loan), Droylsden

2012–13	Fleetwood T	37	1	37	1
2013–14	Mansfield T	27	2		
2014–15	Mansfield T	29	1		
2015–16	Mansfield T	20	0	76	3

MURRAY, Adam (M)   250 18
H: 5 9 W: 10 01 b.Birmingham 30-9-81

1998–99	Derby Co	4	0		
1999–2000	Derby Co	8	0		
2000–01	Derby Co	14	0		
2001–02	Derby Co	6	0		
2001–02	Mansfield T	13	7		
2002–03	Derby Co	24	0	56	0
2003–04	Kidderminster H	22	3	22	3

From Burton Alb

2003–04	Notts Co	3	0	3	0
2004–05	Mansfield T	32	5		
2005–06	Carlisle U	37	1	37	1
2006–07	Torquay U	21	0	21	0
2006–07	Macclesfield U	11	0		
2007–08	Macclesfield T	23	0	34	0

From Oxford U, Luton T

2013–14	Mansfield T	18	1		
2014–15	Mansfield T	14	1		
2015–16	Mansfield T	0	0	77	14

PEARCE, Krystian (D)   208 14
H: 6 1 W: 13 05 b.Birmingham 5-1-90
Internationals: England U17, U19.

2006–07	Birmingham C	0	0		
2007–08	Birmingham C	0	0		
2007–08	Port Vale	12	0	12	0
2007–08	Notts Co	8	1		
2008–09	Birmingham C	0	0		
2008–09	Scunthorpe U	39	0	39	0
2009–10	Birmingham C	0	0		
2009–10	Peterborough U	2	0	2	0
2009–10	Huddersfield T	1	0	1	0
2010–11	Notts Co	27	1		
2011–12	Notts Co	27	3		
2012–13	Notts Co	2	1	64	6
2012–13	Barnet	17	1	17	1
2013–14	Torquay U	35	4	35	4
2015–16	Mansfield T	38	3	38	3

ROSE, Mitchell (M)   40 2
H: 5 9 W: 12 03 b. 4-7-94

2012–13	Rotherham U	5	0		

2013–14	Rotherham U	0	0		
2014–15	Rotherham U	0	0	**5**	**0**
2014–15	*Crawley T*	1	0	**1**	**0**
2015–16	Mansfield T	34	2	**34**	**2**

SHEARER, Scott (G)   **310**   **0**
H: 6 3 W: 12 00 b.Glasgow 15-2-81
Internationals: Scotland B.

2000–01	Albion R	3	0		
2001–02	Albion R	10	0		
2002–03	Albion R	36	0	**49**	**0**
2003–04	Coventry C	30	0		
2004–05	Coventry C	8	0	**38**	**0**
2004–05	*Rushden & D*	13	0	**13**	**0**
2005–06	Bristol R	45	0		
2006–07	Bristol R	2	0	**47**	**0**
2006–07	*Shrewsbury T*	20	0	**20**	**0**
2007–08	Wycombe W	5	0		
2008–09	Wycombe W	29	0		
2009–10	Wycombe W	29	0		
2010–11	Wycombe W	0	0	**63**	**0**
2011–12	Crawley T	25	0	**25**	**0**
2012–13	Rotherham U	19	0		
2013–14	Rotherham U	12	0	**31**	**0**
2014–15	*Crewe Alex*	2	0	**2**	**0**
2014–15	*Burton Alb*	1	0	**1**	**0**
2015–16	Mansfield T	21	0	**21**	**0**

SHIRES, Corbin (D)   **1**   **0**
b. 31-12-97

| 2014–15 | Mansfield T | 1 | 0 | | |
| 2015–16 | Mansfield T | 0 | 0 | **1** | **0** |

SMITH, Cain (M)   **0**   **0**
b. 3-12-98

| 2015–16 | Mansfield T | 0 | 0 | | |

SPENCER, Chris (M)   **0**   **0**
b. 13-11-96

| 2015–16 | Mansfield T | 0 | 0 | | |

TAFAZOLLI, Ryan (D)   **104**   **8**
H: 6 5 W: 12 3 b.Sutton 28-9-91

| 2010–11 | Southampton | 0 | 0 | | |

From Salisbury, Cambridge C, Carshalton Ath

2013–14	Mansfield T	24	2		
2014–15	Mansfield T	36	1		
2015–16	Mansfield T	44	5	**104**	**8**

THOMAS, Jack (M)   **46**   **3**
H: 5 9 W: 10 10 b.Sutton-in-Ashfield 3-6-96

2013–14	Mansfield T	1	0		
2014–15	Mansfield T	12	1		
2015–16	Mansfield T	33	2	**46**	**3**

WESTCARR, Craig (F)   **297**   **61**
H: 5 11 W: 11 04 b.Nottingham 29-1-85
Internationals: England U18.

2001–02	Nottingham F	8	0		
2002–03	Nottingham F	11	1		
2003–04	Nottingham F	3	0		
2004–05	Nottingham F	1	0	**23**	**1**
2004–05	*Lincoln C*	6	1	**6**	**1**
2004–05	*Milton Keynes D*	4	0	**4**	**0**

From Cambridge U, Kettering T.

2009–10	Notts Co	42	9		
2010–11	Notts Co	41	12		
2011–12	Notts Co	4	0	**87**	**21**
2011–12	Chesterfield	38	8		
2012–13	Chesterfield	15	2	**53**	**10**
2012–13	Walsall	24	5		
2013–14	Walsall	43	14	**67**	**19**
2014–15	Portsmouth	33	6	**33**	**6**
2015–16	Mansfield T	24	3	**24**	**3**

YUSSUF, Abdi (F)   **51**   **6**
H: 6 1 W: 11 13 b.Zanzibar 3-10-92

2010–11	Leicester C	0	0		
2011–12	Burton Alb	17	1		
2012–13	Burton Alb	8	0	**25**	**1**

From Lincoln C, Oxford C.

| 2015–16 | Mansfield T | 26 | 5 | **26** | **5** |

Scholars
Bloor, Teddy John; Hakeem, Mohammed Zayn Junayd; Holmes Harrison, Kieran; Marriott, Tom William; Reittie, Devante Paul; Smith, Cain; Wilson, Samuel John.

MIDDLESBROUGH (51)

ADOMAH, Albert (F)   **371**   **59**
H: 6 1 W: 11 08 b.Lambeth 13-12-87
Internationals: Ghana Full caps.

2007–08	Barnet	22	5		
2008–09	Barnet	45	9		
2009–10	Barnet	45	5	**112**	**19**
2010–11	Bristol R	46	5		
2011–12	Bristol C	45	5		
2012–13	Bristol C	40	7		
2013–14	Bristol C	0	0	**131**	**17**
2013–14	Middlesbrough	42	12		
2014–15	Middlesbrough	43	5		
2015–16	Middlesbrough	43	6	**128**	**23**

AGAZZI, Michael (G)   **249**   **0**
H: 6 2 W: 12 08 b.Ponte San Pietro 3-7-84

2005–06	Triestina	5	0		
2006–07	Triestina	0	0		
2006–07	*Sassuolo*	22	0	**22**	**0**
2007–08	Triestina	0	0		
2007–08	*Foggia*	26	0	**26**	**0**
2008–09	Triestina	42	0		
2009–10	Triestina	18	0	**65**	**0**
2009–10	Cagliari	3	0		
2010–11	Cagliari	38	0		
2011–12	Cagliari	36	0		
2012–13	Cagliari	34	0		
2013–14	Cagliari	11	0	**122**	**0**
2013–14	*Chievo*	14	0	**14**	**0**
2014–15	AC Milan	0	0		
2014–15	AC Milan	0	0		

On loan from AC Milan.

| 2015–16 | Middlesbrough | 0 | 0 | | |

AYALA, Daniel (M)   **137**   **12**
H: 6 3 W: 13 03 b.Sevilla 7-11-90
Internationals: Spain U21.

2007–08	Liverpool	0	0		
2008–09	Liverpool	0	0		
2009–10	Liverpool	5	0		
2010–11	Liverpool	0	0	**5**	**0**
2010–11	*Hull C*	12	1	**12**	**1**
2010–11	*Derby Co*	17	0	**17**	**0**
2011–12	Norwich C	7	0		
2012–13	Norwich C	0	0		
2012–13	*Nottingham F*	12	1	**12**	**1**
2013–14	Norwich C	0	0	**7**	**0**
2013–14	Middlesbrough	19	3		
2014–15	Middlesbrough	30	4		
2015–16	Middlesbrough	35	3	**84**	**10**

BAPTISTE, Alex (D)   **426**   **21**
H: 6 0 W: 11 11 b.Sutton-in-Ashfield 31-1-86

2002–03	Mansfield T	4	0		
2003–04	Mansfield T	17	0		
2004–05	Mansfield T	41	1		
2005–06	Mansfield T	41	1		
2006–07	Mansfield T	46	3		
2007–08	Mansfield T	25	0	**174**	**5**
2008–09	Blackpool	21	1		
2009–10	Blackpool	42	3		
2010–11	Blackpool	21	2		
2011–12	Blackpool	43	1		
2012–13	Blackpool	43	1	**170**	**8**
2013–14	Bolton W	39	4		
2014–15	Bolton W	0	0	**39**	**4**
2014–15	*Blackburn R*	32	3	**32**	**3**
2015–16	Middlesbrough	0	0		
2015–16	*Sheffield U*	11	1	**11**	**1**

CARAYOL, Mustapha (F)   **165**   **28**
H: 5 10 W: 11 11 b.Gambia 10-6-89
Internationals: Gambia Full caps.

2007–08	Milton Keynes D	0	0		
2009–10	Torquay U	20	6	**20**	**6**
2010–11	Lincoln C	33	3	**33**	**3**
2011–12	Bristol R	30	4		
2012–13	Bristol R	0	0	**30**	**4**
2012–13	Middlesbrough	18	3		
2013–14	Middlesbrough	32	8		
2014–15	Middlesbrough	0	0		
2014–15	*Brighton & HA*	5	0	**5**	**0**
2015–16	Middlesbrough	0	0	**50**	**11**
2015–16	*Huddersfield T*	15	3	**15**	**3**
2015–16	*Leeds U*	12	1	**12**	**1**

CHAPMAN, Harry (M)   **11**   **1**
H: 5 10 W: 11 00 b.Hartlepool 5-11-97
Internationals: England U18.

| 2015–16 | Middlesbrough | 0 | 0 | | |
| 2015–16 | *Barnsley* | 11 | 1 | **11** | **1** |

CLAYTON, Adam (M)   **257**   **20**
H: 5 9 W: 11 11 b.Manchester 14-1-89
Internationals: England U20.

2007–08	Manchester C	0	0		
2008–09	Manchester C	0	0		
2009–10	Manchester C	0	0		
2009–10	*Carlisle U*	28	1	**28**	**1**
2010–11	Leeds U	4	0		
2010–11	*Peterborough U*	7	0	**7**	**0**
2010–11	*Milton Keynes D*	6	1	**6**	**1**
2011–12	Leeds U	43	6	**47**	**6**
2012–13	Huddersfield T	43	4		
2013–14	Huddersfield T	42	7	**85**	**11**

| 2014–15 | Middlesbrough | 41 | 0 | | |
| 2015–16 | Middlesbrough | 43 | 1 | **84** | **1** |

DE PENA, Carlos (M)   **64**   **15**
b. 11-3-92

2012–13	Nacional	6	1		
2013–14	Nacional	24	3		
2014–15	Nacional	26	9		
2015–16	Nacional	2	2	**58**	**15**
2015–16	Middlesbrough	6	0	**6**	**0**

DE SART, Julien (M)   **64**   **3**
H: 6 0 W: 10 10 b.Waremme 23-12-94
Internationals: Belgium U16, U17, U18, U19, U21.

2013–14	Standard Liege	24	2		
2014–15	Standard Liege	26	1		
2015–16	Standard Liege	12	0	**62**	**3**
2015–16	Middlesbrough	2	0	**2**	**0**

DOWNING, Stewart (M)   **430**   **42**
H: 5 11 W: 10 04 b.Middlesbrough 22-7-84
Internationals: England U21, B, Full caps.

2001–02	Middlesbrough	3	0		
2002–03	Middlesbrough	2	0		
2003–04	Middlesbrough	20	0		
2003–04	*Sunderland*	7	3	**7**	**3**
2004–05	Middlesbrough	35	5		
2005–06	Middlesbrough	12	1		
2006–07	Middlesbrough	34	2		
2007–08	Middlesbrough	38	9		
2008–09	Middlesbrough	37	0		
2009–10	Aston Villa	25	2		
2010–11	Aston Villa	38	7	**63**	**9**
2011–12	Liverpool	36	0		
2012–13	Liverpool	29	3		
2013–14	Liverpool	0	0	**65**	**3**
2013–14	West Ham U	32	1		
2014–15	West Ham U	37	6	**69**	**7**
2015–16	Middlesbrough	45	3	**226**	**20**

FEWSTER, Bradley (F)   **24**   **8**
H: 5 10 W: 11 00 b. 27-1-96
Internationals: England U16, U17, U18, U19.

2013–14	Middlesbrough	0	0		
2014–15	Middlesbrough	0	0		
2014–15	*Preston NE*	0	0		
2015–16	Middlesbrough	0	0		
2015–16	*York C*	24	8	**24**	**8**

FORSHAW, Adam (M)   **153**   **14**
H: 6 1 W: 11 02 b.Liverpool 8-10-91

2009–10	Everton	0	0		
2010–11	Everton	1	0		
2011–12	Everton	0	0	**1**	**0**
2011–12	Brentford	7	0		
2012–13	Brentford	43	3		
2013–14	Brentford	39	8	**89**	**11**
2014–15	Wigan Ath	16	1	**16**	**1**
2014–15	Middlesbrough	18	0		
2015–16	Middlesbrough	29	2	**47**	**2**

FRIEND, George (D)   **256**   **8**
H: 6 2 W: 13 01 b.Barnstaple 19-10-87

2008–09	Exeter C	4	0		
2008–09	Wolverhampton W	6	0		
2009–10	Wolverhampton W	1	0	**7**	**0**
2009–10	*Millwall*	6	0	**6**	**0**
2009–10	*Southend U*	6	1	**6**	**1**
2009–10	*Scunthorpe U*	4	0	**4**	**0**
2009–10	*Exeter C*	13	1	**17**	**1**
2010–11	Doncaster R	32	1		
2011–12	Doncaster R	27	0		
2012–13	Doncaster R	0	0	**59**	**1**
2012–13	Middlesbrough	34	0		
2013–14	Middlesbrough	41	3		
2014–15	Middlesbrough	42	1		
2015–16	Middlesbrough	40	1	**157**	**5**

FRY, Dael (D)   **7**   **0**
b. 30-8-97
Internationals: England U17, U18, U19.

| 2015–16 | Middlesbrough | 7 | 0 | **7** | **0** |

GARCIA, Enrique (F)   **209**   **61**
b.Motilla del Palancar 25-11-89
Internationals: Spain U20.

2008–09	Murcia	3	1		
2009–10	Murcia	30	3		
2010–11	Murcia	34	12		
2011–12	Murcia	2	1		
2012–13	Murcia	36	8		
2013–14	Murcia	43	23	**148**	**48**
2014–15	Middlesbrough	42	9		
2015–16	Middlesbrough	19	4	**61**	**13**

Transferred to Eibar February 2016.

GIBSON, Ben (D)   **143**   **3**
H: 6 1 W: 12 04 b.Nunthorpe 15-1-93
Internationals: England U17, U18, U20, U21.

| 2010–11 | Middlesbrough | 1 | 0 | | |

2011–12	Middlesbrough	0	0		
2011–12	*Plymouth Arg*	13	0	13	0
2012–13	Middlesbrough	1	0		
2012–13	*Tranmere R*	28	1	28	1
2013–14	Middlesbrough	31	1		
2014–15	Middlesbrough	36	0		
2015–16	Middlesbrough	33	1	102	2

HALLIDAY, Bradley (M)   62   1
b.Redcar 10-7-95

2011–12	Middlesbrough	0	0		
2014–15	Middlesbrough	0	0		
2014–15	*York C*	24	1	24	1
2015–16	Middlesbrough	0	0		
2015–16	*Hartlepool U*	6	0	6	0
2015–16	*Accrington S*	32	0	32	0

HUSBAND, James (D)   95   4
H: 5 10   W: 10 00   b.Leeds 3-1-94

2011–12	Doncaster R	3	0		
2012–13	Doncaster R	33	3		
2013–14	Doncaster R	28	1	64	4
2014–15	Middlesbrough	3	0		
2014–15	Fulham	5	0		
2015–16	Middlesbrough	0	0	3	0
2015–16	Fulham	12	0	17	0
2015–16	*Huddersfield T*	11	0	11	0

JACKSON, Adam (D)   29   3
b.Darlington 18-5-94
Internationals: England U16, U17, U18, U19.

2011–12	Middlesbrough	0	0		
2012–13	Middlesbrough	0	0		
2013–14	Middlesbrough	0	0		
2014–15	Middlesbrough	0	0		
2015–16	Middlesbrough	0	0		
2015–16	Coventry C	0	0		
2015–16	*Hartlepool U*	29	3	29	3

JONES, Jordan (M)   12   0
H: 5 8   W: 9 07   b.Kettering 24-10-94

2012–13	Middlesbrough	0	0		
2013–14	Middlesbrough	0	0		
2014–15	Middlesbrough	0	0		
2014–15	*Hartlepool U*	11	0	11	0
2015–16	Middlesbrough	0	0		
2015–16	*Cambridge U*	1	0	1	0

KIKE SOLA, Clemente (F)   126   24
H: 6 0   W: 13 12   b.Tudela 25-2-86
Internationals: Spain U21.

2005–06	Osasuna	0	0		
2006–07	Osasuna	2	2		
2007–08	Osasuna	20	3		
2008–09	Osasuna	16	0		
2009–10	Osasuna	0	0		
2009–10	*Levadiakos*	10	1	10	1
2009–10	*Numancia*	7	1	7	1
2010–11	Osasuna	16	7		
2011–12	Osasuna	7	0		
2012–13	Osasuna	31	9	92	21
2013–14	Athletic Bilbao	5	1		
2014–15	Athletic Bilbao	5	0		
2015–16	Athletic Bilbao	5	0	15	1

On loan from Athletic Bilbao.

2015–16	Middlesbrough	2	0	2	0

KITCHING, Mark (D)   1   0
b.Guisborough 4-9-95

2013–14	Middlesbrough	0	0		
2014–15	Middlesbrough	0	0		
2015–16	Middlesbrough	0	0		
2015–16	*York C*	1	0	1	0

KONSTANTOPOULOS, Dimitrios (G)   312   0
H: 6 4   W: 14 02   b.Kalamata 29-11-78
Internationals: Greece U21, Full caps.

2003–04	Hartlepool U	0	0		
2004–05	Hartlepool U	25	0		
2005–06	Hartlepool U	46	0		
2006–07	Hartlepool U	46	0	117	0
2007–08	Coventry C	21	0		
2008–09	Coventry C	0	0		
2008–09	*Swansea C*	4	0	4	0
2008–09	*Cardiff C*	6	0	6	0
2009–10	Coventry C	3	0	24	0
2010–11	*Kerkyra*	30	0	30	0
2011–12	AEK Athens	9	0		
2012–13	AEK Athens	24	0	33	0
2013–14	Middlesbrough	12	0		
2014–15	Middlesbrough	40	0		
2015–16	Middlesbrough	46	0	98	0

LEADBITTER, Grant (M)   397   49
H: 5 9   W: 11 06   b.Chester-le-Street 7-1-86
Internationals: England U16, U17, U19, U20, U21.

2002–03	Sunderland	0	0		
2003–04	Sunderland	0	0		
2004–05	Sunderland	0	0		
2005–06	Sunderland	12	0		
2005–06	*Rotherham U*	5	1	5	1
2006–07	Sunderland	44	7		
2007–08	Sunderland	31	2		
2008–09	Sunderland	23	2		
2009–10	Sunderland	1	0	111	11
2009–10	Ipswich T	38	3		
2010–11	Ipswich T	44	5		
2011–12	Ipswich T	34	5		
2012–13	Ipswich T	0	0	116	13
2012–13	Middlesbrough	42	3		
2013–14	Middlesbrough	39	6		
2014–15	Middlesbrough	43	11		
2015–16	Middlesbrough	41	4	165	24

MALONEY, Lewis (D)   0   0
b. 5-5-95

2015–16	Middlesbrough	0	0

MEJIAS, Tomas (G)   9   0
H: 6 5   W: 13 02   b.Madrid 30-1-89
Internationals: Spain U19, U20.

2010–11	Real Madrid	0	0		
2011–12	Real Madrid	0	0		
2012–13	Real Madrid	0	0		
2013–14	Real Madrid	0	0	1	0
2013–14	*Middlesbrough*	1	0		
2014–15	Middlesbrough	7	0		
2015–16	Middlesbrough	0	0	8	0

MORRIS, Bryn (M)   17   0
H: 6 0   W: 11 01   b.Hartlepool 25-4-96
Internationals: England U16, U17, U18, U19.

2012–13	Middlesbrough	1	0		
2013–14	Middlesbrough	1	0		
2014–15	Middlesbrough	0	0		
2014–15	*Burton Alb*	5	0	5	0
2015–16	Middlesbrough	0	0	2	0
2015–16	Coventry C	6	0	6	0
2015–16	*York C*	3	0	3	0
2015–16	*Walsall*	1	0	1	0

NSUE, Emilio (F)   279   28
H: 5 10   W: 11 11   b.Palma 30-9-89
Internationals: Spain U16, U17, U19, U20, U21. Equatorial Guinea Full caps.

2007–08	Mallorca	2	0		
2008–09	Mallorca	0	0		
2008–09	*Castellon*	37	7	37	7
2009–10	Mallorca	0	0		
2009–10	*Real Sociedad*	34	5	34	5
2010–11	Mallorca	38	4		
2011–12	Mallorca	30	3		
2012–13	Mallorca	32	2		
2013–14	Mallorca	40	4	142	13
2014–15	Middlesbrough	26	0		
2015–16	Middlesbrough	40	3	66	3

NUGENT, Dave (F)   487   135
H: 5 11   W: 12 13   b.Liverpool 2-5-85
Internationals: England U20, U21, Full caps.

2001–02	Bury	5	0		
2002–03	Bury	31	4		
2003–04	Bury	26	3		
2004–05	Bury	26	11	88	18
2004–05	Preston NE	18	8		
2005–06	Preston NE	32	10		
2006–07	Preston NE	44	15	94	33
2007–08	Portsmouth	15	0		
2008–09	Portsmouth	16	3		
2009–10	Portsmouth	3	0		
2009–10	*Burnley*	30	6	30	6
2010–11	Portsmouth	44	13	78	16
2011–12	Leicester C	42	15		
2012–13	Leicester C	42	14		
2013–14	Leicester C	46	20		
2014–15	Leicester C	29	5	159	54
2015–16	Middlesbrough	38	8	38	8

REACH, Adam (M)   138   16
H: 6 1   W: 11 07   b.Gateshead 3-2-93
Internationals: England U19, U20.

2010–11	Middlesbrough	1	1		
2011–12	Middlesbrough	1	0		
2012–13	Middlesbrough	16	2		
2013–14	Middlesbrough	2	0		
2013–14	*Shrewsbury T*	22	3	22	3
2013–14	*Bradford C*	18	3	18	3
2014–15	Middlesbrough	39	2		
2015–16	Middlesbrough	4	1	63	6
2015–16	*Preston NE*	35	4	35	4

RHODES, Jordan (F)   330   171
H: 6 1   W: 11 03   b.Oldham 5-2-90
Internationals: Scotland U21, Full caps.

2007–08	Ipswich T	8	1		
2008–09	Ipswich T	2	0	10	1
2008–09	*Rochdale*	5	2	5	2
2008–09	*Brentford*	14	7	14	7
2009–10	Huddersfield T	45	19		
2010–11	Huddersfield T	37	16		
2011–12	Huddersfield T	40	35		
2012–13	Huddersfield T	2	2	124	72
2012–13	Blackburn R	43	27		
2013–14	Blackburn R	46	25		
2014–15	Blackburn R	45	21		
2015–16	Blackburn R	25	10	159	83
2015–16	Middlesbrough	18	6	18	6

STUANI, Christian (F)   308   108
H: 6 0   W: 11 05   b. 12-10-86
Internationals: Uruguay Full caps.

2003–04	Danubio	2	0		
2004–05	Danubio	5	0		
2005–06	Danubio	15	4		
2006–07	Danubio	0	0		
2006–07	*Bella Vista*	14	12	14	12
2007–08	Danubio	14	19	36	23
2008–09	Reggina	12	0		
2008–09	Reggina	6	1		
2009–10	Reggina	0	0		
2009–10	*Albacete*	39	23	39	23
2010–11	Reggina	0	0		
2010–11	*Levante*	30	8	30	8
2011–12	Reggina	0	0		
2011–12	*Racing Santander*	32	9	32	9
2012–13	Reggina	0	0	18	1
2012–13	Espanyol	32	7		
2013–14	Espanyol	34	6		
2014–15	Espanyol	37	12	103	25
2015–16	Middlesbrough	36	7	36	7

WILLIAMS, Rhys (M)   145   5
H: 6 2   W: 11 05   b.Perth 14-7-88
Internationals: Wales U21. Australia Full caps.

2006–07	Middlesbrough	0	0		
2007–08	Middlesbrough	0	0		
2008–09	Middlesbrough	0	0		
2008–09	*Burnley*	17	0	17	0
2009–10	Middlesbrough	32	2		
2010–11	Middlesbrough	12	1		
2011–12	Middlesbrough	35	2		
2012–13	Middlesbrough	23	0		
2013–14	Middlesbrough	22	0		
2014–15	Middlesbrough	1	0		
2015–16	Middlesbrough	0	0	125	5
2015–16	*Charlton Ath*	3	0	3	0

WOODGATE, Jonathan (D)   309   8
H: 6 2   W: 12 06   b.Middlesbrough 22-1-80
Internationals: England U16, U18, U21, Full caps.

1996–97	Leeds U	0	0		
1997–98	Leeds U	0	0		
1998–99	Leeds U	25	2		
1999–2000	Leeds U	34	1		
2000–01	Leeds U	14	1		
2001–02	Leeds U	13	0		
2002–03	Leeds U	18	0	104	4
2002–03	Newcastle U	10	0		
2003–04	Newcastle U	18	0	28	0
2004–05	Real Madrid	0	0		
2005–06	Real Madrid	9	0	9	0
2006–07	Middlesbrough	30	0		
2007–08	Middlesbrough	16	0		
2007–08	Tottenham H	12	1		
2008–09	Tottenham H	34	1		
2009–10	Tottenham H	3	0		
2010–11	Tottenham H	0	0	49	2
2011–12	Stoke C	17	0	17	0
2012–13	Middlesbrough	24	1		
2013–14	Middlesbrough	25	0		
2014–15	Middlesbrough	7	1		
2015–16	Middlesbrough	0	0	102	2

Players retained or with offer of contract
Burn, Jonathan David; Cooke, Callum James; Coulson, Hayden Ross; Elsdon, Matthew; Fryer, Joseph Luke; Jakupovic, Arnel; Johnson, Callum Charles; McAloon, Thomas; Mondal, Junior; Morelli, Joao Neto; Osorio, Tomas Mejias; Pattison, Alexander Antony; Ripley, Connor James; Tinkler, Robbie; Wheatley, Josef James.

Scholars
Convery, Nathan Rhys; Cook, James Michael; Curry, Mitchell; Dawson, Thomas James; Hegarty, Liam Michael; Hetherington, Lee; Holdsworth, Brandon Brian; James, Bradley David; Jowers, Jordan; Lambert, Jack; Liddle, Ben George; McGinley, Nathan; McGoldrick, Niall Richard; Pears, Aynsley Alan William; Reading, Patrick James; Renton, Anthony Peter; Storey, Keiran; Tavernier, Marcus Joseph; Wilson, Jay Harry; Wilson, Matthew.

MILLWALL (52)

ABDOU, Nadjim (M)   415 11
H: 5 10   W: 11 02   b.Martigues 13-7-84
Internationals: Comoros Full caps.

2002–03	Martigues	26	1	26	1
2003–04	Sedan	17	0		
2004–05	Sedan	32	2		
2005–06	Sedan	14	0		
2006–07	Sedan	17	0	80	2
2007–08	Plymouth Arg	31	1	31	1
2008–09	Millwall	36	3		
2009–10	Millwall	43	1		
2010–11	Millwall	34	0		
2011–12	Millwall	40	0		
2012–13	Millwall	39	1		
2013–14	Millwall	24	0		
2014–15	Millwall	33	1		
2015–16	Millwall	29	1	278	7

ARCHER, Jordan (G)   79 0
H: 6 1   W: 12 08   b.Walthamstow 12-4-93
Internationals: Scotland U19, U20, U21.

2011–12	Tottenham H	0	0		
2012–13	Tottenham H	0	0		
2012–13	*Wycombe W*	27	0	27	0
2013–14	Tottenham H	0	0		
2014–15	Tottenham H	0	0		
2014–15	*Northampton T*	13	0	13	0
2014–15	*Millwall*	0	0		
2015–16	Millwall	39	0	39	0

BEEVERS, Mark (D)   284 10
H: 6 4   W: 13 00   b.Barnsley 21-11-89
Internationals: England U19.

2006–07	Sheffield W	2	0		
2007–08	Sheffield W	28	0		
2008–09	Sheffield W	34	0		
2009–10	Sheffield W	35	0		
2010–11	Sheffield W	28	2		
2011–12	Sheffield W	7	0		
2011–12	*Milton Keynes D*	14	1	14	1
2012–13	Sheffield W	6	0	140	2
2012–13	Millwall	35	1		
2013–14	Millwall	28	0		
2014–15	Millwall	25	2		
2015–16	Millwall	42	4	130	7

CHESMAIN, Noah (F)   1 0
b. 16-12-97

2015–16	Millwall	1	0	1	0

COWAN-HALL, Paris (F)   105 14
H: 5 8   W: 11 08   b.Portsmouth 5-10-90

2008–09	Portsmouth	0	0		
2009–10	Portsmouth	0	0		
2009–10	*Grimsby T*	3	0	3	0
2010–11	Portsmouth	0	0		
2010–11	*Scunthorpe U*	1	0	1	0
2012–13	Plymouth Arg	40	3	40	3
2013–14	Wycombe W	25	4		
2014–15	Wycombe W	20	6		
2014–15	Millwall	5	0		
2015–16	Millwall	3	0	8	0
2015–16	*Bristol R*	3	0	3	0
2015–16	*Wycombe W*	5	1	50	11

CRAIG, Tony (D)   365 8
H: 6 0   W: 10 03   b.Greenwich 20-4-85

2002–03	Millwall	2	1		
2003–04	Millwall	9	0		
2004–05	Millwall	10	0		
2004–05	*Wycombe W*	14	0	14	0
2005–06	Millwall	28	0		
2006–07	Millwall	30	1		
2007–08	Crystal Palace	13	0	13	0
2007–08	*Millwall*	5	1		
2008–09	Millwall	44	2		
2009–10	Millwall	30	2		
2010–11	Millwall	24	0		
2011–12	Millwall	23	0		
2011–12	*Leyton Orient*	4	0	4	0
2012–13	Brentford	44	0		
2013–14	Brentford	44	0		
2014–15	Brentford	23	0	111	0
2015–16	Millwall	18	1	223	8

CUMMINGS, Shaun (D)   140 2
H: 6 0   W: 11 10   b.Hammersmith 25-2-89
Internationals: Jamaica Full caps.

2007–08	Chelsea	0	0		
2008–09	Chelsea	0	0		
2008–09	*Milton Keynes D*	32	0	32	0
2009–10	Chelsea	0	0		
2009–10	*WBA*	3	0	3	0
2009–10	Reading	8	0		
2010–11	Reading	10	0		
2011–12	Reading	34	0		

2012–13	Reading	9	0		
2013–14	Reading	11	0		
2014–15	Reading	5	1	77	1
2014–15	Millwall	12	0		
2015–16	Millwall	16	1	28	1

EDWARDS, Carlos (M)   497 46
H: 5 8   W: 11 02   b.Port of Spain 24-10-78
Internationals: Trinidad & Tobago Full caps.

2000–01	Wrexham	36	4		
2001–02	Wrexham	26	5		
2002–03	Wrexham	44	8		
2003–04	Wrexham	42	5		
2004–05	Wrexham	18	1	166	23
2005–06	Luton T	42	2		
2006–07	Luton T	26	6	68	8
2006–07	Sunderland	15	5		
2007–08	Sunderland	13	0		
2008–09	Sunderland	22	0		
2008–09	*Wolverhampton W*	6	0	6	0
2009–10	Sunderland	0	0	50	5
2009–10	Ipswich T	28	2		
2010–11	Ipswich T	45	3		
2011–12	Ipswich T	45	0		
2012–13	Ipswich T	43	3		
2013–14	Ipswich T	15	1	176	9
2013–14	*Millwall*	8	1		
2014–15	Millwall	8	0		
2015–16	Millwall	15	0	31	1

FARRELL, Kyron (M)   0 0
b. 17-8-97
Internationals: Republic of Ireland U17, U18, U19.

2015–16	Millwall	0	0		

FERGUSON, Shane (D)   91 4
H: 5 9   W: 10 01   b.Limavady 12-7-91
Internationals: Northern Ireland U17, U19, U21, B, Full caps.

2008–09	Newcastle U	0	0		
2009–10	Newcastle U	0	0		
2010–11	Newcastle U	7	0		
2011–12	Newcastle U	7	0		
2012–13	Newcastle U	9	0		
2012–13	*Birmingham C*	11	1		
2013–14	Newcastle U	0	0		
2013–14	*Birmingham C*	18	0	29	1
2014–15	Newcastle U	0	0		
2014–15	*Rangers*	0	0		
2015–16	Newcastle U	0	0	23	0
2015–16	Millwall	39	3	39	3

FORDE, David (G)   395 0
H: 6 3   W: 13 06   b.Galway 20-12-79
Internationals: Republic of Ireland Full caps.

2001–02	West Ham U	0	0		
2002–03	West Ham U	0	0		
2003–04	West Ham U	0	0		
2004	Derry C	11	0		
2005	Derry C	33	0		
2006	Derry C	29	0	73	0
2006–07	Cardiff C	7	0		
2007–08	Cardiff C	0	0	7	0
2007–08	*Luton T*	5	0	5	0
2007–08	*Bournemouth*	11	0	11	0
2008–09	Millwall	46	0		
2009–10	Millwall	46	0		
2010–11	Millwall	46	0		
2011–12	Millwall	27	0		
2012–13	Millwall	40	0		
2013–14	Millwall	40	0		
2014–15	Millwall	46	0		
2015–16	Millwall	8	0	299	0

GIRLING, Harry (G)   0 0
b. 15-1-98

2015–16	Millwall	0	0		

GREGORY, Lee (F)   80 27
b. 26-8-88

2014–15	Millwall	39	9		
2015–16	Millwall	41	18	80	27

KING, Tom (G)   0 0
b.Plymouth 9-3-95
Internationals: England U17.

2011–12	Crystal Palace	0	0		
2012–13	Crystal Palace	0	0		
2014–15	Millwall	0	0		
2015–16	Millwall	0	0		

MARQUIS, John (F)   138 26
H: 6 1   W: 11 03   b.Lewisham 16-5-92

2009–10	Millwall	1	0		
2010–11	Millwall	11	4		
2011–12	Millwall	17	1		
2012–13	Millwall	10	0		
2013–14	Millwall	2	0		
2013–14	*Portsmouth*	5	1	5	1

2013–14	*Torquay U*	5	3	5	3
2013–14	*Northampton T*	14	2		
2014–15	Millwall	1	0		
2014–15	*Cheltenham T*	13	1	13	1
2014–15	*Gillingham*	21	8	21	8
2015–16	Millwall	10	0	52	5
2015–16	*Leyton Orient*	13	0	13	0
2015–16	*Northampton T*	15	6	29	8

MARTIN, Joe (M)   212 10
H: 6 0   W: 12 13   b.Dagenham 29-11-88
Internationals: England U16, U17.

2005–06	Tottenham H	0	0		
2006–07	Tottenham H	0	0		
2007–08	Tottenham H	0	0		
2007–08	*Blackpool*	1	0		
2008–09	Blackpool	15	0		
2009–10	Blackpool	6	0	22	0
2010–11	Gillingham	17	1		
2011–12	Gillingham	35	1		
2012–13	Gillingham	38	2		
2013–14	Gillingham	46	2		
2014–15	Gillingham	25	2	161	8
2015–16	Millwall	29	2	29	2

MARTIN, Lee (M)   243 14
H: 5 10   W: 10 03   b.Taunton 9-2-87

2004–05	Manchester U	0	0		
2005–06	Manchester U	0	0		
2006–07	Manchester U	0	0		
2006–07	*Rangers*	7	0	7	0
2006–07	*Stoke C*	13	1	13	1
2007–08	Manchester U	0	0		
2007–08	*Plymouth Arg*	12	2	12	2
2007–08	*Sheffield U*	6	0	6	0
2008–09	Manchester U	1	0		
2008–09	*Nottingham F*	13	1	13	1
2009–10	Manchester U	0	0	1	0
2009–10	Ipswich T	16	1		
2010–11	Ipswich T	16	0		
2010–11	*Charlton Ath*	20	2	20	2
2011–12	Ipswich T	34	5		
2012–13	Ipswich T	34	0		
2013–14	Ipswich T	0	0	100	6
2013–14	Millwall	26	1		
2014–15	Millwall	27	1		
2015–16	Millwall	8	0	61	2
2015–16	*Northampton T*	10	0	10	0

MBULU, Christian (D)   0 0
b. 6-8-96

2015–16	Millwall	0	0		

MORISON, Steven (F)   287 76
H: 6 2   W: 13 07   b.Enfield 29-8-83
Internationals: England C. Wales Full caps.

2001–02	Northampton T	1	0		
2002–03	Northampton T	13	1		
2003–04	Northampton T	5	1		
2004–05	Northampton T	4	1	23	3
From Stevenage B.					
2008–09	Millwall	0	0		
2009–10	Millwall	43	20		
2010–11	Millwall	40	15		
2011–12	Norwich C	34	9		
2012–13	Norwich C	19	1	53	10
2012–13	Leeds U	15	3		
2013–14	Leeds U	0	0		
2013–14	*Millwall*	41	8		
2014–15	Leeds U	26	2	41	5
2015–16	Millwall	46	15	170	58

NELSON, Sid (D)   23 0
b. 1-1-96

2013–14	Millwall	0	0		
2014–15	Millwall	14	0		
2015–16	Millwall	9	0	23	0

O'BRIEN, Aiden (F)   74 12
H: 5 8   W: 10 12   b.Islington 4-10-93
Internationals: Republic of Ireland U17, U19, U21.

2010–11	Millwall	0	0		
2011–12	Millwall	0	0		
2012–13	Millwall	0	0		
2012–13	*Crawley T*	9	0	9	0
2013–14	Millwall	0	0		
2013–14	*Torquay U*	3	0	3	0
2014–15	Millwall	19	2		
2015–16	Millwall	43	10	62	12

ONYEDINMA, Fred (M)   65 12
b. 24-11-96

2013–14	Millwall	4	0		
2014–15	Millwall	2	0		
2014–15	*Wycombe W*	25	8	25	8
2015–16	Millwall	34	4	40	4

PAVEY, Alfie (F)   5   0
b. 2-10-95

2013–14	Millwall	0	0		
2014–15	Millwall	1	0		
2015–16	Millwall	4	0	5	0

PHILPOT, Jamie (F)   7   1
b. 2-10-96

2014–15	Millwall	1	1		
2015–16	Millwall	6	0	7	1

POWELL, Jack (M)   6   0
b. 29-1-94

2013–14	Millwall	0	0		
2014–15	Millwall	5	0		
2015–16	Millwall	1	0	6	0

ROMEO, Mahlon (M)   19   1
H: 5 10 W: 11 05 b.Westminster 19-9-95
Internationals: Antigua and Barbuda Full caps.

2012–13	Gillingham	1	0		
2013–14	Gillingham	0	0		
2014–15	Gillingham	0	0	1	0
2015–16	Millwall	18	1	18	1

THOMPSON, Ben (M)   28   1
H: 5 11 W: 12 04 b. 3-10-95

2014–15	Millwall	0	0		
2015–16	Millwall	28	1	28	1

TWARDEK, Kris (M)   0   0
b. 8-3-97
Internationals: Czech Republic U17.

2015–16	Millwall	0	0

UPSON, Edward (M)   206   15
H: 5 10 W: 11 07 b.Bury St Edmunds 21-11-89
Internationals: England U17, U19.

2006–07	Ipswich T	0	0		
2007–08	Ipswich T	0	0		
2008–09	Ipswich T	0	0		
2009–10	Ipswich T	0	0		
2009–10	Barnet	9	1	9	1
2010–11	Yeovil T	23	0		
2011–12	Yeovil T	41	3		
2012–13	Yeovil T	41	2		
2013–14	Yeovil T	24	4	129	9
2013–14	Millwall	10	0		
2014–15	Millwall	26	2		
2015–16	Millwall	32	0	68	2

WEBSTER, Byron (D)   208   18
H: 6 5 W: 12 07 b.Sherburn-in-Elmet 31-3-87

2007–08	Siad Most	23	4		
2008–09	Siad Most	0	0	23	4
2009–10	Doncaster R	5	0		
2010–11	Doncaster R	7	0	12	0
2010–11	Hereford U	2	0	2	0
2010–11	Northampton T	8	0		
2011–12	Northampton T	13	0	21	0
2012–13	Yeovil T	44	5		
2013–14	Yeovil T	41	3		
2014–15	Millwall	11	0		
2014–15	Yeovil T	14	0	99	8
2015–16	Millwall	40	6	51	6

WILLIAMS, Shaun (M)   279   47
H: 5 9 W: 11 11 b.Dublin 19-10-86
Internationals: Republic of Ireland U21, U23.

2007	Drogheda U	1	0		
2007	Dundalk	19	9	19	9
2008	Drogheda U	4	0		
2008	Finn Harps	14	2	14	2
2009	Drogheda U	1	0		
2009	Sporting Fingal	13	7		
2010	Sporting Fingal	32	5	45	12
2011–12	Milton Keynes D	39	8		
2012–13	Milton Keynes D	4	3		
2013–14	Milton Keynes D	25	8	108	19
2013–14	Millwall	17	1		
2014–15	Millwall	38	2		
2015–16	Millwall	33	2	88	5

Players retained or with offer of contract
Sandford, Ryan David Luca.

Scholars
Bray, Rian Edward; Brown, James Dominic; Campbell-Mhlope, Matthew Blair; Chesmain, Noah Litchfield; Day, Matthew George; Donovan, Harry; Ebuzoeme, Ezechukwu Aniere Uzoma; Eze, Eberechi Oluchi; Fitzgerald, James Francis John; Girling, Harry Leonard; Green, Ryan Aaron; Leighton, Noel Stuart; McNamara, Danny John; Mulrooney-Skinner, Alexander Hugo; Mundle-Smith, Kyren Cassius; Ndjoli, Mikael Bongili; O'Donnell, Ronald Richard; White, James Alan; White, Lewis Antonio.

MILTON KEYNES D (53)

BAKER, Carl (M)   310   55
H: 6 2 W: 12 06 b.Prescot 26-12-82
Internationals: England C.

2007–08	Morecambe	42	10	42	10
2008–09	Stockport Co	22	3		
2009–10	Stockport Co	20	9	42	12
2009–10	Coventry C	22	0		
2010–11	Coventry C	32	1		
2011–12	Coventry C	26	1		
2012–13	Coventry C	43	12		
2013–14	Coventry C	37	7	160	21
2014–15	Milton Keynes D	32	9		
2015–16	Milton Keynes D	34	3	66	12

BALDOCK, George (M)   111   5
H: 5 9 W: 10 07 b.Buckingham 26-1-93

2009–10	Milton Keynes D	1	0		
2010–11	Milton Keynes D	2	0		
2011–12	Milton Keynes D	0	0		
2011–12	*Northampton T*	5	0	5	0
2012–13	Milton Keynes D	2	0		
2013–14	Milton Keynes D	38	2		
2014–15	Milton Keynes D	9	0		
2014–15	*Oxford U*	12	1		
2015–16	Milton Keynes D	15	0	67	2
2015–16	*Oxford U*	27	2	39	3

BENAVENTE, Cristian (M)   13   2
b.Alcala de Henares 19-5-94
Internationals: Peru U17, U20, Full caps.

2014–15	Real Madrid	0	0		
2015–16	Milton Keynes D	2	0	2	0
2015–16	Charleroi	11	2	11	2

BOWDITCH, Dean (F)   356   72
H: 5 11 W: 11 05 b.Bishops Stortford 15-6-86
Internationals: England U16, U17, U19.

2002–03	Ipswich T	5	0		
2003–04	Ipswich T	16	4		
2004–05	Ipswich T	21	3		
2004–05	*Burnley*	10	1	10	1
2005–06	Ipswich T	21	0		
2005–06	*Wycombe W*	11	1	11	1
2006–07	Ipswich T	9	1		
2006–07	*Brighton & HA*	3	1		
2007–08	Ipswich T	0	0		
2007–08	*Northampton T*	10	2	10	2
2007–08	*Brighton & HA*	5	0	8	1
2008–09	Ipswich T	1	0	73	8
2008–09	*Brentford*	9	2	9	2
2009–10	Yeovil T	30	10		
2010–11	. Yeovil T	41	15	71	25
2011–12	Milton Keynes D	41	12		
2012–13	Milton Keynes D	39	8		
2013–14	Milton Keynes D	12	1		
2014–15	Milton Keynes D	35	7		
2015–16	Milton Keynes D	37	4	164	32

BRITTAIN, Callum (F)   0   0

2015–16	Milton Keynes D	0	0

BURNS, Charlie (G)   5   0
b. 27-5-95

2012–13	Milton Keynes D	0	0		
2013–14	Milton Keynes D	1	0		
2014–15	Milton Keynes D	0	0		
2015–16	Milton Keynes D	4	0	5	0

CARRUTHERS, Samir (F)   97   5
H: 5 8 W: 11 00 b.Islington 4-4-93
Internationals: Republic of Ireland U19, U21.

2011–12	Aston Villa	3	0		
2012–13	Aston Villa	0	0		
2013–14	Aston Villa	0	0	3	0
2013–14	*Milton Keynes D*	23	2		
2014–15	Milton Keynes D	32	2		
2015–16	Milton Keynes D	39	1	94	5

CHURCH, Simon (F)   238   42
H: 6 0 W: 13 04 b.Amersham 10-12-88
Internationals: Wales U21, Full caps.

2007–08	Reading	3	0		
2007–08	*Crewe Alex*	12	1	12	1
2007–08	*Yeovil T*	6	0	6	0
2008–09	Reading	0	0		
2008–09	*Wycombe W*	9	0	9	0
2008–09	*Leyton Orient*	13	5	13	5
2009–10	Reading	36	10		
2010–11	Reading	37	5		
2011–12	Reading	31	7		
2012–13	Reading	0	0	104	22
2012–13	*Huddersfield T*	7	1	7	1
2013–14	Charlton Ath	38	3		

2014–15	Charlton Ath	17	2	55	5
2015–16	Milton Keynes D	19	2	19	2
2015–16	*Aberdeen*	13	6	13	6

CROPPER, Cody (G)   9   0
H: 6 3 W: 14 05 b.Atlanta 16-2-93
Internationals: USA U20, U23.

2011–12	Ipswich T	0	0		
2012–13	Ipswich T	0	0		
2012–13	Southampton	0	0		
2013–14	Southampton	0	0		
2014–15	Southampton	0	0		
2015–16	Milton Keynes D	9	0	9	0

FURLONG, Connor (M)   1   0
b. 7-2-98

2015–16	Milton Keynes D	1	0	1	0

HITCHCOCK, Tom (F)   78   15
H: 5 11 W: 12 08 b.Hemel Hempstead 1-10-92

2009–10	Blackburn R	0	0		
2010–11	Blackburn R	0	0		
2011–12	Blackburn R	0	0		
2011–12	*Plymouth Arg*	8	0	8	0
2011–12	QPR	0	0		
2012–13	QPR	0	0		
2012–13	*Bristol R*	17	3	17	3
2013–14	QPR	1	1	1	1
2013–14	. *Crewe Alex*	6	3		
2013–14	*Rotherham U*	11	5	11	5
2014–15	Milton Keynes D	12	0		
2014–15	*Fleetwood T*	6	1	6	1
2015–16	Milton Keynes D	0	0	12	0
2015–16	*Stevenage*	10	2	10	2
2015–16	*Crewe Alex*	7	0	13	3

HODSON, Lee (D)   149   3
H: 5 11 W: 11 02 b.Boreham Wood 2-10-91
Internationals: Northern Ireland U19, U21, Full caps.

2008–09	Watford	1	0		
2009–10	Watford	31	0		
2010–11	Watford	29	1		
2011–12	Watford	20	0		
2012–13	Watford	2	0	83	1
2012–13	*Brentford*	13	0	13	0
2013–14	Milton Keynes D	23	1		
2014–15	Milton Keynes D	14	1		
2015–16	Milton Keynes D	3	0	40	2
2015–16	*Kilmarnock*	13	0	13	0

JACKSON, Oran (D)   1   0
b. 16-10-98

2015–16	Milton Keynes D	1	0	1	0

JENNINGS, Dale (F)   83   10
H: 5 7 W: 11 00 b.Liverpool 21-12-92

2010–11	Tranmere R	29	6	29	6
2013–14	Barnsley	27	3		
2013–14	*Milton Keynes D*	6	0		
2014–15	Barnsley	20	1	47	4
2015–16	Milton Keynes D	1	0	7	0

KASUMU, David (M)   0   0
b. 5-10-99

2015–16	Milton Keynes D	0	0

KAY, Antony (D)   493   44
H: 5 11 W: 11 08 b.Barnsley 21-10-82

1999–2000	Barnsley	0	0		
2000–01	Barnsley	7	0		
2001–02	Barnsley	1	0		
2002–03	Barnsley	16	0		
2003–04	Barnsley	43	3		
2004–05	Barnsley	39	6		
2005–06	Barnsley	36	1		
2006–07	Barnsley	32	1	174	11
2007–08	Tranmere R	38	6		
2008–09	Tranmere R	44	11	82	17
2009–10	Huddersfield T	40	6		
2010–11	Huddersfield T	27	3		
2011–12	Huddersfield T	28	1		
2012–13	Huddersfield T	0	0	95	10
2012–13	Milton Keynes D	33	1		
2013–14	Milton Keynes D	30	2		
2014–15	Milton Keynes D	45	1		
2015–16	Milton Keynes D	34	2	142	6

LEWINGTON, Dean (D)   544   20
H: 5 11 W: 11 07 b.Kingston 18-5-84

2002–03	Wimbledon	1	0		
2003–04	Wimbledon	28	1	29	1
2004–05	Milton Keynes D	43	2		
2005–06	Milton Keynes D	44	1		
2006–07	Milton Keynes D	45	0		
2007–08	Milton Keynes D	45	0		
2008–09	Milton Keynes D	40	2		
2009–10	Milton Keynes D	42	1		
2010–11	Milton Keynes D	42	3		

2011–12	Milton Keynes D	46	3
2012–13	Milton Keynes D	38	1
2013–14	Milton Keynes D	43	1
2014–15	Milton Keynes D	41	3
2015–16	Milton Keynes D	46	1 515 19

MARTIN, David E (G)   291   0
H: 6 1   W: 13 04   b.Romford 22-1-86
Internationals: England U16, U17, U18, U19.

2003–04	Wimbledon	2	0 **2 0**
2004–05	Milton Keynes D	15	0
2005–06	Milton Keynes D	0	0
2005–06	Liverpool	0	0
2006–07	Liverpool	0	0
2006–07	Accrington S	10	0 **10 0**
2007–08	Liverpool	0	0
2008–09	Liverpool	0	0
2008–09	Leicester C	25	0 **25 0**
2009–10	Liverpool	0	0
2009–10	Tranmere R	3	0 **3 0**
2009–10	Leeds U	0	0
2009–10	Derby Co	2	0 **2 0**
2010–11	Milton Keynes D	43	0
2011–12	Milton Keynes D	46	0
2012–13	Milton Keynes D	31	0
2013–14	Milton Keynes D	40	0
2014–15	Milton Keynes D	39	0
2015–16	Milton Keynes D	35	0 **249 0**

MAYNARD, Nicky (F)   271   91
H: 5 11   W: 11 00   b.Winsford 11-12-86

2005–06	Crewe Alex	1	1
2006–07	Crewe Alex	31	16
2007–08	Crewe Alex	27	14 **59 31**
2008–09	Bristol C	43	11
2009–10	Bristol C	42	20
2010–11	Bristol C	13	6
2011–12	Bristol C	27	8 **125 45**
2011–12	West Ham U	14	2
2012–13	West Ham U	0	0 **14 2**
2012–13	Cardiff C	4	1
2013–14	Cardiff C	8	0
2013–14	Wigan Ath	16	4 **16 4**
2014–15	Cardiff C	10	1 **22 2**
2015–16	Milton Keynes D	35	7 **35 7**

McFADZEAN, Kyle (D)   176   9
H: 6 1   W: 13 04   b.Sheffield 20-2-87
Internationals: England C.

2004–05	Sheffield U	0	0
2005–06	Sheffield U	0	0
2006–07	Sheffield U	0	0
From Alfreton T			
2011–12	Crawley T	37	2
2012–13	Crawley T	17	3
2013–14	Crawley T	42	1 **96 6**
2014–15	Milton Keynes D	41	3
2015–16	Milton Keynes D	39	0 **80 3**

POTTER, Darren (M)   356   16
H: 6 0   W: 10 08   b.Liverpool 21-12-84
Internationals: Republic of Ireland Full caps.

2001–02	Liverpool	0	0
2002–03	Liverpool	0	0
2003–04	Liverpool	0	0
2004–05	Liverpool	2	0
2005–06	Liverpool	0	0
2005–06	Southampton	10	0 **10 0**
2006–07	Liverpool	0	0 **2 0**
2006–07	Wolverhampton W	38	0
2007–08	Wolverhampton W	18	0
2008–09	Wolverhampton W	0	0 **56 0**
2008–09	Sheffield W	17	2
2009–10	Sheffield W	46	3
2010–11	Sheffield W	33	3 **96 8**
2011–12	Milton Keynes D	40	2
2012–13	Milton Keynes D	46	4
2013–14	Milton Keynes D	40	2
2014–15	Milton Keynes D	29	0
2015–16	Milton Keynes D	37	0 **192 8**

POWELL, Daniel (F)   211   35
H: 5 11   W: 13 03   b.Luton 12-3-91

2008–09	Milton Keynes D	7	1
2009–10	Milton Keynes D	2	1
2010–11	Milton Keynes D	29	9
2011–12	Milton Keynes D	43	6
2012–13	Milton Keynes D	34	7
2013–14	Milton Keynes D	32	1
2014–15	Milton Keynes D	42	8
2015–16	Milton Keynes D	22	2 **211 35**

RASULO, Georgio (M)   13   0
b.Banbury 23-1-97
Internationals: England U16, U17.

2012–13	Milton Keynes D	1	0
2013–14	Milton Keynes D	7	0
2014–15	Milton Keynes D	0	0
2014–15	Oxford U	1	0 **1 0**

2015–16	Milton Keynes D	1	0 **9 0**
2015–16	Oldham Ath	3	0 **3 0**

REEVES, Ben (D)   96   18
H: 5 10   W: 10 07   b.Verwood 19-11-91
Internationals: Northern Ireland Full caps.

2008–09	Southampton	0	0
2009–10	Southampton	0	0
2010–11	Southampton	0	0
2011–12	Southampton	2	0
2011–12	Dagenham & R	5	0 **5 0**
2012–13	Southampton	3	0 **5 0**
2012–13	Southend U	10	1 **10 1**
2013–14	Milton Keynes D	28	7
2014–15	Milton Keynes D	30	7
2015–16	Milton Keynes D	18	3 **76 17**

REVELL, Alex (F)   418   78
H: 6 3   W: 13 00   b.Cambridge 7-7-83

2000–01	Cambridge U	4	0
2001–02	Cambridge U	24	2
2002–03	Cambridge U	9	0
2003–04	Cambridge U	20	3 **57 5**
From Braintree T.			
2006–07	Brighton & HA	38	7
2007–08	Brighton & HA	21	6 **59 13**
2007–08	Southend U	6	0
2008–09	Southend U	23	4
2009–10	Southend U	3	0 **34 4**
2009–10	Swindon T	10	2 **10 2**
2009–10	Wycombe W	15	6 **15 6**
2010–11	Leyton Orient	39	13
2011–12	Leyton Orient	5	0 **44 13**
2011–12	Rotherham U	40	10
2012–13	Rotherham U	41	6
2013–14	Rotherham U	45	8
2014–15	Rotherham U	24	4 **150 28**
2014–15	Cardiff C	16	2
2015–16	Cardiff C	10	0 **26 2**
2015–16	Wigan Ath	6	1 **6 1**
2015–16	Milton Keynes D	17	4 **17 4**

SPENCE, Jordan (D)   161   2
H: 6 2   W: 12 07   b.Woodford 24-5-90
Internationals: England U16, U17, U18, U19, U21.

2007–08	West Ham U	0	0
2008–09	West Ham U	0	0
2008–09	Leyton Orient	20	0 **20 0**
2009–10	West Ham U	1	0
2009–10	Scunthorpe U	9	0 **9 0**
2010–11	West Ham U	2	0
2010–11	Bristol C	11	0
2011–12	West Ham U	0	0
2011–12	Bristol C	10	0 **21 0**
2012–13	West Ham U	4	0
2013–14	West Ham U	4	0 **7 0**
2013–14	Sheffield W	4	0 **4 0**
2013–14	Milton Keynes D	29	2
2014–15	Milton Keynes D	38	0
2015–16	Milton Keynes D	33	0 **100 2**

TSHIMANGA, Kabongo (F)   0   0
b. 31-5-96

2014–15	Milton Keynes D	0	0
2015–16	Milton Keynes D	0	0

UPSON, Matthew (D)   385   14
H: 6 1   W: 11 04   b.Eye 18-4-79
Internationals: England U21, Full caps.

1995–96	Luton T	0	0
1996–97	Luton T	1	0 **1 0**
1996–97	Arsenal	0	0
1997–98	Arsenal	5	0
1998–99	Arsenal	5	0
1999–2000	Arsenal	8	0
2000–01	Arsenal	2	0
2000–01	Nottingham F	1	0 **1 0**
2000–01	Crystal Palace	7	0 **7 0**
2001–02	Arsenal	14	0
2002–03	Arsenal	0	0 **34 0**
2002–03	Reading	14	0 **14 0**
2002–03	Birmingham C	14	0
2003–04	Birmingham C	30	0
2004–05	Birmingham C	36	2
2005–06	Birmingham C	24	1
2006–07	Birmingham C	9	2 **113 5**
2006–07	West Ham U	2	0
2007–08	West Ham U	29	1
2008–09	West Ham U	30	3
2009–10	West Ham U	33	3
2010–11	West Ham U	30	0 **131 4**
2011–12	Stoke C	14	1
2012–13	Stoke C	1	1 **15 2**
2012–13	Brighton & HA	18	1
2013–14	Brighton & HA	43	2 **61 3**
2014–15	Leicester C	5	0 **5 0**
2015–16	Milton Keynes D	3	0 **3 0**

WALSH, Joe (D)   117   9
H: 5 11   W: 11 00   b.Cardiff 15-5-92
Internationals: Wales U17, U19, U21.

2010–11	Swansea C	0	0
2011–12	Swansea C	0	0
2012–13	Crawley T	30	2
2013–14	Crawley T	39	5
2014–15	Crawley T	28	1 **97 8**
2014–15	Milton Keynes D	2	0
2015–16	Milton Keynes D	18	1 **20 1**

Players retained or with offer of contract
Hickford, Harry Samuel; Tilney, Benjamin Rowland.

Scholars
Furlong, Connor Jason; Hadden-Becker, Jack; Hunt, Adam Matthew Samuel; Jackson, Oran Egypt; Kioso, Peter Katako; Logan, Hugo James; McCorkell, Andrew Robert William; Nombe, Samuel Tshiayima; Omar, Juma Abdulla; Osei-Bonsu, Andrew Kwadjo; Owusu, Kevin; Palmiero, Dominic Antonio; Steele, Joseph James; Stratton, Harry; Thomas-Asante, Solomon Brandon Michael; Wyant, Thomas Paul.

MORECAMBE (54)

BAILEY, Charlie (M)   0   0
b. 12-6-97

2015–16	Morecambe	0	0

BARKHUIZEN, Tom (F)   117   23
H: 5 9   W: 11 00   b.Blackpool 4-7-93

2011–12	Blackpool	0	0
2011–12	Hereford U	38	11 **38 11**
2012–13	Blackpool	0	0
2012–13	Fleetwood T	13	1 **13 1**
2013–14	Blackpool	14	1
2014–15	Blackpool	7	0 **21 1**
2014–15	Morecambe	5	0
2015–16	Morecambe	40	10 **45 10**

BEELEY, Shaun (D)   147   0
H: 5 10   W: 11 05   b.Stockport 21-11-88
Internationals: England C.

2012–13	Fleetwood T	34	0 **34 0**
2013–14	Bury	20	0 **20 0**
2013–14	Morecambe	12	0
2014–15	Morecambe	42	0
2015–16	Morecambe	39	0 **93 0**

BONDSWELL, Nathan (M)   0   0
b.Nottingham 10-2-97

2014–15	Morecambe	0	0
2015–16	Morecambe	0	0

DEVITT, Jamie (F)   166   22
H: 5 10   W: 10 05   b.Dublin 6-7-90
Internationals: Republic of Ireland U21.

2007–08	Hull C	0	0
2008–09	Hull C	0	0
2009–10	Hull C	0	0
2009–10	Darlington	6	1 **6 1**
2009–10	Shrewsbury T	9	2 **9 2**
2009–10	Grimsby T	15	5 **15 5**
2010–11	Hull C	16	0
2011–12	Hull C	0	0
2011–12	Bradford C	7	1 **7 1**
2011–12	Accrington S	16	2 **16 2**
2012–13	Hull C	0	0 **16 0**
2012–13	Rotherham U	1	0 **1 0**
2013–14	Chesterfield	7	0 **7 0**
2013–14	Morecambe	14	2
2014–15	Morecambe	36	3
2015–16	Morecambe	39	6 **89 11**

DOYLE, Chris (D)   17   0
H: 6 2   W: 13 05   b.Liverpool 22-7-94

2012–13	Morecambe	4	0
2013–14	Morecambe	3	0
2014–15	Morecambe	2	0
2015–16	Morecambe	8	0 **17 0**

DUGDALE, Adam (D)   166   7
H: 6 3   W: 12 07   b.Liverpool 12-9-87

2006–07	Crewe Alex	0	0
2006–07	Accrington S	2	0 **2 0**
From Southport, Droylsden, Montagnee, Barrow, AFC Telford U.			
2010–11	Crewe Alex	20	1
2011–12	Crewe Alex	43	3
2012–13	Crewe Alex	18	0
2013–14	Crewe Alex	21	1
2013–14	Tranmere R	4	1
2014–15	Crewe Alex	18	1 **120 6**
2014–15	Tranmere R	16	0 **20 1**
2015–16	Morecambe	24	0 **24 0**

EDWARDS, Ryan (D)   117   0
b.Liverpool 7-10-93

2011–12	Blackburn R	0	0		
2012–13	Rochdale	26	0	26	0
2012–13	Blackburn R	0	0		
2012–13	*Fleetwood T*	9	0	9	0
2013–14	Blackburn R	0	0		
2013–14	*Chesterfield*	5	0	5	0
2013–14	*Tranmere R*	0	0		
2013–14	Morecambe	9	0		
2014–15	Morecambe	31	0		
2015–16	Morecambe	37	0	77	0

ELLISON, Kevin (M)   504 104
H: 6 0   W: 12 00   b.Liverpool 23-2-79

2000–01	Leicester C	1	0		
2001–02	Leicester C	0	0	1	0
2001–02	Stockport Co	11	0		
2002–03	Stockport Co	23	1		
2003–04	Stockport Co	14	1	48	2
2003–04	*Lincoln C*	11	0	11	0
2004–05	Chester C	24	9		
2004–05	Hull C	16	1		
2005–06	Hull C	23	1	39	2
2006–07	Tranmere R	34	4	34	4
2007–08	Chester C	36	11		
2008–09	Chester C	39	8	99	28
2008–09	Rotherham U	0	0		
2009–10	Rotherham U	39	8		
2010–11	Rotherham U	23	3	62	11
2010–11	*Bradford C*	7	1	7	1
2011–12	Morecambe	34	15		
2012–13	Morecambe	40	11		
2013–14	Morecambe	42	10		
2014–15	Morecambe	43	11		
2015–16	Morecambe	44	9	203	56

FLEMING, Andy (M)   188 16
H: 6 1   W: 12 00   b.Liverpool 18-2-89
Internationals: England C.

2006–07	Wrexham	2	0		
2007–08	Wrexham	4	0	6	0
2010–11	Morecambe	30	2		
2011–12	Morecambe	17	2		
2012–13	Morecambe	32	5		
2013–14	Morecambe	35	2		
2014–15	Morecambe	35	2		
2015–16	Morecambe	33	3	182	16

GOODALL, Alan (D)   325 20
H: 5 9   W: 11 06   b.Birkenhead 2-12-81

2004–05	Rochdale	34	2		
2005–06	Rochdale	40	3		
2006–07	Rochdale	46	3		
2007–08	Luton T	29	1	29	1
2008–09	Chesterfield	28	3		
2009–10	Chesterfield	17	0	45	3
2010–11	Rochdale	5	0	125	8
2010–11	Stockport Co	13	0	13	0
2012–13	Fleetwood T	29	4		
2013–14	Fleetwood T	19	0	48	4
2014–15	Morecambe	28	0		
2015–16	Morecambe	37	4	65	4

HEDLEY, Ben (M)   0   0

2015–16	Morecambe	0	0		

JONES, Lee (G)   250 0
H: 5 8   W: 12 02   b.Pontypridd 9-8-70

1994–95	Swansea C	1	0		
1995–96	Swansea C	1	0		
1995–96	*Crewe Alex*	1	0	1	0
1996–97	Swansea C	1	0		
1997–98	Swansea C	2	0	6	0
1997–98	Bristol R	8	0		
1998–99	Bristol R	32	0		
1999–2000	Bristol R	36	0	76	0
2000–01	Stockport Co	27	0		
2001–02	Stockport Co	24	0		
2002–03	Stockport Co	24	0	75	0
2003–04	Blackpool	21	0		
2004–05	Blackpool	29	0		
2005–06	Blackpool	31	0		
2006–07	Blackpool	0	0	81	0
2006–07	*Bury*	2	0	2	0
2006–07	Darlington	9	0	9	0
2012–13	Morecambe	0	0		
2013–14	Morecambe	0	0		
2014–15	Morecambe	0	0		
2015–16	Morecambe	0	0		

KELLEHER, Jack (F)   1   0
b. 22-9-97

2015–16	Morecambe	1	0	1	0

KENYON, Alex (M)   105 6
H: 5 11   W: 11 12   b.Preston 17-7-92

2013–14	Morecambe	39	0		
2014–15	Morecambe	37	3		
2015–16	Morecambe	29	3	105	6

MAHER, Niall (G)   0   0

2015–16	Morecambe	0	0		

McGOWAN, Aaron (D)   32 1
b.Maghull 20-9-95

2012–13	Morecambe	1	0		
2013–14	Morecambe	2	0		
2014–15	Morecambe	8	1		
2015–16	Morecambe	21	0	32	1

McKNIGHT, Darren (M)   0   0
b. 27-8-95

2014–15	Barnsley	0	0		
2015–16	Shrewsbury T	0	0		
2015–16	Morecambe	0	0		

MILLER, Shaun (F)   259 61
H: 5 11 08   b.Alsager 25-9-87

2006–07	Crewe Alex	7	3		
2007–08	Crewe Alex	15	1		
2008–09	Crewe Alex	33	4		
2009–10	Crewe Alex	33	5		
2010–11	Crewe Alex	42	18		
2011–12	Crewe Alex	33	5	163	38
2012–13	Sheffield U	15	4		
2013–14	Sheffield U	13	0	28	4
2013–14	*Shrewsbury T*	8	3	8	3
2014–15	Coventry C	12	1	12	1
2014–15	*Crawley T*	5	0	5	0
2014–15	*York C*	6	0	6	0
2015–16	Morecambe	37	15	37	15

MOLYNEUX, Lee (D)   137 18
H: 6 1   W: 12 09   b.Liverpool 24-2-89
Internationals: England U16, U17, U18.

2005–06	Everton	0	0		
2006–07	Everton	0	0		
2007–08	Everton	0	0		
2008–09	Southampton	4	0		
2009–10	Southampton	0	0	4	0
2010–11	Plymouth Arg	9	0	9	0
2012–13	Accrington S	39	8		
2013–14	Crewe Alex	7	0		
2013–14	*Rochdale*	3	0	3	0
2013–14	*Accrington S*	17	6		
2014–15	Crewe Alex	3	0	10	0
2014–15	*Accrington S*	10	1	66	15
2014–15	Tranmere R	11	0	11	0
2015–16	Morecambe	34	3	34	3

MULLIN, Paul (F)   82 17
H: 5 10   W: 11 01   b. 6-11-94

2013–14	Huddersfield T	0	0		
2014–15	Morecambe	42	8		
2015–16	Morecambe	40	9	82	17

MURPHY, Peter (D)   204 26
H: 6 0   W: 11 10   b.Liverpool 13-2-90

2007–08	Accrington S	2	0		
2008–09	Accrington S	3	0		
2009–10	Accrington S	10	0		
2010–11	Accrington S	13	0		
2011–12	Accrington S	38	4		
2012–13	Accrington S	45	5		
2013–14	Accrington S	44	9	155	18
2014–15	Wycombe W	42	7	42	7
2015–16	Morecambe	7	1	7	1

PARRISH, Andy (D)   311 2
H: 6 0   W: 11 00   b.Bolton 22-6-88

2005–06	Bury	8	0		
2006–07	Bury	9	0		
2007–08	Bury	26	1	43	1
2008–09	Morecambe	13	0		
2009–10	Morecambe	35	0		
2010–11	Morecambe	41	0		
2011–12	Morecambe	38	0		
2012–13	Morecambe	25	1		
2013–14	Morecambe	39	0		
2014–15	Morecambe	45	0		
2015–16	Morecambe	32	0	268	1

ROCHE, Barry (G)   456 1
H: 6 5   W: 14 08   b.Dublin 6-4-82
Internationals: Republic of Ireland U17.

1999–2000	Nottingham F	0	0		
2000–01	Nottingham F	2	0		
2001–02	Nottingham F	0	0		
2002–03	Nottingham F	1	0		
2003–04	Nottingham F	8	0		
2004–05	Nottingham F	2	0	13	0
2005–06	Chesterfield	41	0		
2006–07	Chesterfield	40	0		
2007–08	Chesterfield	45	0	126	0
2008–09	Morecambe	46	0		
2009–10	Morecambe	42	0		
2010–11	Morecambe	42	0		
2011–12	Morecambe	44	0		
2012–13	Morecambe	42	0		
2013–14	Morecambe	45	0		

STEWART, Tom (G)   1   0
b. 17-4-96

2014–15	Morecambe	1	0		
2015–16	Morecambe	0	0	1	0

STOCKTON, Cole (F)   82 11
H: 6 1   W: 11 11   b.Huyton 13-3-94

2011–12	Tranmere R	1	0		
2012–13	Tranmere R	31	3		
2013–14	Tranmere R	21	2		
2014–15	Tranmere R	22	4	75	9

On loan from Tranmere R.

2015–16	Morecambe	7	2	7	2

THOMPSON, Tony (G)   1   0
H: 6 0   W: 13 01   b.Liverpool 4-11-94

2012–13	Rotherham U	0	0		
2013–14	Rotherham U	0	0		
2014–15	Rotherham U	0	0		
2015–16	Morecambe	1	0	1	0

WILDIG, Aaron (M)   121 9
H: 5 9   W: 11 02   b.Hereford 15-4-92
Internationals: Wales U16.

2009–10	Cardiff C	11	1		
2010–11	Cardiff C	2	0		
2010–11	*Hamilton A*	3	0	3	0
2011–12	Cardiff C	0	0	13	1
2011–12	Shrewsbury T	12	2		
2012–13	Shrewsbury T	21	1		
2013–14	Shrewsbury T	30	2		
2014–15	Shrewsbury T	1	0	64	5
2014–15	*Morecambe*	9	1		
2015–16	Morecambe	32	2	41	3

WILSON, Laurence (D)   330 17
H: 5 10   W: 10 09   b.Huyton 10-10-86
Internationals: England U18, U19.

2004–05	Everton	0	0		
2005–06	Everton	0	0		
2005–06	*Mansfield T*	15	1	15	1
2006–07	Chester C	41	1		
2007–08	Chester C	40	2		
2008–09	Chester C	34	1	115	4
2009–10	Morecambe	41	3		
2010–11	Morecambe	38	3		
2011–12	Morecambe	30	5		
2012–13	Rotherham U	5	0	5	0
2012–13	Accrington S	19	0		
2013–14	Accrington S	15	0	34	0
2014–15	Morecambe	34	1		
2015–16	Morecambe	18	0	161	12

Scholars
Box, Oliver Tyler; Cowley, Thomas David; Dawson, Paul; Hedley, Ben; Homson-Smith, Morgan; Jenkinson, Robbie Jake; Jordan, Luke Macauley; Livingstone, Matthew Richard; Maher, Niall Michael; Masters, Lewis Robert; Povey, Maxwell Jordan; Taylor, Jack Charles; Tomlinson, Lewis; Townsend, Jake Ryan; Webb, Alexander Lawrence; Yawson, Steven.

NEWCASTLE U (55)

AARONS, Rolando (M)   14 2
H: 5 9   W: 10 08   b.Kingston 16-11-95
Internationals: England U20.

2014–15	Newcastle U	4	1		
2015–16	Newcastle U	10	1	14	2

AMEOBI, Sam (F)   99 4
H: 6 3   W: 10 04   b.Newcastle 1-5-92
Internationals: Nigeria U20. England U21.

2010–11	Newcastle U	1	0		
2011–12	Newcastle U	10	0		
2012–13	Newcastle U	8	0		
2012–13	*Middlesbrough*	9	1	9	1
2013–14	Newcastle U	10	0		
2014–15	Newcastle U	25	2		
2015–16	Newcastle U	0	0	54	2
2015–16	*Cardiff C*	36	1	36	1

ANITA, Vurnon (M)   215 7
H: 5 5   W: 10 04   b.Willemstad 4-4-89
Internationals: Netherlands U15, U17, U19, U20, U21, Full caps.

2005–06	Ajax	1	0		
2006–07	Ajax	1	0		
2008–09	Ajax	16	0		
2009–10	Ajax	26	0		
2010–11	Ajax	31	3		
2011–12	Ajax	33	2		
2012–13	Ajax	1	0	109	5
2012–13	Newcastle U	25	0		

2013–14	Newcastle U	34	1		
2014–15	Newcastle U	19	0		
2015–16	Newcastle U	28	1	106	2

ARMSTRONG, Adam (F)   55 20
H: 5 8 W: 10 12 b.Newcastle 10-2-97
Internationals: England U16, U17, U18, U19.

2013–14	Newcastle U	4	0		
2014–15	Newcastle U	11	0		
2015–16	Newcastle U	0	0	15	0
2015–16	*Coventry C*	40	20	40	20

BARLASER, Daniel (M)   0 0
H: 6 0 W: 9 11 b.Gateshead 18-1-97
Internationals: Turkey U16, U17.

2015–16	Newcastle U	0	0		

BIGIRIMANA, Gael (M)   52 1
H: 5 9 W: 11 09 b.Burundi 22-10-93
Internationals: England U20.

2011–12	Coventry C	26	0		
2012–13	Newcastle U	13	1		
2013–14	Newcastle U	0	0		
2014–15	Newcastle U	0	0		
2014–15	*Rangers*	0	0		
2015–16	Newcastle U	0	0	13	1
2015–16	*Coventry C*	13	0	39	0

CABELLA, Remy (M)   179 33
H: 5 7 W: 9 11 b.Ajaccio 8-3-90
Internationals: France U21, Full caps.

2010–11	Montpellier	0	0		
2010–11	*Avignon*	17	3	17	3
2011–12	Montpellier	29	3		
2012–13	Montpellier	31	7		
2013–14	Montpellier	37	14	97	24
2014–15	Newcastle U	31	1		
2015–16	Newcastle U	0	0	31	1
2015–16	*Marseille*	34	5	34	5

CAMERON, Kyle (D)   18 1
b. 15-1-97
Internationals: England U16, U17. Scotland U17.

2015–16	Newcastle U	0	0		
2015–16	*York C*	18	1	18	1

CISSE, Papiss (F)   359 150
H: 6 0 W: 11 07 b.Dakar 3-6-85
Internationals: Senegal Full caps.

2003–04	AS Douanes	26	23	26	23
2004–05	Metz B	10	3		
2005–06	Metz B	3	0	13	3
2005–06	Metz	1	0		
2005–06	*Cherbourg*	28	11	28	11
2006–07	Metz	32	12		
2007–08	Metz	9	0		
2007–08	*Chateauroux*	15	4	15	4
2008–09	Metz	37	15		
2009–10	Freiburg	16	8	95	35
2009–10	Freiburg	16	6		
2010–11	Freiburg	32	22		
2011–12	Freiburg	17	9	65	37
2011–12	Newcastle U	14	13		
2012–13	Newcastle U	36	8		
2013–14	Newcastle U	24	2		
2014–15	Newcastle U	22	11		
2015–16	Newcastle U	21	3	117	37

COLBACK, Jack (M)   229 13
H: 5 9 W: 11 05 b.Killingworth 24-10-89
Internationals: England U20.

2007–08	Sunderland	0	0		
2008–09	Sunderland	0	0		
2009–10	Sunderland	1	0		
2009–10	*Ipswich T*	37	4		
2010–11	Sunderland	11	0		
2010–11	*Ipswich T*	13	0	50	4
2011–12	Sunderland	35	1		
2012–13	Sunderland	35	0		
2013–14	Sunderland	33	3	115	4
2014–15	Newcastle U	35	4		
2015–16	Newcastle U	29	1	64	5

COLOCCINI, Fabricio (D)   466 22
H: 6 0 W: 12 04 b.Cordoba 22-1-82
Internationals: Argentina Full caps.

1998–99	Boca Juniors	1	1		
1999–2000	Boca Juniors	1	0	2	1
1999–2000	AC Milan	0	0		
2000–01	AC Milan	0	0		
2000–01	San Lorenzo	19	3	19	3
2001–02	Alaves	33	6	33	6
2002–03	Atletico Madrid	27	0	27	0
2003–04	Villarreal	31	1	31	1
2004–05	AC Milan	1	0	1	0
2004–05	La Coruna	15	1		
2005–06	La Coruna	26	0		
2006–07	La Coruna	26	0		
2007–08	La Coruna	38	4	105	5

2008–09	Newcastle U	34	0		
2009–10	Newcastle U	37	2		
2010–11	Newcastle U	35	2		
2011–12	Newcastle U	35	0		
2012–13	Newcastle U	22	0		
2013–14	Newcastle U	27	0		
2014–15	Newcastle U	32	1		
2015–16	Newcastle U	26	1	248	6

DARLOW, Karl (G)   124 0
H: 6 1 W: 12 05 b.Northampton 8-10-90

2009–10	Nottingham F	0	0		
2010–11	Nottingham F	1	0		
2011–12	Nottingham F	0	0		
2012–13	Nottingham F	20	0		
2012–13	*Walsall*	9	0	9	0
2013–14	Nottingham F	43	0		
2014–15	Newcastle U	0	0		
2014–15	*Nottingham F*	42	0	106	0
2015–16	Newcastle U	9	0	9	0

DE JONG, Siem (M)   188 58
H: 6 1 W: 12 00 b.Aigle 28-1-89
Internationals: Netherlands U17, U19, U21, B, Full caps.

2007–08	Ajax	22	2		
2008–09	Ajax	10	1		
2009–10	Ajax	22	10		
2010–11	Ajax	32	12		
2011–12	Ajax	29	13		
2012–13	Ajax	33	12		
2013–14	Ajax	18	7	166	57
2014–15	Newcastle U	4	1		
2015–16	Newcastle U	18	0	22	1

DOUMBIA, Seydou (F)   228 128
H: 6 0 W: 11 09 b.Yamoussoukro 31-12-87
Internationals: Ivory Coast Full caps.

2006	Kashiwa Reysol	6	0		
2007	Kashiwa Reysol	18	3	24	3
2008	Tokushima Vortis	16	7	16	7
2008–09	Young Boys	32	20		
2009–10	Young Boys	32	30	64	50
2010–11	CSKA Moscow	11	5		
2011–12	CSKA Moscow	42	28		
2012–13	CSKA Moscow	7	3		
2013–14	CSKA Moscow	22	18		
2014–15	CSKA Moscow	13	7		
2014–15	Roma	13	2		
2015–16	Roma	0	0	13	2
2015–16	*CSKA Moscow*	13	5	108	66

On loan from Roma.

2015–16	Newcastle U	3	0	3	0

DUMMETT, Paul (D)   96 4
H: 5 10 W: 10 02 b.Newcastle 26-9-91
Internationals: Wales U21, Full caps.

2010–11	Newcastle U	0	0		
2011–12	Newcastle U	0	0		
2012–13	Newcastle U	0	0		
2012–13	*St Mirren*	30	2	30	2
2013–14	Newcastle U	18	1		
2014–15	Newcastle U	25	0		
2015–16	Newcastle U	21	1	66	2

ELLIOT, Rob (G)   143 0
H: 6 3 W: 14 10 b.Chatham 30-4-86
Internationals: Republic of Ireland U19, Full caps.

2004–05	Charlton Ath	0	0		
2004–05	*Notts Co*	4	0	4	0
2005–06	Charlton Ath	0	0		
2006–07	Charlton Ath	0	0		
2006–07	*Accrington S*	7	0	7	0
2007–08	Charlton Ath	1	0		
2008–09	Charlton Ath	23	0		
2009–10	Charlton Ath	33	0		
2010–11	Charlton Ath	35	0		
2011–12	Charlton Ath	4	0	96	0
2011–12	Newcastle U	0	0		
2012–13	Newcastle U	10	0		
2013–14	Newcastle U	2	0		
2014–15	Newcastle U	3	0		
2015–16	Newcastle U	21	0	36	0

GIBSON, Liam (D)   0 0
H: 6 1 W: 12 08 b.Stanley 25-4-97

2015–16	Newcastle U	0	0		

GILLESPHEY, Macaulay (D)   23 2
b. 24-11-95

2015–16	Newcastle U	0	0		
2015–16	*Carlisle U*	23	2	23	2

GILLIEAD, Alex (F)   35 5
H: 6 0 W: 11 00 b.Shotley Bridge 11-2-96
Internationals: England U16, U17, U18, U20.

2014–15	Newcastle U	0	0		
2015–16	Newcastle U	0	0		
2015–16	*Carlisle U*	35	5	35	5

GOOD, Curtis (D)   31 2
H: 6 2 W: 13 05 b.Melbourne 23-3-93
Internationals: Australia U20, U23, Full caps.

2011–12	Melbourne Heart	24	1	24	1
2012–13	Newcastle U	0	0		
2012–13	*Bradford C*	3	0	3	0
2013–14	Newcastle U	0	0		
2013–14	*Dundee U*	4	1	4	1
2014–15	Newcastle U	0	0		
2015–16	Newcastle U	0	0		

GOUFFRAN, Yoan (F)   338 76
H: 5 9 W: 11 11
b.Villeneuve-Saint-Georges 25-5-86
Internationals: France U21.

2004–05	Caen	8	0		
2005–06	Caen	29	8		
2006–07	Caen	37	15		
2007–08	Caen	36	10	110	33
2008–09	Bordeaux	32	3		
2009–10	Bordeaux	32	5		
2010–11	Bordeaux	21	2		
2011–12	Bordeaux	34	14		
2012–13	Bordeaux	20	8	139	32
2012–13	Newcastle U	13	3		
2013–14	Newcastle U	35	6		
2014–15	Newcastle U	31	2		
2015–16	Newcastle U	8	0	89	11

HAIDARA, Massadio (D)   81 0
H: 5 11 W: 11 10 b.Trappes 2-12-92
Internationals: France U19, U20, U21.

2010–11	AS Nancy	8	0		
2011–12	AS Nancy	19	0		
2012–13	AS Nancy	17	0	44	0
2012–13	Newcastle U	0	0		
2013–14	Newcastle U	11	0		
2014–15	Newcastle U	15	0		
2015–16	Newcastle U	7	0	37	0

JANMAAT, Daryl (D)   240 15
H: 6 1 W: 12 13 b.Leidschendam 22-7-89
Internationals: Netherlands U20, U21, Full caps.

2007–08	Den Haag	25	2	25	2
2008–09	Heerenveen	10	0		
2009–10	Heerenveen	28	0		
2010–11	Heerenveen	24	3		
2011–12	Heerenveen	22	2	84	5
2012–13	Feyenoord	32	3		
2013–14	Feyenoord	30	2	62	5
2014–15	Newcastle U	37	1		
2015–16	Newcastle U	32	2	69	3

KRUL, Tim (G)   191 0
H: 6 2 W: 11 08 b.Den Haag 3-4-88
Internationals: Netherlands U15, U16, U17, U19, U20, U21, Full caps.

2005–06	Newcastle U	0	0		
2006–07	Newcastle U	0	0		
2007–08	*Falkirk*	22	0	22	0
2007–08	Newcastle U	0	0		
2008–09	Newcastle U	0	0		
2008–09	*Carlisle U*	9	0	9	0
2009–10	Newcastle U	3	0		
2010–11	Newcastle U	21	0		
2011–12	Newcastle U	38	0		
2012–13	Newcastle U	36	0		
2013–14	Newcastle U	36	0		
2014–15	Newcastle U	30	0		
2015–16	Newcastle U	8	0	160	0

LASCELLES, Jamaal (D)   83 6
H: 6 2 W: 13 01 b.Derby 11-11-93
Internationals: England U18, U19, U20, U21.

2010–11	Nottingham F	0	0		
2011–12	Nottingham F	1	0		
2011–12	*Stevenage*	7	1	7	1
2012–13	Nottingham F	2	0		
2013–14	Nottingham F	29	2		
2014–15	Newcastle U	0	0		
2014–15	*Nottingham F*	26	1	58	3
2015–16	Newcastle U	18	2	18	2

MARVEAUX, Sylvain (M)   164 18
H: 5 8 W: 10 05 b.Vannes 15-4-86
Internationals: France U21.

2006–07	Rennes	28	5		
2007–08	Rennes	24	0		
2008–09	Rennes	5	0		
2009–10	Rennes	35	10		
2010–11	Rennes	10	1	102	16
2011–12	Newcastle U	7	0		
2012–13	Newcastle U	22	1		
2013–14	Newcastle U	9	0		
2014–15	Newcastle U	0	0		
2014–15	*Guingamp*	24	1	24	1
2015–16	Newcastle U	0	0	38	1

MBABU, Kevin (D) 4 0
H: 6 0　W: 12 03　b.Zurich 19-4-95
Internationals: Switzerland U16, U17, U18, U19.

Season	Club				
2012-13	Servette	1	0	1	0
2012-13	Newcastle U	0	0		
2013-14	Newcastle U	0	0		
2014-15	Newcastle U	0	0		
2014-15	*Rangers*	0	0		
2015-16	Newcastle U	3	0	3	0

MBEMBA, Chancel (D) 96 6
H: 6 0　W: 12 00　b.Kinshasa 8-8-94
Internationals: DR Congo Full caps.

2011-12	Anderlecht	0	0		
2012-13	Anderlecht	0	0		
2013-14	Anderlecht	35	5		
2014-15	Anderlecht	28	1	63	6
2015-16	Newcastle U	33	0	33	0

MITROVIC, Aleksandar (F) 156 65
H: 6 2　W: 13 10　b.Smederevo 16-9-94
Internationals: Serbia U19, U21, Full caps.

2011-12	Teleoptik	25	7	25	7
2012-13	Partizan Belgrade	25	10		
2013-14	Partizan Belgrade	3	3	28	13
2013-14	Anderlecht	32	16		
2014-15	Anderlecht	37	20	69	36
2015-16	Newcastle U	34	9	34	9

OBERTAN, Gabriel (F) 141 6
H: 6 1　W: 12 06　b.Paris 26-2-89
Internationals: France U16, U17, U18, U19, U21.

2006-07	Bordeaux	17	1		
2007-08	Bordeaux	26	2		
2008-09	Bordeaux	11	0	54	3
2008-09	*Lorient*	15	1	15	1
2009-10	Manchester U	7	0		
2010-11	Manchester U	7	0	14	0
2011-12	Newcastle U	23	1		
2012-13	Newcastle U	14	0		
2013-14	Newcastle U	3	0		
2014-15	Newcastle U	13	1		
2015-16	Newcastle U	5	0	58	2

PEREZ, Ayoze (F) 116 30
H: 5 10　W: 10 06　b.Santa Cruz de Tenerife 23-7-93
Internationals: Spain U21.

2012-13	Tenerife	16	1		
2013-14	Tenerife	30	16	46	17
2014-15	Newcastle U	36	7		
2015-16	Newcastle U	34	6	70	13

RIVIERE, Emmanuel (F) 187 41
H: 6 0　W: 12 00　b.Lamentin 3-3-90
Internationals: France U16, U17, U18, U19, U21.

2008-09	St Etienne	8	1		
2009-10	St Etienne	30	8		
2010-11	St Etienne	35	8	73	17
2011-12	Toulouse	26	5		
2012-13	Toulouse	18	4	44	9
2012-13	Monaco	14	4		
2013-14	Monaco	30	10	44	14
2014-15	Newcastle U	23	1		
2015-16	Newcastle U	3	0	26	1

ROBERTS, Callum (M) 0 0
b. 1-4-97

2014-15	Newcastle U	0	0		
2015-16	Newcastle U	0	0		

SAIVET, Henri (M) 156 20
H: 5 9　W: 10 08　b.Dakar 26-10-90
Internationals: France U16, U17, U18, U21. Senegal Full caps.

2007-08	Bordeaux	1	0		
2008-09	Bordeaux	1	0		
2009-10	Bordeaux	3	0		
2010-11	Bordeaux	6	0		
2010-11	*Angers*	18	3	18	3
2011-12	Bordeaux	24	1		
2012-13	Bordeaux	34	8		
2013-14	Bordeaux	33	6		
2014-15	Bordeaux	14	0		
2015-16	Bordeaux	18	2	134	17
2015-16	Newcastle U	4	0	4	0

SATKA, Lubomir (D) 6 0
H: 6 1　W: 11 05　b.Ilava 2-12-95
Internationals: Slovakia U17, U18, U19, U21.

2013-14	Newcastle U	0	0		
2014-15	Newcastle U	0	0		
2015-16	Newcastle U	0	0		
2015-16	*York C*	6	0	6	0

SHELVEY, Jonjo (M) 193 25
H: 6 1　W: 11 02　b.Romford 27-2-92
Internationals: England U16, U17, U19, U21, Full caps.

2007-08	Charlton Ath	2	0		
2008-09	Charlton Ath	16	3		
2009-10	Charlton Ath	24	4	42	7
2010-11	Liverpool	15	0		
2011-12	Liverpool	13	1		
2011-12	*Blackpool*	10	6	10	6
2012-13	Liverpool	19	1	47	2
2013-14	Swansea C	32	6		
2014-15	Swansea C	31	3		
2015-16	Swansea C	16	1	79	10
2015-16	Newcastle U	15	0	15	0

SISSOKO, Moussa (M) 308 31
H: 6 2　W: 13 00　b.Le Blanc Mesnil 16-8-89
Internationals: France U16, U17, U18, U19, U21, Full caps.

2007-08	Toulouse	29	1		
2008-09	Toulouse	35	4		
2009-10	Toulouse	37	7		
2010-11	Toulouse	35	5		
2011-12	Toulouse	35	2		
2012-13	Toulouse	19	1	190	20
2012-13	Newcastle U	12	3		
2013-14	Newcastle U	35	3		
2014-15	Newcastle U	34	4		
2015-16	Newcastle U	37	1	118	11

SMITH, Liam (M) 8 0
b.South Shields 28-9-95

2015-16	Newcastle U	0	0		
2015-16	*Blackpool*	8	0	8	0

STERRY, Jamie (D) 1 0
H: 5 11　W: 11 00　b.Newcastle upon Tyne 21-11-95

2014-15	Newcastle U	0	0		
2015-16	Newcastle U	1	0	1	0

TAYLOR, Steven (D) 221 13
H: 6 2　W: 13 01　b.Greenwich 23-1-86
Internationals: England U16, U17, U20, U21, B.

2002-03	Newcastle U	0	0		
2003-04	Newcastle U	1	0		
2003-04	*Wycombe W*	6	0	6	0
2004-05	Newcastle U	13	0		
2005-06	Newcastle U	12	0		
2006-07	Newcastle U	27	2		
2007-08	Newcastle U	31	1		
2008-09	Newcastle U	21	4		
2009-10	Newcastle U	21	1		
2010-11	Newcastle U	14	3		
2011-12	Newcastle U	14	0		
2012-13	Newcastle U	25	0		
2013-14	Newcastle U	10	1		
2014-15	Newcastle U	10	1		
2015-16	Newcastle U	10	0	215	13

THAUVIN, Florian (M) 145 25
H: 5 10　W: 11 00　b.Orleans 23-1-93
Internationals: France U18, U19, U20, U21.

2010-11	Grenoble	3	0	3	0
2011-12	Bastia	13	0		
2012-13	Bastia	19	3		
2012-13	Lille	0	0		
2012-13	Bastia	13	7	45	10
2013-14	Marseille	31	8		
2014-15	Marseille	36	5		
2015-16	Marseille	2	0	84	15
2015-16	Newcastle U	13	0	13	0
2015-16	*Marseille*	15	2		

TIOTE, Cheik (M) 226 4
H: 5 11　W: 12 06　b.Yamoussoukro 21-6-86
Internationals: Ivory Coast Full caps.

2005-06	Anderlecht	2	0		
2006-07	Anderlecht	2	0	4	0
2007-08	Roda JC	26	2	26	2
2008-09	Twente	28	0		
2009-10	Twente	28	1		
2010-11	Twente	2	0	58	1
2010-11	Newcastle U	26	1		
2011-12	Newcastle U	24	0		
2012-13	Newcastle U	24	0		
2013-14	Newcastle U	33	0		
2014-15	Newcastle U	11	0		
2015-16	Newcastle U	20	0	138	1

TONEY, Ivan (F) 70 12
H: 5 10　W: 12 00　b.Northampton 16-3-96

2012-13	Northampton T	0	0		
2013-14	Northampton T	13	3		
2014-15	Northampton T	40	8	53	11
2015-16	Newcastle U	2	0	2	0
2015-16	*Barnsley*	15	1	15	1

TOWNSEND, Andros (M) 164 18
H: 6 0　W: 12 00　b.Chingford 16-7-91
Internationals: England U16, U17, U19, U21, Full caps.

2008-09	Tottenham H	0	0		
2008-09	*Yeovil T*	10	1	10	1
2009-10	Tottenham H	0	0		
2009-10	*Leyton Orient*	22	2	22	2
2009-10	*Milton Keynes D*	9	2	9	2
2010-11	Tottenham H	0	0		
2010-11	*Ipswich T*	13	1	13	1
2010-11	*Watford*	3	0	3	0
2010-11	*Millwall*	11	2	11	2
2011-12	Tottenham H	0	0		
2011-12	*Leeds U*	6	1	6	1
2011-12	*Birmingham C*	15	0	15	0
2012-13	Tottenham H	5	0		
2012-13	*QPR*	12	2	12	2
2013-14	Tottenham H	25	1		
2014-15	Tottenham H	17	2		
2015-16	Tottenham H	3	0	50	3
2015-16	Newcastle U	13	4	13	4

VUCKIC, Haris (F) 71 15
H: 6 2　W: 12 02　b.Ljubljana 21-8-92
Internationals: Slovenia U17, U19, U21, Full caps.

2007-08	Domzale	1	0		
2008-09	Domzale	4	0	5	0
2009-10	Newcastle U	2	0		
2010-11	Newcastle U	0	0		
2011-12	Newcastle U	4	0		
2011-12	*Cardiff C*	5	1	5	1
2012-13	Newcastle U	0	0		
2013-14	Newcastle U	0	0		
2013-14	*Rotherham U*	22	4	22	4
2014-15	Newcastle U	1	0		
2014-15	*Rangers*	17	8	17	8
2015-16	Newcastle U	0	0		
2015-16	*Wigan Ath*	15	2	15	2

WIJNALDUM, Georginio (M) 258 75
H: 5 8　W: 10 10　b.Rotterdam 11-11-90
Internationals: Netherlands U17, U19, U21, Full caps.

2006-07	Feyenoord	3	0		
2007-08	Feyenoord	10	1		
2008-09	Feyenoord	33	4		
2009-10	Feyenoord	31	4		
2010-11	Feyenoord	34	14	111	23
2011-12	PSV Eindhoven	32	9		
2012-13	PSV Eindhoven	33	14		
2013-14	PSV Eindhoven	11	4		
2014-15	PSV Eindhoven	33	14	109	41
2015-16	Newcastle U	38	11	38	11

WILLIAMS, Callum (D) 0 0
b.Bishop Auckland 4-2-97

2015-16	Newcastle U	0	0		

WOODMAN, Freddie (G) 11 0
H: 6 1　W: 10 12　b.London 4-3-97
Internationals: England U16, U17, U18, U19.

2014-15	Newcastle U	0	0		
2014-15	*Hartlepool U*	0	0		
2015-16	Newcastle U	0	0		
2015-16	*Crawley T*	11	0	11	0

Players retained or with offer of contract
Heardman, Tom.

Scholars
Adu-Peprah, Gideon; Aziakonou, Yannick; Bailey, Owen John Edward; Broccoli, Stefan; Cameron, Kyle Milne; Charman, Luke; Gallacher, Owen John; Gibson, Liam Steven; Harker, Nathan; Heaney, Mackenzie; Holmes, Jamie Jason; Hunter, Jack David; Kitchen, Benjamin; Long, Oliver James; Longstaff, Sean David; Lowther, Daniel Robert; McNall, Lewis; Newberry, Michael; Pearson, Brendan Conor; Smith, Ben Joseph; Smith, Callum; Spooner, Craig; Ward, Daniel John; Williams, Callum Dylan; Woolston, Paul Hudson .

NEWPORT CO (56)

ANGEL, Liam (M) 0 0
H: 8-17-3-99
Internationals: Wales U16, U17.

2015-16	Newport Co	0	0		

AYINA, John-Christophe (F) 66 11
b.9-4-91

2010-11	PSV Eindhoven	0	0		
2011-12	Quevilly Rouen	10	2	10	2
2012-13	Cordoba	5	0		
2012-13	Ecija	17	3	17	3

2013–14	Cordoba	3	0	8	0
2013–14	Racing Santander	17	5	17	5
2014–15	Getafe	0	0		
2015–16	Rochdale	0	0		
2015–16	Newport Co	14	1	14	1

BAMFORD, Lewis (M) 1 0
b. 23-11-97

2015–16	Newport Co	1	0	1	0

BARROW, Scott (D) 34 2
H: 5 9 W: 11 00 b.Swansea 19-10-88
From Port Talbot T, Tamworth, Macclesfield T.

2015–16	Newport Co	34	2	34	2

BODEN, Scott (F) 156 28
H: 5 11 W: 11 00 b.Sheffield 19-12-89

2008–09	Chesterfield	11	2		
2009–10	Chesterfield	35	6		
2010–11	Chesterfield	23	3		
2011–12	Chesterfield	26	4		
2011–12	*Macclesfield T*	7	0	7	0
2012–13	Chesterfield	9	0		
2012–13	*Alfreton T*	0	0		
2013–14	Chesterfield	0	0	104	15
2015–16	Newport Co	45	13	45	13

BYRNE, Mark (M) 201 20
H: 5 9 W: 11 00 b.Dublin 9-11-88

2006–07	Nottingham F	0	0		
2007–08	Nottingham F	1	0		
2008–09	Nottingham F	1	0		
2009–10	Nottingham F	0	0		
2010–11	Nottingham F	0	0	2	0
2010–11	*Barnet*	28	6		
2011–12	*Barnet*	43	5		
2012–13	*Barnet*	40	3	111	14
2014–15	Newport Co	42	4		
2015–16	Newport Co	46	2	88	6

DAY, Joe (G) 81 0
H: 6 1 W: 12 00 b.Brighton 13-8-90

2011–12	Peterborough U	0	0		
2012–13	Peterborough U	0	0		
2013–14	Peterborough U	4	0		
2014–15	Peterborough U	0	0	4	0
2014–15	*Newport Co*	36	0		
2015–16	Newport Co	41	0	77	0

ELITO, Medy (M) 196 24
H: 6 2 W: 12 00 b.Kinshasa 20-3-90
Internationals: England U17, U18, U19.

2007–08	Colchester U	11	1		
2008–09	Colchester U	5	0		
2009–10	Colchester U	3	0		
2009–10	*Cheltenham T*	12	3		
2010–11	Colchester U	0	0	19	1
2010–11	*Cheltenham T*	2	0	14	3
2011–12	Dagenham & R	10	2		
2011–12	*Cheltenham T*	24	4		
2012–13	Dagenham & R	46	6		
2013–14	Dagenham & R	45	7	125	19
2015–16	Newport Co	38	1	38	1

FEELY, Kevin (D) 65 2
H: 5 10 W: 11 07 b.Dublin 30-8-92
Internationals: Republic of Ireland U21.

2011	Bohemians	5	0		
2012	Bohemians	23	1	28	1
2012–13	Charlton Ath	0	0		
2013–14	Charlton Ath	0	0		
2013–14	*Carlisle U*	2	0	2	0
2013–14	*AFC Wimbledon*	0	0		
2014–15	Newport Co	10	1		
2014–15	Newport Co	22	0		
2015–16	Newport Co	3	0	35	1

GREEN, Joe (G) 0 0

2015–16	Newport Co	0	0

HOLMES, Danny (D) 227 7
H: 6 0 W: 11 13 b.Birkenhead 6-1-89

2007–08	Tranmere R	11	0		
2008–09	Tranmere R	1	0		
2009–10	The New Saints	32	0		
2010–11	The New Saints	26	3	58	3
2011–12	Tranmere R	26	0		
2012–13	Tranmere R	43	2		
2013–14	Tranmere R	28	0		
2014–15	Tranmere R	36	2	134	4
2015–16	Newport Co	35	0	35	0

HUGHES, Andrew (D) 67 3
b.Cardiff 5-6-92
Internationals: Wales U23.

2013–14	Newport Co	26	2		
2014–15	Newport Co	16	1		
2015–16	Newport Co	25	0	67	0

JOHN-LEWIS, Lemell (M) 183 20
H: 5 10 W: 11 10 b.Hammersmith 17-5-89

2006–07	Lincoln C	0	0		
2007–08	Lincoln C	21	3		
2008–09	Lincoln C	27	4		
2009–10	Lincoln C	24	1	72	8
2010–11	Bury	39	2		
2011–12	Bury	28	5		
2012–13	Bury	16	2	83	9
2015–16	Newport Co	28	3	28	3

JONES, Dafydd (F) 0 0
b. 5-6-98

2015–16	Newport Co	0	0

JONES, Darren (D) 273 12
H: 6 0 W: 14 12 b.Newport 28-8-83

2000–01	Bristol C	0	0		
2001–02	Bristol C	2	0		
2002–03	Bristol C	0	0		
2003–04	Bristol C	0	0	2	0
2003–04	*Cheltenham T*	14	1	14	1

From Forest Green R.

2009–10	Hereford U	41	3	41	3
2010–11	Aldershot T	43	1		
2011–12	Aldershot T	42	0	85	1
2012–13	Shrewsbury T	38	1		
2013–14	Shrewsbury T	15	0	53	1
2013–14	*AFC Wimbledon*	18	1	18	1
2014–15	Newport Co	43	4		

From Forest Green R.

2015–16	Newport Co	17	1	60	5

KLUKOWSKI, Yan (M) 66 5
H: 6 1 W: 13 05 b.Chippenham 1-1-87

2014–15	Newport Co	38	4		
2015–16	Newport Co	28	1	66	5

MEECHAN, Tom (M) 3 0
From St Ives T, Godmanchester R, St Neots T.

2015–16	Newport Co	3	0	3	0

MORGAN, Dean (M) 389 52
H: 5 11 W: 13 00 b.Enfield 3-10-83
Internationals: Montserrat Full caps.

2000–01	Colchester U	4	0		
2001–02	Colchester U	30	0		
2002–03	Colchester U	37	6		
2003–04	Colchester U	0	0	71	6
2003–04	Reading	13	1		
2004–05	Reading	18	2	31	3
2005–06	Luton T	36	6		
2006–07	Luton T	36	4		
2007–08	Luton T	16	1		
2007–08	*Southend U*	8	0	8	0
2007–08	*Crewe Alex*	9	1	9	1
2008–09	Luton T	0	0		
2008–09	*Leyton Orient*	32	5	32	5
2009–10	Luton T	0	0	88	11
2009–10	*Milton Keynes D*	9	1	9	1
2009–10	*Aldershot T*	9	4	9	4
2010–11	Chesterfield	21	1		
2011–12	Chesterfield	17	3	38	4
2011–12	*Oxford U*	10	1	10	1
2012–13	Wycombe W	33	7		
2013–14	Wycombe W	29	8	62	15
2014–15	Crawley T	13	0	13	0
2015–16	Newport Co	9	1	9	1

NANA OFORI-TWUMASI, Seth (D) 38 0
H: 5 8 W: 11 09 b.Accra 15-5-90
Internationals: England U16, U17, U18, U20.

2009–10	*Dagenham & R*	0	0		
2010–11	Peterborough U	0	0		
2011–12	*Northampton T*	0	0		
2012–13	Northampton T	0	0		
2013–14	Yeovil T	3	0		
2014–15	Yeovil T	25	0	28	0
2015–16	Newport Co	10	0	10	0

OWEN-EVANS, Tom (F) 16 0
b. 18-3-97

2014–15	Newport Co	1	0		
2015–16	Newport Co	15	0	16	0

PARSELLE, Kieran (D) 7 0
b. 30-11-96

2015–16	Newport Co	7	0	7	0

PARTRIDGE, Matt (D) 46 1
H: 6 3 W: 13 02 b.Reading 24-10-84

2012–13	Reading	0	0		
2013–14	Reading	0	0		
2014–15	Dagenham & R	24	1		
2015–16	Dagenham & R	2	0	26	1

From Basingstoke T.

2015–16	Newport Co	20	0	20	0

RALPH, Nathan (D) 35 1
H: 5 9 W: 11 00 b.Dunmow 14-2-93

2011–12	Peterborough U	0	0		
2012–13	Yeovil T	14	1		
2013–14	Yeovil T	0	0		
2014–15	Yeovil T	21	0	35	1
2015–16	Newport Co	0	0		

RODMAN, Alex (F) 90 12
H: 6 2 W: 12 08 b.Sutton Coldfield 15-2-87
Internationals: England C.

2010–11	Aldershot T	14	5		
2011–12	Aldershot T	18	1		
2012–13	Aldershot T	11	1	43	7
2012–13	*York C*	18	1	18	1
2015–16	Newport Co	29	4	29	4

SHEPHARD, Corey (D) 0 0
b. 28-12-97

2015–16	Newport Co	0	0

TAYLOR, Matthew (D) 202 11
H: 6 0 W: 12 04 b.Chorley 30-1-82

2008–09	Exeter C	31	2		
2009–10	Exeter C	46	5		
2010–11	Exeter C	28	2	105	9
2011–12	Charlton Ath	41	0		
2012–13	Charlton Ath	12	0	53	0
2013–14	Bradford C	2	0	2	0
2013–14	*Colchester U*	5	1	5	1
2014–15	Cheltenham T	33	1	33	1
2015–16	Newport Co	4	0	4	0

TAYLOR, Rhys (G) 65 0
H: 6 2 W: 12 08 b.Neath 7-4-90
Internationals: Wales U17, U19, U21.

2007–08	Chelsea	0	0		
2008–09	Chelsea	0	0		
2009–10	Chelsea	0	0		
2010–11	Chelsea	0	0		
2010–11	*Crewe Alex*	44	0	44	0
2011–12	Chelsea	0	0		
2011–12	*Rotherham U*	20	0	20	0
2012–13	Chelsea	0	0		
2012–13	*Preston NE*	0	0		
2012–13	*Macclesfield T*	0	0		
2015–16	Newport Co	1	0	1	0

TURLEY, Jamie (D) 0 0
H: 6 1 W: 12 13 b.Reading 7-4-90

2014–15	Swindon T	0	0
2015–16	Newport Co	0	0

Non-Contract
Meechan, Thomas.

Scholars
Bamford, Lewis Paul; Evans, Andrew James; Gray, Nyall James Wade; Hughes, Connah William; James, Samuel Evan; Jones, Dafydd Rhys; Kavanagh, Rhys Michael; Mathias, Nathan; Molyneux, Dion Richard; Mpadi, Cedrick Matondo; Redman, Ellis Anthony David; Shephard, Corey John; Smith, Cairan; Tolland, Kyron; Waterhouse, Harry James; Wood, Finlay; Young, Jake Edward.

NORTHAMPTON T (57)

ADAMS, Nicky (F) 367 33
H: 5 10 W: 11 00 b.Bolton 16-10-86
Internationals: Wales U21.

2005–06	Bury	15	1		
2006–07	Bury	19	1		
2007–08	Bury	43	12		
2008–09	Leicester C	12	0		
2008–09	*Rochdale*	14	1		
2009–10	Leicester C	18	0	30	0
2009–10	*Leyton Orient*	6	0	6	0
2010–11	Brentford	7	0	7	0
2010–11	Rochdale	30	0		
2011–12	Rochdale	41	4	85	5
2012–13	Crawley T	46	8		
2013–14	Crawley T	24	1	70	9
2013–14	*Rotherham U*	15	1	15	1
2013–14	Bury	0	0		
2014–15	Bury	38	1	115	15
2015–16	Northampton T	39	3	39	3

BROWN, Brendan (G) 0 0
b. 15-11-96

2014–15	Northampton T	0	0
2015–16	Northampton T	0	0

BUCHANAN, David (M) 370 2
H: 5 7 W: 11 03 b.Rochdale 6-5-86
Internationals: Northern Ireland U19, U21.

2004–05	Bury	3	0
2005–06	Bury	23	0
2006–07	Bury	41	0

2007–08	Bury	35	0		
2008–09	Bury	46	0		
2009–10	Bury	38	0	186	0
2010–11	Hamilton A	28	1	28	1
2011–12	Tranmere R	41	1	41	1
2012–13	Preston NE	33	0		
2013–14	Preston NE	19	0		
2014–15	Preston NE	17	0	69	0
2015–16	Northampton T	46	0	46	0

BYROM, Joel (M)   151 13
H: 6 0   W: 12 04   b.Accrington 14-9-86
Internationals: England C.

2004–05	Blackburn R	0	0		
2005–06	Blackburn R	0	0		
2006–07	Accrington S	1	0	1	0

From Clitheroe, Southport, Clitheroe, Northwich Vic.

2010–11	Stevenage	7	0		
2011–12	Stevenage	32	4	39	4
2012–13	Preston NE	22	2		
2013–14	Preston NE	11	2	33	4
2013–14	Oldham Ath	4	0	4	0
2014–15	Northampton T	39	3		
2015–16	Northampton T	35	2	74	5

CLARKE, Ryan (G)   219 0
H: 6 3   W: 13 00   b.Bristol 30-4-82

2001–02	Bristol R	1	0		
2002–03	Bristol R	2	0		
2003–04	Bristol R	2	0		
2004–05	Bristol R	18	0	23	0
2004–05	Southend U	1	0	1	0
2004–05	Kidderminster H	6	0	6	0

From Salisbury C.

2010–11	Oxford U	46	0		
2011–12	Oxford U	42	0		
2012–13	Oxford U	24	0		
2013–14	Oxford U	46	0		
2014–15	Oxford U	31	0	189	0
2015–16	Northampton T	0	0		

CLIFTON, Danny (M)   0 0
b.Northampton 8-11-96

2014–15	Northampton T	0	0		
2015–16	Northampton T	0	0		

CORRY, Paul (M)   103 8
H: 6 2   W: 11 12   b.Dublin 3-2-91
Internationals: Republic of Ireland U17.

2010	UCD	28	4		
2011	UCD	36	2		
2012	UCD	17	1	81	7
2012–13	Sheffield W	6	0		
2012–13	Tranmere R	6	0	6	0
2013–14	Sheffield W	1	0		
2014–15	Sheffield W	0	0	7	0
2014–15	Carlisle U	6	1	6	1
2015–16	Northampton T	3	0	3	0

CRESSWELL, Ryan (D)   235 24
H: 5 9   W: 10 05   b.Rotherham 22-12-87

2006–07	Sheffield U	0	0		
2007–08	Sheffield U	0	0		
2007–08	Rotherham U	3	0		
2007–08	Morecambe	2	0	2	0
2007–08	Macclesfield T	19	1	19	1
2008–09	Bury	25	1		
2009–10	Bury	28	0	53	1
2010–11	Rotherham U	22	4		
2011–12	Rotherham U	16	4	41	8
2012–13	Southend U	43	6	43	6
2013–14	Fleetwood T	20	1		
2014–15	Fleetwood T	1	0	21	1
2014–15	Northampton T	32	5		
2015–16	Northampton T	24	2	56	7

D'ATH, Lawson (M)   125 15
H: 5 9   W: 12 02   b.Witney 24-12-92

2010–11	Reading	0	0		
2011–12	Reading	0	0		
2011–12	Yeovil T	14	1	14	1
2012–13	Reading	0	0		
2012–13	Cheltenham T	2	1	2	1
2012–13	Exeter C	8	1	8	1
2013–14	Reading	0	0		
2013–14	Dagenham & R	21	1	21	1
2014–15	Northampton T	41	7		
2015–16	Northampton T	39	4	80	11

DIAMOND, Zander (D)   348 26
H: 6 2   W: 11 07   b.Alexandria 3-12-85
Internationals: Scotland U21.

2003–04	Aberdeen	19	2		
2004–05	Aberdeen	29	3		
2005–06	Aberdeen	33	0		
2006–07	Aberdeen	21	0		
2007–08	Aberdeen	26	3		
2008–09	Aberdeen	28	4		
2009–10	Aberdeen	16	3		
2010–11	Aberdeen	32	1	204	16
2011–12	Oldham Ath	23	2	23	2
2012–13	Burton Alb	37	4		
2013–14	Burton Alb	10	1	47	5
2013–14	*Northampton T*	14	1		
2014–15	Northampton T	21	1		
2015–16	Northampton T	39	1	74	3

HACKETT, Chris (M)   387 25
H: 6 0   W: 12 08   b.Oxford 1-3-83

1999–2000	Oxford U	2	0		
2000–01	Oxford U	16	2		
2001–02	Oxford U	15	0		
2002–03	Oxford U	12	0		
2003–04	Oxford U	22	1		
2004–05	Oxford U	37	4		
2005–06	Oxford U	21	2	125	9
2005–06	Hearts	2	0	2	0
2006–07	Millwall	33	3		
2007–08	Millwall	6	0		
2008–09	Millwall	22	0		
2009–10	Millwall	40	2		
2010–11	Millwall	16	0		
2011–12	Millwall	3	0	120	5
2011–12	Exeter C	5	0	5	0
2011–12	Wycombe W	8	0	8	0
2012–13	Northampton T	41	6		
2013–14	Northampton T	37	2		
2014–15	Northampton T	38	3		
2015–16	Northampton T	6	0	122	11
2015–16	Barnet	5	0	5	0

HOLMES, Ricky (M)   193 31
H: 6 1   W: 11 11   b.Southend 19-6-87
Internationals: England C.

2010–11	Barnet	25	2		
2011–12	Barnet	41	8		
2012–13	Barnet	25	5	91	15
2013–14	Portsmouth	40	2		
2013–14	Portsmouth	13	0	53	2
2014–15	Northampton T	21	5		
2015–16	Northampton T	28	9	49	14

HORWOOD, Evan (D)   295 6
H: 6 0   W: 10 06   b.Billingham 10-3-86

2004–05	Sheffield U	0	0		
2004–05	Stockport Co	10	0	10	0
2005–06	Sheffield U	0	0		
2005–06	Scunthorpe U	0	0		
2005–06	Chester C	1	0	1	0
2006–07	Sheffield U	0	0		
2006–07	Darlington	20	0	20	0
2007–08	Sheffield U	0	0		
2007–08	Gretna	15	1	15	1
2007–08	Carlisle U	19	0		
2008–09	Carlisle U	24	0		
2009–10	Carlisle U	32	0	75	0
2010–11	Hartlepool U	45	2		
2011–12	Hartlepool U	41	1		
2012–13	Hartlepool U	37	2	123	5
2013–14	Tranmere R	18	0	18	0
2013–14	*Northampton T*	8	0		
2014–15	Northampton T	25	0		
2015–16	Northampton T	0	0	33	0

HOSKINS, Sam (F)   87 10
H: 5 8   W: 10 07   b.Dorchester 4-2-93

2011–12	Southampton	0	0		
2011–12	*Preston NE*	0	0		
2011–12	*Rotherham U*	8	2	8	2
2012–13	Southampton	0	0		
2012–13	Stevenage	14	1	14	1
2013–14	Yeovil T	19	0		
2014–15	Yeovil T	12	1	31	1
2015–16	Northampton T	34	6	34	6

JACKSON, Ben (D)   0 0
b. 19-10-96

2014–15	Northampton T	0	0		
2015–16	Northampton T	0	0		

LELAN, Josh (D)   16 0
H: 6 1   W: 11 00   b.Derby 21-12-94

2012–13	Derby Co	0	0		
2013–14	Derby Co	0	0		
2014–15	Derby Co	0	0		
2014–15	*Swindon T*	5	0	5	0
2015–16	Northampton T	11	0	11	0

McDONALD, Rod (D)   23 3
H: 6 3   W: 12 13   b.Crewe 11-4-92

2010–11	Oldham Ath	0	0		

From Colwyn Bay, Nantwich T, Hereford U, AFC Telford U.

2015–16	Northampton T	23	3	23	3

McWILLIAMS, Shaun (M)   0 0
b.Northampton 14-8-98

2014–15	Northampton T	0	0		
2015–16	Northampton T	0	0		

MOLONEY, Brendan (M)   173 4
H: 6 1   W: 11 12   b.Killarney 18-1-89
Internationals: Republic of Ireland U21.

2005–06	Nottingham F	0	0		
2006–07	Nottingham F	0	0		
2007–08	Nottingham F	2	0		
2007–08	*Chesterfield*	9	1	9	1
2008–09	Nottingham F	12	0		
2009–10	Nottingham F	0	0		
2009–10	*Notts Co*	18	1	18	1
2009–10	*Scunthorpe U*	3	0	3	0
2010–11	Nottingham F	6	0		
2011–12	Nottingham F	8	0		
2012–13	Nottingham F	13	0	42	0
2012–13	Bristol C	17	0		
2013–14	Bristol C	32	0	49	0
2014–15	*Yeovil T*	5	0	5	0
2014–15	Northampton T	22	1		
2015–16	Northampton T	25	1	47	2

NEWEY, Tom (D)   428 8
H: 5 10   W: 10 02   b.Sheffield 31-10-82

2000–01	Leeds U	0	0		
2001–02	Leeds U	0	0		
2002–03	Leeds U	0	0		
2002–03	Cambridge U	6	0		
2002–03	Darlington	7	1	7	1
2003–04	Leyton Orient	34	2		
2004–05	Leyton Orient	20	1	54	3
2004–05	Cambridge U	16	0	22	0
2005–06	Grimsby T	38	1		
2006–07	Grimsby T	43	1		
2007–08	Grimsby T	42	1		
2008–09	Grimsby T	24	0		
2008–09	Rochdale	2	0	2	0
2009–10	Grimsby T	0	0	147	3
2009–10	Bury	32	0	32	0
2010–11	Rotherham U	38	0		
2011–12	Rotherham U	20	0	58	0
2012–13	Scunthorpe U	45	0	45	0
2013–14	Oxford U	40	1		
2014–15	Oxford U	12	0	52	1
2014–15	*Northampton T*	9	0		
2015–16	Northampton T	0	0	9	0

O'TOOLE, John (M)   272 43
H: 6 2   W: 13 07   b.Harrow 30-9-88
Internationals: Republic of Ireland U21.

2007–08	Watford	35	3		
2008–09	Watford	22	7		
2008–09	*Sheffield U*	9	1	9	1
2009–10	Watford	0	0	57	10
2009–10	Colchester U	31	2		
2010–11	Colchester U	15	0		
2011–12	Colchester U	15	0		
2012–13	Colchester U	15	0	72	2
2012–13	*Bristol R*	18	3		
2013–14	Bristol R	41	13	59	16
2014–15	Northampton T	35	2		
2014–15	*Southend U*	2	0	2	0
2015–16	Northampton T	38	12	73	14

POTTER, Alfie (M)   183 22
H: 5 7   W: 9 06   b.Islington 9-1-89

2007–08	Peterborough U	2	0	2	0

From Kettering T.

2010–11	Oxford U	38	2		

From Kettering T.

2011–12	Oxford U	25	2		
2012–13	Oxford U	43	10		
2013–14	Oxford U	24	4		
2014–15	Oxford U	15	2	145	20
2014–15	AFC Wimbledon	15	1	15	1
2014–15	Northampton T	0	0		
2015–16	Northampton T	21	1	21	1

RICHARDS, Marc (F)   473 158
H: 6 2   W: 12 06   b.Wolverhampton 8-7-82
Internationals: England U18, U20.

1999–2000	Blackburn R	0	0		
2000–01	Blackburn R	0	0		
2001–02	Blackburn R	0	0		
2001–02	Crewe Alex	4	0	4	0
2001–02	Oldham Ath	5	0	5	0
2001–02	Halifax T	5	0	5	0
2002–03	Blackburn R	0	0		
2002–03	Swansea C	17	7	17	7
2003–04	Northampton T	41	8		
2004–05	Northampton T	12	2		
2004–05	Rochdale	5	2	5	2
2005–06	Northampton T	0	0		
2005–06	Barnsley	38	12		
2006–07	Barnsley	31	6	69	18
2007–08	Port Vale	29	5		
2008–09	Port Vale	30	10		
2009–10	Port Vale	46	20		
2010–11	Port Vale	40	16		
2011–12	Port Vale	36	17	181	68

2012–13	Chesterfield	34	12		
2013–14	Chesterfield	38	8	72	20
2013–14	Northampton T	0	0		
2014–15	Northampton T	31	18		
2015–16	Northampton T	31	15	115	43

ROSE, Danny (M)   131 9
H: 5 7 W: 10 04 b.Bristol 21-2-88
Internationals: England C.

2006–07	Manchester U	0	0		
2007–08	Manchester U	0	0		
From Oxford U, Newport Co					
2012–13	Fleetwood T	0	0		
2012–13	Aldershot T	34	2	34	2
2013–14	Oxford U	40	4		
2014–15	Oxford U	29	2		
2015–16	Oxford U	13	0	82	6
2015–16	Northampton T	15	1	15	1

SMITH, Adam (G)   50 0
H: 5 11 W: 11 00 b.Sunderland 23-11-92

2010–11	Leicester C	0	0		
2011–12	Leicester C	0	0		
2011–12	*Chesterfield*	0	0		
2011–12	*Bristol R*	0	0		
2012–13	Leicester C	0	0		
2013–14	Leicester C	0	0		
2013–14	*Stevenage*	0	0		
2014–15	Leicester C	0	0		
2014–15	*Mansfield T*	4	0	4	0
2015–16	Northampton T	46	0	46	0

TAYLOR, Jason (M)   361 20
H: 6 1 W: 11 03 b.Ashton-under-Lyne 28-1-87

2005–06	Oldham Ath	0	0		
2005–06	Stockport Co	9	0		
2006–07	Stockport Co	45	1		
2007–08	Stockport Co	42	4		
2008–09	Stockport Co	8	1	104	6
2008–09	Rotherham U	15	1		
2009–10	Rotherham U	2 ·	0		
2009–10	Rochdale	23	1	23	1
2010–11	Rotherham U	42	5		
2011–12	Rotherham U	39	2		
2012–13	Rotherham U	20	2	118	10
2012–13	Cheltenham T	16	0		
2013–14	Cheltenham T	33	2		
2014–15	Cheltenham T	16	0	65	2
2014–15	Northampton T	21	0		
2015–16	Northampton T	30	1	51	1

WARBURTON, Sam (D)   0 0
b. 10-10-96

2014–15	*Northampton T*	0	0		
2015–16	*Northampton T*	0	0		

Scholars
Andrews, Charlie Shaun; Andrews-Lamptey, Ethan Jack Nii-Odartei; Carroll, Thomas Edward; Forster, Matthew James Michael; Goff, James William; Hall, Jamie Luke; Hammond, James; Iaciofano, Giuseppe James; Marsden, Ryan John; Master, Shaquille; McCammon, Joshua Lewis; McWilliams, Shaun Daniel; Mushata, Alex; Toseland, Ben; Westwood, Callum Lee.

NORWICH C (58)

ANDREU, Tony (M)   185 44
H: 5 10 W: 11 05 b.Cagnes-Sur-Mer 22-5-88

2009–10	Nyon	29	2		
2010–11	Nyon	21	2		
2011–12	Nyon	27	6	77	10
2012–13	Livingston	33	7	33	7
2013–14	Hamilton A	35	13		
2014–15	Hamilton A	23	12	58	25
2014–15	Norwich C	6	0		
2015–16	Norwich C	0	0	6	0
2015–16	*Rotherham U*	11	2	11	2

BASSONG, Sebastien (D)   285 7
H: 6 2 W: 11 07 b.Paris 9-7-86
Internationals: France U21. Cameroon Full caps.

2005–06	Metz	23	0		
2006–07	Metz	37	1		
2007–08	Metz	19	0	79	1
2008–09	Newcastle U	30	0		
2009–10	Newcastle U	0	0	30	0
2009–10	Tottenham H	28	1		
2010–11	Tottenham H	12	1		
2011–12	Tottenham H	5	0		
2011–12	*Wolverhampton W*	9	0	9	0
2012–13	Tottenham H	0	0	45	2
2012–13	Norwich C	34	3		
2013–14	Norwich C	27	0		
2014–15	Norwich C	18	0		
2014–15	*Watford*	11	0	11	0
2015–16	Norwich C	32	1	111	4

BENNETT, Ryan (M)   259 14
H: 6 2 W: 11 00 b.Thurrock 6-3-90
Internationals: England U18, U21.

2006–07	Grimsby T	5	0		
2007–08	Grimsby T	40	1		
2008–09	Grimsby T	45	5		
2009–10	Grimsby T	13	0	103	6
2009–10	Peterborough U	22	1		
2010–11	Peterborough U	34	4		
2011–12	Peterborough U	32	1	88	6
2011–12	Norwich C	8	0		
2012–13	Norwich C	15	1		
2013–14	Norwich C	16	1		
2014–15	Norwich C	7	0		
2015–16	Norwich C	20	0	68	2

BRADY, Robert (F)   150 13
H: 5 9 W: 10 12 b.Belfast 14-1-92
Internationals: Republic of Ireland Youth, U21, Full caps.

2008–09	Manchester U	0	0		
2009–10	Manchester U	0	0		
2010–11	Manchester U	0	0		
2011–12	Manchester U	0	0		
2011–12	*Hull C*	39	3		
2012–13	Manchester U	0	0		
2012–13	Hull C	32	4		
2013–14	Hull C	16	3		
2014–15	Hull C	27	0	114	10
2015–16	Norwich C	36	3	36	3

DORRANS, Graham (F)   293 45
H: 5 9 W: 11 07 b.Glasgow 5-5-87
Internationals: Scotland U20, U21, Full caps.

2006–07	Livingston	8	0		
2006–07	*Partick Thistle*	15	5	15	5
2006–07	Livingston	34	5		
2007–08	Livingston	34	11	76	16
2008–09	WBA	8	0		
2009–10	WBA	45	13		
2010–11	WBA	21	1		
2011–12	WBA	31	3		
2012–13	WBA	26	1		
2013–14	WBA	14	2		
2014–15	WBA	21	1	166	21
2014–15	*Norwich C*	15	3		
2015–16	Norwich C	21	0	36	3

GODFREY, Ben (M)   12 1
H: 6 0 W: b.York 15-1-98

2014–15	York C	0	0		
2015–16	York C	12	1	12	1
2015–16	Norwich C	0	0		

HOOLAHAN, Wes (M)   464 61
H: 5 6 W: 10 03 b.Dublin 10-8-83
Internationals: Republic of Ireland U21, B, Full caps.

2001–02	Shelbourne	20	3		
2002–03	Shelbourne	23	0		
2004	Shelbourne	31	2		
2005	Shelbourne	29	4	103	9
2005–06	Livingston	16	0	16	0
2006–07	Blackpool	42	8		
2007–08	Blackpool	45	5	87	13
2008–09	Norwich C	32	2		
2009–10	Norwich C	37	11		
2010–11	Norwich C	41	10		
2011–12	Norwich C	33	4		
2012–13	Norwich C	33	3		
2013–14	Norwich C	16	1		
2014–15	Norwich C	36	4		
2015–16	Norwich C	30	4	258	39

HOWSON, Jonathan (M)   323 39
H: 5 11 W: 12 01 b.Morley 21-5-88
Internationals: England U21.

2006–07	Leeds U	9	1		
2007–08	Leeds U	26	3		
2008–09	Leeds U	40	4		
2009–10	Leeds U	45	4		
2010–11	Leeds U	46	10		
2011–12	Leeds U	19	1	185	23
2011–12	Norwich C	11	1		
2012–13	Norwich C	30	2		
2013–14	Norwich C	27	2		
2014–15	Norwich C	34	8		
2015–16	Norwich C	36	3	138	16

IVO PINTO, Daniel (D)   157 0
H: 6 0 W: 11 07 b.Lourosa 7-1-90
Internationals: Portugal U16, U17, U18, U19, U21.

2008–09	Porto	0	0		
2009–10	Porto	0	0		
2009–10	*Vicente*	1	0	1	0
2009–10	*Vitoria Setubal*	2	0	2	0
2010–11	Porto	0	0		
2010–11	*Covilha*	22	0	22	0
2011–12	Rio Ave	0	0		
2011–12	*Uniao Leiria*	25	0	25	0
2012–13	Cluj	27	0	27	0
2013–14	Dinamo Zagreb	28	0		
2014–15	Dinamo Zagreb	29	0		
2015–16	Dinamo Zagreb	13	0	70	0
2015–16	Norwich C	10	0	10	0

JARVIS, Matthew (M)   371 36
H: 5 8 W: 11 10 b.Middlesbrough 22-5-86
Internationals: England Full caps.

2003–04	Gillingham	10	0		
2004–05	Gillingham	30	3		
2005–06	Gillingham	35	3		
2006–07	Gillingham	35	6	110	12
2007–08	Wolverhampton W	26	1		
2008–09	Wolverhampton W	28	3		
2009–10	Wolverhampton W	34	3		
2010–11	Wolverhampton W	37	4		
2011–12	Wolverhampton W	37	8		
2012–13	Wolverhampton W	2	0	164	19
2012–13	West Ham U	32	2		
2013–14	West Ham U	32	2		
2014–15	West Ham U	11	0		
2015–16	West Ham U	3	0	78	4
2015–16	Norwich C	19	1	19	1

JEROME, Cameron (F)   407 91
H: 6 1 W: 13 06 b.Huddersfield 14-8-86
Internationals: England U21.

2004–05	Cardiff C	29	6		
2005–06	Cardiff C	44	18	73	24
2006–07	Birmingham C	38	7		
2007–08	Birmingham C	33	7		
2008–09	Birmingham C	43	9		
2009–10	Birmingham C	32	11		
2010–11	Birmingham C	34	3		
2011–12	Birmingham C	1	0	181	37
2011–12	Stoke C	26	3		
2012–13	Stoke C	26	3		
2013–14	Stoke C	1	0	50	7
2013–14	*Crystal Palace*	28	2	28	2
2014–15	Norwich C	41	18		
2015–16	Norwich C	34	3	75	21

KEAN, Jake (G)   92 0
H: 6 4 W: 11 13 b.Derby 4-2-91
Internationals: England U20.

2010–11	Blackburn R	0	0		
2010–11	*Hartlepool U*	19	0	19	0
2011–12	Blackburn R	1	0		
2011–12	*Rochdale*	14	0	14	0
2012–13	Blackburn R	18	0		
2013–14	Blackburn R	18	0		
2014–15	Blackburn R	0	0	37	0
2014–15	*Yeovil T*	5	0	5	0
2014–15	*Oldham Ath*	11	0	11	0
2015–16	Norwich C	0	0		
2015–16	*Colchester U*	3	0	3	0
2015–16	*Swindon T*	3	0	3	0

KLOSE, Timm (D)   144 10
H: 6 4 W: 13 10 b.Frankfurt am Main 9-5-88
Internationals: Switzerland U21, U23, Full caps.

2009–10	Thun	29	2		
2010–11	Thun	30	3	59	5
2011–12	Nuremburg	13	0		
2012–13	Nuremburg	32	2	45	2
2013–14	Wolfsburg	10	0		
2014–15	Wolfsburg	12	1		
2015–16	Wolfsburg	8	1	30	2
2015–16	Norwich C	10	1	10	1

LAFFERTY, Kyle (F)   294 64
H: 6 4 W: 11 00 b.Northern Ireland 16-9-87
Internationals: Northern Ireland U17, U19, U21, Full caps.

2005–06	Burnley	11	1		
2005–06	*Darlington*	9	3	9	3
2006–07	Burnley	35	4		
2007–08	Burnley	37	5	83	10
2008–09	Rangers	25	6		
2009–10	Rangers	28	7		
2010–11	Rangers	31	11		
2011–12	Rangers	20	7	104	31
2012–13	Sion	25	5	25	5
2013–14	Palermo	34	11	34	11
2014–15	Norwich C	18	1		
2014–15	*Caykur Rizespor*	14	2	14	2
2015–16	Norwich C	1	0	19	1
2015–16	*Birmingham C*	6	1	6	1

LOZA, Jamar (F) 30 2
H: 5 10 W: 11 01 b.Kingston 10-5-94
Internationals: Jamaica Full caps.
2013–14	Norwich C	1	0	
2013–14	Coventry C	1	0	1 0
2013–14	Leyton Orient	3	0	3 0
2013–14	Southend U	7	1	
2014–15	Norwich C	2	1	
2014–15	Yeovil T	5	0	5 0
2015–16	Norwich C	0	0	3 1
2015–16	Stevenage	1	0	1 0
2015–16	Southend U	10	0	17 1

MADDISON, James (M) 35 5
H: 5 10 W: 11 07 b.Coventry 23-11-96
2013–14	Coventry C	0	0	
2014–15	Coventry C	12	2	
2015–16	Norwich C	0	0	
2015–16	Coventry C	23	3	35 5

MARTIN, Russell (M) 414 21
H: 6 0 W: 11 08 b.Brighton 4-1-86
Internationals: Scotland Full caps.
2004–05	Wycombe W	7	0	
2005–06	Wycombe W	23	3	
2006–07	Wycombe W	42	2	
2007–08	Wycombe W	44	0	116 5
2008–09	Peterborough U	46	1	
2009–10	Peterborough U	10	0	56 1
2009–10	Norwich C	26	0	
2010–11	Norwich C	46	5	
2011–12	Norwich C	33	2	
2012–13	Norwich C	31	3	
2013–14	Norwich C	31	0	
2014–15	Norwich C	45	2	
2015–16	Norwich C	30	3	242 15

MATTHEWS, Remi (G) 11 0
H: 6 0 W: 12 04 b.Gorleston 10-2-94
2014–15	Norwich C	0	0	
2014–15	Burton Alb	0	0	
2015–16	Norwich C	0	0	
2015–16	Burton Alb	2	0	2 0
2015–16	Doncaster R	9	0	9 0

MBOKANI, Dieumerci (F) 325 188
H: 6 1 W: 11 11 b.Kinshasa 22-11-85
Internationals: DR Congo Full caps.
2004	Bel'Or	27	21	27 21
2005	Mazembe	40	40	
2006	Mazembe	32	27	72 67
2006–07	Anderlecht	9	0	
2007–08	Standard Liege	32	15	
2008–09	Standard Liege	29	16	
2009–10	Standard Liege	24	7	85 38
2010–11	Monaco	10	1	10 1
2010–11	Wolfsburg	7	0	
2011–12	Anderlecht	26	0	
2012–13	Anderlecht	27	19	62 38
2013–14	Dynamo Kiev	25	13	
2014–15	Dynamo Kiev	8	3	
2015–16	Dynamo Kiev	0	0	33 16

On loan from Dynamo Kiev.
2015–16	Norwich C	29	7	29 7

McGRANDLES, Conor (M) 71 7
H: 6 0 W: 10 00 b.Falkirk 24-9-95
2012–13	Falkirk	26	2	
2013–14	Falkirk	36	5	
2014–15	Falkirk	3	0	
2014–15	Norwich C	1	0	
2015–16	Norwich C	0	0	1 0
2015–16	Falkirk	5	0	70 7

MORRIS, Carlton (F) 48 8
H: 6 1 W: 13 05 b.Cambridge 16-12-95
Internationals: England U19.
2014–15	Norwich C	1	0	
2014–15	Oxford U	7	0	7 0
2014–15	York C	8	0	8 0
2015–16	Norwich C	0	0	1 0
2015–16	Hamilton A	32	8	32 8

MULUMBU, Youssef (M) 240 16
H: 5 9 W: 10 03 b.Kinshasa 25-1-87
Internationals: France U20, U21. DR Congo Full caps.
2006–07	Paris St Germain	12	0	
2007–08	Paris St Germain	1	0	
2007–08	Amiens	23	1	23 1
2008–09	Paris St Germain	0	0	13 0
2008–09	WBA	6	0	
2009–10	WBA	40	3	
2010–11	WBA	34	7	
2011–12	WBA	35	1	
2012–13	WBA	28	2	
2013–14	WBA	37	2	
2014–15	WBA	17	0	197 15
2015–16	Norwich C	7	0	7 0

MURPHY, Jacob (M) 76 16
H: 5 9 W: 11 03 b.Wembley 24-2-95
Internationals: England U18, U19, U20.
2013–14	Norwich C	0	0	
2013–14	Swindon T	6	0	6 0
2013–14	Southend U	7	1	7 1
2014–15	Norwich C	0	0	
2014–15	Blackpool	9	2	9 2
2014–15	Scunthorpe U	3	0	3 0
2014–15	Colchester U	11	4	11 4
2015–16	Norwich C	0	0	
2015–16	Coventry C	40	9	40 9

MURPHY, Josh (F) 69 6
H: 5 8 W: 10 07 b.London 24-2-95
Internationals: England U18, U19, U20.
2012–13	Norwich C	0	0	
2014–15	Norwich C	9	0	
2014–15	Norwich C	13	1	
2014–15	Wigan Ath	5	0	5 0
2015–16	Norwich C	0	0	
2015–16	Milton Keynes D	42	5	42 5

NAISMITH, Steven (F) 316 76
H: 5 10 W: 11 04 b.Irvine 14-9-86
Internationals: Scotland U21, B, Full caps.
2003–04	Kilmarnock	1	0	
2004–05	Kilmarnock	24	1	
2005–06	Kilmarnock	36	13	
2006–07	Kilmarnock	37	15	
2007–08	Kilmarnock	4	0	102 29
2007–08	Rangers	21	5	
2008–09	Rangers	7	0	
2009–10	Rangers	28	3	
2010–11	Rangers	31	11	
2011–12	Rangers	11	9	98 28
2012–13	Everton	31	4	
2013–14	Everton	31	5	
2014–15	Everton	31	6	
2015–16	Everton	10	3	103 18
2015–16	Norwich C	13	1	13 1

O'NEIL, Gary (M) 425 29
H: 5 10 W: 11 00 b.Beckenham 18-5-83
Internationals: England U19, U20, U21.
1999–2000	Portsmouth	1	0	
2000–01	Portsmouth	10	1	
2001–02	Portsmouth	33	1	
2002–03	Portsmouth	31	3	
2003–04	Portsmouth	3	2	
2003–04	Walsall	7	0	7 0
2004–05	Portsmouth	24	2	
2004–05	Cardiff C	9	1	9 1
2005–06	Portsmouth	36	6	
2006–07	Portsmouth	35	1	
2007–08	Portsmouth	2	0	175 16
2007–08	Middlesbrough	26	0	
2008–09	Middlesbrough	29	4	
2009–10	Middlesbrough	36	4	
2010–11	Middlesbrough	18	0	109 8
2010–11	West Ham U	8	0	
2011–12	West Ham U	16	2	
2012–13	West Ham U	24	1	48 3
2013–14	QPR	29	1	29 1
2014–15	Norwich C	21	0	
2015–16	Norwich C	27	0	48 0

ODJIDJA-OFOE, Vadis (M) 205 24
H: 5 11 W: 10 08 b.Gent 21-2-89
Internationals: Belgium U18, U19, U21, Full caps.
2007–08	Anderlecht	3	1	3 1
2008–09	Hamburg	2	0	2 0
2008–09	Club Brugge	16	0	
2009–10	Club Brugge	35	4	
2010–11	Club Brugge	37	6	
2011–12	Club Brugge	29	4	
2012–13	Club Brugge	31	5	
2013–14	Club Brugge	30	3	
2014–15	Club Brugge	3	0	181 22
2014–15	Norwich C	5	0	
2015–16	Norwich C	10	0	15 0
2015–16	Rotherham U	4	1	4 1

OLSSON, Martin (D) 217 5
H: 5 7 W: 12 12 b.Gavle 17-5-88
Internationals: Sweden U19, U21, Full caps.
2005–06	Blackburn R	1	0	
2006–07	Blackburn R	0	0	
2007–08	Blackburn R	2	0	
2008–09	Blackburn R	9	0	
2009–10	Blackburn R	21	1	
2010–11	Blackburn R	29	2	
2011–12	Blackburn R	27	0	
2012–13	Blackburn R	29	0	117 3
2013–14	Norwich C	34	0	
2014–15	Norwich C	42	1	
2015–16	Norwich C	24	1	100 2

REDMOND, Nathan (M) 174 18
H: 5 8 W: 11 11 b.Birmingham 6-3-94
Internationals: England U16, U17, U18, U19, U20, U21.
2011–12	Birmingham C	24	5	
2012–13	Birmingham C	38	2	62 7
2013–14	Norwich C	34	1	
2014–15	Norwich C	43	4	
2015–16	Norwich C	35	6	112 11

RUDD, Declan (G) 81 0
H: 6 3 W: 12 06 b.Diss 16-1-91
Internationals: England U16, U17, U19, U20, U21, Full caps.
2008–09	Norwich C	0	0	
2009–10	Norwich C	7	0	
2010–11	Norwich C	1	0	
2011–12	Norwich C	2	0	
2012–13	Norwich C	0	0	
2012–13	Preston NE	14	0	
2013–14	Norwich C	0	0	
2013–14	Preston NE	46	0	60 0
2014–15	Norwich C	0	0	
2015–16	Norwich C	11	0	21 0

RUDDY, John (G) 342 0
H: 6 3 W: 12 07 b.St Ives 24-10-86
Internationals: England Full caps.
2003–04	Cambridge U	1	0	
2004–05	Cambridge U	38	0	39 0
2005–06	Everton	1	0	
2005–06	Walsall	5	0	5 0
2005–06	Rushden & D	3	0	3 0
2005–06	Chester C	4	0	4 0
2006–07	Everton	0	0	
2006–07	Stockport Co	11	0	
2006–07	Wrexham	5	0	5 0
2006–07	Bristol C	1	0	1 0
2007–08	Everton	0	0	
2007–08	Stockport Co	12	0	23 0
2008–09	Everton	0	0	
2008–09	Crewe Alex	19	0	19 0
2009–10	Everton	0	0	1 0
2009–10	Motherwell	34	0	34 0
2010–11	Norwich C	45	0	
2011–12	Norwich C	37	0	
2012–13	Norwich C	15	0	
2013–14	Norwich C	38	0	
2014–15	Norwich C	46	0	
2015–16	Norwich C	27	0	208 0

TETTEY, Alexander (M) 252 19
H: 5 11 W: 10 09 b.Accra 4-4-86
Internationals: Norway U18, U19, U21, Full caps.
2004–05	Rosenborg	0	0	
2005–06	Rosenborg	10	1	
2006–07	Rosenborg	21	1	
2007–08	Rosenborg	25	4	
2008–09	Rosenborg	28	6	
2009–10	Rosenborg	1	0	85 12
2009–10	Rennes	24	0	
2010–11	Rennes	17	1	
2011–12	Rennes	19	1	60 2
2012–13	Norwich C	27	0	
2013–14	Norwich C	21	1	
2014–15	Norwich C	36	2	
2015–16	Norwich C	23	2	107 5

THOMPSON, Louis (M) 92 6
H: 5 11 W: 11 10 b.Bristol 19-12-94
Internationals: Wales U19, U21.
2012–13	Swindon T	4	0	
2013–14	Swindon T	28	2	
2014–15	Norwich C	0	0	
2014–15	Swindon T	32	2	
2015–16	Norwich C	0	0	
2015–16	Swindon T	28	2	92 6

TOFFOLO, Harry (D) 42 1
H: 6 0 W: 11 03 b. 19-8-95
Internationals: England U18, U19, U20.
2014–15	Norwich C	0	0	
2014–15	Swindon T	28	1	28 1
2015–16	Norwich C	0	0	
2015–16	Rotherham U	7	0	7 0
2015–16	Peterborough U	7	0	7 0

TURNER, Michael (D) 386 24
H: 6 4 W: 13 05 b.Lewisham 9-11-83
2001–02	Charlton Ath	0	0	
2002–03	Charlton Ath	0	0	
2002–03	Leyton Orient	7	1	7 1
2003–04	Charlton Ath	0	0	
2004–05	Brentford	45	1	
2005–06	Brentford	46	2	91 3
2006–07	Hull C	43	3	
2007–08	Hull C	44	5	
2008–09	Hull C	38	4	

2009–10	Hull C	4	0	**129**	**12**
2009–10	Sunderland	29	2		
2010–11	Sunderland	15	0		
2011–12	Sunderland	24	0	**68**	**2**
2012–13	Norwich C	26	3		
2013–14	Norwich C	22	0		
2014–15	Norwich C	23	1		
2014–15	*Fulham*	9	1	**9**	**1**
2015–16	Norwich C	0	0	**71**	**4**
2015–16	*Sheffield W*	11	1	**11**	**1**

VAN WOLFSWINKEL, Ricky (F) **220** **69**
H: 6 1 W: 10 13 b.Amersfoort 27-1-89
Internationals: Netherlands U19, U21, Full caps.

2007–08	Vitesse	1	0		
2008–09	Vitesse	32	8	**33**	**8**
2009–10	FC Utrecht	35	11		
2010–11	FC Utrecht	29	15	**64**	**26**
2011–12	Sporting Lisbon	25	14		
2012–13	Sporting Lisbon	29	14	**54**	**28**
2013–14	Norwich C	25	1		
2014–15	Norwich C	0	0		
2014–15	*St Etienne*	28	5	**28**	**5**
2015–16	Norwich C	0	0	**25**	**1**
2015–16	*Real Betis*	16	1	**16**	**1**

WHITTAKER, Steven (D) **369** **28**
H: 6 1 W: 13 07 b.Edinburgh 16-6-84
Internationals: Scotland U21, Full caps.

2001–02	Hibernian	1	0		
2002–03	Hibernian	6	0		
2003–04	Hibernian	28	1		
2004–05	Hibernian	37	1		
2005–06	Hibernian	34	1		
2006–07	Hibernian	35	1	**141**	**4**
2007–08	Rangers	30	4		
2008–09	Rangers	24	2		
2009–10	Rangers	35	7		
2010–11	Rangers	36	4		
2011–12	Rangers	25	2	**150**	**19**
2012–13	Norwich C	13	1		
2013–14	Norwich C	20	1		
2014–15	Norwich C	37	2		
2015–16	Norwich C	8	1	**78**	**5**

Players retained or with offer of contract
Adams, Ebrima; Cantwell, Todd Owen; Eaton-Collins, Jamie; Efete, Michee; Grant, Raymond Michael; Killip, Ben.

Scholars
Aransibia, Devonte; Ashley-Seal, Bernard Patrick; Crowe, Joe; Da Costa, Rui Giovanni; Ellesley, Callum John; Higgs, Kieran Suthun; Jaiyesimi, Diallang; Lewis, Jamal; McIntosh, Louis; Mututala Sambu, Emersson; Oxborough, Aston Jay; Pollock, Henry; Ramsay, Louis Mark; Syme, Toby; Wallis, Owen.

NOTTINGHAM F (59)

ASSOMBALONGA, Britt (F) **123** **54**
H: 5 9 W: 11 13 b.Kinshasa 6-12-92

2010–11	Watford	0	0		
2011–12	Watford	4	0		
2012–13	Watford	0	0		
2012–13	*Southend U*	43	15	**43**	**15**
2013–14	Watford	0	0	**4**	**0**
2013–14	Peterborough U	43	23	**43**	**23**
2014–15	Nottingham F	29	15		
2015–16	Nottingham F	4	1	**33**	**16**

BLACKSTOCK, Dexter (F) **335** **84**
H: 6 2 W: 13 00 b.Oxford 20-5-86
Internationals: England U18, U19, U20, U21. Antigua and Barbuda Full caps.

2004–05	Southampton	9	1		
2004–05	*Plymouth Arg*	14	4	**14**	**4**
2005–06	Southampton	19	3	**28**	**4**
2005–06	*Derby Co*	9	3	**9**	**3**
2006–07	QPR	39	13		
2007–08	QPR	35	6		
2008–09	QPR	36	11	**110**	**30**
2008–09	*Nottingham F*	6	2		
2009–10	Nottingham F	39	12		
2010–11	Nottingham F	17	5		
2011–12	Nottingham F	22	8		
2012–13	Nottingham F	37	6		
2013–14	Nottingham F	1	0		
2013–14	*Leeds U*	4	1	**4**	**1**
2014–15	Nottingham F	19	5		
2015–16	Nottingham F	29	4	**170**	**42**

BURKE, Chris (M) **383** **58**
H: 5 9 W: 10 10 b.Glasgow 2-12-83
Internationals: Scotland U21, B, Full caps.

2001–02	Rangers	2	1		
2002–03	Rangers	0	0		
2003–04	Rangers	20	3		
2004–05	Rangers	12	0		
2005–06	Rangers	27	3		
2006–07	Rangers	22	2		
2007–08	Rangers	11	2		
2008–09	Rangers	1	0	**95**	**11**
2008–09	Cardiff C	14	1		
2009–10	Cardiff C	44	9		
2010–11	Cardiff C	44	5	**102**	**15**
2011–12	Birmingham C	46	12		
2012–13	Birmingham C	41	8		
2013–14	Birmingham C	44	4	**131**	**24**
2014–15	Nottingham F	41	6		
2015–16	Nottingham F	9	0	**50**	**6**
2015–16	*Rotherham U*	5	2	**5**	**2**

BURKE, Oliver (M) **22** **2**
H: 5 9 W: 11 11 b.Melton Mowbray 7-4-97

2014–15	Nottingham F	2	0		
2014–15	*Bradford C*	2	0	**2**	**0**
2015–16	Nottingham F	18	2	**20**	**2**

CASH, Matty (M) **12** **3**
b. 7-8-97

2015–16	Nottingham F	0	0		
2015–16	*Dagenham & R*	12	3	**12**	**3**

COHEN, Chris (M) **342** **20**
H: 5 11 W: 10 11 b.Norwich 5-3-87

2003–04	West Ham U	7	0		
2004–05	West Ham U	11	0		
2005–06	West Ham U	0	0	**18**	**0**
2005–06	*Yeovil T*	30	1		
2006–07	Yeovil T	44	6	**74**	**7**
2007–08	Nottingham F	41	2		
2008–09	Nottingham F	41	2		
2009–10	Nottingham F	44	3		
2010–11	Nottingham F	42	2		
2011–12	Nottingham F	7	0		
2012–13	Nottingham F	38	2		
2013–14	Nottingham F	16	1		
2014–15	Nottingham F	6	0		
2015–16	Nottingham F	15	1	**250**	**13**

DE VRIES, Dorus (G) **402** **0**
H: 6 1 W: 12 08 b.Bewerwijk 29-12-80

1999–2000	Telstar	1	0		
2000–01	Telstar	27	0		
2001–02	Telstar	27	0		
2002–03	Telstar	26	0	**81**	**0**
2003–04	Den Haag	18	0		
2004–05	Den Haag	32	0		
2005–06	Den Haag	0	0	**50**	**0**
2006–07	Dunfermline Ath	27	0	**27**	**0**
2007–08	Swansea C	46	0		
2008–09	Swansea C	40	0		
2009–10	Swansea C	46	0		
2010–11	Swansea C	46	0	**178**	**0**
2011–12	Wolverhampton W	4	0		
2012–13	Wolverhampton W	10	0	**14**	**0**
2013–14	Nottingham F	3	0		
2014–15	Nottingham F	4	0		
2015–16	Nottingham F	45	0	**52**	**0**

EBECILIO, Kyle (M) **11** **0**
H: 5 11 W: 12 02 b.Rotterdam 17-2-94
Internationals: Netherlands U16, U17, U19, U21.

2010–11	Arsenal	0	0		
2011–12	Arsenal	0	0		
2012–13	Arsenal	0	0		
2015–16	FC Twente	0	0		

On loan from FC Twente.

2015–16	Nottingham F	5	0	**5**	**0**
2015–16	*ADO Den Haag*	6	0	**6**	**0**

ERLANDSSON, Tim (G) **0** **0**
b. 25-12-96
Internationals: Sweden U17, U19.

2014–15	Halmstads	0	0		
2015–16	Nottingham F	0	0		

EVTIMOV, Dimitar (G) **12** **0**
H: 6 3 W: 13 00 b.Plevan 7-9-93
Internationals: Bulgaria U19, U21.

2012–13	Nottingham F	0	0		
2013–14	Nottingham F	1	0		
2014–15	Nottingham F	0	0		
2014–15	*Mansfield T*	10	0	**10**	**0**
2015–16	Nottingham F	1	0	**2**	**0**

FOX, Danny (D) **347** **15**
H: 5 11 W: 12 06 b.Winsford 29-5-86
Internationals: England U21. Scotland Full caps.

2004–05	Everton	0	0		
2004–05	*Stranraer*	11	1	**11**	**1**
2005–06	Walsall	33	0		
2006–07	Walsall	44	3		
2007–08	Walsall	22	3	**99**	**6**
2007–08	Coventry C	18	1		
2008–09	Coventry C	39	5		
2009–10	Coventry C	0	0	**57**	**6**
2009–10	Celtic	15	0	**15**	**0**
2009–10	Burnley	14	1		
2010–11	Burnley	35	0		
2011–12	Burnley	1	0	**50**	**1**
2011–12	Southampton	41	0		
2012–13	Southampton	20	1		
2013–14	Southampton	3	0	**64**	**1**
2013–14	Nottingham F	14	0		
2014–15	Nottingham F	27	0		
2015–16	Nottingham F	10	0	**51**	**0**

FRYATT, Matty (F) **364** **116**
H: 5 10 W: 11 00 b.Nuneaton 5-3-86
Internationals: England U19.

2002–03	Walsall	0	0		
2003–04	Walsall	11	1		
2003–04	*Carlisle U*	10	1	**10**	**1**
2004–05	Walsall	36	15		
2005–06	Walsall	23	11	**70**	**27**
2005–06	Leicester C	19	6		
2006–07	Leicester C	32	3		
2007–08	Leicester C	30	2		
2008–09	Leicester C	46	27		
2009–10	Leicester C	29	11		
2010–11	Leicester C	12	2	**168**	**51**
2010–11	Hull C	22	9		
2011–12	Hull C	46	16		
2012–13	Hull C	4	0		
2013–14	Hull C	10	2	**82**	**27**
2013–14	*Sheffield W*	9	4	**9**	**4**
2014–15	Nottingham F	25	6		
2015–16	Nottingham F	0	0	**25**	**6**

GRANT, Jorge (M) **11** **0**
H: 5 9 W: 11 07 b.Oxford 26-9-94

2013–14	Nottingham F	0	0		
2014–15	Nottingham F	1	0		
2015–16	Nottingham F	10	0	**11**	**0**

HOBBS, Jack (D) **265** **4**
H: 6 3 W: 13 05 b.Portsmouth 18-8-88
Internationals: England U19.

2004–05	Lincoln C	1	0	**1**	**0**
2005–06	Liverpool	0	0		
2006–07	Liverpool	0	0		
2007–08	Liverpool	2	0		
2007–08	*Scunthorpe U*	9	1	**9**	**1**
2008–09	Liverpool	0	0	**2**	**0**
2008–09	Leicester C	44	1		
2009–10	Leicester C	44	0		
2010–11	Leicester C	26	0	**114**	**1**
2010–11	*Hull C*	13	0		
2011–12	Hull C	40	1		
2012–13	Hull C	22	0	**75**	**1**
2013–14	Nottingham F	27	1		
2014–15	Nottingham F	17	0		
2015–16	Nottingham F	20	0	**64**	**1**

IACOVITTI, Alex (D) **0** **0**
b. 2-9-97
Internationals: Scotland U17, U19.

2015–16	Nottingham F	0	0		

JOKIC, Bojan (D) **273** **1**
H: 5 9 W: 11 11 b.Kranj 17-5-86
Internationals: Slovenia U21, Full caps.

2003–04	Triglav Kranj	28	0		
2004–05	Triglav Kranj	29	0	**57**	**0**
2005–06	Gorica	31	1		
2006–07	Gorica	34	0	**65**	**1**
2007–08	Souchaux	17	0		
2008–09	Souchaux	20	0		
2009–10	Souchaux	6	0	**43**	**0**
2009–10	Verona	9	0		
2010–11	Verona	15	0		
2011–12	Verona	20	0		
2012–13	Verona	20	0	**64**	**0**
2013–14	Villareal	15	0		
2014–15	Villareal	7	0	**22**	**0**
2015–16	Villareal	2	0	**2**	**0**

On loan from Villarreal.

2015–16	Nottingham F	20	0	**20**	**0**

LANSBURY, Henri (M) **229** **40**
H: 6 0 W: 13 06 b.Enfield 12-10-90
Internationals: England U16, U17, U19, U21.

2007–08	Arsenal	0	0		
2008–09	Arsenal	0	0		
2008–09	*Scunthorpe U*	16	4	**16**	**4**
2009–10	Arsenal	1	0		
2009–10	*Watford*	37	5	**37**	**5**
2010–11	Arsenal	0	0		
2010–11	*Norwich C*	23	4	**23**	**4**
2011–12	Arsenal	2	0		
2011–12	*West Ham U*	22	1	**22**	**1**

2012–13	Arsenal	0	0	**3 0**
2012–13	Nottingham F	32	5	
2013–14	Nottingham F	29	7	
2014–15	Nottingham F	39	10	
2015–16	Nottingham F	28	4	**128 26**

LICHAJ, Eric (D)   **172 3**
H: 5 11 W: 12 07 b.Chicago 17-11-88
Internationals: USA U17, U20, Full caps.

2007–08	Aston Villa	0	0	
2008–09	Aston Villa	0	0	
2009–10	Aston Villa	0	0	
2009–10	Lincoln C	6	0	**6 0**
2009–10	Leyton Orient	9	1	**9 1**
2010–11	Aston Villa	5	0	
2010–11	Leeds U	16	0	**16 0**
2011–12	Aston Villa	10	1	
2012–13	Aston Villa	17	0	**32 1**
2013–14	Nottingham F	24	0	
2014–15	Nottingham F	42	0	
2015–16	Nottingham F	43	1	**109 1**

MANCIENNE, Michael (D)   **234 0**
H: 6 0 W: 11 09 b.Isleworth 8-1-88
Internationals: England U16, U17, U18, U19, U21.

2005–06	Chelsea	0	0	
2006–07	Chelsea	0	0	
2006–07	QPR	28	0	
2007–08	Chelsea	0	0	
2007–08	QPR	30	0	**58 0**
2008–09	Chelsea	4	0	
2008–09	Wolverhampton W	10	0	
2009–10	Chelsea	0	0	
2009–10	Wolverhampton W	30	0	
2010–11	Chelsea	0	0	**4 0**
2010–11	Wolverhampton W	16	0	**56 0**
2011–12	Hamburg	16	0	
2012–13	Hamburg	21	0	
2013–14	Hamburg	12	0	**49 0**
2014–15	Nottingham F	36	0	
2015–16	Nottingham F	31	0	**67 0**

McDONAGH, Gerry (F)   **1 0**
b. 14-2-98
Internationals: Republic of Ireland U17.

2015–16	Nottingham F	1	0	**1 0**

MENDES, Ryan (F)   **163 29**
H: 5 9 W: 11 07 b.Mindelo 8-1-90
Internationals: Cape Verde U16, U21, Full caps.

2008–09	Le Havre	1	0	
2009–10	Le Havre	14	1	
2010–11	Le Havre	32	4	
2011–12	Le Havre	34	13	
2012–13	Le Havre	3	2	**84 20**
2012–13	Lille	16	3	
2013–14	Lille	19	2	
2014–15	Lille	3	0	**47 7**
On loan from Lille.				
2015–16	Nottingham F	32	2	**32 2**

MILLS, Matthew (D)   **321 22**
H: 6 3 W: 12 12 b.Swindon 14-7-86
Internationals: England U18, U19.

2004–05	Southampton	0	0	
2004–05	Coventry C	4	0	**4 0**
2004–05	Bournemouth	12	3	**12 3**
2005–06	Southampton	4	0	
2005–06	Manchester C	1	0	
2006–07	Manchester C	0	0	
2006–07	Colchester U	9	0	**9 0**
2007–08	Manchester C	0	0	**2 0**
2007–08	Doncaster R	34	3	
2008–09	Doncaster R	41	0	
2009–10	Doncaster R	0	0	**75 3**
2009–10	Reading	23	2	
2010–11	Reading	38	2	**61 4**
2011–12	Leicester C	25	1	**25 1**
2012–13	Bolton W	18	1	
2013–14	Bolton W	32	1	
2014–15	Bolton W	37	4	**87 6**
2015–16	Nottingham F	42	5	**42 5**

NELSON OLIVEIRA, Miguel (F)   **143 26**
H: 6 1 W: 12 13 b.Barcelos 8-8-91
Internationals: Portugal U16, U17, U19, U20, U21, Full caps.

2009–10	Benfica	0	0	
2009–10	Rio Ave	10	0	**10 0**
2010–11	Benfica	0	0	
2010–11	Pacos Ferreira	23	4	**23 4**
2011–12	Benfica	12	0	
2012–13	Benfica	0	0	
2012–13	La Coruna	30	4	**30 4**
2013–14	Benfica	0	0	
2013–14	Rennes	30	8	**30 8**

2014–15	Benfica	0	0	
2014–15	Swansea C	10	1	**10 1**
2015–16	Benfica	0	0	**12 0**
On loan from Benfica.				
2015–16	Nottingham F	28	9	**28 9**

OSBORN, Ben (D)   **81 6**
H: 5 9 W: 11 11 b.Derby 5-8-94
Internationals: England U18, U19, U20.

2011–12	Nottingham F	0	0	
2012–13	Nottingham F	0	0	
2013–14	Nottingham F	8	0	
2014–15	Nottingham F	37	3	
2015–16	Nottingham F	36	3	**81 6**

PATERSON, Jamie (F)   **182 30**
H: 5 9 W: 10 07 b.Coventry 20-12-91

2010–11	Walsall	14	0	
2011–12	Walsall	34	3	
2012–13	Walsall	46	12	**94 15**
2013–14	Nottingham F	32	8	
2014–15	Nottingham F	21	1	
2015–16	Nottingham F	1	0	**54 9**
2015–16	Huddersfield T	34	6	**34 6**

PETRAVICIUS, Deimantas (M)   **2 0**
b. 2-9-95
Internationals: Lithuania U17, U19, U21, Full caps.

2014–15	Nottingham F	0	0	
2015–16	Nottingham F	1	0	**1 0**
2015–16	Stevenage	1	0	**1 0**

PINILLOS, Daniel (D)   **68 1**
H: 6 0 W: 11 09 b.Logrono 22-10-92

2013–14	Ourense	21	0	**21 0**
2013–14	Cordoba	16	1	
2014–15	Cordoba	12	0	**28 1**
2015–16	Nottingham F	19	0	**19 0**

RIERA, Roger (D)   **0 0**
b.El Masnou 17-2-95

2014–15	Nottingham F	0	0	
2015–16	Nottingham F	0	0	

SMITH, Jordan (G)   **0 0**
b. 8-8-94
Internationals: Costa Rica U17, U20, Full caps.

2013–14	Nottingham F	0	0	
2014–15	Nottingham F	0	0	
2015–16	Nottingham F	0	0	

TESCHE, Robert (M)   **183 12**
H: 5 11 W: 11 03 b.Wismar 27-5-87

2006–07	Arminia Bielefeld	7	0	
2007–08	Arminia Bielefeld	15	1	**22 1**
2008–09	Arminia Bielefeld	26	2	**26 2**
2009–10	Hamburg	16	2	
2010–11	Hamburg	11	0	
2011–12	Hamburg	23	2	
2012–13	Hamburg	4	0	
2012–13	Fortuna Dusseldorf	14	0	**14 0**
2013–14	Hamburg	9	0	**63 4**
2014–15	Nottingham F	22	2	
2014–15	Birmingham C	12	2	**12 2**
2015–16	Nottingham F	24	1	**46 3**

VAUGHAN, David (M)   **407 27**
H: 5 7 W: 11 00 b.Abergele 18-2-83
Internationals: Wales U19, U21, Full caps.

2000–01	Crewe Alex	1	0	
2001–02	Crewe Alex	13	0	
2002–03	Crewe Alex	32	3	
2003–04	Crewe Alex	31	0	
2004–05	Crewe Alex	44	6	
2005–06	Crewe Alex	34	5	
2006–07	Crewe Alex	29	4	
2007–08	Crewe Alex	1	0	**185 18**
2007–08	Real Sociedad	7	1	**7 1**
2008–09	Blackpool	33	1	
2009–10	Blackpool	41	1	
2010–11	Blackpool	35	2	**109 4**
2011–12	Sunderland	22	2	
2012–13	Sunderland	24	1	
2013–14	Sunderland	3	0	**49 3**
2013–14	Nottingham F	9	0	
2014–15	Nottingham F	13	0	
2015–16	Nottingham F	35	1	**57 1**

VELDWIJK, Lars (F)   **122 58**
H: 6 5 W: 14 13 b. 21-8-91

2010–11	Voldendam	2	0	**2 0**
2011–12	Utrecht	5	0	**5 0**
2012–13	Dordrecht	31	14	**31 14**
2013–14	Excelsior	38	30	**38 30**
2014–15	Nottingham F	11	0	
2015–16	Nottingham F	0	0	**11 0**
2015–16	PEC Zwolle	35	14	**35 14**

WALKER, Tyler (F)   **27 2**
H: 5 10 W: 9 13 b. 17-10-96
Internationals: England U20.

2013–14	Nottingham F	0	0	
2014–15	Nottingham F	7	1	
2015–16	Nottingham F	14	0	**21 1**
2015–16	Burton Alb	6	1	**6 1**

WARD, Jamie (M)   **333 84**
H: 5 5 W: 9 04 b.Birmingham 12-5-86
Internationals: Northern Ireland U18, U21, Full caps.

2003–04	Aston Villa	0	0	
2004–05	Aston Villa	0	0	
2005–06	Aston Villa	0	0	
2005–06	Stockport Co	9	1	**9 1**
2006–07	Torquay U	25	9	**25 9**
2006–07	Chesterfield	9	3	
2007–08	Chesterfield	35	12	
2008–09	Chesterfield	23	14	**67 29**
2008–09	Sheffield U	16	2	
2009–10	Sheffield U	28	7	
2010–11	Sheffield U	19	0	**63 9**
2010–11	Derby Co	13	5	
2011–12	Derby Co	37	4	
2012–13	Derby Co	25	12	
2013–14	Derby Co	38	7	
2014–15	Derby Co	25	6	**138 34**
2015–16	Nottingham F	31	2	**31 2**

WILSON, Kelvin (D)   **321 4**
H: 6 2 W: 12 01 b.Nottingham 3-9-85

2003–04	Notts Co	3	0	
2004–05	Notts Co	41	2	
2005–06	Notts Co	34	1	**78 3**
2005–06	Preston NE	6	0	
2006–07	Preston NE	21	1	**27 1**
2007–08	Nottingham F	42	0	
2008–09	Nottingham F	36	0	
2009–10	Nottingham F	35	0	
2010–11	Nottingham F	10	0	
2011–12	Celtic	15	0	
2012–13	Celtic	32	0	**47 0**
2013–14	Nottingham F	9	0	
2014–15	Nottingham F	23	0	
2015–16	Nottingham F	14	0	**169 0**

WORRALL, Joe (D)   **14 1**
b. 10-1-97

2015–16	Nottingham F	0	0	
2015–16	Dagenham & R	14	1	**14 1**

WRIGHT, Jordan (G)   **0 0**
2015–16	Nottingham F	0	0	

Players retained or with offer of contract
Lawrence-Gabriel, Jordan Jay; Nielsen, Frederik Fisker; Thorne, James Samuel.

Scholars
Adams, Liam; Ahmedhodzic, Anel; Austin, Aidan Jerry; Boyd, Joseph Alexander; Brereton, Benjamin Anthony; Burns, Dylan John; Crookes, Adam Mark; Dearle, Richard Alexander; Diallo, Ismael; Edser, Toby George; Gambelton, Thomas Anthony; Gomis, Virgil Vayle; Hayes, Kieran; Iacovitti, Alexander; Jemson, Charlie; McClean, Kyle Justin; McDonagh, Gerry Luke; Otim, Elvis Apota; Re, Giuseppe David; Taylor, Jake Jon; Wright, Anthony Paul; Wright, Jordan Ian; Yates, Ryan James.

NOTTS CO (60)

ABORAH, Stanley (M)   **138 13**
H: 5 7 W: 10 08 b. 23-6-87
Internationals: Belgium U19.

2004–05	Ajax	4	0	
2005–06	Ajax	0	0	**4 0**
2005–06	Den Bosch	21	3	
2006–07	Dender	3	0	**3 0**
2007–08	Den Bosch	16	3	
2008–09	Den Bosch	21	3	**58 9**
2009–10	Trencin	0	0	
2010–11	Gillingham	1	0	**1 0**
2010–11	Capellen	14	0	**14 0**
2011–12	Vitesse	13	1	**13 1**
2012–13	Mura 05	12	1	**12 1**
2012–13	Ferencvaros	7	1	**7 1**
Unattached since 2013.				
2015–16	Notts Co	26	1	**26 1**

ADAMS, Blair (D)   **143 1**
H: 5 11 W: 11 05 b.South Shields 8-9-91
Internationals: England U20.

2010–11	Sunderland	0	0	
2011–12	Sunderland	0	0	
2011–12	Brentford	7	0	**7 0**

2011–12	*Northampton T*	22	0	22	0
2012–13	Sunderland	0	0		
2012–13	Coventry C	16	0		
2013–14	Coventry C	36	0	52	0
2014–15	Notts Co	34	1		
2015–16	Notts Co	15	0	49	1
2015–16	*Mansfield T*	13	0	13	0

AMEVOR, Mawouna (D) **117 7**
H: 6 4 W: 13 01 b. 16-12-91
Internationals: Togo Full caps.

2010–11	Dordrecht	12	0		
2011–12	Dordrecht	29	2		
2012–13	Dordrecht	30	2	71	4
2013–14	Go Ahead Eagles	22	1		
2014–15	Go Ahead Eagles	13	1	35	2
2015–16	Notts Co	11	1	11	1

ATKINSON, Wes (M) **19 0**
b.West Bromwich 13-10-94

2014–15	WBA	0	0		
2014–15	*Cambridge U*	2	0	2	0
2015–16	Notts Co	17	0	17	0

AUDEL, Thierry (D) **41 3**
H: 6 2 W: 12 08 b. 15-1-87
Internationals: France U19.

2007–08	Triestina	2	0		
2008–09	Triestina	0	0		
2009–10	Triestina	7	1	9	1
From Macclesfield T.					
2013–14	Crewe Alex	2	0		
2014–15	Crewe Alex	2	0	4	0
From Macclesfield T.					
2015–16	Notts Co	28	2	28	2

BANTON, Jason (F) **82 10**
H: 5 10 W: 11 05 b.Tottenham 15-12-92
Internationals: England U17.

2009–10	Blackburn R	0	0		
2010–11	Blackburn R	0	0		
2010–11	Liverpool	0	0		
2011–12	Liverpool	0	0		
2011–12	*Burton Alb*	1	0	1	0
2012–13	Crystal Palace	0	0		
2012–13	*Plymouth Arg*	14	6		
2013–14	Crystal Palace	0	0		
2013–14	*Milton Keynes D*	11	2	11	2
2013–14	Plymouth Arg	13	1		
2014–15	Plymouth Arg	25	0	52	7
2015–16	Wycombe W	5	1	5	1
2015–16	*Hartlepool U*	4	0	4	0
2015–16	Notts Co	9	0	9	0

BENNETT, Scott (D) **161 18**
H: 5 10 W: 12 10 b.Newquay 30-11-90

2008–09	Exeter C	0	0		
2009–10	Exeter C	0	0		
2010–11	Exeter C	1	0		
2011–12	Exeter C	15	3		
2012–13	Exeter C	43	6		
2013–14	Exeter C	45	6		
2014–15	Exeter C	28	3	132	18
2015–16	Notts Co	6	0	6	0
2015–16	*Newport Co*	12	0	12	0
2015–16	*York C*	11	0	11	0

BISHOP, Colby (M) **4 0**
H: 5 11 W: 11 05 b. 14-11-94

2013–14	Notts Co	0	0		
2014–15	Notts Co	3	0		
2015–16	Notts Co	1	0	4	0

BURKE, Graham (F) **41 3**
H: 5 11 W: 11 11 b.Dublin 21-9-93
Internationals: Republic of Ireland U19, U21.

2010–11	Aston Villa	0	0		
2011–12	Aston Villa	0	0		
2012–13	Aston Villa	0	0		
2013–14	Aston Villa	0	0		
2013–14	*Shrewsbury T*	3	0	3	0
2014–15	Aston Villa	0	0		
2014–15	*Notts Co*	7	1		
2015–16	Notts Co	31	2	38	3

CAMPBELL, Adam (F) **63 6**
H: 5 7 W: 11 07 b.North Shields 1-1-95
Internationals: England U16, U17, U19.

2011–12	Newcastle U	0	0		
2012–13	Newcastle U	3	0		
2013–14	Newcastle U	0	0		
2013–14	*Carlisle U*	1	0	1	0
2013–14	*St Mirren*	11	2	11	2
2014–15	Newcastle U	0	0	3	0
2014–15	*Fleetwood T*	2	0	2	0
2014–15	*Hartlepool U*	2	0	2	0
2015–16	Notts Co	44	4	44	4

CARROLL, Roy (G) **448 0**
H: 6 2 W: 12 09 b.Enniskillen 30-9-77
Internationals: Northern Ireland U21, Full caps.

1995–96	Hull C	23	0		
1996–97	Hull C	23	0	46	0
1996–97	Wigan Ath	0	0		
1997–98	Wigan Ath	29	0		
1998–99	Wigan Ath	43	0		
1999–2000	Wigan Ath	34	0		
2000–01	Wigan Ath	29	0	135	0
2001–02	Manchester U	7	0		
2002–03	Manchester U	10	0		
2003–04	Manchester U	6	0		
2004–05	Manchester U	26	0	49	0
2005–06	West Ham U	19	0		
2006–07	West Ham U	12	0	31	0
2007–08	Rangers	0	0		
2007–08	Derby Co	14	0		
2008–09	Derby Co	16	0	30	0
2009–10	Odense	28	0		
2010–11	Odense	18	0	46	0
2011–12	OFI Crete	16	0	16	0
2011–12	Olympiacos	2	0		
2012–13	Olympiacos	16	0		
2013–14	Olympiacos	0	0	18	0
2014–15	Notts Co	45	0		
2015–16	Notts Co	32	0	77	0

DE SILVA, Kyle (F) **14 0**
H: 5 10 W: 11 05 b.Croydon 29-11-93

2010–11	Crystal Palace	0	0		
2011–12	Crystal Palace	6	0		
2012–13	Crystal Palace	1	0		
2012–13	*Barnet*	3	0	3	0
2013–14	Crystal Palace	0	0		
2014–15	Crystal Palace	0	0	7	0
2015–16	Notts Co	4	0	4	0

EDWARDS, Mike (D) **549 34**
H: 6 0 W: 12 10 b.Hessle 25-4-80

1997–98	Hull C	21	0		
1998–99	Hull C	30	0		
1999–2000	Hull C	40	1		
2000–01	Hull C	42	4		
2001–02	Hull C	39	1		
2002–03	Hull C	6	0	178	6
2002–03	Colchester U	5	0	5	0
2003–04	Grimsby T	33	1	33	1
2004–05	Notts Co	9	0		
2005–06	Notts Co	46	7		
2006–07	Notts Co	45	3		
2007–08	Notts Co	19	1		
2008–09	Notts Co	43	2		
2009–10	Notts Co	40	5		
2010–11	Notts Co	37	1		
2011–12	Notts Co	30	1		
2012–13	Carlisle U	23	0		
2013–14	Carlisle U	1	0	24	0
2014–15	Notts Co	18	3		
2015–16	Notts Co	22	4	309	27

GIBSON, Montel (F) **4 0**

2015–16	Notts Co	4	0	4	0

HEWITT, Elliott (D) **115 1**
H: 5 11 W: 11 10 b.Rhyl 30-5-94
Internationals: Wales U17, U21.

2010–11	Macclesfield T	1	0		
2011–12	Macclesfield T	21	0	22	0
2012–13	Ipswich T	7	0		
2013–14	Ipswich T	4	0		
2013–14	*Gillingham*	20	0	20	0
2014–15	Ipswich T	3	0	14	0
2014–15	*Colchester U*	21	1	21	1
2015–16	Notts Co	38	0	38	0

HOLLIS, Haydn (D) **87 6**
H: 6 4 W: 13 01 b.Selston 14-10-92

2011–12	Notts Co	1	0		
2012–13	Notts Co	6	0		
2013–14	Notts Co	10	4		
2014–15	Notts Co	41	0		
2015–16	Notts Co	29	2	87	6

JENNER, Julian (M) **214 25**
H: 5 11 W: 11 05 b.Delft 28-2-84
Internationals: Netherlands U21.

2003–04	NAC Breda	1	0		
2004–05	NAC Breda	5	1		
2005–06	NAC Breda	29	3		
2006–07	AZ Alkmaar	25	2		
2007–08	AZ Alkmaar	21	3		
2008–09	AZ Alkmaar	0	0	46	5
2008–09	*Vitesse*	21	0		
2009–10	Vitesse	4	0		
2009–10	*Rot Weiss Ahlen*	11	1	11	1
2010–11	Vitesse	14	3		
2010–11	*NAC Breda*	11	2	46	6
2011–12	Vitesse	10	1	49	4
2012–13	Ferencvaros	20	5		
2013–14	Ferencvaros	25	4	45	9
2014–15	Diosgyor	6	0	6	0
2015–16	Notts Co	11	0	11	0

LOACH, Scott (G) **233 0**
H: 6 1 W: 13 01 b.Nottingham 27-5-88
Internationals: England U21.

2006–07	Watford	0	0		
2007–08	Watford	0	0		
2007–08	*Morecambe*	2	0	2	0
2007–08	*Bradford C*	20	0	20	0
2008–09	Watford	31	0		
2009–10	Watford	46	0		
2010–11	Watford	46	0		
2011–12	Watford	31	0	154	0
2012–13	Ipswich T	22	0		
2013–14	Ipswich T	6	0	28	0
2014–15	Rotherham U	2	0	2	0
2014–15	*Bury*	2	0	2	0
2014–15	*Peterborough U*	5	0	5	0
2014–15	*Yeovil T*	6	0	6	0
2015–16	Notts Co	14	0	14	0

McLEOD, Izale (F) **435 142**
H: 6 1 W: 11 02 b.Birmingham 15-10-84
Internationals: England U21.

2002–03	Derby Co	29	3		
2003–04	Derby Co	10	1	39	4
2003–04	*Sheffield U*	7	0	7	0
2004–05	Milton Keynes D	43	16		
2005–06	Milton Keynes D	39	17		
2006–07	Milton Keynes D	34	21		
2007–08	Charlton Ath	18	1		
2007–08	*Colchester U*	2	0	2	0
2008–09	Charlton Ath	2	0		
2008–09	*Millwall*	7	2	7	2
2009–10	Charlton Ath	11	2		
2009–10	*Peterborough U*	4	0	4	0
2010–11	Charlton Ath	0	0	31	3
2010–11	Barnet	29	14		
2011–12	Barnet	44	18	73	32
2012–13	Portsmouth	24	10	24	10
2012–13	Milton Keynes D	13	1		
2013–14	Milton Keynes D	36	7	165	62
2013–14	*Northampton T*	4	1	4	1
2014–15	Crawley T	42	19	42	19
2015–16	Notts Co	37	9	37	9

MILSOM, Robert (M) **131 3**
H: 5 10 W: 11 04 b.Redhill 2-1-87

2005–06	Fulham	0	0		
2006–07	Fulham	0	0		
2007–08	Fulham	0	0		
2007–08	*Brentford*	6	0	6	0
2008–09	Fulham	1	0		
2008–09	*Southend U*	6	0	6	0
2009–10	Fulham	0	0		
2010	*TPS Turku*	14	0	14	0
2010–11	Fulham	0	0	1	0
2010–11	Aberdeen	18	1		
2011–12	Aberdeen	22	1		
2012–13	Aberdeen	13	0	53	2
2013–14	Rotherham U	27	1		
2014–15	Rotherham U	8	0	35	1
2014–15	*Bury*	2	0	2	0
2015–16	Notts Co	14	0	14	0

MURRAY, Ronan (F) **109 14**
H: 5 7 W: 11 00 b.Mayo 12-9-91
Internationals: Republic of Ireland U17, U19, U21.

2010–11	Ipswich T	8	0		
2010–11	*Torquay U*	7	1	7	1
2011–12	Ipswich T	0	0		
2011–12	*Swindon T*	20	3	20	3
2012–13	Ipswich T	1	0	9	0
2012–13	*Plymouth Arg*	13	1		
2013–14	Plymouth Arg	0	0	13	1
2013–14	Notts Co	24	7		
2014–15	Notts Co	20	1		
2015–16	Notts Co	16	1	60	9

NOBLE, Liam (M) **200 33**
H: 5 9 W: 10 05 b.Newcastle 8-5-91

2009–10	Sunderland	0	0		
2010–11	Sunderland	0	0		
2010–11	*Carlisle U*	21	3		
2011–12	Sunderland	0	0		
2011–12	Carlisle U	40	6		
2012–13	Carlisle U	35	6		
2013–14	Carlisle U	34	5	130	20
2014–15	Notts Co	33	5		
2015–16	Notts Co	37	8	70	13

PILKINGTON, Kevin (G) **363 0**
H: 6 1 W: 13 08 b.Hitchin 8-3-74

1992–93	Manchester U	0	0		

1993–94	Manchester U	0	0		
1994–95	Manchester U	1	0		
1995–96	Manchester U	3	0		
1995–96	*Rochdale*	6	0	6	0
1996–97	Manchester U	0	0		
1996–97	*Rotherham U*	17	0	17	0
1997–98	Manchester U	2	0	6	0
1998–99	Port Vale	8	0		
1999–2000	Port Vale	15	0	23	0
2000–01	Mansfield T	2	0		
2001–02	Mansfield T	45	0		
2002–03	Mansfield T	32	0		
2003–04	Mansfield T	46	0		
2004–05	Mansfield T	42	0	167	0
2005–06	Notts Co	45	0		
2006–07	Notts Co	39	0		
2007–08	Notts Co	32	0		
2008–09	Notts Co	25	0		
From Luton T, Mansfield T					
2012–13	Notts Co	1	0		
2013–14	Notts Co	1	0		
2014–15	Notts Co	1	0		
2015–16	Notts Co	0	0	144	0

RICHARDS, Jordan (D)   **0 0**
b. 6-7-97

2015–16	Notts Co	0	0

SARPONG, Lartey (M)   **1 0**
b. 10-1-95

2015–16	Notts Co	1	0	1	0

SHARPE, Rhys (D)   **8 0**
b. 17-10-94
Internationals: Northern Ireland U21.

2013–14	Derby Co	0	0		
2014–15	Derby Co	0	0		
2014–15	*Shrewsbury T*	3	0	3	0
2015–16	Notts Co	5	0	5	0

SMITH, Alan (F)   **435 47**
H: 5 10   W: 12 04   b.Rothwell 28-10-80
Internationals: England U21, B, Full caps.

1997–98	Leeds U	6	2		
1998–99	Leeds U	22	7		
1999–2000	Leeds U	26	4		
2000–01	Leeds U	33	11		
2001–02	Leeds U	23	4		
2002–03	Leeds U	33	3		
2003–04	Leeds U	35	9	172	38
2004–05	Manchester U	31	6		
2005–06	Manchester U	21	1		
2006–07	Manchester U	9	0	61	7
2007–08	Newcastle U	33	0		
2008–09	Newcastle U	6	0		
2009–10	Newcastle U	32	0		
2010–11	Newcastle U	11	0		
2011–12	Newcastle U	2	0	84	0
2011–12	Milton Keynes D	16	1		
2012–13	Milton Keynes D	27	1		
2013–14	Milton Keynes D	24	0	67	2
2014–15	Notts Co	23	0		
2015–16	Notts Co	28	0	51	0

SNIJDERS, Genaro (F)   **108 12**
H: 5 11   W: 10 12   b.Amsterdam 29-7-89

2008–09	Vitesse	2	0		
2009–10	Vitesse	6	0		
2009–10	*Almere C*	11	3	11	3
2010–11	Vitesse	15	0		
2011–12	Vitesse	0	0	23	0
2012–13	Willem II	23	2	23	2
2013–14	Dordrecht	10	2	10	2
2014–15	Oss	27	3	27	3
2015–16	Notts Co	14	2	14	2

SPROCKEL, Civard (D)   **319 5**
H: 5 10   W: 11 11   b.Willemstad 10-5-83
Internationals: Netherlands U20.

2001–02	Feyenoord	6	0		
2002–03	Feyenoord	0	0	6	0
2002–03	Excelsior	13	0		
2003–04	Excelsior	10	1		
2004–05	Excelsior	23	0		
2005–06	Excelsior	38	0	84	1
2006–07	Vitesse	31	0		
2007–08	Vitesse	32	2		
2008–09	Vitesse	30	1		
2009–10	Vitesse	29	1		
2010–11	Vitesse	10	0	132	4
2010–11	An Famagusta	15	0		
2011–12	An Famagusta	25	0	40	0
2011–12	CSKA Sofia	0	0		
2012–13	Botev Plovdiv	12	0		
2013–14	Botev Plovdiv	30	0	42	0
2014–15	Othellos	10	0	10	0
2015–16	Notts Co	5	0	5	0

STEAD, Jon (F)   **461 104**
H: 6 3   W: 13 03   b.Huddersfield 7-4-83
Internationals: England U21.

2001–02	Huddersfield T	0	0		
2002–03	Huddersfield T	42	6		
2003–04	Huddersfield T	26	16		
2003–04	Blackburn R	13	6		
2004–05	Blackburn R	29	2	42	8
2005–06	Sunderland	30	1		
2006–07	Sunderland	5	1	35	2
2006–07	Derby Co	17	3	17	3
2006–07	Sheffield U	14	5		
2007–08	Sheffield U	24	3		
2008–09	Sheffield U	10	0	39	8
2008–09	Ipswich T	39	12		
2009–10	Ipswich T	22	6		
2009–10	Coventry C	10	2	10	2
2010–11	Ipswich T	3	1	64	19
2010–11	Bristol C	27	9		
2011–12	Bristol C	24	6		
2012–13	Bristol C	28	5	79	20
2013–14	Huddersfield T	12	1		
2013–14	Oldham Ath	5	0	5	0
2013–14	Bradford C	8	1		
2014–15	Huddersfield T	7	1	87	24
2014–15	Bradford C	32	6	40	7
2015–16	Notts Co	43	11	43	11

SWERTS, Gill (D)   **294 15**
H: 5 10   W: 11 11   b.Brasschaart 23-2-82
Internationals: Belgium U16, U17, U18, U21, Full caps.

2001–02	Feyenoord	0	0		
2001–02	Excelsior	30	6		
2002–03	Feyenoord	0	0		
2002–03	Excelsior	33	1	63	7
2003–04	Feyenoord	17	0		
2004–05	Feyenoord	0	0		
2004–05	Den Haag	33	1	33	1
2005–06	Vitesse	30	2		
2006–07	Vitesse	2	0		
2007–08	Vitesse	34	3	66	5
2008–09	AZ Alkmaar	27	2		
2009–10	AZ Alkmaar	17	0		
2010–11	AZ Alkmaar	1	0	45	2
2010–11	Feyenoord	10	0		
2011–12	Feyenoord	3	0	30	0
2012–13	SonderjyskE	14	0	14	0
2013–14	NAC Breda	15	0		
2014–15	NAC Breda	16	0	31	0
2015–16	Notts Co	12	0	12	0

THOMPSON, Curtis (M)   **70 2**
H: 5 10   W: 12 06   b.Nottingham 2-9-93

2011–12	Notts Co	0	0		
2012–13	Notts Co	2	0		
2013–14	Notts Co	11	0		
2014–15	Notts Co	31	0		
2015–16	Notts Co	26	2	70	2

VALENCIC, Filip (F)   **134 19**
b. 7-1-92
Internationals: Slovenia U19, U21.

2009–10	Interblock	0	0		
2010–11	Interblock	25	4	31	4
2011–12	Olimpija	25	3		
2012–13	Olimpija	24	6		
2013–14	Olimpija	27	3		
2014–15	Olimpija	12	1	88	13
2014–15	Monza	6	1	6	1
2015–16	Notts Co	9	1	9	1

WILDIN, Luther (M)   **0 0**
b. 3-12-97
Internationals: Antigua U20.

2015–16	Notts Co	0	0

Non-Contract
Pilkington, Kevin William.

Scholars
Beraki, Paulos; Blaney, Kieran James; Brown-Hill, Dominic; Browne, Benjamin James Peter; Clayton-Naute, Tamar Singh; Cobain, Nathan Anthony; Collett-McCartney, George Robert; Dearle, Peter James; Gibbons, Harry Jacob; Gibson, Montel; Layton, Keenan; McMillan, Jack Louie; Parkes, Monty Joshua; Payling, Jake; Richards, Jordon George; Rutty-Smith, Yohan; Searson-Smithard, Joseph Luke; Wildin, Luther Ash.

OLDHAM ATH (61)

BOVE, Jordan (F)   **5 0**
H: 5 9   W: 11 00   b.Manchester 12-12-95

2013–14	Oldham Ath	0	0		
2014–15	Oldham Ath	5	0		
2015–16	Oldham Ath	0	0	5	0

BROWN, Connor (D)   **97 1**
H: 5 8   W: 10 12   b.Sheffield 2-10-91

2010–11	Sheffield U	0	0		
2011–12	Sheffield U	0	0		
2012–13	Oldham Ath	25	0		
2013–14	Oldham Ath	27	1		
2014–15	Oldham Ath	24	0		
2014–15	*Carlisle U*	8	0	8	0
2015–16	Oldham Ath	13	0	89	1

BURN, Jonathan (D)   **12 1**
b. 1-8-95

2014–15	Middlesbrough	0	0		
2014–15	Oldham Ath	12	1	12	1

BYRNES, Danny (F)   **0 0**
b. 17-1-97
Internationals: Wales U17.

2013–14	Oldham Ath	0	0
2014–15	Oldham Ath	0	0
2015–16	Oldham Ath	0	0

CASSIDY, Jake (F)   **129 20**
H: 5 10   W: 11 02   b.Glan Conwy 9-2-93
Internationals: Wales U19, U21.

2010–11	Wolverhampton W	0	0		
2011–12	Wolverhampton W	0	0		
2011–12	Tranmere R	10	5		
2012–13	Wolverhampton W	6	0		
2012–13	Tranmere R	26	11		
2013–14	Wolverhampton W	14	0		
2013–14	Tranmere R	19	1		
2014–15	Wolverhampton W	0	0	20	0
2014–15	Tranmere R	0	0	55	17
2014–15	Notts Co	16	3	16	3
2014–15	Southend U	17	0	17	0
2015–16	Oldham Ath	21	0	21	0

COLEMAN, Joel (G)   **43 0**
H: 6 6   W: 12 13   b.Bolton 26-9-95

2013–14	Oldham Ath	0	0		
2014–15	Oldham Ath	11	0		
2015–16	Oldham Ath	32	0	43	0

CORNELL, David (G)   **44 0**
H: 5 11   W: 11 07   b.Gorseinon 28-3-91
Internationals: Wales U17, U19, U21.

2009–10	Swansea C	0	0		
2010–11	Swansea C	0	0		
2011–12	Swansea C	0	0		
2011–12	*Hereford U*	25	0	25	0
2012–13	Swansea C	0	0		
2013–14	Swansea C	0	0		
2013–14	*St Mirren*	5	0	5	0
2014–15	Swansea C	0	0		
2014–15	*Portsmouth*	0	0		
2015–16	Oldham Ath	14	0	14	0

CROFT, Lee (F)   **265 15**
H: 5 11   W: 13 00   b.Wigan 21-6-85
Internationals: England U20.

2002–03	Manchester C	0	0		
2003–04	Manchester C	0	0		
2004–05	Manchester C	7	0		
2004–05	*Oldham Ath*	12	0		
2005–06	Manchester C	21	1	28	1
2006–07	Norwich C	36	3		
2007–08	Norwich C	41	1		
2008–09	Norwich C	41	5	118	9
2009–10	Derby Co	19	1		
2010–11	Derby Co	0	0		
2010–11	*Huddersfield T*	3	0	3	0
2011–12	Derby Co	8	0		
2011–12	*St Johnstone*	11	3	11	3
2012–13	Derby Co	0	0	27	1
2012–13	Oldham Ath	45	0		
2015–16	Oldham Ath	21	1	78	1

DIENG, Timothee (M)   **66 1**
H: 5 11   W: 12 00   b. 9-4-92

2011–12	Brest	0	0		
2012–13	Brest	2	0		
2013–14	Brest	4	0	6	0
2014–15	Oldham Ath	22	0		
2015–16	Oldham Ath	38	1	60	1

DUNN, David (M)   **382 57**
H: 5 9   W: 12 03   b.Gt Harwood 27-12-79
Internationals: England U18, U21, Full caps.

1997–98	Blackburn R	0	0
1998–99	Blackburn R	15	1

Season	Club	Apps	Gls	Tot Apps	Tot Gls
1999–2000	Blackburn R	22	2		
2000–01	Blackburn R	42	12		
2001–02	Blackburn R	29	7		
2002–03	Blackburn R	28	8		
2003–04	Birmingham C	21	2		
2004–05	Birmingham C	11	2		
2005–06	Birmingham C	15	2		
2006–07	Birmingham C	11	1	58	7
2006–07	Blackburn R	11	0		
2007–08	Blackburn R	31	1		
2008–09	Blackburn R	15	1		
2009–10	Blackburn R	23	9		
2010–11	Blackburn R	27	2		
2011–12	Blackburn R	26	2		
2012–13	Blackburn R	15	1		
2013–14	Blackburn R	23	4		
2014–15	Blackburn R	9	0	316	50
2015–16	Oldham Ath	8	0	8	0

ECKERSLEY, Richard (D)   114 0
H: 6 0 W: 13 05 b.Salford 12-3-89

Season	Club	Apps	Gls	Tot Apps	Tot Gls
2006–07	Manchester U	0	0		
2007–08	Manchester U	0	0		
2008–09	Manchester U	2	0		
2009–10	Manchester U	0	0	2	0
2009–10	Burnley	0	0		
2009–10	Plymouth Arg	7	0	7	0
2010–11	Burnley	0	0		
2010–11	Bradford C	12	0	12	0
2010–11	Bury	3	0	3	0
2011	Toronto	23	0		
2012	Toronto	33	0		
2013	Toronto	16	0	72	0
2014	New York Red Bulls	14	0	14	0
2015–16	Oldham Ath	4	0	4	0

EDMUNDSON, Gerorge (D)   0 0
b. 15-8-97

Season	Club	Apps	Gls
2015–16	Oldham Ath	0	0

EDMUNDSON, Sam (D)   2 0

Season	Club	Apps	Gls	Tot Apps	Tot Gls
2015–16	Oldham Ath	2	0	2	0

FORTE, Jonathan (M)   319 60
H: 6 0 W: 12 02 b.Sheffield 25-7-86
Internationals: England U16, U17, U18.
Barbados Full caps.

Season	Club	Apps	Gls	Tot Apps	Tot Gls
2003–04	Sheffield U	7	0		
2004–05	Sheffield U	22	1		
2005–06	Sheffield U	1	0		
2005–06	Doncaster R	13	4		
2005–06	Rotherham U	11	4	11	4
2006–07	Sheffield U	0	0		
2006–07	Doncaster R	41	5	54	9
2007–08	Scunthorpe U	38	4		
2008–09	Scunthorpe U	8	0		
2008–09	Notts Co	18	8		
2009–10	Scunthorpe U	28	2		
2010–11	Scunthorpe U	24	3	98	9
2010–11	Southampton	10	2		
2011–12	Southampton	1	0		
2011–12	Preston NE	3	0	3	0
2011–12	Notts Co	10	5	28	13
2012–13	Southampton	0	0		
2012–13	Crawley T	12	3	12	3
2012–13	Sheffield U	12	1	42	2
2013–14	Southampton	0	0	11	2
2014–15	Oldham Ath	34	15		
2015–16	Oldham Ath	26	3	60	18

FULLER, Ricardo (F)   441 105
H: 6 3 W: 12 10 b.Kingston, Jamaica
31-10-79
Internationals: Jamaica Full caps.

Season	Club	Apps	Gls	Tot Apps	Tot Gls
2000–01	Crystal Palace	8	0	8	0
2001–02	Hearts	27	8	27	8
From Tivoli Gardens.					
2002–03	Preston NE	18	9		
2003–04	Preston NE	38	17		
2004–05	Preston NE	2	1	58	27
2004–05	Portsmouth	31	1	31	1
2005–06	Southampton	30	9		
2005–06	Ipswich T	3	2	3	2
2006–07	Southampton	1	0	31	9
2006–07	Stoke C	30	10		
2007–08	Stoke C	42	15		
2008–09	Stoke C	34	11		
2009–10	Stoke C	35	3		
2010–11	Stoke C	28	4		
2011–12	Stoke C	13	0	182	43
2012–13	Charlton Ath	31	5		
2013–14	Charlton Ath	10	0	31	5
2013–14	Blackpool	27	6	27	6
2014–15	Millwall	38	4	38	4
2015–16	Oldham Ath	5	0	5	0

GERRARD, Anthony (D)   379 17
H: 6 2 W: 13 07 b.Huyton 6-2-86
Internationals: Republic of Ireland U18.

Season	Club	Apps	Gls	Tot Apps	Tot Gls
2004–05	Everton	0	0		
2004–05	Walsall	8	0		
2005–06	Walsall	34	0		
2006–07	Walsall	35	1		
2007–08	Walsall	44	3		
2008–09	Walsall	42	3	163	7
2009–10	Cardiff C	39	2		
2010–11	Cardiff C	0	0		
2010–11	Hull C	41	5	41	5
2011–12	Cardiff C	20	1		
2012–13	Cardiff C	0	0	59	3
2012–13	Huddersfield T	38	0		
2013–14	Huddersfield T	40	1		
2014–15	Huddersfield T	3	0	81	2
2014–15	Oldham Ath	6	0		
2015–16	Shrewsbury T	11	0	11	0
2015–16	Oldham Ath	18	0	24	0

JACOBS, Devante (F)   2 0
b. 1-1-98

Season	Club	Apps	Gls	Tot Apps	Tot Gls
2014–15	Oldham Ath	2	0		
2015–16	Oldham Ath	0	0	2	0

JONES, Mike (M)   348 35
H: 5 11 W: 12 04 b.Birkenhead 15-8-87

Season	Club	Apps	Gls	Tot Apps	Tot Gls
2005–06	Tranmere R	1	0		
2006–07	Tranmere R	10	0		
2006–07	Shrewsbury T	13	1	13	1
2007–08	Tranmere R	9	1	10	1
2008–09	Bury	46	4		
2009–10	Bury	41	5		
2010–11	Bury	42	8		
2011–12	Bury	24	3	153	20
2011–12	Sheffield W	10	0		
2012–13	Sheffield W	0	0	10	0
2012–13	Crawley T	40	1		
2013–14	Crawley T	42	3	82	4
2014–15	Oldham Ath	45	6		
2015–16	Oldham Ath	35	3	80	9

KELLY, Liam (M)   199 22
H: 6 2 W: 13 11 b.Milton Keynes 10-2-90
Internationals: Scotland U18, U21, Full caps.

Season	Club	Apps	Gls	Tot Apps	Tot Gls
2009–10	Kilmarnock	15	1		
2010–11	Kilmarnock	32	7		
2011–12	Kilmarnock	34	1		
2012–13	Kilmarnock	19	6	100	15
2012–13	Bristol C	19	0		
2013–14	Bristol C	2	0	21	0
2014–15	Oldham Ath	37	1		
2015–16	Oldham Ath	41	6	78	7

MILLS, Joseph (D)   152 3
H: 5 9 W: 11 00 b.Swindon 30-10-89
Internationals: England U17, U18.

Season	Club	Apps	Gls	Tot Apps	Tot Gls
2006–07	Southampton	0	0		
2007–08	Southampton	0	0		
2008–09	Southampton	8	0		
2008–09	Scunthorpe U	14	0	14	0
2009–10	Southampton	16	0		
2010–11	Southampton	2	0		
2010–11	Doncaster R	18	2	18	2
2011–12	Southampton	0	0	26	0
2011–12	Reading	15	0		
2012–13	Reading	0	0	15	0
2012–13	Burnley	10	0		
2013–14	Burnley	0	0	10	0
2013–14	Shrewsbury T	13	0	13	0
2014–15	Oldham Ath	30	0		
2015–16	Oldham Ath	15	1	56	1

MURPHY, Rhys (F)   123 35
H: 6 1 W: 11 13 b.Shoreham 6-11-90
Internationals: England U16, U17, U19.
Republic of Ireland U21.

Season	Club	Apps	Gls	Tot Apps	Tot Gls
2007–08	Arsenal	0	0		
2008–09	Arsenal	0	0		
2009–10	Arsenal	0	0		
2009–10	Brentford	5	0	5	0
2010–11	Arsenal	0	0		
2011–12	Arsenal	0	0		
2011–12	Preston NE	5	0	5	0
2012–13	Arsenal	0	0		
2012–13	Stormvogels Telstar	26	8	26	8
2013–14	Dagenham & R	32	13		
2014–15	Dagenham & R	9	1	41	14
2014–15	Oldham Ath	11	0		
2015–16	Oldham Ath	13	3	24	3
2015–16	Crawley T	15	9	15	9
2015–16	AFC Wimbledon	7	1	7	1

O'CONNELL, Eoghan (D)   7 0
H: 6 1 W: 12 08 b.Cork 13-8-95
Internationals: Republic of Ireland U18, U21.

Season	Club	Apps	Gls	Tot Apps	Tot Gls
2013–14	Celtic	1	0		
2014–15	Celtic	3	0		
2015–16	Celtic	1	0	5	0
On loan from Celtic.					
2015–16	Oldham Ath	2	0	2	0

Transferred to Cork C February 2016.

POLEON, Dominic (F)   103 13
H: 6 3 W: 12 13 b.Newham 7-9-93

Season	Club	Apps	Gls	Tot Apps	Tot Gls
2011–12	Leeds U	6	2		
2012–13	Bury	7	2	7	2
2012–13	Sheffield U	7	0	7	0
2013–14	Leeds U	19	1		
2014–15	Leeds U	4	0	29	3
2014–15	Oldham Ath	35	4		
2015–16	Oldham Ath	25	4	60	8

READ, Alex (M)   0 0
b. 24-10-97

Season	Club	Apps	Gls
2015–16	Oldham Ath	0	0

RENSHAW, Chris (G)   0 0
b. 26-9-97

Season	Club	Apps	Gls
2015–16	Oldham Ath	0	0

TRUELOVE, Jack (D)   1 0
H: 5 11 W: 12 00 b.Burnley 27-12-95

Season	Club	Apps	Gls	Tot Apps	Tot Gls
2012–13	Oldham Ath	1	0		
2013–14	Oldham Ath	0	0		
2014–15	Oldham Ath	0	0		
2015–16	Oldham Ath	0	0	1	0

TUOHY, Jack (M)   2 0
b.Oldham 6-9-96

Season	Club	Apps	Gls	Tot Apps	Tot Gls
2014–15	Oldham Ath	1	0		
2015–16	Oldham Ath	1	0	2	0

TURNER, Rhys (F)   31 4
b.Preston 22-7-95

Season	Club	Apps	Gls	Tot Apps	Tot Gls
2013–14	Oldham Ath	2	0		
2014–15	Oldham Ath	14	3		
2015–16	Oldham Ath	6	0	22	3
2015–16	York C	9	1	9	1

VASSELL, Theo (D)   0 0
b. 2-1-97

Season	Club	Apps	Gls
2014–15	Stoke C	0	0
2015–16	Oldham Ath	0	0

WILSON, Brian (D)   401 16
H: 5 10 W: 11 00 b.Manchester 9-5-83

Season	Club	Apps	Gls	Tot Apps	Tot Gls
2001–02	Stoke C	1	0		
2002–03	Stoke C	3	0		
2003–04	Stoke C	2	0	6	0
2003–04	Cheltenham T	14	0		
2004–05	Cheltenham T	43	3		
2005–06	Cheltenham T	43	9		
2006–07	Cheltenham T	25	2	125	14
2006–07	Bristol C	19	0		
2007–08	Bristol C	18	1		
2008–09	Bristol C	20	0		
2009–10	Bristol C	3	0	60	1
2010–11	Colchester U	26	1		
2011–12	Colchester U	46	0		
2012–13	Colchester U	41	0		
2013–14	Colchester U	38	0	151	1
2014–15	Oldham Ath	33	0		
2015–16	Oldham Ath	26	0	59	0

WILSON, James (D)   162 2
H: 6 2 W: 11 05 b.Chepstow 26-2-89
Internationals: Wales U19. U21, Full caps.

Season	Club	Apps	Gls	Tot Apps	Tot Gls
2005–06	Bristol C	0	0		
2006–07	Bristol C	0	0		
2007–08	Bristol C	0	0		
2008–09	Bristol C	2	0		
2009–10	Bristol C	0	0		
2009–10	Brentford	14	0		
2009–10	Brentford	13	0	27	0
2010–11	Bristol C	2	0		
2011–12	Bristol C	21	0		
2012–13	Bristol C	6	0		
2013–14	Bristol C	0	0	31	0
2013–14	Cheltenham T	4	0	4	0
2013–14	Oldham Ath	16	1		
2014–15	Oldham Ath	41	1		
2015–16	Oldham Ath	43	0	100	2

WINCHESTER, Carl (D)   111 7
H: 5 10 W: 11 08 b.Belfast 12-4-93
Internationals: Northern Ireland U16, U17,
U18, U19, U21, Full caps.

Season	Club	Apps	Gls	Tot Apps	Tot Gls
2010–11	Oldham Ath	6	1		
2011–12	Oldham Ath	12	0		
2012–13	Oldham Ath	9	0		
2013–14	Oldham Ath	12	1		
2014–15	Oldham Ath	41	4		
2015–16	Oldham Ath	31	1	111	7

Scholars
Brown, Ronaldo Mushchario; Fallon, Mason
Kevin; Glackin, Brendan Paul; Hargreaves,

Jake Paul; Kay, Bradley Steven; King, Dylan John Frederick; Knight, Lee David; Leonard, Ryan Michael Raymond; Mantack, Kallum Kevin; Middleton, Rory Michael; Murray, Rio Dennis; O'Neill, Callum Terence; Parmar, Rahul; Read, Alexander Douglas Eldred; Renshaw, Christopher Thomas; Scullion, Callum Patrick; Stott, Jamie Garry.

OXFORD U (62)

ASHBY, Josh (M)   5   0
b.Oxford 3-5-96

2013–14	Oxford U	0	0		
2014–15	Oxford U	2	0		
2015–16	Oxford U	3	0	5	0

ASHDOWN, Jamie (G)   159   0
H: 6 1   W: 13 05   b.Reading 30-11-80

1999–2000	Reading	0	0		
2000–01	Reading	1	0		
2001–02	Reading	1	0		
2001–02	*Arsenal*	0	0		
2002–03	Reading	1	0		
2002–03	*Bournemouth*	2	0	2	0
2003–04	Reading	10	0	13	0
2003–04	*Rushden & D*	19	0	19	0
2004–05	Portsmouth	16	0		
2005–06	Portsmouth	17	0		
2006–07	Portsmouth	0	0		
2006–07	*Norwich C*	2	0	2	0
2007–08	Portsmouth	3	0		
2008–09	Portsmouth	0	0		
2009–10	Portsmouth	6	0		
2010–11	Portsmouth	46	0		
2011–12	Portsmouth	21	0	109	0
2012–13	Leeds U	0	0		
2013–14	Leeds U	0	0		
2014–15	Crawley T	9	0	9	0
2014–15	Oxford U	5	0		
2015–16	Oxford U	0	0	5	0

BOWERY, Jordan (F)   165   22
H: 6 1   W: 12 00   b.Nottingham 2-7-91

2008–09	Chesterfield	3	0		
2009–10	Chesterfield	10	0		
2010–11	Chesterfield	27	1		
2011–12	Chesterfield	40	8		
2012–13	Chesterfield	3	1	83	10
2012–13	Aston Villa	10	0		
2013–14	Aston Villa	9	0	19	0
2013–14	*Doncaster R*	3	0	3	0
2014–15	Rotherham U	33	5		
2015–16	Rotherham U	7	0	40	5
2015–16	*Bradford C*	3	0	3	0
2015–16	Oxford U	17	7	17	7

BUCHEL, Benjamin (G)   23   0
H: 6 2   W: 11 08   b.Ruggel 4-7-89
Internationals: Liechtenstein U17, U19, U21, Full caps.

2012–13	Bournemouth	0	0		
2013–14	Bournemouth	0	0		
2014–15	Bournemouth	0	0		
2015–16	Oxford U	23	0	23	0

CARROLL, Canice (M)   0   0
b. 26-1-99
Internationals: Republic of Ireland U17.

2015–16	Oxford U	0	0		

CAVANAGH, Eddie (G)   0   0
b.Oxford 30-3-97

2014–15	Oxford U	0	0		
2015–16	Oxford U	0	0		

COLLINS, Michael (M)   307   23
H: 6 0   W: 11 00   b.Halifax 30-4-86
Internationals: Republic of Ireland U18, U19, U21.

2004–05	Huddersfield T	8	0		
2005–06	Huddersfield T	17	1		
2006–07	Huddersfield T	43	4		
2007–08	Huddersfield T	41	2		
2008–09	Huddersfield T	36	9		
2009–10	Huddersfield T	28	3	173	19
2010–11	Scunthorpe U	32	1		
2011–12	Scunthorpe U	1	0		
2012–13	Scunthorpe U	29	1		
2013–14	Scunthorpe U	17	0	79	2
2013–14	*AFC Wimbledon*	9	0	9	0
2014–15	Oxford U	39	2		
2015–16	Oxford U	0	0	39	2
2015–16	*York C*	7	0	7	0

CROCOMBE, Max (G)   9   0
H: 6 4   b.Auckland 12-8-93
Internationals: New Zealand U20, U23, Full caps.

2012–13	Oxford U	4	0		
2013–14	Oxford U	0	0		
2014–15	Oxford U	0	0		
2015–16	Oxford U	0	0	4	0
2015–16	*Barnet*	5	0	5	0

CUNDY, Robbie (D)   0   0
b. 30-5-97

2015–16	Oxford U	0	0		

DUNKLEY, Cheyenne (D)   38   4
H: 6 2   W: 13 05   b.Wolverhampton 13-2-92
From Kidderminster H.

2014–15	Oxford U	9	0		
2015–16	Oxford U	29	4	38	4

GAYLE, Cameron (D)   53   2
H: 5 11   W: 11 00   b.Birmingham 22-11-92

2010–11	WBA	0	0		
2011–12	WBA	0	0		
2012–13	WBA	0	0		
2012–13	*Shrewsbury T*	18	1		
2013–14	WBA	0	0		
2013–14	*Shrewsbury T*	3	0		
2014–15	Shrewsbury T	28	0		
2015–16	Shrewsbury T	0	0	49	1
2015–16	Oxford U	0	0		
2015–16	*Cambridge U*	4	1	4	1

GEORGE, Adriel (M)   2   0
b. 6-12-96
Internationals: Antigua and Barbuda Full caps.

2015–16	Oxford U	2	0	2	0

GILES, Jonny (M)   0   0
b. 14-5-94

2015–16	Southport	0	0		
2015–16	Oxford U	0	0		

HAWTIN, Aidan (M)   1   0
b. 13-6-95

2014–15	Oxford U	1	0		
2015–16	Oxford U	0	0	1	0

HOBAN, Patrick (F)   44   3
b.Galway 28-7-91

2014–15	Oxford U	20	1		
2015–16	Oxford U	23	2	43	3
2015–16	*Stevenage*	1	0	1	0

HUMPHREYS, Sam (M)   1   0
b.Oxford 3-11-95

2014–15	Oxford U	1	0		
2015–16	Oxford U	0	0	1	0

HYLTON, Danny (F)   264   61
H: 6 0   W: 11 13   b.Camden 25-2-89

2008–09	Aldershot T	29	5		
2009–10	Aldershot T	21	3		
2010–11	Aldershot T	33	5		
2011–12	Aldershot T	44	13		
2012–13	Aldershot T	27	4	154	30
2013–14	*Rotherham U*	1	0	1	0
2013–14	*Bury*	7	2	7	2
2013–14	*AFC Wimbledon*	17	3	17	3
2014–15	Oxford U	44	14		
2015–16	Oxford U	41	12	85	26

JEACOCK, George (F)   0   0
b. 16-9-97

2015–16	Oxford U	0	0		

LONG, Sam (D)   15   1
H: 5 10   W: 11 11   b.Oxford 16-1-95

2012–13	Oxford U	1	0		
2013–14	Oxford U	3	0		
2014–15	Oxford U	10	1		
2015–16	Oxford U	1	0	15	1

LUNDSTRAM, John (M)   100   5
H: 5 11   W: 11 09   b.Liverpool 18-2-94
Internationals: England U17, U18, U19, U20.

2011–12	Everton	0	0		
2012–13	Everton	0	0		
2012–13	*Doncaster R*	14	0	14	0
2013–14	Everton	0	0		
2013–14	*Yeovil T*	14	2	14	2
2013–14	*Leyton Orient*	7	0		
2014–15	Everton	0	0		
2014–15	*Blackpool*	17	0	17	0
2014–15	*Leyton Orient*	4	0	11	0
2015–16	*Scunthorpe U*	7	0	7	0
2015–16	Oxford U	37	3	37	3

MACDONALD, Alex (F)   192   22
H: 5 7   W: 11 04   b.Warrington 14-4-90
Internationals: Scotland U19, U21.

2007–08	Burnley	2	0		
2008–09	Burnley	3	0		
2009–10	Burnley	0	0		
2009–10	*Falkirk*	11	1	11	1
2010–11	Burnley	0	0		
2010–11	*Inverness CT*	10	1	10	1
2011–12	Burnley	5	0		
2011–12	*Plymouth Arg*	18	4		
2012–13	Burnley	1	0	11	0
2012–13	*Plymouth Arg*	16	1	34	5
2012–13	Burton Alb	15	1		
2013–14	Burton Alb	35	0		
2014–15	Burton Alb	21	6	71	7
2014–15	Oxford U	15	3		
2015–16	Oxford U	40	5	55	8

MAGUIRE, Chris (F)   280   48
H: 5 7   W: 10 05   b.Bellshill 16-1-89
Internationals: Scotland U16, U19, U21, Full caps.

2005–06	Aberdeen	1	0		
2006–07	Aberdeen	19	1		
2007–08	Aberdeen	28	4		
2008–09	Aberdeen	31	3		
2009–10	Aberdeen	17	1		
2009–10	*Kilmarnock*	14	4	14	4
2010–11	Aberdeen	35	7	131	16
2011–12	Derby Co	7	1	7	1
2011–12	Portsmouth	11	3	11	3
2012–13	Sheffield W	10	1		
2013–14	Sheffield W	27	9		
2013–14	*Coventry C*	3	2	3	2
2014–15	Sheffield W	42	8	79	18
2015–16	Rotherham U	14	0	14	0
2015–16	Oxford U	21	4	21	4

MULLINS, John (D)   402   24
H: 5 11   W: 12 07   b.Hampstead 6-11-85

2004–05	Reading	0	0		
2004–05	*Kidderminster H*	21	2	21	2
2005–06	Reading	0	0		
2006–07	Mansfield T	43	2		
2007–08	Mansfield T	43	2	86	4
2008–09	Stockport Co	33	3		
2009–10	Stockport Co	36	1	69	4
2010–11	Rotherham U	35	1		
2011–12	Rotherham U	35	2		
2012–13	Rotherham U	29	4	99	7
2012–13	*Oxford U*	8	2		
2013–14	Oxford U	35	3		
2014–15	Oxford U	44	2		
2015–16	Oxford U	40	0	127	7

O'DOWDA, Callum (M)   87   12
H: 5 11   W: 11 11   b.Oxford 23-4-95
Internationals: Republic of Ireland U21, Full caps.

2012–13	Oxford U	0	0		
2013–14	Oxford U	10	0		
2014–15	Oxford U	39	4		
2015–16	Oxford U	38	8	87	12

ROBERTS, James (F)   31   3
b.Stoke Mandeville 21-6-96

2012–13	Oxford U	0	0		
2013–14	Oxford U	0	0		
2014–15	Oxford U	25	3		
2015–16	Oxford U	4	0	29	3
2015–16	*Barnet*	2	0	2	0

ROOFE, Kemar (M)   73   25
H: 5 10   W: 11 03   b.Walsall 6-1-93

2011–12	WBA	0	0		
2012–13	WBA	0	0		
2012–13	*Northampton T*	6	0	6	0
2013–14	WBA	0	0		
2013–14	*Cheltenham T*	9	1	9	1
2014–15	WBA	0	0		
2014–15	*Colchester U*	2	0	2	0
2014–15	Oxford U	16	6		
2015–16	Oxford U	40	18	56	24

RUFFELS, Joshua (M)   79   1
H: 5 10   W: 11 11   b.Oxford 23-10-93

2011–12	Coventry C	1	0		
2012–13	Coventry C	0	0	1	0
2013–14	Oxford U	29	1		
2014–15	Oxford U	33	0		
2015–16	Oxford U	16	0	78	1

SERCOMBE, Liam (M)   281   37
H: 5 10   W: 10 10   b.Exeter 25-4-90

2008–09	Exeter C	29	2		
2009–10	Exeter C	28	1		
2010–11	Exeter C	42	3		
2011–12	Exeter C	33	7		

Season	Club				
2012–13	Exeter C	20	1		
2013–14	Exeter C	44	5		
2014–15	Exeter C	40	4	236	23
2015–16	Oxford U	45	14	45	14

SKARZ, Joe (D)   350 7
H: 5 10   W: 11 04   b.Huddersfield 13-7-89

Season	Club				
2006–07	Huddersfield T	17	0		
2007–08	Huddersfield T	27	0		
2008–09	Huddersfield T	9	1		
2008–09	Hartlepool U	7	0	7	0
2009–10	Huddersfield T	15	0	68	1
2009–10	Shrewsbury T	20	0	20	0
2010–11	Bury	45	1		
2011–12	Bury	45	1		
2012–13	Bury	39	2	130	4
2012–13	Rotherham U	8	0		
2013–14	Rotherham U	41	2		
2014–15	Rotherham U	17	0	66	2
2014–15	Oxford U	18	0		
2015–16	Oxford U	41	0	59	0

SLOCOMBE, Sam (G)   138 0
H: 6 0   W: 11 11   b.Scunthorpe 5-6-88

Season	Club				
2008–09	Scunthorpe U	0	0		
2009–10	Scunthorpe U	1	0		
2010–11	Scunthorpe U	2	0		
2011–12	Scunthorpe U	28	0		
2012–13	Scunthorpe U	29	0		
2013–14	Scunthorpe U	46	0		
2014–15	Scunthorpe U	9	0	115	0
2015–16	Oxford U	23	0	23	0

STEPHENS, Jack (G)   0 0
b. 2-8-97

Season	Club		
2014–15	Oxford U	0	0
2015–16	Oxford U	0	0

TAYLOR, Ryan (F)   255 41
H: 6 2   W: 10 10   b.Rotherham 4-5-88

Season	Club				
2005–06	Rotherham U	11	0		
2006–07	Rotherham U	10	0		
2007–08	Rotherham U	35	6		
2008–09	Rotherham U	33	4		
2009–10	Rotherham U	19	0		
2009–10	Exeter C	7	0	7	0
2010–11	Rotherham U	34	11	132	21
2011–12	Bristol C	7	1		
2012–13	Bristol C	25	1		
2013–14	Bristol C	7	0	39	2
2013–14	Portsmouth	18	6		
2014–15	Portsmouth	37	9	55	15
2015–16	Oxford U	22	3	22	3

WRIGHT, Jake (D)   229 0
H: 5 10   W: 11 07   b.Keighley 11-3-86

Season	Club				
2005–06	Bradford C	1	0	1	0
From Halifax T, Crawley T					
2009–10	Brighton & HA	6	0	6	0
2010–11	Oxford U	35	0		
2011–12	Oxford U	43	0		
2012–13	Oxford U	42	0		
2013–14	Oxford U	31	0		
2014–15	Oxford U	42	0		
2015–16	Oxford U	29	0	222	0

Scholars
Agboola, Emmanuel Ayomikun; Baptiste, Shandon Harkeem; Diaz-Benitez, Kieran Mark; Graham, Jordan Owen; Hartley, Joseph; Hastings, Luke Paul; Hawtin, Charles Christopher; Hayden, Lewis Scott; Humphries, Seth William Osborne; Jeacock, George Edward; McCormack, Cian Anthony; Napa, Malachi Tyrese Mthokozisi; Ricketts, Drew Anthony; Stevens, Jack Anthony; Tuttle, Charley David; Welch-Hayes, Miles Winfield.

PETERBOROUGH U (63)

ADDISON, Miles (D)   134 5
H: 6 2   W: 13 03   b.Newham 7-1-89
Internationals: England U21.

Season	Club				
2005–06	Derby Co	2	0		
2006–07	Derby Co	0	0		
2007–08	Derby Co	1	0		
2008–09	Derby Co	28	1		
2009–10	Derby Co	13	2		
2010–11	Derby Co	21	0		
2011–12	Derby Co	0	0		
2011–12	Barnsley	11	0	11	0
2011–12	Bournemouth	14	1		
2012–13	Derby Co	0	0	65	3
2012–13	Bournemouth	20	0		
2013–14	Bournemouth	0	0		
2013–14	Rotherham U	6	0	6	0
2014–15	Bournemouth	0	0	34	1
2014–15	Scunthorpe U	3	0	3	0
2014–15	Blackpool	6	0	6	0
2015–16	Peterborough U	3	1	3	1
2015–16	Kilmarnock	6	0	6	0

ADEBAYO-ROWLING, Tobi (M)   4 0
b. 16-11-96

Season	Club				
2014–15	Peterborough U	0	0		
2015–16	Peterborough U	4	0	4	0

ALNWICK, Ben (G)   148 0
H: 6 2   W: 13 12   b.Prudhoe 1-1-87
Internationals: England U16, U17, U18, U19, U21.

Season	Club				
2003–04	Sunderland	0	0		
2004–05	Sunderland	3	0		
2005–06	Sunderland	5	0		
2006–07	Sunderland	11	0	19	0
2006–07	Tottenham H	0	0		
2007–08	Tottenham H	0	0		
2007–08	Luton T	4	0	4	0
2007–08	Leicester C	8	0	8	0
2008–09	Tottenham H	0	0		
2008–09	Carlisle U	6	0	6	0
2009–10	Tottenham H	1	0		
2009–10	Norwich C	3	0	3	0
2010–11	Tottenham H	0	0		
2010–11	Leeds U	0	0		
2010–11	Doncaster R	1	0		
2011–12	Tottenham H	0	0		
2011–12	Leyton Orient	6	0		
2012–13	Tottenham H	0	0	1	0
2012–13	Barnsley	10	0		
2013–14	Barnsley	0	0	10	0
2013–14	Charlton Ath	10	0	10	0
2013–14	Leyton Orient	1	0	7	0
2014–15	Peterborough U	41	0		
2015–16	Peterborough U	39	0	80	0

ANDERSON, Harry (F)   15 0
H: 5 6   W: 9 11   b. 9-1-97

Season	Club				
2014–15	Peterborough U	10	0		
2015–16	Peterborough U	5	0	15	0

ANDERSON, Jermaine (M)   52 5
b. 16-5-96
Internationals: England U18, U20.

Season	Club				
2012–13	Peterborough U	1	0		
2013–14	Peterborough U	13	0		
2014–15	Peterborough U	24	1		
2015–16	Peterborough U	14	4	52	5

ANGOL, Lee (M)   36 11
H: 5 10   W: 11 04   b. 4-8-94

Season	Club				
2012–13	Wycombe W	3	0		
2013–14	Wycombe W	0	0	3	0
2014–15	Luton T	0	0		
2015–16	Peterborough U	33	11	33	11

BALDWIN, Jack (D)   117 5
H: 6 1   W: 11 00   b.Barking 30-6-93

Season	Club				
2011–12	Hartlepool U	17	0		
2012–13	Hartlepool U	32	2		
2013–14	Hartlepool U	28	2	77	4
2013–14	Peterborough U	11	0		
2014–15	Peterborough U	11	0		
2015–16	Peterborough U	18	1	40	1

BEAUTYMAN, Harry (M)   40 5
H: 5 10   W: 11 09   b.Newham 1-4-92
Internationals: England C.

Season	Club				
2010–11	Leyton Orient	0	0		
From Sutton U, Welling U.					
2014–15	Peterborough U	18	2		
2015–16	Peterborough U	22	3	40	5

BOSTWICK, Michael (D)   239 29
H: 6 4   W: 14 00   b.Eltham 17-5-88
Internationals: England C.

Season	Club				
2006–07	Millwall	0	0		
From Rushden & D, Ebbsfleet U					
2010–11	Stevenage	41	2		
2011–12	Stevenage	43	7	84	9
2012–13	Peterborough U	39	5		
2013–14	Peterborough U	42	4		
2014–15	Peterborough U	38	7		
2015–16	Peterborough U	36	4	155	20

BRISLEY, Shaun (M)   234 9
H: 6 2   W: 12 02   b.Macclesfield 6-5-90

Season	Club				
2007–08	Macclesfield T	10	1		
2008–09	Macclesfield T	38	0		
2009–10	Macclesfield T	33	1		
2010–11	Macclesfield T	14	0		
2011–12	Macclesfield T	29	3	124	6
2011–12	Peterborough U	11	0		
2012–13	Peterborough U	28	0		
2013–14	Peterborough U	22	0		
2014–15	Peterborough U	15	1		
2014–15	Scunthorpe U	7	0	7	0
2015–16	Peterborough U	2	0	78	1
2015–16	Northampton T	9	1	9	1
2015–16	Leyton Orient	16	1	16	1

CHETTLE, Callum (M)   5 0
b. 28-8-96
Internationals: England C.
From Ilkeston, Nuneaton T.

Season	Club				
2015–16	Peterborough U	5	0	5	0

COLLISON, Jack (M)   128 11
H: 6 0   W: 13 10   b.Watford 2-10-88
Internationals: Wales U21, Full caps.

Season	Club				
2007–08	West Ham U	2	0		
2008–09	West Ham U	20	3		
2009–10	West Ham U	22	2		
2010–11	West Ham U	3	0		
2011–12	West Ham U	31	4		
2012–13	West Ham U	17	2		
2013–14	West Ham U	10	0		
2013–14	Bournemouth	4	0	4	0
2013–14	Wigan Ath	9	0	9	0
2014–15	West Ham U	0	0	105	11
2015–16	Peterborough U	10	0	10	0

COULIBALY, Souleymane (F)   33 6
b.Anguededou 26-12-94
Internationals: Ivory Coast U17.

Season	Club				
2013–14	Tottenham H	0	0		
2015–16	Peterborough U	27	5	27	5
2015–16	Newport Co	6	1	6	1

COULTHIRST, Shaquile (F)   61 11
H: 5 9   W: 12 02   b.Hackney 2-1-94
Internationals: England U19.

Season	Club				
2012–13	Tottenham H	0	0		
2013–14	Tottenham H	0	0		
2013–14	Leyton Orient	1	1	1	1
2013–14	Torquay U	6	2	6	2
2014–15	Tottenham H	0	0		
2014–15	Southend U	22	4	22	4
2014–15	York C	11	2	11	2
2015–16	Tottenham H	0	0		
2015–16	Wigan Ath	2	0	2	0
2015–16	Peterborough U	19	2	19	2

DA SILVA LOPES, Leonardo (M)   10 0
b. 30-11-98

Season	Club				
2014–15	Peterborough U	2	0		
2015–16	Peterborough U	8	0	10	0

EDWARDS, Jonathan (M)   3 0
H: 5 11   W: 10 01   b.Luton 24-11-96

Season	Club				
2014–15	Peterborough U	3	0		
2015–16	Peterborough U	0	0	3	0

FORRESTER, Chris (M)   35 2
b.Dublin 17-12-92
Internationals: Republic of Ireland U21.
From Bohemians, St Patrick's Ath.

Season	Club				
2015–16	Peterborough U	35	2	35	2

FOX, Andrew (D)   18 1
b. 15-1-93

Season	Club				
2015–16	Peterborough U	18	1	18	1

GORMLEY, Joe (F)   4 0
b. 26-11-89
From Cliftonville.

Season	Club				
2015–16	Peterborough U	4	0	4	0

HENRY, Dion (M)   1 0
H: 5 11   W: 10 03   b.Ipswich 12-9-97

Season	Club				
2014–15	Peterborough U	0	0		
2015–16	Peterborough U	1	0	1	0

JAMES, Luke (M)   152 21
H: 6 0   W: 12 08   b.Amble 4-11-94

Season	Club				
2011–12	Hartlepool U	19	3		
2012–13	Hartlepool U	26	3		
2013–14	Hartlepool U	42	13		
2014–15	Hartlepool U	4	0		
2014–15	Peterborough U	32	1		
2015–16	Peterborough U	0	0	32	1
2015–16	Bradford C	9	0	9	0
2015–16	Hartlepool U	20	1	111	20

LUTO, Oliver (M)   0 0
H: 6 1   W: 12 00   b.Kinshasa 13-2-96

Season	Club		
2014–15	Peterborough U	0	0
2015–16	Peterborough U	0	0

MADDISON, Marcus (M)   68 18
H: 5 9   W: 11 03   b.Sedgefield 26-9-93
Internationals: England C.

Season	Club				
2014–15	Peterborough U	29	7		
2015–16	Peterborough U	39	11	68	18

MASLEN-JONES, Bradley (D)   0 0
b. 12-1-98

Season	Club		
2015–16	Peterborough U	0	0

NABI, Adil (F) **16 3**
H: 5 9 W: 10 10 b.Birmingham 28-2-94
Internationals: England U16, U17.

2010–11	WBA	0	0		
2011–12	WBA	0	0		
2012–13	WBA	0	0		
2013–14	WBA	0	0		
2014–15	WBA	0	0		
2015	*Delhi Dynamos*	10	3	**10**	**3**
2015–16	WBA	0	0		
2015–16	Peterborough U	6	0	**6**	**0**

NICHOLS, Tom (F) **105 33**
H: 5 10 W: 10 10 b.Wellington 1-9-93

2010–11	Exeter C	1	0		
2011–12	Exeter C	7	1		
2012–13	Exeter C	3	0		
2013–14	Exeter C	28	6		
2014–15	Exeter C	36	15		
2015–16	Exeter C	23	10	**98**	**32**
2015–16	Peterborough U	7	1	**7**	**1**

NICHOLSON, Jordan (F) **2 0**
b. 29-9-93
From Histon.

2015–16	Peterborough U	2	0	**2**	**0**

NTLHE, Kgosietsile (D) **76 4**
H: 5 9 W: 10 05 b.Pretoria 21-2-94
Internationals: South Africa U20, Full caps.

2010–11	Peterborough U	0	0		
2011–12	Peterborough U	2	0		
2012–13	Peterborough U	12	1		
2013–14	Peterborough U	27	2		
2014–15	Peterborough U	28	1		
2015–16	Peterborough U	7	0	**76**	**4**

OZTUMER, Erhun (M) **50 7**
b.Greenwich 29-5-91

2014–15	Peterborough U	20	1		
2015–16	Peterborough U	30	6	**50**	**7**

PAYNE, Jack (M) **219 11**
H: 5 9 W: 9 02 b.Gravesend 5-12-91

2008–09	Gillingham	2	0		
2009–10	Gillingham	19	0		
2010–11	Gillingham	31	1		
2011–12	Gillingham	30	2		
2012–13	Gillingham	19	2	**101**	**5**
2012–13	*Peterborough U*	14	0		
2013–14	Peterborough U	32	2		
2014–15	Peterborough U	41	3		
2015–16	Peterborough U	2	0	**89**	**5**
2015–16	*Leyton Orient*	29	1	**29**	**1**

SANTOS, Ricardo (D) **62 1**
H: 6 5 W: 12 02 b.Almada 18-6-95

2012–13	Dagenham & R	0	0		
2013–14	Dagenham & R	0	0		
2013–14	Peterborough U	1	0		
2014–15	Peterborough U	24	0		
2015–16	Peterborough U	37	1	**62**	**1**

SMITH, Michael (D) **357 19**
H: 5 11 W: 11 02 b.Ballyclare 4-9-88
Internationals: Northern Ireland Full caps.

2005–06	Ballyclare Com	1	0		
2006–07	Ballyclare Com	25	2		
2007–08	Ballyclare Com	39	1		
2008–09	Ballyclare Com	27	7	**92**	**10**
2008–09	Ballymena U	12	1		
2009–10	Ballymena U	37	2		
2010–11	Ballymena U	34	3	**83**	**6**
2011–12	Bristol R	20	0		
2012–13	Bristol R	38	1		
2013–14	Bristol R	43	0	**101**	**1**
2014–15	Peterborough U	43	1		
2015–16	Peterborough U	38	1	**81**	**2**

TAYLOR, Jon (M) **201 36**
H: 5 11 W: 12 04 b.Liverpool 23-12-89

2009–10	Shrewsbury T	2	0		
2010–11	Shrewsbury T	20	6		
2011–12	Shrewsbury T	33	0		
2012–13	Shrewsbury T	37	7		
2013–14	Shrewsbury T	41	9	**133**	**22**
2014–15	Peterborough U	24	3		
2015–16	Peterborough U	44	11	**68**	**14**

VASSELL, Kyle (F) **55 6**
H: 6 0 W: 12 04 b.Milton Keynes 7-2-93

2013–14	Peterborough U	6	0		
2014–15	Peterborough U	17	5		
2014–15	*Oxford U*	6	1	**6**	**1**
2015–16	Peterborough U	5	0	**28**	**5**
2015–16	*Dagenham & R*	8	0	**8**	**0**
2015–16	*Shrewsbury T*	13	0	**13**	**0**

WILLIAMS, Aaron (F) **16 2**
H: 5 11 W: 12 05 b. 21-10-93
Internationals: England C.

2012–13	Walsall	6	0		
2013–14	Walsall	0	0	**6**	**0**

From Worcester C, Rushall Olympic, Nuneaton T.

2015–16	Peterborough U	10	2	**10**	**2**

ZAKUANI, Gaby (D) **356 13**
H: 6 1 W: 12 13 b.DR Congo 31-5-86
Internationals: DR Congo Full caps.

2002–03	Leyton Orient	1	0		
2003–04	Leyton Orient	10	2		
2004–05	Leyton Orient	33	0		
2005–06	Leyton Orient	43	1	**87**	**3**
2006–07	Fulham	0	0		
2006–07	*Stoke C*	9	0		
2007–08	Fulham	0	0		
2007–08	*Stoke C*	19	0	**28**	**0**
2008–09	Fulham	0	0		
2008–09	Peterborough U	32	1		
2009–10	Peterborough U	29	0		
2010–11	Peterborough U	30	2		
2011–12	Peterborough U	41	1		
2012–13	Peterborough U	33	1		
2013–14	Peterborough U	15	0		
2013–14	*Kalloni*	15	1	**15**	**1**
2014–15	Peterborough U	22	1		
2015–16	Peterborough U	24	3	**226**	**9**

Scholars
Alban Jones, Hugh Alexander; Baldry, Harry Max; Ferrier, Glenn; Ford, Michael Brendan; Goode, James; Hood, Joseph; Humphrey, Oliver James Victor; Jarvis, Daniel John; Keating, Ben Alex; Lee, Ethan; Maslen-Jones, Bradley; Moore, Deon Ryan; Noble, Luke Melvyn William; Penfold, Morgan Kendall.

PLYMOUTH ARG (64)

BENTLEY, Jordan (D) **1 0**

2015–16	Plymouth Arg	1	0	**1**	**0**

BITTNER, James (G) **2 0**
H: 6 2 W: 12 09 b.Devizes 2-2-82

2001–02	Bournemouth	0	0		

From Exeter C.

2005–06	Torquay U	0	0		

From Woking, Salisbury C, Chippenham T, Forest Green R, Hereford U.

2013–14	Newport Co	0	0		

From Salisbury C.

2014–15	Plymouth Arg	1	0		
2015–16	Plymouth Arg	1	0	**2**	**0**

BRUNT, Ryan (F) **123 20**
H: 6 1 W: 11 11 b.Birmingham 26-5-93

2011–12	Stoke C	0	0		
2011–12	*Tranmere R*	15	1	**15**	**1**
2012–13	Stoke C	0	0		
2012–13	*Leyton Orient*	18	3	**18**	**3**
2012–13	Bristol R	18	5		
2013–14	Bristol R	11	0		
2014–15	Bristol R	0	0	**29**	**5**
2014–15	*York C*	6	0	**6**	**0**
2014–15	*Stevenage*	5	0	**5**	**0**
2014–15	Plymouth Arg	16	2		
2015–16	Plymouth Arg	34	9	**50**	**11**

CAREY, Graham (M) **201 26**
H: 6 0 W: 10 03 b.Dublin 20-5-89
Internationals: Republic of Ireland U21.

2008–09	Celtic	0	0		
2009	*Bohemians*	15	2	**15**	**2**
2009–10	Celtic	0	0		
2009–10	*St Mirren*	15	3		
2010–11	Celtic	0	0		
2010–11	*Huddersfield T*	19	2	**19**	**2**
2011–12	St Mirren	29	2		
2012–13	St Mirren	26	1	**70**	**6**
2013–14	Ross Co	36	3		
2014–15	Ross Co	22	2	**58**	**5**
2015–16	Plymouth Arg	39	11	**39**	**11**

DOREL, Vincent (G) **4 0**
b. 21-3-92

2014–15	Le Poire SV	3	0	**3**	**0**
2015–16	Plymouth Arg	1	0	**1**	**0**

FORSTER, Jordon (D) **80 7**
b.Edinburgh 23-9-93

2010–11	Hibernian	0	0		
2011–12	Hibernian	0	0		
2011–12	*Berwick R*	10	2	**10**	**2**
2012–13	Hibernian	3	0		
2012–13	*East Fife*	12	0	**12**	**0**
2013–14	Hibernian	26	4		
2014–15	Hibernian	17	1		
2015–16	Hibernian	0	0	**46**	**5**

On loan from Hibernian.

2015–16	Plymouth Arg	12	0	**12**	**0**

HALL, Callum (M) **0 0**
b. 23-3-97

2015–16	Plymouth Arg	0	0		

HARTLEY, Peter (D) **291 18**
H: 6 0 W: 12 06 b.Hartlepool 3-4-88

2006–07	Sunderland	1	0		
2007–08	Sunderland	0	0		
2007–08	*Chesterfield*	12	0	**12**	**0**
2008–09	Sunderland	0	0	**1**	**0**
2009–10	Hartlepool U	38	2		
2010–11	Hartlepool U	40	2		
2011–12	Hartlepool U	44	4		
2012–13	Hartlepool U	43	2		
2013–14	Hartlepool U	1	0	**166**	**10**
2013–14	Stevenage	31	2	**31**	**2**
2014–15	Plymouth Arg	39	4		
2015–16	Plymouth Arg	42	2	**81**	**6**

HARVEY, Cory (G) **0 0**
b. 1-8-98

2015–16	Plymouth Arg	0	0		

HARVEY, Tyler (F) **50 5**
H: 5 10 W: 11 05 b.Plymouth 29-6-95

2012–13	Plymouth Arg	10	1		
2013–14	Plymouth Arg	21	1		
2014–15	Plymouth Arg	13	1		
2015–16	Plymouth Arg	6	2	**50**	**5**

JERVIS, Jake (F) **140 32**
H: 6 3 W: 12 13 b.Birmingham 17-9-91

2009–10	Birmingham C	0	0		
2009–10	*Hereford U*	7	2		
2010–11	Birmingham C	0	0		
2010–11	*Notts Co*	10	0	**10**	**0**
2010–11	*Hereford U*	4	0	**11**	**2**
2011–12	Birmingham C	0	0		
2011–12	*Swindon T*	12	3	**12**	**3**
2011–12	*Preston NE*	5	2	**5**	**2**
2012–13	Birmingham C	2	0	**2**	**0**
2012–13	*Carlisle U*	5	3	**5**	**3**
2012–13	*Tranmere R*	4	1	**4**	**1**
2012–13	*Portsmouth*	3	1		
2012–13	Elazigspor	4	1	**4**	**1**
2013–14	Portsmouth	15	4	**18**	**5**
2014–15	Ross Co	27	4	**27**	**4**
2015–16	Plymouth Arg	42	11	**42**	**11**

McCORMICK, Luke (G) **128 0**
H: 6 0 W: 13 12 b.Coventry 15-8-83

2012–13	Oxford U	15	0	**15**	**0**
2013–14	Plymouth Arg	27	0		
2014–15	Plymouth Arg	46	0		
2015–16	Plymouth Arg	40	0	**113**	**0**

McHUGH, Carl (D) **111 7**
H: 5 11 W: 11 05 b.Co. Donegal 5-2-93
Internationals: Republic of Ireland U17, U19, U21.

2011–12	Reading	0	0		
2012–13	Bradford C	16	1		
2013–14	Bradford C	14	1	**30**	**2**
2014–15	Plymouth Arg	44	2		
2015–16	Plymouth Arg	37	3	**81**	**5**

MELLOR, Kelvin (D) **154 4**
H: 5 10 W: 11 09 b.Copenhagen 25-1-91

2007–08	Crewe Alex	0	0		
2008–09	Crewe Alex	0	0		
2009–10	Crewe Alex	0	0		
2010–11	Crewe Alex	1	0		
2011–12	Crewe Alex	12	1		
2012–13	Crewe Alex	35	0		
2013–14	Crewe Alex	28	1	**76**	**2**
2014–15	Plymouth Arg	37	1		
2015–16	Plymouth Arg	41	1	**78**	**2**

NELSON, Curtis (D) **211 8**
H: 6 0 W: 11 07 b.Newcastle-u-Lyme 21-5-93
Internationals: England U18.

2010–11	Plymouth Arg	35	0		
2011–12	Plymouth Arg	17	0		
2012–13	Plymouth Arg	27	3		
2013–14	Plymouth Arg	44	1		
2014–15	Plymouth Arg	42	1		
2015–16	Plymouth Arg	46	3	**211**	**8**

PURRINGTON, Ben (D) **33 0**
H: 5 9 W: 11 07 b.Exeter 5-5-96

2013–14	Plymouth Arg	12	0		
2014–15	Plymouth Arg	8	0		
2015–16	Plymouth Arg	13	0	**33**	**0**

REID, Reuben (F) 306 80
H: 6 0 W: 12 02 b.Bristol 26-7-88

2005–06	Plymouth Arg	1	0	
2006–07	Plymouth Arg	6	0	
2006–07	Rochdale	2	0	2 0
2006–07	Torquay U	7	2	7 2
2007–08	Plymouth Arg	0	0	
2007–08	Wycombe W	11	1	11 1
2007–08	Brentford	10	1	10 1
2008–09	Rotherham U	41	18	41 18
2009–10	WBA	4	0	
2009–10	Peterborough U	13	0	13 0
2010–11	WBA	0	0	4 0
2010–11	Walsall	18	3	18 3
2010–11	Oldham Ath	19	2	
2011–12	Oldham Ath	20	5	39 7
2012–13	Yeovil T	19	4	19 4
2012–13	Plymouth Arg	18	2	
2013–14	Plymouth Arg	46	17	
2014–15	Plymouth Arg	42	18	
2015–16	Plymouth Arg	29	7	142 44

ROONEY, Louis (F) 1 2
b. 28-9-96
Internationals: Northern Ireland U19.

2015–16	Plymouth Arg	1	2	1 2

SAWYER, Gary (D) 270 6
H: 6 0 W: 11 08 b.Bideford 5-7-85

2004–05	Plymouth Arg	0	0	
2005–06	Plymouth Arg	0	0	
2006–07	Plymouth Arg	22	0	
2007–08	Plymouth Arg	31	1	
2008–09	Plymouth Arg	13	3	
2009–10	Plymouth Arg	29	1	
2009–10	Bristol C	2	0	2 0
2010–11	Bristol R	37	0	
2011–12	Bristol R	24	0	61 0
2012–13	Leyton Orient	34	1	
2013–14	Leyton Orient	22	0	
2014–15	Leyton Orient	13	0	69 1
2015–16	Plymouth Arg	43	0	138 5

SIMPSON, Josh (M) 184 13
H: 5 10 W: 12 02 b.Cambridge 6-3-87
Internationals: England C.

2009–10	Peterborough U	21	2	
2010–11	Peterborough U	0	0	21 2
2010–11	Southend U	17	1	17 1
2011–12	Crawley T	40	2	
2012–13	Crawley T	36	4	
2013–14	Crawley T	38	2	
2014–15	Crawley T	8	1	122 9
2015–16	Plymouth Arg	24	1	24 1

SMALLEY, Deane (F) 250 36
H: 6 0 W: 11 10 b.Chadderton 5-9-88

2006–07	Oldham Ath	1	0	
2007–08	Oldham Ath	37	2	
2008–09	Oldham Ath	34	5	
2009–10	Oldham Ath	29	3	
2010–11	Oldham Ath	3	0	105 10
2010–11	Rochdale	3	0	3 0
2010–11	Chesterfield	28	12	28 12
2011–12	Oxford U	22	1	
2011–12	Bradford C	13	0	13 0
2012–13	Oxford U	27	5	
2013–14	Oxford U	32	7	81 13
2014–15	Plymouth Arg	16	1	
2015–16	Plymouth Arg	1	0	17 1
2015–16	Newport Co	3	0	3 0

WYLDE, Gregg (M) 148 14
H: 5 9 W: 11 04 b.Kirkintilloch 23-3-91
Internationals: Scotland U17, U19, U21.

2009–10	Rangers	4	0	
2010–11	Rangers	30	0	
2011–12	Rangers	42	4	76 4
2012–13	Bolton W	0	0	
2012–13	Bury	4	0	4 0
2013–14	Aberdeen	8	1	8 1
2013–14	St Mirren	17	2	17 2
2015–16	Plymouth Arg	43	7	43 7

Scholars
Battle, Alex Martin Jon; Bentley, Jordan David James; Calver, Jack Lee; Fletcher, Alex Samuel; Harvey, Cory Henri; Jones, Owen Martyn; Knowles, Liam Michael; Lane, Ryan Alan John; McAuley, Connor Michael; Miller-Medway, Jake; Palfrey, William Harry; Richards, Joshua Samuel; Roberts, Jamil; Rooney, Daniel Martyn; Rose, Callum Thomas; Ryan, Sam Michael Ellis; Steer, Benjamin George; Taylor, Aaron; Vincent, Jason James.

PORT VALE (65)

ALNWICK, Jak (G) 48 0
H: 6 2 W: 12 13 b.Hexham 17-6-93
Internationals: England U17, U18, U19, U20.

2010–11	Newcastle U	0	0	
2011–12	Newcastle U	0	0	
2012–13	Newcastle U	0	0	
2013–14	Newcastle U	0	0	
2014–15	Newcastle U	6	0	6 0
2014–15	Bradford C	1	0	1 0
2015–16	Port Vale	41	0	41 0

ANDOH, Ebo (M) 49 2
b. 1-1-93
Internationals: Ghana U20.

2012–13	AEL Limassol	20	0	
2013–14	AEL Limassol	17	1	37 1
2014–15	Port Vale	0	0	
2015–16	Port Vale	12	1	12 1

BIRCHALL, Chris (M) 287 18
H: 6 2 W: 12 07 b.Liverpool 5-5-84
Internationals: Trinidad & Tobago Full caps.

2001–02	Port Vale	1	0	
2002–03	Port Vale	2	0	
2003–04	Port Vale	10	0	
2004–05	Port Vale	34	6	
2005–06	Port Vale	31	1	
2006–07	Coventry C	28	2	
2007–08	Coventry C	1	0	
2007–08	St Mirren	9	0	9 0
2008–09	Coventry C	0	0	29 2
2008–09	Carlisle U	2	0	2 0
2008–09	Brighton & HA	9	0	9 0
2009	LA Galaxy	11	0	
2010	LA Galaxy	28	0	
2011	LA Galaxy	27	1	66 1
2012	Columbus Crew	18	1	18 1
2012–13	Port Vale	11	1	
2013–14	Port Vale	27	1	
2014–15	Port Vale	27	3	
2015–16	Port Vale	11	2	154 14

BOOT, Ryan (G) 0 0
H: 6 1 W: 11 03 b.Rocester 9-11-94

2012–13	Port Vale	0	0	
2013–14	Port Vale	0	0	
2014–15	Port Vale	0	0	
2015–16	Port Vale	0	0	

BROWN, Michael (M) 559 42
H: 5 9 W: 12 04 b.Hartlepool 25-1-77
Internationals: England U21.

1994–95	Manchester C	0	0	
1995–96	Manchester C	21	0	
1996–97	Manchester C	11	0	
1996–97	Hartlepool U	6	1	6 1
1997–98	Manchester C	26	0	
1998–99	Manchester C	31	2	
1999–2000	Manchester C	0	0	89 2
1999–2000	Portsmouth	4	0	
1999–2000	Sheffield U	24	3	
2000–01	Sheffield U	36	1	
2001–02	Sheffield U	36	5	
2002–03	Sheffield U	40	16	
2003–04	Sheffield U	15	2	151 27
2003–04	Tottenham H	17	1	
2004–05	Tottenham H	24	1	
2005–06	Tottenham H	9	0	50 2
2005–06	Fulham	7	0	
2006–07	Fulham	34	0	41 0
2007–08	Wigan Ath	31	0	
2008–09	Wigan Ath	25	0	
2009–10	Wigan Ath	2	0	58 0
2009–10	Portsmouth	24	2	
2010–11	Portsmouth	21	2	49 4
2011–12	Leeds U	24	1	
2012–13	Leeds U	24	1	
2013–14	Leeds U	18	0	66 2
2014–15	Port Vale	36	4	
2015–16	Port Vale	13	0	49 4

CAMPION, Achille (F) 18 2
H: 6 2 W: 14 05 b.Levallois-Perret 10-3-90

2014	Norrby	6	1	6 1
2014–15	Port Vale	12	1	
2015–16	Port Vale	0	0	12 1

DANIEL, Colin (M) 224 24
H: 5 11 W: 11 06 b.Eastwood 15-2-88

2006–07	Crewe Alex	0	0	
2007–08	Crewe Alex	1	0	
2008–09	Crewe Alex	13	1	14 1
2008–09	Macclesfield T	8	0	
2009–10	Macclesfield T	38	3	
2010–11	Macclesfield T	43	8	
2011–12	Macclesfield T	36	2	125 13

REID, Reuben continued

2013–14	Mansfield T	28	2	
2014–15	Port Vale	28	4	
2015–16	Port Vale	20	2	48 6
2015–16	Mansfield T	9	2	37 4

DEEN-CONTEH, Aziz (D) 7 0
H: 5 9 W: 11 00 b.Sierra Leone 14-1-93
Internationals: England U16, U19. Sierra Leone Full caps.

2010–11	Chelsea	0	0	
2011–12	Chelsea	0	0	
2013–14	Ergotelis	7	0	7 0
2014–15	Port Vale	0	0	
2015–16	Port Vale	0	0	

DICKINSON, Carl (D) 311 7
H: 6 1 W: 12 04 b.Swadlincote 31-3-87

2004–05	Stoke C	0	0	
2005–06	Stoke C	5	0	
2005–06	Stoke C	13	0	
2006–07	Blackpool	7	0	7 0
2007–08	Stoke C	27	0	
2008–09	Stoke C	5	0	
2008–09	Leeds U	7	0	7 0
2009–10	Stoke C	0	0	
2009–10	Barnsley	28	1	28 1
2010–11	Stoke C	0	0	51 0
2010–11	Portsmouth	36	0	
2011–12	Watford	39	2	
2012–13	Watford	4	0	43 2
2012–13	Portsmouth	6	0	42 0
2012–13	Coventry C	6	0	6 0
2013–14	Port Vale	40	0	
2014–15	Port Vale	43	1	
2015–16	Port Vale	44	3	127 4

DODDS, Louis (M) 342 62
H: 5 10 W: 12 04 b.Sheffield 8-10-86

2005–06	Leicester C	0	0	
2006–07	Leicester C	0	0	
2006–07	Rochdale	12	2	12 2
2007–08	Leicester C	0	0	
2007–08	Lincoln C	41	9	41 9
2008–09	Port Vale	44	7	
2009–10	Port Vale	44	6	
2010–11	Port Vale	33	7	
2011–12	Port Vale	35	8	
2012–13	Port Vale	30	7	
2013–14	Port Vale	29	4	
2014–15	Port Vale	37	4	
2015–16	Port Vale	37	8	289 51

DUFFY, Richard (D) 358 6
H: 5 9 W: 10 03 b.Swansea 30-8-85
Internationals: Wales U17, U19, U21, Full caps.

2002–03	Swansea C	0	0	
2003–04	Swansea C	18	1	
2003–04	Portsmouth	1	0	
2004–05	Portsmouth	0	0	
2004–05	Burnley	7	1	7 1
2004–05	Coventry C	14	0	
2005–06	Portsmouth	32	0	
2006–07	Portsmouth	0	0	
2006–07	Coventry C	13	0	
2006–07	Swansea C	11	0	29 1
2007–08	Portsmouth	0	0	
2007–08	Coventry C	2	0	61 0
2008–09	Portsmouth	0	0	1 0
2008–09	Millwall	12	0	12 0
2009–10	Exeter C	42	1	
2010–11	Exeter C	42	2	
2011–12	Exeter C	28	0	112 3
2012–13	Port Vale	36	0	
2013–14	Port Vale	28	0	
2014–15	Port Vale	27	1	
2015–16	Port Vale	45	0	136 1

FOLEY, Sam (M) 142 13
H: 6 0 W: 11 08 b.St Albans 17-10-86

2012–13	Yeovil T	41	5	
2013–14	Yeovil T	7	0	
2013–14	Shrewsbury T	9	0	9 0
2014–15	Yeovil T	40	2	88 7
2015–16	Port Vale	45	6	45 6

GRANT, Anthony (M) 366 15
H: 5 10 W: 11 01 b.Lambeth 4-6-87
Internationals: England U16, U17, U19.

2004–05	Chelsea	0	0	
2005–06	Chelsea	0	0	
2005–06	Oldham Ath	2	0	2 0
2006–07	Chelsea	0	0	
2006–07	Wycombe W	40	0	40 0
2007–08	Chelsea	0	0	1 0
2007–08	Luton T	4	0	4 0
2007–08	Southend U	10	0	
2008–09	Southend U	35	1	

2009–10	Southend U	38	0		
2010–11	Southend U	43	8		
2011–12	Southend U	33	1	159	10
2012–13	Stevenage	41	0	41	0
2013–14	Crewe Alex	38	2		
2014–15	Crewe Alex	43	2	81	4
2015–16	Crewe Alex	38	1	38	1

HOOPER, JJ (F) — 31 5
b. 9-10-93

2013–14	Northampton T	3	0	3	0

From Havant & Waterlooville.

2015–16	Port Vale	28	5	28	5

JOHNSON, Sam (G) — 23 0
H: 6 6 W: 12 04 b.Newcastle-under-Lyme 1-12-92

2011–12	Port Vale	0	0		
2012–13	Port Vale	0	0		
2013–14	Port Vale	16	0		
2014–15	Port Vale	7	0		
2015–16	Port Vale	0	0	23	0
2015–16	FC Halifax T	0	0		

KELLY, Sam (M) — 28 3
b. 21-10-93

2014–15	Norwich C	0	0		
2015–16	Port Vale	28	3	28	3

LEITCH-SMITH, AJ (F) — 191 36
H: 5 11 W: 12 04 b.Crewe 6-3-90

2008–09	Crewe Alex	0	0		
2009	IBV	18	5	18	5
2009–10	Crewe Alex	1	0		
2010–11	Crewe Alex	16	5		
2011–12	Crewe Alex	38	8		
2012–13	Crewe Alex	28	4		
2013–14	Crewe Alex	20	2	103	19
2014–15	Yeovil T	33	2	33	2
2015–16	Port Vale	37	10	37	10

LLOYD, Ryan (M) — 17 0
H: 5 10 W: 10 03 b.Newcastle-u-Lyme 1-2-94

2010–11	Port Vale	1	0		
2011–12	Port Vale	2	0		
2012–13	Port Vale	6	0		
2013–14	Port Vale	3	0		
2014–15	Port Vale	0	0		
2015–16	Port Vale	5	0	17	0

McGIVERN, Ryan (D) — 177 2
H: 5 10 W: 11 07 b.Newry 8-1-90
Internationals: Northern Ireland U16, U17, U19, U21, B, Full caps.

2007–08	Manchester C	0	0		
2008–09	Manchester C	0	0		
2008–09	Morecambe	5	1	5	1
2009–10	Manchester C	0	0		
2009–10	Leicester C	12	0	12	0
2010–11	Manchester C	1	0		
2010–11	Walsall	15	0	15	0
2011–12	Manchester C	0	0		
2011–12	Crystal Palace	5	0	5	0
2011–12	Bristol C	31	0	31	0
2012–13	Manchester C	0	0	1	0
2012–13	Hibernian	27	1		
2013–14	Hibernian	33	0	60	1
2014–15	Port Vale	20	0		
2015–16	Port Vale	28	0	48	0

MOORE, Byron (M) — 313 34
H: 6 0 W: 10 06 b.Stoke 24-8-88

2006–07	Crewe Alex	0	0		
2007–08	Crewe Alex	33	3		
2008–09	Crewe Alex	36	3		
2009–10	Crewe Alex	32	3		
2010–11	Crewe Alex	38	6		
2011–12	Crewe Alex	42	8		
2012–13	Crewe Alex	41	4		
2013–14	Crewe Alex	40	3	262	30
2014–15	Port Vale	15	1		
2015–16	Port Vale	36	3	51	4

NEAL, Chris (G) — 200 0
H: 6 2 W: 12 04 b.St Albans 23-10-85

2004–05	Preston NE	1	0		
2005–06	Preston NE	0	0		
2006–07	Preston NE	0	0		
2006–07	Shrewsbury T	0	0		
2007–08	Morecambe	0	0		
2007–08	Preston NE	0	0		
2008–09	Preston NE	0	0	1	0
2009–10	Shrewsbury T	7	0		
2010–11	Shrewsbury T	22	0		
2011–12	Shrewsbury T	35	0	64	0
2012–13	Port Vale	46	0		
2013–14	Port Vale	31	0		
2014–15	Port Vale	40	0		
2015–16	Port Vale	6	0	123	0

2015–16	*Doncaster R*	2	0	2	0
2015–16	*Bury*	10	0	10	0

O'CONNOR, Michael (M) — 318 33
H: 6 1 W: 11 08 b.Belfast 6-10-87
Internationals: Northern Ireland U21, B, Full caps.

2005–06	Crewe Alex	2	0		
2006–07	Crewe Alex	29	0		
2007–08	Crewe Alex	23	0		
2008–09	Crewe Alex	23	3	77	3
2008–09	*Lincoln C*	10	1	10	1
2009–10	Scunthorpe U	32	2		
2010–11	Scunthorpe U	32	2		
2011–12	Scunthorpe U	33	1	97	11
2012–13	Rotherham U	35	6		
2013–14	Rotherham U	29	2	64	8
2014–15	Port Vale	44	6		
2015–16	Port Vale	26	4	70	10

PURKISS, Ben (D) — 150 0
H: 6 2 W: 10 13 b.Sheffield 1-4-84

2001–02	Sheffield U	0	0		
2002–03	Sheffield U	0	0		

From Gainsborough T, York C

2010–11	Oxford U	23	0	23	0
2011–12	Hereford U	15	0	15	0
2012–13	Walsall	27	0		
2013–14	Walsall	14	0		
2014–15	Walsall	32	0	73	0
2015–16	Port Vale	39	0	39	0

REEVES, William (M) — 0 0
b. 18-12-96

2015–16	Port Vale	0	0		

ROBINSON, Theo (F) — 299 70
H: 5 9 W: 10 03 b.Birmingham 22-1-89
Internationals: Jamaica Full caps.

2005–06	Watford	1	0		
2006–07	Watford	1	0		
2007–08	Watford	0	0		
2007–08	*Hereford U*	43	13	43	13
2008–09	Watford	3	0	5	0
2008–09	*Southend U*	21	7	21	7
2009–10	Huddersfield T	37	13		
2010–11	Huddersfield T	1	0		
2010–11	Millwall	1	0		
2010–11	Derby Co	13	2		
2011–12	Derby Co	39	10		
2012–13	Derby Co	28	8		
2012–13	*Huddersfield T*	6	0	44	13
2013–14	Millwall	0	0	11	3
2013–14	Derby Co	0	0	80	20
2013–14	Doncaster R	31	5		
2014–15	Doncaster R	32	4	63	9
2014–15	*Scunthorpe U*	8	3	8	3
2015–16	Motherwell	10	0	10	0
2015–16	Port Vale	14	2	14	2

SMITH, Nathan (D) — 0 0
H: 6 0 W: 11 05 b.Madeley 3-4-96

2014–15	Port Vale	0	0		
2015–16	Port Vale	0	0		

STEELE, James (M) — 0 0
H: 6 0 W: 11 05 b.

2014–15	Port Vale	0	0		

STREETE, Remie (D) — 15 0
H: 6 2 W: 12 13 b.Boldon 2-11-94

2011–12	Newcastle U	0	0		
2012–13	Newcastle U	0	0		
2013–14	Newcastle U	0	0		
2014–15	Newcastle U	0	0		
2014–15	*Port Vale*	2	0		
2015–16	Port Vale	13	0	15	0

TURNER, Dan (F) — 1 0
b. 23-6-98

2015–16	Port Vale	1	0	1	0

YATES, Adam (D) — 289 4
H: 5 10 W: 10 07 b.Stoke 28-5-83
Internationals: England C.

2000–01	Crewe Alex	0	0		
2001–02	Crewe Alex	0	0		
2002–03	Crewe Alex	0	0		
2003–04	Crewe Alex	0	0		
2004–05	Crewe Alex	0	0		
2005–06	Crewe Alex	0	0		
2006–07	Crewe Alex	0	0		
2007–08	Morecambe	44	0		
2008–09	Morecambe	32	0	76	0
2009–10	Port Vale	32	0		
2010–11	Port Vale	46	0		
2011–12	Port Vale	38	2		
2012–13	Port Vale	26	0		
2013–14	Port Vale	34	1		
2014–15	Port Vale	25	1		

2015–16	Port Vale	11	0	212	4
2015–16	*Northampton T*	1	0	1	0

Scholars
Ashton, Thomas Michael; Attrell, Taylor Thomas; Barton, Brian William Alan James; Calveley, Michael Thomas; Conlon, Michael Joseph; Dennis, Luke Anthony; Ede, Brad Michael; Faulkner, Mackenzie; Ferrie, Calum John; Fraser, Benjamin Sean Michael; Gibbons, James Andrew; Morris, Alex William; Mottram, Liam Andrew; Pickering, Harry Thomas; Slinn, Joseph Antony; Turner, Daniel Graham; Walford, Charlie.

PORTSMOUTH (66)

AGYEMANG, Patrick (F) — 467 72
H: 6 1 W: 12 00 b.Walthamstow 29-9-80
Internationals: Ghana Full caps.

1998–99	Wimbledon	0	0		
1999–2000	Wimbledon	0	0		
1999–2000	*Brentford*	12	0	12	0
2000–01	Wimbledon	29	4		
2001–02	Wimbledon	33	4		
2002–03	Wimbledon	33	5		
2003–04	Wimbledon	26	7	121	20
2003–04	Gillingham	20	6		
2004–05	Gillingham	13	2	33	8
2004–05	Preston NE	27	4		
2005–06	Preston NE	42	6		
2006–07	Preston NE	31	7		
2007–08	Preston NE	22	4	122	21
2007–08	QPR	17	8		
2008–09	QPR	20	2		
2009–10	QPR	17	3		
2009–10	*Bristol C*	7	0	7	0
2010–11	QPR	19	2		
2011–12	QPR	2	0	75	15
2011–12	*Millwall*	2	0	2	0
2011–12	Stevenage	13	1		
2012–13	Stevenage	14	0	27	1
2012–13	Portsmouth	15	3		
2013–14	Portsmouth	41	4		
2014–15	Portsmouth	8	0		
2014–15	*Dagenham & R*	4	0	4	0
2015–16	Portsmouth	0	0	64	7

ALLSOP, Ryan (G) — 85 0
H: 6 2 W: 12 06 b.Birmingham 17-6-92
Internationals: England U17.

2012–13	Leyton Orient	20	0	20	0
2012–13	Bournemouth	10	0		
2013–14	Bournemouth	12	0		
2014–15	Bournemouth	0	0		
2014–15	Coventry C	24	0	24	0
2015–16	Bournemouth	1	0	23	0
2015–16	Wycombe W	18	0	18	0
2015–16	Portsmouth	0	0		

BARTON, Adam (M) — 129 4
H: 5 11 W: 12 01 b.Clitheroe 7-1-91
Internationals: Republic of Ireland U21. Northern Ireland Full caps.

2008–09	Preston NE	0	0		
2009–10	Preston NE	1	0		
2010–11	Preston NE	33	1		
2011–12	Preston NE	16	0		
2012–13	Preston NE	0	0	50	1
2012–13	Coventry C	22	3		
2013–14	Coventry C	14	0		
2013–14	Fleetwood T	0	0		
2014–15	Coventry C	27	0	63	3
2015–16	Portsmouth	16	0	16	0

BASS, Alex (G) — 0 0
b.Southampton 1-1-97

2014–15	Portsmouth	0	0		
2015–16	Portsmouth	0	0		

BENNETT, Kyle (F) — 212 24
H: 5 5 W: 9 08 b.Telford 9-9-90
Internationals: England U18.

2007–08	Wolverhampton W	0	0		
2008–09	Wolverhampton W	0	0		
2009–10	Wolverhampton W	0	0		
2010–11	Bury	32	2	32	2
2011–12	Doncaster R	36	4		
2012–13	Doncaster R	35	3		
2013–14	Doncaster R	3	0		
2013–14	Crawley T	4	0	4	0
2013–14	Bradford C	18	1	18	1
2014–15	Doncaster R	42	8	116	15
2015–16	Portsmouth	42	6	42	6

BURGESS, Christian (D) — 109 4
H: 6 5 W: 13 02 b. 7-10-91

2012–13	Middlesbrough	1	0		
2013–14	Middlesbrough	0	0	1	0

Season	Club				
2013–14	Hartlepool U	41	0	41	0
2014–15	Peterborough U	30	2	30	2
2015–16	Portsmouth	37	2	37	2

CHAPLIN, Conor (M) 39 9
b. 16-2-97

2014–15	Portsmouth	9	1		
2015–16	Portsmouth	30	8	39	9

CLOSE, Ben (M) 13 0
b.Portsmouth 8-8-96

2013–14	Portsmouth	0	0		
2014–15	Portsmouth	6	0		
2015–16	Portsmouth	7	0	13	0

DAVIES, Ben (M) 430 74
H: 5 7 W: 12 03 b.Birmingham 27-5-81

2000–01	Kidderminster H	3	0		
2001–02	Kidderminster H	9	0	12	0
2004–05	Chester C	44	2		
2005–06	Chester C	45	7	89	9
2006–07	Shrewsbury T	43	12		
2007–08	Shrewsbury T	27	6		
2008–09	Shrewsbury T	42	12	112	30
2009–10	Notts Co	45	15		
2010–11	Notts Co	22	5	67	20
2010–11	Derby Co	13	1		
2011–12	Derby Co	35	2		
2012–13	Derby Co	23	4		
2013–14	Derby Co	4	0	75	7
2013–14	Sheffield U	18	3		
2014–15	Sheffield U	14	4	32	7
2015–16	Portsmouth	43	1	43	1

DOYLE, Micky (M) 539 31
H: 5 10 W: 11 00 b.Dublin 8-7-81
Internationals: Republic of Ireland U21, Full caps.

2003–04	Coventry C	40	5		
2004–05	Coventry C	44	2		
2005–06	Coventry C	44	0		
2006–07	Coventry C	40	3		
2007–08	Coventry C	42	7		
2008–09	Coventry C	37	2		
2009–10	Coventry C	0	0		
2009–10	Leeds U	42	0	42	0
2010–11	Coventry C	18	1	265	20
2010–11	Sheffield U	16	0		
2011–12	Sheffield U	43	3		
2012–13	Sheffield U	43	3		
2013–14	Sheffield U	43	2		
2014–15	Sheffield U	43	1	188	9
2015–16	Portsmouth	44	2	44	2

EVANS, Gary (F) 339 62
H: 6 0 W: 12 08 b.Stockport 26-4-88

2007–08	Macclesfield T	42	7		
2008–09	Macclesfield T	40	12	82	19
2009–10	Bradford C	43	11		
2010–11	Bradford C	36	3	79	14
2011–12	Rotherham U	32	7		
2012–13	Rotherham U	13	2	45	9
2012–13	Fleetwood T	16	1		
2013–14	Fleetwood T	34	6		
2014–15	Fleetwood T	43	3	93	10
2015–16	Portsmouth	40	10	40	10

HAITHAM, Kaleem (D) 0 0
b. 4-6-98

2015–16	Portsmouth	0	0		

HAUNSTRUP, Brandon (D) 1 0
b. 26-10-96

2015–16	Portsmouth	1	0	1	0

HOLLANDS, Danny (M) 370 41
H: 6 0 W: 11 11 b.Ashford (Middlesex) 6-11-85

2003–04	Chelsea	0	0		
2004–05	Chelsea	0	0		
2005–06	Chelsea	0	0		
2005–06	Torquay U	10	1	10	1
2006–07	Bournemouth	33	1		
2007–08	Bournemouth	37	4		
2008–09	Bournemouth	42	6		
2009–10	Bournemouth	39	6		
2010–11	Bournemouth	42	7	193	24
2011–12	Charlton Ath	43	7		
2012–13	Charlton Ath	14	0		
2012–13	Swindon T	10	2	10	2
2013–14	Charlton Ath	0	0	57	7
2013–14	Gillingham	17	1	17	1
2014–15	Portsmouth	7	5		
2014–15	Portsmouth	44	1		
2015–16	Portsmouth	32	0	83	6

JONES, Paul (G) 281 0
H: 6 3 W: 13 00 b.Maidstone 28-6-86

2008–09	Exeter C	46	0		
2009–10	Exeter C	26	0		
2010–11	Exeter C	18	0	90	0
2010–11	Peterborough U	1	0		
2011–12	Peterborough U	35	0	36	0
2012–13	Crawley T	46	0		
2013–14	Crawley T	46	0		
2014–15	Portsmouth	46	0		
2015–16	Portsmouth	9	0	55	0
2015–16	Crawley T	8	0	100	0

JOSEPH-BAUDI, Brandon (D) 0 0
b. 2-10-97

2015–16	Portsmouth	0	0		

MAY, Adam (M) 2 0
b. 6-12-97

2014–15	Portsmouth	1	0		
2015–16	Portsmouth	1	0	2	0

McGURK, Adam (F) 177 27
H: 5 9 W: 12 13 b.Larne 24-1-89
Internationals: Northern Ireland U21.

2005–06	Aston Villa	0	0		
2006–07	Aston Villa	0	0		
2007–08	Aston Villa	0	0		
2008–09	Aston Villa	0	0		
2009–10	Aston Villa	0	0		

From Hednesford T.

2010–11	Tranmere R	21	3		
2011–12	Tranmere R	31	4		
2012–13	Tranmere R	27	3	79	10
2013–14	Burton Alb	34	9		
2014–15	Burton Alb	37	6	71	15
2015–16	Portsmouth	27	2	27	2

MURPHY, Brian (G) 154 0
H: 6 0 W: 13 00 b.Waterford 7-5-83
Internationals: Republic of Ireland U16.

2000–01	Manchester C	0	0		
2001–02	Manchester C	0	0		
2002–03	Manchester C	0	0		
2002–03	Oldham Ath	0	0		
2002–03	Peterborough U	1	0	1	0

From Waterford

2003–04	Swansea C	11	0		
2004–05	Swansea C	2	0		
2005–06	Swansea C	0	0		
2006–07	Swansea C	0	0	13	0
2007	Bohemians	29	0		
2008	Bohemians	33	0		
2009	Bohemians	35	0	97	0
2009–10	Ipswich T	16	0		
2010–11	Ipswich T	4	0		
2011–12	Ipswich T	0	0	20	0
2011–12	QPR	0	0		
2012–13	QPR	0	0		
2013–14	QPR	2	0		
2014–15	QPR	0	0	2	0
2015–16	Portsmouth	21	0	21	0

NAISMITH, Kal (F) 96 17
H: 5 7 W: 13 02 b.Glasgow 18-2-92
Internationals: Scotland U16, U17.

2013–14	Accrington S	38	10		
2014–15	Accrington S	35	4	73	14
2015–16	Portsmouth	19	3	19	3
2015–16	Hartlepool U	4	0	4	0

OXLADE-CHAMBERLAIN, Christian (D) 0 0
b. 24-6-98

2015–16	Portsmouth	0	0		

POKE, Michael (G) 98 0
H: 6 1 W: 13 12 b.Staines 21-11-85

2003–04	Southampton	0	0		
2004–05	Southampton	0	0		
2005–06	Southampton	0	0		
2005–06	Oldham Ath	0	0		
2005–06	Northampton T	0	0		
2006–07	Southampton	0	0		
2007–08	Southampton	4	0		
2008–09	Southampton	0	0		
2009–10	Southampton	0	0	4	0
2009–10	Torquay U	29	0		
2010–11	Brighton & HA	0	0		
2011–12	Brighton & HA	0	0		
2011–12	Bristol R	8	0	8	0
2012–13	Torquay U	43	0		
2013–14	Torquay U	14	0	86	0
2014–15	Portsmouth	0	0		
2015–16	Portsmouth	0	0		

ROBERTS, Gary (F) 380 70
H: 5 10 W: 11 09 b.Chester 18-3-84
Internationals: England C.

2006–07	Accrington S	14	8	14	8
2006–07	Ipswich T	33	2		
2007–08	Ipswich T	21	1	54	3
2007–08	Crewe Alex	0	0		
2008–09	Huddersfield T	43	9		
2009–10	Huddersfield T	43	9		
2010–11	Huddersfield T	37	9		
2011–12	Huddersfield T	39	6	162	31
2012–13	Swindon T	39	4	39	4
2013–14	Chesterfield	40	11		
2014–15	Chesterfield	34	6	74	17
2015–16	Portsmouth	33	7	33	7

STEVENS, Enda (D) 176 2
H: 6 0 W: 12 04 b.Dublin 9-7-90
Internationals: Republic of Ireland U21.

2008	UCD	2	0	2	0
2009	St Patrick's Ath	30	0	30	0
2010	Shamrock R	18	0		
2011	Shamrock R	27	0	45	0
2011–12	Aston Villa	0	0		
2012–13	Aston Villa	7	0		
2013–14	Aston Villa	0	0		
2013–14	Notts Co	2	0	2	0
2013–14	Doncaster R	13	0		
2014–15	Aston Villa	0	0	7	0
2014–15	Northampton T	4	1	4	1
2014–15	Doncaster R	28	1	41	1
2015–16	Portsmouth	45	0	45	0

TOLLITT, Ben (M) 12 1
b. 30-11-94

2015–16	Portsmouth	12	1	12	1

TUBBS, Matt (F) 166 55
H: 5 9 W: 11 00 b.Salisbury 15-7-84
Internationals: England C.

2008–09	Bournemouth	8	1		
2009–10	Bournemouth	0	0		
2011–12	Crawley T	24	12		
2011–12	Bournemouth	7	1		
2012–13	Bournemouth	31	6		
2013–14	Bournemouth	0	0		
2013–14	Rotherham U	17	1	17	1
2013–14	Crawley T	18	8	42	20
2014–15	Bournemouth	0	0	46	8
2014–15	AFC Wimbledon	22	12	22	12
2014–15	Portsmouth	23	9		
2015–16	Portsmouth	16	5	39	14

WEBSTER, Adam (D) 67 5
H: 6 1 W: 11 11 b.West Wittering 4-1-95
Internationals: England U18, U19.

2011–12	Portsmouth	3	0		
2012–13	Portsmouth	18	0		
2013–14	Portsmouth	4	2		
2014–15	Portsmouth	15	1		
2015–16	Portsmouth	27	2	67	5

WHATMOUGH, Jack (D) 36 0
b.Gosport 19-8-96
Internationals: England U18, U19.

2012–13	Portsmouth	0	0		
2013–14	Portsmouth	12	0		
2014–15	Portsmouth	22	0		
2015–16	Portsmouth	2	0	36	0

YATES, Jordi (D) 0 0
b. 25-4-98

2015–16	Portsmouth	0	0		

Scholars
Bass, Alexander Michael; Bedford, Jeremy-Finley Dylan; Bradbury, Harvey Lee; Davies, Calvin Jack; Haitham, Kaleem; Hall, Nicholas Adam; Joseph-Buadi, Brandon Yaw; McDowell, Kyle John; Oxlade-Chamberlain, Christian Benjamin; Saidy, Ousman; Sayers, Liam James; Scutt, Tommy Joel; Wakley, Eddie Mitchell; Widdrington, Theo Jack; Yates, Dory Sean.

PRESTON NE (67)

ANDERTON, Nick (D) 0 0
H: 6 2 W: 12 06 b. 22-4-96

2014–15	Preston NE	0	0		
2015–16	Preston NE	0	0		

BECKFORD, Jermaine (F) 325 126
H: 6 2 W: 13 02 b.Ealing 9-12-83
Internationals: Jamaica Full caps.

2005–06	Leeds U	5	0		
2006–07	Leeds U	5	0		
2006–07	Carlisle U	4	1	4	1
2006–07	Scunthorpe U	18	8	18	8
2007–08	Leeds U	40	20		
2008–09	Leeds U	34	26		
2009–10	Leeds U	42	25	126	71
2010–11	Everton	32	8		
2011–12	Everton	2	0	34	8
2011–12	Leicester C	39	9		
2012–13	Leicester C	4	0	43	9
2012–13	Huddersfield T	21	8	21	8
2013–14	Bolton W	33	7		
2014–15	Bolton W	13	0	46	7

2014–15	Preston NE	23	12		
2015–16	Preston NE	10	2	33	14

BROWNE, Alan (M)   64 7
H: 5 8   W: 11 03   b.Cork 15-4-95
Internationals: Republic of Ireland U19, U21.

2013–14	Preston NE	8	1		
2014–15	Preston NE	20	3		
2015–16	Preston NE	36	3	64	7

BROWNHILL, Josh (M)   67 7
H: 5 10   W: 10 12   b.Warrington 19-12-95

2013–14	Preston NE	24	3		
2014–15	Preston NE	18	2		
2015–16	Preston NE	3	0	45	5
2015–16	*Barnsley*	22	2	22	2

CLARKE, Tom (D)   232 8
H: 6 0   W: 11 02   b.Sowerby Bridge 21-12-87
Internationals: England U18, U19.

2004–05	Huddersfield T	12	0		
2005–06	Huddersfield T	17	1		
2006–07	Huddersfield T	9	0		
2007–08	Huddersfield T	3	0		
2008–09	Huddersfield T	15	1		
2008–09	*Bradford C*	6	0	6	0
2009–10	Huddersfield T	21	0		
2010–11	Huddersfield T	5	1		
2011–12	Huddersfield T	14	0		
2011–12	*Leyton Orient*	10	0	10	0
2012–13	Huddersfield T	0	0	96	3
2013–14	Preston NE	42	4		
2014–15	Preston NE	43	1		
2015–16	Preston NE	35	0	120	5

CUNNINGHAM, Greg (D)   176 6
H: 6 0   W: 11 00   b.Galway 31-1-91
Internationals: Republic of Ireland U17, U21, Full caps.

2008–09	Manchester C	0	0		
2009–10	Manchester C	0	0		
2010–11	Manchester C	0	0		
2010–11	*Leicester C*	13	0	13	0
2011–12	Manchester C	0	0		
2011–12	*Nottingham F*	27	0	27	0
2012–13	Manchester C	0	0	2	0
2012–13	Bristol C	30	1		
2013–14	Bristol C	37	1		
2014–15	Bristol C	24	2	91	4
2015–16	Preston NE	43	2	43	2

DAVIES, Ben (D)   73 0
H: 6 1   W: 11 09   b.Barrow 11-8-95

2012–13	Preston NE	3	0		
2013–14	Preston NE	0	0		
2013–14	*York C*	44	0	44	0
2014–15	Preston NE	4	0		
2014–15	*Tranmere R*	3	0	3	0
2015–16	Preston NE	0	0	7	0
2015–16	*Newport Co*	19	0	19	0

GALLAGHER, Paul (F)   403 75
H: 6 1   W: 11 00   b.Glasgow 9-8-84
Internationals: Scotland U21, B, Full caps.

2002–03	Blackburn R	1	0		
2003–04	Blackburn R	26	3		
2004–05	Blackburn R	16	2		
2005–06	Blackburn R	1	0		
2005–06	Stoke C	37	11		
2006–07	Blackburn R	16	1		
2007–08	Blackburn R	8	0		
2007–08	*Preston NE*	19	1		
2007–08	*Stoke C*	7	0	44	11
2008–09	Blackburn R	0	0		
2008–09	*Plymouth Arg*	40	13	40	13
2009–10	Blackburn R	1	0	61	6
2009–10	Leicester C	41	7		
2010–11	Leicester C	41	10		
2011–12	Leicester C	28	8		
2012–13	Leicester C	0	0		
2012–13	*Sheffield U*	6	1	6	1
2013–14	Leicester C	0	0		
2013–14	*Preston NE*	28	6		
2014–15	Leicester C	0	0	118	25
2014–15	*Preston NE*	46	7		
2015–16	Preston NE	41	5	134	19

GARNER, Joe (F)   298 91
H: 5 10   W: 11 02   b.Blackburn 12-4-88
Internationals: England U16, U17, U19.

2004–05	Blackburn R	0	0		
2005–06	Blackburn R	0	0		
2006–07	Blackburn R	0	0		
2006–07	*Carlisle U*	18	5		
2007–08	*Carlisle U*	31	14		
2008–09	Nottingham F	28	7		
2009–10	Nottingham F	18	2		
2010–11	Nottingham F	0	0		
2010–11	*Huddersfield T*	16	0	16	0

2010–11	*Scunthorpe U*	18	6	18	6
2011–12	Nottingham F	2	0	48	9
2011–12	*Watford*	22	1		
2012–13	*Watford*	2	0	24	1
2012–13	*Carlisle U*	16	7	65	26
2012–13	Preston NE	14	0		
2013–14	Preston NE	35	18		
2014–15	Preston NE	37	25		
2015–16	Preston NE	41	6	127	49

GRIMSHAW, Liam (D)   0 0
b. 2-2-95
Internationals: England U18.

2013–14	Manchester U	0	0
2014–15	Morecambe	0	0
2015–16	Manchester U	0	0
2015–16	Motherwell	0	0
2015–16	Preston NE	0	0

HUDSON, Matthew (G)   1 0
b. 29-7-98

2014–15	Preston NE	0	0		
2015–16	Preston NE	1	0	1	0

HUGILL, Jordan (F)   66 12
H: 6 0   W: 10 01   b.Middlesbrough 4-6-92

2013–14	*Port Vale*	20	4	20	4
2014–15	Preston NE	3	0		
2014–15	*Tranmere R*	6	1	6	1
2014–15	*Hartlepool U*	8	4	8	4
2015–16	Preston NE	29	3	32	3

HUMPHREY, Chris (M)   302 16
H: 5 11   W: 11 07   b.Walsall 19-9-87
Internationals: Jamaica Full caps.

2006–07	Shrewsbury T	12	0		
2007–08	Shrewsbury T	25	0		
2008–09	Shrewsbury T	37	2	74	2
2009–10	Motherwell	28	0		
2010–11	Motherwell	36	3		
2011–12	Motherwell	35	2		
2012–13	Motherwell	33	3	132	8
2013–14	Preston NE	42	2		
2014–15	Preston NE	44	4		
2015–16	Preston NE	10	0	96	6

HUNTINGTON, Paul (D)   265 20
H: 6 3   W: 12 08   b.Carlisle 17-9-87
Internationals: England U18.

2005–06	Newcastle U	0	0		
2006–07	Newcastle U	11	1		
2007–08	Newcastle U	0	0	11	1
2007–08	Leeds U	17	2		
2008–09	Leeds U	4	0		
2009–10	Leeds U	0	0	21	2
2009–10	*Stockport Co*	26	0	26	0
2010–11	Yeovil T	40	5		
2011–12	Yeovil T	37	2	77	7
2012–13	Preston NE	37	3		
2013–14	Preston NE	23	2		
2014–15	Preston NE	32	5		
2015–16	Preston NE	38	0	130	10

JAMES, Steven (G)   0 0
H: 6 2   W: 11 11   b.Southport 19-12-95

2012–13	Preston NE	0	0
2013–14	Preston NE	0	0
2014–15	Preston NE	0	0
2015–16	Preston NE	0	0

JOHNSON, Daniel (M)   85 19
H: 5 8   W: 10 07   b.Kingston, Jam 8-10-92

2011–12	Aston Villa	0	0		
2012–13	Aston Villa	0	0		
2012–13	Aston Villa	0	0		
2012–13	*Yeovil T*	5	0	5	0
2013–14	Aston Villa	0	0		
2014–15	Aston Villa	0	0		
2014–15	*Chesterfield*	11	0	11	0
2014–15	*Oldham Ath*	6	3	6	3
2014–15	Preston NE	20	8		
2015–16	Preston NE	43	8	63	16

KILKENNY, Neil (M)   334 17
H: 5 8   W: 10 08   b.Enfield 19-12-85
Internationals: England U18, U20. Australia U23, Full caps.

2003–04	Birmingham C	0	0		
2004–05	Birmingham C	0	0		
2004–05	*Oldham Ath*	27	4		
2005–06	Birmingham C	18	0		
2006–07	Birmingham C	8	0		
2007–08	Birmingham C	0	0	26	0
2007–08	*Oldham Ath*	20	1	47	5
2007–08	Leeds U	16	1		
2008–09	Leeds U	30	4		
2009–10	Leeds U	35	2		
2010–11	Leeds U	37	1	118	8
2011–12	Bristol C	41	1		
2012–13	Bristol C	24	0		

2013–14	Bristol C	3	0	68	1
2013–14	Preston NE	27	2		
2014–15	Preston NE	35	0		
2015–16	Preston NE	13	1	75	3

KIRKLAND, Chris (G)   284 0
H: 6 5   W: 14 08   b.Barwell 2-5-81
Internationals: England U21, Full caps.

1997–98	Coventry C	0	0		
1998–99	Coventry C	0	0		
1999–2000	Coventry C	0	0		
2000–01	Coventry C	23	0		
2001–02	Coventry C	1	0	24	0
2001–02	Liverpool	1	0		
2002–03	Liverpool	8	0		
2003–04	Liverpool	6	0		
2004–05	Liverpool	10	0		
2005–06	Liverpool	0	0	25	0
2005–06	*WBA*	10	0	10	0
2006–07	Wigan Ath	26	0		
2007–08	Wigan Ath	37	0		
2008–09	Wigan Ath	32	0		
2009–10	Wigan Ath	32	0		
2010–11	Wigan Ath	4	0		
2010–11	*Leicester C*	3	0	3	0
2011–12	Wigan Ath	0	0	131	0
2011–12	*Doncaster R*	1	0	1	0
2012–13	Sheffield W	46	0		
2013–14	Sheffield W	35	0		
2014–15	Sheffield W	4	0	85	0
2015–16	Preston NE	5	0	5	0

LITTLE, Andrew (M)   89 35
H: 6 0   W: 12 00   b.Enniskillen 12-5-89
Internationals: Northern Ireland Youth, U21, B, Full caps.

2008–09	Rangers	0	0		
2009–10	Rangers	6	1		
2010–11	Rangers	0	0		
2011–12	Rangers	10	5		
2011–12	*Port Vale*	7	0	7	0
2012–13	Rangers	28	22		
2013–14	Rangers	21	5	65	33
2014–15	*Preston NE*	12	1		
2015–16	Preston NE	0	0	12	1
2015–16	*Blackpool*	5	1	5	1
2015–16	*Accrington S*	0	0		

MAY, Stevie (F)   163 74
H: 5 3   W: 9 07   b.Perth 3-11-92
Internationals: Scotland U20, U21, Full caps.

2008–09	St Johnstone	1	1		
2009–10	St Johnstone	0	0		
2010–11	St Johnstone	19	2		
2011–12	St Johnstone	1	0		
2011–12	*Alloa Ath*	22	19	22	19
2012–13	St Johnstone	3	0		
2012–13	*Hamilton A*	33	25	33	25
2013–14	St Johnstone	38	20	62	23
2014–15	Sheffield W	39	7		
2015–16	Sheffield W	0	0	39	7
2015–16	Preston NE	7	0	7	0

PEARSON, Ben (M)   60 2
H: 5 5   W: 11 03   b. 4-1-95
Internationals: England U16, U17, U18, U19, U21, Full caps.

2013–14	Manchester U	0	0		
2014–15	Manchester U	0	0		
2014–15	*Barnsley*	22	1		
2015–16	Manchester U	0	0		
2015–16	*Barnsley*	23	1	45	2
2015–16	Preston NE	15	0	15	0

REID, Kyel (M)   247 21
H: 5 10   W: 12 05   b.Deptford 26-11-87
Internationals: England U17, U18, U19.

2004–05	West Ham U	0	0		
2005–06	West Ham U	2	0		
2006–07	West Ham U	0	0		
2006–07	*Barnsley*	26	2	26	2
2007–08	West Ham U	1	0		
2007–08	*Crystal Palace*	2	0	2	0
2008–09	West Ham U	0	0	3	0
2008–09	*Blackpool*	7	0	7	0
2008–09	*Wolverhampton W*	8	1	8	1
2009–10	Sheffield U	7	0	7	0
2009–10	Charlton Ath	17	4		
2010–11	Charlton Ath	32	1	49	5
2011–12	Bradford C	37	4		
2012–13	Bradford C	33	2		
2013–14	Bradford C	26	4		
2014–15	Preston NE	14	0		
2015–16	Preston NE	1	0	15	0
2015–16	*Bradford C*	34	3	130	13

RYAN, Jack (F) — 4 0
H: 6 0 W: 12 06 b.Barrow-in-Furness 5-4-96

Season	Club	A	G		
2013–14	Preston NE	0	0		
2014–15	Preston NE	1	0		
2015–16	Preston NE	0	0	1	0
2015–16	Morecambe	3	0	3	0

SAMPSON, Josh (D) — 0 0
b. 16-9-96

Season	Club	A	G
2014–15	Preston NE	0	0
2015–16	Preston NE	0	0

SMITH, Clive (D) — 0 0
b. 12-12-97
Internationals: Wales U17.

Season	Club	A	G
2015–16	Preston NE	0	0

VERMIJL, Marnick (D) — 67 4
H: 5 11 W: 11 12 b.Overpelt 13-1-92
Internationals: Belgium U17, U18, U19, U21.

Season	Club	A	G		
2010–11	Manchester U	0	0		
2011–12	Manchester U	0	0		
2012–13	Manchester U	0	0		
2013–14	Manchester U	0	0		
2013–14	NEC	28	3	28	3
2014–15	Manchester U	0	0		
2014–15	Sheffield W	11	0	11	0
2015–16	Preston NE	28	1	28	1

WELSH, John (M) — 327 17
H: 5 7 W: 12 02 b.Liverpool 10-1-84
Internationals: England U20, U21.

Season	Club	A	G		
2000–01	Liverpool	0	0		
2001–02	Liverpool	0	0		
2002–03	Liverpool	0	0		
2003–04	Liverpool	1	0		
2004–05	Liverpool	3	0		
2005–06	Liverpool	0	0	4	0
2005–06	Hull C	32	2		
2006–07	Hull C	18	1		
2007–08	Hull C	0	0		
2007–08	Chester C	6	0	6	0
2008–09	Hull C	0	0	50	3
2008–09	Carlisle U	4	0	4	0
2008–09	Bury	5	0	5	0
2009–10	Tranmere R	45	4		
2010–11	Tranmere R	41	4		
2011–12	Tranmere R	44	3	130	11
2012–13	Preston NE	36	1		
2013–14	Preston NE	36	2		
2014–15	Preston NE	32	0		
2015–16	Preston NE	24	0	128	3

WOODS, Calum (D) — 250 11
H: 5 11 W: 11 07 b.Liverpool 5-2-87

Season	Club	A	G		
2006–07	Dunfermline Ath	12	0		
2007–08	Dunfermline Ath	25	0		
2008–09	Dunfermline Ath	30	5		
2009–10	Dunfermline Ath	29	2		
2010–11	Dunfermline Ath	32	3	128	10
2011–12	Huddersfield T	26	0		
2012–13	Huddersfield T	27	0		
2013–14	Huddersfield T	19	1	72	1
2014–15	Preston NE	18	0		
2015–16	Preston NE	32	0	50	0

WRIGHT, Bailey (D) — 161 8
H: 5 9 W: 13 05 b.Melbourne 28-7-92
Internationals: Australia U17, Full caps.

Season	Club	A	G		
2010–11	Preston NE	2	0		
2011–12	Preston NE	13	1		
2012–13	Preston NE	38	2		
2013–14	Preston NE	43	4		
2014–15	Preston NE	27	1		
2015–16	Preston NE	38	0	161	8

Scholars
Barry, Thomas Michael Robinson; Boyd, James Thomas William; Burgoyne, Jack Geoffrey; Davidson, Dylan Gary Iain; Earl, Joshua John Francis; Jagne, Lamin; Kwateng, Akwasi Oduro; Lunney, Jonathan michael; Meulensteen, Melle Reinhard Maria; Roberts, Ben James; Roberts, Lee Callum Thornill; Robinson, Adam James; Robinson, Adam Joseph Thomas; Tait, Callum Joseph; Whelan, Sean Kenneh.

QPR (68)

BLACKWOOD, Tyler (F) — 4 1
b. 24-7-91

Season	Club	A	G		
2015–16	QPR	1	0	1	0
2015–16	Newport Co	3	1	3	1

BRZOZOWSKI, Marcin (G) — 0 0
b. 29-10-98

Season	Club	A	G
2015–16	QPR	0	0

CAULKER, Steven (D) — 196 10
H: 6 3 W: 12 00 b.Feltham 29-12-91
Internationals: England U19 U21, Full caps. Great Britain.

Season	Club	A	G		
2009–10	Tottenham H	0	0		
2009–10	Yeovil T	44	0	44	0
2010–11	Tottenham H	0	0		
2010–11	Bristol C	29	2	29	2
2011–12	Tottenham H	0	0		
2011–12	Swansea C	26	0	26	0
2012–13	Tottenham H	18	2	18	2
2013–14	Cardiff C	38	5	38	5
2014–15	QPR	35	1		
2015–16	QPR	0	0	35	1
2015–16	Southampton	3	0	3	0
2015–16	Liverpool	3	0	3	0

CHERY, Tjaronn (M) — 253 55
H: 5 7 W: 10 10 b.Enschede 4-6-88

Season	Club	A	G		
2008–09	FC Twente	1	0		
2008–09	Cambuur	15	0	15	0
2009–10	FC Twente	0	0	1	0
2009–10	Roosendaal	30	1	30	1
2010–11	Emmen	33	9	33	9
2011–12	Den Haag	34	2		
2012–13	Den Haag	32	8		
2013–14	Den Haag	0	0	66	10
2013–14	Groningen	35	10		
2014–15	Groningen	34	15	69	25
2015–16	QPR	39	10	39	10

COMLEY, Brandon (M) — 13 0
b.Islington 18-11-95

Season	Club	A	G		
2014–15	QPR	1	0		
2015–16	QPR	0	0	1	0
2015–16	Carlisle U	12	0	12	0

DIAKITE, Samba (M) — 131 2
H: 6 1 W: 11 13 b.Montfermeil 24-1-89
Internationals: Mali Full caps.

Season	Club	A	G		
2007–08	Valenciennes B	7	0	7	0
2008–09	Olympique N-le-Sec	28	0	28	0
2009–10	Nancy B	19	0	19	0
2009–10	Nancy	3	0		
2010–11	Nancy	23	0		
2011–12	Nancy	15	0	41	0
2011–12	QPR	9	1		
2012–13	QPR	14	0		
2013–14	QPR	0	0		
2013–14	Watford	6	0	6	0
2014–15	QPR	0	0		
2014–15	Al-Ittihad	7	1	7	1
2015–16	QPR	0	0	23	1

DOUGHTY, Michael (M) — 99 7
H: 6 1 W: 12 10 b.Westminster 20-11-92
Internationals: Wales U19, U21.

Season	Club	A	G		
2010–11	QPR	0	0		
2011–12	QPR	0	0		
2011–12	Crawley T	16	0	16	0
2011–12	Aldershot T	5	0	5	0
2012–13	QPR	0	0		
2012–13	St Johnstone	5	0	5	0
2013–14	QPR	0	0		
2013–14	Stevenage	36	2	36	2
2014–15	QPR	3	0		
2014–15	Gillingham	9	0	9	0
2015–16	QPR	3	0		
2015–16	Swindon T	20	5	20	5

EL KHAYATI, Abdenasser (F) — 85 24
H: 6 1 W: 11 11 b. 7-2-89

Season	Club	A	G		
2008–09	Den Bosh	8	0	8	0
2009–10	Dan Bosh	2	0	2	0
2010–11	Breda	0	0		
2012–13	Olympiacos	0	0		
2014–15	Kozakken Boys	17	12	17	12
2014–15	Burton Alb	18	3		
2015–16	Burton Alb	24	8	42	11
2015–16	QPR	16	1	16	1

EMMANUEL-THOMAS, Jay (M) — 209 43
H: 5 9 W: 11 05 b.Forest Gate 27-12-90
Internationals: England U17, U19.

Season	Club	A	G		
2008–09	Arsenal	0	0		
2009–10	Arsenal	0	0		
2009–10	Blackpool	11	1	11	1
2009–10	Doncaster R	14	5	14	5
2010–11	Arsenal	1	0	1	0
2010–11	Cardiff C	14	2	14	2
2011–12	Ipswich T	42	6		
2012–13	Ipswich T	29	2	71	8
2013–14	Bristol C	46	15		
2014–15	Bristol C	36	9	82	24
2015–16	QPR	12	3	12	3
2015–16	Milton Keynes D	4	0	4	0

FAURLIN, Alejandro (M) — 225 13
H: 6 1 W: 12 06 b.Argentina 9-8-86
Internationals: Argentina U17.

Season	Club	A	G		
2004	Rosario Central	1	0		
2005	Rosario Central	0	0		
2006	Rosario Central	0	0	1	0
2007	Atletico Rafaela	40	1	40	1
2008–09	Instituto	27	7	27	7
2009–10	QPR	41	1		
2010–11	QPR	40	3		
2011–12	QPR	20	1		
2012–13	QPR	11	0		
2012–13	Palermo	6	0	6	0
2013–14	QPR	7	0		
2014–15	QPR	2	0		
2015–16	QPR	30	0	151	5

FER, Leroy (M) — 243 38
H: 6 2 W: 12 05 b.Zortermeer 5-1-90
Internationals: Netherlands U16, U17, U19, U21, Full caps.

Season	Club	A	G		
2007–08	Feyenoord	13	1		
2008–09	Feyenoord	31	6		
2009–10	Feyenoord	31	2		
2010–11	Feyenoord	23	3		
2011–12	Feyenoord	4	2	102	14
2011–12	FC Twente	26	8		
2012–13	FC Twente	26	5	52	13
2013–14	Norwich C	29	3		
2014–15	Norwich C	1	0	30	3
2014–15	QPR	29	6		
2015–16	QPR	19	2	48	8
2015–16	Swansea C	11	0	11	0

FURLONG, Darnell (D) — 34 0
b. 31-10-95

Season	Club	A	G		
2014–15	QPR	3	0		
2015–16	QPR	0	0	3	0
2015–16	Northampton T	10	0	10	0
2015–16	Cambridge U	21	0	21	0

GLADWIN, Ben (D) — 68 10
b.Reading 8-6-92

Season	Club	A	G		
2013–14	Swindon T	13	0		
2014–15	Swindon T	34	8		
2015–16	QPR	7	0	7	0
2015–16	Swindon T	13	2	60	10
2015–16	Bristol C	1	0	1	0

GOBERN, Oscar (M) — 102 4
H: 5 11 W: 10 10 b.Birmingham 26-1-91
Internationals: England U19.

Season	Club	A	G		
2008–09	Southampton	6	0		
2009–10	Southampton	4	0		
2009–10	Milton Keynes D	2	0	2	0
2010–11	Southampton	11	1	21	1
2011–12	Huddersfield T	21	2		
2012–13	Huddersfield T	15	0		
2013–14	Huddersfield T	23	0		
2014–15	Huddersfield T	12	1	71	3
2014–15	Chesterfield	3	0	3	0
2015–16	QPR	0	0		
2015–16	Doncaster R	5	0	5	0

GREEN, Rob (G) — 563 0
H: 6 3 W: 14 09 b.Chertsey 18-1-80
Internationals: England U16, U18, B, Full caps.

Season	Club	A	G		
1997–98	Norwich C	0	0		
1998–99	Norwich C	2	0		
1999–2000	Norwich C	3	0		
2000–01	Norwich C	5	0		
2001–02	Norwich C	41	0		
2002–03	Norwich C	46	0		
2003–04	Norwich C	46	0		
2004–05	Norwich C	38	0		
2005–06	Norwich C	42	0	223	0
2006–07	West Ham U	26	0		
2007–08	West Ham U	38	0		
2008–09	West Ham U	38	0		
2009–10	West Ham U	38	0		
2010–11	West Ham U	37	0		
2011–12	West Ham U	42	0	219	0
2012–13	QPR	16	0		
2013–14	QPR	45	0		
2014–15	QPR	36	0		
2015–16	QPR	24	0	121	0

GREGO-COX, Reece (F) — 4 0
b. 12-11-96
Internationals: Republic of Ireland U17, U19, U21.

Season	Club	A	G		
2014–15	QPR	4	0		
2015–16	QPR	0	0	4	0

HALL, Grant (D) — 86 2
H: 5 9 W: 11 02 b.Brighton 29-10-91

Season	Club	A	G
2009–10	Brighton & HA	0	0
2010–11	Brighton & HA	0	0

Season	Club				
2011–12	Brighton & HA	1	0	1	0
2012–13	Tottenham H	0	0		
2013–14	Tottenham H	0	0		
2013–14	Swindon T	27	0	27	0
2014–15	Tottenham H	0	0		
2014–15	Birmingham C	7	0	7	0
2014–15	Blackpool	12	1	12	1
2015–16	QPR	39	1	39	1

HAMALAINEN, Niko (M)   1 0
b. 3-5-97
Internationals: Finland U18.

Season	Club				
2014–15	QPR	0	0		
2015–16	QPR	0	0		
2015–16	Dagenham & R	1	0	1	0

HENRY, Karl (M)   477 10
H: 6 0   W: 12 00   b.Wolverhampton 26-11-82
Internationals: England U20.

Season	Club				
1999–2000	Stoke C	0	0		
2000–01	Stoke C	0	0		
2001–02	Stoke C	24	0		
2002–03	Stoke C	18	1		
2003–04	Stoke C	20	0		
2003–04	*Cheltenham T*	9	1	9	1
2004–05	Stoke C	34	0		
2005–06	Stoke C	24	0	120	1
2006–07	Wolverhampton W	34	3		
2007–08	Wolverhampton W	40	3		
2008–09	Wolverhampton W	43	0		
2009–10	Wolverhampton W	34	0		
2010–11	Wolverhampton W	29	0		
2011–12	Wolverhampton W	31	0		
2012–13	Wolverhampton W	39	0	250	6
2013–14	QPR	27	1		
2014–15	QPR	33	0		
2015–16	QPR	38	1	98	2

HILL, Clint (D)   525 30
H: 6 0   W: 11 06   b.Liverpool 19-10-78

Season	Club				
1997–98	Tranmere R	14	0		
1998–99	Tranmere R	33	4		
1999–2000	Tranmere R	29	5		
2000–01	Tranmere R	34	5		
2001–02	Tranmere R	30	2	140	16
2002–03	Oldham Ath	17	1	17	1
2003–04	Stoke C	12	0		
2004–05	Stoke C	32	1		
2005–06	Stoke C	13	0		
2006–07	Stoke C	18	2		
2007–08	Stoke C	5	0	80	3
2007–08	Crystal Palace	28	3		
2008–09	Crystal Palace	43	1		
2009–10	Crystal Palace	43	1	114	5
2010–11	QPR	44	2		
2011–12	QPR	22	0		
2011–12	*Nottingham F*	5	0	5	0
2012–13	QPR	31	0		
2013–14	QPR	40	1		
2014–15	QPR	19	1		
2015–16	QPR	13	1	169	5

HOILETT, Junior (M)   226 30
H: 5 8   W: 11 00   b.Ottawa 5-6-90
Internationals: Canada Full caps.

Season	Club				
2007–08	Blackburn R	0	0		
2007–08	Paderborn	12	1	12	1
2008–09	Blackburn R	0	0		
2008–09	St Pauli	21	6	21	6
2009–10	Blackburn R	23	0		
2010–11	Blackburn R	24	5		
2011–12	Blackburn R	34	7	81	12
2012–13	QPR	26	1		
2013–14	QPR	35	4		
2014–15	QPR	22	0		
2015–16	QPR	29	6	112	11

HUDNOTT, Conor (G)   0 0
b. 2-9-96

Season	Club				
2015–16	QPR	0	0		

INGRAM, Matt (G)   128 0
H: 6 3   W: 12 13   b.Croydon 18-12-93

Season	Club				
2011–12	Wycombe W	0	0		
2012–13	Wycombe W	8	0		
2013–14	Wycombe W	46	0		
2014–15	Wycombe W	46	0		
2015–16	Wycombe W	24	0	124	0
2015–16	QPR	4	0	4	0

KAKAY, Osman (D)   10 0
b. 25-8-97

Season	Club				
2015–16	QPR	0	0		
2015–16	*Livingston*	10	0	10	0

KPEKAWA, Cole (D)   21 0
b. 20-5-96
Internationals: England U20.

Season	Club				
2014–15	QPR	1	0		
2014–15	Colchester U	4	0	4	0
2014–15	Portsmouth	2	0	2	0
2015–16	QPR	5	0	6	0
2015–16	Leyton Orient	9	0	9	0

LUMLEY, Joe (G)   6 0
b. 15-2-95

Season	Club				
2013–14	QPR	0	0		
2014–15	QPR	0	0		
2014–15	Accrington S	5	0	5	0
2014–15	Morecambe	0	0		
2015–16	QPR	1	0	1	0
2015–16	Stevenage	0	0		

LUONGO, Massimo (F)   124 13
H: 5 8   W: 11 10   b.Sydney 25-9-92
Internationals: Australia U20, Full caps.

Season	Club				
2010–11	Tottenham H	0	0		
2011–12	Tottenham H	0	0		
2012–13	Tottenham H	0	0		
2012–13	Ipswich T	9	0	9	0
2012–13	Swindon T	7	1		
2013–14	Swindon T	44	6		
2014–15	Swindon T	34	6	85	13
2015–16	QPR	30	0	30	0

MACKIE, Jamie (F)   291 44
H: 5 8   W: 11 00   b.Dorking 22-9-85
Internationals: Scotland Full caps.

Season	Club				
2003–04	Wimbledon	13	0	13	0
2004–05	Milton Keynes D	3	0	3	0
From Exeter C					
2007–08	Plymouth Arg	13	3		
2008–09	Plymouth Arg	43	5		
2009–10	Plymouth Arg	42	8	98	16
2010–11	QPR	25	9		
2011–12	QPR	31	7		
2012–13	QPR	29	2		
2013–14	Nottingham F	45	4	45	4
2014–15	Reading	32	5	32	5
2015–16	QPR	15	1	100	19

MULRANEY, Jake (M)   12 1
b. 5-4-96
Internationals: Republic of Ireland U17, U19.

Season	Club				
2015–16	QPR	0	0		
2015–16	*Dagenham & R*	6	0	6	0
2015–16	Stevenage	6	1	6	1

ONUOHA, Nedum (D)   260 8
H: 6 2   W: 12 04   b.Warri 12-11-86
Internationals: England U20, U21.

Season	Club				
2004–05	Manchester C	17	0		
2005–06	Manchester C	10	0		
2006–07	Manchester C	18	0		
2007–08	Manchester C	16	1		
2008–09	Manchester C	23	1		
2009–10	Manchester C	10	1		
2010–11	Manchester C	0	0		
2010–11	*Sunderland*	31	1	31	1
2011–12	Manchester C	1	0	95	3
2011–12	QPR	16	0		
2012–13	QPR	23	0		
2013–14	QPR	26	2		
2014–15	QPR	23	0		
2015–16	QPR	46	2	134	4

PERCH, James (D)   371 11
H: 5 11   W: 11 05   b.Mansfield 29-9-85

Season	Club				
2002–03	Nottingham F	0	0		
2003–04	Nottingham F	0	0		
2004–05	Nottingham F	22	0		
2005–06	Nottingham F	38	3		
2006–07	Nottingham F	46	5		
2007–08	Nottingham F	30	0		
2008–09	Nottingham F	37	3		
2009–10	Nottingham F	17	1	190	12
2010–11	Newcastle U	13	0		
2011–12	Newcastle U	25	0		
2012–13	Newcastle U	27	1	65	1
2013–14	Wigan Ath	40	0		
2014–15	Wigan Ath	41	3	81	3
2015–16	QPR	35	0	35	0

PETRASSO, Michael (M)   38 5
H: 5 6   W: 10 01   b.Toronto 9-7-95
Internationals: Canada U17, U20, U23, Full caps.

Season	Club				
2013–14	QPR	1	0		
2013–14	Oldham Ath	11	1	11	1
2013–14	Coventry C	7	1	7	1
2014–15	QPR	0	0		
2014–15	Leyton Orient	3	0	3	0
2014–15	Notts Co	8	3	8	3
2015–16	QPR	8	0	9	0

PHILLIPS, Matthew (M)   268 39
H: 6 0   W: 12 10   b.Aylesbury 13-3-91
Internationals: England U19, U20. Scotland Full caps.

Season	Club				
2007–08	Wycombe W	2	0		
2008–09	Wycombe W	37	3		
2009–10	Wycombe W	36	5		
2010–11	Wycombe W	3	0	78	8
2010–11	Blackpool	27	1		
2011–12	Blackpool	33	7		
2011–12	Sheffield U	6	5	6	5
2012–13	Blackpool	34	4		
2013–14	Blackpool	0	0	94	12
2013–14	QPR	21	3		
2014–15	QPR	25	3		
2015–16	QPR	44	8	90	14

POLTER, Sebastian (F)   111 27
H: 6 3   W: 13 01   b.Wilhelmshaven 1-4-91
Internationals: Germany U18, U20, U21.

Season	Club				
2008–09	Wolfsburg	0	0		
2009–10	Wolfsburg	0	0		
2010–11	Wolfsburg	0	0		
2011–12	Wolfsburg	12	2		
2012–13	Wolfsburg	0	0	12	2
2012–13	Nurnberg	26	5	26	5
2013–14	Mainz 05	13	0		
2014–15	Mainz 05	0	0	13	0
2014–15	*Union Berlin*	29	14	29	14
2015–16	QPR	31	6	31	6

PROHOULY, Axel (M)   0 0
b. 30-6-97
Internationals: France U19.

Season	Club				
2015–16	QPR	0	0		

ROBINSON, Jack (D)   79 0
H: 5 11   W: 10 08   b.Warrington 1-9-93
Internationals: England U16, U17, U18, U19, U21.

Season	Club				
2009–10	Liverpool	1	0		
2010–11	Liverpool	2	0		
2011–12	Liverpool	0	0		
2012–13	Liverpool	0	0		
2012–13	*Wolverhampton W*	11	0	11	0
2013–14	Liverpool	0	0	3	0
2013–14	*Blackpool*	34	0	34	0
2014–15	QPR	0	0		
2014–15	*Huddersfield T*	30	0	30	0
2015–16	QPR	1	0	1	0

SANDRO (M)   164 8
H: 6 2   W: 11 11   b.Riachinho 15-3-89
Internationals: Brazil U20, U23, Full caps.

Season	Club				
2008	Internacional	7	2		
2009	Internacional	27	1		
2010	Internacional	9	1	43	4
2010–11	Tottenham H	19	1		
2011–12	Tottenham H	23	0		
2012–13	Tottenham H	22	1		
2013–14	Tottenham H	17	1	81	3
2014–15	QPR	17	1		
2015–16	QPR	11	0	28	1
2015–16	*WBA*	12	0	12	0

SMITHIES, Alex (G)   265 0
H: 6 1   W: 10 01   b.Huddersfield 25-3-90
Internationals: England U16, U17, U18, U19.

Season	Club				
2006–07	Huddersfield T	0	0		
2007–08	Huddersfield T	2	0		
2008–09	Huddersfield T	27	0		
2009–10	Huddersfield T	46	0		
2010–11	Huddersfield T	22	0		
2011–12	Huddersfield T	13	0		
2012–13	Huddersfield T	46	0		
2013–14	Huddersfield T	46	0		
2014–15	Huddersfield T	44	0		
2015–16	Huddersfield T	1	0	247	0
2015–16	QPR	18	0	18	0

SUTHERLAND, Frankie (M)   23 1
H: 5 9   W: 10 00   b.Hillingdon 6-12-93
Internationals: Republic of Ireland U17, U19, U21.

Season	Club				
2010–11	QPR	0	0		
2011–12	QPR	0	0		
2012–13	QPR	0	0		
2012–13	Portsmouth	1	0	1	0
2013–14	QPR	0	0		
2013–14	Leyton Orient	0	0		
2014–15	QPR	0	0		
2014–15	AFC Wimbledon	7	1	7	1
2015–16	QPR	0	0		
2015–16	Dagenham & R	4	0	4	0
2015–16	Crawley T	11	0	11	0

TOZSER, Daniel (M)   319   29
H: 6 1   W: 11 08   b.Szolnok 12-5-85
Internationals: Hungary U21, Full caps.

2002–03	Debrecen	0	0	
2003–04	Debrecen	1	0	1 0
2004–05	Ferencvaros	24	1	
2005–06	Ferencvaros	30	2	54 3
2006–07	AEK Athens	23	2	
2007–08	AEK Athens	12	1	35 3
2008–09	Genk	25	2	
2009–10	Genk	38	5	
2010–11	Genk	39	8	
2011–12	Genk	25	2	127 17
2012–13	Genoa	21	0	
2013–14	Genoa	0	0	21 0
2013–14	*Watford*	20	0	
2014–15	Parma	0	0	
2014–15	*Watford*	45	5	65 5
2015–16	QPR	16	1	16 1

WASHINGTON, Conor (F)   121   31
H: 5 10   W: 11 09   b.Chatham 18-5-92
Internationals: Northern Ireland Full caps.

2013–14	Newport Co	24	4	24 4
2013–14	Peterborough U	17	4	
2014–15	Peterborough U	40	13	
2015–16	Peterborough U	25	10	82 27
2015–16	QPR	15	0	15 0

YUN, Suk-Young (D)   125   6
H: 6 0   W: 11 09   b.Suwon 13-2-90
Internationals: South Korea U17, U20, U23, Full caps.

2009	Jeonnam Dragons	20	1	
2010	Jeonnam Dragons	16	0	
2011	Jeonnam Dragons	19	1	
2012	Jeonnam Dragons	25	3	80 5
2012–13	QPR	0	0	
2013–14	QPR	7	1	
2013–14	*Doncaster R*	3	0	3 0
2014–15	QPR	23	0	
2015–16	QPR	3	0	33 1
2015–16	*Charlton Ath*	9	0	9 0

Players retained or with offer of contract
Manning, Ryan Phelim; Shodipo, Olamide Oluwatimilehin; Wallen, Joshua Thomas.

Scholars
Adams, Brandon Lea; Akinola, Romoluwa Ayomide; Arthur, Jeremy Bernard; Barzey, Brandon James; Bowler, Joshua Luke; Brzozowski, Marcin Maurycy; Clarke, Ruudi Leon; Crichlow, Gianni Dimitri; Darbyshire, Daniel Richard; Donnellan, Leo James; Dos Santos Cardoso, Hugo Alexandre; Eales, Jake Callum; Folkes, Anthony Junior Tyreke; Fox, Charles John; Herdman, Martin John; Klass, Michael Anthony; Komodikis, Andreas; Springer-Downes, Rhys Tre Marlon; Williams, Jack.

READING (69)

AL HABSI, Ali (G)   241   0
H: 6 4   W: 12 06   b.Oman 30-12-81
Internationals: Oman Full caps.

2003	Lyn	13	0	
2004	Lyn	24	0	
2005	Lyn	25	0	62 0
2005–06	Bolton W	0	0	
2006–07	Bolton W	0	0	
2007–08	Bolton W	10	0	
2008–09	Bolton W	0	0	
2009–10	Bolton W	0	0	
2010–11	Bolton W	0	0	10 0
2010–11	*Wigan Ath*	34	0	
2011–12	Wigan Ath	38	0	
2012–13	Wigan Ath	29	0	
2013–14	Wigan Ath	24	0	
2014–15	Wigan Ath	11	0	136 0
2014–15	*Brighton & HA*	1	0	1 0
2015–16	Reading	32	0	32 0

ALEX, Fernandez (M)   47   2
H: 5 11   W: 10 10   b.Madrid 15-10-92
Internationals: Spain U17, U18, U19, U20.

2010–11	Real Madrid	1	0	
2011–12	Real Madrid	0	0	
2012–13	Real Madrid	0	0	1 0
2013–14	Espanyol	24	0	
2014–15	Espanyol	5	0	
2014–15	*Rijeka*	9	2	9 2
2015–16	*Espanyol*	0	0	29 0
2015–16	Reading	8	0	8 0

BARRETT, Josh (F)   3   0
b. 21-6-98
Internationals: Republic of Ireland U17, U21.

2015–16	Reading	3	0	3 0

BOND, Jonathan (G)   47   0
H: 6 3   W: 13 03   b.Hemel Hempstead 19-5-93
Internationals: Wales U17, U19. England U20, U21.

2010–11	Watford	0	0	
2011–12	Watford	1	0	
2011–12	*Dagenham & R*	5	0	5 0
2011–12	*Bury*	6	0	6 0
2012–13	Watford	8	0	
2013–14	Watford	10	0	
2014–15	Watford	3	0	22 0
2015–16	Reading	14	0	14 0

COOPER, Jake (D)   39   4
H: 6 4   W: 13 05   b.Bracknell 3-2-95
Internationals: England U18, U19, U20.

2013–14	Reading	0	0	
2014–15	Reading	15	2	
2015–16	Reading	24	2	39 4

COX, Simon (F)   296   79
H: 5 10   W: 10 12   b.Reading 28-4-87
Internationals: Republic of Ireland Full caps.

2005–06	Reading	2	0	
2006–07	Reading	0	0	
2006–07	*Brentford*	13	0	13 0
2006–07	*Northampton T*	8	3	8 3
2007–08	Reading	0	0	
2007–08	Swindon T	36	15	
2008–09	Swindon T	45	29	81 44
2009–10	WBA	28	9	
2010–11	WBA	19	1	
2011–12	WBA	18	0	
2012–13	WBA	0	0	65 10
2012–13	Nottingham F	39	5	
2013–14	Nottingham F	34	8	73 13
2014–15	Reading	37	8	
2015–16	Reading	13	1	52 9
2015–16	*Bristol C*	4	0	4 0

DICKIE, Rob (D)   1   0
b. 3-3-96
Internationals: England U18, U19.

2015–16	Reading	1	0	1 0

EVANS, George (M)   57   5
H: 6 0   W: 11 12   b.Cheadle 13-1-96
Internationals: England U17, U19, U20.

2012–13	Manchester C	0	0	
2013–14	Manchester C	0	0	
2013–14	*Crewe Alex*	23	1	23 1
2014–15	Manchester C	0	0	
2014–15	*Scunthorpe U*	16	1	16 1
2015–16	Manchester C	0	0	
2015–16	*Walsall*	12	3	12 3
2015–16	Reading	6	0	6 0

FERDINAND, Anton (D)   298   5
H: 6 2   W: 11 00   b.Peckham 18-2-85
Internationals: England U18, U20, U21.

2002–03	West Ham U	0	0	
2003–04	West Ham U	20	0	
2004–05	West Ham U	29	1	
2005–06	West Ham U	33	2	
2006–07	West Ham U	31	0	
2007–08	West Ham U	25	2	
2008–09	West Ham U	0	0	138 5
2008–09	Sunderland	31	0	
2009–10	Sunderland	24	0	
2010–11	Sunderland	27	0	
2011–12	Sunderland	3	0	85 0
2011–12	QPR	31	0	
2012–13	QPR	13	0	
2012–13	*Bursaspor*	7	0	7 0
2013–14	QPR	0	0	44 0
2013–14	*Antalyaspor*	3	0	3 0
2014–15	Reading	2	0	
2015–16	Reading	19	0	21 0

FOSU, Tarique (M)   15   4
b. 5-11-95
Internationals: England U18.

2013–14	Reading	0	0	
2014–15	Reading	1	0	
2015–16	Reading	0	0	1 0
2015–16	*Fleetwood T*	6	1	6 1
2015–16	*Accrington S*	8	3	8 3

GRIFFIN, Shane (D)   0   0
b. 8-9-94
Internationals: Republic of Ireland U19, U21.

2013–14	Reading	0	0	
2014–15	Reading	0	0	

GUNTER, Chris (D)   320   2
H: 5 11   W: 11 02   b.Newport 21-7-89
Internationals: Wales U17, U19, U21, Full caps.

2006–07	Cardiff C	15	0	
2007–08	Cardiff C	13	0	28 0
2007–08	Tottenham H	2	0	
2008–09	Tottenham H	3	0	5 0
2008–09	*Nottingham F*	8	0	
2009–10	Nottingham F	44	1	
2010–11	Nottingham F	43	0	
2011–12	Nottingham F	46	1	141 2
2012–13	Reading	20	0	
2013–14	Reading	44	0	
2014–15	Reading	38	0	
2015–16	Reading	44	0	146 0

HURTADO, Paolo (M)   183   30
H: 5 10   W: 10 08   b.Callao 27-7-90
Internationals: Peru Full caps.

2008	Alianza Lima	20	2	
2009	Alianza Lima	0	0	
2009	*Juan Aurich*	21	3	21 3
2010	Alianza Lima	36	8	
2011	Alianza Lima	26	4	
2012	Alianza Lima	1	0	83 14
2012–13	Pacos de Ferreira	28	8	
2013–14	Pacos de Ferreira	8	0	
2013–14	*Penarol*	10	0	10 0
2014–15	Pacos de Ferreira	21	4	57 12
2015–16	Reading	5	0	5 0
2015–16	*Guimaraes*	7	1	7 1

HYAM, Dominic (D)   16   0
b. 20-12-95
Internationals: Scotland U19, U21.

2014–15	Reading	0	0	
2015–16	Reading	0	0	
2015–16	*Dagenham & R*	16	0	16 0

JOHN, Ola (F)   137   16
H: 5 11   W: 12 08   b.Zwedru 19-5-92
Internationals: Netherlands U17, U19, U21, Full caps.

2010–11	FC Twente	13	1	
2011–12	FC Twente	33	8	46 9
2012–13	Benfica	22	0	
2013–14	Benfica	5	0	
2013–14	*Hamburg*	8	0	8 0
2014–15	Benfica	26	3	
2015–16	Benfica	2	0	55 3
On loan from Benfica.				
2015–16	Reading	28	4	28 4

KELLY, Liam (M)   0   0
b. 22-11-95
Internationals: Republic of Ireland U19, U21.

2014–15	Reading	0	0	
2015–16	Reading	0	0	

KEOWN, Niall (D)   2   0
b. 5-4-95
Internationals: Republic of Ireland U21.

2013–14	Reading	0	0	
2014–15	Reading	2	0	
2015–16	Reading	0	0	2 0

KERMORGANT, Yann (F)   367   103
H: 6 0   W: 13 03   b.Vannes 8-11-81
Internationals: Brittany Full caps.

2004–05	Chatellerault	29	14	29 14
2005–06	Grenoble	26	6	
2006–07	Grenoble	32	10	58 16
2007–08	Reims	33	4	
2008–09	Reims	34	9	67 13
2009–10	Leicester C	20	1	
2010–11	Leicester C	0	0	20 1
2010–11	*Arles-Avignon*	26	3	26 3
2011–12	Charlton Ath	36	12	
2012–13	Charlton Ath	32	12	
2013–14	Charlton Ath	21	5	89 29
2013–14	Bournemouth	0	0	
2014–15	Bournemouth	38	15	
2015–16	Bournemouth	7	0	61 24
2015–16	Reading	17	3	17 3

KUHL, Aaron (M)   11   0
H: 5 8   W: 10 06   b.Paulton 30-1-96
Internationals: England U19, U20.

2014–15	Reading	6	0	
2015–16	Reading	0	0	6 0
2015–16	*Dundee U*	5	0	5 0

LIBURD, Rowan (F)   13   0
b. 28-8-92

2015–16	Reading	3	0	3 0
2015–16	*Wycombe W*	10	0	10 0

LONG, Sean (D) 9 0
H: 5 10   W: 11 00   b.Dublin 2-5-95
Internationals: Republic of Ireland U19, U21.

2013–14	Reading	0	0
2014–15	Reading	0	0
2015–16	Reading	0	0
2015–16	*Luton T*	9	0	9 0

McCLEARY, Garath (M) 244 26
H: 5 10   W: 12 06   b.Oxford 15-5-87
Internationals: Jamaica Full caps.

2007–08	Nottingham F	8	1
2008–09	Nottingham F	39	1
2009–10	Nottingham F	24	0
2010–11	Nottingham F	18	2
2011–12	Nottingham F	22	9	111 13
2011–12	Reading	0	0
2012–13	Reading	31	3
2013–14	Reading	42	5
2014–15	Reading	26	1
2015–16	Reading	34	4	133 13

McSHANE, Paul (D) 273 11
H: 6 0   W: 11 05   b.Wicklow 6-1-86
Internationals: Republic of Ireland U21, Full caps.

2002–03	Manchester U	0	0
2003–04	Manchester U	0	0
2004–05	Manchester U	0	0
2004–05	Walsall	4	1	4 1
2005–06	Manchester U	0	0
2005–06	Brighton & HA	38	3	38 3
2006–07	WBA	32	2	32 2
2007–08	Sunderland	21	0
2008–09	Sunderland	3	0
2008–09	Hull C	17	1
2009–10	Sunderland	0	0	24 0
2009–10	Hull C	27	0
2010–11	Hull C	19	0
2010–11	Barnsley	10	1	10 1
2011–12	Hull C	1	0
2011–12	Crystal Palace	11	0	11 0
2012–13	Hull C	25	2
2013–14	Hull C	10	0
2014–15	Hull C	20	1	119 4
2015–16	Reading	35	0	35 0

MOORE, Stuart (G) 4 0
b. 8-9-94

2013–14	Reading	0	0
2014–15	Reading	0	0
2015–16	Reading	0	0
2015–16	*Peterborough U*	4	0	4 0

NORWOOD, Oliver (M) 200 15
H: 5 11   W: 11 13   b.Burnley 12-4-91
Internationals: England U16, U17. Northern Ireland U19, U21, B, Full caps.

2009–10	Manchester U	0	0
2010–11	Manchester U	0	0
2010–11	Carlisle U	6	0	6 0
2011–12	Manchester U	0	0
2011–12	Scunthorpe U	15	1	15 1
2011–12	Coventry C	18	2	18 2
2012–13	Huddersfield T	39	3
2013–14	Huddersfield T	40	5
2014–15	Huddersfield T	1	0	80 8
2014–15	Reading	38	1
2015–16	Reading	43	3	81 4

NOVAKOVICH, Andrija (F) 2 0
b. 21-9-96
Internationals: USA U17, U18, U20.

2014–15	Reading	2	0
2015–16	Reading	0	0	2 0

OBITA, Jordan (M) 130 5
H: 5 11   W: 11 08   b.Oxford 8-12-93
Internationals: England U18, U19, U21.

2010–11	Reading	0	0
2011–12	Reading	0	0
2011–12	Barnet	5	0	5 0
2011–12	Gillingham	6	3	6 3
2012–13	Reading	0	0
2012–13	Portsmouth	8	1	8 1
2012–13	Oldham Ath	8	0	8 0
2013–14	Reading	34	1
2014–15	Reading	43	0
2015–16	Reading	26	0	103 1

ORLANDO SA, Carlos (F) 162 52
H: 6 2   W: 13 05   b.Barcelos 28-5-88
Internationals: Portugal U20, U21, Full caps.

2007–08	Braga	0	0
2007–08	Maria da Fonte	26	6	26 6
2008–09	Braga	10	3	10 3
2009–10	Porto	2	0
2010–11	Porto	0	0	2 0
2010–11	Nacional	16	3	16 3

QUINN, Stephen (M) 349 25
H: 5 6   W: 9 08   b.Dublin 4-4-86
Internationals: Republic of Ireland U21, Full caps.

2011–12	Fulham	7	1	7 1
2012–13	AEL Limassol	20	5
2013–14	AEL Limassol	19	13	39 18
2013–14	Legia Warsaw	7	1
2014–15	Legia Warsaw	26	13	33 14
2015–16	Reading	19	5	19 5
2015–16	Maccabi Tel-Aviv	10	2	10	2

2005–06	Sheffield U	0	0
2005–06	Milton Keynes D	15	0	15 0
2005–06	Rotherham U	16	0	16 0
2006–07	Sheffield U	15	2
2007–08	Sheffield U	19	2
2008–09	Sheffield U	43	7
2009–10	Sheffield U	44	4
2010–11	Sheffield U	37	1
2011–12	Sheffield U	45	4
2012–13	Sheffield U	3	0	206 20
2012–13	Hull C	42	3
2013–14	Hull C	15	0
2014–15	Hull C	28	1	85 4
2015–16	Reading	27	1	27 1

RAKELS, Deniss (F) 168 72
b.Jekabpils 20-8-92
Internationals: Latvia U17, U19, U21, Full caps.

2009	Metalurgs	14	9
2010	Metalurgs	26	18	40 27
2010–11	Zaglebie Lubin	4	0
2011–12	Zaglebie Lubin	0	0
2011–12	Katowice	20	5
2012–13	Zaglebie Lubin	0	0
2012–13	Katowice	27	11	47 16
2013–14	Zaglebie Lubin	5	0	9 0
2013–14	Cracovia	7	0
2014–15	Cracovia	33	11
2015–16	Cracovia	20	15	60 26
2015–16	Reading	12	3	12 3

ROBSON-KANU, Hal (F) 240 33
H: 5 7   W: 11 08   b.Acton 21-5-89
Internationals: England U19, U20. Wales U21, Full caps.

2007–08	Reading	0	0
2007–08	Southend U	8	3
2008–09	Reading	0	0
2008–09	Southend U	14	2	22 5
2008–09	Swindon T	20	4	20 4
2009–10	Reading	17	0
2010–11	Reading	27	5
2011–12	Reading	36	4
2012–13	Reading	25	7
2013–14	Reading	36	4
2014–15	Reading	29	1
2015–16	Reading	28	3	198 24

SAMUEL, Dominic (F) 43 13
H: 6 0   W: 14 00   b.Southwark 1-4-94
Internationals: England U19.

2011–12	Reading	0	0
2012–13	Reading	1	0
2012–13	Colchester U	2	0	2 0
2013–14	Reading	0	0
2013–14	Dagenham & R	1	0	1 0
2014–15	Reading	0	0
2014–15	Coventry C	13	6	13 6
2015–16	Reading	1	0	2 0
2015–16	Gillingham	25	7	25 7

SEMEDO, Lisandro (M) 0 0
b. 12-3-96
From Sporting Lisbon.

2015–16	Reading	0	0

STACEY, Jack (M) 17 2
H: 6 4   W: 13 05   b.Bracknell 6-4-96

2014–15	Reading	6	0
2015–16	Reading	0	0	6 0
2015–16	Barnet	2	0	2 0
2015–16	Carlisle U	9	2	9 2

TANNER, Craig (F) 64 4
H: 5 7   W: 11 05   b.Reading 27-10-94

2011–12	Reading	0	0
2012–13	Reading	0	0
2013–14	Reading	0	0
2014–15	Reading	0	0
2014–15	AFC Wimbledon	19	0	19 0
2015–16	Reading	0	0
2015–16	Plymouth Arg	42	4	42 4

TAYLOR, Andrew (D) 316 6
H: 5 10   W: 11 04   b.Hartlepool 1-8-86
Internationals: England U16, U17, U18, U19, U20, U21.

2003–04	Middlesbrough	0	0
2004–05	Middlesbrough	0	0
2005–06	Middlesbrough	13	0
2005–06	Bradford C	24	0	24 0
2006–07	Middlesbrough	34	0
2007–08	Middlesbrough	19	0
2008–09	Middlesbrough	26	0
2009–10	Middlesbrough	12	0
2010–11	Middlesbrough	21	3	125 3
2010–11	Watford	19	1	19 1
2011–12	Cardiff C	42	1
2012–13	Cardiff C	43	0
2013–14	Cardiff C	18	0	103 1
2014–15	Wigan Ath	26	1	26 1
2015–16	Reading	19	0	19 0

TSHIBOLA, Aaron (M) 36 0
H: 6 3   W: 11 01   b.Newham 2-1-95
Internationals: England U18.

2011–12	Reading	0	0
2012–13	Reading	0	0
2013–14	Reading	0	0
2014–15	Reading	1	0
2014–15	Hartlepool U	23	0	23 0
2015–16	Reading	12	0	13 0

WATSON, Tennai (D) 0 0
b. 4-3-97

2015–16	Reading	0	0

WILLIAMS, Daniel (M) 152 10
H: 6 0   W: 11 12   b.Karlsruhe 8-3-89
Internationals: USA Full caps.

2009–10	SC Freiburg	5	0
2010–11	SC Freiburg	7	0
2011–12	SC Freiburg	1	0	13 0
2011–12	Hoffenheim	24	0
2012–13	Hoffenheim	21	1	45 1
2013–14	Reading	30	3
2014–15	Reading	25	1
2015–16	Reading	39	5	94 9

Players retained or with offer of contract
Andresson, Axel Oskar; Cardwell, Harry James; Davis, Conor Florin; Jules, Zak Kennedy; Legg, George Jack Adam; Osho, Gabriel Jeremiah Adedayo; Rinomhota, Andrew Farai; Scheving, Sindri; Sheppard, Jake Edwin; Vancooten, Terence Owen; Ward, Lewis Moore.

Scholars
Akinwunmi, Daniel Oladapo Ayoola; Bennett, Harrison George; Chatee, Joshua William; Collings, Billy Paul; Denton, Jack James; Driscoll, Liam Michael-Owen; East, Ryan Henry; Frost, Tyler Jayden; Howe, Teddy William; McIntyre, Thomas Peter; Medford-Smith, Ramarni Nelson; Richards, Omar Tyrell Crawford; Rollinson, Joel Robert Paul; Shokunbi, Ademola Oluwaseyi Abiodun; Smith, Samuel Toby; Southwood, Luke Kevin; Tupper, Joe Daniel.

ROCHDALE (70)

ALESSANDRA, Lewis (F) 254 36
H: 5 9   W: 11 07   b.Heywood 8-2-89

2007–08	Oldham Ath	15	2
2008–09	Oldham Ath	32	5
2009–10	Oldham Ath	1	0
2010–11	Oldham Ath	19	1	67 8
2011–12	Morecambe	42	4
2012–13	Morecambe	40	3	82 7
2013–14	Plymouth Arg	42	7
2014–15	Plymouth Arg	44	11	86 18
2015–16	Rochdale	8	1	8 1
2015–16	York C	11	2	11 2

ALLEN, Jamie (M) 98 9
H: 5 11   W: 11 05   b.Rochdale 29-1-95

2012–13	Rochdale	0	0
2013–14	Rochdale	25	6
2014–15	Rochdale	35	0
2015–16	Rochdale	38	3	98 9

ANDREW, Calvin (F) 258 23
H: 6 0   W: 12 11   b.Luton 19-12-86

2004–05	Luton T	8	0
2005–06	Luton T	1	1
2005–06	Grimsby T	8	1	8 1
2005–06	Bristol C	3	0	3 0
2006–07	Luton T	7	1
2007–08	Luton T	39	2	55 4
2008–09	Crystal Palace	7	0

Season	Club				
2008–09	Brighton & HA	9	2	9	2
2009–10	Crystal Palace	27	1		
2010–11	Crystal Palace	13	0		
2010–11	Millwall	3	0	3	0
2010–11	Swindon T	10	1	10	1
2011–12	Crystal Palace	6	0	53	1
2011–12	Leyton Orient	10	0	10	0
2012–13	Port Vale	22	1		
2013–14	Port Vale	0	0	22	1
2013–14	Mansfield T	15	1	15	1
2013–14	York C	8	1	8	1
2014–15	Rochdale	32	5		
2015–16	Rochdale	30	6	62	11

BARRY-MURPHY, Brian (M) 458 17
H: 5 10 W: 13 01 b.Cork 27-7-78
Internationals: Republic of Ireland U21.

Season	Club				
1995–96	Cork C	13	0		
1996–97	Cork C	25	0		
1997–98	Cork C	15	1		
1998–99	Cork C	27	1	80	2
1999–2000	Preston NE	1	0		
2000–01	Preston NE	14	0		
2001–02	Preston NE	4	0		
2001–02	Southend U	8	1	8	1
2002–03	Preston NE	2	0	21	0
2002–03	Hartlepool U	7	0	7	0
2002–03	Sheffield W	17	0		
2003–04	Sheffield W	41	0	58	0
2004–05	Bury	45	6		
2005–06	Bury	40	3		
2006–07	Bury	14	0		
2007–08	Bury	31	1		
2008–09	Bury	42	2		
2009–10	Bury	46	1	218	13
2010–11	Rochdale	32	0		
2011–12	Rochdale	22	1		
2012–13	Rochdale	8	0		
2013–14	Rochdale	3	0		
2014–15	Rochdale	0	0		
2015–16	Rochdale	1	0	66	1

BELL, Nyal (D) 3 0
b.Manchester 17-1-97

Season	Club				
2014–15	Rochdale	3	0		
2015–16	Rochdale	0	0	3	0

BENNETT, Rhys (D) 96 4
H: 6 3 W: 12 00 b.Manchester 1-9-91

Season	Club				
2011–12	Bolton W	0	0		
2011–12	Falkirk	19	0	19	0
2013–14	Rochdale	22	0		
2014–15	Rochdale	39	2		
2015–16	Rochdale	16	2	77	4

BUNNEY, Joe (F) 73 15
H: 6 1 W: 11 00 b.Manchester 26-9-93
Internationals: England U16, U18.

Season	Club				
2012–13	Rochdale	1	1		
2013–14	Rochdale	21	3		
2014–15	Rochdale	19	2		
2015–16	Rochdale	32	9	73	15

CAMPS, Callum (M) 46 6
b.Stockport 30-11-95
Internationals: Northern Ireland U18, U21.

Season	Club				
2012–13	Rochdale	2	0		
2013–14	Rochdale	0	0		
2014–15	Rochdale	12	1		
2015–16	Rochdale	32	5	46	6

CANNON, Andy (M) 43 0
H: 5 9 W: 11 09 b. 14-3-96

Season	Club				
2014–15	Rochdale	18	0		
2015–16	Rochdale	25	0	43	0

COLLIS, Steve (G) 88 0
H: 6 3 W: 12 05 b.Harrow 18-3-81

Season	Club				
1999–2000	Barnet	0	0		
2000–01	Nottingham F	0	0		
2001–02	Nottingham F	0	0		
2003–04	Yeovil T	11	0		
2004–05	Yeovil T	9	0		
2005–06	Yeovil T	23	0	43	0
2006–07	Southend U	1	0		
2007–08	Southend U	20	0	21	0
2008–09	Crewe Alex	18	0		
2009–10	Crewe Alex	1	0	19	0
2009–10	Bristol C	0	0		
2009–10	Torquay U	1	0	1	0
2010–11	Peterborough U	0	0		
2010–11	Northampton T	4	0	4	0
2011–12	Macclesfield T	0	0		
2012–13	Rochdale	0	0		
2013–14	Rochdale	0	0		
2014–15	Rochdale	0	0		
2015–16	Rochdale	0	0		

DIBA MUSANGU, Jonathan (G) 1 0
H: 6 0 W: 11 09 b.Mbuji-Mayi 12-10-97

Season	Club				
2014–15	Rochdale	1	0		
2015–16	Rochdale	0	0	1	0

EASTHAM, Ashley (D) 155 6
H: 6 3 W: 12 06 b.Preston 22-3-91

Season	Club				
2009–10	Blackpool	1	0		
2009–10	Cheltenham T	20	0		
2010–11	Blackpool	0	0		
2010–11	Cheltenham T	9	0	29	0
2010–11	Carlisle U	0	0		
2011–12	Blackpool	0	0		
2011–12	Bury	25	2		
2012–13	Blackpool	0	0	1	0
2012–13	Fleetwood T	1	0	1	0
2012–13	Notts Co	4	0	4	0
2012–13	Bury	19	0	44	2
2013–14	Rochdale	15	0		
2014–15	Rochdale	41	2		
2015–16	Rochdale	20	2	76	4

HENDERSON, Ian (F) 390 81
H: 5 10 W: 11 06 b.Thetford 25-1-85
Internationals: England U18, U20.

Season	Club				
2002–03	Norwich C	20	1		
2003–04	Norwich C	19	4		
2004–05	Norwich C	3	0		
2005–06	Norwich C	24	1		
2006–07	Norwich C	2	0	68	6
2006–07	Rotherham U	18	1	18	1
2007–08	Northampton T	23	0		
2008–09	Northampton T	3	0	26	0
2008–09	Luton T	19	1	19	1
2009–10	Colchester U	13	2		
2009–10	Ankaragucu	2	0	2	0
2010–11	Colchester U	36	10		
2011–12	Colchester U	46	9		
2012–13	Colchester U	22	3	117	24
2012–13	Rochdale	12	3		
2013–14	Rochdale	45	11		
2014–15	Rochdale	44	22		
2015–16	Rochdale	39	13	140	49

HOLT, Grant (F) 465 154
H: 6 1 W: 14 02 b.Carlisle 12-4-81

Season	Club				
1999–2000	Halifax T	4	0		
2000–01	Halifax T	2	0	6	0
From Sengkang, Barrow					
2002–03	Sheffield W	7	1		
2003–04	Sheffield W	17	2	24	3
2003–04	Rochdale	14	4		
2004–05	Rochdale	40	17		
2005–06	Rochdale	21	14		
2005–06	Nottingham F	19	4		
2006–07	Nottingham F	45	14		
2007–08	Nottingham F	32	3	96	21
2007–08	Blackpool	4	0	4	0
2008–09	Shrewsbury T	43	20	43	20
2009–10	Norwich C	39	24		
2010–11	Norwich C	45	21		
2011–12	Norwich C	36	15		
2012–13	Norwich C	34	8	154	68
2013–14	Wigan Ath	16	2		
2013–14	Aston Villa	10	1	10	1
2014–15	Wigan Ath	0	0		
2014–15	Huddersfield T	15	2	15	2
2014–15	Wigan Ath	4	0	20	2
2015–16	Wolverhampton W	4	0	4	0
2015–16	Rochdale	14	2	89	37

HOOPER, James (D) 2 0
b. 10-2-97

Season	Club				
2014–15	Rochdale	0	0		
2015–16	Rochdale	2	0	2	0

KENNEDY, Tom (D) 427 15
H: 5 10 W: 11 01 b.Bury 24-6-85

Season	Club				
2002–03	Bury	1	0		
2003–04	Bury	27	0		
2004–05	Bury	46	1		
2005–06	Bury	37	0		
2006–07	Bury	33	0		
2007–08	Rochdale	43	2		
2008–09	Rochdale	43	4		
2009–10	Rochdale	44	3		
2010–11	Leicester C	1	0		
2010–11	Rochdale	6	0		
2010–11	Peterborough U	14	0		
2011–12	Leicester C	5	0		
2011–12	Peterborough U	10	0	24	0
2012–13	Leicester C	0	0	6	0
2012–13	Barnsley	24	0		
2013–14	Barnsley	44	1	68	1
2014–15	Rochdale	46	0		
2014–15	Bury	2	0	145	5
2014–15	Blackpool	5	0		
2015–16	Rochdale	18	0	179	9

KISIMBA, Kisimba (M) 0 0
H: 5 9 W: 11 11 b. 23-10-97

Season	Club				
2014–15	Rochdale	0	0		
2015–16	Rochdale	0	0		

LANCASHIRE, Oliver (D) 192 4
H: 6 1 W: 11 10 b.Basingstoke 13-12-88

Season	Club				
2006–07	Southampton	0	0		
2007–08	Southampton	0	0		
2008–09	Southampton	11	0		
2009–10	Southampton	2	0	13	0
2009–10	Grimsby T	25	1	25	1
2010–11	Walsall	29	0		
2011–12	Walsall	20	1	49	1
2012–13	Aldershot T	12	0	12	0
2013–14	Rochdale	38	0		
2014–15	Rochdale	21	0		
2015–16	Rochdale	34	2	93	2

LILLIS, Josh (G) 218 0
H: 6 0 W: 12 08 b.Derby 24-6-87

Season	Club				
2006–07	Scunthorpe U	1	0		
2007–08	Scunthorpe U	3	0		
2008–09	Scunthorpe U	5	0		
2008–09	Notts Co	5	0	5	0
2009–10	Scunthorpe U	8	0		
2009–10	Grimsby T	4	0	4	0
2009–10	Rochdale	1	0		
2010–11	Scunthorpe U	15	0		
2010–11	Rochdale	23	0		
2011–12	Scunthorpe U	6	0	38	0
2012–13	Rochdale	46	0		
2013–14	Rochdale	45	0		
2014–15	Rochdale	16	0		
2015–16	Rochdale	40	0	171	0

LUND, Matthew (M) 131 16
H: 6 0 W: 11 13 b.Manchester 21-11-90
Internationals: Northern Ireland U21.

Season	Club				
2009–10	Stoke C	0	0		
2010–11	Stoke C	0	0		
2010–11	Hereford U	2	0	2	0
2011–12	Stoke C	0	0		
2011–12	Oldham Ath	3	0	3	0
2011–12	Bristol R	13	2		
2012–13	Stoke C	0	0		
2012–13	Bristol R	18	2	31	4
2012–13	Southend U	12	1	12	1
2013–14	Rochdale	40	8		
2014–15	Rochdale	14	2		
2015–16	Rochdale	29	1	83	11

McDERMOTT, Donal (F) 100 9
H: 6 6 W: 12 00 b.Co. Meath 19-10-89
Internationals: Republic of Ireland U17, U18, U19.

Season	Club				
2007–08	Manchester C	0	0		
2008–09	Manchester C	0	0		
2008–09	Milton Keynes D	1	0	1	0
2009–10	Manchester C	0	0		
2009–10	Chesterfield	15	5	15	5
2009–10	Scunthorpe U	9	0	9	0
2010–11	Manchester C	0	0		
2010–11	Bournemouth	9	1		
2011–12	Huddersfield T	9	0	9	0
2011–12	Bournemouth	14	1		
2012–13	Bournemouth	6	0		
2013–14	Bournemouth	0	0	29	2
2014–15	Rochdale	0	0		
2015–16	Rochdale	37	2	37	2

McNULTY, Jim (D) 253 5
H: 6 1 W: 12 00 b.Runcorn 13-2-85
Internationals: Scotland U17, U19.

Season	Club				
2006–07	Macclesfield T	15	0		
2007–08	Macclesfield T	19	1	34	1
2007–08	Stockport Co	11	0		
2008–09	Stockport Co	26	1	37	1
2008–09	Brighton & HA	5	1		
2009–10	Brighton & HA	8	0		
2009–10	Scunthorpe U	3	0		
2010–11	Brighton & HA	0	0	13	1
2010–11	Scunthorpe U	6	0	9	0
2011–12	Barnsley	44	2		
2012–13	Barnsley	12	0		
2013–14	Barnsley	0	0	56	2
2013–14	Tranmere R	12	0	12	0
2013–14	Bury	21	0		
2014–15	Bury	25	0	46	0
2015–16	Rochdale	46	0	46	0

MENDEZ-LAING, Nathaniel (M) 150 18
H: 5 10 W: 11 12 b.Birmingham 15-4-92
Internationals: England U16, U17.

Season	Club				
2009–10	Wolverhampton W	0	0		
2010–11	Wolverhampton W	0	0		
2010–11	Peterborough U	33	5		
2011–12	Wolverhampton W	0	0		
2011–12	Sheffield U	8	1	8	1

2012–13	Peterborough U	21	3		
2012–13	*Portsmouth*	8	0	8	0
2013–14	Peterborough U	16	1		
2013–14	*Shrewsbury T*	6	0	6	0
2014–15	Peterborough U	14	0	84	9
2014–15	*Cambridge U*	11	1	11	1
2015–16	Rochdale	33	7	33	7

NOBLE-LAZARUS, Reuben (F)   79   5
H: 5 11 W: 13 07 b.Huddersfield 16-8-93

2008–09	Barnsley	2	0		
2009–10	Barnsley	2	0		
2010–11	Barnsley	7	1		
2011–12	Barnsley	8	0		
2012–13	Barnsley	14	1		
2013–14	Barnsley	12	1		
2013–14	*Scunthorpe U*	4	0	4	0
2014–15	Barnsley	1	0	46	3
2014–15	Rochdale	19	1		
2015–16	Rochdale	10	1	29	2

RAFFERTY, Joe (D)   114   2
H: 6 0 W: 11 11 b.Liverpool 6-10-93
Internationals: Republic of Ireland U18, U19.

2012–13	Rochdale	21	0		
2013–14	Rochdale	31	0		
2014–15	Rochdale	31	1		
2015–16	Rochdale	31	1	114	2

ROSE, Michael (D)   364   23
H: 5 11 W: 12 04 b.Salford 28-7-82
Internationals: England C.

1999–2000	Manchester U	0	0		
2000–01	Manchester U	0	0		
2001–02	Manchester U	0	0		
From Hereford U					
2004–05	Yeovil T	40	1		
2005–06	Yeovil T	1	0	41	1
2005–06	*Cheltenham T*	3	0	3	0
2005–06	*Scunthorpe U*	15	0	15	0
2006–07	Stockport Co	25	3		
2007–08	Stockport Co	28	3		
2008–09	Stockport Co	27	0		
2009–10	Stockport Co	24	2	104	8
2009–10	*Norwich C*	12	1	12	1
2010–11	Swindon T	35	3	35	3
2010–11	Colchester U	0	0		
2011–12	Colchester U	14	0		
2012–13	Colchester U	22	2	36	2
2012–13	Rochdale	14	0		
2013–14	Rochdale	42	4		
2014–15	Rochdale	32	1		
2015–16	Rochdale	30	1	118	8

SYERS, Dave (M)   141   23
H: 6 0 W: 11 07 b.Leeds 30-11-87

2010–11	Bradford C	37	8		
2011–12	Bradford C	18	2	55	10
2012–13	Doncaster R	32	3		
2013–14	Doncaster R	2	0	34	3
2013–14	Scunthorpe U	37	10		
2014–15	Scunthorpe U	6	0		
2015–16	Scunthorpe U	3	0	46	10
2015–16	Rochdale	6	0	6	0

TANSER, Scott (D)   38   1
b.Blackpool 23-10-94

2012–13	Rochdale	1	0		
2013–14	Rochdale	0	0		
2014–15	Rochdale	30	1		
2015–16	Rochdale	7	0	38	1

VINCENTI, Peter (F)   226   41
H: 6 2 W: 11 13 b.St Peter 7-7-86

2007–08	Millwall	0	0		
2010–11	Stevenage	5	1	5	1
2010–11	Aldershot T	23	6		
2011–12	Aldershot T	42	6		
2012–13	Aldershot T	39	2	104	14
2013–14	Rochdale	42	5		
2014–15	Rochdale	37	13		
2015–16	Rochdale	38	8	117	26

Scholars
Berry, Tyler James; Chea, Rapheal; Coyne, Louis Patrick; Evans, Declan; Gillam, Matthew Rhys; Hollins, Andrew James; Kisimba, Kisimba Arnon; Lenehan, Jack Joseph; Mata Anse, Japhet; Piggott, Joe; Pratt, Harry Partick; Prescott, Jordan Paul; Price, Kieran Thomas; Schorah, Callum Patrick; Smalley, Brandon Joe; Stewart, Jack Mathew.

ROTHERHAM U (71)

BAILEY-KING, Darnell (M)   1   0
b. 17-5-98

2015–16	Rotherham U	1	0	1	0

BECCHIO, Luciano (F)   313   109
H: 6 2 W: 13 05 b.Cordoba 28-12-83

2003–04	Mallorca B	0	0		
2004–05	Mallorca B	0	0		
2004–05	Murcia	16	3	16	3
2005–06	Terrassa	24	2	24	2
2006–07	Barcelona Ath	10	0	10	0
2006–07	Merida	12	5		
2007–08	Merida	38	22	50	27
2008–09	Leeds U	45	15		
2009–10	Leeds U	37	15		
2010–11	Leeds U	41	19		
2011–12	Leeds U	41	11		
2012–13	Leeds U	26	15	190	75
2012–13	Norwich C	8	0		
2013–14	Norwich C	5	0		
2014–15	Norwich C	0	0	13	0
2014–15	*Rotherham U*	5	2		
2015	Belgrano Cordoba	3	0	3	0
2015–16	Rotherham U	2	0	7	2

BELAID, Aymen (D)   99   4
b. 2-1-89
Internationals: Tunisia Full caps.

2010–11	Grenoble	0	0	8	0
2011–12	Etoile du Sahel	13	2		
2012–13	Etoile du Sahel	7	0	20	2
2013–14	Loko Plovdiv	12	1	12	1
2013–14	Levski Sofia	9	0		
2014–15	Levski Sofia	28	0		
2015–16	Levski Sofia	19	1	56	1
2015–16	Rotherham U	3	0	3	0

BEST, Leon (F)   270   58
H: 6 1 W: 13 03 b.Nottingham 19-9-86
Internationals: Republic of Ireland U21, Full caps.

2004–05	Southampton	3	0		
2004–05	*QPR*	5	0	5	0
2005–06	Southampton	3	0		
2005–06	*Sheffield W*	13	2		
2006–07	Southampton	9	4	15	4
2006–07	*Bournemouth*	15	3	15	3
2006–07	*Yeovil T*	15	10	15	10
2007–08	Coventry C	34	8		
2008–09	Coventry C	31	2		
2009–10	Coventry C	27	9	92	19
2009–10	Newcastle U	13	0		
2010–11	Newcastle U	11	6		
2011–12	Newcastle U	18	4	42	10
2012–13	Blackburn R	6	0		
2013–14	Blackburn R	8	2		
2013–14	*Sheffield W*	15	4	28	6
2014–15	Blackburn R	0	0		
2014–15	*Derby Co*	15	0	15	0
2014–15	*Brighton & HA*	13	0	13	0
2015–16	Blackburn R	0	0	14	2
2015–16	Rotherham U	16	4	16	4

BROADFOOT, Kirk (D)   354   17
H: 6 3 W: 13 13 b.Irvine 8-8-84
Internationals: Scotland U21, B, Full caps.

2002–03	St Mirren	23	1		
2003–04	St Mirren	31	3		
2004–05	St Mirren	36	4		
2005–06	St Mirren	27	2		
2006–07	St Mirren	37	3	154	13
2007–08	Rangers	15	1		
2008–09	Rangers	27	0		
2009–10	Rangers	12	0		
2010–11	Rangers	8	0		
2011–12	Rangers	16	0	78	1
2012–13	Blackpool	32	2		
2013–14	Blackpool	33	0	65	2
2014–15	Rotherham U	25	0		
2015–16	Rotherham U	32	1	57	1

BUXTON, Lewis (D)   346   7
H: 6 1 W: 13 11 b.Newport (IW) 10-12-83

2000–01	Portsmouth	0	0		
2001–02	Portsmouth	29	0		
2002–03	Portsmouth	5	0		
2002–03	*Exeter C*	4	0	4	0
2003–04	*Bournemouth*	17	0		
2003–04	Portsmouth	0	0		
2003–04	*Bournemouth*	26	0	43	0
2004–05	Portsmouth	0	0	30	0
2004–05	Stoke C	16	0		
2005–06	Stoke C	32	1		
2006–07	Stoke C	1	0		
2007–08	Stoke C	4	0		
2008–09	Stoke C	0	0	53	1

2008–09	Sheffield W	32	1		
2009–10	Sheffield W	28	0		
2010–11	Sheffield W	30	1		
2011–12	Sheffield W	37	1		
2012–13	Sheffield W	40	0		
2013–14	Sheffield W	20	3		
2014–15	Sheffield W	9	0	196	6
2015–16	Rotherham U	20	0	20	0

CAIRNS, Alex (G)   1   0
H: 6 0 W: 11 05 b.Doncaster 4-1-93

2011–12	Leeds U	1	0		
2012–13	Leeds U	0	0		
2013–14	Leeds U	0	0		
2014–15	Leeds U	0	0	1	0
2015–16	Chesterfield	0	0		
2015–16	Rotherham U	0	0		

CAMP, Lee (G)   429   0
H: 5 11 W: 11 11 b.Derby 22-8-84
Internationals: England U21. Northern Ireland Full caps.

2002–03	Derby Co	1	0		
2003–04	Derby Co	0	0		
2003–04	*QPR*	12	0		
2004–05	Derby Co	45	0		
2005–06	Derby Co	40	0		
2006–07	Derby Co	3	0	89	0
2006–07	*Norwich C*	3	0		
2006–07	QPR	11	0		
2007–08	QPR	46	0		
2008–09	QPR	4	0	73	0
2008–09	Nottingham F	15	0		
2009–10	Nottingham F	45	0		
2010–11	Nottingham F	46	0		
2011–12	Nottingham F	46	0		
2012–13	Nottingham F	26	0	178	0
2012–13	*Norwich C*	3	0	6	0
2013–14	WBA	0	0		
2013–14	*Bournemouth*	33	0		
2014–15	Bournemouth	9	0		
2015–16	Bournemouth	0	0	42	0
2015–16	Rotherham U	41	0	41	0

CLARKE-HARRIS, Jonson (F)   124   21
H: 6 0 W: 11 01 b.Leicester 21-7-94

2012–13	Peterborough U	0	0		
2012–13	*Southend U*	3	0	3	0
2012–13	*Bury*	12	4	12	4
2013–14	Oldham Ath	40	6		
2014–15	Oldham Ath	5	1	45	7
2014–15	Rotherham U	15	3		
2014–15	*Milton Keynes D*	5	0	5	0
2014–15	*Doncaster R*	9	1	9	1
2015–16	Rotherham U	35	6	50	9

COLLIN, Adam (G)   207   0
H: 6 2 W: 12 00 b.Penrith 9-12-84

2003–04	Newcastle U	0	0		
2003–04	*Oldham Ath*	0	0		
From Workington					
2009–10	Carlisle U	29	0		
2010–11	Carlisle U	46	0		
2011–12	Carlisle U	46	0		
2012–13	Carlisle U	12	0	133	0
2013–14	Rotherham U	34	0		
2014–15	Rotherham U	36	0		
2015–16	Rotherham U	1	0	71	0
2015–16	*Aberdeen*	3	0	3	0

COLLINS, Danny (D)   333   12
H: 6 2 W: 11 13 b.Buckley 6-8-80
Internationals: England C. Wales Full caps.

2004–05	Chester C	12	1	12	1
2004–05	Sunderland	14	0		
2005–06	Sunderland	23	1		
2006–07	Sunderland	38	0		
2007–08	Sunderland	36	1		
2008–09	Sunderland	35	1		
2009–10	Sunderland	3	0	149	3
2009–10	Stoke C	25	0		
2010–11	Stoke C	25	0		
2011–12	Stoke C	0	0	50	0
2011–12	*Ipswich T*	16	3	16	3
2011–12	*West Ham U*	11	1	11	1
2012–13	Nottingham F	40	0		
2013–14	Nottingham F	23	1		
2014–15	Nottingham F	8	1	71	2
2015–16	Rotherham U	24	2	24	2

DAWSON, Chris (M)   4   0
b.Dewsbury 2-9-94
Internationals: Wales U21.

2012–13	Leeds U	1	0		
2013–14	Leeds U	0	0		
2014–15	Leeds U	3	0		
2015–16	Leeds U	0	0	4	0
2015–16	Rotherham U	0	0		

DERBYSHIRE, Matt (F) — 273 60
H: 5 10 W: 11 01 b.Gt Harwood 14-4-86
Internationals: England U21.

Season	Club				
2003–04	Blackburn R	0	0		
2004–05	Blackburn R	1	0		
2005–06	Blackburn R	0	0		
2005–06	Plymouth Arg	12	0	12	0
2005–06	Wrexham	16	10	16	10
2006–07	Blackburn R	22	5		
2007–08	Blackburn R	23	3		
2008–09	Blackburn R	17	2	63	10
2008–09	Olympiacos	7	5		
2009–10	Olympiacos	19	6		
2010–11	Olympiacos	0	0	26	11
2010–11	Birmingham C	13	0	13	0
2011–12	Nottingham F	15	1		
2012–13	Nottingham F	0	0		
2012–13	Oldham Ath	18	4	18	4
2012–13	Blackpool	12	0		
2013–14	Blackpool	0	0	12	0
2013–14	Nottingham F	29	7	44	8
2014–15	Rotherham U	34	9		
2015–16	Rotherham U	35	8	69	17

DOYLEY, Lloyd (D) — 398 2
H: 5 10 W: 12 13 b.Whitechapel 1-12-82
Internationals: Jamaica Full caps.

Season	Club				
2000–01	Watford	0	0		
2001–02	Watford	20	0		
2002–03	Watford	22	0		
2003–04	Watford	9	0		
2004–05	Watford	29	0		
2005–06	Watford	44	0		
2006–07	Watford	21	0		
2007–08	Watford	36	0		
2008–09	Watford	37	0		
2009–10	Watford	44	1		
2010–11	Watford	36	0		
2011–12	Watford	34	1		
2012–13	Watford	24	0		
2013–14	Watford	6	0		
2015–16	Watford	0	0	395	2
2015–16	Rotherham U	3	0	3	0

FRECKLINGTON, Lee (M) — 343 52
H: 5 8 W: 11 00 b.Lincoln 8-9-85
Internationals: Republic of Ireland B.

Season	Club				
2003–04	Lincoln C	0	0		
2004–05	Lincoln C	3	0		
2005–06	Lincoln C	18	2		
2006–07	Lincoln C	42	8		
2007–08	Lincoln C	34	4		
2008–09	Lincoln C	27	7	124	21
2008–09	Peterborough U	7	0		
2009–10	Peterborough U	35	2		
2010–11	Peterborough U	9	1		
2011–12	Peterborough U	37	5		
2012–13	Peterborough U	5	0	93	8
2012–13	Rotherham U	31	6		
2013–14	Rotherham U	39	10		
2014–15	Rotherham U	29	2		
2015–16	Rotherham U	27	5	126	23

GREEN, Paul (M) — 439 42
H: 5 9 W: 10 02 b.Pontefract 10-4-83
Internationals: Republic of Ireland Full caps.

Season	Club				
2003–04	Doncaster R	43	8		
2004–05	Doncaster R	42	7		
2005–06	Doncaster R	34	3		
2006–07	Doncaster R	41	2		
2007–08	Doncaster R	38	5	198	25
2008–09	Derby Co	29	3		
2009–10	Derby Co	33	2		
2010–11	Derby Co	36	2		
2011–12	Derby Co	27	1	125	8
2012–13	Leeds U	32	4		
2013–14	Leeds U	9	0	41	4
2013–14	Ipswich T	14	2	14	2
2014–15	Rotherham U	37	3		
2015–16	Rotherham U	24	0	61	3

HALFORD, Greg (D) — 412 45
H: 6 4 W: 12 10 b.Chelmsford 8-12-84
Internationals: England U20.

Season	Club				
2002–03	Colchester U	18	4		
2003–04	Colchester U	44	4		
2004–05	Colchester U	45	7		
2005–06	Colchester U	28	3	136	18
2006–07	Colchester U	1	0		
2006–07	Reading	3	0	3	0
2007–08	Sunderland	8	0		
2007–08	Charlton Ath	16	2	16	2
2008–09	Sunderland	0	0		
2008–09	Sheffield U	41	4	41	4
2009–10	Sunderland	0	0	8	0
2009–10	Wolverhampton W	15	0		
2010–11	Wolverhampton W	2	0	17	0
2010–11	Portsmouth	33	5		
2011–12	Portsmouth	42	7	75	12
2012–13	Nottingham F	37	3		
2013–14	Nottingham F	36	4		
2014–15	Nottingham F	0	0	73	7
2014–15	Brighton & HA	19	0	19	0
2015–16	Rotherham U	21	2	21	2
2015–16	Birmingham C	3	0	3	0

KELLY, Stephen (D) — 257 3
H: 6 0 W: 12 04 b.Dublin 6-9-83
Internationals: Republic of Ireland U16, U20, U21, Full caps.

Season	Club				
2000–01	Tottenham H	0	0		
2001–02	Tottenham H	0	0		
2002–03	Tottenham H	0	0		
2002–03	Southend U	10	0	10	0
2002–03	QPR	7	0	7	0
2003–04	Tottenham H	11	0		
2003–04	Watford	13	0	13	0
2004–05	Tottenham H	17	2		
2005–06	Tottenham H	9	0	37	2
2006–07	Birmingham C	36	0		
2007–08	Birmingham C	38	0		
2008–09	Birmingham C	5	0		
2008–09	Stoke C	6	0	6	0
2009–10	Birmingham C	0	0	79	0
2009–10	Fulham	8	0		
2010–11	Fulham	10	0		
2011–12	Fulham	24	0		
2012–13	Fulham	2	0	44	0
2012–13	Reading	16	0		
2013–14	Reading	15	1		
2014–15	Reading	15	0	46	1
2015–16	Rotherham U	15	0	15	0

KENNY, Paddy (G) — 567 0
H: 6 1 W: 14 01 b.Halifax 17-5-78
Internationals: Republic of Ireland Full caps.

Season	Club				
1998–99	Bury	0	0		
1999–2000	Bury	46	0		
2000–01	Bury	46	0		
2001–02	Bury	41	0		
2002–03	Bury	0	0		
2002–03	Sheffield U	45	0		
2003–04	Sheffield U	27	0		
2004–05	Sheffield U	40	0		
2005–06	Sheffield U	46	0		
2006–07	Sheffield U	34	0		
2007–08	Sheffield U	40	0		
2008–09	Sheffield U	44	0		
2009–10	Sheffield U	2	0	278	0
2010–11	QPR	44	0		
2011–12	QPR	33	0	77	0
2012–13	Leeds U	46	0		
2013–14	Leeds U	30	0	76	0
2014–15	Bolton W	0	0		
2014–15	Oldham Ath	3	0	3	0
2014–15	Ipswich T	0	0		
2015–16	Bury	0	0	133	0
2015–16	Rotherham U	0	0		

LEDESMA, Emmanuel (M) — 136 17
H: 5 11 W: 12 02 b.Quilmes 24-5-88

Season	Club				
2007–08	Genoa	1	0	1	0
2008–09	Salernitana	8	1	8	1
2008–09	QPR	17	1	17	1
2009–10	Novara	8	1	8	1
2010–11	Crotone	10	0	10	0
2010–11	Walsall	10	1		
2011–12	Walsall	10	4	20	5
2012–13	Middlesbrough	28	2		
2013–14	Middlesbrough	27	6		
2014–15	Middlesbrough	1	0	56	8
2014–15	Rotherham U	7	1		
2014–15	Brighton & HA	4	0	4	0
2015–16	Rotherham U	5	0	12	1

LENIGHAN, Simon (M) — 0 0
b. 13-5-94

Season	Club		
2012–13	Leeds U	0	0
2013–14	Leeds U	0	0
2015–16	Rotherham U	0	0

MATTOCK, Joe (D) — 222 5
H: 5 11 W: 12 05 b.Leicester 15-5-90
Internationals: England U17, U19, U21.

Season	Club				
2006–07	Leicester C	4	0		
2007–08	Leicester C	31	0		
2008–09	Leicester C	31	1		
2009–10	Leicester C	0	0	66	1
2009–10	WBA	29	0		
2010–11	WBA	0	0		
2010–11	Sheffield U	13	0	13	0
2011–12	WBA	0	0		
2011–12	Portsmouth	7	0	7	0
2011–12	Brighton & HA	15	1	15	1
2012–13	Sheffield W	7	0		
2013–14	Sheffield W	23	2		
2014–15	Sheffield W	27	0	57	2
2015–16	Rotherham U	35	1	35	1

NEWELL, Joe (M) — 131 8
H: 5 11 W: 11 02 b.Tamworth 15-3-93

Season	Club				
2010–11	Peterborough U	2	0		
2011–12	Peterborough U	14	1		
2012–13	Peterborough U	30	0		
2013–14	Peterborough U	11	0		
2014–15	Peterborough U	39	2	96	3
2015–16	Rotherham U	35	5	35	5

RICHARDSON, Frazer (D) — 318 5
H: 5 11 W: 11 12 b.Rotherham 29-10-82

Season	Club				
1999–2000	Leeds U	0	0		
2000–01	Leeds U	0	0		
2001–02	Leeds U	0	0		
2002–03	Leeds U	0	0		
2002–03	Stoke C	7	0		
2003–04	Leeds U	4	0		
2003–04	Stoke C	6	1	13	1
2004–05	Leeds U	38	1		
2005–06	Leeds U	23	1		
2006–07	Leeds U	22	0		
2007–08	Leeds U	39	1		
2008–09	Leeds U	23	0	149	3
2009–10	Charlton Ath	38	1	38	1
2010–11	Southampton	21	0		
2011–12	Southampton	34	0		
2012–13	Southampton	5	0	60	0
2013–14	Middlesbrough	11	0	11	0
2013–14	Ipswich T	7	0	7	0
2014–15	Rotherham U	23	0		
2015–16	Rotherham U	17	0	40	0

SMALLWOOD, Richard (M) — 163 5
H: 5 11 W: 11 05 b.Redcar 29-12-90
Internationals: England U18.

Season	Club				
2008–09	Middlesbrough	0	0		
2009–10	Middlesbrough	0	0		
2010–11	Middlesbrough	13	1		
2011–12	Middlesbrough	13	0		
2012–13	Middlesbrough	22	2		
2013–14	Middlesbrough	13	0		
2013–14	Rotherham U	18	0		
2014–15	Middlesbrough	0	0	61	3
2014–15	Rotherham U	41	1		
2015–16	Rotherham U	43	1	102	2

THOMAS, Jerome (M) — 237 22
H: 5 9 W: 11 09 b.Wembley 23-3-83
Internationals: England U19, U20, U21.

Season	Club				
2001–02	Arsenal	0	0		
2001–02	QPR	4	1		
2002–03	Arsenal	0	0		
2002–03	QPR	6	2	10	3
2003–04	Arsenal	0	0		
2003–04	Charlton Ath	1	0		
2004–05	Charlton Ath	24	3		
2005–06	Charlton Ath	25	1		
2006–07	Charlton Ath	20	3		
2007–08	Charlton Ath	32	0		
2008–09	Charlton Ath	1	0	103	7
2008–09	Portsmouth	3	0		
2009–10	Portsmouth	0	0	3	0
2009–10	WBA	27	7		
2010–11	WBA	33	3		
2011–12	WBA	29	1		
2012–13	WBA	10	0	99	11
2012–13	Leeds U	6	1	6	1
2013–14	Crystal Palace	9	0		
2014–15	Crystal Palace	1	0	10	0
2015–16	Rotherham U	6	0	6	0

THORPE, Tom (D) — 17 2
H: 6 0 W: 14 00 b.Manchester 13-1-93
Internationals: England U16, U17, U18, U19, U20, U21.

Season	Club				
2010–11	Manchester U	0	0		
2011–12	Manchester U	0	0		
2012–13	Manchester U	0	0		
2013–14	Manchester U	0	0		
2013–14	Birmingham C	6	0	6	0
2014–15	Manchester U	1	0	1	0
2015–16	Rotherham U	7	2	7	2
2015–16	Bradford C	3	0	3	0

WARD, Danny (M) — 209 33
H: 5 11 W: 12 05 b.Bradford 11-12-91

Season	Club				
2008–09	Bolton W	0	0		
2009–10	Bolton W	2	0		
2009–10	Swindon T	28	7	28	7
2010–11	Bolton W	0	0		
2010–11	Coventry C	5	0	5	0
2010–11	Huddersfield T	7	3		
2011–12	Huddersfield T	39	4		
2012–13	Huddersfield T	28	2		
2013–14	Huddersfield T	38	10		
2014–15	Huddersfield T	12	0	124	19

2014–15	*Rotherham U*	16	3		
2015–16	Rotherham U	34	4	**50**	**7**

WARREN, Mason (D)   **0**   **0**
b. 28-3-97

2015–16	Rotherham U	0	0		

WOOD, Richard (D)   **349**   **18**
H: 6 3   W: 12 13   b.Ossett 5-7-85

2002–03	Sheffield W	3	1		
2003–04	Sheffield W	12	0		
2004–05	Sheffield W	34	1		
2005–06	Sheffield W	30	1		
2006–07	Sheffield W	12	0		
2007–08	Sheffield W	27	2		
2008–09	Sheffield W	42	0		
2009–10	Sheffield W	11	2	**171**	**7**
2009–10	Coventry C	24	3		
2010–11	Coventry C	40	1		
2011–12	Coventry C	17	1		
2012–13	Coventry C	36	3	**117**	**8**
2013–14	Charlton Ath	21	0	**21**	**0**
2014–15	Rotherham U	6	0		
2014–15	*Crawley T*	10	3	**10**	**3**
2015–16	Rotherham U	13	0	**19**	**0**
2015–16	*Fleetwood T*	6	0	**6**	**0**
2015–16	*Chesterfield*	5	0	**5**	**0**

YATES, Jerry (M)   **1**   **0**
H: 5 9   W: 10 10   b.Doncaster 10-11-96

2014–15	Rotherham U	1	0		
2015–16	Rotherham U	0	0	**1**	**0**

Players retained or with offer of contract
Bailey, Fabian Paul Richard; Bilboe,
Laurence Sidney; Muskwe, Kudakwashe;
Rose, Thomas Andrew.

Scholars
Abraham, J-Cee; Adeyemi, Trae
Abdulrasheed; Dickinson, Ross; Fidler, Harry
Colin; Peace-McDonald, Bradley William;
Potts, Brandon Russell; Redmayne, Alaster
Kenneth; Saxton, Adam Lewis; Smalley,
Daniel Matthew; Wiles, Benjamin Jack.

SCUNTHORPE U (72)

ADELAKUN, Hakeeb (F)   **83**   **10**
H: 6 3   W: 11 11   b.Hackney 11-6-96

2012–13	Scunthorpe U	2	0		
2013–14	Scunthorpe U	28	2		
2014–15	Scunthorpe U	32	6		
2015–16	Scunthorpe U	21	2	**83**	**10**

ANYON, Joe (G)   **19**   **0**
H: 6 4   W: 14 01   b.Blackpool 29-12-86
Internationals: England U16.

2006–07	Port Vale	0	0		
2010–11	Lincoln C	0	0		
2010–11	*Morecambe*	0	0		
2012–13	Shrewsbury T	0	0		
2013–14	Shrewsbury T	11	0		
2014–15	Shrewsbury T	0	0	**11**	**0**
2014–15	Scunthorpe U	0	0		
2015–16	Scunthorpe U	8	0	**8**	**0**

ASSENSO, Isaac (M)   **0**   **0**
b. 30-5-97

2015–16	Scunthorpe U	0	0

BISHOP, Neil (M)   **363**   **20**
H: 6 1   W: 12 10   b.Stockton 7-8-81
Internationals: England C.

2007–08	Barnet	39	2		
2008–09	Barnet	44	1	**83**	**3**
2009–10	Notts Co	43	1		
2010–11	Notts Co	43	1		
2011–12	Notts Co	41	2		
2012–13	Notts Co	41	7	**168**	**11**
2013–14	Blackpool	35	1	**35**	**1**
2014–15	Scunthorpe U	35	4		
2015–16	Scunthorpe U	42	1	**77**	**5**

BOYCE, Andrew (D)   **42**   **1**
H: 6 3   W: 12 08   b.Doncaster 5-11-89

2013–14	Scunthorpe U	2	0		
2014–15	Scunthorpe U	29	1		
2015–16	Scunthorpe U	0	0	**31**	**1**
2015–16	*Hartlepool U*	8	0	**8**	**0**
2015–16	Notts Co	3	0	**3**	**0**

BURDETT, Noel (F)   **0**   **0**
b. 13-11-97

2013–14	Scunthorpe U	0	0
2014–15	Scunthorpe U	0	0
2015–16	Scunthorpe U	0	0

CANAVAN, Niall (D)   **168**   **16**
H: 6 3   W: 12 00   b.Guiseley 11-4-91
Internationals: Republic of Ireland U21.

2009–10	Scunthorpe U	7	1		
2010–11	Scunthorpe U	8	0		
2010–11	*Shrewsbury T*	3	0	**3**	**0**
2011–12	Scunthorpe U	12	1		
2012–13	Scunthorpe U	40	6		
2013–14	Scunthorpe U	45	4		
2014–15	Scunthorpe U	32	3		
2015–16	Scunthorpe U	10	0	**154**	**15**
2015–16	*Rochdale*	11	1	**11**	**1**

CLARKE, Jordan (D)   **186**   **8**
H: 6 0   W: 11 02   b.Coventry 19-11-91
Internationals: England U19, U20.

2009–10	Coventry C	12	0		
2010–11	Coventry C	21	1		
2011–12	Coventry C	19	1		
2012–13	Coventry C	20	0		
2013–14	Coventry C	41	1		
2014–15	Coventry C	11	1	**124**	**4**
2014–15	*Yeovil T*	5	2	**5**	**2**
2014–15	Scunthorpe U	24	0		
2015–16	Scunthorpe U	33	2	**57**	**2**

DANIELS, Luke (G)   **159**   **0**
H: 6 1   W: 12 10   b.Bolton 5-1-88
Internationals: England U19.

2006–07	WBA	0	0		
2007–08	*Motherwell*	2	0	**2**	**0**
2007–08	WBA	0	0		
2008–09	WBA	0	0		
2008–09	*Shrewsbury T*	38	0	**38**	**0**
2009–10	WBA	0	0		
2009–10	*Tranmere R*	37	0	**37**	**0**
2010–11	WBA	0	0		
2010–11	*Charlton Ath*	0	0		
2010–11	*Rochdale*	1	0	**1**	**0**
2010–11	*Bristol R*	9	0	**9**	**0**
2011–12	WBA	0	0		
2011–12	*Southend U*	9	0	**9**	**0**
2012–13	WBA	0	0		
2013–14	WBA	1	0		
2014–15	WBA	0	0	**1**	**0**
2014–15	Scunthorpe U	23	0		
2015–16	Scunthorpe U	39	0	**62**	**0**

DAWSON, Stephen (M)   **399**   **18**
H: 5 9   W: 11 09   b.Dublin 4-12-85
Internationals: Republic of Ireland U21.

2003–04	Leicester C	0	0		
2004–05	Leicester C	0	0		
2005–06	Mansfield T	40	1		
2006–07	Mansfield T	34	1		
2007–08	Mansfield T	43	2	**117**	**4**
2008–09	Bury	43	2		
2009–10	Bury	45	4	**88**	**6**
2010–11	Leyton Orient	40	2		
2011–12	Leyton Orient	20	1	**60**	**3**
2011–12	Barnsley	12	0		
2012–13	Barnsley	32	4		
2013–14	Barnsley	37	1	**81**	**5**
2014–15	Rochdale	30	0	**30**	**0**
2015–16	Scunthorpe U	23	0	**23**	**0**

DYCHE, Jack (D)   **0**   **0**
b. 11-10-97

2014–15	Scunthorpe U	0	0
2015–16	Scunthorpe U	0	0

GOODE, Charlie (D)   **10**   **1**
b. 3-8-95
Internationals: England C.

2015–16	Scunthorpe U	10	1	**10**	**1**

HOPPER, Tom (F)   **68**   **15**
H: 6 1   W: 12 00   b.Boston 14-12-93
Internationals: England U18.

2011–12	Leicester C	0	0		
2012–13	Leicester C	0	0		
2012–13	*Bury*	22	3	**22**	**3**
2013–14	Leicester C	0	0		
2014–15	Leicester C	0	0		
2014–15	*Scunthorpe U*	12	4		
2015–16	Scunthorpe U	34	8	**46**	**12**

KING, Jack (M)   **114**   **8**
H: 6 0   W: 11 11   b.Oxford 20-8-85

2012–13	Preston NE	36	4		
2013–14	Preston NE	24	2		
2014–15	Preston NE	18	1	**78**	**7**
2015–16	Scunthorpe U	36	1	**36**	**1**

LAIRD, Scott (D)   **206**   **19**
H: 5 11   W: 11 05   b.Taunton 15-5-88
Internationals: Scotland U16. England C.

2006–07	Plymouth Arg	0	0
2007–08	Plymouth Arg	0	0
2010–11	Stevenage	44	4

2011–12	Stevenage	46	8	**90**	**12**
2012–13	Preston NE	19	4		
2013–14	Preston NE	34	1		
2014–15	Preston NE	31	0	**84**	**5**
2015–16	Scunthorpe U	32	2	**32**	**2**

LEDGER, Ben (G)   **0**   **0**
b. 2-12-97

2015–16	Scunthorpe U	0	0

MADDEN, Patrick (F)   **256**   **83**
H: 6 0   W: 11 13   b.Dublin 4-3-90
Internationals: Republic of Ireland U19, U21,
U23, Full caps.

2008	Bohemians	18	4		
2009	Bohemians	2	0		
2009	Shelbourne	13	6	**13**	**6**
2010	Bohemians	34	10	**54**	**14**
2010–11	Carlisle U	13	0		
2011–12	Carlisle U	18	1		
2012–13	Carlisle U	1	1	**32**	**2**
2012–13	Yeovil T	35	22		
2013–14	Yeovil T	9	0	**44**	**22**
2013–14	Scunthorpe U	21	5		
2014–15	Scunthorpe U	46	14		
2015–16	Scunthorpe U	46	20	**113**	**39**

McALLISTER, Sean (M)   **185**   **5**
H: 5 8   W: 10 07   b.Bolton 15-8-87

2005–06	Sheffield W	2	0		
2006–07	Sheffield W	6	1		
2007–08	Sheffield W	8	0		
2007–08	*Mansfield T*	7	0	**7**	**0**
2007–08	*Bury*	0	0		
2008–09	Sheffield W	40	3		
2009–10	Sheffield W	12	0	**68**	**4**
2010–11	Shrewsbury T	18	0		
2011–12	Shrewsbury T	17	1	**35**	**1**
2012–13	Port Vale	2	0	**2**	**0**
2014–15	Scunthorpe U	39	0		
2015–16	Scunthorpe U	11	0	**73**	**0**

McSHEFFREY, Gary (F)   **468**   **103**
H: 5 8   W: 10 06   b.Coventry 13-8-82
Internationals: England U18, U20.

1998–99	Coventry C	1	0		
1999–2000	Coventry C	3	0		
2000–01	Coventry C	0	0		
2001–02	*Stockport Co*	5	1	**5**	**1**
2001–02	Coventry C	8	1		
2002–03	Coventry C	29	4		
2003–04	Coventry C	19	11		
2003–04	Luton T	18	9		
2004–05	Luton T	5	1	**23**	**10**
2004–05	Coventry C	37	12		
2005–06	Coventry C	43	15		
2006–07	Coventry C	3	1		
2006–07	Birmingham C	40	13		
2007–08	Birmingham C	32	3		
2008–09	Birmingham C	6	0		
2008–09	*Nottingham F*	4	0	**4**	**0**
2009–10	Birmingham C	5	0	**83**	**16**
2009–10	*Leeds U*	10	1	**10**	**1**
2010–11	Coventry C	33	8		
2011–12	Coventry C	39	8		
2012–13	Coventry C	32	1		
2013–14	Coventry C	0	0	**247**	**61**
2013–14	Chesterfield	9	1	**9**	**1**
2014–15	Scunthorpe U	13	0		
2014–15	Scunthorpe U	41	7		
2015–16	Scunthorpe U	26	5	**80**	**12**
2015–16	*Doncaster R*	7	1	**7**	**1**

MIRFIN, David (D)   **402**   **18**
H: 6 3   W: 13 00   b.Sheffield 18-4-85

2002–03	Huddersfield T	1	0		
2003–04	Huddersfield T	21	2		
2004–05	Huddersfield T	41	4		
2005–06	Huddersfield T	31	1		
2006–07	Huddersfield T	38	1		
2007–08	Huddersfield T	29	1	**161**	**9**
2008–09	Scunthorpe U	33	0		
2009–10	Scunthorpe U	37	1		
2010–11	Scunthorpe U	23	3		
2011–12	Watford	4	0	**4**	**0**
2011–12	*Scunthorpe U*	19	1		
2012–13	Scunthorpe U	30	0		
2013–14	Scunthorpe U	45	2		
2014–15	Scunthorpe U	0	0		
2014–15	*Hartlepool U*	15	0	**15**	**0**
2015–16	Scunthorpe U	35	2	**222**	**9**

MOSANYA, Reece (M)   **0**   **0**

2014–15	Scunthorpe U	0	0
2015–16	Scunthorpe U	0	0

NESS, Jamie (M)   90   4
H: 6 2   W: 10 13   b.Irvine 2-3-91
Internationals: Scotland U17, U19, U21.

2010–11	Rangers	11	0	
2011–12	Rangers	5	1	16 1
2012–13	Stoke C	0	0	
2013–14	Stoke C	0	0	
2013–14	*Leyton Orient*	13	1	13 1
2014–15	Stoke C	0	0	
2014–15	*Crewe Alex*	34	2	34 2
2015–16	Scunthorpe U	27	0	27 0

SUTTON, Levi (M)   1   0
b.24-3-96

2014–15	Scunthorpe U	0	0	
2015–16	Scunthorpe U	1	0	1 0

TOWNSEND, Conor (D)   75   2
H: 5 4   W: 9 11   b.Hessle 4-3-93

2011–12	Hull C	0	0	
2012–13	Hull C	0	0	
2012–13	*Chesterfield*	20	1	20 1
2013–14	Hull C	0	0	
2013–14	*Carlisle U*	12	0	12 0
2014–15	Hull C	0	0	
2014–15	*Dundee U*	17	0	17 0
2014–15	*Scunthorpe U*	6	0	
2015–16	Hull C	0	0	
2015–16	Scunthorpe U	20	1	26 1

VAN VEEN, Kevin (F)   101   41
H: 6 1   W: 11 11   b.Eindhoven 1-6-91

2013–14	JVC Cuyk	29	20	29 20
2014–15	FC Oss	20	16	20 16
2014–15	Scunthorpe U	20	2	
2015–16	Scunthorpe U	20	2	40 4
2015–16	*Cambuur Leeuwarden*	12	1	12 1

VOSE, Dominic (M)   38   0
H: 5 8   W: 11 03   b.Lambeth 23-11-93

2010–11	West Ham U	0	0	
2011–12	West Ham U	0	0	
2012–13	Barnet	2	0	2 0
2013–14	Colchester U	27	0	
2014–15	Colchester U	7	0	34 0

From Wrexham.

2015–16	Scunthorpe U	2	0	2 0

WEAVER, Pat (G)   0   0
H: 6 0   W: 12 04   b.Kingston upon Hull 4-1-96

2014–15	Scunthorpe U	0	0	
2015–16	Scunthorpe U	0	0	

WILLIAMS, Luke (F)   82   11
H: 6 1   W: 11 08   b.Middlesbrough 11-6-93
Internationals: England U17, U19, U20.

2009–10	Middlesbrough	4	0	
2010–11	Middlesbrough	6	0	
2011–12	Middlesbrough	0	0	
2012–13	Middlesbrough	11	2	
2013–14	Middlesbrough	9	0	
2013–14	*Hartlepool U*	7	2	7 2
2014–15	Middlesbrough	4	0	34 2
2014–15	*Scunthorpe U*	6	2	
2014–15	*Coventry C*	5	0	5 0
2014–15	*Peterborough U*	2	0	2 0
2015–16	Scunthorpe U	28	5	34 7

WISEMAN, Scott (D)   321   5
H: 6 0   W: 11 06   b.Hull 9-10-85
Internationals: England U20. Gilbraltar Full caps.

2003–04	Hull C	2	0	
2004–05	Hull C	3	0	
2004–05	*Boston U*	2	0	2 0
2005–06	Hull C	11	0	
2006–07	Hull C	0	0	16 0
2006–07	*Rotherham U*	18	1	18 1
2006–07	*Darlington*	10	0	
2007–08	Darlington	7	0	17 0
2008–09	Rochdale	32	0	
2009–10	Rochdale	36	1	
2010–11	Rochdale	37	0	105 1
2011–12	Barnsley	43	1	
2012–13	Barnsley	36	0	
2013–14	Barnsley	23	0	102 1
2013–14	*Preston NE*	15	0	
2014–15	Preston NE	22	2	37 2
2015–16	Scunthorpe U	24	0	24 0

WOOTTON, Kyle (M)   32   4
H: 6 2   W: 12 04   b.11-10-96

2014–15	Scunthorpe U	12	1	
2015–16	Scunthorpe U	20	3	32 4

Players retained or with offer of contract
Wallace, Murray.

Scholars
Baker, Riley James; Barmby, George; Butroid, Lewis Malcolm; Cleminshaw, Charles George; Dean-Atkinson, James Peter; Ebraheem, Sami; Ledger, Ben David; McMichael, Lewis; Parker, Joe; Sackey, Leslie Nii Aflah; Shilling, Sonny Joseph; Sithole, Fortunate Chibuzo; Stockill, Matthew Thomas; Watkis, De'Andre Michael.

SHEFFIELD U (73)

ADAMS, Che (F)   46   11
b.Leicester 13-7-96
Internationals: England C, U20.

2014–15	Sheffield U	10	0	
2015–16	Sheffield U	36	11	46 11

BASHAM, Chris (M)   198   9
H: 5 11   W: 12 08   b.Hebburn 20-7-88

2007–08	Bolton W	0	0	
2007–08	*Rochdale*	13	0	13 0
2008–09	Bolton W	11	1	
2009–10	Bolton W	8	0	19 1
2010–11	Blackpool	0	0	
2011–12	Blackpool	17	2	
2012–13	Blackpool	26	1	
2013–14	Blackpool	40	2	85 5
2014–15	Sheffield U	37	0	
2015–16	Sheffield U	44	3	81 3

BAXTER, Jose (F)   157   38
H: 5 10   W: 11 07   b.Bootle 7-2-92
Internationals: England U16, U17.

2008–09	Everton	3	0	
2009–10	Everton	2	0	
2010–11	Everton	1	0	
2011–12	Everton	1	0	
2011–12	*Tranmere R*	14	3	14 3
2012–13	Everton	0	0	7 0
2012–13	Crystal Palace	0	0	
2012–13	*Oldham Ath*	39	13	
2013–14	Oldham Ath	4	2	43 15
2013–14	Sheffield U	35	6	
2014–15	Sheffield U	34	10	
2015–16	Sheffield U	24	4	93 20

BRAYFORD, John (D)   272   7
H: 5 8   W: 11 02   b.Stoke 29-12-87
Internationals: England C.

2008–09	Crewe Alex	36	2	
2009–10	Crewe Alex	45	0	81 2
2010–11	Derby Co	46	1	
2011–12	Derby Co	23	0	
2012–13	Derby Co	40	1	109 2
2013–14	Cardiff C	0	0	
2013–14	*Sheffield U*	15	1	
2014–15	Cardiff C	26	0	26 0
2014–15	*Sheffield U*	22	1	
2015–16	Sheffield U	19	1	56 3

BROOKS, David (M)   0   0
b. 8-7-98

2015–16	Sheffield U	0	0	

CALVERT-LEWIN, Dominic (F)   31   5
b. 16-3-97

2013–14	Sheffield U	0	0	
2014–15	Sheffield U	2	0	
2015–16	Sheffield U	9	0	11 0
2015–16	*Northampton T*	20	5	20 5

CAMPBELL-RYCE, Jamal (M)   414   36
H: 5 7   W: 12 03   b.Lambeth 6-4-83
Internationals: Jamaica Full caps.

2002–03	Charlton Ath	1	0	
2002–03	*Leyton Orient*	17	2	
2003–04	Charlton Ath	2	0	
2003–04	*Wimbledon*	4	0	4 0
2004–05	Charlton Ath	0	0	3 0
2004–05	*Chesterfield*	14	0	
2004–05	Rotherham U	24	0	
2005–06	Rotherham U	7	0	31 0
2005–06	Southend U	13	0	
2005–06	*Colchester U*	4	0	4 0
2006–07	Southend U	43	2	
2007–08	Southend U	2	0	58 2
2007–08	Barnsley	37	3	
2008–09	Barnsley	40	9	
2009–10	Barnsley	13	0	90 12
2009–10	Bristol C	14	0	
2010–11	Bristol C	31	2	
2011–12	Bristol C	17	0	62 2
2011–12	*Leyton Orient*	8	1	25 3
2012–13	Notts Co	37	8	
2013–14	Notts Co	36	3	
2014–15	Sheffield U	19	4	
2014–15	*Notts Co*	4	0	77 11
2015–16	Sheffield U	18	0	37 4
2015–16	*Chesterfield*	9	2	23 2

COLLINS, Neill (D)   456   26
H: 6 3   W: 12 07   b.Irvine 2-9-83
Internationals: Scotland U21, B.

2000–01	Queen's Park	4	0	
2001–02	Queen's Park	28	0	32 0
2002–03	Dumbarton	33	2	
2003–04	Dumbarton	30	2	63 4
2004–05	Sunderland	11	0	
2005–06	Sunderland	0	0	
2005–06	*Hartlepool U*	22	0	22 0
2005–06	*Sheffield U*	2	0	
2006–07	Sunderland	7	1	18 1
2006–07	Wolverhampton W	22	2	
2007–08	Wolverhampton W	39	3	
2008–09	Wolverhampton W	23	4	
2009–10	Wolverhampton W	0	0	84 9
2009–10	*Preston NE*	21	1	21 1
2009–10	Leeds U	9	0	
2010–11	Leeds U	21	0	30 0
2010–11	Sheffield U	14	0	
2011–12	Sheffield U	42	2	
2012–13	Sheffield U	39	3	
2013–14	Sheffield U	44	2	
2014–15	Sheffield U	8	1	
2014–15	*Port Vale*	7	0	7 0
2015–16	Sheffield U	30	3	179 11

COUTTS, Paul (M)   241   7
H: 5 9   W: 11 11   b.Aberdeen 22-7-88
Internationals: Scotland U21.

2008–09	Peterborough U	0	0	
2009–10	Peterborough U	16	0	53 0
2009–10	Preston NE	13	1	
2010–11	Preston NE	23	1	
2011–12	Preston NE	41	2	77 4
2012–13	Derby Co	44	3	
2013–14	Derby Co	8	0	
2013–14	Derby Co	7	0	59 3
2014–15	Sheffield U	20	0	
2015–16	Sheffield U	32	0	52 0

CUVELIER, Florent (M)   59   7
H: 6 0   W: 11 05   b.Brussels 12-9-92
Internationals: Belgium U16, U17, U18, U19, U20, U21.

2009–10	Portsmouth	0	0	
2010–11	Stoke C	0	0	
2011–12	Stoke C	0	0	
2011–12	*Walsall*	18	4	
2012–13	Stoke C	0	0	
2012–13	*Walsall*	19	2	37 6
2012–13	*Peterborough U*	1	0	1 0
2013–14	Stoke C	0	0	
2013–14	*Sheffield U*	7	0	
2013–14	*Port Vale*	1	0	1 0
2014–15	Sheffield U	3	0	
2014–15	*Burton Alb*	1	1	1 1
2015–16	Sheffield U	9	0	19 0

DE GIROLAMO, Diago (F)   20   4
H: 5 10   W: 11 00   b.Chesterfield 5-10-95
Internationals: Italy U18, U19, U20.

2013–14	Sheffield U	2	0	
2013–14	Sheffield U	0	0	
2014–15	Sheffield U	0	0	
2014–15	*York C*	12	4	12 4
2015–16	*Northampton T*	6	0	6 0
2015–16	Sheffield U	0	0	2 0

DONE, Matt (M)   313   31
H: 5 10   W: 10 04   b.Oswestry 22-6-88

2005–06	Wrexham	0	0	
2006–07	Wrexham	34	1	
2007–08	Wrexham	26	0	66 1
2008–09	Hereford U	36	0	
2009–10	Hereford U	20	0	56 0
2010–11	Rochdale	33	5	
2011–12	Barnsley	31	4	
2012–13	Barnsley	13	0	44 4
2012–13	*Hibernian*	7	0	7 0
2013–14	Rochdale	38	0	
2014–15	Rochdale	23	10	94 15
2014–15	*Sheffield U*	15	7	
2015–16	Sheffield U	31	4	46 11

FLYNN, Ryan (M)   222   23
H: 5 8   W: 10 00   b.Falkirk 4-9-88
Internationals: Scotland U19.

2006–07	Liverpool	0	0	
2007–08	*Hereford U*	0	0	
2007–08	Liverpool	0	0	
2008–09	Liverpool	0	0	
2009–10	Liverpool	0	0	
2009–10	Falkirk	36	5	
2010–11	Falkirk	33	5	69 10
2011–12	Sheffield U	26	2	
2012–13	Sheffield U	36	3	
2013–14	Sheffield U	32	5	

2014–15	Sheffield U	32	1		
2015–16	Sheffield U	27	2	**153**	**13**

FREEMAN, Kieron (D) 128 2
H: 5 10 W: 12 05 b.Nottingham 21-3-92
Internationals: Wales U17, U19, U21.

2010–11	Nottingham F	0	0		
2011–12	Nottingham F	0	0		
2011–12	*Notts Co*	19	1		
2012–13	Derby Co	19	0		
2013–14	Derby Co	6	0		
2013–14	*Notts Co*	16	0	**35**	**1**
2013–14	*Sheffield U*	12	0		
2014–15	Derby Co	0	0	**25**	**0**
2014–15	*Mansfield T*	11	0	**11**	**0**
2014–15	Sheffield U	19	1		
2015–16	Sheffield U	19	0	**50**	**1**
2015–16	*Portsmouth*	7	0	**7**	**0**

HARRIS, Robert (D) 230 14
H: 5 8 W: 10 00 b.Glasgow 28-8-87

2004–05	Clyde	1	0		
2005–06	Clyde	20	0		
2006–07	Clyde	24	0	**45**	**0**
2007–08	Queen of the South	26	2		
2008–09	Queen of the South	21	2		
2009–10	Queen of the South	32	4		
2010–11	Queen of the South	31	2	**110**	**10**
2011–12	Blackpool	5	0		
2012–13	Blackpool	4	0		
2012–13	*Rotherham U*	5	1	**5**	**1**
2013–14	Blackpool	4	0	**13**	**0**
2013–14	Sheffield U	11	0		
2014–15	Sheffield U	40	3		
2015–16	Sheffield U	5	0	**56**	**3**
2015–16	*Fleetwood T*	1	0	**1**	**0**

HIGDON, Michael (F) 323 99
H: 6 1 W: 12 08 b.Liverpool 2-9-83

2000–01	Crewe Alex	0	0		
2001–02	Crewe Alex	0	0		
2002–03	Crewe Alex	0	0		
2003–04	Crewe Alex	10	1		
2004–05	Crewe Alex	20	3		
2005–06	Crewe Alex	26	3		
2006–07	Crewe Alex	25	3		
2007–08	Crewe Alex	0	0	**81**	**10**
2007–08	Falkirk	24	4		
2008–09	Falkirk	27	7	**51**	**11**
2009–10	St Mirren	33	3		
2010–11	St Mirren	28	14	**61**	**17**
2011–12	Motherwell	35	14		
2012–13	Motherwell	37	26	**72**	**40**
2013–14	NEC	32	14	**32**	**14**
2014–15	Sheffield U	13	2		
2015–16	Sheffield U	2	0	**15**	**2**
2015–16	*Oldham Ath*	11	5	**11**	**5**

HOWARD, Mark (G) 146 0
H: 6 0 W: 11 13 b.Southwark 21-9-86

2005–06	Falkirk	8	0	**8**	**0**
2006–07	Cardiff C	0	0		
2006–07	Swansea C	0	0		
2007–08	St Mirren	10	0		
2008–09	St Mirren	33	0		
2009–10	St Mirren	2	0	**45**	**0**
2010–11	Aberdeen	9	0	**9**	**0**
2011–12	Blackpool	4	0	**4**	**0**
2011–12	Sheffield U	0	0		
2012–13	Sheffield U	11	0		
2013–14	Sheffield U	19	0		
2014–15	Sheffield U	35	0		
2015–16	Sheffield U	15	0	**80**	**0**

KELLY, Graham (D) 1 0
b. 16-10-97
Internationals: Republic of Ireland U18, U19.

2015–16	Sheffield U	1	0	**1**	**0**

KENNEDY, Terry (D) 21 0
H: 5 10 W: 12 04 b.Barnsley 14-11-93

2010–11	Sheffield U	1	0		
2011–12	Sheffield U	0	0		
2012–13	Sheffield U	1	0		
2013–14	Sheffield U	5	0		
2014–15	Sheffield U	11	0		
2015–16	Sheffield U	1	0	**19**	**0**
2015–16	*Cambridge U*	2	0	**2**	**0**

LONG, George (G) 120 0
H: 6 0 W: 12 05 b.Sheffield 5-11-93
Internationals: England U18.

2010–11	Sheffield U	1	0		
2011–12	Sheffield U	2	0		
2012–13	Sheffield U	36	0		
2013–14	Sheffield U	27	0		
2014–15	Sheffield U	0	0		
2014–15	*Oxford U*	10	0	**10**	**0**
2014–15	*Motherwell*	13	0	**13**	**0**
2015–16	Sheffield U	31	0	**97**	**0**

McEVELEY, James (D) 340 8
H: 6 1 W: 13 03 b.Liverpool 11-2-85
Internationals: England U20, U21. Scotland B, Full caps.

2002–03	Blackburn R	9	0		
2003–04	Blackburn R	0	0		
2003–04	*Burnley*	4	0	**4**	**0**
2004–05	Blackburn R	5	0		
2004–05	*Gillingham*	10	1	**10**	**1**
2005–06	Blackburn R	0	0		
2005–06	*Ipswich T*	19	1	**19**	**1**
2006–07	Blackburn R	4	0	**18**	**0**
2006–07	Derby Co	15	0		
2007–08	Derby Co	29	2		
2008–09	Derby Co	15	0		
2008–09	*Preston NE*	7	0	**7**	**0**
2008–09	*Charlton Ath*	6	0	**6**	**0**
2009–10	Derby Co	33	2	**92**	**4**
2010–11	Barnsley	17	1		
2011–12	Barnsley	29	0	**46**	**1**
2011–12	*Swindon T*	8	0		
2012–13	Swindon T	28	0		
2013–14	Swindon T	32	0	**68**	**0**
2014–15	Sheffield U	34	1		
2015–16	Sheffield U	36	0	**70**	**1**

McFADZEAN, Callum (D) 42 2
b.Sheffield 16-1-94
Internationals: England U16. Scotland U21.

2010–11	Sheffield U	0	0		
2011–12	Sheffield U	0	0		
2012–13	Sheffield U	8	0		
2013–14	Sheffield U	7	0		
2013–14	*Chesterfield*	4	0	**4**	**0**
2013–14	*Burton Alb*	7	1		
2014–15	Sheffield U	0	0		
2014–15	*Burton Alb*	9	1	**16**	**2**
2015–16	Sheffield U	1	0	**16**	**0**
2015–16	*Stevenage*	6	0	**6**	**0**

McGAHEY, Harrison (D) 30 0
b.Preston 26-9-95

2013–14	Blackpool	4	0	**4**	**0**
2014–15	Sheffield U	15	0		
2014–15	*Tranmere R*	4	0	**4**	**0**
2015–16	Sheffield U	7	0	**22**	**0**

McNULTY, Marc (M) 168 57
H: 5 10 W: 11 00 b.Edinburgh 14-9-92

2009–10	Livingston	9	1		
2010–11	Livingston	5	1		
2011–12	Livingston	30	11		
2012–13	Livingston	26	7		
2013–14	Livingston	35	17	**105**	**37**
2014–15	Sheffield U	31	9		
2015–16	Sheffield U	5	1	**36**	**10**
2015–16	*Portsmouth*	27	10	**27**	**10**

PHILLIPS, Jake (D) 0 0
b. 26-10-92

2015–16	Sheffield U	0	0		

RAMSDALE, Aaron (G) 0 0
b. 14-5-98

2015–16	Sheffield U	0	0		

REED, Louis (M) 39 0
b. 25-7-97
Internationals: England U18, U19.

2013–14	Sheffield U	1	0		
2014–15	Sheffield U	19	0		
2015–16	Sheffield U	19	0	**39**	**0**

SCOUGALL, Stefan (M) 61 4
H: 5 7 W: 8 13 b.Edinburgh 7-12-92
Internationals: Scotland U21.

2013–14	Sheffield U	15	2		
2014–15	Sheffield U	25	1		
2015–16	Sheffield U	11	0	**51**	**3**
2015–16	*Fleetwood T*	10	1	**10**	**1**

SHARP, Billy (F) 392 161
H: 5 9 W: 11 00 b.Sheffield 5-2-86

2004–05	Sheffield U	2	0		
2004–05	*Rushden & D*	16	9	**16**	**9**
2005–06	Scunthorpe U	37	23		
2006–07	Scunthorpe U	45	30	**82**	**53**
2007–08	Sheffield U	29	4		
2008–09	Sheffield U	22	4		
2009–10	Sheffield U	0	0		
2009–10	*Doncaster R*	33	15		
2010–11	Doncaster R	29	15		
2011–12	Doncaster R	20	10		
2011–12	Southampton	15	9		
2012–13	Southampton	2	0		
2012–13	*Nottingham F*	39	10	**39**	**10**
2013–14	Southampton	0	0	**17**	**9**
2013–14	*Reading*	10	2	**10**	**2**
2013–14	*Doncaster R*	16	4	**98**	**44**
2014–15	Leeds U	33	5	**33**	**5**
2015–16	Sheffield U	44	21	**97**	**29**

WALLACE, James (M) 93 7
H: 5 11 W: 12 08 b.Fazackerly 19-12-91
Internationals: England U19, U20.

2008–09	Everton	0	0		
2009–10	Everton	0	0		
2010–11	Everton	0	0		
2010–11	*Stockport Co*	14	1	**14**	**1**
2010–11	*Bury*	0	0		
2011–12	Everton	0	0		
2011–12	*Shrewsbury T*	3	0		
2011–12	*Stevenage*	0	0		
2011–12	*Tranmere R*	18	2		
2012–13	Tranmere R	19	2		
2013–14	Everton	0	0		
2013–14	Tranmere R	18	2	**55**	**6**
2014–15	Sheffield U	10	0		
2015–16	Sheffield U	4	0	**14**	**0**
2015–16	*Shrewsbury T*	7	0	**10**	**0**

WALLACE, Kieran (M) 15 0
b. 26-1-95
Internationals: England U16, U17.

2014–15	Sheffield U	4	0		
2015–16	Sheffield U	11	0	**15**	**0**

WHITEMAN, Ben (M) 6 0
b.Rochdale 17-6-96

2014–15	Sheffield U	0	0		
2015–16	Sheffield U	6	0	**6**	**0**

WOOLFORD, Martyn (M) 279 31
H: 6 0 W: 11 09 b.Castleford 13-10-85
Internationals: England C.

2008–09	Scunthorpe U	39	4		
2009–10	Scunthorpe U	40	5		
2010–11	Scunthorpe U	24	6	**103**	**15**
2010–11	Bristol C	15	0		
2011–12	Bristol C	25	1		
2012–13	Bristol C	15	3	**55**	**4**
2012–13	Millwall	15	1		
2013–14	Millwall	40	7		
2014–15	Millwall	38	3	**93**	**11**
2015–16	Sheffield U	28	1	**28**	**1**

Players retained or with offer of contract
Crofts, Nathaniel Wilson; Eastwood, Jake; Hall, Connor Matthew; Smith, Kimarni; Wright, Jake David.

Scholars
Adebowale, Emmanuel; Brown, Alexander Thomas; Burton, Keegan Jon; Charlesworth, Thomas Harry; Cummings, Joseph; Ford, Jake Christopher; Gilmour, Harvey James; Giraud-Hutchinson, O'Shaye Samuel; Gordon, Shea Martin; Hallam, Jordan Paul; Kelly, Graham; Mallon, Stephen; Perryman, Joshua; Ramsey, Daniel Christopher; Semple, Callum Charlie; Slew, Jorome Anthony; Smith, Tyler Gavin Junior.

SHEFFIELD W (74)

BANNAN, Barry (D) 174 6
H: 5 10 W: 10 08 b.Glasgow 1-12-89
Internationals: Scotland U21, Full caps.

2008–09	Aston Villa	0	0		
2008–09	*Derby Co*	10	1	**10**	**1**
2009–10	Aston Villa	0	0		
2009–10	*Blackpool*	20	1	**20**	**1**
2010–11	Aston Villa	12	0		
2010–11	*Leeds U*	7	0	**7**	**0**
2011–12	Aston Villa	28	1		
2012–13	Aston Villa	24	0		
2013–14	Aston Villa	0	0	**64**	**1**
2013–14	Crystal Palace	15	1		
2014–15	Crystal Palace	7	0		
2014–15	*Bolton W*	16	0	**16**	**0**
2015–16	Crystal Palace	0	0	**22**	**1**
2015–16	Sheffield W	35	2	**35**	**2**

BETRA, Franck (F) 0 0
b. 18-12-96

2013–14	Sheffield W	0	0		
2014–15	Sheffield W	0	0		
2015–16	Sheffield W	0	0		

BUS, Sergiu (F) 122 32
H: 6 1 W: 12 13 b.Cluj-Napoca 2-11-92
Internationals: Romania U21.

2009–10	CFR Cluj	1	0		
2010–11	CFR Cluj	12	1		
2010–11	*Unirea Albu Iulia*	12	2	**12**	**2**
2011–12	CFR Cluj	0	0		
2011–12	*Targu Mures*	22	6	**22**	**6**
2012–13	CFR Cluj	6	2		
2012–13	*Gaz Metan Medias*	3	0	**3**	**0**
2013–14	CFR Cluj	0	0	**19**	**3**
2013–14	*Corona Brasov*	28	9	**28**	**9**

2014–15	CSKA Sofia	19	10	19 10
2014–15	Sheffield W	7	1	
2015–16	Sheffield W	2	0	9 1
2015–16	*Salernitana*	10	1	10 1

CLARE, Sean (M) 4 0
b.Sheffield 18-9-96

2015–16	Sheffield W	0	0	
2015–16	*Bury*	4	0	4 0

DAWSON, Cameron (G) 0 0
H: 6 0 W: 10 12 b.Sheffield 7-7-95
Internationals: England U18, U19.

2013–14	Sheffield W	0	0	
2014–15	*Plymouth Arg*	0	0	
2014–15	Sheffield W	0	0	
2015–16	Sheffield W	0	0	

DE HAVILLAND, Will (D) 0 0
H: 6 0 W: 11 00 b.Huntingdon 8-11-94

2013–14	Millwall	0	0	
2014–15	Sheffield W	0	0	
2015–16	Sheffield W	0	0	

DIELNA, Claude (D) 133 4
H: 6 0 W: 12 08 b.Clichy-la-Garenne 14-12-87

2006–07	Lorient	0	0	
2007–08	Lorient	0	0	
2009–10	Istres	21	0	
2010–11	Istres	24	1	
2011–12	Istres	17	0	62 1
2012–13	Olympiacos	0	0	
2012–13	Sedan	25	2	25 2
2013–14	Olympiacos	0	0	
2013–14	AC Ajaccio	22	0	22 0
2014–15	Sheffield W	23	1	
2015–16	Sheffield W	0	0	23 1
2015–16	*Slovan Bratislava*	1	0	1 0

FILIPE MELO, Silva (M) 143 5
H: 6 2 W: 12 13 b.3-11-89

2006–07	Uniao Lamas	0	0	
2007–08	Uniao Lamas	0	0	
2008–09	Uniao Lamas	0	0	
2009–10	Beira-Mar	1	0	
2009–10	Avanca	21	1	21 1
2010–11	Beira-Mar	0	0	
2010–11	Espinho	23	0	23 0
2011–12	Beira-Mar	0	0	1 0
2011–12	Arouca	11	1	11 1
2012–13	Naval	29	1	29 1
2013–14	Moreirense	35	2	
2014–15	Moreirense	17	0	52 2
2014–15	Sheffield W	6	0	
2015–16	Sheffield W	0	0	6 0

FORESTIERI, Fernando (F) 212 48
H: 5 8 W: 10 07 b.Rosario 16-1-90
Internationals: Italy U17, U19, U20, U21.

2006–07	Genoa	1	1	1 1
2007–08	Siena	17	1	
2008–09	Siena	2	0	19 1
2008–09	Vicenza	13	5	13 5
2009–10	Malaga	19	1	19 1
2010–11	Empoli	17	3	17 3
2011–12	Bari	27	2	27 2
2012–13	Udinese	0	0	
2012–13	*Watford*	28	8	
2013–14	Watford	28	7	
2014–15	Watford	24	5	80 20
2015–16	Sheffield W	36	15	36 15

HELAN, Jeremy (M) 142 4
H: 5 11 W: 12 00 b.Paris 9-5-92
Internationals: France U19.

2009–10	Manchester C	0	0	
2010–11	Manchester C	0	0	
2011–12	Manchester C	0	0	
2011–12	Carlisle U	2	0	2 0
2012–13	Manchester C	0	0	
2012–13	Shrewsbury T	3	0	3 0
2012–13	*Sheffield W*	28	1	
2013–14	Sheffield W	43	2	
2014–15	Sheffield W	38	1	
2015–16	Sheffield W	20	0	129 4
2015–16	*Wolverhampton W*	8	0	8 0

HOOPER, Gary (F) 323 152
H: 5 9 W: 11 02 b.Loughton 26-1-88

2006–07	Southend U	19	0	
2006–07	Leyton Orient	4	2	4 2
2007–08	Southend U	3	2	32 2
2007–08	Hereford U	19	11	19 11
2008–09	Scunthorpe U	45	24	
2009–10	Scunthorpe U	35	19	80 43
2010–11	Celtic	26	20	
2011–12	Celtic	37	24	
2012–13	Celtic	32	19	95 63
2013–14	Norwich C	32	6	
2014–15	Norwich C	30	12	
2015–16	Norwich C	2	0	64 18
2015–16	Sheffield W	29	13	29 13

HUNT, Jack (D) 202 2
H: 5 9 W: 11 02 b.Rothwell 6-12-90

2009–10	Huddersfield T	0	0	
2010–11	Huddersfield T	19	1	
2010–11	Chesterfield	20	0	20 0
2011–12	Huddersfield T	43	1	
2012–13	Huddersfield T	40	0	
2013–14	Huddersfield T	2	0	104 2
2013–14	Crystal Palace	0	0	
2013–14	Barnsley	11	0	11 0
2014–15	Crystal Palace	0	0	
2014–15	Nottingham F	17	0	17 0
2014–15	Rotherham U	16	0	16 0
2015–16	Sheffield W	34	0	34 0

HUTCHINSON, Sam (M) 70 2
H: 6 0 W: 11 07 b.Windsor 3-8-89
Internationals: England U18, U19.

2006–07	Chelsea	1	0	
2007–08	Chelsea	0	0	
2008–09	Chelsea	2	0	
2009–10	Chelsea	0	0	
2010–11	Chelsea	2	0	
2011–12	Chelsea	2	0	
2012–13	Nottingham F	9	1	9 1
2013–14	Chelsea	0	0	5 0
2013–14	Vitesse	1	0	1 0
2013–14	Sheffield W	10	1	
2014–15	Sheffield W	20	0	
2015–16	Sheffield W	25	0	55 1

LACHMAN, Darryl (D) 129 0
H: 6 2 W: 11 11 b.11-11-89
Internationals: Curacao Full caps.

2009–10	Groningen	2	0	
2010–11	Groningen	6	0	8 0
2011–12	PEC Zwolle	34	0	
2012–13	PEC Zwolle	33	0	
2013–14	PEC Zwolle	24	0	91 0
2014–15	FC Twente	15	0	15 0
2015–16	Sheffield W	0	0	
2015–16	*C Leeuwarden*	15	0	15 0

LAVERY, Caolan (F) 66 16
H: 5 11 W: 11 12 b.Red Deer 22-10-92
Internationals: Canada U17. Northern Ireland U19, U21.

2012–13	Sheffield W	0	0	
2012–13	Southend U	3	0	3 0
2013–14	Sheffield W	21	4	
2013–14	Plymouth Arg	8	3	8 3
2014–15	Sheffield W	13	2	
2014–15	Chesterfield	8	3	8 3
2015–16	Sheffield W	0	0	34 6
2015–16	Portsmouth	13	4	13 4

LEE, Kieran (D) 250 17
H: 6 1 W: 12 00 b.Stalybridge 22-6-88

2006–07	Manchester U	1	0	
2007–08	Manchester U	0	0	
2007–08	QPR	7	0	7 0
2008–09	Oldham Ath	7	0	
2009–10	Oldham Ath	24	1	
2010–11	Oldham Ath	43	2	
2011–12	Oldham Ath	43	2	117 5
2012–13	Sheffield W	23	0	
2013–14	Sheffield W	26	1	
2014–15	Sheffield W	33	6	
2015–16	Sheffield W	43	5	125 12

LEES, Tom (D) 285 10
H: 6 1 W: 12 04 b.Warwick 28-11-90
Internationals: England U21.

2008–09	Leeds U	0	0	
2009–10	Leeds U	0	0	
2009–10	Accrington S	39	0	39 0
2010–11	Leeds U	0	0	
2010–11	Bury	45	4	45 4
2011–12	Leeds U	42	2	
2012–13	Leeds U	40	1	
2013–14	Leeds U	41	0	123 3
2014–15	Sheffield W	44	0	
2015–16	Sheffield W	34	3	78 3

LOOVENS, Glenn (D) 323 13
H: 5 10 W: 11 08 b.Doetinchem 22-10-83
Internationals: Netherlands U21, Full caps.

2001–02	Feyenoord	8	0	
2002–03	Feyenoord	12	0	
2003–04	Feyenoord	1	0	
2003–04	Excelsior	24	2	24 2
2004–05	Feyenoord	6	0	27 0
2004–05	De Graafschap	11	0	11 0
2005–06	Cardiff C	33	2	
2006–07	Cardiff C	30	1	
2007–08	Cardiff C	36	0	
2008–09	Cardiff C	1	0	100 3
2008–09	Celtic	17	3	
2009–10	Celtic	20	3	
2010–11	Celtic	13	1	
2011–12	Celtic	11	1	61 8
2012–13	Real Zaragoza	21	0	21 0
2013–14	Sheffield W	22	0	
2014–15	Sheffield W	26	0	
2015–16	Sheffield W	31	0	79 0

LOPEZ, Alex (M) 185 17
H: 5 9 W: 10 10 b.Ferrol 11-1-88
Internationals: Spain U16, U17.

2009–10	Celta Vigo	2	0	
2010–11	Celta Vigo	36	3	
2011–12	Celta Vigo	36	6	
2012–13	Celta Vigo	33	2	
2013–14	Celta Vigo	31	5	
2014–15	Celta Vigo	25	1	
2015–16	Celta Vigo	0	0	163 17

On loan from Celta Vigo.

2015–16	Sheffield W	22	0	22 0

LUCAS JOAO, Eduardo (F) 113 24
H: 6 4 W: 12 08 b.4-9-93
Internationals: Portugal U20, U21, U23, Full caps.

2012–13	Nacional	0	0	
2012–13	Mirandela	27	12	27 12
2013–14	Nacional	16	0	
2014–15	Nacional	30	6	46 6
2015–16	Sheffield W	40	6	40 6

MARCO MATIAS, Andre (F) 169 35
H: 5 10 W: 10 08 b.Barreiro 10-5-89
Internationals: Portugal U18, U19, U21.

2008–09	Sporting Lisbon	0	0	
2008–09	Varzim	12	0	12 0
2009–10	Sporting Lisbon	0	0	
2009–10	Fatima	7	2	7 2
2009–10	Real Massama	15	0	15 0
2010–11	Vit Guimaraes	0	0	
2010–11	Freamunde	24	5	
2011–12	Vit Guimaraes	0	0	
2011–12	Freamunde	19	2	43 7
2012–13	Vit Guimaraes	20	0	
2013–14	Vit Guimaraes	22	6	42 6
2014–15	Nacional	33	17	33 17
2015–16	Sheffield W	17	3	17 3

McGUGAN, Lewis (M) 277 56
H: 5 9 W: 11 06 b.Long Eaton 25-10-88
Internationals: England U17, U19.

2006–07	Nottingham F	13	2	
2007–08	Nottingham F	33	6	
2008–09	Nottingham F	33	5	
2009–10	Nottingham F	18	3	
2010–11	Nottingham F	40	13	
2011–12	Nottingham F	35	3	
2012–13	Nottingham F	30	8	202 40
2013–14	Watford	34	10	
2014–15	Watford	6	0	40 10
2014–15	*Sheffield W*	22	3	
2015–16	Sheffield W	13	3	35 6

NUHIU, Atdhe (F) 255 42
H: 6 6 W: 13 05 b.Prishtina 29-7-89
Internationals: Austria U19, U20, U21.

2008–09	Austria Karnten	16	2	
2009–10	Austria Karnten	3	0	19 2
2009–10	SV Ried	27	6	27 6
2010–11	Rapid Vienna	28	5	
2011–12	Rapid Vienna	31	8	59 13
2012–13	Eskisehirspor	28	2	28 2
2013–14	Sheffield W	38	8	
2014–15	Sheffield W	43	8	
2015–16	Sheffield W	41	3	122 19

PALMER, Liam (M) 155 1
H: 6 2 W: 12 10 b.Worksop 19-9-91
Internationals: Scotland U19, U21.

2010–11	Sheffield W	9	0	
2011–12	Sheffield W	14	1	
2011–12	Sheffield W	0	0	
2012–13	Tranmere R	43	0	
2013–14	Tranmere R	0	0	43 0
2013–14	Sheffield W	39	0	
2014–15	Sheffield W	35	0	
2015–16	Sheffield W	15	0	112 1

PRICE, Lewis (G) 130 0
H: 6 3 W: 13 05 b.Bournemouth 19-7-84
Internationals: Wales U19, U21, Full caps.

2002–03	Ipswich T	0	0	
2003–04	Ipswich T	1	0	
2004–05	Ipswich T	8	0	
2004–05	Cambridge U	6	0	6 0
2005–06	Ipswich T	25	0	
2006–07	Ipswich T	34	0	68 0

2007–08	Derby Co	6	0		
2008–09	Derby Co	0	0		
2008–09	Milton Keynes D	2	0	2	0
2008–09	Luton T	1	0	1	0
2009–10	Derby Co	0	0	6	0
2009–10	Brentford	13	0	13	0
2010–11	Crystal Palace	1	0		
2011–12	Crystal Palace	5	0		
2012–13	Crystal Palace	0	0		
2013–14	Crystal Palace	0	0		
2013–14	Mansfield T	5	0	5	0
2014–15	Crystal Palace	0	0	6	0
2014–15	Crawley T	18	0	18	0
2015–16	Sheffield W	5	0	5	0

SASSO, Vincent (D)   70   2
H: 6 3   W: 12 13   b.Saint-Cloud 16-2-91
Internationals: France U16, U17, U18, U19, U20, U21.

2010–11	Nantes	20	0		
2011–12	Nantes	4	0	24	0
2012–13	Beira-Mar	15	2	15	2
2012–13	Braga	5	0		
2013–14	Braga	7	0		
2014–15	Braga	5	0		
2015–16	Braga	0	0	17	0

On loan from Braga.

2015–16	Sheffield W	14	0	14	0

SEMEDO, Jose (D)   324   5
H: 6 0   W: 12 08   b.Setubal 11-1-85
Internationals: Portugal U17, U18, U19, U20, U21, B.

2004–05	Sporting Lisbon	0	0		
2004–05	Casa Pia	34	2	34	2
2005–06	Feirense	18	0	18	0
2006–07	Cagliari	3	0	3	0
2007–08	Charlton Ath	37	0		
2008–09	Charlton Ath	18	0		
2009–10	Charlton Ath	38	1		
2010–11	Charlton Ath	42	1	135	2
2011–12	Sheffield W	46	1		
2012–13	Sheffield W	26	0		
2013–14	Sheffield W	22	0		
2014–15	Sheffield W	30	0		
2015–16	Sheffield W	10	0	134	1

SOUGOU, Moudou (F)   272   44
H: 5 10   W: 10 10   b.Fissel 18-12-84
Internationals: Senegal Full caps.

2004–05	Uniao Leiria	7	0		
2005–06	Victoria Setubal	27	0	27	0
2006–07	Uniao Leiria	15	5		
2007–08	Uniao Leiria	23	1	45	6
2008–09	Academica	23	4		
2009–10	Academica	29	9		
2010–11	Academica	28	6	80	19
2011–12	Cluj	33	10		
2012–13	Cluj	11	1	44	11
2012–13	Marseille	14	0		
2013–14	Marseille	0	0		
2013–14	Evian	29	4		
2014–15	Marseille	0	0	14	0
2014–15	Evian	24	2	53	6
2015–16	Sheffield W	9	2	9	2

STOBBS, Jack (M)   2   0
b. 27-2-97

2013–14	Sheffield W	1	0		
2014–15	Sheffield W	0	0		
2015–16	Sheffield W	1	0	2	0

WALLACE, Ross (M)   359   37
H: 5 6   W: 9 12   b.Dundee 23-5-85
Internationals: Scotland U18, U19, U21, B, Full caps.

2001–02	Celtic	0	0		
2002–03	Celtic	0	0		
2003–04	Celtic	8	1		
2004–05	Celtic	16	0		
2005–06	Celtic	11	0		
2006–07	Celtic	2	0	37	1
2006–07	Sunderland	32	6		
2007–08	Sunderland	21	2		
2008–09	Sunderland	0	0	53	8
2008–09	Preston NE	39	5		
2009–10	Preston NE	41	7	80	12
2010–11	Burnley	40	3		
2011–12	Burnley	44	5		
2012–13	Burnley	36	3		
2013–14	Burnley	14	0		
2014–15	Burnley	15	1	149	12
2015–16	Sheffield W	40	4	40	4

WESTWOOD, Keiren (G)   354   0
H: 6 1   W: 13 10   b.Manchester 23-10-84
Internationals: Republic of Ireland Full caps.

2001–02	Manchester C	0	0		
2002–03	Manchester C	0	0		
2003–04	Manchester C	0	0		
2003–04	Oldham Ath	0	0		
2004–05	Manchester C	0	0		
2005–06	Manchester C	0	0		
2005–06	Carlisle U	35	0		
2006–07	Carlisle U	46	0		
2007–08	Carlisle U	46	0	127	0
2008–09	Coventry C	46	0		
2009–10	Coventry C	44	0		
2010–11	Coventry C	41	0	131	0
2011–12	Sunderland	9	0		
2012–13	Sunderland	0	0		
2013–14	Sunderland	10	0	19	0
2014–15	Sheffield W	43	0		
2015–16	Sheffield W	34	0	77	0

WILDSMITH, Joe (G)   11   0
H: 6 0   W: 10 03   b. 28-12-95
Internationals: England U20.

2013–14	Sheffield W	0	0		
2014–15	Sheffield W	0	0		
2014–15	Barnsley	2	0	2	0
2015–16	Sheffield W	9	0	9	0

Players retained or with offer of contract
Clarke, Warren Eliott; Hirst, George David Eric; Kirby, Connor Alexander; Lee, Jack; Penney, Matthew Luke; Ribeiro Centeno, Jonatas Ian; Vermijl, Marnick Danny.

Scholars
Brown, Spencer Joseph; Conneh, Mike Keita; Cook, Joseph Oliver; Duffy, Mason; McDonagh, Bradley Michael; Nicholson, Jake Thomas; O'Grady, Connor Joseph; Preston, Fraser Thomas; Price, Lewis Alan; Rodney, Devante Darrius; Stachini, Josh; Tracey, Frederick William Robert; Wallis, Daniel Michael.

SHREWSBURY T (75)

AKPA AKPRO, Jean-Louis (F)   320   49
H: 6 0   W: 10 12   b.Toulouse 4-1-85

2004–05	Toulouse	13	0		
2005–06	Toulouse	14	3	27	3
2006–07	Brest	15	2	15	2
2007–08	FC Brussels	3	0	3	0
2008–09	Grimsby T	20	3		
2009–10	Grimsby T	36	5	56	8
2010–11	Rochdale	32	4		
2011–12	Rochdale	41	7	73	11
2012–13	Tranmere R	28	8		
2013–14	Tranmere R	25	2	53	10
2013–14	Bury	10	0	10	0
2014–15	Shrewsbury T	45	9		
2015–16	Shrewsbury T	38	6	83	15

ANDERSON, Kaiman (F)   0   0
b. 15-8-95

2015–16	Shrewsbury T	0	0		

BARNETT, Tyrone (F)   218   56
H: 6 3   W: 13 05   b.Stevenage 28-10-85

2010–11	Macclesfield T	45	13	45	13
2011–12	Crawley T	26	14	26	14
2011–12	Peterborough U	13	4		
2012–13	Peterborough U	18	1		
2012–13	Ipswich T	3	0	3	0
2013–14	Peterborough U	21	6		
2013–14	Bristol C	17	1	17	1
2014–15	Peterborough U	4	0	56	11
2014–15	Oxford U	12	4	12	4
2014–15	Shrewsbury T	18	4		
2015–16	Shrewsbury T	21	4	39	8
2015–16	Southend U	20	5	20	5

BLACK, Ian (M)   332   19
H: 5 8   W: 9 13   b.Edinburgh 14-3-85
Internationals: Scotland B, Full caps.

2002–03	Blackburn R	0	0		
2003–04	Blackburn R	0	0		
2004–05	Inverness CT	13	0		
2005–06	Inverness CT	26	1		
2006–07	Inverness CT	26	0		
2007–08	Inverness CT	33	3		
2008–09	Inverness CT	34	4	132	8
2009–10	Hearts	26	1		
2010–11	Hearts	32	1		
2011–12	Hearts	29	2	87	4
2012–13	Rangers	29	2		
2013–14	Rangers	32	3		
2014–15	Rangers	22	1	83	6
2015–16	Shrewsbury T	30	1	30	1

BROWN, Junior (D)   140   15
H: 5 9   W: 10 09   b.Crewe 7-5-89

2006–07	Crewe Alex	0	0		
2007–08	Crewe Alex	1	0	1	0
2012–13	Fleetwood T	43	11		
2013–14	Fleetwood T	21	1	64	12
2013–14	Tranmere R	9	1	9	1
2014–15	Oxford U	11	0	11	0
2014–15	Mansfield T	24	2	24	2
2015–16	Shrewsbury T	31	0	31	0

BURTON, Callum (G)   1   0
H: 6 2   W: 12 00   b.Newport, Shropshire 15-8-96
Internationals: England U16, U17, U18.

2013–14	Shrewsbury T	0	0		
2014–15	Shrewsbury T	0	0		
2015–16	Shrewsbury T	1	0	1	0

CATON, James (M)   6   0
H: 5 8   W: 10 12   b.Bolton 4-1-94

2012–13	Blackpool	0	0		
2013–14	Blackpool	2	0	2	0
2013–14	Accrington S	2	0	2	0
2014–15	Shrewsbury T	2	0		
2015–16	Shrewsbury T	0	0	2	0
2015–16	Mansfield T	0	0		

CLARK, Jordan (F)   56   5
H: 6 0   W: 11 07   b.Barnsley 22-9-93

2010–11	Barnsley	4	0		
2011–12	Barnsley	2	0		
2012–13	Barnsley	0	0		
2012–13	Chesterfield	2	0	2	0
2013–14	Barnsley	0	0	6	0
2013–14	Scunthorpe U	1	0	1	0
2014–15	Shrewsbury T	27	3		
2015–16	Shrewsbury T	20	2	47	5

COLLINS, James S (F)   253   77
H: 6 2   W: 13 08   b.Coventry 1-12-90
Internationals: Republic of Ireland U19, U21.

2008–09	Aston Villa	0	0		
2009–10	Aston Villa	0	0		
2009–10	Darlington	7	2	7	2
2010–11	Aston Villa	0	0		
2010–11	Burton Alb	10	4	10	4
2011–12	Shrewsbury T	42	14		
2012–13	Swindon T	45	15	45	15
2013–14	Hibernian	36	6	36	6
2014–15	Shrewsbury T	45	15		
2015–16	Shrewsbury T	23	5	134	42
2015–16	Northampton T	21	8	21	8

DEMETRIOU, Mickey (D)   58   3
b.Durrington 12-3-90
Internationals: England C.

2014–15	Shrewsbury T	42	3		
2014–15	Shrewsbury T	1	0	43	3
2015–16	Cambridge U	15	0	15	0

GRANDIN, Elliot (F)   150   19
H: 5 10   W: 10 07   b.Caen 17-10-87
Internationals: France U21.

2004–05	Caen	1	0		
2005–06	Caen	19	3		
2006–07	Caen	23	2		
2007–08	Caen	12	1	55	6
2007–08	Marseille	8	0		
2008–09	Marseille	8	2	16	2
2008–09	Grenoble	8	0	8	0
2009–10	CSKA Sofia	10	4		
2010–11	CSKA Sofia	1	0	11	4
2010–11	Blackpool	23	1		
2011–12	Blackpool	7	2		
2011–12	Nice	9	0	9	0
2012–13	Blackpool	12	3		
2013–14	Crystal Palace	0	0		
2013–14	Blackpool	7	1	49	7
2014–15	Astra Giurgiu	2	0	2	0
2015–16	Shrewsbury T	0	0		

GRANDISON, Jermaine (D)   163   5
H: 6 4   W: 13 03   b.Birmingham 15-12-90

2008–09	Coventry C	2	0		
2009–10	Coventry C	3	0		
2010–11	Coventry C	0	0	5	0
2010–11	Tranmere R	8	0	8	0
2010–11	Shrewsbury T	13	0		
2011–12	Shrewsbury T	38	2		
2012–13	Shrewsbury T	30	1		
2013–14	Shrewsbury T	14	0		
2014–15	Shrewsbury T	36	2		
2015–16	Shrewsbury T	19	0	150	5

HALSTEAD, Mark (G)   20   0
H: 6 4   W: 14 00   b.Blackpool 1-9-90

2009–10	Blackpool	0	0		
2010–11	Blackpool	1	0		
2011–12	Blackpool	0	0		
2012–13	Blackpool	0	0		
2013–14	Blackpool	0	0	3	0
2014–15	Shrewsbury T	1	0		
2015–16	Shrewsbury T	16	0	17	0

JONES, Ethan (F)   1   0
b.Dudley 4-4-98
| 2015–16 | Shrewsbury T | 1 | 0 | 1 | 0 |

KNIGHT-PERCIVAL, Nathaniel (M) 109 7
H: 6 0   W: 11 06   b.Cambridge 31-3-87
2012–13	Peterborough U	31	0		
2013–14	Peterborough U	15	1	46	1
2014–15	Shrewsbury T	28	1		
2015–16	Shrewsbury T	35	5	63	6

LEUTWILER, Jayson (G)   78   0
H: 6 3   W: 12 07   b.Basel 25-4-89
Internationals: Switzerland U16, U17, U18, U19, U20, U21.
2012–13	Middlesbrough	0	0		
2013–14	Middlesbrough	3	0	3	0
2014–15	Shrewsbury T	46	0		
2015–16	Shrewsbury T	29	0	75	0

LEWIS, Harry (G)   0   0
b. 20-12-97
Internationals: England U18.
| 2015–16 | Shrewsbury T | 0 | 0 | | |

MANGAN, Andy (F)   124 26
H: 6 0   W: 11 09   b.Liverpool 30-8-86
Internationals: England C.
2003–04	Blackpool	2	0		
2004–05	Blackpool	0	0	2	0
From Hyde					
2006–07	Accrington S	34	4		
2007–08	Bury	20	4	20	4
2007–08	*Accrington S*	7	1	41	5
From Forest Green R, Wrexham					
2012–13	Fleetwood T	12	4	12	4
From Forest Green R.					
2014–15	Shrewsbury T	30	8		
From Tranmere R.					
2015–16	Shrewsbury T	19	5	49	13

OGOGO, Abu (D)   276 20
H: 5 8   W: 10 02   b.Epsom 3-11-89
2007–08	Arsenal	0	0		
2008–09	Arsenal	0	0		
2008–09	*Barnet*	9	1	9	1
2009–10	Dagenham & R	30	2		
2010–11	Dagenham & R	33	1		
2011–12	Dagenham & R	40	1		
2012–13	Dagenham & R	46	1		
2013–14	Dagenham & R	44	8		
2014–15	Shrewsbury T	32	4	225	17
2015–16	Shrewsbury T	42	2	42	2

PATTERSON, Sam (D)   0   0
H: 5 8   W: 10 10   b.Leeds 29-10-93
2012–13	Barnsley	0	0		
2013–14	Barnsley	0	0		
2014–15	Barnsley	0	0		
2014–15	Bradford P A	0	0		
2015–16	Shrewsbury T	0	0		

ROWLEY, Shaun (G)   0   0
b. 11-1-96
| 2015–16 | Shrewsbury T | 0 | 0 | | |

SADLER, Matthew (D)   334 5
H: 5 11   W: 11 08   b.Birmingham 26-2-85
Internationals: England U17, U18, U19.
2001–02	Birmingham C	0	0		
2002–03	Birmingham C	2	0		
2003–04	Birmingham C	0	0		
2003–04	*Northampton T*	7	0	7	0
2004–05	Birmingham C	0	0		
2005–06	Birmingham C	8	0		
2006–07	Birmingham C	36	0		
2007–08	Birmingham C	5	0	51	0
2007–08	Watford	15	0		
2008–09	Watford	15	0		
2009–10	Watford	0	0		
2009–10	*Stockport Co*	20	0	20	0
2010–11	Watford	0	0	30	0
2010–11	*Shrewsbury T*	46	0		
2011–12	Walsall	46	1	46	1
2012–13	Crawley T	46	1		
2013–14	Crawley T	46	1		
2014–15	Rotherham U	0	0		
2014–15	*Crawley T*	10	0	102	2
2014–15	*Oldham Ath*	8	0	8	0
2014–15	Shrewsbury T	0	0		
2015–16	Shrewsbury T	24	2	70	2

SMITH, Dominic (D)   21   0
H: 6 0   W: 11 11   b.Shewsbury 9-2-96
Internationals: Wales U19, U21.
2012–13	Shrewsbury T	0	0		
2013–14	Shrewsbury T	0	0		
2014–15	Shrewsbury T	0	0		
2015–16	Shrewsbury T	21	0	21	0

TOOTLE, Matt (D)   215 2
H: 5 9   W: 11 00   b.Widnes 11-10-90
2009–10	Crewe Alex	28	1		
2010–11	Crewe Alex	39	0		
2011–12	Crewe Alex	37	0		
2012–13	Crewe Alex	37	1		
2013–14	Crewe Alex	43	0		
2014–15	Crewe Alex	15	0	199	2
2015–16	Shrewsbury T	16	0	16	0

VERNON, Scott (F)   400 89
H: 6 1   W: 11 06   b.Manchester 13-12-83
2002–03	Oldham Ath	8	1		
2003–04	Oldham Ath	45	12		
2004–05	Oldham Ath	22	7	75	20
2004–05	*Blackpool*	4	3		
2005–06	Blackpool	17	1		
2005–06	*Colchester U*	7	1		
2006–07	Blackpool	38	11		
2007–08	Blackpool	15	4	74	19
2007–08	Colchester U	17	5		
2008–09	Colchester U	33	4		
2008–09	*Northampton T*	6	1	6	1
2009–10	Colchester U	7	3	64	13
2009–10	Gillingham	1	0	1	0
2009–10	*Southend U*	17	4	17	4
2010–11	Aberdeen	33	10		
2011–12	Aberdeen	35	11		
2012–13	Aberdeen	35	3		
2013–14	Aberdeen	25	6	128	30
2014–15	Shrewsbury T	22	1		
2015–16	Shrewsbury T	13	1	35	2

WELLENS, Richard (M)   598 40
H: 5 9   W: 11 06   b.Manchester 26-3-80
1996–97	Manchester U	0	0		
1997–98	Manchester U	0	0		
1998–99	Manchester U	0	0		
1999–2000	Manchester U	0	0		
1999–2000	Blackpool	0	0		
2000–01	Blackpool	36	8		
2001–02	Blackpool	36	1		
2002–03	Blackpool	39	1		
2003–04	Blackpool	41	3		
2004–05	Blackpool	28	3	188	16
2005–06	Oldham Ath	45	4		
2006–07	Oldham Ath	46	4		
2007–08	Doncaster R	45	6		
2008–09	Doncaster R	39	3		
2009–10	Leicester C	41	1		
2010–11	Leicester C	45	2		
2011–12	Leicester C	41	1		
2012–13	Leicester C	2	0		
2012–13	*Ipswich T*	7	0	7	0
2013–14	Leicester C	0	0	129	4
2013–14	*Doncaster R*	37	0		
2014–15	Doncaster R	39	3		
2015–16	Doncaster R	12	0	172	12
2015–16	*Oldham Ath*	3	0	90	8
2015–16	Shrewsbury T	12	0	12	0

WESOLOWSKI, James (M)   238 14
H: 5 8   W: 11 11   b.Sydney 25-8-87
Internationals: Australia U20.
2004–05	Leicester C	0	0		
2005–06	Leicester C	5	0		
2006–07	Leicester C	19	0		
2007–08	Leicester C	22	0		
2008–09	Leicester C	0	0		
2008–09	*Dundee U*	8	0	8	0
2008–09	*Cheltenham T*	4	0	4	0
2009–10	Leicester C	0	0	46	0
2009–10	*Hamilton A*	29	4	29	4
2010–11	Peterborough U	32	2	32	2
2011–12	Oldham Ath	21	3		
2012–13	Oldham Ath	33	0		
2013–14	Oldham Ath	39	4	93	7
2014–15	Shrewsbury T	21	1		
2015–16	Shrewsbury T	5	0	26	1

WHALLEY, Shaun (M)   42   9
H: 5 9   W: 10 08   b.Whiston 7-8-87
| 2014–15 | Luton T | 18 | 3 | 18 | 3 |
| 2015–16 | Shrewsbury T | 24 | 6 | 24 | 6 |

WHITBREAD, Zak (D)   198 7
H: 6 2   W: 12 07   b.Houston 4-3-84
Internationals: USA U20.
2002–03	Liverpool	0	0		
2003–04	Liverpool	0	0		
2004–05	Liverpool	0	0		
2005–06	Liverpool	0	0		
2005–06	*Millwall*	25	0		
2006–07	Millwall	14	0		
2007–08	Millwall	23	3		
2008–09	Millwall	38	0		
2009–10	Millwall	0	0	100	3
2009–10	*Norwich C*	9	0		
2010–11	Norwich C	22	1		
2011–12	Norwich C	18	0	44	1
2012–13	Leicester C	16	1		
2013–14	Leicester C	3	0	19	1
2013–14	*Derby Co*	4	1		
2014–15	Derby Co	9	0	13	1
2015–16	Shrewsbury T	22	1	22	1

WOODS, Martin (M)   234 13
H: 5 11   W: 11 13   b.Airdrie 1-1-86
2002–03	Leeds U	0	0		
2003–04	Leeds U	0	0		
2004–05	Leeds U	1	0	1	0
2004–05	*Hartlepool U*	6	0	6	0
2005–06	Sunderland	7	0	7	0
2006–07	Rotherham U	36	4	36	4
2007–08	Doncaster R	15	0		
2007–08	*Yeovil T*	3	0	3	0
2008–09	Doncaster R	41	2		
2009–10	Doncaster R	24	4		
2010–11	Doncaster R	15	1		
2011–12	Doncaster R	4	0		
2012–13	Doncaster R	16	0		
2013–14	Doncaster R	4	0	119	7
2013–14	*Barnsley*	8	0	8	0
2014–15	Ross Co	27	2		
2015–16	Shrewsbury T	4	0	4	0
2015–16	Ross Co	23	0	50	2

Players retained or with offer of contract
Grogan, Callum.

Scholars
Bonner, Joel; Butts, Jack Thomas; Carta, Joel Sebastian; Gallagher, Christopher Paul; Hassall, George Alan; Hughes, George William; Jones, Ethan Anthony; Jones, Mathew George; Kenton, Joseph Lewis; Kerins, Jake Lawrence Ryan; King, Thomas James William; McAtee, John George; Millis, Nathan Darrell; Rammell, Jacob William; Roberts, Callum James; Sears, Ryan Joseph; Wilson, Jordan Reece Keith.

SOUTHAMPTON (76)

AUSTIN, Charlie (F)   225 118
H: 6 2   W: 13 03   b.Hungerford 5-7-89
2009–10	Swindon T	33	19		
2010–11	Swindon T	21	12	54	31
2010–11	Burnley	4	0		
2011–12	Burnley	41	16		
2012–13	Burnley	37	25	82	41
2013–14	QPR	31	17		
2014–15	QPR	35	18		
2015–16	QPR	16	10	82	45
2015–16	Southampton	7	1	7	1

BERTRAND, Ryan (D)   255 4
H: 5 10   W: 11 00   b.Southwark 5-8-89
Internationals: England U17, U18, U19, U20, U21, Full caps. Great Britain.
2006–07	Chelsea	0	0		
2006–07	*Bournemouth*	5	0	5	0
2007–08	Chelsea	0	0		
2007–08	*Oldham Ath*	21	0	21	0
2007–08	*Norwich C*	18	0		
2008–09	Chelsea	0	0		
2008–09	*Norwich C*	38	0	56	0
2009–10	Chelsea	0	0		
2009–10	*Reading*	44	1	44	1
2010–11	Chelsea	1	0		
2010–11	*Nottingham F*	19	0	19	0
2011–12	Chelsea	7	0		
2012–13	Chelsea	19	0		
2013–14	Chelsea	1	0	28	0
2013–14	*Aston Villa*	16	0	16	0
2014–15	Southampton	34	2		
2015–16	Southampton	32	1	66	3

CEDRIC SOARES, Ricardo (D) 115 2
H: 5 8   W: 10 08   b.Gelsenkirchen, Germany 31-8-91
Internationals: Portugal U16, U17, U18, U19, U20, U21, Full caps.
2010–11	Sporting Lisbon	2	0		
2010–11	Sporting Lisbon	0	0		
2011–12	*Academica*	24	0	24	0
2012–13	Sporting Lisbon	13	1		
2013–14	Sporting Lisbon	28	1		
2014–15	Sporting Lisbon	24	0	67	2
2015–16	Southampton	24	0	24	0

CLASIE, Jordy (M)   183 10
H: 5 7   W: 10 12   b.Haarlem 27-7-91
Internationals: Netherlands U17, U18, U19, U21, Full caps.
2010–11	Feyenoord	0	0		
2010–11	*Excelsior*	32	2	32	2
2011–12	Feyenoord	33	3		

2012–13	Feyenoord	33	2	
2013–14	Feyenoord	32	1	
2014–15	Feyenoord	31	2	129 8
2015–16	Southampton	22	0	22 0

DAVIS, Kelvin (G)   614 0
H: 6 1   W: 11 05   b.Bedford 29-9-76
Internationals: England U21.

1993–94	Luton T	1	0	
1994–95	Luton T	9	0	
1994–95	*Torquay U*	2	0	2 0
1995–96	Luton T	6	0	
1996–97	Luton T	1	0	
1997–98	Luton T	32	0	
1997–98	*Hartlepool U*	2	0	2 0
1998–99	Luton T	44	0	92 0
1999–2000	Wimbledon	0	0	
2000–01	Wimbledon	45	0	
2001–02	Wimbledon	40	0	
2002–03	Wimbledon	46	0	131 0
2003–04	Ipswich T	45	0	
2004–05	Ipswich T	39	0	84 0
2005–06	Sunderland	33	0	33 0
2006–07	Southampton	38	0	
2007–08	Southampton	35	0	
2008–09	Southampton	46	0	
2009–10	Southampton	40	0	
2010–11	Southampton	46	0	
2011–12	Southampton	45	0	
2012–13	Southampton	10	0	
2013–14	Southampton	2	0	
2014–15	Southampton	7	0	
2015–16	Southampton	1	0	270 0

DAVIS, Steven (M)   400 32
H: 5 8   W: 11 04   b.Ballymena 1-1-85
Internationals: Northern Ireland U15, U16, U17, U19, U21, U23, Full caps.

2004–05	Aston Villa	28	1	
2005–06	Aston Villa	35	4	
2006–07	Aston Villa	28	0	91 5
2007–08	Fulham	22	0	22 0
2007–08	Rangers	12	0	
2008–09	Rangers	34	6	
2009–10	Rangers	36	3	
2010–11	Rangers	37	4	
2011–12	Rangers	33	5	152 18
2012–13	Southampton	32	2	
2013–14	Southampton	34	2	
2014–15	Southampton	35	0	
2015–16	Southampton	34	5	135 9

DEBAYO, Josh (D)   0 0
H: 6 0   W: 10 10   b.London 17-10-96

2015–16	Southampton	0	0	

FLANNIGAN, Jake (M)   0 0
H: 5 11   W: 11 03   b.Southampton 2-2-96

2014–15	Southampton	0	0	
2015–16	Southampton	0	0	

FONTE, Jose (D)   405 24
H: 6 2   W: 12 08   b.Penafiel 22-12-83
Internationals: Portugal U21, B, Full caps.

2004–05	Felgueiros	28	1	28 1
2005–06	Setubal	15	0	15 0
2005–06	Benfica	1	0	1 0
2005–06	Pacos	11	1	11 1
2006–07	Amadora	25	1	25 1
2007–08	Crystal Palace	22	1	
2008–09	Crystal Palace	38	4	
2009–10	Crystal Palace	22	1	82 6
2009–10	Southampton	21	0	
2010–11	Southampton	43	7	
2011–12	Southampton	42	1	
2012–13	Southampton	27	2	
2013–14	Southampton	36	3	
2014–15	Southampton	37	0	
2015–16	Southampton	37	2	243 15

FORSTER, Fraser (G)   236 0
H: 6 0   W: 12 00   b.Hexham 17-3-88
Internationals: England Full caps.

2007–08	Newcastle U	0	0	
2008–09	Newcastle U	0	0	
2008–09	Stockport Co	6	0	6 0
2009–10	Newcastle U	0	0	
2009–10	Bristol R	4	0	4 0
2009–10	Norwich C	38	0	38 0
2010–11	Newcastle U	0	0	
2010–11	Celtic	36	0	
2011–12	Newcastle U	0	0	
2011–12	Celtic	33	0	
2012–13	Celtic	34	0	
2013–14	Celtic	37	0	140 0
2014–15	Southampton	30	0	
2015–16	Southampton	18	0	48 0

GALLAGHER, Sam (F)   31 1
H: 6 4   b.Crediton 15-9-95
Internationals: Scotland U19, England U19.

2013–14	Southampton	18	1	
2014–15	Southampton	0	0	
2015–16	Southampton	0	0	18 1
2015–16	*Milton Keynes D*	13	0	13 0

GAPE, Dominic (M)   1 0
H: 5 11   W: 10 13   b.Southampton 9-9-94

2012–13	Southampton	0	0	
2013–14	Southampton	0	0	
2014–15	Southampton	1	0	
2015–16	Southampton	0	0	1 0

GARDOS, Florin (D)   143 4
H: 6 4   W: 10 10   b.Satu Mare 29-10-88
Internationals: Romania U19, U21, Full caps.

2008–09	Concordia Chiajna	22	0	
2009–10	Concordia Chiajna	29	1	51 1
2010–11	Steau Bucharest	23	0	
2011–12	Steau Bucharest	8	0	
2012–13	Steau Bucharest	21	1	52 1
2013–14	Steaua Bucuresti	29	2	29 2
2014–15	Southampton	11	0	
2015–16	Southampton	0	0	11 0

GAZZANIGA, Paulo (G)   41 0
H: 6 5   W: 14 02   b.Santa Fe 2-1-92

2011–12	Gillingham	20	0	20 0
2012–13	Southampton	9	0	
2013–14	Southampton	8	0	
2014–15	Southampton	2	0	
2015–16	Southampton	2	0	21 0

HESKETH, Jake (M)   2 0
H: 5 6   W: 9 13   b. 27-3-96

2014–15	Southampton	2	0	
2015–16	Southampton	0	0	2 0

ISGROVE, Lloyd (M)   44 1
H: 5 10   W: 11 05   b.Yeovil 12-1-93
Internationals: Wales U21, Full caps.

2011–12	Southampton	0	0	
2012–13	Southampton	0	0	
2013–14	Southampton	0	0	
2013–14	*Peterborough U*	8	1	8 1
2014–15	Southampton	1	0	
2014–15	*Sheffield W*	8	0	8 0
2015–16	Southampton	0	0	1 0
2015–16	*Barnsley*	27	0	27 0

JUANMI, Jimenez (M)   116 18
H: 5 7   W: 9 13   b.Coin 20-5-93
Internationals: Spain U17, U18, U19, Full caps.

2009–10	Malaga	5	0	
2010–11	Malaga	17	4	
2011–12	Malaga	6	1	
2012–13	Malaga	1	1	
2012–13	*Racing Santander*	19	0	19 0
2013–14	Malaga	22	4	
2014–15	Malaga	34	8	85 18
2015–16	Southampton	12	0	12 0

LONG, Shane (F)   331 82
H: 5 10   W: 11 02   b.Co. Tipperary 22-1-87
Internationals: Republic of Ireland B, U21, Full caps.

2005	Cork C	1	0	1 0
2005–06	Reading	11	3	
2006–07	Reading	21	2	
2007–08	Reading	29	3	
2008–09	Reading	37	9	
2009–10	Reading	31	6	
2010–11	Reading	44	21	
2011–12	Reading	1	0	174 44
2011–12	WBA	32	8	
2012–13	WBA	34	8	
2013–14	WBA	15	3	81 19
2013–14	Hull C	15	4	15 4
2014–15	Southampton	32	5	
2015–16	Southampton	28	10	60 15

MANE, Sadio (F)   152 54
H: 5 9   W: 12 00   b.Sedhiou 10-4-92
Internationals: Senegal U23, Full caps.

2011–12	Metz	19	1	
2012–13	Metz	3	1	22 2
2012–13	Red Bull Salzburg	26	16	
2013–14	Red Bull Salzburg	33	13	
2014–15	Red Bull Salzburg	4	2	63 31
2014–15	Southampton	30	10	
2015–16	Southampton	37	11	67 21

MARTINA, Cuco (D)   189 5
H: 6 1   W: 11 05   b.Rotterdam 25-9-89
Internationals: Curacao Full caps.

2008–09	Roosendaal	14	0	
2009–10	Roosendaal	23	1	
2010–11	Roosendaal	32	1	69 2
2011–12	Waalwijk	23	0	
2012–13	Waalwijk	34	1	57 1
2013–14	FC Twente	16	1	
2014–15	FC Twente	32	0	48 1
2015–16	Southampton	15	1	15 1

McCARTHY, Jason (D)   36 2
H: 6 1   W: 12 08   b.Southampton 7-11-95

2013–14	Southampton	0	0	
2014–15	Southampton	1	0	
2015–16	Southampton	0	0	1 0
2015–16	*Wycombe W*	35	2	35 2

McQUEEN, Sam (M)   18 2
H: 5 9   W: 11 00   b.Southampton 6-2-95

2011–12	Southampton	0	0	
2012–13	Southampton	0	0	
2013–14	Southampton	0	0	
2014–15	Southampton	0	0	
2015–16	Southampton	0	0	
2015–16	*Southend U*	18	2	18 2

OLOMOLA, Olufela (F)   0 0
H: 5 7   b.London 5-9-97

PELLE, Graziano (F)   308 108
H: 6 4   W: 13 03   b.Lecce 15-7-85
Internationals: Italy U20, U21, U23, Full caps.

2003–04	Leece	1	0	
2004–05	Leece	0	0	
2004–05	Catania	15	0	15 0
2005–06	Leece	10	0	
2005–06	Crotone	17	6	17 6
2006–07	Leece	0	0	11 0
2006–07	Cesena	38	10	38 10
2007–08	AZ Alkmaar	27	3	
2008–09	AZ Alkmaar	20	3	
2009–10	AZ Alkmaar	13	2	
2010–11	AZ Alkmaar	18	6	78 14
2011–12	Parma	11	1	
2011–12	Sampdoria	12	4	12 4
2012–13	Parma	1	0	12 1
2012–13	Feyenoord	29	27	
2013–14	Feyenoord	28	23	57 50
2014–15	Southampton	38	12	
2015–16	Southampton	30	11	68 23

RAMIREZ, Gaston (M)   145 26
H: 6 0   W: 12 00   b.Montevideo 2-12-90
Internationals: Uruguay U20, U23, Full caps.

2010–11	Bologna	24	4	
2011–12	Bologna	33	8	57 12
2012–13	Southampton	26	5	
2013–14	Southampton	18	1	
2014–15	Southampton	1	0	
2014–15	*Hull C*	22	1	22 1
2015–16	Southampton	3	0	48 6
2015–16	*Middlesbrough*	18	7	18 7

REED, Harrison (M)   14 0
H: 5 9   W: 11 09   b.Worthing 27-1-95
Internationals: England U19, U20.

2012–13	Southampton	0	0	
2013–14	Southampton	0	0	
2013–14	Southampton	4	0	
2014–15	Southampton	9	0	
2015–16	Southampton	1	0	14 0

RODRIGUEZ, Jay (F)   202 56
H: 6 0   W: 12 00   b.Burnley 29-7-89
Internationals: England U21, Full caps.

2007–08	Burnley	1	0	
2007–08	*Stirling Alb*	11	3	11 3
2008–09	Burnley	25	2	
2009–10	Burnley	0	0	
2009–10	*Barnsley*	6	1	6 1
2010–11	Burnley	42	14	
2011–12	Burnley	37	15	105 31
2012–13	Southampton	35	6	
2013–14	Southampton	33	15	
2014–15	Southampton	0	0	
2015–16	Southampton	12	0	80 21

ROMEU, Oriol (M)   141 2
H: 6 0   W: 12 06   b.Ulldecona 24-9-91
Internationals: Spain U17, U19, U20, U21, U23.

2008–09	Barcelona B	5	0	
2009–10	Barcelona B	26	0	
2010–11	Barcelona B	18	1	49 1
2010–11	Barcelona	1	0	1 0
2011–12	Chelsea	16	0	
2012–13	Chelsea	6	0	
2013–14	Chelsea	0	0	
2013–14	Valencia	13	0	13 0
2014–15	Chelsea	0	0	22 0
2014–15	*Stuttgart*	27	0	27 0
2015–16	Southampton	29	1	29 1

SEAGER, Ryan (F) — 5 1
H: 5 11 W: 11 00 b.Southampton 5-2-96
Internationals: England U17.

Season	Club	Apps	Gls	Tot	Tot
2014–15	Southampton	1	0		
2015–16	Southampton	0	0	1	0
2015–16	*Crewe Alex*	4	1	4	1

STEPHENS, Jack (D) — 69 1
H: 6 1 W: 13 03 b.Torpoint 27-1-94
Internationals: England U18, U19, U20, U21.

Season	Club	Apps	Gls	Tot	Tot
2010–11	Plymouth Arg	5	0	5	0
2010–11	Southampton	0	0		
2011–12	Southampton	0	0		
2012–13	Southampton	0	0		
2013–14	Southampton	0	0		
2013–14	*Swindon T*	10	0		
2014–15	Southampton	0	0		
2014–15	*Swindon T*	37	1	47	1
2015–16	Southampton	0	0		
2015–16	*Middlesbrough*	1	0	1	0
2015–16	*Coventry C*	16	0	16	0

TADIC, Dusan (M) — 306 82
H: 5 11 W: 12 00 b.Backa Topola 20-11-88
Internationals: Serbia Full caps.

Season	Club	Apps	Gls	Tot	Tot
2006–07	Vojvodina	23	3		
2007–08	Vojvodina	28	7		
2008–09	Vojvodina	29	9		
2009–10	Vojvodina	27	10	107	29
2010–11	Groningen	34	7		
2011–12	Groningen	34	7	68	14
2012–13	FC Twente	33	12		
2013–14	FC Twente	33	16	66	28
2014–15	Southampton	31	4		
2015–16	Southampton	34	7	65	11

TARGETT, Matt (D) — 20 0
H: 6 0 W: 12 11 b.Edinburgh 18-9-95
Internationals: Scotland U19, England U19, U20, U21.

Season	Club	Apps	Gls	Tot	Tot
2013–14	Southampton	0	0		
2014–15	Southampton	6	0		
2015–16	Southampton	14	0	20	0

VAN DIJK, Virgil (D) — 172 19
H: 6 4 W: 14 07 b.Breda 8-7-91
Internationals: Netherlands U19, U21, Full caps.

Season	Club	Apps	Gls	Tot	Tot
2010–11	Groningen	5	2		
2011–12	Groningen	23	3		
2012–13	Groningen	34	2	62	7
2013–14	Celtic	36	5		
2014–15	Celtic	35	4		
2015–16	Celtic	5	0	76	9
2015–16	Southampton	34	3	34	3

WANYAMA, Victor (M) — 195 16
H: 6 2 W: 11 12 b.Nairobi 25-6-91
Internationals: Kenya Full caps.

Season	Club	Apps	Gls	Tot	Tot
2009–10	Beerschot	19	0		
2010–11	Beerschot	30	2	49	2
2011–12	Celtic	29	4		
2012–13	Celtic	32	6	61	10
2013–14	Southampton	23	0		
2014–15	Southampton	32	3		
2015–16	Southampton	30	1	85	4

WARD-PROWSE, James (M) — 107 3
H: 5 8 W: 10 06 b.Portsmouth 1-11-94
Internationals: England U17, U19, U20, U21.

Season	Club	Apps	Gls	Tot	Tot
2011–12	Southampton	0	0		
2012–13	Southampton	15	0		
2013–14	Southampton	34	0		
2014–15	Southampton	25	1		
2015–16	Southampton	33	2	107	3

YOSHIDA, Maya (D) — 136 8
H: 6 2 W: 12 03 b.Nagasaki 24-8-88
Internationals: Japan U23, Full caps.

Season	Club	Apps	Gls	Tot	Tot
2010–11	VVV	20	0		
2011–12	VVV	32	5		
2012–13	VVV	2	0	54	5
2012–13	Southampton	32	0		
2013–14	Southampton	8	1		
2014–15	Southampton	22	1		
2015–16	Southampton	20	1	82	3

Players retained or with offer of contract
Barnes, Marcus Thomas; Lewis, Harry Charles John; Little, Armani; Mugabi, Bevis Kristofer Kizito; Sims, Joshua Samuel; Slattery, Callum; Turnbull, Jordan Robert; Valery, Yan; Willard, Harley Bryn; Wood, William Nicholas.

Scholars
Bakary, Mohamed Richard; Cook, Oliver David Paul; Cull, Benjamin Simon; Johnson, Tyreke Martin; Jones, Alfie; Langan, Connor John; Mdlalose, Siphesihle Thembinkosi; Musendo, Rugare David; Nlundulu, Dan; O'Connor, Thomas James; Olomola, Olufela; Osborn, Neal Paul Sean; Rowthorn, Ben John; Thomas, Archie Alexander.

SOUTHEND U (77)

ADEYEYE, Emmanuel (D) — 0 0

Season	Club	Apps	Gls
2015–16	Southend U	0	0

ALAWODE-WILLIAMS, Jordan (D) — 0 0

Season	Club	Apps	Gls
2015–16	Southend U	0	0

ATKINSON, Will (M) — 254 19
H: 5 10 W: 10 07 b.Beverley 14-10-88

Season	Club	Apps	Gls	Tot	Tot
2006–07	Hull C	0	0		
2007–08	Hull C	0	0		
2007–08	*Port Vale*	4	0	4	0
2007–08	*Mansfield T*	12	0	12	0
2008–09	Hull C	0	0		
2009–10	Hull C	2	1		
2009–10	*Rochdale*	15	3		
2010–11	Hull C	4	0		
2010–11	*Rotherham U*	3	1	3	1
2010–11	*Rochdale*	21	2	36	5
2011–12	Hull C	0	0	6	1
2011–12	*Plymouth Arg*	22	4	22	4
2011–12	*Bradford C*	12	1		
2012–13	*Bradford C*	42	1	54	2
2013–14	Southend U	45	2		
2014–15	Southend U	36	2		
2015–16	Southend U	36	2	117	6

BARRETT, Adam (D) — 626 45
H: 5 10 W: 12 00 b.Dagenham 29-11-79

Season	Club	Apps	Gls	Tot	Tot
1998–99	Plymouth Arg	11	0		
1999–2000	Plymouth Arg	42	3		
2000–01	Plymouth Arg	9	0	52	3
2000–01	Mansfield T	8	1		
2001–02	Mansfield T	29	0	37	1
2002–03	Bristol R	45	1		
2003–04	Bristol R	45	4	90	5
2004–05	Southend U	43	11		
2005–06	Southend U	45	3		
2006–07	Southend U	28	3		
2007–08	Southend U	45	6		
2008–09	Southend U	45	2		
2009–10	Southend U	41	2		
2010–11	Crystal Palace	7	0	7	0
2010–11	*Leyton Orient*	14	0	14	0
2011–12	Bournemouth	21	1	21	1
2012–13	Gillingham	43	1		
2013–14	Gillingham	45	2		
2014–15	*AFC Wimbledon*	23	1	23	1
2014–15	Southend U	10	0		
2015–16	Southend U	37	4	294	31

BENTLEY, Daniel (G) — 141 0
H: 6 2 W: 11 05 b.Wickford 13-7-93

Season	Club	Apps	Gls	Tot	Tot
2011–12	Southend U	1	0		
2012–13	Southend U	9	0		
2013–14	Southend U	46	0		
2014–15	Southend U	42	0		
2015–16	Southend U	43	0	141	0

BOLGER, Cian (D) — 107 3
H: 6 4 W: 12 05 b.Co. Kildare 12-3-92
Internationals: Republic of Ireland U19, U21.

Season	Club	Apps	Gls	Tot	Tot
2009–10	Leicester C	0	0		
2010–11	Leicester C	0	0		
2010–11	*Bristol R*	6	0		
2011–12	Leicester C	0	0		
2011–12	*Bristol R*	39	2		
2012–13	Leicester C	0	0		
2012–13	*Bristol R*	3	0	48	2
2012–13	Bolton W	0	0		
2013–14	Bolton W	0	0		
2013–14	*Colchester U*	4	0	4	0
2013–14	*Southend U*	1	0		
2014–15	Southend U	23	1		
2015–16	Southend U	22	0	46	1
2015–16	*Bury*	9	0	9	0

BRIDGE, Jack (M) — 2 0
H: 5 10 W: 11 07 b. 21-9-95

Season	Club	Apps	Gls	Tot	Tot
2013–14	Southend U	0	0		
2014–15	Southend U	0	0		
2015–16	Southend U	2	0	2	0

COKER, Ben (D) — 158 4
H: 5 11 W: 11 09 b.Hatfield 17-6-89

Season	Club	Apps	Gls	Tot	Tot
2010–11	Colchester U	20	0		
2011–12	Colchester U	20	0		
2012–13	Colchester U	1	0	41	0
2013–14	Southend U	45	2		
2014–15	Southend U	32	1		
2015–16	Southend U	40	1	117	4

COTTON, Nico (M) — 0 0

Season	Club	Apps	Gls
2015–16	Southend U	0	0

DEEGAN, Gary (M) — 236 18
H: 5 9 W: 11 11 b.Dublin 28-9-87

Season	Club	Apps	Gls	Tot	Tot
2005–06	Shelbourne				
2006	Kilkenny City	18	4	18	4
2007	Longford Town	30	3	30	3
2008	Galway U	17	0	17	0
2008	Bohemians	12	3	12	3
2009	Bohemians	23	2	23	2
2009–10	Coventry C	17	2		
2010–11	Coventry C	1	0		
2011–12	Coventry C	24	3	42	5
2012–13	Hibernian	20	0	20	0
2013–14	Northampton T	27	1	27	1
2014–15	Southend U	22	0		
2015–16	Southend U	25	0	47	0

GARD, Frederick (M) — 0 0

Season	Club	Apps	Gls
2015–16	Southend U	0	0

HUNT, Noel (F) — 341 71
H: 5 8 W: 11 05 b.Waterford 26-12-82
Internationals: Republic of Ireland U21, B, Full caps.

Season	Club	Apps	Gls	Tot	Tot
2002–03	Dunfermline Ath	12	1		
2003–04	Dunfermline Ath	13	2		
2004–05	Dunfermline Ath	23	1		
2005–06	Dunfermline Ath	32	4	80	8
2006–07	Dundee U	28	10		
2007–08	Dundee U	36	13	64	23
2008–09	Reading	37	11		
2009–10	Reading	10	2		
2010–11	Reading	33	10		
2011–12	Reading	41	8		
2012–13	Reading	24	3	145	33
2013–14	Leeds U	19	0		
2014–15	Leeds U	1	0	20	0
2014–15	*Ipswich T*	11	3	11	3
2015–16	Southend U	21	4	21	4

HURST, Kevan (M) — 368 35
H: 5 10 W: 11 07 b.Chesterfield 27-8-85

Season	Club	Apps	Gls	Tot	Tot
2003–04	Boston U	7	1	7	1
2004–05	Sheffield U	1	0		
2004–05	*Stockport Co*	14	1	14	1
2005–06	Sheffield U	0	0		
2005–06	*Chesterfield*	37	4		
2006–07	Sheffield U	0	0	1	0
2006–07	*Chesterfield*	25	3	62	7
2006–07	*Scunthorpe U*	4	0		
2007–08	Scunthorpe U	33	1		
2008–09	Scunthorpe U	20	2	66	3
2009–10	Carlisle U	33	2		
2010–11	Carlisle U	2	0	35	2
2010–11	*Morecambe*	21	2	21	2
2011–12	Walsall	34	2	34	2
2012–13	Southend U	44	5		
2013–14	Southend U	42	11		
2014–15	Southend U	28	1		
2015–16	Southend U	14	0	128	17

JOHNSON, Ross (M) — 0 0
b. 17-12-96

Season	Club	Apps	Gls
2015–16	Southend U	0	0

KEATING, Macauley (M) — 0 0

Season	Club	Apps	Gls
2015–16	Southend U	0	0

KYPRIANOU, Harry (D) — 0 0
b. 16-3-97

Season	Club	Apps	Gls
2013–14	Watford	0	0
2014–15	Watford	0	0
2015–16	Watford	0	0
2015–16	Southend U	0	0

LEONARD, Ryan (D) — 161 13
H: 6 0 W: 11 01 b.Plympton 24-5-92

Season	Club	Apps	Gls	Tot	Tot
2009–10	Plymouth Arg	1	0		
2010–11	Plymouth Arg	0	0	1	0
2011–12	Southend U	17	1		
2012–13	Southend U	22	2		
2013–14	Southend U	43	5		
2014–15	Southend U	41	3		
2015–16	Southend U	37	2	160	13

MATSUZAKA, Daniel (D) — 0 0
b. 1-8-98

Season	Club	Apps	Gls
2014–15	Southend U	0	0
2015–16	Southend U	0	0

McLAUGHLIN, Stephen (M) — 107 15
H: 5 9 W: 11 12 b.Derry 14-6-90

Season	Club	Apps	Gls	Tot	Tot
2011	Derry C	33	3		
2012	Derry C	24	10	57	13
2012–13	Nottingham F	13	0		
2013–14	Nottingham F	3	0		
2013–14	*Bristol C*	5	0	5	0
2014–15	Nottingham F	6	0	9	0
2014–15	*Notts Co*	13	0	13	0

| 2014–15 | Southend U | 6 | 1 | | |
| 2015–16 | Southend U | 17 | 1 | **23** | **2** |

MOONEY, David (F)   **353 106**
H: 6 2 W: 12 06 b.Dublin 30-10-84
Internationals: Republic of Ireland U23.

2005	Longford T	13	4		
2005	Shamrock R	14	2	**14**	**2**
2006	Longford T	21	3		
2007	Longford T	32	19	**66**	**26**
2008	Cork C	22	15	**22**	**15**
2008–09	Reading	0	0		
2008–09	Stockport Co	2	0	**2**	**0**
2008–09	Norwich C	9	3	**9**	**3**
2009–10	Reading	0	0		
2009–10	Charlton Ath	28	5	**28**	**5**
2010–11	Reading	0	0		
2010–11	Colchester U	39	9	**39**	**9**
2011–12	Leyton Orient	37	5		
2012–13	Leyton Orient	32	5		
2013–14	Leyton Orient	38	19		
2014–15	Leyton Orient	33	9	**140**	**38**
2015–16	Southend U	33	8	**33**	**8**

MOUSSA, Franck (M)   **229 34**
H: 5 8 W: 10 08 b.Brussels 24-7-89

2005–06	Southend U	1	0		
2006–07	Southend U	4	0		
2007–08	Southend U	16	0		
2008–09	Southend U	26	2		
2008–09	Wycombe W	9	0	**9**	**0**
2009–10	Southend U	43	5		
2010–11	Leicester C	8	1		
2010–11	Doncaster R	14	2	**14**	**2**
2011–12	Leicester C	0	0	**8**	**1**
2011–12	Chesterfield	10	4	**10**	**4**
2012–13	Nottingham F	0	0		
2012–13	Coventry C	38	6		
2013–14	Coventry C	39	12	**77**	**18**
2014–15	Charlton Ath	14	1		
2015–16	Charlton Ath	6	0	**20**	**1**
2015–16	Southend U	1	1	**91**	**8**

NORMAN, Harry (M)   **0 0**

| 2015–16 | Southend U | 0 | 0 | | |

O'NEILL, Luke (D)   **57 1**
H: 6 0 W: 11 04 b.Slough 20-8-91
Internationals: England U17.

| 2009–10 | Leicester C | 1 | 0 | **1** | **0** |
| 2009–10 | Tranmere R | 4 | 0 | **4** | **0** |

From Kettering T (loan), Mansfield T

2012–13	Burnley	1	0		
2012–13	Burnley	0	0		
2013–14	York C	15	1	**15**	**1**
2013–14	Southend U	0	0		
2014–15	Burnley	0	0		
2014–15	Scunthorpe U	13	0	**13**	**0**
2014–15	Leyton Orient	8	0	**8**	**0**
2015–16	Southend U	14	0	**15**	**0**

PAYNE, Jack (M)   **77 15**
H: 5 5 W: 9 06 b.Tower Hamlets 25-10-94

2013–14	Southend U	11	0		
2014–15	Southend U	34	6		
2015–16	Southend U	32	9	**77**	**15**

PROSSER, Luke (D)   **172 9**
H: 6 2 W: 12 04 b.Waltham Cross 28-5-88

2005–06	Port Vale	0	0		
2006–07	Port Vale	0	0		
2007–08	Port Vale	5	0		
2008–09	Port Vale	26	1		
2009–10	Port Vale	2	1	**33**	**2**
2010–11	Southend U	17	1		
2011–12	Southend U	21	1		
2012–13	Southend U	25	0		
2013–14	Southend U	25	3		
2014–15	Southend U	30	0		
2015–16	Southend U	13	2	**131**	**7**
2015–16	Northampton T	8	0	**8**	**0**

SCOTT, Brandon (M)   **0 0**

| 2015–16 | Southend U | 0 | 0 | | |

SMITH, Paul (G)   **266 0**
H: 6 3 W: 14 00 b.Epsom 17-12-79

1998–99	Charlton Ath	0	0		
1998–99	Brentford	0	0		
1999–2000	Charlton Ath	0	0		

From Carshalton Ath.

2000–01	Brentford	2	0		
2001–02	Brentford	18	0		
2002–03	Brentford	43	0		
2003–04	Brentford	24	0	**87**	**0**
2004–05	Southampton	0	0		
2005–06	Southampton	6	0		
2006–07	Southampton	9	0	**15**	**0**
2006–07	Nottingham F	45	0		
2007–08	Nottingham F	46	0		

2008–09	Nottingham F	28	0		
2009–10	Nottingham F	1	0		
2010–11	Nottingham F	0	0		
2010–11	Middlesbrough	10	0	**10**	**0**
2011–12	Nottingham F	0	0	**120**	**0**
2012–13	Southend U	34	0		
2013–14	Southend U	0	0		
2014–15	Southend U	0	0		
2015–16	Southend U	0	0	**34**	**0**

SMITH, Ted (G)   **7 0**
b.Benfleet 18-1-96
Internationals: England U18, U19, U20.

2012–13	Southend U	0	0		
2013–14	Southend U	0	0		
2014–15	Southend U	4	0		
2015–16	Southend U	3	0	**7**	**0**

THOMPSON, Adam (D)   **106 3**
H: 6 2 W: 12 10 b.Harlow 28-9-92
Internationals: Northern Ireland U17, U19, U21, Full caps.

2010–11	Watford	10	1		
2011–12	Watford	0	0		
2011–12	Brentford	20	0	**20**	**0**
2012–13	Watford	4	0		
2012–13	Wycombe W	2	0	**2**	**0**
2012–13	Barnet	1	0	**1**	**0**
2013–14	Watford	0	0	**14**	**1**
2013–14	Southend U	16	0		
2014–15	Southend U	28	0		
2015–16	Southend U	25	2	**69**	**2**

TIMLIN, Michael (M)   **284 18**
H: 5 8 W: 11 08 b.New Cross 19-3-85
Internationals: Republic of Ireland U17, U21.

2002–03	Fulham	0	0		
2003–04	Fulham	0	0		
2004–05	Fulham	0	0		
2005–06	Fulham	0	0		
2005–06	Scunthorpe U	1	0	**1**	**0**
2005–06	Doncaster R	3	0	**3**	**0**
2006–07	Fulham	0	0		
2006–07	Swindon T	24	1		
2007–08	Swindon T	0	0		
2007–08	Swindon T	10	1		
2008–09	Swindon T	41	2		
2009–10	Swindon T	21	0		
2010–11	Swindon T	22	2		
2010–11	Southend U	8	1		
2011–12	Swindon T	1	0	**119**	**6**
2011–12	Southend U	39	4		
2012–13	Southend U	25	0		
2013–14	Southend U	36	2		
2014–15	Southend U	32	3		
2015–16	Southend U	21	2	**161**	**12**

WESTON, Myles (M)   **308 27**
H: 5 11 W: 12 05 b.Lewisham 12-3-88
Internationals: England U16, U17, U18, U19. Antigua and Barbuda Full caps.

2006–07	Charlton Ath	0	0		
2006–07	Notts Co	4	0		
2007–08	Notts Co	25	0		
2008–09	Notts Co	44	3	**73**	**3**
2009–10	Brentford	40	8		
2010–11	Brentford	42	3		
2011–12	Brentford	26	1	**108**	**12**
2012–13	Gillingham	37	8		
2013–14	Gillingham	39	2	**76**	**10**
2014–15	Southend U	34	2		
2015–16	Southend U	17	0	**51**	**2**

WHITE, John (D)   **344 2**
H: 6 0 W: 12 01 b.Maldon 26-7-86

2004–05	Colchester U	20	0		
2005–06	Colchester U	35	0		
2006–07	Colchester U	16	0		
2007–08	Colchester U	21	0		
2008–09	Colchester U	26	0		
2009–10	Colchester U	39	0		
2009–10	Southend U	5	0		
2010–11	Colchester U	22	0		
2011–12	Colchester U	26	0		
2012–13	Colchester U	22	0	**227**	**0**
2013–14	Colchester U	41	1		
2014–15	Colchester U	42	0		
2015–16	Colchester U	29	1	**117**	**2**

WILLIAMS, Jason (F)   **6 0**
H: 6 0 W: 12 06 b. 1-11-95

2013–14	Southend U	2	0		
2014–15	Southend U	2	0		
2015–16	Southend U	2	0	**6**	**0**

WORDSWORTH, Anthony (M)   **240 46**
H: 6 1 W: 12 00 b.Camden 3-1-89

2007–08	Colchester U	3	0		
2008–09	Colchester U	30	3		
2009–10	Colchester U	41	11		

2010–11	Colchester U	35	5		
2011–12	Colchester U	44	13		
2012–13	Colchester U	24	3	**177**	**35**
2012–13	Ipswich T	7	1		
2013–14	Ipswich T	10	1		
2014–15	Ipswich T	1	0	**18**	**2**
2014–15	Rotherham U	6	1	**6**	**1**
2014–15	Crawley T	18	4	**18**	**4**
2015–16	Southend U	21	4	**21**	**4**

WORRALL, David (M)   **270 22**
H: 6 0 W: 11 03 b.Manchester 12-6-90

2006–07	Bury	0	0		
2007–08	Bury	0	0		
2007–08	WBA	0	0		
2008–09	Accrington S	4	0	**4**	**0**
2008–09	Shrewsbury T	9	0	**9**	**0**
2009–10	WBA	0	0		
2009–10	Bury	40	4		
2010–11	Bury	40	2		
2011–12	Bury	41	3		
2012–13	Bury	42	2	**163**	**11**
2013–14	Rotherham U	3	1	**3**	**1**
2013–14	Oldham Ath	18	1	**18**	**1**
2014–15	Southend U	38	6		
2015–16	Southend U	35	3	**73**	**9**

Scholars
Adeyeye, Emmanuel Adekunle; Alawode-Williams, Jordan; Batlokwa, Wedu Reneilwe; Bedford, Joseph; Bexon, Josh Andrew; Bwomono, Elvis Okello; Clark, Alex; Clifford, Thomas; Cotton, Nico Lewis; Coutts, Sonny Joseph; Dias, Damani Joseph; Gard, Frederick Jack; Gard, Lewis Thomas; Johnson, Ross Anthony; Keating, Macauley Anthony; Mackenzie, Joseph Peter Uduakobong; Macree, James Terence; Matsuzaka, Daniel Lewis; Matthews, Imani Anthony George; Musselwhite, Benjamin George John; Norman, Harry Alan; Phillips, Harry; Pitoula Wabo, Fotsing Norman Arthur; Ripsher, Tommy Michael; Salami, Abdus-Salam Efosa Uhunoma; Scott, Brandon Montel; Walker, Daniel Charles.

STEVENAGE (78)

ADAMS, Charlie (M)   **36 2**
H: 5 6 W: 9 10 b.London 16-5-94

2012–13	Brentford	1	0		
2013–14	Brentford	3	0		
2014–15	Brentford	0	0	**4**	**0**
2014–15	*Stevenage*	9	0		
2015	Louisville C	21	2	**21**	**2**
2015–16	Stevenage	2	0	**11**	**0**

AKINYEMI, Dipo (F)   **14 1**
b. 10-6-97

| 2014–15 | Stevenage | 0 | 0 | | |
| 2015–16 | Stevenage | 14 | 1 | **14** | **1** |

CASEY, George (M)   **0 0**
H: 6 0 W: 11 00 b. 8-9-97

| 2014–15 | Stevenage | 0 | 0 | | |
| 2015–16 | Stevenage | 0 | 0 | | |

CONLON, Tom (M)   **46 2**
H: 5 8 W: 9 11 b.Stoke-on-Trent 3-2-96

2013–14	Peterborough U	1	0	**1**	**0**
2014–15	Stevenage	13	0		
2015–16	Stevenage	32	2	**45**	**2**

COX, Lee (M)   **153 4**
H: 6 1 W: 12 02 b.Leicester 26-6-90

2007–08	Leicester C	0	0		
2008–09	Leicester C	0	0		
2008–09	Yeovil T	0	0		
2009–10	Inverness CT	35	2		
2010–11	Inverness CT	27	1		
2011–12	Inverness CT	7	0	**69**	**3**
2011–12	Swindon T	7	0		
2012–13	Swindon T	0	0		
2012–13	Oxford U	14	0	**14**	**0**
2012–13	*Plymouth Arg*	10	0		
2013–14	*Plymouth Arg*	0	0		
2013–14	Swindon T	5	1	**12**	**1**
2014–15	Plymouth Arg	32	0		
2015–16	Plymouth Arg	4	0	**46**	**0**
2015–16	Stevenage	0	0	**12**	**0**

DAY, Chris (G)   **390 0**
H: 6 2 W: 13 07 b.Whipps Cross 28-7-75
Internationals: England U18, U21.

1992–93	Tottenham H	0	0		
1993–94	Tottenham H	0	0		
1994–95	Tottenham H	0	0		
1995–96	Tottenham H	0	0		
1996–97	Crystal Palace	24	0	**24**	**0**

1997–98	Watford	0	0		
1998–99	Watford	0	0		
1999–2000	Watford	11	0		
2000–01	Watford	0	0	11	0
2000–01	Lincoln C	14	0	14	0
2001–02	QPR	16	0		
2002–03	QPR	12	0		
2003–04	QPR	29	0		
2004–05	QPR	30	0	87	0
2004–05	*Preston NE*	6	0	6	0
2005–06	Oldham Ath	30	0	30	0
2006–07	Millwall	5	0		
2007–08	Millwall	5	0	10	0
2010–11	Stevenage	46	0		
2011–12	Stevenage	44	0		
2012–13	Stevenage	17	0		
2013–14	Stevenage	44	0		
2014–15	Stevenage	38	0		
2015–16	Stevenage	19	0	208	0

FRANKS, Fraser (D) 55 3
H: 6 0　W: 10 12　b.Hammersmith 22-11-90
Internationals: England C.

2009–10	Brentford	0	0		
2011–12	AFC Wimbledon	4	0	4	0
2014–15	Luton T	13	0	13	0
2015–16	Stevenage	38	3	38	3

GORDAN, Rohdell (M) 7 0
b. 28-3-96

2013–14	Stevenage	3	0		
2014–15	Stevenage	0	0		
2015–16	Stevenage	4	0	7	0

GORMAN, Dale (D) 13 0
H: 5 11　W: 11 00　b.Letterkenny 28-6-96
Internationals: Northern Ireland U19.

| 2014–15 | Stevenage | 0 | 0 | | |
| 2015–16 | Stevenage | 13 | 0 | 13 | 0 |

HENRY, Ronnie (D) 154 0
H: 5 11　W: 11 10　b.Hemel Hempstead 2-1-84
Internationals: England C.

2002–03	Tottenham H	0	0		
2002–03	*Southend U*	3	0	3	0
2004	Dublin C	12	0	12	0
2010–11	Stevenage	42	0		
2011–12	Stevenage	32	0		
2014–15	Stevenage	34	0		
2015–16	Stevenage	31	0	139	0

JACKSON, Ben (G) 0 0
b. 3-12-97

| 2015–16 | Stevenage | 0 | 0 | | |

JEBB, Jack (M) 14 0
H: 6 0　W: 11 09　b.London 11-9-95
Internationals: England U16, U17.

2012–13	Arsenal	0	0		
2013–14	Arsenal	0	0		
2014–15	Arsenal	0	0		
2014–15	*Stevenage*	9	0		
2015–16	Arsenal	0	0		
2015–16	Stevenage	5	0	14	0

JOHNSON, Ryan (D) 12 0
H: 6 2　W: 13 05　b. 2-10-96
Internationals: Northern Ireland U21.

2013–14	Stevenage	1	0		
2014–15	Stevenage	4	0		
2015–16	Stevenage	7	0	12	0

JONES, Jamie (G) 219 0
H: 6 2　W: 14 05　b.Kirkby 18-2-89

2007–08	Everton	0	0		
2008–09	Leyton Orient	20	0		
2009–10	Leyton Orient	36	0		
2010–11	Leyton Orient	35	0		
2011–12	Leyton Orient	6	0		
2012–13	Leyton Orient	26	0		
2013–14	Leyton Orient	28	0	151	0
2014–15	Preston NE	17	0		
2014–15	*Coventry C*	4	0	4	0
2014–15	*Rochdale*	13	0	13	0
2015–16	Preston NE	0	0	17	0
2015–16	*Colchester U*	17	0	17	0
2015–16	Stevenage	17	0	17	0

KENNEDY, Ben (F) 37 6
H: 5 10　W: 11 00　b. 12-1-97
Internationals: Northern Ireland U17, U19.

| 2014–15 | Stevenage | 15 | 4 | | |
| 2015–16 | Stevenage | 22 | 3 | 37 | 6 |

KERR, Nathan (D) 0 0
b. 20-1-98

| 2015–16 | Stevenage | 0 | 0 | | |

LEE, Charlie (M) 331 37
H: 5 11　W: 11 07　b.Whitechapel 5-1-87

2005–06	Tottenham H	0	0		
2006–07	Tottenham H	0	0		
2006–07	Millwall	5	0	5	0
2007–08	Peterborough U	42	6		
2008–09	Peterborough U	44	5		
2009–10	Peterborough U	33	2		
2010–11	Peterborough U	34	1	153	14
2010–11	Gillingham	4	1		
2011–12	Gillingham	33	6		
2012–13	Gillingham	31	2		
2013–14	Gillingham	31	2	99	11
2014–15	Stevenage	44	9		
2015–16	Stevenage	30	3	74	12

MARRIOTT, Adam (F) 19 3
H: 5 9　W: 11 03　b.Brandon 14-4-91

| 2014–15 | Stevenage | 13 | 3 | | |
| 2015–16 | Stevenage | 6 | 0 | 19 | 3 |

McALLISTER, David (M) 171 30
H: 5 10　W: 11 09　b.Dublin 29-12-88

2008	Drogheda U	0	0		
2008	*Shelbourne*	16	7		
2009	Shelbourne	30	16	46	23
2010	St Patrick's Ath	32	3	32	3
2010–11	Sheffield U	2	1		
2011–12	Sheffield U	4	0		
2011–12	*Shrewsbury T*	15	0		
2012–13	Sheffield U	14	1	20	2
2012–13	Shrewsbury T	15	1		
2013–14	Shrewsbury T	26	1	56	2
2014–15	Stevenage	16	0		
2015–16	Stevenage	1	0	17	0

McCOMBE, Jamie (D) 396 27
H: 6 5　W: 12 05　b.Scunthorpe 1-1-83

2001–02	Scunthorpe U	17	0		
2002–03	Scunthorpe U	31	1		
2003–04	Scunthorpe U	15	0	63	1
2003–04	Lincoln C	8	0		
2004–05	Lincoln C	41	3		
2005–06	Lincoln C	38	4	87	7
2006–07	Bristol C	41	4		
2007–08	Bristol C	34	3		
2008–09	Bristol C	28	1		
2009–10	Bristol C	16	1	119	9
2010–11	Huddersfield T	34	5		
2011–12	Huddersfield T	20	3		
2011–12	*Preston NE*	6	0	6	0
2012–13	Huddersfield T	0	0	54	8
2012–13	Doncaster R	33	1		
2013–14	Doncaster R	2	0		
2014–15	Doncaster R	18	1	53	2
2015–16	Stevenage	14	0	14	0

O'CONNOR, Aaron (F) 59 12
b.Nottingham 9-8-83

| 2002–03 | Scunthorpe U | 3 | 0 | 3 | 0 |

From Ilkeston T, Gresley, Grays Ath, Mansfield T, Rushden & D, Luton T.

| 2013–14 | Newport Co | 4 | 1 | | |
| 2014–15 | Newport Co | 39 | 10 | 43 | 11 |

From Forest Green R.

| 2015–16 | Stevenage | 13 | 1 | 13 | 1 |

OGILVIE, Connor (D) 21 1
b. 14-2-96
Internationals: England U16, U17.

2013–14	Tottenham H	0	0		
2014–15	Tottenham H	0	0		
2015–16	Stevenage	21	1	21	1

OKIMO, Jerome (D) 42 1
H: 6 0　W: 12 00　b. 8-6-88

| 2014–15 | Stevenage | 29 | 0 | | |
| 2015–16 | Stevenage | 13 | 1 | 42 | 1 |

PARRETT, Dean (M) 103 11
H: 5 10　W: 11 04　b.Hampstead 16-11-91
Internationals: England U16, U17, U19, U20.

2008–09	Tottenham H	0	0		
2009–10	Tottenham H	0	0		
2009–10	*Aldershot T*	4	0	4	0
2010–11	Tottenham H	0	0		
2010–11	*Plymouth Arg*	8	1	8	1
2010–11	*Charlton Ath*	9	1	9	1
2011–12	Tottenham H	0	0		
2011–12	*Yeovil T*	10	1	10	1
2012–13	Tottenham H	0	0		
2012–13	*Swindon T*	3	0	3	0
2013–14	Stevenage	12	1		
2014–15	Stevenage	30	4		
2015–16	Stevenage	27	3	69	8

PETT, Tom (M) 74 8
H: 5 8　W: 11 00　b. 3-12-91

| 2014–15 | Stevenage | 34 | 7 | | |
| 2015–16 | Stevenage | 40 | 1 | 74 | 8 |

READING, Tyler (G) 0 0
H: 5 10　W: 11 11　b. 21-5-97

| 2014–15 | Stevenage | 0 | 0 | | |
| 2015–16 | Stevenage | 0 | 0 | | |

SCHUMACHER, Steven (M) 387 50
H: 5 10　W: 11 00　b.Liverpool 30-4-84

2000–01	Everton	0	0		
2001–02	Everton	0	0		
2002–03	Everton	0	0		
2003–04	Everton	0	0		
2003–04	*Carlisle U*	4	0	4	0
2004–05	Bradford C	43	6		
2005–06	Bradford C	30	1		
2006–07	Bradford C	44	6	117	13
2007–08	Crewe Alex	26	1		
2008–09	Crewe Alex	15	2		
2009–10	Crewe Alex	32	4	73	7
2010–11	Bury	43	9		
2011–12	Bury	32	6		
2012–13	Bury	39	8	114	23
2013–14	Fleetwood T	32	5		
2014–15	Fleetwood T	32	0	64	5
2015–16	Stevenage	15	2	15	2

SMYTH, Matthew (D) 0 0
b. 8-5-98
Internationals: Northern Ireland U16, U17.

| 2015–16 | Stevenage | 0 | 0 | | |

STORER, Jack (F) 1 0
b. 2-1-98

| 2014–15 | Stevenage | 0 | 0 | | |
| 2015–16 | Stevenage | 1 | 0 | 1 | 0 |

TONGE, Michael (M) 417 30
H: 6 0　W: 11 10　b.Manchester 7-4-83
Internationals: England U20, U21.

2000–01	Sheffield U	2	0		
2001–02	Sheffield U	30	3		
2002–03	Sheffield U	44	6		
2003–04	Sheffield U	46	4		
2004–05	Sheffield U	34	2		
2005–06	Sheffield U	30	3		
2006–07	Sheffield U	27	2		
2007–08	Sheffield U	45	1		
2008–09	Sheffield U	4	0	262	21
2008–09	Stoke C	10	0		
2009–10	Stoke C	0	0		
2009–10	*Preston NE*	7	0		
2009–10	*Derby Co*	18	2	18	2
2010–11	Stoke C	2	0		
2010–11	*Preston NE*	5	1	12	1
2011–12	Stoke C	0	0		
2011–12	*Barnsley*	10	0	10	0
2012–13	Stoke C	0	0	12	0
2012–13	*Leeds U*	35	4		
2013–14	Leeds U	23	0		
2014–15	Leeds U	10	0	68	4
2014–15	*Millwall*	6	0	6	0
2015–16	Stevenage	29	2	29	2

WELLS, Dean (D) 71 6
H: 6 1　W: 13 03　b.Isleworth 25-5-85

| 2014–15 | Stevenage | 43 | 4 | | |
| 2015–16 | Stevenage | 28 | 2 | 71 | 6 |

WHELPDALE, Chris (M) 293 50
H: 6 0　W: 12 08　b.Harold Wood 27-1-87

2007–08	Peterborough U	35	3		
2008–09	Peterborough U	39	7		
2009–10	Peterborough U	29	1		
2010–11	Peterborough U	22	1	125	12
2010–11	*Gillingham*	4	2		
2011–12	Gillingham	39	12		
2012–13	Gillingham	41	7		
2013–14	Gillingham	24	1	108	23
2014–15	Gillingham	39	7		
2015–16	Stevenage	21	8	60	15

WILKINSON, Luke (D) 146 15
H: 6 2　W: 11 09　b.Wells 2-12-92

2009–10	Portsmouth	0	0		
2010–11	Dagenham & R	0	0		
2011–12	Dagenham & R	0	0		
2012–13	Dagenham & R	43	6		
2013–14	Dagenham & R	22	0	65	6
2014–15	Luton T	40	2		
2015–16	Luton T	20	3	62	7
2015–16	Stevenage	19	2	19	2

WILLIAMS, Brett (F) 44 7
H: 6 2　W: 12 07　b.Southampton 1-12-87

2010–11	Reading	0	0		
2011–12	Reading	0	0		
2011–12	*Rotherham U*	11	2	11	2
2011–12	*Northampton T*	18	3	18	3

From Woking, Aldershot T.

| 2015–16 | Stevenage | 15 | 2 | 15 | 2 |

YAMFAM, Louis (F)   0   0
b. 24-3-98
2014-15   Stevenage   0   0
2015-16   Stevenage   0   0

Scholars
Brady, Liam Aiden; Cregan, Michael James; Croud, Jacob William; Gray, Jamie; Guerfi, Zakary Zidane; Jackson, Benjamin Edward Alan; Kanda-Botaka, Norley; McKee, Mark Anthony; Schmid, Ryan Stephen; Smyth, Matthew Mervyn; Sweeney, Robbie-Lee; Wade Slater, Luke Keith; Yamfam, Louis-Michel.

STOKE C (79)

ADAM, Charlie (M)   326   70
H: 6 1   W: 12 00   b.Dundee 10-12-85
Internationals: Scotland U21, B, Full caps.

Season	Club	App	Gls	App	Gls
2004-05	Rangers	1	0		
2004-05	Ross Co	10	2	10	2
2005-06	Rangers	1	0		
2005-06	St Mirren	29	5	29	5
2006-07	Rangers	32	11		
2007-08	Rangers	16	2		
2008-09	Rangers	9	0	59	13
2008-09	Blackpool	13	2		
2009-10	Blackpool	43	16		
2010-11	Blackpool	35	12	91	30
2011-12	Liverpool	28	2	28	2
2012-13	Stoke C	27	3		
2013-14	Stoke C	31	7		
2014-15	Stoke C	29	7		
2015-16	Stoke C	22	1	109	18

AFELLAY, Ibrahim (M)   240   44
H: 5 11   W: 10 10   b.Utrecht 2-4-86
Internationals: Netherlands Full caps.

Season	Club	App	Gls	App	Gls
2003-04	PSV Eindhoven	2	0		
2004-05	PSV Eindhoven	7	2		
2005-06	PSV Eindhoven	23	2		
2006-07	PSV Eindhoven	27	6		
2007-08	PSV Eindhoven	24	2		
2008-09	PSV Eindhoven	28	13		
2009-10	PSV Eindhoven	29	4		
2010-11	PSV Eindhoven	19	6	159	35
2010-11	Barcelona	16	1		
2011-12	Barcelona	4	0		
2012-13	Barcelona	0	0		
2012-13	Schalke 04	10	2	10	2
2013-14	Barcelona	1	0		
2014-15	Barcelona	0	0	21	1
2014-15	Olympiacos	19	4	19	4
2015-16	Stoke C	31	2	31	2

ARNAUTOVIC, Marko (F)   212   42
H: 6 4   W: 13 00   b.Floridsdorf 19-4-89
Internationals: Austria U18, U19, U21, Full caps.

Season	Club	App	Gls	App	Gls
2006-07	FC Twente	2	0		
2007-08	FC Twente	14	0		
2008-09	FC Twente	28	12		
2009-10	FC Twente	0	0	44	12
2009-10	Inter Milan	3	0	3	0
2010-11	Werder Bremen	25	3		
2011-12	Werder Bremen	19	6		
2012-13	Werder Bremen	26	5		
2013-14	Werder Bremen	2	0	72	14
2013-14	Stoke C	30	4		
2014-15	Stoke C	29	1		
2015-16	Stoke C	34	11	93	16

BACHMANN, Daniel (G)   9   0
H: 6 3   W: 12 11   b.Vienna 9-7-94
Internationals: Austria U16, U17, U18, U19, U21.

Season	Club	App	Gls	App	Gls
2011-12	Stoke C	0	0		
2012-13	Stoke C	0	0		
2013-14	Stoke C	0	0		
2014-15	Stoke C	0	0		
2015-16	Stoke C	0	0		
2015-16	Ross Co	1	0	1	0
2015-16	Bury	8	0	8	0

BARDSLEY, Phillip (D)   258   8
H: 5 11   W: 11 13   b.Salford 28-6-85
Internationals: Scotland Full caps.

Season	Club	App	Gls	App	Gls
2003-04	Manchester U	0	0		
2004-05	Manchester U	0	0		
2005-06	Manchester U	8	0		
2005-06	Burnley	6	0	6	0
2006-07	Manchester U	0	0		
2006-07	Rangers	5	1	5	1
2006-07	Aston Villa	13	0	13	0
2007-08	Manchester U	0	0	8	0
2007-08	Sheffield U	16	0	16	0
2007-08	Sunderland	11	0		
2008-09	Sunderland	28	0		
2009-10	Sunderland	26	0		
2010-11	Sunderland	34	3		
2011-12	Sunderland	31	1		
2012-13	Sunderland	18	1		
2013-14	Sunderland	26	2	174	7
2014-15	Stoke C	25	0		
2015-16	Stoke C	11	0	36	0

BOJAN, Krkic (F)   223   50
H: 5 8   W: 10 03   b.Linyola 28-8-90
Internationals: Spain U17, U21, Full caps.

Season	Club	App	Gls	App	Gls
2007-08	Barcelona	31	10		
2008-09	Barcelona	23	2		
2009-10	Barcelona	23	8		
2010-11	Barcelona	27	6		
2011-12	Roma	33	7		
2011-12	Roma	0	0	33	7
2012-13	AC Milan	19	3	19	3
2013-14	Barcelona	0	0	104	26
2013-14	Ajax	24	3	24	3
2014-15	Stoke C	16	4		
2015-16	Stoke C	27	7	43	11

BUTLAND, Jack (G)   142   0
H: 6 4   W: 12 00   b.Clevedon 10-3-93
Internationals: England U16, U17, U19, U20, U21, Full caps.

Season	Club	App	Gls	App	Gls
2009-10	Birmingham C	0	0		
2010-11	Birmingham C	0	0		
2011-12	Birmingham C	0	0		
2011-12	Cheltenham T	24	0	24	0
2012-13	Birmingham C	46	0	46	0
2012-13	Stoke C	0	0		
2013-14	Stoke C	3	0		
2013-14	Barnsley	13	0	13	0
2013-14	Leeds U	16	0	16	0
2014-15	Stoke C	3	0		
2014-15	Derby Co	6	0	6	0
2015-16	Stoke C	31	0	37	0

CAMERON, Geoff (D)   253   12
H: 6 3   W: 13 02   b.Attleboro 11-7-85
Internationals: USA Full caps.

Season	Club	App	Gls	App	Gls
2008	Houston D	24	1		
2009	Houston D	32	2		
2010	Houston D	16	3		
2011	Houston D	37	5		
2012	Houston D	15	0	124	11
2012-13	Stoke C	35	0		
2013-14	Stoke C	37	2		
2014-15	Stoke C	27	0		
2015-16	Stoke C	30	0	129	2

CROUCH, Peter (F)   498   128
H: 6 7   W: 13 03   b.Macclesfield 30-1-81
Internationals: England U20, U21, B, Full caps.

Season	Club	App	Gls	App	Gls
1998-99	Tottenham H	0	0		
1999-2000	Tottenham H	0	0		
2000-01	QPR	42	10	42	10
2001-02	Portsmouth	37	18		
2001-02	Aston Villa	7	2		
2002-03	Aston Villa	14	0		
2003-04	Aston Villa	16	4	37	6
2003-04	Norwich C	15	4	15	4
2004-05	Southampton	27	12	27	12
2005-06	Liverpool	32	8		
2006-07	Liverpool	32	9		
2007-08	Liverpool	21	5	85	22
2008-09	Portsmouth	38	11		
2009-10	Portsmouth	0	0	75	29
2009-10	Tottenham H	38	8		
2010-11	Tottenham H	34	4		
2011-12	Tottenham H	1	0	73	12
2011-12	Stoke C	32	10		
2012-13	Stoke C	34	7		
2013-14	Stoke C	34	8		
2014-15	Stoke C	33	8		
2015-16	Stoke C	11	0	144	33

DIONATAN, Teixeira (D)   47   3
H: 6 4   W: 12 04   b.Londrina 24-7-92
Internationals: Brazil U17. Slovakia U21.

Season	Club	App	Gls	App	Gls
2009-10	Kosice	2	0		
2010-11	Kosice	0	0		
2011-12	Kosice	0	0	2	0
2012-13	Duckla	13	0	13	0
2013-14	Dukla	22	3	22	3
2014-15	Stoke C	1	0		
2015-16	Stoke C	1	0	2	0
2015-16	Fleetwood T	8	0	8	0

DIOUF, Mame (F)   221   78
H: 6 1   W: 12 00   b.Dakar 16-12-87
Internationals: Senegal Full caps.

Season	Club	App	Gls	App	Gls
2007	Molde	21	9		
2008	Molde	23	7		
2009	Molde	29	16	73	32
2009-10	Manchester U	5	1		
2010-11	Manchester U	0	0		
2010-11	Blackburn R	26	3	26	3
2011-12	Manchester U	0	0	5	1
2011-12	Hannover 96	10	6		
2012-13	Hannover 96	28	12		
2013-14	Hannover 96	19	8	57	26
2014-15	Stoke C	34	11		
2015-16	Stoke C	26	5	60	16

EL OURIACHI, Moha (M)   0   0
H: 5 11   W: 11 07   b.Nador 13-1-96
Internationals: Spain U17. Morocco U23.

Season	Club	App	Gls
2014-15	Barcelona	0	0
2015-16	Stoke C	0	0

GIVEN, Shay (G)   484   0
H: 6 0   W: 13 03   b.Lifford 20-4-76
Internationals: Republic of Ireland U21, Full caps.

Season	Club	App	Gls	App	Gls
1994-95	Blackburn R	0	0		
1994-95	Swindon T	0	0		
1995-96	Blackburn R	0	0		
1995-96	Swindon T	5	0	5	0
1995-96	Sunderland	17	0	17	0
1996-97	Blackburn R	2	0	2	0
1997-98	Newcastle U	24	0		
1998-99	Newcastle U	31	0		
1999-2000	Newcastle U	14	0		
2000-01	Newcastle U	34	0		
2001-02	Newcastle U	38	0		
2002-03	Newcastle U	38	0		
2003-04	Newcastle U	38	0		
2004-05	Newcastle U	36	0		
2005-06	Newcastle U	38	0		
2006-07	Newcastle U	22	0		
2007-08	Newcastle U	19	0		
2008-09	Newcastle U	22	0	354	0
2008-09	Manchester C	15	0		
2009-10	Manchester C	35	0		
2010-11	Manchester C	0	0	50	0
2011-12	Aston Villa	32	0		
2012-13	Aston Villa	2	0		
2013-14	Aston Villa	0	0		
2013-14	Middlesbrough	16	0	16	0
2014-15	Aston Villa	3	0	37	0
2015-16	Stoke C	3	0	3	0

HAUGAARD, Jakob (G)   49   0
b. 1-5-92
Internationals: Denmark U18, U20.

Season	Club	App	Gls	App	Gls
2010-11	Akademisk BK	14	0	14	0
2011-12	Midtjylland	6	0		
2012-13	Midtjylland	6	0		
2013-14	Midtjylland	1	0		
2014-15	Midtjylland	23	0	30	0
2015-16	Stoke C	5	0	5	0

IMBULA, Giannelli (M)   181   9
H: 6 0   W: 12 02   b.Vilvoorde 12-9-92
Internationals: France U20, U21.

Season	Club	App	Gls	App	Gls
2009-10	Guingamp	2	0		
2010-11	Guingamp	28	2		
2011-12	Guingamp	27	0		
2012-13	Guingamp	34	2	91	4
2013-14	Marseille	29	1		
2014-15	Marseille	37	4	66	3
2015-16	FC Porto	10	0	10	0
2015-16	Stoke C	14	2	14	2

IRELAND, Stephen (F)   242   19
H: 5 8   W: 10 07   b.Cork 22-8-86
Internationals: Republic of Ireland U21, Full caps.

Season	Club	App	Gls	App	Gls
2005-06	Manchester C	24	0		
2006-07	Manchester C	24	1		
2007-08	Manchester C	33	4		
2008-09	Manchester C	35	9		
2009-10	Manchester C	22	2		
2010-11	Manchester C	0	0	138	16
2010-11	Aston Villa	10	0		
2010-11	Newcastle U	2	0	2	0
2011-12	Aston Villa	24	1		
2012-13	Aston Villa	13	0		
2013-14	Aston Villa	0	0	47	1
2013-14	Stoke C	25	2		
2014-15	Stoke C	17	0		
2015-16	Stoke C	13	0	55	2

JOHNSON, Glen (D)   334   15
H: 6 0   W: 13 04   b.Greenwich 23-8-84
Internationals: England U20, U21, Full caps.

Season	Club	App	Gls	App	Gls
2001-02	West Ham U	0	0		
2002-03	West Ham U	15	0	15	0
2002-03	Millwall	8	0	8	0
2003-04	Chelsea	19	3		
2004-05	Chelsea	17	0		
2005-06	Chelsea	4	0		
2006-07	Chelsea	0	0		

Season	Club	A	G	Tot A	Tot G
2006–07	*Portsmouth*	26	0		
2007–08	Chelsea	2	0	42	3
2007–08	Portsmouth	29	1		
2008–09	Portsmouth	29	3		
2009–10	Portsmouth	0	0	84	4
2009–10	Liverpool	25	3		
2010–11	Liverpool	28	2		
2011–12	Liverpool	23	1		
2012–13	Liverpool	36	1		
2013–14	Liverpool	29	0		
2014–15	Liverpool	19	1	160	8
2015–16	Stoke C	25	0	25	0

JOSELU, Mato (F)   128 31
H: 6 3   W: 12 08   b.Stuttgart, Germany 27-3-90
Internationals: Spain U19, U20, U21.

Season	Club	A	G	Tot A	Tot G
2008–09	Celta Vigo	2	0		
2009–10	Real Madrid	0	0		
2009–10	*Celta Vigo*	24	4	26	4
2010–11	Real Madrid	1	1		
2011–12	Real Madrid	0	0	1	1
2012–13	Hoffenheim	25	5		
2013–14	Hoffenheim	0	0	25	5
2013–14	*Eintracht Frankfurt*	24	9	24	9
2014–15	Hannover 96	30	8	30	8
2015–16	Stoke C	22	4	22	4

LECYGNE, Eddy (M)   1 0
H: 5 11   W: 10 08   b.Pabu 6-8-96
Internationals: France U19.

Season	Club	A	G	Tot A	Tot G
2013–14	Stoke C	0	0		
2014–15	Stoke C	0	0		
2015–16	Stoke C	0	0		
2015–16	*Doncaster R*	1	0	1	0

MUNIESA, Marc (D)   49 0
H: 5 10   W: 11 04   b.Lloret de Mar 27-3-92
Internationals: Spain U16, U17, U19, U21.

Season	Club	A	G	Tot A	Tot G
2008–09	Barcelona	1	0		
2009–10	Barcelona	0	0		
2010–11	Barcelona	0	0		
2011–12	Barcelona	1	0		
2012–13	Barcelona	0	0	2	0
2013–14	Stoke C	13	0		
2014–15	Stoke C	19	0		
2015–16	Stoke C	15	0	47	0

ODEMWINGIE, Peter (F)   330 91
H: 6 0   W: 11 09   b.Tashkent 15-7-81
Internationals: Nigeria Full caps.

Season	Club	A	G	Tot A	Tot G
2002–03	La Louviere	14	2		
2003–04	La Louviere	27	5		
2004–05	La Louviere	3	2	44	9
2004–05	Lille	20	4		
2005–06	Lille	26	14		
2006–07	Lille	29	5	75	23
2007	Loko Moscow	14	4		
2008	Loko Moscow	26	10		
2009	Loko Moscow	25	7		
2010	Loko Moscow	10	0	75	21
2010–11	WBA	32	15		
2011–12	WBA	30	10		
2012–13	WBA	25	5	87	30
2013–14	Cardiff C	15	1	15	1
2013–14	Stoke C	15	5		
2014–15	Stoke C	7	0		
2015–16	Stoke C	5	0	27	5
2015–16	*Bristol C*	7	2	7	2

PIETERS, Erik (D)   246 3
H: 6 0   W: 13 00   b.Tiel 7-8-88
Internationals: Netherlands U17, U19, U21, Full caps.

Season	Club	A	G	Tot A	Tot G
2006–07	FC Utrecht	20	0		
2007–08	FC Utrecht	31	2	51	2
2008–09	PSV Eindhoven	17	0		
2009–10	PSV Eindhoven	27	0		
2010–11	PSV Eindhoven	31	0		
2011–12	PSV Eindhoven	16	0		
2012–13	PSV Eindhoven	2	0	93	0
2013–14	Stoke C	36	1		
2014–15	Stoke C	31	0		
2015–16	Stoke C	35	0	102	1

SHAQIRI, Xherdan (M)   186 33
H: 5 7   W: 11 05   b.Gnjilane 10-10-91
Internationals: Switzerland U17, U18, U19, U21, Full caps.

Season	Club	A	G	Tot A	Tot G
2009–10	Basel	32	4		
2010–11	Basel	29	5		
2011–12	Basel	31	9	92	18
2012–13	Bayern Munich	26	4		
2013–14	Bayern Munich	17	6		
2014–15	Bayern Munich	9	1	52	11
2014–15	Inter Milan	15	1	15	1
2015–16	Stoke C	27	3	27	3

SHAWCROSS, Ryan (D)   297 19
H: 6 3   W: 13 13   b.Buckley 4-10-87
Internationals: England U21, Full caps.

Season	Club	A	G	Tot A	Tot G
2006–07	Manchester U	0	0		
2007–08	Manchester U	0	0		
2007–08	Stoke C	41	7		
2008–09	Stoke C	30	3		
2009–10	Stoke C	28	2		
2010–11	Stoke C	36	1		
2011–12	Stoke C	36	2		
2012–13	Stoke C	37	1		
2013–14	Stoke C	37	1		
2014–15	Stoke C	32	2		
2015–16	Stoke C	20	0	297	19

SHENTON, Oliver (M)   1 0
H: 6 0   W: 12 02   b.Stoke-on-Trent 6-11-97

Season	Club	A	G	Tot A	Tot G
2014–15	Stoke C	1	0		
2015–16	Stoke C	0	0	1	0

SIDWELL, Steve (M)   391 56
H: 5 10   W: 11 00   b.Wandsworth 14-12-82
Internationals: England U20, U21.

Season	Club	A	G	Tot A	Tot G
2001–02	Arsenal	0	0		
2001–02	*Brentford*	30	4	30	4
2002–03	Arsenal	0	0		
2002–03	*Brighton & HA*	12	5		
2002–03	Reading	13	2		
2003–04	Reading	43	8		
2004–05	Reading	44	5		
2005–06	Reading	33	10		
2006–07	Reading	35	4	168	29
2007–08	Chelsea	15	0	15	0
2008–09	Aston Villa	16	3		
2009–10	Aston Villa	25	0		
2010–11	Aston Villa	4	0	45	3
2010–11	Fulham	12	2		
2011–12	Fulham	14	1		
2012–13	Fulham	28	4		
2013–14	Fulham	38	7	92	14
2014–15	Stoke C	12	0		
2015–16	Stoke C	1	0	13	0
2015–16	*Brighton & HA*	16	1	28	6

WALTERS, Jon (F)   466 90
H: 6 0   W: 12 06   b.Birkenhead 20-9-83
Internationals: Republic of Ireland U21, B, Full caps.

Season	Club	A	G	Tot A	Tot G
2001–02	Bolton W	0	0		
2002–03	Bolton W	4	0		
2002–03	*Hull C*	11	5		
2003–04	Bolton W	0	0	4	0
2003–04	Crewe Alex	0	0		
2003–04	*Barnsley*	8	0	8	0
2003–04	*Hull C*	16	1		
2004–05	Hull C	21	1	48	7
2004–05	*Scunthorpe U*	3	0	3	0
2005–06	Wrexham	38	5	38	5
2006–07	Chester C	26	9	26	9
2006–07	Ipswich T	16	4		
2007–08	Ipswich T	40	13		
2008–09	Ipswich T	36	5		
2009–10	Ipswich T	43	8		
2010–11	Ipswich T	1	0	136	30
2010–11	Stoke C	36	6		
2011–12	Stoke C	38	7		
2012–13	Stoke C	38	8		
2013–14	Stoke C	32	5		
2014–15	Stoke C	32	8		
2015–16	Stoke C	27	5	203	39

WARING, George (F)   33 7
b.Chester 2-2-94

Season	Club	A	G	Tot A	Tot G
2013–14	Stoke C	0	0		
2014–15	Stoke C	0	0		
2014–15	*Barnsley*	19	6	19	6
2015–16	Stoke C	0	0		
2015–16	*Oxford U*	14	1	14	1

WHELAN, Glenn (M)   416 17
H: 5 11   W: 12 07   b.Dublin 13-1-84
Internationals: Republic of Ireland U16, U21, B, Full caps.

Season	Club	A	G	Tot A	Tot G
2000–01	Manchester C	0	0		
2001–02	Manchester C	0	0		
2002–03	Manchester C	0	0		
2003–04	Manchester C	0	0		
2003–04	*Bury*	13	0	13	0
2004–05	Sheffield W	36	2		
2005–06	Sheffield W	43	1		
2006–07	Sheffield W	38	7		
2007–08	Sheffield W	25	2	142	12
2007–08	Stoke C	14	1		
2008–09	Stoke C	26	1		
2009–10	Stoke C	33	2		
2010–11	Stoke C	29	0		
2011–12	Stoke C	30	1		
2012–13	Stoke C	32	0		
2013–14	Stoke C	32	0		
2014–15	Stoke C	28	0		
2015–16	Stoke C	37	0	261	5

WILSON, Marc (M)   213 4
H: 6 2   W: 12 07   b.Lisburn 17-8-87
Internationals: Republic of Ireland U18, U19, U21, Full caps.

Season	Club	A	G	Tot A	Tot G
2005–06	Portsmouth	0	0		
2005–06	*Yeovil T*	2	0	2	0
2006–07	Portsmouth	0	0		
2006–07	*Bournemouth*	19	3		
2007–08	Portsmouth	0	0		
2007–08	*Bournemouth*	7	0	26	3
2007–08	*Luton T*	4	0	4	0
2008–09	Portsmouth	3	0		
2009–10	Portsmouth	28	0		
2010–11	Portsmouth	4	0	35	0
2010–11	Stoke C	28	1		
2011–12	Stoke C	35	0		
2012–13	Stoke C	19	0		
2013–14	Stoke C	33	0		
2014–15	Stoke C	27	0		
2015–16	Stoke C	4	0	146	1

WOLLSCHEID, Philipp (D)   216 11
H: 6 4   W: 13 03   b.Wadern 6-3-89
Internationals: Germany U20, Full caps.

Season	Club	A	G	Tot A	Tot G
2006–07	Noswendel-Wadern	8	2	8	2
2007–08	Hasborn-Dautweiler	18	0	18	0
2007–08	Saarbrucken	7	1		
2008–09	Saarbrucken	23	2	30	3
2009–10	Nuremberg II	26	1		
2010–11	Nuremberg II	14	0	40	1
2010–11	Nuremberg	19	3		
2011–12	Nuremberg	2	0	21	3
2012–13	Bayer Leverkusen	31	2		
2013–14	Bayer Leverkusen	20	0		
2014–15	Bayer Leverkusen	0	0	51	2
2014–15	Mainz	5	0	5	0
2014–15	Stoke C	12	0		
2015–16	Stoke C	31	0	43	0

Players retained or with offer of contract
Edwards, Liam; Gyollai, Daniel; Isted, Harvey James Duke; Jarvis, Daniel Adam; Marques De Almeida, Luis; Mato Sanmartin, Jose Luis; Molina Beloqui, Sergio; Ngoy Bin Cibambi, Julien Fontaine; Renee-Pringle, Johnville Isaacs Joseph; Sadiki, Kosovar; Taylor, Joel; Telford, Dominic; Waddington, Mark Thomas.

Scholars
Ayoola, Olusola Adeola; Banks, Lewis; Dunwoody, Jake; Dyche, Thomas; Edwards, Thomas Adam; Read, Harvey Stafford; Verlinden, Thibaud.

SUNDERLAND (80)

BEADLING, Tom (D)   0 0
H: 6 1   W: 12 08   b.Barrow-in-Furness 16-1-96

Season	Club	A	G	Tot A	Tot G
2014–15	Sunderland	0	0		
2015–16	Sunderland	0	0		

BORINI, Fabio (F)   120 29
H: 5 10   W: 11 08   b.Bentivoglio 23-3-91
Internationals: Italy U17, U19, U21, Full caps.

Season	Club	A	G	Tot A	Tot G
2008–09	Chelsea	0	0		
2009–10	Chelsea	4	0		
2010–11	Chelsea	0	0	4	0
2010–11	Swansea C	9	6	9	6
2011–12	Roma	24	9	24	9
2012–13	Liverpool	13	1		
2013–14	Liverpool	0	0		
2013–14	*Sunderland*	32	7		
2014–15	Liverpool	12	1		
2015–16	Liverpool	0	0	25	2
2015–16	Sunderland	26	5	58	12

BRIDCUTT, Liam (M)   216 2
H: 5 9   W: 11 07   b.Reading 8-5-89
Internationals: Scotland Full caps.

Season	Club	A	G	Tot A	Tot G
2007–08	Chelsea	0	0		
2007–08	*Yeovil T*	9	0	9	0
2008–09	Chelsea	0	0		
2008–09	*Watford*	6	0	6	0
2009–10	Chelsea	0	0		
2009–10	*Stockport Co*	15	0	15	0
2010–11	Chelsea	0	0		
2010–11	Brighton & HA	37	2		
2011–12	Brighton & HA	43	0		
2012–13	Brighton & HA	41	0		
2013–14	Brighton & HA	11	0	132	2
2013–14	Sunderland	12	0		
2014–15	Sunderland	18	0		
2015–16	Sunderland	0	0	30	0
2015–16	*Leeds U*	24	0	24	0

BROWN, Wes (D)   308 4
H: 6 1   W: 13 08   b.Manchester 13-10-79
Internationals: England U21, Full caps.

Season	Club				
1996–97	Manchester U	0	0		
1997–98	Manchester U	2	0		
1998–99	Manchester U	14	0		
1999–2000	Manchester U	0	0		
2000–01	Manchester U	28	0		
2001–02	Manchester U	17	0		
2002–03	Manchester U	22	0		
2003–04	Manchester U	17	0		
2004–05	Manchester U	21	1		
2005–06	Manchester U	19	0		
2006–07	Manchester U	22	0		
2007–08	Manchester U	36	1		
2008–09	Manchester U	8	1		
2009–10	Manchester U	19	0		
2010–11	Manchester U	7	0	232	3
2011–12	Sunderland	20	1		
2012–13	Sunderland	0	0		
2013–14	Sunderland	25	0		
2014–15	Sunderland	25	0		
2015–16	Sunderland	6	0	76	1

BUCKLEY, Will (F)   230 38
H: 6 0   W: 13 00   b.Oldham 12-8-88

Season	Club				
2007–08	Rochdale	7	0		
2008–09	Rochdale	37	10		
2009–10	Rochdale	15	3	59	13
2009–10	Watford	6	1		
2010–11	Watford	33	4	39	5
2011–12	Brighton & HA	29	8		
2012–13	Brighton & HA	36	8		
2013–14	Brighton & HA	30	3		
2014–15	Brighton & HA	1	0	96	19
2014–15	Sunderland	22	0		
2015–16	Sunderland	0	0	22	0
2015–16	*Leeds U*	4	0	4	0
2015–16	*Birmingham C*	10	1	10	1

CATTERMOLE, Lee (M)   263 6
H: 5 10   W: 11 13   b.Stockton 21-3-88
Internationals: England U16, U17, U18, U19, U21.

Season	Club				
2005–06	Middlesbrough	14	1		
2006–07	Middlesbrough	31	1		
2007–08	Middlesbrough	24	1	69	3
2008–09	Wigan Ath	33	1		
2009–10	Wigan Ath	0	0	33	1
2009–10	Sunderland	22	0		
2010–11	Sunderland	23	0		
2011–12	Sunderland	23	0		
2012–13	Sunderland	10	0		
2013–14	Sunderland	24	1		
2014–15	Sunderland	28	1		
2015–16	Sunderland	31	0	161	2

COATES, Sebastian (D)   105 5
H: 6 5   W: 13 12   b.Montevideo 7-10-90
Internationals: Uruguay U20, U23, Full caps.

Season	Club				
2008–09	Nacional	6	1		
2009–10	Nacional	21	2		
2010–11	Nacional	27	1		
2011–12	Nacional	1	0	55	4
2011–12	Liverpool	7	1		
2012–13	Liverpool	5	0		
2013–14	Liverpool	0	0		
2014–15	Liverpool	0	0	12	1
2014–15	*Sunderland*	10	0		
2015–16	Sunderland	10	0	26	0
2015–16	*Sporting Lisbon*	12	0	12	0

DEFOE, Jermain (F)   498 183
H: 5 7   W: 10 04   b.Beckton 7-10-82
Internationals: England U16, U18, U21, B, Full caps.

Season	Club				
1999–2000	West Ham U	0	0		
2000–01	West Ham U	1	0		
2000–01	Bournemouth	29	18	29	18
2001–02	West Ham U	35	10		
2002–03	West Ham U	38	8		
2003–04	West Ham U	19	11	93	29
2003–04	Tottenham H	15	7		
2004–05	Tottenham H	35	13		
2005–06	Tottenham H	36	9		
2006–07	Tottenham H	34	10		
2007–08	Tottenham H	19	4		
2007–08	Portsmouth	12	8		
2008–09	Portsmouth	19	7	31	15
2008–09	Tottenham H	8	3		
2009–10	Tottenham H	34	18		
2010–11	Tottenham H	14	11		
2011–12	Tottenham H	25	11		
2012–13	Tottenham H	34	11		
2013–14	Tottenham H	14	1	276	91
2014	Toronto	19	11	19	11
2014–15	Sunderland	17	4		
2015–16	Sunderland	33	15	50	19

FLETCHER, Steven (F)   358 98
H: 6 1   W: 12 00   b.Shrewsbury 26-3-87
Internationals: Scotland U20, U21, B, Full caps.

Season	Club				
2003–04	Hibernian	5	0		
2004–05	Hibernian	20	5		
2005–06	Hibernian	34	8		
2006–07	Hibernian	31	6		
2007–08	Hibernian	32	13		
2008–09	Hibernian	34	11	156	43
2009–10	Burnley	35	8	35	8
2010–11	Wolverhampton W	29	10		
2011–12	Wolverhampton W	32	12	61	22
2012–13	Sunderland	28	11		
2013–14	Sunderland	20	3		
2014–15	Sunderland	30	5		
2015–16	Sunderland	14	4	94	23
2015–16	*Marseille*	12	2	12	2

GIACCHERINI, Emanuele (M)   197 35
H: 5 3   W: 10 07   b.Forli 5-5-85
Internationals: Italy Full caps.

Season	Club				
2008–09	Cesena	29	5		
2009–10	Cesena	32	8		
2010–11	Cesena	36	7	97	20
2011–12	Juventus	23	1		
2012–13	Juventus	17	3	40	4
2013–14	Sunderland	24	4		
2014–15	Sunderland	8	0		
2015–16	Sunderland	0	0	32	4
2015–16	*Bologna*	28	7	28	7

GOMEZ, Jordi (M)   248 36
H: 5 10   W: 11 09   b.Barcelona 24-5-85
Internationals: Spain U17.

Season	Club				
2006–07	Espanyol B	21	0	21	0
2007–08	Espanyol	2	0	2	0
2008–09	Swansea C	44	12	44	12
2009–10	Wigan Ath	23	1		
2010–11	Wigan Ath	13	1		
2011–12	Wigan Ath	28	5		
2012–13	Wigan Ath	32	3		
2013–14	Wigan Ath	31	7	127	17
2014–15	Sunderland	29	4		
2015–16	Sunderland	6	0	35	4
2015–16	*Blackburn R*	19	3	19	3

GOOCH, Lynden (M)   10 0
H: 5 8   W: 10 12   b.Santa Cruz 24-12-95
Internationals: USA U20.

Season	Club				
2015–16	Sunderland	0	0		
2015–16	*Doncaster R*	10	0	10	0

GRAHAM, Danny (F)   386 108
H: 5 11   W: 12 05   b.Gateshead 12-8-85
Internationals: England U20.

Season	Club				
2003–04	Middlesbrough	0	0		
2003–04	*Darlington*	9	2	9	2
2004–05	Middlesbrough	11	1		
2005–06	Middlesbrough	3	0		
2005–06	*Derby Co*	14	0	14	0
2005–06	*Leeds U*	3	0	3	0
2006–07	Middlesbrough	1	0		
2006–07	*Blackpool*	4	1	4	1
2006–07	Carlisle U	11	7		
2007–08	Carlisle U	45	14		
2008–09	Carlisle U	44	15	100	36
2009–10	Watford	46	14		
2010–11	Watford	45	23	91	37
2011–12	Swansea C	36	12		
2012–13	Swansea C	18	3	54	15
2012–13	Sunderland	13	0		
2013–14	Sunderland	0	0		
2013–14	*Hull C*	18	1	18	1
2013–14	*Middlesbrough*	18	6	33	7
2014–15	Sunderland	14	1		
2014–15	*Wolverhampton W*	5	1	5	1
2015–16	Sunderland	10	0	37	1
2015–16	*Blackburn R*	18	7	18	7

GREENWOOD, Rees (F)   1 0
b. 2-1-96

Season	Club				
2015–16	Sunderland	1	0	1	0

HARPER, Steve (G)   225 0
H: 6 2   W: 13 10   b.Easington 14-3-75

Season	Club				
1993–94	Newcastle U	0	0		
1994–95	Newcastle U	0	0		
1995–96	Newcastle U	0	0		
1995–96	*Bradford C*	1	0	1	0
1996–97	Newcastle U	0	0		
1996–97	*Stockport Co*	0	0		
1997–98	Newcastle U	0	0		
1997–98	*Hartlepool U*	15	0	15	0
1997–98	*Huddersfield T*	24	0	24	0
1998–99	Newcastle U	8	0		
1999–2000	Newcastle U	18	0		
2000–01	Newcastle U	5	0		
2001–02	Newcastle U	0	0		
2002–03	Newcastle U	0	0		
2003–04	Newcastle U	0	0		
2004–05	Newcastle U	2	0		
2005–06	Newcastle U	0	0		
2006–07	Newcastle U	18	0		
2007–08	Newcastle U	21	0		
2008–09	Newcastle U	16	0		
2009–10	Newcastle U	45	0		
2010–11	Newcastle U	18	0		
2011–12	Newcastle U	0	0		
2011–12	*Brighton & HA*	5	0	5	0
2012–13	Newcastle U	6	0	157	0
2013–14	Hull C	13	0		
2014–15	Hull C	10	0	23	0
2015–16	Sunderland	0	0		

HONEYMAN, George (M)   1 0
H: 5 8   W: 11 05   b.Prudhoe 8-9-94

Season	Club				
2014–15	Sunderland	0	0		
2015–16	Sunderland	1	0	1	0

JOHNSON, Adam (M)   308 48
H: 5 8   W: 10 00   b.Sunderland 14-7-87
Internationals: England U19, U21, Full caps.

Season	Club				
2004–05	Middlesbrough	0	0		
2005–06	Middlesbrough	13	1		
2006–07	Middlesbrough	12	0		
2006–07	*Leeds U*	5	0	5	0
2007–08	Middlesbrough	19	1		
2007–08	*Watford*	12	5	12	5
2008–09	Middlesbrough	26	0		
2009–10	Middlesbrough	26	11	96	13
2009–10	Manchester C	16	1		
2010–11	Manchester C	31	4		
2011–12	Manchester C	26	6		
2012–13	Manchester C	0	0	73	11
2012–13	Sunderland	35	5		
2013–14	Sunderland	36	8		
2014–15	Sunderland	32	4		
2015–16	Sunderland	19	2	122	19

JONES, Billy (M)   396 23
H: 5 11   W: 13 00   b.Shrewsbury 24-3-87
Internationals: England U16, U17, U19, U20.

Season	Club				
2003–04	Crewe Alex	27	1		
2004–05	Crewe Alex	20	0		
2005–06	Crewe Alex	44	6		
2006–07	Crewe Alex	41	1	132	8
2007–08	Preston NE	29	0		
2008–09	Preston NE	44	3		
2009–10	Preston NE	44	4		
2010–11	Preston NE	43	6	160	13
2011–12	WBA	18	0		
2012–13	WBA	27	1		
2013–14	WBA	21	0	66	1
2014–15	Sunderland	14	0		
2015–16	Sunderland	24	1	38	1

KABOUL, Younes (D)   224 13
H: 6 2   W: 13 07   b.Annemasse 4-1-86
Internationals: France U21, Full caps.

Season	Club				
2004–05	Auxerre	12	1		
2005–06	Auxerre	9	0		
2006–07	Auxerre	31	2	52	3
2007–08	Tottenham H	21	3		
2008–09	Portsmouth	20	1		
2009–10	Portsmouth	19	3	39	4
2009–10	Tottenham H	10	0		
2010–11	Tottenham H	21	1		
2011–12	Tottenham H	33	1		
2012–13	Tottenham H	1	0		
2013–14	Tottenham H	13	1		
2014–15	Tottenham H	11	0	110	6
2015–16	Sunderland	23	0	23	0

KHAZRI, Wahbi (M)   238 47
H: 6 0   W: 12 04   b.Ajaccio 8-2-91
Internationals: France U21. Tunisia U20, Full caps.

Season	Club				
2008–09	Bastia	13	3		
2009–10	Bastia	31	2		
2010–11	Bastia	34	4		
2011–12	Bastia	33	9		
2012–13	Bastia	29	7		
2013–14	Bastia	32	6	172	31
2014–15	Bordeaux	32	9		
2015–16	Bordeaux	20	5	52	14
2015–16	Sunderland	14	2	14	2

KIRCHHOFF, Jan (D)   95 0
H: 6 4   W: 12 04   b.Frankfurt am Main 1-10-90
Internationals: Germany U18, U19, U21.

Season	Club				
2010–11	Mainz	10	0		
2011–12	Mainz	29	0		
2012–13	Mainz	18	0	57	0
2013–14	Bayern Munich	7	0		
2013–14	Schalke 04	2	0		
2014–15	Bayern Munich	0	0		

2014–15	Schalke 04	14	0	16	0
2015–16	Bayern Munich	0	0	7	0
2015–16	Sunderland	15	0	15	0

KONE, Lamine (D)   215 13
H: 6 2   W: 13 01   b.Paris 1-2-89
Internationals: France U17, U18, U19, U20. Ivory Coast Full caps.

2006–07	Chateauroux	5	0		
2007–08	Chateauroux	16	0		
2008–09	Chateauroux	27	1		
2009–10	Chateauroux	26	3	74	4
2010–11	Lorient	7	1		
2011–12	Lorient	21	1		
2012–13	Lorient	32	3		
2013–14	Lorient	18	1		
2014–15	Lorient	30	1		
2015–16	Lorient	18	0	126	7
2015–16	Sunderland	15	2	15	2

LARSSON, Sebastian (M)   342 31
H: 5 11   W: 11 02   b.Eskilstuna 6-6-85
Internationals: Sweden U16, U17, U19, U21, Full caps.

2002–03	Arsenal	0	0		
2003–04	Arsenal	0	0		
2004–05	Arsenal	0	0		
2005–06	Arsenal	3	0		
2006–07	Arsenal	0	0	3	0
2006–07	Birmingham C	43	4		
2007–08	Birmingham C	35	6		
2008–09	Birmingham C	38	1		
2009–10	Birmingham C	33	4		
2010–11	Birmingham C	35	4	184	19
2011–12	Sunderland	32	7		
2012–13	Sunderland	38	1		
2013–14	Sunderland	31	1		
2014–15	Sunderland	36	3		
2015–16	Sunderland	18	0	155	12

LENS, Jeremain (F)   252 74
H: 5 10   W: 12 08   b.Amsterdam 24-11-87
Internationals: Netherlands U19, U20, U21, Full caps.

2005–06	AZ Alkmaar	2	0		
2006–07	AZ Alkmaar	14	1		
2007–08	AZ Alkmaar	0	0		
2007–08	NEC	31	13	31	13
2008–09	AZ Alkmaar	8	1		
2009–10	AZ Alkmaar	32	12	56	14
2010–11	PSV Eindhoven	33	10		
2011–12	PSV Eindhoven	33	9		
2012–13	PSV Eindhoven	30	15	96	34
2013–14	Dynamo Kiev	28	5		
2014–15	Dynamo Kiev	21	5	49	10
2015–16	Sunderland	20	3	20	3

M'VILA, Yann (M)   195 3
H: 5 7   W: 8 11   b.Amiens 29-6-90
Internationals: France U16, U17, U18, U19, U21, Full caps.

2007–08	Rennes	0	0		
2008–09	Rennes	0	0		
2009–10	Rennes	35	0		
2010–11	Rennes	37	2		
2011–12	Rennes	38	0		
2012–13	Rennes	16	0	126	2
2012–13	Rubin Kazan	5	0		
2013–14	Rubin Kazan	19	0		
2014–15	Rubin Kazan	0	0		
2014–15	Inter Milan	8	0	8	0
2015–16	Rubin Kazan	0	0	24	0

On loan from Rubin Kazan.

2015–16	Sunderland	37	1	37	1

MANDRON, Mikael (F)   22 1
H: 6 3   W: 12 13   b.Boulogne 11-10-94

2011–12	Sunderland	0	0		
2012–13	Sunderland	2	0		
2013–14	Sunderland	0	0		
2013–14	Fleetwood T	11	1	11	1
2014–15	Sunderland	1	0		
2014–15	Shrewsbury T	3	0	3	0
2015–16	Sunderland	0	0		
2015–16	Hartlepool U	5	0	5	0

MANNONE, Vito (G)   106 0
H: 6 0   W: 11 08   b.Milan 2-3-88
Internationals: Italy U21.

2005–06	Arsenal	0	0		
2006–07	Arsenal	0	0		
2006–07	Barnsley	2	0	2	0
2007–08	Arsenal	0	0		
2008–09	Arsenal	1	0		
2009–10	Arsenal	5	0		
2010–11	Arsenal	0	0		
2010–11	Hull C	10	0		
2011–12	Arsenal	0	0		
2011–12	Hull C	21	0	31	0
2012–13	Arsenal	9	0	15	0
2013–14	Sunderland	29	0		
2014–15	Sunderland	10	0		
2015–16	Sunderland	19	0	58	0

MATTHEWS, Adam (D)   151 5
H: 5 10   W: 11 02   b.Swansea 13-1-92
Internationals: Wales U17, U19, U21, Full caps.

2008–09	Cardiff C	0	0		
2009–10	Cardiff C	32	1		
2010–11	Cardiff C	8	0	40	1
2011–12	Celtic	27	0		
2012–13	Celtic	22	2		
2013–14	Celtic	23	1		
2014–15	Celtic	29	1	101	4
2015–16	Sunderland	1	0	1	0
2015–16	Bristol C	9	0	9	0

N'DOYE, Dame (F)   294 117
H: 6 1   b.Thies 21-2-85
Internationals: Senegal Full caps.

2005–06	Al-Sadd	27	12	27	12
2006–07	Academica Coimbra	25	4	25	4
2007–08	Panathaniakos	19	2	19	2
2008–09	Irakliou	15	7	15	7
2008–09	Copenhagen	11	2		
2009–10	Copenhagen	32	14		
2010–11	Copenhagen	31	25		
2011–12	Copenhagen	30	18	104	59
2012–13	Lokomotiv Moscow	25	10		
2013–14	Lokomotiv Moscow	27	13		
2014–15	Lokomotiv Moscow	14	4	66	27
2014–15	Hull C	15	5	15	5
2015–16	Trabzonspor	12	0	12	0

On loan from Trabzonspor.

2015–16	Sunderland	11	1	11	1

O'SHEA, John (D)   427 14
H: 6 3   W: 13 07   b.Waterford 30-4-81
Internationals: Republic of Ireland U21, Full caps.

1998–99	Manchester U	0	0		
1999–2000	Manchester U	0	0		
1999–2000	Bournemouth	10	1	10	1
2000–01	Manchester U	9	0		
2001–02	Manchester U	0	0		
2002–03	Manchester U	32	0		
2003–04	Manchester U	33	2		
2004–05	Manchester U	23	2		
2005–06	Manchester U	34	1		
2006–07	Manchester U	32	4		
2007–08	Manchester U	30	0		
2008–09	Manchester U	30	0		
2009–10	Manchester U	15	1		
2010–11	Manchester U	20	0	256	10
2011–12	Sunderland	34	0		
2012–13	Sunderland	34	2		
2013–14	Sunderland	33	1		
2014–15	Sunderland	37	0		
2015–16	Sunderland	28	0	161	3

PICKFORD, Jordan (G)   89 0
H: 6 1   b.Washington 7-3-94
Internationals: England U16, U17, U18, U19, U20, U21.

2010–11	Sunderland	0	0		
2011–12	Sunderland	0	0		
2012–13	Sunderland	0	0		
2013–14	Sunderland	0	0		
2013–14	Burton Alb	12	0	12	0
2013–14	Carlisle U	18	0	18	0
2014–15	Sunderland	0	0		
2014–15	Bradford C	33	0	33	0
2015–16	Sunderland	2	0	2	0
2015–16	Preston NE	24	0	24	0

ROBERGE, Valentin (D)   123 2
H: 6 1   W: 11 06   b.Montreuil 9-6-87

2008–09	Aris Thessaloniki	20	0		
2009–10	Aris Thessaloniki	5	0	25	0
2010–11	Maritimo	25	1		
2011–12	Maritimo	25	0		
2012–13	Maritimo	27	1	77	2
2013–14	Sunderland	9	0		
2014–15	Sunderland	1	0		
2014–15	Reims	11	0	11	0
2015–16	Sunderland	0	0	10	0

ROBSON, Josh (D)   0 0
H: 5 11   W: 11 07   b.Bedlington 3-2-98

2015–16	Sunderland	0	0	

ROBSON, Tom (M)   1 0
H: 5 10   W: 11 11   b.Stanley 9-11-95

2015–16	Sunderland	0	0		
2015–16	Sunderland	1	0	1	0

RODWELL, Jack (D)   146 10
H: 6 2   W: 12 08   b.Southport 11-3-91
Internationals: England U16, U17, U19, U21, Full caps.

2007–08	Everton	2	0		
2008–09	Everton	19	0		
2009–10	Everton	26	2		
2010–11	Everton	24	0		
2011–12	Everton	14	2	85	4
2012–13	Manchester C	11	2		
2013–14	Manchester C	5	0	16	2
2014–15	Sunderland	23	3		
2015–16	Sunderland	22	1	45	4

SMITH, Martin (M)   2 0
H: 5 10   W: 11 00   b.Sunderland 25-1-96

2013–14	Sunderland	0	0		
2014–15	Sunderland	0	0		
2015–16	Carlisle U	2	0	2	0

STRYJEK, Maksymilian (G)   0 0
H: 6 2   W: 12 11   b.Warsaw 18-7-96
Internationals: Poland U17, U18, U19.

2014–15	Sunderland	0	0	
2015–16	Sunderland	0	0	

TOIVONEN, Ola (M)   314 106
H: 6 3   W: 11 11   b.Degerfors 3-3-86
Internationals: Sweden U17, U19, U21, Full caps.

2003	Degerfors	2	0		
2004	Degerfors	12	3		
2005	Degerfors	27	5	41	8
2006	Orgryte	25	6	25	6
2007	Malmo	24	3		
2008	Malmo	27	14	51	17
2008–09	PSV Eindhoven	14	6		
2009–10	PSV Eindhoven	33	13		
2010–11	PSV Eindhoven	28	15		
2011–12	PSV Eindhoven	33	18		
2012–13	PSV Eindhoven	17	8		
2013–14	PSV Eindhoven	14	1	139	61
2013–14	Rennes	15	7		
2014–15	Rennes	30	7		
2015–16	Rennes	1	0	46	14

On loan from Rennes.

2015–16	Sunderland	12	0	12	0

VAN AANHOLT, Patrick (D)   172 10
H: 5 9   W: 10 08   b.Den Bosch 3-7-88
Internationals: Netherlands U16, U17, U18, U19, U20, U21, Full caps.

2007–08	Chelsea	0	0		
2008–09	Chelsea	0	0		
2009–10	Chelsea	2	0		
2009–10	Coventry C	20	0	20	0
2009–10	Newcastle U	7	0	7	0
2010–11	Chelsea	0	0		
2010–11	Leicester C	12	1	12	1
2011–12	Chelsea	0	0		
2011–12	Wigan Ath	3	0	3	0
2011–12	Vitesse	9	0		
2012–13	Vitesse	31	1		
2013–14	Chelsea	0	0	2	0
2013–14	Vitesse	27	4	67	5
2014–15	Sunderland	28	0		
2015–16	Sunderland	33	4	61	4

VERGINI, Santiago (D)   169 6
H: 6 3   W: 13 00   b.Maximo Paz 3-8-88
Internationals: Argentina Full caps.

2008–09	Olimpia	0	0		
2009–10	Olimpia	0	0		
2010–11	Olimpia	4	0	4	0
2010–11	Verona	15	1	15	1
2011–12	Newell's Old Boys	32	3		
2012–13	Newell's Old Boys	34	1	66	4
2013–14	Estudiantes	17	1		
2013–14	*Sunderland*	11	0		
2014–15	Estudiantes	0	0	17	1
2014–15	*Sunderland*	31	0		
2015–16	*Sunderland*	0	0	42	0
2015–16	Getafe	25	0	25	0

WATMORE, Duncan (F)   32 4
H: 5 9   W: 11 05   b.Cheadle Hulme 8-3-94
Internationals: England U20, U21.

2013–14	Sunderland	0	0		
2013–14	*Hibernian*	9	1	9	1
2014–15	Sunderland	0	0		
2015–16	Sunderland	23	3	23	3

Players retained or with offer of contract
Blinco, Jordan William; Brady, George; Casey, Dan Patrick; Lawson, Carl; Ledger, Michael; Mavrias, Charalampos; Pybus, Daniel Joseph; Robson, Ethan; Talbot, James; Wright, Daniel.

Scholars
Allan, Christopher Mark; Asoro, Joel Joshghene; Bale, Adam James; Embleton, Elliot John; Gamble, Owen Jay; Hume, Denver Jay; Krusnell, Oscar; Maja, Joshua Erowoli; McCulloch, Cameron James; Molyneux, Luke; Nelson, Andrew George Robert; Poame, Jean-Yves; Storey, Alexander Michael; Taylor, Brandon Lewis; Woud, Michael Cornelis.

SWANSEA C (81)

ALFEI, Daniel (D) 39 0
H: 5 11 W: 12 02 b.Swansea 23-2-92
Internationals: Wales U17, U19, U21.

Season	Club	Apps	Gls	Tot Apps	Tot Gls
2010–11	Swansea C	1	0		
2011–12	Swansea C	0	0		
2012–13	Swansea C	0	0		
2013–14	Swansea C	0	0		
2013–14	Portsmouth	15	0	15	0
2014–15	Swansea C	0	0		
2014–15	Northampton T	11	0	11	0
2015–16	Swansea C	0	0		
2015–16	Mansfield T	12	0	12	0

AMAT, Jordi (D) 103 1
H: 6 0 W: 12 03 b.Barcelona 21-3-92
Internationals: Spain U16, U17, U18, U19, U20, U21.

Season	Club	Apps	Gls	Tot Apps	Tot Gls
2009–10	Espanyol	6	0		
2010–11	Espanyol	26	0		
2011–12	Espanyol	9	0		
2012–13	Espanyol	0	0	41	0
2012–13	Rayo Vallecano	27	1	27	1
2013–14	Swansea C	17	0		
2014–15	Swansea C	10	0		
2015–16	Swansea C	8	0	35	0

AYEW, Andre (F) 34 12
H: 5 9 W: 11 05 b.Seclin 17-12-89
Internationals: Ghana U20, Full caps.

Season	Club	Apps	Gls	Tot Apps	Tot Gls
2015–16	Swansea C	34	12	34	12

BARROW, Modou (F) 129 41
H: 5 9 W: 9 13 b.Banjul 13-10-92
Internationals: Gambia Full caps.

Season	Club	Apps	Gls	Tot Apps	Tot Gls
2010	Mjolby AI	15	6	15	6
2011	Mjolby Sodra	19	23	19	23
2012	Norrkping	7	0	7	0
2013	Varbergs	28	2	28	2
2014	Ostersunds FK	19	9	19	9
2014–15	Swansea C	11	0		
2014–15	Nottingham F	4	0	4	0
2015–16	Swansea C	22	1	33	1
2015–16	Blackburn R	4	0	4	0

BARTLEY, Kyle (D) 92 4
H: 5 11 W: 11 00 b.Stockport 22-5-91
Internationals: England U16, U17.

Season	Club	Apps	Gls	Tot Apps	Tot Gls
2008–09	Arsenal	0	0		
2009–10	Arsenal	0	0		
2009–10	Sheffield U	14	0		
2010–11	Arsenal	0	0		
2010–11	Sheffield U	21	0	35	0
2010–11	Rangers	5	1		
2011–12	Arsenal	0	0		
2011–12	Rangers	19	0	24	1
2012–13	Arsenal	0	0		
2012–13	Swansea C	2	0		
2013–14	Swansea C	2	0		
2013–14	Birmingham C	17	3	17	3
2014–15	Swansea C	7	0		
2015–16	Swansea C	5	0	16	0

BLAIR, Ryan (M) 7 0
b.Glasgow 23-2-96

Season	Club	Apps	Gls	Tot Apps	Tot Gls
2013–14	Falkirk	0	0		
2014–15	Falkirk	0	0		
2015–16	Falkirk	7	0	7	0
2015–16	Swansea C	0	0		

BRAY, Alex (M) 1 0
H: 5 10 W: 10 06 b.Bath 25-7-95
Internationals: Wales U19.

Season	Club	Apps	Gls	Tot Apps	Tot Gls
2013–14	Swansea C	0	0		
2014–15	Swansea C	0	0		
2014–15	Plymouth Arg	1	0	1	0
2015–16	Swansea C	0	0		

BRITTON, Leon (M) 464 11
H: 5 6 W: 10 00 b.Merton 16-9-82
Internationals: England U16.

Season	Club	Apps	Gls	Tot Apps	Tot Gls
1999–2000	West Ham U	0	0		
2000–01	West Ham U	0	0		
2001–02	West Ham U	0	0		
2002–03	West Ham U	0	0		
2002–03	Swansea C	25	0		
2003–04	Swansea C	42	3		
2004–05	Swansea C	30	1		
2005–06	Swansea C	38	4		
2006–07	Swansea C	41	2		
2007–08	Swansea C	40	0		
2008–09	Swansea C	43	0		
2009–10	Swansea C	36	0		
2010–11	Sheffield U	24	0	24	0
2010–11	Swansea C	17	1		
2011–12	Swansea C	36	0		
2012–13	Swansea C	33	0		
2013–14	Swansea C	25	0		
2014–15	Swansea C	9	0		
2015–16	Swansea C	25	0	440	11

CORK, Jack (D) 319 10
H: 6 0 W: 10 12 b.Carshalton 25-6-89
Internationals: England U17, U18, U19, U20, U21. Great Britain.

Season	Club	Apps	Gls	Tot Apps	Tot Gls
2006–07	Chelsea	0	0		
2006–07	Bournemouth	7	0	7	0
2007–08	Chelsea	0	0		
2007–08	Scunthorpe U	34	2	34	2
2008–09	Chelsea	0	0		
2008–09	Southampton	23	0		
2008–09	Watford	19	0	19	0
2009–10	Chelsea	0	0		
2009–10	Coventry C	21	0	21	0
2009–10	Burnley	11	1		
2010–11	Chelsea	0	0		
2010–11	Burnley	40	3	51	4
2011–12	Southampton	46	0		
2012–13	Southampton	28	0		
2013–14	Southampton	28	0		
2014–15	Southampton	12	2	137	2
2014–15	Swansea C	15	1		
2015–16	Swansea C	35	1	50	2

DYER, Nathan (M) 314 28
H: 5 5 W: 9 00 b.Trowbridge 29-11-87

Season	Club	Apps	Gls	Tot Apps	Tot Gls
2005–06	Southampton	17	0		
2005–06	Burnley	5	2	5	2
2006–07	Southampton	18	0		
2007–08	Southampton	17	1		
2008–09	Southampton	4	0	56	1
2008–09	Sheffield U	7	1	7	1
2008–09	Swansea C	17	2		
2009–10	Swansea C	40	2		
2010–11	Swansea C	46	2		
2011–12	Swansea C	34	5		
2012–13	Swansea C	37	3		
2013–14	Swansea C	27	6		
2014–15	Swansea C	32	3		
2015–16	Swansea C	1	0	234	23
2015–16	Leicester C	12	1	12	1

EDER, Antonio (F) 211 55
H: 6 3 W: 12 11 b.Bissau 22-12-87
Internationals: Portugal Full caps.

Season	Club	Apps	Gls	Tot Apps	Tot Gls
2006–07	Tourizense	7	1		
2007–08	Tourizense	34	10		
2008–09	Tourizense	1	0	42	11
2008–09	Academica	24	1		
2009–10	Academica	22	4		
2010–11	Academica	21	2		
2011–12	Academica	16	5	83	12
2012–13	Braga	18	13		
2013–14	Braga	13	3		
2014–15	Braga	29	10	60	26
2015–16	Swansea C	13	0	13	0
2015–16	Lille	13	6	13	6

EMNES, Marvin (M) 228 36
H: 5 11 W: 10 06 b.Rotterdam 27-5-88
Internationals: Netherlands U16, U17, U19, U20, U21.

Season	Club	Apps	Gls	Tot Apps	Tot Gls
2005–06	Sparta Rotterdam	11	1		
2006–07	Sparta Rotterdam	16	0		
2007–08	Sparta Rotterdam	29	8	56	9
2008–09	Middlesbrough	15	0		
2009–10	Middlesbrough	16	1		
2010–11	Middlesbrough	23	3		
2010–11	Swansea C	4	2		
2011–12	Middlesbrough	42	14		
2012–13	Middlesbrough	24	5		
2013–14	Middlesbrough	22	1	142	24
2013–14	Swansea C	7	1		
2014–15	Swansea C	17	0		
2015–16	Swansea C	2	0	30	3

EVANS, Sam (M) 0 0
b.Swansea 12-5-95
Internationals: Wales U19.

Season	Club	Apps	Gls	Tot Apps	Tot Gls
2013–14	Swansea C	0	0		
2014–15	Swansea C	0	0		
2015–16	Swansea C	0	0		

FABIANSKI, Lukasz (G) 159 0
H: 6 3 W: 13 01 b.Costrzyn nad Odra 18-4-85
Internationals: Poland U21, Full caps.

Season	Club	Apps	Gls	Tot Apps	Tot Gls
2005–06	Legia	30	0		
2006–07	Legia	23	0	53	0
2007–08	Arsenal	3	0		
2008–09	Arsenal	6	0		
2009–10	Arsenal	4	0		
2010–11	Arsenal	14	0		
2011–12	Arsenal	0	0		
2012–13	Arsenal	4	0		
2013–14	Arsenal	1	0	32	0
2014–15	Swansea C	37	0		
2015–16	Swansea C	37	0	74	0

FERNANDEZ, Federico (D) 177 5
H: 6 3 W: 13 01 b.Tres Algarrobos 21-2-89
Internationals: Argentina U20, Full caps.

Season	Club	Apps	Gls	Tot Apps	Tot Gls
2008–09	Estudiantes	14	2		
2009–10	Estudiantes	12	0		
2010–11	Estudiantes	33	1	59	3
2011–12	Napoli	16	0		
2012–13	Napoli	2	0		
2012–13	Getafe	14	1	14	1
2013–14	Napoli	26	0	44	0
2014–15	Swansea C	28	0		
2015–16	Swansea C	32	1	60	1

FULTON, Jay (M) 17 0
H: 5 10 W: 10 08 b.Bolton 4-4-94
Internationals: Scotland U18, U19, U21.

Season	Club	Apps	Gls	Tot Apps	Tot Gls
2013–14	Swansea C	2	0		
2014–15	Swansea C	2	0		
2015–16	Swansea C	2	0	6	0
2015–16	Oldham Ath	11	0	11	0

GOMIS, Bafetimbi (F) 397 123
H: 6 0 W: 12 02 b.Seyne-sur-Mer 6-8-85
Internationals: France U17, Full caps.

Season	Club	Apps	Gls	Tot Apps	Tot Gls
2003–04	St Etienne	11	2		
2004–05	St Etienne	6	0		
2004–05	Troyes	13	6	13	6
2005–06	St Etienne	24	2		
2006–07	St Etienne	30	10		
2007–08	St Etienne	35	16		
2008–09	St Etienne	36	10	142	40
2009–10	Lyon	37	10		
2010–11	Lyon	35	10		
2011–12	Lyon	36	14		
2012–13	Lyon	37	16		
2013–14	Lyon	33	14	178	64
2014–15	Swansea C	31	7		
2015–16	Swansea C	33	6	64	13

GORRE, Kenji (M) 6 0
H: 5 10 W: 11 03 b.Paramaribo 29-9-94

Season	Club	Apps	Gls	Tot Apps	Tot Gls
2013–14	Swansea C	0	0		
2014–15	Swansea C	1	0		
2015–16	Swansea C	0	0	1	0
2015–16	ADO Den Haag	5	0	5	0

GRIMES, Matt (M) 75 5
H: 5 10 W: 11 00 b.Exeter 15-7-95
Internationals: England U20, U21.

Season	Club	Apps	Gls	Tot Apps	Tot Gls
2013–14	Exeter C	35	1		
2014–15	Exeter C	23	4	58	5
2014–15	Swansea C	3	0		
2015–16	Swansea C	1	0	4	0
2015–16	Blackburn R	13	0	13	0

HEDGES, Ryan (M) 23 2
b.Swansea 7-9-95
Internationals: Wales U19, U21.

Season	Club	Apps	Gls	Tot Apps	Tot Gls
2013–14	Swansea C	0	0		
2014–15	Swansea C	0	0		
2014–15	Leyton Orient	17	2	17	2
2015–16	Swansea C	0	0		
2015–16	Stevenage	6	0	6	0

JAMES, Daniel (M) 0 0
b. 10-11-97
Internationals: Wales U17.

Season	Club	Apps	Gls	Tot Apps	Tot Gls
2015–16	Swansea C	0	0		

KI, Sung-Yeung (M) 184 22
H: 6 2 W: 11 10 b.Gwangju 24-1-89
Internationals: South Korea U17, U20, U23, Full caps.

Season	Club	Apps	Gls	Tot Apps	Tot Gls
2009–10	Celtic	10	0		
2010–11	Celtic	26	3		
2011–12	Celtic	30	6	66	9
2012–13	Swansea C	29	0		
2013–14	Swansea C	1	0		
2013–14	Sunderland	27	3	27	3
2014–15	Swansea C	33	8		
2015–16	Swansea C	28	2	91	10

KING, Adam (M) **26** **4**
H: 5 11 W: 11 10 b.Edinburgh 11-10-95
Internationals: Scotland U18, U19, U21.

2012–13	Hearts	0	0		
2013–14	Hearts	2	0	**2**	**0**
2013–14	Swansea C	0	0		
2014–15	Swansea C	0	0		
2015–16	Swansea C	0	0		
2015–16	*Crewe Alex*	24	4	**24**	**4**

KINGSLEY, Stephen (D) **116** **1**
H: 5 10 W: 10 09 b.Stirling 23-7-94
Internationals: Scotland U18, U19, U21, Full caps.

2010–11	Falkirk	3	0		
2011–12	Falkirk	15	0		
2012–13	Falkirk	35	0		
2013–14	Falkirk	35	1	**88**	**1**
2014–15	Swansea C	0	0		
2014–15	*Yeovil T*	12	0	**12**	**0**
2015–16	Swansea C	4	0	**4**	**0**
2015–16	*Crewe Alex*	12	0	**12**	**0**

LOVERIDGE, James (F) **14** **0**
H: 6 2 W: 13 04 b.Swansea 16-5-94
Internationals: Wales U17, U19.

2012–13	Swansea C	0	0		
2013–14	Swansea C	0	0		
2013–14	*Milton Keynes D*	7	0	**7**	**0**
2014–15	Swansea C	0	0		
2014–15	*Newport Co*	7	0	**7**	**0**
2015–16	Swansea C	0	0		

McBURNIE, Oliver (F) **23** **3**
H: 6 2 W: 10 04 b.Bradford 6-4-96
Internationals: Scotland U19, U21.

2013–14	Bradford C	8	0		
2014–15	Bradford C	7	0	**15**	**0**
2015–16	Swansea C	0	0		
2015–16	*Newport Co*	3	3	**3**	**3**
2015–16	*Bristol R*	5	0	**5**	**0**

MICHU, Miguel (M) **176** **50**
H: 6 1 W: 12 07 b.Oviedo 21-3-86
Internationals: Spain Full caps.

2007–08	Celta Vigo	12	1		
2008–09	Celta Vigo	18	1		
2009–10	Celta Vigo	27	6		
2010–11	Celta Vigo	30	7	**87**	**15**
2011–12	Rayo Vallecano	37	15	**37**	**15**
2012–13	Swansea C	35	18		
2013–14	Swansea C	17	2		
2014–15	Swansea C	0	0		
2014–15	Napoli	0	0		
2015–16	Swansea C	0	0	**52**	**20**

MONTERO, Jefferson (M) **226** **34**
H: 5 8 W: 11 00 b.Babahoyo 1-9-89
Internationals: Ecuador Full caps.

2007	Emelec	22	2	**22**	**2**
2008	Independiente de Valle	25	8		
2008–09	*Dorados*	5	1	**5**	**1**
2009	Independiente de Valle	12	11	**37**	**19**
2010–11	Villareal	9	1		
2010–11	*Levante*	11	0	**11**	**0**
2011–12	Villareal	0	0	**9**	**1**
2011–12	*Real Betis*	32	1	**32**	**1**
2012–13	Morelia	32	4		
2013–14	Morelia	25	5	**57**	**9**
2014–15	Swansea C	30	1		
2015–16	Swansea C	23	0	**53**	**1**

NAUGHTON, Kyle (M) **218** **6**
H: 5 11 W: 11 07 b.Sheffield 11-11-88
Internationals: England U21.

2006–07	Sheffield U	0	0		
2007–08	*Gretna*	18	0	**18**	**0**
2007–08	Sheffield U	0	0		
2008–09	Sheffield U	40	1		
2009–10	Sheffield U	0	0	**40**	**1**
2009–10	Tottenham H	1	0		
2009–10	*Middlesbrough*	15	0	**15**	**0**
2010–11	Tottenham H	0	0		
2010–11	*Leicester C*	34	5	**34**	**5**
2011–12	Tottenham H	0	0		
2011–12	*Norwich C*	32	0	**32**	**0**
2012–13	Tottenham H	14	0		
2013–14	Tottenham H	22	0		
2014–15	Tottenham H	5	0	**42**	**0**
2014–15	Swansea C	10	0		
2015–16	Swansea C	27	0	**37**	**0**

NORDFELDT, Kristoffer (G) **216** **0**
H: 6 3 W: 13 05 b. 23-6-89
Internationals: Sweden U19, U21, Full caps.

2006	Brommapojkarna	0	0		
2007	Brommapojkarna	0	0		
2008	Brommapojkarna	29	0		
2009	Brommapojkarna	21	0		
2010	Brommapojkarna	25	0		
2011	Brommapojkarna	28	0	**103**	**0**
2011–12	Heerenveen	6	0		
2012–13	Heerenveen	33	0		
2013–14	Heerenveen	35	0		
2014–15	Heerenveen	38	0	**112**	**0**
2015–16	Swansea C	1	0	**1**	**0**

PALOSCHI, Alberto (F) **230** **63**
H: 5 9 W: 10 10 b.Chiari 4-1-90
Internationals: Italy U17, U19, U20, U21.

2007–08	AC Milan	7	2	**7**	**2**
2008–09	Parma	39	11		
2009–10	Parma	17	4		
2010–11	Parma	1	0	**57**	**15**
2010–11	Genoa	12	2	**12**	**2**
2011–12	Chievo	32	5		
2012–13	Chievo	20	7		
2013–14	Chievo	34	13		
2014–15	Chievo	37	9		
2015–16	Chievo	21	8	**144**	**42**
2015–16	Swansea C	10	2	**10**	**2**

RANGEL, Angel (D) **340** **10**
H: 5 11 W: 11 09 b.Barcelona 28-10-82

2006–07	Terrassa	34	2	**34**	**2**
2007–08	Swansea C	43	2		
2008–09	Swansea C	40	1		
2009–10	Swansea C	38	0		
2010–11	Swansea C	38	2		
2011–12	Swansea C	34	0		
2012–13	Swansea C	33	3		
2013–14	Swansea C	30	0		
2014–15	Swansea C	27	0		
2015–16	Swansea C	23	0	**306**	**8**

ROBERTS, Connor (D) **45** **0**
b. 23-9-95
Internationals: Wales U19, U21.

2014–15	Swansea C	0	0		
2015–16	Swansea C	0	0		
2015–16	*Yeovil T*	45	0	**45**	**0**

RODON, Joe (D) **0** **0**
b.Swansea 22-10-97

2015–16	Swansea C	0	0		

ROUTLEDGE, Wayne (M) **417** **36**
H: 5 6 W: 11 02 b.Sidcup 7-1-85
Internationals: England U20, U21.

2001–02	Crystal Palace	2	0		
2002–03	Crystal Palace	26	4		
2003–04	Crystal Palace	44	6		
2004–05	Crystal Palace	38	0	**110**	**10**
2005–06	Tottenham H	3	0		
2005–06	*Portsmouth*	13	0	**13**	**0**
2006–07	Tottenham H	0	0		
2006–07	*Fulham*	24	0	**24**	**0**
2007–08	Tottenham H	2	0	**5**	**0**
2007–08	Aston Villa	1	0		
2008–09	Aston Villa	1	0	**2**	**0**
2008–09	*Cardiff C*	9	2	**9**	**2**
2008–09	QPR	19	1		
2009–10	QPR	25	2		
2009–10	Newcastle U	17	3		
2010–11	Newcastle U	17	0	**34**	**3**
2010–11	*QPR*	20	5	**64**	**8**
2011–12	Swansea C	28	1		
2012–13	Swansea C	36	5		
2013–14	Swansea C	35	2		
2014–15	Swansea C	29	3		
2015–16	Swansea C	28	2	**156**	**13**

SHEEHAN, Josh (M) **26** **2**
H: 6 0 W: 11 11 b.Pembrey 30-3-95
Internationals: Wales U19, U21.

2013–14	Swansea C	0	0		
2014–15	Swansea C	0	0		
2014–15	*Yeovil T*	13	0		
2015–16	Swansea C	0	0		
2015–16	*Yeovil T*	13	2	**26**	**2**

SHEPHARD, Liam (D) **26** **0**
H: 5 10 W: 10 08 b.Rhondda 22-11-94
Internationals: Wales U21.

2013–14	Swansea C	0	0		
2014–15	Swansea C	0	0		
2014–15	*Yeovil T*	20	0		
2015–16	Swansea C	0	0		
2015–16	*Yeovil T*	6	0	**26**	**0**

SIGURDSSON, Gylfi (M) **240** **64**
H: 6 1 W: 12 02 b.Reykjavik 9-9-89
Internationals: Iceland U17, U18, U19, U21, Full caps.

2007–08	Reading	0	0		
2008–09	Reading	0	0		
2008–09	*Shrewsbury T*	5	1	**5**	**1**
2008–09	*Crewe Alex*	15	3	**15**	**3**
2009–10	Reading	38	16		
2010–11	Reading	4	2	**42**	**18**
2010–11	Hoffenheim	28	9		
2011–12	Hoffenheim	6	0	**34**	**9**
2011–12	*Swansea C*	18	7		
2012–13	Tottenham H	33	3		
2013–14	Tottenham H	25	5	**58**	**8**
2014–15	Swansea C	32	7		
2015–16	Swansea C	36	11	**86**	**25**

TABANOU, Franck (M) **214** **19**
H: 5 10 W: 11 00 b.Thiais 30-1-89
Internationals: France U20, U21.

2008–09	Toulouse	5	0		
2009–10	Toulouse	33	4		
2010–11	Toulouse	34	4		
2011–12	Toulouse	32	3		
2012–13	Toulouse	34	4	**138**	**15**
2013–14	St Etienne	34	3		
2014–15	St Etienne	31	1		
2015–16	Swansea C	0	0		
2015–16	*St Etienne*	11	0	**76**	**4**

TAYLOR, Neil (D) **175** **0**
H: 5 9 W: 10 02 b.Ruthin 7-2-89
Internationals: Wales U17, U19, U21, Full caps. Great Britain.

2007–08	Wrexham	26	0	**26**	**0**
2010–11	Swansea C	29	0		
2011–12	Swansea C	36	0		
2012–13	Swansea C	6	0		
2013–14	Swansea C	10	0		
2014–15	Swansea C	34	0		
2015–16	Swansea C	34	0	**149**	**0**

TIENDALLI, Dwight (D) **188** **5**
H: 5 9 W: 11 08 b.Surinam 21-10-85
Internationals: Netherlands U21, Full caps.

2004–05	FC Utrecht	10	1		
2005–06	FC Utrecht	29	2		
2006–07	FC Utrecht	1	0	**40**	**3**
2006–07	Feyenoord	13	0		
2007–08	*S Rotterdam*	13	0	**13**	**0**
2008–09	Feyenoord	22	0	**35**	**0**
2009–10	FC Twente	26	1		
2010–11	FC Twente	18	0		
2011–12	FC Twente	27	0	**71**	**1**
2012–13	Swansea C	14	1		
2013–14	Swansea C	10	0		
2014–15	Swansea C	3	0		
2014–15	*Middlesbrough*	2	0	**2**	**0**
2015–16	Swansea C	0	0	**27**	**1**

TREMMEL, Gerhard (G) **122** **0**
H: 6 3 W: 14 00 b.Munich 16-11-78

2006–07	Energie Cottbus	1	0		
2007–08	Energie Cottbus	24	0		
2008–09	Energie Cottbus	34	0		
2009–10	Energie Cottbus	34	0	**93**	**0**
2011–12	Swansea C	1	0		
2012–13	Swansea C	14	0		
2013–14	Swansea C	12	0		
2014–15	Swansea C	2	0		
2015–16	Swansea C	0	0	**29**	**0**
2015–16	*Werder Bremen*	0	0		

VICKERS, Josh (G) **0** **0**
H: 6 0 W: 11 05 b.Billericay 1-12-95
From Arsenal.

2015–16	Swansea C	0	0		

WILLIAMS, Ashley (D) **484** **17**
H: 6 0 W: 11 02 b.Wolverhampton 23-8-84
Internationals: Wales Full caps.

2003–04	Stockport Co	10	0		
2004–05	Stockport Co	44	1		
2005–06	Stockport Co	36	1		
2006–07	Stockport Co	46	1		
2007–08	Stockport Co	26	0	**162**	**3**
2007–08	*Swansea C*	3	0		
2008–09	Swansea C	46	2		
2009–10	Swansea C	46	5		
2010–11	Swansea C	46	3		
2011–12	Swansea C	37	1		
2012–13	Swansea C	37	0		
2013–14	Swansea C	34	1		
2014–15	Swansea C	37	0		
2015–16	Swansea C	36	2	**322**	**14**

ZABRET, Gregor (G) **0** **0**
H: 6 2 W: 12 11 b.Ljubljana 18-8-95
Internationals: Slovenia U16, U17, U19, U21.

2013–14	Swansea C	0	0		
2014–15	Swansea C	0	0		
2015–16	Swansea C	0	0		

Players retained or with offer of contract
Bia Bi, Botti Boulenin; Cullen, Liam Jamie; Davies, Keston Ellis; Davies, Thomas Oliver; Evans, Keiran; Garrick, Jordon D'Andre; Holland, Thomas; Jones, Owain Rhys; Maric,

Adnan; Samuel, Alexander Kinloch; Thomas, Lewis Rhys.

Scholars
Darame, Causso; Davies, Mael Daniel; Dulca, Marco-Alexandru; Dyson, Thomas Jonathan; Edwards, Liam Rhys; Evans, Jack; Hanbury, Sean; Jefferies, Daniel Rhys; Jones, Jordan Levi; Lewis, Aaron James; Morgan, Ben; Treacy, Ross Anthony.

SWINDON T (82)

AJOSE, Nicholas (F) 193 65
H: 5 8 W: 11 00 b.Bury 7-10-91
Internationals: England U16, U17. Nigeria U20.

Season	Club				
2009–10	Manchester U	0	0		
2010–11	Manchester U	0	0		
2010–11	Bury	28	13		
2011–12	Peterborough U	2	0		
2011–12	Scunthorpe U	7	0	7	0
2011–12	Chesterfield	12	1	12	1
2012–13	Crawley T	19	2	19	2
2012–13	Peterborough U	0	0		
2012–13	Bury	19	4	47	17
2013–14	Peterborough U	22	7	24	7
2013–14	Swindon T	16	6		
2014–15	Leeds U	3	0		
2014–15	Crewe Alex	27	8	27	8
2015–16	Leeds U	0	0	3	0
2015–16	Swindon T	38	24	54	30

BALMY, Jeremy (M) 14 0
H: 5 8 W: 10 10 b. 19-4-94

Season	Club				
2013–14	Notts Co	1	0		
2014–15	Notts Co	1	0	2	0
2014–15	Oxford U	0	0		
2015–16	Swindon T	12	0	12	0

BANGOURA, Momar (M) 3 0
H: 5 9 W: 10 03 b.Dakar 24-2-94

Season	Club				
2011–12	Marseille	2	0		
2012–13	Marseille	0	0		
2013–14	Marseille	0	0		
2014–15	Marseille	0	0	2	0
2015–16	Swindon T	1	0	1	0

BARRY, Bradley (D) 35 0
b. 13-12-95

Season	Club				
2013–14	Brighton & HA	0	0		
2014–15	Brighton & HA	0	0		
2015–16	Swindon T	35	0	35	0

BELFORD, Tyrell (G) 15 0
H: 6 0 W: 12 00 b.Nuneaton 6-5-94
Internationals: England U16, U17.

Season	Club				
2011–12	Liverpool	0	0		
2012–13	Liverpool	0	0		
2013–14	Swindon T	5	0		
2014–15	Swindon T	2	0		
2015–16	Swindon T	8	0	15	0

BRANCO, Raphael Rossi (D) 80 4
b. 25-7-90

Season	Club				
2013–14	Swindon T	15	0		
2014–15	Swindon T	29	3		
2015–16	Swindon T	36	1	80	4

BROPHY, James (D) 28 0
b. 25-7-94
From Harrow Bor, Woodlands U, Broadfields U.

Season	Club				
2015–16	Swindon T	28	0	28	0

CALVIN, Jamie (F) 0 0
b. 8-10-95

Season	Club				
2014–15	Oxford U	0	0		
2015–16	Swindon T	0	0		

COOKE, Josh (F) 4 0
b. 4-2-97

Season	Club				
2014–15	Swindon T	2	0		
2015–16	Swindon T	2	0	4	0

EVANS, Jake (M) 1 0
b. 8-4-98

Season	Club				
2015–16	Swindon T	1	0	1	0

GODDARD, John (M) 0 0
H: 5 10 W: 11 09 b.Sandhurst 2-6-93
Internationals: England C.

Season	Club				
2011–12	Reading	0	0		
2014–15	Woking	0	0		
2015–16	Swindon T	0	0		

HENRY, Will (G) 2 0
b. 6-7-98

Season	Club				
2015–16	Swindon T	2	0	2	0

HOLLAND, Tom (M) 0 0
Internationals: Republic of Ireland U17.

Season	Club				
2014–15	Swindon T	0	0		
2015–16	Swindon T	0	0		

HYLTON, Jermaine (F) 27 1
H: 5 10 W: 11 00 b.Birmingham 28-6-93

Season	Club				
2014–15	Swindon T	11	1		
2015–16	Swindon T	16	0	27	1

IANDOLO, Ellis (M) 12 0
b. 22-8-97
From Maidstone U.

Season	Club				
2015–16	Swindon T	12	0	12	0

JOHNS, Connor (G) 0 0
b. 22-6-98

Season	Club				
2014–15	Swindon T	0	0		
2015–16	Swindon T	0	0		

KASIM, Yaser (M) 100 5
H: 5 11 W: 11 07 b.Bagdad 10-5-91
Internationals: Iraq U23, Full caps.

Season	Club				
2010–11	Brighton & HA	1	0		
2011–12	Brighton & HA	0	0		
2012–13	Brighton & HA	0	0	1	0
2013–14	Swindon T	37	2		
2014–15	Swindon T	35	2		
2015–16	Swindon T	27	1	99	5

MARSHALL, Lee (M) 4 0
H: 5 10 W: 11 03 b. 21-11-97

Season	Club				
2014–15	Swindon T	2	0		
2015–16	Swindon T	2	0	4	0

OBIKA, Jonathan (F) 186 42
H: 6 0 W: 12 00 b.Enfield 12-9-90
Internationals: England U19, U20.

Season	Club				
2008–09	Tottenham H	0	0		
2008–09	Yeovil T	10	4		
2009–10	Tottenham H	0	0		
2009–10	Yeovil T	22	6		
2010–11	Millwall	12	2	12	2
2010–11	Tottenham H	0	0		
2010–11	Crystal Palace	7	0	7	0
2010–11	Peterborough U	1	1	1	1
2010–11	Swindon T	5	0		
2010–11	Yeovil T	11	3		
2011–12	Tottenham H	0	0		
2011–12	Yeovil T	27	4	70	17
2012–13	Tottenham H	0	0		
2012–13	Charlton Ath	10	3		
2013–14	Tottenham H	0	0		
2013–14	Brighton & HA	5	0	5	0
2013–14	Charlton Ath	12	0	22	3
2014–15	Tottenham H	0	0		
2014–15	Swindon T	32	8		
2015–16	Swindon T	32	11	69	19

OJAMAA, Henrik (F) 171 21
H: 5 9 W: 11 11 b.Tallinn 20-5-91
Internationals: Estonia U19, U21, Full caps.

Season	Club				
2009–10	Derby Co	0	0		
2010–11	Aachen	1	0	1	0
2010–11	Fortuna Sittard	12	1	12	1
2011	RoPS Rovaniemi	17	2	17	2
2011–12	Motherwell	18	7		
2012–13	Motherwell	36	4		
2013–14	Legia Warsaw	33	2		
2014–15	Legia Warsaw	1	0	34	2
2014–15	Motherwell	18	3	72	14
2015	Sarpsborg 08	10	0	10	0
2015–16	Swindon T	9	0	9	0
2015–16	Wacker Innsbruck	16	2	16	2

ORMONDE-OTTEWILL, Brandon (D) 28 1
b.London 21-12-95
Internationals: England U16, U19.

Season	Club				
2012–13	Arsenal	0	0		
2013–14	Arsenal	0	0		
2014–15	Arsenal	0	0		
2015–16	Swindon T	28	1	28	1

OULDRIDGE, Tom (M) 0 0

Season	Club				
2014–15	Swindon T	0	0		
2015–16	Swindon T	0	0		

ROBERT, Fabien (F) 110 10
H: 5 8 W: 10 07 b.Hennebont 6-1-89
Internationals: France U20.

Season	Club				
2007–08	Lorient	11	0		
2008–09	Lorient	11	1		
2009–10	Boulogne	16	1	16	1
2010–11	Lorient	4	1		
2011–12	Lorient	1	0		
2011–12	Doncaster R	13	2	13	2
2012–13	Lorient	4	1		
2013–14	Lorient	12	0		
2014–15	Lorient	3	0	46	3
2015–16	Swindon T	35	4	35	4

RODGERS, Anton (M) 55 4
H: 5 7 W: 10 02 b.Reading 26-1-93
Internationals: Republic of Ireland U19.

Season	Club				
2011–12	Brighton & HA	0	0		
2012–13	Exeter C	2	0	2	0
2013–14	Oldham Ath	7	0	7	0
2014–15	Swindon T	10	2		
2015–16	Swindon T	36	2	46	4

SENDLES-WHITE, Jamie (D) 24 0
H: 6 2 W: 13 05 b.Kingston 10-4-94
Internationals: Northern Ireland U19, U20, U21.

Season	Club				
2011–12	QPR	0	0		
2012–13	QPR	0	0		
2013–14	QPR	0	0		
2013–14	Colchester U	0	0		
2014–15	QPR	0	0		
2014–15	Mansfield T	7	0	7	0
2015–16	Hamilton A	7	0	7	0
2015–16	Swindon T	10	0	10	0

SMITH, Michael (F) 131 38
H: 6 4 W: 11 02 b.Wallsend 17-10-91

Season	Club				
2011–12	Charlton Ath	0	0		
2011–12	Accrington S	6	3	6	3
2012–13	Charlton Ath	0	0		
2012–13	Colchester U	8	1	8	1
2013–14	Charlton Ath	0	0		
2013–14	AFC Wimbledon	23	9	23	9
2013–14	Swindon T	20	8		
2014–15	Swindon T	40	13		
2015–16	Swindon T	5	0	65	21
2015–16	Barnsley	13	0	13	0
2015–16	Portsmouth	16	4	16	4

SMITH, Tom (M) 2 1
H: 5 10 W: 11 00 b. 25-1-98

Season	Club				
2014–15	Swindon T	1	0		
2015–16	Swindon T	1	1	2	1

STEWART, Jordan (F) 1 0
b. 31-3-95
Internationals: Northern Ireland U19, U21.
From Glentoran.

Season	Club				
2015–16	Swindon T	1	0	1	0

STOREY, Miles (F) 105 19
H: 5 11 W: 11 00 b.West Bromwich 4-1-94
Internationals: England U19.

Season	Club				
2010–11	Swindon T	2	0		
2011–12	Swindon T	4	0		
2012–13	Swindon T	8	1		
2013–14	Swindon T	18	3		
2013–14	Shrewsbury T	6	0	6	0
2014–15	Portsmouth	17	2	17	2
2014–15	Newport Co	18	2	18	2
2015–16	Swindon T	2	0	34	4
2015–16	Inverness CT	30	11	30	11

THOMPSON, Nathan (M) 133 2
H: 5 7 W: 11 02 b.Chester 9-11-90

Season	Club				
2009–10	Swindon T	0	0		
2010–11	Swindon T	3	0		
2011–12	Swindon T	5	0		
2012–13	Swindon T	26	0		
2013–14	Swindon T	41	1		
2014–15	Swindon T	35	0		
2015–16	Swindon T	23	1	133	2

TRAORE, Drissa (M) 33 0
H: 5 9 W: 11 11 b. 25-3-92

Season	Club				
2012–13	Le Havre	5	0		
2013–14	Le Havre	0	0	5	0
2014–15	Notts Co	4	0	4	0
2015–16	Swindon T	24	0	24	0

TURNBULL, Jordan (D) 86 1
H: 6 1 W: 11 05 b.Trowbridge 30-10-94
Internationals: England U19, U20.

Season	Club				
2014–15	Southampton	0	0		
2014–15	Swindon T	44	1		
2015–16	Swindon T	42	0	86	1

TWINE, Scott (F) 0 0

Season	Club				
2015–16	Swindon T	0	0		

VIGOUROUX, Lawrence (G) 33 0
b.London 19-11-93

Season	Club				
2012–13	Tottenham H	0	0		
2013–14	Tottenham H	0	0		
2015–16	Swindon T	33	0	33	0

WOOD, Ryan (D) 0 0

Season	Club				
2013–14	Swindon T	0	0		
2014–15	Swindon T	0	0		
2015–16	Swindon T	0	0		

YOUNG, Jordan (F)   3   1
b. 31-7-99

Season	Club	A	G	A	G
2015-16	Swindon T	3	1	3	1

Scholars
Christopher, William Ernest Francis;
Frimpong, Christian Addei; Georgaklis,
James; Gunner, Callum Andrew Barry;
Hathaway, Mason John; Johns, Connor
Jason; Marks, Nathan James; Martinez,
Ramon Sebastian; Ouldridge, Thomas Neil;
Simpson, Jordan Tyler; Smith, Thomas;
Stanley, Jack Peter; Twine, Scott Edward;
Wood, Ryan Anthony; Young, Jordan John.

TOTTENHAM H (83)

ALDERWEIRELD, Toby (D)   203   13
H: 6 1   W: 11 11   b.Wilrijk 2-3-89
Internationals: Belgium U26, U17, U18, U19, U21, Full caps.

Season	Club	A	G	A	G
2008-09	Ajax	5	0		
2009-10	Ajax	31	2		
2010-11	Ajax	26	2		
2011-12	Ajax	29	1		
2012-13	Ajax	32	2		
2013-14	Ajax	4	0	127	7
2013-14	Atletico Madrid	12	1	12	1
2014-15	Southampton	26	1	26	1
2015-16	Tottenham H	38	4	38	4

ALLI, Bamidele (M)   105   32
H: 6 1   W: 11 12   b.Watford 11-4-96
Internationals: England U17, U18, U19, U21, Full caps.

Season	Club	A	G	A	G
2012-13	Milton Keynes D	1	0		
2013-14	Milton Keynes D	33	6		
2014-15	Milton Keynes D	39	16	72	22
2015-16	Tottenham H	33	10	33	10

BALL, Dominic (D)   32   0
b.Welwyn Garden City 2-8-95
Internationals: Northern Ireland U16, U17, U19, U21. England U20.

Season	Club	A	G	A	G
2013-14	Tottenham H	0	0		
2014-15	Tottenham H	0	0		
2014-15	Cambridge U	11	0	11	0
2015-16	Tottenham H	0	0		
2015-16	Rangers	21	0	21	0

BENTALEB, Nabil (M)   46   0
H: 6 2   W: 10 09   b.Lille, France 24-11-94
Internationals: France U18. Algeria Full caps.

Season	Club	A	G	A	G
2012-13	Tottenham H	0	0		
2013-14	Tottenham H	15	0		
2014-15	Tottenham H	26	0		
2015-16	Tottenham H	5	0	46	0

CARROLL, Tommy (M)   89   2
H: 5 10   W: 10 00   b.Watford 28-5-92
Internationals: England U19, U21.

Season	Club	A	G	A	G
2010-11	Tottenham H	0	0		
2010-11	Leyton Orient	12	0	12	0
2011-12	Tottenham H	0	0		
2011-12	Derby Co	12	1	12	1
2012-13	Tottenham H	7	0		
2013-14	Tottenham H	0	0		
2013-14	QPR	26	0	26	0
2014-15	Tottenham H	0	0		
2014-15	Swansea C	13	0	13	0
2015-16	Tottenham H	19	1	26	1

CARTER-VICKERS, Cameron (D)   0   0
H: 6 1   W: 13 08   b.Westcliff on Sea 31-12-97
Internationals: USA U20.

Season	Club	A	G	A	G
2015-16	Tottenham H	0	0		

CHADLI, Nacer (M)   264   68
H: 6 2   W: 12 07   b.Liege 3-6-88
Internationals: Morocco Full caps. Belgium Full caps.

Season	Club	A	G	A	G
2007-08	AGOVV	19	2		
2008-09	AGOVV	34	9		
2009-10	AGOVV	39	17	92	28
2010-11	FC Twente	33	7		
2011-12	FC Twente	25	6		
2012-13	FC Twente	26	12	84	25
2013-14	Tottenham H	24	1		
2014-15	Tottenham H	35	11		
2015-16	Tottenham H	29	3	88	15

DAVIES, Ben (D)   102   3
H: 5 7   W: 12 00   b.Neath 24-4-93
Internationals: Wales U19, Full caps.

Season	Club	A	G	A	G
2011-12	Swansea C	0	0		
2012-13	Swansea C	37	1		
2013-14	Swansea C	34	2	71	3
2014-15	Tottenham H	14	0		
2015-16	Tottenham H	17	0	31	0

DEMBELE, Mousa (F)   346   45
H: 5 9   W: 10 01   b.Wilrijk 17-7-87
Internationals: Belgium U16, U17, U18, U19, Full caps.

Season	Club	A	G	A	G
2003-04	Beerschot	1	0		
2004-05	Beerschot	19	1	20	1
2005-06	Willem II	33	9	33	9
2006-07	AZ	33	6		
2007-08	AZ	33	4		
2008-09	AZ	23	10		
2009-10	AZ	29	4	118	24
2010-11	Fulham	24	3		
2011-12	Fulham	36	2		
2012-13	Fulham	2	0	62	5
2012-13	Tottenham H	30	1		
2013-14	Tottenham H	28	1		
2014-15	Tottenham H	21	1		
2015-16	Tottenham H	29	3	113	6

DIER, Eric (D)   92   6
H: 6 3   W: 13 08   b.Cheltenham 15-1-94
Internationals: England U18, U19, U20, U21, Full caps.

Season	Club	A	G	A	G
2012-13	Sporting Lisbon	14	1		
2013-14	Sporting Lisbon	13	0	27	1
2014-15	Tottenham H	28	2		
2015-16	Tottenham H	37	3	65	5

ERIKSEN, Christian (M)   211   48
H: 5 9   W: 10 02   b.Middelfart 14-2-92
Internationals: Denmark U17, U18, U19, U21, Full caps.

Season	Club	A	G	A	G
2009-10	Ajax	15	0		
2010-11	Ajax	28	6		
2011-12	Ajax	33	7		
2012-13	Ajax	33	10		
2013-14	Ajax	4	2	113	25
2013-14	Tottenham H	25	7		
2014-15	Tottenham H	38	10		
2015-16	Tottenham H	35	6	98	23

GLOVER, Tom (G)   0   0
b.Sydney 24-11-97

Season	Club	A	G	A	G
2015-16	Tottenham H	0	0		

KANE, Harry (F)   139   63
H: 6 0   W: 10 00   b.Chingford 28-7-93
Internationals: England U17, U19, U20, U21, Full caps.

Season	Club	A	G	A	G
2010-11	Tottenham H	0	0		
2010-11	Leyton Orient	18	5	18	5
2011-12	Tottenham H	0	0		
2011-12	Millwall	22	7	22	7
2012-13	Tottenham H	1	0		
2012-13	Norwich C	3	0	3	0
2012-13	Leicester C	13	2	13	2
2013-14	Tottenham H	10	3		
2014-15	Tottenham H	34	21		
2015-16	Tottenham H	38	25	83	49

LAMELA, Erik (F)   171   30
H: 6 0   W: 10 13   b.Buenos Aires 4-3-92
Internationals: Argentina U20, Full caps.

Season	Club	A	G	A	G
2008-09	River Plate	1	0		
2009-10	River Plate	1	0		
2010-11	River Plate	32	4	34	4
2011-12	Roma	29	4		
2012-13	Roma	32	15	61	19
2013-14	Tottenham H	23	0		
2014-15	Tottenham H	33	2		
2015-16	Tottenham H	34	5	76	7

LLORIS, Hugo (G)   354   0
H: 6 2   W: 12 03   b.Nice 26-12-86
Internationals: France U18, U19, U20, U21, Full caps.

Season	Club	A	G	A	G
2005-06	Nice	5	0		
2006-07	Nice	37	0		
2007-08	Nice	30	0	72	0
2008-09	Lyon	35	0		
2009-10	Lyon	36	0		
2010-11	Lyon	37	0		
2011-12	Lyon	36	0		
2012-13	Lyon	2	0	146	0
2012-13	Tottenham H	27	0		
2013-14	Tottenham H	37	0		
2014-15	Tottenham H	35	0		
2015-16	Tottenham H	37	0	136	0

MAGHOMA, Christian (D)   0   0
b. 8-11-97

Season	Club	A	G	A	G
2015-16	Tottenham H	0	0		
2015-16	Yeovil T	0	0		

MASON, Ryan (M)   123   13
H: 5 9   W: 10 00   b.Enfield 13-6-91
Internationals: England U19, U20, Full caps.

Season	Club	A	G	A	G
2007-08	Tottenham H	0	0		
2008-09	Tottenham H	0	0		
2009-10	Tottenham H	0	0		
2009-10	Yeovil T	28	6	28	6
2010-11	Tottenham H	0	0		
2010-11	Doncaster R	15	0		
2011-12	Tottenham H	0	0		
2011-12	Doncaster R	4	0	19	0
2011-12	Millwall	5	0	5	0
2012-13	Tottenham H	0	0		
2012-13	Lorient	0	0		
2013-14	Tottenham H	0	0		
2013-14	Swindon T	18	5	18	5
2014-15	Tottenham H	31	1		
2015-16	Tottenham H	22	1	53	2

McGEE, Luke (G)   0   0
H: 6 2   W: 12 08   b.Edgware 9-2-95
Internationals: England U17.

Season	Club	A	G	A	G
2014-15	Tottenham H	0	0		
2015-16	Tottenham H	0	0		

N'JIE, Clinton (F)   45   7
H: 5 9   W: 10 10   b.Douala 15-8-93
Internationals: Cameroon U20, Full caps.

Season	Club	A	G	A	G
2012-13	Lyon	4	0		
2013-14	Lyon	3	0		
2014-15	Lyon	30	7	37	7
2015-16	Tottenham H	8	0	8	0

ODUWA, Nathan (F)   28   0
H: 6 1   W: 11 11   b.London 5-3-96
Internationals: England U17, U18, U20.

Season	Club	A	G	A	G
2013-14	Tottenham H	0	0		
2014-15	Tottenham H	0	0		
2014-15	Luton T	11	0	11	0
2015-16	Tottenham H	0	0		
2015-16	Rangers	15	1	15	1
2015-16	Colchester U	2	0	2	0

ONOMAH, Joshua (M)   8   0
H: 5 11   W: 10 01   b.Enfield 27-4-97
Internationals: England U16, U17, U18, U19.

Season	Club	A	G	A	G
2013-14	Tottenham H	0	0		
2014-15	Tottenham H	0	0		
2015-16	Tottenham H	8	0	8	0

PRITCHARD, Alex (M)   91   18
H: 5 7   W: 9 11   b.Grays 3-5-93
Internationals: England U20, U21.

Season	Club	A	G	A	G
2011-12	Tottenham H	0	0		
2012-13	Tottenham H	0	0		
2012-13	Peterborough U	6	0	6	0
2013-14	Tottenham H	1	0		
2013-14	Swindon T	36	6	36	6
2014-15	Tottenham H	0	0		
2014-15	Brentford	45	12	45	12
2015-16	Tottenham H	1	0	2	0
2015-16	WBA	2	0	2	0

ROSE, Danny (M)   141   7
H: 5 8   W: 11 11   b.Doncaster 2-6-90
Internationals: England U17, U19, U21, Full caps. Great Britain.

Season	Club	A	G	A	G
2007-08	Tottenham H	0	0		
2008-09	Tottenham H	0	0		
2008-09	Watford	7	0	7	0
2009-10	Tottenham H	1	1		
2010-11	Tottenham H	4	0		
2010-11	Bristol C	17	0	17	0
2011-12	Tottenham H	11	0		
2012-13	Tottenham H	0	0		
2012-13	Sunderland	27	1	27	1
2013-14	Tottenham H	22	1		
2014-15	Tottenham H	28	3		
2015-16	Tottenham H	24	1	90	6

SON, Heung-Min (M)   163   45
H: 6 0   W: 12 00   b.Chuncheon 8-7-92
Internationals: South Korea U17, U23, Full caps.

Season	Club	A	G	A	G
2010-11	Hamburg	13	3		
2011-12	Hamburg	27	5		
2012-13	Hamburg	33	12	73	20
2013-14	Bayer Leverkusen	31	10		
2014-15	Bayer Leverkusen	30	11		
2015-16	Bayer Leverkusen	1	0	62	21
2015-16	Tottenham H	28	4	28	4

TRIPPIER, Keiran (D)   218   7
H: 5 10   W: 11 00   b.Bury 19-9-90
Internationals: England U18, U19, U20, U21.

Season	Club	A	G	A	G
2007-08	Manchester C	0	0		
2008-09	Manchester C	0	0		
2009-10	Manchester C	0	0		
2009-10	Barnsley	3	0		
2010-11	Manchester C	0	0		
2010-11	Barnsley	39	2	42	2
2011-12	Manchester C	0	0		
2011-12	Burnley	46	3		
2012-13	Burnley	45	0		

2013–14	Burnley	41	1		
2014–15	Burnley	38	0	170	4
2015–16	Tottenham H	6	1	6	1

VERTONGHEN, Jan (D)   285   30
H: 6 2   W: 12 05   b.Sint-Niklaas 24-4-87
Internationals: Belgium U16, U21, Full caps.

2006–07	Ajax	3	0		
2006–07	RKC	12	3	12	3
2007–08	Ajax	31	2		
2008–09	Ajax	26	4		
2009–10	Ajax	32	3		
2010–11	Ajax	32	6		
2011–12	Ajax	31	8	155	23
2012–13	Tottenham H	34	4		
2013–14	Tottenham H	23	0		
2014–15	Tottenham H	32	0		
2015–16	Tottenham H	29	0	118	4

VORM, Michel (G)   265   0
H: 6 0   W: 13 03   b.Nieuwegein 20-10-83
Internationals: Netherlands Full caps.

2005–06	Den Bosch	35	0	35	0
2006–07	Utrecht	33	0		
2007–08	Utrecht	11	0		
2008–09	Utrecht	26	0		
2009–10	Utrecht	33	0		
2010–11	Utrecht	33	0	136	0
2011–12	Swansea C	37	0		
2012–13	Swansea C	26	0		
2013–14	Swansea C	26	0	89	0
2014–15	Tottenham H	4	0		
2015–16	Tottenham H	1	0	5	0

VOSS, Harry (G)   0   0
b. 11-1-97

2015–16	Tottenham H	0	0		
2015–16	Stevenage	0	0		

WALKER, Kyle (D)   222   5
H: 5 10   W: 11 07   b.Sheffield 28-5-90
Internationals: England U19, U21, Full caps.

2008–09	Sheffield U	2	0		
2008–09	Northampton T	9	0	9	0
2009–10	Tottenham H	2	0		
2009–10	Sheffield U	26	0	28	0
2010–11	Tottenham H	1	0		
2010–11	QPR	20	0	20	0
2010–11	Aston Villa	15	1	15	1
2011–12	Tottenham H	37	2		
2012–13	Tottenham H	36	0		
2013–14	Tottenham H	26	1		
2014–15	Tottenham H	15	0		
2015–16	Tottenham H	33	1	150	4

WALKER-PETERS, Kyle (F)   0   0
b. 13-4-97
Internationals: England U18, U19.

2015–16	Tottenham H	0	0		

WARD, Grant (M)   74   3
b. 5-12-94

2013–14	Tottenham H	0	0		
2014	Chicago Fire	23	1	23	1
2014–15	Tottenham H	0	0		
2014–15	Coventry C	11	0	11	0
2015–16	Tottenham H	0	0		
2015–16	Rotherham U	40	2	40	2

WIMMER, Kevin (D)   105   6
H: 6 2   W: 13 05   b.Wels 15-11-92
Internationals: Austria U18, U21, Full caps.

2011–12	LASK Linkz	28	4	28	4
2012–13	Cologne	9	0		
2013–14	Cologne	26	2		
2014–15	Cologne	32	0	67	2
2015–16	Tottenham H	10	0	10	0

WINKS, Harry (M)   0   0
H: 5 10   W: 10 03   b.Hemel Hempstead 2-2-96
Internationals: England U17, U18, U19, U20.

2013–14	Tottenham H	0	0		
2014–15	Tottenham H	0	0		
2015–16	Tottenham H	0	0		

YEDLIN, DeAndre (D)   86   2
H: 5 9   W: 11 07   b.Seattle 9-7-93
Internationals: USA U20, Full caps.

2013	Seattle Sounders	33	2		
2014	Seattle Sounders	29	0	62	2
2014–15	Tottenham H	0	0		
2015–16	Tottenham H	0	0	1	0
2015–16	Sunderland	23	0	23	0

Players retained or with offer of contract
Amos, Luke Ayodele; Fazio, Federico;
Georgiou, Anthony Michael; Goddard, Cy;
Harrison, Shayon; Lesniak, Filip; Miller,
William; Ogilvie, Connor Stuart; Pritchard,
Joe Cameron; Tracey, Shilow; Walkes, Anton.

Scholars
Austin, Brandon Anthony; Bennetts, Keanan
Chidozie; Brown, Jaden; Duncan, Dylan;
Edwards, Marcus; Loft, Ryan; Marsh, George
Owen; Mcdermott, Thomas William;
Mukena, Joy-Richard; Muscatt, Joseph Luis;
Oteh, Aramide Jay; Owens, Charlie; Roles,
Jack; Shashoua, Samuel; Sterling, Kazaiah;
Stylianides, Zenon; Tanganga, Japhat
Manzambi; Tsaroulla, Nicholas; Whiteman,
Alfie.

WALSALL (84)

BAKAYOKO, Amadou (F)   13   0
H: 6 4   W: 13 05   b. 1-1-96

2013–14	Walsall	6	0		
2014–15	Walsall	7	0		
2015–16	Walsall	0	0	13	0

BRADSHAW, Tom (F)   159   51
H: 5 5   W: 11 02   b.Shrewsbury 27-7-92
Internationals: Wales U19, U21, Full caps.

2009–10	Shrewsbury T	6	3		
2010–11	Shrewsbury T	26	6		
2011–12	Shrewsbury T	8	1		
2012–13	Shrewsbury T	21	0		
2013–14	Shrewsbury T	28	7	89	17
2014–15	Walsall	29	17		
2015–16	Walsall	41	17	70	34

CHAMBERS, Adam (D)   444   12
H: 5 10   W: 11 12   b.Sandwell 20-11-80

1998–99	WBA	0	0		
1999–2000	WBA	0	0		
2000–01	WBA	11	1		
2001–02	WBA	32	0		
2002–03	WBA	13	0		
2003–04	WBA	0	0		
2003–04	Sheffield W	11	0	11	0
2004–05	WBA	0	0	56	1
2004–05	Kidderminster H	2	0	2	0
2006–07	Leyton Orient	38	4		
2007–08	Leyton Orient	45	3		
2008–09	Leyton Orient	33	1		
2009–10	Leyton Orient	29	1		
2010–11	Leyton Orient	29	0	174	9
2011–12	Walsall	29	2		
2012–13	Walsall	37	0		
2013–14	Walsall	45	0		
2014–15	Walsall	45	0		
2015–16	Walsall	45	0	201	2

COOK, Jordan (F)   107   13
H: 5 10   W: 10 10   b.Hetton-le-Hole 20-3-90

2007–08	Sunderland	0	0		
2008–09	Sunderland	0	0		
2009–10	Sunderland	0	0		
2009–10	Darlington	5	0	5	0
2010–11	Sunderland	3	0		
2010–11	Walsall	8	1		
2011–12	Sunderland	0	0	3	0
2011–12	Carlisle U	14	4	14	4
2012–13	Charlton Ath	7	0		
2012–13	Yeovil T	1	0	1	0
2013–14	Charlton Ath	3	0	10	0
2014–15	Walsall	32	5		
2015–16	Walsall	34	3	74	9

DEMETRIOU, Jason (D)   287   18
H: 5 11   W: 10 08   b.Newham 18-11-87
Internationals: Cyprus Full caps.

2005–06	Leyton Orient	3	0		
2006–07	Leyton Orient	15	2		
2007–08	Leyton Orient	43	3		
2008–09	Leyton Orient	43	4		
2009–10	Leyton Orient	39	1	143	10
2010–11	AEK Larnaca	15	0		
2011–12	AEK Larnaca	23	1		
2012–13	AEK Larnaca	19	3	57	4
2013–14	An Famagusta	19	1		
2014–15	An Famagusta	25	0	44	1
2015–16	Walsall	43	3	43	3

DOWNING, Paul (D)   188   6
H: 6 1   W: 12 06   b.Taunton 26-10-91

2009–10	WBA	0	0		
2009–10	Hereford U	6	0		
2010–11	WBA	0	0		
2010–11	Hereford U	0	0	6	0
2010–11	Swansea C	0	0		
2011–12	WBA	0	0		
2011–12	Barnet	26	0	26	0
2012–13	Walsall	31	1		
2013–14	Walsall	44	1		
2014–15	Walsall	35	1		
2015–16	Walsall	46	3	156	6

ETHERIDGE, Neil (G)   60   0
H: 6 3   W: 14 00   b.Enfield 7-2-90
Internationals: England U16. Philippines Full caps.

2008–09	Fulham	0	0		
2009–10	Fulham	0	0		
2010–11	Fulham	0	0		
2011–12	Fulham	0	0		
2012–13	Fulham	0	0		
2012–13	Bristol R	12	0	12	0
2013–14	Fulham	0	0		
2013–14	Crewe Alex	4	0	4	0
2014–15	Oldham Ath	0	0		
2014–15	Charlton Ath	4	0	4	0
2015–16	Walsall	40	0	40	0

FLANAGAN, Reece (M)   30   0
b. 19-10-94

2013–14	Walsall	0	0		
2014–15	Walsall	16	0		
2015–16	Walsall	14	0	30	0

FORDE, Anthony (M)   107   7
H: 5 9   W: 10 10   b.Limerick 16-11-93
Internationals: Republic of Ireland U19, U21.

2011–12	Wolverhampton W	6	0		
2012–13	Wolverhampton W	12	0		
2012–13	Scunthorpe U	8	0	8	0
2013–14	Wolverhampton W	3	0	21	0
2014–15	Walsall	37	3		
2015–16	Walsall	41	4	78	7

HENRY, Rico (D)   44   2
b. 8-7-97
Internationals: England U19.

2014–15	Walsall	9	0		
2015–16	Walsall	35	2	44	2

JEZEPH, Dan (G)   0   0
b. 25-12-97

2015–16	Walsall	0	0		

KINSELLA, Liam (M)   11   1
b.Colchester 23-2-96
Internationals: Republic of Ireland U19.

2013–14	Walsall	0	0		
2014–15	Walsall	4	0		
2015–16	Walsall	7	1	11	1

KOUHYAR, Maz (D)   0   0

2015–16	Walsall	0	0		

LALKOVIC, Milan (F)   117   13
H: 5 9   W: 10 01   b.Kosice 9-12-92
Internationals: Slovakia U17, U19, U21.

2010–11	Chelsea	0	0		
2011–12	Chelsea	0	0		
2011–12	Doncaster R	6	0	6	0
2011–12	Den Haag	2	0	2	0
2012–13	Chelsea	0	0		
2012–13	Vitoria Guimaraes	8	0	8	0
2013–14	Chelsea	0	0		
2013–14	Walsall	38	6		
2014–15	Mlada Boleslav	6	0	6	0
2014–15	Barnsley	17	0	17	0
2015–16	Walsall	40	7	78	13

MACGILLIVRAY, Craig (G)   7   0
H: 6 2   W: 12 04   b.Harrogate 12-1-93

2014–15	Walsall	0	0		
2015–16	Walsall	5	0	7	0

MANTOM, Sam (M)   140   18
H: 5 9   W: 11 00   b.Stourbridge 20-2-92
Internationals: England U17.

2010–11	WBA	0	0		
2010–11	Tranmere R	2	0	2	0
2010–11	Oldham Ath	4	0	4	0
2011–12	WBA	0	0		
2011–12	Walsall	13	3		
2012–13	WBA	0	0		
2012–13	Walsall	29	2		
2013–14	Walsall	43	5		
2014–15	Walsall	12	0		
2015–16	Walsall	37	8	134	18

MORRIS, Kieron (M)   49   5
H: 5 10   W: 11 01   b.Hereford 3-6-94

2012–13	Walsall	0	0		
2013–14	Walsall	2	0		
2014–15	Walsall	14	2		
2015–16	Walsall	33	3	49	5

MURPHY, Jordan (F)   2   0
H: 5 6   W: 10 01   b.Birmingham 5-6-96

2014–15	Walsall	2	0		
2015–16	Walsall	0	0	2	0

O'CONNOR, James (D)   364   8
H: 5 10   W: 12 05   b.Birmingham 20-11-84

2003–04	Aston Villa	0	0		

2004–05	Aston Villa	0	0		
2004–05	Port Vale	13	0	13	0
2004–05	Bournemouth	6	0		
2005–06	Bournemouth	39	1	45	1
2006–07	Doncaster R	40	1		
2007–08	Doncaster R	40	0		
2008–09	Doncaster R	32	1		
2009–10	Doncaster R	38	0		
2010–11	Doncaster R	34	2		
2011–12	Doncaster R	28	0	212	4
2012–13	Derby Co	22	1		
2013–14	Derby Co	0	0	22	1
2013–14	Bristol C	3	0	3	0
2014–15	Walsall	32	1		
2015–16	Walsall	37	1	69	2

OSBOURNE, Isaiah (M)   156   3
H: 6 2   W: 12 06   b.Birmingham 5-11-87
Internationals: England U16.

2005–06	Aston Villa	0	0		
2006–07	Aston Villa	11	0		
2007–08	Aston Villa	8	0		
2008–09	Aston Villa	0	0		
2008–09	Nottingham F	8	0	8	0
2009–10	Aston Villa	0	0		
2009–10	Middlesbrough	9	0	9	0
2010–11	Aston Villa	0	0	19	0
2010–11	Sheffield W	10	0	10	0
2011–12	Hibernian	30	1	30	1
2012–13	Blackpool	28	1		
2013–14	Blackpool	24	1	52	2
2014–15	Scunthorpe U	28	0	28	0
2015–16	Walsall	0	0		

PRESTON, Matt (D)   11   2
b. 16-3-95

2013–14	Walsall	0	0		
2014–15	Walsall	1	0		
2015–16	Walsall	10	2	11	2

ROBERTS, Liam (G)   1   0
H: 6 0   W: 12 13   b.Walsall 24-11-94

2012–13	Walsall	0	0		
2013–14	Walsall	0	0		
2014–15	Walsall	0	0		
2015–16	Walsall	1	0	1	0

ROWLEY, Kyle (M)   0   0
b. 4-5-97

2014–15	Walsall	0	0		
2015–16	Walsall	0	0		

SANGHA, Jordan (M)   0   0
b. 4-1-98

2015–16	Walsall	0	0		

SAWYERS, Romaine (M)   144   16
H: 5 9   W: 11 00   b.Birmingham 2-11-91
Internationals: St Kitts and Nevis U23, Full caps.

2009–10	WBA	0	0		
2010–11	WBA	0	0		
2010–11	Port Vale	1	0	1	0
2011–12	WBA	0	0		
2011–12	Shrewsbury T	7	0	7	0
2012–13	WBA	0	0		
2012–13	Walsall	4	0		
2013–14	Walsall	44	6		
2014–15	Walsall	42	4		
2015–16	Walsall	46	6	136	16

TAYLOR, Andy (D)   266   7
H: 5 11   W: 11 07   b.Blackburn 14-3-86
Internationals: England U16, U17, U18, U19, U20.

2004–05	Blackburn R	0	0		
2005–06	Blackburn R	0	0		
2005–06	QPR	3	0	3	0
2005–06	Blackpool	3	0	3	0
2006–07	Blackburn R	0	0		
2006–07	Crewe Alex	4	0	4	0
2006–07	Huddersfield T	8	0	8	0
2007–08	Blackburn R	0	0		
2007–08	Tranmere R	30	2		
2008–09	Tranmere R	39	1	69	3
2009–10	Sheffield U	26	0		
2010–11	Sheffield U	9	0		
2011–12	Sheffield U	4	0		
2012–13	Sheffield U	0	0	39	0
2012–13	Nottingham F	0	0		
2012–13	Walsall	34	0		
2013–14	Walsall	33	1		
2014–15	Walsall	39	1		
2015–16	Walsall	34	2	140	4

Scholars

Caswell, Bradley William; Cela, Lezion; Cockerill-Mollett, Callum David; Hayles-Docherty, Tobias Martin; Jezeph, Daniel George Alfred; King, Kyle Malik Omar;

Maddocks, Ashley Francis; Oliver, Rory Benjamin; Owen, Nathan Paul; Peters, Cameron James; Pooni, Brendan Dharshan; Roberts, Kory Paul; Shorrock, William John; Smith, Jamie Patrick; Smith, Raekwon Amari; Tonks, Samuel George; Vann, Daniel Jordan.

WATFORD (85)

ABDI, Almen (M)   296   56
H: 5 11   W: 12 11   b.Prizren 21-10-86
Internationals: Switzerland, U21, Full caps.

2003–04	FC Zurich	11	0		
2004–05	FC Zurich	5	0		
2005–06	FC Zurich	12	0		
2006–07	FC Zurich	28	5		
2007–08	FC Zurich	31	7		
2008–09	FC Zurich	32	19		
2009–10	FC Zurich	8	0	127	31
2009–10	Le Mans	13	0	13	0
2010–11	Udinese	19	0		
2011–12	Udinese	22	0	41	0
2012–13	Watford	38	12		
2013–14	Watford	13	2		
2014–15	Watford	32	9		
2015–16	Watford	32	2	115	25

AMRABAT, Nordin (F)   269   48
H: 5 10   W: 12 02   b.Naarden 31-3-87
Internationals: Netherlands U21, Morocco Full caps.

2006–07	Omniworld	36	14	36	14
2007–08	VVV-Venlo	33	10	33	10
2008–09	PSV Eindhoven	25	5		
2009–10	PSV Eindhoven	25	3		
2010–11	PSV Eindhoven	6	1	56	9
2010–11	Kayserispor	14	1		
2011–12	Kayserispor	25	5	39	6
2012–13	Galatasaray	30	1		
2013–14	Galatasaray	4	0		
2013–14	Malaga	15	2		
2014–15	Galatasaray	0	0	34	1
2014–15	Malaga	31	6		
2015–16	Malaga	13	0	59	8
2015–16	Watford	12	0	12	0

ANGELLA, Gabriele (D)   181   15
H: 6 2   W: 12 05   b.Firenze 28-4-89
Internationals: Italy U21.

2008–09	Empoli	11	0		
2009–10	Empoli	35	0		
2010–11	Empoli	2	0	48	0
2010–11	Udinese	8	0		
2011–12	Udinese	0	0		
2011–12	Siena	0	0		
2011–12	Reggina	19	1	19	1
2012–13	Udinese	14	4	22	4
2013–14	Watford	40	7		
2014–15	Watford	35	2		
2015–16	Watford	0	0	75	9
2015–16	QPR	17	1	17	1

ANYA, Ikechi (M)   156   11
H: 5 5   W: 11 04   b.Glasgow 3-1-88
Internationals: Scotland Full caps.

2004–05	Wycombe W	3	0		
2005–06	Wycombe W	2	0		
2006–07	Wycombe W	13	0		
2007–08	Wycombe W	0	0	18	0
2008–09	Northampton T	14	3	14	3
2010–11	Celta Vigo	1	0	1	0
	From Cadiz				
2012–13	Watford	25	3		
2013–14	Watford	35	5		
2014–15	Watford	35	0		
2015–16	Watford	28	0	123	8

ARLAUSKIS, Giedrius (G)   124   0
H: 6 0   W: 12 08   b.Telsiai 1-12-87
Internationals: Lithuania Full caps.

2006	Siauliai	14	0		
2007	Siauliai	19	0	33	0
2007–08	Unirea Urziceni	4	0		
2008–09	Unirea Urziceni	30	0		
2009–10	Unirea Urziceni	18	0		
2010–11	Unirea Urziceni	3	0	55	0
2010–11	Rubin Kazan	2	0		
2011–12	Rubin Kazan	3	0		
2012–13	Rubin Kazan	2	0		
2013–14	Rubin Kazan	0	0	7	0
2014–15	Steau Bucharest	25	0	25	0
2015–16	Watford	1	0	1	0
2015–16	Espanyol	3	0	3	0

BEHRAMI, Valon (M)   327   11
H: 6 1   W: 12 04   b.Titova Mitrovika 19-4-85
Internationals: Switzerland Full caps.

2002–03	Lugano	2	0	2	0
2003–04	Genoa	24	0		
2004–05	Genoa	0	0	24	0
2004–05	Verona	33	3	33	3
2005–06	Lazio	26	2		
2006–07	Lazio	17	1		
2007–08	Lazio	22	1	65	4
2008–09	West Ham U	24	1		
2009–10	West Ham U	27	1		
2010–11	West Ham U	7	2	58	4
2010–11	Fiorentina	17	0		
2011–12	Fiorentina	31	0	48	0
2012–13	Napoli	33	0		
2013–14	Napoli	21	0	54	0
2014–15	Hamburg	22	0	22	0
2015–16	Watford	21	0	21	0

BELKALEM, Essaïd (D)   73   5
H: 6 3   W: 13 04   b.Mekla 1-1-89
Internationals: Algeria U20, U23, Full caps.

2009–10	JS Kabylie	19	1		
2010–11	JS Kabylie	12	0		
2011–12	JS Kabylie	12	2		
2012–13	JS Kabylie	22	2	65	5
2013–14	Granada	0	0		
2013–14	Watford	8	0		
2015–16	Watford	0	0	8	0

BERGHUIS, Steven (F)   103   22
H: 5 11   W: 11 11   b.Apeldoorn 19-12-91
Internationals: Netherlands U19, U20, U21, Full caps.

2010–11	FC Twente	1	0		
2011–12	FC Twente	7	1	8	1
2011–12	VVV Venlo	16	2	16	2
2012–13	AZ Alkmaar	20	0		
2013–14	AZ Alkmaar	25	8		
2014–15	AZ Alkmaar	22	11	70	19
2015–16	Watford	9	0	9	0

BRITOS, Miguel (D)   234   11
H: 6 2   W: 12 13   b.Montevideo 17-7-85

2004–05	Fenix	12	0	12	0
2005–06	Juventud	33	3	33	3
2006–07	Montevideo Wanderers	26	1	26	1
2008–09	Bologna	24	1		
2009–10	Bologna	23	0		
2010–11	Bologna	34	3	71	4
2011–12	Napoli	11	1		
2012–13	Napoli	22	0		
2013–14	Napoli	16	1		
2014–15	Napoli	19	1	68	3
2015–16	Watford	24	0	24	0

CAPOUE, Etienne (M)   231   14
H: 6 2   W: 11 10   b.Niort 11-7-88
Internationals: France U18, U19, U21, Full caps.

2006–07	Toulouse	0	0		
2007–08	Toulouse	5	0		
2008–09	Toulouse	32	1		
2009–10	Toulouse	33	0		
2010–11	Toulouse	37	2		
2011–12	Toulouse	33	3		
2012–13	Toulouse	34	7	174	13
2013–14	Tottenham H	12	1		
2014–15	Tottenham H	12	0	24	1
2015–16	Watford	33	0	33	0

CATHCART, Craig (D)   232   10
H: 6 2   W: 11 06   b.Belfast 6-2-89
Internationals: Northern Ireland U16, U17, U20, U21, Full caps.

2005–06	Manchester U	0	0		
2006–07	Manchester U	0	0		
2007–08	Manchester U	0	0		
2007–08	Antwerp	13	2	13	2
2008–09	Manchester U	0	0		
2008–09	Plymouth Arg	31	1	31	1
2009–10	Manchester U	0	0		
2009–10	Watford	12	0		
2010–11	Blackpool	30	1		
2011–12	Blackpool	27	0		
2012 13	Blackpool	25	1		
2013–14	Blackpool	30	1	112	3
2014–15	Watford	29	3		
2015–16	Watford	35	1	76	4

DEENEY, Troy (F)   366   118
H: 5 11   W: 12 00   b.Solihull 29-6-88

2006–07	Walsall	1	0		
2007–08	Walsall	35	1		
2008–09	Walsall	45	12		
2009–10	Walsall	42	14	123	27
2010–11	Watford	36	3		

2011–12	Watford	43	11		
2012–13	Watford	40	19		
2013–14	Watford	44	24		
2014–15	Watford	42	21		
2015–16	Watford	38	13	243	91

DIAMANTI, Alessandro (M)   368   65
H: 5 10 W: 11 09 b.Prato 2-5-83
Internationals: Italy Full caps.

1999–2000	Prato	1	0		
2000–01	Prato	0	0		
2000–01	Empoli	0	0		
2001–02	Prato	0	0		
2001–02	Fucecchio	24	2	24	2
2002–03	Prato	2	0		
2002–03	Fiorentina	3	0		
2003–04	Prato	20	4		
2004–05	Prato	0	0		
2004–05	Albinoleffe	18	0		
2005–06	Prato	11	4		
2005–06	Albinoleffe	8	0	26	0
2006–07	Prato	25	10	59	18
2007–08	Livorno	26	4		
2008–09	Livorno	32	1		
2009–10	Livorno	1	0	59	5
2009–10	West Ham U	27	7		
2010–11	West Ham U	1	0	28	7
2010–11	Brescia	32	6	32	6
2011–12	Bologna	30	8		
2012–13	Bologna	34	7		
2013–14	Bologna	19	5	83	20
2014–15	Guangzhou E	24	4		
2014–15	*Fiorentina*	11	2	14	2
2015–16	Guangzhou E	0	0	24	4

On loan from Guangzhou Evergrande.

2015–16	Watford	3	0	3	0
2015–16	*Atalanta*	16	1	16	1

DOUCOURE, Abdoulaye (M)   90   12
b.Meulan-en-Yvelines 1-1-93
Internationals: France U17, U18, U19, U20, U21.

2012–13	Rennes	4	1		
2013–14	Rennes	20	6		
2014–15	Rennes	35	3		
2015–16	Rennes	16	2	75	12
2015–16	Watford	0	0		
2015–16	*Granada*	15	0	15	0

EKSTRAND, Joel (D)   175   3
H: 6 2 W: 12 00 b.Lund 4-2-89
Internationals: Sweden U17, U19, U21, Full caps.

2007–08	Helsingborgs IF	12	0		
2008–09	Helsingborgs IF	24	0		
2009–10	Helsingborgs IF	25	1		
2010–11	Helsingborgs IF	12	0	73	1
2010–11	Udinese	1	0		
2011–12	Udinese	12	0	13	0
2012–13	*Watford*	32	1		
2013–14	Watford	33	0		
2014–15	Watford	24	1		
2015–16	Watford	0	0	89	2

GILMARTIN, Rene (G)   64   0
H: 6 5 W: 13 06 b.Dublin 31-5-87
Internationals: Republic of Ireland U21.

2005–06	Walsall	2	0		
2006–07	Walsall	0	0		
2007–08	Walsall	0	0		
2008–09	Walsall	11	0		
2009–10	Walsall	22	0	35	0
2010–11	Watford	0	0		
2011–12	Watford	2	0		
2011–12	*Yeovil T*	8	0	8	0
2011–12	*Crawley T*	6	0	6	0
2012–13	Plymouth Arg	13	0		
2013–14	Plymouth Arg	0	0	13	0
2014–15	Watford	0	0		
2015–16	Watford	0	0	2	0

GOMES, Heurelho (G)   373   0
H: 6 3 W: 12 13 b.Minas Gerais 15-2-81
Internationals: Brazil U23, Full caps.

2001	Cruzeiro	0	0		
2002	Cruzeiro	14	0		
2003	Cruzeiro	40	0		
2004	Cruzeiro	5	0	59	0
2004–05	PSV Eindhoven	30	0		
2005–06	PSV Eindhoven	32	0		
2006–07	PSV Eindhoven	32	0		
2007–08	PSV Eindhoven	34	0	128	0
2008–09	Tottenham H	34	0		
2009–10	Tottenham H	31	0		
2010–11	Tottenham H	30	0		
2011–12	Tottenham H	0	0		
2012–13	Tottenham H	0	0		
2012–13	*Hoffenheim*	9	0	9	0
2013–14	Tottenham H	0	0	95	0

2014–15	Watford	44	0		
2015–16	Watford	38	0	82	0

GUEDIOURA, Adlene (M)   238   20
H: 6 1 W: 12 08 b.La Roche-sur-Yon 12-11-85
Internationals: Algeria Full caps.

2004–05	Sedan	0	0		
2005–06	Noisy-Le-Sec	15	1	15	1
2006–07	L'Entente	21	3	21	3
2007–08	Creteil	24	6	24	6
2008–09	Kortrijk	10	0	10	0
2008–09	Charleroi	12	0		
2009–10	Charleroi	13	1	25	1
2009–10	Wolverhampton W	14	1		
2010–11	Wolverhampton W	10	1		
2011–12	Wolverhampton W	10	0	34	2
2011–12	*Nottingham F*	19	1		
2012–13	Nottingham F	35	3		
2013–14	Nottingham F	5	0	59	4
2013–14	Crystal Palace	8	0		
2014–15	Crystal Palace	7	0		
2014–15	*Watford*	17	3		
2015–16	Crystal Palace	0	0	15	0
2015–16	Watford	18	0	35	3

HOBAN, Tommie (D)   54   2
H: 6 2 W: 11 13 b.Walthamstow 24-1-94
Internationals: Republic of Ireland U17, U19, U21.

2010–11	Watford	1	0		
2011–12	Watford	0	0		
2012–13	Watford	19	2		
2013–14	Watford	7	0		
2014–15	Watford	27	0		
2015–16	Watford	0	0	54	2

HOLEBAS, Jose (M)   236   32
H: 6 0 W: 12 06 b.Aschaffenburg 27-6-84
Internationals: Greece Full caps.

2005–06	Viktoria Kahl	33	15	33	15
2006–07	1860 Munich	0	0		
2007–08	1860 Munich	19	2		
2008–09	1860 Munich	24	1		
2009–10	1860 Munich	31	4	74	7
2010–11	Olympiacos	24	1		
2011–12	Olympiacos	23	2		
2012–13	Olympiacos	28	4		
2013–14	Olympiacos	19	2	94	9
2014–15	Roma	24	1	24	1
2015–16	Watford	11	0	11	0

IBARBO, Victor (F)   244   22
H: 6 2 W: 12 06 b.Tumaco 19-5-90
Internationals: Colombia U20, Full caps.

2008	Atletico Nacional	16	0		
2009	Atletico Nacional	30	1		
2010	Atletico Nacional	40	3		
2011	Atletico Nacional	16	2		
2011–12	Cagliari	38	3		
2012–13	Cagliari	34	6		
2013–14	Cagliari	30	4		
2014–15	Cagliari	13	2		
2015–16	Cagliari	0	0	115	15
2015–16	Roma	2	0	12	0

On loan from Cagliari.

2015–16	Watford	4	0	4	0
2015–16	*Atletico Nacional*	11	1	113	7

IGHALO, Odion Jude (F)   196   62
H: 6 2 W: 11 00 b.Lagos 16-6-89
Internationals: Nigeria U20, Full caps.

2007	Lyn	7	3		
2008	Lyn	13	6	20	9
2008–09	Udinese	6	1		
2009–10	Udinese	0	0		
2010–11	Udinese	0	0		
2010–11	Cesena	3	0	3	0
2010–11	Granada	21	4		
2011–12	Udinese	0	0		
2011–12	Granada	30	6		
2012–13	Udinese	0	0		
2012–13	Granada	28	5		
2013–14	Udinese	0	0		
2013–14	Granada	16	2	95	17
2014–15	Udinese	0	0	6	1
2014–15	Watford	35	20		
2015–16	Watford	37	15	72	35

IKPEAZU, Uche (F)   72   11
H: 6 3 W: 12 04 b.London 28-2-95

2013–14	Watford	0	0		
2013–14	*Crewe Alex*	15	4		
2014–15	Watford	0	0		
2014–15	*Crewe Alex*	17	2	32	6
2014–15	*Doncaster R*	7	0	7	0
2015–16	Watford	0	0		
2015–16	*Port Vale*	21	5	21	5
2015–16	*Blackpool*	12	0	12	0

JAKUBIAK, Alex (F)   33   5
H: 5 10 W: 10 06 b.Westminster 27-8-96
Internationals: Scotland U19.

2013–14	Watford	1	0		
2014–15	Watford	0	0		
2014–15	*Oxford U*	9	1	9	1
2014–15	*Dagenham & R*	23	4	23	4
2015–16	Watford	0	0	1	0

JUANFRAN, Moreno (D)   105   3
H: 5 10 W: 10 12 b.Madrid 11-9-88

2007–08	Getafe	1	0	1	0
2008–09	Villarreal	0	0		
2009–10	Real Madrid	1	0		
2010–11	Real Madrid	0	0		
2012–13	Real Madrid	0	0	1	0
2013–14	Real Betis	34	1		
2014–15	Real Betis	0	0	34	1
2014–15	Deportivo La Coruna	34	1		
2015–16	Watford	0	0		
2015–16	*Deportivo La Coruna*	35	1	69	2

JURADO, Jose Manuel (M)   265   36
H: 5 8 W: 11 05 b.Sanlucar de Barrameda 29-6-86
Internationals: Spain U16, U17, U19, U21.

2003–04	Real Madrid	0	0		
2004–05	Real Madrid	0	0		
2005–06	Real Madrid	3	0	3	0
2006–07	Atletico Madrid	33	0		
2007–08	Atletico Madrid	16	2		
2008–09	Atletico Madrid	0	0		
2008–09	*Mallorca*	35	9	35	9
2009–10	Atletico Madrid	38	7		
2010–11	Atletico Madrid	1	1	88	10
2010–11	Schalke 04	28	3		
2011–12	Schalke 04	18	0		
2012–13	Schalke 04	0	0	46	3
2012–13	*Spartak Moscow*	18	3		
2013–14	Spartak Moscow	29	8		
2014–15	Spartak Moscow	18	3		
2015–16	Spartak Moscow	1	0	66	14
2015–16	Watford	27	0	27	0

LAYUN, Miguel (D)   242   21
H: 5 10 W: 10 01 b.Cordoba 25-6-88
Internationals: Mexico Full caps.

2006–07	Veracruz	1	0		
2007–08	Veracruz	30	0		
2008–09	Veracruz	27	1	58	1
2009–10	Bergamo	2	0	2	0
2009–10	Club America	8	0		
2010–11	Club America	33	1		
2011–12	Club America	11	0		
2012–13	Club America	33	2		
2013–14	Club America	33	5		
2014–15	Club America	17	6	135	14
2014–15	Watford	17	0		
2015–16	Watford	3	1	20	1
2015–16	*FC Porto*	27	5	27	5

LEWIS, Dennon (M)   0   0
b. 9-5-97

2015–16	Watford	0	0		

MARIO SUAREZ, Mata (M)   258   15
H: 6 1 W: 12 02 b.Madrid 24-2-87
Internationals: Spain U16, U17, U19, U20, U21, Full caps.

2005–06	Atletico Madrid	4	0		
2006–07	Atletico Madrid	0	0		
2006–07	*Real Valladolid*	23	3	23	3
2007–08	Atletico Madrid	0	0		
2007–08	*Celta Vigo*	26	2	26	2
2008–09	Mallorca	26	0		
2009–10	Mallorca	34	5	60	5
2010–11	Atletico Madrid	27	2		
2011–12	Atletico Madrid	28	0		
2012–13	Atletico Madrid	29	1		
2013–14	Atletico Madrid	17	0		
2014–15	Atletico Madrid	20	1	125	4
2015–16	Fiorentina	9	1	9	1
2015–16	Watford	15	0	15	0

MURRAY, Sean (M)   82   11
H: 5 9 W: 10 10 b.Abbots Langley 11-10-93
Internationals: Republic of Ireland U17, U19, U21.

2010–11	Watford	2	0		
2011–12	Watford	18	7		
2012–13	Watford	15	1		
2013–14	Watford	34	3		
2014–15	Watford	6	0		
2015–16	Watford	0	0	75	11
2015–16	*Wigan Ath*	7	0	7	0

NYOM, Allan (D) 247 2
H: 5 7 W: 12 11 b.Neuilly-sur-Seine 10-5-88
Internationals: Cameroon Full caps.

2008–09	Arles-Avignon	37	0	37 0
2009–10	Udinese	0	0	
2010–11	Udinese	0	0	
2010–11	*Granada*	43	1	
2011–12	Udinese	0	0	
2011–12	*Granada*	32	0	
2012–13	Udinese	0	0	
2012–13	*Granada*	35	0	
2013–14	Udinese	0	0	
2013–14	*Granada*	34	0	
2014–15	Udinese	0	0	
2014–15	*Granada*	34	1	178 2
2015–16	Watford	32	0	32 0

OULARE, Obbi (F) 27 4
H: 6 5 W: 15 02 b.Waregem 8-1-96
Internationals: Belgium U18, U19, U21.

2014–15	Club Brugge	19	3	
2015–16	Club Brugge	6	1	25 4
2015–16	Watford	2	0	2 0

PANTILIMON, Costel (G) 154 0
H: 6 5 W: 15 02 b.Bacau 1-2-87
Internationals: Romania U17, U19, U21, Full caps.

2005–06	Aerostar Bacau	9	0	9 0
2006–07	Poli Timisoara	8	0	
2007–08	Poli Timisoara	5	0	13 0
2008–09	Timisoara	31	0	
2009–10	Timisoara	21	0	
2010–11	Timisoara	28	0	80 0
2011–12	*Manchester C*	0	0	
2012–13	Manchester C	2	0	
2013–14	Manchester C	7	0	7 0
2014–15	Sunderland	28	0	
2015–16	Sunderland	17	0	45 0
2015–16	Watford	0	0	

PAREDES, Juan Carlos (D) 277 14
H: 5 10 W: 11 05 b.Esmeraldas 8-7-87
Internationals: Ecuador Full caps.

2006–07	Barcelona	5	0	
2007–08	Deportivo Cuena	19	1	
2007–08	*Rocafuerte*	29	2	29 2
2008–09	Deportivo Cuena	32	3	51 4
2009–10	Deportivo Quito	38	4	
2010–11	Deportivo Quito	36	3	
2011–12	Deportivo Quito	19	0	93 7
2012–13	Barcelona	35	1	
2013–14	Barcelona	8	0	48 1
2014–15	Watford	39	0	
2015–16	Watford	17	0	56 0

PENARANDA, Adalberto (F) 60 9
b.El Vigia 31-5-97
Internationals: Venezuela U17, U20, Full caps.

2013–14	Dep La Guaira	18	1	
2014–15	Dep La Guaira	19	3	37 4
2015–16	Udinese	0	0	
2015–16	Watford	0	0	
2015–16	*Granada*	23	5	23 5

PRODL, Sebastien (D) 213 16
H: 6 4 W: 13 05 b.Graz 21-6-87
Internationals: Austria U19, U20, Full caps.

2006–07	Sturm Graz	16	1	
2007–08	Sturm Graz	27	3	43 4
2008–09	Werder Bremen	22	0	
2009–10	Werder Bremen	9	1	
2010–11	Werder Bremen	25	1	
2011–12	Werder Bremen	16	2	
2012–13	Werder Bremen	28	1	
2013–14	Werder Bremen	27	2	
2014–15	Werder Bremen	22	3	149 10
2015–16	Watford	21	2	21 2

PUDIL, Daniel (D) 270 26
H: 6 1 W: 12 11 b.Prague 27-9-85
Internationals: Czech Republic U19, U21, Full caps.

2003–04	Blsany	2	2	2 2
2005–06	Liberec	3	4	
2006–07	Liberec	3	3	6 7
2007–08	Slavia Prague	16	6	16 6
2008–09	Genk	29	4	
2009–10	Genk	27	1	
2010–11	Genk	32	0	
2011–12	Genk	18	0	106 5
2011–12	Cesena	7	1	7 1
2012–13	Watford	37	1	
2013–14	Watford	37	2	
2014–15	Watford	23	0	
2015–16	Watford	0	0	97 3
2015–16	*Sheffield W*	36	2	36 2

VYDRA, Matej (F) 153 46
H: 5 10 W: 11 09 b.Chotebor 1-5-92
Internationals: Czech Republic U16, U17, U18, U19, U21, Full caps.

2009–10	Banik Ostrava	13	4	13 4
2010–11	Udinese	2	0	
2011–12	Udinese	0	0	
2011–12	*Club Brugge*	1	0	1 0
2012–13	Udinese	0	0	
2012–13	*Watford*	41	20	
2013–14	Udinese	0	0	
2013–14	*WBA*	23	3	23 3
2014–15	Udinese	0	0	2 0
2014–15	*Watford*	42	16	
2015–16	Watford	0	0	83 36
2015–16	*Reading*	31	3	31 3

WATSON, Ben (M) 358 36
H: 5 10 W: 10 11 b.Camberwell 9-7-85
Internationals: England U21.

2002–03	Crystal Palace	5	0	
2003–04	Crystal Palace	16	1	
2004–05	Crystal Palace	21	0	
2005–06	Crystal Palace	42	4	
2006–07	Crystal Palace	25	3	
2007–08	Crystal Palace	42	5	
2008–09	Crystal Palace	18	5	169 18
2008–09	Wigan Ath	10	2	
2009–10	Wigan Ath	5	1	
2009–10	*QPR*	16	2	16 2
2009–10	*WBA*	7	1	7 1
2010–11	Wigan Ath	29	3	
2011–12	Wigan Ath	21	3	
2012–13	Wigan Ath	12	1	
2013–14	Wigan Ath	25	2	
2014–15	Wigan Ath	9	1	111 13
2014–15	Watford	20	0	
2015–16	Watford	35	2	55 2

Players retained or with offer of contract
Adeyemo, Ola; Cholevas, Chose Loint; Folivi, Michael Kwaku; Nyom, Allan; Obi, Ogochukwu Alexander; Ovenden, Rhyle; Ranegie, Mathias.

Scholars
Charles, Ashley James; Eleftheriou, Andrew; Gartside, Nathan James; Johnson, Treon Joval; Mason, Brandon Alexander; Pereira, Dion Enrico; Roe, Joshua Dylan; Rogers, Louis Ronald; Rowan, Charles Alfred; Ryan, Maximillian Medwyn Richard; Sesay, David Junior Deen; Stevens, Connor John .

WBA (86)

ANICHEBE, Victor (F) 186 23
H: 6 1 W: 13 00 b.Nigeria 23-4-88
Internationals: Nigeria U23, Full caps.

2005–06	Everton	2	1	
2006–07	Everton	19	3	
2007–08	Everton	27	1	
2008–09	Everton	17	1	
2009–10	Everton	11	1	
2010–11	Everton	16	0	
2011–12	Everton	12	4	
2012–13	Everton	26	6	
2013–14	Everton	1	0	131 17
2013–14	WBA	24	3	
2014–15	WBA	21	3	
2015–16	WBA	10	0	55 6

BERAHINO, Saido (F) 133 35
H: 5 10 W: 11 13 b.Burundi 4-8-93
Internationals: England U16, U17, U18, U19, U20, U21.

2010–11	WBA	0	0	
2011–12	WBA	0	0	
2011–12	*Northampton T*	14	6	14 6
2011–12	*Brentford*	8	4	8 4
2012–13	WBA	0	0	
2012–13	*Peterborough U*	10	2	10 2
2013–14	WBA	32	5	
2014–15	WBA	38	14	
2015–16	WBA	31	4	101 23

BRUNT, Chris (M) 426 62
H: 6 1 W: 13 04 b.Belfast 14-12-84
Internationals: Northern Ireland U19, U21, U23, Full caps.

2002–03	Middlesbrough	0	0	
2003–04	Middlesbrough	0	0	
2003–04	Sheffield W	9	2	
2004–05	Sheffield W	42	4	
2005–06	Sheffield W	44	7	
2006–07	Sheffield W	44	11	
2007–08	WBA	1	0	140 24
2007–08	WBA	34	4	

2008–09	WBA	34	8	
2009–10	WBA	40	13	
2010–11	WBA	34	4	
2011–12	WBA	29	2	
2012–13	WBA	31	2	
2013–14	WBA	28	3	
2014–15	WBA	34	2	
2015–16	WBA	22	0	286 38

CAMPBELL, Tahvon (F) 17 1
b. 10-1-97

2015–16	WBA	0	0	
2015–16	*Yeovil T*	17	1	17 1

CHESTER, James (D) 195 9
H: 5 11 W: 11 04 b.Warrington 23-1-89
Internationals: Wales Full caps.

2007–08	Manchester U	0	0	
2008–09	Manchester U	0	0	
2008–09	*Peterborough U*	5	0	5 0
2009–10	Manchester U	0	0	
2009–10	*Plymouth Arg*	3	0	3 0
2010–11	Manchester U	0	0	
2010–11	*Carlisle U*	18	2	18 2
2010–11	Hull C	21	1	
2011–12	Hull C	44	2	
2012–13	Hull C	44	1	
2013–14	Hull C	24	1	
2014–15	Hull C	23	2	156 7
2015–16	WBA	13	0	13 0

DAWSON, Craig (D) 191 29
H: 6 0 W: 12 04 b.Rochdale 6-5-90
Internationals: England U21. Great Britain.

2008–09	Rochdale	0	0	
2009–10	Rochdale	42	9	
2010–11	WBA	0	0	
2010–11	*Rochdale*	45	10	87 19
2011–12	WBA	8	0	
2012–13	WBA	1	0	
2012–13	*Bolton W*	16	4	16 4
2013–14	WBA	12	0	
2014–15	WBA	29	2	
2015–16	WBA	38	4	88 6

DONNELLAN, Shaun (D) 0 0
b. 22-5-97
Internationals: Republic of Ireland U19.

2015–16	WBA	0	0	

EDWARDS, Kyle (M) 0 0
H: 5 8 W: 10 01 b.Dudley 17-2-98
Internationals: England U16, U17.

2015–16	WBA	0	0	

EVANS, Jonny (D) 208 8
H: 6 2 W: 12 02 b.Belfast 3-1-88
Internationals: Northern Ireland U16, U17, U21, Full caps.

2004–05	Manchester U	0	0	
2005–06	Manchester U	0	0	
2006–07	Manchester U	0	0	
2006–07	*Antwerp*	14	2	14 2
2006–07	*Sunderland*	18	1	
2007–08	Manchester U	0	0	
2007–08	*Sunderland*	15	0	33 1
2008–09	Manchester U	17	0	
2009–10	Manchester U	18	0	
2010–11	Manchester U	13	0	
2011–12	Manchester U	29	1	
2012–13	Manchester U	23	3	
2013–14	Manchester U	17	0	
2014–15	Manchester U	14	0	
2015–16	Manchester U	0	0	131 4
2015–16	WBA	30	1	30 1

FIELD, Sam (M) 1 0
b. 8-5-98

2015–16	WBA	1	0	1 0

FITZWATER, Jack (D) 1 0
H: 6 2 W: 11 00 b.Solihull 23-9-97

2015–16	WBA	0	0	
2015–16	*Chesterfield*	1	0	1 0

FLETCHER, Darren (M) 276 20
H: 6 0 W: 11 09 b.Edinburgh 1-2-84
Internationals: Scotland U20, U21, B, Full caps.

2000–01	Manchester U	0	0	
2001–02	Manchester U	0	0	
2002–03	Manchester U	0	0	
2003–04	Manchester U	22	0	
2004–05	Manchester U	18	3	
2005–06	Manchester U	27	1	
2006–07	Manchester U	24	3	
2007–08	Manchester U	16	0	
2008–09	Manchester U	26	3	
2009–10	Manchester U	30	4	
2010–11	Manchester U	26	2	
2011–12	Manchester U	8	1	

2012–13	Manchester U	3	1		
2013–14	Manchester U	12	0		
2014–15	Manchester U	11	0	223	18
2014–15	WBA	15	1		
2015–16	WBA	38	1	53	2

FOSTER, Ben (G)   276   0
H: 6 2 W: 12 08 b.Leamington Spa 3-4-83
Internationals: England Full caps.

2000–01	Stoke C	0	0		
2001–02	Stoke C	0	0		
2002–03	Stoke C	0	0		
2003–04	Stoke C	0	0		
2004–05	Stoke C	0	0		
2004–05	*Kidderminster H*	2	0	2	0
2004–05	*Wrexham*	17	0	17	0
2005–06	Manchester U	0	0		
2005–06	*Watford*	44	0		
2006–07	Manchester U	0	0		
2006–07	*Watford*	29	0	73	0
2007–08	Manchester U	1	0		
2008–09	Manchester U	2	0		
2009–10	Manchester U	9	0	12	0
2010–11	Birmingham C	38	0		
2011–12	Birmingham C	0	0	38	0
2011–12	*WBA*	37	0		
2012–13	WBA	30	0		
2013–14	WBA	24	0		
2014–15	WBA	28	0		
2015–16	WBA	15	0	134	0

GAMBOA, Cristian (D)   146   1
H: 5 9 W: 10 08 b.Liberia 24-10-89
Internationals: Costa Rica Full caps.

2006–07	Municipal Liberia	16	0	16	0
2007–08	Liberia Mia	26	0		
2008–09	Liberia Mia	13	0	39	0
2009–10	Aguilas Guanacastercas	13	0	13	0
2010–11	Fredrikstad	11	1		
2011–12	Fredrikstad	16	0	27	1
2012	Rosenborg	10	0		
2013	Rosenborg	28	0		
2014	Rosenborg	2	0	40	0
2014–15	WBA	10	0		
2015–16	WBA	1	0	11	0

GARDNER, Craig (M)   251   31
H: 5 10 W: 11 13 b.Solihull 25-11-86
Internationals: England U21.

2004–05	Aston Villa	0	0		
2005–06	Aston Villa	8	0		
2006–07	Aston Villa	13	2		
2007–08	Aston Villa	23	3		
2008–09	Aston Villa	14	0		
2009–10	Aston Villa	1	0	59	5
2009–10	Birmingham C	13	1		
2010–11	Birmingham C	29	8	42	9
2011–12	Sunderland	30	3		
2012–13	Sunderland	33	6		
2013–14	Sunderland	18	2	81	11
2014–15	WBA	35	3		
2015–16	WBA	34	3	69	6

JONES, Callum (M)   0   0
H: 6 0 W: 11 12 b.London 31-1-96
Internationals: England U16, U17.

2013–14	WBA	0	0
2014–15	WBA	0	0
2015–16	WBA	0	0

LAMBERT, Ricky (F)   588   215
H: 6 2 W: 14 08 b.Liverpool 16-2-82
Internationals: England Full caps.

1999–2000	Blackpool	3	0		
2000–01	Blackpool	0	0	3	0
2000–01	Macclesfield T	9	0		
2001–02	Macclesfield T	35	8	44	8
2001–02	Stockport Co	0	0		
2002–03	Stockport Co	29	2		
2003–04	Stockport Co	40	12		
2004–05	Stockport Co	29	4	98	18
2004–05	Rochdale	15	6		
2005–06	Rochdale	46	22		
2006–07	Rochdale	3	0	64	28
2006–07	Bristol R	36	8		
2007–08	Bristol R	46	14		
2008–09	Bristol R	45	29		
2009–10	Bristol R	1	1	128	52
2009–10	Southampton	45	30		
2010–11	Southampton	45	21		
2011–12	Southampton	42	27		
2012–13	Southampton	38	15		
2013–14	Southampton	37	13	207	106
2014–15	Liverpool	25	2	25	2
2015–16	WBA	19	1	19	1

LEKO, Jonathan (M)   5   0
H: 6 0 W: 11 11 b.Kinshasa 24-4-99
Internationals: England U16, U17.

2015–16	WBA	5	0	5	0

LINDEGAARD, Anders (G)   105   0
H: 6 4 W: 12 08 b.Odense 13-4-84
Internationals: Denmark U19, U20, Full caps.

2003–04	Odense	0	0		
2004–05	Odense	0	0		
2005–06	Odense	0	0		
2006–07	Odense	1	0		
2007–08	Odense	1	0		
2008–09	*Kolding*	10	0	10	0
2009	*Aalesund*	26	0		
2009	Odense	4	0	6	0
2010	*Aalesund*	30	0	56	0
2010–11	Manchester U	0	0		
2011–12	Manchester U	8	0		
2012–13	Manchester U	10	0		
2013–14	Manchester U	1	0		
2014–15	Manchester U	0	0		
2015–16	Manchester U	0	0	19	0
2015–16	WBA	0	0		
2015–16	*Preston NE*	14	0	14	0

McAULEY, Gareth (D)   419   29
H: 6 3 W: 13 00 b.Larne 5-12-79
Internationals: Northern Ireland B, Full caps.

2004–05	Lincoln C	37	3		
2005–06	Lincoln C	35	5	72	8
2006–07	Leicester C	30	3		
2007–08	Leicester C	44	2	74	5
2008–09	Ipswich T	35	0		
2009–10	Ipswich T	41	5		
2010–11	Ipswich T	39	2	115	7
2011–12	WBA	32	2		
2012–13	WBA	36	3		
2013–14	WBA	32	2		
2014–15	WBA	24	1		
2015–16	WBA	34	1	158	9

McCLEAN, James (M)   240   36
H: 5 11 W: 11 00 b.Derry 22-4-89
Internationals: Northern Ireland U21.
Republic of Ireland Full caps.

2009	Derry C	27	1		
2010	Derry C	30	10		
2011	Derry C	16	7	73	18
2011–12	Sunderland	23	5		
2012–13	Sunderland	36	2		
2013–14	Sunderland	0	0	59	7
,2013–14	Wigan Ath	37	3		
2014–15	Wigan Ath	36	6	73	9
2015–16	WBA	35	2	35	2

McMANAMAN, Callum (F)   113   12
H: 5 9 W: 11 03 b.Huyton 25-4-91
Internationals: England U20.

2008–09	Wigan Ath	1	0		
2009–10	Wigan Ath	0	0		
2010–11	Wigan Ath	3	0		
2011–12	Wigan Ath	2	0		
2011–12	*Blackpool*	14	2	14	2
2012–13	Wigan Ath	20	2		
2013–14	Wigan Ath	30	3		
2014–15	Wigan Ath	23	5	79	10
2014–15	WBA	8	0		
2015–16	WBA	12	0	20	0

MORRISON, James (M)   322   31
H: 5 10 W: 10 06 b.Darlington 25-5-86
Internationals: England U17, U18, U19, U20.
Scotland Full caps.

2003–04	Middlesbrough	1	0		
2004–05	Middlesbrough	14	0		
2005–06	Middlesbrough	24	1		
2006–07	Middlesbrough	28	2	67	3
2007–08	WBA	35	4		
2008–09	WBA	30	3		
2009–10	WBA	11	1		
2010–11	WBA	31	4		
2011–12	WBA	30	5		
2012–13	WBA	35	5		
2013–14	WBA	32	1		
2014–15	WBA	33	2		
2015–16	WBA	18	3	255	28

MYHILL, Boaz (G)   380   0
H: 6 4 W: 14 06 b.California 9-11-82
Internationals: England U20. Wales Full caps.

2000–01	Aston Villa	0	0		
2001–02	Aston Villa	0	0		
2001–02	Stoke C	0	0		
2002–03	Aston Villa	0	0		
2002–03	Bristol C	0	0		
2002–03	*Bradford C*	2	0	2	0
2003–04	Aston Villa	0	0		
2003–04	*Macclesfield T*	15	0	15	0

2003–04	*Stockport Co*	2	0	2	0
2003–04	Hull C	23	0		
2004–05	Hull C	45	0		
2005–06	Hull C	45	0		
2006–07	Hull C	46	0		
2007–08	Hull C	43	0		
2008–09	Hull C	28	0		
2009–10	Hull C	27	0	257	0
2010–11	WBA	6	0		
2011–12	WBA	0	0		
2011–12	*Birmingham C*	42	0	42	0
2012–13	WBA	8	0		
2013–14	WBA	14	0		
2014–15	WBA	11	0		
2015–16	WBA	23	0	62	0

OLSSON, Jonas (D)   386   18
H: 6 4 W: 12 08 b.Landskrona 10-3-83
Internationals: Sweden U21, Full caps.

2002	Landskrona	0	0		
2003	Landskrona	22	0		
2004	Landskrona	22	1		
2005	Landskrona	12	0	56	1
2005–06	NEC Nijmegen	34	0		
2006–07	NEC Nijmegen	32	2		
2007–08	NEC Nijmegen	27	3	93	5
2008–09	WBA	28	2		
2009–10	WBA	43	4		
2010–11	WBA	24	1		
2011–12	WBA	33	2		
2012–13	WBA	36	0		
2013–14	WBA	32	1		
2014–15	WBA	13	1		
2015–16	WBA	28	1	237	12

PALMER, Alex (G)   0   0
b. 10-8-96
Internationals: England U16.

2014–15	WBA	0	0
2015–16	WBA	0	0

POCOGNOLI, Sebastien (D)   241   8
H: 5 11 W: 11 07 b.Liege 1-8-87
Internationals: Belgium U16, U17, U19, U21, U23, Full caps.

2003–04	Genk	1	0		
2004–05	Genk	0	0		
2005–06	Genk	15	1		
2006–07	Genk	30	0	46	1
2007–08	AZ Alkmaar	28	2		
2008–09	AZ Alkmaar	25	2		
2009–10	AZ Alkmaar	11	1	64	5
2009–10	Standard Liege	10	1		
2010–11	Standard Liege	34	1		
2011–12	Standard Liege	32	0		
2012–13	Standard Liege	9	0	85	2
2012–13	Hannover 96	11	0		
2013–14	Hannover 96	19	0	30	0
2014–15	WBA	15	0		
2015–16	WBA	1	0	16	0

ROBERTS, Tyler (F)   1   0
H: 5 11 W: 11 11 b.Gloucester 12-1-98
Internationals: Wales U16, U17.

2014–15	WBA	0	0		
2015–16	WBA	1	0	1	0

RONDON, Jose Salomon (F)   269   94
H: 6 1 W: 13 08 b.Caracas 16-9-89
Internationals: Venezuela U20, Full caps.

2006–07	Aragua	21	7		
2007–08	Aragua	28	8	49	15
2008–09	Las Palmas	10	0		
2009–10	Las Palmas	36	12	46	12
2010–11	Malaga	30	14		
2011–12	Malaga	37	11	67	25
2012–13	Rubin Kazan	25	7		
2013–14	Rubin Kazan	11	6	36	13
2013–14	Zenit St Petersburg	14	7		
2014–15	Zenit St Petersburg	26	13		
2015–16	Zenit St Petersburg	3	0	37	20
2015–16	WBA	34	9	34	9

ROSE, Jack (G)   9   0
H: 6 0 W: 11 11 b.Solihull 31-1-95

2014–15	WBA	0	0		
2014–15	*Accrington S*	4	0	4	0
2015–16	WBA	0	0		
2015–16	*Crawley T*	5	0	5	0

SESSEGNON, Stephane (M)   374   49
H: 5 8 W: 11 05 b.Allahe 1-6-84
Internationals: Benin Full caps.

2003–04	Requins	2	0	2	0
2004–05	Creteil	35	5		
2005–06	Creteil	33	5	68	10
2006–07	Le Mans	31	0		
2007–08	Le Mans	30	5	61	6
2008–09	Paris St Germain	34	5		
2009–10	Paris St Germain	29	3		

2010–11	Paris St Germain	14	0	77 8
2010–11	Sunderland	14	3	
2011–12	Sunderland	36	7	
2012–13	Sunderland	35	7	
2013–14	Sunderland	2	0	87 17
2013–14	WBA	26	5	
2014–15	WBA	28	1	
2015–16	WBA	25	2	79 8

WARD, Joe (M)   0 0
H: 6 0   W: 12 02   b. 27-9-96

2015–16	WBA	0	0

YACOB, Claudio (M)   236 5
H: 5 11   W: 11 06   b.Carcarana 18-7-87
Internationals: Argentina U20, Full caps.

2006–07	Racing Club	12	0	
2007–08	Racing Club	24	0	
2008–09	Racing Club	25	1	
2009–10	Racing Club	26	0	
2010–11	Racing Club	21	2	
2011–12	Racing Club	17	1	125 4
2012–13	WBA	30	0	
2013–14	WBA	27	1	
2014–15	WBA	20	0	
2015–16	WBA	34	0	111 1

Players retained or with offer of contract
Barbir, Daniel; Elbouzedi, Zachary; Gardner, Craig; Howkins, Kyle; McCourt, Robbie; McManaman, Callum Henry; Ross, Ethan Walker.

Scholars
Artymatas, Panagiotis; Bradley, Alex; Campbell, Tahvon; Dool, Sameron; Edwards, Kyle Hakeem; Field, Samuel; Fitzwater, Jack Joseph; Forss, Marcus; House, Bradley Roy; Leko, Jonathan Kisolokele; Melbourne, Max; Nabi, Rahis; O'Shea, Dara; Pierce, Evan; Piggott, Jordan Christian John; Pritchatt, Callum George; Scrivens, Chay; Smith, James; Sweeney, Bradley Stuart; Ward, Joseph; Wright, Andre .

WEST HAM U (87)

ADRIAN (G)   122 0
H: 6 2   W: 12 00   b.Seville 3-1-87

2008–09	Real Betis	0	0	
2009–10	Real Betis	0	0	
2010–11	Real Betis	0	0	
2011–12	Real Betis	0	0	
2012–13	Real Betis	32	0	32 0
2013–14	West Ham U	20	0	
2014–15	West Ham U	38	0	
2015–16	West Ham U	32	0	90 0

ANTONIO, Michael (M)   234 49
H: 6 0   W: 11 11   b.Wandsworth 28-3-90

2008–09	Reading	0	0	
2008–09	Cheltenham T	9	0	9 0
2009–10	Reading	1	0	
2009–10	Southampton	28	3	28 3
2010–11	Reading	21	1	
2011–12	Reading	1	06	
2011–12	Colchester U	15	4	15 4
2011–12	Sheffield W	14	5	
2012–13	Reading	0	0	28 1
2012–13	Sheffield W	37	8	
2013–14	Sheffield W	27	4	78 17
2014–15	Nottingham F	46	14	
2015–16	Nottingham F	4	2	50 16
2015–16	West Ham U	26	8	26 8

BROWNE, Marcus (M)   0 0
b. 18-12-97

2015–16	West Ham U	0	0

BURKE, Reece (D)   39 2
H: 6 2   W: 12 11   b.London 2-9-96
Internationals: England U18, U19, U20.

2013–14	West Ham U	0	0	
2014–15	West Ham U	5	0	
2015–16	West Ham U	0	0	5 0
2015–16	Bradford C	34	2	34 2

BYRAM, Samuel (M)   134 9
H: 5 11   W: 11 04   b.Thurrock 16-9-93

2012–13	Leeds U	44	3	
2013–14	Leeds U	25	0	
2014–15	Leeds U	39	3	
2015–16	Leeds U	22	3	130 9
2015–16	West Ham U	4	0	4 0

CARROLL, Andy (F)   215 61
H: 6 4   W: 11 00   b.Gateshead 6-1-89
Internationals: England U19, U21, Full caps.

2006–07	Newcastle U	4	0
2007–08	Newcastle U	0	0

2007–08	*Preston NE*	11	1	11 1
2008–09	Newcastle U	14	3	
2009–10	Newcastle U	39	17	
2010–11	Newcastle U	19	11	80 31
2010–11	Liverpool	7	2	
2011–12	Liverpool	35	4	
2012–13	Liverpool	2	0	44 6
2012–13	West Ham U	24	7	
2013–14	West Ham U	15	2	
2014–15	West Ham U	14	5	
2015–16	West Ham U	27	9	80 23

CHAMBERS, Leo (D)   6 0
H: 6 1   W: 13 00   b.London 5-8-95
Internationals: England U16, U17, U18, U19.

2012–13	West Ham U	0	0	
2013–14	West Ham U	0	0	
2014–15	West Ham U	0	0	
2015–16	West Ham U	0	0	
2015–16	*Colchester U*	6	0	6 0

COLLINS, James M (D)   310 11
H: 6 2   W: 14 05   b.Newport 23-8-83
Internationals: Wales U19, U20, U21, Full caps.

2000–01	Cardiff C	3	0	
2001–02	Cardiff C	7	1	
2002–03	Cardiff C	2	0	
2003–04	Cardiff C	20	1	
2004–05	Cardiff C	34	1	66 3
2005–06	West Ham U	14	2	
2006–07	West Ham U	16	0	
2007–08	West Ham U	3	0	
2008–09	West Ham U	18	0	
2009–10	West Ham U	3	0	
2009–10	Aston Villa	27	1	
2010–11	Aston Villa	32	3	
2011–12	Aston Villa	32	1	91 5
2012–13	West Ham U	29	0	
2013–14	West Ham U	24	1	
2014–15	West Ham U	27	0	
2015–16	West Ham U	19	0	153 3

CRESSWELL, Aaron (D)   277 15
H: 5 7   W: 10 05   b.Liverpool 15-12-89

2008–09	Tranmere R	13	1	
2009–10	Tranmere R	14	0	
2010–11	Tranmere R	43	4	70 5
2011–12	Ipswich T	44	1	
2012–13	Ipswich T	46	3	
2013–14	Ipswich T	42	2	132 6
2014–15	West Ham U	38	2	
2015–16	West Ham U	37	2	75 4

CULLEN, Josh (M)   16 0
H: 5 8   W: 11 00   b.Southend-on-Sea 4-7-96
Internationals: England U16. Republic of Ireland U19, U21.

2014–15	West Ham U	0	0	
2015–16	West Ham U	1	0	1 0
2015–16	*Bradford C*	15	0	15 0

DOBSON, George (M)   0 0
H: 6 1   b.Harold Wood 15-11-97
From Arsenal.

2015–16	West Ham U	0	0

EMENIKE, Emmanuel (F)   195 78
H: 6 0   W: 12 13   b.Otuocha 10-5-87
Internationals: Nigeria Full caps.

2007–08	*Mpumalanga Black Aces*	7	3	7 3
2008–09	*Cape Town*	16	1	16 1
2009–10	Karabukspor	28	16	
2010–11	Karabukspor	23	14	51 30
2011–12	Fenerbahce	0	0	
2011–12	Spartak Moscow	22	13	
2012–13	Spartak Moscow	16	5	
2013–14	Spartak Moscow	4	3	42 21
2013–14	Fenerbahce	28	12	
2014–15	Fenerbahce	27	4	
2015–16	Fenerbahce	0	0	55 16
2015–16	*Al-Ain*	11	7	11 7

On loan from Fenerbahce.

2015–16	West Ham U	13	0	13 0

HENDRIE, Stephen (D)   105 1
H: 5 10   W: 11 00   b.Glasgow 8-1-95
Internationals: Scotland U17, U19, U21.

2010–11	Hamilton A	1	0	
2011–12	Hamilton A	25	0	
2012–13	Hamilton A	23	0	
2013–14	Hamilton A	22	0	
2013–14	Hamilton A	30	0	100 0
2015–16	West Ham U	0	0	
2015–16	*Southend U*	5	1	5 1

HENRY, Doneil (D)   74 2
H: 6 2   W: 12 13   b.Brampton 20-4-93
Internationals: Canada U20, U23, Full caps.

2010	Toronto	1	0

2011	Toronto	10	0	
2012	Toronto	18	1	
2013	Toronto	20	0	49 1
2014	Toronto FC	21	1	21 1
2014–15	West Ham U	0	0	
2014–15	*Blackburn R*	3	0	
2015–16	West Ham U	0	0	
2015–16	*Blackburn R*	1	0	4 0

HOWES, Sam (G)   0 0
H: 6 3   W: 13 05   b.London 10-11-97
Internationals: England U16, U18, U19.

JELAVIC, Nikica (F)   291 93
H: 6 2   W: 13 12   b.Capljina 27-8-85
Internationals: Croatia U17, U18, Full caps.

2002–03	Hajduk Split	2	0	
2003–04	Hajduk Split	2	0	
2004–05	Hajduk Split	9	0	
2005–06	Hajduk Split	9	0	
2006–07	Hajduk Split	22	5	35 5
2007–08	Waregem	23	3	23 3
2008–09	Rapid Vienna	34	7	
2009–10	Rapid Vienna	33	17	
2010–11	Rapid Vienna	3	1	70 25
2010–11	Rangers	23	16	
2011–12	Rangers	22	14	45 30
2011–12	Everton	13	9	
2012–13	Everton	37	7	
2013–14	Everton	9	0	59 16
2013–14	Hull C	16	4	
2014–15	Hull C	26	8	
2015–16	Hull C	4	1	46 13
2015–16	West Ham U	13	1	13 1

Transferred to Beijing Renhe February 2016.

KNOYLE, Kyle (D)   9 0
b. 24-9-96
Internationals: England U18.

2015–16	West Ham U	0	0	
2015–16	*Dundee U*	9	0	9 0

KOUYATE, Cheikhou (M)   254 16
H: 6 3   W: 11 11   b.Dakar 21-12-89
Internationals: Senegal U20, Full caps.

2007–08	Brussels	10	0	
2008–09	Brussels	0	0	10 0
2008–09	Kortrijk	26	3	26 3
2009–10	Anderlecht	21	1	
2010–11	Anderlecht	23	1	
2011–12	Anderlecht	38	0	
2012–13	Anderlecht	33	1	
2013–14	Anderlecht	38	1	153 4
2014–15	West Ham U	31	4	
2015–16	West Ham U	34	5	65 9

LANZINI, Manuel (M)   162 29
H: 5 7   W: 11 00   b.Ituzaingo 15-2-93
Internationals: Argentina U20.

2010–11	River Plate	22	0	
2010–11	Fluminense	22	2	
2011–12	River Plate	0	0	
2011–12	Fluminense	6	1	28 3
2012–13	River Plate	26	8	26 8
2013–14	River Plate	36	4	58 4
2014–15	Al-Jazira	24	8	
2015–16	Al-Jazira	0	0	24 8

On loan from Al-Jazira.

2015–16	West Ham U	26	6	26 6

LEE, Elliot (F)   36 6
H: 5 11   W: 11 05   b.Co. Durham 16-12-94

2011–12	West Ham U	0	0	
2012–13	West Ham U	0	0	
2013–14	West Ham U	1	0	
2013–14	*Colchester U*	4	1	
2014–15	West Ham U	1	0	
2014–15	*Southend U*	0	0	
2014–15	*Luton T*	11	3	11 3
2015–16	West Ham U	0	0	2 0
2015–16	*Blackpool*	4	0	4 0
2015–16	*Colchester U*	15	2	19 3

MAIGA, Modibo (F)   226 55
H: 6 1   W: 12 07   b.Bamako 3-9-87
Internationals: Mali Full caps.

2007–08	Le Mans	19	0	
2008–09	Le Mans	37	8	
2009–10	Le Mans	32	7	88 15
2010–11	Sochaux	36	15	
2011–12	Sochaux	23	9	59 24
2012–13	West Ham U	17	2	
2013–14	West Ham U	14	1	
2013–14	*QPR*	8	1	8 1
2014–15	West Ham U	0	0	
2014–15	Metz	25	9	25 9
2015–16	West Ham U	3	1	34 4
2015–16	Al-Nasr	12	2	12 2

NOBLE, Mark (M) 335 39
H: 5 11　W: 12 00　b.West Ham 8-5-87
Internationals: England U16, U17, U18, U19, U21.

Season	Club	App	Gls	App	Gls
2004–05	West Ham U	13	0		
2005–06	West Ham U	5	0		
2005–06	*Hull C*	5	0	5	0
2006–07	West Ham U	10	2		
2006–07	*Ipswich T*	13	1	13	1
2007–08	West Ham U	31	3		
2008–09	West Ham U	29	3		
2009–10	West Ham U	27	2		
2010–11	West Ham U	26	4		
2011–12	West Ham U	45	8		
2012–13	West Ham U	28	4		
2013–14	West Ham U	38	3		
2014–15	West Ham U	28	2		
2015–16	West Ham U	37	7	317	38

O'BRIEN, Joey (M) 160 5
H: 5 11　W: 10 13　b.Dublin 17-2-86
Internationals: Republic of Ireland U19, U21, Full caps.

Season	Club	App	Gls	App	Gls
2004–05	Bolton W	1	0		
2004–05	*Sheffield W*	15	2		
2005–06	Bolton W	23	0		
2006–07	Bolton W	0	0		
2007–08	Bolton W	19	0		
2008–09	Bolton W	7	0		
2009–10	Bolton W	0	0		
2010–11	Bolton W	0	0	50	0
2010–11	*Sheffield W*	4	0	19	2
2011–12	West Ham U	32	1		
2012–13	West Ham U	33	2		
2013–14	West Ham U	17	0		
2014–15	West Ham U	9	0		
2015–16	West Ham U	0	0	91	3

OBIANG, Pedro (M) 156 4
H: 6 1　W: 12 13　b.Alcala de Henares 13-5-90
Internationals: Spain U17, U19, U20, U21.

Season	Club	App	Gls	App	Gls
2008–09	Sampdoria	0	0		
2009–10	Sampdoria	0	0		
2010–11	Sampdoria	4	0		
2011–12	Sampdoria	33	0		
2012–13	Sampdoria	34	1		
2013–14	Sampdoria	27	0		
2014–15	Sampdoria	34	3	132	4
2015–16	West Ham U	24	0	24	0

OGBONNA, Angelo (D) 238 1
H: 6 2　W: 13 08　b.Cassino 23-5-88
Internationals: Italy U21, Full caps.

Season	Club	App	Gls	App	Gls
2006–07	Torino	4	0		
2007–08	Torino	0	0		
2007–08	*Crotone*	22	0	22	0
2008–09	Torino	19	0		
2009–10	Torino	28	1		
2010–11	Torino	35	0		
2011–12	Torino	39	0		
2012–13	Torino	22	0	147	1
2013–14	Juventus	16	0		
2014–15	Juventus	25	0	41	0
2015–16	West Ham U	28	0	28	0

ONARIASE, Manny (D) 0 0
b. 29-1-95

Season	Club	App	Gls	App	Gls
2014–15	West Ham U	0	0		
2015–16	West Ham U	0	0		

OXFORD, Reece (D) 7 0
H: 6 3　W: 13 08　b.Edmonton 16-12-98
Internationals: England U16, U17, U18, U19.

Season	Club	App	Gls	App	Gls
2014–15	West Ham U	0	0		
2015–16	West Ham U	7	0	7	0

PAGE, Lewis (D) 6 0
b. 20-5-96

Season	Club	App	Gls	App	Gls
2014–15	West Ham U	0	0		
2015–16	West Ham U	0	0		
2015–16	*Cambridge U*	6	0	6	0

PARFITT-WILLIAMS, Djair (F) 0 0
b. 1-10-96

Season	Club	App	Gls	App	Gls
2015–16	West Ham U	0	0		

PASK, Josh (D) 5 0
b. 1-11-97

Season	Club	App	Gls	App	Gls
2015–16	West Ham U	0	0		
2015–16	*Dagenham & R*	5	0	5	0

PAYET, Dimitri (M) 335 66
H: 5 9　W: 11 00　b.Saint-Pierre 29-3-87
Internationals: France U21, Full caps.

Season	Club	App	Gls	App	Gls
2005–06	Nantes	3	1		
2006–07	Nantes	30	4	33	5
2007–08	St Etienne	31	0		
2008–09	St Etienne	30	4		
2009–10	St Etienne	35	2		
2010–11	St Etienne	33	13	129	19
2011–12	Lille	33	6		
2012–13	Lille	38	12	71	18
2013–14	Marseille	36	8		
2014–15	Marseille	36	7	72	15
2015–16	West Ham U	30	9	30	9

PIKE, Alex (D) 0 0
b. 8-2-97

Season	Club	App	Gls	App	Gls
2015–16	West Ham U	0	0		

POYET, Diego (M) 49 0
H: 6 0　W: 11 09　b. 8-4-95
Internationals: England U16, U17. Uruguay U20.

Season	Club	App	Gls	App	Gls
2011–12	Charlton Ath	0	0		
2012–13	Charlton Ath	0	0		
2013–14	Charlton Ath	20	0		
2014–15	West Ham U	3	0		
2014–15	*Huddersfield T*	2	0	2	0
2015–16	West Ham U	0	0	3	0
2015–16	*Milton Keynes D*	18	0	18	0
2015–16	*Charlton Ath*	6	0	26	0

RANDOLPH, Darren (G) 252 0
H: 6 1　W: 12 02　b.Dublin 12-5-87
Internationals: Republic of Ireland U21, B, Full caps.

Season	Club	App	Gls	App	Gls
2004–05	Charlton Ath	0	0		
2005–06	Charlton Ath	0	0		
2006–07	Charlton Ath	1	0		
2006–07	*Gillingham*	3	0	3	0
2007–08	Charlton Ath	1	0		
2007–08	*Bury*	14	0	14	0
2008–09	Charlton Ath	1	0		
2008–09	*Hereford U*	13	0	13	0
2009–10	Charlton Ath	11	0	14	0
2010–11	Motherwell	37	0		
2011–12	Motherwell	38	0		
2012–13	Motherwell	36	0	111	0
2013–14	Birmingham C	46	0		
2014–15	Birmingham C	45	0	91	0
2015–16	West Ham U	6	0	6	0

REID, Winston (D) 230 9
H: 6 3　W: 13 10　b.North Shore 3-7-88
Internationals: Denmark U19, U20, U21. New Zealand Full caps.

Season	Club	App	Gls	App	Gls
2005–06	Midtjylland	9	0		
2006–07	Midtjylland	11	0		
2007–08	Midtjylland	9	0		
2008–09	Midtjylland	25	2		
2009–10	Midtjylland	29	0	83	2
2010–11	West Ham U	7	0		
2011–12	West Ham U	28	3		
2012–13	West Ham U	36	1		
2013–14	West Ham U	22	1		
2014–15	West Ham U	30	1		
2015–16	West Ham U	24	1	147	7

SAKHO, Diafra (F) 165 59
H: 6 0　W: 12 06　b.Guediawaye 24-12-89
Internationals: Senegal Full caps.

Season	Club	App	Gls	App	Gls
2009–10	Metz	5	0		
2010–11	Metz	30	5		
2011–12	Metz	9	0		
2011–12	*Boulogne*	7	0	7	0
2012–13	Metz	33	19		
2013–14	Metz	37	20	114	44
2014–15	West Ham U	23	10		
2015–16	West Ham U	21	5	44	15

SAMUELSEN, Martin (F) 17 1
b. 17-4-97
Internationals: Norway U16, U17, U18, U21.

Season	Club	App	Gls	App	Gls
2015–16	West Ham U	0	0		
2015–16	*Peterborough U*	17	1	17	1

SONG, Alex (M) 229 8
H: 5 11　W: 12 04　b.Douala 9-9-87
Internationals: France Youth. Cameroon Youth, Full caps.

Season	Club	App	Gls	App	Gls
2005–06	Arsenal	5	0		
2006–07	Arsenal	2	0		
2006–07	*Charlton Ath*	12	0	12	0
2007–08	Arsenal	9	0		
2008–09	Arsenal	31	1		
2009–10	Arsenal	26	1		
2010–11	Arsenal	31	4		
2011–12	Arsenal	34	1	138	7
2012–13	Barcelona	20	1		
2013–14	Barcelona	19	0		
2014–15	Barcelona	0	0		
2014–15	*West Ham U*	28	0		
2015–16	Barcelona	0	0	39	1

On loan from Barcelona.

Season	Club	App	Gls	App	Gls
2015–16	West Ham U	12	0	40	0

SPIEGEL, Raphael (G) 19 0
H: 6 5　W: 15 00　b.Zurich 19-12-92
Internationals: Switzerland U17, U19, U21.

Season	Club	App	Gls	App	Gls
2011–12	Grasshoppers	0	0		
2011–12	*Bruhl*	17	0	17	0
2012–13	Grasshoppers	0	0		
2012–13	West Ham U	0	0		
2013–14	West Ham U	0	0		
2014–15	West Ham U	0	0		
2014–15	*Carlisle U*	2	0	2	0
2015–16	West Ham U	0	0		

TOMKINS, James (D) 215 8
H: 6 3　W: 11 10　b.Basildon 29-3-89
Internationals: England U16, U17, U18, U19, U20, U21. Great Britain.

Season	Club	App	Gls	App	Gls
2005–06	West Ham U	0	0		
2006–07	West Ham U	0	0		
2007–08	West Ham U	6	0		
2008–09	West Ham U	12	1		
2008–09	*Derby Co*	7	0	7	0
2009–10	West Ham U	23	0		
2010–11	West Ham U	19	1		
2011–12	West Ham U	44	4		
2012–13	West Ham U	26	1		
2013–14	West Ham U	31	0		
2014–15	West Ham U	22	1		
2015–16	West Ham U	25	0	208	8

VALENCIA, Enner (F) 204 53
H: 5 10　W: 11 05　b.San Lorenzo 11-4-89
Internationals: Ecuador Full caps.

Season	Club	App	Gls	App	Gls
2010	Emelec	25	1		
2011	Emelec	30	9		
2012	Emelec	40	13		
2013	Emelec	35	4	130	27
2013–14	Pachuca	23	18	23	18
2014–15	West Ham U	32	4		
2015–16	West Ham U	19	4	51	8

WESTLEY, Sam (D) 1 0
b. 4-2-94

Season	Club	App	Gls	App	Gls
2015–16	West Ham U	0	0		
2015–16	*VVV*	1	0	1	0

ZARATE, Mauro (F) 297 80
H: 5 8　W: 10 10　b.Haedo 18-3-87
Internationals: Argentina U21.

Season	Club	App	Gls	App	Gls
2003–04	Velez Sarsfield	4	1		
2004–05	Velez Sarsfield	14	2		
2005–06	Velez Sarsfield	33	3		
2006–07	Velez Sarsfield	32	16		
2007–08	*Al-Sadd*	6	0	6	0
2007–08	*Birmingham C*	14	4	14	4
2008–09	Al-Saad	0	0		
2008–09	Lazio	36	13		
2009–10	Lazio	32	3		
2010–11	Lazio	35	9		
2011–12	Lazio	0	0		
2011–12	*Inter Milan*	22	2	22	2
2012–13	Lazio	1	0	104	25
2013–14	Velez Sarsfield	29	19	112	41
2014–15	West Ham U	7	2		
2014–15	*QPR*	4	0	4	0
2015–16	West Ham U	15	3	22	5
2015–16	Fiorentina	13	3	13	3

Players retained or with offer of contract
Belic, Luka; Diangana, Grady; Ford, Samuel George; Gordon, Jaanai Derece; Makasi, Kusu Moses.

Scholars
Akinola, Olatunji Oluwasehun; Carter, Matthew James; Hector-Ingram, Jahmal Justin; Kemp, Daniel; Matrevics, Rihards; Neufville, Vashon; Powell, Joe; Rice, Declan; Scully, Anthony Richard; Sylvestre, Noha; Trott, Nathan Wallace Newman.

WIGAN ATH (88)

ANSON, Adam (D) 0 0
b. 4-2-97

Season	Club	App	Gls	App	Gls
2015–16	Wigan Ath	0	0		

BARNETT, Leon (D) 263 13
H: 6 0　W: 12 04　b.Stevenage 30-11-85

Season	Club	App	Gls	App	Gls
2003–04	Luton T	0	0		
2004–05	Luton T	0	0		
2005–06	Luton T	20	0		
2006–07	Luton T	39	3	59	3
2007–08	WBA	32	3		
2008–09	WBA	11	0		
2009–10	WBA	2	0		
2009–10	*Coventry C*	20	0	20	0
2010–11	WBA	0	0	45	3
2010–11	*Norwich C*	25	1		
2011–12	Norwich C	17	1		

Season	Club				
2012–13	Norwich C	8	0		
2012–13	*Cardiff C*	8	0	8	0
2013–14	Norwich C	0	0	50	2
2013–14	Wigan Ath	41	4		
2014–15	Wigan Ath	20	0		
2015–16	Wigan Ath	20	1	81	5

BURKE, Luke (D)   0 0
b. 22-2-98

2015–16	Wigan Ath	0	0		

CHOW, Tim (M)   15 1
H: 5 11 W: 11 06 b.Wigan 18-1-94

2011–12	Wigan Ath	0	0		
2012–13	Wigan Ath	0	0		
2013–14	Wigan Ath	0	0		
2014–15	Wigan Ath	4	1		
2015–16	Wigan Ath	11	0	15	1

COLCLOUGH, Ryan (F)   70 14
H: 6 3 W: 13 01 b.Budapest 27-12-94

2012–13	Crewe Alex	18	1		
2013–14	Crewe Alex	8	2		
2014–15	Crewe Alex	7	2		
2015–16	Crewe Alex	27	7	60	12
2015–16	Wigan Ath	10	2	10	2

COSGROVE, Sam (F)
b.Beverley 2-12-96

2014–15	Wigan Ath	0	0		
2015–16	Wigan Ath	0	0		

COWIE, Don (M)   446 44
H: 5 5 W: 8 05 b.Inverness 15-2-83
Internationals: Scotland Full caps.

2000–01	Ross Co	1	0		
2001–02	Ross Co	18	0		
2002–03	Ross Co	30	1		
2003–04	Ross Co	23	0		
2004–05	Ross Co	34	5		
2005–06	Ross Co	32	4		
2006–07	Ross Co	28	7	166	17
2007–08	Inverness CT	37	9		
2008–09	Inverness CT	22	3	59	12
2008–09	Watford	10	3		
2009–10	Watford	41	2		
2010–11	Watford	37	4	88	9
2011–12	Cardiff C	43	4		
2012–13	Cardiff C	25	2		
2013–14	Cardiff C	18	0	86	6
2014–15	Wigan Ath	32	0		
2015–16	Wigan Ath	5	0	37	0
2015–16	Hearts	10	0	10	0

DANIELS, Donervorn (D)   86 6
H: 6 1 W: 14 05 b.Montserrat 24-11-93
Internationals: England U20.

2011–12	WBA	0	0		
2012–13	WBA	0	0		
2012–13	*Tranmere R*	13	1	13	1
2013–14	WBA	0	0		
2013–14	*Gillingham*	3	1	3	1
2014–15	WBA	0	0		
2014–15	*Blackpool*	19	1	19	1
2014–15	*Aberdeen*	9	0	9	0
2015–16	Wigan Ath	42	3	42	3

DAVIES, Craig (F)   368 90
H: 6 2 W: 13 05 b.Burton-on-Trent 9-1-86
Internationals: Wales U17, U19, U21, Full caps.

2004–05	Oxford U	28	6		
2005–06	Oxford U	20	2	48	8
2005–06	Verona	0	0		
2006–07	Wolverhampton W	23	0	23	0
2007–08	Oldham Ath	32	10		
2008–09	Oldham Ath	12	0	44	10
2008–09	*Stockport Co*	9	5	9	5
2008–09	Brighton & HA	16	1		
2009–10	Brighton & HA	5	0	21	1
2009–10	*Yeovil T*	4	0	4	0
2009–10	Port Vale	24	7	24	7
2010–11	Chesterfield	41	23	41	23
2011–12	Barnsley	40	11		
2012–13	Barnsley	20	8	60	19
2012–13	Bolton W	18	4		
2013–14	Bolton W	8	0		
2013–14	*Preston NE*	15	5	15	5
2014–15	Bolton W	27	6	53	10
2015–16	Wigan Ath	26	2	26	2

FLORES, Jordan (F)   4 1
b.Wigan 4-10-95

2014–15	Wigan Ath	1	0		
2015–16	Wigan Ath	3	1	4	1

GRIGG, Will (M)   217 77
H: 5 11 W: 11 00 b.Solihull 3-7-91
Internationals: Northern Ireland U19, U21, Full caps.

2008–09	Walsall	1	0		
2009–10	Walsall	0	0		
2010–11	Walsall	28	4		
2011–12	Walsall	29	4		
2012–13	Walsall	41	19	99	27
2013–14	Brentford	34	5		
2014–15	Brentford	0	0	34	5
2014–15	*Milton Keynes D*	44	20	44	20
2015–16	Wigan Ath	40	25	40	25

HENDRY, Jack (D)   10 0
b. 7-5-95

2014–15	Partick Thistle	1	0		
2015–16	Partick Thistle	3	0	4	0
2015–16	Wigan Ath	0	0		
2015–16	*Shrewsbury T*	6	0	6	0

HUWS, Emyr (M)   73 7
H: 5 10 W: 11 07 b.Llanelli 30-9-93
Internationals: Wales U17, U19, U21, Full caps.

2010–11	Manchester C	0	0		
2011–12	Manchester C	0	0		
2012–13	Manchester C	0	0		
2012–13	*Northampton T*	10	0	10	0
2013–14	Manchester C	0	0		
2013–14	*Birmingham C*	17	2	17	2
2014–15	Wigan Ath	16	0		
2015–16	Wigan Ath	0	0	16	0
2015–16	*Huddersfield T*	30	5	30	5

JAASKELAINEN, Jussi (G)   684 0
H: 6 3 W: 12 10 b.Vaasa 19-4-75
Internationals: Finland U21, Full caps.

1992	MP	6	0		
1993	MP	6	0		
1994	MP	26	0		
1995	MP	26	0	64	0
1996	VPS	27	0		
1997	VPS	27	0	54	0
1997–98	Bolton W	0	0		
1998–99	Bolton W	34	0		
1999–2000	Bolton W	34	0		
2000–01	Bolton W	27	0		
2001–02	Bolton W	34	0		
2002–03	Bolton W	38	0		
2003–04	Bolton W	38	0		
2004–05	Bolton W	36	0		
2005–06	Bolton W	38	0		
2006–07	Bolton W	38	0		
2007–08	Bolton W	28	0		
2008–09	Bolton W	38	0		
2009–10	Bolton W	38	0		
2010–11	Bolton W	35	0		
2011–12	Bolton W	18	0	474	0
2012–13	West Ham U	38	0		
2013–14	West Ham U	18	0		
2014–15	West Ham U	1	0	57	0
2015–16	Wigan Ath	35	0	35	0

JACOBS, Michael (M)   210 32
H: 5 9 W: 11 08 b.Rothwell 23-3-92

2009–10	Northampton T	0	0		
2010–11	Northampton T	41	5		
2011–12	Northampton T	46	6	87	11
2012–13	Derby Co	38	2		
2013–14	Derby Co	3	0	41	2
2013–14	Wolverhampton W	30	8		
2014–15	Wolverhampton W	12	0	42	8
2014–15	*Blackpool*	5	1	5	1
2015–16	Wigan Ath	35	10	35	10

JAMES, Reece (D)   40 2
H: 5 6 b.Bacup 7-11-93

2012–13	Manchester U	0	0		
2013–14	Manchester U	0	0		
2013–14	*Carlisle U*	1	0	1	0
2014–15	Manchester U	0	0		
2014–15	*Rotherham U*	7	0	7	0
2014–15	*Huddersfield T*	6	1	6	1
2015–16	Wigan Ath	26	1	26	1

JENNINGS, Ryan (F)   0 0
b.Manchester 8-7-95

2013–14	Wigan Ath	0	0		
2014–15	Wigan Ath	0	0		
2014–15	*Accrington S*	0	0		
2015–16	Wigan Ath	0	0		

KELLETT, Andy (D)   25 3
H: 5 8 b.Bolton 10-11-93

2012–13	Bolton W	0	0		
2013–14	Bolton W	3	0		
2014–15	Bolton W	1	0		
2014–15	*Plymouth Arg*	12	1	12	1
2014–15	*Manchester U*	0	0		
2015–16	Bolton W	0	0	4	0
2015–16	Wigan Ath	9	2	9	2

LANGFORD, Liam (D)   0 0
b. 10-12-96

2015–16	Wigan Ath	0	0		

LAVERCOMBE, Dan (G)   0 0
H: 6 3 W: 11 03 b.Torquay 16-5-96

2013–14	Torquay U	0	0		
2015–16	Wigan Ath	0	0		

McCANN, Chris (M)   320 35
H: 6 1 W: 11 11 b.Dublin 21-7-87
Internationals: Republic of Ireland U19.

2005–06	Burnley	23	2		
2006–07	Burnley	38	5		
2007–08	Burnley	35	5		
2008–09	Burnley	44	6		
2009–10	Burnley	7	0		
2010–11	Burnley	4	1		
2011–12	Burnley	46	4		
2012–13	Burnley	41	4	238	27
2013–14	Wigan Ath	27	2		
2014–15	Wigan Ath	17	2		
2015–16	Wigan Ath	38	4	82	8

McKAY, Billy (F)   234 79
H: 5 7 W: 10 10 b.Corby 22-10-88
Internationals: Northern Ireland U18, U20, U21, Full caps.

2007–08	Leicester C	0	0		
2008–09	Leicester C	0	0		
2009–10	Northampton T	40	8		
2010–11	Northampton T	34	5	74	13
2011–12	Inverness CT	22	3		
2012–13	Inverness CT	38	23		
2013–14	Inverness CT	38	18		
2014–15	Inverness CT	23	10	121	54
2014–15	Wigan Ath	9	0		
2015–16	Wigan Ath	1	0	10	0
2015–16	*Dundee U*	29	12	29	12

McNALLY, Reece (D)   0 0
b. 3-1-97

2015–16	Wigan Ath	0	0		

McNAUGHTON, Kevin (D)   454 5
H: 5 10 W: 10 06 b.Dundee 28-8-82
Internationals: Scotland B, Full caps.

1999–2000	Aberdeen	0	0		
2000–01	Aberdeen	33	0		
2001–02	Aberdeen	34	0		
2002–03	Aberdeen	22	1		
2003–04	Aberdeen	17	0		
2004–05	Aberdeen	35	2		
2005–06	Aberdeen	34	0	175	3
2006–07	Cardiff C	42	0		
2007–08	Cardiff C	35	1		
2008–09	Cardiff C	39	0		
2009–10	Cardiff C	21	0		
2010–11	Cardiff C	44	0		
2011–12	Cardiff C	42	0		
2012–13	Cardiff C	27	0		
2013–14	Cardiff C	5	0		
2013–14	*Bolton W*	13	1		
2014–15	Cardiff C	0	0	255	1
2014–15	Bolton W	9	0	22	1
2015–16	Wigan Ath	2	0	2	0

MORGAN, Craig (D)   398 11
H: 6 0 W: 11 04 b.Flint 18-6-85
Internationals: Wales U17, U19, U21, Full caps.

2001–02	Wrexham	2	0		
2002–03	Wrexham	6	1		
2003–04	Wrexham	18	0		
2004–05	Wrexham	26	0		
2005–06	Milton Keynes D	40	0		
2006–07	Milton Keynes D	3	0	43	0
2006–07	*Wrexham*	1	0	53	1
2006–07	Peterborough U	23	1		
2007–08	Peterborough U	41	2		
2008–09	Peterborough U	27	0		
2009–10	Peterborough U	34	1	125	4
2010–11	Preston NE	31	2		
2011–12	Preston NE	19	1		
2012–13	Preston NE	0	0	50	3
2012–13	Rotherham U	21	1		
2013–14	Rotherham U	35	0		
2014–15	Rotherham U	35	0	91	1
2015–16	Wigan Ath	36	2	36	2

MORSY, Sam (M)   186 12
H: 5 9 W: 12 06 b.Wolverhampton 10-9-91

2009–10	Port Vale	1	0		
2010–11	Port Vale	16	1		
2011–12	Port Vale	26	1		
2012–13	Port Vale	28	2	71	4
2013–14	Chesterfield	34	1		
2014–15	Chesterfield	39	2		
2015–16	Chesterfield	26	4	99	7
2015–16	Wigan Ath	16	1	16	1

NICHOLLS, Lee (G) **79 0**
H: 6 3 W: 13 05 b.Huyton 5-10-92
Internationals: England U19.

2009–10	Wigan Ath	0	0		
2010–11	Wigan Ath	0	0		
2010–11	*Hartlepool U*	0	0		
2010–11	*Shrewsbury T*	0	0		
2010–11	*Sheffield W*	0	0		
2011–12	Wigan Ath	0	0		
2011–12	*Accrington S*	9	0	**9**	**0**
2012–13	Wigan Ath	0	0		
2012–13	*Northampton T*	46	0	**46**	**0**
2013–14	Wigan Ath	6	0		
2014–15	Wigan Ath	1	0		
2015–16	Wigan Ath	2	0	**9**	**0**
2015–16	*Bristol R*	15	0	**15**	**0**

ODELUSI, Sanmi (F) **33 3**
H: 6 0 W: 11 11 b.London 11-6-93

2012–13	Bolton W	1	0		
2013–14	Bolton W	5	0		
2013–14	*Milton Keynes D*	10	0	**10**	**0**
2014–15	Bolton W	0	0	**6**	**0**
2014–15	*Coventry C*	14	3	**14**	**3**
2015–16	Wigan Ath	3	0	**3**	**0**

PEARCE, Jason (D) **351 15**
H: 5 11 W: 12 00 b.Hillingdon 6-12-87

2006–07	Portsmouth	0	0		
2007–08	Bournemouth	33	1		
2008–09	Bournemouth	44	2		
2009–10	Bournemouth	39	1		
2010–11	Bournemouth	46	3	**162**	**7**
2011–12	Portsmouth	43	2	**43**	**2**
2011–12	Leeds U	0	0		
2012–13	Leeds U	33	0		
2013–14	Leeds U	45	2		
2014–15	Leeds U	21	0	**99**	**2**
2014–15	Wigan Ath	16	2		
2015–16	Wigan Ath	31	2	**47**	**4**

PERKINS, David (D) **373 14**
H: 5 6 W: 11 06 b.Heysham 21-6-82
Internationals: England C.

2006–07	Rochdale	18	0		
2007–08	Rochdale	40	4	**58**	**4**
2008–09	Colchester U	38	5		
2009–10	Colchester U	5	1		
2009–10	*Chesterfield*	13	1	**13**	**1**
2009–10	*Stockport Co*	22	0	**22**	**0**
2010–11	Colchester U	36	1	**79**	**7**
2011–12	Barnsley	33	1		
2012–13	Barnsley	35	1		
2013–14	Barnsley	23	0	**91**	**2**
2013–14	Blackpool	20	0		
2014–15	Blackpool	45	0	**65**	**0**
2015–16	Wigan Ath	45	0	**45**	**0**

POWER, Max (M) **153 18**
H: 5 11 W: 11 13 b.Bebington 27-7-93

2010–11	Tranmere R	0	0		
2011–12	Tranmere R	4	0		
2012–13	Tranmere R	27	3		
2013–14	Tranmere R	33	2		
2014–15	Tranmere R	45	7	**109**	**12**
2015–16	Wigan Ath	44	6	**44**	**6**

PURZYCKI, Adrian (M) **0 0**
b. 2-8-97
Internationals: Poland U18, U19.

2015–16	Wigan Ath	0	0		

WABARA, Reece (D) **127 3**
H: 6 0 W: 12 06 b.Birmingham 28-12-91
Internationals: England U19, U20.

2008–09	Manchester C	0	0		
2009–10	Manchester C	0	0		
2010–11	Manchester C	1	0		
2011–12	Manchester C	0	0		
2011–12	*Ipswich T*	6	0	**6**	**0**
2012–13	Manchester C	0	0		
2012–13	*Oldham Ath*	25	0	**25**	**0**
2012–13	*Blackpool*	1	0	**1**	**0**
2013–14	Manchester C	0	0	**1**	**0**
2013–14	*Doncaster R*	13	0		
2014–15	Doncaster R	43	1	**56**	**1**
2015–16	Barnsley	19	1	**19**	**1**
2015–16	Wigan Ath	19	1	**19**	**1**

WHITEHEAD, Danny (M) **2 0**
H: 5 10 W: 10 11 b.Trafford 23-10-93

2013–14	West Ham U	0	0		
2014–15	West Ham U	0	0		
2014–15	Accrington S	2	0	**2**	**0**

From Macclesfield T.

2015–16	Wigan Ath	0	0		

WILDSCHUT, Yanic (F) **169 22**
H: 6 2 W: 13 08 b. 1-11-91
Internationals: Netherlands U21.

2010–11	Zwolle	33	3	**33**	**3**
2011–12	VVV	29	7		
2012–13	VVV	32	1	**61**	**8**
2013–14	Heerenveen	18	2		
2013–14	*Den Haag*	7	0	**7**	**0**
2014–15	Heerenveen	4	0	**22**	**2**
2014–15	Middlesbrough	11	2		
2015–16	Middlesbrough	1	0	**12**	**2**
2015–16	Wigan Ath	34	7	**34**	**7**

Players retained or with offer of contract
Evans, Owen Rhys; O'Brien, Daniel William; Taylor, Andrew Derek.

Scholars
Absalom, Kelland Ellis; Barrigan, James Patrick; Baxendale, Arnold Spencer; Beaumont, Joshua Jack; Burke, Luke; Carroll-Burgess, Luke Eugene; Fitton, Remell Scott; Forecast, Charlie Joe; Gregory, Joshua James; Lang, Callum Joseph; Lingard, Alex Matthew; Merrie, Christopher Francis; Powell, Thomas david; Randell, Nathan; Rimmer, Matthew Luke; Sang, Christopher Neil; Stubbs, Sam Alan; Taylor, Matthew William; White, Jack Kincaid.

WOLVERHAMPTON W (89)

BATTH, Danny (D) **212 12**
H: 6 3 W: 13 05 b.Brierley Hill 21-9-90

2009–10	Wolverhampton W	0	0		
2009–10	*Colchester U*	17	1	**17**	**1**
2010–11	Wolverhampton W	0	0		
2010–11	*Sheffield U*	1	0	**1**	**0**
2010–11	*Sheffield W*	10	0		
2011–12	Wolverhampton W	0	0		
2011–12	*Sheffield W*	44	2	**54**	**2**
2012–13	Wolverhampton W	12	1		
2013–14	Wolverhampton W	46	2		
2014–15	Wolverhampton W	44	4		
2015–16	Wolverhampton W	38	2	**140**	**9**

BRESLIN, Anthony (D) **0 0**
b. 13-2-97
Internationals: Republic of Ireland U19, U21.

2015–16	Wolverhampton W	0	0		

BURGOYNE, Harry (G) **0 0**
b. 28-12-96

2015–16	Wolverhampton W	0	0		

BYRNE, Nathan (D) **146 13**
H: 5 10 W: 10 10 b.St Albans 5-6-92

2010–11	Tottenham H	0	0		
2010–11	*Brentford*	11	0	**11**	**0**
2011–12	Tottenham H	0	0		
2011–12	*Bournemouth*	9	0	**9**	**0**
2012–13	Tottenham H	0	0		
2012–13	*Crawley T*	12	1	**12**	**1**
2012–13	*Swindon T*	7	0		
2013–14	Swindon T	36	4		
2014–15	Swindon T	42	3		
2015–16	Swindon T	5	3	**90**	**10**
2015–16	Wolverhampton W	24	2	**24**	**2**

COADY, Conor (D) **122 8**
H: 6 1 W: 11 05 b.Liverpool 25-2-93
Internationals: England U16, U17, U18, U19, U20.

2010–11	Liverpool	0	0		
2011–12	Liverpool	0	0		
2012–13	Liverpool	1	0		
2013–14	Liverpool	0	0	**1**	**0**
2013–14	*Sheffield U*	39	5	**39**	**5**
2014–15	Huddersfield T	45	3	**45**	**3**
2015–16	Wolverhampton W	37	0	**37**	**0**

COLLINS, Aaron (F) **20 2**
b. 27-5-97
Internationals: Wales U19.

2014–15	Newport Co	2	0		
2015–16	Newport Co	18	2	**20**	**2**
2015–16	Wolverhampton W	0	0		

DESLANDES, Sylvain (D) **3 0**
b. 25-4-97
Internationals: France U16, U17, U18.

2014–15	Caen	0	0		
2015–16	Wolverhampton W	3	0	**3**	**0**

DICKO, Nouha (M) **147 53**
H: 5 8 W: 11 00 b.Paris 14-5-92
Internationals: Mali Full caps.

2009–10	Strasbourg B	18	4		
2010–11	Strasbourg B	24	8	**42**	**12**
2010–11	Strasbourg	3	0	**3**	**0**
2011–12	Wigan Ath	0	0		
2011–12	*Blackpool*	10	4		
2012–13	Wigan Ath	0	0		
2012–13	*Blackpool*	22	5	**32**	**9**
2012–13	*Wolverhampton W*	4	1		
2013–14	Wigan Ath	0	0		
2013–14	*Rotherham U*	5	5	**5**	**5**
2013–14	Wolverhampton W	19	12		
2014–15	Wolverhampton W	37	14		
2015–16	Wolverhampton W	5	0	**65**	**27**

DOHERTY, Matthew (M) **129 7**
H: 6 0 W: 12 08 b.Dublin 17-1-92
Internationals: Republic of Ireland U19, U21.

2010–11	Wolverhampton W	0	0		
2011–12	Wolverhampton W	1	0		
2011–12	*Hibernian*	13	2	**13**	**2**
2012–13	Wolverhampton W	13	1		
2012–13	*Bury*	17	1	**17**	**1**
2013–14	Wolverhampton W	18	1		
2014–15	Wolverhampton W	33	0		
2015–16	Wolverhampton W	34	2	**99**	**4**

EBANKS-LANDELL, Ethan (M) **66 5**
H: 5 6 W: 11 02 b.Oldbury 16-12-92

2009–10	Wolverhampton W	0	0		
2010–11	Wolverhampton W	0	0		
2011–12	Wolverhampton W	0	0		
2012–13	Wolverhampton W	0	0		
2012–13	*Bury*	24	0	**24**	**0**
2013–14	Wolverhampton W	7	2		
2014–15	Wolverhampton W	14	2		
2015–16	Wolverhampton W	21	1	**42**	**5**

EDWARDS, Dave (M) **361 47**
H: 5 11 W: 11 04 b.Shrewsbury 3-2-86
Internationals: Wales U21, Full caps.

2002–03	Shrewsbury T	1	0		
2003–04	Shrewsbury T	0	0		
2004–05	Shrewsbury T	27	5		
2005–06	Shrewsbury T	30	2		
2006–07	Shrewsbury T	45	5	**103**	**12**
2007–08	Luton T	19	4	**19**	**4**
2007–08	Wolverhampton W	10	1		
2008–09	Wolverhampton W	44	3		
2009–10	Wolverhampton W	20	1		
2010–11	Wolverhampton W	15	1		
2011–12	Wolverhampton W	26	3		
2012–13	Wolverhampton W	24	2		
2013–14	Wolverhampton W	30	9		
2014–15	Wolverhampton W	41	6		
2015–16	Wolverhampton W	29	5	**239**	**31**

ENOBAKHARE, Bright (F) **7 0**
b. 8-2-98

2015–16	Wolverhampton W	7	0	**7**	**0**

EVANS, Lee (M) **79 7**
H: 6 1 W: 13 12 b.Newport 24-7-94
Internationals: Wales U21.

2012–13	Wolverhampton W	0	0		
2013–14	Wolverhampton W	26	2		
2014–15	Wolverhampton W	18	1		
2015–16	Wolverhampton W	0	0	**44**	**3**
2015–16	*Bradford C*	35	4	**35**	**4**

FLATT, Jonathan (G) **0 0**
H: 6 1 W: 13 12 b.Wolverhampton 12-9-94

2013–14	Wolverhampton W	0	0		
2014–15	Wolverhampton W	0	0		
2014–15	*Chesterfield*	0	0		
2015–16	Wolverhampton W	0	0		
2015–16	*Cheltenham T*	0	0		

GRAHAM, Jordan (M) **19 1**
H: 6 0 W: 10 10 b.Coventry 5-3-95
Internationals: England U16, U17.

2011–12	Aston Villa	0	0		
2012–13	Aston Villa	0	0		
2013–14	Aston Villa	0	0		
2013–14	*Ipswich T*	2	0	**2**	**0**
2013–14	*Bradford C*	1	0	**1**	**0**
2014–15	Wolverhampton W	0	0		
2015–16	Wolverhampton W	11	1	**11**	**1**
2015–16	*Oxford U*	5	0	**5**	**0**

HAUSE, Kortney (D) **79 3**
H: 6 2 W: 13 03 b.Goodmayes 16-7-95
Internationals: England U20, U21.

2012–13	Wycombe W	9	1		
2013–14	Wycombe W	14	1	**23**	**2**
2013–14	Wolverhampton W	0	0		
2014–15	Wolverhampton W	17	0		
2014–15	*Gillingham*	14	1	**14**	**1**
2015–16	Wolverhampton W	25	0	**42**	**0**

HAYDEN, Aaron (D) **5 0**
b. 16-1-97

2015–16	Wolverhampton W	0	0		
2015–16	*Newport Co*	5	0	**5**	**0**

HENRY, James (M)   279 44
H: 6 1 W: 11 11 b.Reading 10-6-89
Internationals: Scotland U16, U19. England U18, U19.

Season	Club				
2006-07	Reading	0	0		
2006-07	Nottingham F	1	0	1	0
2007-08	Reading	0	0		
2007-08	Bournemouth	11	4	11	4
2007-08	Norwich C	3	0	3	0
2008-09	Reading	7	0		
2008-09	Millwall	16	3		
2009-10	Reading	3	0	10	0
2009-10	Millwall	9	5		
2010-11	Millwall	42	5		
2011-12	Millwall	39	0		
2012-13	Millwall	35	5		
2013-14	Millwall	5	0	146	18
2013-14	Wolverhampton W	32	10		
2014-15	Wolverhampton W	37	5		
2015-16	Wolverhampton W	39	7	108	22

HUNTE, Connor (M)   2 0
b. 12-9-96
Internationals: England U16, U17.

Season	Club				
2014-15	Wolverhampton W	0	0		
2015-16	Wolverhampton W	2	0	2	0

IKEME, Carl (G)   222 0
H: 6 2 W: 13 09 b.Sutton Coldfield 8-6-86

Season	Club				
2005-06	Wolverhampton W	0	0		
2005-06	Stockport Co	9	0	9	0
2006-07	Wolverhampton W	1	0		
2007-08	Wolverhampton W	0	0		
2008-09	Wolverhampton W	12	0		
2009-10	Wolverhampton W	0	0		
2009-10	Charlton Ath	4	0	4	0
2009-10	Sheffield U	2	0	2	0
2009-10	QPR	17	0	17	0
2010-11	Wolverhampton W	0	0		
2010-11	Leicester C	5	0	5	0
2011-12	Wolverhampton W	1	0		
2011-12	Middlesbrough	10	0	10	0
2011-12	Doncaster R	15	0	15	0
2012-13	Wolverhampton W	38	0		
2013-14	Wolverhampton W	41	0		
2014-15	Wolverhampton W	33	0		
2015-16	Wolverhampton W	34	0	160	0

IORFA, Dominic (D)   69 0
H: 6 2 W: 12 04 b.Southend-on-Sea 24-6-95
Internationals: England U18, U20, U21.

Season	Club				
2013-14	Wolverhampton W	0	0		
2013-14	Shrewsbury T	7	0	7	0
2014-15	Wolverhampton W	20	0		
2015-16	Wolverhampton W	42	0	62	0

ISMAIL, Zeli (M)   64 8
H: 5 8 W: 11 12 b.Kukes 12-12-93
Internationals: England U16, U17.

Season	Club				
2010-11	Wolverhampton W	0	0		
2011-12	Wolverhampton W	0	0		
2012-13	Wolverhampton W	0	0		
2012-13	Milton Keynes D	7	0	7	0
2013-14	Wolverhampton W	9	0		
2013-14	Burton Alb	15	3		
2014-15	Wolverhampton W	0	0		
2014-15	Notts Co	14	4	14	4
2015-16	Wolverhampton W	0	0	9	0
2015-16	Burton Alb	3	0	18	3
2015-16	Oxford U	5	0	5	0
2015-16	Cambridge U	11	1	11	1

LE FONDRE, Adam (F)   424 160
H: 5 9 W: 11 04 b.Stockport 2-12-86

Season	Club				
2004-05	Stockport Co	20	4		
2005-06	Stockport Co	22	6		
2006-07	Stockport Co	21	7	63	17
2006-07	Rochdale	7	4		
2007-08	Rochdale	46	16		
2008-09	Rochdale	44	18		
2009-10	Rochdale	1	0	98	38
2009-10	Rotherham U	44	25		
2010-11	Rotherham U	45	23		
2011-12	Rotherham U	4	4	93	52
2011-12	Reading	32	12		
2012-13	Reading	34	12		
2013-14	Reading	38	15	104	39
2014-15	Cardiff C	23	3	23	3
2014-15	Bolton W	17	8	17	8
2015-16	Wolverhampton W	26	3	26	3

LEACOCK-McLEOD, Mekhi (M)   0 0
b. 15-9-96

Season	Club		
2015-16	Wolverhampton W	0	0

MASON, Joe (F)   194 45
H: 5 9 W: 11 11 b.Plymouth 13-5-91
Internationals: Republic of Ireland U19, U21.

Season	Club				
2009-10	Plymouth Arg	19	3		
2010-11	Plymouth Arg	34	7	53	10
2011-12	Cardiff C	39	9		
2012-13	Cardiff C	28	6		
2013-14	Cardiff C	0	0		
2013-14	Bolton W	16	6		
2014-15	Cardiff C	7	1		
2014-15	Bolton W	12	4	28	10
2015-16	Cardiff C	23	6	97	22
2015-16	Wolverhampton W	16	3	16	3

McALINDEN, Liam (F)   56 9
H: 6 1 W: 11 10 b.Cannock 26-9-93
Internationals: Northern Ireland U21. Republic of Ireland U21.

Season	Club				
2010-11	Wolverhampton W	0	0		
2011-12	Wolverhampton W	0	0		
2012-13	Wolverhampton W	1	0		
2013-14	Wolverhampton W	7	1		
2013-14	Shrewsbury T	9	3		
2014-15	Wolverhampton W	6	0		
2014-15	Fleetwood T	19	4	19	4
2015-16	Wolverhampton W	0	0	14	1
2015-16	Shrewsbury T	8	0	17	3
2015-16	Crawley T	6	1	6	1

McCAREY, Aaron (G)   31 0
H: 6 1 W: 11 09 b.Monaghan 14-1-92
Internationals: Republic of Ireland U17, U18, U19, U21.

Season	Club				
2009-10	Wolverhampton W	0	0		
2010-11	Wolverhampton W	0	0		
2011-12	Wolverhampton W	0	0		
2012-13	Wolverhampton W	0	0		
2012-13	Walsall	14	0	14	0
2013-14	Wolverhampton W	5	0		
2013-14	York C	5	0	5	0
2014-15	Wolverhampton W	0	0		
2015-16	Wolverhampton W	0	0	5	0
2015-16	Portsmouth	6	0	6	0
2015-16	Bury	1	0	1	0

McDONALD, Kevin (M)   355 30
H: 6 2 W: 13 03 b.Carnoustie 4-11-88
Internationals: Scotland U19, U21.

Season	Club				
2005-06	Dundee	26	3		
2006-07	Dundee	31	2		
2007-08	Dundee	34	9	91	14
2008-09	Burnley	25	1		
2009-10	Burnley	26	1		
2010-11	Burnley	0	0	51	2
2010-11	Scunthorpe U	5	1	5	1
2010-11	Notts Co	11	0	11	0
2011-12	Sheffield U	31	3		
2012-13	Sheffield U	45	1		
2013-14	Sheffield U	1	1	77	5
2013-14	Wolverhampton W	41	5		
2014-15	Wolverhampton W	46	0		
2015-16	Wolverhampton W	33	3	120	8

ODOFIN, Hakeem (D)   1 0
b. 13-4-98

Season	Club				
2015-16	Barnet	1	0	1	0
2015-16	Wolverhampton W	0	0		

PRICE, Jack (M)   84 2
H: 6 3 W: 13 10 b.Shrewsbury 19-12-92

Season	Club				
2011-12	Wolverhampton W	0	0		
2012-13	Wolverhampton W	0	0		
2013-14	Wolverhampton W	26	0		
2014-15	Wolverhampton W	23	1		
2014-15	Yeovil T	5	0	6	0
2014-15	Leyton Orient	5	0	5	0
2015-16	Wolverhampton W	24	1	73	2

RAINEY, Ryan (M)
b. 11-10-96
Internationals: Republic of Ireland U16.

Season	Club		
2015-16	Wolverhampton W	0	0

RANDALL, Will (M)   9 0
H: 5 11 W: 10 03 b.Swindon 2-5-97

Season	Club				
2013-14	Swindon T	1	0		
2014-15	Swindon T	4	0		
2015-16	Swindon T	4	0	9	0
2015-16	Wolverhampton W	0	0		

REID, Bradley (F)   0 0
b. 15-10-95
Internationals: Wales U19, U21.

Season	Club		
2013-14	Wolverhampton W	0	0
2014-15	Wolverhampton W	0	0
2015-16	Wolverhampton W	0	0

RONAN, Connor (M)   0 0
b. 6-3-98
Internationals: England U17. Republic of Ireland U17, U19.

Season	Club		
2015-16	Wolverhampton W	0	0

ROWE, Tommy (M)   288 40
H: 5 11 W: 12 11 b.Manchester 1-5-89

Season	Club				
2006-07	Stockport Co	4	0		
2007-08	Stockport Co	24	6		
2008-09	Stockport Co	44	7	72	13
2008-09	Peterborough U	32	2		
2009-10	Peterborough U	12	0		
2010-11	Peterborough U	35	5		
2011-12	Peterborough U	43	4		
2012-13	Peterborough U	31	5		
2013-14	Peterborough U	34	7	175	23
2014-15	Wolverhampton W	14	0		
2015-16	Wolverhampton W	3	0	17	0
2015-16	Scunthorpe U	14	1	14	1
2015-16	Doncaster R	10	3	10	3

SAVILLE, George (M)   88 9
H: 5 9 W: 11 07 b.Camberley 1-6-93

Season	Club				
2010-11	Chelsea	0	0		
2011-12	Chelsea	0	0		
2012-13	Chelsea	0	0		
2012-13	Millwall	3	0		
2013-14	Chelsea	0	0		
2013-14	Brentford	40	3	40	3
2014-15	Wolverhampton W	7	0		
2014-15	Bristol C	7	1	7	1
2015-16	Wolverhampton W	19	5	26	5
2015-16	Millwall	12	0	15	0

SIGURDARSON, Bjorn (F)   168 28
H: 6 1 W: 12 09 b.Akranes 26-12-91
Internationals: Iceland U17, U19, U21, Full caps.

Season	Club				
2008-09	Lillestrom	5	0		
2009-10	Lillestrom	19	4		
2010-11	Lillestrom	22	4		
2011-12	Lillestrom	24	9	70	17
2012-13	Wolverhampton W	37	5		
2013-14	Wolverhampton W	18	2		
2014-15	Wolverhampton W	0	0		
2014-15	Molde	15	3	15	3
2014-15	Copenhagen	14	1	14	1
2015-16	Wolverhampton W	14	0	69	7

SIMPSON, Aaron (D)   0 0
b. 4-7-97

Season	Club		
2015-16	Wolverhampton W	0	0

UPTON, Regan (D)   0 0
b. 17-9-96

Season	Club		
2015-16	Wolverhampton W	0	0

WALLACE, Jed (M)   131 28
b.Reading 15-12-93
Internationals: England U19.

Season	Club				
2011-12	Portsmouth	0	0		
2012-13	Portsmouth	22	6		
2013-14	Portsmouth	44	7		
2014-15	Portsmouth	44	14	110	27
2015-16	Wolverhampton W	9	0	9	0
2015-16	Millwall	12	1	12	1

WILLIAMSON, Mike (D)   333 14
H: 6 4 W: 13 03 b.Stoke 8-11-83

Season	Club				
2001-02	Torquay U	3	0		
2002-03	Southampton	0	0		
2003-04	Southampton	0	0		
2003-04	Torquay U	11	0	14	0
2003-04	Doncaster R	0	0		
2004-05	Southampton	0	0		
2004-05	Wycombe W	37	2		
2005-06	Wycombe W	39	5		
2006-07	Wycombe W	33	1		
2007-08	Wycombe W	12	0		
2008-09	Wycombe W	22	3	143	11
2008-09	Watford	17	1		
2009-10	Watford	4	1	21	2
2009-10	Portsmouth	0	0		
2009-10	Newcastle U	16	0		
2010-11	Newcastle U	29	0		
2011-12	Newcastle U	22	0		
2012-13	Newcastle U	19	0		
2013-14	Newcastle U	33	0		
2014-15	Newcastle U	31	1		
2015-16	Newcastle U	0	0	150	1
2015-16	Wolverhampton W	5	0	5	0

WILSON, Donovan (F)   0 0
b.Yate 14-3-97

Season	Club		
2014-15	Wolverhampton W	0	0
2015-16	Wolverhampton W	0	0

ZYRO, Michal (M)   103 16
b.Warsaw 20-9-92
Internationals: Poland U19, U21, Full caps.

2009–10	Legia Warsaw	1	0		
2010–11	Legia Warsaw	6	0		
2011–12	Legia Warsaw	25	1		
2012–13	Legia Warsaw	9	2		
2013–14	Legia Warsaw	23	4		
2014–15	Legia Warsaw	27	5		
2015–16	Legia Warsaw	5	1	96	13
2015–16	Wolverhampton W	7	3	7	3

Players retained or with offer of contract
Armstrong, Daniel Charles; O'Hanlon, Ben Joseph; Van La Parra, Rajiv.

Scholars
Allan, Jordan Scott; Ball, Brandon Levi; Beasley, Harry Alexander; Bills, Rhys Mason; Carnat, Nicolae; Delacoe, Joseph Dennis Leigh; Ennis, Niall Nathan Michael; Finnie, Ross Steven; Herc, Christian; John, Cameron Bradley; Johnson, Connor William; Leak, Ryan David; Levingston, Conor Thomas; Lindsey, Bradley Carl; Osbourne, Adam; Phillips, Sam; Rehman, Akeal; Sibley, Michael Robert; Sinclair, Nyeko.

WYCOMBE W (90)

AINSWORTH, Gareth (M)   539 105
H: 5 10   W: 12 05   b.Blackburn 10-5-73

1991–92	Preston NE	5	0		
1992–93	Cambridge U	4	1	4	1
1992–93	Preston NE	26	0		
1993–94	Preston NE	38	11		
1994–95	Preston NE	16	1		
1995–96	Preston NE	2	0		
1995–96	Lincoln C	31	12		
1996–97	Lincoln C	46	22		
1997–98	Lincoln C	6	3	83	37
1997–98	Port Vale	40	5		
1998–99	Port Vale	15	5	55	10
1998–99	Wimbledon	8	0		
1999–2000	Wimbledon	2	2		
2000–01	Wimbledon	12	2		
2001–02	Wimbledon	2	0		
2001–02	*Preston NE*	5	1	92	13
2002–03	Wimbledon	12	2	36	6
2002–03	Walsall	5	1	5	1
2002–03	Cardiff C	9	0	9	0
2003–04	QPR	29	6		
2004–05	QPR	22	2		
2005–06	QPR	43	9		
2006–07	QPR	22	1		
2007–08	QPR	24	3		
2008–09	QPR	0	0		
2009–10	QPR	1	0	141	21
2009–10	Wycombe W	14	2		
2010–11	Wycombe W	43	10		
2011–12	Wycombe W	32	2		
2012–13	Wycombe W	25	2		
2013–14	Wycombe W	0	0		
2014–15	Wycombe W	0	0		
2015–16	Wycombe W	0	0	114	16

AMADI-HOLLOWAY, Aaron (D)   66 8
H: 6 2   W: 13 00   b.Newark 21-2-93
Internationals: Wales U17, U19.

2012–13	Bristol C	0	0		
2013–14	Bristol C	0	0		
2013–14	Newport Co	4	0	4	0
2014–15	Wycombe W	29	3		
2015–16	Wycombe W	23	3	52	6
2015–16	*Oldham Ath*	10	2	10	2

BEAN, Marcus (M)   385 25
H: 5 11   W: 11 06   b.Hammersmith 2-11-84
Internationals: Jamaica Full caps.

2002–03	QPR	7	0		
2003–04	QPR	31	1		
2004–05	QPR	20	1		
2004–05	Swansea C	8	0		
2005–06	QPR	9	0	67	2
2005–06	Swansea C	9	1	17	1
2005–06	Blackpool	17	1		
2006–07	Blackpool	6	0		
2007–08	Blackpool	0	0	23	1
2007–08	*Rotherham U*	12	1	12	1
2008–09	Brentford	44	9		
2009–10	Brentford	31	0		
2010–11	Brentford	37	3		
2011–12	Brentford	32	2	144	14
2012–13	Colchester U	31	0		
2013–14	Colchester U	35	5		
2014–15	Colchester U	3	0	69	5
2014–15	Portsmouth	6	1	6	1

2014–15	Wycombe W	17	0
2015–16	Wycombe W	30	0	47	0

BLOOMFIELD, Matt (M)   346 26
H: 5 9   W: 11 00   b.Felixstowe 8-2-84
Internationals: England U19.

2001–02	Ipswich T	0	0		
2002–03	Ipswich T	0	0		
2003–04	Ipswich T	0	0		
2003–04	Wycombe W	12	1		
2004–05	Wycombe W	26	2		
2005–06	Wycombe W	39	5		
2006–07	Wycombe W	41	4		
2007–08	Wycombe W	35	4		
2008–09	Wycombe W	20	0		
2009–10	Wycombe W	14	2		
2010–11	Wycombe W	34	3		
2011–12	Wycombe W	31	2		
2012–13	Wycombe W	2	1		
2013–14	Wycombe W	32	0		
2014–15	Wycombe W	33	1		
2015–16	Wycombe W	27	1	346	26

EPHRAIM, Hogan (F)   175 11
H: 5 9   W: 10 06   b.Islington 31-3-88
Internationals: England U16, U17, U18, U19.

2004–05	West Ham U	0	0		
2005–06	West Ham U	0	0		
2006–07	West Ham U	0	0		
2006–07	*Colchester U*	21	1	21	1
2007–08	West Ham U	0	0		
2007–08	QPR	29	3		
2008–09	QPR	27	1		
2009–10	QPR	22	0		
2009–10	*Leeds U*	3	0	3	0
2010–11	QPR	28	3		
2011–12	QPR	2	0		
2011–12	*Charlton Ath*	5	1	5	1
2011–12	*Bristol C*	5	1	5	1
2012–13	QPR	0	0		
2012–13	*Toronto FC*	11	0	11	0
2013–14	QPR	0	0	108	7
2013–14	*Peterborough U*	8	0	8	0
2014–15	Wycombe W	14	1		
2015–16	Wycombe W	0	0	14	1

HARRIMAN, Michael (D)   136 9
H: 5 6   W: 11 10   b.Chichester 23-10-92
Internationals: Republic of Ireland U18, U19, U21.

2010–11	QPR	0	0		
2011–12	QPR	1	0		
2012–13	QPR	1	0		
2012–13	*Wycombe W*	20	0		
2013–14	QPR	0	0		
2013–14	*Gillingham*	34	1	34	1
2014–15	QPR	0	0	2	0
2014–15	*Luton T*	35	1	35	1
2015–16	Wycombe W	45	7	65	7

HAYES, Paul (F)   494 111
H: 6 0   W: 12 12   b.Dagenham 20-9-83

2002–03	Scunthorpe U	18	8		
2003–04	Scunthorpe U	35	2		
2004–05	Scunthorpe U	46	18		
2005–06	Barnsley	45	6		
2006–07	Barnsley	30	5		
2006–07	*Huddersfield T*	4	1	4	1
2007–08	Scunthorpe U	40	8		
2008–09	Scunthorpe U	44	17		
2009–10	Scunthorpe U	45	9		
2010–11	Preston NE	23	2	23	2
2010–11	*Barnsley*	7	0	82	11
2011–12	Charlton Ath	19	3	19	3
2011–12	*Wycombe W*	6	6		
2012–13	Brentford	23	4		
2012–13	*Crawley T*	11	2	11	2
2013–14	Brentford	0	0	23	4
2013–14	*Plymouth Arg*	6	0	6	0
2013–14	*Scunthorpe U*	14	4	244	66
2014–15	Wycombe W	39	12		
2015–16	Wycombe W	37	4	82	22

JACOBSON, Joe (D)   308 15
H: 5 11   W: 12 06   b.Cardiff 17-11-86
Internationals: Wales U21.

2005–06	Cardiff C	1	0		
2006–07	Cardiff C	0	0	1	0
2006–07	*Accrington S*	6	1		
2006–07	*Bristol R*	11	0		
2007–08	Bristol R	40	1		
2008–09	Bristol R	22	0	73	1
2009–10	Oldham Ath	15	0		
2010–11	Oldham Ath	1	0	16	0
2010–11	*Accrington S*	26	2	32	3
2011–12	Shrewsbury T	39	1		
2012–13	Shrewsbury T	30	2		
2013–14	Shrewsbury T	41	4	110	7

2014–15	Wycombe W	42	3
2015–16	Wycombe W	34	1	76	4

JOMBATI, Sido (D)   185 5
H: 6 0   W: 11 11   b.Lisbon 20-8-87

2011–12	Cheltenham T	36	2		
2012–13	Cheltenham T	37	1		
2013–14	Cheltenham T	43	1	116	4
2014–15	Wycombe W	35	0		
2015–16	Wycombe W	34	1	69	1

KRETZSCHMAR, Max (M)   73 8
H: 5 9   W: 11 03   b.Kingston upon Thames 12-10-93

2011–12	Wycombe W	0	0		
2012–13	Wycombe W	0	0		
2013–14	Wycombe W	35	6		
2014–15	Wycombe W	16	0		
2015–16	Wycombe W	22	2	73	8

LYNCH, Alex (G)   4 0
H: 5 11   W: 9 08   b.Holyhead 4-4-95
Internationals: Wales U17.

2013–14	Peterborough U	0	0		
2014–15	Wycombe W	1	0		
2015–16	Wycombe W	3	0	4	0

McGINN, Stephen (M)   198 13
H: 5 9   W: 10 01   b.Glasgow 2-12-88
Internationals: Scotland U19, U21.

2006–07	St Mirren	4	1		
2007–08	St Mirren	25	2		
2008–09	St Mirren	26	1		
2009–10	St Mirren	18	3	73	7
2009–10	Watford	9	0		
2010–11	Watford	29	2		
2011–12	Watford	0	0		
2012–13	Watford	0	0	38	2
2012–13	*Shrewsbury T*	18	2	18	2
2013–14	Sheffield U	30	0		
2014–15	Sheffield U	0	0	30	0
2014–15	*Dundee*	13	1	13	1
2015–16	Wycombe W	26	1	26	1

O'NIEN, Luke (M)   36 5
b. 21-11-94

2013–14	Watford	1	0		
2014–15	Watford	0	0	1	0
2015–16	Wycombe W	35	5	35	5

PIERRE, Aaron (D)   90 7
H: 6 1   W: 13 12   b.Southall 17-2-93
Internationals: Grenada Full caps.

2011–12	Brentford	0	0		
2012–13	Brentford	0	0		
2013–14	Brentford	0	0		
2013–14	*Wycombe W*	8	1		
2014–15	Wycombe W	42	4		
2015–16	Wycombe W	40	2	90	7

RICHARDSON, Barry (G)   308 0
H: 6 1   W: 12 01   b.Willington Quay 5-8-69

1987–88	Sunderland	0	0		
1988–89	Scunthorpe U	0	0		
1989–90	Scarborough	24	0		
1990–91	Scarborough	6	0	30	0
1991–92	Northampton T	27	0		
1992–93	Northampton T	42	0		
1993–94	Northampton T	27	0	96	0
1994–95	Preston NE	17	0		
1995–96	Preston NE	3	0	20	0
1995–96	Lincoln C	34	0		
1996–97	Lincoln C	36	0		
1997–98	Lincoln C	26	0		
1998–99	Lincoln C	13	0		
1999–2000	Lincoln C	22	0		
1999–2000	*Mansfield T*	6	0	6	0
1999–2000	*Sheffield W*	0	0		
2000–01	Lincoln C	0	0	131	0
	From Doncaster R.				
2001–02	Halifax T	24	0	24	0
	From Gainsborough T.				
2003–04	Doncaster R	0	0		
2004–05	Nottingham F	0	0		
	From Cheltenham T, Peterborough U.				
2015–16	Wycombe W	1	0	1	0

ROWE, Daniel (D)   35 1
H: 6 2   W: 12 08   b.Middlesbrough 24-10-95

2012–13	Rotherham U	0	0		
2013–14	Rotherham U	0	0		
2013–14	*Wycombe W*	7	0		
2014–15	Rotherham U	0	0		
2014–15	Wycombe W	16	0		
2015–16	Wycombe W	12	1	35	1

SELLARS, Jerell (F)   8 0
b. 28-4-95

2015–16	Aston Villa	0	0		
2015–16	Wycombe W	8	0	8	0

SELLERS, Ryan (D) 15 0
b.London 13-10-95

2014–15	Bolton W	0	0		
2015–16	Wycombe W	15	0	15	0

STEWART, Anthony (D) 93 5
H: 5 10　W: 12 03　b.Brixton 18-9-92

2011–12	Wycombe W	4	0		
2012–13	Wycombe W	19	1		
2013–14	Wycombe W	33	3		
2014–15	Crewe Alex	10	0	10	0
2015–16	Wycombe W	27	1	83	5

THOMPSON, Gary (M) 320 54
H: 6 0　W: 14 02　b.Kendal 24-11-80

2007–08	Morecambe	40	7	40	7
2008–09	Scunthorpe U	24	3		
2009–10	Scunthorpe U	36	9		
2010–11	Scunthorpe U	12	1		
2011–12	Scunthorpe U	39	7	111	20
2012–13	Bradford C	41	6		
2013–14	Bradford C	44	2	85	8
2014–15	Notts Co	41	12	41	12
2015–16	Wycombe W	43	7	43	7

UGWU, Chigozie (F) 93 18
H: 6 2　W: 12 00　b.Oxford 22-4-93

2011–12	Reading	0	0		
2012–13	Reading	0	0		
2012–13	Yeovil T	15	3		
2012–13	Plymouth Arg	6	0	6	0
2013–14	Reading	0	0		
2013–14	Shrewsbury T	7	1	7	1
2014–15	Dunfermline Ath	14	7	14	7
2014–15	Yeovil T	22	5	37	8
2015–16	Wycombe W	29	2	29	2

WOOD, Sam (M) 284 17
H: 6 0　W: 11 05　b.Sidcup 9-8-86

2008–09	Brentford	40	1		
2009–10	Brentford	43	2		
2010–11	Brentford	20	1		
2011–12	Brentford	5	0	108	4
2011–12	Rotherham U	26	1	26	1
2012–13	Wycombe W	35	3		
2013–14	Wycombe W	43	2		
2014–15	Wycombe W	44	5		
2015–16	Wycombe W	28	2	150	12

Non-Contract
Ainsworth, Gareth; Richardson, Barry.

YEOVIL T (91)

ALLEN, Iffy (M) 14 0
H: 5 9　W: 10 12　b.Lambeth 15-3-94

2012–13	Barnet	2	0	2	0
2015–16	Yeovil T	12	0	12	0

BASSETT, Ollie (F) 2 0
b. 6-3-98

2015–16	Yeovil T	2	0	2	0

BECK, Mark (F) 74 7
H: 6 5　W: 12 08　b.Sunderland 2-2-94
Internationals: Scotland U19.

2011–12	Carlisle U	2	0		
2012–13	Carlisle U	27	4		
2013–14	Carlisle U	10	0		
2014–15	Carlisle U	27	3	66	7
2015–16	Yeovil T	8	0	8	0

BIRD, Ryan (F) 86 19
H: 6 4　W: 12 06　b.Slough 15-11-87

2013–14	Portsmouth	18	3		
2014–15	Portsmouth	2	0	20	3
2014–15	Cambridge U	24	6	24	6
2014–15	Hartlepool U	6	2	6	2
2015–16	Yeovil T	36	8	36	8

BURROWS, Jamie (F) 1 0
b.Jersey 24-3-95

2014–15	Rangers	0	0		
2015–16	Yeovil T	1	0	1	0

COMPTON, Jack (M) 145 11
H: 5 8　W: 10 07　b.Torquay 2-9-88

2008–09	Brighton & HA	0	0		

From Havant & Waterloovlle,
Weston-Super-Mare.

2010–11	Falkirk	24	3		
2011–12	Falkirk	13	0	37	3
2011–12	Bradford C	14	0	14	0
2011–12	St Johnstone	0	0		
2012–13	Portsmouth	12	0	12	0
2012–13	Colchester U	7	0	7	0
2013–14	Hartlepool U	34	4		
2014–15	Hartlepool U	21	0	55	4
2015–16	Yeovil T	20	4	20	4

DAWSON, Kevin (M) 133 8
H: 5 10　W: 12 08　b.Dublin 30-6-90
Internationals: Republic of Ireland U18.

2011	Shelbourne	26	2		
2012	Shelbourne	25	2	51	4
2012–13	Yeovil T	20	2		
2013–14	Yeovil T	35	1		
2014–15	Yeovil T	17	1		
2015–16	Yeovil T	10	0	82	4

DICKSON, Ryan (M) 254 10
H: 5 10　W: 11 05　b.Saltash 14-12-86

2004–05	Plymouth Arg	3	0		
2005–06	Plymouth Arg	0	0		
2006–07	Plymouth Arg	2	0		
2006–07	Torquay U	9	1	9	1
2007–08	Plymouth Arg	0	0	5	0
2007–08	Brentford	31	0		
2008–09	Brentford	39	1		
2009–10	Brentford	27	2	97	3
2010–11	Southampton	23	1		
2011–12	Southampton	0	0		
2011–12	Yeovil T	5	1		
2011–12	Leyton Orient	9	0	9	0
2012–13	Southampton	0	0	23	1
2012–13	Bradford C	5	1	5	1
2013–14	Colchester U	32	0	32	0
2014–15	Crawley T	32	1	32	1
2015–16	Yeovil T	37	2	42	3

DOLAN, Matthew (M) 93 6
b.Hartlepool 11-2-93

2010–11	Middlesbrough	0	0		
2011–12	Middlesbrough	0	0		
2012–13	Middlesbrough	0	0		
2012–13	Yeovil T	8	1		
2013–14	Middlesbrough	0	0		
2013–14	Hartlepool U	20	2		
2013–14	Bradford C	11	0		
2014–15	Bradford C	13	0	24	0
2014–15	Hartlepool U	20	0	22	2
2015–16	Yeovil T	39	3	47	4

FOGDEN, Wes (F) 97 6
H: 5 8　W: 10 04　b.Brighton 12-4-88

2006–07	Brighton & HA	0	0		
2007–08	Brighton & HA	3	0	3	0

From Dorchester T, Havant & Waterlooville.

2011–12	Bournemouth	27	3		
2012–13	Bournemouth	26	1		
2013–14	Bournemouth	0	0	53	4
2013–14	Portsmouth	19	2		
2014–15	Portsmouth	9	0	28	2
2015–16	Yeovil T	13	0	13	0

GIBBONS, Jordan (M) 4 0
H: 5 10　W: 10 12　b.London 18-11-93

2011–12	QPR	0	0		
2012–13	QPR	0	0		
2012–13	Inverness CT	1	0	1	0
2013–14	QPR	0	0		
2014–15	QPR	0	0		
2015–16	Yeovil T	3	0	3	0

GILLETT, Simon (M) 230 9
H: 5 6　W: 11 07　b.Oxford 6-11-85

2003–04	Southampton	0	0		
2004–05	Southampton	0	0		
2005–06	Southampton	0	0		
2005–06	Walsall	2	0	2	0
2006–07	Southampton	0	0		
2006–07	Blackpool	31	1	31	1
2006–07	Bournemouth	7	1	7	1
2007–08	Southampton	4	0		
2007–08	Yeovil T	4	0		
2008–09	Southampton	27	0		
2009–10	Southampton	2	0	31	0
2009–10	Doncaster R	11	0		
2010–11	Doncaster R	22	1		
2011–12	Doncaster R	46	3		
2012–13	Doncaster R	0	0	79	4
2012–13	Nottingham F	25	0		
2013–14	Nottingham F	0	0	25	0
2013–14	Bristol C	23	2	23	2
2014–15	Yeovil T	17	1		
2015–16	Yeovil T	6	0	27	1
2015–16	Peterborough U	5	0	5	0

JEFFERS, Shaun (F) 97 5
H: 6 1　W: 11 03　b.Bedford 14-4-92
Internationals: England U19.

2009–10	Coventry C	4	0		
2010–11	Coventry C	0	0		
2010–11	Cheltenham T	22	1	22	1
2011–12	Coventry C	3	0		
2012–13	Coventry C	0	0	7	0
2013–14	Peterborough U	8	1	8	1
2013–14	Newport Co	14	0		
2014–15	Newport Co	21	2	35	2
2015–16	Yeovil T	25	1	25	1

KRYSIAK, Artur (G) 225 0
H: 6 1　W: 12 00　b.Lodz 11-8-89
Internationals: Poland U19.

2006–07	Birmingham C	0	0		
2007–08	Gretna	4	0	4	0
2007–08	Birmingham C	0	0		
2008–09	Birmingham C	0	0		
2008–09	Motherwell	1	0	1	0
2008–09	Swansea C	2	0	2	0
2009–10	Birmingham C	0	0		
2009–10	Burton Alb	38	0	38	0
2010–11	Exeter C	10	0		
2011–12	Exeter C	38	0		
2012–13	Exeter C	42	0		
2013–14	Exeter C	37	0	127	0
2014–15	Yeovil T	15	0		
2015–16	Yeovil T	38	0	53	0

LACEY, Alex (D) 38 0
b.Milton Keynes 31-5-93

2014–15	Luton T	18	0	18	0
2015–16	Yeovil T	20	0	20	0

LAIRD, Marc (M) 220 12
H: 6 1　W: 10 07　b.Edinburgh 23-1-86

2003–04	Manchester C	0	0		
2004–05	Manchester C	0	0		
2005–06	Manchester C	0	0		
2006–07	Manchester C	0	0		
2006–07	Northampton T	6	0	6	0
2007–08	Manchester C	0	0		
2007–08	Port Vale	7	1	7	1
2007–08	Millwall	17	1		
2008–09	Millwall	38	5		
2009–10	Millwall	20	0		
2010–11	Millwall	1	0	76	6
2010–11	Brentford	4	1	4	1
2010–11	Walsall	8	0	8	0
2011–12	Leyton Orient	22	2		
2012–13	Leyton Orient	1	0		
2012–13	Southend U	23	1		
2013–14	Leyton Orient	0	0	23	2
2013–14	Southend U	19	0	42	1
2014–15	Tranmere R	34	1	34	1
2015–16	Yeovil T	20	0	20	0

LITA, Leroy (F) 353 96
H: 5 7　W: 11 12　b.DR Congo 28-12-84
Internationals: England U21.

2002–03	Bristol C	15	2		
2003–04	Bristol C	26	5		
2004–05	Bristol C	44	24	85	31
2005–06	Reading	26	11		
2006–07	Reading	33	7		
2007–08	Reading	14	1		
2007–08	Charlton Ath	8	3	8	3
2008–09	Reading	10	1	83	20
2008–09	Norwich C	16	7	16	7
2009–10	Middlesbrough	40	8		
2010–11	Middlesbrough	38	12	78	20
2011–12	Swansea C	16	2		
2012–13	Swansea C	0	0		
2012–13	Birmingham C	10	3	10	3
2012–13	Sheffield W	17	6	17	6
2013–14	Swansea C	2	0	18	2
2013–14	Brighton & HA	5	1	5	1
2014–15	Barnsley	19	2	19	2
2014–15	Notts Co	6	0	6	0
2015–16	Yeovil T	8	1	8	1

MELANSON, Max (M) 0 0
b. 5-10-97

2015–16	Yeovil T	0	0	

NEEDLE, James (D) 0 0
b. 18-11-97

2015–16	Yeovil T	0	0	

SMITH, Nathan (D) 262 2
H: 5 11　W: 12 00　b.Enfield 11-1-87
Internationals: Jamaica Full caps.

2007–08	Yeovil T	31	0		
2008–09	Yeovil T	33	1		
2009–10	Yeovil T	34	0		
2010–11	Yeovil T	40	0		
2011–12	Chesterfield	25	0		
2012–13	Chesterfield	29	0		
2013–14	Chesterfield	13	0	67	0
2014–15	Yeovil T	41	0		
2015–16	Yeovil T	40	1	195	2

SOKOLIK, Jakub (D) 56 1
H: 5 6　W: 12 02　b.Ostrava 28-8-93
Internationals: Czech Republic U16, U17, U18.

2010–11	Liverpool	0	0	
2011–12	Liverpool	0	0	
2012–13	Liverpool	0	0	
2013–14	Liverpool	0	0	

2013–14	Southend U	10	0		
2014–15	Yeovil T	11	0		
2014–15	Southend U	1	0	11	0
2015–16	Yeovil T	34	1	45	1

SOWUNMI, Omar (D)   5   1
H: 6 6   W: 14 09   b.Colchester 7-11-95

2015–16	Yeovil T	5	1	5	1

TOZER, Ben (D)   203   6
H: 6 1   W: 12 11   b.Plymouth 1-3-90

2007–08	Swindon T	2	0	2	0
2007–08	Newcastle U	0	0		
2008–09	Newcastle U	0	0		
2009–10	Newcastle U	1	0		
2010–11	Newcastle U	0	0	1	0
2010–11	Northampton T	31	3		
2011–12	Northampton T	45	3		
2012–13	Northampton T	46	0		
2013–14	Northampton T	29	0		
2013–14	Colchester U	1	0	1	0
2014–15	Northampton T	22	0	173	6
2015–16	Yeovil T	26	0	26	0

WARD, Darren (D)   538   18
H: 6 3   W: 11 04   b.Harrow 13-9-78

1995–96	Watford	1	0		
1996–97	Watford	7	0		
1997–98	Watford	0	0		
1998–99	Watford	1	0		
1999–2000	Watford	9	1		
1999–2000	QPR	14	0	14	0
2000–01	Watford	40	1		
2001–02	Watford	1	0		
2001–02	Millwall	14	0		
2002–03	Millwall	39	1		
2003–04	Millwall	46	3		
2004–05	Millwall	43	0		
2005–06	Crystal Palace	43	5		
2006–07	Crystal Palace	20	0	63	5
2007–08	Wolverhampton W	30	0		
2008–09	Wolverhampton W	1	0	31	0
2008–09	Watford	9	1	68	3
2008–09	Charlton Ath	16	0	16	0
2009–10	Millwall	31	1		
2010–11	Millwall	31	1		
2011–12	Millwall	30	0		
2012–13	Millwall	1	0	235	6
2012–13	Swindon T	39	2		
2013–14	Swindon T	36	0		
2014–15	Swindon T	0	0	75	2
2014–15	Crawley T	18	1	18	1
2015–16	Yeovil T	18	1	18	1

WEALE, Chris (G)   295   1
H: 6 2   W: 13 03   b.Chard 9-2-82
Internationals: England C.

2003–04	Yeovil T	35	0		
2004–05	Yeovil T	38	0		
2005–06	Yeovil T	25	0		
2006–07	Bristol C	1	0		
2007–08	Hereford U	1	0		
2007–08	Bristol C	3	0		
2008–09	Bristol C	5	0	9	0
2008–09	Hereford U	1	0	2	0
2008–09	Yeovil T	10	1		
2009–10	Leicester C	45	0		
2010–11	Leicester C	29	0		
2011–12	Leicester C	1	0	75	0
2011–12	Northampton T	3	0	3	0
2012–13	Shrewsbury T	46	0		
2013–14	Shrewsbury T	35	0	81	0
2014–15	Yeovil T	8	0		
2014–15	Burton Alb	0	0		
2015–16	Yeovil T	9	0	125	1

ZOKO, Francois (F)   440   79
H: 6 0   W: 11 05   b.Daloa 13-9-83
Internationals: Ivory Coast U20, U23.

2001–02	Nancy	24	3		
2002–03	Nancy	28	2		
2003–04	Nancy	19	3	71	8
2004–05	Laval	27	7		
2005–06	Laval	33	2	60	9
2006–07	Mons	23	4		
2007–08	Mons	32	8	55	12
2008–09	Hacettepe	27	1	27	1
2009–10	Ostend	11	4	11	4
2010–11	Carlisle U	44	6		
2011–12	Carlisle U	45	13		
2012–13	Carlisle U	0	0	89	19
2012–13	Notts Co	38	7		
2013–14	Notts Co	1	0	39	7
2013–14	Stevenage	33	10	33	10
2014–15	Blackpool	14	1	14	1
2014–15	Bradford C	16	1	16	1
2015–16	Yeovil T	25	7	25	7

Scholars
Akinuli, Paul Oluwarotimi; Corbridge, Jayden Shaun Alan; Ismail, Samyan hassan; Iwyeh Nwabudike, Prince; Latham, Kingsley Finn; Macfoy Johnston, Dion Thomas Nyake; Melanson, Max Stanford; Nyman, Luis James Antonio; Warren, Arthur James Reuben Lewis.

YORK C (92)

BERRETT, James (M)   269   30
H: 5 10   W: 10 13   b.Halifax 13-1-89
Internationals: Republic of Ireland U18, U19, U21.

2006–07	Huddersfield T	2	0		
2007–08	Huddersfield T	15	1		
2008–09	Huddersfield T	9	1		
2009–10	Huddersfield T	9	0	35	2
2010–11	Carlisle U	46	10		
2011–12	Carlisle U	42	9		
2012–13	Carlisle U	42	2		
2013–14	Carlisle U	40	2	170	23
2014–15	Yeovil T	28	1	28	1
2015–16	York C	36	4	36	4

CARSON, Josh (M)   111   12
H: 5 9   W: 11 00   b.Ballymena 3-6-93
Internationals: Northern Ireland U16, U17, U18, U19, U21, Full caps.

2010–11	Ipswich T	9	3		
2011–12	Ipswich T	16	2		
2012–13	York C	5	0		
2013–14	Ipswich T	0	0	31	5
2013–14	York C	31	4		
2014–15	York C	22	2		
2015–16	York C	22	1	80	7

COULSON, Michael (F)   162   25
H: 5 10   W: 10 00   b.Scarborough 4-4-88
Internationals: England C.

2006–07	Barnsley	2	0		
2007–08	Barnsley	12	0		
2008–09	Barnsley	2	0		
2009–10	Barnsley	0	0	16	0
2009–10	Grimsby T	29	5	29	5
2012–13	York C	19	4		
2013–14	York C	33	7		
2014–15	York C	43	4		
2015–16	York C	22	5	117	20

DIXON, Matty (M)   7   0
b. 19-12-94

2013–14	Hull C	0	0		
2014–15	Hull C	0	0		
2015–16	Hull C	0	0		
2015–16	York C	7	0	7	0

FLINDERS, Scott (G)   347   1
H: 6 4   W: 13 00   b.Rotherham 12-6-86
Internationals: England U20.

2004–05	Barnsley	11	0		
2005–06	Barnsley	3	0	14	0
2006–07	Crystal Palace	8	0		
2006–07	Gillingham	9	0	9	0
2006–07	Brighton & HA	12	0	12	0
2007–08	Crystal Palace	0	0		
2007–08	Yeovil T	9	0	9	0
2008–09	Crystal Palace	0	0	8	0
2009–10	Hartlepool U	46	0		
2010–11	Hartlepool U	26	1		
2011–12	Hartlepool U	45	0		
2012–13	Hartlepool U	46	0		
2013–14	Hartlepool U	43	0		
2014–15	Hartlepool U	46	0	252	1
2015–16	York C	43	0	43	0

GALBRAITH, Danny (M)   115   4
b. 19-8-90

2009–10	Hibernian	14	1		
2010–11	Hibernian	22	0		
2011–12	Hibernian	16	0	52	1
2013	Limerick	27	0		
2014	Limerick	8	2	35	2
2014–15	Gillingham	7	0	7	0
2015–16	York C	21	1	21	1

GREENING, Jonathan (M)   425   15
H: 5 11   W: 11 00   b.Scarborough 2-1-79
Internationals: England U21.

1996–97	York C	5	0		
1997–98	York C	20	2		
1997–98	Manchester U	3	0		
1998–99	Manchester U	3	0		
1999–2000	Manchester U	4	0		
2000–01	Manchester U	7	0	14	0
2001–02	Middlesbrough	36	1		
2002–03	Middlesbrough	38	2		
2003–04	Middlesbrough	25	1	99	4
2004–05	WBA	34	0		
2005–06	WBA	38	2		
2006–07	WBA	42	2		
2007–08	WBA	46	1		
2008–09	WBA	34	2		
2009–10	WBA	2	0	196	7
2009–10	Fulham	23	1		
2010–11	Fulham	10	0	33	1
2011–12	Nottingham F	31	0		
2012–13	Nottingham F	5	0		
2012–13	Barnsley	6	1	6	1
2013–14	Nottingham F	13	0		
2014–15	Nottingham F	0	0	49	0
2015–16	York C	3	0	28	2

HARE, Taron (D)   0   0
H: 6 1   W: 11 00   b.Bottesford 4-10-96

2014–15	Scunthorpe U	0	0		
2015–16	York C	0	0		

HYDE, Jake (F)   154   38
H: 6 1   W: 13 02   b.Slough 1-7-90
Internationals: England C.

2009–10	Barnet	34	6		
2010–11	Dundee	2	3		
2010–11	Dunfermline Ath	2	0	2	0
2011–12	Dundee	26	6	28	9
2012–13	Barnet	40	14	74	20
2014–15	York C	39	9		
2015–16	York C	11	0	50	9

ILESANMI, Femi (D)   187   1
H: 6 1   W: 11 13   b.Southwark 18-4-91

2010–11	Dagenham & R	25	0		
2011–12	Dagenham & R	17	0		
2012–13	Dagenham & R	46	1		
2013–14	Dagenham & R	29	0	117	1
2014–15	York C	33	0		
2015–16	York C	37	0	70	0

INGHAM, Michael (G)   217   0
H: 6 4   W: 13 08   b.Preston 9-7-80
Internationals: Northern Ireland U18, U21, Full caps.

1998–99	Cliftonville	18	0	18	0
1999–2000	Sunderland	0	0		
1999–2000	Carlisle U	7	0	7	0
2000–01	Sunderland	0	0		
2001–02	Sunderland	0	0		
2001–02	Stoke C	0	0		
2002–03	Sunderland	0	0		
2002–03	Darlington	3	0	3	0
2002–03	York C	17	0		
2003–04	Sunderland	0	0		
2003–04	Wrexham	11	0		
2004–05	Sunderland	2	0	2	0
2004–05	Doncaster R	1	0	1	0
2005–06	Wrexham	40	0		
2006–07	Wrexham	31	0	82	0
2012–13	York C	46	0		
2013–14	York C	19	0		
2014–15	York C	19	0		
2015–16	York C	3	0	104	0

LOWE, Keith (D)   300   20
H: 6 2   W: 13 03   b.Wolverhampton 13-9-85

2004–05	Wolverhampton W	11	0		
2005–06	Wolverhampton W	3	0		
2005–06	Burnley	16	0	16	0
2005–06	QPR	1	0	1	0
2005–06	Swansea C	4	0	4	0
2006–07	Wolverhampton W	0	0		
2006–07	Brighton & HA	0	0		
2006–07	Cheltenham T	16	1		
2007–08	Wolverhampton W	0	0		
2007–08	Port Vale	28	3	28	3
2008–09	Wolverhampton W	0	0	14	0
2009–10	Hereford U	19	1	19	1
2010–11	Cheltenham T	36	1		
2011–12	Cheltenham T	30	1		
2012–13	Cheltenham T	31	4		
2013–14	Cheltenham T	13	1	126	8
2013–14	York C	30	1		
2014–15	York C	46	6		
2015–16	York C	16	1	92	8

McCOMBE, John (D)   286   20
H: 6 2   W: 13 00   b.Pontefract 7-5-85

2002–03	Huddersfield T	1	0		
2003–04	Huddersfield T	0	0		
2004–05	Huddersfield T	5	0		
2005–06	Huddersfield T	1	0		
2005–06	Torquay U	0	0		
2006–07	Huddersfield T	7	0	14	0
2007–08	Hereford U	27	0	27	0
2008–09	Port Vale	31	2		
2009–10	Port Vale	40	3		

2010–11	Port Vale	42	4		
2011–12	Port Vale	40	4		
2012–13	Port Vale	32	1		
2013–14	Port Vale	0	0	185	14
2013–14	Mansfield T	5	2	5	2
2013–14	York C	19	3		
2014–15	York C	31	0		
2015–16	York C	5	1	55	4

McCOY, Marvin (D) 136 0
H: 5 11 W: 11 00 b.Walthamstow 2-10-88
Internationals: Antigua and Barbuda Full caps.

2007–08	Hereford U	0	0		
From Leyton, Wealdstone.					
2010–11	Wycombe W	21	0		
2011–12	Wycombe W	28	0		
2012–13	Wycombe W	9	0		
2013–14	Wycombe W	33	0	91	0
2014–15	York C	31	0		
2015–16	York C	14	0	45	0

McEVOY, Kenneth (M) 28 3
H: 5 9 W: 10 01 b.Waterford 4-9-94
Internationals: Republic of Ireland U17, U19, U21.

2013–14	Tottenham H	0	0		
2014–15	Tottenham H	0	0		
2014–15	*Peterborough U*	7	1	7	1
2014–15	*Colchester U*	1	0	1	0
2015–16	Tottenham H	0	0		
2015–16	*Stevenage*	1	0	1	0
2015–16	York C	19	2	19	2

NOLAN, Eddie (D) 206 3
H: 6 0 W: 13 05 b.Waterford 5-8-88
Internationals: Republic of Ireland U21, B, Full caps.

2005–06	Blackburn R	0	0		
2006–07	Blackburn R	0	0		
2006–07	Stockport Co	4	0	4	0
2007–08	Blackburn R	0	0		
2007–08	Hartlepool U	11	0	11	0
2008–09	Blackburn R	0	0		
2008–09	Preston NE	21	0		
2009–10	Preston NE	19	0		
2009–10	*Sheffield W*	14	1	14	1
2010–11	Preston NE	0	0	40	0
2010–11	Scunthorpe U	35	0		
2011–12	Scunthorpe U	30	1		
2012–13	Scunthorpe U	12	0		
2013–14	Scunthorpe U	39	0		
2014–15	Scunthorpe U	6	0	122	1
2015–16	York C	15	1	15	1

OLIVER, Vadaine (F) 101 17
H: 6 2 W: 12 04 b.Sheffield 21-10-91

2010–11	Sheffield W	0	0		
2011–12	Sheffield W	0	0		
2013–14	Crewe Alex	25	2		
2014–15	Crewe Alex	9	1	34	3
2014–15	*Mansfield T*	30	7	30	7
2015–16	York C	37	7	37	7

PENN, Russ (M) 286 14
H: 5 11 W: 12 13 b.Dudley 8-11-85
Internationals: England C.

2009–10	Burton Alb	40	4		
2010–11	Burton Alb	41	3	81	7
2011–12	Cheltenham T	43	1		
2012–13	Cheltenham T	43	1		
2013–14	Cheltenham T	19	0	105	2
2013–14	York C	21	0		
2014–15	York C	45	2		
2015–16	York C	34	3	100	5

PLATT, Tom (M) 47 0
H: 6 1 W: 12 13 b.Pontefract 1-10-93

2012–13	York C	7	0		
2013–14	York C	20	0		
2014–15	York C	20	0		
2015–16	York C	0	0	47	0

RIORDAN, Derek (F) 270 99
H: 6 2 W: 10 03 b.Edinburgh 16-1-83
Internationals: Scotland U21, Full caps.

2001–02	Hibernian	6	0		
2002–03	Hibernian	10	3		
2002–03	*Cowdenbeath*	2	3	2	3
2003–04	Hibernian	34	15		
2004–05	Hibernian	37	20		
2005–06	Hibernian	36	16		
2006–07	Celtic	16	4		
2007–08	Celtic	8	1	24	5
2008–09	Hibernian	32	12		
2009–10	Hibernian	37	13		
2010–11	Hibernian	33	11	225	90
2011–12	Shanghai S	1	1	1	1
2011–12	St Johnstone	4	0	4	0
2012–13	Bristol R	11	0		
2013–14	Bristol R	0	0	11	0
2015–16	York C	3	0	3	0

RZONCA, Callum (M) 1 0
b. 7-1-97

2015–16	York C	1	0	1	0

SINCLAIR, Emile (F) 238 35
H: 6 0 W: 11 04 b.Leeds 29-12-87

2007–08	Nottingham F	12	1		
2007–08	*Brentford*	4	0	4	0
2008–09	Nottingham F	3	0	15	1
2008–09	*Macclesfield T*	17	1		
2009–10	Macclesfield T	42	7		
2010–11	Macclesfield T	31	5		
2011–12	Macclesfield T	5	1	95	14
2011–12	Peterborough U	35	10		
2012–13	Peterborough U	12	3		
2012–13	*Barnsley*	4	0	4	0
2012–13	*Doncaster R*	4	0	4	0
2013–14	Peterborough U	0	0	47	13
2013–14	*Crawley T*	15	2	15	2
2013–14	*Northampton T*	20	2		
2014–15	Northampton T	10	1	30	3
2014–15	York C	12	0		
2015–16	York C	12	0	24	2

STRAKER, Anthony (D) 257 8
H: 5 9 W: 11 11 b.Ealing 23-9-88
Internationals: England U18. Grenada Full caps.

2008–09	Aldershot T	32	0		
2009–10	Aldershot T	37	2		
2010–11	Aldershot T	38	2		
2010–11	*Wycombe W*	4	0	4	0
2011–12	Aldershot T	44	2	151	6
2012–13	Southend U	28	0		
2013–14	Southend U	39	2	67	2
2014–15	York C	12	0		
2014–15	*Motherwell*	12	0	12	0
2015–16	York C	11	0	23	0

SUMMERFIELD, Luke (M) 271 23
H: 6 0 W: 11 00 b.Ivybridge 6-12-87

2004–05	Plymouth Arg	1	0		
2005–06	Plymouth Arg	0	0		
2006–07	Plymouth Arg	23	1		
2006–07	*Bournemouth*	8	1	8	1
2007–08	Plymouth Arg	7	0		
2008–09	Plymouth Arg	29	2		
2009–10	Plymouth Arg	12	0		
2009–10	*Leyton Orient*	14	0	14	0
2010–11	Plymouth Arg	7	1	79	4
2011–12	Cheltenham T	41	4	41	4
2012–13	Shrewsbury T	36	2		
2013–14	Shrewsbury T	28	1	64	3
2014–15	York C	31	4		
2015–16	York C	34	7	65	11

SWANN, George (D) 4 0
H: 6 3 b.Plymouth 10-9-91

2012–13	Manchester C	0	0		
2013–14	Manchester C	0	0		
2013–14	*Sheffield W*	0	0		
2014–15	Wolverhampton W	0	0		
2015–16	York C	4	0	4	0

THOMPSON, Reece (F) 13 3
b. 11-11-93

2015–16	York C	13	3	13	3

WINFIELD, Dave (D) 197 12
H: 6 3 W: 13 08 b.Aldershot 24-3-88

2008–09	Aldershot T	10	0		
2009–10	Aldershot T	25	2	35	2
2010–11	Wycombe W	37	2		
2011–12	Wycombe W	25	2		
2012–13	Wycombe W	29	2		
2013–14	Wycombe W	0	0	91	6
2013–14	Shrewsbury T	17	0	17	0
2014–15	York C	10	2		
2014–15	*AFC Wimbledon*	7	0	7	0
2015–16	York C	37	2	47	4

Scholars
Breslin, Reece Michael; Brettell, Aaron Andrew; Bruton, Alex; Caulfield, Ryan Peter; Cooney, Robert James; De Groot, Richard Oshiro; Fielding, Samuel Harry; Freer, Bradley Linden; Jefferson, Sam David; Kennedy, Nicholas John Steve; Leen, Declan Dennis; Parker, Matthew Keith; Price, Kieran Richard Roderick; Salmon, Christopher; Tranter, Kyle; Wilson, Cameron James.

ENGLISH LEAGUE PLAYERS – INDEX

NATIONAL LIST OF REFEREES FOR SEASON 2016–17

Adcock, JG (James) – Nottinghamshire
Atkinson, M (Martin) – West Yorkshire
Attwell, SB (Stuart) – Warwickshire
Bankes, P (Peter) – Merseyside
Bond, D (Darren) – Lancashire
Boyeson, C (Carl) – East Yorkshire
Breakspear, C (Charles) – Surrey
Brooks, J (John) – Leicestershire
Brown, M (Mark) – East Yorkshire
Busby, J (John) – Oxfordshire
Clark, R (Richard) – Northumberland
Clattenburg, M (Mark) – County Durham
Collins, LM (Lee) – Surrey
Coote, D (David) – West Yorkshire
Davies, A (Andy) – Hampshire
Deadman, D (Darren) – Cambridgeshire
Dean, ML (Mike) – Merseyside
Drysdale, D (Darren) – Lincolnshire
Duncan, S (Scott) – Northumberland
East, R (Roger) – Wiltshire
Eltringham, G (Geoff) – Tyne & Wear
England, D (Darren) – South Yorkshire
Friend, KA (Kevin) – Leicestershire
Haines, A (Andy) – Tyne & Wear
Handley, D (Darren) – Lancashire

Harrington, T (Tony) – Cleveland
Haywood, M (Mark) – West Yorkshire
Heywood, M (Mark) – Cheshire
Hill, K (Keith) – Hertfordshire
Hooper, SA (Simon) – Wiltshire
Horwood, G (Graham) – Bedfordshire
Huxtable, B (Brett) – Devon
Ilderton, EL (Eddie) – Tyne & Wear
Johnson, K (Kevin) – Somerset
Jones, MJ (Michael) – Cheshire
Jones, RJ (Robert) – Merseyside
Joyce, R (Ross) – Cleveland
Kavanagh, C (Chris) – Lancashire
Kettle, TM (Trevor) – Leicestershire
Kinseley, N (Nick) – Essex
Langford, O (Oliver) – West Midlands
Lewis, RL (Rob) – Shropshire
Linington, JJ (James) – Isle of Wight
Madley, AJ (Andy) – West Yorkshire
Madley, RJ (Bobby) – West Yorkshire
Malone, BJ (Brendan) – Wiltshire
Marriner, AM (André) – West Midlands
Martin, S (Stephen) – Staffordshire
Mason, LS (Lee) – Lancashire
Miller, NS (Nigel) – County Durham
Moss, J (Jon) – West Yorkshire

Oliver, M (Michael) – Northumberland
Pawson, CL (Craig) – South Yorkshire
Probert, LW (Lee) – Wiltshire
Robinson, T (Tim) – West Sussex
Russell, MP (Mick) – Hertfordshire
Salisbury, G (Graham) – Lancashire
Salisbury, M (Michael) – Lancashire
Sarginson, CD (Chris) – Staffordshire
Scott, GD (Graham) – Oxfordshire
Simpson, J (Jeremy) – Lancashire
Stockbridge, S (Seb) – Tyne & Wear
Stroud, KP (Keith) – Hampshire
Sutton, GJ (Gary) – Lincolnshire
Swabey, L (Lee) – Devon
Swarbrick, ND (Neil) – Lancashire
Taylor, A (Anthony) – Cheshire
Tierney, P Paul) – Lancashire
Toner, B (Ben) – Lancashire
Ward, GL (Gavin) – Surrey
Webb, D (David) – County Durham
Whitestone, D (Dean) – Northamptonshire
Woolmer, KA (Andy) – Northamptonshire
Wright, KK (Kevin) – Merseyside
Yates, O (Ollie) – Staffordshire

ASSISTANT REFEREES

Akers, C (Chris) – South Yorkshire
Amey, JR (Justin) – Dorset
Amphlett, MJ (Marvyn) – Worcestershire
Aspinall, N (Natalie) – Lancashire
Atkin, R (Robert) – Lincolnshire
Avent, D (David) – Northamptonshire
Aylott, A (Andrew) – Bedfordshire
Barnard, N (Nicholas) – Cheshire
Barratt, W (Wayne) – Worcestershire
Bartlett, R (Richard) – Cheshire
Beck, S (Simon) – Bedfordshire
Bell, J (James) – South Yorkshire
Bennett, A (Andrew) – Devon
Bennett, S (Simon) – Staffordshire
Benton, DK (David) – South Yorkshire
Beswick, G (Gary) – County Durham
Betts, L (Lee) – Norfolk
Blunden, D (Darren) – Kent
Bristow, M (Matthew) – Manchester
Bromley, A (Adam) – Devon
Bryan, D (Dave) – Lincolnshire
Bull, W (William) – Hampshire

Burt, S (Stuart) – Northamptonshire
Bushell, DD (David) – London
Butler, S (Stuart) – Kent
Byrne, H (Helen) – Durham
Cann, D (Darren) – Norfolk
Cheosiaua D-R (Dumitru-Ravel) – Worcestershire
Child, S (Stephen) – Kent
Clark, J (Joseph) – West Midlands
Clayton, A (Alan) – Cheshire
Clayton, S (Simon) – County Durham
Collin, J (Jake) – Merseyside
Cook, D (Dan) – Hampshire
Cook, D (Daniel) – Essex
Cooke, B (Ben) – Warwickshire
Cooper, IJ (Ian) – Kent
Cooper, N (Nicholas) – Suffolk
Steven (Copeland) – Merseyside
Cropp, B (Barry) – Lancashire
Crysell, A (Adam) – Northamptonshire
Dabbs, R (Robert) – Dorset
Da Costa, A (Anthony) – Cambridgeshire
D'aguilar, M (Michael) – Staffordshire

Daly, SDJ (Stephen) – Middlesex
Davies, N (Neil) – London
Degnarain, A (Ashvin) – London
Denton, MJ (Michael) – Lancashire
Dermott, P (Philip) – Lancashire
Derrien, M (Mark) – Dorset
Dudley, IA (Ian) – Nottinghamshire
Duncan, M (Mark) – Cheshire
Durie, B (Brian) – Gloucestershire
Dwyer, M (Mark) – West Yorkshire
Eaton, D (Derek) – Gloucestershire
Edwards, M (Marc) – Durham
Eva, M (Matt) – Surrey
Farries, J (John) – Oxfordshire
Fearn, AE (Amy) – Derbyshire
Finch, S (Steven) – Suffolk
Fissenden, I (Ian) – Kent
Fitch-Jackson, C (Carl) – Suffolk
Flynn, J (John) – Oxfordshire
Foley, MJ (Matt) – Hertfordshire
Ford, D (Declan) – Lincolnshire
Fox, A (Andrew) – Warwickshire
Fyvie, G (Graeme) – Tyne & Wear
Ganfield, R (Ron) – Somerset
Garratt, A (Andy) – West Midlands

George, M (Mike) – Norfolk
Gibbons, P (Peter) – Cheshire
Gooch, P (Peter) – Lancashire
Gordon, B (Barry) – County Durham
Graham, P (Paul) – Manchester
Gratton, D (Danny) – Staffordshire
Greenhalgh, N (Nick) – Lancashire
Greenwood, AH (Alf) –
  North Yorkshire
Griffiths, M (Mark) – West Midlands
Grunnill, W (Wayne) –
  East Yorkshire
Halliday, A (Andy) –
  North Yorkshire
Hanley, M (Michael) – Merseyside
Harris, P (Paul) – Kent
Hart, G (Glen) – County Durham
Harty, T (Thomas) – West Midlands
Hatzidakis, C (Constantine) – Kent
Haycock, KW (Ken) –
  South Yorkshire
Hendley, AR (Andy) –
  West Midlands
Hicks, C (Craig) – Surrey
Hilton, G (Gary) – Lancashire
Hobbis, N (Nick) – West Midlands
Hobday, P (Paul) – West Midlands
Hodskinson, P (Paul) – Lancashire
Holmes, A (Adrian) –
  West Yorkshire
Hopkins, AJ (Adam) – Devon
Hopton, N (Nicholas) – Derbyshire
Howick, K (Kevin) – Oxfordshire
Howson, A (Akil) – Leicestershire
Hudson, S (Shaun) – Tyne & Wear
Hulme, R (Richard) – Somerset
Hunt, J (Jonathan) – Merseyside
Husband, C (Christopher) –
  Worcestershire
Hussin, I (Ian) – Merseyside
Hyde, RA (Robert) – Essex
Isherwood, C (Chris) – Lancashire
Johnson, RL (Ryan) – Manchester
Jones, MT (Mark) – Nottinghamshire
Jones, M (Matthew) – Staffordshire
Kane, G (Graham) – East Sussex
Kelly, P (Paul) – Kent
Kendall, R (Richard) – Bedfordshire
Kettlewell, PT (Paul) – Lancashire
Khatib, B (Billy) – County Durham
Kidd, C (Chris) – Oxfordshire
Kirkup, P (Peter) – Northamptonshire
Knapp, SC (Simon) – Bristol
Laver, AA (Andrew) – Hampshire

Law, J (John) – Worcestershire
Leach, D (Daniel) – Oxfordshire
Ledger, S (Scott) – South Yorkshire
Lee, M (Matthew) – West Sussex
Lennard, H (Harry) – East Sussex
Liddle, G (Geoff) – County Durham
Long, S (Simon) – Cornwall
Lugg, N (Nigel) – Surrey
Lymer, C (Colin) – Hampshire
Mcdonough, M (Mick) –
  Northumberland
Mcgrath, M (Matt) – East Yorkshire
Mackay, R (Rob) – Bedfordshire
Mainwaring, J (James) – Lancashire
Markham, DR (Danny) –
  Tyne & Wear
Marks, L (Louis) – Hampshire
Marsden, PR (Paul) – Lancashire
Maskell, G (Garry) – London
Massey-Ellis, R (Rob) –
  West Midlands
Massey-Ellis, S (Sian) –
  West Midlands
Matthews, A (Adam) –
  Gloucestershire
Mattocks, KJ (Kevin) – Lancashire
Meeson, DP (Daniel) – Staffordshire
Mellor, G (Gareth) – West Yorkshire
Mellor, JM (Mark) – Hertfordshire
Merchant, R (Rob) – Staffordshire
Meredith, S (Steven) –
  Nottinghamshire
Metcalfe, RL (Lee) – Lancashire
Moore, A (Anthony) – Manchester
Morris, K (Kevin) – Herefordshire
Muge, G (Gavin) – Bedfordshire
Mulraine, K (Kevin) – Cumbria
Newbold, AM (Andy) –
  Leicestershire
Newhouse, P (Paul) –
  County Durham
Nunn, A (Adam) – Wiltshire
O'brien, J (John) – London
Parry, MJ (Matthew) – Merseyside
Pashley, A (Alix) – Derbyshire
Peart, T (Tony) – North Yorkshire
Perry, M (Marc) – West Midlands
Plane, S (Steven) – Worcestershire
Plowright, DP (David) –
  Nottinghamshire
Pottage, M (Mark) – Dorset
Powell, CI (Chris) – Dorset
Purkiss, S (Sam) – London
Quin, A (Andrew) – Devon

Radford, N (Neil) – Worcestershire
Ramsey, T (Thomas) – Essex
Rashid, L (Lisa) – West Midlands
Rathbone, I (Ian) –
  Northamptonshire
Rees, P (Paul) – Somerset
Robathan, DM (Daniel) –
  Bedfordshire
Roberts, B (Bob) – Lancashire
Rushton, S (Steven) – Staffordshire
Russell, GR (Geoff) –
  Northamptonshire
Russell, M (Mark) – Somerset
Sannerude, A (Adrian) – Suffolk
Scholes, M (Mark) –
  Buckinghamshire
Sharp, N (Neil) – Cleveland
Siddall, I (Iain) – Manchester
Simpson, J (Joe) – Manchester
Slaughter, A (Ashley) – West Sussex
Smallwood, W (William) – Cheshire
Smart, E (Eddie) – West Midlands
Smedley, I (Ian) – Derbyshire
Smith, J (Josh) – Lincolnshire
Smith, M (Michael) – Essex
Smith, N (Nigel) – Derbyshire
Smith, R (Rob) – Hertfordshire
Smith, W (Wade) – Cheshire
Strain, D (Darren) – Cheshire
Street, DR (Duncan) –
  West Yorkshire
Taylor, C (Craig) – West Midlands
Thompson, PI (Paul) – Derbyshire
Tranter, A (Adrian) – Dorset
Treleaven, D (Dean) – West Sussex
Tyas, J (Jason) – West Yorkshire
Venamore, L (Lee) – Kent
Wade, C (Christopher) – Hampshire
Wade, S (Stephen) – East Yorkshire
Ward, C (Chris) – South Yorkshire
Warren, (George) – London
Waters, A (Adrian) – London
Webb, MP (Michael) – Surrey
West, R (Richard) – East Riding
Wigglesworth, RJ (Richard) –
  South Yorkshire
Wild, R (Richard) – Lancashire
Wilkes, M (Matthew) – West
  Midlands
Wilson, J (James) – Cheshire
Wilson, M (Marc) – Cambridgeshire
Wood, T (Tim) – Gloucestershire
Wootton, R (Ricky) – West Yorkshire
Young, A (Alan) – Cambridgeshire

MANAGERS – IN AND OUT 2015–16

JULY 2015
13   Claudio Ranieri appointed manager of Leicester City.

SEPTEMBER 2015
6   Dave Robertson sacked as manager of Peterborough United after winning only one of their first six league games to become the first managerial casualty of the season.
8   Paul Dickov sacked as manager of Doncaster Rovers. Defender Rob Jones takes temporary charge.
12   Darren Kelly sacked as manager of Oldham Athletic.
13   David Dunn, former Blackburn Rovers midfielder, appointed interim manager of Oldham Athletic.
21   Graham Westley appointed manager of Peterborough United.
28   Marinus Dijkhuizen sacked as manager of Brentford after only nine games in charge. Development squad manager Lee Carsley takes temporary charge. Rotherham United and Steve Evans part company with the club and manager 'wished to head in a different direction'. First-team coach Eric Black takes temporary charge.
30   Graham Alexander sacked as manager of Fleetwood Town.

OCTOBER 2015
1   Terry Butcher sacked as manager of Newport County with the club bottom of the Football League.
2   John Sheridan appointed manager of Newport County.
4   Dick Advocaat resigned as manager of Sunderland with the team yet to win after eight games in the Premier League. First-team coach Paul Bracewell and youth team coach Robbie Stockdale take temporary charge. Brendan Rodgers sacked as manager of Liverpool.
6   Steven Pressley appointed manager of Fleetwood Town.
7   David Dunn appointed full-time manager of Oldham Athletic after being in temporary charge.
8   Jurgen Klopp appointed manager of Liverpool.
9   Sam Allardyce appointed manager of Sunderland. Neil Redfearn appointed manager of Rotherham United.
16   Darren Ferguson appointed manager of Doncaster Rovers.
17   Mark Cooper sacked as manager of Swindon Town with chairman Lee Power taking temporary charge.
19   Uwe Rosler sacked as manager of Leeds United. Steve Evans appointed new manager.
24   Guy Luzon sacked as manager of Charlton Athletic. Karel Fraeye takes temporary charge.
25   Tim Sherwood sacked as manager of Aston Villa. Under-21 manager Kevin McDonald takes temporary charge.
26   Russ Wilcox sacked as manager of York City. First-team coach Richard Cresswell takes temporary charge.

NOVEMBER 2015
2   Remi Garde appointed manager of Aston Villa. Richard Money sacked as manager of Cambridge United. Assistant manager Joe Dunne takes temporary charge.
3   Martin Ling appointed manager of Swindon Town.
4   Chris Ramsey sacked as manager of Queens Park Rangers. Former manager Neil Warnock takes temporary charge. Chris Powell sacked as manager of Huddersfield Town. Academy manager Mark Lillis takes temporary charge. Jackie McNamara appointed manager of York City.
5   David Wagner appointed manager of Huddersfield Town.
8   Kit Symons sacked as manager of Fulham. First-team coach Peter Grant takes temporary charge.
10   Gary Bower sacked as manager of Blackburn Rovers.
12   Shaun Derry appointed manager of Cambridge United.
15   Paul Lambert appointed manager of Blackburn Rovers.
26   Tony Humes leaves as manager of Colchester United by mutual consent. Assistant manager Richard Hall and Under-21 manager John McGreal take temporary charge.
28   Dean Saunders sacked as manager of Chesterfield. Academy manager Mark Smith takes temporary charge.
30   Dean Smith leaves as manager of Walsall to take over as manager of Brentford. John Ward, Jon Whitney and Neil Cutler take temporary charge.

DECEMBER 2015
1   Paul Sturrock sacked as manager of Yeovil Town. Darren Way takes temporary charge.
4   Steve Clark sacked as manager of Reading. Under-21 manager Martin Kuhl takes temporary charge. Jimmy Floyd Hasselbaink leaves Burton Albion to take over as manager of Queens Park Rangers.
7   Nigel Clough appointed manager of Burton Albion.
9   Garry Monk sacked as manager of Swansea City. First-team coach Alan Curtis takes temporary charge.
17   Jose Mourinho sacked as manager of Chelsea. Assistant First-team coach Steve Holland takes temporary charge. John Still sacked as manager of Luton Town. Academy manager Andy Awford takes temporary charge. Brian McDermott appointed manager of Reading.
18   Sean O'Driscoll appointed manager of Walsall.
19   Gus Hiddink appointed Chelsea manager until the end of the season.
21   Kevin Keen appointed manager of Colchester United. Wayne Burnett sacked as manager of Dagenham & Redbridge. Coaches Darren Currie and Warren Hackett take temporary charge.
24   Danny Wilson appointed manager of Chesterfield.
27   Slavisa Jokanovic appointed manager of Fulham.
29   Martin Ling resigns as manager of Swindon Town due to health reasons. First-team coach Luke Williams takes temporary charge. Ricardo Moniz sacked as manager of Notts County. Academy manager Mick Halsall and Under-21 coach Richard Dryden take temporary charge.
31   Darren Way appointed permanent manager of Yeovil Town after being in temporary charge. John Still appointed manager of Dagenham & Redbridge.

JANUARY 2016
6   Nathan Jones appointed manager of Luton Town.
7   Alan Curtis appointed manager of Swansea City until the end of the season. He had been in temporary charge since the sacking of Garry Monk.
10   Jamie Fullarton appointed manager of Notts County.
12   David Dunn sacked as manager of Oldham Athletic.

13	John Sheridan leaves as manager of Newport County to become manager at Oldham Athletic.
14	Steve Cotterill sacked as manager of Bristol City. Assistant manager John Pemberton and Under-21 manager Wade Elliott take temporary charge. Jose Riga appointed manager of Charlton Athletic.
15	Warren Feeney appointed manager of Newport County.
18	Francesco Guidolin appointed manager of Swansea City to take over from Alan Curtis. Ian Hendon sacked as manager of Leyton Orient. Mark Robins sacked as manager of Scunthorpe United. Coaches Andy Dawson and Nick Daws take temporary charge.
21	Kevin Nolan appointed player-manager of Leyton Orient. Luke Williams appointed manager of Swindon Town after being in temporary charge.

FEBRUARY 2016

1	Teddy Sheringham sacked as manager of Stevenage. First-team coach Darren Sarll takes temporary charge.
6	Lee Johnson leaves as manager of Barnsley to take charge at Bristol City. Assistant manager Tommy Wright and coach Paul Heckingbottom take temporary charge of Barnsley.
8	Paul Clement sacked as manager of Derby County. Academy director Darren Wassall takes charge until the end of the season. Neil Redfearn sacked as manager of Rotherham United. Assistant manager Nicky Eaden takes temporary charge and will be assisted by Paul Warne and Andy Dibble.
10	Ronnie Moore sacked as manager of Hartlepool United. Craig Hignett appointed as his replacement.
11	Neil Warnock appointed manager of Rotherham United.
22	Nick Daws appointed manager of Scunthorpe United after being in temporary charge.

MARCH 2016

6	Sean O'Driscoll sacked as manager of Walsall. Jon Witney takes temporary charge.
11	Steve McClaren sacked as manager of Newcastle United. Rafael Benitez appointed as his replacement.
13	Dougie Freedman sacked as manager of Nottingham Forest. First-team coach Paul Williams takes charge until the end of the season.
15	Neil Lennon leaves as manager of Bolton Wanderers by mutual consent. Academy manager Jimmy Phillips takes temporary charge.
19	Jamie Fullarton sacked as manager of Notts County after only 69 days in charge.
20	Mark Cooper appointed manager of Notts County.
22	Graham Alexander appointed manager of Scunthorpe United and replaces Nick Daws who becomes his assistant.
29	Remi Garde leaves as manager of Aston Villa by mutual consent. First-team coach Eric Black takes temporary charge.

APRIL 2016

12	Kevin Nolan relieved of his duties as manager of Leyton Orient. Nolan remains as an Orient player. Andy Hessenthaler appointed termporary manager.
23	Graham Westley sacked as manager of Peterborough United. Coach Grant McCann takes charge until the end of the season.
25	Mark Yates sacked as manager of Crawley Town.
26	Kevin Keen sacked as manager of Colchester United. David Wright takes charge until the end of the season.
27	Dermot Drummy appointed manager of Crawley Town.

MAY 2016

4	John McGreal appointed manager of Colchester United.
6	Russell Slade to move from manager of Cardiff City to a new role as Head of Football at the end of the season. Jose Riga resigns as manager of Charlton Athletic.
7	Mark Cooper resigns as manager of Notts County.
8	Darren Sarll appointed manager of Stevenage after being in temporary charge.
12	Nigel Adkins sacked as manager of Sheffield United. Chris Wilder leaves Northampton Town to become new manager. Roberto Martinez sacked as manager of Everton.
13	Quique Sanchez Flores announces that he will leave as manager of Watford at the end of the season.
16	Grant McCann appointed manager of Peterborough United after being in temporary charge.
18	Paul Trollope appointed manager of Cardiff City. Neil McDonald sacked as manager of Blackpool.
19	Rob Page leaves Port Vale and is appointed manager of Northampton Town.
21	Walter Mazzarri will become Watford manager on 1 July.
23	Louis van Gaal sacked as manager of Manchester United.
27	Jose Mourinho appointed manager of Manchester United. Brian McDermott sacked as manager of Reading. John Sheridan leaves as manager of Oldham Athletic to become manager of Notts County. Nigel Pearson appointed manager of Derby County and replaces Darren Wassell who had been in charge until the end of the season.
31	Steve Evans sacked as manager of Leeds United.

JUNE 2016

1	Alan Stubbs appointed manager of Rotherham United. Gary Bowyer appointed manager of Blackpool.
2	Roberto Di Matteo appointed manager of Aston Villa. Garry Monk appointed manager of Leeds United. Owen Coyle appointed manager of Blackburn Rovers. Jon Whitney confirmed as manager of Walsall after being in temporary charge.
3	Andy Hessethaler confirmed as manager of Leyton Orient after being in temporary charge.
6	Russell Slade appointed as manager of Charlton Athletic.
10	Phil Parkinson leaves Bradford City to become manager of Bolton Wanderers.
13	Jaap Stam appointed manager of Reading.
14	Ronald Koeman leaves Southampton to be appointed manager of Everton.
15	Paul Heckingbottom appointed manager of Barnsley after being in temporary charge.
20	Bruno Ribeiro appointed manager of Port Vale. Stuart McCall appointed manager of Bradford City.
27	Philippe Montanier appointed manager of Nottingham Forest.
30	Claude Puel appointed manager of Southampton.

JULY 2016

9	Stephen Robinson appointed manager of Oldham Athletic.

TRANSFERS 2015–16

JUNE 2015	From	To	Fee in £
18 Ajayi, Semi	Arsenal	Cardiff C	Free
8 Alessandra, Lewis	Plymouth Arg	Rochdale	Free
23 Archer, Jordan	Tottenham H	Millwall	Free
29 Arnason, Kari	Rotherham U	Malmo	Undisclosed
4 Assenso, Isaac	Leeds U	Scunthorpe U	Free
4 Atkinson, David	Middlesbrough	Carlisle U	Free
29 Ba, El Hadji	Sunderland	Charlton Ath	Undisclosed
19 Baird, Chris	WBA	Derby Co	Free
30 Balanta, Angelo	Bristol R	Carlisle U	Free
30 Banton, Jason	Plymouth Arg	Wycombe W	Free
24 Barton, Adam	Coventry C	Portsmouth	Free
5 Beardsley, Chris	Stevenage	Mansfield T	Free
8 Beckford, Jermaine	Bolton W	Preston NE	Free
8 Bent, Darren	Aston Villa	Derby Co	Free
23 Berrett, James	Yeovil T	York C	Free
15 Berry, Luke	Barnsley	Cambridge U	Undisclosed
12 Bogdan, Adam	Bolton W	Liverpool	Free
2 Boyata, Dedryck	Manchester C	Celtic	£1.5m
22 Briggs, Matthew	Millwall	Colchester U	Free
2 Brindley, Richard	Rotherham U	Colchester U	Free
24 Brown, Junior	Mansfield T	Shrewsbury T	Free
25 Burgess, Christian	Peterborough U	Portsmouth	Undisclosed
15 Butcher, Calum	Dundee U	Burton Alb	Free
25 Buxton, Lewis	Sheffield W	Rotherham U	Free
26 Cairney, Tom	Blackburn R	Fulham	Undisclosed
25 Carr, Danny	Huddersfield T	Cambridge U	Free
12 Carroll, Jake	Huddersfield T	Hartlepool U	Free
12 Carson, Scott	Wigan Ath	Derby Co	Undisclosed
15 Carson, Trevor	Cheltenham T	Hartlepool U	Undisclosed
23 Cassidy, Jake	Wolverhampton W	Oldham Ath	Free
29 Cech, Petr	Chelsea	Arsenal	£10m
19 Charles, Darius	Stevenage	Burton Alb	Free
30 Church, Simon	Charlton Ath	Milton Keynes D	Free
2 Clarke, Leon	Wolverhampton W	Bury	Free
1 Clarke, Peter	Blackpool	Bury	Free
5 Cleverley, Tom	Manchester U	Everton	Free
9 Clohessy, Sean	Colchester U	Leyton Orient	Free
8 Collins, Lee	Northampton T	Mansfield T	Free
17 Compton, Jack	Hartlepool U	Yeovil T	Free
2 Corr, Barry	Southend U	Cambridge U	Free
30 Cropper, Cody	Southampton	Milton Keynes D	Free
30 Cullen, Mark	Luton T	Blackpool	£180,000
10 Dagnall, Chris	Leyton Orient	Kerala Blasters	Free
30 Daniels, Donervon	WBA	Wigan Ath	Free
26 Davidson, Jason	WBA	Huddersfield T	Free
30 Davies, Andrew	Bradford C	Ross Co	Free
30 Davies, Steven	Blackpool	Bradford C	Free
23 Dembele, Bira	Stevenage	Barnet	Free
17 Dolan, Matt	Bradford C	Yeovil T	Free
8 Doyle, Colin	Birmingham C	Blackpool	Free
6 Ebanks-Blake, Sylvan	Preston NE	Chesterfield	Free
23 Egbo, Mandela	Crystal Palace	Borussia Moenchengladbach	Undisclosed
12 Emmanuel-Thomas, Jay	Bristol C	QPR	Free
10 Erwin, Lee	Motherwell	Leeds U	Undisclosed
29 Etheridge, Ross	Derby Co	Accrington S	Free
23 Fenelon, Shamir	Brighton & HA	Crawley T	Free
27 Fletcher, Wes	York C	Motherwell	Free
23 Flinders, Scott	Hartlepool U	York C	Free
18 Foley, Sam	Yeovil T	Port Vale	Free
18 Franks, Jonathan	Hartlepool U	Ross Co	Free
16 Gallagher, Paul	Leicester C	Preston NE	Free
15 Garmston, Bradley	WBA	Gillingham	Free
22 Gibbons, Jordan	QPR	Yeovil T	Free
20 Gomez, Joe	Charlton Ath	Liverpool	£3.5m
19 Green, George	Everton	Oldham Ath	Free
24 Herron, John	Celtic	Blackpool	Free
24 Hery, Bastien	Rochdale	Carlisle U	Free
15 Holden, Darren	Hartlepool U	Ross Co	Free
24 Holmes, Danny	Tranmere R	Newport Co	Free
26 Hopper, Tom	Leicester C	Scunthorpe U	Free
9 Horton, Charlie	Cardiff C	Leeds U	Free
11 Hoyte, Gavin	Gillingham	Barnet	Free
22 Hunt, Nicky	Accrington S	Mansfield T	Free
24 Huth, Robert	Stoke C	Leicester C	Undisclosed
25 Ibehre, Jabo	Colchester U	Carlisle U	Free
8 Ings, Danny	Burnley	Liverpool	Undisclosed
23 Jeffers, Shaun	Newport Co	Yeovil T	Free
30 Jennings, Dale	Barnsley	Milton Keynes D	Free
24 Jensen, Brian	Crawley T	Mansfield T	Free
29 Jervis, Jake	Ross Co	Plymouth Arg	Free

19 Kakuta, Gael	Chelsea	Sevilla	Undisclosed
27 Kee, Billy	Scunthorpe U	Accrington S	Free
15 Kelly, Sam	Norwich C	Port Vale	Free
22 Kiernan, Rob	Wigan Ath	Rangers	Undisclosed
30 Laing, Louis	Nottingham F	Motherwell	Free
19 Laird, Marc	Tranmere R	Yeovil T	Free
11 Laird, Scott	Preston NE	Scunthorpe U	Free
27 Legzdins, Adam	Leyton Orient	Birmingham C	Free
2 Lelan, Josh	Derby Co	Northampton T	Free
1 Lepoint, Christophe	Charlton Ath	Zulte-Waregem	Undisclosed
12 Letheren, Kyle	Dundee	Blackpool	Free
30 Lines, Chris	Port Vale	Bristol R	Undisclosed
19 Lonergan, Andy	Bolton W	Fulham	Free
22 Lowton, Matthew	Aston Villa	Burnley	Undisclosed
30 MacKenzie, Gary	Blackpool	Doncaster R	Free
16 Mackie, Jamie	Nottingham F	QPR	Free
23 Martin, Joe	Gillingham	Millwall	Free
12 Mattock, Joe	Sheffield W	Rotherham U	Free
30 Mawson, Alfie	Brentford	Barnsley	Free
19 McCallum, Paul	West Ham U	Leyton Orient	Free
22 McClean, James	Wigan Ath	WBA	£1.5m
25 McConville, Sean	Chester	Accrington S	Undisclosed
2 McGeehan, Cameron	Norwich C	Luton T	Undisclosed
24 McGurk, Adam	Burton Alb	Portsmouth	Free
2 McNulty, Jim	Bury	Rochdale	Free
30 McQueen, Alexander	Tottenham H	Carlisle U	Free
29 McQuoid, Josh	Bournemouth	Luton T	Free
23 Meades, Jon	Oxford U	Wimbledon	Free
30 Mellis, Jacob	Blackpool	Bury	Free
4 Milner, James	Manchester C	Liverpool	Free
16 Milsom, Rob	Rotherham U	Notts Co	Free
26 Mings, Tyrone	Ipswich T	Bournemouth	Undisclosed
9 Moore, Sammy	AFC Wimbledon	Leyton Orient	Free
4 Morgan, Adam	Yeovil T	Accrington S	Free
12 Morgan, Craig	Rotherham U	Wigan Ath	Free
22 Mulumbu, Youssouf	WBA	Norwich C	Free
17 Murdoch, Stewart	Fleetwood T	Ross Co	Free
8 Murphy, Peter	Wycombe W	Morecambe	Free
29 Naylor, Tom	Derby Co	Burton Alb	Free
30 Nosworthy, Nyron	Blackpool	Dagenham & R	Free
11 Nutall, Joe	Manchester C	Aberdeen	Free
22 O'Donnell, Stephen	Partick Thistle	Luton T	Free
1 Ogogo, Abu	Dagenham & R	Shrewsbury T	Free
2 Olejnik, Bobby	Peterborough U	Exeter C	Free
12 Omozusi, Elliot	Leyton Orient	Cambridge U	Free
29 Paulinho	Tottenham H	Guangzhou Evergrande	£9.9m
27 Paynter, Billy	Carlisle U	Hartlepool U	Free
8 Pearce, Alex	Reading	Derby Co	Free
26 Pitman, Brett	Bournemouth	Ipswich T	Undisclosed
9 Pope, Tom	Port Vale	Bury	Free
11 Potts, Brad	Carlisle U	Blackpool	Undisclosed
9 Pringle, Ben	Rotherham U	Fulham	Free
30 Quinn, Stephen	Hull C	Reading	Free
5 Reilly, Callum	Birmingham C	Burton Alb	Free
17 Richards, Micah	Manchester C	Aston Villa	Free
30 Riera, Oriol	Wigan Ath	Deportivo La Coruna	Undisclosed
17 Roberts, Gary	Chesterfield	Portsmouth	Undisclosed
30 Robertson, Chris	Port Vale	Ross Co	Free
15 Robertson, Clark	Aberdeen	Blackpool	Free
23 Rosenior, Liam	Hull C	Brighton & HA	Free
30 Rowe, Danny	Rotherham U	Wycombe W	Free
17 Ryan, Jimmy	Chesterfield	Fleetwood T	Free
25 Sawyer, Gary	Leyton Orient	Plymouth Arg	Free
24 Schumacher, Steven	Fleetwood T	Stevenage	Free
15 Sellers, Ryan	Bolton W	Wycombe W	Free
2 Sharpe, Rhys	Derby Co	Notts Co	Free
24 Shearer, Scott	Crewe Alex	Mansfield T	Free
12 Slocombe, Sam	Scunthorpe U	Oxford U	Free
26 Smith, Adam	Leicester C	Northampton T	Free
24 Sowunmi, Omar	Ipswich T	Yeovil T	Free
15 Stevens, Enda	Aston Villa	Portsmouth	Free
26 Stewart, Anthony	Crewe Alex	Wycombe W	Free
15 Streete, Remie	Newcastle U	Port Vale	Free
10 Stuckmann, Thorsten	Preston NE	Doncaster R	Free
11 Swan, George	Wolverhampton W	York C	Free
22 Sylla, Yacouba	Aston Villa	Stade Rennais	Undisclosed
12 Taarabt, Adel	QPR	Benfica	Free
15 Theophile-Catherine, Kevin	Cardiff C	Saint-Etienne	Undisclosed
3 Thomas, Nathan	Motherwell	Mansfield T	Free
15 Thompson, Garry	Notts Co	Wycombe W	Free
16 Tootle, Matt	Crewe Alex	Shrewsbury T	Free
19 Tozer, Ben	Northampton T	Yeovil T	Free
19 Trippier, Kieran	Burnley	Tottenham H	Undisclosed
19 Turgott, Blair	Coventry C	Leyton Orient	Free
18 Walton, Simon	Stevenage	Crawley T	Free
5 Watkins, Marley	Inverness CT	Barnsley	Free

18 Weimann, Andreas	Aston Villa	Derby Co	Undisclosed
12 Westcarr, Craig	Portsmouth	Mansfield T	Free
6 Whalley, Shaun	Luton T	Shrewsbury T	Free
10 White, Aidy	Leeds U	Rotherham U	Free
23 Whitehead, Dean	Middlesbrough	Huddersfield T	Free
8 Wildig, Aaron	Shrewsbury T	Morecambe	Free
19 Williams, Andy	Swindon T	Doncaster R	Free
11 Williams, Ryan	Morecambe	Brentford	Free
15 Williamson, Ben	Port Vale	Gillingham	Free
8 Worley, Harry	Stevenage	Hartlepool U	Free
30 Wylde, Gregg	St Mirren	Plymouth Arg	Free
23 Yorwerth, Josh	Cardiff C	Ipswich T	Free

JULY 2015

29 Agyei, Dan	AFC Wimbledon	Burnley	Undisclosed
14 Al-Habsi, Ali	Wigan Ath	Reading	Free
28 Allen, Iffy	Barnet	Yeovil T	Free
1 Amoo, David	Carlisle U	Partick Thistle	Free
1 Amos, Ben	Manchester U	Bolton W	Free
20 Angol, Lee	Luton T	Peterborough U	Undisclosed
8 Ashton, Jon	Stevenage	Crawley T	Free
20 Atkinson, Wesley	WBA	Notts Co	Free
6 Baptiste, Alex	Bolton W	Middlesbrough	Undisclosed
1 Barcham, Andy	Portsmouth	AFC Wimbledon	Free
28 Barnard, Lee	Southend U	Crawley T	Free
9 Batt, Shaun	Leyton Orient	Barnet	Free
4 Beasant, Sam	Stevenage	Cambridge U	Free
24 Beck, Mark	Carlisle U	Yeovil T	Free
13 Begovic, Asmir	Stoke C	Chelsea	£8m
22 Benteke, Christian	Aston Villa	Liverpool	£32.5m
6 Bingham, Billy	Dagenham & R	Crewe Alex	Free
14 Bird, Ryan	Cambridge U	Yeovil T	Free
4 Bond, Jonathan	Watford	Reading	Undisclosed
2 Bong, Gaetan	Wigan Ath	Brighton & HA	Free
29 Brady, Robbie	Hull C	Norwich C	£7m
3 Brown, Troy	Cheltenham T	Exeter	Free
9 Bunn, Mark	Norwich C	Aston Villa	Free
6 Burke, Graham	Aston Villa	Notts Co	Free
3 Burrows, Jamie	Rangers	Yeovil T	Free
6 Campbell, Adam	Newcastle U	Notts Co	Free
6 Capoue, Etienne	Tottenham H	Watford	Undisclosed
3 Carey, Graham	Ross Co	Plymouth Arg	Free
23 Ceballos, Cristian	Tottenham H	Charlton Ath	Free
6 Chaplow, Richard	Millwall	Doncaster R	Free
29 Chester, James	Hull C	WBA	£8m
30 Chiriches, Vlad	Tottenham H	Napoli	Undisclosed
27 Cisak, Alex	Burnley	Leyton Orient	Undisclosed
28 Clarke, Nathan	Leyton Orient	Bradford C	Free
2 Clarke, Ryan	Oxford U	Northampton T	Free
27 Clucas, Sam	Chesterfield	Hull C	£1.3m
1 Clyne, Nathaniel	Southampton	Liverpool	£12.5m
3 Coady, Conor	Huddersfield T	Wolverhampton W	£2m
1 Coates, Sebastian	Liverpool	Sunderland	Undisclosed
3 Collins, Danny	Nottingham F	Rotherham U	Free
10 Cornell, David	Swansea C	Oldham Ath	Free
4 Craig, Tony	Brentford	Millwall	Free
22 Cranie, Martin	Barnsley	Huddersfield T	Free
27 Cunningham, Greg	Bristol C	Preston NE	Undisclosed
30 Darikwa, Tendayi	Chesterfield	Burnley	Undisclosed
7 Davies, Craig	Bolton W	Wigan Ath	Free
6 De Silva, Kyle	Crystal Palace	Notts Co	Free
28 Deacon, Roarie	Stevenage	Crawley T	Free
22 Della-Verde, Lyle	Fulham	Fleetwood T	Free
2 Delort, Andy	Wigan Ath	Caen	Undisclosed
17 Delph, Fabian	Aston Villa	Manchester C	£8m
10 Dempsey, Kyle	Carlisle U	Huddersfield T	Undisclosed
13 Denton, Peter	Rotherham U	Hartlepool U	Free
28 Diaby, Abou	Arsenal	Marseille	Free
1 Dickson, Ryan	Crawley T	Yeovil T	Undisclosed
1 Distin, Sylvain	Everton	Bournemouth	Free
13 Donaldson, Coll	QPR	Dundee U	Free
16 Downing, Stewart	West Ham U	Middlesbrough	£5.5m
6 Doyle, Michael	Sheffield U	Portsmouth	Free
27 Drogba, Didier	Chelsea	Montreal Impact	Free
30 Dunn, David	Blackburn R	Oldham Ath	Free
27 Dunne, Alan	Millwall	Leyton Orient	Free
6 Edwards, Joe	Yeovil T	Colchester U	Free
2 Ehmer, Max	QPR	Gillingham	Free
2 Elliott, Tom	Cambridge U	AFC Wimbledon	Free
3 Elokobi, George	Oldham Ath	Colchester U	Free
2 Etheridge, Neil	Charlton Ath	Walsall	Free
28 Evans, Gareth	Fleetwood T	Portsmouth	Free
17 Fogden, Wes	Portsmouth	Yeovil T	Free
14 Fox, David	Colchester U	Crewe Alex	Free
17 Franks, Fraser	Luton T	Stevenage	Free
31 Gestede, Rudy	Blackburn R	Aston Villa	Undisclosed

10 Given, Shay	Aston Villa	Stoke C	Free
22 Grant, Bobby	Blackpool	Fleetwood T	Free
4 Green, Danny	Milton Keynes D	Luton T	Free
14 Grigg, Will	Brentford	Wigan Ath	Undisclosed
11 Guidetti, John	Manchester C	Celta Vigo	Free
6 Halford, Greg	Nottingham F	Rotherham U	Free
31 Hare, Taron	Scunthorpe U	York C	Free
24 Henderson, Darius	Leyton Orient	Scunthorpe U	Free
17 Hiwula, Jordy	Manchester C	Huddersfield T	Undisclosed
1 Holtby, Lewis	Tottenham H	Hamburg	Undisclosed
30 Hoskins, Will	Oxford U	Exeter C	Free
13 Hughes, Aaron	Brighton & HA	Melbourne C	Free
15 Hughes, Jeff	Fleetwood T	Cambridge U	Free
3 Ince, Thomas	Hull C	Derby Co	£4.75m
27 Jacobs, Michael	Wolverhampton W	Wigan Ath	Free
21 James, Reece	Manchester U	Wigan Ath	Undisclosed
1 Janko, Saidy	Manchester U	Celtic	£200,000
12 Johnson, Glen	Liverpool	Stoke C	Free
31 Jovetic, Stevan	Manchester C	Inter Milan	Undisclosed
16 Kaboul, Younes	Tottenham H	Sunderland	Undisclosed
16 Kennedy, Kieran	Leicester C	Motherwell	Free
1 Kuszczak, Tomasz	Wolverhampton W	Birmingham C	Free
22 Lacey, Alex	Luton T	Yeovil T	Free
16 Lalkovic, Milan	Barnsley	Walsall	Free
31 Lambert, Rickie	Liverpool	WBA	Undisclosed
2 Ledesma, Emmanuel	Middlesbrough	Rotherham U	Free
20 Leitch-Smith, AJ	Yeovil T	Port Vale	Free
1 Loach, Scott	Rotherham U	Notts Co	Free
28 Long, Chris	Everton	Burnley	Undisclosed
28 Luis, Filipe	Chelsea	Atletico Madrid	Undisclosed
12 Lussey, Jordan	Liverpool	Bolton W	Free
1 Madine, Gary	Sheffield W	Bolton W	Free
24 Maguire, Chris	Sheffield W	Rotherham U	Free
14 Marshall, Mark	Port Vale	Bradford C	Free
30 McAlister, Jim	Dundee	Blackpool	Free
13 McBurnie, Ollie	Bradford C	Swansea C	Undisclosed
23 McCarthy, Alex	QPR	Crystal Palace	Undisclosed
16 McClure, Matt	Wycombe W	Dagenham & R	Free
1 McCourt, Paddy	Brighton & HA	Luton T	Free
10 McEachran, Josh	Chelsea	Brentford	£750,000
16 McGugan, Lewis	Watford	Sheffield W	Undisclosed
3 McMahon, Tony	Blackpool	Bradford C	Free
2 McShane, Paul	Hull C	Reading	Free
1 Mills, Matt	Bolton W	Nottingham F	Free
2 Mooney, David	Leyton Orient	Southend U	Free
1 Mooney, Jason	York C	Accrington S	Free
1 Morris, Josh	Blackburn R	Bradford C	Free
6 Nani	Manchester U	Fenerbahce	£4.25m
10 Ness, Jamie	Stoke C	Scunthorpe U	Free
17 Newton, Conor	Rotherham U	Cambridge U	Free
30 N'Guessan, Dany	Port Vale	Doncaster R	Free
6 Nolan, Eddie	Scunthorpe U	York C	Free
9 Nzonzi, Steven	Stoke C	Sevilla	£7m
9 O'Brien, Mark	Derby Co	Luton T	Free
18 O'Connor, Anthony	Plymouth Arg	Burton Alb	Undisclosed
9 Odelusi, Sanmi	Bolton W	Wigan Ath	Undisclosed
7 O'Hara, Jamie	Blackpool	Fulham	Free
1 Okuonghae, Magnus	Colchester U	Luton T	Free
25 O'Nien, Luke	Watford	Wycombe W	Free
2 Ormonde-Ottewill, Brandon	Arsenal	Swindon T	Free
6 Oyenuga, Kudus	Dundee U	Hartlepool U	Free
6 Palmer, Ollie	Mansfield T	Leyton Orient	Undisclosed
23 Parish, Elliot	Blackpool	Colchester U	Free
16 Passley, Josh	Fulham	Dagenham & R	Free
10 Pearce, Krystian	Torquay U	Mansfield T	Free
31 Perch, James	Wigan Ath	QPR	Undisclosed
4 Podolski, Lukas	Arsenal	Galatasaray	£1.8m
29 Preston, Callum	Birmingham C	Crawley T	Free
10 Price, Lewis	Crystal Palace	Sheffield W	Free
13 Pugh, Danny	Coventry C	Bury	Free
10 Redshaw, Jack	Morecambe	Blackpool	Undisclosed
28 Richards, Dave	Bristol C	Crewe Alex	Free
2 Richards, Jazz	Swansea C	Fulham	Undisclosed
6 Ricketts, Sam	Wolverhampton W	Coventry C	Free
19 Roberts, Patrick	Fulham	Manchester C	Undisclosed
7 Ruiz, Bryan	Fulham	Sporting Lisbon	Undisclosed
20 Sadlier, Kieran	St Mirren	Peterborough U	Free
13 Schneiderlin, Morgan	Southampton	Manchester U	£25m
23 Shackell, Jason	Burnley	Derby Co	Undisclosed
25 Sharp, Billy	Leeds U	Sheffield U	Undisclosed
6 Simpson, Josh	Crawley T	Plymouth Arg	Free
21 Stambouli, Benjamin	Tottenham H	Paris Saint-Germain	£6m
2 Stead, Jon	Huddersfield T	Notts Co	Free
14 Sterling, Raheem	Liverpool	Manchester C	£44m (rising to £49m)
14 Taylor, Lyle	Scunthorpe U	AFC Wimbledon	Undisclosed
6 Taylor, Matt	Cheltenham T	Newport Co	Free

27 Taylor, Ryan	Newcastle U	Hull C	Free
20 Taylor-Sinclair, Aaron	Wigan Ath	Doncaster R	Free
31 Thompson, Joe	Bury	Carlisle U	Free
3 Thorpe, Tom	Manchester U	Rotherham U	Free
13 Traore, Drissa	Notts Co	Swindon T	Free
15 Turnbull, Ross	Barnsley	Leeds U	Free
30 Upson, Matthew	Leicester C	Milton Keynes D	Free
14 van Persie, Robin	Manchester U	Fenerbahce	Undisclosed
8 Vincelot, Romain	Leyton Orient	Coventry C	Undisclosed
10 Wallace, Ross	Burnley	Sheffield W	Free
2 Ward, Jamie	Derby Co	Nottingham F	Free
2 Williams, Luke	Middlesbrough	Scunthorpe U	Free
26 Williams, Ryan	Fulham	Barnsley	Undisclosed
1 Wood, Chris	Leicester C	Leeds U	Undisclosed
14 Woolford, Martyn	Millwall	Sheffield U	Free
3 Wordsworth, Anthony	Ipswich T	Southend U	Free
27 Wright-Phillips, Shaun	QPR	New York Red Bulls	Free

AUGUST 2015

21 Abeid, Mehdi	Newcastle U	Panathinaikos	Undisclosed
11 Akpan, Hope	Reading	Blackburn R	Free
6 Ambrose, Darren	Ipswich T	Colchester U	Free
1 Anderson, Paul	Ipswich T	Bradford C	Free
31 Angel Pozo, Jose	Manchester C	Almeria	Undisclosed
31 Bannan, Barry	Crystal Palace	Sheffield W	Undisclosed
10 Barry, Bradley	Brighton & HA	Swindon T	Free
27 Barton, Joey	QPR	Burnley	Free
11 Battocchio, Cristian	Watford	Brest	Undisclosed
17 Biabi, Botti	Falkirk	Swansea C	Undisclosed
1 Bodin, Billy	Northampton T	Bristol R	Free
31 Borini, Fabio	Liverpool	Sunderland	£10m
5 Boyce, Emmerson	Wigan Ath	Blackpool	Free
6 Cairns, Alex	Leeds U	Chesterfield	Free
7 Cambiasso, Esteban	Leicester C	Olympiacos	Free
3 Coke, Giles	Sheffield W	Ipswich T	Free
28 Cole, Devante	Manchester C	Bradford C	Free
3 Corry, Paul	Sheffield W	Northampton T	Free
4 Dallas, Stuart	Brentford	Leeds U	Undisclosed
6 Davies, Ben	Sheffield U	Portsmouth	Free
6 Delfouneso, Nathan	Blackpool	Blackburn R	Free
6 Di Maria, Angel	Manchester U	Paris Saint-Germain	£44.3m
5 Dobbie, Stephen	Crystal Palace	Bolton W	Free
4 Douglas, Jonathan	Brentford	Ipswich T	Free
21 Eisfeld, Thomas	Fulham	Vfl Bochum	Undisclosed
29 Evans, Jonny	Manchester U	WBA	Undisclosed
6 Ferdinand, Kane	Peterborough U	Dagenham & R	Free
29 Fieri, Fernando	Watford	Sheffield W	Undisclosed
25 Flanagan, Tom	Milton Keynes D	Burton Alb	Free
6 Fredericks, Ryan	Tottenham H	Bristol C	Undisclosed
31 Fredericks, Ryan	Bristol C	Fulham	Undisclosed
27 Garvan, Owen	Crystal Palace	Colchester U	Free
10 Ginnelly, Josh	Shrewsbury T	Burnley	Undisclosed
6 Gobern, Oscar	Huddersfield T	QPR	Free
19 Goldson, Connor	Shrewsbury T	Brighton & HA	Free
21 Grant, Joel	Yeovil T	Exeter	Free
21 Gray, Andre	Brentford	Burnley	£9m
31 Guerra, Javi	Cardiff C	Rayo Vallecano	Undisclosed
6 Gunning, Gavin	Birmingham C	Oldham Ath	Free
5 Guthrie, Danny	Reading	Blackburn R	Free
7 Hall, Grant	Tottenham H	QPR	Undisclosed
6 Hendrie, Luke	Derby Co	Burnley	Free
31 Hernandez, Javier	Manchester U	Bayer Leverkusen	£7.3m
4 Hewitt, Elliott	Ipswich T	Notts Co	Free
13 Holgate, Mason	Barnsley	Everton	Undisclosed
1 Hoskins, Sam	Yeovil T	Northampton T	Free
1 Hunt, Noel	Ipswich T	Southend	Free
31 Ideye, Brown	WBA	Olympiacos	Undisclosed
11 Jaaskelainen, Jussi	West Ham U	Wigan Ath	Free
17 Jones, Brad	Liverpool	Bradford C	Free
1 Kean, Jake	Blackburn R	Norwich C	Free
31 Kemen, Olivier	Newcastle U	Lyon	£550,000
12 Kirkland, Chris	Sheffield W	Preston NE	Free
21 Lee, Olly	Birmingham C	Luton T	Free
6 Leigh, Greg	Manchester C	Bradford C	Free
31 Lindegaard, Anders	Manchester U	WBA	Free
28 Lopes, Marcos	Manchester C	Monaco	Undisclosed
13 Lundstram, John	Everton	Oxford U	Free
1 Mackail-Smith, Craig	Brighton & HA	Luton T	Free
31 Maiga, Modibo	West Ham U	Al Nassr	Undisclosed
16 Martinez, Angel	Millwall	Chesterfield	Free
31 Mayuka, Emmanuel	Southampton	Metz	Undisclosed
6 Mbulu, Christian	Brentwood	Millwall	Free
7 McCombe, Jamie	Doncaster R	Stevenage	Free
4 McGinn, Stephen	Dundee	Wycombe W	Free
28 McLaughlin, Stephen	Nottingham F	Southend	Undisclosed
19 Mclean, Aaron	Bradford C	Barnet	Free

22 McLeod, Izale	Crawley T	Notts Co	Undisclosed
4 McNaughton, Kevin	Cardiff C	Wigan Ath	Free
27 Mendez-Laing, Nathaniel	Peterborough U	Rochdale	Free
21 Mesca	Fulham	AEL Limassol	Undisclosed
5 Miller, Shaun	Coventry C	Morecambe	Free
4 Morison, Steve	Leeds U	Millwall	Undisclosed
8 Murphy, Brian	QPR	Portsmouth	Free
14 Murphy, Jamie	Sheffield U	Brighton & HA	Undisclosed
10 N'Doye, Dame	Hull C	Trabzonspor	£2.2m
31 Nego, Loic	Charlton Ath	Videoton	Undisclosed
3 Nelson, Michael	Cambridge U	Barnet	Free
5 Newell, Joe	Peterborough U	Rotherham U	Undisclosed
3 Nugent, Ben	Cardiff C	Crewe Alex	Free
14 Nugent, David	Leicester C	Middlesbrough	Undisclosed
7 Odubajo, Moses	Brentford	Hull C	£3.5m
24 O'Neil, Liam	WBA	Chesterfield	Undisclosed
3 Pogba, Mathias	Crawley T	Partick Thistle	Free
27 Pogrebnyak, Pavel	Reading	Dynamo Moscow	Free
20 Ream, Tim	Bolton W	Fulham	Undisclosed
3 Richards, Matt	Cheltenham T	Dagenham & R	Free
3 Robinson, Paul	Portsmouth	AFC Wimbledon	Free
28 Robinson, Theo	Doncaster R	Motherwell	Free
12 Romeu, Oriol	Chelsea	Southampton	£5m
31 Saadi, Idriss	Clermont Foot	Cardiff C	Undisclosed
5 Sako, Bakary	Wolverhampton W	Crystal Palace	Free
7 Smith, Renny	Arsenal	Burnley	Free
20 Smithies, Alex	Huddersfield T	QPR	Undisclosed
18 Soldado, Roberto	Tottenham H	Villarreal	£7m
6 Stephens, Jamie	Newport Co	Barnet	Free
6 Thompson, Tony	Rotherham U	Morecambe	Free
4 Tomlin, Lee	Middlesbrough	Bournemouth	£3m
27 Tonev, Aleksandar	Aston Villa	Frosinone	Undisclosed
6 Toney, Ivan	Northampton T	Newcastle U	Undisclosed
31 Velikonja, Etien	Cardiff C	Lierse	Undisclosed
12 Vickers, Josh	Arsenal	Swansea C	Free
31 Vossen, Jelle	Burnley	Club Brugge	Undisclosed
15 Wabara, Reece	Doncaster R	Barnsley	Free
7 Wakefield, Liam	Doncaster R	Accrington S	Free
3 Wickham, Connor	Sunderland	Crystal Palace	£7m
5 Wiggins, Rhoys	Charlton Ath	Sheffield W	Undisclosed
5 Wilson, Lawrie	Charlton Ath	Bolton W	Free
31 Woods, Martin	Shrewsbury T	Ross Co	Free
7 Wright, Josh	Leyton Orient	Gillingham	Free
25 Yeates, Mark	Bradford C	Oldham Ath	Free
3 Zamora, Bobby	QPR	Brighton & HA	Free

SEPTEMBER 2015

1 Antonio, Michail	Nottingham F	West Ham U	Undisclosed
1 Butterfield, Jacob	Huddersfield T	Derby Co	Undisclosed
1 Byrne, Nathan	Swindon T	Wolverhampton W	Undisclosed
1 Camp, Lee	Bournemouth	Rotherham U	Free
1 Drury, Adam	Manchester C	Bristol R	Free
1 Guedioura, Adlene	Crystal Palace	Watford	Undisclosed
1 Hector, Michael	Reading	Chelsea	£4m
1 Hendry, Jack	Partick Thistle	Wigan Ath	Undisclosed
1 Jebb, Jack	Arsenal	Stevenage	Free
1 Jelavic, Nikica	Hull C	West Ham U	£3m
1 Johnson, Bradley	Norwich C	Derby Co	Undisclosed
1 Kellett, Andy	Bolton W	Wigan Ath	Undisclosed
1 Lennon, Aaron	Tottenham H	Everton	Undisclosed
1 Lescott, Joleon	WBA	Aston Villa	£2m
1 May, Stevie	Sheffield W	Preston NE	Undisclosed
1 Murray, Glenn	Crystal Palace	Bournemouth	£4m
1 O'Neill, Luke	Burnley	Southend	Free
1 Partridge, Matt	Dagenham & R	Newport Co	Free
1 Poole, Regan	Newport Co	Manchester U	Undisclosed
1 Stearman, Richard	Wolverhampton W	Fulham	Undisclosed
1 Townsend, Nick	Birmingham C	Barnsley	Undisclosed
1 van Dijk, Virgil	Celtic	Southampton	£11.5m
1 Woods, Ryan	Shrewsbury T	Brentford	Undisclosed

NOVEMBER 2015

26 Maguire, Chris	Rotherham U	Oxford U	Undisclosed

JANUARY 2016

10 Afobe, Benik	Wolverhampton W	Bournemouth	£9m
14 Aimson, Will	Hull C	Blackpool	Undisclosed
7 Alcock, Craig	Sheffield U	Doncaster R	Undisclosed
20 Atangana, Nigel	Portsmouth	Leyton Orient	Undisclosed
16 Austin, Charlie	QPR	Southampton	£4m
5 Bennett, Elliott	Norwich C	Blackburn R	Undisclosed
6 Blackman, Nick	Reading	Derby Co	£2.5m
30 Boco, Romuald	Portsmouth	Accrington S	Free
22 Bowery, Jordan	Rotherham U	Oxford U	Free
27 Brown, Scott	Grimsby T	Accrington S	Free
20 Byram, Sam	Leeds U	West Ham U	Undisclosed

8 Cairns, Alex	Chesterfield	Rotherham U	Free
23 Chettle, Callum	Nuneaton T	Peterborough U	Undisclosed
28 Colclough, Ryan	Crewe Alex	Wigan Ath	Undisclosed
22 Cole, Devante	Bradford C	Fleetwood T	Undisclosed
7 Cole, Joe	Aston Villa	Coventry C	Free
22 Collins, Aaron	Newport Co	Wolverhampton W	Undisclosed
22 Coulthirst, Shaquile	Tottenham H	Peterborough U	Undisclosed
29 Cox, Lee	Plymouth Arg	Stevenage	Free
19 Cubero, Jose Miguel	Blackpool	Herediano	Undisclosed
11 Davis, Joe	Leicester C	Fleetwood T	Undisclosed
6 Dawkins, Simon	Derby Co	San Jose Earthquakes	Undisclosed
28 Dawson, Chris	Leeds U	Rotherham U	Free
25 Diagouraga, Toumani	Brentford	Leeds U	Undisclosed
15 Dixon, Matt	Hull C	York C	Free
8 Ellis, Mark	Shrewsbury T	Carlisle U	Free
19 Evans, George	Manchester C	Reading	Undisclosed
27 Fabbrini, Diego	Watford	Birmingham C	£1.5m
26 Ferguson, Shane	Newcastle U	Millwall	Undisclosed
2 Foulds, Matthew	Bury	Everton	Undisclosed
14 Gaffney, Rory	Cambridge U	Bristol R	Undisclosed
26 Gerrard, Anthony	Shrewsbury T	Oldham Ath	Free
22 Gnanduillet, Armand	Chesterfield	Leyton Orient	Undisclosed
15 Godfrey, Ben	York C	Norwich C	Undisclosed
8 Golbourne, Scott	Wolverhampton W	Bristol C	Undisclosed
11 Grabban, Lewis	Norwich C	Bournemouth	£7m
4 Gray, Demarai	Birmingham C	Leicester C	£3.7m
18 Grimshaw, Liam	Manchester U	Preston NE	Undisclosed
21 Guttridge, Luke	Luton T	Dagenham & R	Free
6 Harriman, Michael	QPR	Wycombe W	Undisclosed
15 Hawkins, Oliver	Hemel Hempstead T	Dagenham & R	Undisclosed
22 Hooper, Gary	Norwich C	Sheffield W	Undisclosed
29 Hughes, Mark	Stevenage	Accrington S	Free
13 Hunt, Jack	Crystal Palace	Sheffield W	Undisclosed
22 Ingram, Matt	Wycombe W	QPR	Undisclosed
2 Jarvis, Matt	West Ham U	Norwich C	Undisclosed
25 Jones, Darren	Forest Green R	Newport Co	Free
29 Jones, Jamie	Preston NE	Stevenage	Free
20 Kermorgant, Yann	Bournemouth	Reading	Undisclosed
25 Khan, Otis	Sheffield U	Barnsley	Free
6 Lavercombe, Dan	Torquay U	Wigan Ath	Undisclosed
7 Lawrence, Liam	Shrewsbury T	Bristol R	Free
27 Lowry, Shane	Birmingham C	Perth Glory	Free
7 Mangan, Andy	Tranmere R	Shrewsbury T	Undisclosed
28 Mason, Joe	Cardiff C	Wolverhampton W	Undisclosed
19 Maxwell, Luke	Kidderminster H	Birmingham C	£75,000
29 McCourt, Jak	Leicester C	Barnsley	Undisclosed
5 McEvoy, Kenny	Tottenham H	York C	Free
11 McKay, Jack	Doncaster R	Leeds U	Undisclosed
11 McKay, Paul	Doncaster R	Leeds U	Undisclosed
19 Monakana, Jeffrey	Brighton & HA	FC Voluntari	Free
28 Morsy, Sam	Chesterfield	Wigan Ath	Undisclosed
21 Nabi, Adil	WBA	Peterborough U	Undisclosed
19 Naismith, Steven	Everton	Norwich C	£8.5m
29 Odoffin, Hakeem	Barnet	Wolverhampton W	Undisclosed
26 Olsson, Marcus	Blackburn R	Derby Co	Undisclosed
19 Pantilimon, Costel	Sunderland	Watford	£500,000
13 Parr, Jonathan	Ipswich T	Stromsgodset	Free
11 Pearson, Ben	Manchester U	Preston NE	Undisclosed
7 Philliskirk, Danny	Oldham Ath	Blackpool	Undisclosed
27 Ramires	Chelsea	Jiangsu Suning	£25m
14 Randall, Mark	Milton Keynes D	Barnet	Free
12 Randall, Will	Swindon T	Wolverhampton W	Undisclosed
25 Robinson, Theo	Motherwell	Port Vale	Free
26 Sa, Orlando	Reading	Maccabi Tel Aviv	Undisclosed
15 Sesay, Alie	Leicester C	Barnet	Undisclosed
12 Shelvey, Jonjo	Swansea C	Newcastle U	£12m
22 Smith, Connor	Watford	AFC Wimbledon	Free
30 Spencer, Jimmy	Notts Co	Cambridge U	Free
18 Syers, David	Scunthorpe U	Rochdale	Free
26 Taggart, Adam	Fulham	Perth Glory	Undisclosed
27 Taylor, Jack	Reading	Exeter C	Free
20 Thomas, Luke	Cheltenham T	Derby Co	Undisclosed
12 Thomas, Nathan	Hartlepool U	Mansfield T	Undisclosed
27 Townsend, Andros	Tottenham H	Newcastle U	£12m
6 Townsend, Conor	Hull C	Scunthorpe U	Free
20 Walker, Lewis	Ilkeston	Derby Co	Undisclosed
2 Wallace, Murray	Huddersfield T	Scunthorpe U	Undisclosed
20 Ward, Elliott	Bournemouth	Blackburn R	Undisclosed
19 Washington, Conor	Peterborough U	QPR	Undisclosed
8 Wellens, Richie	Doncaster R	Shrewsbury T	Free
8 White, Aidy	Rotherham U	Barnsley	Free
8 Whitehead, Danny	Macclesfield T	Wigan Ath	Undisclosed
9 Wildschut, Yanic	Middlesbrough	Wigan Ath	Undisclosed
22 Wilkinson, Luke	Luton T	Stevenage	Undisclosed
23 Williams, Aaron	Nuneaton T	Peterborough U	Undisclosed
15 Williamson, Ben	Gillingham	Cambridge U	Undisclosed

29 Williamson, Mike	Newcastle U	Wolverhampton W	Undisclosed
7 Yeates, Mark	Oldham Ath	Blackpool	Free
21 Zarate, Mauro	West Ham U	Fiorentina	Undisclosed
2 Zyro, Michal	Legia Warsaw	Wolverhampton W	Undisclosed

FEBRUARY 2016

12 Ameobi, Shola	Bolton W	Fleetwood T	Free
13 Banton, Jason	Wycombe W	Notts Co	Free
1 Baxendale, James	Walsall	Mansfield T	Free
1 Cowie, Don	Wigan Ath	Hearts	Free
1 Dicker, Gary	Carlisle U	Kilmarnock	Free
1 Dimaio, Connor	Sheffield U	Chesterfield	Free
1 El Khayati, Abdenasser	Burton Alb	QPR	Undisclosed
1 Harris, Charlie	Brighton & HA	Barnsley	Undisclosed
5 Henderson, Darius	Scunthorpe U	Coventry C	Free
18 Holt, Grant	Wigan Ath	Rochdale	Free
1 Hunt, Nicky	Mansfield T	Leyton Orient	Undisclosed
16 Jelavic, Nikica	West Ham U	Beijing Renhe	Around £2m
3 Kike	Middlesbrough	Eibar	Undisclosed
1 Laurent, Josh	Brentford	Hartlepoo U	Free
1 Liddle, Gary	Bradford C	Chesterfield	Undisclosed
1 Maddison, James	Coventry C	Norwich C	Undisclosed
(loaned back to Coventry for rest of season)			
1 Maguire, Chris	Rotherham U	Oxford U	Free
1 Nichols, Tom	Exeter C	Peterborough U	Undisclosed
1 O'Donnell, Richard	Wigan Ath	Bristol C	Undisclosed
1 Petshi, Sacha	Blackburn R	US Creteil-Lusitanos	Undisclosed
1 Proctor, Jamie	Fleetwood T	Bradford C	Free
1 Revell, Alex	Cardiff C	Milton Keynes D	Free
1 Rhodes, Jordan	Blackburn R	Middlesbrough	£9m
1 Rose, Danny	Oxford U	Northampton T	Free
1 Tarkowski, James	Brentford	Burnley	Undisclosed
1 Tuton, Shaun	Halifax T	Barnsley	Undisclosed
1 Vose, Dominic	Wrexham	Scunthorpe U	Undisclosed
1 Wiggins, Rhoys	Sheffield W	Bournemouth	Undisclosed

MARCH 2016

3 Jones, Rob	Doncaster R	Hartlepool U	Free
8 Rooney, Luke	Crawley T	Arizona U	Free

APRIL 2016

12 Storer, Jack	Stevenage	Birmingham C	Undisclosed

MAY 2016

24 Adams, Nicky	Northampton T	Carlisle U	Free
24 Banton, Jason	Notts Co	Crawley T	Free
24 Barton, Joey	Burnley	Rangers	Free
27 Baudry, Mathieu	Leyton Orient	Doncaster R	Free
24 Blair, Matty	Mansfield T	Doncaster R	Free
22 Bolger, Cian	Southend U	Fleetwood T	Free
25 Cairns, Alex	Rotherham U	Fleetwood T	Free
31 Canavan, Niall	Scunthorpe U	Rochdale	Free
31 Charles, Darius	Burton Alb	AFC Wimbledon	Free
26 Deegan, Gary	Southend U	Shrewsbury T	Free
27 Dodds, Louis	Port Vale	Shrewsbury T	Free
20 Eastham, Ashley	Rochdale	Fleetwood T	Free
25 Etheridge, Ross	Accrington S	Doncaster R	Free
25 Holloway, Aaron	Wycombe W	Fleetwood T	Undisclosed
31 Hylton, Danny	Oxford U	Luton T	Free
23 Jackson, Kayden	Wrexham	Barnsley	Free
25 James, Lloyd	Leyton Orient	Exeter C	Free
10 Jones, Jodi	Dagenham & R	Coventry	Undisclosed
20 Lancashire, Oliver	Rochdale	Shrewsbury T	Free
26 Lowe, Ryan	Bury	Crewe Alex	Free
24 Martin, James	Queen of the South	Hartlepool U	Free
16 Maxwell, Chris	Fleetwood T	Preston NE	Free
31 McAlinden, Liam	Wolverhampton W	Exeter C	Free
25 McCarey, Aaron	Wolverhampton W	Ross Co	Free
24 McKee, Joe	Greenock Morton	Carlisle U	Undisclosed
25 Morris, Glenn	Gillingham	Crawley T	Free
31 Mullins, Johnny	Oxford U	Luton T	Free
25 Neal, Chris	Port Vale	Fleetwood T	Free
25 Nolan, Jon	Grimsby T	Chesterfield	Free
27 Penn, Russell	York C	Carlisle U	Free
24 Pollock, Ben	Newcastle U	Hartlepool U	Free
31 Randall, Mark	Barnet	Newport Co	Free
25 Rose, Danny	Bury	Mansfield T	Undisclosed
13 Rossiter, Jordan	Liverpool	Rangers	Undisclosed
25 Routis, Christopher	Bradford C	Ross Co	Free
18 Rowe, Tommy	Wolverhampton W	Doncaster R	Undisclosed
28 Sarcevic, Antoni	Fleetwood T	Shrewsbury R	Free
25 Sheehan, Alan	Bradford C	Luton T	Free

25 Simpson, Robbie	Cambridge U	Exeter C	Free
11 Stockley, Jayden	Bournemouth	Aberdeen	Free
17 Storey, Miles	Swindon T	Aberdeen	Undisclosed
26 Taft, George	Burton Alb	Mansfield T	Free
30 Warnock, Stephen	Derby Co	Wigan Ath	Free
16 White, Hayden	Bolton W	Peterborough U	Free
27 Yamfam, Louis-Michel	Stevenage	Charlton Ath	Undisclosed
16 Yiadom, Andy	Barnet	Barnsley	Free

THE NEW FOREIGN LEGION 2015–16

JUNE 2015	From	To	Fee in £
4 Arlauskis, Giedrius	Steaua Bucharest	Watford	Free
9 Ayew, Andre	Marseille	Swansea C	Free
24 Bamba, Sol	Palermo	Leeds U	Undisclosed
25 Barbet, Yoann	Chamois Niortais	Brentford	Undisclosed
23 Bauer, Patrick	Maritimo	Charlton Ath	Undisclosed
12 Depay, Memphis	PSV Eindhoven	Manchester U	£31m
25 Deulofeu, Gerard	Barcelona	Everton	£4.3m
2 Erlandsson, Tim	Halmstad	Nottingham F	Undisclosed
24 Firmino, Roberto	Hoffenheim	Liverpool	£29m
3 Fuchs, Christian	Schalke 04	Leicester C	Free
24 Hemed, Tomer	Almeria	Brighton & HA	Undisclosed
16 Joselu	Hannover 96	Stoke C	£5.75m
16 Juanmi	Malaga	Southampton	£5m
25 Lachman, Darryl	FC Twente	Sheffield W	Undisclosed
23 Nordfeldt, Kristoffer	Heerenveen	Swansea C	Undisclosed
10 Obiang, Pedro	Sampdoria	West Ham U	Undisclosed
26 Okazaki, Shinji	1.FSV Mainz	Leicester C	Undisclosed
26 Payet, Dimitri	Marseille	West Ham U	Undisclosed
1 Prodl, Sebastian	Werder Bremen	Watford	Free
29 Sa, Orlando	Legia Warsaw	Reading	Undisclosed
18 Soares, Cedric	Sporting Lisbon	Southampton	£4.7m
25 Swerts, Gill	NAC Breda	Notts Co	Free
19 Tabanou, Franck	Saint-Etienne	Swansea C	Undisclosed
30 Thiele, Timmy	Borussia Dortmund	Burton Alb	Free
30 Sasso, Vincent	Braga	Sheffield W	Loan

JULY 2015			
27 Afellay, Ibrahim	Barcelona	Stoke C	Free
31 Aguza, Sergio	Real Madrid	Milton Keynes D	Free
8 Alderweireld, Toby	Atletico Madrid	Tottenham H	Undisclosed
18 Amavi, Jordan	Nice	Aston Villa	Undisclosed
3 Amevor, Mawouna	Go Ahead Eagles	Notts Co	Free
27 Ayew, Jordan	Lorient	Aston Villa	Undisclosed
11 Behrami, Valon	Hamburg	Watford	Undisclosed
17 Benavente, Cristian	Real Madrid Castilla	Milton Keynes D	Free
23 Bergdich, Zakarya	Real Valladolid	Charlton Ath	Undisclosed
27 Berghuis, Steven	AZ Alkmaar	Watford	£4.6m
2 Bjelland, Andreas	FC Twente	Brentford	£2.1m
24 Blaise, Jordan	Bordeaux	Cardiff C	Free
22 Britos, Miguel	Napoli	Watford	Free
10 Cabaye, Yohan	Paris Saint-Germain	Crystal Palace	£10m
12 Ceberio, Jon	Real Sociedad	Bolton W	Free
20 Chery, Tjaronn	FC Groningen	QPR	Undisclosed
15 Clasie, Jordy	Feyenoord	Southampton	£8m
28 Crespo, Jose Angel	Cordoba	Aston Villa	Undisclosed
11 Darmian, Matteo	Torino	Manchester U	£12.7m
1 Demetriou, Jason	Anorthosis Famagusta	Walsall	Free
1 Eder	Braga	Swansea C	Undisclosed
15 El Ouriachi, Moha	Barcelona	Stoke C	Undisclosed
10 Gueye, Idrissa	Lille	Aston Villa	Undisclosed
22 Hambo, Vahid	Inter Turku	Brighton & HA	Undisclosed
23 Harper, Jack	Real Madrid	Brighton & HA	Undisclosed
23 Hofmann, Philipp	Kaiserslautern	Brentford	Undisclosed
2 Holebas, Jose	Roma	Watford	£1.8m
7 Jenner, Julian	Disogyor	Notts Co	Free
31 Joao, Lucas	Nacional	Sheffield W	Undisclosed
8 Jonsson, Eggert	FC Vestsjaelland	Fleetwood T	Free
22 Jurado, Jose	Spartak Moscow	Watford	Undisclosed
21 Kashi, Ahmed	Metz	Charlton Ath	Undisclosed
1 Kerschbaumer, Konstantin	Admira Wacker Modling	Brentford	Undisclosed
27 Kieftenbeld, Maikel	Groningen	Birmingham C	Undisclosed
31 Knudsen, Jonas	Esbjerg	Ipswich T	Undisclosed
20 Kodjia, Jonathan	Angers	Bristol C	£2.1m
21 Koita, Bangaly-Fode	Caen	Blackburn R	Free
15 Lens, Jeremain	Dynamo Kyiv	Sunderland	£8m
6 Maenpaa, Niki	VVV-Venlo	Brighton & HA	Free
7 Martina, Cuco	FC Twente	Southampton	Undisclosed
9 Matias, Marco	Nacional	Sheffield W	Undisclosed

26 Mbemba, Chancel	Anderlecht	Newcastle U	Undisclosed
21 Mitrovic, Aleksandar	Anderlecht	Newcastle U	£13m
14 Nyom, Allan	Udinese	Watford	Undisclosed
10 Ogbonna, Angelo	Juventus	West Ham U	£10m
6 Osede, Derik	Real Madrid	Bolton W	Free
23 Pantic, Danilo	Partizan Belgrade	Chelsea	Undisclosed
21 Petchi, Sacha	CA Bastia	Blackburn R	Free
30 Pinillos, Daniel	Cordoba	Nottingham F	Free
2 Polter, Sebastian	1.FSV Mainz	QPR	Undisclosed
30 Robert, Fabien	Lorient	Swindon T	Free
27 Romero, Sergio	Sampdoria	Manchester U	Free
28 Sarr, Naby	Sporting Lisbon	Charlton Ath	Undisclosed
13 Schweinsteiger, Bastian	Bayern Munich	Manchester U	£14.4m
6 Snijders, Genaro	FC Oss	Notts Co	Free
6 Unal, Enes	Bursaspor	Manchester C	Undisclosed
8 Valencic, Filip	Monza	Notts Co	Free
31 Veretout, Jordan	Nantes	Aston Villa	Undisclosed
24 Vibe, Lasse	IFK Gothenburg	Brentford	Undisclosed
7 Vossen, Jelle	Genk	Burnley	Undisclosed
1 Vydra, Matej	Udinese	Watford	Undisclosed
11 Wijnaldum, Georginio	PSV Eindhoven	Newcastle U	£14.5m
13 Costa, Filippo	Chievo	Bournemouth	Loan
3 Falcao, Radamel	Monaco	Chelsea	Loan
22 Lanzini, Manuel	Al Jazira	West Ham U	Loan
10 Lopez, Alex	Celta Vigo	Sheffield W	Loan
1 Makienok, Simon	Palermo	Charlton Ath	Loan

AUGUST 2015

3 Benalouane, Yohan	Atalanta	Leicester C	Undisclosed
21 Brock-Madsen, Nicolai	Randers	Birmingham C	£500,000
27 Casado, Jose Manuel	Almeria	Bolton W	Free
14 Colin, Maxime	Anderlecht	Brentford	Undisclosed
30 De Bruyne, Kevin	Wolfsburg	Manchester C	£55m
11 Dikamona, Clevid	Poire-sur-Vie	Dagenham & R	Free
4 Gradel, Max	Saint-Etienne	Bournemouth	Undisclosed
14 Hennings, Rouwen	Karlsruher	Burnley	Undisclosed
28 Heung-min, Son	Bayer Leverkusen	Tottenham H	£22m
12 Hunemeier, Uwe	Paderborn 07	Brighton & HA	Undisclosed
13 Hurtado, Paolo	Pacos de Ferreira	Reading	Undisclosed
19 Inler, Gokhan	Napoli	Leicester C	Undisclosed
5 Joachim, Aurelien	CSKA Sofia	Burton Alb	Free
3 Kante, N'Golo	Caen	Leicester C	Undisclosed
22 Kenedy	Fluminense	Chelsea	Undisclosed
28 Malarczyk, Piotr	Korona Kielce	Ipswich T	Undisclosed
27 Maloney, Shaun	Chicago Fire	Hull C	Undisclosed
29 Manu, Elvis	Feyenoord	Brighton & HA	Undisclosed
4 Mattila, Sakari	Aalesunds	Fulham	Undisclosed
14 N'Jie, Clinton	Lyon	Tottenham H	Undisclosed
29 Oar, Tommy	Utrecht	Ipswich T	Free
20 Otamendi, Nicolas	Valencia	Manchester C	£32m
20 Pedro	Barcelona	Chelsea	£21m
2 Pisano, Francesco	Cagliari	Bolton W	Free
16 Rahman, Baba	Augsburg	Chelsea	Undisclosed
28 Rodriguez, Leandro	River Plate	Everton	£500,000
20 Rondon, Salomon	Zenit St Petersburg	WBA	£12m
11 Shaqiri, Xherdan	Inter Milan	Stoke C	£12m
5 Sougou, Modou	Marseille	Sheffield W	Free
6 Sprockel, Civard	Othellos	Notts Co	Free
7 Stuani, Cristhian	Espanyol	Middlesbrough	£2.8m
19 Thauvin, Florian	Marseille	Newcastle U	£12m
3 Toure, Larsen	Arles-Avignon	Ipswich T	Free
28 Tozser, Daniel	Parma	QPR	Free
14 Traore, Adama	Barcelona	Aston Villa	£7m
7 Van Den Bogaert, Bryan	Royal Antwerp	Crawley T	Free
29 Agazzi, Michael	AC Milan	Middlesbrough	Loan
17 Diamanti, Alessandro	Guangzhou Evergrande	Watford	Loan
31 Djuricin, Marco	Red Bull Salzburg	Brentford	Loan
20 Ebecilio, Kyle	FC Twente	Nottingham F	Loan
8 Fernandez, Alex	Espanyol	Reading	Loan
6 Gouano, Prince-Desir	Atalanta	Bolton W	Loan
31 Mbokani, Dieumerci	Dynamo Kyiv	Norwich C	Loan
6 M'Vila, Yann	Rubin Kazan	Sunderland	Loan
28 Toivonen, Ola	Stade Rennais	Sunderland	Loan

SEPTEMBER 2015

1 Botaka, Jordan	Excelsior	Leeds U	Undisclosed
1 de Pena, Carlos	Nacional	Middlesbrough	Undisclosed
1 Diomande, Adama	Stabaek	Hull C	Undisclosed
1 Djilobodji, Papy	Nantes	Chelsea	£4m
1 Elford-Alliyu, Lateef	Valletta	Coventry C	Free
1 Funes Mori, Ramiro	River Plate	Everton	£9.5m
1 Ibarbo, Victor	Cagliari	Watford	Undisclosed
1 Martial, Anthony	Monaco	Manchester U	£36m
1 Oulare, Obbi	Club Brugge	Watford	Undisclosed
1 Sarkic, Matija	Anderlecht	Aston Villa	Undisclosed
1 Andrade, Tomas	River Plate	Bournemouth	Loan

1 John, Ola	Benfica	Reading	Loan
4 Mendes, Ryan	Lille	Nottingham F	Loan
4 Oliveira, Nelson	Benfica	Nottingham F	Loan
1 Song, Alex	Barcelona	West Ham U	Loan

JANUARY 2016

22 Amartey, Daniel	FC Copenhagen	Leicester C	£6m
18 Amrabat, Nordin	Malaga	Watford	Undisclosed
8 Belaid, Aimen	Levski Sofia	Rotherham U	Free
15 Caceres, Anthony	Central Coast Mariners	Manchester C	Undisclosed
4 Camara, Abdoul	Angers	Derby Co	Undisclosed
14 Elneny, Mohamed	FC Basel	Arsenal	£5m
6 Grujic, Marko	Red Star Belgrade	Liverpool	£5.1m
30 Khazri, Wahbi	Bordeaux	Sunderland	Undisclosed
7 Kirchhoff, Jan	Bayern Munich	Sunderland	Undisclosed
18 Klose, Timm	Wolfsburg	Norwich C	Undisclosed
7 Knockaert, Anthony	Standard Liege	Brighton & HA	Undisclosed
27 Kone, Lamine	Lorient	Sunderland	Undisclosed
30 Miazga, Matt	New York Red Bulls	Chelsea	Undisclosed
29 Paloschi, Alberto	Chievo	Swansea C	Undisclosed
8 Pinto, Ivo	Dinamo Zagreb	Norwich C	Undisclosed
28 Rakels, Deniss	Cracovia	Reading	Undisclosed
27 Brattan, Luke	Brisbane Roar	Manchester C	Free
11 Saivet, Henri	Bordeaux	Newcastle U	Undisclosed
30 Suarez, Mario	Fiorentina	Watford	Undisclosed
7 Tarashaj, Shani	Grasshoppers Zurich	Everton	Undisclosed
19 Teixeira, Jorge	Standard Liege	Charlton Ath	Undisclosed
28 Adamonis, Marius	FK Atlantas	Bournemouth	Loan
31 Emenike, Emmanuel	Fenerbahce	West Ham U	Loan
28 Hurtado, Paolo	Vitoria Guimares	Reading	Loan
21 Immers, Lex	Feyenoord	Cardiff C	Loan
2 Iturbe, Juan	Roma	Bournemouth	Loan
8 Jokic, Bojan	Villarreal	Nottingham F	Loan
29 Madl, Michael	Sturn Graz	Fulham	Loan
14 N'Doye, Dame	Trabzonspor	Sunderland	Loan
29 Pato, Alexandre	Corinthians	Chelsea	Loan
15 Sola, Kike	Athletic Bilbao	Middlesbrough	Loan

FEBRUARY 2016

1 De Sart, Julien	Standard Liege	Middlesbrough	Undisclosed
1 Doucoure, Abdoulaye	Stade Rennais	Watford	£8m
(loaned to Granada for rest of season)			
1 Imbula, Giannelli	Porto	Stoke C	£18.3m
1 Kuciak, Dusan	Legia Warsaw	Hull C	Undisclosed
1 Penaranda, Adalberto	Udinese	Watford	Undisclosed
(loaned to Granada for rest of season)			
1 Skalak, Jiri	Mlada Boleslav	Brighton & HA	Undisclosed
1 Doumbia, Seydou	Roma	Newcastle U	Loan
1 Fanni, Rod	Al-Arabi SC	Charlton Ath	Loan
1 Labyad, Zakaria	Sporting Lisbon	Fulham	Loan
1 O'Neill, Shane	Apollon Limassol	Cambridge U	Loan
1 Zohore, Kenneth	Kortrijk	Cardiff C	Loan

MAY 2016

16 Boldewijn, Enzio	Almere City	Crawley T	Free
25 Gravenberch, Danzell	FC Dordrecht	Reading	Undisclosed
12 Immers, Lex	Feyenoord	Cardiff C	Undisclosed
24 Karius, Loris	1.FSV Mainz	Liverpool	£4.7m
20 Madl, Michael	Sturm Graz	Fulham	Undisclosed
16 Nordtveit, Havard	Borussia Moenchengladbach	West Ham U	Free
25 Xhaka, Granit	Borussia Moenchengladbach	Arsenal	Undisclosed

ENGLISH LEAGUE HONOURS 1888–2016

*Won or placed on goal average (ratio), goal difference or most goals scored. ‡Not promoted after play-offs.
No official competition during 1915–19 and 1939–46, regional leagues operated.*

FOOTBALL LEAGUE (1888–89 to 1891–92) – TIER 1

MAXIMUM POINTS: a 44; b 60.

1	1888–89a	Preston NE	40	Aston Villa	29	Wolverhampton W	28
1	1889–90a	Preston NE	33	Everton	31	Blackburn R	27
1	1890–91a	Everton	29	Preston NE	27	Notts Co	26
1	1891–92b	Sunderland	42	Preston NE	37	Bolton W	36

DIVISION 1 (1892–93 to 1991–92)

MAXIMUM POINTS: a 44; b 52; c 60; d 68; e 76; f 84; g 126; h 120; k 114.

1	1892–93c	Sunderland	48	Preston NE	37	Everton	36
1	1893–94c	Aston Villa	44	Sunderland	38	Derby Co	36
1	1894–95c	Sunderland	47	Everton	42	Aston Villa	39
1	1895–96c	Aston Villa	45	Derby Co	41	Everton	39
1	1896–97c	Aston Villa	47	Sheffield U*	36	Derby Co	36
1	1897–98c	Sheffield U	42	Sunderland	37	Wolverhampton W*	35
1	1898–99d	Aston Villa	45	Liverpool	43	Burnley	39
1	1899–1900d	Aston Villa	50	Sheffield U	48	Sunderland	41
1	1900–01d	Liverpool	45	Sunderland	43	Notts Co	40
1	1901–02d	Sunderland	44	Everton	41	Newcastle U	37
1	1902–03d	The Wednesday	42	Aston Villa*	41	Sunderland	41
1	1903–04d	The Wednesday	47	Manchester C	44	Everton	43
1	1904–05d	Newcastle U	48	Everton	47	Manchester C	46
1	1905–06e	Liverpool	51	Preston NE	47	The Wednesday	44
1	1906–07e	Newcastle U	51	Bristol C	48	Everton*	45
1	1907–08e	Manchester U	52	Aston Villa*	43	Manchester C	43
1	1908–09e	Newcastle U	53	Everton	46	Sunderland	44
1	1909–10e	Aston Villa	53	Liverpool	48	Blackburn R*	45
1	1910–11e	Manchester U	52	Aston Villa	51	Sunderland*	45
1	1911–12e	Blackburn R	49	Everton	46	Newcastle U	44
1	1912–13e	Sunderland	54	Aston Villa	50	Sheffield W	49
1	1913–14e	Blackburn R	51	Aston Villa	44	Middlesbrough*	43
1	1914–15e	Everton	46	Oldham Ath	45	Blackburn R*	43
1	1919–20f	WBA	60	Burnley	51	Chelsea	49
1	1920–21f	Burnley	59	Manchester C	54	Bolton W	52
1	1921–22f	Liverpool	57	Tottenham H	51	Burnley	49
1	1922–23f	Liverpool	60	Sunderland	54	Huddersfield T	53
1	1923–24f	Huddersfield T*	57	Cardiff C	57	Sunderland	53
1	1924–25f	Huddersfield T	58	WBA	56	Bolton W	55
1	1925–26f	Huddersfield T	57	Arsenal	52	Sunderland	48
1	1926–27f	Newcastle U	56	Huddersfield T	51	Sunderland	49
1	1927–28f	Everton	53	Huddersfield T	51	Leicester C	48
1	1928–29f	Sheffield W	52	Leicester C	51	Aston Villa	50
1	1929–30f	Sheffield W	60	Derby Co	50	Manchester C*	47
1	1930–31f	Arsenal	66	Aston Villa	59	Sheffield W	52
1	1931–32f	Everton	56	Arsenal	54	Sheffield W	50
1	1932–33f	Arsenal	58	Aston Villa	54	Sheffield W	51
1	1933–34f	Arsenal	59	Huddersfield T	56	Tottenham H	49
1	1934–35f	Arsenal	58	Sunderland	54	Sheffield W	49
1	1935–36f	Sunderland	56	Derby Co*	48	Huddersfield T	48
1	1936–37f	Manchester C	57	Charlton Ath	54	Arsenal	52
1	1937–38f	Arsenal	52	Wolverhampton W	51	Preston NE	49
1	1938–39f	Everton	59	Wolverhampton W	55	Charlton Ath	50
1	1946–47f	Liverpool	57	Manchester U*	56	Wolverhampton W	56
1	1947–48f	Arsenal	59	Manchester U*	52	Burnley	52
1	1948–49f	Portsmouth	58	Manchester U*	53	Derby Co	53
1	1949–50f	Portsmouth*	53	Wolverhampton W	53	Sunderland	52
1	1950–51f	Tottenham H	60	Manchester U	56	Blackpool	50
1	1951–52f	Manchester U	57	Tottenham H*	53	Arsenal	53
1	1952–53f	Arsenal*	54	Preston NE	54	Wolverhampton W	51
1	1953–54f	Wolverhampton W	57	WBA	53	Huddersfield T	51
1	1954–55f	Chelsea	52	Wolverhampton W*	48	Portsmouth*	48
1	1955–56f	Manchester U	60	Blackpool*	49	Wolverhampton W	49
1	1956–57f	Manchester U	64	Tottenham H*	56	Preston NE	56
1	1957–58f	Wolverhampton W	64	Preston NE	59	Tottenham H	51
1	1958–59f	Wolverhampton W	61	Manchester U	55	Arsenal*	50
1	1959–60f	Burnley	55	Wolverhampton W	54	Tottenham H	53
1	1960–61f	Tottenham H	66	Sheffield W	58	Wolverhampton W	57
1	1961–62f	Ipswich T	56	Burnley	53	Tottenham H	52
1	1962–63f	Everton	61	Tottenham H	55	Burnley	54
1	1963–64f	Liverpool	57	Manchester U	53	Everton	52
1	1964–65f	Manchester U*	61	Leeds U	61	Chelsea	56

1	1965–66f	Liverpool	61	Leeds U*	55	Burnley	55
1	1966–67f	Manchester U	60	Nottingham F*	56	Tottenham H	56
1	1967–68f	Manchester C	58	Manchester U	56	Liverpool	55
1	1968–69f	Leeds U	67	Liverpool	61	Everton	57
1	1969–70f	Everton	66	Leeds U	57	Chelsea	55
1	1970–71f	Arsenal	65	Leeds U	64	Tottenham H*	52
1	1971–72f	Derby Co	58	Leeds U*	57	Liverpool*	57
1	1972–73f	Liverpool	60	Arsenal	57	Leeds U	53
1	1973–74f	Leeds U	62	Liverpool	57	Derby Co	48
1	1974–75f	Derby Co	53	Liverpool*	51	Ipswich T	51
1	1975–76f	Liverpool	60	QPR	59	Manchester U	56
1	1976–77f	Liverpool	57	Manchester C	56	Ipswich T	52
1	1977–78f	Nottingham F	64	Liverpool	57	Everton	55
1	1978–79f	Liverpool	68	Nottingham F	60	WBA	59
1	1979–80f	Liverpool	60	Manchester U	58	Ipswich T	53
1	1980–81f	Aston Villa	60	Ipswich T	56	Arsenal	53
1	1981–82g	Liverpool	87	Ipswich T	83	Manchester U	78
1	1982–83g	Liverpool	82	Watford	71	Manchester U	70
1	1983–84g	Liverpool	80	Southampton	77	Nottingham F*	74
1	1984–85g	Everton	90	Liverpool*	77	Tottenham H	77
1	1985–86g	Liverpool	88	Everton	86	West Ham U	84
1	1986–87g	Everton	86	Liverpool	77	Tottenham H	71
1	1987–88h	Liverpool	90	Manchester U	81	Nottingham F	73
1	1988–89k	Arsenal*	76	Liverpool	76	Nottingham F	64
1	1989–90k	Liverpool	79	Aston Villa	70	Tottenham H	63
1	1990–91k	Arsenal¹	83	Liverpool	76	Crystal Palace	69
1	1991–92g	Leeds U	82	Manchester U	78	Sheffield W	75

¹*Arsenal deducted 2pts due to player misconduct in match on 20/10/1990 v Manchester U at Old Trafford.*

FA PREMIER LEAGUE (1992–93 to 2015–16)

MAXIMUM POINTS: a 126; b 114.

1	1992–93a	Manchester U	84	Aston Villa	74	Norwich C	72
1	1993–94a	Manchester U	92	Blackburn R	84	Newcastle U	77
1	1994–95a	Blackburn R	89	Manchester U	88	Nottingham F	77
1	1995–96b	Manchester U	82	Newcastle U	78	Liverpool	71
1	1996–97b	Manchester U	75	Newcastle U*	68	Arsenal*	68
1	1997–98b	Arsenal	78	Manchester U	77	Liverpool	65
1	1998–99b	Manchester U	79	Arsenal	78	Chelsea	75
1	1999–2000b	Manchester U	91	Arsenal	73	Leeds U	69
1	2000–01b	Manchester U	80	Arsenal	70	Liverpool	69
1	2001–02b	Arsenal	87	Liverpool	80	Manchester U	77
1	2002–03b	Manchester U	83	Arsenal	78	Newcastle U	69
1	2003–04b	Arsenal	90	Chelsea	79	Manchester U	75
1	2004–05b	Chelsea	95	Arsenal	83	Manchester U	77
1	2005–06b	Chelsea	91	Manchester U	83	Liverpool	82
1	2006–07b	Manchester U	89	Chelsea	83	Liverpool*	68
1	2007–08b	Manchester U	87	Chelsea	85	Arsenal	83
1	2008–09b	Manchester U	90	Liverpool	86	Chelsea	83
1	2009–10b	Chelsea	86	Manchester U	85	Arsenal	75
1	2010–11b	Manchester U	80	Chelsea*	71	Manchester C	71
1	2011–12b	Manchester C*	89	Manchester U	89	Arsenal	70
1	2012–13b	Manchester U	89	Manchester C	78	Chelsea	75
1	2013–14b	Manchester C	86	Liverpool	84	Chelsea	82
1	2014–15b	Chelsea	87	Manchester C	79	Arsenal	75
1	2015–16b	Leicester C	81	Arsenal	71	Tottenham H	70

DIVISION 2 (1892–93 to 1991–92) – TIER 2

MAXIMUM POINTS: a 44; b 56; c 60; d 68; e 76; f 84; g 126; h 132; k 138.

2	1892–93a	Small Heath	36	Sheffield U	35	Darwen	30
2	1893–94b	Liverpool	50	Small Heath	42	Notts Co	39
2	1894–95c	Bury	48	Notts Co	39	Newton Heath*	38
2	1895–96c	Liverpool*	46	Manchester C	46	Grimsby T*	42
2	1896–97c	Notts Co	42	Newton Heath	39	Grimsby T	38
2	1897–98c	Burnley	48	Newcastle U	45	Manchester C	39
2	1898–99d	Manchester C	52	Glossop NE	46	Leicester Fosse	45
2	1899–1900d	The Wednesday	54	Bolton W	52	Small Heath	46
2	1900–01d	Grimsby T	49	Small Heath	48	Burnley	44
2	1901–02d	WBA	55	Middlesbrough	51	Preston NE*	42
2	1902–03d	Manchester C	54	Small Heath	51	Woolwich A	48
2	1903–04d	Preston NE	50	Woolwich A	49	Manchester U	48
2	1904–05d	Liverpool	58	Bolton W	56	Manchester U	53
2	1905–06e	Bristol C	66	Manchester U	62	Chelsea	53
2	1906–07e	Nottingham F	60	Chelsea	57	Leicester Fosse	48
2	1907–08e	Bradford C	54	Leicester Fosse	52	Oldham Ath	50
2	1908–09e	Bolton W	52	Tottenham H*	51	WBA	51
2	1909–10e	Manchester C	54	Oldham Ath*	53	Hull C*	53
2	1910–11e	WBA	53	Bolton W	51	Chelsea	49
2	1911–12e	Derby Co*	54	Chelsea	54	Burnley	52

2	1912–13e	Preston NE	53	Burnley	50	Birmingham	46
2	1913–14e	Notts Co	53	Bradford PA*	49	Woolwich A	49
2	1914–15e	Derby Co	53	Preston NE	50	Barnsley	47
2	1919–20f	Tottenham H	70	Huddersfield T	64	Birmingham	56
2	1920–21f	Birmingham*	58	Cardiff C	58	Bristol C	51
2	1921–22f	Nottingham F	56	Stoke C*	52	Barnsley	52
2	1922–23f	Notts Co	53	West Ham U*	51	Leicester C	51
2	1923–24f	Leeds U	54	Bury*	51	Derby Co	51
2	1924–25f	Leicester C	59	Manchester U	57	Derby Co	55
2	1925–26f	Sheffield W	60	Derby Co	57	Chelsea	52
2	1926–27f	Middlesbrough	62	Portsmouth*	54	Manchester C	54
2	1927–28f	Manchester C	59	Leeds U	57	Chelsea	54
2	1928–29f	Middlesbrough	55	Grimsby T	53	Bradford PA*	48
2	1929–30f	Blackpool	58	Chelsea	55	Oldham Ath	53
2	1930–31f	Everton	61	WBA	54	Tottenham H	51
2	1931–32f	Wolverhampton W	56	Leeds U	54	Stoke C	52
2	1932–33f	Stoke C	56	Tottenham H	55	Fulham	50
2	1933–34f	Grimsby T	59	Preston NE	52	Bolton W*	51
2	1934–35f	Brentford	61	Bolton W*	56	West Ham U	56
2	1935–36f	Manchester U	56	Charlton Ath	55	Sheffield U*	52
2	1936–37f	Leicester C	56	Blackpool	55	Bury	52
2	1937–38f	Aston Villa	57	Manchester U*	53	Sheffield U	53
2	1938–39f	Blackburn R	55	Sheffield U	54	Sheffield W	53
2	1946–47f	Manchester C	62	Burnley	58	Birmingham C	55
2	1947–48f	Birmingham C	59	Newcastle U	56	Southampton	52
2	1948–49f	Fulham	57	WBA	56	Southampton	55
2	1949–50f	Tottenham H	61	Sheffield W*	52	Sheffield U*	52
2	1950–51f	Preston NE	57	Manchester C	52	Cardiff C	50
2	1951–52f	Sheffield W	53	Cardiff C*	51	Birmingham C	51
2	1952–53f	Sheffield U	60	Huddersfield T	58	Luton T	52
2	1953–54f	Leicester C*	56	Everton	56	Blackburn R	55
2	1954–55f	Birmingham C*	54	Luton T*	54	Rotherham U	54
2	1955–56f	Sheffield W	55	Leeds U	52	Liverpool*	48
2	1956–57f	Leicester C	61	Nottingham F	54	Liverpool	53
2	1957–58f	West Ham U	57	Blackburn R	56	Charlton Ath	55
2	1958–59f	Sheffield W	62	Fulham	60	Sheffield U*	53
2	1959–60f	Aston Villa	59	Cardiff C	58	Liverpool*	50
2	1960–61f	Ipswich T	59	Sheffield U	58	Liverpool	52
2	1961–62f	Liverpool	62	Leyton Orient	54	Sunderland	53
2	1962–63f	Stoke C	53	Chelsea*	52	Sunderland	52
2	1963–64f	Leeds U	63	Sunderland	61	Preston NE	56
2	1964–65f	Newcastle U	57	Northampton T	56	Bolton W	50
2	1965–66f	Manchester C	59	Southampton	54	Coventry C	53
2	1966–67f	Coventry C	59	Wolverhampton W	58	Carlisle U	52
2	1967–68f	Ipswich T	59	QPR*	58	Blackpool	58
2	1968–69f	Derby Co	63	Crystal Palace	56	Charlton Ath	50
2	1969–70f	Huddersfield T	60	Blackpool	53	Leicester C	51
2	1970–71f	Leicester C	59	Sheffield U	56	Cardiff C*	53
2	1971–72f	Norwich C	57	Birmingham C	56	Millwall	55
2	1972–73f	Burnley	62	QPR	61	Aston Villa	50
2	1973–74f	Middlesbrough	65	Luton T	50	Carlisle U	49
2	1974–75f	Manchester U	61	Aston Villa	58	Norwich C	53
2	1975–76f	Sunderland	56	Bristol C*	53	WBA	53
2	1976–77f	Wolverhampton W	57	Chelsea	55	Nottingham F	52
2	1977–78f	Bolton W	58	Southampton	57	Tottenham H*	56
2	1978–79f	Crystal Palace	57	Brighton & HA*	56	Stoke C	56
2	1979–80f	Leicester C	55	Sunderland	54	Birmingham C*	53
2	1980–81f	West Ham U	66	Notts Co	53	Swansea C*	50
2	1981–82g	Luton T	88	Watford	80	Norwich C	71
2	1982–83g	QPR	85	Wolverhampton W	75	Leicester C	70
2	1983–84g	Chelsea*	88	Sheffield W	88	Newcastle U	80
2	1984–85g	Oxford U	84	Birmingham C	82	Manchester C*	74
2	1985–86g	Norwich C	84	Charlton Ath	77	Wimbledon	76
2	1986–87g	Derby Co	84	Portsmouth	78	Oldham Ath‡	75
2	1987–88h	Millwall	82	Aston Villa*	78	Middlesbrough	78
2	1988–89k	Chelsea	99	Manchester C	82	Crystal Palace	81
2	1989–90k	Leeds U*	85	Sheffield U	85	Newcastle U‡	80
2	1990–91k	Oldham Ath	88	West Ham U	87	Sheffield W	82
2	1991–92k	Ipswich T	84	Middlesbrough	80	Derby Co	78

FIRST DIVISION (1992–93 to 2003–04)

MAXIMUM POINTS: 138

2	1992–93	Newcastle U	96	West Ham U*	88	Portsmouth‡	88
2	1993–94	Crystal Palace	90	Nottingham F	83	Millwall‡	74
2	1994–95	Middlesbrough	82	Reading‡	79	Bolton W	77
2	1995–96	Sunderland	83	Derby Co	79	Crystal Palace‡	75
2	1996–97	Bolton W	98	Barnsley	80	Wolverhampton W‡	76
2	1997–98	Nottingham F	94	Middlesbrough	91	Sunderland‡	90

2	1998–99	Sunderland	105	Bradford C	87	Ipswich T‡	86
2	1999–2000	Charlton Ath	91	Manchester C	89	Ipswich T	87
2	2000–01	Fulham	101	Blackburn R	91	Bolton W	87
2	2001–02	Manchester C	99	WBA	89	Wolverhampton W‡	86
2	2002–03	Portsmouth	98	Leicester C	92	Sheffield U‡	80
2	2003–04	Norwich C	94	WBA	86	Sunderland‡	79

FOOTBALL LEAGUE CHAMPIONSHIP (2004–05 to 2015–16)

MAXIMUM POINTS: 138

2	2004–05	Sunderland	94	Wigan Ath	87	Ipswich T‡	85
2	2005–06	Reading	106	Sheffield U	90	Watford	81
2	2006–07	Sunderland	88	Birmingham C	86	Derby Co	84
2	2007–08	WBA	81	Stoke C	79	Hull C	75
2	2008–09	Wolverhampton W	90	Birmingham C	83	Sheffield U‡	80
2	2009–10	Newcastle U	102	WBA	91	Nottingham F‡	79
2	2010–11	QPR	88	Norwich C	84	Swansea C*	80
2	2011–12	Reading	89	Southampton	88	West Ham U	86
2	2012–13	Cardiff C	87	Hull C	79	Watford‡	77
2	2013–14	Leicester C	102	Burnley	93	Derby Co‡	85
2	2014–15	Bournemouth	90	Watford	89	Norwich C	86
2	2015–16	Burnley	93	Middlesbrough*	89	Brighton & HA‡	89

DIVISION 3 (1920–1921) – TIER 3

MAXIMUM POINTS: *a* 84.

| 3 | 1920–21*a* | Crystal Palace | 59 | Southampton | 54 | QPR | 53 |

DIVISION 3—SOUTH (1921–22 to 1957–58)

MAXIMUM POINTS: *a* 84; *b* 92.

3	1921–22*a*	Southampton*	61	Plymouth Arg	61	Portsmouth	53
3	1922–23*a*	Bristol C	59	Plymouth Arg*	53	Swansea T	53
3	1923–24*a*	Portsmouth	59	Plymouth Arg	55	Millwall	54
3	1924–25*a*	Swansea T	57	Plymouth Arg	56	Bristol C	53
3	1925–26*a*	Reading	57	Plymouth Arg	56	Millwall	53
3	1926–27*a*	Bristol C	62	Plymouth Arg	60	Millwall	56
3	1927–28*a*	Millwall	65	Northampton T	55	Plymouth Arg	53
3	1928–29*a*	Charlton Ath*	54	Crystal Palace	54	Northampton T*	52
3	1929–30*a*	Plymouth Arg	68	Brentford	61	QPR	51
3	1930–31*a*	Notts Co	59	Crystal Palace	51	Brentford	50
3	1931–32*a*	Fulham	57	Reading	55	Southend U	53
3	1932–33*a*	Brentford	62	Exeter C	58	Norwich C	57
3	1933–34*a*	Norwich C	61	Coventry C*	54	Reading*	54
3	1934–35*a*	Charlton Ath	61	Reading	53	Coventry C	51
3	1935–36*a*	Coventry C	57	Luton T	56	Reading	54
3	1936–37*a*	Luton T	58	Notts Co	56	Brighton & HA	53
3	1937–38*a*	Millwall	56	Bristol C	55	QPR*	53
3	1938–39*a*	Newport Co	55	Crystal Palace	52	Brighton & HA	49
3	1946–47*a*	Cardiff C	66	QPR	57	Bristol C	51
3	1947–48*a*	QPR	61	Bournemouth	57	Walsall	51
3	1948–49*a*	Swansea T	62	Reading	55	Bournemouth	52
3	1949–50*a*	Notts Co	58	Northampton T*	51	Southend U	51
3	1950–51*b*	Nottingham F	70	Norwich C	64	Reading*	57
3	1951–52*b*	Plymouth Arg	66	Reading*	61	Norwich C	61
3	1952–53*b*	Bristol R	64	Millwall*	62	Northampton T	62
3	1953–54*b*	Ipswich T	64	Brighton & HA	61	Bristol C	56
3	1954–55*b*	Bristol C	70	Leyton Orient	61	Southampton	59
3	1955–56*b*	Leyton Orient	66	Brighton & HA	65	Ipswich T	64
3	1956–57*b*	Ipswich T*	59	Torquay U	59	Colchester U	58
3	1957–58*b*	Brighton & HA	60	Brentford*	58	Plymouth Arg	58

DIVISION 3—NORTH (1921–22 to 1957–58)

MAXIMUM POINTS: *a* 76; *b* 84; *c* 80; *d* 92.

3	1921–22*a*	Stockport Co	56	Darlington*	50	Grimsby T	50
3	1922–23*a*	Nelson	51	Bradford PA	47	Walsall	46
3	1923–24*b*	Wolverhampton W	63	Rochdale	62	Chesterfield	54
3	1924–25*b*	Darlington	58	Nelson*	53	New Brighton	53
3	1925–26*b*	Grimsby T	61	Bradford PA	60	Rochdale	59
3	1926–27*b*	Stoke C	63	Rochdale	58	Bradford PA	55
3	1927–28*b*	Bradford PA	63	Lincoln C	55	Stockport Co	54
3	1928–29*b*	Bradford C	63	Stockport Co	62	Wrexham	52
3	1929–30*b*	Port Vale	67	Stockport Co	63	Darlington*	50
3	1930–31*b*	Chesterfield	58	Lincoln C	57	Wrexham*	54
3	1931–32*c*	Lincoln C*	57	Gateshead	57	Chester	50
3	1932–33*b*	Hull C	59	Wrexham	57	Stockport Co	54
3	1933–34*b*	Barnsley	62	Chesterfield	61	Stockport Co	59
3	1934–35*b*	Doncaster R	57	Halifax T	55	Chester	54
3	1935–36*b*	Chesterfield	60	Chester*	55	Tranmere R	55

3	1936–37b	Stockport Co	60	Lincoln C	57	Chester	53
3	1937–38b	Tranmere R	56	Doncaster R	54	Hull C	53
3	1938–39b	Barnsley	67	Doncaster R	56	Bradford C	52
3	1946–47b	Doncaster R	72	Rotherham U	64	Chester	56
3	1947–48b	Lincoln C	60	Rotherham U	59	Wrexham	50
3	1948–49b	Hull C	65	Rotherham U	62	Doncaster R	50
3	1949–50b	Doncaster R	55	Gateshead	53	Rochdale*	51
3	1950–51d	Rotherham U	71	Mansfield T	64	Carlisle U	62
3	1951–52d	Lincoln C	69	Grimsby T	66	Stockport Co	59
3	1952–53d	Oldham Ath	59	Port Vale	58	Wrexham	56
3	1953–54d	Port Vale	69	Barnsley	58	Scunthorpe U	57
3	1954–55d	Barnsley	65	Accrington S	61	Scunthorpe U*	58
3	1955–56d	Grimsby T	68	Derby Co	63	Accrington S	59
3	1956–57d	Derby Co	63	Hartlepools U	59	Accrington S*	58
3	1957–58d	Scunthorpe U	66	Accrington S	59	Bradford C	57

DIVISION 3 (1958–59 to 1991–92)

MAXIMUM POINTS: 92; 138 FROM 1981–82.

3	1958–59	Plymouth Arg	62	Hull C	61	Brentford*	57
3	1959–60	Southampton	61	Norwich C	59	Shrewsbury T*	52
3	1960–61	Bury	68	Walsall	62	QPR	60
3	1961–62	Portsmouth	65	Grimsby T	62	Bournemouth*	59
3	1962–63	Northampton T	62	Swindon T	58	Port Vale	54
3	1963–64	Coventry C*	60	Crystal Palace	60	Watford	58
3	1964–65	Carlisle U	60	Bristol C*	59	Mansfield T	59
3	1965–66	Hull C	69	Millwall	65	QPR	57
3	1966–67	QPR	67	Middlesbrough	55	Watford	54
3	1967–68	Oxford U	57	Bury	56	Shrewsbury T	55
3	1968–69	Watford*	64	Swindon T	64	Luton T	61
3	1969–70	Orient	62	Luton T	60	Bristol R	56
3	1970–71	Preston NE	61	Fulham	60	Halifax T	56
3	1971–72	Aston Villa	70	Brighton & HA	65	Bournemouth*	62
3	1972–73	Bolton W	61	Notts Co	57	Blackburn R	55
3	1973–74	Oldham Ath	62	Bristol R*	61	York C	61
3	1974–75	Blackburn R	60	Plymouth Arg	59	Charlton Ath	55
3	1975–76	Hereford U	63	Cardiff C	57	Millwall	56
3	1976–77	Mansfield T	64	Brighton & HA	61	Crystal Palace*	59
3	1977–78	Wrexham	61	Cambridge U	58	Preston NE*	56
3	1978–79	Shrewsbury T	61	Watford*	60	Swansea C	60
3	1979–80	Grimsby T	62	Blackburn R	59	Sheffield W	58
3	1980–81	Rotherham U	61	Barnsley*	59	Charlton Ath	59
3	1981–82	Burnley*	80	Carlisle U	80	Fulham	78
3	1982–83	Portsmouth	91	Cardiff C	86	Huddersfield T	82
3	1983–84	Oxford U	95	Wimbledon	87	Sheffield U*	83
3	1984–85	Bradford C	94	Millwall	90	Hull C	87
3	1985–86	Reading	94	Plymouth Arg	87	Derby Co	84
3	1986–87	Bournemouth	97	Middlesbrough	94	Swindon T	87
3	1987–88	Sunderland	93	Brighton & HA	84	Walsall	82
3	1988–89	Wolverhampton W	92	Sheffield U*	84	Port Vale	84
3	1989–90	Bristol R	93	Bristol C	91	Notts Co	87
3	1990–91	Cambridge U	86	Southend U	85	Grimsby T*	83
3	1991–92	Brentford	82	Birmingham C	81	Huddersfield T‡	78

SECOND DIVISION (1992–93 to 2003–04)

MAXIMUM POINTS: 138

3	1992–93	Stoke C	93	Bolton W	90	Port Vale‡	89
3	1993–94	Reading	89	Port Vale	88	Plymouth Arg*‡	85
3	1994–95	Birmingham C	89	Brentford‡	85	Crewe Alex‡	83
3	1995–96	Swindon T	92	Oxford U	83	Blackpool‡	82
3	1996–97	Bury	84	Stockport Co	82	Luton T‡	78
3	1997–98	Watford	88	Bristol C	85	Grimsby T	72
3	1998–99	Fulham	101	Walsall	87	Manchester C	82
3	1999–2000	Preston NE	95	Burnley	88	Gillingham	85
3	2000–01	Millwall	93	Rotherham U	91	Reading‡	86
3	2001–02	Brighton & HA	90	Reading	84	Brentford*‡	83
3	2002–03	Wigan Ath	100	Crewe Alex	86	Bristol C*‡	83
3	2003–04	Plymouth Arg	90	QPR	83	Bristol C‡	82

FOOTBALL LEAGUE 1 (2004–05 to 2015–16)

MAXIMUM POINTS: 138

3	2004–05	Luton T	98	Hull C	86	Tranmere R‡	79
3	2005–06	Southend U	82	Colchester U	79	Brentford‡	76
3	2006–07	Scunthorpe U	91	Bristol C	85	Blackpool	83
3	2007–08	Swansea C	92	Nottingham F	82	Doncaster R*	80
3	2008–09	Leicester C	96	Peterborough U	89	Milton Keynes D‡	87
3	2009–10	Norwich C	95	Leeds U	86	Millwall	85
3	2010–11	Brighton & HA	95	Southampton	92	Huddersfield T‡	87
3	2011–12	Charlton Ath	101	Sheffield W	93	Sheffield U‡	90
3	2012–13	Doncaster R	84	Bournemouth	83	Brentford‡	79

3	2013–14	Wolverhampton W	103	Brentford	94	Leyton Orient‡	86
3	2014–15	Bristol C	99	Milton Keynes D	91	Preston NE	89
3	2015–16	Wigan Ath	87	Burton Alb	85	Walsall‡	84

DIVISION 4 (1958–59 to 1991–92) – TIER 4

MAXIMUM POINTS: 92; 138 FROM 1981–82.

4	1958–59	Port Vale	64	Coventry C*	60	York C	60	Shrewsbury T	58
4	1959–60	Walsall	65	Notts Co*	60	Torquay U	60	Watford	57
4	1960–61	Peterborough U	66	Crystal Palace	64	Northampton T*	60	Bradford PA	60
4	1961–62[2]	Millwall	56	Colchester U	55	Wrexham	53	Carlisle U	52
4	1962–63	Brentford	62	Oldham Ath*	59	Crewe Alex	59	Mansfield T*	57
4	1963–64	Gillingham*	60	Carlisle U	60	Workington	59	Exeter C	58
4	1964–65	Brighton & HA	63	Millwall*	62	York C	62	Oxford U	61
4	1965–66	Doncaster R*	59	Darlington	59	Torquay U	58	Colchester U*	56
4	1966–67	Stockport Co	64	Southport*	59	Barrow	59	Tranmere R	58
4	1967–68	Luton T	66	Barnsley	61	Hartlepools U	60	Crewe Alex	58
4	1968–69	Doncaster R	59	Halifax T	57	Rochdale*	56	Bradford C	56
4	1969–70	Chesterfield	64	Wrexham	61	Swansea C	60	Port Vale	59
4	1970–71	Notts Co	69	Bournemouth	60	Oldham Ath	59	York C	56
4	1971–72	Grimsby T	63	Southend U	60	Brentford	59	Scunthorpe U	57
4	1972–73	Southport	62	Hereford U	58	Cambridge U	57	Aldershot*	56
4	1973–74	Peterborough U	65	Gillingham	62	Colchester U	60	Bury	59
4	1974–75	Mansfield T	68	Shrewsbury T	62	Rotherham U	59	Chester*	57
4	1975–76	Lincoln C	74	Northampton T	68	Reading	60	Tranmere R	58
4	1976–77	Cambridge U	65	Exeter C	62	Colchester U*	59	Bradford C	59
4	1977–78	Watford	71	Southend U	60	Swansea C*	56	Brentford	56
4	1978–79	Reading	65	Grimsby T*	61	Wimbledon*	61	Barnsley	61
4	1979–80	Huddersfield T	66	Walsall	64	Newport Co	61	Portsmouth*	60
4	1980–81	Southend U	67	Lincoln C	65	Doncaster R	56	Wimbledon	55
4	1981–82	Sheffield U	96	Bradford C*	91	Wigan Ath	91	Bournemouth	88
4	1982–83	Wimbledon	98	Hull C	90	Port Vale	88	Scunthorpe U	83
4	1983–84	York C	101	Doncaster R	85	Reading*	82	Bristol C	82
4	1984–85	Chesterfield	91	Blackpool	86	Darlington	85	Bury	84
4	1985–86	Swindon T	102	Chester C	84	Mansfield T	81	Port Vale	79
4	1986–87	Northampton T	99	Preston NE	90	Southend U	80	Wolverhampton W‡	79
4	1987–88	Wolverhampton W	90	Cardiff C	85	Bolton W	78	Scunthorpe U*‡	77
4	1988–89	Rotherham U	82	Tranmere R	80	Crewe Alex	78	Scunthorpe U*‡	77
4	1989–90	Exeter C	89	Grimsby T	79	Southend U	75	Stockport Co‡	74
4	1990–91	Darlington	83	Stockport Co*	82	Hartlepool U	82	Peterborough U	80
4	1991–92[3]	Burnley	83	Rotherham U*	77	Mansfield T	77	Blackpool	76

[2]*Maximum points:* 88 owing to Accrington Stanley's resignation.
[3]*Maximum points:* 126 owing to Aldershot being expelled (and only 23 teams started the competition).

THIRD DIVISION (1992–93 to 2003–04)

MAXIMUM POINTS: a 126; b 138.

4	1992–93a	Cardiff C	83	Wrexham	80	Barnet	79	York C	75
4	1993–94a	Shrewsbury T	79	Chester C	74	Crewe Alex	73	Wycombe W	70
4	1994–95a	Carlisle U	91	Walsall	83	Chesterfield	81	Bury‡	80
4	1995–96b	Preston NE	86	Gillingham	83	Bury	79	Plymouth Arg*	78
4	1996–97b	Wigan Ath*	87	Fulham	87	Carlisle U	84	Northampton T	72
4	1997–98b	Notts Co	99	Macclesfield T	82	Lincoln C	72	Colchester U*	74
4	1998–99b	Brentford	85	Cambridge U	81	Cardiff C	80	Scunthorpe U	74
4	1999–2000b	Swansea C	85	Rotherham U	84	Northampton T	82	Darlington‡	79
4	2000–01b	Brighton & HA	92	Cardiff C	82	Chesterfield[4]	80	Hartlepool U‡	77
4	2001–02b	Plymouth Arg	102	Luton T	97	Mansfield T	79	Cheltenham T	78
4	2002–03b	Rushden & D	87	Hartlepool U	85	Wrexham	84	Bournemouth	74
4	2003–04b	Doncaster R	92	Hull C	88	Torquay U*	81	Huddersfield T	81

[4]*Chesterfield deducted 9pts for irregularities.*

FOOTBALL LEAGUE 2 (2004–05 to 2015–16)

MAXIMUM POINTS: 138

4	2004–05	Yeovil T	83	Scunthorpe U*	80	Swansea C	80	Southend U	80
4	2005–06	Carlisle U	86	Northampton T	83	Leyton Orient	81	Grimsby T‡	78
4	2006–07	Walsall	89	Hartlepool U	88	Swindon T	85	Milton Keynes D‡	84
4	2007–08	Milton Keynes D	97	Peterborough U	92	Hereford U	88	Stockport Co	82
4	2008–09	Brentford	85	Exeter C	79	Wycombe W*	78	Bury‡	78
4	2009–10	Notts Co	93	Bournemouth	83	Rochdale	82	Morecambe*‡	73
4	2010–11	Chesterfield	86	Bury	81	Wycombe W	80	Shrewsbury T‡	79
4	2011–12	Swindon T	93	Shrewsbury T	88	Crawley T	84	Southend U‡	83
4	2012–13	Gillingham	83	Rotherham U	79	Port Vale	78	Burton Alb	76
4	2013–14	Chesterfield	84	Scunthorpe U*	81	Rochdale	81	Fleetwood T	76
4	2014–15	Burton Alb	94	Shrewsbury T	89	Bury	85	Wycombe W*‡	84
4	2015–16	Northampton T	99	Oxford U	86	Bristol R*	85	Accrington S‡	85

LEAGUE TITLE WINS

DIVISION 1 (1888–89 to 1991–92) – TIER 1
Liverpool 18, Arsenal 10, Everton 9, Aston Villa 7, Manchester U 7, Sunderland 6, Newcastle U 4, Sheffield W 4 (2 as The Wednesday), Huddersfield T 3, Leeds U 3, Wolverhampton W 3, Blackburn R 2, Burnley 2, Derby Co 2, Manchester C 2, Portsmouth 2, Preston NE 2, Tottenham H 2, Chelsea 1, Ipswich T 1, Nottingham F 1, Sheffield U 1, WBA 1.

FA PREMIER LEAGUE (1992–93 to 2015–16) – TIER 1
Manchester U 13, Chelsea 4, Arsenal 3, Manchester C 2, Blackburn R 1, Leicester C 1.

DIVISION 2 (1892–93 TO 1991–92) – TIER 2
Leicester C 6, Manchester C 6, Sheffield W 5 (1 as The Wednesday), Birmingham C 4 (1 as Small Heath), Derby Co 4, Liverpool 4, Ipswich T 3, Leeds U 3, Middlesbrough 3, Notts Co 3, Preston NE 3, Aston Villa 2, Bolton W 2, Burnley 2, Chelsea 2, Grimsby T 2, Manchester U 2, Norwich C 2, Nottingham F 2, Stoke C 2, Tottenham H 2, WBA 2, West Ham U 2, Wolverhampton W 2, Blackburn R 1, Blackpool 1, Bradford C 1, Brentford 1, Bristol C 1, Bury 1, Coventry C 1, Crystal Palace 1, Everton 1, Fulham 1, Huddersfield T 1, Luton T 1, Millwall 1, Newcastle U 1, Oldham Ath 1, Oxford U 1, QPR 1, Sheffield U 1, Sunderland 1.

FIRST DIVISION (1992–93 to 2003–04) – TIER 2
Sunderland , Bolton W, Charlton Ath 1, Crystal Palace 1, Fulham 1, Manchester C 1, Middlesbrough 1, Newcastle U 1, Norwich C 1, Nottingham F 1, Portsmouth 1.

FOOTBALL LEAGUE CHAMPIONSHIP (2004–05 to 2015–16) – TIER 2
Reading 2, Sunderland 2, Bournemouth 1, Burnley 1, Cardiff C 1, Leicester C 1, Newcastle U 1, QPR 1, WBA 1, Wolverhampton W 1.

DIVISION 3—SOUTH (1920–21 to 1957–58) – TIER 3
Bristol C 3, Charlton Ath 2, Ipswich T 2, Millwall 2, Notts Co 2, Plymouth Arg 2, Swansea T 2, Brentford 1, Brighton & HA 1, Bristol R 1, Cardiff C 1, Coventry C 1, Crystal Palace 1, Fulham 1, Leyton Orient 1, Luton T 1, Newport Co 1, Norwich C 1, Nottingham F 1, Portsmouth 1, QPR 1, Reading 1, Southampton 1.

DIVISION 3—NORTH (1921–22 to 1957–58) – TIER 3
Barnsley 3, Doncaster R 3, Lincoln C 3, Chesterfield 2, Grimsby T 2, Hull C 2, Port Vale 2, Stockport Co 2, Bradford C 1, Bradford PA 1, Darlington 1, Derby Co 1, Nelson 1, Oldham Ath 1, Rotherham U 1, Scunthorpe U 1, Stoke C 1, Tranmere R 1, Wolverhampton W 1.

DIVISION 3 (1958–59 to 1991–92) – TIER 3
Oxford U 2, Portsmouth 2, Aston Villa 1, Blackburn R 1, Bolton W 1, Bournemouth 1, Bradford C 1, Brentford 1, Bristol R 1, Burnley 1, Bury 1, Cambridge U 1, Carlisle U 1, Coventry C 1, Grimsby T 1, Hereford U 1, Hull C 1, Mansfield T 1, Northampton T 1, Oldham Ath 1, Orient 1, Plymouth Arg 1, Preston NE 1, QPR 1, Reading 1, Rotherham U 1, Shrewsbury T 1, Southampton 1, Sunderland 1, Watford 1, Wolverhampton W 1, Wrexham 1.

SECOND DIVISION (1992–93 to 2003–04) – TIER 3
Birmingham C 1, Brighton & HA 1, Bury 1, Fulham 1, Millwall 1, Plymouth Arg 1, Preston NE 1, Reading 1, Stoke C 1, Swindon T 1, Watford 1, Wigan Ath 1.

FOOTBALL LEAGUE 1 (2004–05 to 2015–16) – TIER 3
Brighton & HA 1, Bristol C 1, Charlton Ath 1, Doncaster R 1, Leicester C 1, Luton T 1, Norwich C 1, Scunthorpe U 1, Southend U 1, Swansea C 1, Wigan Ath 1, Wolverhampton W 1.

DIVISION 4 (1958–59 to 1991–92) – TIER 4
Chesterfield 2, Doncaster R 2, Peterborough U 2, Brentford 1, Brighton & HA 1, Burnley 1, Cambridge U 1, Darlington 1, Exeter C 1, Gillingham 1, Grimsby T 1, Huddersfield T 1, Lincoln C 1, Luton T 1, Mansfield T 1, Millwall 1, Northampton T 1, Notts Co 1, Port Vale 1, Reading 1, Rotherham U 1, Sheffield U 1, Southend U 1, Southport 1, Stockport Co 1, Swindon T 1, Walsall 1, Watford 1, Wimbledon 1, Wolverhampton W 1, York C 1.

THIRD DIVISION (1992–93 to 2003–04) – TIER 4
Brentford 1, Brighton & HA 1, Cardiff C 1, Carlisle U 1, Doncaster R 1, Notts Co 1, Plymouth Arg 1, Preston NE 1, Rushden & D 1, Shrewsbury T 1, Swansea C 1, Wigan Ath 1.

FOOTBALL LEAGUE 2 (2004–05 to 2015–16) – TIER 4
Chesterfield 2, Brentford 1, Burton Alb 1, Carlisle U 1, Gillingham 1, Milton Keynes D 1, Northampton T 1, Notts Co 1, Swindon T 1, Walsall 1, Yeovil T 1.

PROMOTED AFTER PLAY-OFFS

1986–87	Charlton Ath to Division 1; Swindon T to Division 2; Aldershot to Division 3
1987–88	Middlesbrough to Division 1; Walsall to Division 2; Swansea C to Division 3
1988–89	Crystal Palace to Division 1; Port Vale to Division 2; Leyton Orient to Division 3
1989–90	Sunderland to Division 1; Notts Co to Division 2; Cambridge U to Division 3
1990–91	Notts Co to Division 1; Tranmere R to Division 2; Torquay U to Division 3
1991–92	Blackburn R to Premier League; Peterborough U to First Division; Blackpool to Second Division
1992–93	Swindon T to Premier League; WBA to First Division; York C to Second Division
1993–94	Leicester C to Premier League; Burnley to First Division; Wycombe W to Second Division
1994–95	Bolton W to Premier League; Huddersfield T to First Division; Wycome Wanderers to Second Division
1995–96	Leicester C to Premier League; Bradford C to First Division; Plymouth Arg to Second Division
1996–97	Crystal Palace to Premier League; Crewe Alex to First Division; Northampton T to Second Division
1997–98	Charlton Ath to Premier League; Grimsby T to First Division; Colchester U to Second Division
1998–99	Watford to Premier League; Manchester C to First Division; Scunthorpe U to Second Division
1999–2000	Ipswich to Premier League; Gillingham to First Division; Peterborough U to Second Division
2000–01	Bolton W to Premier league; Walsall to First Division; Blackpool to Second Division
2001–02	Birmingham C to Premier League; Stoke C to First Division; Cheltenham T to Second Division
2002–03	Wolverhampton W to Premier League; Cardiff C to First Division; Bournemouth to Second Division
2003–04	Crystal Palace to Premier League; Brighton & HA to First Division; Huddersfield T to Second Division
2004–05	West Ham U to Premier League; Sheffield W to Championship; Southend U to Football League 1
2005–06	Watford to Premier League; Barnsley to Championship; Cheltenham T to Football League 1
2006–07	Derby Co to Premier League; Blackpool to Championship; Bristol R to Football League 1
2007–08	Hull C to Premier League; Doncaster R to Championship; Stockport Co to Football League 1
2008–09	Burnley to Premier League; Scunthorpe U to Championship; Gillingham to Football League 1
2009–10	Blackpool to Premier League; Millwall to Championship; Dagenham & R to Football League 1
2010–11	Swansea C to Premier League; Peterborough U to Championship; Stevenage to Football League 1
2011–12	West Ham U to Premier League; Huddersfield T to Championship; Crewe Alex to Football League 1
2012–13	Crystal Palace to Premier League; Yeovil T to Championship; Bradford C to Football League 1
2013–14	QPR to Premier League; Rotherham U to Championship; Fleetwood T to Football League 1
2014–15	Norwich C to Premier League; Preston NE to Championship; Southend U to Football League 1
2015–16	Hull C to Premier League; Barnsley to Championship; AFC Wimbledon to Football League 1

RELEGATED CLUBS

1891–92   League extended. Newton Heath, Sheffield W and Nottingham F admitted. *Second Division formed* including Darwen.
1892–93   In Test matches, Sheffield U and Darwen won promotion in place of Notts Co and Accrington S.
1893–94   In Tests, Liverpool and Small Heath won promotion. Newton Heath and Darwen relegated.
1894–95   After Tests, Bury promoted, Liverpool demoted.
1895–96   After Tests, Liverpool promoted, Small Heath relegated.
1896–97   After Tests, Notts Co promoted, Burnley relegated.
1897–98   Test system abolished after success of Stoke C and Burnley. League extended. Blackburn R and Newcastle U elected to First Division. *Automatic promotion and relegation introduced.*

DIVISION 1 TO DIVISION 2 (1898–99 to 1991–92)

1898–99 Bolton W and Sheffield W	1952–53 Stoke C and Derby Co
1899–1900 Burnley and Glossop	1953–54 Middlesbrough and Liverpool
1900–01 Preston NE and WBA	1954–55 Leicester C and Sheffield W
1901–02 Small Heath and Manchester C	1955–56 Huddersfield T and Sheffield U
1902–03 Grimsby T and Bolton W	1956–57 Charlton Ath and Cardiff C
1903–04 Liverpool and WBA	1957–58 Sheffield W and Sunderland
1904–05 League extended. Bury and Notts Co, two	1958–59 Portsmouth and Aston Villa
bottom clubs in First Division, re-elected.	1959–60 Luton T and Leeds U
1905–06 Nottingham F and Wolverhampton W	1960–61 Preston NE and Newcastle U
1906–07 Derby Co and Stoke C	1961–62 Chelsea and Cardiff C
1907–08 Bolton W and Birmingham C	1962–63 Manchester C and Leyton Orient
1908–09 Manchester C and Leicester Fosse	1963–64 Bolton W and Ipswich T
1909–10 Bolton W and Chelsea	1964–65 Wolverhampton W and Birmingham C
1910–11 Bristol C and Nottingham F	1965–66 Northampton T and Blackburn R
1911–12 Preston NE and Bury	1966–67 Aston Villa and Blackpool
1912–13 Notts Co and Woolwich Arsenal	1967–68 Fulham and Sheffield U
1913–14 Preston NE and Derby Co	1968–69 Leicester C and QPR
1914–15 Tottenham H and Chelsea*	1969–70 Sunderland and Sheffield W
1919–20 Notts Co and Sheffield W	1970–71 Burnley and Blackpool
1920–21 Derby Co and Bradford PA	1971–72 Huddersfield T and Nottingham F
1921–22 Bradford C and Manchester U	1972–73 Crystal Palace and WBA
1922–23 Stoke C and Oldham Ath	1973–74 Southampton, Manchester U, Norwich C
1923–24 Chelsea and Middlesbrough	1974–75 Luton T, Chelsea, Carlisle U
1924–25 Preston NE and Nottingham F	1975–76 Wolverhampton W, Burnley, Sheffield U
1925–26 Manchester C and Notts Co	1976–77 Sunderland, Stoke C, Tottenham H
1926–27 Leeds U and WBA	1977–78 West Ham U, Newcastle U, Leicester C
1927–28 Tottenham H and Middlesbrough	1978–79 QPR, Birmingham C, Chelsea
1928–29 Bury and Cardiff C	1979–80 Bristol C, Derby Co, Bolton W
1929–30 Burnley and Everton	1980–81 Norwich C, Leicester C, Crystal Palace
1930–31 Leeds U and Manchester U	1981–82 Leeds U, Wolverhampton W, Middlesbrough
1931–32 Grimsby T and West Ham U	1982–83 Manchester C, Swansea C, Brighton & HA
1932–33 Bolton W and Blackpool	1983–84 Birmingham C, Notts Co, Wolverhampton W
1933–34 Newcastle U and Sheffield U	1984–85 Norwich C, Sunderland, Stoke C
1934–35 Leicester C and Tottenham H	1985–86 Ipswich T, Birmingham C, WBA
1935–36 Aston Villa and Blackburn R	1986–87 Leicester C, Manchester C, Aston Villa
1936–37 Manchester U and Sheffield W	1987–88 Chelsea**, Portsmouth, Watford, Oxford U
1937–38 Manchester C and WBA	1988–89 Middlesbrough, West Ham U, Newcastle U
1938–39 Birmingham C and Leicester C	1989–90 Sheffield W, Charlton Ath, Millwall
1946–47 Brentford and Leeds U	1990–91 Sunderland and Derby Co
1947–48 Blackburn R and Grimsby T	1991–92 Luton T, Notts Co, West Ham U
1948–49 Preston NE and Sheffield U	***Relegated after play-offs.*
1949–50 Manchester C and Birmingham C	**Subsequently re-elected to Division 1 when League was*
1950–51 Sheffield W and Everton	* extended after the War.*
1951–52 Huddersfield T and Fulham	

FA PREMIER LEAGUE TO DIVISION 1 (1992–93 to 2003–04)

1992–93 Crystal Palace, Middlesbrough, Nottingham F	1998–99 Charlton Ath, Blackburn R, Nottingham F
1993–94 Sheffield U, Oldham Ath, Swindon T	1999–2000 Wimbledon, Sheffield W, Watford
1994–95 Crystal Palace, Norwich C, Leicester C, Ipswich T	2000–01 Manchester C, Coventry C, Bradford C
1995–96 Manchester C, QPR, Bolton W	2001–02 Ipswich T, Derby Co, Leicester C
1996–97 Sunderland, Middlesbrough, Nottingham F	2002–03 West Ham U, WBA, Sunderland
1997–98 Bolton W, Barnsley, Crystal Palace	2003–04 Leicester C, Leeds U, Wolverhampton W

FA PREMIER LEAGUE TO CHAMPIONSHIP (2004–05 to 2015–16)

2004–05 Crystal Palace, Norwich C, Southampton	2010–11 Birmingham C, Blackpool, West Ham U
2005–06 Birmingham C, WBA, Sunderland	2011–12 Bolton W, Blackburn R, Wolverhampton W
2006–07 Sheffield U, Charlton Ath, Watford	2012–13 Wigan Ath, Reading, QPR
2007–08 Reading, Birmingham C, Derby Co	2013–14 Norwich C, Fulham, Cardiff C
2008–09 Newcastle U, Middlesbrough, WBA	2014–15 Hull C, Burnley, QPR
2009–10 Burnley, Hull C, Portsmouth	2015–16 Newcastle U, Norwich C, Aston Villa

DIVISION 2 TO DIVISION 3 (1920–21 to 1991–92)

1920–21 Stockport Co	1923–24 Nelson and Bristol C
1921–22 Bradford PA and Bristol C	1924–25 Crystal Palace and Coventry C
1922–23 Rotherham Co and Wolverhampton W	1925–26 Stoke C and Stockport Co

1926–27 Darlington and Bradford C
1927–28 Fulham and South Shields
1928–29 Port Vale and Clapton Orient
1929–30 Hull C and Notts Co
1930–31 Reading and Cardiff C
1931–32 Barnsley and Bristol C
1932–33 Chesterfield and Charlton Ath
1933–34 Millwall and Lincoln C
1934–35 Oldham Ath and Notts Co
1935–36 Port Vale and Hull C
1936–37 Doncaster R and Bradford C
1937–38 Barnsley and Stockport Co
1938–39 Norwich C and Tranmere R
1946–47 Swansea T and Newport Co
1947–48 Doncaster R and Millwall
1948–49 Nottingham F and Lincoln C
1949–50 Plymouth Arg and Bradford PA
1950–51 Grimsby T and Chesterfield
1951–52 Coventry C and QPR
1952–53 Southampton and Barnsley
1953–54 Brentford and Oldham Ath
1954–55 Ipswich T and Derby Co
1955–56 Plymouth Arg and Hull C
1956–57 Port Vale and Bury
1957–58 Doncaster R and Notts Co
1958–59 Barnsley and Grimsby T
1959–60 Bristol C and Hull C
1960–61 Lincoln C and Portsmouth
1961–62 Brighton & HA and Bristol R
1962–63 Walsall and Luton T

1963–64 Grimsby T and Scunthorpe U
1964–65 Swindon T and Swansea T
1965–66 Middlesbrough and Leyton Orient
1966–67 Northampton T and Bury
1967–68 Plymouth Arg and Rotherham U
1968–69 Fulham and Bury
1969–70 Preston NE and Aston Villa
1970–71 Blackburn R and Bolton W
1971–72 Charlton Ath and Watford
1972–73 Huddersfield T and Brighton & HA
1973–74 Crystal Palace, Preston NE, Swindon T
1974–75 Millwall, Cardiff C, Sheffield W
1975–76 Oxford U, York C, Portsmouth
1976–77 Carlisle U, Plymouth Arg, Hereford U
1977–78 Blackpool, Mansfield T, Hull C
1978–79 Sheffield U, Millwall, Blackburn R
1979–80 Fulham, Burnley, Charlton Ath
1980–81 Preston NE, Bristol C, Bristol R
1981–82 Cardiff C, Wrexham, Orient
1982–83 Rotherham U, Burnley, Bolton W
1983–84 Derby Co, Swansea C, Cambridge U
1984–85 Notts Co, Cardiff C, Wolverhampton W
1985–86 Carlisle U, Middlesbrough, Fulham
1986–87 Sunderland**, Grimsby T, Brighton & HA
1987–88 Huddersfield T, Reading, Sheffield U**
1988–89 Shrewsbury T, Birmingham C, Walsall
1989–90 Bournemouth, Bradford C, Stoke C
1990–91 WBA and Hull C
1991–92 Plymouth Arg, Brighton & HA, Port Vale

FIRST DIVISION TO SECOND DIVISION (1992–93 to 2003–04)

1992–93 Brentford, Cambridge U, Bristol R
1993–94 Birmingham C, Oxford U, Peterborough U
1994–95 Swindon T, Burnley, Bristol C, Notts Co
1995–96 Millwall, Watford, Luton T
1996–97 Grimsby T, Oldham Ath, Southend U
1997–98 Manchester C, Stoke C, Reading

1998–99 Bury, Oxford U, Bristol C
1999–2000 Walsall, Port Vale, Swindon T
2000–01 Huddersfield T, QPR, Tranmere R
2001–02 Crewe Alex, Barnsley, Stockport Co
2002–03 Sheffield W, Brighton & HA, Grimsby T
2003–04 Walsall, Bradford C, Wimbledon

FOOTBALL LEAGUE CHAMPIONSHIP TO FOOTBALL LEAGUE 1 (2004–05 to 2015–16)

2004–05 Gillingham, Nottingham F, Rotherham U
2005–06 Crewe Alex, Millwall, Brighton & HA
2006–07 Southend U, Luton T, Leeds U
2007–08 Leicester C, Scunthorpe U, Colchester U
2008–09 Norwich C, Southampton, Charlton Ath
2009–10 Sheffield W, Plymouth Arg, Peterborough U

2010–11 Preston NE, Sheffield U, Scunthorpe U
2011–12 Portsmouth, Coventry C, Doncaster R
2012–13 Peterborough U, Wolverhampton W, Bristol C
2013–14 Doncaster R, Barnsley, Yeovil T
2014–15 Millwall, Wigan Ath, Blackpool
2015–16 Charlton Ath, Milton Keynes D, Bolton W

DIVISION 3 TO DIVISION 4 (1958–59 to 1991–92)

1958–59 Stockport Co, Doncaster R, Notts Co, Rochdale
1959–60 York C, Mansfield T, Wrexham, Accrington S
1960–61 Tranmere R, Bradford C, Colchester U,
 Chesterfield
1961–62 Torquay U, Lincoln C, Brentford, Newport Co
1962–63 Bradford PA, Brighton & HA, Carlisle U,
 Halifax T
1963–64 Millwall, Crewe Alex, Wrexham, Notts Co
1964–65 Luton T, Port Vale, Colchester U, Barnsley
1965–66 Southend U, Exeter C, Brentford, York C
1966–67 Swansea T, Darlington, Doncaster R, Workington
1967–68 Grimsby T, Colchester U, Scunthorpe U,
 Peterborough U (demoted)
1968–69 Northampton T, Hartlepool, Crewe Alex,
 Oldham Ath
1969–70 Bournemouth, Southport, Barrow, Stockport Co
1970–71 Reading, Bury, Doncaster R, Gillingham
1971–72 Mansfield T, Barnsley, Torquay U, Bradford C
1972–73 Rotherham U, Brentford, Swansea C,
 Scunthorpe U
1973–74 Cambridge U, Shrewsbury T, Southport,
 Rochdale

1974–75 Bournemouth, Tranmere R, Watford,
 Huddersfield T
1975–76 Aldershot, Colchester U, Southend U, Halifax T
1976–77 Reading, Northampton T, Grimsby T, York C
1977–78 Port Vale, Bradford C, Hereford U, Portsmouth
1978–79 Peterborough U, Walsall, Tranmere R, Lincoln C
1979–80 Bury, Southend U, Mansfield T, Wimbledon
1980–81 Sheffield U, Colchester U, Blackpool, Hull C
1981–82 Wimbledon, Swindon T, Bristol C, Chester
1982–83 Reading, Wrexham, Doncaster R, Chesterfield
1983–84 Scunthorpe U, Southend U, Port Vale, Exeter C
1984–85 Burnley, Orient, Preston NE, Cambridge U
1985–86 Lincoln C, Cardiff C, Wolverhampton W,
 Swansea C
1986–87 Bolton W**, Carlisle U, Darlington, Newport Co
1987–88 Rotherham U**, Grimsby T, York C, Doncaster R
1988–89 Southend U, Chesterfield, Gillingham, Aldershot
1989–90 Cardiff C, Northampton T, Blackpool, Walsall
1990–91 Crewe Alex, Rotherham U, Mansfield T
1991–92 Bury, Shrewsbury T, Torquay U, Darlington

** *Relegated after play-offs.*

SECOND DIVISION TO THIRD DIVISION (1992–93 to 2003–04)

1992–93 Preston NE, Mansfield T, Wigan Ath, Chester C
1993–94 Fulham, Exeter C, Hartlepool U, Barnet
1994–95 Cambridge U, Plymouth Arg, Cardiff C,
 Chester C, Leyton Orient
1995–96 Carlisle U, Swansea C, Brighton & HA, Hull C

1996–97 Peterborough U, Shrewsbury T, Rotherham U,
 Notts Co
1997–98 Brentford, Plymouth Arg, Carlisle U, Southend U
1998–99 York C, Northampton T, Lincoln C,
 Macclesfield T

1999–2000 Cardiff C, Blackpool, Scunthorpe U, Chesterfield	2002–03 Cheltenham T, Huddersfield T, Mansfield T Northampton T
2000–01 Bristol R, Luton T, Swansea C, Oxford U	2003–04 Grimsby T, Rushden & D, Notts Co, Wycombe W
2001–02 Bournemouth, Bury, Wrexham, Cambridge U	

FOOTBALL LEAGUE 1 TO FOOTBALL LEAGUE 2 (2004–05 to 2015–16)

2004–05 Torquay U, Wrexham, Peterborough U, Stockport Co	2010–11 Dagenham & R, Bristol R, Plymouth Arg, Swindon T
2005–06 Hartlepool U, Milton Keynes D, Swindon T, Walsall	2011–12 Wycombe W, Chesterfield, Exeter C, Rochdale
2006–07 Chesterfield, Bradford C, Rotherham U, Brentford	2012–13 Scunthorpe U, Bury, Hartlepool U, Portsmouth
	2013–14 Tranmere R, Carlisle U, Shrewsbury T, Stevenage
2007–08 Bournemouth, Gillingham, Port Vale, Luton T	2014–15 Notts Co, Crawley T, Leyton Orient, Yeovil T
2008–09 Northampton T, Crewe Alex, Cheltenham T, Hereford U	2015–16 Doncaster R, Blackpool, Colchester U, Crewe Alex
2009–10 Gillingham, Wycombe W, Southend U, Stockport Co	

LEAGUE STATUS FROM 1986–87

RELEGATED FROM LEAGUE

1986–87 Lincoln C	1987–88 Newport Co
1988–89 Darlington	1989–90 Colchester U
1990–91 —	1991–92 —
1992–93 Halifax T	1993–94 —
1994–95 —	1995–96 —
1996–97 Hereford U	1997–98 Doncaster R
1998–99 Scarborough	1999–2000 Chester C
2000–01 Barnet	2001–02 Halifax T
2002–03 Shrewsbury T, Exeter C	
2003–04 Carlisle U, York C	
2004–05 Kidderminster H, Cambridge U	
2005–06 Oxford U, Rushden & D	
2006–07 Boston U, Torquay U	
2007–08 Mansfield T, Wrexham	
2008–09 Chester C, Luton T	
2009–10 Grimsby T, Darlington	
2010–11 Lincoln C, Stockport Co	
2011–12 Hereford U, Macclesfield T	
2012–13 Barnet, Aldershot T	
2013–14 Bristol R, Torquay U	
2014–15 Cheltenham T, Tranmere R	
2015–16 Dagenham & R, York C	

PROMOTED TO LEAGUE

1986–87 Scarborough	1987–88 Lincoln C
1988–89 Maidstone U	1989–90 Darlington
1990–91 Barnet	1991–92 Colchester U
1992–93 Wycombe W	1993–94 —
1994–95 —	1995–96 —
1996–97 Macclesfield T	1997–98 Halifax T
1998–99 Cheltenham T	1999–2000 Kidderminster H
2000–01 Rushden & D	2001–02 Boston U
2002–03 Yeovil T, Doncaster R	
2003–04 Chester C, Shrewsbury T	
2004–05 Barnet, Carlisle U	
2005–06 Accrington S, Hereford U	
2006–07 Dagenham & R, Morecambe	
2007–08 Aldershot T, Exeter C	
2008–09 Burton Alb, Torquay U	
2009–10 Stevenage B, Oxford U	
2010–11 Crawley T, AFC Wimbledon	
2011–12 Fleetwood T, York C	
2012–13 Mansfield T, Newport Co	
2013–14 Luton T, Cambridge U	
2014–15 Barnet, Bristol R	
2015–16 Cheltenham T, Grimsby T	

APPLICATIONS FOR RE-ELECTION

FOURTH DIVISION

Eleven: Hartlepool U.
Seven: Crewe Alex.
Six: Barrow (lost League place to Hereford U 1972), Halifax T, Rochdale, Southport (lost League place to Wigan Ath 1978), York C.
Five: Chester C, Darlington, Lincoln C, Stockport Co, Workington (lost League place to Wimbledon 1977).
Four: Bradford PA (lost League place to Cambridge U 1970), Newport Co, Northampton T.
Three: Doncaster R, Hereford U.
Two: Bradford C, Exeter C, Oldham Ath, Scunthorpe U, Torquay U.
One: Aldershot, Colchester U, Gateshead (lost League place to Peterborough U 1960), Grimsby T, Swansea C, Tranmere R, Wrexham, Blackpool, Cambridge U, Preston NE.
Accrington S resigned and Oxford U were elected 1962.
Port Vale were forced to re-apply following expulsion in 1968.
Aldershot expelled March 1992. Maidstone U resigned August 1992.

THIRD DIVISIONS NORTH & SOUTH

Seven: Walsall.
Six: Exeter C, Halifax T, Newport Co.
Five: Accrington S, Barrow, Gillingham, New Brighton, Southport.
Four: Rochdale, Norwich C.
Three: Crystal Palace, Crewe Alex, Darlington, Hartlepool U, Merthyr T, Swindon T.
Two: Aberdare Ath, Aldershot, Ashington, Bournemouth, Brentford, Chester, Colchester U, Durham C, Millwall, Nelson, QPR, Rotherham U, Southend U, Tranmere R, Watford, Workington.
One: Bradford C, Bradford PA, Brighton & HA, Bristol R, Cardiff C, Carlisle U, Charlton Ath, Gateshead, Grimsby T, Mansfield T, Shrewsbury T, Torquay U, York C.

LEAGUE ATTENDANCES SINCE 1946–47

Season	Matches	Total	Div. 1	Div. 2	Div. 3 (S)	Div. 3 (N)
1946–47	1848	35,604,606	15,005,316	11,071,572	5,664,004	3,863,714
1947–48	1848	40,259,130	16,732,341	12,286,350	6,653,610	4,586,829
1948–49	1848	41,271,414	17,914,667	11,353,237	6,998,429	5,005,081
1949–50	1848	40,517,865	17,278,625	11,694,158	7,104,155	4,440,927
1950–51	2028	39,584,967	16,679,454	10,780,580	7,367,884	4,757,109
1951–52	2028	39,015,866	16,110,322	11,066,189	6,958,927	4,880,428
1952–53	2028	37,149,966	16,050,278	9,686,654	6,704,299	4,708,735
1953–54	2028	36,174,590	16,154,915	9,510,053	6,311,508	4,198,114
1954–55	2028	34,133,103	15,087,221	8,988,794	5,996,017	4,051,071
1955–56	2028	33,150,809	14,108,961	9,080,002	5,692,479	4,269,367
1956–57	2028	32,744,405	13,803,037	8,718,162	5,622,189	4,601,017
1957–58	2028	33,562,208	14,468,652	8,663,712	6,097,183	4,332,661

Season	Matches	Total	Div. 1	Div. 2	Div. 3	Div. 4
1958–59	2028	33,610,985	14,727,691	8,641,997	5,946,600	4,276,697
1959–60	2028	32,538,611	14,391,227	8,399,627	5,739,707	4,008,050
1960–61	2028	28,619,754	12,926,948	7,033,936	4,784,256	3,874,614
1961–62	2015	27,979,902	12,061,194	7,453,089	5,199,106	3,266,513
1962–63	2028	28,885,852	12,490,239	7,792,770	5,341,362	3,261,481
1963–64	2028	28,535,022	12,486,626	7,594,158	5,419,157	3,035,081
1964–65	2028	27,641,168	12,708,752	6,984,104	4,436,245	3,512,067
1965–66	2028	27,206,980	12,480,644	6,914,757	4,779,150	3,032,429
1966–67	2028	28,902,596	14,242,957	7,253,819	4,421,172	2,984,648
1967–68	2028	30,107,298	15,289,410	7,450,410	4,013,087	3,354,391
1968–69	2028	29,382,172	14,584,851	7,382,390	4,339,656	3,075,275
1969–70	2028	29,600,972	14,868,754	7,581,728	4,223,761	2,926,729
1970–71	2028	28,194,146	13,954,337	7,098,265	4,377,213	2,764,331
1971–72	2028	28,700,729	14,484,603	6,769,308	4,697,392	2,749,426
1972–73	2028	25,448,642	13,998,154	5,631,730	3,737,252	2,081,506
1973–74	2027	24,982,203	13,070,991	6,326,108	3,421,624	2,163,480
1974–75	2028	25,577,977	12,613,178	6,955,970	4,086,145	1,992,684
1975–76	2028	24,896,053	13,089,861	5,798,405	3,948,449	2,059,338
1976–77	2028	26,182,800	13,647,585	6,250,597	4,152,218	2,132,400
1977–78	2028	25,392,872	13,255,677	6,474,763	3,332,042	2,330,390
1978–79	2028	24,540,627	12,704,549	6,153,223	3,374,558	2,308,297
1979–80	2028	24,623,975	12,163,002	6,112,025	3,999,328	2,349,620
1980–81	2028	21,907,569	11,392,894	5,175,442	3,637,854	1,701,379
1981–82	2028	20,006,961	10,420,793	4,750,463	2,836,915	1,998,790
1982–83	2028	18,766,158	9,295,613	4,974,937	2,943,568	1,552,040
1983–84	2028	18,358,631	8,711,448	5,359,757	2,729,942	1,557,484
1984–85	2028	17,849,835	9,761,404	4,030,823	2,667,008	1,390,600
1985–86	2028	16,488,577	9,037,854	3,551,968	2,490,481	1,408,274
1986–87	2028	17,379,218	9,144,676	4,168,131	2,350,970	1,715,441
1987–88	2030	17,959,732	8,094,571	5,341,599	2,751,275	1,772,287
1988–89	2036	18,464,192	7,809,993	5,887,805	3,035,327	1,791,067
1989–90	2036	19,445,442	7,883,039	6,867,674	2,803,551	1,891,178
1990–91	2036	19,508,202	8,618,709	6,285,068	2,835,759	1,768,666
1991–92	2064*	20,487,273	9,989,160	5,809,787	2,993,352	1,694,974

Season	Matches	Total	FA Premier	Div. 1	Div. 2	Div. 3
1992–93	2028	20,657,327	9,759,809	5,874,017	3,483,073	1,540,428
1993–94	2028	21,683,381	10,644,551	6,487,104	2,972,702	1,579,024
1994–95	2028	21,856,020	11,213,168	6,044,293	3,037,752	1,560,807
1995–96	2036	21,844,416	10,469,107	6,566,349	2,843,652	1,965,308
1996–97	2036	22,783,163	10,804,762	6,931,539	3,195,223	1,851,639
1997–98	2036	24,692,608	11,092,106	8,330,018	3,503,264	1,767,220
1998–99	2036	25,435,542	11,620,326	7,543,369	4,169,697	2,102,150
1999–2000	2036	25,341,090	11,668,497	7,810,208	3,700,433	2,161,952
2000–01	2036	26,030,167	12,472,094	7,909,512	3,488,166	2,160,395
2001–02	2036	27,756,977	13,043,118	8,352,128	3,963,153	2,398,578
2002–03	2036	28,343,386	13,468,965	8,521,017	3,892,469	2,460,935
2003–04	2036	29,197,510	13,303,136	8,772,780	4,146,495	2,975,099

Season	Matches	Total	FA Premier	Championship	League 1	League 2
2004–05	2036	29,245,870	12,878,791	9,612,761	4,270,674	2,483,644
2005–06	2036	29,089,084	12,871,643	9,719,204	4,183,011	2,315,226
2006–07	2036	29,541,949	13,058,115	10,057,813	4,135,599	2,290,422
2007–08	2036	29,914,212	13,708,875	9,397,036	4,412,023	2,396,278
2008–09	2036	29,881,966	13,527,815	9,877,552	4,171,834	2,304,765
2009–10	2036	30,057,892	12,977,251	9,909,882	5,043,099	2,127,660
2010–11	2036	29,459,105	13,406,990	9,595,236	4,150,547	2,306,332
2011–12	2036	29,454,401	13,148,465	9,784,100	4,091,897	2,429,939
2012–13	2036	29,225,443	13,653,958	9,662,232	3,485,290	2,423,963
2013–14	2036	29,629,309	13,930,810	9,168,922	4,126,701	2,402,876
2014–15	2036	30,052,575	13,746,753	9,838,940	3,884,414	2,582,468
2015–16	2036	30,207,923	13,852,291	9,705,865	3,955,385	2,694,382

*Figures include matches played by Aldershot.
Football League official total for their three divisions in 2001–02 was 14,716,162.

ENGLISH LEAGUE ATTENDANCES 2015–16

BARCLAYS PREMIER LEAGUE ATTENDANCES

	Average Gate			Season 2015–16	
	2014–15	2015–16	+/–%	Highest	Lowest
Arsenal	59,992	59,944	–0.08	60,084	59,257
Aston Villa	34,133	33,690	–1.30	42,200	28,245
Bournemouth	10,265	11,189	+9.00	11,386	10,863
Chelsea	41,546	41,500	–0.11	41,642	40,945
Crystal Palace	24,421	24,636	+0.88	25,295	23,528
Everton	38,406	38,124	–0.73	39,598	35,736
Leicester C	31,693	32,021	+1.03	32,242	31,733
Liverpool	44,659	43,910	–1.68	44,228	43,210
Manchester C	45,365	54,041	+19.12	54,693	53,052
Manchester U	75,335	75,279	–0.07	75,415	74,363
Newcastle U	50,359	49,754	–1.20	52,311	46,424
Norwich C	26,343	26,972	+2.39	27,137	26,279
Southampton	30,652	30,782	+0.42	31,688	28,399
Stoke City	27,081	27,534	+1.67	27,833	26,747
Sunderland	43,157	43,071	–0.20	47,653	38,852
Swansea C	20,555	20,711	+0.76	20,972	20,044
Tottenham H	35,728	35,776	+0.14	36,084	34,882
Watford	16,664	20,594	+23.58	21,012	20,011
WBA	25,064	24,631	–1.73	26,313	22,062
West Ham U	34,871	34,910	+0.11	34,977	34,602

TOTAL ATTENDANCES: 13,852,291 (380 games)
Average 36,453 (+0.77%)
HIGHEST: 75,415 Manchester U v Swansea C
LOWEST: 10,863 Bournemouth v Stoke C
HIGHEST AVERAGE: 75,279 Manchester U
LOWEST AVERAGE: 11,189 Bournemouth

SKY BET FOOTBALL LEAGUE: CHAMPIONSHIP ATTENDANCES

	Average Gate			Season 2015–16	
	2014–15	2015–16	+/–%	Highest	Lowest
Birmingham C	16,111	17,603	+9.26	21,380	14,366
Blackburn R	14,930	14,131	–5.35	21,029	12,002
Bolton W	15,413	15,056	–2.32	18,423	12,257
Brentford	10,822	10,310	–4.73	12,301	8,363
Brighton & HA	25,660	25,583	–0.30	30,292	21,397
Bristol C	12,056	15,292	+26.83	15,854	14,291
Burnley	19,131	16,709	–12.66	20,478	12,430
Cardiff C	21,124	16,463	–22.06	28,680	12,729
Charlton Ath	16,708	15,632	–6.44	21,506	12,294
Derby Co	29,232	29,663	+1.47	33,010	26,834
Fulham	18,276	17,566	–3.89	20,316	14,283
Huddersfield T	13,613	12,755	–6.30	17,118	10,167
Hull C	23,557	17,199	–26.99	21,842	15,139
Ipswich T	19,603	18,989	–3.13	23,615	16,488
Leeds U	24,052	22,446	–6.68	29,311	17,103
Middlesbrough	19,562	24,627	+25.89	33,806	19,966
Milton Keynes D	9,452	13,158	+39.20	21,345	9,402
Nottingham F	23,492	19,676	–16.25	27,551	16,449
Preston NE	10,852	13,035	+20.11	19,852	9,963
QPR	17,809	15,994	–10.19	18,031	14,007
Reading	17,022	17,285	+1.55	21,581	12,949
Rotherham U	10,240	10,025	–2.10	11,658	8,534
Sheffield W	21,993	22,641	+2.95	31,843	18,706
Wolverhampton W	22,419	20,157	–10.09	25,488	17,387

TOTAL ATTENDANCES: 9,705,865 (552 games)
Average 17,583 (–1.53%)
HIGHEST: 33,806 Middlesbrough v Brighton & HA
LOWEST: 8,363 Brentford v Cardiff C
HIGHEST AVERAGE: 29,663 Derby Co
LOWEST AVERAGE: 10,025 Rotherham U

Premier League and Football League attendance averages and highest crowd figures for 2015–16 are unofficial.

SKY BET FOOTBALL LEAGUE: DIVISION 1 ATTENDANCES

	Average Gate			Season 2015–16	
	2014–15	*2015–16*	*+/–%*	*Highest*	*Lowest*
Barnsley	9,768	9,499	–2.76	13,571	8,227
Blackpool	10,928	7,052	–35.47	9,226	5,960
Bradford C	13,353	18,090	+35.47	20,807	16,786
Burton Alb	3,237	4,089	+26.34	5,512	2,666
Bury	3,774	3,751	–0.60	6,470	2,180
Chesterfield	6,925	6,676	–3.59	9,402	5,227
Colchester U	3,886	4,136	+6.42	9,222	2,493
Coventry C	9,332	12,570	+34.70	17,779	9,942
Crewe Alex	4,732	4,551	–3.81	6,751	3,094
Doncaster R	6,884	6,553	–4.82	10,168	4,693
Fleetwood T	3,522	3,308	–6.08	5,123	2,133
Gillingham	5,694	6,316	+10.91	9,375	4,823
Millwall	10,902	9,108	–16.46	12,419	7,657
Oldham Ath	4,349	4,361	+0.27	6,117	3,301
Peterborough U	6,227	5,447	–12.53	7,153	3,544
Port Vale	5,313	4,993	–6.02	8,595	3,256
Rochdale	3,309	3,098	–6.38	5,690	1,767
Scunthorpe U	3,646	3,907	+7.14	7,275	2,596
Sheffield U	19,805	19,803	–0.01	24,777	17,623
Shrewsbury T	5,343	5,407	+1.21	7,019	4,057
Southend U	6,024	7,001	+16.21	10,279	5,212
Swindon T	7,940	7,409	–6.69	9,240	6,311
Walsall	4,392	5,382	+22.54	7,176	3,868
Wigan Ath	12,882	9,467	–26.51	18,730	7,794

TOTAL ATTENDANCES: 3,955,385 (552 games)
Average 7,166 (+1.83%)
HIGHEST: 24,777 Sheffield U v Bradford C
LOWEST: 1,767 Rochdale v Fleetwood T
HIGHEST AVERAGE: 19,803 Sheffield U
LOWEST AVERAGE: 3,098 Rochdale

SKY BET FOOTBALL LEAGUE: DIVISION 2 ATTENDANCES

	Average Gate			Season 2015–16	
	2014–15	*2015–16*	*+/–%*	*Highest*	*Lowest*
Accrington S	1,478	1,834	+24.08	4,386	1,073
AFC Wimbledon	4,073	4,138	+1.60	4,805	3,525
Barnet	1,961	2,358	+20.27	4,008	1,322
Bristol R	6,629	8,096	+22.13	11,130	5,819
Cambridge U	5,108	5,274	+3.25	6,714	3,941
Carlisle U	4,376	4,838	+10.56	7,461	3,336
Crawley T	2,709	2,405	–11.21	4,003	1,543
Dagenham & R	2,041	1,979	–3.00	3,336	1,233
Exeter C	3,873	4,008	+3.47	7,177	2,883
Hartlepool U	3,736	3,890	+4.12	5,046	3,124
Leyton Orient	5,042	5,332	+5.76	6,526	4,209
Luton T	8,702	8,226	–5.48	9,676	6,997
Mansfield T	3,064	3,439	+12.24	6,357	2,435
Morecambe	1,998	1,572	–21.33	3,070	1,027
Newport Co	3,213	2,731	–15.01	4,903	2,032
Northampton T	4,599	5,279	+14.77	7,664	3,642
Notts Co	5,351	4,860	–9.18	10,074	3,098
Oxford U	6,154	7,211	+17.19	11,815	5,273
Plymouth Arg	7,412	8,798	+18.70	14,008	6,071
Portsmouth	15,242	16,391	+7.54	18,746	13,616
Stevenage	3,180	3,349	+5.32	4,782	2,415
Wycombe W	4,044	3,984	–1.48	5,816	2,812
Yeovil T	4,346	3,936	–9.43	6,051	2,954
York C	3,555	3,218	–9.46	4,890	2,559

TOTAL ATTENDANCES: 2,694,382 (552 games)
Average 4,881 (+4.34%)
HIGHEST: 18,746 Portsmouth v Northampton T
LOWEST: 1,027 Morecambe v Dagenham & R
HIGHEST AVERAGE: 16,391 Portsmouth
LOWEST AVERAGE: 1,572 Morecambe

LEAGUE CUP FINALS 1961–2016

Played as a two-leg final until 1966. All subsequent finals played at Wembley except between 2001 and 2007 (inclusive) which were played at Millennium Stadium, Cardiff.

FOOTBALL LEAGUE CUP

1961	Rotherham U v Aston Villa	2-0
	Aston Villa v Rotherham U	3-0*
	Aston Villa won 3-2 on aggregate.	
1962	Rochdale v Norwich C	0-3
	Norwich C v Rochdale	1-0
	Norwich C won 4-0 on aggregate.	
1963	Birmingham C v Aston Villa	3-1
	Aston Villa v Birmingham C	0-0
	Birmingham C won 3-1 on aggregate.	
1964	Stoke C v Leicester C	1-1
	Leicester C v Stoke C	3-2
	Leicester C won 4-3 on aggregate.	
1965	Chelsea v Leicester C	3-2
	Leicester C v Chelsea	0-0
	Chelsea won 3-2 on aggregate.	
1966	West Ham U v WBA	2-1
	WBA v West Ham U	4-1
	WBA won 5-3 on aggregate.	
1967	QPR v WBA	3-2
1968	Leeds U v Arsenal	1-0
1969	Swindon T v Arsenal	3-1*
1970	Manchester C v WBA	2-1*
1971	Tottenham H v Aston Villa	2-0
1972	Stoke C v Chelsea	2-1
1973	Tottenham H v Norwich C	1-0
1974	Wolverhampton W v Manchester C	2-1
1975	Aston Villa v Norwich C	1-0
1976	Manchester C v Newcastle U	2-1
1977	Aston Villa v Everton	0-0
Replay	Aston Villa v Everton	1-1*
	(at Hillsborough)	
Replay	Aston Villa v Everton	3-2*
	(at Old Trafford)	
1978	Nottingham F v Liverpool	0-0*
Replay	Nottingham F v Liverpool	1-0
	(at Old Trafford)	
1979	Nottingham F v Southampton	3-2
1980	Wolverhampton W v Nottingham F	1-0
1981	Liverpool v West Ham U	1-1*
Replay	Liverpool v West Ham U	2-1
	(at Villa Park)	

MILK CUP

1982	Liverpool v Tottenham H	3-1*
1983	Liverpool v Manchester U	2-1*
1984	Liverpool v Everton	0-0*
Replay	Liverpool v Everton	1-0
	(at Maine Road)	
1985	Norwich C v Sunderland	1-0
1986	Oxford U v QPR	3-0

LITTLEWOODS CUP

1987	Arsenal v Liverpool	2-1
1988	Luton T v Arsenal	3-2
1989	Nottingham F v Luton T	3-1
1990	Nottingham F v Oldham Ath	1-0

RUMBELOWS LEAGUE CUP

1991	Sheffield W v Manchester U	1-0
1992	Manchester U v Nottingham F	1-0

COCA-COLA CUP

1993	Arsenal v Sheffield W	2-1
1994	Aston Villa v Manchester U	3-1
1995	Liverpool v Bolton W	2-1
1996	Aston Villa v Leeds U	3-0
1997	Leicester C v Middlesbrough	1-1*
Replay	Leicester C v Middlesbrough	1-0*
	(at Hillsborough)	
1998	Chelsea v Middlesbrough	2-0*

WORTHINGTON CUP

1999	Tottenham H v Leicester C	1-0
2000	Leicester C v Tranmere R	2-1
2001	Liverpool v Birmingham C	1-1*
	Liverpool won 5-4 on penalties.	
2002	Blackburn R v Tottenham H	2-1
2003	Liverpool v Manchester U	2-0

CARLING CUP

2004	Middlesbrough v Bolton W	2-1
2005	Chelsea v Liverpool	3-2*
2006	Manchester U v Wigan Ath	4-0
2007	Chelsea v Arsenal	2-1
2008	Tottenham H v Chelsea	2-1*
2009	Manchester U v Tottenham H	0-0*
	Manchester U won 4-1 on penalties.	
2010	Manchester U v Aston Villa	2-1
2011	Birmingham C v Arsenal	2-1
2012	Liverpool v Cardiff C	2-2*
	Liverpool won 3-2 on penalties.	

CAPITAL ONE CUP

2013	Swansea C v Bradford C	5-0
2014	Manchester C v Sunderland	3-1
2015	Chelsea v Tottenham H	2-0
2016	Manchester C v Liverpool	1-1*
	Manchester C won 3-1 on penalties.	

*After extra time.

LEAGUE CUP WINS
Liverpool 8, Aston Villa 5, Chelsea 5, Manchester C 4, Manchester U 4, Nottingham F 4, Tottenham H 4, Leicester C 3, Arsenal 2, Birmingham C 2, Norwich C 2, Wolverhampton W 2, Blackburn R 1, Leeds U 1, Luton T 1, Middlesbrough 1, Oxford U 1, QPR 1, Sheffield W 1, Stoke C 1, Swansea C 1, Swindon T 1, WBA 1.

APPEARANCES IN FINALS
Liverpool 12, Aston Villa 8, Manchester U 8, Tottenham H 8, Arsenal 7, Chelsea 7, Nottingham F 6, Leicester C 5, Manchester C 5, Norwich C 4, Birmingham C 3, Middlesbrough 3, WBA 3, Bolton W 2, Everton 2, Leeds U 2, Luton T 2, QPR 2, Sheffield W 2, Stoke C 2, Sunderland 2, West Ham U 2, Wolverhampton W 2, Blackburn R 1, Bradford C 1, Cardiff C 1, Newcastle U 1, Oldham Ath 1, Oxford U 1, Rochdale 1, Rotherham U 1, Southampton 1, Swansea C 1, Swindon T 1, Tranmere R 1, Wigan Ath 1.

APPEARANCES IN SEMI-FINALS
Liverpool 16, Arsenal 14, Aston Villa 14, Tottenham H 14, Manchester U 13, Chelsea 12, Manchester C 9, West Ham U 9, Blackburn R 6, Nottingham F 6, Birmingham C 5, Everton 5, Leeds U 5, Leicester C 5, Middlesbrough 5, Norwich C 5, Bolton W 4, Burnley 4, Crystal Palace 4, Ipswich T 4, Sheffield W 4, Sunderland 4, WBA 4, QPR 3, Stoke C 3, Swindon T 3, Wolverhampton W 3, Bristol C 2, Cardiff C 2, Coventry C 2, Derby Co 2, Luton T 2, Oxford U 2, Plymouth Arg 2, Sheffield U 2, Southampton 2, Tranmere R 2, Watford 2, Wimbledon 2, Blackpool 1, Bradford C 1, Bury 1, Carlisle U 1, Chester C 1, Huddersfield T 1, Newcastle U 1, Oldham Ath 1, Peterborough U 1, Rochdale 1, Rotherham U 1, Shrewsbury T 1, Stockport Co 1, Swansea C 1, Walsall 1, Wigan Ath 1, Wycombe W 1.

CAPITAL ONE CUP 2015–16

* *Denotes player sent off.*

FIRST ROUND

Tuesday, 11 August 2015

Accrington S (0) 2 *(Crooks 105, Gornell 115)*
Hull C (0) 2 *(Akpom 92, Luer 108)*   2118
Accrington S: (4411) Mooney; Wakefield (Gornell 98), Davies, Winnard, Pearson; Mingoia, Crooks, Barry (Conneely 81), Bruna (McConville 61); Windass; Kee.
Hull C: (442) Jakupovic; Odubajo (Luer 71), Davies, Maguire, Robertson; Elmohamady, Meyler, Huddlestone, Clucas; Jelavic (Akpom 60), Aluko (Dixon 96).
aet; Hull C won 4-3 on penalties.
Referee: David Webb.

Blackburn R (1) 1 *(Delfouneso 30)*
Shrewsbury T (2) 2 *(Collins 9, Barnett 32)*   5280
Blackburn R: (442) Steele; Nyambe, Lenihan, Kilgallon, Spurr; O'Sullivan (Barrow 57), Evans (Guthrie 65), Williamson, Marshall; Brown (Koita 56), Delfouneso.
Shrewsbury T: (442) Leutwiler; Tootle, Grandison, Goldson, Sadler; Lawrence, Ogogo, Woods R, Woods M (Brown 85); Collins (Akpa Akpro 76), Barnett.
Referee: Geoff Eltringham.

Bolton W (0) 0
Burton Alb (0) 1 *(Palmer 87)*   5842
Bolton W: (41212) Amos; Wilson (Walker 90), Dervite, Holding, Moxey; Vela; Danns, Davies; Clough (Dobbie 69); Feeney (Heskey 89), Madine.
Burton Alb: (4411) Matthews; Edwards, Mousinho, O'Connor, McCrory; Akins (Naylor 62), Reilly, Butcher, Binnom-Williams; Thiele (Joachim 86); Palmer (Cansdell-Sherriff 90).
Referee: Richard Clark.

Brentford (0) 0
Oxford U (3) 4 *(Sercombe 5, Hylton 9, Roofe 12, Mullins 54)*   5177
Brentford: (4411) Bonham; O'Connell, Barbet, Bjelland (Bidwell 46), Yennaris (McCormack 53); Laurent, Williams, Clarke, Udumaga; Vibe; Senior (Gogia 75).
Oxford U: (442) Slocombe; Baldock, Mullins, Wright, Skarz; Rose, Roofe (O'Dowda 46), Sercombe, Hylton; MacDonald (Ruffels 59), Taylor (Hoban 65).
Referee: Dean Whitestone.

Bristol R (0) 1 *(Harrison 65)*
Birmingham C (0) 2 *(Maghoma 57, Shinnie 68)*   5650
Bristol R: (442) Mildenhall; Leadbitter, Clarke J (Broom 81), Parkes, Brown; Sinclair, Clarke O, Lockyer, Gosling (Montano 64); Harrison, Easter (Taylor 64).
Birmingham C: (442) Legzdins; Eardley, Morrison (Spector 71), Robinson, Grounds; Shinnie, Maghoma (Gray 81), Gleeson, Davis; Thomas (Arthur 90), Novak.
Referee: Andy Davies.

Cardiff C (1) 1 *(Noone 45)*
AFC Wimbledon (0) 0   6314
Cardiff C: (442) Wilson; Peltier, Morrison, Connolly, Da Silva; Noone, Gunnarsson, O'Keefe, Ameobi (Harris 73); Doyle, Revell (Jones 68).
AFC Wimbledon: (343) Shea; Fuller, Robinson, Kennedy; Francomb (Barcham 69), Bulman, Nightingale, Meades; Akinfenwa (Elliott 69), Rigg, Taylor (Azeez 69).
Referee: Brendan Malone.

Carlisle U (0) 3 *(Ibehre 75, 108, Osei 120)*
Chesterfield (0) 1 *(Dieseruvwe 84)*   2950
Carlisle U: (352) Gillespie; Raynes, Grainger, Atkinson (Miller 74); McQueen, Hery, Dicker, Balanta, Brough (Osei 65); Wyke (Ibehre 65), Rigg.
Chesterfield: (442) Lee; Raglan, Hird, Evatt, Jones; Gardner, Morsy, Banks (Onovwigun 96), Ariyibi (Orrell 81); O'Shea, Gnanduillet (Dieseruvwe* 73).
aet.
Referee: Seb Stockbridge.

Charlton Ath (2) 4 *(Watt 26, Ahearne-Grant 40, Bergdich 57, Ghoochannejhad 77)*
Dagenham & R (0) 1 *(Doidge 69)*   5100
Charlton Ath: (442) Pope; Charles, Sarr, Bauer, Fox; Ceballos (Holmes-Dennis 74), Ba, Jackson, Bergdich (Gudmundsson 62); Watt (Ghoochannejhad 62), Ahearne-Grant.
Dagenham & R: (433) Cousins; Partridge (Passley 75), Dikamona, Widdowson, Boucaud; Nosworthy, Ferdinand, Hamalainen (Hemmings 58); McClure (Doidge 58), Jones, Chambers.
Referee: Stuart Attwell.

Colchester U (0) 0
Reading (0) 1 *(Gunter 115)*   2706
Colchester U: (4231) Walker (Parish 59); Brindley, Eastman, Wynter, Briggs; Gilbey, Edwards; Sembie-Ferris, Moncur (Szmodics 75), Massey (Wright 68); Bonne.
Reading: (442) Al Habsi; Gunter, McShane, Ferdinand, Taylor; Robson-Kanu (Samuel 82 (Tshibola 96)), Williams, Norwood, Quinn; Blackman, Orlando Sa (Cox 82).
aet.
Referee: Darren Drysdale.

Fleetwood T (0) 0
Hartlepool U (0) 1 *(Paynter 58)*   1892
Fleetwood T: (442) Maxwell; McLaughlin, Jonsson, Jordan, Andrew; Della Verde (Grant R 68), Ryan, Sarcevic, Bell (Sanogo 80); Proctor (Ball 67), McManus.
Hartlepool U: (433) Bartlett; Duckworth, Harrison S, Worley, Carroll; Woods, Magnay, Featherstone; Bingham, Paynter (Oates 85), Fenwick.
Referee: Gary Sutton.

Huddersfield T (1) 1 *(Wallace 35)*
Notts Co (1) 2 *(Noble 42, 56)*   4238
Huddersfield T: (343) Murphy; Cranie, Lynch, Wallace; Smith (Hiwula 65), Dempsey (Butterfield 65), Whitehead, Davidson (Hammill 82); Wells, Miller, Bunn.
Notts Co: (433) Carroll; Swerts*, Bennett, Sprockel, Audel; Thompson, Aborah, Noble; Jenner, Stead (Spencer 83), De Silva.
Referee: Jeremy Simpson.

Ipswich T (0) 2 *(Yorwerth 55, Tabb 76)*
Stevenage (1) 1 *(Berra 34 (og))*   10,449
Ipswich T: (442) Gerken; Chambers, Berra, Yorwerth, Kenlock (Smith 77); Toure (Fraser 46), Coke, Douglas, Tabb; Pitman, McGoldrick.
Stevenage: (451) Day; Franks, McCombe, Wells, Okimo; Pett, McAllister (Gorman 46), Parrett, Schumacher (Conlon 78), Lee; Akinyemi (Williams 46).
Referee: Fred Graham.

Luton T (1) 3 *(Marriott 44, 63, Benson 59)*
Bristol C (0) 1 *(Robinson 71)*   3948
Luton T: (442) Tyler; Cuthbert, McNulty, Wilkinson, Potts; O'Donnell (Griffiths 79), McGeehan, O'Brien (Doyle 76), Ruddock; Benson, Marriott (McQuoid 80).
Bristol C: (352) Hamer; Ayling, Flint, Williams; Fredericks (Burns 58), Smith, Pack (Reid 74), Freeman, Robinson; Wilbraham, Kodjia (Agard 67).
Referee: James Linington.

Millwall (0) 1 *(Morison 76)*
Barnet (1) 2 *(Akinde 11 (pen), Yiadom 102)*   4454
Millwall: (442) Archer; Nelson, Webster, Craig, Ferguson; Onyedinma (Beevers 97), Upson, Williams, Martin L (Cowan-Hall 67); Morison, Marquis (Gregory 66).
Barnet: (442) Stack; Hoyte, Dembele, Nelson (N'Gala 89), Johnson; Yiadom, Weston (Gash 63), Togwell, Champion; Akinde, Gambin (Vilhete 69).
aet.
Referee: Andrew Madley.

Milton Keynes D (0) 2 *(Baudry 90 (og), Baker 90)*
Leyton Orient (1) 1 *(Lewington 36 (og))*　　　5444
Milton Keynes D: (4231) Cropper; Hodson, Upson (McFadzean 77), Walsh, Lewington; Aguza, Rasulo; Baker, Benavente (Gallagher 76), Jennings (Reeves 67); Church.
Leyton Orient: (442) Cisak; Clohessy, Essam, Baudry, Dunne (Shaw 82); Turgott, Pritchard, Moore, Cox; Palmer (Simpson 81), Kashket.
Referee: Simon Hooper.

Morecambe (0) 0
Sheffield U (0) 1 *(Collins 90)*　　　2168
Morecambe: (4231) Roche; Beeley, Parrish, Edwards, Wilson; Fleming (Ellison 71), Goodall; Devitt, Wildig (Kenyon 57), Molyneux (Miller 80); Mullin.
Sheffield U: (442) Howard; Wallace K, McEveley, Edgar (Collins 84), Freeman; Woolford (Adams 46), Basham, Wallace J (Reed 90), Scougall; Sammon, McNulty.
Referee: Stephen Martin.

Northampton T (3) 3 *(Hackett 20, Calvert-Lewin 24, Hoskins 29)*
Blackpool (0) 0　　　2549
Northampton T: (442) Clarke; Lelan, Diamond, Cresswell, Buchanan; Hackett (Potter 75), Taylor (O'Toole 60), Byrom, D'Ath (Holmes 66); Hoskins, Calvert-Lewin.
Blackpool: (433) Letheren; Aldred, Robertson, Jones, Ferguson; Cubero (Oliver 55), Potts (Cameron 46), McAlister; Thomas, Cullen, Redshaw (Samuel 46).
Referee: James Adcock.

Nottingham F (1) 3 *(Walker 32, Antonio 81, 90)*
Walsall (2) 4 *(Bradshaw 11, 14, 90 (pen), Sawyers 79)* 5237
Nottingham F: (4411) De Vries; Lichaj, Wilson, Hobbs, Fox; Burke C (Burke O 78), Mancienne, Vaughan, Ward (Antonio 78); Paterson (Blackstock 71); Walker.
Walsall: (451) Etheridge; Demetriou, O'Connor, Downing, Henry; Flanagan, Mantom, Chambers (Sawyers 54), Morris K (Cook 84), Lalkovic (Forde 73); Bradshaw.
Referee: Darren Handley.

Peterborough U (1) 2 *(Washington 2, Maddison 49)*
Crawley T (0) 0　　　2500
Peterborough U: (442) Alnwick; Adebayo-Rowling, Zakuani, Davey, Nthle; Anderson H, Bostwick, Collison, Maddison (Taylor 88); Washington (Vassell 74), Gormley (Coulibaly 74).
Crawley T: (433) Woodman; Donnelly, McNerney, Bradley, Van Den Bogaert; Smith J, Rooney, Young (Bawling 81); Fenelon (Edwards 62); Harrold, Deacon (Barnard 58).
Referee: Rob Lewis.

Plymouth Arg (0) 1 *(Tanner 78)*
Gillingham (0) 2 *(Dack 85, Hessenthaler 87)*　　　5120
Plymouth Arg: (4231) McCormick; Mellor, Nelson, Hartley, Sawyer; McHugh, Boateng; Jervis (Tanner 11), Carey, Wylde (Brunt 78); Reid (Simpson 84).
Gillingham: (442) Nelson; Jackson, Egan, Oshilaja, Dickenson; McGlashan (Garmston 59), Hessenthaler, Dack, Houghton; Norris (Donnelly 84), Williamson (Wright 69).
Referee: Kevin Johnson.

Port Vale (0) 1 *(Moore 82)*
Burnley (0) 0　　　4634
Port Vale: (4411) Alnwick; Purkiss, Streete (Inniss 46), Duffy, Dickinson; Moore, Foley, Grant, Andoh (Kelly 81); Dodds; Leitch-Smith (Ikpeazu 70).
Burnley: (442) Gilks; Darikwa, Duff, Mee, Ward; Boyd, Arfield, Taylor (Jutkiewicz 84), Kightly; Vossen (Sordell 65), Vokes.
Referee: Trevor Kettle.

Rochdale (1) 1 *(McDermott 45)*
Coventry C (0) 1 *(Tudgay 84)*　　　1986
Rochdale: (4141) Lillis; Rafferty, Lancashire, McNulty, Kennedy; Allen; Vincenti, McDermott (Noble-Lazarus 64), Camps (Rose 96), Bunney (Andrew 46); Henderson.
Coventry C: (451) Charles-Cook; Phillips, Martin, Ricketts, Stokes; O'Brien (Thomas G 76), Vincelot (Maddison 51), Fleck, Morris, Lameiras; Tudgay.
aet; Rochdale won 5-3 on penalties.
Referee: Eddie Ilderton.

Rotherham U (1) 1 *(Bowery 45)*
Cambridge U (0) 0　　　4568
Rotherham U: (442) Roos; Buxton (Richardson 76), Collins, Halford, Newell (Ward G 73); Ledesma, Frecklington, Smallwood, White; Bowery (Ward D 80), Derbyshire.
Cambridge U: (3412) Dunn; Roberts, Coulson, Taft; Omozusi, Berry, Keane, Taylor (Dunk 64); Simpson (Donaldson 64); Carr (Newton 64), Slew.
Referee: Christopher Sarginson.

Scunthorpe U (0) 1 *(Madden 52 (pen))*
Barnsley (0) 1 *(Scowen 47 (pen))*　　　3003
Scunthorpe U: (532) Anyon; Wiseman (Adelakun 80), Mirfin, King, Clarke, Laird; McAllister, Bishop, Dawson (van Veen 83); Madden, Henderson (Hopper 69).
Barnsley: (532) Townsend; Bree, Roberts, Nyatanga, Mawson, Smith (Templeton 101); Pearson, Rothwell (Hourihane 89), Scowen; Watkins, Wilkinson (Winnall 64).
aet; Barnsley won 7-6 on penalties.
Referee: Graham Salisbury.

Sheffield W (2) 4 *(Lucas Joao 13, Semedo 19, Lee 53, Sougou 84)*
Mansfield T (1) 1 *(Tafazolli 45)*　　　14,021
Sheffield W: (4231) Wildsmith; Palmer, Lees, Sasso, Wiggins; Loge (Hutchinson 57), Semedo; Lavery (Marco Matias 51), Lee, Sougou (Lucas Joao (Helan 76).
Mansfield T: (4141) Shearer; Hunt, Tafazolli, Shires, Benning; Chapman; Westcarr (Yussuf 59), Clements, Thomas J (Lambe 59), Thomas N (Caton 57); Beardsley.
Referee: Mark Brown.

Southend U (0) 0
Brighton & HA (0) 1 *(LuaLua 90)*　　　4485
Southend U: (442) Bentley; White, Bolger, Prosser, Coker; Worrall, Leonard, Deegan (Wordsworth 80), Timlin; Hunt (Mooney 70), Pigott (Weston 76).
Brighton & HA: (451) Maenpaa; Rosenior, Greer, Rea, Bong; Calderon, Forster-Caskey (Hemed 73), Ince, Holla, LuaLua; O'Grady (Baldock 73).
Referee: Iain Williamson.

Swindon U (0) 1 *(Obika 65)*
Exeter C (2) 2 *(Nicholls 37, Wheeler 42)*　　　4693
Swindon T: (433) Vigouroux; Thompson N, Branco, Turnbull, Ormonde-Ottewill (Brophy 85); Kasim, Stewart, Williams; Byrne, Obika, Robert (Randall 62).
Exeter C: (433) Olejnik; Butterfield (Oakley 73), Ribeiro, Brown, McAllister; Harley, Davies, Nicholls (Hoskins 80); Wheeler, Nichols (Woodman 75), Tillson.
Referee: Charles Breakspear.

Wigan Ath (0) 1 *(Grigg 46 (pen))*
Bury (0) 2 *(Clarke L 63, 89 (pen))*　　　5484
Wigan Ath: (4231) O'Donnell; McNaughton, Barnett, Morgan, James; Perkins, Power; Jacobs, Odelusi (Jennings 70), Flores (McKay 90); Grigg (Davies 78).
Bury: (4231) Walton; Riley, Cameron, Clarke P, Hussey; Tutte, Etuhu (Pugh 82); Mayor (Pope 46), Soares, Hope (Mellis 54); Clarke L.
Referee: Mark Heywood.

Wolverhampton W (1) 2 *(Dicko 16, Afobe 58 (pen))*
Newport Co (1) 1 *(Boden 6)*　　　9586
Wolverhampton W: (442) Martinez; Iorfa, Ebanks-Landell, Hause, Golbourne; Doherty (van La Parra 67), Price, Coady, Ojo; Afobe (Le Fondre 67), Dicko.
Newport Co: (451) Day; Holmes, Poole, Parselle, Barrow; Rodman (Collins 70), Byrne, Nana Ofori-Twumasi, Klukowski, Elito (Russell-Jones 90); Boden (Owen-Evans 70).
Referee: Darren Bond.

Wycombe W (0) 0
Fulham (0) 1 *(Kacaniklic 69)*　　　4012
Wycombe W: (442) Ingram; Jombati, Stewart, Rowe, Jacobson; Harriman, Bean, McGinn, Wood (Sellers 79); Thompson (Banton 74), Amadi-Holloway (Hayes 83).
Fulham: (442) Bettinelli; Hutchinson, Bodurov, Voser, Grimmer (Richards 62); Cairney, O'Hara (Mattila 83), Pringle, Kacaniklic; Woodrow (Smith 68), McCormack.
Referee: Gavin Ward.

Yeovil T (0) 0

QPR (2) 3 *(Polter 16, Emmanuel-Thomas 20,*
Onuoha 56)   4058
Yeovil T: (541) Krysiak; Roberts, Arthurworrey, Sokolik,
Lacey, Smith; Allen (Fogden 46), Dolan, Laird (Burrows
63), Cornick; Jeffers (Beck 46).
QPR: (4231) Green; Perch, Onuoha, Hall, Kpekawa;
Doughty, Gobern (Hoilett 77); Phillips (Blackwood 70),
Emmanuel-Thomas, Gladwin (Henry 59); Polter.
Referee: Oliver Langford.

York C (0) 2 *(Summerfield 49 (pen), Berrett 85)*

Bradford C (1) 2 *(Routis 21, Hanson 90)*   4201
York C: (352) Flinders; Lowe, Winfield, Zubar; McCoy,
Summerfield (Carson 98), Penn, Berrett, Tutonda;
Thompson, Oliver (Hyde 91).
Bradford C: (442) Williams; McMahon, McArdle, Clarke
N, Sheehan; Anderson (Morris 61), Liddle, Routis,
Marshall; Davies (Hanson 80), James (Clarke B 66).
aet; York C won 4-2 on penalties.
Referee: Mark Haywood.

Wednesday, 12 August 2015

Crewe Alex (1) 1 *(King 36)*

Preston NE (2) 3 *(Hugill 5 (pen), Keane 13,*
Brownhill 86)   2852
Crewe Alex: (433) Garratt; Turton, Ray, Nugent,
Guthrie; Fox, King, Bingham; Haber (Colclough 63),
Dalla Valle, Inman (Cooper 63).
Preston NE: (532) Pickford; Vermijl (Davies 74), Wright
(Humphrey 53), Huntington, Woods, Cunningham;
Brownhill, Browne, Kilkenny; Hugill (Garner 81), Keane.
Referee: Scott Duncan.

Oldham Ath (0) 1 *(Philliskirk 90)*

Middlesbrough (2) 3 *(Wildschut 23, Stuani 41, 61)* 4182
Oldham Ath: (4231) Cornell; Wilson B, Wilson J,
Gunning, Mills; Kelly, Philliskirk; Croft, Winchester
(Poleon 60), Forte (Dunn 60); Cassidy (Turner 84).
Middlesbrough: (4231) Mejias; Nsue, Ayala (Fry 84),
Stephens, Husband; Clayton (Leadbitter 69), Forshaw;
Adomah, Fabbrini (Downing 73), Wildschut; Stuani.
Referee: Carl Boyeson.

Portsmouth (0) 2 *(McGurk 49, Chaplin 76)*

Derby Co (0) 1 *(Shackell 73)*   11,573
Portsmouth: (4231) Jones; Davies, Webster, Clarke,
Haunstrup (Chaplin 71); Hollands, Close; Evans,
McGurk (Stevens 55), Bennett (Tollitt 74); Stockley.
Derby Co: (4231) Grant; Ssewankambo (Thorne 70),
Pearce, Shackell, Forsyth; Baird, Hendrick, Russell,
Dawkins (Ince 61); Weimann; Bent (Martin 60).
Referee: Paul Tierney.

Thursday, 13 August 2015

Doncaster R (1) 1 *(Williams 31 (pen))*

Leeds U (1) 1 *(Cook 14)*   8361
Doncaster R: (4411) Stuckmann; McCullough, Jones,
Butler, Taylor-Sinclair; Evina (Tyson 73), Middleton
(Main 101), Wellens, Forrester; Coppinger; Williams.
Leeds U: (433) Turnbull; Berardi, Bellusci, Cooper,
Taylor; Cook■, Wootton, Mowatt (Byram 75); Doukara
(Murphy 67), Antenucci, Dallas (Wood 67).
aet; Doncaster R won 4-2 on penalties.
Referee: Keith Hill.

SECOND ROUND

Tuesday, 25 August 2015

Aston Villa (1) 5 *(Traore 24, Sinclair 50, 78 (pen), 99,*
Bennett 111)

Notts Co (2) 3 *(Snijders 16, Stead 45 (pen), Burke 56)*
                                                             21,430
Aston Villa: (433) Bunn; Hutton, Sanchez, Baker,
Richardson; Gil (Bennett 100), Veretout, Grealish;
Traore (Cole 60), Ayew (Kozak 72), Sinclair.
Notts Co: (442) Carroll; Swerts, Amevor (Audel 71),
Sprockel, Hewitt; Snijders, Campbell (Jenner 55),
Aborah, Burke; Stead, McLeod (Spencer 82).
aet.
Referee: Robert Madley.

Birmingham C (1) 2 *(Thomas 35, 72)*

Gillingham (0) 0   9275
Birmingham C: (4231) Legzdins; Eardley, Spector,
Robinson, Hancox; Kieftenbeld, Davis; Arthur
(Solomon-Otabor 77), Shinnie (Brown 84), Maghoma;
Thomas (Brock-Madsen 77).
Gillingham: (4231) Nelson; Jackson (Egan 74), Oshilaja,
Ehmer, Garmston; Houghton (Dack 78), Wright;
Donnelly, McGlashan, Hessenthaler; Williamson
(McDonald 62).
Referee: Graham Salisbury.

Burton Alb (1) 1 *(Friend 24 (og))*

Middlesbrough (0) 2 *(Stuani 70, 109)*   3414
Burton Alb: (4411) Matthews; Naylor (El Khayati 101),
O'Connor, Cansdell-Sherriff, Binnom-Williams; Akins
(Edwards 75), Weir, Butcher, Reilly; Palmer; Joachim
(Thiele 83).
Middlesbrough: (352) Mejias; Stephens (Fabbrini 46),
Gibson, Woodgate (Nsue 98); Kalas, Forshaw, Reach
(Downing 65), Leadbitter, Friend; Garcia, Stuani.
aet.
Referee: Mark Brown.

Bury (0) 1 *(Mayor 49)*

Leicester C (2) 4 *(Dodoo 25, 86, 90, Kramaric 41)*   4914
Bury: (442) Walton; Riley, Clarke P, Cameron, Hussey
(Foulds 48); Pugh, Tutte, Soares (Rose 49), Mellis (Jones
62); Pope, Mayor.
Leicester C: (442) Schwarzer; Benalouane, Moore (De
Laet 90), Wasilewski, Fuchs; Dodoo, Inler, Hammond,
Kante; Ulloa, Kramaric (Schlupp 65).
Referee: Andrew Madley.

Crystal Palace (1) 4 *(Gayle 41 (pen), Murray 95 (pen),*
Lee 97, Zaha 111)

Shrewsbury T (1) 1 *(Tootle 9)*   10,978
Crystal Palace: (442) Hennessey; Ward (Souare 46),
Hangeland, Kelly, Mariappa; Zaha, Jedinak (Mutch 50),
Ledley, Lee; Gayle, Bamford (Murray 74).
Shrewsbury T: (442) Leutwiler; Tootle, Grandison, Ellis,
Sadler; Ogogo, Woods R, Lawrence (Wesolowski 91),
Brown; Collins (Whalley 103), Akpa Akpro (Barnett 86).
aet.
Referee: Darren Bond.

Doncaster R (1) 1 *(Williams 23)*

Ipswich T (0) 4 *(Pitman 58, McGoldrick 102, Alabi 105,*
Fraser 113)   3729
Doncaster R: (442) Stuckmann; McCullough (Lund 19),
Butler, Jones (Whitehouse 46), Taylor-Sinclair;
Coppinger, Wellens, Chaplow (Middleton 100), Evina;
Main, Williams.
Ipswich T: (442) Gerken; Emmanuel, Smith (Chambers
79), Yorwerth, Kenlock; Coke, Tabb, McDonnell (Fraser
99), Toure; McGoldrick, Pitman (Alabi 70).
aet.
Referee: Scott Duncan.

Fulham (0) 3 *(McCormack 62 (pen), 75, Dembele 90)*

Sheffield U (0) 0   5927
Fulham: (442) Lonergan; Richards, Ream (Bodurov 80),
Burn, Voser; Kacaniklic (Cairney 64), Tunnicliffe,
Christensen, Pringle; McCormack, Dembele.
Sheffield U: (442) Long; Alcock (Adams 84), McGahey,
Wallace K■, McFadzean; De Girolamo (Baxter■ 66),
Reed, Wallace J (Dimaio 67), Woolford; McNulty,
Higdon.
Referee: Dean Whitestone.

Hartlepool U (0) 0

Bournemouth (3) 4 *(Kermorgant 30, Gosling 34,*
Stanislas 44, 64)   4890
Hartlepool U: (433) Bartlett; Duckworth, Harrison S,
Boyce, Carroll; Magnay, Featherstone, Woods (Walker
66); Oates (Smith 66), Paynter (Fenwick 46), Bingham.
Bournemouth: (442) Federici; Smith (Butcher 77),
Cargill, Distin, Mings; Stanislas, Gosling, MacDonald,
Atsu (Ritchie 77); Tomlin, Kermorgant (Rantie 67).
Referee: Carl Boyeson.

Hull C (1) 1 *(Luer 9)*
Rochdale (0) 0   10,430
Hull C: (4312) Jakupovic; Taylor (Elmohamady 68), Bruce, Maguire, Robertson; Meyler, Hayden, Clucas; Diame (Odubajo 59); Hernandez (Jahraldo-Martin 78), Luer.
Rochdale: (4231) Lillis; Rafferty, McNulty, Eastham, Kennedy; Allen, Cannon; Henderson, Vincenti (Bennett 58), Noble-Lazarus (McDermott 66); Andrew (Alessandra 65).
Referee: Mark Haywood.

Luton T (0) 1 *(McGeehan 90)*
Stoke C (0) 1 *(Walters 67)*   6099
Luton T: (433) Justham; O'Donnell, Cuthbert, Wilkinson, Griffiths; Lee, O'Brien, Smith; Green (McGeehan 60), McQuoid (Benson 71), Ruddock (Hall 61).
Stoke C: (4231) Given; Bardsley, Wollscheid, Wilson, Pieters; Sidwell, Ireland; Walters, Krkic (Cameron 87), Arnautovic (Diouf 96); Crouch (Joselu 63).
aet; Stoke C won 8-7 on penalties.
Referee: Paul Tierney.

Milton Keynes D (0) 2 *(Baker 78, Murphy 108)*
Cardiff C (0) 1 *(Revell 53)*   5617
Milton Keynes D: (4231) Cropper; Spence, Upson, McFadzean, Hodson; Aguza (Carruthers 62), Poyet; Baker, Benavente (Hall 61), Murphy; Powell (Gallagher 62).
Cardiff C: (442) Moore; Connolly, Morrison, Ecuele Manga, Da Silva; Ameobi, Ralls (Dikgacoi 71), O'Keefe (Peltier 91), Noone; Doyle, Revell (Macheda 82).
aet. Referee: Keith Stroud.

Newcastle U (2) 4 *(Thauvin 3, De Jong 8, Janmaat 56, Williamson 63)*
Northampton T (1) 1 *(Richards 10 (pen))*   26,923
Newcastle U: (4231) Darlow; Janmaat, Lascelles, Williamson, Haidara (Toney 78); Tiote, Gouffran; Aarons, De Jong, Thauvin (Mitrovic 65); Perez (Colback 72).
Northampton T: (4231) Clarke; Watson (Hoskins 62), Taylor, Yates, Buchanan; Potter (D'Ath 62), Adams; Byrom, McDonald, Cresswell; Richards (Calvert-Lewin 75).
Referee: David Coote.

Peterborough U (0) 1 *(Anderson J 90)*
Charlton Ath (1) 4 *(Kennedy 3, Ahearne-Grant 53 (pen), Kashi 76, Vetokele 87)*   2771
Peterborough U: (352) Alnwick; Brisley (Bostwick 46), Santos, Davey; Taylor, Anderson J, Collison, Sadlier (Anderson H 61), Maddison; Washington, Coulibaly (Gormley 80).
Charlton Ath: (442) Pope; Charles, Bauer, Sarr, Lennon; Harriott (Vetokele 59), Ba, Cousins (Kashi 66), Bergdich (Muldoon 78); Ahearne-Grant, Kennedy.
Referee: Gary Sutton.

Portsmouth (1) 1 *(Chaplin 40)*
Reading (0) 2 *(Blackman 64, McCleary 84)*   18,190
Portsmouth: (442) Jones; Evans, Webster, Clarke, Haunstrup; McGurk (Dunne 79), Bennett (Tubbs 89), Close, Hollands; Chaplin (Tollitt 83), Stockley.
Reading: (442) Al Habsi; Gunter, Hector, Ferdinand, Obita; Quinn, Williams (Tshibola 90), Norwood, Blackman (McShane 89); Robson-Kanu, Cox (McCleary 69).
Referee: Gavin Ward.

Preston NE (1) 1 *(Vermijl 8)*
Watford (0) 0   6250
Preston NE: (442) Pickford; Clarke, Huntington, Wright, Woods; Vermijl, Brownhill, Kilkenny, Browne; Garner (Beckford 84), Reid (Humphrey 84).
Watford: (4231) Arlauskis; Paredes, Britos*, Angella, Ake; Watson, Smith (Berghuis 59); Forestieri, Abdi, Layun; Vydra.
Referee: Stephen Martin.

QPR (1) 1 *(Emmanuel-Thomas 40)*
Carlisle U (1) 2 *(Asamoah 37, Kennedy 79)*   5501
QPR: (4231) Smithies; Furlong, Hall, Hill, Kpekawa; Doughty, Gobern (Comley 67); Grego-Cox (Chery 83), Hoilett (Luongo 74), Emmanuel-Thomas; Polter.
Carlisle U: (442) Gillespie; Miller, Raynes, McQueen, Grainger (Archibald-Henville 55); Joyce, Sweeney, Dicker, Brough (Ibehre 84); Asamoah, Balanta (Kennedy 72).
Referee: James Linington.

Rotherham U (0) 1 *(Green 80)*
Norwich C (1) 2 *(Howson 22, van Wolfswinkel 68)*   5648
Rotherham U: (41212) Collin; Buxton, Halford, Collins, Richardson; Newell; Ledesma (White 76), Ward G (Green 76); Frecklington (Maguire 16); Derbyshire, Clarke-Harris.
Norwich C: (4411) Rudd; Wisdom, Bennett R, Bassong, Toffolo; Odjidja-Ofoe, O'Neil, Dorrans (Bennett E 80), Johnson; Howson (Andreu 74); van Wolfswinkel.
Referee: Kevin Wright.

Sheffield W (0) 1 *(Nuhiu 55)*
Oxford U (0) 0   11,799
Sheffield W: (4141) Price; Hunt, Lees, Sasso, Helan; Semedo; Wallace (Sougou 64), Lee, Lopez, Lavery (Marco Matias 64); Nuhiu.
Oxford U: (442) Slocombe; Long (Sercombe 45), Mullins, Dunkley, Skarz; MacDonald, Ruffels, Lundstram (Rose 70), O'Dowda; Hoban (Hylton 77), Taylor.
Referee: David Webb.

Sunderland (3) 6 *(Rodwell 12, 64, Defoe 16, 39, 87, Watmore 78)*
Exeter C (3) 3 *(Oyeleke 19, Wheeler 31, McCready 43)*   14,360
Sunderland: (451) Pantilimon; Van Aanholt, Jones, Coates, Matthews (Gooch 58); Larsson, Rodwell, M'Vila, Cattermole, Defoe; Graham (Fletcher 46 (Watmore 54)).
Exeter C: (451) Olejnik; Butterfield, Brown, Tillson, McAllister; Davies, Oyeleke, Noble (Morrison 67), McCready, Holmes (Grant 74); Wheeler (Hoskins 75).
Referee: Stuart Attwell.

Swansea C (1) 3 *(Dyer 2, Grimes 64, Emnes 88)*
York C (0) 0   10,174
Swansea C: (4231) Nordfeldt; Rangel, Bartley, Amat, Tabanou; Britton, Ki (Shelvey 81); Dyer (Ayew 87), Grimes (Emnes 76), Routledge; Eder.
York C: (352) Flinders; McCoy, Lowe, Winfield; Nolan, Ilesanmi, Summerfield, Penn (Carson 78), Berrett (Godfrey 71); Oliver (Rzonca 71), Thompson.
Referee: James Adcock.

Walsall (0) 2 *(Lalkovic 65, Henry 86)*
Brighton & HA (1) 1 *(Forster-Caskey 39 (pen))*   2968
Walsall: (4411) Etheridge; Demetriou, Downing (Preston 58), O'Connor, Henry; Lalkovic (Cook 76), Mantom, Chambers, Morris K; Flanagan (Sawyers 62); Bradshaw.
Brighton & HA: (433) Maenpaa; Calderon, Rea, Dunk, Rosenior; Ince, Holla (Baldock 88), Forster-Caskey; O'Grady (Hemed 73); Murphy (LuaLua 88), March.
Referee: Peter Banks.

WBA (0) 0
Port Vale (0) 0   13,915
WBA: (442) Myhill; Chester, McAuley, Olsson, Brunt (Dawson 13); Gnabry (McManaman 57), Yacob, Fletcher, McClean; Lambert, Ideye (Rondon 57).
Port Vale: (4411) Alnwick; Purkiss, Duffy, Inniss, Dickinson; Moore, Grant, Foley, Andoh (Daniel 94); Dodds (Kelly 106); Ikpeazu (Leitch-Smith 67).
aet; WBA won 5-3 on penalties. Referee: Keith Stroud.

Wolverhampton W (1) 2 *(Enobakhare 3, Ojo 58)*
Barnet (0) 1 *(Dembele 76)*   7384
Wolverhampton W: (442) Martinez; Doherty, Ebanks-Landell, Hause, Deslandes (Iorfa 73); Wallace, Saville (Rowe 72), Price, Ojo; Enobakhare (Henry 46), Le Fondre.
Barnet: (532) Stephens; Johnson, Dembele, N'Gala, Nelson, Vilhete; Muggleton (Weston 46), Champion (Gambin 54), Tomlinson; Batt (Akinde 46), Mclean.
Referee: Mark Haywood.

Wednesday, 26 August 2015

Barnsley (2) 3 *(Winnall 22, Watkins 28, Crowley 60)*
Everton (0) 5 *(Mirallas 51, Naismith 59, Lukaku 78, 115, Roberts 96 (og))*   12,290
Barnsley: (4231) Davies; Wabara (Rothwell 90), Roberts, Mawson, Nyatanga; Scowen, Pearson; Watkins (Smith 105), Crowley, Hourihane; Winnall (Wilkinson 83).
Everton: (4231) Robles; Pennington (Barkley 46), Stones, Jagielka, Oviedo; Besic, Cleverley; McGeady (Deulofeu 46), Naismith, Mirallas (McCarthy 110); Lukaku.
aet. Referee: Simon Hooper.

THIRD ROUND

Tuesday, 22 September 2015

Aston Villa (0) 1 *(Gestede 62)*

Birmingham C (0) 0   34,442

Aston Villa: (433) Guzan; Bacuna, Richards, Lescott (Grealish 46), Amavi; Westwood, Clark, Veretout; Agbonlahor (Ayew 46), Gestede, Sinclair.
Birmingham C: (433) Kuszczak; Caddis, Morrison, Spector, Grounds; Davis (Toral 66), Gleeson, Kieftenbeld; Maghoma (Solomon-Otabor 81), Donaldson (Brock-Madsen 81), Gray.
Referee: Robert Madley.

Fulham (0) 0

Stoke C (1) 1 *(Crouch 33)*   9100

Fulham: (442) Lewis; Richards, Stearman, Burn, Ream; Kacaniklic (Tunnicliffe 66), Mattila (Hyndman 82), Christensen, Pringle; McCormack, Woodrow (Dembele 66).
Stoke C: (4231) Given; Bardsley, Wollscheid, Wilson, Pieters; Sidwell, Cameron; Odemwingie (Shaqiri 84), Ireland (Arnautovic 76), Afellay; Crouch.
Referee: Stuart Attwell.

Hull C (1) 1 *(Meyler 41)*

Swansea C (0) 0   16,286

Hull C: (4411) Jakupovic; Taylor (Odubajo 59), Dawson, Davies, Robertson; Elmohamady, Meyler, Livermore (Clucas 69), Hayden (Huddlestone 85); Maloney, Akpom.
Swansea C: (4231) Nordfeldt; Amat, Tabanou (Naughton 72), Bartley, Rangel; Britton, Sigurdsson; Routledge, Ki, Grimes (Shelvey 57); Eder (Gomis 64).
Referee: James Linington.

Leicester C (1) 2 *(Dodoo 6, King 116)*

West Ham U (1) 1 *(Zarate 27)*   21,268

Leicester C: (442) Schwarzer; Simpson, Benalouane, Wasilewski, Fuchs; Albrighton (Schlupp 68), Inler, King, Dodoo (Kante 82); Ulloa, Kramaric (Mahrez 82).
West Ham U: (4231) Adrian; Jenkinson, Tomkins, Collins, Cresswell; Noble, Obiang (Reid 113); Moses, Lanzini, Zarate (Kouyate 76); Carroll (Payet 63).
aet.
Referee: Peter Bankes.

Middlesbrough (1) 3 *(Adomah 37, 64, Fabbrini 57)*

Wolverhampton W (0) 0   13,368

Middlesbrough: (352) Mejias; Amorebieta, Kalas, Friend (Stephens 74); Adomah, Nsue, Leadbitter (Clayton 68), De Pena (Reach 79), Forshaw; Fabbrini, Garcia.
Wolverhampton W: (4231) Ikeme; Doherty, Deslandes, Ebanks-Landell, Iorfa; McDonald, Saville (Henry 81); Price, van La Parra (Le Fondre 60), Wallace; Enobakhare (Afobe 60).
Referee: Kevin Wright.

Preston NE (0) 2 *(Hugill 84, Johnson 118 (pen))*

Bournemouth (1) 2 *(MacDonald 23, Pugh 96)*   5643

Preston NE: (442) Pickford; Woods, Clarke, Wright, Cunningham; Humphrey (Vermijl 78), Johnson, Welsh (Reid 74), Browne; Keane, May (Hugill 74).
Bournemouth: (442) Federici; Francis, Cargill, Cook, Smith; Atsu (Tomlin 81), MacDonald (Gosling 90), O'Kane, Stanislas; King, Kermorgant (Pugh 81).
aet; Bournemouth won 3-2 on penalties.
Referee: Nigel Miller.

Reading (1) 1 *(Blackman 36)*

Everton (0) 2 *(Barkley 62, Deulofeu 73)*   19,435

Reading: (4132) Al Habsi; Gunter, Cooper, Hector, Taylor; Tshibola; John (Williams 77), Hurtado (McCleary 65), Piazon; Alex, Blackman.
Everton: (352) Robles; Stones (Galloway 49), Jagielka, Funes Mori; Lennon, Osman, Barkley, McCarthy, Deulofeu; Kone (Barry 46), Lukaku.
Referee: Keith Hill.

Sunderland (0) 1 *(Toivonen 83)*

Manchester C (4) 4 *(Aguero 9 (pen), De Bruyne 25, Mannone 33 (og), Sterling 36)*   21,644

Sunderland: (4231) Mannone; Yedlin, Coates, O'Shea, Van Aanholt; M'Vila, Rodwell (Cattermole 46); Johnson, Toivonen, Lens; Borini.
Manchester C: (4231) Caballero; Sagna, Demichelis, Otamendi, Kolarov; Toure (Evans 89), Fernando; Jesus Navas (Roberts 55), De Bruyne, Sterling; Aguero (Garcia M 74).
Referee: Roger East.

Wednesday, 23 September 2015

Crystal Palace (0) 4 *(Campbell 51, Gayle 59 (pen), 74 (pen), 86)*

Charlton Ath (0) 1 *(Sarr 65)*   16,576

Crystal Palace: (442) Hennessey; Kelly, Mariappa, Delaney (Hangeland 34), Souare; Lee, McArthur (Cabaye 75), Ledley, Zaha; Campbell (Bamford 60), Gayle.
Charlton Ath: (4411) Pope; Solly, Sarr, Diarra■, Fox; Kennedy (Gudmundsson 60), Ba, Cousins (Kashi 65), Bergdich; McAleny (Watt 75); Ahearne-Grant.
Referee: Neil Swarbrick.

Liverpool (1) 1 *(Ings 23)*

Carlisle U (1) 1 *(Asamoah 35)*   42,518

Liverpool: (343) Bogdan; Can, Skrtel, Lovren; Clyne (Ibe 86), Milner, Allen (Coutinho 64), Moreno; Firmino (Origi 35), Ings, Lallana.
Carlisle U: (3511) Gillespie; Miller, Raynes, Grainger; McQueen, Dicker, Joyce, Kennedy (Gillesphey 73), Sweeney (Ibehre 64); Hery; Asamoah (Gilliead 64).
aet; Liverpool won 3-2 on penalties.
Referee: Andrew Madley.

Manchester U (1) 3 *(Rooney 23, Andreas Pereira 60, Martial 90)*

Ipswich T (0) 0   56,607

Manchester U: (4231) De Gea; Valencia, Smalling (Jones 70), Blind, Young; Schweinsteiger, Ander Herrera; Mata (Martial 70), Rooney (Depay 81), Andreas Pereira; Fellaini.
Ipswich T: (4411) Bialkowski; Emmanuel, Yorwerth, Malarczyk, Parr; Bru, Coke, Tabb (Toure 75), Oar; McGoldrick (Sears 61); Murphy (Pitman 61).
Referee: Simon Hooper.

Milton Keynes D (0) 0

Southampton (3) 6 *(Rodriguez 5, 48 (pen), Mane 10, 25, Long 68, 75)*   10,189

Milton Keynes D: (4231) Martin; Hodson, McFadzean, Kay, Lewington; Poyet, Aguza (Reeves 57); Baker, Benavente (Hall 36), Powell; Church (Maynard 58).
Southampton: (4231) Stekelenburg; Cedric, Fonte, van Dijk (Yoshida 79), Targett (Bertrand 55); Davis S, Romeu; Juanmi, Rodriguez, Mane (Ramirez 65); Long.
Referee: Keith Stroud.

Newcastle U (0) 0

Sheffield W (0) 1 *(McGugan 76)*   33,986

Newcastle U: (4231) Krul; Janmaat (Mbabu 46), Lascelles, Williamson, Mbemba; Anita, Wijnaldum; Thauvin (Perez 46), Sissoko, Obertan (Toney 71); De Jong.
Sheffield W: (451) Wildsmith; Palmer, Loovens, Lees, Wiggins; Sougou (Bannan 86), Semedo, McGugan, Helan, Marco Matias (Bus 65); Lucas Joao (Nuhiu 80).
Referee: Chris Kavanagh.

Norwich C (0) 3 *(Jarvis 62, Lafferty 85, Pocognoli 90 (og))*

WBA (0) 0   19,015

Norwich C: (442) Rudd; Wisdom, Bennett R, Bassong, Olsson; Bennett E, O'Neil, Dorrans (Howson 46), Jarvis; Grabban (Hoolahan 59), Mbokani (Lafferty 76).
WBA: (433) Lindegaard; Chester, Dawson, Olsson, Pocognoli; Gamboa, Anichebe (McClean 76), Gardner; Sessegnon (Leko 77), Lambert, Gnabry (McManaman 68).
Referee: Craig Pawson.

Tottenham H (0) 1 *(Chambers 56 (og))*
Arsenal (1) 2 *(Flamini 26, 78)* 35,687
Tottenham H: (4231) Vorm; Trippier, Fazio, Wimmer, Rose; Dier (N'Jie 85), Carroll; Townsend (Son 67), Eriksen, Chadli (Alli 75); Kane.
Arsenal: (4231) Ospina; Debuchy, Chambers, Mertesacker, Gibbs; Flamini, Arteta; Campbell (Sanchez 67), Ramsey, Oxlade-Chamberlain (Walcott 89); Giroud.
Referee: Andre Marriner.

Walsall (1) 1 *(O'Connor 45)*

Chelsea (2) 4 *(Ramires 10, Remy 41, Kenedy 52, Pedro 90)* 10,525
Walsall: (4231) Etheridge; Demetriou, Downing, O'Connor, Henry; Chambers (Flanagan 73), Mantom; Morris K, Sawyers, Lalkovic (Forde 73); Cook (Baxendale 86).
Chelsea: (4231) Begovic; Ivanovic, Terry, Cahill, Baba; Mikel, Loftus-Cheek (Matic 72); Ramires, Kenedy (Pedro 70), Remy; Falcao (Djilobodji 90).
Referee: Lee Mason.

FOURTH ROUND

Tuesday, 27 October 2015

Everton (0) 1 *(Osman 68)*
Norwich C (0) 1 *(Bassong 51)* 31,694
Everton: (442) Robles; Browning (Barkley 62), Stones, Funes Mori, Oviedo; Mirallas (Naismith 98), Gibson, McCarthy, Osman; Kone (Deulofeu 62), Lukaku.
Norwich C: (4231) Rudd; Wisdom (Whittaker 91), Bennett R, Bassong, Olsson; O'Neil, Mulumbu (Dorrans 76); Redmond, Odjidja-Ofoe (Jarvis 69), Hoolahan; Grabban.
aet; Everton won 4-3 on penalties.
Referee: Roger East.

Hull C (0) 1 *(Hernandez 105)*
Leicester C (0) 1 *(Mahrez 99)* 16,818
Hull C: (3511) Jakupovic; Maguire, Dawson, Taylor (Hernandez 79); Odubajo, Hayden, Huddlestone, Diame (Meyler 110), Robertson; Maloney; Luer (Akpom 74).
Leicester C: (4411) Schwarzer; De Laet, Wasilewski, Benalouane, Chilwell; Inler, Dodoo (Mahrez 84), King, Albrighton; Okazaki (Vardy 65); Kramaric (Drinkwater 65).
aet; Hull C won 5-4 on penalties.
Referee: Stuart Attwell.

Sheffield W (2) 3 *(Wallace 27, Lucas Joao 40, Hutchinson 51)*
Arsenal (0) 0 35,065
Sheffield W: (4141) Wildsmith; Hunt, Lees, Loovens, Pudil; Hutchinson (McGugan 80); Wallace, Lee, Bannan (Semedo 75), Helan; Lucas Joao (Nuhiu 85).
Arsenal: (4231) Cech; Debuchy, Chambers, Mertesacker, Gibbs; Flamini, Kamara (Bielik 60); Campbell, Oxlade-Chamberlain (Walcott 5 (Bennacer 19)), Iwobi; Giroud.
Referee: Graham Scott.

Stoke C (0) 1 *(Walters 52)*
Chelsea (0) 1 *(Remy 90)* 24,886
Stoke C: (4231) Butland; Bardsley■, Shawcross, Wollscheid, Muniesa (Wilson 49); Whelan, Adam; Diouf, Afellay (Shaqiri 76), Arnautovic; Walters (Odemwingie 90).
Chelsea: (4231) Begovic; Zouma, Cahill, Terry, Baba (Kenedy 70); Ramires (Traore 80), Mikel; Willian, Oscar, Hazard; Costa (Remy 33).
aet; Stoke C won 5-4 on penalties.
Referee: Kevin Friend.

Wednesday, 28 October 2015

Liverpool (1) 1 *(Clyne 17)*
Bournemouth (0) 0 41,948
Liverpool: (4231) Bogdan; Randall, Toure (Skrtel 33), Lovren, Clyne; Brannagan (Lucas 65), Allen; Ibe, Firmino (Lallana 87), Teixeira; Origi.
Bournemouth: (433) Federici; Smith, Francis, Distin, Daniels; Arter (King 71), MacDonald, Stanislas (Rantie 82); Ritchie, Kermorgant (Tomlin 71), Pugh.
Referee: Mike Jones.

Manchester C (2) 5 *(Bony 22, De Bruyne 44, Iheanacho 59, Toure 76 (pen), Garcia M 90)*
Crystal Palace (0) 1 *(Delaney 89)* 40,585
Manchester C: (442) Caballero; Zabaleta (Sagna 56), Demichelis, Mangala, Kolarov; Jesus Navas, Fernando, Toure, De Bruyne (Roberts 75); Bony (Garcia M 84), Iheanacho.
Crystal Palace: (4231) Hennessey; Mariappa (Ward 85), Dann, Delaney, Kelly; Jedinak, Ledley; Zaha, Mutch (Lee 75), Bolasie; Bamford (Gayle 77).
Referee: Paul Tierney.

Manchester U (0) 0
Middlesbrough (0) 0 67,258
Manchester U: (4231) Romero; Darmian, Smalling, Blind, Rojo (Young 61); Carrick, Fellaini; Lingard, Andreas Pereira, Depay (Martial 71); Wilson (Rooney 46).
Middlesbrough: (4231) Mejias; Kalas, Stephens (Clayton 114), Ayala, Friend; Gibson, Leadbitter; Nsue, De Pena (Zuculini 78), Downing; Garcia (Nugent 84).
aet; Middlesbrough won 3-1 on penalties.
Referee: Lee Mason.

Southampton (0) 2 *(Yoshida 51, Pelle 77)*
Aston Villa (0) 1 *(Sinclair 90 (pen))* 31,314
Southampton: (4231) Stekelenburg; Yoshida, Caulker, van Dijk, Targett; Ward-Prowse, Wanyama; Ramirez (Davis S 68), Juanmi (Tadic 69), Romeu; Pelle.
Aston Villa: (442) Guzan; Hutton, Crespo, Clark, Richardson; Bacuna (Ayew 63), Westwood, Sanchez, Amavi (Grealish 64); Agbonlahor, Gestede (Sinclair 72).
Referee: Keith Stroud.

QUARTER-FINALS

Tuesday, 1 December 2015

Manchester C (1) 4 *(Bony 12, Iheanacho 80, De Bruyne 82, 87)*
Hull C (0) 1 *(Robertson 90)* 38,246
Manchester C: (4231) Caballero; Sagna, Otamendi, Mangala, Clichy; Fernandinho, Delph; Jesus Navas (Sterling 62), Silva (Demichelis 83), De Bruyne; Bony (Iheanacho 71).
Hull C: (352) Jakupovic; Odubajo, Maguire, Bruce; Elmohamady, Livermore, Hayden, Taylor (Diame 58), Robertson; Aluko (Snodgrass 73), Akpom (Hernandez 68).
Referee: Neil Swarbrick.

Middlesbrough (0) 0
Everton (2) 2 *(Deulofeu 20, Lukaku 28)* 31,628
Middlesbrough: (4231) Mejias; Nsue, Ayala, Gibson (Friend 83), Amorebieta; Clayton (Adomah 73), Leadbitter; Stuani, Downing, De Pena (Forshaw 46); Garcia.
Everton: (4231) Robles; Coleman, Stones, Funes Mori, Galloway (Baines 73); Cleverley, Barry; Deulofeu (Mirallas 81), Barkley, Osman; Lukaku (Naismith 86).
Referee: Roger East.

Stoke C (1) 2 *(Afellay 30, Bardsley 75)*
Sheffield W (0) 0 26,779
Stoke C: (4231) Butland; Johnson (Bardsley 46), Wilson, Wollscheid, Pieters; Cameron, van Ginkel; Walters, Afellay, Arnautovic (Whelan 88); Crouch (Joselu 13).
Sheffield W: (442) Wildsmith; Hunt (McGugan 46), Lees (Pudil 38), Loovens (Nuhiu 77), Wiggins; Wallace, Lee, Hutchinson, Sougou; Hooper, Lucas Joao.
Referee: Mark Clattenburg.

Wednesday, 2 December 2015

Southampton (1) 1 *(Mane 1)*
Liverpool (3) 6 *(Sturridge 25, 29, Origi 45, 68, 86, Ibe 73)* 31,592
Southampton: (4231) Stekelenburg; Cedric (Ward-Prowse 63), Caulker, van Dijk, Bertrand; Clasie (Long 63), Wanyama; Tadic, Mane, Davis S (Romeu 77); Pelle.
Liverpool: (4312) Bogdan; Randall, Skrtel, Lovren, Moreno (Smith 77); Can, Lucas, Allen (Henderson 74); Lallana; Sturridge (Ibe 59), Origi.
Referee: Robert Madley.

SEMI-FINALS FIRST LEG

Tuesday, 5 January 2016

Stoke C (0) 0

Liverpool (1) 1 *(Ibe 37)*   27,369

Stoke C: (4231) Butland; Johnson, Shawcross, Wollscheid, Pieters; Cameron (Walters 46), Whelan; Shaqiri (Crouch 83), Afellay, Arnautovic; Krkic (Joselu 69).
Liverpool: (433) Mignolet; Clyne, Toure, Lovren (Milner 34), Moreno; Can, Lucas, Allen (Benteke 79); Lallana, Firmino, Coutinho (Ibe 18).
Referee: Anthony Taylor.

Wednesday, 6 January 2016

Everton (1) 2 *(Funes Mori 45, Lukaku 78)*

Manchester C (0) 1 *(Jesus Navas 76)*   34,027

Everton: (4231) Robles; Coleman, Stones, Funes Mori, Baines; Besic, Barry; Deulofeu (Mirallas 68), Barkley, Cleverley (Osman 46); Lukaku (Kone 82).
Manchester C: (4231) Caballero; Sagna, Otamendi, Mangala (Demichelis 46), Clichy; Fernandinho, Delph (Jesus Navas 54); De Bruyne (Fernando 90), Toure, Silva; Aguero.
Referee: Robert Madley.

SEMI-FINALS SECOND LEG

Tuesday, 26 January 2016

Liverpool (0) 0

Stoke C (1) 1 *(Arnautovic 45)*   43,091

Liverpool: (433) Mignolet; Flanagan (Ibe 106), Toure (Allen 85), Sakho, Moreno; Henderson (Benteke 58), Lucas, Can; Milner, Firmino, Lallana.
Stoke C: (4231) Butland; Johnson, Wollscheid, Muniesa, Pieters; Whelan, Afellay; Walters, Krkic (Adam 71 (van Ginkel 98)), Arnautovic (Shaqiri 78); Crouch.
aet; Liverpool won 6-5 on penalties.
Referee: Jon Moss.

Wednesday, 27 January 2016

Manchester C (1) 3 *(Fernandinho 24, De Bruyne 70, Aguero 76)*

Everton (1) 1 *(Barkley 18)*   50,048

Manchester C: (4231) Caballero; Zabaleta, Otamendi, Demichelis, Clichy; Fernandinho, Delph (Jesus Navas 46); Silva (Fernando 80), Toure (De Bruyne 66), Sterling; Aguero.
Everton: (4231) Robles; Stones (Coleman 77), Jagielka, Funes Mori, Baines; Cleverley, Barry; Deulofeu (Kone 60), Barkley, Osman (McCarthy 60); Lukaku.
Manchester C won 4-3 on aggregate.
Referee: Martin Atkinson.

CAPITAL ONE CUP FINAL 2016

Sunday, 28 February 2016

(at Wembley Stadium, attendance 86,206)

Liverpool (0) 1   **Manchester C (0) 1**

aet; Manchester C won 3-1 on penalties

Liverpool: (4411) Mignolet; Clyne, Lucas, Sakho (Toure 25), Moreno (Lallana 72); Milner, Henderson, Can, Coutinho; Firmino (Origi 80); Sturridge.
Scorer: Coutinho 83.

Manchester C: (4231) Caballero; Sagna (Zabaleta 91), Kompany, Otamendi, Clichy; Toure, Fernando (Jesus Navas 91); Fernandinho, Silva (Bony 110), Sterling; Aguero.
Scorer: Fernandinho 49.

Referee: Michael Oliver.

Manchester City's Willy Caballero saves a penalty by Liverpool's Philippe Coutinho during the penalty shoot-out which decided the Capital One Cup final in City's favour. The game finished 1-1 after extra time.
(Reuters/Eddie Keogh Livepic)

LEAGUE CUP ATTENDANCES 1960–2016

Season	Attendances	Games	Average
1960–61	1,204,580	112	10,755
1961–62	1,030,534	104	9,909
1962–63	1,029,893	102	10,097
1963–64	945,265	104	9,089
1964–65	962,802	98	9,825
1965–66	1,205,876	106	11,376
1966–67	1,394,553	118	11,818
1967–68	1,671,326	110	15,194
1968–69	2,064,647	118	17,497
1969–70	2,299,819	122	18,851
1970–71	2,035,315	116	17,546
1971–72	2,397,154	123	19,489
1972–73	1,935,474	120	16,129
1973–74	1,722,629	132	13,050
1974–75	1,901,094	127	14,969
1975–76	1,841,735	140	13,155
1976–77	2,236,636	147	15,215
1977–78	2,038,295	148	13,772
1978–79	1,825,643	139	13,134
1979–80	2,322,866	169	13,745
1980–81	2,051,576	161	12,743
1981–82	1,880,682	161	11,681
1982–83	1,679,756	160	10,498
1983–84	1,900,491	168	11,312
1984–85	1,876,429	167	11,236
1985–86	1,579,916	163	9,693
1986–87	1,531,498	157	9,755
1987–88	1,539,253	158	9,742
1988–89	1,552,780	162	9,585
1989–90	1,836,916	168	10,934
1990–91	1,675,496	159	10,538
1991–92	1,622,337	164	9,892
1992–93	1,558,031	161	9,677
1993–94	1,744,120	163	10,700
1994–95	1,530,478	157	9,748
1995–96	1,776,060	162	10,963
1996–97	1,529,321	163	9,382
1997–98	1,484,297	153	9,701
1998–99	1,555,856	153	10,169
1999–2000	1,354,233	153	8,851
2000–01	1,501,304	154	9,749
2001–02	1,076,390	93	11,574
2002–03	1,242,478	92	13,505
2003–04	1,267,729	93	13,631
2004–05	1,313,693	93	14,216
2005–06	1,072,362	93	11,531
2006–07	1,098,403	93	11,811
2007–08	1,332,841	94	14,179
2008–09	1,329,753	93	14,298
2009–10	1,376,405	93	14,800
2010–11	1,197,917	93	12,881
2011–12	1,209,684	93	13,007
2012–13	1,210,031	93	13,011
2013–14	1,362,360	93	14,649
2014–15	1,274,413	93	13,690
2015–16	1,430,554	93	15,382

CAPITAL ONE CUP 2015–16

Round	Aggregate	Games	Average
One	180,835	36	5,023
Two	224,876	24	9,370
Three	366,289	16	22,893
Four	289,568	8	36,196
Quarter-finals	128,245	4	32,061
Semi-finals	154,535	4	38,634
Final	86,206	1	86,206
Total	1,430,554	93	15,382

FOOTBALL LEAGUE TROPHY
FINALS 1984–2016

The 1984 final was played at Boothferry Park, Hull. All subsequent finals played at Wembley except between 2001 and 2007 (inclusive) which were played at Millennium Stadium, Cardiff.

ASSOCIATE MEMBERS' CUP
1984	Bournemouth v Hull C	2-1

FREIGHT ROVER TROPHY
1985	Wigan Ath v Brentford	3-1
1986	Bristol C v Bolton W	3-0
1987	Mansfield T v Bristol C	1-1*
	Mansfield T won 5-4 on penalties	

SHERPA VANS TROPHY
1988	Wolverhampton W v Burnley	2-0
1989	Bolton W v Torquay U	4-1

LEYLAND DAF CUP
1990	Tranmere R v Bristol R	2-1
1991	Birmingham C v Tranmere R	3-2

AUTOGLASS TROPHY
1992	Stoke C v Stockport Co	1-0
1993	Port Vale v Stockport Co	2-1
1994	Swansea C v Huddersfield T	1-1*
	Swansea C won 3-1 on penalties	

AUTO WINDSCREENS SHIELD
1995	Birmingham C v Carlisle U	1-0*
1996	Rotherham U v Shrewsbury T	2-1
1997	Carlisle U v Colchester U	0-0*
	Carlisle U won 4-3 on penalties	
1998	Grimsby T v Bournemouth	2-1
1999	Wigan Ath v Millwall	1-0
2000	Stoke C v Bristol C	2-1

LDV VANS TROPHY
2001	Port Vale v Brentford	2-1
2002	Blackpool v Cambridge U	4-1
2003	Bristol C v Carlisle U	2-0
2004	Blackpool v Southend U	2-0
2005	Wrexham v Southend U	2-0*

FOOTBALL LEAGUE TROPHY
2006	Swansea C v Carlisle U	2-1

JOHNSTONE'S PAINT TROPHY
2007	Doncaster R v Bristol R	3-2*
2008	Milton Keynes D v Grimsby T	2-0
2009	Luton T v Scunthorpe U	3-2*
2010	Southampton v Carlisle U	4-1
2011	Carlisle U v Brentford	1-0
2012	Chesterfield v Swindon T	2-0
2013	Crewe Alex v Southend U	2-0
2014	Peterborough U v Chesterfield	3-1
2015	Bristol C v Walsall	2-0
2016	Barnsley v Oxford U	3-2

After extra time.

FOOTBALL LEAGUE TROPHY WINS

Bristol C 3, Birmingham C 2, Blackpool 2, Carlisle U 2, Port Vale 2, Stoke C 2, Swansea C 2, Wigan Ath 2, Barnsley 1, Bolton W 1, Bournemouth 1, Chesterfield 1, Crewe Alex 1, Doncaster R 1, Grimsby T 1, Luton T 1, Mansfield T 1, Milton Keynes D 1, Peterborough U 1, Rotherham U 1, Southampton 1, Tranmere R 1, Wolverhampton W 1, Wrexham 1.

APPEARANCES IN FINALS

Carlisle U 6, Bristol C 5, Brentford 3, Southend U 3, Birmingham C 2, Blackpool 2, Bolton W 2, Bournemouth 2, Bristol R 2, Chesterfield 2, Grimsby T 2, Port Vale 2, Stockport Co 2, Stoke C 2, Swansea C 2, Tranmere R 2, Wigan Ath 2, Barnsley 1, Burnley 1, Cambridge U 1, Colchester U 1, Crewe Alex 1, Doncaster R 1, Huddersfield T 1, Hull C 1, Luton T 1, Mansfield T 1, Millwall 1, Milton Keynes D 1, Oxford U 1, Peterborough U 1, Rotherham U 1, Scunthorpe U 1, Shrewsbury T 1, Southampton 1, Swindon T 1, Torquay U 1, Walsall 1, Wolverhampton W 1, Wrexham 1.

JOHNSTONE'S PAINT TROPHY 2015–16

■ *Denotes player sent off.*

NORTHERN SECTION FIRST ROUND

Tuesday, 1 September 2015
Accrington S (0) 1 *(Bruna 83)*
Bury (0) 2 *(Hope 46, Tutte 70)*   1344
Accrington S: (442) Etheridge; Wakefield, Davies, Winnard, Pearson; Mingoia (Bruna 68), Barry, Conneely (Procter 2), McConville; Morgan (Phillips 54), Kee.
Bury: (4141) Lainton; Riley, Cameron, Foulds, Hussey; Pugh (Brown 46); Mayor (Pope 46), Tutte (Soares 76), Mellis, Jones; Hope.
Referee: Tony Harrington.

Doncaster R (0) 0
Burton Alb (0) 0   2956
Doncaster R: (442) Stuckmann (Marosi 46); Lund, Butler, McKay, Evina; Stewart, Keegan (Chaplow 46), Middleton, Whitehouse; Mandeville (Williams 71), Main.
Burton Alb: (442) Matthews; Naylor, O'Connor, Flanagan, McCrory; Akins, Butcher (Reilly 52), Weir, Duffy (Binnom-Williams 60); Palmer, Joachim.
Doncaster R won 5-3 on penalties.
Referee: Ross Joyce.

Hartlepool U (0) 1 *(Fenwick 51)*
Sheffield U (1) 1 *(Flynn 7)*   2221
Hartlepool U: (343) Bartlett; Harrison S, Worley, Jones; Duckworth (Nearney 65), Hawkins (Nelson-Addy 90), Featherstone, Carroll; Bingham, Fenwick, Oates.
Sheffield U: (442) Long; Alcock, McGahey, Kennedy (Sharp 86), McEveley; Woolford, Wallace K, Basham, Flynn (Campbell-Ryce 72); McNulty, Higdon.
Sheffield U won 4-3 on penalties.
Referee: Scott Duncan.

Morecambe (0) 2 *(Devitt 57, Barkhuizen 72)*
Walsall (0) 0   1332
Morecambe: (4231) Roche; McGowan, Devitt, Dugdale, Molyneux; Kenyon (Bailey 71), Goodall; Barkhuizen (Bondswell 90), Fleming, Mullin; Ryan (Miller 68).
Walsall: (4141) MacGillivray; Kinsella, O'Connor, Preston, Taylor; Chambers; Morris K (Forde 66), Mantom, Baxendale (Sawyers 65); Lalkovic (Cook 65); Bradshaw.
Referee: Seb Stockbridge.

Notts Co (0) 3 *(McLeod 52, Edwards 79, Stead 90)*
Mansfield T (0) 1 *(Westcarr 90 (pen))*   2696
Notts Co: (442) Loach; Atkinson, Swerts (Edwards 46), Hollis (Jenner 88), Audel; Snijders, Aborah (Smith 74), Burke, Campbell; Stead, McLeod.
Mansfield T: (4411) Jensen; Marsden, Pearce, Collins, Benning; Rose (Thomas J 46), McGuire, Chapman (Clements 61), Yussuf; Thomas N; Beardsley (Westcarr 65).
Referee: Richard Clark.

Port Vale (0) 1 *(Ikpeazu 60)*
Carlisle U (0) 0   2571
Port Vale: (4411) Alnwick; Purkiss, Duffy, Streete, Dickinson; Birchall, McCourt, Grant, Andoh (Daniel 77); Dodds; Ikpeazu (Hooper 86).
Carlisle U: (352) Hanford; Miller, Raynes, Grainger; Thompson (Brough 87), Dicker, Sweeney, Hery, McQueen; Balanta (Asamoah 68), Rigg (Ibehre 69).
Referee: Darren England.

Scunthorpe U (0) 1 *(Goode 90)*
Barnsley (0) 2 *(Nyatanga 62, Watkins 76)*   1796
Scunthorpe U: (442) Daniels; Wiseman, King (McSheffrey 66), Goode, Laird; Adelakun, McAllister, Bishop, Wallace; Hopper (Madden 68), Wootton (van Veen 72).
Barnsley: (451) Townsend; Wabara (Bree 56), Nyatanga, Mawson, Smith; Harris, Scowen, Rothwell (Digby 81), Crowley (Wilkinson 87), Watkins; Winnall.
Referee: Ben Toner.

Shrewsbury T (1) 2 *(McAlinden 40, Barnett 49)*
Oldham Ath (0) 0   1817
Shrewsbury T: (352) Leutwiler; Ellis, Knight-Percival (Sadler 78), Grandison; Patterson, Wesolowski (Lawrence 72), Ogogo, Clark, Brown; Barnett, McAlinden (Whalley 68).
Oldham Ath: (4231) Cornell; Dieng, Wilson, Edmundson, Brown (Murphy 62); Philliskirk, Jones; Croft, Green (Tuohy 85), Yeates; Turner (Forte 72).
Referee: Stephen Martin.

SOUTHERN SECTION FIRST ROUND

Tuesday, 1 September 2015
AFC Wimbledon (2) 2 *(Azeez 7, Taylor 25)*
Plymouth Arg (1) 3 *(Jervis 38, Brunt 54, McHugh 57)*   1251
AFC Wimbledon: (442) Shea; Fuller, Nightingale, Osborne, Harrison; Rigg, Reeves, Beere (Gallagher 34 (Francomb 52)), Barcham (Fitzpatrick 46); Taylor, Azeez.
Plymouth Arg: (4231) McCormick; Mellor, Nelson, Hartley, Sawyer; McHugh, Boateng; Jervis, Carey, Wylde (Threlkeld 83); Brunt (Tanner 74).
Referee: Charles Breakspear.

Cambridge U (0) 0
Dagenham & R (2) 2 *(Hemmings 20, McClure 27)*   1618
Cambridge U: (352) Beasant; Roberts (Carr 46), Coulson, Taft; Newton, Hughes J (Simpson 46), Morrissey (Hughes L 65), Berry, Demetriou; Slew, Blyth.
Dagenham & R: (442) O'Brien; Passley, Obileye, Dikamona, Connors; Chambers (Raymond 88), Richards, Ferdinand, Hemmings; McClure (Hines 73), Doidge.
Referee: Darren Drysdale.

Exeter C (0) 2 *(Harley 54 (pen), Nicholls 72)*
Portsmouth (0) 0   2323
Exeter C: (451) Olejnik; Butterfield, Moore-Taylor, Tillson, Woodman; Holmes (Reid 75), Harley (Jay 60), McCready, Oyeleke, Nicholls; Wheeler (Morrison 61).
Portsmouth: (4231) Jones; Davies, Webster, Barton, Haunstrup (Haitham 82); Close, May; Tollitt, Chaplin, Joseph-Baudi (Naismith 66); McGurk (Oxlade-Chamberlain 76).
Referee: Lee Swabey.

Luton T (1) 2 *(Green 29, O'Donnell 90)*
Leyton Orient (0) 1 *(James 59 (pen))*   1953
Luton T: (451) Tyler; O'Donnell, McNulty, Cuthbert (Okuonghae 59), Griffiths; Ruddock (Hall 72), Guttridge, Smith, Green (McQuoid 85), Lee; Marriott**■**.
Leyton Orient: (442) Grainger; Clohessy (Moncur 46), Maguire, Essam, Shaw; Turgott, James (Judd 83), Moore, Pritchard; Kashket, Palmer (Semedo 87).
Referee: Nick Kinseley.

Millwall (0) 1 *(Williams 90)*
Peterborough U (0) 0   2050
Millwall: (442) Archer; Edwards, Nelson, Beevers, Craig; Onyedinma (Webster 90), Williams, Upson, O'Brien (Cowan-Hall 81); Thompson, Marquis (Gregory 69).
Peterborough U: (442) Alnwick; Davey (Beautyman 20), Bostwick, Santos (Smith 63), Elder; Taylor, Anderson J, Forrester, Maddison; Washington, Vassell (Coulibaly 76).
Referee: Keith Hill.

Newport Co (0) 1 *(Collins 72)*
Swindon T (1) 1 *(Rodgers 19)*   1434
Newport Co: (442) Taylor; Rodman (Collins 57), Hayden, Parselle, Barrow; Owen-Evans, Byrne, Laurent (Klukowski 73), Nana Ofori-Twumasi; Boden, John-Lewis (Ansah 86).
Swindon T: (433) Belford; Barry, Turnbull, Brophy, Stewart (Iandolo 79); Traore, Branco, Rodgers; Marshall (Smith T 71), Randall, Robert.
Swindon T won 7-6 on penalties.
Referee: Kevin Johnson.

Northampton T (1) 3 *(Calvert-Lewin 9, Watson 49, Richards 85)*

Colchester U (1) 2 *(Bonne 32, 82)*   1366

Northampton T: (442) Clarke; Yates (Lelan 46), McDonald, Cresswell, Buchanan; Potter, Watson, Corry (Taylor 73), D'Ath; Calvert-Lewin (Richards 80), Hoskins.
Colchester U: (451) Parish; Wynter, Kent, Elokobi, Briggs; Sembie-Ferris (Wright 60), Moncur, Garvan, Szmodics, Harriott; Bonne.
Referee: Darren Deadman.

Yeovil T (1) 1 *(Dembele 37 (og))*

Barnet (0) 0   1203

Yeovil T: (442) Krysiak; Roberts, Lacey, Arthurworrey, Smith; Cornick, Dolan, Wakefield (Gibbons 35), Compton (Allen 81); Jeffers, Sowunmi (Bird 65).
Barnet: (442) Stephens; Hoyte, Nelson, Dembele, Johnson (Muggleton 9); Batt (Gondoh 56), Weston, Champion, Tomlinson; Akinde (Stevens 46), Mclean.
Referee: Tim Robinson.

NORTHERN SECTION SECOND ROUND

Tuesday, 6 October 2015

Bury (0) 0

Morecambe (0) 1 *(Miller 81)*   1508

Bury: (442) Lainton; Riley (Jones 46), Brown, Cameron, Hussey (Pugh 46); Mayor, Sedgwick (Soares 58), Burgess, Rose; Pope, Hope.
Morecambe: (4231) Roche; Beeley, Edwards, Parrish, McGowan; Kenyon, Goodall; Devitt, Mullin (Ryan 78), Molyneux (Miller 46); Ellison.
Referee: Mark Brown.

Crewe Alex (2) 2 *(Haber 6, Colclough 36)*

Wigan Ath (1) 3 *(Hiwula 10, 70, Wildschut 76)*   2168

Crewe Alex: (4231) Garratt; Turton, Ray (Baillie 62), Nugent, Guthrie; Fox, Atkinson; Colclough, Inman (Dalla Valle 87), Cooper (Ainley 67); Haber.
Wigan Ath: (532) Jaaskelainen; Kellett, McCann (Cowie 28), Barnett, Hendry, Daniels; Power, Wildschut (Chow 84), Junior; Hiwula, Odelusi (Holt 54).
Referee: James Adcock.

Fleetwood T (0) 2 *(Hunter 69, Grant R 90)*

Shrewsbury T (1) 1 *(Brown 25)*   1267

Fleetwood T: (442) Maxwell; Hornby-Forbes, Wood, Teixeira, Bell; Sarcevic, Nirennold (Grant R 88), Ryan, Haughton (Davis 90); Proctor, Matt (Hunter 63).
Shrewsbury T: (3142) Leutwiler; Ellis, Grandison, Sadler; Black (Ogogo 67); Patterson, Cole, Clark, Brown; McAlinden (KaiKai 73), Barnett.
Referee: Kevin Wright.

Port Vale (0) 1 *(Grant 52 (pen))*

Blackpool (1) 2 *(Rivers 44, Robertson 56)*   2720

Port Vale: (4411) Alnwick; Purkiss, Streete (McGivern 38), Duffy, Dickinson; Moore, Grant, Brown (Ikpeazu 61), Andoh; Daniel (Leitch-Smith 77); Dodds.
Blackpool: (442) Doyle; Higham, Robertson, Aldred, Dunne; Rivers, Oliver, Cubero, Samuel; Paterson (Herron 67), Thomas.
Referee: Mark Heywood.

Rochdale (1) 2 *(Tanser 18, Alessandra 66)*

Chesterfield (0) 1 *(Eastham 65 (og))*   1042

Rochdale: (4231) Lillis; Cannon (Bennett 22 (Noble-Lazarus 54)), Eastham, McNulty, Tanser; Lund, Camps; Vincenti, Alessandra, McDermott (Barry-Murphy 84); Mendez-Laing.
Chesterfield: (4231) Lee; Talbot (O'Shea 46), Hird, Raglan, Jones; O'Neil, Donohue; Simons (Banks 80), Gnanduillet (Ebanks-Blake 46), Orrell; Dieseruvwe.
Referee: Jeremy Simpson.

Sheffield U (3) 5 *(Baxter 20 (pen), 36 (pen), Done 23, Scougall 67, Adams 74 (pen))*

Notts Co (0) 1 *(Stead 62)*   5497

Sheffield U: (4411) Long; Freeman, McGahey, McEveley, Woolford; Campbell-Ryce (Sammon 84), Scougall, Reed, Adams; Baxter (Coutts 71); Done (Wallace K 71).
Notts Co: (451) Loach; Hewitt, Edwards (Swerts 46), Hollis*, Audel; Campbell, Noble, Aborah (Smith 58), Burke (Stead 46), Barmby; McLeod.
Referee: Carl Boyeson.

York C (1) 2 *(Oliver 5, 50)*

Doncaster R (0) 0   1627

York C: (352) Flinders; Lowe, McCombe, Ilesanmi; McCoy, Berrett, Penn, Collins, Straker; Coulson (Carson 68), Oliver (Thompson 80).
Doncaster R: (451) Stuckmann; Horsfield, Butler, Taylor-Sinclair, Evina; N'Guessan, Coppinger, Wellens, Middleton, Williams (Mandeville 64); Anderson (Forrester 73).
Referee: Geoff Eltringham.

Tuesday, 13 October 2015

Bradford C (1) 1 *(Knott 22)*

Barnsley (1) 2 *(Watkins 45, Mawson 69)*   4127

Bradford C: (442) Williams; Darby, Clarke N, McArdle, Leigh; Marshall, Liddle (Evans 73), Knott, McMahon; Hanson (Davies 64), James (Cole 63).
Barnsley: (541) Davies; Wabara (Bree 59), Roberts, Mawson, Nyatanga, Smith; Watkins, Pearson, Hourihane (Digby 80), Harris (White H 65); Winnall.
Referee: Trevor Kettle.

SOUTHERN SECTION SECOND ROUND

Tuesday, 6 October 2015

Bristol R (2) 2 *(Taylor 4, Easter 11)*

Wycombe W (0) 0   3243

Bristol R: (442) Nicholls; Leadbitter, Parkes, McChrystal, Brown; Bodin, Lines, Sinclair (Clarke O 74), Montano (Lyttle 90); Taylor, Easter (Blissett 88).
Wycombe W: (442) Ingram; Jombati, Pierre, Kretzschmar (Jacobson 88), Banton; Rowe, Bloomfield, McGinn, Wood; Sellers (O'Nien 73), Amadi-Holloway (Thompson 88).
Referee: Oliver Langford.

Crawley T (0) 0

Southend U (2) 3 *(Weston 26, Pigott 39, 87)*   1139

Crawley T: (442) Preston; Donnelly (Young 46), Bradley, McNerney, Hancox; Smith J, Walton, Rooney (Fenelon 55), Edwards; Barnard (Tomlin 70), Deacon.
Southend U: (433) Bentley; White, Bolger, Prosser, Coker; Atkinson, Deegan, Wordsworth (Timlin 58); Weston (Worrall 82), Payne (Mooney 75), Pigott.
Referee: Tim Robinson.

Gillingham (0) 2 *(Ehmer 65, Dack 83)*

Luton T (1) 1 *(McGeehan 41)*   3428

Gillingham: (41212) Nelson; Morris, Lennon, Ehmer, Dickenson (Garmston 74); Hessenthaler; McGlashan, Houghton (Dack 66); Osaoabe; Norris (Williamson 63), McDonald.
Luton T: (4231) Tyler; Lawless, Okuonghae, O'Brien, Potts; Doyle, Lee (Griffiths 46); McGeehan (Green 46), Guttridge (Hall 46), McQuoid; Marriott.
Referee: Michael Bull.

Millwall (0) 2 *(O'Brien 71, Gregory 75)*

Northampton T (0) 0   2254

Millwall: (433) Archer; Cummings, Craig, Beevers, Martin J; Saville, Powell (Thompson 60), Martin L (Onyedinma 60); Gregory, O'Brien, Morison.
Northampton T: (433) Clarke; Furlong, Cresswell, Brisley, Buchanan; Watson, Taylor (Adams 66), O'Toole; Hackett (Hoskins 66), Calvert-Lewin, D'Ath.
Referee: Iain Williamson.

586 Johnstone's Paint Trophy 2015–16

Oxford U (1) 2 *(Roofe 41, 53)*
Swindon T (0) 0 9013
Oxford U: (442) Buchel; Baldock, Mullins, Wright, Skarz; Roofe (Ruffels 90), Sercombe, Lundstram, O'Dowda; Taylor (Hoban 82), Graham (MacDonald 75).
Swindon T: (4231) Vigouroux; Barry (Bangoura 70), Branco, Turnbull■, Ormonde-Ottewill; Traore, Rodgers; Ajose, Hylton (Ojamaa 43 (Balmy 80)), Brophy; Obika.
Referee: Gavin Ward.

Plymouth Arg (1) 2 *(Boateng 32, Tanner 49)*
Exeter C (0) 0 9441
Plymouth Arg: (4231) McCormick; Mellor, Nelson, Hartley, Purrington; Simpson (Cox 89), Boateng; Jervis, Tanner (Harvey T 90), Wylde; Reid (Brunt 86).
Exeter C: (433) Olejnik; McCready (Ribeiro 65), Brown, Tillson (Morrison 54), Moore-Taylor; Butterfield, Harley, Davies; Grant, Wheeler (Nichols 54), Nicholls.
Referee: Brendan Malone.

Yeovil T (0) 0
Coventry C (0) 0 1605
Yeovil T: (451) Krysiak; Roberts, Arthurworrey, Smith, Dickson; Cornick, Dolan, Laird, Fogden, Howells; Bird.
Coventry C: (4231) Charles-Cook; Phillips, Ricketts, Martin, Haynes; Thomas C (Lawton 76), Fleck; Murphy, O'Brien (Elford-Alliyu 85), Lameiras (Thomas G 55); Tudgay.
Yeovil T won 4-3 on penalties.
Referee: Kevin Johnson.

Wednesday, 7 October 2015

Stevenage (0) 1 *(Kennedy 79 (pen))*
Dagenham & R (0) 2 *(Cureton 53, Chambers 55)* 1401
Stevenage: (442) Day; Henry (Franks 19), Wells, Hughes, Ogilvie; Conlon, Schumacher, Parrett (Whelpdale 54), Kennedy; Williams, Loza (Hitchcock 90).
Dagenham & R: (442) O'Brien; Passley, Nosworthy, Dikamona (Obileye 46), Hoyte; Jones (Mulraney 54), Raymond, Ferdinand, Hemmings; Cureton (Doidge 82), Chambers.
Referee: James Linington.

NORTHERN SECTION QUARTER-FINALS

Tuesday, 10 November 2015

Barnsley (0) 2 *(Pearson 67, Hammill 83)*
York C (1) 1 *(Coulson 40)* 3360
Barnsley: (4411) Davies; Wabara, Mawson, Nyatanga, Smith; Isgrove, Pearson, Hourihane, Hammill; Toney (White H 83); Jackson (Winnall 69).
York C: (442) Flinders; McCoy, Swann, Godfrey (Tutonda 50), Ilesanmi; Coulson, Nolan, Berrett, Collins; Oliver (Hyde 75), Sinclair (Straker 65).
Referee: David Webb.

Fleetwood T (0) 0
Sheffield U (0) 0 1587
Fleetwood T: (433) Maxwell; Davis, Bell, Pond, Teixeira; Jonsson, Ryan, Haughton; Matt (Ball 58), McManus (Hunter 72), Hornby-Forbes (Grant R 84).
Sheffield U: (433) Long; Wallace K, McGahey, Kennedy, McEveley; Wallace J (Hammond 71), Scougall, Reed (Baxter 80); Woolford, Sammon (Sharp 71), Done.
Fleetwood T won 4-1 on penalties.
Referee: Chris Kavanagh.

Rochdale (0) 0
Morecambe (1) 1 *(Mullin 17)* 1428
Rochdale: (4141) Castro; Cannon, McNulty (Kennedy 34), Eastham, Tanser; Rose; Bennett, Lund (Alessandra 46), McDermott (Ayina 61), Mendez-Laing; Andrew.
Morecambe: (4231) Roche; McGowan, Edwards, Parrish, Wilson; Kenyon, Fleming; Devitt, Wildig (Ellison 64), Molyneux (Barkhuizen 64); Mullin (Hilton 73).
Referee: David Coote.

Wigan Ath (1) 4 *(Hiwula 20, 78 (pen), Murray 63, Wildschut 71)*
Blackpool (0) 0 5224
Wigan Ath: (352) Jaaskelainen; Pearce, Barnett, Hendry; Kellett, Flores (Vuckic 79), Chow, Murray (Daniels 73), Cowie; Davies (Wildschut 66), Hiwula.
Blackpool: (4411) Letheren (Boney 77); Dunne, Aimson, Higham, Ferguson; Rivers (McAlister 70), Oliver, Cubero, Samuel; Herron (Redshaw 70); Thomas.
Referee: Andrew Madley.

SOUTHERN SECTION QUARTER-FINALS

Tuesday, 10 November 2015

Gillingham (1) 1 *(Garmston 43)*
Yeovil T (1) 1 *(Cornick 13)* 1832
Gillingham: (532) Nelson; Jackson, Egan, Lennon, Oshilaja (Osaoabe 46), Garmston; Loft, Wright (McGlashan 74), Dack; McDonald (Williamson 80), Donnelly.
Yeovil T: (442) Weale; Roberts, Ward, Lacey, Smith; Cornick, Dolan, Tozer, Fogden; Jeffers (Allen 90), Sowunmi (Bird 66).
Yeovil T won 5-4 on penalties.
Referee: Dean Whitestone.

Plymouth Arg (1) 3 *(Jervis 34, 85, Carey 56)*
Millwall (2) 5 *(Gregory 21, 43, 49, 58 (pen), O'Brien 66)* 5869
Plymouth Arg: (4231) McCormick; Mellor, Nelson, Hartley (Purrington 83), Sawyer; Threlkeld, McHugh; Tanner (Brunt 62), Carey, Wylde (Simpson 69); Jervis.
Millwall: (442) Archer; Edwards (Nelson 34), Webster, Beevers, Martin J; Onyedinma (Thompson 88), Saville, Williams, O'Brien (Upson 83); Morison, Gregory.
Referee: James Linington.

Wednesday, 11 November 2015

Dagenham & R (0) 0
Oxford U (1) 2 *(Hoban 1, MacDonald 47)* 1011
Dagenham & R: (442) Cousins; Passley, Obileye (Dikamona 37), Widdowson (Cureton 62), Pask; Chambers, Dunne, Labadie, Hemmings; Doidge (Mulraney 46), McClure.
Oxford U: (442) Buchel; Gayle, Dunkley, George, Skarz; MacDonald (Humphreys 82), Sercombe, Rose, Cundy; Hoban, Hylton (Ashby 71).
Referee: A Davies.

Southend U (1) 1 *(White 11)*
Bristol R (0) 0 3495
Southend U: (442) Bentley; White, Thompson, Barrett, Coker; Hurst, Leonard, Atkinson, Worrall; Payne, Mooney (Pigott 82).
Bristol R: (442) Nicholls; Clarke J, Parkes, McChrystal, Brown; Gosling (Montano 57), Sinclair, Lines, Bodin; Taylor, Easter (Lucas 72).
Referee: Andy Woolmer.

NORTHERN SECTION SEMI-FINALS

Saturday, 5 December 2015

Wigan Ath (0) 2 *(Grigg 48, 82)*
Barnsley (1) 2 *(Hammill 42, Toney 53)* 6628
Wigan Ath: (352) Jaaskelainen; Hendry, Barnett, Pearce; James (Wildschut 46), Perkins, Power, Jacobs (Flores 61), Kellett; Grigg, Revell (Davies 61).
Barnsley: (442) Davies; White A, Nyatanga, Mawson, Wabara; Hammill, Hourihane, Pearson (Bree 90), Watkins; Toney, Winnall.
Barnsley won 4-2 on penalties.
Referee: Keith Hill.

Tuesday, 8 December 2015

Fleetwood T (0) 2 *(Ball 63, Ryan 76)*
Morecambe (0) 0 1715
Fleetwood T: (433) Maxwell; McLaughlin, Pond, Davis, Bell; Ryan (Haughton 86), Jonsson, Sarcevic; Grant R (Proctor 82), Henen, Fosu (Ball 59).

Morecambe: (352) Thompson; Dugdale, Edwards (Wilson 66), Parrish; Barkhuizen (Molyneux 80), Murphy, Wildig, Mullin (Devitt 67), Beeley; Ellison, Forrester.
Referee: Paul Tierney.

SOUTHERN SECTION SEMI-FINALS

Tuesday, 8 December 2015

Oxford U (2) 3 *(Evans 5, O'Dowda 42, Maguire 54)*
Yeovil T (1) 2 *(Fogden 37, Jeffers 90)* 2532

Oxford U: (442) Slocombe; Long, Dunkley, Wright, Ruffels; O'Dowda, Lundstram (Sercombe 85), Maguire (Hoban 77), MacDonald; Hylton, Evans.
Yeovil T: (442) Weale; Tozer, Ward, Roberts, Smith; Sokolik, Fogden, Dolan, Sheehan (Jeffers 55); Zoko, Cornick.
Referee: Keith Stroud.

Southend U (0) 0
Millwall (1) 2 *(Morison 34, Williams 65)* 5972

Southend U: (442) Bentley; White (Rea 73), Thompson, Barrett, Coker; Hurst (Pigott 58), Leonard, Atkinson, Worrall; Mooney, Payne.
Millwall: (433) Archer; Edwards, Beevers, Webster, Martin J; Upson, Williams, Saville; O'Brien (Nelson 90), Gregory, Morison (Ferguson 71).
Referee: Simon Hooper.

NORTHERN FINAL FIRST LEG

Saturday, 9 January 2016

Barnsley (0) 1 *(Fletcher 73)*
Fleetwood T (0) 1 *(Davies 61 (og))* 11,403

Barnsley: (4411) Davies; Wabara, Mawson, Long, White A; Isgrove, Abbott, Hourihane, Hammill; Williams R (Fletcher 68); Winnall.
Fleetwood T: (451) Maxwell; McLaughlin, Jonsson, Pond, Bell; Hunter (Haughton 76), Ryan, Sarcevic, Davis, Proctor; Grant R (Hornby-Forbes 71).
Referee: Fred Graham.

NORTHERN FINAL SECOND LEG

Thursday, 4 February 2016

Fleetwood T (0) 1 *(Hunter 81)*
Barnsley (0) 1 *(Hourihane 67)* 3705

Fleetwood T: (433) Maxwell; McLaughlin, Bell, Pond, Davis; Nirennold, Jonsson, Haughton (Ball 80); Grant R, Matt (Hunter 65), Henen (Hornby-Forbes 65).
Barnsley: (442) Davies; Bree, Long, Mawson, White A (Scowen 90); Isgrove (Fletcher 85), Hourihane, Brownhill (Roberts 90), Hammill; Winnall, Watkins.
Barnsley won 4-2 on penalties.
Referee: Eddie Ilderton.

SOUTHERN FINAL FIRST LEG

Thursday, 14 January 2016

Millwall (0) 0
Oxford U (2) 2 *(Roofe 15, 43)* 7275

Millwall: (442) Forde; Cummings, Webster, Beevers, Martin J (O'Brien 64); Wallace, Williams (Upson 78), Abdou, Ferguson; Gregory (Onyedinma 85), Morison.
Oxford U: (442) Buchel; Kenny, Mullins, Wright, Evans; MacDonald, Lundstram, Sercombe, Maguire; Roofe (Hylton 87), Hoban (O'Dowda 77).
Referee: Stuart Attwell.

SOUTHERN FINAL SECOND LEG

Tuesday, 2 February 2016

Oxford U (0) 0
Millwall (0) 1 *(Gregory 54)* 10,138

Oxford U: (442) Buchel; Kenny, Mullins, Wright, Skarz; MacDonald (Bowery 81), Lundstram, Sercombe, O'Dowda (Ismail 89); Roofe, Hylton.
Millwall: (343) Archer; Cummings (Martin J 68), Beevers*, Webster; Ferguson, Wallace, Abdou, Upson (Onyedinma 82); O'Brien, Morison, Gregory.
Oxford U won 2-1 on aggregate.
Referee: Scott Duncan.

JOHNSTONE'S PAINT TROPHY FINAL 2016

Sunday, 3 April 2016

(at Wembley Stadium, attendance 59,230)

Barnsley (0) 3   Oxford U (1) 2

Barnsley: (442) Davies; Williams G, Roberts, Mawson, White A; Isgrove (Scowen 77), Brownhill, Hourihane, Hammill; Fletcher (Chapman 90), Winnall (Toney 66).
Scorers: Dunkley 52 (og), Fletcher 68, Hammill 74.

Oxford U: (442) Buchel; Kenny, Mullins, Dunkley, Evans; MacDonald (Maguire 65), Ruffels, Sercombe, O'Dowda (Waring 85); Roofe, Hylton (Bowery 80).
Scorers: O'Dowda 29, Hylton 76.

Referee: Andy Woolmer.

JOHNSTONE'S PAINT TROPHY
ATTENDANCES 2015–16

Round	*Aggregate*	*Games*	*Average*
One	29,931	16	1,871
Two	51,480	16	3,218
Area Quarter-finals	23,806	8	2,976
Area Semi-finals	16,847	4	4,212
Area finals	32,521	4	8,130
Final	59,230	1	59,230
Total	213,815	49	4,364

FA CUP FINALS 1872–2016

VENUES

1872 and 1874–92	Kennington Oval		1895–1914	Crystal Palace
1873	Lillie Bridge		1915	Old Trafford, Manchester
1893	Fallowfield, Manchester		1920–22	Stamford Bridge
1894	Everton		2001–06	Millennium Stadium, Cardiff
1923–2000	Wembley Stadium (old)		2007 to date	Wembley Stadium (new)

THE FA CUP

1872	Wanderers v Royal Engineers	1-0
1873	Wanderers v Oxford University	2-0
1874	Oxford University v Royal Engineers	2-0
1875	Royal Engineers v Old Etonians	1-1*
Replay	Royal Engineers v Old Etonians	2-0
1876	Wanderers v Old Etonians	1-1*
Replay	Wanderers v Old Etonians	3-0
1877	Wanderers v Oxford University	2-1*
1878	Wanderers v Royal Engineers	3-1

Wanderers won the cup outright, but it was restored to the Football Association.

1879	Old Etonians v Clapham R	1-0
1880	Clapham R v Oxford University	1-0
1881	Old Carthusians v Old Etonians	3-0
1882	Old Etonians v Blackburn R	1-0
1883	Blackburn Olympic v Old Etonians	2-1*
1884	Blackburn R v Queen's Park, Glasgow	2-1
1885	Blackburn R v Queen's Park, Glasgow	2-0
1886	Blackburn R v WBA	0-0
Replay	Blackburn R v WBA	2-0
	(at Racecourse Ground, Derby Co)	

A special trophy was awarded to Blackburn R for third consecutive win.

1887	Aston Villa v WBA	2-0
1888	WBA v Preston NE	2-1
1889	Preston NE v Wolverhampton W	3-0
1890	Blackburn R v The Wednesday	6-1
1891	Blackburn R v Notts Co	3-1
1892	WBA v Aston Villa	3-0
1893	Wolverhampton W v Everton	1-0
1894	Notts Co v Bolton W	4-1
1895	Aston Villa v WBA	1-0

FA Cup was stolen from a shop window in Birmingham and never found.

1896	The Wednesday v Wolverhampton W	2-1
1897	Aston Villa v Everton	3-2
1898	Nottingham F v Derby Co	3-1
1899	Sheffield U v Derby Co	4-1
1900	Bury v Southampton	4-0
1901	Tottenham H v Sheffield U	2-2
Replay	Tottenham H v Sheffield U	3-1
	(at Burnden Park, Bolton W)	
1902	Sheffield U v Southampton	1-1
Replay	Sheffield U v Southampton	2-1
1903	Bury v Derby Co	6-0
1904	Manchester C v Bolton W	1-0
1905	Aston Villa v Newcastle U	2-0
1906	Everton v Newcastle U	1-0
1907	The Wednesday v Everton	2-1
1908	Wolverhampton W v Newcastle U	3-1
1909	Manchester U v Bristol C	1-0
1910	Newcastle U v Barnsley	1-1
Replay	Newcastle U v Barnsley	2-0
	(at Goodison Park, Everton)	
1911	Bradford C v Newcastle U	0-0
Replay	Bradford C v Newcastle U	1-0
	(at Old Trafford, Manchester U)	

Trophy was given to Lord Kinnaird – he made nine FA Cup Final appearances – for services to football.

1912	Barnsley v WBA	0-0
Replay	Barnsley v WBA	1-0
	(at Bramall Lane, Sheffield U)	

1913	Aston Villa v Sunderland	1-0
1914	Burnley v Liverpool	1-0
1915	Sheffield U v Chelsea	3-0
1920	Aston Villa v Huddersfield T	1-0*
1921	Tottenham H v Wolverhampton W	1-0
1922	Huddersfield T v Preston NE	1-0
1923	Bolton W v West Ham U	2-0
1924	Newcastle U v Aston Villa	2-0
1925	Sheffield U v Cardiff C	1-0
1926	Bolton W v Manchester C	1-0
1927	Cardiff C v Arsenal	1-0
1928	Blackburn R v Huddersfield T	3-1
1929	Bolton W v Portsmouth	2-0
1930	Arsenal v Huddersfield T	2-0
1931	WBA v Birmingham	2-1
1932	Newcastle U v Arsenal	2-1
1933	Everton v Manchester C	3-0
1934	Manchester C v Portsmouth	2-1
1935	Sheffield W v WBA	4-2
1936	Arsenal v Sheffield U	1-0
1937	Sunderland v Preston NE	3-1
1938	Preston NE v Huddersfield T	1-0*
1939	Portsmouth v Wolverhampton W	4-1
1946	Derby Co v Charlton Ath	4-1*
1947	Charlton Ath v Burnley	1-0*
1948	Manchester U v Blackpool	4-2
1949	Wolverhampton W v Leicester C	3-1
1950	Arsenal v Liverpool	2-0
1951	Newcastle U v Blackpool	2-0
1952	Newcastle U v Arsenal	1-0
1953	Blackpool v Bolton W	4-3
1954	WBA v Preston NE	3-2
1955	Newcastle U v Manchester C	3-1
1956	Manchester C v Birmingham C	3-1
1957	Aston Villa v Manchester U	2-1
1958	Bolton W v Manchester U	2-0
1959	Nottingham F v Luton T	2-1
1960	Wolverhampton W v Blackburn R	3-0
1961	Tottenham H v Leicester C	2-0
1962	Tottenham H v Burnley	3-1
1963	Manchester U v Leicester C	3-1
1964	West Ham U v Preston NE	3-2
1965	Liverpool v Leeds U	2-1*
1966	Everton v Sheffield W	3-2
1967	Tottenham H v Chelsea	2-1
1968	WBA v Everton	1-0*
1969	Manchester C v Leicester C	1-0
1970	Chelsea v Leeds U	2-2*
Replay	Chelsea v Leeds U	2-1
	(at Old Trafford, Manchester U)	
1971	Arsenal v Liverpool	2-1*
1972	Leeds U v Arsenal	1-0
1973	Sunderland v Leeds U	1-0
1974	Liverpool v Newcastle U	3-0
1975	West Ham U v Fulham	2-0
1976	Southampton v Manchester U	1-0
1977	Manchester U v Liverpool	2-1
1978	Ipswich T v Arsenal	1-0
1979	Arsenal v Manchester U	3-2
1980	West Ham U v Arsenal	1-0
1981	Tottenham H v Manchester C	1-1*
Replay	Tottenham H v Manchester C	3-2

1982	Tottenham H v QPR	1-1*
Replay	Tottenham H v QPR	1-0
1983	Manchester U v Brighton & HA	2-2*
Replay	Manchester U v Brighton & HA	4-0
1984	Everton v Watford	2-0
1985	Manchester U v Everton	1-0*
1986	Liverpool v Everton	3-1
1987	Coventry C v Tottenham H	3-2*
1988	Wimbledon v Liverpool	1-0
1989	Liverpool v Everton	3-2*
1990	Manchester U v Crystal Palace	3-3*
Replay	Manchester U v Crystal Palace	1-0
1991	Tottenham H v Nottingham F	2-1*
1992	Liverpool v Sunderland	2-0
1993	Arsenal v Sheffield W	1-1*
Replay	Arsenal v Sheffield W	2-1*
1994	Manchester U v Chelsea	4-0

THE FA CUP SPONSORED BY LITTLEWOODS POOLS

1995	Everton v Manchester U	1-0
1996	Manchester U v Liverpool	1-0
1997	Chelsea v Middlesbrough	2-0
1998	Arsenal v Newcastle U	2-0

THE AXA-SPONSORED FA CUP

1999	Manchester U v Newcastle U	2-0
2000	Chelsea v Aston Villa	1-0
2001	Liverpool v Arsenal	2-1
2002	Arsenal v Chelsea	2-0

THE FA CUP

2003	Arsenal v Southampton	1-0
2004	Manchester U v Millwall	3-0
2005	Arsenal v Manchester U	0-0*
	Arsenal won 5-4 on penalties.	
2006	Liverpool v West Ham U	3-3*
	Liverpool won 3-1 on penalties.	

THE FA CUP SPONSORED BY E.ON

2007	Chelsea v Manchester U	1-0*
2008	Portsmouth v Cardiff C	1-0
2009	Chelsea v Everton	2-1
2010	Chelsea v Portsmouth	1-0
2011	Manchester C v Stoke C	1-0

THE FA CUP WITH BUDWEISER

2012	Chelsea v Liverpool	2-1
2013	Wigan Ath v Manchester C	1-0
2014	Arsenal v Hull C	3-2*

THE FA CUP

2015	Arsenal v Aston Villa	4-0

THE EMIRATES FA CUP

2016	Manchester U v Crystal Palace	2-1*

*After extra time.

FA CUP WINS

Arsenal 12, Manchester U 12, Tottenham H 8, Aston Villa 7, Chelsea 7, Liverpool 7, Blackburn R 6, Newcastle U 6, Everton 5, Manchester C 5, The Wanderers 5, WBA 5, Bolton W 4, Sheffield U 4, Wolverhampton W 4, Sheffield W 3, West Ham U 3, Bury 2, Nottingham F 2, Old Etonians 2, Portsmouth 2, Preston NE 2, Sunderland 2, Barnsley 1, Blackburn Olympic 1, Blackpool 1, Bradford C 1, Burnley 1, Cardiff C 1, Charlton Ath 1, Clapham R 1, Coventry C 1, Derby Co 1, Huddersfield T 1, Ipswich T 1, Leeds U 1, Notts Co 1, Old Carthusians 1, Oxford University 1, Royal Engineers 1, Southampton 1, Wigan Ath 1, Wimbledon 1.

APPEARANCES IN FINALS

Arsenal 19, Manchester U 19, Liverpool 14, Everton 13, Newcastle U 13, Aston Villa 11, Chelsea 11, Manchester C 10, WBA 10, Tottenham H 9, Blackburn R 8, Wolverhampton W 8, Bolton W 7, Preston NE 7, Old Etonians 6, Sheffield U 6, Sheffield W 6, Huddersfield T 5, Portsmouth 5, *The Wanderers 5, West Ham U 5, Derby Co 4, Leeds U 4, Leicester C 4, Oxford University 4, Royal Engineers 4, Southampton 4, Sunderland 4, Blackpool 3, Burnley 3, Cardiff C 3, Nottingham F 3, Barnsley 2, Birmingham C 2, *Bury 2, Charlton Ath 2, Clapham R 2, Crystal Palace 2, Notts Co 2, Queen's Park (Glasgow) 2, *Blackburn Olympic 1, *Bradford C 1, Brighton & HA 1, Bristol C 1, *Coventry C 1, Fulham 1, Hull C 1, *Ipswich T 1, Luton T 1, Middlesbrough 1, Millwall 1, *Old Carthusians 1, QPR 1, Stoke C 1, Watford 1, *Wigan Ath 1, *Wimbledon 1.
* *Denotes undefeated in final.*

APPEARANCES IN SEMI-FINALS

Arsenal 28, Manchester U 28, Everton 26, Liverpool 24, Aston Villa 21, Chelsea 21, WBA 20, Tottenham H 19, Blackburn R 18, Newcastle U 17, Sheffield W 16, Bolton W 14, Sheffield U 14, Wolverhampton W 14, Derby Co 13, Manchester C 12, Nottingham F 12, Sunderland 12, Southampton 11, Preston NE 10, Birmingham C 9, Burnley 8, Leeds U 8, Huddersfield T 7, Leicester C 7, Portsmouth 7, West Ham U 7, Old Etonians 6, Fulham 6, Oxford University 6, Watford 6, Millwall 5, Notts Co 5, The Wanderers 5, Cardiff C 4, Crystal Palace (professional club) 4, Luton T 4, Queen's Park (Glasgow) 4, Royal Engineers 4, Stoke C 4, Barnsley 3, Blackpool 3, Clapham R 3, Ipswich T 3, Middlesbrough 3, Norwich C 3, Old Carthusians 3, Oldham Ath 3, The Swifts 3, Blackburn Olympic 2, Bristol C 2, Bury 2, Charlton Ath 2, Grimsby T 2, Hull C 2, Reading 2, Swansea T 2, Swindon T 2, Wigan Ath 2, Wimbledon 2, Bradford C 1, Brighton & HA 1, Cambridge University 1, Chesterfield 1, Coventry C 1, Crewe Alex 1, Crystal Palace (amateur club) 1, Darwen 1, Derby Junction 1, Glasgow R 1, Marlow 1, Old Harrovians 1, Orient 1, Plymouth Arg 1, Port Vale 1, QPR 1, Shropshire W 1, Wycombe W 1, York C 1.

FA CUP ATTENDANCES 1969–2016

	1st Round	2nd Round	3rd Round	4th Round	5th Round	6th Round	Semi-finals & Final	Total	No. of matches	Average per match
1969–70	345,229	195,102	925,930	651,374	319,893	198,537	390,700	3,026,765	170	17,805
1970–71	329,687	230,942	956,683	757,852	360,687	304,937	279,644	3,220,432	162	19,879
1971–72	277,726	236,127	986,094	711,399	486,378	230,292	248,546	3,158,562	160	19,741
1972–73	259,432	169,114	938,741	735,825	357,386	241,934	226,543	2,928,975	160	18,306
1973–74	214,236	125,295	840,142	747,909	346,012	233,307	273,051	2,779,952	167	16,646
1974–75	283,956	170,466	914,994	646,434	393,323	268,361	291,369	2,968,903	172	17,261
1975–76	255,533	178,099	867,880	573,843	471,925	206,851	205,810	2,759,941	161	17,142
1976–77	379,230	192,159	942,523	631,265	373,330	205,379	258,216	2,982,102	174	17,139
1977–78	258,248	178,930	881,406	540,164	400,751	137,059	198,020	2,594,578	160	16,216
1978–79	243,773	185,343	880,345	537,748	243,683	263,213	249,897	2,604,002	166	15,687
1979–80	267,121	204,759	804,701	507,725	364,039	157,530	355,541	2,661,416	163	16,328
1980–81	246,824	194,502	832,578	534,402	320,530	288,714	339,250	2,756,800	169	16,312
1981–82	236,220	127,300	513,185	356,987	203,334	124,308	279,621	1,840,955	160	11,506
1982–83	191,312	150,046	670,503	452,688	260,069	193,845	291,162	2,209,625	154	14,348
1983–84	192,276	151,647	625,965	417,298	181,832	185,382	187,000	1,941,400	166	11,695
1984–85	174,604	137,078	616,229	320,772	269,232	148,690	242,754	1,909,359	157	12,162
1985–86	171,142	130,034	486,838	495,526	311,833	184,262	192,316	1,971,951	168	11,738
1986–87	209,290	146,761	593,520	349,342	263,550	119,396	195,533	1,877,400	165	11,378
1987–88	204,411	104,561	720,121	443,133	281,461	119,313	177,585	2,050,585	155	13,229
1988–89	212,775	121,326	690,199	421,255	206,781	176,629	167,353	1,966,318	164	12,173
1989–90	209,542	133,483	683,047	412,483	351,423	123,065	277,420	2,190,463	170	12,885
1990–91	194,195	121,450	594,592	530,279	276,112	124,826	196,434	2,038,518	162	12,583
1991–92	231,940	117,078	586,014	372,576	270,537	155,603	201,592	1,935,340	160	12,095
1992–93	241,968	174,702	612,494	377,211	198,379	149,675	293,241	2,047,670	161	12,718
1993–94	190,683	118,031	691,064	430,234	172,196	134,705	228,233	1,965,146	159	12,359
1994–95	219,511	125,629	640,017	438,596	257,650	159,787	174,059	2,015,249	161	12,517
1995–96	185,538	115,669	748,997	391,218	274,055	174,142	156,500	2,046,199	167	12,252
1996–97	209,521	122,324	651,139	402,293	199,873	67,035	191,813	1,843,998	151	12,211
1997–98	204,803	130,261	629,127	455,557	341,290	192,651	172,007	2,125,696	165	12,883
1998–99	191,954	132,341	609,486	431,613	359,398	181,005	202,150	2,107,947	155	13,599
1999–2000	181,485	127,728	514,030	374,795	182,511	105,443	214,921	1,700,913	158	10,765
2000–01	171,689	122,061	577,204	398,241	256,899	100,663	177,778	1,804,535	151	11,951
2001–02	198,369	119,781	566,284	330,434	249,190	173,757	171,278	1,809,093	148	12,224
2002–03	189,905	104,103	577,494	404,599	242,483	156,244	175,498	1,850,326	150	12,336
2003–04	162,738	117,967	624,732	347,964	292,521	156,780	167,401	1,870,103	149	12,551
2004–05	161,197	98,702	602,152	477,472	339,082	127,914	193,233	1,999,752	146	13,697
2005–06	188,876	107,456	654,570	388,339	286,225	163,449	177,723	1,966,638	160	12,291
2006–07	168,884	113,924	708,628	478,924	340,612	230,064	177,810	2,218,846	158	14,043
2007–08	175,195	99,528	704,300	356,404	276,903	142,780	256,210	2,011,320	152	13,232
2008–09	161,526	96,923	631,070	529,585	297,364	149,566	264,635	2,131,669	163	13,078
2009–10	147,078	100,476	613,113	335,426	288,604	144,918	254,806	1,884,421	151	12,480
2010–11	169,259	101,291	637,202	390,524	284,311	164,092	250,256	1,996,935	150	13,313
2011–12	155,858	92,267	640,700	391,214	250,666	194,971	262,064	1,987,740	151	13,164
2012–13	135,642	115,965	645,676	373,892	288,509	221,216	234,210	2,015,110	156	12,917
2013–14	144,709	75,903	668,242	346,706	254,084	156,630	243,350	1,889,624	149	12,682
2014–15	156,621	111,434	609,368	515,229	208,908	233,341	258,780	2,093,681	153	13,684
2015–16	134,914	94,855	755,187	397,217	235,433	227,262	253,793	2,098,661	149	14,085

THE EMIRATES FA CUP 2015–16

PRELIMINARY AND QUALIFYING ROUNDS

EXTRA PRELIMINARY ROUND

Penrith v Jarrow Roofing Boldon CA	1-2
Silsden v West Allotment Celtic	2-1
Ashington v Alb Sports	2-2, 3-2
AFC Darwen v Washington	1-2
Newcastle Benfield v Yorkshire Amateur	4-2
Nelson v Newton Aycliffe	0-4
Bedlington Terriers v West Auckland T	1-1, 0-4
Barnoldswick T v Colne	0-5
Billingham Synthonia v Consett	0-0, 0-8
Hebburn T v Tadcaster Alb	1-3
Bishop Auckland v Shildon	1-1, 4-2
Sunderland RCA v Guisborough T	4-4, 2-3
Crook T v Dunston UTS	0-6
Holker Old Boys v Liversedge	4-0
Pickering T v Thornaby	4-0
Seaham Red Star v Marske U	2-2, 1-3
Garforth T v Morpeth T	1-4
Heaton Stannington v Norton & Stockton Ancients	3-1
Bridlington T v North Shields	0-5
Whitley Bay v Sunderland Ryhope CW	1-1, 3-2
Whickham v Padiham	1-2
Durham C v Thackley	1-3
Glasshoughton Welfare v Runcorn Linnets	2-2, 1-6
Chadderton v AFC Liverpool	2-9
Congleton T v Nostell MW	0-0, 4-0
Alsager T v Athersley Recreation	1-0
Winsford U v AFC Blackpool	1-1, 2-3
AFC Emley v Parkgate	7-1
Ashton Ath v Maltby Main	2-2, 2-3
Penistone Church v Pontefract Collieries	0-2
Maine Road v St Helens T	2-1
Handsworth Parramore v Staveley MW	6-0
1874 Northwich v West Didsbury & Chorlton	3-0
Barton T Old Boys v Squires Gate	2-2, 4-2
aet; 2-2 at the end of normal time.	
Abbey Hey v Worksop T	3-1
Runcorn T v Bacup Bor	3-0
Hemsworth MW v Armthorpe Welfare	1-2
Bootle v Atherton Collieries	0-2
Hanley T v Shawbury U	4-2
Continental Star v Bolehall Swifts	2-2, 3-1
Boldmere St Michaels v Rocester	3-3, 0-4
Hinckley v Walsall Wood	0-0, 3-1
Brocton v Stourport Swifts	1-5
Southam U v AFC Wulfrunians	0-2
Alvechurch v Heath Hayes	3-0
Tipton T v Cadbury Ath	0-2
AFC Bridgnorth v Wolverhampton Casuals	1-0
Malvern T v Sporting Khalsa	0-5
Westfields v Pegasus Juniors	1-0
Gornal Ath v Bromsgrove Sporting	1-2
Lye T v Coventry Sphinx	2-2, 1-2
aet; 1-1 at the end of normal time.	
Coleshill T v Ellesmere Rangers	11-0
Cleethorpes T v Brigg T	5-1
Harborough T v Shirebrook T	3-2
South Normanton Ath v AFC Mansfield	2-1
Shepshed Dynamo v Retford U	1-0
Bottesford T v Rainworth MW	2-2, 5-1
Kirby Muxloe v Heanor T	3-1
Long Eaton U v Harrowby U	2-1
Loughborough University v Barrow T	4-1
St Andrews v Clipstone Welfare	2-3
Radford v Sleaford T	3-2
Quorn v Oadby T	1-3
Bardon Hill Sports v Dunkirk	0-1
Ellistown & Ibstock U v Holwell Sports	0-5
Blaby & Whetstone Ath v Leicester Nirvana	0-5
Walsham Le Willows v Godmanchester R	0-3
Wisbech T v Diss T	1-0
Yaxley v Gorleston	2-1
Peterborough Northern Star v Newmarket T	1-2
Haverhill R v Mildenhall T	0-1
Fakenham T v Huntingdon T	0-0, 6-0
Eynesbury R v Peterborough Sports	0-1
Swaffham T v Thetford T	2-4
Great Yarmouth T v Norwich U	0-3
Deeping Rangers v Boston T	6-1

Holbeach U v Ely C	1-1, 4-0
Welwyn Garden C v Haverhill Bor	3-1
Hoddesdon T v Sawbridgeworth T	4-0
FC Romania v Whitton U	0-3
Southend Manor v Codicote	3-1
Wivenhoe T v Tower Hamlets	1-5
Cockfosters v Burnham Ramblers	4-0
Hadley v Saffron Walden T	1-2
Hertford T v Kirkley & Pakefield	2-2, 1-2
Debenham LC v Ipswich W	0-1
Bowers & Pitsea v Ilford	0-1
Basildon U v Sporting Bengal U	3-1
FC Broxbourne Bor v Brantham Ath	1-2
Long Melford v London Bari	3-0
FC Clacton v Eton Manor	3-1
Hullbridge Sports v Hadleigh U	2-1
Clapton v Stanway R	1-2
Stansted v Takeley	2-1
Enfield 1893 v London Colney	0-4
Felixstowe & Walton U v Barking	1-1, 1-3
aet; 1-1 at the end of normal time.	
Waltham Forest v St Margaretsbury	0-3
AFC Hayes v Flackwell Heath	3-2
Wellingborough T v Ashford T (Middlesex)	1-8
Berkhamsted v Hanworth Villa	3-2
Oxhey Jets v AFC Kempston R	0-0, 2-3
Spelthorne Sports v Stotfold	2-1
Windsor v AFC Dunstable	0-1
Ampthill T v Risborough Rangers	0-3
Rothwell Corinthians v Thrapston T	1-2
Hillingdon Bor v Wembley	1-1, 1-2
Northampton Sileby Rangers v Sun Postal Sports	2-1
Wellingborough Whitworths v Northampton Spencer	0-3
Newport Pagnell T v Holmer Green	6-2
Biggleswade U v Desborough T	2-1
Potton U v Bedfont Sports	0-2
London Tigers v Bedfont & Feltham	1-1, 2-2
aet; Bedfont & Feltham won 8-7 on penalties.	
Tring Ath v Leverstock Green	2-1
Bedford v Cogenhoe U	0-6
Raunds T v Crawley Green	1-0
Harefield U v Long Buckby	2-2, 0-1
Royal Wootton Bassett T v Bracknell T	0-2
Ardley U v Tuffley R	1-4
Binfield v Westfield	1-1, 1-0
Ascot U v Kidlington	1-2
Holyport v Milton U	1-3
Hook Norton v Frimley Green	5-0
Reading T v Chertsey T	0-5
Knaphill v Highworth T	1-3
Chinnor v Hartley Wintney	0-2
Thame U v Farnham T	1-1, 1-1
aet; Farnham T won 4-3 on penalties.	
Abingdon U v Brimscombe & Thrupp	0-3
Cheltenham Saracens v Winterbourne U	1-0
Tadley Calleva v Guildford C	2-3
Highmoor Ibis v Thatcham T	1-2
Badshot Lea v Camberley T	2-1
Cove v Shrivenham	5-4
Banstead Ath v Rochester U	1-1, 1-2
Hailsham T v Eastbourne U	2-3
Worthing U v Deal T	0-0, 1-7
Arundel v Raynes Park Vale	3-1
Horsham YMCA v AFC Croydon Ath	2-0
Fisher v Corinthian	0-3
Crawley Down Gatwick v Chichester C	1-3
Tunbridge Wells v Glebe	
Walkover for Tunbridge Wells – Glebe not accepted	
into the competition.	
Shoreham v St Francis Rangers	8-0
East Preston v Littlehampton T	1-2
Horsham v Lancing	1-0
Colliers Wood U v Eastbourne T	0-2
Redhill v Pagham	1-2
Holmesdale v Mile Oak	2-0
Selsey v Erith T	1-5
Croydon v Sutton Common R	5-1
Sevenoaks T v Seven Acre & Sidcup	1-1, 1-1
aet; Seven Acre & Sidcup won 4-2 on penalties.	

Cray Valley (PM) v Ashford U	5-1
Chessington & Hook U v Crowborough Ath	1-1, 2-1
aet; 1-1 at the end of normal time.	
Bexhill U v Loxwood	3-1
Ringmer v Beckenham T	1-4
Lingfield v Canterbury C	0-3
Greenwich Bor v Lordswood	1-0
Epsom & Ewell v Erith & Belvedere	0-4
Horley T v Wick & Barnham U	7-0
Christchurch v Cadbury Heath	2-1
Melksham T v Cowes Sports	2-2, 1-3
Longwell Green Sports v Folland Sports	2-1
Andover T v Gillingham T	3-0
Lymington v Bitton	0-3
Alresford T v Bridport	0-1
Hamworthy U v Hallen	1-1, 1-0
Amesbury T v Bemerton Heath Harlequins	1-2
Hythe & Dibden v Moneyfields	1-4
Team Solent v Blackfield & Langley	3-4
Bradford T v U Services Portsmouth	2-0
Cribbs v Bristol Manor Farm	0-5
Verwood T v Newport (IW)	2-0
Almondsbury UWE v Fawley	3-2
Brockenhurst v Fareham T	2-0
Bournemouth v AFC Portchester	0-3
Sherborne T v New Milton T	2-0
Whitchurch U v Wincanton T	1-1, 1-3
Horndean v Sholing	1-3
Buckland Ath v Clevedon T	3-0
Saltash U v AFC St Austell	0-4
Bishop Sutton v Street	0-6
Witheridge v Welton R	2-0
Shepton Mallet v Plymouth Parkway	0-2
Bodmin T v Brislington	3-1
Odd Down v Ashton & Backwell U	3-1
Barnstaple T v Willand R	2-0

PRELIMINARY ROUND

Whitley Bay v Heaton Stannington	2-1
West Auckland T v Washington	2-3
Ashington v Thackley	1-2
Pickering T v Clitheroe	1-5
North Shields v Kendal T	1-1, 0-2
Bishop Auckland v Jarrow Roofing Boldon CA	1-2
Silsden v Padiham	0-2
Guisborough T v Newcastle Benfield	4-2
Marske U v Lancaster C	1-1, 0-1
Harrogate Railway Ath v Spennymoor T	0-0, 0-2
Holker Old Boys v Dunston UTS	0-2
Consett v Scarborough Ath	2-0
Tadcaster Alb v Colne	2-5
Newton Aycliffe v Morpeth T	2-0
Congleton T v Handsworth Parramore	4-3
Runcorn Linnets v Pontefract Collieries	6-0
Armthorpe Welfare v New Mills	1-0
Runcorn T v Northwich Vic	2-3
Alsager T v Shaw Lane Aquaforce	2-1
Ossett Alb v Maine Road	3-0
Mossley v Bamber Bridge	1-1, 1-3
Burscough v AFC Emley	3-1
Barton T Old Boys v Droylsden	1-2
1874 Northwich v Maltby Main	1-2
Abbey Hey v Warrington T	3-2
AFC Blackpool v Ossett T	1-0
Brighouse T v Atherton Collieries	1-1, 2-1
AFC Liverpool v Radcliffe Bor	3-2
Stocksbridge Park Steels v Farsley Celtic	1-1, 0-3
Glossop North End v Prescot Cables	2-1
Goole v Sheffield	1-1, 3-0
Trafford v Witton Alb	1-2
Market Drayton T v AFC Bridgnorth	2-0
Bromsgrove Sporting v Hinckley	2-6
Newcastle T v Continental Star	4-0
Leek T v Rocester	1-1, 2-1
Rugby T v Coventry Sphinx	1-0
Coleshill T v Stafford Rangers	2-1
Sporting Khalsa v Cadbury Ath	4-0
Chasetown v Evesham U	2-0
Westfields v Kidsgrove Ath	1-1, 6-5
aet; 4-4 at the end of normal time.	
Stourport Swifts v Alvechurch	1-0
AFC Wulfrunians v Romulus	2-0
Tividale v Hanley T	1-0
Carlton T v Shepshed Dynamo	1-2
Harborough T v Oadby T	0-2

Kirby Muxloe v Holwell Sports	0-0, 0-1
Loughborough Dynamo v Basford U	1-3
Radford v Spalding U	1-2
Dunkirk v Bottesford T	4-1
South Normanton Ath v Lincoln U	1-1, 1-2
Gresley v Coalville T	2-2, 0-5
Leicester Nirvana v Belper T	2-4
Loughborough University v Long Eaton U	1-2
Clipstone Welfare v Cleethorpes T	1-0
Mildenhall T v Soham T Rangers	5-2
Yaxley v Godmanchester R	4-1
Deeping Rangers v Dereham T	1-0
Thetford T v Bury T	3-5
Wroxham v Fakenham T	3-2
Wisbech T v Holbeach U	0-1
St Ives T v Norwich U	1-1, 6-2
Newmarket T v Peterborough Sports	3-5
London Colney v Potters Bar T	1-3
St Margaretsbury v AFC Hornchurch	1-5
Welwyn Garden C v Waltham Abbey	1-0
Ilford v Stanway R	0-2
Hullbridge Sports v Maldon & Tiptree	2-0
Harlow T v Southend Manor	5-1
Barkingside v Ipswich W	1-2
Barking v Haringey Bor	0-0, 1-2
AFC Sudbury v Ware	4-0
Whitton U v Kirkley & Pakefield	0-3
Hoddesdon T v Romford	0-0, 1-1
aet; Hoddesdon T won 5-4 on penalties.	
Stansted v Tilbury	0-0, 0-3
Redbridge v Heybridge Swifts	1-2
Cockfosters v Tower Hamlets	3-3, 5-1
Saffron Walden T v Cheshunt	2-0
Great Wakering R v Brantham Ath	0-2
Basildon U v Long Melford	1-0
Thurrock v Royston T	2-2, 3-1
Witham T v Brightlingsea Regent	1-1, 3-2
FC Clacton v Aveley	2-6
Ashford T (Middlesex) v AFC Kempston R	1-0
Long Buckby v Daventry T	2-1
Beaconsfield SYCOB v Raunds T	3-0
Barton R v Berkhamsted	3-1
Biggleswade U v Chalfont St Peter	5-3
Risborough Rangers v Aylesbury	0-3
Wembley v North Greenford U	1-1, 1-5
Northampton Sileby Rangers v Leighton T	0-3
Bedfont & Feltham v AFC Hayes	1-1, 3-1
Newport Pagnell T v AFC Dunstable	1-1, 1-2
Bedfont Sports v Hanwell T	1-2
Uxbridge v Northampton Spencer	1-0
Aylesbury U v Northwood	1-2
Bedford T v Thrapston T	2-1
Cogenhoe U v Spelthorne Sports	3-0
Tring Ath v Arlesey T	0-2
Kings Langley v AFC Rushden & Diamonds	0-1
Wantage T v Didcot T	3-4
Chertsey T v Kidlington	1-4
Binfield v Shortwood U	1-2
Badshot Lea v Fleet T	2-4
Marlow v Godalming T	1-1, 1-2
aet; 1-1 at the end of normal time.	
Brimscombe & Thrupp v Bracknell T	2-2, 0-1
Tuffley R v Bishop's Cleeve	1-0
Cheltenham Saracens v Milton U	1-0
Cove v North Leigh	0-7
Egham T v Slimbridge	2-2, 2-3
aet; 2-2 at the end of normal time.	
Thatcham T v Guildford C	3-2
Hartley Wintney v Banbury U	5-2
Farnham T v Highworth T	4-2
Hook Norton v Burnham	1-1, 4-2
aet; 2-2 at the end of normal time.	
Molesey v East Grinstead T	7-1
Chipstead v Rochester U	0-1
Deal T v Horsham	1-1, 2-1
Seven Acre & Sidcup v Sittingbourne	1-2
Ramsgate v Tooting & Mitcham U	0-1
Folkestone Invicta v Corinthian	3-1
Herne Bay v Peacehaven & Telscombe	3-0
Hythe v Chessington & Hook U	0-2
Tunbridge Wells v Croydon	1-1, 1-2
Cray Valley (PM) v Hastings U	1-0
Holmesdale v South Park	1-10
Whitstable T v Walton Casuals	3-0
Three Bridges v Cray W	0-1
Bexhill U v Faversham T	0-5

Eastbourne U v Arundel	1-1, 4-1
Littlehampton T v Thamesmead T	0-1
Chichester C v Chatham T	0-4
Shoreham v Horley T	1-1, 3-2
Beckenham T v Greenwich Bor	0-4
Pagham v Corinthian-Casuals	3-0
Erith T v Horsham YMCA	2-4
Worthing v Walton & Hersham	4-2
Eastbourne T v Whyteleafe	1-1, 3-2
Phoenix Sports v Guernsey	2-2, 2-1
Dorking W v Canterbury C	6-2
Erith & Belvedere v Carshalton Ath	1-2
Winchester C v Wincanton T	5-1
Hamworthy U v Andover T	4-1, 2-1
Tie ordered to be replayed after Hamworthy U found to	
have fielded an ineligible player.	
Longwell Green Sports v Cinderford T	0-1
Brockenhurst v Yate T	2-1
Sholing v Swindon Supermarine	2-4
Bradford T v Christchurch	6-3
Cowes Sports v Wimborne T	0-5
Bristol Manor Farm v Bitton	3-2
AFC Portchester v AFC Totton	3-1
Bashley v Mangotsfield U	0-4
Almondsbury UWE v Verwood T	3-1
Moneyfields v Petersfield T	1-2
Blackfield & Langley v Bemerton Heath Harlequins	1-0
Bridport v Sherborne T	3-3, 1-0
aet; 0-0 at the end of normal time.	
Plymouth Parkway v Tiverton T	4-1
Larkhall Ath v Buckland Ath	3-2
AFC St Austell v Bodmin T	0-1
Barnstaple T v Bridgwater T	2-0
Street v Witheridge	1-2
Taunton T v Odd Down	5-1

FIRST QUALIFYING ROUND

Jarrow Roofing Boldon CA v Congleton T	3-4
Buxton v Ramsbottom U	2-1
Washington v Runcorn Linnets	1-0
Padiham v Lancaster C	0-2
Spennymoor T v Blyth Spartans	2-1
Droylsden v Ossett Alb	2-1
Northwich Vic v AFC Blackpool	4-0
Workington v Colwyn Bay	5-0
Consett v Colne	3-1
Matlock T v Whitley Bay	0-0, 3-3
aet; Whitley Bay won 4-2 on penalties.	
Kendal T v Dunston UTS	5-2
Glossop North End v Skelmersdale U	1-1, 1-2
aet; 1-1 at the end of normal time.	
Maltby Main v Frickley Ath	0-2
Salford C v Whitby T	1-1, 5-0
Darlington 1883 v Hyde U	1-3
AFC Liverpool v Armthorpe Welfare	3-4
Ashton U v Guisborough T	0-0, 3-2
Thackley v Abbey Hey	2-2, 0-1
Alsager T v Burscough	1-2
Witton Alb v Farsley Celtic	2-1
Brighouse T v Newton Aycliffe	0-2
Marine v Clitheroe	2-0
Goole v Bamber Bridge	2-2, 2-4
Spalding U v Nantwich T	1-0
Hinckley v Redditch U	2-1
Ilkeston v Rugby T	2-3
Tividale v Stourbridge	0-1
Leamington v Stamford	1-1, 1-2
Market Drayton T v Kettering T	0-5
Coleshill T v Newcastle T	3-3, 3-1
Sutton Coldfield T v Oadby T	0-1
Sporting Khalsa v AFC Wulfrunians	3-2
Clipstone Welfare v Lincoln U	1-2
Shepshed Dynamo v Rushall Olympic	0-0, 1-4
Holwell Sports v Bedworth U	2-2, 0-2
aet; 0-0 at the end of normal time.	
Barwell v Westfields	4-1
Halesowen T v Mickleover Sports	2-1
Basford U v Long Eaton U	1-0
Chasetown v Grantham T	3-0
Stratford T v Coalville T	0-2
Holbeach U v Stourport Swifts	2-2, 1-0
aet; 0-0 at the end of normal time.	
Belper T v Dunkirk	1-3
Leek T v Deeping Rangers	2-2, 2-4
Beaconsfield SYCOB v Kirkley & Pakefield	1-2

Long Buckby v Wingate & Finchley	0-4
Thurrock v Witham T	1-2
Hanwell T v Saffron Walden T	1-0
Cogenhoe U v Leighton T	3-2
Billericay v Enfield T	1-1, 0-2
Heybridge Swifts v Uxbridge	1-3
Potters Bar T v Haringey Bor	3-0
Northwood v Harrow Bor	0-0, 1-0
Yaxley v East Thurrock U	0-0, 1-3
First match abandoned after 85 mins due to player	
injury 0-0.	
Leiston v AFC Dunstable	1-0
Peterborough Sports v Hitchin T	1-1, 2-4
aet; 2-2 at the end of normal time.	
Harlow T v Bedford T	5-1
AFC Sudbury v Hendon	3-1
Bury T v Cockfosters	2-1
Bedfont & Feltham v AFC Rushden & Diamonds	1-2
Basildon U v Hullbridge Sports	0-1
AFC Hornchurch v Cambridge C	2-1
Ipswich W v Canvey Island	1-0
Dunstable T v Barton R	2-1
Brantham Ath v Biggleswade T	1-2
Brentwood T v Arlesey T	2-0
Hoddesdon T v Ashford T (Middlesex)	3-1
Histon v Aveley	1-5
North Greenford U v Mildenhall T	0-0, 0-1
Welwyn Garden C v St Ives T	0-1
Tilbury v St Neots T	1-1, 2-5
Tie ordered to be replayed to a conclusion at Tilbury	
after St Neots T were found to have fielded an ineligible	
player in the first match.	
King's Lynn T v Wroxham	4-1
Chesham U v Aylesbury	0-0, 2-1
Needham Market v Stanway R	1-1, 0-3
Grays Ath v Biggleswade U	5-0
Tooting & Mitcham U v Farnham T	2-1
Worthing v Thamesmead T	2-1
Metropolitan Police v Sittingbourne	0-0, 0-1
Pagham v Carshalton Ath	1-2
Rochester U v Herne Bay	1-3
Greenwich Bor v Slimbridge	2-3
Croydon v Molesey	1-0
Horsham YMCA v Burgess Hill T	1-2
South Park v Leatherhead	1-1, 3-1
Eastbourne U v Hook Norton	0-1
Godalming T v Kidlington	0-1
Shoreham v Eastbourne T	2-3
Tonbridge Angels v Folkestone Invicta	1-1, 2-1
Hampton & Richmond Bor v Dulwich Hamlet	0-1
Phoenix Sports v Lewes	2-0
Whitstable T v Deal T	1-1, 0-2
Dorking W v Slough T	0-1
Bognor Regis T v Merstham	2-1
VCD Ath v Didcot T	1-1, 3-4
Staines T v Faversham T	2-2, 3-1
Chessington & Hook U v North Leigh	2-3
Kingstonian v Farnborough	1-1, 3-2
Hartley Wintney v Fleet T	1-1, 4-0
Hastings U v Thatcham T	1-0
Chatham T v Cray W	1-0
Swindon Supermarine v Winchester C	0-4
Wimborne T v Witheridge	3-2
Shortwood U v Bracknell T	4-3
Cinderford T v Paulton R	1-2
Taunton T v Tuffley R	3-0
Dorchester T v Cirencester T	1-1, 1-3
Bridport v Larkhall Ath	2-5
Bristol Manor Farm v AFC Portchester	0-3
Hungerford T v Bradford T	1-1, 0-2
Poole T v Barnstaple T	1-0
Frome T v Chippenham T	0-0, 0-1
Brockenhurst v Mangotsfield U	3-0
Plymouth Parkway v Merthyr T	0-2
Cheltenham Saracens v Blackfield & Langley	1-2
Bodmin T v Almondsbury UWE	2-0
Petersfield v Weymouth	3-1
Bideford v Hamworthy U	3-1

SECOND QUALIFYING ROUND

Chorley v Frickley Ath	2-0
Salford C v Curzon Ashton	2-1
Spennymoor T v Burscough	0-2
Abbey Hey v Ashton U	0-5
Workington v Harrogate T	0-1

Bamber Bridge v Skelmersdale U	2-0
Kendal T v Stalybridge Celtic	2-3
FC United of Manchester v Witton Alb	3-1
Hyde U v Northwich Vic	0-1, 1-2

Tie ordered to be replayed after Northwich Vic were found to have fielded an ineligible player in the first match.

Whitley Bay v Congleton T	2-1
Droylsden v Lancaster C	2-0
Consett v Bradford Park Avenue	1-2
Marine v Washington	3-3, 3-2

aet; 1-1 at the end of normal time.

Armthorpe Welfare v Buxton	1-6
AFC Fylde v Stockport Co	1-0
Newton Aycliffe v North Ferriby U	0-0, 0-3
Holbeach U v Worcester C	1-1, 0-2
Barwell v Cogenhoe U	5-0
Basford U v Sporting Khalsa	2-3
Rugby T v Lincoln U	3-2
Deeping Rangers v AFC Rushden & Diamonds	0-3
Halesowen T v Nuneaton T	0-2
Kettering T v AFC Telford U	2-1
Gainsborough Trinity v Boston U	2-0
Coalville T v Spalding U	0-3
Corby T v Rushall Olympic	1-1, 1-2
Chasetown v Hinckley	5-2
Solihull Moors v Oadby T	3-1
Hednesford T v Bedworth U	2-0
Tamworth v Alfreton T	2-3
Stourbridge v Dunkirk	3-1
Coleshill T v Stamford	2-0
Grays Ath v Hullbridge Sports	6-0
Maidstone U v South Park	6-2
Hanwell T v Mildenhall T	1-0
Chelmsford C v Ebbsfleet U	0-0, 2-1
Phoenix Sports v AFC Hornchurch	3-5
Dunstable T v Kingstonian	2-0
St Albans C v Deal T	2-1
Dartford v Uxbridge	0-1
St Ives T v Harlow T	0-3
St Neots T v Worthing	1-1, 2-2

aet; Worthing won 6-5 on penalties.

Carshalton Ath v East Thurrock U	0-5
Wealdstone v Biggleswade T	1-1, 2-0
Potters Bar T v Margate	1-5
Wingate & Finchley v Concord Rangers	2-1
Eastbourne Bor v AFC Sudbury	2-1
Bognor Regis T v Lowestoft T	2-1
Tooting & Mitcham U v Brackley T	1-3
Whitehawk v Dulwich Hamlet	4-2
Bury T v Hemel Hempstead T	0-3
Horsham YMCA v Aveley	2-2, 1-4
Stanway R v Staines T	0-1
Chatham T v Eastbourne T	1-2
Brentwood T v Croydon	3-1
Sittingbourne v Hoddesdon T	1-2
Enfield T v Ipswich W	1-0
Bishop's Stortford v Sutton U	0-2
King's Lynn T v Witham T	1-0
Kirkley & Pakefield v Hitchin T	0-2
Leiston v Tonbridge Angels	3-1
Northwood v Didcot T	1-2
Herne Bay v Hastings U	1-1, 2-3
North Leigh v Slimbridge	4-1
Hook Norton v Weston-super-Mare	1-2
Larkhall Ath v Havant & Waterlooville	1-1, 2-4
Merthyr T v Hartley Wintney	0-1
Bradford T v Chippenham T	2-3
Brockenhurst v AFC Portchester	1-0
Paulton R v Chesham U	0-2
Bodmin T v Bath C	1-2
Gosport Bor v Bideford	7-0
Winchester C v Maidenhead U	1-1, 2-4
Taunton T v Truro C	2-2, 1-3
Oxford C v Shortwood U	3-1
Hayes & Yeading U v Poole T	2-3
Wimborne T v Blackfield & Langley	1-6
Gloucester C v Kidlington	4-2
Basingstoke T v Slough T	4-2
Petersfield T v Cirencester T	3-1

THIRD QUALIFYING ROUND

Harrogate T v Burscough	3-0
Salford C v Bradford Park Avenue	1-1, 1-0

aet; 0-0 at the end of normal time.

Whitley Bay v Chorley	2-3
Stourbridge v Rushall Olympic	1-0
Solihull Moors v Worcester C	1-1, 0-1
FC United of Manchester v Buxton	1-1, 2-0
Marine v Northwich Vic	2-4
Chasetown v Stalybridge Celtic	1-1, 0-2
North Ferriby U v Nuneaton T	2-1
AFC Fylde v Coleshill T	9-0
Barwell v King's Lynn T	1-0
Hednesford T v Alfreton T	2-4
Droylsden v Gainsborough Trinity	3-4
Sporting Khalsa v Spalding U	1-1, 2-1
Brackley T v Rugby T	1-1, 2-0
Kettering T v Bamber Bridge	1-1, 2-3
AFC Rushden & Diamonds v Ashton U	2-0
Harlow T v Bath C	2-2, 2-1
East Thurrock U v Staines T	3-6
Bognor Regis T v Oxford C	4-2
Basingstoke T v Chelmsford C	4-2
Maidstone U v Dunstable T	2-0
Eastbourne Bor v Hartley Wintney	3-2
Leiston v Gloucester C	1-3
Hastings U v Poole T	0-2
Hoddesdon T v Brentwood T	0-0, 1-2
Didcot T v Eastbourne T	4-1
Whitehawk v Gosport Bor	2-2, 2-1
Enfield T v Hitchin T	0-0, 2-1
Wingate & Finchley v Weston-super-Mare	1-3
Chesham U v North Leigh	2-0
Hanwell T v Grays Ath	1-2
Margate v Truro C	4-1
Brockenhurst v Wealdstone	1-5
Uxbridge v Chippenham T	0-3
Hemel Hempstead T v Sutton U	1-1, 1-2
Petersfield T v St Albans C	0-1
Aveley v Havant & Waterlooville	0-2
Worthing v AFC Hornchurch	1-4
Blackfield & Langley v Maidenhead U	0-1

FOURTH QUALIFYING ROUND

Gateshead v Worcester C	1-2
AFC Fylde v Barrow	1-0
Wrexham v Gainsborough Trinity	0-1
Northwich Vic v Chorley	0-0, 2-1
Harrogate T v Grimsby T	1-4
Barwell v AFC Rushden & Diamonds	2-2, 1-0
Salford C v Southport	1-0
Sporting Khalsa v FC United of Manchester	1-3
Stalybridge Celtic v North Ferriby U	1-1, 0-0

aet; Stalybridge Celtic won 8-7 on penalties.

FC Halifax T v Guiseley	2-2, 2-1
Tranmere R v Lincoln C	0-0, 0-2
Stourbridge v Kidderminster H	3-0
Macclesfield T v Alfreton T	3-2
Brackley T v Bamber Bridge	3-0
Altrincham v Chester FC	1-0
Whitehawk v Poole T	2-0
Maidenhead U v Woking	3-0
Basingstoke T v Torquay U	3-0
Grays Ath v Welling U	1-1, 0-4
Boreham Wood v AFC Hornchurch	2-1
Wealdstone v Bognor Regis T	2-1
Didcot T v Brentwood T	4-2
Eastbourne Bor v Dover Ath	1-2
Chesham U v Enfield T	2-1
Staines T v Gloucester C	2-1
Aldershot T v Sutton U	1-0
Bromley v Eastleigh	1-2
Margate v Forest Green R	1-2
Braintree T v Harlow T	2-0
Havant & Waterlooville v Cheltenham T	3-3, 0-1
Chippenham T v Maidstone U	0-2
St Albans C v Weston-super-Mare	2-1

THE EMIRATES FA CUP 2015–16
COMPETITION PROPER

■ *Denotes player sent off.*

FIRST ROUND

Friday, 6 November 2015

Salford City (0) 2 *(Webber 46, Allen 73)*
Notts Co (0) 0   1400

Salford City: (4231) Lynch J; Lynch C, O'Halloran, Dawson, Howson; Burton, Hulme; Hardcastle (Moses 90), Stopforth, Poole (Mwasile 81); Webber (Allen 70).
Notts Co: (442) Carroll; Hewitt (Jenner 82), Audel, Edwards, Sheehan; Smith (Spencer 65), Aborah, Noble, De Silva (Campbell 56); Stead, McLeod.
Referee: Andrew Madley.

Saturday, 7 November 2015

Accrington S (2) 3 *(McConville 29, Crooks 36, Windass 48 (pen))*
York C (1) 2 *(Oliver 34, Coulson 90)*   1475

Accrington S: (442) Mooney; Halliday, Wright, Davies, Pearson; Mingoia, Crooks, Conneely, McConville; Kee, Windass (Gornell 88).
York C: (433) Flinders; McCoy, Lowe (Winfield 46), Ilesanmi, Nolan; Collins, Godfrey (Turner 77), Morris; Sinclair (Hyde 59), Oliver, Coulson.
Referee: Fred Graham.

AFC Wimbledon (1) 1 *(Kennedy 24)*
Forest Green R (1) 2 *(Carter 6, Frear 90)*   2465

AFC Wimbledon: (442) Wilson; Fuller, Robinson, Osborne, Meades; Rigg, Bulman (Toonga 68), Reeves, Kennedy (Beere 77); Taylor, Elliott (Azeez 69).
Forest Green R: (433) Arnold; Bennett, Clough, Racine, Jennings; Wedgbury, Sinclair (Pipe 89), Carter; Marsh-Brown (Kelly 82), Parkin (Guthrie 74), Frear.
Referee: Graham Horwood.

Altrincham (0) 1 *(Reeves 46)*
Barnsley (0) 0   2571

Altrincham: (451) Deasy; Sinnott, Leather, Havern (Heathcote 65), Griffin; Lawrie, Richman, Moult, O'Keefe, Crowther (Clee 76); Reeves (Rankine 89).
Barnsley: (41212) Davies; Wabara, Roberts (Isgrove 53), Nyatanga, Smith; Mawson; Pearson, Scowen (Hourihane 53); Maris (Wilkinson 53); Watkins, Winnall.
Referee: Andy Haines.

Barnet (2) 2 *(Champion 36, Gash 41)*
Blackpool (0) 0   1869

Barnet: (442) Stephens; Champion, Nelson, N'Gala, Johnson; Yiadom, Weston, Muggleton (Hoyte 67), Gambin (Bailey 82); Gash, Akinde (Batt 75).
Blackpool: (442) Doyle (Letheren 32); Higham, Robertson, Aldred, Dunne; Rivers, Herron (Oliver 65), Cubero, Cameron; Thomas, Paterson (Cullen 65).
Referee: Kevin Johnson.

Barwell (0) 0
Welling U (1) 2 *(Wellard 34, Bakare 90)*   843

Barwell: (442) Castle; Lower, Kay, Towers D, Nisevic; Hickey (Brennan 79), Woodward (Gaunt 71), Lavery, Tomlinson; Christie (Towers J 59), Carney.
Welling U: (451) McEntegart; Williams, Lokko, Chambers, Jefford; Harris, Vidal (Bakare 72), Corne, Wellard, Taylor; Porter.
Referee: Steven Rushton.

Burton Alb (0) 0
Peterborough U (1) 3 *(Washington 41, 71, Anderson J 84)*
                                                      2517

Burton Alb: (4411) Matthews; Edwards, Mousinho, Flanagan, Binnom-Williams; Akins (Beavon 55), Butcher, Palmer (Reilly 72), El Khayati; Duffy; Thiele (Joachim 55).

Peterborough U: (41212) Alnwick; Bostwick, Zakuani (Smith 36), Santos, Elder; Anderson J; Taylor, Forrester; Oztumer (Fox 64); Washington, Angol (Baldwin■ 90).
Referee: David Webb.

Bury (3) 4 *(Pope 18, Mayor 34, Cameron 45, Clarke L 65)*
Wigan Ath (0) 0   3856

Bury: (442) Bachmann; Riley, Clarke P, Cameron, Hussey; Pugh, Mellis (Burgess 85), Soares (Brown 80), Mayor; Rose (Clarke L 60), Pope.
Wigan Ath: (532) O'Donnell; Love, Daniels, Morgan, McCann, James; Junior (Power 61), Perkins, Vuckic (Wildschut 46); Davies, Grigg (Jacobs 46).
Referee: David Coote.

Cambridge U (1) 1 *(Hughes J 19)*
Basingstoke T (0) 0   2974

Cambridge U: (442) Dunn; Omozusi (Demetriou 77), Sesay, Roberts, Taylor; Donaldson, Hughes J (Newton 70), Berry, Dunk; Corr, Simpson (Gaffney 62).
Basingstoke T: (451) Howe; Salmon, Gasson, Ray, Bird; Soares, Southam, Harper, Gilkes (Macklin 66), McAuley (Enver-Marum 64); Flood.
Referee: John Brooks.

Coventry C (1) 1 *(Murphy 10)*
Northampton T (2) 2 *(Diamond 5, Richards 18)*   9124

Coventry C: (4231) Burge; Phillips (Haynes 46), Martin, Ricketts, Stokes; Thomas C (Sambou 58), Fleck; Lameiras, Murphy, O'Brien; Fortune (Elford-Alliyu 71).
Northampton T: (4231) Smith; Moloney, Diamond, McDonald, Buchanan; Taylor, O'Toole; D'Ath (Watson 68), Potter, Adams (Hoskins 83); Richards (Calvert-Lewin 63).
Referee: Darren Handley.

Crawley T (0) 1 *(Harrold 63)*
Luton T (0) 2 *(McQuoid 54, 89)*   1929

Crawley T: (442) Flahavan; Young, Yorwerth, Bradley, Scales; Edwards, Walton (Rooney 85), Smith J, Deacon (Fenelon 88); Harrold, Murphy (Barnard 83).
Luton T: (4411) Justham; Long, Cuthbert, Wilkinson, Griffiths; Lawless (Green 69), Lee, Smith, McQuoid; Guttridge; Marriott (Benson 60).
Referee: Nick Kinseley.

Crewe Alex (0) 0
Eastleigh (0) 1 *(Strevens 75 (pen))*   3008

Crewe Alex: (442) Garratt■; Turton, Ray, Nugent, Guthrie (Dalla Valle 84); Colclough (Cooper 35 (Nizic 64)), King, Jones, Inman; Haber, Saunders.
Eastleigh: (442) Flitney; Partington, Turley, Evans, Harding (Green 71); Reason, Drury, Payne, Strevens; Constable (Lafayette 70), Odubade.
Referee: Carl Boyeson.

Dagenham & R (0) 0
Morecambe (0) 0   900

Dagenham & R: (442) Cousins; Hoyte, Obileye, Nosworthy, Connors; Mulraney (Jones 80), Dunne, Labadie, Hemmings; Cureton (McClure 79), Vassell.
Morecambe: (4231) Roche; Beeley, Edwards, Parrish, McGowan; Kenyon, Goodall (Devitt 59); Barkhuizen (Molyneux 67), Wildig, Ellison; Miller (Mullin 77).
Referee: Tim Robinson.

Doncaster R (1) 2 *(Williams 3, 68)*
Stalybridge Celtic (0) 0   3991

Doncaster R: (352) Stuckmann; Lund, Butler, Taylor-Sinclair; Felipe Mattioni, Coppinger (Wellens 87), Middleton, Grant, Evina; Williams, Tyson (Anderson 57).
Stalybridge Celtic: (442) McMillan; Crowley, Hughes, Higgins, Wylie; Farrell, Wisdom (Chippendale 67), Chalmers, Dixon; Tames (Wright 55), Johnson (Simm 67).
Referee: Martin Coy.

Dover Ath (1) 1 *(Thomas 33)*
Stourbridge (1) 2 *(Lait 8, Hawley 69 (pen))*   1392
Dover Ath: (532) Walker■; Magri, Orlu, Grimes, Raggett, Thomas; Modeste (Ofori-Acheampong 78), Parkinson, Deverdics (Ajala 65); Miller (Rafferty 68), Payne.
Stourbridge: (442) Solly; Green, Scarr, Pierpiont, Smickle; Dodd, Tonks, Broadhurst, Lait; Hawley, Richards.
Referee: Richard Martin.

Grimsby T (2) 5 *(Townsend 30, Amond 45, 90, Pittman 71, Marshall 84)*
St Albans C (0) 1 *(Theophanous 62)*   2263
Grimsby T: (442) McKeown; Tait, Pearson, Gowling, Townsend; Arnold, Brown, Clay, Monkhouse (Robertson 78); Pittman (Marshall 74), Bogle (Amond 43).
St Albans C: (442) Welch; Nunn, Martin, Comley, Chappell; Corcoran (Green 76), Thomas, Gibson, Montgomery (Crawford 54); Krans, Theophanous (Sow 86).
Referee: Ryan Johnson.

Hartlepool U (1) 1 *(Oyenuga 45)*
Cheltenham T (0) 0   2287
Hartlepool U: (442) Carson; Duckworth, Bates, Jackson, Carroll; Oates, Featherstone, Gray (Woods 82), Oyenuga (Banton 71); Paynter (Bingham 41), Fenwick.
Cheltenham T: (352) Phillips; Parslow, Downes, Dickie; Barthram (Dayton 54), Pell, Munns (Hall 62), Storer, McLennan (Vaughan 71); Wright, Waters.
Referee: James Adcock.

Leyton Orient (4) 6 *(Palmer 8, 13, Cox 12, 33, Marquis 89, Clohessy 90)*
Staines T (1) 1 *(Purse 23)*   2287
Leyton Orient: (442) Cisak; Clohessy, Baudry, Dunne, Shaw; Turgott, Payne (Moncur 63), James, Cox; Palmer (Marquis 76), Simpson (Kashket 69).
Staines T: (4141) Turner; Felix, Purse, Gough, Bennett; Brewer (Boakye 72); Wanadio, Abdulla (Vancooten 90), Lodge, Hutchinson (Kalu 46); Cox.
Referee: Rob Jones.

Mansfield T (0) 0
Oldham Ath (0) 0   2886
Mansfield T: (4411) Jensen; Hunt, Collins, Tafazolli, Adams; Rose (Thomas N 64), Clements, Chapman, Lambe (Blair 81); Westcarr; Green (Yussuf 82).
Oldham Ath: (442) Coleman; Dummigan, Dieng, Wilson B, Mills; Yeates, Winchester, Philliskirk, Poleon (Rasulo 73); Fuller (Croft 56 (Eckersley 79)), Higdon.
Referee: Tony Harrington.

Millwall (0) 3 *(O'Brien 54, Gregory 60, Morison 88)*
AFC Fylde (0) 1 *(Whittle 62)*   3445
Millwall: (442) Forde; Cummings, Webster, Beevers, Martin J; Cowan-Hull (O'Brien 46), Thompson, Williams (Powell 90), Onyedinma; Morison (Pavey 90), Gregory.
AFC Fylde: (4411) Urwin; Hughes C, Hannigan, Collins, Whittle; Hughes M (Lloyd 83), Charles, Wilson (Finley 71), Baker; Rowe; Blinkhorn.
Referee: Stephen Martin.

Northwich Vic (1) 1 *(Williams 12)*
Boreham Wood (1) 1 *(Morias 23)*   502
Northwich Vic: (442) Springthorpe; Byrne, Clarke, Asltes, Duxbury; Summerskill, Krou, Ball, Williams (Cook 87); Bennett (Amis 64), Howard.
Boreham Wood: (442) Russell; Woodards D, Clifford Conor, Doe, Morias; Vilhete, Kamdjo (Cox 87), Jeffrey, Tiryaki; Stephens, Devera.
Referee: Wayne Barratt.

Plymouth Arg (0) 0
Carlisle U (2) 2 *(Sweeney 23, Hope 41)*   6005
Plymouth Arg: (4231) McCormick; Mellor, Nelson, Hartley, Sawyer; Simpson (Wylde 73), McHugh; Jervis, Carey, Tanner (Threlkeld 86); Brunt (Harvey T 85).
Carlisle U: (442) Hanford; Atkinson, Raynes, Ellis, Grainger (Miller 78); Gilliead (Thompson 84), Sweeney (Hery 74), Dicker, Kennedy; Hope, Asamoah.
Referee: Charles Breakspear.

Portsmouth (2) 2 *(McGurk 3, 45)*
Macclesfield T (1) 1 *(Dennis 15)*   9834
Portsmouth: (4231) Murphy; Davies, Burgess, Webster, Stevens; Hollands, Doyle; Evans, McGurk (Boco 90), Bennett (Naismith 68); Chaplin (McNulty 65).
Macclesfield T: (433) Jalal; Halls, Pilkington (Byrne 46), Diagne, Fitzpatrick; Whitaker, Turnbull (Sampson 74), Whitehead (Lewis 75); Holroyd, Dennis, Rowe.
Referee: Lee Swabey.

Rochdale (1) 3 *(Mendez-Laing 24, 46, 69 (pen))*
Swindon T (0) 1 *(Ajose 71 (pen))*   2060
Rochdale: (4231) Lillis; Cannon, Eastham, McNulty, Tanser; Lund, Rose; Vincenti, Camps (Bennett 80), Bunney (Andrew 81); Mendez-Laing (McDermott 90).
Swindon T: (433) Vigouroux; Barry, El-Abd, Branco, Turnbull; Rodgers (Balmy 70), Kasim, Thompson L; Ojamaa (Robert 55), Ajose, Obika (Hylton 81).
Referee: Christopher Sarginson.

Scunthorpe U (1) 2 *(Madden 16, 78)*
Southend U (1) 1 *(Leonard 30)*   3335
Scunthorpe U: (433) Daniels; Wiseman (Clarke 60), Mirfin, Goode (Boyce 75), Laird; King, Williams (Henderson 56), Bishop; Madden, van Veen, McSheffrey.
Southend U: (442) Bentley; O'Neill, Bolger, Prosser, Coker; Leonard, Timlin, Rea (Hurst 80), McLaughlin (Worrall 13); Pigott (Mooney 73), Weston.
Referee: Peter Bankes.

Sheffield U (1) 3 *(Baxter 19 (pen), Sammon 81, Freeman 90)*
Worcester C (0) 0   11,108
Sheffield U: (442) Long; Freeman, Collins, Basham (McGahey 85), Harris; Campbell-Ryce, Coutts (Reed 88), Hammond, Baxter; Adams (Scougall 32), Sammon.
Worcester C: (4231) Vaughan; Minihan (Weir 51), Thomas, Sharpe, Gudger; Gater (Dunkley 60), Deeney; Nti, Jackman, Vincent (Harrad 74); Burton.
Referee: Simon Bennett.

Stevenage (2) 3 *(Schumacher 13, Whelpdale 29, Gnanduillet 90)*
Gillingham (0) 0   1619
Stevenage: (442) Joronen (Day 78); Henry, Wells, Franks, Ogilvie; Pett, Parrett, Schumacher (Conlon 75), Whelpdale; Gnanduillet, Kennedy (Hughes 87).
Gillingham: (442) Nelson; Jackson, Ehmer, Morris, Dickenson (Garmston 61); Loft, Houghton (Hessenthaler 61), Egan, Osaoabe; McDonald (Williamson 67), Donnelly.
Referee: Trevor Kettle.

Walsall (1) 2 *(Evans 19, Forde 90)*
Fleetwood T (0) 0   2532
Walsall: (4411) Etheridge (MacGillivray 46); Demetriou, Downing, Preston, Henry; Morris K, Evans, Chambers, Lalkovic (Forde 46); Sawyers; Bradshaw (Cook 74).
Fleetwood T: (451) Maxwell; McLaughlin, Pond, Davis, Bell; Hornby-Forbes, Sarcevic, Jonsson (Haughton 71); Ball (McManus 78), Ryan; Proctor (Matt 46).
Referee: Ross Joyce.

Wealdstone (2) 2 *(Louis 31 (pen), Hudson-Odoi 38)*
Colchester U (2) 6 *(Bonne 26, 44, 47, 68, Moncur 82, Sordell 90)*   2440
Wealdstone: (4141) North; Urquhart, Parker, Hamblin, Duffy; Corcoran (McGleish 80); Lucien (Wright 56), Davies, Lowe (Ball 66), Hudson-Odoi; Louis.
Colchester U: (4222) Parish; Edwards, Kent, Eastman, Briggs; Lapslie, Gilbey; Bonne (Curtis 90), Harriott; Moncur (Massey 88), Sordell.
Referee: Brendan Malone.

Sunday, 8 November 2015
Aldershot T (0) 0
Bradford C (0) 0 2640
Aldershot T: (442) Smith; Alexander, Beckles, Saville, McGinty; Walker D, Stevenson, Lathrope, Browne (Richards 73); Walker C, Brodie.
Bradford C: (442) Williams; Darby, McArdle, Burke, Meredith; McMahon, Knott, Liddle, Reid (Marshall 84); Hanson, Clarke B (Cole 70).
Referee: Ben Toner.

Brackley T (0) 2 *(Graham 59, McDonald 90)*
Newport Co (2) 2 *(John-Lewis 15 (pen), Bennett 41)* 1707
Brackley T: (442) Hornby; Hawtin (Smith 90), Graham, Mills, McDonald; Odhiambo (Moyo 81), Batchelor, Clarke, Walker (Winters 81); Diggin, Akintunde.
Newport Co: (352) Day; Bennett, Donacien, Partridge; Barnum-Bobb (Holmes 73), Byrne, Elito, O'Sullivan (Rodman 78), Barrow; Ansah, John-Lewis (Boden 46).
Referee: Mark Haywood.

Braintree T (0) 1 *(Davis 63)*
Oxford U (1) 1 *(Taylor 15)* 1248
Braintree T: (4141) Norris; Clerima (Miles 36), Phillips, Paine, Habergham; Davis; Brundle, Woodyard, Isaac, Sparkes (Marks 68); Cheek (List 89).
Oxford U: (442) Buchel; Gayle, Mullins▪, Skarz, Baldock; MacDonald (Sercombe 77), Rose, Lundstram, O'Dowda; Taylor (Hylton 77), Hoban.
Referee: Phil Gibbs.

Bristol R (0) 0
Chesham U (0) 1 *(Blake 77)* 5181
Bristol R: (442) Nicholls; Leadbitter (Clarke J 73), Lockyer, McChrystal, Brown; Gosling, Mansell (Lines 62), Sinclair, Bodin; Harrison, Taylor (Easter 62).
Chesham U: (442) Gore; Smtih, Beasant, Ujah, Fenton; Pearce (Hayles 72), Youngs, Taylor (Hamilton-Forbes 90), Little; Blake (Casey 86), Wadkins.
Referee: Andy Davies.

Didcot T (0) 0
Exeter C (0) 3 *(Morrison 48, Nichols 73, Nicholls 78)* 2707
Didcot T: (4411) Bedwell; Heapy (Williams 87), Carnell, Leoroyd, Organ; Longford, Ballard, Self (Francis 65), Dutton-Black; Martin (Powell 90); Janes.
Exeter C: (442) Olejnik; Davies, Brown, Moore-Taylor, McAllister; Wheeler, Oyeleke (Nicholls 62), Noble, Harley; Morrison (Grant 78), Nichols (Watkins 80).
Referee: Chris Kavanagh.

FC Halifax T (0) 0
Wycombe W (1) 4 *(Thompson 17, Jombati 65, Kretzschmar 84, Amadi-Holloway 90)* 1789
FC Halifax T: (4231) Griffiths; Bolton, O'Brien, Brown N, McManus; Miller (Tuton 57), Wroe; Roberts (Sadlier 74), James, Walker; Burrow.
Wycombe W: (442) Ingram; Jombati, Pierre, McCarthy, Jacobson; O'Nien, Bean, Bloomfield (Kretzschmar 66), Wood; Thompson (Ugwu 87), Hayes (Amadi-Holloway 66).
Referee: Graham Salisbury.

Gainsborough Trinity (0) 0
Shrewsbury T (0) 1 *(Collins 71)* 2180
Gainsborough Trinity: (433) Budtz; Lacey, Roma, Picton, Brogan; Russell, Binns (Bignall 76), D'Laryea; Jarman, Newsham (Stamp 82), Drury (Yates 83).
Shrewsbury T: (433) Leutwiler; Smith, Gerrard, Whitbread, Sadler; Ogogo, Black, Cole (McAlinden 74); Clark (Vernon 62), Collins, Brown (Whalley 46).
Referee: Darren Bond.

Maidstone U (0) 0
Yeovil T (0) 1 *(Fogden 55)* 2811
Maidstone U: (4411) Worgan; Driver, Parry, Coyle, Mills; Bodkin, Paxman, Rogers, Osborn (Akrofi 63); Flisher (Birchall 81); May (Collin 74).
Yeovil T: (442) Krysiak▪; Ward, Sokolik▪, Roberts, Smith; Fogden, Tozer, Sheehan (Weale 58), Dickson; Sowunmi (Lacey 18), Bird.
Referee: Michael Bull.

Port Vale (1) 1 *(Moore 31)*
Maidenhead U (0) 1 *(Mulley 90)* 3977
Port Vale: (4411) Alnwick; Purkiss, Duffy, McGivern, Dickinson; Moore, O'Connor, Grant (Streete 90), Daniel (Foley 51); Dodds; Leitch-Smith (Ikpeazu 51).
Maidenhead U: (442) Pentney; Peters, Massey, Inman, Steer; Forbes, Upward, Tarpey, Pritchard (Mulley 76); Wright (Huggins 61), Reid (James 76).
Referee: Adrian Holmes.

Whitehawk (2) 5 *(Mills 6, Robinson 27, Deering 58, 90 (pen), Martin 86)*
Lincoln C (1) 3 *(Rhead 45 (pen), 63, 90)* 1342
Whitehawk: (4141) Ross; Arnold, Van Den Bogaert (Sessegnon 24), Cruz Gotta, Leacock; Mendy; Robinson, Torres (Ijaha 66), Martin, Deering; Mills (Neilson 86).
Lincoln C: (4411) Farman; Beevers, Howe, Waterfall, Bush; Muldoon (Hodge 79), Wood (Hearn 58), Sparrow, Hawkridge (Tempest 62); Power▪; Rhead.
Referee: Constantine Hatzidakis.

Monday, 9 November 2015
FC United of Manchester (0) 0 *(Ashworth 90)*
Chesterfield (2) 4 *(Ariyibi 7, Novak 12, Simons 68, Banks 87)* 2916
FC United of Manchester: (4141) Carnell; Brownhill, Lynch, Ashworth, Wright; Stott; Fallon (Daniels 46), Thurston, Sheridan (Byrne 80), Lindfield (Patterson 76); Greaves.
Chesterfield: (442) Lee; Talbot, Evatt, Wood, Jones; Ariyibi, Herd (Banks 55), Morsy (Raglan 72), O'Shea; Novak, Ebanks-Blake (Simons 56).
Referee: Oliver Langford.

FIRST ROUND REPLAYS

Monday, 16 November 2015
Boreham Wood (0) 1 *(MacDonald 90)*
Northwich Vic (1) 2 *(Williams 28, Asltes 52)* 512
Boreham Wood: (442) Russell; Devera, Stephens, Doe, Woodards D (Clifford B 62); Jeffrey (Shakes 83), Kamdjo, Cox, Vilhete; Tiryaki (MacDonald 62), Morias.
Northwich Vic: (442) Springthorpe; Byrne, Krou, Clarke, Duxbury; Summerskill, Asltes, Ball (Cook 82), Williams (Ali 86); Bennett (Amis 67), Howard.
Referee: Andy Woolmer.

Tuesday, 17 November 2015
Morecambe (2) 2 *(Barkhuizen 6, Wildig 7)*
Dagenham & R (2) 4 *(Vassell 13 (pen), 50, Dunne 37, Labadie 70)* 1176
Morecambe: (4231) Roche; McGowan, Edwards, Parrish, Wilson; Kenyon, Fleming; Barkhuizen, Wildig (Mullin 58), Devitt (Ellison 58); Miller.
Dagenham & R: (442) O'Brien; Passley, Nosworthy, Dikamona, Widdowson; Chambers, Labadie, Dunne, Hemmings; Cureton, Vassell.
Referee: Geoff Eltringham.

Newport Co (2) 4 *(John-Lewis 1, Klukowski 17, Rodman 63, Hawtin 71 (og))*
Brackley T (1) 1 *(Hawtin 39)* 1511
Newport Co: (442) Day; Barnum-Bobb (Hughes 58), Bennett, Partridge, Holmes; Elito, Klukowski (Owen-Evans 67), Rodman, Byrne; John-Lewis (Collins 69), Boden.
Brackley T: (442) Hornby; Hawtin, Graham, Mills, McDonald; Odhiambo, Clarke, Walker, Batchelor (Winters 76); Akintunde (Moyo 73), Diggin (Smith 78).
Referee: Stuart Attwell.

Oldham Ath (0) 2 *(Philliskirk 70, Poleon 78)*
Mansfield T (0) 0 1893
Oldham Ath: (4231) Coleman; Eckersley, Wilson B, Wilson J, Mills; Dieng, Kelly; Poleon (Fuller 87), Philliskirk, Yeates; Higdon (Rasulo 59).
Mansfield T: (451) Shearer; Tafazolli, Pearce, Collins, Adams; Thomas N, Chapman, Thomas J (Yussuf 76), McGuire, Blair (Rose 65); Green.
Referee: Lee Collins.

Oxford U (1) 3 *(Sercombe 42, Hoban 64, 80 (pen))*
Braintree T (1) 1 *(Davis 33 (pen))* 3265
Oxford U: (442) Buchel; Baldock, Dunkley, Mullins (Ruffels 82), Skarz; MacDonald (George 90), Sercombe (Rose 74), Lundstram, O'Dowda; Roofe, Hoban.
Braintree T: (442) Norris; Clerima (Miles 78), Paine, Fry, Habergham; Isaac (Brundle 53), Woodyard, Davis, Sparkes; Cheek (Sekajja 82), Marks.
Referee: Darren England.

Wednesday, 18 November 2015

Bradford C (0) 2 *(Leigh 61, McMahon 76 (pen))*
Aldershot T (0) 0 2930
Bradford C: (442) Williams; Darby, McArdle, Clarke N, Leigh; McMahon, Liddle (Routis 81), Knott, Marshall; Hanson (Clarke B 59), Cole (James 70).
Aldershot T: (442) Smith; Alexander, Oliver, Beckles, McGinty; Walker D, Stevenson, Lathrope (Browne 66), Hatton (Richards 84); Walker C, Brodie.
Referee: Keith Hill.

Thursday, 19 November 2015

Maidenhead U (1) 1 *(Massey 15)*
Port Vale (1) 3 *(O'Connor 35, Leitch-Smith 49, 57)* 2212
Maidenhead U: (4411) Pentney; Peters, Inman, Massey (Nisbet 58), Steer; Tarpey, Upward (Barratt 81), Forbes, Pritchard; Reid; Wright (Huggins 66).
Port Vale: (4411) Alnwick; Yates, Duffy, McGivern, Dickinson; Moore, O'Connor, Grant, Foley (Daniel 74); Dodds; Leitch-Smith (Ikpeazu 79).
Referee: Dean Whitestone.

SECOND ROUND

Friday, 4 December 2015

Salford City (1) 1 *(O'Halloran 23)*
Hartlepool U (1) 1 *(Oates 8 (pen))* 1400
Salford City: (4231) Lynch J; Lynch C, Dawson, Howson, O'Halloran; Hardcastle, Burton; Allen (Mwasile 85), Stopforth, Poole; Webber (Hulme 79).
Hartlepool U: (433) Carson; Duckworth, Bates, Jackson, Carroll; Gray, Featherstone, Magnay; Oates (Walker 87), Mandron (Bingham 55), Fenwick.
Referee: Gavin Ward.

Saturday, 5 December 2015

Barnet (0) 0
Newport Co (0) 1 *(Boden 59)* 1767
Barnet: (442) Stephens; Dembele, N'Gala, Nelson, Yiadom; Akinde, Muggleton (Johnson 46), Gash, Odofin (Gambin 75); Batt (Lisbie 46), Bailey.
Newport Co: (442) Day; Holmes, Bennett, Partridge, Hughes; O'Sullivan (Klukowski 90), Elito, Byrne, Rodman; John-Lewis, Boden (Ansah 90).
Referee: Dean Whitestone.

Chesterfield (0) 1 *(Morsy 89)*
Walsall (1) 1 *(Demetriou 19)* 4126
Chesterfield: (352) Lee; Hird, Evatt, Wood (Raglan 70); Talbot, Morsy, O'Neil, Donohue (Gardner 64), O'Shea (Banks 65); Ebanks-Blake, Novak.
Walsall: (4231) Etheridge; Demetriou, O'Connor, Downing, Henry; Chambers, Evans (Mantom 77); Lalkovic (Bakayoko 85), Sawyers, Morris K (Forde 61); Cook.
Referee: Richard Clark.

Leyton Orient (0) 0
Scunthorpe U (0) 0 2540
Leyton Orient: (442) Grainger; Clohessy, Baudry, Mvoto, Shaw; Pritchard (Kashket 61), Payne, James, Turgott; McAnuff, Palmer (Adeboyejo 86).
Scunthorpe U: (442) Daniels; Wiseman, Canavan, King, Laird; Adelakun (van Veen 68), McAllister (Ness 68), Goode, Williams; Henderson, Madden.
Referee: James Linington.

Millwall (0) 1 *(Thompson 57)*
Wycombe W (0) 2 *(Hayes 50, Harriman 90)* 3960
Millwall: (442) Archer; Edwards, Nelson, Webster, Martin J; Upson (Onyedinma 69 (Pavey 90)), Thompson, Williams, O'Brien (Martin L 83); Gregory, Morison.
Wycombe W: (442) Ingram; McCarthy, Stewart, Pierre, Jombati; Harriman, O'Nien, Bloomfield, Wood; Hayes, Amadi-Holloway (Thompson 75).
Referee: Fred Graham.

Northampton T (0) 3 *(Hoskins 83, Taylor 85, Calvert-Lewin 87)*
Northwich Vic (1) 2 *(Ball 44, Bennett 63)* 3837
Northampton T: (4231) Smith; Moloney, Diamond, Cresswell (Hoskins 68), Buchanan; Taylor, Byrom; D'Ath (Holmes 59), Potter (Richards 46); Adams; Calvert-Lewin.
Northwich Vic: (4231) Springthorpe; Byrne, Clarke, Asltes, Duxbury; Ball (Ali 82), Krou; Summerskill, Howard, Williams (Sanogo 75); Bennett (Amis 75).
Referee: Paul Tierney.

Portsmouth (1) 1 *(McGurk 21)*
Accrington S (0) 0 9258
Portsmouth: (4411) Murphy; Davies, Webster, Clarke, Stevens; Evans, Hollands, Doyle, Bennett (Burgess 90); McNulty (Chaplin 90); McGurk (Stockley 75).
Accrington S: (4231) Mooney; Halliday, Wright, Davies, Pearson; Barry (Buxton 67), Crooks; Mingoia (McCartan 76), Windass (Gornell 83), McConville; Kee.
Referee: Kevin Johnson.

Sheffield U (0) 1 *(Done 47)*
Oldham Ath (0) 0 6938
Sheffield U: (4411) Long; Brayford, Collins, McEveley, Harris (Wallace K 45); Coutts, Basham, Hammond, Adams**ª**; Done (Sammon 85); Sharp (Scougall 46).
Oldham Ath: (4231) Cornell; Dieng, Wilson J, Wilson B, Mills; Kelly, Jones; Yeates (Rasulo 77), Winchester, Philliskirk (Poleon 72); Cassidy.
Referee: Eddie Ilderton.

Stourbridge (0) 0
Eastleigh (0) 2 *(Constable 59, Payne 77)* 2086
Stourbridge: (442) Solly; Green, Scarr, Pierpiont, Smickle; Dodd, Tonks, Broadhurst (Billingham 55), Lait (Wright 82); Hawley, Richards.
Eastleigh: (442) Flitney; Partington, Reid, Evans, Green; Strevens, Payne, Drury, Reason; Constable, Midson.
Referee: Ben Toner.

Yeovil T (0) 1 *(Tozer 86)*
Stevenage (0) 0 2264
Yeovil T: (442) Weale; Roberts, Sokolik, Ward, Smith; Cornick, Dolan, Sheehan (Tozer 74), Dickson; Bird (Zoko 71), Jeffers.
Stevenage: (442) Day; Henry, Franks (McCombe 38), Wells, Ogilvie; Whelpdale, Cox, Tonge, Gnanduillet (Marriott 87); Pett, Kennedy (Lee 87).
Referee: Christopher Sarginson.

Sunday, 6 December 2015

Bradford C (2) 4 *(Reid 22, Hanson 43, Liddle 90, Cole 90)*
Chesham U (0) 0 6047
Bradford C: (451) Williams; Darby, McArdle, Burke, Leigh; Knott (Liddle 88), Evans, McMahon, Reid (Marshall 77), Clarke B (Cole 76); Hanson.
Chesham U: (442) Gore; Smtih, Fenton, Beasant, Ujah; Little (Pearce 62), Taylor, Youngs, Wilson (Hamilton-Forbes 71); Wadkins (Hayles 66), Blake.
Referee: Scott Duncan.

Cambridge U (1) 1 *(Berry 23)*
Doncaster R (0) 3 *(Grant 46, 57, Lund 56)* 3951
Cambridge U: (4231) Beasant; Taylor, Roberts, Legge, Demetriou; Ledson (Hughes L 78), Newton; Donaldson (Simpson 69), Berry, Dunk; Corr.
Doncaster R: (532) Stuckmann; Lund, Alcock, Butler, Taylor-Sinclair, Evina; Coppinger (Keegan 67), Middleton, Grant; Tyson (Stewart 46), Williams.
Referee: Mark Brown.

Colchester U (1) 3 *(Harriott 14, 90, Lapslie 53)*
Altrincham (1) 2 *(Moult 3, Rankine 46)* 2592
Colchester U: (4231) Jones; Brindley (Olufemi 81),
Eastman, Elokobi, Briggs; Lapslie (Szmodics 69), Gilbey;
Massey (Porter 83), Moncur, Harriott; Sordell.
Altrincham: (442) Deasy; Sinnott, Leather, Heathcote,
Griffin; Lawrie, Richman, Moult, Crowther (Clee 66);
Rankine, Reeves (Bowerman 87).
Referee: Andy Davies.

Dagenham & R (1) 1 *(Cureton 5)*
Whitehawk (0) 1 *(Rose 90)* 1983
Dagenham & R: (451) Cousins; Passley, Nosworthy,
Dikamona, Connors; Vassell (Chambers 81), Labadie,
Boucaud, Dunne, Jones; Cureton (Doidge 90).
Whitehawk: (442) Ross; Arnold, Lorraine (Rose 74),
Leacock (Cruz Gotta 49), Braham-Barrett; Deering,
Mendy, Torres, Neilson (Martin 67); Robinson, Mills.
Referee: Lee Swabey.

Exeter C (1) 2 *(Tillson 19, Watkins 89)*
Port Vale (0) 0 3565
Exeter C: (442) Olejnik; Moore-Taylor, Brown, Tillson,
Woodman; Wheeler, Davies, Nicholls, Holmes (Watkins
84); Grant (Nichols 90), Reid (Oakley 88).
Port Vale: (4411) Alnwick; Purkiss, Streete (Hooper 78),
Duffy, McGivern; Birchall, O'Connor, Grant, Foley
(Kelly 61); Dodds (Ikpeazu 52); Leitch-Smith.
Referee: Trevor Kettle.

Oxford U (0) 1 *(Roofe 76)*
Forest Green R (0) 0 4618
Oxford U: (442) Buchel; Baldock, Dunkley, Mullins,
Skarz; Roofe, Sercombe, Rose (Lundstram 78),
O'Dowda; Hylton (Evans 77), Hoban.
Forest Green R: (4411) Arnold; Bennett (Pipe 41),
Racine, Clough, Jennings; Guthrie (Marsh-Brown 79),
Sinclair, Wedgbury, Frear; Carter (Williams 79); Parkin.
Referee: Rob Lewis.

Peterborough U (1) 2 *(Washington 35, Maddison 82)*
Luton T (0) 0 8329
Peterborough U: (442) Alnwick; Smith, Bostwick, Santos,
Elder; Forrester, Anderson J (Beautyman 5), Oztumer
(Fox 90), Taylor (Maddison 46); Washington, Angol.
Luton T: (433) Tyler; Lawless (Griffiths 78), Okuonghae,
Wilkinson, Long; Lee (McGeehan 62), Doyle, Smith;
McQuoid, Mackail-Smith, McCourt (Green 72).
Referee: Nigel Miller.

Rochdale (0) 0
Bury (1) 1 *(Rose 8)* 4887
Rochdale: (4231) Castro; Bennett (Rose 70), Lancashire,
McNulty, Tanser; Camps, McDermott (Cannon 56);
Andrew, Hooper, O'Sullivan (Vincenti 57); Henderson.
Bury: (442) Bachmann; Jones, Cameron, Clarke P,
Hussey; Dodoo (Eagles 64), Soares, Etuhu, Mayor (Pugh
26); Rose (Brown 74), Clarke L.
Referee: Darren Drysdale.

Welling (0) 0
Carlisle U (2) 5 *(Wyke 18, 71, 90, Sweeney 45,*
Grainger 67 (pen)) 2028
Welling U: (433) McEntegart; Williams, Osborne■,
Chambers, Jefford; Corne, Fagan (Lee 57), Wellard;
Porter, St Aimie (Harris 62), Bakare (Kabba 77).
Carlisle U: (442) Hanford; McQueen, Raynes, Ellis,
Grainger; Gilliead (Brough 72), Joyce, Kennedy,
Sweeney (Dicker 68); Ibehre (Asamoah 68), Wyke.
Referee: Simon Hooper.

Monday, 7 December 2015

Grimsby T (0) 0
Shrewsbury T (0) 0 3366
Grimsby T: (442) McKeown; Tait, Nsiala, Gowling,
Townsend; Arnold (Jones 86), Clay, Disley, Monkhouse;
Amond (Alabi 86), Pittman (Bogle 76).

Shrewsbury T: (442) Leutwiler (Halstead 45); Grandison,
Gerrard, Knight-Percival, Brown; Whalley, Ogogo,
Lawrence, KaiKai; Vernon (Akpa Akpro 80), Collins
(Barnett 80).
Referee: Seb Stockbridge.

SECOND ROUND REPLAYS

Tuesday, 15 December 2015

Hartlepool U (0) 2 *(Fenwick 97, Mandron 120)*
Salford City (0) 0 4374
Hartlepool U: (442) Carson; Magnay (Harrison S 85),
Bates, Jackson, Carroll; Oates, Featherstone, Gray
(Walker 66), Smith (Mandron 67); Bingham, Fenwick.
Salford City: (433) Lynch J; Lynch C, Dawson, Howson,
O'Halloran; Hardcastle (Mwasile 106), Stopforth,
Burton; Poole (Seddon 82), Webber (Allen 78), Hulme.
aet.
Referee: Jeremy Simpson.

Scunthorpe U (0) 3 *(Mvoto 55 (og), King 60, Adelakun 90)*
Leyton Orient (0) 0 3082
Scunthorpe U: (4231) Daniels; Wiseman, Goode,
Canavan, Laird; King, Bishop; Ness (McAllister 78),
Williams, Madden; Wootton (Adelakun 83).
Leyton Orient: (442) Cisak; Clohessy, Baudry, Mvoto,
Shaw; Pritchard, Payne, James (Turgott 63), McAnuff
(Adeboyejo 72); Palmer (Marquis 62), Simpson.
Referee: David Webb.

Shrewsbury T (0) 1 *(Ogogo 90)*
Grimsby T (0) 0 2730
Shrewsbury T: (442) Halstead; Grandison (Smith 36),
Whitbread (Knight-Percival 53), Gerrard, Brown;
Barnett (Black 77), Ogogo, Lawrence, KaiKai; Collins,
Vernon.
Grimsby T: (442) McKeown; Tait, Gowling, Nsiala,
Townsend; Arnold, Disley, Clay, Monkhouse; Pittman
(Bogle 22), Amond.
Referee: Dean Whitestone.

Walsall (0) 0
Chesterfield (0) 0 2953
Walsall: (352) Etheridge; Downing, O'Connor, Taylor;
Chambers, Demetriou, Evans, Mantom (Lalkovic 68),
Forde (Baxendale 106); Sawyers, Cook (Morris K 85).
Chesterfield: (442) Lee; O'Neil, Evatt, Raglan, Talbot;
O'Shea, Morsy, Banks (Donohue 103), Gardner (Ariyibi
46); Novak, Dieseruvwe (Ebanks-Blake 77).
aet; Walsall won 5-3 on penalties.
Referee: Charles Breakspear.

Wednesday, 16 December 2015

Whitehawk (0) 1 *(Mills 32, Cruz Gotta 90)*
Dagenham & R (1) 3 *(Vassell 44, Passley 77, Obileye 100)*
2174
Whitehawk: (442) Ross; Arnold, Lorraine (Rose 48),
Leacock (Cruz Gotta 44), Braham-Barrett; Deering,
Torres, Mendy, Martin (Neilson 56); Robinson, Mills.
Dagenham & R: (442) Cousins; Hoyte, Nosworthy,
Obileye, Widdowson; Passley (Chambers 84), Dunne■,
Labadie, Hemmings; Cureton (Doidge 88), Vassell
(Boucaud 118).
aet.
Referee: Keith Stroud.

THIRD ROUND

Friday, 8 January 2016

Exeter C (2) 2 *(Nichols 9, Holmes 45)*
Liverpool (1) 2 *(Sinclair 12, Smith 73)* 8298
Exeter C: (4132) Olejnik; Ribeiro (Davies 66), Brown,
Moore-Taylor, Woodman; Tillson; Nicholls, Noble
(Oakley 62), Holmes (Grant 84); Read, Nichols.
Liverpool: (442) Bogdan; Randall, Tiago Ilori (Maguire
77), Jose Enrique, Smith; Kent (Chirivella 57),
Brannagan, Stewart, Teixeira; Sinclair (Ojo 71), Benteke.
Referee: Stuart Attwell.

Saturday, 9 January 2016

Arsenal (1) 3 *(Campbell 25, Ramsey 72, Giroud 75)*
Sunderland (1) 1 *(Lens 17)* 59,349
Arsenal: (4231) Cech; Bellerin, Gabriel, Koscielny, Gibbs; Oxlade-Chamberlain, Chambers (Arteta 67); Campbell (Reine-Adelaide 81), Iwobi (Ramsey 67), Walcott; Giroud.
Sunderland: (4231) Pickford; Yedlin, Coates, O'Shea (Jones 65), Van Aanholt; Cattermole (M'Vila 57), Toivonen; Watmore, Lens, Graham; Fletcher (Mavrias 76).
Referee: Martin Atkinson.

Birmingham C (1) 1 *(Morrison 40)*
Bournemouth (1) 2 *(Tomlin 44 (pen), Murray 85)* 13,140
Birmingham C: (442) Legzdins; Eardley (Lowry 46), Morrison, Spector, Grounds; Cotterill (Maghoma 46), Davis, Kieftenbeld, Solomon-Otabor (Toral 68); Shinnie, Vaughan.
Bournemouth: (442) Federici; Lee (Cook 84), Cargill, Distin, Butcher; Pugh, MacDonald, O'Kane, Tomlin; Kermorgant (Murray 78), Rantie (Ritchie 39).
Referee: Mike Jones.

Brentford (0) 0
Walsall (1) 1 *(Mantom 34)* 7950
Brentford: (4231) Button; Yennaris, Dean, O'Connell, Bidwell; McEachran (Judge 46), McCormack (Kerschbaumer 60); Woods, Canos, Swift; Hofmann (Djuricin 70).
Walsall: (442) Etheridge; O'Connor, Downing, Evans, Henry (Taylor 75); Sawyers, Chambers, Mantom■, Kinsella; Lalkovic (Forde 76), Bradshaw (Morris K 86).
Referee: Andy Davies.

Bury (0) 0
Bradford C (0) 0 6962
Bury: (451) Lawlor; Riley (Pugh 64), Cameron, Brown, Hussey; Jones (Lowe 20 (Rose 79)), Tutte, Soares, Etuhu; Mayor; Clarke L.
Bradford C: (442) Williams; Darby, Routis, McArdle, Meredith; McMahon, Evans (Marshall 87), Liddle, Reid (Morris 83); Hanson, Clarke B (James 67).
Referee: Rob Lewis.

Colchester U (2) 2 *(Moncur 28, Sordell 41)*
Charlton Ath (0) 1 *(Ghoochannejhad 90)* 5742
Colchester U: (442) Kean; Brindley, Wynter, Eastman, Briggs; Massey, Moncur (Vincent-Young 87), Gilbey, Garvan (Edwards 73); Porter, Sordell (Bonne 82).
Charlton Ath: (4132) Pope; Charles, Sarr, Johnson (Vaz Te 61), Fox; Poyet, Moussa, Ceballos (Williams 46), Cousins (Vetokele 38); Makienok Christoffersen, Ghoochannejhad.
Referee: Chris Kavanagh.

Doncaster R (1) 1 *(Tyson 25)*
Stoke C (1) 2 *(Crouch 15, Walters 57)* 13,299
Doncaster R: (532) Stuckmann; Alcock, McCullough, Butler, Taylor-Sinclair (Main 76), Evina; Middleton (MacKenzie 89), Keegan (Chaplow 77), Grant; Tyson, Williams.
Stoke C: (4411) Haugaard; Bardsley (Johnson 61), Shawcross, Wollscheid, Wilson; Walters, van Ginkel, Adam (Sidwell 87), Diouf; Joselu; Crouch (Whelan 66).
Referee: Keith Stroud.

Eastleigh (0) 1 *(Dervite 51 (og))*
Bolton W (0) 1 *(Pratley 87)* 5250
Eastleigh: (4141) Flitney; Partington, Reid, Evans, Harding; Strevens; Odubade (Mohamed 35), Payne, Drury, Reason; Constable.
Bolton W: (4231) Amos; Holding, Dervite, Wheater, Moxey; Danns (Trotter 85), Vela (Ameobi 71); Feeney, Wellington Silva, Pratley; Madine (Woolery 85).
Referee: Iain Williamson.

Everton (1) 2 *(Kone 32, Mirallas 85 (pen))*
Dagenham & R (0) 0 30,918
Everton: (4231) Robles; Oviedo, Jagielka, Funes Mori (Pennington 45), Galloway; Gibson, Besic; Lennon (Rodriguez 89), Mirallas, Pienaar (Osman 77); Kone.
Dagenham & R: (352) Cousins; Passley, Worrall, Hemmings (Connors 75); Dikamona, Nosworthy, Raymond, Muldoon, Doidge (Cureton 66); Chambers (Jones 62), Labadie.
Referee: Paul Tierney.

Hartlepool U (0) 1 *(Gray 61)*
Derby Co (0) 2 *(Butterfield 67, Bent 85)* 4860
Hartlepool U: (433) Carson; Richards, Harrison S, Jackson, Carroll; Featherstone (Bingham 87), Woods, Gray (Walker 80); Hawkins, Oates, Fenwick.
Derby Co: (433) Mitchell; Baird, Pearce, Buxton, Warnock; Bryson (Butterfield 66), Hanson (Russell 46), Shotton; Camara, Bent, Blackman (Weimann 76).
Referee: Darren Bond.

Huddersfield T (0) 2 *(Paterson 57, Wells 90 (pen))*
Reading (0) 2 *(Vydra 71, Robson-Kanu 87)* 9236
Huddersfield T: (4231) Murphy; Smith (Dempsey 27), Hudson, Lynch, Davidson (Miller 89); Hogg, Paterson; Scannell (Husband 84), Lolley, Bunn; Wells.
Reading: (442) Al Habsi; Gunter, Ferdinand, Cooper, Taylor; McCleary, Norwood, Williams, Quinn (Piazon 68); Vydra, Robson-Kanu.
Referee: Jeremy Simpson.

Hull C (1) 1 *(Snodgrass 41 (pen))*
Brighton & HA (0) 0 10,706
Hull C: (442) Jakupovic; Odubajo, Davies, Maguire, Robertson; Taylor, Huddlestone, Hayden, Snodgrass; Diomande (Luer 51), Aluko (Clucas 85).
Brighton & HA: (3421) Maenpaa; Calderon (LuaLua 63), Chicksen, Ridgewell; Dunk, Goldson, Towell, Holla (Baldock 57); Ince, Manu (Hemed 76); Crofts.
Referee: Geoff Eltringham.

Ipswich T (0) 2 *(Oar 53, Fraser 88)*
Portsmouth (0) 2 *(Bennett 55, Chaplin 86)* 17,020
Ipswich T: (442) Bialkowski; Chambers, Malarczyk, Digby (Smith 63), Knudsen; Maitland-Niles (Fraser 58), Skuse, Hyam, Oar; Varney (Sears 74), Pitman.
Portsmouth: (4231) Murphy; Davies, Barton, Webster, Stevens; Hollands (Haunstrup 81), Close (May 74); Roberts (Chaplin 78), Ince, Manu (Bennett; McGurk.
Referee: David Coote.

Leeds U (1) 2 *(Carayol 45, Doukara 90)*
Rotherham U (0) 0 16,039
Leeds U: (442) Silvestri; Taylor, Bellusci (Bamba 79), Cooper, Coyle; Carayol (Dallas 74), Bridcutt, Murphy (Cook 88), Byram; Antenucci, Doukara.
Rotherham U: (541) Camp; Mattock, Broadfoot, Facey (Clarke-Harris 46), Belaid, Richardson; Ward G (Derbyshire 78), Newell, Smallwood, Green; Ward D (Ledesma 57).
Referee: Andy Woolmer.

Manchester U (0) 1 *(Rooney 90 (pen))*
Sheffield U (0) 0 74,284
Manchester U: (4231) De Gea; Darmian, Smalling, Blind, Borthwick-Jackson; Fellaini (Andreas Pereira 78), Schweinsteiger; Mata (Depay 60), Ander Herrera (Lingard 60), Martial; Rooney.
Sheffield U: (442) Long; Brayford, Edgar, Collins, McEveley (Reed 78); Coutts, Hammond, Basham, Woolford; Sammon (Done 90), Sharp (Flynn 64).
Referee: Andre Marriner.

Middlesbrough (1) 1 *(Fabbrini 36)*
Burnley (1) 2 *(Hennings 45, Ward 71)* 18,286
Middlesbrough: (4231) Mejias; Kalas, Amorebieta (Nsue 54), Ayala, Friend; Forshaw, Clayton; Adomah, De Pena (Stuani 76), Fabbrini (Garcia 76); Nugent.

Burnley: (4231) Heaton; Darikwa, Keane, Mee, Ward; Ulvestad, Jones (Barton 76); Boyd, Hennings, Kightly (Arfield 69); Vokes (Long 90).
Referee: Simon Hooper.

Northampton T (0) 2 *(Holmes 49, 58)*
Milton Keynes D (1) 2 *(Cresswell 13 (og), Maynard 82)*
                                                        5878
Northampton T: (4231) Smith; Moloney, McDonald, Cresswell, Buchanan; Byrom, O'Toole; Adams (Taylor 89), Hoskins (Hackett 77), Holmes (D'Ath 64); Richards.
Milton Keynes D: (4231) Cropper; Spence, McFadzean (Upson 61), Walsh, Hodson; Forster-Caskey, Reeves; Bowditch, Hall, Murphy (Maynard 61); Church (Carruthers 61).
Referee: Darren Drysdale.

Norwich C (0) 0
Manchester C (2) 3 *(Aguero 16, Iheanacho 31, De Bruyne 78)*   24,507
Norwich C: (541) Ruddy; Wisdom, Bennett R, Martin, Bassong (Lafferty 72), Olsson; Howson (Redmond 63), Mulumbu (O'Neil 64), Dorrans, Odjidja-Ofoe; Jerome.
Manchester C: (442) Caballero; Zabaleta, Otamendi, Demichelis, Kolarov; Jesus Navas, Fernando, Delph, Sterling (De Bruyne 61); Iheanacho (Celina 85), Aguero (Clichy 70).
Referee: Mike Dean.

Nottingham F (1) 1 *(Ward 24)*
QPR (0) 0   14,197
Nottingham F: (433) De Vries; Mancienne, Hobbs, Wilson, Cohen (Lichaj 71); Tesche, Gardner (Lansbury 62 (Jokic 79)), Osborn; Burke O, Blackstock, Ward.
QPR: (451) Lumley; Onuoha, Hall, Hill (Perch 67); Angella; Mackie (Petrasso 61), Doughty, Luongo, Tozser, Gladwin (Chery 52); Emmanuel-Thomas.
Referee: Oliver Langford.

Peterborough U (1) 2 *(Samuelsen 7, Washington 52)*
Preston NE (0) 0   7665
Peterborough U: (4132) Alnwick; Smith, Baldwin, Santos, Wilson; Forrester; Oztumer (Maddison 72), Beautyman, Samuelsen (Fox 90); Washington, Angol (Coulibaly 72).
Preston NE: (352) Kirkland; Clarke, Huntington, Cunningham; Vermijl, Brownhill (Robinson 56), Welsh (Gallagher 48), Browne, Reach; Doyle (Hugill 75), Garner.
Referee: Tony Harrington.

Sheffield W (1) 2 *(Bannan 42, Nuhiu 73)*
Fulham (1) 1 *(Dembele 43)*   15,244
Sheffield W: (442) Wildsmith; Palmer, Loovens, Sougou (Nuhiu 59), Pudil; Lopez (Helan 46), Lee, Sasso, Bannan; Lucas Joao, Wallace (Semedo 77).
Fulham: (442) Lonergan; Richards, Hutchinson, Burn, Garbutt (Ream 71); Cairney, Christensen, O'Hara, Kacaniklic (Mattila 71); Woodrow (Dembele 25), McCormack.
Referee: Gavin Ward.

Southampton (0) 1 *(Romeu 51)*
Crystal Palace (1) 2 *(Ward 29, Zaha 68)*   30,763
Southampton: (3421) Stekelenburg; Fonte, van Dijk, Yoshida (Juanmi 46); Martina, Romeu, Clasie (Ward-Prowse 76), Targett; Davis S (Tadic 46), Mane; Long.
Crystal Palace: (442) Hennessey; Ward, Dann, Delaney, Souare; Zaha, Cabaye (Jedinak 83), Ledley, Puncheon; Campbell (Chamakh 76), Mutch (Sako 57).
Referee: Lee Mason.

Watford (1) 1 *(Deeney 44)*
Newcastle U (0) 0   18,259
Watford: (442) Gomes; Nyom, Prodl, Cathcart, Holebas; Jurado (Ighalo 73), Guedioura, Watson, Berghuis (Abdi 63); Deeney, Oulare (Anya 46).
Newcastle U: (352) Elliot; Mbemba, Coloccini (Lascelles 46), Dummett; Janmaat, Sissoko, Tiote (De Jong 82), Wijnaldum, Mbabu (Thauvin 52); Perez, Mitrovic.
Referee: Roger East.

WBA (0) 2 *(Berahino 67, Morrison 90)*
Bristol C (0) 2 *(Kodjia 74, Agard 83)*   24,917
WBA: (4321) Foster; Chester (Dawson 63), McAuley, Evans, Brunt; Morrison, Fletcher, McClean (McManaman 63); Sessegnon, Rondon; Lambert (Berahino 63).
Bristol C: (352) Fielding (O'Leary 46); Ayling, Flint, Baker; Little, Smith, Pack, Freeman, Bryan; Wilbraham (Burns 82), Kodjia (Agard 83).
Referee: Graham Scott.

West Ham U (0) 1 *(Jelavic 84)*
Wolverhampton W (0) 0   34,547
West Ham U: (4231) Randolph; Reid, Cresswell, Song, Zarate (Carroll 72); Jenkinson, Obiang; Noble (Payet 67), Collins, Jelavic (Oxford 87); Antonio.
Wolverhampton W: (4411) Ikeme; Doherty, Edwards, Batth, McDonald; Coady, van La Parra (Henry 81), Iorfa, Sigurdarson (Le Fondre 57); Ebanks-Landell; Zyro (Graham 81).
Referee: Anthony Taylor.

Wycombe W (0) 1 *(Jacobson 50 (pen))*
Aston Villa (1) 1 *(Richards 22)*   9298
Wycombe W: (442) Lynch; McCarthy, Stewart, Pierre, Jacobson; Harriman, Bloomfield (McGinn 82), O'Nien, Wood; Thompson, Amadi-Holloway (Ugwu 70).
Aston Villa: (4411) Bunn; Richards (Lyden 83), Okore, Clark, Richardson; Bacuna, Gana, Westwood, Sinclair (Ayew 71); Gil (Veretout 71); Gestede.
Referee: Michael Oliver.

Sunday, 10 January 2016

Cardiff C (0) 0
Shrewsbury T (0) 1 *(Mangan 62)*   4782
Cardiff C: (442) Moore; Da Silva (Noone 74), Ecuele Manga, Tamas, Malone; Ameobi, Dikgacoi (Kennedy 63), O'Keefe, Whittingham; Revell (Mason 79), Macheda.
Shrewsbury T: (352) Halstead; Gerrard, Whitbread, Knight-Percival; Grimmer, Clark, Black, Cole, Sadler; Vernon (Grandison 83), Mangan (Akpa Akpro 83).
Referee: Peter Bankes.

Carlisle U (1) 2 *(Grainger 25, Ellis 76)*
Yeovil T (0) 2 *(Zoko 71, Jeffers 90)*   3357
Carlisle U: (442) Hanford; Atkinson, Raynes, Ellis, Gillesphey; Gilliead (Hope 83), Dicker, Joyce, Grainger; Ibehre (Asamoah 90), Wyke (Hery 77).
Yeovil T: (433) Krysiak; Roberts, Ward, Sokolik, Dickson; Walsh (Bird 86), Tozer, Dolan; Compton (Allen 70), Zoko, Campbell (Jeffers 58).
Referee: Andrew Madley.

Chelsea (1) 2 *(Costa 13, Loftus-Cheek 68)*
Scunthorpe U (0) 0   41,625
Chelsea: (4231) Begovic; Ivanovic, Zouma, Cahill, Azpilicueta; Fabregas, Ramires; Willian, Oscar (Loftus-Cheek 46), Pedro (Kenedy 72); Costa (Traore 86).
Scunthorpe U: (451) Daniels; Clarke, Mirfin, Wallace, Laird; Madden, Dawson (King 79), Ness, Bishop, van Veen (Wootton 81); Williams (Adelakun 79).
Referee: Craig Pawson.

Oxford U (1) 3 *(Sercombe 45 (pen), Roofe 49, 59)*
Swansea C (1) 2 *(Montero 23, Gomis 66)*   11,673
Oxford U: (442) Slocombe; Baldock, Mullins, Wright, Skarz; MacDonald (O'Dowda 71), Sercombe, Lundstram, Maguire; Taylor (Hylton 80), Roofe (Hoban 90).
Swansea C: (4231) Nordfeldt; Shephard, Bartley, Amat, Tabanou (Kingsley 60); Cork, Grimes (Barrow 76); Emnes, Shelvey, Montero; Gomis.
Referee: Kevin Friend.

Tottenham H (1) 2 *(Eriksen 8, Kane 89 (pen))*
Leicester C (1) 2 *(Wasilewski 19, Okazaki 48)*					35,805
Tottenham H: (4231) Vorm; Trippier, Alderweireld, Wimmer, Rose; Dier (Bentaleb 68), Carroll (Kane 68); Chadli (Alli 73), Eriksen, Onomah; Son.
Leicester C: (451) Schmeichel; De Laet, Wasilewski, Benalouane, Chilwell; Dyer, Inler, King, Kante (Okazaki 46), Gray (Albrighton 65); Ulloa.
Referee: Robert Madley.

Monday, 18 January 2016
Newport Co (1) 1 *(Byrne 30)*
Blackburn R (1) 2 *(Marshall 8 (pen), Rhodes 75)*					5083
Newport Co: (532) Day■; Holmes, Donacien, Hughes, Davies, Barrow (Green 90); Dymond (Taylor 83), Byrne, Elito (Owen-Evans 14); Boden, Collins.
Blackburn R: (442) Steele; Marshall, Evans (Henley 90), Hanley, Spurr; Bennett (Rhodes 46), Taylor, Lenihan, Lawrence (Conway 77); Brown■, Akpan.
Referee: Charles Breakspear.

THIRD ROUND REPLAYS

Tuesday, 19 January 2016
Aston Villa (0) 2 *(Clark 75, Gana 90)*
Wycombe W (0) 0					20,706
Aston Villa: (442) Guzan; Grealish (Gil 73), Richards, Clark, Richardson; Sanchez (Gana 46), Westwood, Sinclair, Lyden; Ayew, Gestede.
Wycombe W: (442) Ingram; Jacobson, Thompson (Ugwu 80), Hayes (Amadi-Holloway 73), Stewart; Bloomfield (McGinn 54), Pierre, Wood, McCarthy; O'Nien, Harriman.
Referee: Craig Pawson.

Bolton W (2) 3 *(Madine 39, Moxey 43, Pratley 58)*
Eastleigh (2) 2 *(Partington 11, Mohamed 45)*					8287
Bolton W: (442) Rachubka; Vela, Holding, Dervite, Moxey; Feeney, Pratley, Trotter, Davies; Madine (Ameobi 52), Wellington Silva (Woolery 86).
Eastleigh: (4141) Flitney; Partington, Reid, Evans, Harding; Strevens (Midson 75); Mohamed (Lafayette 86), Payne, Drury, Reason (Cook 79); Constable.
Referee: Mark Clattenburg.

Bradford C (0) 0
Bury (0) 0					6227
Bradford C: (442) Williams; Darby, Clarke N, McArdle, Meredith; McMahon, Evans, Routis (Clarke B 66), Marshall (Davies 85); James (Morris 66), Cole.
Bury: (442) Lawlor; Soares, Cameron■, Brown, Hussey; Tutte, Etuhu (Mellis 120), Pugh, Mayor (Lowe 115); Pope (Clarke P 42), Clarke L.
aet; Bury won 4-2 on penalties.
Referee: Geoff Eltringham.

Bristol C (0) 0
WBA (0) 1 *(Rondon 52)*					15,185
Bristol C: (433) O'Leary; Little (Ayling 78), Flint, Baker, Williams; Reid, Pack, Freeman (Kodjia 66); Burns, Wilbraham, Wagstaff (Agard 85).
WBA: (442) Foster; Dawson, McAuley, Evans, Brunt (Pocognoli 17); Sessegnon, Gardner, Yacob, McClean; Rondon (Chester 87), Anichebe (Lambert 90).
Referee: Jon Moss.

Milton Keynes D (0) 3 *(Reeves 53 (pen), Murphy 61, Church 89 (pen))*
Northampton T (0) 0					15,133
Milton Keynes D: (4231) Martin; Hodson, Upson (Walsh 38), Kay, Lewington; Carruthers, Forster-Caskey; Hall, Reeves (Powell 74), Bowditch (Murphy 54); Church.
Northampton T: (4231) Smith; Moloney, Diamond (Cresswell 88), McDonald, Buchanan; Byrom, O'Toole; Holmes, Hoskins, Adams; Richards.
Referee: Tony Harrington.

Portsmouth (2) 2 *(Roberts 32 (pen), McNulty 37)*
Ipswich T (0) 1 *(Maitland-Niles 60)*					15,179
Portsmouth: (4231) Murphy; Davies, Burgess (Close 85), Webster, Stevens; Doyle, Barton; Evans, Roberts (Chaplin 81), Bennett; McNulty.
Ipswich T: (442) Bialkowski; Emmanuel, Malarczyk■, Digby, Kenlock; Maitland-Niles (Robinson 89), Hyam, Tabb (Coke 71), Oar; Varney (Toure 76), Pitman.
Referee: Andy Woolmer.

Reading (1) 5 *(Piazon 29, Vydra 57, 61, 90, Alex 90)*
Huddersfield T (2) 2 *(Paterson 8, Smith 15)*					8119
Reading: (442) Al Habsi; Gunter, Ferdinand, Cooper, Taylor; McCleary (John 43), Norwood, Piazon (Alex 79), Williams; Vydra (Orlando Sa 90), Robson-Kanu.
Huddersfield T: (442) Murphy; Smith, Hudson, Lynch, Davidson; Huws, Dempsey (Miller 77), Hogg■, Paterson; Wells, Lolley (Whitehead 28 (Cranie 76)).
Referee: Oliver Langford.

Yeovil T (1) 1 *(Compton 31)*
Carlisle U (0) 1 *(Sweeney 77)*					4114
Yeovil T: (433) Krysiak; Roberts, Sokolik, Lacey■, Dickson; Tozer, Dolan, Walsh (Smith 100); Jeffers, Zoko, Compton (Dawson 87).
Carlisle U: (442) Gillespie; Atkinson, Ellis, Raynes, Grainger (Gillesphey 46); Gilliead (Ibehre 46), Joyce■, Sweeney, Kennedy; Wyke, Hope (Asamoah 65).
aet; Carlisle U won 5-4 on penalties.
Referee: Tim Robinson.

Wednesday, 20 January 2016
Leicester C (0) 0
Tottenham H (1) 2 *(Son 39, Chadli 66)*					30,006
Leicester C: (433) Schmeichel; Simpson (Albrighton 63), Wasilewski, Benalouane, Chilwell; King, Inler, Drinkwater (Okazaki 46); Dyer (Vardy 74), Ulloa, Gray.
Tottenham H: (4231) Vorm; Walker, Dier, Wimmer, Davies; Carroll, Bentaleb; Lamela (Kane 60), Eriksen, Chadli (Onomah 73); Son (Alli 84).
Referee: Anthony Taylor.

Liverpool (1) 3 *(Allen 10, Ojo 74, Teixeira 82)*
Exeter C (0) 0					43,292
Liverpool: (433) Mignolet; Randall (Flanagan 51), Tiago Ilori, Jose Enrique, Smith; Brannagan, Stewart, Allen (Ojo 65); Ibe (Chirivella 79), Benteke, Teixeira.
Exeter C: (4141) Olejnik; Ribeiro, Brown, Moore-Taylor, Woodman; Butterfield (Hoskins 46), Nicholls, Oakley (Wheeler 64), Davies, Holmes; Morrison (Nichols 46).
Referee: Neil Swarbrick.

FOURTH ROUND

Friday, 29 January 2016
Derby Co (1) 1 *(Thorne 37)*
Manchester U (1) 3 *(Rooney 16, Blind 65, Mata 83)*	31,134
Derby Co: (4141) Carson; Christie, Keogh, Shackell, Warnock; Thorne (Russell 76); Ince, Butterfield, Johnson (Hendrick 76), Blackman (Camara 59); Martin.
Manchester U: (4231) De Gea; Varela, Smalling, Blind, Borthwick-Jackson; Schneiderlin (Carrick 74), Fellaini; Lingard, Mata (Ander Herrera 84), Martial; Rooney.
Referee: Anthony Taylor.

Saturday, 30 January 2016
Arsenal (1) 2 *(Chambers 19, Sanchez 53)*
Burnley (1) 1 *(Vokes 30)*					59,932
Arsenal: (4231) Ospina; Chambers, Gabriel, Koscielny, Gibbs; Coquelin (Arteta 71), El-Nenny; Oxlade-Chamberlain, Iwobi (Rosicky 71), Sanchez (Walcott 78); Giroud.
Burnley: (442) Heaton; Darikwa, Keane, Mee, Ward; Boyd (Kightly 80), Jones (Barton 67), Ulvestad, Arfield, Vokes (Hennings 75), Gray.
Referee: Roger East.

Aston Villa (0) 0

Manchester C (2) 4 *(Iheanacho 4, 24 (pen), 74,*
Sterling 76) 23,636
Aston Villa: (433) Guzan; Bacuna, Richards, Clark,
Cissokho; Veretout, Gana, Westwood (Okore 46); Gil
(Grealish 80), Ayew, Sinclair (Agbonlahor 65).
Manchester C: (433) Caballero; Zabaleta, Sagna, Otamendi
(Humphreys 88), Clichy (Tasende 81); Fernandinho (Celina
78), Fernando, Delph; Jesus Navas, Iheanacho, Sterling.
Referee: Mike Jones.

Bolton W (0) 1 *(Pratley 80)*

Leeds U (2) 2 *(Doukara 8, Diagouraga 39)* 17,336
Bolton W: (4231) Amos; Vela, Holding, Dervite, Moxey;
Trotter, Davies (Spearing 70); Feeney, Pratley,
Wellington Silva (Woolery 70); Madine.
Leeds U: (442) Silvestri; Taylor, Bamba (Coyle 89),
Bellusci, Wootton; Cook (Adeyemi 90), Bridcutt,
Diagouraga, Dallas; Antenucci (Carayol 86), Doukara.
Referee: Andre Marriner.

Bury (0) 1 *(Jones 86)*

Hull C (1) 3 *(Akpom 14, 57 (pen), 69)* 7064
Bury: (442) Lawlor; Soares, Cameron, Brown, Hussey;
Tutte (Jones 51), Etuhu (Riley 10), Pugh, Mayor; Rose
(Lowe 51), Pope.
Hull C: (442) Jakupovic; Taylor, Huddlestone, Bruce,
Dawson; Tymon, Aluko (Maguire 85), Meyler, Akpom;
Diomande (Clucas 68), Elmohamady.
Referee: Darren Bond.

Colchester U (0) 1 *(Davies 80 (og))*

Tottenham H (1) 4 *(Chadli 27, 78, Dier 64, Carroll 82)*
9920
Colchester U: (4231) Kean; Brindley, Wynter (Kent 6),
Eastman (Briggs 21), Vincent-Young; Gilbey, Garvan;
Massey, Moncur, Ambrose (Sordell 61); Porter.
Tottenham H: (4231) Vorm; Trippier, Dier, Wimmer,
Davies; Bentaleb, Carroll; Lamela (Dembele 56), Eriksen
(Onomah 76), Chadli; Kane (Son 67).
Referee: Michael Oliver.

Crystal Palace (1) 1 *(Zaha 19)*

Stoke C (0) 0 17,062
Crystal Palace: (433) Hennessey; Ward, Dann, Delaney,
Souare; Ledley (Jedinak 46), Puncheon, Cabaye (Mutch
46); Zaha, Campbell (Chamakh 81), Lee.
Stoke C: (442) Haugaard; Bardsley, Wollscheid, Wilson,
Pieters; Ireland, van Ginkel, Krkic (Crouch 75), Shaqiri;
Joselu, Odemwingie (Diouf 75).
Referee: Mark Clattenburg.

Liverpool (0) 0

West Ham U (0) 0 44,006
Liverpool: (433) Mignolet; Clyne, Caulker, Lovren,
Smith; Brannagan (Sinclair 86), Stewart, Allen; Ibe (Ojo
80), Benteke, Teixeira (Jose Enrique 90).
West Ham U: (433) Randolph; Tomkins (O'Brien 35),
Reid, Ogbonna, Cresswell; Kouyate (Jelavic 37), Song,
Obiang; Moses (Antonio 70), Valencia, Payet.
Referee: Martin Atkinson.

Nottingham F (0) 0

Watford (0) 1 *(Ighalo 89)* 24,703
Nottingham F: (4141) De Vries; Lichaj, Hobbs, Wilson,
Cohen; Vaughan; Burke O, Gardner, Grant (Oliveira
83), Ward (Osborn 68); Blackstock.
Watford: (4411) Pantilimon; Nyom, Prodl, Cathcart, Ake;
Anya (Jurado 72), Watson, Guedioura, Abdi; Deeney
(Ighalo 72); Amrabat (Paredes 86).
Referee: Neil Swarbrick.

Oxford U (0) 0

Blackburn R (2) 3 *(Marshall 36 (pen), 76, Watt 45)* 11,647
Oxford U: (442) Slocombe; Baldock (Kenny 86), Mullins,
Wright, Skarz (Evans 77); MacDonald, Sercombe,
Lundstram, O'Dowda; Roofe, Bowery (Hylton 62).
Blackburn R: (442) Steele; Marshall, Hanley, Ward,
Spurr; Bennett, Lenihan (Taylor 71), Evans, Conway;
Jackson, Watt (Lawrence 61).
Referee: Andy Davies.

Portsmouth (1) 1 *(Roberts 43)*

Bournemouth (0) 2 *(King 71, Pugh 83)* 18,901
Portsmouth: (4231) Fulton; Davies, Burgess (Webster
62), Clarke, Stevens; Close, Doyle; McGurk (Tollitt 77),
Roberts (Evans 62), Bennett; McNulty.
Bournemouth: (442) Federici; Smith, Elphick (Francis
76), Distin, Cargill; Iturbe (Pugh 62), O'Kane,
MacDonald, King; Murray (Ritchie 62), Grabban.
Referee: Mike Dean.

Reading (2) 4 *(Robson-Kanu 37, Vydra 40, 89, Williams 75)*

Walsall (0) 0 13,367
Reading: (433) Al Habsi; Gunter, Cooper, Ferdinand
(McShane 68), Obita; Norwood, Tshibola (Hector 10),
Williams; Quinn (John 79), Robson-Kanu, Vydra.
Walsall: (3511) Etheridge (MacGillivray 78); Taylor,
O'Connor, Downing; Demetriou, Chambers (Cook 64),
Mantom, Forde, Henry; Sawyers; Bradshaw.
Referee: Peter Bankes.

Shrewsbury T (0) 3 *(Akpa Akpro 56, Whalley 87,*
Grimmer 90)

Sheffield W (1) 2 *(McGugan 19, 76)* 5699
Shrewsbury T: (352) Leutwiler; Smith (Wallace 78),
Whitbread, Knight-Percival; Grimmer, Cole, Black
(Whalley 79), Clark, Brown; Akpa Akpro (Vernon 90),
Mangan.
Sheffield W: (442) Price; Palmer, Turner, Sasso, Bennett;
Sougou (Wallace 71), Semedo, McGugan, Marco Matias
(Lee 78); Hooper (Nuhiu 61), Lucas Joao.
Referee: Paul Tierney.

WBA (1) 2 *(Berahino 14, 84)*

Peterborough U (0) 2 *(Coulthirst 79, Taylor 86)* 22,517
WBA: (442) Myhill; Dawson, McAuley, Evans,
Pocognoli; Sessegnon (Anichebe 67), Yacob, Gardner,
McClean; Lambert (Rondon 63), Berahino.
Peterborough U: (41212) Alnwick; Smith, Bostwick,
Santos, Wilson (Samuelsen 46); Baldwin; Beautyman
(Taylor 46), Forrester; Oztumer (Maddison 61); Angol,
Coulthirst.
Referee: Kevin Friend.

Sunday, 31 January 2016

Carlisle U (0) 0

Everton (2) 3 *(Kone 2, Lennon 14, Barkley 65)* 17,101
Carlisle U: (3421) Gillespie; Atkinson, Raynes, Ellis;
Miller, Comley (Ibehre 63), Dicker (Gilliead 46),
Gillesphey (Hope 46); Sweeney, Kennedy; Asamoah.
Everton: (4231) Robles; Coleman (Galloway 83),
Jagielka, Funes Mori, Oviedo; Cleverley, McCarthy;
Lennon, Barkley (Gibson 75), Pienaar (Osman 62);
Kone.
Referee: Lee Mason.

Milton Keynes D (1) 1 *(Potter 21)*

Chelsea (3) 5 *(Oscar,15, 32, 44, Hazard 55 (pen),*
Traore 62) 28,127
Milton Keynes D: (4231) Martin; Spence, McFadzean,
Walsh, Lewington; Potter, Forster-Caskey; Hall,
Carruthers (Powell 82), Murphy (Williams 67); Bowditch
(Maynard 76).
Chelsea: (4231) Courtois; Ivanovic, Cahill, Terry, Baba;
Matic, Fabregas; Oscar (Willian 64), Loftus-Cheek,
Hazard (Pedro 64); Costa (Traore 57).
Referee: Jon Moss.

FOURTH ROUND REPLAYS

Tuesday, 9 February 2016

West Ham U (1) 2 *(Antonio 45, Ogbonna 120)*

Liverpool (0) 1 *(Coutinho 48)* 34,433
West Ham U: (433) Randolph; O'Brien (Moses 83), Reid
(Collins 65), Ogbonna, Cresswell; Kouyate (Carroll 75),
Obiang, Noble; Antonio, Valencia, Payet.
Liverpool: (433) Mignolet; Flanagan, Tiago Ilori, Lucas,
Smith; Chirivella (Milner 101), Stewart, Teixeira (Origi
59); Ibe, Benteke, Coutinho (Sturridge 59).
aet.
Referee: Roger East.

Wednesday, 10 February 2016

Peterborough U (0) 1 *(Taylor 55)*

WBA (0) 1 *(Fletcher 71)*   10,632

Peterborough U: (41212) Alnwick; Baldwin, Bostwick, Zakuani, Fox; Forrester, Samuelsen, Taylor (Oztumer 106); Beautyman (Maddison 99); Coulthirst (Coulibaly 89), Angol.
WBA: (352) Foster; McAuley (Pocognoli 19), Olsson, Chester; Gamboa, Fletcher, Yacob (Sessegnon 62), Gardner, McClean; Rondon, Berahino.
aet; WBA won 4-3 on penalties.
Referee: Mike Jones.

FIFTH ROUND

Saturday, 20 February 2016

Arsenal (0) 0

Hull C (0) 0   59,830

Arsenal: (4231) Ospina; Chambers, Mertesacker, Koscielny, Gibbs; Flamini, El-Nenny; Campbell (Giroud 67), Iwobi (Oxlade-Chamberlain 73), Welbeck (Sanchez 67); Walcott.
Hull C: (3511) Jakupovic; Maguire, Bruce, Davies; Elmohamady, Maloney, Taylor (Huddleston 55), Meyler, Tymon (Odubajo 55); Powell (Aluko 78); Diomande.
Referee: Mike Dean.

Bournemouth (0) 0

Everton (0) 2 *(Barkley 55, Lukaku 76)*   11,404

Bournemouth: (4141) Federici; Francis, Elphick, Distin, Daniels; O'Kane, Iturbe (Murray 71), Gosling (Smith 77), MacDonald (Ritchie 63), Stanislas; King.
Everton: (4231) Robles; Coleman, Jagielka, Funes Mori, Oviedo; McCarthy, Barry; Lennon, Barkley (Mirallas 81), Cleverley; Lukaku (Niasse 81).
Referee: Martin Atkinson.

Reading (0) 3 *(McShane 59, Hector 72, Piazon 90)*

WBA (0) 1 *(Fletcher 54)*   19,566

Reading: (442) Al Habsi; Gunter, McShane, Cooper, Obita; Robson-Kanu, Norwood, Hector, Quinn (Piazon 90); Rakels (John 59), Cox (Vydra 59).
WBA: (442) Foster; Chester, Evans, Olsson, Brunt; Sessegnon, Fletcher, Sandro (Pritchard 82), McClean (Anichebe 75); Berahino, Rondon.
Referee: Anthony Taylor.

Watford (0) 1 *(Wootton 53 (og))*

Leeds U (0) 0   18,336

Watford: (433) Pantilimon; Paredes, Cathcart, Britos, Holebas; Capoue (Anya 90), Mario Suarez, Watson; Abdi (Guedioura 77), Deeney, Amrabat (Ighalo 67).
Leeds U: (442) Silvestri; Wootton, Bamba, Bellusci, Taylor; Dallas (Mowatt 61), Diagouraga (Botaka 86), Bridcutt, Cook; Antenucci (Erwin 83), Doukara.
Referee: Michael Oliver.

Sunday, 21 February 2016

Blackburn R (1) 1 *(Marshall 20)*

West Ham U (2) 5 *(Moses 26, Payet 36, 90, Emenike 64, 85)*   18,793

Blackburn R: (4231) Steele; Marshall, Duffy, Ward, Henley; Akpan, Lenihan; Taylor[■], Bennett, Conway (Jackson 59); Brown (Watt 78).
West Ham U: (433) Randolph; Antonio, Collins, Ogbonna (Oxford 78), Cresswell; Noble (Song 73), Kouyate[■], Obiang (Lanzini 67); Moses, Emenike, Payet.
Referee: Jon Moss.

Chelsea (1) 5 *(Costa 35, Willian 48, Cahill 53, Hazard 67, Traore 89)*

Manchester C (1) 1 *(Faupala 37)*   41,594

Chelsea: (4231) Courtois; Azpilicueta, Cahill, Ivanovic, Baba; Fabregas, Mikel (Matic 82); Pedro (Oscar 70), Willian, Hazard; Costa (Traore 70).
Manchester C: (442) Caballero; Zabaleta, Adarabioyo, Demichelis, Kolarov; Garcia M, Garcia A, Fernando (Humphreys 78), Celina (Barker 53); Iheanacho, Faupala.
Referee: Andre Marriner.

Tottenham H (0) 0

Crystal Palace (1) 1 *(Kelly 45)*   35,547

Tottenham H: (4231) Vorm; Walker, Dier, Wimmer, Rose; Bentaleb, Dembele (Eriksen 46); Son (Chadli 67), Alli (Mason 80), Onomah; Kane.
Crystal Palace: (442) Hennessey; Kelly, Dann, Delaney, Ward; Zaha, Cabaye (Jedinak 81), Ledley, Mutch; Adebayor (Bolasie 76), Wickham.
Referee: Craig Pawson.

Monday, 22 February 2016

Shrewsbury T (0) 0

Manchester U (2) 3 *(Smalling 37, Mata 45, Lingard 61)*   9370

Shrewsbury T: (352) Leutwiler; Grandison, Whitbread, Knight-Percival (Cole 46); Grimmer, Whalley, Ogogo, Black, Brown; Mangan, Akpa Akpro (Clark 81).
Manchester U: (4231) Romero; Varela, Smalling, Blind, Borthwick-Jackson (Riley 46); Ander Herrera, Schneiderlin; Lingard, Mata (Andreas Pereira 65), Depay; Martial (Keane 71).
Referee: Robert Madley.

FIFTH ROUND REPLAY

Tuesday, 8 March 2016

Hull C (0) 0

Arsenal (1) 4 *(Giroud 41, 71, Walcott 77, 88)*   20,993

Hull C: (3511) Jakupovic; Maguire, Bruce, Davies; Elmohamady, Diame, Huddlestone, Meyler (Aluko 58), Odubajo (Robertson 81); Powell; Diomande (Taylor 88).
Arsenal: (4231) Ospina; Chambers, Mertesacker (Monreal 33), Gabriel (Ramsey 57 (Reine-Adelaide 73)), Gibbs; El-Nenny, Flamini; Campbell, Iwobi, Walcott; Giroud.
Referee: Kevin Friend.

SIXTH ROUND

Friday, 11 March 2016

Reading (0) 0

Crystal Palace (0) 2 *(Cabaye 86 (pen), Campbell 90)*   23,110

Reading: (4141) Al Habsi; Gunter, McShane, Cooper[■], Obita (Rakels 90); Hector; Robson-Kanu, Norwood (Williams 75), Quinn, John; Cox (Vydra 60).
Crystal Palace: (442) Hennessey; Ward, Dann, Delaney, Souare; Zaha, Cabaye, Jedinak, Ledley (Sako 79); Bolasie (Campbell 90), Adebayor.
Referee: Mike Dean.

Saturday, 12 March 2016

Everton (0) 2 *(Lukaku 77, 82)*

Chelsea (0) 0   37,283

Everton: (4231) Robles; Coleman, Jagielka, Funes Mori, Baines; McCarthy, Barry[■]; Lennon (Stones 88), Barkley (Besic 90), Cleverley; Lukaku (Niasse 90).
Chelsea: (4231) Courtois; Azpilicueta, Cahill, Ivanovic, Kenedy (Terry 85); Mikel, Matic (Remy 82); Willian (Oscar 73), Fabregas, Pedro; Costa[■].
Referee: Michael Oliver.

Sunday, 13 March 2016

Arsenal (0) 1 *(Welbeck 88)*

Watford (0) 2 *(Ighalo 50, Guedioura 63)*   58,436

Arsenal: (4231) Ospina; Chambers, Mertesacker, Gabriel, Gibbs; El-Nenny (Iwobi 67), Coquelin; Campbell (Welbeck 68), Ozil, Sanchez; Giroud (Walcott 68).
Watford: (433) Pantilimon; Nyom, Prodl, Cathcart, Ake; Behrami, Watson, Capoue (Anya 73); Guedioura (Abdi 77), Ighalo (Amrabat 82), Deeney.
Referee: Andre Marriner.

Manchester U (0) 1 *(Martial 83)*

West Ham U (0) 1 *(Payet 68)* 74,928

Manchester U: (4141) De Gea; Varela (Darmian 87), Smalling, Blind, Rojo; Carrick; Lingard, Ander Herrera, Fellaini (Schweinsteiger 76), Martial; Rashford (Depay 76).
West Ham U: (433) Randolph; Antonio, Reid (Obiang 62), Ogbonna, Cresswell; Noble, Kouyate, Lanzini; Emenike (Sakho 64), Carroll (Valencia 82), Payet.
Referee: Martin Atkinson.

SIXTH ROUND REPLAY

Wednesday, 13 April 2016

West Ham U (0) 1 *(Tomkins 79)*

Manchester U (0) 2 *(Rashford 54, Fellaini 67)* 33,505

West Ham U: (4231) Randolph; Antonio, Tomkins, Ogbonna, Cresswell; Kouyate, Noble, Valencia 62), Lanzini (Emenike 74), Payet; Carroll.
Manchester U: (4141) De Gea; Fosu-Mensah, Smalling, Blind, Rojo (Valencia 68); Carrick; Lingard, Fellaini, Ander Herrera (Schneiderlin 76), Martial; Rashford (Rooney 90).
Referee: Roger East.

SEMI-FINALS (at Wembley)

Saturday, 23 April 2016

Everton (0) 1 *(Smalling 75 (og))*

Manchester U (1) 2 *(Fellaini 34, Martial 90)* 86,064

Everton: (4231) Robles; Besic, Stones, Jagielka, Baines; McCarthy, Gibson (Mirallas 90); Lennon (Deulofeu 70), Barkley, Cleverley; Lukaku.
Manchester U: (4141) De Gea; Fosu-Mensah (Valencia 62), Smalling, Blind, Rojo; Carrick; Lingard, Fellaini (Ander Herrera 87), Rooney, Martial; Rashford.
Referee: Anthony Taylor.

Sunday, 24 April 2016

Crystal Palace (1) 2 *(Bolasie 6, Wickham 61)*

Watford (0) 1 *(Deeney 55)* 79,110

Crystal Palace: (4231) Hennessey; Ward, Dann, Delaney, Souare; Jedinak, Cabaye; Zaha, Bolasie (McArthur 74), Puncheon (Sako 81); Wickham (Adebayor 86).
Watford: (442) Pantilimon; Nyom (Anya 82), Cathcart, Britos, Ake; Abdi (Guedioura 55), Capoue (Mario Suarez 32), Watson, Jurado; Ighalo, Deeney.
Referee: Craig Pawson.

THE FA CUP FINAL 2016

Saturday, 21 May 2016

(at Wembley Stadium, attendance 88,619)

Crystal Palace (0) 1   Manchester U (0) 2

Crystal Palace: (4231) Hennessey; Ward, Dann (Mariappa 90), Delaney, Souare; Cabaye (Puncheon 72), Jedinak; Zaha, McArthur, Bolasie; Wickham (Gayle 86).
Scorer: Puncheon 78.

Manchester U: (4141) De Gea; Valencia, Smalling■, Blind, Rojo (Darmian 66); Carrick; Mata (Lingard 90), Fellaini, Rooney, Martial; Rashford (Young 72).
Scorers: Mata 81, Lingard 110.

aet.

Referee: Mark Clattenburg.

Manchester United's Wayne Rooney and Michael Carrick hold the FA Cup aloft.
(Mike Egerton/PA Wire)

606

VANARAMA NATIONAL LEAGUE 2015–16

(P) *Promoted into division at end of 2014–15 season.*   (R) *Relegated into division at end of 2014–15 season.*

			Home				Away				Total					
		P	W	D	L	F	A	W	D	L	F	A	W	D	L	F	A	GD	Pts
1	Cheltenham T (R)	46	17	5	1	49	13	13	6	4	38	17	30	11	5	87	30	57	101
2	Forest Green R	46	15	3	5	37	17	11	8	4	32	25	26	11	9	69	42	27	89
3	Braintree T	46	13	6	4	24	12	10	6	7	32	26	23	12	11	56	38	18	81
4	Grimsby T¶	46	13	6	4	44	17	9	8	6	38	28	22	14	10	82	45	37	80
5	Dover Ath	46	13	5	5	43	22	10	6	7	32	31	23	11	12	75	53	22	80
6	Tranmere R (R)	46	12	2	9	31	23	10	10	3	30	21	22	12	12	61	44	17	78
7	Eastleigh	46	13	5	5	32	23	8	7	8	32	30	21	12	13	64	53	11	75
8	Wrexham	46	13	4	6	48	27	7	5	11	23	29	20	9	17	71	56	15	69
9	Gateshead	46	9	4	10	33	39	10	6	7	26	31	19	10	17	59	70	–11	67
10	Macclesfield T	46	10	5	8	28	21	9	4	10	32	27	19	9	18	60	48	12	66
11	Barrow (P)	46	11	8	4	38	26	6	6	11	26	45	17	14	15	64	71	–7	65
12	Woking	46	9	7	7	36	29	8	3	12	35	39	17	10	19	71	68	3	61
13	Lincoln C	46	10	7	6	37	25	6	6	11	32	43	16	13	17	69	68	1	61
14	Bromley (P)	46	11	4	8	38	26	6	5	12	29	46	17	9	20	67	72	–5	60
15	Aldershot T	46	7	4	12	23	31	9	4	10	31	41	16	8	22	54	72	–18	56
16	Southport	46	6	7	10	34	44	8	6	9	18	21	14	13	19	52	65	–13	55
17	Chester FC	46	9	8	6	43	29	5	4	14	24	42	14	12	20	67	71	–4	54
18	Torquay U	46	7	5	11	26	33	6	7	10	28	43	13	12	21	54	76	–22	51
19	Boreham Wood (P)	46	5	7	11	18	24	7	7	9	26	25	12	14	20	44	49	–5	50
20	Guiseley (P)	46	8	7	8	33	38	3	9	11	14	32	11	16	19	47	70	–23	49
21	FC Halifax T	46	6	10	7	35	43	6	2	15	20	39	12	12	22	55	82	–27	48
22	Altrincham	46	8	9	6	34	30	2	5	16	14	43	10	14	22	48	73	–25	44
23	Kidderminster H	46	5	7	11	21	29	4	6	13	28	42	9	13	24	49	71	–22	40
24	Welling U	46	5	6	12	21	33	3	5	15	14	40	8	11	27	35	73	–38	35

¶*Grimsby T promoted via play-offs.*

VANARAMA NATIONAL LEAGUE PLAY-OFFS 2015–16

■ *Denotes player sent off.*

SEMI-FINALS FIRST LEG

Wednesday 4 May 2016

Dover Ath (0) 0

Forest Green R (1) 1 *(Williams 35)*   2071

Dover Ath: Walker; Magri, Kinnear, Orlu, Modeste, Miller, Deverdics, Parkinson, Payne, Thomas (Sterling 85), Essam.
Forest Green R: Arnold; Jennings (Pipe 68), Clough, Bennett, Marsh-Brown, Kelly (Williams 15), Frear, Racine, Guthrie, Sinclair (Parkin 90), Carter.
Referee: Adrian Holmes.

Thursday 5 May 2016

Grimsby T (0) 0

Braintree T (0) 1 *(Davis 53 (pen))*   5271

Grimsby T: McKeown; Tait, Gowling, Disley, Bogle (Hoban 69), Amond, Monkhouse, Arnold (East 79), Nsiala, Nolan, Monkhouse.
Braintree T: King; Habergham, Paine, Fry, Brundle, Davis, Akinola (Sparkes 83), Phillips, Long, Cheek (Marks 77), Woodyard.
Referee: John Brooks.

SEMI-FINALS SECOND LEG

Saturday 7 May 2016

Forest Green R (0) 1 *(Marsh-Brown 54)*

Dover Ath (0) 1 *(Miller 50)*   2755

Forest Green R: Arnold; Clough, Bennett, Marsh-Brown, Frear (Moore K 51), Racine, Guthrie, Sinclair, Carter (Kamdjo 88), Williams (Parkin 77), Jefford.

Dover Ath: Walker; Magri (Marsh 90), Kinnear, Raggett, Orlu, Modeste, Miller, Deverdics, Parkinson, Thomas, Payne.
Referee: Michel Salisbury.
Forest Green R won on 2-1 on aggregate.

Sunday 8 May 2016

Braintree T (0) 0

Grimsby T (0) 2 *(Amond 75 (pen), Bogle 110)*   3102

Braintree T: King; Long, Phillips■, Fry, Habergham, Brundle, Paine (Cardwell 86), Davis, Woodyard, Akinola (Sparkes 70), Cheek (Marks 68).
Grimsby T: McKeown; Tait, Robertson, Gowling, Disley, Bogle, Amond, Clay (Marshall 73), Pittman (Arnold 63), Nsiala (Pearson 114), Nolan.
Referee: Simon Bennett.
aet; Grimsby T won on 2-1 on aggregate.

FINAL

Wembley, Sunday 15 May 2016

Grimsby T (2) 3 *(Bogle 42, 44, Arnold 90))*

Forest Green R (0) 1 *(Marsh-Brown 60)*   17,198

Grimsby T: McKeown; Tait, Nsiala, Gowling, Robertson, Arnold (Pearson 90), Disley, Clay, Nolan, Bogle (Hoban 89), Amond (Pittman 80).
Forest Green R: Arnold; Bennett, Clough, Racine, Jefford (Jennings 71); Marsh-Brown, Pipe, Carter, Frear; Guthrie (Jeffrey 78), Williams (Parkin 46).
Referee: Robert Jones.

VANARAMA NATIONAL LEAGUE PROMOTED TEAMS ROLL CALL 2015–16

CHELTENHAM TOWN

Player	H	W	DOB
Barthram, Jack (D)	5 8	11 10	13/10/1993
Bowen, James (M)	5 11	12 02	4/2/1996
Cranston, Jordan (D)	5 11	13 01	11/11/1993
Dayton, James (M)	5 8	10 01	12/12/1988
Downes, Aaron (D)	6 1	12 13	15/5/1985
Hall, Asa (M)	6 1	11 00	29/11/1986
Hanks, Joe (M)	6 2	11 05	2/3/1995
Holman, Dan (F)	5 11	11 03	5/6/1990
Kitscha, Calum (G)	6 2	12 13	6/4/1993
McLennan, George (D)	5 9	10 06	10/12/1995
Morgan-Smith, Amari (F)	6 0	13 05	3/4/1986
Munns, Jack (M)	5 5	10 01	18/11/1993
Parslow, Daniel (D)	5 11	12 06	11/9/1985
Pell, Harry (M)	6 4	13 05	21/10/1991
Rowe, James (M)	5 11	10 03	21/10/1991
Storer, Kyle (M)	5 11	11 11	30/4/1987
Waters, Billy (M)	5 9	11 07	15/10/1994
Wright, Danny (F)	6 2	13 08	10/9/1984

GRIMSBY TOWN

Player	H	W	DOB
Amond, Padraig (F)	5 11	11 11	15/4/1988
Bogle, Omar (F)	6 2	13 07	26/7/1992
Clay, Craig (M)	5 11	11 07	5/5/1992
Disley, Craig (M)	5 11	11 00	24/8/1981
East, Danny (D)	5 10	11 03	26/12/1991
Henderson, Conor (M)	6 1	11 09	8/9/1991
Mackreth, Jack (M)	5 11	10 10	13/4/1992
Marshall, Marcus (M)	5 10	11 06	17/10/1989
McKeown, James (G)	6 1	14 00	24/7/1989
Monkhouse, Andy (M)	6 2	13 01	23/10/1980
Nolan, Jon (M)	5 11	11 05	22/4/1992
Nsiala, Aristote (D)	6 4	13 01	25/3/1992
Pearson, Shaun (D)	6 0	12 04	28/4/1989
Pittman, Jon-Paul (F)	5 9	11 00	24/10/1986
Robertson, Gregor (D)	6 0	12 08	19/1/1984
Straker, Anthony (D)	5 9	11 11	23/9/1988
Tait, Richard (D)	5 11	11 00	2/12/1989
Venney, Josh (M)	5 5	09 05	9/2/1997
Warrington, Andy (G)	6 3	12 13	10/6/1976

VANARAMA NATIONAL LEAGUE ATTENDANCES BY CLUB 2015–16

	Aggregate 2015–16	Average 2015–16	Highest Attendance 2015–16
Tranmere R	119,932	5,214	7,541 v Wrexham
Wrexham	106,177	4,616	6,706 v Tranmere R
Grimsby T	99,941	4,345	7,650 v Lincoln C
Cheltenham T	69,132	3,006	5,449 v Forest Green R
Lincoln C	59,657	2,594	5,848 v Grimsby T
Chester FC	50,573	2,199	3,741 v Wrexham
Eastleigh	45,326	1,971	3,292 v Barrow
Torquay U	42,477	1,847	2,874 v Barrow
Kidderminster H	41,497	1,804	3,459 v Grimsby T
Forest Green R	40,581	1,764	3,127 v Cheltenham T
Woking	37,522	1,631	3,708 v Aldershot T
Aldershot T	37,031	1,610	3,150 v Woking
Macclesfield T	36,746	1,598	3,037 v Tranmere R
FC Halifax T	35,553	1,546	3,131 v Grimsby T
Bromley	32,041	1,393	2,455 v Barrow
Barrow	30,709	1,335	2,285 v Dover Ath
Altrincham	28,281	1,230	2,460 v Tranmere R
Southport	26,065	1,133	2,827 v Tranmere R
Dover Ath	23,670	1,029	1,957 v Grimsby T
Gateshead	21,821	949	2,174 v Grimsby T
Guiseley	21,304	926	1,915 v Torquay U
Braintree T	17,786	773	1,803 v Altrincham
Welling U	15,684	682	1,337 v Grimsby T
Boreham Wood	12,509	544	1,293 v Grimsby T

VANARAMA NATIONAL LEAGUE LEADING GOALSCORERS 2015–16

Player	Club	League	FA Cup	FA Trophy	Play-Offs	Total
Padraig Amond	Grimsby T	30	4	2	1	37
Dan Holman	Cheltenham T	30	0	0	0	30
(Includes 14 league goals for Woking)						
Kristian Dennis	Macclesfield T	22	3	4	0	29
Ross Hannah	Chester FC	23	0	3	0	26
Andy Cook	Barrow	24	0	0	0	24
Daniel Wright	Cheltenham T	22	1	0	0	23
Matt Rhead	Lincoln C	20	3	0	0	23
Stefan Payne	Dover Ath	18	1	4	0	23
Ricky Miller	Dover Ath	20	0	0	1	21
James Norwood	Tranmere R	19	0	2	0	21
Moses Emmanuel	Bromley	20	0	0	0	20
Ryan Bowman	Gateshead	16	1	3	0	20
Jordan Burrow	FC Halifax T	14	0	4	0	18
John Goddard	Woking	17	0	0	0	17
Michael Cheek	Braintree T	15	2	0	0	17
James Constable	Eastleigh	15	1	1	0	17
Nicky Deverdics	Dover Ath	14	0	2	0	16
Connor Jennings	Wrexham	14	0	0	0	14
Jon Parkin	Forest Green R	14	0	0	0	14
Charlie Walker	Aldershot T	14	0	0	0	14

VANARAMA NATIONAL LEAGUE NORTH 2015–16

(P) *Promoted into division at end of 2014–15 season.* (R) *Relegated into division at end of 2014–15 season.*

		Home						Away					Total						
		P	W	D	L	F	A	W	D	L	F	A	W	D	L	F	A	GD	Pts
1	Solihull Moors	42	14	1	6	39	21	11	9	1	45	27	25	10	7	84	48	36	85
2	North Ferriby U¶	42	13	5	3	41	14	9	5	7	41	35	22	10	10	82	49	33	76
3	AFC Fylde	42	11	4	6	41	26	11	5	5	35	27	22	9	11	76	53	23	75
4	Harrogate T	42	11	6	4	42	21	10	3	8	31	25	21	9	12	73	46	27	72
5	Boston U	42	12	3	6	37	27	10	2	9	36	33	22	5	15	73	60	13	71
6	Nuneaton T* (R)	42	8	9	4	27	17	12	4	5	44	29	20	13	9	71	46	25	70
7	Tamworth	42	9	9	3	28	18	7	6	8	27	27	16	15	11	55	45	10	63
8	Chorley	42	11	5	5	36	21	7	4	10	28	34	18	9	15	64	55	9	63
9	Stockport Co	42	6	7	8	24	28	9	7	5	26	21	15	14	13	50	49	1	59
10	Alfreton T (R)	42	6	6	9	26	29	9	7	5	32	25	15	13	14	58	54	4	58
11	Curzon Ashton (P)	42	9	6	6	29	25	5	9	7	26	27	14	15	13	55	52	3	57
12	Stalybridge Celtic	42	7	7	7	35	38	7	4	10	27	37	14	11	17	62	75	−13	53
13	FC United of Manchester (P)	42	8	4	9	38	37	7	4	10	22	38	15	8	19	60	75	−15	53
14	Bradford PA	42	10	6	5	37	28	3	5	13	14	31	13	11	18	51	59	−8	50
15	Gloucester C	42	7	5	9	20	23	5	9	7	19	26	12	14	16	39	49	−10	50
16	Gainsborough Trinity	42	8	6	7	24	27	6	2	13	22	35	14	8	20	46	62	−16	50
17	Worcester C	42	7	7	7	34	27	5	5	11	21	34	12	12	18	55	61	−6	48
18	AFC Telford U (R)	42	9	4	8	28	27	4	4	13	19	33	13	8	21	47	60	−13	47
19	Brackley T	42	7	6	8	27	27	4	7	10	18	27	11	13	18	45	54	−9	46
20	Lowestoft T	42	8	6	7	28	27	4	4	13	20	42	12	10	20	48	69	−21	46
21	Hednesford T	42	5	6	10	26	38	3	8	10	24	39	8	14	20	50	77	−27	38
22	Corby T (P)	42	4	3	14	27	51	3	8	10	20	42	7	11	24	47	93	−46	32

¶*North Ferriby U promoted via play-offs.* **Nuneaton T deducted 3 points for fielding an ineligible player.*

VANARAMA NATIONAL LEAGUE NORTH PLAY-OFFS 2015–16

SEMI-FINALS FIRST LEG

Wednesday 4 May 2016

Boston U (1) 2 *(Roberts 23, Mills 90)*
North Ferriby U (0) 0   2592
Boston U: Spiess; Mills, McEvoy, Roberts, Brown, Piergianni (Burgess 77), Felix, Garner, Southwell, Hilliard, Rollins.
North Ferriby U: Nicklin; Middleton, Wilde, King, Palmer, Hone, Clarke, Fry, Denton, Hotte (Brooksby 51), Bateson.
Referee: Simon Barrow.

Harrogate T (0) 0
AFC Fylde (0) 1 *(Rowe 53)*   1694
Harrogate T: Crook; Turner, Swain, Thirlwell, Ellis, Shiels, Colbeck (Burrell 69), Kerry, Clayton (Knowles 69), Thewlis (Emmett 55), Daniels.
AFC Fylde: Urwin; Hughes C, Hannigan, Langley, Crainey, Barnes, Baker, Finley (Dixon 90), Hughes M (Lloyd 86), Hardy (Charles 73), Rowe.
Referee: Dave Richardson

SEMI-FINALS SECOND LEG

Sunday 8 May 2016

North Ferriby U (2) 3 *(King 11 (pen), Denton 16, Clarke 54)*
Boston U (0) 0   2027
North Ferriby U: Nicklin; Topliss, Hone, Palmer, Wilde, Brooksby (Emerton 87), Bolder (Fry 70), Clarke, King, Bateson, Denton.
Boston U: Spiess; Mills, Brown, Piergianni (Johnson 82), Garner, Roberts (Burgess 60), Hilliard, Felix (Jones 60), Southwell, Rollins.
Referee: Andrew Miller.
North Ferriby U won on 3-2 on aggregate.

AFC Fylde (1) 1 *(Finley 11)*
Harrogate T (1) 1 *(Knowles 15)*   1384
AFC Fylde: Urwin; Hughes C (Charles 35), Langley, Hannigan, Crainey, Barnes, Baker, Finley, Hughes M (Lloyd 74), Hardy (Dixon 50), Rowe.
Harrogate T: Crook; Platt, McWilliams, Burrell (Clayton 71), Ellis, Shiels, Colbeck, Kerry (Thirlwell 75), Emmett (Cadman 64), Knowles, Daniels.
Referee: Jonathan Hunt.
AFC Fylde won on 2-1 on aggregate.

FINAL

Saturday 14 May 2016

North Ferriby U (1) 2 *(Brooksby 45, Hone 95)*
AFC Fylde (1) 1 *(Finley 23)*   1829
North Ferriby U: Nicklin; Topliss (Middleton 105), Wilde, King, Palmer, Hone, Clarke, Bolder, Denton, Brooksby, Bateson (Fry 31 (Emerton 90)).
AFC Fylde: Unwin; Hughes C, Crainey, Langley, Hannigan, Barnes (Dixon 97), Hughes M (Lloyd 86), Finley, Rowe, Baker, Hardy (Charles 46).
Referee: Anthony Backhouse.
aet.

VANARAMA NATIONAL LEAGUE SOUTH 2015–16

(P) *Promoted into division at end of 2014–15 season.*   (R) *Relegated into division at end of 2014–15 season.*

		Home					Away					Total						
		P	W	D	L	F	A	W	D	L	F	A	W	D	L	F	A	GD	Pts
1	Sutton U	42	11	8	2	42	19	15	4	2	41	13	26	12	4	83	32	51	90
2	Ebbsfleet U	42	11	6	4	40	22	13	6	2	33	14	24	12	6	73	36	37	84
3	Maidstone U¶ (P)	42	12	2	7	29	22	12	3	6	26	18	24	5	13	55	40	15	77
4	Truro C (P)	42	10	4	7	34	32	7	10	4	28	23	17	14	11	62	55	7	65
5	Whitehawk	42	9	3	9	32	23	9	7	5	43	39	18	10	14	75	62	13	64
6	Hemel Hempstead T	42	7	7	7	33	30	9	6	6	39	36	16	13	13	72	66	6	61
7	Maidenhead U	42	11	7	3	36	21	5	4	12	30	41	16	11	15	66	62	4	59
8	Dartford (R)	42	8	7	6	35	27	8	4	9	23	29	16	11	15	58	56	2	59
9	Gosport Bor	42	8	6	7	31	34	7	5	9	22	29	15	11	16	53	63	–10	56
10	Concord Rangers	42	6	4	11	29	32	9	6	6	37	36	15	10	17	66	68	–2	55
11	Bishop's Stortford	42	10	1	2	9	30	26	5	8	8	26	37	15	10	17	56	63	–7	55
12	Oxford C	42	6	9	6	36	30	7	6	8	34	30	13	15	14	70	60	10	54
13	Wealdstone	42	6	10	5	37	31	6	7	8	26	33	12	17	13	63	64	–1	53
14	Bath C	42	8	5	8	25	26	6	6	9	25	35	14	11	17	50	61	–11	53
15	Chelmsford C	42	9	2	10	42	35	6	5	10	24	29	15	7	20	66	64	2	52
16	Weston–super–Mare	42	8	3	10	31	38	6	6	9	32	38	14	9	19	63	76	–13	51
17	Eastbourne Bor	42	7	8	6	32	25	6	3	12	28	38	13	11	18	60	63	–3	50
18	St Albans C	42	9	5	7	41	26	4	5	12	17	39	13	10	19	58	65	–7	49
19	Margate (P)	42	7	4	10	25	34	6	4	11	26	39	13	8	21	51	73	–22	47
20	Havant & Waterlooville	42	10	4	7	30	25	2	7	12	22	50	12	11	19	52	75	–23	47
21	Hayes & Yeading U	42	3	9	9	25	45	8	4	9	26	31	11	13	18	51	76	–25	46
22	Basingstoke T	42	6	6	9	24	27	3	5	13	22	42	9	11	22	46	69	–23	38

¶*Maidstone U promoted via play-offs.*

VANARAMA NATIONAL LEAGUE SOUTH PLAY-OFFS 2015–16

SEMI-FINALS FIRST LEG

Wednesday 4 May 2016
Whitehawk (0) 1 *(Mills 82)*
Ebbsfleet U (1) 2 *(Lewis 28, Kedwell 74)*   1055
Whitehawk: Ross; Graham (Sessegnon 80), Rents, M'Boungou, Rose, Mendy (Ijaha 73), Arnold, Torres, Robinson, Mills, Martin.
Ebbsfleet U: Ashmore; Pooley, Howe, Lewis, Acheampong, Clark, Deering, Rance, Kedwell, Godden (Sheringham 87), Cook.
Referee: Andrew Laver.

Truro C (0) 0
Maidstone U (1) 2 *(Healy 27, Flisher 56)*   1011
Truro C: Rice; White, Brett, Bentley (Knowles 75), Richards, Pugh, Adelsbury, Green, Wright, Jay, Cooke (Afful 57).
Maidstone U: Worgan, Driver, Mills, Coyle, Parry, Rogers, Karagiannis (Sweeney 77), Healy, May (Dumaka 80), Taylor, Flisher.
Referee: Tim Wood.

SEMI-FINALS SECOND LEG

Sunday 8 May 2016
Ebbsfleet U (1) 1 *(Clark 23)*
Whitehawk (1) 2 *(Arnold 4, Mills 49)*   1942
Ebbsfleet U: Ashmore; Pooley (Parkes 66), Howe, Lewis, Acheampong, Clark, Deering (Bonner 91), Rance, Kedwell, Godden, Cook (Sheringham 91).
Whitehawk: Ross; Sessegnon, Rents, M'Boungou, Rose (Graham 82), Mendy (Ijaha 66), Arnold, Torres, Robinson, Mills (Gotta 111), Martin.
Referee: Anthony Serrano.
aet; 3-3 on aggregate, Ebbsfleet U won 3-2 on penalties.

Maidstone U (0) 1 *(Flischer 73)*
Truro C (0) 0   2508
Maidstone U: Worgan; Driver, Mills, Coyle, Parry, Rogers, Karagiannis (Sweeney 74), Healy, Dumaka (May 62), Taylor (Paxman 78), Flisher.
Truro C: Rice; Dawson, Riley-Lowe (Afful 62), Brett, Bentley, Pugh (Richards 48), Knowles, Green, Wright, Jay, Cooke (Adelsbury 69).
Referee: Carl Brook.
Maidstone U won on 3-0 on aggregate.

FINAL

Sunday 15 May 2016
Ebbsfleet U (1) 2 *(Kedwell 19 (pen), 109 (pen))*
Maidstone U (0) 2 *(Taylor 47, Dumaka 120)*   3,800
Ebbsfleet U: Ashmore; Bonner, Howe, Lewis (Sheringham 120), Acheampong, Clark, Deering (Kissock 57), Rance, Kedwell, Godden, Parkes.
Maidstone U: Worgan; Driver, Mills, Coyle, Parry, Rogers (Paxman 111), Karagiannis (Dumaka 81), Healy, May (Sweeney 87), Taylor, Flisher.
Referee: Chris O'Donnell.
aet; Maidstone U won 4-3 on penalties.

ALDERSHOT TOWN

Ground: The EBB Stadium at the Recreation Ground, High Street, Aldershot, Hampshire GU11 1TW.
Tel: (01252) 320211. *Website:* www.theshots.co.uk *Email:* admin@theshots.co.uk *Year Formed:* 1926.
Record Attendance: 19,138 v Carlisle U, FA Cup 4th rd (replay), 28 January 1970. *Nickname:* 'The Shots'.
Manager: Gary Waddock. *Colours:* Red shirts with white trim, blue shorts with white trim, red socks.

ALDERSHOT TOWN – VANARAMA NATIONAL 2015–16 LEAGUE RECORD

Match No.	Date	Venue	Opponents	Result	H/T Score	Lg Pos.	Goalscorers	Attendance
1	Aug 8	H	Gateshead	L	1-2	1-0	15	Browne [22]	1749
2	11	A	Cheltenham T	D	0-0	0-0	19		2552
3	15	A	Wrexham	L	0-3	0-1	21		4951
4	18	H	Dover Ath	D	1-1	1-1	21	Brodie [37]	1559
5	22	A	Guiseley	W	4-0	2-0	16	Brodie 2 [22, 80], Stevenson [33], Alexander [49]	782
6	29	H	Eastleigh	L	1-2	0-1	18	Walker, C [64]	1778
7	31	A	Braintree T	W	2-1	0-1	13	Harris [70], Brodie [86]	707
8	Sept 5	H	FC Halifax T	W	3-2	2-0	12	Stevenson [18], Walker, C 2 [24, 51]	1603
9	12	A	Grimsby T	L	1-4	1-0	14	Walker, C [30]	3869
10	15	H	Welling U	W	1-0	0-0	12	Brodie [49]	1256
11	19	A	Barrow	W	3-1	1-1	11	Walker, C 2 [32, 60], Alexander [66]	1564
12	22	A	Tranmere R	L	1-3	1-1	13	Hatton [5]	4126
13	26	H	Macclesfield T	L	0-3	0-2	15		1579
14	Oct 3	A	Torquay U	W	2-0	2-0	13	Hatton [21], Walker, C [34]	1946
15	7	H	Forest Green R	L	0-3	0-2	15		1353
16	10	A	Altrincham	W	2-0	1-0	14	Saville [33], Browne [63]	1412
17	13	A	Boreham Wood	W	1-0	1-0	12	Walker, C [10]	581
18	17	H	Bromley	D	1-1	1-1	12	Walker, C [38]	1617
19	31	A	Southport	D	1-1	1-0	12	Stevenson [11]	845
20	Nov 11	H	Lincoln C	L	1-2	0-1	13	Akinyemi [65]	1367
21	14	A	Kidderminster H	L	0-2	0-0	14		1790
22	21	H	Wrexham	L	0-1	0-0	15		1483
23	28	H	Cheltenham T	L	0-2	0-2	17		1493
24	Dec 5	A	Dover Ath	L	2-5	0-2	17	Stevenson [46], Walker, C [49]	1012
25	19	A	Guiseley	W	1-0	0-0	16	Richards [79]	1325
26	26	H	Woking	L	0-1	0-1	16		3150
27	28	A	Eastleigh	D	1-1	1-1	16	Hatton (pen) [26]	2107
28	Jan 2	A	Woking	L	1-2	0-2	17	Browne [74]	3708
29	9	H	Chester FC	W	3-1	0-0	15	McGinty [51], Pavey [52], Stevenson [89]	1617
30	23	A	Macclesfield T	W	2-0	1-0	14	Pavey [19], Lathrope [65]	1515
31	30	H	Kidderminster H	W	1-0	0-0	13	Walker, C [50]	1768
32	Feb 13	A	Tranmere R	D	0-0	0-0	13		1882
33	20	A	Gateshead	L	2-3	2-2	13	Browne [6], Gallagher [42]	1074
34	27	A	Welling U	W	1-0	0-0	13	Lafayette (pen) [76]	704
35	Mar 5	A	Lincoln C	L	0-2	0-1	14		2398
36	8	A	Chester FC	L	2-8	1-6	14	Lafayette [23], Walker, D [67]	1425
37	12	H	Torquay U	D	0-0	0-0	15		1771
38	19	A	Altrincham	L	0-4	0-1	15		1292
39	25	A	Forest Green R	D	0-0	0-0	15		2272
40	28	H	Braintree T	W	2-1	1-1	15	Beckles [40], Ralph [69]	1539
41	Apr 2	H	Barrow	L	0-1	0-0	15		1488
42	5	H	Grimsby T	L	3-4	2-0	15	Walker, C [33], Rasulo [43], Browne [69]	1397
43	9	A	FC Halifax T	W	2-0	0-0	14	Stevenson [46], Browne [83]	1714
44	16	H	Boreham Wood	L	1-2	1-1	15	Gallagher [11]	1389
45	23	A	Southport	L	1-2	1-2	16	Walker, D [9]	1456
46	30	A	Bromley	W	3-1	1-1	15	Walker, C 2 [11, 75], Francis (og) [64]	1445

Final League Position: 15

GOALSCORERS

League (54): Walker, C 14, Browne 6, Stevenson 6, Brodie 5, Hatton 3 (1 pen), Alexander 2, Gallagher 2, Lafayette 2 (1 pen), Pavey 2, Walker, D 2, Akinyemi 1, Beckles 1, Harris 1, Lathrope 1, McGinty 1, Ralph 1, Rasulo 1, Richards 1, Saville 1, own goal 1.
FA Cup (1): Browne 1.
FA Trophy (0).

Smith 39	Lathrope 18+3	Beckles 45	Alexander 46	Oliver 14+4	Richards 12+13	Hatton 21+9	Stevenson 38+7	Browne 31+6	Barnes-Homer 7+8	Walker D 26+10	Saville 21+3	Walker C 31+9	Anderton 11	Gallagher 34+2	Brodie 17+5	Harris 2+2	Thomas 7+2	McGinty 24	Akinyemi 2+2	Barker 3	Carr 5+2	Harness —+2	Oastler 12	Pavey 7+8	Lafayette 13+3	Ralph 9+3	Rasulo 11	Match No.
1	2²	3	4	5	6	7¹	8	9	10	11	12	13																1
1	6	3	2	4	12		7	8¹	11	10		13	5	9²														2
1	7	4	2	3	12		6	8²	10²	11		14	5	9¹	13													3
1	7²	5	2	3	13	6	8	12	10¹	9	4			11														4
1		3	2	4	12	6³	8		9¹	13	11	5	14				7	10²										5
1		4	2	3	12		7	9	10	11	6	8¹		5														6
1		3	2	4			8¹	9²	13	6		11	5	7	10	12												7
1	12	4	2	3			6		13	9²	14	10	5	7	11¹	8³												8
1²		4	2	3		13	7		14	9		10³	5	8	11	6¹	12											9
	7	2				6	3	5¹	12	13	4	11	10	8	9²		1											10
	14	4	2			6²	7	9¹		12	3	10	5²	8	11	13	1											11
		3	2			6¹	8	9²	13	12	4	11	5	7	10		1											12
1	14	4	2			6³	7	13	12	9	3	10²	5	8⁴	11¹													13
1	7	4	2			6	8	9	11²	13	3	10	5	12														14
1	6	3	4		12	7¹	8	9	10²	14	2	11	5³		13													15
1	8	4	2	5		7	9	12	6	3		11		10¹														16
1	6¹	3	2	5	12	8	7	9²				4	11	13	10													17
1	6	5	14	4³	13	7	8²	12	3	10¹				9⁴	11					2								18
1	7	4	2	12	13	8	6¹	9		3²		10		11				5										19
1	7	4	2	12	9	13	8¹	6		3²		10						5	11									20
1	7	3	2	4³	13	14	8	9²	6			12		10				5	11¹									21
1		3	2					9²		8	12	6		11¹			7⁴	10	5		13	4						22
1	8	7		6²	4	5	9		11³				3	14				10¹	2				12	13				23
1	8	4	2			9¹	7	6		3		10²						5	12		11							24
1	7		2	4	13	9	8²		6¹			10¹					12	14	5	3	11							25
1	3	2		9	6¹	8		13		12		7	11					5			10²	4						26
1	3	2		9²	6¹	8	13	12		10		7					5		8¹	12	2							27
1	3	2		9²	6¹	8	13	12		10		7					5		11	4								28
1²	7	4	2			13	9	6		11³		8		12	5	14				3	10¹							29
1	7	4	2		14		13	6¹	9			10³		8				5				3	11²	12				30
1	7	4	2		14		12	9	6²			10		8¹				5				3	11³	13				31
1	7	4	3			14	8	5¹		11¹		9		8				6			2	10	13	12				32
1	4¹	6	3			14	9	7²		11³				8				5			2	13	10	12				33
1		2	4			7	8			11¹				9				6			5	12	10	3				34
1	4	2		13		8	6	12				7						5			3	10¹	11	9²				35
1	4	2		12	6²	7	11	14		8				7				5			3	13	10¹	9³				36
1	6	5		4	9		12	13	2			7									10	11	3²	8¹				37
1	4	2		5	7²	13	14			3	12			6				5			10¹	11	9	8³				38
1	4	2	3			8	9							7				5			12	11¹	10	6				39
1	3	2	4			7	9							8				5			12	11¹	10	6				40
1	4	2	3	10		7²	8					12		9				5			13	11	6¹					41
1	3	2		12²		8	9					4¹	11	7				5			13	10	6					42
	3	2			14	7	9					10	8			1	5²		4		13	11¹	12	6³				43
	5	4	12			2	6					3¹	7			1		9⁴				10	11	8				44
	3	5		13	12	6²		9	2	11		7				1					10	4	8¹					45
	5	4		12	7	6		10	2	11		8¹				1					3	9						46

FA Cup

Fourth Qualifying	Sutton U	(h)	1-0
First Round	Bradford C	(h)	0-0
Replay	Bradford C	(a)	0-2

FA Trophy

First Round	Eastleigh	(h)	0-1

ALTRINCHAM

Ground: J. Davidson Stadium, Moss Lane, Altrincham WA15 8AP.   *Tel:* (0161) 928 1045.   *Website:* altrinchamfc.co.uk
Email: see website.   *Year Formed:* 1903.   *Record Attendance:* 10,275 (Altrincham Boys v Sunderland Boys, ESFA
Shield, 28 February 1925).   *Nickname:* 'The Robins'.   *Manager:* Neil Young.   *Colours:* Red and white striped shirts,
red shorts with black trim, red socks with black and white trim.

ALTRINCHAM – VANARAMA NATIONAL 2015–16 LEAGUE RECORD

Match No.	Date	Venue	Opponents	Result	H/T Score	Lg Pos.	Goalscorers	Atten- dance
1	Aug 8	H	Forest Green R	L 0-1	0-0	17		975
2	11	A	Guiseley	L 0-1	0-1	22		797
3	15	A	Woking	L 0-2	0-1	24		1297
4	18	H	Grimsby T	W 2-1	1-1	19	Rankine [13], Bowerman [60]	1680
5	22	A	Dover Ath	L 1-2	1-1	21	Bowerman [41]	711
6	29	H	Tranmere R	W 2-1	2-0	17	Bowerman [7], Rankine [29]	2460
7	31	A	Southport	L 0-3	0-2	19		1143
8	Sept 5	H	Cheltenham T	W 2-1	0-0	16	Crowther [59], Heathcote [90]	1206
9	12	A	Wrexham	L 1-3	0-2	19	Rankine [50]	4628
10	15	H	Eastleigh	D 1-1	1-0	19	Lawrie [29]	677
11	19	H	Braintree T	L 0-4	0-2	19		861
12	22	A	Lincoln C	D 1-1	1-1	19	Crowther [17]	1893
13	26	A	Boreham Wood	W 1-0	1-0	19	Rankine (pen) [11]	351
14	Oct 3	H	Barrow	W 1-0	0-0	19	Reeves [61]	1384
15	6	H	FC Halifax T	L 1-3	0-1	19	Reeves [56]	1119
16	10	A	Aldershot T	L 0-2	0-1	19		1412
17	13	H	Kidderminster H	D 2-2	1-1	19	Lawrie [21], Rankine [90]	869
18	17	A	Gateshead	D 2-2	0-0	19	Rankine [77], Bowerman [79]	911
19	31	H	Torquay U	D 1-1	0-1	19	Moult [66]	1060
20	Nov 10	A	Macclesfield T	L 0-3	0-2	19		1801
21	14	A	Bromley	W 3-1	1-1	19	Reeves 2 [19, 51], O'Keefe [50]	1737
22	21	H	Boreham Wood	W 1-0	0-0	17	Clee [76]	1002
23	28	A	Forest Green R	L 0-2	0-2	18		1292
24	Dec 19	A	Cheltenham T	L 0-1	0-0	19		2591
25	28	H	Tranmere R	L 0-1	0-1	20		5414
26	Jan 2	A	Chester FC	D 1-1	0-1	19	Rankine [60]	2155
27	23	A	Grimsby T	L 0-5	0-2	21		4323
28	26	H	Woking	W 3-1	2-0	19	Rankine (pen) [13], Ginnelly [43], Margetts [71]	826
29	Feb 6	A	Welling U	D 1-1	0-0	19	Rankine [58]	551
30	9	H	Wrexham	D 1-1	1-1	19	Ginnelly [11]	1261
31	13	H	Lincoln C	D 3-3	2-2	19	Margetts [3], Ginnelly [11], Reeves [65]	1293
32	16	A	Chester FC	L 0-3	0-2	19		1442
33	20	H	Guiseley	D 1-1	1-0	19	Rankine [41]	1137
34	Mar 5	H	Macclesfield T	D 0-0	0-0	21		2014
35	8	H	Gateshead	L 2-3	0-1	21	Holness [47], Moult (pen) [90]	805
36	12	A	Barrow	L 2-3	1-1	21	Sinnott [19], Lawrie [69]	1019
37	19	H	Aldershot T	W 4-0	1-0	20	Reeves [32], Ginnelly [47], Moult (pen) [61], Sinnott [69]	1292
38	26	A	FC Halifax T	L 0-1	0-0	20		1747
39	28	H	Southport	D 1-1	0-0	21	Ginnelly [60]	1480
40	Apr 2	A	Kidderminster H	D 1-1	1-0	21	Reeves [9]	1402
41	5	A	Dover Ath	L 1-2	1-0	22	Rankine [37]	1007
42	9	H	Bromley	D 0-0	0-0	22		1035
43	12	A	Torquay U	L 0-2	0-1	22		1995
44	16	A	Eastleigh	L 0-2	0-0	22		2034
45	23	H	Welling U	W 5-0	2-0	22	Sinnott [33], Rankine 2 (1 pen) [45 (p), 90], Lawrie [50], Reeves [66]	1396
46	30	A	Braintree T	L 0-3	0-2	22		1803

Final League Position: 22

GOALSCORERS

League (48): Rankine 13 (3 pens), Reeves 8, Ginnelly 5, Bowerman 4, Lawrie 4, Moult 3 (2 pens), Sinnott 3, Crowther
2, Margetts 2, Clee 1, Heathcote 1, Holness 1, O'Keefe 1.
FA Cup (4): Reeves 2, Moult 1, Rankine 1.
FA Trophy (4): Rankine 2 (1 pen), Lawrie 1, Reeves 1.

Coburn 5	Densmore 12 + 2	Griffin 44	Moult 44	Havern 30 + 1	Marshall 4	Lawrie 38 + 5	O'Keefe 16 + 11	Rankine 30 + 10	Reeves 27 + 14	Sinnott 42 + 2	Bowerman 14 + 14	Leather 41 + 3	Crowther 19 + 12	Richman 35 + 2	Clee 3 + 12	Parry 10	Deasy 41	Griffith — + 1	Heathcote 9 + 7	Swift — + 1	Mottley-Henry 1 + 4	Ginnelly 19 + 1	Margetts 6	Holness 14	Phillips 2 + 2	Saville — + 3	Williams C — + 1	Match No.
1	2	3	4	5	6	7	8^2	9	10^1	11	12	13																1
1	2	3	4	5^2	6	7^1	8	9	10^2	11	13	12	14															2
1	2	5	7						10^2	13	8	11^1	3		6	12												3
1	2	5	7		3^3	9	13	10	14		6^2	11^1	4		8	12												4
1	2	5^1	7			9	14	11^3	12	6	10^2	4		8	13	3												5
	2	5	7			9^2	14	10	12	6^3	11^1	4		8		3	1	13										6
	2	5	4			6	12	13	10	9	11	3	8^1	7^2			1											7
	2	5	7			6	8^2	10	13	9	11^1	3	12^3			4	1		14									8
	2	5	7^2	13		9		10	14	8	11^3	3	12			4	1		6^1									9
	2	5	7	4		11		10		6^1	9^2	3	12			8	1		13									10
5^1	9		3			8	14	10^1	11	6	13	2	12	7		4^3	1											11
	5	6^2	4			9		11	13	8	12	2	10^1	7		3	1											12
	5	7	4			10		11^2	12	6	13	2	9^1	8		3	1											13
13	5	7	3			9			11^2	8^1	12	2	10^3	6	14	4	1											14
12	5	7	3			9			11	8^2	13	2		6	10^3	4^1	1		14									15
2^2	5	6	3			9	14	12	11	13	10^3	4		7	8^1		1											16
		4	2			7	8^1	9	11	6	5	3			10		1		12									17
	5	7	3			9	8^2	10^1	11^3	2	12	4		6	13		1		14									18
	4	5	3			9.8		10	7	11^1	2	12	6				1											19
	2	5					7^2	13	10	9	11	4	8^1	6	12		1		3									20
	2	3					7	13	11^1	9	10^3	4	8^2	5	12		1		6	14								21
	2	6				13	5	14	11^2	9	10^3	3	8^1	7	12		1		4									22
	5^1	8	3^4			6	9^4	12	10^1	2	14	4	11^3	7	13		1											23
	2	5	3			11		9	10^1	8	13	4	7^2	6	12		1											24
	5	7	3			6		11^2	10	2	13	4	9^1	8	12		1											25
	5	6	3			10	8^1	9	11^2	2	13	4		7	12^3		1		14									26
	5	3				12	14	10^2		2		4	13	7^3			1		8			6^1	9	11				27
	5	3				12	14	10		6		2	9^3	7			1				13	8^1	11^2	4				28
	5	8				9		10		2		3		7			1				12	6	11^1	4				29
	3	7						10		2		4	9^1	8			1				12	6	11	5				30
	5	6				12			10^2	2		4	9^1	8			1				13	7	11	3				31
	5	7				14	12	10	13			3	6^3	8^2			1		2			9	11^1	4				32
	3^1	7	4			10	8	11	13	2		12	6^2				1					9	5					33
	5	6	3			10		11	12	2			7^1	8			1					9	4					34
	5	7	3			10^1	6		11	2	12			8			1					9	4					35
	5	7	4			10			11	6	13	2^1	12	8			1					9^2	3					36
	5	7	3			11			14	10^2	6^1	2	13	8			1					9^3	4	12				37
	5	7	3			6^3	14	12	10	2		4		11^1			1		8^3			9		13				38
	5	7	3			10	8	13	11^1	2		4	12				1					6		9^2				39
	5	9	3			10	7	12	11^2			2	13	6			1					8^1	4					40
	6	5				11^3		10	12	2		3	13	7			1		14			8^1	4	9^3				41
	5	7^1	3			10	12	11	13	2		4	6^2	8			1					9						42
	5^2		3			10	7	11^1	12	6		4	9	8^3		$·1$		2				13				14		43
	5	8	3			7		10	11	12		4	9^2			1		2^1				6				13		44
	5	7^1	3			6		10	11^3	8		2		14		1^2						9	4			13	12	45
	5	6	4			11^1		10	9	8		3		12			1					7	2					46

FA Cup

Fourth Qualifying	Chester FC	(h)	1-0	
First Round	Barnsley	(h)	1-0	
Second Round	Colchester U	(a)	2-3	

FA Trophy

First Round	Leamington	(h)	1-1	
Replay	Leamington	(a)	2-1	
aet.				
Second Round	Bognor Regis T	(a)	1-2	

BARROW

Ground: Furness Building Society Stadium, Wilkie Road, Barrow-in-Furness, Cumbria LA14 5UW.
Tel: (01229) 666010.   *Website:* www.barrowafc.com   *Email:* office@barrowafc.com   *Year Formed:* 1901.
Record Attendance: 16,854 v Swansea T, FA Cup 3rd rd, 9 January 1954.   *Nickname:* 'The Bluebirds'.
Manager: Paul Cox.   *Colours:* White shirts with blue trim, blue shorts, white socks with blue trim.

BARROW – VANARAMA NATIONAL 2015–16 LEAGUE RECORD

Match No.	Date		Venue	Opponents	Result		H/T Score	Lg Pos.	Goalscorers	Atten- dance
1	Aug	8	H	Dover Ath	W	2-1	2-1	4	Cook 2 24, 34	2285
2		11	A	Grimsby T	L	1-4	0-2	15	Newby, E 90	5047
3		15	A	Forest Green R	L	0-4	0-2	18		1217
4		18	H	Guiseley	D	1-1	1-1	17	Walker 36	1440
5		22	A	Cheltenham T	L	1-2	1-0	20	Downes (og) 44	2209
6		29	H	Southport	W	1-0	1-0	16	Cook 39	1343
7		31	A	FC Halifax T	L	1-3	0-0	18	Cook 53	1490
8	Sept	5	H	Eastleigh	W	1-0	0-0	15	Walker (pen) 3	1448
9		12	A	Braintree T	D	1-1	0-0	15	Pilkington 81	710
10		15	H	Lincoln C	W	1-0	0-0	13	Cook 56	1233
11		19	H	Aldershot T	L	1-3	1-1	16	Walker (pen) 40	1564
12		22	A	Macclesfield T	W	2-1	1-0	14	Cook 2 (1 pen) 55, 86 (p)	1215
13		26	H	Kidderminster H	D	1-1	0-1	15	Cook 51	1323
14	Oct	3	A	Altrincham	L	0-1	0-0	17		1384
15		6	H	Chester FC	W	3-2	1-1	12	Haworth 35, Cook 47, Cowperthwaite 77	1345
16		10	A	Bromley	L	0-5	0-2	15		2455
17		13	A	Tranmere R	W	1-0	1-0	15	Haworth 37	4624
18		17	H	Welling U	D	1-1	0-1	15	Cook 53	1327
19		31	A	Wrexham	L	1-4	0-1	15	Symington 74	3892
20	Nov	7	A	Guiseley	L	1-3	1-2	16	Cook (pen) 45	749
21		10	H	Grimsby T	L	1-3	1-1	17	Khan 31	1255
22		14	H	Torquay U	W	4-0	2-0	15	Khan 2 9, 41, Walker 63, Haworth 90	1119
23		21	A	Dover Ath	L	1-3	0-3	16	Cook 77	847
24		28	H	Woking	W	2-1	1-0	14	Cook 4, Williams, S 73	1115
25	Dec	19	A	Lincoln C	D	2-2	1-2	15	Walker 2 (1 pen) 44, 62 (p)	2540
26		28	A	Southport	L	1-2	1-1	17	Khan 26	1528
27	Jan	2	A	Gateshead	D	1-1	0-1	16	Williams, J 84	892
28		9	H	Tranmere R	L	3-4	0-1	17	Walker (pen) 67, Grand 82, Cook 87	1766
29		23	A	Welling U	W	2-1	1-1	16	Livesey 45, Grimes 55	542
30		30	A	Woking	D	2-2	2-2	16	Griffiths (og) 18, Cook 29	1713
31	Feb	2	H	Gateshead	D	0-0	0-0	16		939
32		6	A	Cheltenham T	L	1-2	0-1	16	Grand 77	1202
33		27	A	Forest Green R	D	2-2	1-1	17	Livesey 73, Williams, J 83	1233
34	Mar	5	A	Boreham Wood	W	2-0	2-0	15	Tomlinson 13, Cook 45	332
35		8	H	Boreham Wood	D	0-0	0-0	16		881
36		12	H	Altrincham	W	3-2	1-1	14	Livesey 44, Cook 61, Tomlinson 67	1019
37		19	H	Bromley	D	1-1	0-0	14	Walker 82	1123
38		26	A	Chester FC	W	2-1	0-1	14	Williams, J 2 55, 85	2020
39		28	H	FC Halifax T	W	4-1	1-0	13	Williams, J 31, Cook 48, Walker 81, Tomlinson 90	1466
40	Apr	2	A	Aldershot T	W	1-0	0-0	13	Cook 64	1488
41		5	H	Braintree T	W	2-0	1-0	12	Walker 7, Cook 81	1039
42		9	H	Macclesfield T	D	1-1	1-1	13	Walker (pen) 43	1516
43		12	A	Eastleigh	L	1-3	0-2	13	Cook 60	3292
44		16	A	Kidderminster H	D	0-0	0-0	12		1517
45		23	A	Torquay U	D	2-2	1-0	11	Tomlinson 34, Cook 90	2874
46		30	H	Wrexham	W	2-0	1-0	11	Cook 2 43, 77	1728

Final League Position: 11

GOALSCORERS

League (64): Cook 24 (2 pens), Walker 11 (5 pens), Williams, J 5, Khan 4, Tomlinson 4, Haworth 3, Livesey 3, Grand 2, Cowperthwaite 1, Grimes 1, Newby, E 1, Pilkington 1, Symington 1, Williams, S 1, own goals 2.
FA Cup (0).
FA Trophy (1): Van den Broek 1.

Dixon 46	Cowperthwaite 21 + 3	Grand 37 + 3	Livesey 39	Ashton 22	Haworth 32 + 5	Fofana 6 + 3	Mellor 17 + 3	Pilkington 14 + 10	Cook 45	Grimes 8 + 9	Symington 21 + 6	Walker 20 + 14	Harvey 21 + 11	Newby E 2 + 11	Williams S 16 + 2	Williams G 15	Cosgrove 1 + 4	Lacey 20 + 3	van den Broek 6 + 4	Wilson 1 + 5	Khan 6 + 2	Anderton 21	O'Reilly 1 + 2	Hearn 1	Rigg — + 1	Newby A — + 1	Williams J 19 + 1	Parry 17	Donohue 6	Rowe 3	Tomlinson 11 + 3	Sutton 10	Abbott 1 + 4	Match No.
1	2	3	4	5	6^3	7	8	9^1	10	11^2	12	13	14																					1
1	2	4	3	5	6	7	8^2	11				9^1	12	10	13																			2
1	2	12	3^4	5	9^2	7	8	11^1	14	6^3	10	13				4^4																		3
1		3	4	5	9	7^2	8	11^2	13	10^1	6	12			2	14																		4
1	12	4	3^2	5	9	13	7					10^1	6	14	2	11	8^2																	5
1		5	4	3	6			11^2	13			10^2	8	12	2	14	9	7^1																6
1		5	4	3	6^1			10	12	13	11^3	8			2	14	7	9^2																7
1	14	4	3	5	6	12	7^2		10		13				2	8	9	9^3																8
1	13	5	4	3	8		7^3	12	10^2		9				2	14	6	11^1																9
1	8	12	3	5	9^1	14		6^3	11		10			13	4^2	2		7																10
1	8	4	3	5	9			6^3	10^1	12	11	13			2			7^2	14															11
1	8	4	3	5	9			11	12		10^1	13			2			7	6^2															12
1	7	4	3	5	9			10	14	2	11^1	12						8^2	6^3	13														13
1	7	4	3	5	9		6^1	11		2	10^1	12	14					8^2		13														14
1	7		4	5	9	13		6^2	11^2	10^1	2	14	8		3				12															15
1	6		4	3	8^1		13	11	10	9^1	14				7^2		5	2		12														16
1	6		4	3	8^3		7	14	10	9	13				5	2^1		12		11^4														17
1	8		3	5	6^2		7^3	9	10	11^1		12	13	14	4	2																		18
1	8		3	5^1	7		4^3	11	13	9		14	10^2	6	2			12																19
1	6		4		8^2		7^4	11		10^1	12		9^3	5	2		14	13	3^4															20
1	8	12	4		6^2			10	14	5	11^3		13	3^1	2		7		9															21
1	8^1	3	4		6			13	11^2	2	10	12						7	14	9^3	5													22
1	8^4	4	3		7^2		5	12	11	2	10^1							6	13	9														23
1		3			9^2	8		6	11	2	14		5		8				6	4	11^1	13^3												24
1		3		8			6	11	2	10^2	7		4		13				9^1	5^4	12													25
1		3	5		7			6^2	11	2	10	8	12	4					9^1			13												26
1	2	4		5			7	9^2	10	6	12	8^1	13	3								11												27
1	8	4		5	13		7	6^1	11	2	14	9^3		3^2								10							12					28
1	2	4	3		6		5	7^1	8			12										11	9											29
1	6^3	5	4		13		12	11	10	9^2	2	14							3			8^1	7											30
1		4	3		13			7	9^1	11	10^2	2	12						5			8	6											31
1		4	3					8^1	12	10	13	2			5^2			7				6						11	9					32
1		3	4					10	11^1	2	12								5			13	7	6	8	9^2								33
1		4	3					12	10										5			11	6	7^1	8	9	2							34
1		4	3					10				12							5			9	8	6	7^1	11	2							35
1		4	3		13			10		12									5			9	7^1	6^2		11	2							36
1		4	3		12			10			13	7							5			9		6^2		11^1	2							37
1		4	3		12			10				7							5			9	6	8^1		11	2							38
1		4	3^1		6			11^2				10	7	12					5			9	8			13	2							39
1		4	3		6^1			11				7							5			9	8			10	2					12		40
1		4	3		6^2			11				10^1	7					12	5			9	8			13	2							41
1		4	3		6^1			14	11		12	10^2	8						5			9	7			13	2^3							42
1		4	3		6^1			11		12		7							5			9	8			10	2^2	13						43
1		3	2^2		5^1			13	11			7					8		4			9	6			10		12						44
1		3	6^2					10				13	7	4^1			2		5			8	9			11		12						45
1		4	6^1					11				12	8				2		5			9	3			10		7						46

FA Cup
Fourth Qualifying   AFC Fylde   (a)   0-1

FA Trophy
First Round   Sutton Coldfield T   (a)   1-0
Second Round   FC Halifax T   (a)   0-1

BOREHAM WOOD

Ground: Meadow Park, Broughinge Road, Borehamwood, Hertfordshire WD6 5AL.   *Tel:* (02089) 535097.
Website: borehamwoodfootballclub.co.uk   *Email:* see website.   *Year Formed:* 1948.
Record Attendance: 4,030 v Arsenal, Friendly, 13 July 2001.   *Nickname:* 'The Wood'   *Manager:* Luke Garrard
Colours: White shirts, black shorts, white socks.

BOREHAM WOOD – VANARAMA NATIONAL 2015–16 LEAGUE RECORD

Match No.	Date		Venue	Opponents	Result		H/T Score	Lg Pos.	Goalscorers	Atten- dance
1	Aug	8	H	FC Halifax T	W	3-1	1-1	2	Shakes ³⁷, Lucas ⁶¹, Crawford ⁹⁰	701
2		11	A	Eastleigh	L	0-1	0-0	7		1427
3		15	A	Gateshead	L	1-2	1-0	15	Lucas ³⁰	760
4		18	H	Forest Green R	L	0-1	0-0	18		464
5		22	A	Tranmere R	W	2-0	0-0	15	Montgomery ⁵⁸, Crawford ⁹⁰	4832
6		29	H	Woking	D	1-1	0-1	13	Morias ⁸³	601
7		31	A	Dover Ath	L	1-2	1-2	15	Crawford ⁹	1012
8	Sept	5	H	Grimsby T	L	1-3	0-1	20	MacDonald ⁸⁰	1293
9		12	A	Lincoln C	L	1-3	1-0	20	Whichelow ³⁵	2272
10		15	H	Bromley	L	2-3	0-1	20	Doe ⁵⁷, Morias ⁹⁰	364
11		19	H	Wrexham	L	0-1	0-1	21		685
12		22	A	Torquay U	W	2-1	1-0	20	Montgomery ⁸, Tiryaki ⁵⁵	1735
13		26	H	Altrincham	L	0-1	0-1	20		351
14	Oct	3	A	Macclesfield T	D	0-0	0-0	20		1186
15		6	A	Kidderminster H	D	1-1	0-1	20	Clifford, Conor ⁷⁷	1294
16		10	H	Welling U	W	2-0	1-0	20	Lucas ¹⁹, Devera ⁶⁴	543
17		13	A	Aldershot T	L	0-1	0-1	20		581
18		17	A	Guiseley	D	1-1	0-0	20	Kamdjo ⁵⁹	749
19		31	H	Gateshead	L	2-3	1-2	20	Clifford, B (pen) ²⁶, Vilhete ⁷⁵	344
20	Nov	10	A	Bromley	W	2-1	2-1	20	Howell 2 ³, ¹¹	939
21		14	H	Chester FC	D	0-0	0-0	20		589
22		21	A	Altrincham	L	0-1	0-0	20		1002
23		25	H	Lincoln C	D	1-1	1-1	20	Kamdjo ²⁶	661
24		28	H	Tranmere R	D	0-0	0-0	20		640
25	Dec	19	A	Forest Green R	L	0-1	0-0	21		1156
26		26	H	Braintree T	W	1-0	1-0	20	Jeffrey ⁷	443
27		28	A	Woking	D	0-0	0-0	19		2097
28	Jan	9	H	Cheltenham T	D	0-0	0-0	20		647
29		23	A	Eastleigh	D	1-1	1-0	20	Lucas ⁴³	406
30	Feb	6	H	Kidderminster H	L	0-2	0-1	21		366
31		13	A	Grimsby T	D	0-0	0-0	21		3927
32		16	A	Braintree T	W	2-0	0-0	20	Doe ⁴⁸, Howell ⁵⁴	628
33		20	H	Torquay U	L	0-1	0-0	21		555
34		27	A	Southport	W	3-0	2-0	19	Howell 2 ¹⁶, ²⁹, Stephens ⁷⁵	815
35	Mar	5	H	Barrow	L	0-2	0-2	20		332
36		8	A	Barrow	D	0-0	0-0	19		881
37		12	A	Wrexham	L	0-1	0-1	19		3470
38		19	H	Macclesfield T	D	0-0	0-0	21		306
39		25	A	Cheltenham T	L	1-4	0-2	21	Haynes ⁶³	3243
40		28	H	Dover Ath	W	3-0	2-0	19	Lucas 2 ³, ⁸¹, Haynes ⁴⁵	602
41	Apr	2	A	Chester FC	D	2-2	1-1	19	Doe ¹⁶, White, H ⁹⁰	1444
42		5	A	FC Halifax T	L	2-3	0-2	21	White, H ⁵⁷, Lucas ⁸³	1309
43		9	H	Southport	L	0-2	0-2	21		434
44		16	A	Aldershot T	W	2-1	1-1	20	Shakes ⁹, Clifford, Conor (pen) ⁷⁷	1389
45		23	A	Guiseley	W	1-0	1-0	19	Sam-Yorke ²³	601
46		30	H	Welling U	W	3-0	2-0	19	Lokko (og) ³¹, Howell ⁴¹, Kamdjo ⁶¹	577

Final League Position: 19

GOALSCORERS

League (44): Lucas 7, Howell 6, Crawford 3, Doe 3, Kamdjo 3, Clifford, Conor 2 (1 pen), Haynes 2, Montgomery 2, Morias 2, Shakes 2, White, H 2, Clifford, B 1 (1 pen), Devera 1, Jeffrey 1, MacDonald 1, Sam-Yorke 1, Stephens 1, Tiryaki 1, Vilhete 1, Whichelow 1, own goal 1.
FA Cup (4): Jeffrey 1, MacDonald 1, Morias 1, Tiryaki 1.
FA Trophy (1): Tiryaki 1.

Russell 40	Nunn 23 + 3	Doe 45	Reynolds 28 + 3	Shakes 41 + 4	Montgomery 10 + 1	Howell 32 + 5	Clifford B 14 + 7	Woodards D 38 + 1	Clifford Conor 44	Lucas 19 + 5	Crawford 2 + 8	Whichelow 2 + 7	Morias 8 + 21	Edwards 6	Cox 21 + 1	MacDonald 12 + 6	Hill 1 + 1	Devera 26 + 1	Kandjo 28 + 3	Tiryaki 6 + 2	Banton — + 2	Jeffrey 14 + 6	Stephens 18	Vilhete 6 + 3	Chiedozie 1	Sam-Yorke 8 + 8	Connors — + 1	Haynes 6 + 2	White H 7 + 1	Match No.
1	2	3	4	5	6	7	8[2]	9	10	11[1]	12	13																		1
1	2	4	5	6	8	7	11[3]	3	10[1]	9[2]	12	13	14																	2
1	2	6	4	7	8	3	11[3]	5	10[2]	9[1]	13	14	12																	3
1	2[2]	3	4	7	9[3]	10	11	5	8	6[1]	12	13	14																	4
	2	3	4	7		9	8[1]	5	10	11[2]	12	13			1	6														5
	2[2]	3	4	7	8	9	10	5	6		13	12	14		1	11[1]														6
	2	3	4	6	14	12		5[1]	10		13	11[2]	8	9	1	7[3]														7
	2[2]	5	6	7		9	8	3	10	12	13	11[3]	14		1	4[1]														8
	2	4	3	8	12	9[2]	5	10		6[3]	13		14	7	1	11[1]														9
	12	4	3	6		9	11	5[2]	8		2	13	14		1	7[1]		10[3]												10
1		3	4	7	10	6	12	9			13	14			2[1]	11[3]	8[2]	5												11
1		3	5	7	6	9[1]	10[2]	4		12					2	8		11	13											12
1	2[2]	3	5	6	10	9[1]	14		12	7					4	8		11[3]	13											13
1		3	9	6		5	7	11[1]	12						2	10[2]		4	8			13								14
1	4	14	6		9	5	7[1]	11[2]	10						2[3]	12		3	8			13								15
1	4		6		10	5	7	9[1]	11[1]						2	12		3	8			13								16
1		3	8[2]		9	5	7	11[3]	10[1]						2	12		4	6	14		13								17
1		4	6		9	5	7	10	12						2	11[1]		3	8											18
1		3	5		6[3]	2	7	13	14							11[1]		8	10[2]			9	4	12						19
1		3	7		9[1]	2	8		13						12	11		5	6			4	10							20
1		4	7		8[2]	2	9	13							5	11[1]		6				12	3	10						21
1		3	14	7[2]	8[3]	2[1]	9	13							6	11		4				10	5	12						22
1		4	5	13	11[3]	8		12	10[1]						2	7	14					9	3	6[2]						23
1		3	5	13	10[1]	14	8		12						11[2]	2	7					9	4	6[1]						24
1		4	5	7[1]	11[3]	12	8	13	6						2[2]	10						9	3	14						25
1	2	4	5	6	12		3	7							8			9[1]				11	10							26
1	2	4	3	6	12		5	7							8			9				11	10[1]							27
1	2	3	4	6	12		5	8							7			9				10			11[1]					28
1	5	7		8		9	4	6	10	11[1]						3			2			12								29
1	2	3		7		12	9	6	11						8			5	4			10[1]								30
1		3		9		11		5	7	10[2]					8			4	13			6[1]	2			12				31
1		4		7		8		5	9	11[1]					3			10				6	2			12				32
1		3	13	10		5	6[1]	8[2]	11[3]						7			2	14			9	4			12				33
1	13	4		9		8	5	11							3[2]			7	12			6[1]	2			10				34
1		3		6		9	5	8	14			13						2	7[1]			10[3]	4			11[12]	12			35
1		3		6	7	5	11								2	8		12	4			9			10[1]					36
1	12	3[1]		6	9	13	5	7	14						2	8		4				11[3]	10[2]							37
1	2	3	4	13	9[1]	5	8		10[2]						6	7												12	11	38
1		3		6	8[2]	2	9	13					12		4	7						5						10	11[1]	39
1	2	3	4	9		5	8	6[2]					10		13	7										12	11[1]			40
1	2	3	4	6		5	7	11	9[2]						8											13	10[1]	12		41
1	2	3	4	8	13	5	9	7[1]							11											12	6[1]	10		42
1	2	3	4	6[1]	7	5	8	10[2]				12			9											13	11			43
1		3	12	4	5	2[1]	7								11	9						10				6	8			44
1	2	3	5	6	9[1]	8	12	4							7											10	11			45
1	2	4	3	9	6[1]	7	12	14							5	8										11[2]	13	10[3]		46

FA Cup

Fourth Qualifying	AFC Hornchurch	(h)	2-1
First Round	Northwich Vic	(a)	1-1
Replay	Northwich Vic	(h)	1-2

FA Trophy

| First Round | Woking | (h) | 1-2 |

BRAINTREE TOWN

Ground: The Avanti Stadium, Clockhouse Way, Braintree, Essex CM7 3RD.   *Tel:* (01376) 345 617.
Website: www.braintreetownfc.org.uk   *Email:* braintreeTFC@aol.com   *Year Formed:* 1898.
Record Attendance: 4,000 v Tottenham H, Friendly, 8 May 1952.   *Nickname:* 'The Iron'.   *Manager:* Danny Cowley.
Colours: Orange shirts with white trim, blue shorts, orange socks.

BRAINTREE TOWN – VANARAMA NATIONAL 2015–16 LEAGUE RECORD

Match No.	Date		Venue	Opponents	Result	H/T Score	Lg Pos.	Goalscorers	Atten- dance
1	Aug	8	A	Chester FC	L 0-1	0-1	17		2256
2		11	H	Lincoln C	L 1-3	0-0	23	Akinola 63	657
3		15	H	Tranmere R	D 0-0	0-0	20		838
4		18	A	Bromley	W 2-1	1-0	16	Sparkes 23, Chiedozie 48	755
5		22	H	Southport	W 1-0	1-0	13	Sparkes 23	504
6		29	A	Welling U	W 2-1	1-1	9	Cheek 14, Sparkes 76	521
7		31	H	Aldershot T	L 1-2	1-0	10	Chiedozie 42	707
8	Sept	5	A	Kidderminster H	W 1-0	1-0	8	Davis (pen) 43	1670
9		12	H	Barrow	D 1-1	0-0	9	Akinola 56	710
10		15	A	Dover Ath	D 0-0	0-0	9		638
11		19	A	Altrincham	W 4-0	2-0	7	Cheek 9, Davis (pen) 42, Miles 90, Edgar 90	861
12		22	H	Woking	W 2-1	0-0	5	Akinola 62, Cheek 74	652
13		26	H	Guiseley	L 0-1	0-0	9		679
14	Oct	3	A	Eastleigh	W 2-0	1-0	6	Davis (pen) 32, Cheek 60	1330
15		6	A	Cheltenham T	D 1-1	0-0	8	Edgar 90	2097
16		10	H	Grimsby T	D 0-0	0-0	9		1394
17		13	H	Dover Ath	W 1-0	1-0	6	Cheek 45	637
18		17	A	Lincoln C	L 0-2	0-0	8		2565
19		31	H	Macclesfield T	W 1-0	0-0	5	Szmodics 75	687
20	Nov	10	A	Woking	D 1-1	0-0	7	Marks 23	1182
21		14	A	FC Halifax T	W 6-3	4-3	5	Woodyard 4, Cheek 3 18, 24, 49, Davis (pen) 30, Szmodics 57	1065
22		28	H	Torquay U	D 0-0	0-0	9		773
23	Dec	5	A	Tranmere R	W 2-1	2-1	6	Sparkes 5, Akinola 24	4224
24		26	A	Boreham Wood	L 0-1	0-1	10		443
25	Jan	23	A	Forest Green R	L 0-1	0-0	12		1507
26		26	H	Wrexham	W 1-0	0-0	11	Miles 74	484
27		30	H	Chester FC	W 2-0	2-0	10	Phillips 11, Paine 35	727
28	Feb	2	H	Welling U	W 1-0	1-0	7	Sparkes 9	461
29		13	A	Southport	D 1-1	1-0	6	Sparkes 30	827
30		16	H	Boreham Wood	L 0-2	0-0	7		628
31		23	H	FC Halifax T	W 2-0	1-0	7	Davis 1, Cheek 67	506
32		27	A	Guiseley	D 1-1	1-0	6	Cheek 42	788
33	Mar	1	H	Kidderminster H	W 2-1	1-0	4	Isaac 29, Paine 61	502
34		5	H	Eastleigh	W 2-0	1-0	4	Akinola 2 35, 85	666
35		8	A	Torquay U	D 0-0	0-0	4		1462
36		15	H	Gateshead	D 0-0	0-0	5		572
37		19	H	Cheltenham T	W 1-0	0-0	5	Cheek 63	1138
38		25	H	Bromley	W 1-0	1-0	4	Akinola 45	1321
39		28	A	Aldershot T	L 1-2	1-1	6	Akinola 34	1539
40	Apr	2	A	Macclesfield T	L 1-3	0-1	6	Akinola 76	1222
41		5	A	Barrow	L 0-2	0-1	6		1039
42		9	H	Forest Green R	D 1-1	1-1	6	Davis (pen) 34	740
43		12	A	Grimsby T	W 1-0	0-0	6	Miles 77	3010
44		16	A	Gateshead	W 3-2	2-1	5	Miles 2 4, 16, Brundle 48	588
45		23	A	Wrexham	W 3-2	2-2	5	Cheek 2 3, 43, Brundle 81	4507
46		30	H	Altrincham	W 3-0	2-0	3	Cheek 2 17, 42, Brundle 63	1803

Final League Position: 3

GOALSCORERS

League (56): Cheek 15, Akinola 9, Davis 6 (5 pens), Sparkes 6, Miles 5, Brundle 3, Chiedozie 2, Edgar 2, Paine 2, Szmodics 2, Isaac 1, Marks 1, Phillips 1, Woodyard 1.
FA Cup (4): Cheek 2, Davis 2 (1 pen).
FA Trophy (1): Marks 1.
Vanarama National Play-Offs (1): Davis 1 (pen).

Norris 24	Brundle 24 + 10	Clerima 27	Fry 26 + 1	Habergham 45	Woodyard 44	Isaac 30 + 8	Davis 43 + 1	Miles 10 + 29	Akinola 41	Sparkes 30 + 6	Cheek 28 + 12	Marks 11 + 21	Walker J — + 4	Phillips 38 + 1	Paine 33 + 2	Dallison 4	Chiedozie 4 + 1	Edgar 4 + 17	Cox — + 2	O'Shaughnessy — + 1	Walker A — + 1	Miller — + 1	Szmodics 3	Sekajja — + 2	Powell 3 + 4	Crowe 6	Anderson 1 + 1	Gardner — + 6	King 16	Long 9	Cardwell 2 + 2	Match No.
1	2^1	3	4	5	6^3	7	8	9^2	10	11	12	13	14																			1
1	2^4	3	4	5	6	7^2	8	12	11	9^1	10^2	13		14																		2
		2	4^2	5	8	6^1	10	13	11	9^2		12	14	3	7																	3
1	14	2		5	6	12	7		11^1	9^2			13	3	8		4	10^3														4
1		3		5	8	12	7^2	14	9^1	11	13			4	6		2	10^3														5
1		2		5	7	12		9^1	10^2			8	11^3	3	6		4	13	14													6
1	2			5	8	6^2	12		10^3	9	13			4	7	3	11^1	14														7
1	13	2		5	8^4	6	7	14	11^1	9^2	12	10^1		3	4																	8
1	12	2			6	8			10	7^2	13	11		4	5		9^1															9
1	2			5		6	7	8^1	11	9^2	12	10^1		4	3		14	13														10
1		2		5	6	8	7	12	10^3	9^1	11^2	14		4	3		13															11
1	2			5^3	7	9	8	6^1	11	12	10^2	14		4	3					13												12
1		2		5	8	6^1	7	13	11	9^2	10^2			3	4		14	12														13
1	13	2		5	6	7^1	8	12	10	9^1	11^2	14		4	3																	14
1	2	3		5^3	8	6^2	7	12	10	9	11^1	14			4		13															15
1	6	2		5	8			7^2	13	10		11^3	12	14			9^1															16
1	2	3		5	8	7^2		6	10^1		11	12	13	4			9^3			14												17
1	2	4		5	8	6	7^2			9^1	11	14		3			10^3				13											18
1	14	2	5		9	6^1	8		10^2	12	11^3	13		3	4							7										19
1	6	2	3	5	7	9		8^1			12	11^2		4								10		13								20
1	2	3	12	5^3	8	6	7	13		9^1	10^3	14										11										21
1		2	4	5	8		7	12	10	9^1	11^3	13		3											14	6^2						22
1	13	2	3	5	6		7	12	11^2	8^3	9	14		4											10^1							23
1		4		5	9	6^3	7	8	11		10	12		3	2^2		13								14							24
	5	9	2	7				8	12	10	6^1	11^2		4	3^3		14									1	13					25
	2	4	5	8	14	7^1	9				11^2	12		3	6											1	10^3					26
	2	4	5	6	13	8^1	14	10	11^3	12		9^2		3	7											1						27
	2	4	5	6	12	8	13	11^1	10^2		9^4			3	7											1						28
	2	4	5	6	7	13	11		9^1		10^2			3	8		14									1		12				29
2^2		4^3	5	10	13	7	6^1	9			11			3	8^4		12									1		14				30
13	2	4	5	7	6^3	8	14	10^2	9^1	11				3												1		12	1			31
11			2	10	3^2	5	14	6		9^3	13			7	4		8^1											12	1			32
2			5	8	6	7	12	9^3	11^1	10^2	13			3	4													14	1			33
2		4^4	5	8	6^1	10^3	12	9^2		11				3	7		14											13	1			34
2			5	7	6	8^2	14	11		9^1	12	10^3		3	4		13												1			35
14		4	5	8	6	10^2	12	9			13	11^3		3	7^1												1	2				36
13		4	5	8	7	6		11	9^1	10^2	12^3			3			14										1	2				37
2		4	5	8	7^2	6	14	9^1	10^1					3			13								12		1			11		38
2^3		4	5	7	12	8	13	11	9^2					3			14								6^1		1			10		39
13		4^3	5	6	7	9	14	8	10^1	11^1				3			12										1				2	40
8	6		5	9	7^1	10^3		4	13	12	11^2			3											14		1				2	41
7	4		5	8	6	10^1		9	13	12	11^2			3													1				2	42
7	4		5	8	6^1	10	12		9^2	11				3			13										1				2	43
4	6		5	8	10^2	7^3	9		11^1					3	13		12										1			14	2	44
7	4		5	9^3	8	6^1	10	13	11^2					3	12												1			14	2	45
6	4		5	9	8^3	13	10^1	14	11^2	12				3	7												1				2	46

FA Cup

Fourth Qualifying	Harlow T	(h)	2-0
First Round	Oxford U	(h)	1-1
Replay	Oxford U	(a)	1-3

FA Trophy

First Round	Bromley	(h)	1-0
Second Round	Stourbridge	(h)	0-1

Vanarama National Play-Offs

Semi-Finals 1st leg	Grimsby T	(a)	1-0
Semi-Finals 2nd leg	Grimsby T	(h)	0-2

aet; Grimsby T won 2-1 on aggregate.

BROMLEY

Ground: Hayes Lane, Bromley BR2 9EF. *Tel:* (02084) 605291. *Website:* bromleyfc.tv *Email:* info@bromleyfc.co.uk
Year Formed: 1892. *Record Attendance:* 10,798 v Nigeria, Friendly, 24 September 1949.
Nickname: 'The Ravens', 'The Lillywhites'. *Manager:* Neil Smith. *Colours:* White shirts, black shorts, black socks.

BROMLEY – VANARAMA NATIONAL 2015–16 LEAGUE RECORD

Match No.	Date		Venue	Opponents	Result		H/T Score	Lg Pos.	Goalscorers	Atten-dance
1	Aug	8	H	Wrexham	W	3-1	3-1	2	Francis 24, Wall 29, Emmanuel 43	2083
2		11	A	Woking	L	0-2	0-1	11		1507
3		15	A	Grimsby T	L	1-4	1-3	17	Davies 40	4731
4		18	H	Braintree T	L	1-2	0-1	20	Emmanuel 67	755
5		22	A	FC Halifax T	D	2-2	0-0	19	Emmanuel 75, Joseph-Dubois 90	1107
6		29	H	Dover Ath	D	1-1	0-0	19	Goldberg 88	1273
7		31	A	Forest Green R	L	1-2	1-2	20	Wall 7	1764
8	Sept	5	H	Gateshead	W	3-0	0-0	18	Emmanuel 2 76, 90, Dennis 85	1411
9		12	H	Macclesfield T	W	1-0	0-0	13	May 76	955
10		15	A	Boreham Wood	W	3-2	1-0	11	May 31, Emmanuel 53, Goldberg 63	364
11		19	A	Torquay U	W	7-3	3-2	9	Emmanuel 3 8, 13, 30, Holland 59, Dennis 69, Cook (pen) 72, Fuseini 80	1653
12		22	H	Kidderminster H	W	3-2	1-1	8	Dennis 37, Emmanuel 48, Cook (pen) 59	736
13		26	H	Chester FC	W	3-0	3-0	4	Emmanuel 2 19, 45, Dennis 29	1610
14	Oct	3	A	Tranmere R	L	0-4	0-1	9		4817
15		6	A	Welling U	W	2-1	1-1	5	Fuseini 25, Holland 62	1127
16		10	H	Barrow	W	5-0	2-0	4	Holland 18, Cook 25, Prestedge 49, Emmanuel 64, Dennis 88	2455
17		13	H	Cheltenham T	L	1-2	0-0	5	Cook (pen) 88	1500
18		17	A	Aldershot T	D	1-1	1-1	6	Holland 41	1617
19		31	A	Lincoln C	W	1-0	0-0	4	Emmanuel 81	2550
20	Nov	10	H	Boreham Wood	L	1-2	1-2	6	Emmanuel 39	939
21		14	H	Altrincham	L	1-3	1-1	9	Emmanuel 37	1737
22		21	A	Macclesfield T	L	0-2	0-0	11		1632
23		28	A	Guiseley	L	0-2	0-1	12		787
24	Dec	19	A	Southport	L	3-5	2-2	13	Minshull 36, Swaine 45, Francis 78	751
25		26	H	Eastleigh	D	2-2	0-0	13	Emmanuel 36, Rodgers 46	1708
26		28	H	Dover Ath	W	3-2	1-1	13	Cunnington 37, Holland 65, Prestedge 79	1537
27	Jan	9	H	Southport	D	0-0	0-0	13		1317
28		23	H	Tranmere R	L	0-1	0-0	13		2219
29		30	A	Cheltenham T	L	1-4	0-2	14	Wall 85	2662
30	Feb	9	H	Grimsby T	L	1-2	1-1	14	Francis 6	1074
31		13	A	Wrexham	L	0-2	0-2	15		3511
32		20	H	Woking	W	2-1	2-1	14	Emmanuel (pen) 24, Cunnington 30	1227
33		27	A	Kidderminster H	W	1-0	0-0	14	Anderson 86	1539
34	Mar	1	H	Welling U	W	2-0	1-0	13	Gordon 9, Emmanuel (pen) 56	1110
35		5	A	Chester FC	D	1-1	0-1	13	Emmanuel 53	2058
36		8	H	FC Halifax T	W	1-0	0-0	11	Cunnington 75	706
37		12	H	Guiseley	W	2-0	0-0	11	Goldberg 2 70, 83	1044
38		15	A	Eastleigh	L	0-2	0-2	11		1520
39		19	A	Barrow	D	1-1	0-0	11	Cunnington 57	1123
40		25	A	Braintree T	L	0-1	0-1	11		1321
41		28	H	Forest Green R	D	2-2	0-2	12	Joseph-Dubois 61, Holland 90	1455
42	Apr	2	H	Lincoln C	W	2-0	1-0	11	Cunnington 33, Goldberg 75	1202
43		9	A	Altrincham	D	0-0	0-0	12		1035
44		16	H	Torquay U	L	0-2	0-1	13		2080
45		23	A	Gateshead	L	1-3	0-2	13	Coombes 51	865
46		30	H	Aldershot T	L	1-3	1-1	14	Fuseini 16	1445

Final League Position: 14

GOALSCORERS

League (67): Emmanuel 20 (2 pens), Holland 6, Cunnington 5, Dennis 5, Goldberg 5, Cook 4 (3 pens), Francis 3, Fuseini 3, Wall 3, Joseph-Dubois 2, May 2, Prestedge 2, Anderson 1, Coombes 1, Davies 1, Gordon 1, Minshull 1, Rodgers 1, Swaine 1.
FA Cup (1): Dennis 1.
FA Trophy (0).

Julian 32	Udoji 14 + 2	Swaine 37	Francis 26 + 5	Anderson 44 + 1	Cook 19 + 1	Minshull 27 + 2	Fuseini 37 + 4	Emmanuel 41 + 2	Wall 9 + 9	Goldberg 17 + 15	Joseph-Dubois 14 + 16	May 6 + 10	Prestedge 12 + 5	Holland 43 + 1	Dennis 13 + 10	Davies 7	Porter 7 + 3	Chorley 29 + 2	Rodgers 14 + 7	Kettings 14	Tumwa 2 + 3	Kiernan 1	O'Connor — + 5	Ajakaiye — + 1	Pinau 3	Cunnington 19 + 1	Coombes 10 + 5	Allassani 2 + 1	Gordon 11 + 4	Higgs 2 + 2	Stanic-Stewart — + 1	Match No.
1	2	3	4	5	6	7	8	9²	10¹	11	12	13																				1
1	2	4³	3	5	9	7²	8	6¹	11	10			12	13	14																	2
1	2	3	6	10		4							8	13	11³	7²	5	12	9¹	14												3
1	2²		4	5	6		8	9	10¹	11	13			7³	3	14		12														4
1		3	5	9		8	6	13	11²	12	10¹		2		7	4³	14															5
1		5	4	6		7	8	12	10	13	11¹	9²	2		3																	6
1		3	5	9		8	10	11	12	6²	13	7¹	4		2																	7
1	3		5	9²		7	6	10³	11¹		14	13	2	12	8	4																8
1	4		5			3	14	11²	9	13	12	7	10	8³	6	2¹																9
1	3		5	12		4	7		11¹		10		9	8	6	2																10
1	3	13	5	9		7	11²		10³		2		6	8	4¹	12	1	14														11
1	12	3		5	6		7	11		13		10	9¹	8	4	2²	1															12
	2³	3²	12	5	6		8	11		14		10	7¹	9	4	13	1															13
	2	3		5	9	14	8	11	12		13		7¹	10⁵	6²		4			1												14
	12	3		5	9		8	10	11¹		7	2	6		4					1												15
	2³	4	14	5	9¹		7	11²		13	12		8	6	10		3			1												16
	2¹	4³	12	9	8		3	10		13	6²		7	5			11			1	14											17
	2		5	3	8	12	6	11		7¹	9	10		4						1												18
	2	3		5	6	8	7	10		11	9		4							1												19
	2	4		5¹		7	9	11		10	8	12		3²			1	13	6													20
	2¹	3		5	8	9	6²	11		13	12		7	10			4			1												21
		4		5	8	9	6³	11		13		7²	2	10¹		12	3	14		1												22
	2²	4			10	6	11	12		8		9³	7		5			1	3¹		13	14										23
	4¹	13	3		7	8³	11	12		6¹		2		5	14	1		9	10													24
1		3	4	12		7		10		13		2		8	6²		5¹		9	11												25
1	2³	4¹		5		6		10	13	12		14	8	3	7		11²	9														26
1		4	3	5		7		11	12	8²		13	2	9	6		10¹															27
1		3	4¹	5		8	14	11	12	9²		2⁴	7	6		10	13															28
1		3	4	5		7	12	9	10	13		2	8¹	6³		11²	14															29
1			4	5		7	8	11	13	14	12		3	2		10¹	6²	9³														30
1			4	5		7	8	11	10¹	14	12		3	2		13	9³	6²														31
1		3	4	5		8	7	10²	13	12		2		11¹	9	6																32
1		4	3	5		7	8	11²	13	12		2	14	9¹	10³	6																33
1		3	4	5		7¹	8	11²	14	2	13	10	9⁹	12	6																	34
1		3	4	5		7	10³	13	12	2	8¹	14	11	9¹	6																	35
1		3	4	5		8	14	11³	12	6²	2	13	7	10¹	9																	36
1		3	4	5		8		10¹	12	9²	13	2	14	7	11³	6																37
1		3	4	5		7	12	13	10³	6	2	14	8¹	11	9²																	38
1		3	4	5		7	8	11¹	14	6	13	2	12	10²	9³																	39
1		3	2	5		8	7	11²	12	6	10¹	4	9³	13	14																	40
1		2		3		8	5	10²	13	7¹	6	12	4⁴	9	11³	14																41
1		4	5			3	8¹	11	9	6	2		13	10	7¹	12																42
1		3	4¹	5		8	7	10	11	6	2			9²	12	13																43
1		3		8		9³	2⁸	10	6	5²	4		14	7	11¹	13	12															44
1		3		5				10	6¹	4	8²	2	13	11³	12	9	7	14														45
1		2²	4	5		6		10	12	7	3	13	14	11	8³	9¹																46

FA Cup
Fourth Qualifying   Eastleigh   (h)   1-2

FA Trophy
First Round   Braintree T   (a)   0-1

CHELTENHAM TOWN

Ground: The Abbey Business Stadium, Whaddon Road, Cheltenham, Gloucestershire GL52 5NA.
Tel: (01242) 573558.   *Website:* www.ctfc.com   *Email:* info@ctfc.com   *Year Formed:* 1892.
Record Attendance: 10,389 v Blackpool, FA Cup 3rd rd, 13 January 1934 (at Cheltenham Athletic Ground);
8,326 v Reading, FA Cup 1st rd, 17 November 1956 (at Whaddon Road).   *Nickname:* 'The Robins'.
Manager: Gary Johnson.   *Colours:* Red and white striped shirts, white shorts, white socks.

CHELTENHAM TOWN – VANARAMA NATIONAL 2015–16 LEAGUE RECORD

Match No.	Date		Venue	Opponents	Result	H/T Score	Lg Pos.	Goalscorers	Attendance
1	Aug	8	A	Lincoln C	D 1-1	1-0	17	Munns [26]	2767
2		11	H	Aldershot T	D 0-0	0-0	11		2552
3		15	H	Southport	W 3-0	0-0	11	Downes [51], Morgan-Smith 2 [76, 82]	2251
4		18	A	Chester FC	D 1-1	0-1	7	Storer [48]	2304
5		22	H	Barrow	W 2-1	0-1	6	Storer [72], Dickie [88]	2209
6		29	A	Torquay U	W 3-0	1-0	5	Downes [30], Wright 2 (1 pen) [61, 85 (p)]	2018
7		31	H	Wrexham	W 2-1	0-0	6	Parslow [59], Morgan-Smith [84]	2827
8	Sept	5	A	Altrincham	L 1-2	0-0	4	Downes [82]	1206
9		12	H	Dover Ath	W 3-2	1-2	3	Waters 2 [38, 84], Wright (pen) [55]	2021
10		15	H	Macclesfield T	W 2-0	2-0	2	Pell [17], Wright [43]	1962
11		19	A	Woking	W 1-0	0-0	2	Wright [67]	2035
12		22	A	Forest Green R	D 2-2	1-0	3	Morgan-Smith [45], Pell [77]	3127
13		26	H	Tranmere R	L 0-1	0-0	2		2556
14	Oct	3	A	FC Halifax T	W 7-1	2-1	1	Munns 3 (1 pen) [12, 90 (p), 90], Morgan-Smith [40], Wright [47], Pell [58], Waters [80]	1267
15		6	H	Braintree T	D 1-1	1-1	2	Waters [90]	2097
16		10	A	Gateshead	D 1-1	0-1	2	Wright [50]	1238
17		13	A	Bromley	W 2-1	0-0	2	Waters [78], Hall [90]	1500
18		17	H	Eastleigh	D 1-1	1-0	1	Munns [20]	2802
19		30	A	Grimsby T	W 1-0	0-0	1	Downes [68]	5218
20	Nov	10	H	Guiseley	W 5-0	2-0	1	Waters 2 [1, 62], Dickie [9], Munns [80], Rowe, J [90]	2237
21		14	A	Southport	W 4-0	3-0	1	Pell [4], Waters 2 [8, 14], Parslow [53]	947
22		21	H	Forest Green R	D 1-1	0-0	1	Pell [52]	5449
23		28	A	Aldershot T	W 2-0	2-0	1	Pell [7], Munns [28]	1493
24	Dec	5	H	Chester FC	W 3-1	1-1	1	Waters 2 [18, 60], Wright [88]	2501
25		19	H	Altrincham	W 1-0	0-0	1	Wright (pen) [58]	2591
26		26	A	Kidderminster H	W 2-1	1-1	1	Wright [26], Downes [67]	3238
27		28	H	Torquay U	W 1-0	0-0	1	Munns [59]	3781
28	Jan	9	A	Boreham Wood	D 0-0	0-0	1		647
29		24	A	Dover Ath	W 2-1	0-0	1	Wright 2 (1 pen) [88 (p), 89]	1184
30		30	H	Bromley	W 4-1	2-0	2	Holman 2 [20, 25], Wright 2 [49, 63]	2662
31	Feb	6	A	Barrow	W 2-1	1-0	1	Wright [2], Hall [82]	1202
32		13	H	Welling U	W 2-0	1-0	1	Wright [17], Holman [51]	2549
33		16	H	Kidderminster H	W 2-0	0-0	1	Wright (pen) [50], Holman [57]	3387
34		20	A	Tranmere R	W 1-0	1-0	1	Wright [3]	5418
35		23	H	Gateshead	D 0-0	0-0	1		2201
36	Mar	1	A	Eastleigh	L 0-1	0-1	1		1982
37		5	A	Welling U	D 1-1	1-1	1	Holman [90]	604
38		12	H	Woking	W 4-0	2-0	1	Holman 4 [32, 38, 58, 64]	2951
39		19	A	Braintree T	L 0-1	0-0	1		1138
40		25	H	Boreham Wood	W 4-1	2-0	1	Wright 2 (2 pens) [17, 51], Holman 2 [41, 90]	3243
41		28	A	Wrexham	L 1-2	1-1	1	Dayton [41]	4463
42	Apr	1	H	Grimsby T	W 3-1	1-0	1	Dayton [35], Pell [58], Wright [77]	4003
43		9	A	Guiseley	W 2-0	0-0	1	Dickie [80], Holman [89]	1058
44		16	H	FC Halifax T	W 2-0	2-0	1	Holman 2 (1 pen) [24, 33 (p)]	5245
45		23	A	Macclesfield T	W 1-0	1-0	1	Holman [7]	1895
46		30	H	Lincoln C	W 3-1	1-1	1	Wright [39], Storer [62], Holman [78]	5055

Final League Position: 1

GOALSCORERS

League (87): Wright 22 (7 pens), Holman 16 (1 pen), Waters 11, Munns 8 (1 pen), Pell 7, Downes 5, Morgan-Smith 5, Dickie 3, Storer 3, Dayton 2, Hall 2, Parslow 2, Rowe, J 1.
FA Cup (4): Hayter 1, Paterson 1, Strugnell 1, Wright 1.
FA Trophy (5): Dickie 3 (1 pen), Dale 1, Rowe.

Phillips 36	Barthram 38+4	Downes 28	Parslow 46	McLennan 34+4	Pell 34+5	Storer 46	Munns 31+11	Waters 18+19	Wright 43	Morgan-Smith 21+6	Hanks —+1	Hall 18+16	Cooke —+6	Bowen —+1	Dickie 26+1	Rowe J 12+16	Vaughan 2+8	Dayton 13+9	Jennings 6+3	Novakovich 1+3	Harries —+1	Holman 18	Burgess 17	Cranston 8+7	Kitscha —+1	Flatt 10	Match No.
1	2	3	4	5	6²	7	8	9	10	11¹	12	13															1
1	2	4	5	3	7	6	11	8³	9	10¹	12	13															2
1	2	3	4	5¹	6	7	8	9³	10²	11	12		14		13												3
1	2	3	4	5	6	7	8	9¹	10	11	12																4
1	2	3	4	5	6²	7	8	9¹	10³	11	12		14		13												5
1	5	4	3	9⁴	6	7	8²	10³	11¹	12	14				2	13											6
1	5	4	3		6	7	9³	13	10²	11	8¹	14			2		12										7
1	5	3	4		7²	6	9	12	11	10	8¹	14			2²		13										8
1	5	4	3		7	6	8¹	9²	10	11					2	13	12										9
1	6²	4	5	14	7¹	8	12	9¹	11	10					3	13	2										10
1	2	3	5	6	7	8	9²	13	10¹	11	12				4												11
1	2	5	6	3	7	4	10		8	9					11												12
1	14	4	3	9		8	13	12	10	11				6³	2	7²	5¹										13
1	5¹	3	4	8	6²	7³	9	13	10	11	14				2		12										14
1	2²	4	5	6	7	8	9¹	12	11	10					3	13											15
1	5²	3	2	9	6	8	7¹	12	10	11					4		13										16
1	2³	5	6	3	7¹	4	10	12	8	9²	14				11		13										17
1	5¹	4	3	6	7	8	9³	12	10	11²					2	13	14										18
1	2²	4	5	3	7	8	9¹	10	11						6	12	13										19
1	12	3	4	5	7³	8¹	9	10	11				13		2	14		6²									20
1	6	4¹	5	3	9	8	7²	10	11						2	14		12³	13								21
1	6¹	3	4²	5	7	8	9	10	11						2		13		12								22
1		3	4	5	8	7	9²	10³	11¹				14		2	13			6	12							23
1		3	4	5	7	6	8²	9¹	10				13		2	14			11³	12							24
1	2	3	4	5	7	8	9²	10³	11				14			12		6¹	13								25
1	2	3	4	5	8	7	9¹	12	10				14			13		6²	11³								26
1	2²	3	4	5	7	8	9³	10	11				14			2		13	6²								27
1		3	4	5	8	9	7³	11¹	10				12			2		13	6²		14						28
1	2		4	5	8	7	9¹	6²	11				3			12		14	13³			10					29
1	2²		3	7			8	13	14	10			6			9¹		5³				11	4	12			30
1	2²		3	5³	12	8		14	10	7						9¹		6				11	4	13			31
1	2		3		12³	7	13	14	10				8¹			9		6²				11	4	5			32
1	2		3	5		7	13	12	11				8²			9³		6¹				10	4	14			33
1	2²		3	5		7	13		10				8			9		6¹				11	4	12			34
1	2¹		3	13		7		12	10				8			9		6²				11	4	5			35
1³	2		3	5²		8	12		10	7			9			6¹		11	4	13	14						36
	2		3	12	13	7	9		11¹	14			8³		5²			10	4	6						1	37
	2		4	12	13	8	9	14	11				7²		6¹			10	3	5³						1	38
	2		3	5	12	8	6²		11	13			7		9¹			10	4							1	39
			4		6	8	13		10¹	14			7²		2	12		9³		11	3	5				1	40
	14		3		9	7			10²	13			8¹		2	12		6³		11	4	5				1	41
	14		3	5	7	8¹	12		10	9²					2			6³		11	4	13				1	42
	2¹		3	6	8⁴	7	9³	12		10²			13		4		14			11	5					1	43
	6³		3	5		7²	12	13		10			8		2			9¹		11	4	14				1	44
	5		3		7	6	14	11²		13					4	12		9³		10	2	8¹				1	45
	5¹		4		8	9	12			10³	14				6²			13			11	3	7			1	46

FA Cup

Fourth Qualifying	Havant & Waterlooville	(a)	3-3
Replay	Havant & Waterlooville	(h)	1-0
First Round	Hartlepool U	(a)	0-1

FA Trophy

First Round	Chelmsford C	(h)	3-1
Second Round	Oxford C	(a)	2-2
Replay	Oxford C	(h)	0-3

CHESTER FC

Ground: Lookers Vauxhall Stadium, Bumpers Lane, Chester CH1 4LT. *Tel:* (01244) 371376.
Website: www.chesterfc.com *Email:* info@chesterfc.com *Year Formed:* 1885, renamed Chester City 1983, reformed
as Chester FC 2010. *Record Attendance:* 20,500 v Chelsea, FA Cup 3rd rd (replay), 16 January 1952 (at Sealand
Road). *Nickname:* 'The Blues'. *Manager:* Jon McCarthy. *Colours:* Blue shirts with white sleeves, blue shorts with
white trim, white socks with blue trim.

CHESTER FC – VANARAMA NATIONAL 2015–16 LEAGUE RECORD

Match No.	Date	Venue	Opponents	Result	H/T Score	Lg Pos.	Goalscorers	Attendance
1	Aug 8	H	Braintree T	W 1-0	1-0	6	Hunt [4]	2256
2	11	A	FC Halifax T	W 1-0	1-0	3	Chappell [34]	1732
3	15	A	Dover Ath	D 0-0	0-0	5		801
4	18	H	Cheltenham T	D 1-1	1-0	8	Hannah [8]	2304
5	22	A	Woking	L 2-5	0-1	11	Sharps [65], Rooney [89]	1503
6	29	A	Macclesfield T	W 2-1	0-0	7	Hobson [90], Peers [90]	2062
7	31	H	Guiseley	D 1-1	0-0	8	Rooney (pen) [65]	2304
8	Sept 5	H	Forest Green R	L 1-2	0-1	11	George [61]	2163
9	12	A	Tranmere R	L 0-2	0-2	12		7433
10	15	H	Grimsby T	D 1-1	0-0	15	Hannah (pen) [73]	1964
11	19	H	Eastleigh	W 1-0	1-0	13	Heneghan [11]	1922
12	22	A	Welling U	L 1-2	0-1	15	Hannah [90]	564
13	26	A	Bromley	L 0-3	0-3	17		1610
14	Oct 3	H	Wrexham	W 3-2	1-1	14	Rooney [34], Shaw [58], Richards [69]	3741
15	6	A	Barrow	L 2-3	1-1	16	Chappell [30], Shaw [72]	1345
16	10	H	Lincoln C	L 2-3	1-2	16	Chappell [26], Hannah [67]	2224
17	13	A	Southport	W 2-1	0-1	16	Kay [79], Mahon [84]	1326
18	17	H	FC Halifax T	W 2-1	1-0	14	Roberts [44], Hunt [55]	2088
19	31	A	Forest Green R	L 1-2	1-2	14	Hannah [12]	1561
20	Nov 10	H	Kidderminster H	W 3-1	1-1	14	Hannah 2 [42, 82], Rooney [46]	1956
21	14	A	Boreham Wood	D 0-0	0-0	13		589
22	21	H	Woking	L 1-2	0-1	13	Hannah [90]	1837
23	24	A	Dover Ath	D 1-1	1-1	14	Hannah [45]	1479
24	28	A	Gateshead	L 0-1	0-0	15		842
25	Dec 5	A	Cheltenham T	L 1-3	1-1	15	Hannah [45]	2501
26	19	H	Torquay U	W 4-1	3-0	14	Hannah 3 [1, 40, 72], Higgins [38]	2160
27	28	H	Macclesfield T	L 0-2	0-2	14		2791
28	Jan 2	A	Altrincham	D 1-1	1-0	15	Hannah [20]	2155
29	9	A	Aldershot T	L 1-3	0-0	16	Rooney [78]	1617
30	23	H	Southport	D 0-0	0-0	17		2228
31	30	A	Braintree T	L 0-2	0-2	17		727
32	Feb 16	H	Altrincham	W 3-0	2-0	16	O'Brien [26], Astles [45], Hannah [76]	1442
33	20	A	Kidderminster H	D 2-2	0-2	15	Hannah (pen) [66], Alabi [76]	2067
34	28	H	Tranmere R	L 0-1	0-0	15		3494
35	Mar 5	A	Bromley	D 1-1	1-0	17	Hannah [16]	2058
36	8	H	Aldershot T	W 8-2	6-1	15	Hughes 2 [5, 38], Alabi 4 [13, 35, 42, 45], Hannah 2 [54, 73]	1425
37	12	A	Eastleigh	L 0-1	0-0	16		1831
38	19	A	Wrexham	L 0-3	0-0	16		6459
39	26	H	Barrow	L 1-2	1-0	17	Hannah [37]	2020
40	28	A	Guiseley	D 3-3	1-0	17	Hannah [39], Richards [83], Shaw [90]	1186
41	Apr 2	H	Boreham Wood	D 2-2	1-1	17	Rooney 2 [11, 65]	1444
42	5	A	Torquay U	L 0-2	0-1	17		1831
43	9	A	Lincoln C	L 1-2	0-1	17	Alabi [73]	2001
44	16	H	Welling U	W 4-0	1-0	18	Rooney 2 [17, 47], Richards [66], Shaw [84]	2237
45	23	A	Grimsby T	W 2-1	0-0	17	Rooney [48], Astles [61]	4575
46	30	H	Gateshead	W 4-2	0-0	17	Richards [60], Higgins [62], Hannah 2 [76, 80]	2323

Final League Position: 17

GOALSCORERS

League (67): Hannah 23 (2 pens), Rooney 10 (1 pen), Alabi 6, Richards 4, Shaw 4, Chappell 3, Astles 2, Higgins 2,
Hughes 2, Hunt 2, George 1, Heneghan 1, Hobson 1, Kay 1, Mahon 1, O'Brien 1, Peers 1, Roberts 1, Sharps 1.
FA Cup (0).
FA Trophy (6): Hannah 3, Chappell 1, Gilchrist 1, Hunt 1.

Wornsop 34	Higgins 41 + 3	Heneghan 42 + 1	Sharps 32 + 1	Hunt 43 + 1	Shaw 35 + 5	George 21 + 2	Rooney 36 + 5	Chappel 29 + 7	Hannah 40 + 2	Hobson 10 + 18	Mahon 20 + 19	Peers — + 7	Tonge 1 + 2	Kay 9 + 3	Thomson 5 + 7	Richards 5 + 13	O'Hanlon 2	Hughes 12 + 7	Roberts 6	McDonagh — + 1	Dyson 2 + 2	Woodland — + 1	Whitmore 5	Lloyd 21 + 1	Hattersley 6	Hewitt 1 + 1	Gilchrist — + 2	Astles 16	Alabi 13 + 3	Thompson 12	O'Brien 7 + 2	Bell — + 3	Match No.
1	2	3	4	5	6[3]	7	8	9[1]	10	11[2]	12	13	14																				1
1	3	4	2	5	7	6	8	10[1]	11[2]		9[3]	14			12	13																	2
1	2	3	4	5	7	8	10	6[2]	11	12	9[1]				13																		3
1	2	3	4	5	7	6	9[2]	10	11	12	8[1]				13																		4
1	2	3[4]	4	5	7[2]	8	6	9[3]	11[1]	10	12			14	13																		5
1	2		4	5	7[3]	6	8	9[2]		10	11[1]	14			3	12	13																6
1	5	3	4	8	13		7	9[1]		10[2]	12	14			2	6[3]	11																7
1	9	3	4	5	8	6[1]	7	13		11[2]	12	2			14			10[3]															8
1	6	3	4	5	8		7		10[1]	14	9[3]			2	13	11[2]		12															9
1	2	3	4	5	6		7	9[1]	10	11[2]		14			8[3]	13		12															10
1	2	3	4	5	6		7	9	10	11[2]	12				8[1]			13															11
1	2	9	4	3	5		6[1]	7	11	10[3]	12				8[2]	13		14															12
1	2	3[4]	4	5	8		9	7	11	10[2]	6	13			12																		13
1	2	3	5	6	7		8	13	10	11[1]					4			12			9[2]												14
1	2	6	4	5	7		8	9[2]	10	12					3[1]	14	13	13															15
1	2	8[1]	4	5	7		9	6	11	10[2]					3	12		13															16
1	5[2]	2	3	9	8		6	7	11	14	12				4	10[3]		13															17
1	5	2	3	9	6		7[3]		10[1]	14	8				4	12		13	11[2]														18
1	2	13	5[2]	3	8	6		9	10		7				4			11[1]	12														19
1	2	4	3	5	6	7	8[1]	12	10	14	9[3]							11[2]	13														20
1	2	4	3	5	7	6	8[2]	13	11	14	12							9[3]	10[1]														21
1	2	3	4	5	7		8[1]	9[2]	10	13	6							11[1]	12	14													22
1	2	4		5	6	7	8	12	10	13	9[2]								11[1]				3										23
1	2	3		5	6[1]	8	7	13	10		12													4	9[2]	11							24
1	2		3	5	7	8		6	11		12													4	9	10							25
1	2	3	4	5	8[1]	6		13		10[2]	14	12												7	9[3]	11							26
1	5	2	3[2]	9	6	7[3]		13		10	14	12												4	8[1]	11							27
1	2	3	4	5	8		7[2]		10	13	6													9	11[1]	12							28
1	2	3	4[1]	5	12		8	13		10					6									7[3]	11	9[3]	14						29
1	2	3		5		6	7	8	11		9				10													4					30
1	2	3	14	5		7	8	9[1]	10		6[3]							13										12	4	11[2]			31
12	4	2				7	11	10[1]		5[2]								13	6					8				3	14	1	9[3]		32
12	2	3				7[3]	10	11		9[1]								14	8					6				4	13	1	5[2]		33
	2	3[4]	12			6	9	10[1]		13								8						7				4	11	1	5[2]	14	34
	2	3	5		12		9[1]	10		14								8						7				4	11[2]	1	6[3]	13	35
	2	3	5	13			9	10		14								8[1]						7				4	11[2]	1	6[3]	12	36
	2	3	5	12			9[2]	10	14	13								8						4				6	11[1]	1	7[3]		37
	2	3	5	13		14	9[2]	10		12[3]								8						7				4[1]	11	1	6[1]		38
	2	3	4	5	7	6		10										8						9[1]					11	1	12		39
1	3	6	4	7	5			11							12			9						8				2	10[1]				40
1	5	2[3]	9	7	12	6		10		14					13	3								8[1]				4	11[2]				41
1			4	5	8[2]	9[3]	7		11	12	10				14	2								13				3	6[1]				42
12	4[1]		5	9	8	7	14	11		6[2]						2[3]								10				3	13	1			43
	2	3	5	7		6	9[2]	13	12		10[1]													8				4	11[3]	1	14		44
	2	4	5	7	14	6	9[2]	12	13		10[2]													8				3	11[1]	1			45
	2	3	5	7		9	6[2]	13	14	12	10[1]				10[1]									8				4	11[3]	1			46

FA Cup

Fourth Qualifying	Altrincham		(a)	0-1

FA Trophy

First Round	AFC Telford U	(a)	2-0
Second Round	Hungerford T	(h)	4-0
Third Round	FC Halifax T	(a)	0-1

DOVER ATHLETIC

Ground: Crabbie Athletic Ground, Lewisham Road, River, Dover, Kent CT17 0JB. *Tel:* (01304) 822373.
Website: doverathletic.com *Email:* enquiries@doverathletic.com *Year Formed:* 1894 as Dover FC, reformed as
Dover Ath 1983. *Record Attendance:* 7,000 v Folkestone, 13 October 1951 (Dover FC); 5,645 v Crystal Palace,
FA Cup 3rd rd, 4 January 2015 (Dover Ath). *Nickname:* 'The Whites'. *Manager:* Chris Kinnear.
Colours: White shirts with black trim, black shorts with white trim, black socks.

DOVER ATHLETIC – VANARAMA NATIONAL 2015–16 LEAGUE RECORD

Match No.	Date	Venue	Opponents	Result	H/T Score	Lg Pos.	Goalscorers	Attendance
1	Aug 8	A	Barrow	L	1-2	1-2	15	Deverdics [18]	2285
2	11	H	Kidderminster H	W	3-2	2-0	9	Grimes [40], Miller [45], Payne [83]	906
3	15	H	Chester FC	D	0-0	0-0	13		801
4	18	A	Aldershot T	D	1-1	1-1	13	Payne [7]	1559
5	22	H	Altrincham	W	2-1	1-1	10	Ofori-Acheampong [22], Raggett [90]	711
6	29	A	Bromley	D	1-1	0-0	12	Deverdics [70]	1273
7	31	H	Boreham Wood	W	2-1	2-1	7	Parkinson [15], Grimes [17]	1012
8	Sept 5	A	Southport	D	0-0	0-0	7		957
9	12	A	Cheltenham T	L	2-3	2-1	11	Deverdics (pen) [4], Payne [31]	2021
10	15	H	Braintree T	D	0-0	0-0	10		638
11	19	H	Guiseley	D	0-0	0-0	14		823
12	22	A	Eastleigh	W	5-2	1-1	10	Miller 2 [18, 86], Deverdics 2 (2 pens) [48, 63], Murphy [83]	1360
13	25	H	Woking	W	2-0	1-0	5	Payne 2 [3, 76]	864
14	Oct 3	A	Gateshead	W	3-2	1-2	5	Payne [4], Thomas [62], Parkinson [80]	949
15	6	A	Torquay U	W	3-2	1-1	4	Payne 2 [15, 90], Parkinson [69]	1210
16	10	H	Wrexham	W	2-1	1-0	3	Miller [31], Ajala [51]	1253
17	13	A	Braintree T	L	0-1	0-1	3		637
18	17	H	Macclesfield T	W	2-1	1-1	3	Payne [6], Deverdics (pen) [56]	1012
19	31	A	Tranmere R	W	1-0	1-0	3	Miller [42]	4486
20	Nov 10	H	Eastleigh	L	1-2	0-0	3	Modeste [62]	913
21	14	A	Forest Green R	L	1-3	1-0	6	Deverdics [38]	1661
22	21	H	Barrow	W	3-1	3-0	4	Modeste [11], Orlu [19], Miller [35]	847
23	24	A	Chester FC	D	1-1	1-1	3	Miller [37]	1479
24	28	A	FC Halifax T	L	2-4	1-3	6	Miller [19], Payne [63]	1067
25	Dec 5	H	Aldershot T	W	5-2	2-0	3	Deverdics [1], Parkinson [35], Payne [61], Raggett 2 [69, 75]	1012
26	19	A	Grimsby T	L	0-1	0-0	5		4266
27	26	A	Welling U	W	2-1	1-0	4	Modeste [13], Deverdics [68]	1006
28	28	H	Bromley	L	2-3	1-1	5	Miller 2 [8, 71]	1537
29	Jan 9	A	Lincoln C	W	3-2	1-1	4	Miller 2 [42, 65], Deverdics (pen) [55]	2402
30	24	H	Cheltenham T	L	1-2	0-0	5	Deverdics [83]	1184
31	Feb 13	H	Gateshead	W	4-0	3-0	5	Miller 2 [24, 45], Deverdics [31], Payne [56]	638
32	Mar 1	H	Southport	L	1-2	0-1	9	Miller [62]	588
33	5	A	Woking	W	1-0	1-0	7	Parkinson [35]	1305
34	8	H	Welling U	W	2-1	1-1	6	Payne [23], Raggett [50]	726
35	12	A	Tranmere R	D	0-0	0-0	7		1460
36	15	H	Lincoln C	W	4-1	1-0	4	Payne 2 [3, 60], Miller 2 [58, 72]	743
37	19	A	Guiseley	W	1-0	1-0	4	Payne [6]	690
38	26	H	Torquay U	W	5-0	4-0	4	Modeste [34], Deverdics (pen) [39], Miller [41], Payne [45], Kinnear [85]	1367
39	28	A	Boreham Wood	L	0-3	0-2	5		602
40	Apr 2	H	FC Halifax T	W	1-0	1-0	4	Deverdics [8]	1027
41	5	A	Altrincham	W	2-1	0-1	4	Miller [67], Payne [74]	1007
42	9	A	Wrexham	W	1-0	0-0	3	Modeste [61]	4931
43	12	A	Macclesfield T	D	0-0	0-0	3		1022
44	16	H	Grimsby T	D	1-1	0-1	3	Parkinson [56]	1957
45	23	H	Kidderminster H	D	1-1	1-1	4	Miller [45]	1410
46	30	H	Forest Green R	L	0-1	0-0	5		1651

Final League Position: 5

GOALSCORERS
League (75): Miller 20, Payne 18, Deverdics 14 (6 pens), Parkinson 6, Modeste 5, Raggett 4, Grimes 2, Ajala 1, Kinnear 1, Murphy 1, Ofori-Acheampong 1, Orlu 1, Thomas 1.
FA Cup (3): Payne 1, Raggett 1, Thomas 1.
FA Trophy (11): Payne 4, Deverdics 2, Miller 1, Ofori-Acheampong 1, Orlu 1, Parkinson 1, Raggett 1.
Vanarama National Play-Offs (1): Miller 1.

Walker 34	Raggett 43	Orlu 42	Grimes 26+5	Magri 42+1	Bellamy 22+3	Murphy 6+15	Deverdics 45	Sterling 23+6	Payne 42	Miller 45	Young —+2	Modeste 24+5	Otori-Acheampong 6+13	Wynter —+4	Diallo 2+8	Parkinson 36+3	Thomas 21+3	Gibbs 3+2	Ajala 7+9	Rafferty 12	Pinnock —+2	Marsh 1+7	Crawford —+6	Kinnear 9+2	Braham-Barrett 11	Essam 4+4	Paxman —+1	Match No.
1	2	3	4	5¹	6	7²	8	9	10	11¹	12	13	14															1
1	5	3	4	2¹	8	7¹	9	6	10	11²	13	12	14															2
1	5	3	4	2¹	8		9	6	10	11¹			7	12	13													3
1	3	5	4	2¹	7		8	6²	11	10			9³	13	12	14												4
1	5	3	4	2	8		9	6	7¹	11		10²	13	14	12													5
1	3	4	5	2	7		8	6	11	9¹		10²	13		12													6
1	5	3	4	2	8		9	6	11	10¹		12			7													7
1	5	3	4	2	8		9	6²	11¹	10						13	7	12										8
1	3	4	5	2¹	8		7	6²	11■	10¹		14				9	13	12										9
1	3	2	4	5	7		8	6²		10		12⁹				11¹	8■	13	14									10
1	3	4	5	2	7		8		11	9¹		10				6			12									11
1	3	4	5	2	7	12	9		11²	10¹					13	6	8											12
1	5	3	4	2	7³	12	9		10	11¹		13		14		6	8²											13
1	5	3	4	2		12	9	13	10	11¹		14				7	6²	8²										14
1	4	3			8	12	9	13	11	10²		14				5	7	2³	6¹									15
1	6	3	4			12	9		10	11¹	13					7	5	2	8²									16
	2	3	12			14	7	4	11	10¹	13					6	9	5³	8²									17
1	4	6	3	2		13	9		11	10¹	12					8	5	7²										18
1	3	2	4	5		12	6	14	11²	10¹	9¹					7	8	13										19
	5	3	4	2			9		11	10	7					8	6					1						20
	3		2	5			8	4	10	11	6					7	9					1						21
	5	3	4	2		13	9		11	10¹	7²					8	6	12				1						22
	7	4	3	2			6		11¹	10	9					8	5	12				1						23
	2	4	3	5⁶		13	6		11	10	9¹					7	8	12				1						24
	5	3	4	2		13	9		11³	10¹	7²		14			8	6	12				1						25
	3	4		2			8	7	11	6	5					9	10¹	12				1						26
	3	4		2	12	8	7	11¹	6²	5						9	10	13				1						27
	4	3		2⁶	12	8	5	11■	10	9¹						7	6	13				1						28
	5	6	12	4²		7¹	8	2	10	11		13	9	3								1						29
	4	3		2	12	11¹	9	5		10	7	13				8	6²					1						30
1	4	3		2	6		9	5	11¹	10³	7²					8							12	13	14			31
1	4	3		2	6¹		8	5	10	11	7					9							12					32
1	2	3	5		8	7	4	9	10¹	11						6								12				33
1	4	3		2	6³		9	5²	11	10¹	7					8							13	14	12			34
1	4	3	12	2			8		11	9¹	10					6							13	14	7	5²		35
1	5	3	12	2		7		9	11¹	10²						4							13	14	8	6³		36
1	4	5	13	2	12		8		10	7	6²					9								3¹	11			37
1	5	3¹		2	12		9		11³	10²	7					4							13	8	6	14		38
1	4	5		2	12³		6		10	11	9²					7							14	8	3¹	13		39
1	4	5		2	6		8	13	10¹	7²		12				9									3	11		40
1	5	3		2	9		8	13	11	10³		12				4									7¹	6²	14	41
1	2	4	5			7	14	11	10²	8¹	13					3									6³	9	12	42
1	4¹	6■		3	12		7		11	10²	9	13				8									5	2		43
1	5²		13	2	8		9		11	10	7¹					4							12		6	3		44
1				2	7		8	5	11	10	9					3									12	6¹	4	45
			3		8	9¹		4				11²		6		5					1		12	10	13	7³	2 14	46

EASTLEIGH

Ground: The Silverlake Stadium, Stoneham Lane, Eastleigh, Hampshire SO50 9HT.   *Tel:* (02380) 613361.
Website: eastleighfc.com   *Email:* admin@eastleighfc.com   *Year Formed:* 1946.
Record Attendance: 4,216 v Macclesfield, Vanarama Conference, 28 February 2015.   *Nickname:* 'Spitfires'.
Manager: Chris Todd.   *Colours:* Blue shirts with white trim, white shorts, blue socks.

EASTLEIGH – VANARAMA NATIONAL 2015–16 LEAGUE RECORD

Match No.	Date		Venue	Opponents	Result		H/T Score	Lg Pos.	Goalscorers	Atten-dance
1	Aug	8	A	Southport	W	4-0	1-0	1	Reason [41], Turley [53], Strevens (pen) [74], Constable [90]	1017
2		11	H	Boreham Wood	W	1-0	0-0	1	Constable [90]	1427
3		15	H	Lincoln C	D	1-1	0-1	3	Constable [77]	1354
4		18	A	Welling U	D	2-2	1-1	6	Constable [22], Strevens [78]	545
5		22	H	Macclesfield T	W	1-0	0-0	4	Lafayette [66]	1928
6		29	A	Aldershot T	W	2-1	1-0	3	Constable [34], Cook [90]	1778
7		31	H	Torquay U	W	3-2	2-0	2	Odubade [4], Cook [29], Payne [71]	1819
8	Sept	5	A	Barrow	L	0-1	0-1	2		1448
9		12	H	Gateshead	L	1-2	0-2	6	Ramsden (og) [79]	2264
10		15	A	Altrincham	D	1-1	0-1	6	Odubade [87]	677
11		19	A	Chester FC	L	0-1	0-1	6		1922
12		22	H	Dover Ath	L	2-5	1-1	11	Lafayette [30], Cook [50]	1360
13		26	A	Wrexham	W	3-2	2-0	10	Reason [20], Drury [40], Strevens [87]	4708
14	Oct	3	H	Braintree T	L	0-2	0-1	11		1330
15		10	A	Tranmere R	W	2-1	0-0	11	Partington [47], Constable [54]	5133
16		13	H	Forest Green R	W	3-2	1-2	8	Odubade 2 [2, 50], Lafayette [90]	2884
17		17	A	Cheltenham T	D	1-1	0-1	10	Lafayette [77]	2802
18		31	H	FC Halifax T	W	2-1	0-1	7	Drury [48], Payne [70]	1890
19	Nov	10	A	Dover Ath	W	2-1	0-0	4	Constable 2 [53, 66]	913
20		14	A	Guiseley	W	4-1	2-1	3	Drury 2 [22, 72], Partington [30], Reason [90]	699
21		21	H	Grimsby T	L	0-1	0-1	7		2057
22		28	H	Southport	W	1-0	0-0	5	Drury [84]	1755
23	Dec	8	A	Macclesfield T	W	2-1	1-1	4	Constable 2 [6, 61]	1087
24		19	H	Kidderminster H	W	3-1	1-0	3	Constable [42], Drury [72], Cook [85]	1862
25		26	A	Bromley	D	2-2	0-1	3	Strevens 2 [55, 59]	1708
26		28	H	Aldershot T	D	1-1	1-1	4	Payne (pen) [8]	2107
27	Jan	23	A	Boreham Wood	D	1-1	0-1	4	Drury [90]	406
28		30	H	Wrexham	D	1-1	1-1	4	Drury [10]	1904
29	Feb	6	A	Lincoln C	L	0-3	0-3	5		2085
30		9	A	Kidderminster H	L	2-3	0-1	5	Constable 2 [61, 69]	1335
31		16	A	Gateshead	L	1-2	0-2	8	Payne [80]	648
32		20	A	Forest Green R	L	1-2	0-0	10	Constable [64]	2221
33	Mar	1	H	Cheltenham T	W	1-0	1-0	8	Burgess (og) [13]	1982
34		5	A	Braintree T	L	0-2	0-1	10		666
35		8	H	Woking	W	2-1	0-1	9	Reason [68], Evans [90]	1630
36		12	H	Chester FC	W	1-0	0-0	8	Tubbs (pen) [70]	1831
37		15	H	Bromley	W	2-0	2-0	8	Odubade [24], Reason [32]	1520
38		25	H	Welling U	D	0-0	0-0	7		2037
39		28	A	Torquay U	W	1-0	1-0	7	Cook [4]	2081
40	Apr	2	H	Guiseley	D	1-1	1-0	7	Lockwood (og) [2]	1790
41		9	A	Grimsby T	D	0-0	0-0	7		4011
42		12	H	Barrow	W	3-1	2-0	7	Coulson [9], Constable [26], Strevens [90]	3292
43		16	H	Altrincham	W	2-0	0-0	6	Reason [59], Coulson [70]	2034
44		19	A	FC Halifax T	D	0-0	0-0	6		1337
45		23	H	Tranmere R	L	0-1	0-0	7		3269
46		30	A	Woking	L	1-2	0-2	7	Tubbs [74]	1853

Final League Position: 7

GOALSCORERS

League (64): Constable 15, Drury 8, Reason 6, Strevens 6 (1 pen), Cook 5, Odubade 5, Lafayette 4, Payne 4 (1 pen), Coulson 2, Partington 2, Tubbs 2 (1 pen), Evans 1, Turley 1, own goals 3.
FA Cup (8): Constable 1, Mohamed 1, Odubade 1, Partington 1, Payne 1, Reason 1, Strevens 1 (1 pen), own goal 1.
FA Trophy (2): Constable 1, Odubade 1.

Poke 12	Partington 43	Evans 32+2	Turley 34+1	Harding 30+1	Reason 40+3	Strevens 27+4	Drury 33+2	Midson 20+18	Lafayette 13+9	Odubade 22+18	Constable 32+4	Cook 21+15	Green 22+12	Payne 32+6	Reid 21+1	Noice 4+2	Todd —+1	Flitney 30	Davies 1	Fanimo 2+6	Atkinson 2	Willmott —+1	Mohamed 3+2	Coulson 16	Lee —+1	Tubbs 14+2	Match No.
1	2	3	4	5^2	6^1	7	8	9	10	11^3	12	13	14														1
1	2	3	4	11	6	9^3	10	8^1	7^2	13	5	14		12													2
1	4	2	3	5^2	7	6	8			13	9^1	10	14	12^b	11^3												3
1	3	2	4	5	12	13	7	6	10^1	14	11	9^2		8^3													4
1	4		3	6^2	7	9	2	8^2	10^1	14	11	12	13		5												5
1	2		3	5	7^2	6^1	8	9	10^3	12	11	14			13	4											6
1	2		3	5	13	12	8	11^3	14	7^2	10	9^1			6	4											7
1	2		3	5^2	7	9		10^3	8	14	11^1	13	12	6		4											8
1^3	2	14	3^1	5^2	9	8^b		11		6	10		12	7	4	13											9
	2	8	4	3^2	9			13	11^1	12	10^2	6	5	7		14		1									10
	2	7^3	3^2	5	9			12	14	11	13	10	6	4	8^1			1									11
	2				5	14		8	6	11^3	13	10	9^4	4	7^1	12		1		3^b							12
	2	4		5	6^2	8	7	12	13	11^1	10^3	9	3	14				1									13
	2	6		5	9^1	7	11	12	10	8^2		3	4	13				1									14
	2	4	3	12	10	9	7	6^2		13	11^b		5^1	8				1									15
	2	6	3	4	8^1	7	5	11	12	10		9						1									16
	3	4	5	2	6	10	8	11^2	13	9		7^1						1		12							17
	2	4	3	5		7	11	13	10^3	8^2	12		14	9				1		6^1							18
		2	3		9	8	7		12	10^1	11		5	6	4			1									19
	6	4	3^2		9		7	12	13	11^3	10		5^2	2	8	14		1									20
	3	4			9	8^1	7	13	12	6^2	10		5	11				1			2						21
	2	4			9^1	6	7	11^2		12	10		5	8	3			1				13					22
	2				6	13	7	11^1		12	10		9^2	5	8	3		1					4				23
	2	3				9^1		7	10^2	12		11	8	5	6	4		1		13							24
	2	3				6^1	9	7		11^2	12	10	13	5	6	4		1									25
	2	4		5	6^1		7	11^2		13	10	9		8	3		1			12							26
	8		2	4^2	7	10	5	11			13	12	6	3				1					9^1				27
	2^1	4	3	5	7	12	8	10			13		6					1					9^2	11			28
1		4	3	2^1	7	10	8^3	12		11		13	6										9^2	5	14		29
1	2	4	3	5^1		8		13			10		9	7									12^2	6		11	30
1	8	3			9		14			6^1	10	12	5^2	7	4								13	2^3		11	31
	2	3			9^1	6^b	8			11	12	5	7	4				1						10			32
	2	3		5	8		7	13		12	10^2	9^1		4				1						6		10	33
	2	13	3^1	5	6^2		7			14	11	9^1		12	4			1						8		10^3	34
	5	6		2^2	8		13			11^1	10	9	12	7	4^b			1						3			35
	4	2	3	5	8		12		6^1			9^2	13	7				1						10		11	36
	2	3	4^1	5	8		13		10^3	12		9^2	14	7				1						6		11	37
	3	4^2	14	5	8		10^3		6	13	9^1		7				1		12				2		11		38
	2		3	5	8			6^2	11	9^1	13	7	4				1						10		12		39
	2		3	5	7	12			10^1	11	9^2		8^3	4			1		14				6^1		13		40
	2		3		8	6	9			12	10		5	7^b	4			1								11^1	41
	2	4	3		8	9	7	13		12	11^1		5					1						6		10^2	42
	2	4	3		8	9^2	7	12		10^1		14	5					1		13				6		11^3	43
	2	3	4		9	8	7	12		11^1		13	5					1						6^2		10	44
	2	4	3		8	9	7^3	11^2		14		13	5	12				1						6^1		10	45
	2	3			8			13	10	9			12	5	7	4^2		1		6^1						11	46

FA Cup

Fourth Qualifying	Bromley	(a)	2-1
First Round	Crewe Alex	(a)	1-0
Second Round	Stourbridge	(a)	2-0
Third Round	Bolton W	(h)	1-1
Replay	Bolton W	(a)	2-3

FA Trophy

First Round	Aldershot T	(a)	1-0
Second Round	Gateshead	(h)	1-2

FOREST GREEN ROVERS

Ground: The New Lawn, Another Way, Nailsworth, Gloucestershire GL6 0FG.   *Tel:* (01453) 834 860.
Website: www.forestgreenroversfc.com   *Email:* see website.   *Year Formed:* 1890.
Record Attendance: 4,836 v Derby Co, FA Cup 3rd rd, 3 January 2009.   *Nickname:* 'The Rovers'.
Manager: Mark Cooper.   *Colours:* Green shirts with black trim, green shorts with black trim, black socks with green trim.

FOREST GREEN ROVERS – VANARAMA NATIONAL 2015–16 LEAGUE RECORD

Match No.	Date		Venue	Opponents	Result	H/T Score	Lg Pos.	Goalscorers	Attendance
1	Aug	8	A	Altrincham	W 1-0	0-0	6	Parkin [73]	975
2		11	H	Welling U	W 1-0	1-0	3	O'Connor [45]	1076
3		15	H	Barrow	W 4-0	2-0	1	O'Connor 2 (1 pen) [19 lpl, 65], Guthrie [28], Racine [72]	1217
4		18	A	Boreham Wood	W 1-0	0-0	1	Guthrie [77]	464
5		22	H	Lincoln C	W 3-1	2-0	1	Jennings [24], O'Connor [40], Parkin [87]	1385
6		29	A	Kidderminster H	W 2-0	0-0	1	Marsh-Brown [64], Parkin [72]	1905
7		31	H	Bromley	W 2-1	2-1	1	Jennings 2 [6, 42]	1764
8	Sept	5	A	Chester FC	W 2-1	1-0	1	Frear [40], O'Connor [78]	2163
9		12	H	Southport	W 2-1	2-0	1	O'Connor [11], Marsh-Brown [21]	1535
10		15	A	Woking	L 1-2	0-1	1	Guthrie [74]	1775
11		19	A	Macclesfield T	L 1-4	1-2	1	Parkin [2]	1311
12		22	H	Cheltenham T	D 2-2	0-1	1	Pipe [64], Guthrie [82]	3127
13		26	H	Gateshead	L 0-1	0-1	1		1256
14	Oct	3	A	Grimsby T	D 1-1	1-1	1	Parkin [34]	5034
15		7	A	Aldershot T	W 3-0	2-0	1	Carter [38], Guthrie [43], O'Connor [85]	1353
16		10	H	Guiseley	W 3-0	1-0	1	Frear [25], Parkin (pen) [57], O'Connor [78]	1749
17		13	A	Eastleigh	L 2-3	2-1	1	O'Connor [21], Frear [45]	2884
18		17	H	Tranmere R	L 0-2	0-2	1		2133
19		31	H	Chester FC	W 2-1	2-1	1	Parkin [31], Marsh-Brown [33]	1561
20	Nov	10	A	Welling U	D 1-1	0-0	2	Guthrie [83]	660
21		14	H	Dover Ath	W 3-1	0-1	2	Jennings [53], Carter [58], Frear [71]	1661
22		21	A	Cheltenham T	D 1-1	0-0	2	Carter [70]	5449
23		28	H	Altrincham	W 2-0	2-0	2	Parkin 2 [1, 19]	1292
24	Dec	19	H	Boreham Wood	W 1-0	0-0	2	Guthrie [67]	1156
25		26	A	Torquay U	L 1-4	1-2	2	Marsh-Brown [20]	2051
26		28	H	Kidderminster H	W 3-0	1-0	2	Parkin (pen) [16], Williams [58], Guthrie [90]	2110
27	Jan	1	H	Torquay U	W 3-1	0-0	2	Gerring (og) [66], Carter (pen) [84], Marsh-Brown [90]	1907
28		16	A	Lincoln C	W 1-0	0-0	2	Marsh-Brown [77]	1975
29		23	H	Braintree T	W 1-0	0-0	1	Parkin [52]	1507
30		26	A	Southport	W 1-0	0-0	1	Guthrie [90]	707
31		30	H	Macclesfield T	W 2-1	0-0	1	Jennings [77], Clough [90]	1617
32	Feb	6	A	Wrexham	D 2-2	1-0	2	Carter [21], Williams [90]	3891
33		13	A	FC Halifax T	W 2-0	2-0	2	Parkin [20], Frear [30]	1329
34		20	H	Eastleigh	W 2-1	0-0	2	Parkin 2 [67, 88]	2221
35		23	A	Guiseley	W 1-0	0-0	2	Williams [82]	550
36		27	A	Barrow	D 2-2	1-0	2	Moore, K [36], Marsh-Brown [60]	1233
37	Mar	4	A	Grimsby T	L 0-1	0-0	2		2242
38		12	H	Gateshead	W 1-0	1-0	2	Jennings [13]	887
39		19	A	Tranmere R	D 1-1	1-0	2	Carter [5]	5073
40		25	H	Aldershot T	D 0-0	0-0	2		2272
41		28	A	Bromley	D 2-2	2-0	2	Guthrie 2 [4, 45]	1455
42	Apr	2	H	Wrexham	D 0-0	0-0	2		2246
43		9	A	Braintree T	D 1-1	1-1	2	Carter [37]	740
44		16	H	Woking	L 1-2	1-0	2	Moore, K [10]	1605
45		23	H	FC Halifax T	L 0-1	0-0	2		1942
46		30	A	Dover Ath	W 1-0	0-0	2	Williams [52]	1651

Final League Position: 2

GOALSCORERS

League (69): Parkin 14 (2 pens), Guthrie 11, O'Connor 9 (1 pen), Carter 7 (1 pen), Marsh-Brown 7, Jennings 6, Frear 5, Williams 4, Moore, K 2, Clough 1, Pipe 1, Racine 1, own goal 1.
FA Cup (4): Carter 1, Frear 1, Guthrie 1, Marsh-Brown 1.
FA Trophy (0):
Vanarama National Play-Offs (3): Marsh-Brown 2, Williams 1

Maxted 20	Pipe 22 + 8	Bennett 42	Racing 41	Kelly 18 + 11	Wedgbury 34 + 4	Frear 43 + 3	O'Connor 13 + 7	Sinclair 37	Parkin 30 + 9	Guthrie 28 + 12	Sam-Yorke 1 + 15	Marsh-Brown 37 + 6	Jennings 30 + 1	Kamdjo — + 4	Bender — + 2	Clough 28 + 8	Jones 8 + 2	Carter 32 + 1	Arnold 26	Williams 6 + 16	Moore K 7 + 9	Jeffrey 1 + 3	Jefford 1 + 1	Stokes 1	Match No.
1	2	3	4	5	6	7^2	8^1	9	10	11	12	13													1
1	3	4	2	5	8	9	11	7	10^2	6^1	13	12													2
1	2	3	4	14	8^3	9	10^2	7^1		11	12	6	5	13											3
1	2	3	4		8	9^2	10^3	7		11	12	6^3	5	14	13										4
1	2	3	4		8	9^2	10^3	7^1	13	6	12	11	5	14											5
1	2	3	4	12	8	9^1	10	7^2	13	11	14	6^3	5												6
1	2	3^1	4	8	7	9	10^3		11		6	14	5^2			12	13								7
1	2	4	3	5	8	9^2	12	7	10^2	11	13	6^1		14											8
1	2	3	4	5	8	9^1	11^2	7	13	10	12	6^4		14											9
1	2	4	3	12^2	7	9^1	10^2	8	13	11	14	6	5^3												10
1	5	2	4		7	13	11	8^1	10^1	6^2	12	9^2	14				3								11
1	2^1	4	9	7		8	5^3	13	10	12	6^2			14		3	11								12
1		2^3	3	5		9	10^1	7	12	11^2	13	6				14	4	8							13
1	12	3	4	6		7		8	11	10		5^1					2	9							14
1		3	4	6		7	13	8	11	10^2	12	5^1				14	2^2	9							15
1		2	4	5	13	7	14	8^1	11	10^2		6				12	3^1	9							16
1	5	2	4			9^1	11	7		10	12	6				3		8							17
1	2^1	3	4	5	6	9		7^2		11	12	10				13		8							18
1		2	4	12	8	10		6	11		9^1	5	13			3		7^1							19
1		2		6	11		7	10	12		9^1	5				4	3	8							20
13	5	3		8	9	14	7^3	10^2	11			2				12	4^1	6	1						21
	2	4		8	9	12	7	11^1	6			5				3		10	1						22
12	2^2	3	5	7	9	14		11^3	10^2		6^1					4		8	1	13					23
2		5		6	10		7	11^1	12		10^1	9				4		8^2	1	13					24
2		4	8	7	6	12		10^1	9		11^2					3		5	1	13					25
13	5^2	3	2	9	6^2		7	10	14		12					4		8^1	1	11					26
	2	4		7	11		8	10^2	13		12	5				3		6	1	9^1					27
13	2	4^1		6	8^1		7	11^2	12		10	5				3		9^3	1	14					28
14	5			8	9^1		7	10^3	12		11	2				4		6^2	1	13	3				29
14	2			7	10		6^2	11^3	13		8	5				4		9^1	1	12	3				30
	2	13		6	8		7	14	10^3		9^1	5				3		12	1	11^2	4				31
	2	4		8^1	9		7	10^1	13		6^1	5				3		11^2	1	14	12				32
7	2	3			10^1		6^2	11^3	13		8	5				4		9	1	14	12				33
6	2	4	12	13	10		8^1	11			7	5^2				3		9^1	1	14					34
6	2	4	14		10^2		8	11^3			7	5				3		9^1	1	13	12				35
6	2	4		12	10^2		8^1		13		7	5				3		9	1	14	11^2				36
5	3			6	8^2		7	11^1	14		10	2				4		9^3	1	13	12				37
	2	4	13	7	9^3		8	11^1			6	5				3		10^2	1	14	12				38
	2	3	13	7	9^3		8	11^2			6^1	5				4		10^4	1	12	14				39
	2	3		7	9^1		8	11^3	12		6	5				4			1	13	10^2	14			40
	2	5	9	12	13		8^1	10			6^1	3				4		7	1	11^2	14				41
	2	4	8	6	10^1		12	11			7^1	5				3		9	1	13					42
	2	3	14	8	9^3			10^1	11		6^2	5				4		7	1	13		12			43
5		3	14	8	6			11^1			9^2					4		7^3	1	13	10	12			44
12	2^1		7	8^2	14			11	9			13				4			1	10	3	6^3	5		45
2		4	8		10^2			13	11^3		12	5				3		7	1	9^1			14	6	46

FA Cup

Fourth Qualifying	Margate	(a)	2-1
First Round	AFC Wimbledon	(a)	2-1
Second Round	Oxford U	(a)	0-1

FA Trophy

First Round	Havant & Waterlooville	(a)	0-2

Vanarama National Play-Offs

Semi-Finals 1st leg	Dover Ath	(a)	1-0
Semi-Finals 2nd leg	Dover Ath	(h)	1-1
Forest Green R won 2-1 on aggregate.			
Final	Grimsby T	Wembley	1-3

GATESHEAD

Ground: Gateshead International Stadium, Neilson Road, Gateshead, Tyne and Wear NE10 0EF.
Tel: (0191) 4783883.　*Website:* www.gateshead-fc.com　*Email:* info@gateshead-fc.com
Year Formed: 1889 (Reformed 1977).　*Record Attendance:* 20,752 v Lincoln C, Division 3N (at Redheugh Park),
25 September 1937.　*Nickname:* 'The Tynesiders', 'The Heed'.　*Manager:* Neil Aspin.
Colours: White shirts, black shorts, white socks with black trim.

GATESHEAD – VANARAMA NATIONAL 2015–16 LEAGUE RECORD

Match No.	Date		Venue	Opponents	Result		H/T Score	Lg Pos.	Goalscorers	Attendance
1	Aug	8	A	Aldershot T	W	2-1	0-1	4	Bowman 2 [77, 80]	1749
2		11	H	Tranmere R	L	1-4	1-3	15	Shaw [45]	1589
3		15	H	Boreham Wood	W	2-1	0-1	10	Bowman 2 [67, 81]	760
4		18	A	Southport	W	2-1	1-1	5	Bowman [5], Gillies (pen) [69]	806
5		22	H	Kidderminster H	D	1-1	0-1	6	Bowman [83]	801
6		29	A	Guiseley	W	2-0	1-0	5	Johnson 2 [39, 47]	603
7		31	H	Lincoln C	W	2-0	1-0	4	Curtis [40], Clark [80]	1248
8	Sept	5	A	Bromley	L	0-3	0-0	5		1411
9		12	A	Eastleigh	W	2-1	2-0	3	Johnson [20], Phillips [34]	2264
10		15	H	Wrexham	W	2-1	1-1	2	Gillies [17], Bowman [58]	1113
11		19	H	Welling U	L	1-2	1-2	4	Buddle [36]	822
12		22	A	FC Halifax T	L	1-0	1-0	4	Shaw [27]	1001
13		26	A	Forest Green R	W	1-0	1-0	2	Phillips [5]	1256
14	Oct	3	H	Dover Ath	L	2-3	2-1	4	Ramsden [16], Buddle [36]	949
15		6	A	Grimsby T	L	1-2	1-1	6	Baxter [10]	3835
16		10	H	Cheltenham T	D	1-1	0-0	6	Cranston [35]	1238
17		13	A	Macclesfield T	L	0-1	0-0	9		1223
18		17	H	Altrincham	D	2-2	0-0	11	Bowman [49], Phillips [90]	911
19		31	A	Boreham Wood	W	3-2	2-1	8	Mafuta [2], Johnson [11], Honeyman [77]	344
20	Nov	14	A	Wrexham	L	0-4	0-0	11		4055
21		21	H	FC Halifax T	L	1-4	1-3	12	Bowman (pen) [38]	853
22		28	H	Chester FC	W	1-0	0-0	11	Whitmore (og) [83]	842
23	Dec	5	A	Kidderminster H	W	1-0	0-0	10	McLaughlin [90]	1489
24		8	H	Southport	L	0-1	0-0	10		582
25		19	H	Woking	L	1-5	1-2	11	McLaughlin [17]	573
26		28	H	Guiseley	W	3-0	0-0	12	Bowman 2 [46, 58], Johnson [88]	679
27	Jan	2	H	Barrow	D	1-1	1-0	10	Bowman (pen) [40]	892
28		23	A	Torquay U	W	2-0	1-0	9	Bowman [29], Johnson [52]	1721
29		30	H	Grimsby T	W	1-0	1-0	9	Johnson [3]	2174
30	Feb	2	A	Barrow	D	0-0	0-0	9		939
31		13	A	Dover Ath	L	0-4	0-3	11		638
32		16	H	Eastleigh	W	2-1	2-0	6	McLaughlin [19], Bowman [24]	648
33		20	H	Aldershot T	W	3-2	2-2	5	Bowman [34], Hamilton [37], McLaughlin [51]	1074
34		23	A	Cheltenham T	D	0-0	0-0	5		2201
35	Mar	5	A	Tranmere R	L	1-3	0-2	9	Johnson [68]	4668
36		8	A	Altrincham	W	3-2	1-0	7	Johnson 2 [11, 51], Hamilton [86]	805
37		12	H	Forest Green R	L	0-1	0-1	9		887
38		15	H	Braintree T	D	0-0	0-0	9		572
39		19	A	Welling U	W	1-0	1-0	9	Whitmore [45]	500
40		25	H	Macclesfield T	L	0-3	0-2	9		948
41		28	A	Lincoln C	D	1-1	0-1	9	Johnson [78]	2142
42	Apr	2	H	Torquay U	L	1-2	1-0	9	Shaw [20]	785
43		9	A	Woking	D	1-1	1-1	9	Bowman (pen) [45]	1005
44		16	H	Braintree T	L	2-3	1-2	10	Clark [13], Whitmore [64]	588
45		23	H	Bromley	W	3-1	2-0	9	Johnson [12], Gillies 2 [24, 75]	865
46		30	A	Chester FC	L	2-4	0-0	9	Ramshaw [51], Johnson [86]	2323

Final League Position: 9

GOALSCORERS

League (59): Bowman 16 (3 pens), Johnson 13, Gillies 4 (1 pen), McLaughlin 4, Phillips 3, Shaw 3, Buddle 2, Clark 2, Hamilton 2, Whitmore 2, Baxter 1, Cranston 1, Curtis 1, Honeyman 1, Mafuta 1, Ramsden 1, Ramshaw 1, own goal 1.
FA Cup (1): Bowman 1.
FA Trophy (10): Bowman 3, Gillies 2, Johnson 2, Buddle 1, Mafuta 1, McLaughlin 1.

Russell 44	Baxter 32+3	Chandler 17+9	Curtis 31+4	Cranston 24	Ramsden 24	Johnson 20+16	Clark 44	Gillies 21+2	Phillips 14+5	Shaw 23+12	Bowman 38+3	Ramshaw 14+13	McLaughlin 31+4	Buddle 11+4	Pattison 18+7	Marwood 5+5	Mafuta 25+6	Allen 3+1	Honeyman 6+3	MacDonald 2	Wrightson 2+4	Gibson 1	Smith 1	Hamilton 21+4	Whitmore 19	Bennett 9+2	Holden 5+2	Onorwigun 1+2	Kanda —+1	Match No.
1	2	3	4	5	6	7^2	8	9	10^1	11	12	13																		1
1	2	8	3	5	7^3	13	4	6	9^2	11^1	10	12	14																	2
1	2	8	3	5	7	13		9		10	11	12		6^2	4															3
1	2	7^1		5	8	14	3	6	13	11	10	12	9^2	4^3	13															4
1	2	4	5	3	7^3	14	6	8	12	10^1	11		9^2		13															5
1	2	8^1	4	6	3	11^2	5	7	14		10	13	9^3		12															6
1	2	8	3	5	7	13	4	6	9^2	10^3	11^1		14	12																7
1	2		3		7	11^2	4	6	8^1	13	10	12	9		5															8
1	2	7	3		8	11^1	4	6	9		10	12^2		5	13															9
1	2	8		7			4	6	9	11^1	10			3	5	12														10
1	2	8		7^2		4	6^1	9^3	12	11	14		3	5	10	13														11
1	2	7^1	5	8		3		6	10	11	14	13	4	9^2	12															12
1	2	7	5	6		4		8	12	11^1		9	3		10^2		13													13
1	2	6^1	5	9		4	7	8^2	13	11		10	3		12															14
1		3		8	2		4		7^1	11	10	13	9^2	5		12	14	6^3												15
1	2	12	5	7	14	4			9^2	10	11			3^3		6	13	8^1												16
1	2		3	5	6	12	4		8^2	10^3	11		14		9	13	7^1													17
1		8	3^3	5	2	11	4	12		10		13	14		6^1	7		9^2												18
			5	2	10^1	4			13	11^2		9	3	8		7		6	1	12										19
1	13		5	2	11^3	3	12	14	10^1		6^4	4	8		7^2	9														20
1			5^2	2	11	4		9^1	14	10		12	8		6	13	3^3	7												21
1	2		3	5	7		4		10^1	9		8			6	13	11^2		12											22
1	2		3	6	4	13	5		11		8				10	7^1	12		9^2											23
1	2		3	5	7^2	13	4		10				7	8	6	9	12	11^1												24
	2		3	5	6		10	4				7	8	13	6	12	1	9^1	11^2											25
1	2		3	5		14	4		10^1	11	6	9	8^3		7^2	13		12												26
1	2		3	5		13	4		10^1	11	6	7	8^2	12			9													27
1	14		13	2		8^2	3		10	7^1	4		6^3	5										12	9	11				28
1		13	13	3		9	4		6	7^1	7		11^2	8^1										12	5	2				29
1			3			6	12		11	9	7^1	4		8										10	5	2				30
1	12	3^3				4	10^2		13	11	7	9		8^1										6	2	5	14			31
1		3				4	10^1		12	11	6	7		8										9	2		5			32
1		12				13	4		10^1	11^3	6	7	14	8										9	3	2	5^1			33
1	13	3				14	4		12	10	9^2	7	8^3	6^1										11	2	5				34
1	12	3				11	4	6	10		7^1	8	13											9^2	5	2				35
1	13	3				10	4		11^2	12	8	9^1		7										6	5	2				36
1	12	7^3	3			11	4		10^1	13	8	14		6										9	5	2^2				37
1	2	12	3			11^2	4	6^1		13	10		8	7										9	5					38
1	2		3			11^1	4	6		10	8	12	7											9	5					39
1	2	4^2				12	5	6	14	11^3	8		10											9	3	13		7^1		40
1	4		3			12	5	13	10		6^2	8	11^1											9	2			7^2	14	41
1	2	12	3			11^2	10	4	13	6^1	8^3	7		9		5								9	5	14				42
1	2	7	3			12	4		10^1	11			6	8^2										9	5^1			13	14	43
1	2	7	3^4			11^1	4		10	6^2	8	13												9	5	12				44
1	2	13				11	3^2	6	10^1	12	8	7		9		4	5							9	4	5				45
1	2	13	12			11	4^1	6	10^3	14	8	7^2	9			5								9	5	3				46

FA Cup

Fourth Qualifying	Worcester C	(h)	1-2

FA Trophy

First Round	Stocksbridge Park Steels	(h)	4-1
Second Round	Eastleigh	(a)	2-1
Third Round	AFC Fylde	(h)	1-0
Fourth Round	FC Halifax T	(a)	0-0
Replay	FC Halifax T	(h)	3-3

aet; Halifax T won 5-4 on penalties.

GRIMSBY TOWN

Ground: Blundell Park, Cleethorpes, NE Lincolnshire DN35 7PY.   *Tel:* (01472) 605 050.
Website: www.grimsby-townfc.co.uk   *Email:* webmaster@gtfc.co.uk   *Year Formed:* 1878.
Record Attendance: 31,651 v Wolverhampton W, FA Cup 5th rd, 20 February 1937.   *Nickname:* 'The Mariners'.
Manager: Paul Hurst.   *Colours:* Black and white striped shirts, black shorts with white trim, red socks with white trim.

GRIMSBY TOWN – VANARAMA NATIONAL 2015–16 LEAGUE RECORD

Match No.	Date		Venue	Opponents	Result	H/T Score	Lg Pos.	Goalscorers	Atten-dance
1	Aug	8	A	Kidderminster H	D 2-2	1-0	11	Amond [43], Monkhouse [67]	3459
2		11	H	Barrow	W 4-1	2-0	5	Monkhouse 2 [16, 59], Bogle [22], Nsiala [66]	5047
3		15	H	Bromley	W 4-1	3-1	2	Amond 2 [3, 25], Bogle (pen) [7], Clay [89]	4731
4		18	A	Altrincham	L 1-2	1-1	9	Bogle [42]	1680
5		22	H	Torquay U	D 2-2	0-2	8	Robinson [68], Amond [80]	4290
6		29	A	Lincoln C	D 1-1	0-1	10	Bogle [66]	5848
7		31	H	Macclesfield T	L 0-2	0-1	11		4251
8	Sept	5	A	Boreham Wood	W 3-1	1-0	9	Doe (og) [8], Bogle [69], Arnold [76]	1293
9		12	H	Aldershot T	W 4-1	0-1	7	Bogle 2 (1 pen) [53 (p), 81], Amond [60], Arnold [85]	3869
10		15	A	Chester FC	D 1-1	0-0	7	Amond [90]	1964
11		18	H	Tranmere R	D 1-1	1-0	7	Pittman [9]	4368
12		22	A	Wrexham	D 0-0	0-0	9		4818
13		26	A	Southport	W 4-0	3-0	7	Clay [18], Disley [29], Pittman [34], Gowling [46]	1320
14	Oct	3	H	Forest Green R	D 1-1	1-1	10	Pittman [31]	5034
15		6	H	Gateshead	W 2-1	1-1	7	Arnold 2 [19, 49]	3835
16		10	A	Braintree T	D 0-0	0-0	7		1394
17		13	H	FC Halifax T	W 7-0	4-0	4	Bogle 2 [10, 42], Amond 4 [35, 45, 77, 83], Clay [55]	3806
18		17	A	Torquay U	D 1-1	0-1	4	Bogle (pen) [79]	2003
19		30	H	Cheltenham T	L 0-1	0-0	4		5218
20	Nov	10	A	Barrow	W 3-1	1-1	5	Amond 2 [36, 85], Gowling [60]	1255
21		14	H	Welling U	W 3-1	2-1	4	Arnold [8], Townsend [12], Mackreth [90]	4108
22		21	A	Eastleigh	W 1-0	1-0	3	Amond [29]	2057
23		28	H	Kidderminster H	W 1-0	0-0	3	Amond [66]	3894
24	Dec	19	A	Dover Ath	W 1-0	0-0	4	Amond (pen) [90]	4266
25		28	H	Lincoln C	W 2-0	1-0	3	Amond [21], Arnold [79]	7650
26	Jan	2	H	Guiseley	D 1-1	0-1	3	Amond [72]	5093
27		9	A	Welling U	W 4-0	0-0	3	Amond 3 [64, 70, 77], Disley [82]	1337
28		23	H	Altrincham	W 5-0	2-0	3	Monkhouse 2 [2, 52], Bogle [19], Amond [62], Arnold [90]	4323
29		30	A	Gateshead	L 0-1	0-1	3		2174
30	Feb	9	A	Bromley	W 2-1	1-1	3	Nolan [32], Pittman [84]	1074
31		13	H	Boreham Wood	D 0-0	0-0	3		3927
32		20	A	FC Halifax T	L 2-4	0-3	3	Amond [87], Nolan [90]	3131
33		23	H	Woking	W 3-1	3-1	3	Pittman [4], Amond 2 [37, 42]	2874
34	Mar	4	A	Forest Green R	W 1-0	0-0	3	Disley [71]	2242
35		8	H	Southport	W 1-0	1-0	3	Amond [1]	3180
36		15	A	Guiseley	D 2-2	1-1	3	Disley [19], Amond [55]	1842
37		26	H	Wrexham	W 1-0	1-0	3	Disley [7]	4581
38		28	H	Macclesfield T	L 1-2	0-1	3	Nolan [58]	2326
39	Apr	1	A	Cheltenham T	L 1-3	0-1	3	Monkhouse [92]	4003
40		5	A	Aldershot T	W 4-3	0-2	3	Amond [53], Bogle [56], Arnold [67], Nolan [87]	1397
41		9	H	Eastleigh	D 0-0	0-0	4		4011
42		12	H	Braintree T	L 0-1	0-0	4		3010
43		16	A	Dover Ath	D 1-1	1-0	4	Bogle (pen) [17]	1957
44		19	A	Woking	W 3-1	1-0	3	Amond 3 [15, 60, 85]	1394
45		23	H	Chester FC	L 1-2	0-0	3	Disley [83]	4575
46		30	A	Tranmere R	L 0-1	0-1	4		6637

Final League Position: 4

GOALSCORERS

League (82): Amond 30 (1 pen), Bogle 13 (4 pens), Arnold 8, Disley 6, Monkhouse 6, Pittman 5, Nolan 4, Clay 3, Gowling 2, Mackreth 1, Nsiala 1, Robinson 1, Townsend 1, own goal 1.
FA Cup (9): Amond 4, Arnold 1, Bogle 1, Marshall 1, Pittman 1, Townsend 1.
FA Trophy (15): Arnold 3, Alabi 2 (1 pen), Amond 2 (1 pen), Bogle 2, Pittman 2, Henderson 1, Mackreth 1, Nolan 1, own goal 1.
Vanarama National Play-Offs (5): Bogle 3, Amond 1 (pen), Arnold 1.

McKeown 45	Nsiala 36+3	Pearson 21+8	Gowling 37	East 19+6	Arnold 38+2	Clay 29+6	Disley 42+1	Monkhouse 38	Amond 37+3	Bogle 29+12	Mackreth 5+10	Tait 33+4	Venney —+2	Robertson 21+3	Robinson 6+1	Marshall 3+13	Pittman 8+20	Tomlinson 5+2	Townsend 9	Brown —+3	Jones 3+1	Alabi —+2	Henderson 1+2	Nolan 17+1	Horwood 11	Straker —+2	Jennings 3+6	Hoban 8+2	Stewart 1+1	Warrington 1	Match No.
1	2	3	4	5	6	7	8	9	10^1	11	12																				1
1	4	3		3	5	6	8^2	7	9	11^1	10	12	2	13																	2
1	3	13	4	5	6	10	7	8^2	11^1	9	12	2																			3
1	3	13	4	5	6	8	7	9^2	11	10	12	2^1																			4
1	3^1	5	4	12	10		8	9^3	13	11		2^2		6	7	14															5
1	12	3	4^4	5	9^1		8	6	11	10^2	13		2	7^3		14															6
1	4	3			12	7	14		11	10	6	2^2		5	8^3	9^1	13														7
1	3	4		2	6		7	9	11^1	10^2	13			5	8		12														8
1	3	4		2	6^1	12	7	9	11^3	10			14	5	8^2		13														9
1	3	4^2		2	6	12	7	9^2	10	11	13			5	8^1		14														10
1	3		5	4	7^2	6	8	9		10	13		2				11^1	12													11
1	3		5	2		9^3	7	8		11^1	6			4	14	12	13	10^2													12
1		4	5	2		9	8	7^3		12	6^1		14	3		13	10^2	11													13
1		4	5	3		9	7	8	13	12	6^1			2		14	10^3	11^2													14
1		3	4	9	8	7	5	6	13	12				2			10^2	11^1													15
1	12	4	3^1	2	6^3	7	8	9		11		13		5^2		14	10														16
1	4	3			6	7	8^2	9^3	11	10^1		2		12	14	5	13														17
1	4	3			6	7	8		11^2	10	12	2		9^1	13		5														18
1	4	3		9	8	7^2	6		11	10^3		2^1		12	13		5	14													19
1	3		4	13	6^2	7	8	9^1	10			2	14	11^3			5	12													20
1	4		3		6^2	7	8	9	11		12	2		13			5	10^1													21
1	3		4	13	6	8	7	9	11			2		12		5^1	10^2														22
1	3				6^3	8	7	9	10^2	12		2		14		5	11^1	13													23
1	10	14	3		9^3	8	4	7^2	6	5^1		2		13		11	12														24
1	4		3		6^3	8	7	9	11	10^1		2		12	13	14	5^2														25
1	4		3		6^2	7^1	8	9^3	11	10		2		5		12	14	13													26
1	11		4	12	10^2	9^3	5	8	7^1	6		2		3			13							14							27
1	4	12	3		6	8^2	7	9	11	10		2		5^3									14	13							28
1	3		4	5	6		8	9	11^1	10		2			13	12								7							29
1	3	13	4		6^1		8	9	11	10^2		2				12								7	5						30
1	5		4		6^3	14	8	9	10	12		2				11^1								7	3^2	13					31
1	3		5	13	7		6^1	10	9^3			2		4		12								8		14	11^2				32
1		3	4	9	8		6	10^1	12			2				11^2								7	5	13					33
1	13		3	4	6		7	9	10^1			2				12								8	5			11^3			34
1	4		3	14	6	12	7	9^3	10^1			2												8^2	5		13	11			35
1		3	4		6		5		11	12		2												7	8		9	10^1			36
1	4	13	3		6	8	7		11	10^1		2												9	5			11^1			37
1	4	14	3		6	8^3	7		11	10^1		2^2		5										9			12	13			38
1	2	4	3		6^2		7	9	11	12			13											8	5^1			10			39
1	4		3		6	14	8	9	10^2	12		2		5										7			11^3	13			40
1	3		4		6		7^1		10	11^2		2		5										8		12	13	9^1			41
1	4		5	6		7	9	10^2	13	3		2				12								8			14	11^1			42
1	4		3	12		8	7	9		10		2				11^1								6	5						43
1	3	13	4	6		12	7	9^2	11^3	10^1				14										8	5						44
1	4^3		3		6		7	9^1	11	10^2		2	14			12								8	5	13					45
	4		5		9^1	7			14			2	13	3		12	10^2		8								6	11^3		1	46

FA Cup

Fourth Qualifying	Harrogate T	(a)	4-1
First Round	St Albans C	(h)	5-1
Second Round	Shrewsbury T	(h)	0-0
Replay	Shrewsbury T	(a)	0-1

Vanarama National Play-Offs

Semi-Finals 1st leg	Braintree T	(h)	0-1
Semi-Finals 2nd leg	Braintree T	(a)	2-0

aet; Grimsby T won 2-1 on aggregate.

Final	Forest Green R	Wembley	3-1

FA Trophy

First Round	Solihull Moors	(h)	1-1
Replay	Solihull Moors	(a)	3-2
Second Round	Weston-super-Mare	(h)	3-1
Third Round	Havant & Waterlooville	(h)	3-0
Fourth Round	Woking	(h)	2-0
Semi-Final 1st leg	Bognor Regis T	(a)	1-0
Semi-Final 2nd leg	Bognor Regis T	(h)	2-1

Grimsby T won 3-1 on aggregate.

Final	FC Halifax T	Wembley	0-1

GUISELEY

Ground: Nethermoor Park, Otley Road, Guiseley, Leeds LS20 8BT. *Tel:* (01943) 873223. *Website:* guiseleyafc.co.uk
Email: see website. *Year Formed:* 1909. *Record Attendance:* 6,548 v Carlisle U, FA Cup 1st rd, 13 November 1994
(at Valley Parade); 2,486 v Bridlington T, FA Vase Semi-Final 1st leg, 24 March 1990 (at Nethermoor Park).
Nickname: 'The Lions'. *Manager:* Mark Bower. *Colours:* White shirts with blue trim, blue shorts with white trim,
blue socks with white trim.

GUISELEY – VANARAMA NATIONAL 2015–16 LEAGUE RECORD

Match No.	Date		Venue	Opponents	Result		H/T Score	Lg Pos.	Goalscorers	Atten- dance
1	Aug	8	A	Welling U	L	0-1	0-1	17		505
2		11	H	Altrincham	W	1-0	1-0	12	Atkinson, R [16]	797
3		15	H	Kidderminster H	W	1-0	0-0	8	Boyes [85]	756
4		18	A	Barrow	D	1-1	1-1	10	Boshell, N [45]	1440
5		22	H	Aldershot T	L	0-4	0-2	14		782
6		29	H	Gateshead	L	0-2	0-1	15		603
7		31	A	Chester FC	D	1-1	0-0	14	Boyes [84]	2304
8	Sept	5	A	Torquay U	D	1-1	1-1	17	Dickinson, L (pen) [28]	1558
9		12	H	Woking	D	4-4	2-3	17	Atkinson, R [33], Boshell, N [41], Craddock [67], Lawlor [90]	643
10		15	H	FC Halifax T	W	2-1	1-1	16	Hatfield [27], Dickinson, L (pen) [81]	1184
11		19	A	Dover Ath	D	0-0	0-0	15		823
12		22	H	Southport	D	1-1	1-0	16	Dickinson, L [19]	748
13		26	A	Braintree T	W	1-0	0-0	13	Craddock [80]	679
14	Oct	2	A	Lincoln C	L	0-1	0-1	13		1279
15		6	H	Macclesfield T	L	0-3	0-2	18		653
16		10	A	Forest Green R	L	0-3	0-0	18		1749
17		14	A	Wrexham	D	3-3	1-2	18	Rothery [3], Dickinson, L [70], Boyes [81]	3633
18		17	H	Boreham Wood	D	1-1	0-0	18	Boshell, N (pen) [90]	749
19		31	H	Welling U	W	2-0	2-0	17	Dudley 2 [9, 43]	653
20	Nov	7	H	Barrow	W	3-1	2-1	14	Boshell, D [5], Atkinson, R [36], Dudley [73]	749
21		10	A	Cheltenham T	L	0-5	0-2	15		2237
22		14	H	Eastleigh	L	1-4	1-2	16	Boyes [40]	699
23		21	A	Tranmere R	L	1-2	1-1	18	Boshell, D [24]	4352
24		28	H	Bromley	W	2-0	1-0	16	Norburn [45], Dudley [89]	787
25	Dec	5	A	FC Halifax T	D	1-1	0-0	16	Dudley [48]	1355
26		19	A	Aldershot T	L	0-1	0-0	17		1325
27		28	A	Gateshead	L	0-3	0-0	18		679
28	Jan	2	A	Grimsby T	D	1-1	1-0	18	Norburn [40]	5093
29		23	A	Kidderminster H	W	1-0	0-0	18	Dickinson, L [79]	1431
30		30	A	Lincoln C	L	0-1	0-1	18		2265
31	Feb	13	A	Woking	W	1-0	1-0	17	Dickinson,.L [9]	1182
32		20	A	Altrincham	D	1-1	0-1	17	Atkinson, R [56]	1137
33		23	H	Forest Green R	L	0-1	0-0	18		550
34		27	H	Braintree T	D	1-1	0-1	18	Norburn [73]	788
35	Mar	8	H	Tranmere R	D	2-2	1-1	18	Hurst 2 [38, 60]	1147
36		12	A	Bromley	L	0-2	0-0	18		1044
37		15	H	Grimsby T	D	2-2	1-1	18	Atkinson, R [6], Boshell, N [50]	1842
38		19	A	Dover Ath	L	0-1	0-1	18		690
39		26	A	Southport	L	0-2	0-1	18		983
40		28	H	Chester FC	D	3-3	0-1	18	Sinclair 2 [74, 90], Hatfield [81]	1186
41	Apr	2	A	Eastleigh	D	1-1	0-1	18	Hurst [55]	1790
42		9	H	Cheltenham T	L	0-2	0-0	19		1058
43		12	H	Wrexham	W	3-1	3-0	18	Johnson [14], Boyes 2 [17, 26]	1046
44		16	A	Macclesfield T	L	0-1	0-0	19		1408
45		23	A	Boreham Wood	L	0-1	0-1	21		601
46		30	A	Torquay U	W	4-3	3-0	20	Johnson [5], Hatfield [11], Dudley 2 [30, 73]	1915

Final League Position: 20

GOALSCORERS

League (47): Dudley 7, Boyes 6, Dickinson, L 6 (2 pens), Atkinson, R 5, Boshell, N 4 (1 pen), Hatfield 3, Hurst 3,
Norburn 3, Boshell, D 2, Craddock 2, Johnson 2, Sinclair 2, Lawlor 1, Rothery 1.
FA Cup (3): Boyes 3.
FA Trophy (9): Craddock 2, Dudley 1, Hatfield 1, Hurst 1, Lowe 1, Rothbury 1 (pen), Rothery 1, own goal 1.

Drench 37	Atkinson R 38	Boshell N 15 + 16	Lockwood 24 + 2	Lowe 44	Lawlor 44 + 2	Thompson 9 + 2	Hatfield 36 + 2	Craddock 11 + 19	Boyes 28 + 14	Brooksby 15 + 5	Toulson 33 + 5	Dickinson L 12 + 19	Rothery 20 + 13	Boshell D 24 + 4	Atkinson D 9	Parker 18 + 2	Porritt — + 3	Maris 7	Dudley 16	Smith 8 + 3	Marsden — + 1	Hall 11 + 1	Norburn 17 + 3	Hurst 18	Sinclair 7 + 4	Johnson 5 + 7	Match No.
1	2	3[1]	4	5	6	7[3]	8[2]	9	10	11	12	13	14														1
1	11	9[1]	3	2	4	10[2]	8	7[3]	6	5	13	14	12														2
1	4	9[2]	3	5	7	8[1]	2	11[3]	10	6	14	13	12														3
1	4	9[2]	3	5	8[1]		2	11[3]	10	6	13	14	12		7												4
1	4	9[2]	3	5	8[1]		2	11[3]	10	6	13	14	12		7												5
	5	11[1]	4[2]	3	6		8	7	10[3]	13	9	2	14		1	12											6
1	4	8[3]	3	9	7[2]	10	12	14	6	2	11[1]	13			5												7
1	4	14	3	6	7[3]	8	13	9	10[2]	2	11[1]	12			5												8
1	4	6[1]	3	7	10[1]	8	13	9[2]	12	2	11				5	14											9
1	4	14	3	7	9[2]	6	10[1]	13	12	2	11			8[3]	5												10
1	4	13	3	7	14	6[3]	11[3]	12	9[1]	2	10			8	5												11
1	5	4	3	7	9		12		6	2	10[1]			8		11											12
1	4	12	3	5	6		13	9	14	8	2					10[2]		11[1]							7[3]		13
1	5	14	4	3	6		8	12	13	9	2					10[2]		11[1]							7[3]		14
1	4		3	5	6	8[2]	7	9[3]	13	12	2	14				10[1]		11									15
1	4	13	3	2	6		5	14	11[2]	7	12			9[3]		10[1]		8									16
1	4		3	5	12		9		11	6	2	13		7[8]		10[1]		8[1]									17
1	3	12	4	5		8	7	11[2]	10	6[1]	2							13	9								18
1	4		3	5	6		12	8[1]		2		9	7	10[2]	13	11											19
1	6		5	4	7		13	11[2]		2	14	9	7	3[1]		10[3]	12										20
1	4[3]	3[8]	5	6			11[1]		2	13	9	7	10			8[2]	12	14									21
1			3	4		13	6[3]	12	2	14	7	5[1]		10[2]	9		8	11									22
1		12	5	3			11	14		13	9	7		8[2]	10[1]		4[1]	6	2								23
1	12	3	2	5	7	13	11[1]			6				9	8[2]			10	4								24
1	13	3	5	4	7		11		12	14	9[2]			10	6[3]			8	2[1]								25
1	13	3	5	4	7	12	11[1]		2[2]		9	6						8				10					26
1	12	3	5	4		2	13	11			9	7[2]				6[1]		8	10								27
1		3	5	4		8	10[1]	13		2	12	11	7						9	6[2]							28
1		5	4	12			11[3]		2	13	9[2]	6	14	10					3	7[1]	8						29
1	4	12	5	7		9		11		2	13			6[1]		8[2]			3		10						30
1	3	12	5	8		7	14		2	10[2]	9[1]	13				4					6	11[3]					31
	4	6[2]		2	7		12		10[2]	13	8	1		9[1]						9[1]	3	14	5	11			32
	3	10		5	6	14	12		13	7[3]	1		9			4				8[3]	2	11[1]	12				33
	8	6		2	3		13		14	12	4[2]	1		9[1]						9[1]	5	10	11	7[3]			34
	5	9[1]		3	4	7		14		2	8[2]	12	1			6				10[3]	11				13		35
	4	10[1]		5	6	7[2]		2	11	9[3]	13	1						3			8	12	14				36
	4	11		6	7	12	10[2]	2		8[1]	1		5		9[3]	3					14	13					37
	4			3	5	9[2]	10	14	8	2	13	7[3]	1	3[1]					11	6[8]		12					38
	4	8		3	6	9	14	11[2]	2				1	5[3]			12			7				13	10[1]		39
1	2	6			7[3]	9		4		8[1]		5							11[2]		14	12	3	10	13		40
1	4		3	5	14	6	13	2		10		9[3]		5							7	8[2]	11[1]	12			41
1	3		4	6	9[2]	14	12	2		10		5									7	8[1]	11[3]	13			42
1	4	14	3	7	6	13	10	2		12	5			9[3]						8[1]						11[2]	43
1	4	14	5	8[1]	11	13	10	2		12	3		9[2]							7[3]					6		44
1	3	14	5	7	6	13	11	2[1]	9	4			8[2]						12						10[3]		45
1	3	14	4	7	6	11	2	12	5				9[1]	8[3]									13	10[2]			46

FA Cup

Fourth Qualifying	FC Halifax T	(a)	2-2
Replay	FC Halifax T	(h)	1-2
aet.			

FA Trophy

First Round	Burscough	(a)	2-2
Replay	Burscough	(h)	3-2
Second Round	Dulwich Hamlet	(a)	2-1
Third Round	Dover Ath	(a)	2-2
Replay	Dover Ath	(h)	0-3

FC HALIFAX TOWN

Ground: The MBi Shay Stadium, Halifax, West Yorkshire HX1 2 YT.   *Tel:* (01422) 341222.
Website: www.halifaxafc.co.uk   *Email:* mikesharman@fchalifaxtown.com   *Year Formed:* 1911.
Record Attendance: 36,855 v Tottenham H, FA Cup 5th rd, 15 February 1953.   *Nickname:* 'The Shaymen'.
Manager: Jim Harvey.   *Colours:* Blue shirts with white trim, blue shorts with white trim, blue socks with white trim.

FC HALIFAX TOWN – VANARAMA NATIONAL 2015–16 LEAGUE RECORD

Match No.	Date	Venue	Opponents	Result		H/T Score	Lg Pos.	Goalscorers	Atten- dance
1	Aug 8	A	Boreham Wood	L	1-3	1-1	22	Burrow (pen) [45]	701
2	11	H	Chester FC	L	0-1	0-1	23		1732
3	15	H	Torquay U	L	2-3	1-2	23	Burrow 2 [24, 48]	1199
4	18	A	Tranmere R	L	0-1	0-0	24		5235
5	22	H	Bromley	D	2-2	0-0	23	Burrow (pen) [90], Hughes [90]	1107
6	29	A	Wrexham	L	1-3	1-2	23	Burrow [26]	5662
7	31	H	Barrow	W	3-1	0-0	21	Tuton [81], Hamilton [83], Burrow [90]	1490
8	Sept 5	A	Aldershot T	L	2-3	0-2	23	Hattersley [80], Brooks [83]	1603
9	12	H	Kidderminster H	D	1-1	0-1	22	Hamilton [67]	1128
10	15	A	Guiseley	L	1-2	1-1	23	Hamilton [9]	1184
11	19	H	Southport	D	2-2	0-1	23	Burrow 2 (1 pen) [74 (p), 89]	1211
12	22	H	Gateshead	D	1-1	0-1	23	Bolton [53]	1001
13	26	A	Welling U	L	0-2	0-2	23		653
14	Oct 3	H	Cheltenham T	L	1-7	1-2	23	James [29]	1267
15	6	A	Altrincham	W	3-1	1-0	22	Burrow 2 [22, 60], James (pen) [90]	1119
16	10	H	Woking	L	0-3	0-1	23		1155
17	13	A	Grimsby T	L	0-7	0-4	23		3806
18	17	A	Chester FC	L	1-2	0-1	23	Burrow [73]	2088
19	31	A	Eastleigh	L	1-2	1-0	24	James [15]	1890
20	Nov 14	H	Braintree T	L	3-6	3-4	24	Burrow [5], Tuton 2 [32, 42]	1065
21	21	A	Gateshead	W	4-1	3-1	24	Smith (og) [22], James [40], Tuton 2 [44, 79]	853
22	28	H	Dover Ath	W	4-2	3-1	23	Tuton 2 [7, 75], Wroe [13], Burrow [42]	1067
23	Dec 5	H	Guiseley	D	1-1	0-0	23	Walker [84]	1355
24	19	H	Tranmere R	D	1-1	1-1	22	Wroe [44]	1684
25	26	A	Lincoln C	W	1-0	0-0	22	Walker [70]	3558
26	28	H	Wrexham	W	2-0	2-0	22	Tuton [16], James [38]	2243
27	Jan 2	H	Lincoln C	D	2-2	1-1	21	Tuton [27], James [89]	1932
28	9	A	Macclesfield T	W	1-0	0-0	19	Tuton [77]	2055
29	23	A	Woking	D	1-1	1-1	19	Walker [38]	1484
30	30	H	Welling U	D	1-1	0-0	19	James [56]	1407
31	Feb 13	H	Forest Green R	L	0-2	0-2	20		1329
32	20	H	Grimsby T	W	4-2	3-0	20	Whitehouse, B [10], Bolton [25], Wroe [28], Hibbs [89]	3131
33	23	A	Braintree T	L	0-2	0-1	20		506
34	Mar 5	A	Southport	W	1-0	0-0	19	McDonald [90]	1148
35	8	A	Bromley	L	0-1	0-0	20		706
36	15	A	Torquay U	D	0-0	0-0	19		1664
37	26	H	Altrincham	W	1-0	0-0	19	Hughes [68]	1747
38	28	A	Barrow	L	1-4	0-1	20	Hughes [87]	1466
39	Apr 2	A	Dover Ath	L	0-1	0-1	22		1027
40	5	H	Boreham Wood	W	3-2	2-0	20	Burrow [20], Bolton [23], Hughes [90]	1309
41	9	H	Aldershot T	L	0-2	0-0	20		1714
42	12	A	Kidderminster H	L	0-1	0-0	20		1340
43	16	A	Cheltenham T	L	0-2	0-2	21		5245
44	19	H	Eastleigh	D	0-0	0-0	21		1337
45	23	A	Forest Green R	W	1-0	0-0	21	McDonald [70]	1942
46	30	H	Macclesfield T	D	1-1	1-0	21	McManus [45]	2943

Final League Position: 21

GOALSCORERS

League (55): Burrow 14 (3 pens), Tuton 10, James 7 (1 pen), Hughes 4, Bolton 3, Hamilton 3, Walker 3, Wroe 3, McDonald 2, Brooks 1, Hattersley 1, Hibbs 1, McManus 1, Whitehouse, B 1, own goal 1.
FA Cup (4): Walker 2, Bolton 1, James 1.
FA Trophy (17): Burrow 4 (1 pen), James 3, Hughes 2, McDonald 2, Fairhurst 1, Tuton 1, Wroe 1, McManus 2, own goal 1.

Glennon 20	Bolton 45	Bencherif 38 + 3	Brown M 29	McManus 42 + 1	James 45	Whitehouse E 3 + 1	Tuton 24 + 3	Burrow 43 + 2	MacDonald 16 + 25	Hibbs 19 + 12	Hughes 7 + 26	Bishop 2 + 2	Hutchison 5	Hattersley 2 + 10	Roberts 38 + 1	Walker 12 + 5	Hamilton 6 + 3	Racchi 3 + 1	Brooks 3 + 2	Banton 9	Sadlier 5 + 3	Wroe 30	Brown N 3	O'Brien 6	Miller 1	Griffiths 1	Porter —+ 1	Johnson 25	Clappison 1 + 1	McDonald 4 + 11	Fazlic 1 + 1	Peniket 12 + 5	Fairhurst 3 + 5	Whitehouse B 2	Kingsley 1	Match No.
1	2	3	4	5	6	7	8	9	10^1	11^2	12	13																								1
1	2	6		4	5	7^3	11	10^1	9^2	8	13	14	3	12																						2
1	2	6		3	5	9	11	7^2	8	12	10^1		4	13																						3
1	4	7^2	3	5	6	8^1	10	11	13	9	12				2																					4
1	3	7^2	4	5	6	14	8	10	9^1	12	11^3	13			2																					5
1	4	7		5	6			10	9	11^3	8^2	13		3^1	2	12	14																			6
1	2	4		6				10	9	12	8^1			5^1	11^1	3																				7
1	3	4	12	6		7^1	11		14					2^2	13	5		9	8^3	10																8
1	3	8^2	4	5	9			11	13	12	14			6^1	2		10		7^3																	9
1	2		4	9	7^1			10	12	6	13			5^2		11		8	3																	10
1	2	14	4	5	7		6^1	11	13	8^2	10^3						9		12	3																11
1	4	8^1	3	6	7		10	11^2	14					13	2	9^3		12		5																12
1	4	8	3	6^2	7		10	9	12	13				14	2^1	11^2				5																13
1	2	10^1	3		8		14	11	6^3		7			12	5	13		9^2		4																14
1	2	8	4	6	7		10^1	11^2	13	12	14			5	9^3					3																15
1	2	7^1	3	9^3	6		11^2	10	14	12				5	13					4	8															16
1	2		3		8			9^1	10	12				5		11				4	6	7														17
1	2	14	3	6	8			13	11					12		10^2				5^1	7^3	9	4													18
1	3	13		5	7			12	10						9						11^2	6	8	2	4^1											19
1	2			5	8			10	11	12					9^1						6	7	4	3												20
	2	8^3	4	9	7			10^2	11^1	13				5							14	6		3			1^a	12								21
	5	2	4^1	9	7			10	11	12				8^2							13	6		3				1								22
	2	6		5	9^2			10	11	7^3	14				13						12	8		3^1				1	4							23
	2	7	4	5^2	8			10^3	11^1	12			14		9	13						6		3^1				1								24
	2	4	3	5	7			11^3		14			10^1		6	8^2						9						1		13	12					25
	2	4	3	5	8			10	11^3	12	14	13			6	9^2						7^1						1		11	14					26
	3	4	2	9	7			11	10	13			12		5^1	8^2						6						1		14						27
	2	3	8	4	5			10^1	6^2	14	12	13			9	7^1						11						1		14						28
	2	4	3	9	6^2			11	10	13					5^1	7^3						8						1				12	14			29
	2	4	3	9	7				10		13	12			5^1							8						1		14		6^3	11^2			30
	3	4^2	5	6	9				11	7^3	14				2	10^1						8						1		12		13				31
	3	6	2	4	8				13	9^2	12				5							7^3						1		14		11^1		10		32
	2	4	3	8	7				10^2	9^3	13	14			5^4							6						1		12		11		11^1		33
	2	4	3	6	8				11^2	12	9	10^3			5							7^1						1		13		14				34
	2	3	4	5	9^3				10^1	12	7	13			6^2							8						1		11		14				35
	2	4	7	5	3^3				11^2	12	14				8	13						9						1				6	10^1			36
	2^a	4	3^2	5	8				11	7^3	12	13			6							9						1		14			10^1			37
		4		5	6				12	13	2	10			3	8^1						7						1		9^1		11^2	14			38
	2	6		4	8				10	12	5	11^2			3							7						1		13		9^1				39
	3	4		5	8				11	10^1	2	12			6							9						1		14		7^2				40
	3	4		5	7				10	11^2	2	12			6							8^1						1		14		9^3	13			41
	3	4		5	8				11	13	6^3	12			2							7						1		14		10^2	9^1			42
	5	3^1		2	8				10	6	7	12			4							9						1		13		11^2				43
	3			4	8				11	6^1	2	12		14	5							7						1		10^3		9^2	13			44
	2	3^2		5					10	9^1	8	13		14	4							6						1		12		11^3		7		45
	3			5	7				10	6^2	2	12		14	4							8						1		11^1		9^3	13			46

FA Cup

Fourth Qualifying	Guiseley		(h)	2-2
Replay	Guiseley		(a)	2-1
aet.				
First Round	Wycombe W		(h)	0-4

FA Trophy

First Round	Tamworth		(h)	5-0
Second Round	Barrow		(h)	1-0
Third Round	Chester		(h)	1-0
Fourth Round	Gateshead		(h)	0-0
Replay	Gateshead		(a)	3-3
aet; FC Halifax T won 5-4 on penalties.				
Semi-Final 1st leg	Nantwich T		(a)	4-2
Semi-Final 2nd leg	Nantwich T		(h)	2-2
Final	Grimsby T	Wembley		1-0

KIDDERMINSTER HARRIERS

Ground: Aggborough Stadium, Hoo Road, Kidderminster DY10 1NB. *Tel:* (01562) 823 931.
Website: www.harriers.co.uk *Email:* info@harriers.co.uk *Year Formed:* 1886. *Record Attendance:* 9,155 v Hereford U,
FA Cup 1st rd, 27 November 1948. *Nickname:* 'The Harriers'. *Manager:* Colin Gordon. *Colours:* Red and white
halved shirts with white sleeves, white shorts with red trim, red socks with white trim.

KIDDERMINSTER HARRIERS – VANARAMA NATIONAL 2015–16 LEAGUE RECORD

Match No.	Date	Venue	Opponents	Result	H/T Score	Lg Pos.	Goalscorers	Attendance
1	Aug 8	H	Grimsby T	D	2-2	0-1	11	Styche 60, Verma 90	3459
2	11	A	Dover Ath	L	2-3	0-2	18	Dawson 61, Singh 72	906
3	15	A	Guiseley	L	0-1	0-0	19		756
4	18	H	Wrexham	L	1-3	0-1	22	Wright 80	2620
5	22	A	Gateshead	D	1-1	1-0	22	Singh 26	801
6	29	H	Forest Green R	L	0-2	0-0	22		1905
7	31	A	Tranmere R	D	2-2	0-2	24	Singh 84, Styche 90	4622
8	Sept 5	H	Braintree T	L	0-1	0-1	24		1670
9	12	A	FC Halifax T	D	1-1	1-0	24	Singh 11	1128
10	15	H	Torquay U	D	2-2	0-1	24	Verma 57, Styche (pen) 90	1493
11	19	H	Lincoln C	L	0-2	0-2	24		1581
12	22	A	Bromley	L	2-3	1-1	24	Jones 2 20, 65	736
13	26	A	Barrow	D	1-1	1-0	24	Styche 5	1323
14	Oct 3	H	Welling U	L	0-1	0-0	24		1438
15	6	H	Boreham Wood	D	1-1	1-0	24	Francis-Angol 9	1294
16	10	A	Macclesfield T	L	1-2	0-2	24	Murphy 77	1652
17	13	A	Altrincham	D	2-2	1-1	24	Hassan 38, Whitfield 75	869
18	17	H	Southport	L	0-1	0-0	24		1593
19	31	H	Woking	W	1-0	0-0	23	Murphy 87	1449
20	Nov 10	A	Chester FC	L	1-3	1-1	23	Langmead 40	1956
21	14	H	Aldershot T	W	2-0	0-0	23	McQuilkin 53, Whitfield 60	1790
22	28	A	Grimsby T	L	0-1	0-0	24		3894
23	Dec 5	A	Gateshead	L	0-1	0-0	24		1489
24	19	A	Eastleigh	L	1-3	0-1	24	Whitfield 60	1862
25	26	H	Cheltenham T	L	1-2	1-1	24	Howkins 30	3238
26	28	A	Forest Green R	L	0-3	0-1	24		2110
27	Jan 23	H	Guiseley	L	0-1	0-0	24		1431
28	30	A	Aldershot T	L	0-1	0-0	24		1768
29	Feb 6	A	Boreham Wood	W	2-0	1-0	24	Whitfield 21, Ngwatala (pen) 75	366
30	9	H	Eastleigh	W	3-2	1-0	23	Maxwell 3, White 52, Gnahoua 74	1335
31	13	A	Macclesfield T	W	3-1	3-0	23	Lowe 10, White 16, Gnahoua 23	1693
32	16	A	Cheltenham T	L	0-2	0-0	23		3387
33	20	A	Chester FC	D	2-2	2-0	23	Gnahoua 22, White (pen) 26	2067
34	23	A	Wrexham	L	0-2	0-2	24		3899
35	27	H	Bromley	L	0-1	0-0	24		1539
36	Mar 1	A	Braintree T	L	1-2	0-1	24	Maxwell 49	502
37	5	A	Torquay U	L	2-3	0-2	24	Langmead 52, Gnahoua 63	2021
38	19	A	Lincoln C	W	2-1	0-1	24	McQuilkin 2 72, 83	2178
39	26	A	Woking	D	1-1	0-1	24	McQuilkin 79	1730
40	28	H	Tranmere R	L	0-2	0-1	24		2744
41	Apr 2	H	Altrincham	D	1-1	0-1	24	Whitfield 89	1402
42	9	A	Welling U	W	2-1	0-1	24	Langmead 82, McQuilkin 85	565
43	12	H	FC Halifax T	W	1-0	0-0	23	Whitfield 49	1340
44	16	H	Barrow	D	0-0	0-0	23		1517
45	23	H	Dover Ath	D	1-1	1-1	23	Lowe 14	1410
46	30	A	Southport	W	4-3	2-1	23	McQuilkin 9, Ngwatala 39, Williams 77, Garnett 84	1473

Final League Position: 23

GOALSCORERS

League (49): McQuilkin 6, Whitfield 6, Gnahoua 4, Singh 4, Styche 4 (1 pen), Langmead 3, White 3 (1 pen), Jones 2,
Lowe 2, Maxwell 2, Murphy 2, Ngwatala 2 (1 pen), Verma 2, Dawson 1, Francis-Angol 1, Garnett 1, Hassan 1, Howkins
1, Williams 1, Wright 1.
FA Cup (0).
FA Trophy (1): Singh 1.

Match No.	Snecker 30	Hodgkiss 40 + 3	Tunnicliffe 15	Langmead 39	Rowe-Turner 15 + 4	Verma 11 + 3	Garnett 4 + 12	Clarke 16 + 1	Maxwell 33 + 4	Styche 14 + 3	Wright 4 + 8	White 7	Dawson 8	Green 3 + 8	Reid 1 + 3	Kinsella 13	Campbell 11 + 4	Singh 11 + 9	Fox 6	Palmer 11	O'Leary 5	Dinsley 4 + 5	Jones 11 + 7	Spencer — + 2	Toner 6	Francis-Angol 23 + 3	Murphy 7	Hassan 2 + 1	Whitfield 28 + 1	Ward 1	Sweeney 3 + 1	Young 6 + 2	Howkins 8	Barnes-Homer 6 + 2	Fazlic 4 + 1	McQuilkin 13 + 7	Obosu — + 2	Patrick 6 + 12	Ngwatala 12 + 3	Lowe 20	Fane 20	Gnahoua 14 + 2	Williams 15 + 3
1	1	2	3	4^1	5	6	7	8^3	9	10^2	11	12	13	14																													
2	1	2	3	4		6	7	8^3	10^2	13	11		5	12	9^1		14																										
3	1	2	3	4				8	7	11		9	5	10^1	6		12																										
4	1	2^2	3	4		9^1	7	8	10*	13	11			14	6^1	12	5																										
5		2	3	4		8	7	6		10^2	9	13		12	11^1	5	1																										
6		2	4	3		8^3	6	7^1	12	14	11			9	10^2	5	1	13																									
7		2	5	11	12	4	3	6	7^2	10			8^1	13	9	1																											
8		2	4	3		8	7	6*	10		9			12	11^1	5^2	1	13																									
9		2		3	4	9	6		11^1	12		13		10^2	8^3	5	1	7	14																								
10		2		3	4	9	7		8	12		5		10^2	11	1	6^1	13																									
11		2	3	4		7	6		9^1	10^3				12	11	1	8^2	14	13	5																							
12		2	4	3		13	8	7^1	11^3	12				9	10^2	1	14	6		5																							
13		2	4	3		11^1	8	7	10^2	12		13		9	1	14	6^1			5																							
14		2	3*	4	12	6	7^1	8	10			13		9^3	1	11^2				5	14																						
15		2	3	4		7	8	11^1	13		14	10^2		1	12	6				5	9^3																						
16	1	2	5	3	13	12	9	8^1	10					6^3	4^2	7	11	14																									
17	1	2	4	3	5		14	7	13		12				9^1	10^3	11		6^2	8																							
18	1	2	3	5			7	12					8			11	9^1	10	6		4																						
19	1	2	4	5^2		6^1			14					7		9^3	11		8		12	3	10	13																			
20	1	2	4					12						6^2		9	11		8		5^3	10	7	13	14																		
21	1	2	3			7								12		9	10		11^2		5^1	4	8	6	13																		
22	1	2	3	14		8^3							13			12	5	10^1	7		4	11^2	6	9																			
23	1	2	4			8							10			6^3	5	11^1	14	3	13	7^2	9	12																			
24	1	7	4	12		6^3							10^1			5	11	2	3	13	9^2		8	14																			
25	1	7	5	3^2		8							12			6	9	2	4	10^1		11	13																				
26	1	9	4			12							13			10	5	11^3	2*	3	8^1	14	6	7^2																			
27	1	2	4			12							13			5	10^3		11^1	9	14	6	3	7	8^2																		
28	1	2^3	3					14	6							5	8			12	10^1	9	4	7	11	13																	
29	1	2	3					12	6		10^1					5	9					7	4	8	11																		
30	1	2	4					14	10		11^3					5^1	7			13		9^2	3	6	8	12																	
31	1	2	4					12	9		11^1					5	8^2			14		13		3	7	9	8																
32	1	2	4					12	6		11					5^1	10					13		3	7	9	8																
33	1	2	4					13	6		10^2		5			9						12		4	7	11^1	8																
34	1	2	4					12	7^3		9^2		5			11^1						13	14	3	8	10	6																
35	1	2	4					13	14		10^2		5			12						7^3	9^1	3	6	11	8																
36	1	2	4					10	8				5			11					6^2		13	3	7^1	9	12																
37	1	2	3					11	8				5			12^2	9					13	4	7	10	6^1																	
38		2^2	3					11^1	9				5			1	13					14	8^3		12	4	7	10															
39		5^1	3					12	7^2				8			1	13					11	9	14	2	6	10^3	4															
40		12	4^2	11				13	14				5			1	6^1					8	10^3	9	3	7		2															
41		5	3	11				6^1	9				1				13					7	2	8	12	4^2																	
42			4	13									5	6^1	1		8		11^2	10		12	7	3	9		2															
43	1	13	4										5	10^2		9	11^3		12	8		14	7^1	3	6		2															
44	1		4										5			9	11	10^1	8		12	7	3	6		2																
45	1		4										5			9	11	10^1	8^2		13	6	3	7	12		2															
46	1	14	4		13								5^1			10^3	11^2		7		12	6	3	8	9		2															

FA Cup
Fourth Qualifying Stourbridge (a) 0-3

FA Trophy
First Round Stourbridge (a) 1-2

LINCOLN CITY

Ground: Sincil Bank Stadium, Sincil Bank, Lincoln LN5 8LD. *Tel:* (01522) 880 011.
Website: www.redimps.com *Email:* info@lincolncityfc.co.uk *Year Formed:* 1884.
Record Attendance: 23,196 v Derby Co, League Cup 4th rd (replay), 15 November 1967. *Nickname:* 'The Red Imps'.
Manager: Chris Moyses. *Colours:* Red and white striped shirts, black shorts, red socks with white trim.

LINCOLN CITY – VANARAMA NATIONAL 2015–16 LEAGUE RECORD

Match No.	Date	Venue	Opponents	Result	H/T Score	Lg Pos.	Goalscorers	Attendance
1	Aug 8	H	Cheltenham T	D 1-1	0-1	13	Hearn [73]	2767
2	11	A	Braintree T	W 3-1	0-0	6	Rhead 2 (1 pen) [47, 73 (p)], Stanley [81]	657
3	15	A	Eastleigh	D 1-1	1-0	12	Muldoon [13]	1354
4	18	H	Macclesfield T	W 5-3	3-2	7	Hearn 3 [10, 24, 73], Rhead 2 [26, 49]	2320
5	22	A	Forest Green R	L 1-3	0-2	9	Simmons [70]	1385
6	29	H	Grimsby T	D 1-1	1-0	11	Rhead (pen) [32]	5848
7	31	A	Gateshead	L 0-2	0-1	12		1248
8	Sept 5	H	Wrexham	D 1-1	0-0	13	Rhead [70]	2628
9	12	H	Boreham Wood	W 3-1	0-1	10	Rhead 2 (1 pen) [64 (p), 88], Simmons [90]	2272
10	15	A	Barrow	L 0-1	0-0	14		1233
11	19	A	Kidderminster H	W 2-0	2-0	12	Power [22], Muldoon [27]	1581
12	22	A	Altrincham	D 1-1	1-1	12	Power [8]	1893
13	26	H	Torquay U	W 2-0	2-0	11	Hearn [35], Rhead [39]	2467
14	Oct 2	A	Guiseley	W 1-0	1-0	7	Rhead [17]	1279
15	10	A	Chester FC	W 3-2	2-1	8	Rhead [4], Everington [28], Power [54]	2224
16	13	A	Welling U	L 1-2	0-1	10	Hearn [48]	702
17	17	H	Braintree T	W 2-0	0-0	7	Hawkridge [53], Hearn [54]	2565
18	31	H	Bromley	L 0-1	0-0	11		2550
19	Nov 11	A	Aldershot T	W 2-1	1-0	8	Wootton [38], Muldoon [80]	1367
20	14	H	Tranmere R	W 1-0	1-0	7	Waterfall [44]	3176
21	21	A	Torquay U	W 3-1	2-0	5	Waterfall 2 [16, 74], Hearn [25]	1752
22	25	A	Boreham Wood	D 1-1	1-1	5	Rhead [18]	661
23	28	H	Welling U	D 1-1	0-1	4	Muldoon [72]	2528
24	Dec 5	A	Woking	L 1-3	0-2	7	Rhead [76]	1432
25	19	H	Barrow	D 2-2	2-1	7	Rhead 2 [28, 43]	2540
26	26	H	FC Halifax T	L 0-1	0-0	7		3558
27	28	A	Grimsby T	L 0-2	0-1	9		7650
28	Jan 2	A	FC Halifax T	D 2-2	1-1	8	Stanley [16], Hearn [69]	1932
29	9	H	Dover Ath	L 2-3	1-1	9	Waterfall [36], Hearn [48]	2402
30	16	H	Forest Green R	L 0-1	0-0	9		1975
31	23	A	Wrexham	L 1-3	1-1	11	Rhead (pen) [14]	3853
32	30	H	Guiseley	W 1-0	1-0	11	Bush [26]	2265
33	Feb 6	H	Eastleigh	W 3-0	3-0	9	Rhead [22], Caton [40], Muldoon [45]	2085
34	13	A	Altrincham	D 3-3	2-2	10	Rhead 2 (1 pen) [7, 33 (p)], Muldoon [56]	1293
35	20	H	Southport	W 3-1	1-0	8	Caton 2 [31, 59], McDaid [89]	2581
36	Mar 5	H	Aldershot T	W 2-0	1-0	8	McCombe [8], Oastler (og) [61]	2398
37	12	A	Macclesfield T	D 1-1	1-0	10	McCombe [16]	1676
38	15	H	Dover Ath	L 1-4	0-1	10	Muldoon [62]	743
39	19	H	Kidderminster H	L 1-2	1-0	10	Muldoon [27]	2178
40	25	A	Tranmere R	L 2-3	1-2	10	Maris [41], McDaid [73]	5366
41	28	H	Gateshead	D 1-1	1-1	11	Waterfall [37]	2142
42	Apr 2	A	Bromley	L 0-2	0-1	12		1202
43	9	H	Chester FC	W 2-1	1-0	11	McDaid [38], Maris [81]	2001
44	16	A	Southport	D 2-2	1-1	11	McDaid [45], Wood [89]	961
45	23	H	Woking	L 2-3	0-2	12	Rhead [47], Muldoon [48]	2518
46	30	A	Cheltenham T	L 1-3	1-1	13	Waterfall [45]	5055

Final League Position: 13

GOALSCORERS

League (69): Rhead 20 (5 pens), Hearn 10, Muldoon 9, Waterfall 6, McDaid 4, Caton 3, Power 3, Maris 2, McCombe 2, Simmons 2, Stanley 2, Bush 1, Everington 1, Hawkridge 1, Wood 1, Wootton 1, own goal 1.
FA Cup (5): Rhead 3 (1 pen), Hearn 1, Robinson 1.
FA Trophy (1): Muldoon 1.

Farman 45	Wood 39+1	Waterfall 35+1	Howe 27	Beevers 43+1	Stanley 26+3	Sparrow 22+5	Muldoon 45+1	Power 32+6	Simmons 5+13	Rhead 41+2	Hearn 13+7	Nolan 6+1	Hodge Elliot 5+3	Bush 29+2	Robinson 4+13	Everington 1+12	Tempest 17+3	Brown 2	Hawkridge 34+4	Wootton 1+4	Grant 1	Blissett 1+2	Reid 2	Brough 4	McDaid 3+13	McCombe 8	Caton 8+4	Maris 6+7	Wildin 1+3	Match No.
1	2	3	4	5	6	7^2	8^3	9	10^1	11	12	13	14																	1
1		3	4	2	6^1	13	10^2	9		11	8^3	7		5	12	14														2
1		3	4	2	7	8	6^2	12		10	11^1	9		5	13															3
1		3	9	7	2	8	11^1	13		10	5^3	6^2		4	12		14													4
1	12	3	4	2	7	9^2	6^1	13	14	10		8		5^3	11															5
1	2	3		5	7	12	11^2	6^2	13	10		8	14			9^1			4											6
1	2^3	3		5	6^2		8^1	9	13	11	7			14	10	12			4											7
1	2		4	5	7	8	6	12		10	11^1			3					9											8
1	2	3		5	8^2	9	6^1			11	10			4	12	13			7											9
1	2	3		5	13	8	12			11	10			4	9^2	7^1			6											10
1		3	4	2	7	9	11^3	6^1	14	10	13			5	12				8^2											11
1	2	3		5	7	6^2		10	9	12	11	13		4					8^1											12
1	6	3	4	2	7^2			10	12	11^3	8^1		13	5	14				9											13
1	2	3	6	5	7^1			10	8^2	13	11	12		4					9											14
1	8	3	4	2	7^3			6^2	9	14	11^3	13		5	12				10											15
1	2^4		4	5	3			8	7	12	11		9^1	6					10											16
1		3	4	2				6	8	10	11			5	12	7^1			9											17
1	8	3	4	2				6^2	7	10	11^1			5	13		✓		9	12										18
	7	3	4	2	8^1	9	6^2	10		12				13	5		14		11^3	1										19
1	2	3	4	5	7^3	8	6^2	12		11	10^1								9	14	13									20
1	5	3	4	2	7^3		6	8		10	11^1					14	9^2		12	13										21
1	2	3	4	5	7^2	13	6	8		10	11^3					14	9^1		12											22
1	2	3	4	5	7^2	8	6	10		11						9^1	12					13								23
1	2	3	4	5	13	8	6	7^3		11				14		12	9^2					10^1								24
1	2	3	4				8	7^1	6	11				5	12	13			9					10^2						25
1	2	3	4				9	7^3	6	12				5		8			13	10^1										26
1	2	3^4	6	9^2	4^1			7	8	10			13	12	14	5	11^3													27
1	2		5				6	8	11	13				12		5^1	9^2								10					28
1	3	4		2	8		11^1	5		10	9			13					6^2						7	12				29
1	8	4	3	2	7^2		6	10^1		11				12	13				9						5					30
1	8^1	3	4	2	13	9	6	7		10	11^2														5	12				31
1	2		5				6^2	13	11	9^1				4		7	10								12	3	8			32
1	2		5					10^1	7	11				3		6	8								13	4	9^2	12		33
1	2		5					10^1	7	11				4		8	6^2								13	3	9	12		34
1	2		5					10^3	8^2	11^1				3	14		7		6						12	4	9		13	35
1	2		5					10^1	7	11^2				4		8^3	6								13	3	9	14	12	36
1	2		5				14	9^1	6	11				3		8^3	10								13	4	7^2	12		37
1	2		5					10	7	11				4		8^2	9								13	3^3	6^1	12	14	38
1	2	3		12			8^1	9	7	10				4			6^2						11				13	5		39
1	2^4		5				7	10	13	11^3				4			8^1		6						12		9			40
1		4		2			6^1	10	7	9			8^2	3	13		5										12	11		41
1		3	2				8	9	5	10^2			7	4			6								13		12	11^1		42
1	2		4	5			8	11		14	13		6^3	3			7								10^1		9^2	12		43
1	4	12	2	5			8	10^1		14	13		6	3^3			9								11^2		7			44
1	3^2	4	8	2			7	9^1	12	11			6				5								14		13	10^1		45
1	2	3		5				11	7	10				8			6^2								13	4	12	9^1		46

FA Cup
Fourth Qualifying   Tranmere R   (a)   0-0
Replay   Tranmere R   (h)   2-0
First Round   Whitehawk   (a)   3-5

FA Trophy
First Round   Bradford Park Avenue   (a)   1-2

MACCLESFIELD TOWN

Ground: Moss Rose Stadium, London Road, Macclesfield, Cheshire SK11 7SP.   *Tel:* (01625) 264 686.
Website: www.mtfc.co.uk   *Email:* see website.   *Year Formed:* 1874.
Record Attendance: 9,008 v Winsford U, Cheshire Senior Cup 2nd rd, 4 February 1948.
Nickname: 'The Silkmen'.   *Manager:* John Askey.   *Colours:* Blue shirts with white trim, white shorts, blue socks with white trim.

MACCLESFIELD TOWN – VANARAMA NATIONAL 2015–16 LEAGUE RECORD

Match No.	Date	Venue	Opponents	Result	H/T Score	Lg Pos.	Goalscorers	Attendance
1	Aug 8	A	Torquay U	L	0-1	0-0	17		2066
2	11	H	Southport	D	0-0	0-0	20		1472
3	15	H	Welling U	W	2-1	1-0	14	Whitaker 24, Dennis 46	1236
4	18	A	Lincoln C	L	3-5	2-3	15	Dennis 2 3,90, Lewis 6	2320
5	22	A	Eastleigh	L	0-1	0-0	18		1928
6	29	H	Chester FC	L	1-2	0-0	21	Whitehead 52	2062
7	31	A	Grimsby T	W	2-0	1-0	16	Dennis 2 45,68	4251
8	Sept 5	H	Woking	W	2-1	1-0	14	Dennis 14, Byrne 62	1285
9	12	A	Bromley	L	0-1	0-0	16		955
10	15	A	Cheltenham T	L	0-2	0-2	17		1962
11	19	H	Forest Green R	W	4-1	2-1	17	Dennis 2 (1 pen) 15,45(p), Lewis 64, Whitaker 83	1311
12	22	H	Barrow	L	1-2	0-0	17	Lewis 58	1215
13	26	A	Aldershot T	W	3-0	2-0	16	Rowe 2 3,41, Dennis 69	1579
14	Oct 3	H	Boreham Wood	D	0-0	0-0	18		1186
15	6	A	Guiseley	W	3-0	2-0	14	Turnbull 24, Whitehead 44, Whitaker 58	653
16	10	A	Kidderminster H	W	2-1	2-0	13	Diagne 31, Rowe 38	1652
17	13	H	Gateshead	W	1-0	0-0	11	Dennis 59	1223
18	17	A	Dover Ath	L	1-2	1-1	13	Whitehead 4	1012
19	31	A	Braintree T	L	0-1	0-0	13		687
20	Nov 10	H	Altrincham	W	3-0	2-0	11	Dennis 13, Whitaker 40, Holroyd 81	1801
21	14	A	Woking	W	5-2	2-0	10	Whitehead 13, Dennis 3 26,61,80, Byrne 49	1324
22	21	H	Bromley	W	2-0	0-0	9	Lewis 49, Dennis 80	1632
23	28	A	Wrexham	W	3-2	1-1	7	Dennis 2 23,48, Whitaker 71	4591
24	Dec 5	A	Southport	L	1-3	1-1	9	Whitaker (pen) 45	861
25	8	H	Eastleigh	L	1-2	1-1	9	Diagne 8	1087
26	19	A	Welling U	W	1-0	1-0	6	Dennis 6	577
27	26	H	Tranmere R	L	1-2	1-1	6	Dennis 45	3037
28	28	A	Chester FC	W	2-0	2-0	6	Sharps (og) 25, Dennis (pen) 31	2791
29	Jan 2	A	Tranmere R	W	1-0	1-0	5	Sampson 31	4923
30	9	H	FC Halifax T	L	0-1	0-0	7		2055
31	23	H	Aldershot T	L	0-2	0-1	7		1515
32	30	A	Forest Green R	L	1-2	0-0	8	Sampson 69	1617
33	Feb 13	A	Kidderminster H	L	1-3	0-3	12	Dennis 90	1693
34	27	H	Wrexham	D	0-0	0-0	12		2406
35	Mar 1	H	Torquay U	L	1-2	1-1	12	Dennis 43	1022
36	5	A	Altrincham	D	0-0	0-0	12		2014
37	12	H	Lincoln C	D	1-1	0-1	12	Whitehead 50	1676
38	19	A	Boreham Wood	D	0-0	0-0	12		306
39	26	A	Gateshead	W	3-0	2-0	12	Styche 3 7,23,87	948
40	28	H	Grimsby T	W	2-1	1-0	10	Sampson 26, Styche 68	2326
41	Apr 2	H	Braintree T	W	3-1	1-0	10	Whitaker (pen) 25, Rowe 47, McCombe 65	1222
42	9	A	Barrow	D	1-1	1-1	10	Whitehead 24	1516
43	12	H	Dover Ath	D	0-0	0-0	10		1022
44	16	H	Guiseley	W	1-0	0-0	9	Lewis 76	1408
45	23	H	Cheltenham T	L	0-1	0-1	10		1895
46	30	A	FC Halifax T	D	1-1	0-1	10	Rowe 60	2943

Final League Position: 10

GOALSCORERS

League (60): Dennis 22 (2 pens), Whitaker 7 (2 pens), Whitehead 6, Lewis 5, Rowe 5, Styche 4, Sampson 3, Byrne 2, Diagne 2, Holroyd 1, McCombe 1, Turnbull 1, own goal 1.
FA Cup (4): Dennis 3, Turnbull 1.
FA Trophy (11): Dennis 4 (2 pens), Lewis 2, Byrne 1, Sampson 1, Turner 1, Whitaker 1, Whitehead 1.

Jalal 37	Halls 39 + 2	Byrne 25 + 2	Pilkington 39 + 1	Diagne 25 + 7	Whitehead 31 + 5	Lewis 23 + 2	Whitaker 43 + 1	Holroyd 39 + 3	Rowe 30 + 11	Dennis 32 + 7	Sampson 31 + 8	Turnbull 31 + 7	Bailey-Jones — + 4	Cowan 10 + 9	Marsden — + 2	Branagan 9 + 2	Fitzpatrick 36 + 1	Meikle 2 + 4	Adarabioyo 1 + 2	Styche 8 + 7	Churchman — + 1	Turner 1 + 1	Sutherland 2 + 6	Robles — + 1	Phillips 1 + 2	McCombe 11 + 1	Templeton — + 1	Match No.
1	2	3	4	5	6^2	7	8	9^3	10^1	11	12	13	14															1
1	$2▪$	3	4	5	8	7	6	9^1	11^2	10^3	12		13	14														2
1		3	4	5		7	6	9		11	10	8																3
1^3	5	4	3		14	7	8	9^1	12	11	10	6^2		2		13												4
	2	3	4	5	13	7	8	9^1	12	11	10^2	6^3			14	1												5
	2	3	4	5	8		7	9	12	10^1	6^1	13				1												6
1	2	3	4	5	12	7	11	8	9^1	10				6														7
1	2	3	4	5			8	9	6	10	11					7												8
1	2	3	4	5	9	6	7	11^2	8^1	10	12			13														9
1	2	3	4	5^2	8^2	7	9	6	10^1	11	13			14			12											10
1	2	3^4	4	13	8	7	6	9	12	11^1	10						5											11
1	2	3	4		8	7	9	6^1	12	11	10						5											12
1	2^3		4	5	6		7	10	8^1	11^2	9			14			3	12	13									13
1	2	3	4		8	7	6	9		11							5	12	10^1									14
1	2	3	4			7	8	9		10	11	6					5											15
1	5	4	3	6		7		9^1	11^2	12	10	8		2			13											16
1	4	5	2		8		9	7	11^1	10^2		6					3	12	13									17
1	2^1	3	4		8		6		11	10		7		12			5	9										18
1	2	3	4	9	12	8	6^2		11			7^1					5	10		13								19
1		5		3	8	7^2	9	10	12	11^1		6				2	4			13								20
1		4		3	9^2	7^1	10	6	12	11^3	13	8		2			5	14										21
1		3		4	8^2	7	9	10	13	11^1	12	6		2			5											22
1	13	3		4	8^1	7^3	9	6	12	11^2	14	10		2			5											23
1	$4▪$	12	5	9^2		10	7	8^1		11	6			2			3					13						24
1	12		3	4		8	9	7	10		11	6		2^1			5											25
1	2	3			8	7	9	6	10^1	11	12	4					5											26
1	2	12	3		13	$7▪$	9^1	10	8	11	14	6^2	4^3				5											27
1	2	4	3	12			6^1	11		9	10	7	8				5											28
1^2	2	3	4	14			9^3	13	6	8	8^1	11	10	7			12	5										29
	2	3	4		12		11	7^1	9	10	8^2	5				1	6						13					30
	2	4	3	7^3	10		6	12	9^3	11	8^1					1	5							13	14			31
1	2	4	3	6^2	7^1		8	10^3	9	11	12						5						13		14			32
1	2	4	3		8	12^3	13	10	7		14	5	9^2				11^1	6										33
1	2	4^3	3	9^1			8	7		11	10^2	6					5			14					13			34
1	2	3	4^1	8	7^3	9^2			11		10^2	6					5			13					10	14		35
1	2	3		9	8^2		13		11	10	6						5					7^1	12	4				36
1	2		4	8^1			9	7	12	11	10	6					5									3		37
1	2		4	6^3			7^2	9	12	10	11^1	8	14				5			13						3		38
1	2		5	13			8	9	7^2		10	6^3	12				3			11^1		14				4		39
1	2^2		4	13	8		7	6	9		10		12				5			11^1						3		40
1	2		4		8		7	6	9	9^3		14	10^2	13			5			11^1						3	12	41
	2		4		8		7^1	11	6	13	9	12		1			5			10^2						3		42
	2		5		7^2		8	9^3	6	13	10	12		$1▪$			3			11^1		14				4		43
	2	12	4^2		13		8	6	9	14	10^1	7		1			5			11^3						3		44
	2	4^1			8^3		6	9	12	10	7	14		1			5			11^2		13				3		45
	2	4		14			9	11^2	6	8^1	10	3^3	12	1			7			13						5		46

FA Cup

Fourth Qualifying   Alfreton T   (h)   3-2
First Round   Portsmouth   (a)   1-2

FA Trophy

First Round   Ashton U   (h)   A-A
Abandoned at half-time due to waterlogged pitch.
First Round   Ashton U   (h)   4-0
Second Round   Truro C   (a)   2-2
Replay   Truro C   (h)   2-0
Third Round   Torquay U   (a)   3-3
Replay   Torquay U   (h)   0-1

SOUTHPORT

Ground: Merseyrail Community Stadium, Haig Avenue, Southport, Lancashire PR8 6JZ.   *Tel:* (01704) 533 422.
Website: southportfc.net   *Email:* secretary@southportfc.net   *Year Formed:* 1881.
Record Attendance: 20,010 v Newcastle U, FA Cup 4th rd (replay), 26 January 1932.   *Nickname:* 'The Sandgrounders'.
Manager: Andy Bishop.   *Colours:* Yellow shirts with black trim, yellow shorts with black trim, yellow socks with black trim.

SOUTHPORT – VANARAMA NATIONAL 2015–16 LEAGUE RECORD

Match No.	Date		Venue	Opponents		Result	H/T Score	Lg Pos.	Goalscorers	Atten- dance
1	Aug	8	H	Eastleigh	L	0-4	0-1	24		1017
2		11	A	Macclesfield T	D	0-0	0-0	21		1472
3		15	A	Cheltenham T	L	0-3	0-0	22		2251
4		18	H	Gateshead	L	1-2	1-1	23	Almond [39]	806
5		22	A	Braintree T	L	0-1	0-1	24		504
6		29	A	Barrow	L	0-1	0-1	24		1343
7		31	H	Altrincham	W	3-0	2-0	23	Jones, G (pen) [12], Nolan [24], McCarthy [85]	1143
8	Sept	5	H	Dover Ath	D	0-0	0-0	22		957
9		12	A	Forest Green R	L	1-2	0-2	23	Wright [75]	1535
10		15	H	Tranmere R	D	2-2	2-0	22	Jones, G [15], Phenix [20]	2827
11		19	A	FC Halifax T	D	2-2	1-0	22	Brown, M (og) [35], Stockton [66]	1211
12		22	A	Guiseley	D	1-1	0-1	22	Almond [87]	748
13		26	H	Grimsby T	L	0-4	0-3	22		1320
14	Oct	3	A	Woking	W	2-1	2-0	21	Stockton 2 [8, 17]	1510
15		10	H	Torquay U	L	0-1	0-1	22		1104
16		13	H	Chester FC	L	1-2	1-0	22	Almond [36]	1326
17		17	A	Kidderminster H	W	1-0	0-0	22	Bishop [83]	1593
18		31	H	Aldershot T	D	1-1	0-1	22	Foster [54]	845
19	Nov	14	H	Cheltenham T	L	0-4	0-3	22		947
20		21	A	Welling U	W	1-0	0-0	21	Phenix [74]	603
21		28	A	Eastleigh	L	0-1	0-0	21		1755
22	Dec	5	H	Macclesfield T	W	3-1	1-1	21	Almond 2 (1 pen) [27, 73 (p)], Thompson [77]	861
23		8	A	Gateshead	W	1-0	0-0	20	Almond [56]	582
24		19	H	Bromley	W	5-3	2-2	18	Wright [20], Jones, G [45], Phenix [47], Almond (pen) [59], Allen [76]	751
25		26	A	Wrexham	W	1-0	1-0	17	Blakeman [19]	5508
26		28	H	Barrow	W	2-1	1-1	15	Jones, G [23], Allen [50]	1528
27	Jan	2	H	Wrexham	W	3-2	1-1	14	Almond 2 (1 pen) [41, 85 (p)], Foster [51]	2148
28		9	A	Bromley	D	0-0	0-0	14		1317
29		23	A	Chester FC	D	0-0	0-0	15		2228
30		26	H	Forest Green R	L	0-1	0-0	15		707
31	Feb	6	A	Tranmere R	L	0-1	0-0	15		5199
32		13	H	Braintree T	D	1-1	0-1	14	Almond [57]	827
33		20	A	Lincoln C	L	1-3	0-1	16	Almond [67]	2581
34		27	H	Boreham Wood	L	0-3	0-2	16		815
35	Mar	1	A	Dover Ath	W	2-1	1-0	15	Allen [26], Bishop [74]	588
36		5	H	FC Halifax T	L	0-1	0-0	16		1148
37		8	A	Grimsby T	L	0-1	0-1	17		3180
38		12	H	Welling U	D	3-3	1-0	17	Phenix [37], Thompson [57], O'Brien [59]	746
39		19	A	Torquay U	L	0-1	0-0	17		1783
40		26	H	Guiseley	W	2-0	1-0	16	Margetts [37], Westcarr [66]	983
41		28	A	Altrincham	D	1-1	0-0	16	Jones, G [62]	1480
42	Apr	2	H	Woking	D	2-2	0-1	16	Margetts [76], Westcarr [84]	825
43		9	A	Boreham Wood	W	2-0	2-0	16	Rutherford 2 [10, 37]	434
44		16	H	Lincoln C	D	2-2	1-1	16	Bishop [44], Allen [86]	961
45		23	A	Aldershot T	W	2-1	2-1	15	Nolan [18], Wright [39]	1456
46		30	H	Kidderminster H	L	3-4	1-2	16	Almond (pen) [5], Phenix [64], Ryan [90]	1473

Final League Position: 16

GOALSCORERS

League (52): Almond 12 (4 pens), Jones, G 5 (1 pen), Phenix 5, Allen 4, Bishop 3, Stockton 3, Wright 3, Foster 2, Margetts 2, Nolan 2, Rutherford 2, Thompson 2, Westcarr 2, Blakeman 1, McCarthy 1, O'Brien 1, Ryan 1, own goal 1.
FA Cup (0).
FA Trophy (4): Almond 1 (pen), Ryan 1, Thompson 1, Wright 1.

Coughlin 15	Challoner 34+1	Beesley 9	Thompson 36+1	Foster 29	Wright 35+3	Brodie 1	Jones G 43	McCarthy 2+7	Almond 41+1	Jones A 15+5	Joyce 7+10	Allen 15+17	Nolan 35+7	Cameron 4+6	Phenix 33+3	Blakeman 27+1	Rutherford 32+8	Bishop 13+10	Davies 9	Stockton 10	Viscosi 6	Crocombe 25	Ryan 1+12	Grimshaw —+3	Giles 2+2	Hewitt 5+7	Cartwright 2	O'Brien 7	Westcarr 4+7	Margetts 3	Whittle 6+1	Match No.
1	2	3	4	5	6	7[1]	8	9	10[2]	11■	12	13																				1
1	2	5	3	4			10		9			7	12	6	8[1]	11																2
1	2	6	3	4			9	13	10			8	12	5	7[1]	11[2]																3
1	2	5	3	4			8	12	10[1]			13	7		6[3]	11[2]	9	14														4
1	2[1]	5	3	4[2]	6		8				7		13	9	12	11	10[3]	14														5
1	2		3■	5	6		8	13		9■			12		7[1]	10[3]	4[2]	14	11													6
1	2	5	3	4			7[1]	12	11[2]			14	13	8	9[3]		6	10														7
1	2	5		4	3		7	12	10			8		6		9	11[1]															8
1	2		3		5		8	11	10[2]		12	7	13	6		9			4													9
1	2		3■	4			8		10[1]			13	12	7	6	9	11[2]		5													10
1	2	3	4				8		9			12	13	7	11■	6[1]			5	10[2]												11
	2[1]		3	4			7		10	9		12	8	13	6[2]				5	11	1											12
	2[3]		6	7			11■					4	8	13	12	10	14	9[1]	3	5[2]	1											13
1	12	8	3	2			9[1]					5	6	13	7	11				4	10[2]											14
1	6[1]		5	4			10	2				9	7	13	8[2]	12				3	11											15
1		12	3	4			9	2[1]				7	8	6		13	10[2]			5	11											16
	2		3	4	7		6					8	9	12[2]		13	11			5	10[1]											17
	3		4		6		8[2]		10			12	2		5	9	7	11[1]				1	13									18
	4		5		2		9[2]		10[3]			7	6		8	12	13	11[1]				1	14									19
	2		3	4	5[1]		7		10			13	11[3]		8	9	12	6[2]				1	14									20
	2		3	4			9		10			13	8[2]	14	6	5	7[1]	11[3]				1	12									21
	2		5	4	8[1]		9					7[3]	12	14	10	3	6[2]	11■				1	13									22
	2		5	4	8		9		10			12	13		11[2]	3	6	7[1]				1										23
	2		5	4			9[3]		13			14	10	6	11[2]	3	8[1]					1				12						24
	2		3	4	8[3]		7		11			13	9[2]	12	10[1]	5	6	14				1										25
	2		4	3			7	12	10			11[1]	8		6	5	9					1										26
	4		5		6		9[1]		10	2		11	12		7	3	8					1										27
	2		3	4	7[1]		8		10			11	12		9	5	6					1										28
	2		3	4	8[1]		7		10[2]			11	12		9	5	6					1	13									29
	2		4	3	7[3]		12		10	13		11[2]	8		6[1]	5	9					1	14									30
	4		3		2		8[2]		10[1]			11	7		6[3]	5	9	12				1		14	13							31
	2		3	4			7		11[2]			10[1]	8		5		9	12				1	13		6							32
	2		3	4[2]	12		7		8			14	9		11	5	6[3]	13				1				10[1]						33
	2[1]		4		8		7		10[3]			11[2]	3		9	5	6	12				1				13	14					34
	2		4[2]		10		8			12		11	3		9	13	7					1						6[1]	5■			35
	2[1]				8		7					11	4		5	9	10[2]					1	14	13				6[1]	3	12		36
	2				8		7		13			10[2]	4	12	5[1]		14					1						6[1]	9	3	11	37
	2		3		9		8		10[2]			13	12		7[1]	5	6[3]					1						14	4	11		38
	2		4		7		8		10[2]	11[3]		9[1]			6	5	14					1						13	3	12		39
	4						8					11	5		7	9[1]	2[3]	6				1				14		3	13	10[2]	12	40
	3		13				9[3]			2					8		6					1		14		10[1]		4	12	11[2]	5	41
	4				12		7		10	2		8			6[1]		9[2]					1						3	13	11	5	42
	2		4		7		9		8			12	3		13	6[3]	11[2]					1				14		10			5[1]	43
	2		4		5		9		7			8			13	6[3]	11[1]					1				14		10[2]	3			44
1	3		4		7				11	2		10[3]	8		9[1]		12						14					6[2]	13		5	45
	4		3		7				10	2		6[1]	11		8		9[2]					1	13					12	14		5[3]	46

FA Cup
Fourth Qualifying   Salford C   (a)   0-1

FA Trophy
First Round   Worcester C   (h)   0-0
Replay   Worcester C   (a)   3-2
Second Round   Dover Ath   (a)   1-2

TORQUAY UNITED

Ground: The Launa Windows Stadium, Plainmoor, Torquay, Devon TQ1 3PS.   *Tel:* (01803) 328666.
Website: www.torquayunited.com   *Email:* reception@torquayunited.com
Year Formed: 1899.   *Record Attendance:* 21,908 v Huddersfield T, FA Cup 4th rd, 29 January 1955.
Nickname: 'The Gulls'.   *Manager:* Kevin Nicholson.   *Colours:* Yellow shirts with blue trim, yellow shorts with blue trim, yellow socks.

TORQUAY UNITED – VANARAMA NATIONAL 2015–16 LEAGUE RECORD

Match No.	Date		Venue	Opponents	Result	H/T Score	Lg Pos.	Goalscorers	Attendance
1	Aug	8	H	Macclesfield T	W 1-0	0-0	6	Fisher, A [61]	2066
2		11	A	Wrexham	L 1-3	1-0	14	Carmichael [42]	4734
3		15	A	FC Halifax T	W 3-2	2-1	9	MacDonald [20], Hurst [31], Fisher, A [63]	1199
4		18	H	Woking	L 0-1	0-0	12		1936
5		22	A	Grimsby T	D 2-2	2-0	12	Quigley [19], Robinson (og) [33]	4290
6		29	H	Cheltenham T	L 0-3	0-1	14		2018
7		31	A	Eastleigh	L 2-3	0-2	17	Hurst [84], Fisher, A [90]	1819
8	Sept	5	H	Guiseley	D 1-1	1-1	19	Geohaghon [34]	1558
9		12	A	Welling U	D 1-1	1-1	18	Butler [20]	659
10		15	A	Kidderminster H	D 2-2	1-0	18	Hurst 2 [16, 68]	1493
11		19	H	Bromley	L 3-7	2-3	18	Hurst [5], Marsh 2 [45, 85]	1653
12		22	H	Boreham Wood	L 1-2	0-1	21	Fisher, A [59]	1735
13		26	A	Lincoln C	L 0-2	0-2	21		2467
14	Oct	3	H	Aldershot T	L 0-2	0-2	22		1946
15		6	H	Dover Ath	L 2-3	1-1	23	Hurst 2 [40, 88]	1210
16		10	A	Southport	W 1-0	1-0	21	Fisher, A [2]	1104
17		13	A	Woking	D 2-2	0-1	21	Richards, C [46], Marsh (pen) [77]	1556
18		17	H	Grimsby T	D 1-1	1-0	21	Marsh [38]	2003
19		31	A	Altrincham	D 1-1	1-0	21	Marsh [24]	1060
20	Nov	14	A	Barrow	L 0-4	0-2	21		1119
21		21	H	Lincoln C	L 1-3	0-2	22	Butler [75]	1752
22		28	A	Braintree T	D 0-0	0-0	22		773
23	Dec	5	A	Wrexham	L 0-1	0-0	22		1512
24		19	A	Chester FC	L 1-4	0-3	23	Wright [68]	2160
25		26	H	Forest Green R	W 4-1	2-1	23	Marsh 2 [22, 37], Berry [83], Wright [88]	2051
26		28	A	Cheltenham T	L 0-1	0-0	23		3781
27	Jan	1	A	Forest Green R	L 1-3	0-0	23	Verma [48]	1907
28		23	A	Gateshead	L 0-2	0-1	23		1721
29		30	A	Tranmere R	L 1-2	0-1	23	Harrad [82]	5053
30	Feb	20	A	Boreham Wood	W 1-0	0-0	24	Blissett [58]	555
31		23	H	Welling U	W 2-0	0-0	23	Smith [60], Allen [70]	1341
32	Mar	1	H	Macclesfield T	W 2-1	1-1	22	Blissett 2 [20, 47]	1022
33		5	H	Kidderminster H	W 3-2	2-0	22	Snedker (og) [10], Blissett [43], Smith [82]	2021
34		8	H	Braintree T	D 0-0	0-0	22		1462
35		12	A	Aldershot T	D 0-0	0-0	22		1771
36		15	H	FC Halifax T	D 0-0	0-0	21		1664
37		19	H	Southport	W 1-0	0-0	19	Blissett [80]	1783
38		26	A	Dover Ath	L 0-5	0-4	21		1367
39		28	H	Eastleigh	L 0-1	0-1	22		2081
40	Apr	2	A	Gateshead	W 2-1	0-0	20	Allen [49], Wright [71]	785
41		5	H	Chester FC	W 2-0	1-0	18	Blissett [3], Allen [90]	1831
42		9	H	Tranmere R	L 0-1	0-0	18		2264
43		12	H	Altrincham	W 2-0	1-0	17	Young [17], Harrad [59]	1995
44		16	A	Bromley	W 2-0	1-0	17	MacDonald [11], Richards, C [85]	2080
45		23	H	Barrow	D 2-2	0-1	18	Richards, C [61], Blissett [81]	2874
46		30	A	Guiseley	L 3-4	0-3	18	Blissett [53], Ajala [60], Harrad [77]	1915

Final League Position: 18

GOALSCORERS

League (54): Blissett 8, Hurst 7, Marsh 7 (1 pen), Fisher, A 5, Allen 3, Harrad 3, Richards, C 3, Wright 3, Butler 2, MacDonald 2, Smith 2, Ajala 1, Berry 1, Carmichael 1, Geohaghon 1, Quigley 1, Verma 1, Young 1, own goals 2.
FA Cup (0).
FA Trophy (7): Wright 2, Allen 1, Butler 1, Murombedzi 1, Rees 1, Smith 1.

Spiess 17	Smith 39	MacDonald 41	Geoghaghon 16+2	Butler 45	Carmichael 12+2	Richards C 35+1	Fenwick 4+3	Murombedzi 7+12	Fisher A 16+5	Quigley 8+2	Lavelle-Moore 3+6	Fairhurst —+3	Chaney 5+9	Marsh 11+7	Hurst 17	Briscoe 14+7	Heslop 19+1	Lavercombe 17+1	Bell 2+4	Berry 26	Yeoman —+4	Hickford 2	Nicholson 16	Campion 2+1	Verma 20+3	Wright 10+12	Gerring 10+3	Finch —+2	Ajala 12+6	Harrad 15+3	Blissett 16+1	Rees 16+2	Racchi 12+2	Allen 5+8	Moore 12	Young 4+4	Match No.
1	2	3	4	5	6	7	8	9	10^{1}	11^{2}	12	13																									1
1	2	3	8	5	7	4	6^{3}	11	10^{2}	9^{1}	12		13	14																							2
1	6	3	4	5	8	7	12^{*}		10	11^{1}	14	13			2^{2}	9^{1}																					3
1	5	3	4	11	6	7			10^{1}	9^{2}	14			13	2	8^{3}	12																				4
1	4	3	5	6	9^{1}	7		14	11^{3}	10^{2}				12	2	13	8																				5
4^{1}	2	3	9	6	7			13	10	11^{3}				14	5	12	8^{2}																				6
1	6	3	4	8^{1}	9				14	11^{2}	13			10^{3}	5	12	7																				7
1	4	3	5	2	7				10	12	11^{1}				6	9	8																				8
1^{*}	4	5	6	3	8				11^{2}	13	9^{1}				2	10	7	12																			9
1	9	3	4	5	8		12		10^{1}	11^{2}	13				2	7	6^{*}																				10
7	3	4	5	9			6^{3}	14	13		11^{1}					8	2	10^{2}	1	12																	11
1	9	3	4	5	7^{1}				11						10^{2}	6	12		1	8	2	13															12
1	5	4	3^{1}	9				13	12						11^{2}	7	10		8^{3}	2	14	6															13
1	4	3		8					11^{2}	12					10^{3}	6	9^{1}	7	13	2	14		5														14
1	4	3		9			7^{3}	12	13	10					6	11^{1}	8	14	2				5^{2}														15
1	5	4		6			8		13	10					12	7^{2}	11^{1}	9		2			3														16
1	4			8			9^{2}	13	10						12	6^{3}	11^{1}	7	14	2		3	5														17
1	4	3		9			7		12	11^{2}					10	6^{1}		8		2	13		5														18
4	3		9	7					12	10^{3}					11^{*}	6^{1}	14	8^{2}	1	2			5	13													19
4^{*}	3		9	8					12						11^{1}	6	1		2			5	10	7^{2}	13											20
	3		9	7		6						13			10^{2}	8	1		2			5	11^{1}		12	4										21
	3	4		9		8		6								7	1		2			5	10	11												22
	4	3		9		7		11^{1}						12	13	8^{2}	1		2			5	6	10												23
	3	4		8	12			6^{1}	10^{3}				14		11	2	1		2			5^{1}	7	9	13											24
	4			6	13	7									10^{1}	12	8	1		2			5^{2}	9	11^{3}	3	14									25
	3	14		8		7^{1}	12								11^{1}		6	1		2			5	9^{2}	10^{3}	4	13									26
	3	6		7^{1}			12								11			1		2			5	9	10	4										27
	4	3		6		8		14							10^{3}			1		2			5^{2}	9	11^{1}			7	12	13						28
	4	3	14	9		6							12^{3}					1		2			5^{1}		13			8	10	11^{2}	7						29
	3	4		5		6							12					1		2								8^{1}	10	11	9	7					30
	4	3		5		7							14					1		2				13				6^{2}	10^{3}	11^{1}	9	8	12				31
	5	4		3		8												1		2				13	12			7^{2}	11	10	9^{1}	6					32
	4	3		5		7							13					1		2					12			9^{2}	11^{1}	10	6	8					33
	4	3		5		7												1		2				14	12			6^{2}	11	10^{3}	9^{1}	8	13				34
	4	5		2		7^{1}												3						8	11			13	10^{2}		9	6	12	1			35
	4	3		5		8							14					2						6	11^{1}			13	10^{3}		9^{2}	7	12	1			36
	4	3		5		8												2						6^{3}	13			9	10^{1}	11	14	7^{1}	12	1			37
	6^{1}	3		5		8												2^{2}						7		13		9	10	11^{3}	4		12	1	14		38
		3		5		8^{2}							9^{3}											2	10	4		14		11	7^{1}	6	13	1	12		39
		3		5		8^{1}							6											2	14	9			10^{3}	11	4	7^{2}	12	1	13		40
	4	3		5		13							8^{2}											2		14		9^{3}	12	11^{1}	6	7	10	1			41
	4	3		5									9^{1}											2	14			10^{2}	13	11	7	8^{3}	6	1	12		42
		3		5		8																		2	12	4		13	10^{1}	11	6		9^{2}	1	7		43
		4		5		8							13											2	14	3		12	11^{1}	10	7		9^{3}	1	6^{2}		44
		4	5			8							14											2		3		12	11	10	9^{1}	13	6^{2}	1	7^{3}		45
		4	5			8							3^{1}											6	13	2		9^{2}	10	11	14	12		1	7^{3}		46

FA Cup

Fourth Qualifying	Basingstoke T	(a)	0-3

FA Trophy

First Round	Chesham U	(h)	0-0
Replay	Chesham U	(a)	2-0
Second Round	Wrexham	(h)	1-0
Third Round	Macclesfield T	(h)	3-3
Replay	Macclesfield T	(a)	1-0
Fourth Round	Bognor Regis T	(a)	0-1

TRANMERE ROVERS

Ground: Prenton Park, Prenton Road West, Prenton, Wirral CH42 9PY.   *Tel:* (03330) 144452.
Website: www.tranmererovers.co.uk   *Email:* customerservice@tranmererovers.co.uk   *Year Formed:* 1884.
Record Attendance: 4,424 v Stoke C, FA Cup 4th rd, 5 February 1972.   *Nickname:* 'Rovers'   *Manager:* Gary Brabin.
Colours: White shirts with blue and green trim, white shorts with green trim, white socks with blue and green trim.

TRANMERE ROVERS – VANARAMA NATIONAL 2015–16 LEAGUE RECORD

Match No.	Date	Venue	Opponents	Result	H/T Score	Lg Pos.	Goalscorers	Attendance
1	Aug 8	H	Woking	W 1-0	0-0	6	Harris 58	5583
2	11	A	Gateshead	W 4-1	3-1	2	Ridehalgh 30, Sutton 39, Ihiekwe 44, Hill 66	1589
3	15	A	Braintree T	D 0-0	0-0	4		838
4	18	H	FC Halifax T	W 1-0	0-0	2	Mangan 74	5235
5	22	H	Boreham Wood	L 0-2	0-0	5		4832
6	29	A	Altrincham	L 1-2	0-2	8	Maynard 85	2460
7	31	H	Kidderminster H	D 2-2	2-0	9	Hogan 20, Mangan 26	4622
8	Sept 5	A	Welling U	D 1-1	0-0	10	Maynard 46	1012
9	12	H	Chester FC	W 2-0	2-0	8	Hogan 6, Norwood 37	7433
10	15	A	Southport	D 2-2	0-2	8	Harris 46, Norwood 57	2827
11	18	A	Grimsby T	D 1-1	0-1	8	Blissett 54	4368
12	22	H	Aldershot T	W 3-1	1-1	7	Norwood 45, Mekki 69, Mangan 90	4126
13	26	A	Cheltenham T	W 1-0	0-0	6	Mangan 90	2556
14	Oct 3	H	Bromley	W 4-0	1-0	3	Mangan 2 (1 pen) 28, 80 (p), Margetts 2 52, 90	4817
15	6	A	Wrexham	D 2-2	1-1	3	Maynard 25, Mangan 52	6706
16	10	H	Eastleigh	L 1-2	0-0	5	Jennings 79	5133
17	13	H	Barrow	L 0-1	0-1	7		4624
18	17	A	Forest Green R	W 2-0	2-0	5	Taylor-Fletcher 5, Norwood 22	2133
19	31	H	Dover Ath	L 0-1	0-1	10		4486
20	Nov 14	A	Lincoln C	L 0-1	0-1	12		3176
21	21	H	Guiseley	W 2-1	1-1	10	Norwood 2 (1 pen) 45, 90 (p)	4352
22	24	A	Woking	L 1-4	0-2	10	Norwood 90	1477
23	28	A	Boreham Wood	D 0-0	0-0	10		640
24	Dec 5	H	Braintree T	L 1-2	1-2	12	Mekki 3	4224
25	19	A	FC Halifax T	D 1-1	1-1	12	Norwood 40	1684
26	26	A	Macclesfield T	W 2-1	1-1	11	McNulty 5, Ihiekwe 77	3037
27	28	H	Altrincham	W 1-0	1-0	8	Norwood 28	5414
28	Jan 2	H	Macclesfield T	L 0-1	0-1	9		4923
29	9	A	Barrow	W 4-3	1-0	8	Mekki (pen) 18, Maynard 90, Hughes 90, Kirby 90	1766
30	23	A	Bromley	W 1-0	0-0	8	Vaughan 54	2219
31	30	H	Torquay U	W 2-1	1-0	5	Taylor-Fletcher 37, Norwood 79	5053
32	Feb 6	A	Southport	W 1-0	0-0	4	Norwood (pen) 63	5199
33	13	H	Aldershot T	D 0-0	0-0	4		1882
34	20	A	Cheltenham T	L 0-1	0-1	4		5418
35	28	A	Chester FC	W 1-0	0-0	4	Norwood (pen) 69	3494
36	Mar 5	A	Gateshead	W 3-1	2-0	5	Norwood 2 (2 pens) 27, 44, Higdon 53	4668
37	8	A	Guiseley	D 2-2	1-1	5	Atkinson, R (og) 35, Kirby 58	1147
38	12	A	Dover Ath	D 0-0	0-0	4		1460
39	19	H	Forest Green R	D 1-1	0-1	6	Harris 48	5073
40	25	H	Lincoln C	W 3-2	2-0	5	Norwood (pen) 38, Kirby 45, Mekki 87	5366
41	28	A	Kidderminster H	W 2-0	1-0	4	Norwood 2 15, 90	2744
42	Apr 2	H	Welling U	L 1-2	1-1	5	Vaughan 18	5173
43	9	A	Torquay U	W 1-0	0-0	5	Higdon 59	2264
44	16	H	Wrexham	L 1-2	0-1	7	Norwood (pen) 78	7541
45	23	A	Eastleigh	W 1-0	0-0	6	Norwood 87	3269
46	30	H	Grimsby T	W 1-0	1-0	6	Jennings 24	6637

Final League Position: 6

GOALSCORERS

League (61): Norwood 19 (7 pens), Mangan 7 (1 pen), Maynard 4, Mekki 4 (1 pen), Harris 3, Kirby 3, Higdon 2, Hogan 2, Ihiekwe 2, Jennings 2, Margetts 2, Taylor-Fletcher 2, Vaughan 2, Blissett 1, Hill 1, Hughes 1, McNulty 1, Ridehalgh 1, Sutton 1, own goal 1.
FA Cup (0).
FA Trophy (2): Norwood 2.

Davies S 45	Hogan 17+1	Sutton 20+5	Ihiekwe 34+1	Hill 31	Maynard 31+4	Jennings 40+2	Harris 40+1	Ridehalgh 25+1	Stockton 4+2	Norwood 36+2	Mekki 28+11	Mangan 16+6	Holness 1+3	Riley 12+4	Margetts 6+4	Blissett 2+3	Jackson 2+9	Dawson 8+1	Taylor-Fletcher 15+6	Turner 1	McNulty 27	Tomlinson 5+5	Vaughan 24	Kirby 9+6	Hughes 18	Mackreth 1+7	Higdon 8+1	Fenwick —+3	Match No.
1	2	3	4	5	6	7	8	9	10	11^1	12																		1
1	4	3	2	5	6	7	8	9^1	10^2		12	11	13																2
1	4^3	3	2	5	8	6	7	9	11^2	13	14	10^1		12															3
1		2	5	7	4	9	8	3				11		6	10														4
1		3	2	5	6^2	8	7	9				13	11	4	10^1	12													5
1	4				8	6	7	9^1	10^1	5	13	2	3	11^3	12	14													6
1	10	2	13		6	4	5	3				7^2	8		9		11^1	12											7
1	4	2^4	6	7	5	8	9	3				10		11^1	12														8
1	4	3	2	5	13	8	7					10^2	6	11^3	14		12	9^1											9
1	3	4	2	5		7	8					10	9	11^1		12	6												10
1	6^2	2	3	5	14	4	7					10	8^3	12		13	11^1	9											11
1		2	3	4	8	7	6					11	9	12		13	10^1		5^2										12
1	3	4	2	5	6	8	7					11	10^1		13		12	9^2											13
1	3	2	4^2	5	7		8					9	10	12	11		13	6^1											14
1	4	2		5	7	12	8					13	6	10^2		3	11^3	14	9^1										15
1	3	2^2		5	7^4	12	8	14				10	7		11		4	6^3	9^1										16
1	3	2			6			8	4	9^1		10	7		5	11		12											17
1	4	12		2	8	6	7	5^1				10^2	9	3			13		11										18
	2			5	8	7		9^1				11		3	12				10	1	4	6							19
	2			5		7	8					11	12	10	4				9		3	6^1							20
1	3			5	12	7	8					9	6^2	11		2^1			10		4	13							21
1	4	13		5	2	7	8					9	6^1	11^2					10		3	12							22
1	3^3	13		5	7	8	6^2					9	12	14					10^1		4	11	2						23
1		4			5	8	7					11	6	10				12			3		2						24
1	12	4			9	6	7	5^2				10	8^1	14					11^3		3	13	2						25
1			4	5	3	7	8					11	9						10^1		6	12	2						26
1			4	5		7	8	9				11	6^2	12							3	10^5	2	13					27
1			3	4	8	7	9		13	11	5^1										2	12	6				10^2		28
1			4	5	9	7	6		12		11^1										3	8^2	2	13	10				29
1			4	5	6	8	7					10	9^1					12			3		2		11				30
1	12	4			9	6	7	5				11	8^2						10		3^1		2		13				31
1			4		9	6	7	5				11									8^1	3	2	10	12				32
1			5		4		7	2				11									12	3	6		9	8^1	10		33
1			4		8		7	5				10	12								6^1	3	2	13	9^2		11		34
1			3			6		5				11	7								13	4	2	10^2	8	12	9^1		35
1			4			7		5				11	6^1			14					13	3	2	9^2	8	12	10^5		36
1			6			3		2				5	7	12					10^1			4	9	8		11			37
1			4		13	7	12	5				11	6^1								3		2	9	8		10^2		38
1			3	5			7					11	6						10		4		2	8^1	9	12			39
1			4	5		8	7					11	12						10^2		3		2	6^1	9			13	40
1			7	8		2	4					6							5^2		11		3	10^1	9	13		12	41
1			4	5		7	8					11							10^1		3		2	6^3	9^2	12	14	13	42
1			4		10^2	7	8	5				9^1	12								3		2	13	6		11		43
1			4			7	8	5				10	6						13		3		2	12	9^1	11^2			44
1			3		10	7	8^1	5				11	13	12					14			4^3	2	6^2	9				45
1	12		4		10^2	7	8	5				11	6						3				2^1	13	9				46

FA Cup
Fourth Qualifying Lincoln C (h) 0-0
Replay Lincoln C (a) 0-2

FA Trophy
First Round Wrexham (h) 2-4

WELLING UNITED

Ground: Park View Road, Welling, Kent DA16 1SY. *Tel:* (0208) 3011196. *Website:* www.wellingunited.com
Email: info@wellingunited.com *Year Formed:* 1963. *Record Attendance:* 4,100 v Gillingham, FA Cup 1st rd (replay),
22 November 1989. *Nickname:* 'The Wings'. *Manager:* Mark Goldberg. *Colours:* Red shirts with white trim, red
shorts, white socks.

WELLING UNITED – VANARAMA NATIONAL 2015–16 LEAGUE RECORD

Match No.	Date		Venue	Opponents	Result		H/T Score	Lg Pos.	Goalscorers	Attendance
1	Aug	8	H	Guiseley	W	1-0	1-0	6	Kabba [40]	505
2		11	A	Forest Green R	L	0-1	0-1	12		1076
3		15	A	Macclesfield T	L	1-2	0-1	16	Kabba [90]	1236
4		18	H	Eastleigh	D	2-2	1-1	14	Turley (og) [31], Vidal [71]	545
5		22	A	Wrexham	L	0-1	0-0	17		5277
6		29	H	Braintree T	L	1-2	1-1	20	Obafemi [6]	521
7		31	A	Woking	L	0-2	0-0	22		1675
8	Sept	5	H	Tranmere R	D	1-1	0-0	21	Corne [87]	1012
9		12	H	Torquay U	D	1-1	1-1	21	Vidal [9]	659
10		15	A	Aldershot T	L	0-1	0-0	21		1256
11		19	A	Gateshead	W	2-1	2-1	20	Vidal 2 [24, 29]	822
12		22	H	Chester FC	W	2-1	1-0	18	Harris [43], Wellard [70]	564
13		26	H	FC Halifax T	W	2-0	2-0	18	Kabba 2 [44, 45]	653
14	Oct	3	A	Kidderminster H	W	1-0	0-0	15	Porter [49]	1438
15		6	H	Bromley	L	1-2	1-1	17	Chambers [4]	1127
16		10	A	Boreham Wood	L	0-2	0-1	17		543
17		13	H	Lincoln C	W	2-1	1-0	17	Corne [43], Obafemi [85]	702
18		17	A	Barrow	D	1-1	1-0	17	Williams, S (og) [42]	1327
19		31	A	Guiseley	L	0-2	0-2	18		653
20	Nov	10	H	Forest Green R	D	1-1	0-0	18	Bakare [63]	660
21		14	A	Grimsby T	L	1-3	1-2	18	Corne [6]	4108
22		21	H	Southport	L	0-1	0-0	19		603
23		28	A	Lincoln C	D	1-1	1-0	19	Harris [45]	2528
24	Dec	19	H	Macclesfield T	L	0-1	0-1	20		577
25		26	H	Dover Ath	L	1-2	0-1	21	Corne [90]	1006
26	Jan	9	H	Grimsby T	L	0-4	0-0	22		1337
27		23	H	Barrow	L	1-2	1-1	22	Vidal (pen) [28]	542
28		30	A	FC Halifax T	D	1-1	0-0	22	Daniel [80]	1407
29	Feb	2	A	Braintree T	L	0-1	0-1	22		461
30		6	H	Altrincham	D	1-1	0-0	22	Kabba [90]	551
31		13	A	Cheltenham T	L	0-2	0-1	22		2549
32		20	H	Wrexham	L	0-2	0-2	22		620
33		23	A	Torquay U	L	0-2	0-0	22		1341
34		27	H	Aldershot T	L	0-1	0-0	22		704
35	Mar	1	A	Bromley	L	0-2	0-1	23		1110
36		5	H	Cheltenham T	D	1-1	0-0	23	Wanadio [90]	604
37		8	A	Dover Ath	L	1-2	1-1	23	Bakare [2]	726
38		12	A	Southport	D	3-3	0-1	23	Bakare [74], Kabba [82], Gayle [89]	746
39		19	H	Gateshead	L	0-1	0-1	23		500
40		25	A	Eastleigh	D	0-0	0-0	23		2037
41		28	H	Woking	W	2-1	1-0	23	Lokko [28], Nortey [62]	550
42	Apr	2	A	Tranmere R	W	2-1	1-1	23	Gayle [20], Daniel [72]	5173
43		9	H	Kidderminster H	L	1-2	1-0	23	Daniel [7]	565
44		16	A	Chester FC	L	0-4	0-1	24		2237
45		23	A	Altrincham	L	0-5	0-2	24		1396
46		30	H	Boreham Wood	L	0-3	0-2	24		577

Final League Position: 24

GOALSCORERS

League (35): Kabba 6, Vidal 5 (1 pen), Corne 4, Bakare 3, Daniel 3, Gayle 2, Harris 2, Obafemi 2, Chambers 1, Lokko 1, Nortey 1, Porter 1, Wanadio 1, Wellard 1, own goals 2.
FA Cup (7): Vidal 4, Bakare 1, Corne 1, Wellard 1.
FA Trophy (5): Porter 2, Harris 1, St Aimie 1, Wellard 1.

King 20	Lokko 36+2	Jefford 24+1	Chambers 35	Wellard 23+5	Corne 31	Fazakerley 1	Harris 38+3	Vidal 24+3	Kabba 14+19	Adeyinka 3+8	Porter 23+6	Obafemi 4+8	Awotwi —+3	Osborne 10+4	Fagan 8+2	Nortey 26+6	Lee 29+1	McEntegart 9	Williams 25+2	Semedo 2+1	Taylor 6+3	Bakare 13+8	Cumberbatch —+1	St Aimie 1+1	Rodak 17	Daniel 10+4	Chesmain 12	Ferry 7	Gayle 16	Kadell 1+1	Wanadio 11+6	Yusuff 6+1	Adeloye 4+2	Kargbo 10	Kashket 6+1	Faggers —+2	Zapata-Caicedo 1+2	Match No.
1	2	3	4	5	6	7³	8	9	10¹	11²	12	13	14																									1
1	4	5	3	6			9	8	11³	10²	13	14			2¹	7	12																					2
1	4	5	3	6	7¹		9	8	12	11³	10				2²	14			13																			3
1	4	5	3	6	8		10	9	12		11¹				2		7																					4
1	4	5	3	10³	9		6	7	13	14	11²	12			2		8¹																					5
1	3	5	4	12	7		9	6¹	13	11²	10				2		8																					6
1	4	5	3	9	8		6	10			11	13	12	2			7²																					7
1	5²	2	4		8		9	10	11¹	13	6	12			3		7																					8
	4³	2	5	13	8		9	10		14	6	11			3¹				7²	1	12																	9
	8	5	4	13	9		10	3¹		12	6	2²				14			7³	1	11■																	10
1	4	5	3	9	7		6	10	11						2	8																						11
1	5	2	3	8	9		10	11¹	12		6				4	7																						12
1	4	5	3	8	7		6	10¹		11		12			2	9																						13
1	3	5	4	10	7		12	13	11²	6					2	8			9¹																			14
1	2	3	4³	6	7¹		9	13	14	10				12	5	8			11²																			15
1	4	5		10¹	7		9	6²	11			13			3■	2	8		12																			16
1	5	2	3	7	8		9	10	11¹			12			4	6																						17
1	12	5	4	8	7		10	6	11¹			13			3²	2	9																					18
1	3	13		8			9					10			4¹	6	7		2		5²	11	12															19
1	3	5	4	8			9¹	7	14		10				13	6	2		11			10³																20
1	3	5	4	9	8		6	14		10				12		7³	2²	13	11¹																			21
7	2³	3	6²	8			9	11	13	4			14			5¹	1	10				12																22
1			4	9	7		6				10				3	8	2		5			11¹	12															23
8	2			7³	9		10	13	12	4					3		5¹	1	11			14	6²															24
6²	2	3	5	7			8	10	14	4					12³	13		1	9			11¹																25
		3	6	8			9	11	5¹	4			2		7		1	10				12																26
	2	4	8²				12	11	7	5			3		6		9¹	13						1	10												27
		4	14				9	10¹	11²				3³	12	7		2		13					1	6	5	8										28
		4	13				10³	9¹					12	7			2		11					1		5	6	3¹	8	14							29
	3						6¹	13					4	7			2		12					1	9	5	8		10	11²							30
	3						12	11					6³	10			2		8²					1	9¹	5	7	4	14	13							31
	5						8	13					14	6²			3							1	11¹	2	7	4	9	10³	12						32
12	3¹		8				9	13					6				2							1		5	7²	4	14	10³	11						33
3							6	12					2				4							1	13	11	8			5	9¹	10²	7				34
4							8	13					9				2		12					1	6¹	5	3		10		11²	7					35
7							8	13					4				9		12					1		2	6	3	11²	10	5¹						36
3							9	12					7				2		11²					1	14	5	3		6³	13	8	10¹					37
3							9	12					8				2		11					1	5	4		6¹			7	10					38
4							9²	12					7				2		11					1	13	5	3		6¹			8	10				39
5	4		9				6	10²					7		1	2	8¹	11■							3	13			12								40
4³			8				11¹	14					6		1	2	5		12			3	9		7	10²	13										41
5	3	7		6			13						8			2	9²		12			1	10		4	12		11¹									42
3	2	8		9			14						5		4²	12						1	11		7	6¹	10³	—		13							43
3	4¹	8		11³	13		12						6			5	10²					1	9		2	14		7									44
4		2			13		6¹							7			5	11³				1			3	14	9	10²	8				12				45
4	3	6					9						5³	7	1	13	14						10		2²			8			12	11¹					46

FA Cup

Fourth Qualifying	Grays Ath	(a)	1-1
Replay	Grays Ath	(h)	4-0
First Round	Barwell	(a)	2-0
Second Round	Carlisle U	(h)	0-5

FA Trophy

| First Round | Tilbury | (a) | 4-3 |
| Second Round | Havant & Waterlooville | (a) | 1-2 |

WOKING

Ground: The Laithwaite Community Stadium, Kingfield, Woking, Surrey GU22 9AA.   *Tel:* (01483) 722 470.
Website: wokingfc.co.uk   *Email:* admin@wokingfc.co.uk   *Year Formed:* 1889.   *Record Attendance:* 6,064 v Coventry C,
FA Cup 3rd rd, 4 February 1997.   *Nickname:* 'The Cardinals'.   *Manager:* Garry Hill.   *Colours:* Red and white halved
shirts, black shorts with white trim, white socks with red trim.

WOKING – VANARAMA NATIONAL 2015–16 LEAGUE RECORD

Match No.	Date	Venue	Opponents	Result	H/T Score	Lg Pos.	Goalscorers	Attendance
1	Aug 8	A	Tranmere R	L	0-1	0-0	17		5583
2	11	H	Bromley	W	2-0	1-0	8	Goddard 2 36, 52	1507
3	15	H	Altrincham	W	2-0	1-0	7	Sole 32, Holman 75	1297
4	18	A	Torquay U	W	1-0	0-0	4	Yakubu 90	1936
5	22	H	Chester FC	W	5-2	1-0	2	Goddard (pen) 24, Holman 47, Daniel 63, Jones 76, Pattie 90	1503
6	29	A	Boreham Wood	D	1-1	1-0	4	Daniel 40	601
7	31	H	Welling U	W	2-0	0-0	3	Goddard 62, Keohane 78	1675
8	Sept 5	A	Macclesfield T	L	1-2	0-1	3	Jones 86	1285
9	12	A	Guiseley	D	4-4	3-2	5	Goddard 2 8, 13, Saah 45, Holman 75	643
10	15	H	Forest Green R	W	2-1	1-0	4	Goddard 43, Keohane 70	1775
11	19	H	Cheltenham T	L	0-1	0-0	5		2035
12	22	A	Braintree T	L	1-2	0-0	6	Murtagh 67	652
13	25	A	Dover Ath	L	0-2	0-1	9		864
14	Oct 3	H	Southport	L	1-2	0-2	12	Murtagh 78	1510
15	10	A	FC Halifax T	W	3-0	1-0	12	Holman 2 11, 60, Goddard 58	1155
16	13	H	Torquay U	D	2-2	1-0	13	Daniel 2, Holman 85	1556
17	17	H	Wrexham	L	0-1	0-1	16		1778
18	31	A	Kidderminster H	L	0-1	0-0	16		1449
19	Nov 10	H	Braintree T	D	1-1	0-1	16	Goddard 78	1182
20	14	H	Macclesfield T	L	2-5	0-2	17	Holman 74, Jones 86	1324
21	21	A	Chester FC	W	2-1	1-0	14	Holman 15, Goddard 90	1837
22	24	H	Tranmere R	W	4-1	2-0	12	Holman 2 27, 55, Goddard 40, Quigley 73	1477
23	28	A	Barrow	L	1-2	0-1	13	Jones 48	1115
24	Dec 5	H	Lincoln C	W	3-1	2-0	11	Holman 2 6, 68, Quigley 40	1432
25	19	A	Gateshead	W	5-1	2-1	10	Holman 2 3, 41, Andrade 68, Robinson, M 77, Quigley 90	573
26	26	A	Aldershot T	W	1-0	1-0	9	Goddard 78	3150
27	28	H	Boreham Wood	D	0-0	0-0	7		2097
28	Jan 2	H	Aldershot T	W	2-1	2-0	7	Quigley 25, Goddard 45	3708
29	9	A	Wrexham	W	3-1	1-1	6	Taylor (og) 13, Quigley 49, Andrade 83	4030
30	23	H	FC Halifax T	D	1-1	1-1	6	Andrade 35	1484
31	26	A	Altrincham	L	1-3	0-2	6	Sole 57	826
32	30	A	Barrow	D	2-2	2-2	6	Goddard 22, Sole 45	1713
33	Feb 13	A	Guiseley	L	0-1	0-1	9		1182
34	20	A	Bromley	L	1-2	1-2	11	Goddard 6	1227
35	23	A	Grimsby T	L	1-3	1-3	11	Sole 34	2874
36	Mar 5	H	Dover Ath	L	0-1	0-1	11		1305
37	8	A	Eastleigh	L	1-2	1-0	12	Jones 25	1630
38	12	A	Cheltenham T	L	0-4	0-2	13		2951
39	26	H	Kidderminster H	D	1-1	1-0	13	Carr 14	1730
40	28	A	Welling U	L	1-2	0-1	14	Gayle (og) 55	550
41	Apr 2	H	Southport	D	2-2	1-0	14	Butcher 2 37, 47	825
42	9	H	Gateshead	D	1-1	1-1	15	Robinson, M 31	1005
43	16	A	Forest Green R	W	2-1	0-1	14	Carr (pen) 69, Norman 90	1605
44	19	H	Grimsby T	L	1-3	0-1	14	Andrade 71	1394
45	23	A	Lincoln C	W	3-2	2-0	14	Murtagh 19, Andrade 22, Goddard 87	2518
46	30	H	Eastleigh	W	2-1	2-0	12	Murtagh 13, Goddard 15	1853

Final League Position: 12

GOALSCORERS

League (71): Goddard 17 (1 pen), Holman 14, Andrade 5, Jones 5, Quigley 5, Murtagh 4, Sole 4, Daniel 3, Butcher 2,
Carr 2 (1 pen), Keohane 2, Robinson, M 2, Norman 1, Pattie 1, Saah 1, Yakubu 1, own goals 2.
FA Cup (0).
FA Trophy (9): Murtagh 2, Quigley 2, Sole 2, Arthur 1, Saah 1, own goal 1.

Cole 44	Caprice 33+9	Saah 42	Yakubu 6	Arthur 30+7	Ricketts 36	Jones 37+6	Murtagh 31+7	Andrade 28+15	Rendell 1	Goddard 40+1	Sole 12+23	Daniel 9+12	Beckles —+1	Poku 6+12	Newton —+1	Holman 25	Pattie —+9	Thomas T 11+1	Keohane 7+8	Mills —+2	Cardwell 4+1	Braham-Barrett 4	Hamann 2	Norman 23+4	Robinson M 24+2	Cunnington 3	Quigley 15+4	Smith A 3+4	Griffiths 3	Jeffers 3	Smith S 1	Robinson J 5+1	Butcher 10	Carr 9+1	Match No.
1	2¹	3	4	5	6	7	8	9²	10³	11	12	13	14																						1
1	2³	3	4	5	7	6	8	12		9	10¹	11²		13	14	10																			2
1	2	3	4	5	6	7³	8	13		9²	11¹	12		14		10																			3
1	2	5	6	3	4	7	8	13		9¹	10¹	12						11²	14																4
1	2	3	4	5	6¹	8	7	12		9²		10²		13				11	14																5
1	2	3		4¹	5	6²	7¹	8		13	9	10		12				11	14																6
1	2	3		5		7	6	8¹		9¹		10²						11	13	4	12	14													7
1	2	3		5	6	7²	11	8¹		13	9³							10	14	4	12														8
1	2¹	3		5				6³		9	13	12			7			11²	14	4	10	8													9
1	2	3		5¹		7	6⁴			9	13	12			14			11		4	8	10³													10
1	2²	3			12	7	8			9	13	14						10		4	6	11³	5												11
1			4		2²	7	6²			9	11	12			8¹			10	14	3	13		5												12
1	2	3			7³	12	8	6		9²	13							11		4¹	10	14	5												13
1	5	2			3	4	7	13		8	12							11¹	14			6³	10²	9											14
1	2	3			5	7²	8	6³		11	12	9		13		10¹			14	4															15
1	2	3			5	6¹	7	9		12	8¹	13		10		11			4																16
1	2²	3⁴			5	6		12		10	13	7¹		8³				11	14	4				9											17
	3	5²	2	7	8	13				9¹	12	14				10¹							1	4		6	11								18
1		4		5	8	3		12		9		6¹				10		13						2	7²		11								19
1	13	4		5		7		14		9						10		3³	8					2	6¹		11²								20
1	12	3			5	7	4	6¹		9		14				10²		13						2	8		11³								21
1	12	3			5	7³	4	6²		9		14				11		13						2	8		10¹								22
1	14	3			5	7	4	6¹		9		12				10		13						2²	8¹		11³								23
1	2	4		6	3	13	7²			9						10¹		12						5	8		11								24
1	2	3			13	8	4	14		9		12		6		11²								5¹	7³		10								25
1	2	3			13	8	4	12		9		14		6¹		11								5	7		10³								26
1	2	4			13	6	5	14		9		12		8		10								3³	7¹		11²								27
1	2	4			13	6	5	14		9		12		8¹		10²								3	7		11¹								28
1	2¹	3			12	7	4	8		9		10²	13						14					5			11								29
1	13	4		5¹	8	3	7	6¹		9		10²												2	12		11								30
1	2	3³			8	4	6¹	9²		10		11			14									5	7		12	13							31
1	14	4			6	5	12	8³		9		12												2	7		11	13	3³						32
1	14	3			7	4²	8¹	13		9		12												2	6		10	5		11³					33
1	2	3³			5	7	13	12		9				6										4	8²		11	14		10¹					34
	2				12			3²		6	9¹			11³	7								1	14	8		13	10	5		4				35
1	12				5	8	3	7		9		13												2²			11³	14		4		6	10¹		36
1	13				5	4	6¹			8		10¹			7									2			12			3		11	9²		37
1	2				5²	3¹	4	6³		9		11												14	7		10					12	8		38
1	2	4			5	7³	3	8²		9		13		12											12	14						11¹	10		39
1		3			13	4³				9		12			14	10¹	8¹							5	6					7	2	11			40
1	2	4		5	6¹	14	8	12				13			7												10³			3		9	11²		41
1	2	4			5	6	3³			9		12			14									13	8		10²					7	11¹		42
1	2	3			5	7				6		10			12									4	8							9	11¹		43
1	2	4			5	6	13	7		8		12			14									3²	9								10³	11¹	44
1	2	4			5	6	13	7		9		14		12										3²	8								11²	10¹	45
1	2	4			5	7	3	8		11²	9¹	10³			14									13	6									12	46

FA Cup
Fourth Qualifying   Maidenhead U   (a)   0-3

FA Trophy
First Round   Boreham Wood   (a)   2-1
Second Round   Maidenhead U   (h)   6-1
Third Round   Oxford C   (h)   1-0
Fourth Round   Grimsby T   (a)   0-2

WREXHAM

Ground: Racecourse Ground, Mold Road, Wrexham, Wales LL11 2AH.   *Tel:* (01978) 891 864.
Website: wrexhamafc.co.uk   *Email:* see website.   *Year Formed:* 1872.
Record Attendance: 34,445 v Manchester U, FA Cup 4th rd, 26 January 1957.
Nickname: 'Red Dragons'.   *Manager:* Gary Mills.
Colours: Red shirts with white trim, white shorts with red trim, red socks.

WREXHAM – VANARAMA NATIONAL 2015–16 LEAGUE RECORD

Match No.	Date	Venue	Opponents	Result	H/T Score	Lg Pos.	Goalscorers	Attendance
1	Aug 8	A	Bromley	L	1-3	1-3	22	York [22]	2083
2	11	H	Torquay U	W	3-1	0-1	9	Vose [57], Jennings [64], Gray (pen) [80]	4734
3	15	H	Aldershot T	W	3-0	1-0	6	York [20], Gray [52], Vose (pen) [90]	4951
4	18	A	Kidderminster H	W	3-1	1-0	3	Smith, M [21], Newton [55], Smith, A [90]	2620
5	22	A	Welling U	W	1-0	0-0	3	Vose [90]	5277
6	29	H	FC Halifax T	W	3-1	2-1	2	Vidal [8], Vose [24], York [55]	5662
7	31	A	Cheltenham T	L	1-2	0-0	6	Gray [54]	2827
8	Sept 5	A	Lincoln C	D	1-1	0-0	4	Gray [55]	2628
9	12	H	Altrincham	W	3-1	2-0	2	Leather (og) [20], Hudson [43], Gray [58]	4628
10	15	A	Gateshead	L	1-2	1-1	5	Newton [29]	1113
11	19	A	Boreham Wood	W	1-0	0-0	3	Jennings [12]	685
12	22	H	Grimsby T	D	0-0	0-0	3		4818
13	26	H	Eastleigh	L	2-3	0-2	5	York [54], Newton [75]	4708
14	Oct 3	A	Chester FC	L	2-3	1-1	7	Vose (pen) [39], Jennings [90]	3741
15	6	H	Tranmere R	D	2-2	1-1	9	Evans [17], Quigley [82]	6706
16	10	A	Dover Ath	L	1-2	1-1	10	Jennings (pen) [39]	1253
17	14	H	Guiseley	D	3-3	2-1	13	Vose 2 [23, 37], Jennings [90]	3633
18	17	A	Woking	W	1-0	1-0	9	Jennings [28]	1778
19	31	H	Barrow	W	4-1	1-0	6	Jennings 2 [45, 90], York 2 [58, 78]	3892
20	Nov 14	A	Gateshead	W	4-0	0-0	8	Evans [55], Hudson [66], Vose 2 [70, 75]	4055
21	21	A	Aldershot T	W	1-0	0-0	6	York [63]	1483
22	28	H	Macclesfield T	L	2-3	1-1	8	Jennings [32], Gray [76]	4591
23	Dec 5	A	Torquay U	W	1-0	0-0	5	Carrington [78]	1512
24	26	H	Southport	L	0-1	0-1	8		5508
25	28	A	FC Halifax T	L	0-2	0-2	10		2243
26	Jan 2	A	Southport	L	2-3	1-1	11	York [18], Gray [71]	2148
27	9	H	Woking	L	1-3	1-1	11	Vose [16]	4030
28	23	H	Lincoln C	W	3-1	1-0	10	York [36], Jennings [48], Heslop [86]	3853
29	26	A	Braintree T	L	0-1	0-0	10		484
30	30	A	Eastleigh	D	1-1	1-1	12	Newton [18]	1904
31	Feb 6	A	Forest Green R	D	2-2	0-1	12	Hudson 2 [62, 68]	3891
32	9	A	Altrincham	D	1-1	1-1	12	Heslop [29]	1261
33	13	H	Bromley	W	2-0	2-0	8	Fowler [31], Jennings (pen) [38]	3511
34	20	A	Welling U	W	2-0	2-0	6	Fowler [33], Jennings (pen) [44]	620
35	23	H	Kidderminster H	W	2-0	2-0	4	Jackson 2 [14, 29]	3899
36	27	A	Macclesfield T	D	0-0	0-0	4		2406
37	Mar 12	H	Boreham Wood	W	1-0	1-0	6	Jennings (pen) [13]	3470
38	19	A	Chester FC	W	3-0	0-0	7	Jennings (pen) [64], Jackson [77], Evans [84]	6459
39	26	A	Grimsby T	L	0-1	0-1	8		4581
40	28	H	Cheltenham T	W	2-1	1-1	8	Vidal [16], York [90]	4463
41	Apr 2	A	Forest Green R	D	0-0	0-0	8		2246
42	9	H	Dover Ath	L	0-1	0-0	8		4931
43	12	A	Guiseley	L	1-3	0-3	8	Newton [68]	1046
44	16	A	Tranmere R	W	2-1	1-0	8	Jackson [15], Newton [85]	7541
45	23	H	Braintree T	L	2-3	2-2	8	Heslop [11], Fowler [38]	4507
46	30	A	Barrow	L	0-2	0-1	8		1728

Final League Position: 8

GOALSCORERS

League (71): Jennings 14 (5 pens), Vose 10 (2 pens), York 10, Gray 7 (1 pen), Newton 6, Hudson 4, Jackson 4, Evans 3, Fowler 3, Heslop 3, Vidal 2, Carrington 1, Quigley 1, Smith, A 1, Smith, M 1, own goal 1.
FA Cup (0).
FA Trophy (4): Newton 1, Smith, M 1, Vose 1, York 1.

Belford 19	Watkins-Clark 1	Smith M 44	Hudson 34 + 4	Newton 46	Vidal 20 + 3	Jennings 45	Vose 26 + 2	York 27 + 15	Gray 15 + 12	Moke 26 + 6	Logan — + 3	Fyfield 41 + 2	Jackson 17 + 19	Royle 1	Evans 41 + 3	Smith A 2 + 10	Fowler 11 + 7	Carrington 26 + 6	Nolan 3 + 3	Quigley 2 + 2	White 4 + 1	Walsh — + 1	Taylor 27	Caton — + 4	O'Brien — + 2	Cofie 1 + 1	Heslop 20	Beck 7 + 4	Briscoe — + 4	Smith J — + 1	O'Reilly — + 1	Match No.
1	2^2	3	4	5	6	7	8^1	9	10^3	11	12	13	14																			1
1		3		5	2	8	9	11^2	10	6		4			7^1	12	13															2
1		3		5	2	8	11	9^1	10^2	7		4	13		6	12																3
1			4	5	2	6	11	9^1	10^2	7		3	13		8	12																4
1		3		5	2	8^3	11	9^1	10	7^2		4	14		6	13	12															5
1		3		5	2	8	11^3	9	10^1	7^2		4	12		6	13	14															6
1		3	13	5	2	7	10	6^1	11^3	8^2		4	14		9	12																7
1		3	14	5	2^3	6	11	9	10^1	7^2		4	13		8	12																8
1	2	3		5		7	11^3	9^1	10^2	8	13	4	14		6	12																9
1	2	3		5		7	11	9^2	10^3	8	14	4			6^1	12	13															10
1	2	3		5		8	11^1	9^2	10^3	7		4	12		6	14	13															11
1		3	4	2		10	8	6^1	9	11		5			7	12																12
1	2	3		5	12		8	11	9	7^2		$4^■$			6^1	10^3	13	14														13
1		3	4	5	2	9	11	13	7^2			6			12		14	8^3	10^1													14
1		3		5	2	10	11^2	9		7^1		4	13		6			8^3	14	12												15
1		3	4	6		10	14	7^1		5	13	9			8^3		12	11	2^2													16
1	2	3^2		5	6	9	10	8^1		4	14	7			11^3		12	13														17
1		3	4	6	2	11	9	14		5		10^1			8^2		7	13	12^3													18
		3	13	5	2^1	10	11	9^2		12		4	14		7^7		6	8			1											19
		2	3	5		10^1	11	9	14	7		4			6^2		12	8^3			1	13										20
1		3	4	2		7	6	11		8		5			10		9															21
		2	3	5		10	11	9^3	13	7		4			8^1		6^2					1	14	12								22
		2	3	5		11	10^3	6^2	14	7^1		4			9		8					1	12	13								23
		3	4^2	7		8	11^1	9	14	5		12			6		2			1	13	10^3										24
		2	3^3	5		8	9^2	11	10	6^1		$4^■$	13		7		14			1	12											25
		4	5^3	3		11	13	7	14	8^2		6	12		10		9^1			2	1											26
		2	3^2	9		11	6^3	10	12	14		4	13		8^1		5					1				7						27
		3		5		8	11^2	9	10^1	13		4	12		6		2					1				7						28
		3	13	5		8		9				4	11^{12}		6		$2^■$					1				7	10^1	12				29
		6	3	5	2	9		13	10^2			4	12		8							1				7	11^1					30
		2	3	9	5^1	8		10^2		12		4	11		6							1				7	13					31
		3	4	6		10				7^1		5	11		8		2					1				9	12					32
		3		5		9		13	14	6^2		4	11		12		7^3	2				1				8	10^1					33
		3		5		6						4	11		8		9	2				1				7	10					34
		3	4	5		6		12	13			11^1			8^2		9^3	2				1				7	10	14				35
		3	4	5		10		12		9		8			7^1		2					1				6	11^{12}	13				36
		3	4	5		11		12		8^3		13	10		6^2		9^1	2				1				7	14					37
		2	3	9		11		12	13			4	10^2		8		6^1	5				1				7						38
		3	4	5	13	10		12				7	11		8^2		9^1	2^3				1				6	14					39
		2	3	9	6^1	11		12				4	10		7		5					1				8						40
		3	$4^■$	5	2^1	$11^■$		12				9	10^2		7		6					1				8		13				41
		3		5	7^2	11		13	12			4	9		6^3		14	2				1				8	10^1					42
		7	3^1	5	2^2	8		12	13			4	10		6		14	9				1				11^3						43
		4	3^3	6	12	11		13				5	10		7		9^1	2				1				8^2	14					44
		2	3^1	9		11		14	13			4	10		8		6^3	5				1				7^2	12					45
		3	5^2	7	2^1	11		13		14		6	12		9		10	4				1				8^3						46

FA Cup
Fourth Qualifying Gainsborough T (h) 0-1

FA Trophy
First Round Tranmere R (a) 4-2
Second Round Torquay U (a) 0-1

SCOTTISH LEAGUE TABLES 2015–16

(P) *Promoted into division at end of 2014–15 season.*   (R) *Relegated into division at end of 2014–15 season.*

SPFL LADBROKES PREMIERSHIP 2015–16

			Home				Away				Total					
		P	W	D	L	F	A	W	D	L	F	A	W	D	L	F	A	GD	Pts
1	Celtic	38	14	4	1	55	12	12	4	3	38	19	26	8	4	93	31	62	86
2	Aberdeen	38	12	4	3	30	19	10	1	8	32	29	22	5	11	62	48	14	71
3	Hearts (P)	38	11	5	3	37	22	7	6	6	22	18	18	11	9	59	40	19	65
4	St Johnstone	38	8	6	5	27	22	8	2	9	31	33	16	8	14	58	55	3	56
5	Motherwell	38	8	3	8	27	27	7	2	10	20	36	15	5	18	47	63	−16	50
6	Ross Co	38	9	0	10	29	33	5	6	8	26	28	14	6	18	55	61	−6	48
7	Inverness CT	38	7	5	7	25	20	7	5	7	29	28	14	10	14	54	48	6	52
8	Dundee	38	7	7	5	30	23	4	8	7	23	34	11	15	12	53	57	−4	48
9	Partick Thistle	38	6	4	9	21	29	6	6	7	20	21	12	10	16	41	50	−9	46
10	Hamilton A	38	4	6	9	21	28	7	4	8	21	35	11	10	17	42	63	−21	43
11	Kilmarnock	38	4	4	11	19	37	5	5	9	22	27	9	9	20	41	64	−23	36
12	Dundee U*	38	3	4	12	22	35	5	3	11	23	35	8	7	23	45	70	−25	28

Top 6 teams split after 33 games, teams in the bottom six cannot pass teams in the top six after the split.
*Dundee U deducted 3 points for fielding an ineligible player. Kilmarnock not relegated after play-offs.

SPFL LADBROKES CHAMPIONSHIP 2015–16

			Home				Away				Total					
		P	W	D	L	F	A	W	D	L	F	A	W	D	L	F	A	GD	Pts
1	Rangers	36	16	2	0	48	13	9	4	5	40	21	25	6	5	88	34	54	81
2	Falkirk	36	13	3	2	33	13	6	10	2	28	21	19	13	4	61	34	27	70
3	Hibernian	36	14	3	1	37	15	7	4	7	22	19	21	7	8	59	34	25	70
4	Raith R	36	10	4	4	31	19	8	4	6	21	27	18	8	10	52	46	6	62
5	Greenock Morton (P)	36	7	4	7	17	17	4	6	8	22	25	11	10	15	39	42	−3	43
6	St Mirren (R)	36	5	6	7	24	28	6	3	9	20	25	11	9	16	44	53	−9	42
7	Queen of the South	36	8	4	6	27	26	4	2	12	19	30	12	6	18	46	56	−10	42
8	Dumbarton	36	8	3	7	26	34	2	4	12	9	32	10	7	19	35	66	−31	37
9	Livingston®	36	3	6	9	14	19	5	1	12	23	32	8	7	21	37	51	−14	31
10	Alloa Ath	36	1	6	11	12	30	3	3	12	10	37	4	9	23	22	67	−45	21

Falkirk not promoted after play-offs. ®Livingston relegated via play-offs.

SPFL LADBROKES LEAGUE ONE 2015–16

			Home				Away				Total					
		P	W	D	L	F	A	W	D	L	F	A	W	D	L	F	A	GD	Pts
1	Dunfermline Ath	36	12	4	2	45	15	12	3	3	38	15	24	7	5	83	30	53	79
2	Ayr U¶	36	11	2	5	38	22	8	2	8	27	25	19	4	13	65	47	18	61
3	Peterhead	36	9	6	3	39	20	7	5	6	33	27	16	11	9	72	47	25	59
4	Stranraer	36	8	2	8	21	25	7	4	7	22	24	15	6	15	43	49	−6	51
5	Airdrieonians	36	5	5	8	19	21	9	2	7	29	29	14	7	15	48	50	−2	49
6	Albion R (P)	36	7	5	6	25	21	6	5	7	15	23	13	10	13	40	44	−4	49
7	Brechin C	36	8	4	6	29	24	4	2	12	18	35	12	6	18	47	59	−12	42
8	Stenhousemuir	36	6	3	9	25	42	5	4	9	21	38	11	7	18	46	80	−34	40
9	Cowdenbeath (R)®	36	7	3	8	27	28	4	3	11	19	44	11	6	19	46	72	−26	39
10	Forfar Ath	36	5	3	10	24	28	3	7	8	24	32	8	10	18	48	60	−12	34

¶Ayr U promoted via play-offs. ®Cowdenbeath relegated via play-offs.

SPFL LADBROKES LEAGUE TWO 2015–16

			Home				Away				Total					
		P	W	D	L	F	A	W	D	L	F	A	W	D	L	F	A	GD	Pts
1	East Fife	36	10	4	4	30	17	8	4	6	32	24	18	8	10	62	41	21	62
2	Elgin C	36	12	5	1	36	15	5	3	10	23	31	17	8	11	59	46	13	59
3	Clyde	36	9	3	6	29	22	8	3	7	27	23	17	6	13	56	45	11	57
4	Queen's Park¶	36	7	5	6	21	18	8	6	4	25	14	15	11	10	46	32	14	56
5	Annan Ath	36	9	6	3	39	29	7	2	9	30	28	16	8	12	69	57	12	56
6	Berwick Rangers	36	10	4	4	29	22	4	3	11	16	28	14	7	15	45	50	−5	49
7	Stirling Alb (R)	36	9	3	6	27	21	4	6	8	20	25	13	9	14	47	46	1	48
8	Montrose	36	9	4	5	30	31	2	6	10	20	39	11	10	15	50	70	−20	43
9	Arbroath	36	5	4	9	19	21	6	2	10	23	30	11	6	19	42	51	−9	39
10	East Stirlingshire®	36	6	1	11	21	40	3	4	11	20	39	9	5	22	41	79	−38	32

¶Queen's Park promoted via play-offs. ®East Stirlingshire relegated after play-off with Edinburgh C who are promoted into SPFL League 2.

SCOTTISH LEAGUE ATTENDANCES 2015–16

SPFL LADBROKES PREMIERSHIP ATTENDANCES

	Average Gate			Season 2015–16	
	2014–15	*2015–16*	*+/–%*	*Highest*	*Lowest*
Aberdeen	13,359	13,094	–1.98	20,385	10,003
Celtic	44,585	44,850	+0.59	49,050	41,396
Dundee	6,966	6,122	–12.11	11,025	4,335
Dundee U	8,113	7,969	–1.77	11,835	4,689
Hamilton A	2,877	3,027	+5.21	5,017	1,516
Hearts	15,985	16,423	+2.74	16,995	15,438
Inverness CT	3,733	3,839	+2.84	6,410	2,775
Kilmarnock	4,076	3,993	–2.04	6,867	2,633
Motherwell	4,286	4,912	+14.62	9,123	3,279
Partick Thistle	3,586	3,800	+5.96	7,238	2,320
Ross Co	3,525	4,034	+14.44	6,042	2,976
St Johnstone	4,592	3,880	–15.51	6,418	2,157

SPFL LADBROKES CHAMPIONSHIP ATTENDANCES

	Average Gate			Season 2015–16	
	2014–15	*2015–16*	*+/–%*	*Highest*	*Lowest*
Alloa Ath	1,429	1,121	–21.52	3,100	492
Dumbarton	1,072	1,041	–2.90	1,978	468
Falkirk	4,661	4,670	+0.19	7,804	3,550
Greenock Morton	1,728	2,731	+58.01	7,392	1,175
Hibernian	10,170	9,339	–8.17	14,412	6,686
Livingston	2,364	1,765	–25.33	6,505	787
Queen of the South	2,778	2,115	–23.86	5,858	1,047
Raith R	2,598	2,317	–10.85	6,943	1,064
Rangers	32,798	45,325	+38.19	50,349	37,182
St Mirren	3,869	3,549	–8.28	5,933	2,321

SPFL LADBROKES LEAGUE ONE ATTENDANCES

	Average Gate			Season 2015–16	
	2014–15	*2015–16*	*+/–%*	*Highest*	*Lowest*
Airdrieonians	830	861	+3.82	1,371	547
Albion R	552	555	+0.59	1,413	210
Ayr U	1,123	1,297	+15.50	2,190	763
Brechin C	552	540	–2.08	1,214	376
Cowdenbeath	1,462	596	–59.26	2,335	269
Dunfermline Ath	2,523	3,497	+38.58	6,236	2,361
Forfar Ath	735	698	–5.03	1,618	434
Peterhead	580	637	+9.75	1,115	423
Stenhousemuir	584	566	–3.06	1,554	213
Stranraer	546	507	–7.25	1,178	328

SPFL LADBROKES LEAGUE TWO ATTENDANCES

	Average Gate			Season 2015–16	
	2014–15	*2015–16*	*+/–%*	*Highest*	*Lowest*
Annan Ath	393	447	+13.69	640	354
Arbroath	721	651	–9.66	1,146	334
Berwick R	466	461	–1.12	721	238
Clyde	525	612	+16.54	1,123	373
East Fife	557	625	+12.18	1,360	345
East Stirling	315	320	+1.82	523	234
Elgin C	544	737	+35.46	1,193	502
Montrose	419	566	+35.06	1,387	262
Queen's Park	608	518	–14.76	1,270	339
Stirling Alb	770	616	–19.95	796	415

ABERDEEN

Year Formed: 1903. *Ground & Address:* Pittodrie Stadium, Pittodrie St, Aberdeen AB24 5QH. *Telephone:* 01224 650400. *Fax:* 01224 644173. *E-mail:* feedback@afc.co.uk *Website:* www.afc.co.uk
Ground Capacity: 22,199 (all seated). *Size of Pitch:* 105m × 66m.
Chairman: Stewart Milne. *Chief Executive:* Duncan Fraser.
Manager: Derek McInnes. *Assistant Manager:* Tony Docherty. *U-20 Coach:* Paul Sheerin.
Club Nicknames: 'The Dons', 'The Reds', 'The Dandies'.
Previous Grounds: None.
Record Attendance: 45,061 v Hearts, Scottish Cup 4th rd, 13 March 1954.
Record Transfer Fee received: £1,750,000 for Eoin Jess to Coventry C (February 1996).
Record Transfer Fee paid: £1,000,000+ for Paul Bernard from Oldham Ath (September 1995).
Record Victory: 13-0 v Peterhead, Scottish Cup 3rd rd, 10 February 1923.
Record Defeat: 0-9 v Celtic, Premier League, 6 November 2010.
Most Capped Player: Alex McLeish, 77 (Scotland).
Most League Appearances: 556: Willie Miller, 1973-90.
Most League Goals in Season (Individual): 38: Benny Yorston, Division I, 1929-30.
Most Goals Overall (Individual): 199: Joe Harper, 1969-72; 1976-81.

ABERDEEN – SCOTTISH PREMIERSHIP 2015–16 LEAGUE RECORD

Match No.	Date	Venue	Opponents	Result	H/T Score	Lg Pos.	Goalscorers	Atten- dance
1	Aug 2	A	Dundee U	W 1-0	0-0	4	McLean [82]	10,706
2	9	H	Kilmarnock	W 2-0	1-0	2	Shinnie [37], Rooney (pen) [56]	11,305
3	15	A	Motherwell	W 2-1	1-1	3	McGinn [25], Taylor [62]	5437
4	22	H	Dundee	W 2-0	0-0	3	Rooney 2 (1 pen) [66, 90 (p)]	13,621
5	29	A	Partick Thistle	W 2-0	0-0	2	Rooney [49], McLean [58]	4940
6	Sept 12	H	Celtic	W 2-1	0-1	1	Rooney (pen) [56], Quinn [86]	20,385
7	15	H	Hamilton A	W 1-0	1-0	1	Rooney [23]	13,246
8	20	A	Hearts	W 3-1	3-0	1	Goodwillie 2 [9, 45], McGinn [23]	16,702
9	26	A	Inverness CT	L 1-2	1-2	1	Taylor [35]	6410
10	Oct 3	H	St Johnstone	L 1-5	1-3	1	Taylor [12]	13,405
11	16	A	Ross Co	L 0-2	0-1	1		5543
12	24	H	Motherwell	D 1-1	1-0	2	Rooney [43]	12,389
13	31	A	Celtic	L 1-3	0-1	3	Rooney [89]	48,161
14	Nov 7	H	Dundee U	W 2-0	0-0	3	Rooney [52], Hayes [73]	12,805
15	22	A	Hamilton A	D 1-1	1-0	3	McLean [4]	2434
16	28	H	Ross Co	W 3-1	0-1	2	Rooney [51], Hayes [53], McGinn [80]	10,843
17	Dec 5	A	Dundee	W 2-0	2-0	2	McGinn [9], Rooney [25]	6327
18	12	H	Hearts	W 1-0	0-0	2	Rooney (pen) [87]	13,110
19	19	A	Kilmarnock	W 4-0	2-0	2	McGinn [9], Rooney [35], Hayes [46], Logan [80]	3928
20	26	H	Inverness CT	D 2-2	0-1	2	McGinn [73], Rooney (pen) [90]	15,142
21	30	H	Partick Thistle	D 0-0	0-0	2		12,583
22	Jan 17	A	Ross Co	W 3-2	2-1	2	Rooney (pen) [33], Logan 2 [36, 60]	4107
23	22	H	Dundee	W 1-0	1-0	2	Rooney [14]	11,805
24	Feb 3	H	Celtic	W 2-1	2-0	2	Hayes [31], Church [37]	19,003
25	6	A	St Johnstone	W 4-3	2-0	2	Rooney 2 [5, 77], Pawlett [20], McGinn [71]	5712
26	15	A	Inverness CT	L 1-3	1-1	2	Rooney [7]	4544
27	27	H	St Johnstone	D 1-1	1-0	2	Church [35]	12,563
28	Mar 2	A	Dundee U	W 1-0	1-0	2	Church [29]	9737
29	8	A	Partick Thistle	W 2-1	0-0	2	Considine [74], Church [76]	3915
30	12	H	Kilmarnock	W 2-1	1-0	2	Taylor [37], Logan [71]	13,725
31	19	A	Motherwell	L 1-2	1-0	2	McLean (pen) [44]	6251
32	Apr 3	A	Hamilton A	W 3-0	3-0	2	Church [5], McGinn [15], McLean [33]	12,509
33	8	A	Hearts	L 1-2	1-1	2	Church [4]	16,995
34	22	A	St Johnstone	L 0-3	0-2	2		3990
35	30	H	Motherwell	W 4-1	2-0	2	McLean (pen) [6], McGinn [26], Rooney [54], Hayes [78]	10,259
36	May 8	A	Celtic	L 2-3	0-2	2	McGinn [57], Considine [64]	47,877
37	12	H	Hearts	L 0-1	0-0	2		10,087
38	15	H	Ross Co	L 0-4	0-2	2		10,003

Final League Position: 2

Honours
League Champions: Division I 1954-55. Premier Division 1979-80, 1983-84, 1984-85; *Runners-up:* Premiership 2014-15, 2015-16. Division I 1910-11, 1936-37, 1955-56, 1970-71, 1971-72. Premier Division 1977-78, 1980-81, 1981-82, 1988-89, 1989-90, 1990-91, 1992-93, 1993-94.
Scottish Cup Winners: 1947, 1970, 1982, 1983, 1984, 1986, 1990; *Runners-up:* 1937, 1953, 1954, 1959, 1967, 1978, 1993, 2000.
League Cup Winners: 1955-56, 1976-77, 1985-86, 1989-90, 1995-96, 2013-14; *Runners-up:* 1946-47, 1978-79, 1979-80, 1987-88, 1988-89, 1992-93, 1999-2000.
Drybrough Cup Winners: 1971, 1980.

European: *European Cup:* 12 matches (1980-81, 1984-85, 1985-86); *Cup Winners' Cup:* 39 matches (1967-68, 1970-71, 1978-79, 1982-83 winners, 1983-84 semi-finals, 1986-87, 1990-91, 1993-94); *UEFA Cup:* 56 matches (*Fairs Cup:* 1968-69. *UEFA Cup:* 1971-72, 1972-73, 1973-74, 1977-78, 1979-80, 1981-82, 1987-88, 1988-89, 1989-90, 1991-92, 1994-95, 1996-97, 2000-01, 2002-03, 2007-08). *Europa League:* 14 matches (2009-10, 2014-15, 2015-16).

Club colours: All red with white trim.

Goalscorers: *League (62):* Rooney 20 (7 pens), McGinn 10, Church 6, McLean 6 (2 pens), Hayes 5, Logan 4, Taylor 4, Considine 2, Goodwillie 2, Pawlett 1, Quinn 1, Shinnie 1.
William Hill Scottish FA Cup (0).
Scottish League Cup (0).
UEFA Europa League (8): McLean 3, McGinn 2, Considine 1, Hayes 1, Pawlett 1.

Ward D 21	Quinn P 9+4	Considine A 26+6	Taylor A 36+1	Logan S 35+2	Flood W 18+4	Smith C 2+12	Shinnie G 37	Hayes J 35	McLean K 38	Rooney A 22+5	McGinn N 33+3	Goodwillie D 7+10	Jack R 26+2	Parker J 1+6	Robson B 3+9	McLaughlin R 1+3	Pawlett P 9+9	Wright S 1+3	Reynolds M 19+3	Storie C 6+4	Ross F —+2	Brown S 13	Church S 13	McKenna S 2+1	Harvie D —+2	Rose M 1	McLennan C —+1	Collin A 3	Nuttall J —+2	Lennox A 1	Match No.
1	2	3¹	4	5	6	7¹	8	9¹	10	11	12	13	14																		1
1	4	12	3	2	6	13	5	10²	9¹	11	8¹	14	7																		2
1	13	4	3	2	7¹		5	9	8	12	10	11²	6																		3
1	13	4	3	2			5	8²	9	10	6	11¹	7	12																	4
1		4	3	2	12		5	9¹	8	11²	7	10³	6	13	14																5
1	3	4	2	5	13		8	9¹	10	11¹	6²		7	12																	6
1		4	3	13	8		5	9¹	10³	11	6		7	12		2⁴	14														7
1	4	5	3	2			7		9	12	8¹	11²	6	13		14	10¹														8
1	4²	5	3	2			7	10	9	12	8¹	14	6	11³			13														9
1		4	3	2			5	8³	9²	11	6	12	7		13		10¹	14													10
1	2	5	4	12	6¹		7	10	9	13	8	11³		14					3²												11
1	12		3¹	2			5	9	8	11	6³	13	7			14	10²		4												12
1	12	5¹	3	2			9	6	8	11	10²	13	7³				14		4												13
1		3	2	7			5	6¹	9¹	11	13		8		12	14	10²		4												14
1		12	3	2⁴	7	13	5	6	9	11	10						8¹		4												15
1	3²	5	13	2	7¹	14	6	10	8	11	9²								4	12											16
1		5	4	2	7		9	6³	8	11²	10¹	13					12			3		14									17
1		5	3	2	7		8	9	10	11		13	12				6²		4¹												18
1	4		3	2	6	12	5	8	9	11³	10²	14	7¹				13														19
1	4¹	5	3	2			8	9	10	11	6	12	7																		20
1		3	2	7	13		5	10	9	11	8²		6¹				12		4												21
	12	4	5		2	6	7	11²	9³	10¹			13		14		3⁴	8		1											22
	4	3	2	12	5	6	8	10	9	11¹							13		4	7		1									23
	12	3	2	14	5	6	8	11	9¹							13	4	7		1	10²										24
		3	2	9²	5	8	7	10	12					6¹		4	13			1	11¹³	14									25
		3	2	13	5	9¹	8	6	10					12		4	7		1	11²											26
		5	3		7	8		10	9	2				6¹	12	4			1	11											27
	4	3	2	13	5		9	10²	6		7³		8¹	12	14	1	11														28
	5	3		7	10	9			6		12²			4	8¹		1	11	13												29
	4	3	2		12	5	6	10		9²		7		8¹		13			1	11											30
	5¹	3	2		9	6	7		10	8	12			4			1	11													31
	12	3	2	8²	5	6	10	9		7³				4	13	14	1	11													32
	14	3²	2	12	13	5	8	9	10	6¹				4	7²	1	11														33
		4		5	10	9	8²	6	12					3		1	11	7¹	13												34
	4	3	2	7	5	6	10	12³	9²	8	13	14					11¹							1							35
	3	4	2	6²	5	10	9	8	7	13	12						11¹							1							36
	4	3	2	8²	12	5	6	10	11	7				9¹			1	13													37
	5	3	2	7	12	6	10	9¹		8²	11			4³	14			13	1												38

AIRDRIEONIANS

Year Formed: 2002. *Ground & Address:* Excelsior Stadium, New Broomfield, Craigneuk Avenue, Airdrie ML6 8QZ.
Telephone: (Stadium) 01236 622000. *Fax:* 01236 626002. *Postal Address:* 60 St Enoch Square, Glasgow G1 4AG.
E-mail: annmarie@ballantyneand.co.uk *Website:* www.airdriefc.com
Ground Capacity: 10,171 (all seated). *Size of Pitch:* 105m × 67m.
Chairman: Tom Wotherspoon. *Secretary:* Ann Marie Ballantyne.
Head Coach: Eddie Wolecki Black. *First Team Coach:* Kevin McBride.
Club Nickname: 'The Diamonds'.
Record Attendance: 9,044 v Rangers, League 1, 23 August 2013.
Record Victory: 11-0 v Gala Fairydean, Scottish Cup 3rd rd, 19 November 2011.
Record Defeat: 0-7 v Partick Thistle, First Division, 20 October 2012.
Most League Appearances: 222, Paul Lovering 2004-12.
Most League Goals in Season (Individual): 21: Ryan Donnelly, 2011-12.
Most Goals Overall (Individual): 43: Bryan Prunty, 2005-08, 2015-16.

AIRDRIEONIANS – SCOTTISH LEAGUE ONE 2015–16 LEAGUE RECORD

Match No.	Date	Venue	Opponents	Result	H/T Score	Lg Pos.	Goalscorers	Attendance
1	Aug 8	H	Forfar Ath	L 0-1	0-1	8		856
2	15	A	Stenhousemuir	L 1-2	0-1	8	Crighton [49]	731
3	22	A	Brechin C	W 2-1	2-0	6	Prunty 2 [36, 39]	464
4	29	H	Peterhead	W 1-0	0-0	7	Bain [71]	676
5	Sept 5	H	Cowdenbeath	W 3-2	1-1	4	Cox [30], Hunter [77], Watt [81]	773
6	12	A	Albion R	W 3-1	2-0	4	Morgan [11], Dunlop, M (og) [19], Cox [67]	1120
7	19	H	Ayr U	L 1-2	1-1	4	Watt [5]	1141
8	26	A	Dunfermline Ath	D 1-1	1-0	4	Hunter [18]	3391
9	Oct 3	H	Stranraer	L 0-1	0-0	4		847
10	17	A	Brechin C	W 1-0	0-0	3	Watt [47]	729
11	24	A	Peterhead	L 0-2	0-1	4		553
12	31	H	Albion R	D 1-1	1-1	4	Prunty [23]	1156
13	Nov 7	A	Forfar Ath	W 3-2	3-1	3	Lithgow [14], Cox [22], Fitzpatrick [29]	555
14	14	H	Dunfermline Ath	L 0-2	0-1	3		1371
15	21	A	Ayr U	L 0-3	0-2	5		1403
16	Dec 12	A	Stranraer	W 3-1	1-0	5	Prunty [40], Morgan [49], Watt [70]	428
17	19	A	Cowdenbeath	L 0-3	0-1	5		366
18	26	H	Peterhead	L 3-4	2-1	5	Cox [8], Watt [29], Cadden (pen) [78]	745
19	29	H	Stenhousemuir	L 0-1	0-0	7		724
20	Jan 2	A	Albion R	W 2-1	0-1	5	Reid (og) [67], Lister [87]	1104
21	23	A	Brechin C	D 3-3	3-1	6	Lister [13], Crighton 2 [43, 45]	476
22	29	A	Dunfermline Ath	W 1-0	1-0	4	Bain [30]	2545
23	Feb 6	H	Cowdenbeath	W 2-0	1-0	4	Fitzpatrick [14], Lister [89]	717
24	13	A	Stenhousemuir	L 2-3	1-1	4	Cadden [5], Lister [46]	472
25	20	H	Stranraer	D 1-1	0-0	4	Watt [68]	704
26	27	H	Ayr U	L 0-1	0-1	5		1000
27	Mar 5	A	Cowdenbeath	W 3-1	1-0	4	Thompson [5], Lister 2 [69, 78]	338
28	8	H	Forfar Ath	D 1-1	0-1	4	Cadden [60]	547
29	12	H	Brechin C	L 0-2	0-1	4		671
30	19	A	Peterhead	L 0-1	0-0	5		633
31	26	H	Albion R	D 1-1	0-0	5	Fitzpatrick [55]	1104
32	Apr 2	A	Stranraer	L 0-4	0-2	6		461
33	9	H	Stenhousemuir	D 1-1	0-0	6	Lithgow [90]	614
34	16	A	Forfar Ath	W 2-0	2-0	6	Lithgow [10], Lister [43]	577
35	23	H	Dunfermline Ath	W 3-0	3-0	5	Fitzpatrick [2], Mackin [20], Lister [27]	1131
36	30	A	Ayr U	W 3-0	2-0	5	Lithgow [3], Mackin [10], Crighton [79]	1594

Final League Position: 5

Honours
League Champions: Second Division 2003-04; *Runners-up:* Second Division 2007-08.
League Challenge Cup Winners: 2008-09; *Runners-up:* 2003-04.

Club colours: Shirt: White with red diamond. Shorts: White with red trim. Socks: White with red trim.

Goalscorers: *League (48):* Lister 8, Watt 6, Cox 4, Crighton 4, Fitzpatrick 4, Lithgow 4, Prunty 4, Cadden 3 (1 pen), Bain 2, Hunter 2, Mackin 2, Morgan 2, Thompson 1, own goals 2.
William Hill Scottish FA Cup (3): Morgan 2, Prunty 1.
Scottish League Cup (1): Morton 1.
Petrofac Training Cup (1): Crighton 1.

Parry N 35	Bain J 21+9	Crighton S 36	Lithgow A 36	O'Neil C 22+1	Cox D 26+2	Gilfillan B 2+1	McBride K 4	Morton J 4+5	Prunty B 14+14	Morgan T 12+6	Watt L 21+4	Sumsky N 3+3	Stewart S 8+10	van Zanten D 9	McAleer C 5+4	Smith S 9	Brown A 6+6	Hunter G 6+4	Fitzpatrick M 29+1	Cadden N 22+2	Lister J 13+4	Ferguson R 1+1	Ferguson D 9	Faria H 14	Mackin D 7+4	McCue J —+1	MacDonald K 15	Esposito J —+6	Thompson J 7	McIntosh S —+1	McLaughlin C —+1	Leighton R —+1	Match No.
1	2	3	4	5	6	7	8	9¹	10	11²	12	13																					1
1	2	4	8	5	9	7³	3¹	13	14	11	6	10⁵	12																				2
1	12	4	8	5	11	13		9	10¹		7			3	2¹	6⁴																	3
1	12	3	4	5	11			9¹	10²	13	6					8	2		7														4
1	12	3	4	5	11			10³	13	9				2⁶	6¹	7			8	14													5
1	2	3	4	5	10¹				14	9²	6	13				7		8²	11	12													6
1	2	3	4	5¹	10				14	11²	6	13				9¹		7	12	8													7
1	2	3	4	5	6			9		11²	12	13				7			10¹	8													8
1	2	3	4	5	6			9	10¹		12	13				7			11²	8													9
1	13	3	4	2	7			9	10	11	12				6¹				8²	5													10
1	14	3	4	2	11	7²		10	13	9					6¹			8²	12	5													11
1	14	3	4	5	11				10¹		12	13		2	6²	7			8	9³													12
1	13	3	4	2	11				10¹		12				5	8		6²	7	9													13
1	6²	3	4	2	11				14	10		13			5	7¹		12	8³	9													14
1	13	3	4	2⁴	11				14	12				5	6	7			8³	10¹	9²												15
1	2	3	4	8	10²				11¹		7				5	13			8	9	12												16
1	2	3	4	6²	10				11¹		7	13			5	14			8	9³	12												17
1¹	2	4	6	5	9				14	10¹	7	13							8²	3	11¹	12											18
1	2	4	7	5	11²				13	10	8	12							9¹	3	6												19
1	2	3	4	5	11				6²			13							10¹	8¹	12		7		9	1	2	8	11	12			20
		3	4	5								13							6¹	7	9		10²			1	2	8	11	12			21
1	6	3	4	12	11				9										8	10³	2		7	13			5²						22
1	6¹	3	4	10					14										9³	8	12		11²	2	7	13	5						23
1	7²	3	4	9⁴					12										8	6	10		2	11¹	5	13							24
1	6¹	3	4						11		12								8	9	2		7	10²	5	13							25
1	6³	3	4						14									12	8	9	11		2	7	5²	13	10¹						26
1		3	4		10¹				14										8	9¹	11		2	7²	5	13	6						27
1		3	4	12	10²				13										8	9	11		2	7	5		6¹						28
1	14	3	4	9⁵					13										8	11³	10		2	7	5	12	6¹						29
1		3	4	2	11¹				12									9	8	10			7²	5	13	6							30
1		3	4	2	6¹				11²								12		7	9	10		8	13	5								31
1		3	4	2	9²				11								13		7	12	10³		8¹	14	5	6							32
1	2	3	4		13				14		7							6³	8	9²	12		11¹	5	10								33
1	2	3	4															6	12	7	9		10¹	8	11	5							34
1	2	3	4						13									6	14	8	9		10²	7	11³	5	12						35
1	2	3	4						12									6	8	9¹	10²		7	11³	5	13	14						36

ALBION ROVERS

Year Formed: 1882. *Ground & Address:* Cliftonhill Stadium, Main St, Coatbridge ML5 3RB. *Telephone/Fax:* 01236 606334.
E-mail: general@albionroversfc.co.uk *Website:* albionroversfc.co.uk
Ground capacity: 1,572 (seated: 489). *Size of Pitch:* 101m × 66m.
Chairman John Devlin. *Secretary:* Paul Reilly.
Manager: Darren Young. *Assistant Manager:* Billy Stark.
Club Nickname: 'The Wee Rovers'.
Previous Grounds: Cowheath Park, Meadow Park, Whifflet.
Record Attendance: 27,381 v Rangers, Scottish Cup 2nd rd, 8 February 1936.
Record Transfer Fee received: £40,000 from Motherwell for Bruce Cleland (1979).
Record Transfer Fee paid: £7000 for Gerry McTeague to Stirling Alb, September 1989.
Record Victory: 12-0 v Airdriehill, Scottish Cup 1st rd, 3 September 1887.
Record Defeat: 1-11 v Partick Thistle, League Cup 2nd rd, 11 August 1993.
Most Capped Player: Jock White, 1 (2), Scotland.
Most League Appearances: 399: Murdy Walls, 1921-36.
Most League Goals in Season (Individual): 41: Jim Renwick, Division II, 1932-33.
Most Goals Overall (Individual): 105: Bunty Weir, 1928-31.

ALBION ROVERS – SCOTTISH LEAGUE ONE 2015–16 LEAGUE RECORD

Match No.	Date		Venue	Opponents	Result		H/T Score	Lg Pos.	Goalscorers	Atten-dance
1	Aug	8	H	Ayr U	W	3-0	2-0	2	Davidson [2], Love 2 [45, 69]	781
2		15	A	Forfar Ath	L	0-4	0-0	5		608
3		22	A	Cowdenbeath	L	0-1	0-1	7		406
4		29	H	Brechin C	W	3-1	2-1	6	Dunlop, R [23], Gemmell (pen) [33], Barrowman [46]	470
5	Sept	5	A	Peterhead	D	1-1	1-1	6	Love [45]	550
6		12	H	Airdrieonians	L	1-3	0-2	7	Young [46]	1120
7		19	A	Stranraer	W	1-0	0-0	5	McBride [79]	412
8		26	H	Stenhousemuir	W	2-0	1-0	5	Barrowman 2 [30, 56]	406
9	Oct	3	A	Dunfermline Ath	L	0-3	0-1	5		3086
10		17	H	Peterhead	W	1-0	0-0	4	Gemmell [89]	341
11		24	A	Brechin C	W	1-0	1-0	3	Willis [25]	414
12		31	A	Airdrieonians	D	1-1	1-1	3	Love [41]	1156
13	Nov	14	A	Ayr U	L	0-1	0-1	4		1389
14		21	H	Dunfermline Ath	D	1-1	1-1	4	Mullin [20]	1041
15		24	H	Cowdenbeath	W	2-1	0-0	3	McBride [50], Mullin [66]	287
16	Dec	12	A	Stenhousemuir	W	1-0	0-0	3	Fisher [69]	354
17		19	A	Forfar Ath	D	1-1	1-0	3	Willis [42]	346
18	Jan	2	H	Airdrieonians	L	1-2	1-0	4	Gemmell [26]	1104
19		23	H	Ayr U	L	1-3	0-3	4	Love [90]	427
20		30	A	Peterhead	L	1-5	1-1	5	McBride (pen) [1]	522
21	Feb	2	H	Stranraer	L	0-2	0-0	7		241
22		9	A	Cowdenbeath	W	2-1	1-1	5	McBride 2 [13, 47]	292
23		13	A	Stranraer	D	0-0	0-0	5		432
24		23	H	Brechin C	W	4-1	3-0	4	McBride [33], Barrowman [38], Love 2 (1 pen) [41, 90 (p)]	210
25		27	A	Forfar Ath	L	0-1	0-0	4		538
26	Mar	1	H	Stenhousemuir	D	1-1	0-0	4	Love [78]	275
27		5	H	Peterhead	D	1-1	1-0	5	Love [16]	409
28		8	A	Dunfermline Ath	D	1-1	0-0	5	Davidson [77]	2729
29		12	A	Stranraer	L	0-1	0-1	5		408
30		19	A	Brechin C	L	1-2	1-0	6	Love [12]	461
31		26	A	Airdrieonians	D	1-1	0-0	6	Love [80]	1104
32	Apr	2	H	Dunfermline Ath	L	0-1	0-0	5		1413
33		9	A	Ayr U	W	1-0	0-0	5	Dunlop, M [73]	1044
34		16	A	Cowdenbeath	D	0-0	0-0	5		356
35		23	H	Forfar Ath	W	3-2	2-1	6	Love [7], McBride [18], Dunlop, M [76]	352
36		30	A	Stenhousemuir	W	3-1	0-0	6	McBride 2 [49, 74], Love [66]	662

Final League Position: 6

Honours
League Champions: Division II 1933-34, Second Division 1988-89. League Two 2014-15; *Runners-up:* Division II 1913-14, 1937-38, 1947-48. *Promoted to Second Division:* 2010-11 (play-offs).
Scottish Cup Runners-up: 1920.

Club colours: Shirt: Yellow with white trim. Shorts: Red. Socks: Red.

Goalscorers: *League (40):* Love 13 (1 pen), McBride 9 (1 pen), Barrowman 4, Gemmell 3 (1 pen), Davidson 2, Dunlop, M 2, Mullin 2, Willis 2, Dunlop, R 1, Fisher 1, Young 1.
William Hill Scottish FA Cup (0).
Scottish League Cup (0).
Petrofac Training Cup (1): Love 1.

Stewart R 36	Reid A 30+3	Dunlop M 36	Dunlop R 35	Turnbull K 34	Mullin J 18+1	Young D 7+3	Davidson R 32+3	Willis P 21+3	Barrowman A 15+7	Love A 29+6	Gemmell J 4+8	Ferry M 14+11	McRobbie C 4+11	Fisher G 28+5	Cappie B —+1	Tate R 13+8	McBride S 21+9	Archibald P 8+6	Petrie D 3+4	Georgiev S 8+4	Kerjean Y —+2	Match No.
1	2	3	4	5	6^3	7	8	9^2	10^1	11	12	13	14									1
1	2	4	3	5	6	7	8^1	9		11			10^2	12	13							2
1	2^3	4	3	5	6		8	11^{12}	12	9	10^1	13	14	7^1								3
1	2	3	4	5^4	6	8	7^3	11^{12}	12	9	10^1		14	13								4
1	5	3	4		6	8	7^2	10	11	9^3		13		14		2^1	12					5
1	2	3	4	5	6	8	7^2	11	10^1	9^3	13		14				12					6
1	2	3	4	5	6		7	10	11^2	9^3	12	14	8^1				13					7
1	2^1	3	4	5	6		8	11	10^2	9^3		13	7	12	14							8
1		4	3	5	6	13^4	8	10^1	11	9^2		14		7^3		2	12					9
1		4	3	5	6		8^2	10	11^1	9^3	13	14		7		2	12					10
1	14	3	4	5	6^3		8	10	11^1	9^2				7		2	12					11
1		3	4	5	8^1		7	9	11^3	10^2	14^4	13		6		2	12					12
1	2	4	3	5	13		8	9	11^3	10^1		6^2	14	7			12					13
1	2	3	4	5	6		8	10^2	11	12		9^1		7		13						14
1	4	3		5	6		13	12		9^2	14	11^3	10^1	7		2	8					15
1	2	4	3		6^3	14		7	11^2		12		13	10^1	8		5	9				16
1	2	4	3	5	6		8	10^3		13	12	14	11^1	7			9^2					17
1	2	3	4	5	6		8^1	10		12	11		13	7			9^2					18
1	2	4	3	5	6		7	10^1		14	11^2	13	12^3	8			9					19
1	2	4	3	5		7^1	8		10^2		9^3	12	6			13	11	14				20
1	5	4	3	2		7	10		9^4		8	13	6^1			12	11					21
1	14	6	5	3	4			13	10^2		7^1			8		2	9	11^3	12			22
1	14	3	4	5	6			12	8^2		10^3			7		2	9	11^1	13			23
1	2	3	4	5			12		11^3	9		6^2	13	7			10^1		8	14		24
1	2	3	4	5			13		10	9^1		6^3		7		14	11^4	12	8^2			25
1	2	3	4	5			8		11	9		6^1	13	7^3		14		10^2		12		26
1	2	3	4	5			8		11	9^2			13	7		10	12	6^1				27
1	2	4	3	5			7		12^3	13		14		6		10	11^2	8^1	9			28
1	2^1	3	4	5			8			9			$11^■$	7^2		10	12	13	6			29
1	2	4	3	5	12		8		10^2		11^3	14		7^1		9	13		6			30
1	2	4	3	5	9			7				6		10	11		8					31
1	2	3	4	5	8	12		9				7		10	11^1		6					32
1	2	3	4	5	8			9^2				7	13	11	10		6^1	12				33
1	2	3	4	5	8	12		9^1				7		10	11^2		6	13				34
1	2	3	4	5	8	10^3	14	9^2		6^1	7			11	12		13					35
1	2	4	3	5	8	11^3	14	9		6^2	7^1			10	13		12					36

ALLOA ATHLETIC

Year Formed: 1878. *Ground & Address:* Indodrill Stadium, Recreation Park, Clackmannan Rd, Alloa FK10 1RY.
Telephone: 01259 722695. *Fax:* 01259 210886. *E-mail:* fcadmin@alloaatheltic.co.uk *Website:* www.alloaathletic.co.uk
Ground Capacity: 3,100 (seated: 919). *Size of Pitch:* 102m × 69m.
Honorary President: George Ormiston. *Chairman:* Mike Mulraney. *Secretary:* Ewen G. Cameron.
Manager: Jack Ross. *Assistant Manager:* Paddy Connolly. *Physio:* Gerry Docherty.
Club Nicknames: 'The Wasps', 'The Hornets'.
Previous Grounds: West End Public Park, Gabberston Park, Bellevue Park.
Record Attendance: 13,000 v Dunfermline Ath, Scottish Cup 3rd rd replay, 26 February 1939.
Record Transfer Fee received: £100,000 for Martin Cameron to Bristol R.
Record Transfer Fee paid: £26,000 for Ross Hamilton from Stenhousemuir.
Record Victory: 9-0 v Selkirk, Scottish Cup 1st rd, 28 November 2005.
Record Defeat: 0-10 v Dundee, Division II, 8 March 1947; v Third Lanark, League Cup, 8 August 1953.
Most Capped Player: Jock Hepburn, 1, Scotland.
Most League Appearances: 239: Peter Smith 1960-69.
Most League Goals in Season (Individual): 49: 'Wee' Willie Crilley, Division II, 1921-22.
Most Goals Overall (Individual): 91: Willie Irvine, 1996-2001.

ALLOA ATHLETIC – SCOTTISH CHAMPIONSHIP 2015–16 LEAGUE RECORD

Match No.	Date	Venue	Opponents	Result	H/T Score	Lg Pos.	Goalscorers	Attendance
1	Aug 8	A	Queen of the South	L	1-3	0-3	8	Flannigan [49]	1726
2	16	H	Rangers	L	1-5	1-4	10	Chopra [7]	3047
3	22	A	Raith R	L	0-3	0-0	10		1458
4	29	H	Greenock Morton	L	0-1	0-0	10		825
5	Sept 5	A	Dumbarton	W	2-0	0-0	9	Holmes [59], Ferns [90]	715
6	12	A	Hibernian	L	0-3	0-1	9		7774
7	19	H	Falkirk	D	1-1	0-0	9	Hamilton [90]	1572
8	26	H	Livingston	L	0-3	0-1	10		622
9	Oct 3	A	St Mirren	D	1-1	0-0	9	Marr [75]	2994
10	17	H	Raith R	L	0-1	0-0	9		808
11	24	A	Greenock Morton	L	0-1	0-0	10		1716
12	31	A	Queen of the South	L	1-2	1-0	10	Holmes [1]	616
13	Nov 7	A	Rangers	L	0-4	0-3	10		43,242
14	14	A	Falkirk	L	0-5	0-3	10		3550
15	21	H	Hibernian	L	0-1	0-0	10		1952
16	Dec 5	H	Dumbarton	L	0-2	0-0	10		492
17	12	A	Livingston	W	1-0	0-0	10	Crawford, R [64]	937
18	19	H	St Mirren	L	0-2	0-1	10		912
19	Jan 2	H	Falkirk	L	0-1	0-1	10		1176
20	12	A	Raith R	W	1-0	0-0	10	Flannigan (pen) [86]	1064
21	23	A	Queen of the South	L	0-1	0-1	10		1559
22	30	A	St Mirren	L	1-3	1-1	10	Layne (pen) [9]	2589
23	Feb 9	H	Greenock Morton	D	2-2	1-2	10	Hamilton [19], Hill [71]	535
24	13	H	Rangers	D	1-1	0-0	10	Marr [61]	3100
25	21	A	Hibernian	L	0-3	0-2	10		8765
26	27	H	Livingston	L	1-3	1-3	10	Duffy [19]	619
27	Mar 5	A	Falkirk	L	0-2	0-2	10		3774
28	8	A	Dumbarton	L	1-3	1-2	10	Megginson [31]	468
29	12	H	Raith R	D	1-1	0-0	10	Hetherington [64]	762
30	19	A	Greenock Morton	L	1-4	1-2	10	McAusland [39]	1513
31	26	H	St Mirren	L	0-1	0-0	10		753
32	Apr 2	A	Livingston	D	0-0	0-0	10		927
33	9	H	Hibernian	W	1-0	1-0	10	Duffy [45]	1364
34	16	H	Queen of the South	D	2-2	1-0	10	Flannigan (pen) [37], McManus [76]	512
35	23	A	Rangers	D	1-1	1-1	10	Duffy [8]	50,349
36	May 1	H	Dumbarton	D	1-1	1-0	10	Layne [7]	515

Final League Position: 10

Honours
League Champions: Division II 1921-22; Third Division 1997-98, 2011-12; *Runners-up:* Division II 1938-39.
Second Division 1976-77, 1981-82, 1984-85, 1988-89, 1999-2000, 2001-02, 2009-10; *Runners-up:* 2012-13 (promoted via play-offs).
League Challenge Cup Winners: 1999-2000; *Runners-up:* 2001-02, 2014-15.

Club colours: Shirt: Gold and black hoops. Shorts: Black. Socks: Black.

Goalscorers: *League (22):* Duffy 3, Flannigan 3 (2 pens), Hamilton 2, Holmes 2, Layne 2 (1 pen), Marr 2, Chopra 1, Crawford, R 1, Ferns 1, Hetherington 1, Hill 1, McAusland 1, McManus 1, Megginson 1.
William Hill Scottish FA Cup (0).
Scottish League Cup (2): Flannigan 2.
Petrofac Training Cup (1): Mitchell 1.

Crawford D 8+2	Williams M 6+6	Reintam M 11+1	Hamilton C 34	Hill D 29	McAusland K 24+8	O'Brien B 27	McManus C 26+6	Flannigan I 19+4	Duffy M 31+3	Mitchell G 4	Chopra M 12+3	Ferns E 3+23	Marr J 26+2	McNeil A 13	Holmes G 23+3	Hetherington S 12+6	Layne I 7+10	Lynas A —+1	Kader O —+1	Crawford R 20+5	Paun C —+1	Doyle M 13	Hoggan R —+1	Hynd S 1+5	Hardie M —+1	McKenna S 4	Gallacher S 15	Megginson M 15	Finnie R 7	Caddis L 6+2	Match No.
1	2	3^1	4	5^8	6	7	8^2	9	10	11	12	13	14																		1
			5	4	2	8	7		6^1	11^2	10		3	1	9^3	12	13	14													2
1	7^2		5	4	2	8	6^3		9	10^1	11	13	3		12		14														3
1	5^2	3	9		2	7^3	6		8	11^1	10	12	4			14		13													4
1	7^2		5	3	2	6	8			11^1	12	4			9^3	13			10	14											5
1			5	3	2	8^1	7	14	12		11	13	4		9^2	10^1			6												6
1	12		5	4	2	8^1	7	10	11^3		13	14	3^4		9^2				6												7
1	13	3	5	4	2^2	7^1	6	8^1	11		9	12		14					10												8
		13	3^1	5	2	6	8^2	9	11^1		14	12	4	1	7				10												9
		3	5		6		8	11^1			9^2	12	4	1	7	13			10	2											10
		4	5		2^2	7		12	11^1		10^3	14	3	1	6	13			9	8											11
12		3	5		14	6^2	8^3		13		11	7	4	1	9				10	2^1											12
		3	5		7	6^2	8		12		11^1	10^4	4	1	9^3	14					2	13									13
	2^1	4		5	3	8^2	9		11				1	7	12		10^3			6		13	14								14
12		4	3^5	5^4		8	13	9		10			1^1	7^2	14		11			6		2									15
	2	4	5			7^2	6	12	10		11		1	8			9^1			3		13									16
12		5	4	13	6	8^2	7	11			12	3^3		9^1						10		2									17
	14	5	4	8	6	9^1	7	11			12	3^3					10^1			2		13									18
		5	4	6	7	9^1	8	11			12		1				10^1			2				3							19
13		5	4^2	8^1	7	12	6	11			14		1			10^3				9		2		3							20
		5^3	4	12	7	9		10			13			8^1	11		6^2			2		14	3	1							21
		5^3	4^2		6	7		8			14	13		9^1	11		12			2			3	1	10						22
		5	4	12	7	8		6			13	3		9^1	10^2					1		11			2						23
		5	4	13	6	7		8			3	12		9^2	11^1					1		10			2						24
		5	3	12	7	8		6			14	4^1		9	11^2					1		10			2^3	13					25
		5^2	4	12	9	7	13	6			3			10						1		11			2^1	8^3					26
		5	4	2^1		8^3	7	6			12	3		10^2	9^1	13				14					1	11					27
			4		7	6^2	8	11			12	3			5	13									1	10	2	9^1			28
		5	3	12	7^1	8	10	6			13	4		9											1	11^2	2				29
		5^1	4	8		7^2	6	10			3			9	12					13					1	11	2				30
		5	4	2		6	10				12	3		8^1	9					7					1	11					31
		5^2	4	2			9	10			14	3		7^3	6^4	12				8^1					1	11		13			32
12		3	5	2	13	9	6					4		7						11^2						1^1	10	8			33
1		3	5	2	12	9	11				4			7	13					6^1					1		8²				34
		5	3	2	12	10^3	11				14	4		6^1	8	13				1		9					7^2				35
		4	3	2	12	8	9				6	7		10^1	13	14				1					14		11^3	5^2			36

ANNAN ATHLETIC

Year Formed: 1942. *Ground & Address:* Galabank, North Street, Annan DG12 5DQ. *Telephone:* 01461 204108.
E-mail: annanathletic.enquiries@btconnect.com *Website:* www.annanathleticfc.com
Ground capacity: 2,517 (seated: 500). *Size of Pitch:* 100m × 62m.
Chairman: Henry McClelland.
Secretary: Alan Irving.
Manager: Jim Chapman.
Assistant Manager: John Joyce.
Coaches: Peter Weatherson and Bill Bentley.
Club Nicknames: 'Galabankies', 'Black and Golds'.
Previous Ground: Mafeking Park.
Record attendance: 2,517, v Rangers, Third Division, 15 September 2012.
Record Victory: 6-0 v Elgin C, Third Division, 7 March 2009.
Record Defeat: 1-8 v Inverness CT, Scottish Cup 3rd rd, 24 January 1998.
Most League Appearances: 218: Peter Watson, 2008-16.
Most League Goals in Season (Individual): 22: Peter Weatherson, 2014-15.
Most Goals Overall (Individual): 50: Peter Weatherson, 2013-16.

ANNAN ATHLETIC – SCOTTISH LEAGUE TWO 2015–16 LEAGUE RECORD

Match No.	Date	Venue	Opponents	Result	H/T Score	Lg Pos.	Goalscorers	Attendance
1	Aug 8	A	Queen's Park	W 1-0	0-0	3	Flynn [64]	495
2	15	H	Stirling Alb	D 1-1	0-0	2	Osadolor [46]	489
3	22	A	East Stirling	L 1-3	1-1	7	Osadolor [34]	294
4	29	H	Montrose	W 3-2	2-0	3	Osadolor 2 [12, 83], Flynn [21]	372
5	Sept 5	H	East Fife	W 2-0	1-0	1	Todd [38], Omar [89]	510
6	12	A	Clyde	L 2-4	1-3	3	Flynn [24], Gilfillan [86]	506
7	19	A	Berwick R	W 2-0	1-0	1	Omar [13], Osadolor [57]	405
8	26	H	Elgin C	D 1-1	1-0	3	Black [40]	414
9	Oct 3	A	Arbroath	W 2-0	2-0	1	Weatherson [11], Little (og) [23]	492
10	17	H	Queen's Park	W 3-1	2-0	1	Osadolor [36], Weatherson [42], Todd [90]	414
11	31	A	East Fife	W 1-0	1-0	1	Weatherson [15]	517
12	Nov 7	A	Elgin C	L 2-3	1-2	1	McHardy (og) [29], Flynn [90]	644
13	14	H	Berwick R	W 1-0	0-0	1	McColm [81]	486
14	21	H	Arbroath	D 2-2	1-0	1	Weatherson [35], Osadolor [60]	424
15	Dec 12	H	East Stirling	W 3-1	2-0	1	Flynn [6], Weatherson 2 [36, 50]	357
16	15	A	Montrose	D 1-1	1-0	1	Finnie [27]	262
17	19	A	Stirling Alb	L 0-1	0-0	1		624
18	26	H	Clyde	L 2-3	1-2	1	Weatherson [21], Osadolor [90]	549
19	Jan 16	H	East Fife	L 2-4	0-4	4	McDonald [85], Weatherson [90]	481
20	23	A	Arbroath	L 1-2	0-0	4	Weatherson (pen) [88]	616
21	30	H	Elgin C	W 4-2	2-0	4	Todd [33], Flynn 2 [36, 46], Jago [82]	399
22	Feb 13	H	Montrose	D 3-3	1-1	5	McStay [43], Gilfillan (pen) [57], Flynn [74]	354
23	16	A	Berwick R	L 2-3	0-2	5	McStay [53], McColm [90]	238
24	20	A	East Stirling	W 1-0	0-0	4	Todd [52]	248
25	27	H	Stirling Alb	D 2-2	1-0	5	Guy [29], Todd [49]	426
26	Mar 5	H	Clyde	D 3-3	2-0	5	Todd 2 [23, 30], Weatherson [85]	491
27	12	A	East Fife	L 2-4	0-2	5	Weatherson [49], Osadolor [81]	600
28	15	A	Queen's Park	W 3-1	3-0	5	Weatherson 2 [15, 27], Flynn [33]	339
29	19	H	Berwick R	W 1-0	0-0	5	Flynn [83]	430
30	22	A	Clyde	L 1-2	0-1	5	Flynn [78]	373
31	26	A	Montrose	W 5-0	2-0	4	Weatherson 2 (1 pen) [21 (p), 45], Flynn [60], Todd 2 [68, 90]	452
32	Apr 2	A	Elgin C	D 2-2	0-0	4	Todd [62], Osadolor [73]	861
33	9	H	Arbroath	W 4-1	2-1	2	Todd 2 [22, 46], Guy [26], Osadolor [88]	414
34	16	A	East Stirling	L 1-3	0-1	4	Osadolor [60]	398
35	23	A	Stirling Alb	L 1-2	0-1	5	Todd [86]	545
36	30	H	Queen's Park	W 1-0	1-0	5	Weatherson [43]	640

Final League Position: 5

Honours
League Two Runners-up: 2013-14.
League Challenge Cup: Semi-finals: 2009-10, 2011-12.

Club colours: Shirt: Gold with black trim. Shorts: Black. Socks: Gold with black and white rings.

Goalscorers: *League (69):* Weatherson 16 (2 pens), Todd 13, Flynn 12, Osadolor 12, Gilfillan 2 (1 pen), Guy 2, McColm 2, McStay 2, Omar 2, Black 1, Finnie 1, Jago 1, McDonald 1, own goals 2.
William Hill Scottish FA Cup (14): Weatherson 5 (1 pen), Omar 3, Flynn 2, Todd 2, McColm 1, Swinglehurst 1.
Scottish League Cup (3): Weatherson 2, Osadolor 1.
Petrofac Training Cup (4): Todd 3, Weatherson 1 (1 pen).

Hart J 30	Black S 22+2	Watson P 31+1	Swinglehurst S 23+2	McNiff M 36	Osadolor S 15+17	Sloan S 23+4	Flynn M 32	McColm S 8+14	Todd J 33	Weatherson P 24+2	Norman S 1+3	Ogen J —+1	Omar R 27+3	Park L —+12	Watson J —+3	McDonald G 1+8	Ferguson D 5+4	McStay R 8+4	Gilfillan B 10+2	Finnie R 10+3	Morton J 5+3	Jago B 12+1	Currie B 6	Nicoll K 6	Guy L 13+1	Cuddihy B 10	Breslin J 5+1	Match No.
1	2	3	4	5	6	7¹	8	9²	10	11	12	13																1
1	3	2⁴	4	8	10	6¹	7	12	9	11			5²	13														2
1	2¹		3	4	10	6²	7	8³	9	11	5		13	12	14													3
1	3	2	4	11	6	7¹	12	9	10				5															4
1	3²	2	4	8	11		7	6¹	14	9	10³	13	5				12											5
1	3	2	4	5³	11		8	9²	10	.			7¹			14	6	12	13									6
1	3	2	4	9	11²	7	6	13	8				5¹			14	12		10³									7
1	3	2	4	8	11	6	7		9	12			5						10¹									8
1	3	2	4	9	11¹		7		8	10²			5³	14		13		6	12									9
1	2¹		4	11²	6	7³	13	9	10				5				12	14	3	8								10
1		12	4		6	8	11²	10	9⁴	13			7³	14			3		2¹	5								11
1	5	12	4	2	10³	8²	7	11	9					14		13	3¹			6								12
1	2	3	4	5		6¹	7	12	10				11	14		13		8²		9¹								13
1	3	2	4	9	11	7²	8	13	6¹	10			5							12								14
1	12	3	5	9	14	7	8	11²		10			6	13					4¹	2³								15
1	2	3	5	4	13	7	8	9¹		11			10	12					6²									16
1	3	2⁴	4	5	14		8	12	11³	10			9¹	13		7			6									17
1			4	8	12		7	10¹	9	11⁴			6			2	13	3	5²									18
1	3	2		4	12	6¹		10	11				8³	14		13		7		5²	9							19
1	5²	3	2¹	4	14	6	7		10	11			8			9³		12	13									20
1		3		5	13	7	8²	11					9				6¹	4	2	10	12							21
1			4	10¹		7	12	9									6	2		8	5⁴	1	3	11				22
1		2		5	10²			12	7				6	14		13	8	4	9¹		1	3	11³					23
1		4		3	10¹	6	8	12	11				9				7²			2	1	5	13					24
1		3		8	12	7	10		9				5				6¹		13	2	1	4	11²					25
1		3		5		7³	6¹		10	13			9			14		8²		12	2	1	4	11				26
	13	4³	12	5	14		8			10			6¹						9	2	1	3²	11	7				27
1	9	3	4	2		14	7¹		8	10³			12						13	5				11²	6			28
1		3		8	13	14	7²		9	10			5				12			2²				11¹	6	4	29
1	4	3	5²	9	13		8	14	6	11			12							2¹				10²	7		30
1	4	3		9	12	13	7²		6	11			5³	14						2				10¹	8		31
1	3¹	4		9	13	7	10⁴		6				5							2				11²	8	12	32
1		3	4	8	12	7			9	10²			13							5				11¹	6	2	33
1		2¹	4	8	12		14		9	10			6	13						5²				11³	7	3	34
1	2¹	4	5³	3	13	12	6		9	10			14											11²	8	7	35
1	4	3¹	5	9	12	6²	8	13	10	11																7	2	36

ARBROATH

Year Formed: 1878. *Ground & Address:* Gayfield Park, Arbroath DD11 1QB. *Telephone:* 01241 872157. *Fax:* 01241 431125. *E-mail:* afc@gayfield.fsnet.co.uk *Website:* www.arbroathfc.co.uk
Ground Capacity: 6,600 (seated: 861). *Size of Pitch:* 105m × 65m.
Chairman: John Christison. *Secretary:* Dr Gary Callon. *Administrator:* Mike Cargill.
Manager: Dick Campbell. *Assistant Manager:* Ian Campbell. *Physio:* Ross Grant.
Club Nickname: 'The Red Lichties'.
Previous Grounds: Lesser Gayfield.
Record Attendance: 13,510 v Rangers, Scottish Cup 3rd rd, 23 February 1952.
Record Transfer Fee received: £120,000 for Paul Tosh to Dundee (August 1993).
Record Transfer Fee paid: £20,000 for Douglas Robb from Montrose (1981).
Record Victory: 36-0 v Bon Accord, Scottish Cup 1st rd, 12 September 1885.
Record Defeat: 0-8 v Kilmarnock, Division II, 3 January 1949; 1-9 v Celtic, League Cup 3rd rd, 25 August 1993.
Most Capped Player: Ned Doig, 2 (5), Scotland.
Most League Appearances: 445: Tom Cargill, 1966-81.
Most League Goals in Season (Individual): 45: Dave Easson, Division II, 1958-59.
Most Goals Overall (Individual): 120: Jimmy Jack, 1966-71.

ARBROATH – SCOTTISH LEAGUE TWO 2015–16 LEAGUE RECORD

Match No.	Date		Venue	Opponents	Result	H/T Score	Lg Pos.	Goalscorers	Attendance
1	Aug	8	H	Elgin C	L	0-3	0-2	10		683
2		15	A	Montrose	L	0-3	0-2	10		1100
3		22	H	Queen's Park	L	1-2	0-1	10	Vitoria [89]	604
4		29	A	Berwick R	D	2-2	1-2	10	Ryan [18], Ramsay [88]	721
5	Sept	5	A	Clyde	L	0-1	0-1	10		662
6		12	A	East Fife	W	1-0	0-0	10	Linn [80]	518
7		19	H	Stirling Alb	W	2-0	0-0	9	Cecilia [49], Linn [51]	638
8		26	A	East Stirling	W	4-0	1-0	8	Ryan 2 [7, 56], Linn (pen) [53], Grehan [78]	291
9	Oct	3	A	Annan Ath	L	0-2	0-2	8		492
10		17	H	Montrose	W	3-1	1-0	8	Linn 2 [23, 66], Rutherford, G [79]	1146
11		31	A	Elgin C	L	0-2	0-1	8		627
12	Nov	7	H	East Fife	D	1-1	0-1	9	Watson [53]	596
13		14	A	Stirling Alb	L	1-3	1-0	9	Linn [21]	763
14		21	A	Annan Ath	D	2-2	0-1	9	Linn [64], Rutherford, G [79]	424
15	Dec	12	A	Queen's Park	L	0-1	0-1	9		458
16		15	H	Berwick R	W	3-1	0-1	8	Linn [74], Wilson, C [76], Ramsay [90]	451
17		19	A	Clyde	W	2-0	0-0	7	Hester 2 [83, 84]	520
18	Jan	2	A	Montrose	W	2-0	1-0	7	Linn [31], Whatley [64]	1387
19		9	H	Elgin C	L	2-3	1-1	7	Rutherford, G [30], Ramsay [47]	624
20		23	H	Annan Ath	W	2-1	0-0	7	Watson [46], McNiff (og) [58]	616
21		30	A	East Stirling	W	3-0	1-0	6	Skelly [11], Cecilia [64], Linn [68]	306
22	Feb	6	A	Stirling Alb	D	1-1	0-0	5	Hester [70]	638
23		13	A	East Fife	L	1-2	0-1	6	Stewart [89]	533
24		20	H	Queen's Park	L	0-1	0-1	8		593
25		23	H	East Stirling	D	0-0	0-0	7		334
26		27	H	Clyde	L	0-1	0-0	7		588
27	Mar	5	A	Stirling Alb	L	0-1	0-0	8		652
28		8	A	Berwick R	L	0-3	0-1	9		302
29		12	H	East Stirling	W	3-0	1-0	9	Wilson, C [11], Whatley [69], Williams [73]	609
30		19	A	Queen's Park	L	1-2	0-1	9	Hester [54]	474
31		26	A	Clyde	W	2-1	0-1	8	Linn (pen) [56], Little [58]	697
32	Apr	2	H	East Fife	L	0-1	0-1	8		816
33		9	A	Annan Ath	L	1-4	1-2	8	Reid [25]	414
34		16	A	Berwick R	L	1-2	0-0	9	Hester [69]	558
35		23	H	Montrose	D	0-0	0-0	9		1073
36		30	A	Elgin C	L	1-4	0-2	9	Skelly [85]	1193

Final League Position: 9

Honours
League Champions: Third Division 2010-11; *Runners-up:* Division II 1934-35, 1958-59, 1967-68, 1971-72; Second Division 2000-01; Third Division 1997-98, 2007-08. *Promoted to Second Division:* 2007-08 (play-offs). *Scottish Cup:* Quarter-finals 1993.

Club colours: Shirt: Maroon with white trim. Shorts: Maroon. Socks: Maroon with white tops.

Goalscorers: *League (42):* Linn 11 (2 pens), Hester 5, Ramsay 3, Rutherford, G 3, Ryan 3, Cecilia 2, Skelly 2, Watson 2, Whatley 2, Wilson 2, Grehan 1, Little 1, Reid 1, Stewart 1, Vitoria 1, Williams 1, own goal 1.
William Hill Scottish FA Cup (5): Linn 2, Grehan 1 (1 pen), Ramsay 1, Whatley 1.
Scottish League Cup (2): Gold 1, Grehan 1.
Petrofac Training Cup (1): Grehan 1.

Fleming A 36	Wilson C 24 + 1	Hay G 2	Little R 33	Lowdon J 21 + 4	Linn R 33	Stewart K 13 + 7	Clarke J 9 + 5	Cecilia S 11 + 3	Gold D 16 + 8	Coull L 1	Munro A 23 + 2	Grehan M 8 + 5	Jones M — + 1	Ramsay D 28 + 5	Ryan A 8 + 5	Hester K 3 + 21	Johnstone C 13	Reid J 11 + 1	Whatley M 33 + 1	Vitoria J — + 5	Watson C 20	Rutherford G 20 + 5	Skelly J 10 + 4	Rutherford S 6	Henry J 4 + 1	Williams M 10 + 1	Match No.
1	2⁴	3	4	5²	6	7	8	9¹	10	11²	12	13	14														1
1		3	2	5	8	6	4²	9¹	10		7	11³		12	13	14											2
1	2	3		6	8⁶				7		4	10³		12	11		5	9¹	13	14							3
1	2³		4	9¹			13		7²		3	10		6	11		5	12	8	14							4
1	2³		3	6¹			8		14		10			9²	11		5	13	7	12	4						5
1	2		3	6	8	12	10¹					14		9²	11³		5	13	7		4						6
1			3	6³	7¹	11				2	13			9	11¹		5	14	7		4						7
1			3	6³	7¹	11				2	13			9	10¹²		5	14	8		4						8
1			3	6	8²		11	13		2	12			9	10¹		5²		7	14	4						9
1		3	14	6³	8¹	11			12					2	10²		9		5	7		4	13				10
1		4				13	9²	6¹	7		3	11³			10			5		8	14	2	12				11
1		3		6¹			10		7		2	11²			9	12		5		8		4	13				12
1	12	2⁸		11		6			8²		3	10³			9		14	5¹		7		4	13				13
1	2		5	10		12		6¹	8	4				9						7		3	11				14
1	2	3	5	7		8		12			10²	13	14		9¹	6		4³	11								15
1	2	3	12	10	6²		13				9		14	5¹	8³	7		4	11								16
1	2	3	5	8²	12	7¹					10	14	13		9	6		4	11³								17
1	2	3	5	8	6						10	12	13		9¹	7		4	11²								18
1	2	3	5	6	8¹	13					9	11²			12		7		4	10							19
1	2	3	5	8					7		10				12		6		4	11	9¹						20
1	2	4	3	6			12	8¹			11				13	14	7		5	9²	10³						21
1	2	3		6¹			8³				9				13	12	7		4	10	11²	5	14				22
1	2	3		14		8²					9				12	6²	7		4	10¹	13	5	11				23
1	2	3	12	6					13		9¹				10	14	7		4²		11	5²	8⁸				24
1	2	3	9	6	14		8²		4		12	11			10³	7			13	5¹							25
1	2	4⁸	5	6					3		9²	12			7			11	13		10	8					26
1	2		5	6	7²	14			4		9	12			8		10¹	13		11²	3						27
1	2	4	5	6	8²	12			3		13	14			7		10³	11			9¹						28
1	2		5	6			14		4		9²	12			13	8	10¹	11	3		7³						29
1	2	3	11¹	6			14		4		9	12			7³		13	10²	5		8						30
1	2	3	5	6			12		4		14	13			9	7		10²	11³			8¹					31
1	2²	3	5	6			8		4		9	12			14	7		10³	11¹		13						32
1		3	5	6	12		7¹		4		11				9	8		10				2					33
1		3	5	6	13		7²		4		9¹	12			11	8		10				2					34
1		3	5	6	13		7		4		9	11¹			12	8		10²				2					35
1		3	12	6			7		4		13	5			11	8		10²	9			2¹					36

AYR UNITED

Year Formed: 1910. *Ground & Address:* Somerset Park, Tryfield Place, Ayr KA8 9NB. *Telephone:* 01292 263435.
Fax: 01292 281314. *E-mail:* info@ayrunitedfc.co.uk *Website:* ayrunitedfc.co.uk
Ground Capacity: 10,185 (seated: 1,597). *Size of Pitch:* 101m × 66m.
Chairman: Lachlan Cameron.
Managing Director: Lewis Grant.
Manager: Ian McCall. *Assistant Manager:* John Henry. *Physio:* Steven Maguire.
Club Nickname: 'The Honest Men'.
Previous Grounds: None.
Record Attendance: 25,225 v Rangers, Division I, 13 September 1969.
Record Transfer Fee received: £300,000 for Steven Nicol to Liverpool (October 1981).
Record Transfer Fee paid: £90,000 for Mark Campbell from Stranraer (March 1999).
Record Victory: 11-1 v Dumbarton, League Cup, 13 August 1952.
Record Defeat: 0-9 in Division I v Rangers (1929); v Hearts (1931); B Division v Third Lanark (1954).
Most Capped Player: Jim Nisbet, 3, Scotland.
Most League Appearances: 459: John Murphy, 1963-78.
Most League League and Cup Goals in Season (Individual): 66: Jimmy Smith, 1927-28.
Most League and Cup Goals Overall (Individual): 213: Peter Price, 1955-61.

AYR UNITED – SCOTTISH LEAGUE ONE 2015–16 LEAGUE RECORD

Match No.	Date	Venue	Opponents	Result	H/T Score	Lg Pos.	Goalscorers	Attendance
1	Aug 8	A	Albion R	L	0-3	0-2	9		781
2	15	H	Brechin C	W	2-1	1-0	6	Forrest [21], Trouten (pen) [73]	1074
3	22	A	Stranraer	W	2-1	1-0	4	Moore [4], Trouten [77]	882
4	29	H	Forfar Ath	D	2-2	1-1	5	Moore [45], Forrest [58]	1243
5	Sept 1	A	Stenhousemuir	W	5-2	3-1	2	Preston 2 [3, 47], Moore [26], Barclay (og) [35], Caldwell [86]	1046
6	12	H	Dunfermline Ath	W	2-0	1-0	2	Forrest [23], Preston [59]	3596
7	19	A	Airdrieonians	W	2-1	1-1	1	Moore [45], Gilmour [66]	1141
8	26	H	Peterhead	D	1-1	0-0	1	Devlin [55]	1304
9	Oct 3	H	Cowdenbeath	W	5-0	2-0	1	Preston [1], Forrest [19], McLauchlan [48], Gilmour [57], Moore [72]	1171
10	17	A	Forfar Ath	D	2-2	0-2	2	Graham [54], Caldwell [72]	745
11	24	A	Stenhousemuir	W	1-0	1-0	2	Caldwell [9]	767
12	31	H	Stranraer	W	3-1	2-1	1	Crawford [15], Adams [39], Preston [83]	1415
13	Nov 7	A	Brechin C	D	1-1	1-0	1	Adams [43]	541
14	14	H	Albion R	W	1-0	1-0	1	Trouten [38]	1389
15	21	H	Airdrieonians	W	3-0	2-0	1	Preston [26], Donald [45], Trouten (pen) [61]	1403
16	Dec 12	H	Dunfermline Ath	L	1-2	1-1	2	McLauchlan [36]	2076
17	19	A	Peterhead	L	0-3	0-0	2		612
18	26	H	Brechin C	W	2-1	2-0	2	Forrest [4], Moore [13]	1485
19	29	A	Cowdenbeath	L	2-4	1-3	2	Caldwell [2], Preston [59]	640
20	Jan 2	A	Stranraer	L	0-1	0-0	2		1178
21	23	A	Albion R	W	3-1	3-0	2	Preston 2 [2, 43], Stevenson [5]	427
22	Feb 6	H	Peterhead	L	1-2	1-2	3	Moore [25]	1155
23	13	A	Dunfermline Ath	L	2-3	2-1	3	Graham [41], Moore (pen) [44]	3319
24	20	H	Forfar Ath	W	2-1	1-0	3	Stevenson 2 [39, 75]	763
25	27	A	Airdrieonians	W	1-0	1-0	3	Moore [45]	1000
26	Mar 1	A	Cowdenbeath	W	4-1	3-0	3	McCrorie [15], Stevenson 2 [17, 60], Moore [36]	856
27	5	A	Brechin C	L	0-1	0-0	3		491
28	8	H	Stenhousemuir	W	4-1	0-0	3	Moore [65], Malcolm (og) [77], Stevenson [84], Trouten [90]	889
29	12	H	Dunfermline Ath	L	0-2	0-0	3		2190
30	19	A	Forfar Ath	L	1-3	1-1	3	Stevenson [14]	614
31	26	H	Stranraer	W	2-1	1-0	3	Trouten [17], Wardrobe [61]	1244
32	Apr 2	A	Cowdenbeath	L	0-1	0-0	3		429
33	9	H	Albion R	L	0-1	0-0	3		1044
34	16	A	Stenhousemuir	W	4-0	1-0	3	Donald [1], Moore [47], Preston 2 (1 pen) [79 (p), 88]	652
35	23	A	Peterhead	W	4-0	2-0	2	Moore 2 [24, 81], McCrorie [45], Preston [54]	617
36	30	H	Airdrieonians	L	0-3	0-2	2		1594

Final League Position: 2

Honours

League Champions: Division II 1911-12, 1912-13, 1927-28, 1936-37, 1958-59, 1965-66. Second Division 1987-88, 1996-97; *Runners-up:* Division II 1910-11, 1955-56, 1968-69. Second Division 2008-09. League One 2015-16. *Promoted to First Division:* 2008-09 (play-offs). *Promoted to First Division:* 2010-11 (play-offs). *Promoted to Championship:* 2015-16 (play-offs).
Scottish Cup: Semi-finals 2002.
League Cup: Runners-up: 2001-02.
League Challenge Cup Runners-up: 1990-91, 1991-92.

Club colours: Shirt: White with black hoops. Shorts: Black. Socks: White.

Goalscorers: *League (65):* Moore 14 (1 pen), Preston 12 (1 pen), Stevenson 7, Trouten 6 (2 pens), Forrest 5, Caldwell 4, Adams 2, Donald 2, Gilmour 2, Graham 2, McCrorie 2, McLauchlan 2, Crawford 1, Devlin 1, Wardrobe 1, own goals 2.
William Hill Scottish FA Cup (0).
Scottish League Cup (2): Boyle 1, McLauchlan 1.
Petrofac Training Cup (3): Caldwell 1, Devlin 1, Trouten 1 (1 pen).
Championship Play-Offs (7): Crawford 2, Preston 2, Devlin 1, Docherty 1, Donald 1.

Fleming G 36	Adams J 17 + 3	Campbell M 1	Murphy P 29 + 1	Boyle P 27 + 1	Gilmour B 19 + 4	Docherty R 25 + 1	Crawford R 15 + 12	Donald M 16 + 15	Caldwell R 6 + 11	Trouten A 25 + 6	Forrest A 22 + 12	Nisbet R — + 1	McKenzie S — + 5	Devlin N 33 + 1	McLauchlan G 21 + 3	Moore C 23 + 2	Preston J 28 + 6	Graham A 22 + 3	Stevenson R 16 + 2	McCracken C — + 1	Muir A 1 + 1	Wardrobe M 4 + 6	McCrorie R 10 + 1	McGuffie C — + 1	Match No.
1	2	3	4	5	6²	7	8	9³	10¹	11	12	13	14												1
1	12		4	5	9²	7	8	13	14	10	6³					2	3	11¹							2
1	8		4	5	14	7⁴	6	12		13	11²					2	3	9¹	10¹						3
1	7		4	5	6		8	12			9¹					2	3	11	10						4
1	7¹		4	5	6³	8	13	12	14		9					2	3	11¹	10						5
1	8		3	5	6³	7		14	12	13	9¹					2	4	11²	10						6
1	7³		4	5	6	8		12	14	13	9¹					2	3	11	10²						7
1			4	5	6	7	8¹	12		9						2	3	11	10²	13					8
1			4	5	8¹	7²	13		12	9	6					2	3	11³	14						9
1	9³			5	8	6	12	14	13	11	7¹			2³	3		10²	4							10
1	13			5	9¹	7	8	12	11	6²	14			2	4		10²	3							11
1	6¹	14	5		7	8	12	11²	9³	13				2	3		10	4							12
1	6		5		8	7¹	12	11²	9	13				2	4		10	3							13
1	6		5		7	8	13	12	9	10²				2	3		11¹	4							14
1	8		4	5	14	7¹	12	6	13	10	9			2	3²		11³								15
1			4	8	5	7¹	6	12	14	9²	10		13	2²			11	3							16
1	8		4¹	5	9			14		6	13					2	3	11²	10³	7					17
1			3	6			13	5	12	8²	9			2	14	10¹	11	4	7²						18
1			8			6	5	11	10¹	9¹				2	4	12	3²	7	13	14					19
1			4			6²	8	11	12	9³		14		2	3	10	13	7				5¹			20
1			4			5	6	9		12				2	11¹	10	3	7				8			21
1	7		4		6²		5	9		12				2	3	11¹	10	8				13			22
1	8¹		3	12	6⁴		14	5		9						10²	11³	4	7			13			23
1			3	5			12	9		13	6²			2		11	10¹	4	7			8			24
1			3	5	6²	14		9³		12	10			2		11	13	4	7¹			8			25
1			3	5	10	9⁵	14		6						11³	12	4	8				13	7¹		26
1	13		3	5	11¹	9				6³	12			2	4	14	10		8			7²			27
1	8¹		3	5	13	7²				9	12			2		10	14	4	11			6²			28
1	8²		3	5	9¹	7³	14			6	12			2		11	13		10			4			29
1		5²				8	14	12		6	9			2	13	10	11	3	7³			4¹			30
1	8			13	5			9	12		14			3	11²	10¹	2	7³				6			31
1	4			7	14	5		6	12		13			2	11³	3	10¹					9²	8		32
1	4			6			11	9²						2	10³	12	3	7				13	8¹	14	33
1			7	5	3	8¹	9			6²				2	10³	11	4						13	12	34
1			7	5	4¹	8	9			12				2	13	11	10	3²					14	6³	35
1				5	14	7²	8	9		10	6¹			2	3	13	11²		12				4		36

BERWICK RANGERS

Year Formed: 1881. *Ground & Address:* Shielfield Park, Tweedmouth, Berwick-upon-Tweed TD15 2EF. *Telephone:*
01289 307424. *Fax:* 01289 309424. *Email:* club@berwickrangersfc.co.uk *Website:* berwickrangersfc.com
Ground Capacity: 4,131 (seated: 1,366). *Size of Pitch:* 101m × 64m.
Chairman: Len Eyre. *Vice-Chairman:* John Bell. *Football Secretary:* Dennis McCleary.
Manager: John Coughlin. *Assistant Manager:* Arthur Bell.
Club Nicknames: 'The Borderers', 'Black and Gold', 'The Wee Gers'.
Previous Grounds: Bull Stob Close, Pier Field, Meadow Field, Union Park, Old Shielfield.
Record Transfer Fee received: £80,000 for John Hughes to Swansea C (November 1989).
Record Transfer Fee paid: £27,000 for Sandy Ross from Cowdenbeath (March 1991).
Record Attendance: 13,283 v Rangers, Scottish Cup 1st rd, 28 January 1967.
Record Victory: 8-1 v Forfar Ath, Division II, 25 December 1965; v Vale of Leithen, Scottish Cup, December 1966.
Record Defeat: 1-9 v Hamilton A, First Division, 9 August 1980.
Most League Appearances: 439: Eric Tait, 1970-87.
Most League Goals in Season (Individual): 33: Ken Bowron, Division II, 1963-64.
Most Goals Overall (Individual): 114: Eric Tait, 1970-87.

BERWICK RANGERS – SCOTTISH LEAGUE TWO 2015–16 LEAGUE RECORD

Match No.	Date	Venue	Opponents	Result	H/T Score	Lg Pos.	Goalscorers	Attendance
1	Aug 8	H	Montrose	W 2-1	1-1	2	Henderson 2 [12, 71]	479
2	15	A	East Fife	L 0-5	0-3	8		516
3	22	A	Stirling Alb	W 3-1	2-0	6	Comrie (og) [39], Graham, F [41], Henderson [66]	601
4	29	H	Arbroath	D 2-2	2-1	4	Lavery [3], McKenna [15]	721
5	Sept 5	H	Queen's Park	W 1-0	1-0	2	Lavery (pen) [19]	533
6	12	A	Elgin C	L 1-4	1-1	4	McNeil [36]	627
7	19	H	Annan Ath	L 0-2	0-1	7		405
8	26	A	Clyde	D 1-1	0-1	7	Henderson [68]	504
9	Oct 3	H	East Stirling	W 2-1	0-1	7	Henderson [47], Lavery [51]	423
10	17	H	East Fife	D 1-1	0-0	5	Graham, F [59]	531
11	31	A	Montrose	L 1-4	0-2	7	Graham, F [57]	418
12	Nov 7	H	Stirling Alb	L 1-2	0-0	8	McNeil [70]	438
13	14	A	Annan Ath	L 0-1	0-0	8		486
14	21	H	Clyde	L 0-5	0-1	10		411
15	Dec 12	H	Elgin C	L 2-3	1-2	10	McKenna [16], Lavery [87]	394
16	15	A	Arbroath	L 1-3	1-0	10	Henderson (pen) [28]	451
17	19	A	East Stirling	W 4-0	2-0	9	Graham, F 2 [26, 37], Coultress [71], Lavery [88]	241
18	26	A	Queen's Park	W 1-0	0-0	8	Lavery [90]	547
19	Jan 9	A	East Fife	L 0-1	0-0	8		445
20	23	A	Elgin C	L 0-1	0-1	9		752
21	Feb 6	H	East Stirling	D 2-2	1-1	9	McGregor [3], Lavery [69]	359
22	13	A	Stirling Alb	L 1-2	1-2	10	Henderson [9]	618
23	16	H	Annan Ath	W 3-2	2-0	9	Henderson [32], Lavery (pen) [43], Walker, A [89]	238
24	20	A	Clyde	L 1-2	0-2	9	McNeil [70]	539
25	23	A	Queen's Park	D 1-1	1-1	9	Martin [40]	326
26	27	H	Montrose	W 1-0	0-0	9	Henderson [72]	380
27	Mar 5	A	Queen's Park	D 0-0	0-0	9		409
28	8	H	Arbroath	W 3-0	1-0	8	Henderson 2 [4, 51], Lavery [60]	302
29	12	H	Stirling Alb	W 1-0	1-0	7	Henderson [1]	502
30	19	A	Annan Ath	L 0-1	0-0	8		430
31	26	H	Elgin C	W 2-0	1-0	7	Henderson 2 (1 pen) [5 (p), 88]	512
32	Apr 2	A	East Stirling	D 0-0	0-0	7		304
33	9	H	Clyde	W 3-0	1-0	7	Henderson 2 [21, 85], McGregor [88]	637
34	16	A	Arbroath	W 2-1	0-0	6	Notman [79], McKenna [90]	558
35	23	H	East Fife	W 2-0	0-0	6	Henderson [72], Lavery [90]	707
36	30	A	Montrose	L 0-1	0-1	6		937

Final League Position: 6

Honours
League Champions: Second Division 1978-79. Third Division 2006-07; *Runners-up:* Second Division 1993-94. Third Division 1999-2000, 2005-06 (not promoted).
Scottish Cup: Quarter-finals 1953-54, 1979-80.
League Cup: Semi-finals 1963-64.
League Challenge Cup: Quarter-finals 2004-05.

Club colours: Shirt: Black with gold vertical stripes. Shorts: Black. Socks: Black.

Goalscorers: *League (45):* Henderson 17 (2 pens), Lavery 10 (2 pens), Graham, F 5, McKenna 3, McNeil 3, McGregor 2, Coultress 1, Martin 1, Notman 1, Walker, A 1, own goal 1.
William Hill Scottish FA Cup (1): Coultress 1.
Scottish League Cup (4): Lavery 2, Banjo 1, Morris 1.
Petrofac Training Cup (1): Henderson 1.

Walker K 33	McNeil E 30+3	Fairbairn J 31	Wilson R 16+5	Beveridge G 19+4	McKenna M 32+2	Graham F 31+3	Banjo D 5+3	Coultress D 8+6	Henderson B 31+3	Lavery D 31+3	Morris D 6+10	Russell A —+10	Drummond R 7+5	Graham R 4+3	Walters M 3+3	Ainslie K 4	Cameron C 5+1	Notman S 27+2	Hogg B 1+4	Halkett C 4	Crane C 20	Stevenson D 8+7	McGregor J 15+1	Walker A 7+2	Martin B 14+1	Cunningham A 4+5	Duthie C —+1	Watt D —+1	Match No.
1	2	3	4	5	6³	7	8	9¹	10	11²	12	13	14																1
1¹	2	4	3¹	5	6	7	8	13	10	11¹	9²			12	14														2
	2	4		5	11	8	13		9	10	7¹		12		14	1	3³	6²											3
1	2	4		5	7	8	13³	9¹	10	11	14		12		3	6²													4
1	2	4		6	7	8		13	10³	11²	9¹	14	5		3	12													5
1	2	4		9²	7	8			10³	11	12	14	5		3	6¹	13												6
1	2	4	12	9²	7	8		14	10	11		5			6¹	3³	13												7
1	2	3		5²	8	7		12	11	9		13	4			6	10¹												8
1	2	3		6	7			9¹	10	11²	12	13	5	4		8													9
1	2	3	12	6	8			9	10	11¹		5⁴	4		13	7²													10
1	2			6³	8			9¹	11	10	12	14	5		7²	4	13	3											11
1	2	4		5	6	8		10²	11	12	13	9¹			7	3													12
1	2	4		5	6	9	8¹		10	11		12			7	3													13
1	2	4		5	9³	8¹	6		11²	10	14	13	12		7	3													14
1	2	4	3	9²	10³	8	6¹		14	11	12		13		7			5											15
1	2	4	3		10	6²	13		11		8	12	9¹		7			5											16
1	2	4	3		10¹	6			9		11	8			7			5	12										17
1	2	4	3		10	6			9¹		11	8			7			5	12										18
1	2²		3	13					10³	11		9¹	14		7			5	6	4	8	12							19
1	2	4ᵃ			9	12		14	11¹		13				7			5	6³	3	8²	10							20
1			3	2	9²	6			13	10	12							5	8¹	4	7		11						21
1	12		4	2	10	6²			11³	13								8	9	7¹	3⁴		5		14				22
1¹	2¹	4	3		9				11³	10²			12		7				5	13	6	8	14						23
	2		3		11²	12			9³	10			1		7				5	13	4	6¹	8	14					24
1	2	4			13	9			11	10					7				5	6¹	3		8²	12					25
1	2³	4	13	14	12	6			10	11					7				5		3²		8	9¹					26
	2	4	12		10	8			13	11			1		7²				5	6¹	3		9						27
1	14	4	2	5	8¹	7			13	11³	10				9	12	3			6²									28
1	5	3	2		9¹	6			10	11					7				8		12	4ᵃ							29
1	5	3	2¹		9	6²			11	10					7				8	13	4			12					30
1	5	3			13	9	12		11	14					6¹				8	7²	2		4	10³					31
1	2³	4	14	7²	9	6			11	10									8¹	3	12	5	13						32
1		3		5	9	6			10	11					7				8		2	4							33
1¹	14		5		9	6²			10	11¹			12		7				8ᵃ		2	13	4						34
1	5¹	3	2	12	10	8²			11³	13					6	14			4ᵃ		7	9							35
1		4	3	2²		7¹			11	10									6³	12	5	14		9	8		13		36

BRECHIN CITY

Year Formed: 1906. *Ground & Address:* Glebe Park, Trinity Rd, Brechin, Angus DD9 6BJ. *Telephone:* 01356 622856.
Fax: 01382 206331. *E-mail:* secretary@brechincityfc.com *Website:* www.brechincity.com
Ground Capacity: 4,123 (seated: 1,528). *Size of Pitch:* 101m × 61m.
Chairman: Kenneth Ferguson. *Vice-Chairman:* Martin Smith. *Secretary:* Gus Fairlie.
Manager: Darren Dods. *Assistant Manager:* Lee Bailey.
Club Nicknames: 'The City', 'The Hedgemen'.
Previous Grounds: Nursery Park.
Record Attendance: 8,122 v Aberdeen, Scottish Cup 3rd rd, 3 February 1973.
Record Transfer Fee received: £100,000 for Scott Thomson to Aberdeen (1991) and Chris Templeman to Morton (2004).
Record Transfer Fee paid: £16,000 for Sandy Ross from Berwick R (1991).
Record Victory: 12-1 v Thornhill, Scottish Cup 1st rd, 28 January 1926.
Record Defeat: 0-10 v Airdrieonians, Albion R and Cowdenbeath, all in Division II, 1937-38.
Most League Appearances: 459: David Watt, 1975-89.
Most League Goals in Season (Individual): 26: Ronald McIntosh, Division II, 1959-60.
Most Goals Overall (Individual): 131: Ian Campbell, 1977-85.

BRECHIN CITY – SCOTTISH LEAGUE ONE 2015–16 LEAGUE RECORD

Match No.	Date	Venue	Opponents	Result	H/T Score	Lg Pos.	Goalscorers	Attendance
1	Aug 8	H	Dunfermline Ath	L	1-6	0-4	10	Weatherston [89]	1214
2	15	A	Ayr U	L	1-2	0-1	9	Thomson [68]	1074
3	22	H	Airdrieonians	L	1-2	0-2	10	Jackson, A [72]	464
4	29	A	Albion R	L	1-3	1-2	10	Johnston (pen) [25]	470
5	Sept 5	A	Stranraer	L	0-1	0-0	10		366
6	12	H	Forfar Ath	L	0-2	0-1	10		602
7	19	A	Peterhead	W	3-2	2-2	10	Thomson 2 [11, 83], Shields [31]	554
8	26	H	Cowdenbeath	W	2-0	0-0	10	Bates [49], Tiffoney [64]	408
9	Oct 3	A	Stenhousemuir	D	2-2	0-1	9	Jackson, A [71], Weatherston [75]	348
10	17	A	Airdrieonians	L	0-1	0-0	10		729
11	24	H	Albion R	L	0-1	0-1	10		414
12	31	A	Forfar Ath	W	1-0	0-0	10	Jackson, A [67]	728
13	Nov 7	A	Ayr U	D	1-1	0-1	10	Layne [47]	541
14	14	A	Cowdenbeath	L	0-3	0-1	10		386
15	21	H	Stenhousemuir	L	1-2	0-1	10	Layne [71]	376
16	Dec 5	A	Dunfermline Ath	L	1-3	0-2	10	Layne [66]	2361
17	12	H	Peterhead	D	1-1	0-1	10	Thomson [80]	403
18	19	H	Stranraer	W	2-0	2-0	9	Shields [20], Layne [26]	401
19	26	A	Ayr U	L	1-2	0-2	10	Thomson [90]	1485
20	Jan 23	H	Airdrieonians	D	3-3	1-3	10	Spence [24], Thomson [50], Dods [80]	476
21	30	A	Stranraer	L	0-2	0-1	10		435
22	Feb 2	A	Stenhousemuir	L	0-1	0-0	10		213
23	13	H	Cowdenbeath	D	2-2	1-1	10	Tiffoney [38], Shepherd [90]	404
24	20	H	Dunfermline Ath	L	1-2	1-2	10	Thomson [17]	1053
25	23	A	Albion R	L	1-4	0-3	10	McLean (pen) [76]	210
26	27	A	Peterhead	L	1-4	0-2	10	Watt [64]	680
27	Mar 1	H	Forfar Ath	W	4-0	2-0	10	Watt 2 [24, 59], Dods [31], Thomson [81]	633
28	5	H	Ayr U	W	1-0	0-0	10	Thomson [74]	491
29	12	A	Airdrieonians	W	2-0	1-0	10	Jackson, A [43], Spence [66]	671
30	19	A	Albion R	W	2-1	0-1	9	Thomson [80], Coogans [86]	461
31	26	A	Dunfermline Ath	L	1-3	1-2	10	Thomson [25]	4402
32	Apr 2	H	Stenhousemuir	W	1-0	0-0	10	Thomson [49]	454
33	9	A	Cowdenbeath	L	1-2	0-1	10	Spence [70]	455
34	16	H	Peterhead	W	5-1	4-1	9	Jackson, A [5], Thomson 3 [21, 45, 66], Watt [42]	481
35	23	H	Stranraer	W	1-0	0-0	8	Robson [81]	452
36	30	A	Forfar Ath	W	2-1	1-0	7	McCormack [45], Robson [88]	928

Final League Position: 7

Honours
League Champions: Second Division 1982-83, 1989-90, 2004-05. Third Division 2001-02. C Division 1953-54;
Runners-up: Second Division 1992-93, 2002-03. Third Division 1995-96.
League Challenge Cup Runners-up: 2002-03.

Club colours: Shirt: Red with white trim. Shorts: White. Socks: Red.

Goalscorers: *League (47):* Thomson 15, Jackson, A 5, Layne 4, Watt 4, Spence 3, Dods 2, Robson 2, Shields 2, Tiffoney 2, Weatherston 2, Bates 1, Coogans 1, Johnston 1 (1 pen), McCormack 1, McLean 1 (1 pen), Shepherd 1.
William Hill Scottish FA Cup (1): Jackson, A 1.
Scottish League Cup (0).
Petrofac Training Cup (0).

Smith G 34	McLean P 28 + 1	McCormack D 23 + 2	Perry R 7 + 1	Buchan K 1 + 2	Molloy C 23 + 4	Smith E 9 + 14	Johnston C 4 + 11	Dale J 22 + 2	Jackson A 34	Thomson R 28 + 4	Weatherston D 11 + 5	Montgomery J 4 + 8	Dods D 19 + 2	Tiffoney J 22 + 7	Fusco G 30 + 1	Finnie R — + 3	O'Neil P 2 + 1	Dyer W 31	Bates D 10	Shields D 7 + 1	Layne I 8	Spence L 13	Shepherd S 3 + 5	Culjak L 5 + 1	Watt L 10	Coogans L — + 5	Robson J 6	Sukar J 2	Match No.
1	2	3	4	5	6	7	8	9[1]	10	11	12																		1
1■		3			8	9	6[1]		10	11			2[2]	4	5	7	12	13											2
		3			7	8	6		10	11		9[1]	4	5	2	12	1												3
			4		7	9[2]	6[1]	12	10	11			3	2	8	13	1	5											4
1		3		13	8	9[2]	12		10	11	6[1]		4	2	7			5											5
1	13	3		14	8		12	9[2]	10	11	6[3]			2[1]	7			5	4										6
1	2				8	13	12		10	11			3	6[1]	7			5	4	9[2]									7
1	2	13			8[3]	12	14			11		9[1]	3	6[2]	7			5	4	10									8
1	2		12		7				10	11	13		3[2]	6[1]	8			5	4	9									9
1	2	14	4		6[2]			13	9	8[3]	12		10[1]		7			5	3	11									10
1	2	7	4		6	13			10		9[1]	12	11[2]		8			5	3										11
1	5	8	4		7				10				3		6			9	2			11							12
1	5	8[2]	3		7	12			10				4		6[1]	13		9	2			11							13
1	5	8	4		7	6[1]			10				3[2]		12			9	2			11							14
1	5		3		7			12	10	13			4		8[1]	6[2]		9■	2			11							15
1	2	3					12		8	10[1]	9[2]	6	14	4	5	7[3]				13		11							16
1	2	3			7				8	9	13	6[2]		12	4[1]			5				11	10						17
1	2	3			7				8	9	12	6[1]		13	4			5				11	6						18
1	3	4			8	7[1]			10[2]	14	9[3]	13		12	2			5			6	11							19
1	4[1]	3			13			14	8	9	11	6	12		2			5					7[3]	10[2]					20
1		3						12	9	10	11	7[1]	13	4	2			5					8	6[2]					21
1		3[2]						14	7	10	11	6[1]	12	13	2			5					8	9[3]	4				22
1								13	8	10	11	9[1]		3	6[2]	2		5					7	12	4				23
1	3				7[1]	14			8	10	11	12[3]	6		9[2]	2		5					13		4				24
1	3				12	14			8	10[3]	11		6[2]		9[1]	2		5					7	13	4				25
1	2	3			12				8		10		14		6	7[3]		5				11[1]	13		4	9[2]			26
1	2	3			7	13			8[1]	9[2]	10		14	4	6			5					12		11[3]				27
1	2	3[1]			8				7		9			4	6			5				10		12	11				28
1	3				8	13			7	10[2]	11		14	4	6[1]	2		5					9[3]		12				29
1	3				7[3]	14			6[1]	11[1]	10		4	12	2			5					8		9	13			30
1	2				8[2]	12			4	10	11		3[1]		7			5							9	13	6		31
1	4				13	12			7	10[2]	11			6■	2			5					8		9		5[1]	3	32
1	2				12				7[1]	10	11				3			5					8[2]		6	13	9	4	33
1	3	4			12				7	10	11[3]		13		2			5					8[2]		9	14	6[1]		34
1	2	3			12				8	10	11				4			5					7[1]		9		6		35
1	4	3			12■	9[1]			7	10	11	13			2			5					8[2]				6		36

CELTIC

Year Formed: 1888. *Ground & Address:* Celtic Park, Glasgow G40 3RE. *Telephone:* 0871 226 1888. *Fax:* 0141 551 8106.
E-mail: customerservices@celticfc.co.uk *Website:* www.celticfc.net
Ground Capacity: 60,832 (all seated). *Size of Pitch:* 105m × 68m.
Chairman: Ian Bankier. *Chief Executive:* Peter Lawwell. *Secretary:* Michael Nicholson.
Manager: Brendan Rodgers. *Assistant Manager:* Chris Davies. *First Team Coach:* John Kennedy. *Physio:* Graham Parsons.
Club Nicknames: 'The Bhoys', 'The Hoops', 'The Celts'. *Previous Grounds:* None.
Record Attendance: 92,000 v Rangers, Division I, 1 January 1938.
Record Transfer Fee received: £12,500,000 for Victor Wanyama to Southampton (July 2013).
Record Transfer Fee paid: £6,000,000 for Chris Sutton from Chelsea (July 2000) and for John Hartson from Coventry C (August 2001).
Record Victory: 11-0 Dundee, Division I, 26 October 1895. *Record Defeat:* 0-8 v Motherwell, Division I, 30 April 1937.
Most Capped Player: Pat Bonner 80, Republic of Ireland. *Most League Appearances:* 486: Billy McNeill, 1957-75.
Most League Goals in Season (Individual): 50: James McGrory, Division I, 1935-36.
Most Goals Overall (Individual): 397: James McGrory, 1922-39.

Honours
League Champions: (47 times) Division I 1892-93, 1893-94, 1895-96, 1897-98, 1904-05, 1905-06, 1906-07, 1907-08, 1908-09, 1909-10, 1913-14, 1914-15, 1915-16, 1916-17, 1918-19, 1921-22, 1925-26, 1935-36, 1937-38, 1953-54, 1965-66, 1966-67, 1967-68, 1968-69, 1969-70, 1970-71, 1971-72, 1972-73, 1973-74. Premier Division 1976-77, 1978-79, 1980-81, 1981-82, 1985-86, 1987-88, 1997-98, 2000-01, 2001-02, 2003-04, 2005-06, 2006-07, 2007-08, 2011-12, 2012-13; Premiership 2013-14, 2014-15, 2015-16. *Runners-up:* 31 times.
Scottish Cup Winners: (36 times) 1892, 1899, 1900, 1904, 1907, 1908, 1911, 1912, 1914, 1923, 1925, 1927, 1931, 1933, 1937, 1951, 1954, 1965, 1967, 1969, 1971, 1972, 1974, 1975, 1977, 1980, 1985, 1988, 1989, 1995, 2001, 2004, 2005, 2007, 2011, 2013. *Runners-up:* 18 times.

CELTIC – SCOTTISH PREMIERSHIP 2015–16 LEAGUE RECORD

Match No.	Date		Venue	Opponents	Result		H/T Score	Lg Pos.	Goalscorers	Attendance
1	Aug	1	H	Ross Co	W	2-0	2-0	2	Griffiths (pen) [4], Johansen [35]	45,197
2		9	A	Partick Thistle	W	2-0	1-0	1	Rogic [28], Commons [63]	7088
3		12	A	Kilmarnock	D	2-2	1-1	2	Griffiths [3], Bitton [55]	6090
4		15	H	Inverness CT	W	4-2	2-0	2	Lustig [8], Griffiths [12], Armstrong 2 [55, 69]	42,727
5		22	A	Dundee U	W	3-1	2-1	2	Griffiths [17], Durnan (og) [44], McGregor [74]	10,605
6		29	H	St Johnstone	W	3-1	2-1	1	Griffiths [18], Rogic [45], Mulgrew [67]	42,507
7	Sept	12	A	Aberdeen	L	1-2	1-0	2	Griffiths (pen) [35]	20,385
8		20	H	Dundee	W	6-0	2-0	2	Rogic [14], Griffiths [16], Izaguirre 2 [54, 61], Brown [87], Ciftci [87]	48,558
9		26	H	Hearts	D	0-0	0-0	2		46,297
10	Oct	4	A	Hamilton A	W	2-1	2-1	2	Boyata [26], Griffiths [31]	4910
11		17	A	Motherwell	W	1-0	1-0	1	Ciftci [15]	8888
12		25	H	Dundee U	W	5-0	3-0	1	Griffiths [23], Boyata [40], Commons 2 (1 pen) [45 (pl), 53], Kuhl (og) [89]	42,718
13		31	H	Aberdeen	W	3-1	1-0	1	Griffiths 2 (1 pen) [44, 53 (pl)], Forrest [60]	48,161
14	Nov	8	A	Ross Co	W	4-1	1-0	1	Rogic [38], Griffiths 2 [54, 56], Bitton [75]	6042
15		21	H	Kilmarnock	D	0-0	0-0	1		42,770
16		29	A	Inverness CT	W	3-1	1-1	1	McGregor [7], Griffiths [59], Devine (og) [85]	5976
17	Dec	13	A	St Johnstone	W	3-0	1-0	1	Ciftci 2 [35, 67], Boyata [49]	6418
18		19	H	Motherwell	L	1-2	0-0	1	Bitton [49]	42,603
19		27	A	Hearts	D	2-2	1-1	1	Bitton [42], Rogic [70]	16,844
20	Jan	2	A	Partick Thistle	W	1-0	0-0	1	Griffiths [90]	46,067
21		15	A	Dundee U	W	4-1	2-1	1	Griffiths 2 [21, 48], Simunovic [27], Commons [56]	10,848
22		19	A	Hamilton A	W	8-1	5-0	1	Lustig [4], Bitton [9], Rogic [10], Griffiths 3 [22, 34, 54], Forrest [53], McGregor [89]	45,659
23		23	H	St Johnstone	W	3-1	2-1	1	Mackay-Steven 2 [9, 55], Armstrong [43]	43,948
24	Feb	3	A	Aberdeen	L	1-2	0-2	1	Griffiths [90]	19,003
25		13	A	Ross Co	W	2-0	1-0	1	Griffiths [45], Boyata [57]	42,550
26		20	A	Inverness CT	W	3-0	0-0	1	Mackay-Steven [54], Griffiths 2 [59, 90]	43,600
27		26	A	Hamilton A	D	1-1	1-0	1	Griffiths (pen) [35]	5017
28	Mar	2	A	Dundee	D	0-0	0-0	1		41,451
29		12	A	Partick Thistle	W	2-1	1-0	1	Griffiths [45], McGregor [54]	7238
30		19	A	Kilmarnock	W	1-0	0-0	1	Rogic [90]	6867
31	Apr	2	H	Hearts	W	3-1	2-1	1	Mackay-Steven [15], Roberts 2 [35, 49]	49,009
32		5	A	Dundee	D	0-0	0-0	1		9566
33		9	A	Motherwell	W	2-1	1-0	1	Griffiths 2 [44, 75]	9123
34		24	H	Ross Co	D	1-1	1-0	1	Griffiths [23]	41,396
35		30	A	Hearts	W	3-1	1-0	1	Kazim-Richards [17], Roberts [66], Griffiths [85]	16,527
36	May	8	H	Aberdeen	W	3-2	2-0	1	Roberts 2 [7, 20], Lustig [49]	47,877
37		11	A	St Johnstone	L	1-2	1-0	1	Griffiths [53]	5959
38		15	H	Motherwell	W	7-0	3-0	1	Tierney [21], Rogic [26], Lustig [39], Armstrong [50], Roberts [54], Christie [59], Aitchison [77]	49,050

Final League Position: 1

League Cup Winners: (15 times) 1956-57, 1957-58, 1965-66, 1966-67, 1967-68, 1968-69, 1969-70, 1974-75, 1982-83, 1997-98, 1999-2000, 2000-01, 2005-06, 2008-09, 2014-15; *Runners-up:* 15 times.

European: *European Cup/Champions League:* 176 matches (1966-67 winners, 1967-68, 1968-69, 1969-70 runners-up, 1970-71, 1971-72, 1972-73, 1973-74 semi-finals, 1974-75, 1977-78, 1979-80, 1981-82, 1982-83, 1986-87, 1988-89, 1998-99, 2001-02, 2002-03, 2003-04, 2004-05, 2005-06, 2006-07, 2007-08, 2008-09, 2009-10, 2010-11, 2012-13, 2013-14, 2014-15, 2015-16). *Cup Winners' Cup:* 38 matches (1963-64 semi-finals, 1965-66 semi-finals, 1975-76, 1980-81, 1984-85, 1985-86, 1989-90, 1995-96). *UEFA Cup:* 75 matches (*Fairs Cup:* 1962-63, 1964-65. *UEFA Cup:* 1976-77, 1983-84, 1987-88, 1991-92, 1992-93, 1993-94, 1996-97, 1997-98, 1998-99, 1999-2000, 2000-01, 2001-02, 2002-03 runners-up, 2003-04 quarter-finals). *Europa League:* 30 matches (2009-10, 2010-11, 2011-12, 2014-15, 2015-16).

Club colours: Shirt: Green and white hoops. Shorts: White. Socks: White with green hoop.

Goalscorers: *League (93):* Griffiths 31 (4 pens), Rogic 8, Roberts 6, Bitton 5, Armstrong 4, Boyata 4, Ciftci 4, Commons 4 (1 pen), Lustig 4, Mackay-Steven 4, McGregor 4, Forrest 2, Izaguirre 2, Aitchison 1, Brown 1, Christie 1, Johansen 1, Kazim-Richards 1, Mulgrew 1, Simunovic 1, Tierney 1, own goals 3.
William Hill Scottish FA Cup (10): Griffiths 4, Cole 1, Kazim-Richards 1, Mackay-Steven 1, McGregor 1, Rogic 1, Sviatchenko 1.
Scottish League Cup (5): Commons 1, Griffiths 1, Johansen 1, Mackay-Steven 1, Rogic 1.
UEFA Champions League (10): Griffiths 3, Bitton 2, Boyata 2, Johansen 2, Mulgrew 1.
UEFA Europa League (8): Commons 4, Bitton 1, Griffiths 1, Lustig 1, McGregor 1.

Gordon C 35	Ambrose E 15 + 6	Boyata D 25 + 1	van Dijk V 5	Tierney K 23	Brown S 22	Johansen S 22 + 1	Forrest J 10 + 9	Armstrong S 19 + 6	Mackay-Steven G 15 + 10	Griffiths L 32 + 2	Scepovic S — +1	Commons K 16 + 5	Janko S 6 + 4	Lustig M 29 + 1	Izaguirre E 14 + 3	Bitton N 28 + 2	Rogic T 24 + 6	McGregor C 15 + 12	Henderson L — +1	Mulgrew C 8 +5	Bailly L 3	O'Connell E 1	Stokes A 1	Allan S 2 + 11	Thomson J — +1	Blacket T 3	Ciftci N 5 + 6	Simunovic J 11	Cole C — + 4	Christie R 2 + 3	Sviatchenko E 14	Kazim-Richards C 4 + 7	Roberts P 9 + 2	Ralston A — +1	Aitchison J — +1	Match No.
1	2	3	4	5²	6	7³	8	9	10	11¹	12	13	14																							1
1		3	4			9		10¹	13	11		8¹		2	5	6	7²	12	14																	2
1	3	4			7	10²		12	11		8¹	2		5	6²	9	14		13																3
1		3	4		7¹	9		10¹	8	11		13	2²	5	6		14		12																4
	3							8	11²		9	2		5		6³	12		7¹	1	4	10	13	14											5
1		3	4		7¹			10	11		8¹	2		5	6³	9	14	12					13												6
1	12	3			7	9	13		10³	11			2²		6	8¹		5						4	14										7
1	3	4			6		10²		13	11¹		8²	2		5	7	9	14					12												8
1	4¹	3			7		10			11		8		2	5	6	9¹						12												9
	3				7		10¹	12	13	11		8	2²	14	5	6	9³						4												10
1	2	3			7			9²	13	12		10		5	8³	6	14						4	11¹											11
1	2	3		5	6	7		9³	10	11⁷		8¹				13	14						12	4											12
1	14	3		5²		7	10¹	12		11		8		2	13	6	9							4³											13
1	4	3			6¹	8	10	12	11²			2	5	7	9³	14						13												14
1		3		7		8	10¹	12	11			2	5³	6			14						13	4										15
1	4		5	6		8¹	14	11³			2		7	9²	10		12							3	13										16
1	3			6	8	9¹			12		2	5		7²	10		14					11³	4	13											17
1	3	5			10¹				8		2		6	9²	7		12					11	4	13											18
1	13	3²		5	7	12	10¹	14			2		6	9³	8							11	4												19
1	3			5		7	13		14	12		8²	2		6⁸	9²	10						11¹	4											20
1	3		5³		7	12	10²		11		8		2	14		9¹	6					13		4											21
1	3				13	10	8	11³			2	5	6	9¹	7						12			4²	14										22
1	3		5		9	13	10³	8²	11		2	6		7¹			12					4		14											23
1	4		5	6		13	10³	8	11		2²	7		9²			14							3	12										24
1	3		5	7	9¹	14	10³	8	11²		2		6	12										4	13										25
1		3		5	7	9²		10¹	8³	11		2	6					12								13	4		14							26
		3⁴		5	6	7		8²	11		9¹		2		12	1		10³							13	4	14								27
1	3	5		6		12	10¹		11	14	2³			9²			7								13	4	13	8							28
1	14		5	6		13	10³	11³	9¹		2	7		8	4									3	12										29
1	12		5¹	7			10	9²		2	8³	14	6		3									4	11	13									30
1	3		5	6	7		10²	11³		2	12	9¹	13										4	14	8										31
1	3		5	6	7	14	10³	11		2⁵	9			12										4¹	13	8									32
1	3		5	6	9¹	14		11		2	7	12	13		4								10²	8³										33
1	14		5	7			11	13	2	6	9¹	12		4³									3	10²	8										34
1	4		5	8³		13		11²	14	2	7	12	9											3	10	6¹									35
1	12		5		14	10		11		13	2²		6	9¹	7		4¹							3		8									36
	3				6¹			11		2²		5	12	14	7			1		9³					10	4		8	13						37
1	4		2¹		7		10³			14	5	12		9²	6									11	3		8		13						38

CLYDE

Year Formed: 1877. *Ground & Address:* Broadwood Stadium, Cumbernauld, G68 9NE. *Telephone:* 01236 451511.
Fax: 01236 733490. *E-mail:* info@clydefc.co.uk *Website:* www.clydefc.co.uk
Ground Capacity: 8,006 (all seated). *Size of Pitch:* 100m × 68m.
Chairman: John Alexander. *Vice Chairman:* John Taylor. *Secretary:* Gordon Thomson.
Manager: Barry Ferguson. *Assistant Manager:* Robert Malcolm. *Physio:* Imran Alam.
Club Nickname: 'The Bully Wee'.
Previous Grounds: Barrowfield Park 1877-98, Shawfield Stadium 1898-1986, Firhill Stadium 1986-91, Douglas Park 1991-94.
Record Attendance: 52,000 v Rangers, Division I, 21 November 1908.
Record Transfer Fee received: £200,000 from Blackburn R for Gordon Greer (May 2001).
Record Transfer Fee paid: £14,000 for Harry Hood from Sunderland (1966).
Record Victory: 11-1 v Cowdenbeath, Division II, 6 October 1951.
Record Defeat: 0-11 v Dumbarton, Scottish Cup 4th rd, 22 November, 1879; v Rangers, Scottish Cup 4th rd, 13 November 1880.
Most Capped Player: Tommy Ring, 12, Scotland.
Most League Appearances: 420: Brian Ahern, 1971-81; 1987-88.
Most League Goals in Season (Individual): 32: Bill Boyd, 1932-33.
Most Goals Overall (Individual): 124: Tommy Ring, 1950-60.

CLYDE – SCOTTISH LEAGUE TWO 2015–16 LEAGUE RECORD

Match No.	Date	Venue	Opponents	Result	H/T Score	Lg Pos.	Goalscorers	Attendance
1	Aug 8	A	Stirling Alb	W 1-0	0-0	3	Linton (pen) [75]	796
2	15	H	Queen's Park	L 0-2	0-0	6		783
3	22	A	Montrose	L 0-2	0-0	8		460
4	29	H	East Stirling	W 3-1	0-0	7	Higgins, S 2 [53, 73], Greene (og) [55]	502
5	Sept 5	A	Arbroath	W 1-0	1-0	6	Smith [9]	662
6	12	H	Annan Ath	W 4-2	3-1	2	Bolochoweckyj [5], Gormley [15], Linton (pen) [33], Marsh [81]	506
7	19	A	East Fife	L 0-1	0-1	6		669
8	26	H	Berwick R	D 1-1	1-1	5	Higgins, S [17]	504
9	Oct 3	A	Elgin C	D 1-1	1-1	6	Andrews [28]	672
10	17	H	Stirling Alb	L 0-1	0-1	7		628
11	31	A	Queen's Park	D 1-1	1-0	6	Higgins, S [35]	684
12	Nov 7	H	Montrose	W 3-1	2-0	5	Marsh [26], Bolochoweckyj [36], McLaughlin, S [71]	477
13	14	H	Elgin C	W 4-2	2-2	3	Gordon (og) [2], Ferguson, S [27], Gormley [50], Linton [84]	528
14	21	A	Berwick R	W 5-0	1-0	2	Gormley 4 [22, 50, 82, 84], Linton [58]	411
15	Dec 12	H	East Fife	W 2-0	1-0	3	Ferguson, S 2 [34, 84]	527
16	19	H	Arbroath	L 0-2	0-0	3		520
17	26	A	Annan Ath	W 3-2	2-1	2	Linton [5], McLaughlin, S [18], Marsh [64]	549
18	Jan 2	H	Queen's Park	L 0-1	0-1	4		907
19	23	A	Montrose	L 1-2	1-1	5	McLaughlin, M [22]	500
20	30	A	East Fife	L 0-2	0-0	5		522
21	Feb 13	A	Elgin C	L 0-1	0-1	7		728
22	20	H	Berwick R	W 2-1	2-0	6	Linton (pen) [33], Gemmell [34]	539
23	23	A	Stirling Alb	W 2-1	0-1	5	Linton 2 (2 pens) [50, 70]	601
24	27	A	Arbroath	W 1-0	0-0	4	Wilson, C (og) [72]	588
25	Mar 1	H	East Stirling	L 0-1	0-1	4		453
26	5	A	Annan Ath	D 3-3	0-2	4	Higgins, S 2 [60, 72], McLaughlin, S [68]	491
27	8	A	East Stirling	W 3-0	1-0	4	Marsh [44], Higgins, S [62], Durie [74]	326
28	12	H	Elgin C	W 1-0	1-0	3	Marsh [15]	611
29	19	A	East Stirling	W 4-2	2-1	3	Cairnie (og) [7], McLaughlin, S [40], Higgins, S 2 [71, 90]	394
30	22	A	Annan Ath	W 2-1	1-0	2	Gormley [40], McGovern [48]	373
31	26	H	Arbroath	L 1-2	1-0	2	Kirkpatrick [8]	697
32	Apr 2	H	Montrose	D 3-3	1-1	2	Kirkpatrick [19], Durie [66], Linton (pen) [90]	638
33	9	A	Berwick R	L 0-3	0-1	3		637
34	16	H	East Fife	D 0-0	0-0	2		1123
35	23	A	Queen's Park	L 1-2	0-1	4	Gemmell [60]	1270
36	30	H	Stirling Alb	W 3-1	2-0	3	Marsh 2 [14, 41], Gormley [62]	704

Final League Position: 3

Honours
League Champions: Division II 1904-05, 1951-52, 1956-57, 1961-62, 1972-73. Second Division 1977-78, 1981-82, 1992-93, 1999-2000; *Runners-up:* Division II 1903-04, 1905-06, 1925-26, 1963-64. First Division 2002-03, 2003-04.
Scottish Cup Winners: 1939, 1955, 1958; *Runners-up:* 1910, 1912, 1949.
League Challenge Cup Runners-up: 2006-07.

Club colours: Shirt: White with red sleeves and black trim. Shorts: Black. Socks: Red.

Goalscorers: *League (56):* Higgins, S 9, Linton 9 (6 pens), Gormley 8, Marsh 7, McLaughlin, S 4, Ferguson, S 3, Bolochoweckyj 2, Durie 2, Gemmell 2, Kirkpatrick 2, Andrews 1, McGovern 1, McLaughlin, M 1, Smith 1, own goals 4.
William Hill Scottish FA Cup (0).
Scottish League Cup (0).
Petrofac Training Cup (1): Bolochoweckyj 1.
League One Play-Offs (7): Linton 3 (1 pen), Gemmell 2, Kirkpatrick 1, McLaughlin, M 1.

Gibson J 24	Mitchell C 14+1	Bolochoweckyj M 23+2	Smith C 36	Linton S 34+1	McLaughlin S 34+1	Murray H 1+3	Brisbane S 3+4	Higgins S 24+6	Campbell A 8+8	Gormley D 34	Marsh D 28+4	Ferguson S 13+6	McQueen B —+7	Lynass C —+1	McGovern J 27+1	McLaughlin M 23+1	Andrews M 8+5	Durie S 18+4	Higgins A —+1	Capuano F —+1	Watson J 2+9	Millen R 14+1	McMillan M —+1	Waters M 12	Gemmell J 5+5	Slane P 1+4	Glackin R —+1	Kirkpatrick J 6	McMann S 4+2	Match No.
1	2	3	4	5	6	7¹	8²	9	10	11³	12	13	14																	1
1	2²	3	7	5	6		9¹	10	11	8	4	12	13																	2
1	2	3	6	5	7			10	11¹	9	4	8	12																	3
1	2	3	7	5	6		12	9	10³	11¹	4	8²	13	14																4
1	2	3	5	8				11²	9¹	10	4	12	13		6															5
1	2	3²	4	5	7			9	10¹	11	6	12			8	13														6
1	2²	3	4	5	7			11	9	10	6¹	12	13		8															7
1	2	3	4	5	8			11	9²	10	6¹	12	13		7															8
1	2		4	5	8			9¹	13	10²	12	11			7	6	3													9
1	5		4	9¹	7		12	8	13	10	14	11			6²	3	2²													10
1	5	2	4	14	8		9³	10	12	11¹	7				6	3²	13													11
1	5	2	4	9	8	12			11³	7¹	10²				6	3	13	14												12
1	5²	2	4	9	8				11	7	10¹				6	3	12													13
1		3	5	9	8	13		12	11	7²	6¹				10	4	2³	14												14
1		4	5	9	7²	13		12	14	11	8¹	6³			10	3	2													15
1	8	4¹	11	6				13	12	10⁵	9	5			7	3	2													16
1		4	5	9	7			12		10	8¹	6			11	3	2													17
1		3²	5	10	9			13	12	11	8¹	7			6	4	2													18
1		4⁴	8	5	6			9¹		7	12	10			11	3	2²				13									19
1	13		2	8				10	12³	11	6	9¹			7	3	5²				14	4								20
1¹		3	5	9	6		12	10⁴		11	7³				8	4	2⁴				14		13							21
		13	5	9	6			8¹		10					7	4	3²				2			1	11	12				22
		3	4	5	6			8		11	7²				9⁴		2				12	13		1	10¹					23
		3	5	11	8²			6		9³	7³				12		4	2			14			1	10¹	13				24
		3	2	10	9			11			6				7	13	5		12	4²		3	1			8¹				25
		12	5	11	6			10			8				7	9	4¹	2			3	1								26
			4	5	6			11¹		10²	8				9	3	2				7²			1	12	14	13			27
			4	8	5			9¹		10	2				7	3²	13	11			6			1	12					28
			3	4	9	8		11		10	2⁴				6		5				7			1						29
			3²	5	9	8		10¹		11					7	4	13	2			12	6		1						30
			5	8	9			11¹							6	3	4	2⁴			14	7³		1	12			10	13	31
1			4	9	6¹			12		11	2				7²	3	5					10³			14			8	13	32
		2	4	8	13			14		11	5				6¹	3		12			7²			1	10			9³		33
			4	7				10		11	2				3				6	5⁵		1	13	12	8¹	9				34
1			4	9	8			11							3	12			7¹	2		10			6	5				35
1			4	9	8	14		11³		2					3²	13			12	7		10¹			6	5				36

COWDENBEATH

Year Formed: 1882. *Ground & Address:* Central Park, Cowdenbeath KY4 9QQ. *Telephone:* 01383 610166. *Fax:* 01383 512132.
E-mail: office@cowdenbeathfc.com *Website:* www.cowdenbeathfc.com
Ground Capacity: 4,370 (seated: 1,431). *Size of Pitch:* 98m × 59m.
Chairman: Donald Findlay QC. *Finance Director:* David Allan. *Operations:* John Cameron.
Club Nicknames: 'The Blue Brazil', 'Cowden', 'The Miners'.
Head Coach: Liam Fox. *First Team Coach:* Jason Dair. *Physio:* Grant McLeod.
Previous Grounds: North End Park.
Record Attendance: 25,586 v Rangers, League Cup quarter-final, 21 September 1949.
Record Transfer Fee received: £30,000 for Nicky Henderson to Falkirk (March 1994).
Record Victory: 12-0 v Johnstone, Scottish Cup 1st rd, 21 January 1928.
Record Defeat: 1-11 v Clyde, Division II, 6 October 1951; 0-10 v Hearts, Championship, 28 February 2015.
Most Capped Player: Jim Paterson, 3, Scotland.
Most League and Cup Appearances: 491, Ray Allan 1972-75, 1979-89.
Most League Goals in Season (Individual): 54, Rab Walls, Division II, 1938-39.
Most Goals Overall (Individual): 127, Willie Devlin, 1922-26, 1929-30.

COWDENBEATH – SCOTTISH LEAGUE ONE 2015–16 LEAGUE RECORD

Match No.	Date	Venue	Opponents	Result	H/T Score	Lg Pos.	Goalscorers	Attendance
1	Aug 8	H	Stranraer	L	1-2	0-1	7	Brett [62]	380
2	15	A	Dunfermline Ath	L	1-7	0-4	10	Scullion [89]	4009
3	22	H	Albion R	W	1-0	1-0	9	Spence [2]	406
4	29	A	Stenhousemuir	L	2-4	0-2	9	El-Zubaidi [54], Spence [63]	509
5	Sept 5	A	Airdrieonians	L	2-3	1-1	9	Buchanan (pen) [42], Murdoch [58]	773
6	12	H	Peterhead	D	2-2	1-1	9	Smith [15], Spence [83]	301
7	19	H	Forfar Ath	W	2-1	1-0	8	Smith [29], Spence [71]	443
8	26	A	Brechin C	L	0-2	0-0	9		408
9	Oct 3	A	Ayr U	L	0-5	0-2	10		1171
10	17	H	Stenhousemuir	D	2-2	1-0	9	Donaldson [24], Spence [70]	349
11	24	A	Stranraer	W	3-0	1-0	9	Donaldson [11], Miller [58], Buchanan [85]	345
12	31	H	Dunfermline Ath	D	0-0	0-0	8		2097
13	Nov 14	H	Brechin C	W	3-0	1-0	8	Brett (pen) [10], McLean (og) [76], Spence [90]	386
14	21	A	Peterhead	L	0-7	0-4	8		535
15	24	A	Albion R	L	1-2	0-0	8	Spence [46]	287
16	Dec 12	A	Forfar Ath	W	1-0	1-0	7	Spence [31]	493
17	19	H	Airdrieonians	W	3-0	1-0	7	Spence 2 [45, 70], Murdoch [60]	366
18	29	A	Ayr U	W	4-2	3-1	6	Brett [4], Spence 2 [11, 65], Smith [41]	640
19	Jan 2	A	Dunfermline Ath	L	1-2	1-1	7	Spence [37]	5641
20	23	H	Stranraer	L	0-2	0-0	7		402
21	Feb 6	A	Airdrieonians	L	0-2	0-1	8		717
22	9	H	Albion R	L	1-2	1-1	8	Spence [28]	292
23	13	A	Brechin C	D	2-2	1-1	8	Kane [6], Brett [84]	404
24	20	H	Peterhead	L	2-3	1-2	8	McDaid [28], Beaumont [51]	359
25	23	H	Forfar Ath	L	1-4	1-2	8	Brett (pen) [27]	269
26	27	A	Stenhousemuir	W	3-2	0-0	8	Caldwell [51], Byrne [55], Milne [79]	370
27	Mar 1	A	Ayr U	L	1-4	0-3	8	Hughes [52]	856
28	5	H	Airdrieonians	L	1-3	0-1	8	Milne [71]	338
29	12	A	Forfar Ath	D	1-1	1-1	8	Spence [4]	525
30	19	H	Dunfermline Ath	L	0-1	0-0	10		2335
31	26	A	Peterhead	W	1-0	1-0	8	Spence [31]	703
32	Apr 2	H	Ayr U	W	1-0	0-0	8	McKenzie (og) [55]	429
33	9	H	Brechin C	W	2-1	1-0	7	Spence [1], Kane [85]	455
34	16	A	Albion R	D	0-0	0-0	7		356
35	23	H	Stenhousemuir	L	1-3	1-0	9	Sives [42]	474
36	30	A	Stranraer	L	0-1	0-0	9		523

Final League Position: 9

Honours
League Champions: Division II 1913-14, 1914-15, 1938-39. Second Division 2011-12. Third Division 2005-06. *Runners-up:* Division II 1921-22, 1923-24, 1969-70. Second Division 1991-92. Third Division 2000-01, 2008-09. *Promoted to First Division:* 2009-10 (play-offs).
Scottish Cup: Quarter-finals 1931.
League Cup: Semi-finals 1959-60, 1970-71.

Club colours: Shirt: Royal blue with white trim. Shorts: White. Socks: Red.

Goalscorers: *League (46):* Spence 17, Brett 5 (2 pens), Smith 3, Buchanan 2 (1 pen), Donaldson 2, Kane 2, Milne 2, Murdoch 2, Beaumont 1, Byrne 1, Caldwell 1, El-Zubaidi 1, Hughes 1, McDaid 1, Miller 1, Scullion 1, Sives 1, own goals 2.
William Hill Scottish FA Cup (6): Brett 3 (1 pen), Callaghan 1, Johnston 1, Spence 1.
Scottish League Cup (1): Hughes 1.
Petrofac Training Cup (0).
League One Play-Offs (1): Spence 1.

Andrews M 4	Brett D 32	Scullion P 24+3	Donaldson B 21+2	Yaqub M 13+2	Buchanan R 7+3	Kane C 14+7	Hughes D 21+4	Milne L 11+4	Nish C 4	Spence G 35+1	Johnston C 3+18	Orritt S 3+4	Armstrong L —+6	Adamson K 25+1	Miller K 13+6	Armstrong J 3	El-Zubaidi A 23+4	Smith G 14+2	Sneddon J 15	Murdoch A 13	Callaghan L 15+4	Kerr F 13	Adam G 12	Caldwell R 5+11	McDaid D 16+1	Gibbons K 12+1	Beaumont J 9+2	Roman A 5	Byrne D 4+4	Sives C 7	Match No.
2	3	4	5		6¹	7	8			9²	10³	11	12	13	14																1
1	2	12	3	5	9	8				10	11	6¹				4¹	7														2
1	2	4	14		11	8				12	10²	9		6³	13		5	7¹	3												3
1	2	8¹		13	11	7	14			10³	9			5⁶	6	3⁴	4	12													4
	2	3		5	11		8¹			10	9²	13	12			5⁶	6	1	7												5
	2	3		5¹	11³		7			10	9²	12		13	14		4	6¹	1	8											6
	2	3		13	14	8¹				11		9²		5	10³		4	6	1	7	12										7
2⁸	3			11		7				10³	13	9²	12	5	8¹		4	6	1	14											8
	12	2				14	6²			11			13	5	8	3¹	4	10¹	1	7	9										9
	6	3	2			12	13			10				5	7²		4	11¹	1	8	9										10
	6	3	2		12	14				10¹	13			5	7³		4	11²	1	8	9										11
	6	3	2		12					11²	13			5	7		4	10¹	1	8	9										12
	6	3	2¹							11	13	12		5	7		4	10²	1	8	9										13
	6	3	2²			13				11	14		12	5	8		4	10¹	1	7²	9										14
		3	5			7	8			9²	14			6	10¹		4	12	1	11³	13	2									15
	6	4	2			8				10²	13			5			12	11¹	1	7	9	3									16
	6	4	2			7				11	13			5			12	10²	1	8	9¹	3									17
	6	4	2			7				11	12			5				10¹	1	8	9	3									18
	4	2			6¹	7	8²			11	12			5			13	10	1	9	3										19
	6	2				7	8¹			11	13			5			4				9²	3	1	10	12						20
	6	4	2²				13			11	12			3			5						1	10	9	7	8¹				21
	6	3	2¹		7²		13			10	12			5			4				11		1	9	8³	14					22
	9	4	2		7	12				11¹				5			14				3		1	13	10	8¹	6²				23
	6	4	2	12	7					11				5²							3			13	10	8¹	9	1			24
	2	4			6¹	13				11	12			5							3			10²	9	7¹	8	1			25
	2		4		8	6	13			11¹	14			3			5				12			10	7³	1	9²				26
	4	3	12		5	7				14				8							11	9¹	13	6³	1	10²					27
	7¹		2	3	4	6	9			11				5							12	10	8²	1	13						28
		4	2	6		8	9			11	14			5¹			3				12		1	13	10³	7²					29
	2		5			6	9			11				4			8¹				1	13	10	7²				12	3		30
	2		5			7	10			11¹			13	4			9³				1	14	6²	8	12				3		31
	2		5			14	7	10		11¹			12	4			9³				1		6²	8					3		32
	2		5			12	7	10		11³			13	4			9¹				1		6²	8			14		3		33
	2	14	5			9	10²			11			12	4							1	13	7	8³		6¹	3				34
	2		5			10				11			12	4							1	13	9	8	7²	6¹	3				35
	6	2			7³					11	14		5	10	4						1	13	9²	8¹	12	3					36

DUMBARTON

Year Formed: 1872. *Ground:* Dumbarton Football Stadium, Castle Road, Dumbarton G82 1JJ. *Telephone/Fax:* 01389 762569. *E-mail:* enquiries@dumbartonfc.com *Website:* www.dumbartonfootballclub.com
Ground Capacity: total: 2,025. *Size of Pitch:* 104m × 69m.
Chairman: Alan Jardine. *Vice-Chairman:* Colin Hosie.
Manager: Stephen Aitken. *Assistant Manager:* Stephen Farrell. *Physio:* Claire Mitchell.
Club Nickname: 'The Sons', 'Sons of the Rock'.
Previous Grounds: Broadmeadow, Ropework Lane, Townend Ground, Boghead Park, Cliftonhill Stadium.
Record Attendance: 18,000 v Raith R, Scottish Cup, 2 March 1957.
Record Transfer Fee received: £300,000 for Neill Collins to Sunderland (July 2004).
Record Transfer Fee paid: £50,000 for Charlie Gibson from Stirling Alb (1989).
Record Victory: 13-1 v Kirkintilloch Central, Scottish Cup 1st rd, 1 September 1888.
Record Defeat: 1-11 v Albion R, Division II, 30 January 1926: v Ayr U, League Cup, 13 August 1952.
Most Capped Player: James McAulay, 9, Scotland.
Most League Appearances: 298: Andy Jardine, 1957-67.
Most Goals in Season (Individual): 38: Kenny Wilson, Division II, 1971-72. *(League and Cup):* 46 Hughie Gallacher, 1955-56.
Most Goals Overall (Individual): 202: Hughie Gallacher, 1954-62

DUMBARTON – SCOTTISH CHAMPIONSHIP 2015–16 LEAGUE RECORD

Match No.	Date		Venue	Opponents		Result	H/T Score	Lg Pos.	Goalscorers	Atten- dance
1	Aug	8	H	Hibernian	W	2-1	1-1	4	Buchanan [3], Gibson [55]	1552
2		15	H	St Mirren	W	2-1	1-0	2	Gibson [26], Fleming (pen) [85]	3806
3		22	H	Queen of the South	L	0-2	0-1	5		943
4		28	A	Falkirk	L	1-2	1-2	5	Barr [27]	3600
5	Sept	5	H	Alloa Ath	L	0-2	0-0	7		715
6		12	A	Greenock Morton	D	0-0	0-0	7		2016
7		19	H	Rangers	L	1-2	0-0	7	Fleming (pen) [90]	1978
8		26	A	Raith R	L	0-1	0-0	7		1440
9	Oct	3	H	Livingston	W	2-1	1-1	7	Cawley [40], Brophy [82]	819
10		17	A	Hibernian	L	2-4	1-3	8	Gallagher [22], Craig [74]	8221
11		24	H	Falkirk	L	0-5	0-3	8		963
12		31	H	Greenock Morton	L	1-2	0-1	9	Barr [53]	1110
13	Nov	7	A	Queen of the South	L	0-1	0-0	9		1465
14		21	H	Raith R	D	3-3	0-2	9	Saunders 2 [81, 83], Fleming (pen) [87]	707
15	Dec	1	A	Rangers	L	0-4	0-0	9		37,182
16		5	A	Alloa Ath	W	2-0	0-0	7	Docherty [71], Gallagher [87]	492
17		12	H	St Mirren	W	1-0	0-0	7	Fleming [50]	1142
18		19	A	Livingston	D	1-1	0-1	7	Saunders [89]	911
19		26	A	Falkirk	L	0-1	0-1	7		4013
20	Jan	2	H	Rangers	L	0-6	0-1	8		1894
21		23	A	Raith R	D	0-0	0-0	7		1397
22		30	H	Livingston	W	1-0	0-0	7	Docherty [56]	760
23	Feb	13	A	Greenock Morton	L	0-2	0-0	8		1595
24		20	A	St Mirren	L	0-1	0-0	8		2792
25		27	H	Hibernian	W	3-2	2-0	8	Cawley [21], Nade [42], Barr [49]	1345
26	Mar	5	A	Livingston	L	0-2	0-1	8		828
27		8	H	Alloa Ath	W	3-1	2-1	8	Nade 3 [9, 32, 47]	468
28		12	H	Falkirk	D	1-1	0-0	8	Fleming (pen) [90]	734
29		19	A	Queen of the South	L	0-6	0-2	8		1459
30	Apr	2	H	Greenock Morton	D	0-0	0-0	8		994
31		5	A	Rangers	L	0-1	0-0	8		48,568
32		12	H	Queen of the South	W	4-2	1-2	8	Nade 2 [4, 50], Walsh [48], Fleming (pen) [86]	573
33		16	H	Raith R	L	2-3	1-0	8	Nade [12], Saunders [90]	655
34		23	H	St Mirren	W	2-1	1-1	8	Watson (og) [40], Fleming [54]	1387
35		26	A	Hibernian	L	0-4	0-2	8		6686
36	May	1	A	Alloa Ath	D	1-1	0-1	8	McCallum, D [51]	515

Final League Position: 8

Honours
League Champions: Division I 1890-91 (shared with Rangers), 1891-92. Division II 1910-11, 1971-72. Second Division 1991-92. Third Division 2008-09; *Runners-up:* First Division 1983-84. Division II 1907-08. Second Division 1994-95. Third Division 2001-02.
Scottish Cup Winners: 1883; *Runners-up:* 1881, 1882, 1887, 1891, 1897.

Club colours: Shirt: White with yellow and black horizontal stripe. Shorts: White. Socks: White.

Goalscorers: *League (35):* Fleming 7 (5 pens), Nade 7, Saunders 4, Barr 3, Cawley 2, Docherty 2, Gallagher 2, Gibson 2, Brophy 1, Buchanan 1, Craig 1, McCallum, D 1, Walsh 1, own goal 1.
William Hill Scottish FA Cup (7): Fleming 3, Kirkpatrick 2, McCallum, D 1, Waters 1.
Scottish League Cup (1): Cawley 1.
Petrofac Training Cup (3): Gallagher 2, Fleming 1.

Brown M 21	Taggart S 8+5	Graham A 1+1	Buchanan G 29+1	Docherty M 31+3	Cawley K 25+7	Gallagher G 24+7	Routledge J 30+1	Gibson W 13+5	Fleming G 30+5	Craig S 7+4	Kirkpatrick J 7+15	Lindsay J 20+3	Smith G —+2	Barr D 30+1	Waters C 9+7	Brown S 12+4	Wright F 26+1	Ross S 1+4	McCallum C —+1	Brophy E 5+5	McCallum D 3+11	Saunders S 25	Ewings J 15	Walsh T 10+4	Heh K —+4	Nade C 10+2	Heffernan P 4+4	Match No.
1	2	3	4	5	6^1	7	8	9	10^3	11^2	12	13	14															1
1	2	13	4	5	9^3	7	8	6^2	10	11^1	12			3	14													2
1	2		3	5	6^1	7^3	8	9	10	11^2	14	13		4		12												3
1			4	5	6^1	7^3	8		10	11	12		14	2	9^2	3	13											4
1			3	5	12	7	8	11	9	10^2				2	8^1	4			13									5
1	2^2		4	12	11	7	6	14	10				9^3	3	5^1	8						13						6
1	4^8		5^3	6^2	2	7	9		10		12			3	14	8	13					11^1						7
1			5	6	2	8	9^2	7^1			12			3		11	4	13				10^3	14					8
1			3		11^1	6^2	7^3	9	10		13			4		8	5					12	14	2				9
1			3	12		7	5	10^2	11	14	9^3			8		6	4^1	13					2					10
1			3	5		9	7^1	10^3	8	11^2	14			4		6	12					13	2					11
1			4	5		8	12	9	10		6^2	13		3		7						11^3	14	2^1				12
1			4	5^3	14	9	2	13	12		8^2			3	6	7		10^1				11						13
1			4		9	12	10^3	8	14	13	7			3	5^2	6^1						11	2					14
1			5	6^1	7	8^2	9	11	10^3		12			4	13	3						14	2^4					15
1			5	6	12	7	9^3	11	10^2		8^1			3	14	2	4					13						16
1			5	9	6^2	7	13	11^1	12	14	8			3		4						10^3	2					17
1			5	7^1	9	8^2	12	11	13	14	6			3		4						10^3	2^1					18
1			5	9^2	7	8		11			10^3	6		3	14	12	4					13	2^1					19
1	2^3		12	5	9	6	7		11		13	8		3^1		14	4					10^2						20
12			3	5	11^1	8	7		10^3	13	6					4						14	2	1		9^2		21
12			3	5	10^1	8	6		11		9^2			13		4							2	1		7^3	14	22
	2		9		6^3	12	7		10^2					3		4						13	5	1	8	14	11^1	23
1	5^1		2	9	13	10	7^3		11^2					3		4						12	6		8	14		24
13			3	5	8^3			12		14		9		6	10		4						2	1		7^2	11^1	25
			3	5	8^3			12		13		9		6	10^2		4					14	2	1		7^1	11	26
13			3	5	9^1		7^*		10			14	6^3	8	12		4						2	1			11^2	27
			3	5^4	6^2				10			7^1	9^2	8	12		4						2	1	13	11	14	28
			3^1		7^3	12			11			8^2	9	6	5		4						2	1	13	10	14	29
			3	5	12	14	7		9			8^2	6^3				4						2	1	13	10	11^1	30
6			3	5	13	12	7		8^3			9^1			10^2		4					14	2	1		11		31
14			3	5	6^1	12	7		10			8^3					4						2	1	9	11^2	13	32
			3	5	13	6^2	7		10			8^2					4					14	2	1	9	11^1	12	33
			3	5	13		7		8			9^2		4	14	6							2	1	10^2	12	11^1	34
			3	5	6	9^2	7		12			8	10^3	4									2	1	14	13	11^1	35
	5		3	13	6^3				10^1			7		4	8							12	2	1	9^2	14	11	36

DUNDEE

Year Formed: 1893. *Ground & Address:* Dens Park Stadium, Sandeman St, Dundee DD3 7JY. *Telephone:* 01382 889966.
Fax: 01382 832284. *E-mail:* reception@dundeefc.co.uk *Website:* www.dundeefc.co.uk
Ground Capacity: 11,850 (all seated). *Size of Pitch:* 101m × 66m.
Chairman: Tim Keyes. *Managing Director:* John Nelms.
Manager: Paul Hartley. *Assistant Manager:* Gerry McCabe. *Youth Development:* Jimmy Boyle.
Physio: Karen Gibson.
Club Nicknames: 'The Dark Blues' or 'The Dee'.
Previous Grounds: Carolina Port 1893-98.
Record Attendance: 43,024 v Rangers, Scottish Cup 2nd rd, 7 February 1953.
Record Transfer Fee received: £1,500,000 for Robert Douglas to Celtic (October 2000).
Record Transfer Fee paid: £600,000 for Fabian Caballero from Sol de América (Paraguay) (July 2000).
Record Victory: 10-0 Division II v Alloa Ath, 9 March 1947 and v Dunfermline Ath, 22 March 1947.
Record Defeat: 0-11 v Celtic, Division I, 26 October 1895.
Most Capped Player: Alex Hamilton, 24, Scotland.
Most League Appearances: 400: Barry Smith, 1995-2006.
Most League Goals in Season (Individual): 52: Alan Gilzean, 1960-64.
Most Goals Overall (Individual): 113: Alan Gilzean 1960-64.

DUNDEE – SCOTTISH PREMIERSHIP 2015–16 LEAGUE RECORD

Match No.	Date	Venue	Opponents	Result	H/T Score	Lg Pos.	Goalscorers	Atten- dance
1	Aug 1	A	Kilmarnock	W 4-0	2-0	1	Stewart 2 [34, 78], Loy 2 [45, 47]	5207
2	8	H	Hearts	L 1-2	1-0	2	Hemmings [5]	8222
3	11	A	Dundee U	D 2-2	0-0	4	Stewart [81], McPake [90]	11,835
4	15	H	St Johnstone	W 2-1	2-0	4	McPake [16], Hemmings [39]	6176
5	22	A	Aberdeen	L 0-2	0-0	6		13,621
6	29	H	Inverness CT	D 1-1	0-0	6	Hemmings [90]	4767
7	Sept 12	A	Partick Thistle	W 1-0	0-0	5	Stewart [77]	2946
8	20	A	Celtic	L 0-6	0-2	6		48,558
9	26	H	Ross Co	D 3-3	1-3	6	Stewart [20], Loy 2 (1 pen) [54 (p), 69]	5128
10	Oct 3	H	Motherwell	W 2-1	0-0	6	Loy [58], Holt [70]	5152
11	17	A	Hamilton A	D 1-1	0-0	6	Holt [47]	2862
12	24	A	Kilmarnock	L 1-2	0-1	7	Healey [76]	4970
13	31	A	Inverness CT	D 1-1	0-0	7	Loy (pen) [50]	2940
14	Nov 7	H	Partick Thistle	D 1-1	0-1	7	Hemmings [85]	5067
15	21	A	Hearts	D 1-1	0-1	6	Loy [67]	16,736
16	27	A	St Johnstone	D 1-1	1-1	6	Hemmings [3]	4598
17	Dec 5	H	Aberdeen	L 0-2	0-2	7		6327
18	12	A	Motherwell	L 1-3	0-2	9	Harkins [68]	3512
19	19	H	Hamilton A	W 4-0	4-0	6	Hemmings 3 [5, 21, 26], Stewart [19]	4568
20	26	A	Ross Co	L 2-5	1-1	7	Hemmings 2 [5, 53]	3687
21	Jan 2	H	Dundee U	W 2-1	1-1	7	Hemmings [41], Ross [62]	11,025
22	16	A	Partick Thistle	W 4-2	4-1	6	Hemmings (pen) [7], Harkins 2 [10, 37], Stewart [15]	3222
23	22	A	Aberdeen	L 0-1	0-1	6		11,805
24	30	H	Motherwell	D 2-2	1-2	6	McGowan [6], Hemmings (pen) [88]	4960
25	Feb 12	H	St Johnstone	W 2-0	1-0	5	Hemmings 2 [21, 51]	4876
26	20	A	Kilmarnock	D 0-0	0-0	6		3688
27	27	H	Inverness CT	D 1-1	0-1	6	Hemmings [86]	5048
28	Mar 2	A	Celtic	D 0-0	0-0	5		41,451
29	12	H	Hearts	L 0-1	0-0	7		6195
30	20	A	Dundee U	D 2-2	2-0	7	Hemmings 2 [34, 45]	11,603
31	Apr 2	H	Ross Co	W 5-2	3-2	6	Stewart 2 [7, 90], Hemmings [9], Loy [38], Wighton [65]	5095
32	5	H	Celtic	D 0-0	0-0	6		9566
33	9	A	Hamilton A	L 1-2	0-2	7	Harkins [63]	2764
34	23	A	Partick Thistle	W 2-1	1-0	7	Hemmings 2 [34, 81]	2769
35	May 2	H	Dundee U	W 2-1	0-0	7	Gadzhalov [77], Wighton [90]	10,088
36	7	H	Hamilton A	L 0-1	0-1	7		4757
37	11	H	Kilmarnock	D 1-1	1-0	8	Loy [18]	4335
38	14	A	Inverness CT	L 0-4	0-0	8		3794

Final League Position: 8

Honours
League Champions: Division I 1961-62. First Division 1978-79, 1991-92, 1997-98. Division II 1946-47; Championship 2013-14.
Runners-up: Division I 1902-03, 1906-07, 1908-09, 1948-49. First Division 1980-81, 2007-08, 2009-10, 2011-12.
Scottish Cup Winners: 1910; *Runners-up:* 1925, 1952, 1964, 2003.
League Cup Winners: 1951-52, 1952-53, 1973-74; *Runners-up:* 1967-68, 1980-81, 1995-96.
League Challenge Cup Winners: 1990-91, 2009-10.

European: *European Cup:* 8 matches (1962-63 semi-finals). *Cup Winners' Cup:* 2 matches: (1964-65).
UEFA Cup: 22 matches: (*Fairs Cup:* 1967-68 semi-finals. *UEFA Cup:* 1971-72, 1973-74, 1974-75, 2003-04).

Club colours: Shirt: Navy blue with white trim. Shorts: White with navy trim. Socks: Navy blue with red top.

Goalscorers: *League (53):* Hemmings 21 (2 pens), Loy 9 (2 pens), Stewart 9, Harkins 4, Holt 2, McPake 2, Wighton 2, Gadzhalov 1, Healey 1, McGowan 1, Ross 1.
William Hill Scottish FA Cup (8): Hemmings 3, Stewart 2, Harkins 1, Holt 1, McGinn 1.
Scottish League Cup (1): Hemmings 1.

Bain S 27	McGinn P 33+1	Konrad T 20+7	Etxabeguren Leanizbarrutia J 20+3	Holt K 34	Ross N 36+1	Harkins G 22+8	Thomson K 11+1	Stewart G 36+1	Hemmings K 34+3	Loy R 21+8	McGowan P 27+3	Ferry S —+1	McPake J 16	Low N 15+6	Megatt D 2+4	Tankulic L —+1	Carreiro D —+2	Irvine G 6+1	Calder R 3+8	Healey R 4+3	Curran J —+3	Gadzhalov K 8+6	Kerr C 7+3	O'Dea D 16	Arturo P —+3	Wighton C 7+6	Mitchell D 1+1	Colquhoun C 2+1	Black A —+1	Match No.
1	2	3	4	5	6	7	8^1	9	10^2	11	12	13																		1
1	2		4	5	6	9		11	10		8		3																	2
1	2	12	4^1	5	8	6	7^2	9	11^3	10	13		3	14																3
1	2	12	3	5	6	9		11	10^3		7		4^1	8^2	13	14														4
1	2	9^1	3	5	6	10^4		7	11		8		4				12													5
1	2	3^1		8		7		10	11		6		4	9	12		13	5^2												6
1	2	4	12		8	7		11	10	14		3^1	6^2				5	13												7
1	2	4		9	8	7^1	10	11^3	13		3	6				5	12	14												8
1	2	13	4	5	7	12	8^1	6	10^5	11		3^2				9	14													9
1	2	3	4	5	6	12	7^2	9^1	10	11^3		8				14	13													10
1	2	4	3^2	5	8	7		6	10			12	13			9^1	11^3	14												11
1	2		5	8	7^3		6	9^2	10	14		3	13	4^1		11	12													12
1	2	4		5	6		7	12	11^2	8		9^1				13	10	3												13
1	2	4		5	6		11	12	10	7		8^2				13	9^1	3												14
1	2	12	3^2	5	9		8	6	10	11	7	4^1						13												15
1	2	13	4^2	5	7^1	12		11	10	9	8	6^3				14		13												16
1	2		4	5	6^1	12		9	11	10^2	7	3	8				13													17
1	2	12	4^1		13	7	8	11	10^6	9		3	6^2			5	14													18
1	13	4		5	12	8		7	10	11^3	14	6	3	9		2^2														19
1		4		5	7^1	8		10	11	12	6	3	9^2			2	13													20
1	2	4		5	8	10^2	13	11			7	3^1	9				14			12		6^3								21
1	5	4		2	6	9		10	11^3	14	7	8^1						13	12	3^2										22
1	5	3		2^1	7	10		9	11	13	8	6^2						12	4											23
1	2	4		5	6^2	9		8	11	10^1	7							3	12	13										24
1	2	4	13	5	6	8^2		11	10	9	7^1	12						3												25
1	2	3		5	7	9^1		8	11	10	6							4	12											26
1	2	3		5	6	9		8	10^2	7								12	4^1	13										27
1	2	3		5	9	13		14	12	11^1	8		7^2					4	6			10^3								28
1	2			5	7	9^2		6	11	13	8							4^1	10	3		12								29
1^1	2	12^2		5	6	9		8	11		7				13^3			4^1	10	3			14							30
	2	3^1	8	7		9^3		11	10^2	6		12					14	5	4	13^1	1									31
1	2	3	9	8	13		7	10^1	11^2	6								5	4	12										32
1	4	5^2	2	7	12	9		11	8	13								6	3	10^1										33
1	2			5	6	9^2		8	11	7								3	12	4		10^1	13							34
1	2	12		5	8	9		10	6		7^1							3	4	11										35
1	5	3^1	8	7		11	10	12		6								2	4	9		10^3								36
1	2	3	5	6		9^1		11^1	10								13		4	12	8	7								37
1	2^3	3	5	8		6^2		11	10				13					4	12	9		7^1	14							38

DUNDEE UNITED

Year Formed: 1909 (1923). *Ground & Address:* Tannadice Park, Tannadice St, Dundee DD3 7JW. *Telephone:* 01382
833166. *Fax:* 01382 889398. *E-mail:* enquiries@dundeeunited.co.uk *Website:* www.dufc.co
Ground Capacity: 14,223 (all seated). *Size of Pitch:* 100m × 66m.
Chairman: Stephen Thompson, OBE. *Vice-Chair:* Justine Mitchell. *Secretary:* Spence Anderson.
Manager: Ray McKinnon. *Assistant Manager:* Laurie Ellis. *Physio:* Jeff Clarke.
Club Nicknames: 'The Terrors', 'The Arabs'.
Previous Grounds: None.
Record Attendance: 28,000 v Barcelona, Fairs Cup, 16 November 1966.
Record Transfer Fee received: £4,000,000 for Duncan Ferguson from Rangers (July 1993).
Record Transfer Fee paid: £750,000 for Steven Pressley from Coventry C (July 1995).
Record Victory: 14-0 v Nithsdale Wanderers, Scottish Cup 1st rd, 17 January 1931.
Record Defeat: 1-12 v Motherwell, Division II, 23 January 1954.
Most Capped Player: Maurice Malpas, 55, Scotland.
Most League Appearances: 618, Maurice Malpas, 1980-2000.
Most Appearances in European Matches: 76, Dave Narey (record for Scottish player).
Most League Goals in Season (Individual): 40: John Coyle, Division II, 1955-56.
Most Goals Overall (Individual): 199: Peter McKay, 1947-54.

DUNDEE UNITED – SCOTTISH PREMIERSHIP 2015–16 LEAGUE RECORD

Match No.	Date	Venue	Opponents	Result	H/T Score	Lg Pos.	Goalscorers	Attendance
1	Aug 2	H	Aberdeen	L	0-1	0-0	9		10,706
2	8	A	Motherwell	W	2-0	0-0	4	Laing (og) [83], Murray [90]	4859
3	11	H	Dundee	D	2-2	0-0	5	Spittal 2 [64, 67]	11,835
4	15	A	Hamilton A	L	0-4	0-3	7		2173
5	22	H	Celtic	L	1-3	1-2	8	Erskine (pen) [45]	10,605
6	29	A	Ross Co	L	1-2	0-2	9	Dillon [61]	4014
7	Sept 12	A	Kilmarnock	L	1-2	0-1	11	McKay (pen) [66]	8264
8	19	H	Inverness CT	D	1-1	1-0	11	McKay [7]	6235
9	26	A	St Johnstone	L	1-2	1-0	11	McKay (pen) [24]	4634
10	Oct 3	A	Partick Thistle	L	0-3	0-1	12		3675
11	18	H	Hearts	L	0-1	0-1	12		7461
12	25	A	Celtic	L	0-5	0-3	12		42,718
13	31	H	Ross Co	W	1-0	0-0	12	McKay (pen) [81]	5549
14	Nov 7	A	Aberdeen	L	0-2	0-0	12		12,805
15	21	H	St Johnstone	L	1-2	1-2	12	McKay [33]	7020
16	28	H	Hamilton A	L	1-2	1-0	12	McKay [29]	5788
17	Dec 5	A	Kilmarnock	D	1-1	1-1	12	McKay (pen) [24]	2828
18	12	H	Partick Thistle	L	0-1	0-0	12		6256
19	19	A	Inverness CT	D	2-2	1-0	12	Rankin [26], McKay [81]	2981
20	30	A	Hearts	L	2-3	2-3	12	McKay (pen) [2], Fraser [45]	16,721
21	Jan 2	A	Dundee	L	1-2	1-1	12	Spittal [15]	11,025
22	15	H	Celtic	L	1-4	1-2	12	Murray [31]	10,848
23	23	H	Kilmarnock	W	5-1	4-0	12	Spittal 2 [8, 39], Durnan [32], Rankin [44], Dillon [78]	7729
24	Feb 13	A	Hamilton A	D	0-0	0-0	12		3902
25	16	H	Motherwell	L	0-3	0-1	12		6251
26	20	H	Hearts	W	2-1	1-0	12	Demel [43], Paton [88]	8031
27	27	A	Ross Co	W	3-0	1-0	12	Paton [10], McKay [71], Dow [76]	3564
28	Mar 2	A	Aberdeen	L	0-1	0-1	12		9737
29	11	A	Motherwell	L	1-2	1-1	12	Anier [22]	4210
30	20	H	Dundee	D	2-2	0-2	12	McKay 2 (1 pen) [53 (p), 90]	11,603
31	Apr 2	A	St Johnstone	W	1-0	1-0	12	Dow [22]	5784
32	5	A	Partick Thistle	L	0-1	0-0	12		4533
33	9	H	Inverness CT	L	0-2	0-1	12		6927
34	24	H	Hamilton A	L	1-3	0-1	12	Murray [89]	5884
35	May 2	A	Dundee	L	1-2	0-0	12	Ofere [54]	10,088
36	6	A	Inverness CT	W	3-2	2-0	12	Murray 2 [6, 45], Ofere [55]	3587
37	10	H	Partick Thistle	D	3-3	0-2	12	Frans (og) [67], Ofere [86], Johnson [90]	4689
38	14	A	Kilmarnock	W	4-2	1-2	12	Durnan [12], Murray 2 [73, 82], Soutar [86]	2702

Final League Position: 12

Honours: *League Champions:* Premier Division 1982-83.
Division II 1924-25, 1928-29.
Runners-up: Division II 1930-31, 1959-60. First Division 1995-96.
Scottish Cup Winners: 1994, 2010; *Runners-up:* 1974, 1981, 1985, 1987, 1988, 1991, 2005, 2014.
League Cup Winners: 1979-80, 1980-81; *Runners-up:* 1981-82, 1984-85, 1997-98, 2007-08, 2014-15.
League Challenge Cup Runners-up: 1995-96.

European: *European Cup:* 8 matches (1983-84, semi-finals). *Cup Winners' Cup:* 10 matches (1974-75, 1988-89, 1994-95).
UEFA Cup: 86 matches (*Fairs Cup:* 1966-67, 1969-70, 1970-71. *UEFA Cup:* 1975-76, 1977-78, 1978-79, 1979-80, 1980-81, 1981-82, 1982-83, 1984-85, 1985-86, 1986-87 runners-up, 1987-88, 1989-90, 1990-91, 1993-94, 1997-98, 2005-06). *Europa League:* 6 matches (2010-2011, 2011-12, 2012-13).

Club colours: Shirt: Tangerine with black trim. Shorts: Black. Socks: Tangerine.

Goalscorers: *League (45):* McKay 12 (6 pens), Murray 7, Spittal 5, Ofere 3, Dillon 2, Dow 2, Durnan 2, Paton 2, Rankin 2, Anier 1, Demel 1, Erskine 1 (1 pen), Fraser 1, Johnson 1, Soutar 1, own goals 2.
William Hill Scottish FA Cup (5): Anier 2, Fraser 1, McKay 1, Spittal 1.
Scottish League Cup (3): Fraser 1, Morris 1, Spittal 1.

DUNFERMLINE ATHLETIC

Year Formed: 1885. *Ground & Address:* East End Park, Halbeath Road, Dunfermline KY12 7RB.
Telephone: 01383 724295. *Fax:* 01383 745 959. *E-mail:* enquiries@dafc.co.uk
Website: www.dafc.co.uk
Ground Capacity: 11,380 (all seated). *Size of Pitch:* 105m × 65m.
Chairman: Bob Garmony. *Football matters:* Kip McBay.
Manager: Allan Johnston. *Assistant Manager:* Sandy Clark. *Head Coach:* John Potter. *Physio:* Kenny Murray.
Club Nickname: 'The Pars'.
Previous Grounds: None.
Record Attendance: 27,816 v Celtic, Division I, 30 April 1968.
Record Transfer Fee received: £650,000 for Jackie McNamara to Celtic (October 1995).
Record Transfer Fee paid: £540,000 for Istvan Kozma from Bordeaux (September 1989).
Record Victory: 11-2 v Stenhousemuir, Division II, 27 September 1930.
Record Defeat: 1-13 v St. Bernard's, Scottish Cup, 1st rd; 15 September 1883.
Most Capped Player: Colin Miller 16 (61), Canada.
Most League Appearances: 497: Norrie McCathie, 1981-96.
Most League Goals in Season (Individual): 53: Bobby Skinner, Division II, 1925-26.
Most Goals Overall (Individual): 212: Charles Dickson, 1954-64.

DUNFERMLINE ATHLETIC – SCOTTISH LEAGUE ONE 2015–16 LEAGUE RECORD

Match No.	Date	Venue	Opponents	Result	H/T Score	Lg Pos.	Goalscorers	Atten- dance
1	Aug 8	A	Brechin C	W 6-1	4-0	1	El Bakhtaoui 2 [6, 44], Moffat [23], Cardle [31], Wallace [80], Falkingham [90]	1214
2	15	H	Cowdenbeath	W 7-1	4-0	1	El Bakhtaoui 2 [2, 8], Moffat [13], Cardle 2 [32, 88], Hopkirk [65], Wallace [73]	4009
3	22	A	Peterhead	L 1-2	1-1	3	Moffat [44]	996
4	29	H	Stranraer	W 3-1	2-0	2	El Bakhtaoui [14], Talbot [22], Geggan [51]	3330
5	Sept 5	A	Forfar Ath	W 4-0	2-0	1	Cardle 3 [4, 45, 69], Geggan [90]	1618
6	12	H	Ayr U	L 0-2	0-1	3		3596
7	19	A	Stenhousemuir	W 5-0	3-0	2	Cardle [11], El Bakhtaoui 2 [24, 52], Byrne [44], Antoine-Curier [85]	1554
8	26	H	Airdrieonians	D 1-1	0-1	2	Moffat [74]	3391
9	Oct 3	H	Albion R	W 3-0	1-0	2	Cardle [43], McCabe [62], El Bakhtaoui [75]	3086
10	17	A	Stranraer	W 3-0	2-0	1	Moffat [4], Richards-Everton [32], Antoine-Curier [72]	667
11	24	H	Forfar Ath	W 4-0	1-0	1	Hopkirk [8], Cardle [63], Wallace 2 [75, 84]	3198
12	31	A	Cowdenbeath	D 0-0	0-0	2		2097
13	Nov 7	H	Peterhead	D 0-0	0-0	2		2915
14	14	A	Airdrieonians	W 2-0	1-0	2	Moffat [7], Byrne [54]	1371
15	21	A	Albion R	D 1-1	1-1	2	Geggan [15]	1041
16	Dec 5	H	Brechin C	W 3-1	2-0	1	El Bakhtaoui [34], Paton [41], Hopkirk [71]	2361
17	12	A	Ayr U	W 2-1	1-1	1	Moffat [34], Hopkirk [69]	2076
18	19	H	Stenhousemuir	W 1-0	0-0	1	Rooney [78]	2952
19	26	A	Forfar Ath	W 4-2	1-1	1	El Bakhtaoui 2 [18, 49], Cardle [60], Wallace [79]	1443
20	Jan 2	H	Cowdenbeath	W 2-1	1-1	1	Moffat 2 (1 pen) [18, 65 (p)]	5641
21	23	A	Peterhead	D 0-0	0-0	1		1115
22	29	H	Airdrieonians	L 0-1	0-1	1		2545
23	Feb 6	A	Stenhousemuir	W 3-0	0-0	1	El Bakhtaoui [41], Geggan 2 [52, 78]	1328
24	13	H	Ayr U	W 3-2	1-2	1	Moffat (pen) [45], Devlin (og) [56], El Bakhtaoui [65]	3319
25	20	A	Brechin C	W 2-1	2-1	1	Falkingham [6], Richards-Everton [41]	1053
26	27	H	Stranraer	W 6-1	2-0	1	El Bakhtaoui 2 [24, 54], Cardle 3 [42, 57, 73], McKay [52]	3016
27	Mar 5	H	Stenhousemuir	W 5-0	2-0	1	Falkingham [28], Paton [31], El Bakhtaoui [54], Wallace 2 [69, 79]	3017
28	8	H	Albion R	D 1-1	0-0	1	Wallace [75]	2729
29	12	A	Ayr U	W 2-0	0-0	1	El Bakhtaoui 2 [62, 68]	2190
30	19	A	Cowdenbeath	W 1-0	0-0	1	McCabe [81]	2335
31	26	H	Brechin C	W 3-1	2-1	1	El Bakhtaoui 3 [7, 24, 90]	4402
32	Apr 2	A	Albion R	W 1-0	0-0	1	El Bakhtaoui [87]	1413
33	9	H	Forfar Ath	D 2-2	1-1	1	Moffat 2 [30, 60]	3201
34	16	A	Stranraer	L 1-4	1-0	1	McKay [35]	545
35	23	A	Airdrieonians	L 0-3	0-3	1		1131
36	30	H	Peterhead	W 1-0	1-0	1	Cardle [17]	6236

Final League Position: 1

Honours
League Champions: First Division 1988-89, 1995-96, 2010-11. Division II 1925-26. Second Division 1985-86. League One 2015-16. *Runners-up:* First Division 1986-87, 1993-94, 1994-95, 1999-2000. Division II 1912-13, 1933-34, 1954-55, 1957-58, 1972-73. Second Division 1978-79. League One 2013-14.
Scottish Cup Winners: 1961, 1968; *Runners-up:* 1965, 2004, 2007.
League Cup Runners-up: 1949-50, 1991-92, 2005-06.
League Challenge Cup Runners-up: 2007-08.

European: *Cup Winners' Cup:* 14 matches (1961-62, 1968-69 semi-finals). *UEFA Cup:* 32 matches (*Fairs Cup:* 1962-63, 1964-65, 1965-66, 1966-67, 1969-70. *UEFA Cup:* 2004-05, 2007-08).

Club colours: Shirt: White with black stripes. Shorts: White with black trim. Socks: White with black trim.

Goalscorers: *League (83):* El Bakhtaoui 22, Cardle 14, Moffat 12 (2 pens), Wallace 8, Geggan 5, Hopkirk 4, Falkingham 3, Antoine-Curier 2, Byrne 2, McCabe 2, McKay 2, Paton 2, Richards-Everton 2, Rooney 1, Talbot 1, own goal 1.
William Hill Scottish FA Cup (3): El Bakhtaoui 1, Geggan 1, McKay 1.
Scottish League Cup (9): El Bakhtaoui 4, Byrne 2, Cardle 1, Paton 1, Wallace 1 (1 pen).
Petrofac Training Cup (7): El Bakhtaoui 3, Moffat 3 (1 pen), Wallace 1.

Murdoch S 34	Williamson R 5+1	Fordyce C 6	Richards-Everton B 34	Martin L 18	Paton M 30+2	Geggan A 29+1	Byrne S 14+8	Cardle J 27+2	Moffat M 29+5	El Bakhtaoui F 31+1	Talbot J 33+1	Wallace R 11+23	Falkingham J 23+5	Hopkirk D 11+18	Rooney S 7+4	Antoine-Curier M 1+8	McCabe R 7+8	McAusland M 13	McKay B 16	Reid C 11+2	Crossan P —+2	Hutton D 2	Robinson S 2	Duthie C 2+1	Match No.
1	2	3^1	4	5	6	7	8^3	9	10	11^2	12	13	14												1
1	2	3	4	5	6^3	8	7	9	10^1	11^2		12	13	14											2
1		3	4	2	6^1	7	8^1	9^2	10	11	5	12	13	14											3
1		3	4	2^3	6	7	14	9^2	11^{11}	10	5	12	8		13										4
1		3	4	2	6^3	7	14	9^1	10	11	5	12	8^2		13										5
1		3^1	4	2	6^2	8		9	10^3	11	5	14	7		12	13									6
1		4	3		6^3	8	7	9^1		11	5	10		13	2^2	14	12								7
1		4	5		2	7^1	9	13	11		10	8^2		12	6	3									8
1		4		6	7		9^1	10^3	11	5	14		13	2^2	12	8	3								9
1		4	2	6^3	7	8	9^2	10		5	13		11^1		12	14	3								10
1		4	2	14	7	6	8^2	10^3	11^2	5	12		9		13		3								11
1		4	2	14	6	9	8	10^1	11^2	5	12		7^2		13		3								12
1		4	2	6^2	8	14	9	13	11	5	12				10^1	7^3	3								13
1		4	2	9	7	12		10	11	5	6					8^1	3								14
1		4	2	6	7^1	8		10	11	5		12	9				3								15
1		4	2	6		7	9^2	10^3	11^1	5	13	8	12		14		3								16
1		4	2	6		8	9^1	10^1	11	5		7	12				3								17
1		3		6^3	2	8	12	9^2	10	5	14	7	11	13			4^1								18
1		4		6^2	8		11	10^1	9	5	12	7	13	2			3								19
1		4		6	7	12	9^2	10	11^3	5	14	8	13	2			3^1								20
1		4		6^2	7		9	11^1	10	5	13	8	12				3								21
1		4		6	7	13		10	11	5	12	8^1	9^2	2^9		14	3								22
1		4		6^3	7^1		9	10^2	11	5	12	8	13				14			3	2				23
1		4		6	7		9^1	10	11^2	5	12	8	13							3	2				24
1		4		6^1	7		9^2	10	11	5	13	8	12							3	2				25
1		4		6	8		9^2	10^1	11^3	5	13	7	14							3	2	12			26
1		4		6		8	9	10^3	11^3	5	12	7^2	14			13				3	2				27
1		4		6	7^1		9^2	10^3	11	5	12	8	13				14			3	2				28
1		4		6^2	7		9	12	11^1	5	10^3	8	13				14			3	2				29
1		4		6^1	7		9		11	5	10	8^2	12				13			3	2				30
1		4		6	7			12	11	5	10^2	8	9^1							3	2	13			31
		4		7	6		13	14	11	5	10^2		9^2	12		8			3	2^1	1				32
1	2^1		4	6				10		5	11	12			8			3	13				7^2	9	33
	2		4^2		12		11		5	10	8	9						3	13		1	7	6^1		34
1	2^1		4		12			10^2		5	6	9	11	7		8		3						13	35
1	14		4		7	13	9	10	12	5	11^2	8^1	6					3	2^3						36

EAST FIFE

Year Formed: 1903. *Ground & Address:* Bayview Stadium, Harbour View, Methil, Fife KY8 3RW. *Telephone:* 01333 426323. *Fax:* 01333 426376. *E-mail:* office@eastfifefc.info. *Website:* www.eastfifefc.info
Ground Capacity: 1,992. *Size of Pitch:* 105m × 65m.
Chairman: Jim Stevenson. *Vice-Chairman:* David Marshall.
Manager: Gary Naysmith. *Assistant Manager:* Douglas Anderson. *Physio:* George Good.
Club Nickname: 'The Fifers'.
Previous Ground: Bayview Park.
Record Attendance: 22,515 v Raith Rovers, Division I, 2 January 1950 (Bayview Park); 4,700 v Rangers, League One, 26 October 2013 (Bayview Stadium).
Record Transfer Fee received: £150,000 for Paul Hunter from Hull C (March 1990).
Record Transfer Fee paid: £70,000 for John Sludden from Kilmarnock (July 1991).
Record Victory: 13-2 v Edinburgh C, Division II, 11 December 1937.
Record Defeat: 0-9 v Hearts, Division I, 5 October 1957.
Most Capped Player: George Aitken, 5 (8), Scotland.
Most League Appearances: 517: David Clarke, 1968-86.
Most League Goals in Season (Individual): 41: Jock Wood, Division II; 1926-27 and Henry Morris, Division II, 1947-48.
Most Goals Overall (Individual): 225: Phil Weir, 1922-35.

EAST FIFE – SCOTTISH LEAGUE TWO 2015–16 LEAGUE RECORD

Match No.	Date		Venue	Opponents	Result		H/T Score	Lg Pos.	Goalscorers	Atten-dance
1	Aug	8	A	East Stirling	L	0-1	0-0	7		382
2		15	H	Berwick R	W	5-0	3-0	3	Austin, N [4], Smith [24], Wilkie 2 [35, 50], Sutherland [75]	516
3		22	H	Elgin C	W	2-1	1-1	2	Page [9], Austin, N [60]	538
4		29	A	Queen's Park	W	2-0	1-0	1	Murray [27], Austin, N [62]	505
5	Sept	5	A	Annan Ath	L	0-2	0-1	4		510
6		12	H	Arbroath	L	0-1	0-0	6		518
7		19	H	Clyde	W	1-0	1-0	5	Smith [13]	669
8		26	A	Montrose	W	4-1	1-1	1	Austin, N 3 [40, 48, 78], Mercer [59]	572
9	Oct	3	H	Stirling Alb	D	1-1	1-0	2	Austin, N [32]	673
10		17	A	Berwick R	D	1-1	0-0	2	Wilkie [89]	531
11		31	H	Annan Ath	L	0-1	0-1	3		517
12	Nov	7	A	Arbroath	D	1-1	1-0	3	Page [11]	596
13		14	H	East Stirling	W	5-3	1-2	2	Wilkie [11], Insall [54], Austin, N 2 [61, 90], Slattery [65]	543
14		21	A	Elgin C	L	2-4	2-2	5	Wilkie [10], Austin, N [37]	654
15	Dec	8	H	Queen's Park	L	0-2	0-0	5		345
16		12	A	Clyde	L	0-2	0-1	6		527
17		19	H	Montrose	D	1-1	1-1	6	Insall [35]	419
18		26	A	Stirling Alb	W	3-1	2-1	6	Austin, N 3 [21, 45, 80]	645
19	Jan	2	H	Elgin C	L	0-2	0-0	6		591
20		9	H	Berwick R	W	1-0	0-0	5	Austin, N [47]	445
21		16	A	Annan Ath	W	4-2	4-0	3	Insall [8], Austin, N [35], Kerr [39], Wilkie [43]	481
22		23	A	East Stirling	W	3-1	2-1	3	Wilkie [17], Austin, N [24], Coote [87]	356
23		30	H	Clyde	W	2-0	0-0	2	Insall [54], Wilkie [66]	522
24	Feb	6	A	Montrose	D	2-2	1-0	2	Wilkie [10], Kerr [58]	501
25		13	H	Arbroath	W	2-1	1-0	2	Austin, N [45], Insall [64]	533
26		20	A	Stirling Alb	W	1-0	0-0	1	Smith [72]	707
27		27	A	Queen's Park	L	0-3	0-0	2		561
28	Mar	5	A	Elgin C	W	3-1	2-1	1	Austin, N 2 [6, 24], Smith [76]	977
29		12	H	Annan Ath	W	4-2	2-0	1	Insall 2 [4, 69], Page 2 [6, 58]	600
30		19	A	Stirling Alb	W	6-0	2-0	1	Brown [3], Smith [16], Austin, N 2 [73, 78], Campbell [85], Coote [87]	709
31		26	H	Queen's Park	D	1-1	1-1	1	Insall [2]	901
32	Apr	2	A	Arbroath	W	1-0	1-0	1	Kerr [26]	816
33		9	H	Montrose	W	3-0	3-0	1	Page [13], Campbell [16], Austin, N [24]	854
34		16	A	Clyde	D	0-0	0-0	1		1123
35		23	A	Berwick R	L	0-2	0-0	1		707
36		30	H	East Stirling	D	1-1	0-0	1	Smith [53]	1360

Final League Position: 1

Honours
League Champions: Division II 1947-48. Third Division 2007-08. League Two 2015-16.
Runners-up: Division II 1929-30, 1970-71. Second Division 1983-84, 1995-96. Third Division 2002-03.
Scottish Cup Winners: 1938; *Runners-up:* 1927, 1950.
League Cup Winners: 1947-48, 1949-50, 1953-54.

Club colours: Shirt: Gold with black sleeves. Shorts: White. Socks: Black.

Goalscorers: *League (62):* Austin, N 22, Wilkie 9, Insall 8, Smith 6, Page 5, Kerr 3, Campbell 2, Coote 2, Brown 1, Mercer 1, Murray 1, Slattery 1, Sutherland 1.
William Hill Scottish FA Cup (0).
Scottish League Cup (2): Austin, N 2.
Petrofac Training Cup (1): Smith 1.

Goodfellow R 19	MacGregor G 2+1	Page J 36	O'Kane D 10+4	Mullen F 12+12	Smith K 20+6	Murray C 11+10	Wilkie K 36	Slattery P 31+2	Austin N 33+2	Sutherland C —+5	Brown R 22+7	Walker A 7+6	Kerr J 33+1	Naysmith G 26+3	MacDonald K 5+1	Leyden Jordan 2+2	Jones R —+1	Campbell S 21+1	Insall J 15+6	Austin J —+7	Hill D 1	Kelly L 16	Coote A 1+5	McManus P 1+3	Gray B —+1	Match No.
1	2³	3	4	5	6	7²	8¹	9	10	11	12	13	14													1
1		3	2³	14	10	13	8	9	11	12	6¹	7	4	5²												2
1		3	2	14	11³	13	8	9	10²	12	6¹	7	4	5												3
1		3		5	2²	9¹	8	6	12	11		13	7	10	4											4
1		4		2		11	6¹	8³	9	10	13	12	7	3	5											5
1		4		2		11	12	8	9²	10	13	6¹	7	3	5											6
1		4	5²	2	8	11³	6¹	7	9	10		12	14	3	13											7
1	13	4	2	5	7³	11	6²	9	8¹	10		14	12	3												8
1		4	2³	5	6²	10	8¹	9	7	11		12	13	3	14											9
1		3		7	12	11		8	2	10		6		4	5	9¹										10
1	7¹	4	3	2	8	12		11		10		6²		5	9³	13	14									11
1		5		2	14		8²	11	9	10			3	13	6³	7		4¹	12							12
1		4	14	2	12		6	9	8³	11		3²	5					7¹	13	10⁴						13
1		4	8²	2	7³	12	6	9		10		14	3	5				11¹	13							14
1		4	14	2	6	11²	5¹	9		10		7	12		8			3³	13							15
1		4	6²	2	13		9	12	10		7³		8	5	14			3¹	11							16
	2	3	7	5		13		9	4¹	10	6²	12	8	11							1					17
1		4	9	7	2		12	10	5	11²	6		8					3¹	11							18
1		4	7	9	6¹	13	11	8³	10	5²	2		3					12	14							19
		4	2				9	11	8	10	6¹			3	5			7	12			1				20
		4	12	2	13		11	8	10³		6			3¹	5			7	9²	14		1				21
		3		5			8	6	11		7			4	9			2	10¹			1		12		22
		4		2			9	8	11		6			3	5			7	10			1				23
		4		2		12	9	8	10		6			3	5			7	11¹			1				24
		4		2	14	12	9	8³	10		6			3	5			7	11²	13		1		6¹		25
		4		2		12	9	8	10		6			3	5			7	11¹			1				26
		4		2		12	14	8	9	10	7³			3	5			6¹	11²			1		13		27
		4		2		11²	13	9³	7	10¹	6			3	5			8	14	12		1				28
		4		2		11	12	9	8		6			3	5			7¹	10²	13		1				29
		3		2	13		11	9	6	12	7³			4	5²			8	10¹			1		14		30
		4		2		11	9	8	12		6¹			3	5			7	10²			1			13	31
		4		2	13		11	12	9	8	10³	7¹		6	5²			3				1			14	32
		4		2		12	9	6	8	10	14			3	5¹			7³	11²			1			13	33
		4		2		9	10	8	11		6¹			3	5			7	12			1				34
1		4		2	7	11¹	14	6	8	10				3	5³								13	9²	12	35
		4	12	2			11	8	7	10³				5	3			6¹	9²	13		1			14	36

EAST STIRLINGSHIRE

Year Formed: 1880. *Grounds:* Ochilview Park (with Stenhousemuir). *Contact address:* 81d Main Street, Bainsford, Falkirk FK2 7NZ. *Telephone/Fax:* 01324 629 942.
E-mail: fceaststirlingshire@gmail.com *Website:* www.eaststirlingshirefc.co.uk
Ground Capacity: 3,776 (seated 626). *Size of Pitch:* 100m × 66m.
Chairman: Alan Archibold. *Secretary:* Tadek Kopszywa.
Head Coach: John Sludden. *Assistant Head Coach:* Martin Mooney.
Club Nickname: 'The Shire'.
Previous Grounds: Burnhouse, Randyford Park, Merchiston Park, New Kilbowie Park, Firs Park.
Record Attendance: 12,000 v Partick Thistle, *Scottish Cup* 3rd rd, 21 February 1921.
Record Transfer Fee received: £35,000 for Jim Docherty to Chelsea (1978).
Record Transfer Fee paid: £6,000 for Colin McKinnon from Falkirk (March 1991).
Record Victory: 11-2 v Vale of Bannock, *Scottish Cup* 2nd rd, 22 September 1888.
Record Defeat: 1-12 v Dundee U, Division II, 13 April 1936.
Most Capped Player: Humphrey Jones, 5 (14), Wales.
Most League Appearances: 415: Gordon Russell, 1983-2001.
Most League Goals in Season (Individual): 36: Malcolm Morrison, Division II, 1938-39.

EAST STIRLINGSHIRE – SCOTTISH LEAGUE TWO 2015–16 LEAGUE RECORD

Match No.	Date		Venue	Opponents	Result	H/T Score	Lg Pos.	Goalscorers	Atten- dance
1	Aug	8	H	East Fife	W 1-0	0-0	3	Kinnaird 73	382
2		15	A	Elgin C	L 0-4	0-2	7		502
3		22	H	Annan Ath	W 3-1	1-1	5	Faulds 40, Shepherd 2 76, 84	294
4		29	A	Clyde	L 1-3	0-0	8	Shepherd 72	502
5	Sept	5	H	Stirling Alb	L 2-3	1-2	8	Shepherd 14, Roy 89	511
6		12	H	Queen's Park	L 1-5	0-2	9	Roy 64	404
7		19	A	Montrose	L 1-2	0-2	10	Wright 86	469
8		26	H	Arbroath	L 0-4	0-1	10		291
9	Oct	3	A	Berwick R	L 1-2	1-0	10	Shepherd 15	423
10		17	H	Elgin C	W 2-0	1-0	10	Court 19, Roy 87	241
11		31	A	Stirling Alb	D 0-0	0-0	10		618
12	Nov	7	H	Queen's Park	W 2-1	0-0	10	McKenna 57, Wright 90	316
13		14	A	East Fife	L 3-5	2-1	10	Gilmour 33, McKenna 40, Donaldson 63	543
14		21	H	Montrose	W 3-1	1-0	8	Cairnie 11, Kay 46, McKenna 58	238
15	Dec	12	A	Annan Ath	L 1-3	0-2	8	Roy 78	357
16		19	H	Berwick R	L 0-4	0-2	10		241
17	Jan	2	H	Stirling Alb	W 3-2	2-0	10	McKenna 2 2, 68, Orr 20	523
18		9	A	Montrose	L 2-3	2-0	10	Faulds 21, Orr 36	378
19		23	H	East Fife	L 1-3	1-2	10	Naysmith (og) 8	356
20		30	H	Arbroath	L 0-3	0-1	10		306
21	Feb	6	A	Berwick R	D 2-2	1-1	10	McCabe 16, Orr 70	359
22		13	A	Queen's Park	W 3-0	2-0	9	Orr 36, McKenna 42, Ferries 68	461
23		20	A	Annan Ath	L 0-1	0-0	10		248
24		23	A	Arbroath	D 0-0	0-0	10		334
25		27	A	Elgin C	L 0-2	0-0	10		697
26	Mar	1	A	Clyde	W 1-0	1-0	10	McKenna 2	453
27		5	A	Montrose	L 2-4	0-1	10	McKenna 52, Cairnie 85	251
28		8	H	Clyde	L 0-3	0-1	10		326
29		12	A	Arbroath	L 0-3	0-1	10		609
30		19	H	Clyde	L 2-4	1-2	10	Orr 3, Faulds 81	394
31		26	A	Stirling Alb	L 0-3	0-1	10		602
32	Apr	2	H	Berwick R	D 0-0	0-0	10		304
33		9	H	Queen's Park	L 0-3	0-3	10		312
34		16	A	Annan Ath	W 3-1	1-0	10	Wright 21, Faulds 79, McMillan 82	398
35		23	H	Elgin C	L 0-3	0-2	10		234
36		30	A	East Fife	D 1-1	0-0	10	McMullin 51	1360

Final League Position: 10

Honours
League Champions: Division II 1931-32; C Division 1947-48.
Runners-up: Division II 1962-63. Second Division 1979-80. Division Three 1923-24.

Club colours: Shirt: Black and white hoops. Shorts: Black. Socks: Red.

Goalscorers: *League (41):* McKenna 8, Orr 5, Shepherd 5, Faulds 4, Roy 4, Wright 3, Cairnie 2, Court 1, Donaldson 1, Ferries 1, Gilmour 1, Kay 1, Kinnaird 1, McCabe 1, McMillan 1, McMullin 1, own goal 1.
William Hill Scottish FA Cup (1): McKenna 1 (1 pen).
Scottish League Cup (0).
Petrofac Training Cup (2): Donaldson 1, McKenna 1.
League Two Play-Offs (1): Wright 1.

Barnard R 23	Kinnaird L 26 + 3	Tully J 7 + 2	Donaldson R 24	Wright M 14 + 10	Greene C 23 + 3	Carruthers K 3 + 1	Faulds K 25 + 7	Shepherd N 17	Roy A 5 + 9	McKenna D 28 + 4	Court J 9 + 4	Kay A 13 + 7	Wallace M 2 + 10	McCabe N 26	Murray A 2 + 3	Vidler W 2 + 3	Townsley C 21	Dolan D 13	Lynas A 12 + 3	Cairnie J 16 + 3	Gilmour R 10	McMullin M 16	Orr T 18 + 2	Fisher R 15 + 1	Russell A 12 + 4	Ferries S 6	McMillan G 3 + 10	Fraser J 4	Marsh D 1	White S — + 1	Grant David — + 1	Peddie L — + 1	Match No.
1	2	3	4	5	6		7²	8	9	10¹	11³	12	13	14																			1
1	2	3²	4	5	6			8	9	10	11¹	13		12	7																		2
1	5	3	4	6²	2	12	10	9			11		8¹	13	7																		3
1	5	3	4	6²	2	8¹	10	9	12		11			13	7																		4
1	2	3	4	6	8		9	5	12	11	10²	14	13	7³																		5
1	5	14	3³	10	7		8	9	12	13	11¹	4³			2	6²																	6
1	2	4		9	8		6	5	13	11	10²			7	12		3¹																7
1	5	2	9³	6²	3⁴		8	4	10¹	11		13		7	14	12																	8
	2	3			7¹	6	5	10	11	12	9		8					1	4														9
	2		12	3		6	5	13	11²	10¹	9		7					1	8	4													10
	2	6¹	12	13			5	14	11³	10²			7					3	1	8	4	9											11
	2	6	12				14	9		11³	10¹		13	7				3	1	8	4	5²											12
	2	5⁴	12				14	9	13	11	10¹			8³				3	1	7⁴	4	6²											13
	2		11²	12			8	5³	13	10	14	6¹		7				3	1		4	9											14
	2		10	4			12	5	14	11³		6²	13	7				3	1	8¹		9											15
	2	13		10³			11	5	6	14			12	7				3	1	8¹	4	9²											16
1		9³	13				6	5		11				7				3		12	8	2	4	10²									17
1	12	9	13				6			11				7				3		5²	8	2¹	4	10									18
1	12		5¹	13			6			11		7²	14					3		9	8		4	10³	2								19
1	2				7			10						8				5			4¹		3	12	6	9	11						20
1	8			2	7			11²		14		6			3		5³					12	4	10¹	9	13							21
1	5			3	8			11²		13		7	12	4									10³	2	6	9	14						22
1	5			2	8			11				7		3									10	4	6	9¹	12						23
1		5		2	10¹			13				8		3		7						9³	11²	4	12	6	14						24
1		5		2	8¹			11³				7		4		12						9²	10	3	13	6	14						25
1		5		2				11		12		7		3		13						9	10	4	8¹			6²					26
1	13	5		2	14			6				7		3¹				12			9	10	4²	11			8³						27
1	2	5		3	8			6		12												9	10²	4	11¹		13		7⁸				28
1	5		9	12	2			11¹		7	14							4				8	10³	3	6²		13						29
	2		5	11⁴	4		9			7	6					1			8			10¹	3	12		13							30
	2		5²	11³	13		9			14		7	6¹			12		1			8	4	10	3									31
		5	14	2			13			7	6					1				11²		4	9	3	10³		12	8¹					32
1		5	13	2			12			10	6				4					7²		8³	9	3	11¹		14						33
	5		9⁸				12			11³		4¹		7		8	1		13	2²	3	10		14	6								34
	2				7			11				8¹		14	4	1			13	5²	3	10	12	9³	6								35
1				5										2³	9²				7	4		3	10		11			6	8¹		12	13	14	36

ELGIN CITY

Year Formed: 1893. *Ground and Address:* Borough Briggs, Borough Briggs Road, Elgin IV30 1AP.
Telephone: 01343 551114. *Fax:* 01343 547921. *E-mail:* office@elgincity.com *Website:* www.elgincity.net
Ground Capacity: 3,927 (seated: 478). *Size of pitch:* 102m × 68m.
Chairman: Graham Tatters. *Secretary:* Kate Taylor.
Manager: Jim Weir. *Assistant Manager:* Gavin Price. *Physio:* Andy Jones.
Previous names: 1900-03 Elgin City United.
Club Nicknames: 'City', 'The Black & Whites'.
Previous Grounds: Association Park 1893-95; Milnfield Park 1895-1909; Station Park 1909-19; Cooper Park 1919-21.
Record Attendance: 12,608 v Arbroath, Scottish Cup, 17 February 1968.
Record Transfer Fee received: £32,000 for Michael Teasdale to Dundee (January 1994).
Record Transfer Fee paid: £10,000 for Russell McBride from Fraserburgh (July 2001).
Record Victory: 18-1 v Brora Rangers, North of Scotland Cup, 6 February 1960.
Record Defeat: 1-14 v Hearts, Scottish Cup, 4 February 1939.
Most League Appearances: 274: Mark Nicholson, 2007-16.
Most League Goals in Season (Individual): 21: Craig Gunn, 2015-16.
Most Goals Overall (Individual): 120: Craig Gunn, 2009-16.

ELGIN CITY – SCOTTISH LEAGUE TWO 2015–16 LEAGUE RECORD

Match No.	Date		Venue	Opponents	Result	H/T Score	Lg Pos.	Goalscorers	Attendance
1	Aug	8	A	Arbroath	W 3-0	2-0	1	Gunn 2 (1 pen) 4, 30 (p), Nicolson 76	683
2		15	H	East Stirling	W 4-0	2-0	1	Moore 23, MacLeod 36, Gunn 52, McHardy 54	502
3		22	A	East Fife	L 1-2	1-1	1	Gunn 21	538
4		29	H	Stirling Alb	W 1-0	1-0	1	MacLeod 12	720
5	Sept	5	A	Montrose	L 0-2	0-1	4		584
6		12	H	Berwick R	W 4-1	1-1	1	McLaren 31, Drummond (og) 52, Gunn 56, Nicolson 79	627
7		19	A	Queen's Park	L 1-3	0-1	2	McLaren 72	439
8		26	A	Annan Ath	D 1-1	0-1	4	Gunn 90	414
9	Oct	3	H	Clyde	D 1-1	1-1	5	McHardy 13	672
10		17	A	East Stirling	L 0-2	0-1	6		241
11		31	H	Arbroath	W 2-0	1-0	4	Gunn 6, Cameron 82	627
12	Nov	7	H	Annan Ath	W 3-2	2-1	2	McHardy 6, Cameron 44, Gunn (pen) 56	644
13		14	A	Clyde	L 2-4	2-2	4	Gunn 2 (2 pens) 12, 23	528
14		21	H	East Fife	W 4-2	2-2	3	Cameron 1, Gunn 4, McHardy 66, Moore 90	654
15	Dec	5	A	Stirling Alb	L 1-3	1-0	3	Gunn (pen) 21	452
16		12	A	Berwick R	W 3-2	2-1	4	McHardy 26, Cameron 37, Gunn 77	394
17		19	H	Queen's Park	D 0-0	0-0	4		732
18		26	H	Montrose	W 2-0	0-0	3	Gunn 60, Reilly 70	697
19	Jan	2	A	East Fife	W 2-0	0-0	1	Reilly 55, MacLeod 87	591
20		9	A	Arbroath	W 3-2	1-1	1	McLaren 27, Gunn (pen) 53, Easton 77	624
21		23	H	Berwick R	W 1-0	1-0	1	Gunn 12	752
22		30	A	Annan Ath	L 2-4	0-2	1	MacLeod 63, Gilfillan (og) 80	399
23	Feb	6	A	Queen's Park	D 0-0	0-0	1		529
24		13	H	Clyde	W 1-0	1-0	1	Gunn (pen) 4	728
25		20	A	Montrose	L 1-3	0-1	2	Martyniuk (og) 90	515
26		27	H	East Stirling	W 2-0	0-0	1	Gunn (pen) 65, Cameron 87	697
27	Mar	5	H	East Fife	L 1-3	1-2	2	Easton 22	977
28		8	H	Stirling Alb	W 2-1	1-1	1	Gunn 14, Cameron (pen) 90	503
29		12	A	Clyde	L 0-1	0-1	2		611
30		19	H	Montrose	D 1-1	1-0	2	Gunn 24	784
31		26	A	Berwick R	L 0-2	0-1	3		512
32	Apr	2	H	Annan Ath	D 2-2	0-0	3	MacLeod 77, Cameron (pen) 87	861
33		9	A	Stirling Alb	D 0-0	0-0	5		578
34		16	A	Queen's Park	D 1-1	1-1	5	McKenzie 18	887
35		23	A	East Stirling	W 3-0	2-0	3	Cameron 2 9, 75, Easton 27	234
36		30	H	Arbroath	W 4-1	2-0	2	MacLeod 5, Cameron 2 (1 pen) 32 (p), 64, Gunn 90	1193

Final League Position: 2

Honours
Runners-up: League Two 2015-16.
Scottish Cup: Quarter-finals 1968.
Highland League Champions: winners 15 times.
Scottish Qualifying Cup (North): winners 7 times.
North of Scotland Cup: winners 17 times.
Highland League Cup: winners 5 times.
Inverness Cup: winners twice.

Club colours: Shirt: Black and white stripes. Shorts: Black. Socks: Black with white tops.

Goalscorers: *League (59):* Gunn 21 (8 pens), Cameron 11 (3 pens), MacLeod 6, McHardy 5, Easton 3, McLaren 3, Moore 2, Nicolson 2, Reilly 2, McKenzie 1, own goals 3.
William Hill Scottish FA Cup (2): Halsman 1, MacPhee 1.
Scottish League Cup (0).
Petrofac Training Cup (6): Gunn 2 (2 pens), Cameron 1, Duff 1, McHardy 1, McKenzie 1 (1 pen).
League One Play-Offs (1): MacLeod 1.

Hurst M 35	Cooper M 33 + 1	Gordon L 12	Duff J 17 + 1	McHardy D 30	McKenzie M 17 + 13	Nicolson M 30 + 2	Cameron B 36	Moore D 27 + 8	Gunn C 32 + 4	MacLeod K 17 + 16	MacPhee A 30 + 5	Hunter G — + 4	Bruce R — + 3	McLean C 2 + 11	Halsman J 2 + 6	McLaren C 17 + 12	Reilly T 28 + 2	Black S 1	Allan J — + 1	Easton D 21 + 2	MaCaulay C — + 1	Dryden S 4	Ross S 5 + 8	Lander K — + 4	Match No.
1	2	3	4	5	6^3	7	8	9^1	10^2	11	12	13	14												1
1	2	3	4	5	6^2	8	7	9	10^3	11^1	12	13		14											2
1	2	3	4^1	5	6	7	8	9^3	10^2	11	12	13			14										3
1	2	4^3	3	5	6	8	7	9	10^2	11	12	13													4
1	2		4	3		7^1	8	9	10	11^2	5	13		6	14	12									5
1	2	4	3	5		8	7	9^3	10^2	11				13	14	6^3	12								6
1	2	3^1	5		8^a	7	9	10^2	11	13				14		6^3	12								7
1	2	4	3	5	12	7	9	13	10	8^2				14		6^1	11								8
2	3	4	5	6^3	14	7	9	10^2	11^1	8				13				1	12						9
1	2	4		3	12	8	7		14	10	9			5^2	6^1	11^3				13					10
1	2	3		4	6^1		8	9^3	10		5			13	14	12	7			11^2					11
1	2	3		4	14		7	9^1	11^2	13	5			12		6	8			10^1					12
1	2	3^1		4		12	7	9	10	13	5					6^2	8			11					13
1	2			4	12	3	7	9	11^3	14	5			13		6^1	8			10^2					14
1	2			3	6^3	4	7	12	11	13	5			14	9^1		8			10^2					15
1	2			3	12	4	7	13	11	10^2	5			6^1		14	9			8^3					16
1	2			4	6^2	3	7	9^1	11^3	13	5			14		8				10^1	12				17
1	2			4	12	3	7	9	11^2	13	5	14				6^1	8			10^1					18
1	2			4	13	3	7	9^2	11^3	12	5			14		6	8			10^1					19
1	2			3	12	4	8	9	10^2	13	5			14		6^1	7			11^3					20
1	2			4	6^1	3	7	9	11^2	13	5			14		12	8			10^3					21
1	2^3		14	3	6^2	4	7	9^1	11	12	5			13		8				10^4					22
1				4	12	3	7	5	10	11	8			6^1		9					2				23
1		3	4^a	6^2		7	9	10^3	11^1	5			14	13		8					2	12			24
1	13	3		6^1	4	8	9	11	12	5				7			10^2				2^3	14			25
1	2			4	14	3	7	9	11^2	13	5			6^3		8				10^1		12			26
1	2			4	12	3	7	9^2	11	14	5			6^1		8				10^3		13			27
1	2			3	9^1	4	7	12	10^3	5				6		8				11^2			13	14	28
1	2			3	6^1	4	10	12	11^3	5				9^2		8				7			13	14	29
1	2			4	12	3	7	13	11^3	14	5			6^1		8				10^2			9		30
1	2^3	4			3	7	13	11^2	6^1	5				12		8				10			9	14	31
1	2	4		13^a	3	7	9^2	11^3	14	5				6		8				12			10^1		32
1	2	4			3	7	13	10^3	11^2	9				12		8					5^1	6	14		33
1	2	4	5	6^1	3	7	14	11	13	9^3				12		8				10^2					34
1	2	4		6^1	3	8	9	14	10^3	5				12		7				11^3			13		35
1	2	4		10^2	3	6	8	12	11^1	5				13		7				9^3			14		36

FALKIRK

Year Formed: 1876. *Ground & Address:* The Falkirk Stadium, 4 Stadium Way, Falkirk FK2 9EE. *Telephone:* 01324 624121. *Fax:* 01324 612418. *Email:* feedback@falkirkfc.co.uk *Website:* www.falkirkfc.co.uk
Ground Capacity: 8,750 (all seated). *Size of Pitch:* 105m × 68m.
Chairman: Doug Henderson. *Secretary:* Robert Bateman.
Manager: Peter Houston. *Assistant Manager:* Alan Maybury.
Club Nickname: 'The Bairns'.
Previous Grounds: Randyford 1876-81; Blinkbonny Grounds 1881-83; Brockville Park 1883-2003.
Record Attendance: 23,100 v Celtic, Scottish Cup 3rd rd, 21 February 1953.
Record Transfer Fee received: £945,000 for Conor McGrandles to Norwich C (August 2014).
Record Transfer Fee paid: £225,000 to Chelsea for Kevin McAllister (August 1991).
Record Victory: 11-1 v Tillicoultry, Scottish Cup 1st rd, 7 Sep 1889.
Record Defeat: 1-11 v Airdrieonians, Division I, 28 April 1951.
Most Capped Player: Alex Parker, 14 (15), Scotland.
Most League Appearances: 451: Tom Ferguson, 1919-32.
Most League Goals in Season (Individual): 43: Evelyn Morrison, Division I, 1928-29.
Most Goals Overall (Individual): 154: Kenneth Dawson, 1934-51.

FALKIRK – SCOTTISH CHAMPIONSHIP 2015–16 LEAGUE RECORD

Match No.	Date		Venue	Opponents	Result		H/T Score	Lg Pos.	Goalscorers	Atten-dance
1	Aug	8	A	Greenock Morton	D	1-1	1-0	5	Watson [19]	2782
2		15	H	Raith R	W	1-0	0-0	3	Kerr [80]	3753
3		22	A	Livingston	W	2-1	1-0	2	Leahy [16], Vaulks [62]	1211
4		28	H	Dumbarton	W	2-1	2-1	1	Alston [5], Sibbald [14]	3600
5	Sept	12	A	St Mirren	W	3-2	0-2	2	Leahy [55], Baird 2 (1 pen) [72 (p), 90]	3412
6		19	H	Alloa Ath	D	1-1	0-0	2	Baird (pen) [68]	1572
7		25	H	Queen of the South	D	0-0	0-0	2		3757
8	Oct	3	A	Rangers	L	1-3	1-1	4	Vaulks [17]	45,135
9		17	H	Greenock Morton	W	1-0	0-0	4	Miller [90]	3946
10		20	H	Hibernian	L	0-1	0-1	4		5429
11		24	A	Dumbarton	W	5-0	3-0	3	Baird 3 [5, 23, 48], McHugh [43], Alston [71]	963
12		31	H	St Mirren	W	3-0	2-0	3	Sibbald [18], Baird [43], Vaulks [76]	4239
13	Nov	7	A	Raith R	W	2-1	1-1	3	Alston [42], Baird [60]	2160
14		14	H	Alloa Ath	W	5-0	3-0	3	Baird 3 [12, 31, 44], McHugh [63], Leahy [81]	3550
15		21	H	Queen of the South	D	2-2	1-1	3	Vaulks [17], Miller [83]	1728
16	Dec	12	A	Hibernian	D	1-1	0-0	3	Miller [84]	9459
17		19	H	Rangers	W	2-1	1-1	3	Baird (pen) [3], Vaulks [55]	7488
18		26	A	Dumbarton	W	1-0	1-0	3	Alston [36]	4013
19		29	H	Livingston	W	2-0	0-0	2	Miller 2 [56, 60]	4245
20	Jan	2	A	Alloa Ath	W	1-0	1-0	2	Baird [15]	1176
21		17	H	Hibernian	D	1-1	0-0	2	Alston [49]	7081
22		23	A	Livingston	D	1-1	1-0	3	Sibbald [44]	1536
23		30	A	Rangers	L	0-1	0-0	3		46,980
24	Feb	13	H	Raith R	D	2-2	2-1	3	Alston [14], McCracken [20]	3956
25		20	A	Greenock Morton	W	1-0	1-0	3	Baird [27]	1991
26		27	H	Queen of the South	W	3-1	0-1	3	Baird [53], Dowie (og) [65], Alston [85]	3918
27	Mar	1	A	St Mirren	D	0-0	0-0	3		2321
28		5	H	Alloa Ath	W	2-0	2-0	2	Watson [28], Kerr [36]	3774
29		12	A	Dumbarton	D	1-1	0-0	2	Baird (pen) [65]	734
30		18	H	Rangers	W	3-2	0-2	2	Alston [72], Hippolyte [77], McHugh [90]	7804
31		26	A	Livingston	L	1-2	0-0	2	Vaulks [90]	3897
32	Apr	2	A	Queen of the South	D	2-2	1-0	2	Alston [45], Baird [52]	1530
33		9	H	St Mirren	W	3-2	1-0	2	Miller [9], McHugh [70], Alston [90]	4331
34		12	A	Hibernian	D	2-2	0-1	2	McCracken [87], McHugh [90]	10,277
35		23	A	Raith R	D	2-2	0-1	2	Sibbald [56], McHugh [88]	2602
36	May	1	H	Greenock Morton	W	1-0	0-0	2	Watson [48]	5271

Final League Position: 2

Honours
League Champions: Division II 1935-36, 1969-70, 1974-75. First Division 1990-91, 1993-94, 2002-03, 2004-05. Second Division 1979-80;
Runners-up: Division I 1907-08, 1909-10. First Division 1985-86, 1988-89, 1997-98, 1998-99. Division II 1904-05, 1951-52, 1960-61. Championship: 2015-16.
Scottish Cup Winners: 1913, 1957; *Runners-up:* 1997, 2009, 2015. *League Cup Runners-up:* 1947-48. *League Challenge Cup Winners:* 1993-94, 1997-98, 2004-05, 2011-12.

European: *Europa League:* 2 matches (2009-10).

Club colours: Shirt: Navy blue with red and white vertical stripes. Shorts: White. Socks: Navy blue.

Goalscorers: *League (61):* Baird 17 (4 pens), Alston 10, McHugh 6, Miller 6, Vaulks 6, Sibbald 4, Leahy 3, Watson 3, Kerr 2, McCracken 2, Hippolyte 1, own goal 1.
William Hill Scottish FA Cup (5): Miller 3, Vaulks 1, Watson 1.
Scottish League Cup (6): Alston 1, Baird 1, Grant 1, McHugh 1, Muirhead 1, own goal 1.
Petrofac Training Cup (6): Baird 1, Cooper 1, Grant 1, McHugh 1, Smith 1, Watson 1.
Premiership Play-Offs (6): McHugh 2, Alston 1, Leahy 1, Miller 1, Vaulks 1.

Rogers D 35	Muirhead A 29 + 2	Grant P 23	Watson P 25 + 2	Leahy L 36	Taiwo T 15 + 5	Vaulks W 35	Kerr M 34 + 1	Sibbald C 34 + 2	Baird J 35 + 1	McHugh B 9 + 13	Alston B 32 + 4	Smith D 7 + 8	Shepherd S — + 4	Miller L 16 + 13	Blair R — + 7	McCracken D 20 + 1	Sinnamon R — + 3	O'Hara K 3 + 11	McGrandles C 2 + 3	Hippolyte M 4 + 8	McCann K 1 + 1	Mehmet D 1	Match No.
1	2	3	4	5	6^1	7	8^2	9	10	11	12	13											1
1		4	3	5	13	2	8	9	10^2	11	7	6^1	12										2
1	12	4	3	5		7	2	8	9	10		6	11^1										3
1	12	4	3	5		7		9^1	10	11^3	8	6^2	14	13									4
1		4	3	5		7	2	6^2	9	11		8^1	10	12	13								5
1		4	3	5		7^3	2	8	9	10	13	12	6^1	11^2	14								6
1	2		4		5	7^3	8	14	9	11^2	10^1	12	6	13		3							7
1	2		4		5	8^1	6	9^2	10	11		7	12	13		3							8
1	5		4		2	6^1	8	7^2	10	11		9^3	13	14	12	3							9
1	2	4	3	5		8	7	10	12	13	9^2	6^1		11									10
1	2^3	4	13	5		6	7	8	9	12	10			11^1		3^2	14						11
1	2	4	3	5		7	6	8^3	9^2	11	10^1	12		14		13							12
1	2	4	3^1	5		7	6	8	10^2	11	9			13	12								13
1	2	3	4^2	5		8	7	6^1	11	10	9^1	12		14	13								14
1	2	4		5		6	7	9	10	11^1	8		12			3^2	13						15
1	2	3	14	5		7	8	9^2	11^3	6	13	12	4					10^1					16
1	2	3		5		7	8	9	11^2	6	13	12	4					10^1					17
1	2	4		5		7	8	9^2	11^3	6	13	12	14	3				10^1					18
1	2	4	3	5		7	8	9	11^1	6		10						12					19
1	2	4	3	5		7	8	9^1	11^2	6	12	10						13					20
1	2	4	3	5		7	8	9	11	6^2		10^1				13	12						21
1	8	4	3	5		2	7	9^1	11	14	12	10^1				13	6^2						22
1	2	4	3	5	12	9	6	10^7	11^3	8						14	7^1	13					23
1	2		3	5	14	7	8^3	9	11^1		6^2			10		4			12	13			24
1	2		3	5	13	7	8	9	10	12	6^3			11^1		4^2		14					25
1	2		4	5	13	7	8	9	11^3	6				12		3^1		14		10^2			26
1	2		3	5	7^1	4	8	9	11^2	13	6			10^3				14		12			27
1	2		4	5		8	7	9	10^2	11^1	6			12		3				13			28
1		3	5			7	8	9^1	10^2	13	6			11		4				12	2		29
1	2	4	5	9	7			8^1	10^3	14	6			11^1		3		13		12			30
	2^2	4	5			7	8	9	10	11^1	6			12		3				13	1		31
1	2		4^1	5	9^5	7	8	13	10	14	6			11^2		3				12			32
1	2			5	7	4	8	13	11^1	12	6			10		3				9^2			33
1	2^a			5	7^1	4	8	9	10^2	13	6			12		3		14		11^3			34
1			5	6^3	4	7	8	10^1	12	2		13		11		3		14		9^2			35
1	2		3	5	6^1		8	9	10^2	13	7			11		4				12			36

FORFAR ATHLETIC

Year Formed: 1885. *Ground & Address:* Station Park, Carseview Road, Forfar DD8 3BT. *Telephone:* 01307 463576.
Fax: 01307 466956. *E-mail:* pat@ramsayladders.co.uk *Website:* www.forfarathletic.co.uk
Ground Capacity: 6,777 (seated: 739). *Size of Pitch:* 103m × 64m.
Chairman: Alastair Donald. *Vice-Chairman:* Dennis Fenton. *Secretary:* David McGregor.
Manager: Gary Bollan. *Assistant Manager:* Stuart Balmer. *Physio:* Duncan Sangster.
Club Nicknames: 'The Loons', 'The Sky Blues'.
Previous Grounds: None.
Record Attendance: 10,780 v Rangers, Scottish Cup 2nd rd, 2 February 1970.
Record Transfer Fee received: £65,000 for David Bingham to Dunfermline Ath (September 1995).
Record Transfer Fee paid: £50,000 for Ian McPhee from Airdrieonians (1991).
Record Victory: 14-1 v Lindertis, Scottish Cup 1st rd, 1 September 1888.
Record Defeat: 2-12 v King's Park, Division II, 2 January 1930.
Most League Appearances: 463: Ian McPhee, 1978-88 and 1991-98.
Most League Goals in Season (Individual): 46: Dave Kilgour, Division II, 1929-30.
Most Goals Overall: 125: John Clark, 1978-91.

FORFAR ATHLETIC – SCOTTISH LEAGUE ONE 2015–16 LEAGUE RECORD

Match No.	Date	Venue	Opponents	Result	H/T Score	Lg Pos.	Goalscorers	Atten- dance
1	Aug 8	A	Airdrieonians	W 1-0	1-0	4	Templeman [2]	856
2	15	H	Albion R	W 4-0	0-0	2	Nicoll [57], Denholm [60], Hay 2 [77, 79]	608
3	22	H	Stenhousemuir	W 4-1	4-1	1	Denholm 2 [15, 27], Hay [34], Travis [37]	610
4	29	A	Ayr U	D 2-2	1-1	1	Allan [26], Travis [90]	1243
5	Sept 5	H	Dunfermline Ath	L 0-4	0-2	2		1618
6	12	A	Brechin C	W 2-0	1-0	1	Young [35], Kader [48]	602
7	19	A	Cowdenbeath	L 1-2	0-1	3	Swankie [49]	443
8	26	H	Stranraer	L 1-2	0-1	3	Travis [76]	562
9	Oct 3	A	Peterhead	D 2-2	0-1	3	Swankie [48], Campbell [70]	573
10	17	H	Ayr U	D 2-2	2-0	5	Denholm [2], Campbell [45]	745
11	24	A	Dunfermline Ath	L 0-4	0-1	5		3198
12	31	H	Brechin C	L 0-1	0-0	5		728
13	Nov 7	H	Airdrieonians	L 2-3	1-3	7	Martin 2 [45, 52]	555
14	14	A	Stenhousemuir	D 2-2	1-0	6	Campbell (pen) [31], Denholm [51]	438
15	21	A	Stranraer	D 0-0	0-0	7		411
16	Dec 8	H	Peterhead	L 0-2	0-1	7		434
17	12	H	Cowdenbeath	L 0-1	0-1	8		493
18	19	A	Albion R	D 1-1	0-1	8	Hay [76]	346
19	26	H	Dunfermline Ath	L 2-4	1-1	8	Campbell (pen) [41], Travis [73]	1443
20	Jan 23	H	Stenhousemuir	L 0-1	0-1	9		532
21	Feb 6	H	Stranraer	D 1-1	0-1	9	Ryan [54]	485
22	13	A	Peterhead	L 2-3	2-2	9	Craig [15], Ryan [18]	667
23	20	A	Ayr U	L 1-2	0-1	9	Ryan [68]	763
24	23	A	Cowdenbeath	W 4-1	2-1	9	Ryan (pen) [38], Rodger [41], Craig [69], Hay [85]	269
25	27	H	Albion R	W 1-0	0-0	9	Craig [90]	538
26	Mar 1	A	Brechin C	L 0-4	0-2	9		633
27	5	A	Stranraer	L 0-1	0-0	9		442
28	8	A	Airdrieonians	D 1-1	1-0	9	Kader [37]	547
29	12	H	Cowdenbeath	D 1-1	1-1	9	Ryan [3]	525
30	19	H	Ayr U	W 3-1	1-1	8	Ryan 2 [4, 71], Craig [75]	614
31	26	A	Stenhousemuir	L 1-2	0-1	9	Craig [81]	429
32	Apr 2	H	Peterhead	W 2-0	0-0	9	Denholm [48], Craig [54]	570
33	9	A	Dunfermline Ath	D 2-2	1-1	9	Swankie [13], Ryan [50]	3201
34	16	H	Airdrieonians	L 0-2	0-2	10		577
35	23	A	Albion R	L 2-3	1-2	10	Denholm [1], Ryan (pen) [60]	352
36	30	H	Brechin C	L 1-2	0-1	10	Denholm [90]	928

Final League Position: 10

Honours
League Champions: Second Division 1983-84. Third Division 1994-95; C Division 1948-49.
Runners-up: Third Division 1996-97, 2009-10. *Promoted to Second Division:* 2009-10 (play-offs).
Scottish Cup: Semi-finals 1982.
League Cup: Semi-finals 1977-78.
League Challenge Cup: Semi-finals 2004-05.

Club colours: All navy blue with sky blue trim.

Goalscorers: *League (48):* Ryan 9 (2 pens), Denholm 8, Craig 6, Hay 5, Campbell 4 (2 pens), Travis 4, Swankie 3, Kader 2, Martin 2, Allan 1, Nicoll 1, Rodger 1, Templeman 1, Young 1.
William Hill Scottish FA Cup (6): Travis 2, Campbell 1 (1 pen), Denholm 1, Swankie 1, Templeman 1.
Scottish League Cup (3): Denholm 1, Dunlop 1, Young 1.
Petrofac Training Cup (1): Campbell 1.

Douglas R 14	Baxter M 13	Nicoll K 15 + 1	O'Brien T 26	Campbell J 22 + 1	Fotheringham M 12 + 13	Young D 20 + 4	Hodge B 24 + 4	Denholm D 27 + 6	Swankie G 32	Templeman C 9 + 6	Smith C 2 + 12	Malin G — + 3	Hay K 8 + 12	Allan L 4 + 3	Travis M 11 + 1	Dunlop M 9 + 2	Black A 11 + 3	Kader O 10 + 4	Gallacher S 4	Martin S 24	Kennedy M 12 + 2	Rose M 7	Hill D 18	Ryan A 16	Spark E 13 + 1	Rodger G 15	Craig S 13 + 1	Smith S 5 + 2	Yeates J — + 1	Aitken M — + 1	Match No.
1	2	3	4	5	6^1	7^2	8	9	10	11	12	13																			1
1	2	3	4	5	6^3	7^1	8	9	10	11^2	13	14	12																		2
1	2^3	3	4^2	5			8	7	9	10^1	12				6	11	13	14													3
1				5	13	7^4	8	9		10^3	12	14	6^2	11	4	3	2														4
1				4	5	14	7	8	9	10^1			12	11		3	13	2^3	6^2												5
		3	4	5	10^1	7^3	8	9		14			13	11	2			12	6^2	1											6
		3	4	5	7^1		8	9^3	11	10^2	14		13	12	2			6		1											7
			4	5			7^1	8	9	11^2	12	10^3	13	14	3	2		6		1											8
	2	8^2	7^1	5	10^3			9	11			14		13	12	4	3	6		1											9
1	2	3	8	5	14		7	9^2	11	10^1	13		12		4^3			6													10
1	2		4	5	7		8^1	9		10	11^3	14	13					6^2				3	12								11
1	2^3	3	4^1	5	14	10^1	8	9^1	11	12			6^1				13					7									12
1		3			5^2	6^1	8	9	11	10	12					2						7	13	4							13
1	2^1	3		5	6^2	12	8	9^1	11	10			14				13					7		4							14
1	2	3^1	6	5	12	8^2	9	10	11		13											7		4							15
1	2	3		5	13		7	6	9	12				4^1			10^2					11		8							16
1	2^1	3		7	14			9	11^2	13	12		10^3									8	6	5	4						17
1	4^2			9	7^3	13	6	8^1	11		14		12		2		5					10	3								18
	4			5	8	12	7^2	9	11		13		6^1		2							10	3	1							19
	2	12	4	5		7		13	9			11^3	14		3^2		6^1					8		1	10						20
				4	5		8	9	11						3		6							1	10	2	7				21
		2^2		8			7	13	12	9					3		6							1	10	5	4	11^1			22
		3			7^1		12	11^2									8	13			6	5		1	9	2	4	10			23
		8			12		13	11					7				3^2				6	5		1	9^1	2	4	10			24
		4			13	7^1	12	10					8^2								6	5		1	11	2	3	9			25
		4			5^2	7	13	9	8									12			6			1	11	2	3^4	10			26
		3	4			7^1	8	12	9								13				6	5		1	11	2		10^2			27
		3			7^1	12		11	9								8				6	5		1	10	2	4				28
		4				7^1	12	9^2	10								6				8	5		1	11	2	3	13			29
		3				7^1	9	8									5				6			1	11	2^2	4	10	12	13	30
		3			2			9	11								6^1				8	5		1	10		4	7	12		31
		3	13			12	9	8					14				6				2	5^2		1	11		4	10^1	7^3		32
		3^4				5	9	11									6				7			1	8	12	4	10^1	2		33
					12		5	9	8				11^1				3				6			1		2	4	10^2	7	13	34
		12	13				9	11									3^1				6	5^2		1	10	2	4	8	7		35
		13			7^2	8	11										12				5	4		1	10^4	2	3	9	6^1		36

GREENOCK MORTON

Year Formed: 1874. *Ground & Address:* Cappielow Park, Sinclair St, Greenock PA15 2TY. *Telephone:* 01475 723571.
Fax: 01475 781084. *E-mail:* info@gmfc.net *Website:* www.gmfc.net
Ground Capacity: 11,612 (seated: 6,062). *Size of Pitch:* 100m × 65m.
Chairman: Douglas Rae. *Chief Executive:* Gillian Donaldson. *Company Secretary:* Mary Davidson.
Manager: Jim Duffy. *Assistant Manager:* Craig McPherson. *Physio:* Alyson Fielding.
Club Nickname: 'The Ton'.
Previous Grounds: Grant Street 1874, Garvel Park 1875, Cappielow Park 1879, Ladyburn Park 1882, Cappielow Park 1883.
Record Attendance: 23,500 v Celtic, 29 April 1922.
Record Transfer Fee received: £500,000 for Derek Lilley to Leeds U (March 1997).
Record Transfer Fee paid: £250,000 for Janne Lindberg and Marko Rajamäki from MyPa, Finland (November 1994).
Record Victory: 11-0 v Carfin Shamrock, Scottish Cup 4th rd, 13 November 1886.
Record Defeat: 1-10 v Port Glasgow Ath, Division II, 5 May, 1894 and v St Bernards, Division II, 14 October 1933.
Most Capped Player: Jimmy Cowan, 25, Scotland.
Most League Appearances: 534: Derek Collins, 1987-98, 2001-05.
Most League Goals in Season (Individual): 58: Allan McGraw, Division II, 1963-64.
Most Goals Overall (Individual): 136: Andy Ritchie, 1976-83.

GREENOCK MORTON – SCOTTISH CHAMPIONSHIP 2015–16 LEAGUE RECORD

Match No.	Date	Venue	Opponents	Result	H/T Score	Lg Pos.	Goalscorers	Attendance
1	Aug 8	H	Falkirk	D 1-1	0-1	5	MacDonald 60	2782
2	15	A	Hibernian	L 0-1	0-0	7		8923
3	21	H	St Mirren	D 0-0	0-0	7		5343
4	29	A	Alloa Ath	W 1-0	0-0	7	O'Ware 72	825
5	Sept 5	A	Livingston	W 4-2	1-0	4	McCluskey 31, Johnstone 52, Barr 66, Scullion 82	1186
6	12	H	Dumbarton	D 0-0	0-0	4		2016
7	19	A	Queen of the South	D 2-2	1-1	5	Higgins, C (og) 7, Johnstone 65	1565
8	27	H	Rangers	L 0-4	0-3	6		7392
9	Oct 3	A	Raith R	L 1-2	0-1	6	O'Ware 82	1754
10	10	A	Queen of the South	L 0-1	0-1	6		1583
11	17	A	Falkirk	L 0-1	0-0	7		3946
12	24	H	Alloa Ath	W 1-0	0-0	6	Forbes 55	1716
13	31	A	Dumbarton	W 2-1	1-0	6	McKee 41, Johnstone 85	1110
14	Nov 7	H	Livingston	W 1-0	1-0	6	Johnstone (pen) 6	1758
15	14	H	Queen of the South	W 2-0	0-0	4	Johnstone 2 51, 62	1849
16	20	A	St Mirren	D 1-1	0-1	4	Samuel 90	4163
17	Dec 12	A	Rangers	D 2-2	1-1	4	Tavernier (og) 31, McCluskey 82	41,816
18	18	A	Raith R	L 1-2	1-0	5	Samuel 23	1264
19	Jan 2	H	St Mirren	L 0-1	0-1	6		4736
20	25	H	Rangers	L 0-2	0-1	6		5778
21	Feb 2	H	Hibernian	L 0-1	0-0	6		2696
22	9	A	Alloa Ath	D 2-2	2-1	6	McManus 14, McCluskey 17	535
23	13	H	Dumbarton	W 2-0	0-0	6	Johnstone 64, McKee 88	1595
24	20	H	Falkirk	L 0-1	0-1	6		1991
25	24	A	Hibernian	W 3-0	1-0	5	O'Ware 36, Johnstone 51, Forbes 63	8655
26	27	A	Raith R	L 2-3	0-1	5	McManus 2 73, 87	1633
27	Mar 1	A	Livingston	D 0-0	0-0	6		787
28	11	A	Rangers	L 1-3	1-1	6	Johnstone 22	45,072
29	15	H	Queen of the South	W 3-2	3-0	5	Johnstone 2 8, 22, McMullan 29	1175
30	19	H	Alloa Ath	W 4-1	2-1	5	Marr (og) 15, Forbes 17, McManus 78, Johnstone 81	1513
31	26	A	Raith R	L 0-1	0-0	5		1778
32	Apr 2	A	Dumbarton	D 0-0	0-0	5		994
33	9	H	Livingston	W 2-1	0-1	5	Johnstone (pen) 51, O'Ware 82	1463
34	16	A	St Mirren	L 1-3	0-1	5	Johnstone 59	4299
35	23	H	Hibernian	D 0-0	0-0	5		2308
36	May 1	A	Falkirk	L 0-1	0-0	5		5271

Final League Position: 5

Honours
League Champions: First Division 1977-78, 1983-84, 1986-87. Division II 1949-50, 1963-64, 1966-67. Second Division 1994-95, 2006-07. League One: 2014–15. Third Division 2002-03.
Runners-up: Division 1 1916-17. First Division 2012-13. Division II 1899-1900, 1928-29, 1936-37.
Scottish Cup Winners: 1922; *Runners-up:* 1948. *League Cup Runners-up:* 1963-64.
League Challenge Cup Runners-up: 1992-93.

European: *UEFA Cup:* 2 matches (*Fairs Cup:* 1968-69).

Club colours: Shirt: Blue and white hoops. Shorts: White with blue trim. Socks: White.

Goalscorers: *League (39):* Johnstone 14 (2 pens), McManus 4, O'Ware 4, Forbes 3, McCluskey 3, McKee 2, Samuel 2, Barr 1, MacDonald 1, McMullan 1, Scullion 1, own goals 3.
William Hill Scottish FA Cup (7): McCluskey 3, McKee 2, Johnstone 1, O'Ware 1.
Scottish League Cup (10): Forbes 2 (1 pen), Johnstone 2, Samuel 2, Scullion 2, McCluskey 1, Tidser 1.
Petrofac Training Cup (2): Kilday 1, MacDonald 1 (1 pen).

Gaston D 26	Pepper C 21+1	Kilday L 33	Lamie R 16+3	Russell M 29+1	Barr B 31+3	Miller M 21+4	Forbes R 31+5	McCluskey S 24+7	MacDonald P 4+4	Johnstone D 35	Scullion J —+8	Orr T 1+1	Gasparotto L 19+1	Stevenson D —+3	Sabajo R 2+5	O'Ware T 32+1	Adam G 8+1	Tidser M 11+5	Samuel A 6+20	McKee J 21+5	Quitongo J —+6	McManus D 17	McGowan J 1	McNeil A 1	McMullan P 6+5	Tennant J —+1	Match No.
1	2	3	4	5	6²	7	8	9	10¹	11	12	13															1
1	6	2	4	5¹	12	7	8¹	9³	10	11			3	13	14												2
1³	5	2	4		6	7	8	9²	11	10			3¹		13	12	14										3
	6	2	5		9	7¹	8	10²		11	12		3		13	4	1										4
	5	2	3		6	7	8¹	10		11²	13					9³	4	1	12	14							5
1	5¹	2	4		6	7	8	10³	13		12	14				3				9¹	11²						6
1		2	5		6	8	7	10	13	11²			3			4				9¹	12						7
1	5	2	4		6³	7	8¹	13	12	10			14			3				9	11²						8
1	2	3		5	6	7²	13	9¹	10³	11	14					4				8	12						9
1		2	4	5¹	6	7²	9¹			10	12		14			3				8	11	13					10
1	13	2	4	5	6¹	7	8	10²		11						3				9	12						11
1	2	3		5	12		8			10	13	11²	4		6¹	7				9⁵	14						12
	2	3		5	6¹		13	10²		11			4			8	1		9	12	7						13
	2	3		5	6³	14	12	13		11			4			8	1	9	10²	7¹							14
	2	3		5	6		8	11²		10			4			7	1	9¹	13	12							15
	2	3		5	9		6	10¹		11			4			7	1	8²	12	13							16
	2	3	12	5	6³	7¹	9	10²		11				14		4	1		13	8							17
	2	3		5	9³	12	6	13		10			4			7	1	11²	8¹	14							18
1	2	3		5		8¹	9			10			4			7			12	6		11					19
1	2	3		5	6³		8	9¹		10²	14		4			12	13	7		11							20
1	2	3		5	9¹		8²			11			4			13	12	7	14	10							21
	2	4	5	12	7		8¹	11		9²			3			13	6		10	1							22
	2	3	4	5	6²		12	9¹		10³			8			13	14	7		11		1					23
1	2	3¹	4	5	6		12	9²		10			8			13		7		11							24
1	2¹	3	12	5	6³		8	13		10			4					7	14	9					11²		25
1		2	4	5	13		8²	6		10			3			4		7	12	11					9¹		26
1		3		5	6¹	2	8	12		11			4					7	13	10					9²		27
1		3		5	6	2	7³	9	13	11¹			4					8		10²					12	14	28
1	2¹		5	9	12	8	13			10¹			4			3		14	7		11				6²		29
1		4¹	5	7²	2	8	9			10³			3			6		14	12		11				13		30
1			5	9²	2	8	6¹			10			4			3		13	7		11				12		31
1	2		5	9		8				10			3			4		12	7		11¹				6		32
1		13	5	9³	2	8		14		10			3			4		11²	7	12					6¹		33
1		3¹	5	9	2	8				10			4			7		13	6²	11					12		34
1		3	5	6	2	9	12			10²			4			8		13	7	11¹							35
1		3	5	12	9²	2¹	8	6³		10			4					13	7	11					14		36

HAMILTON ACADEMICAL

Year Formed: 1874. *Ground:* New Douglas Park, Cadzow Avenue, Hamilton ML3 0FT. *Telephone:* 01698 368652.
Fax: 01698 285422. *E-mail:* office@acciesfc.co.uk *Website:* www.hamiltonacciesfc.co.uk
Ground Capacity: 6,078 (all seated). *Size of Pitch:* 105m × 68m.
Chairman: Les Gray. *Secretary:* Scott Struthers.
Player Manager: Martin Canning. *First Team Coach:* Guillaume Beuzelin. *Physio:* Victoria McIntyre.
Club Nickname: 'The Accies'.
Previous Grounds: Bent Farm, South Avenue, South Haugh, Douglas Park, Cliftonhill Stadium, Firhill Stadium.
Record Attendance: 28,690 v Hearts, Scottish Cup 3rd rd, 3 March 1937 (at Douglas Park); 5,895 v Rangers, 28 February 2009 (at New Douglas Park).
Record Transfer Fee received: £1,200,000 for James McCarthy to Wigan Ath (July 2009).
Record Transfer Fee paid: £180,000 for Tomas Cerny from Sigma Olomouc (July 2009).
Record Victory: 10-2 v Greenock Morton, Scottish Championship, 3 May 2014.
Record Defeat: 1-11 v Hibernian, Division I, 6 November 1965.
Most Capped Player: Colin Miller, 29 (61), Canada, 1988-94.
Most League Appearances: 452: Rikki Ferguson, 1974-88.
Most League Goals in Season (Individual): 35: David Wilson, Division I; 1936-37.
Most Goals Overall (Individual): 246: David Wilson, 1928-39.

HAMILTON ACADEMICAL – SCOTTISH PREMIERSHIP 2015–16 LEAGUE RECORD

Match No.	Date		Venue	Opponents	Result	H/T Score	Lg Pos.	Goalscorers	Atten- dance
1	Aug	1	H	Partick Thistle	D	0-0	0-0	4		2872
2		8	A	Ross Co	L	0-2	0-2	11		3479
3		15	H	Dundee U	W	4-0	3-0	5	Crawford [19], Tagliapietra [36], Morris [39], Nade [90]	2173
4		22	A	Inverness CT	W	2-0	1-0	4	Morris [18], Longridge [90]	3003
5		29	H	Hearts	W	3-2	1-0	4	Kurtaj [45], Crawford [83], Garcia Tena [88]	4745
6	Sept	12	A	St Johnstone	L	1-4	0-3	6	Tagliapietra [67]	2648
7		15	A	Aberdeen	L	0-1	0-1	6		13,246
8		19	H	Motherwell	W	1-0	0-0	5	Imrie [72]	3325
9		26	A	Kilmarnock	W	2-1	0-1	4	Imrie [49], Crawford [64]	3308
10	Oct	4	H	Celtic	L	1-2	1-2	4	Kurtaj [4]	4910
11		17	H	Dundee	D	1-1	0-0	5	Imrie [87]	2862
12		24	A	Partick Thistle	D	1-1	0-0	5	Imrie [78]	3122
13		31	H	St Johnstone	L	2-4	0-1	6	Garcia Tena 2 (1 pen) [81, 89 (p)]	2216
14	Nov	7	A	Hearts	L	0-2	0-2	6		16,121
15		22	A	Aberdeen	D	1-1	0-1	6	Imrie [70]	2434
16		28	H	Dundee U	W	2-1	0-1	5	Gunning (og) [70], Gordon [79]	5788
17	Dec	12	H	Ross Co	L	1-3	1-0	6	Kurtaj [26]	2120
18		19	A	Dundee	L	0-4	0-4	8		4568
19		26	H	Kilmarnock	L	0-1	0-0	9		2006
20		30	A	Inverness CT	L	3-4	0-1	10	Morris [66], Gordon [81], Nade [90]	1555
21	Jan	2	A	Motherwell	D	3-3	2-1	10	Tagliapietra [25], MacKinnon [28], Crawford (pen) [90]	5734
22		16	A	St Johnstone	D	0-0	0-0	10		2685
23		19	A	Celtic	L	1-8	0-5	10	Brophy [73]	45,659
24		24	H	Hearts	D	0-0	0-0	10		2684
25		30	A	Kilmarnock	W	1-0	0-0	8	Morris [71]	3076
26	Feb	13	H	Dundee U	D	0-0	0-0	8		3902
27		20	A	Ross Co	L	1-2	0-1	9	Imrie [66]	3059
28		26	A	Celtic	D	1-1	0-1	9	Brophy [73]	5017
29	Mar	5	H	Motherwell	L	0-1	0-1	10		3755
30		12	A	Inverness CT	W	1-0	0-0	10	Morris [59]	3510
31		19	H	Partick Thistle	L	1-2	1-0	10	Docherty [10]	3055
32	Apr	3	A	Aberdeen	L	0-3	0-3	10		12,509
33		9	H	Dundee	W	2-1	2-0	10	Crawford [30], Garcia Tena (pen) [41]	2764
34		24	A	Dundee U	W	3-1	1-0	10	Gillespie [12], Morris 2 [52, 73]	5884
35		30	H	Kilmarnock	L	0-4	0-2	10		3595
36	May	7	H	Dundee	W	1-0	1-0	10	Morris [8]	4757
37		11	H	Inverness CT	L	0-1	0-1	10		1516
38		14	A	Partick Thistle	D	2-2	2-2	10	Brophy 2 (1 pen) [10 (p), 20]	2971

Final League Position: 10

Honours
League Champions: Division II 1903-04. First Division 1985-86, 1987-88, 2007-08; Third Division 2000-01.
Runners-up: Division II 1952-53, 1964-65; Second Division 1996-97, 2003-04; Championship 2013-14 (promoted via play-offs).
Scottish Cup Runners-up: 1911, 1935. *League Cup:* Semi-finalists three times.
League Challenge Cup Winners: 1991-92, 1992-93. *Runners-up:* 2005-06, 2011-12.

Club colours: Shirt: Red and white hoops. Shorts: White. Socks: White.

Goalscorers: *League (42):* Morris 8, Imrie 6, Crawford 5 (1 pen), Brophy 4 (1 pen), Garcia Tena 4 (2 pens), Kurtaj 3, Tagliapietra 3, Gordon 2, Nade 2, Docherty 1, Gillespie 1, Longridge 1, MacKinnon 1, own goal 1.
William Hill Scottish FA Cup (1): Docherty 1.
Scottish League Cup (1): Nade 1.

McGovern M 37	Gordon Z 38	Garcia Tena J 20+3	Tagliapietra L 34	Kurakins A 35	Gillespie G 28+2	Imrie D 34+1	Turner C 3	Crawford A 32+1	Longridge L 6+9	Nade C 4+13	Kurtaj G 28+6	Morris C 27+5	Docherty G 16+18	MacKinnon D 30+1	Watson C —+1	D'Acol A 3+12	Lyon D 9+3	Canning M 1+2	Sendles-White J 4+3	Boyd S 2+3	Brophy E 7+7	Redmond D 1+10	Devlin M 16	Diaby O 1+5	Agustien K 1+1	Hughes R —+2	Martin A 1	Cunningham R —+1	Match No.
1	2	3	4	5	6	7^1	8^3	9	10	11^2	12	13	14																1
1	2	3	4	5	6	7^2	8^1	9	10^3	11		13	14	12															2
1	2	3	4^1	5	6	7^3		9	14	13	10	11^2	9		8	12													3
1	2	3	4	5	6^1	7		8	14	13	10^3	11^2	12	9															4
1	2	3	4	5	6	7^1		9	13	12	10^2	11^3	14	8															5
1	2	3	4	5	7	8^1		9	14	11^2	10	11^3	13	6^2															6
1	2^3	3	4	5	6	8		9	14	11^2	10		12	7^1	13														7
1	3	13	4	5	7	6		8	14	12	9	11^1	10^3			2^2													8
1	2	3	4	5	6	7		9		12	10	11^1	8^2			13													9
1	2	3	4	5	6	7^3		9^2		12	10	11^1	13	8	14														10
1	2	3	4	5	7	6^3		10^1	12	13	9	11^2	8^1																11
1	2	3	4^1	5	6	7		8^3	13	10	11^2	9^1		14	12														12
1	2	3		5	6	7		10	9^2	11^1	8^3	12	14	13	4														13
1	2	3^1	4	5		7^3	6^2	13	14	9	11	10	8	12															14
1	2		4	5	9	6		8	11^1	10^2	7		12	3^1	13														15
1	2		4	5	7	10^1		8	14	6^2	11^3	13	9	12	3														16
1	2		4	5^2	6	7		9	12	14	10	11^1	13	8^2	3														17
1	2	12	4	5	6	7		10		13	11^3	9^2	8	3^1	14														18
1	2	3	4^1	5	6	7^3		9	10^2		11		8	12	13	14													19
1	2	3	4	5	6	7^3		9	10^1	13		12		8	11^2	14													20
1	3		4^3	5	2	8^1		10		11^2	6	7	13	14	9	12													21
1	2		4	5	12			10		9	13	7	6	11^1	8^2		3												22
1	2		4	5	8^3	12		10		9^1	7	6	11^2	14	13	3													23
1	2	13^4	4^2	5		8		9		10	12	7^1	11	6^3	14	3													24
1	2		4	5		7		9		10^2	11^1	13	6	12	8	3													25
1	2		4	5	8^2	10		9		7^3	11^1	13	12	6	14	3^4													26
1	2	3	4	5		6		10		8^3	11^2	14	7	12	9^1	13													27
1	2		4	9		10		7		8^2	11^3	13	6	5^1	12	3	14												28
1	2		4	5		7		9^2		10^1	11	12	8	6^3	13	3	14												29
1	2		4	5	7^1	6^3		9^2	11	10	8	12		14	13	3													30
1	2		4	8	6	12		10^1		5^2	7	9^3		11	13	3	14												31
1	2	4		5	8^3	9		14	10	6				13	12	3	14	7^1											32
1	2	5	4			6		7		9^1	11^3	8			13	10^2	14		3	12									33
1	5	3	2	8	9^2	10^1		13	11^3	6	7				12	4	14												34
1	2		4	5	6	10		9		12	11	7^1	8^2			13	3												35
1	2	5	4		14	9		7^3		6	10^2	12	8	13		11^1	3												36
1	2	4^2		5	8			9^1	11	12	7^4				6^3	10	13	3			14								37
	3			5	2			8^3		9^1	6			12			10	11	7^4	4					14	1	13		38

HEART OF MIDLOTHIAN

Year Formed: 1874. *Ground & Address:* Tynecastle Stadium, McLeod Street, Edinburgh EH11 2NL. *Telephone:* 0871 663 1874. *Fax:* 0131 200 7222. *E-mail:* supporterservices@homplc.co.uk *Website:* www.heartsfc.co.uk
Ground Capacity: 17,529. *Size of Pitch:* 100m × 64m.
Chief Executive and Chairwoman: Ann Budge. *Director of Football:* Craig Levein.
Head Coach: Robbie Neilson. *Assistant Head Coach:* Stevie Crawford. *Physio:* Rob Marshall.
Club Nicknames: 'Hearts', 'Jambos', 'Jam Tarts'.
Previous Grounds: The Meadows 1874, Powderhall 1878, Old Tynecastle 1881 Tynecastle Park, 1886.
Record Attendance: 53,396 v Rangers, Scottish Cup 3rd rd, 13 February 1932 (57,857 v Barcelona, 28 July 2007 at Murrayfield).
Record Transfer Fee received: £9,000,000 for Craig Gordon to Sunderland (August 2008).
Record of Transfer paid: £850,000 for Mirsad Beslija to Genk (January 2006).
Record Victory: 15-0 v King's Park, Scottish Cup 2nd rd, 13 February 1937 (21-0 v Anchor, EFA Cup, 30 October 1880).
Record Defeat: 1-8 v Vale of Leven, Scottish Cup 3rd rd, 1883; 0-7 v Celtic, Scottish Cup 4th rd, 1 December 2013.
Most Capped Player: Steven Pressley, 32, Scotland.
Most League Appearances: 515: Gary Mackay, 1980-97.
Most League Goals in Season (Individual): 44: Barney Battles, 1930-31.
Most Goals Overall (Individual): 214: John Robertson, 1983-98.

HEART OF MIDLOTHIAN – SCOTTISH PREMIERSHIP 2015–16 LEAGUE RECORD

Match No.	Date		Venue	Opponents	Result	H/T Score	Lg Pos.	Goalscorers	Attendance
1	Aug	2	H	St Johnstone	W 4-3	1-0	3	Delgado [4], Walker [53], Paterson [62], Nicholson [80]	16,334
2		8	A	Dundee	W 2-1	0-1	1	Delgado 2 (1 pen) [56 (p), 63]	8222
3		12	H	Motherwell	W 2-0	1-0	1	Reilly (pen) [32], King [64]	16,645
4		15	A	Ross Co	W 2-1	2-1	1	Sow [11], Ozturk [14]	4806
5		22	H	Partick Thistle	W 3-0	1-0	1	Sow [29], Nicholson [69], Delgado [71]	16,657
6		29	A	Hamilton A	L 2-3	0-1	3	King [53], Paterson [71]	4745
7	Sept	11	A	Inverness CT	L 0-2	0-0	3		4160
8		20	H	Aberdeen	L 1-3	0-3	3	Igor Rossi [52]	16,702
9		26	A	Celtic	D 0-0	0-0	3		46,297
10	Oct	3	H	Kilmarnock	D 1-1	1-0	3	Walker (pen) [40]	16,461
11		18	A	Dundee U	W 1-0	1-0	3	Delgado [16]	7461
12		24	H	Ross Co	W 2-0	1-0	3	Paterson [15], Sow [67]	16,264
13		31	A	Partick Thistle	W 4-0	1-0	2	Delgado 2 (1 pen) [38, 64 (p)], Sow 2 (1 pen) [51, 86 (p)]	4776
14	Nov	7	H	Hamilton A	W 2-0	2-0	2	Buaben [27], Djoum [38]	16,121
15		21	H	Dundee	D 1-1	1-0	2	Djoum [24]	16,736
16		28	A	Motherwell	D 2-2	1-1	3	Delgado [9], Sow [69]	5141
17	Dec	12	A	Aberdeen	L 0-1	0-0	3		13,110
18		19	A	St Johnstone	D 0-0	0-0	3		4780
19		27	H	Celtic	D 2-2	1-1	3	Nicholson [45], Sow [90]	16,844
20		30	A	Dundee U	W 3-2	3-2	3	Reilly [17], Buaben [26], Sow (pen) [30]	16,721
21	Jan	2	A	Kilmarnock	D 2-2	1-1	3	Reilly [45], Paterson [56]	5388
22		16	H	Motherwell	W 6-0	3-0	3	Igor Rossi [11], Sow [16], Reilly (pen) [22], Paterson [77], Delgado [87], Djoum (pen) [90]	16,574
23		24	A	Hamilton A	D 0-0	0-0	3		2684
24	Feb	10	A	Ross Co	W 3-0	0-0	3	Davies (og) [53], Dauda 2 [86, 89]	3391
25		20	A	Dundee U	L 1-2	0-1	3	Walker [48]	8031
26		27	H	Kilmarnock	W 1-0	1-0	3	Walker [7]	16,354
27	Mar	1	H	Inverness CT	W 2-0	1-0	3	Walker [35], Dauda [53]	15,767
28		5	H	Partick Thistle	W 1-0	1-0	3	Djoum [25]	16,558
29		12	A	Dundee	W 1-0	0-0	3	Walker [52]	6195
30		19	H	St Johnstone	L 0-3	0-2	3		16,295
31	Apr	2	A	Celtic	L 1-3	1-2	3	Walker [5]	49,009
32		8	H	Aberdeen	W 2-1	1-1	3	Delgado 2 [33, 61]	16,995
33		12	A	Inverness CT	D 0-0	0-0	3		3202
34		23	A	Motherwell	L 0-1	0-1	3		5125
35		30	H	Celtic	L 1-3	0-1	3	Dauda [57]	16,527
36	May	7	H	Ross Co	D 1-1	0-0	3	Delgado [84]	15,438
37		12	A	Aberdeen	W 1-0	0-0	3	Dauda [64]	10,087
38		15	H	St Johnstone	D 2-2	2-2	3	Djoum [17], Shaughnessy (og) [20]	16,046

Final League Position: 3

Honours
League Champions: Division I 1894-95, 1896-97, 1957-58, 1959-60. First Division 1979-80. Championship 2014-15.
Runners-up: Division I 1893-94, 1898-99, 1903-04, 1905-06, 1914-15, 1937-38, 1953-54, 1956-57, 1958-59, 1964-65. Premier Division 1985-86, 1987-88, 1991-92, 2005-06. First Division 1977-78, 1982-83.
Scottish Cup Winners: 1891, 1896, 1901, 1906, 1956, 1998, 2006, 2012; *Runners-up:* 1903, 1907, 1968, 1976, 1986, 1996.
League Cup Winners: 1954-55, 1958-59, 1959-60, 1962-63; *Runners-up:* 1961-62, 1996-97, 2012-13.

European: *European Cup:* 8 matches (1958-59, 1960-61, 2006-07). *Cup Winners' Cup:* 10 matches (1976-77, 1996-97, 1998-99). *UEFA Cup:* 46 matches (*Fairs Cup:* 1961-62, 1963-64, 1965-66. *UEFA Cup:* 1984-85, 1986-87, 1988-89, 1990-91, 1992-93, 1993-94, 2000-01, 2003-04, 2004-05, 2006-07). *Europa League:* 8 matches (2010-11, 2011-12, 2012-13).

Club colours: Shirt: Maroon. Shorts: White with maroon trim. Socks: Maroon.

Goalscorers: *League (59):* Delgado 12 (2 pens), Sow 9 (2 pens), Walker 7 (1 pen), Dauda 5, Djoum 5 (1 pen), Paterson 5, Reilly 4 (2 pens), Nicholson 3, Buaben 2, Igor Rossi 2, King 2, Ozturk 1, own goals 2.
William Hill Scottish FA Cup (3): Djoum 1, Nicholson 1, Paterson 1.
Scottish League Cup (10): Sow 2 (1 pen), Delgado 1, Djoum 1, McGhee 1, McHattie 1, Nicholson 1, Ozturk 1, Reilly 1, own goal 1.

Alexander N 35	Paterson C 27+2	Ozturk A 24	Augustyn B 21+1	Igor Rossi B 28+1	Walker J 20+2	Buaben P 33+3	Gomis M 12+5	Nicholson S 28+8	Delgado J 28+5	Sow O 22+1	McHattie K —+1	McGhee J 10+12	Reilly G 11+17	Oshaniwa J 24	King B 7+8	Oliver G —+1	McKirdy S 1+1	Morrison C —+1	Swanson D 4+4	Pallardo M 10+6	Djoum A 24+4	Smith L 5+5	Zanatta D 3+10	Souttar J 14+1	Cowie D 7+3	Dauda A 7+6	Kitchen P 9+1	Hamilton J 3	Moore L 1	Match No.
1	2	3	4	5	6²	7	8	9	10¹	11³	12	13	14																	1
1	2	6	3	4	9	7	8	12	11³	10¹			14	5²13																2
1	2	3	4²			8	7	9	12	10⁵	13	11	5	6³14																3
1	2	3	4	6	7¹	8	9³	10	11²		12	13	5	14																4
1	2	4	3		7²	8	9	10³	6¹		11	5	12		13	14														5
1	2⁴	4	3		9	8²	6	13	11	10¹		12	14	5	7³															6
1	2	3		4	13	6		8	11	9¹		14	5⁴	12	7³	10²														7
1	2	3	4	5	10	6²		12	11	8		9¹	13							7										8
1	2		4	3	9³	12	6	8	11²	10¹		13	5							7	14									9
1	2		3	4	9²	8	7	6	10	11¹		13⁴	5							12										10
1			3	4	12	8	13	9	11	10		2		5²						6¹	7³		14							11
1	2	3⁴	4		6³	7	13	9²	11³	10		5								14	8	12								12
1	2		4		8	12	9³	11²	10		3		5	13						6¹		7	14							13
1	2	3	4		7	8	9³	11¹	10			5	12							14	13	6²								14
1	2	3	4		7²	12	9		10			13	5	11¹						14	8	6³								15
1	2	3	4		13			10	8	11		12		5¹						9²	7	6								16
1	2	3	4			8	12	9³	10	11		5			13					7¹	6									17
1	2	3	4		7¹	8	9	11⁴	10²			14	13	5						12	6³									18
1	2	3	4		6	8²	9		11			10²	5	13						12	7¹	14								19
1		3	4		7	8¹	6³		10²			2	11	5	9			13		12		14								20
1	2	3	4		8			9	10	12		11²	5	6¹						7		13								21
1	2	3	4	5³	8			12	10¹			14	11²		9					7	6	13								22
1	2	3	4	5⁴		9			14	10³		12	11¹		6²					7	8	13								23
1	5				9²			6	11				4³		2					8	10¹14	13	3	7	12					24
1		4	3	13	6	7³		9				2⁴		5¹						14		11¹12	8	10						25
1	2³	3	14	5	6	8¹		9	13			10²								7			4	12	11					26
1	3		5³	9¹	7			6				14	10							8	2	12	4	13	11²					27
1	3		5¹	10	7			8	11³			13	14							9¹	2		4	6	12					28
1	3		10³	9		6¹	11²					5	13						14	8	2		4	7		12				29
1		4³		9	12	13	10		5			14								8	2		3	6¹	11²	7				30
1	3		4²	8¹	6³		10	11	12			5¹	9							13	2			14	7					31
1	3	4	5	8²	6¹		10	11³		13		12	9		14					2	7									32
1	12	3	4		11			14	10				5³						7¹	9	6²	2		13	8					33
1	2	3		8	6³			10¹11²			13								9	5		4	14	12	7				34
1	12	3	4²	6	7³			14	10			9							11			2	5¹	13	8				35
	2	3		6			9³13					10²	5							12		14	4	8¹	11	7	1			36
	2	3		7			12	10³				14	13	5						11		9¹	4		6²	8	1			37
	2	3		8			13	10³				14	5¹		6					12		3		11¹	7	1	9²			38

HIBERNIAN

Year Formed: 1875. *Ground & Address:* Easter Road Stadium, 12 Albion Place, Edinburgh EH7 5QG. *Telephone:* 0131 661 2159. *Fax:* 0131 659 6488. *E-mail:* club@hibernianfc.co.uk *Website:* www.hibernianfc.co.uk
Ground Capacity: 20,421 (all seated). *Size of Pitch:* 102m × 67m.
Chairman: Rod Petrie. *Chief Executive:* Leean Dempster.
Head Coach: Neil Lennon. *Assistant Head Coach:* Garry Parker. *Physio:* Kitty MacKinnon.
Club Nickname: 'Hibs', 'Hibees'.
Previous Grounds: Meadows 1875-78, Powderhall 1878-79, Mayfield 1879-80, First Easter Road 1880-92, Second Easter Road 1892-.
Record Attendance: 65,860 v Hearts, Division I, 2 January 1950.
Record Transfer Fee received: £4,400,000 for Scott Brown from Celtic (2007).
Record of Transfer paid: £700,000 for Ulises de la Cruz to LDU Quito (2001).
Record Victory: 15-1 v Pebbles Rovers, Scottish Cup 2nd rd, 11 February 1961.
Record Defeat: 0-10 v Rangers, Division I, 24 December 1898.
Most Capped Player: Lawrie Reilly, 38, Scotland.
Most League Appearances: 446: Arthur Duncan, 1969-84.
Most League Goals in Season (Individual): 42: Joe Baker, 1959-60.
Most Goals Overall (Individual): 233: Lawrie Reilly, 1945-58.

HIBERNIAN – SCOTTISH CHAMPIONSHIP 2015–16 LEAGUE RECORD

Match No.	Date		Venue	Opponents	Result		H/T Score	Lg Pos.	Goalscorers	Atten- dance
1	Aug	8	A	Dumbarton	L	1-2	1-1	7	Malonga [14]	1552
2		15	H	Greenock Morton	W	1-0	0-0	6	Cummings [58]	8923
3		23	A	Rangers	L	0-1	0-0	6		49,220
4		29	H	Raith R	W	2-0	1-0	5	Keatings [22], Cummings [50]	8484
5	Sept	12	H	Alloa Ath	W	3-0	1-0	3	Henderson [44], Cummings [50], McGinn [65]	7774
6		19	A	Livingston	W	1-0	0-0	3	Henderson [50]	3007
7		26	H	St Mirren	D	1-1	1-1	4	Boyle [42]	8911
8	Oct	3	A	Queen of the South	W	3-0	2-0	3	Cummings [3], Henderson [41], Boyle [89]	2745
9		17	H	Dumbarton	W	4-2	3-1	3	Malonga [21], Fontaine [26], Cummings (pen) [43], Keatings [60]	8221
10		20	A	Falkirk	W	1-0	1-0	2	Cummings (pen) [40]	5429
11		24	A	Raith R	W	2-1	2-0	2	McGinn [4], Cummings [26]	4114
12	Nov	1	H	Rangers	W	2-1	1-0	2	Cummings [11], Hanlon [73]	14,412
13		7	A	St Mirren	W	4-1	3-1	2	Cummings [10], Keatings 3 (1 pen) [37, 41, 78 (p)]	4503
14		17	H	Livingston	W	2-1	0-0	2	Keatings 2 [52, 69]	7801
15		21	A	Alloa Ath	W	1-0	0-0	2	Cummings [60]	1952
16	Dec	12	H	Falkirk	D	1-1	0-0	2	Boyle [90]	9459
17		19	H	Queen of the South	W	1-0	0-0	2	Malonga [90]	9163
18		28	A	Rangers	L	2-4	1-2	2	Cummings [23], Malonga [86]	49,995
19	Jan	2	H	Raith R	W	1-0	0-0	3	Cummings [50]	10,994
20		17	A	Falkirk	D	1-1	0-0	3	Cummings [73]	7081
21		23	H	St Mirren	W	3-1	2-1	2	Henderson [10], McGinn [44], Stokes [90]	10,160
22	Feb	2	A	Greenock Morton	W	1-0	0-0	2	Stokes [47]	2696
23		13	A	Livingston	D	0-0	0-0	2		2663
24		21	H	Alloa Ath	W	3-0	2-0	2	Boyle 2 [5, 77], Carmichael [40]	8765
25		24	H	Greenock Morton	L	0-3	0-1	2		8655
26		27	A	Dumbarton	L	2-3	0-2	2	Henderson [57], El Alagui [71]	1345
27	Mar	1	A	Queen of the South	L	0-1	0-0	2		2017
28		19	A	Raith R	L	1-2	1-1	3	Stokes [25]	2386
29	Apr	2	A	St Mirren	D	2-2	1-1	3	Cummings [27], El Alagui [89]	3765
30		5	H	Livingston	W	2-1	0-1	3	Stokes [75], Boyle [78]	7289
31		9	A	Alloa Ath	L	0-1	0-1	3		1364
32		12	H	Falkirk	D	2-2	1-0	3	Cummings 2 (1 pen) [10, 81 (p)]	10,277
33		20	H	Rangers	W	3-2	2-1	3	Cummings [5], Foderingham (og) [18], Gunnarsson [58]	12,231
34		23	A	Greenock Morton	D	0-0	0-0	3		2308
35		26	H	Dumbarton	W	4-0	2-0	3	Keatings 2 [7, 13], Cawley (og) [75], Stokes [90]	6686
36	May	1	H	Queen of the South	W	2-0	0-0	3	Gunnarsson [67], Cummings [79]	9900

Final League Position: 3

Honours
League Champions: Division I 1902-03, 1947-48, 1950-51, 1951-52. First Division 1980-81, 1998-99. Division II 1893-94, 1894-95, 1932-33; *Runners-up:* Division I 1896-97, 1946-47, 1949-50, 1952-53, 1973-74, 1974-75. Championship 2014-15.
Scottish Cup Winners: 1887, 1902, 2016; *Runners-up:* 1896, 1914, 1923, 1924, 1947, 1958, 1972, 1979, 2001, 2012, 2013.
League Cup Winners: 1972-73, 1991-92, 2006-07; *Runners-up:* 1950-51, 1968-69, 1974-75, 1985-86, 1993-94, 2003-04, 2015-16.
Drybrough Cup Winners: 1972-73, 1973-74.

European: *European Cup:* 6 matches (1955-56 semi-finals). *Cup Winners' Cup:* 6 matches (1972-73). *UEFA Cup:* 64 matches (*Fairs Cup:* 1960-61 semi-finals, 1961-62, 1962-63, 1965-66, 1967-68, 1968-69, 1970-71. *UEFA Cup:* 1973-74, 1974-75, 1975-76, 1976-77, 1978-79, 1989-90, 1992-93, 2001-02, 2005-06. *Europa League:* 4 matches 2010-11, 2013-14).

Club colours: Shirt: Green with white sleeves. Shorts: White. Socks: Green.

Goalscorers: *League (59):* Cummings 18 (3 pens), Keatings 9 (1 pen), Boyle 6, Henderson 5, Stokes 5, Malonga 4, McGinn 3, El Alagui 2, Gunnarsson 2, Carmichael 1, Fontaine 1, Hanlon 1, own goals 2.
William Hill Scottish FA Cup (11): Stokes 4, Cummings 2, Gray 1, Hanlon 1, Keatings 1, Malonga 1, McGregor 1.
Scottish League Cup (12): Cummings 4 (2 pens), Allan, S 1, Fontaine 1, Gray 1, Malonga 1, Martin 1, McGinn 1, Stevenson 1, own goal 1.
Petrofac Training Cup (2): Cummings 1 (1 pen), Stanton 1.
Premiership Play-Offs (6): Keatings 2 (1 pen), McGregor 2, Henderson 1, McGinn 1.

Oxley M 34	Gray D 30 + 1	Hanlon P 28 + 1	Fontaine L 22 + 4	Stevenson L 35	Bartley M 20 + 5	Fyvie F 20 + 1	Martin S 1 + 1	Allan S 1	Malonga D 13 + 6	Cummings J 31 + 2	McGinn J 33 + 3	Stanton S — + 4	Boyle M 12 + 13	Carmichael D 4 + 2	Henderson L 27 + 5	McGeouch D 14 + 5	Keatings J 18 + 10	McGregor D 24 + 4	Feruz I — + 6	El Alagui F 1 + 5	Anier H — + 3	Dagnall C 3 + 8	Stokes A 13 + 1	Gunnarsson N 8 + 2	Thomson K 2 + 3	Logan C 2	Match No.
1	2	3	4	5	6^3	7	8^1	9	10	11^2	12	13	14														1
1	2	3	4	5	6^1	9			10	12	8	14	7^2	11^2	13												2
1	2^1	3	4	5		7			13	11	6	14	8	10^2	9^3	12											3
1	2	3	4	5	7^3		13		12	11	6				9	8^2	10^1	14									4
1	2	3	4	5		7			14	11^3	8		12		9^2	6	10^1		13								5
1	2	3	4	5		7			10^1	11	9		12		8^2	6			13								6
1	2	3	4	5		7			12	4^1	8		10^1	13	9^2	6											7
1	2	3		5		7			10	11	8^2	14	12	13	9^3	6		4									8
1	2		4	5	12	7^2			10	11^3	8				9	13	6^1	3	14								9
1	2	4	13	5		7			10	11	8		12		6	9^2	3										10
1	5	3	4	9	13	14			10^1	11	6^3				8^2	7	12	2									11
1	2	4		5	12	7			10^3	11	9				8^2	6^1	13	3	14								12
1	2	4	13	5	6				11^2	10^1	7		12		9	8^3	3	14									13
1	2	4	5	13		7				11^3	9		6^1		8^2	12	10	3	14								14
1	2	3		5	6	7			10^1	11^3	8		14		13	9^2	4					12					15
1	6	3^4	4	5		7			10^1	11	8		13		12	9^2	2					14					16
1	2		4	5		7			12	10^2	9		6^1		8	11^3	3	14			13						17
1	2^1	4	12	5		7			13	11	8^3		14		9	6	10^2	3									18
1	2	3	4	5	7^1				10	11^2	9				6	8	12				13						19
1		3	4	5		7			10^2	11	8		12		6	9^1	2					13					20
1	2	3	4	5	7	6				11^2	8				9^3		13	14					10^1	12			21
1	14	12	4^1	5		6					8				9	7	11	3					13	10^2	2^3		22
1	2	3		5	6				10^3	8		13			7^2		14	4					11^1	9		12	23
1		4	3		7^2				12			5	9		8	6^1	11	14					10^3		2	13	24
1	2	4		5	13				10	8			7		9^2	12	3	14					11^3			6^1	25
1	4^3	14		5	6^1				11	8			9	7		10^2	3				12				2		26
1	2	4		5	6				11^1	7	8		9		12	3						13	10^2				27
1	2	4		5	7				11^1	8			6		9^2	3					12	13	10				28
1	2	3		5	7^2				11	8			6^1		9			4			13	12	10				29
1	2	4		5					10^3	8	13		6		12	3			11^1			9	14	7^2			30
1	2	4		5	6				11^2	8			7		9^1							13	10	3			31
1	2^1	4		5	8^3	7			11	9^2		6	13			3							10	12	14		32
1	5	4		9	7	6			11^1	8					12	3						13	10^2	2			33
1	5	4		9	7^1	6			11	13	12				8^3	14	3						10	2^2			34
		4	5		8				9	6	7		10	3								11	2			1	35
	3	4	5		6^1				12	9	7		8^2	13	11^3							14	10	2		1	36

INVERNESS CALEDONIAN THISTLE

Year Formed: 1994. *Ground & Address:* Tulloch Caledonian Stadium, Stadium Road, Inverness IV1 1FF. *Telephone:* 01463 222880. *Fax:* 01463 227479. *E-mail:* info@ictfc.co.uk *Website:* www.ictfc.co.uk
Ground Capacity: 7,780 (all seated). *Size of Pitch:* 105m × 68m.
Chairman: Kenny Cameron. *Club Secretary:* Ian MacDonald.
Club Nicknames: 'Caley Thistle', 'Caley Jags', 'ICT'.
Manager: Richie Foran. *Assistant Manager:* Brian Rice. *Physio:* John McCreadie.
Record Attendance: 7,753 v Rangers, SPL, 20 January 2008.
Record Transfer Fee received: £400,000 for Marius Niculae to Dinamo Bucharest (July 2008).
Record of Transfer paid: £65,000 for John Rankin from Ross Co (July 2006).
Record Victory: 8-1 v Annan Ath, Scottish Cup 3rd rd, 24 January 1998; 7-0 v Ayr U, First Division, 24 April 2010.
Record Defeats: 0-6 v Airdrieonians, First Division, 21 Sep 2000; 0-6 v Celtic, League Cup 3rd rd, 22 Sep 2010; 0-6 v Celtic, Scottish Premiership, 27 April 2014.
Most Capped Player: Richard Hastings, 38 (59), Canada.
Most League Appearances: 490: Ross Tokely, 1995-2012.
Most League Goals in Season: 27: Iain Stewart, 1996-97; Denis Wyness, 2002-03.
Most Goals Overall (Individual): 118: Denis Wyness, 2000-03, 2005-08.

INVERNESS CALEDONIAN TH – SCOTTISH PREMIERSHIP 2015–16 LEAGUE RECORD

Match No.	Date		Venue	Opponents	Result	H/T Score	Lg Pos.	Goalscorers	Attendance
1	Aug	1	H	Motherwell	L 0-1	0-1	10		3307
2		8	A	St Johnstone	D 1-1	1-0	10	Christie [9]	2959
3		12	H	Partick Thistle	D 0-0	0-0	9		3141
4		15	A	Celtic	L 2-4	0-2	11	Christie [71], Lopez [78]	42,727
5		22	H	Hamilton A	L 0-2	0-1	11		3003
6		29	A	Dundee	D 1-1	0-0	10	Raven [60]	4767
7	Sept	11	H	Hearts	W 2-0	0-0	7	Vincent [49], Storey [89]	4160
8		19	A	Dundee U	D 1-1	0-1	9	Meekings [56]	6235
9		26	H	Aberdeen	W 2-1	2-1	8	Storey [8], Christie [29]	6410
10	Oct	3	A	Ross Co	W 2-1	2-0	8	Storey [42], Vincent [45]	5473
11		17	A	Kilmarnock	L 0-2	0-1	8		3234
12		24	H	St Johnstone	L 0-1	0-0	9		3471
13		31	H	Dundee	D 1-1	0-0	9	Tansey (pen) [64]	2940
14	Nov	7	A	Motherwell	W 3-1	2-0	8	Tansey (pen) [11], Storey [46], Vigurs [53]	3569
15		21	H	Partick Thistle	L 1-2	1-1	8	Storey [6]	2864
16		29	H	Celtic	L 1-3	1-1	8	Storey [39]	5976
17	Dec	12	H	Kilmarnock	W 2-1	2-0	7	Vigurs 2 [14, 32]	2775
18		19	H	Dundee U	D 2-2	0-1	9	Polworth [46], Horner [90]	2981
19		26	A	Aberdeen	D 2-2	1-0	8	Polworth [41], Tansey (pen) [47]	15,142
20		30	A	Hamilton A	W 4-3	1-0	6	Tansey 2 [18, 88], Polworth 2 [51, 90]	1555
21	Jan	2	H	Ross Co	W 2-0	2-0	6	Storey [26], Tansey [45]	5388
22		16	H	Kilmarnock	L 1-2	1-1	7	Draper [41]	2937
23		23	H	Partick Thistle	D 0-0	0-0	6		3556
24	Feb	15	A	Aberdeen	W 3-1	1-1	6	Vigurs [18], Tansey (pen) [51], Tremarco [65]	4544
25		20	A	Celtic	L 0-3	0-0	7		43,600
26		27	A	Dundee	D 1-1	1-0	7	Draper [13]	5048
27	Mar	1	A	Hearts	L 0-2	0-1	7		15,767
28		9	A	St Johnstone	L 0-1	0-0	9		2157
29		12	H	Hamilton A	L 0-1	0-0	9		3510
30		19	A	Ross Co	W 3-0	2-0	9	Polworth [32], Draper [37], Storey [48]	5912
31	Apr	2	H	Motherwell	L 1-2	0-0	9	Vigurs (pen) [70]	3348
32		9	A	Dundee U	W 2-0	1-0	9	Storey [13], Vigurs [50]	6927
33		12	H	Hearts	D 0-0	0-0	9		3202
34		24	H	Kilmarnock	W 3-1	0-1	8	Tansey (pen) [55], Draper [73], Williams, D [76]	2228
35		30	A	Partick Thistle	W 4-1	1-0	7	Tremarco [14], Storey [46], Meekings [76], Roberts [85]	2609
36	May	6	A	Dundee U	L 2-3	0-2	8	Roberts [56], Polworth [69]	3587
37		11	A	Hamilton A	W 1-0	1-0	7	Devine [41]	1516
38		14	H	Dundee	W 4-0	0-0	7	Storey [61], Devine [69], Draper [71], Foran (pen) [84]	3794

Final League Position: 7

Honours
League Champions: First Division 2003-04, 2009-10. Third Division 1996-97. *Runners-up:* Second Division 1998-99.
Scottish Cup Winners: 2015; Semi-finals 2003, 2004; Quarter-finals 1996.
League Cup Runners-up: 2013-14.
League Challenge Cup Winners: 2003-04; *Runners-up:* 1999-2000, 2009-10.

European: *Europa League:* 4 matches (2015-16).

Club colours: Shirt: Blue with vertical red stripes. Shorts: Blue. Socks: Blue with red hoops.

Goalscorers: *League (54):* Storey 11, Tansey 8 (5 pens), Polworth 6, Vigurs 6 (1 pen), Draper 5, Christie 3, Devine 2, Meekings 2, Roberts 2, Tremarco 2, Vincent 2, Foran 1 (1 pen), Horner 1, Lopez 1, Raven 1, Williams, D 1.
William Hill Scottish FA Cup (6): Mbuyi-Mutombo 2, Vigurs 2, Roberts 1, Storey 1.
Scottish League Cup (3): Devine 1, Storey 1, Tansey 1.
UEFA Europa League (0).

Fon Williams O 38	Raven D 18 + 1	Warren G 23 + 2	Meekings J 21	Devine D 37	Wedderburn N 8 + 7	Tansey G 37	Draper R 31 + 1	Williams D 25 + 9	Lopez D 5 + 2	Christie R 12 + 1	Mbuyi-Mutombo A 12 + 13	Polworth L 33 + 3	Horner L 11 + 5	Sutherland A — + 5	Vigurs I 24 + 6	Tremarco C 28 + 4	Vincent J 14 + 2	Storey M 29 + 1	Sho-Silva T — + 5	Foran R — + 7	Fisher A — + 1	Roberts J 8 + 1	Hughes L 4 + 5	Williams R — + 8	Match No.
1	2	3[3]	4[3]	5	6[1]	7	8	9	10	11	12	13	14												1
1	2		4	13	8	3	9	10[1]	7	11[2]	6	5	12												2
1	2		3		7	4	5	11	10	6	8	9[1]			12										3
1	2		3	14	6	4	11	13	12	10	8[1]	9				7[3]	5[2]								4
1	2		4	13	6[1]	3	5	11[3]	9	8	7		14			10[2]	12								5
1	2		4	12	6	3	10	11	9	8[4]	7[1]					5									6
1	2	3	4			7	6	10		9[1]		13			5	8[2]	11	12							7
1	2	3	4			7	6	10[1]		9		13			5	8	11[2]	12							8
1	2	4	3	13		7	6	5		9[4]	12					8[1]	10	11[2]							9
1	2	4	3			6	7	5[2]		9[1]		8			13	12	10	11							10
1	2[3]	4	3			10	6[1]	7[2]		9	13	8		14	12	5		11							11
1	2	4	3			6		10[1]		9	7[2]	13			12	5	8	11							12
1	2[8]	13	4			3	6	10[2]		11	7			12	8[1]	5	9								13
1	13	4	3	14		8					12	10[1]			6	2	9[3]	5	7	11[2]					14
1		4	3			8	14	10[1]			12				6[3]	2	9	5	7	11[2]	13				15
1		3	2	4		6	7	5		13	8[3]	14			10[2]	9[1]	11	12							16
1		3	2	4		6[2]	7	5			12	8			10[3]	13	9	11[1]	14						17
1		3		4		7[2]	6	5			12	8	2		10[1]	13	9[3]	11	14						18
1	2	3	4			7	6	10		13	12	8[1]			5	9	11[2]								19
1	2	3	4			7[1]	6	9		12	8				5	10	11								20
1	2	3	4			7[1]	6	9		13	14	8		12	5[2]	10[3]	11								21
1	2[3]	4	3[2]			8	6	9		12	7[1]		14		10	5	11				13				22
1	2	3	4			6	9	10		8[1]	12	7			5	11									23
1		3	4			6	7	12		8	2[2]	10			5	11[3]						9[1]	13	14	24
1		3	4			6[3]	7	12		8	2[2]	9			5	11		10[1]				13	14		25
1		3	4			7	6	12		8[1]	2	10			5	11[2]						9	13		26
1		3	4			7	9			6	2[2]	8			5	10						11[1]	13	14	27
1		3[4]		4	12	8	7	6		2[2]	13				9	5						10[1]	11		28
1			4	3		7	6	5		8[3]	2	10				13		12				9[1]	11		29
1		3	2	4		6	7	14		9[3]		8[1]	5		11	13		10[2]	12						30
1		3	2[3]	4		6	12	9		8	14	7	5		10[2]			11[1]	13						31
1		3	2	4		6	7	13		11[1]	9	8	5		12	10[2]									32
1		3	2	4		7	6	13		11[1]	9	8	5		12	10[2]									33
1		3	2	4		7	6	9		12	10	8[1]	5		11										34
1		3	2	4		7	6			10[2]	8	5			11			9[3]	14	13					35
1		3	2	4[3]		8	7	13		10	6[1]	5			11	12		9	14						36
1		3	2	4		7	6	10[2]		8		9	5		11[1]	13		12							37
1	13	3	2[2]	4		8	7	9[3]		6		10	5		11[1]	12					14				38

KILMARNOCK

Year Formed: 1869. *Ground & Address:* Rugby Park, Kilmarnock KA1 2DP. *Telephone:* 01563 545300. *Fax:* 01563 522181. *Email:* info@kilmarnockfc.co.uk *Website:* www.kilmarnockfc.co.uk
Ground Capacity: 18,128 (all seated). *Size of Pitch:* 102m × 67m.
Chairman: Jim Mann. *Secretary:* Michael Johnston.
Manager: Lee Clark. *Assistant Manager:* Lee McCulloch. *Physio:* Alex MacQueen.
Club Nickname: 'Killie'.
Previous Grounds: Rugby Park (Dundonald Road); The Grange; Holm Quarry; Rugby Park 1899.
Record Attendance: 35,995 v Rangers, Scottish Cup Quarter-final, 10 March 1962.
Record Transfer Fee received: £1,900,000 for Steven Naismith to Rangers (2007).
Record Transfer Fee paid: £340,000 for Paul Wright from St Johnstone (1995).
Record Victory: 11-1 v Paisley Academical, Scottish Cup 1st rd, 18 January 1930.
Record Defeat: 1-9 v Celtic, Division I, 13 August 1938.
Most Capped Player: Joe Nibloe, 11, Scotland.
Most League Appearances: 481: Alan Robertson, 1972-88.
Most League Goals in Season (Individual): 34: Harry 'Peerie' Cunningham 1927-28; Andy Kerr 1960-61.
Most Goals Overall (Individual): 148: Willy Culley, 1912-23.

KILMARNOCK – SCOTTISH PREMIERSHIP 2015–16 LEAGUE RECORD

Match No.	Date	Venue	Opponents	Result	H/T Score	Lg Pos.	Goalscorers	Attendance
1	Aug 1	H	Dundee	L	0-4	0-2	12		5207
2	9	A	Aberdeen	L	0-2	0-1	12		11,305
3	12	H	Celtic	D	2-2	1-1	12	Magennis 44, Higginbotham (pen) 88	6090
4	15	A	Partick Thistle	D	2-2	1-1	12	McKenzie 38, Boyd 85	3600
5	22	H	Ross Co	L	0-4	0-4	12		3604
6	29	A	Motherwell	L	0-1	0-1	12		4136
7	Sept 12	H	Dundee U	W	2-1	1-0	10	Higginbotham (pen) 44, McHattie 88	8264
8	19	H	St Johnstone	W	2-1	1-1	8	Magennis 40, Easton, B (og) 60	3165
9	26	H	Hamilton A	L	1-2	1-0	10	Kiltie 34	3308
10	Oct 3	A	Hearts	D	1-1	0-1	10	Balatoni 79	16,461
11	17	H	Inverness CT	W	2-0	1-0	9	Kiltie 45, Magennis 66	3234
12	24	A	Dundee	W	2-1	1-0	8	Magennis 9, Smith 48	4970
13	31	H	Motherwell	L	0-1	0-0	8		3931
14	Nov 7	A	St Johnstone	L	1-2	1-1	9	Smith 2	3475
15	21	A	Celtic	D	0-0	0-0	9		42,770
16	28	H	Partick Thistle	L	2-5	1-2	10	Magennis 23, Connolly 72	3860
17	Dec 5	H	Dundee U	D	1-1	1-1	10	Boyd 4	2828
18	12	A	Inverness CT	L	1-2	0-2	11	Connolly 87	2775
19	19	A	Aberdeen	L	0-4	0-2	11		3928
20	26	A	Hamilton A	W	1-0	0-0	11	Obadeyi 69	2006
21	29	A	Ross Co	L	2-3	1-1	11	Obadeyi 33, Magennis 48	3518
22	Jan 2	H	Hearts	D	2-2	1-1	11	Balatoni 43, Magennis 80	5388
23	16	A	Inverness CT	W	2-1	1-1	11	Kiltie 9, Slater 51	2937
24	23	A	Dundee U	L	1-5	0-4	11	Magennis 82	7729
25	30	H	Hamilton A	L	0-1	0-0	11		3076
26	Feb 13	A	Motherwell	W	2-0	0-0	10	Kiltie 56, Slater 61	3764
27	20	H	Dundee	D	0-0	0-0	11		3688
28	27	H	Hearts	L	0-1	0-1	11		16,354
29	Mar 1	H	Ross Co	L	0-2	0-1	11		2633
30	12	A	Aberdeen	L	1-2	0-1	11	Magennis 47	13,725
31	19	H	Celtic	L	0-1	0-0	11		6867
32	Apr 2	A	Partick Thistle	D	0-0	0-0	11		4359
33	9	H	St Johnstone	W	3-0	1-0	11	Boyd 2 (1 pen) 25, 88 (p), Higginbotham 65	3693
34	24	A	Inverness CT	L	1-3	1-0	11	Higginbotham 44	2228
35	30	A	Hamilton A	W	4-0	2-0	11	Kiltie 2 11, 32, Boyd (pen) 58, Magennis 77	3595
36	May 7	H	Partick Thistle	L	0-2	0-1	11		5729
37	11	A	Dundee	D	1-1	0-1	11	Balatoni 55	4335
38	14	H	Dundee U	L	2-4	2-1	11	Higginbotham 27, Obadeyi 34	2702

Final League Position: 11

Honours
League Champions: Division I 1964-65. Division II 1897-98, 1898-99; *Runners-up:* Division I 1959-60, 1960-61, 1962-63, 1963-64. First Division 1975-76, 1978-79, 1981-82, 1992-93. Division II 1953-54, 1973-74. Second Division 1989-90.
Scottish Cup Winners: 1920, 1929, 1997; *Runners-up:* 1898, 1932, 1938, 1957, 1960.
League Cup Winners: 2011-12; *Runners-up:* 1952-53, 1960-61, 1962-63, 2000-01, 2006-07.

European: *European Cup:* 4 matches (1965-66). *Cup Winners' Cup:* 4 matches (1997-98). *UEFA Cup:* 32 matches (*Fairs Cup:* 1964-65, 1966-67 semi-finals, 1969-70, 1970-71. *UEFA Cup:* 1998-99, 1999-2000, 2001-02).

Club colours: Shirts: White and blue stripes. Shorts: Blue. Socks: White.

Goalscorers: *League (41):* Magennis 10, Kiltie 6, Boyd 5 (2 pens), Higginbotham 5 (2 pens), Balatoni 3, Obadeyi 3, Connolly 2, Slater 2, Smith 2, McHattie 1, McKenzie 1, own goal 1.
William Hill Scottish FA Cup (2): McKenzie 1, Slater 1.
Scottish League Cup (6): Magennis 2, Boyd 1 (1 pen), Higginbotham 1, McKenzie 1, Slater 1.
Premiership Play-Offs (4): Kiltie 2, Addison 1, Boyd 1.

MacDonald J 37	Westlake D 7+1	Connolly M 10	Findlay S 21+1	Smith S 21+1	Johnston C 1	Hamil J 14+2	Robinson S 6+6	Higginbotham K 23+4	Boyd K 15+14	Magennis J 32+2	McKenzie R 23+5	O'Hara M 23+6	Carrick D 1+10	Ashcroft L 14+1	Kiltie G 30+5	Splaine A 1+6	Mclean S —+1	McCulloch L 1	Barbour R 1+1	Slater C 23+3	Obadeyi T 15+15	McHattie K 18+3	Brennan C 1+2	Balatoni C 30	Frizzell A 6+4	Syme D 4+1	Hodson L 13	Dicker G 12	Faubert J 7+2	Addison M 6	Henshall A 1+1	Taylor G 1	Clark L —+1	Match No.
1	2	3	4	5	6³	7¹	8	9	10	11¹	12	13	14																					1
1	2		4			6	8	9	7¹¹	11	12	10			3¹					5	13													2
1	2	3		5		8	9²	10	7	11	12		4¹	6³	13	14																		3
1	2	3		5		6²		10	12	11	9	7		4	8¹	13																		4
1	2²	3¹	12	5				9	11	6	10	7		4		14			8³	13														5
1	12		3	5¹		2		9¹	11	10³	6	7		4	14					8	13													6
1	2		3			7	14	9¹	13	11²	6		4	10						8¹	12	5												7
1¹	2¹		4			7		9		11	10	12		3	6²					8	14	5	13											8
1			6²	12²		8	13	11		2			3⁴	9	14					7	10¹	5		4										9
1		3	14	6²				9³	13	11	12	2		8						7	10¹	5		4										10
1		4	5					10	13	11²	8³	2		9¹						6	12	7		3	14									11
1		3	6				14	10	13	11²	8³	2		9¹						7	12	5		4										12
1		3	6					10²	13	11	8	2		9¹						7	12	5		4										13
1		3	7					10²	13	11	6	2	14	9¹						8³	12	5		4										14
1	3		9			13	7	10²		11		6¹		2						8	5			4										15
1	3		8			7	10¹	12	11			2	14	9						13	6²	5¹		4										16
1	3	5¹	9¹	8			10³	11			2	14	13							7	6²	12		4										17
1	3		6			7³	14	11	8		2	12	13							9¹	10¹	5		4										18
1	3	5	7³	6¹				11²	8	13		10	9	2	12	14				4														19
1		4	7					11		2	13		9¹	12						6	10	5		3	8²									20
1		4	7					13	11		2¹	14	8²							6	10	5		3	9³	12								21
1			7					13	11	12			3	8						6²	10¹	5		4	9	2								22
1		5		6		13	10²				11	3	9							7	12			4	8¹	2								23
1		2	6¹	7			10³	11					3²	8						9	14	13		4	12	5								24
1			12	8		10	11	6²		14	3	9			7	13	5¹			4		2												25
1		4	5			14		11	8²		13	9			7³	10¹				3	12			2	6									26
1		4				12	13	11	8		9¹				6	10²	5			3		2	7											27
1		3					13	11		2¹		9			6²	10	5			8		7	12											28
1		4				12		10	6²	14	13	7			9¹	11				3		2	8	5³										29
1		4	5			12	13	10	6¹	14					7³	9²				3		2	8	11										30
1						8	11²	10¹	5		3	9	12		13					4		2	7	6										31
1						10¹	11	12	8²	5		6			3	13				2	7	9	4											32
1						9¹	11	10	12	2		6			4					5	8	7	3											33
1⁴						9¹	11		8	2		14	10³		13					12	4²	5	7	6	3									34
						11	8¹	9	2		10				6	12	1	4		5	7		3											35
1						13	11	8	9	2		10¹			6¹	12				4³		5	7		3	14								36
1	3¹					11	8		12			10			13					4	9	5	6	7²	2									37
1						10³		6		3					7	11	14			4¹	9		5²	13		8	2	12						38

LIVINGSTON

Year Formed: 1974. *Ground:* Tony Macaroni Arena, Almondvale Stadium, Alderstone Road, Livingston EH54 7DN.
Telephone: 01506 417000. *Fax:* 01506 429 948.
Email: lfcreception@livingstonfc.co.uk *Website:* www.livingstonfc.co.uk
Ground Capacity: 9,865 (all seated). *Size of Pitch:* 98m × 69m.
Chairman (Interim): Robert Wilson. *Secretary:* Carolyn Sumner.
Head Coach: David Hopkin. *First Team Coach:* Ian McCaldon. *Physio:* Andy Mackenzie.
Club Nickname: 'Livi Lions'.
Previous Grounds: Meadowbank Stadium (as Meadowbank Thistle).
Record Attendance: 10,024 v Celtic, Premier League, 18 August 2001.
Record Transfer Fee received: £1,000,000 for David Fernandez to Celtic (June 2002).
Record Transfer Fee paid: £120,000 for Wes Hoolahan from Shelbourne (December 2005).
Record Victory: 8-0 v Stranraer, League Cup, 1st rd, 31 July 2012.
Record Defeat: 0-8 v Hamilton A. Division II, 14 December 1974.
Most Capped Player (under 18): Ian Little.
Most League Appearances: 446: Walter Boyd, 1979-89.
Most League Goals in Season (Individual): 22: Leigh Griffiths, 2008-09; Iain Russell, 2010-11.
Most Goals Overall (Individual): 64: David Roseburgh, 1986-93.

LIVINGSTON – SCOTTISH CHAMPIONSHIP 2015–16 LEAGUE RECORD

Match No.	Date		Venue	Opponents		Result	H/T Score	Lg Pos.	Goalscorers	Atten- dance
1	Aug	8	A	Raith R	L	0-3	0-2	10		1560
2		15	H	Queen of the South	L	0-1	0-0	10		856
3		22	H	Falkirk	L	1-2	0-1	9	Mullen 52	1211
4		29	A	St Mirren	D	1-1	1-1	9	Buchanan (pen) 22	3018
5	Sept	5	A	Greenock Morton	L	2-4	0-1	10	White 85, Sheerin 89	1186
6		12	H	Rangers	L	0-3	0-2	10		44,832
7		19	H	Hibernian	L	0-1	0-0	10		3007
8		26	A	Alloa Ath	W	3-0	1-0	9	Buchanan 2 23, 78, Sheerin 59	622
9	Oct	3	A	Dumbarton	L	1-2	1-1	10	Glen 44	819
10		17	H	St Mirren	L	0-1	0-1	10		1199
11		24	A	Queen of the South	W	4-1	0-1	9	Pitman 50, White 67, Buchanan 2 75, 85	1485
12		31	H	Raith R	W	3-0	1-0	7	White 2 6, 64, Gallagher 61	957
13	Nov	7	A	Greenock Morton	L	0-1	0-1	7		1758
14		17	A	Hibernian	L	1-2	0-0	7	Sheerin 87	7801
15		21	H	Rangers	D	1-1	0-1	7	Hippolyte 51	6505
16	Dec	12	A	Alloa Ath	L	0-1	0-0	9		937
17		19	H	Dumbarton	D	1-1	1-0	9	Pitman 14	911
18		26	A	St Mirren	W	4-1	2-1	8	Buchanan 2 23, 66, Gordon 32, Glen 54	2952
19		29	A	Falkirk	L	0-2	0-0	8		4245
20	Jan	2	H	Queen of the South	L	0-2	0-0	9		958
21		16	A	Rangers	L	1-4	0-4	9	Buchanan 55	42,906
22		23	H	Falkirk	D	1-1	0-1	9	Buchanan 51	1536
23		30	A	Dumbarton	L	0-1	0-0	9		760
24	Feb	13	H	Hibernian	D	0-0	0-0	9		2663
25		20	A	Raith R	L	0-2	0-1	9		1617
26		27	A	Alloa Ath	W	3-1	3-1	9	Longridge 11, White 14, Stanton 39	619
27	Mar	1	H	Greenock Morton	D	0-0	0-0	9		787
28		5	H	Dumbarton	W	2-0	1-0	9	Buchanan 29, White 83	828
29		19	H	St Mirren	L	2-3	1-2	9	Buchanan 16, White 53	1228
30		26	A	Falkirk	W	2-1	0-0	9	White 76, Stanton 90	3897
31	Apr	2	H	Alloa Ath	D	0-0	0-0	9		927
32		5	A	Hibernian	L	1-2	1-0	9	White 23	7289
33		9	A	Greenock Morton	L	1-2	1-0	9	White 33	1463
34		23	A	Queen of the South	L	1-3	1-0	9	Stanton 29	1421
35		26	H	Rangers	W	1-0	1-0	9	Halkett 45	5021
36	May	1	H	Raith R	L	0-1	0-0	9		1049

Final League Position: 9

Honours
League Champions: First Division 2000-01. Second Division 1986-87, 1998-99, 2010-11. Third Division 1995-96, 2009-10; *Runners-up:* Second Division 1982-83. First Division 1987-88.
Scottish Cup: Semi-finals 2001, 2004.
League Cup Winners: 2003-04. Semi-finals 1984-85. *B&Q Cup:* Semi-finals 1992-93, 1993-94, 2001.
League Challenge Cup Winners: 2014-15. *Runners-up:* 2000-01.

European: *UEFA Cup:* 4 matches (2002-03).

Club colours: Shirt: Yellow with black trim. Shorts: Black with yellow trim. Socks: Yellow with black tops.

Goalscorers: *League (37):* Buchanan 11 (1 pen), White 10, Sheerin 3, Stanton 3, Glen 2, Pitman 2, Gallagher 1, Gordon 1, Halkett 1, Hippolyte 1, Longridge 1, Mullen 1.
William Hill Scottish FA Cup (3): White 2, Glen 1.
Scottish League Cup (4): Buchanan 1, Gallagher 1, Mullen 1, White 1.
Petrofac Training Cup (3): Hippolyte 1, Mullen 1, White 1.
Championship Play-Offs (6): Buchanan 2, White 2, Halkett 1, Mullen 1.

Jamieson D 10	Cole D 19 + 1	Gallagher D 23	Sives C 5	Longridge J 29 + 1	Hippolyte M 11 + 6	Pitman S 30 + 2	Gibbons K 15 + 3	Mullen D 12 + 7	Buchanan L 26 + 9	White J 25 + 9	Glen G 17 + 5	Georgiev S 2 + 6	Sheerin J 8 + 21	Millan R 7 + 2	Gordon B 28	Faria H 15 + 3	Neill M 17 + 6	McCallum M 26	Currie R 1 + 7	Knox M 2 + 5	Fotheringham M 14	Stanton S 12 + 1	Halkett C 15	Kakay O 10	Telfer C 10 + 3	Mullin J 7 + 2	Match No.
1	2	4	5^{1}	6	7	8	9^{2}	10^{3}	11	12	13	14															1
1	4	3	2	11	8	7^{1}	6^{2}	10	12	9	13	14	5^{3}														2
1	6	2	4	9^{2}	8		10	14	11^{3}	12	5^{1}	13		3	7												3
1	6	2	3	5	10	9^{1}	7		11^{3}	14	12	8^{2}			4	13											4
1	8	3		5^{1}	6		7	11^{2}	10^{3}	12	9		14	2	4^{4}	13											5
1	6	3	4^{1}	5	10	7^{3}	14	13	11^{2}		8			2	9	12											6
1		3		5	10	8	7^{1}		11^{3}	12	6^{2}	13	14	2		9	4										7
7	3			5	9^{1}	8			10	13	6^{2}	14	11^{3}	2	4	12		1									8
7^{1}	4		5^{2}	12^{8}	6	14		11		9		10^{3}	2	3	8	13	1										9
	3		9	7	5^{1}		10	12	8^{2}	13^{1}	11			4	6	2	1										10
	3		5		9^{2}	8^{3}		12	10	6		11^{1}	14	4	7	2	1	13									11
	2		9	12	7	6^{3}		10^{1}	11	5^{2}		13		3	8	4	1	14									12
	4		5		7	9^{1}		10	11	6		12		3	8	2	1										13
	3		5	9^{1}	10	7		12	11^{2}	13	14	6	4	8^{3}	2	1											14
	4		9	5^{3}	7	6		13	11^{2}	12		10^{1}	14	3	8	2	1										15
	4		9	12	7	6^{1}		10	11	5		13		3	8^{2}	2	1										16
	4		9		7	8	12		11	5		10^{1}		3	6	2	1										17
	3		5	12	7		9^{1}	10^{3}	11^{2}	8		13		4	6^{2}	2	1	14									18
1	2		14	9^{3}	7	8^{1}	12	11^{2}	13	6		10		3	5^{4}	4											19
1	2		9^{3}	12	6	14	8^{1}	11^{2}	10	5		13		3	7	4											20
	3		5		7	8^{2}	12	13	11^{3}	9^{1}				4		2	1	14		6	10						21
	3		5	12	7		9^{1}	11	10					4		1		8	6	2							22
6^{1}	4			8^{3}		10^{2}	7	9	11	13				12	1			3	2	5	14						23
7			5^{1}	8		11^{3}	10	12				4		1	14		6		3	2	13	9^{2}					24
4				8^{1}	12	11^{2}	10			14		3		1		7	9	2	5	13	6^{3}						25
3			5	13		11^{1}	12	10^{2}				4		1	14	8	9	2	6^{2}	8	7						26
3			5	14		10^{1}	13	11^{2}				4		1		8	9	2	6^{2}	7	12						27
4			5	8		10^{2}	13			12		3		1		14	7	9^{2}	2	11^{1}	6						28
4^{1}					14	10	11			13		3		12	1		7	9	2	5^{2}	8	6^{3}					29
4			5^{8}	9		11^{3}	10			13		3		14	1		7	12	2	8^{2}	6^{1}						30
4				6^{2}		10	11			13		3		5^{3}	1		14	7	8	2	9^{1}	12					31
4			5	8		10^{1}	11			12		3			1	13	14	7		2	9^{2}	6^{3}					32
4			5	6		11	10			14		3^{1}		12	1		13	7^{3}	9	2	8^{2}						33
			5	11^{2}		13	6	10		12				4	1		8	9	2	3	7^{1}						34
			5	8		10^{2}	12	11^{1}		14				4	1	13	7^{3}	9	3	2		6					35
1	13					6^{3}	12	14		11^{1}				2		10	7	3		4^{2}	5	8	9				36

MONTROSE

Year Formed: 1879. *Ground & Address:* Links Park, Wellington St, Montrose DD10 8QD. *Telephone:* 01674 673200.
Fax: 01674 677311. *E-mail:* office@montrosefc.co.uk *Website:* www.montrosefc.co.uk
Ground Capacity: total: 4,936, (seated: 1,338). *Size of Pitch:* 103m × 64m.
Chairman: Derek Sim. *Vice-Chairman:* John Crawford. *Secretary:* Brian Petrie.
Manager: Paul Hegarty. *Assistant Manager:* John Holt. *Physio:* George Stewart.
Club Nickname: 'The Gable Endies'.
Previous Grounds: None.
Record Attendance: 8,983 v Dundee, Scottish Cup 3rd rd, 17 March 1973.
Record Transfer Fee received: £50,000 for Gary Murray to Hibernian (December 1980).
Record Transfer Fee paid: £17,500 for Jim Smith from Airdrieonians (February 1992).
Record Victory: 12-0 v Vale of Leithen, Scottish Cup 2nd rd, 4 January 1975.
Record Defeat: 0-13 v Aberdeen, 17 March 1951.
Most Capped Player: Alexander Keillor, 2 (6), Scotland.
Most League Appearances: 432: David Larter, 1987-98.
Most League Goals in Season (Individual): 28: Brian Third, Division II, 1972-73.
Most Goals Overall (Individual): 126: Bobby Livingstone, 1967-79.

MONTROSE – SCOTTISH LEAGUE TWO 2015–16 LEAGUE RECORD

Match No.	Date	Venue	Opponents	Result	H/T Score	Lg Pos.	Goalscorers	Attendance
1	Aug 8	A	Berwick R	L 1-2	1-1	6	Watson (pen) [20]	479
2	15	H	Arbroath	W 3-0	2-0	4	Fraser 2 [20, 39], Campbell, R [56]	1100
3	22	H	Clyde	W 2-0	0-0	3	Webster [78], Fraser [81]	460
4	29	A	Annan Ath	L 2-3	0-2	5	Webster [50], McCord (pen) [90]	372
5	Sept 5	H	Elgin C	W 2-0	1-0	3	Webster [36], Fraser [59]	584
6	12	H	Stirling Alb	L 0-1	0-0	5		529
7	19	A	East Stirling	W 2-1	2-0	3	Webster [8], Fraser [21]	469
8	26	H	East Fife	L 1-4	1-1	6	Fraser [20]	572
9	Oct 3	A	Queen's Park	W 1-0	0-0	4	Webster [50]	342
10	17	A	Arbroath	L 1-3	0-1	4	Webster [82]	1146
11	31	H	Berwick R	W 4-1	2-0	2	Fraser 2 (1 pen) [17 (pl, 80], Campbell, R [45], Webster [60]	418
12	Nov 7	A	Clyde	L 1-3	0-2	4	Fraser [54]	477
13	17	H	Queen's Park	L 1-6	1-3	7	Mallagaray [6]	346
14	21	A	East Stirling	L 1-3	0-1	7	Fraser [66]	238
15	Dec 12	H	Stirling Alb	L 1-3	0-1	7	Mallagaray [82]	384
16	15	H	Annan Ath	D 1-1	0-1	7	Webster [51]	262
17	19	A	East Fife	D 1-1	1-1	8	Fraser [40]	419
18	26	H	Elgin C	L 0-2	0-0	9		697
19	Jan 2	A	Arbroath	L 0-2	0-1	9		1387
20	9	H	East Stirling	W 3-2	0-2	8	Webster [54], Pascazio [76], Comrie [84]	378
21	16	A	Queen's Park	D 1-1	1-0	8	Fraser [42]	407
22	23	H	Clyde	W 2-1	1-1	8	Clarke [45], Mallagaray [76]	500
23	Feb 6	H	East Fife	D 2-2	0-1	8	Fraser [70], Masson [89]	501
24	9	A	Stirling Alb	L 0-7	0-3	8		415
25	13	A	Annan Ath	D 3-3	1-1	8	Mallagaray [32], Campbell, R (pen) [82], Fraser (pen) [90]	354
26	20	H	Elgin C	W 3-1	1-0	7	Templeman [42], Fraser [55], Mallagaray [60]	515
27	27	A	Berwick R	L 0-1	0-0	8		380
28	Mar 5	A	East Stirling	W 4-2	1-0	7	Templeman 2 [13, 89], Fraser [58], Mallagaray [79]	251
29	12	H	Queen's Park	D 1-1	0-1	8	Fraser [47]	454
30	19	A	Elgin C	D 1-1	0-1	7	Campbell, R [62]	784
31	26	H	Annan Ath	L 0-5	0-2	9		452
32	Apr 2	A	Clyde	D 3-3	1-1	9	Mallagaray [12], Masson [74], Fraser [90]	638
33	9	A	East Fife	L 0-3	0-3	9		854
34	16	H	Stirling Alb	D 1-1	0-0	8	Webster [58]	463
35	23	A	Arbroath	D 0-0	0-0	8		1073
36	30	H	Berwick R	W 1-0	1-0	8	Fraser [43]	937

Final League Position: 8

Honours
League Champions: Second Division 1984-85; *Runners-up:* Second Division 1990-91. Third Division 1994-95.
Scottish Cup: Quarter-finals 1973, 1976.
League Cup: Semi-finals 1975-76.
League Challenge Cup: Semi-finals 1992-93, 1996-97.

Club colours: Shirt: Blue. Shorts: Blue. Socks: Blue.

Goalscorers: *League (50):* Fraser 19 (2 pens), Webster 10, Mallagaray 7, Campbell, R 4 (1 pen), Templeman 3, Masson 2, Clarke 1, Comrie 1, McCord 1 (1 pen), Pascazio 1, Watson 1 (1 pen).
William Hill Scottish FA Cup (2): Campbell, R 1, Masson 1.
Scottish League Cup (0).
Petrofac Training Cup (0).

Salmon R 9+1	Masson T 21+4	Reoch J 2+1	Allan M 16	Steeves A 27	Johnston S 18	McCord R 9+2	Watson P 4	Ferguson R 19+9	Fraser G 35	Campbell R 34+2	Milne D —+16	Millar J 24	Pascazio G 29	Webster G 29+3	Reid D —+2	Malin G 10+3	Kenneth R 7+5	Mallagaray A 25+5	Harwood A 8+4	McLeod K 1+3	Howlett J 3	Curran J 3	Comrie A 21	Buist S 2	Clarke J 12+1	Templeman C 11+2	Tokarczyk A 3	Martyniuk N 7+3	McWalter K 7+1	Hester L —+2	Match No.
1	2	3	4	5	6	7	8	9	10	11^1	12																				1
			4	5	9	7	8^1	2	10^2	11	12		1	3	6	13															2
			4	5	6	7	8	2	10	11^1	12		1	3	9																3
14	12	13	5	3	7	6	8^1	2	10	11			1^3	4^2	9																4
1			4	5	6	7		2	10	11				3	9	8															5
1			4	5	6	7		2	10	11^1	12			3	9	8^2	13														6
1	12		4		6	7^1		2	11	10				3	9	8^2	5	13													7
1	12		4	5	6	7^1		2	11	10^3				3^4	9	8^2	14	13													8
	7	3	4		6	12		2	10	11^1			1	9^2		13	5	8													9
	7	3	4		6	12		2	10^2	11^3	13		1	9		14	5	8^1													10
1	7		4		6^1		8		5	10^3	11^2			3	9	13		12	2	14											11
1			10						5^1	11	12	13		3	6			9^2	2				4	8							12
1			4			9			12	11		13	14	2	6	7^1		10^3	5				3		8^2						13
1	8			5					6^3	10	11	14		4	9	7^2		12	13				2		3^1						14
	4			8					6^2	10	3	12	1	2	7	13		5	9		11^1										15
	3				6				11	7			1	4	6	8	9	10	2				5								16
	5				6				10	9^1			1	3	8		7	12	11			2	4								17
8	4					5			12	10	7		1	3	6	11		9^1					2								18
8						9			13	11^3	7	14	1	3	6		12	10^2	2				5		4						19
8	4								9	10			1	2	6	5		11					7	3							20
7^1	3		4						8	10^2	11	12	1	2				9	6^1	13			5								21
	4								9	11	8		1	3	6			10	2^1				5		7	12					22
12	4								5^2	11	8^1		1	3	6			9	2				7			10	1	13			23
7	4								5^2	10	11	14		3	6^3			9^1	2				8			12	1	13			24
7	4								12	10	8				6^1			9	2				3		11	1	5				25
7	4								12	11^3	8		1	2				9^2	14			6			3	10^1		5	13		26
7	4								12	10^1	8		1	2				9^2				6			3	11		5		13	27
7	4								10^2	9			1	8^1				12				6			3	11		5	2		28
8	4								10^2	9			1	2^1	13			6	12			7			3	11		5			29
7	4								11	9			1	12				6^1	13			8			3	10		5^2	2		30
8	4								11^1	9			1	12				6	13			7			3	10		5^2	2^3	14	31
7	5								10	11	12		1	4	8			9				2			3				6^1		32
7	5								13	10^3	11	14	1	4	8			9	12			2			3^1		–		6^2		33
7	8								11	4			1	3	6			9	5^1			2				10		12			34
7	5								13	11	4	12	1	3	8^2			9				2				10			9		35
8	4^1								14	11^3	5	13	1	3	6			9				2				12	10^2		7		36

MOTHERWELL

Year Formed: 1886. *Ground & Address:* Fir Park Stadium, Motherwell ML1 2ON. *Telephone:* 01698 333333. *Fax:* 01698 338001.
E-mail: mfcenquiries@motherwellfc.co.uk *Website:* www.motherwellfc.co.uk
Ground Capacity: 13,742 (all seated). *Size of Pitch:* 100m × 68m.
Chairman: Brian McCafferty. *Vice-Chairman:* Les Hutchinson. *Secretary:* Graham Keys.
Manager: Mark McGhee. *Physio:* Aileen Anderson.
Club Nicknames: 'The Well', 'The Steelmen'.
Previous Grounds: The Meadows, Dalziel Park.
Record Attendance: 35,632 v Rangers, Scottish Cup 4th rd replay, 12 March 1952.
Record Transfer Fee received: £1,750,000 for Phil O'Donnell to Celtic (September 1994).
Record Transfer Fee paid: £500,000 for John Spencer from Everton (January 1999).
Record Victory: 12-1 v Dundee U, Division II, 23 January 1954.
Record Defeat: 0-8 v Aberdeen, Premier Division, 26 March 1979.
Most Capped Player: Stephen Craigan, 54, Northern Ireland.
Most League Appearances: 626: Bobby Ferrier, 1918-37.
Most League Goals in Season (Individual): 52: Willie McFadyen, Division I, 1931-32.
Most Goals Overall (Individual): 283: Hugh Ferguson, 1916-25.

MOTHERWELL – SCOTTISH PREMIERSHIP 2015–16 LEAGUE RECORD

Match No.	Date	Venue	Opponents	Result	H/T Score	Lg Pos.	Goalscorers	Atten- dance
1	Aug 1	A	Inverness CT	W	1-0	1-0	3	Fletcher.⁴	3307
2	8	H	Dundee U	L	0-2	0-0	7		4859
3	12	A	Hearts	L	0-2	0-1	7		16,645
4	15	H	Aberdeen	L	1-2	1-1	9	Johnson ⁵	5437
5	22	A	St Johnstone	L	1-2	1-0	9	Moult ¹¹	3361
6	29	H	Kilmarnock	W	1-0	1-0	7	Moult (pen) ¹³	4136
7	Sept12	H	Ross Co	D	1-1	0-1	8	Moult ⁹⁰	3545
8	19	A	Hamilton A	L	0-1	0-0	10		3325
9	26	H	Partick Thistle	W	2-1	1-0	9	Frans (og) ²², McDonald ⁶⁹	3963
10	Oct 3	A	Dundee	L	1-2	0-0	9	Pearson ⁸³	5152
11	17	H	Celtic	L	0-1	0-1	10		8888
12	24	A	Aberdeen	D	1-1	0-1	10	McDonald ⁷³	12,389
13	31	A	Kilmarnock	W	1-0	0-0	10	Moult ⁸⁷	3931
14	Nov 7	H	Inverness CT	L	1-3	0-2	10	Moult ⁵⁸	3569
15	21	A	Ross Co	L	0-3	0-1	11		3378
16	28	H	Hearts	D	2-2	1-1	11	Moult ², Johnson ⁶⁵	5141
17	Dec 12	H	Dundee	W	3-1	2-0	10	McDonald ⁶, Moult ³², Pearson ⁹⁰	3512
18	19	A	Celtic	W	2-1	0-0	10	Moult 2 (1 pen) ⁵³, ⁵⁹ ⁽ᵖ⁾	42,603
19	30	H	St Johnstone	W	2-0	2-0	8	Hall ³⁸, Pearson ⁴⁵	4055
20	Jan 2	H	Hamilton A	D	3-3	1-2	8	McDonald 2 ⁹, ⁴⁶, Moult ⁵⁷	5734
21	16	A	Hearts	L	0-6	0-3	8		16,574
22	23	H	Ross Co	L	1-2	0-1	9	Pearson ⁸⁷	3279
23	30	A	Dundee	D	2-2	2-1	9	Cadden ⁴, Pearson ²³	4960
24	Feb 2	A	Partick Thistle	L	0-1	0-0	10		2487
25	13	H	Kilmarnock	L	0-2	0-0	11		3764
26	16	A	Dundee U	W	3-0	1-0	8	McManus ⁴⁵, McDonald 2 ⁷², ⁸⁰	6251
27	20	A	St Johnstone	L	1-2	1-1	8	Moult ³³	3006
28	27	H	Partick Thistle	W	3-1	1-0	8	Moult 2 (1 pen) ³⁷ ⁽ᵖ⁾, ⁵², Johnson ⁶⁹	4302
29	Mar 5	A	Hamilton A	W	1-0	1-0	7	Laing ⁴⁵	3755
30	11	H	Dundee U	W	2-1	1-1	6	Johnson ⁴⁵, Moult ⁶⁵	4210
31	19	H	Aberdeen	W	2-1	0-1	5	McDonald ⁷³, Moult ⁷⁵	6251
32	Apr 2	A	Inverness CT	W	2-1	0-0	4	Ainsworth ⁶², Johnson ⁹⁰	3348
33	9	H	Celtic	L	1-2	0-1	4	McDonald ⁶⁰	9123
34	23	H	Hearts	W	1-0	1-0	4	Ainsworth ²⁸	5125
35	30	A	Aberdeen	L	1-4	0-2	5	Cadden ⁶⁴	10,259
36	May 7	H	St Johnstone	L	1-2	1-2	5	McDonald ⁴	4441
37	11	A	Ross Co	W	3-1	2-0	5	Pearson 2 ⁴, ⁹⁰, Lasley ¹⁶	2976
38	15	A	Celtic	L	0-7	0-3	5		49,050

Final League Position: 5

Honours
League Champions: Division I 1931-32. First Division 1981-82, 1984-85. Division II 1953-54, 1968-69.
Runners-up: Premier Division 1994-95, 2012-13. Premiership 2013-14. Division I 1926-27, 1929-30, 1932-33, 1933-34. Division II 1894-95, 1902-03.
Scottish Cup: 1952, 1991; *Runners-up:* 1931, 1933, 1939, 1951, 2011.
League Cup Winners: 1950-51; *Runners-up:* 1954-55, 2004-05.

European: *Champions League:* 2 matches (2012-13). *Cup Winners' Cup:* 2 matches (1991-92). *UEFA Cup:* 8 matches (1994-95, 1995-96, 2008-09). *Europa League:* 18 matches (2009-10, 2010-11, 2012-13, 2013-14, 2014-15).

Club colours: Shirt: Amber with diagonal maroon band. Shorts: Maroon. Socks: Maroon with amber band.

Goalscorers: *League (47):* Moult 15 (3 pens), McDonald 10, Pearson 7, Johnson 5, Ainsworth 2, Cadden 2, Fletcher 1, Hall 1, Laing 1, Lasley 1, McManus 1, own goal 1.
William Hill Scottish FA Cup (6): McDonald 2, Pearson 2, Johnson 1, Moult 1.
Scottish League Cup (5): McDonald 2, Moult 2, Ainsworth 1.

Ripley C 36	Chalmers J 11+6	Laing L 13+2	McManus S 37	Hammell S 25+2	Law J 28+1	Lasley K 30	Pearson S 25+1	Johnson M 34+4	Fletcher W 5+9	McDonald S 34+3	Leitch J 3+8	Moult L 34+4	Clarkson D —+7	Thomas D 2+12	Ainsworth L 17+12	Taylor J 6+1	Cadden C 16+4	Kennedy K 18+4	Robinson T 2+8	Grimshaw L 13+1	Hall B 16+2	Mackin D —+1	Watt L 1+1	McFadden J 2+1	Gomis M 8+2	Samson C 2	Match No.
1	2	3	4	5	6	7	8¹	9	10²	11³	12	13	14														1
1	6²	3	4	5	2	7		9	11¹	10		8³	12	14	13												2
1		3	4	5	2	7		9		10³	12	11¹	14	14	13	6	7										3
1		3	4	5	2	7		9¹		10		11²	13	12		6	8³	14									4
1	12	3	4	5¹	2	7		9		10³	13	11		14		6²	8⁴										5
1	5	14	4		2	7		13		10		8³	11¹		9	6²			3	12							6
1		3	4	5	2³	7		13		10¹		11		9²	6	8			12	14							7
1	5		3		2	7²		12		13		11		14	9²	8	4	10¹	6								8
1	5		4			7	8	9²	14	11³	12	10¹		13	6		3	2									9
1	5		4		2	7³	8	12	14	10²		11			6¹		3	13	9								10
1	6	3	4		2		8	9³	11²	13		10¹		14	12		5	7									11
1	5		4		2	7¹	8	9	10²	13		11³		12			3	14	6								12
1	5		4		2		8	9	13	11²		12			7³	14	3	10¹	6								13
1	5		4¹		2		8	9²	12	10¹		11			6		3	13	7								14
1	3		2			8	9	10	11				6²	4¹	13	5	12	7									15
1		4	5	2	7	8	9¹	10²	11	12		3	13	6													16
1		4	5	2	7	8	9²	10¹	11³	13	12				6	3	14										17
1	13	4²	5	2	7	8	9	10	11	12³				6¹	3	14											18
1		4	5	2	7	8	9²	10	11³	13	12				6	3											19
1		4	5	2	8⁴	9	6²	10	11¹					13	12	7	3										20
1	5		4	2	7³		8	9	13	11		10²	14	12	6¹		3										21
1	12		4	5¹		7	8	9		10²		11		13	6³	2	3				14						22
1		4	5	2	7	8	9	12	11¹	10					6	3											23
1		4	5	2	7	8	9	10	11¹			14			6³	12	3²						13				24
1		4	5	2	8	9	11	12		13	6¹		7	3							10²						25
1	2	4	13	12	6	9²	14	10³	11				5		3	7¹	8										26
1	2	3	12	6	13	8	9³	11			14	5		4	10¹	7²											27
1		2	4	5	7	8	9	10	11	6				3													28
1	2	3	7		6	9	5	11	10¹			8	12	4													29
1		4	5	2¹	7²	8¹	9	10	11	13		6	14	3							12						30
1		4	5	2		9	13	10	7	11²		12		6¹							8						31
1		4	5	2	7³	9	14	11	13	10		12		6¹	3						8²						32
1		4	5	2	7¹	9	13	11	14	12		6²	3								8³						33
14		4	5	2¹	8²	6		10	13	11		7³	9	3	12									1			34
1	3¹	4	5	7⁴	9	6	10	11		8²		13	2	12													35
1	12	4		7¹	8	9³	10	14	11	13		5²	6	3	2												36
1	12	4	2¹		7	9	5	11	10			6		3			8	1									37
1	12	3		6	2	10		11		9¹		8	13	4	5²	7											38

PARTICK THISTLE

Year Formed: 1876. *Ground & Address:* Firhill Stadium, 80 Firhill Rd, Glasgow G20 7AL. *Telephone:* 0141 579 1971.
Fax: 0141 945 1525. *E-mail:* mail@ptfc.co.uk *Website:* ptfc.co.uk
Ground Capacity: 10,102 (all seated). *Size of Pitch:* 105m × 69m.
Chairman: David Beattie. *Managing Director:* Ian Maxwell.
Manager: Alan Archibald. *Assistant Manager:* Scott Paterson. *Head of Youth Development:* Gerry Britton.
Club Nickname: 'The Jags'.
Previous Grounds: Overnewton Park; Jordanvale Park; Muirpark; Inchview; Meadowside Park.
Record Attendance: 49,838 v Rangers, Division I, 18 February 1922. *Ground Record:* 54,728, Scotland v Ireland, 25
February 1928.
Record Transfer Fee received: £200,000 for Mo Johnston to Watford (July 1981).
Record Transfer Fee paid: £85,000 for Andy Murdoch from Celtic (February 1991).
Record Victory: 16-0 v Royal Albert, Scottish Cup 1st rd, 17 January 1931.
Record Defeat: 0-10 v Queen's Park, Scottish Cup 5th rd, 3 December 1881.
Most Capped Player: Alan Rough, 51 (53), Scotland.
Most League Appearances: 410: Alan Rough, 1969-82.
Most League Goals in Season (Individual): 41: Alex Hair, Division I, 1926-27.
Most Goals Overall (Individual): 229: Willie Sharp, 1939-57.

PARTICK THISTLE – SCOTTISH PREMIERSHIP 2015–16 LEAGUE RECORD

Match No.	Date	Venue	Opponents	Result	H/T Score	Lg Pos.	Goalscorers	Attendance
1	Aug 1	A	Hamilton A	D 0-0	0-0	4		2872
2	9	H	Celtic	L 0-2	0-1	10		7088
3	12	A	Inverness CT	D 0-0	0-0	10		3141
4	15	H	Kilmarnock	D 2-2	1-1	8	Doolan 2 [9, 78]	3600
5	22	A	Hearts	L 0-3	0-1	10		16,657
6	29	H	Aberdeen	L 0-2	0-0	11		4940
7	Sept 12	H	Dundee	L 0-1	0-0	12		2946
8	19	A	Ross Co	L 0-1	0-1	12		3531
9	26	A	Motherwell	L 1-2	0-1	12	Amoo [78]	3963
10	Oct 3	H	Dundee U	W 3-0	1-0	11	Amoo [15], Dumbuya [55], Bannigan [65]	3675
11	17	A	St Johnstone	W 2-1	2-0	11	Miller [28], Lawless [34]	3414
12	24	H	Hamilton A	D 1-1	0-0	11	Pogba [60]	3122
13	31	H	Hearts	L 0-4	0-1	11		4776
14	Nov 7	A	Dundee	D 1-1	1-0	11	Lindsay [5]	5067
15	21	H	Inverness CT	W 2-1	1-1	10	Doolan [42], Stevenson [90]	2864
16	28	A	Kilmarnock	W 5-2	2-1	9	Doolan 2 [7, 15], Fraser [52], Muirhead 2 [62, 75]	3860
17	Dec 12	A	Dundee U	W 1-0	0-0	8	Doolan [51]	6256
18	19	H	Ross Co	W 1-0	0-0	7	Davies (og) [52]	2762
19	30	A	Aberdeen	D 0-0	0-0	7		12,583
20	Jan 2	A	Celtic	L 0-1	0-0	9		46,067
21	16	H	Dundee	L 2-4	1-4	9	Amoo [23], Doolan [90]	3222
22	23	A	Inverness CT	D 0-0	0-0	8		3556
23	Feb 2	H	Motherwell	W 1-0	0-0	8	Lawless [90]	2487
24	23	H	St Johnstone	W 2-0	0-0	8	Doolan [72], Amoo [87]	2320
25	27	A	Motherwell	L 1-3	0-1	9	Booth [76]	4302
26	Mar 2	A	St Johnstone	W 2-1	2-0	7	Booth [6], Lawless [13]	2569
27	5	A	Hearts	L 0-1	0-1	8		16,558
28	8	H	Aberdeen	L 1-2	0-0	8	Lawless [60]	3915
29	12	H	Celtic	L 1-2	0-1	8	Welsh (pen) [85]	7238
30	19	A	Hamilton A	W 2-1	0-1	7	Pogba [50], Edwards [84]	3055
31	Apr 2	H	Kilmarnock	D 0-0	0-0	8		4359
32	5	H	Dundee U	W 1-0	0-0	7	Doolan [71]	4533
33	9	A	Ross Co	L 0-1	0-1	8		3603
34	23	H	Dundee	L 1-2	0-1	8	Doolan [70]	2769
35	30	H	Inverness CT	L 1-4	0-1	9	Doolan [83]	2609
36	May 7	A	Kilmarnock	W 2-0	1-0	9	Lawless [32], Doolan [66]	5729
37	10	A	Dundee U	D 3-3	2-0	9	Frans [6], Doolan [34], Edwards [76]	4689
38	14	H	Hamilton A	D 2-2	2-2	9	Doolan [3], Amoo [19]	2971

Final League Position: 9

Honours
League Champions: First Division 1975-76, 2001-02, 2012-13; Division II 1896-97, 1899-1900, 1970-71; Second Division 2000-01; *Runners-up:* First Division 1991-92, 2008-09. Division II 1901-02. *Promoted to First Division:* 2005-06 (play-offs).
Scottish Cup Winners: 1921; *Runners-up:* 1930.
League Cup Winners: 1971-72; *Runners-up:* 1953-54, 1956-57, 1958-59.
League Challenge Cup Runners-up: 2012-13.

European: *Fairs Cup:* 4 matches (1963-64). *UEFA Cup:* 2 matches (1972-73). *Intertoto Cup:* 4 matches (1995-96).

Club colours: Shirt: Yellow with red front panel and black trim. Shorts: Black. Socks: Black.

Goalscorers: *League (41):* Doolan 14, Amoo 5, Lawless 5, Booth 2, Edwards 2, Muirhead 2, Pogba 2, Bannigan 1, Dumbuya 1, Frans 1, Fraser 1, Lindsay 1, Miller 1, Stevenson 1, Welsh 1 (pen), own goal 1.
William Hill Scottish FA Cup (2): Amoo 1, Seaborne 1.
Scottish League Cup (0).

Cerny T 28	Miller G 20 + 1	Frans F 17 + 4	Lindsay L 25	Booth C 34	Amoo D 27 + 10	Osman A 32 + 1	Stevenson R 6 + 4	Welsh S 32 + 2	Bannigan S 26	Doolan K 24 + 12	Hendry J 1 + 2	McDaid D 1 + 3	Wilson D 4 + 7	Lawless S 36 + 1	Pogba M 13 + 15	Fraser G 7 + 5	Seaborne D 31 + 1	Dumbuya M 19 + 2	Muirhead R 4 + 4	Nisbet K — + 8	Edwards R 10 + 7	Scully R 9 + 1	Gallacher P 1	Elliot C 5 + 7	Nesbitt A 4 + 3	German A — + 2	Penrice J 2	Mcinally M — + 1	Match No.
1	2	3^8	4	5	6^2	7	8^1	9^3	10	11	12	13	14																1
1	2		4	5	13	6	11^2	7^3	9			3		8	10^1	12	14												2
1	2	3	4	5	10^2	7		9	8	12				13	6	11^1													3
1	2	3	4^4	5	8			9^2	6	7	11			10^1		12	13												4
1	2	4		5	10^3	13	8^1	7^2	6	11		14		12		9	3												5
1	2	3^1	4	5		9	13	7^2	6	14	12	8		10^1	11^3														6
1		3	4	5	12	6	9^2	14	7	11		13		8^1					2	10^3									7
1		3		5	13	6	9^1	10	7^2	11^3				8			4	2	12	14									8
1		3		5	14	6		8	9^3	11^1				10	13		4	2	7^2	12									9
1			3	5	8^1	6		9	7	13				12	10^1	11^2	4	2		14									10
1	2	13	3	5	6^2	8^4		7	9	12				10	11^1	4													11
1^1		3	5	8				6	7	14				10	11^3	4	2	13		9^2	12								12
	14	3	5	8	7	12	9^2	6						10^1	11		4^3	2	13		1^8								13
		3	5	9	8	13	6	7	10^2					11^1		12	4	2				1							14
		3	5	8^1	7	14	9		11^2					10	13	6^8	4	2	12			1							15
		3	5	12	10		13	7^2	11^3					9	14	8	4	2	6^1			1							16
1	13	3	5	9^2	6			8	7	11				12	10^1		4	2											17
1		3	5	12	6			7	10	11^2				8	13		4	2	9^1										18
1		3	5	9^2	6			10	11					13	8	12	4	2		7^1									19
1	12	3	5	6	7			8^2	10^3	11				14	9	13	4	2											20
1	14	9^4	4	5^2				3	6	10				11^1	7^3		2	8	12			13							21
1		3		5	9	7		6	8	10				11^1			4	2				12							22
1	2	3		5	13	7		9^1	6	11^3				8	12	14	4					10^2							23
1	2	3		5	13	6		7		12				8^3	11^1		4			14		10	9^2						24
1	2^2	3		5	13	6		7		11^3				9	12		4					8	10^1	14					25
1	2		3	5	6^1	7		9	8	13				10^1	11^2	4				14		12							26
1	2		3	5	8^2	6		7	9^1	14				10	11^3	4				12			13						27
1			3	5	8	6		7		13				10^3	11^2	9^1	4			12			2	14					28
1	2		3	5	8	6		7		11^1				10^3	12	9^2	4			14			13						29
1	2			5	6	7		8		13				10	11^2	9^1	3	12		4									30
1	2	3		5	6^3	8		9		13				10	11^2	12	4			7^1			14						31
1	2	3^2		5	8	6		7		11^3				10	12	9^1	4	13		14									32
	3			5	9^2	6		8^3		12				11	10^1		4	2		13	7	1		14					33
	3	4			12	6		7		11^3				10	13		5		14	8^2	1		2	9^1					34
	3			5^2	8^3	7		6		11				14	10^1	12	4	2		9^1	1		13						35
	2	3			8^1	6		7		11^2				10			4	5	13	9^1	1		12						36
		2	3		8^3			7		11^2				6^1	10^1	13	4			14	9^1	1		12	5				37
	2^3	3			8^1					11^2				6	10^1	13	4			14	9^1	1		7		5	14		38

PETERHEAD

Year Formed: 1891. *Ground and Address:* Balmoor Stadium, Balmoor Terrace, Peterhead AB42 1EU.
Telephone: 01779 478256. *Fax:* 01779 490682. *E-mail:* office@peterheadfc.co.uk *Website:* www.peterheadfc.com
Ground Capacity: 4,000 (seated: 1,000). *Size of Pitch:* 101m × 64m.
Chairman: Rodger Morrison. *Vice-Chairman:* Ian Grant. *Secretary:* Brian McCombie.
Manager: Jim McInally. *Assistant coach:* David Nicholls. *Physio:* Greig Smith.
Club Nickname: 'Blue Toon'.
Previous Ground: Recreation Park.
Record Attendance: 8,643 v Raith R, Scottish Cup 4th rd replay, 25 February 1987 (Recreation Park); 4,855 v Rangers, Third Division, 19 January 2013 (at Balmoor).
Record Victory: 8-0 v Forfar Athletic, Second Division, 30 Sep 2006.
Record Defeat: 0-13 v Aberdeen, Scottish Cup 3rd rd, 10 February 1923.
Most League Appearances: 275: Martin Bavidge, 2003-13.
Most League Goals in Season (Individual): 32: Rory McAllister, 2013-14.
Most Goals Overall (Individual): 119: Rory McAllister, 2011-16.

PETERHEAD – SCOTTISH LEAGUE ONE 2015–16 LEAGUE RECORD

Match No.	Date		Venue	Opponents	Result	H/T Score	Lg Pos.	Goalscorers	Atten-dance
1	Aug	8	H	Stenhousemuir	D 2-2	0-2	5	McAllister (pen) [61], Brown [74]	530
2		15	A	Stranraer	W 4-0	1-0	3	McAllister 2 [5, 57], Brown [79], McIntosh [80]	328
3		22	H	Dunfermline Ath	W 2-1	1-1	2	McAllister (pen) [30], McIntosh [89]	996
4		29	A	Airdrieonians	L 0-1	0-0	3		676
5	Sept	5	H	Albion R	D 1-1	1-1	5	Brown [25]	550
6		12	A	Cowdenbeath	D 2-2	1-1	6	McAllister (pen) [2], Sutherland [62]	301
7		19	H	Brechin C	L 2-3	2-2	7	Sutherland [25], McAllister [38]	554
8		26	A	Ayr U	D 1-1	0-0	6	Redman [87]	1304
9	Oct	3	H	Forfar Ath	D 2-2	1-0	7	Riley [28], McIntosh [78]	573
10		17	A	Albion R	L 0-1	0-0	8		341
11		24	H	Airdrieonians	W 2-0	1-0	6	McAllister [42], McIntosh [80]	553
12		31	A	Stenhousemuir	L 3-4	3-1	7	McAllister 3 (1 pen) [13, 31, 38 (p)]	292
13	Nov	7	H	Dunfermline Ath	D 0-0	0-0	6		2915
14		17	A	Stranraer	D 1-1	1-1	6	McAllister [45]	423
15		21	H	Cowdenbeath	W 7-0	4-0	6	McIntosh 3 [16, 43, 55], Brown 2 [17, 32], McAllister [59], Ferries [88]	535
16	Dec	8	A	Forfar Ath	W 2-0	1-0	4	Brown [38], Stevenson [85]	434
17		12	A	Brechin C	D 1-1	1-0	4	McIntosh [7]	403
18		19	H	Ayr U	W 3-0	0-0	4	Dzierzawski [62], Sutherland 2 [81, 85]	612
19		26	A	Airdrieonians	W 4-3	1-2	3	McAllister (pen) [25], Strachan [84], Brown [88], Gilchrist [90]	745
20	Jan	2	H	Stenhousemuir	W 4-1	1-1	3	Redman [5], Stevenson [53], McAllister [77], Dzierzawski [82]	588
21		16	A	Stranraer	W 5-1	3-0	3	Sutherland 2 [17, 36], Stevenson [41], Gilchrist [76], McIntosh [88]	406
22		23	H	Dunfermline Ath	D 0-0	0-0	3		1115
23		30	H	Albion R	W 5-1	1-1	3	Redman [9], McAllister 2 (1 pen) [52, 54 (p)], Sutherland 2 [63, 67]	522
24	Feb	6	A	Ayr U	W 2-1	2-1	2	Sutherland [22], McAllister [41]	1155
25		13	H	Forfar Ath	W 3-2	2-2	2	McAllister [4], Sutherland [42], McIntosh [75]	667
26		20	A	Cowdenbeath	W 3-2	2-1	2	Strachan [15], McIntosh [30], Redman [76]	359
27		27	H	Brechin C	W 4-1	2-0	2	McAllister 3 [25, 45, 75], Sutherland [90]	680
28	Mar	5	A	Albion R	D 1-1	0-1	2	McAllister (pen) [90]	409
29		12	A	Stenhousemuir	W 4-1	2-0	2	Stevenson [13], Sutherland 2 (1 pen) [43, 54 (p)], McIntosh [67]	369
30		15	H	Stranraer	D 0-0	0-0	2		607
31		19	H	Airdrieonians	W 1-0	0-0	2	Rodgers [76]	633
32		26	H	Cowdenbeath	L 0-1	0-1	2		703
33	Apr	2	A	Forfar Ath	L 0-2	0-0	2		570
34		16	A	Brechin C	L 1-5	1-4	2	Blockley [30]	481
35		23	H	Ayr U	L 0-4	0-2	3		617
36		30	A	Dunfermline Ath	L 0-1	0-1	3		6236

Final League Position: 3

Honours
League Champions League Two: 2013-14.
Third Division Runners up: 2004-05, 2012-13.
Scottish Cup: Quarter-finals 2001.
League Challenge Cup: Runners up: 2015-16.

Club colours: Shirt: Royal blue with white trim. Shorts: Royal blue. Socks: White.

Goalscorers: *League (72):* McAllister 22 (7 pens), Sutherland 13 (1 pen), McIntosh 12, Brown 7, Redman 4, Stevenson 4, Dzierzawski 2, Gilchrist 2, Strachan 2, Blockley 1, Ferries 1, Riley 1, Rodgers 1.
William Hill Scottish FA Cup (1): McAllister 1 (1 pen).
Scottish League Cup (0).
Petrofac Training Cup (13): McAllister 8 (1 pen), Brown 2, McIntosh 1, Noble 1, Redman 1.
Championship Play-Offs (2): McIntosh 1, own goal 1.

Smith G 36	Blockley N 15+8	Strachan R 34+1	Gilchrist A 27+1	Baptie R 1	Dzierzawski K 29+2	Brown J 23+9	Stevenson J 20+8	McAllister R 32+1	Sutherland S 26+9	Rodgers A 1+21	Riley N 21+9	Ferries S 2+9	Noble S 27	McIntosh L 11+20	Redman J 33+1	Kerr C 10	Ross S 19+3	Ferry S 24	Sukar J 2	Lawrence M 3+4	Match No.
1	2^2	3	4	5^1	6	7	8	9^3	10	11	12	13	14								1
1	2	3	4		6	5	7	9^2	10^1	11^2	14	12	13	8							2
1	5^3	4	3		8	7	6^1	9	10	11^2	14	13	12	2							3
1		4	3		8	7		9	10	11^3	14		12	2^2	5	6	13				4
1		3	4		7	8		9	10	11^3	14		12	13	6^2	5	2				5
1		7	4		8	9^1	13	12	10	11^3			14		6^2	5	2	3			6
1		7	4		14		6^2	9^3	10	11	12			13	5	2	$3^{\bullet}$	8^1			7
1	14	4	3		13		6^2	9^3	10	11			12	7	5	2		8^1			8
1		3	4			12	6^1	9^3	10	11	14		13	8	5	2		7^2			9
1		2	4		7	9^1	6	12	10	11^2	13			8		5	3				10
1	12	3	4			9^3	5^1	11^2	10	14			13	7		8	2	6			11
1	12	8	4^3			11		9^2	10	14			13	7	5	$2^{\bullet}$	3	6^1			12
1		7			11	12			10^2	13	14	5	9^1	8	4		3	6^2	2		13
1	8	13	4		7				10	14	11^3		12	6	9	5	2^1			3^2	14
1	2	4	12		9	8		10			14	13	11^3	6	5		3^1	7^2			15
1	2	4	3		7^1	6^2	13	10	12		14	11^2	8	5			9				16
1	2	4	3^2		7	8	14	10	13			11^3	9	5		12	6^1				17
1	2	4			9	8^2	14	13	10	12			11^1	6	5		3^3	7			18
1	2^3	4	3		7	11	13	14	10	12				9^1	8	$5^{\bullet}$		6^2			19
1		3	4		6	7^3	5	9^3	10^1	11	14	12		2		13	8				20
1		3	4		7	14	2	13	10^3	11				12	6	5	8^1	9			21
1		3	4		8	13	5^3	14	11^1	10				12	6	9	2	7^2			22
1		3^1	4		8^2	6	12	7^3	10	11	14			13	5	9	2				23
1		2	4		7	6^1	12	14	10^3	11^2				13	9	5	$3^{\bullet}$	8			24
1	13	3	4		7	14	2	9	10^2	11				12	6	$5^{\bullet}$		8			25
1	4	3	2		6		5	12	10^2	11^1	13		9^3	8			7			14	26
1	13	3	4		8^2	12	5	9^3	10^3	11	14			6			2	7			27
1	5^2	4			6	11	2^1		10	9	14	12		8			3	7^3		13	28
1		9	4		6	13	2^2	8^3		10	14			12	11	5	3			7^1	29
1	13	3	4^1		6	7^2		14	11	10^3				12	5	9	2	8			30
1	2	4				12		9	10	11^3	14		13	8	5		3^1	7		6^2	31
1	2^1	3	4		7	9	12	10^2	11	14	13			8		5		6^2			32
1	2	3			4	8	6	12	10^3	13	9^3	11^1		4	5			7			33
1	2				3	7	6	9^1		11	13	14	10^2	8	5		4^3			12	34
1	13	4			6	9	2	10^1	$11^{\bullet}$	8			12	3	5			7^3			35
1	12	3			8^1	6	2^2	9^1		10	14		11	4	5			7		13	36

QUEEN OF THE SOUTH

Year Formed: 1919. *Ground & Address:* Palmerston Park, Dumfries DG2 9BA. *Telephone:* 01387 254853.
Fax: 01387 240470. *E-mail:* admin@qosfc.com *Website:* www.qosfc.com
Ground Capacity: 8,690 (seated: 3,377) *Size of Pitch:* 102m × 66m.
Chairman: Billy Hewitson. *Vice-Chairman:* Craig Paterson. *Football Administration:* Ewan Lithgow.
Manager: Gavin Skelton. *Coach:* Kenny Arthur. *Physio:* Ross Goodwin.
Club Nickname: 'The Doonhamers'.
Previous Grounds: None.
Record Attendance: 26,552 v Hearts, Scottish Cup 3rd rd, 23 February 1952.
Record Transfer Fee received: £250,000 for Andy Thomson to Southend U (July 1994).
Record Transfer Fee paid: £30,000 for Jim Butter from Alloa Ath (1995).
Record Victory: 11-1 v Stranraer, Scottish Cup 1st rd, 16 January 1932.
Record Defeat: 2-10 v Dundee, Division I, 1 December 1962.
Most Capped Player: Billy Houliston, 3, Scotland.
Most League Appearances: 731: Allan Ball, 1963-82.
Most League Goals in Season (Individual): 37: Jimmy Gray, Division II, 1927-28.
Most Goals in Season: 41: Jimmy Rutherford, 1931-32; Nicky Clark, 2012-13.
Most Goals Overall (Individual): 251: Jim Patterson, 1949-63.

QUEEN OF THE SOUTH – SCOTTISH CHAMPIONSHIP 2015–16 LEAGUE RECORD

Match No.	Date	Venue	Opponents	Result	H/T Score	Lg Pos.	Goalscorers	Attendance
1	Aug 8	H	Alloa Ath	W 3-1	3-0	2	Lyle [5], Russell 2 [29, 38]	1726
2	15	A	Livingston	W 1-0	0-0	1	Kidd [65]	856
3	22	A	Dumbarton	W 2-0	1-0	1	Russell [41], Lyle [68]	943
4	30	H	Rangers	L 1-5	0-1	3	Smith, A [81]	5858
5	Sept 5	H	St Mirren	L 0-2	0-2	3		2001
6	12	A	Raith R	L 0-1	0-0	6		1527
7	19	H	Greenock Morton	D 2-2	1-1	6	Lyle [45], Gasparotto (og) [81]	1565
8	25	A	Falkirk	D 0-0	0-0	5		3757
9	Oct 3	H	Hibernian	L 0-3	0-2	5		2745
10	10	H	Greenock Morton	W 1-0	1-0	5	Lyle [14]	1583
11	17	A	Rangers	L 1-2	1-0	5	Lyle [35]	44,133
12	24	H	Livingston	L 1-4	1-0	5	Hilson [27]	1485
13	31	A	Alloa Ath	W 2-1	0-1	5	Oliver 2 [46, 55]	616
14	Nov 7	H	Dumbarton	W 1-0	0-0	5	Heffernan [52]	1465
15	14	A	Greenock Morton	L 0-2	0-0	6		1849
16	21	H	Falkirk	D 2-2	1-1	6	Lyle (pen) [35], Russell [84]	1728
17	Dec 11	H	Raith R	D 1-1	0-1	6	Russell [48]	1047
18	19	A	Hibernian	L 0-1	0-0	6		9163
19	Jan 2	A	Livingston	W 2-0	0-0	5	Lyle [65], Russell [77]	958
20	23	H	Alloa Ath	W 1-0	1-0	5	Russell [41]	1559
21	Feb 6	A	St Mirren	L 0-1	0-1	5		2706
22	13	H	St Mirren	W 1-0	0-0	4	Harris [65]	1923
23	21	H	Rangers	L 0-1	0-0	5		5449
24	27	A	Falkirk	L 1-3	1-0	6	Higgins [43]	3918
25	Mar 1	A	Hibernian	W 1-0	0-0	5	Murdoch [78]	2017
26	8	A	Raith R	L 0-2	0-2	5		1398
27	12	A	St Mirren	L 1-2	0-1	5	Oliver [62]	3888
28	15	A	Greenock Morton	L 2-3	0-3	6	Hilson [69], Oliver [78]	1175
29	19	H	Dumbarton	W 6-0	2-0	6	Brownlie [34], Lyle 2 [43, 52], Harris 2 [69, 73], Russell [88]	1459
30	26	A	Rangers	L 3-4	1-1	6	Russell (pen) [25], Oliver [57], Millar [90]	46,117
31	Apr 2	H	Falkirk	D 2-2	0-1	6	Lyle [73], Russell [90]	1530
32	9	H	Raith R	L 1-2	0-1	6	Hilson [53]	1511
33	12	A	Dumbarton	L 2-4	2-1	6	Russell [28], Harris [43]	573
34	16	A	Alloa Ath	D 2-2	0-1	7	Lyle (pen) [67], Hilson [85]	512
35	23	H	Livingston	W 3-1	0-1	6	Lyle 2 (1 pen) [60 (p), 69], Oliver [79]	1421
36	May 1	A	Hibernian	L 0-2	0-0	7		9900

Final League Position: 7

Honours
League Champions: Division II 1950-51. Second Division 2001-02, 2012-13.
Runners-up: Division II 1932-33, 1961-62, 1974-75. Second Division 1980-81, 1985-86.
Scottish Cup Runners-up: 2007-08.
League Cup: semi-finals 1950-51, 1960-61.
League Challenge Cup Winners: 2002-03, 2012-13; *Runners-up:* 1997-98, 2010-11.

European: *UEFA Cup:* 2 matches (2008-09).

Club colours: Shirt: Royal blue with white trim. Shorts: Royal blue. Socks: Royal blue.

Goalscorers: *League (46):* Lyle 13 (3 pens), Russell 11 (1 pen), Oliver 6, Harris 4, Hilson 4, Brownlie 1, Heffernan 1, Higgins 1, Kidd 1, Millar 1, Murdoch 1, Smith, A 1, own goal 1.
William Hill Scottish FA Cup (1): Lyle 1.
Scottish League Cup (4): Lyle 2, Conroy 1, Hilson 1.
Petrofac Training Cup (2): Conroy 1, Lyle 1.

Thomson R 30	Kidd L 21+6	Dowie A 29	Higgins C 32+1	Marshall J 29	Conroy R 20+8	Pickard J 12+8	Jacobs K 23+3	Russell I 22+9	Lyle D 29+3	Hooper S 5+1	Tapping C 11+2	Brownlie D 25+4	Smith A 3+13	Millar M 19+8	Hilson D 11+3	Hutton K 24+6	Harris A 20+6	Atkinson J 6+1	Oliver G 15+13	Heffernan P 3+2	Moxon O —+1	Coogans L —+3	Rutherford S —+1	Murdoch A 7+3	Match No.
1	2[1]	3	4	5	6[2]	7	8	9	10[3]	11	12	13	14												1
1	2	4	3	5	6		8	9[3]	10[1]				14		13	7	11[2]	12							2
1[1]	14	2	3	4	5	7[2]			11	10			8		6	13	9[3]	12							3
1		2	4	5	6[1]	14	7[2]		11	10			3	12	8[3]	13	9								4
1		2	7	3	6[1]		11	8	10				5[2]	9	4[3]				12	13	14				5
1	13	2	4	5	9		7[3]	8[2]	11				3	14		12	6[1]		10						6
1	6[1]	2	4	5	9	–		8	11				3		12		7[2]		10				13		7
1	6	2	4	5	9[2]			8	11				3		12	13	7[1]		10						8
1	6	2	4	5	10			9	11[2]				3[1]	12	7[3]		8		13	14					9
1	5	3[1]	4	9	6	14		8[3]	10[2]				2	11	13		7	12							10
1			4	5	9	8	2		11[1]	3			10[2]		7	6[3]	12			13	14				11
1			4	5	9	8[2]	2	12	10	3			13	11[1]	7	6[3]	14								12
1	2		4	5	12	13		9	11[3]	14			3		8[2]	7	6	10[1]							13
1	5		3	4	12	14		8[1]	11[3]				2	13	6	7	9	10[2]							14
1	2		4	5	9[1]			12	10				3		7	8	13	6[3]	11[2]		14				15
1		3	4	9	12	14	7	10[3]	11[2]				2		6	8	5[1]		13						16
1	12	2	4	8	14			9	10[3]	11			3[1]		6[2]	7	5		13						17
1	2	3	4	5			9[3]	13	6	10[1]	11[2]		14	12	8		7								18
1	2	3	4		5	14	13	7	10	12			8[2]			9	6[1]		11[3]						19
1	5	2		4	12	6	13	11	10[2]				3		7[1]	8	9								20
1	2[3]	3		5	12	9		10[1]	11				4	14	7	6	8[2]		13						21
	2	3	4	5	9[1]	11	14	12	10[2]				3			7	6	1	13				8[3]		22
	2	3	4	5	9	10	–	12	11[1]				14	7[2]		8	6[3]	1	13						23
		3	4	5	9	11	2	10[3]					13		14	8	6[1]	1	12				7[2]		24
1	6	3	4	8	7[2]	10		11[3]		9[1]	2	13	14	5									12		25
1	5	3	4	9	8	11		13	12	7[1]	2[2]		10[3]	6				14							26
1	2[2]	3	4	5[1]		8	13	11	9[3]	12			14	10		6							7		27
1		3	4		8[1]	7[2]	14	10		13	2		11[3]	5	12	9							6		28
1		4		14	5	12	11[3]	7[2]	3	13	9[1]	6	8	10					2						29
1	2	3		8[2]	14	5	7	9[3]	4	13	12	6	10[1]	11									7		30
1	13	3	4		12	10	8[2]	2[2]		14	11	5	6[1]	9									7		31
1	2	3	5		11	12	7[2]	4		14	10	6[3]	13	9[1]					8						32
1	13	3	5	10	2[0]	9	8[3]	4		7	11	6[1]	12						14						33
	2	3	13	5[2]	6	11[3]	9[1]	4		7	10	8	14	1	12										34
12[1]	3	4	5	14	9[2]	11[3]	2[1]	8	7	10	13	1	6												35
	4		5	9	10[2]	2	8[1]	3	14	7[4]	11	12	1	6[3]					13						36

QUEEN'S PARK

Year Formed: 1867. *Ground & Address:* Hampden Park, Mount Florida, Glasgow G42 9BA. *Telephone:* 0141 632 1275.
Fax: 0141 636 1612. *E-mail:* secretary@queensparkfc.co.uk *Website:* queensparkfc.co.uk
Ground Capacity: 52,025 (all seated). *Size of Pitch:* 105m × 68m.
President: Ron Jack. *Secretary:* Christine Wright. *Treasurer:* David Gordon.
Head Coach: Gus MacPherson. *Assistant Head Coach:* Chris Hillcoat. *Physio:* Andy Harrison.
Club Nickname: 'The Spiders'.
Previous Grounds: 1st Hampden (Recreation Ground); (Titwood Park was used as an interim measure between 1st &
2nd Hampdens); 2nd Hampden (Cathkin); 3rd Hampden.
Record Attendance: 95,772 v Rangers, Scottish Cup 1st rd, 18 January 1930.
Record for Ground: 149,547 Scotland v England, 1937.
Record Transfer Fee received: Not applicable due to amateur status.
Record Transfer Fee paid: Not applicable due to amateur status.
Record Victory: 16-0 v St. Peter's, Scottish Cup 1st rd, 12 Sep 1885.
Record Defeat: 0-9 v Motherwell, Division I, 26 April 1930.
Most Capped Player: Walter Arnott, 14, Scotland.
Most League Appearances: 532: Ross Caven, 1982-2002.
Most League Goals in Season (Individual): 30: William Martin, Division I, 1937-38.
Most Goals Overall (Individual): 163: James B. McAlpine, 1919-33.

QUEEN'S PARK – SCOTTISH LEAGUE TWO 2015–16 LEAGUE RECORD

Match No.	Date		Venue	Opponents	Result	H/T Score	Lg Pos.	Goalscorers	Attendance
1	Aug	8	H	Annan Ath	L 0-1	0-0	7		495
2		15	A	Clyde	W 2-0	0-0	5	McKernon [53], Woods [65]	783
3		22	A	Arbroath	W 2-1	1-0	4	Woods [4], Burns [48]	604
4		29	H	East Fife	L 0-2	0-1	6		505
5	Sept	5	A	Berwick R	L 0-1	0-1	7		533
6		12	H	East Stirling	W 5-1	2-0	7	McGeever [21], Duggan [22], Woods (pen) [69], Galt [83], Carter [86]	404
7		19	H	Elgin C	W 3-1	1-0	3	Galt [29], McKernon [60], Hurst (og) [81]	439
8		26	A	Stirling Alb	W 2-1	1-1	2	Carter [23], Ralston [57]	671
9	Oct	3	H	Montrose	L 0-1	0-0	3		342
10		17	A	Annan Ath	L 1-3	0-2	3	Woods [69]	414
11		31	H	Clyde	D 1-1	0-1	5	Carter [55]	684
12	Nov	7	A	East Stirling	L 1-2	0-0	6	Burns [79]	316
13		17	A	Montrose	W 6-1	3-1	5	Woods 2 [15, 80], Salmon (og) [24], McGeever [27], McKernon [83], Burns [90]	346
14		21	H	Stirling Alb	W 1-0	0-0	4	Carter [69]	514
15	Dec	8	A	East Fife	W 2-0	0-0	2	Mitchell [53], Woods [65]	345
16		12	H	Arbroath	W 1-0	1-0	2	Duggan [11]	458
17		19	A	Elgin C	D 0-0	0-0	2		732
18		26	H	Berwick R	L 0-1	0-0	4		547
19	Jan	2	A	Clyde	W 1-0	1-0	2	Mitchell [23]	907
20		16	H	Montrose	D 1-1	0-1	2	Carter [50]	407
21		23	A	Stirling Alb	D 0-0	0-0	2		671
22	Feb	6	H	Elgin C	D 0-0	0-0	3		529
23		13	H	East Stirling	L 0-3	0-2	4		461
24		20	A	Arbroath	W 1-0	1-0	3	Carter [5]	593
25		23	A	Berwick R	D 1-1	1-1	3	McGeever [27]	326
26		27	H	East Fife	W 3-0	0-0	3	Carter [55], Woods [90], Duggan [90]	561
27	Mar	5	A	Berwick R	D 0-0	0-0	3		409
28		12	A	Montrose	D 1-1	1-0	4	Woods [16]	454
29		15	H	Annan Ath	L 1-3	0-3	4	Carter [90]	339
30		19	H	Arbroath	W 2-1	1-0	4	Woods [32], McGeever [90]	474
31		26	A	East Fife	D 1-1	1-1	5	Duggan [21]	901
32	Apr	2	H	Stirling Alb	D 1-1	1-0	5	Duggan [43]	494
33		9	A	East Stirling	W 3-0	3-0	4	McKernon (pen) [13], Berry [40], Woods [45]	312
34		16	A	Elgin C	D 1-1	1-1	3	Brown [29]	887
35		23	H	Clyde	W 2-1	1-0	2	Duggan (pen) [22], Berry [50]	1270
36		30	A	Annan Ath	L 0-1	0-1	4		640

Final League Position: 4

Honours
League Champions: Division II 1922-23. B Division 1955-56. Second Division 1980-81. Third Division 1999-2000.
Runners-up: Third Division 2011-12. League Two 2014-15. *Promoted to Second Division:* 2006-07 (play-offs). *Promoted to League One:* 2015-16 (play-offs).
Scottish Cup Winners: 1874, 1875, 1876, 1880, 1881, 1882, 1884, 1886, 1890, 1893; *Runners-up:* 1892, 1900.
FA Cup Runners-up: 1884, 1885.
FA Charity Shield: 1899 (shared with Aston Villa).

Club colours: Shirt: Black and white thin hoops. Shorts: White. Socks: Black.

Goalscorers: *League (46):* Woods 11 (1 pen), Carter 8, Duggan 6 (1 pen), McGeever 4, McKernon 4 (1 pen), Burns 3, Berry 2, Galt 2, Mitchell 2, Brown 1, Ralston 1, own goals 2.
William Hill Scottish FA Cup (4): Woods 2, Duggan 1, McKernon 1.
Scottish League Cup (0).
Petrofac Training Cup (4): Bradley 1, Duggan 1, McLeish 1, Woods 1 (1 pen).
League One Play-Offs (5): Duggan 2 (1 pen), Berry 1, Burns 1 (1 pen), Galt 1.

Muir W 36	Baty J 6+3	Gibson S 23+3	Wharton B 24+1	McVey C 7+4	Berry V 33	McKernon J 32	McLeish C 22+8	Woods P 34+1	Mortimer W 2+2	Bradley J 12+19	Galt D 25+9	Marlow C 1+6	Carter J 12+17	Ralston A 10	McGeever R 28	Burns S 32	Duggan C 25+5	McElroy C 3+9	Mitchell G 17+1	Innes R —+6	Hynes R —+6	Brennan G —+1	Mackay K —+1	Brown L 6+3	Foy C —+1	Hooper S 6	Match No.
1	2	3	4	5^1	6	7^1	8^2	9	10	11	12	13	14														1
1	13		4		7	8	9	6	10^1	11^2			12		2	3	5										2
1	11	3	4		7	8^1	13	6		9^2	14		12		2		5	10^3									3
1	2	3	4^2		6	7		9		11^3	14	13	12	5	8	10^1											4
1			4^4		6	8^1	7	9^3	11^2		13		12	2		5	10	14									5
1	3				6	7	5	8^2		12	9	10^1	14	4	2	11^3	13										6
1		4	2	6	7	5	8^2		13	9^3	14	12		3		11^1	10^1										7
1		4		7	8	5	6		12	11^2	13	10	2	3			9^1										8
1		4		7^2	8	5	6^1		12	11	14	13	2	3		10	9^3										9
1		4		7^2	8	5^3	6		11	13		12	2	3	9	10^1	14									10
1	4			6	7	10^2	8		14	9^3		11^1	2	3	5	12	13									11
1	8	4	3^2	7	9		6		13	12	10^1	2	5	11^3	14											12
1		4	6	7	8	5		12	10^1	2^2	3	11^3	14	13												13
1		4		6	7	10	8		9^1		12		3	5	11^2	13	2									14
1	3	4	6^1		7	12	9^2	14	11		2	8	10^3	13	5											15
1		4		13	6	7	10	8^1		9^2	12		3	5	11	2										16
1		4		6	7	10	8^1	12		9^2		3	5	11^3	13	2	14									17
1	12	4		6	7	14	8		9^2	10^3		3^1	5	11	2	13										18
6^1	4	3		7	8	12	9		14	10^3	11^2		5		2	13											19
1	4	3	6^2	7	10^1	8		12	9^3	11			5		2	13	14									20
1	4	2	12	7^1	8	9	6^2		13	11^3	10		3	5		14										21
1	4			6	7	8^1		12	10	14	9^2		3	5	11^3	2		13								22
1		4	3^3		7		8	13	9^2	10	12		5	11^1	2				6	14						23
1	5		7	8	13	12		10^1	11^3	4	9	14	2						6^2	3						24
1	5		7^1	8	6^2		14	11^3	10	4	9	13	2						12	3						25
1	4		6	8	11^3		12	13	10^2	3	9	14	5						7^1	2						26
1	4		6^1	8	12	10	7^4	14	11	3	9	13	5^3							2						27
1	4	8^1	6		11		13	7	12	3	9^2	10	5							2						28
1	3^2	12	6	7	13	8^3	9	10	14	2	5	11								4						29
1		4	7	8	5	6		12	11^2	13		3	9^1	10	2	13										30
1	5	4		7	8	14	6^3		12	11^1	13	3	9^2	10	2											31
1	12	4	6^2	7	10	9^3		8	14	3^1	5	11	2							13						32
1	3	4	13	7	8^2	2	6	11^1	9	14		5	10^3							12						33
1	14	4	7	6^3	5	8		10^1	12	3	2^1	11^2		13		9										34
1	14	4	13	7	5	6	12	9^2	10^1	3	2	11					8^3									35
1	13	4	11	7	5	6	12	9^1		3	2	10^2					8									36

RAITH ROVERS

Year Formed: 1883. *Ground & Address:* Stark's Park, Pratt St, Kirkcaldy KY1 1SA. *Telephone:* 01592 263514. *Fax:* 01592 642833. *E-mail:* info@raithrovers.net *Website:* www.raithrovers.net
Ground Capacity: 8,473 (all seated). *Size of Pitch:* 103m × 64m.
Chairman: Alan Young. *Chief Executive:* Eric Drysdale.
Manager: Gary Locke. *Coach:* Darren Jackson. *Physio:* Stuart Phin.
Club Nickname: 'Rovers'.
Previous Grounds: Robbie's Park.
Record Attendance: 31,306 v Hearts, Scottish Cup 2nd rd, 7 February 1953.
Record Transfer Fee received: £900,000 for Steve McAnespie to Bolton W (September 1995).
Record Transfer Fee paid: £225,000 for Paul Harvey from Airdrieonians (July 1996).
Record Victory: 10-1 v Coldstream, Scottish Cup 2nd rd, 13 February 1954.
Record Defeat: 2-11 v Morton, Division II, 18 March 1936.
Most Capped Player: David Morris, 6, Scotland.
Most League Appearances: 430: Willie McNaught, 1946-51.
Most League Goals in Season (Individual): 38: Norman Haywood, Division II, 1937-38.
Most Goals Overall (Individual): 154: Gordon Dalziel (League), 1987-94.

RAITH ROVERS – SCOTTISH CHAMPIONSHIP 2015–16 LEAGUE RECORD

Match No.	Date		Venue	Opponents	Result		H/T Score	Lg Pos.	Goalscorers	Attendance
1	Aug	8	H	Livingston	W	3-0	2-0	1	Stewart [8], McCord (pen) [35], Megginson [90]	1560
2		15	A	Falkirk	L	0-1	0-0	4		3753
3		22	H	Alloa Ath	W	3-0	0-0	4	Craigen [55], Wighton [60], Stewart [84]	1458
4		29	A	Hibernian	L	0-2	0-1	4		8484
5	Sept	5	A	Rangers	L	0-5	0-2	6		44,050
6		12	H	Queen of the South	W	1-0	0-0	5	Benedictus [78]	1527
7		18	A	St Mirren	W	2-1	1-1	3	Craigen [12], Anderson [87]	2877
8		26	H	Dumbarton	W	1-0	0-0	3	Toshney [56]	1440
9	Oct	3	H	Greenock Morton	W	2-1	1-0	2	Stewart [45], Thomson [90]	1754
10		17	A	Alloa Ath	W	1-0	0-0	2	Anderson [79]	808
11		24	H	Hibernian	L	1-2	0-2	4	Daly [64]	4114
12		31	A	Livingston	L	0-3	0-1	4		957
13	Nov	7	H	Falkirk	L	1-2	1-1	4	Stewart [39]	2160
14		21	A	Dumbarton	D	3-3	2-0	5	Craigen [4], Routledge (og) [44], Robertson [56]	707
15		24	H	St Mirren	D	1-1	1-0	5	Stewart [39]	1264
16	Dec	11	A	Queen of the South	D	1-1	1-0	4	Thomson (og) [22]	1047
17		18	A	Greenock Morton	W	2-1	0-1	4	Callachan [48], Craigen (pen) [90]	1264
18	Jan	2	A	Hibernian	L	0-1	0-0	4		10,994
19		12	H	Alloa Ath	L	0-1	0-0	4		1064
20		23	H	Dumbarton	D	0-0	0-0	4		1397
21	Feb	2	H	Rangers	L	0-1	0-1	4		5493
22		13	A	Falkirk	D	2-2	1-2	5	Craigen [16], Stewart [68]	3956
23		20	H	Livingston	W	2-0	1-0	4	Stewart [37], Connolly [48]	1617
24		27	H	Greenock Morton	W	3-2	1-0	4	McKeown [7], Connolly [74], Hardie [89]	1633
25	Mar	1	A	Rangers	L	0-2	0-1	4		40,662
26		5	H	St Mirren	W	4-3	2-1	4	Hardie 3 [3, 53, 55], Stewart [24]	1888
27		8	H	Queen of the South	W	2-0	2-0	4	Stewart [32], Craigen (pen) [44]	1398
28		12	A	Alloa Ath	D	1-1	0-0	4	Benedictus [90]	762
29		19	H	Hibernian	W	2-1	1-1	4	Toshney [38], Stewart [53]	2386
30		22	A	St Mirren	W	2-1	2-1	4	Connolly [22], Callachan [36]	2381
31		26	A	Greenock Morton	W	1-0	0-0	4	Craigen [53]	1778
32	Apr	2	H	Rangers	D	3-3	2-2	4	Longridge [25], Craigen [38], Panayiotou [90]	6943
33		9	A	Queen of the South	W	2-1	1-0	4	Benedictus [8], Barr [63]	1511
34		16	A	Dumbarton	W	3-2	0-1	4	Hardie [49], Connolly [60], Craigen [70]	655
35		23	H	Falkirk	D	2-2	1-0	4	Thomas [7], Hardie [70]	2602
36	May	1	A	Livingston	W	1-0	0-0	4	Connolly [50]	1049

Final League Position: 4

Honours
League Champions: First Division 1992-93, 1994-95. Second Division 2002-03, 2008-09. Division II 1907-08, 1909-10 (shared), 1937-38, 1948-49; *Runners-up:* Division II 1908-09, 1926-27, 1966-67. Second Division 1975-76, 1977-78, 1986-87.
Scottish Cup Runners-up: 1913.
League Cup Winners: 1994-95. *Runners-up:* 1948-49.
League Challenge Cup Winners: 2013-14.

European: *UEFA Cup:* 6 matches (1995-96).

Club colours: Shirt: Navy with white sleeves. Shorts: White with navy trim. Socks: Navy.

Goalscorers: *League (52):* Stewart 10, Craigen 9 (2 pens), Hardie 6, Connolly 5, Benedictus 3, Anderson 2, Callachan 2, Toshney 2, Barr 1, Daly 1, Longridge 1, McCord 1 (1 pen), McKeown 1, Megginson 1, Panayiotou 1, Robertson 1, Thomas 1, Thomson 1, Wighton 1, own goals 2.
William Hill Scottish FA Cup (2): Anderson 1, McCord 1 (1 pen).
Scottish League Cup (5): Benedictus 2, Davidson 1, McKeown 1, Vaughan 1 (1 pen).
Petrofac Training Cup (1): Vaughan 1.
Premiership Play-Offs (1): Panayiotou 1.

Cuthbert K 36	Thomson J 25 + 1	Toshney L 31	Bates D 7 + 3	McKeown R 36	Anderson G 14 + 12	Callachan R 21 + 4	McCord R 17 + 2	Craigen J 31 + 3	Stewart M 26 + 3	Wighton C 7 + 9	Megginson M 4 + 13	Davidson I 27 + 2	Petrie D — + 4	Benedictus K 30	Campbell K — + 1	Mackie S — + 1	Daly J 13 + 2	Matthews R 4 + 10	Robertson S 17 + 2	Longridge L 9 + 4	Court J — + 1	Connolly A 13 + 3	Panayiotou H 8 + 6	Barr C 11 + 1	Hardie R 7 + 3	Thomas J 2 + 6	Match No.
1	2	3	4	5	6²	7	8¹	9	10³	11	12	13	14														1
1	2	3	13	5	6³	8	7¹	9	11	10²	12	14		4⁴													2
1	2	3		5²	6¹	7	8	9	10	11²	12			4	13	14											3
1	2	4¹		5	6	7		9²	11	12	13	8		3			10										4
1	2		4	5	6²	8¹	7		10	13	9			3			11	12									5
1	2	3		5	6³	8¹	9	12	11²	13	7			4			10	14									6
1	2	4		5	6	7²	9	10	13	8¹				3			11	12									7
1	2	3		5	8²	6¹	7	11	9¹	13	14			4			10	12									8
1	2	3		5	6¹	8³	9¹	11	14	13	7			4			10		12								9
1	2	3¹		5	13	12	8³	10	9²	14	7			4			11		6								10
1	2	3		5	14		9¹	10	13²	12	7			4			11	6⁶	8								11
1	2¹	3		5	6	9²		11	12	13	7			4			10		8								12
1	2		5¹		13	7²	9	11³	14	6	3	12		4			10		8								13
1	2		5		13	7²	6	10	11³	9¹	3	12		4			14		8								14
1	2¹		5	6	12	7	9	11²	13		3			4			10		8								15
1	2¹	13	5	6¹	8	7	10	11³	12		3			4			14		9								16
1	2¹	12	5		6	7²	9	10³	14	3				4			11	13	8								17
1		4	5	13⁴	8	7¹	9		12	11²				3			10	2	6								18
1	2	5		7			9	12	11¹	3				4			6	8²	10	13							19
1	2	5	12	7		9¹	10		13	3				4			8	6	11²								20
1	3	2	5	14	9²	13³	11¹			6				4			7	10	8	12							21
1	12	3	2¹	5		9		6²	10					4⁴			14	7³	13	8	11						22
1	2			5	13	7		9	11					3			8			6²	10¹	4	12				23
1	2	3		5	13	7	14	9¹	10³					4			8			6²	11		12				24
1	2	4		5	6³		10¹	7						8			9¹	12		14	11	3		13			25
1	2	3		5	12	7			11					8		4	13			6¹	9²		10				26
1	2	3		5		8		9	10²					7¹	4				14	6³	13	12	11				27
1	2	7		5				9²	10³					4					13	6¹	14	3	11	12			28
1	2	7		5	12	6			13	10²				8		4			9¹			3	11				29
1	2	8¹		5	14	7		10						4			12		9	6³	11²	3		13			30
1	2	8		5		7³		10	11¹		9			4			14		13	6²		3		12			31
1	2	7		5	13	6		10²						8		4			9¹	14	12	3		11³			32
1	2	3		5	13			9²						4			8	10¹	7	12	6	11³	14				33
1	2	8		5	6¹	7		12						4³			14		9	10²	3	11	13				34
1	2			5		13		8³						7		4		6²	9	14	10	3	12	11¹			35
1	5	3		2		8		9¹	12					7				11²		6	13	4	10				36

RANGERS

Year Formed: 1873. *Ground & Address:* Ibrox Stadium, 150 Edmiston Drive, Glasgow G51 2XD.
Telephone: 0871 702 1972. *Fax:* 0870 600 1978. *Website:* www.rangers.co.uk
Ground Capacity: 51,082 (all seated). *Size of Pitch:* 105m × 68m.
Chairman: Dave King. *Secretary:* James Blair.
Manager: Mark Warburton. *Assistant Manager:* David Weir. *Managing Director:* Stewart Robinson.
Club Nickname: 'The Gers', 'The Teddy Bears'.
Previous Grounds: Flesher's Haugh, Burnbank, Kinning Park, Old Ibrox.
Record Attendance: 118,567 v Celtic, Division I, 2 January 1939.
Record Transfer Fee received: £8,500,000 for Giovanni van Bronckhorst to Arsenal (July 2001).
Record Transfer Fee paid: £12,000,000 for Tore Andre Flo from Chelsea (November 2000).
Record Victory: 14-2 v Blairgowrie, Scottish Cup 1st rd, 20 January, 1934.
Record Defeat: 1-7 v Celtic, League Cup Final, 19 October 1957.
Most Capped Player: Ally McCoist, 60, Scotland.
Most League Appearances: 496: John Greig, 1962-78.
Most League Goals in Season (Individual): 44: Sam English, Division I, 1931-32.
Most Goals Overall (Individual): 355: Ally McCoist; 1985-98.

Honours
League Champions: (54 times) Division I 1890-91 (shared), 1898-99, 1899-1900, 1900-01, 1901-02, 1910-11, 1911-12, 1912-13, 1917-18, 1919-20, 1920-21, 1922-23, 1923-24, 1924-25, 1926-27, 1927-28, 1928-29, 1929-30, 1930-31, 1932-33, 1933-34, 1934-35, 1936-37, 1938-39, 1946-47, 1948-49, 1949-50, 1952-53, 1955-56, 1956-57, 1958-59, 1960-61, 1962-63, 1963-64, 1974-75. Premier Division: 1975-76, 1977-78, 1986-87, 1988-89, 1989-90, 1990-91, 1991-92, 1992-93, 1993-94, 1994-95, 1995-96, 1996-97, 1998-99, 1999-2000, 2002-03, 2004-05, 2008-09, 2009-10, 2010-11. *Runners-up:* 30 times. Championship 2015-16. League One 2013-14. Third Division 2012-13.
Scottish Cup Winners: (33 times) 1894, 1897, 1898, 1903, 1928, 1930, 1932, 1934, 1935, 1936, 1948, 1949, 1950, 1953, 1960, 1962, 1963, 1964, 1966, 1973, 1976, 1978, 1979, 1981, 1992, 1993, 1996, 1999, 2000, 2002, 2003, 2008, 2009; *Runners-up:* 18 times.

RANGERS – SCOTTISH CHAMPIONSHIP 2015–16 LEAGUE RECORD

Match No.	Date		Venue	Opponents	Result		H/T Score	Lg Pos.	Goalscorers	Atten- dance
1	Aug	7	H	St Mirren	W	3-1	2-1	1	Wallace 2 [4, 26], Shiels [90]	49,216
2		16	A	Alloa Ath	W	5-1	4-1	1	Tavernier [4], Waghorn (pen) [9], Holt [39], Miller 2 [43, 85]	3047
3		23	H	Hibernian	W	1-0	0-0	1	Tavernier [66]	49,220
4		30	A	Queen of the South	W	5-1	1-0	1	Halliday [28], Waghorn 2 (2 pens) [52, 76], Holt [59], McKay [64]	5858
5	Sept	5	H	Raith R	W	5-0	2-0	1	Wallace [4], Tavernier [45], McKay [55], Waghorn 2 (2 pens) [64, 69]	44,050
6		12	H	Livingston	W	3-0	2-0	1	Wallace [16], Waghorn [41], Law [80]	44,832
7		19	A	Dumbarton	W	2-1	0-0	1	Waghorn 2 (1 pen) [64, 73 (p)]	1978
8		27	A	Greenock Morton	W	4-0	3-0	1	Waghorn 3 (1 pen) [12 (p), 22, 81], Tavernier [34]	7392
9	Oct	3	H	Falkirk	W	3-1	1-1	1	Shiels [3], Tavernier [81], Wallace [90]	45,135
10		17	H	Queen of the South	W	2-1	0-1	1	Holt [53], Waghorn [90]	44,133
11		25	A	St Mirren	W	1-0	1-0	1	Holt [25]	5477
12	Nov	1	A	Hibernian	L	1-2	0-1	1	McGregor (og) [47]	14,412
13		7	H	Alloa Ath	W	4-0	3-0	1	Waghorn 2 [10, 44], Tavernier [14], Clark [90]	43,242
14		21	A	Livingston	D	1-1	1-0	1	Holt [22]	6505
15	Dec	1	H	Dumbarton	W	4-0	0-0	1	Holt [47], Waghorn [60], Oduwa [81], Halliday (pen) [88]	37,182
16		12	H	Greenock Morton	D	2-2	1-1	1	Miller [2], Waghorn [84]	41,816
17		19	A	Falkirk	L	1-2	1-1	1	McKay [15]	7488
18		28	H	Hibernian	W	4-2	2-1	1	Holt 2 [33, 43], Clark [65], Waghorn [89]	49,995
19	Jan	2	A	Dumbarton	W	6-0	1-0	1	Miller 3 [42, 59, 64], Waghorn [71], Halliday [81], Tavernier [88]	1894
20		16	H	Livingston	W	4-1	4-0	1	Wilson [8], Waghorn 2 (1 pen) [22 (p), 41], Miller [35]	42,906
21		25	A	Greenock Morton	W	2-0	1-0	1	Miller [26], McKay [70]	5778
22		30	H	Falkirk	W	1-0	0-0	1	King [90]	46,980
23	Feb	2	A	Raith R	W	1-0	1-0	1	Halliday [44]	5493
24		13	A	Alloa Ath	D	1-1	0-0	1	O'Halloran [83]	3100
25		21	A	Queen of the South	W	1-0	0-0	1	Miller [64]	5449
26		27	H	St Mirren	W	1-0	0-0	1	Forrester [86]	46,366
27	Mar	1	H	Raith R	W	2-0	1-0	1	Forrester [27], Wallace [51]	40,662
28		11	H	Greenock Morton	W	3-1	1-1	1	Miller 2 [43, 48], Wallace [56]	45,072
29		18	A	Falkirk	L	2-3	2-0	1	Miller [7], McKay [9]	7804
30		26	H	Queen of the South	W	4-3	1-1	1	Forrester [14], O'Halloran [46], Halliday [51], Tavernier [55]	46,117
31	Apr	2	A	Raith R	D	3-3	2-2	1	Forrester [30], O'Halloran [35], Miller [49]	6943
32		5	H	Dumbarton	W	1-0	0-0	1	Tavernier [50]	48,568
33		20	A	Hibernian	L	2-3	1-2	1	Holt [41], McKay [85]	12,231
34		23	H	Alloa Ath	D	1-1	1-1	1	Tavernier [45]	50,349
35		26	A	Livingston	L	0-1	0-1	1		5021
36	May	1	A	St Mirren	D	2-2	0-1	1	Miller [54], Holt [88]	5933

Final League Position: 1

League Cup Winners: (27 times) 1946-47, 1948-49, 1960-61, 1961-62, 1963-64, 1964-65, 1970-71, 1975-76, 1977-78, 1978-79, 1981-82, 1983-84, 1984-85, 1986-87, 1987-88, 1988-89, 1990-91, 1992-93, 1993-94, 1996-97, 1998-99, 2001-02, 2002-03, 2004-05, 2007-08, 2009-10, 2010-11; *Runners-up:* 7 times.
League Challenge Cup Winners: 2015-16. *Runners-up:* 2013-14.

European: *European Cup:* 161 matches (1956-57, 1957-58, 1959-60 semi-finals, 1961-62, 1963-64, 1964-65, 1975-76, 1976-77, 1978-79, 1987-88, 1989-90, 1990-91, 1991-92, 1992-93 final pool, 1993-94, 1994-95, 1995-96; 1996-97, 1997-98, 1999-2000, 2000-01, 2001-02, 2003-04, 2004-05, 2005-06, 2007-08, 2008-09, 2009-10, 2010-11, 2011-12).
Cup Winners' Cup: 54 matches (1960-61 runners-up, 1962-63, 1966-67 runners-up, 1969-70, 1971-72 winners, 1973-74, 1977-78, 1979-80, 1981-82, 1983-84).
UEFA Cup: 88 matches (*Fairs Cup:* 1967-68, 1968-69 semi-finals, 1970-71. *UEFA Cup:* 1982-83, 1984-85, 1985-86, 1986-87, 1988-89, 1997-98, 1998-99, 1999-2000, 2000-01, 2001-02, 2002-03, 2004-05, 2006-07, 2007-08 runners-up). *Europa League:* 6 matches (2010-11, 2011-12).

Club colours: Shirt: Royal blue with red and white trim. Shorts: White with blue trim. Socks: Black with red tops.

Goalscorers: *League (88):* Waghorn 20 (8 pens), Miller 14, Holt 10, Tavernier 10, Wallace 7, McKay 6, Halliday 5 (1 pen), Forrester 4, O'Halloran 3, Clark 2, Shiels 2, King 1, Law 1, Oduwa 1, Wilson 1, own goal 1.
William Hill Scottish FA Cup (15): Waghorn 4 (3 pens), Halliday 2, McKay 2, Miller 2, Wallace 2, Clark 1, Forrester 1, Holt 1.
Scottish League Cup (9): Tavernier 3, Clark 1, Halliday 1, Miller 1, Shiels 1, Templeton 1, Waghorn 1.
Petrofac Training Cup (17): Miller 4, Waghorn 3, Clark 2, Halliday 2 (1 pen), Tavernier 2, Holt 1, McKay 1, own goals 2.

Foderingham W 36	Tavernier J 36	Kiernan R 33	Wilson D 30	Wallace L 36	Holt J 31 + 1	Halliday A 35	Law N 10 + 8	McKay B 33 + 1	Waghorn M 25	Walsh T 1	Clark N 5 + 17	Shiels D 5 + 26	Templeton D — + 1	Miller K 22 + 10	Oduwa N 7 + 8	Zelalem G 15 + 6	Ball D 15 + 6	Aird F — + 3	Hardie R — + 3	Thompson J — + 2	Forrester H 6 + 5	King B 6 + 6	O'Halloran M 9 + 3	Burt L — + 2	Match No.
1	2	3	4	5	6²	7	8	9¹	10	11¹	12	13	14												1
1	2	3	4	5		7	8	9³	6¹	11²		13	14	10	12										2
1	2	3	4	5	6²	7	8	9¹	10		14	13		11³	12										3
1	2³	3	4	5¹	7	8		6	10					11²	13	9	12	14							4
1	2	3	4	5	8¹	7	12	9	10			13		11³	6²		14								5
1	2	3	4	5	8²	7	12	9	10		14			13	11	6³									6
1	2³		4	5		8		6²11¹	9			13		10	12	7	3	14							7
1	2	3	4	5	8²	7	14	9³	10		13			12	11	6¹									8
1	2	3	4	5	8²	7	13	11	10		6¹			12	9¹		14								9
1	2	3		5	6	7	12	9³	10		14	8²		11¹	13		4								10
1	2	3		5	8	7		11³	10		12	13		9²		6¹	4	14							11
1	5	2	4²	9	8³	6		7	11		10¹	14				13	12	3							12
1	2	4		5	8¹	7³		11	10		12	13			9²	6	3		14						13
1	2	3		5	8	7²		10	11			13		12	6¹	9	4								14
1	2	4		5	8	7		10²	9³		11			12	14	6¹	3		13						15
1	2	4		5	8	7		11³	9		12	13		10¹	14	6²	3								16
1	2	3	4³	5	8	7	12	9	11		14	10²		13	6¹										17
1	2	3	4	5	6	7¹	8²11³	9			12	13		10¹				14							18
1	2	3	4	5	7²	8	6¹	11			12	13		10¹	14										19
1	2	3	4	5	6³	7	8²11	9¹			12	14		10	13										20
1	2	3	4	5		7¹	8²	9				13		10²		6¹	14				12				21
1	2	3	4	5			6²11	9			8²			10¹		14	7				13	12			22
1	2	3	4	5		9		10¹ 11			14			7²		8³	6				12	13			23
1	2	3	4	5	8¹	6		7	11²		12			14								9³	13	10		24
1	2	3	4	5	8	7		9			11² 12			13								6¹	10		25
1	2	3	4	5	6³	7	8² 11¹				13			10							14	12	9		26
1	2	3	4	5	6³	7²					11 12			13							8¹	10	9	14	27
1	2		4	5	6	7		11			14	12		10³		3					8¹	13	9²		28
1	2	3	4	5	8	6		11¹			14			10³		7					12	9²	13		29
1	2	3	4	5	6³	8	14				13	12		10			7¹				11²		9		30
1	2	3	4	5	8	7		9²			13			10	14						6³	12	11¹		31
1	2	3	4	5	8	7		11¹			14	13		10¹							6²	9	12		32
1	2	3	4	5	9	8		10				14		11³		12	6¹					13	7²		33
1	2	3	4	5	8¹	7		11			10² 12			13		6						9³		14	34
1	2		4	5	13	8	14	12				7²		10		6¹	3					9³	11		35
1	2	3	4	5	8	7		11	9¹		13	14		10³			6²	12							36

ROSS COUNTY

Year Formed: 1929. *Ground & Address:* The Global Energy Stadium, Victoria Park, Dingwall IV15 9QZ. *Telephone:* 01349 860860. *Fax:* 01349 866277. *E-mail:* info@rosscountyfootballclub.co.uk
Website: www.rosscountyfootballclub.co.uk
Ground Capacity: 6,700 (all seated). *Size of Ground:* 105 × 68m.
Chairman: Rory MacGregor. *Secretary:* Fiona MacBean.
Manager: Jim McIntyre. *Assistant Manager:* Billy Dodds. *Physio:* Crawford Quinn.
Club Nickname: 'The Staggies'.
Record Attendance: 6,110 v Celtic, Premier League, 18 August 2012.
Record Transfer Fee received: £200,000 for Neil Tarrant to Aston Villa (April 1999).
Record Transfer Fee paid: £50,000 for Derek Holmes from Hearts (October 1999).
Record Victory: 11-0 v St Cuthbert Wanderers, Scottish Cup 1st rd, 11 December 1993.
Record Defeat: 0-7 v Kilmarnock, Scottish Cup 3rd rd, 17 February 1962.
Most League Appearances: 230: Mark McCulloch, 2002-09.
Most League Goals in Season: 24: Andrew Barrowman, 2007-08.
Most League Goals (Overall): 47: Sean Higgins, 2002-09.

ROSS COUNTY – SCOTTISH PREMIERSHIP 2015–16 LEAGUE RECORD

Match No.	Date	Venue	Opponents	Result	H/T Score	Lg Pos.	Goalscorers	Atten- dance
1	Aug 1	A	Celtic	L	0-2	0-2	11		45,197
2	8	H	Hamilton A	W	2-0	2-0	6	Curran 2 [10, 41]	3479
3	11	A	St Johnstone	D	1-1	1-0	6	Curran [17]	3065
4	15	H	Hearts	L	1-2	1-2	6	Boyce (pen) [39]	4806
5	22	A	Kilmarnock	W	4-0	4-0	5	Boyce 2 [2, 29], Franks [4], Davies [35]	3604
6	29	H	Dundee U	W	2-1	2-0	5	Boyce (pen) [17], Davies [28]	4014
7	Sept 12	A	Motherwell	D	1-1	1-0	4	Gardyne [33]	3545
8	19	H	Partick Thistle	W	1-0	1-0	4	Boyce [18]	3531
9	26.	A	Dundee	D	3-3	3-1	5	Boyce [19], McPake (og) [37], Gardyne [43]	5128
10	Oct 3	H	Inverness CT	L	1-2	0-2	5	Boyce [90]	5473
11	16	H	Aberdeen	W	2-0	1-0	3	Graham 2 [36, 49]	5543
12	24	A	Hearts	L	0-2	0-1	4		16,264
13	31	A	Dundee U	L	0-1	0-0	5		5549
14	Nov 8	H	Celtic	L	1-4	0-1	5	Dingwall [59]	6042
15	21	H	Motherwell	W	3-0	1-0	5	Curran [22], Dingwall [69], Boyce (pen) [90]	3378
16	28	A	Aberdeen	L	1-3	1-0	6	Curran [14]	10,843
17	Dec 5	H	St Johnstone	L	2-3	0-2	6	Boyce [68], Davidson (og) [74]	3229
18	12	A	Hamilton A	W	3-1	0-1	5	Curran [58], Murdoch [86], Boyce [90]	2120
19	19	A	Partick Thistle	L	0-1	0-0	5		2762
20	26	H	Dundee	W	5-2	1-1	5	Boyce 3 [29, 69, 85], Gardyne [55], Irvine [60]	3687
21	29	H	Kilmarnock	W	3-2	1-1	5	Curran [12], Gardyne 2 [50, 56]	3518
22	Jan 2	A	Inverness CT	L	0-2	0-2	5		5388
23	17	H	Aberdeen	L	2-3	1-2	5	McShane 2 [27, 82]	4107
24	23	A	Motherwell	W	2-1	1-0	4	Irvine [20], Graham [69]	3279
25	Feb 10	H	Hearts	L	0-3	0-0	4		3391
26	13	A	Celtic	L	0-2	0-1	4		42,550
27	20	H	Hamilton A	W	2-1	1-0	4	Schalk [45], McShane [78]	3059
28	27	A	Dundee U	L	0-3	0-1	5		3564
29	Mar 1	A	Kilmarnock	W	2-0	1-0	4	Schalk [8], Graham [90]	2633
30	16	A	St Johnstone	D	1-1	0-1	4	Graham (pen) [65]	2501
31	19	H	Inverness CT	L	0-3	0-2	6		5912
32	Apr 2	A	Dundee	L	2-5	2-3	7	Davies [15], Schalk [45]	5095
33	9	H	Partick Thistle	W	1-0	1-0	6	Schalk [14]	3603
34	24	A	Celtic	D	1-1	0-1	6	Murdoch [64]	41,396
35	30	H	St Johnstone	L	0-1	0-0	6		3329
36	May 7	A	Hearts	D	1-1	0-0	6	Goodwillie [88]	15,438
37	11	H	Motherwell	L	1-3	0-2	6	Boyce [69]	2976
38	15	A	Aberdeen	W	4-0	2-0	6	Graham (pen) [23], Schalk [45], Boyce [68], Woods, M [78]	10,003

Final League Position: 6

Honours
League Champions: First Division 2011-12. Second Division 2007-08. Third Division 1998-99.
Scottish Cup Runners-up: 2010.
League Cup Winners: 2015-16.
League Challenge Cup Winners: 2006-07, 2010-11; *Runners-up:* 2004-05, 2008-09.

Club colours: Shirt: Navy blue with vertical white stripe. Shorts: Navy blue. Socks: Navy blue.

Goalscorers: *League (55):* Boyce 15 (3 pens), Curran 7, Graham 6 (2 pens), Gardyne 5, Schalk 5, Davies 3, McShane 3, Dingwall 2, Irvine 2, Murdoch 2, Franks 1, Goodwillie 1, Woods, M 1, own goals 2.
William Hill Scottish FA Cup (9): Graham 4 (2 pens), Schalk 2, Boyce 1, De Vita 1, Quinn, P 1.
Scottish League Cup (16): Boyce 4, Gardyne 3, Schalk 2, De Vita 1, Franks 1, Graham 1, Holden 1, Irvine 1, Quinn, P 1, Woods, M 1 (1 pen).

Fox S 27	Fraser M 29	Davies A 31	Boyd S 12+3	Foster R 28+4	McShane I 16+2	Quinn R 5+5	Gardyne M 34+1	Irvine J 34+2	Murdoch S 14+15	Curran C 15+4	De Vita R 8+11	Boyce L 29+6	Graham B 10+13	Bachmann D —+1	Robertson C 21+2	Dingwall T 5+7	Reckord J 14+2	Franks J 18+11	Woods M 23+3	Woods G 11+1	Schalk A 14+11	Morrison G —+2	Quinn P 14	Goodwillie D 4+5	McLaughlin C 2	Match No.
1	2	3	4	5	6³	7	8	9	10¹	11²	12	13	14													1
1²	2	4	3	5	7	12	6	8	10³	9	11¹	14	13													2
1	2	4		5	8³	14	6	7		10	9¹	11²	13		3	12										3
1	2	3		5³	8¹	12	6	7		11	9²	10			4	13	14									4
1	2	3			9	6	7	13	10¹	14	11²	12			4		5	8³								5
1	2	4			13	12	9	6³	7	14	11¹	10			3		5	8²								6
1	2	4		12		8²	9	7		10¹	11	14			3		5	6³	13							7
1	2	3			6¹	7	14		9	10	11²	4	13	5	12	8³										8
1	2	4¹	13	14		8	6	12	9³	10	11²	3	5	7¹												9
1¹	2		4	5		6	7	8	14	11	10²	3	13	9¹												10
	2	3		9		6²	7	8	12	10³	11¹	4		5	13		1	14								11
	2	4		5		6	7	8²	14	10	11³	3		9¹	12	13	1									12
	2	4¹	12	5		6	7	13	10³	11	3	9²			8	1	14									13
	2	4	5	9¹		7	8²14	12		11²	3	10			6	1	13									14
	2	3	4	5		7	14	10²	12	11		9¹			6³	8	1	13								15
	2	4	3	5		8	6¹	10³	13	11		9²			12	7	1	14								16
	2	3	4	5		7	9²	11		10		6¹			13	8	1	12								17
1		4		2		12	7	14	10²	9¹	11				3		5	6³	8	13						18
1		4		2		6²	7	12	10³		11				3	14	5	9¹	8	13						19
1		4	12	2		14	9	13	8²	11		10			3¹		5	6³	7							20
1		4	3	2		13	6	7	12	11		10³	14				5	9²	8¹							21
1		4	3	2		6³	9	7		11¹	14		12				5	13	8	10³						22
1	5¹	3		6	7		9	13	8²			12		10	4	2			11³	14						23
1	2	4	3	5	8		6	7	12	13		11²					9¹			10³	14					24
1	5	3		2	6		9	8²		10					13	7		12			4		11¹			25
1	2³			5	8	10	7	13		11¹		3		14	9	6		12			4²		4	14		26
1		3		2	6		9¹	7	12		10³		13	5⁴		8		11²			4		4	14		27
1	2	3			7¹		9	6				10³	13			12	8		11²			4	14	5		28
	5	4	2				9	6	14	12	13				7³	8	1	10¹			3	11²				29
	4	2	14	8		5	6		12	10²					9³	7	1	13			3	11¹				30
	2	4²	5	8		6³	7	9		11	12				10		1	10			3	14				31
	2	4	5¹	6		9		12		11	13		14		7³	8	1	10²			3					32
1	2	4	9	13		6		8		12	10¹				14	7		11²			3		5³			33
1	2		7			6	8	9	13	11¹	14				5²			10³			4	12				34
1	2	3		6¹			5³	7	8	11²	13			14	9	12					4					35
1		4	5	11³		6	7	13	12	2					9²	8		10¹			3	14				36
1		4		9		6	8¹	12	13	14					2	5²		7	11		3	10³				37
1		3		9²		8¹	12		5	7	10		4		13	11		6			2					38

ST JOHNSTONE

Year Formed: 1884. *Ground & Address:* McDiarmid Park, Crieff Road, Perth PH1 2SJ. *Telephone:* 01738 459090. *Fax:* 01738 625 771. *Email:* enquiries@perthsaints.co.uk *Website:* www.perthstjohnstonefc.co.uk
Ground Capacity: 10,673 (all seated). *Size of Pitch:* 105m × 68m.
Chairman: Steve Brown. *Football Administrator:* Paul Smith.
Manager: Tommy Wright. *Assistant Manager:* Callum Davidson. *Physio:* Scott Williams.
Club Nickname: 'Saints'.
Previous Grounds: Recreation Grounds, Muirton Park.
Record Attendance: 29,972 v Dundee, Scottish Cup 2nd rd, 10 February 1951 (Muirton Park): 10,545 v Dundee, Premier Division, 23 May 1999 (McDiarmid Park).
Record Transfer Fee received: £1,750,000 for Callum Davidson to Blackburn R (March 1998).
Record Transfer Fee paid: £400,000 for Billy Dodds from Dundee (January 1994).
Record Victory: 9-0 v Albion R, League Cup, 9 March 1946.
Record Defeat: 1-10 v Third Lanark, Scottish Cup 1st rd, 24 January 1903.
Most Capped Player: Nick Dasovic, 26, Canada.
Most League Appearances: 298: Drew Rutherford, 1976-85.
Most League Goals in Season (Individual): 36: Jimmy Benson, Division II, 1931-32.
Most Goals Overall (Individual): 140: John Brogan, 1977-83.

ST JOHNSTONE – SCOTTISH PREMIERSHIP 2015–16 LEAGUE RECORD

Match No.	Date	Venue	Opponents	Result	H/T Score	Lg Pos.	Goalscorers	Attendance
1	Aug 2	A	Hearts	L	3-4	0-1	8	Lappin [56], Sutton [75], Cummins [78]	16,334
2	8	H	Inverness CT	D	1-1	0-1	9	Cummins [90]	2959
3	11	A	Ross Co	D	1-1	0-1	8	Cummins [52]	3065
4	15	A	Dundee	L	1-2	0-2	10	MacLean [54]	6176
5	22	H	Motherwell	W	2-1	0-1	7	MacLean 2 [62, 79]	3361
6	29	A	Celtic	L	1-3	1-2	8	Boyata (og) [11]	42,507
7	Sept 12	A	Hamilton A	W	4-1	3-0	7	Craig [22], MacLean 3 (1 pen) [25 (p), 43, 54]	2648
8	19	A	Kilmarnock	L	1-2	1-1	7	Wotherspoon [17]	3165
9	26	H	Dundee U	W	2-1	0-1	7	Cummins [63], Lappin [80]	4634
10	Oct 3	A	Aberdeen	W	5-1	3-1	7	Easton [5], Shaughnessy [10], Craig [30], MacLean 2 [47, 51]	13,405
11	17	H	Partick Thistle	L	1-2	0-2	7	MacLean [48]	3414
12	24	A	Inverness CT	W	1-0	0-0	6	Craig (pen) [90]	3471
13	31	A	Hamilton A	W	4-2	1-0	4	Cummins 2 [40, 49], Wotherspoon [63], O'Halloran [67]	2216
14	Nov 7	H	Kilmarnock	W	2-1	1-1	4	O'Halloran [23], Kane [49]	3475
15	21	A	Dundee U	W	2-1	2-1	4	Kane [43], Davidson [45]	7020
16	27	H	Dundee	D	1-1	1-1	4	Wotherspoon [13]	4598
17	Dec 5	A	Ross Co	W	3-2	2-0	4	Wotherspoon 2 [3, 43], Mackay [88]	3229
18	13	H	Celtic	L	0-3	0-1	4		6418
19	19	H	Hearts	D	0-0	0-0	4		4780
20	30	A	Motherwell	L	0-2	0-2	4		4055
21	Jan 16	H	Hamilton A	D	0-0	0-0	4		2685
22	23	A	Celtic	L	1-3	1-2	5	MacLean [12]	43,948
23	Feb 6	H	Aberdeen	L	3-4	0-2	5	Wotherspoon [52], Anderson [79], Scobbie [89]	5712
24	12	A	Dundee	L	0-2	0-1	6		4876
25	20	H	Motherwell	W	2-1	1-1	5	Wotherspoon [43], Scobbie [90]	3006
26	23	A	Partick Thistle	L	0-2	0-0	5		2320
27	27	A	Aberdeen	D	1-1	0-1	4	Craig (pen) [88]	12,563
28	Mar 2	H	Partick Thistle	L	1-2	0-2	6	Kane [67]	2569
29	9	H	Inverness CT	W	1-0	0-0	4	Kane [84]	2157
30	16	H	Ross Co	D	1-1	1-0	4	Wotherspoon [11]	2501
31	19	A	Hearts	W	3-0	2-0	4	Davidson 2 [11, 21], Fisher [88]	16,295
32	Apr 2	H	Dundee U	L	0-1	0-1	5		5784
33	9	A	Kilmarnock	L	0-3	0-1	5		3693
34	22	H	Aberdeen	W	3-0	2-0	4	Wotherspoon [14], MacLean [38], Craig [55]	3990
35	30	A	Ross Co	W	1-0	0-0	4	MacLean [56]	3329
36	May 7	A	Motherwell	W	2-1	2-1	4	MacLean [34], Swanson [45]	4441
37	11	H	Celtic	W	2-1	0-0	4	MacLean [56], Cummins [77]	5959
38	15	A	Hearts	D	2-2	2-2	4	Craig (pen) [9], Cummins [12]	16,046

Final League Position: 4

Honours
League Champions: First Division 1982-83, 1989-90, 1996-97, 2008-09. Division II 1923-24, 1959-60, 1962-63;
Runners-up: Division II 1931-32. First Division 2005-06, 2006-07. Second Division 1987-88.
Scottish Cup Winners: 2014.
League Cup Runners-up: 1969-70, 1998-99.
League Challenge Cup Winners: 2007-08; *Runners-up:* 1996-97.

European: *UEFA Cup:* 20 matches (1971-72, 1999-2000, 2012-13, 2013-14, 2014-15).

Club colours: Shirt: Blue with white trim. Short: White. Socks: Blue.

Goalscorers: *League (58):* MacLean 14 (1 pen), Wotherspoon 9, Cummins 8, Craig 6 (3 pens), Kane 4, Davidson 3, Lappin 2, O'Halloran 2, Scobbie 2, Anderson 1, Easton 1, Fisher 1, Mackay 1, Shaughnessy 1, Sutton 1, Swanson 1, own goal 1.
William Hill Scottish FA Cup (0).
Scottish League Cup (7): O'Halloran 2, Davidson 1, Kane 1, Lappin 1, MacLean 1 (1 pen), Shaughnessy 1.
UEFA Europa League (2): McKay 1, O'Halloran 1.

Mannus A 33	Shaughnessy J 35+2	McKay B 2	Scobbie T 28+2	Easton B 26+3	Millar C 20	Wotherspoon D 32+3	O'Halloran M 19+1	Craig L 24+11	Lappin S 14+9	Sutton J 5+16	Brown S 2+3	Cummins G 23+9	Kane C 10+19	Wright F 1	Davidson M 30	MacLean S 29+4	Mackay D 17	Fisher D 22+1	Thomson C 2+8	Anderson S 23+1	Clark Z 5+1	Hurst G ——+2	Caddis L ——+5	Swanson D 14	Krachunov P 1+1	Doyle M ——+2	Gordon L 1	Match No.
1	2	3	4	5	6¹	7³	8	9	10²	11	12	13	14															1
1	2	3		5		6	11	9	8²	10¹		13		4	7	12												2
1	2	3	4	5		6²	9	8	13	11³		10¹	12			7	14											3
1	2		4	5	6		9	8¹	12	13		11¹	14			7	10³	3										4
1	2		4	5	7	12	6³	14	9¹			10²	13			8	11	3										5
1	2		4	5	7	6	9	12		13		10¹	14			8¹	11²	3										6
1	4			5	7	8	9	12		14		11³			6¹	10³	3	2	13									7
1	4			5	7	6	9	8²	13	11³		10	14			3	2¹	12										8
1*	2		4	5	6²	13	9¹	8	14		11				7	10³	3		12									9
	2		4	5		6¹		8	9	13		10²			7	11³	3	12		1	14							10
1	2		4	5		6²	12	9	8¹	14		11¹			7	10	3					13						11
1	2		5	12		10³	13	7			9	14		6	11²	4¹	8	3										12
1	2		3	5		10²	7³	9		12		11¹	14	8			6	13	4									13
1	14		3	5		13	6³	9⁴				11¹	12	7	10	2	8²	4										14
1	4			5	6	8¹	9			13		11²			7	10	2		3			12						15
1	2			5	7	9	6			12			10¹		8	11²	3		13	4								16
1	2		5	13	7	6¹	11²	9						8	10	3	4					12						17
1	2			5	7¹	6	10	9				13		8	11²	3		4				12						18
1	13			5		9	6	8		11¹		12		7³	8²	10	3	2²	4									19
1		13	5	6		11¹	9		14			7³		8²	10	3	2	12	4									20
1	2		5		6		13	8²	14			11¹	12	7	10³	3		9	4									21
1	2	4	5		10	8	12	7	13			9¹			6³	11²		3		14								22
1	2		5		7²	9		8	14			11	12		10¹		3	13	4				6³					23
1	2		5			9¹		12	7	13		11²	14	8	10³	3		4					6					24
1	3		5		6	9		8¹	14	13		12			7	11²		2	10¹	4			6³					25
1	3		5		6²	9		12	8	14		11			7¹			2³	4					10	13			26
1	3		5			9		12	8		7¹	11	14		10³			2	13	4				6²				27
1	3		5		6²			9	14			10¹	12		8	11³		2	13	4				7				28
1	4		5			9		13	8			12	11		7	10¹		2		3				6²				29
1	5	3	2		9			13	7			12	11¹		8	10			4					6²				30
1	4		5		7³	10		9	14			13	11²		8	12		2		3				6¹				31
1	3	4	5	7¹	9			12				14	11		8²	10³		2	13					6				32
1	5	3		7	6		9	8	12			13	11¹			2								10²	4			33
	3		5		8³	6		9	12			10³	13		7¹	11		2		4	1						14	34
	4		5	13	8¹	9		11			12	6³	14			10		2		3	1			7²				35
	3	14	5		9		10			12	6²	13			8¹	11		2		4	1			7¹				36
	2	4	5		6		8			7	12	11¹			10			3	1					9²	13			37
1	4		7	5		6		8			11	10¹			13			2					12	9		3²		38

ST MIRREN

Year Formed: 1877. *Ground & Address:* St Mirren Park, Greenhill Road, Paisley PA3 1RU. *Telephone:* 0141 889 2558.
Fax: 0141 848 6444. *E-mail:* info@saintmirren.net *Website:* www.saintmirren.net
Ground Capacity: 8,023 (all seated). *Size of Pitch:* 100m × 64m.
Chairman: Stewart Gilmour. *Vice-Chairman:* George Campbell. *Secretary:* Chris Stewart.
Manager: Alex Rae. *Assistant Manager:* David Farrell. *Physio:* Gavin Lee.
Club Nickname: 'The Buddies'.
Previous Grounds: Shortroods 1877-79, Thistle Park Greenhill 1879-83, Westmarch 1883-94, Love Street 1894-2009.
Record Attendance: 47,438 v Celtic, League Cup, 20 August 1949.
Record Transfer Fee received: £850,000 for Ian Ferguson to Rangers (February 1988).
Record Transfer Fee paid: £400,000 for Thomas Stickroth from Bayer Uerdingen (March 1990).
Record Victory: 15-0 v Glasgow University, Scottish Cup 1rst rd, 30 January 1960.
Record Defeat: 0-9 v Rangers, Division I, 4 December 1897.
Most Capped Player: Godmundur Torfason, 29, Iceland.
Most League Appearances: 399: Hugh Murray, 1997-2012.
Most League Goals in Season (Individual): 45: Dunky Walker, Division I, 1921-22.
Most Goals Overall (Individual): 221: David McCrae, 1923-34.

ST MIRREN – SCOTTISH CHAMPIONSHIP 2015–16 LEAGUE RECORD

Match No.	Date		Venue	Opponents	Result		H/T Score	Lg Pos.	Goalscorers	Attendance
1	Aug	7	A	Rangers	L	1-3	1-2	10	Howieson [28]	49,216
2		15	H	Dumbarton	L	1-2	0-1	9	Agnew [63]	3806
3		21	A	Greenock Morton	D	0-0	0-0	8		5343
4		29	H	Livingston	D	1-1	1-1	8	McMullan [4]	3018
5	Sept	5	A	Queen of the South	W	2-0	2-0	8	Kelly [7], Thompson [29]	2001
6		12	H	Falkirk	L	2-3	2-0	8	Agnew [3], Mallan [38]	3412
7		18	H	Raith R	L	1-2	1-1	8	Shankland [45]	2877
8		26	A	Hibernian	D	1-1	1-1	8	Gallagher [18]	8911
9	Oct	3	A	Alloa Ath	D	1-1	0-0	8	Shankland [68]	2994
10		17	A	Livingston	W	1 0	1 0	6	Mallan [12]	1199
11		25	H	Rangers	L	0-1	0-1	7		5477
12		31	A	Falkirk	L	0-3	0-2	7		4239
13	Nov	7	H	Hibernian	L	1-4	1-3	8	Kelly [8]	4503
14		20	H	Greenock Morton	D	1-1	1-0	7	Baird [11]	4163
15		24	A	Raith R	D	1-1	0-1	7	Mallan [88]	1264
16	Dec	12	A	Dumbarton	L	0-1	0-0	8		1142
17		19	A	Alloa Ath	W	2-0	1-0	8	Shankland [13], Gallagher [59]	912
18		26	H	Livingston	L	1-4	1-2	9	Shankland [41]	2952
19	Jan	2	A	Greenock Morton	W	1-0	1-0	7	Shankland [39]	4736
20		23	A	Hibernian	L	1-3	1-2	8	Mallan [45]	10,160
21		30	H	Alloa Ath	W	3-1	1-1	8	Watson [37], Gallagher [59], Mallan [90]	2589
22	Feb	6	H	Queen of the South	W	1-0	1-0	7	Mallan [25]	2706
23		13	A	Queen of the South	L	0-1	0-0	7		1923
24		20	H	Dumbarton	W	1-0	0-0	7	Shankland [63]	2792
25		27	A	Rangers	L	0-1	0-0	7		46,366
26	Mar	1	H	Falkirk	D	0-0	0-0	7		2321
27		5	A	Raith R	L	3-4	1-2	7	Watson 2 [41, 76], Clarkson [61]	1888
28		12	H	Queen of the South	W	2-1	1-0	7	Mallan (pen) [30], Tapping (og) [63]	3888
29		19	A	Livingston	W	3-2	2-1	7	Mallan (pen) [15], Shankland 2 [35, 72]	1228
30		22	H	Raith R	L	1-2	1-2	7	Cooper [43]	2381
31		26	A	Alloa Ath	W	1-0	0-0	7	Watson [85]	753
32	Apr	2	H	Hibernian	D	2-2	1-1	7	Quinn [35], Shankland [57]	3765
33		9	A	Falkirk	L	2-3	0-1	7	Mallan 2 [56, 82]	4331
34		16	H	Greenock Morton	W	3-1	1-0	6	Shankland [7], Gallagher [62], Mallan [90]	4299
35		23	A	Dumbarton	L	1-2	1-1	7	Gallagher [10]	1387
36	May	1	H	Rangers	D	2-2	1-0	6	Gallagher [40], Morgan [90]	5933

Final League Position: 6

Honours
League Champions: First Division 1976-77, 1999-2000, 2005-06. Division II 1967-68;
Runners-up: First Division 2004-05; Division II 1935-36.
Scottish Cup Winners: 1926, 1959, 1987; *Runners-up:* 1908, 1934, 1962.
League Cup Winners: 2012-13; *Runners-up:* 1955-56, 2009-10.
League Challenge Cup Winners: 2005-06.
B&Q Cup Runners-up: 1993-94. *Anglo-Scottish Cup:* 1979-80.

European: *Cup Winners' Cup:* 4 matches (1987-88). *UEFA Cup:* 10 matches (1980-81, 1983-84, 1985-86).

Club colours: Shirt: Black and thin vertical white stripes. Shorts: White with black trim. Socks: White with black trim.

Goalscorers: *League (44):* Mallan 11 (2 pens), Shankland 10, Gallagher 6, Watson 4, Agnew 2, Kelly 2, Baird 1, Clarkson 1, Cooper 1, Howieson 1, McMullan 1, Morgan 1, Quinn 1, Thompson 1, own goal 1.
William Hill Scottish FA Cup (1): Watson 1.
Scottish League Cup (2): Gallagher 1, Mallan 1.
Petrofac Training Cup (9): Agnew 3, Mallan 2, Gallagher 1, Gow 1, Stewart 1, Thompson 1 (1 pen).

Ridgers M 2	Naismith J 5	Conlan L 3	Baird J 30 + 1	Kelly S 23 + 3	McMullan P 12 + 5	Howieson C 10 + 5	Carswell S 15 + 5	Agnew S 22 + 1	Mallan S 32 + 2	Thompson S 9 + 20	Morgan L 1 + 17	Gallagher C 33 + 3	Gow A 2 + 6	Cuddihy B 1 + 2	Langfield J 34	Watson K 26	Goodwin J 11 + 5	Stewart J 6 + 7	Webster A 32	Shankland L 27 + 4	McGrath J — + 2	McLean L 1 + 2	Reid C 6	Quinn R 13	Clarkson D 12	Cooper A 11 + 1	Irvine G 15 + 1	McAllister K 2 + 2	Match No.
1	2	3	4	5	6	7^1	8	9	10^3	11^2	12	13	14																1
1	2^1	5^3	4	3	7		6	9	14	13	10	11	8^2	12															2
		5^3	3	4	7	10^3	8	9^1		11^2	14	13			1	2	6	12											3
			2	4	6			9	7	13	12	10^2	14		1		8^1	5^2	3	11									4
			5	4	6^3	12		8^2	7	10^1	13	11			1	9	3		2		14								5
			3	5	7^1			9^2	8	11		10			1	2	6		4	13	12								6
			3	5			9	6		7		12	10^1		1	2	8		4	11									7
			3	5	8^1	9	6		13	12	14	11^3			1	2	7		4	10^2									8
			3	5				8^1		6	10	12	9		1	2	7		4	11									9
			3	5	12	6^1	13	8^2	9	10^3		11		2	1		7		4			14							10
			3	5	12		9^1	13	8	6	10	11^3			1	2	7^2		4	14									11
		12	3^1	5	12	9^1		8^2	6	10^3	14	11			1		7		4	13			2						12
			4	5	10^3	12		7^2	9	11	14	8^1			1		6	2	3	13									13
			3	5	9^1	14	7	8^3	6	13		10			1				4	11^2	12	2							14
			3	5	12		6	9^2	8		13	7			1				4	11^1	10	2							15
			4	5			8	9	7	13	12	10			1	2			3	11^2			6^1						16
				5	6^2	12	8^1	9	7		11		13		1	3			4	10			2						17
		12	5	6			8	9^2	7	14	13	11^3			1	3			4	10			2^1						18
			3	5	8^1	10	6	7	9			12			1	2			4	11									19
			3	5	14	9^1		7^2	8	13		11^3			1	2		12	4	10					6				20
			3	5		9^1		7	14		8				1	2			4	10^3					6	11^2	12	13	21
			3	12		14		7	13		6				1	2			4^1	11^2					8	10	9^3	5	22
			3	4				7^8	13		6^1				1	2				10					8	11	9^2	5	23
			3	4			8^2			14		10^1			1		13	12	2	11				7	6^3		5	9	24
			3	14				7	13			11^3			1	2		12	4	9				8	10^2		5	6^1	25
			4					7	13		9	12			1	2		6^1	3	10				8	11^2		5		26
			4			12	7	14			6^2	13			1	2		9^2	3	10				8^1	11		5		27
					14	8^1	7				6	12			1	3	13	5	4	11					10^1	9^2	2		28
			3		12	8^1	7	14			6	13			1	2			4	10					11^3	9^2	5		29
			3^2		8	7	14				6^3	10^1			1	2		13	4	11							9	5	30
				14		10	8^1	7	13	12	6				1	3		5^2	4	11							9^2	2	31
			3			7		10	12		8				1	5			4	11				6^1		9	2		32
			3			7^2		10		14	8^3				1	5^1	13	12	4	11				6		9	2		33
	2		3			14		7		12	6^2				1		13		4	11					8^3	10^1	9	5	34
	2							8	14	12	6^1				1	5		13	4	10					11	7^1	9^3	3	35
	2							8	14	12	6^3				1	3	13		4	10					7	11^2	9^1	5	36

STENHOUSEMUIR

Year Formed: 1884. *Ground & Address:* Ochilview Park, Gladstone Rd, Stenhousemuir FK5 4QL. *Telephone:* 01324 562992. *Fax:* 01324 562980. *E-mail:* info@stenhousemuirfc.com *Website:* www.stenhousemuirfc.com
Ground Capacity: 3,776 (seated: 626). *Size of Pitch:* 101m × 66m.
Chairman: Gordon Thompson. *Vice-Chairman:* David Reid. *Secretary/General Manager:* Margaret Kilpatrick.
Manager: Brown Ferguson. *First-Team Coach:* David Irons. *Physio:* Melanie Stewart.
Club Nickname: 'The Warriors'.
Previous Grounds: Tryst Ground 1884-86, Goschen Park 1886-90.
Record Attendance: 12,500 v East Fife, Scottish Cup Quarter-final, 11 March 1950.
Record Transfer Fee received: £70,000 for Euan Donaldson to St Johnstone (May 1995).
Record Transfer Fee paid: £20,000 to Livingston for Ian Little (June 1995); £20,000 to East Fife for Paul Hunter (September 1995).
Record Victory: 9-2 v Dundee U, Division II, 16 April 1937.
Record Defeat: 2-11 v Dunfermline Ath, Division II, 27 September 1930.
Most League Appearances: 434: Jimmy Richardson, 1957-73.
Most League Goals in Season (Individual): 32: Robert Taylor, Division II, 1925-26.

STENHOUSEMUIR – SCOTTISH LEAGUE ONE 2015–16 LEAGUE RECORD

Match No.	Date		Venue	Opponents	Result		H/T Score	Lg Pos.	Goalscorers	Atten- dance
1	Aug	8	A	Peterhead	D	2-2	2-0	5	Murray [4], Smith [10]	530
2		15	H	Airdrieonians	W	2-1	1-0	4	Cook [42], Eddington [90]	731
3		22	A	Forfar Ath	L	1-4	1-4	5	Robertson, J [36]	610
4		29	H	Cowdenbeath	W	4-2	2-0	4	McMenamin [9], Henderson [14], Smith [47], Cook [60]	509
5	Sept	1	A	Ayr U	L	2-5	1-3	5	Boyle (og) [17], McCroary [88]	1046
6		12	H	Stranraer	W	1-0	0-0	5	Smith [66]	357
7		19	H	Dunfermline Ath	L	0-5	0-3	6		1554
8		26	A	Albion R	L	0-2	0-1	7		406
9	Oct	3	A	Brechin C	D	2-2	1-0	8	Cook [34], Martinez [90]	348
10		17	A	Cowdenbeath	D	2-2	0-1	7	McMenamin [87], Small [90]	349
11		24	H	Ayr U	L	0-1	0-1	7		767
12		31	H	Peterhead	W	4-3	1-3	6	McMenamin [43], Scotland 2 [59, 66], Millar [68]	292
13	Nov	7	A	Stranraer	W	2-1	1-0	5	Gilhaney [18], Scotland [56]	414
14		14	A	Forfar Ath	D	2-2	0-1	5	McMenamin [78], Scotland (pen) [85]	438
15		21	A	Brechin C	W	2-1	1-0	3	Cook [29], McMenamin [80]	376
16	Dec	12	H	Albion R	L	0-1	0-0	6		354
17		19	A	Dunfermline Ath	L	0-1	0-0	6		2952
18		26	H	Stranraer	L	1-5	1-3	6	Meechan [13]	346
19		29	A	Airdrieonians	W	1-0	0-0	5	Murray [88]	724
20	Jan	2	A	Peterhead	L	1-4	1-1	6	Cook [33]	588
21		23	A	Forfar Ath	W	1-0	1-0	5	Stirling [45]	532
22	Feb	2	H	Brechin C	D	0-0	0-0	6		213
23		6	H	Dunfermline Ath	L	0-3	0-1	6		1328
24		13	H	Airdrieonians	W	3-2	1-1	6	Summers [18], McCormack 2 [53, 90]	472
25		27	H	Cowdenbeath	L	2-3	0-0	7	McMenamin 2 [59, 61]	370
26	Mar	1	A	Albion R	D	1-1	0-0	6	Meechan [63]	275
27		5	A	Dunfermline Ath	L	0-5	0-2	7		3017
28		8	A	Ayr U	L	1-4	0-0	7	McCormack [69]	889
29		12	H	Peterhead	L	1-4	0-2	7	Martinez [81]	369
30		19	A	Stranraer	L	1-3	0-3	7	Scotland (pen) [62]	446
31		26	H	Forfar Ath	W	2-1	1-0	7	Gilhaney [12], McMenamin [88]	429
32	Apr	2	A	Brechin C	L	0-1	0-0	7		454
33		9	A	Airdrieonians	D	1-1	0-0	8	Cook [60]	614
34		16	A	Ayr U	L	0-4	0-1	8		652
35		23	A	Cowdenbeath	W	3-1	0-1	7	Cook 2 [69, 78], Robertson, J [74]	474
36		30	H	Albion R	L	1-3	0-0	8	McCormack [88]	662

Final League Position: 8

Honours
League Champions: Third Division runners-up: 1998-99. *Promoted to Second Division:* 2008-09 (play-offs).
Scottish Cup: Semi-finals 1902-03. Quarter-finals 1948-49, 1949-50, 1994-95.
League Cup: Quarter-finals 1947-48, 1960-61, 1975-76.
League Challenge Cup Winners: 1995-96.

Club colours: Shirt: Maroon with light blue trim. Shorts: Maroon with light blue trim. Socks: Maroon.

Goalscorers: *League (46):* Cook 8, McMenamin 8, Scotland 5 (2 pens), McCormack 4, Smith 3, Gilhaney 2, Martinez 2, Meechan 2, Murray 2, Robertson, J 2, Eddington 1, Henderson 1, McCroary 1, Millar 1, Small 1, Stirling 1, Summers 1, own goal 1.
William Hill Scottish FA Cup (3): Malcolm 1, McMenamin 1, Scotland 1.
Scottish League Cup (0).
Petrofac Training Cup (5): Stirling 3, Cook 1, McMenamin 1.

Barclay J 15+1	Meechan R 35	Malcolm S 25+2	Murray E 26+2	Summers C 12+1	Millar K 18+3	Robertson J 28+4	Stirling S 30+1	Cook A 25+6	McMenamin C 32+3	Smith A 7	McCormack J 29+3	Henderson L 5+6	McShane J 3+3	Gilhaney M 31+9	Eddington F 1+9	Martinez C 6+16	McCroary L 1+6	Marenghi A 5+6	Paterson J 14	Small I 9+14	Scotland J 12+3	Robertson S —+1	Gould M 6	Monaghan H 1+1	Bowman G 2	McCabe C 13	Beith A 5	Match No.
1	2	3	4	5	6	7	8	9[1]	10[2]	11[3]	12	13	14															1
1	3		4	5[2]		8	7	9	10[3]	11	2	12	13		6[1]	14												2
1	7	3	4			8	6	9[1]	12	10	2[1]	5	11[2]		14	13												3
1	2	3	4			8	6[2]	9	10	7[1]		5	11[3]	14	13	12												4
1	2[3]	4	3			8	6	9[1]	10	7		5	11[2]	12	14		13											5
1	2	3	4			8	7	9	10	11[2]		5		6[1]	12	13												6
1	2	3	4		7[2]	8	6[1]		10	11	13	5[3]		9		12	14											7
1	5	3	4		13	7	8	9[1]	10		2			6[2]	12	11												8
1	5	3	4[1]			7	8	9			2[2]	12	13	6	10[3]	11		14										9
1	4	3			13	7	8[1]	9[1]	10		2	12		6		11		5[2]	14									10
1	4	3	12		7	8		9	10		2[1]			6		14		5[2]	11[3]	13								11
1	2	3				7[3]		6[2]	8	10	5			9	13		14	12	4	11[1]								12
1	2	3				7		6[1]	8	10	5	13		9		12	4	14	11[2]									13
1[1]	4	3			7	14	8[2]	9	10		2			6		13		5[1]	11[3]	12								14
	4	3	13		8	12	7[2]	9	10		2[3]			6		5		11		1	14							15
	4	3			7	8		12	10		2			6[1]	13	9[3]	5[2]	14	11	1								16
	4	3			9	8[2]		14	12		2			6	10[1]	5	13	11[3]	1	7								17
	4	3			7	13	8[2]	12	10		2			6	9[1]	5	11	1										18
		3	4		7	8		9	10		2			6	12	5	11[1]	1										19
	4		3		7	8[2]	14	9	10		2	12		6	13	5[2]	11[1]	1										20
	4		3		8	7	11	9[1]	10[1]		2			6	12	5	14	13[3]	1									21
	4		3		8	11	9[1]	10			2			6	12	7[2]	5	13	1									22
		3	4	5	7[3]	8	9	10[2]	11[1]		2			6	13			14	12						1			23
	3		4	5	6[1]	9	7[2]	11			2	10		6	13	8								1				24
3	14		4	5	9	6[3]	7[1]		10[2]		2	8		13	12	11								1				25
4		3	5	8	7	6	12	10[2]			2	9		13	11[1]									1				26
14	6	4	3	5		8	10[1]	12			2	13	7[2]		9[3]	11								1				27
1	7	3	4	5		12	8[2]	9[3]	10		2	6				13	11[1]											28
6	3[2]	4	5		8	7[1]		10			2	9	12			13	11[1]							1				29
3	14	4	5			9[1]	10				2	8	6[1]	7	13	12	11[3]							1				30
	3	4	5		2	8	13	10						9	12	6[1]		11[2]							1	7		31
2	3	4	5[1]		7	6[2]			14		9	13	12[3]				11[1]							1	8			32
3	4			6	7	12	10	2			9	13				5[3]	11[1]							1	8			33
3		4	12		2[1]	8[3]	9	10[2]	5					14	13	11								1	7			34
4	3	5	12		8	7	10[1]	11	2				6											1	9			35
4	3	5		11[2]	7	8	9[1]	10	2				6			12			13				1					36

STIRLING ALBION

Year Formed: 1945. *Ground & Address:* Forthbank Stadium, Springkerse, Stirling FK7 7UJ. *Telephone:* 01786 450399.
Fax: 01786 448592. *Email:* office@stirlingalbionfc.co.uk *Website:* www.stirlingalbionfc.co.uk
Ground Capacity: 3,808 (seated: 2,508). *Size of Pitch:* 101m × 68m.
Chairman: Stuart Brown. *Administrator:* Neil Mackay.
Manager: Stuart McLaren. *Assistant Manager:* Martyn Corrigan. *Physio:* Kenny Crichton.
Club Nickname: 'The Binos'.
Previous Grounds: Annfield 1945-92.
Record Attendance: 26,400 v Celtic, Scottish Cup 4th rd, 14 March 1959 (Annfield); 3,808 v Aberdeen, Scottish Cup
4th rd, 15 February 1996 (Forthbank).
Record Transfer Fee received: £90,000 for Stephen Nicholas to Motherwell (March 1999).
Record Transfer Fee paid: £25,000 for Craig Taggart from Falkirk (August 1994).
Record Victory: 20-0 v Selkirk, Scottish Cup 1st rd, 8 December 1984.
Record Defeat: 0-9 v Dundee U, Division I, 30 December 1967; 0-9 v Ross Co, Scottish Cup 5th rd, 6 February 2010.
Most League Appearances: 504: Matt McPhee, 1967-81.
Most League Goals in Season (Individual): 27: Joe Hughes, Division II, 1969-70.
Most Goals Overall (Individual): 129: Billy Steele, 1971-83.

STIRLING ALBION – SCOTTISH LEAGUE TWO 2015–16 LEAGUE RECORD

Match No.	Date		Venue	Opponents	Result	Score	H/T Score	Lg Pos.	Goalscorers	Attendance
1	Aug	8	H	Clyde	L	0-1	0-0	7		796
2		15	A	Annan Ath	D	1-1	0-0	9	Dickson (pen) 57	489
3		22	H	Berwick R	L	1-3	0-2	9	Robertson 70	601
4		29	A	Elgin C	L	0-1	0-1	9		720
5	Sept	5	A	East Stirling	W	3-2	2-1	9	Cunningham 4, Doris 7, McMillan 75	511
6		12	H	Montrose	W	1-0	0-0	8	McMillan 69	529
7		19	A	Arbroath	L	0-2	0-0	8		638
8		26	H	Queen's Park	L	1-2	1-1	9	Doris 24	671
9	Oct	3	A	East Fife	D	1-1	0-1	9	Robertson, W 63	673
10		17	A	Clyde	W	1-0	1-0	9	Cunningham 30	628
11		31	H	East Stirling	D	0-0	0-0	9		618
12	Nov	7	A	Berwick R	W	2-1	0-0	7	Verlaque 54, Doris 59	438
13		14	H	Arbroath	W	3-1	0-1	6	Robertson, W 55, Smith, R 78, Doris (pen) 82	763
14		21	A	Queen's Park	L	0-1	0-0	6		514
15	Dec	5	H	Elgin C	W	3-1	0-1	6	Lamont 53, Doris 80, Smith, D 86	452
16		12	A	Montrose	W	3-1	1-0	5	Smith, D 3 12, 51, 64	384
17		19	A	Annan Ath	W	1-0	0-0	5	Johnston 77	624
18		26	H	East Fife	L	1-3	1-2	5	Kerr (og) 9	645
19	Jan	2	A	East Stirling	L	2-3	0-2	5	McKinlay 49, Beattie 77	523
20		23	H	Queen's Park	D	0-0	0-0	6		671
21	Feb	6	A	Arbroath	D	1-1	0-0	7	Smith, D 76	638
22		9	H	Montrose	W	7-0	3-0	6	Doris 2 31, 84, Smith, D 3 42, 45, 46, McLear 48, Dickson 83	415
23		13	H	Berwick R	W	2-1	2-1	3	Smith, R 13, Dickson (pen) 16	618
24		20	A	East Fife	L	0-1	0-0	5		707
25		23	H	Clyde	L	1-2	1-0	6	Doris 31	601
26		27	A	Annan Ath	D	2-2	0-1	6	McLear 57, Dickson (pen) 77	426
27	Mar	5	H	Arbroath	W	1-0	0-0	6	Beattie 82	652
28		8	A	Elgin C	L	1-2	1-1	6	McGeachie 29	503
29		12	A	Berwick R	L	0-1	0-1	6		502
30		19	H	East Fife	L	0-6	0-2	6		709
31		26	H	East Stirling	W	3-0	1-0	6	Olanrewaju 17, Smith, D 64, Johnston 88	602
32	Apr	2	A	Queen's Park	D	1-1	0-1	6	Doris 63	494
33		9	H	Elgin C	D	0-0	0-0	6		578
34		16	A	Montrose	D	1-1	0-0	7	Beattie 89	463
35		23	H	Annan Ath	W	2-1	1-0	7	Olanrewaju 7, Kavanagh 76	545
36		30	A	Clyde	L	1-3	0-2	7	Burns 84	704

Final League Position: 7

Honours
League Champions: Division II 1952-53, 1957-58, 1960-61, 1964-65. Second Division 1976-77, 1990-91, 1995-96, 2009-10; *Runners-up:* Division II 1948-49, 1950-51. Second Division 2006-07. Third Division 2003-04. *Promoted to First Division:* 2006-07 (play-offs). *Promoted to League One:* 2013-14 (play-offs).
League Cup: Semi-finals 1961-62.
League Challenge Cup: Semi-finals 1995-96, 1999-2000.

Club colours: Shirt: Red with white trim. Shorts: Red. Socks: Red with white trim.

Goalscorers: *League (47):* Doris 9 (1 pen), Smith, D 9, Dickson 4 (3 pens), Beattie 3, Robertson 3, Cunningham 2, Johnston 2, McLear 2, McMillan 2, Olanrewaju 2, Smith, R 2, Burns 1, Kavanagh 1, Lamont 1, McGeachie 1, McKinlay 1, Verlaque 1, own goal 1.
William Hill Scottish FA Cup (7): Doris 3, Beattie 2, Dickson 1, Lander 1.
Scottish League Cup (0).
Petrofac Training Cup (2): Beattie 1, Cunningham 1.

Smith C 34	Hamilton L 8 + 4	McGeachie R 25 + 3	Staunton M 1	Forsyth R 29 + 3	Johnston P 17 + 5	Comrie C 16 + 2	Robertson W 27	Dickson S 28 + 4	McGovern J 2	Beattie C 6 + 12	Cunningham A 11 + 5	Doris S 33 + 3	McKinlay K 13 + 3	McMillan R 20 + 4	McKenzie C — + 2	Smith R 21 + 3	Kouider-Aisser S — + 3	McAllister T — + 1	Davidson Scott 6 + 2	Lander K 2 + 5	Lamont Mark 19 + 5	Mazel A 20 + 6	Verlaque D 15 + 2	McNabb R — + 1	Sinclair D — + 1	Smith D 19 + 5	Binnie C 2 + 1	Buist S 5	McLear L 12	Olanrewaju M 4 + 8	Burns S 1 + 2	Kavanagh R — + 4	Stevenson S — + 2	Herron J — + 1	Davidson Sam — + 1	Match No.
1	2	3	4■	5	6	7^1	8	9^3	10	11^2	12	13	14																							1
1	2	3		12	7^2	8	6	10^3	9	11^1		13	5■	4	14																					2
1	2			5^3	8^2	6	7	10		11^1	9	12		4	13	3	14																			3
1	8^2	2		5^3		7	6	10			9^1	11		4		3	12	13	14																	4
1	9^2	2		8		5	6	7			11^1	10^3	13	4		3				12	14															5
1	5	2■		8		6	7	11			9^2	10^3	12	3		4^1				13		14														6
1	6^3			5		7	8	11			9^1	10	3	4						12	13	2^2	14													7
1	5	2		4		6^2	7				13	10	8	3		14				9^1	11^3	12														8
1		2		8		6	7■				11	10		3		4				9^1	12	5														9
1		3		8		6■		13			10^1	11^3	7			4				12	9^2	2	5	14												10
1				4				7			11^3	10	8^2	3		2■				12	9^1	6	5		13	14										11
1		2		4		7	6	12			9^2	10	8								11^1	3	5			13										12
1■		2				6	7	13			11^2	10^3	8			4					9^1	3	5			14	12									13
		2		12		7^2	6	11^1			9	10	8^3			4					14	3	5			13	1									14
1		3		4			7	9^1		12	13	10^3	5			14					6	8	2			11^2										15
1	13	3		4			8^1	9		12	14	10	5								6^3	7	2^2			11										16
1	14	3			12		8	9^3				10	5			4			13		6^1	7	2			11^2										17
1		3			12		8	9^1				10	5			4	13				6	7^2	2			11										18
1		3		4	14	12	8	9^2		13		10	5								6	7^3	2^1			11										19
1		2		4	5^3		7^1	8		10^2	14	11				3					9	12	13			6										20
1	14			4	5			8				10		13		3					11^1	7^2				6		2^3	9	12						21
1				5	2		8	9				10		12		3					6^3	14				11		4^1	7^2	13						22
1				5	2		8	6^3				10		12		3^1					9^2	14				11		4	7	13						23
1				5	2		7	9		12		10		14		4					8^2	13				11		3^3	6^1							24
1				4	5		7	8		13		11		3		2^2					12	6^1				10			9							25
1		13		5	2		8	9		14		10		4		3^1					6^2					11			7^3	12						26
1	14	4		5	9		8			13		11		3							6^3		2			10^2				12	7^1					27
1		4		5	9^2		3	7^3		10		11^1		8							6		2			12				13	14					28
1		2^3		13	8	12	6^1	7		11		10		3		4							5^2			9				14						29
1		12		5	2		7	8^2		14		10		4							9					11^3		3^1	6	13						30
1		2		5	12	7				13		11^2		4					3			6				10			9^3	8^1		14				31
1		2		5	12	8		13		14		10		3					7			4^2				9			11^3	6^1						32
1		2		5	6^2			7		14		10^3		3					4			8				9^1			11			12	13			33
1		2^2		5	6	8^1		9		12		10		4^3		14			3			7				11							13			34
		14		5	9^1			8				10				3			4			7	2				1		6^2	11^3		12		13		35
1		3						9^3				10		7		4■			5			8^2	2						11^1	6	13	12			14	36

STRANRAER

Year Formed: 1870. *Ground & Address:* Stair Park, London Rd, Stranraer DG9 8BS. *Telephone and Fax:* 01776 703271.
E-mail: secretary@stranraerfc.org *Website:* www.stranraerfc.org
Ground Capacity: 6,250 (seated: 1,830). *Size of Pitch:* 103m × 64m.
Chairman: Iain Dougan. *Vice-Chairman:* David Broadfoot. *Secretary:* Hilde Law.
Manager: Brian Reid. *Assistant Manager:* Chris Aitken. *Physio:* Matthew Wallace.
Club Nicknames: 'The Blues', 'The Clayholers'.
Previous Grounds: None.
Record Attendance: 6,500 v Rangers, Scottish Cup 1st rd, 24 January 1948.
Record Transfer Fee received: £90,000 for Mark Campbell to Ayr U (1999).
Record Transfer Fee paid: £35,000 for Michael Moore from St Johnstone (March 2005).
Record Victory: 9-0 v St Cuthbert Wanderers, Scottish Cup 2nd rd, 23 October 2010; 9-0 v Wigtown & Bladnoch, Scottish Cup 2nd rd, 22 October 2011.
Record Defeat: 1-11 v Queen of the South, Scottish Cup 1st rd, 16 January 1932.
Most League Appearances: 301: Keith Knox, 1986-90; 1999-2001.
Most League Goals in Season (Individual): 27: Derek Frye, 1977-78.
Most Goals Overall (Individual): 115: Jim Campbell, 1965-75.

STRANRAER – SCOTTISH LEAGUE ONE 2015–16 LEAGUE RECORD

Match No.	Date		Venue	Opponents	Result	H/T Score	Lg Pos.	Goalscorers	Atten- dance
1	Aug	8	A	Cowdenbeath	W 2-1	1-0	3	Thomson [4], Malcolm (pen) [90]	380
2		15	H	Peterhead	L 0-4	0-1	7		328
3		22	H	Ayr U	L 1-2	0-1	8	Stirling [90]	882
4		29	A	Dunfermline Ath	L 1-3	0-2	8	Longworth [56]	3330
5	Sept	5	H	Brechin C	W 1-0	0-0	8	Longworth [51]	366
6		12	A	Stenhousemuir	L 0-1	0-0	8		357
7		19	H	Albion R	L 0-1	0-0	9		412
8		26	A	Forfar Ath	W 2-1	1-0	8	McGuigan [20], Aitken (pen) [56]	562
9	Oct	3	A	Airdrieonians	W 1-0	0-0	6	Thomson [83]	847
10		17	H	Dunfermline Ath	L 0-3	0-2	6		667
11		24	H	Cowdenbeath	L 0-3	0-1	8		345
12		31	A	Ayr U	L 1-3	1-2	9	Robertson [29]	1415
13	Nov	7	H	Stenhousemuir	L 1-2	0-1	9	Thomson [90]	414
14		17	A	Peterhead	D 1-1	1-1	9	Malcolm (pen) [13]	423
15		21	H	Forfar Ath	D 0-0	0-0	9		411
16	Dec	12	H	Airdrieonians	L 1-3	0-1	9	Malcolm [55]	428
17		19	A	Brechin C	L 0-2	0-2	10		401
18		26	A	Stenhousemuir	W 5-1	3-1	9	Malcolm 3 (1 pen) [30, 51, 82 (p)], Longworth [31], McCloskey [33]	346
19	Jan	2	H	Ayr U	W 1-0	0-0	8	Longworth [57]	1178
20		16	H	Peterhead	L 1-5	0-3	8	Malcolm [68]	406
21		23	A	Cowdenbeath	W 2-0	0-0	8	Gibson [63], Malcolm (pen) [83]	402
22		30	H	Brechin C	W 2-0	1-0	7	Stirling [45], Gibson [79]	435
23	Feb	2	A	Albion R	W 2-0	0-0	5	Malcolm [53], Stirling [54]	241
24		6	A	Forfar Ath	D 1-1	1-0	5	Longworth [35]	485
25		13	H	Albion R	D 0-0	0-0	7		432
26		20	A	Airdrieonians	D 1-1	0-0	6	McGuigan [60]	704
27		27	A	Dunfermline Ath	L 1-6	0-2	6	McGuigan [48]	3016
28	Mar	5	H	Forfar Ath	W 1-0	0-0	6	Pettigrew [61]	442
29		12	A	Albion R	W 1-0	1-0	6	Longworth [38]	408
30		15	A	Peterhead	D 0-0	0-0	4		607
31		19	H	Stenhousemuir	W 3-1	3-0	4	McGuigan 2 [5, 37], Robertson [15]	446
32		26	A	Ayr U	L 1-2	0-1	4	Thomson [75]	1244
33	Apr	2	H	Airdrieonians	W 4-0	2-0	4	Malcolm [11], Gibson [31], Stirling [78], Turner [88]	461
34		16	H	Dunfermline Ath	W 4-1	0-1	4	McGuigan [49], Malcolm 2 [62, 85], Stirling [68]	545
35		23	H	Brechin C	L 0-1	0-0	4		452
36		30	H	Cowdenbeath	W 1-0	0-0	4	McGuigan [48]	523

Final League Position: 4

Honours
League Champions: Second Division 1993-94, 1997-98. Third Division 2003-04.
Runners-up: Second Division 2004-05, Third Division 2007-08. League One: 2014-15. Promoted to Second Division 2011-12 (play-offs).
Scottish Cup: Quarter-finals 2003
League Challenge Cup Winners: 1996-97. Semi-finals: 2000-01, 2014-15.

Club colours: Shirt: Blue with white trim. Shorts: White. Socks: Blue.

Goalscorers: *League (43):* Malcolm 12 (4 pens), McGuigan 7, Longworth 6, Stirling 5, Thomson 4, Gibson 3, Robertson 2, Aitken 1 (1 pen), McCloskey 1, Pettigrew 1, Turner 1.
William Hill Scottish FA Cup (3): McGuigan 1, Nequecaur 1, Thomson 1.
Scottish League Cup (2): Malcolm 2.
Petrofac Training Cup (0).
Championship Play-Offs (9): McGuigan 3, Cairney 1, Dick 1, Gibson 1, Longworth 1, Stirling 1, own goal 1.

Brennan C 3	Robertson S 30 + 2	Rumsby S 26 + 1	Keenan D 13 + 2	Pettigrew C 36	McGuigan M 27 + 8	Bell S 30 + 1	Thomson R 24 + 5	Stirling A 28 + 4	Longworth J 16 + 16	Malcolm C 23 + 4	Cairney P 32 + 3	McCloskey S 2 + 14	Aitken C 5 + 9	McGill P 3 + 6	McGurn D 15	Mair L 9	Turner K 5 + 12	McCluskey J 4	Dick L 23 + 1	Nequecaur L 4 + 3	Asghar A — + 1	Barron D 3 + 1	Currie M 2 + 1	Gibson W 16	Belford C 16	Stoney D — + 2	Kemp C — + 5	Schmidt K 1 + 1	Match No.
1	2	3	4	5	6	7	8	9[1]	10[2]	11	12	13																	1
1	2[1]	3	4	5	6[2]	8	7	9	11	10	12		13																2
1	2	3	4	5	6[2]	8	7[1]	9	12	11	10[3]		14	13															3
	2[1]	3	13	5	6	7		9[2]	12	10	11[3]	8	14		1	4													4
12	2	9[2]	3	14		8	6[1]	5	10	11[3]		7	13		1	4													5
	2	5	4	12	7		6[3]	9	11[2]	10	13		8[1]		1	3	14												6
	3	5	2	13	6		12	11[1]	10	9[2]		8	14		1	4	7[3]												7
	3[1]	5	2	11[2]	7	10	9	14		6[3]		12	8		1	4	13												8
	4	5	2	11	7	10	9	13		6		12	8[1]		1		3[2]												9
14	3	5	2	11	7[3]	8	9	12		10[2]		13	6[1]		1	4													10
6	3	5[2]	2	11		7	9	8[1]		10[3]		13	12		1	4	14												11
2	3		5	11		8	10	12		7[3]	14	9[2]			1	4	13		6[1]										12
2	3	14	5	6[3]		8	9	12		7	13				1		10[1]	4	11[2]										13
2	3	5	4	13		8		12	10	7[3]					1		6[2]	9	11[1]	14									14
7	3	4[1]	2	13	12	8		14	10	9[3]					1		6[2]	5	11										15
7	3	4	2	6[2]	8		13	10	9[3]	12		14	1					5	11[1]										16
7	3[1]		2	11	4	8[2]		12	10	6			1		13		9[1]	14		5									17
2	4		3	8	7		13	10	11[2]	6	9[1]		12	14			5[3]	1											18
4	3		2	6[3]	7		12	11	10	8	9[2]		11[1]	14			5			13									19
7[3]	3		2	6[2]	4	13	12	11[1]	10	8	14							5				1		9					20
4	3		2	13	8	12	6[1]	11[2]	10	7	14							5						9[1]	1				21
7	3		2	13	4	12	6	11[1]	10[1]	8								5	14					9[2]	1				22
8	2		5	12	4		7	11[1]	10[2]	9[3]	13							3						6	1	14			23
7	4[1]		2	6[2]	3		9	11[1]	10	8	13							5							1	12			24
7			2		4	12	6	11	10[1]	8	13							5					3[2]	9	1				25
7	3		2	11[3]	4	12	6	10[1]		8[2]			14					5						9	1		13		26
7[3]	4		2	11	3	10	8[2]		6[1]	12			14					5						9	1		13		27
3			2	10	4[2]	7	6		8[3]	13			14					5						9	1		12	11[1]	28
3			2	11	4		6[2]	10[1]	12	7[3]	13	14					8	5						9	1				29
2			2	10[2]	4	11	6[1]		13	8	12						7	5						9	1				30
3			2	11	4	9	6		12	8[1]	13						7[2]							10[1]	1		14		31
4			2	10[3]	3	11	6	13	12	7[2]			14				8[1]							9	1				32
3			2	11[1]	4	7[2]	6	13	10[3]	8			14					5						9	1		12		33
3[1]	14		2	11[2]	4	7	6	13	10	8								5						9[1]	1		12		34
3			2	11	4	9[2]	8	14	10[1]	7[3]			12					5		13				6	1				35
3			2	11[1]	4	7[3]	9	12	10	8[2]			14	13				5						6	1				36

SCOTTISH LEAGUE HONOURS 1890–2016

=Until 1921–22 season teams were equal if level on points, unless a play-off took place. §Not promoted after play-offs.
*Won or placed on goal average (ratio), goal difference or most goals scored (goal average from 1921–22 until 1971–72 when it was replaced by goal difference). No official competition during 1939–46; Regional Leagues operated.

DIVISION 1 (1890–91 to 1974–75) – TIER 1

Tier	Season	Max Pts	First	Pts	Second	Pts	Third	Pts
1	1890–91	36	Dumbarton=	29	Rangers=	29	Celtic	21

Dumbarton and Rangers held title jointly after indecisive play-off ended 2-2. Celtic deducted 4 points for fielding an ineligible player.

Tier	Season	Max Pts	First	Pts	Second	Pts	Third	Pts
1	1891–92	44	Dumbarton	37	Celtic	35	Hearts	34
1	1892–93	36	Celtic	29	Rangers	28	St Mirren	20
1	1893–94	36	Celtic	29	Hearts	26	St Bernard's	23
1	1894–95	36	Hearts	31	Celtic	26	Rangers	22
1	1895–96	36	Celtic	30	Rangers	26	Hibernian	24
1	1896–97	36	Hearts	28	Hibernian	26	Rangers	25
1	1897–98	36	Celtic	33	Rangers	29	Hibernian	22
1	1898–99	36	Rangers	36	Hearts	26	Celtic	24
1	1899–1900	36	Rangers	32	Celtic	25	Hibernian	24
1	1900–01	40	Rangers	35	Celtic	29	Hibernian	25
1	1901–02	36	Rangers	28	Celtic	26	Hearts	22
1	1902–03	44	Hibernian	37	Dundee	31	Rangers	29
1	1903–04	52	Third Lanark	43	Hearts	39	Celtic / Rangers=	38
1	1904–05	52	Celtic=	41	Rangers=	41	Third Lanark	35

Celtic won title after beating Rangers 2-1 in play-off.

Tier	Season	Max Pts	First	Pts	Second	Pts	Third	Pts
1	1905–06	60	Celtic	49	Hearts	43	Airdrieonians	38
1	1906–07	68	Celtic	55	Dundee	48	Rangers	45
1	1907–08	68	Celtic	55	Falkirk	51	Rangers	50
1	1908–09	68	Celtic	51	Dundee	50	Clyde	48
1	1909–10	68	Celtic	54	Falkirk	52	Rangers	46
1	1910–11	68	Rangers	52	Aberdeen	48	Falkirk	44
1	1911–12	68	Rangers	51	Celtic	45	Clyde	42
1	1912–13	68	Rangers	53	Celtic	49	Hearts / Airdrieonians=	41
1	1913–14	76	Celtic	65	Rangers	59	Hearts / Morton=	54
1	1914–15	76	Celtic	65	Hearts	61	Rangers	50
1	1915–16	76	Celtic	67	Rangers	56	Morton	51
1	1916–17	76	Celtic	64	Morton	54	Rangers	53
1	1917–18	68	Rangers	56	Celtic	55	Kilmarnock / Morton=	43
1	1918–19	68	Celtic	58	Rangers	57	Morton	47
1	1919–20	84	Rangers	71	Celtic	68	Motherwell	57
1	1920–21	84	Rangers	76	Celtic	66	Hearts	50
1	1921–22	84	Celtic	67	Rangers	66	Raith R	51
1	1922–23	76	Rangers	55	Airdrieonians	50	Celtic	46
1	1923–24	76	Rangers	59	Airdrieonians	50	Celtic	46
1	1924–25	76	Rangers	60	Airdrieonians	57	Hibernian	52
1	1925–26	76	Celtic	58	Airdrieonians*	50	Hearts	50
1	1926–27	76	Rangers	56	Motherwell	51	Celtic	49
1	1927–28	76	Rangers	60	Celtic*	55	Motherwell	55
1	1928–29	76	Rangers	67	Celtic	51	Motherwell	50
1	1929–30	76	Rangers	60	Motherwell	55	Aberdeen	53
1	1930–31	76	Rangers	60	Celtic	58	Motherwell	56
1	1931–32	76	Motherwell	66	Rangers	61	Celtic	48
1	1932–33	76	Rangers	62	Motherwell	59	Hearts	50
1	1933–34	76	Rangers	66	Motherwell	62	Celtic	47
1	1934–35	76	Rangers	55	Celtic	52	Hearts	50
1	1935–36	76	Celtic	66	Rangers*	61	Aberdeen	61
1	1936–37	76	Rangers	61	Aberdeen	54	Celtic	52
1	1937–38	76	Celtic	61	Hearts	58	Rangers	49
1	1938–39	76	Rangers	59	Celtic	48	Aberdeen	46
1	1946–47	60	Rangers	46	Hibernian	44	Aberdeen	39
1	1947–48	60	Hibernian	48	Rangers	46	Partick Thistle	36
1	1948–49	60	Rangers	46	Dundee	45	Hibernian	39
1	1949–50	60	Rangers	50	Hibernian	49	Hearts	43
1	1950–51	60	Hibernian	48	Rangers*	38	Dundee	38
1	1951–52	60	Hibernian	45	Rangers	41	East Fife	37
1	1952–53	60	Rangers*	43	Hibernian	43	East Fife	39
1	1953–54	60	Celtic	43	Hearts	38	Partick Thistle	35
1	1954–55	60	Aberdeen	49	Celtic	46	Rangers	41
1	1955–56	68	Rangers	52	Aberdeen	46	Hearts*	45
1	1956–57	68	Rangers	55	Hearts	53	Kilmarnock	42
1	1957–58	68	Hearts	62	Rangers	49	Celtic	46
1	1958–59	68	Rangers	50	Hearts	48	Motherwell	44
1	1959–60	68	Hearts	54	Kilmarnock	50	Rangers*	42
1	1960–61	68	Rangers	51	Kilmarnock	50	Third Lanark	42
1	1961–62	68	Dundee	54	Rangers	51	Celtic	46
1	1962–63	68	Rangers	57	Kilmarnock	48	Partick Thistle	46

1	1963–64	68	Rangers	55	Kilmarnock	49	Celtic*	47
1	1964–65	68	Kilmarnock*	50	Hearts	50	Dunfermline Ath	49
1	1965–66	68	Celtic	57	Rangers	55	Kilmarnock	45
1	1966–67	68	Celtic	58	Rangers	55	Clyde	46
1	1967–68	68	Celtic	63	Rangers	61	Hibernian	45
1	1968–69	68	Celtic	54	Rangers	49	Dunfermline Ath	45
1	1969–70	68	Celtic	57	Rangers	45	Hibernian	44
1	1970–71	68	Celtic	56	Aberdeen	54	St Johnstone	44
1	1971–72	68	Celtic	60	Aberdeen	50	Rangers	44
1	1972–73	68	Celtic	57	Rangers	56	Hibernian	45
1	1973–74	68	Celtic	53	Hibernian	49	Rangers	48
1	1974–75	68	Rangers	56	Hibernian	49	Celtic*	45

PREMIER DIVISION (1975–76 to 1997–98)

1	1975–76	72	Rangers	54	Celtic	48	Hibernian	43
1	1976–77	72	Celtic	55	Rangers	46	Aberdeen	43
1	1977–78	72	Rangers	55	Aberdeen	53	Dundee U	40
1	1978–79	72	Celtic	48	Rangers	45	Dundee U	44
1	1979–80	72	Aberdeen	48	Celtic	47	St Mirren	42
1	1980–81	72	Celtic	56	Aberdeen	49	Rangers*	44
1	1981–82	72	Celtic	55	Aberdeen	53	Rangers	43
1	1982–83	72	Dundee U	56	Celtic*	55	Aberdeen	55
1	1983–84	72	Aberdeen	57	Celtic	50	Dundee U	47
1	1984–85	72	Aberdeen	59	Celtic	52	Dundee U	47
1	1985–86	72	Celtic*	50	Hearts	50	Dundee U	47
1	1986–87	88	Rangers	69	Celtic	63	Dundee U	60
1	1987–88	88	Celtic	72	Hearts	62	Rangers	60
1	1988–89	72	Rangers	56	Aberdeen	50	Celtic	46
1	1989–90	72	Rangers	51	Aberdeen*	44	Hearts	44
1	1990–91	72	Rangers	55	Aberdeen	53	Celtic*	41
1	1991–92	88	Rangers	72	Hearts	63	Celtic	62
1	1992–93	88	Rangers	73	Aberdeen	64	Celtic	60
1	1993–94	88	Rangers	58	Aberdeen	55	Motherwell	54
1	1994–95	108	Rangers	69	Motherwell	54	Hibernian	53
1	1995–96	108	Rangers	87	Celtic	83	Aberdeen*	55
1	1996–97	108	Rangers	80	Celtic	75	Dundee U	60
1	1997–98	108	Celtic	74	Rangers	72	Hearts	67

PREMIER LEAGUE (1998–99 to 2012–13)

1	1998–99	108	Rangers	77	Celtic	71	St Johnstone	57
1	1999–2000	108	Rangers	90	Celtic	69	Hearts	54
1	2000–01	114	Celtic	97	Rangers	82	Hibernian	66
1	2001–02	114	Celtic	103	Rangers	85	Livingston	58
1	2002–03	114	Rangers*	97	Celtic	97	Hearts	63
1	2003–04	114	Celtic	98	Rangers	81	Hearts	68
1	2004–05	114	Rangers	93	Celtic	92	Hibernian*	61
1	2005–06	114	Celtic	91	Hearts	74	Rangers	73
1	2006–07	114	Celtic	84	Rangers	72	Aberdeen	65
1	2007–08	114	Celtic	89	Rangers	86	Motherwell	60
1	2008–09	114	Rangers	86	Celtic	82	Hearts	59
1	2009–10	114	Rangers	87	Celtic	81	Dundee U	63
1	2010–11	114	Rangers	93	Celtic	92	Hearts	63
1	2011–12	114	Celtic	93	Rangers	73	Motherwell	62

Rangers deducted 10 points for entering administration.

1	2012–13	114	Celtic	79	Motherwell	63	St Johnstone	56

SPFL SCOTTISH PREMIERSHIP (2013–14 to 2015–16)

Tier	Season	Max Pts	First	Pts	Second	Pts	Third	Pts
1	2013–14	114	Celtic	99	Motherwell	70	Aberdeen	68
1	2014–15	114	Celtic	92	Aberdeen	75	Inverness CT	65
1	2015–16	114	Celtic	86	Aberdeen	71	Hearts	65

DIVISION 2 (1893–93 to 1974–75) – TIER 2

2	1893–94	36	Hibernian	29	Cowlairs	27	Clyde	24
2	1894–95	36	Hibernian	30	Motherwell	22	Port Glasgow Ath	20
2	1895–96	36	Abercorn	27	Leith Ath	23	Renton / Kilmarnock=	21
2	1896–97	36	Partick Thistle	31	Leith Ath	27	Airdrieonians / Kilmarnock=	21
2	1897–98	36	Kilmarnock	29	Port Glasgow Ath	25	Morton	22
2	1898–99	36	Kilmarnock	32	Leith Ath	27	Port Glasgow Ath	25
2	1899–1900	36	Partick Thistle	29	Morton	28	Port Glasgow Ath	20
2	1900–01	36	St Bernard's	26	Airdrieonians	23	Abercorn	21
2	1901–02	44	Port Glasgow Ath	32	Partick Thistle	30	Motherwell	26
2	1902–03	44	Airdrieonians	35	Motherwell	28	Ayr U / Leith Ath=	27
2	1903–04	44	Hamilton A	37	Clyde	29	Ayr U	28
2	1904–05	44	Clyde	32	Falkirk	28	Hamilton A	27
2	1905–06	44	Leith Ath	34	Clyde	31	Albion R	27

2	1906–07	44	St Bernard's	32	Vale of Leven=	27	Arthurlie=	27
2	1907–08	44	Raith R	30	Dumbarton=	27	Ayr U=	27

Dumbarton deducted 2 points for registration irregularities.

2	1908–09	44	Abercorn	31	Raith R=	28	Vale of Leven=	28
2	1909–10	44	Leith Ath=	33	Raith R=	33	St Bernard's	27

Leith Ath and Raith R held title jointly, no play-off game played.

2	1910–11	44	Dumbarton	31	Ayr U	27	Albion R	25
2	1911–12	44	Ayr U	35	Abercorn	30	Dumbarton	27
2	1912–13	52	Ayr U	34	Dunfermline Ath	33	East Stirling	32
2	1913–14	44	Cowdenbeath	31	Albion R	27	Dunfermline Ath / Dundee U=	26
2	1914–15	52	Cowdenbeath=	37	St Bernard's=	37	Leith Ath=	37

Cowdenbeath won title after a round robin tournament between the three tied clubs.

2	1921–22	76	Alloa Ath	60	Cowdenbeath	47	Armadale	45
2	1922–23	76	Queen's Park	57	Clydebank	50	St Johnstone	48

Clydebank and St Johnstone both deducted 2 points for fielding an inelligible player.

2	1923–24	76	St Johnstone	56	Cowdenbeath	55	Bathgate	44
2	1924–25	76	Dundee U	50	Clydebank	48	Clyde	47
2	1925–26	76	Dunfermline Ath	59	Clyde	53	Ayr U	52
2	1926–27	76	Bo'ness	56	Raith R	49	Clydebank	45
2	1927–28	76	Ayr U	54	Third Lanark	45	King's Park	44
2	1928–29	72	Dundee U	51	Morton	50	Arbroath	47
2	1929–30	76	Leith Ath*	57	East Fife	57	Albion R	54
2	1930–31	76	Third Lanark	61	Dundee U	50	Dunfermline Ath	47
2	1931–32	76	East Stirling*	55	St Johnstone	55	Raith R*	46
2	1932–33	76	Hibernian	54	Queen of the South	49	Dunfermline Ath	47

Armadale and Bo'ness were expelled for failing to meet match guarantees. Their records were expunged.

2	1933–34	68	Albion R	45	Dunfermline Ath*	44	Arbroath	44
2	1934–35	68	Third Lanark	52	Arbroath	50	St Bernard's	47
2	1935–36	68	Falkirk	59	St Mirren	52	Morton	48
2	1936–37	68	Ayr U	54	Morton	51	St Bernard's	48
2	1937–38	68	Raith R	59	Albion R	48	Airdrieonians	47
2	1938–39	68	Cowdenbeath	60	Alloa Ath*	48	East Fife	48
2	1946–47	52	Dundee	45	Airdrieonians	42	East Fife	31
2	1947–48	60	East Fife	53	Albion R	42	Hamilton A	40
2	1948–49	60	Raith R*	42	Stirling Alb	42	Airdrieonians*	41
2	1949–50	60	Morton	47	Airdrieonians	44	Dunfermline Ath*	36
2	1950–51	60	Queen of the South*	45	Stirling Alb	45	Ayr U*	36
2	1951–52	60	Clyde	44	Falkirk	43	Ayr U	39
2	1952–53	60	Stirling Alb	44	Hamilton A	43	Queen's Park	37
2	1953–54	60	Motherwell	45	Kilmarnock	42	Third Lanark*	36
2	1954–55	60	Airdrieonians	46	Dunfermline Ath	42	Hamilton A	39
2	1955–56	72	Queen's Park	54	Ayr U	51	St Johnstone	49
2	1956–57	72	Clyde	64	Third Lanark	51	Cowdenbeath	45
2	1957–58	72	Stirling Alb	55	Dunfermline Ath	53	Arbroath	47
2	1958–59	72	Ayr U	60	Arbroath	51	Stenhousemuir	46
2	1959–60	72	St Johnstone	53	Dundee U	50	Queen of the South	49
2	1960–61	72	Stirling Alb	55	Falkirk	54	Stenhousemuir	50
2	1961–62	72	Clyde	54	Queen of the South	53	Morton	44
2	1962–63	72	St Johnstone	55	East Stirling	49	Morton	48
2	1963–64	72	Morton	67	Clyde	53	Arbroath	46
2	1964–65	72	Stirling Alb	59	Hamilton A	50	Queen of the South	45
2	1965–66	72	Ayr U	53	Airdrieonians	50	Queen of the South	47
2	1966–67	76	Morton	69	Raith R	58	Arbroath	57
2	1967–68	72	St Mirren	62	Arbroath	53	East Fife	49
2	1968–69	72	Motherwell	64	Ayr U	53	East Fife*	48
2	1969–70	72	Falkirk	56	Cowdenbeath	55	Queen of the South	50
2	1970–71	72	Partick Thistle	56	East Fife	51	Arbroath	46
2	1971–72	72	Dumbarton*	52	Arbroath	52	Stirling Alb*	50
2	1972–73	72	Clyde	56	Dunfermline Ath	52	Raith R*	47
2	1973–74	72	Airdrieonians	60	Kilmarnock	58	Hamilton A	55
2	1974–75	76	Falkirk	54	Queen of the South*	53	Montrose	53

Elected to First Division: 1894 Clyde; 1895 Hibernian; 1896 Abercorn; 1897 Partick Thistle; 1899 Kilmarnock; 1900 Morton and Partick Thistle; 1902 Port Glasgow and Partick Thistle; 1903 Airdrieonians and Motherwell; 1905 Falkirk and Aberdeen; 1906 Clyde and Hamilton A; 1910 Raith R; 1913 Ayr U and Dumbarton.

FIRST DIVISION (1975–76 to 2012–13)

2	1975–76	52	Partick Thistle	41	Kilmarnock	35	Montrose	30
2	1976–77	78	St Mirren	62	Clydebank	58	Dundee	51
2	1977–78	78	Morton*	58	Hearts	58	Dundee	57
2	1978–79	78	Dundee	55	Kilmarnock*	54	Clydebank	54
2	1979–80	78	Hearts	53	Airdrieonians	51	Ayr U*	44
2	1980–81	78	Hibernian	57	Dundee	52	St Johnstone	51
2	1981–82	78	Motherwell	61	Kilmarnock	51	Hearts	50
2	1982–83	78	St Johnstone	55	Hearts	54	Clydebank	50
2	1983–84	78	Morton	54	Dumbarton	51	Partick Thistle	46
2	1984–85	78	Motherwell	50	Clydebank	48	Falkirk	45
2	1985–86	78	Hamilton A	56	Falkirk	45	Kilmarnock*	44
2	1986–87	88	Morton	57	Dunfermline Ath	56	Dumbarton	53
2	1987–88	88	Hamilton A	56	Meadowbank Thistle	52	Clydebank	49

2	1988–89	78	Dunfermline Ath	54	Falkirk	52	Clydebank	48
2	1989–90	78	St Johnstone	58	Airdrieonians	54	Clydebank	44
2	1990–91	78	Falkirk	54	Airdrieonians	53	Dundee	52
2	1991–92	88	Dundee	58	Partick Thistle*	57	Hamilton A	57
2	1992–93	88	Raith R	65	Kilmarnock	54	Dunfermline Ath	52
2	1993–94	88	Falkirk	66	Dunfermline Ath	65	Airdrieonians	54
2	1994–95	108	Raith R	69	Dunfermline Ath*	68	Dundee	68
2	1995–96	108	Dunfermline Ath	71	Dundee U*	67	Greenock Morton	67
2	1996–97	108	St Johnstone	80	Airdrieonians	60	Dundee*	58
2	1997–98	108	Dundee	70	Falkirk	65	Raith R*	60
2	1998–99	108	Hibernian	89	Falkirk	66	Ayr U	62
2	1999–2000	108	St Mirren	76	Dunfermline Ath	71	Falkirk	68
2	2000–01	108	Livingston	76	Ayr U	69	Falkirk	56
2	2001–02	108	Partick Thistle	66	Airdrieonians	56	Ayr U*	52
2	2002–03	108	Falkirk	81	Clyde	72	St Johnstone	67
2	2003–04	108	Inverness CT	70	Clyde	69	St Johnstone	57
2	2004–05	108	Falkirk	75	St Mirren*	60	Clyde	60
2	2005–06	108	St Mirren	76	St Johnstone	66	Hamilton A	59
2	2006–07	108	Gretna	66	St Johnstone	65	Dundee*	53
2	2007–08	108	Hamilton A	76	Dundee	69	St Johnstone	58
2	2008–09	108	St Johnstone	65	Partick Thistle	55	Dunfermline Ath	51
2	2009–10	108	Inverness CT	73	Dundee	61	Dunfermline Ath	58
2	2010–11	108	Dunfermline Ath	70	Raith R	60	Falkirk	58
2	2011–12	108	Ross Co	79	Dundee	55	Falkirk	52
2	2012–13	108	Partick Thistle	78	Greenock Morton	67	Falkirk	53

SPFL SCOTTISH CHAMPIONSHIP (2013–14 to 2015–16)

Tier	Season	Max Pts	First	Pts	Second	Pts	Third	Pts
2	2013–14	108	Dundee	69	Hamilton A	67	Falkirk§	66
2	2014–15	108	Hearts	91	Hibernian§	70	Rangers§	67
2	2015–16	108	Rangers	81	Falkirk*§	70	Hibernian§	70

SECOND DIVISION (1975–76 to 2012–13) – TIER 3

3	1975–76	52	Clydebank*	40	Raith R	40	Alloa Ath	35
3	1976–77	78	Stirling Alb	55	Alloa Ath	51	Dunfermline Ath	50
3	1977–78	78	Clyde*	53	Raith R	53	Dunfermline Ath*	48
3	1978–79	78	Berwick R	54	Dunfermline Ath	52	Falkirk	50
3	1979–80	78	Falkirk	50	East Stirling	49	Forfar Ath	46
3	1980–81	78	Queen's Park	50	Queen of the South	46	Cowdenbeath	45
3	1981–82	78	Clyde	59	Alloa Ath*	50	Arbroath	50
3	1982–83	78	Brechin C	55	Meadowbank Thistle	54	Arbroath	49
3	1983–84	78	Forfar Ath	63	East Fife	47	Berwick R	43
3	1984–85	78	Montrose	53	Alloa Ath	50	Dunfermline Ath	49
3	1985–86	78	Dunfermline Ath	57	Queen of the South	55	Meadowbank Thistle	49
3	1986–87	78	Meadowbank Thistle	55	Raith R*	52	Stirling Alb*	52
3	1987–88	78	Ayr U	61	St Johnstone	59	Queen's Park	51
3	1988–89	78	Albion R	50	Alloa Ath	45	Brechin C	43
3	1989–90	78	Brechin C	49	Kilmarnock	48	Stirling Alb	47
3	1990–91	78	Stirling Alb	54	Montrose	46	Cowdenbeath	45
3	1991–92	78	Dumbarton	52	Cowdenbeath	51	Alloa Ath	50
3	1992–93	78	Clyde	54	Brechin C*	53	Stranraer	53
3	1993–94	78	Stranraer	56	Berwick R	48	Stenhousemuir*	47
3	1994–95	108	Greenock Morton	64	Dumbarton	60	Stirling Alb	58
3	1995–96	108	Stirling Alb	81	East Fife	67	Berwick R	60
3	1996–97	108	Ayr U	77	Hamilton A	74	Livingston	64
3	1997–98	108	Stranraer	61	Clydebank	60	Livingston	59
3	1998–99	108	Livingston	77	Inverness CT	72	Clyde	53
3	1999–2000	108	Clyde	65	Alloa Ath	64	Ross Co	62
3	2000–01	108	Partick Thistle	75	Arbroath	58	Berwick R*	54
3	2001–02	108	Queen of the South	67	Alloa Ath	59	Forfar Ath	53
3	2002–03	108	Raith R	59	Brechin C	55	Airdrie U	54
3	2003–04	108	Airdrie U	70	Hamilton A	62	Dumbarton	60
3	2004–05	108	Brechin C	72	Stranraer	63	Greenock Morton	62
3	2005–06	108	Gretna	88	Greenock Morton§	70	Peterhead*§	57
3	2006–07	108	Greenock Morton	77	Stirling Alb	69	Raith R§	62
3	2007–08	108	Ross Co	73	Airdrie U	66	Raith R§	60
3	2008–09	108	Raith R	76	Ayr U	74	Brechin C§	62
3	2009–10	108	Stirling Alb*	65	Alloa Ath§	65	Cowdenbeath	59
3	2010–11	108	Livingston	82	Ayr U*	59	Forfar Ath§	59
3	2011–12	108	Cowdenbeath	71	Arbroath§	63	Dumbarton	58
3	2012–13	108	Queen of the South	92	Alloa Ath	67	Brechin C	61

SPFL SCOTTISH LEAGUE ONE (2013–14 to 2015–16)

Tier	Season	Max Pts	First	Pts	Second	Pts	Third	Pts
3	2013–14	108	Rangers	102	Dunfermline Ath§	63	Stranraer§	51
3	2014–15	108	Greenock Morton	69	Stranraer§	67	Forfar Ath	66
2	2015–16	108	Dunfermline Ath	79	Ayr U	61	Peterhead§	59

THIRD DIVISION (1994–95 to 2012–13) – TIER 4

4	1994–95	108	Forfar Ath	80	Montrose	67	Ross Co	60
4	1995–96	108	Livingston	72	Brechin C	63	Inverness CT	57
4	1996–97	108	Inverness CT	76	Forfar Ath*	67	Ross Co	67
4	1997–98	108	Alloa Ath	76	Arbroath	68	Ross Co	67
4	1998–99	108	Ross Co	77	Stenhousemuir	64	Brechin C	59
4	1999–2000	108	Queen's Park	69	Berwick R	66	Forfar Ath	61
4	2000–01	108	Hamilton A*	76	Cowdenbeath	76	Brechin C	72
4	2001–02	108	Brechin C	73	Dumbarton	61	Albion R	59
4	2002–03	108	Greenock Morton	72	East Fife	71	Albion R	70
4	2003–04	108	Stranraer	79	Stirling Alb	77	Gretna	68
4	2004–05	108	Gretna	98	Peterhead	78	Cowdenbeath	51
4	2005–06	108	Cowdenbeath*	76	Berwick R§	76	Stenhousemuir§	73
4	2006–07	108	Berwick R	75	Arbroath§	70	Queen's Park	68
4	2007–08	108	East Fife	88	Stranraer	65	Montrose§	59
4	2008–09	108	Dumbarton	67	Cowdenbeath	63	East Stirling§	61
4	2009–10	108	Livingston	78	Forfar Ath	63	East Stirling§	61
4	2010–11	108	Arbroath	66	Albion R	61	Queen's Park*§	59
4	2011–12	108	Alloa Ath	77	Queen's Park§	63	Stranraer	58
4	2012–13	108	Rangers	83	Peterhead§	59	Queen's Park§	56

SPFL SCOTTISH LEAGUE TWO (2013–14 to 2015–16)

Tier	Season	Max Pts	First	Pts	Second	Pts	Third	Pts
4	2013–14	108	Peterhead	76	Annan Ath§	63	Stirling Alb	57
3	2014–15	108	Albion R	71	Queen's Park§	61	Arbroath§	56
2	2015–16	108	East Fife	62	Elgin C§	59	Clyde§	56

RELEGATED CLUBS

RELEGATED FROM DIVISION I (1921–22 to 1973–74)

1921–22 *Dumbarton, Queen's Park, Clydebank
1922–23 Albion R, Alloa Ath
1923–24 Clyde, Clydebank
1924–25 Ayr U, Third Lanark
1925–26 Raith R, Clydebank
1926–27 Morton, Dundee U
1927–28 Bo'ness, Dunfermline Ath
1928–29 Third Lanark, Raith R
1929–30 Dundee U, St Johnstone
1930–31 Hibernian, East Fife
1931–32 Dundee U, Leith Ath
1932–33 Morton, East Stirling
1933–34 Third Lanark, Cowdenbeath
1934–35 St Mirren, Falkirk
1935–36 Airdrieonians, Ayr U
1936–37 Dunfermline Ath, Albion R
1937–38 Dundee, Morton
1938–39 Queen's Park, Raith R
1946–47 Kilmarnock, Hamilton A
1947–48 Airdrieonians, Queen's Park
1948–49 Morton, Albion R
1949–50 Queen of the South, Stirling Alb
1950–51 Clyde, Falkirk

1951–52 Morton, Stirling Alb
1952–53 Motherwell, Third Lanark
1953–54 Airdrieonians, Hamilton A
1954–55 *No clubs relegated as league extended to 18 teams*
1955–56 Clyde, Stirling Alb
1956–57 Dunfermline Ath, Ayr U
1957–58 East Fife, Queen's Park
1958–59 Falkirk, Queen of the South
1959–60 Stirling Alb, Arbroath
1960–61 Clyde, Ayr U
1961–62 St Johnstone, Stirling Alb
1962–63 Clyde, Raith R
1963–64 Queen of the South, East Stirling
1964–65 Airdrieonians, Third Lanark
1965–66 Morton, Hamilton A
1966–67 St Mirren, Ayr U
1967–68 Motherwell, Stirling Alb
1968–69 Falkirk, Arbroath
1969–70 Raith R, Partick Thistle
1970–71 St Mirren, Cowdenbeath
1971–72 Clyde, Dunfermline Ath
1972–73 Kilmarnock, Airdrieonians
1973–74 East Fife, Falkirk

Season 1921–22 – only 1 club promoted, 3 clubs relegated.

RELEGATED FROM PREMIER DIVISION (1974–75 to 1997–98)

1974–75 *No relegation due to League reorganization*
1975–76 Dundee, St Johnstone
1976–77 Hearts, Kilmarnock
1977–78 Ayr U, Clydebank
1978–79 Hearts, Motherwell
1979–80 Dundee, Hibernian
1980–81 Kilmarnock, Hearts
1981–82 Partick Thistle, Airdrieonians
1982–83 Morton, Kilmarnock
1983–84 St Johnstone, Motherwell
1984–85 Dumbarton, Morton
1985–86 *No relegation due to League reorganization*

1986–87 Clydebank, Hamilton A
1987–88 Falkirk, Dunfermline Ath, Morton
1988–89 Hamilton A
1989–90 Dundee
1990–91 *No clubs relegated*
1991–92 St Mirren, Dunfermline Ath
1992–93 Falkirk, Airdrieonians
1993–94 *See footnote.* St Johnstone, Raith R, Dundee
1994–95 Dundee U
1995–96 Partick Thistle, Falkirk
1996–97 Raith R
1997–98 Hibernian

RELEGATED FROM PREMIER LEAGUE (1998–99 to 2012–13)

1998–99 Dunfermline Ath
1999–2000 *No relegation due to League reorganization*
2000–01 St Mirren
2001–02 St Johnstone
2002–03 *No clubs relegated*
2003–04 Partick Thistle
2005–06 Livingston
2006–07 Dunfermline Ath

2007–08 Gretna
2008–09 Inverness CT
2009–10 Falkirk
2010–11 Hamilton A
2011–12 Dunfermline Ath, Rangers (demoted to third division)
2012–13 Dundee

RELEGATED FROM SPFL SCOTTISH PREMIERSHIP (2013–14 to 2015–16)

2013–14 Hibernian, Hearts
2014–15 St Mirren

2015–16 Dundee U

RELEGATED FROM FIRST DIVISION (1975–76 to 2013–14)

1975–76 Dunfermline Ath, Clyde
1976–77 Raith R, Falkirk
1977–78 Alloa Ath, East Fife
1978–79 Montrose, Queen of the South
1979–80 Arbroath, Clyde
1980–81 Stirling Alb, Berwick R
1981–82 East Stirling, Queen of the South
1982–83 Dunfermline Ath, Queen's Park
1983–84 Raith R, Alloa Ath
1984–85 Meadowbank Thistle, St Johnstone
1985–86 Ayr U, Alloa Ath
1986–87 Brechin C, Montrose
1987–88 East Fife, Dumbarton
1988–89 Kilmarnock, Queen of the South
1989–90 Albion R, Alloa Ath
1990–91 Clyde, Brechin C
1991–92 Montrose, Forfar Ath
1992–93 Meadowbank Thistle, Cowdenbeath
1993–94 *See footnote.* Dumbarton, Stirling Alb, Clyde, Morton, Brechin C

1994–95 Ayr U, Stranraer
1995–96 Hamilton A, Dumbarton
1996–97 Clydebank, East Fife
1997–98 Partick Thistle, Stirling Alb
1998–99 Hamilton A, Stranraer
1999–2000 Clydebank
2000–01 Greenock Morton, Alloa Ath
2001–02 Raith R
2002–03 Alloa Ath, Arbroath
2003–04 Ayr U, Brechin C
2004–05 Partick Thistle, Raith R
2005–06 Stranraer, Brechin C
2006–07 Airdrie U, Ross Co
2007–08 Stirling Alb
2008–09 Livingstone *(for breaching rules)*, Clyde
2009–10 Airdrie U, Ayr U
2010–11 Cowdenbeath, Stirling Alb
2011–12 Ayr U, Queen of the South
2012–13 Dunfermline Ath, Airdrie U

RELEGATED FROM SPFL SCOTTISH CHAMPIONSHIP (2013–14 to 2015–16)

2013–14 Greenock Morton
2014–15 Cowdenbeath

2015–16 Livingston, Alloa Ath

RELEGATED FROM SECOND DIVISION (1993–94 to 2012–13)

1993–94 *See footnote.* Alloa Ath, Forfar Ath, East Stirlingshire, Montrose, Queen's Park, Arbroath, Albion R, Cowdenbeath
1994–95 Meadowbank Thistle, Brechin C
1995–96 Forfar Ath, Montrose
1996–97 Dumbarton, Berwick R
1997–98 Stenhousemuir, Brechin C
1998–99 East Fife, Forfar Ath
1999–2000 Hamilton A *(after being deducted 15 points)*
2000–01 Queen's Park, Stirling Alb
2001–02 Greenock Morton
2002–03 Stranraer, Cowdenbeath
2003–04 East Fife, Stenhousemuir

2004–05 Arbroath, Berwick R
2005–06 Dumbarton
2006–07 Stranraer, Forfar Ath
2007–08 Cowdenbeath, Berwick R
2008–09 Queen's Park, Stranraer
2009–10 Arbroath, Clyde
2010–11 Alloa Ath, Peterhead
2011–12 Stirling Alb
2012–13 Albion R

RELEGATED FROM SPFL SCOTTISH LEAGUE ONE (2013–14 to 2015–16)

2013–14 East Fife, Arbroath
2014–15 Stirling Alb

2015–16 Cowdenbeath, Forfar Ath

RELEGATED FROM SPFL SCOTTISH LEAGUE TWO (2013–14 to 2015–16)

2015–16 East Stirlingshire

SCOTTISH LEAGUE CHAMPIONSHIP WINS

Rangers 54, Celtic 47, Aberdeen 4, Hearts 4, Hibernian 4, Dumbarton 2, Dundee 1, Dundee U 1, Kilmarnock 1, Motherwell 1, Third Lanark 1.
The totals for Rangers and Dumbarton each include the shared championship of 1890–91.

Since the formation of the Scottish Football League in 1890, there have been periodic reorganisations of the leagues to allow for expansion, improve competition and commercial aspects of the game. The table below lists the league names by tier and chronology. This table can be used to assist when studying the records.

Tier	Division		Tier	Division	
1	Scottish League Division I	1890–1939	3	Scottish League Division III	1923–1926
	Scottish League Division A	1946–1956		Scottish League Division C	1946–1949
	Scottish League Division I	1956–1975		Second Division	1975–2013
	Premier Division	1975–1998		SPFL League One	2013–
	Scottish Premier League	1998–2013			
	SPFL Premiership	2013–	4	Third Division	1994–2013
				SPFL League Two	2013–
2	Scottish League Division II	1893–1939			
	Scottish League Division B	1946–1956			
	Scottish League Division II	1956–1975			
	First Division	1975–2013			
	SPFL Championship	2013–			

In 2013–14 the SPFL introduced play-offs to determine a second promotion/relegation place for the Premiership, Championship and League One.

In each division, the team finishing second bottom plays two legs against the team from the lower division that won the eliminator games played between the teams finishing second, third and fourth.

In 2014–15 a play-off was introduced for promotion/relegation from League Two. The team finishing bottom of League Two plays two legs against the victors of the eliminator games between the winners of the Highland and Lowland leagues.

SCOTTISH LEAGUE PLAY-OFFS 2015–16

 Denotes player sent off.

PREMIERSHIP QUARTER-FINAL FIRST LEG

Wednesday, 4 May 2016

Raith R (0) 1 *(Panayiotou 75)*

Hibernian (0) 0 5330

Raith R: (451) Cuthbert; Thomson, Benedictus, Barr, McKeown; Connolly (Panayiotou 65), Callachan, Toshney, Davidson, Craigen (Longridge 65); Hardie (Stewart 90).
Hibernian: (352) Logan; McGregor, Fontaine (Henderson 84), Hanlon; Gray, Fyvie (Keatings 81), Bartley, McGinn, Stevenson; Cummings (McGeouch 80), Stokes.
Referee: Kevin Clancy.

PREMIERSHIP QUARTER-FINAL SECOND LEG

Saturday, 7 May 2016

Hibernian (2) 2 *(McGinn 8, McGregor 12)*

Raith R (0) 0 11,133

Hibernian: (442) Logan; Gray, McGregor, Hanlon, Stevenson; Henderson (Fontaine 82), Fyvie, McGeouch (Bartley 66), McGinn; Cummings (Keatings 81), Stokes.
Raith R: (451) Cuthbert; Thomson, Barr, Toshney, McKeown; Callachan, Davidson, Benedictus, Craigen (Panayiotou 52), Longridge (Stewart 65); Hardie (Thomas 75).
Hibernian won 2-1 on aggregate.
Referee: John McKendrick.

PREMIERSHIP SEMI-FINAL FIRST LEG

Tuesday, 10 May 2016

Hibernian (0) 2 *(Henderson 57, McGregor 66)*

Falkirk (1) 2 *(Miller 34, McHugh 80)* 11,830

Hibernian: (41212) Logan; Gray, McGregor, Hanlon, Stevenson; McGeouch; Fyvie, McGinn; Henderson (Boyle 89); Stokes, Cummings (Keatings 73).
Falkirk: (442) Rogers; Muirhead, McCracken, Vaulks, Leahy; Alston, Kerr, Taiwo (Hippolyte 78), Sibbald; Baird (O'Hara 71), Miller (McHugh 59).
Referee: Alan Muir.

PREMIERSHIP SEMI-FINAL SECOND LEG

Friday, 13 May 2016

Falkirk (1) 3 *(Alston 13, Leahy 79, McHugh 90)*

Hibernian (2) 2 *(Keatings 31 (pen), 34)* 7851

Falkirk: (442) Rogers; Muirhead, McCracken, Watson, Leahy; Alston (Shepherd 71), Kerr (Hippolyte 58), Vaulks, Sibbald; Baird (Miller 58), McHugh.
Hibernian: (41212) Logan; Gray, McGregor, Hanlon, Stevenson; McGeouch (Bartley 38); Fyvie, McGinn; Henderson; Stokes, Keatings (Cummings 82).
Falkirk won 5-4 on aggregate.
Referee: Chris Thomson.

PREMIERSHIP FINAL FIRST LEG

Thursday, 19 May 2016

Falkirk (0) 1 *(Vaulks 90)*

Kilmarnock (0) 0 7636

Falkirk: (442) Rogers; Muirhead, Watson, McCracken, Leahy; Alston (Shepherd 61), Kerr, Vaulks, Sibbald; Baird (Hippolyte 78), McHugh.
Kilmarnock: (4231) MacDonald; O'Hara, Addison, Ashcroft, Hodson; Slater, Dicker; Obadeyi, McKenzie, Kiltie; Boyd.
Referee: John Beaton.

PREMIERSHIP FINAL SECOND LEG

Sunday, 22 May 2016

Kilmarnock (2) 4 *(Kiltie 3, 62, Addison 8, Boyd 65)*

Falkirk (0) 0 11,013

Kilmarnock: (4231) MacDonald; Hodson, Addison, Ashcroft, Taylor; Slater, Dicker; Magennis (O'Hara 75), Obadeyi, Kiltie (McKenzie 90); Boyd.
Falkirk: (442) Rogers; Muirhead, Watson, McCracken, Leahy; Taiwo (Alston 53), Kerr, Vaulks, Sibbald (Hippolyte 64); Baird (Miller 58), McHugh.
Kilmarnock won 4-1 on aggregate.
Referee: Willie Collum.

CHAMPIONSHIP SEMI-FINALS FIRST LEG

Tuesday, 3 May 2016

Peterhead (1) 1 *(McIntosh 35)*

Ayr U (2) 4 *(Donald 18, Preston 41, 59, Crawford 74)* 807

Peterhead: (4231) Smith; Blockley, Redman, Strachan, Noble; Ferry, Dzierzawski; McIntosh, Brown (Lawrence 77), Riley; Sutherland (Rodgers 63).
Ayr U: (442) Fleming; Devlin, Graham, Murphy, Boyle; McCrorie, Docherty, Crawford, Donald (Gilmour 72); Preston, Moore (Trouten 75).
Referee: Stephen Finnie.

Wednesday, 4 May 2016

Stranraer (3) 5 *(McGuigan 14, 70, Stirling 17, Gibson 40, Cole 81 (og))*

Livingston (1) 2 *(White 10, Buchanan 68)* 589

Stranraer: (442) Belford; Pettigrew, Robertson, Bell, Dick; Gibson, Thomson, Cairney (Turner 88), Stirling; Malcolm (Kemp 84), McGuigan (Longworth 82).
Livingston: (442) McCallum; Kakay, Halkett, Neill (Cole 72), Longridge; Mullin (Fotheringham 46), Buchanan, Pitman, Stanton; White, Mullen (Telfer 46).
Referee: Steven McLean.

CHAMPIONSHIP SEMI-FINALS SECOND LEG

Saturday, 7 May 2016

Ayr U (1) 2 *(Crawford 26, Devlin 57)*

Peterhead (1) 1 *(Donald 31 (og))* 1848

Ayr U: (442) Fleming; Devlin, Adams, Murphy, Boyle; McCrorie (Forrest 70), Docherty, Crawford, Donald (Gilmour 58); Preston, Moore (Stevenson 64).
Peterhead: (4312) Smith; Blockley, Ross, Strachan, Noble; Redman (Sutherland 60), Dzierzawski (Riley 55), Ferry; Brown (Lawrence 73); McAllister, McIntosh.
Ayr U won 6-2 on aggregate.
Referee: Crawford Allan.

Livingston (2) 4 *(Buchanan 18, White 45, Mullen 89, Halkett 90)*

Stranraer (0) 3 *(Cairney 62, Dick 109, Longworth 120)* 1018

Livingston: (442) McCallum; Halkett, Cole (Mullen 71), Neill, Kakay; Telfer (Sheerin 79), Fotheringham, Pitman, Stanton; White, Buchanan.
Stranraer: (442) Belford; Pettigrew, Robertson, Bell, Dick; Gibson, Thomson, Cairney, Stirling (Kemp 88); Malcolm (Barron 59), McGuigan (Longworth 73).
aet.
Stranraer won 8-6 on aggregate.
Referee: Craig Thomson.

CHAMPIONSHIP FINAL FIRST LEG

Wednesday, 11 May 2016

Stranraer (0) 1 *(McGuigan 54)*

Ayr U (0) 1 *(Docherty 90)* 1652

Stranraer: (442) Belford; Dick, Bell, Robertson, Pettigrew; Stirling, Cairney, Thomson, Gibson; Malcolm (Longworth 65), McGuigan (Barron 76).

Ayr U: (442) Fleming; Boyle, Murphy, Adams, Devlin; Donald (Trouten 80), Crawford, Docherty, McCrorie (Gilmour 61); Moore (Stevenson 61), Preston.
Referee: Bobby Madden.

CHAMPIONSHIP FINAL SECOND LEG

Sunday, 15 May 2016
Ayr U (0) 0
Stranraer (0) 0   4581
Ayr U: (442) Fleming; Devlin, Adams, Murphy, Boyle; Gilmour (McCrorie 75), Docherty, Crawford, Donald (Graham 46); Stevenson (Trouten 97), Preston.
Stranraer: (442) Belford; Pettigrew, Bell, Robertson, Dick; Gibson, Cairney, Thomson, Stirling; Malcolm (Longworth 60), McGuigan (Barron 102).
aet; Ayr U won 3-1 on penalties.
Referee: Andrew Dallas.

LEAGUE ONE SEMI-FINALS FIRST LEG

Tuesday, 3 May 2016
Clyde (2) 3 *(Gemmell 19, Linton 41, McLaughlin M 67)*
Elgin C (0) 1 *(MacLeod 49)*   804
Clyde: (442) Gibson; Millen, McLaughlin M, Smith, McMann; Linton, Marsh (Brisbane 76), McLaughlin S, Kirkpatrick; Gemmell (Higgins S 78), Gormley (Watson 83).
Elgin C: (4312) Hurst; Cooper, Nicolson, Duff, MacPhee; Cameron, Reilly, Moore (Ross 85); Easton; McKenzie (McLaren 70), MacLeod (Gunn 76).
Referee: John McKendrick.

Wednesday, 4 May 2016
Queen's Park (1) 2 *(Duggan 1, 66 (pen))*
Cowdenbeath (0) 0   572
Queen's Park: (4231) Muir; Burns, McGeever, Wharton, McLeish; Berry, Brown (McVey 77); Woods, Bradley, Galt (Carter 86); Duggan.
Cowdenbeath: (442) Adam; Donaldson, Sives, El-Zubaidi (Milne 54), Adamson; Brett, Kane, Gibbons, McDaid (Caldwell 73); Spence, Miller (Hughes 58).
Referee: Greg Aitken.

LEAGUE ONE SEMI-FINALS SECOND LEG

Saturday, 7 May 2016
Cowdenbeath (0) 1 *(Spence 54)*
Queen's Park (0) 0   585
Cowdenbeath: (4411) Adam; Brett, Sives, Kane, Adamson; Johnston (Nish 73), Hughes, Milne, Swan (McDaid 83); Caldwell; Spence.
Queen's Park: (4231) Muir; Burns, McGeever, Wharton, McLeish; Berry, Brown (Galt 64); Woods (Baty 71), McVey, Bradley; Duggan (Carter 23).
Queen's Park won 2-1 on aggregate.
Referee: Craig Charleston.

Elgin C (0) 0
Clyde (0) 2 *(Kirkpatrick 62, Linton 90)*   1371
Elgin C: (4312) Hurst; Cooper, Nicolson, Duff, MacPhee; Cameron, Reilly, Moore (McLaren 63); Easton (Ross 18); Gunn (McKenzie 71), MacLeod.
Clyde: (442) Gibson; Brisbane, McLaughlin M (Andrews 46), Smith, McMann; Linton, Marsh, McLaughlin S, Kirkpatrick; Gemmell (Higgins S 65), Gormley (Watson 71).
Clyde won 5-1 on aggregate.
Referee: Euan Anderson.

LEAGUE ONE FINAL FIRST LEG

Tuesday, 10 May 2016
Clyde (1) 1 *(Gemmell 15)*
Queen's Park (1) 3 *(Burns 5 (pen), Berry 63, Galt 84)*   1312
Clyde: (442) Gibson; Brisbane, Andrews, Smith, McMann; Linton, Marsh (Higgins S 70), McLaughlin S, Kirkpatrick; Gemmell (Watson 73), Gormley (Millen 79).

Queen's Park: (4411) Muir; Mitchell, McGeever, Wharton, McLeish; Woods (Bradley 73), Berry, Brown (McVey 73), Burns; Galt; Carter (Mortimer 87).
Referee: Kevin Clancy.

LEAGUE ONE FINAL SECOND LEG

Saturday, 14 May 2016
Queen's Park (0) 0
Clyde (1) 1 *(Linton 33 (pen))*   2107
Queen's Park: (4231) Muir; Mitchell, McGeever, Wharton, McLeish; Berry, Brown; Woods (Bradley 74), Galt (McVey 80), Burns; Carter.
Clyde: (442) Gibson; Brisbane (Andrews 84), Bolochoweckyj■, Smith, Linton; Millen, Marsh (Gormley 65), McLaughlin S, Kirkpatrick; Higgins S (Watson 77), Gemmell.
Queen's Park won 3-2 on aggregate.
Referee: Steven McLean.

LEAGUE TWO SEMI-FINAL FIRST LEG

Saturday, 23 April 2016
Cove R (0) 0
Edinburgh C (3) 3 *(Allum 22, 44, Donaldson 42)*
Cove R: (442) McKenzie; Redford, Milne, Yule, Watson; Kelly, Campbell, Duff, Nicol; Smith J, Scully.
Edinburgh C: (442) Amos; Dunsmore, Donaldson, Paterson, McKee (Caddow 83); Mbu, Gair, Allum (Vanson 86), Dunn; MacDonald, McConnell (Gibson 59).
Referee: Gavin Ross.

LEAGUE TWO SEMI-FINAL SECOND LEG

Saturday, 30 April 2016
Edinburgh C (1) 1 *(Gair 32)*
Cove R (0) 1 *(Watt 84)*   839
Edinburgh C: (442) Amos; Dunsmore (Caddow 65), Donaldson (Guthrie 58), McConnell, Paterson; Mbu, Harrison, Gair, Allum (Vanson 77); Dunn, MacDonald.
Cove R: (442) McCafferty; Redford, Lawrie, Yule, Watson (Donaldson 69); Kelly, Burnett, Campbell, Nicol (Scully 48); Smith J, Milne (Watt 72).
Edinburgh C won 4-1 on aggregate.
Referee: Colin Steven.

LEAGUE TWO FINAL FIRST LEG

Saturday, 7 May 2016
Edinburgh C (1) 1 *(Gair 12)*
East Stirlingshire (1) 1 *(Wright 39)*   1090
Edinburgh C: (442) Amos; Dunsmore (Gibson 82); Paterson, Mbu■, Donaldson; McConnell, Gair, McKee, MacDonald; Allum (Harrison 77), Dunn (Guthrie 48).
East Stirlingshire: (442) Dolan; Kinnaird, McMullin, Fisher, Donaldson■; Faulds, McCabe, Townsley, Wright; Orr (McKenna 70), Kay (Lynas 57).
Referee: Gavin Duncan.

LEAGUE TWO FINAL SECOND LEG

Saturday, 14 May 2016
East Stirlingshire (0) 0
Edinburgh C (0) 1 *(Gair 87 (pen))*   1286
East Stirlingshire: (442) Dolan; Kinnaird, McMullin, Townsley, Donaldson■; Faulds (Lynas 67), McCabe, Fisher, Wright; Orr (McMillan 63), McKenna.
Edinburgh C: (4132) Amos; Dunsmore, Mbu, Paterson (Harrison 54), McKee; McConnell; McFarland, Gair, MacDonald; Guthrie (Muhsin 75), Allum.
Edinburgh C won 2-1 on aggregate.
Referee: Don Robertson.

SCOTTISH LEAGUE CUP FINALS 1946–2016

SCOTTISH LEAGUE CUP

1946–47	Rangers v Aberdeen	4-0
1947–48	East Fife v Falkirk	0-0*
Replay	East Fife v Falkirk	4-1
1948–49	Rangers v Raith R	2-0
1949–50	East Fife v Dunfermline Ath	3-0
1950–51	Motherwell v Hibernian	3-0
1951–52	Dundee v Rangers	3-2
1952–53	Dundee v Kilmarnock	2-0
1953–54	East Fife v Partick Thistle	3-2
1954–55	Hearts v Motherwell	4-2
1955–56	Aberdeen v St Mirren	2-1
1956–57	Celtic v Partick Thistle	0-0*
Replay	Celtic v Partick Thistle	3-0
1957–58	Celtic v Rangers	7-1
1958–59	Hearts v Partick Thistle	5-1
1959–60	Hearts v Third Lanark	2-1
1960–61	Rangers v Kilmarnock	2-0
1961–62	Rangers v Hearts	1-1*
Replay	Rangers v Hearts	3-1
1962–63	Hearts v Kilmarnock	1-0
1963–64	Rangers v Morton	5-0
1964–65	Rangers v Celtic	2-1
1965–66	Celtic v Rangers	2-1
1966–67	Celtic v Rangers	1-0
1967–68	Celtic v Dundee	5-3
1968–69	Celtic v Hibernian	6-2
1969–70	Celtic v St Johnstone	1-0
1970–71	Rangers v Celtic	1-0
1971–72	Partick Thistle v Celtic	4-1
1972–73	Hibernian v Celtic	2-1
1973–74	Dundee v Celtic	1-0
1974–75	Celtic v Hibernian	6-3
1975–76	Rangers v Celtic	1-0
1976–77	Aberdeen v Celtic	2-1*
1977–78	Rangers v Celtic	2-1*
1978–79	Rangers v Aberdeen	2-1

BELL'S LEAGUE CUP

1979–80	Dundee U v Aberdeen	0-0*
Replay	Dundee U v Aberdeen	3-0
1980–81	Dundee U v Dundee	3-0

SCOTTISH LEAGUE CUP

1981–82	Rangers v Dundee U	2-1
1982–83	Celtic v Rangers	2-1
1983–84	Rangers v Celtic	3-2*

SKOL CUP

1984–85	Rangers v Dundee U	1-0
1985–86	Aberdeen v Hibernian	3-0
1986–87	Rangers v Celtic	2-1
1987–88	Rangers v Aberdeen	3-3*
	Rangers won 5-3 on penalties.	
1988–89	Rangers v Aberdeen	3-2
1989–90	Aberdeen v Rangers	2-1*
1990–91	Rangers v Celtic	2-1*
1991–92	Hibernian v Dunfermline Ath	2-0
1992–93	Rangers v Aberdeen	2-1*

SCOTTISH LEAGUE CUP

1993–94	Rangers v Hibernian	2-1

COCA-COLA CUP

1994–95	Raith R v Celtic	2-2*
	Raith R won 6-5 on penalties.	
1995–96	Aberdeen v Dundee	2-0
1996–97	Rangers v Hearts	4-3
1997–98	Celtic v Dundee U	3-0

SCOTTISH LEAGUE CUP

1998–99	Rangers v St Johnstone	2-1

CIS INSURANCE CUP

1999–2000	Celtic v Aberdeen	2-0
2000–01	Celtic v Kilmarnock	3-0
2001–02	Rangers v Ayr U	4-0
2002–03	Rangers v Celtic	2-1
2003–04	Livingston v Hibernian	2-0
2004–05	Rangers v Motherwell	5-1
2005–06	Celtic v Dunfermline Ath	3-0
2006–07	Hibernian v Kilmarnock	5-1
2007–08	Rangers v Dundee U	2-2*
	Rangers won 3-2 on penalties.	

CO-OPERATIVE INSURANCE CUP

2008–09	Celtic v Rangers	2-0*
2009–10	Rangers v St Mirren	1-0
2010–11	Rangers v Celtic	2-1*

SCOTTISH COMMUNITIES LEAGUE CUP

2011–12	Kilmarnock v Celtic	1-0
2012–13	St Mirren v Hearts	3-2
2013–14	Aberdeen v Inverness CT	0-0*
	Aberdeen won 4-2 on penalties.	

SCOTTISH LEAGUE CUP PRESENTED BY QTS

2014–15	Celtic v Dundee U	2-0
2015–16	Ross Co v Hibernian	2-1

*After extra time.

SCOTTISH LEAGUE CUP WINS

Rangers 27, Celtic 15, Aberdeen 6, Hearts 4, Dundee 3, East Fife 3, Hibernian 3, Dundee U 2, Kilmarnock 1, Livingston 1, Motherwell 1, Partick Thistle 1, Raith R 1, Ross Co 1, St Mirren 1.

APPEARANCES IN FINALS

Rangers 34, Celtic 30 Aberdeen 13, Hibernian 10, Dundee U 7, Hearts 7, Dundee 6, Kilmarnock 6, Partick Thistle 4, Dunfermline Ath 3, East Fife 3, Motherwell 3, St Mirren 3, Raith R 2, St Johnstone 2, Ayr U 1, Falkirk 1, Inverness CT 1, Livingston 1, Morton 1, Ross Co 1, Third Lanark 1.

SCOTTISH LEAGUE CUP
PRESENTED BY QTS 2015–16

■ *Denotes player sent off.*

FIRST ROUND

Thursday, 30 July 2015

Hearts (0) 4 *(McGhee 57, Sow 60, 61 (pen),*
Wilson 90 (og))

Arbroath (1) 2 *(Gold 40, Grehan 85)*   6240

Hearts: (442) Hamilton; Paterson, McGhee, Ozturk,
McHattie; King, McKirdy, Gomis (Delgado 66),
Nicholson; Sow (Igor Rossi 77), Oliver (Walker 54).
Arbroath: (442) Fleming; Wilson C, Hay, Little, Lowdon;
Linn, Clarke, Stewart, Cecilia (Hester 83); Coult (Grehan
58), Gold.
Referee: Alan Muir.

Friday, 31 July 2015

Falkirk (1) 5 *(Muirhead 17, Baird 57, Vidler 68 (og),*
McHugh 70, Alston 78)

East Stirling (0) 0   881

Falkirk: (442) Rogers; Muirhead, Grant, Watson, Leahy;
Smith (Cooper 80), Alston, Vaulks, Sibbald; McHugh,
Baird (Shepherd 72).
East Stirling: (352) Barnard; Greene, Tully, Donaldson;
Kinnaird, Wallace (Roy 70), McCabe, Faulds, Shepherd;
Wright, Vidler (Kay 82).
Referee: George Salmond.

Saturday, 1 August 2015

Annan Ath (0) 3 *(Osadolor 59, Weatherson 63, 72)*

Queen of the South (1) 4 *(Conroy 42, Lyle 65, 100,*
Hilson 90)   1359

Annan Ath: (352) Hart; Black■, Watson P, Swinglehurst
(Watson J 117); Omar■, Sloan (Liddell 116), Flynn
(Norman 105), Osadolor, McNiff; Weatherson, McColm.
Queen of the South: (433) Thomson; Kidd (Hooper 84),
Dowie, Higgins, Marshall (Pickard 84); Jacobs, Millar,
Conroy; Hilson, Lyle, Russell (Smith A 77).
aet.
Referee: Kevin Graham.

Ayr U (1) 2 *(McLauchlan 12, Boyle 64)*

Brechin C (0) 0   976

Ayr U: (4411) Fleming; Devlin, McLauchlan, Campbell
(McCracken 85), Boyle; Crawford, Gilmour (Forrest 57),
Docherty, Donald (Nisbet 77); Trouten; Caldwell.
Brechin C: (4132) Smith G; McLean, McCormack, Perry,
Buchan; Fusco (Molloy 66); Smith E (Weatherston 82),
Dale, Montgomery (Johnston 46); Thomson, Jackson A.
Referee: Euan Anderson.

Berwick R (0) 3 *(Lavery 56, Morris 77, Banjo 97)*

Alloa Ath (2) 2 *(Flannigan 6, 21)*   405

Berwick R: (442) Walker K; McNeil, Wilson, Fairbairn,
Beveridge; McKenna, Banjo, Graham F, Coultress
(Morris 69); Henderson (Drummond 106), Lavery
(Russell 106).
Alloa Ath: (3511) McNeil; Reintam, Paun, Hill; Ferns
(Williams 67), McManus, O'Brien (Kader 100),
Flannigan, Hamilton; Duffy; Mitchell (Layne 67).
aet.
Referee: Craig Charleston.

Dunfermline Ath (0) 5 *(El Bakhtaoui 49, 90, Byrne 56, 78,*
Wallace 74 (pen))

Cowdenbeath (0) 1 *(Hughes 58)*   2756

Dunfermline Ath: (442) Murdoch; Williamson, Fordyce,
Richards-Everton, Martin; Paton, Geggan, Byrne
(Falkingham 79), Cardle (Hopkirk 77); Moffat (Wallace
66), El Bakhtaoui.

Cowdenbeath: (442) Andrews■; Brett, Armstrong J,
Donaldson, Yaqub; Orritt (Kane 24), Milne, Hughes,
Johnston (Sneddon 73); Spence, Armstrong L (Nish 61).
Referee: Andrew Dallas.

East Fife (0) 1 *(Austin N 48)*

Dumbarton (0) 1 *(Cawley 65)*   461

East Fife: (442) Goodfellow; MacGregor (Naysmith 75),
Page, O'Kane, Slattery; Mullen, Brown, Mercer, Wilkie;
Murray (Walker 63), Austin N (Sutherland 109).
Dumbarton: (442) Brown; Taggart, Buchanan, Barr
(Graham 105), Waters; Lindsay (Kirkpatrick 82),
Gallagher, Routledge, Gibson; Fleming (Craig 61),
Cawley.
aet; East Fife won 4-3 on penalties.
Referee: Steven Kirkland.

Greenock Morton (0) 5 *(McCluskey 48, Johnstone 68,*
Scullion 70, 83, Forbes 74 (pen))

Elgin C (0) 0   1052

Greenock Morton: (4411) Gaston; Pepper, Kilday, Lamie,
Russell; Barr (McKeown 82), Miller (Stevenson 75),
Forbes, McCluskey; Scullion; Johnstone (Orr 80).
Elgin C: (4411) Black; Cooper, Gordon, Duff, McHardy;
McKenzie (MacPhee 63), McLean (Hunter 64), Nicolson,
Moore (Halsman 76); Cameron; Gunn.
Referee: Barry Cook.

Hibernian (1) 3 *(Martin 33, Allan S 71, Cummings 82)*

Montrose (0) 0   5933

Hibernian: (442) Oxley; Gray, Hanlon, Fontaine,
Stevenson; Martin, Fyvie, Bartley (Allan S 66), Stanton
(Sinclair 84); Harris (Shaw 75), Cummings.
Montrose: (442) Salmon; Ferguson, Reoch, McCord
(Milne 83), Steeves; Johnston, Allan, Watson, Webster;
Fraser, Campbell R (Reid 60).
Referee: John Beaton.

Livingston (0) 1 *(White 110)*

Clyde (0) 0   664

Livingston: (442) Jamieson; Sives, Gallagher (Millen
107), Gordon, Longridge; Georgiev (Neill 120), Pitman,
Gibbons, Mullen; White, Buchanan (Sheerin 85).
Clyde: (451) Gibson; Bolochoweckyj, McLaughlin M
(Ferguson 58), Smith, Linton; Mitchell, Brisbane
(Campbell 79), Murray (McQueen 80), Higgins S,
McLaughlin S; Gormley.
aet.
Referee: John McKendrick.

Queen's Park (0) 0

Forfar Ath (2) 2 *(Young 16, Denholm 29)*   441

Queen's Park: (4231) Muir; McVey, Quinn (Mortimer
58), Wharton, Burns (Gibson 68); Berry, McLeish
(McKernon 46); Woods, Bradley, Galt; Carter.
Forfar Ath: (442) Douglas; Baxter, Young (Travis 85),
O'Brien, Campbell; Fotheringham, Nicoll, Hodge,
Denholm (Kennedy 69); Templeman (Malin 81),
Swankie.
Referee: Gavin Duncan.

Raith R (2) 3 *(Vaughan 16 (pen), Benedictus 38,*
McKeown 54)

Albion R (0) 0   1163

Raith R: (433) Cuthbert; Thomson, Benedictus, Bates,
McKeown; Callachan, McCord (Craigen 77), Petrie;
Vaughan (Anderson 30), Stewart (Megginson 66),
Wighton.
Albion R: (433) Stewart; Reid (Ferry 74), Dunlop R,
Dunlop M, Turnbull; Fisher, Young, Davidson
(McRobbie 61); Mullin, Barrowman (Willis 61), Love.
Referee: Nick Walsh.

Stirling Alb (0) 0
Airdrieonians (1) 1 *(Morton 41)* 799
Stirling Alb: (4231) Smith C; Hamilton, Staunton, Smith R, Forsyth; McGovern, Robertson; Johnston, Comrie (Cunningham 69), Dickson (Doris 79); Beattie (Kouider-Aisser 57).
Airdrieonians: (442) Parry; Bain, Crighton, Lithgow, van Zanten; Cox (Watt 86), O'Neil (Gilfillan 50), McBride, Morton; Morgan, Prunty (Stewart 86).
Referee: Mike Roncone.

Stranraer (1) 2 *(Malcolm 15, 90)*
Stenhousemuir (0) 0 345
Stranraer: (442) Brennan; Robertson, Rumsby, Pettigrew, Keenan; McGuigan, Bell, Thomson, Stirling (McCloskey 90); Longworth (Aitken 84), Malcolm.
Stenhousemuir: (442) Barclay; Meechan, Malcolm, Murray, Henderson; Cook, Stirling (Robertson J 62), Millar, Martinez (Eddington 86); McMenamin, Smith (McShane 77).
Referee: Don Robertson.

Sunday, 2 August 2015
Rangers (1) 3 *(Templeton 41, Miller 76, Tavernier 82)*
Peterhead (0) 0 25,608
Rangers: (433) Foderingham; Tavernier, Kiernan, Wilson, Wallace; Shiels, Halliday, McKay (Clark 71), Waghorn, Templeton (Miller 58).
Peterhead: (4411) Smith; Blockley, Ross, Strachan, Noble; Stevenson (McIntosh 54), Brown (Ferries 67), Redman (Rodgers 76), Sutherland; Dzierzawski; McAllister.
Referee: Greg Aitken.

SECOND ROUND

Tuesday, 25 August 2015
Dunfermline Ath (1) 3 *(El Bakhtaoui 11, 90, Cardle 86)*
Dundee (0) 1 *(Hemmings 48)* 3806
Dunfermline Ath: (442) Murdoch; Martin, Fordyce, Richards-Everton, Talbot; Paton, Geggan, Falkingham, Cardle (Hopkirk 90); Moffat (Wallace 74), El Bakhtaoui.
Dundee: (4312) Bain; McGinn, McPake, Konrad, Holt; Ross, Etxabeguren Leanizbarrutia (Carreiro 60), McGowan; Harkins; Hemmings, Stewart.
Referee: Stephen Finnie.

East Fife (0) 1 *(Austin N 60)*
Motherwell (0) 3 *(Moult 80, McDonald 103, Ainsworth 107)* 1158
East Fife: (442) Goodfellow; MacGregor (Naysmith 82), Page, O'Kane, Mercer; Brown (Murray 94), Walker, Wilkie, Slattery; Austin N (Sutherland 89), Smith.
Motherwell: (442) Ripley; Law (Watt 105), Laing, Kennedy, Chalmers; Ainsworth, Lasley, Leitch, Johnson (Thomas 46); Clarkson (McDonald 62), Moult.
aet.
Referee: Barry Cook.

Forfar Ath (0) 1 *(Dunlop 84)*
Hearts (2) 2 *(McHattie 74, Reilly 105)* 1844
Forfar Ath: (4411) Douglas; Dunlop, Nicoll[*], Travis, Campbell; Hay (Allan 57), Hodge, Young (Malin 46), Denholm[*]; Fotheringham; Templeman (Smith 64).
Hearts: (41212) Hamilton; McGhee, Igor Rossi, Smith, McHattie; Gomis, King (Morrison 63), Nicholson; McKirdy (Paterson 73); Reilly, Oliver (Delgado 60).
aet.
Referee: Greg Aitken.

Kilmarnock (1) 4 *(Boyd 16 (pen), McKenzie 70, Slater 77, Higginbotham 90)*
Berwick R (0) 1 *(Lavery 55)* 1484
Kilmarnock: (4411) MacDonald; Hamill, Ashcroft, Findlay, Smith; Slater (Hawkshaw 88), Splaine (Obadeyi 80), O'Hara, Kiltie (Higginbotham 79); McKenzie; Boyd.
Berwick R: (4132) Walker K; McNeil, Ainslie, Fairbairn, Beveridge; Cameron (Graham R 73); Lavery, Graham F (Hogg 90), Coultress; Henderson, McKenna (Morris 81).
Referee: John McKendrick.

Partick Thistle (0) 0
Falkirk (1) 1 *(Grant 32)* 2221
Partick Thistle: (4231) Cerny; Miller, Hendry, Seaborne, Booth; Osman, Fraser (McDaid 83); Lawless, Stevenson (Wilson 75), Amoo (Pogba 46); Doolan.
Falkirk: (442) Rogers; Taiwo, Watson, Grant, Leahy; Alston, Vaulks, Kerr, Sibbald; Baird, Smith (Muirhead 85).
Referee: Craig Thomson.

Queen of the South (0) 0
Greenock Morton (0) 1 *(Forbes 69)* 1034
Queen of the South: (442) Thomson; Dowie, Brownlie, Higgins, Marshall (Heffernan 81); Kidd (Smith A 65), Hutton (Moxon 76), Millar, Conroy; Lyle, Russell.
Greenock Morton: (4411) Adam; Kilday, O'Ware, Lamie, Pepper; Barr, Miller, Forbes, McCluskey; Sabajo (MacDonald 86); Johnstone.
Referee: Andrew Dallas.

Raith R (1) 2 *(Davidson 3, Benedictus 81)*
Hamilton A (0) 1 *(Nade 66)* 1470
Raith R: (442) Cuthbert; Thomson, Benedictus, Toshney, McKeown; Anderson (Daly 70), Davidson, McCord, Craigen; Megginson (Wighton 70), Stewart.
Hamilton A: (433) McGovern; Gordon, Tagliapietra, Garcia Tena, Kurakins; Docherty (Boyd 71), MacKinnon, Crawford; Longridge (Imrie 46), Nade, Kurtaj.
Referee: Don Robertson.

Ross Co (1) 2 *(Boyce 3, Gardyne 50)*
Ayr U (0) 0 1743
Ross Co: (442) Bachmann; Fraser, Boyd, Davies, Reckord; Gardyne (Holden 78), Irvine, McShane, De Vita (Dingwall 62); Graham, Boyce (Quinn R 82).
Ayr U: (451) Fleming; Devlin, McLauchlan, McCracken, Boyle; Gilmour, Docherty, Adams (Moore 58), Trouten (Forrest 23), Donald; Caldwell (Preston 46).
Referee: Craig Charleston.

St Mirren (2) 2 *(Gallagher 16, Mallan 45)*
Livingston (2) 3 *(Buchanan 41, Mullen 45, Gallagher 84)* 1568
St Mirren: (442) Langfield; Watson (Cuddihy 46), Baird, Kelly, Stewart; Morgan, Mallan, Goodwin (Carswell 44), Howieson (McMullan 59); Gallagher, Thompson.
Livingston: (4231) Jamieson; Millen (Sives 90), Gallagher, Gordon, Longridge (Georgiev 77); Cole, Hippolyte; Pitman, Mullen[*], Gibbons; Buchanan (White 90).
Referee: Brian Colvin.

Wednesday, 26 August 2015
Airdrieonians (0) 0
Rangers (3) 5 *(Clark 5, Halliday 14, Waghorn 15, Shiels 84, Tavernier 88)* 7006
Airdrieonians: (4411) Parry; Bain, Crighton, Lithgow, O'Neil; Stewart, Watt, Smith (Brown 72), Morton; Cox (Morgan 78); Prunty (Sumsky 60).
Rangers: (433) Foderingham; Tavernier, Kiernan, Ball, Wallace; Zelalem, Halliday (McKay 72), Shiels; Clark, Waghorn (Hardie 62), Oduwa.
Referee: Euan Anderson.

Hibernian (0) 1 *(Rumsby 54 (og))*
Stranraer (0) 0 5224
Hibernian: (4231) Oxley; McGregor, Hanlon, Fontaine, Stevenson; McGinn, Fyvie (Carmichael 63); Boyle, Henderson, McGeouch; Cummings (Keatings 84).
Stranraer: (4411) Brennan; Robertson, Rumsby, Mair, Pettigrew; McGuigan, Bell, Thomson (Aitken 67), Stirling; Cairney (Longworth 71); Malcolm (McGill 78).
Referee: Kevin Clancy.

THIRD ROUND

Tuesday, 22 September 2015

Dundee U (1) 3 *(Morris 35, Fraser 96, Spittal 99)*
Dunfermline Ath (1) 1 *(Paton 10)*   5174
Dundee U: (442) Zwick; McGowan, Morris, Durnan, Robson; Telfer (Spittal 61), Kuhl (Taggart 73), Fraser, Rankin; McKay, Bodul (Murray 73).
Dunfermline Ath: (442) Murdoch; Geggan, Martin, Richards-Everton, Talbot (McCabe 81); Paton, Falkingham, Byrne (Hopkirk 46), Cardle; Wallace (Moffat 68), El Bakhtaoui.
aet.
Referee: John Beaton.

Greenock Morton (1) 3 *(Samuel 11, 100, Tidser 112)*
Motherwell (0) 2 *(McDonald 90, Moult 116)*   2539
Greenock Morton: (442) Gaston; Kilday, O'Ware, Gasparotto, Pepper; Tidser, Miller (Lamie 86), Forbes, Sabajo (Barr 99); MacDonald (Johnstone 76), Samuel.
Motherwell: (451) Ripley; Law, McManus, Kennedy, Chalmers; Johnson, Grimshaw, Leitch, Taylor (Ainsworth 80), Thomas (McDonald 57); Robinson (Moult 57).
aet.
Referee: Greg Aitken.

Livingston (0) 0
Inverness CT (2) 2 *(Storey 12, Devine 43)*   644
Livingston: (442) Jamieson; Millen, Gallagher, Neill, Longridge; Glen (Currie 83), Pitman, Cole, Hippolyte (Georgiev 73); White (Buchanan 74), Mullen.
Inverness CT: (4231) Fon Williams; Raven, Devine, Meekings, Tremarco (Polworth 76); Draper, Tansey; Vincent (Mbuyi-Mutombo 87), Christie, Williams D; Storey (Lopez 87).
Referee: Alan Muir.

Rangers (0) 1 *(Tavernier 62)*
St Johnstone (2) 3 *(Davidson 19, Lappin 29, O'Halloran 46)*   27,094
Rangers: (433) Foderingham; Tavernier, Kiernan, Wilson, Wallace; Zelalem (McKay 75), Halliday (Law 75), Holt (Shiels 53); Miller, Waghorn, Oduwa.
St Johnstone: (4411) Mannus; Shaughnessy, Mackay, Scobbie, Easton; Wotherspoon, Davidson, Millar, Lappin (Craig 67); O'Halloran (Cummins 73); MacLean.
Referee: Kevin Clancy.

Ross Co (3) 7 *(Boyce 30, 35, 40, De Vita 46, Franks 54, Graham 58, Holden 81)*
Falkirk (0) 0   1341
Ross Co: (4411) Fox; Foster, Robertson, Boyd, Reckord; Franks (Holden 58), Irvine (Dingwall 72), Murdoch, De Vita; Boyce (McShane 63); Graham.
Falkirk: (442) Rogers; Vaulks, Watson, Grant, Leahy; Alston, Taiwo, Kerr (Muirhead 67), Sibbald; Blair (McHugh 46), Baird (Miller 46).
Referee: Stephen Finnie.

Wednesday, 23 September 2015

Celtic (1) 2 *(Commons 32, Johansen 87)*
Raith R (0) 0   13,591
Celtic: (4231) Gordon; Janko, Ambrose, Blackett, Tierney; Brown, Johansen; McGregor (Forrest 66), Commons (Rogic 66), Mackay-Steven; Ciftci (Nesbitt 89).
Raith R: (4411) Cuthbert; Thomson, Benedictus, Toshney, McKeown; Anderson (Megginson 75), Davidson (Daly 70), Matthews (McCord 79), Craigen; Wighton; Stewart.
Referee: John McKendrick.

Hibernian (0) 2 *(Cummings 82, Malonga 88)*
Aberdeen (0) 0   11,092
Hibernian: (352) Oxley; McGregor, Hanlon, Fontaine; Gray, McGeouch, McGinn, Henderson (Carmichael 62), Stevenson; Boyle (Bartley 89), Cummings (Malonga 85).
Aberdeen: (442) Ward; Logan, Considine, Taylor, Shinnie (McLaughlin 27); Flood (Pawlett 18), Jack, McLean, McGinn; Goodwillie (Parker 84), Rooney.
Referee: Steven McLean.

Kilmarnock (1) 2 *(Magennis 13, 80)*
Hearts (0) 3 *(Ozturk 74, Delgado 90, Nicholson 90)*   3249
Kilmarnock: (4231) Ridgers; O'Hara, Ashcroft, Balatoni, Findlay (Smith 26); Hamill, Slater; Higginbotham, Kiltie (Boyd 85), Obadeyi (Robinson 73); Magennis.
Hearts: (4231) Alexander; Paterson, Ozturk, Augustyn, Igor Rossi; Gomis, Buaben; Nicholson, Swanson (Delgado 58), King (Walker 52); Sow.
Referee: Craig Thomson.

QUARTER-FINALS

Tuesday, 27 October 2015

Greenock Morton (0) 1 *(Johnstone 52)*
St Johnstone (0) 3 *(MacLean 61 (pen), O'Halloran 63, Kane 83)*   2433
Greenock Morton: (442) Gaston; Russell, Kilday, Gasparotto, Pepper (Tidser 81); Miller, O'Ware, Forbes (Orr 86), Barr (Scullion 80); Johnstone, McCluskey.
St Johnstone: (442) Mannus; Shaughnessy, Easton, Anderson, Scobbie; O'Halloran (Wotherspoon 87), Craig, Davidson, Lappin; Cummins (Kane 76), MacLean.
Referee: Craig Thomson.

Inverness CT (0) 1 *(Tansey 78)*
Ross Co (1) 2 *(Irvine 41, Gardyne 48)*   3004
Inverness CT: (4231) Fon Williams; Raven (Sutherland 83), Devine, Meekings, Tremarco; Tansey, Polworth; Vincent, Christie, Vigurs (Williams D 62); Storey.
Ross Co: (442) Woods G; Fraser, Robertson, Davies, Reckord; Dingwall (Murdoch 80), Woods M, Irvine, Gardyne (Foster 86); Boyce, Curran (Schalk 87).
Referee: Steven McLean.

Wednesday, 28 October 2015

Hearts (0) 1 *(Djoum 90)*
Celtic (0) 2 *(Griffiths 71, Rogic 82)*   11,598
Hearts: (4231) Alexander; Paterson, Augustyn, Igor Rossi, McGhee; Buaben (Djoum 81), Gomis; King (Walker 53), Sow, Nicholson; Delgado (Reilly 87).
Celtic: (4141) Gordon; Lustig, Simunovic, Boyata, Izaguirre; Commons; Forrest (Rogic 59), Bitton, Johansen, Armstrong; Griffiths (Ciftci 83).
Referee: John Beaton.

Wednesday, 4 November 2015

Hibernian (1) 3 *(Gray 20, Cummings 61 (pen), Stevenson 90)*
Dundee U (0) 0   11,891
Hibernian: (442) Oxley; Gray, Fontaine, Hanlon, Stevenson; Keatings (Boyle 83), Fyvie, Henderson, McGinn (McGregor 68); Cummings, Malonga (El Alagui 86).
Dundee U: (451) Szromnik; Souttar, McGowan, Durnan, Dillon; Spittal, Rankin, Fraser, Kuhl (Murray 71), Taggart; McKay.
Referee: Willie Collum.

SEMI-FINALS

Saturday, 30 January 2016

Hibernian (1) 2 *(Cummings 29 (pen), McGinn 74)*

St Johnstone (1) 1 *(Shaughnessy 33)*   16,971

Hibernian: (4132) Oxley; Gray, Fontaine, Hanlon, Stevenson; Fyvie; McGinn, McGeouch, Henderson (McGregor 90); Dagnall, Cummings (Keatings 87).
St Johnstone: (442) Mannus; Shaughnessy, Mackay, Anderson, Easton (Scobbie 53); Wotherspoon (Sutton 78), Millar (Craig 71), Davidson, Lappin; O'Halloran, MacLean.
Referee: Steven McLean.

Sunday, 31 January 2016

Ross Co (1) 3 *(Woods M 15 (pen), Quinn P 48, Schalk 63)*

Celtic (1) 1 *(Mackay-Steven 1)*   22,130

Ross Co: (4141) Fox; Fraser, Quinn P, Davies, Foster; McShane; Murdoch (Franks 28), Irvine, Woods M, Gardyne (Boyce 83); Schalk (Graham 71).
Celtic: (4231) Gordon; Lustig, Ambrose■, Boyata, Tierney; Bitton (Brown 67), Johansen; Mackay-Steven, McGregor (Sviatchenko 14), Armstrong (Forrest 79); Griffiths.
Referee: Craig Thomson.

SCOTTISH LEAGUE CUP PRESENTED BY QTS FINAL 2016

Sunday, 13 March 2016

(at Hampden Park, attendance 38,796)

Hibernian (1) 1   Ross Co (1) 2

Hibernian: (442) Oxley; Gray, McGregor, Fontaine, Stevenson; Henderson, Bartley (Boyle 90), Thomson (Keatings 76), McGinn; Cummings, Stokes.
Scorer: Fontaine 45.

Ross Co: (442) Woods G; Fraser, Quinn P, Davies, Foster (Franks 85); Gardyne, Irvine, Woods M, McShane (Murdoch 79); Boyce (Graham 59), Schalk.
Scorers: Gardyne 25, Schalk 90.

Referee: Kevin Clancy.

Ross County's players celebrate winning the Scottish League Cup at Hampden Park on 13 March, the club's first
major trophy in senior football. Hibernian were defeated 2-1 in the final, courtesy of a last-minute winner.
(Jeff Holmes/PA Wire/Press Association Images)

PETROFAC TRAINING SCOTTISH LEAGUE CHALLENGE CUP 2015–16

■ *Denotes player sent off.*

FIRST ROUND NORTH

Saturday, 25 July 2015

Arbroath (0) 1 *(Grehan 72)*
Dunfermline Ath (3) 4 *(El Bakhtaoui 9, 28, Moffat 20,*   914
Wallace 62)
Arbroath: (442) Fleming; Wilson C, Hay, Little, Lowdon; Gold, Stewart, Clarke, Reid (Cecilia 63); Coult (Grehan 62), Linn.
Dunfermline Ath: (442) Murdoch; Williamson, Fordyce, Richards-Everton, Martin; Paton, Byrne, Geggan (Spence 80), Cardle; El Bakhtaoui (Wallace 55), Moffat (Thomas 70).
Referee: Nick Walsh.

Brechin C (0) 0
Peterhead (0) 3 *(Brown 57, 67, McAllister 75)*   346
Brechin C: (433) Smith G; Buchan, McCormack, Dods, McLean; Smith E, Molloy (Johnston 71), Dale; Thomson, Jackson A, Shields.
Peterhead: (442) Smith; Strachan, Ross, Gilchrist, Noble; Riley (Ferries 79), Dzierzawski, Brown, Stevenson (Blockley 71); McAllister, Sutherland (McIntosh 76).
Referee: Colin Steven.

Brora (0) 0
Alloa Ath (0) 1 *(Mitchell 49)*   265
Brora: (4411) Malin; Williamson, Munro, Houston, Macdonald; Maclean (Brindle 79), Gillespie, Kettlewell (Brittain 86), Graham (Greig 71); Mackay; Sutherland.
Alloa Ath: (4411) Crawford D; Williams, Paun, Hill, Hamilton; O'Brien, McManus, Flannigan (McAusland 79), Duffy; Mitchell; Ferns (Kader 80).
Referee: Matt Northcroft.

Cowdenbeath (0) 0
Raith R (1) 1 *(Vaughan 23)*   711
Cowdenbeath: (442) Andrews; Brett, Armstrong J, Donaldson, Yaqub; Orritt (Milne 67), Kane (Nish 78), Hughes, Johnston (Miller 84); Spence, Armstrong L.
Raith R: (4411) Cuthbert; Thomson, Toshney (Ford 67), Bates, McKeown; Anderson, McCord, Callachan, Craigen; Vaughan (Wighton 46); Stewart.
Referee: Kevin Clancy.

East Stirling (1) 2 *(Donaldson 30, McKenna 77)*
Stenhousemuir (2) 3 *(Stirling 35, 45, McMenamin 59)* 304
East Stirling: (352) Barnard; Greene, Townsley (Tully 40), Donaldson; Kinnaird, Wallace, McCabe, Faulds, Shepherd; McKenna, Carruthers (Wright 63).
Stenhousemuir: (442) Barclay; Meechan, Malcolm, Murray, Henderson; Cook, Stirling, Millar, Gilhaney; McMenamin, Smith (McShane 87).
Referee: Stephen Finnie.

Elgin C (1) 3 *(Gunn 42 (pen), Duff 60, Cameron 83)*
Stirling Alb (1) 2 *(Beattie 19, Cunningham 54)*   612
Elgin C: (442) Hurst; McLean, Gordon, Duff, McHardy; McKenzie, Nicolson (Bruce 62), Cameron, Moore; Gunn, MacLeod.
Stirling Alb: (4231) Smith C; Hamilton, Staunton, Smith R, Forsyth (Kouider-Aisser 90); Robertson, McGovern; Johnston (Comrie 72), Cunningham, Dickson (McKenzie 90); Beattie.
Referee: Ryan Milne.

Falkirk (1) 3 *(Grant 2, Baird 90, McHugh 90)*
East Fife (1) 1 *(Smith 14)*   1175
Falkirk: (442) Rogers; Muirhead, Watson, Grant, Leahy; Taiwo, Vaulks (Alston 54), Kerr, Sibbald (Smith 55); McHugh, Baird.

East Fife: (442) Goodfellow; Mullen, Page, MacGregor, Wilkie; Murray, Smith, Brown (Slattery 80), O'Kane; Austin N (Sutherland 72), Mercer.
Referee: Euan Anderson.

Forfar Ath (0) 1 *(Campbell 79)*
Montrose (0) 0   579
Forfar Ath: (442) Douglas; Baxter, Travis, O'Brien, Campbell; Malin (Templeman 58), Young, Nicoll, Denholm (Hodge 58); Smith (Hay 70), Swankie.
Montrose: (442) Millar; Masson, Reoch, Allan, Steeves; Ferguson, McCord, Watson, Reid (Milne 70); Johnston, Fraser.
Referee: Alan Newlands.

FIRST ROUND SOUTH

Saturday, 25 July 2015

Annan Ath (0) 3 *(Todd 51, 72, 74)*
Airdrieonians (1) 1 *(Crighton 11)*   553
Annan Ath: (343) Hart; Black, Watson P, Swinglehurst, Omar, McNiff, Sloan, Flynn; McColm (Osadolor 80), Weatherson, Todd.
Airdrieonians: (4312) Parry; Bain, Crighton, Lithgow, van Zanten; Stewart, McBride, Watt (McAleer 78); Sumsky (Morton 67); Morgan (Prunty 75), Cox.
Referee: David Munro.

Ayr U (1) 3 *(Trouten 39 (pen), Devlin 50, Caldwell 71)*
Albion R (0) 1 *(Love 90)*   1003
Ayr U: (4411) Fleming; Devlin, McLauchlan, Murphy (Nisbet 73), Boyle; Crawford, Docherty, Adams (Donald 57), Gilmour; Trouten (McCracken 74); Caldwell.
Albion R: (442) Lochhead; Reid, Dunlop R, Dunlop M, Turnbull; Willis (Love 63), Young, Fisher, Mullin; Barrowman (Gemmell 63), McBride (Ferry 72).
Referee: Gavin Ross.

Edinburgh City (0) 0
Queen's Park (0) 0   344
Edinburgh City: (442) Amos; McConnell, McKee, Mbu, Donaldson; Dunn (Carse 113), Guthrie (Muhsin 64), Gair, MacDonald; Osborne, Allum (Deniran 85).
Queen's Park: (442) Muir; McVey, Quinn, Gibson, Burns; Woods, Wharton, Berry, McLeish (McElroy 120); McKernon (Mortimer 103), Carter (Galt 68).
aet; Queen's Park won 3-1 on penalties.
Referee: Mike Roncone.

Greenock Morton (0) 2 *(Kilday 73, MacDonald 83 (pen))*
Dumbarton (2) 3 *(Gallagher 6, 30, Fleming 65)*   1418
Greenock Morton: (4411) Gaston; Pepper, Kilday, O'Ware (Cairnie 46), Russell; McCluskey, McKee (Stevenson 59), Forbes, Barr; Scullion (Orr 80); MacDonald.
Dumbarton: (4231) Brown; Taggart, Barr, Buchanan, Waters; Routledge, Gallagher (Smith 70); Lindsay, Cawley, Gibson; Fleming.
Referee: Craig Charleston.

Hibernian (1) 2 *(Stanton 14, Cummings 61 (pen))*
Rangers (2) 6 *(Tavernier 39, Waghorn 44, 47, Halliday 62,*   11,225
Miller 77, 82)
Hibernian: (352) Oxley; Fontaine, Hanlon, Forster (Allan S 53); Gray, Martin, Fyvie, Stanton, Stevenson; Cummings, Malonga (Allan L 24).
Rangers: (442) Foderingham; Tavernier, Kiernan, Wilson, Wallace; McKay, Halliday, Holt (Shiels 61), Templeton (Miller 62); Law, Waghorn (Clark 74).
Referee: Willie Collum.

Livingston (2) 2 *(Mullen 4, Hippolyte 17)*
Clyde (1) 1 *(Bolochoweckyj 35)* 741
Livingston: (4231) Jamieson; Millen, Sives, Gordon, Longridge; Gibbons, Pitman; Mullen (Neill 90), Buchanan (Glen 82), Hippolyte; White.
Clyde: (442) Gibson; Smith, McLaughlin M, Bolochoweckyj, Linton; Brisbane, Murray, McLaughlin S (Ferguson S 69), Mitchell (McQueen 89); Gormley (Campbell 72), Higgins S.
Referee: Crawford Allan.

Queen of the South (1) 2 *(Lyle 20, Conroy 90)*
Stranraer (0) 0 1229
Queen of the South: (442) Thomson; Kidd, Dowie, Higgins, Marshall; Conroy (Pickard 90), Jacobs, Millar, Russell (Smith A 90); Lyle (Hooper 77), Hilson.
Stranraer: (442) Brennan; Robertson, Keenan, Rumsby, Pettigrew; Stirling, Bell, Thomson, Cairney (Longworth 53); Malcolm (Rowan 79), McGuigan.
Referee: Bobby Madden.

St Mirren (1) 3 *(Thompson 19 (pen), Agnew 50, 61)*
Berwick R (1) 1 *(Henderson 6)* 2394
St Mirren: (4411) Ridgers; Naismith, Kelly, Baird, Conlan; Agnew, Carswell (Howieson 74), Mallan (Goodwin 67), Morgan; McMullan; Thompson (McLear 68).
Berwick R: (442) Walker K; McNeil, Wilson, Fairbairn, Beveridge; Banjo (Lavery 63), Cameron (Drummond 72), Graham, Coultress; Henderson, McKenna.
Referee: Alan Muir.

SECOND ROUND NORTH

Tuesday, 18 August 2015
Falkirk (2) 3 *(Smith 13, Watson 20, Cooper 76)*
Peterhead (3) 5 *(McAllister 22, 27, 43, 81, 87 (pen))* 1004
Falkirk: (442) Bowman; Muirhead (Cooper 75), Watson, McCracken, Leahy; Alston, Taiwo, Vaulks, Smith; Miller, McHugh (Baird 57).
Peterhead: (442) Smith; Blockley (Rodgers 70), Ross, Strachan, Gilchrist; Stevenson (Adams 77), Redman, Dzierzawski, Brown (Ferries 64); McAllister, McIntosh.
Referee: Brian Colvin.

Forfar Ath (0) 0
Dunfermline Ath (2) 3 *(Moffat 32 (pen), El Bakhtaoui 44, Moffat 82)* 1027
Forfar Ath: (442) Douglas; Baxter (Dunlop 54), Nicoll■, O'Brien, Campbell; Fotheringham, Young, Hodge, Denholm (Travis 35); Templeman (Hay 65), Swankie.
Dunfermline Ath: (442) Murdoch; Williamson, Fordyce, Richards-Everton, Martin; Paton (Falkingham 65), Geggan, Byrne, Cardle (Hopkirk 46); Moffat, El Bakhtaoui (Wallace 54).
Referee: Crawford Allan.

Stenhousemuir (0) 2 *(Cook 67, Stirling 71)*
Raith R (0) 0 449
Stenhousemuir: (4141) Barclay; McCormack, Malcolm, Murray, Henderson; Meechan; Cook, Stirling (McCroary 90), Robertson J, Smith (Eddington 90); McShane (McMenamin 79).
Raith R: (442) Cuthbert; Thomson■, Bates, Benedictus, Petrie; Anderson, Matthews (Stewart 65), Davidson, McCord (Callachan 72); Megginson, Wighton.
Referee: Greg Aitken.

Wednesday, 19 August 2015
Alloa Ath (0) 0
Elgin C (0) 2 *(Gunn 104 (pen), McKenzie 111 (pen))* 240
Alloa Ath: (4141) Crawford D; Williams, Reintam, Hill, Hoggan; Paun (Holmes 69); Ferns, Kader (Mitchell 60), McManus, Duffy; Layne (Chopra 82).

Elgin C: (442) Hurst; Cooper, Gordon, McHardy, MacPhee; McKenzie, Cameron, Nicolson, Moore (Halsman 114); Gunn (McLean 107), MacLeod (Bruce 120).
aet.
Referee: George Salmond.

SECOND ROUND SOUTH

Tuesday, 18 August 2015
Annan Ath (1) 1 *(Weatherson 1 (pen))*
St Mirren (0) 2 *(Stewart 50, Gow 66)* 794
Annan Ath: (3421) Hart; Black, Swinglehurst, McNiff; Omar, Sloan, Flynn (McDonald 83), McColm (Watson J 83); Todd, Osadolor; Weatherson.
St Mirren: (3412) Langfield; Kelly, Goodwin, Baird; Gow, McLear (McMullan 68), Mallan (Agnew 85), Howieson (Morgan 90); Cuddihy; Gallagher, Stewart.
Referee: Don Robertson.

Queen of the South (0) 0
Livingston (0) 1 *(White 115)* 1189
Queen of the South: (352) Thomson; Kidd, Brownlie, Higgins; Conroy, Pickard (Marshall 46), Hutton, Millar, Jacobs; Heffernan (Lyle 58), Hilson (Smith A 48).
Livingston: (442) Jamieson; Sives, Gordon, Gallagher, Longridge (Glen 102); Georgiev (Mullen 64), Pitman, Cole, Hippolyte; White, Sheerin (Buchanan 64).
aet.
Referee: Kevin Graham.

Queen's Park (0) 1 *(Bradley 95)*
Dumbarton (0) 0 587
Queen's Park: (343) Muir; Baty, Gibson, Wharton; Ralston, Berry, McKernon, Burns; Woods (McElroy 87), Mortimer (Bradley 46), Marlow (Carter 30).
Dumbarton: (433) Brown; Taggart, Graham, Buchanan, Waters (Docherty 58); Kirkpatrick (Craig 58), Routledge, Gallagher; Cawley, Smith (Gibson 59), Fleming.
aet.
Referee: Nick Walsh.

Wednesday, 19 August 2015
Ayr U (0) 0
Rangers (2) 2 *(Clark 15, McKay 43)* 7468
Ayr U: (4411) Fleming; Devlin, McLauchlan, Murphy, Boyle; Caldwell (Forrest 46), Docherty, Gilmour (Nisbet 75), Donald (Crawford 60); Trouten; Moore.
Rangers: (433) Foderingham; Tavernier (Aird 81), Ball, Wilson, Wallace; Holt, Oduwa, Shiels; Walsh (Law 59), Clark, McKay (Waghorn 73).
Referee: Stephen Finnie.

QUARTER-FINALS

Saturday, 10 October 2015
Peterhead (3) 3 *(Redman 17, McAllister 38, Noble 45)*
Stenhousemuir (0) 0 561
Peterhead: (442) Smith; Kerr, Strachan, Gilchrist, Noble; Redman, Dzierzawski, Brown (Ferries 63), Blockley (McIntosh 51); McAllister, Sutherland (Rodgers 70).
Stenhousemuir: (442) Barclay; McCormack, Malcolm, Paterson (Millar 77), Meechan; Gilhaney, Robertson J, Stirling (Marenghi 88), Cook; McShane (Eddington 12), Martinez.
Referee: Alan Muir.

Queen's Park (2) 2 *(McLeish 2, Duggan 18)*
Elgin C (0) 1 *(McHardy 50)* 497
Queen's Park: (433) Muir; Ralston, McGeever, Wharton, McLeish; McKernon, Berry, Galt (Burns 69); Woods, Duggan (Marlow 90), Carter (Bradley 78).
Elgin C: (442) Hurst; Cooper, Duff, Gordon, McHardy; McKenzie (McLaren 65), Cameron, MacPhee, Moore (Nicolson 46); Reilly (Gunn 46), MacLeod.
Referee: Nick Walsh.

St Mirren (3) 4 *(Gallagher 10, Mallan 23, 88, Agnew 37)*
Dunfermline Ath (0) 0 2339
St Mirren: (442) Langfield; Watson, Baird, Webster, Kelly; Mallan, Goodwin (Cuddihy 83), Agnew, Howieson; Thompson (McLear 71), Gallagher (Stewart 79).
Dunfermline Ath: (442) Murdoch; Rooney (McCabe 64), McAusland, Richards-Everton, Talbot; Paton, Geggan, Byrne, Cardle; Wallace (Hopkirk 46), El Bakhtaoui (Moffat 39).
Referee: George Salmond.

Tuesday, 20 October 2015
Rangers (0) 1 *(Clark 75)*
Livingston (0) 0 17,386
Rangers: (433) Foderingham; Tavernier, Ball, Kiernan, Wallace; Holt, Halliday, Law; Oduwa (Clark 46), Waghorn, McKay.
Livingston: (3412) McCallum; Neill, Gallagher, Gordon; Millen (Georgiev 85), Faria, Gibbons, Longridge; Glen (Currie 86); White, Buchanan (Sheerin 77).
Referee: Andrew Dallas.

SEMI-FINALS
Saturday, 14 November 2015
Queen's Park (1) 1 *(Woods 22 (pen))*
Peterhead (2) 2 *(McAllister 17, McIntosh 27)* 917
Queen's Park: (4231) Muir; Ralston, McGeever, Gibson (Galt 68), Burns; Berry, McKernon■; Baty (McLeish 59), Woods, Bradley; Duggan (Carter 85).
Peterhead: (442) Smith; Strachan, Ross, Sukar, Noble; Brown, Dzierzawski, Redman, Riley (Ferries 72); McAllister (Rodgers 90), McIntosh (Sutherland 76).
Referee: Don Robertson.

Saturday, 28 November 2015
Rangers (1) 4 *(Holt 34, Miller 77, Waghorn 84, Kelly 90 (og))*
St Mirren (0) 0 22,369
Rangers: (433) Foderingham; Tavernier, Kiernan, Wilson, Wallace; Holt (Shiels 63), Halliday, Zelalem; Waghorn, Miller (Hardie 78), McKay (Clark 63).
St Mirren: (4141) Langfield; Reid, Webster, Baird, Kelly; Carswell; McMullan (Morgan 46), Agnew, Mallan (Stewart 85), McLear (Thompson 72); Gallagher.
Referee: Bobby Madden.

PETROFAC TRAINING SCOTTISH LEAGUE CHALLENGE CUP FINAL 2016

Sunday, 10 April 2016

(at Hampden Park, attendance 48,133)

Rangers (2) 4   Peterhead (0) 0

Rangers: (433) Foderingham; Tavernier, Kiernan, Wilson, Wallace (O'Halloran 67); Holt, Ball, Halliday; Forrester (King 67), Miller, McKay (Shiels 78).
Scorers: Gilchrist 17 (og), Tavernier 40, Halliday 85 (pen), Miller 89.

Peterhead: (451) Smith; Strachan (Stevenson 26), Ross, Gilchrist, Noble; Redman (McIntosh 64), Ferry, Dzierzawski, Brown, Sutherland (Riley 58); McAllister.

Referee: George Salmond.

LEAGUE CHALLENGE FINALS 1991–2016

B&Q CENTENARY CUP

1990–91	Dundee v Ayr U	3-2*

B&Q CUP

1991–92	Hamilton A v Ayr U	1-0
1992–93	Hamilton A v Morton	3-2
1993–94	Falkirk v St Mirren	3-0
1994–95	Airdrieonians v Dundee	3-2*

SCOTTISH LEAGUE CHALLENGE CUP

1995–96	Stenhousemuir v Dundee U	0-0*
	Stenhousemuir won 5-4 on penalties.	
1996–97	Stranraer v St Johnstone	1-0
1997–98	Falkirk v Queen of the South	1-0
1998–99	*No competition.*	
	Suspended due to lack of sponsorship.	

BELL'S CHALLENGE CUP

1999–2000	Alloa Ath v Inverness CT	4-4*
	Alloa Ath won 5-4 on penalties.	
2000–01	Airdrieonians v Livingston	2-2*
	Airdrieonians won 3-2 on penalties.	
2001–02	Airdrieonians v Alloa Ath	2-1

BELL'S CUP

2002–03	Queen of the South v Brechin C	2-0
2003–04	Inverness CT v Airdrie U	2-0
2004–05	Falkirk v Ross Co	2-1
2005–06	St Mirren v Hamilton A	2-1

SCOTTISH LEAGUE CHALLENGE CUP

2006–07	Ross Co v Clyde	1-1*
	Ross Co won 5-4 on penalties.	
2007–08	St Johnstone v Dunfermline Ath	3-2

ALBA CHALLENGE CUP

2008–09	Airdrie U v Ross Co	2-2*
	Airdrie U won 3-2 on penalties.	
2009–10	Dundee v Inverness CT	3-2
2010–11	Ross Co v Queen of the South	2-0

RAMSDENS CUP

2011–12	Falkirk v Hamilton A	1-0
2012–13	Queen of the South v Partick Thistle	1-1*
	Queen of the South won 6-5 on penalties.	
2013–14	Raith R v Rangers	1-0*

PETROFAC TRAINING SCOTTISH LEAGUE CHALLENGE CUP

2014–15	Livingston v Alloa Athletic	4-0
2015–16	Rangers v Peterhead	4-0

*After extra time.

SCOTTISH CUP FINALS 1874–2016

SCOTTISH FA CUP

Year	Match	Score
1874	Queen's Park v Clydesdale	2-0
1875	Queen's Park v Renton	3-0
1876	Queen's Park v Third Lanark	1-1
Replay	Queen's Park v Third Lanark	2-0
1877	Vale of Leven v Rangers	1-1
Replay	Vale of Leven v Rangers	1-1
2nd Replay	Vale of Leven v Rangers	3-2
1878	Vale of Leven v Third Lanark	1-0
1879	Vale of Leven v Rangers	1-1
	Vale of Leven awarded cup, Rangers failing to appear for replay.	
1880	Queen's Park v Thornliebank	3-0
1881	Queen's Park v Dumbarton	2-1
Replay	Queen's Park v Dumbarton	3-1
	After Dumbarton protested the first game.	
1882	Queen's Park v Dumbarton	2-2
Replay	Queen's Park v Dumbarton	4-1
1883	Dumbarton v Vale of Leven	2-2
Replay	Dumbarton v Vale of Leven	2-1
1884	Queen's Park v Vale of Leven	
	Queen's Park awarded cup, Vale of Leven failing to appear.	
1885	Renton v Vale of Leven	0-0
Replay	Renton v Vale of Leven	3-1
1886	Queen's Park v Renton	3-1
1887	Hibernian v Dumbarton	2-1
1888	Renton v Cambuslang	6-1
1889	Third Lanark v Celtic	3-0
Replay	Third Lanark v Celtic	2-1
	Replay by order of Scottish FA because of playing conditions in first match.	
1890	Queen's Park v Vale of Leven	1-1
Replay	Queen's Park v Vale of Leven	2-1
1891	Hearts v Dumbarton	1-0
1892	Celtic v Queen's Park	1-0
Replay	Celtic v Queen's Park	5-1
	After mutually protested first match.	
1893	Queen's Park v Celtic	0-1
Replay	Queen's Park v Celtic	2-1
	Replay by order of Scottish FA because of playing conditions in first match.	
1894	Rangers v Celtic	3-1
1895	St Bernard's v Renton	2-1
1896	Hearts v Hibernian	3-1
1897	Rangers v Dumbarton	5-1
1898	Rangers v Kilmarnock	2-0
1899	Celtic v Rangers	2-0
1900	Celtic v Queen's Park	4-3
1901	Hearts v Celtic	4-3
1902	Hibernian v Celtic	1-0
1903	Rangers v Hearts	1-1
Replay	Rangers v Hearts	0-0
2nd Replay	Rangers v Hearts	2-0
1904	Celtic v Rangers	3-2
1905	Third Lanark v Rangers	0-0
Replay	Third Lanark v Rangers	3-1
1906	Hearts v Third Lanark	1-0
1907	Celtic v Hearts	3-0
1908	Celtic v St Mirren	5-1
1909	Celtic v Rangers	2-2
Replay	Celtic v Rangers	1-1
	Owing to riot, the cup was withheld.	
1910	Dundee v Clyde	2-2
Replay	Dundee v Clyde	0-0*
2nd Replay	Dundee v Clyde	2-1
1911	Celtic v Hamilton A	0-0
Replay	Celtic v Hamilton A	2-0
1912	Celtic v Clyde	2-0
1913	Falkirk v Raith R	2-0
1914	Celtic v Hibernian	0-0
Replay	Celtic v Hibernian	4-1
1920	Kilmarnock v Albion R	3-2
1921	Partick Thistle v Rangers	1-0
1922	Morton v Rangers	1-0
1923	Celtic v Hibernian	1-0
1924	Airdrieonians v Hibernian	2-0
1925	Celtic v Dundee	2-1
1926	St Mirren v Celtic	2-0
1927	Celtic v East Fife	3-1
1928	Rangers v Celtic	4-0
1929	Kilmarnock v Rangers	2-0
1930	Rangers v Partick Thistle	0-0
Replay	Rangers v Partick Thistle	2-1
1931	Celtic v Motherwell	2-2
Replay	Celtic v Motherwell	4-2
1932	Rangers v Kilmarnock	1-1
Replay	Rangers v Kilmarnock	3-0
1933	Celtic v Motherwell	1-0
1934	Rangers v St Mirren	5-0
1935	Rangers v Hamilton A	2-1
1936	Rangers v Third Lanark	1-0
1937	Celtic v Aberdeen	2-1
1938	East Fife v Kilmarnock	1-1
Replay	East Fife v Kilmarnock	4-2*
1939	Clyde v Motherwell	4-0
1947	Aberdeen v Hibernian	2-1
1948	Rangers v Morton	1-1*
Replay	Rangers v Morton	1-0*
1949	Rangers v Clyde	4-1
1950	Rangers v East Fife	3-0
1951	Celtic v Motherwell	1-0
1952	Motherwell v Dundee	4-0
1953	Rangers v Aberdeen	1-1
Replay	Rangers v Aberdeen	1-0
1954	Celtic v Aberdeen	2-1
1955	Clyde v Celtic	1-1
Replay	Clyde v Celtic	1-0
1956	Hearts v Celtic	3-1
1957	Falkirk v Kilmarnock	1-1
Replay	Falkirk v Kilmarnock	2-1*
1958	Clyde v Hibernian	1-0
1959	St Mirren v Aberdeen	3-1
1960	Rangers v Kilmarnock	2-0
1961	Dunfermline Ath v Celtic	0-0
Replay	Dunfermline Ath v Celtic	2-0
1962	Rangers v St Mirren	2-0
1963	Rangers v Celtic	1-1
Replay	Rangers v Celtic	3-0
1964	Rangers v Dundee	3-1
1965	Celtic v Dunfermline Ath	3-2
1966	Rangers v Celtic	0-0
Replay	Rangers v Celtic	1-0
1967	Celtic v Aberdeen	2-0
1968	Dunfermline Ath v Hearts	3-1
1969	Celtic v Rangers	4-0
1970	Aberdeen v Celtic	3-1
1971	Celtic v Rangers	1-1
Replay	Celtic v Rangers	2-1
1972	Celtic v Hibernian	6-1
1973	Rangers v Celtic	3-2
1974	Celtic v Dundee U	3-0
1975	Celtic v Airdrieonians	3-1
1976	Rangers v Hearts	3-1
1977	Celtic v Rangers	1-0
1978	Rangers v Aberdeen	2-1
1979	Rangers v Hibernian	0-0
Replay	Rangers v Hibernian	0-0*
2nd Replay	Rangers v Hibernian	3-2*
1980	Celtic v Rangers	1-0*
1981	Rangers v Dundee U	0-0*
Replay	Rangers v Dundee U	4-1
1982	Aberdeen v Rangers	4-1*
1983	Aberdeen v Rangers	1-0*
1984	Aberdeen v Celtic	2-1*
1985	Celtic v Dundee U	2-1
1986	Aberdeen v Hearts	3-0
1987	St Mirren v Dundee U	1-0*
1988	Celtic v Dundee U	2-1
1989	Celtic v Rangers	1-0

TENNENTS SCOTTISH CUP

1990	Aberdeen v Celtic	0-0*
	Aberdeen won 9-8 on penalties.	
1991	Motherwell v Dundee U	4-3*
1992	Rangers v Airdrieonians	2-1
1993	Rangers v Aberdeen	2-1
1994	Dundee U v Rangers	1-0
1995	Celtic v Airdrieonians	1-0
1996	Rangers v Hearts	5-1
1997	Kilmarnock v Falkirk	1-0
1998	Hearts v Rangers	2-1
1999	Rangers v Celtic	1-0
2000	Rangers v Aberdeen	4-0
2001	Celtic v Hibernian	3-0
2002	Rangers v Celtic	3-2
2003	Rangers v Dundee	1-0
2004	Celtic v Dunfermline Ath	3-1
2005	Celtic v Dundee U	1-0
2006	Hearts v Gretna	1-1*
	Hearts won 4-2 on penalties.	
2007	Celtic v Dunfermline Ath	1-0

SCOTTISH FA CUP

2008	Rangers v Queen of the South	3-2

HOMECOMING SCOTTISH CUP

2009	Rangers v Falkirk	1-0

ACTIVE NATION SCOTTISH CUP

2010	Dundee U v Ross Co	3-0

SCOTTISH FA CUP

2011	Celtic v Motherwell	3-0

WILLIAM HILL SCOTTISH CUP

2012	Hearts v Hibernian	5-1
2013	Celtic v Hibernian	3-0
2014	St Johnstone v Dundee U	2-0
2015	Inverness CT v Falkirk	2-1
2016	Hibernian v Rangers	3-2

After extra time.

SCOTTISH CUP WINS

Celtic 36, Rangers 33, Queen's Park 10, Hearts 8, Aberdeen 7, Clyde 3, Hibernian 3, Kilmarnock 3, St Mirren 3, Vale of Leven 3, Dundee U 2, Dunfermline Ath 2, Falkirk 2, Motherwell 2, Renton 2, Third Lanark 2, Airdrieonians 1, Dumbarton 1, Dundee 1, East Fife 1, Inverness CT 1, Morton 1, Partick Thistle 1, St Bernard's 1, St Johnstone 1.

APPEARANCES IN FINAL

Celtic 54, Rangers 51, Aberdeen 15, Hearts 14, Hibernian 14, Queen's Park 12, Dundee U 10, Kilmarnock 8, Motherwell 7, Vale of Leven 7, Clyde 6, Dumbarton 6, St Mirren 6, Third Lanark 6, Dundee 5, Dunfermline Ath 5, Falkirk 5, Renton 5, Airdrieonians 4, East Fife 3, Hamilton A 2, Morton 2, Partick Thistle 2, Albion R 1, Cambuslang 1, Clydesdale 1, Gretna 1, Inverness CT 1, Queen of the South 1, Raith R 1, Ross Co 1, St Bernard's 1, St Johnstone 1, Thornliebank 1.

WILLIAM HILL SCOTTISH CUP 2015–16

Denotes player sent off.

FIRST PRELIMINARY ROUND

Civil Service Strollers v Newton Stewart	3-0
Golspie Sutherland v Cove Rangers	1-6
Harestanes v Girvan	0-3
St Cuthbert Wndrs v Burntisland Shipyard	3-1
Wigtown & Bladnoch v Vale of Leithen	1-0

SECOND PRELIMINARY ROUND

Civil Service Strollers v Kelty Hearts	0-4
Hermes v Auchinleck Talbot	0-4
Wigton & Bladnoch v Hawick Royal Albert	2-3
Lothian Thistle v Girvan	2-2, 5-2
Cove Rangers v St Cuthbert Wanderers	7-2

FIRST ROUND

Banks O'Dee v Cove Rangers	2-3
BSC Glasgow v Auchinleck Talbot	2-2, 0-5
Buckie Thistle v Rothes	7-0
Deveronvale v Clachnacuddin	0-5
Formartine United v Gretna 2008	3-1
Fraserburgh v Dalbeattie Star	3-2
Gala Fairydean v Linlithgow Rose	0-2
Hawick Royal Albert v Huntly	0-3
Keith v Inverurie Loco Works	1-5
Lossiemouth v Forres Mechanics	1-4
Lothian Thistle v Kelty Hearts	3-0
Nairn County v Selkirk	5-1
Preston Athletic v Fort William	2-3
Spartans v Coldstream	5-1
Strathspey Thistle v Edinburgh University	1-2
Threave Rovers v Stirling University	1-3
Wick Academy v Whitehill Welfare	2-2, 3-2
Cumbernauld Colts v Glasgow Univ	3-0

SECOND ROUND

Annan Ath v Berwick R	4-1
Brora Rangers v Arbroath	1-2
Clachnacuddin v Linlithgow Rose	1-3
Cumbernauld Colts v Auchinleck Talbot	2-0
East Fife v Stirling Alb	0-0, 0-1
East Kilbride v Forres Mechanics	1-1, 3-2
Edinburgh City v Buckie Thistle	1-2
Elgin C v Spartans	1-0
Formartine United v Clyde	2-0
Huntly v East Stirling	2-1
Inverurie Loco Works v Edinburgh University	2-1
Lothian Thistle v Montrose	1-1, 2-1
Nairn County v Wick Academy	2-2, 1-5
Stirling University v Queen's Park	0-2
Turriff United v Fraserburgh	2-3
Fort William v Cove Rangers	0-4

THIRD ROUND

Saturday, 28 November 2015

Airdrieonians (2) 3 *(Morgan 5, 25, Prunty 70)*
Brechin C (1) 1 *(Jackson A 13)*   532
Airdrieonians: (442) Parry; Bain, Crighton, Lithgow, van Zanten; Cox, Watt, Fitzpatrick, Cadden; Prunty (Brown 89), Morgan (Hunter 82).
Brechin C: (352) Smith G; Dods, McCormack, Perry (Fusco 38); McLean, Dale (Thomson 69), Molloy, Tiffoney (Smith E 82), Dyer; Layne, Jackson A.
Referee: Euan Anderson.

Albion R (0) 0
Greenock Morton (1) 2 *(Johnstone 41, McKee 88)*   505
Albion R: (451) Stewart; Reid, Dunlop M, Dunlop R, Turnbull; Willis, McBride, Davidson, Fisher, Love (Gemmell 75); Barrowman (McRobbie 83).
Greenock Morton: (442) Adam; Pepper, O'Ware, Gasparotto, Russell; McKee, Miller (Kilday 46), Forbes, Barr; Johnstone, Samuel (Orr 79).
Referee: Greg Aitken.

Ayr U (0) 0
Dunfermline Ath (1) 1 *(Geggan 22)*   1576
Ayr U: (442) Fleming; Muir, McLauchlan, Graham, Boyle; Donald (Crawford 55), Docherty, Adams, Forrest (Caldwell 46); Preston (Gilmour 62), Trouten.

Dunfermline Ath: (442) Murdoch; Martin, McAusland, Richards-Everton, Talbot; Paton, Geggan, Falkingham, Cardle; Moffat, El Bakhtaoui.
Referee: Kevin Clancy.

Cowdenbeath (0) 1 *(Johnston 73)*
Arbroath (0) 1 *(Whatley 56)*   409
Cowdenbeath: (442) Sneddon; Donaldson, Kerr, El-Zubaidi, Adamson; Brett (Johnston 66), Miller, Murdoch, Callaghan (Kane 67); Smith, Spence.
Arbroath: (451) Fleming; Wilson C, Little, Munro, Lowdon; Linn, Gold (Clarke 84), Whatley, Watson, Ramsay; Rutherford G.
Referee: Brian Colvin.

Elgin C (0) 1 *(Halsman 90)*
Raith R (1) 2 *(McCord 39 (pen), Anderson 54)*   853
Elgin C: (4411) Black; Cooper, Nicolson, McHardy, MacPhee; McLaren (McKenzie 64), Cameron, Reilly, Moore (McLean 64); Easton (Halsman 87); Gunn.
Raith R: (442) Cuthbert; Bates, Davidson, Benedictus, McKeown; Anderson (Callachan 65), McCord (Matthews 89), Robertson, Craigen; Daly, Stewart.
Referee: George Salmond.

Falkirk (1) 4 *(Miller 16, 74, 84, Vaulks 70)*
Fraserburgh (0) 1 *(Lawrence 67)*   1825
Falkirk: (442) Tokarczyk; Sinnamon, Grant, Muirhead, Leahy (Gallacher 85); Sibbald, Vaulks, Blair (Smith 68), Alston; Baird (O'Hara 80), Miller.
Fraserburgh: (4411) Barbour; Dickson, Hay, McBride, Cowie R; Cowie D, Christie, Chalmers (Cooper 82), Lawrence (Davidson 76); West; Johnston (Noble 86).
Referee: Alan Newlands.

Formartine United (1) 1 *(Barbour 45)*
Cove Rangers (0) 1 *(Nicol 79)*   376
Formartine United: (442) Reid; Dingwall, Crawford*, Lawson, Smith; Rodger (Michie 88), Wood, Anderson, Barbour (Bagshaw 88); Keith (Gauld 80), Masson.
Cove Rangers: (442) McKenzie; Redford, Watson, Kelly, Walker; Scully, Yule, Duff, Nicol; Watt (Milne 61), Park (Smith S 88).
Referee: Scott Millar.

Huntly (1) 1 *(Booth 39)*
Lothian Thistle (0) 1 *(Gormley 70)*   239
Huntly: (442) Hobday; Allan, Clark, Wood, Urquhart; Thoirs, McCulloch, Cruickshank, Murison; Booth, Donaldson (Dorrat 64).
Lothian Thistle: (451) Swain; Moore, Wilkes, Crawford, Taylor-Mackenzie; Brown (Kerr 75), Cummings, Mearns*, Smith (O'Donnell 66), Hare; Gormley (Hendry 81).
Referee: Gavin Ross.

Inverurie Loco Works (1) 4 *(McLean 37, 90, Hunter 53, Laing 68)*
Annan Ath (1) 4 *(Weatherson 3, 89, Swinglehurst 70, McColm 73)*   340
Inverurie Loco Works: (442) Mathieson; Jeffrey, Adams, Broadhurst, Forsyth; Laing, Begg (Souter 76), McLean, Maitland; Hunter (McCabe 75), Mitchell.
Annan Ath: (352) Hart; Watson P, Black (McDonald 61), Swinglehurst; McColm, Watson J (Sloan 61), Finnie, Flynn, McNiff; Omar, Weatherson.
Referee: Steven Reid.

Peterhead (0) 1 *(McAllister 90 (pen))*
Livingston (2) 3 *(Glen 14, White 25, 74)*   587
Peterhead: (442) Smith; Blockley, Redman, Strachan, Noble; Brown (Ferries 75), Dzierzawski, Ferry, Riley (Sutherland 60); McAllister, McIntosh (Rodgers 75).
Livingston: (442) McCallum; Neill, Gordon, Gallagher, Longridge (Currie 83); Pitman, Faria (Hippolyte 76), Gibbons, Glen (Sheerin 83); Buchanan, White.
Referee: Crawford Allan.

Queen's Park (1) 1 *(Duggan 30)*

Forfar Ath (0) 1 *(Denholm 60)* 418

Queen's Park: (4231) Muir; Mitchell, McGeever, Gibson, Burns; Berry, McKernon; Woods (McElroy 88), Galt, McLeish; Duggan (Bradley 88).
Forfar Ath: (442) Douglas; Baxter, Nicoll, O'Brien, Campbell; Fotheringham (Smith 46), Young, Hodge, Denholm (Kennedy 88); Templeman (Hay 77), Swankie.
Referee: John McKendrick.

Stenhousemuir (0) 2 *(Scotland 73, Malcolm 90)*

East Kilbride (1) 2 *(Coll 36, Winter 59)* 502

Stenhousemuir: (442) Gould; McCormack (Small 72), Malcolm, Meechan, Paterson; Gilhaney, Millar, Stirling (Robertson J 72), Cook (Marenghi 72); McMenamin, Scotland.
East Kilbride: (442) McGinley; Lachlan, Russell, Howie, Coll; Hastings, McBride, Winter (Gebbie 87), Johnstone (Templeton 80); Smith J (Gormley 71), Smith R.
Referee: Kevin Graham.

Stranraer (1) 3 *(Nequecaur 13, McGuigan 54, Thomson 72)*

Buckie Thistle (0) 1 *(Napier 55)* 415

Stranraer: (442) McGurn; Pettigrew, Rumsby, Bell, Barron (McCloskey 85); McGuigan (McGill 77), Robertson, Thomson, Cairney (Turner 80); Malcolm, Nequecaur.
Buckie Thistle: (442) Sim; Wood (Hodge 56), Hegarty, MacKinnon, Carroll; Fraser K, Munro, Angus■, Napier (Taylor 81); Wyness (Copeland 73), Ross.
Referee: Barry Cook.

Tuesday, 1 December 2015

Stirling Alb (2) 6 *(Doris 15, 49, Dickson 22, Beattie 73, 90, Lander 83)*

Cumbernauld Colts (0) 0 511

Stirling Alb: (442) Smith C; Verlaque, McGeachie, Forsyth, McKinlay; Lamont, Robertson, Mazel (Comrie 61), Dickson; Doris (Beattie 69), Smith D (Lander 75).
Cumbernauld Colts: (442) Doohan; Duncan, Kirwan, Munn (Black 52), Oliver; Ward, Ballantyne (Brown 73), Barclay, Broadfoot (Tilley 57); Selkirk, O'Neill.
Referee: Don Robertson.

Tuesday, 8 December 2015

Dumbarton (2) 5 *(McCallum D 1, Fleming 14, Kirkpatrick 78, 90, Waters 90)*

Alloa Ath (0) 0 274

Dumbarton: (442) Brown; Buchanan, Barr, Wright, Docherty; Gallagher, Routledge, Lindsay, Cawley (Hopkins 87); Fleming (Waters 80), McCallum D (Kirkpatrick 67).
Alloa Ath: (442) McNeil; Doyle, Reintam, Hill, Hamilton; Flannigan, McManus, Holmes, Hetherington (Ferns 60); Crawford R (Chopra 29 (McAusland 87)), Duffy.
Referee: Stephen Finnie.

Wednesday, 16 December 2015

Wick Academy (1) 2 *(Macadie 41 (pen), Allan D 90)*

Linlithgow Rose (1) 2 *(Strickland 27, Kelbie 50)* 634

Wick Academy: (442) McCarthy; Mackay D, Farquhar, Steven M, Campbell; Anderson, Mackay S, Pickles, Macadie (Allan R 69); Weir, Allan D.
Linlithgow Rose: (433) Adams; Thom, Baptie, McKenzie, Gray; MacLennan, Robertson, Kelbie; Strickland, Shirra, Coyne.
Referee: Don Robertson.

THIRD ROUND REPLAYS

Saturday, 5 December 2015

Cove Rangers (2) 4 *(Watt 17, Park 41, Yule 72, Milne 82)*

Formartine United (0) 1 *(Gauld 52)* 450

Cove Rangers: (442) McCafferty; Redford, Watson, Kelly, Duff; Park, Yule, Scully (Burnett 70), Watt (Milne 77); Walker, Nicol (Smith J 87).
Formartine United: (442) Reid; Michie, Smith, Anderson, Dingwall; Rodger (Bagshaw 77), Wood, Masson, Barbour; Gauld, Keith.
Referee: Alan Newlands.

East Kilbride (1) 2 *(Smith J 6, 101)*

Stenhousemuir (1) 1 *(McMenamin 31)* 488

East Kilbride: (442) McGinley; Lachlan, Howie, Russell, Coll; Winter, McBride, Smith R, Brady (Gormley 103); Smith J (Gebbie 115), Hastings.
Stenhousemuir: (442) Barclay; Meechan, Malcolm, Murray, Paterson; Gilhaney (Small 75), Robertson J, Millar, Cook■; McMenamin, Scotland.
aet.
Referee: Kevin Graham.

Forfar Ath (1) 2 *(Travis 45, Templeman 77)*

Queen's Park (0) 1 *(McKernon 52)* 520

Forfar Ath: (442) Douglas; Baxter, Nicoll, Travis (Kennedy 68), Campbell; Denholm, Young, Hodge, Swankie; Hay (Fotheringham 85), Templeman (Smith 90).
Queen's Park: (3421) Muir; Wharton, McGeever, Gibson (Bradley 84); Mitchell, McKernon, Berry, Burns; Woods (Hynes 87), Galt; Duggan (McElroy 89).
Referee: John McKendrick.

Monday, 7 December 2015

Arbroath (1) 2 *(Linn 42, 51)*

Cowdenbeath (4) 4 *(Spence 14, Callaghan 21, Brett 37, 40 (pen))* 500

Arbroath: (442) Fleming; Wilson C, Little, Munro, Lowdon (Reid 85); Gold (Hester 79), Whatley, Watson, Ramsay; Linn, Rutherford G (Grehan 59).
Cowdenbeath: (442) Sneddon; Donaldson, Scullion, Kerr, Adamson; Miller (Hughes 23), Brett, Murdoch, Callaghan; Spence (Beaumont 89), Smith (Johnston 90).
Referee: Craig Charleston.

Lothian Thistle (1) 3 *(Taylor-Mackenzie 22, Kerr 54, Smith 83 (pen))*

Huntly (0) 0 365

Lothian Thistle: (442) Swain; Moore, Smith, Crawford, Taylor-Mackenzie; Brown, Wilkes, Cummings, Hare (Hendry 79); Gormley (O'Donnell 79), Kerr (McDonagh 73).
Huntly: (442) Hobday■; Allan, Wood, McCulloch, Urquhart; Murison (Scoular 65), Clark, Cruickshank (Grant 84), Davidson; Booth (Duguid 84), Donaldson.
Referee: Grant Irvine.

Tuesday, 8 December 2015

Annan Ath (1) 1 *(Weatherson 44)*

Inverurie Loco Works (0) 0 287

Annan Ath: (3412) Hart; Watson P, Black, Swinglehurst; Finnie, Sloan, Flynn, McNiff; Gilfillan; Weatherson, Osadolor (McColm 74).
Inverurie Loco Works: (442) Mathieson; Jeffrey (Crisp 82), Adams, Souter, Forsyth; Laing, Begg (McCabe 72), McLean, Maitland; Hunter, Mitchell.
Referee: Steven Reid.

Tuesday, 22 December 2015

Linlithgow Rose (3) 5 *(Weir 20, Baptie 32, Strickland 36, MacLennan 52, 66)*

Wick Academy (1) 1 *(Mackay S 4)* 1200

Linlithgow Rose: (41212) Adams; Thom, McKenzie, Leiper, Baptie; MacLennan; Weir (Kelbie 71), Batchelor; Shirra; Strickland, Coyne (Robertson 77).
Wick Academy: (4141) McCarthy; Steven M, Steven G, Farquhar, Mackay D; Campbell■; Allan D■, Mackay S, Manson (Macadie 78), Anderson (Hughes 85); Weir (MacGregor 67).
Referee: Nick Walsh.

FOURTH ROUND

Friday, 8 January 2016

St Mirren (0) 1 *(Watson 88)*

Partick Thistle (0) 2 *(Seaborne 62, Amoo 73)* 4572

St Mirren: (4231) Langfield; Watson, Baird, Webster, Kelly; Carswell (Stewart 29), Agnew; McMullan (Gallagher 46), Mallan, Howieson (Thompson 77); Shankland.
Partick Thistle: (4231) Cerny; Miller, Lindsay, Seaborne, Booth; Osman, Welsh; Amoo, Bannigan, Lawless; Doolan (Nisbet 86).
Referee: Craig Thomson.

Saturday, 9 January 2016

Airdrieonians (0) 0

Dundee U (0) 1 *(Spittal 79)*　　　　　　2330

Airdrieonians: (442) Ferguson; Bain, Lithgow, Crighton, O'Neil; Cox (Morgan 83), Watt, Fitzpatrick, Cadden; Lister (Mackin 59), Prunty (Brown 83).
Dundee U: (3421) Kawashima; Donaldson (Paton 87), Dillon, Durnan; Spittal, Demel, Rankin, Dixon; Fraser, Erskine (Riski 67); McKay.
Referee: Greg Aitken.

Annan Ath (1) 4 *(Flynn 6, Todd 47, Omar 66, 71)*
Hamilton A (0) 1 *(Docherty 65)*　　　　　817

Annan Ath: (3142) Hart; Black, Watson P, McNiff; McStay (Osadolor 68); Finnie, Sloan, Flynn (Park 90), Omar; Todd, Weatherson (McDonald 88).
Hamilton A: (442) McGovern; Gillespie, Gordon, Garcia Tena, Devlin; Docherty (Lyon 86), MacKinnon, Redmond (Mandiangu 57), Crawford; D'Acol (Morris 71), Brophy.
Referee: Barry Cook.

Dumbarton (1) 2 *(Fleming 17, 57)*
Queen of the South (0) 1 *(Lyle 52)*　　　680

Dumbarton: (451) Brown; Saunders, Buchanan, Wright, Waters (Taggart 75); Cawley (Kirkpatrick 86), Gallagher, Routledge, Lindsay, Docherty; Fleming (Craig 89).
Queen of the South: (352) Thomson; Dowie, Higgins (Brownlie 67), Marshall; Kidd (Pickard 83), Hutton, Millar, Jacobs (Harris 72), Russell; Lyle, Oliver.
Referee: George Salmond.

Dunfermline Ath (1) 2 *(El Bakhtaoui 15, McKay 56)*
Ross Co (2) 2 *(Schalk 4, Graham 27 (pen))*　3439

Dunfermline Ath: (442) Murdoch; Rooney, McKay, Richards-Everton, Talbot; Paton, Geggan, Falkingham, Cardle; Moffat, El Bakhtaoui.
Ross Co: (442) Fox; Fraser (Foster 62), Boyd, Davies, Reckord; Gardyne, Woods M, Irvine, De Vita (Franks 62); Graham, Schalk (McShane 73).
Referee: Alan Muir.

Hearts (1) 1 *(Paterson 3)*
Aberdeen (0) 0　　　　　　　　　　　13,595

Hearts: (4231) Alexander; Paterson, Ozturk, Augustyn, Igor Rossi; Pallardo, Buaben; Nicholson (King 70), Djoum, Sow (McGhee 88); Reilly (Delgado 80).
Aberdeen: (442) Ward; Logan, Taylor, Reynolds, Considine (Goodwillie 71); Hayes, McLean, Flood (Pawlett 38), Shinnie; Rooney, McGinn.
Referee: John Beaton.

Linlithgow Rose (1) 3 *(MacLennan 39, McKenzie 65, Weir 66)*
Forfar Ath (1) 3 *(Travis 32, Campbell 50 (pen), Swankie 53)*　　　　　　　　　　　2153

Linlithgow Rose: (4132) Adams; Thom■, McKenzie, Leiper, Baptie (Tyrell 56); MacLennan; Weir (Gray 75), Shirra, Batchelor; Kelly (Kelbie 90), Coyne.
Forfar Ath: (4411) Hill; Travis, Nicoll, O'Brien, Campbell; Martin, Hodge, Fotheringham (Young 73), Denholm (Kader 73); Swankie; Smith.
Referee: Stephen Finnie.

Livingston (0) 0
Greenock Morton (0) 1 *(O'Ware 65)*　　873

Livingston: (442) Jamieson; Neill, Gordon, Gallagher, Longridge; Pitman (Knox 83), Fotheringham, Mullen (Currie 85), Stanton; Sheerin (White 67), Buchanan.
Greenock Morton: (433) Gaston; Pepper, Kilday, Gasparotto, Russell; McKee, O'Ware, Forbes (Lamie 86); Samuel, Johnstone, McManus.
Referee: Craig Charleston.

Motherwell (4) 5 *(Moult 2, McDonald 6, Johnson 34, Pearson 44, 61)*
Cove Rangers (0) 0　　　　　　　　　3833

Motherwell: (4411) Ripley; Law, Hall, McManus, Hammell; Grimshaw, Lasley, Pearson (Thomas 71), Johnson (Ainsworth 53); McDonald; Moult (McFadden 54).
Cove Rangers: (4141) McKenzie; Redford, Kelly, Watson (Burnett 76), Walker; Duff; Park (Smith J 67), Yule, Smith S, Scully (Watt 83); Nicol.
Referee: Euan Anderson.

Raith R (0) 0
Hibernian (0) 2 *(McGregor 61, Malonga 64)*　5203

Raith R: (442) Cuthbert; Matthews (Anderson 65), Benedictus, Davidson, McKeown; Robertson, Callachan, Craigen, Bates; Daly, Megginson (McCord 79).
Hibernian: (442) Oxley; Gunnarsson (McGregor 54), Hanlon, Fontaine, Stevenson; McGeouch, Bartley (Henderson 59), Keatings, McGinn; Malonga (Boyle 84), Dagnall.
Referee: Willie Collum.

St Johnstone (0) 0
Kilmarnock (1) 1 *(Slater 6)*　　　　　3147

St Johnstone: (442) Mannus; Shaughnessy, Mackay, Anderson, Easton; Wotherspoon, Millar, Davidson, O'Halloran (Thomson 79); Kane (Cummins 66), MacLean (Sutton 66).
Kilmarnock: (451) MacDonald; Syme, Ashcroft, Balatoni, McHattie; McKenzie (Findlay 82), Slater, Frizzell, Smith, Kiltie (Higginbotham 75); Magennis.
Referee: Kevin Clancy.

Stirling Alb (0) 0
Inverness CT (0) 0　　　　　　　　　1224

Stirling Alb: (4321) Smith C; Mazel, Smith R, Forsyth, McKinlay (McGeachie 13); Comrie (Beattie 80), Robertson, Dickson; Johnston (Lamont 62), Smith D; Doris.
Inverness CT: (4132) Fon Williams; Raven, Warren, Devine, Wedderburn (Fisher 46); Tansey; Williams D, Draper, Polworth; Vigurs (Mbuyi-Mutombo 80), Storey.
Referee: Matt Northcroft.

Sunday, 10 January 2016

Rangers (2) 5 *(Wallace 19, McKay 33, Waghorn 48, 55 (pen), 78 (pen))*
Cowdenbeath (1) 1 *(Brett 40)*　　　20,915

Rangers: (433) Foderingham; Tavernier, Ball, Wilson, Wallace; Zelalem (Forrester 62), Halliday (Shiels 62), Holt; Waghorn, Miller (Hardie 71), McKay.
Cowdenbeath: (442) Sneddon; Donaldson, Kerr, Scullion, Adamson; Brett, Hughes (El-Zubaidi 79), Milne (Kane 56), Callaghan; Smith (Johnston 72), Spence.
Referee: Steven McLean.

Stranraer (0) 0
Celtic (2) 3 *(Griffiths 18, 84, Cole 42)*　4051

Stranraer: (442) Currie; Dick, Bell, Rumsby, Pettigrew; McCloskey (Gibson 61), Cairney, Robertson, McGuigan (Stirling 61); Malcolm, Longworth (Thomson 80).
Celtic: (442) Bailly; Tierney (Blackett 77), Simunovic, Ambrose, Lustig; McGregor, Johansen, Bitton, Commons (Rogic 74); Griffiths, Cole (Allan 69).
Referee: Andrew Dallas.

Wednesday, 20 January 2016

East Kilbride (1) 2 *(Smith J 40, Winter 87)*
Lothian Thistle (0) 0　　　　　　　　696

East Kilbride: (442) McGinley; Gebbie, Stevenson, Russell, Coll; Winter, McBride, Smith R (Johnstone 25), Brady; Smith J, Hastings (Gormley 79).
Lothian Thistle: (442) Gibb; Moore, Joint, Mearns, Taylor-Mackenzie; Smith (Fox 74), Crawford, Kerr (Moffat 61), Hare (O'Donnell 77); Brown, Gormley.
Referee: Nick Walsh.

Tuesday, 26 January 2016

Dundee (1) 3 *(Hemmings 39, 60, Harkins 74)*
Falkirk (1) 1 *(Watson 41)*　　　　　　4279

Dundee: (4231) Bain; McGinn, Konrad, Gadzhalov (Etxabeguren Leanizbarrutia 76), Holt; Ross, McGowan; Stewart, Harkins, Low (Loy 71); Hemmings.
Falkirk: (4411) Rogers; Muirhead, McCracken, Watson, Leahy; Alston, Vaulks, Kerr, Taiwo (McHugh 67); Sibbald; Baird.
Referee: Willie Collum.

FOURTH ROUND REPLAYS

Tuesday, 12 January 2016

Ross Co (0) 1 *(De Vita 70)*
Dunfermline Ath (0) 0　　　　　　　2041

Ross Co: (442) Fox; Fraser, Davies, Robertson, Foster; Franks (De Vita 46), Irvine (McShane 68), Murdoch, Gardyne; Graham, Schalk (Quinn R 75).

Dunfermline Ath: (442) Murdoch; Rooney, McKay, Richards-Everton (McCabe 76), Talbot; Paton, Geggan, Falkingham, Cardle (Hopkirk 66); Moffat (Wallace 79), El Bakhtaoui.
Referee: Alan Muir.

Tuesday, 19 January 2016

Inverness CT (1) 2 *(Mbuyi-Mutombo 28, Vigurs 61)*
Stirling Alb (0) 0   1231
Inverness CT: (4141) Fon Williams; Raven, Warren, Devine, Williams D; Tansey; Polworth (Fisher 76), Draper (Foran 83), Vigurs, Mbuyi-Mutombo (Roberts 83); Storey.
Stirling Alb: (4411) Smith C; Mazel, McGeachie, Smith R (Beattie 76), Forsyth; Johnston (Cunningham 70), Comrie (Lamont 51), Robertson, Dickson; Smith D; Doris.
Referee: Matt Northcroft.

Tuesday, 26 January 2016

Forfar Ath (0) 0
Linlithgow Rose (0) 1 *(Kelbie 115)*   1168
Forfar Ath: (442) Hill; Baxter, Dunlop, O'Brien, Campbell; Kader (Hay 114), Young, Hodge, Denholm (Smith 98); Martin, Swankie.
Linlithgow Rose: (442) Adams; Batchelor, McKenzie, Leiper, Baptie; Kelbie, Weir, Shirra, Kelly; Strickland (Jones 103), Coyne.
aet.
Referee: John Beaton.

FIFTH ROUND

Saturday, 6 February 2016

Annan Ath (0) 1 *(Flynn 76)*
Greenock Morton (2) 4 *(McCluskey 21, 65, 68, McKee 45)*   736
Annan Ath: (4411) Hart; Breslin (Jago 39), Watson P, Gilfillan, McNiff; Sloan (Osadolor 54), Flynn, McStay (Guy 54), Morton; Todd; Omar.
Greenock Morton: (442) Gaston; Pepper, Kilday, O'Ware (Lamie 87), Russell; Barr (Samuel 90), McKee, Forbes, McCluskey (Tidser 82); Johnstone, McManus.
Referee: John Beaton.

Dumbarton (0) 0
Dundee (0) 0   1410
Dumbarton: (352) Ewings; Buchanan, Barr, Wright; Saunders, Gallagher (Taggart 81), Routledge, Walsh, Docherty; Fleming, Nade (Cawley 76).
Dundee: (4411) Bain; McGinn, O'Dea, Konrad, Holt; Stewart, McGowan, Ross (Arturo 73), Loy (Low 80); Harkins; Hemmings.
Referee: Stephen Finnie.

Dundee U (0) 1 *(Fraser 85)*
Partick Thistle (0) 0   5803
Dundee U: (352) Kawashima; Donaldson, Gunning, Dillon; Spittal, Rankin, Demel (Dixon 77), Paton, Dow (Fraser 74); McKay (Durnan 89), Murray.
Partick Thistle: (4411) Cerny; Miller, Frans, Seaborne, Booth; Bannigan, Osman, Welsh (Fraser 64), Lindsay; Lawless (Amoo 81); Doolan (Pogba 64).
Referee: Willie Collum.

Motherwell (0) 1 *(McDonald 67)*
Inverness CT (1) 2 *(Storey 39, Roberts 90)*   3907
Motherwell: (4411) Ripley; Law, Kennedy, McManus, Hammell; Cadden, Lasley (Moult 83), Pearson, Gomis; Johnson; McDonald (Ainsworth 88).
Inverness CT: (4231) Fon Williams; Raven, Warren, Devine, Tremarco; Tansey; Vigurs (Hughes 89); Mbuyi-Mutombo (Roberts 57), Draper, Williams D; Storey (Polworth 70).
Referee: Steven McLean.

Rangers (0) 0
Kilmarnock (0) 0   33,581
Rangers: (433) Foderingham; Tavernier, Kiernan (Law 74), Wilson, Wallace; Zelalem (Holt 61), Ball, Halliday; Waghorn, Miller (Forrester 60), McKay.
Kilmarnock: (4231) MacDonald; Hodson, Balatoni, Findlay, Smith; Dicker (O'Hara 65), Slater; Kiltie, McKenzie, Obadeyi (Higginbotham■ 74); Magennis.
Referee: Bobby Madden.

Ross Co (1) 4 *(Quinn P 4, Graham 58, 78, Schalk 63)*
Linlithgow Rose (1) 2 *(Reckord 44 (og), MacLennan 76)*
                                                          2208
Ross Co: (442) Woods G; Fraser, Boyd, Quinn P, Reckord (Foster 46); De Vita, Irvine, McShane, Franks (Gardyne 46); Graham, Schalk (Boyce 65).
Linlithgow Rose: (442) Adams; Tyrell, MacLennan, Leiper (Gray 75), Baptie; Batchelor, McKenzie, Thom (Strickland 73), Weir; Kelly, Coyne (Kelbie 73).
Referee: Euan Anderson.

Sunday, 7 February 2016

East Kilbride (0) 0
Celtic (1) 2 *(Griffiths 21, Kazim-Richards 50)*   7767
East Kilbride: (451) McGinley; Stevenson, Howie, Russell, Coll; Hastings (Gormley 63), Lachlan, Brady (Millar 90), McBride, Johnstone (Templeton 85); Smith J.
Celtic: (442) Bailly; Ambrose, Sviatchenko, Boyata, Tierney; Mackay-Steven (Allan 69), Brown, Mulgrew (Bitton 77), Forrest; Griffiths (Christie 81), Kazim-Richards.
Referee: George Salmond.

Hearts (2) 2 *(Djoum 32, Nicholson 44)*
Hibernian (0) 2 *(Cummings 80, Hanlon 90)*   16,845
Hearts: (4231) Alexander; Paterson, Augustyn, Ozturk (Oshaniwa 50), McGhee; Buaben (Cowie 10), Pallardo; Reilly, Djoum (Walker 82), Nicholson; Dauda.
Hibernian: (4132) Oxley; Gray (Gunnarsson 54), McGregor, Hanlon, Stevenson; Bartley; McGeouch (Thomson 31), McGinn, Henderson; Stokes, Cummings.
Referee: Craig Thomson.

FIFTH ROUND REPLAYS

Tuesday, 16 February 2016

Hibernian (1) 1 *(Cummings 4)*
Hearts (0) 0   19,433
Hibernian: (4132) Oxley; Gray, McGregor, Hanlon, Stevenson; Bartley; Henderson (Boyle 88), Thomson (Carmichael 69), McGinn; Stokes (Keatings 90), Cummings■.
Hearts: (442) Alexander; Paterson, Augustyn■, Igor Rossi (Souttar 77), McGhee; Cowie, Djoum, Pallardo (Nicholson 59), Walker (Zanatta 84); Dauda, Delgado.
Referee: John Beaton.

Kilmarnock (1) 1 *(McKenzie 7)*
Rangers (1) 2 *(Waghorn 3 (pen), Clark 90)*   13,179
Kilmarnock: (4231) MacDonald; Hodson, Balatoni, Findlay, Smith (Ashcroft 28); Dicker, Slater; Kiltie, McKenzie, Obadeyi (Frizzell 79); Magennis.
Rangers: (433) Foderingham; Tavernier, Kiernan, Wilson, Wallace; Holt, Ball (Shiels 59), Halliday; Waghorn (Clark 7), Miller (Forrester 71), McKay.
Referee: Bobby Madden.

Tuesday, 23 February 2016

Dundee (2) 5 *(McGinn 16, Hemmings 29, Stewart 51, 90, Holt 79)*
Dumbarton (0) 0   3532
Dundee: (4231) Bain; McGinn, Konrad, O'Dea (Etxabeguren Leanizbarrutia 76), Holt; Ross, McGowan; Stewart, Harkins (Wighton 59), Loy; Hemmings (Arturo 59).
Dumbarton: (442) Brown; Taggart, Buchanan, Wright, Docherty; Barr, Kirkpatrick (Lindsay 60), Routledge, Walsh; Heh (Fleming 58), Nade (Cawley 72).
Referee: Stephen Finnie.

QUARTER-FINALS

Saturday, 5 March 2016

Rangers (1) 4 *(Forrester 1, Holt 47, Halliday 54, Wallace 84)*
Dundee (0) 0   30,944
Rangers: (433) Foderingham; Tavernier, Kiernan, Wilson, Wallace; Holt (Law 78), Ball, Halliday; Forrester (Shiels 73), Miller, McKay (Clark 73).
Dundee: (442) Bain; McGinn, Konrad (Kerr 68), O'Dea, Holt; Ross, McGowan, Stewart, Harkins; Hemmings, Loy (Wighton 55).
Referee: Alan Muir.

Ross Co (1) 2 *(Boyce 24, Graham 60 (pen))*
Dundee U (0) 3 *(Anier 57, 65, McKay 89)*   3052
Ross Co: (442) Woods G; Fraser, Quinn P, Davies,
Foster; Franks (De Vita 76), Irvine, Woods M (McShane
61), Gardyne; Boyce, Graham (Schalk 68).
Dundee U: (352) Zwick; Donaldson, Durnan■, Dillon;
Spittal, Paton (Knoyle 66), Dow, Dixon, Rankin; McKay,
Anier (Erskine 83).
Referee: Craig Thomson.

Sunday, 6 March 2016

Celtic (3) 3 *(Griffiths 14, Mackay-Steven 25, McGregor 35)*
Greenock Morton (0) 0   14,858
Celtic: (4231) Gordon; Lustig, Sviatchenko, Mulgrew,
Tierney; Brown, McGregor; Commons (Armstrong 73),
Johansen (Kazim-Richards 46), Mackay-Steven; Griffiths
(Roberts 60).
Greenock Morton: (352) Gaston; Kilday, O'Ware, Lamie;
McCluskey (Gasparotto 76), McKee, Miller (Barr 52),
Forbes, Russell; Johnstone (Quitongo 89), McManus.
Referee: Willie Collum.

Hibernian (0) 1 *(Keatings 54)*
Inverness CT (0) 1 *(Mbuyi-Mutombo 77)*   9884
Hibernian: (442) Oxley; Gray, McGregor, Fontaine,
Stevenson; Henderson, McGeouch (Gunnarsson 26),
Thomson, McGinn; Keatings (Dagnall 86), Stokes.
Inverness CT: (451) Fon Williams; Polworth (Horner 72),
Warren, Devine, Tremarco; Roberts, Tansey, Draper,
Vigurs (Mbuyi-Mutombo 73); Williams D; Storey.
Referee: Crawford Allan.

QUARTER-FINAL REPLAY
Wednesday, 16 March 2016
Inverness CT (0) 1 *(Vigurs 77)*
Hibernian (2) 2 *(Stokes 36, 41)*   3207
Inverness CT: (442) Fon Williams; Meekings, Warren,
Devine, Tremarco (Polworth 73); Horner (Storey 62),
Draper, Wedderburn (Williams D 62), Vigurs; Foran,
Hughes.
Hibernian: (442) Oxley (Virtanen 88); Gray, McGregor,
Fontaine, Stevenson; Keatings (Gunnarsson 80), Bartley,
Henderson, McGinn; Stokes, Cummings.
Referee: Stephen Finnie.

SEMI-FINALS (at Hampden Park)
Saturday, 16 April 2016
Hibernian (0) 0
Dundee U (0) 0   19,651
Hibernian: (41212) Logan; Gray, McGregor, Hanlon,
Stevenson; Bartley; Fyvie, McGinn; Henderson (Boyle
85); Stokes (El Alagui 79 Dagnall 96)), Cummings.
Dundee U: (4231) Kawashima; Knoyle, Morris (Dixon
34), Donaldson (Demel 74), Dillon; Paton, Rankin;
Spittal, Dow, Erskine (Anier 76); McKay.
aet; Hibernian won 4-2 on penalties.
Referee: John Beaton.

Sunday, 17 April 2016
Rangers (1) 2 *(Miller 16, McKay 96)*
Celtic (0) 2 *(Sviatchenko 50, Rogic 106)*   50,069
Rangers: (4141) Foderingham; Tavernier, Kiernan
(Zelalem 88), Wilson, Wallace; Ball; Shiels (Law 66),
Halliday, Holt, McKay; Miller (Clark 91).
Celtic: (4231) Gordon; Lustig, Boyata (Sviatchenko 25),
Mulgrew, Tierney; Brown, Bitton; Roberts, Johansen
(Rogic 84), Mackay-Steven (McGregor 71); Griffiths.
aet; Rangers won 5-4 on penalties.
Referee: Craig Thomson.

WILLIAM HILL SCOTTISH CUP FINAL 2016
Saturday, 21 May 2016
(at Hampden Park, attendance 50,701)

Rangers (1) 2   Hibernian (1) 3

Rangers: (433) Foderingham; Tavernier, Kiernan, Wilson, Wallace; Zelalem (Shiels 63), Halliday, Holt; Waghorn
(Clark 75), Miller, McKay.
Scorers: Miller 27, Halliday 64.

Hibernian: (352) Logan; McGregor, Hanlon (Gunnarsson 83), Fontaine (Henderson 70); Gray, Fyvie, McGeouch,
McGinn, Stevenson; Stokes, Cummings (Keatings 65).
Scorers: Stokes 3, 80, Gray 90.

Referee: Steven McLean.

Hibernian's Anthony Stokes
wheels away after scoring the
first of his two goals in the
Edinburgh club's 3-2 victory over
Rangers in the Scottish FA Cup
final at Hampden Park on 21 May.
It was Hibernian's first triumph in
the competition since 1902.
(Reuters/Russell Cheyne Livepic)

SCOTTISH FOOTBALL PYRAMID 2015–16

PRESS & JOURNAL HIGHLAND LEAGUE

	P	W	D	L	F	A	GD	Pts
Cove Rangers*	34	29	2	3	98	28	70	89
Formartine U	34	27	4	3	137	35	102	85
Brora Rangers	34	27	4	3	128	35	93	85
Turriff U	34	20	8	6	88	31	57	68
Wick Academy	34	18	6	10	76	42	34	60
Inverurie Loco Works	34	18	4	12	71	43	28	58
Buckie Thistle	34	18	4	12	80	77	3	58
Nairn Co	34	17	6	11	75	55	20	57
Fraserburgh	34	15	8	11	63	49	14	53
Keith	34	17	1	16	70	76	–6	52
Forres Mechanics	34	15	4	15	60	65	–5	49
Lossiemouth	34	12	2	20	46	70	–24	38
Deveronvale	34	8	8	18	46	64	–18	32
Clachnacuddin	34	10	2	22	59	80	–21	32
Huntly	34	7	5	22	49	89	–40	26
Strathspey Thistle	34	6	2	26	38	118	–80	20
Fort William	34	5	1	28	38	116	–78	16
Rothes	34	1	1	32	16	165	–149	4

Edinburgh C won play-off with Cove Rangers (4-1 on aggregate) for the right to play in a further play-off with East Stirlingshire, the winners of which would play in Scottish League Two in 2016–17.

SCOTTISH SUN LOWLAND LEAGUE

	P	W	D	L	F	A	GD	Pts
Edinburgh C*	28	24	1	3	74	28	46	73
Spartans	28	18	4	6	74	36	38	58
Stirling University	28	17	5	6	65	32	33	56
Cumbernauld Colts	28	15	6	7	60	42	18	51
East Kilbride	28	14	7	7	68	44	24	49
Edinburgh University	28	13	3	12	51	46	5	42
BSC Glasgow	28	12	5	11	54	51	3	41
Whitehill Welfare	28	12	4	12	47	43	4	40
Dalbeattie Star	28	10	6	12	54	50	4	36
Gretna 2008	28	11	3	14	38	50	–12	36
Gala Fairydean R	28	10	2	16	53	61	–8	32
Selkirk	28	9	2	17	52	70	–18	29
Vale of Leithen	28	7	5	16	38	67	–29	26
Preston Ath	28	6	4	18	28	70	–42	22
Threave R	28	3	1	24	30	96	–66	10

Edinburgh C promoted to Scottish League Two after play-off with East Stirlingshire (2-1 on aggregate).

CENTRAL TAXIS EAST OF SCOTLAND LEAGUE

	P	W	D	L	F	A	GD	Pts
Leith Athletic	28	24	0	4	103	23	80	72
Lothian Thistle Hutchison Vale	28	20	3	5	99	42	57	63
Civil Service Strollers	28	18	1	9	74	49	25	55
Tynecastle	28	16	4	8	72	71	1	52
Hawick Royal Albert	28	15	3	10	70	50	20	48
Peebles R	28	13	4	11	57	60	–3	43
Spartans*	28	14	2	12	67	61	6	41
Ormiston	28	12	5	11	70	70	0	41
Stirling University	28	10	5	13	65	55	10	35
Heriot Watt University	28	9	6	13	61	65	–4	33
Coldstream	28	10	2	16	63	87	–24	32
Craigroyston	28	10	2	16	48	74	–26	32
Burntisland Shipyard	28	8	3	17	43	67	–24	27
Eyemouth U	28	5	2	21	39	115	–76	17
Duns	28	4	2	22	46	88	–42	14

Kelso U resigned membership, record expunged.
Spartans deducted 3 points

SOUTH OF SCOTLAND FOOTBALL LEAGUE

	P	W	D	L	F	A	GD	Pts
St Cuthbert W	26	24	1	1	120	34	86	73
Edusport Academy	26	20	3	3	96	22	74	63
Wigtown & Bladnoch	26	15	4	7	67	49	18	49
Crichton	26	14	5	7	76	54	22	47
Heston R	26	13	5	8	68	52	16	44
Upper Annandale	26	13	1	12	54	57	–3	40
Lochar Thistle	26	12	2	12	68	56	12	38
Mid-Annandale	26	10	4	12	57	51	6	34
Newton Stewart	26	10	3	13	54	62	–8	33
Creetown	26	9	2	15	54	68	–14	29
Abbey Vale	26	8	2	16	48	76	–28	26
Nithsdale W	26	7	5	14	43	74	–31	26
Fleet Star	26	5	3	18	43	87	–44	18
Dumfries YMCA	26	2	0	24	32	138	–106	6

EDINBURGH CITY

Year formed: 1928 (disbanded 1955, reformed from Postal United in 1986).
Ground & Address: Meadowbank Stadium, London Road, Edinburgh EH7 6AE.
Telephone: 0845 463 1932. *Postal Address:* 74 Lochend Road South, Edinburgh EH7 6DR.
E-mail: admin@edinburghcityfc.com *Website:* edinburghcityfc.com
Ground Capacity: 16,000 (all seated).
Chairman: Jim Lumsden. *Secretary:* Gavin Kennedy.
Manager: Gary Jardine. *Coach:* Ross MacNamara.
Previous names: Postal United.
Club Nickname: 'The Citizens'.
Previous Grounds: City Park 1928-55; Fernieside 1986-95.

Honours
Scottish Lowland League Champions: 2014-15, 2015-16 (promoted to League Two via play-offs).

Club colours: Shirt: White with diagonal black band. Shorts: Black. Socks: White.

WELSH FOOTBALL 2015–16

THE DAFABET WELSH PREMIER LEAGUE 2015–16

		P	Home					Away					Total					GD	Pts
			W	D	L	F	A	W	D	L	F	A	W	D	L	F	A		
1	The New Saints	32	10	5	1	34	9	8	5	3	38	15	18	10	4	72	24	48	64
2	Bala T	32	10	5	1	28	10	5	7	4	20	17	15	12	5	48	27	21	57
3	Llandudno	32	7	3	6	22	25	8	4	4	31	21	15	7	10	53	46	7	52
4	Connah's Quay Nomads	32	10	1	5	30	18	5	2	9	20	24	15	3	14	50	42	8	48
5	Newtown	32	4	5	7	23	34	7	4	5	23	20	11	9	12	46	54	-8	42
6	Airbus UK Broughton	32	7	3	6	27	27	5	3	8	19	28	12	6	14	46	55	-9	42
7	Carmarthen T	32	6	3	7	19	25	8	2	6	26	27	14	5	13	45	52	-7	47
8	Aberystwyth T	32	6	2	8	28	28	7	5	4	23	19	13	7	12	51	47	4	46
9	Bangor C	32	7	3	6	27	24	6	3	7	22	28	13	6	13	49	52	-3	45
10	Port Talbot T	32	4	5	7	20	27	6	4	6	19	29	10	9	13	39	56	-17	39
11	Rhyl	32	3	6	7	20	23	2	6	8	16	27	5	12	15	36	50	-14	27
12	Haverfordwest Co	32	2	5	9	11	23	3	1	12	16	34	5	6	21	27	57	-30	21

Top 6 teams split after 22 games.

PREVIOUS WELSH LEAGUE WINNERS

1993	Cwmbran Town	1999	Barry Town	2005	TNS	2011	Bangor C
1994	Bangor City	2000	TNS	2006	TNS	2012	The New Saints
1995	Bangor City	2001	Barry Town	2007	TNS	2013	The New Saints
1996	Barry Town	2002	Barry Town	2008	Llanelli	2014	The New Saints
1997	Barry Town	2003	Barry Town	2009	Rhyl	2015	The New Saints
1998	Barry Town	2004	Rhyl	2010	The New Saints	2016	The New Saints

NATHANIEL CARS WELSH LEAGUE 2015–16

		P	Home					Away					Total					GD	Pts
			W	D	L	F	A	W	D	L	F	A	W	D	L	F	A		
1	Cardiff Met University	30	12	1	2	38	10	7	4	4	25	16	19	5	6	63	26	37	62
2	Barry T	30	8	5	2	38	21	8	5	2	24	12	16	10	4	62	33	29	58
3	Goytre	30	10	3	2	44	18	7	2	6	28	18	17	5	8	72	36	36	56
4	Caerau (Ely)	30	8	4	3	33	20	7	1	7	26	23	15	5	10	59	43	16	50
5	Cambrian & Clydach Vale	30	8	2	5	30	23	7	3	5	18	16	15	5	10	48	39	9	50
6	Taff's Well	30	8	3	4	28	20	6	2	7	29	31	14	5	11	57	51	6	47
7	Goytre U	30	6	3	6	23	21	7	1	7	22	26	13	4	13	45	47	-2	43
8	Afan Lido	30	4	6	5	24	23	7	3	5	29	30	11	9	10	53	53	0	42
9	Ton Pentre	30	6	2	7	21	22	6	2	7	24	30	12	4	14	45	52	-7	40
10	Risca U	30	6	1	8	24	22	6	2	7	24	26	12	3	15	48	48	0	39
11	Penybont	30	6	3	6	32	27	5	3	7	21	29	11	6	13	53	56	-3	39
12	Monmouth T	30	6	3	6	23	27	4	6	5	33	33	10	9	11	56	60	-4	39
13	Briton Ferry	30	8	4	3	26	21	2	5	8	15	28	10	9	11	41	49	-8	39
14	Aberdare T	30	7	1	7	16	22	4	3	8	18	34	11	4	15	34	56	-22	37
15	Aberbargoed Buffs	30	5	3	7	28	28	3	0	12	14	35	8	3	19	42	63	-21	27
16	Garden Village	30	1	1	13	13	39	0	3	12	14	54	1	4	25	27	93	-66	7

HUWS GRAY CYMRU ALLIANCE LEAGUE 2015–16

		P	Home					Away					Total					GD	Pts
			W	D	L	F	A	W	D	L	F	A	W	D	L	F	A		
1	Caernarfon T	30	11	1	3	51	17	13	2	0	44	6	24	3	3	95	23	72	75
2	Cefn Druids	30	9	1	5	27	21	12	2	1	35	12	21	3	6	62	33	29	66
3	Denbigh T	30	9	2	4	33	24	11	1	3	39	22	20	3	7	72	46	26	63
4	Guilsfield	30	8	0	7	28	22	9	2	4	32	22	17	2	11	60	44	16	53
5	Holywell T	30	9	4	2	34	14	6	3	6	21	20	15	7	8	55	34	21	52
6	Gresford Ath	30	8	1	6	20	17	7	3	5	25	27	15	4	11	45	44	1	49
7	Holyhead Hotspur	30	8	4	3	25	16	5	3	7	19	24	13	7	10	44	40	4	46
8	Prestatyn T	30	6	2	7	27	22	8	1	6	34	28	14	3	13	61	50	11	45
9	Flint Town U	30	7	1	7	23	20	6	2	7	31	25	13	3	14	54	45	9	42
10	Porthmadog	30	7	0	8	23	27	6	2	7	24	27	13	2	15	47	54	-7	41
11	Conwy Borough	30	6	2	7	30	28	5	1	9	17	26	11	3	16	47	54	-7	36
12	Buckley T	30	4	2	9	26	35	5	3	7	19	30	9	5	16	45	65	-20	32
13	Mold Alexandra	30	4	3	8	18	33	5	1	9	20	26	9	4	17	38	59	-21	31
14	Caersws	30	1	1	12	18	41	7	0	8	22	26	8	2	20	40	67	-27	26
15	Llanfair U	30	3	0	12	15	35	4	0	11	20	35	7	0	23	35	70	-35	21
16	Rhayader T	30	3	2	10	15	39	1	1	13	9	57	4	3	23	24	96	-72	15

Caernarfon T failed to gain Domestic licence. Cefn Druids promoted.

WELSH FA CUP 2015–16

After extra time.

FIRST QUALIFYING ROUND – CENTRAL

Aberaeron v Abermule	6-1
Berriew v Newbridge on Wye	11-2
Hay St Mary v Llansantffraid Village	2-2*
(1-1 at full time; Hay St Mary won 5-4 on penalties)	
Knighton T v Kerry	4-0
Llanfyllin T v Machynlleth	2-4
Montgomery T v Pontrhydfendigaid	3-0
Presteigne St. Andrews v Tywyn Bryncrug	2-4
Welshpool T v Borth U	5-4

FIRST QUALIFYING ROUND – NORTH

Aberffraw v Gaerwen	4-1*
Amlwch T v Meliden	3-2*
Aston Park Rangers v Llandyrnog U	0-6
Blaenau Ffestiniog v Prestatyn Sports	0-6
Brymbo v Halkyn U	4-1
Caerwys v Castell Alun Colts	1-3
Cefn Alb v Llanuwchllyn	5-2
CPD Sychdyn v Argoed U	2-1
Ewloe Harriers v Lex Glyndwr	2-3
Greenfield v Overton Recreational	2-1
Llanerch y Medd v Talysarn Celts	8-0
Llanfairpwll v Llanberis	2-4
Llangollen T v Llay Miners Welfare	9-1
Llanystumdwy v Dyffryn Nantlle Vale	0-1
Mochdre Sports v Llanllyfni	3-2
Penley v Brickfield Rangers	4-3
Penmaenmawr Phoenix v Pwllheli	3-1
Pentraeth v Menai Bridge Tigers	7-1
Penyffordd v Coedpoeth U	8-0
Rhostyllen v AFC Brynford	6-0
Saltney T v Queens Park	1-4
St Asaph C v Llanrwst U	0-2
Trearddur Bay U v Glan Conwy	5-2*

FIRST QUALIFYING ROUND – SOUTH

Panteg v Newport YMCA	2-1
(First match abandoned after 90 minutes due to bad light, 4-4)	
AFC Butetown v Blaenrhondda	4-1
AFC Perthcelyn v Llantwit Fardre	1-2
Bettws v Newcastle Emlyn	6-2
Brecon Corries v Penrhiwfer	3-0
Bridgend Street v Cardiff Corinthians	2-3
Canton Liberal v Pontypridd T	1-2
Cardiff Hibernians v Treharris Ath Western	3-5
Carnetown v Pontyclun	1-7
Cornelly U v Penlan	2-4
Cwmbach Royal Stars v Ely Rangers	2-0
FC Tredegar v Dynamo Aber	4-4*
(Dynamo Aber won 4-1 on penalties)	
Garw v Ynysygerwn	3-0
Graig v Cwm Welfare	2-4
Llangynwyd Rangers v Trefelin	4-2
Llantwit Major v Cefn Cribwr	5-0
Lliswerry v Newport Civil Service	1-1*
(Newport Civil Service won 4-3 on penalties)	
Merthyr Saints v Cogan Coronation	5-2
Penrhiwceiber Constitutional Ath v Clwb Cymric	2-1
Porthcawl T Ath v Caerau	3-1
RTB Ebbw Vale v Aberfan	6-2
STM Sports v West of St Julians	6-0
Sully Sports v Treforest	3-0
Tredegar T v Caerleon	0-2
Treowen Stars v Aber Valley YMCA	3-2
Trethomas Bluebirds v Cwmbran T	2-3*
Ynysddu Welfare v Machen AFC	4-0

SECOND QUALIFYING ROUND – CENTRAL

Aberaeron v Montgomery T	4-2
Berriew v Machynlleth	2-1
Bow Street v Hay St Mary	2-1
Carno v Llanrhaeadr Ym Mochant	5-0
Knighton T v Welshpool T	2-1
Penrhyncoch v Llanidloes T	5-1
Waterloo R v Tywyn Bryncrug	3-1

SECOND QUALIFYING ROUND – NORTH

Barmouth & Dyffryn U v Llandudno Junction	1-1*
(Llandudno Junction won 3-1 on penalties)	
Cefn Alb v Llannerch y Medd	3-2

Dyffryn Nantlle Vale v Penley	4-3*
Gwalchmai v Greenfield	5-3*
(3-3 at full time)	
Lex Glyndwr v Ruthin T	1-2
Llangefni T v Glantraeth	0-1
Llangollen T v Chirk AAA	0-1
Llanrug U v Llanberis	3-1
Llanrwst U v Aberffraw	1-2
Mochdre Sports v FC Nomads of Connah's Quay	1-7
Penrhyndeudraeth v Abergele T	2-0
Pentraeth v Castell Alun Colts	3-1
Penycae v Penmaenmawr Phoenix	2-5
Penyffordd v Corwen	1-3
Prestatyn Sports v CPD Sychdyn	3-1
Queens Park v Llandyrnog U	2-1
Rhostyllen v Brymbo	1-0*
Trearddur Bay U v Amlwch T	8-1

SECOND QUALIFYING ROUND – SOUTH

AFC Butetown v Chepstow T	5-0
AFC Llwydcoed v Bettws	5-2
AFC Porth v Undy Ath	1-4
Cardiff Corinthians v West End	2-3*
(2-2 at full time)	
Croesyceiliog v Llanelli T AFC	0-4
Cwm Welfare v Brecon Corries	1-2
Cwmamman U v Garw	4-2
Cwmbach Royal Stars v Newport Civil Service	3-2*
Cwmbran Celtic v Llanwern	3-0
Cwmbran T v Penrhiwceiber Rangers	7-3
Dynamo Aber v Treowen Stars	4-5
(3-3 at full time)	
Llantwit Fardre v Merthyr Saints	1-1
(Llantwit Fardre won 6-5 on penalties)	
Llantwit Major v Tata Steel	3-2
Panteg v Ammanford	2-1*
Penlan v Caldicot T	1-2*
(1-1 at full time)	
Penrhiwceiber Constitutional Ath v Llandrindod Wells	2-4
Pontardawe T v RTB Ebbw Vale	1-2
Pontyclun v Caerleon	1-2*
Pontypridd T v Sully Sports	4-2
STM Sports v Porthcawl T Ath	5-1
Treharris Ath Western v Llangynwyd Rangers	2-0
Ynysddu Welfare v Dinas Powys	2-6

FIRST ROUND – NORTH

Aberffraw v Penrhyncoch	0-5
Caersws v Llandudno Junction	1-6
Carno v Flint Town U	0-4
Cefn Druids v Gresford Ath	4-0
Chirk AAA v Prestatyn Sports	5-0
Conwy Borough v Cefn Alb	5-3
Corwen v Prestatyn T	2-3
Dyffryn Nantlle Vale v Knighton T	1-2
FC Nomads of Connah's Quay v Denbigh T	1-3
Guilsfield v Glantraeth	4-2*
(1-1 at full time)	
Gwalchmai v Mold Alexandra	0-3
Hawarden Rangers v Llanfair U	0-4
Holyhead Hotspur v Pentraeth	8-0
Llanrug U v Caernarfon T	2-3*
(2-2 at full time)	
Penmaenmawr Phoenix v Buckley T	0-1
Penrhyndeudraeth v Queens Park	2-0
Porthmadog v Bow Street	3-1
Rhostyllen v Berriew	2-1
Ruthin T v Holywell T	0-1
Waterloo R v Trearddur Bay U	1-7

FIRST ROUND – SOUTH

Aberaman v Brecon Corries	0-1
Afan Lido v AFC Butetown	5-1
Briton Ferry Llansawel v Barry Town U	2-3
Caerau Ely v Undy Ath	4-0
Caerleon v Treharris Ath Western	2-1*
(1-1 at full time)	
Cambrian & Clydach Vale v AFC Llwydcoed	3-0
Cwmamman U v Taffs Well	2-1
Cwmbach Royal Stars v Aberdare T	0-3
Dinas Powys v Cwmbran T	4-1
Garden Village v Rhayader T	2-1
Goytre (Gwent) v Llantwit Major	2-0

Goytre U v Monmouth T   4-2*
(2-2 at full time)
Llandrindod Wells v Cwmbran Celtic   0-3
Llanelli T AFC v Panteg   6-3
Llantwit Fardre v Cardiff Metropolitan   0-1
Pontypridd T v Penybont   0-2
Ton Pentre v STM Sports   0-4
Treowen Stars v West End   2-3
Risca U v Aberbargoed Buds   2-3
RTB Ebbw Vale v Caldicot T   1-1*
(Caldicot T won 5-4 on penalties)

SECOND ROUND – NORTH
Caernarfon T v Llandudno Junction   4-0
Cefn Druids v Porthmadog   2-0
Denbigh T v Conwy Borough   4-1
Guilsfield v Penrhyndeudraeth   3-2
Holyhead Hotspur v Chirk AAA   4-0
Holywell T v Knighton T   6-3
Llanfair U v Prestatyn T   3-5
Mold Alexandra v Buckley T   0-1
Penrhyncoch v Trearddur Bay U   4-0
Rhostyllen v Flint Town U   0-2

SECOND ROUND – SOUTH
Afan Lido v Caerleon   2-0
Barry Town U v Aberdare T   7-2
Brecon Corries v Aberbargoed Buds   3-0
Cardiff Metropolitan v Penybont   4-2
Cwmamman U v Caldicot T   4-2
Garden Village v STM Sports   1-4
Goytre (Gwent) v Dinas Powys   4-1
Goytre U v Caerau Ely   1-4
West End v Cwmbran Celtic   2-3
Llanelli T AFC v Cambrian & Clydach Vale   0-2

THIRD ROUND
Cwmamman U v Guilsfield   0-3
Goytre (Gwent) v Caernarfon T   4-2
Holyhead Hotspur v Bangor C   2-1
Afan Lido v Holywell T   1-0
Barry Town U v Denbigh T   6-1
Caerau Ely v Brecon Corries   4-0
Cardiff Metropolitan v STM Sports   2-0
Carmarthen T v Bala T   1-3

Cefn Druids v Rhyl   1-0*
Flint Town U v Newtown   0-2
Haverfordwest Co v Airbus UK Broughton   0-2
MBi Llandudno v Buckley T   0-0*
(Buckley T won 4-3 on penalties)
Penrhyncoch v Cwmbran Celtic   2-3
Prestatyn T v Gap Connahs Quay   0-3
The New Saints v Aberystwyth T   3-0
Port Talbot T v Cambrian & Clydach Vale   2-1*
(1-1 at full time)

FOURTH ROUND
Airbus UK Broughton v Guilsfield   3-0
Cwmbran Celtic v Goytre (Gwent)   5-3
Afan Lido v Cardiff Metropolitan   0-2
Barry Town U v The New Saints   2-5
Holyhead Hotspur v Bala T   1-3
Newtown v Cefn Druids   6-0
Port Talbot T v Caerau Ely   3-0
Gap Connahs Quay v Buckley T   4-1

QUARTER-FINALS
Airbus UK Broughton v Bala T   3-0
Cardiff Metropolitan v Gap Connahs Quay   0-2
Cwmbran Celtic v Port Talbot T   1-2
The New Saints v Newtown   1-0

SEMI-FINALS
Port Talbot T v Airbus UK Broughton   0-7
The New Saints v Gap Connahs Quay   5-0

WELSH FA CUP FINAL 2016
Wrexham, Monday 2 May 2016
The New Saints (1) 2 *(Brobbel 33, Quigley 51)*
Airbus UK Broughton (0) 0   1402
The New Saints: Harrison; Spender, Marriott, Edwards
K, Seargeant (Baker 66), Brobbel, Williams (Wilde 46),
Rawlinson, Ciesslewicz, Quigley, Edwards A.
Airbus UK Broughton: Coates; Pearson, Kearney,
Budrys, Gray, Wignall, Williams, Owen (Barrow 61),
McGinn (Jackson 60), Owens, Murphy (Fraughan 81).
Referee: Bryn Markham-Jones.

PREVIOUS WELSH CUP WINNERS

1878	Wrexham	1911	Wrexham	1954	Flint Town United	1987	Merthyr Tydfil
1879	Newtown White Star	1912	Cardiff City	1955	Barry Town	1988	Cardiff City
1880	Druids	1913	Swansea Town	1956	Cardiff City	1989	Swansea City
1881	Druids	1914	Wrexham	1957	Wrexham	1990	Hereford United
1882	Druids	1915	Wrexham	1958	Wrexham	1991	Swansea City
1883	Wrexham	1920	Cardiff City	1959	Cardiff City	1992	Cardiff City
1884	Oswestry White Stars	1921	Wrexham	1960	Wrexham	1993	Cardiff City
1885	Druids	1922	Cardiff City	1961	Swansea Town	1994	Barry Town
1886	Druids	1923	Cardiff City	1962	Bangor City	1995	Wrexham
1887	Chirk	1924	Wrexham	1963	Borough United	1996	TNS
1888	Chirk	1925	Wrexham	1964	Cardiff City	1997	Barry Town
1889	Bangor	1926	Ebbw Vale	1965	Cardiff City	1998	Bangor City
1890	Chirk	1927	Cardiff City	1966	Swansea Town	1999	Inter Cable-Tel
1891	Shrewsbury Town	1928	Cardiff City	1967	Cardiff City	2000	Bangor City
1892	Chirk	1929	Connah's Quay	1968	Cardiff City	2001	Barry Town
1893	Wrexham	1930	Cardiff City	1969	Cardiff City	2002	Barry Town
1894	Chirk	1931	Wrexham	1970	Cardiff City	2003	Barry Town
1895	Newtown	1932	Swansea Town	1971	Cardiff City	2004	Rhyl
1896	Bangor	1933	Chester	1972	Wrexham	2005	TNS
1897	Wrexham	1934	Bristol City	1973	Cardiff City	2006	Rhyl
1898	Druids	1935	Tranmere Rovers	1974	Cardiff City	2007	Carmarthen Town
1899	Druids	1936	Crewe Alexandra	1975	Wrexham	2008	Bangor City
1900	Aberystwyth Town	1937	Crewe Alexandra	1976	Cardiff City	2009	Bangor City
1901	Oswestry United	1938	Shrewsbury Town	1977	Shrewsbury Town	2010	Bangor City
1902	Wellington Town	1939	South Liverpool	1978	Wrexham	2011	Llanelli
1903	Wrexham	1940	Wellington Town	1979	Shrewsbury Town	2012	The New Saints
1904	Druids	1947	Chester	1980	Newport County	2013	Prestatyn Town
1905	Wrexham	1948	Lovell's Athletic	1981	Swansea City	2014	The New Saints
1906	Wellington Town	1949	Merthyr Tydfil	1982	Swansea City	2015	The New Saints
1907	Oswestry United	1950	Swansea Town	1983	Swansea City	2016	The New Saints
1908	Chester	1951	Merthyr Tydfil	1984	Shrewsbury Town		
1909	Wrexham	1952	Rhyl	1985	Shrewsbury Town		
1910	Wrexham	1953	Rhyl	1986	Wrexham		

WELSH THEWORD LEAGUE CUP 2015–16

*After extra time.

FIRST ROUND

Aberystwyth T v Goytre U	5-1
Bangor C v Caernarfon T	0-1
Carmarthen T v Briton Ferry Llansawel	4-4*
Carmarthen T won 5-4 on penalties.	
Cefn Druids v Airbus UK Broughton	0-2
Guilsfield v Gap Connah's Quay	0-3*
Holyhead Hotspur v Llandudno	2-0
Holywell T v Buckley T	2-1
Penrhyncoch v Newtown	2-2*
Penrhyncoch won 9-8 on penalties.	
Penybont v Haverfordwest Co	0-4
Pontypridd T v Taffs Well	2-1
Rhyl v Denbigh T	2-4
Ton Pentre v Cardiff	1-0

SECOND ROUND

Airbus UK Broughton v Penrhyncoch	2-0
Caernarfon T v Bala T	2-1
Carmarthen T v Pontypridd T	4-2
Haverfordwest Co v Aberystwyth T	4-1
Holyhead Hotspur v Denbigh T	0-4
Prestatyn T v Gap Connah's Quay	1-3

The New Saints v Holywell T	7-1
Ton Pentre v Port Talbot T	1-3

THIRD ROUND

The New Saints v Haverfordwest Co	3-1
Denbigh T v Airbus UK Broughton	2-1*
Carmarthen T v Port Talbot T	3-1
Gap Connah's Quay v Caernarfon T	5-3*

SEMI-FINALS

The New Saints v Carmarthen T	4-1
Denbigh T v Gap Connah's Quay	1-0

WELSH THEWORD CUP FINAL

Llandudno, 23 January 2016

The New Saints (1) 2 *(Williams 25, Wilde 57)*

Denbigh T (0) 0   1158

The New Saints: Harrison; Spender, Marriott, Rawlinson, Edwards K, Seargeant, Edwards A (Gossett 80), Mullan, Wilde, Williams (Draper 86), Cieslewicz (Quigley 80).
Denbigh T: Power; Sharples, Freeman, Davies (Lloyd 46), Duckett (Cronshaw 80), Hughes, Williams, Pierce, Macintyre (Hart 72), Tate, Roberts.
Referee: Lee Evans.

THE FAW TROPHY 2015–16

*After extra time.

THIRD ROUND – NORTH

Brymbo v Llandrindod Wells	1-0
Carno v Penycae	3-3*
(2-2 at full-time; Carno won on penalties)	
Cefn Alb v Castell Alun Colts	2-4*
(2-2 at full-time)	
Corwen v Llangollen T	1-0
Gaerwen v Llandudno Junction	3-8
Glan Conwy v Y Felinheli	4-0
Greenfield v Knighton T	3-2*
(2-2 at full-time)	
Gwalchmai v Meliden	6-1
Llanberis v Dyffryn Nantlle Vale	2-1
Llanfairfechan v Aberffraw	1-3*
(1-1 at full-time)	
Llanidloes T v Queens Park	2-4
Llanllyfni v Glantraeth	3-4
Llanrhaeadr Ym Mochant v Chirk AAA	4-1
Llanrug U v Trearddur Bay U	3-3*
(2-2 at full-time; Trearddur Bay won 4-3 on penalties)	
Llanystumdwy v Penrhyndeudraeth	0-3
Penrhyncoch v Llannerch y Medd	3-2
Rhos Aelwyd v New Brighton Villa	2-1
Ruthin T v Penyffordd	5-4
Saltney T v Rhostyllen	2-3
Tywyn Bryncrug v Pentraeth	1-5

THIRD ROUND – SOUTH

Abergavenny T v Tonyrefail BGC	3-0
Bwlch Rangers v Sully Sports	2-4*
(2-2 at full-time)	
Canton Liberal v Penlan	4-1
Cardiff Draconians v Cefn Cribwr	2-0
Clydach Wasps v AC Pontymister	0-2
Llanbradach v Llantwit Fardre	2-0
Maltsters Sports v Grange Alb	1-0
Morriston Olympic v Hakin U	1-2
North End v Llangynwyd Rangers	1-3
Sporting Marvels v Abertillery Excelsiors	5-1
Team Swansea v Hirwaun Sports	6-2
Trefelin v Cogan Coronation	2-2*
(Cogan Coronation won 6-5 on penalties)	

FOURTH ROUND – NORTH

Brymbo v Llanrhaeadr Ym Mochant	1-2
Carno v Castell Alun Colts	6-0
Glantraeth v Corwen	2-3
Greenfield v Llanberis	4-1
Gwalchmai v Trearddur Bay U	2-3

Llandudno Junction v Aberffraw	6-1
Penrhyncoch v Penrhyndeudraeth	1-0
Queens Park v Rhos Aelwyd	4-3
Rhostyllen v Pentraeth	3-1
Ruthin T v Glan Conwy	2-1

FOURTH ROUND – SOUTH

Cardiff Draconians v Sporting Marvels	1-2
AC Pontymister v Hakin U	5-1
Llanbradach v Sully Sports	1-5
Llangynwyd Rangers v Canton Liberal	1-0
Maltsters Sports v Cogan Coronation	3-2
Team Swansea v Abergavenny T	3-4

FIFTH ROUND – NORTH

Greenfield v Llanrhaeadr Ym Mochant	2-3
Llandudno Junction v Corwen	3-2
Queens Park v Penrhyncoch	1-0
Rhostyllen v Ruthin T	2-0
Trearddur Bay U v Carno	2-5

FIFTH ROUND – SOUTH

Llangynwyd Rangers v AC Pontymister	1-2
Maltsters Sports v Sully Sports	2-4
Sporting Marvels v Abergavenny T	1-2

QUARTER-FINALS

Carno v Sully Sports	0-2*
(Original match abandoned after 70 minutes; 0-1)	
Abergavenny T v Llanrhaeadr Ym Mochant	6-1
AC Pontymister v Rhostyllen	3-4*
(3-3 at full-time)	
Queens Park v Llandudno Junction	3-1

SEMI-FINALS

Abergavenny T v Queens Park	7-0
Sully Sports v Rhostyllen	1-0

THE FAW TROPHY FINAL 2016

Newport, Saturday 16 April 2016

Abergavenny T (1) 0 *(Norman C 2)*

Sully Sports (0) 0

Abergavenny T: Indge; Morgan, Evans, Brewer, Summers, Norman A (Laurent 74), Jones (Bull 81), Norman C, Jenkins, Morgan, Jeremiah.
Sully Sports: Davie; Lamb, Harding, Constant, Hopkins, Townsend (Rees 46), Brown (Barnett 46), Lewis, McInery, Long (Gale 72), Boyles.
Referee: Iwan Griffith (Conwy).

NORTHERN IRISH FOOTBALL 2015–16

NORTHERN IRISH DANSKE BANK PREMIERSHIP 2015–16

		Home					Away					Total						
		P	W	D	L	F	A	W	D	L	F	A	W	D	L	F	A	GD	Pts
1	Crusaders	38	14	3	1	42	10	14	4	2	37	18	28	7	3	79	28	51	91
2	Linfield	38	13	4	2	49	13	13	1	5	42	22	26	5	7	91	35	56	83
3	Glenavon	38	10	4	5	35	19	10	5	4	37	21	20	9	9	72	40	32	69
4	Cliftonville	38	11	4	5	35	24	7	6	5	23	29	18	10	10	58	53	5	64
5	Coleraine	38	9	3	6	23	17	9	1	10	24	29	18	4	16	47	46	1	58
6	Glentoran	38	8	3	8	20	25	7	4	8	26	30	15	7	16	46	55	−9	52
7	Dungannon Swifts	38	8	1	10	32	31	4	6	9	19	35	12	7	19	51	66	−15	43
8	Ballymena U	38	5	4	10	27	40	6	3	10	30	41	11	7	20	57	81	−24	40
9	Portadown	38	6	4	9	29	34	5	1	13	14	33	11	5	22	43	67	−24	38
10	Carrick Rangers	38	4	5	11	23	39	4	6	8	20	29	8	11	19	43	68	−25	35
11	Ballinamallard U	38	5	3	10	19	23	4	4	12	20	36	9	7	22	39	59	−20	34
12	Warrenpoint T	38	5	5	10	25	37	4	2	12	20	36	9	7	22	45	73	−28	34

Top 6 teams split after 33 games. Ballinamallard U not relegated after 5-4 aggregate play-off win over Institute.

LEADING GOALSCORERS (League goals only)

22	Paul Heatley	Crusaders
22	Andy Waterworth	Linfield
19	Aaron Burns	Linfield
18	Jordan Owens	Crusaders
18	Curtis Allen	Glentoran
17	Eoin Bradley	Glenavon
16	Andrew Mitchell	Dungannon Swifts
13	Miguel Chines	Carrick Rangers
12	David McDaid	Cliftonville
12	James McLaughlin	Coleraine
11	David Cushley	Ballymena U
11	Allan Jenkins	Ballymena U
11	Jay Donnelly	Cliftonville
11	Darren Murray	Cliftonville
9	Matthew Tipton	Ballymena U
9	Jordan Forsythe	Crusaders
9	Ryan Harpur	Dungannon Swifts
8	Kevin Braniff	Glenavon
8	Jonathan Smith	Glentoran

IRISH LEAGUE CHAMPIONSHIP WINNERS

1891	Linfield	1914	Linfield	1949	Linfield	1973	Crusaders	1997	Crusaders
1892	Linfield	1915	Belfast Celtic	1950	Linfield	1974	Coleraine	1998	Cliftonville
1893	Linfield	1920	Belfast Celtic	1951	Glentoran	1975	Linfield	1999	Glentoran
1894	Glentoran	1921	Glentoran	1952	Glenavon	1976	Crusaders	2000	Linfield
1895	Linfield	1922	Linfield	1953	Glentoran	1977	Glentoran	2001	Linfield
1896	Distillery	1923	Linfield	1954	Linfield	1978	Linfield	2002	Portadown
1897	Glentoran	1924	Queen's Island	1955	Linfield	1979	Linfield	2003	Glentoran
1898	Linfield	1925	Glentoran	1956	Linfield	1980	Linfield	2004	Linfield
1899	Distillery	1926	Belfast Celtic	1957	Glentoran	1981	Glentoran	2005	Glentoran
1900	Belfast Celtic	1927	Belfast Celtic	1958	Ards	1982	Linfield	2006	Linfield
1901	Distillery	1928	Belfast Celtic	1959	Linfield	1983	Linfield	2007	Linfield
1902	Linfield	1929	Belfast Celtic	1960	Glenavon	1984	Linfield	2008	Linfield
1903	Distillery	1930	Linfield	1961	Linfield	1985	Linfield	2009	Glentoran
1904	Linfield	1931	Glentoran	1962	Linfield	1986	Linfield	2010	Linfield
1905	Glentoran	1932	Linfield	1963	Distillery	1987	Linfield	2011	Linfield
1906	Cliftonville/	1933	Belfast Celtic	1964	Glentoran	1988	Glentoran	2012	Linfield
	Distillery (shared)	1934	Linfield	1965	Derry City	1989	Linfield	2013	Cliftonville
1907	Linfield	1935	Linfield	1966	Linfield	1990	Portadown	2014	Cliftonville
1908	Linfield	1936	Belfast Celtic	1967	Glentoran	1991	Portadown	2015	Crusaders
1909	Linfield	1937	Belfast Celtic	1968	Glentoran	1992	Glentoran	2016	Crusaders
1910	Cliftonville	1938	Belfast Celtic	1969	Linfield	1993	Linfield		
1911	Linfield	1939	Belfast Celtic	1970	Glentoran	1994	Linfield		
1912	Glentoran	1940	Belfast Celtic	1971	Linfield	1995	Crusaders		
1913	Glentoran	1948	Belfast Celtic	1972	Glentoran	1996	Portadown		

BELFAST TELEGRAPH CHAMPIONSHIP ONE 2015–16

			Home				Away					Total					
		P	W	D	L	F	A	W	D	L	F	A	W	D	L	F	A	GD	Pts
1	Ards	26	8	3	2	27	15	9	0	4	32	20	17	3	6	59	35	24	54
2	H&W Welders	26	10	1	2	29	10	5	5	3	25	18	15	6	5	54	28	26	51
3	Armagh C	26	8	2	3	36	16	5	3	5	28	20	13	5	8	64	36	28	44
4	Knockbreda	26	6	6	1	24	15	6	1	6	24	17	12	7	7	48	32	16	43
5	Institute	26	7	4	2	22	6	5	2	6	18	14	12	6	8	40	20	20	42
6	Larne	26	6	4	3	28	23	6	2	5	36	22	12	6	8	64	45	19	42
7	Lurgan Celtic	24	4	4	5	20	22	7	2	4	20	18	11	6	9	40	40	0	39
8	Ballyclare Comrades	26	6	4	3	25	21	3	6	4	19	19	9	10	7	44	40	4	37
9	Loughgall	26	7	2	4	25	28	3	4	6	20	26	10	6	10	45	54	–9	36
10	Bangor	26	6	2	5	23	18	4	3	6	21	22	10	5	11	44	40	4	35
11	Dergview	26	4	5	4	19	20	5	3	5	22	20	9	8	9	41	40	1	35
12	Annagh U	26	2	2	9	17	35	5	4	4	20	22	7	6	13	37	57	–20	27
13	Donegal Celtic	26	0	0	13	12	41	2	4	7	22	39	2	4	20	34	80	–46	10
14	Lisburn Distillery	26	0	2	11	5	50	2	2	9	13	35	2	4	20	18	85	–67	10

Teams finishing 2nd, 3rd and 4th did not apply for promotion licence.

BELFAST TELEGRAPH CHAMPIONSHIP (Previously First Division)

1996	Coleraine	2003	Dungannon Swifts	2010	Loughgall
1997	Ballymena United	2004	Loughgall	2011	Carrick Rangers
1998	Newry Town	2005	Armagh City	2012	Ballinamallard U
1999	Distillery	2006	Crusaders	2013	Ards
2000	Omagh Town	2007	Institute	2014	Institute
2001	Ards	2008	Loughgall	2015	Carrick Rangers
2002	Lisburn Distillery	2009	Portadown	2016	Ards

BELFAST TELEGRAPH CHAMPIONSHIP TWO 2015–16

			Home				Away					Total					
		P	W	D	L	F	A	W	D	L	F	A	W	D	L	F	A	GD	Pts
1	Limavady U*	26	9	4	0	34	12	9	1	3	32	15	18	5	3	66	27	39	59
2	PSNI	26	12	1	0	43	8	6	4	3	16	15	18	5	3	59	23	36	59
3	Sport & Leisure Swifts	26	5	4	4	23	14	8	4	1	36	14	13	8	5	59	28	31	47
4	Tobermore U	26	7	2	4	18	12	6	3	4	20	19	13	5	8	38	31	7	44
5	Moyola Park	26	5	5	3	20	14	7	0	6	20	20	12	5	9	40	34	6	41
6	Banbridge T	26	4	3	6	14	20	5	2	2	21	14	9	9	8	35	34	1	36
7	Queen's University	26	5	2	6	20	22	5	4	4	15	15	10	6	10	35	37	–2	36
8	Dundela	26	6	1	6	22	22	5	2	6	16	25	11	3	12	38	47	–9	36
9	Newington Youth	26	6	2	5	21	16	3	5	5	17	22	9	7	10	38	38	0	34
10	Dollingstown	26	5	4	4	25	20	4	3	6	21	31	9	7	10	46	51	–5	34
11	Glebe Rangers	26	6	1	6	19	26	3	4	6	15	20	9	5	12	34	46	–12	32
12	Coagh U	26	4	3	6	13	20	2	1	10	15	34	6	4	16	28	54	–26	22
13	Portstewart	26	3	3	7	22	30	3	0	10	12	28	6	3	17	34	58	–24	21
14	Wakehurst	26	0	3	10	13	32	1	1	11	12	35	1	4	21	25	67	–42	7

*Limavardy U not promoted – second tier licence application refused.

IFA YOUTH LEAGUE 2015–16

SECTION A

	P	W	D	L	F	A	GD	Pts
Linfield Rangers	22	19	2	1	87	16	71	59
Crusaders Colts	22	11	7	4	58	28	30	40
Cliftonville Strollers	22	12	4	6	63	39	24	40
Ballymena U III	22	11	5	6	51	38	13	38
Institute Colts	22	11	3	8	43	50	–7	36
Glentoran Colts	22	9	3	10	45	41	4	30
Portadown III	22	8	5	9	50	54	–4	29
Glenavon III	22	7	2	13	37	47	–10	23
Lisburn Distillery III	22	7	2	13	30	45	–15	23
Dungannon Swifts Youth	22	5	7	10	33	53	–20	22
Ballyclare Comrades Colts	22	4	2	16	33	77	–44	14
Coleraine Colts	22	4	1	17	22	69	–47	13

SECTION B

	P	W	D	L	F	A	GD	Pts
Ballinamallard U Youth	20	17	2	1	80	25	55	53
St Oliver Plunkett U	20	14	1	5	67	38	29	43
Ards Youth	20	13	2	5	63	46	17	41
Warrenpoint T Youth	20	11	3	6	56	35	21	36
Dundela Youth	20	9	3	8	52	43	9	30
Moyola Park Youth	20	9	2	9	41	41	0	29
Knockbreda Youth	20	7	2	11	38	53	–15	23
Carrick Rangers Colts	20	6	4	10	35	53	–18	22
Lurgan Celtic Youth	20	5	3	12	46	71	–25	18
Carniny Youth	20	4	1	15	34	63	–29	13
Annagh U Youth	20	2	1	17	24	74	–50	7

IFA RESERVE LEAGUE 2015–16

	P	W	D	L	F	A	GD	Pts
Cliftonville Olympic	33	28	1	4	101	39	62	85
Linfield Swifts	33	26	1	6	103	28	75	79
Crusaders	33	19	6	8	86	45	41	63
Ballymena U	33	18	4	11	81	57	24	58
Glenavon	33	14	4	15	81	73	8	46
Coleraine	33	14	3	16	62	55	7	45
Glentoran II	33	12	6	15	60	68	–8	42
Portadown	33	12	1	20	66	98	–32	37
Ballinamallard U II	33	10	4	19	60	89	–29	34
Carrick Rangers	33	9	6	18	45	71	–26	33
Dungannon Swifts	33	10	1	22	65	107	–42	31
Warrenpoint T	33	7	1	25	45	125	–80	22

TENNENT'S NORTHERN IRISH FA CUP 2015–16

After extra time.

FIRST ROUND

Newcastle v Ballynahinch Olympic	3-2
Drumaness Mills v Dunloy	1-4
Ballynure OB v Sirocco Works	1-2
Abbey Mills v UUJ	4-1
Ardstraw v Newry C AFC	1-5
Ballynahinch U v Valley Rangers	2-4
Ballywalter Rec. v Iveagh U	4-2
Bloomfield v Desertmartin	1-4
Chimney Corner v Downshire YM	3-3*

Downshire YM won 5-4 on penalties.

Comber Rec. v Windmill Stars	3-0
Craigavon C v Lower Maze	3-4
Crumlin Star v Shorts	3-0
Crumlin U v Nortel	3-2
Derriaghy CC v Orangefield OB	4-1
Donard Hospital v Shankill U	2-4
Dromara Village v Colin Valley	2-1
Dromore Amateurs v Lisburn Rangers	0-3
Dundonald v Broomhill	3-2
Dungiven v Newtowne	1-5
Dunmurry YM v Laurelvale	8-1
East Belfast v Ards Rangers	1-2
Fivemiletown U v St. Mary's YC	2-3
Grove U v Malachians	0-1
Hanover v Ballymoney U	5-1
Immaculata v 1st Bangor	2-1
Killyleagh YC v Bryansburn Rangers	3-2
Lurgan T v Wellington Rec.	0-1
Magherafelt Sky Blues v Brantwood	1-2
Moneyslane v Barn U	2-1
Mossley v 18th Newtownabbey OB	1-3
Newbuildings U v Crewe U	2-3
Oxford Sunnyside v Rosario YC	2-7
Portaferry R v Banbridge Rangers	0-3
Rathcoole v Ballymacash Rangers	3-2
Rathfern Rangers v Richhill	4-2
Saintfield U v Ardglass	1-2
Seapatrick v Killymoon Rangers	1-0
St Patrick's YM v Markethill Swifts	2-1
Strabane Ath v Kilmore Rec.	11-0
Tandragee R v Albert Foundry	1-0
Trojans v Islandmagee	2-1

Byes: Downpatrick, Dunmurry Rec., Groomsport, Larne Tech OB, Oxford U Stars, Rathfriland Rangers, Seagoe.

SECOND ROUND

18th Newtownabbey OB v Abbey Villa	1-3
Ardglass v Killyleagh YC	3-1
Ards Rangers v Strabane Ath	4-1
Ballywalter Rec. v Tandragee R	0-4
Banbridge Rangers v Seapatrick	2-0
Brantwood v Sirocco Works	2-3
Crumlin Star v Newry C AFC	2-1
Crumlin U v Seagoe	9-1
Derriaghy CC v Trojans	1-6
Desertmartin v Lisburn Rangers	1-2
Downshire YM v Moneyslane	4-2
Dromara Village v Newcastle	2-1
Dunloy v Dundonald	2-10
Dunmurry Rec. v Hanover	5-3
Groomsport v Newtowne	1-4
Immaculata v Dunmurry YM	10-0
Larne Tech. OB v Oxford U Stars	2-2*

Oxord U Stars won 5-4 on penalties.

Malachians v Comber Rec.	0-1
Rathcoole v Lower Maze	1-2
Rathfriland Rangers v Crewe U	1-0
St. Mary's YC v Downpatrick	3-1
St Patrick's YM v Shankill U	4-1
Valley Rangers v Rathfern Rangers	3-1
Wellington Rec. v Rosario YC	2-1

THIRD ROUND

Abbey Villa v Dunmurry Rec.	1-1*

Abbey Villa won 4-2 on penalties.

Ards Rangers v St. Mary's YC	4-1
Comber Rec. v Ardglass	3-4
Crumlin Star v Dundonald	5-0
Downshire YM v Crumlin U	2-3
Immaculata v Lower Maze	4-2
Lisburn Rangers v Tandragee R	3-0
Newtowne v Dromara Village	3-2

Oxford U Stars v St Patrick's YM	1-0
Rathfriland Rangers v Sirocco Works	4-2
Trojans v Banbridge Rangers	5-1
Valley Rangers v Wellington Rec.	0-2

FOURTH ROUND

Annagh U v Dollingstown	2-1
Ards v Donegal Celtic	7-0
Ards Rangers v Oxford U Stars	2-3
Armagh C v Lisburn Rangers	3-0
Ballyclare Comrades v Crumlin Star	0-1
Banbridge T v Crumlin U	3-3*

Banbridge T won 3-2 on penalties.

Dundela v Immaculata	0-2
H&W Welders v Wellington Rec.	3-2
Loughgall v Trojans	2-1
Lurgan Celtic v Ardglass	4-0
Newington v PSNI	1-2*
Queen's University v Tobermore U	1-2
Wakehurst v Glebe Rangers	1-1*

Wakehurst won on 3-2 on penalties.

Bangor v Coagh U	5-0
Institute v Newtowne	1-1*

Institute won on 5-4 on penalties.

Dergview v Sport & Leisure Swifts	1-6
Larne v Limavady U	2-0
Lisburn Distillery v Knockbreda	2-3*
Portstewart v Moyola Park	3-1
Abbey Villa v Rathfriland Rangers	0-4

FIFTH ROUND

Armagh C v Portstewart	2-2*

Armagh C won on 4-1 on penalties.

Banbridge T v Carrick Rangers	0-2
Cliftonville v Immaculata	2-0
Coleraine v Ballinamallard U	2-2*

Coleraine won on 4-2 on penalties.

Crumlin Star v Oxford U Stars	3-2
Crusaders v Rathfriland Rangers	3-0
Dungannon Swifts v Warrenpoint T	4-3
H&W Welders v Glenavon	1-4
Linfield v Ballymena U	2-1*
Loughgall v Larne	5-2
Lurgan Celtic v Bangor	2-1
Portadown v Wakehurst	6-1
Sport & Leisure Swifts v Institute	3-2*
Tobermore U v PSNI	0-2
Annagh U v Knockbreda	1-5
Glentoran v Ards	4-1

SIXTH ROUND

Cliftonville v Sport & Leisure Swifts	4-0
Dungannon Swifts v Crusaders	1-3
Glentoran v Glenavon	1-4
Linfield v Armagh C	7-0
Loughgall v PSNI	2-0
Lurgan Celtic v Knockbreda	1-0
Portadown v Coleraine	3-1
Carrick Rangers v Crumlin Star	1-0

QUARTER-FINALS

Carrick Rangers v Crusaders	0-3
Cliftonville v Linfield	0-3
Glenavon v Loughgall	2-1
Portadown v Lurgan Celtic	2-3

SEMI-FINALS

Linfield v Lurgan Celtic	3-0
Glenavon v Crusaders	4-3

TENNENTS NORTHERN IRISH FA CUP FINAL 2016

Windsor Park, Belfast, Saturday 7 May 2016

Glenavon (1) 2 *(Braniff 45, Hall 48)*

Linfield (0) 0   11,500

Glenavon: Tuffey; Kelly, Dillon, Kilmartin, Marshall, Cooper (Kearns 90), Bradley (Hamilton 85), Hall, Patton, Braniff, Martyn (Sykes 68).
Linfield: Deane; Haughey, Callacher (Quinn 77), Waterworth, Lowry, Burns, Ward, Clarke M (Millar 56), Mulgrew, Gaynor, Smyth.
Referee: Raymond Hetherington.

IRISH CUP FINALS (from 1946–47)

1946–47 Belfast Celtic 1, Glentoran 0	1983–84 Ballymena U 4, Carrick Rangers 1
1947–48 Linfield 3, Coleraine 0	1984–85 Glentoran 1:1, Linfield 1:0
1948–49 Derry City 3, Glentoran 1	1985–86 Glentoran 2, Coleraine 1
1949–50 Linfield 2, Distillery 1	1986–87 Glentoran 1, Larne 0
1950–51 Glentoran 3, Ballymena U 1	1987–88 Glentoran 1, Glenavon 0
1951–52 Ards 1, Glentoran 0	1988–89 Ballymena U 1, Larne 0
1952–53 Linfield 5, Coleraine 0	1989–90 Glentoran 3, Portadown 0
1953–54 Derry City 1, Glentoran 0	1990–91 Portadown 2, Glenavon 1
1954–55 Dundela 3, Glenavon 0	1991–92 Glenavon 2, Linfield 1
1955–56 Distillery 1, Glentoran 0	1992–93 Bangor 1:1:1, Ards 1:1:0
1956–57 Glenavon 2, Derry City 0	1993–94 Linfield 2, Bangor 0
1957–58 Ballymena U 2, Linfield 0	1994–95 Linfield 3, Carrick Rangers 1
1958–59 Glenavon 2, Ballymena U 0	1995–96 Glentoran 1, Glenavon 0
1959–60 Linfield 5, Ards 1	1996–97 Glenavon 1, Cliftonville 0
1960–61 Glenavon 5, Linfield 1	1997–98 Glentoran 1, Glenavon 0
1961–62 Linfield 4, Portadown 0	1998–99 *Portadown awarded trophy after Cliftonville*
1962–63 Linfield 2, Distillery 1	*were eliminated for using an ineligible player in*
1963–64 Derry City 2, Glentoran 0	*semi-final.*
1964–65 Coleraine 2, Glenavon 1	1999–2000 Glentoran 1, Portadown 0
1965–66 Glentoran 2, Linfield 0	2000–01 Linfield 1, Linfield 0
1966–67 Crusaders 3, Glentoran 1	2001–02 Linfield 2, Portadown 1
1967–68 Crusaders 2, Linfield 0	2002–03 Coleraine 1, Glentoran 0
1968–69 Ards 4, Distillery 2	2003–04 Glentoran 1, Coleraine 0
1969–70 Linfield 2, Ballymena U 1	2004–05 Portadown 5, Larne 1
1970–71 Distillery 3, Derry City	2005–06 Linfield 2, Glentoran 1
1971–72 Coleraine 2, Portadown 1	2006–07 Linfield 2, Dungannon Swifts 2
1972–73 Glentoran 3, Linfield 2	*(aet; Linfield won 3-2 on penalties).*
1973–74 Ards 2, Ballymena U 1	2007–08 Linfield 2, Coleraine 1
1974–75 Coleraine 1:0:1, Linfield 1:0:0	2008–09 Crusaders 1, Cliftonville 0
1975–76 Carrick Rangers 2, Linfield 1	2009–10 Linfield 2, Portadown 1
1976–77 Coleraine 4, Linfield 1	2010–11 Linfield 2, Crusaders 1
1977–78 Linfield 3, Ballymena U 1	2011–12 Linfield 4, Crusaders 1
1978–79 Cliftonville 3, Portadown 2	2012–13 Glentoran 3, Cliftonville 1
1979–80 Linfield 2, Crusaders 0	2013–14 Glentoran 1, Ballymena U 1
1980–81 Ballymena U 1, Glenavon 0	2014–15 Glentoran 1, Portadown 0
1981–82 Linfield 2, Coleraine 1	2015–16 Glenavon 2, Linfield 0
1982–83 Glentoran 1:2, Linfield 1:1	

JBE LEAGUE CUP 2015–16

After extra time.

FIRST ROUND

Ballyclare Comrades v Wakehurst	2-1
Glebe Rangers v Coagh U	1-0
Larne v Loughgall	3-1
Moyola Park v Donegal Celtic	2-0
Banbridge T v Armagh City	3-1
Portstewart v Knockbreda	0-3
Queens University v S&L Swifts	1-7
Tobermore U v Newington YC	0-2

SECOND ROUND

Glenavon v Annagh U	3-3*

3-3 at the end of normal time; Annagh U won 3-2 on penalties.

Cliftonville v Dundela	2-1
Newington YC v Dungannon Swifts	0-3
Warrenpoint T v Lisburn Distillery	5-1
Ballinamallard U v Banbridge T	5-0
Carrick Rangers v Lurgan Celtic	1-1*

0-0 at the end of normal time; Carrick Rangers won 5-4 on penalties.

Coleraine v Ballyclare Comrades	3-1
Crusaders v Knockbreda	3-1
Dergview v Ards	1-2
Glentoran v PSNI	1-0
Institute v S&L Swifts	5-2
Larne v Portadown	1-4*

1-1 at the end of normal time.

Limavady U v Bangor	2-1
Linfield v Glebe Rangers	5-0
Moyola Park v Ballymena U	1-4*

1-1 at the end of normal time.

Dollingstown v H&W Welders	0-4

THIRD ROUND

Annagh U v Ards	0-2
Coleraine v H&W Welders	1-1*

1-1 at the end of normal time; Coleraine won 3-1 on penalties.

Crusaders v Institute	3-4*

3-3 at the end of normal time.

Dungannon Swifts v Cliftonville	3-3*

1-1 at the end of normal time; Cliftonville won 4-3 on penalties.

Glentoran v Carrick Rangers	3-1
Limavady U v Ballymena U	0-1
Linfield v Ballinamallard U	0-1
Portadown v Warrenpoint T	1-2

QUARTER-FINALS

Ards v Ballinamallard U	2-2*

1-1 at the end of normal time; Ards won 7-6 on penalties.

Ballymena U v Coleraine	1-2
Cliftonville v Glentoran	3-2
Institute v Warrenpoint T	1-2

SEMI-FINALS

Ards v Coleraine	3-2*

2-2 at the end of normal time; Ards won 5-3 on penalties.

Warrenpoint T v Cliftonville	0-1*

0-0 at the end of normal time.

JBE LEAGUE CUP FINAL 2016

Solitude, Saturday February 13 2016

Cliftonville (1) 3 *(Donnelly M 35, McDaid 62, Garrett 83)*

Ards (0) 0

Cliftonville: Devlin, Cosgrove, Smyth, McGovern (Flynn 77), Ives, Donnelly M, Catney, Knowles, Curran (George 86), Donnelly J, McDaid (Garrett 81).
Ards: Brown, Hall, Gage, Cully, Lambe, Dorrian (O'Neill 46), McMillen (McAllister E 73), Arthurs, McAllister D, Baker, Carson.
Referee: Andrew Davey.

ROLL OF HONOUR SEASON 2015–16

Competition	Winner	Runner-up
Northern Irish Danske Bank Premier League	Crusaders	Linfield
Tennents Northern Irish FA Cup	Glenavon	Linfield
Belfast Telegraph Irish Championship Division One	Ards	H&W Welders
Belfast Telegraph Irish Championship Division Two	Limavady U	PSNI
JBE League Cup	Cliftonville	Ards
County Antrim Shield	Ballymena U	Linfield
Steel & Sons Cup	H&W Welders	Albert Foundry
Co Antrim Junior Shield	Harryville Homers	Ballyvea
Irish Junior Cup	Harryville Homers	Rosemount Rec
Mid Ulster Cup (Senior)	Dungannon Swifts	Armagh C
Harry Cavan Youth Cup	Crusaders Colts	Ballymena U III
George Wilson Memorial Cup	Crusaders Reserves	Cliftonville Olympic
North West Senior Cup	Limavady U	Coleraine
The Fermanagh Mulhern Cup	Strathroy Harps	Lisbellaw U
Intermediate Cup	Institute	Ards

NORTHERN IRELAND FOOTBALL WRITERS ASSOCIATION AWARDS 2015–16

MANAGER OF THE YEAR
Stephen Baxter (Crusaders)

PLAYER OF THE YEAR
Billy Joe Burns (Crusaders)

CHAMPIONSHIP PLAYER OF THE YEAR
Scott Davidson (H&W Welders)

YOUNG PLAYER OF THE YEAR
Joel Cooper (Glenavon)

INTERNATIONAL PERSONALITY OF THE YEAR
Michael O'Neill (Northern Ireland manager)

NON-SENIOR TEAM OF THE YEAR
Harryville Homers

MERIT AWARD
Billy and Graham Heslip (*Crusaders season ticket holders*)

DR MALCOLM BRODIE HALL OF FAME
Ronnie McFall, Mal Donaghy

TEAM OF THE SEASON
John Tuffey (Glenavon)
Billy Joe Burns (Crusaders)
Jimmy Callacher (Linfield)
Colin Coates (Crusaders)
Craig McClean (Crusaders)
Andy Hall (Glenavon)
Matthew Snoddy (Crusaders)
Aaron Burns (Linfield)
Paul Heatley (Crusaders)
Andrew Waterworth (Linfield)
Jordan Owens (Crusaders)

NIFWA @BTSPORT PREMIERSHIP PLAYER OF THE MONTH 2015–16

Month	Player	Team
August	Aaron Burns	Linfield
September	Andy Waterworth	Linfield
October	Keke Guillaume	Larne
November	Jordan Forsythe	Crusaders
December	Jonny Tuffey	Glenavon
January	Martin Murray	Warrenpoint Town (Cliftonville)
February	Josh Robinson	Crusaders
March	Ross Gaynor	Linfield
April	Gavin Whyte	Crusaders

NIFWA MANAGER OF THE MONTH 2015–16

Month	Player	Team
August	Warren Feeney	Linfield
September	Glen Ferguson	Ballymena United
October	Whitey Anderson	Ballinamallard United
November	Oran Kearney	Coleraine
December	David Healy	Linfield
January	Barry Gray	Warrenpoint Town
February	Rodney McAree	Dungannon Swifts
March	David Healy	Linfield
April	Stephen Baxter	Crusaders

NIFWA CHAMPIONSHIP 1 PLAYER OF THE MONTH 2015–16

Month	Player	Team
August	Michael McLellan	H&W Welders
September	Michael Dougherty	H&W Welders
October	Michael Doherty	Coleraine
November	Chris Trussell	Ballyclare Comrades
December	Danny McKee	Ards (Glenavon)
January	Warner Mullen	Loughgall
February	Shane McGinty	Institute
March	Stephen O'Neill	Ards
April	Stefan Lavery	Dungannon Swifts

EUROPEAN CUP FINALS

EUROPEAN CUP FINALS 1956–1992

Year	Winners v Runners-up		Venue	Attendance	Referee
1956	Real Madrid v Reims	4-3	Paris	38,239	A. Ellis (England)
1957	Real Madrid v Fiorentina	2-0	Madrid	124,000	L. Horn (Netherlands)
1958	Real Madrid v AC Milan	3-2*	Brussels	67,000	A. Alsteen (Belgium)
1959	Real Madrid v Reims	2-0	Stuttgart	72,000	A. Dutsch (West Germany)
1960	Real Madrid v Eintracht Frankfurt	7-3	Glasgow	127,621	J. Mowat (Scotland)
1961	Benfica v Barcelona	3-2	Berne	26,732	G. Dienst (Switzerland)
1962	Benfica v Real Madrid	5-3	Amsterdam	61,257	L. Horn (Netherlands)
1963	AC Milan v Benfica	2-1	Wembley	45,715	A. Holland (England)
1964	Internazionale v Real Madrid	3-1	Vienna	71,333	J. Stoll (Austria)
1965	Internazionale v Benfica	1-0	Milan	89,000	G. Dienst (Switzerland)
1966	Real Madrid v Partizan Belgrade	2-1	Brussels	46,745	R. Kreitlein (West Germany)
1967	Celtic v Internazionale	2-1	Lisbon	45,000	K. Tschenscher (West Germany)
1968	Manchester U v Benfica	4-1*	Wembley	92,225	C. Lo Bello (Italy)
1969	AC Milan v Ajax	4-1	Madrid	31,782	J. Ortiz de Mendibil (Spain)
1970	Feyenoord v Celtic	2-1*	Milan	53,187	C. Lo Bello (Italy)
1971	Ajax v Panathinaikos	2-0	Wembley	90,000	J. Taylor (England)
1972	Ajax v Internazionale	2-0	Rotterdam	61,354	R. Helies (France)
1973	Ajax v Juventus	1-0	Belgrade	89,484	M. Guglovic (Yugoslavia)
1974	Bayern Munich v Atletico Madrid	1-1	Brussels	48,722	V. Loraux (Belgium)
Replay	Bayern Munich v Atletico Madrid	4-0	Brussels	23,325	A. Delcourt (Belgium)
1975	Bayern Munich v Leeds U	2-0	Paris	48,374	M. Kitabdjian (France)
1976	Bayern Munich v Saint-Etienne	1-0	Glasgow	54,864	K. Palotai (Hungary)
1977	Liverpool v Moenchengladbach	3-1	Rome	52,078	R. Wurtz (France)
1978	Liverpool v Club Brugge	1-0	Wembley	92,500	C. Corver (Netherlands)
1979	Nottingham F v Malmo	1-0	Munich	57,500	E. Linemayr (Austria)
1980	Nottingham F v Hamburger SV	1-0	Madrid	51,000	A. Garrido (Portugal)
1981	Liverpool v Real Madrid	1-0	Paris	48,360	K. Palotai (Hungary)
1982	Aston Villa v Bayern Munich	1-0	Rotterdam	46,000	G. Konrath (France)
1983	Hamburg v Juventus	1-0	Athens	73,500	N. Rainea (Romania)
1984	Liverpool v Roma	1-1*	Rome	69,693	E. Fredriksson (Sweden)
	(Liverpool won 4-2 on penalties)				
1985	Juventus v Liverpool	1-0	Brussels	58,000	A. Daina (Switzerland)
1986	Steaua Bucharest v Barcelona	0-0*	Seville	70,000	M. Vautrot (France)
	(Steaua won 2-0 on penalties)				
1987	FC Porto v Bayern Munich	2-1	Vienna	57,500	A. Ponnet (Belgium)
1988	PSV Eindhoven v Benfica	0-0*	Stuttgart	68,000	L. Agnolin (Italy)
	(PSV won 6-5 on penalties)				
1989	AC Milan v Steaua Bucharest	4-0	Barcelona	97,000	K.-H. Tritschler (West Germany)
1990	AC Milan v Benfica	1-0	Vienna	57,500	H. Kohl (Austria)
1991	Crvena Zvezda v Olympique Marseille	0-0*	Bari	56,000	T. Lanese (Italy)
	(Crvena Zvezda won 5-3 on penalties)				
1992	Barcelona v Sampdoria	1-0*	Wembley	70,827	A. Schmidhuber (Germany)

UEFA CHAMPIONS LEAGUE FINALS 1993–2016

1993	Marseille† v AC Milan	1-0	Munich	64,400	K. Rothlisberger (Switzerland)
1994	AC Milan v Barcelona	4-0	Athens	70,000	P. Don (England)
1995	Ajax v AC Milan	1-0	Vienna	49,730	I. Craciunescu (Romania)
1996	Juventus v Ajax	1-1*	Rome	70,000	M. D. Vega (Spain)
	(Juventus won 4-2 on penalties)				
1997	Borussia Dortmund v Juventus	3-1	Munich	59,000	S. Puhl (Hungary)
1998	Real Madrid v Juventus	1-0	Amsterdam	48,500	H. Krug (Germany)
1999	Manchester U v Bayern Munich	2-1	Barcelona	90,245	P. Collina (Italy)
2000	Real Madrid v Valencia	3-0	Paris	80,000	S. Braschi (Italy)
2001	Bayern Munich v Valencia	1-1*	Milan	79,000	D. Jol (Netherlands)
	(Bayern Munich won 5-4 on penalties)				
2002	Real Madrid v Leverkusen	2-1	Glasgow	50,499	U. Meier (Switzerland)
2003	AC Milan v Juventus	0-0*	Manchester	62,315	M. Merk (Germany)
	(AC Milan won 3-2 on penalties)				
2004	FC Porto v Monaco	3-0	Gelsenkirchen	53,053	K. M. Nielsen (Denmark)
2005	Liverpool v AC Milan	3-3*	Istanbul	65,000	M. M. González (Spain)
	(Liverpool won 3-2 on penalties)				
2006	Barcelona v Arsenal	2-1	Paris	79,610	T. Hauge (Norway)
2007	AC Milan v Liverpool	2-1	Athens	74,000	H. Fandel (Germany)
2008	Manchester U v Chelsea	1-1*	Moscow	67,310	L. Michel (Slovakia)
	(Manchester U won 6-5 on penalties)				
2009	Barcelona v Manchester U	2-0	Rome	62,467	M. Busacca (Switzerland)
2010	Internazionale v Bayern Munich	2-0	Madrid	73,490	H. Webb (England)
2011	Barcelona v Manchester U	3-1	Wembley	87,695	V. Kassai (Hungary)
2012	Chelsea v Bayern Munich	1-1*	Munich	62,500	P. Proença (Portugal)
	(Chelsea won 4-3 on penalties)				
2013	Bayern Munich v Borussia Dortmund	2-1	Wembley	86,298	N. Rizzoli (Italy)
2014	Real Madrid v Atletico Madrid	4-1*	Lisbon	60,000	B. Kuipers (Netherlands)
2015	Barcelona v Juventus	3-1	Berlin	70,442	C. Cakir (Turkey)
2016	Real Madrid v Atletico Madrid	1-1*	Milan	71,942	M. Clattenburg (England)
	(Real Madrid won 5-3 on penalties)				

†*Subsequently stripped of title.*
*After extra time.

UEFA CHAMPIONS LEAGUE 2015-16

* *Denotes player sent off.*

FIRST QUALIFYING ROUND FIRST LEG

Tuesday, 30 June 2015

Crusaders (0) 0
Levadia Tallinn (0) 0 1748
Crusaders: (442) O'Neill; Burns, Coates, Robinson, McClean; Mitchell, Caddell (Forsyth 76), Clarke, Heatley; Owens (O'Flynn 85), Carvill.
Levadia Tallinn: (442) Pikker; Rakhmanaw, Laitinen, Kruglov, Pikk; Rahn, Pecha, El Hussieny, Luts; Marin (Antonov 61), Teever (Saag 85).

Lincoln (0) 0
Santa Coloma (0) 0 1520
Lincoln: (442) Navas; Sambruno (Bardon 82), Casciaro R, Chipolina J, Chipolina R; Garcia, Chietino, Walker, Pegalajar (Yome 75); Casciaro K, Casciaro L.
Santa Coloma: (442) Casals; Lima, Wagner, Ramos A, Ramos R; Pujol, Juvenal, Riera (Juanfer 61), Rebes (Rodriguez 74); Parra, Martinez C (Toscano 83).

Pyunik (1) 2 *(Satunyan 45, Romero 48)*
Folgore/Falciano (0) 1 *(Hirsch 71)* 4000
Pyunik: (442) Ayvazov; Satunyan, Hayrapetyan, Haroyan, Hovhannisyan G (Shahinyan 79); Voskanyan, Yuspashyan, Badoyan, Hovhannisyan K; Jeremiah (Hakobyan 65), Hovsepyan (Romero 46).
Folgore/Falciano: (442) Bicchirelli; Hirsch (Amici 90), Bollini F, Mazzola, Berardi; Bollini G, Pacini (Casadei 72), Muccini, Perrotta (Della Valle 80); Ceschi*, Tardini.

Wednesday, 1 July 2015

B36 Torshavn (1) 1 *(Samuelsen 7)*
The New Saints (1) 2 *(Quigley 9, Wilde 90)* 1050
B36 Torshavn: (4141) Thomsen; Eysturoy, Eriksen, Faero, Heinesen; Jakobsen (Mellemgaard 81); Nielsen, Borg (Dam 62), Thorleifsson (Petersen P 90), Samuelsen; Cieslewicz.
The New Saints: (433) Harrison; Spender, Edwards K, Rawlinson, Marriott; Edwards A, Seargeant, Finley (Williams 81); Cieslewicz (Mullan 74), Wilde, Quigley (Draper 83).

FIRST QUALIFYING ROUND SECOND LEG

Tuesday, 7 July 2015

Folgore/Falciano (0) 1 *(Traini 66)*
Pyunik (2) 2 *(Hovhannisyan K 6, Satunyan 44)* 821
Folgore/Falciano: (442) Bicchirelli; Traini, Bollini G (Casadei 83), Mazzola, Berardi; Genestreti, Bollini F (Rossi 71), Pacini, Nucci (Della Valle 59); Muccini, Hirsch.
Pyunik: (442) Ayvazov; Hovhannisyan K (Hovhannisyan G 71), Satunyan, Hayrapetyan, Haroyan; Voskanian, Yuspashyan, Badoyan, Gagik Poghosyan (Hovsepyan 65); Hakobyan (Jeremiah 73), Romero.

Levadia Tallinn (1) 1 *(Luts 22)*
Crusaders (1) 1 *(Carvill 4)* 1230
Levadia Tallinn: (451) Pikker; Laitinen, Rahn, Rakhmanaw, Pikk; El Hussieny (Subbotin 88), Antonov, Pecha (Saag 72), Luts, Kruglov; Teever.
Crusaders: (4321) O'Neill; McClean, Magowan, Mitchell, Burns; Robinson, Forsyth, Caddell (Clarke 79); Carvill (O'Carroll 90), Owens (O'Flynn 70); Heatley.
Crusaders won on away goals.

Santa Coloma (1) 1 *(Lima 44)*
Lincoln (0) 2 *(Bardon 48, Casciaro L 64)* 700
Santa Coloma: (442) Casals; Lima, Wagner (Mercade 68), Ramos A, Ramos R; Pujol, Juvenal, Juanfer (Toscano 52), Rebes; Parra, Martinez C (Martinez J 76).
Lincoln: (442) Bardon; Casciaro L (Chrayeh 90), Navas, Sambruno, Chipolina J; Chipolina R, Casciaro R, Chietino, Walker; Pegalajar (Calderon 46), Casciaro K (Garcia 78).

The New Saints (2) 4 *(Wilde 15, 27, 47, Williams 89)*
B36 Torshavn (0) 1 *(Cieslewicz 90)* 1148
The New Saints: (433) Harrison; Spender, Edwards K, Rawlinson, Marriott; Edwards A (Williams 83), Finley, Seargeant; Cieslewicz (Mullan 62), Wilde (Draper 74), Quigley.
B36 Torshavn: (4411) Thomsen; Eysturoy, Eriksen, Faero (Mellemgaard 37), Heinesen; Thorleifsson, Nielsen, Jakobsen (Petersen B 85), Samuelsen; Dam (Petersen P 76); Cieslewicz.

SECOND QUALIFYING ROUND FIRST LEG

Tuesday, 14 July 2015

APOEL Nicosia (0) 0
Vardar (0) 0 14,531
APOEL Nicosia: (532) Waterman; Carlao (Joao Guilherme 41), Antoniades, Astiz, Mario Sergio, Morais; Makrides (Efrem 60), Vinicius, De Vincenti, Leal, Sotiriou (Piatkowski 66).
Vardar: (451) Pacovski; Popov, Mijuskovic, Grncarov, Hambardzumyan; Velkovski, Blazevski (Asani 88), Nikolov, Gligorov, Juan Felipe (Dashyan 64); Ivanovski (Stojkov 75).

Hibernians (0) 2 *(Jorginho 74, Lima 85)*
Maccabi Tel Aviv (1) 1 *(Igiebor 22)* 1470
Hibernians: (433) Borg; Soares, Agius, Da Garcia, Dias; Kristensen, Lima, Failla; Cohen (Bezzina 90), Gilmar (Silva 64), Jorginho (Mbong 90).
Maccabi Tel Aviv: (433) Juan Pablo; Ben Haim, Tibi, Mitrovic (Ben Haroush 46), Carlos Garcia; Igiebor, Vermouth (Itzhaki 59), Alberman; Micha, Ben Chaim, Ben Basat.

Ludogorets Razgrad (0) 0
Milsami (1) 1 *(Antoniuc 41)* 5120
Ludogorets Razgrad: (442) Moti; Stoyanov, Angulo, Aleksandrov A, Minev; Dyakov, Aleksandrov M (Cicinho 63), Sasha, Andrianantenaina (Prepelita 46); Quixada (Chunchukov 46), Misidjan.
Milsami: (442) Antoniuc; Mitu, Rassulov, Erhan, Monday; Rhaili, Cojocari, Patras, Andronic (Zarichnyuk 90); Belak (Bolohan 69), Surdu (Bud 59).

Maribor (1) 1 *(Suler 5)*
Astana (0) 0 10,458
Maribor: (4231) Handanovic; Stojanovic, Rajcevic, Suler, Viler; Mertelj, Kabha (Filipovic 66); Ibraimi, Tavares, Vrsic (Bohar 66); Volas (Zahovic 74).
Astana: (442) Loginovskiy; Ilic, Anicic, Postnikov, Shomko; Dzholchiev (Kethevoama 90), Canas, Maksimovic, Twumasi; Nuserbaev (Kabananga 72), Zhukov (Dedechko 82).

Midtjylland (1) 1 *(Rasmussen 33)*
Lincoln (0) 0 5291
Midtjylland: (442) Dahlin; Hansen, Sviatchenko, Lauridsen, Romer; Poulsen, Sparv, Royer, Larsen; Urena Porras, Rasmussen.
Lincoln: (442) Navas; Sambruno, Chipolina J, Casciaro R, Garcia; Chietino, Walker, Bardon, Pegalajar (Yome 78); Casciaro K, Casciaro L (Bosio 90).

Molde (2) 5 *(Elyounoussi 36, 45, Kamara 84, 90, Mostrom 90)*
Pyunik (0) 0 5650
Molde: (433) Horvath; Toivio, Gabrielsen, Forren, Rindaroy; Linnes (Mostrom 66), Singh (Berg Hestad 81), Hussain; Elyounoussi, Kamara, Svendsen (Hoiland 68).
Pyunik: (442) Ayvazov; Hovhannisyan G (Jeremiah 59), Voskanian, Haroyan, Hayrapetyan; Hovhannisyan K, Yuspashyan, Gagik Poghosyan, Badoyan (Hakobyan 71); Satunyan, Romero.

Partizan Belgrade (0) 1 *(Babovic 83)*
Dila Gori (0) 0   11,746
Partizan Belgrade: (442) Zivkovic Z; Babovic, Balazic, Vulicevic, Cirkovic; Petrovic, Brasanac, Jevtovic, Ninkovic (Ilic 72); Bojinov (Saponjic 77), Oumarou (Zivkovic A 60).
Dila Gori: (442) Shevchenko; Kvirkvelia, Navalovsky, Kvakhadze, Khurtsilava; Razmadze, Gvalia, Palavandishvili■, Papava; Martsvaladze (Dzaria 83), Iluridze (Ghonghadze 90).

Sarajevo (0) 0
Lech Poznan (1) 2 *(Hamalainen 40, Thomalla 62)* 16,500
Sarajevo: (4411) Ostrakovic; Hebibovic, Stepanov, Barbaric, Puzigaca; Duljevic, Radovac (Rustemovic 78), Cimirot, Velkoski (Amer Bekic 73); Stojcev (Alispahic 66); Benko.
Lech Poznan: (4411) Buric; Kedziora, Kaminski, Kadar, Douglas; Kownacki (Formella 38), Tralka, Linetty (Dudka 7), Pawlowski (Jevtic 78); Hamalainen; Thomalla.

Skenderbeu (2) 4 *(Nimaga 15, Salihi 34, 83, Berisha 76)*
Crusaders (0) 1 *(Owens 48)*   5500
Skenderbeu: (433) Shehi; Arapi, Osmani, Vangjeli, Radas; Progni (Latifi 74), Nimaga, Shkembi; Salihi (Abilaliaj 90), Hristov (Esquerdinha 79), Berisha.
Crusaders: (451) O'Neill; Burns, Magowan, Robinson, McClean; Carvill (Forsyth 59 (Snoddy 72)), Heatley, Caddell, Mitchell, Clarke (O'Carroll 88); Owens.

The New Saints (0) 0
Videoton (0) 1 *(Gyurcso 77)*   1068
The New Saints: (442) Harrison; Spender, Marriott, Edwards K, Rawlinson; Seargeant (Williams 81), Finley, Edwards A, Cieslewicz (Mullan 57); Quigley, Wilde (Draper 84).
Videoton: (442) Gabor; Vinicius, Fejes, Juhasz, Szolnoki; Kovacs, Patkai (Trebotic 70), Simon, Oliveira (Luyckx 83); Koltai (Pajac 66), Gyurcso.

Trencin (0) 0
Steaua Bucharest (0) 2 *(Stanciu 63, Hamroun 70)* 6936
Trencin: (433) Semrinec; Cogley, Ramon, Rundic, Madu; Ibrahim (Koolwijk 79), Lobotka, Bero; Guba (Ferreira Da Silva 59), Jairo, Van Kessel.
Steaua Bucharest: (4411) Cojocaru; Papp, Tamas, Varela, Guilherme; Popa, Sulley, Breeveld (Tahar 81), Chipciu (Hamroun 59); Stanciu; Tade (Tudorie 87).

Ventspils (0) 1 *(Jemelins 63)*
HJK Helsinki (0) 3 *(Zeneli 75 (pen), Jallow 86, Tanaka 90)*   2450
Ventspils: (442) Melnicenko; Krjauklis, Barinovs, Jemelins, Sinelnikovs; Zigajevs (Doric 71), Zulevs, Paulius, Rugins (Mordatenko 86); Mujeci (Turkovs 82), Karlsons.
HJK Helsinki: (442) Orlund; Baah, Heikkila, Heikkinen, Sorsa; Savage, Schuller, Zeneli, Moussi; Tanaka, Havenaar (Jallow 84).

Wednesday, 15 July 2015

BATE Borisov (2) 2 *(Karnitskiy 11, Yablonskiy 38)*
Dundalk (1) 1 *(McMillan 32)*   11,421
BATE Borisov: (442) Chernik; Mladenovic, Dubra, Zhavnerchik, Milunovic; Stasevich, Baha (Nikolic 64), Yablonskiy, Karnitskiy; Gordeichuk (Ryas 80), Rodionov.
Dundalk: (442) Rogers; Towell, Gartland, Boyle, Massey; Shields, Gannon, O'Donnell, Horgan (Byrne 88); Mountney (Meenan 70), McMillan (Finn 77).

Celtic (1) 2 *(Boyata 44, Johansen 56)*
Stjarnan (0) 0   37,969
Celtic: (4411) Gordon; Lustig, Boyata (Ambrose 82), Mulgrew, Izaguirre; Forrest (Griffiths 58), Brown, Bitton, Armstrong; Johansen; Ciftci (Stokes 74).
Stjarnan: (4231) Nielsen; Aegisson, Gudjonsson, Laxdal, Arnason; Praest, Johannsson (Runarsson 73); Bjorgvinsson (Palsson 86), Finsen, Bjornsson (Gunnarson 81); Hansen.

Dinamo Zagreb (1) 1 *(Henriquez 36)*
Fola Esch (1) 1 *(Hadji 25)*   9100
Dinamo Zagreb: (442) Eduardo; Henriquez, Taravel (Hodzic 80), Goncalo (Cekici 69), Pivaric; Ivo Pinto, Simunovic, Paulo Machado (Pamic 59), Rog; Soudani, Pjaca.
Fola Esch: (442) Hym; Martino, Klein, Kirch, Martin; Payal, Ronny■, Dallevedove, Bensi (Hornuss 9); Francoise (Rani 78), Hadji (Camerling 82).

Malmo (0) 0
Zalgiris (0) 0   12,436
Malmo: (442) Azinovic; Bengtsson, Yotun, Tinnerholm, Brorsson; Eikrem (Mehmeti 82), Lewicki, Kroon (Rakip 69), Cibicki (Sana 46); Rosenberg, Berget.
Zalgiris: (442) Vitkauskas; Vaitkunas, Kerla, Semberas, Pilibaitis; Luksa (Janusauskas 78), Kuklys, Kendysh, Svrljuga; Sernas (Goncalves 86), Chula (Nyuiadzi 24).

Qarabag (0) 0
Rudar Pljevlja (0) 0   28,854
Qarabag: (4231) Sehic; Garayev (Diniyev 72), Medvedev, Sadygov, Guseynov; Quintana, Almeida; Agolli, El Jadeyaoui, Tagiyev; Reynaldo.
Rudar Pljevlja: (442) Radanovic; Djuric, Nestorovic, Zivkovic (Tomasevic 66), Jovanovic (Reljic 60); Ivanovic, Radisic, Brnovic, Vlahovic; Vukovic, Knezevic (Soppo 86).

SECOND QUALIFYING ROUND SECOND LEG

Tuesday, 21 July 2015

Crusaders (0) 3 *(O'Flynn 50, Mitchell 90, Snoddy 90)*
Skenderbeu (0) 2 *(Berisha 69, Latifi 77)*   1548
Crusaders: (442) O'Neill; Burns, Coates, Robinson, McClean; Mitchell, Caddell (Clarke 73), Snoddy, O'Flynn (O'Carroll 67); Owens, Carvill.
Skenderbeu: (442) Shehi; Arapi■, Jashanica, Vangjeli, Radas; Nimaga, Berisha, Latifi (Progni 85), Shkembi; Salihi (Hristov 90), Esquerdinha.

Dila Gori (0) 0
Partizan Belgrade (1) 2 *(Brasanac 37, Oumarou 64)* 700
Dila Gori: (442) Shevchenko; Khurtsilava, Kvakhadze, Bagaev, Navalovsky; Papava (Kvirkvia 46), Gvalia, Dzaria, Iluridze (Mashukov 46); Martsvaladze (Eristavi 82), Modebadze.
Partizan Belgrade: (442) Zivkovic Z; Vulicevic, Balazic, Cirkovic, Petrovic; Babovic, Brasanac (Ilic 80), Jevtovic, Zivkovic A; Oumarou (Saponjic 87), Bojinov (Ninkovic 68).

HJK Helsinki (0) 1 *(Havenaar 83)*
Ventspils (0) 0   6562
HJK Helsinki: (442) Orlund; Baah, Heikkila, Sorsa (Peiponen 87), Tanaka (Klinga 67); Zeneli (Jallow 85), Heikkinen, Schuller, Moussi; Savage, Havenaar.
Ventspils: (442) Melnicenko; Sinelnikovs, Krjauklis, Jemelins, Zulevs (Bezusconoks 90); Rugins, Paulius, Doric, Turkovs (Karlsons 81); Barinovs, Mujeci (Mordatenko 77).

Lincoln (0) 0
Midtjylland (1) 2 *(Pusic 44, Duelund 89)*   1950
Lincoln: (442) Navas; Sambruno (Yome 72), Chipolina J (Jolly 82), Chipolina R, Casciaro R; Chietino, Walker, Bardon, Pegalajar (Parker 86); Casciaro K, Casciaro L.
Midtjylland: (442) Andersen; Pusic, Hansen, Sviatchenko (Banggaard 46), Lauridsen; Romer, Poulsen, Sparv, Larsen (Duelund 69); Olsson, Sisto (Gemmer 54).

Maccabi Tel Aviv (1) 5 *(Jorginho 32 (og), Zahavi 58 (pen), 90, Ben Chaim 61, Igiebor 82)*
Hibernians (0) 1 *(Soares 52)*   13,125
Maccabi Tel Aviv: (442) Juan Pablo; Ben Haroush (Ziv 62), Carlos Garcia, Ben Haim, Spungin; Ben Chaim (Itzhaki 81), Alberman, Mitrovic, Micha (Ben Basat 86); Igiebor, Zahavi.
Hibernians: (3142) Borg; Soares, Agius, Da Garcia; Lima; Dias (Mbong 88), Kristensen, Cohen, Failla; Gilmar (Silva 63), Jorginho.

Milsami (1) 2 *(Andronic 26, Racu 89)*
Ludogorets Razgrad (1) 1 *(Wanderson 25)* 2970
Milsami: (442) Mitu; Rhaili, Erhan, Shedrack, Rassulov; Patras, Belak, Andronic (Bolohan 76), Cojocari■; Antoniuc (Zarichnyuk 77), Bud (Racu 87).
Ludogorets Razgrad: (442) Stoyanov; Aleksandrov A, Angulo, Minev, Moti; Dyakov, Prepelita (Lukoki 63), Quixada, Marcelinho; Wanderson, Misidjan.

Pyunik (0) 1 *(Badoyan 75)*
Molde (0) 0 2500
Pyunik: (442) Ayvazov; Hayrapetyan, Haroyan, Voskanyan, Yuspashyan; Hovhannisyan K, Badoyan, Gagik Poghosyan, Hovsepyan; Satumyan (Ghukas Poghosyan 70), Jeremiah.
Molde: (442) Linde; Forren, Flo, Toivio, Gabrielsen; Hussain (Bendiksen 67), Hestad E, Kamara (Hoiland 61), Mostrom (Agnaldo 73); Elyounoussi, Svendsen.

Vardar (0) 1 *(Ljamchevski 90)*
APOEL Nicosia (0) 1 *(De Vincenti 60)* 22,540
Vardar: (4231) Pacovski; Popov, Mijuskovic, Grncarov, Hambardzumyan; Velkovski (Stojkov 64), Gligorov; Dashyan (Ivanovski 79), Juan Felipe, Grozdanoski (Ljamchevski 71); Blazevski.
APOEL Nicosia: (4231) Waterman; Mario Sergio, Vinicius, Astiz, Antoniades; Makrides, Morais; De Vincenti (Ioannou 85), Sotiriou (Stilic 57), Vander (Alexandrou 72); Leal.
APOEL Nicosia won on away goals.

Zalgiris (0) 0
Malmo (0) 1 *(Tinnerholm 55)* 4933
Zalgiris: (442) Vitkauskas; Vaitkunas, Kerla■, Semberas, Kendysh; Svrljuga, Luksa (Lucas Gaucho 64), Pilibaitis, Kuklys (Janusauskas 34); Sernas (Chula 77), Nyuiadzi.
Malmo: (442) Azinovic (Johansson 50); Tinnerholm, Yotun, Bengtsson, Brorsson; Rakip, Lewicki, Eikrem (Vindheim 90), Sana (Adu 75); Berget, Rosenberg.

Wednesday, 22 July 2015

Astana (2) 3 *(Dzholchiev 12, Canas 43, Twumasi 58)*
Maribor (1) 1 *(Rajcevic 39)* 23,650
Astana: (442) Loginovskiy, Ilic, Anicic, Postnikov, Shomko; Dzholchiev, Canas■, Maksimovic (Kethevoama 46), Twumasi (Beisebekov 83); Nuserbaev (Dedechko 71), Zhukov.
Maribor: (442) Handanovic; Stojanovic, Rajcevic, Suler, Viler; Ibraimi, Mertelj (Filipovic 60), Kabha, Bohar (Vrsic 77); Mendy, Tavares.

Dundalk (0) 0
BATE Borisov (0) 0 3103
Dundalk: (442) Rogers; Gartland, Towell, Boyle, Massey; O'Donnell, Gannon, Horgan (Byrne 82), Finn (Mountney 76); Meenan (Shields 56), McMillan.
BATE Borisov: (442) Chernik; Milunovic, Zhavnerchik, Dubra, Mladenovic; Karnitskiy (Signevich 90), Aleksiyevich (Nikolic 68), Stasevich, Baha; Gordeichuk (Ryas 85), Rodionov.

Fola Esch (0) 0
Dinamo Zagreb (2) 3 *(Pjaca 29, 40, Rog 75)* 3300
Fola Esch: (433) Hym; Martino, Klein, Martin, Kirch; Rani (Klapp 68), Payal, Dallevedoe; Hornuss (Camerling 57), Hadji, Francoise (Rachid 79).
Dinamo Zagreb: (4321) Eduardo; Matel, Sigali (Benkovic 78), Simunovic, Taravel; Soudani (Fernandes 69), Ademi, Pivaric; Pjaca, Paulo Machado; Henriquez (Rog 59).

Lech Poznan (1) 1 *(Douglas 6)*
Sarajevo (0) 0 12,205
Lech Poznan: (442) Buric; Kaminski, Douglas, Kedziora, Kadar; Dudka (Tetteh 72), Tralka, Hamalainen (Jevtic 69), Pawlowski (Lovrencsics 78); Thomalla, Formella.
Sarajevo: (442) Ostrakovic; Puzigaca, Tatomirovic, Stepanov, Barbaric; Alispahic, Duljevic (Velkoski 54), Cimirot, Radovac (Stojcev 77); Almir Bekic (Hebibovic 85), Benko.

Rudar Pljevlja (0) 0
Qarabag (0) 1 *(Reynaldo 57)* 1400
Rudar Pljevlja: (442) Radanovic; Nestorovic, Zivkovic, Jovanovic (Soppo 81), Radisic; Brnovic, Djuric, Vlahovic, Vukovic (Reljic 78); Ivanovic, Knezevic.
Qarabag: (442) Sehic; Guseynov, Medvedev, Sadygov, Agolli (Gurbanov 64); Quintana, Garayev, Almeida, El Jadeyaoui (Tagiyev 56); Diniyev (Mammadov 79), Reynaldo.

Steaua Bucharest (0) 2 *(Sulley 57, Tade 60 (pen))*
Trencin (2) 3 *(Ferreira Da Silva 13, 84, Bero 21)*
Steaua Bucharest: (4231) Cojocaru; Papp, Varela (Rapa 35), Tosca, Guilherme; Breeveld, Sulley; Popa, Stanciu (Hamroun 19), Chipciu; Tade (Tahar 82).
Trencin: (433) Semrinec; Cogley (Ibrahim 73), Ramon, Rundic■, Madu; Lobotka, Koolwijk, Bero; Jairo (Klescik 87), Ferreira Da Silva, Van Kessel (Guba 64).
Behind closed doors.

Stjarnan (1) 1 *(Finsen 7)*
Celtic (1) 4 *(Bitton 33, Mulgrew 49, Griffiths 88, Johansen 90)* 1022
Stjarnan: (433) Nielsen; Aegisson, Laxdal, Gudjonsson, Arnason; Runarsson (Gunnarson 58), Praest, Punyed; Bjorgvinsson (Bjornsson 46), Hansen (Barddal 80), Finsen.
Celtic: (4231) Gordon; Lustig (Ambrose 52), van Dijk, Boyata, Mulgrew; Bitton, Brown; Armstrong (Griffiths 62), Johansen, Mackay-Steven; Ciftci (Rogic 81).

Videoton (0) 1 *(Gyurcso 107)*
The New Saints (0) 1 *(Williams 78)* 3268
Videoton: (4141) Danilovic; Luyckx (Simon 86), Fejes, Lang, Juhasz (Vinicius 67); Szolnoki; Gyurcso, Patkai, Trebotic, Oliveira; Ivanovski (Kovacs 56).
The New Saints: (433) Harrison; Spender, Edwards K, Rawlinson, Marriott; Finley■, Seargeant (Williams 72), Edwards A; Mullan (Draper 109), Wilde, Cieslewicz (Quigley 66).
aet.

THIRD QUALIFYING ROUND FIRST LEG

Tuesday, 28 July 2015

CSKA Moscow (1) 2 *(Dzagoev 14, Tosic 53)*
Sparta Prague (1) 2 *(Fatai 15, Krejci 57)* 10,500
CSKA Moscow: (451) Akinfeev; Fernandes, Ignashevich, Berezutski A, Nababkin (Schennikov 46); Wernbloom, Tosic (Strandberg 86), Dzagoev (Milanov 72), Eremenko, Natcho; Musa.
Sparta Prague: (451) Bicik; Holek, Nhamoinesu, Hybs, Vacha; Matejovsky, Dockal (Brabec 90), Marecek, Frydek, Krejci (Paixao 84); Fatai (Konate 57).

Dinamo Zagreb (1) 1 *(Henriquez 18)*
Molde (1) 1 *(Kamara 21)* 9327
Dinamo Zagreb: (451) Eduardo; Taravel (Fernandes 73), Simunovic, Sigali, Matel (Ivo Pinto 56); Pivaric, Pjaca, Ademi, Paulo Machado■ (Rog 64); Soudani; Henriquez.
Molde: (451) Horvath; Linnes, Toivio, Forren, Rindaroy (Gabrielsen 80); Mostrom (Flo 72), Hussain (Hestad D 67), Singh, Hestad E, Elyounoussi; Kamara.

Fenerbahce (0) 0
Shakhtar Donetsk (0) 0 37,342
Fenerbahce: (442) Demirel; Kaldirim, Bruno Alves, Kjaer, Erkin; Nani, Topal (Meireles 64), Souza, Diego (Stoch 84); Fernandao, Sow (van Persie 68).
Shakhtar Donetsk: (4411) Pyatov; Srna, Ordets, Rakitskiy, Shevchuk; Marlos (Eduardo 77), Fred (Malyshev 90), Stepanenko, Taison (Kovalenko 79); Alex Teixeira; Gladkyy.

Maccabi Tel Aviv (0) 1 *(Itzhaki 79)*
Viktoria Plzen (2) 2 *(Mahmutovic 17, Petrzela 21)* 13,420
Maccabi Tel Aviv: (4411) Juan Pablo; Spungin, Carlos Garcia, Ben Haim, Ziv; Micha (Vermouth 46), Igiebor, Alberman, Ben Chaim (Itzhaki 64); Zahavi; Ben Basat (Rikan 46).
Viktoria Plzen: (4411) Kozacik; Rajtoral, Hubnik, Prochazka, Limbersky; Petrzela (Kopic 86), Vanek, Horava, Kovarik; Kolar (Hrosovsky 70); Mahmutovic (Holenda 75).

Midtjylland (0) 1 *(Poulsen 87)*
APOEL Nicosia (2) 2 *(De Vincenti 30, 33)* 8253
Midtjylland: (451) Dahlin; Romer, Hansen, Sviatchenko, Lauridsen; Sisto, Poulsen, Sparv, Andersson (Royer 27), Olsson (Urena Porras 63); Pusic (Rasmussen 71).
APOEL Nicosia: (541) Waterman; Mario Sergio, Astiz, Carlao, Alexandrou, De Vincenti (Charalambidis 84); Morais, Vinicius, Makrides, Vander (Sotiriou 63); Leal (Efrem 78).

Milsami (0) 0
Skenderbeu (0) 2 *(Salihi 46, 73 (pen))* 7227
Milsami: (451) Mitu; Rassulov, Shedrack, Rhaili, Erhan; Patras (Suvorov 57), Bolohan (Banovic 74), Zarichnyuk (Antoniuc 51), Belak, Andronic; Bud.
Skenderbeu: (451) Shehi; Vangjeli, Radas, Jashanica, Esquerdinha; Latifi (Progni 86), Lilaj, Shkembi, Nimaga, Berisha (Ademir 90); Salihi (Abilaliaj 90).

Panathinaikos (1) 2 *(Berg 37, Karelis 65 (pen))*
Club Brugge (1) 1 *(Bolingoli Mbombo 10)* 12,874
Panathinaikos: (4312) Kotsolis; Wemmer, Tavlaridis, Sergio Sanchez■, Pranjic; Koutroubis, Ajagun (Lagos 46), Zeca; Ninis (Triantafyllopoulos 46); Berg, Karelis (Lod 74).
Club Brugge: (433) Bruzzese; De Fauw (Cools 80), Duarte, Mechele, De Bock; Vormer, Simons, Bolingoli Mbombo (De Sutter 71); Vanaken, Vazquez (Izquierdo 59), Diaby.

Videoton (0) 1 *(Vinicius 89)*
BATE Borisov (0) 1 *(Milunovic 56)* 3118
Videoton: (4411) Danilovic; Mareval (Fejes 73), Vinicius, Juhasz (Lang 29), Szolnoki; Oliveira, Trebotic, Luyckx, Gyurcso; Kovacs (Soumah 59); Ivanovski.
BATE Borisov: (4411) Chernik; Zhavnerchik, Dubra, Milunovic, Mladenovic; Gordeichuk (Volodko M 85), Nikolic, Baha, Aleksiyevich; Karnitskiy (Ryas 64); Rodionov (Signevich 74).

Young Boys (0) 1 *(Nuzzolo 74)*
Monaco (0) 3 *(Kurzawa 64, Carrillo 72, Pasalic 75)* 16,079
Young Boys: (4231) Mvogo; Benito (Lecjaks 51), von Bergen, Vilotic, Sutter; Sanogo (Zakaria 60), Gajic; Kubo, Nuzzolo, Hoarau (Affum 76); Sulejmani.
Monaco: (451) Subasic; Fabinho, Raggi, Carvalho, Kurzawa; Dirar (Bahlouli 90), Joao Moutinho, Toulalan, Pasalic, Ivan Cavaleiro (Carrillo 70); Martial (El Shaarawy 83).

Wednesday, 29 July 2015
Celtic (0) 1 *(Boyata 82)*
Qarabag (0) 0 43,011
Celtic: (4231) Gordon; Lustig, Boyata, van Dijk, Izaguirre; Bitton (Griffiths 69), Brown; Armstrong (Forrest 62), Johansen, Mackay-Steven; Ciftci (Commons 80).
Qarabag: (451) Sehic; Gurbanov, Guseynov, Sadygov, Agolli; El Jadeyaoui (Poepon 87), Almeida, Garayev, Quintana (Diniyev 82), Tagiyev (Mammadov 73); Reynaldo.

HJK Helsinki (0) 0
Astana (0) 0 9788
HJK Helsinki: (442) Orlund; Sorsa, Moren, Heikkinen, Baah; Savage, Moussi, Schuller, Zeneli; Tanaka, Havenaar (Jallow 90).
Astana: (442) Eric; Ilic, Anicic, Postnikov, Shomko; Dzholchiev, Zhukov, Maksimovic, Twumasi (Beisebekov 90); Nuserbaev (Schetkin 88), Kethevoama (Muzhikov 80).

Lech Poznan (1) 1 *(Thomalla 36)*
FC Basel (1) 3 *(Lang 34, Janko 77, Calla 90)* 25,478
Lech Poznan: (4231) Buric; Kedziora■, Kadar, Kaminski, Douglas; Tralka, Linetty; Formella (Ceesay 69), Hamalainen (Lovrencsics 75), Pawlowski; Thomalla (Robak 55).
FC Basel: (4231) Vaclik; Lang, Hoegh, Suchy, Safari; Kuzmanovic (El-Nenny 86), Xhaka■; Bjarnason, Zuffi, Gashi (Calla 75); Embolo (Janko 61).

Rapid Vienna (0) 2 *(Kainz 48, Beric 76)*
Ajax (2) 2 *(Klaassen 25, 43)* 43,200
Rapid Vienna: (4231) Novota; Auer, Sonnleitner, Hofmann M, Stangl; Petsos, Schwab; Kainz (Huspek 84), Hofmann S (Grahovac 60), Schobesberger (Schaub■ 69); Beric.
Ajax: (433) Cillessen; Tete, Veltman, Riedewald, Dijks; Bazoer, Klaassen, Gudelj; El Ghazi (Fischer 74), Milik (Sanogo 84), Sinkgraven.

Red Bull Salzburg (0) 2 *(Ulmer 51, Hinteregger 89 (pen))*
Malmo (0) 0 15,027
Red Bull Salzburg: (442) Stankovic; Schmitz, Paulo Miranda, Hinteregger, Ulmer; Berisha, Keita, Leitgeb, Atanga (Lainer 90); Djuricin (Nielsen 76), Oberlin (Pires 63).
Malmo: (442) Wiland; Tinnerholm, Arnason, Carvalho, Yotun; Rodic (Eikrem 77), Lewicki, Adu, Sana (Berget 61); Rosenberg, Djurdjic.

Steaua Bucharest (0) 1 *(Varela 81)*
Partizan Belgrade (0) 1 *(Vulicevic 62)*
Steaua Bucharest: (4231) Cojocaru; Alcenat, Papp, Varela, Tosca; Popa (Tudorie 65), Sulley; Breeveld (Tahar 75), Chipciu, Hamroun (Mihalcea 90); Tade.
Partizan Belgrade: (433) Zivkovic Z; Vulicevic, Balazic, Fabricio, Petrovic; Brasanac, Jevtovic, Babovic (Ilic 83); Oumarou (Ninkovic 70), Zivkovic A, Bojinov (Saponjic 19).
Behind closed doors.

THIRD QUALIFYING ROUND SECOND LEG
Tuesday, 4 August 2015
Ajax (0) 2 *(Milik 52, Gudelj 75)*
Rapid Vienna (2) 3 *(Beric 12, Schaub 39, 77)* 43,200
Ajax: (442) Cillessen; Veltman (Sanogo 71), Riedewald, Tete, Dijks; Bazoer, Sinkgraven (Schone 87), Klaassen, Fischer (Gudelj 59); Milik, El Ghazi.
Rapid Vienna: (442) Novota; Sonnleitner, Dibon, Stangl, Auer; Petsos, Schaub (Alar 88), Hofmann S (Schobesberger 58); Kainz; Grahovac, Beric (Prosenik 90).

APOEL Nicosia (0) 0
Midtjylland (1) 1 *(Sviatchenko 3)* 16,070
APOEL Nicosia: (442) Waterman; Morais, Carlao, Astiz, Mario Sergio; Alexandrou, Makrides, Vinicius■, De Vincenti (Sotiriou 90); Leal (Artymatas 84), Piatkowski (Vander 46).
Midtjylland: (442) Dahlin; Hansen, Sviatchenko, Lauridsen, Bak Nielsen (Onuachu 81); Sparv, Poulsen, Andersson (Larsen 89), Sisto; Royer (Pusic 65), Rasmussen.
APOEL Nicosia won on away goals.

Molde (1) 3 *(Hussain 43, Elyounoussi 52 (pen), Kamara 75)*
Dinamo Zagreb (3) 3 *(Pjaca 17, Ademi 20, Rog 22)* 7017
Molde: (451) Horvath; Linnes, Rindaroy, Forren■, Toivio; Singh, Hestad E (Gabrielsen 77), Hussain (Hestad D 87), Mostrom (Svendsen 75), Kamara; Elyounoussi.
Dinamo Zagreb: (4231) Eduardo; Pivaric, Simunovic, Ivo Pinto, Sigali; Goncalo, Pjaca; Ademi, Rog (Coric 75), Soudani (Hodzic 62); Henriquez (Antolic 54).
Dinamo Zagreb won on away goals.

Monaco (0) 4 *(Ivan Cavaleiro 54, Kurzawa 64, Martial 70, El Shaarawy 77)*
Young Boys (0) 0 10,457
Monaco: (442) Subasic; Fabinho, Kurzawa, Carvalho, Raggi; Dirar, Joao Moutinho, Pasalic (Traore 80), Toulalan, Ivan Cavaleiro (El Shaarawy 74), Martial (Carrillo 70).
Young Boys: (442) Mvogo; Vilotic (Rochat 46), von Bergen, Lecjaks, Sutter (Hadergjonaj 65); Bertone, Gajic, Nuzzolo (Gonzalez 71), Kubo; Affum, Sulejmani.

Wednesday, 5 August 2015
Astana (1) 4 *(Twumasi 44, Canas 47 (pen), Postnikov 56, 90)*
HJK Helsinki (2) 3 *(Jallow 4, Baah 41, Zeneli 86 (pen))* 27,937
Astana: (442) Eric; Ilic (Kabananga 46), Postnikov, Shomko, Zhukov (Kethevoama 88); Anicic, Maksimovic, Dzholchiev, Nuserbaev (Beisebekov 60); Canas, Twumasi■.
HJK Helsinki: (442) Orlund; Sorsa, Moren, Baah, Tanaka (Heikkila 90); Zeneli, Heikkinen, Schuller, Moussi; Havenaar, Jallow (Mendy 78).

BATE Borisov (0) 1 *(Nikolic 82)*

Videoton (0) 0   12,498

BATE Borisov: (4411) Chernik; Zhavnerchik, Dubra, Milunovic, Mladenovic; Gordeichuk, Aleksiyevich (Yablonskiy 65), Nikolic, Volodko M; Karnitskiy (Baha 75); Rodionov (Signevich 89).
Videoton: (442) Danilovic; Szolnoki, Vinicius, Lang, Mareval (Fejes 50); Gyurcso (Patkai 61), Trebotic, Luyckx■, Oliveira; Kovacs (Soumah 74), Ivanovski.

Club Brugge (0) 3 *(Cools 53, Vazquez 58, Oulare 82)*

Panathinaikos (0) 0   27,038

Club Brugge: (442) Bruzzese; Duarte, Cools, De Bock, Mechele; Simons, Vazquez (Vanaken 84), Vormer, De Sutter (Oulare 77); Diaby, Dierckx (Bolingoli Mbombo 66).
Panathinaikos: (442) Kotsolis; Pranjic, Wemmer, Koutroubis (Petric 60), Triantafyllopoulos; Tavlaridis, Lagos, Zeca, Ninis (Lod 73); Berg, Karelis (Klonaridis 73).

FC Basel (0) 1 *(Bjarnason 90)*

Lech Poznan (0) 0   18,196

FC Basel: (4231) Vaclik; Lang, Hoegh, Suchy, Safari (Traore 89); Kuzmanovic, El-Nenny; Calla, Delgado (Zuffi 77), Bjarnason; Janko (Embolo 70).
Lech Poznan: (4141) Buric; Ceesay, Kaminski, Dudka, Douglas; Tralka; Formella (Lovrencsics 69), Jevtic (Thomalla 73), Linetty, Pawlowski; Hamalainen (Robak 84).

Malmo (3) 3 *(Djurdjic 7, Rosenberg 14, Rodic 42)*

Red Bull Salzburg (0) 0   19,522

Malmo: (442) Wiland; Tinnerholm, Yotun, Bengtsson, Arnason; Lewicki, Adu■, Rodic (Carvalho 55), Rosenberg; Berget, Djurdjic (Rakip 69).
Red Bull Salzburg: (442) Stankovic; Schmitz, Paulo Miranda (Lainer 78), Ulmer, Hinteregger; Keita, Pires, Berisha, Atanga (Reyna 85); Leitgeb, Oberlin (Prevljak 77).

Partizan Belgrade (1) 4 *(Babovic 8, Jevtovic 60, Zivkovic A 69, Trujic 90)*

Steaua Bucharest (2) 2 *(Sulley 11, Hamroun 33)*   26,775

Partizan Belgrade: (442) Zivkovic Z; Vulicevic, Petrovic, Balazic, Fabricio; Brasanac, Babovic (Trujic 90), Zivkovic A, Jevtovic; Oumarou, Bojinov (Ilic 60).
Steaua Bucharest: (442) Cojocaru; Popa, Papp, Tosca, Varela■; Chipciu (Guilherme 51), Sulley, Alcenat, Hamroun (Iancu 70); Breeveld (Tudorie 72), Tade.

Qarabag (0) 0

Celtic (0) 0   31,850

Qarabag: (433) Sehic; Gurbanov, Guseynov, Sadygov, Agolli; Quintana (Tagiyev 84), Garayev, Almeida; El Jadeyaoui (Mammadov 73), Poepon (Ismayilov 64), Reynaldo.
Celtic: (4231) Gordon; Lustig, Boyata, van Dijk, Izaguirre; Brown, Bitton; Mackay-Steven (Commons 79), Johansen, Armstrong (Forrest 83); Ciftci (Griffiths 67).

Shakhtar Donetsk (1) 3 *(Gladkyy 25, Srna 65 (pen), Alex Teixeira 68)*

Fenerbahce (0) 0   33,179

Shakhtar Donetsk: (4411) Pyatov; Srna, Ordets (Kucher 83), Rakitskiy, Shevchuk; Marlos (Kovalenko 87), Fred, Stepanenko, Taison; Alex Teixeira; Gladkyy (Eduardo 82).
Fenerbahce: (4411) Demirel; Ozbayrakli (Topal 88), Bruno Alves, Kjaer■, Erkin; Nani (Stoch 88), Souza, Meireles (Potuk 78), Sow; Fernandao; Diego.

Skenderbeu (1) 2 *(Salihi 16, Progni 55)*

Milsami (0) 0   7800

Skenderbeu: (433) Shehi; Vangjeli, Radas, Jashanica, Esquerdinha (Abazi 46); Lilaj, Shkembi, Nimaga; Progni (Ademir 75), Salihi (Hristov 78), Berisha.
Milsami: (424) Mitu; Rassulov, Shedrack, Racu, Erhan (Gheti 57); Banovic, Cojocari; Patras, Belak (Bud 46), Andronic■, Antoniuc (Zarichnyuk 67).

Sparta Prague (2) 2 *(Krejci 6, Fatai 16)*

CSKA Moscow (1) 3 *(Musa 34, 51, Dzagoev 76)*   16,580

Sparta Prague: (352) Bicik; Marecek, Holek (Konate 64), Hybs; Frydek, Matejovsky■, Vacha, Dockal, Nhamoinesu; Krejci (Husbauer 87), Fatai (Lafata 54).
CSKA Moscow: (4411) Akinfeev; Fernandes, Berezutski V, Berezutski A, Nababkin; Tosic (Milanov 83), Wernbloom, Natcho (Ignashevich 80), Dzagoev (Golovin 90); Eremenko; Musa.

Viktoria Plzen (0) 0

Maccabi Tel Aviv (0) 2 *(Zahavi 76 (pen), 83)*   11,242

Viktoria Plzen: (433) Kozacik; Rajtoral, Hubnik, Prochazka, Limbersky; Vanek, Kolar (Holenda 85), Horava; Petrzela (Kopic 83), Mahmutovic (Duris 58), Kovarik.
Maccabi Tel Aviv: (424) Juan Pablo; Spungin, Tibi, Ben Haim, Ben Haroush; Alberman, Igiebor; Rikan (Vermouth 65), Itzhaki (Micha 73), Zahavi, Ben Chaim (Mitrovic 59).

PLAY-OFF ROUND FIRST LEG

Tuesday, 18 August 2015

Astana (1) 1 *(Dzholchiev 14)*

APOEL Nicosia (0) 0   30,000

Astana: (442) Eric; Ilic, Anicic, Postnikov, Shomko; Dzholchiev, Canas, Maksimovic, Kethevoama (Muzhikov 90); Zhukov (Beisebekov 86), Nuserbaev (Kabananga 68).
APOEL Nicosia: (4411) Waterman; Mario Sergio, Carlao, Astiz, Antoniades; Efrem (Stilic 63), Alexandrou (Piatkowski 46), Morais, De Vincenti; Makrides (Sotiriou 86); Leal.

BATE Borisov (0) 1 *(Gordeichuk 75)*

Partizan Belgrade (0) 0   11,628

BATE Borisov: (433) Chernik; Mladenovic, Palyakow, Milunovic, Zhavnerchik; Aleksiyevich, Yablonskiy (Signevich 71), Gordeichuk; Hleb (Baha 86), Volodko M (Stasevich 64), Rodionov.
Partizan Belgrade: (442) Zivkovic Z; Vulicevic, Petrovic, Balazic, Fabricio; Brasanac, Babovic, Zivkovic A (Ilic 89), Jevtovic■; Oumarou, Bojinov (Trnic 54).

Lazio (0) 1 *(Keita Balde 77)*

Bayer Leverkusen (0) 0   38,917

Lazio: (442) Berisha; de Vrij (Gentiletti 89), Basta, Mauricio, Lulic; Felipe Anderson, Parolo, Biglia, Onazi (Milinkovic-Savic 53); Candreva, Klose (Keita Balde 46).
Bayer Leverkusen: (451) Leno; Tah, Papadopoulos, Hilbert, Wendell; Bender, Calhanoglu (Brandt 84), Kramer, Bellarabi, Son (Mehmedi 46); Kiessling (Kruse 90).

Manchester U (2) 3 *(Depay 13, 43, Fellaini 90)*

Club Brugge (1) 1 *(Carrick 8 (og))*   75,312

Manchester U: (4231) Romero; Darmian, Smalling, Blind, Shaw; Carrick (Schweinsteiger 46), Schneiderlin; Mata, Januzaj (Hernandez 72), Depay; Rooney (Fellaini 83).
Club Brugge: (4132) Bruzzese; Cools, Mechele■, Duarte, De Bock; Simons (Claudemir 40); Vormer, Vazquez (Vanaken 78), Bolingoli Mbombo; Dierckx, Diaby (Oulare 55).

Sporting Lisbon (1) 2 *(Gutierrez 12, Slimani 82)*

CSKA Moscow (1) 1 *(Doumbia 40)*   41,826

Sporting Lisbon: (442) Rui Patricio; Jefferson, Paulo Oliveira, Joao Pereira, Naldo; Joao Mario (Carlos Mane 76), Carrillo, Adrien Silva, Slimani; Gutierrez (Gelson Martins 76), Ruiz (Aquilani 65).
CSKA Moscow: (442) Akinfeev; Fernandes, Ignashevich, Nababkin (Berezutski A 90), Berezutski V; Wernbloom, Tosic (Milanov 79), Dzagoev, Eremenko; Musa, Doumbia (Natcho 90).

Wednesday, 19 August 2015

Celtic (2) 3 *(Griffiths 3, 62, Bitton 10)*

Malmo (0) 2 *(Berget 52, 90)*   52,412

Celtic: (4411) Gordon; Lustig (Ambrose 80), van Dijk, Boyata, Izaguirre; Forrest, Brown, Bitton, Johansen; Armstrong (Mackay-Steven 63); Griffiths (Ciftci 73).
Malmo: (442) Wiland; Tinnerholm, Arnason, Bengtsson, Yotun; Rodic, Lewicki, Rakip (Sana 81), Berget; Eikrem (Carvalho 72), Djurdjic.

FC Basel (1) 2 *(Delgado 39 (pen), Embolo 88)*

Maccabi Tel Aviv (1) 2 *(Zahavi 31, 90)*   15,620

FC Basel: (442) Vaclik; Lang, Suchy, Hoegh, Safari (Degen 74); Embolo, El-Nenny, Zuffi, Bjarnason; Delgado (Boetius 68), Janko (Gashi 15).
Maccabi Tel Aviv: (4411) Juan Pablo; Spungin, Ben Haim, Tibi, Ben Haroush; Rikan (Micha 89), Igiebor (Peretz 71), Alberman, Ben Chaim; Zahavi; Ben Basat (Mitrovic 51).

Rapid Vienna (0) 0

Shakhtar Donetsk (1) 1 *(Marlos 44)*   46,400

Rapid Vienna: (442) Novota; Sonnleitner, Dibon, Pavelic, Auer; Petsos, Schaub, Hofmann S (Alar 84), Kainz (Schobesberger 80); Grahovac, Beric (Prosenik 89).
Shakhtar Donetsk: (442) Pyatov; Kucher, Rakitskiy, Azevedo, Fred; Stepanenko (Malyshev 46), Srna, Marlos (Eduardo 80), Taison (Bernard 86); Alex Teixeira, Gladkyy.

Skenderbeu (1) 1 *(Shkembi 37)*

Dinamo Zagreb (0) 2 *(Soudani 66, Pivaric 90)*   12,163

Skenderbeu: (451) Shehi; Vangjeli (Ademir 87), Radas, Jashanica, Esquerdinha; Latifi (Progni 79), Lilaj, Shkembi, Nimaga, Berisha (Abazi 90); Salihi.
Dinamo Zagreb: (4231) Eduardo; Ivo Pinto, Sigali, Taravel, Pivaric; Goncalo, Paulo Machado (Coric 61); Soudani (Fernandes 78), Rog (Antolic 71), Pjaca; Hodzic.

Valencia (1) 3 *(Rodrigo 4, Parejo 59, Feghouli 86)*

Monaco (0) 1 *(Pasalic 49)*   45,633

Valencia: (442) Ryan; Barragan, Mustafi, Ruben Vezo, Gaya; Perez (Negredo 76), Feghouli, Parejo, De Paul (Piatti 56); Rodrigo, Alcacer (Javi Fuego 66).
Monaco: (442) Subasic; Fabinho, Raggi, Wallace Santos, Carvalho; Echiejile, Toulalan, Bernardo Silva (El Shaarawy 78), Pasalic (Bahlouli 76); Ivan Cavaleiro (Dirar 63), Martial.

PLAY-OFF ROUND SECOND LEG

Tuesday, 25 August 2015

Dinamo Zagreb (2) 4 *(Soudani 9, 80, Hodzic 15, Taravel 55)*

Skenderbeu (1) 1 *(Esquerdinha 10)*   16,888

Dinamo Zagreb: (442) Eduardo; Ivo Pinto, Sigali, Taravel, Pivaric; Soudani, Paulo Machado, Goncalo■, Pjaca (Fernandes 77); Coric (Rog 67), Hodzic (Antolic 52).
Skenderbeu: (442) Shehi; Esquerdinha, Berisha (Olayinka 58), Latifi (Hristov 78), Progni (Nimaga 65); Arapi, Shkembi, Lilaj, Vangjeli; Jashanica, Radas.

Maccabi Tel Aviv (1) 1 *(Zahavi 24)*

FC Basel (1) 1 *(Zuffi 11)*   13,350

Maccabi Tel Aviv: (442) Juan Pablo; Spungin, Ben Haim, Tibi, Ben Haroush; Ben Chaim (Micha 83), Alberman, Igiebor (Peretz 70), Rikan; Mitrovic (Itzhaki 90), Zahavi.
FC Basel: (442) Vaclik; Bjarnason (Boetius 68), Zuffi, Embolo, Calla (Ajeti 83); Safari, Xhaka, El-Nenny (Gashi 76), Lang; Samuel, Suchy.
Maccabi Tel Aviv won on away goals.

Malmo (1) 2 *(Rosenberg 23, Boyata 55 (og))*

Celtic (0) 0   20,500

Malmo: (442) Wiland; Tinnerholm, Arnason, Bengtsson (Carvalho 46), Yotun; Rodic (Rakip 82), Lewicki, Adu, Berget (Mehmeti 90); Rosenberg; Djurdjic.
Celtic: (4231) Gordon; Janko, Boyata, van Dijk, Mulgrew; Brown, Bitton (Ciftci 72); Forrest (Mackay-

Steven 79), Johansen, Armstrong (Commons 46); Griffiths.

Monaco (1) 2 *(Raggi 17, Echiejile 75)*

Valencia (1) 1 *(Negredo 4)*   13,165

Monaco: (433) Subasic; Fabinho, Raggi, Carvalho, Kurzawa (Echiejile 62); Pasalic (Lemar 52), Toulalan, Bernardo Silva; Dirar, Martial, Ivan Cavaleiro (Carrillo 64).
Valencia: (433) Ryan; Barragan, Mustafi, Ruben Vezo, Gaya; Perez (Danilo 77), Javi Fuego, Parejo; Feghouli, Negredo (Alcacer 60), Rodrigo (Piatti 65).

Shakhtar Donetsk (2) 2 *(Marlos 10, Gladkyy 27)*

Rapid Vienna (2) 2 *(Schaub 13, Hofmann S 22)*   28,417

Shakhtar Donetsk: (4411) Pyatov; Srna, Kryvtsov, Rakitskiy, Azevedo; Marlos, Fred, Stepanenko, Taison (Bernard 87); Alex Teixeira; Gladkyy (Eduardo 83).
Rapid Vienna: (4411) Novota; Pavelic, Sonnleitner■, Dibon, Auer; Schaub (Prosenik 85), Petsos, Grahovac (Schwab 70), Kainz; Hofmann S (Schobesberger 63); Beric.

Wednesday, 26 August 2015

APOEL Nicosia (0) 1 *(Stilic 60)*

Astana (0) 1 *(Maksimovic 84)*   17,699

APOEL Nicosia: (4231) Waterman; Carlao (Joao Guilherme 83), Antoniades (Piatkowski 86), Astiz, Mario Sergio; Morais, Makrides (Charalambidis 55); Stilic, Vander, De Vincenti; Leal.
Astana: (442) Eric; Shomko, Ilic, Postnikov, Maksimovic; Zhukov (Beisebekov 89), Kethevoama (Schetkin 90), Anicic, Dzholchiev; Canas, Nuserbaev (Kabananga 68).

Bayer Leverkusen (1) 3 *(Calhanoglu 40, Mehmedi 48, Bellarabi 88)*

Lazio (0) 0   28,222

Bayer Leverkusen: (4411) Leno; Hilbert, Tah, Papadopoulos, Wendell; Bellarabi (Ramalho Silva 89), Kramer, Bender, Mehmedi (Brandt 76); Calhanoglu (Kruse 80); Kiessling.
Lazio: (532) Berisha; Basta, Mauricio■, de Vrij, Radu (Kishna 56), Lulic; Onazi (Morrison 82), Parolo, Candreva; Keita Balde, Felipe Anderson (Gentiletti 70).

Club Brugge (0) 0

Manchester U (1) 4 *(Rooney 20, 49, 57, Ander Herrera 63)*   28,733

Club Brugge: (4132) Bolat; De Fauw, Castelletto, Duarte, De Bock; Claudemir; Vormer, Vazquez (Vanaken 62), Bolingoli Mbombo (Cools 77); De Sutter, Diaby (Dierckx 62).
Manchester U: (4231) Romero; Darmian, Smalling, Blind, Shaw; Ander Herrera (Hernandez 64), Carrick; Mata (Young 62), Januzaj (Schweinsteiger 46), Depay; Rooney.

CSKA Moscow (0) 3 *(Doumbia 49, 72, Musa 85)*

Sporting Lisbon (1) 1 *(Gutierrez 36)*   17,259

CSKA Moscow: (4231) Akinfeev; Fernandes (Nababkin 34), Ignashevich, Berezutski V, Schennikov; Wernbloom, Tosic; Dzagoev, Eremenko, Musa (Milanov 90); Doumbia (Berezutski A 89).
Sporting Lisbon: (442) Rui Patricio; Silva, Paulo Oliveira, Joao Pereira, Naldo; Adrien (Montero 90), Joao Mario■, Adrien Silva, Gutierrez (Slimani 68); Carrillo, Ruiz (Carlos Mane 89).

Partizan Belgrade (0) 2 *(Zhavnerchik 74 (og), Saponjic 90)*

BATE Borisov (1) 1 *(Stasevich 25)*   27,234

Partizan Belgrade: (4411) Zivkovic Z; Vulicevic, Balazic, Fabricio, Petrovic; Zivkovic A, Brasanac, Babovic, Oumarou; Lukic (Ilic 63); Bojinov (Saponjic 38).
BATE Borisov: (451) Chernik; Zhavnerchik, Palyakow, Milunovic, Mladenovic; Stasevich, Aleksiyevich, Volodko A, Hleb (Karnitskiy 75), Gordeichuk (Ryas 90); Rodionov (Signevich 16).
BATE Borisov won on away goals.

GROUP STAGE

GROUP A

Tuesday, 15 September 2015

Paris Saint-Germain (1) 2 *(Di Maria 4, Cavani 61)*
Malmo (0) 0   46,612
Paris Saint-Germain: (433) Trapp; van der Wiel, Thiago Silva, Luiz, Maxwell; Verratti, Thiago Motta, Matuidi; Di Maria (Lavezzi 84), Ibrahimovic (Pastore 75), Cavani.
Malmo: (523) Wiland; Tinnerholm, Arnason, Bengtsson, Carvalho (Rodic 46), Yotun; Adu (Rakip 85), Lewicki; Rosenberg, Berget, Djurdjic.

Real Madrid (1) 4 *(Benzema 30,
Ronaldo 55 (pen), 64 (pen), 81)*
Shakhtar Donetsk (0) 0   66,389
Real Madrid: (4231) Navas; Carvajal, Varane (Pepe 46), Sergio Ramos (Nacho 59), Marcelo; Modric, Kroos; Isco, Bale (Kovacic 31), Ronaldo; Benzema.
Shakhtar Donetsk: (4231) Pyatov; Srna, Kucher, Rakitskiy, Azevedo; Fred, Stepanenko■; Marlos (Kovalenko 74), Alex Teixeira, Taison (Malyshev 67); Gladkyy (Bernard 83).

Wednesday, 30 September 2015

Malmo (0) 0
Real Madrid (1) 2 *(Ronaldo 29, 90)*   20,500
Malmo: (442) Wiland; Tinnerholm, Arnason, Bengtsson, Yotun■; Rodic (Eikrem 67), Lewicki, Adu, Berget; Rosenberg, Djurdjic (Carvalho 81).
Real Madrid: (433) Navas; Carvajal, Varane, Nacho, Arbeloa; Casemiro, Kroos, Isco (Cheryshev 83); Kovacic (Lucas 73), Benzema (Modric 68), Ronaldo.

Shakhtar Donetsk (0) 0
Paris Saint-Germain (2) 3 *(Aurier 7, Luiz 23, Srna 90 (og))*
                                                            32,730
Shakhtar Donetsk: (4411) Pyatov; Srna, Kucher, Rakitskiy, Shevchuk; Marlos (Kovalenko 71), Fred, Malyshev, Taison (Bernard 71); Alex Teixeira; Gladkyy (Dentinho 85).
Paris Saint-Germain: (433) Trapp; Aurier, Thiago Silva, Luiz, Maxwell; Verratti, Thiago Motta, Matuidi; Di Maria (Pastore 81), Ibrahimovic (Lavezzi 90), Cavani (Lucas Moura 80).

Wednesday, 21 October 2015

Malmo (1) 1 *(Rosenberg 17)*
Shakhtar Donetsk (0) 0   20,500
Malmo: (442) Wiland; Tinnerholm, Arnason, Bengtsson, Konate; Rodic (Rakip 78), Lewicki, Adu, Berget; Rosenberg, Djurdjic (Mehmeti 88).
Shakhtar Donetsk: (4411) Pyatov; Srna, Kucher, Rakitskiy, Ismaily; Marlos (Eduardo 71), Fred, Stepanenko, Bernard; Alex Teixeira; Gladkyy (Kovalenko 81).

Paris Saint-Germain (0) 0
Real Madrid (0) 0   46,858
Paris Saint-Germain: (433) Trapp; Aurier, Marquinhos, Thiago Silva, Maxwell; Verratti (Lavezzi 79), Thiago Motta, Matuidi; Di Maria (Lucas Moura 66), Cavani (Pastore 66), Ibrahimovic.
Real Madrid: (442) Navas; Danilo, Sergio Ramos, Varane, Marcelo; Lucas, Casemiro, Kroos, Isco (Modric 69); Jese (Cheryshev 73), Ronaldo.

Tuesday, 3 November 2015

Real Madrid (1) 1 *(Nacho 35)*
Paris Saint-Germain (0) 0   78,300
Real Madrid: (433) Navas; Danilo, Sergio Ramos, Varane, Marcelo (Nacho 32); Modric, Casemiro, Kroos; Jese (Lucas 63), Ronaldo, Isco (Kovacic 82).
Paris Saint-Germain: (433) Trapp; Aurier, Thiago Silva, Luiz, Maxwell; Verratti (Rabiot 17), Thiago Motta, Matuidi (Lucas Moura 75); Di Maria, Ibrahimovic, Cavani.

Shakhtar Donetsk (1) 4 *(Gladkyy 29, Srna 48 (pen), Eduardo 55, Alex Teixeira 73)*
Malmo (0) 0   23,712
Shakhtar Donetsk: (442) Kanibolotskiy; Srna, Kucher, Rakitskiy, Azevedo; Marlos, Fred (Taison 68), Stepanenko, Bernard (Kovalenko 75); Alex Teixeira, Gladkyy (Eduardo 46).
Malmo: (442) Wiland; Tinnerholm, Arnason■, Bengtsson, Konate; Rodic, Lewicki (Rakip 11), Adu, Berget (Yotun 46); Djurdjic (Eikrem 74), Rosenberg.

Wednesday, 25 November 2015

Malmo (0) 0
Paris Saint-Germain (2) 5 *(Rabiot 3, Di Maria 14, 68, Ibrahimovic 50, Lucas Moura 82)*   20,500
Malmo: (442) Wiland; Konate, Tinnerholm, Bengtsson, Brorsson; Lewicki, Adu (Rakip 81), Rodic (Fikrem 59), Rosenberg; Berget, Djurdjic (Kroon 69).
Paris Saint-Germain: (433) Trapp; Thiago Silva, Marquinhos, Maxwell, van der Wiel; Thiago Motta (Lucas Moura 69), Di Maria (Stambouli 69), Matuidi; Rabiot, Cavani, Ibrahimovic (Augustin 85).

Shakhtar Donetsk (0) 3 *(Alex Teixeira 77 (pen), 88, Dentinho 83)*
Real Madrid (1) 4 *(Ronaldo 18, 70, Modric 50, Carvajal 52)*   33,990
Shakhtar Donetsk: (4411) Pyatov; Kobin, Ordets, Rakitskiy, Azevedo (Dentinho 64); Marlos (Taison 62), Fred, Stepanenko, Bernard; Alex Teixeira; Gladkyy (Ferreyra 74).
Real Madrid: (433) Casilla; Carvajal, Pepe, Varane (Danilo 32), Nacho; Modric (Kroos 62), Casemiro, Kovacic; Bale (Benzema 71), Ronaldo, Isco.

Tuesday, 8 December 2015

Paris Saint-Germain (0) 2 *(Lucas Moura 57, Ibrahimovic 86)*
Shakhtar Donetsk (0) 0   44,408
Paris Saint-Germain: (433) Trapp; van der Wiel, Marquinhos, Luiz, Kurzawa; Stambouli, Rabiot, Matuidi (Di Maria 68); Lucas Moura (Nkunku 87), Ibrahimovic, Lavezzi (Cavani 68).
Shakhtar Donetsk: (4411) Kanibolotskiy; Srna, Kucher, Rakitskiy, Ismaily; Marlos (Kovalenko 74), Fred, Stepanenko, Taison (Bernard 69); Alex Teixeira; Eduardo (Dentinho 78).

Real Madrid (3) 8 *(Benzema 13, 24, 73, Ronaldo 38, 47, 50, 59, Kovacic 70)*
Malmo (0) 0   60,663
Real Madrid: (433) Casilla; Danilo, Pepe (Marcelo 53), Nacho, Arbeloa; Kovacic (Cheryshev 76), Casemiro, Isco; Rodriguez (Jese 64), Benzema, Ronaldo.
Malmo: (442) Wiland; Tinnerholm, Arnason, Carvalho, Yotun; Rakip (Kroon 77), Lewicki, Adu, Sana (Mehmeti 64); Berget, Djurdjic (Rodic 46).

Group A Table	P	W	D	L	F	A	GD	Pts
Real Madrid	6	5	1	0	19	3	16	16
Paris Saint-Germain	6	4	1	1	12	1	11	13
Shakhtar Donetsk	6	1	0	5	7	14	–7	3
Malmo	6	1	0	5	1	21	–20	3

GROUP B

Tuesday, 15 September 2015

PSV Eindhoven (1) 2 *(Moreno 45, Narsingh 57)*
Manchester U (1) 1 *(Depay 41)*   35,292
PSV Eindhoven: (451) Zoet; Arias, Bruma, Moreno, Brenet; Narsingh, Propper, Hendrix, Guardado (Schaars 71), Lestienne (Locadia 85); de Jong.
Manchester U: (4231) De Gea; Darmian, Smalling, Blind, Shaw (Rojo 24); Schweinsteiger, Ander Herrera (Fellaini 75); Young (Valencia 86), Mata, Depay; Martial.

Wolfsburg (1) 1 *(Draxler 40)*
CSKA Moscow (0) 0   20,126
Wolfsburg: (4132) Benaglio; Trasch, Naldo, Dante, Rodriguez; Gustavo; Caligiuri (Guilavogui 85), Draxler, Schurrle (Arnold 76); Kruse, Dost (Bendtner 46).
CSKA Moscow: (442) Akinfeev; Fernandes, Berezutski V, Schennikov; Dzagoev, Wernbloom, Natcho (Doumbia 64), Tosic (Milanov 78); Musa, Eremenko.

Wednesday, 30 September 2015

CSKA Moscow (3) 3 *(Musa 7, Doumbia 21, 36 (pen))*
PSV Eindhoven (0) 2 *(Lestienne 60, 68)*   16,152
CSKA Moscow: (4411) Akinfeev; Fernandes, Berezutski A, Ignashevich, Schennikov; Tosic (Milanov 70), Natcho (Eremenko 66), Wernbloom, Musa; Dzagoev; Doumbia (Panchenko 90).

PSV Eindhoven: (433) Zoet; Arias■, Bruma, Moreno, Brenet (Poulsen 77); Propper, Hendrix, Maher (Vloet 89); Narsingh, Locadia, Lestienne (Pereiro 78).

Manchester U (1) 2 *(Mata 34 (pen), Smalling 53)*
Wolfsburg (1) 1 *(Caligiuri 4)*   74,811
Manchester U: (4231) De Gea; Valencia (Young 46), Smalling, Blind, Darmian; Schneiderlin, Schweinsteiger (Jones 72); Mata, Rooney, Depay (Andreas Pereira 62); Martial.
Wolfsburg: (4231) Benaglio; Trasch (Jung 77), Naldo, Dante, Rodriguez; Guilavogui, Arnold (Schurrle 69); Caligiuri, Kruse, Draxler; Dost (Bendtner 69).

Wednesday, 21 October 2015
CSKA Moscow (1) 1 *(Doumbia 15)*
Manchester U (0) 1 *(Martial 65)*   18,456
CSKA Moscow: (4411) Akinfeev; Fernandes, Berezutski V (Berezutski A 41), Ignashevich, Schennikov; Tosic, Wernbloom, Eremenko (Panchenko 83), Musa; Dzagoev (Cauna 86); Doumbia.
Manchester U: (4231) De Gea; Valencia, Jones, Smalling, Rojo (Blind 64); Schweinsteiger (Fellaini 46), Schneiderlin; Lingard (Depay 79), Rooney, Ander Herrera; Martial.

Wolfsburg (0) 2 *(Dost 47, Kruse 57)*
PSV Eindhoven (0) 0   23,375
Wolfsburg: (4411) Benaglio; Trasch, Naldo, Dante, Rodriguez; Caligiuri (Vieirinha 72), Gustavo, Guilavogui (Arnold 84), Draxler (Schurrle 79); Kruse; Dost.
PSV Eindhoven: (433) Zoet; Brenet, Bruma, Moreno, Poulsen (De Wijs 74); Propper, Hendrix (Locadia 73), Guardado; Narsingh, de Jong (Pereiro 80), Maher.

Tuesday, 3 November 2015
Manchester U (0) 1 *(Rooney 79)*
CSKA Moscow (0) 0   75,165
Manchester U: (4231) De Gea; Young, Smalling, Blind, Rojo; Schweinsteiger (Ander Herrera 89), Carrick; Lingard, Mata (Depay 74), Martial (Fellaini 66); Rooney.
CSKA Moscow: (4231) Akinfeev; Fernandes, Berezutski A, Ignashevich, Schennikov; Wernbloom, Natcho (Doumbia 55); Tosic (Golovin 75), Dzagoev (Panchenko 85), Milanov; Musa.

PSV Eindhoven (0) 2 *(Locadia 55, de Jong 86)*
Wolfsburg (0) 0   35,000
PSV Eindhoven: (433) Zoet; Arias, Bruma, Moreno, Brenet; Propper, Guardado, Narsingh (Pereiro 83); Maher (Hendrix 74), Locadia (Isimat-Mirin 75), de Jong.
Wolfsburg: (4411) Benaglio; Jung, Naldo, Klose, Rodriguez; Caligiuri, Gustavo, Guilavogui (Draxler 69), Schurrle (Vieirinha 64); Arnold; Dost (Bendtner 69).

Wednesday, 25 November 2015
CSKA Moscow (0) 0
Wolfsburg (0) 2 *(Akinfeev 67 (og), Schurrle 88)* 16,450
CSKA Moscow: (4411) Akinfeev; Fernandes, Berezutski A, Ignashevich (Vasin 46), Nababkin (Natcho 75); Tosic, Wernbloom, Dzagoev (Panchenko 90), Milanov; Musa; Doumbia.
Wolfsburg: (442) Benaglio; Trasch, Naldo, Dante, Schafer; Vieirinha, Guilavogui, Arnold, Caligiuri (Schurrle 61); Kruse (Jung 81), Dost (Bendtner 86).

Manchester U (0) 0
PSV Eindhoven (0) 0   75,321
Manchester U: (4411) De Gea; Darmian (Mata 84), Smalling, Blind, Rojo; Lingard, Schneiderlin, Schweinsteiger (Fellaini 58), Depay (Young 58); Rooney; Martial.
PSV Eindhoven: (433) Zoet; Arias, Bruma, Moreno, Brenet; Propper, Hendrix (Isimat-Mirin 60), Guardado; Narsingh (Pereiro 18), de Jong, Locadia.

Tuesday, 8 December 2015
PSV Eindhoven (0) 2 *(de Jong 78, Propper 85)*
CSKA Moscow (0) 1 *(Ignashevich 76 (pen))*   34,000
PSV Eindhoven: (4141) Zoet; Brenet, Moreno, Bruma, Isimat-Mirin; Hendrix; Locadia, Guardado, Propper, Pereiro (Bergwijn 85); de Jong.

CSKA Moscow: (4411) Akinfeev; Cauna, Ignashevich, Berezutski A, Nababkin; Dzagoev, Wernbloom, Natcho, Tosic; Musa; Doumbia.

Wolfsburg (2) 3 *(Naldo 14, 84, Vieirinha 29)*
Manchester U (1) 2 *(Martial 10, Guilavogui 82 (og))* 26,400
Wolfsburg: (4231) Benaglio; Trasch, Naldo, Dante, Rodriguez (Schafer 16); Vieirinha (Klose 78), Guilavogui; Arnold, Draxler (Caligiuri 85), Kruse; Schurrle.
Manchester U: (4231) De Gea; Darmian (Jackson 43), Smalling, Blind, Varela; Fellaini, Schweinsteiger (Carrick 69); Lingard, Mata (Powell 90), Depay; Martial.

Group B Table	P	W	D	L	F	A	GD	Pts
Wolfsburg	6	4	0	2	9	6	3	12
PSV Eindhoven	6	3	1	2	8	7	1	10
Manchester U	6	2	2	2	7	7	0	8
CSKA Moskow	6	1	1	4	5	9	–4	4

GROUP C

Tuesday, 15 September 2015
Benfica (0) 2 *(Gaitan 51, Mitroglou 62)*
Astana (0) 0   35,000
Benfica: (442) Julio Cesar; Semedo, Luisao, Jardel, Eliseu; Goncalo Guedes, Samaris (Fejsa 84), Anderson Talisca (Jimenez 76), Gaitan; Mitroglou, Jonas (Pizzi 72).
Astana: (4411) Eric; Ilic (Dedechko 90), Postnikov, Anicic, Shomko; Dzholchiev (Beisebekov 80), Canas, Maksimovic, Kethevoama; Zhukov; Kabananga (Schetkin 46).

Galatasaray (0) 0
Atletico Madrid (2) 2 *(Griezmann 18, 25)*   33,469
Galatasaray: (4141) Muslera; Sarioglu (Oztekin 46), Kaya, Denayer, Carole; Balta; Podolski (Gumus 72), Inan, Colak (Bulut 33), Sneijder; Yilmaz.
Atletico Madrid: (442) Oblak; Juanfran, Gimenez, Godin, Siqueira; Koke, Saul (Torres O 80), Tiago, Griezmann; Vietto (Gabi 62), Martinez (Torres F 60).

Wednesday, 30 September 2015
Astana (0) 2 *(Balta 77 (og), Canas 89)*
Galatasaray (1) 2 *(Kisa 31, Eric 86 (og))*   27,264
Astana: (4411) Eric; Ilic, Anicic, Postnikov, Shomko; Dzholchiev (Nuserbaev 78), Maksimovic, Canas, Kethevoama (Muzhikov 82); Zhukov (Schetkin 89); Kabananga.
Galatasaray: (4411) Muslera; Denayer, Balta, Kaya, Carole; Podolski (Rodriguez 68), Inan, Kisa (Gumus 81), Oztekin (Sarioglu 90); Sneijder; Bulut.

Atletico Madrid (1) 1 *(Correa 23)*
Benfica (1) 2 *(Gaitan 36, Goncalo Guedes 51)*   40,938
Atletico Madrid: (442) Oblak; Juanfran, Gimenez, Godin, Filipe Luis; Torres O (Saul 63), Gabi, Tiago, Correa (Torres F 77); Griezmann (Vietto 71), Martinez.
Benfica: (442) Julio Cesar; Semedo, Luisao, Jardel, Eliseu; Goncalo Guedes, Andre Almeida, Samaris (Fejsa 73), Gaitan; Jonas (Pizzi 79), Jimenez (Mitroglou 71).

Wednesday, 21 October 2015
Atletico Madrid (2) 4 *(Saul 23, Martinez 29, Torres O 63, Dedechko 89 (og))*
Astana (0) 0   33,853
Atletico Madrid: (442) Oblak; Juanfran, Savic, Godin, Siqueira; Carrasco, Tiago (Torres O 46), Gabi, Saul; Martinez (Torres F 67), Griezmann (Correa 58).
Astana: (541) Eric; Beisebekov, Postnikov, Dedechko, Ilic, Akhnetov; Schetkin (Kulbekov 80), Muzhikov (Kozhamberdy 83), Zhukov (Pikalkin 65), Kethevoama; Kabananga.

Galatasaray (2) 2 *(Inan 20 (pen), Podolski 33)*
Benfica (1) 1 *(Gaitan 2)*   33,615
Galatasaray: (451) Muslera; Sarioglu, Chedjou, Balta, Carole; Podolski, Kisa (Rodriguez 90), Sneijder, Inan, Oztekin (Adin 58); Bulut (Yilmaz 77).
Benfica: (442) Julio Cesar; Eliseu (Pizzi 66), Jardel, Luisao, Silvio (Mitroglou 81); Goncalo Guedes (Victor Andrade 76), Samaris, Andre Almeida, Gaitan; Jimenez, Jonas.

Tuesday, 3 November 2015

Astana (0) 0

Atletico Madrid (0) 0 29,231

Astana: (442) Eric; Ilic, Postnikov, Anicic, Shomko; Canas, Maksimovic, Dzholchiev (Beisebekov 89), Kethevoama; Kabananga (Schetkin 80), Muzhikov (Zhukov 77).
Atletico Madrid: (442) Oblak; Juanfran, Godin, Gimenez, Siqueira; Tiago, Gabi, Saul (Carrasco 73), Koke (Torres O 82); Torres F (Martinez 64), Griezmann.

Benfica (0) 2 *(Jonas 52, Luisao 67)*

Galatasaray (0) 1 *(Podolski 58)* 35,726

Benfica: (442) Julio Cesar; Silvio, Jardel, Luisao, Eliseu; Goncalo Guedes (Carcela-Gonzalez 73), Andre Almeida, Anderson Talisca (Cristante 90), Gaitan■; Jimenez, Jonas (Pizzi 81).
Galatasaray: (4411) Muslera; Denayer (Colak 74), Chedjou, Balta, Adin; Sarioglu, Inan, Kisa (Oztekin 69), Podolski; Sneijder; Yilmaz (Bulut 74).

Wednesday, 25 November 2015

Astana (2) 2 *(Twumasi 19, Anicic 31)*

Benfica (1) 2 *(Jimenez 40, 72)* 15,089

Astana: (442) Eric; Ilic, Postnikov, Anicic, Shomko; Twumasi (Dedechko 90), Canas, Maksimovic, Kethevoama (Zhukov 87); Muzhikov, Kabananga (Schetkin 83).
Benfica: (4231) Julio Cesar; Silvio (Andre Almeida 64), Lopez, Jardel, Eliseu; Sanches, Samaris (Anderson Talisca 64); Goncalo Guedes, Jonas (Cristante 80), Pizzi; Jimenez.

Atletico Madrid (1) 2 *(Griezmann 12, 65)*

Galatasaray (0) 0 35,753

Atletico Madrid: (442) Oblak; Jesus Gamez, Gimenez, Godin, Filipe Luis; Carrasco (Torres O 71), Tiago (Saul 75), Gabi, Koke; Griezmann (Vietto 68), Torres F.
Galatasaray: (4231) Muslera; Denayer (Adin 25), Chedjou, Kaya, Balta (Gumus 78); Kisa (Bulut 63), Karacan; Sarioglu, Sneijder, Oztekin; Podolski.

Tuesday, 8 December 2015

Benfica (0) 1 *(Mitroglou 75)*

Atletico Madrid (1) 2 *(Saul 33, Vietto 55)* 47,630

Benfica: (4411) Julio Cesar; Andre Almeida, Lopez, Jardel, Eliseu; Pizzi, Fejsa, Sanches, Goncalo Guedes (Mitroglou 46); Gaitan (Carcela-Gonzalez 76); Jonas (Jimenez 61).
Atletico Madrid: (442) Oblak; Juanfran, Savic, Godin, Filipe Luis; Koke, Saul, Gabi, Carrasco (Torres O 73); Vietto (Torres F 62), Griezmann (Gimenez 90).

Galatasaray (0) 1 *(Inan 64)*

Astana (0) 1 *(Twumasi 62)* 26,464

Galatasaray: (4411) Muslera; Sarioglu, Kaya, Balta, Chedjou; Podolski, Adin (Rodriguez 82), Inan, Oztekin (Bulut 87); Sneijder; Yilmaz.
Astana: (4411) Eric; Ilic, Postnikov, Anicic, Shomko; Twumasi, Canas, Maksimovic, Kethevoama (Nuserbaev 74); Muzhikov (Zhukov 88); Kabananga (Dzholchiev 73).

Group C Table	P	W	D	L	F	A	GD	Pts
Atletico Madrid	6	4	1	1	11	3	8	13
Benfica	6	3	1	2	10	8	2	10
Galatasaray	6	1	2	3	6	10	–4	5
Astana	6	0	4	2	5	11	–6	4

GROUP D

Tuesday, 15 September 2015

Manchester C (0) 1 *(Chiellini 57 (og))*

Juventus (0) 2 *(Mandzukic 70, Morata 81)* 50,363

Manchester C: (4231) Hart; Sagna, Kompany (Otamendi 74), Mangala, Kolarov; Fernandinho, Toure; Silva, Sterling (De Bruyne 72), Nasri (Aguero 83); Bony.
Juventus: (442) Buffon; Lichtsteiner, Bonucci, Chiellini, Evra; Cuadrado, Pogba, Hernanes, Sturaro; Morata (Barzagli 85), Mandzukic (Dybala 78).

Sevilla (0) 3 *(Gameiro 47 (pen), Banega 66 (pen), Konoplyanka 84)*

Borussia Moenchengladbach (0) 0 36,959

Sevilla: (4231) Sergio Rico; Coke, Andreolli, Kolodzieczak, Tremoulinas; Krychowiak, Nzonzi; Vitolo, Banega (Krohn-Dehli 75), Reyes (Konoplyanka 83); Gameiro (Immobile 71).

Borussia Moenchengladbach: (442) Sommer; Korb, Brouwers, Jantschke, Wendt; Hahn (Schulz N 72), Stindl (Dahoud 67), Nordtveit, Traore; Raffael (Drmic 83), Hazard.

Wednesday, 30 September 2015

Borussia Moenchengladbach (0) 1 *(Stindl 54)*

Manchester C (0) 2 *(Otamendi 66, Aguero 90 (pen))* 46,279

Borussia Moenchengladbach: (442) Sommer; Korb (Traore 78), Christensen, Dominguez, Wendt; Herrmann (Hahn 72), Dahoud (Nordtveit 84), Xhaka, Johnson; Raffael, Stindl.
Manchester C: (4231) Hart; Sagna, Demichelis, Otamendi, Kolarov; Toure (Fernando 46), Fernandinho; De Bruyne, Silva (Jesus Navas 64), Sterling (Zabaleta 90); Aguero.

Juventus (1) 2 *(Morata 41, Zaza 87)*

Sevilla (0) 0 36,499

Juventus: (433) Buffon; Barzagli, Bonucci, Chiellini, Evra; Khedira (Alex Sandro 76), Hernanes, Pogba; Cuadrado, Morata (Zaza 80), Dybala (Rugani 88).
Sevilla: (442) Sergio Rico; Coke, Andreolli, Kolodzieczak, Tremoulinas; Konoplyanka, Nzonzi (Iborra 66), Krychowiak, Krohn-Dehli; Gameiro (Immobile 66), Reyes (Munoz 79).

Wednesday, 21 October 2015

Juventus (0) 0

Borussia Moenchengladbach (0) 0 40,940

Juventus: (352) Buffon; Barzagli, Bonucci, Chiellini; Cuadrado (Pereyra 60), Khedira, Marchisio, Pogba, Alex Sandro; Mandzukic (Zaza 70), Morata (Dybala 80).
Borussia Moenchengladbach: (442) Sommer; Korb, Christensen, Dominguez, Wendt; Traore (Hahn 82), Dahoud (Nordtveit 87), Xhaka, Johnson; Stindl, Raffael (Hazard 74).

Manchester C (1) 2 *(Rami 36 (og), De Bruyne 90)*

Sevilla (1) 1 *(Konoplyanka 30)* 45,595

Manchester C: (442) Hart; Zabaleta (Kolarov 60), Otamendi, Mangala, Sagna; Jesus Navas, Toure, Fernandinho, De Bruyne (Kompany 90); Sterling, Bony (Fernando 76).
Sevilla: (4411) Sergio Rico; Coke (Mariano 84), Rami, Kolodzieczak, Tremoulinas; Vitolo, Iborra, Krychowiak, Konoplyanka (Nzonzi 78); Banega (Krohn-Dehli 69); Gameiro.

Tuesday, 3 November 2015

Borussia Moenchengladbach (1) 1 *(Johnson 18)*

Juventus (1) 1 *(Lichtsteiner 44)* 46,217

Borussia Moenchengladbach: (442) Sommer; Wendt, Dominguez, Christensen, Nordtveit; Johnson (Hazard 85), Xhaka, Dahoud, Traore; Stindl, Raffael.
Juventus: (442) Buffon; Evra, Bonucci, Chiellini, Lichtsteiner; Pogba, Marchisio, Sturaro (Lemina 87); Hernanes■; Morata (Barzagli 75), Dybala (Cuadrado 62).

Sevilla (1) 1 *(Tremoulinas 25)*

Manchester C (3) 3 *(Sterling 8, Fernandinho 11, Bony 36)* 39,261

Sevilla: (4231) Sergio Rico; Coke (Mariano 56), Rami, Kolodzieczak, Tremoulinas; Iborra (Krohn-Dehli 46), Krychowiak; Vitolo, Banega, Konoplyanka; Llorente (Immobile 65).
Manchester C: (451) Hart; Sagna, Kompany, Otamendi, Kolarov; Jesus Navas, Toure, Fernando, Fernandinho (Demichelis 90), Sterling (De Bruyne 73); Bony (Delph 86).

Wednesday, 25 November 2015

Borussia Moenchengladbach (1) 4 *(Stindl 29, 83, Johnson 68, Raffael 78)*

Sevilla (0) 2 *(Vitolo 82, Banega 90 (pen))* 45,177

Borussia Moenchengladbach: (442) Sommer; Korb, Christensen, Nordtveit, Wendt; Traore (Drmic 14), Dahoud (Schulz M 79), Xhaka, Johnson (Elvedi 87); Raffael, Stindl.
Sevilla: (451) Sergio Rico; Coke (Mariano 83), Rami, Kolodzieczak, Tremoulinas; Vitolo, Krychowiak, Banega, Krohn-Dehli (Nzonzi 64), Konoplyanka; Gameiro (Llorente 76).

Juventus (1) 1 *(Mandzukic 18)*
Manchester C (0) 0   38,193
Juventus: (352) Buffon; Barzagli, Bonucci, Chiellini;
Lichtsteiner, Sturaro, Marchisio, Pogba, Alex Sandro
(Evra 77); Mandzukic (Morata 54), Dybala (Cuadrado
82).
Manchester C: (442) Hart (Caballero 81); Sagna,
Demichelis, Otamendi, Clichy; Fernando, Fernandinho
(Delph 60), Jesus Navas, Toure; De Bruyne, Aguero
(Sterling 68).

Tuesday, 8 December 2015
Manchester C (1) 4 *(Silva 16, Sterling 79, 81, Bony 85)*
Borussia Moenchengladbach (2) 2 *(Korb 18, Raffael 42)*
                                                                                    41,829
Manchester C: (4411) Hart; Clichy (Sagna 80), Otamendi,
Mangala, Kolarov; De Bruyne (Jesus Navas 65), Delph
(Bony 65), Fernandinho, Silva; Toure; Sterling.
Borussia Moenchengladbach: (442) Sommer; Elvedi,
Christensen, Nordtveit, Wendt (Hazard 84); Korb,
Dahoud (Schulz M 66), Xhaka, Johnson (Drmic 72);
Stindl, Raffael.

Sevilla (0) 1 *(Llorente 65)*
Juventus (0) 0   35,583
Sevilla: (4231) Sergio Rico; Coke, Rami, Kolodzieczak
(Mariano 57), Tremoulinas; Nzonzi, Krychowiak; Vitolo,
Konoplyanka (Krohn-Dehli 68), Banega; Llorente
(Gameiro 77).
Juventus: (352) Buffon; Barzagli, Bonucci, Chiellini;
Lichtsteiner (Cuadrado 76), Sturaro, Marchisio, Pogba,
Alex Sandro; Morata, Dybala.

Group D Table	P	W	D	L	F	A	GD	Pts
Manchester C	6	4	0	2	12	8	4	12
Juventus	6	3	2	1	6	3	3	11
Sevilla	6	2	0	4	8	11	–3	6
Borussia Moenchengladbach	6	1	2	3	8	12	–4	5

GROUP E

Wednesday, 16 September 2015
Bayer Leverkusen (1) 4 *(Mehmedi 4,*
Calhanoglu 47, 75 (pen), Hernandez 59)
BATE Borisov (1) 1 *(Milunovic 13)*   24,280
Bayer Leverkusen: (442) Leno; Hilbert, Papadopoulos,
Tah, Wendell; Bellarabi, Kampl, Bender (Kramer 43),
Mehmedi; Calhanoglu (Brandt 77), Hernandez (Kiessling
72).
BATE Borisov: (4231) Chernik; Palyakow, Dubra,
Milunovic, Mladenovic; Baha (Karnitskiy 60),
Aleksiyevich; Stasevich, Hleb (Volodko A 30),
Gordeichuk (Volodko M 78); Signevich.

Roma (1) 1 *(Florenzi 31)*
Barcelona (1) 1 *(Suarez 21)*   57,836
Roma: (433) Szczesny (De Sanctis 49); Florenzi
(Torosidis 85), Manolas, Rudiger, Digne; Nainggolan, De
Rossi, Keita; Falque (Iturbe 81), Salah, Dzeko.
Barcelona: (433) ter Stegen; Sergi Roberto, Pique,
Mathieu, Jordi Alba; Rakitic (Rafinha 61 (Mascherano
64)), Busquets, Iniesta; Messi, Neymar, Suarez.

Tuesday, 29 September 2015
Barcelona (0) 2 *(Sergi Roberto 81, Suarez 82)*
Bayer Leverkusen (1) 1 *(Papadopoulos 23)*   68,694
Barcelona: (433) ter Stegen; Dani Alves, Pique,
Mascherano, Mathieu; Rakitic (Sergi Roberto 72),
Busquets, Iniesta (Jordi Alba 60); Sandro (Munir 63),
Suarez, Neymar.
Bayer Leverkusen: (4231) Leno; Donati (Hilbert 76),
Tah, Papadopoulos, Wendell; Kramer, Bender; Kampl,
Calhanoglu, Bellarabi (Brandt 65); Hernandez (Kiessling
55).

BATE Borisov (3) 3 *(Stasevich 8, Mladenovic 12, 31)*
Roma (0) 2 *(Gervinho 66, Torosidis 82)*   12,767
BATE Borisov: (4231) Chernik; Palyakow, Dubra,
Milunovic, Mladenovic; Nikolic (Volodko A 86),
Yablonskiy; Stasevich, Gordeichuk (Hleb 72), Volodko
M (Ryas 84); Signevich.

Roma: (433) Szczesny; Florenzi (Soleri 90), Manolas, De
Rossi, Digne; Pjanic, Nainggolan, Vainqueur (Falque 39);
Iturbe (Torosidis 46), Gervinho, Salah.

Tuesday, 20 October 2015
BATE Borisov (0) 0
Barcelona (0) 2 *(Rakitic 48, 65)*   13,074
BATE Borisov: (4411) Chernik; Palyakow, Hayduchyk,
Milunovic, Mladenovic; Stasevich, Volodko A, Nikolic
(Yablonskiy 66), Volodko M (Karnitskiy 62);
Gordeichuk; Signevich (Mozolewski 80).
Barcelona: (433) ter Stegen; Dani Alves, Pique, Bartra,
Jordi Alba; Busquets (Gumbau 72), Mascherano, Sergi
Roberto (Rakitic 17); Munir (Sandro 69), Suarez,
Neymar.

Bayer Leverkusen (2) 4 *(Hernandez 4 (pen), 19,*
Kampl 84, Mehmedi 86)
Roma (2) 4 *(De Rossi 30, 38, Pjanic 54, Falque 73)* 29,412
Bayer Leverkusen: (442) Leno; Donati, Tah,
Papadopoulos, Wendell; Bellarabi (Mehmedi 56),
Toprak (Yurchenko 79), Kramer (Brandt 66), Kampl;
Hernandez, Calhanoglu.
Roma: (442) Szczesny; Torosidis, Rudiger, Manolas,
Digne; Florenzi (Iturbe 90), Nainggolan, De Rossi,
Pjanic; Salah (Falque 62), Gervinho (Dzeko 85).

Wednesday, 4 November 2015
Barcelona (1) 3 *(Neymar 31 (pen), 83, Suarez 60)*
BATE Borisov (0) 0   68,502
Barcelona: (433) ter Stegen; Dani Alves, Mascherano,
Vermaelen, Adriano; Rakitic (Munir 20), Busquets
(Gumbau 75), Sergi Roberto; Suarez, Iniesta (Bartra 68),
Neymar.
BATE Borisov: (4411) Chernik; Palyakow, Hayduchyk,
Milunovic, Mladenovic; Stasevich, Volodko A (Nikolic
67), Yablonskiy, Volodko M (Ryas 78); Gordeichuk;
Mozolewski (Hleb 60).

Roma (2) 3 *(Salah 2, Dzeko 29, Pjanic 80 (pen))*
Bayer Leverkusen (0) 2 *(Mehmedi 46, Hernandez 51)*
                                                                                    38,361
Roma: (433) Szczesny; Florenzi (Maicon 56 (Torosidis
76)), Manolas, Rudiger, Digne; Pjanic, De Rossi,
Nainggolan; Salah, Dzeko, Gervinho (Iturbe 67).
Bayer Leverkusen: (442) Leno; Donati, Tah,
Papadopoulos, Wendell; Mehmedi (Brandt 88), Toprak▪,
Kampl, Calhanoglu; Kiessling (Bellarabi 46 (Kramer
73)), Hernandez.

Tuesday, 24 November 2015
Barcelona (3) 6 *(Suarez 15, 44, Messi 18, 61, Pique 56,*
Adriano 77)
Roma (0) 1 *(Dzeko 90)*   71,433
Barcelona: (433) ter Stegen; Dani Alves, Pique (Bartra
57), Vermaelen, Jordi Alba; Rakitic, Busquets (Samper
46), Sergi Roberto (Adriano 64); Messi, Neymar, Suarez.
Roma: (433) Szczesny; Maicon, Manolas, Rudiger, Digne;
Pjanic (Ucan 75), Keita, Nainggolan (Iturbe 46); Florenzi
(Vainqueur 58), Falque, Dzeko.

BATE Borisov (1) 1 *(Gordeichuk 2)*
Bayer Leverkusen (0) 1 *(Mehmedi 68)*   12,601
BATE Borisov: (433) Chernik; Zhavnerchik, Palyakow,
Milunovic, Mladenovic; Volodko A (Nikolic 78),
Yablonskiy, Hleb (Karnitskiy 73); Ryas (Volodko M 46),
Mozolewski, Gordeichuk.
Bayer Leverkusen: (4231) Leno; Donati, Tah, Ramalho
Silva, Wendell; Kramer, Kampl; Bellarabi, Calhanoglu
(Brandt 78), Mehmedi (Yurchenko 88); Hernandez.

Wednesday, 9 December 2015
Bayer Leverkusen (1) 1 *(Hernandez 23)*
Barcelona (1) 1 *(Messi 20)*   29,412
Bayer Leverkusen: (4231) Leno; Hilbert, Tah, Toprak,
Wendell; Kramer (Papadopoulos 90), Kampl; Bellarabi,
Calhanoglu (Brandt 79), Mehmedi (Kiessling 70);
Hernandez.
Barcelona: (433) ter Stegen; Adriano, Bartra, Vermaelen,
Jordi Alba (Camara 74); Rakitic, Kaptoum (Gumbau
62), Samper; Sandro, Messi, Munir.

Roma (0) 0

BATE Borisov (0) 0 29,489

Roma: (433) Szczesny; Florenzi, Manolas, Digne, Rudiger; Nainggolan, De Rossi, Pjanic; Iturbe (Salah 59), Dzeko, Falque (Ucan 83).
BATE Borisov: (4411) Chernik; Zhavnerchik, Palyakow (Dubra 56), Milunovic, Mladenovic, Stasevich, Yablonskiy, Nikolic (Karnitskiy 79), Gordeichuk; Hleb; Mozolewski (Volodko M 60).

Group E Table	P	W	D	L	F	A	GD	Pts
Barcelona	6	4	2	0	15	4	11	14
Roma	6	1	3	2	11	16	–5	6
Bayer Leverkusen	6	1	3	2	13	12	1	6
BATE Borisov	6	1	2	3	5	12	–7	5

GROUP F

Wednesday, 16 September 2015

Dinamo Zagreb (1) 2 *(Pivaric 29, Fernandes 58)*

Arsenal (0) 1 *(Walcott 79)* 17,840

Dinamo Zagreb: (4411) Eduardo; Ivo Pinto, Sigali, Taravel, Pivaric; Soudani, Paulo Machado, Ademi, Antolic (Rog 82), Fernandes (Coric 73); Pjaca (Benkovic 88).
Arsenal: (4411) Ospina; Debuchy, Gabriel, Koscielny, Gibbs (Campbell 65); Oxlade-Chamberlain (Walcott 64), Cazorla, Arteta (Coquelin 64), Sanchez; Ozil; Giroud*.

Olympiacos (0) 0

Bayern Munich (0) 3 *(Muller 52, 90 (pen), Gotze 89)*
31,688

Olympiacos: (433) Roberto; Elabdellaoui, da Costa, Siovas, Masuaku; Leandro Salino, Cambiasso (Fortounis 66), Kasami; Pardo (Seba 82), Dominguez (Hernani 61), Ideye.
Bayern Munich: (433) Neuer; Lahm, Boateng, Alaba, Bernat; Vidal (Gotze 78), Alonso (Kimmich 76), Thiago; Muller, Lewandowski (Coman 59), Douglas Costa.

Tuesday, 29 September 2015

Arsenal (1) 2 *(Walcott 35, Sanchez 65)*

Olympiacos (2) 3 *(Pardo 32, Ospina 40 (og), Finnbogason 66)* 59,428

Arsenal: (451) Ospina; Bellerin (Campbell 86), Gabriel, Koscielny (Mertesacker 57), Gibbs; Sanchez, Ozil, Coquelin (Ramsey 60), Cazorla, Oxlade-Chamberlain; Walcott.
Olympiacos: (442) Roberto; Elabdellaoui, Botia, Siovas, Leandro Salino; Pardo, Kasami, Cambiasso, Seba (Hernani 72); Fortounis (Vouros 87), Ideye (Finnbogason 46).

Bayern Munich (4) 5 *(Douglas Costa 13, Lewandowski 21, 28, 55, Gotze 25)*

Dinamo Zagreb (0) 0 70,000

Bayern Munich: (433) Neuer; Lahm, Boateng (Rafinha 64), Alaba, Bernat (Javi Martinez 46); Kimmich, Thiago; Gotze; Coman, Lewandowski, Douglas Costa.
Dinamo Zagreb: (4231) Eduardo; Matel, Benkovic (Goncalo 46), Taravel, Pivaric; Paulo Machado (Rog 61), Ademi; Soudani, Antolic, Fernandes; Pjaca (Henriquez 69).

Tuesday, 20 October 2015

Arsenal (0) 2 *(Giroud 77, Ozil 90)*

Bayern Munich (0) 0 49,824

Arsenal: (4231) Cech; Bellerin, Mertesacker, Koscielny, Monreal; Coquelin, Cazorla; Ramsey (Oxlade-Chamberlain 57), Ozil, Sanchez (Gibbs 82); Walcott (Giroud 74).
Bayern Munich: (4231) Neuer; Lahm, Alaba, Boateng, Bernat; Vidal (Rafinha 71), Alonso (Kimmich 71); Muller, Thiago, Douglas Costa; Lewandowski.

Dinamo Zagreb (0) 0

Olympiacos (0) 1 *(Ideye 79)* 13,678

Dinamo Zagreb: (433) Eduardo; Matel, Goncalo, Taravel, Pivaric; Soudani, Paulo Machado, Antolic; Rog (Coric 87), Fernandes (Henriquez 72), Hodzic (Pjaca 61).
Olympiacos: (4411) Roberto; Elabdellaoui, Siovas, Botia, Masuaku; Pardo (Leandro Salino 83), Milivojevic, Kasami, Seba (da Costa 90); Fortounis (Dominguez 72); Ideye.

Wednesday, 4 November 2015

Bayern Munich (3) 5 *(Lewandowski 11, Muller 29, 89, Alaba 44, Robben 55)*

Arsenal (0) 1 *(Giroud 69)* 70,000

Bayern Munich: (451) Neuer; Lahm, Boateng (Benatia 68), Javi Martinez, Alaba; Alonso, Coman (Robben 54), Muller, Thiago, Douglas Costa; Lewandowski (Vidal 71).
Arsenal: (4231) Cech; Debuchy, Mertesacker, Gabriel, Monreal; Coquelin, Cazorla (Chambers 87); Campbell (Gibbs 58), Ozil, Sanchez; Giroud (Iwobi 84).

Olympiacos (0) 2 *(Pardo 65, 90)*

Dinamo Zagreb (1) 1 *(Hodzic 21)* 31,473

Olympiacos: (4231) Roberto; Elabdellaoui, Siovas, Botia (da Costa 51), Masuaku; Milivojevic, Kasami (Finnbogason 80); Hernani (Pardo 63), Fortounis, Seba; Ideye.
Dinamo Zagreb: (433) Eduardo; Matel, Goncalo, Taravel, Pivaric*; Paulo Machado, Rog, Antolic; Fernandes (Musa 88), Hodzic (Henriquez 57), Pjaca (Sigali 80).

Tuesday, 24 November 2015

Arsenal (2) 3 *(Ozil 29, Sanchez 33, 69)*

Dinamo Zagreb (0) 0 58,978

Arsenal: (4231) Cech; Bellerin (Debuchy 82), Mertesacker, Koscielny, Monreal; Flamini, Cazorla (Chambers 82); Campbell, Ozil, Sanchez; Giroud (Ramsey 67).
Dinamo Zagreb: (433) Eduardo; Ivo Pinto, Sigali, Taravel, Matel; Paulo Machado (Coric 84), Goncalo, Antolic (Henriquez 71); Pjaca, Rog, Fernandes (Soudani 57).

Bayern Munich (3) 4 *(Douglas Costa 8, Lewandowski 16, Muller 20, Coman 70)*

Olympiacos (0) 0 70,000

Bayern Munich: (451) Neuer; Lahm, Boateng, Badstuber*, Rafinha; Robben (Kimmich 33), Muller, Vidal, Douglas Costa (Javi Martinez 72), Coman; Lewandowski (Benatia 56).
Olympiacos: (433) Roberto; Elabdellaoui (Leandro Salino 78), da Costa, Siovas, Masuaku; Kasami (Fortounis 67), Cambiasso, Milivojevic; Pardo (Hernani 67), Ideye, Seba.

Wednesday, 9 December 2015

Dinamo Zagreb (0) 0

Bayern Munich (0) 2 *(Lewandowski 61, 64)* 19,681

Dinamo Zagreb: (433) Eduardo; Ivo Pinto, Sigali, Taravel, Pivaric; Rog (Pavicic 81), Goncalo, Antolic; Soudani, Coric (Pjaca 61), Fernandes (Paulo Machado 74).
Bayern Munich: (433) Ulreich; Lahm, Javi Martinez, Benatia (Boateng 46), Rafinha; Kimmich, Alonso, Rode; Green (Vidal 62), Ribery (Muller 46), Lewandowski.

Olympiacos (0) 0

Arsenal (1) 3 *(Giroud 29, 49, 67 (pen))* 31,388

Olympiacos: (4231) Roberto; Elabdellaoui, da Costa, Siovas, Masuaku; Kasami (Dominguez 71), Milivojevic; Seba (Hernani 77), Fortounis, Pardo (Finnbogason 86); Ideye.
Arsenal: (4231) Cech; Bellerin, Mertesacker, Koscielny, Monreal; Ramsey, Flamini; Walcott (Gibbs 72), Ozil, Campbell (Oxlade-Chamberlain 90); Giroud (Chambers 90).

Group F Table	P	W	D	L	F	A	GD	Pts
Bayern Munich	6	5	0	1	19	3	16	15
Arsenal	6	3	0	3	12	10	2	9
Olympiacos	6	3	0	3	6	13	–7	9
Dinamo Zagreb	6	1	0	5	3	14	–11	3

GROUP G

Wednesday, 16 September 2015

Chelsea (2) 4 *(Willian 15, Oscar 45 (pen), Costa 58, Fabregas 78)*

Maccabi Tel Aviv (0) 0 40,684

Chelsea: (451) Begovic; Azpilicueta, Zouma, Cahill, Baba; Willian (Costa 23), Fabregas, Loftus-Cheek (Traore 77), Oscar (Ramires 65); Hazard; Remy.
Maccabi Tel Aviv: (451) Rajkovic; Spungin (Peretz 71), Ben Haim, Tibi, Ben Haroush; Ben Chaim (Micha 64), Mitrovic, Alberman, Igiebor, Rikan (Radonjic 64); Zahavi.

Dynamo Kyiv (1) 2 *(Gusev 21, Buyalsky 89)*
Porto (1) 2 *(Aboubakar 23, 81)*   52,369
Dynamo Kyiv: (4231) Rybka; Danilo Silva, Khacheridi, Dragovic, Antunes; Rybalka, Garmash; Gusev (Buyalsky 67), Veloso (Kravets 87), Gonzalez (Belhanda 70); Junior Moraes.
Porto: (442) Casillas; Maxi Pereira, Maicon, Martins Indi, Layun; Andre Andre, Danilo Pereira, Ruben Neves, Herrera (Tello 65); Brahimi (Corona 78), Aboubakar (Osvaldo 90).

Tuesday, 29 September 2015
Maccabi Tel Aviv (0) 0
Dynamo Kyiv (1) 2 *(Yarmolenko 4, Junior Moraes 50)*
                                                       27,100
Maccabi Tel Aviv: (451) Rajkovic; Dasa, Tibi, Ben Haim, Rikan; Vermouth (Micha 79), Mitrovic (Itzhaki 61), Alberman, Peretz, Zahavi; Ben Basat (Ben Chaim 46).
Dynamo Kyiv: (4231) Shovkovskiy; Danilo Silva, Khacheridi, Dragovic, Antunes; Sydorchuk, Rybalka; Gonzalez (Vida 78), Veloso (Buyalsky 69), Yarmolenko; Junior Moraes (Kravets 81).

Porto (1) 2 *(Andre Andre 39, Maicon 52)*
Chelsea (1) 1 *(Willian 45)*   46,120
Porto: (4411) Casillas; Maxi Pereira, Maicon, Marcano, Martins Indi; Andre Andre (Layun 80), Danilo Pereira, Ruben Neves (Evandro 78), Imbula; Brahimi (Osvaldo 86); Aboubakar.
Chelsea: (4231) Begovic; Ivanovic, Cahill, Zouma, Azpilicueta; Mikel (Hazard 62), Fabregas; Ramires (Matic 73), Willian, Pedro (Kenedy 73); Costa.

Tuesday, 20 October 2015
Dynamo Kyiv (0) 0
Chelsea (0) 0   60,291
Dynamo Kyiv: (4231) Shovkovskiy; Danilo Silva, Khacheridi, Dragovic, Vida; Sydorchuk, Rybalka; Yarmolenko, Buyalsky (Garmash 82), Gonzalez; Kravets (Junior Moraes 78).
Chelsea: (4231) Begovic; Zouma, Cahill, Terry, Azpilicueta; Matic, Fabregas (Oscar 75); Ramires, Hazard, Willian; Costa.

Porto (2) 2 *(Aboubakar 37, Brahimi 41)*
Maccabi Tel Aviv (0) 0   35,209
Porto: (451) Casillas; Maxi Pereira, Martins Indi, Marcano, Layun; Corona (Tello 54), Andre Andre, Ruben Neves, Imbula (Danilo Pereira 54), Brahimi (Herrera 84); Aboubakar.
Maccabi Tel Aviv: (451) Rajkovic; Tibi, Carlos Garcia, Ben Haim, Ben Haroush; Micha (Vermouth 73), Mitrovic (Rikan 56), Alberman, Peretz, Ben Chaim (Itzhaki 84); Zahavi.

Wednesday, 4 November 2015
Chelsea (1) 2 *(Dragovic 34 (og), Willian 83)*
Dynamo Kyiv (0) 1 *(Dragovic 78)*   41,241
Chelsea: (4231) Begovic; Azpilicueta, Zouma, Terry, Baba; Ramires, Matic; Willian (Cahill 90), Fabregas (Pedro 79), Oscar (Hazard 79); Costa.
Dynamo Kyiv: (4231) Shovkovskiy; Vida, Khacheridi, Dragovic, Antunes; Sydorchuk (Garmash 46), Rybalka; Yarmolenko, Buyalsky, Gonzalez; Kravets (Junior Moraes 56).

Maccabi Tel Aviv (0) 1 *(Zahavi 75 (pen))*
Porto (1) 3 *(Tello 19, Andre Andre 49, Layun 72)* 26,646
Maccabi Tel Aviv: (4321) Rajkovic; Tibi, Carlos Garcia, Ben Haim, Ben Haroush (Ben Basat 46); Vermouth (Mitrovic 46), Alberman, Peretz (Igiebor 82); Ben Chaim, Rikan; Zahavi.
Porto: (433) Casillas; Maxi Pereira, Martins Indi, Marcano, Layun; Danilo Pereira, Evandro (Herrera 62), Ruben Neves; Tello (Varela 76), Aboubakar, Andre Andre (Imbula 89).

Tuesday, 24 November 2015
Maccabi Tel Aviv (0) 0
Chelsea (1) 4 *(Cahill 21, Willian 73, Oscar 77, Zouma 90)*
                                                       29,121
Maccabi Tel Aviv: (433) Rajkovic; Dasa, Ben Haim■, Carlos Garcia, Ben Haroush; Igiebor, Alberman (Azulay 85), Peretz; Ben Chaim (Ben Basat 80), Zahavi (Itzhaki 89), Rikan.

Chelsea: (433) Begovic; Azpilicueta, Cahill, Terry (Zouma 72), Baba; Fabregas, Matic, Oscar; Willian (Remy 78), Costa, Hazard (Pedro 68).

Porto (0) 0
Dynamo Kyiv (1) 2 *(Yarmolenko 35 (pen), Gonzalez 64)*
                                                       31,220
Porto: (433) Casillas; Maxi Pereira (Andre Andre 46), Marcano, Martins Indi, Layun; Ruben Neves, Danilo Pereira, Imbula (Corona 67); Tello, Aboubakar, Brahimi (Osvaldo 67).
Dynamo Kyiv: (4231) Shovkovskiy; Danilo Silva, Khacheridi, Dragovic, Antunes; Sydorchuk (Buyalsky 84), Garmash; Rybalka, Yarmolenko, Junior Moraes (Teodorczyk 87); Gonzalez (Belhanda 78).

Wednesday, 9 December 2015
Chelsea (1) 2 *(Marcano 12 (og), Willian 52)*
Porto (0) 0   41,096
Chelsea: (4231) Courtois; Ivanovic, Zouma, Terry, Azpilicueta; Ramires, Matic; Willian, Oscar (Pedro 81), Hazard (Remy 90); Costa (Mikel 86).
Porto: (433) Casillas; Maxi Pereira (Ruben Neves 57), Marcano, Maicon, Martins Indi; Herrera (Tello 71), Danilo Pereira, Imbula (Aboubakar 56); Corona, Brahimi, Layun.

Dynamo Kyiv (1) 1 *(Garmash 16)*
Maccabi Tel Aviv (0) 0   475
Dynamo Kyiv: (4231) Shovkovskiy; Danilo Silva, Khacheridi, Dragovic, Antunes; Sydorchuk, Rybalka; Yarmolenko (Gusev 18), Garmash (Veloso 63), Gonzalez; Junior Moraes (Teodorczyk 89).
Maccabi Tel Aviv: (4231) Rajkovic; Dasa, Carlos Garcia, Tibi, Ben Haroush; Igiebor (Peretz 72), Rikan; Micha (Vermouth 70), Alberman, Ben Chaim (Itzhaki 83); Zahavi.

Group G Table	P	W	D	L	F	A	GD	Pts
Chelsea	6	4	1	1	13	3	10	13
Dynamo Kyiv	6	3	2	1	8	4	4	11
Porto	6	3	1	2	9	8	1	10
Maccabi Tel Aviv	6	0	0	6	1	16	–15	0

GROUP H

Wednesday, 16 September 2015
KAA Gent (0) 1 *(Milicevic 68)*
Lyon (0) 1 *(Jallet 58)*   ·   19,601
KAA Gent: (343) Sels; Nielsen, Mitrovie, Asare; Foket■, Kums, Renato Neto, Dejaegere■; Milicevic (Matton 81), Depoitre, Simon (Raman 69 (Rafinha 90)).
Lyon: (41212) Lopes; Da Silva (Jallet 45), Yanga-Mbiwa, Umtiti, Morel; Gonalons, Ferri (Malbranque 81), Tolisso; Valbuena; Lacazette, Beauvue (Kalulu 69).

Valencia (0) 2 *(Joao Cancelo 55, Andre Gomes 73)*
Zenit St Petersburg (2) 3 *(Hulk 9, 44, Witsel 76)* 28,005
Valencia: (451) Jaume; Joao Cancelo, Mustafi, Abdennour, Gaya; Feghouli (Rodrigo 70), Perez, Parejo, Javi Fuego (Alcacer 46), Piatti (Andre Gomes 46); Negredo.
Zenit St Petersburg: (532) Lodygin; Smolnikov (Shatov 69), Garay, Lombaerts, Criscito, Aniukov (Luis Neto 76); Javi Garcia, Danny, Witsel; Dzjuba (Fayzulin 58), Hulk.

Tuesday, 29 September 2015
Lyon (0) 0
Valencia (1) 1 *(Feghouli 42)*   33,534
Lyon: (442) Lopes; Bisevac, Morel (Ghezzal 78), Umtiti, Tolisso; Darder (Ferri 44), Valbuena, Jallet, Gonalons; Kalulu, Lacazette (Beauvue 74).
Valencia: (442) Jaume; Joao Cancelo, Mustafi, Orban, Abdennour (Aderlan Santos 59); Feghouli, Parejo, Perez (Danilo 84), Javi Fuego; Negredo (Rodrigo 71), Piatti.

Zenit St Petersburg (1) 2 *(Dzjuba 35, Shatov 67)*
KAA Gent (0) 1 *(Matton 56)*   18,095
Zenit St Petersburg: (4231) Kerzhakov; Smolnikov, Garay, Lombaerts (Luis Neto 62), Aniukov; Witsel, Javi Garcia; Danny, Hulk, Shatov (Ryazantsev 88); Dzjuba (Yusupov 71).
KAA Gent: (4231) Sels; Rafinha (Coulibaly 90), Nielsen, Mitrovic, Asare; Saief, Kums, Renato Neto, Milicevic (Pedersen 80), Matton (Raman 84); Depoitre.

Tuesday, 20 October 2015
Valencia (1) 2 *(Nielsen 15 (og), Mitrovic 73 (og))*
KAA Gent (1) 1 *(Foket 40)*   38,207
Valencia: (451) Jaume; Gaya, Aderlan Santos, Mustafi, Joao Cancelo; Santi Mina (Piatti 61), Andre Gomes, Javi Fuego, Parejo (Rodrigo 68), Feghouli; Alcacer (Danilo 82).
KAA Gent: (3421) Sels; Asare, Mitrovic, Nielsen; Saief, Kums, Renato Neto, Foket; Milicevic, Matton (Simon 84); Depoitre.

Zenit St Petersburg (1) 3 *(Dzjuba 2, Hulk 56, Danny 82)*
Lyon (0) 1 *(Lacazette 49)*   17,517
Zenit St Petersburg: (451) Kerzhakov; Aniukov, Lombaerts, Garay, Criscito; Danny (Ryazantsev 89), Witsel, Javi Garcia (Luis Neto 84), Shatov, Hulk; Dzjuba (Yusupov 75).
Lyon: (433) Lopes; Jallet, Yanga-Mbiwa, Umtiti, Morel; Ferri (Ghezzal 71), Gonalons, Tolisso; Da Silva (Cornet 84), Lacazette (Beauvue 80), Valbuena.

Wednesday, 4 November 2015
KAA Gent (0) 1 *(Kums 49 (pen))*
Valencia (0) 0   19,452
KAA Gent: (343) Sels; Nielsen, Mitrovic, Asare; Foket, Kums, Renato Neto, Saief (Raman 55 (Rafinha 85)); Milicevic, Depoitre, Dejaegere (Coulibaly 90).
Valencia: (433) Jaume; Barragan, Aderlan Santos, Mustafi, Gaya; Parejo, Javi Fuego (Andre Gomes 63), Perez; Feghouli (Joao Cancelo 70), Alcacer, Santi Mina (Piatti 46).

Lyon (0) 0
Zenit St Petersburg (1) 2 *(Dzjuba 25, 57)*   30,173
Lyon: (4231) Lopes; Jallet (Da Silva 61), Yanga-Mbiwa, Umtiti, Bedimo; Gonalons[■], Tolisso; Valbuena, Lacazette, Darder (Ferri 77); Beauvue (Cornet 69).
Zenit St Petersburg: (442) Lodygin; Aniukov[■], Lombaerts, Luis Neto, Criscito (Smolnikov 73); Danny, Javi Garcia (Yusupov 80), Witsel, Shatov; Dzjuba (Ryazantsev 83), Hulk.

Tuesday, 24 November 2015
Lyon (1) 1 *(Ferri 7)*
KAA Gent (1) 2 *(Milicevic 32, Coulibaly 90)*   30,206
Lyon: (4312) Lopes; Da Silva, Bisevac, Yanga-Mbiwa, Bedimo; Malbranque (Darder 64), Tolisso, Ghezzal (Beauvue 74); Ferri (Cornet 85); Lacazette, Valbuena.

KAA Gent: (3421) Sels; Nielsen, Mitrovic, Asare; Foket, Renato Neto, Kums, Saief (Raman 67); Dejaegere (Rafinha 82), Milicevic; Depoitre (Coulibaly 90).

Zenit St Petersburg (1) 2 *(Shatov 15, Dzjuba 74)*
Valencia (0) 0   17,002
Zenit St Petersburg: (4411) Lodygin; Smolnikov (Yusupov 64), Garay, Lombaerts, Criscito; Shatov (Ryazantsev 83), Luis Neto (Evseev 86), Witsel, Hulk; Danny; Dzjuba.
Valencia: (442) Jaume; Joao Cancelo (De Paul 79), Ruben Vezo[■], Abdennour, Gaya; Feghouli, Parejo, Perez (Danilo 73), Andre Gomes; Alcacer, Mir (Santi Mina 56).

Wednesday, 9 December 2015
KAA Gent (1) 2 *(Depoitre 18, Milicevic 78)*
Zenit St Petersburg (0) 1 *(Dzjuba 65)*   19,978
KAA Gent: (343) Sels; Mitrovic, Nielsen, Rafinha; Asare, Kums, Renato Neto, Foket; Simon (Saief 88), Milicevic (Dejaegere 82), Depoitre (Coulibaly 90).
Zenit St Petersburg: (532) Lodygin; Criscito, Lombaerts, Luis Neto, Garay, Aniukov (Bogaev 83); Yusupov, Javi Garcia (Troyanov 86), Ryazantsev (Dolgov 61); Dzjuba, Danny.

Valencia (0) 0
Lyon (1) 2 *(Cornet 37, Lacazette 76)*   32,494
Valencia: (433) Jaume; Joao Cancelo, Mustafi, Abdennour, Gaya; Danilo (Negredo 52), Parejo, Perez (Javi Fuego 23); Santi Mina, Alcacer, De Paul (Piatti 75).
Lyon: (433) Lopes; Da Silva, Morel, Yanga-Mbiwa, Bedimo; Darder (Kone 77), Gonalons, Tolisso; Cornet, Lacazette (Beauvue 77), Grenier (Ghezzal 69).

Group H Table	P	W	D	L	F	A	GD	Pts
Zenit St Petersburg	6	5	0	1	13	6	7	15
KAA Gent	6	3	1	2	8	7	1	10
Valencia	6	2	0	4	5	9	–4	6
Lyon	6	1	1	4	5	9	–4	4

KNOCK-OUT STAGE

ROUND OF 16 FIRST LEG
Tuesday, 16 February 2016
Benfica (0) 1 *(Jonas 90)*
Zenit St Petersburg (0) 0   48,615
Benfica: (4231) Julio Cesar; Andre Almeida, Lindelof, Jardel, Eliseu; Samaris, Renato Sanches; Pizzi (Carcela-Gonzalez 71), Jonas, Gaitan; Mitroglou (Jimenez 63).
Zenit St Petersburg: (4231) Lodygin; Aniukov, Garay, Lombaerts, Criscito[■]; Witsel, Javi Garcia; Shatov (Zhirkov 81), Hulk, Danny (Mauricio 87); Dzjuba (Kokorin 73).

Paris Saint-Germain (1) 2 *(Ibrahimovic 39, Cavani 78)*
Chelsea (1) 1 *(Mikel 45)*   46,505
Paris Saint-Germain: (433) Trapp; Marquinhos, Thiago Silva, Luiz, Maxwell; Verratti (Rabiot 80), Thiago Motta, Matuidi (Pastore 81); Di Maria, Ibrahimovic, Lucas Moura (Cavani 74).
Chelsea: (433) Courtois; Ivanovic, Cahill, Baba, Azpilicueta; Fabregas, Mikel, Pedro; Willian, Costa, Hazard (Oscar 71).

Wednesday, 17 February 2016
KAA Gent (0) 2 *(Kums 80, Coulibaly 89)*
Wolfsburg (1) 3 *(Draxler 44, 54, Kruse 60)*   19,978
KAA Gent: (352) Sels; Nielsen, Mitrovic, Asare; Foket, Milicevic (Saief 62), Renato Neto, Kums, Dejaegere; Depoitre (Coulibaly 79), Simon (Matton 61).
Wolfsburg: (4231) Casteels; Jung (Schurrle 45), Dante, Knoche, Rodriguez; Trasch, Gustavo; Vieirinha (Schafer 79), Arnold, Draxler; Kruse (Putaro 90).

Roma (0) 0
Real Madrid (0) 2 *(Ronaldo 57, Jese 86)*   55,612
Roma: (433) Szczesny; Florenzi (Totti 87), Manolas, Rudiger, Digne; Pjanic, Vainqueur (De Rossi 77), Nainggolan; Salah, Perotti, El Shaarawy (Dzeko 63).
Real Madrid: (433) Navas; Carvajal, Sergio Ramos, Varane, Marcelo; Modric, Kroos, Isco (Kovacic 64); Rodriguez (Jese 82), Benzema, Ronaldo (Casemiro 89).

Tuesday, 23 February 2016
Arsenal (0) 0
Barcelona (0) 2 *(Messi 71, 84 (pen))*   59,889
Arsenal: (4231) Cech; Bellerin, Mertesacker, Koscielny, Monreal; Coquelin (Flamini 82), Ramsey; Oxlade-Chamberlain (Walcott 50), Ozil, Sanchez; Giroud (Welbeck 73).
Barcelona: (433) ter Stegen; Dani Alves, Pique, Mascherano, Jordi Alba; Busquets, Rakitic, Iniesta; Suarez, Messi, Neymar.

Juventus (0) 2 *(Dybala 63, Sturaro 76)*
Bayern Munich (1) 2 *(Muller 43, Robben 55)*   41,332
Juventus: (442) Buffon; Lichtsteiner, Barzagli, Bonucci, Evra; Cuadrado, Khedira (Sturaro 69), Marchisio (Hernanes 46), Pogba; Mandzukic, Dybala (Morata 75).
Bayern Munich: (451) Neuer; Lahm, Kimmich, Alaba, Bernat (Benatia 74); Robben, Muller, Vidal, Thiago, Douglas Costa (Ribery 84); Lewandowski.

Wednesday, 24 February 2016
Dynamo Kyiv (0) 1 *(Buyalsky 58)*
Manchester C (2) 3 *(Aguero 15, Silva 40, Toure 89)* 53,691
Dynamo Kyiv: (4141) Shovkovskiy; Danilo Silva (Makarenko 66), Khacheridi, Dragovic, Vida; Rybalka; Yarmolenko, Garmash (Veloso 31), Buyalsky, Gonzalez; Teodorczyk (Junior Moraes 46).
Manchester C: (4231) Hart; Sagna, Kompany, Otamendi, Clichy, Fernando, Fernandinho; Silva, Toure, Sterling; Aguero (Iheanacho 90).

PSV Eindhoven (0) 0
Atletico Madrid (0) 0 34,948
PSV Eindhoven: (451) Zoet; Arias, Bruma, Moreno, Willems; Narsingh (Isimat-Mirin 65), van Ginkel, Propper, Guardado (Hendrix 74), Locadia (Lestienne 85); Pereiro■.
Atletico Madrid: (442) Oblak; Juanfran, Savic, Godin, Filipe Luis; Torres O, Gabi, Saul (Correa 74), Koke; Griezmann, Vietto (Torres F 61).

ROUND OF 16 SECOND LEG

Tuesday, 8 March 2016
Real Madrid (0) 2 *(Ronaldo 64, Rodriguez 68)*
Roma (0) 0 76,654
Real Madrid: (433) Navas; Danilo, Sergio Ramos, Pepe, Marcelo; Modric (Jese 75), Casemiro (Kovacic 83), Kroos; Bale (Lucas 61), Rodriguez, Ronaldo.
Roma: (4321) Szczesny; Florenzi, Manolas, Zukanovic, Digne; Pjanic (Vainqueur 46), Keita (Maicon 86), Perotti; Salah, El Shaarawy (Totti 74); Dzeko.

Wolfsburg (0) 1 *(Schurrle 74)*
KAA Gent (0) 0 23,457
Wolfsburg: (4231) Casteels; Trasch, Knoche, Dante, Rodriguez; Guilavogui, Gustavo; Arnold (Vieirinha 83), Draxler (Caligiuri 77), Schurrle (Schafer 88); Kruse.
KAA Gent: (424) Sels; Rafinha (Foket 78), Nielsen, Gershon, Asare; Renato Neto, Kums; Milicevic, Dejaegere, Matton (Saief 68), Simon (Coulibaly 70).

Wednesday, 9 March 2016
Chelsea (1) 1 *(Costa 27)*
Paris Saint-Germain (1) 2 *(Rabiot 16, Ibrahimovic 67)*
37,591
Chelsea: (4231) Courtois; Azpilicueta, Ivanovic, Cahill, Kenedy; Mikel, Fabregas; Pedro, Willian, Hazard (Oscar 77); Costa (Traore 60).
Paris Saint-Germain: (433) Trapp; Marquinhos, Thiago Silva, Luiz, Maxwell; Rabiot, Thiago Motta, Matuidi (van der Wiel 87); Di Maria (Cavani 82), Ibrahimovic, Lucas Moura (Pastore 77).

Zenit St Petersburg (0) 1 *(Hulk 69)*
Benfica (0) 2 *(Gaitan 86, Anderson Talisca 90)* 17,688
Zenit St Petersburg: (4231) Lodygin; Aniukov (Smolnikov 59), Lombaerts, Luis Neto, Zhirkov; Mauricio (Yusupov 82), Witsel; Hulk, Danny, Kokorin (Shatov 58); Dzjuba.
Benfica: (442) Ederson; Semedo, Eliseu, Lindelof, Fejsa; Renato Sanches, Pizzi (Salvio 73), Gaitan, Samaris; Jonas (Anderson Talisca 90), Mitroglou (Jimenez 67).

Tuesday, 15 March 2016
Atletico Madrid (0) 0
PSV Eindhoven (0) 0 50,135
Atletico Madrid: (442) Oblak; Juanfran, Gimenez, Godin (Lucas 89), Filipe Luis; Koke, Fernandez (Torres F 56), Gabi, Griezmann; Saul, Carrasco (Kranevitter 75).
PSV Eindhoven: (532) Zoet; Arias, Bruma, Isimat-Mirin, Moreno, Willems (Brenet 74); Propper, Guardado, van Ginkel; de Jong (Narsingh 118), Locadia (Lestienne 86).
aet; Atletico Madrid won 8-7 on penalties.

Manchester C (0) 0
Dynamo Kyiv (0) 0 43,630
Manchester C: (4231) Hart; Zabaleta, Kompany (Mangala 6), Otamendi (Demichelis 23), Clichy; Fernando, Fernandinho; Jesus Navas, Toure, Silva (Sterling 79); Aguero.

Dynamo Kyiv: (4141) Shovkovskiy; Vida, Khacheridi, Dragovic, Antunes; Veloso; Yarmolenko, Garmash (Sydorchuk 64), Buyalsky, Gusev (Yakovenko 62); Teodorczyk (Gonzalez 46).

Wednesday, 16 March 2016
Barcelona (1) 3 *(Neymar 18, Suarez 65, Messi 88)*
Arsenal (0) 1 *(Elneny 51)* 76,092
Barcelona: (433) ter Stegen; Dani Alves, Mascherano, Mathieu, Jordi Alba; Rakitic (Turan 77), Busquets, Iniesta (Sergi Roberto 72); Messi, Suarez, Neymar.
Arsenal: (4231) Ospina; Bellerin, Koscielny, Gabriel, Monreal; Flamini (Coquelin 45), Elneny; Iwobi (Giroud 73), Ozil, Sanchez; Welbeck (Walcott 73).

Bayern Munich (0) 4 *(Lewandowski 73, Muller 90, Thiago 108, Coman 110)*
Juventus (2) 2 *(Pogba 5, Cuadrado 28)* 70,000
Bayern Munich: (4141) Neuer; Lahm, Kimmich, Benatia (Bernat 46), Alaba; Alonso (Coman 60); Douglas Costa, Muller, Vidal, Ribery (Thiago 101); Lewandowski.
Juventus: (4231) Buffon; Lichtsteiner, Barzagli, Bonucci, Evra; Khedira (Sturaro 67), Pogba; Cuadrado (Pereyra 89), Hernanes, Alex Sandro; Morata (Mandzukic 71).
aet.

QUARTER-FINALS FIRST LEG

Tuesday, 5 April 2016
Barcelona (0) 2 *(Suarez 63, 74)*
Atletico Madrid (1) 1 *(Torres F 25)* 88,534
Barcelona: (433) ter Stegen; Dani Alves, Pique, Mascherano, Jordi Alba; Rakitic (Rafinha 64), Busquets (Sergi Roberto 81), Iniesta (Turan 83); Messi, Suarez, Neymar.
Atletico Madrid: (4312) Oblak; Juanfran, Lucas, Godin, Filipe Luis; Koke, Gabi, Saul (Correa 90); Griezmann (Thomas 75); Carrasco (Fernandez 53), Torres F■.

Bayern Munich (1) 1 *(Vidal 2)*
Benfica (0) 0 70,000
Bayern Munich: (4141) Neuer; Lahm, Kimmich (Javi Martinez 59), Alaba, Bernat; Vidal; Douglas Costa (Coman 71), Muller (Gotze 85), Thiago, Ribery; Lewandowski.
Benfica: (442) Ederson; Andre Almeida, Lindelof, Jardel, Eliseu; Pizzi (Samaris 90), Fejsa, Renato Sanches, Gaitan; Jonas (Salvio 82), Mitroglou (Jimenez 72).

Wednesday, 6 April 2016
Paris Saint-Germain (1) 2 *(Ibrahimovic 41, Rabiot 60)*
Manchester C (1) 2 *(De Bruyne 38, Fernandinho 73)* 47,228
Paris Saint-Germain: (433) Trapp; Aurier (van der Wiel 78), Thiago Silva, Luiz, Maxwell; Rabiot (Lucas Moura 78), Thiago Motta, Matuidi; Di Maria, Ibrahimovic, Cavani.
Manchester C: (451) Hart; Sagna, Mangala, Otamendi, Clichy; Jesus Navas, Fernandinho, De Bruyne (Delph 77), Fernando, Silva (Bony 88); Aguero (Kolarov 90).

Wolfsburg (2) 2 *(Rodriguez 18 (pen), Arnold 25)*
Real Madrid (0) 0 26,400
Wolfsburg: (4231) Benaglio; Vieirinha, Naldo, Dante, Rodriguez; Guilavogui, Gustavo; Bruno Henrique (Trasch 80), Arnold, Draxler (Schafer 90); Schurrle (Kruse 84).
Real Madrid: (433) Navas; Danilo, Pepe, Sergio Ramos, Marcelo; Modric (Isco 64), Casemiro, Kroos (Rodriguez 85); Bale, Benzema (Jese 41), Ronaldo.

QUARTER-FINALS SECOND LEG

Tuesday, 12 April 2016
Manchester C (0) 1 *(De Bruyne 76)*
Paris Saint-Germain (0) 0 53,039
Manchester C: (4231) Hart; Sagna, Otamendi, Mangala, Clichy; Fernandinho, Fernando; Jesus Navas, De Bruyne (Toure 84), Silva (Delph 87); Aguero (Iheanacho 90).
Paris Saint-Germain: (433) Trapp; van der Wiel, Aurier (Pastore 61), Thiago Silva, Maxwell; Rabiot, Marquinhos, Thiago Motta (Lucas Moura 44); Di Maria, Ibrahimovic, Cavani.

Real Madrid (2) 3 *(Ronaldo 16, 17, 77)*
Wolfsburg (0) 0   76,684
Real Madrid: (433) Navas; Carvajal, Sergio Ramos, Pepe,
Marcelo; Modric (Varane 90), Casemiro, Kroos; Bale,
Benzema (Jese 84), Ronaldo.
Wolfsburg: (4231) Benaglio; Vieirinha, Naldo, Dante,
Rodriguez; Guilavogui (Dost 79), Gustavo; Bruno Henrique
(Caligiuri 73), Arnold, Draxler (Kruse 32); Schurrle.

Wednesday, 13 April 2016
Atletico Madrid (1) 2 *(Griezmann 36, 88 (pen))*
Barcelona (0) 0   52,851
Atletico Madrid: (442) Oblak; Juanfran, Godin, Lucas,
Filipe Luis; Koke, Fernandez (Savic 90), Gabi, Saul;
Carrasco (Thomas 73), Griezmann (Correa 89).
Barcelona: (433) ter Stegen; Dani Alves (Sergi Roberto
64), Pique, Mascherano, Jordi Alba; Rakitic (Turan 64),
Busquets, Iniesta; Messi, Suarez, Neymar.

Benfica (1) 2 *(Jimenez 27, Anderson Talisca 77)*
Bayern Munich (1) 2 *(Vidal 38, Muller 52)*   63,235
Benfica: (4411) Ederson; Andre Almeida, Lindelof,
Jardel, Eliseu (Jovic 88); Salvio (Anderson Talisca 68),
Fejsa, Renato Sanches, Carcela-Gonzalez; Pizzi (Goncalo
Guedes 58); Jimenez.
Bayern Munich: (433) Neuer; Lahm, Kimmich, Javi Marti-
nez, Alaba; Vidal, Alonso (Bernat 90), Thiago; Douglas
Costa, Muller (Lewandowski 83), Ribery (Gotze 90).

SEMI-FINALS FIRST LEG

Tuesday, 26 April 2016
Manchester C (0) 0
Real Madrid (0) 0   52,221
Manchester C: (4231) Hart; Sagna, Kompany, Otamendi,
Clichy; Fernandinho, Fernando; Jesus Navas (Sterling
76), De Bruyne, Silva (Iheanacho 40); Aguero.

Real Madrid: (433) Navas; Carvajal, Sergio Ramos, Pepe,
Marcelo; Modric, Casemiro, Kroos (Isco 89); Lucas,
Benzema (Jese 46), Bale.

Wednesday, 27 April 2016
Atletico Madrid (1) 1 *(Saul 11)*
Bayern Munich (0) 0   52,127
Atletico Madrid: (442) Oblak; Juanfran, Gimenez, Savic,
Filipe Luis; Saul (Thomas 85), Gabi, Fernandez, Koke;
Griezmann, Torres F.
Bayern Munich: (4141) Neuer; Lahm, Javi Martinez, Alaba,
Bernat (Benatia 77); Alonso; Douglas Costa, Thiago
(Muller 70), Vidal, Coman (Ribery 64); Lewandowski.

SEMI-FINALS SECOND LEG

Tuesday, 3 May 2016
Bayern Munich (1) 2 *(Alonso 31, Lewandowski 74)*
Atletico Madrid (0) 1 *(Griezmann 54)*   70,000
Bayern Munich: (4141) Neuer; Lahm, Boateng, Javi
Martinez, Alaba; Alonso; Douglas Costa (Coman 73),
Muller, Vidal, Ribery; Lewandowski.
Atletico Madrid: (442) Oblak; Juanfran, Godin, Gimenez,
Filipe Luis; Saul, Gabi, Fernandez (Carrasco 46), Koke
(Savic 90); Torres F, Griezmann (Thomas 82).
Atletico Madrid won on away goals.

Wednesday, 4 May 2016
Real Madrid (1) 1 *(Fernando 20 (og))*
Manchester C (0) 0   78,300
Real Madrid: (433) Navas; Carvajal, Pepe, Sergio Ramos,
Marcelo; Modric (Kovacic 88), Kroos, Isco (Rodriguez
67); Jese (Lucas 55), Ronaldo, Bale.
Manchester C: (4141) Hart; Sagna, Kompany (Mangala
10), Otamendi, Clichy; Fernando; Jesus Navas
(Iheanacho 69), Fernandinho, Toure (Sterling 61), De
Bruyne; Aguero.

CHAMPIONS LEAGUE FINAL 2016

Saturday, 28 May 2016

(in Milan, 71,942)

Real Madrid (1) 1 *(Sergio Ramos 15)*   **Atletico Madrid (0) 1** *(Carrasco 80)*

Real Madrid: (433) Navas; Carvajal (Danilo 52), Sergio Ramos, Pepe, Marcelo; Modric, Casemiro, Kroos (Isco 72);
Bale, Benzema (Lucas 77), Ronaldo.

Atletico Madrid: (4411) Oblak; Juanfran, Savic, Godin, Filipe Luis (Lucas 109); Saul, Gabi, Fernandez (Carrasco 46),
Koke (Thomas 116); Griezmann; Torres F.

aet; Real Madrid won 5-3 on penalties.

Referee: Mark Clattenburg.

Real Madrid's Cristiano Ronaldo
scores the winning penalty in the
shoot-out to beat city rivals
Atletico in the Champions League
final at the San Siro Stadium in
Milan on 28 May.
(Reuters/Stefano Rellandini Livepic)

EUROPEAN CUP-WINNERS' CUP
FINALS 1961–99

Year	Winners v Runners-up		Venue	Attendance	Referee
1961	1st Leg Fiorentina v Rangers	2-0	Glasgow	80,000	C. E. Steiner (Austria)
	2nd Leg Fiorentina v Rangers	2-1	Florence	50,000	V. Hernadi (Hungary)
1962	Atletico Madrid v Fiorentina	1-1	Glasgow	27,389	T. Wharton (Scotland)
Replay	Atletico Madrid v Fiorentina	3-0	Stuttgart	38,000	K. Tschenscher (West Germany)
1963	Tottenham Hotspur v Atletico Madrid	5-1	Rotterdam	49,000	A. van Leuwen (Netherlands)
1964	Sporting Lisbon v MTK Budapest	3-3*	Brussels	3,208	L. van Nuffel (Belgium)
Replay	Sporting Lisbon v MTK Budapest	1-0	Antwerp	13,924	G. Versyp (Belgium)
1965	West Ham U v Munich 1860	2-0	Wembley	7,974	I. Zsolt (Hungary)
1966	Borussia Dortmund v Liverpool	2-1*	Glasgow	41,657	P. Schwinte (France)
1967	Bayern Munich v Rangers	1-0*	Nuremberg	69,480	C. Lo Bello (Italy)
1968	AC Milan v Hamburg	2-0	Rotterdam	53,000	J. Ortiz de Mendibil (Spain)
1969	Slovan Bratislava v Barcelona	3-2	Basle	19,000	L. van Ravens (Netherlands)
1970	Manchester C v Gornik Zabrze	2-1	Vienna	7,968	P. Schiller (Austria)
1971	Chelsea v Real Madrid	1-1*	Athens	45,000	R. Scheurer (Switzerland)
Replay	Chelsea v Real Madrid	2-1*	Athens	19,917	R. Scheurer (Switzerland)
1972	Rangers v Dynamo Moscow	3-2	Barcelona	24,701	J. Ortiz de Mendibil (Spain)
1973	AC Milan v Leeds U	1-0	Salonika	40,154	C. Mihas (Greece)
1974	Magdeburg v AC Milan	2-0	Rotterdam	4,641	A. van Gemert (Netherlands)
1975	Dynamo Kyiv v Ferencvaros	3-0	Basle	13,000	R. Davidson (Scotland)
1976	Anderlecht v West Ham U	4-2	Brussels	51,296	R. Wurtz (France)
1977	Hamburger SV v Anderlecht	2-0	Amsterdam	66,000	P. Partridge (England)
1978	Anderlecht v Austria/WAC	4-0	Paris	48,679	H. Adlinger (West Germany)
1979	Barcelona v Fortuna Dusseldorf	4-3*	Basel	58,000	K. Palotai (Hungary)
1980	Valencia v Arsenal	0-0*	Brussels	40,000	V. Christov (Czechoslovakia)
	(Valencia won 5-4 on penalties)				
1981	Dinamo Tbilisi v Carl Zeiss Jena	2-1	Dusseldorf	4,750	R. Lattanzi (Italy)
1982	Barcelona v Standard Liege	2-1	Barcelona	80,000	W. Eschweiler (West Germany)
1983	Aberdeen v Real Madrid	2-1*	Gothenburg	17,804	G. Menegali (Italy)
1984	Juventus v Porto	2-1	Basel	55,000	A. Prokop (Egypt)
1985	Everton v Rapid Vienna	3-1	Rotterdam	38,500	P. Casarin (Italy)
1986	Dynamo Kyiv v Atletico Madrid	3-0	Lyon	50,000	F. Wohrer (Austria)
1987	Ajax v Lokomotiv Leipzig	1-0	Athens	35,107	L. Agnolin (Italy)
1988	Mechelen v Ajax	1-0	Strasbourg	39,446	D. Pauly (West Germany)
1989	Barcelona v Sampdoria	2-0	Berne	42,707	G. Courtney (England)
1990	Sampdoria v Anderlecht	2-0*	Gothenburg	20,103	B. Galler (Switzerland)
1991	Manchester U v Barcelona	2-1	Rotterdam	43,500	B. Karlsson (Sweden)
1992	Werder Bremen v Monaco	2-0	Lisbon	16,000	P. D'Elia (Italy)
1993	Parma v Antwerp	3-1	Wembley	37,393	K.-J. Assenmacher (Germany)
1994	Arsenal v Parma	1-0	Copenhagen	33,765	V. Krondl (Czech Republic)
1995	Real Zaragoza v Arsenal	2-1	Paris	42,424	P. Ceccarini (Italy)
1996	Paris Saint-Germain v Rapid Vienna	1-0	Brussels	37,000	P. Pairetto (Italy)
1997	Barcelona v Paris Saint-Germain	1-0	Rotterdam	52,000	M. Merk (Germany)
1998	Chelsea v VfB Stuttgart	1-0	Stockholm	30,216	S. Braschi (Italy)
1999	Lazio v Mallorca	2-1	Villa Park	33,021	G. Benko (Austria)

INTER-CITIES FAIRS CUP FINALS 1958–71

Year	1st Leg		Attendance	2nd Leg	Attendance	Agg	Winner
1958	London XI v Barcelona	2-2	45,466	0-6	70,000	2-8	Barcelona
1960	Birmingham C v Barcelona	0-0	40,524	1-4	70,000	1-4	Barcelona
1961	Birmingham C v Roma	2-2	21,005	0-2	60,000	2-4	Roma
1962	Valencia v Barcelona	6-2	65,000	1-1	60,000	7-3	Valencia
1963	Dinamo Zagreb v Valencia	1-2	40,000	0-2	55,000	1-4	Valencia
1964	Real Zaragoza v Valencia	2-1	50,000 (in Barcelona, one match only)				Real Zaragoza
1965	Ferencvaros v Juventus	1-0	25,000 (in Turin, one match only)				Ferencvaros
1966	Barcelona v Real Zaragoza	0-1	70,000	4-2*	70,000	4-3	Barcelona
1967	Dinamo Zagreb v Leeds U	2-0	40,000	0-0	35,604	2-0	Dynamo Zagreb
1968	Leeds U v Ferencvaros	1-0	25,368	0-0	70,000	1-0	Leeds U
1969	Newcastle U v Ujpest Dozsa	3-0	60,000	3-2	37,000	6-2	Newcastle U
1970	Anderlecht v Arsenal	3-1	37,000	0-3	51,612	3-4	Arsenal
1971	Juventus v Leeds U	0-0	*(abandoned 51 minutes)*		42,000		
	Juventus v Leeds U	2-2	42,000	1-1	42,483	3-3	Leeds U
	Leeds U won on away goals rule.						

Trophy Play-Off – *between first and last winners to decide who would have possession of the original trophy*

1971	Barcelona v Leeds U	2-1	50,000 (in Barcelona, one match only)				

*After extra time.

UEFA CUP FINALS 1972–97

Year	1st Leg		Attendance	2nd Leg	Attendance	Agg	Winner
1972	Wolverhampton W v Tottenham H	1-2	38,562	1-1	54,303	2-3	Tottenham H
1973	Liverpool v Moenchengladbach	0-0	*(abandoned after 27 minutes)*		44,967		
	Liverpool v Moenchengladbach	3-0	41,169	0-2	35,000	3-2	Liverpool
1974	Tottenham H v Feyenoord	2-2	46,281	0-2	59,317	2-4	Feyenoord
1975	Moenchengladbach v FC Twente	0-0	42,368	5-1	21,767	5-1	Moenchengladbach
1976	Liverpool v Club Brugge	3-2	49,981	1-1	29,423	4-3	Liverpool
1977	Juventus v Athletic Bilbao	1-0	66,000	1-2	39,700	2-2	Juventus
	Juventus won on away goals rule.						
1978	Bastia v PSV Eindhoven	0-0	8,006	0-3	28,000	0-3	PSV Eindhoven
1979	RS Belgrade v Moenchengladbach	1-1	65,000	0-1	45,000	1-2	Moenchengladbach
1980	Moenchengladbach v E. Frankfurt	3-2	25,000	0-1	59,000	3-3	E. Frankfurt
	Eintracht Frankfurt won on away goals rule.						
1981	Ipswich T v AZ 67 Alkmaar	3-0	27,532	2-4	22,291	5-4	Ipswich T
1982	IFK Gothenburg v Hamburger SV	1-0	42,548	3-0	57,312	4-0	IFK Gothenburg
1983	Anderlecht v Benfica	1-0	55,000	1-1	70,000	2-1	Anderlecht
1984	Anderlecht v Tottenham H	1-1	33,000	1-1*	46,258	2-2	Tottenham H
	Tottenham H won 4-3 on penalties.						
1985	Videoton v Real Madrid	0-3	30,000	1-0	80,000	1-3	Real Madrid
1986	Real Madrid v Cologne	5-1	60,000	0-2	22,000	5-3	Real Madrid
1987	IFK Gothenburg v Dundee U	1-0	48,614	1-1	20,900	2-1	IFK Gothenburg
1988	Espanol v Bayer Leverkusen	3-0	31,180	0-3*	21,600	3-3	Bayer Leverkusen
	Bayer Leverkusen won 3-2 on penalties.						
1989	Napoli v VfB Stuttgart	2-1	81,093	3-3	64,000	5-4	Napoli
1990	Juventus v Fiorentina	3-1	47,519	0-0	30,999	3-1	Juventus
1991	Internazionale v Roma	2-0	68,887	0-1	70,901	2-1	Internazionale
1992	Torino v Ajax	2-2	65,377	0-0	40,000	2-2	Ajax
	Ajax won on away goals rule.						
1993	Borussia Dortmund v Juventus	1-3	37,000	0-3	62,781	1-6	Juventus
1994	Salzburg v Internazionale	0-1	43,000	0-1	80,345	0-2	Internazionale
1995	Parma v Juventus	1-0	22,057	1-1	80,000	2-1	Parma
1996	Bayern Munich v Bordeaux	2-0	63,000	3-1	30,000	5-1	Bayern Munich
1997	Schalke 04 v Internazionale	1-0	57,000	0-1*	81,675	1-1	Schalke 04
	Schalke 04 won 4-1 on penalties.						

UEFA CUP FINALS 1998–2009

Year	Winners v Runners-up		Venue	Attendance	Referee
1998	Internazionale v Lazio	3-0	Paris	44,412	A. L. Nieto (Spain)
1999	Parma v Olympique Marseille	3-0	Moscow	61,000	H. Dallas (Scotland)
2000	Galatasaray v Arsenal	0-0*	Copenhagen	38,919	A. L. Nieto (Spain)
	Galatasaray won 4-1 on penalties.				
2001	Liverpool v Alaves	5-4*	Dortmund	48,050	G. Veissiere (France)
	Liverpool won on sudden death 'golden goal'.				
2002	Feyenoord v Borussia Dortmund	3-2	Rotterdam	45,611	V. M. M. Pereira (Portugal)
2003	FC Porto v Celtic	3-2*	Seville	52,140	L. Michel (Slovakia)
2004	Valencia v Olympique Marseille	2-0	Gothenburg	39,000	P. Collina (Italy)
2005	CSKA Moscow v Sporting Lisbon	3-1	Lisbon	47,085	G. Poll (England)
2006	Sevilla v Middlesbrough	4-0	Eindhoven	32,100	H. Fandel (Germany)
2007	Sevilla v Espanyol	2-2*	Glasgow	47,602	M. Busacca (Switzerland)
	Sevilla won 3-1 on penalties.				
2008	Zenit St Petersburg v Rangers	2-0	Manchester	43,878	P. Fröjdfeldt (Sweden)
2009	Shakhtar Donetsk v Werder Bremen	2-1*	Istanbul	37,357	L. M. Chantalejo (Spain)

UEFA EUROPA LEAGUE FINALS 2010–16

Year	Winners v Runners-up		Venue	Attendance	Referee
2010	Atletico Madrid v Fulham	2-1*	Hamburg	49,000	N. Rizzoli (Italy)
2011	FC Porto v Braga	1-0	Dublin	45,391	V. Carballo (Spain)
2012	Atletico Madrid v Athletic Bilbao	3-0	Bucharest	52,347	W. Stark (Germany)
2013	Chelsea v Benfica	2-1	Amsterdam	46,163	B. Kuipers (Netherlands)
2014	Sevilla v Benfica	0-0*	Turin	33,120	F. Brych (Germany)
	Sevilla won 4-2 on penalties.				
2015	Sevilla v Dnipro Dnipropetrovsk	3-2	Warsaw	45,000	M. Atkinson (England)
2016	Sevilla v Liverpool	3-1	Basel	34,429	J. Eriksson (Sweden)

*After extra time.

UEFA EUROPA LEAGUE 2015–16

■ *Denotes player sent off.*

FIRST QUALIFYING ROUND FIRST LEG
Tuesday, 30 June 2015

Balzan (0) 0
Zeljeznicar Sarajevo (2) 2 *(Bajic 4 (pen), 13)*   627
Balzan: (442) Cassar; Grioli, Micallef (Cipriott 90), Bilbao, Grima (Darmanin 84); Bezzina, Sciberras (Arab 78), Brincat, Agius; Serrano, Guobadia.
Zeljeznicar Sarajevo: (442) Antolovic; Kvesic, Kosoric, Bajic, Blagojevic; Djelmic, Livaja, Hadziahmetovic (Sadikovic E 76), Beganovic (Sadikovic D 56); Bogdanovic, Kokot (Diatta 84).

Progres Niederkorn (0) 0
Shamrock R (0) 0   1451
Progres Niederkorn: (4231) Flauss; Rigo (Ferino 40), Bouzid, Dog, Soares; Garos, Thill S; Menai (Rougeaux 68), Cassan, Poinsignon (Fiorani 80); Rossini.
Shamrock R: (4231) Hyland; Byrne, Webster, Clancy, Madden; Brennan G, McCabe; Miele (Kavanagh C 81), Cregg, Waters (Kavanagh D 74); Drennan.

Renova (0) 0
Dacia (1) 1 *(Rosca 12)*   1500
Renova: (442) Mustafi; Memedi, Miskovski, Mecinovic (Skenderi 70), Musliu; Velija (Neziri 46), Nuhiu, Gafuri, Mojsov; Emini, Ramadan (Selmani 79).
Dacia: (442) Gaiduchevici; Cojocari (Gavrylenko 46), Rosca, Posmac, Pidnebennoy (Zaginaylov 46); Zastavnyi, Lozoviy, Mani, Mamah; Cociuc, Pavlov (Mihaliov 64).

Thursday, 2 July 2015

Airbus UK Broughton (1) 1 *(Riley 28)*
Lokomotiva Zagreb (0) 3 *(Sovsic 48, Maric 61, Kolar 68)*   543
Airbus UK Broughton: (442) Coates; Pearson, Owens, Field, McGinn; Jones, Riley, Wignall (Healing 84), Owen; Budrys (Evans 83), Gray (Wade 75).
Lokomotiva Zagreb: (442) Zelenika; Bartolec, Mrcela, Capan, Brucic; Andrijasevic, Sovsic (Coric 84), Leko, Fiolic; Misic (Grzan 75), Maric (Kolar 63).

Aktobe (0) 0
Nomme Kalju (0) 1 *(Purje 72)*   10,870
Aktobe: (442) Pokatilov■; Adeleye, Dmitrenko, Miroshnichenko, Deac; Khairullin, Logvinenko, Pizzelli (Bekbaev 78), Zulpa; Danilo Neco (Zhalmukan 87), Danilo (Khizhnichenko 91).
Nomme Kalju: (442) Teles; Barengrub, Kallaste, Topic (Neemelo 82), Rodrigues; Puri, Wakui (Lindpere 58), Purje, Mool; Kimbaloula (Listmann 90), Dmitrijev.

Alashkert (0) 1 *(Manasyan 60)*
St Johnstone (0) 0   4000
Alashkert: (343) Kasparov; Fofana, Arakelyan, Poghosyan; Usenya (Manasyan 58), Minasyan, Muradyan, Veranyan; Bareghamyan, Grigoryan (Hovhannisyan 90), Gyozalyan (Dos Santos 80).
St Johnstone: (4411) Mannus; Scobbie, Shaughnessy, McKay, Easton; Lappin, Davidson (Brown 45), Wotherspoon, MacLean; Sutton (Kane 61); O'Halloran.

Atlantas (0) 0
Beroe (0) 2 *(Delev 60, Bozhilov 84)*   3000
Atlantas: (442) Malinauskas; Gnedojus, Epifanov, Joksas, Baravykas (Baranauskas 69); Vezevicius, Bartkus (Zukauskas 46), Norvilas (Beneta 17), Virksas; Panyukov, Maksimov.
Beroe: (442) Makendzhiev; Penev, Elias, Vasilev, Ivanov; Djoman, Milisavljevic, Zehirov, Mapuku (Andonov 81); Bozhilov, Delev (Kokonov 69).

Birkirkara (0) 0
Ulisses (0) 0   1895
Birkirkara: (442) Haber (Akpan 37); Zerafa, Vucanac, Mazzetti Latini, Agius (Miccoli 72); Fenech, Muscat Z, Camenzuli, Plut (Murga 65); Muscat R, Liliu.

Ulisses: (442) Beglaryan; Morozov, Chezhiya, Jarkava, Dugalic; Mamakhanov, Piliev (Tshibamba 62), Aleksanyan, Khubua (Belomyttsev 79); Khurtsidze, Geperidze (Kalimullin 84).

Botosani (0) 1 *(Ivanovici 21)*
Tskhinvali (0) 1 *(Katcharava 46)*   6031
Botosani: (442) Iliev; Cordos, Dimitrov, Plamada, Croitoru (Brata 74); Costin, Vasvari, Ivanovici (Batin 86), Hadnagy (Roman 46); Martinus, Browne.
Tskhinvali: (442) Nadiradze; Kakubava, Kilasonia, Kardava, Bachiashvili; Ivanishvili (Katchkatchishvili 89), Lekvtadze (Shulaia 63), Gigauri (Burdzenadze 77), Tsatskrialashvili; Tsertvadze, Katcharava.

Brondby (6) 9 *(Elmander 6, 16, Da Silva 14, Pukki 22, Holst 23, Larsson 35, Rashani 56, 88, Corlu 66)*
Juvenes/Dogana (0) 0   8408
Brondby: (442) Hradecky; Dumic, Larsson, Holst, Da Silva; Örnskov Nielsen, Szymanowski, Hjulsager, Phiri (Stuckler 63); Elmander (Rashani 46), Pukki (Corlu 63).
Juvenes/Dogana: (442) Manzaroli; Cavalli (Canini 53), Merlini, Villa, Mantovani; Santini, Gasperoni, Maccagno, Battistini; Bagli (Ugolini 76), Mariotti (Bernardi 59).

Buducnost Podgorica (1) 1 *(Raicevic 6)*
Spartaks Jurmala (2) 3 *(Bulvitis 22, 74 (pen), Mickevics 42)*   4072
Buducnost Podgorica: (442) Agovic; Simovic, Raspopovic, Tomkovic, Vukcevic (Milosevic 71); Flavio Beck, Pavicevic, Raicevic, Hocko (Raickovic 77); Ilincic (Gazivoda 60), Nikac.
Spartaks Jurmala: (442) Kolinko; Bulvitis, Mezs, Nazarenko, Maksymenko; Slampe (Stuglis 90), Mickevics, Kazacoks, Ulimbashevs (Bespalovs 90); Vivacqua (Mena 81), Takyi.

Celje (0) 0
Slask Wroclaw (1) 1 *(Pich 32)*   4900
Celje: (442) Kotnik; Vidmajer, Soria, Klemencic, Jakolic; Bajde (Vrhovec 63), Miskic, Klapan, Mrsic (Tezak 70); Ahmedi (Omoregie 46), Firer.
Slask Wroclaw: (442) Pawalek; Zielinski, Celeban, Pawelec, Dudu Paraiba; Flavio Paixao (Ostrowski 79), Holota, Hateley, Pich (Danielewicz 90); Grajciar (Machaj 69), Kielb.

Europa (0) 0
Slovan Bratislava (5) 6 *(Meszaros 5, 25, 30, Simovic 32, 90, Stefanik 40)*   754
Europa: (442) Cafer; Merino, Plazanic, Pinero, Jukic (Mouelhi 45); Chacon, Catalan, Sokol (Ortega 72), Akrapovic; Toncheff, Ledesma (Fernandez 51).
Slovan Bratislava: (442) Krnac; Salata, Dobrotka, Podany, Sekulic; Milinkovic, Simovic, Meszaros (Kubik 64), Stefanik (Orsula 70); Priskin, Zrelak (Peltier 65).

Cork C (1) 1 *(Bennett 19)*
KR Reykjavik (1) 1 *(Hauksson 28)*   4641
Cork C: (433) McNulty; Gaynor (Dunleavy 46), Bennett, Dennehy D, Forde; Healy (Murray 66), Buckley, Horgan; Sheppard, O'Flynn (O'Sullivan 59), Dennehy B.
KR Reykjavik: (433) Magnusson S; Gudjonsson (Josepsson 31), Fridgeirsson, Christiansen, Ormarsson (Ragnarsson 74); Gunnarsson, Saevarsson, Palmason; Schoop, Hauksson (Martin 68), Frederiksen.

Crvena Zvezda (0) 0
Kairat Almaty (1) 2 *(Gohou 45, Kuantayev 64)*   25,211
Crvena Zvezda: (442) Rajkovic; Rendulic, Andjelkovic, Pavicevic■, Cvetkovic; Vered, Kovacevic (Jovanovic 5), Savicevic, Parker; Katai (Ristic 77), Orlandic (Jovic 60).
Kairat Almaty: (442) Plotnikov; Markovic, Gorman, Bruno, Kuantayev; Isael (Darabayev 81), Kuat (Kukeev 85), Islamkhan (Serginho 62), Sito Riera; Gohou, Lunin.

Debrecen (1) 3 *(Mihelic 16, Brkovic 71, Sidibe 74)*
Sutjeska (0) 0 5744
Debrecen: (442) Verpecz; Meszaros, Korhut, Brkovic, Szakaly; Varga, Mihelic, Jovanovic, Bodi (Zsidai 85); Kulcsar (Horvath 66), Balogh (Sidibe 46).
Sutjeska: (442) Radovic; Ognjanovic, Lukic, Sofranac, Stijepovic; Nikolic, Bozovic, Kovacevic, Milos Vucic (Marko Vucic 59); Vujovic, Fukui.

Differdange 03 (3) 3 *(Er Rafik 4, Caron 7, Sinani 26)*
Bala Town (1) 1 *(Sheridan 36)* 1223
Differdange 03: (4141) Weber; Rodrigues, Siebenaler (Caillet 76), Bukvic, Franzoni; Lebresne (May 46); Luisi, Sinani (Almeida 69), Er Rafik, Pedro Ribeiro; Caron.
Bala Town: (4231) Morris; Valentine, Bell, Artell, Stephens; Murtagh, Pearson (Hayes[■] 46); Jones, Smith, Connolly (Brown 79); Sheridan.

Dinamo Batumi (1) 1 *(Tetunashvili 40)*
Omonia Nicosia (0) 0 3589
Dinamo Batumi: (442) Alavidze; Sukhiashvili, Makharadze, Tetunashvili, Shonia; Kavtaradze (Chirikashvili 83), Gogitidze, Poniava, Beriashvili (Varshanidze 87); Tatanashvili (Tevdoradze 75), Gabedava.
Omonia Nicosia: (442) Georgallides; Mendy (Margaca 46), Lobjanidze, Runje, Economides; Goulon, Fofana (Kirm 58), Cristovao, Nuno Assis; Pote, Schembri (Okeuhie 70).

Dinamo Tbilisi (0) 2 *(Jigauri 65, Papunashvili 84)*
Gabala (0) 1 *(Huseynov 74)* 7500
Dinamo Tbilisi: (442) Hrdlicka; Tchelidze, Totadze, Gvelesiani[■], Tvildiani; Tsintsadze, Jigauri, Papunashvili, Kiteishvili (Rene 54); Tchanturishvili (Parunashvili 14), Kvilitaia (Iashvili 62).
Gabala: (442) Bezotosnyi; Ricardinho, Rafael Santos, Vernydub, Abbasov; Florescu (Sadiqov 72), Huseynov, Dashdemirov (Dodo 73); Gai; Antonov, Zenjov.

Domzale (0) 0
Cukaricki Belgrade (1) 1 *(Matic 43)* 1200
Domzale: (442) Vidmar; Zec, Dobrovoljc[■], Trajkovski, Korun; Juninho (Horvat 46), Horic, Pozeg, Majer (Kous 92); Morel, Vuk (Podlogar 46).
Cukaricki Belgrade: (442) Stevanovic; Lucas, Brezancic, Ostojic, Stojkovic; Matic (Jovanovic 82), Jankovic B (Mirosavljevic 89), Bojic, Srnic S; Pavlovic (Radovanovic 90), Srnic D.

Flora Tallinn (0) 1 *(Gussev 59)*
Rabotnicki (0) 0 1236
Flora Tallinn: (442) Toom; Jaager, Kams, Jurgenson, Baranov; Frolov, Gussev, Slein (Luigend 80), Alliku; Logua (Tamm 72), Sappinen (Beglarishvili 53).
Rabotnicki: (442) Efremov; Ilievski, Siljanovski, Trajcevski (Jovanovski 72), Cikarski; Petrovic, Altiparmakovski, Mitrov (Anene 46), Vujcic; Sahiti (Markoshi 62), Ilijoski.

Glenavon (0) 1 *(Patton 89)*
Shakhtyor Soligorsk (2) 2 *(Afanasyev 3, Komarovski 30)* 640
Glenavon: (442) McGrath; Kelly, Marshall, Dillon, Elebert (Lindsay 64); Singleton, Kilmartin (Patton 67), Hall (Hamilton 83), Martyn; Bradley, Braniff.
Shakhtyor Soligorsk: (442) Bushma; Rybak, Yanushkevich, Yurevich, Kuzmyanok; Matsveychyk, Afanasyev (Covic 73), Starhorodskyi, Mikoliunas (Kovalev 52); Komarovski (Martynyuk 84), Yanush.

Glentoran (0) 1 *(McMenamin 66)*
Zilina (2) 4 *(Jelic 13, Paur 20, Cmelik 59, Mabouka 81)* 1676
Glentoran: (361) Morris; Holland, Birney, Gibson; Magee, Kane, McCaffrey (McAlorum 82), Gordon, McCullough, McMenamin; Stewart (Addis 63).
Zilina: (352) Volesak; Vavro, Letic, Mabouka; Skriniar, Kacer, Paur (Mihalik 63), Pecovsky, Benes; Jelic (Willian 89), Cmelik (Spalek 78).

Go Ahead Eagles (1) 1 *(Vriends 45)*
Ferencvaros (1) 1 *(Gera 4)* 6248
Go Ahead Eagles: (433) Cummins; Nieuwpoort, Vriends, Schenk, Teijsse; Duits (Lambooij 74), van Ewijk (Rijsdijk 62), Turuc; Van Overbeek, ten Den (Schalk 83), Wolters.
Ferencvaros: (433) Dibusz; Ramirez, Nalepa, Mateos, De Almeida; Lamah (Ugrai 79), Gera, Gyomber; Somalia (Busai 86), Varga (Nagy 79), Bode.

Jelgava (0) 1 *(Malasenoks 83)*
Litex Lovech (0) 1 *(Bozhikov 50)* 1560
Jelgava: (442) Ikstens; Bogdaskins, Gubins, Freimanis, Oss; Diallo, Latka, Kluskins (Jaudzems 83), Eriba (Kirilins 69); Sosranovs, Sushkin (Malasenoks 70).
Litex Lovech: (442) Vinicius; Perez, Popov, Bozhikov, Malinov; Goranov, Kolev, Arsenio (Angelov 77), Rumenov (Boumal 57); Moreno Asprilla (Georgiev 90), Johnsen.

Kruoja (0) 0
Jagiellonia Bialystock (0) 1 *(Swiderski 90)* 2354
Kruoja: (442) Matuzas; Skroblas, Strockis, Crisan, Navikas; Tautvydas Eliosius, Pocevicius, Jankauskas, Salamanavicius (Diarra 85); Beniusis (Birskys 80), Bagocius (Tadas Eliosius 75).
Jagiellonia Bialystock: (442) Dragowski; Madera, Tomasik, Modelski, Grzyb[■]; Tarasovs, Vassiljev (Romanchuk 64), Dzalamidze (Swiderski 80), Gajos; Mackiewicz, Tuszynski (Sekulski 63).

Kukesi (1) 2 *(Jean Carioca 9, Pejic 54)*
Torpedo Zhodino (0) 0 1500
Kukesi: (442) Stajila; Jean Carioca, Pejic, Hallaci, Mici; Malota, Muca, Flores Bonfim, Hasani (Musolli 46); Birungueta (Lopes 68), Moreira (Hysa 60).
Torpedo Zhodino: (442) Stepanov; Pankavets, Serdyuk (Selyava 79), Melnyk, Burko; Platonaw (Matveenko 75), Maksimovs, Datsenko, Hleb; Kontsevoy (Vaskow 67), Yatskevich.

La Fiorita (0) 0
Vaduz (3) 5 *(Hasler 5, Sutter 26, Pergl 42, Abbeglen 79, Ciccone 90)* 649
La Fiorita: (442) Pazzini; Mascerata, Martini, Bugli, Gasperoni; Tommasi, Zafferani (Casadei 88), Cangini (Righi 78), Ricchiuti (Cavalli 70); Selva, Rinaldi.
Vaduz: (442) Jehle; Stahel, Pergl, Von Niederhausern (Abbeglen 46), Aliji; Ciccone, Neumayr, Schurpf, Lang; Hasler (Kamber 66), Sutter (Kuzmanovic 72).

Laci (1) 1 *(Meto 20)*
Inter Baku (0) 1 *(Kvekveskiri 47)* 850
Laci: (442) Vujadinovic; Doku (Nimani 56), Cela, Sefgjinaj, Sheta; Vucaj, Veliaj, Meto (Mitraj 78), Teqja; Mustafa, Adeniyi.
Inter Baku: (442) Agayev; Khizanishvili, Juanfran, Kasradze, Huseynov; Kvekveskiri, Seyidov, Bayramov, Abbasov (Sadiqov 74); Aliyev (Nahavandi 90), Fomenko (Haciyev 43).

Lahti (1) 2 *(Lagerblom 25, Matheus Alves 61)*
Elfsborg (1) 2 *(Rohden 15, Prodell 59)* 3152
Lahti: (4141) Moisander; Hauhia, Joenmaki, Pasanen, Lansitalo; Karkkainen; Paananen, Gela, Lagerblom (Sesay 41), Shala (Ristola 78); Matheus Alves (Rafael 72).
Elfsborg: (442) Stuhr-Ellegaard; Klarstrom (Manns 74), Jonsson, Svensson, Lundqvist; Hedlund, Hauger, Rohden, Lundevall; Claesson, Prodell (Frick 69).

Linfield (0) 2 *(Waterworth 57, Bates 73)*
NSI Runavik (0) 0 1824
Linfield: (442) Ross Glendinning; Hegarty (Reece Glendinning 65), Haughey, Ward, Clarke M; Lowry, Burns, Waterworth, Sproule; Kee, Bates (Millar 90).
NSI Runavik: (442) Gango; Langgaard, Jacobsen M, Joensen (Edmundsson 75), Justinussen; Jacobsen C, Frederiksberg A, Frederiksberg J (Hojgaard J 69), Magnus Olsen; Hojgaard H (Mortensen 63), Olsen K.

MTK Budapest (0) 0

Vojvodina (0) 0   902

MTK Budapest: (442) Hegedus; Vadnai, Vukmir, Grgic, Vass; Strestik (Ramos 46), Kanta, Thian, Varga (Szatmari 59); Torghelle (Schrammel 57), Bese.
Vojvodina: (442) Žakula; Djuric, Vasilic, Nastic, Dinga; Stanisavljevic, Puskaric, Sekulic, Palocevic (Stamenic 64); Ivanic (Kordic 90), Mrdakovic (Maksimovic 89).

Neftchi (1) 2 *(Qurbanov R 36, Abdullayev A 55)*

Mladost Podgorica (1) 2 *(Lagator 34, Mirkovic 87)* 9866

Neftchi: (442) Mammadov; Melli, Ailton, Qurbanov K, Abdullayev A (Nacafzada 77); Haciyev, Badalov, Qurbanov R, Abdullayev E (Abbasov 73); Qurbanov M, Masimov (Gurbanov 80).
Mladost Podgorica: (442) Mileta Radulovic; Pejovic, Lakic, Milos M Radulovic (Adzovic 94), Milos B Radulovic; Novovic, Lagator (Mirkovic 15), Raicevic, Igumanovic; Vukovic, Djurisic (Scepanovic 61).

Newtown (1) 2 *(Boundford 40, Oswell 90)*

Valletta (0) 1 *(Jhonnattann 73)*   1420

Newtown: (451) Jones; Edwards, Mills-Evans, Sutton (Cadwallader 90), Williams; Goodwin, Owen (Evans 78), Mitchell (Price 70), Oswell, Hearsey; Boundford.
Valletta: (442) Vella; Azzopardi■, Cruz, Focsa, Camilleri R; Umeh (Jhonnattann 62), Pani, Cremona, Nafti (Camilleri D 87); Montebello (Triganza 54), Falzon.

Olimpic Sarajevo (1) 1 *(Pandza 14)*

Spartak Trnava (0) 1 *(Halilovic 70)*   2622

Olimpic Sarajevo: (442) Hamzic; Muharemovic, Bogicevic, Regoje, Merajic; Gligorov, Handzic, Jusufovic (Karic 80), Rascic; Pandza (Stefan 80), Brkovic.
Spartak Trnava: (442) Knezevic; Nikolic, Gressak (Jose Casado 46), Conka, Bortel; Godal, Vlasko, Sabo, Harba; Mikovic (Cleber 63), Schranz (Halilovic 70).

Ordabasy (0) 0

Beitar Jerusalem (0) 0   11,600

Ordabasy: (442) Sidelnikov; Simcevic, Abdulin, Maly, Suyumbayev; Kasyanov, Nurgaliev, Ashirbekov (Tolebek 75), Geynrikh (Petrov 90); Bozic, Adyrbekov.
Beitar Jerusalem: (442) Klaiman; Matovic, Kachila, Askling, Yerucham; Zhairi, Claudemir, Majabi (Cohen I 73), Cohen L (Zamir 54); Atzili (Nachmani 64), Gabay.

Sant Julia (0) 0

Randers (1) 1 *(Borring 22)*   350

Sant Julia: (442) Coca; Varela, Ruis, Brito, Vigo; Spano (Javier Castellano 63), Bruninho, Barcelo, Rodriguez (Peppe 67); Quirino (Gandara 57), Alves.
Randers: (442) Johnsson; Thomsen, Fenger, Keller, Fischer; Borring (Marxen 82), Amini, Poulsen (Allansson 62), Tverskov■; Lundberg■, Brock-Madsen (Thygesen 85).

Saxan (0) 0

Apollon Limassol (1) 2 *(Joao Pedro 32, Papoulis 89)* 2535

Saxan: (442) Chirinciuc; Popovici, Arabadji, Kouadja, Kone; Truhanov (Fofana 79), Bamba, Ne (Doumbia 89), Catan; Puntus (Bogdanov 63), Dao.
Apollon Limassol: (442) Bruno Vale; Elizio, Freire, Nuno Lopes, Gullon; Stojanovic (Reynolds 71), Kyriakou, Sachetti, Joao Pedro; Kolokoudias (Josephides 90), Papoulis.

Seinajoki (0) 0

Hafnarfjordur (0) 1 *(Lennon 56)*   2678

Seinajoki: (442) Aksalu; Laaksonen, Milosavljevic, Savic, Gogoua; Vasara (Atajic 64), Hetemaj, Brown (Tahvanainen 82), Dorman; Lehtinen (Nguekam 67), Pelvas.
Hafnarfjordur: (442) Oskarsson; Vidarsson P, Thorisson, Doumbia, Gudmundsson; Bodvarsson, Vidarsson D, Palsson, Gudnason (Vidarsson B 77); Lennon (Finnbogason KF 82), Valdimarsson.

Sheriff (0) 0

Odd (3) 3 *(Bentley 2, Johnsen 11, Hagen 28)*   6628

Sheriff: (442) Mitrev; Metoua, Potirniche, Dupovac (Novicov 19), Ernandes; Susic, Jugovic (Sharpar 63), Cadu, Yahaya; Potiguar (Crnov 33), Ricardinho.

Odd: (442) Rossbach; Ruud, Jonassen (Grogaard 52), Hagen, Eriksen; Gashi, Berg, Samuelsen, Halvorsen; Bentley (Storbaek 73), Johnsen (Occean 18).

Shirak (1) 2 *(Bougouhi 18, 67)*

Zrinjski Mostar (0) 0   2774

Shirak: (442) Ermakov; Hovanisian, Stamenkovic, Hovhannisyan, Malakyan E; Davtyan, Hakobyan (Barikian 59), Davoyan, Malakyan G; Diarrassouba (Ayvazyan 80), Bougouhi (Muradyan 86).
Zrinjski Mostar: (442) Dujkovic; Radeljic, Stojkic, Blaic, Graovac; Todorovic, Muminovic, Zeravica, Filipovic (Stojanovic 71); Simeunovic (Scepanovic 46), Nikolic (Acimovic 86).

Sillamae Kalev (1) 1 *(Silich 40)*

Hajduk Split (1) 1 *(Caktas 6 (pen))*   750

Sillamae Kalev: (442) Starodubtsev; Sisov, Cinikas, Cheminava, Dudarev; Toomet, Vnukov (Ratnikov 65), Silich, Tjapkin; Russo, Kvasov.
Hajduk Split: (442) Kalinic; Nizic, Milovic, Mikanovic, Caktas; Roguljic (Bilyi 74), Vlasic, Balic (Maglica 81), Tudor; Ohandza, Maloku (Radchenko 58).

Skendija Tetovo (0) 1 *(Kirovski 84)*

Aberdeen (0) 1 *(McGinn 79)*   7040

Skendija Tetovo: (442) Jovanovski; Dzemaili (Kirovski 83), Cuculi, Alimi, Demiri; Polozani, Todorovski, Junior, Juffo (Bejtulai 80); Vrucina (Besar 46), Hasani.
Aberdeen: (442) Ward; Logan, Taylor, Reynolds (Quinn 69), Considine; Flood (Pawlett 64), Jack, Shinnie, Hayes; McGinn, Rooney (Goodwillie 64).

Skonto (1) 2 *(Karasausks 38, Gutkovskis 65)*

St Patrick's Ath (1) 1 *(Greene 21)*   1780

Skonto: (442) Pavlovs; Timofejevs, Rode, Smirnovs, Murillo (Tatiefang 90); Visnakovs (Isajevs 72), Kozlovs, Jermolajevs, Kovalovs; Gutkovskis (Lukanyuk 83), Karasausks.
St Patrick's Ath: (442) Clarke; O'Brien, Bermingham, Hoare (McGuinness 67); Browne; Bolger, Greene, Brennan, Chambers; Forrester, Fagan (McGrath 73).

Stromsgodset (1) 3 *(Vilsvik 21, 72, Ogunjimi 66)*

Partizani (0) 1 *(Fazliu 68)*   3273

Stromsgodset: (442) Pettersen; Madsen, Vilsvik, Hanin, Hoibraten; Storflor, Abu, Wikheim (Kastrati 79), Fossum; Boateng, Ogunjimi (Kovacs 84).
Partizani: (442) Hoxha (Xhika 30); Vrapi, Kalari, Bicaj, Fejzullahu; Ibrahimi, Vila, Trashi, Batha; Plaku (Fazliu 60), Racic (Tafili 89).

Trakai (1) 3 *(Bychenok 19, Arshakiyan 60, Solomin 86)*

Torshavn (0) 0   1070

Trakai: (442) Rapalis; Klimavicius, Janusevskis, Cesnauskis, Mamaev; Silenas, Bychenok, Kochanauskas (Segzda 40), Solomin; Zasavitchi, Arshakiyan.
Torshavn: (442) Gestsson; Johan Davidsen (Haraldsen 64), Alex■, Holm, Jogvan Davidsen; Joensen, Hanssen, Benjaminsen, Mouritsen (Wardum 74); Vatnsdal, Hansen (Jacobsen 79).

University College Dublin (1) 1 *(Swan 45)*

F91 Dudelange (0) 0   1075

University College Dublin: (433) Corbet; Langtry, Leahy, Boyle, McLaughlin; Watts (Watson 90), O'Neill, Benson; Mullhall, Swan, Doyle.
F91 Dudelange: (433) Joubert; Moreira, Schnell, Prempeh, Ney; Pedro, Adler (Turpel 58), Nakache; Ibrahimovic, Benzouien, Da Mota Alves (Lauriente 74).

Vaasa (1) 2 *(Catovic 45, Seabrook 65)*

AIK Solna (0) 2 *(Bahoui 70, 83 (pen))*   2180

Vaasa: (442) Sillanpaa; Niemi, Lahti, Koskimaa, Engstrom; Abdulahi, Bjork (Kula 84), Catovic, Soiri; Seabrook (Tamminen 68), Makela.
AIK Solna: (442) Carlgren (Linner 29); Ofori, Karlsson, Johansson, Hauksson; Sundberg, Blomberg, Etuhu (Saletros 78), Brustad (Bangura 64); Goitom, Bahoui.

Vikingur (0) 0
Rosenborg (0) 2 *(Soderlund 82, 90)*   1057
Vikingur: (4321) Turi; Hansen B, Gregersen, Jacobsen E, Jacobsen H; Justinussen, Djurhuus, Djordjevic (Lervig 89); Vatnhamar S, Hansen H (Vatnhamar G 80); Olsen (Hansen G 87).
Rosenborg: (442) Andre Hansen; Svensson, Eyjolfsson, Skjelvik, Dorsin; Mikkelsen, Selnaes, Riski (Helmersen 80), Jensen; Midtsjoe, Malec (Soderlund 64).

Vikingur Reykjavik (0) 0
Koper (0) 1 *(Pucko 77)*   1010
Vikingur Reykjavik: (442) Nielsen; Lowing, Zivkovic, Olafsson, Baldvinsson; Taskovic, Snorrason (Steingrimsson 52), Atlason, Bjarnason (Arnarson 85); Jonssan, Toft (Kristinsson 64).
Koper: (442) Simcic; Galesic (Blazic 90), Halilovic, Hadzic, Sme; Tomic, Guberac, Pucko, Palcic (Rahmanovic 67); Crnigoj, Ivancic (Lotric 82).

West Ham U (2) 3 *(Sakho 41, 45, Tomkins 58)*
Lusitanos (0) 0   34,966
West Ham U: (442) Randolph; Burke, Oxford, Tomkins, Page; Amalfitano, O'Brien (Cullen 59), Poyet, Jarvis; Sakho (Lee 61), Zarate (Parfitt-Williams 74).
Lusitanos: (532) Gerardo; Acosta, San Nicolas M, Munoz, Maciel, Molina; San Nicolas L (Conteh-Lacalle 46), Soares (Sonejee 54), Romero; dos Reis, Aguilar (Moya 54).

FIRST QUALIFYING ROUND SECOND LEG

Tuesday, 7 July 2015
Shamrock R (2) 3 *(Webster 21, Waters 41, 57)*
Progres Niederkorn (0) 0   2800
Shamrock R: (451) Hyland; Madden, Webster, Clancy, Byrne; Brennan G, Cregg, Miele, McCabe, Waters (Brennan R 74); Drennan (North 87).
Progres Niederkorn: (451) Flauss; Ferino, Bouzid, Dog, Fiorani (Bossi 75); Menai, Garos, Cassan, Thill S (Thill O 77), Rougeaux (Poinsignon 67); Rossini.

Thursday, 9 July 2015
Aberdeen (0) 0
Skendija Tetovo (0) 0   14,112
Aberdeen: (442) Ward; Shinnie, Considine, Taylor, Logan; Hayes (Robson 79), Jack, Flood (Goodwillie 79), McLean (Pawlett 67); McGinn, Rooney.
Skendija Tetovo: (442) Jovanovski; Todorovski, Polozani, Cuculi, Abdula (Kirovski 80); Juffo (Bejtulai 71), Alimi, Demiri, Junior (Vrucina 84); Hasani, Ibraimi.
Aberdeen won on away goals.

AIK Solna (1) 4 *(Goitom 14, 59, Bangura 54, Ofori 85)*
Vaasa (0) 0   8430
AIK Solna: (442) Linner; Johansson, Hauksson (Lundholm 70), Pereira (Saletros 71), Sundberg; Blomberg, Ofori, Etuhu, Eliasson; Goitom (Nikolic 77), Bangura.
Vaasa: (451) Sillanpaa; Lahti, Koskimaa, Viitikko, Engstrom; Abdulahi (Alanko 77), Bjork (Hertsi 63), Kula, Catovic, Soiri; Seabrook (Tamminen 46).

Apollon Limassol (1) 2 *(Stojanovic 2, Papoulis 61)*
Saxan (0) 0   3800
Apollon Limassol: (442) Bruno Vale; Elizio, Freire, Nuno Lopes, Gullon; Stojanovic (Rosa 57), Kyriakou, Sachetti, Joao Pedro (Wheeler 42); Kolokoudias (Josephides 53), Papoulis.
Saxan: (442) Chirinciuc; Popovici, Arabadji, Kouadja, Kone; Truhanov, Bamba (Fofana 80), Ne, Catan (Bogdanov 58); Sebai (Puntus 62), Dao.

Bala Town (0) 2 *(Murtagh 49, Sheridan 83)*
Differdange 03 (0) 1 *(Er Rafik 90)*   1049
Bala Town: (442) Morris; Valentine, Stephens, Connolly, Thompson; Davies, Murtagh, Jones (Lunt 90), Pearson; Sheridan, Smith.
Differdange 03: (442) Weber; Rodrigues, Siebenaler, Bukvic, Janisch; Yeye (Almeida 63), Pedro Ribeiro (Sinani 72), Lebresne (Luisi 85), Er Rafik; Caron, Franzoni.

Beitar Jerusalem (1) 2 *(Atzili 17, Gabay 60)*
Ordabasy (0) 1 *(Petrov 66)*   14,000
Beitar Jerusalem: (442) Klaiman; Dasa (Yerucham 67), Kachila, Matovic, Askling; Atzili, Freda (Cohen L 53), Zhairi, Claudemir; Nachmani (Magbo 74), Gabay.
Ordabasy: (442) Sidelnikov; Suyumbayev, Abdulin, Maly, Simcevic; Nurgaliev, Ashirbekov (Tungyshbayev 62), Kasyanov■, Adyrbekov (Petrov 58); Tazhimbetov, Geynrikh.

Beroe (2) 3 *(Delev 7, 45, 67)*
Atlantas (0) 1 *(Vezevicius 65)*   7432
Beroe: (442) Makendzhiev; Penev, Ivanov, Vasilev, Milisavljevic; Elias, Djoman (Tom 63), Zehirov (Filipov 54), Delev; Mapuku (Kostov 69), Bozhilov.
Atlantas: (442) Malinauskas; Gnedojus, Baravykas, Joksas, Zarskis; Verbickas, Norvilas (Sveikauskas 55), Vezevicius, Virksas (Beneta 57); Maksimov, Panyukov (Baranauskas 77).

Cukaricki Belgrade (0) 0
Domzale (0) 0   1800
Cukaricki Belgrade: (442) Stevanovic; Lucas, Brezancic, Ostojic, Stojkovic; Matic (Mandic 69), Jankovic B, Bojic (Mirosavljevic 90), Srnic S; Pavlovic (Stoiljkovic 81), Srnic D.
Domzale: (442) Vidmar; Skubic, Trajkovski, Korun■, Husmani (Sisic 81); Horic, Pozeg (Grvala 60), Majer (Vuk 67), Horvat; Podlogar, Morel.

Dacia (1) 4 *(Cociuc 9, Jardan 55, Pavlov 60, Lozoviy 88)*
Renova (1) 1 *(Emini 32)*   800
Dacia: (442) Gaiduchevici; Mamah, Posmac, Zastavnyi, Rosca; Mihaliov, Mani (Lozoviy 52), Gavrylenko, Frunza (Jardan 52); Cociuc, Pavlov (Bejan 75).
Renova: (442) Mustafi; Memedi, Miskovski, Mecinovic (Skenderi 71), Musliu; Gafuri, Mojsov (Jusufi 71), Sadiki, Emini; Neziri, Ramadan (Redzepi 80).

Elfsborg (3) 5 *(Svensson 11, Claesson 21 (pen), Rohden 33, Prodell 70, Nilsson 81)*
Lahti (0) 0   3304
Elfsborg: (442) Stuhr-Ellegaard; Holmen, Klarstrom, Lundqvist, Rohden (Jonsson 59); Svensson, Zeneli, Hedlund (Lundevall 68), Claesson; Frick (Nilsson 68), Prodell.
Lahti: (541) Moisander; Sesay (Rafael 55), Hauhia, Joenmaki, Toivomaki, Pasanen; Gela, Karkkainen, Shala (Mboma 46), Paananen; Matheus Alves (Ristola 68).

F91 Dudelange (2) 2 *(Pedro 43, Nakache 45)*
University College Dublin (1) 1 *(Swan 17)*   1245
F91 Dudelange: (451) Joubert; Moreira (Ibrahimovic 65), Ney, Schnell, Prempeh; Pedro, Stelvio Cruz, Nakache, Da Mota Alves (Lauriente 76), Benzouien (Adler 71); Turpel.
University College Dublin: (433) Corbet; Coyne■, Langtry, Leahy (Harney 79), Boyle; O'Neill, Benson, Watts (Kougun 31); Mulfhall, Swan (Belhout 67), Doyle.
University College Dublin won on away goals.

Ferencvaros (3) 4 *(Gera 4, Bode 20, Busai 45, Haraszti 89)*
Go Ahead Eagles (0) 1 *(Turuc 90)*
Ferencvaros: (442) Dibusz; Leandro, Busai (Hajnal 72), Nalepa, Dilaver (Gyomber 28); Ramirez, Bode, Gera, Lamah; Somalia, Varga (Haraszti 79).
Go Ahead Eagles: (442) Cummins; Vriends, Schenk, Teijsse, Nieuwpoort (Lambooij 76); Duits (van Ewijk 73), Van Overbeek, Turuc, Rijsdijk; Schalk (ten Den 59), Wolters.
Behind closed doors.

Gabala (0) 2 *(Mammadov 89, Antonov 90)*
Dinamo Tbilisi (0) 0   4400
Gabala: (442) Bezotosnyi; Ricardinho, Rafael Santos, Vernydub, Abbasov (Dashdemirov 21); Florescu (Dodo 77), Sadiqov (Mammadov 82), Huseynov, Gai; Antonov, Zenjov.
Dinamo Tbilisi: (442) Hrdlicka; Tchelidze, Totadze, Rene, Tvildiani (Janelidze 84); Jigauri, Tsintsadze, Papunashvili, Iashvili (Kiteishvili 13); Tchanturishvili, Kvilitaia (Guruli 74).

Hafnarfjordur (0) 1 *(Finnbogason KF 90)*
Seinajoki (0) 0 1473
Hafnarfjordur: (442) Oskarsson; Vidarsson P, Thorisson, Doumbia, Hendrickx; Bodvarsson, Vidarsson D, Palsson, Gudnason; Lennon (Vidarsson B 73), Valdimarsson (Finnbogason KF 81).
Seinajoki: (442) Aksalu; Aalto, Laaksonen, Milosavljevic, Gogoua; Hetemaj, Brown (Vasara 65), Tahvanainen, Lehtinen (Atajic 45); Pelvas (Lidman 89), Nguekam.

Hajduk Split (2) 6 *(Balic 15, Caktas 45, Ohandza 56, 63, Vlasic 72, Maglica 88)*
Sillamae Kalev (2) 2 *(Russo 36, 41)* 4500
Hajduk Split: (442) Kalinic; Nizic, Milovic (Bilyi 81), Pejic, Caktas; Roguljic, Vlasic (Kis 87), Balic, Ohandza (Maglica 74); Tudor, Maloku.
Sillamae Kalev: (442) Usikov; Sisov (Ivanjusin 61), Cinikas (Aleksejev 78), Cheminava, Dudarev; Ratnikov, Toomet (Kvasov 70), Vnukov, Silich; Tjapkin, Russo.

Inter Baku (0) 0
Laci (0) 0 3000
Inter Baku: (442) Agayev; Khizanishvili, Juanfran, Kasradze, Huseynov; Kvekveskiri, Seyidov, Bayramov, Abbasov (Nahavandi 90); Haciyev (Sadiqov 80), Aliyev (Denis Silva 90).
Laci: (442) Vujadinovic; Doku (Mitraj 76), Cela, Sefgjinaj, Sheta; Veliaj, Meto, Nimani (Bardhi 82), Vucaj; Teqja, Adeniyi.
Inter Baku won on away goals.

Jagiellonia Bialystock (4) 8 *(Gajos 3, Swiderski 8, Tuszynski 18, 45, 49 (pen), Frankowski 64, 75, 81)*
Kruoja (0) 0 13,274
Jagiellonia Bialystock: (442) Gajos; Swiderski (Vassiljev 55), Tuszynski (Sekulski 74), Dragowski, Madera; Tomasik, Modelski, Tarasovs, Dzalamidze; Romanchuk, Grzelczak (Frankowski 62).
Kruoja: (442) Matuzas; Skroblas, Strockis, Tarasenko, Navikas; Tautvydas Eliosius, Pocevicius, Jankauskas, Salamanavicius (Tadas Eliosius 46); Beniusis (Barba 59), Bagocius (Birskys 21).

Juvenes/Dogana (0) 0
Brondby (0) 2 *(Elmander 49, Rashani 59)* 814
Juvenes/Dogana: (442) Manzaroli; Merlini, Villa, Mantovani, Santini (Zafferani 65); Canini (Bagli 85), Gasperoni, Maccagno, Battistini; Ugolini, Mariotti (Zonzini 76).
Brondby: (442) Hradecky; Albrechtsen, Dumic, Larsson, Durmisi, Rashani, Szymanowski (Corlu 46), Hjulsager (Stuckler 71), Phiri (Crone 82); Elmander, Pukki.

Kairat Almaty (1) 2 *(Islamkhan 29, Kuat 47)*
Crvena Zvezda (0) 1 *(Savicevic 85 (pen))* 21,550
Kairat Almaty: (442) Plotnikov; Bruno, Gorman, Markovic, Kuantayev; Kuat (Darabayev 84), Islamkhan (Serginho 66), Isael, Gohou (Kukeev 90); Sito Riera, Lunin.
Crvena Zvezda: (433) Rajkovic; Petkovic (Cvetkovic 46), Mbodj, Andjelkovic, Rendulic; Parker (Orlandic 60), Stojanovic, Savicevic; Vered (Gavric 70), Katai, Jovic.

Koper (1) 2 *(Pucko 18, Palcic 61)*
Vikingur Reykjavik (0) 0 *(Kristinsson 51, 76)* 1500
Koper: (442) Simcic; Galesic (Krivicic 90), Hadzic, Sme, Blazic; Tomic, Guberac, Pucko, Palcic; Crnigoj, Ivancic (Stromajer 58).
Vikingur Reykjavik: (442) Nielsen; Gudmundsson, Zivkovic, Olafsson (Sigurdsson 77), Baldvinsson; Taskovic, Kristinsson, Snorrason, Atlason (Toft 57); Bjarnason (Steingrimsson 73), Jonsson.

KR Reykjavik (0) 2 *(Palmason 75, Schoop 99)*
Cork C (1) 1 *(O'Sullivan 13)* 1145
KR Reykjavik: (442) Magnusson S; Josepsson, Christiansen, Fridgeirsson■, Gunnarsson (Ragnarsson 71); Frederiksen, Saevarsson (Ormarsson 53), Palmason, Hauksson; Schoop, Martin (Sigurdsson 104).
Cork C: (4231) McNulty; Dunleavy, Bennett, Murray,

O'Connor; Buckley, Healy; Sheppard (O'Flynn 80), Miller (Kearney 65), Gaynor; O'Sullivan (Morrissey 107). *aet.*

Litex Lovech (1) 2 *(Johnsen 25, 56)*
Jelgava (1) 2 *(Oss 11, Diallo 60)* 1235
Litex Lovech: (442) Vinicius; Perez, Popov, Bozhikov, Malinov (Angelov 86); Goranov, Kolev (Georgiev 72), Boumal, Arsenio (Diogo Viana 61); Moreno Asprilla, Johnsen.
Jelgava: (442) Ikstens; Bogdaskins (Eriba 22), Gubins, Freimanis, Redjko (Sushkin 59); Oss, Diallo, Latka, Kluskins; Sosranovs, Malasenoks (Kirilins 74).
Jelgava won on away goals.

Lokomotiva Zagreb (0) 2 *(Fiolic 65, Sovsic 73)*
Airbus UK Broughton (0) 2 *(Budrys 46, Jones 75)* 650
Lokomotiva Zagreb: (442) Zelenika; Bartolec, Mamic, Mrcela, Capan; Sovsic (Puljic 90), Begonja, Andrijasevic, Maric; Fiolic (Grzan 70), Misic (Kolar 46).
Airbus UK Broughton: (442) Coates; Pearson, McGinn, Owens, Field (Barrow 66); Jones, Riley (Spittle 90), Wignall, Owen; Budrys, Gray (Wade 74).

Lusitanos (0) 0
West Ham U (1) 1 *(Lee 21)* 837
Lusitanos: (442) Gerardo; Maciel, San Nicolas M, Munoz, Acosta (Moya 52); Soares, Molina, San Nicolas L (Pinto 74), Aguilar; dos Reis, Romero (Conteh-Lacalle 76).
West Ham U: (442) Randolph; Tomkins, Oxford, Page, O'Brien (Burke 61); Jarvis, Amalfitano (Parfitt-Williams 75), Poyet, Cullen (Nasha 86); Sakho■, Lee.

Mladost Podgorica (0) 1 *(Vukovic 90)*
Neftchi (0) 1 *(Abdullayev A 71)* 4000
Mladost Podgorica: (442) Mileta Radulovic; Pejovic, Lakic, Mirkovic (Novovic 31), Milos M Radulovic■ (Muhovic 80); Milos B Radulovic, Raicevic, Igumanovic, Scepanovic (Adzovic 69); Vukovic, Djurisic.
Neftchi: (442) Mammadov; Melli, Ailton■, Qurbanov K, Caue; Haciyev, Badalov, Qurbanov R, Abdullayev A; Qurbanov M (Abdullayev E 63), Masimov (Gurbanov 78).
Mladost Podgorica won on away goals.
Mladost Podgorica's Milos M Radulovic was shown a red card after he had been substituted. Neftchi player Vailo was also shown a red card although he was an unused substitute.

Nomme Kalju (0) 0
Aktobe (0) 0 844
Nomme Kalju: (442) Teles; Barengrub, Kallaste, Topic (Mbu Alidor 57), Rodrigues; Puri, Purje, Wakui (Lindpere 20), Mool; Kimbaloula, Dmitrijev (Neemelo 74).
Aktobe: (442) Bekbaev; Adeleye, Miroshnichenko, Deac, Korobkin; Logvinenko, Pizzelli (Khairullin 78), Zulpa, Danilo (Zhalmukan 62); Danilo Neco, Khizhnichenko.

NSI Runavik (3) 4 *(Olsen K 17, Justinussen 19, 85, Joensen 45)*
Linfield (2) 3 *(Reece Glendinning 13, Bates 33, Waterworth 69)* 550
NSI Runavik: (442) Gango; Jacobsen M, Joensen, Hansen E, Justinussen; Frederiksberg A, Frederiksberg J (Mortensen 68), Magnus Olsen (Meinhard Olsen 81), Jacobsen C; Hojgaard H (Hansen K 55), Olsen K.
Linfield: (442) Ross Glendinning; Hegarty, Ward, Clarke M, Reece Glendinning; Lowry, Burns (Murray 83), Kee, Waterworth; Bates (Clarke R 71), Sproule.

Odd (0) 0
Sheriff (0) 0 3981
Odd: (442) Rossbach; Ruud, Grogaard, Hagen, Eriksen; Gashi, Berg, Samuelsen (Zehninki 83), Halvorsen; Occean (Bergan 73), Bentley (Storbaek 66).
Sheriff: (442) Mitrev; Novicov, Potirniche, Ernandes, Macritchii V (Ginsari 67); Susic (Macritchii A 71), Cakic, Yahaya, Sharpar; Ricardinho, Potiguar (Balima 72).

Omonia Nicosia (0) 2 *(Goulon 56, Schembri 61)*
Dinamo Batumi (0) 0   13,532
Omonia Nicosia: (442) Panagi; Lobjanidze, Runje, Economides, Cristovao; Nuno Assis (Perez 88), Margaca, Goulon, Kirm (Fofana 46); Schembri (Okeuhie 79), Sheridan.
Dinamo Batumi: (442) Alavidze; Sukhiashvili, Makharadze, Tetunashvili■, Shonia; Kavtaradze (Chirikashvili 80), Gogitidze, Poniava (Varshanidze 52), Beriashvili; Tatanashvili (Koridze 59), Gabedava.

Partizani (0) 0
Stromsgodset (0) 1 *(Moen 90)*   4200
Partizani: (442) Hoxha; Fejzullahu, Vrapi, Bicaj, Kalari (Bylykbashi 89); Vila, Batha, Mazrekaj (Nedzipi 61), Fazliu; Racic, Plaku (Trashi 77).
Stromsgodset: (442) Pettersen; Hamoud, Vilsvik, Madsen, Valsvik; Abu (Jradi 84), Ovenstad, Fossum, Wikheim; Kastrati (Moen 58), Ogunjimi (Sorum 87).

Rabotnicki (0) 2 *(Anene 48, Altiparmakovski 54)*
Flora Tallinn (0) 0   1690
Rabotnicki: (442) Bozinovski; Ilievski, Siljanovski, Ristevski, Cikarski; Petrovic, Altiparmakovski (Trajcevski 80), Anene, Vujcic; Sahiti (Jovanovski 85), Ilijoski (Mitrov 75).
Flora Tallinn: (442) Toom; Jaager, Kams, Jurgenson, Baranov (Aloe 68); Frolov, Slein, Alliku, Logua (Gussev 55); Sappinen, Tukiainen (Tamm 46).

Randers (1) 3 *(Amini 42, Babayan 72, Ishak 90)*
Sant Julia (0) 0   1456
Randers: (442) Johnsson; Thomsen (Bager 75), Fenger, Marxen, Keller; Thygesen (Kallesoe 72), Fischer, Borring, Allansson (Babayan 59); Ishak, Amini.
Sant Julia: (442) Coca; Varela, Ruis, Brito, Vigo; Spano (Alves 78), Bruninho, Barcelo, Rodriguez (Peppe 61); Gandara, Quirino (Javier Castellano 71).

Rosenborg (0) 0
Vikingur (0) 0   4572
Rosenborg: (442) Alexander Hansen; Dorsin, Eyjolfsson, Skjelvik, Svensson; Midtsjoe (Helmersen 84), Selnaes (Jensen 66), Saeter, Riski (Soderlund 74); Nielsen, Malec.
Vikingur: (442) Tamas; Gregersen, Djurhuus, Jacobsen E, Jacobsen H; Hjartvard Hansen, Vatnhamar S, Hansen H (Hansen G 75), Djordjevic (Vatnhamar G 64); Olsen (Joensen 85), Justinussen.

Shakhtyor Soligorsk (1) 3 *(Yurevich 8, Yanush 66, Komarovski 83)*
Glenavon (0) 0   3200
Shakhtyor Soligorsk: (442) Bushma; Matsveychyk, Kuzmyanok (Kozeka 75), Rybak, Yanushkevich; Afanasyev (Mikoliunas 59), Yurevich, Starhorodskyi, Kovalev (Shlbun 82); Komarovski, Yanush.
Glenavon: (442) Tuffey; Marshall, Kelly, Lindsay (Caldwell 66), Singleton; Hall (Patton 35), Kilmartin (Hamilton 62), Martyn, Dillon; Bradley, Braniff.

Slask Wroclaw (0) 3 *(Ostrowski 46, Kielb 56, 90)*
Celje (0) 1 *(Firer 80)*   12,364
Slask Wroclaw: (442) Pawalek; Celeban, Dudu Paraiba, Pawelec, Zielinski; Hateley, Holota, Kielb (Dankowski 90), Flavio Paixao (Ostrowski 11); Grajciar (Bartowiak 76), Pich.
Celje: (442) Kotnik; Klemencic, Jakolic, Soria, Vidmajer; Vrhovec, Mrsic (Spremo 69), Klapan, Firer; Omoregie, Miskic (Ahmedi 79).

Slovan Bratislava (2) 3 *(Gorosito 21, Zrelak 35, Vittek 67 (pen))*
Europa (0) 0   2145
Slovan Bratislava: (442) Krnac; Dobrotka, Podany, Gorosito (Salata 43), Sekulic; Milinkovic, Simovic, Kubik, Lasik (Meszaros 46); Vittek (Priskin 75), Zrelak.

Europa: (442) Camara; Merino, Plazanic, Pinero, Jukic (Ortega 64); Pacheco, Catalan, Fernandez, Rodriguez (Sokol 71); Akrapovic, Toncheff (Morgan 86).

Spartak Trnava (0) 0
Olimpic Sarajevo (0) 0   3011
Spartak Trnava: (442) Jakubech; Toth, Nikolic, Conka, Godal; Vlasko (Gressak 90), Sabo, Halilovic (Schranz 58), Jose Casado; Cleber (Harba 10), Mikovic.
Olimpic Sarajevo: (442) Hamzic; Muharemovic, Bogicevic, Regoje, Merajic; Gligorov, Smajic (Karic 55), Handzic (Jusufovic 80), Rascic; Pandza, Brkovic (Stefan 65).
Spartak Trnava won on away goals.

Spartaks Jurmala (0) 0
Buducnost Podgorica (0) 0   1018
Spartaks Jurmala: (442) Kolinko; Bulvitis, Mezs, Nazarenko, Maksymenko; Slampe, Mickevics, Kazacoks, Ulimbashevs; Vivacqua (Abdultaofik 90), Takyi (Stuglis 82).
Buducnost Podgorica: (442) Agovic; Simovic, Raspopovic■, Tomkovic, Vukcevic (Milosevic 74); Flavio Beck, Pavicevic (Gazivoda 65), Raicevic, Raickovic (Burzanovic 56); Ilincic, Nikac.

St Johnstone (1) 2 *(O'Halloran 34, McKay 86)*
Alashkert (0) 1 *(Gyozalyan 73)*   5764
St Johnstone: (424) Mannus; Shaughnessy, Anderson (Caddis 71), Wright (McKay 65), Scobbie; Brown, Easton; O'Halloran, Sutton (Cummins 80), MacLean, Kane.
Alashkert: (4141) Kasparov; Fofana, Arakelyan, Usenya, Muradyan■; Bareghamyan (Dos Santos 90); Grigoryan, Veranyan (Voskanyan 90), Poghosyan, Minasyan; Gyozalyan (Manasyan 75).
Alashkert won on away goals.

St Patrick's Ath (0) 0
Skonto (1) 2 *(Sorokins 37, Karasausks 59 (pen))* 2354
St Patrick's Ath: (433) Clarke; O'Brien, Desmond, Browne, Bermingham; Greene (McGrath 65), Bolger, Brennan; Byrne, Fagan (Langley 65), Forrester.
Skonto: (433) Pavlovs; Timofejevs, Rode, Smirnovs, Sorokins; Kozlovs, Murillo (Isajevs 77), Kovalovs; Jermolajevs, Karasausks (Ivanovs 83), Gutkovskis (Visnakovs 64).

Sutjeska (0) 2 *(Fukui 53, Bozovic 81 (pen))*
Debrecen (0) 0   1214
Sutjeska: (442) Radovic; Ognjanovic, Lukic, Sofranac, Stijpreovic (Marko Vucic 84); Nikolic, Bozovic, Kovacevic, Vujovic (Vorotovic 90); Fukui, Milos Vucic (Karadzic 71).
Debrecen: (442) Verpecz; Meszaros, Korhut, Brkovic, Szakaly (Morozov 90); Varga, Jovanovic, Bodi, Sidibe; Kulcsar (Balogh 73), Horvath (Szecsi 46).

Torpedo Zhodino (0) 0
Kukesi (0) 0   2950
Torpedo Zhodino: (442) Chesnovskiy; Burko, Melnyk, Pankavets, Serdyuk; Selyava, Maksimovs (Kibuk 61), Datsenko, Vaskow (Kontsevoy 67); Hleb, Yatskevich (Platonaw 59).
Kukesi: (442) Stajila; Shameti (Hasani 56), Hallaci, Malota, Mici; Flores Bonfim, Lopes (Musolli 87), Muca, Jean Carioca; Pejic, Moreira (Birungueta 70).

Torshavn (0) 1 *(Hanssen 90)*
Trakai (2) 4 *(Arshakiyan 30, 90, Solomin 38, Bychenok 83)* 313
Torshavn: (442) Gestsson; Haraldsen, Holm■, Jogvan Davidsen, Joensen; Wardum, Hanssen, Benjaminsen, Vatnsdal; Jacobsen (Justinussen 67), Hansen (Ingason 74).
Trakai: (442) Rapalis; Klimavicius (Apakidze 55), Janusevskis, Cesnauskis, Mamaev (Masenzovas 63); Silenas, Bychenok, Solomin, Arshakiyan; Zasavitchi (Stanulevicius 70), Segzda.

Tskhinvali (0) 1 *(Kilasonia 65 (pen))*

Botosani (1) 3 *(Roman 6, 59, Batin 68)* 4500

Tskhinvali: (442) Nadiradze; Kakubava, Kilasonia, Kardava (Lobjanidze 71), Bachiashvili; Ivanishvili, Gigauri (Shulaia 63), Tsatskrialashvili (Burdzenadze 78), Tsertvadze; Makharoblidze, Katcharava■.
Botosani: (442) Iliev; Cordos, Patache, Plamada■, Costin; Vasvari, Cucu, Ivanovici (Batin 46), Roman (Hadnagy 74); Martinus (Croitoru 53), Browne.

Ulisses (0) 1 *(Morozov 71)*

Birkirkara (2) 3 *(Miccoli 21, Mazzetti Latini 44, Fenech 80)* 3500

Ulisses: (442) Beglaryan; Morozov, Jarkava (Janashia 70), Dugalic, Mamakhanov; Mesaki (Aleksanyan■, Paderin, Khubua, Khurtsidze; Tshibamba (Piliev 53), Geperidze.
Birkirkara: (442) Akpan; Zerafa, Vucanac, Mazzetti Latini, Fenech; Muscat Z, Camenzuli, Miccoli (Agius 65), Muscat R; Liliu (Plut 68), Murga (Vella■ 71).

Vaduz (3) 5 *(Kamber 25, 33, Schurpf 41, Muntwiler 71, Lang 84)*

La Fiorita (0) 1 *(Tommasi 74)* 727

Vaduz: (442) Hirzel; Grippo, Von Niederhausern, Buhler, Muntwiler; Ciccone (Kuzmanovic 57), Neumayr, Schurpf (Sutter 46), Lang; Cecchini, Kamber (Hasler 58).
La Fiorita: (442) Pazzini; Mascerata, Martini, Gasperoni, Tommasi; Cavalli (Guidi 70), Zafferani, Righi (Casadei 60), Cangini; Ricchiuti, Rinaldi (De Biagi 82).

Valletta (0) 1 *(Fidjeu 46)*

Newtown (1) 2 *(Oswell 7, Owen 85)* 1914

Valletta: (451) Vella; Camilleri R■, Cruz, Caruana, Briffa; Jhonnattann, Pani, Cremona, Falzon, Nafti (Umeh 87); Fidjeu (Triganza 63).
Newtown: (442) Jones; Sutton, Mills-Evans, Edwards, Hearsey (Cook■ 68); Williams, Owen (Price 89), Goodwin, Mitchell (Partridge 88); Boundford, Oswell.

Vojvodina (2) 3 *(Stanisavljevic 14, Mrdakovic 40, Ivanic 51)*

MTK Budapest (1) 1 *(Strestik 3)* 8460

Vojvodina: (442) Zakula; Djuric, Vasilic, Nastic, Pankov; Stanisavljevic, Maksimovic (Puskaric 55), Sekulic, Ivanic; Mrdakovic (Palocevic 90), Stamenic (Babic 77).
MTK Budapest: (442) Hegedus; Vadnai, Vukmir, Grgic, Vass (Gera 90); Strestik (Szatmari 63), Kanta, Thian, Varga (Ramos 53); Torghelle, Bese.

Zeljeznicar Sarajevo (0) 1 *(Sadikovic D 68)*

Balzan (0) 0 5500

Zeljeznicar Sarajevo: (442) Antolovic; Kvesic, Kosoric, Bogdanovic, Memija; Djelmic, Blagojevic (Sadikovic E 70), Bajic, Hadziahmetovic; Kokot (Hiros 84), Beganovic (Sadikovic D 64).
Balzan: (442) Senatore; Serrano, Bezzina, Arab, Grioli; Brincat, Fenech, Grima (Darmanin 79), Guobadia (Borg 90); Agius (Micallef 73), Bilbao.

Zilina (1) 3 *(Jelic 44, 55, 66)*

Glentoran (0) 0 2897

Zilina: (451) Volesak; Mabouka, Vavro, Skriniar, Letic; Spalek (Kacer 59), Benes, Pecovsky (Cmelik 59), Skvarka, Mihalik; Jelic (Paur 79).
Glentoran: (433) Morris; Holland, Birney, Magee (Garrett 79), Kane; Gordon, Gibson, McCullough; McAlorum (Nelson 67), McCaffrey (Addis 76), McMenamin.

Zrinjski Mostar (0) 2 *(Mesanovic 80 (pen), Filipovic 85)*

Shirak (0) 1 *(Bougouhi 90)* 4800

Zrinjski Mostar: (442) Dujkovic; Stojanovic, Radeljic, Blaic, Graovac; Todorovic (Filipovic 69), Zeravica, Radulovic (Muminovic 90), Zakaric (Scepanovic 76); Nikolic, Mesanovic.
Shirak: (442) Ermakov; Hovanisian, Stamenkovic, Hovhannisyan, Malakyan E; Davtyan (Aleksanyan 15), Hakobyan, Davoyan, Malakyan G■ Diarrassouba (Barikian 46), Bougouhi.

SECOND QUALIFYING ROUND FIRST LEG

Thursday, 16 July 2015

AIK Solna (1) 2 *(Goitom 29, 83 (pen))*

Shirak (0) 0 7315

AIK Solna: (442) Stamatopoulos; Karlsson (Lundholm 89), Johansson, Sundberg, Ofori; Etuhu, Pavey, Ishizaki, Eliasson (Blomberg 67); Goitom, Bangura (Brustad 67).
Shirak: (352) Yermakov; Hovhannisyan■, Stamenkovic, Malakyan E; Hovanisian, Malakyan G■, Hakobyan (Barikian■ 78), Aleksanyan, Davoyan; Diarrassouba (Davtyan 90), Bougouhi (Ayvazyan 90).

Apollon Limassol (1) 4 *(Kolokoudias 20, 62 (pen), Stojanovic 52, Rosa 87)*

Trakai (0) 0 3720

Apollon Limassol: (442) Bruno Vale; Elizio, Nuno Lopes (Stylianou 80), Freire, Sachetti; Gullon, Jaime, Joao Pedro, Stojanovic (Alex 72); Papoulis (Rosa 68), Kolokoudias.
Trakai: (442) Rapalis; Klimavicius, Cesnauskis, Arshakiyan, Solomin; Stanulevicius (Segzda 68), Janusevskis, Silenas, Zasavitchi (Apakidze 88); Bychenok, Mamaev.

Beroe (0) 0

Brondby (0) 1 *(Albrechtsen 85)* 8256

Beroe: (433) Makendzhiev; Vasilev, Ivanov, Penev, Zehirov; Milisavljevic (Kokonov 86), Elias, Djoman (Tom 89); Mapuku (Andonov 71), Bozhilov, Delev.
Brondby: (433) Hradecky; Albrechtsen, Larsson, Durmisi, Dumic; Ornskov Nielsen, Phiri, Norgaard (Holst 85); Rashani (Hjulsager 60), Pukki, Elmander (Eriksson 73).

Charleroi (1) 5 *(Pollet 10, 68, Kebano 47, 90, Stevance 88)*

Beitar Jerusalem (1) 1 *(Gabay 35)* 10,175

Charleroi: (442) Penneteau; Dewaest, Tainmont, Martos, Pollet (Stevance 80); Marinos, Marcq, Saglik (Ferber 89), N'Ganga; Ndongala (Francois 90), Kebano.
Beitar Jerusalem: (442) Klaiman; Dasa■, Kachila, Atzili (Cohen L 75), Claudemir; Freda (De Lucas■ 55), Gabay, Zhairi, Nachmani (Zamir 30); Matovic, Askling.

Cherno More (1) 1 *(Coureur 11)*

Dinamo Minsk (0) 1 *(Politevich 72)* 3650

Cherno More: (442) Canovic; Venkov, Stanchev, Coulibaly, Klok; Raykov, Burkhardt (Stenio 67), Coureur (Vasev 72), Bijev (Varea 58); Bourabia, Palankov.
Dinamo Minsk: (442) Gutor; Vitus, Politevich, Bykov, Rassadkin (Voronkov 87); Bangura, Korzun, Beqiraj, Begunov; Yedigaryan (Udoji 60), Adamovic (Korytko 77).

Cukaricki Belgrade (0) 0 *(Stoiljkovic 53 (pen))*

Gabala (0) 0 3550

Cukaricki Belgrade: (442) Stevanovic; Piasentin, Srnic D, Jankovic N, Stoiljkovic (Mirosavljevic 85); Pavlovic (Mandic 67), Srnic S, Stojkovic, Ostojic; Bojic (Jovanovic 90), Brezancic.
Gabala: (442) Bezotosnyi; Florescu (Dodo 36), Sadiqov, Zenjov (Mammadov 88), Huseynov; Vernydub, Gai, Ricardinho, Abbasov; Rafael Santos, Antonov (Dashdemirov 46).

Dacia (0) 2 *(Gavrylenko 35, Mihaliov 80)*

Zilina (0) 2 *(Jelic 53, 59)* 3800

Dacia: (442) Gaiduchevici; Rosca, Jardan (Frunza 68), Posmac, Lozoviy; Mani (Mihaliov 46), Cociuc, Gavrylenko, Zastavnyi; Pavlov (Stjepanovic 57), Mamah.
Zilina: (442) Volesak; Skriniar, Kacer, Paur (Mihalik 66), Jelic; Pecovsky, Cmelik (Spalek 85), Vavro, Letic; Benes (Skvarka 89), Mabouka.

FC Copenhagen (1) 2 *(Verbic 3, Kusk 74)*

Newtown (0) 0 8104

FC Copenhagen: (442) Andersen; Augustinsson, Nilsson, Ankersen, Toutouh; Delaney, Kusk, Amartey, Verbic (Olsen 90); Jorgensen N, Pourie (Hogli 82).
Newtown: (442) Jones; Boundford, Mills-Evans (Cadwallader 78), Sutton, Williams; Goodwin, Edwards, Mitchell, Oswell; Owen (Price 80), Hearsey (Evans 69).

Ferencvaros (0) 0
Zeljeznicar Sarajevo (0) 1 *(Beganovic 90)*　　　8853
Ferencvaros: (442) Dibusz; Busai (Hajnal 46), Nalepa, Dilaver, Ramirez (Sestak 46); Bode, Leandro, Gera, Lamah (Gyomber 68); Somalia, Varga.
Zeljeznicar Sarajevo: (442) Antolovic; Kosoric, Memija, Bogdanovic, Kvesic; Blagojevic, Hadziahmetovic (Beganovic 53), Sadıkovıc D, Delmic (Sadıkovıc E 71); Kokot (Diatta 87), Bajic.

Hafnarfjordur (1) 1 *(Gudnason 39 (pen))*
Inter Baku (0) 2 *(Kvekveskiri 54 (pen), Martins 61)*　1020
Hafnarfjordur: (442) Oskarsson▪; Vidarsson P, Palsson (Kristjan Finnbogason 52), Valdimarsson (Bjornsson 83), Vidarsson D; Gudnason, Vidarsson B (Finnbogason KF 70), Thorisson, Doumbia; Bodvarsson, Hendrickx.
Inter Baku: (442) Agayev; Juanfran, Kasradze, Kvekveskiri, Haciyev (Poljak 80); Aliyev, Abbasov (Martins 46), Khizanishvili, Seyidov; Bayramov (Denis Silva 69), Huseynov.

Hapoel Beer Sheva (1) 1 *(Hoban 26)*
Thun (0) 1 *(Frontino 87)*　　　　　11,796
Hapoel Beer Sheva: (352) Goresh; Tzedek, Davidadze, William Soares; Radi (Gordana 88), Buzaglo, Biton, Hoban, Melikson (Nwakaeme 77); Ogu, Barda (Sahar 61).
Thun: (451) Faivre; Burki, Sulmoni, Siegfried (Sutter 18 (Schirinzi 67)), Glarner; Wittwer, Frontino, Rojas, Hediger, Ferreira; Buess (Rapp 62).

Inverness CT (0) 0
Astra Giurgiu (1) 1 *(Budescu 24)*　　　　5534
Inverness CT: (4411) Fon Williams; Meekings (Raven 80), Warren, Devine, Williams D; Tansey, Draper (Roberts 80), Wedderburn, Doran; Christie; Lopez (Foran 84).
Astra Giurgiu: (442) Lung Jr; Pedro Queiros, Gaman (Oros 47), Geraldo Alves, Junior Morais; Enache (Stan 70), Boldrin, Seto, William Amorim; Teixeira, Budescu (Florea 82).

Jagiellonia Bialystock (0) 0
Omonia Nicosia (0) 0　　　　　16,067
Jagiellonia Bialystock: (442) Dragowski; Modelski, Romanchuk (Vassiljev 23 (Sekulski 85)), Madera, Tuszynski; Dzalamidze, Tarasovs, Gajos, Frankowski (Swiderski 78); Grzyb, Tomasik.
Omonia Nicosia: (442) Panagi; Lobjanidze, Sheridan, Cristovao, Nuno Assis (Bebe 89); Economides, Fofana (Demetriou 81), Schembri (Kirm 65), Margaca; Runje, Goulon.

Jelgava (0) 1 *(Kluskins 87)*
Rabotnicki (0) 0　　　　　1510
Jelgava: (442) Ikstens; Freimanis (Redjko 86), Sosranovs, Latka, Bogdaskins; Diallo, Gubins, Eriba (Kirilins 56), Oss; Kluskins, Sushkin (Malasenoks 63).
Rabotnicki: (442) Bozinovski; Vujcic, Anene, Ilijoski (Sahiti 65), Siljanovski; Ristevski, Petrovic, Altiparmakovski (Jovanovski 79), Trajcevski; Cikarski (Mitrov 88), Ilievski.

Kairat Almaty (1) 3 *(Islamkhan 14 (pen), Gohou 55, Despotovic 69)*
Alashkert (0) 0　　　　　22,100
Kairat Almaty: (442) Plotnikov; Bruno, Markovic, Kuantayev, Kuat (Despotovic 64); Islamkhan (Kukeev 90), Isael, Tymoschuk, Gohou (Gorman 87); Sito Riera, Lunin.
Alashkert: (442) Kasparov; Fofana, Arakelyan, Poghosyan, Usenya; Minasyan, Veranyan, Bareghamyan (Karapetyan 77), Grigoryan; Manasyan (Ghazaryan 57), Gyozalyan (Dos Santos 73).

Koper (3) 3 *(Halilovic 7, Rahmanovic 17, 41)*
Hajduk Split (1) 2 *(Milovic 29, Nizic 90)*　　2590
Koper: (442) Simcic; Sme, Guberac, Rahmanovic (Pucko 60), Ivancic (Stromajer 71); Galesic, Halilovic, Crnigoj, Krivicic; Hadzic, Palcic.

Hajduk Split: (442) Kalinic; Milovic, Jefferson, Vlasic, Maglica (Radchenko 74); Caktas, Nizic, Pejic, Tudor; Roguljic (Maloku 70), Balic (Kis 46).

KR Reykjavik (0) 0
Rosenborg (0) 1 *(Helland 56 (pen))*　　　1550
KR Reykjavik: (442) Magnusson S; Christiansen, Schoop, Gunnarsson, Josepsson; Sigurdsson, Sacvarsson, Palmason, Hauksson (Ormarsson 80); Ragnarsson (Martin 29), Frederiksen (Fridjonsson 66).
Rosenborg: (442) Andre Hansen; Dorsin, Eyjolfsson, Jensen, Skjelvik; Selnaes, Midtsjoe, Svensson, Mikkelsen; Helland (Riski 78), Soderlund.

Kukesi (0) 0
Mladost Podgorica (0) 1 *(Lakic 52)*　　　2500
Kukesi: (442) Stajila; Muca, Mici, Flores Bonfim, Hallaci; Birungueta (Hasani 36), Moreira (Granado 61), Jean Carioca (Halili 89), Pejic; Malota, Jefferson.
Mladost Podgorica: (442) Mileta Radulovic; Pejovic, Raicevic, Igumanovic (Muhovic 77), Djurisic; Novovic, Lakic, Vukovic, Milos M Radulovic; Milos B Radulovic, Scepanovic (Mirkovic 74).

Legia Warsaw (0) 1 *(Duda 78)*
Botosani (0) 0　　　　　10,446
Legia Warsaw: (442) Kuciak; Pazdan, Jodlowiec, Guilherme (Zyro 68), Duda (Maslowski 90); Nikolic (Prijovic 68), Brzyski, Kucharczyk, Rzezniczak; Broz, Furman.
Botosani: (442) Iliev; Cordos, Miron, Brata (Ivanovici 69), Vasvari (Robertson 64); Cucu, Acsinte, Roman, Batin; Costin (Croitoru 84), Dimitrov.

Lokomotiva Zagreb (2) 2 *(Kolar 30, Andrijasevic 45)*
PAOK Salonika (0) 1 *(Mak 90)*　　　1000
Lokomotiva Zagreb: (442) Zelenika; Bartolec, Mrcela, Prenga, Brucic; Sovsic (Capan 90), Begonja, Andrijasevic, Leko; Kolar (Dolezal 65), Maric (Misic 73).
PAOK Salonika: (442) Olsen; Skondras (Rat 79), Maduro Vitor, Ricardo Costa, Tzavelas; Kitsiou, Tziolis (Maduro 61), Mak, Kace; Pelkas, Salpingidis (Mystakidis 68).

Mlada Boleslav (1) 1 *(Bartl 39)*
Stromsgodset (1) 2 *(Sorum 44, Jradi 85)*　　4756
Mlada Boleslav: (442) Veselovsky; Krapka, Mendy, Kudela, Scuk; Zahustel, Klobasa (Stohanzl 77), Rada, Bartl (Cermak 64); Chramostra (Magera 64), Kysela.
Stromsgodset: (442) Pettersen; Hoibraten, Valsvik, Abu, Moen (Jradi 61); Fossum, Vilsvik, Storflor (Kastrati 85), Hamoud; Wikheim, Sorum (Olsen 53).

Randers (0) 0
Elfsborg (0) 0　　　　　3151
Randers: (442) Johnsson; Fenger, Thomsen, Tverskov, Fischer; Amini, Borring (Marxen 78), Poulsen, Keller; Ishak (Babayan 75), Brock-Madsen.
Elfsborg: (442) Stuhr-Ellegaard; Holmen, Manns (Klarstrom 19), Lundqvist, Rohden; Svensson, Zeneli (Lundevall 61), Hedlund (Nilsson 75), Hauger; Claesson, Frick.

Rijeka (0) 0
Aberdeen (1) 3 *(Considine 38, Pawlett 52, McLean 75)*　　　9000
Rijeka: (4141) Vargic; Tomecak, Samardzic, Leskovic, Leovac; Radosevic (Bezjak 55); Bradaric (Mocinic 74), Moises, Sharbini, Tomasov (Kvrzic 46); Balaj.
Aberdeen: (4141) Ward; Logan, Considine, Taylor, Shinnie; Quinn; Pawlett (Flood 63), Jack, Goodwillie (Rooney 83), Hayes; McGinn (McLean 70).

Shakhtyor Soligorsk (0) 0
Wolfsburger (0) 1 *(Jacobo 62)*　　　2500
Shakhtyor Soligorsk: (442) Bushma; Afanasyev (Trubila 63), Yanushkevich, Yurevich, Rybak; Kuzmyanok, Matsveychyk, Starhorodskyi, Kovalev (Mikoliunas 72); Yanush, Komarovski (Kozaka 80).
Wolfsburger: (442) Kofler; Zundel (Wernitznig 82), Berger, Palla, Sollbauer; Drescher, Weber (Huttenbrenner 90), Jacobo, Putsche; Hellqvist, Silvio (Trdina 71).

Shamrock R (0) 0

Odd (0) 2 *(Occean 53 (pen), 67)*   2900

Shamrock R: (442) Hyland; Byrne, Kenna, Webster, Madden; Brennan R (Kavanagh C 86), Brennan G (North 80), Cregg, McCabe; Waters (Miele 67), Drennan.
Odd: (442) Rossbach; Ruud, Jonassen, Hagen, Eriksen; Gashi (Jensen 46), Samuelsen, Nordkvelle, Halvorsen; Occean (Bergan 85), Bentley (Storbaek 82).

Skonto (1) 2 *(Karasausks 27, 47)*

Debrecen (1) 2 *(Tisza 9, Castillon 72)*   2200

Skonto: (442) Pavlovs; Timofejevs, Rode, Murillo, Visnakovs (Lukanyuk 71); Kozlovs, Jermolajevs, Gutkovskis (Isajevs 57), Kovalovs; Karasausks, Sorokins.
Debrecen: (442) Verpecz; Balogh (Horvath 90), Meszaros, Brkovic, Sidibe (Castillon 71); Bodi, Varga, Tisza (Szecsi 80), Szakaly; Korhut, Jovanovic.

Slask Wroclaw (0) 0

IFK Gothenburg (0) 0   16,978

Slask Wroclaw: (442) Pawalek; Celeban, Dudu Paraiba, Pawelec, Kokoszka (Gecov 59); Zielinski, Hateley (Bilinski 67), Holota, Kielb (Flavio Paixao 77); Grajciar, Pich.
IFK Gothenburg: (442) Alvbage; Aleesami, Rogne (Jonsson 86), Bjarsmyr, Salomonsson; Ankersen, Eriksson, Smedberg-Dalence (Rieks 78), Svensson; Vibe, Boman (Engvall 78).

Slovan Bratislava (0) 1 *(Zrelak 84)*

University College Dublin (0) 0   3050

Slovan Bratislava: (442) Mucha; Sekulic, Gorosito■, Salata, Podany; Milinkovic, Stefanik, Simovic (Hudak 44), Zrelak; Priskin (Zahumensky 90), Vittek (Kubik 46).
University College Dublin: (442) Corbet; Langtry, Leahy, Benson, Boyle; Kougun, Mullhall, Swan, O'Neill; Watts (Cannon 85), Doyle.

Spartak Trnava (2) 2 *(Sabo 16 (pen), Mikovic 35)*

Linfield (1) 1 *(Kee 21)*   3220

Spartak Trnava: (442) Jakubech; Toth, Conka, Godal, Baez; Mikovic, Jose Casado (Mikinic 65), Nikolic■, Sabo; Halilovic, Harba (Bortel 46 (Gressak 70)).
Linfield: (442) Ross Glendinning; Hegarty, Haughey, Clarke M, Reece Glendinning; Lowry, Burns (Clarke R 57), Kee, Waterworth; Bates, Sproule.

Trabzonspor (1) 1 *(Ekici 44)*

Differdange 03 (0) 0   9254

Trabzonspor: (442) Kivrak; Medjani, Demirok, Yumlu, Dursun; Nizam, Ekici (Atik 84), Yilmaz S, Aydogdu; Zengin (Erdogan 64), Waris (Yavru 81).
Differdange 03: (442) Weber; Rodrigues, Siebenaler, Bukvic, Janisch; Franzoni, Pedro Ribeiro (May 90), Sinani (Lebresne 63), Er Rafik; Caron (Meligner 76), Yeye.

Vaduz (1) 3 *(Ciccone 20, Neumayr 53, 90)*

Nomme Kalju (0) 1 *(Wakui 86)*   912

Vaduz: (442) Jehle; Grippo, Pergl, Lang (Schurpf 84), Ciccone; Messaoud (Caballero 66), Stahel, Neumayr, Kukuruzovic (Kamber 75); Muntwiler, Aliji.
Nomme Kalju: (442) Teles; Barengrub, Rodrigues, Mbu Alidor, Dmitrijev (Lindpere 63); Purje (Neemelo 70), Kimbaloula, Kallaste, Topic (Puri 46); Mool, Wakui.

Vojvodina (2) 3 *(Stanisavljevic 6, Mrdakovic 16, Mickevics 88 (og))*

Spartaks Jurmala (0) 0   9000

Vojvodina: (442) Zakula; Vasilic, Ivanic, Stanisavljevic, Mrdakovic (Ozegovic 74); Pankov, Nastic, Djuric, Sekulic; Maksimovic (Puskaric 79), Stamenic (Palocevic 72).
Spartaks Jurmala: (442) Kolinko; Maksymenko, Nazarenko, Ulimbashevs, Kazacoks (Mezs 46); Stuglis (Takyi 21), Mickevics, Vivacqua, Bulvitis; Abdultaofik (Punculs 75), Slampe.

West Ham U (0) 1 *(Tomkins 90)*

Birkirkara (0) 0   33,048

West Ham U: (433) Adrian; O'Brien, Reid, Tomkins, Cresswell; Amalfitano (Samuelsen 59), Noble, Jarvis; Nolan (Poyet 79), Maiga (Lee 70), Zarate.
Birkirkara: (442) Haber; Fenech (Zammit 49), Vucanac, Mazzetti Latini, Camenzuli; Zerafa, Muscat R, Liliu (Plut 65), Muscat Z; Murga (Agius 45), Miccoli.

SECOND QUALIFYING ROUND SECOND LEG

Tuesday, 21 July 2015

Elfsborg (0) 1 *(Lundevall 94)*

Randers (0) 0   5197

Elfsborg: (442) Stuhr-Ellegaard; Holmen, Klarstrom (Lundevall 90), Lundqvist, Rohden; Svensson, Zeneli (Prodell 72), Hedlund, Hauger; Claesson, Frick (Nilsson 106).
Randers: (442) Johnsson; Thomsen, Marxen (Babayan 54), Fenger, Fischer; Tverskov, Amini, Borring (Thygesen 79), Poulsen; Keller, Brock-Madsen■.
aet.

Thursday, 23 July 2015

Aberdeen (0) 2 *(McGinn 64, Hayes 72)*

Rijeka (0) 2 *(Tomasov 58, Kvrzic 63)*   15,803

Aberdeen: (3511) Ward; Taylor, Quinn, Considine; Logan, Hayes, Jack, McGinn (Flood 83), Shinnie; McLean (Pawlett 73); Goodwillie (Rooney 75).
Rijeka: (4411) Sluga; Bradaric (Balaj 74), Samardzic, Mitrovic, Leovac; Tomasov, Radosevic, Ristovski, Roshi (Kvrzic 52); Moises; Bezjak.

Alashkert (1) 2 *(Arakelyan 28, Dos Santos 90)*

Kairat Almaty (1) 1 *(Gohou 45)*   2500

Alashkert: (442) Kasparov; Fofana, Arakelyan, Usenya, Minasyan; Muradyan (Hovsepyan 78), Veranyan (Poghosyan 58), Bareghamyan, Grigoryan; Dos Santos, Gyozalyan (Manasyan 58).
Kairat Almaty: (433) Plotnikov; Kuantayev, Markovic (Gorman 85), Bruno, Lunin; Tymoschuk, Islamkhan, Kuat (Konysbayev 67); Isael, Gohou, Sito Riera (Despotovic 71).

Astra Giurgiu (0) 0

Inverness CT (0) 0   3067

Astra Giurgiu: (442) Lung Jr; Geraldo Alves, Junior Morais, Gaman, Pedro Queiros; Seto, Enache (Florea 80), Boldrin (Dandea 84), Teixeira; William Amorim, Budescu (Lovin 89).
Inverness CT: (442) Fon Williams; Raven, Warren, Meekings, Devine; Wedderburn (Draper 79), Doran, Tansey, Williams D (Foran 78); Lopez, Christie.

Beitar Jerusalem (1) 1 *(Atzili 16)*

Charleroi (1) 4 *(Kebano 43, Saglik 53, Ndongala 76, Stevance 90)*   6500

Beitar Jerusalem: (442) Klaiman; Kapiloto, Kachila, Atzili, Cohen A (Cohen L 61); Claudemir, Freda (Zamir 61), Gabay, Zhairi (Cohen I 46); Magbo, Matovic.
Charleroi: (442) Penneteau; Dewaest, Martos, Pollet, Marinos; Galvez-Lopez (Geraerts 57), Marcq, Saglik (Stevance 78), N'Ganga; Ndongala, Kebano (Boulenger 68).

Birkirkara (1) 1 *(Miccoli 15)*

West Ham U (0) 0   14,571

Birkirkara: (433) Haber; Muscat Z, Vucanac, Mazzetti Latini■, Zerafa; Muscat R (Agius 70), Emerson (Zammit 96), Camenzuli; Liliu, Fenech, Miccoli (Plut 77).
West Ham U: (442) Adrian; O'Brien, Collins, Tomkins■, Cresswell; Amalfitano (Maiga 59), Kouyate, Noble, Jarvis (Samuelsen 120); Nolan (Poyet 59), Zarate.
aet; West Ham U won 5-3 on penalties.

Botosani (0) 0

Legia Warsaw (2) 3 *(Guilherme 7, Nikolic 38 (pen), Prijovic 84)*   5353

Botosani: (442) Iliev; Cordos (Vasvari 46), Plamada, Brata, Croitoru; Cucu, Patache (Martinus 33), Acsinte, Costin (Robertson 73); Hadnagy, Dimitrov.
Legia Warsaw: (442) Kuciak; Pazdan, Jodlowiec (Maslowski 80), Guilherme, Duda; Nikolic (Prijovic 70), Brzyski (Zyro 46), Kucharczyk, Rzezniczak; Broz, Furman.

Brondby (0) 0
Beroe (0) 0　　　　　　　　　　　　　9550
Brondby: (451) Hradecky; Larsson, Ornskov Nielsen, Albrechtsen, Durmisi; Hjulsager, Norgaard, Phiri, Elmander, Rashani (Eriksson 58); Pukki (Holst 79).
Beroe: (4411) Makendzhiev; Vasilev, Elias, Ivanov, Penev, Mapuku, Zchirov, Djoman, Milisavljevic; Delev; Bozhilov (Kokonov 79).

Debrecen (5) 9 *(Tisza 7, 45, Balogh 12, Sidibe 29, 31, Brkovic 51, Szakaly 54 (pen), Bodi 58, Castillon 70)*
Skonto (0) 2 *(Gutkovskis 59, Rode 65)*　　8532
Debrecen: (442) Verpecz; Balogh (Castillon 56), Meszaros, Brkovic, Sidibe; Bodi (Horvath 62), Varga (Zsidai 46), Tisza, Szakaly; Korhut, Jovanovic.
Skonto: (442) Pavlovs; Timofejevs, Rode, Murillo (Indrans 54), Visnakovs (Berenfelds 46); Kozlovs, Jermolajevs, Gutkovskis, Kovalovs*; Karasausks (Lukanyuk 61), Sorokins.

Differdange 03 (0) 1 *(Er Rafik 81)*
Trabzonspor (1) 2 *(Dursun 19, Aydogdu 90)*　3455
Differdange 03: (433) Weber; Rodrigues (Lebresne 70), Siebenaler, Bukvic, Franzoni; Sinani (Luisi 57), Janisch, Pedro Ribeiro (Bettmer 79); Yeye, Er Rafik, Caron.
Trabzonspor: (4231) Kivrak; Dursun, Yumlu, Demirok, Nizam; Medjani (Kara 90), Constant; Yilmaz S, Ekici (Aydogdu 59), Erdogan (Zengin 72); Waris.

Dinamo Minsk (1) 4 *(Korytko 41, Adamovic 58, Beqiraj 86, 90)*
Cherno More (0) 0　　　　　　　　　　2616
Dinamo Minsk: (442) Gutor; Vitus, Politevich, Rassadkin, Korytko (Voronkov 88); Bangura, Korzun, Beqiraj, Begunov; El Monir (Neacsa 58), Adamovic (Bykov 63).
Cherno More: (442) Canovic; Venkov, Stanchev, Coulibaly, Klok (Georgiev 46); Raykov, Burkhardt (Stenio 46), Coureur, Bijev (Vasev 65); Bourabia, Palankov*.

Gabala (1) 2 *(Zenjov 39, 53)*
Cukaricki Belgrade (0) 0　　　　　　　8500
Gabala: (442) Bezotosnyi; Stankovic, Sadiqov, Zenjov, Huseynov; Gai, Ricardinho, Abbasov, Rafael Santos; Zargarov (Dashdemirov 70), Antonov (Dodo 90).
Cukaricki Belgrade: (442) Stevanovic; Piasentin, Srnic D (Obeng 55), Jankovic B (Matic 76), Stoiljkovic; Pavlovic, Srnic S (Mandic 81), Stojkovic, Ostojic; Bojic, Brezancic.

Hajduk Split (2) 4 *(Kis 2, Jefferson 40, Caktas 62, Maglica 69)*
Koper (1) 1 *(Palcic 45)*　　　　　　　22,800
Hajduk Split: (442) Kalinic; Milovic, Jefferson, Vlasic, Caktas; Nizic, Pejic, Tudor, Kis (Maglica 69); Roguljic (Maloku 53), Balic (Susic 77).
Koper: (442) Simcic; Sme (Pucko 71), Guberac, Rahmanovic (Radujko 77), Ivancic; Galesic, Halilovic, Crnigoj, Hadzic; Tomic (Vekic 81), Palcic.

IFK Gothenburg (0) 2 *(Engvall 55, Boman 59)*
Slask Wroclaw (0) 0　　　　　　　　10,823
IFK Gothenburg: (442) Alvbage; Aleesami, Rogne, Bjarsmyr, Salomonsson; Rieks, Eriksson, Svensson, Ankersen; Boman (Smedberg-Dalence 79), Engvall (Pettersson 87).
Slask Wroclaw: (442) Pawalek; Zielinski (Machaj 88), Celeban, Kokoszka, Dudu Paraiba; Paixao (Gecov 76), Holota, Hateley, Pich; Kielb, Grajciar (Bilinski 68).

Inter Baku (1) 2 *(Huseynov 45, Aliyev 91)*
Hafnarfjordur (0) 2 *(Valdimarsson 47, Kristjan Floki Finnbogason 52)*　　　　3500
Inter Baku: (442) Agayev; Juanfran, Kasradze, Kvekveskiri, Haciyev; Aliyev, Khizanishvili, Seyidov (Poljak 72), Martins (Abbasov 55); Bayramov, Huseynov (Qirtimov 87).

Hafnarfjordur: (442) Finnbogason K; Tillen (Bodvarsson 78), Vidarsson P, Palsson, Valdimarsson; Vidarsson D, Gudnason (Gudmundsson 97), Vidarsson B (Finnbogason KF* 38), Doumbia; Serwy, Hendrickx.
aet.

Linfield (1) 1 *(Lowry 34)*
Spartak Trnava (0) 3 *(Sabo 54, 84, Vojtus 60)*　3001
Linfield: (442) Ross Glendinning; Reece Glendinning, Haughey (Ward 76), Hegarty, Clarke M; Sproule (Clarke R 63), Kee, Lowry, Burns; Bates, Waterworth.
Spartak Trnava: (442) Jakubech; Toth, Bortel*, Gressak, Conka; Mikovic, Sabo, Jose Casado, Halilovic (Baez 76); Harba (Mikinic 70), Vojtus (Jirka 88).

Mladost Podgorica (0) 2 *(Scepanovic 62, Adzovic 87)*
Kukesi (3) 4 *(Moreira 13, Pejic 19, 72, Flores Bonfim 32)*　　　　　　　　　　　4500
Mladost Podgorica: (442) Mileta Radulovic; Pejovic, Lagator (Mirkovic 70), Raicevic, Djurisic; Novovic, Lakic, Vukovic, Milos M Radulovic (Muhovic 57); Milos B Radulovic (Adzovic 80), Scepanovic.
Kukesi: (442) Stajila; Muca, Mici, Flores Bonfim, Hallaci; Hasani (Musolli 73), Moreira (Birungueta 60), Jean Carioca, Pejic (Granado 79); Malota, Jefferson.

Newtown (0) 1 *(Goodwin 70)*
FC Copenhagen (2) 3 *(Pourie 28, 51, Jorgensen N 40 (pen))*　　　　　　　　1400
Newtown: (4141) Jones; Williams, Sutton, Mills-Evans, Edwards; Goodwin (Cook 73); Hearsey (Harris 82), Boundford, Mitchell, Owen (Price 73); Oswell.
FC Copenhagen: (442) Andersen; Ankersen, Jorgensen M, Nilsson, Augustinsson; Kusk (Henriksen 65), Delaney, Toutouh (Hogli 46), Verbic; Jorgensen N (Remmer 46), Pourie.

Nomme Kalju (0) 0
Vaduz (0) 2 *(Caballero 59, Aliji 74)*　　1030
Nomme Kalju: (442) Teles; Barengrub, Rodrigues, Dmitrijev (Voskoboinikov 74), Purje; Kimbaloula, Puri (Neemelo 63), Kallaste, Lindpere (Topic 72); Mool, Wakui.
Vaduz: (442) Klaus; Grippo, Sutter, Cecchini, Von Niederhausern (Ciccone 62); Stahel, Neumayr (Kukuruzovic 71), Muntwiler, Buhler; Caballero, Kamber (Aliji 62).

Odd (0) 2 *(Halvorsen 72, Hagen 86)*
Shamrock R (0) 1 *(Brennan G 90)*　　3814
Odd: (451) Rossbach; Ruud, Eriksen (Bergan 78), Hagen, Jonassen; Halvorsen, Berg, Gashi, Nordkvelle (Samuelsen 62), Zehninki; Bentley (Occean 46).
Shamrock R: (433) Hyland; Madden, Kenna, Webster, Byrne; Brennan R, Cregg (Kavanagh C 67), McCabe; Brennan G, Miele (North 79), Drennan.

Omonia Nicosia (1) 1 *(Sheridan 8)*
Jagiellonia Bialystock (0) 0　　　　17,481
Omonia Nicosia: (442) Panagi; Lobjanidze, Sheridan, Bebe (Fofana 56), Cristovao; Nuno Assis, Economides, Schembri (Kirm 84), Margaca; Runje, Goulon (Fylaktou 79).
Jagiellonia Bialystock: (442) Dragowski; Modelski, Romanchuk (Swiderski 75), Madera, Tuszynski; Dzalamidze (Grzelczak 46), Tarasovs, Gajos, Frankowski (Sekulski 62); Grzyb, Tomasik.

PAOK Salonika (4) 6 *(Lucas Perez 3, Mak 7, 84, Pelkas 14, Kitsiou 34, Andrijasevic 60 (og))*
Lokomotiva Zagreb (0) 0　　　　　11,923
PAOK Salonika: (442) Olsen; Miguel Vitor, Ricardo Costa, Tzavelas, Kitsiou; Tziolis (Maduro 46), Mak, Kace, Pelkas; Lucas Perez (Mystakidis 82), Koulouris (Rat 60).
Lokomotiva Zagreb: (442) Zelenika; Bartolec, Brucic, Mrcela, Prenga (Misic 25); Sovsic, Begonja, Kolar, Andrijasevic; Leko (Dolezak 46), Maric (Capan 56).

Rabotnicki (2) 2 *(Ilijoski 6, Sahiti 17)*
Jelgava (0) 0 2300
Rabotnicki: (442) Bozinovski; Sahiti, Vujcic, Anene (Trajcevski 68), Ilijoski (Markoshi 90); Siljanovski, Ristevski, Petrovic, Altiparmakovski (Jovanovski 86); Cikarski, Ilievski.
Jelgava: (442) Ikstens; Freimanis, Redjko, Sosranovs, Latka; Bogdaskins, Diallo, Gubins (Kirilins 60), Oss; Kluskins (Jaudzems 84), Sushkin (Malasenoks 79).

Rosenborg (3) 3 *(Midtsjoe 4, Helland 7, Soderlund 18)*
KR Reykjavik (0) 0 6371
Rosenborg: (442) Andre Hansen; Dorsin, Eyjolfsson, Jensen, Skjelvik; Selnaes (Riski 37), Helland (Nielsen 72), Midtsjoe, Svensson; Mikkelsen, Soderlund (Helmersen 79).
KR Reykjavik: (442) Magnusson S; Christiansen, Fridgeirsson, Gunnarsson, Josepsson; Saevarsson (Sigurdsson 46), Palmason, Ormarsson, Hauksson (Balbi 61); Martin, Fridjonsson (Magnusson K 46).

Shirak (0) 0
AIK Solna (2) 2 *(Goitom 14, Ishizaki 25)* 2820
Shirak: (442) Yermakov; Mikaelyan, Stamenkovic, Hovanisian, Davtyan; Hakobyan (Ayvazyan 58), Aleksanyan (Kaba 70), Malakyan E, Davoyan; Diarrassouba, Bougouhi (Muradyan 76).
AIK Solna: (442) Stamatopoulos; Karlsson (Pereira 13), Johansson, Hauksson, Sundberg; Blomberg, Ofori, Etuhu (Saletros 59), Ishizaki; Brustad (Eliasson 46), Goitom.

Spartaks Jurmala (0) 0 *(Vivacqua 90)*
Vojvodina (0) 1 *(Kordic 86)* 650
Spartaks Jurmala: (442) Davidovs; Maksymenko, Nazarenko, Mezs, Ulimbashevs; Bespalovs (Punculs 54), Vivacqua, Takyi (Stuglis 71), Bulvitis; Abdultaofik (Mickevics 46), Šlampe.
Vojvodina: (442) Zakula; Ivanic (Palocevic 69), Stanisavljevic (Stamenic 73), Pankov, Lakicevic; Nastic, Babic, Djuric, Sekulic; Maksimovic, Ozegovic (Kordic 80).

Stromsgodset (0) 0
Mlada Boleslav (1) 1 *(Cermak 31)* 4371
Stromsgodset: (442) Pettersen; Madsen, Hanin, Abu, Valsvik; Moen (Ovenstad 70), Fossum, Storflor (Kastrati 86), Wikheim; Sorum (Olsen 69), Thomas.
Mlada Boleslav: (442) Veselovsky; Boril, Krapka, Cermak (Scuk 79), Kudela; Zahustel, Rada, Kysela, Malpon (Chramostra 77); Magera, Klobasa (Skalak 67).

Thun (1) 2 *(Ferreira 40, 72)*
Hapoel Beer Sheva (1) 1 *(Ogu 6)* 4017
Thun: (4141) Faivre; Glarner (Schirinzi 60), Reinmann, Sulmoni, Wittwer; Hediger; Rojas (Burki 90), Frontino (Munsy 85), Zino, Ferreira; Rapp.
Hapoel Beer Sheva: (4411) Goresh; Bitton, William Soares, Tzedek■, Davidadze; Melikson (Nwakaeme 83), Radi, Ogu, Buzaglo; Hoban (Sahar 75); Barda (Taha 39).

Trakai (0) 0
Apollon Limassol (0) 0 930
Trakai: (442) Rapalis; Klimavicius, Cesnauskis, Arshakiyan, Solomin (Gaurilovas 75); Janusevskis, Silenas, Zasavitchi (Stanulevicius 78), Bychenok; Mamaev, Segzda (Apakidze 59).
Apollon Limassol: (442) Bruno Vale; Elizio, Freire, Sachetti, Gullon (Alex 63); Rosa (Thuram 73), Jaime, Joao Paulo, Stojanovic; Stylianou, Kolokoudias (Josephides 87).

University College Dublin (0) 1 *(Swan 57)*
Slovan Bratislava (1) 5 *(Vittek 41, 90, 90, Milinkovic 49, Salata 81)* 1361
University College Dublin: (433) Corbet; Leahy, Kougun, Boyle, Langtry; Watts (Cannon 56), O'Neill, Benson; Mulhall (Belhout 88), Swan, Doyle (Kirwan 76).
Slovan Bratislava: (4411) Mucha; Sekulic, Dobrotka (Hudak 69), Salata, Podany; Milinkovic (Gasparovic 83), Stefanik, Lasik, Kubik (Orsula 67); Zrelak; Vittek.

Wolfsburger (1) 2 *(Sollbauer 19, Hellqvist 90)*
Shakhtyor Soligorsk (0) 0 6400
Wolfsburger: (4231) Kofler; Berger, Sollbauer, Drescher (Huttenbrenner 59), Palla; Weber (Tschernegg 45), Putsche; Zundel (Wernitznig 85), Silvio, Jacobo; Hellqvist.
Shakhtyor Soligorsk: (442) Bushma; Matsveychyk (Covic 82), Kuzmyanok, Rybak, Yanushkevich; Kovalev (Afanasyev 65), Yurevich, Starhorodskyi, Martynyuk (Vergeychik 52); Komarovski, Yanush.

Zeljeznicar Sarajevo (1) 2 *(Kokot 23, Delmic 90)*
Ferencvaros (0) 0 16,000
Zeljeznicar Sarajevo: (442) Antolovic; Kosoric, Memija, Bogdanovic, Kvesic; Blagojevic, Hadziahmetovic (Sadikovic E 57), Sadikovic D (Beganovic 72), Delmic; Bajic, Kokot (Stokic 86).
Ferencvaros: (433) Dibusz; Leandro, Nalepa, Dilaver, Hajnal (Sestak 46); Gyomber, Bode (Busai 58), Gera; Lamah, Somalia, Varga (Rado 41).

Zilina (1) 4 *(Vavro 15, Kacer 50, Skvarka 62, Paur 85)*
Dacia (0) 2 *(Cociuc 64, Leuca 87)* 3856
Zilina: (442) Volesak; Skriniar, Kacer, Jelic, Pecovsky; Cmelik (Paur 73), Vavro, Skvarka (Benes 66), Letic; Mihalik (Spalek 81), Mabouka.
Dacia: (442) Gaiduchevici; Rosca, Posmac, Frunza (Gavrylenko 55), Lozoviy■; Mihaliov, Mani (Leuca 55), Cociuc, Pidnebennoy (Pavlov 55); Zastavnyi, Mamah.

THIRD QUALIFYING ROUND FIRST LEG

Wednesday, 29 July 2015
Jablonec (0) 0
FC Copenhagen (0) 1 *(Verbic 51)* 4830
Jablonec: (451) Hruby; Karavaev, Pernica, Benes, Novak; Masopust (Tecl■ 62), Pospisil (Travnik 63), Hubschman, Gregus, Crnkic; Wagner (Dolezal 77).
FC Copenhagen: (442) Andersen; Ankersen, Jorgensen M, Antonsson, Augustinsson; Toutouh (Kvist Jorgensen 63), Amartey, Delaney, Verbic (Kusk 81); Santander (Pourie 88), Jorgensen N.

Thursday, 30 July 2015
AIK Solna (0) 1 *(Goitom 70 (pen))*
Atromitos (2) 3 *(Napoleoni 3, Marcelinho 15, Umbides 80 (pen))* 9771
AIK Solna: (442) Carlgren; Pavey, Sundberg■, Johansson, Pereira; Blomberg (Eliasson 57), Ofori, Etuhu, Ishizaki; Bangura, Brustad (Goitom 57).
Atromitos: (4231) Gorbunov; Kivrakidis, Fitanidis, Lazaridis, Bittolo; Usero, Godoy; Umbides, Pitu (M'Bow 75), Marcelinho (Brito 85); Napoleoni (Ballas 90).

Apollon Limassol (1) 1 *(Kolokoudias 14)*
Gabala (0) 1 *(Huseynov 90 (pen))* 4540
Apollon Limassol: (442) Bruno Vale; Elizio, Nuno Lopes, Freire, Jaime; Sachetti, Gullon, Alex (Thuram 76), Pedro Silva (Stylianou 89); Papoulis, Kolokoudias (Guie Guie 63).
Gabala: (442) Bezotosnyi; Stankovic, Ricardinho, Abbasov (Dashdemirov 85), Rafael Santos; Sadiqov, Huseynov, Gai, Zargarov (Dodo 35); Zenjov, Antonov (Zec 76).

Athletic Bilbao (1) 2 *(Eraso 12, 49)*
Inter Baku (0) 0 32,823
Athletic Bilbao: (442) Herrerin; Etxeita, Gurpegi, Balenziaga, Eraso; Benat, Iturraspe (Elustondo 46), De Marcos, Susaeta (Viguera 81); Ibai (Aketxe 70), Aduriz.
Inter Baku: (442) Agayev; Juanfran (Huseynov 46), Kasradze, Denis Silva, Khizanishvili; Qirtimov (Abatsiyev 87), Kvekveskiri, Haciyev, Poljak (Fomenko 46); Bayramov, Aliyev.

AZ Alkmaar (1) 2 *(van der Linden 17 (pen), Janssen 63)*
Istanbul Basaksehir (0) 0 11,723
AZ Alkmaar: (442) Rochet; Johansson, Gouweleeuw, van der Linden, Haps; Haye, Ortiz, Henriksen, dos Santos Souza (Muhren 86); van Overeem (Johannsson 46), Janssen (Tankovic 74).
Istanbul Basaksehir: (433) Babacan■; Ucar, Ayhan, Cansev (Emre 65), Oztorun; Badji, Mossoro (Ceylan 16), Tekdemir; Visca, Cikalleshi, Doka Madureira (Alkilic 77).

Belenenses (2) 2 *(Carlos Martins 23, 41)*
IFK Gothenburg (0) 1 *(Aleesami 58)*   5671
Belenenses: (442) Hugo Ventura; Andre Geraldes, Tonel, Brandao, Andre Teixeira; Miguel Rosa, Andre Sousa (Ricardo Dias 67), Joao Meira, Fabio Sturgeon; Carlos Martins (Tiago Silva 87), Abel Camara (Fabio Nunes 67).
IFK Gothenburg: (442) Alvbage; Aleesami, Eriksson, Rogne, Bjarsmyr; Salomonsson, Smedberg-Dalence (Ankersen 46), Svensson, Rieks; Boman (Pettersson 72), Engvall (Skold 81).

Bordeaux (0) 3 *(Biyogo Poko 53, Diabate 74 (pen), Maurice-Belay 80)*
AEK Larnaca (0) 0   30,174
Bordeaux: (433) Carasso; Guilbert, Sertic, Pallois, Poundje; Chantome, Biyogo Poko, Saivet; Toure (Maulun 84), Diabate (Thelin 89), Khazri (Maurice-Belay 65).
AEK Larnaca: (4411) Ramirez; Mintikkis, Ninu, Catala, Marciniak; Monteiro, Boljevic, Larena (Ortiz 57), Tete (Kante 90); Tomas; Dos Santos (Mitidis 69).

Brondby (0) 0
Omonia Nicosia (0) 0   7427
Brondby: (451) Hradecky; Larsson, Dumic, Albrechtsen (Johansen 43), Durmisi; Eriksson (Hjulsager 81), Holst, Phiri, Elmander (Schwartz 62), Rashani; Pukki.
Omonia Nicosia: (451) Panagi; Cristovao, Runje, Lobjanidze, Margaca; Fofana (Fylaktou 75), Nuno Assis, Economides, Bebe (Roushias 89), Schembri (Kirm 61); Sheridan.

Charleroi (0) 0
Zorya Luhansk (0) 2 *(Malinovsky 70, 89)*   9415
Charleroi: (433) Penneteau; Dewaest, Martos, Marinos, N'Ganga; Marcq, Saglik, Ndongala (Ferber 79); Kebano, Stevance (Galvez-Lopez 74), Pollet.
Zorya Luhansk: (442) Shevchenko M; Gordienko (Ljubenovic 63), Opanasenko, Pylyavskyi, Kamenyuka; Khomchenovskiy, Sivakov, Chaykovsky (Grenchyskin 81), Malinovsky; Karavayev (Petryak 78), Budkivsky.

Debrecen (1) 2 *(Balogh 33, Bodi 90)*
Rosenborg (0) 3 *(Mikkelsen 52, 87, Helland 58)*   10,532
Debrecen: (442) Verpecz; Mate, Brkovic, Korhut, Jovanovic; Bodi, Varga, Szakaly (Zsidai 84), Balogh; Sidibe (Castillon 64), Tisza (Mihelic 84).
Rosenborg: (442) Andre Hansen; Dorsin, Eyjolfsson, Jensen, Skjelvik; Selnaes, Midtsjoe, Helland (de Lanlay 73), Svensson; Mikkelsen (Riski 90), Soderlund (Vilhjalmsson 80).

Elfsborg (1) 2 *(Prodell 43, Lundevall 76)*
Odd (1) 1 *(Occean 21 (pen))*   4232
Elfsborg: (442) Stuhr-Ellegaard; Lundqvist, Holmen, Svensson, Klarstrom; Zeneli, Hauger, Rohden, Hedlund (Lundevall 69); Claesson (Nilsson 87), Prodell (Frick 80).
Odd: (451) Rossbach; Ruud, Eriksen, Hagen, Grogaard; Halvorsen, Samuelsen, Jensen, Nordkvelle (Berg 43), Diouf (Bentley 68); Occean.

FC Zurich (0) 0
Dinamo Minsk (0) 1 *(Beqiraj 63 (pen))*   3587
FC Zurich: (442) Brecher; Djimsiti, Nef, Koch, Kleiber (Brunner 12); Chermiti (Gavranovic 66), Buff, Cabral, Schneuwly; Sadiku, Chiumiento (Chikhaoui 46).
Dinamo Minsk: (424) Gutor; Begunov, Politevich, Bangura, Veretilo; Adamovic (Vitus 90), Korzun; Korytko (Neacsa 75), El Monir (Tigorev 55), Rassadkin, Beqiraj.

Hajduk Split (0) 2 *(Balic 67, Kis 90)*
Stromsgodset (0) 0   28,000
Hajduk Split: (442) Kalinic; Pejic, Nizic, Milovic, Tudor; Caktas, Jefferson, Balic (Susic 74), Roguljic (Maloku 61); Ohandza (Kis 78), Vlasic.
Stromsgodset: (433) Pettersen; Vilsvik, Madsen, Valsvik, Hamoud; Ovenstad (Moen 82), Abu, Fossum; Kastrati (Jradi 72), Olsen (Sorum 66), Wikheim.

Kairat Almaty (2) 2 *(Bakaev 13, Islamkhan 22)*
Aberdeen (0) 1 *(McLean 68)*   23,500
Kairat Almaty: (451) Plotnikov; Bruno, Gorman (Serginho 79), Markovic, Kuantayev; Bakaev, Islamkhan, Isael, Tymoschuk, Lunin; Despotovic (Konysbayev 67).
Aberdeen: (451) Ward; Logan, Shinnie, Considine, Taylor; Quinn (Robson 84), Hayes, Pawlett (Rooney 45), Jack, McGinn; Goodwillie (McLean 64).

Krasnodar (1) 2 *(Granqvist 45, Mamaev 59 (pen))*
Slovan Bratislava (0) 0   10,420
Krasnodar: (451) Dykan; Jedrzejczyk, Sigurdsson, Granqvist, Kaleshin; Smolov (Laborde 62), Mamaev (Ahmedov 68), Gazinski (Strandberg 81), Pereyra, Wanderson; Ari.
Slovan Bratislava: (4411) Mucha; Kotula, Hudak, Salata, Podany; Meszaros (Orsula 60), Sekulic, Gonzalez (Stefanik 80), Zrelak (Kubik 73); Milinkovic; Vittek.

Kukesi (1) 1
Legia Warsaw (1) 2   5000
Match abandoned due to crowd distuburbance – Legia Warsaw awarded a 3-0 win.

PAOK Salonika (0) 1 *(Lucas Perez 82)*
Spartak Trnava (0) 0   12,427
PAOK Salonika: (442) Olsen; Miguel Vitor■, Ricardo Costa, Tzavelas, Kitsiou; Tziolis (Savvidis 73), Mak (Mystakidis 78), Kace, Pelkas; Koulouris (Skondras 5), Lucas Perez.
Spartak Trnava: (442) Kamenar; Nikolic, Janecka, Toth, Gressak; Mikovic (Steinhubel 21), Jose Casado, Sabo, Halilovic (Baez 86); Mikinic, Vojtus (Harba 74).

Rabotnicki (1) 1 *(Ilijoski 23)*
Trabzonspor (0) 0   6200
Rabotnicki: (4411) Bozinovski; Cikarski, Ilievski, Ristevski, Siljanovski; Anene, Petrovic, Vujcic, Sahiti (Mitrov 85); Ilijoski (Trajcevski 63); Altiparmakovski (Markoshi 82).
Trabzonspor: (4231) Cakir; Dursun, Yumlu, Demir (Yokuslu 75), Uludag; Medjani, Constant; Yilmaz S (Hurmaci 62), Waris (Zengin 80), Erdogan; Cardozo.

Sampdoria (0) 0
Vojvodina (1) 4 *(Ivanic 4, Stanisavljevic 49, Ozegovic 58, 90)*   4200
Sampdoria: (433) Viviano; Cassani, Palombo (Regini 59), Silvestre, Zukanovic; Barreto, Fernando, Soriano; Eder, Muriel (Bonazzoli 73), Krsticic (Wszolek 59).
Vojvodina: (433) Zakula; Vasilic, Pankov, Djuric, Nastic; Sekulic, Maksimovic, Ivanic (Babic 87); Stanisavljevic (Stamenic 85), Ozegovic, Puskaric (Palocevic 71).

SCR Altach (1) 2 *(Ngwat-Mahop 24, Aigner 50 (pen))*
Vitoria (0) 1 *(Toze 71)*   3267
SCR Altach: (442) Lukse; Zech, Lienhart, Zwischenbrugger, Cesar; Netzer, Luxbacher, Prokopic (Jager 90), Aigner (Harrer 78); Seeger (Barrera 78), Ngwat-Mahop.
Vitoria: (442) Douglas; Luis Rocha, Joao Afonso, Arrondel, Moreno; Cafu, Bruno Alves, Montoya (Toze 52), Ricardo Valente (Henrique 70); Tomane, Alex (Lica 90).

Slovan Liberec (1) 2 *(Delarge 43, Shala 84)*
Hapoel Kiryat Shmona (0) 1 *(Abed 89)*   5400
Slovan Liberec: (424) Koubek; Bartosak, Svejdik, Hovorka, Coufal; Sackey, Pavelka; Sural, Rabusic (Bakos 73), Kerbr (Shala 53), Delarge (Fleisman 86).
Hapoel Kiryat Shmona: (4411) Haimov; Elkayami, Gutierrez, Kassio, Borchal; Abed, Brown, Shukrani (Rochet 51), Bruno Cantanhede; Ostvind (Mizrachi 75); Exbard (Chukwuma 46).

Southampton (2) 3 *(Pelle 37, Tadic 45 (pen), Long 84)*
Vitesse (0) 0   30,850
Southampton: (433) Stekelenburg; Targett, Cedric Soares, Yoshida, Fonte; Clasie (Juanmi 62), Wanyama, Davis S; Mane (Reed 85), Pelle, Tadic (Long 62).

Vitesse: (433) Room; Diks (Lelieveld 90), Leerdam, Kashia, Achenteh; Nakamba, Baker, Kazaishvili (Pantic 67); Brown, Djurdjevic (Rashica 61), Oliynyk.

Standard Liege (2) 2 *(Kosoric 16 (og), Knockaert 28)*
Zeljeznicar Sarajevo (0) 1 *(Delmic 64)*   11,608
Standard Liege: (433) Thuram-Ulien; Milec, Scholz, Van Damme, Faty; Knockaert (Yattara 85), De Sart J (de Sart A 54), Enoh; Trebel, Badibanga (Kasami 67), Santini.
Zeljeznicar Sarajevo: (442) Antolovic; Kosoric, Bogdanovic, Memija, Mladenovic; Blagojevic, Hadziahmetovic (Sadikovic E 90), Sadikovic D (Diatta 90), Delmic; Kokot (Beganovic 78), Bajic.

Sturm Graz (1) 2 *(Avdijaj 21, Piesinger 56)*
Rubin Kazan (2) 3 *(Kanunnikov 14, Karadeniz 25, Portnyagin 61)*   9765
Sturm Graz: (4411) Esser; Klem, Kamavuaka, Madl, Ehrenreich; Dobras, Piesinger, Hadzic (Horvath 75), Schick (Gruber 68); Avdijaj■; Tadic (Kienast 63).
Rubin Kazan: (4411) Ryzhikov; Kuzmin, Kvirkvelia, Cotugno, Nabiullin; Bilyaletdinov (Kislyak 66), Kambolov (Portnyagin 46), Ozdoev, Karadeniz; Carlos Eduardo; Kanunnikov (Georgiev 46).

Targu Mures (0) 0
Saint-Etienne (1) 3 *(Diomande 24, Hamouma 75, 83)* 6498
Targu Mures: (442) Stancioiu; Balic, Gonzalez, Bejan, Muresan (Costa 67); Golanski, Jazvic, Brandan (Pedro 61), Gorobsov; N'Doye, Axente (Manolov 79).
Saint-Etienne: (442) Ruffier; Theophile-Catherine, Assou-Ekotto (Brison 61), Pogba, Perrin; Bayal Sall, Clement, Diomande, Gradel; Hamouma, Roux (Mollo 74).

Thun (0) 0
Vaduz (0) 0   3407
Thun: (4411) Faivre; Schirinzi, Reinmann, Sulmoni, Wittwer; Rojas (Munsy 89), Hediger, Wieser, Ferreira; Frontino (Buess 56); Rapp.
Vaduz: (352) Klaus; Von Niederhausern, Pergl, Grippo; Cecchini (Messaoud 72), Muntwiler, Aliji, Ciccone, Kukuruzovic; Costanzo (Kamber 78), Caballero (Neumayr 66).

West Ham U (1) 2 *(Valencia 23, Zarate 51)*
Astra Giurgiu (0) 2 *(Boldrin 71, Ogbonna 82 (og))* 33,858
West Ham U: (433) Adrian; Cresswell, Kouyate, Collins■, Ogbonna; Oxford, Noble, O'Brien (Burke 35); Valencia (Maiga 37), Zarate (Jarvis 76), Payet.
Astra Giurgiu: (4231) Lung Jr; Geraldo Alves, Junior Morais, Gaman, Pedro Queiros; Seto, Enache; Boldrin (Dandea 86), Teixeira, William Amorim (Florea 76); Budescu (Lovin 90).

Wolfsburger (0) 0
Borussia Dortmund (1) 1 *(Hofmann 14)*   30,250
Wolfsburger: (451) Kofler; Berger, Sollbauer, Huttenbrenner, Palla; Zundel, Seidl, Standfest (Tschernegg 90), Putsche (Trdina 70), Wernitznig (Jacobo 81); Silvio.
Borussia Dortmund: (4231) Burki; Piszczek, Papastathopoulos, Hummels, Schmelzer; Gundogan, Weigl (Castro 66); Hofmann (Kagawa 66), Mkhitaryan, Reus (Kampl 79); Aubameyang.

Zilina (1) 2 *(Jelic 26, Paur 73)*
Vorskla (0) 0   4757
Zilina: (451) Volesak; Mabouka (Spalek 20), Vavro, Skriniar, Letic; Paur, Benes (Skvarka 90), Pecovsky, Kacer, Mihalik (Willian 83); Jelic.
Vorskla: (424) Bogush■; Sapai, Dallku, Tkachuk Y, Siminin; Tursunov, Sklyar (Tkachuk A 85); Chesnakov, Gromov (Bartulovic 77), Shynder, Kovpak (Barannik 80).

THIRD QUALIFYING ROUND SECOND LEG

Thursday, 6 August 2015

Aberdeen (0) 1 *(McLean 84)*
Kairat Almaty (0) 1 *(Gohou 59)*   20,317
Aberdeen: (442) Ward; Logan, Taylor, Considine, Shinnie; Pawlett (Rooney 68), Jack, McLean, Hayes (Flood 81); McGinn, Goodwillie (Quinn 81).
Kairat Almaty: (442) Plotnikov; Markovic, Bruno, Gorman, Kuantayev; Isael (Serginho 82), Bakaev, Tymoschuk, Islamkhan; Lunin (Kuat 90), Gohou (Despotovic 73).

AEK Larnaca (0) 0
Bordeaux (1) 1 *(Thelin 29)*   2500
AEK Larnaca: (442) Ramirez; Catala, Ortiz■, Ninu, Charalambous (Dos Santos 75); Tete, Boljevic, Monteiro (Kante 84), Tomas; Mitidis, Laban.
Bordeaux: (442) Carrasso; Gajic, Contento, Yambere (Biyogo Poko 78), Pallois; Traore (Sertic 63), Chantome■, Maulun, Thelin; Maurice-Belay, Khazri (Toure 54).

Astra Giurgiu (2) 2 *(Budescu 32, 36)*
West Ham U (1) 1 *(Lanzini 3)*   6300
Astra Giurgiu: (4231) Lung Jr; Pedro Queiros, Gaman, Geraldo Alves (Oros 19), Junior Morais; Seto, Boldrin; Enache, Teixeira (Alibec 67), William Amorim; Budescu (Lovin 83).
West Ham U: (442) Randolph; Knoyle, Jenkinson, Henry, Page (Pike 90); Lanzini, Cullen, Poyet, Nolan; Lee (Brown 80), Maiga.

Atromitos (0) 1 *(Marcelinho 67)*
AIK Solna (0) 0   2587
Atromitos: (4321) Gorbunov; Bittolo, Lazaridis, Fitanidis, Kivrakidis; Usero, Godoy, Marcelinho; Pitu (Brito 75), Umbides (Limnios 90); Napoleoni (Le Tallec 85).
AIK Solna: (442) Carlgren; Hauksson, Etuhu, Johansson, Pereira (Blomberg 11); Pavey, Saletros, Ishizaki, Eliasson (Bangura 46); Brustad (Nikolic 79), Goitom.

Borussia Dortmund (0) 5 *(Reus 48, Aubameyang 64, Mkhitaryan 73, 82, 86)*
Wolfsburger (0) 0   65,190
Borussia Dortmund: (442) Weidenfeller; Hummels, Papastathopoulos, Piszczek, Schmelzer; Weigl, Gundogan (Bender 77), Reus (Hofmann 77), Kagawa (Castro 65); Mkhitaryan, Aubameyang.
Wolfsburger: (442) Kofler; Palla, Berger, Standfest (Tschernegg 85), Sollbauer; Weber, Wernitznig (Zulj 75), Jacobo, Huttenbrenner; Putsche (Trdina 67), Silvio.

Dinamo Minsk (0) 1 *(Beqiraj 118)*
FC Zurich (1) 1 *(Buff 4)*   9437
Dinamo Minsk: (442) Gutor; Politevich, Veretilo, Begunov, Korytko (Voronkov 102); Bangura, Korzun, Tigorev (Neacsa 36), Adamovic (El Monir 81); Rassadkin, Beqiraj.
FC Zurich: (4411) Brecher; Djimsiti, Nef, Koch, Cabral; Schneuwly (Simonyan 102), Buff (Sadiku 73), Kukeli, Grgic; Gavranovic (Sarr 110); Chermiti.
aet.

FC Copenhagen (0) 2 *(Jorgensen N 72, Santander 88)*
Jablonec (1) 3 *(Wagner 14, Gregus 53, Pospisil 83)* 14,142
FC Copenhagen: (442) Andersen (Nilsson 86); Augustinsson, Jorgensen M, Antonsson, Ankersen; Verbic■, Delaney, Amartey, Kvist Jorgensen (Kusk 61); Jorgensen N, Santander.
Jablonec: (4141) Hruby; Karavaev, Pernica, Benes, Novak; Hubschman; Masopust (Mingazov 72), Pospisil, Gregus, Crnkic (Rossi 88); Wagner (Dolezal 82).
Jablonec won on away goals.

Gabala (0) 1 *(Huseynov 80 (pen))*
Apollon Limassol (0) 0   9500
Gabala: (442) Bezotosnyi; Stankovic, Abbasov■, Rafael Santos, Sadiqov; Huseynov, Dashdemirov, Gai, Dodo; Zenjov, Antonov (Zec 71).
Apollon Limassol: (442) Bruno Vale; Elizio, Nuno Lopes (Thuram 61), Freire, Jaime (Rosa 81); Sachetti, Gullon, Alex, Joao Pedro; Papoulis, Kolokoudias (Guie Guie 61).

Hapoel Kiryat Shmona (0) 0
Slovan Liberec (2) 3 *(Pavelka 33, Sural 44, Bakos 52)*
1200
Hapoel Kiryat Shmona: (451) Haimov; Borchal, Kassio, Gutierrez, Elkayami; Ostvind (Mizrachi 54), Brown (Shamir 61), Rochet (Shukrani 78), Abed, Chukwuma; Bruno Cantanhede.
Slovan Liberec: (433) Koubek; Coufal, Hovorka, Bartosak, Pokorny; Pavelka, Shala (Kerbr 82), Folprecht; Delarge (Sackey 76), Sural, Bakos (Rabusic 80).

IFK Gothenburg (0) 0
Belenenses (0) 0 12,976
IFK Gothenburg: (442) Alvbage; Aleesami, Rogne, Bjarsmyr, Salomonsson; Ankersen, Eriksson (Pettersson 75), Rieks, Svensson; Boman (Smedberg-Dalence 75), Engvall.
Belenenses: (442) Hugo Ventura; Joao Amorim, Tonel, Andre Geraldes, Brandao; Ruben Pinto, Miguel Rosa (Dalcio 68), Andre Sousa, Carlos Martins (Tiago Silva 78); Fabio Sturgeon, Abel Camara (Joao Afonso 89).

Inter Baku (0) 0
Athletic Bilbao (0) 0 4000
Inter Baku: (442) Agayev; Kasradze, Denis Silva, Khizanishvili, Qirtimov; Kvekveskiri, Haciyev (Abatsiyev 76), Seyidov, Bayramov; Aliyev, Martins (Fomenko 77).
Athletic Bilbao: (442) Herrerin; Laporte, San Jose, Etxeita, Balenziaga; Eraso (Sabin 67), Benat (Elustondo 90), Susaeta (Ibai 86), Aketxe; De Marcos, Aduriz.

Istanbul Basaksehir (1) 1 *(Doka Madureira 45)*
AZ Alkmaar (1) 2 *(Henriksen 21, van Overeem 75)* 5289
Istanbul Basaksehir: (442) Ceylan; Ucar (Alkilic 46), Ayhan, Cansev, Oztorun; Visca, Mossoro (Batdal 74), Emre (Tekdemir 64), Badji; Doka Madureira, Cikalleshi.
AZ Alkmaar: (451) Rochet; Johansson, Gouweleeuw, van der Linden, Haps; van Overeem (Hupperts 86), Henriksen, Ortiz, Haye, dos Santos Souza (Vaarnold 78); Janssen (Muhren 68).

Legia Warsaw (0) 1 *(Kucharczyk 47)*
Kukesi (0) 0 11,847
Legia Warsaw: (352) Kuciak; Pazdan (Makowski 61), Lewczuk, Rzezniczak; Brzyski, Bereszynski, Duda, Zyro (Guilherme 45), Furman; Kucharczyk (Bartczak 68), Prijovic.
Kukesi: (442) Koci; Mici, Hallaci, Malota, Hasani (Halili 50); Birungueta, Moreira (Qafa 90), Jean Carioca (Shameti 83), Musolli; Flores Bonfim, Muca.

Odd (1) 2 *(Occean 27, Bentley 71)*
Elfsborg (0) 0 6106
Odd: (433) Rossbach; Ruud, Eriksen, Hagen, Grogaard; Samuelsen (Gashi 82), Jensen, Nordkvelle (Berg 84); Bentley, Diouf (Halvorsen 46), Occean.
Elfsborg: (442) Stuhr-Ellegaard; Klarstrom (Lans 46), Svensson, Holmen, Lundqvist; Hedlund (Frick 79), Rohden, Hauger, Zeneli; Claesson, Prodell (Nilsson 78).

Omonia Nicosia (2) 2 *(Sheridan 15 (pen), 45 (pen))*
Brondby (2) 2 *(Pukki 2, 39)* 6106
Omonia Nicosia: (442) Panagi; Lobjanidze, Runje, Bebe, Nuno Assis; Economides (Fylaktou 82), Margaca, Fofana (Roushias 69), Demetriou (Mendy 90); Sheridan, Schembri.
Brondby: (433) Hradecky■; Albrechtsen, Holst, Larsson, Durmisi; Dumic, Da Silva (Johansen 84), Ornskov Nielsen; Pukki (Rashani 90), Eriksson, Elmander (Phiri 56).
Brondby won on away goals.

Rosenborg (2) 3 *(Soderlund 27, Jensen 40, Vilhjalmsson 86)*
Debrecen (1) 1 *(Castillon 43)* 12,919
Rosenborg: (433) Andre Hansen; Svensson, Bjordal, Eyjolfsson, Skjelvik; Jensen (Solli 90), Selnaes, Midtsjoe (Saeter 82); Helland, Mikkelsen, Soderlund (Vilhjalmsson 77).
Debrecen: (433) Verpecz; Jovanovic, Meszaros, Mate■, Korhut; Bodi, Varga, Tisza (Morozov 52); Balogh (Zsidai 62), Castillon, Sidibe (Mihelic 77).

Rubin Kazan (0) 1 *(Kuzmin 85)*
Sturm Graz (0) 1 *(Tadic 68)* 9346
Rubin Kazan: (442) Ryzhikov; Kuzmin, Kvirkvelia, Lemos, Nabiullin (Batov 79); Kambolov, Georgiev, Ozdoev, Karadeniz (Cotugno 89); Portnyagin, Dyadyun (Kanunnikov 60).
Sturm Graz: (361) Esser; Spendlhofer, Madl, Lykogiannis (Ehrenreich 45); Potzmann, Kamavuaka, Offenbacher, Dobras (Kienast 80), Schick, Schmerbock (Edomwonyi 46); Tadic.

Saint-Etienne (0) 1 *(Gonzalez 72 (og))*
Targu Mures (1) 2 *(Pedro 39, Gonzalez 62)* 27,284
Saint-Etienne: (442) Ruffier; Pogba, Clerc (Theophile-Catherine 77), Brison, Perrin; Bayal Sall, Clement, Diomande (Lemoine 67), Mollo; Roux, Monnet-Paquet (Hamouma 55).
Targu Mures: (442) Stancioiu; Velayos, Balic, Gonzalez, Muresan; Golanski, Hanca (Jazvic 61), Gorobsov, Pedro (Costa 72); Jurado (Brandan 46), Axente.

Slovan Bratislava (0) 3 *(Vittek 54, 60, 77)*
Krasnodar (2) 3 *(Mamaev 8 (pen), 11, Smolov 90)* 2852
Slovan Bratislava: (442) Mucha; Sekulic, Hudak, Gorosito, Salata; Podany, Gonzalez (Stefanik 81), Milinkovic, Peltier (Meszaros 46); Kubik (Orsula 74), Vittek.
Krasnodar: (442) Dykan; Jedrzejczyk, Granqvist, Sigurdsson, Mamaev (Torbinski 46); Gazinski (Strandberg 64), Ahmedov, Laborde (Wanderson 78), Petrov; Ari, Smolov.

Spartak Trnava (1) 1 *(Sabo 35 (pen))*
PAOK Salonika (0) 1 *(Konstantinidis 48)* 3555
Spartak Trnava: (442) Kamenar; Nikolic, Janecka, Bortel, Toth; Gressak, Mikovic, Jose Casado (Baez 79), Sabo; Halilovic (Mikinic 79), Vojtus (Harba 62).
PAOK Salonika: (442) Olsen; Skondras■, Ricardo Costa, Korovesis, Konstantinidis; Tzavelas, Tziolis, Mak, Kace (Savvidis 81); Mystakidis (Koulouris 57 (Poungouras 69)), Pelkas.

Stromsgodset (0) 0
Hajduk Split (0) 2 *(Caktas 55, Ohandza 77)* 5330
Stromsgodset: (433) Pettersen; Vilsvik, Hoibraten, Valsvik, Hanin (Hamoud 30); Jradi (Storflor 61), Abu, Fossum; Kastrati, Olsen (Sorum 72), Wikheim.
Hajduk Split: (4411) Kalinic; Tudor, Nizic■, Milovic, Pejic; Balic (Juranovic 70), Jefferson, Caktas (Susic 83), Maloku; Vlasic; Ohandza (Maglica 80).

Trabzonspor (0) 1 *(Yokuslu 55)*
Rabotnicki (0) 1 *(Markoshi 112)* 13,704
Trabzonspor: (4231) Kivrak; Cavanda, Yumlu, Medjani, Constant; Yokuslu (Kara 86), Mbia; Erdogan (Yilmaz S 105), Hurmaci (Yilmaz D 77), Zengin; Cardozo.
Rabotnicki: (433) Bozinovski; Siljanovski, Ristevski, Ilievski, Cikarski; Petrovic, Trajcevski■, Vujcic; Sahiti (Altiparmakovski 61), Ilijoski (Mitrov 74), Anene (Markoshi 90).
aet.

Vaduz (2) 2 *(Costanzo 32, Neumayr 45)*
Thun (1) 2 *(Rojas 38, Buess 65)* 2788
Vaduz: (442) Klaus; Grippo, Pergl, Buhler, Aliji; Ciccone, Messaoud (Cecchini 77), Neumayr, Kukuruzovic; Kamber (Hasler 69), Costanzo.
Thun: (442) Faivre; Burki, Sulmoni, Reinmann, Schirinzi; Wittwer, Wieser, Frontino (Sutter 80), Rojas; Hediger, Buess.
Thun won on away goals.

Vitesse (0) 0
Southampton (1) 2 *(Pelle 4, Mane 89)* 20,515
Vitesse: (442) Room; Van der Werff (Achenteh 73), Leerdam, Diks, Kashia; Kazaishvili, Nakamba, Baker (Pantic 81), Brown (Nathan 69); Oliynyk, Rashica.
Southampton: (442) Stekelenburg; Yoshida, Fonte, Martina, Caulker; Davis S (Reed 78), Wanyama, Ward-Prowse, Tadic (Juanmi 65); Pelle (Rodriguez 72), Mane.

Vitoria (0) 1 *(Tomane 67)*
SCR Altach (1) 4 *(Netzer 31, Bruno Alves 59 (og),*
Prokopic 63, Lienhart 90)   20,181
Vitoria: (442) Douglas; Luis Rocha (Tomane 59), Joao Afonso, Pedro Correia■, Moreno; Cafu, Bruno Alves (Otavio 46), Toze, Lica (Ricardo Valente 69); Alex, Henrique.
SCR Altach: (442) Lukse; Lienhart, Zwischenbrugger, Cesar, Jager; Netzer (Roth 63), Luxbacher (Hofbauer 86), Zech, Prokopic; Seeger (Aigner 67), Ngwat-Mahop.

Vojvodina (0) 0
Sampdoria (1) 2 *(Eder 15, Muriel 70)*   10,763
Vojvodina: (442) Zakula; Vasilic, Pankov, Nastic, Djuric; Ivanic (Babic 90), Stanisavljevic (Lakicevic 87), Puskaric (Palocevic 78), Sekulic; Maksimovic, Ozegovic.
Sampdoria: (442) Viviano; Cassani, Coda, Silvestre, Zukanovic; Fernando, Barreto, Krsticic (Ivan 79), Soriano (Wszolek 85); Eder, Muriel (Bonazzoli 72).

Vorskla (0) 3 *(Shynder 67, Tkachuk Y 90,*
Tursunov 101 (pen))
Zilina (0) 1 *(Willian 120)*   12,500
Vorskla: (4411) Nepogodov; Sapai, Tkachuk Y, Dallku, Siminin (Perduta 46); Tursunov, Tkachuk A, Sklyar (Mishchenko 87), Bartulovic (Barannik 60); Kovpak; Shynder.
Zilina: (451) Volesak; Spalek■, Vavro, Skriniar, Letic (Hucko 118); Paur, Benes (Skvarka 73), Pecovsky, Kacer, Mihalik (Willian 78); Jelic.
aet; Zilina won on away goals.

Zeljeznicar Sarajevo (0) 0
Standard Liege (0) 1 *(Van Damme 68)*   19,721
Zeljeznicar Sarajevo: (442) Antolovic; Kosoric, Bogdanovic, Memija, Mladenovic; Blagojevic, Hadziahmetovic (Sadikovic E 60), Sadikovic D (Beganovic 66), Delmic; Kokot (Stokic 76), Bajic.
Standard Liege: (442) Thuram-Ulien; El Messaouoi (De Sart J 59), Teixeira, Milec, Van Damme; Faty, Knockaert, Enoh, Trebel; Badibanga (Andrade 79), Santini (Yattara 70).

Zorya Luhansk (0) 3 *(Ljubenovic 57, 68 (pen),*
Malinovsky 90)
Charleroi (0) 0   4000
Zorya Luhansk: (4411) Shevchenko M; Kamenyuka, Pylyavskyi, Sivakov, Opanasenko; Khomchenovskiy, Gordienko, Chaykovsky (Ljubenovic 46), Karavayev (Grenchyskin 59); Malinovsky; Budkivskiy (Petryak 70).
Charleroi: (4411) Penneteau; Marinos, Dewaest, Willems, Boulenger (N'Ganga 57); Saglik, Marcq, Geraerts (Stevance 63), Ferber (Ndongala 42); Kebano; Pollet.

PLAY-OFF ROUND FIRST LEG

Thursday, 20 August 2015

Ajax (0) 1 *(Milik 54)*
Jablonec (0) 0   30,898
Ajax: (433) Cillessen; Tete, Veltman, Riedewald, Dijks; Bazoer, Klaassen, Gudelj; El Ghazi (Cerny 85), Sinkgraven (Schone 71), Milik.
Jablonec: (451) Hruby; Karavaev, Pernica, Novak, Benes; Gregus, Hubschman, Crnkic, Mingazov (Masopust 67); Pospisil (Travnik 72); Wagner (Dolezal 84).

Astra Giurgiu (3) 3 *(Boldrin 26, Alibec 42, Dandea 45)*
AZ Alkmaar (2) 2 *(Henriksen 12, Janssen 14)*   3712
Astra Giurgiu: (4231) Lung Jr; Pedro Queiros, Gaman, Oros, Junior Morais; Lovin, Boldrin (Dandea 36); Enache, Budescu, William Amorim (Stan 84); Alibec (Florea 68).
AZ Alkmaar: (4231) Rochet; Johansson, Gouweleeuw, van der Linden, Haps; Luckassen, Ortiz (Haye 66); Hupperts (Lewis 46), Henriksen, van Overeem; Janssen (Muhren 79).

Atromitos (0) 0
Fenerbahce (0) 1 *(van Persie 90)*   3328
Atromitos: (4231) Gorbunov; Kivrakidis, Fitanidis, Lazaridis, Bittolo; Godoy, Usero (M'Bow 90); Umbides, Pitu (Le Tallec 85), Marcelinho (Brito 76); Napoleoni.
Fenerbahce: (424) Demirel; Ozbayrakli, Ba, Bruno Alves, Erkin; Souza, Meireles (Topal 71); Nani (Sen 89), Fernandao, Sow (van Persie 80), Diego.

Bordeaux (1) 1 *(Khazri 27)*
Kairat Almaty (0) 0   24,795
Bordeaux: (442) Prior; Contento (Poundje 14), Pallois, Yambere, Guilbert; Traore (Maurice-Belay 71), Biyogo Poko, Khazri, Rolan (Crivelli 85); Saivet, Thelin.
Kairat Almaty: (442) Plotnikov; Bruno, Gorman, Kuantayev, Kuat; Bakaev, Islamkhan (Serginho 68), Isael, Tymoschuk (Rudosselskiy 90); Gohou, Sito Riera (Despotovic 83).

Dinamo Minsk (0) 2 *(Rassadkin 57, Adamovic 90)*
Red Bull Salzburg (0) 0   9952
Dinamo Minsk: (442) Gutor; Begunov, Politevich, Bangura, Vitus; Udoji (Adamovic 53), Korzun, Korytko, Neacsa (El Monir 70); Beqiraj, Rassadkin (Voronkov 90).
Red Bull Salzburg: (442) Walke; Schwegler, Paulo Miranda, Caleta-Car, Ulmer; Berisha, Keita, Leitgeb, Minamino (Lazaro 74); Reyna, Oberlin (Atanga 59).

Gabala (0) 0
Panathinaikos (0) 0   10,950
Gabala: (4231) Bezotosnyi; Dashdemirov, Stankovic, Rafael Santos, Ricardinho; Gai, Sadiqov; Zenjov, Zec (Zargarov 58), Dodo; Antonov (Mammadov 90).
Panathinaikos: (4411) Steele; Wemmer, Tavlaridis, Koutroubis, Nano; Lod (Ajagun 67), Zeca, Pranjic, Kaltsas (Lagos 76); Petric; Karelis (Berg 58).

Krasnodar (2) 5 *(Ojala 8 (og), Mamaev 10 (pen),*
Smolov 57 (pen), Wanderson 62, Gazinski 64)
HJK Helsinki (1) 1 *(Jallow 18)*   15,425
Krasnodar: (451) Dykan; Petrov, Granqvist, Sigurdsson, Kaleshin; Mamaev, Gazinski, Strandberg, Ahmedov (Ari 58), Bystrov (Wanderson 58); Smolov (Torbinski 74).
HJK Helsinki: (4411) Orlund; Peiponen, Ojala, Heikkinen, Baah (Heikkila 60); Mendy (Malolo 84), Moussi, Schuller, Zeneli; Tanaka (Kolehmainen 22); Jallow.

Lech Poznan (1) 3 *(Linetty 11, Thomalla 57, Tralka 68)*
Videoton (0) 0   14,133
Lech Poznan: (442) Buric; Kaminski, Douglas, Kedziora, Dudka; Tralka, Linetty, Hamalainen (Formella 83), Pawlowski; Lovrencsics (Robak 79 (Holman 89)), Thomalla.
Videoton: (442) Danilovic; Vinicius, Fejes, Lang, Szolnoki; Patkai (Trebotic 71), Simon, Oliveira, Ivanovski; Soumah (Kovacs 57), Gyurcso (Sejben 89).

Milsami (0) 1 *(Bud 57)*
Saint-Etienne (1) 1 *(Hamouma 40)*   6072
Milsami: (442) Mitu; Rhaili, Erhan (Gheti 64), Racu, Shedrack; Rassulov (Bolohan 73), Patras, Belak (Zarichnyuk 69), Banovic; Cojocari, Bud.
Saint-Etienne: (442) Ruffier; Assou-Ekotto, Theophile-Catherine, Pogba, Bayal Sall; Corgnet (Bamba 80), Lemoine, Hamouma■, Diomande; Bahebeck (Monnet-Paquet 62), Roux (Brison 87).

Molde (2) 2 *(Hoiland 24, Elyounoussi 28)*
Standard Liege (0) 0   3940
Molde: (451) Horvath; Linnes, Gabrielsen, Toivio, Flo; Mostrom, Singh, Hestad D, Hestad E (Svendsen 80), Elyounoussi; Hoiland (Simonsen 90).
Standard Liege: (4321) Thuram-Ulien; Milec (Yattara 46), Faty, Teixeira, Van Damme; Andrade, Enoh, Knockaert; Trebel, El Messaouoi (de Sart A 52); Santini (Badibanga 65).

Odd (3) 3 *(Samuelsen 2, Nordkvelle 20, Ruud 22)*
Borussia Dortmund (1) 4 *(Aubameyang 34, 76,
Kagawa 47, Mkhitaryan 85)*   12,436
Odd: (442) Rossbach; Ruud, Bergan, Grogaard, Hagen;
Samuelsen (Berg 57), Nordkvelle, Jensen, Occean (Flo
77); Zehninki, Bentley (Halvorsen 65).
Borussia Dortmund: (442) Weidenfeller; Hummels,
Ginter, Schmelzer, Castro (Papastathopoulos 46); Bender
(Weigl 68), Gundogan, Mkhitaryan, Kagawa; Kampl
(Ramos 63), Aubameyang.

PAOK Salonika (2) 5 *(Mak 17, 80, 83, Pelkas 36,
Rodrigues 51)*
Brøndby (0) 0   20,106
PAOK Salonika: (352) Olsen; Malezas, Ricardo Costa,
Miguel Vitor; Tziolis, Kace, Konstantinidis, Pelkas
(Savvidis 66), Kitsiou; Rodrigues (Mystakidis 71), Mak.
Brøndby: (433) Ronnow; Larsson, Albrechtsen, Agger,
Durmisi; Holst (Dumic 42), Ornskov Nielsen, Phiri;
Eriksson, Elmander (Schwartz 58), Pukki.

Rabotnicki (0) 1 *(Ristevski 85)*
Rubin Kazan (0) 1 *(Karadeniz 69)*   10,000
Rabotnicki: (433) Bozinovski (Siskovski 90); Cikarski,
Ilievski, Ristevski, Siljanovski; Jovanovski (Ristovski 70),
Vujcic, Petrovic■; Altiparmakovski, Anene (Nastevski
86), Markoshi.
Rubin Kazan: (4231) Ryzhikov; Cotugno, Kvirkvelia,
Kambolov, Kuzmin; Georgiev, Ozdoev; Bilyaletdinov
(Portnyagin 58), Carlos Eduardo (Kislyak 81), Karadeniz
(Batov 72); Kanunnikov.

SCR Altach (0) 0
Belenenses (1) 1 *(Tiago Caeiro 13)*   4572
SCR Altach: (424) Lukse; Lienhart, Cesar,
Zwischenbrugger, Zech; Netzer, Prokopic; Ngwat-
Mahop, Aigner (Harrer 72), Seeger (Barrera 80),
Salomon (Hofbauer 65).
Belenenses: (433) Hugo Ventura; Andre Geraldes,
Brandao, Tonel, Joao Amorim; Fabio Sturgeon, Andre
Sousa (Ricardo Dias 64), Miguel Rosa; Tiago Silva
(Fabio Nunes 77), Tiago Caeiro (Abel Camara 66),
Ruben Pinto.

Slovan Liberec (0) 1 *(Pokorny 79)*
Hajduk Split (0) 0   8530
Slovan Liberec: (451) Koubek; Bartosak, Pokorny,
Hovorka, Coufal; Folprecht, Delarge (Kerbr 90), Shala
(Sackey 79), Sural, Bakos (Rabusic 62); Pavelka.
Hajduk Split: (451) Kalinic; Juranovic, Milovic, Bilyi,
Milic; Jefferson, Susic, Balic (Maloku 66), Ohandza,
Caktas; Vlasic.

Southampton (0) 1 *(Rodriguez 56 (pen))*
Midtjylland (1) 1 *(Sparv 45)*   28,890
Southampton: (433) Stekelenburg; Fonte, Caulker,
Targett, Yoshida; Ward-Prowse (Juanmi 83), Wanyama,
Romeu; Pelle, Mane, Rodriguez (Long 76).
Midtjylland: (4132) Dahlin; Romer, Hansen,
Sviatchenko, Lauridsen; Sparv; Sisto (Hassan 71),
Poulsen, Royer; Andersson (Olsson 78), Rasmussen
(Onuachu 89).

Sparta Prague (2) 3 *(Nhamoinesu 43, Dockal 45, 90)*
Thun (1) 1 *(Sutter 5)*   12,448
Sparta Prague: (442) Bicik; Marecek, Holek,
Nhamoinesu, Hybs; Dockal, Vacha (Frydek 29),
Husbauer (Konate 55), Krejci; Fatai, Lafata.
Thun: (451) Faivre; Bigler, Sulmoni, Reinmann, Wittwer;
Rapp (Munsy 82), Frontino, Hediger, Ferreira, Sutter;
Buess (Zarate 56).

Steaua Bucharest (0) 0
Rosenborg (0) 3 *(Mikkelsen 61, Helland 67, Jensen 90)*
                                                    21,204
Steaua Bucharest: (4231) Cojocaru; Alcenat (Iancu 75),
Papp, Tosca, Guilherme; Sully, Sulley (Tahar 68); Popa,
Hamroun (Stanciu 46), Chipciu; Tade.
Rosenborg: (4141) Andre Hansen; Svensson, Bjordal,
Eyjolfsson, Skjelvik; Selnaes; Helland (de Lanlay 76),
Jensen, Midtsjoe, Mikkelsen; Soderlund.

Viktoria Plzen (1) 3 *(Kopic 25, 82, Vanek 51)*
Vojvodina (0) 0   10,769
Viktoria Plzen: (442) Kozacik; Hubnik, Limbersky,
Prochazka, Rajtoral; Vanek, Kopic, Hrosovsky, Kovarik
(Petrzela 78); Kolar (Horava 69), Duris (Holenda 86).
Vojvodina: (442) Zakula; Vasilic, Pankov, Nastic, Djuric;
Ivanic, Stanisavljevic (Babic 88), Puskaric (Palocevic 68),
Sekulic; Maksimovic, Ozegovic (Pavkov 88).

Young Boys (0) 0
Qarabag (0) 1 *(Almeida 67)*   6700
Young Boys: (442) Mvogo; Vilotic, von Bergen, Lecjaks,
Sutter; Bertone (Zakaria 80), Gajic, Nuzzolo (Gonzalez
69), Kubo (Tabakovic 85); Sulejmani, Hoarau.
Qarabag: (442) Sehic; Sadygov, Guseynov, Garayev,
Agolli; Quintana (Diniyev 75), Gurbanov, Almeida, El
Jadeyaoui (Yunuszadze 87); Tagiyev (Ismayilov 80),
Reynaldo.

Zilina (0) 3 *(Paur 66, Willian 77, 90)*
Athletic Bilbao (2) 2 *(Sabin 16, Kike Sola 33)* 10,175
Zilina: (451) Volesak; Mabouka (Willian 57), Vavro,
Skriniar, Letic; Paur, Kacer, Pecovsky, Benes (Skvarka
88), Cmelik (Mihalik 72); Jelic.
Athletic Bilbao: (451) Herrerin; Boveda, Gurpegi,
Laporte, Lekue; Sabin (Williams 74 (De Marcos 82)),
Mikel Rico (Benat 70), Aketxe, Elustondo, Ibai; Kike
Sola.

Zorya Luhansk (0) 0
Legia Warsaw (0) 1 *(Kucharczyk 48)*   16,000
Zorya Luhansk: (4231) Shevchenko M; Opanasenko,
Checher, Sivakov, Kamenyuka; Karavayev (Lipartia 70),
Gordienko; Chaykovsky, Petryak, Malinovsky;
Budkivskiy.
Legia Warsaw: (442) Kuciak; Pazdan, Jodlowiec, Brzyski,
Bereszynski; Rzezniczak, Guilherme, Furman, Nikolic
(Saganowski 89); Kucharczyk, Prijovic (Duda 75).

PLAY-OFF ROUND SECOND LEG

Thursday, 27 August 2015
Athletic Bilbao (1) 1 *(Elustondo 24)*
Zilina (0) 0   38,688
Athletic Bilbao: (4231) Herrerin; De Marcos, Gurpegi,
Laporte, Lekue; Elustondo, Benat; Susaeta (Mikel Rico
85), Eraso (Aketxe 73), Viguera (Sabin 57); Aduriz.
Zilina: (451) Volesak; Mabouka (Mihalik 81), Vavro,
Skriniar, Mazan; Paur, Kacer (Spalek 88), Pecovsky,
Benes, Jelic (Cmelik 67); Willian.
Athletic Bilbao won on away goals.

AZ Alkmaar (0) 2 *(van der Linden 80, Muhren 85)*
Astra Giurgiu (0) 0   9679
AZ Alkmaar: (433) Rochet; Johansson, Gouweleeuw,
van der Linden, Haps; Luckassen (Tankovic 78),
Henriksen, Haye; Hupperts, Janssen (Muhren 78), dos
Santos Souza (Wuytens 89).
Astra Giurgiu: (433) Lung Jr; Pedro Queiros, Gaman,
Oros, Junior Morais; Dandea, Enache (Ionita II 83),
Lovin (Florea 84); Budescu, Alibec (Boldrin 62), William
Amorim.

Belenenses (0) 0
SCR Altach (0) 0   5940
Belenenses: (442) Hugo Ventura; Joao Amorim,
Brandao, Tonel, Andre Geraldes; Miguel Rosa, Andre
Sousa, Ruben Pinto (Ricardo Dias 90), Fabio Sturgeon;
Tiago Caeiro (Joao Afonso 87), Abel Camara (Tiago
Silva 69).
SCR Altach: (4141) Lukse; Lienhart, Cesar (Harrer 83),
Zwischenbrugger, Zech; Pollhuber; Ngwat-Mahop,
Netzer (Roth 64), Prokopic, Salomon (Aigner 57);
Seeger.

Borussia Dortmund (4) 7 *(Mkhitaryan 25, Reus 27, 32, 57, Kagawa 40, 90, Gundogan 51)*
Odd (1) 2 *(Halvorsen 19, Berg 64)* 64,200

Borussia Dortmund: (4141) Weidenfeller; Ginter, Hummels, Papastathopoulos (Piszczek 64), Schmelzer; Weigl; Hofmann, Kagawa, Gundogan (Bender 66), Mkhitaryan (Aubameyang 64); Reus.
Odd: (4141) Rossbach; Hurme, Bergan, Hagen, Grogaard; Jensen; Halvorsen, Nordkvelle (Gashi 65), Berg, Zehnnki (Bentley 76); Occean (Flo 46).

Brondby (1) 1 *(Rashani 27)*
PAOK Salonika (1) 1 *(Ricardo Costa 21)* 6630

Brondby: (451) Ronnow; Larsson, Ornskov Nielsen, Albrechtsen, Durmisi; Hjulsager, Norgaard, Phiri (Holst 81), Eriksson (Pukki 72), Rashani; Schwartz (Elmander 60).
PAOK Salonika: (4411) Glykos; Miguel Vitor, Tzavelas, Ricardo Costa, Konstantinidis (Savvidis 64); Kitsiou, Kace, Tziolis (Mak 64), Mystakidis; Koulouris (Deligiannidis 76); Rodrigues.

Fenerbahce (1) 3 *(Fernandao 7, 78, Erkin 59)*
Atromitos (0) 0 33,121

Fenerbahce: (433) Demirel; Ozbayrakli, Kjaer, Ba, Erkin; Souza, Topal (Sen 77), Diego (Meireles 67); van Persie (Potuk 67), Fernandao, Nani.
Atromitos: (4411) Gorbunov; Kivrakidis, Fitanidis, Lazaridis, Bittolo (Kouros 82); Umbides, Godoy (Ballas 62), Usero, Marcelinho; Napoleoni; Pitu (Le Tallec 62).

Hajduk Split (0) 0
Slovan Liberec (1) 1 *(Sural 23)* 33,000

Hajduk Split: (4141) Kalinic; Milic, Nizic, Milovic, Tudor (Juranovic 73); Jefferson; Vlasic, Balic (Maloku 34), Caktas (Roguljic 49), Susic; Ohandza.
Slovan Liberec: (451) Koubek; Coufal, Hovorka, Pokorny, Bartosak; Sural, Pavelka, Sackey (Fleisman 75), Shala (Soungole 63), Delarge (Kerbr 49); Bakos.

HJK Helsinki (0) 0
Krasnodar (0) 0 2953

HJK Helsinki: (4411) Dahne; Peiponen, Heikkila, Ojala (Heikkinen 64), Lehtinen; Mendy, Moussi, Schuller, Zeneli, Klinga (Lingman 77); Jallow (Tanaka 68).
Krasnodar: (433) Dykan; Kaleshin (Jedrzejczyk 70), Sigurdsson, Granqvist, Petrov; Torbinski, Strandberg, Ahmedov; Wanderson (Laborde 67), Ari (Smolov 75), Markov.

Jablonec (0) 0
Ajax (0) 0 6040

Jablonec: (4141) Hruby; Karavaev, Pernica, Benes, Novak; Hubschman; Mingazov, Gregus (Travnik 75), Pospisil, Crnkic (Dolezal 68); Wagner (Tecl 46).
Ajax: (433) Cillessen; Tete, Veltman, Riedewald, Dijks; Bazoer[a], Klaassen, Gudelj; El Ghazi, Milik (Van Rhijn 69), Sinkgraven (Fischer 46).

Kairat Almaty (1) 2 *(Yambere 1 (og), Kuat 66)*
Bordeaux (0) 1 *(Crivelli 76)* 23,800

Kairat Almaty: (4231) Plotnikov; Kuat, Bruno, Markovic, Kuantayev (Kukeev 87); Bakaev, Tymoschuk; Sito Riera, Isael, Islamkhan (Despotovic 83); Gohou.
Bordeaux: (4231) Prior; Guilbert, Traore (Maurice-Belay 69), Pallois, Poundje; Biyogo Poko, Yambere; Khazri, Saivet, Rolan (Crivelli 69); Thelin.
·*Bordeaux won on away goals.*

Legia Warsaw (1) 3 *(Rzezniczak 16, Guilherme 62, Duda 90 (pen))*
Zorya Luhansk (1) 2 *(Khomchenovskiy 39, Ljubenovic 66)* 23,163

Legia Warsaw: (442) Kuciak; Bereszynski, Rzezniczak, Pazdan (Lewczuk 7), Brzyski; Guilherme, Jodlowiec, Furman, Kucharczyk; Prijovic (Saganowski 90), Nikolic (Duda 67).
Zorya Luhansk: (4231) Shevchenko M; Opanasenko, Sivakov, Pylyavskyi (Checher 83), Kamenyuka; Gordienko, Ljubenovic (Lipartia 87); Karavayev, Malinovsky, Khomchenovskiy (Budkivsky 58); Petryak.

Midtjylland (1) 1 *(Rasmussen 28)*
Southampton (0) 0 9481

Midtjylland: (4141) Dahlin; Bak Nielsen (Romer 83), Hansen, Sviatchenko, Lauridsen; Sparv; Royer, Poulsen, Andersson (Pusic 80), Sisto (Hassan 68); Rasmussen.
Southampton: (4312) Stekelenburg; Yoshida, Fonte, Caulker (Tadic 56), Targett; Ward-Prowse, Martina, Romeu; Davis S (Juanmi 82); Pelle, Rodriguez (Long 75).

Panathinaikos (1) 2 *(Berg 34, Nano 78)*
Gabala (1) 2 *(Dodo 6, 60)* 13,956

Panathinaikos: (4312) Steele; Bourbos (Lagos 77), Sergio Sanchez, Tavlaridis, Nano; Zeca, Koutroubis, Pranjic (Petric 66); Ninis; Berg, Karelis (Klonaridis 67).
Gabala: (4231) Bezotosnyi; Dashdemirov, Vernydub, Stankovic, Ricardinho; Gai, Sadiqov; Zenjov, Antonov, Dodo; Zec (Jamalov 86).
Gabala won on away goals.

Qarabag (2) 3 *(Almeida 4 (pen), Reynaldo 43, Ismayilov 61)*
Young Boys (0) 0 29,620

Qarabag: (4231) Sehic; Gurbanov, Guseynov, Sadygov, Agolli; Garayev (Mustafayev 85), Almeida; Ismayilov (Poepon 71), Quintana, Tagiyev (Diniyev 78); Reynaldo.
Young Boys: (4231) Mvogo; Sutter, Vilotic, von Bergen[a], Hadergjonaj; Gonzalez, Kubo (Gajic 80); Bertone, Sulejmani (Nuzzolo 65), Zakaria; Hoarau (Affum 54).

Red Bull Salzburg (1) 2 *(Minamino 11, Soriano 58)*
Dinamo Minsk (0) 0 7849

Red Bull Salzburg: (442) Walke; Lainer, Caleta-Car, Hinteregger, Ulmer (Sorensen 106); Reyna (Atanga 77), Schmitz, Leitgeb (Schwegler 91), Minamino; Berisha, Soriano.
Dinamo Minsk: (442) Gutor; Begunov, Politevich, Bangura, Vitus; Adamovic, Korytko, Voronkov (Veretilo 77), Neacsa (Premudrov 84); Beqiraj, Rassadkin (El Monir 62).
aet; Dinamo Minsk won 3-2 on penalties.

Rosenborg (0) 0
Steaua Bucharest (0) 1 *(Popa 54)* 14,640

Rosenborg: (433) Andre Hansen; Midtsjoe, Bjordal, Eyjolfsson, Svensson; Jensen, Selnaes (Vilhjalmsson 29), Konradsen; Helland, Soderlund, Mikkelsen.
Steaua Bucharest: (4411) Nita; Alcenat (Papp 46), Varela, Tosca, Guilherme; Popa, Filip (Enceanu 75), Sulley, Chipciu; Stanciu; Iancu (Tade 46).

Rubin Kazan (1) 1 *(Carlos Eduardo 35)*
Rabotnicki (0) 0 4231

Rubin Kazan: (4411) Ryzhikov; Cotugno, Lemos, Kvirkvelia, Kuzmin; Bilyaletdinov, Ozdoev, Georgiev, Kanunnikov; Carlos Eduardo (Portnyagin 79); Dyadyun (Batov 90).
Rabotnicki: (424) Bozinovski; Cikarski, Ilievski, Vujcic, Siljanovski; Trajcevski (Jovanovski 87), Ristevski, Sahiti (Markoshi 46), Altiparmakovski, Ilijoski, Anene.

Saint-Etienne (1) 1 *(Corgnet 15)*
Milsami (0) 0 22,456

Saint-Etienne: (4411) Ruffier; Assou-Ekotto, Perrin, Bayal Sall, Theophile-Catherine; Monnet-Paquet (Polomat 89), Lemoine, Clement, Corgnet (Bamba 63); Eysseric; Roux (Maupay 74).
Milsami: (532) Mitu; Gheti, Racu, Rhaili, Erhan, Patras; Antoniuc, Cojocari, Banovic (Slivca 78); Belak (Zarichnyuk 62), Bud (Bolohan 70).

Standard Liege (1) 3 *(Knockaert 26, Santini 48, Trebel 90)*
Molde (1) 1 *(Hussain 42)* 12,568

Standard Liege: (442) Thuram-Ulien; Andrade, Faty, Fiore, Van Damme; Bruls (Legear 74), Enoh, Trebel, Knockaert; Santini, Yattara.
Molde: (451) Horvath; Linnes, Gabrielsen, Forren, Flo; Mostrom (Toivio 70), Hussain, Hestad D, Singh, Elyounoussi; Kamara (Hoiland 77).
Molde won on away goals.

Thun (1) 3 *(Ferreira 33, 81, Munsy 50)*
Sparta Prague (2) 3 *(Dockal 10, Husbauer 21,*
Nhamoinesu 71)   6024
Thun: (451) Faivre; Wittwer, Schindelholz, Sulmoni, Bigler; Rojas (Schirinzi 46), Frontino (Munsy 46), Zino (Zarate 55), Hediger, Rapp; Ferreira.
Sparta Prague: (4411) Bicik; Steinhofer, Holek, Nhamoinesu, Hybs (Breznanik[■] 68); Dockal, Frydek, Marecek, Krejci; Husbauer (Litsingi 27); Lafata (Fatai 82).

Videoton (0) 0
Lech Poznan (0) 1 *(Kedziora 57)*   2815
Videoton: (4411) Danilovic; Szolnoki, Juhasz, Vinicius, Fejes; Koltai (Gyurcso 58), Luyckx (Simon 57), Trebotic, Ivanovski; Kovacs; Feczesin (Rudolf 70).
Lech Poznan: (4231) Buric; Kedziora, Kaminski, Kadar, Douglas; Tralka, Dudka; Formella, Hamalainen (Holman 72), Pawlowski (Lovrencsics 74); Thomalla (Kurbiel 81).

Vojvodina (0) 0
Viktoria Plzen (1) 2 *(Djuric 19 (og), Duris 60)*   7617
Vojvodina: (4411) Zakula; Vasilic, Djuric, Pekaric, Nastic (Radovic 66); Palocevic, Maksimovic, Sekulic, Babic; Ivanic (Stamenic 80); Ozegovic.
Viktoria Plzen: (4411) Kozacik; Rajtoral, Hubnik (Baranek 54), Prochazka, Limbersky; Petrzela (Vuch 72), Hrosovsky, Vanek, Kopic; Kolar (Mahmutovic 81); Duris.

GROUP STAGE

GROUP A

Thursday, 17 September 2015
Ajax (1) 2 *(Fischer 25, Schone 84)*
Celtic (2) 2 *(Bitton 8, Lustig 42)*   47,455
Ajax: (433) Cillessen; Tete, Veltman, Riedewald, Dijks; Gudelj, Fischer (Schone 75), Sinkgraven (Serero 63); El Ghazi, Younes (Milik 62), Klaassen.
Celtic: (4141) Gordon; Lustig (Ambrose 68), Simunovic, Boyata, Izaguirre[■]; Johansen; Brown, Bitton, Forrest (Blackett 75), Commons (Janko 83); Griffiths.

Fenerbahce (1) 1 *(Nani 41)*
Molde (1) 3 *(Hoiland 37 (pen), Elyounoussi 52,*
Linnes 64)   35,500
Fenerbahce: (451) Fabiano; Ozbayrakli, Bruno Alves, Kadlec, Erkin; Sen, Tufan, Topal (Fernandao 57); Meireles (Zeybek 68), Nani; van Persie (Potuk 68).
Molde: (451) Horvath; Linnes, Gabrielsen, Forren, Rindaroy; Mostrom (Toivio 88), Singh, Hestad D, Hestad E (Hussain 81), Elyounoussi[■]; Hoiland (Kamara 66).

Thursday, 1 October 2015
Celtic (2) 2 *(Griffiths 28, Commons 32)*
Fenerbahce (1) 2 *(Fernandao 43, 48)*   41,330
Celtic: (451) Gordon; Lustig, Boyata, Ambrose, Tierney (Blackett 82); Commons, Brown, Bitton, Forrest (Armstrong 90), Johansen (Rogic 82); Griffiths.
Fenerbahce: (433) Fabiano; Ozbayrakli, Kjaer, Bruno Alves, Kaldirim; Sen (Fernandao 40), Tufan (Diego 46), Topal; Meireles (Ba 78), Nani, van Persie.

Molde (1) 1 *(Hestad E 7)*
Ajax (1) 1 *(Fischer 18)*   7890
Molde: (442) Horvath; Linnes (Toivio 61), Gabrielsen, Forren, Rindaroy; Mostrom, Singh, Hestad D, Hussain; Hestad E (Svendsen 59), Hoiland (Kamara 80).
Ajax: (433) Cillessen; Tete, Veltman, Riedewald, Dijks; Bazoer (Serero 89), Klaassen, Gudelj; El Ghazi, Milik (Younes 81), Fischer.

Thursday, 22 October 2015
Fenerbahce (0) 1 *(Fernandao 89)*
Ajax (0) 0   47,000
Fenerbahce: (4231) Fabiano; Gonul, Kjaer, Ba, Erkin; Topal, Souza; Markovic (Potuk 84), Diego (Tufan 72), Nani; van Persie (Fernandao 72).
Ajax: (4231) Cillessen; Van Rijn (Tete 63), Veltman, Riedewald, Dijks; Gudelj, Bazoer; Schone, Klaassen, Fischer (Younes 63); El Ghazi (Sinkgraven 77).

Molde (2) 3 *(Kamara 11, Forren 19, Elyounoussi 56)*
Celtic (0) 1 *(Commons 55)*   9166
Molde: (433) Horvath; Linnes, Toivio, Forren, Rindaroy (Flo 52); Hestad D, Singh, Hussain; Mostrom, Kamara (Hestad E 74), Elyounoussi (Bakenga 84).
Celtic: (4231) Gordon; Lustig, Ambrose, Boyata, Izaguirre; Brown, Bitton; Commons (Ciftci 76), Johansen, Armstrong (Mackay-Steven 74); Griffiths.

Thursday, 5 November 2015
Ajax (0) 0
Fenerbahce (0) 0   48,990
Ajax: (433) Cillessen; Tete, Veltman, Viergever, Riedewald; Bazoer, Klaassen, Gudelj (Serero 76); El Ghazi (Schone 32), Milik, Fischer (Younes 53).
Fenerbahce: (433) Demirel; Gonul, Kjaer, Bruno Alves, Kaldirim; Topal, Diego (Tufan 74), Souza; Potuk, van Persie (Sen 80), Nani (Fernandao 63).

Celtic (1) 1 *(Commons 26)*
Molde (2) 2 *(Elyounoussi 21, Hestad D 37)*   37,071
Celtic: (4411) Gordon; Lustig, Boyata, Simunovic (Blackett 9 (Ciftci 69)), Tierney; Armstrong, Bitton[■], Johansen, Commons (Forrest 46); Rogic; Griffiths.
Molde: (433) Horvath; Linnes, Toivio, Forren, Rindaroy; Singh, Hestad D, Hussain (Gabrielsen 90); Mostrom (Hestad E 62), Hoiland (Kamara 46), Elyounoussi.

Thursday, 26 November 2015
Celtic (1) 1 *(McGregor 3)*
Ajax (1) 2 *(Milik 22, Cerny 87)*   44,118
Celtic: (451) Gordon; Lustig, Boyata, Simunovic, Tierney (Izaguirre 78); Forrest, Armstrong, Rogic (Mulgrew 66), McGregor, Mackay-Steven (Allan 71); Griffiths.
Ajax: (433) Cillessen; Tete, van der Hoorn (Sanogo 80), Riedewald, Dijks; Schone (van de Beek 72), Klaassen, Gudelj; Fischer (Cerny 68), Milik, Younes.

Molde (0) 0
Fenerbahce (0) 2 *(Fernandao 68, Tufan 84)*   8235
Molde: (451) Horvath; Linnes, Toivio, Forren, Rindaroy[■]; Svendsen (Gabrielsen 85), Singh, Hestad D (Hestad E 76), Hussain, Elyounoussi; Gulbrandsen (Kamara 46).
Fenerbahce: (433) Fabiano; Gonul, Kjaer, Bruno Alves, Kaldirim (Kadlec 73); Tufan, Souza, Diego; Nani (Sen 81), Fernandao (van Persie 86), Potuk.

Thursday, 10 December 2015
Ajax (1) 1 *(van de Beek 14)*
Molde (1) 1 *(Singh 29)*   48,041
Ajax: (433) Cillessen; Van Rijhn, Veltman, Riedewald, Dijks; van de Beek (Bazoer 64), Klaassen, Gudelj[■]; Younes (El Ghazi 62), Milik, Fischer (Schone 77).
Molde: (433) Horvath; Linnes, Toivio (Hestad D 19), Forren, Flo; Singh, Gabrielsen, Hussain; Mostrom (Hestad E 76), Kamara (Gulbrandsen 52), Elyounoussi.

Fenerbahce (1) 1 *(Markovic 39)*
Celtic (0) 1 *(Commons 75)*   35,372
Fenerbahce: (4411) Fabiano; Gonul, Ba, Bruno Alves, Kaldirim; Markovic (Tufan 82), Souza, Topal, Potuk; Diego[■]; Fernandao (Erkin 86).
Celtic: (4411) Gordon; Lustig, Boyata, Simunovic, Tierney; McGregor, Bitton, Johansen (Rogic 74), Armstrong (Forrest 63); Allan (Commons 74); Ciftci.

Group A Table	P	W	D	L	F	A	GD	Pts
Molde	6	3	2	1	10	7	3	11
Fenerbahce	6	2	3	1	7	6	1	9
Ajax	6	1	4	1	6	6	0	7
Celtic	6	0	3	3	8	12	–4	3

GROUP B

Thursday, 17 September 2015

Bordeaux (0) 1 *(Jussie 81)*

Liverpool (0) 1 *(Lallana 65)*   35,328

Bordeaux: (442) Carasso; Gajic (Guilbert 86), Pablo, Pallois, Poundje; Chantome, Maurice-Belay, Khazri (Jussie 69), Rolan; Saivet (Biyogo Poko 76), Crivelli.
Liverpool: (433) Mignolet; Toure (Chirivella 27), Gomez, Sakho, Moreno; Coutinho, Lallana, Can; Ibe, Rossiter (Brannagan 80), Origi (Ings 73).

Sion (1) 2 *(Konate 11, 82)*

Rubin Kazan (0) 1 *(Kanunnikov 65)*   7000

Sion: (451) Vanins; Zverotic, Lacroix, Ziegler, Jagne; Assifuah (Mujangi Bia 68), Kouassi, Salatic, Fernandes, Carlitos; Konate (Ndoye 90).
Rubin Kazan: (451) Ryzhikov; Kuzmin, Kambolov, Kvirkvelia, Nabiullin; Kanunnikov, Carlos Eduardo (Dyadyun 90), Georgiev, Bilyaletdinov (Ozdoev 46), Karadeniz (Devic 86); Portnyagin.

Thursday, 1 October 2015

Liverpool (1) 1 *(Lallana 4)*

Sion (1) 1 *(Assifuah 17)*   37,252

Liverpool: (433) Mignolet; Clyne (Moreno 46), Can, Toure (Sakho 76), Gomez; Allen, Rossiter, Lallana; Ibe, Origi, Ings (Coutinho 61).
Sion: (433) Vanins; Zverotic, Lacroix, Ziegler, Jagne; Kouassi, Salatic, Fernandes; Assifuah (Ndoye 86), Konate (Mujangi Bia 89), Carlitos.

Rubin Kazan (0) 0

Bordeaux (0) 0   17,642

Rubin Kazan: (451) Ryzhikov; Kuzmin, Kvirkvelia, Kambolov, Nabiullin; Kanunnikov, Kislyak■, Devic (Bilyaletdinov 46), Carlos Eduardo; Portnyagin (Dyadyun 73).
Bordeaux: (442) Carasso; Guilbert, Yambere (Sane 88), Pallois, Contento; Biyogo Poko (Khazri 57), Chantome, Saivet, Jussie (Plasil 58); Crivelli, Maurice-Belay.

Thursday, 22 October 2015

Bordeaux (0) 0

Sion (1) 1 *(Lacroix 21)*   18,313

Bordeaux: (433) Carasso; Biyogo Poko, Sane, Pallois, Poundje; Chantome, Saivet, Plasil (Khazri■ 64); Diabate (Crivelli 65), Rolan, Toure (Ounas 77).
Sion: (433) Vanins; Zverotic, Lacroix, Ziegler, Jagne; Ndoye, Salatic, Fernandes; Assifuah (Follonier 77), Konate, Carlitos.

Liverpool (1) 1 *(Can 37)*

Rubin Kazan (1) 1 *(Devic 15)*   42,951

Liverpool: (433) Mignolet; Clyne, Skrtel, Sakho, Moreno; Can, Allen (Lucas 46), Milner; Coutinho (Benteke 63), Origi (Firmino 74), Lallana.
Rubin Kazan: (4231) Ryzhikov; Kuzmin■, Kvirkvelia, Kambolov, Nabiullin; Georgiev, Ozdoev; Kanunnikov, Carlos Eduardo (Portnyagin 64), Karadeniz (Dyadyun 81); Devic (Cotugno 46).

Thursday, 5 November 2015

Rubin Kazan (0) 0

Liverpool (0) 1 *(Ibe 52)*   41,585

Rubin Kazan: (4231) Ryzhikov; Cotugno (Ustinov 81), Kambolov, Kvirkvelia, Nabiullin; Georgiev, Kislyak (Akhmetov 69); Kanunnikov, Carlos Eduardo (Ozdoev 46), Karadeniz; Devic.
Liverpool: (433) Mignolet; Clyne, Sakho, Lovren, Moreno; Milner (Lallana 60), Allen, Can (Skrtel 90); Firmino (Lucas 81), Benteke, Ibe.

Sion (0) 1 *(Ruefli 90)*

Bordeaux (0) 1 *(Toure 67)*   9000

Sion: (4231) Vanins; Ruefli, Lacroix, Ziegler, Zverotic; Ndoye (Follonier 87), Salatic; Assifuah (Karlen 87), Fernandes, Carlitos (Zeman 74); Konate.
Bordeaux: (541) Carasso; Biyogo Poko, Sane, Yambere, Pallois, Contento; Toure (Saivet 90), Plasil, Chantome, Jussie (Maurice-Belay 66); Diabate (Crivelli 79).

Thursday, 26 November 2015

Liverpool (2) 2 *(Milner 38 (pen), Benteke 45)*

Bordeaux (1) 1 *(Saivet 34)*   9000

Liverpool: (433) Mignolet; Clyne, Toure, Lovren, Moreno; Milner, Lucas, Allen (Can 67); Ibe (Origi 90), Benteke, Firmino (Lallana 74).
Bordeaux: (442) Carasso; Biyogo Poko, Sane, Yambere, Contento; Plasil (Ounas 84), Chantome, Saivet, Rolan; Crivelli (Diabate 67), Jussie (Maurice-Belay 76).

Rubin Kazan (0) 2 *(Georgiev 72, Devic 90)*

Sion (0) 0   14,500

Rubin Kazan: (451) Ryzhikov; Ustinov, Kambolov, Kvirkvelia, Nabiullin; Kanunnikov, Georgiev, Kislyak (Dyadyun 46), Ozdoev, Carlos Eduardo (Bilyaletdinov 70); Devic (Akhmetov 90).
Sion: (451) Vanins; Zverotic, Lacroix, Ziegler, Ruefli; Assifuah (Follonier 80), Ndoye■, Salatic (Mujangi Bia 87), Fernandes, Carlitos; Konate (Karlen 81).

Thursday, 10 December 2015

Bordeaux (0) 2 *(Laborde 58, Rolan 63)*

Rubin Kazan (1) 2 *(Kanunnikov 31, Ustinov 76)*   13,640

Bordeaux: (433) Prior; Poundje, Yambere, Guilbert■, Biyogo Poko; Vada, Traore (Soni 65), Maulun; Laborde (Khazri 72), Thelin, Rolan (Crivelli 83).
Rubin Kazan: (4132) Ryzhikov; Nabiullin, Kambolov, Kvirkvelia, Kuzmin (Ustinov 75); Kislyak (Bilyaletdinov 45 (Dyadyun 78)); Georgiev, Ozdoev, Carlos Eduardo; Devic, Kanunnikov.

Sion (0) 0

Liverpool (0) 0   10,000

Sion: (433) Vanins; Zverotic, Lacroix, Ziegler, Jagne; Kouassi, Salatic, Fernandes; Ruefli (Adao 90), Assifuah (Mujangi Bia 73), Carlitos.
Liverpool: (433) Mignolet; Clyne, Toure, Lovren, Smith; Henderson (Rossiter 76), Milner (Coutinho 60), Can; Lallana, Origi, Firmino (Brannagan 89).

Group B Table	P	W	D	L	F	A	GD	Pts
Liverpool	6	2	4	0	6	4	2	10
Sion	6	2	3	1	5	5	0	9
Rubin Kazan	6	1	3	2	6	6	0	6
Bordeaux	6	0	4	2	5	7	–2	4

GROUP C

Thursday, 17 September 2015

Borussia Dortmund (1) 2 *(Ginter 45, Park 90)*

Krasnodar (1) 1 *(Mamaev 12)*   58,000

Borussia Dortmund: (4231) Weidenfeller; Ginter, Hummels, Papastathopoulos, Schmelzer (Kagawa 46); Castro (Weigl 61), Gundogan; Januzaj, Mkhitaryan, Park; Aubameyang (Ramos 72).
Krasnodar: (433) Dykan; Jedrzejczyk, Sigurdsson, Granqvist, Petrov; Kabore (Gazinski 70), Strandberg, Ahmedov; Pereyra (Laborde 60), Smolov, Mamaev (Ari 81).

Gabala (0) 0

PAOK Salonika (0) 0   4800

Gabala: (4231) Bezotosnyi; Stankovic, Vernydub, Ricardinho, Dashdemirov; Dodo (Zargarov 83), Gai; Meza, Zec (Pereyra 46), Zenjov; Antonov.
PAOK Salonika: (433) Olsen; Miguel Vitor, Ricardo Costa, Tzavelas, Kitsiou; Tziolis, Mak, Rodrigues; Sabo (Jairo 84), Pelkas (Golasa 76), Athanasiadis (Berbatov 59).

Thursday, 1 October 2015
Krasnodar (1) 2 *(Wanderson 8, Smolov 84)*
Gabala (0) 1 *(Dodo 51)*   8901
Krasnodar: (451) Sinitsyn; Jedrzejczyk, Strandberg, Granqvist, Kaleshin; Kabore, Gazinski (Joaozinho 76), Ahmedov, Wanderson, Ari (Smolov 60); Mamaev (Laborde 66).
Gabala: (451) Bezotosnyi; Dashdemirov, Vernydub, Stankovic, Ricardinho; Gai, Meza (Sadiqov 46 (Zargarov 90)), Zenjov, Antonov (Zec 74), Dodo; Pereyra.

PAOK Salonika (1) 1 *(Mak 34)*
Borussia Dortmund (0) 1 *(Castro 72)*   20,000
PAOK Salonika: (343) Olsen; Ricardo Costa, Miguel Vitor, Tzavelas, Konstantinidis, Kace (Charisis 85), Tziolis, Rodrigues; Mak (Jairo 73), Berbatov (Pelkas 89), Sabo.
Borussia Dortmund: (4141) Weidenfeller; Piszczek, Subotic, Bender, Park; Weigl (Schmelzer 65); Hofmann, Castro, Mkhitaryan (Ramos 65), Reus; Januzaj (Leitner 84).

Thursday, 22 October 2015
Gabala (0) 1 *(Dodo 90)*
Borussia Dortmund (2) 3 *(Aubameyang 31, 38, 72)* 9000
Gabala: (442) Bezotosnyi; Stankovic, Vernydub, Ricardinho, Dashdemirov; Dodo, Gai, Meza (Sadiqov 83), Zenjov (Zec 79); Pereyra (Zargarov 60), Antonov.
Borussia Dortmund: (442) Weidenfeller; Park (Schmelzer 69), Hummels (Piszczek 63), Papastathopoulos, Ginter; Weigl, Hofmann, Gundogan (Bender 63), Reus; Kagawa, Aubameyang.

PAOK Salonika (0) 0
Krasnodar (0) 0   9325
PAOK Salonika: (4411) Glykos; Skondras, Miguel Vitor (Leovac 46), Ricardo Costa, Malezas; Jairo■, Sabo, Rodrigues, Kace; Pelkas (Mak 72); Athanasiadis (Berbatov 57).
Krasnodar: (451) Dykan; Jedrzejczyk■, Strandberg, Granqvist, Kaleshin; Laborde, Ahmedov (Mamaev 65), Torbinski (Gazinski 81), Joaozinho, Kabore; Smolov (Ari 63).

Thursday, 5 November 2015
Borussia Dortmund (2) 4 *(Reus 28, Aubameyang 45, Zenjov 68 (og), Mkhitaryan 70)*
Gabala (0) 0   57,009
Borussia Dortmund: (4231) Weidenfeller; Piszczek, Ginter (Gundogan 62), Hummels, Schmelzer; Weigl, Bender; Castro, Mkhitaryan, Reus (Januzaj 46); Aubameyang (Ramos 68).
Gabala: (4231) Pietrzkiewicz; Vernydub, Stankovic, Rafael Santos, Ricardinho; Gai, Meza (Jamalov 76); Dashdemirov, Antonov (Pereyra 68), Dodo; Zenjov (Zargarov 86).

Krasnodar (1) 2 *(Ari 33, Joaozinho 68 (pen))*
PAOK Salonika (0) 1 *(Mak 90)*   15,550
Krasnodar: (451) Dykan; Kaleshin (Mamaev 70), Sigurdsson, Granqvist, Petrov; Laborde (Smolov 62), Torbinski, Kabore, Ahmedov (Gazinski 77), Joaozinho; Ari.
PAOK Salonika: (3421) Glykos; Skondras, Ricardo Costa, Malezas; Golasa (Athanasiadis 68), Tziolis, Charisis, Tzavelas (Kitsiou 82); Rodrigues, Sabo (Pelkas 57); Mak.

Thursday, 26 November 2015
Krasnodar (1) 1 *(Mamaev 2 (pen))*
Borussia Dortmund (0) 0   30,150
Krasnodar: (4231) Dykan; Jedrzejczyk, Granqvist, Sigurdsson, Kaleshin; Ahmedov (Torbinski 85), Kabore; Smolov, Pereyra (Gazinski 74), Mamaev (Laborde 84); Ari.
Borussia Dortmund: (4231) Weidenfeller; Piszczek (Ginter 79), Bender, Hummels, Schmelzer; Gundogan, Weigl (Leitner 86); Hofmann (Januzaj 68), Castro, Mkhitaryan; Ramos.

PAOK Salonika (0) 0
Gabala (0) 0   6131
PAOK Salonika: (352) Glykos; Skondras, Malezas, Tzavelas; Kitsiou (Athanasiadis 78), Pelkas (Sabo 46), Tziolis, Kace, Rodrigues; Berbatov (Mystakidis 71), Mak.
Gabala: (433) Bezotosnyi; Dashdemirov, Rafael Santos, Stankovic, Ricardinho; Zenjov (Javadov 77), Sadiqov (Jamalov 87), Zargarov (Mirzabekov 83); Gai, Zec, Antonov.

Thursday, 10 December 2015
Borussia Dortmund (0) 0
PAOK Salonika (1) 1 *(Mak 33)*   55,200
Borussia Dortmund: (4231) Weidenfeller; Ginter, Subotic, Hummels, Park; Stenzel, Bender (Weigl 46); Januzaj, Kagawa (Aubameyang 66), Reus (Mkhitaryan 46); Ramos.
PAOK Salonika: (532) Glykos; Mystakidis (Rodrigues 77), Konstantinidis, Skondras, Malezas, Tzavelas; Tziolis, Kace, Cimirot; Berbatov (Sabo 71), Mak (Leovac 66).

Gabala (0) 0
Krasnodar (2) 3 *(Sigurdsson 26, Pereyra 40, Wanderson 75)*   3050
Gabala: (4231) Popovich; Stankovic, Ricardinho, Dashdemirov, Rafael Santos; Dodo, Gai (Sadiqov 76); Meza, Zenjov (Zargarov 57), Pereyra (Zec 61); Antonov.
Krasnodar: (433) Dykan; Granqvist, Kaleshin (Laborde 65), Sigurdsson, Mamaev; Ahmedov, Joaozinho, Pereyra (Gazinski 69); Kabore, Petrov, Wanderson (Smolov 77).

Group C Table	P	W	D	L	F	A	GD	Pts
Krasnodar	6	4	1	1	9	4	5	13
Borussia Dortmund	6	3	1	2	10	5	5	10
PAOK Salonika	6	1	4	1	3	3	0	7
Gabala	6	0	2	4	2	12	–10	2

GROUP D

Thursday, 17 September 2015
Midtjylland (0) 1 *(Rasmussen 61)*
Legia Warsaw (0) 0   6798
Midtjylland: (442) Andersen; Hansen, Sviatchenko, Bak Nielsen, Novak; Sparv, Poulsen, Andersson (Olsson 46), Sisto (Onuachu 81); Royer, Rasmussen (Pusic 88).
Legia Warsaw: (442) Kuciak; Bereszynski, Rzezniczak, Lewczuk, Brzyski; Guilherme, Vranjes (Makowski 83), Furman■, Kucharczyk (Trickovski 75); Nikolic, Prijovic.

Napoli (3) 5 *(Callejon 5, 77, Mertens 19, 25, Hamsik 53)*
Club Brugge (0) 0   13,043
Napoli: (451) Reina; Hisaj, Albiol, Koulibaly, Ghoulam; Callejon, David Lopez, Jorginho, Hamsik (Allan 62), Mertens (Insigne 75); Higuain (Gabbiadini 71).
Club Brugge: (433) Bolat; Meunier, Mechele, Duarte, De Bock; Vormer, Simons, Vazquez (De Fauw 69); Leandro Pereira, Diaby (Claudemir 60), Bolingoli Mbombo (Izquierdo 46).

Thursday, 1 October 2015
Club Brugge (0) 1 *(Meunier 79)*
Midtjylland (0) 3 *(Sisto 51, Onuachu 67, Novak 74)* 14,126
Club Brugge: (451) Bruzzese; De Fauw (Meunier 70), Duarte, De Bock, Mechele; Claudemir, Vanaken, Vormer, Diaby (Vossen 63), Leandro Pereira; Izquierdo (Dierckx 71).
Midtjylland: (451) Andersen; Hansen, Sviatchenko, Bak Nielsen (Romer 31), Novak; Sparv, Poulsen, Olsson, Sisto (Urena Porras 79), Royer; Rasmussen (Onuachu 53).

Legia Warsaw (0) 0
Napoli (0) 2 *(Mertens 53, Higuain 84)*   26,357
Legia Warsaw: (433) Kuciak; Bereszynski, Rzezniczak, Lewczuk, Brzyski; Guilherme, Pazdan (Makowski 89), Jodlowiec; Trickovski (Duda 62), Kucharczyk (Nikolic 62), Prijovic.
Napoli: (433) Gabriel; Maggio, Chiriches, Koulibaly, Ghoulam; Allan (Chalobah 85), Valdifiori, David Lopez; Callejon (Higuain 77), Gabbiadini, Mertens (El Kaddouri 72).

Thursday, 22 October 2015

Legia Warsaw (0) 1 *(Kucharczyk 52)*

Club Brugge (1) 1 *(De Fauw 39)* 16,320

Legia Warsaw: (451) Kuciak; Broz, Rzezniczak, Lewczuk, Brzyski; Guilherme (Duda 46), Pazdan, Jodlowiec, Furman (Trickovski 46), Kucharczyk; Nikolic (Prijovic 76).
Club Brugge: (433) Bruzzese; Meunier, Denswil, Mechele, De Fauw; Diaby (Dierckx 71), Bolingoli Mbombo (De Bock 68), Simons; Vanaken, Izquierdo, Vossen (Leandro Pereira 80).

Midtjylland (1) 1 *(Pusic 43)*

Napoli (3) 4 *(Callejon 19, Gabbiadini 31, 40, Higuain 90)* 9210

Midtjylland: (442) Andersen; Romer, Hansen, Sviatchenko, Novak; Duelund (Mabil 73), Sparv, Poulsen, Royer; Rasmussen (Larsen 73), Pusic (Onuachu 62).
Napoli: (433) Reina; Maggio, Chiriches, Koulibaly, Ghoulam (Strinic 80); Allan (Hamsik 59), Valdifiori, David Lopez; Callejon (Higuain 64), Gabbiadini, El Kaddouri.

Thursday, 5 November 2015

Club Brugge (1) 1 *(Meunier 38)*

Legia Warsaw (0) 0 16,349

Club Brugge: (442) Bruzzese; Meunier, Denswil, Mechele, De Bock; Felipe Gedoz, Claudemir, Simons, Vazquez (Vanaken 90); Diaby (Bolingoli Mbombo 82), Leandro Pereira (Vossen 74).
Legia Warsaw: (433) Kuciak; Bereszynski (Kucharczyk 67), Rzezniczak, Lewczuk, Brzyski; Vranjes, Pazdan, Jodlowiec (Guilherme 62); Duda, Saganowski (Prijovic 59), Trickovski.

Napoli (3) 5 *(El Kaddouri 13, Gabbiadini 23, 38, Maggio 54, Callejon 77)*

Midtjylland (0) 0 18,475

Napoli: (433) Reina; Maggio, Chiriches, Koulibaly, Strinic (Hisaj 69); David Lopez, Valdifiori, Hamsik (Allan 53); El Kaddouri, Gabbiadini, Insigne (Callejon 57).
Midtjylland: (4231) Andersen; Romer, Banggaard, Sviatchenko, Novak; Olsson (Sisto 69), Hansen (Urena Porras 46); Sparv, Royer, Poulsen; Onuachu (Pusic 62).

Thursday, 26 November 2015

Club Brugge (0) 0

Napoli (1) 1 *(Chiriches 41)* 180

Club Brugge: (433) Bruzzese; Meunier, Mechele, Denswil, De Fauw; Vormer, Simons (Leandro Pereira 88), Vazquez (Vanaken 81); Felipe Gedoz (Diaby 81), Vossen, Izquierdo.
Napoli: (433) Gabriel; Maggio, Chiriches, Koulibaly, Strinic; David Lopez, Valdifiori, Chalobah (Allan 80); Hamsik (Hisaj 69), Callejon (Ghoulam 77), El Kaddouri.

Legia Warsaw (1) 1 *(Prijovic 34)*

Midtjylland (0) 0 9468

Legia Warsaw: (442) Malarz; Bereszynski, Jodlowiec, Lewczuk, Broz; Trickovski (Zyro 82), Vranjes, Duda, Kucharczyk; Prijovic (Guilherme 64), Nikolic (Saganowski 90).
Midtjylland: (451) Andersen; Romer, Hansen, Sviatchenko, Novak; Sisto (Mabil 46), Olsson (Pusic 70), Poulsen, Sparv, Royer; Rasmussen (Onuachu 36).

Thursday, 10 December 2015

Midtjylland (1) 1 *(Sisto 27)*

Club Brugge (0) 1 *(Vossen 68)* 8624

Midtjylland: (451) Andersen; Romer, Hansen, Sviatchenko, Novak; Sparv, Poulsen, Olsson (Lauridsen 90), Sisto (Urena Porras 74), Royer; Pusic (Onuachu 81).
Club Brugge: (451) Bruzzese; Meunier, Denswil, Mechele (Engels 81), De Fauw; Simons, Vazquez, Felipe Gedoz (Rafaelov 46), Vormer, Izquierdo (Leandro Pereira 62); Vossen.

Napoli (2) 5 *(Chalobah 32, Insigne 39, Callejon 57, Mertens 65, 90)*

Legia Warsaw (0) 2 *(Vranjes 62, Prijovic 90)* 7922

Napoli: (433) Gabriel; Maggio, Chiriches (Luperto 79), Koulibaly (Albiol 68), Strinic; David Lopez, Valdifiori, Chalobah; El Kaddouri, Insigne (Callejon 55), Mertens.
Legia Warsaw: (433) Kuciak; Bereszynski, Lewczuk, Pazdan, Broz; Vranjes, Jodlowiec, Duda (Trickovski 71); Guilherme, Nikolic (Prijovic 60), Kucharczyk (Pablo Dyego 79).

Group D Table	P	W	D	L	F	A	GD	Pts
Napoli	6	6	0	0	22	3	19	18
Midtjylland	6	2	1	3	6	12	–6	7
Club Brugge	6	1	2	3	4	11	–7	5
Legia Warsaw	6	1	1	4	4	10	–6	4

GROUP E

Thursday, 17 September 2015

Rapid Vienna (0) 2 *(Schwab 50, Hofmann S 54 (pen))*

Villarreal (1) 1 *(Leo Baptistao 45)* 36,200

Rapid Vienna: (4231) Novota; Pavelic, Dibon, Hofmann M, Stangl (Auer 90); Grahovac, Schwab; Schaub (Schobesberger 63), Hofmann S, Kainz (Huspek 72); Prosenik.
Villarreal: (442) Barbosa; Rukavina, Bonera, Victor Ruiz, Jokic; Samuel (Castillejo 46), Jonathan, Bruno, Suarez (Nahuel 79); Leo Baptistao, Adrian (Bakambu 69).

Viktoria Plzen (1) 2 *(Horava 36, Petrzela 75)*

Dinamo Minsk (0) 0 10,784

Viktoria Plzen: (442) Kozacik; Limbersky, Prochazka, Baranek, Rajtoral; Horava (Kucera 90), Vanek, Kopic, Hrosovsky; Kovarik (Petrzela 73), Duris (Holenda 83).
Dinamo Minsk: (442) Gutor; Begunov, Vitus, Politevich, Bangura; Voronkov (Tigorev 78), Korytko (Yarotsky 60), Korzun, Adamovic; Beqiraj, Neacsa (Rassadkin 73).

Thursday, 1 October 2015

Dinamo Minsk (0) 0

Rapid Vienna (0) 1 *(Hofmann S 54)* 5800

Dinamo Minsk: (442) Gutor; Vitus, Politevich, Bangura, Begunov (Veretilo 90); Voronkov (El Monir 66), Korytko, Udoji, Korzun; Adamovic (Rassadkin 72), Beqiraj.
Rapid Vienna: (4231) Novota; Pavelic, Sonnleitner, Dibon, Stangl; Schaub (Schobesberger 46), Grahovac; Schwab, Kainz, Hofmann S (Alar 75); Jelic (Prosenik 85).

Villarreal (0) 1 *(Leo Baptistao 54)*

Viktoria Plzen (0) 0 14,000

Villarreal: (442) Barbosa; Rukavina, Bailly, Victor Ruiz, Jaume; Castillejo, Jonathan (Trigueros 75), Bruno, Nahuel (Samuel 83); Soldado, Leo Baptistao.
Viktoria Plzen: (442) Kozacik; Rajtoral, Baranek, Prochazka[a], Limbersky; Petrzela (Mahmutovic 75), Horava, Hrosovsky, Kovarik (Vuch 88); Kopic (Hejda 81), Duris.

Thursday, 22 October 2015

Rapid Vienna (1) 3 *(Hofmann S 34, Schaub 52, Petsos 67)*

Viktoria Plzen (1) 2 *(Duris 12, Hrosovsky 76)* 29,400

Rapid Vienna: (4231) Novota; Pavelic, Dibon, Hofmann M, Stangl; Petsos, Schwab; Schaub (Huspek 80), Hofmann S (Grahovac 62); Kainz; Prosenik (Jelic 70).
Viktoria Plzen: (4231) Kozacik; Rajtoral, Baranek, Hejda, Limbersky; Hrosovsky, Vanek (Holenda 80); Kopic (Petrzela 58), Horava (Kolar 58), Kovarik; Duris.

Villarreal (2) 4 *(Bakambu 17, 32, Soldado 61, Bailly 71)*

Dinamo Minsk (0) 0 17,481

Villarreal: (442) Barbosa; Rukavina, Bailly, Victor Ruiz, Jokic; Samuel, Jonathan, Pina (Trigueros 62), Suarez (Castillejo 67); Soldado, Bakambu (Leiva 46).
Dinamo Minsk: (433) Gutor; Begunov, Politevich, Bangura, Vitus; Korytko (Adamovic 46), Udoji (Voronkov 74), Korzun; Premudrov, Rassadkin, Beqiraj (El Monir 66).

Thursday, 5 November 2015
Dinamo Minsk (0) 1 *(Vitus 69)*
Villarreal (0) 2 *(Soldado 72 (pen), 86)*   6000
Dinamo Minsk: (442) Ignatovich; Begunov, Politevich, Bangura, El Monir; Adamovic (Vitus 67), Premudrov, Voronkov (Korytko 73), Beqiraj; Rassadkin, Udoji (Yedigaryan 78).
Villarreal: (4411) Barbosa; Rukavina, Mario, Victor Ruiz, Jokic; Samuel, Trigueros, Pina (Jonathan 62), Castillejo (Suarez 73); Leiva (Soldado 46); Bakambu.

Viktoria Plzen (0) 1 *(Holenda 72)*
Rapid Vienna (1) 2 *(Schobesberger 13, 78)*   11,691
Viktoria Plzen: (4231) Kozacik; Rajtoral (Mahmutovic 81), Hejda, Prochazka, Limbersky; Hrosovsky, Horava; Petrzela (Kopic 64), Kolar (Holenda 70), Kovarik; Duris.
Rapid Vienna: (4231) Novota; Pavelic, Sonnleitner, Dibon (Hofmann M 67), Stangl; Petsos, Schwab; Schobesberger, Hofmann S (Grahovac 51), Kainz; Prosenik (Jelic 80).

Thursday, 26 November 2015
Dinamo Minsk (0) 1 *(Adamovic 90)*
Viktoria Plzen (0) 0   4250
Dinamo Minsk: (442) Gutor; Veretilo■, Politevich, Bangura, Begunov; Korytko (El Monir 66), Premudrov, Korzun, Udoji; Rassadkin (Adamovic 76), Beqiraj.
Viktoria Plzen: (4231) Bolek; Mateju, Baranek, Prochazka, Limbersky; Kucera, Hrosovsky; Kopic (Rajtoral 72), Kolar, Kovarik (Holenda 83); Mahmutovic (Duris 63).

Villarreal (0) 1 *(Bruno 79)*
Rapid Vienna (0) 0   12,000
Villarreal: (442) Barbosa; Rukavina, Mario, Victor Ruiz, Jaume; Castillejo (Leiva 83), Jonathan (Trigueros 73), Bruno, Suarez; Soldado, Bakambu (Samuel 51).
Rapid Vienna: (4231) Novota (Strebinger 61); Pavelic, Sonnleitner, Dibon (Hofmann M 6), Stangl; Petsos, Schwab; Schobesberger, Hofmann S, Kainz; Prosenik (Jelic 87).

Thursday, 10 December 2015
Rapid Vienna (1) 2 *(Hofmann M 29, Jelic 59)*
Dinamo Minsk (0) 1 *(El Monir 64)*   34,800
Rapid Vienna: (4231) Strebinger; Pavelic, Sonnleitner, Hofmann M, Auer; Petsos, Schwab; Alar (Stangl 80), Hofmann S (Grahovac 65), Kainz; Jelic (Prosenik 71).
Dinamo Minsk: (442) Gutor; Begunov, Politevich, Bangura, Vitus; Korytko (Bulyga 85), Korzun, Premudrov (Voronkov 60), Udoji; Adamovic (El Monir 64), Beqiraj.

Viktoria Plzen (1) 3 *(Kolar 9 (pen), Kovarik 65, Horava 90)*
Villarreal (1) 3 *(Bakambu 40, Jonathan 63, Bruno 90)*   10,071
Viktoria Plzen: (433) Bolek; Mateju, Baranek, Hejda, Limbersky; Kucera (Prochazka 89), Horava, Kopic (Petrzela 83); Kolar, Kovarik, Holenda (Mahmutovic 71).
Villarreal: (424) Barbosa; Rukavina, Musacchio, Victor Ruiz, Jokic (Marin 43); Trigueros, Bruno; Samuel (Jonathan 56), Bakambu, Soldado, Castillejo (Suarez 73).

Group E Table	P	W	D	L	F	A	GD	Pts
Rapid Vienna	6	5	0	1	10	6	4	15
Villarreal	6	4	1	1	12	6	6	13
Viktoria Plzen	6	1	1	4	8	10	−2	4
Dinamo Minsk	6	1	0	5	3	11	−8	3

GROUP F

Thursday, 17 September 2015
FC Groningen (0) 0
Marseille (2) 3 *(Nkoudou 25, Ocampos 39, Alessandrini 61)*   22,550
FC Groningen: (433) Padt; Hateboer, Kappelhof, Lindgren, Tamata; Maduro, De Leeuw, Tibbling; Linssen, Hoesen (Mahi 66), Rusnak (Drost 70).
Marseille: (433) Mandanda; Isla, Sparagna, Rekik, Mendy (De Ceglie 66); Zambo Anguissa, Lucas Silva (Rolando 82), Romao; Alessandrini (Sarr 75), Ocampos, Nkoudou.

Slovan Liberec (0) 0
Braga (0) 1 *(Rafa 60)*   8132
Slovan Liberec: (4411) Koubek; Coufal, Hovorka, Pokorny, Bartosak; Sural, Pavelka, Soungole (Sykora 65), Bartl; Shala (Rabusic 65); Bakos (Kerbr 75).
Braga: (442) Matheus Magalhaes; Baiano, Boly, Andre Pinto, Djavan; Alan (Filipe Augusto 75), Vukcevic, Mauro Sousa, Rafa; Crislan (Eduardo 62), Rui Fonte (Ricardo Ferreira 86).

Thursday, 1 October 2015
Braga (1) 1 *(Hassan 5)*
FC Groningen (0) 0   9150
Braga: (442) Matheus Magalhaes; Marcelo Goiano, Boly, Arghus (Mauro Sousa 40), Djavan (Pedro Santos 82); Alan, Luiz Carlos, Vukcevic, Rafa; Hassan, Rui Fonte (Eduardo 71).
FC Groningen: (4231) Padt; Hateboer, Kappelhof, Reijnen, Tamata; Maduro, Tibbling; Linssen, De Leeuw (Hoesen 82), Rusnak (Larsen 32); Mahi (Antonia 82).

Marseille (0) 0
Slovan Liberec (0) 1 *(Coufal 84)*   10,040
Marseille: (4231) Mandanda; Isla (Djadjedje 67), Rolando, Rekik, Mendy; Romao, Lucas Silva; Alessandrini (Sarr 82), Cabella (Barrada 71), Ocampos; Batshuayi.
Slovan Liberec: (433) Koubek; Coufal, Hovorka, Pokorny, Bartosak; Shala (Bartl 73), Pavelka, Sykora; Sural (Kerbr 89), Rabusic (Bakos 46), Efremov.

Thursday, 22 October 2015
Braga (0) 3 *(Hassan 61, Wilson Eduardo 77, Alan 88)*
Marseille (0) 2 *(Alessandrini 84, Batshuayi 87)*   10,495
Braga: (442) Matheus Magalhaes; Marcelo Goiano, Ricardo Ferreira, Boly, Djavan; Alan, Mauro Sousa, Vukcevic, Rafa (Luiz Carlos 84); Hassan (Crislan 75), Rui Fonte (Wilson Eduardo 65).
Marseille: (433) Mandanda; Djadjedje (Cabella 64), Rekik, Sparagna, Mendy; Isla, Diarra (Ocampos 83), Lucas Silva; Alessandrini, Batshuayi, Barrada (Nkoudou 74).

Slovan Liberec (0) 1 *(Luckassen 87)*
FC Groningen (0) 1 *(Hoesen 90)*   8793
Slovan Liberec: (4141) Koubek; Coufal, Svejdik, Pokorny, Bartosak; Pavelka; Efremov, Shala (Bartl 84), Folprecht, Sural (Sackey 89); Bakos (Luckassen 61).
FC Groningen: (451) Padt; Hateboer, Kappelhof, Larsen (Antonia 88), Tamata; Linssen (Hoesen 70), Maduro (De Leeuw■ 78), Reijnen, Tibbling, Rusnak; Mahi.

Thursday, 5 November 2015
FC Groningen (0) 0
Slovan Liberec (0) 1 *(Padt 83 (og))*   18,693
FC Groningen: (4231) Padt; Burnet, Larsen, Reijnen, Kappelhof; Tibbling (Hateboer 84), Maduro (Drost 78); Rusnak, Linssen, Hoesen (Bacuna 67); Antonia.
Slovan Liberec: (4141) Koubek; Bartosak (Sykora 60), Pokorny, Svejdik, Coufal; Pavelka; Efremov (Kerbr 90), Shala, Folprecht, Sural; Bakos (Rabusic 73).

Marseille (1) 1 *(Nkoudou 39)*
Braga (0) 0   12,793
Marseille: (4231) Mandanda; Isla, N'Koulou, Rekik, Mendy; Lucas Silva (Sparagna 69), Romao; Nkoudou (Barrada 82), Cabella, Ocampos; Batshuayi (Manquillo 90).
Braga: (442) Matheus Magalhaes; Baiano, Boly, Ricardo Ferreira, Marcelo Goiano; Alan (Wilson Eduardo 78), Mauro Sousa (Luiz Carlos 53), Vukcevic, Rafa; Rui Fonte, Hassan (Crislan 67).

Thursday, 26 November 2015
Braga (1) 2 *(Alan 42, Crislan 90)*
Slovan Liberec (1) 1 *(Efremov 35)*   10,000
Braga: (442) Matheus Magalhaes; Marcelo Goiano, Ricardo Ferreira, Boly, Djavan; Alan (Pedro Santos 87), Vukcevic, Luiz Carlos, Rafa; Hassan (Eduardo 90), Rui Fonte (Crislan 59).
Slovan Liberec: (451) Koubek; Coufal (Sykora 85), Pokorny, Hovorka, Bartosak; Kerbr (Mudra 76), Folprecht, Pavelka, Shala, Efremov (Rabusic 62); Bakos.

Marseille (1) 2 *(Nkoudou 28, Batshuayi 88)*
FC Groningen (0) 1 *(Maduro 50)* 9107
Marseille: (4231) Mandanda; Djadjedje, N'Koulou, Rolando (Barrada 87), Mendy; Diarra, Isla (Lucas Silva 65); Ocampos (Alessandrini 57), Cabella, Nkoudou; Batshuayi.
FC Groningen: (433) Padt; Hateboer, Reijnen, Larsen, Tamata; Rusnak, Kappelhof, Maduro; Antonia (Drost 84), Hoesen, Linssen (Tibbling 71).

Thursday, 10 December 2015
FC Groningen (0) 0
Braga (0) 0 15,000
FC Groningen: (433) Padt; Hateboer, Reijnen, Larsen, Tamata; Tibbling, Kappelhof, Maduro; Linssen (Antonia 74), Hoesen (De Leeuw 74), Rusnak.
Braga: (442) Matheus Magalhaes; Baiano, Boly, Andre Pinto, Marcelo Goiano; Luiz Carlos, Vukcevic, Alan (Pedro Santos 80), Rafa; Wilson Eduardo (Rui Fonte 90), Hassan (Crislan 65).

Slovan Liberec (0) 2 *(Bakos 75 (pen), Sural 76)*
Marseille (2) 4 *(Batshuayi 14, Nkoudou 43, Barrada 48, Ocampos 90)* 9900
Slovan Liberec: (4141) Koubek; Coufal, Hovorka, Svejdik, Bartosak; Pavelka; Efremov, Folprecht (Rabusic 60), Shala (Sural 66), Sykora (Kerbr 89); Bakos.
Marseille: (4411) Mandanda; Manquillo, N'Koulou, Rolando, Mendy; Barrada, Isla, Romao, Nkoudou (Sparagna 65); Cabella (Lucas Silva 54); Batshuayi (Ocampos 72).

Group F Table	P	W	D	L	F	A	GD	Pts
Braga	6	4	1	1	7	4	3	13
Marseille	6	4	0	2	12	7	5	12
Slovan Liberec	6	2	1	3	6	8	−2	7
FC Groningen	6	0	2	4	2	8	−6	2

GROUP G

Thursday, 17 September 2015
Dnipro Dnipropetrovsk (0) 1 *(Seleznyov 90)*
Lazio (1) 1 *(Milinkovic-Savic 34)* 6000
Dnipro Dnipropetrovsk: (4411) Boyko; Fedetskiy (Ruiz 61), Douglas, Gueye, Anderson Pico; Matheus, Fedorchuk (Danilo 46); Edmar (Bruno Gama 86), Leo Matos; Rotan; Seleznyov.
Lazio: (4231) Marchetti; Konko, Hoedt, Gentiletti, Radu; Onazi, Parolo; Felipe Anderson, Milinkovic-Savic (Mauri 89), Kishna (Candreva 76); Matri (Keita Balde 76).

Saint-Etienne (1) 2 *(Beric 4, Roux 87 (pen))*
Rosenborg (1) 2 *(Mikkelsen 16, Svensson 79)* 10,734
Saint-Etienne: (442) Ruffier; Clerc, Bayal Sall, Perrin, Assou-Ekotto; Monnet-Paquet (Bamba 71), Lemoine (Pajot 76), Clement, Eysseric (Corgnet 64); Beric, Roux.
Rosenborg: (433) Andre Hansen; Svensson, Eyjolfsson, Skjelvik, Midtsjoe; Jensen, Selnaes, Konradsen; Helland (de Lanlay 76), Soderlund, Mikkelsen.

Thursday, 1 October 2015
Lazio (1) 3 *(Onazi 22, Hoedt 48, Biglia 80)*
Saint-Etienne (1) 2 *(Bayal Sall 6, Monnet-Paquet 84)* 11,039
Lazio: (4231) Berisha; Basta, Mauricio (Gentiletti 46), Hoedt, Radu; Biglia, Onazi (Cataldi 74); Felipe Anderson, Milinkovic-Savic, Keita Balde; Mauri (Matri 64).
Saint-Etienne: (433) Ruffier; Clerc, Bayal Sall■, Perrin, Polomat; Corgnet (Diomande 63), Pajot, Lemoine; Hamouma (Bahebeck 63), Beric■, Roux (Monnet-Paquet 74).

Rosenborg (0) 0
Dnipro Dnipropetrovsk (0) 1 *(Seleznyov 80)* 13,939
Rosenborg: (433) Andre Hansen; Svensson, Bjordal, Eyjolfsson, Skjelvik; Konradsen, Selnaes, Midtsjoe (Jensen 71); Helland (de Lanlay 46), Mikkelsen, Soderlund.
Dnipro Dnipropetrovsk: (4321) Boyko; Fedetskiy, Douglas, Gueye, Leo Matos; Tomecak (Luchkevych 71), Fedorchuk, Matheus (Cheberyachko 90); Edmar, Rotan; Seleznyov (Bruno Gama 84).

Thursday, 22 October 2015
Dnipro Dnipropetrovsk (0) 0
Saint-Etienne (1) 1 *(Hamouma 44)* 4900
Dnipro Dnipropetrovsk: (4231) Boyko; Leo Matos, Gueye, Douglas, Fedetskiy (Bruno Gama 46); Fedorchuk (Bezus 59), Edmar; Matheus (Anderson Pico 78), Rotan, Tomecak; Seleznyov.
Saint-Etienne: (4141) Ruffier; Assou-Ekotto, Pogba, Perrin, Clerc; Hamouma (Bahebeck 81); Lemoine, Pajot, Eysseric (Diomande 80), Monnet-Paquet (Polomat 87); Roux.

Lazio (1) 3 *(Matri 28, Felipe Anderson 54, Candreva 80)*
Rosenborg (0) 1 *(Soderlund 69)* 8630
Lazio: (4231) Berisha; Konko, Mauricio■, Hoedt, Radu; Cataldi, Onazi (Gentiletti 10); Candreva, Mauri (Milinkovic-Savic 74), Felipe Anderson (Lulic 70); Matri.
Rosenborg: (451) Andre Hansen; Svensson (Konradsen 75), Bjordal, Eyjolfsson, Dorsin (Mikkelsen 62); de Lanlay, Jensen, Selnaes (Vilhjalmsson 89), Midtsjoe, Skjelvik; Soderlund.

Thursday, 5 November 2015
Rosenborg (0) 0
Lazio (2) 2 *(Djordjevic 9, 29)* 16,038
Rosenborg: (433) Andre Hansen; Svensson, Reginiussen (Bjordal 32), Eyjolfsson, Skjelvik; Jensen, Selnaes, Midtsjoe (Konradsen 61); Helland, Soderlund (Vilhjalmsson 65), Mikkelsen.
Lazio: (4321) Berisha; Konko, Gentiletti, Hoedt, Radu; Cataldi, Kishna, Onazi; Morrison (Mauri 75), Candreva (Keita Balde■ 46); Djordjevic (Matri 66).

Saint-Etienne (1) 3 *(Monnet-Paquet 38, Beric 52, Hamouma 65)*
Dnipro Dnipropetrovsk (0) 0 38,000
Saint-Etienne: (442) Ruffier; Clerc, Perrin, Pogba, Assou-Ekotto; Monnet-Paquet (Hamouma 61), Lemoine, Pajot (Clement 70); Eysseric (Corgnet 80); Roux, Beric.
Dnipro Dnipropetrovsk: (4231) Boyko; Fedetskiy, Douglas, Gueye, Leo Matos; Edmar, Cheberyachko (Bezus 46); Tomecak (Luchkevych 63), Rotan, Matheus; Seleznyov (Bruno Gama 78).

Thursday, 26 November 2015
Lazio (1) 3 *(Candreva 4, Parolo 68, Djordjevic 90)*
Dnipro Dnipropetrovsk (0) 1 *(Bruno Gama 65)* 3000
Lazio: (433) Berisha; Konko, Gentiletti, Mauricio, Radu; Parolo, Cataldi, Candreva; Matri (Djordjevic 70), Klose (Milinkovic-Savic 66), Kishna (Lulic 81).
Dnipro Dnipropetrovsk: (4141) Boyko; Fedetskiy (Shakhov 74), Gueye, Douglas, Leo Matos; Chygrynskiy; Danilo, Bezus (Zozulya 57), Bruno Gama, Matheus (Anderson Pico 41); Seleznyov.

Rosenborg (1) 1 *(Soderlund 40)*
Saint-Etienne (0) 1 *(Roux 80 (pen))* 16,000
Rosenborg: (433) Alexander Hansen; Svensson, Bjordal, Eyjolfsson, Skjelvik; Jensen, Selnaes, Konradsen (Vilhjalmsson 82); Helland (de Lanlay 82), Soderlund, Mikkelsen.
Saint-Etienne: (433) Ruffier; Clerc, Perrin, Polomat, Assou-Ekotto; Pajot, Clement, Cohade (Maupay 71); Hamouma, Roux (Diomande 86), Monnet-Paquet.

Thursday, 10 December 2015
Dnipro Dnipropetrovsk (1) 3 *(Matheus 35, 60, Shakhov 80)*
Rosenborg (0) 0 4541
Dnipro Dnipropetrovsk: (442) Boyko; Chygrynskiy, Gueye, Fedetskiy, Edmar; Leo Matos, Cheberyachko, Bruno Gama (Luchkevych 77), Ruiz (Tomecak 86); Shakhov (Bezus 81), Matheus.
Rosenborg: (442) Andre Hansen; Dorsin (Saeter 84), Svensson, Jensen, Skjelvik; Selnaes, Midtsjoe, Vilhjalmsson, de Lanlay (Konradsen 68); Helland (Mikkelsen 68), Soderlund.

Saint-Etienne (0) 1 *(Eysseric 76)*
Lazio (0) 1 *(Matri 52)*   29,000
Saint-Etienne: (442) Moulin; Polomat, Pogba, Brison, Karamoko (Bayal Sall 27); Clement, Corgnet (Bamba 64), Eysseric, Diomande (Pinheiro 57); Bahebeck, Maupay.
Lazio: (442) Berisha; Hoedt, Basta, Konko, Mauricio; Felipe Anderson, Parolo, Cataldi, Oikonomidis (Candreva 84); Djordjevic, Matri (Morrison 74).

Group F Table	P	W	D	L	F	A	GD	Pts
Lazio	6	4	2	0	13	6	7	14
Saint-Etienne	6	2	3	1	10	7	3	9
Dnipro Dnipropetrovsk	6	2	1	3	6	8	–2	7
Rosenborg	6	0	2	4	4	12	–8	2

GROUP H

Thursday, 17 September 2015
Skenderbeu (0) 0
Besiktas (1) 1 *(Sosa 28)*   8000
Skenderbeu: (442) Shehi; Arapi, Ademir (Vangjeli 71), Radas, Abazi; Latifi (Nimaga 46), Esquerdinha, Lilaj, Shkembi; Berisha, Olayinka (Salihi 72).
Besiktas: (442) Zengin; Koybasi, Gulum, Beck, Rhodolfo; Sosa, Hutchinson, Uysal, Frei (Tore 55); Quaresma (Pektemek 84), Tosun (Gomez 61).

Sporting Lisbon (0) 1 *(Montero 50)*
Lokomotiv Moscow (1) 3 *(Samedov 12, 56, Niasse 65)*
                                                           25,400
Sporting Lisbon: (442) Rui Patricio; Jefferson, Paulo Oliveira, Joao Pereira, Figueiredo; Aquilani (Andre Martins 71), Adrien Silva, Gelson Martins, Montero (Slimani 63); Gutierrez, Carlos Mane (Ruiz 63).
Lokomotiv Moscow: (442) Guilherme; Pejcinovic, Corluka, Denisov, Shishkin; Fernandes (Kolomeytsev 81), Samedov, Tarasov (Mykhalyk 86), Ndinga; Maicon (Grigorev 82), Niasse.

Thursday, 1 October 2015
Besiktas (0) 1 *(Tore 61)*
Sporting Lisbon (1) 1 *(Ruiz 16)*   25,827
Besiktas: (4231) Zengin; Beck, Rhodolfo, Gulum, Koybasi; Uysal (Ozyakup 46), Hutchinson; Tore (Tosun 68), Quaresma (Frei 90); Gomez.
Sporting Lisbon: (442) Rui Patricio; Joao Pereira, Naldo, Figueiredo, Silva; Carlos Mane, Aquilani (Martins 78), William Carvalho, Pereira (Adrien Silva 55); Gutierrez (Slimani 70), Ruiz.

Lokomotiv Moscow (1) 2 *(Niasse 35, Samedov 73)*
Skenderbeu (0) 0   10,340
Lokomotiv Moscow: (4231) Guilherme; Logashov, Corluka, Pejcinovic, Yanbaev; Kolomeytsev (Ndinga 66), Tarasov; Samedov, Fernandes (Miranchuk 46), Maicon; Niasse (Skuletic 81).
Skenderbeu: (4231) Shehi; Vangjeli, Radas, Jashanica, Abazi (Arapi 77); Lilaj, Nimaga; Latifi (Shkembi 71), Olayinka (Progni 87), Berisha; Salihi.

Thursday, 22 October 2015
Lokomotiv Moscow (0) 1 *(Maicon 54)*
Besiktas (0) 1 *(Gomez 64)*   19,124
Lokomotiv Moscow: (4411) Guilherme; Shishkin, Corluka■, Mykhalyk, Denisov; Samedov, Ndinga, Kolomeytsev, Maicon (Kasaev 79); Fernandes (Durica 73); Niasse (Grigorev 88).
Besiktas: (4411) Zengin; Beck, Rhodolfo, Gulum, Koybasi; Tore (Tosun 65), Ozyakup, Hutchinson, Quaresma (Frei 87); Sosa (Uysal 57); Gomez.

Sporting Lisbon (2) 5 *(Aquilani 38 (pen), Montero 41 (pen), Pereira 64, 77, Figueiredo 69)*
Skenderbeu (0) 1 *(Jashanica 89)*   20,000
Sporting Lisbon: (4231) Rui Patricio; Ricardo Esgaio, Ewerton, Figueiredo, Silva; Paulista, Aquilani (William Carvalho 72); Andre Martins (Slimani 59), Carlos Mane (Martins 65), Pereira; Montero.
Skenderbeu: (451) Shehi; Vangjeli, Jashanica, Osmani, Arapi; Progni (Latifi 67), Esquerdinha (Abazi 76), Lilaj, Nimaga (Shkembi 66), Berisha; Salihi■.

Thursday, 5 November 2015
Besiktas (0) 1 *(Quaresma 58)*
Lokomotiv Moscow (0) 1 *(Niasse 76)*   23,000
Besiktas: (451) Zengin; Beck, Gulum, Rhodolfo, Koybasi; Tore, Sosa (Uysal 71), Hutchinson, Ozyakup (Tosun 83), Sahan (Quaresma 46); Gomez.
Lokomotiv Moscow: (4411) Guilherme; Yanbaev, Shishkin, Durica, Denisov; Samedov, Ndinga, Kolomeytsev, Maicon (Grigorev 90); Fernandes (Miranchuk 73); Niasse (Skuletic 90).

Skenderbeu (2) 3 *(Lilaj 15, 20 (pen), Nimaga 56)*
Sporting Lisbon (0) 0   3000
Skenderbeu: (433) Shehi; Vangjeli, Radas, Jashanica, Abazi; Lilaj, Nimaga, Esquerdinha (Shkembi 90); Latifi (Progni 82), Olayinka, Berisha (Arapi 90).
Sporting Lisbon: (4141) Rui Patricio■; Ricardo Esgaio, Ewerton (Paulo Oliveira 70), Figueiredo, Silva; Adrien Silva (Joao Mario 59); Pereira, Paulista, Carlos Mane, Tanaka (Marcelo 19); Montero.

Thursday, 26 November 2015
Besiktas (1) 2 *(Tosun 35, 78)*
Skenderbeu (0) 0   11,500
Besiktas: (4231) Zengin; Koybasi, Rhodolfo, Gulum (Tosic 33), Beck; Hutchinson, Uysal; Frei (Quaresma 68), Ozyakup, Tore (Sahan 84); Tosun.
Skenderbeu: (4231) Shehi; Vangjeli, Radas, Jashanica, Abazi; Lilaj, Esquerdinha; Latifi (Progni 80), Olayinka, Berisha (Arapi 46); Salihi (Djair 83).

Lokomotiv Moscow (1) 2 *(Maicon 5, Miranchuk 86)*
Sporting Lisbon (3) 4 *(Montero 20, Ruiz 38, Gelson Martins 43, Matheus Pereira 60)*   11,043
Lokomotiv Moscow: (4411) Guilherme; Shishkin, Mykhalyk, Durica, Denisov; Samedov, Tarasov (Kolomeytsev 65), Ndinga, Maicon (Kasaev 81); Fernandes (Miranchuk 79); Niasse.
Sporting Lisbon: (442) Marcelo; Ricardo Esgaio, Ewerton, Naldo, Silva; Joao Mario (Aquilani 79), Adrien Silva, Ruiz, Gelson Martins; Montero (Slimani 71), Matheus Pereira (Andre Martins 67).

Thursday, 10 December 2015
Skenderbeu (0) 0
Lokomotiv Moscow (1) 3 *(Tarasov 18, Niasse 88, Samedov 90)*   4500
Skenderbeu: (4411) Shehi; Ademir, Radas, Jashanica, Abazi; Latifi (Progni 72), Lilaj, Esquerdinha (Djair 83), Berisha; Olayinka; Salihi.
Lokomotiv Moscow: (4411) Guilherme; Shishkin, Mykhalyk (Durica 82), Pejcinovic, Denisov; Samedov, Tarasov, Ndinga, Kasaev (Maicon 75); Kolomeytsev; Niasse (Miranchuk 90).

Sporting Lisbon (0) 3 *(Slimani 67, Ruiz 72, Gutierrez 77)*
Besiktas (0) 1 *(Gomez 58)*   28,211
Sporting Lisbon: (4141) Rui Patricio; Joao Pereira, Paulo Oliveira, Naldo, Jefferson; William Carvalho; Joao Mario, Ruiz, Adrien Silva (Gutierrez 65), Montero (Gelson Martins 46); Slimani (Matheus Pereira 87).
Besiktas: (433) Zengin; Beck, Rhodolfo, Tosic, Koybasi (Frei 85); Sosa (Tosun 80), Hutchinson, Ozyakup; Sahan (Uysal 72), Quaresma, Gomez.

Group H Table	P	W	D	L	F	A	GD	Pts
Lokomotiv Moscow	6	3	2	1	12	7	5	11
Sporting Lisbon	6	3	1	2	14	11	3	10
Besiktas	6	2	3	1	7	6	1	9
Skenderbeu	6	1	0	5	4	13	–9	3

GROUP I

Thursday, 17 September 2015
Fiorentina (1) 1 *(Kalinic 3)*
FC Basel (0) 2 *(Bjarnason 71, El-Nenny 79)*   15,269
Fiorentina: (442) Sepe; Rodriguez■, Astori (Tomovic 68), Alonso, Roncaglia; Badelj, Valero, Fernandez (Pasqual 68), Blaszczykowski; Kalinic, Ilicic (El Babacar 46).
FC Basel: (442) Vaclik; Lang, Suchy, Hoegh, Zuffi; Bjarnason, El-Nenny, Xhaka, Embolo; Boetius (Delgado 72), Janko (Calla 86).

Lech Poznan (0) 0

Belenenses (0) 0   7934

Lech Poznan: (442) Buric; Kadar, Dudka, Ceesay, Arajuuri; Kaminski, Tralka (Linetty 46), Lovrencsics (Pawlowski 67), Thomalla; Kownacki (Hamalainen 59), Formella.
Belenenses: (442) Hugo Ventura; Joao Amorim, Tonel, Andre Geraldes, Brandao; Ruben Pinto, Miguel Rosa, Andre Sousa (Ricardo Dias 80), Carlos Martins (Dalcio 88); Fabio Sturgeon (Kuca 62), Leal.

Thursday, 1 October 2015

Belenenses (0) 0

Fiorentina (2) 4 *(Bernarderschi 18, El Babacar 45, Tonel 83 (og), Rossi 90)*   6886

Belenenses: (4141) Hugo Ventura; Andre Geraldes, Tonel, Brandao, Filipe Ferreira; Ruben Pinto; Fabio Sturgeon (Dalcio 40), Carlos Martins (Tiago Caeiro 78), Andre Sousa, Kuca (Fabio Nunes 63); Leal.
Fiorentina: (352) Sepe; Tomovic, Astori, Alonso; Bernarderschi (Badelj 60), Vecino, Mario Suarez, Fernandez, Rebic (Blaszczykowski 81); El Babacar (Verdu 78), Rossi.

FC Basel (0) 2 *(Bjarnason 55, Embolo 90)*

Lech Poznan (0) 0   17,567

FC Basel: (442) Vaclik; Xhaka, Suchy, Samuel, Lang; Zuffi, El-Nenny, Bjarnason, Calla (Gashi 80); Embolo, Janko.
Lech Poznan: (4411) Gostomski; Ceesay, Arajuuri, Kaminski, Kadar; Formella, Tetteh, Linetty■, Jevtic (Tralka 53); Kownacki (Hamalainen 46); Gajos (Lovrencsics 69).

Thursday, 22 October 2015

FC Basel (1) 1 *(Lang 15)*

Belenenses (2) 2 *(Leal 27, Kuca 45)*   17,275

FC Basel: (433) Vailati; Lang, Suchy, Samuel, Safari; Xhaka, Kuzmanovic (Ajeti 77), Gashi; Delgado (Zuffi 67), Janko, Embolo (Bjarnason 58).
Belenenses: (451) Hugo Ventura; Filipe Ferreira, Joao Afonso, Brandao, Joao Amorim; Kuca, Tiago Silva (Oliveira Silva 90), Ruben Pinto, Andre Sousa (Ricardo Dias 84), Fabio Sturgeon; Leal (Tiago Caeiro 87).

Fiorentina (0) 1 *(Rossi 90)*

Lech Poznan (0) 2 *(Kownacki 65, Gajos 82)*   14,293

Fiorentina: (433) Sepe; Tomovic, Roncaglia, Astori, Pasqual (Bernarderschi 68); Fernandez, Mario Suarez (Ilicic 73), Verdu (Vecino 65); Babacar, Rossi.
Lech Poznan: (4411) Buric; Kedziora, Dudka, Kaminski, Kadar; Lovrencsics, Tetteh, Tralka, Formella; Holman (Hamalainen 67); Thomalla (Kownacki 62 (Gajos 77)).

Thursday, 5 November 2015

Belenenses (0) 0

FC Basel (1) 2 *(Janko 45 (pen), Embolo 64)*   4802

Belenenses: (4141) Hugo Ventura; Joao Amorim, Oliveira Silva, Brandao (Tonel 28), Filipe Ferreira; Ruben Pinto, Fabio Sturgeon, Tiago Silva, Andre Sousa (Tiago Caeiro 67), Kuca (Fabio Nunes 83); Leal.
FC Basel: (4231) Vaclik; Lang, Suchy, Akanji, Safari; Xhaka, El-Nenny; Embolo, Zuffi, Bjarnason; Janko.

Lech Poznan (0) 0

Fiorentina (1) 2 *(Ilicic 42, 83)*   22,343

Lech Poznan: (4231) Buric; Kedziora, Dudka, Kaminski, Kadar; Tetteh (Thomalla 73), Tralka; Formella (Lovrencsics 60), Linetty, Pawlowski; Hamalainen (Gajos 77).
Fiorentina: (4231) Sepe; Tomovic, Rodriguez, Astori, Bernarderschi; Vecino, Mario Suarez (Badelj 80); Blaszczykowski (Alonso 72), Fernandez, Ilicic; Rossi (Kalinic 63).

Thursday, 26 November 2015

Belenenses (0) 0

Lech Poznan (0) 0   1987

Belenenses: (451) Hugo Ventura; Filipe Ferreira, Brandao, Tonel, Andre Geraldes; Kuca, Ruben Pinto,

Ricardo Dias, Tiago Silva (Carlos Martins 67), Fabio Sturgeon (Dalcio 79); Tiago Caeiro (Leal 76).
Lech Poznan: (442) Buric; Kedziora, Dudka, Kadar, Douglas; Formella (Pawlowski 65), Linetty, Tralka (Tetteh 46), Lovrencsics; Gajos, Thomalla (Hamalainen 73).

FC Basel (1) 2 *(Suchy 40, El-Nenny 74)*

Fiorentina (2) 2 *(Bernarderschi 23, 36)*   22,550

FC Basel: (451) Vailati; Xhaka, Lang, Suchy, Safari; Embolo, Bjarnason (Kuzmanovic 88), El-Nenny, Zuffi, Boetius (Calla 60); Janko.
Fiorentina: (451) Sepe; Roncaglia■, Rodriguez, Astori, Alonso; Bernarderschi (El Babacar 85), Vecino, Badelj (Gilberto 85), Valero, Ilicic (Tomovic 33); Kalinic.

Thursday, 10 December 2015

Fiorentina (0) 1 *(El Babacar 67)*

Belenenses (0) 0   13,282

Fiorentina: (442) Sepe; Gilberto (Bernarderschi 56), Tomovic, Astori, Pasqual; Alonso, Badelj (Mario Suarez 79), Valero (Vecino 61), Verdu; Rossi, El Babacar.
Belenenses: (442) Hugo Ventura; Joao Amorim, Joao Afonso, Filipe Ferreira, Oliveira Silva; Ruben Pinto (Fabio Nunes 79), Andre Sousa (Kuca 56), Ricardo Dias, Carlos Martins; Fabio Sturgeon (Tiago Caeiro 83), Leal.

Lech Poznan (0) 0

FC Basel (0) 1 *(Boetius 50)*   10,457

Lech Poznan: (442) Buric; Kedziora, Kadar, Arajuuri, Kaminski; Tralka (Tetteh 46), Linetty (Formella 61), Jevtic (Hamalainen 73), Gajos; Kownacki, Pawlowski.
FC Basel: (442) Vailati (Salvi 45); Traore, Lang (Adjeti 46), Samuel, Zuffi; Bjarnason (Huser 79), El-Nenny, Xhaka, Calla; Boetius, Ajeti.

Group I Table	P	W	D	L	F	A	GD	Pts
FC Basel	6	4	1	1	10	5	5	13
Fiorentina	6	3	1	2	11	6	5	10
Lech Poznan	6	1	2	3	2	6	-4	5
Belenenses	6	1	2	3	2	8	-6	5

GROUP J

Thursday, 17 September 2015

Anderlecht (1) 1 *(Gillet 11)*

Monaco (0) 1 *(Traore L 85)*   15,576

Anderlecht: (433) Proto; Najar, Dendoncker, Deschacht, Obradovic; Defour (Heylen 84), Gillet, Tielemans (Ezekiel 88); Praet, Okaka, Suarez (Acheampong 74).
Monaco: (433) Subasic; Toure, Raggi, Wallace Santos, Echiejile (El Shaarawy 61); Fabinho, Joao Moutinho, Pasalic (Traore L 46); Ivan Cavaleiro (Lemar 76), Bernardo Silva, Fabio Coentrao.

Tottenham H (2) 3 *(Son 27, 30, Lamela 86)*

Qarabag (1) 1 *(Almeida 7 (pen))*   26,463

Tottenham H: (451) Lloris; Trippier, Wimmer, Alderweireld, Rose; Lamela, Carroll, Dier (Winks 75), Alli, Townsend (N'Jie 68); Son (Kane 68).
Qarabag: (451) Sehic; Medvedev, Guseynov, Sadygov, Agolli; Ismayilov (El Jadeyaoui 79), Quintana (Michel 79), Garayev, Almeida, Tagiyev (Armenteros 67); Reynaldo.

Thursday, 1 October 2015

Monaco (0) 1 *(El Shaarawy 81)*

Tottenham H (1) 1 *(Lamela 35)*   7216

Monaco: (442) Subasic; Fabinho, Raggi, Carvalho (Dirar 76), Fabio Coentrao; Joao Moutinho, Toulalan, Traore A, Lemar (El Shaarawy 60); Bernardo Silva, Traore L (Carrillo 67).
Tottenham H: (4231) Lloris; Trippier, Alderweireld, Vertonghen, Rose; Alli, Dier; Chadli (Townsend 70), Eriksen (Carroll 90), Lamela (N'Jie 65); Kane.

Qarabag (1) 1 *(Almeida 36)*

Anderlecht (0) 0   20,000

Qarabag: (442) Sehic; Medvedev, Guseynov, Sadygov, Agolli; Garayev, Almeida, El Jadeyaoui (Yunuszade

77), Quintana (Diniyev 67); Reynaldo, Armenteros (Ismayilov 61).
Anderlecht: (424) Proto; Najar, Mbodji S, Deschacht, Obradovic (Acheampong 64); Dendoncker, Defour; Gillet (Tielemans 72), Okaka, Ezekiel, Praet (Suarez 72).

Thursday, 22 October 2015
Anderlecht (1) 2 *(Gillet 13, Okaka 75)*
Tottenham H (1) 1 *(Eriksen 4)*   18,504
Anderlecht: (433) Proto; Deschacht, Obradovic, Mbodji S, Praet (Conte 90); Defour, Gillet, Tielemans; Dendoncker, Ezekiel (Acheampong 66), Okaka (Sylla 88).
Tottenham H: (4231) Lloris; Trippier, Vertonghen, Alderweireld, Davies; Dier, Dembele (Alli 65); Lamela, Eriksen, Townsend (Onomah 80); N'Jie (Kane 59).

Monaco (0) 1 *(Traore L 70)*
Qarabag (0) 0   4000
Monaco: (442) Subasic; Fabinho, Carvalho, Wallace Santos, Raggi; Bernardo Silva (Pasalic 56), Toulalan, Joao Moutinho, Lemar (Dirar 79); El Shaarawy, Traore L (Carrillo 90).
Qarabag: (4141) Sehic; Medvedev, Guseynov, Sadygov, Agolli; Almeida, Garayev, Ismayilov (Poepon 71), El Jadeyaoui (Mammadov 77), Quintana (Chumbinho 59); Armenteros.

Thursday, 5 November 2015
Qarabag (1) 1 *(Armenteros 39)*
Monaco (0) 1 *(Ivan Cavaleiro 72)*   30,200
Qarabag: (451) Sehic; Medvedev, Guseynov, Sadygov, Agolli; Ismayilov (Poepon 64), Garayev, Almeida, Quintana (Chumbinho 69), El Jadeyaoui; Armenteros.
Monaco: (433) Subasic; Fabinho, Carvalho, Wallace Santos, Raggi; Toulalan, Joao Moutinho, Pasalic (Ivan Cavaleiro 61); Bernardo Silva, Traore L (Echiejile 78), El Shaarawy (Carrillo 70).

Tottenham H (1) 2 *(Kane 29, Dembele 87)*
Anderlecht (0) 1 *(Ezekiel 72)*   33,479
Tottenham H: (4231) Lloris; Trippier, Alderweireld, Vertonghen, Davies; Mason (Dembele 73), Dier; Alli (Onomah 77), Eriksen (Son 58), Lamela; Kane.
Anderlecht: (4411) Proto; Gillet, Mbodji S, Deschacht, N'Sakala (Conte 82); Najar, Dendoncker, Defour, Acheampong (Sylla 89); Tielemans (Ezekiel 68); Okaka.

Thursday, 26 November 2015
Monaco (0) 0
Anderlecht (1) 2 *(Gillet 45, Acheampong 78)*   5913
Monaco: (433) Subasic; Fabinho, Raggi, Carvalho, Fabio Coentrao; Pasalic (Carrillo 61), Toulalan (Toure 28 (Echiejile 84)), Joao Moutinho; Bernardo Silva, Traore L, El Shaarawy.
Anderlecht: (442) Proto; Gillet, Mbodji S, Deschacht, N'Sakala; Najar (Ezekiel 66), Defour, Dendoncker, Praet (Acheampong 76); Tielemans, Okaka (Suarez 84).

Qarabag (0) 0
Tottenham H (0) 1 *(Kane 78)*   28,000
Qarabag: (433) Sehic; Medvedev, Guseynov, Sadygov, Agolli; Garayev, Quintana, Almeida; Tagiyev (Chumbinho 65), Poepon (Armenteros 54), Ismayilov (Mammadov 80).
Tottenham H: (4231) Lloris; Trippier, Alderweireld, Vertonghen, Davies; Dier, Mason (Carroll 73); Alli, Eriksen (Onomah 90), Son (N'Jie 79); Kane.

Thursday, 10 December 2015
Anderlecht (2) 2 *(Najar 28, Okaka 31)*
Qarabag (1) 1 *(Quintana 26)*   16,075
Anderlecht: (442) Proto; Najar, Mbodji K, Deschacht, N'Sakala; Praet (Kawaya 90), Gillet, Tielemans, Ezekiel (Lukebakio 66); Suarez, Okaka (Sylla 81).
Qarabag: (4231) Sehic; Medvedev, Guseynov, Sadygov, Gurbanov; Garayev (Poepon 75), Almeida; Quintana, Ismayilov (Tagiyev 63), Chumbinho (Michel 71); Armenteros.

Tottenham H (3) 4 *(Lamela 2, 15, 37, Carroll 78)*
Monaco (0) 1 *(El Shaarawy 61)*   34,122
Tottenham H: (4231) Lloris; Trippier, Alderweireld, Wimmer, Davies; Dier (Bentaleb 42), Carroll; Onomah, N'Jie (Alli 79), Lamela (Chadli 62); Son.
Monaco: (352) Subasic; Wallace Santos, Toulalan, Echiejile; Bernardo Silva (Diarra 65), Pasalic, Bakayoko, Dirar, Traore L (Mbappe-Lottin 56); Joao Moutinho (Lemar 46), El Shaarawy.

Group J Table	P	W	D	L	F	A	GD	Pts
Tottenham H	6	4	1	1	12	6	6	13
Anderlecht	6	3	1	2	8	6	2	10
Monaco	6	1	3	2	5	9	–4	6
Qarabag	6	1	1	4	4	8	–4	4

GROUP K

Thursday, 17 September 2015
APOEL Nicosia (0) 0
Schalke 04 (2) 3 *(Matip 28, Huntelaar 35, 71)*   15,000
APOEL Nicosia: (442) Waterman; Carlao, Antoniades (Artymatas 23), Astiz, Mario Sergio; Makrides, Vinicius (Stilic 61), Morais, De Vincenti[1]; Sotiriou (Cavenaghi 56), Vander.
Schalke 04: (442) Fahrmann; Junior Caicara, Aogo, Matip, Geis (Hoger 61); Meyer, Goretzka, Sane (Sam 80), Neustadter; Di Santo, Huntelaar (Hojbjerg 74).

Asteras Tripolis (1) 1 *(Mazza 2)*
Sparta Prague (0) 1 *(Lafata 56)*   5000
Asteras Tripolis: (442) Kosicky; Alloco, Giannoulis, Lluy, Goian; Bertoglio (Fernandez 71), Iglesias, Ederson (Hamdani 77), Mazza; Fountas (Dimoutsos 66), Giannou.
Sparta Prague: (442) Bicik; Holek, Nhamoinesu, Hybs, Matejovsky; Dockal, Frydek, Husbauer (Fatai 66), Krejci; Jiracek (Marecek 83), Lafata.

Thursday, 1 October 2015
Schalke 04 (3) 4 *(Di Santo 28, 36, 44 (pen), Huntelaar 84)*
Asteras Tripolis (0) 0   42,447
Schalke 04: (451) Fahrmann; Riether, Matip, Howedes, Kolasinac; Di Santo (Choupo-Moting 63), Hojbjerg, Geis (Ayhan 46), Goretzka (Meyer 74), Sane; Huntelaar.
Asteras Tripolis: (451) Theodoropoulos; Zisopoulos, Goian (Fountas 70), Sankare, Giannoulis; Lluy, Iglesias, Ederson (Kourmpelis 79), Hamdani, Mazza (Tsokanis 59); Giannou.

Sparta Prague (1) 2 *(Fatai 24, Brabec 60)*
APOEL Nicosia (0) 0   9130
Sparta Prague: (433) Bicik; Marecek, Brabec, Nhamoinesu, Frydek; Matejovsky, Dockal, Fatai (Konate 86); Krejci (Steinhofer 90), Jiracek, Lafata.
APOEL Nicosia: (433) Waterman; Mario Sergio, Anastasiou, Carlao, Antoniades; Morais, Artymatas, Makrides (Charalambidis 80); Efrem, Piatkowski (Cavenaghi 66), Vander (Stilic 53).

Thursday, 22 October 2015
APOEL Nicosia (1) 2 *(Cavenaghi 43 (pen), Carlao 59)*
Asteras Tripolis (1) 1 *(Lluy 8)*   12,783
APOEL Nicosia: (442) Waterman; Artymatas, Joao Guilherme, Carlao, Antoniades; Vander (Charalambidis 78), Morais, Vinicius, Efrem; Stilic (Astiz 87), Cavenaghi (Piatkowski 63).
Asteras Tripolis: (4231) Theodoropoulos; Lluy, Sankare, Alloco, Giannoulis; Iglesias, Kourmpelis (Lanzarote 74); Mazza (Shkurtaj 88), Dimoutsos (Fernandez 62), Bertoglio; Giannou.

Schalke 04 (1) 2 *(Di Santo 6, Sane 73)*
Sparta Prague (0) 2 *(Fatai 50, Lafata 63)*   51,244
Schalke 04: (442) Fahrmann; Junior Caicara, Howedes, Ayhan (Geis 61), Kolasinac (Aogo 83); Hojbjerg (Sane 61), Goretzka, Neustadter, Meyer; Di Santo, Choupo-Moting.
Sparta Prague: (451) Bicik; Marecek, Brabec, Nhamoinesu, Hybs, Konate (Lafata 62), Dockal, Jiracek, Matejovsky (Husbauer 90), Krejci; Fatai (Holek 88).

Thursday, 5 November 2015

Asteras Tripolis (2) 2 *(Bertoglio 2, Giannou 45)*

APOEL Nicosia (0) 0 3624

Asteras Tripolis: (4231) Theodoropoulos; Lluy, Sankare, Zisopoulos, Panteliadis; Iglesias, Kourmpelis; Lanzarote (Fountas 62), Bertoglio (Hamdani 63), Mazza; Giannou (Alloco 90).
APOEL Nicosia: (433) Waterman; Mario Sergio, Astiz, Carlao, Antoniades (Alexandrou 64); Artymatas (Charalambidis 90), Morais, Vinicius; Stilic, Piatkowski (Cavenaghi 46), Vander.

Sparta Prague (1) 1 *(Lafata 6)*

Schalke 04 (1) 1 *(Geis 21 (pen))* 17,350

Sparta Prague: (451) Bicik; Marecek, Brabec, Nhamoinesu, Hybs; Fatai (Konate 87), Dockal, Jiracek, Matejovsky, Krejci; Lafata (Julis 90).
Schalke 04: (442) Fahrmann; Junior Caicara, Neustadter, Ayhan, Aogo; Sane (Meyer 83), Goretzka (Kolasinac 87), Hojbjerg, Geis; Huntelaar (Di Santo 77), Choupo-Moting.

Thursday, 26 November 2015

Schalke 04 (0) 1 *(Choupo-Moting 87)*

APOEL Nicosia (0) 0 40,000

Schalke 04: (442) Fahrmann; Junior Caicara (Riether 83), Matip, Neustadter, Aogo; Di Santo (Meyer 62), Goretzka, Geis (Hojbjerg 79), Sane; Huntelaar, Choupo-Moting.
APOEL Nicosia: (451) Waterman; Mario Sergio, Joao Guilherme, Carlao, Antoniades (Astiz 30); Charalambidis (Vander 76), Artymatas, Morais, Vinicius, De Vincenti; Sotiriou (Makrides 54).

Sparta Prague (1) 1 *(Brabec 33)*

Asteras Tripolis (0) 0 10,065

Sparta Prague: (451) Bicik; Marecek, Brabec, Nhamoinesu, Hybs; Fatai (Konate 80), Dockal (Holek 85), Vacha, Frydek (Julis 90), Krejci*; Lafata.
Asteras Tripolis: (4231) Theodoropoulos; Lluy, Sankare, Zisopoulos, Giannoulis; Iglesias (Panteliadis 81), Kourmpelis (Dimoutsos 66); Fountas (Lanzarote 77), Fernandez, Mazza; Giannou.

Thursday, 10 December 2015

APOEL Nicosia (1) 1 *(Cavenaghi 6)*

Sparta Prague (0) 3 *(Julis 63, Lafata 77, 87)* 10,000

APOEL Nicosia: (433) Waterman; Mario Sergio, Joao Guilherme, Carlao (Vinicius 35), Alexandrou; Artymatas, Stilic, Morais; De Vincenti, Cavenaghi (Piatkowski 80), Vander (Efrem 60).
Sparta Prague: (343) Stech; Brabec, Nhamoinesu, Holek; Konate, Vacha (Lafata 74), Marecek, Frydek; Fatai (Matejovsky 46), Dockal, Julis (Litsingi 85).

Asteras Tripolis (0) 0

Schalke 04 (2) 4 *(Di Santo 30, Choupo-Moting 38, 78, Meyer 86)* 5500

Asteras Tripolis: (4411) Theodoropoulos; Lluy, Goian (Zisopoulos 62), Sankare, Panteliadis; Lanzarote (Bertoglio 65), Iglesias (Dimoutsos 69), Hamdani, Tsokanis; Fernandez; Giannou.
Schalke 04: (442) Fahrmann; Junior Caicara, Howedes (Friedrich 79), Neustadter, Kolasinac; Sam, Geis (Ayhan 65), Hojbjerg, Choupo-Moting; Di Santo, Huntelaar (Meyer 79).

Group K Table	P	W	D	L	F	A	GD	Pts
Schalke 04	6	4	2	0	15	3	12	14
Sparta Prague	6	3	3	0	10	5	5	12
Asteras Tripolis	6	1	1	4	4	12	–8	4
APOEL Nicosia	6	1	0	5	3	12	–9	3

GROUP L

Thursday, 17 September 2015

Athletic Bilbao (0) 3 *(Aduriz 55, 66, Susaeta 90)*

Augsburg (1) 1 *(Altintop 15)* 38,000

Athletic Bilbao: (442) Herrerin; Laporte, Etxeita, Lekue, Elustondo (Mikel Rico 46); Benat, De Marcos, Susaeta, Ibai (Merino 64); Aduriz, Raul Garcia (Gurpegi 80).

Augsburg: (442) Hitz; Verhaegh, Klavan, Callsen-Bracker, Feulner; Baier, Kohr (Trochowski 72), Altintop (Koo 59), Esswein; Ji, Matavz (Werner 66).

Partizan Belgrade (2) 3 *(Oumarou 11, 39, Zivkovic A 89)*

AZ Alkmaar (1) 2 *(van der Linden 34, Henriksen 90)* 12,000

Partizan Belgrade: (442) Zivkovic Z; Lekovic, Vulicevic, Balazic, Fabricio; Brasanac, Babovic, Zivkovic A (Ninkovic 90), Jevtovic; Oumarou (Ilic 83), Saponjic (Bojinov 66).
AZ Alkmaar: (442) Rochet; Johansson, Gouweleeuw, Brezancic, van der Linden; van Overeem (dos Santos Souza 64), Henriksen, Rienstra, Haye (Tankovic 73); Hupperts*, Janssen (Muhren 73).

Thursday, 1 October 2015

Augsburg (0) 1 *(Bobadilla 57)*

Partizan Belgrade (1) 3 *(Zivkovic A 31, 62, Ji 53 (og))* 22,948

Augsburg: (4132) Hitz; Verhaegh, Hong, Callsen-Bracker (Max 46), Feulner (Trochowski 75); Baier; Koo, Altintop, Ji; Bobadilla, Matavz (Esswein 46).
Partizan Belgrade: (451) Zivkovic Z; Vulicevic, Balazic (Ostojic 46), Fabricio, Subic*; Zivkovic A, Babovic, Jevtovic, Brasanac, Stevanovic; Oumarou (Bojinov 21 (Petrovic 66)).

AZ Alkmaar (0) 2 *(Henriksen 55, Boveda 65 (og))*

Athletic Bilbao (0) 1 *(Aduriz 75)* 11,434

AZ Alkmaar: (433) Coutinho; Johansson, Gouweleeuw, van der Linden, Haps; van Overeem, Rienstra, dos Santos Souza (Haye 87); Janssen (Jahanbakhsh 78), Henriksen, Tankovic (Luckassen 78).
Athletic Bilbao: (4231) Herrerin; Boveda, Gurpegi, Laporte, Lekue; Iturraspe (Raul Garcia 63), Mikel Rico; Aketxe (Williams 57), Eraso, Viguera; Kike Sola (Aduriz 63).

Thursday, 22 October 2015

AZ Alkmaar (0) 0

Augsburg (1) 1 *(Trochowski 43)* 16,511

AZ Alkmaar: (4231) Coutinho; Johansson (Hupperts 77), Gouweleeuw, van der Linden, Haps; Luckassen, Rienstra (Haye 61); van Overeem, Henriksen, dos Santos Souza (Tankovic 69); Janssen.
Augsburg: (4231) Hitz; Verhaegh, Callsen-Bracker, Klavan, Max; Trochowski (Feulner 70), Baier (Kohr 58); Bobadilla (Esswein 80), Koo, Werner; Caiuby.

Partizan Belgrade (0) 0

Athletic Bilbao (1) 2 *(Raul Garcia 32, Benat 85)* 17,000

Partizan Belgrade: (451) Zivkovic Z; Vulicevic, Ostojic, Fabricio, Lekovic; Zivkovic A, Lukic, Petrovic, Ninkovic (Trujic 85), Stevanovic (Saponjic 79); Bojinov (Grbic 64).
Athletic Bilbao: (451) Herrerin; De Marcos, Etxeita, Laporte, Balenziaga; Williams (Boveda 86), San Jose, Raul Garcia, Benat (Elustondo 90), Susaeta (Merino 55); Aduriz.

Thursday, 5 November 2015

Athletic Bilbao (3) 5 *(Williams 16, 19, Benat 40, Aduriz 71, Elustondo 81)*

Partizan Belgrade (1) 1 *(Oumarou 17)* 45,000

Athletic Bilbao: (4231) Herrerin; Boveda, Etxeita, Laporte, Balenziaga; Benat (Elustondo 73), San Jose; Williams (De Marcos 63), Raul Garcia (Eraso 66); Susaeta; Aduriz.
Partizan Belgrade: (4141) Kljajic; Vulicevic, Fabricio, Balazic (Cirkovic 26), Subic; Jevtovic; Oumarou (Saponjic 46), Babovic, Lukic, Stevanovic (Ninkovic 74); Grbic.

Augsburg (2) 4 *(Bobadilla 24, 33, 74, Ji 66)*

AZ Alkmaar (1) 1 *(Janssen 45)* 21,241

Augsburg: (4231) Hitz; Verhaegh, Janker, Klavan, Max; Kohr, Baier (Feulner 65); Caiuby, Ji, Bobadilla (Werner 78); Matavz (Koo 55).
AZ Alkmaar: (4231) Coutinho; Johansson, Gouweleeuw, van der Linden, Haps; Rienstra (Ortiz 52), Luckassen; van Overeem, Henriksen (Haye 37), Jahanbakhsh (Hupperts 76); Janssen.

Thursday, 26 November 2015

Augsburg (1) 2 *(Trochowski 41, Bobadilla 60)*
Athletic Bilbao (1) 3 *(Susaeta 10, Aduriz 84, 86)* 23,741
Augsburg: (4231) Hitz; Verhaegh, Janker, Klavan, Stafylidis; Kohr, Baier; Esswein (Koo 76), Altintop (Bobadilla 56), Trochowski (Caiuby 55); Ji.
Athletic Bilbao: (4231) Herrerin; Boveda, Gurpegi, Laporte, Balenziaga; San Jose (Iturraspe 73), Mikel Rico; Susaeta, Eraso (Raul Garcia 58), Merino (Williams 58); Aduriz.

AZ Alkmaar (0) 1 *(dos Santos Souza 48)*
Partizan Belgrade (0) 2 *(Oumarou 65, Zivkovic A 89)*
15,000
AZ Alkmaar: (433) Coutinho; Johansson, Gouweleeuw, Luckassen, Brezancic; van Overeem (Tankovic 75), Ortiz (Hupperts 88), dos Santos Souza; Janssen, Henriksen, Jahanbakhsh (Muhren 80).
Partizan Belgrade: (4231) Kljajic; Vulicevic, Bandalovski, Cirkovic, Subic; Jevtovic, Babovic (Ilic 75); Zivkovic A (Grbic 90), Brasanac, Ninkovic (Bojinov 85); Oumarou.

Thursday, 10 December 2015

Athletic Bilbao (1) 2 *(Kike Sola 41, San Jose 47 (pen))*
AZ Alkmaar (1) 2 *(van Overeem 26, Janssen 89)* 29,483
Athletic Bilbao: (4231) Herrerin; Boveda, Elustondo, Gurpegi, Saborit; San Jose (Iturraspe 71), Susaeta; Mikel Rico, Eraso (Aketxe 81), Kike Sola (Viguera 77); Merino.

AZ Alkmaar: (4231) Coutinho; Johansson, Gouweleeuw, Luckassen, Ouwejan (Hatzidiakos 75); Ortiz, Rienstra; van Overeem (Muhren 81), Haye, Hupperts (Tankovic 64); Janssen.

Partizan Belgrade (1) 1 *(Oumarou 11)*
Augsburg (1) 3 *(Hong 45, Verhaegh 51, Bobadilla 89)*
29,644
Partizan Belgrade: (442) Zivkovic Z; Bandalovski, Cirkovic, Subic (Petrovic 64), Fabricio; Brasanac, Babovic, Ninkovic (Grbic 83), Zivkovic A▪; Jevtovic, Oumarou.
Augsburg: (442) Hitz; Verhaegh, Stafylidis (Max 80), Janker, Callsen-Bracker (Hong 40); Baier, Trochowski, Koo (Caiuby 61), Ji; Matavz, Bobadilla.

Group L Table	P	W	D	L	F	A	GD	Pts
Athletic Bilbao	6	4	1	1	16	8	8	13
Augsburg	6	3	0	3	12	11	1	9
Partizan Belgrade	6	3	0	3	10	14	–4	9
AZ Alkmaar	6	1	1	4	8	13	–5	4

KNOCKOUT STAGE

ROUND OF 32 FIRST LEG

Tuesday, 16 February 2016

Fenerbahce (1) 2 *(Souza 18, 72)*
Lokomotiv Moscow (0) 0 47,000
Fenerbahce: (433) Fabiano; Gonul, Kjaer, Bruno Alves, Erkin; Tufan, Topal, Souza (Kadlec 84); Nani, van Persie (Fernandao 77), Sen (Potuk 78).
Lokomotiv Moscow: (4231) Guilherme; Yanbaev, Pejcinovic, Durica, Denisov; Ndinga, Tarasov; Samedov, Fernandes, Kasaev (Maicon 62 (Mykhalyk 74)); Skuletic (Miranchuk 79).

Thursday, 18 February 2016

Anderlecht (0) 1 *(Mbodji S 67)*
Olympiacos (0) 0 15,397
Anderlecht: (442) Proto; Najar, Deschacht, Mbodji S, Buttner (Nuytinck 89); Acheampong, Defour (Suarez 88), Badji, Praet; Djuricic (Tielemans 73), Okaka.
Olympiacos: (4321) Roberto; Leandro Salino, da Costa, Botia, Masuaku; Milivojevic, Zdjelar (Kasami 69), Durmaz (Dominguez 83); Fortounis, Seba (Pulido 80); Ideye.

Augsburg (0) 0
Liverpool (0) 0 25,000
Augsburg: (4411) Hitz; Verhaegh, Janker, Klavan, Stafylidis; Bobadilla (Caiuby 23), Kohr, Feulner, Werner (Ji 80); Altintop (Koo 87); Esswein.
Liverpool: (433) Mignolet; Clyne, Toure, Sakho, Moreno; Henderson, Milner (Ibe 81), Can; Coutinho, Firmino, Sturridge (Origi 68).

Borussia Dortmund (1) 2 *(Piszczek 6, Reus 71)*
Porto (0) 0 65,851
Borussia Dortmund: (451) Burki; Piszczek, Papastathopoulos, Hummels, Schmelzer; Mkhitaryan, Sahin (Leitner 57), Weigl, Kagawa (Ginter 87), Reus (Pulisic 86); Aubameyang.
Porto: (451) Casillas; Varela, Layun, Martins Indi, Jose Angel; Brahimi (Andre Andre 59), Ruben Neves, Herrera, Sergio Oliveira (Evandro 76), Marega; Aboubakar (Suk 87).

Fiorentina (0) 1 *(Bernardeschi 59)*
Tottenham H (1) 1 *(Chadli 37 (pen))* 15,200
Fiorentina: (4411) Tatarusanu; Tomovic, Rodriguez, Astori, Alonso; Blaszczykowski (Kalinic 62), Tino Costa (Vecino 67), Valero, Bernarderschi; Ilicic (Badelj 61); Zarate.
Tottenham H: (4231) Vorm; Trippier, Alderweireld, Wimmer, Davies; Chadli (Dier 79), Mason; Eriksen, Carroll (Dembele 46), Alli; Son (Kane 68).

Galatasaray (1) 1 *(Sarioglu 12)*
Lazio (1) 1 *(Milinkovic-Savic 22)* 33,353
Galatasaray: (4231) Muslera; Denayer, Balta, Gunter, Carole (Adin 71); Chedjou, Donk; Sarioglu (Bulut 78), Inan, Sneijder (Oztekin 89); Podolski.
Lazio: (433) Marchetti; Konko, Mauricio, Hoedt, Radu; Milinkovic-Savic, Biglia, Parolo; Felipe Anderson (Candreva 58), Lulic (Mauri 90), Matri (Klose 69).

Marseille (0) 0
Athletic Bilbao (0) 1 *(Aduriz 54)* 29,727
Marseille: (4231) Mandanda; Isla, Rolando, N'Koulou, Manquillo; Diarra, Romao; Alessandrini (Batshuayi 59), Barrada (Thauvin 59), Nkoudou (Sarr 82); Fletcher.
Athletic Bilbao: (4231) Herrerin; De Marcos, Etxeita, Laporte, Balenziaga; San Jose, Eraso (Mikel Rico 58); Benat (Elustondo 90), Williams, Aduriz; Merino (Boveda 74).

Midtjylland (1) 2 *(Sisto 44, Onuachu 77)*
Manchester U (1) 1 *(Depay 37)* 9182
Midtjylland: (4231) Andersen; Romer, Hansen, Bodurov, Novak; Hassan (Urena 67), Sparv; Kadlec (Royer 86), Sisto, Olsson; Pusic (Onuachu 61).
Manchester U: (4231) Romero; Love, Smalling, McNair, Blind; Ander Herrera (Schneiderlin 72), Carrick; Lingard, Mata (Andreas Pereira 78), Depay; Martial.

Saint-Etienne (2) 3 *(Bayal Sall 9, Monnet-Paquet 38, Bahebeck 76)*
FC Basel (1) 2 *(Samuel 44, Janko 55 (pen))* 27,013
Saint-Etienne: (4231) Ruffier; Theophile-Catherine, Bayal Sall, Pogba, Tabanou; Lemoine, Clement (Pajot 66); Monnet-Paquet (Hamouma 75), Cohade, Tannane; Roux (Bahebeck 71).
FC Basel: (433) Vaclik; Lang, Suchy, Samuel, Safari; Xhaka, Zuffi, Embolo (Calla 90); Bjarnason, Steffen (Boetius 63), Janko.

Sevilla (1) 3 *(Llorente 35, 49, Gameiro 72)*
Molde (0) 0 28,920
Sevilla: (442) Soria; Coke, Carrico, Kolodzieczak, Escudero; Vitolo, Nzonzi, Cristoforo (Iborra 68), Krohn-Dehli (Konoplyanka 73); Banega, Llorente (Gameiro 57).
Molde: (442) Horvath; Toivio, Gabrielsen, Forren, Flo; Mostrom, Aursnes (Svendsen 80), Hestad D, Elyounoussi (Hestad E 63); Diouf, Gulbrandsen (Agnaldo 73).

Shakhtar Donetsk (0) 0

Schalke 04 (0) 0   23,615

Shakhtar Donetsk: (4411) Pyatov; Srna, Kucher▪, Rakitskiy, Ismaily; Marlos (Wellington Nem 74), Malyshev (Kryvtsov 89), Stepanenko, Taison (Eduardo 80); Kovalenko; Gladkyy.
Schalke 04: (442) Fahrmann; Junior Caicara, Kolasinac, Neustadter, Matip; Sane (Sam 87), Belhanda (Huntelaar 88), Geis, Choupo-Moting; Meyer (Schopf 81), Goretzka.

Sion (0) 1 *(Konate 54)*

Braga (1) 2 *(Stoiljkovic 13, Rafa 61)*   9000

Sion: (451) Vanins; Ruefli, Lacroix (Assifuah 24), Ziegler, Jagne; Carlitos, Fernandes, Salatic, Ndoye, Mujangi Bia (Follonier 70); Konate (Gekas 77).
Braga: (442) Matheus Magalhaes; Wilson Eduardo, Andre Pinto, Boly, Baiano; Alan (Pedro Santos 66), Luiz Carlos, Vukcevic▪, Rafa; Hassan (Josue 84), Stoiljkovic (Ricardo Ferreira 90).

Sparta Prague (0) 1 *(Julis 64)*

Krasnodar (0) 0   14,120

Sparta Prague: (4231) Bicik; Zahustel, Brabec, Holek, Nhamoinesu; Marecek, Vacha, Fatai (Jiracek 89), Dockal (Matejovsky 80), Krejci; Julis (Konate 78).
Krasnodar: (451) Dykan; Kaleshin, Sigurdsson, Granqvist, Petrov; Smolov (Wanderson 68), Mamaev, Ahmedov, Pereyra (Gazinski 66), Joaozinho (Bystrov 82); Ari.

Sporting Lisbon (0) 0

Bayer Leverkusen (1) 1 *(Bellarabi 26)*   26,201

Sporting Lisbon: (442) Rui Patricio; Joao Pereira, Coates (Ewerton 73), Semedo▪, Jefferson; Joao Mario, Aquilani (Adrien Silva 61), William Carvalho, Carlos Mane; Gutierrez (Slimani 62), Ruiz.
Bayer Leverkusen: (433) Leno; Jedvaj (Hilbert 84), Toprak, Tah, Wendell; Calhanoglu, Kramer, Brandt (Papadopoulos 66); Mehmedi (Henrichs 79), Kiessling, Bellarabi.

Valencia (5) 6 *(Santi Mina 4, 25, Parejo 10, Negredo 29, Andre Gomes 35, Rodrigo 89)*

Rapid Vienna (0) 0   25,000

Valencia: (4141) Ryan; Joao Cancelo (Barragan 76), Filipe Souza, Ruben Vezo, Gaya; Danilo; Santi Mina, Parejo (Javi Fuego 59), Andre Gomes (Rodrigo 68), Piatti; Negredo.
Rapid Vienna: (4231) Strebinger; Pavelic, Sonnleitner, Hofmann M, Stangl; Petsos, Schwab; Schobesberger (Alar 87), Hofmann S (Grahovac 45), Kainz (Murg 46); Jelic.

Villarreal (0) 1 *(Suarez 82)*

Napoli (0) 0   17,686

Villarreal: (442) Areola; Mario, Musacchio, Victor Ruiz, Jaume; Jonathan (Castillejo 36), Bruno, Trigueros (Pina 74), Suarez; Soldado, Leo Baptistao (Bakambu 61).
Napoli: (433) Reina; Hysaj, Chiriches, Koulibaly, Strinic; Callejon (Insigne 73), Hamsik, Valdifiori; David Lopez (Allan 85), Mertens, Gabbiadini (Higuain 67).

ROUND OF 32 SECOND LEG

Wednesday, 24 February 2016

Braga (1) 2 *(Josue 27 (pen), Stoiljkovic 48)*

Sion (2) 2 *(Gekas 16, 30)*   5000

Braga: (442) Matheus Magalhaes; Boly, Baiano, Ricardo Ferreira, Marcelo Goiano; Luiz Carlos, Rafa, Josue (Pedro Santos 62), Mauro Sousa; Stoiljkovic (Rui Fonte 80), Hassan (Andre Pinto 90).
Sion: (4231) Vanins; Vanczak, Ruefli, Ndoye, Salatic; Jagne, Fernandes; Carlitos, Konate, Assifuah (Mujangi Bia 76); Gekas (Zeman 88).

Thursday, 25 February 2016

Athletic Bilbao (0) 1 *(Merino 81)*

Marseille (1) 1 *(Batshuayi 40)*   38,259

Athletic Bilbao: (4411) Herrerin; De Marcos, Etxeita, Laporte, Balenziaga; Susaeta (Mikel Rico 88), Iturraspe, San Jose, Lekue (Muniain 58); Raul Garcia (Merino 75); Aduriz.
Marseille: (4411) Mandanda; Manquillo (Thauvin 85), N'Koulou, Rekik (Alessandrini 87), Mendy; Nkoudou, Diarra, Isla, Cabella; Fletcher; Batshuayi.

Bayer Leverkusen (1) 3 *(Bellarabi 29, 65, Calhanoglu 87)*

Sporting Lisbon (1) 1 *(Joao Mario 38)*   26,954

Bayer Leverkusen: (442) Leno; Jedvaj, Tah, Papadopoulos (Kruse 88), Wendell; Bellarabi, Calhanoglu, Kramer, Brandt (Mehmedi 46); Kiessling (Ramalho Silva 62), Hernandez.
Sporting Lisbon: (442) Rui Patricio; Joao Pereira, Naldo, Ewerton, Jefferson; Bruno Cesar (Martins 79), William Carvalho, Aquilani, Joao Mario; Gutierrez (Slimani 67), Carlos Mane (Ruiz 62).

FC Basel (1) 2 *(Zuffi 15, 90)*

Saint-Etienne (0) 1 *(Bayal Sall 89)*   20,976

FC Basel: (451) Vaclik; Lang, Suchy, Samuel (Fransson 89), Safari (Traore 72); Embolo▪, Xhaka, Delgado (Steffen 68), Zuffi, Bjarnason; Janko.
Saint-Etienne: (433) Ruffier; Theophile-Catherine, Bayal Sall, Pogba, Tabanou; Lemoine (Eysseric▪ 75), Clement, Cohade; Monnet-Paquet, Bahebeck (Roux 57), Tannane (Hamouma 60).
FC Basel won on away goals.

Krasnodar (0) 0

Sparta Prague (0) 3 *(Marecek 51, Frydek 57, Fatai 70)*   14,850

Krasnodar: (451) Dykan; Petrov, Strandberg, Granqvist, Kaleshin; Smolov (Torbinski 75), Ahmedov, Kabore▪, Pereyra (Wanderson 62), Mamaev (Joaozinho 62); Ari.
Sparta Prague: (451) Bicik; Zahustel, Brabec, Holek, Nhamoinesu; Frydek, Marecek (Matejovsky 78), Vacha, Dockal (Konate 83), Krejci; Fatai (Julis 76).

Lazio (0) 3 *(Parolo 58, Felipe Anderson 60, Klose 71)*

Galatasaray (0) 1 *(Oztekin 62)*   14,019

Lazio: (433) Marchetti; Konko, Mauricio, Bisevac, Radu; Milinkovic-Savic, Biglia, Parolo; Felipe Anderson, Matri (Klose 69), Lulic (Candreva 57).
Galatasaray: (4231) Muslera; Sarioglu (Bulut 65), Denayer, Balta, Carole; Donk (Kisa 85), Chedjou; Oztekin (Adin 75), Inan, Sneijder; Podolski.

Liverpool (1) 1 *(Milner 5 (pen))*

Augsburg (0) 0   43,081

Liverpool: (433) Mignolet; Clyne, Lucas, Sakho, Moreno; Can, Henderson, Milner; Firmino, Sturridge (Origi 66), Coutinho (Teixeira 79).
Augsburg: (4231) Hitz; Verhaegh, Janker (Parker 90), Klavan, Stafylidis; Esswein, Altintop; Werner (Bobadilla 72), Koo (Moravek 80), Caiuby; Kohr.

Lokomotiv Moscow (1) 1 *(Samedov 45)*

Fenerbahce (0) 1 *(Topal 83)*   15,695

Lokomotiv Moscow: (451) Guilherme; Pejcinovic, Corluka, Durica, Denisov; Samedov, Ndinga (Mykhalyk 13), Fernandes (Skuletic 73), Kolomeytsev, Kasaev (Zhemaletdinov 81); Miranchuk.
Fenerbahce: (4141) Fabiano; Gonul (Ozbayrakli 44), Kjaer, Bruno Alves, Kaldirim; Topal; Nani (Potuk 79), Tufan (Kadlec 74), Souza, Sen; van Persie.

Manchester U (1) 5 *(Boduruv 32 (og), Rashford 64, 75, Ander Herrera 88 (pen), Depay 90)*

Midtjylland (1) 1 *(Sisto 27)*   58,609

Manchester U: (4231) Romero; Varela, Carrick, Blind, Riley (Rojo 79); Schneiderlin, Ander Herrera (Poole 90); Lingard (Andreas Pereira 86), Mata, Depay; Rashford.
Midtjylland: (4141) Andersen; Romer▪, Hansen, Bodurov, Novak; Sparv; Hassan (Kadlec 66), Poulsen, Olsson (Pusic 79), Sisto; Urena (Onuachu 46).

Molde (1) 1 *(Hestad E 43)*

Sevilla (0) 0	7284

Molde: (433) Horvath; Toivio, Gabrielsen, Forren, Flo; Hestad E, Hestad D (Strande 90), Aursnes; Mostrom (Strand 80), Svendsen (Diop 68), Elyounoussi.

Sevilla: (4231) Soria; Mariano, Fazio, Kolodzieczak, Escudero; Carrico, Iborra; Konoplyanka (Diogo Figueiras 81), Banega, Reyes (Krohn-Dehli 55); Llorente (Gameiro 62).

Napoli (1) 1 *(Hamsik 17)*

Villarreal (0) 1 *(Pina 59)*	23,928

Napoli: (433) Reina; Hysaj, Albiol, Chiriches, Strinic (Maggio 64); David Lopez (Gabbiadini 79), Valdifiori (Jorginho 75), Hamsik; Mertens, Higuain, Insigne.

Villarreal: (442) Areola; Mario, Musacchio, Victor Ruiz, Jaume; Rukavina (Castillejo 78), Pina (Trigueros 84), Bruno, Suarez; Soldado (Adrian 70), Bakambu.

Olympiacos (1) 1 *(Fortounis 30 (pen))*

Anderlecht (0) 2 *(Acheampong 103, 112)*	32,500

Olympiacos: (433) Roberto; Elabdellaoui, Botia, da Costa, Masuaku; Milivojevic, Fortounis, Cambiasso (Zdjelar 67); Durmaz (Dominguez 49), Ideye, Pulido (Seba 83).

Anderlecht: (442) Proto; Najar, Mbodji K, Deschacht, Buttner (Nuytinck 91); Praet, Badji, Dendoncker (Defour 97), Acheampong; Djuricic (Suarez 81), Okaka. *aet.*

Porto (0) 0

Borussia Dortmund (1) 1 *(Casillas 23 (og))*	32,707

Porto: (4231) Casillas; Maxi Pereira, Layun, Marcano, Jose Angel; Ruben Neves, Danilo Pereira; Varela (Brahimi 65), Evandro (Herrera 71), Marega; Aboubakar (Suk 56).

Borussia Dortmund: (4411) Burki; Ginter, Bender, Hummels (Subotic 46), Schmelzer; Mkhitaryan, Gundogan (Sahin 46), Weigl, Reus (Ramos 69); Kagawa; Aubameyang.

Rapid Vienna (0) 0

Valencia (0) 4 *(Rodrigo 59, Feghouli 63, Piatti 72, Ruben Vezo 88)*	39,800

Rapid Vienna: (4411) Strebinger; Sonnleitner, Hofmann M, Pavelic, Wober; Petsos, Schwab, Grahovac, Murg (Schaub 82); Alar (Schobesberger 69); Prosenik (Jelic 64).

Valencia: (4231) Ryan; Ruben Vezo, Mustafi, Gaya (Latorre 46), Barragan; Feghouli, Danilo; Javi Fuego (Tropi 79), Negredo (Mir 65), Piatti; Rodrigo.

Schalke 04 (0) 0

Shakhtar Donetsk (1) 3 *(Marlos 27, Ferreyra 63, Kovalenko 77)*	45,308

Schalke 04: (4231) Fahrmann; Junior Caicara, Matip, Neustadter, Kolasinac (Aogo 46); Sane, Geis; Goretzka (Di Santo 45), Schopf (Sam 58), Belhanda; Huntelaar.

Shakhtar Donetsk: (433) Pyatov; Srna, Kryvtsov, Rakitskiy, Ismaily; Marlos (Wellington Nem 74), Malyshev, Stepanenko; Taison (Eduardo 80), Kovalenko, Ferreyra (Boriachuk 89).

Tottenham H (1) 3 *(Mason 25, Lamela 63, Rodriguez 81 (og))*

Fiorentina (0) 0	34,880

Tottenham H: (4231) Lloris; Trippier, Alderweireld, Wimmer, Davies; Dier, Mason (Winks 87); Lamela (Onomah 76), Alli (Bentaleb 84), Eriksen; Chadli.

Fiorentina: (433) Tatarusanu; Tomovic, Rodriguez, Astori, Alonso; Vecino, Badelj (Fernandez 83), Valero (Blaszczykowski 74); Bernarderschi, Kalinic, Ilicic (Zarate 61).

ROUND OF 16 FIRST LEG

Thursday, 10 March 2016

Athletic Bilbao (1) 1 *(Raul Garcia 21)*

Valencia (0) 0	53,289

Athletic Bilbao: (4231) Herrerin; De Marcos, Etxeita, Laporte, Balenziaga; Iturraspe (Mikel Rico 82), Benat; Susaeta (Elustondo 73), Raul Garcia, Muniain (Merino 54); Aduriz.

Valencia: (4231) Ryan; Barragan, Mustafi, Abdennour, Gaya; Javi Fuego, Danilo; Rodrigo (Feghouli 86), Parejo (Alcacer 82), Piatti (Andre Gomes 70); Negredo.

Borussia Dortmund (1) 3 *(Aubameyang 30, Reus 61, 70)*

Tottenham H (0) 0	65,848

Borussia Dortmund: (4141) Weidenfeller; Bender (Subotic 57), Hummels, Piszczek, Weigl; Schmelzer; Durm, Mkhitaryan, Castro, Reus (Ramos 82); Aubameyang (Kagawa 82).

Tottenham H: (4231) Lloris; Trippier, Alderweireld, Wimmer, Davies; Carroll, Mason; Onomah, Eriksen (Lamela 65), Son (Kane 76); Chadli (Dembele 58).

FC Basel (0) 0

Sevilla (0) 0	22,403

FC Basel: (4411) Vaclik; Lang (Traore 47), Suchy, Samuel (Hoegh 90), Safari; Bjarnason, Xhaka, Zuffi, Steffen; Delgado (Fransson 82); Janko.

Sevilla: (4231) Soria; Coke, Rami, Kolodziejczak, Tremoulinas; Nzonzi■, Cristoforo; Vitolo (Konoplyanka 64), Banega (Carrico 90), Krohn-Dehli; Gameiro (Llorente 73).

Fenerbahce (0) 1 *(Topal 82)*

Braga (0) 0	40,197

Fenerbahce: (433) Demirel; Ozbayrakli, Kjaer, Bruno Alves, Erkin; Topal, Tufan (Meireles 72), Souza; Potuk (Fernandao 79), van Persie, Sen (Nani 65).

Braga: (442) Matheus Magalhaes; Baiano, Ricardo Ferreira (Boly 15), Andre Pinto, Marcelo Goiano; Josue, Luiz Carlos, Vukcevic, Rafa (Pedro Santos 85); Wilson Eduardo (Stoiljkovic 72), Hassan.

Liverpool (1) 2 *(Sturridge 20 (pen), Firmino 73)*

Manchester U (0) 0	43,228

Liverpool: (433) Mignolet; Clyne, Lovren, Sakho, Moreno; Henderson, Can, Lallana; Coutinho, Sturridge (Allen 64), Firmino (Origi 84).

Manchester U: (433) De Gea; Varela, Smalling, Blind, Rojo; Fellaini, Mata (Ander Herrera 79), Schneiderlin (Schweinsteiger 79); Martial, Rashford (Carrick 46), Depay.

Shakhtar Donetsk (2) 3 *(Taison 22, Kucher 24, Eduardo 79)*

Anderlecht (0) 1 *(Acheampong 68)*	23,621

Shakhtar Donetsk: (4411) Pyatov; Srna, Kucher, Rakitskiy, Ismaily; Marlos (Wellington Nem 74), Kovalenko, Malyshev, Taison (Bernard 46); Eduardo (Dentinho 87); Ferreyra.

Anderlecht: (442) Proto; Najar, Mbodji S, Nuytinck, Deschacht; Suarez (Djuricic 67), Badji (Tielemans 74), Defour, Acheampong; Praet (Conte 68), Okaka.

Sparta Prague (1) 1 *(Frydek 13)*

Lazio (1) 1 *(Parolo 39)*	17,482

Sparta Prague: (433) Bicik; Zahustel, Brabec, Holek, Nhamoinesu; Frydek, Vacha, Marecek; Dockal (Fatai 59), Lafata (Julis 61), Krejci.

Lazio: (433) Marchetti; Konko (Basta 46 (Mauricio 66)), Bisevac, Hoedt, Radu; Milinkovic-Savic, Biglia, Parolo; Candreva, Matri (Lulic 55), Keita Balde.

Villarreal (1) 2 *(Bakambu 4, 56)*

Bayer Leverkusen (0) 0	16,211

Villarreal: (442) Areola; Mario, Bailly, Victor Ruiz, Rukavina; Castillejo (Leiva 80), Trigueros, Bruno, Suarez; Soldado (Leo Baptistao 76), Bakambu (Adrian 82).

Bayer Leverkusen: (442) Leno; Jedvaj■, Papadopoulos, Tah, Wendell; Brandt, Kramer (Frey 63), Calhanoglu, Bellarabi (Mehmedi 86); Hernandez, Kiessling (Kruse 67).

ROUND OF 16 SECOND LEG

Thursday, 17 March 2016

Anderlecht (0) 0

Shakhtar Donetsk (0) 1 *(Eduardo 90)*   16,000

Anderlecht: (442) Proto; Najar, Mbodji S■, Nuytinck (Sylla 77), Deschacht; Praet, Badji (Tielemans 70), Defour, Acheampong; Ezekiel (Trezeguet 70), Okaka.
Shakhtar Donetsk: (4231) Pyatov; Srna, Kucher■, Rakitskiy, Ismaily; Malyshev, Stepanenko; Marlos (Eduardo 90), Kovalenko (Ordets 87), Taison (Dentinho 83); Ferreyra.

Bayer Leverkusen (0) 0

Villarreal (0) 0   23,409

Bayer Leverkusen: (4411) Leno; Frey, Tah, Papadopoulos (Ramalho Silva 80), Wendell; Bellarabi, Calhanoglu, Kramer (Yurchenko 67), Brandt; Mehmedi (Kruse 59); Hernandez.
Villarreal: (442) Sergio Asenjo; Mario, Bailly, Victor Ruiz, Rukavina; Suarez (Alfonso Criado 89), Pina, Bruno, Castillejo (Trigueros 60); Soldado (Adrian 73), Bakambu.

Braga (1) 4 *(Hassan 11, Josue 69 (pen), Stoiljkovic 74, Rafa 83)*

Fenerbahce (1) 1 *(Potuk 45)*   16,431

Braga: (442) Matheus Magalhaes; Baiano, Andre Pinto, Boly, Marcelo Goiano; Josue, Mauro Sousa, Vukcevic (Pedro Santos 73), Rafa; Hassan, Stoiljkovic (Filipe Augusto 90).
Fenerbahce: (4231) Demirel; Ozbayrakli, Kjaer, Bruno Alves, Erkin; Souza, Topal■; Nani (Sen■ 72), Diego (Kadlec 72), Potuk■; van Persie (Fernandao 78).

Lazio (0) 0

Sparta Prague (3) 3 *(Dockal 10, Krejci 12, Juls 44)* 18,827

Lazio: (4231) Marchetti; Konko (Mauricio 67), Bisevac, Hoedt, Lulic; Biglia, Parolo; Candreva, Mauri (Felipe Anderson 58), Keita Balde; Klose (Matri 58).
Sparta Prague: (4411) Bicik; Zahustel, Brabec, Holek, Nhamoinesu; Dockal, Marecek, Vacha (Matejovsky 70), Krejci (Fatai 83); Frydek; Juls (Konate 58).

Manchester U (1) 1 *(Martial 32 (pen))*

Liverpool (1) 1 *(Coutinho 45)*   75,180

Manchester U: (4231) De Gea; Varela (Valencia 46), Smalling, Blind, Rojo (Darmian 63); Carrick (Schweinsteiger 70), Fellaini; Lingard, Mata, Martial; Rashford.
Liverpool: (433) Mignolet; Milner, Lovren, Sakho, Clyne; Coutinho, Can, Henderson (Allen 71); Firmino (Benteke 84), Sturridge (Origi 67), Lallana.

Sevilla (3) 3 *(Rami 35, Gameiro 44, 45)*

FC Basel (0) 0   35,546

Sevilla: (4231) Soria; Mariano, Rami, Kolodzieczak, Tremoulinas; Cristofon, Iborra (Krychowiak 60); Reyes, Banega, Krohn-Dehli (Escudero 51); Gameiro (Llorente 69).
FC Basel: (4141) Vaclik; Lang, Hoegh, Suchy, Safari; Xhaka; Bjarnason (Fransson 60), Zuffi, Delgado (Embolo 60), Steffen; Janko (Itten 71).

Tottenham H (0) 1 *(Son 73)*

Borussia Dortmund (1) 2 *(Aubameyang 24, 70)* 36,284

Tottenham H: (4231) Lloris; Trippier, Alderweireld, Wimmer, Davies (Rose 13); Dier, Mason; Lamela (Onomah 74), Alli (Carroll 69), Son; Chadli.
Borussia Dortmund: (433) Weidenfeller; Piszczek, Subotic, Papastathopoulos (Durm 54), Schmelzer; Ginter, Castro, Weigl; Mkhitaryan (Kagawa 71), Aubameyang, Reus (Pulisic 46).

Valencia (2) 2 *(Santi Mina 13, Aderlan Santos 38)*

Athletic Bilbao (0) 1 *(Aduriz 76)*   31,681

Valencia: (433) Ryan; Ruben Vezo, Aderlan Santos, Mustafi, Gaya; Danilo, Andre Gomes (Alcacer 83), Javi Fuego (Parejo 68); Santi Mina, Negredo, Rodrigo (Feghouli 74).

Athletic Bilbao: (4231) Herrerin; De Marcos, Etxeita, Laporte, Balenziaga (Lekue 75); San Jose, Benat; Merino (Iturraspe 75), Raul Garcia, Muniain (Susaeta 25); Aduriz.
Athletic Bilbao won on away goals.

QUARTER-FINALS FIRST LEG

Thursday, 7 April 2016

Athletic Bilbao (0) 1 *(Aduriz 48)*

Sevilla (0) 2 *(Kolodzieczak 56, Iborra 83)* 40,856

Athletic Bilbao: (4231) Herrerin; De Marcos, Boveda, Etxeita, Balenziaga; San Jose, Benat; Williams (Susaeta 62), Eraso (Viguera 69), Muniain (Lekue 62); Aduriz.
Sevilla: (4231) Soria; Coke, Rami, Kolodzieczak, Tremoulinas (Fazio 12); Nzonzi, Krychowiak; Vitolo, Banega (Iborra 74), Krohn-Dehli (Konoplyanka 68); Gameiro.

Borussia Dortmund (0) 1 *(Hummels 48)*

Liverpool (1) 1 *(Origi 36)*   65,848

Borussia Dortmund: (4141) Weidenfeller; Piszczek, Bender (Papastathopoulos 76), Hummels, Schmelzer; Weigl; Durm (Sahin 46), Castro, Mkhitaryan, Reus; Aubameyang (Pulisic 76).
Liverpool: (4231) Mignolet; Clyne, Lovren, Sakho, Moreno; Henderson (Allen 46), Can; Lallana (Firmino 77), Coutinho, Milner; Origi (Sturridge 84).

Braga (0) 1 *(Wilson Eduardo 89)*

Shakhtar Donetsk (1) 2 *(Rakitskiy 45, Ferreyra 75)* 21,645

Braga: (442) Matheus Magalhaes; Baiano, Boly, Ricardo Ferreira, Goiano; Pedro Santos, Luiz Carlos, Vukcevic (Filipe Augusto 87), Rafa; Stoiljkovic (Wilson Eduardo 74), Hassan.
Shakhtar Donetsk: (4231) Pyatov; Srna, Ordets, Rakitskiy, Ismaily; Marlos (Eduardo 82), Malyshev; Stepanenko, Taison (Dentinho 78), Kovalenko (Bernard 88); Ferreyra.

Villarreal (1) 2 *(Bakambu 3, 63)* ·

Sparta Prague (1) 1 *(Brabec 45)*   15,803

Villarreal: (442) Sergio Asenjo; Mario, Bailly, Victor Ruiz, Jaume (Marin 77); Suarez, Trigueros, Bruno, Castillejo (Leo Baptistao 62); Soldado, Bakambu (Adrian 82).
Sparta Prague: (3142) Bicik; Brabec, Holek (Kovac 29), Nhamoinesu; Marecek; Dockal, Frydek, Matejovsky (Lafata 88), Krejci; Konate, Juls (Fatai 73).

QUARTER-FINALS SECOND LEG

Thursday, 14 April 2016

Liverpool (0) 4 *(Origi 48, Coutinho 66, Sakho 78, Lovren 90)*

Borussia Dortmund (2) 3 *(Mkhitaryan 5, Aubameyang 9, Reus 57)*   44,000

Liverpool: (4411) Mignolet; Clyne, Lovren, Sakho, Moreno; Lallana (Allen 62), Milner, Can (Lucas 80); Coutinho; Firmino (Sturridge 63); Origi.
Borussia Dortmund: (4411) Weidenfeller; Piszczek, Papastathopoulos, Hummels, Schmelzer; Mkhitaryan, Castro (Gundogan 83), Weigl, Reus (Ramos 83); Kagawa (Ginter 77); Aubameyang.

Sevilla (0) 1 *(Gameiro 59)*

Athletic Bilbao (0) 2 *(Aduriz 57, Raul Garcia 80)* 38,567

Sevilla: (4231) Soria; Mariano (Coke 100), Rami, Kolodzieczak, Escudero; Krychowiak, Nzonzi; Vitolo, Iborra (Cristofon 66), Krohn-Dehli (Konoplyanka 51); Gameiro.
Athletic Bilbao: (4231) Herrerin; De Marcos, Boveda (Iturraspe 60), Etxeita, Balenziaga; San Jose, Benat; Susaeta, Raul Garcia, Lekue (Muniain 54); Aduriz (Viguera 70).
aet; Sevilla won 5-4 on penalties.

Shakhtar Donetsk (2) 4 *(Srna 25 (pen),*
Ricardo Ferreira 42 (og), 74 (og), Kovalenko 50)
Braga (0) 0   33,617
Shakhtar Donetsk: (4411) Pyatov; Srna, Kucher, Ordets,
Ismaily; Marlos (Eduardo 78), Malyshev, Stepanenko,
Taison (Dentinho 78); Kovalenko (Bernard 86);
Ferreyra.
Braga: (442) Matheus Magalhaes; Goiano, Ricardo
Ferreira, Boly (Andre Pinto 78), Djavan; Josue, Luiz
Carlos (Mauro Sousa 78), Vukcevic, Rafa; Hassan,
Eduardo (Stoiljkovic 57).

Sparta Prague (0) 2 *(Dockal 65, Krejci 71)*
Villarreal (3) 4 *(Bakambu 5, 49, Castillejo 43,*
Lafata 45 (og))   18,201
Sparta Prague: (442) Bicik; Konate, Marecek, Kovac,
Frydek; Fatai, Matejovsky, Dockal, Krejci; Lafata, Julis.
Villarreal: (442) Areola; Mario (Jaume 56), Bailly, Victor
Ruiz, Rukavina; Suarez (Leo Baptistao 66), Trigueros
(Jonathan 61), Bruno, Castillejo; Soldado, Bakambu.

SEMI-FINALS FIRST LEG

Thursday, 28 April 2016

Shakhtar Donetsk (2) 2 *(Marlos 23, Stepanenko 36)*
Sevilla (1) 2 *(Vitolo 6, Gameiro 82 (pen))*   34,267
Shakhtar Donetsk: (4231) Pyatov; Srna, Kucher,
Rakitskiy, Ismaily; Malyshev, Stepanenko; Marlos
(Bernard 90), Kovalenko, Taison (Wellington Nem 90);
Ferreyra (Eduardo 90).
Sevilla: (4231) Soria; Mariano, Rami, Carrico, Escudero;
Krychowiak, Nzonzi; Vitolo, Banega, Konoplyanka
(Krohn-Dehli 59 (Coke 72)); Gameiro.

Villarreal (0) 1 *(Adrian 90)*
Liverpool (0) 0   21,606
Villarreal: (442) Sergio Asenjo; Mario, Bailly (Musacchio
76), Victor Ruiz, Jaume; Jonathan (Castillejo 72), Pina,
Bruno, Suarez; Soldado (Adrian 74), Bakambu.
Liverpool: (442) Mignolet; Clyne, Toure, Lovren,
Moreno; Lallana, Allen, Lucas, Milner; Firmino
(Benteke 89), Coutinho (Ibe 46).

SEMI-FINALS SECOND LEG

Thursday, 5 May 2016

Liverpool (1) 3 *(Bruno 8 (og), Sturridge 63, Lallana 81)*
Villarreal (0) 0   43,074
Liverpool: (4132) Mignolet; Clyne, Lallana, Milner,
Moreno; Can; Lallana, Milner, Coutinho (Allen 83);
Sturridge (Lucas 90), Firmino (Benteke 89).
Villarreal: (442) Areola; Mario, Musacchio, Victor Ruiz■,
Jaume; Jonathan (Bonera 73), Pina (Trigueros 59),
Bruno, Suarez; Soldado (Adrian 68), Bakambu.

Sevilla (1) 3 *(Gameiro 9, 47, Mariano 59)*
Shakhtar Donetsk (1) 1 *(Eduardo 44)*   41,286
Sevilla: (451) Soria; Mariano, Rami, Carrico,
Tremoulinas (Escudero 73); Coke, Krychowiak, Banega
(Cristoforo 89), Nzonzi, Vitolo; Gameiro (Iborra 82).
Shakhtar Donetsk: (451) Pyatov; Srna, Kucher, Rakitskiy,
Ismaily; Marlos (Wellington Nem 84), Malyshev,
Kovalenko, Stepanenko, Taison (Bernard 76); Eduardo
(Dentinho 84).

EUROPA LEAGUE FINAL 2016

Wednesday, 18 May 2016

(in Basel, attendance 34,429)

Liverpool (1) 1   Sevilla (0) 3

Liverpool: (4231) Mignolet; Clyne, Lovren, Toure (Benteke 82), Moreno; Milner, Can; Lallana (Allen 73), Firmino
(Origi 69), Coutinho; Sturridge.
Scorer: Sturridge 35.

Sevilla: (4231) Soria; Mariano, Rami (Kolodzieczak 78), Carrico, Escudero; Krychowiak, Nzonzi; Coke, Banega
(Cristoforo 90), Vitolo; Gameiro (Iborra 89).
Scorers: Gameiro 46, Coke 64, 70.)

Referee: Jonas Eriksson (Sweden).

Man of the Match Andujar Coke drives home Sevilla's third goal as they beat Liverpool 3-1 in the UEFA Europa
League final at St Jakob-Park in Basel on 18 May. (Adam Davy/PA Wire/Press Association Images)

UEFA CHAMPIONS LEAGUE 2016–17

PARTICIPATING CLUBS
The list below is provisional and is subject to pending legal proceedings and final confirmation from UEFA.

GROUP STAGE
Real Madrid (ESP, holders)
Barcelona (ESP)
Leicester C (ENG)
Bayern Munich (GER)
Juventus (ITA)
Benfica (POR)
Paris Saint-Germain (FRA)
CSKA Moscow (RUS)
Atletico Madrid (ESP)
Borussia Dortmund (GER)
Arsenal (ENG)
Sevilla (ESP)
Napoli (ITA)
Bayer Leverkusen (GER)
FC Basel (SUI)
Tottenham H (ENG)
Dynamo Kyiv (UKR)
Lyon (FRA)
PSV Eindhoven (NED)
Sporting Lisbon (POR)
Club Brugge (BEL)
Besiktas (TUR)
10 play-off winners

PLAY-OFF – CHAMPIONS ROUTE
10 third qualifying round winners

PLAY-OFF – LEAGUE ROUTE
Manchester C (ENG)
Porto (POR)
Villarreal (ESP)
Borussia Munchengladbach (GER)
Roma (ITA)
10 third qualifying round winners

THIRD QUALIFYING ROUND – CHAMPIONS ROUTE
Olympiacos (GRE)
Viktoria Plzen (CZE)
Astra Giurgiu (ROU)
17 third qualifying round winners

THIRD QUALIFYING ROUND – LEAGUE ROUTE
Shakhtar Donetsk (UKR)
Ajax (NED)
Anderlecht (BEL)

Fenerbahce (TUR)
Sparta Prague (CZE)
PAOK (GRE)
Steaua Bucharest (ROU)
Monaco (FRA)
Young Boys (SUI)
Rostov (RUS)

SECOND QUALIFYING ROUND
FC Salzburg (AUT)
Celtic (SCO)
APOEL (CYP)
BATE Borisov (BLR)
Legia Warsaw (POL)
Dinamo Zagreb (CRO)
Ludogorets Razgrad (BUL)
FC Copenhagen (DEN)
Qarabag (AZE)
Rosenborg (NOR)
Astana (KAZ)
Sheriff (MDA)
Skenderbeu (ALB)
Crvena Zvezda (SRB)
Dinamo Tbilisi (GEO)
FH Hafnarfjordur (ISL)
Trencin (SVK)
F91 Dudelange (LUX)
Zalgiris Vilnius (LTU)
Hapoel Beer Sheva (ISR)
Olimpija Ljubljana (SVN)
Vardar (MKD)
Norrkoping (SWE)
Ferencvaros (HUN)
Crusaders (NIR)
Zrinjski (BIH)
Dundalk (IRL)
Mladost Podgorica (MNE)
SJK Seinajoki (FIN)
Liepaja (LVA)
4 first qualifying round winners

FIRST QUALIFYING ROUND
The New Saints (WAL)
Valletta (MLT)
Flora (EST)
FC Santa Coloma (AND)
B36 Torshavn (FRO)
Lincoln (GIB)
Alashkert (ARM)
Tre Penne (SMR)

UEFA EUROPA LEAGUE 2016–17

PARTICIPATING CLUBS
The list below is provisional and is subject to pending legal proceedings and final confirmation from UEFA.

GROUP STAGE
Schalke 04 (GER)
Zenit St Petersburg (RUS)
Manchester U (ENG)
Athletic Bilbao (ESP)
Inter Milan (ITA)
Fiorentina (ITA)
Braga (POR)
Standard Liege (BEL)
Celta Vigo (ESP)
Feyenoord (NED)

Mainz (GER)
FC Zurich (SUI)
Southampton (ENG)
Nice (FRA)
Zorya Luhansk (UKR)
Konyaspor (TUR)

PLAY-OFFS
29 third qualifying round winners
15 transfer from UEFA Champions League second qualifying round

THIRD QUALIFYING ROUND
AZ Alkmaar (NED)
Lille (FRA)

Saint-Etienne (FRA)
KAA Gent (BEL)
Krasnodar (RUS)
Rapid Vienna (AUT)
Slovan Liberec (CZE)
Spartak Moscow (RUS)
West Ham U (ENG)
Hertha Berlin (GER)
Panathinaikos (GRE)
Rijeka (CRO)
Sassuolo (ITA)
Rio Ave (POR)
Vorskala Poltava (UKR)
Arouca (POR)
Apollon Limassol (CYP)
Mlada Boleslav (CZE)
Olexandriya (UKR)
Luzern (SUI)
AEK Athens (GRE)
Istanbul Basaksehir (TUR)
Heracles (NED)
Pandurii Targu Jiu (ROU)
Viitorul Constanta (ROU)
33 second qualifying round winners

SECOND QUALIFYING ROUND
Genk (BEL)
Maribor (SVN)
Austria Vienna (AUT)
Partizan (SRB)
Maccabi Haifa (ISR)
Hajduk Split (CRO)
Grasshoppers (SUI)
Stromsgodset (NOR)
Osmanlispor (TUR)*
Slavia Prague (CZE)
Hacken (SWE)
Giannina (GRE)
CSMS Iasi (ROU)
Piast Gliwice (POL)
Levski Sofia (BUL)
Torpedo-Zhodino (BLR)
Hibernian (SCO)
SonderjyskE (DEN)
48 second qualifying round winners

FIRST QUALIFYING ROUND
Maccabi Tel Aviv (ISR)
Midtjylland (DEN)
HJK Helsinki (FIN)
Dinamo Minsk (BLR)
Omonia (CYP)
Neftci PFK (AZE)
AEK Larnaca (CYP)
AIK Solna (SWE)
Slovan Bratislava (SVK)
Videoton (HUN)
Aktobe (KAZ)
Vojvodina (SRB)
Shakhtyor Soligorsk (BLR)
Spartak Trnava (SVK)
Brondby (DEN)
IFK Gothenburg (SWE)
Debrecen (HUN)
Hearts (SCO)
Ventspils (LVA)
Admira Wacker Modling (AUT)
Lokomotiva Zagreb (CRO)
KR Reykjavik (ISL)
Dila Gori (GEO)
Aberdeen (SCO)
Odd (NOR)

Qabala (AZE)
Rabotnicki (MKD)
Vaduz (LIE)
Kairat Almaty (KAZ)
Differdange 03 (LUX)
Shamrock R (IRL)
St Patrick's Ath (IRL)
Zaglebie Lubin (POL)
Cracovia Krakow (POL)
Linfield (NIR)
Dacia Chisinau (MDA)
Beitar Jerusalem (ISR)
Stabaek (NOR)
Kukesi (ALB)
Cukaricki (SRB)
Levadia Tallinn (EST)
Nomme Kalju (EST)
Zimbru Chisinau (MDA)
Pyunik (ARM)
Breidablik (ISL)
Siroki Brijeg (BIH)
Beroe Stara Zagora (BUL)
Domzale (SVN)
Ordabasy Shymkent (KAZ)
Fola Esch (LUX)
Cliftonville (NIR)
Rudar Pljevlja (MNE)
HB Torshavn (FRO)
Gorica (SVN)
Chikhura Sachkhere (GEO)
Shirak (ARM)
Kapaz (AZE)
Buducnost Podgorica (MNE)
Birkirkara (MLT)
Shkendija (MKD)
Víkingur (FRO)
Slavia Sofia (BUL)
MTK Budapest (HUN)
Hibernians (MLT)
Spartak Myjava (SVK)
Suduva (LTU)
Jeunesse Esch (LUX)
RoPS Rovaniemi (FIN)
Zaria Balti (MDA)
Teuta (ALB)
Jelgava (LVA)
Valur Reykjavik (ISL)
IFK Mariehamn (FIN)
Lusitanos (AND)
Atlantas (LTU)
Samtredia (GEO)
Partizani (ALB)
Spartaks Jurmala (LVA)
Banants (ARM)
NSI Runavik (FRO)
Radnik Bijeljina (BIH)
Sloboda Tuzla (BIH)
Trakai (LTU)
Glenavon (NIR)
Cork C (IRL)
La Fiorita (SMR)
Sileks (MKD)
Bala T (WAL)
Santa Coloma (AND)
FK Bokelj (MNE)
Balzan (MLT)
Infonet Tallinn (EST)
Folgore (SMR)
Llandudno T (WAL)
Connah's Quay Nomads (WAL)
Europa (GIB)

BRITISH AND IRISH CLUBS IN EUROPE

SUMMARY OF APPEARANCES

EUROPEAN CUP AND CHAMPIONS LEAGUE (1955–2016)

(Winners in brackets) (SE = seasons entered).

ENGLAND	SE	P	W	D	L	F	A
Manchester U (3)	26	261	145	64	52	483	248
Liverpool (5)	21	181	100	41	40	322	153
Arsenal	20	193	97	41	55	312	202
Chelsea (1)	14	152	77	43	32	257	130
Manchester C	6	42	16	10	16	64	56
Leeds U	4	40	22	6	12	76	41
Nottingham F (2)	3	20	12	4	4	32	14
Newcastle U	3	24	11	3	10	33	33
Everton	3	10	2	5	3	14	10
Tottenham H	2	20	9	4	7	46	32
Aston Villa (1)	2	15	9	3	3	24	10
Derby Co	2	12	6	2	4	18	12
Wolverhampton W	2	8	2	2	4	12	16
Ipswich T	1	4	3	0	1	16	5
Burnley	1	4	2	0	2	8	8
Blackburn R	1	6	1	1	4	5	8

SCOTLAND	SE	P	W	D	L	F	A
Rangers	30	161	62	40	59	232	218
Celtic (1)	30	176	85	28	63	261	194
Aberdeen	3	12	5	4	3	14	12
Hearts	3	8	2	1	5	8	16
Dundee U	1	8	5	1	2	14	5
Dundee	1	8	5	0	3	20	14
Hibernian	1	6	3	1	2	9	5
Kilmarnock	1	4	1	2	1	4	7
Motherwell	1	2	0	0	2	0	5

WALES	SE	P	W	D	L	F	A
The New Saints	9	22	4	3	15	19	39
Barry T	6	14	4	1	9	11	38
Rhyl	2	4	0	0	4	1	19
Cwmbran T	1	2	1	0	1	4	4
Llanelli	1	2	1	0	1	1	4
Bangor C	1	2	0	0	2	0	13

NORTHERN IRELAND	SE	P	W	D	L	F	A
Linfield	27	63	6	22	35	55	112
Glentoran	12	28	3	7	18	20	59
Crusaders	4	10	1	2	7	7	34
Portadown	3	6	0	1	5	3	24
Cliftonville	3	6	0	1	5	1	20
Glenavon	1	2	0	1	1	0	3
Lisburn Distillery	1	2	0	1	1	3	8
Ards	1	2	0	0	2	3	10
Coleraine	1	2	0	0	2	1	11

REPUBLIC OF IRELAND	SE	P	W	D	L	F	A
Shamrock R	9	20	1	6	13	9	33
Dundalk	8	20	3	5	12	14	43
Shelbourne	6	20	4	8	8	21	31
Bohemians	6	18	4	4	10	13	29
Waterford U	6	14	3	0	11	15	47
Derry C	4	9	1	1	7	9	26
St Patrick's Ath	4	8	0	3	5	2	23
Dublin U	3	6	1	0	5	3	25
Cork C	2	8	2	1	5	7	12
Athlone T	2	4	0	2	2	7	14
Sligo R	2	4	0	0	4	0	9
Limerick	2	4	0	0	4	4	16
Drogheda U	1	4	2	1	1	6	5
Cork Hibernians	1	2	0	0	2	1	7
Cork Celtic	1	2	0	0	2	1	7

UEFA CUP AND EUROPA LEAGUE 1971–2016

ENGLAND	SE	P	W	D	L	F	A
Tottenham H (2)	14	138	78	35	25	276	118
Aston Villa	13	56	24	14	18	77	60
Liverpool (3)	14	124	66	34	24	186	94
Ipswich T (1)	10	52	30	10	12	98	53
Newcastle U	8	72	42	17	13	123	60
Manchester C	8	52	28	13	11	84	51
Leeds U	8	46	20	10	16	66	48
Everton	8	42	23	6	13	75	48
Manchester U	8	28	8	11	9	32	29
Arsenal	6	25	12	4	9	45	32
Blackburn R	6	22	7	8	7	27	26
Southampton	6	16	4	7	5	17	16
Chelsea (1)	4	17	10	2	5	28	20
Wolverhampton W	4	20	13	3	4	41	23
Fulham	3	39	21	10	8	64	31
Nottingham F	3	20	10	5	5	18	16
Stoke C	3	16	8	4	4	21	16
WBA	3	12	5	2	5	15	13
West Ham U	3	12	5	2	5	14	12
Leicester C	2	4	0	1	3	3	8
Middlesbrough	2	25	13	4	8	36	24
Bolton W	2	18	6	10	2	18	14
QPR	2	12	8	1	3	39	18
Derby Co	2	10	5	2	3	32	17
Birmingham C	1	8	4	2	2	11	8
Norwich C	1	6	2	2	2	6	4
Portsmouth	1	6	2	2	2	11	10
Watford	1	6	2	1	3	10	12
Wigan Ath	1	6	1	2	3	6	7
Sheffield W	1	4	2	1	1	13	7
Millwall	1	2	0	1	1	2	4
Hull C	1	4	2	1	1	4	3

SCOTLAND	SE	P	W	D	L	F	A
Celtic	19	99	40	25	34	155	112
Dundee U	19	82	33	25	24	134	89
Aberdeen	18	66	19	23	24	83	89
Rangers	16	76	31	23	22	99	77
Hearts	13	46	19	9	18	54	57
Hibernian	11	32	11	9	12	40	51
Motherwell	8	26	8	2	16	33	34
St Johnstone	6	22	7	7	8	24	27
Dundee	4	14	6	0	8	24	24
Kilmarnock	3	12	4	2	6	17	14
St Mirren	3	10	2	3	5	9	12
Dunfermline Ath	2	4	0	2	2	4	6
Raith R	1	6	2	1	3	10	8
Livingston	1	4	1	2	1	7	9
Falkirk	1	2	1	0	1	1	2
Gretna	1	2	0	1	1	3	7
Queen of the South	1	2	0	0	2	2	4
Partick Thistle	1	2	0	0	2	0	4
Inverness CT	1	2	0	1	1	0	1

WALES	SE	P	W	D	L	F	A
Bangor C	9	20	2	2	16	10	57
The New Saints	8	18	1	2	15	12	49
Llanelli	5	12	3	3	6	12	24
Rhyl	3	8	2	1	5	9	12
UWIC Inter Cardiff	3	6	1	0	5	1	18
Cwmbran T	3	6	0	0	6	0	21
Newtown	3	8	2	1	5	6	21
Air UK Broughton	3	6	0	4	2	6	9
Barry T	2	8	2	2	4	10	16
Carmarthen T	2	6	1	0	5	8	21
Bala T	2	4	2	0	2	5	7
Prestatyn T	1	4	1	0	3	3	11
Afan Lido	1	2	0	1	1	1	2
Cefn Druids	1	2	0	1	1	0	5
Port Talbot T	1	2	0	0	2	1	7
Neath	1	2	0	0	2	1	6
Haverfordwest Co	1	2	0	0	2	1	4
Swansea C	1	12	4	4	4	17	10
Aberystwith T	1	2	0	0	2	0	9

NORTHERN IRELAND	SE	P	W	D	L	F	A
Glentoran	18	40	3	8	29	22	97
Portadown	11	28	3	7	18	16	62
Linfield	11	32	9	7	16	36	61
Crusaders	8	18	3	3	12	16	45
Coleraine	7	14	1	3	10	8	36
Glenavon	7	16	1	2	13	6	35
Cliftonville	4	10	2	2	6	4	22
Ards	1	2	1	0	1	4	8
Ballymena U	1	2	1	0	1	2	4
Dungannon Swifts	1	2	1	0	1	1	4
Lisburn Distillery	1	2	0	0	2	1	11
Bangor	1	2	0	0	2	0	6

REPUBLIC OF IRELAND

Bohemians	14	30	3	9	18	16	56
St Patrick's Ath	9	34	9	6	19	31	53
Derry C	7	22	6	5	11	26	32
Cork C	7	18	2	5	11	10	29
Shelbourne	6	12	0	2	10	8	28
Dundalk	6	16	4	2	10	12	35
Shamrock R	6	24	5	3	16	21	47
Drogheda U	4	12	3	4	5	10	24
Sligo R	4	10	2	4	4	11	13
Longford T	3	6	1	1	4	6	12
Finn Harps	3	6	0	0	6	3	33
Athlone T	1	4	1	2	1	4	5
Limerick	1	2	0	1	1	1	4
Sporting Fingal	1	2	0	0	2	4	6
Galway U	1	2	0	0	2	2	8
Bray W	1	2	0	0	2	0	8
University College Dublin	1	4	1	0	3	3	8

EUROPEAN CUP WINNERS' CUP 1960–1999

ENGLAND

	SE	P	W	D	L	F	A
Tottenham H (1)	6	33	20	5	8	65	34
Chelsea (2)	5	39	23	10	6	81	28
Liverpool	5	29	16	5	8	57	29
Manchester U (1)	5	31	16	9	6	55	35
West Ham U (1)	4	30	15	6	9	58	42
Arsenal (1)	3	27	15	10	2	48	20
Everton (1)	3	17	11	4	2	25	9
Manchester C (1)	2	18	11	2	5	32	13
Ipswich T	1	6	3	2	1	6	3
Leeds U	1	9	5	3	1	13	3
Leicester C	1	4	2	1	1	8	5
Newcastle U	1	2	1	0	1	2	2
Southampton	1	6	4	0	2	16	8
Sunderland	1	4	3	0	1	5	3
WBA	1	6	2	2	2	8	5
Wolverhampton W	1	4	1	1	2	6	5

SCOTLAND

Rangers (1)	10	54	27	11	16	100	62
Aberdeen (1)	8	39	22	5	12	79	37
Celtic	8	38	21	4	13	75	37
Dundee U	3	10	3	3	4	9	10
Hearts	3	10	3	3	4	16	14
Dunfermline Ath	2	14	7	2	5	34	14
Airdrieonians	1	2	0	0	2	1	3
Dundee	1	2	0	1	1	3	4
Hibernian	1	6	3	1	2	19	10
Kilmarnock	1	4	1	2	1	5	6
Motherwell	1	2	1	0	1	3	3
St Mirren	1	4	1	2	1	1	2

WALES

Cardiff C	14	49	16	14	19	67	61
Wrexham	8	28	10	8	10	34	35
Swansea C	7	18	3	4	11	32	37
Bangor C	3	9	1	2	6	5	12
Barry T	1	2	0	0	2	0	7
Borough U	1	4	1	1	2	2	4
Cwmbran T	1	2	0	0	2	2	12
Merthyr Tydfil	1	2	1	0	1	2	3
Newport Co	1	6	2	3	1	12	3
The New Saints (Llansantffraid)	1	2	0	1	1	1	6

NORTHERN IRELAND

Glentoran	9	22	3	7	12	18	46
Glenavon	5	10	1	3	6	11	25
Ballymena U	4	8	0	0	8	1	25
Coleraine	4	8	0	1	7	7	34
Crusaders	3	6	0	2	4	5	18
Derry C	3	6	1	1	4	1	11
Linfield	3	6	2	0	4	6	11
Ards	2	4	0	1	3	2	17
Bangor	2	4	0	1	3	2	8
Carrick Rangers	1	4	1	0	3	7	12
Cliftonville	1	2	0	0	2	0	8
Distillery	1	2	0	0	2	1	7
Portadown	1	2	1	0	1	4	7

REPUBLIC OF IRELAND

Shamrock R	6	16	5	2	9	19	27
Shelbourne	4	10	1	1	8	9	20
Bohemians	3	8	2	2	4	6	13
Dundalk	3	8	2	1	5	7	14
Limerick U	3	6	0	1	5	2	11
Waterford U	3	8	1	1	6	6	14
Cork C	2	4	1	0	3	2	9
Cork Hibernians	2	6	2	1	3	7	8
Galway U	2	4	0	0	4	2	11
Sligo R	2	6	1	1	4	5	11
Bray W	1	2	0	1	1	1	3
Cork Celtic	1	2	0	1	1	1	3
Finn Harps	1	2	0	1	1	2	4
Home Farm	1	2	0	1	1	1	7
St Patrick's Ath	1	2	0	0	2	1	8
University College Dublin	1	2	0	0	1	0	1

INTER-CITIES FAIRS CUP 1955–1970

ENGLAND

	SE	P	W	D	L	F	A
Leeds U (2)	5	53	28	17	8	92	40
Birmingham C	4	25	14	6	5	51	38
Liverpool	4	22	12	4	6	46	15
Arsenal (1)	3	24	12	5	7	46	19
Chelsea	3	20	10	5	5	33	24
Everton	3	12	7	2	3	22	15
Newcastle U (1)	3	24	13	6	5	37	21
Nottingham F	2	6	3	0	3	8	9
Sheffield W	2	10	5	0	5	25	18
Burnley	1	8	4	3	1	16	5
Coventry C	1	4	3	0	1	9	8
London XI	1	8	4	1	3	14	13
Manchester U	1	11	6	3	2	29	10
Southampton	1	6	2	3	1	11	6
WBA	1	4	1	1	2	7	9

SCOTLAND

Hibernian	7	36	18	5	13	66	60
Dunfermline Ath	5	28	16	3	9	49	31
Kilmarnock	4	20	8	3	9	34	32
Dundee U	3	10	5	1	4	11	12
Hearts	3	12	4	4	4	20	20
Rangers	3	18	8	4	6	27	17
Celtic	2	6	1	3	2	9	10
Aberdeen	1	4	2	1	1	4	4
Dundee	1	8	5	1	2	14	6
Morton	1	2	0	0	2	3	9
Partick Thistle	1	4	3	0	1	10	7

NORTHERN IRELAND

Glentoran	4	8	1	1	6	7	22
Coleraine	2	8	2	1	5	15	23
Linfield	2	4	1	0	3	3	11

REPUBLIC OF IRELAND

Drumcondra	2	6	2	0	4	8	19
Dundalk	2	6	1	1	4	4	25
Shamrock R	2	4	0	2	2	4	6
Cork Hibernians	1	2	0	0	2	1	6
Shelbourne	1	5	1	2	2	3	4
St Patrick's Ath	1	2	0	0	2	4	9

FIFA CLUB WORLD CUP 2015

Formerly known as the FIFA Club World Championship, this tournament is played annually between the champion clubs from all 6 continental confederations, although since 2007 the champions of Oceania must play a qualifying play-off against the champion club of the host country.

(Finals in Japan)

PLAY-OFF FOR QUARTER FINALS
Thursday 10 December 2015
Sanfrecce Hiroshima (1) 2 *(Minagawa 9, Shiotani 70)*
Auckland City (0) 0   19,421
Sanfrecce Hiroshima: Hayashi; Chiba, Mizumoto, Shiotani, Aoyama, Shimizu (Sasaki 65), Marutani, Kashiwa, Notsuda (Shibasaki 14 (Douglas 53)), Asano, Minagawa.
Auckland City: Spoonley; Dordevic, Angel Berlanga, Iwata, Bilen (Tade 71), Mikel Alvaro, Dae-Uk Kim (White 78), Hudson, Lea'alafa, Joao Moreira (Lewis 84), De Vries.
Referee: Sidi Alioum (Cameroon).

QUARTER FINALS
Sunday 13 December 2015
America (0) 1 *(Peralta 55)*
Guangzhou Evergrande (0) 2 *(Zheng Long 80,*
Paulinho 90)   18,772
America: Munoz; Goltz, Pablo Aguilar, Paul Aguilar, Samudio, Sambueza, Guerrero, Andrade, Peralta, Quintero (Arroyo 83), Benedetto (Martinez 81).
Guangzhou Evergrande: Li Shuai; Feng Xiaoting, Young-Gwon Kim, Zhang Linpeng, Zheng Zhi, Huang Bowen (Gao Lin 66), Zou Zheng, Paulinho, Robinho (Zheng Long 46), Elkeson (Yu Hanchao 79), Ricardo Goulart.
Referee: Jonas Eriksson (Sweden).

TP Mazembe (0) 0
Sanfrecce Hiroshima (1) 3 *(Shiotani 44, Chiba 56,*
Asono 78)   23,609
TP Mazembe: Gbohouo; Frimpong, Kimwaki, Boateng (Bolingi 69), Coulibaly, Singuluma (Ulimwengu 46), Sinkala (Kalaba 63), Diarra, Samatta, Assale, Traore.
Sanfrecce Hiroshima: Hayashi; Chiba, Shiotani, Sasaki, Aoyama, Kazuyuki Morisaki, Mikic (Mizumoto 82), Kashiwa, Chajima, Sato (Asano 75), Douglas (Minagawa 88).
Referee: Wilmar Roldan (Colombia).

SEMI-FINALS
Wednesday 16 December 2015
Sanfrecce Hiroshima (0) 0
River Plate (0) 1 *(Alario 72)*   20,133
Sanfrecce Hiroshima: Hayashi; Chiba, Shiotani, Sasaki, Aoyama, Kazuyuki Morisaki, Shimizu, Kashiwa (Mikic 61), Chajima (Sato 76), Douglas, Minagawa (Asano 66).
River Plate: Barovero; Maidana, Vangioni, Mercado (Mayada 85), Alvarez, Ponzio (Gonzalez 57), Pisculichi (Viudez 64), Sanchez, Kranevitter, Mora, Alario.
Referee: Jonas Eriksson (Sweden).

Thursday 17 December 2014
Barcelona (1) 3 *(Suarez 39, 50, 67 (pen))*
Guangzhou Evergrande (0) 0   63,870
Barcelona: Bravo; Dani Alves, Pique, Jordi Alba (Adriano Correia 76), Mascherano, Iniesta (Sergi Samper 81), Rakitic, Busquets, Sergi Roberto (Sandro Ramirez 72), Suarez, Munir.
Guangzhou Evergrande: Li Shuai; Feng Xiaoting, Young-Gwon Kim, Zhang Linpeng, Zheng Zhi, Huang Bowen, Zheng Long (Yu Hanchao 56), Zou Zheng (Li Xuepeng 35), Paulinho, Elkeson (Gao Lin 67), Ricardo Goulart.
Referee: Joel Aguilar (El Salvador).

MATCH FOR FIFTH PLACE
Wednesday 16 December 2015
America (2) 2 *(Benedetto 19, Zuniga 28)*
TP Mazembe (1) 1 *(Kalaba 43)*   11,686
America: Munoz; Paul Aguilar, Mares, Pimentel, Alvarado, Martinez, Arroyo, Guerrero, Andrade (Goltz 84), Peralta (Sambueza 66), Benedetto (Zuniga 21).
TP Mazembe: Gbohouo; Frimpong (Chongo 61), Kimwaki, Mwepu, Coulibaly, Bokadi (Diarra 46), Adjei Nii, Kalaba, Samatta, Ulimwengu (Assale 72), Traore.
Referee: Alireza Faghani (Iran).

MATCH FOR THIRD PLACE
Sunday 20 December 2015
Sanfrecce Hiroshima (0) 2 *(Douglas 70, 83)*
Guangzhou Evergrande (1) 1 *(Paulinho 4)*   47,968
Sanfrecce Hiroshima: Hayashi; Mizumoto, Shiotani, Aoyama, Mikic (Kashiwa 67), Shimizu (Sasaki 87), Marutani, Miyahara, Chajima, Sato (Douglas 58), Asano.
Guangzhou Evergrande: Li Shuai; Li Xuepeng, Young-Gwon Kim, Zhang Linpeng, Mei Fang, Zheng Zhi, Huang Bowen (Yu Hanchao 86), Paulinho, Gao Lin, Elkeson (Zheng Long 46), Ricardo Goulart (Liu Jian 81).
Referee: Matt Conger (New Zealand).

FIFA CLUB WORLD CUP FINAL 2015
Yokohama, Sunday 20 December 2015 (attendance 66,853)

River Plate (0) 0   Barcelona (1) 3 *(Messi 36, Suarez 49, 68)*

River Plate: Barovero; Maidana, Vangioni, Mercado, Alvarez, Ponzio (Gonzalez 46), Sanchez, Kranevitter, Mora (Martinez 46), Viudez (Driussi 56), Alario.
Barcelona: Bravo; Dani Alves, Pique, Jordi Alba, Mascherano (Vermaelen 81), Iniesta, Rakitic (Sergi Roberto 67), Busquets, Messi, Suarez, Neymar (Mathieu 89).
Referee: Alireza Faghani (Iran).

PREVIOUS FINALS

2000 Corinthians beat Vasco da Gama 4-3 on penalties after 0-0 draw
2001–04 Not contested
2005 Sao Paulo beat Liverpool 1-0
2006 Internacional beat Barcelona 1-0
2007 AC Milan beat Boca Juniors 4-2
2008 Manchester U beat Liga De Quito 1-0
2009 Barcelona beat Estudiantes 2-1
2010 Internazionale beat TP Mazembe Englebert 3-0
2011 Barcelona beat Santos 4-0
2012 Corinthians beat Chelsea 1-0
2013 Bayern Munich beat Raja Casablanca 2-0
2014 Real Madrid beat San Lorenzo 2-0
2015 Barcelona beat River Plate 3-0

WORLD CLUB CHAMPIONSHIP

Played annually up to 1974 and intermittently since then between the winners of the European Cup and the winners of the South American Champions Cup — known as the Copa Libertadores. In 1980 the winners were decided by one match arranged in Tokyo in February 1981 which remained the venue until 2004, when the match was superseded by the FIFA Club World Championship. AC Milan replaced Marseille who had been stripped of their European Cup title in 1993.

1960 Real Madrid beat Penarol 0-0, 5-1	1985 Juventus beat Argentinos Juniors 4-2 on penalties
1961 Penarol beat Benfica 0-1, 5-0, 2-1	after a 2-2 draw
1962 Santos beat Benfica 3-2, 5-2	1986 River Plate beat Steaua Bucharest 1-0
1963 Santos beat AC Milan 2-4, 4-2, 1-0	1987 FC Porto beat Penarol 2-1 after extra time
1964 Inter-Milan beat Independiente 0-1, 2-0, 1-0	1988 Nacional (Uru) beat PSV Eindhoven 7-6 on
1965 Inter-Milan beat Independiente 3-0, 0-0	penalties after 1-1 draw
1966 Penarol beat Real Madrid 2-0, 2-0	1989 AC Milan beat Atletico Nacional (Col) 1-0 after
1967 Racing Club beat Celtic 0-1, 2-1, 1-0	extra time
1968 Estudiantes beat Manchester United 1-0, 1-1	1990 AC Milan beat Olimpia 3-0
1969 AC Milan beat Estudiantes 3-0, 1-2	1991 Crvena Zvezda beat Colo Colo 3-0
1970 Feyenoord beat Estudiantes 2-2, 1-0	1992 Sao Paulo beat Barcelona 2-1
1971 Nacional beat Panathinaikos* 1-1, 2-1	1993 Sao Paulo beat AC Milan 3-2
1972 Ajax beat Independiente 1-1, 3-0	1994 Velez Sarsfield beat AC Milan 2-0
1973 Independiente beat Juventus* 1-0	1995 Ajax beat Gremio Porto Alegre 4-3 on penalties
1974 Atlético Madrid* beat Independiente 0-1, 2-0	after 0-0 draw
1975 Independiente and Bayern Munich could not agree	1996 Juventus beat River Plate 1-0
dates; no matches.	1997 Borussia Dortmund beat Cruzeiro 2-0
1976 Bayern Munich beat Cruzeiro 2-0, 0-0	1998 Real Madrid beat Vasco da Gama 2-1
1977 Boca Juniors beat Borussia Moenchengladbach*	1999 Manchester U beat Palmeiras 1-0
2-2, 3-0	2000 Boca Juniors beat Real Madrid 2-1
1978 Not contested	2001 Bayern Munich beat Boca Juniors 1-0 after extra
1979 Olimpia beat Malmö* 1-0, 2-1	time
1980 Nacional beat Nottingham Forest 1-0	2002 Real Madrid beat Olimpia 2-0
1981 Flamengo beat Liverpool 3-0	2003 Boca Juniors beat AC Milan 3-1 on penalties after
1982 Penarol beat Aston Villa 2-0	1-1 draw
1983 Gremio Porto Alegre beat SV Hamburg 2-1	2004 Porto beat Once Caldas 8-7 on penalties after 0-0
1984 Independiente beat Liverpool 1-0	draw

*European Cup runners-up; winners declined to take part.

EUROPEAN SUPER CUP 2015

Played annually between the winners of the European Champions' Cup and the European Cup-Winners' Cup (UEFA Cup from 2000; UEFA Europa League from 2010). AC Milan replaced Marseille in 1993–94.

Tbilisi, Tuesday 11 August 2015, attendance 51,940

Barcelona (3) 5 *(Messi 7, 15, Rafinha 44, Suarez 52, Pedro 115)*

Sevilla (1) 4 *(Banega 3, Reyes 57, Gameiro 72 (pen), Konoplyanka 81)*

Barcelona: (4123) ter Stegen; Dani Alves, Pique, Mascherano (Pedro 93), Mathieu; Rakitic; Busquets, Iniesta (Sergi 63); Messi, Suarez, Rafinha (Bartra 78).
Sevilla: (4231) Beto; Andujar Moreno, Rami, Krychowiak, Tremoulinas; Krohn-Dehli; Banega; Reyes (Konoplyanka 68), Iborra (Ferreira Filho 80), Machin Perez; Gameiro (Immobile 80).
aet.
Referee: William Collum.

PREVIOUS MATCHES

1972 Ajax beat Rangers 3-1, 3-2	1994 AC Milan beat Arsenal 0-0, 2-0
1973 Ajax beat AC Milan 0-1, 6-0	1995 Ajax beat Zaragoza 1-1, 4-0
1974 Not contested	1996 Juventus beat Paris St Germain 6-1, 3-1
1975 Dynamo Kyiv beat Bayern Munich 1-0, 2-0	1997 Barcelona beat Borussia Dortmund 2-0, 1-1
1976 Anderlecht beat Bayern Munich 4-1, 1-2	1998 Chelsea beat Real Madrid 1-0
1977 Liverpool beat Hamburg 1-1, 6-0	1999 Lazio beat Manchester U 1-0
1978 Anderlecht beat Liverpool 3-1, 1-2	2000 Galatasaray beat Real Madrid 2-1
1979 Nottingham F beat Barcelona 1-0, 1-1	2001 Liverpool beat Bayern Munich 3-2
1980 Valencia beat Nottingham F 1-0, 1-2	2002 Real Madrid beat Feyenoord 3-1
1981 Not contested	2003 AC Milan beat Porto 1-0
1982 Aston Villa beat Barcelona 0-1, 3-0	2004 Valencia beat Porto 2-1
1983 Aberdeen beat Hamburg 0-0, 2-0	2005 Liverpool beat CSKA Moscow 3-1
1984 Juventus beat Liverpool 2-0	2006 Sevilla beat Barcelona 3-0
1985 Juventus v Everton not contested due to UEFA ban	2007 AC Milan beat Sevilla 3-1
on English clubs	2008 Zenit beat Manchester U 2-1
1986 Steaua Bucharest beat Dynamo Kyiv 1-0	2009 Barcelona beat Shakhtar Donetsk 1-0
1987 FC Porto beat Ajax 1-0, 1-0	2010 Atletico Madrid beat Internazionale 2-0
1988 KV Mechelen beat PSV Eindhoven 3-0, 0-1	2011 Barcelona beat Porto 2-0
1989 AC Milan beat Barcelona 1-1, 1-0	2012 Atletico Madrid beat Chelsea 4-1
1990 AC Milan beat Sampdoria 1-1, 2-0	2013 Bayern Munch beat Chelsea 5-4 on penalties after
1991 Manchester U beat Crvena Zvezda 1-0	2-2 draw
1992 Barcelona beat Werder Bremen 1-1, 2-1	2014 Real Madrid beat Sevilla 2-0
1993 Parma beat AC Milan 0-1, 2-0	2015 Barcelona beat Sevilla 5-4

INTERNATIONAL DIRECTORY

The latest available information has been given regarding numbers of clubs and players registered with FIFA, the world governing body. Where known, official colours are listed. With European countries, League tables show a number of signs: * team relegated, *+ team relegated after play-offs, + team not relegated after play-offs.

There are 211 member associations in the six FIFA Confederations, indicated in brackets after the regional heading. The four home countries, England, Scotland, Northern Ireland and Wales, are dealt with elsewhere in the Yearbook; but basic details appear in this directory. Gibraltar was admitted to full UEFA membership in 2013; Northern Cyprus is not a member of FIFA or UEFA and is the subject of an international territorial dispute. From March 2014 FIFA permitted Kosovo to play friendlies against full member nations; Kosovo was granted full membership of both FIFA and UEFA in May 2016 and will enter World Cup 2018 qualification in September 2016. Gozo is included here for its close links with Maltese football. *N.B. In this edition international results for 2015–16 include matches played from 5 July 2015 to 10 July 2016.*

There are a number of associate members and others who have affiliation to their confederations; the most recent admission to full membership was South Sudan in 2011. The current associate members are as follows: AFC: Northern Mariana Islands; CAF: Reunion, Zanzibar; CONCACAF: Bonaire, French Guiana, Guadeloupe, Martinique, Saint-Martin, Sint Maarten; OFC: Kiribati, Niue, Tuvalu. Matches between full members and associate members are indicated with †; matches between full members and Kosovo are indicated with ‡.

EUROPE (UEFA)

ALBANIA

Football Association of Albania, Rruga e Elbasanit, 1000 Tirana.
Founded: 1930. *FIFA:* 1932; *UEFA:* 1954. *National Colours:* Red shirts with white trim, black shorts, red socks.

International matches 2015–16
Denmark (a) 0-0, Portugal (h) 0-1, Serbia (h) 0-2, Armenia (a) 3-0, Kosovo‡ (a) 2-2, Georgia (h) 2-2, Austria (a) 1-2, Luxembourg (a) 2-0, Qatar (n) 3-1, Ukraine (n) 1-3, Switzerland (n) 0-1, France (a) 0-2, Romania (n) 1-0.

League Championship wins (1930–37; 1945–2016)
KF Tirana 24 (formerly SK Tirana; includes 17 Nentori 8); Dinamo Tirana 18; Partizani Tirana 15; Vllaznia 9; Skenderbeu 7; Elbasani 2 (including Labinoti 1); Flamurtari 1; Teuta 1.

Cup wins (1948–2016)
Partizani Tirana 15; KF Tirana 15 (formerly SK Tirana; includes 17 Nentori 8); Dinamo Tirana 13; Vllaznia 6; Flamurtari 4; Teuta 3; Elbasani 2 (including Labinoti 1); Besa 2; Laci 2; Apolonia 1; Kukesi 1.

Final League Table 2015–16

	P	W	D	L	F	A	GD	Pts
Skenderbeu	36	25	4	7	73	27	46	79
Partizani	36	21	11	4	51	21	30	74
Kukesi	36	18	9	9	41	25	16	63
Teuta	36	18	9	9	43	28	15	63
KF Tirana	36	13	14	9	37	25	12	53
Vllaznia	36	11	6	19	36	42	–6	39
Laci	36	8	12	16	30	48	–18	36
Flamurtari (–3)	36	9	11	16	34	44	–10	35
Bylis Ballsh*	36	8	8	20	27	53	–26	32
Terbuni Puke*	36	4	6	26	22	81	–59	18

Top scorer: Salihi (Skenderbeu) 27.
Cup Final: Laci 1, Kukesi 1.
aet; Kukesi won 5-3 on penalties.

ANDORRA

Federacio Andorrana de Futbol, Avda Carlemany 67, 3er Pis, Apartado postal 65, Escaldes-Engordany.
Founded: 1994. *FIFA:* 1996; *UEFA:* 1996. *National Colours:* All red.

International matches 2015–16
Israel (a) 0-4, Bosnia-Herzegovina (a) 0-3, Belgium (h) 1-4, Wales (a) 0-2, St Kitts & Nevis (h) 0-1, Moldova (n) 0-1, Azerbaijan (n) 0-0, Estonia (a) 0-2.

League Championship wins (1996–2016)
FC Santa Coloma 10; Principat 8; Encamp 2; Sant Julia 2; Ranger's 2; Lusitanos 2; Constel-lacio 1.

Cup wins (1991, 1994–2016)
FC Santa Coloma 9*; Principat 6*; Sant Julia 5; UE Santa Coloma 2; Constel-lacio 1; Lusitanos 1.
* *Includes one unofficial title.*

Qualifying League Table 2015–16

	P	W	D	L	F	A	GD	Pts
FC Santa Coloma	14	12	1	1	41	7	34	37
Lusitanos	14	10	0	4	28	18	10	30
UE Santa Coloma	14	8	3	3	31	11	20	27
Sant Julia	14	7	3	4	30	14	16	24
Engordany	14	5	2	7	18	22	–4	17
Encamp	14	3	2	9	15	41	–26	11
Ordino	14	3	1	10	15	35	–20	10
Penya Encarnada	14	1	2	11	6	36	–30	5

Championship Round

	P	W	D	L	F	A	GD	Pts
FC Santa Coloma	20	14	5	1	44	8	36	47
Lusitanos	20	12	3	5	37	28	9	39
Sant Julia	20	9	5	6	41	20	21	32
UE Santa Coloma	20	8	6	6	34	20	14	30

Relegation Round

	P	W	D	L	F	A	GD	Pts
Engordany	20	9	2	9	37	34	3	29
Ordino	20	8	2	10	42	44	–12	26
Encamp+	20	4	4	12	22	50	–28	16
Penya Encarnada*	20	1	3	16	15	58	–43	3

Top scorers (joint): Aguilar (Lusitanos), Bernat (UE Santa Coloma) 12.
Cup Final: UE Santa Coloma 3, Engordany 0.

ARMENIA

Football Federation of Armenia, Khanjyan Street 27, 0010 Yerevan.
Founded: 1992. *FIFA:* 1992; *UEFA:* 1993. *National Colours:* Red shirts with white trim, red shorts, red socks.

International matches 2015–16
Serbia (a) 0-2, Denmark (h) 0-0, France (a) 0-4, Albania (h) 0-3, Belarus (h) 0-0, Guatemala (n) 7-1, El Salvador (n) 4-0.

League Championship wins (1992–2016)
Pyunik 14 (including Homenetmen 1); Shirak 5*; Ararat Yerevan 2*; Araks 2 (including Tsement 1); FK Yerevan 1; Ulisses 1; Banants 1; Alashkert 1.
* *Includes one unofficial shared title.*

Cup wins (1992–2016)
Pyunik (including Homenetmen 1) 8; Mika 6; Ararat Yerevan 5; Banants 3; Tsement 2; Shirak 1.

Final League Table 2015–16

	P	W	D	L	F	A	GD	Pts
Alashkert	28	16	7	5	50	24	26	55
Shirak	28	15	7	6	41	27	14	52
Pyunik	28	13	9	6	44	21	23	48
Gandzasar	28	11	12	5	35	27	8	45
Ararat	28	9	10	9	28	31	–3	37
Banants	28	7	12	9	36	34	2	33
Mika	28	9	5	14	30	32	–2	32
Ulisses†	28	0	2	26	8	76	–68	2

† *Expelled for breaches of financial and league rules; matches from Round 16 awarded 3-0 to opponents.*
Top scorers (joint): Heber (Alashkert), Manasyan (Alashkert) 16.
Cup Final: Banants 2, Mika 0.

AUSTRIA

Oesterreichischer Fussball-Bund, Ernst-Happel Stadion, Sektor A/F, Meiereistrasse 7, Wien 1021.
Founded: 1904. *FIFA:* 1905; *UEFA:* 1954. *National Colours:* Red shirts, white shorts, red socks.

International matches 2015–16
Moldova (h) 1-0, Sweden (a) 4-1, Montenegro (a) 3-2, Liechtenstein (h) 3-0, Switzerland (h) 1-2, Albania (h) 2-1, Turkey (h) 1-2, Malta (h) 2-1, Netherlands (n) 0-2, Hungary (n) 0-2, Portugal (n) 0-0, Iceland (n) 1-2.

League Championship wins (1912–2016)
Rapid Vienna 32; FK Austria Vienna (formerly Amateure) 24; Wacker Innsbruck 10 (incl. Svarowski Tirol 2, Tirol Innsbruck 3); Red Bull Salzburg 10 (incl. Austria Salzburg 3); Admira Vienna (now Admira Wacker Modling) 9 (incl. Wacker Vienna 1); First Vienna 6; Wiener Sportklub 3; Sturm Graz 3; WAF 1; WAC 1; Florisdorfer 1; Hakoah 1; Linz ASK 1; Voest Linz 1; Graz 1.

Cup wins (1919–2016)
FK Austria Vienna (formerly Amateure) 27; Rapid Vienna 14; Wacker Innsbruck 7 (incl. Svarowski Tirol 1, Tirol Innsbruck); Admira Vienna 6 (including Wacker Vienna 1); Graz 4; Sturm Graz 4; Red Bull Salzburg 4; First Vienna 3; WAC 2; Ried 2; WAF 1; Wiener Sportklub 1; Linz ASK 1; Kremser 1; Stockerau 1; Karnten 1; Horn 1; Pasching 1.

Final League Table 2015–16
	P	W	D	L	F	A	GD	Pts
Red Bull Salzburg	36	21	11	4	71	33	38	74
Rapid Vienna	36	20	5	11	66	42	24	65
Austria Vienna	36	17	8	11	65	48	17	59
Admira Wacker Modling	36	13	11	12	45	51	–6	50
Sturm Graz	36	12	12	12	40	40	0	48
Wolfsberger	36	11	10	15	33	36	–3	43
Ried	36	11	9	16	36	52	–16	42
Rheindorf Altach	36	11	7	18	39	49	–10	40
Mattersburg	36	10	9	17	40	70	–30	39
Grodig	36	9	8	19	42	56	–14	35

Top scorer: Soriano (Red Bull Salzburg) 21.
Cup Final: Red Bull Salzburg 5, Admira Wacker Modling 0.

AZERBAIJAN
Association of Football Federations of Azerbaijan, 2208 Nobel prospekti, 1025 Baku.
Founded: 1992. *FIFA:* 1994; *UEFA:* 1994. *National Colours:* All red.

International matches 2015–16
Croatia (h) 0-0, Malta (a) 2-2, Italy (h) 1-3, Bulgaria (a) 0-2, Moldova (h) 2-1, Kazakhstan (n) 0-1, Andorra (n) 0-0, FYR Macedonia (n) 1-3, Canada (n) 1-1.

League Championship wins (1992–2015)
Neftchi 8; Qarabag 3; Kapaz 3; Shamkir 3*; FK Baku 2; Inter Baku 2; Turan 1; Khazar Lankaran 1.
* *Includes one unofficial title.*

Cup wins (1992–2016)
Neftchi 7*; Qarabag 5; Kapaz 4; FK Baku 3; Khazar Lankaran 3; Inshatchi 1; Shafa 1.
* *Includes one title awarded by forfeit.*

Final League Table 2015–16
	P	W	D	L	F	A	GD	Pts
Qarabag	36	26	6	4	66	21	45	84
Zira	36	17	11	8	42	31	11	62
Qabala	36	16	11	9	44	28	16	59
Inter Baku	36	16	11	9	39	28	11	59
Kapaz	36	15	11	10	48	40	8	56
Neftci	36	13	10	13	41	41	0	49
AZAL-Olympik Suvalan	36	13	7	16	26	38	–12	46
Sumqayıt	36	9	12	15	41	49	–8	39
Ravan (–6)	36	5	9	22	27	63	–36	18
Khazar Lankaran*	36	3	6	27	16	51	–35	15

Top scorer: Dani Quintana (Qarabag) 15.
Cup Final: Qarabag 1, Neftchi 0 *aet.*

BELARUS
Belarus Football Federation, Prospekt Pobeditelei 20/3, 220020 Minsk.
Founded: 1989. *FIFA:* 1992; *UEFA:* 1993. *National Colours:* All red with white trim.

International matches 2015–16
Ukraine (a) 1-3, Luxembourg (h) 2-0, Slovakia (a) 1-0, FYR Macedonia (h) 0-0, Armenia (a) 0-0, Montenegro (a) 0-0, Northern Ireland (a) 0-3, Republic of Ireland (a) 2-1.

League Championship wins (1992–2015)
BATE Borisov 12; Dinamo Minsk 7; Slavia Mozyr (incl. MPKC Mozyr 1) 2; Dnepr Mogilev 1; Belshina Bobruisk 1; Gomel 1; Shakhtyor Soligorsk 1.

Cup wins (1992–2016)
Dinamo Minsk 3; Belshina Bobruisk 3; BATE Borisov 3; Slavia Mozyr (formerly MPKC Mozyr) 2; Gomel 2; Shakhtyor Soligorsk 2; MTZ-RIPA (now Partizan Minsk) 2; Naftan Novopolotsk 2; Neman Grodno 1; Dinamo 93 Minsk 1; Lokomotiv 96 1; Dinamo Brest 1; FC Minsk 1; Torpedo Zhodino 1.

Final League Table 2015
	P	W	D	L	F	A	GD	Pts
BATE Borisov	26	20	5	1	44	11	33	65
Dinamo Minsk	26	15	8	3	36	13	23	53
Shakhtyor Soligorsk	26	14	7	5	47	27	20	49
Belshina Bobruisk	26	12	7	7	39	19	20	43
Granit	26	12	6	8	30	32	–2	42
Dinamo Minsk	26	12	4	10	29	28	1	40
Torpedo Zhodino	26	10	6	10	31	29	2	36
Neman Grodno	26	8	8	10	21	32	–11	32
Naftan Novopolotsk	26	8	6	12	34	35	–1	30
Slavia Mozyr	26	7	5	14	33	50	–17	26
Slutsk	26	6	7	13	26	30	–4	25
Dinamo Brest	26	7	3	16	23	42	–19	24
Vitebsk	26	4	9	13	21	47	–26	21
Gomel*	26	5	3	18	22	41	–19	18

Top scorer: Yanush (Shakhtyor Soligorsk) 15.
Cup Final: BATE Borisov 0, Torpedo Zhodino 0.
aet; Torpedo Zhodino won 3-2 on penalties.

BELGIUM
Union Royale Belge des Societes de Football-Association, 145 Avenue Houba de Strooper, B-1020 Bruxelles.
Founded: 1895. *FIFA:* 1904; *UEFA:* 1954. *National Colours:* All red.

International matches 2015–16
Bosnia-Herzegovina (h) 3-1, Cyprus (a) 1-0, Andorra (a) 4-1, Israel (h) 3-1, Italy (h) 3-1, Portugal (h) 1-2, Switzerland (a) 2-1, Finland (h) 1-1, Norway (h) 3-2, Italy (n) 0-2, Republic of Ireland (n) 3-0, Sweden (n) 1-0, Hungary (n) 4-0, Wales (n) 1-3.

League Championship wins (1896–2016)
Anderlecht 33; Club Brugge 14; Union St Gilloise 11; Standard Liege 10; Beerschot VAC (became Germinal) 7; RC Brussels 6; RFC Liege 5; Daring Brussels 5; Antwerp 4; Lierse 4; Mechelen 4; Cercle Brugge 3; Genk 3; Beveren 2; RWD Molenbeek 1; KAA Gent 1.

Cup wins (1912–14; 1927; 1935; 1954–2016)
Club Brugge 11; Anderlecht 9; Standard Liege 7; Genk 4; KAA Gent 3; Union St Gilloise 2; Waterschei (became Racing Genk) 2; Beveren 2; Cercle Brugge 2; Antwerp 2; Lierse 2; Beerschot VAC (became Germinal) 2; Beerschot Antwerpen Club (incl. Germinal Ekeren) 2; Lokeren 2; Racing 1; Daring 1; Tournai 1; Waregem 1; Mechelen 1; FC Liege 1; Westerlo 1; La Louviere 1; Zulte-Waregem 1.

Qualifying League Table 2015–16
	P	W	D	L	F	A	GD	Pts
Club Brugge	30	21	1	8	64	30	34	64
KAA Gent	30	17	9	4	56	29	27	60
Anderlecht	30	15	10	5	51	29	22	55
Oostende	30	14	7	9	55	44	11	49
Genk	30	14	6	10	42	30	12	48
Zulte-Waregem	30	12	7	11	51	50	1	43
Standard Liege	30	12	5	13	41	51	–10	41
Sporting Charleroi	30	10	9	11	36	39	–3	39
Kortrijk	30	10	9	11	31	35	–4	39
Mechelen	30	10	7	13	48	50	–2	37
Lokeren	30	8	10	12	35	40	–5	34
Waasland-Beveren	30	9	6	15	40	57	–17	33
Sint-Truiden	30	8	6	16	28	47	–19	30
Mouscron-Peruwelz	30	7	9	14	39	51	–12	30
Westerlo	30	7	9	14	35	59	–24	30
OH Leuven*	30	7	8	15	42	53	–11	29

NB: Points earned in Qualifying phase are halved and rounded up at start of Championship Play-off phase.

Championship Play-off
	P	W	D	L	F	A	GD	Pts
Club Brugge	10	7	1	2	25	9	16	54
Anderlecht	10	6	1	3	15	16	–1	47
Gent	10	3	3	4	10	15	–5	42
Genk	10	5	1	4	20	13	7	40
KV Oostende	10	3	2	5	14	19	–5	36
Zulte-Waregem	10	1	2	7	11	23	–12	27

Europa League Qualifying Table A
	P	W	D	L	F	A	GD	Pts
Kortrijk	6	4	2	0	13	5	8	14
Standard Liege	6	3	1	2	8	5	3	10

Mouscron Peruwelz	6	1	2	3	5	8 –3	5
Waasland-Beveren	6	1	1	4	3	11 –8	4

Europa League Qualifying Table B

	P	W	D	L	F	A GD	Pts
Sporting Charleroi	6	3	2	1	13	6	7	11
Lokeren	6	3	2	1	12	7	5	11
Mechelen	6	2	1	3	7	14 –7	7
Sint-Truiden	6	0	3	3	4	9 –5	3

Europa League Qualifying Play-off
Sporting Charleroi 1, 2, Kortrijk 0, 1 (agg 3-1).

Europa League Testmatch
Played between Europa League Play-off winners and fifth-placed team in Championship Play-off.
Sporting Charleroi 2, 1, Genk 0, 5 (agg 3-5).
Top scorer: Perbet (Sporting Charleroi) 24.
Cup Final: Standard Liege 2, Club Brugge 1.

BOSNIA-HERZEGOVINA

Football Federation of Bosnia & Herzegovina, Ferhadija 30, 71000 Sarajevo.
Founded: 1992. *FIFA:* 1996; *UEFA:* 1998. *National Colours:* Blue shirts, blue shorts, blue socks with white tops.

International matches 2015–16
Belgium (a) 1-3, Andorra (h) 3-0, Wales (h) 2-0, Cyprus (a) 3-2, Republic of Ireland (h) 1-1, Republic of Ireland (a) 0-2, Luxembourg (a) 3-0, Switzerland (a) 2-0, Spain (n) 1-3, Denmark (n) 2-2 (4-3p), Japan (a) 2-1.

League Championship wins (1998–2016)
Zeljeznicar 6; Zrinjski 4; FK Sarajevo 3; Siroki Brijeg 2; Brotnjo 1; Leotar 1; Modrica 1; Borac Banja Luka 1.

Cup wins (1998; 2000–16)
Zeljeznicar 5; FK Sarajevo 4; Siroki Brijeg 2; Modrica 1; Orasje 1; Zrinjski 1; Slavija 1; Borac Banja Luka 1; Olimpic Sarajevo 1; Radnik Bijeljina 1.

Final League Table 2015–16

	P	W	D	L	F	A GD	Pts
Zrinjski	30	21	6	3	52	17	35	69
Sloboda Tuzla	30	19	5	6	44	23	21	62
Siroki Brijeg	30	18	7	5	56	21	35	61
FK Sarajevo	30	18	3	9	56	28	28	57
Zeljeznicar	30	16	7	7	36	20	16	55
Celik Zenica	30	12	10	8	35	28	7	46
Radnik Bijeljina	30	13	6	11	25	25	0	45
Olimpic Sarajevo	30	11	6	13	36	33	3	39
Vitez	30	11	6	13	36	41	–5	39
Mladost Doboj Kakanj	30	10	9	11	29	39	–10	39
Borac Banja Luka*	30	10	6	14	27	33	–6	36
Slavija*	30	8	11	11	25	37	–12	35
Travnik*	30	8	5	17	36	47	–11	29
Rudar Prijedor*	30	5	10	15	24	38	–14	25
Drina Zvornik*	30	7	1	22	24	66	–42	22
Velez Mostar*	30	1	6	23	10	55	–45	9

Top scorer: Benko (FK Sarajevo) 18.
Cup Final: Radnik Bijeljina 1, 3, Sloboda Tuzla 1, 0 (agg. 4-1).

BULGARIA

Bulgarian Football Union, 26 Tzar Ivan Assen II Str., 1124 Sofia.
Founded: 1923. *FIFA:* 1992; *UEFA:* 1954. *National Colours:* White shirts, green shorts, red socks.

International matches 2015–16
Norway (h) 0-1, Italy (a) 0-1, Croatia (a) 0-3, Azerbaijan (h) 2-0, Portugal (a) 1-0, FYR Macedonia (a) 2-0, Japan (a) 2-7, Denmark (n) 0-4.

League Championship wins (1925–2016)
CSKA Sofia 31; Levski Sofia 26; Slavia Sofia 7; Ludogorets Razgrad 5; Lokomotiv Sofia 4; Litex Lovech 4; Vladislav Varna 3; Botev Plovdiv (includes Trakija) 2; AC 23 Sofia 1; Sokol (Spartak) Varna 1; Sportklub Sofia 1; Ticha Varna 1; Spartak Plovdiv 1; Beroe Stara Zagora 1; Etar 1; Lokomotiv Plovdiv 1.

Cup wins (1946–2016)
Levski Sofia 24; CSKA Sofia 20; Slavia Sofia 7; Lokomotiv Sofia 4; Litex Lovech 4; Botev Plovdiv (includes Trakija) 2; Beroe Stara Zagora 2; Ludogorets Razgrad 2; Spartak Plovdiv 1; Septemvri Sofia 1; Spartak Sofia 1; Marek Dupnica 1; Sliven 1; Cherno More Varna 1.

Final League Table 2015–16

	P	W	D	L	F	A GD	Pts
Ludogorets Razgrad	31	21	7	3	54	19	35	70
Levski Sofia	31	16	8	7	35	16	19	56
Beroe Stara Zagora	31	13	11	7	35	26	9	50
Slavia Sofia	31	13	7	11	33	28	5	46
Lokomotiv Plovdiv	31	14	4	13	38	44	–6	46
Cherno More Varna	32	10	8	14	36	45	–9	38
Botev Plovdiv	31	7	9	15	25	43	–18	30
OFK Pirin	31	5	11	15	26	43	–17	26
Montana+	31	4	9	18	22	40	–18	21
Litex Lovech†	0	0	0	0	0	0	0	0

† *Litex Lovech expelled for player indiscipline, record expunged.*
Top scorer: Kamburov (Lokomotiv Plovdiv) 18.
Cup Final: CSKA Sofia 1, Montana 0.

CHANNEL ISLANDS

Guernsey

League Championship wins (1894–2016)
Northerners 32; Guernsey Rangers 17; Vale Recreation 15; St Martin's 13; Sylvans 10; Belgrave Wanderers 8; 2nd Bn Manchesters 3; 2nd Bn Royal Irish Regt 2; 2nd Bn Wiltshires 2; 10th Comp W Div Royal Artillery 1; 2nd Bn Leicesters 1; 2nd Bn PA Somerset Light Infantry 1; 2nd Middlesex Regt 1; Athletics 1; Band Comp 2nd Bn Royal Fusiliers 1; G&H Comp Royal Fusiliers 1; Grange 1; Yorkshire Regt (Green Howards) 1.

Final League Table 2015–16

	P	W	D	L	F	A GD	Pts
Northerners	18	15	1	2	69	24	45	46
Rovers	18	13	1	4	53	25	28	40
Vale Recreation	18	12	2	4	57	25	32	38
Sylvans	18	8	0	10	31	49	–18	24
St Martins	18	7	1	10	29	44	–15	22
Belgrave Wanderers	18	5	0	13	29	53	–24	15
Guernsey Rangers	18	0	1	17	18	66	–48	1

Jersey

League Championship wins (1894–2016)
Jersey Wanderers 20; First Tower United 19; St Paul's 17; Jersey Scottish 10; Beeches Old Boys 5; Magpies 4; 2nd Bn King's Own Royal Regt 3; Oaklands 3; St Peter 3; 1st Batt Devon Regt 2; 1st Bn East Surrey Regt 2; Georgetown 2; Mechanics 2; YMCA 2; 2nd Bn East Surrey Regt 1; 20th Comp Royal Garrison Artillery 1; National Rovers 1; Sporting Academics 1; Trinity 1.

Qualifying League Table 2015–16

	P	W	D	L	F	A GD	Pts
Jersey Scottish	14	14	0	0	62	11	51	42
St Paul's	14	12	1	1	90	13	77	37
Jersey Wanderers	14	11	2	1	66	17	49	35
St Ouen	14	9	2	3	37	17	20	29
Trinity	14	9	1	4	50	25	25	28
St Peter	14	7	2	5	39	27	12	23
St Clement	14	7	1	6	34	25	9	22
St John	14	7	1	6	20	28	–8	22
Jersey Portuguese	14	6	0	8	33	36	–3	18
Rozel Rovers	14	5	2	7	23	31	–8	17
Grouville	14	4	1	9	16	44	–28	13
St Brelade	14	4	0	10	24	33	–9	12
Sporting Academics	14	2	1	11	19	80	–61	7
St Lawrence	14	1	0	13	15	46	–31	3
Beeches OB	14	0	0	14	5	100	–95	0

Premiership Round

	P	W	D	L	F	A GD	Pts
St Paul's (P)	14	11	1	2	47	14	33	34
Jersey Scottish (P)	14	11	1	2	42	16	26	34
Jersey Wanderers	14	7	3	4	30	21	9	24
St Ouen	14	7	1	6	32	21	11	22
Trinity	14	6	2	6	29	26	3	20
St Peter	14	4	3	7	20	31	–11	15
St John*	14	2	2	10	12	44	–32	8
St Clement*	14	1	1	12	12	51	–39	4

(P) *Qualified for Premiership Play-off.*

Championship Round

	P	W	D	L	F	A GD	Pts
Rozel Rovers (P)	18	15	1	2	69	16	56	46
Jersey Portuguese (P)	18	14	1	3	63	17	46	43
Grouville	18	10	4	4	38	18	10	34
St Brelade	18	10	0	8	52	28	24	30
St Lawrence	18	4	3	11	22	32	–10	15
Sporting Academics	18	3	3	12	23	72	–49	12
Beeches OB	18	1	0	17	10	87	–77	3

Premiership Play-off
Jersey Scottish 2, St Paul's 2.
aet; St Paul's won 5-4 on penalties.

Upton Park Trophy 2016 (For Guernsey & Jersey League Champions)
St Paul's 3, Northerners 1.

Upton Park Trophy wins (1907–2016)
Northerners 17 (including 1 shared); First Tower United 12; Jersey Wanderers 11 (including 1 shared); St Martin's 11; St Paul's 9; Jersey Scottish 6; Guernsey Rangers 5; Vale Recreation 4; Belgrave Wanderers 4; Beeches Old Boys 3; Old St Paul's 3; Magpies 3; Sylvans 3; St Peter 2; Jersey Mechanics 1; Jersey YMCA 1; National Rovers 1; Sporting Academics 1; Trinity 1.

CROATIA

Croatian Football Federation, Vukovarska 269A, 10000 Zagreb.
Founded: 1912. *FIFA:* 1992; *UEFA:* 1993. *National Colours:* Red and white check shirts, white shorts, blue socks.

International matches 2015–16
Azerbaijan (a) 0-0, Norway (a) 0-2, Bulgaria (h) 3-0, Malta (a) 1-0, Russia (a) 3-1, Israel (h) 2-0, Hungary (a) 1-1, Moldova (h) 1-0, San Marino (h) 10-0, Turkey (n) 1-0, Czech Republic (n) 2-2, Spain (n) 2-1, Portugal (n) 0-1.

League Championship wins (1941–46; 1992–2016)
Dinamo Zagreb (formerly Croatia Zagreb) 17; Hajduk Split 8; Concordia 1; Gradjanski 1; NK Zagreb 1.

Cup wins (1992–2016)
Dinamo Zagreb (formerly Croatia Zagreb) 14; Hajduk Split 6; Rijeka 3; Inter Zapresic 1; Osijek 1.

Final League Table 2015–16

	P	W	D	L	F	A	GD	Pts
Dinamo Zagreb	36	26	7	3	67	19	48	85
Rijeka	36	21	14	1	56	20	36	77
Hajduk Split	36	17	10	9	46	28	18	61
Lokomotiva Zagreb	36	16	4	16	56	53	3	52
Inter Zapresic	36	11	14	11	39	48	–9	47
RNK Split	36	10	16	10	28	29	–1	46
Slaven Koprivnica	36	10	12	14	41	42	–1	42
Osijek	36	7	13	16	27	49	–22	34
Istra 1961+	36	4	12	20	23	58	–35	24
Zagreb*	36	3	8	25	27	64	–37	17

Top scorer: Nestorovski (Inter Zapresic) 25.
Cup Final: Dinamo Zagreb 2, Slaven Koprivnica 1.

CYPRUS

Cyprus Football Association, 10 Achaion Street, 2413 Engomi, PO Box 25071, 1306 Nicosia.
Founded: 1934. *FIFA:* 1948; *UEFA:* 1962. *National Colours:* All blue with white trim.

International matches 2015–16
Wales (h) 0-1, Belgium (h) 0-1, Israel (a) 2-1, Bosnia-Herzegovina (h) 2-3, Ukraine (a) 0-1, Serbia (a) 1-2.

League Championship wins (1935–2016)
APOEL 25; Omonia 20; Anorthosis 13; AEL Limassol 6; EPA Larnaca 3; Olympiakos Nicosia 3; Apollon Limassol 3; Pezoporikos Larnaca 2; Trast 1; Cetinkaya 1.

Cup wins (1935–2016)
APOEL 21; Omonia 14; Anorthosis 10; Apollon Limassol 8; AEL Limassol 6; EPA Larnaca 5; Trast 3; Cetinkaya 2; Pezoporikos Larnaca 1; Olympiakos Nicosia 1; Nea Salamis Famagusta 1; AEK Larnaca 1; APOP Kinyras 1.

Qualifying League Table 2015–16

	P	W	D	L	F	A	GD	Pts
APOEL	26	20	2	4	72	18	54	62
AEK Larnaca	26	19	4	3	47	17	30	61
Anorthosis Famagusta	26	15	7	4	48	22	26	52
Omonia	26	14	7	5	46	24	22	49
Apollon Limassol	26	14	5	7	41	24	17	49
Nea Salamis Famagusta	26	8	9	9	37	52	–15	33
Aris	26	8	7	11	29	31	–2	31
AEL Limassol	26	9	4	13	22	32	–10	31
Doxa Katokopia	26	7	9	10	31	41	–10	30
Paphos	26	6	9	11	35	47	–12	27
Ethnikos Achnas	26	5	9	12	27	43	–16	24
Ermis Aradippou	26	6	6	14	22	40	–18	24
Enosis*	26	4	8	14	28	47	–19	20
Ayia Napa*	26	0	6	20	17	64	–47	6

Championship Round

	P	W	D	L	F	A	GD	Pts
APOEL	36	26	5	5	91	26	65	83
AEK Larnaca	36	23	6	7	61	34	27	75
Apollon Limassol	36	19	11	6	61	36	25	68
Omonia Nicosia	36	20	7	9	63	34	29	67
Anorthosis Famagusta	36	16	11	9	57	41	16	59
Nea Salamis Famagusta	36	9	10	17	44	72	–28	37

Relegation Round

	P	W	D	L	F	A	GD	Pts
AEL Limassol (–2)	36	14	7	15	38	43	–5	47
Ermis	36	11	9	16	36	52	–16	42
Doxa Katokopia	36	10	11	15	46	59	–13	41
Aris	36	10	11	15	43	46	–3	41
Ethnikos Achnas	36	9	12	15	43	57	–14	39
Paphos*	36	8	12	16	41	58	–17	36

Top scorers (joint): Alves (AEK Larnaca), Cavenaghi (APOEL), Makriev (Nea Salamis Famagusta) 19.
Cup Final: Apollon Limassol 2, Omonia 1.

CZECH REPUBLIC

Fotbalova Asociace Ceske Republiky, Diskarska 2431/4, PO Box 11, Praha 6 16017.
Founded: 1901. *FIFA:* 1907; *UEFA:* 1954. *National Colours:* All red.

International matches 2015–16
Kazakhstan (h) 2-1, Latvia (a) 2-1, Turkey (h) 0-2, Netherlands (a) 3-2, Serbia (h) 4-1, Poland (a) 1-3, Scotland (h) 0-1, Sweden (a) 1-1, Malta (n) 6-0, Russia (n) 2-1, Korea Republic (h) 1-2, Spain (h) 0-1, Croatia (n) 2-2, Turkey (n) 0-2.

League Championship wins – Czechoslovakia (1925–93)
Sparta Prague 21; Slavia Prague 13; Dukla Prague (prev. UDA, now Marila Pribram) 11; Slovan Bratislava (formerly NV Bratislava) 8; Spartak Trnava 5; Banik Ostrava 3; Viktoria Zizkov 1; Inter-Bratislava 1; Spartak Hradec Kralove 1; Zbrojovka Brno 1; Bohemians 1; Vitkovice 1.

Cup wins – Czechoslovakia (1961–93)
Dukla Prague 8; Sparta Prague 8; Slovan Bratislava 5; Spartak Trnava 4; Banik Ostrava 3; Lokomotiva Kosice 2; TJ Gottwaldov 1; Lokomotiva Kosice 1; Dunajska Streda 1.

League Championship wins – Czech Republic (1994–2016)
Sparta Prague 12; Viktoria Plzen 4; Slavia Prague 3; Slovan Liberec 3; Banik Ostrava 1.

Cup wins – Czech Republic (1994–2016)
Sparta Prague 6; Slavia Prague 3; Viktoria Zizkov 2; Jablonec 2; Slovan Liberec 2; Teplice 2; Mlada Boleslav 2; Hradec Kralove (formerly Spartak) 1; Banik Ostrava 1; Viktoria Plzen 1; Sigma Olomouc 1.

Final League Table 2015–16

	P	W	D	L	F	A	GD	Pts
Viktoria Plzen	30	23	2	5	57	25	32	71
Sparta Prague	30	20	4	6	61	24	37	64
Slovan Liberec	30	17	7	6	51	35	16	58
Mlada Boleslav	30	16	9	5	63	37	26	57
Slavia Prague	30	14	10	6	48	26	22	52
Zbrojovka Brno	30	14	5	11	37	38	–1	47
Jablonec	30	10	11	9	46	39	7	41
Slovacko	30	12	4	14	37	51	–14	40
Bohemians 1905	30	8	13	9	35	37	–2	37
Dukla Prague	30	8	11	11	44	41	3	35
Vysocina Jihlava	30	8	7	15	31	54	–23	31
Teplice	30	8	7	15	37	52	–15	30
Zlin	30	7	9	14	34	50	–16	30
Pribram	30	7	6	17	33	53	–20	27
Sigma Olomouc*	30	6	9	15	35	49	–14	27
Banik Ostrava*	30	4	2	24	27	65	–38	14

Top scorer: Lafata (Sparta Prague) 20.
Cup Final: Mlada Boleslav 2, Jablonec 0.

DENMARK

Dansk Boldspil-Union, Idraettens Hus, DBU Alle 1, DK-2605, Brondby.
Founded: 1889. *FIFA:* 1904; *UEFA:* 1954. *National Colours:* Red shirts, white shorts, red socks.

International matches 2015–16
Albania (h) 0-0, Armenia (a) 0-0, Portugal (a) 0-1, France (h) 1-2, Sweden (a) 1-2, Sweden (h) 2-2, Iceland (h) 2-1, Scotland (a) 0-1, Bosnia-Herzegovina (n) 2-2 (3-4p), Bulgaria (n) 4-0.

League Championship wins (1913–2016)
KB Copenhagen 15; FC Copenhagen 11; Brondby 10; B 93 Copenhagen 9; AB (Akademisk) 9; B 1903 Copenhagen 7; Frem 6; AGF Aarhus 5; Vejle 5; Esbjerg 5; AaB Aalborg 4; Hvidovre 3; OB Odense 3; Koge 2; B 1909 Odense 2; Lyngby 2; Silkeborg 1; Herfolge 1; Nordsjaelland 1; Midtjylland 1.

Cup wins (1955–2016)
AGF Aarhus 9; FC Copenhagen 7; Vejle 6; Brondby 6; OB Odense 5; Esbjerg 3; AaB Aalborg 3; Randers Freja 3; Lyngby 3; Frem 2; B 1909 Odense 2; B 1903 Copenhagen 2; Nordsjaelland 2; B 1913 Odense 1; KB Copenhagen 1; Vanlose 1; Hvidovre 1; B 93 Copenhagen 1; AB (Akademisk) 1; Viborg 1; Silkeborg 1; Randers 1.

Final League Table 2015–16
	P	W	D	L	F	A	GD	Pts
FC Copenhagen	33	21	8	4	62	28	33	71
SonderjyskE	33	19	5	9	56	36	20	62
Midtjylland	33	17	8	8	57	33	24	59
Brondby	33	16	6	11	43	37	6	54
AaB Aalborg	33	15	5	13	56	44	13	50
Randers	33	13	8	12	45	43	2	47
OB Odense	33	14	4	15	50	52	−2	46
Viborg	33	11	7	15	34	42	−8	40
Nordsjaelland	33	11	5	17	35	51	−16	38
AGF Aarhus	32	8	13	12	47	49	−2	37
Esbjerg	32	7	9	17	38	64	−26	30
Hobro*	32	4	6	23	26	70	−44	18
Top scorers: Spalvis (AaB Aalborg) 18.
Cup Final: FC Copenhagen 2, AGF Aarhus 1.

ENGLAND
The Football Association, Wembley Stadium, PO Box 1966, London SW1P 9EQ.
Founded: 1863. *FIFA:* 1905; *UEFA:* 1954. *National Colours:* All white.

ESTONIA
Eesti Jalgpalli Liit, A. Le Coq Arena, Asula 4c, 11312 Tallinn.
Founded: 1921. *FIFA:* 1923; *UEFA:* 1992. *National Colours:* Blue shirts, black shorts, white socks.

International matches 2015–16
Lithuania (h) 1-0, Slovenia (a) 0-1, England (a) 0-2, Switzerland (a) 0-1, Georgia (h) 3-0, St Kitts & Nevis (h) 3-0, Sweden (n) 1-1, Norway (h) 0-0, Serbia (h) 0-1, Lithuania (a) 0-2, Andorra (h) 2-0, Latvia (h) 0-0, Portugal (a) 0-7.

League Championship wins (1921–40; 1992–2015)
Flora 10; Levadia Tallinn (formerly Levadia Maardu) 9; Estonia 5; Tallinn JK 2; Norma 2; Lantana (formerly Nikol) 2; Sillamae Kalev 2; Olimpia Tartu 1; TVMK Tallinn 1; Nomme Kalju 1.

Cup wins (1993–2016)
Levadia Tallinn (formerly Levadia Maardu) 8; Flora 7; Tallinna Sadam 2; TVMK Tallinn 2; Lantana (formerly Nikol) 1; Norma 1; Narva Trans 1; Levadia Tallinn (pre-2004) 1; Nomme Kalju 1.

Final League Table 2015
	P	W	D	L	F	A	GD	Pts
Flora Tallinn	36	27	3	6	72	24	48	84
Levadia Tallinn	36	22	10	4	78	32	46	76
Nomme Kalju	36	22	5	9	69	36	33	71
Infonet Tallinn	36	17	11	8	50	32	18	62
Sillamae Kalev	36	17	8	11	63	43	20	59
Narva Trans	36	14	7	15	50	46	4	49
Paide Linnameeskond	36	9	6	21	50	73	−23	33
Parnu Linnameeskond	36	6	8	22	38	87	−49	26
Tartu Tammeka+	36	7	4	25	39	96	−57	25
Viljandi Tulevik*	36	6	4	26	35	75	−40	22
Top scorer: Teever (Levadia Tallinn) 24.
Cup Final: Flora Tallinn 3, Sillamae Kalev 0 *aet*.

FAROE ISLANDS
Fotboltssamband Foroya, Gundadalur, PO Box 3028, 110 Torshavn.
Founded: 1979. *FIFA:* 1988; *UEFA:* 1990. *National Colours:* White shirts with blue trim, white shorts, white socks.

International matches 2015–16
Northern Ireland (h) 1-3, Finland (a) 0-1, Hungary (a) 1-2, Romania (h) 0-3, Liechtenstein (n) 3-2, Kosovo (n) 0-2.

League Championship wins (1942–2015)
HB Torshavn 22; KI Klaksvik 17; B36 Torshavn 11; TB Tvoroyri 7; GI Gota 6; B68 Toftir 3; EB/Streymur 2; SI Sorvagur 1; IF Fuglafjordur 1; B71 Sandur 1; VB Vagur 1; NSI Runavik 1.

Cup wins (1955–2015)
HB Torshavn 26; GI Gota 6; TB Tvoroyri 5; B36 Torshavn 5; KI Klaksvik 5; Vikingur 5; EB/Streymur 4; NSI Runavik 2; VB Vagur 1; B71 Sandur 1.

Final League Table 2015
	P	W	D	L	F	A	GD	Pts
B36 Torshavn	27	18	7	2	60	25	35	61
NSI Runavik	27	16	6	5	73	37	36	54
Vikingur	27	15	8	4	68	35	33	53
HB Torshavn	27	11	10	6	43	31	12	43
KI Klaksvik	27	11	8	8	50	41	9	41
IF Fuglafjordur	27	5	12	10	44	56	−12	27
TB Tvoroyri	27	4	14	9	36	47	−11	26
AB Argir	27	4	12	11	34	42	−8	24
Suduroy*	27	6	4	17	39	68	−29	22
EB/Streymur*	27	2	5	20	27	92	−65	11
Top scorer: Olsen (NSI Runavik) 21.
Cup Final: Víkingur 3, NSI Runavik 0.

FINLAND
Suomen Palloliitto Finlands Bollfoerbund, Urheilukatu 5, PO Box 191, 00251 Helsinki.
Founded: 1907. *FIFA:* 1908; *UEFA:* 1954. *National Colours:* White shirts with blue trim, white shorts, white socks.

International matches 2015–16
Greece (a) 1-0, Faroe Islands (h) 1-0, Romania (a) 1-1, Northern Ireland (h) 1-1, Sweden (n) 0-3, Iceland (n) 0-1, Poland (a) 0-5, Norway (a) 0-2, Belgium (a) 1-1, Italy (a) 0-2.

League Championship wins (1908–2015)
HJK Helsinki 27; HPS Helsinki 9; Haka Valkeakoski 9; TPS Turku 8; HIFK Helsinki 7; KuPS Kuopio 5; Kuusysi Lahti 5; KIF Helsinki 4; AIFK Turku 3; VIFK Vaasa 3; Reipas Lahti 3; Tampere United 3; VPS Vaasa 2; KTP Kotka 2; OPS Oulu 2; Jazz Pori 2; Unitas Helsinki 1; PUS Helsinki 1; Sudet Viipuri 1; HT Helsinki 1; Ilves-Kissat 1; Pyrkiva Turku 1; KPV Kokkola 1; Ilves Tampere 1; TPV Tampere 1; MyPa Anjalankoski (renamed MYPA-47) 1; Inter Turku 1; SJK Seinajoki 1.

Cup wins (1955–2015)
Haka Valkeakoski 12; HJK Helsinki 12; Reipas Lahti 7; KTP Kotka 4; TPS Turku 3; MyPa Anjalankoski (renamed MYPA-47) 3; KuPS Kuopio 2; Mikkeli 2; Ilves Tampere 2; Kuusysi Lahti 2; RoPS Rovaniemi 2; Pallo-Pojat 1; Drott (renamed Jaro) 1; HPS Helsinki 1; AIFK Turku 1; Jokerit (formerly PK-35) 1; Atlantis 1; Tampere United 1; Inter Turku 1; FC Honka 1; IFK Mariehamn 1.

Final League Table 2015
	P	W	D	L	F	A	GD	Pts
SJK Seinajoki	33	18	6	9	50	22	28	60
RoPS Rovaniemi	33	17	8	8	44	29	15	59
HJK Helsinki	33	16	10	7	45	30	15	58
Inter Turku	33	13	10	10	45	35	10	49
Lahti	33	12	12	9	38	36	2	48
IFK Mariehamn	33	11	12	10	30	36	−6	45
HIFK Helsinki	33	10	13	10	42	42	0	43
Ilves	33	11	7	15	32	48	−16	40
KuPS Kuopio	33	9	11	13	32	40	−8	38
VPS Vaasa	33	8	9	16	36	43	−7	33
KTP Kotka*+	33	7	11	15	27	44	−17	32
FF Jaro*	33	6	11	16	27	43	−16	29
Top scorers: Kokko (RoPS Rovaniemi) 17.
Cup Final: IFK Mariehamn 2, Inter Turku 1.

FRANCE
Federation Francaise de Football, 87 Boulevard de Grenelle, 75738 Paris Cedex 15.
Founded: 1919. *FIFA:* 1904; *UEFA:* 1954. *National Colours:* Blue shirts, white shorts, red socks.

International matches 2015–16
Portugal (a) 1-0, Serbia (h) 2-1, Armenia (h) 4-0, Denmark (a) 2-1, Germany (h) 2-0, England (a) 0-2, Netherlands (a) 3-2, Russia (h) 4-2, Cameroon (h) 3-2, Scotland (h) 3-0, Romania (h) 2-1, Albania (h) 2-0, Switzerland (h) 0-0, Republic of Ireland (h) 2-1, Iceland (h) 5-2, Germany (h) 2-0, Portugal (h) 0-1.

League Championship wins (1933–2016)
Saint-Etienne 10; Olympique Marseille 9; Nantes 8; AS Monaco 7; Olympique Lyonnais 7; Stade de Reims 6; Bordeaux 6; Paris Saint-Germain 6; OGC Nice 4; Lille OSC (includes Olympique Lillois) 4; FC Sete 2; Sochaux 2; Racing Club Paris 1; Roubaix-Tourcoing 1; Strasbourg 1; Auxerre 1; Lens 1; Montpellier 1.

Cup wins (1918–2016)
Olympique Marseille 10; Paris Saint-Germain 10; Lille OSC 6; Saint-Etienne 6; Red Star 5; Racing Club Paris 5; AS Monaco 5; Olympique Lyonnais 5; Bordeaux 4; Auxerre 4; Strasbourg 3; OGC Nice 3; Nantes 3; CAS Genereaux 2; Montpellier 2; FC Sete 2; Sochaux 2; Stade de Reims 2; Sedan 2; Stade Rennais 2; Metz 2; Guingamp 2; Olympique de Pantin 1; CA Paris 1; Club Français 1; AS Cannes 1; Excelsior Roubaix 1; EF Nancy-Lorraine 1; Toulouse 1; Le Havre 1; AS Nancy 1; Bastia 1; Lorient 1.

Final League Table 2015–16
	P	W	D	L	F	A	GD	Pts
Paris Saint-Germain	38	30	6	2	102	19	83	96
Olympique Lyonnais	38	19	8	11	67	43	24	65
AS Monaco	38	17	14	7	57	50	7	65
Nice	38	18	9	11	58	41	17	63
Lille OSC	38	15	15	8	39	27	12	60
Saint-Etienne	38	17	7	14	42	37	5	58
Caen	38	16	6	16	39	52	–13	54
Stade Rennais	38	13	13	12	52	54	–2	52
Angers	38	13	11	14	40	38	2	50
Bastia	38	14	8	16	36	42	–6	50
Bordeaux	38	12	14	12	50	57	–7	50
Montpellier	38	14	7	17	49	47	2	49
Olympique Marseille	38	10	18	10	48	42	6	48
Nantes	38	12	12	14	33	44	–11	48
Lorient	38	11	13	14	47	58	–11	46
Guingamp	38	11	11	16	47	56	–9	44
Toulouse	38	9	13	16	45	55	–10	40
Stade de Reims*	38	10	9	19	44	57	–13	39
Gazelec Ajaccio*	38	8	13	17	37	58	–21	37
Troyes*	38	3	9	26	28	83	–55	18

Top scorer: Ibrahimovic (Paris Saint-Germain) 38.
Cup Final: Paris Saint-Germain 4, Olympique Marseille 2.

FYR MACEDONIA
Football Federation of the Former Yugoslav Republic of Macedonia, 8-ma Udarna Brigada 31-A, PO Box 84, 1000 Skopje.
Founded: 1948. *FIFA:* 1994; *UEFA:* 1994. *National Colours:* All red.

International matches 2015–16
Luxembourg (a) 0-1, Spain (h) 0-1 Ukraine (h) 0-2, Belarus (a) 0-0, Montenegro (h) 4-1, Lebanon (h) 0-1, Slovenia (a) 0-1, Bulgaria (h) 0-2, Azerbaijan (n) 3-1, Iran (h) 1-3.

League Championship wins (1992–2016)
Vardar 9; Rabotnicki 4; Sileks 3; Sloga Jugomagnat 3; Pobeda 2; Renova 1; Makedonija 1; Shkendija 1.

Cup wins (1992–2016)
Vardar 5; Rabotnicki 4; Sloga Jugomagnat 3; Sileks 2; Teteks 1; Pellster 1; Pobeda 1; Cementarnica 55 1; Bashkimi 1; Makedonija 1; Metalurg 1; Renova 1; Shkendija 1.

Qualifying League Table 2015–16
	P	W	D	L	F	A	GD	Pts
Vardar	27	20	5	2	59	15	44	65
Shkendija	27	19	6	2	62	21	41	63
Sileks	27	11	7	9	32	32	0	40
Shkupi	27	9	11	7	28	25	3	38
Rabotnicki	27	8	12	7	32	26	6	36
Bregalnica Stip	27	9	6	12	38	43	–5	33
Turnovo	27	8	9	10	32	42	–10	33
Renova	27	8	7	12	33	37	–4	31
Metalurg Skopje	27	4	4	19	20	48	–28	16
Mladost	27	5	1	21	18	65	–47	16

Championship Round
	P	W	D	L	F	A	GD	Pts
Vardar	32	25	5	2	67	17	50	80
Shkendija	32	23	6	3	74	24	50	75
Sileks	32	12	8	12	35	40	–5	44
Rabotnicki	32	10	13	9	36	30	6	43
Shkupi	32	9	11	12	29	34	–5	38
Bregalnica Stip	32	10	8	14	42	49	–7	38

Relegation Round
	P	W	D	L	F	A	GD	Pts
Renova	33	13	8	12	49	42	7	47
Turnovo*+	33	12	10	11	45	43	2	46
Metalurg Skopje*	33	5	4	24	27	66	–39	19
Mladost*	33	6	1	26	22	81	–59	19

Top scorer: Ibraimi (Shkendija) 25.
Cup Final: Shkendija 2, Rabotnicki 0.

GEORGIA
Georgian Football Federation, 76A Chavchavadze Avenue, 0179 Tbilisi.
Founded: 1990. *FIFA:* 1992; *UEFA:* 1992. *National Colours:* All white with red trim.

International matches 2015–16
Scotland (h) 1-0, Republic of Ireland (a) 0-1, Gibraltar (h) 4-0, Germany (a) 1-2, Estonia (a) 0-3, Albania (a) 2-2, Kazakhstan (h) 1-1, Slovakia (n) 1-3, Romania (a) 1-5, Spain (a) 1-0.

League Championship wins (1990–2016)
Dinamo Tbilisi 16; Torpedo Kutaisi 3; WIT Georgia 2; Metalurgi Rustavi (formerly Olimpi) 2; Zestafoni 2; Sioni Bolnisi 1; Dila Gori 1.

Cup wins (1990–2016)
Dinamo Tbilisi 13; Lokomotivi 3; Torpedo Kutaisi 2; Ameri 2; Guria Lanchkhuti 1; Dinamo Batumi 1; Zestafoni 1; WIT Georgia 1; Gagra 1; Dila Gori 1.

Final League Table 2015–16
	P	W	D	L	F	A	GD	Pts
Dila Gori	30	19	7	4	50	21	29	64
Dinamo Batumi	30	18	4	8	40	24	16	58
Dinamo Tbilisi	30	15	5	4	74	29	45	76
Samtredia	30	20	3	7	66	32	34	63
Dila Gori	30	19	5	6	51	25	26	62
Chikhura Sachkhere	30	17	6	7	53	26	27	57
Sioni Bolnisi	30	14	8	8	50	34	16	50
Torpedo Kutaisi	30	14	6	10	50	42	8	48
Tskhinvali	30	12	10	8	51	36	15	46
Dinamo Batumi	30	12	8	10	41	32	9	44
Saburtalo	30	11	6	13	47	61	–14	39
Shukura Kobuleti	30	8	9	13	28	39	–11	33
Guria Lanchkhuti	30	6	9	15	28	49	–21	27
Kolkheti Poti	30	7	6	17	21	41	–20	27
Lokomotivi Tbilisi	30	5	10	15	26	37	–11	25
Zugdidi+	30	5	8	17	30	60	–30	23
Merani Martvili*	30	5	8	17	28	62	–34	23
Sapovnela Terjola*	30	5	6	19	24	63	–39	21

Top scorer: Kvilitaia (Dinamo Tbilisi) 24.
Cup Final: Dinamo Tbilisi 1, Sioni Bolnisi 0.

GERMANY
Deutscher Fussball-Bund, Hermann-Neuberger-Haus, Otto-Fleck-Schneise 6, 60528 Frankfurt Am Main.
Founded: 1900. *FIFA:* 1904; *UEFA:* 1954. *National Colours:* White shirts with red and black trim, white shorts, white socks with red tops.

International matches 2015–16
Poland (h) 3-1, Scotland (a) 3-2, Republic of Ireland (a) 0-1, Georgia (h) 2-1, France (a) 0-2, England (h) 2-3, Italy (h) 4-1, Slovakia (h) 1-3, Hungary (h) 2-0, Ukraine (n) 2-0, Poland (n) 0-0, Northern Ireland (n) 1-0, Slovakia (n) 3-0, Italy (n) 1-1 (6-5p), France (a) 0-2.

League Championship wins (1903–2016)
Bayern Munich 26; 1.FC Nuremberg 9; Borussia Dortmund 8; Schalke 04 7; Hamburger SV 6; VfB Stuttgart 5; Borussia Moenchengladbach 5; 1.FC Kaiserslautern 4; Werder Bremen 4; 1.FC Lokomotive Leipzig 3; SpVgg Greuther Furth 3; 1.FC Cologne 3; Viktoria Berlin 2; Hertha Berlin 2; Hannover 96 2; Dresden SC 2; Union Berlin 1; Freiburger FC 1; Phoenix Karlsruhe 1; Karlsruher FV 1; Holstein Kiel 1; Fortuna Dusseldorf 1; Rapid Vienna 1; VfR Mannheim 1; Rot-Weiss Essen 1; Eintracht Frankfurt 1; Munich 1860 1; Eintracht Braunschweig 1; VfL Wolfsburg 1.

Cup wins (1935–2016)
Bayern Munich 18; Werder Bremen 6; Schalke 04 5; 1.FC Nuremberg 4; 1.FC Cologne 4; Eintracht Frankfurt 4; VfB Stuttgart 3; Borussia Moenchengladbach 3; Hamburger SV 3; Borussia Dortmund 3; Dresden SC 2; Munich 1860 2; Karlsruhe SC 2; Fortuna Dusseldorf 2; 1.FC Kaiserslautern 2; 1.FC Lokomotive Leipzig 1; Rapid Vienna 1; First Vienna 1; Rot-Weiss Essen 1; SW Essen 1; Kickers Offenbach 1; Bayer Uerdingen 1; Hannover 96 1; Bayer Leverkusen 1; VfLWolfsburg 1.

Final League Table 2015–16

	P	W	D	L	F	A	GD	Pts
Bayern Munich	34	28	4	2	80	17	63	88
Borussia Dortmund	34	24	6	4	82	34	48	78
Bayer Leverkusen	34	18	6	10	56	40	16	60
Borussia M'gladbach	34	17	4	13	67	50	17	55
Schalke 04	34	15	7	12	51	49	2	52
1.FSV Mainz 05	34	14	8	12	46	42	4	50
Hertha Berlin	34	14	8	12	42	42	0	50
VfL Wolfsburg	34	12	9	13	47	49	–2	45
1.FC Cologne	34	10	13	11	38	42	–4	43
Hamburger SV	34	11	8	15	40	46	–6	41
Ingolstadt	34	10	10	14	33	42	–9	40
Augsburg	34	9	11	14	42	52	–10	38
Werder Bremen	34	10	8	16	50	65	–15	38
Darmstadt 98	34	9	11	14	38	53	–15	38
TSG 1899 Hoffenheim	34	9	10	15	39	54	–15	37
Eintracht Frankfurt+	34	9	9	16	34	52	–18	36
VfB Stuttgart*	34	9	6	19	50	75	–25	33
Hannover 96*	34	7	4	23	31	62	–31	25

Top scorer: Lewandowski (Bayern Munich) 30.
Cup Final: Bayern Munich 0, Borussia Dortmund 0.
aet; Bayern Munich won 4-3 on penalties.

GIBRALTAR

Gibraltar Football Association, Bayside Sports Complex, PO Box 513, Gibraltar GX11 1AA.
Founded: 1895. *UEFA:* 2013. *National Colours:* Red shirts with white trim, red shorts, red socks.

International matches 2015–16
Republic of Ireland (n) 0-4, Poland (a) 1-8, Georgia (a) 0-4, Scotland (n) 0-6, Liechtenstein (h) 0-0, Latvia (h) 0-5.

League Championship wins (1896–2016)
Lincoln 22 (incl. Newcastle United 5; 1 title shared); Prince of Wales 19; Glacis United 17 (incl. 1 shared); Britannia (now Britannia XI) 14; Gibraltar United 11; Manchester United (now Manchester 62) 7; Europa 6; St Theresa's 3; Chief Construction 2; Jubilee 2; Exiles 2; South United 2; Gibraltar FC 2; Albion 1; Athletic 1; Royal Sovereign 1; Commander of the Yard 1; St Joseph's 1.

Cup wins (1895–2016)
Lincoln (incl. Newcastle United 4) 17; St Joseph's 9; Europa 5; Glacis United 5; Britannia (now Britannia XI) 3; Gibraltar United 3; Manchester United (now Manchester 62) 3; Gibraltar FC 1; HMS Hood 1; 2nd Bn The King's Regt 1; AARA 1; RAF New Camp 1; 4th Bn Royal Scots 1; Prince of Wales 1; Manchester United Reserves 1; 2nd Bn Royal Green Jackets 1; RAF Gibraltar 1; St Theresa's 1.

Final League Table 2015–16

	P	W	D	L	F	A	GD	Pts
Lincoln	27	25	1	1	130	9	121	76
Europa	27	21	2	4	82	18	64	65
St Joseph's	27	14	3	10	50	37	13	45
Lions Gibraltar	27	14	3	10	49	44	5	45
Lynx	27	11	2	14	37	40	–3	35
Manchester 62	27	9	5	13	41	49	–8	32
Glacis United	27	10	2	15	40	67	–27	32
Gibraltar United	27	9	2	16	28	57	–29	29
Britannia XI*+	27	8	2	17	35	84	–49	26
Angels*	27	3	0	24	20	107	–87	9

Top scorer: Padial (Europa) 29.
Cup Final: Lincoln 2, Europa 0.

GOZO

Gozo Football Association, GFA Headquarters, Mgarr Road, Xewkija, XWK 9014, Malta. (Not a member of FIFA or UEFA.)
Founded: 1936.

League Championship wins (1938–2016)
Victoria Hotspurs 11; Nadur Youngsters 11; Sannat Lions 10; Ghajnsielem 7; Xewkija Tigers 7; Xaghra United 6 (incl. Xaghra Blue Stars 1, Xaghra Young Stars 1); Salesian Youths (renamed Oratory Youths) 6; Victoria Athletics 4; Victoria Stars 1; Victoria City 1; Calypcians 1; Kercem Ajax 1; Victoria United (renamed Victoria Wanderers) 1; Zebbug Rovers 1.

Cup wins (1972–2016)
Xewkija Tigers 10; Sannat Lions 9; Nadur Youngsters 8; Ghajnsielem 4; Xaghra United 4; Kercem Ajax 2; Calypsians 1; Calypsians Bosco Youths 1; Victoria Hotspurs 1; Qala St Joseph 1; Victoria Wanderers 1.

Final League Table 2015–16

	P	W	D	L	F	A	GD	Pts
Xewkija Tigers (P)	18	14	2	2	52	21	31	44
Ghajnsielem (P)	18	14	2	2	45	17	28	44
Kercem Ajax	18	11	2	5	36	24	12	35
Victoria Hotspurs	18	8	2	8	27	33	–6	26
Victoria Wanderers	18	4	2	12	14	29	–15	14
Oratory Youths	18	4	2	12	17	28	–11	14
St Lawrence Spurs*	18	1	2	15	8	47	–39	5

(P) *Qualified for Championship play-off.*

Championship Play-off
Ghajnsielem 3, Xewkija Tigers 2 *aet.*
Top scorer: Bogdanovic (Xewkija Tigers) 14.
Cup Final: Xewkija Tigers 2, Ghajnsielem 0.

GREECE

Hellenic Football Federation, Parko Goudi, PO Box 14161, 11510 Athens.
Founded: 1926. *FIFA:* 1927; *UEFA:* 1954. *National Colours:* All white.

International matches 2015–16
Finland (h) 0-1, Romania (a) 0-0, Northern Ireland (a) 1-3, Hungary (h) 4-3, Luxembourg (h) 0-1, Turkey (a) 0-0, Montenegro (h) 2-1, Iceland (h) 2-3, Australia (a) 0-1, Australia (a) 2-1.

League Championship wins (1928–2016)
Olympiacos 43; Panathinaikos 20; AEK Athens 11; Aris Salonika 3; PAOK Salonika 2; Larissa 1.

Cup wins (1932–2016)
Olympiacos 27; Panathinaikos 18; AEK Athens 15; PAOK Salonika 4; Panionios 2; Larissa 2; Ethnikos 1; Aris Salonika 1; Iraklis 1; Kastoria 1; OFI Crete 1.

Final League Table 2015–16

	P	W	D	L	F	A	GD	Pts
Olympiacos	30	28	1	1	81	16	65	85
Panathinaikos (–3)	30	18	4	8	52	26	26	55
AEK Athens (–3)	30	17	6	7	43	21	22	54
PAOK (–3)	30	13	9	8	45	32	13	45
Panionios	30	12	8	10	33	27	6	44
PAS Giannina	30	12	6	12	36	40	–4	42
Asteras Tripolis	30	11	8	11	31	30	1	41
Platanias	30	10	9	11	32	30	2	39
Atromitos (–3)	30	12	6	12	26	31	–5	39
Levadiakos	30	9	10	11	27	36	–9	37
Panaitolikos	30	9	8	13	30	46	–16	35
Iraklis	30	8	11	11	24	32	–8	35
Xanthi	30	6	15	9	27	32	–5	33
Veria	30	5	12	13	19	33	–14	27
Panthrakikos*	30	3	8	19	18	58	–40	17
AEL Kalloni*	30	3	7	20	19	53	–34	16

Top scorer: Fortounis (Olympiacos) 18.
Cup Final: AEK Athens 2, Olympiacos 1.

HUNGARY

Magyar Labdarugo Szovetseg, Kanai ut 2. D, 1112 Budapest.
Founded: 1901. *FIFA:* 1907; *UEFA:* 1954. *National Colours:* Red shirts, white shorts, green socks.

International matches 2015–16
Romania (h) 0-0, Northern Ireland (a) 1-1, Faroe Islands (h) 2-1, Greece (a) 3-4, Norway (a) 1-0, Norway (h) 2-1, Croatia (h) 1-1, Ivory Coast (h) 0-0, Germany (a) 0-2, Austria (n) 2-0, Iceland (n) 1-1, Portugal (n) 3-3, Belgium (n) 0-4.

League Championship wins (1901–2016)
Ferencvaros 29; MTK-Hungaria Budapest 23; Ujpest 20; Budapest Honved 13 (incl. Kispest Honved); Debrecen 7; Vasas Budapest 6; Csepel 4; Gyor 4; Budapest TC 2; Videoton 2; Nagyvarad 1; Vac 1; Dunaferr (renamed Dunaujvaros) 1; Zalaegerszeg 1.

Cup wins (1910–2016)
Ferencvaros 22; MTK-Hungaria Budapest 12; Ujpest 9; Budapest Honved 7 (inc. Kispest Honved); Debrecen 6; Vasas Budapest 4; Gyor 4; Diosgyor 2; Bocskai 1; III Ker 1; Soroksar 1; Szolnoki MAV 1; Siofoki Banyasz 1; Bekescsaba 1; Pecsi 1; Sopron 1; Fehervar (renamed Videoton) 1; Kecskemet 1.
Cup not regularly held until 1964.

Final League Table 2015–16

	P	W	D	L	F	A	GD	Pts
Ferencvaros	33	24	4	5	69	23	46	76
Videoton	33	17	4	12	42	29	13	55

Debrecen	33	14	11	8	48	34	14	53
MTK Budapest	33	14	9	10	39	37	2	51
Szombathelyi Haladas	33	13	11	9	33	37	−4	50
Ujpest	33	11	13	9	42	37	5	46
Paks	33	12	7	14	41	40	1	43
Budapest Honved	33	12	7	14	40	39	1	43
Diosgyor	33	10	8	15	37	47	−10	38
Vasas Budapest	33	9	5	19	32	54	−22	32
Puskas Akademia*	33	7	10	16	35	51	−16	31
Bekescsaba*	33	6	9	18	25	55	−30	27

Top scorer: Bode (Ferencvaros) 17.
Cup Final: Ferencvaros 1, Ujpest 0.

ICELAND

Knattspyrnusamband Islands, Laugardal, 104 Reykjavik.
Founded: 1947. *FIFA:* 1947; *UEFA:* 1954. *National Colours:* All blue.

International matches 2015–16
Netherlands (a) 1-0, Kazakhstan (h) 0-0, Latvia (h) 2-2, Turkey (a) 0-1, Poland (a) 2-4, Slovakia (a) 1-3, Finland (n) 1-0, UAE (a) 1-2, USA (a) 2-3, Denmark (a) 1-2, Greece (a) 3-2, Norway (a) 2-3, Liechtenstein (h) 4-0, Portugal (n) 1-1, Hungary (n) 1-1, Austria (n) 2-1, England (n) 2-1, France (n) 2-5.

League Championship wins (1912–2015)
KR Reykjavik 26; Valur 20; Fram 18; IA Akranes 18; FH Hafnarfjordur 7; Vestmannaeyjar 5; IBK Keflavik 4; IBV Vestmannaeyjar 3; KA Akureyri 1; Breidablik 1; Stjarnan 1.

Cup wins (1960–2015)
KR Reykjavik 14; Valur 10; IA Akranes 9; Fram 8; IBV Vestmannaeyjar 4; IBK Keflavik 4; Fylkir 2; FH Hafnarfjordur 2; IBA Akureyri 1; Vikingur 1; Breidablik 1.

Final League Table 2015

	P	W	D	L	F	A	GD	Pts
FH Hafnarfjordur	22	15	3	4	47	26	21	48
Breidablik	22	13	7	2	34	13	21	46
KR Reykjavik	22	12	6	4	36	21	15	42
Stjarnan	22	9	6	7	32	24	8	33
Valur	22	9	6	7	38	31	7	33
Fjolnir	22	9	6	7	36	35	1	33
IA Akranes	22	7	8	7	31	31	0	29
Fylkir	22	7	8	7	26	31	−5	29
Vikingur	22	5	8	9	32	36	−4	23
IBV Vestmannaeyjar	22	5	4	13	26	37	−11	19
Leiknir*	22	3	6	13	20	34	−14	15
IBK Keflavik*	22	2	4	16	22	61	−39	10

Top scorer: Pedersen (Valur) 13.
Cup Final: Valur 2, KR Reykjavik 0.

ISRAEL

Israel Football Association, Ramat Gan Stadium, 299 Aba Hilell Street, PO Box 3591, Ramat Gan 52134.
Founded: 1928. *FIFA:* 1929; *UEFA:* 1994. *National Colours:* Blue shirts with white trim, blue shorts, blue socks.

International matches 2015–16
Andorra (h) 4-0, Wales (a) 0-0, Cyprus (h) 1-2, Belgium (a) 1-3, Croatia (a) 0-2, Serbia (a) 1-3.

League Championship wins (1932–2016)
Maccabi Tel Aviv 21; Hapoel Tel Aviv 13; Maccabi Haifa 12; Hapoel Petah Tikva 6; Beitar Jerusalem 6; Maccabi Netanya 5; Hapoel Be'er Sheba 3; Hakoah Ramat Gan 2; British Police 1; Hapoel Ramat Gan 1; Hapoel Kfar Saba 1; Bnei Yehuda 1; Hapoel Haifa 1; Ironi Kiryat Shmona 1.

Cup wins (1928–2016)
Maccabi Tel Aviv 23; Hapoel Tel Aviv 15; Beitar Jerusalem 7; Maccabi Haifa 6; Hapoel Haifa 3; Hapoel Kfar Saba 3; Maccabi Petah Tikva 2; Beitar Tel Aviv 2; Hapoel Petah Tikva 2; Bnei Yehuda 2; Hakoah Amidar Ramat Gan 2; Hapoel Ramat Gan 2; Maccabi Hashmonai Jerusalem 1; British Police 1; Hapoel Jerusalem 1; Maccabi Netanya 1; Hapoel Yehud 1; Hapoel Lod 1; Hapoel Be'er Sheba 1; Bnei Sakhnin 1; Ironi Kiryat Shmona 1.

Qualifying League Table 2015–16

	P	W	D	L	F	A	GD	Pts
Hapoel Be'er Sheva	26	20	4	2	48	17	31	64
Maccabi Tel Aviv	26	19	4	3	59	20	39	61
Beitar Jerusalem	26	15	6	5	38	19	19	51
Maccabi Haifa	26	10	8	8	33	25	8	38

Bnei Sakhnin	26	10	6	10	32	25	7	36
Hapoel Ra'anana	26	10	6	10	29	31	−2	36
Bnei Yehuda	26	9	6	11	27	35	−8	33
Maccabi Petah Tikva	26	8	6	12	23	30	−7	30
Hapoel Kfar Saba	26	7	8	11	19	31	−12	29
Hapoel Acre	26	8	5	13	18	36	−18	29
Ironi Kiryat Shmona	26	6	10	10	25	31	−6	28
Hapoel Tel Aviv	26	6	9	11	17	31	−14	27
Hapoel Haifa	26	5	10	11	27	37	−10	25
Maccabi Netanya	26	1	8	17	10	37	−27	11

Championship Round

	P	W	D	L	F	A	GD	Pts
Hapoel Be'er Sheva	36	25	8	3	66	24	42	83
Maccabi Tel Aviv	36	24	9	3	76	24	52	81
Beitar Jerusalem	36	18	6	12	46	37	9	58
Maccabi Haifa	36	14	11	11	45	42	3	53
Bnei Sakhnin	36	13	9	14	46	40	6	48
Hapoel Ra'anana	36	11	9	16	38	48	−10	42

Relegation Round

	P	W	D	L	F	A	GD	Pts
Maccabi Petah Tikva	33	13	7	13	34	35	−1	46
Bnei Yehuda	33	13	7	13	37	43	−6	46
Hapoel Tel Aviv	33	10	12	11	30	37	−7	42
Hapoel Kfar Saba	33	9	11	13	23	37	−14	38
Ironi Kiryat Shmona	33	8	12	13	32	39	−7	36
Hapoel Haifa	33	7	13	13	38	48	−10	34
Hapoel Acre*	33	9	7	17	27	48	−21	34
Maccabi Netanya*	33	1	9	23	14	50	−36	12

Top scorer: Zahavi (Maccabi Tel Aviv) 35.
Cup Final: Maccabi Haifa 1, Maccabi Tel Aviv 0.

ITALY

Federazione Italiana Giuoco Calcio, Via Gregorio Allegri 14, 00198 Roma.
Founded: 1898. *FIFA:* 1905; *UEFA:* 1954. *National Colours:* Blue shirts, white shorts, blue socks with white tops.

International matches 2015–16
Malta (h) 1-0, Bulgaria (h) 1-0, Azerbaijan (a) 3-1, Norway (h) 2-1, Belgium (a) 1-3, Romania (h) 2-2, Spain (h) 1-1, Germany (a) 1-4, Scotland (n) 1-0, Finland (h) 2-0, Belgium (n) 2-0, Sweden (n) 1-0, Republic of Ireland (n) 0-1, Spain (n) 2-0, Germany (n) 1-1 (5-6p).

League Championship wins (1898–2016)
Juventus 32 (excludes two titles revoked); AC Milan 18; Internazionale 18 (includes one title awarded); Genoa 9; Pro Vercelli 7; Bologna 7; Torino 7 (excludes one title revoked); Roma 3; Fiorentina 2; Lazio 2; Napoli 2; Casale 1; Novese 1; Cagliari 1; Verona 1; Sampdoria 1.

Cup wins (1928–2016)
Juventus 11; Roma 9; Internazionale 7; Fiorentina 6; Lazio 6; Torino 5; Napoli 5; AC Milan 5; Sampdoria 4; Parma 3; Bologna 2; Vado 1; Genoa 1; Venezia 1; Atalanta 1; Vicenza 1.

Final League Table 2015–16

	P	W	D	L	F	A	GD	Pts
Juventus	38	29	4	5	75	20	55	91
Napoli	38	25	7	6	80	32	48	82
Roma	38	23	11	4	83	41	42	80
Internazionale	38	20	7	11	50	38	12	67
Fiorentina	38	18	10	10	60	42	18	64
Sassuolo	38	16	13	9	49	40	9	61
AC Milan	38	15	12	11	49	43	6	57
Lazio	38	15	9	14	52	52	0	54
Chievo	38	13	11	14	43	45	−2	50
Empoli	38	12	10	16	40	49	−9	46
Genoa	38	13	7	18	45	48	−3	46
Torino	38	12	9	17	52	55	−3	45
Atalanta	38	11	12	15	41	47	−6	45
Bologna	38	9	18	33	45	−12	42	
Sampdoria	38	10	10	18	48	61	−13	40
Palermo	38	10	9	19	38	65	−27	39
Udinese	38	10	9	19	35	60	−25	39
Carpi*	38	9	11	18	37	57	−20	38
Frosinone*	38	8	7	23	35	76	−41	31
Hellas Verona*	38	5	13	20	34	63	−29	28

Top scorers: Higuain (Napoli) 36.
Cup Final: Juventus 1, AC Milan 0 *aet*.

KAZAKHSTAN

Football Federation of Kazakhstan, 29 Syganak Street, 9th floor, 010000 Astana.
Founded: 1914. *FIFA:* 1994; *UEFA:* 2002. *National Colours:* All yellow.

International matches 2015–16
Czech Republic (a) 1-2, Iceland (a) 0-0, Netherlands (h) 1-2, Latvia (a) 1-0, Azerbaijan (n) 1-0, Georgia (a) 1-1, China PR (a) 1-0.

League Championship wins (1992–2015)
Irtysh (includes Ansat) 5; Aktobe 5; Yelimay (renamed Spartak Semey) 3; FC Astana-64 (includes Zhenis) 3; Kairat 2; Shakhter Karagandy 2; Astana 2; Taraz 1; Tobol 1.

Cup wins (1992–2015)
Kairat 7; FC Astana-64 (incl. Zhenis) 3; Astana (incl. Lokomotiv) 2; Dostyk 1; Vostok 1; Yelimay (renamed Spartak Semey) 1; Irtysh 1; Kaisar 1; Taraz 1; Almaty 1; Tobol 1; Aktobe 1; Atirau 1; Ordabasy 1; Shakhter Karagandy 1.

Qualifying League Table 2015

	P	W	D	L	F	A	GD	Pts
Kairat	22	13	5	4	43	14	29	44
Aktobe	22	12	8	2	27	12	15	44
Astana	22	12	7	3	40	19	21	43
Atyrau	22	9	10	3	25	19	6	37
Ordabasy	22	9	8	5	21	18	3	35
Irtysh	22	7	9	6	26	23	3	30
Okzhetpes	22	8	2	12	24	33	–9	26
Tobol	22	7	4	11	22	32	–10	25
Taraz	22	7	3	12	17	25	–8	24
Shakhter Karagandy	22	5	3	14	16	38	–22	18
Zhetysu	22	4	5	13	17	32	–15	17
Kaisar	22	3	8	11	12	25	–13	17

NB: Points earned in Qualifying phase are halved and rounded up at start of Championship and Relegation Play-off phase.

Championship Round

	P	W	D	L	F	A	GD	Pts
Astana	32	20	7	5	55	26	29	46
Kairat	32	20	7	5	60	19	41	45
Aktobe	32	15	9	8	35	25	10	32
Ordabasy	32	12	10	10	32	31	1	29
Atyrau	32	11	12	9	31	33	–2	27
Irtysh	32	10	10	12	37	39	–2	25

Relegation Round

	P	W	D	L	F	A	GD	Pts
Tobol	32	12	6	14	32	42	–10	30
Okzhetpes	32	12	6	14	36	41	–5	29
Taraz	32	10	8	14	25	33	–8	26
Shakhter Karagandy	32	9	5	18	27	47	–20	23
Zhetysu*	32	8	6	18	28	46	–18	22
Kaisar*	32	4	12	16	20	36	–16	16

Top scorer: Gohou (Kairat) 22.
Cup Final: Kairat 2, Astana 1.

KOSOVO

Football Federation of Kosovo, Rruga Agim Ramadani 45, Prishtina, Kosovo 10000. *Founded:* 1946. *FIFA:* 2016; *UEFA:* 2016. *National Colours:* All blue.

International matches 2015–16
Equatorial Guinea‡ (h) 2-0, Albania‡ (h) 2-2, Faroe Islands (n) 2-0.

League Championship wins (1945–2016)
Prishtina 14; Vellaznimi 9; KF Trepca 7; Liria 5; Buduqnosti 4; Rudari 3; Red Star 3; Besa 3; Jedinstvo 2; Kosova Prishtina 2; Slloga 2; Obiliqi 2; Fushe-Kosova 2; Feronikeli 2; Proletari 1; KXEK Kosova 1; Rudniku 1; KNI Ramiz Sadiku 1; Dukagjini 1; Besiana 1; Drita 1; Hysi 1; Kosova Vushtrri 1.

Cup wins (1992–2016)
Prishtina 4; Liria 3; Flamurtari 2; Besa 2; Feronikeli 2; KF Trepca 1; KF 2 Korriku 1; Gjilani 1; Drita 1; Besiana 1; KEK-u 1; Kosova Prishtina 1; Vellaznimi 1; Hysi 1; Trepca'89 1.

Final League Table 2015–16

	P	W	D	L	F	A	GD	Pts
Feronikeli	33	21	6	6	53	27	26	69
Hajvalia	33	17	8	8	44	26	18	59
Trepca '89	33	16	8	9	53	30	23	56
Besa Peje	33	16	5	12	37	27	10	53
Gjilani	33	14	7	12	29	27	2	49
Llapi	33	12	8	13	44	44	0	44
Liria Prizren	33	12	8	13	45	55	–10	44
Prishtina	33	12	7	14	29	34	–5	43
Drenica Skenderaj+	33	12	4	17	38	48	–10	40
Drita+	33	9	9	15	33	43	–10	36
Istogu*	33	10	4	19	24	40	–16	34
Kosova Vushtrri*	33	6	8	19	24	52	–28	26

Cup Final: Prishtina 2, Drita 1.

LATVIA

Latvijas Futbola Federacija, Olympic Sports Centre, Grostonas Street 6B, 1013 Riga.
Founded: 1921. *FIFA:* 1922; *UEFA:* 1992. *National Colours:* All carmine red.
International matches 2015–16
Turkey (a) 1-1, Czech Republic (h) 1-2, Iceland (a) 2-2, Kazakhstan (h) 0-1, Northern Ireland (a) 0-1, Slovakia (a) 0-0, Gibraltar (a) 5-0, Lithuania (h) 2-1, Estonia (a) 0-0.

League Championship wins (1922–2015)
Skonto Riga 15; ASK Riga (incl. AVN 2) 11; RFK Riga 8; Sarkanais Metalurgs Liepaja 7; Olympija Liepaja 7; VEF Riga 6; Ventspils 6; Energija Riga (incl. ESR Riga 2) 4; Elektrons Riga (incl. Alfa 1) 4; Torpedo Riga 3; Keisermezhs Riga 2; Khimikis Daugavpils 2; RAF Yelgava 2; Daugava Liepaja 2; Liepajas Metalurgs 2; Dinamo Riga 1; Zhmilyeva Team 1; Darba Rezervi 1; RER Riga 1; Starts Brotseni 1; Venta Ventspils 1; Jumieks Riga 1; Gauja Valmiera 1; Daugava Daugavpils 1; Liepaja 1.

Cup wins (1937–2016)
Skonto Riga 8; ASK Riga 7 (includes AVN 3); Elektrons Riga 7; Ventspils 6; Sarkanais Metalurgs Liepaja 4; Jelgava 4; VEF Riga 3; Tseltnieks Riga 3; RAF Yelgava 3; RFK Riga 2; Daugava Liepaja 2; Starts Brotseni 2; Selmash Liepaya 2; Yurnieks Riga 2; Khimikis Daugavpils 2; Rigas Vilki 1; Dinamo Liepaya 1; Dinamo Riga 1; RER Riga 1; Voulkan Kouldiga 1; Baltika Liepaja 1; Venta Ventspils 1; Pilots Riga 1; Lielupe Yurmala 1; Energija Riga (formerly ESR Riga)1; Torpedo Riga 1; Daugava SKIF Riga 1; Tseltnieks Daugavpils 1; Olympija Riga 1; FK Riga 1; Liepajas Metalurgs 1; Daugava Daugavpils 1.

Final League Table 2015

	P	W	D	L	F	A	GD	Pts
Liepaja	24	15	7	2	48	23	25	52
Skonto†	24	13	6	5	43	23	20	45
Ventspils	24	11	10	3	39	16	23	43
Jelgava	24	11	8	5	26	18	8	41
Spartaks Jurmala	24	5	6	13	20	36	–16	21
BFC Daugavpils	24	2	8	14	14	37	–23	14
Metta/LU+	24	3	3	18	19	56	–37	12
Gulbene*	0	0	0	0	0	0	0	0

* Gulbene excluded, results expunged. † Skonto denied a licence for 2016 season.
Top scorer: Ikaunieks (Liepaja) 15.
Cup Final: Jelgava 2, Spartaks Jurmala 0.

LIECHTENSTEIN

Liechtensteiner Fussballverband, Landstrasse 149, 9494 Schaan.
Founded: 1934. *FIFA:* 1974; *UEFA:* 1974. *National Colours:* Blue shirts, red shorts, blue socks.

International matches 2015–16
Montenegro (a) 0-2, Russia (h) 0-7, Sweden (h) 0-2, Austria (a) 0-3, Gibraltar (a) 0-0, Faroe Islands (n) 2-3, Iceland (a) 0-4.
Liechtenstein has no national league. Teams compete in Swiss regional leagues.

Cup wins (1937–2016)
Vaduz 44; Balzers 11; Triesen 8; 5; FC Schaan 3.
Cup Final: Vaduz 11, FC Schaan 0.

LITHUANIA

Lietuvos Futbolo Federacija, Stadiono g. 2, 02106 Vilnius.
Founded: 1922. *FIFA:* 1923; *UEFA:* 1992. *National Colours:* Yellow shirts, green shorts, yellow socks.

International matches 2015–16
Estonia (a) 0-1, San Marino (h) 2-1, Slovenia (a) 1-1, England (h) 0-3, Romania (a) 0-1, Russia (a) 0-3, Estonia (h) 2-0, Latvia (a) 1-2, Poland (a) 0-0.

League Championship wins (1990–2015)
FBK Kaunas 8 (including Zalgiris Kaunas 1); Ekranas 7; Zalgiris Vilnius 6; Inkaras Kaunas 2; Kareda 2; Sirijus Klaipeda 1; Mazeikiai 1.

Cup wins (1990–2016)
Zalgiris Vilnius 10; Ekranas 4; FBK Kaunas 4; Kareda 2; Atlantas 2; Suduva 2; Sirijus Klaipeda 1; Lietuvos Makabi Vilnius 1; Inkaras Kaunas 1.

Final League Table 2015

	P	W	D	L	F	A	GD	Pts
Zalgiris Vilnius	36	31	1	4	104	25	79	94
Trakai	36	27	3	6	92	33	59	84
Atlantas	36	21	7	8	65	34	31	70
Suduva	36	21	4	11	76	34	42	67
Kauno Zalgiris	36	13	6	17	47	74	–27	45
Utenis Utena	36	11	9	16	41	50	–9	42
Stumbras	36	11	8	17	51	74	–23	41
Klaipedos Granitas†	36	6	9	21	37	83	–46	27
Siauliai	36	5	5	26	37	94	–57	20
Kruoja‡	36	4	8	24	23	72	–49	20

† *Demoted after Round 34 for rule breaches; remaining matches awarded 0-3.*
‡ *Withdrew after Round 24 after match-fixing allegations; remaining matches awarded 0-3.*
Top scorer: Radzinevicius (Suduva) 28.
Cup Final: Zalgiris Vilnius 1, Trakai 0 *aet.*

LUXEMBOURG

Federation Luxembourgeoise de Football, BP 5 Rue de Limpach, 3932 Mondercange.
Founded: 1908. *FIFA:* 1910; *UEFA:* 1954. *National Colours:* White shirts with blue trim, white shorts, white socks.

International matches 2015–16
FYR Macedonia (h) 1-0, Belarus (a) 0-2, Spain (a) 0-4, Slovakia (h) 2-4, Greece (h) 1-0, Portugal (h) 0-2, Bosnia-Herzegovina (h) 0-3, Albania (h) 0-2, Nigeria (h) 1-3.

League Championship wins (1910–2016)
Jeunesse Esch 28; F91 Dudelange 12; Spora Luxembourg 11; Stade Dudelange 10; Fola Esch 7; Red Boys Differdange 6; Union Luxembourg 6; Avenir Beggen 6; US Hollerich-Bonnevoie 5; Progres Niedercorn 3; Aris Bonnevoie 3; Sporting Club 2; Racing Club 1; National Schifflange 1; Grevenmacher 1.

Cup wins (1922–2016)
Red Boys Differdange 15; Jeunesse Esch 13; Union Luxembourg 10; Spora Luxembourg 8; Avenir Beggen 7; F91 Dudelange 6; Progres Niedercorn 4; Stade Dudelange 4; Grevenmacher 4; Differdange 03 4; Fola Esch 3; Alliance Dudelange 2; US Rumelange 2; Racing Club 1; US Dudelange 1; SC Tetange 1; National Schifflange 1; Aris Bonnevoie 1; Jeunesse Hautcharage 1; Swift Hesperange 1; Etzella Ettelbruck 1; CS Petange 1.

Final League Table 2014–16

	P	W	D	L	F	A	GD	Pts
F91 Dudelange	26	19	5	2	65	21	44	62
Fola Esch	26	19	5	2	61	23	38	62
Differdange 03	26	17	4	5	63	32	31	55
Jeunesse Esch	26	13	7	6	48	30	18	46
UNA Strassen	26	11	5	10	50	50	0	38
Progres Niederkorn	26	10	6	10	41	30	·11	36
Mondorf-les-Bains	26	10	6	10	36	34	2	36
Racing FC Union	26	10	5	11	45	54	–9	35
RM Hamm Benfica	26	9	7	10	52	49	3	34
Rumelange	26	8	4	14	38	52	–14	28
Victoria Rosport	26	7	5	14	46	49	–3	26
Wiltz	26	5	6	15	22	60	38	21
Etzella Ettelbruck	26	4	5	17	25	70	–45	17
Grevenmacher	26	3	4	19	15	53	–38	13

Top scorer: Jahier (Racing FC Union) 18.
Cup Final: F91 Dudelange 1, US Mondorf-Les-Bains 0.

MALTA

Malta Football Association, Millennium Stand, Floor 2, National Stadium, Ta'Qali ATD4000.
Founded: 1900. *FIFA:* 1959; *UEFA:* 1960. *National Colours:* Red shirts, white shorts, red socks.

International matches 2015–16
Italy (a) 0-1, Azerbaijan (h) 2-2, Norway (a) 0-2, Croatia (h) 0-1, Jordan (n) 0-2, Moldova (h) 0-0, Czech Republic (n) 0-6, Austria (a) 1-2.

League Championship wins (1910–2016)
Sliema Wanderers 26; Floriana 25; Valletta 23; Hibernians 11; Hamrun Spartans 7; Birkirkara 4; Rabat Ajax 2; St George's 1; KOMR 1; Marsaxlokk 1.

Cup wins (1935–2016)
Sliema Wanderers 21; Floriana 19; Valletta 13; Hibernians 10; Hamrun Spartans 6; Birkirkara 5; Melita 1; Gzira United 1; Zurrieq 1; Rabat Ajax 1.

Qualifying League Table 2015–16

	P	W	D	L	F	A	GD	Pts
Valletta	22	17	2	3	49	21	28	53
Hibernians	22	15	5	2	53	25	28	50
Balzan	22	14	3	5	42	21	21	45
Birkirkara	22	12	6	4	41	20	21	42
Floriana	22	12	3	7	36	25	11	39
Tarxien Rainbows	22	10	7	5	37	17	20	37
Mosta	22	8	6	8	29	33	–4	30
Pembroke Athleta	22	7	4	11	33	39	–6	25
Sliema Wanderers	22	7	3	12	31	36	–5	24
Naxxar Lions	22	4	2	16	22	54	–32	14
Qormi	22	2	3	17	19	49	–30	9
St Andrews	22	1	2	19	14	66	–52	5

NB: Points earned in first phase are halved and rounded up at start of second round during which teams play each other once.

Second Round

	P	W	D	L	F	A	GD	Pts
Valletta	33	25	4	4	69	27	42	53
Hibernians	33	22	8	3	85	33	52	49
Birkirkara	33	20	8	5	64	29	35	47
Balzan	33	20	6	7	69	33	36	44
Floriana	33	18	4	11	60	42	18	39
Tarxien Rainbows	33	15	8	10	59	31	28	35
Sliema Wanderers	33	12	6	15	49	51	–2	30
Pembroke Athleta	33	10	6	17	48	61	–13	24
Mosta	33	10	7	16	42	60	–18	22
St Andrews+	33	4	3	26	32	90	–58	13
Naxxar Lions*	33	5	4	24	29	95	–66	12
Qormi*	33	3	4	26	26	80	–54	9

Top scorer: Fontanella (Floriana) 20.
Cup Final: Sliema Wanderers 0, Balzan 0.
aet; Sliema Wanderers won 5-4 on penalties.

MOLDOVA

Federatia Moldoveneasca de Fotbal, Str. Tricolorului 39, 2012 Chisinau.
Founded: 1990. *FIFA:* 1994; *UEFA:* 1993. *National Colours:* All blue.

International matches 2015–16
Austria (a) 0-1, Montenegro (h) 0-2, Russia (h) 1-2, Sweden (a) 0-2, Azerbaijan (a) 1-2, Malta (a) 0-0, Andorra (n) 1-0, Croatia (a) 0-1, Switzerland (a) 1-2.

League Championship wins (1992–2016)
Sheriff 14; Zimbru Chisinau 8; Constructorul 1; Dacia Chisinau 1; Milsami Orhei 1.

Cup wins (1992–2016)
Sheriff 8; Zimbru Chisinau 6; Tiligul 3; Tiraspol 3 (incl. Constructorul 2); Comrat 1; Nistru Otaci 1; Iskra-Stal 1; Milsami Orhei 1; Zaria Balti 1.

Final League Table 2015–16

	P	W	D	L	F	A	GD	Pts
Dacia Chisinau (P)	27	20	5	2	44	12	32	65
Sheriff (P)	27	20	5	2	50	11	39	65
Zimbru Chisinau	27	15	4	8	42	26	16	49
Zaria Balti	27	12	6	9	36	29	7	42
Dinamo-Auto	27	12	5	10	33	34	–1	41
Milsami Orhei	27	10	6	11	33	23	10	36
Speranta Nisporeni	27	8	7	12	24	36	–12	31
Petrocub	27	6	3	18	21	53	–32	21
Academia Chisinau	27	5	6	16	18	42	–24	21
Saxan*	27	1	5	21	10	45	–35	8

(P) Qualified for Championship play-off.

Championship Play-off
Sheriff 1, Dacia Chisinau 0.
Top scorer: Subotic (Sheriff) 12.
Cup Final: Zaria Balti 1, Milsami Orhei 0 *aet.*

MONTENEGRO

Fudbalski Savez Crne Gore, Ulica 19. Decembar 13, PO Box 275, 81000 Podgorica.
Founded: 1931 *FIFA:* 2007; *UEFA:* 2007. *National Colours:* All red with gold trim.

International matches 2015–16
Liechtenstein (h) 2-0, Moldova (a) 2-0, Austria (h) 2-3, Russia (h) 0-2, FYR Macedonia (h) 1-4, Greece (a) 1-2, Belarus (h) 0-0, Turkey (a) 0-1.

League Championship wins (2006–16)
Buducnost Podgorica 2; Mogren 2; Rudar Pljevlja 2; Sutjeska 2; Zeta 1; Mladost Podgorica 1.

Cup wins (2006–16)
Rudar Pljevlja 4; Mogren 1; Petrovac 1; Celik 1; Buducnost Podgorica 1; Lovcen 1: Mladost Podgorica 1.

Final League Table 2015–16

	P	W	D	L	F	A	GD	Pts
Mladost Podgorica	32	21	4	7	53	27	26	67
Buducnost Podgorica	32	18	6	8	47	21	26	60
Rudar Pljevlja	32	16	9	7	38	25	13	57
Bokelj	32	17	5	10	43	27	16	56
Sutjeska	32	14	9	9	42	30	12	51
Grbalj	32	11	5	16	37	46	–9	38
Zeta	32	10	8	14	37	41	–4	38
Decic	32	10	6	16	35	48	–13	36
Lovcen	32	9	9	14	31	38	–7	36
Petrovac+	32	8	8	16	32	50	–18	32
Iskra+	32	6	13	13	28	51	–23	31
Mornar*	32	8	6	18	29	48	–19	30

Top scorer: Scepanovic (Mladost Podgorica) 19.
Cup Final: Rudar Pljevlja 0, Buducnost Podgorica 0.
aet; Rudar Pljevlja won 4-3 on penalties.

NETHERLANDS

Koninklijke Nederlandse Voetbalbond, Woudenbergseweg 56–58, Postbus 515, 3700 AM Zeist.
Founded: 1889. *FIFA:* 1904; *UEFA:* 1954. *National Colours:* Orange shirts, white shorts, orange socks.

International matches 2015–16
Iceland (a) 0-1, Turkey (a) 0-3, Kazakhstan (a) 2-1, Czech Republic (h) 2-3, Wales (a) 3-2, France (h) 2-3, England (a) 2-1, Republic of Ireland (a) 1-1, Poland (a) 2-1, Austria (a) 2-0.

League Championship wins (1889–2016)
Ajax Amsterdam 33; PSV Eindhoven 23; Feyenoord 14; HVV The Hague 10; Sparta Rotterdam 6; RAP Amsterdam 5; Go Ahead Eagles Deventer 4; HFC Haarlem 3; HBS Craeyenhout 3; Willem II Tilburg 3; RCH Heemstede 2; Heracles 2; ADO Den Haag 2; AZ 67 Alkmaar 2; VV Concordia 1; Quick Den Haag 1; Be Quick Groningen 1; NAC Breda 1; SC Enschede 1; Volewijckers Amsterdam 1; Haarlem 1; BVV Den Bosch 1; Schiedam 1; Limburgia 1; EVV Eindhoven 1; SVV Rapid JC Den Heerlen 1; DOS Utrecht 1; DWS Amsterdam 1; FC Twente 1.

Cup wins (1899–2016)
Ajax Amsterdam 18; Feyenoord 12; PSV Eindhoven 9; Quick The Hague 4; AZ 67 Alkmaar 4; HFC Haarlem 3; Sparta Rotterdam 3; Twente 3; Utrecht 3; Haarlem 2; VOC 2; HBS Craeyenhout 2; DFC 2; RCH Haarlem 2; Wageningen 2; Willem II Tilburg 2; Fortuna 54 2; FC Den Haag (includes ADO) 2; Roda JC 2; RAP Amsterdam 1; Velocitas Breda 1; HVV Den Haag 1; Concordia Delft 1; CVV 1; Schoten 1; ZFC Zaandam 1; Longa 1; VUC 1; Velocitas Groningen 1; Roermond 1; FC Eindhoven 1; VSV 1; Quick 1888 Nijmegen 1; VVV Groningen 1; NAC Breda 1; Heerenveen 1; PEC Zwolle 1; FC Groningen 1.

Final League Table 2015–16

	P	W	D	L	F	A	GD	Pts
PSV Eindhoven	34	26	6	2	88	32	56	84
Ajax	34	25	7	2	81	21	60	82
Feyenoord	34	19	6	9	62	40	22	63
AZ Alkmaar	34	18	5	11	70	53	17	59
Utrecht	34	15	8	11	57	48	9	53
Heracles Almelo	34	14	9	11	47	49	–2	51
FC Groningen	34	14	8	12	41	48	–7	50
PEC Zwolle	34	14	6	14	56	54	2	48
Vitesse	34	12	10	12	55	38	17	46
NEC	34	13	7	14	37	42	–5	46
ADO Den Haag	34	10	13	11	48	49	–1	43
Heerenveen	34	11	9	14	46	61	–15	42
FC Twente (–3)	34	12	7	15	49	64	–15	40
Roda JC	34	8	10	16	34	55	–21	34
SBV Excelsior	34	7	9	18	34	60	–26	30
Willem II Tilburg+	34	6	11	17	35	53	–18	29
De Graafschap*	34	5	8	21	39	66	–27	23
Cambuur*	34	3	9	22	33	79	–46	18

Top scorer: Janssen (AZ Alkmaar) 27.
Cup Final: Feyenoord 2, Utrecht 1.

NORTHERN CYPRUS

Cyprus Turkish Football Federation, 7 Memduh Asaf Street, 107 Kosklucíftlik, Lefkosa. (Not a member of FIFA or UEFA.)
Founded: 1955; *National Colours:* Red shirts with white trim, red shorts, red socks.

League Championship wins (1956–63; 1969–74; 1976–2016)
Cetinkaya 14; Gonyeli 9; Magusa 8; Dogan 7; Yenicami Agdelen 7; Baf Ulku 4; Kucuk Kaymakli 4; Akincilar Genclik 1; Binatli 1.

Cup wins (1956–2016)
Cetinkaya 17; Gonyeli 8; Yenicami Agdelen 7; Kucuk Kaymakli 7; Magusa 5; Turk Ocagi 4; Dogan 2; Lefke 2; Akincilar Genclik 1; Yalova 1; Binatli 1.

Final League Table 2015–16

	P	W	D	L	F	A	GD	Pts
Magusa	26	15	5	6	52	33	19	50
Cetinkaya	26	13	10	3	62	35	27	49
Binatli	26	13	7	6	53	37	16	46
Gencler Birligi	26	13	6	7	51	34	17	45
Lefke	26	11	7	8	43	34	9	40
Yenicami Agdelen	26	10	9	7	45	37	8	39
Kucuk Kaymakli	26	11	6	9	41	36	5	39
Turk Ocagi	26	10	8	8	44	36	8	38
Dogan	26	9	7	10	56	51	5	34
Cihangir	26	10	4	12	45	46	–1	34
Degirmenlik	26	7	5	14	39	63	–24	26
Mormenekse	26	6	6	14	30	46	–16	24
Yeni Bogazici*	26	4	7	15	33	67	–34	19
Bostanci Bagcil*	26	2	9	15	18	57	–39	15

Top scorer: Turan (Yenicami Agdelen) 26.
Cup Final: Kucuk Kaymakli 2, Yenicami Agdelen 2.
aet; Kucuk Kaymakli won 4-3 on penalties.

NORTHERN IRELAND

Irish Football Association, 20 Windsor Avenue, Belfast BT9 6EG.
Founded: 1880. *FIFA:* 1911; *UEFA:* 1954. *National Colours:* Green shirts, white shorts, green socks.

NORWAY

Norges Fotballforbund, Ullevaal Stadion, Serviceboks 1, 0840 Oslo.
Founded: 1902. *FIFA:* 1908; *UEFA:* 1954. *National Colours:* Red shirts, white shorts, red socks.

International matches 2015–16
Bulgaria (a) 1-0, Croatia (h) 2-0, Malta (h) 2-0, Italy (a) 1-2, Hungary (h) 0-1, Hungary (a) 1-2, Estonia (a) 0-0, Finland (h) 2-0, Portugal (a) 0-3, Iceland (h) 3-2, Belgium (a) 2-3.

League Championship wins (1938–2015)
Rosenborg 23; Fredrikstad 9; Viking Stavanger 8; Lillestrom 5; Valerenga 5; Larvik Turn 3; Brann 3; Molde 3; Lyn Oslo 2; Stromsgodset 2; IK Start 2; Freidig 1; Fram 1; Skeid 1; Moss 1; Stabaek 1.

Cup wins (1902–2015)
Odd Grenland 12; Fredrikstad 11; Rosenborg 10; Lyn Oslo 8; Skeid 8; Sarpsborg 6; Brann 6; Viking Stavanger 5; Stromsgodset 5; Lillestrom 5; Orn-Horten 4; Valerenga 4; Molde 4; Frigg 3; Mjondalen 3; Mercantile 2; Bodo/Glimt 2; Tromso 2; Aalesund 2; Grane Nordstrand 1; Kvik Halden 1; Sparta 1; Gjovik/Lyn 1; Moss 1; Bryne 1; Stabaek 1; Hodd 1.
(Known as the Norwegian Championship for HM The King's Trophy.)

Final League Table 2015

	P	W	D	L	F	A	GD	Pts
Rosenborg	30	21	6	3	73	27	46	69
Stromsgodset	30	17	6	7	67	44	23	57
Stabaek	30	17	5	8	54	43	11	56
Odd	30	15	10	5	61	41	20	55
Viking	30	17	2	11	53	39	14	53
Molde	30	15	7	8	62	31	31	52
Valerenga	30	14	7	9	49	41	8	49
Lillestrom (–1)	30	12	9	9	45	43	2	44
Bodo/Glimt	30	12	4	14	53	56	–3	40
Aalesund	30	11	5	14	42	57	–15	38
Sarpsborg 08	30	8	10	12	37	49	–12	34
Haugesund	30	8	7	15	33	52	–19	31
Tromso	30	7	8	15	36	50	–14	29
Start	30	5	7	18	35	64	–29	22
Mjondalen	30	4	9	17	38	69	–31	21
Sandefjord	30	4	4	22	36	68	–32	16

Top scorer: Soderlund (Rosenborg) 22.
Cup Final: Rosenborg 2, Sarpsborg 08 0.

POLAND

Polski Zwiazek Pilki Noznej, ul. Bitwy Warszawskiej 1920r. 7, 02-366 Warszawa.
Founded: 1919. *FIFA:* 1923; *UEFA:* 1954. *National Colours:* White shirts with red vertical band, red shorts, white socks.

International matches 2015–16
Germany (a) 1-3, Gibraltar (h) 8-1, Scotland (a) 2-2, Republic of Ireland (h) 2-1, Iceland (h) 4-2, Czech Republic (h) 3-1, Serbia (h) 1-0, Finland (h) 5-0, Netherlands (h) 1-2, Lithuania (h) 0-0, Northern Ireland (n) 1-0, Germany (n) 0-0, Ukraine (n) 1-0, Switzerland (n) 1-1 (5-4p), Portugal (n) 1-1 (3-5p).

League Championship wins (1921–2016)
Ruch Chorzow 14; Gornik Zabrze 14; Wisla Krakow 13; Legia Warsaw 11; Lech Poznan 7; Cracovia 5; Pogon Lwow 4; Widzew Lodz 4; Warta Poznan 2; Polonia Warsaw 2; Polonia Bytom 2; LKS Lodz 2; Stal Mielec 2; Slask Wroclaw 2; Zaglebie Lubin 2; Garbarnia Krakow 1; Szombierki Bytom 1.

Cup wins (1926; 1951–2016)
Legia Warsaw 18; Gornik Zabrze 6; Lech Poznan 5; Wisla Krakow 4; Zaglebie Sosnowiec 4; Ruch Chorzow 3; GKS Katowice 3; Amica Wronki 3; Polonia Warsaw 2; Slask Wroclaw 2; Dyskobolia Grodzisk 2; Gwardia Warsaw 1; LKS Lodz 1; Stal Rzeszow 1; Arka Gdynia 1; Lechia Gdansk 1; Widzew Lodz 1; Miedz Legnica 1; Wisla Plock 1; Jagiellonia Bialystok 1; Zawisza Bydgoszcz 1.

Qualifying League Table 2015–16
	P	W	D	L	F	A	GD	Pts
Legia Warsaw	30	17	9	4	58	28	30	60
GKS Piast Gliwice	30	17	7	6	49	36	13	58
Pogon Szczecin	30	10	16	4	36	30	6	46
Zaglebie Lubin	30	12	9	9	41	37	4	45
Cracovia Krakow	30	12	9	9	57	42	15	45
Lech Poznan	30	13	4	13	37	38	–1	43
Lechia Gdansk (–1)	30	10	9	11	45	37	8	38
Ruch Chorzow (–1)	30	11	6	13	37	46	–9	38
Podbeskidzie	30	9	11	10	37	46	–9	38
Korona Kielce	30	9	10	11	32	37	–5	37
Wisla Krakow (–1)	30	8	13	9	45	35	10	36
Jagiellonia Bialystok	30	10	5	15	37	54	–17	35
Slask Wroclaw	30	8	10	12	28	37	–9	34
Nieciecza	30	8	9	13	33	43	–10	33
Gornik Leczna	30	8	7	15	30	43	–13	31
Gornik Zabrze (–1)	30	4	14	12	33	46	–13	25

NB: Points earned in Qualifying phase are halved and rounded up at start of Championship and Relegation Play-off phase.

Championship Round
	P	W	D	L	F	A	GD	Pts
Legia Warsaw	37	21	10	6	70	32	38	43
GKS Piast Gliwice	37	20	9	8	60	45	15	40
Zaglebie Lubin	37	17	9	11	55	42	13	38
Cracovia Krakow	37	16	10	11	66	50	16	36
Lechia Gdansk	37	14	10	13	53	44	9	32
Pogon Szczecin	37	12	17	8	43	43	0	30
Lech Poznan	37	14	6	17	42	47	–5	27
Ruch Chorzow	37	11	8	18	40	60	–20	21

Relegation Round
	P	W	D	L	F	A	GD	Pts
Wisla Krakow	37	12	15	10	61	45	16	32
Slask Wroclaw	37	12	12	13	41	46	–5	31
Jagiellonia Bialystok	37	13	6	18	46	62	–16	28
Korona Kielce	37	10	15	12	39	45	–6	27
Nieciecza	37	10	12	15	39	50	–11	26
Gornik Leczna	37	10	9	18	40	53	–13	24
Gornik Zabrze*	37	6	18	13	38	51	–13	23
Podbeskidzie*	37	9	12	16	45	63	–18	20

Top scorer: Nikolic (Legia Warsaw 28.
Cup Final: Legia Warsaw 1, Lech Poznan 0.

PORTUGAL

Federacao Portuguesa de Futebol, Rua Alexandre Herculano No. 58, Apartado postal 24013, Lisboa 1250-012.
Founded: 1914. *FIFA:* 1923; *UEFA:* 1954. *National Colours:* Carmine shirts with , red shorts, red and green socks.

International matches 2015–16
France (h) 0-1, Albania (a) 1-0, Denmark (h) 1-0, Serbia (a) 2-1, Russia (a) 0-1, Luxembourg (a) 2-0, Bulgaria (h) 0-1, Belgium (a) 2-1, Norway (h) 3-0, England (a) 0-1, Estonia (h) 7-0, Iceland (n) 1-1, Austria (n) 0-0, Hungary

(n) 3-3, Croatia (n) 1-0, Poland (n) 1-1 (5-3p), Wales (n) 2-0, France (a) 1-0.

League Championship wins (1935–2016)
Benfica 35; FC Porto 27; Sporting Lisbon 18; Belenenses 1; Boavista 1.

Cup wins (1939–2016)
Benfica 25; Sporting Lisbon 16; FC Porto 16; Boavista 5; Belenenses 3; Vitoria de Setubal 3; Academica de Coimbra 2; Braga 2; Leixoes 1; Estrela da Amadora 1; Beira-Mar 1; Vitoria de Guimaraes 1.

Final League Table 2015–16
	P	W	D	L	F	A	GD	Pts
Benfica	34	29	1	4	88	22	66	88
Sporting Lisbon	34	27	5	2	79	21	58	86
FC Porto	34	23	4	7	67	30	37	73
Braga	34	16	10	8	54	35	19	58
Arouca	34	13	15	6	47	38	9	54
Rio Ave	34	14	8	12	44	44	0	50
Pacos de Ferreira	34	13	10	11	43	42	1	49
Estoril	34	13	8	13	40	41	–1	47
Belenenses	34	10	11	13	44	66	–22	41
Vitoria Guimaraes	34	9	13	12	45	53	–8	40
Nacional	34	10	8	16	40	56	–16	38
Moreirense	34	9	9	16	38	54	–16	36
Maritimo	34	10	5	19	45	63	–18	35
Boavista	34	8	9	17	24	41	–17	33
Vitoria Setubal	34	6	12	16	40	61	–21	30
Tondela	34	8	6	20	34	54	–20	30
Uniao Madeira*	34	7	8	19	27	50	–23	29
Academica de Coimbra*	34	5	10	19	32	60	–28	25

Top scorer: Jonas (Benfica) 32.
Cup Final: Braga 2, Sporting Lisbon 2.
aet; Braga won 4-2 on penalties.

REPUBLIC OF IRELAND

Football Association of Ireland (Cumann Peile na hEireann), National Sports Campus, Abbotstown, Dublin 15.
Founded: 1921. *FIFA:* 1923; *UEFA:* 1954. *National Colours:* Green shirts, green shorts, green socks with white tops.

League Championship wins (1922–2015)
Shamrock Rovers 17; Shelbourne 13; Bohemians 11; Dundalk 11; St Patrick's Athletic 8; Cork Athletic (formerly Cork United) 7; Waterford United 6; Drumcondra 5; Sligo Rovers 3; St James's Gate 2; Limerick 2; Athlone Town 2; Derry City 2; Cork City 2; Dolphin 1; Cork Hibernians 1; Cork Celtic 1; Drogheda United 1.

Cup wins (1922–2015)
Shamrock Rovers 24; Dundalk 10; Bohemians 7; Shelbourne 7; Drumcondra 5; Sligo Rovers 5; Derry City 5; St Patrick's Athletic 3; St James's Gate 2; Cork (incl. Fordsons 1) 2; Waterford United 2; Cork United 2; Cork Athletic 2; Limerick 2; Cork Hibernians 2; Bray Wanderers 2; Cork City 2; Longford Town 2; Alton United 1; Athlone Town 1; Transport 1; Finn Harps 1; Home Farm 1; UC Dublin 1; Galway United 1; Drogheda United 1; Sporting Fingal 1.

Final League Table 2015
	P	W	D	L	F	A	GD	Pts
Dundalk	33	23	9	1	78	23	55	78
Cork City	33	19	10	4	57	25	32	67
Shamrock Rovers	33	18	11	4	56	27	29	65
St Patrick's Athletic	33	18	4	11	52	34	18	58
Bohemians	33	15	8	10	49	42	7	53
Longford Town	33	10	14	41	53	–12		39
Derry City	33	9	8	16	32	42	–10	35
Bray Wanderers	33	9	6	18	27	51	–24	33
Sligo Rovers	33	7	10	16	39	55	–16	31
Galway United	33	9	4	20	39	61	–22	31
Limerick*+	33	7	8	18	46	73	–27	29
Drogheda United*	33	7	7	19	32	62	–30	28

Top scorers: Towell (Dundalk) 25.
Cup Final: Dundalk 1, Cork City 0 *aet.*

ROMANIA

Federatia Romana de Fotbal, House of Football, Str. Sergent Serbanica Vasile 12, 22186 Bucuresti.
Founded: 1909. *FIFA:* 1923; *UEFA:* 1954. *National Colours:* All yellow.

International matches 2015–16
Hungary (a) 0-0, Greece (h) 0-0, Finland (h) 1-1, Faroe Islands (a) 3-0, Italy (a) 2-2, Lithuania (h) 1-0, Spain (h)

0-0, Congo DR (n) 1-1, Ukraine (n) 3-4, Georgia (h) 5-1, France (n) 1-2, Switzerland (n) 1-1, Albania (n) 0-1.

League Championship wins (1910–2016)

Steaua Bucharest 26; Dinamo Bucharest 18; Venus Bucharest 8; Chinezul Timisoara 6; UTA Arad 6; Petrolul Ploiesti 4; Ripensia Timisoara 4; Universitatea Craiova 4; Rapid Bucharest 3; CFR Cluj 3; Olimpia Bucharest 2; Colentina Bucharest 2; Arges Pitesti 2; United Ploiesti 1; Romano-Americana Bucharest 1; Prahova Ploiesti 1; Coltea Brasov 1; Metalochimia Resita 1; Unirea Tricolor 1; CA Oradea 1; Unirea Urziceni 1; Otelul Galati 1; Astra Giurgiu 1.

Cup wins (1934–2016)

Steaua Bucharest 23; Rapid Bucharest 13; Dinamo Bucharest 13; Universitatea Craiova 6; CFR Cluj 4; Petrolul Ploiesti 3; Ripensia Timisoara 2; UTA Arad 2; Politehnica Timisoara 2; CFR Turnu Severin 1; Metalochimia Resita 1; Universitatea Cluj (includes Stiinta) 1; Progresul Oradea (formerly ICO) 1; Progresul Bucharest 1; Ariesul Turda 1; Chimia Ramnicu Vilcea 1; Jiul Petrosani 1; Gloria Bistrita 1; Astra Giurgiu 1.

Qualifying League Table 2015–16

	P	W	D	L	F	A	GD	Pts
Astra Giurgiu	26	14	9	3	42	29	13	51
Dinamo Bucharest	26	13	9	4	36	24	12	48
Pandurii Targu Jiu	26	13	8	5	35	26	9	47
Viitorul Constanta	26	13	7	6	49	30	19	46
Steaua Bucharest	26	12	8	6	35	25	10	44
Targu Mures	26	9	11	6	27	21	6	38
CSMS Iasi	26	9	10	7	22	25	–3	37
Universitatea Craiova	26	8	7	11	26	27	–1	31
CFR Cluj	26	9	10	7	31	25	6	27
Botosani	26	6	8	12	30	35	–5	26
ACS Poli Timisoara	26	5	10	11	24	35	–11	25
Voluntari	26	5	9	12	28	42	–14	24
Concordia Chiajna	26	3	8	15	22	46	–24	17
Petrolul Ploiesti	26	2	8	16	17	34	–17	8

Championship Round

	P	W	D	L	F	A	GD	Pts
Astra Giurgiu	10	7	1	2	20	9	11	48
Steaua Bucharest	10	6	3	1	18	8	10	43
Pandurii Targu Jiu	10	3	6	1	12	7	5	39
Dinamo Bucharest	10	2	6	2	12	15	–3	36
Viitorul Constanta	10	1	3	6	14	21	–7	29
Targu Mures	10	0	3	7	8	24	–16	22

Relegation Round

	P	W	D	L	F	A	GD	Pts
Universitatea Craiova	14	7	2	5	19	17	2	39
CSMS Iasi	14	5	5	4	17	15	2	39
Botosani	14	7	4	3	29	19	10	38
CFR Cluj	14	6	4	4	25	13	12	36
Concordia Chiajna	14	7	5	2	19	13	6	35
Voluntari+	14	5	2	7	19	20	–1	29
ACS Poli Timisoara*	14	1	4	9	14	36	–22	20
Petrolul Ploiesti*	14	4	2	8	9	18	–9	18

Top scorer: Hora (Pandurii Targu Jiu) 19.
Cup Final: CFR Cluj 2, Dinamo Bucharest 2.
aet; CFR Cluj won 5-4 on penalties.

RUSSIA

Russian Football Union, Ulitsa Narodnaya 7, 115 172 Moscow.
Founded: 1912. *FIFA:* 1912; *UEFA:* 1954. *National Colours:* All brick red.

International matches 2015–16

Sweden (h) 1-0, Liechtenstein (a) 7-0, Moldova (a) 2-1, Montenegro (h) 2-0, Portugal (h) 1-0, Croatia (h) 1-3, Lithuania (h) 3-0, France (a) 2-4, Czech Republic (n) 1-2, Serbia (n) 1-1, England (n) 1-1, Slovakia (n) 1-2, Wales (n) 0-3.

League Championship wins (1936–2016)

Spartak Moscow 21; Dynamo Kyiv 13; CSKA Moscow 13; Dynamo Moscow 11; Zenit St Petersburg (formerly Zenit Leningrad) 5; Torpedo Moscow 3; Dinamo Tbilisi 2; Dnepr Dnepropetrovsk 2; Lokomotiv Moscow 2; Rubin Kazan 2; Saria Voroshilovgrad 1; Ararat Erevan 1; Dynamo Minsk 1; Spartak Vladikavkaz (renamed Alania) 1.

Cup wins (1936–2016)

Spartak Moscow 13; CSKA Moscow 12; Dynamo Kyiv 9; Lokomotiv Moscow 8; Torpedo Moscow 7; Dynamo Moscow 7; Zenit St Petersburg (formerly Zenit Leningrad) 4; Shakhtar Donetsk 4; Dinamo Tbilisi 2; Ararat Erevan 2;

Karpaty Lvov 1; SKA Rostov-on-Don 1; Metalist Kharkov 1; Dnepr 1; Terek Grozny 1; Rubin Kazan 1; Rostov 1.

Final League Table 2015–16

	P	W	D	L	F	A	GD	Pts
CSKA Moscow	30	20	5	5	51	25	26	65
Rostov	30	19	6	5	41	20	21	63
Zenit St Petersburg	30	17	8	5	61	32	29	59
Krasnodar	30	16	8	6	54	25	29	56
Spartak Moscow	30	15	5	10	48	39	9	50
Lokomotiv Moscow	30	14	8	8	43	33	10	50
Terek Grozny	30	11	11	8	35	30	5	44
Ural Sverdlovsk Oblast	30	10	9	11	39	46	–7	39
Krylya Sovetov	30	9	8	13	19	31	–12	35
Rubin Kazan	30	9	6	15	33	39	–6	33
Amkar Perm	30	7	10	13	22	33	–11	31
Ufa	30	6	9	15	25	44	–19	27
Anzhi+	30	6	8	16	28	50	–22	26
Kuban Krasnodar*+	30	5	11	14	34	44	–10	26
Dynamo Moscow*	30	5	10	15	28	55	–27	25
Mordovia Saransk*	30	4	12	14	30	50	–20	24

Top scorer: Smolov (Krasnodar) 20.
Cup Final: Zenit St Petersburg 4, CSKA Moscow 1.

SAN MARINO

Federazione Sammarinese Giuoco Calcio, Strada di Montecchio 17, 47890 San Marino.
Founded: 1931. *FIFA:* 1988; *UEFA:* 1988. *National Colours:* Cobalt blue shirts with white trim, white shorts, cobalt blue socks.

International matches 2015–16

England (h) 0-6, Lithuania (a) 1-2, Switzerland (a) 0-7, Slovenia (h) 0-2, Croatia (a) 0-10.

League Championship wins (1986–2016)

Tre Fiori 7; Domagnano 4; Folgore/Falciano 4; Faetano 3; La Fiorita 3; Murata 3; Tre Penne 3; Montevito 1; Libertas 1; Cosmos 1; Pennarossa 1.

Cup wins (1937–2016)

Libertas 11; Domagnano 8; Tre Fiori 6; Juvenes 5; Tre Penne 5; Cosmos 4; La Fiorita 4; Faetano 3; Murata 3; Dogana 2; Pennarossa 2; Juvenes/Dogana 2; Folgore/Falciano 1.

Qualifying League Table 2015–16

Group A

	P	W	D	L	F	A	GD	Pts
La Fiorita	21	13	2	6	56	25	31	41
Pennarossa	21	9	8	4	32	20	12	35
Juvenes/Dogana	21	9	4	8	34	27	7	31
Libertas	21	7	6	8	23	26	–3	27
Cosmos	21	3	8	10	25	37	–12	17
Cailungo	21	4	4	13	19	50	–31	16
Faetano	21	3	6	12	18	35	–17	15
San Giovanni	21	1	3	17	13	63	–50	6

Group B

	P	W	D	L	F	A	GD	Pts
Tre Penne	20	15	3	2	50	14	36	48
Tre Fiori	20	13	1	6	37	27	10	40
Folgore/Falciano	20	12	3	5	44	25	19	39
Fiorentino	20	11	2	7	30	24	6	35
Domagnano	20	9	3	8	33	32	1	30
Virtus	20	8	4	8	37	36	1	28
Murata	20	7	3	10	35	45	–10	24

Play-offs

(Top three in each group qualify for Play-offs; double-elimination format; group winners receive byes in first two rounds.)
Rnd 1: Pennarossa 0, Folgore/Falciano 3; Tre Fiori 1, Juvenes/Dogana 0
Rnd 2: Tre Fiori 2, Folgore/Falciano 3; Juvenes/Dogana 2, Pennarossa 2 (aet; 7-6p)
Rnd 3: La Fiorita 1, Tre Penne 2; Juvenes/Dogana 1, Tre Fiore 0
Rnd 4: Tre Penne 1, Folgore/Falciano 1 (aet; 3-0p); Juvenes/Dogana 0, La Fiorita 3
Rnd 5: Juvenes/Dogana 0, La Fiorita 0 (aet; 4-2p)
Semi-final: Folgore/Falciano 1, La Fiorita 2
Final: Tre Penne 3, La Fiorita 1
Top scorer: Martini (La Fiorita) 19.
Cup Final: La Fiorita 2, Pennarossa 0.

SCOTLAND

Scottish Football Association, Hampden Park, Glasgow G42 9AY.
Founded: 1873. *FIFA:* 1910; *UEFA:* 1954. *National Colours:* Dark blue shirts, dark blue shorts, red socks.

SERBIA

Football Association of Serbia, Terazije 35, PO Box 263, 11000 Beograd.
Founded: 1919. *FIFA:* 1921; *UEFA:* 1954. *National Colours:* Red shirts, blue shorts, white socks.

International matches 2015–16
Armenia (h) 2-0, France (a) 1-2, Albania (a) 2-0, Portugal (h) 1-2, Czech Republic (a) 1-4, Poland (a) 0-1, Estonia (a) 1-0, Cyprus (h) 2-1, Israel (h) 3-1, Russia (n) 1-1.

League Championship wins (1923–2016)
Crvena Zvezda (Red Star Belgrade) 27; Partizan Belgrade 26; Hajduk Split 9; Gradjanski Zagreb 5; BSK Belgrade (renamed OFK) 5; Dinamo Zagreb 4; Jugoslavija Belgrade 2; Concordia Zagreb 2; FC Sarajevo 2; Vojvodina Novi Sad 2; HASK Zagreb 1; Zeljeznicar 1; Obilic 1.

Cup wins (1947–2016)
Crvena Zvezda (Red Star Belgrade) 24; Partizan Belgrade 13; Hajduk Split 9; Dinamo Zagreb 8; OFK Belgrade (incl. BSK 3) 5; Rijeka 2; Velez Mostar 2; Vardar Skopje 1; Borac Banjaluka 1; Sartid 1; Zeleznik 1; Jagodina 1; Vojvodina 1; Cukaricki 1.

Qualifying League Table 2015–16

	P	W	D	L	F	A	GD	Pts
Crvena Zvezda	30	26	4	0	82	19	63	82
Partizan Belgrade	30	16	6	8	59	37	22	54
Cukaricki	30	15	8	7	37	22	15	53
Borac Cacak	30	12	10	8	37	29	8	46
Vojvodina	30	12	10	8	44	38	6	46
Radnicki Nis	30	12	9	9	26	23	3	45
Vozdovac	30	10	10	10	30	29	1	40
Radnik Surdulica	30	9	11	10	34	46	–12	38
Javor Ivanjica	30	8	11	11	21	24	–3	35
Metalac GM	30	8	11	11	29	35	–6	35
Mladost Lucani	30	7	12	11	25	38	–13	33
Novi Pazar	30	7	10	13	21	39	–18	31
OFK Belgrade	30	8	4	18	27	44	–17	28
Spartak Subotica	30	6	10	14	20	37	–17	26
Jagodina	30	5	11	14	22	43	–21	26
Rad	30	5	11	14	30	41	–11	26

NB: Points earned in Qualifying phase are halved and rounded up at start of Championship and Relegation Play-off phase.

Championship Round

	P	W	D	L	F	A	GD	Pts
Crvena Zvezda	37	30	5	2	97	27	70	54
Partizan Belgrade	37	20	7	10	72	44	28	40
Cukaricki	37	19	8	10	48	35	13	39
Vojvodina	37	16	11	10	57	44	13	36
Radnicki Nis	37	16	9	12	40	35	5	35
Borac Cacak	37	14	11	12	46	43	3	30
Vozdovac	37	11	12	14	34	36	–2	25
Radnik Surdulica	37	11	11	15	41	65	–24	25

Relegation Round

	P	W	D	L	F	A	GD	Pts
Mladost Lucani	37	11	14	12	34	44	–10	31
Spartak Subotica	37	11	11	15	37	42	–5	29
Metalac GM	37	10	15	12	41	48	–7	28
Rad	37	9	13	15	40	47	–7	27
Javor Ivanjica	37	10	13	14	25	29	–4	26
Novi Pazar	37	10	10	17	29	50	–21	25
OFK Belgrade*	37	9	5	23	38	58	–20	18
Jagodina*	37	5	13	19	29	61	–32	15

Top scorers (joint): Katai (Crvena Zvezda), Vieira (Crvena Zvezda) 21.
Cup Final: Partizan Belgrade 2, Jafor Ivanjica 0.

SLOVAKIA

Slovensky Futbalovy Zvaz, Trnavska cesta 100, 821 01 Bratislava.
Founded: 1938. *FIFA:* 1994; *UEFA:* 1993. *National Colours:* White shirts with blue trim, white shorts, white socks.

International matches 2015–16
Spain (a) 0-2, Ukraine (h) 0-0, Belarus (h) 0-1, Luxembourg (a) 4-2, Switzerland (h) 3-2, Iceland (h) 3-1,

Latvia (h) 0-0, Republic of Ireland (a) 2-2, Georgia (n) 3-1, Germany (a) 3-1, Northern Ireland (h) 0-0, Wales (n) 1-2, Russia (n) 2-1, England (n) 0-0, Germany (n) 0-3.

League Championship wins (1939–44; 1994–2016)
Slovan Bratislava 12; Zilina 6; Kosice 2; Inter Bratislava 2; Artmedia Petrzalka 2; Trencin 2; Dukla Banska Bystrica 1; OAP Bratislava 1; Ruzomberok 1.
See also Czech Republic section for Slovak club honours in Czechoslovak era 1925–93.

Cup wins (1994–2016)
Slovan Bratislava 6; Inter Bratislava 3; Artmedia Petrzalka 2; Kosice 2; Trencin 2; Humenne 1; Spartak Trnava 1; Koba Senec 1; Matador Puchov 1; Dukla Banska Bystrica 1; Ruzomberok 1; ViOn Zlate Moravce 1; Zilina 1.

Final League Table 2015–16

	P	W	D	L	F	A	GD	Pts
Trencin	33	24	4	73	28	45	81	
Slovan Bratislava	33	20	9	4	50	25	25	69
Spartak Myjava	33	18	6	9	41	33	8	60
Spartak Trnava	33	16	6	11	49	41	8	54
Zilina	33	14	6	13	58	46	12	48
Ruzomberok	33	12	9	12	42	41	1	45
DAC Dunajska Streda	33	12	7	14	38	42	–4	43
Sport Podbrezova	33	10	7	16	43	46	–3	37
ViOn Zlate Moravce	33	7	10	16	38	57	–19	31
Senica	33	7	9	17	30	48	–18	30
Zemplin Michalovce	33	7	8	18	32	55	–23	29
Skalica*	33	6	6	21	30	62	–32	24

Top scorer: van Kessel (Trencin) 17.
Cup Final: Trencin 3, Slovan Bratislava 1.

SLOVENIA

Nogometna Zveza Slovenije, Brnciceva 41g, PP 3986, 1001 Ljubljana.
Founded: 1920. *FIFA:* 1992; *UEFA:* 1992. *National Colours:* White shirts with blue trim, white shorts, white socks.

International matches 2015–16
Switzerland (a) 2-3, Estonia (h) 1-0, Lithuania (h) 1-1, San Marino (a) 2-0, Ukraine (a) 0-2, Ukraine (h) 1-1, FYR Macedonia (h) 1-0, Northern Ireland (a) 0-1, Sweden (a) 0-0, Turkey (h) 0-1.

League Championship wins (1992–2016)
Maribor 13; Olimpija (pre-2005) 4; Gorica 4; Domzale 2; Koper 1; Olimpija Ljubljana 1.

Cup wins (1992–2016)
Maribor 9; Olimpija (pre-2005) 4; Gorica 3; Koper 3; Interblock 2; Mura (pre-2004) 1; Rudar Velenje 1; Celje 1; Domzale 1.

Final League Table 2015–16

	P	W	D	L	F	A	GD	Pts
Olimpija Ljubljana	36	22	8	6	75	25	50	74
Maribor	36	19	11	6	78	37	41	68
Domzale	36	14	13	9	46	31	15	55
Gorica	36	15	7	14	48	49	–1	52
Celje	36	11	12	13	32	46	–14	45
Krsko	36	11	11	15	24	48	–24	41
Rudar Velenje	36	11	8	17	34	52	–18	41
Koper	36	11	7	18	40	54	–14	40
Zavrc*+	36	9	13	14	32	41	–9	40
Krka*	36	8	10	18	30	56	–26	34

Top scorers (joint): Kronaveter (Olimpija Ljubljana), Sporar (Olimpija Ljubljana), Mendy (Maribor) 17.
Cup Final: Maribor 2, Celje 2.
aet; Maribor won 7-6 on penalties.

SPAIN

Real Federacion Espanola de Futbol, Calle Ramon y Cajal s/n, Apartado postale 385, 28230 Las Rozas, Madrid.
Founded: 1913. *FIFA:* 1913; *UEFA:* 1954. *National Colours:* All red with yellow trim.

International matches 2015–16
Slovakia (h) 2-0, FYR Macedonia (a) 1-0, Luxembourg (h) 4-0, Ukraine (a) 1-0, England (h) 2-0, Italy (a) 1-1, Romania (h) 0-0, Bosnia-Herzegovina (n) 3-1, Korea Republic (n) 6-1, Georgia (h) 0-1, Czech Republic (n) 1-0, Turkey (n) 3-0, Croatia (n) 1-2, Italy (n) 0-2.

League Championship wins (1929–36; 1940–2016)
Real Madrid 32; Barcelona 24; Atletico Madrid 10; Athletic Bilbao 8; Valencia 6; Real Sociedad 2; Real Betis 1; Sevilla 1; Deportivo La Coruna 1.

Cup wins (1903–2016)

Barcelona 28; Athletic Bilbao (includesVizcaya Bilbao 1) 23; Real Madrid 19; Atletico Madrid 10; Valencia 7; Real Zaragoza 6; Sevilla 5; Espanyol 4; Real Union de Irun 3; Real Betis 2; Real Sociedad (includes Ciclista) 2; Deportivo La Coruna 2; Arenas 1; Racing de Irun 1; Mallorca 1.

Final League Table 2015–16

	P	W	D	L	F	A	GD	Pts
Barcelona	38	29	4	5	112	29	83	91
Real Madrid	38	28	6	4	110	34	76	90
Atletico Madrid	38	28	4	6	63	18	45	88
Villarreal	38	18	10	10	44	35	9	64
Athletic Bilbao	38	18	8	12	58	45	13	62
Celta Vigo	38	17	9	12	51	59	–8	60
Sevilla	38	14	10	14	51	50	1	52
Malaga	38	12	12	14	38	35	3	48
Real Sociedad	38	13	9	16	45	48	–3	48
Real Betis	38	11	12	15	34	52	–18	45
Las Palmas	38	12	8	18	45	53	–8	44
Valencia	38	11	11	16	46	48	–2	44
Espanyol	38	12	7	19	40	74	–34	43
Eibar	38	11	10	17	49	61	–12	43
Deportivo La Coruna	38	8	18	12	45	61	–16	42
Granada	38	10	9	19	46	69	–23	39
Sporting Gijon	38	10	9	19	40	62	–22	39
Rayo Vallecano*	38	9	11	18	52	73	–21	38
Getafe*	38	9	9	20	37	67	–30	36
Levante*	38	8	8	22	37	70	–33	32

Top scorer: Suarez (Barcelona) 40.
Cup Final: Barcelona 2, Sevilla 0 *aet.*

SWEDEN

Svenska Fotbollfoerbundet, Evenemangsgatan 31, PO Box 1216, SE-171 23 Solna.
Founded: 1904. *FIFA:* 1904; *UEFA:* 1954. *National Colours:* Yellow shirts with blue trim, blue shorts, yellow socks.

International matches 2015–16

Russia (a) 0-1, Austria (h) 1-4, Liechtenstein (a) 2-0, Moldova (h) 2-0, Denmark (h) 2-1, Denmark (a) 2-2, Estonia (n) 1-1, Finland (n) 3-0, Turkey (a) 1-2, Czech Republic (n) 1-1, Slovenia (h) 0-0, Wales (h) 3-0, Republic of Ireland (n) 1-1, Italy (n) 0-1, Belgium (n) 0-1.

League Championship wins (1896–2016)

IFK Gothenburg 18; Malmo 18; IFK Norrkoping 13; Orgryte 12; AIK Stockholm 11; Djurgaarden 11; IF Elfsborg 6; Helsingborg 5; GAIS Gothenburg 4; Oster Vaxjo 4; Halmstad 4; Atvidaberg 3; IF Gothenburg 1; IFK Eskilstuna 1; Fassbergs 1; IF Gavic Brynas 1; IK Sleipner 1; Hammarby 1; Kalmar 1.
(Played in cup format from 1896–1925.)

Cup wins (1941–2016)

Malmo 14; AIK Stockholm 8; IFK Gothenburg 7; IFK Norrkoping 6; Helsingborg 5; Djurgaarden 4; Kalmar 3; IF Elfsborg 3; Atvidaberg 2; GAIS Gothenburg 1; IFK Raa 1; Landskrona 1; Oster Vaxjo 1; Degerfors 1; Halmstad 1; Orgryte 1; Hacken 1.

Final League Table 2015

	P	W	D	L	F	A	GD	Pts
IFK Norrkoping	30	20	6	4	60	33	27	66
IFK Gothenburg	30	18	9	3	52	22	30	63
AIK Solna	30	18	7	5	54	34	20	61
Elfsborg	30	16	7	7	59	42	17	55
Malmo	30	15	9	6	54	34	20	54
Djurgarden	30	14	9	7	52	37	15	51
Hacken	30	13	6	11	45	39	6	45
Helsingborg	30	11	4	15	43	45	–2	37
Orebro	30	9	10	11	36	50	–14	37
Gefle	30	10	6	14	35	50	–15	36
Hammarby	30	8	9	13	35	39	–4	33
GIF Sundsvall	30	9	5	16	34	52	–18	32
Kalmar	30	8	7	15	31	42	–11	31
Falkenberg+	30	7	4	19	38	56	–18	25
Halmstad*	30	4	9	17	21	44	–23	21
Atvidaberg*	30	4	9	19	25	55	–30	15

Top scorer: Kujovic (IFK Norrkoping) 21.
Cup Final: Hacken 2, Orebro 1.
aet; Hacken won 6-5 on penalties.

SWITZERLAND

Schweizerisher Fussballverband, Worbstrasse 48, Postfach 3000, Bern 15.
Founded: 1895. *FIFA:* 1904; *UEFA:* 1954. *National Colours:* Red shirts, white shorts, red socks.

International matches 2015–16

Slovenia (h) 3-2, England (a) 0-2, San Marino (h) 7-0, Estonia (a) 1-0, Slovakia (a) 2-3, Austria (a) 2-1, Republic of Ireland (a) 0-1, Bosnia-Herzegovina (h) 0-2, Belgium (n) 1-2, Moldova (h) 2-1, Albania (n) 1-0, Romania (n) 1-1, France (n) 0-0, Poland (n) 1-1 (4-5p).

League Championship wins (1897–2016)

Grasshoppers 27; FC Basel 19; Servette 17; FC Zurich 12; Young Boys 11; Lausanne-Sport 7; Winterthur 3; Aarau 3; Lugano 3; La Chaux-de-Fonds 3; St Gallen 2; Neuchatel Xamax 2; Sion 2; Anglo-American Club 1; Brühl 1; Cantonal-Neuchatel 1; Etoile La Chaux-de-Fonds 1; Biel-Bienne 1; Bellinzona 1; Luzern 1.

Cup wins (1926–2016)

Grasshoppers 19; Sion 13; FC Basel 11; Lausanne-Sport 9; FC Zurich 9; Servette 7; Young Boys 6; La Chaux-de-Fonds 6; Lugano 3; Luzern 2; FC Grenchen 1; St Gallen 1; Urania Geneva 1; Young Fellows Zurich 1; Aarau 1; Wil 1.

Final League Table 2015–16

	P	W	D	L	F	A	GD	Pts
FC Basel	36	26	5	5	88	38	50	83
Young Boys	36	20	9	7	78	47	31	69
Luzern	36	15	9	12	59	50	9	54
Grasshoppers	36	15	8	13	65	56	9	53
Sion	36	14	8	14	52	49	3	50
Thun	36	10	11	15	45	54	–9	41
St Gallen	36	10	8	18	41	66	–25	38
Vaduz	36	7	15	14	44	60	–16	36
Lugano	36	9	8	19	46	75	–29	35
FC Zurich*	36	7	13	16	48	71	–23	34

Top scorer: Dabour (Grasshoppers) 19.
Cup Final: FC Zurich 1, Lugano 0.

TURKEY

Turkiye Futbol Federasyonu, Hasan Dogan Milli Takimlar, Kamp ve Egitim Tesisleri, Riva, Beykoz, Istanbul.
Founded: 1923. *FIFA:* 1923; *UEFA:* 1962. *National Colours:* All red.

International matches 2015–16

Denmark (a) 2-1, Iceland (a) 0-3, Czech Republic (h) 1-2, Latvia (a) 1-1, Brazil (a) 0-4, Kazakhstan (h) 3-1, Netherlands (a) 1-1, Luxembourg (a) 2-1, Bulgaria (h) 4-0, Kazakhstan (a) 1-0, Latvia (h) 1-1, Netherlands (h) 3-0, Czech Republic (a) 2-0, Iceland (h) 1-0, Qatar (a) 2-1, Greece (h) 0-0, Sweden (h) 2-1, Austria (a) 2-1, England (a) 1-2, Montenegro (h) 1-0, Slovenia (a) 1-0, Croatia (n) 0-1, Spain (n) 0-3, Czech Republic (n) 2-0.

League Championship wins (1959–2016)

Galatasaray 20; Fenerbahce 19; Besiktas 12; Trabzonspor 6; Bursaspor 1.

Cup wins (1963–2016)

Galatasaray 17; Besiktas 9; Trabzonspor 8; Fenerbahce 6; Altay Izmir 2; Goztepe Izmir 2; Ankaragucu 2; Genclerbirligi 2; Kocaelispor 2; Eskisehirspor 1; Bursaspor 1; Sakaryaspor 1; Kayseri 1.

Final League Table 2015–16

	P	W	D	L	F	A	GD	Pts
Besiktas	34	25	4	5	75	35	40	79
Fenerbahce	34	22	8	4	60	27	33	74
Konyaspor	34	19	9	6	44	33	11	66
Istanbul Basaksehir	34	16	11	7	54	36	18	59
Osmanlispor	34	14	10	10	52	36	16	52
Galatasaray	34	13	12	9	69	49	20	51
Kasimpasa	34	14	8	12	50	40	10	50
Akhisar Belediyespor	34	11	13	10	42	41	1	46
Antalyaspor	34	12	9	13	53	52	1	45
Genclerbirligi	34	13	6	15	42	42	0	45
Bursaspor	34	13	5	16	47	55	–8	44
Trabzonspor	34	12	4	18	40	59	–19	40
Rizespor	34	9	10	15	39	48	–9	37
Gaziantepspor	34	9	9	16	31	50	–19	36
Kayserispor	34	7	13	14	25	41	–16	34
Sivasspor*	34	6	13	15	34	48	–14	31
Eskisehirspor*	34	6	8	20	39	64	–25	30
Mersin Idman Yurdu*	34	5	6	23	31	71	–40	21

Top scorer: Gomez (Besiktas) 26.
Cup Final: Galatasaray 1, Fenerbahce 0.

UKRAINE

Football Federation of Ukraine, Provulok Laboratornyi 7-A, PO Box 55, 01133 Kyiv.
Founded: 1991. *FIFA:* 1992; *UEFA:* 1992. *National Colours:* All yellow with blue trim.

International matches 2015–16
Belarus (h) 3-1, Slovakia (a) 0-0, FYR Macedonia (a) 2-0, Spain (h) 0-1, Slovenia (h) 2-0, Slovenia (a) 1-1, Cyprus (h) 1-0, Wales (a) 1-0, Romania (n) 4-3, Albania (n) 3-1, Germany (n) 0-2, Northern Ireland (n) 0-2, Poland (n) 0-1.

League Championship wins (1992–2016)
Dynamo Kyiv 15; Shakhtar Donetsk 9; Tavriya Simferopol 1.

Cup wins (1992–2016)
Dynamo Kyiv 11; Shakhtar Donetsk 10; Chornomorets Odessa 2; Vorskla 1; Tavriya Simferopol 1.

Final League Table 2015–16

	P	W	D	L	F	A	GD	Pts
Dynamo Kyiv	26	23	1	2	54	11	43	70
Shakhtar Donetsk	26	20	3	3	76	25	51	63
Dnipro Dnipropropetrovsk	26	16	5	5	50	22	28	53
Zorya Luhansk	26	14	6	6	51	26	25	48
Vorskla Poltava	26	11	9	6	32	26	6	42
Oleksandria	26	10	8	8	30	29	1	38
Karpaty Lviv	26	8	6	12	26	37	–11	30
Stal Dnipropropetrovsk	26	7	8	11	22	31	–9	29
Olimpik Donetsk	26	6	7	13	22	35	–13	25
Metalist Kharkiv†	26	5	9	12	19	46	–27	24
Chornomorets Odessa	26	4	10	12	20	39	–19	22
Volyn Lutsk (–18)	26	10	8	8	36	36	0	20
Hoverla Uzhhorod† (–9)	26	3	7	16	13	45	–32	7
Metalurh Zaporizhya‡	26	0	3	23	7	50	–43	3

† *Expelled for financial irregularities.* † *Expelled for breach of rules; matches from Round 17 forfeited.*
Top scorer: Alex Teixera (Shakhtar Donetsk) 22.
Cup Final: Shakhtar Donetsk 2, Zorya Luhansk 0.

WALES

Football Association of Wales, 11/12 Neptune Court, Vanguard Way, Cardiff CF24 5PJ.
Founded: 1876. *FIFA:* 1910; *UEFA:* 1954. *National Colours:* All red with green trim.

SOUTH AMERICA (CONMEBOL)

ARGENTINA
Asociacion del Futbol Argentina, Viamonte 1366/76, Buenos Aires 1053.
Founded: 1893. *FIFA:* 1912; *CONMEBOL:* 1916.
National Colours: Light blue and white vertical striped shirts, white shorts, white socks.

International matches 2015–16
Colombia (n) 0-0 (5-4p), Paraguay (n) 6-1, Chile (a) 0-0 (1-4p), Bolivia (n) 7-0, Mexico (n) 2-2, Ecuador (h) 0-2, Paraguay (a) 0-0, Brazil (h) 1-1, Colombia (a) 1-0, Chile (a) 2-1, Bolivia (h) 2-0, Honduras (h) 1-0, Chile (n) 2-1, Panama (n) 5-0, Bolivia (n) 3-0, Venezuela (n) 4-1, USA (a) 4-0, Chile (n) 0-0 (2-4p).

BOLIVIA
Federacion Boliviana de Futbol, Avenida Libertador Bolivar 1168, Casilla 484, Cochabamba.
Founded: 1925. *FIFA:* 1926; *CONMEBOL:* 1926.
National Colours: Green shirts, white shorts, white socks.

International matches 2015–16
Argentina (n) 0-7, Uruguay (h) 0-2, Ecuador (a) 0-2, Venezuela (h) 4-2, Paraguay (a) 1-2, Colombia (h) 2-3, Argentina (a) 0-2, USA (a) 0-4, Panama (n) 1-2, Chile (n) 2-1, Argentina (n) 0-3.

BRAZIL
Confederacao Brasileira de Futebol, Avenida Luis Carlos Prestes 130, Barra da Tijuca, Rio de Janeiro 22775-055.
Founded: 1914. *FIFA:* 1923; *CONMEBOL:* 1916.
National Colours: Yellow shirts with green collar and cuffs, blue shorts, white socks.

International matches 2015–16
Costa Rica (n) 1-0, USA (n) 4-1, Chile (a) 0-2, Venezuela (h) 3-1, Argentina (a) 1-1, Peru (h) 3-0, Uruguay (h) 2-2, Paraguay (a) 2-2, Panama (n) 2-0, Ecuador (n) 0-0, Haiti (n) 7-1, Peru (n) 0-1.

CHILE
Federacion de Futbol de Chile, Avenida Quilin 5635, Comuna Penalolen, Casilla 3733, Santiago de Chile.
Founded: 1895. *FIFA:* 1913; *CONMEBOL:* 1916.
National Colours: Red shirts with blue collars, blue shorts, white socks.

International matches 2015–16
Paraguay (h) 3-2, Brazil (h) 2-0, Peru (a) 4-3, Colombia (h) 1-1, Uruguay (a) 0-3, Argentina (h) 1-2, Venezuela (a) 4-1, Jamaica (h) 1-2, Mexico (n) 0-1, Argentina (n) 1-2, Bolivia (n) 2-1, Panama (n) 4-2, Mexico (n) 7-0, Colombia (h) 2-0, Argentina (n) 0-0 (4-2p).

COLOMBIA
Federacion Colombiana de Futbol, Avenida 32 No. 16–22, Bogota.
Founded: 1924. *FIFA:* 1936; *CONMEBOL:* 1936.
National Colours: Yellow shirts with blue trim, white shorts, white socks.

International matches 2015–16
Argentina (n) 0-0 (4-5p), Peru (n) 1-1, Peru (h) 2-0, Uruguay (a) 0-3, Chile (a) 1-1, Argentina (h) 0-1, Bolivia (a) 3-2, Ecuador (h) 3-1, Haiti (n) 3-1, USA (a) 2-0, Paraguay (n) 2-1, Costa Rica (n) 2-3, Peru (n) 0-0 (4-2p), Chile (n) 0-2, USA (a) 1-0.

ECUADOR
Federacion Ecuatoriana del Futbol, Avenida Las Aguas y Calle Alianza, PO Box 09-01-7447, Guayaquil 593.
Founded: 1925. *FIFA:* 1927; *CONMEBOL:* 1927.
National Colours: Yellow shirts, blue shorts, red socks.

International matches 2015–16
Honduras (h) 2-0, Argentina (a) 2-0, Bolivia (h) 2-0, Uruguay (h) 2-1, Venezuela (a) 3-1, Paraguay (h) 2-2, Colombia (a) 1-3, USA (a) 0-1, Brazil (n) 0-0, Peru (n) 2-2, Haiti (n) 4-0, USA (a) 1-2.

PARAGUAY
Asociacion Paraguaya de Futbol, Calle Mayor Martinez 1393, Asuncion.
Founded: 1906. *FIFA:* 1925; *CONMEBOL:* 1921.
National Colours: Red and white stroped shirts, blue shorts, blue socks.

International matches 2015–16
Chile (a) 2-3, Venezuela (a) 1-0, Argentina (h) 0-0, Peru (a) 0-1, Bolivia (h) 2-1, Ecuador (a) 2-2, Brazil (h) 2-2, Mexico (n) 0-1, Costa Rica (n) 0-0, Colombia (n) 1-2, USA (a) 0-1.

PERU
Federacion Peruana de Futbol, Avenida Aviacion 2085, San Luis, Lima 30.
Founded: 1922. *FIFA:* 1924; *CONMEBOL:* 1925.
National Colours: White shirts with red sash, white shorts, white socks.

International matches 2015–16
USA (a) 1-2, Colombia (n) 1-1, Colombia (a) 0-2, Chile (h) 3-4, Paraguay (h) 1-0, Brazil (a) 0-3, Venezuela (h) 2-2, Uruguay (h) 0-1, Trinidad & Tobago (h) 4-0, El Salvador (n) 3-1, Haiti (n) 1-0, Peru (n) 2-2, Brazil (n) 1-0, Colombia (n) 0-0 (2-4p).

URUGUAY
Asociacion Uruguaya de Futbol, Guayabo 1531, Montevideo 11200.
Founded: 1900. *FIFA:* 1923; *CONMEBOL:* 1916.
National Colours: Sky blue shirts, black shorts, black socks with sky blue tops.

International matches 2015–16
Panama (a) 1-0, Costa Rica (a) 0-1, Bolivia (a) 2-0, Colombia (h) 3-0, Ecuador (a) 1-2, Chile (h) 3-0, Brazil (a) 2-2, Peru (h) 1-0, Trinidad & Tobago (h) 3-1, Mexico (n) 1-3, Venezuela (n) 0-1, Jamaica (n) 3-0.

VENEZUELA
Federacion Venezolana de Futbol, Avenida Santos Erminy 1ra Calle las Delicias, Torre Mega II, P.H.B. Sabana Grande, 1050 Caracas.
Founded: 1926. *FIFA:* 1952; *CONMEBOL:* 1952.
National Colours: All burgundy.

International matches 2015–16
Honduras (h) 0-3, Panama (h) 1-1, Paraguay (h) 0-1, Brazil (a) 1-3, Bolivia (a) 2-4, Ecuador (h) 1-3, Costa Rica (h) 1-0, Peru (a) 2-2, Chile (h) 1-4, Panama (a) 0-0, Costa Rica (a) 1-2, Guatemala (n) 1-1, Jamaica (n) 1-0, Uruguay (n) 1-0, Mexico (n) 1-1, Argentina (n) 1-4.

ASIA (AFC)

AFGHANISTAN
Afghanistan Football Federation, PO Box 128, Kabul.
Founded: 1933. *FIFA:* 1948; *AFC:* 1954. *National Colours:* All red.

International matches 2015–16
Thailand (a) 0-2, Japan (n) 0-6, Singapore (a) 0-1, Syria (n) 2-5, Cambodia (n) 3-0, Bangladesh (n) 4-0, Bhutan (n) 3-0, Maldives (n) 4-1, Sri Lanka (n) 5-0, India (a) 1-2, Japan (a) 0-5, Singapore (n) 2-1.

AUSTRALIA
Football Federation Australia Ltd, Locked Bag A4071, Sydney South, NSW 1235.
Founded: 1961. *FIFA:* 1963; *AFC:* 2006. *National Colours:* Gold shirts, green shorts, white socks.

International matches 2015–16
Bangladesh (h) 5-0, Tajikistan (a) 3-0, Jordan (a) 0-2, Kyrgyzstan (h) 3-0, Bangladesh (a) 4-0, Tajikistan (h) 7-0, Jordan (h) 5-1, England (a) 1-2, Greece (h) 1-0, Greece (h) 1-2.

BAHRAIN
Bahrain Football Association, PO Box 5464, Building 315, Road 2407, Block 934, East Riffa.
Founded: 1957. *FIFA:* 1968; *AFC:* 1969. *National Colours:* All red.

International matches 2015–16
Kuwait (a) 1-0, Uzbekistan (n) 0-0, Iraq (h) 0-0, Korea DPR (h) 2-2, Singapore (h) 2-0, Yemen (n) 0-0, Saudi Arabia (a) 0-3, Qatar (n) 0-0, Saudi Arabia (n) 4-1, Jordan (n) 1-0, Iran (n) 0-2, UAE (n) 1-2, Qatar (n) 2-1, Colombia (h) 0-6, Philippines (h) 2-1, Oman (h) 0-0, Thailand (a) 1-1, Philippines (h) 1-2, Korea DPR (h) 0-1, Yemen (n) 4-0, Uzbekistan (h) 0-4, Philippines (h) 2-0, Korea DPR (a) 0-2, Lebanon (h) 2-0, Yemen (h) 3-0, Uzbekistan (a) 0-1.

BANGLADESH
Bangladesh Football Federation, BFF House, Motijheel Commercial Area, Dhaka 1000.
Founded: 1972. *FIFA:* 1976; *AFC:* 1974. *National Colours:* Green shirts, white shorts, green socks.

International matches 2015–16
Malaysia (a) 0-0, Australia (a) 0-5, Jordan (h) 0-4, Kyrgyzstan (a) 0-2, Tajikistan (a) 0-5, Australia (h) 0-4, Nepal (h) 1-0, Afghanistan (n) 0-4, Maldives (n) 1-3, Bhutan (n) 3-0, Sri Lanka (h) 4-2, Nepal (h) 0-0, UAE (a) 1-6, Jordan (a) 0-8, Tajikistan (a) 0-5, Tajikistan (h) 0-1.

BHUTAN
Bhutan Football Federation, PO Box 365, Changiiji, Thimphu 11001.
Founded: 1983. *FIFA:* 2000; *AFC:* 2000. *National Colours:* Yellow and orange shirts, white shorts, orange socks.

International matches 2015–16
Cambodia (a) 0-2, Qatar (a) 0-15, Maldives (h) 3-4, Hong Kong (h) 0-1, China PR (a) 0-12, Qatar (h) 0-3, Maldives (n) 1-3, Afghanistan (n) 0-3, Bangladesh (n) 0-3, Maldives (a) 2-4.

BRUNEI
National Football Association of Brunei Darussalam, NFABD House, Jalan Pusat Persidangan, Bandar Seri Begawan BB4313.
Founded: 1959. *FIFA:* 1972; *AFC:* 1969. *National Colours:* Yellow and black shirts, white shorts, yellow socks.

International matches 2015–16
Cambodia (a) 1-6.

CAMBODIA
Football Federation of Cambodia, National Football Centre, Road Kabsrov Sangkat Samrongkrom, Khan Dangkor, Phnom Penh 2327 PPT3.
Founded: 1933. *FIFA:* 1954; *AFC:* 1954. *National Colours:* Red and blue shirts, blue shorts, red socks.

International matches 2015–16
Bhutan (h) 2-0, Laos (n) 1-2, Japan (a) 0-3, Syria (h) 0-6, Singapore (a) 1-2, Brunei (h) 6-1, Afghanistan (n) 0-3, Japan (h) 0-2, Maldives (n) 2-3, Syria (n) 0-6, Timor-Leste (h) 2-0, Chinese Taipei (a) 2-2, Chinese Taipei (h) 2-0.

CHINA PR
Football Association of the People's Republic of China, Building A, Dongjiudasha Mansion, Xizhaosi Street, Dongcheng, Beijing 100061.
Founded: 1924. *FIFA:* 1931, rejoined 1980; *AFC:* 1974. *National Colours:* All red.

International matches 2015–16
Korea Republic (h) 0-2, Korea DPR (h) 2-0, Japan (h) 1-1, Hong Kong (h) 0-0, Maldives (a) 3-0*, Qatar (a) 0-1, Bhutan (h) 12-0, Hong Kong (a) 0-0, Maldives (h) 4-0, Qatar (h) 2-0, Trinidad & Tobago (n) 4-2, Kazakhstan (n) 0-1.
* *Match played in China.*

CHINESE TAIPEI
Chinese Taipei Football Association, Room 210, 2F, 55 Chang Chi Street, Tatung, Taipei 10363.
Founded: 1936. *FIFA:* 1954; *AFC:* 1954. *National Colours:* All blue with white trim.

International matches 2015–16
Iraq (n) 1-5, Vietnam (h) 1-2, Macau (h) 5-1, Thailand (a) 2-4, Iraq (h) 0-2, Guam (h) 3-2, Vietnam (a) 1-4, Cambodia (h) 2-2, Cambodia (a) 0-2, Northern Mariana Islands† (n) 8-1, Mongolia (n) 2-0, Macau (h) 3-2.

GUAM
Guam Football Association, PO Box 20008, Barrigada, Guam 96921.
Founded: 1975. *FIFA:* 1996; *AFC:* 1996. *National Colours:* Blue shirts with white sleeves, blue shorts, blue socks.

International matches 2015–16
Iran (a) 0-6, Oman (h) 0-0, Turkmenistan (a) 0-1, India (a) 0-1, Iran (h) 0-6, Chinese Taipei (a) 2-3, Oman (a) 0-1.

HONG KONG
Hong Kong Football Association Ltd, 55 Fat Kwong Street, Ho Man Tin, Kowloon, Hong Kong.
Founded: 1914. *FIFA:* 1954; *AFC:* 1954. *National Colours:* All red with white trim.

International matches 2015–16
China PR (a) 0-0, Qatar (h) 2-3, Thailand (a) 0-1, Bhutan (a) 1-0, Myanmar (h) 5-0, Maldives (a) 1-0, Macau (h) 2-0, China PR (h) 0-0, Qatar (a) 0-2, Vietnam (a) 2-2 (3-4p), Myanmar (h) 0-3.

INDIA
All India Football Federation, Football House, Sector 19, Phase 1 Dwarka, New Delhi 110075.
Founded: 1937. *FIFA:* 1948; *AFC:* 1954. *National Colours:* Sky blue and navy shirts, navy shorts, sky blue and navy socks.

International matches 2015–16
Nepal (h) 0-0, Iran (h) 0-3, Turkmenistan (a) 1-2, Oman (a) 0-3, Guam (h) 1-0, Sri Lanka (h) 2-1, Nepal (h) 4-1, Maldives (h) 3-2, Afghanistan (h) 2-1, Iran (a) 0-4, Turkmenistan (h) 1-2, Laos (a) 1-0, Laos (a) 6-1.

INDONESIA
Football Association of Indonesia, Gelora Bung Karno Pintu X–XI, PO Box 2305, Senayan, Jakarta 10023.
Founded: 1930. *FIFA:* 1952; *AFC:* 1954. *National Colours:* Red shirts with green trim, red shorts, red socks.

International matches 2015–16
None played.

IRAN
Football Federation IR Iran, No. 4 Third St., Seoul Avenue, Tehran 19958-73591.
Founded: 1920. *FIFA:* 1948; *AFC:* 1954. *National Colours:* All white.

International matches 2015–16
Guam (h) 6-0, India (a) 3-0, Oman (a) 1-1, Japan (h) 1-1, Turkmenistan (h) 3-1, Guam (a) 6-0, India (h) 4-0, Oman (h) 2-0, FYR Macedonia (a) 3-1, Kyrgyzstan (h) 6-0.

IRAQ
Iraq Football Association, Al-Shaab Stadium, PO Box 484, Baghdad.
Founded: 1948. *FIFA:* 1950; *AFC:* 1970. *National Colours:* All white.

International matches 2015–16
Lebanon (a) 3-2, Chinese Taipei (n) 5-1, Thailand (a) 2-2, Jordan (a) 0-3, Vietnam (a) 1-1, Chinese Taipei (a) 2-0, Syria (n) 0-1, Thailand (n) 2-2, Vietnam (n) 1-0.

JAPAN
Japan Football Association, JFA House, Football Ave., Bunkyo-ku, Tokyo 113-8311.
Founded: 1921. *FIFA:* 1929, rejoined 1950; *AFC:* 1954. *National Colours:* Blue shirts, white shorts, blue socks.

International matches 2015–16
Korea DPR (n) 1-2, Korea Republic (n) 1-1, China PR (a) 1-1, Cambodia (a) 3-0, Afghanistan (n) 6-0, Syria (n) 3-0, Iran (a) 1-1, Singapore (a) 3-0, Cambodia (a) 2-0, Afghanistan (h) 5-0, Syria (n) 5-0, Bulgaria (h) 7-2, Bosnia-Herzegovina (h) 1-2.

JORDAN
Jordan Football Association, PO Box 962024, Al-Hussein Youth City, Amman 11196.
Founded: 1949. *FIFA:* 1956; *AFC:* 1970. *National Colours:* All white with red trim.

International matches 2015–16
Kyrgyzstan (h) 0-0, Bangladesh (a) 4-0, Iraq (h) 3-0, Australia (h) 2-0, Tajikistan (h) 3-0, Malta (n) 2-0, Kyrgyzstan (a) 0-1, Egypt (a) 1-0, Bangladesh (h) 8-0, Australia (a) 1-5, UAE (n) 3-1, Thailand (a) 0-2.

KOREA DPR
DPR Korea Football Association, Kumsongdong, Kwangbok Street, Mangyongdae, PO Box 818, Pyongyang.
Founded: 1945. *FIFA:* 1958; *AFC:* 1974. *National Colours:* All red.

International matches 2015–16
Japan (n) 2-1, China PR (a) 0-2, Korea Republic (n) 0-0, Bahrain (a) 1-0, Philippines (h) 0-0, Yemen (h) 1-0, Uzbekistan (a) 1-3, Bahrain (h) 2-0, Philippines (a) 2-3.

KOREA REPUBLIC
Korea Football Association, KFA House 21, Gyeonghuigung-gil 46, Jongno-Gu, Seoul 110-062.
Founded: 1933, 1948. *FIFA:* 1948; *AFC:* 1954. *National Colours:* Red shirts, blue shorts, red socks.

International matches 2015–16
China PR (a) 2-0, Japan (n) 1-1, Korea DPR (n) 0-0, Laos (h) 8-0, Lebanon (a) 3-0, Kuwait (a) 1-0, Jamaica (h) 3-0, Myanmar (h) 4-0, Laos (a) 5-0, Lebanon (h) 1-0, Thailand (a) 1-0, Kuwait (h) 3-0*, Spain (n) 1-6, Czech Republic (a) 2-1.
* *Match awarded 3-0 due to breach of FIFA rule.*

KUWAIT
Kuwait Football Association, Block 5, Street 101, Building 141A, Jabriya, PO Box Hawalli 4020, Kuwait 32071.
Founded: 1952. *FIFA:* 1964; *AFC:* 1964. *National Colours:* All blue with white trim.

International matches 2015–16
Myanmar (n) 9-0, Laos (a) 2-0, Korea Republic (h) 1-0, Lebanon (h) 0-0, Myanmar (n) 0-3*, Laos (h) 0-3*, Korea Republic (a) 0-3*.
* *Awarded to opponents due to breach of FIFA rule.*

KYRGYZSTAN
Football Federation of Kyrgyz Republic, Mederova Street 1 'B', PO Box 1484, Bishkek 720082.
Founded: 1992. *FIFA:* 1994; *AFC:* 1994. *National Colours:* Red shirts, red shorts, red socks with yellow tops.

International matches 2015–16
Jordan (a) 0-0, Tajikistan (h) 2-2, Bangladesh (h) 2-0, Australia (a) 0-3, Jordan (h) 1-0, Tajikistan (a) 1-0, Iran (a) 0-6.

LAOS
Lao Football Federation, FIFA Training Centre, Ban Houayhong, Chanthabuly, PO Box 1800, Vientiane 856-21.
Founded: 1951. *FIFA:* 1952; *AFC:* 1968. *National Colours:* All red with white trim.

International matches 2015–16
Cambodia (n) 2-1, Korea Republic (a) 0-8, Kuwait (n) 0-2, Malaysia (n) 1-3, Myanmar (n) 1-3, Lebanon (a) 0-7,

Korea Republic (h) 0-5, Kuwait (h) 3-0*, Nepal (h) 1-1, India (h) 0-1, India (a) 1-6.
* *Match awarded 3-0 due to breach of FIFA rule.*

LEBANON
Association Libanaise de Football, Verdun Street, Bristol Radwan Centre, PO Box 4732, Beirut.
Founded: 1933. *FIFA:* 1936; *AFC:* 1964. *National Colours:* All red.

International matches 2015–16
Iraq (h) 2-3, Palestine (h) 0-0, Korea Republic (h) 0-3, Myanmar (n) 2-0, Kuwait (a) 0-0, Laos (h) 7-0, FYR Macedonia (a) 1-0, Bahrain (a) 0-2, Uzbekistan (n) 0-2, Korea Republic (a) 0-1, Myanmar (h) 1-1.

MACAU
Associacao de Futebol de Macau, Avenida Wai Leong, Taipa University of Science and Technology, Football Field Block 1, Taipa.
Founded: 1939. *FIFA:* 1978; *AFC:* 1978. *National Colours:* White shirts, black shorts, green socks.

International matches 2015–16
Chinese Taipei (a) 1-5, Hong Kong (a) 0-2, Malaysia (a) 0-0, Mongolia (n) 2-2, Northern Mariana Islands† (n) 3-1, Chinese Taipei (n) 2-3.

MALAYSIA
Football Association of Malaysia, 3rd Floor, Wisma FAM, Jalan SS5A/9, Kelana Jaya, Petaling Jaya 47301, Selangor Darul Ehsan.
Founded: 1933. *FIFA:* 1954; *AFC:* 1954. *National Colours:* Yellow and black shirts, black shorts, black socks.

International matches 2015–16
Bangladesh (h) 0-0, UAE (a) 0-10, Saudi Arabia (h) 0-3, Laos (n) 3-1, Timor-Leste (a) 1-0, Palestine (n) 0-6, UAE (h) 1-2, Saudi Arabia (a) 0-2, Macau (h) 0-0, Myanmar (h) 0-0, Timor-Leste (h) 3-0, Timor-Leste (a) 3-0*, Papua New Guinea (a) 0-2, New Caledonia (a) 2-1, Fiji (a) 1-1.
* *Match played in Malaysia.*

MALDIVES
Football Association of Maldives, FAM House, Ujaalahingun, Male 20388.
Founded: 1982. *FIFA:* 1986; *AFC:* 1984. *National Colours:* Red and white shirts, white shorts, red socks.

International matches 2015–16
Seychelles (n) 2-1, Madagascar (n) 0-4, Philippines (a) 0-2, China PR (h) 0-3*, Bhutan (h) 4-3, Qatar (a) 0-4, Hong Kong (h) 0-1, Bhutan (n) 3-1, Bangladesh (n) 3-1, Afghanistan (n) 1-4, India (a) 2-3, Cambodia (n) 3-2, China PR (a) 0-4, Bhutan (h) 4-2, Yemen (h) 0-2, Yemen (n) 0-2.
* *Match played in China.*

MONGOLIA
Mongolian Football Federation, PO Box 259, 15th Khoroo, Khan-Uul, Ulan Bator 210646.
Founded: 1959. *FIFA:* 1998; *AFC:* 1998. *National Colours:* Red shirts, blue shorts, red socks.

International matches 2015–16
Macau (n) 3-2, Chinese Taipei (n) 0-2, Northern Mariana Islands† (n) 8-0.

MYANMAR
Myanmar Football Federation, National Football Training Centre, Waizayanta Road, Thuwunna, Thingankyun Township, Yangon 11070.
Founded: 1947. *FIFA:* 1948; *AFC:* 1954. *National Colours:* All red.

International matches 2015–16
Laos (h) 2-2*, Korea Republic (n) 0-2*, UAE (a) 0-1, Kuwait (n) 0-9, New Zealand (h) 1-1, Lebanon (n) 0-2, Laos (n) 3-1, Hong Kong (a) 0-5, Korea Republic (a) 0-4, Kuwait (n) 3-0†, Singapore (a) 1-2, Lebanon (a) 1-1, Malaysia (h) 0-0, Singapore (h) 0-1, Hong Kong (h) 3-0.
* *Played 11/16.06.2015, results omitted from last edition.*
† *Match awarded 3-0 due to breach of FIFA rule.*

NEPAL
All Nepal Football Association, ANFA House, Satdobato, Lalitpur-17, PO Box 12582, Kathmandu.
Founded: 1951. *FIFA:* 1972; *AFC:* 1954. *National Colours:* All red with white trim.

International matches 2015–16
India (a) 0-0, Bangladesh (a) 0-1, Sri Lanka (n) 0-1, India (a) 1-4, Sri Lanka (n) 1-0, Bangladesh (a) 0-0, Laos (a) 1-1.

OMAN
Oman Football Association, Seeb Sports Stadium, PO Box 3462, 112 Ruwi, Muscat.
Founded: 1978. *FIFA:* 1980; *AFC:* 1980. *National Colours:* All red.

International matches 2015–16
Yemen (h) 1-0, Turkmenistan (h) 3-1, Guam (a) 0-0, Syria (h) 2-1, Iran (h) 1-1, India (h) 3-0, New Zealand (h) 0-1, Turkmenistan (a) 1-2, Guam (h) 1-0, Iran (a) 0-2.

PAKISTAN
Pakistan Football Federation, PFF Football House, Ferozepur Road, Lahore 54600, Punjab.
Founded: 1947. *FIFA:* 1948; *AFC:* 1954. *National Colours:* All green and white.

International matches 2015–16
None played.

PALESTINE
Palestinian Football Association, Nr. Faisal Al-Husseini Stadium, PO Box 4373, Jerusalem-al-Ram.
Founded: 1928. *FIFA:* 1998; *AFC:* 1998. *National Colours:* All red with white trim.

International matches 2015–16
Lebanon (a) 0-0, UAE (h) 0-0, Timor-Leste (a) 1-1, Saudi Arabia (n) 0-0, Malaysia (n) 6-0, UAE (a) 0-2, Timor-Leste (h) 7-0.

PHILIPPINES
Philippine Football Federation, 27 Danny Floro–corner Capt. Henry Javier Streets, Oranbo, Pasig City 1600.
Founded: 1907. *FIFA:* 1930; *AFC:* 1954. *National Colours:* All blue with white trim.

International matches 2015–16
Maldives (h) 2-0, Uzbekistan (h) 1-5, Korea DPR (a) 0-0, Bahrain (a) 0-2, Yemen (h) 0-1, Uzbekistan (a) 0-1, Korea DPR (h) 3-2.

QATAR
Qatar Football Association, 28th Floor, Al Bidda Tower, Corniche Street, West Bay, PO Box 5333, Doha.
Founded: 1960. *FIFA:* 1972; *AFC:* 1974. *National Colours:* All burgundy.

International matches 2015–16
Singapore (h) 4-0, Bhutan (h) 15-0, Hong Kong (a) 3-2, China PR (h) 1-0, Maldives (h) 4-0, Turkey (h) 1-2, Bhutan (a) 3-0, Hong Kong (h) 2-0, China PR (a) 0-2, Albania (a) 1-3.

SAUDI ARABIA
Saudi Arabian Football Federation, Al Mather Quarter, Prince Faisal Bin Fahad Street, PO Box 5844, Riyadh 11432.
Founded: 1956. *FIFA:* 1956; *AFC:* 1972. *National Colours:* White shirts with green trim, white shorts, white socks.

International matches 2015–16
Timor-Leste (h) 7-0, Malaysia (a) 3-0, UAE (h) 2-1, Palestine (n) 0-0, Timor-Leste (a) 10-0, Malaysia (h) 2-0, UAE (a) 1-1.

SINGAPORE
Football Association of Singapore, Jalan Besar Stadium, 100 Tyrwhitt Road, Singapore 207542.
Founded: 1892. *FIFA:* 1956; *AFC:* 1954. *National Colours:* All red.

International matches 2015–16
Qatar (a) 0-4, Syria (n) 0-1, Afghanistan (h) 1-0, Cambodia (h) 2-1, Japan (h) 0-3, Syria (h) 1-2, Myanmar (h) 2-1, Afghanistan (n) 1-2, Myanmar (a) 1-0, Vietnam (n) 0-3.

SRI LANKA
Football Federation of Sri Lanka, 100/9 Independence Avenue, Colombo 07.
Founded: 1939. *FIFA:* 1952; *AFC:* 1954. *National Colours:* All red with white trim.

International matches 2015–16
Nepal (n) 1-0, India (a) 0-2, Afghanistan (n) 0-5, Bangladesh (a) 2-4, Nepal (n) 0-1.

SYRIA
Syrian Arab Federation for Football, Al Faihaa Sports Complex, PO Box 421, Damascus.
Founded: 1936. *FIFA:* 1937; *AFC:* 1970. *National Colours:* All red.

International matches 2015–16
Singapore (n) 1-0, Cambodia (a) 6-0, Oman (a) 1-2, Japan (n) 0-3, Afghanistan (n) 5-2, Singapore (a) 2-1, Iraq (n) 1-0, Cambodia (n) 6-0, Japan (a) 0-5, Vietnam (a) 0-2, Thailand (h) 2-2 (6-7p), UAE (n) 1-0.

TAJIKISTAN
Tajikistan Football Federation, 14/3 Ayni Street, Dushanbe 734 025.
Founded: 1936. *FIFA:* 1994; *AFC:* 1994. *National Colours:* Red, white and green shirts, white and red shorts, red and green socks.

International matches 2015–16
Australia (h) 0-3, Kyrgyzstan (a) 2-2, Jordan (a) 0-3, Bangladesh (h) 5-0, Australia (a) 0-7, Kyrgyzstan (h) 0-1, Bangladesh (h) 5-0, Bangladesh (a) 1-0.

THAILAND
Football Association of Thailand, National Stadium, Gate 3, Rama 1 Road, Patumwan, Bangkok 10330.
Founded: 1916. *FIFA:* 1925; *AFC:* 1954. *National Colours:* All red.

International matches 2015–16
Afghanistan (h) 2-0, Iraq (h) 2-2, Hong Kong (h) 1-0, Vietnam (a) 3-0, Chinese Taipei (h) 4-2, Iraq (n) 2-2, Korea Republic (h) 0-1, Syria (h) 2-2 (7-6p), Jordan (h) 2-0.

TIMOR-LESTE
Federacao Futebol de Timor-Leste, Campo Democracia, Avenida Bairro Formosa, Dili.
Founded: 2002. *FIFA:* 2005; *AFC:* 2005. *National Colours:* Red shirts with black trim, red shorts, red socks.

International matches 2015–16
Saudi Arabia (a) 0-7, Palestine (h) 1-1, Malaysia (h) 0-1, UAE (a) 0-8, Saudi Arabia (h) 0-10, Palestine (a) 0-7, Cambodia (a) 0-2, Malaysia (a) 0-3, Malaysia (h) 0-3*.
* *Match played in Malaysia.*

TURKMENISTAN
Football Federation of Turkmenistan, Stadium Kopetdag, 245 A. Niyazov Street, Ashgabat 744 001.
Founded: 1992. *FIFA:* 1994; *AFC:* 1994. *National Colours:* All white.

International matches 2015–16
Oman (a) 1-3, India (h) 2-1, Guam (h) 1-0, UAE (a) 1-5, Iran (a) 1-3, Oman (h) 2-1, India (a) 2-1.

UNITED ARAB EMIRATES
United Arab Emirates Football Association, Zayed Sports City, PO Box 916, Abu Dhabi.
Founded: 1971. *FIFA:* 1974; *AFC:* 1974. *National Colours:* All white with red trim.

International matches 2015–16
Myanmar (h) 1-0, Malaysia (h) 10-0, Palestine (a) 0-0, Saudi Arabia (a) 1-2, Turkmenistan (h) 5-1, Timor-Leste (h) 8-0, Malaysia (a) 2-1, Iceland (a) 2-1, Bangladesh (h) 6-1, Palestine (h) 2-0, Saudi Arabia (h) 1-1, UAE (n) 1-1, Jordan (n) 1-3, Syria (h) 0-1.

UZBEKISTAN
Uzbekistan Football Federation, Massiv Almazar Furkat Street 15/1, Tashkent 700 003.
Founded: 1946. *FIFA:* 1994; *AFC:* 1994. *National Colours:* All white with blue trim.

International matches 2015–16
Yemen (h) 1-0, Philippines (a) 5-1, Bahrain (a) 4-0, Korea DPR (h) 3-1, Yemen (n) 3-1, Lebanon (a) 2-0, Philippines (h) 1-0, Bahrain (a) 1-0, Canada (a) 1-2.

VIETNAM
Vietnam Football Federation, Le Quang Dao Street, Phu Do Ward, Nam Tu Liem District, Hanoi 844.
Founded: 1960 (NV). *FIFA:* 1952 (SV), 1964 (NV); *AFC:* 1954 (SV), 1978 (SRV). *National Colours:* All red.

International matches 2015–16
Chinese Taipei (a) 2-1, Iraq (h) 1-1, Thailand (h) 0-3, Chinese Taipei (h) 4-1, Iraq (n) 0-1, Syria (h) 2-0, Hong Kong (n) 2-2 (4-3p), Singapore (h) 3-0.

YEMEN

Yemen Football Association, Quarter of Sport Al Jeraf (Ali Mohsen Al-Muraisi Stadium), PO Box 908, Al-Thawra City, Sana'a.
Founded: 1940 (SY), 1962 (NY). *FIFA:* 1967 (SY), 1980 (NY); *AFC:* 1972 (SY), 1980 (NY). *National Colours:* Red shirts, white shorts, black socks.

International matches 2015–16
Oman (a) 0-1, Uzbekistan (a) 0-1, Bahrain (n) 0-4, Korea DPR (a) 0-1, Philippines (a) 1-0, Uzbekistan (n) 1-3, Bahrain (a) 0-3, Maldives (a) 2-0, Maldives (n) 2-0.

NORTH AND CENTRAL AMERICA AND CARIBBEAN (CONCACAF)

ANGUILLA

Anguilla Football Association, 2 Queen Elizabeth Avenue, PO Box 1318, The Valley, AI-2640.
Founded: 1990. *FIFA:* 1996; *CONCACAF:* 1996. *National Colours:* Turquoise and white shirts, orange and blue and shorts, turquoise and orange socks.

International matches 2015–16
Guyana (a) 0-7, Puerto Rico (h) 0-4.

ANTIGUA & BARBUDA

Antigua & Barbuda Football Association, Ground Floor, Sydney Walling Stand, Antigua Recreation Ground, PO Box 773, St John's.
Founded: 1928. *FIFA:* 1970; *CONCACAF:* 1972. *National Colours:* Yellow shirts with black, red and blue stripe, yellow shorts, yellow socks.

International matches 2015–16
Guatemala (h) 1-0, Guatemala (a) 0-2, St Vincent/Grenadines (a) 1-2, Aruba (h) 2-1, St Kitts & Nevis (a) 0-1, Puerto Rico (h) 1-2, Grenada (h) 5-1.

ARUBA

Arubaanse Voetbal Bond, Technical Centre Angel Botta, Shaba 24, PO Box 376, Noord.
Founded: 1932. *FIFA:* 1988; *CONCACAF:* 1986. *National Colours:* Yellow shirts with sky blue sleeves, yellow shorts, yellow socks.

International matches 2015–16
St Vincent/Grenadines (a) 0-2, St Vincent/Grenadines (h) 2-1, Antigua & Barbuda (a) 1-2, St Kitts & Nevis (h) 0-2.

BAHAMAS

Bahamas Football Association, Rosetta Street, PO Box N-8434, Nassau, NP.
Founded: 1967. *FIFA:* 1968; *CONCACAF:* 1981. *National Colours:* Yellow shirts, black shorts, yellow socks.

International matches 2015–16
None played.

BARBADOS

Barbados Football Association, Bottom Floor, ABC Marble Complex, PO Box 1362, Fontabelle, St Michael.
Founded: 1910. *FIFA:* 1968; *CONCACAF:* 1967. *National Colours:* Gold shirts with royal blue sleeves, gold shorts, white socks with gold tops.

International matches 2015–16
St Vincent/Grenadines (a) 2-2, Curacao (h) 1-0, Dominican Republic (a) 0-2.

BELIZE

Football Federation of Belize, 26 Hummingbird Highway, Belmopan, PO Box 1742, Belize City.
Founded: 1980. *FIFA:* 1986; *CONCACAF:* 1986. *National Colours:* Blue shirts with white trim, red shorts, blue socks with white tops.

International matches 2015–16
Canada (a) 0-3, Canada (h) 1-1.

BERMUDA

Bermuda Football Association, 48 Cedar Avenue, PO Box HM 745, Hamilton HM11.
Founded: 1928. *FIFA:* 1962; *CONCACAF:* 1967. *National Colours:* All red.

International matches 2015–16
St Kitts & Nevis (a) 0-3, Cuba (a) 1-2, French Guiana† (h) 2-1, Dominican Republic (h) 0-1, French Guiana† (a) 0-3.

BRITISH VIRGIN ISLANDS

British Virgin Islands Football Association, Botanic Station, PO Box 4269, Road Town, Tortola VG 1110.
Founded: 1974. *FIFA:* 1996; *CONCACAF:* 1996. *National Colours:* Green shirts with gold trim, gold shorts, green socks.

International matches 2015–16
Martinique† (a) 0-3, Dominica (h) 0-7.

US VIRGIN ISLANDS

USVI Soccer Federation Inc., 498D Strawberry, PO Box 2346, Christiansted, St Croix 00851.
Founded: 1987. *FIFA:* 1998; *CONCACAF:* 1987. *National Colours:* Gold shirts with royal blue trim, gold shorts, gold socks.

International matches 2015–16
Sint Maarten† (a) 2-1, Grenada (h) 1-2, Guyana (n) 0-7, Curacao (n) 0-7.

CANADA

Canadian Soccer Association, Place Soccer Canada, 237 Metcalfe Street, Ottawa, Ontario K2P 1R2.
Founded: 1912. *FIFA:* 1912; *CONCACAF:* 1961. *National Colours:* All red.

International matches 2015–16
El Salvador (n) 0-0, Jamaica (n) 0-1, Costa Rica (h) 0-0, Belize (h) 3-0, Belize (a) 1-1, Ghana (n) 1-1, Honduras (h) 1-0, El Salvador (a) 0-0, USA (a) 0-1, Mexico (h) 0-3, Mexico (a) 0-2, Azerbaijan (n) 1-1, Uzbekistan (n) 2-1.

CAYMAN ISLANDS

Cayman Islands Football Association, PO Box 178, Poindexter Road, Prospect, George Town, Grand Cayman KY1-1104.
Founded: 1966. *FIFA:* 1992; *CONCACAF:* 1990. *National Colours:* Red and white shirts, red shorts, red socks with white tops.

International matches 2015–16
None played.

COSTA RICA

Federacion Costarricense de Futbol, 600 mts sur del Cruce de la Panasonic, San Rafael de Alajuela, Radial a Santa Ana, San Jose 670-1000.
Founded: 1921. *FIFA:* 1927; *CONCACAF:* 1961. *National Colours:* Red shirts, blue shorts, white socks.

International matches 2015–16
Jamaica (n) 2-2, El Salvador (n) 1-1, Canada (a) 0-0, Mexico (n) 0-1, Brazil (h) 0-1, Uruguay (h) 1-0, South Africa (h) 0-1, USA (a) 1-0, Haiti (h) 1-0, Panama (a) 2-1, Nicaragua (h) 1-0, Venezuela (a) 0-1, Jamaica (a) 1-1, Jamaica (h) 3-0, Venezuela (h) 2-1, Paraguay (n) 0-0, USA (a) 0-4, Colombia (n) 3-2.

CUBA

Asociacion de Futbol de Cuba, Estadio Pedro Marrero Escuela Nacional de
Futbol – Mario Lopez, Avenida 41 no. 44 y 46, La Habana.
Founded: 1924. *FIFA:* 1932; *CONCACAF:* 1961. *National Colours:* All red.

International matches 2015–16
Mexico (n) 0-6, Trinidad & Tobago (n) 0-2, Guatemala (n) 1-0, USA (a) 0-6, Nicaragua (a) 0-5, Nicaragua (a) 0-1, Honduras (a) 0-2, Panama (h) 0-4*, Bermuda (h) 2-1, French Guiana† (a) 0-3.
* *Match played in Panama.*

CURACAO

Curacao Football Federation, Bonamweg 49, PO Box 341, Willemstad.
Founded: 1921 (Netherlands Antilles), 2010. *FIFA:* 1932, 2010; *CONCACAF:* 1961, 2010. *National Colours:* All blue.

International matches 2015–16
El Salvador (h) 0-1, El Salvador (a) 0-1, Barbados (a) 0-1, Dominican Republic (h) 2-1, Guyana (a) 5-2*, US Virgin Islands (h) 7-0.
* *Match played in Curacao.*

DOMINICA

Dominica Football Association, Patrick John Football House, Bath Estate, PO Box 1080, Roseau.
Founded: 1970. *FIFA:* 1994; *CONCACAF:* 1994. *National Colours:* Emerald green shirts with black sleeves, black shorts, emerald green socks.

International matches 2015–16
British Virgin Islands (a) 7-0, Martinique† (h) 1-4, Guadeloupe† (a) 1-2, Martinique† (h) 0-4.

DOMINICAN REPUBLIC
Federacion Dominicana de Futbol, Centro Olimpico Juan Pablo Duarte, Apartado Postal 1953, Santo Domingo.
Founded: 1953. *FIFA:* 1958; *CONCACAF:* 1964. *National Colours:* All navy blue.

International matches 2015–16
Curacao (a) 1-2, Barbados (h) 2-0, Bermuda (a) 2-2, French Guiana† (h) 1-1.

EL SALVADOR
Federacion Salvadorena de Futbol, Avenida Jose Matias Delgado, Frente al Centro Espanol Colonia Escalon, Zona 10, San Salvador 1029.
Founded: 1935. *FIFA:* 1938; *CONCACAF:* 1961. *National Colours:* All blue.

International matches 2015–16
Canada (n) 0-0, Costa Rica (n) 1-1, Jamaica (n) 0-1, Curacao (a) 1-0, Curacao (h) 1-0, Haiti (n) 1-3, Guatemala (n) 1-1 (2-4p), Mexico (a) 0-3, Canada (n) 0-0, Panama (a) 0-1, Guatemala (a) 0-1, Nicaragua (a) 1-1, Honduras (h) 2-2, Honduras (a) 0-2, Peru (n) 1-3, Armenia (n) 0-4.

GRENADA
Grenada Football Association, National Stadium, PO Box 326, St George's.
Founded: 1924. *FIFA:* 1978; *CONCACAF:* 1969. *National Colours:* Yellow shirts, yellow shorts, green socks.

International matches 2015–16
Haiti (h) 1-3, Haiti (a) 0-3, Trinidad & Tobago (h) 2-2, Sint Maarten† (h) 5-0, US Virgin Islands (a) 2-1, Puerto Rico (h) 3-3 (3-4p), Antigua & Barbuda (a) 1-5.

GUATEMALA
Federacion Nacional de Futbol de Guatemala, 2a Calle 15-57, Zona 15, Boulevard Vista Hermosa, Guatemala City 01015.
Founded: 1919. *FIFA:* 1946; *CONCACAF:* 1961. *National Colours:* Blue shirts with white sash, blue shorts, blue socks.

International matches 2015–16
Trinidad & Tobago (n) 1-3, Mexico (n) 0-0, Cuba (n) 0-1, Antigua & Barbuda (a) 0-1, Antigua & Barbuda (h) 2-0, Honduras (a) 1-1, El Salvador (n) 2-1 (4-2p), Trinidad & Tobago (h) 1-2, St Vincent/Grenadines (a) 4-0, Honduras (h) 3-1, El Salvador (h) 1-0, USA (h) 2-0, USA (a) 0-4, Armenia (n) 1-7, Venezuela (n) 1-1.

GUYANA
Guyana Football Federation, Lot 17, Dadanawa Street Section 'K', Campbellville, PO Box 10727, Georgetown.
Founded: 1902. *FIFA:* 1970; *CONCACAF:* 1961. *National Colours:* Green shirts with white trim, green shorts, green socks.

International matches 2015–16
Suriname (h) 2-0, Anguilla (h) 7-0, Puerto Rico (a) 1-0, Curacao (a) 2-5, US Virgin Islands (a) 7-0.

HAITI
Federation Haitienne de Football, Stade Sylvio Cator, Rue Oswald Durand, Port-au-Prince.
Founded: 1904. *FIFA:* 1933; *CONCACAF:* 1961. *National Colours:* Blue shirts, red shorts, blue socks.

International matches 2015–16
Panama (n) 1-1, USA (a) 0-1, Honduras (n) 1-0, Jamaica (n) 0-1, Grenada (a) 3-1, Grenada (h) 3-0, El Salvador (n) 3-1, Costa Rica (n) 0-1, Jamaica (h) 0-1, Trinidad & Tobago (n) 1-0, Panama (h) 0-0, Panama (a) 0-1, Colombia (n) 1-3, Peru (n) 0-1, Brazil (n) 1-7, Ecuador (n) 0-4.

HONDURAS
Federacion Nacional Autonoma de Futbol de Honduras, Colonia Florencia Norte, Edificio Plaza America Ave. Roble, 1 y 2 Nivle, PO Box 827, Tegucigalpa 504.
Founded: 1935. *FIFA:* 1946; *CONCACAF:* 1961. *National Colours:* All white.

International matches 2015–16
USA (a) 1-2, Panama (n) 1-1, Haiti (n) 0-1, Venezuela (a) 3-0, Ecuador (a) 0-2, Guatemala (h) 1-1, South Africa

(h) 1-1, Canada (a) 0-1, Mexico (h) 0-2, Cuba (h) 2-0, Nicaragua (a) 3-1, Guatemala (a) 1-3, El Salvador (a) 2-2, El Salvador (h) 2-0, Argentina (a) 0-1.

JAMAICA
Jamaica Football Federation Ltd, 20 St Lucia Crescent, Kingston 5.
Founded: 1910. *FIFA:* 1962; *CONCACAF:* 1963. *National Colours:* Gold shirts, black shorts, gold socks with green tops.

International matches 2015–16
Argentina (n) 0-1*, Costa Rica (n) 2-2, Canada (n) 1-0, El Salvador (n) 1-0, Haiti (n) 1-0, USA (a) 2-1, Mexico (n) 1-3, Nicaragua (h) 2-3, Nicaragua (a) 2-0, Korea Republic (a) 0-3, Panama (h) 0-2, Haiti (a) 1-0, Costa Rica (h) 1-1, Costa Rica (a) 0-3, Chile (a) 2-1, Venezuela (n) 0-1, Mexico (n) 0-2, Uruguay (n) 0-3.
* *Played 20.06.2015, result omitted from last edition.*

MEXICO
Federacion Mexicana de Futbol Asociacion, A.C., Colima No. 373, Colonia Roma, Delegacion Cuauhtemoc, Mexico DF 06700.
Founded: 1927. *FIFA:* 1929; *CONCACAF:* 1961. *National Colours:* All black with green trim.

International matches 2015–16
Cuba (n) 6-0, Guatemala (n) 0-0, Trinidad & Tobago (n) 4-4, Costa Rica (n) 1-0, Panama (n) 2-1, Jamaica (n) 3-1, Trinidad & Tobago (n) 3-3, Argentina (n) 2-2, USA (a) 3-2, Panama (n) 1-0, El Salvador (h) 3-0, Honduras (a) 2-0, Senegal (n) 2-0, Canada (a) 3-0, Canada (h) 2-0, Paraguay (n) 1-0, Chile (n) 1-0, Uruguay (n) 3-1, Jamaica (h) 2-0, Venezuela (n) 1-1, Chile (n) 0-7.

MONTSERRAT
Montserrat Football Association Inc., PO Box 505, Blakes, Montserrat.
Founded: 1994. *FIFA:* 1996; *CONCACAF:* 1996. *National Colours:* Black shirts with red stripes, black shorts, black socks.

International matches 2015–16
None played.

NICARAGUA
Federacion Nicaraguense de Futbol, Porton Principal del Hospital Bautista 1 Cuadra Abajo, 1 Cuadra al Sur y 1/2 Cuadra Abajo, Apartado Postal 976, Managua.
Founded: 1931. *FIFA:* 1950; *CONCACAF:* 1961. *National Colours:* All blue.

International matches 2015–16
Jamaica (a) 3-2, Jamaica (h) 0-2, Trinidad & Tobago (a) 0-0, Cuba (h) 5-0, Cuba (h) 1-0, Costa Rica (a) 0-1, Honduras (h) 1-3, El Salvador (h) 1-1, Panama (h) 1-0.

PANAMA
Federacion Panamena de Futbol, Ciudad Deportiva Irving Saladino, Corregimiento de Juan Diaz, Apartado Postal 0827-00391, Zona 8, Panama City.
Founded: 1937. *FIFA:* 1938; *CONCACAF:* 1961. *National Colours:* All red.

International matches 2015–16
Haiti (n) 1-1, Honduras (n) 1-1, USA (a) 1-1, Trinidad & Tobago (n) 1-1 (6-5p), Mexico (n) 1-2, USA (a) 1-1 (3-2p), Uruguay (n) 0-1, Venezuela (a) 1-1, Trinidad & Tobago (h) 1-2, Mexico (a) 0-1, Jamaica (a) 2-0, Costa Rica (h) 1-2, Cuba (a) 4-0*, El Salvador (h) 1-0, Nicaragua (a) 0-1, Haiti (a) 0-0, Haiti (h) 1-0, Venezuela (h) 0-0, Brazil (n) 0-2, Bolivia (n) 2-1, Argentina (n) 0-5, Chile (n) 2-4.
* *Match played in Panama.*

PUERTO RICO
Federacion Puertorriquena de Futbol, PO Box 367567, San Juan 00936.
Founded: 1940. *FIFA:* 1960; *CONCACAF:* 1961. *National Colours:* Red and white striped shirts, blue shorts, blue socks.

International matches 2015–16
Anguilla (a) 4-0, Guyana (h) 0-1, USA (h) 1-3, Grenada (a) 3-3 (4-3p), Antigua & Barbuda (h) 2-1.

ST KITTS & NEVIS
St Kitts & Nevis Football Association, PO Box 465, Lozack Road, Basseterre.
Founded: 1932. *FIFA:* 1992; *CONCACAF:* 1992. *National Colours:* Green and red shirts, red shorts, green socks.

International matches 2015–16
Andorra (a) 1-0, Estonia (a) 0-3, Bermuda (h) 3-0, Aruba (a) 2-0, Antigua & Barbuda (h) 1-0, Suriname (h) 1-0, St Vincent/Grenadines (a) 1-0.

ST LUCIA
St Lucia National Football Association, Barnard Hill, PO Box 255, Castries.
Founded: 1979. *FIFA:* 1988; *CONCACAF:* 1986. *National Colours:* Sky blue shirts with yellow sleeves, sky blue shorts, white socks.

International matches 2015–16
None played.

ST VINCENT & THE GRENADINES
St Vincent & the Grenadines Football Federation, PO Box 1278, Nichols Building (2nd Floor), Bentinck Square, Victoria Park, Kingstown.
Founded: 1979. *FIFA:* 1988; *CONCACAF:* 1986. *National Colours:* Yellow shirts, blue shorts, blue socks.

International matches 2015–16
Barbados (h) 2-2, Aruba (h) 2-0, Aruba (a) 1-2, Antigua & Barbuda (h) 2-1, USA (a) 1-6, Guatemala (h) 0-4, Trinidad & Tobago (h) 2-3, Trinidad & Tobago (a) 0-6, Suriname (a) 1-2, St Kitts & Nevis (h) 0-1.

SURINAME
Surinaamse Voetbal Bond, Letitia Vriesdelaan 7, PO Box 1223, Paramaribo.
Founded: 1920. *FIFA:* 1929; *CONCACAF:* 1961. *National Colours:* White shirts with green cuffs, white shorts, white socks.

International matches 2015–16
Guyana (a) 0-2, Guadeloupe† (a) 0-0, Guadeloupe† (h) 3-2, St Kitts & Nevis (a) 0-1, St Vincent/Grenadines (h) 2-1.

TRINIDAD & TOBAGO
Trinidad & Tobago Football Association, 24–26 Dundonald Street, PO Box 400, Port of Spain.
Founded: 1908. *FIFA:* 1964; *CONCACAF:* 1962. *National Colours:* Red shirts with black trim, black shorts with red trim, red socks.

International matches 2015–16
Guatemala (n) 3-1, Cuba (n) 2-0, Mexico (n) 4-4, Panama (n) 1-1 (5-6p), Mexico (n) 3-3, Panama (a) 2-1, Nicaragua (h) 0-0, Guatemala (a) 2-1, USA (h) 0-0, Haiti (n) 0-1, Grenada (a) 2-2, St Vincent/Grenadines (a) 3-2, St Vincent/Grenadines (h) 6-0, Peru (a) 0-4, Uruguay (n) 1-3, China PR (a) 2-4.

TURKS & CAICOS ISLANDS
Turks & Caicos Islands Football Association, TCIFA National Academy, Venetian Road, PO Box 626, Providenciales.
Founded: 1996. *FIFA:* 1998; *CONCACAF:* 1996. *National Colours:* All white.

International matches 2015–16
None played.

UNITED STATES
US Soccer Federation, US Soccer House, 1801 S. Prairie Avenue, Chicago, IL 60616.
Founded: 1913. *FIFA:* 1914; *CONCACAF:* 1961. *National Colours:* All white.

International matches 2015–16
Honduras (h) 2-1, Haiti (h) 1-0, Panama (h) 1-1, Cuba (h) 6-0, Jamaica (h) 1-2, Panama (h) 1-1 (2-3p), Peru (h) 2-1, Brazil (h) 1-4, Mexico (h) 2-3, Costa Rica (h) 0-1, St Vincent/Grenadines (h) 6-1, Trinidad & Tobago (a) 0-0, Iceland (h) 3-2, Canada (h) 1-0, Guatemala (a) 0-2, Guatemala (h) 4-0, Puerto Rico (a) 3-1, Ecuador (h) 1-0, Bolivia (h) 4-0, Colombia (h) 0-2, Costa Rica (h) 4-0, Paraguay (h) 1-0, Ecuador (h) 2-1, Argentina (n) 0-4, Colombia (h) 0-1.

OCEANIA (OFC)

AMERICAN SAMOA
Football Federation American Samoa, PO Box 982 413, Pago Pago AS 96799.
Founded: 1984. *FIFA:* 1998; *OFC:* 1998. *National Colours:* Navy blue shirts, red shorts, white socks.

International matches 2015–16
Fiji (a) 0-6, Samoa (n) 2-3, Tonga (a) 2-1, Cook Islands (n) 2-0.

COOK ISLANDS
Cook Islands Football Association, Matavera Main Road, PO Box 29, Avarua, Rarotonga.
Founded: 1971. *FIFA:* 1994; *OFC:* 1994. *National Colours:* Green shirts with white trim, green shorts, white socks.

International matches 2015–16
Tonga (a) 3-0, Samoa (n) 1-0, American Samoa (n) 0-2.

FIJI
Fiji Football Association, PO Box 2514, Government Buildings, Suva.
Founded: 1938. *FIFA:* 1964; *OFC:* 1966. *National Colours:* White shirts, black shorts, white socks.

International matches 2015–16
Tahiti (n) 0-0, New Caledonia (n) 1-2, Papua New Guinea (a) 1-2, Tonga (h) 5-0, American Samoa (h) 6-0, Vanuatu (a) 1-1, Vanuatu (a) 1-2, New Zealand (n) 1-3, Solomon Islands (n) 1-0, Vanuatu (n) 2-3, Malaysia (h) 1-1.

NEW CALEDONIA
Federation Caledonienne de Football, 7 bis, Rue Suffren Quartier latin, BP 560, Noumea 99845.
Founded: 1928. *FIFA:* 2004; *OFC:* 2004. *National Colours:* Grey shirts, red shorts, grey socks.

International matches 2015–16
Solomon Islands (n) 1-0, New Zealand (n) 0-5, Fiji (n) 2-1, Tahiti (n) 2-0, Vanuatu (a) 1-2, Papua New Guinea (a) 1-1, Samoa (n) 7-0, Tahiti (n) 1-1, New Zealand (n) 0-1, Malaysia (h) 1-2.

NEW ZEALAND
New Zealand Football, PO Box 301-043, Albany, Auckland.
Founded: 1891. *FIFA:* 1948; *OFC:* 1966. *National Colours:* All white.

International matches 2015–16
Solomon Islands (n) 2-0, Papua New Guinea (a) 1-0, New Caledonia (n) 5-0, Myanmar (a) 1-2, Oman (a) 1-0, Fiji (n) 3-1, Vanuatu (n) 5-0, Solomon Islands (n) 1-0, New Caledonia (n) 1-0, Papua New Guinea (a) 0-0 (4-2p).

PAPUA NEW GUINEA
Papua New Guinea Football Association, PO Box 957, Lae 411, Morobe Province.
Founded: 1962. *FIFA:* 1966; *OFC:* 1966. *National Colours:* Red shirts with black trim, red shorts, yellow socks.

International matches 2015–16
New Zealand (h) 0-1, Solomon Islands (h) 2-1, Tahiti (h) 1-2, Fiji (h) 2-1, Solomon Islands (a) 0-2, Solomon Islands (a) 2-1, New Caledonia (h) 1-1, Tahiti (h) 2-2, Samoa (h) 8-0, Solomon Islands (h) 2-1, New Zealand (h) 0-0 (2-4p), Malaysia (h) 2-0.

SAMOA
Football Federation Samoa, PO Box 1682, Tuanimato, Apia.
Founded: 1968. *FIFA:* 1986; *OFC:* 1986. *National Colours:* Blue, white and red shirts, blue and white shorts, red and blue socks.

International matches 2015–16
American Samoa (n) 3-2, Cook Islands (n) 0-1, Tonga (a) 3-0, Tahiti (n) 0-4, New Caledonia (n) 0-7, Papua New Guinea (a) 0-8.

SOLOMON ISLANDS
Solomon Islands Football Federation, Allan Boso Complex, Panatina Academy, PO Box 584, Honiara.
Founded: 1978. *FIFA:* 1988; *OFC:* 1988. *National Colours:* Green, gold and blue shirts, blue and white shorts, white and blue socks.

International matches 2015–16
New Zealand (n) 0-2, New Caledonia (n) 0-1, Papua New Guinea (a) 1-2, Papua New Guinea (h) 2-0, Papua New Guinea (h) 1-2, Vanuatu (n) 1-0, Fiji (n) 0-1, New Zealand (n) 0-1, Papua New Guinea (a) 1-2.

TAHITI
Federation Tahitienne de Football, Rue Gerald Coppenrath, Complexe de Fautaua, PO Box 50358, Pirae 98716.
Founded: 1989. *FIFA:* 1990; *OFC:* 1990. *National Colours:* White shirts with red trim, white shorts, white socks.

International matches 2015–16
Vanuatu (n) 2-1, Fiji (n) 0-0, Papua New Guinea (a) 2-1, New Caledonia (n) 0-2, Samoa (n) 4-0, Papua New Guinea (a) 2-2, New Caledonia (n) 1-1.

TONGA
Tonga Football Association, Loto-Tonga Soka Centre, Valungafulu Road, Atele, PO Box 852, Nuku'alofa.
Founded: 1965. *FIFA:* 1994; *OFC:* 1994. *National Colours:* All red.

International matches 2015–16
Fiji (a) 0-5, Cook Islands (n) 0-3, American Samoa (h) 1-2, Samoa (h) 0-3.

VANUATU
Vanuatu Football Federation, VFF House, Lini Highway, PO Box 266, Port Vila.
Founded: 1934. *FIFA:* 1988; *OFC:* 1988. *National Colours:* Gold and white shirts with green sleeves, green shorts, black socks with white tops.

International matches 2015–16
Tahiti (n) 1-2, Fiji (h) 1-1, Fiji (h) 2-1, New Caledonia (h) 2-1, Solomon Islands (n) 0-1, New Zealand (n) 0-5, Fiji (n) 3-2.

AFRICA (CAF)

ALGERIA
Federation Algerienne De Football, Chemin Ahmed Ouaked, BP 39, Dely-Ibrahim, Algiers 16000.
Founded: 1962. *FIFA:* 1963; *CAF:* 1964. *National Colours:* All white.

International matches 2015–16
Lesotho (a) 3-1, Guinea (h) 1-2, Senegal (h) 1-0, Tanzania (a) 2-2, Tanzania (h) 7-0, Ethiopia (h) 7-1, Ethiopia (a) 3-3, Seychelles (a) 2-0.

ANGOLA
Federacao Angolana de Futetbol, Senado de Compl. da Cidadela Desportiva, BP 3449, Luanda.
Founded: 1979. *FIFA:* 1980; *CAF:* 1980. *National Colours:* Red shirts with yellow trim, black shorts, red socks.

International matches 2015–16
Madagascar (a) 0-0, South Africa (a) 2-0, South Africa (h) 1-2, South Africa (h) 1-3, South Africa (h) 0-1, Cameroon (n) 0-1, Congo DR (n) 2-4, Ethiopia (n) 2-1, Congo DR (a) 1-2, Congo DR (h) 0-2, Central African Republic (a) 1-3, Malawi (n) 0-3, Lesotho (n) 0-2, Mauritius (n) 0-2.

BENIN
Federation Beninoise de Football, Rue du boulevard Djassain, BP 112, 3-eme Arrondissement de Porto-Novo 01.
Founded: 1962. *FIFA:* 1962; *CAF:* 1962. *National Colours:* All yellow.

International matches 2015–16
Mali (h) 1-1, Congo (a) 1-2, Burkina Faso (h) 2-1, Burkina Faso (a) 0-2, South Sudan (a) 2-1, South Sudan (h) 4-1, Equatorial Guinea (h) 2-1.

BOTSWANA
Botswana Football Association, PO Box 1396, Gaborone.
Founded: 1970. *FIFA:* 1978; *CAF:* 1976. *National Colours:* Blue, white and black shirts, blue shorts, blue socks.

International matches 2015–16
Burkina Faso (h) 1-0, Ethiopia (h) 2-3, Eritrea (a) 2-0, Eritrea (h) 3-1, Mali (h) 2-1, Mali (a) 0-2, Comoros (a) 0-1, Comoros (h) 2-1, Lesotho (h) 2-1, Uganda (h) 1-2, Namibia (h) 1-1 (5-4p), Congo DR (n) 0-0 (5-4p), South Africa (n) 2-3.

BURKINA FASO
Federation Burkinabe de Foot-Ball, Centre Technique National Ouaga 2000, BP 57, Ouagadougou 01.
Founded: 1960. *FIFA:* 1964; *CAF:* 1964. *National Colours:* Green shirts with red sleeves, green shorts, green socks.

International matches 2015–16
Niger (a) 0-0, Botswana (a) 0-1, Mali (n) 1-4, Nigeria (a) 0-2, Nigeria (h) 0-0, Benin (a) 1-2, Benin (h) 2-0, Egypt (a) 0-2, Uganda (h) 1-0, Uganda (a) 0-0, Comoros (a) 1-0.

BURUNDI
Federation de Football du Burundi, Avenue Muyinga, BP 3426, Bujumbura.
Founded: 1948. *FIFA:* 1972; *CAF:* 1972. *National Colours:* All red with white trim.

International matches 2015–16
Niger (h) 2-0, Seychelles (a) 1-0, Seychelles (h) 2-0, Ethiopia (h) 2-0, Ethiopia (a) 0-3, Congo DR (h) 2-3, Congo DR (a) 2-2, Zanzibar† (n) 1-0, Kenya (n) 1-1, Uganda (n) 0-1, Namibia (h) 1-3, Namibia (a) 3-1, Senegal (h) 0-2.

CAMEROON
Federation Camerounaise de Football, Avenue du 27 aout 1940, Tsinga-Yaounde, BP 1116, Yaounde.
Founded: 1959. *FIFA:* 1962; *CAF:* 1963. *National Colours:* Green shirts, red shorts, yellow socks.

International matches 2015–16
Gambia (a) 1-0, Nigeria (n) 0-3, Congo (h) 0-0, Congo (a) 1-0, Niger (a) 3-0, Niger (h) 0-0, Rwanda (a) 1-1, Angola (n) 1-0, Ethiopia (n) 0-0, Congo DR (n) 3-1, Ivory Coast (n) 0-3, South Africa (h) 2-2, South Africa (a) 0-0, France (a) 2-3, Mauritania (a) 1-0.

CAPE VERDE ISLANDS
Federacao Caboverdiana de Futebol, Praia Cabo Verde, FCF CX, PO Box 234, Praia.
Founded: 1982. *FIFA:* 1986; *CAF:* 2000. *National Colours:* All blue with white trim.

International matches 2015–16
Libya (n) 2-1, Kenya (a) 0-1, Kenya (h) 2-0, Morocco (h) 0-1, Morocco (a) 0-2, Sao Tome & Principe (a) 2-1.

CENTRAL AFRICAN REPUBLIC
Federation Centrafricaine de Football, Avenue des Martyrs, BP 344, Bangui.
Founded: 1961. *FIFA:* 1964; *CAF:* 1965. *National Colours:* All white with blue trim.

International matches 2015–16
Congo DR (h) 2-0, Madagascar (h) 0-3, Madagascar (a) 2-2, Madagascar (a) 1-1, Madagascar (h) 2-1, Angola (h) 3-1.

CHAD
Federation Tchadienne de Football, BP 886, N'Djamena.
Founded: 1962. *FIFA:* 1964; *CAF:* 1964. *National Colours:* Blue shirts, yellow shorts, red socks.

International matches 2015–16
Sierra Leone (h) 1-0, Sierra Leone (n) 1-2, Gabon (h) 0-2, Gabon (a) 1-0, Egypt (h) 1-0, Egypt (a) 0-4.

COMOROS
Federation Comorienne de Football, Route d'Itsandra, BP 798, Moroni.
Founded: 1979. *FIFA:* 2005; *CAF:* 2003. *National Colours:* All green.

International matches 2015–16
Uganda (h) 0-1, Lesotho (h) 0-0, Lesotho (a) 1-1, Ghana (h) 0-0, Ghana (a) 0-2, Botswana (h) 1-0, Botswana (a) 1-2, Burkina Faso (h) 0-1.

CONGO
Federation Congolaise de Football, 80 Rue Eugene Etienne, Centre Ville, BP Box 11, Brazzaville 00 242.
Founded: 1962. *FIFA:* 1964; *CAF:* 1965. *National Colours:* Green shirts, yellow shorts, red socks.

International matches 2015–16
Ghana (n) 2-3, Guinea-Bissau (a) 4-2, Benin (h) 2-1, Cameroon (a) 0-0, Cameroon (h) 0-1, Ethiopia (a) 4-3, Ethiopia (h) 2-1, Zambia (a) 1-1, Zambia (h) 1-1, Morocco (a) 0-2, Kenya (a) 1-2.

CONGO DR
Federation Congolaise de Football-Association, 31 Avenue de la Justice Kinshasa-Gombe, BP 1284, Kinshasa 1.
Founded: 1919. *FIFA:* 1964; *CAF:* 1964. *National Colours:* Blue shirts with red sleeves, blue shorts, blue socks.

International matches 2015–16
Central African Republic (a) 0-2, Nigeria (n) 2-0, Gabon (n) 2-1, Burundi (a) 3-2, Burundi (h) 2-2, Rwanda (a) 0-1, Ethiopia (n) 3-0, Angola (n) 4-2, Cameroon (n) 1-3, Rwanda (a) 2-1, Guinea (n) 1-1 (5-4p), Mali (n) 3-0,

Angola (h) 2-1, Angola (a) 2-0, Romania (n) 1-1, Madagascar (a) 6-1, Mozambique (n) 1-0, Botswana (n) 0-0 (4-5p), Swaziland (n) 0-1.

DJIBOUTI

Federation Djiboutienne de Football, Centre Technique National, BP 2694, Ville de Djibouti.
Founded: 1979. *FIFA:* 1994; *CAF:* 1994. *National Colours:* Green shirts, white shorts, blue socks.

International matches 2015–16
Togo (h) 0-2, Swaziland (h) 0-6, Swaziland (a) 1-2, South Sudan (n) 0-2, Malawi (n) 0-3, Sudan (n) 0-4, Liberia (h) 0-1, Liberia (a) 0-5, Tunisia (h) 0-3.

EGYPT

Egyptian Football Association, 5 Gabalaya Street, Gezira El Borg Post Office, Cairo.
Founded: 1921. *FIFA:* 1923; *CAF:* 1957. *National Colours:* Red shirts with white trim, white shorts, black socks.

International matches 2015–16
Zambia (n) 3-0, Chad (a) 0-1, Chad (h) 4-0, Jordan (h) 0-1, Libya (h) 2-0, Burkina Faso (h) 2-0, Nigeria (a) 1-1, Nigeria (h) 1-0, Tanzania (a) 2-0.

EQUATORIAL GUINEA

Federacion Ecuatoguineana de Futbol, Avenida de Hassan II, Apartado de correo 1017, Malabo.
Founded: 1957. *FIFA:* 1986; *CAF:* 1986. *National Colours:* All red.

International matches 2015–16
South Sudan (a) 0-1, Kosovo‡ (a) 0-2, Morocco (a) 0-2, Morocco (h) 1-0, Mali (a) 0-1, Mali (h) 0-1, Benin (a) 1-2.

ERITREA

Eritrean National Football Federation, Sematat Avenue 29–31, PO Box 3665, Asmara.
Founded: 1996. *FIFA:* 1998; *CAF:* 1998. *National Colours:* Blue shirts, red shorts, green socks.

International matches 2015–16
Botswana (h) 0-2, Botswana (h) 1-3.

ETHIOPIA

Ethiopia Football Federation, Addis Ababa Stadium, PO Box 1080, Addis Ababa.
Founded: 1943. *FIFA:* 1952; *CAF:* 1957. *National Colours:* Green shirts, yellow shorts, red socks.

International matches 2015–16
Rwanda (a) 1-3, Seychelles (a) 1-1, Botswana (a) 3-2, Sao Tome & Principe (a) 0-1, Sao Tome & Principe (h) 3-0, Burundi (a) 0-2, Burundi (h) 3-0, Congo (h) 3-4, Congo (a) 1-2, Rwanda (h) 0-1, Somalia (h) 2-0, Tanzania (h) 1-1, Tanzania (h) 1-1 (4-3p), Uganda (h) 0-0 (3-5p), Sudan (h) 1-1 (5-4p), Congo DR (n) 0-3, Cameroon (n) 0-0, Angola (n) 1-2, Algeria (a) 1-7, Algeria (h) 3-3, Lesotho (a) 2-1.

GABON

Federation Gabonaise de Football, BP 181, Libreville.
Founded: 1962. *FIFA:* 1966; *CAF:* 1967. *National Colours:* Yellow shirts, blue shorts with yellow trim, blue socks with yellow tops.

International matches 2015–16
Sudan (h) 4-0, Zambia (a) 1-1, Rwanda (a) 1-0, Tunisia (a) 3-3, Congo DR (n) 1-2, Chad (a) 2-0, Chad (h) 0-1, Mozambique (a) 0-1, Mozambique (h) 1-0 (4-3p), Uganda (a) 1-1, Morocco (n) 0-2, Rwanda (a) 1-2, Ivory Coast (n) 1-4, Sierra Leone (h) 2-1, Sierra Leone (a) 0-1, Mauritania (n) 0-2, Ivory Coast (a) 1-2.

GAMBIA

Gambia Football Association, Kafining Layout, Bakau, PO Box 523, Banjul.
Founded: 1952. *FIFA:* 1968; *CAF:* 1966. *National Colours:* Red shirts, blue shorts, green socks.

International matches 2015–16
Cameroon (h) 0-1, Namibia (h) 1-1, Namibia (a) 1-2, Mauritania (a) 1-2, Mauritania (h) 0-0, Zambia (h) 0-0, South Africa (h) 2-1.

GHANA

Ghana Football Association, General Secretariat, South East Ridge, PO Box AN 19338, Accra.
Founded: 1957. *FIFA:* 1958; *CAF:* 1958. *National Colours:* All white.

International matches 2015–16
Congo (a) 3-2, Rwanda (a) 1-0, Canada (n) 1-1, Ivory Coast (h) 2-1, Ivory Coast (a) 0-1, Comoros (a) 0-0, Comoros (h) 2-0, Mozambique (h) 3-1, Mozambique (a) 0-0, Mauritius (h) 2-0.

GUINEA

Federation Guineenne de Football, Annexe 1 du Palais du Peuple, PO Box 3645, Conakry.
Founded: 1960. *FIFA:* 1962; *CAF:* 1963. *National Colours:* Red shirts, yellow shorts, green socks.

International matches 2015–16
Liberia (n) 1-1, Zimbabwe (a) 1-1, Algeria (a) 2-1, Morocco (a) 1-1, Senegal (n) 2-0, Senegal (a) 1-3, Namibia (a) 1-0, Namibia (n) 2-0, Tunisia (n) 2-2, Niger (n) 2-2, Nigeria (n) 1-0, Zambia (n) 0-0 (5-4p), Congo DR (n) 1-1 (4-5p), Ivory Coast (n) 1-2, Malawi (h) 0-0, Malawi (a) 2-1, Swaziland (h) 0-1.

GUINEA-BISSAU

Federacao de Futebol da Guine-Bissau, Alto Bandim (Nova Sede), BP 375, Bissau 1035.
Founded: 1974. *FIFA:* 1986; *CAF:* 1986. *National Colours:* Red shirts with green and yellow trim, red shorts, red socks.

International matches 2015–16
Mali (a) 1-3, Congo (h) 2-4, Liberia (a) 1-1, Liberia (h) 1-3, Kenya (h) 1-0, Kenya (a) 1-0, Zambia (h) 3-2.

IVORY COAST

Federation Ivoirienne de Football, Treichville Avenue 1, 01, BP 1202, Abidjan 01.
Founded: 1960. *FIFA:* 1964; *CAF:* 1960. *National Colours:* All orange.

International matches 2015–16
Sierra Leone (n) 0-0, Morocco (a) 1-0, Ghana (a) 1-2, Ghana (h) 1-0, Liberia (a) 1-0, Liberia (h) 3-0, Rwanda (a) 0-1, Morocco (a) 1-0, Gabon (n) 4-1, Cameroon (n) 3-0, Mali (n) 0-1, Guinea (n) 2-1, Sudan (n) 1-0, Sudan (a) 1-1, Hungary (a) 0-0, Gabon (a) 2-1.

KENYA

Football Kenya Federation, Nyayo Sports Complex, Kasarani, PO Box 12705, 00400 Nairobi.
Founded: 1960 (KFF); 2011 (FKF). *FIFA:* 1960 (2012); *CAF:* 1968 (2012). *National Colours:* All red.

International matches 2015–16
Zambia (n) 1-2, Mauritius (a) 5-2, Mauritius (h) 0-0, Cape Verde Islands (h) 1-0, Cape Verde Islands (a) 0-2, Uganda (n) 2-0, Burundi (n) 1-1, Zanzibar† (n) 1-3, Rwanda (n) 0-0 (5-3p), Guinea-Bissau (a) 0-1, Guinea-Bissau (h) 0-1, Tanzania (h) 1-1, Sudan (h) 1-1, Congo (h) 2-1.

LESOTHO

Lesotho Football Association, Bambatha Tsita Sports Arena, Old Polo Ground, PO Box 1879, Maseru 100.
Founded: 1932. *FIFA:* 1964; *CAF:* 1964. *National Colours:* Blue shirts, green shorts, white socks.

International matches 2015–16
Algeria (h) 1-3, Comoros (a) 0-0, Comoros (h) 1-1, Zimbabwe (a) 1-3, Zimbabwe (h) 1-1, Seychelles (a) 0-2, Seychelles (h) 2-1, Botswana (a) 1-2, Ethiopia (h) 1-2, Mauritius (n) 3-0, Angola (n) 2-0, Malawi (n) 1-0, South Africa (n) 1-1 (2-4p), Zambia (n) 2-3.

LIBERIA

Liberia Football Association, Professional Building, Benson Street, PO Box 10-1066, Monrovia 1000.
Founded: 1936. *FIFA:* 1964; *CAF:* 1960. *National Colours:* Red and white shirts with black trim, red shorts, red socks with blue.

International matches 2015–16
Guinea (n) 1-1, Tunisia (h) 1-0, Guinea-Bissau (h) 1-1, Guinea-Bissau (a) 3-1, Ivory Coast (h) 0-1, Ivory Coast (a) 0-3, Djibouti (a) 1-0, Djibouti (h) 5-0, Togo (h) 2-2.

LIBYA

Libyan Football Federation, General Sports Federation Building, Sports City, Goriji, PO Box 5137, Tripoli.
Founded: 1962. *FIFA:* 1964; *CAF:* 1965. *National Colours:* Red shirts, black shorts, black socks.

International matches 2015–16
Tanzania (n) 2-1, Cape Verde Islands (n) 1-2, Tunisia (a)

0-1, Morocco (n) 0-4, Rwanda (n) 1-0, Rwanda (a) 3-1, Egypt (a) 0-2, Sao Tome & Principe (a) 1-2, Sao Tome & Principe (n) 4-0, Morocco (n) 1-1.

MADAGASCAR
Federation Malagasy de Football, 29 Rue de Russie Isoraka, PO Box 4409, Antananarivo 101.
Founded: 1961. *FIFA:* 1964; *CAF:* 1963. *National Colours:* All green and white.

International matches 2015–16
Maldives (n) 4-0, Angola (h) 0-0, Central African Republic (a) 3-0, Central African Republic (h) 2-2, Senegal (h) 2-2, Senegal (a) 0-3, Central African Republic (h) 1-1, Central African Republic (a) 1-2, Congo DR (h) 1-6, Seychelles (n) 1-0, Zimbabwe (n) 0-0, Swaziland (n) 0-1.

MALAWI
Football Association of Malawi, Chiwembe Technical Centre, Off Chiwembe Road, PO Box 51657, Limbe.
Founded: 1966. *FIFA:* 1968; *CAF:* 1968. *National Colours:* All red.

International matches 2015–16
Uganda (a) 1-0, Swaziland (a) 2-2, Tanzania (a) 0-2, Tanzania (h) 1-0, Sudan (n) 2-1, Djibouti (n) 3-0, South Sudan (n) 0-2, Uganda (n) 0-2, Guinea (a) 0-0, Guinea (h) 1-2, Zimbabwe (a) 0-3, Namibia (a) 0-0, Angola (n) 3-0, Mauritius (n) 1-0, Lesotho (n) 2-0.

MALI
Federation Malienne de Football, Avenue du Mali, Hamdallaye ACI 2000, BP 1020, Bamako 0000.
Founded: 1960. *FIFA:* 1964; *CAF:* 1963. *National Colours:* All yellow.

International matches 2015–16
Guinea-Bissau (h) 3-1, Benin (a) 1-1, Burkina Faso (n) 4-1, Mauritania (h) 2-1, Mauritania (a) 1-1, Botswana (a) 1-2, Botswana (h) 2-0, Uganda (n) 2-2, Zimbabwe (n) 1-0, Zambia (n) 0-0, Tunisia (n) 2-1, Ivory Coast (n) 1-0, Congo DR (n) 0-3, Equatorial Guinea (h) 1-0, Equatorial Guinea (a) 1-0, Nigeria (n) 0-1, South Sudan (a) 3-0.

MAURITANIA
Federation de Foot-Ball de la Rep. Islamique de Mauritanie, Route de l'Espoire, BP 566, Nouakchott.
Founded: 1961. *FIFA:* 1970; *CAF:* 1968. *National Colours:* All green with yellow trim.

International matches 2015–16
South Africa (h) 3-1, South Sudan (a) 1-1, South Sudan (h) 4-0, Mali (a) 1-2, Mali (h) 1-1, Tunisia (h) 1-2, Tunisia (a) 1-2, Gambia (h) 2-1, Gambia (a) 0-0, Gabon (n) 2-0, Cameroon (h) 0-1.

MAURITIUS
Mauritius Football Association, Sepp Blatter House, Trianon.
Founded: 1952. *FIFA:* 1964; *CAF:* 1963. *National Colours:* All white with red trim.

International matches 2015–16
South Africa (h) 0-2, Mozambique (h) 1-0, Kenya (h) 2-5, Kenya (a) 0-0, Rwanda (h) 1-0, Rwanda (a) 0-5, Ghana (h) 0-2, Lesotho (n) 0-3, Malawi (n) 0-1, Angola (n) 2-0.

MOROCCO
Federation Royale Marocaine de Football, 51 bis, Avenue Ibn Sina, Agdal BP 51, Rabat 10 000.
Founded: 1955. *FIFA:* 1960; *CAF:* 1959. *National Colours:* Red shirts with green trim, white shorts, red socks with green trim.

International matches 2015–16
Sao Tome & Principe (a) 3-0, Ivory Coast (h) 0-1, Guinea (h) 1-1, Libya (n) 4-0, Tunisia (a) 3-2, Equatorial Guinea (h) 2-0, Equatorial Guinea (a) 0-1, Gabon (n) 0-0, Ivory Coast (h) 0-1, Rwanda (a) 4-1, Cape Verde Islands (a) 1-0, Cape Verde Islands (h) 2-0, Congo (h) 2-0, Libya (n) 1-1.

MOZAMBIQUE
Federacao Mocambicana de Futebol, Avenida Samora Machel 11, Caixa Postal 1467, Maputo.
Founded: 1976. *FIFA:* 1980; *CAF:* 1980. *National Colours:* Red shirts, black shorts, black socks with red tops.

International matches 2015–16
Mauritius (a) 0-1, Zambia (a) 0-3, Zambia (h) 1-1, Gabon (h) 1-0, Gabon (a) 0-1 (3-4p), Ghana (a) 1-3, Ghana (h) 0-0, Rwanda (a) 3-2, Congo DR (n) 0-1, Namibia (a) 0-3.

NAMIBIA
Namibia Football Association, Richard Kamuhuka Str., Soccer House, Katutura, PO Box 1345, Windhoek 9000.
Founded: 1990. *FIFA:* 1992; *CAF:* 1992. *National Colours:* All red.

International matches 2015–16
Senegal (h) 0-2, Gambia (a) 1-1, Gambia (h) 2-1, Guinea (a) 0-1, Guinea (n) 0-2, Burundi (a) 3-1, Burundi (h) 1-3, Niger (h) 1-0, Malawi (h) 0-0, Botswana (n) 1-1 (4-5p), Mozambique (h) 3-0, Zambia (h) 1-0.

NIGER
Federation Nigerienne de Football, Avenue Francois Mitterand, BP 10299, Niamey.
Founded: 1961. *FIFA:* 1964; *CAF:* 1964. *National Colours:* White shirts, white shorts, orange socks.

International matches 2015–16
Burkina Faso (h) 0-0, Burundi (a) 0-2, Nigeria (a) 0-2, Somalia (n) 2-0, Somalia (h) 4-0, Togo (h) 2-0, Togo (a) 1-1, Cameroon (h) 0-3, Cameroon (a) 0-0, Nigeria (n) 1-4, Guinea (n) 2-2, Tunisia (n) 0-5, Senegal (a) 0-2, Senegal (h) 1-2, Namibia (a) 0-1.

NIGERIA
Nigeria Football Federation, Plot 2033, Olusegun Obasanjo Way, Zone 7, Wuse Abuja, PO Box 5101 Garki, Abuja.
Founded: 1945. *FIFA:* 1960; *CAF:* 1960. *National Colours:* All green with white trim.

International matches 2015–16
Tanzania (a) 0-0, Niger (h) 2-0, Congo DR (n) 0-2, Cameroon (n) 3-0, Burkina Faso (h) 2-0, Burkina Faso (a) 0-0, Swaziland (a) 0-0, Swaziland (h) 2-0, Niger (n) 4-1, Tunisia (n) 1-1, Guinea (n) 0-1, Egypt (h) 1-1, Egypt (a) 0-1, Mali (n) 1-0, Luxembourg (a) 3-1.

RWANDA
Federation Rwandaise de Football Association, BP 2000, Kigali.
Founded: 1972. *FIFA:* 1978; *CAF:* 1976. *National Colours:* Green and yellow hooped shirts, blue shorts, green socks.

International matches 2015–16
Ethiopia (h) 3-1, Ghana (h) 0-1, Gabon (h) 0-1, Libya (n) 0-1, Libya (h) 1-3, Ethiopia (a) 1-0, Tanzania (n) 1-2, Somalia (n) 3-0, Kenya (n) 0-0 (5-3p), Sudan (n) 1-1 (4-2p), Uganda (n) 0-1, Cameroon (h) 1-1, Congo DR (h) 1-0, Ivory Coast (h) 1-0, Gabon (h) 2-1, Morocco (h) 1-4, Congo DR (h) 1-2, Mauritius (a) 0-1, Mauritius (h) 5-0, Senegal (h) 0-2, Mozambique (h) 2-3.

SAO TOME & PRINCIPE
Federacao Santomense de Futebol, Rua Ex-Joao de Deus No. QXXIII-426/26, BP 440, Sao Tome.
Founded: 1975. *FIFA:* 1986; *CAF:* 1986. *National Colours:* Green and red shirts, black shorts, green socks.

International matches 2015–16
Morocco (h) 0-3, Ethiopia (h) 1-0, Ethiopia (a) 0-3, Libya (h) 2-1, Libya (h) 0-4, Cape Verde Islands (h) 1-2.

SENEGAL
Federation Senegalaise de Football, VDN Ouest-Foire en face du Cicesi, BP 13021, Dakar.
Founded: 1960. *FIFA:* 1964; *CAF:* 1964. *National Colours:* All white with yellow trim.

International matches 2015–16
Namibia (h) 2-0, South Africa (a) 0-1, Algeria (a) 0-1, Guinea (n) 0-2, Guinea (h) 3-1, Madagascar (a) 2-2, Madagascar (h) 3-0, Mexico (n) 0-2, Niger (h) 2-0, Niger (a) 2-1, Rwanda (a) 2-0, Burundi (a) 2-0.

SEYCHELLES
Seychelles Football Federation, Maison Football, Roche Caiman, PO Box 843, Mahe.
Founded: 1979. *FIFA:* 1986; *CAF:* 1986. *National Colours:* Red shirts, blue shorts, blue socks.

International matches 2015–16
Maldives (a) 1-2, Ethiopia (h) 1-1, Burundi (h) 0-1, Burundi (a) 0-2, Lesotho (h) 2-0, Lesotho (a) 1-2, Algeria (h) 0-2, Madagascar (n) 0-1, Swaziland (n) 0-4, Zimbabwe (n) 0-5.

SIERRA LEONE
Sierra Leone Football Association, 21 Battery Street, Kingtom, PO Box 672, Freetown.
Founded: 1960. *FIFA:* 1960; *CAF:* 1960. *National Colours:* Green shirts, white shorts, blue socks.

International matches 2015–16
Ivory Coast (n) 0-0, Chad (a) 0-1, Chad (h) 2-1, Gabon (a) 1-2, Gabon (h) 1-0, Sudan (h) 1-0.

SOMALIA
Somali Football Federation, Mogadishu BN 03040 (DHL only).
Founded: 1951. *FIFA:* 1962; *CAF:* 1968. *National Colours:* All blue with white trim.

International matches 2015–16
Niger (n) 0-2, Niger (a) 0-4, Tanzania (n) 0-4, Ethiopia (h) 0-2*, Rwanda (n) 0-3.
* Match played in Ethiopia.

SOUTH AFRICA
South African Football Association, 76 Nasrec Road, Nasrec, Johannesburg 2000.
Founded: 1991. *FIFA:* 1992; *CAF:* 1992. *National Colours:* Yellow shirts with green trim, green shorts with yellow trim, yellow socks with green tops.

International matches 2015–16
Mauritius (a) 2-0, Mauritania (h) 1-3, Senegal (h) 1-0, Costa Rica (n) 1-0, Honduras (a) 1-1, Angola (h) 0-2, Angola (a) 2-1, Angola (a) 3-1, Angola (h) 1-0, Cameroon (a) 2-2, Cameroon (h) 0-0, Gambia (h) 4-0, Lesotho (a) 1-1 (4-2p), Swaziland (n) 5-1, Botswana (n) 3-2.

SOUTH SUDAN
South Sudan Football Association, Juba National Stadium, Hai Himra, Talata, Juba.
Founded: 2011. *FIFA:* 2012; *CAF:* 2012. *National Colours:* All blue.

International matches 2015–16
Equatorial Guinea (h) 1-0, Mauritania (h) 1-1, Mauritania (h) 0-4, Djibouti (n) 2-0, Sudan (n) 0-0, Malawi (n) 2-0, Sudan (n) 0-0 (3-5p), Benin (h) 1-2, Benin (a) 1-4, Mali (h) 0-3.

SUDAN
Sudan Football Association, Baladia Street, PO Box 437, 11111 Khartoum.
Founded: 1936. *FIFA:* 1948; *CAF:* 1957. *National Colours:* All red.

International matches 2015–16
Gabon (a) 0-4, Uganda (a) 0-2, Uganda (h) 0-2, Zambia (h) 0-1, Zambia (a) 0-2, Malawi (n) 1-2, South Sudan (n) 0-0, Djibouti (n) 4-0, South Sudan (n) 0-0 (5-3p), Rwanda (n) 1-1 (2-4p), Ethiopia (a) 1-1 (4-5p), Ivory Coast (a) 0-1, Ivory Coast (h) 1-1, Sierra Leone (h) 1-0.

SWAZILAND
National Football Association of Swaziland, Sigwaca House, Plot 582, Sheffield Road, PO Box 641, Mbabane H100.
Founded: 1968. *FIFA:* 1978; *CAF:* 1976. *National Colours:* Blue and red shirts, blue shorts, blue socks.

International matches 2015–16
Malawi (h) 2-2, Djibouti (a) 6-0, Djibouti (h) 2-1, Nigeria (h) 0-0, Nigeria (a) 0-2, Zimbabwe (h) 1-1, Zimbabwe (a) 0-4, Guinea (h) 1-0, Zimbabwe (n) 2-2, Seychelles (n) 4-0, Madagascar (n) 1-0, Zambia (n) 0-0 (4-2p), South Africa (n) 1-5, Congo DR (n) 1-0.

TANZANIA
Tanzania Football Federation, Karume Memorial Stadium, Uhuru/Shauri Moyo Road, PO Box 1574, Ilala/Dar Es Salaam.
Founded: 1930. *FIFA:* 1964; *CAF:* 1964. *National Colours:* Blue shirts, black shorts, blue socks.

International matches 2015–16
Libya (n) 1-2, Nigeria (h) 0-0, Malawi (h) 2-0, Malawi (a) 0-1, Algeria (h) 2-2, Algeria (a) 0-7, Somalia (n) 4-0, Rwanda (n) 2-1, Ethiopia (a) 1-1, Ethiopia (a) 1-1 (3-4p), Kenya (a) 1-1, Egypt (h) 0-2.

TOGO
Federation Togolaise de Football, Route de Kegoue, BP 05, Lome.
Founded: 1960. *FIFA:* 1964; *CAF:* 1964. *National Colours:* Yellow shirts, green shorts, yellow socks.

International matches 2015–16
Djibouti (a) 2-0, Niger (a) 0-2, Niger (h) 1-1, Uganda (h) 0-1, Uganda (a) 0-3, Tunisia (a) 0-1, Tunisia (h) 0-0, Zambia (h) 1-0, Liberia (a) 2-2.

TUNISIA
Federation Tunisienne de Football, Stade Annexe d'El Menzah, Cite Olympique, El Menzah 1003.
Founded: 1957. *FIFA:* 1960; *CAF:* 1960. *National Colours:* All white with red trim.

International matches 2015–16
Liberia (a) 0-1, Gabon (h) 3-3, Libya (h) 1-0, Morocco (h) 2-3, Mauritania (a) 2-1, Mauritania (h) 2-1, Guinea (n) 2-2, Nigeria (n) 1-1, Niger (h) 5-0, Mali (n) 1-2, Togo (h) 1-0, Togo (a) 0-0, Djibouti (a) 3-0.

UGANDA
Federation of Uganda Football Associations, FUFA House, Plot No. 879, Wakaliga Road, Mengo, PO Box 22518, Kampala.
Founded: 1924. *FIFA:* 1960; *CAF:* 1960. *National Colours:* Yellow shirts, black shorts, yellow socks.

International matches 2015–16
Malawi (a) 0-1, Comoros (a) 1-0, Sudan (h) 2-0, Sudan (a) 2-0, Togo (a) 1-0, Togo (h) 3-0, Kenya (n) 0-2, Zanzibar† (n) 4-0, Burundi (n) 1-0, Malawi (n) 2-0, Ethiopia (a) 0-0 (5-3p), Rwanda (n) 1-0, Gabon (h) 1-1, Mali (n) 2-2, Zambia (n) 0-1, Zimbabwe (n) 1-1, Burkina Faso (a) 0-1, Burkina Faso (h) 0-0, Zimbabwe (a) 0-2, Botswana (a) 2-1.

ZAMBIA
Football Association of Zambia, Football House, Alick Nkhata Road, Long Acres, PO Box 34751, Lusaka.
Founded: 1929. *FIFA:* 1964; *CAF:* 1964. *National Colours:* Green shirts, green shorts, green and orange socks.

International matches 2015–16
Kenya (a) 2-1, Gabon (h) 1-1, Egypt (n) 0-3, Mozambique (h) 3-0, Mozambique (a) 1-1, Sudan (a) 1-0, Sudan (h) 2-0, Zimbabwe (n) 1-0, Uganda (n) 1-0, Mali (n) 0-0, Guinea (n) 0-0 (4-5p), Congo (h) 1-1, Congo (a) 1-1, Togo (a) 0-1, Gambia (a) 0-0, Guinea-Bissau (a) 2-3, Swaziland (n) 0-0 (2-4p), Lesotho (n) 3-2, Namibia (a) 0-1.

ZIMBABWE
Zimbabwe Football Association, ZIFA House, 53 Livingstone Avenue, PO Box CY 114, Causeway, Harare.
Founded: 1965. *FIFA:* 1965; *CAF:* 1980. *National Colours:* Gold shirts, gold shorts, green socks.

International matches 2015–16
Guinea (h) 1-1, Lesotho (h) 3-1, Lesotho (a) 1-1, Zambia (n) 0-1, Mali (n) 0-1, Uganda (n) 1-1, Swaziland (a) 1-1, Swaziland (h) 4-0, Uganda (h) 2-0, Malawi (h) 3-0, Swaziland (n) 2-2, Madagascar (n) 0-0, Seychelles (n) 5-0.

EURO 2016 QUALIFYING COMPETITION

■ *Denotes player sent off.*

GROUP A

Tuesday, 9 September 2014

Czech Republic (1) 2 *(Dockal 22, Pilar 90)*

Holland (0) 1 *(de Vrij 55)*   17,946

Czech Republic: (442) Cech; Kaderabek, Prochazka, Kadlec M, Limbersky; Dockal, Darida, Krejci (Pilar 66), Vacha (Kolar 81); Rosicky, Lafata (Vydra 72).
Holland: (532) Cillessen; Janmaat, Veltman (Narsingh 39), de Vrij, Martins Indi, Blind; Wijnaldum, Sneijder, de Jong; van Persie, Depay.
Referee: Gianluca Rocchi.

Iceland (1) 3 *(Bodvarsson 18, Sigurdsson G 76, Sigthorsson 78)*

Turkey (0) 0   7000

Iceland: (442) Halldorsson; Bjarnason T, Arnason, Sigurdsson R, Skulason A; Bjarnason B (Gislason 70), Gunnarsson, Sigurdsson G (Skulason O 89), Hallfredsson; Bodvarsson (Kjartansson 90), Sigthorsson.
Turkey: (343) Kivrak; Toprak■, Topal (Calhanoglu 77), Gulum; Gonul, Emre, Inan (Tufan 65), Erkin; Adin (Pektemek 64), Yilmaz, Turan.
Referee: Ivan Bebek.

Kazakhstan (0) 0

Latvia (0) 0   10,000

Kazakhstan: (523) Sidelnikov; Miroshnichenko S, Vorotnikov, Abdulin, Logvinenko, Shomko; Bogdanov, Smakov; Nuserbaev (Dzholchiev 73), Islamkhan (Nurgaliev 82), Khizhnichenko.
Latvia: (442) Kolinko; Gabovs, Bulvitis, Gorkss, Maksimenko; Kovalovs, Zjuzins, Lazdins (Fertovs 27), Laizans; Sabala, Rudnevs (Visnakovs E 79).
Referee: Ivan Kruzliak.

Friday, 10 October 2014

Holland (0) 3 *(Huntelaar 62, Afellay 82, van Persie 89 (pen))*

Kazakhstan (1) 1 *(Abdulin 18)*   45,000

Holland: (433) Cillessen; van der Wiel, de Vrij, Martins Indi (Fer 81), Blind; Sneijder, de Jong (Huntelaar 56), Afellay; Robben, van Persie, Lens.
Kazakhstan: (541) Mokin; Miroshnichenko D, Dmitrenko (Gorman 72), Vorotnikov, Abdulin, Suyumbayev; Dzholchiev■, Bogdanov, Karpovich (Korobkin 79), Shomko; Khizhnichenko (Nurgaliev 90).
Referee: Matej Jug.

Latvia (0) 0

Iceland (0) 3 *(Sigurdsson G 66, Gunnarsson 77, Gislason 90)*   6354

Latvia: (352) Kolinko; Bulvitis, Dubra, Gabovs; Gorkss, Morozs, Kovalovs (Visnakovs A 81), Rugins (Freimanis 63), Fertovs; Sabala (Visnakovs E 81), Rudnevs■.
Iceland: (442) Halldorsson; Sigurdsson R, Arnason, Skulason A, Bjarnason B; Sigurdsson G (Skulason O 80), Gunnarsson, Bjarnason T, Hallfredsson (Gislason 87); Bodvarsson (Finnbogason 78), Sigthorsson.
Referee: Robert Schorgenhofer.

Turkey (1) 1 *(Bulut 8)*

Czech Republic (1) 2 *(Sivok 16, Dockal 58)*   25,000

Turkey: (433) Zengin; Gonul, Topal, Kaya, Erkin; Tufan, Inan (Ozyakup 79), Turan; Sahan (Demir 66), Bulut, Tore (Adin 68).
Czech Republic: (4231) Cech; Kaderabek, Sivok, Kadlec M, Limbersky; Darida, Vacha; Dockal (Plasil 90), Rosicky, Krejci (Pilar 68); Lafata (Vydra 84).
Referee: Jonas Eriksson.

Monday, 13 October 2014

Iceland (2) 2 *(Sigurdsson G 10 (pen), 42)*

Holland (0) 0   10,000

Iceland: (442) Halldorsson; Bjarnason T, Arnason, Sigurdsson R, Skulason A (Saevarsson 46); Bjarnason B, Gunnarsson, Sigurdsson G, Hallfredsson; Bodvarsson (Gislason 89), Sigthorsson.
Holland: (433) Cillessen; van der Wiel, de Vrij, Martins Indi, Blind; Afellay (Fer 78), de Jong, Sneijder (Huntelaar 46); Robben, van Persie, Lens (Promes 68).
Referee: Carlos Velasco Carballo.

Kazakhstan (0) 2 *(Logvinenko 84, 90)*

Czech Republic (2) 4 *(Dockal 13, Lafata 44, Krejci 56, Necid 88)*   24,000

Kazakhstan: (532) Sidelnikov; Miroshnichenko D (Beisebekov 83), Vorotnikov, Abdulin, Logvinenko, Shomko; Tagybergen, Karpovich (Konysbayev 57), Islamkhan; Nuserbaev, Khizhnichenko (Nurgaliev 70).
Czech Republic: (4411) Cech; Kaderabek, Sivok (Prochazka 81), Kadlec M, Limbersky; Dockal, Vacha, Darida, Krejci (Pilar 69); Kolar; Lafata (Necid 79).
Referee: Mattias Gestranius.

Latvia (0) 1 *(Sabala 54 (pen))*

Turkey (0) 1 *(Kisa 47)*   6432

Latvia: (4411) Kolinko; Gabovs (Freimanis■ 37), Dubra, Gorkss, Kurakins; Ikaunieks, Zjuzins (Morozs 83), Fertovs, Visnakovs A; Sabala; Visnakovs E (Rakels 79).
Turkey: (4321) Babacan; Gonul, Topal, Kaya, Erkin; Tufan, Ozyakup (Kisa 40), Turan; Sahan (Sari 59), Tore (Altintop 70); Bulut.
Referee: Bobby Madden.

Sunday, 16 November 2014

Czech Republic (1) 2 *(Kaderabek 45, Bodvarsson 61 (og))*

Iceland (1) 1 *(Sigurdsson R 9)*   11,354

Czech Republic: (4411) Cech; Kaderabek, Sivok, Kadlec M, Pudil; Dockal, Plasil, Darida, Krejci (Pilar 65); Rosicky (Prochazka 90); Lafata (Necid 81).
Iceland: (442) Halldorsson; Bjarnason T (Saevarsson 63), Sigurdsson R, Arnason, Skulason A; Hallfredsson (Gislason 64), Sigurdsson G, Gunnarsson, Bjarnason B (Gudmundsson 77); Bodvarsson, Sigthorsson.
Referee: Wolfgang Stark.

Holland (3) 6 *(van Persie 6, Robben 35, 82, Huntelaar 42, 89, Bruma 78)*

Latvia (0) 0   50,000

Holland: (433) Cillessen; van der Wiel, Bruma, de Vrij, Willems; Afellay (Depay 69), Blind (Clasie 20), Sneijder; Robben, Huntelaar, van Persie (Wijnaldum 79).
Latvia: (4411) Kolinko; Gabovs, Dubra, Gorkss, Kurakins; Ikaunieks (Laizans 46), Zjuzins (Cauna 54), Fertovs, Visnakovs A; Sabala; Visnakovs E (Rudnevs 70).
Referee: Liran Liany.

Turkey (2) 3 *(Yilmaz 27 (pen), 29, Aziz 83)*

Kazakhstan (0) 1 *(Smakov 87 (pen))*   27,547

Turkey: (532) Babacan; Tufan, Aziz, Inan, Kaya, Erkin; Sen (Tore 80), Turan, Sahan (Ekici 84); Bulut (Topal 74), Yilmaz.
Kazakhstan: (343) Mokin; Gorman, Abdulin (Maliy 76), Logvinenko; Lunin (Shchetkin 73), Tagybergen, Smakov, Shomko; Konysbayev, Khizhnichenko (Nurgaliev 82), Islamkhan.
Referee: Aleksei Eskov.

Saturday, 28 March 2015

Czech Republic (0) 1 *(Pilar 90)*

Latvia (1) 1 *(Visnakovs A 30)*   13,700

Czech Republic: (4231) Cech; Gebre Selassie, Kadlec M, Prochazka, Limbersky; Darida, Plasil (Pilar 46); Dockal, Rosicky, Krejci (Necid 57); Lafata (Kadlec V 81).
Latvia: (442) Vanins; Dubra, Gorkss, Freimanis, Maksimenko; Laizans (Ikaunieks 66), Visnakovs A (Fertovs 81), Tarasovs, Zjuzins (Zigajevs 87); Sabala, Rakels.
Referee: Javier Estrada Fernandez.

Holland (0) 1 *(Huntelaar 90)*
Turkey (1) 1 *(Yilmaz 37)*   49,500
Holland: (433) Cillessen; van der Wiel, de Vrij, Martins
Indi (Willems 77), Blind; Wijnaldum (Narsingh 46), de
Jong (Dost 63), Sneijder; Afellay, Huntelaar, Depay.
Turkey: (433) Babacan; Gonul, Aziz (Gulum 69), Balta,
Erkin; Tufan, Topal, Inan; Tore, Yilmaz (Kazim-
Richards 79), Sen (Calhanoglu 60).
Referee: Felix Brych.

Kazakhstan (0) 0
Iceland (2) 3 *(Gudjohnsen 20, Bjarnason B 33, 90)* 13,182
Kazakhstan: (541) Sidelnikov; Gorman (Kuantayev 67),
Vorotnikov, Abdulin (Shchetkin 80), Loginovskiy,
Suyumbayev; Islamkhan, Tagybergen, Smakov,
Nurgaliev (Konysbayev 55); Tazhimbetov.
Iceland: (442) Halldorsson; Saevarsson, Arnason,
Sigurdsson R, Skulason A; Bjarnason B, Gunnarsson
(Hallfredsson 72), Sigurdsson G, Gudmundsson;
Gudjohnsen (Finnbogason 83), Sigthorsson (Bodvarsson
70).
Referee: Tasos Sidiropoulos.

Friday, 12 June 2015
Iceland (0) 2 *(Gunnarsson 60, Sigthorsson 76)*
Czech Republic (0) 1 *(Dockal 55)*   15,500
Iceland: (442) Halldorsson; Saevarsson, Sigurdsson R,
Arnason, Skulason A; Bjarnason B, Sigurdsson G,
Gunnarsson, Hallfredsson (Bodvarsson 63);
Gudmundsson, Sigthorsson (Gislason 90).
Czech Republic: (442) Cech; Kaderabek, Prochazka,
Sivok, Limbersky; Dockal (Darida 84), Rosicky, Pilar
(Krejci 68), Plasil; Vacha (Skoda 79), Necid.
Referee: William Collum.

Kazakhstan (0) 0
Turkey (0) 1 *(Turan 83)*   12,000
Kazakhstan: (541) Pokatilov; Maliy, Gorman
(Tagybergen 78), Abdulin, Logvinenko, Shomko;
Smakov (Beisebekov 67), Konysbayev, Islamkhan
(Kukeev 85), Schmidtgal; Khizhnichenko.
Turkey: (433) Babacan; Kaya (Tasdemir 75), Balta, Aziz,
Gonul; Tufan (Bulut 65), Calhanoglu, Inan; Turan, Topal
(Sen 46), Yilmaz.
Referee: Michael Oliver.

Latvia (0) 0
Holland (0) 2 *(Wijnaldum 67, Narsingh 71)*   9500
Latvia: (442) Vanins; Gorkss, Freimanis (Gabovs 37),
Maksimenko, Jagodinskis; Visnakovs A (Karasausks 75),
Ikaunieks, Tarasovs, Zjuzins; Sabala (Visnakovs E 61),
Rakels.
Holland: (433) Cillessen; van der Wiel, de Vrij, Martins
Indi, Willems (Janmaat 77); Blind, Sneijder, Narsingh;
Huntelaar, van Persie (Wijnaldum 63), Depay (Lens 87).
Referee: Svein Oddvar Moen.

Thursday, 3 September 2015
Czech Republic (0) 2 *(Skoda 74, 86)*
Kazakhstan (1) 1 *(Logvinenko 21)*   10,572
Czech Republic: (4231) Cech; Kaderabek, Suchy,
Prochazka, Limbersky; Dockal, Pavelka; Darida (Sural
68), Krejci (Kopic 84), Skalak (Skoda 46); Lafata.
Kazakhstan: (343) Pokatilov; Gorman, Maliy,
Logvinenko; Kuat, Islamkhan (Suyumbayev 78),
Smakov, Shomko; Dzholchiev, Nuserbaev
(Khizhnichenko 72), Konysbayev (Kukeev 87).
Referee: Martin Strombergsson.

Netherlands (0) 0
Iceland (0) 1 *(Sigurdsson G 52 (pen))*   47,000
Netherlands: (4231) Cillessen; van der Wiel, de Vrij,
Martins Indi*, Blind; Wijnaldum (Promes 80), Klaassen;
Robben (Narsingh 31), Sneijder, Depay; Huntelaar
(Bruma 40).
Iceland: (442) Halldorsson; Saevarsson, Arnason,
Sigurdsson R, Skulason A; Bodvarsson (Finnbogason
78), Sigurdsson G, Gunnarsson (Skulason O 86),
Bjarnason; Gudmundsson, Sigthorsson (Gudjohnsen 64).
Referee: Milorad Mazic.

Turkey (0) 1 *(Inan 77)*
Latvia (0) 1 *(Sabala 90)*   35,900
Turkey: (4141) Babacan; Tufan, Aziz, Balta, Erkin; Inan;
Tore (Ozbayrakli 58), Calhanoglu, Turan, Sen (Bulut 55);
Yilmaz (Topal 83).
Latvia: (442) Vanins; Gabovs, Jagodinskis, Dubra,
Maksimenko; Laizans (Visnakovs E 82), Cauna (Zjuzins
60), Tarasovs, Visnakovs A; Karasausks (Sabala 85),
Rakels.
Referee: Stefan Johannesson.

Sunday, 6 September 2015
Iceland (0) 0
Kazakhstan (0) 0   9767
Iceland: (424) Halldorsson; Skulason A, Sigurdsson R,
Arnason, Saevarsson; Sigurdsson G, Gunnarsson*;
Bjarnason, Sigthorsson, Bodvarsson (Kjartansson 85),
Gudmundsson.
Kazakhstan: (433) Pokatilov; Gorman, Logvinenko,
Maliy, Suyumbayev; Kuat, Smakov, Islamkhan;
Dzholchiev (Merkel 46), Nuserbaev (Shchetkin 76),
Konysbayev.
Referee: Yevhen Aranovskiy.

Latvia (0) 1 *(Zjuzins 73)*
Czech Republic (2) 2 *(Limbersky 13, Darida 25)*   7913
Latvia: (442) Vanins; Freimanis (Gabovs 32), Gorkss,
Dubra, Maksimenko; Kamess (Visnakovs A 29), Fertovs,
Tarasovs, Zjuzins; Rakels, Karasausks (Cauna 66).
Czech Republic: (442) Cech; Kaderabek, Suchy,
Prochazka, Limbersky; Dockal (Gebre Selassie 90),
Darida, Pavelka, Sural (Vanek 77); Kolar (Krejci 54),
Skoda.
Referee: Deniz Aytekin.

Turkey (2) 3 *(Ozyakup 8, Turan 26, Yilmaz 85)*
Netherlands (0) 0   41,007
Turkey: (433) Babacan; Ozbayrakli, Aziz, Balta, Erkin;
Tufan, Inan, Ozyakup (Sahan 82); Calhanoglu (Topal
65), Yilmaz, Turan (Sen 56).
Netherlands: (4231) Cillessen; van der Wiel, de Vrij
(Wijnaldum 46), Riedewald, Blind (de Jong 75);
Klaassen, Bruma; Narsingh (Promes 69), Sneijder,
Depay; van Persie.
Referee: Antonio Miguel Mateu Lahoz.

Saturday, 10 October 2015
Czech Republic (0) 0
Turkey (0) 2 *(Inan 62 (pen), Calhanoglu 80)*   17,190
Czech Republic: (4411) Vaclik; Kaderabek, Suchy,
Prochazka, Novak; Dockal (Petrzela 78), Darida,
Pavelka, Krejci (Skalak 54); Sural (Skoda 68); Lafata.
Turkey: (41212) Babacan; Ozbayrakli, Aziz, Balta, Erkin;
Inan; Tufan, Ozyakup (Topal 87); Turan (Tore 86);
Calhanoglu, Tosun (Sen 64).
Referee: Martin Atkinson.

Iceland (2) 2 *(Sigthorsson 6, Sigurdsson G 27)*
Latvia (0) 2 *(Cauna 49, Sabala 68)*   9767
Iceland: (442) Halldorsson; Saevarsson, Arnason
(Ottesen 17), Sigurdsson R, Skulason A; Gudmundsson,
Sigurdsson G, Hallfredsson, Bjarnason; Finnbogason
(Gudjohnsen 65), Sigthorsson.
Latvia: (451) Vanins; Gorkss, Dubra, Gabovs,
Maksimenko; Rakels, Zjuzins (Ikaunieks 84), Tarasovs
(Laizans 78), Cauna, Sinelnikovs (Karasausks 64);
Sabala.
Referee: Aleksei Eskov.

Kazakhstan (0) 1 *(Kuat 90)*
Netherlands (1) 2 *(Wijnaldum 33, Sneijder 50)*   20,716
Kazakhstan: (541) Pokatilov; Engel, Maliy, Smakov,
Logvinenko, Suyumbayev; Konysbayev, Kuat, Islamkhan
(Geteriev 16), Dosmagambetov (Nurgaliev 81);
Shchetkin (Khizhnichenko 63).
Netherlands: (433) Krul (Zoet 83); Tete, Bruma, van
Dijk, Riedewald; Wijnaldum, Blind, Sneijder (Afellay
80); El Ghazi, Huntelaar (van Persie 87), Depay.
Referee: Clement Turpin.

Tuesday, 13 October 2015
Latvia (0) 0
Kazakhstan (0) 1 *(Kuat 65)* 7027

Latvia: (442) Vanins; Gorkss, Maksimenko, Gabovs, Dubra; Cauna (Visnakovs E 72), Laizans, Zjuzins (Ikaunieks 83), Visnakovs A (Karasausks 57); Sabala, Rakels.
Kazakhstan: (442) Pokatilov; Engel, Maliy, Logvinenko, Shomko; Dosmagambetov (Konysbayev 68), Kuat, Smakov, Suyumbayev; Nuserbaev (Gorman 82), Khizhnichenko (Shchetkin 90).
Referee: Steven Mclean.

Netherlands (0) 2 *(Huntelaar 70, van Persie 83)*
Czech Republic (2) 3 *(Kaderabek 24, Sural 35,*
van Persie 66 (og)) 48,000

Netherlands: (433) Zoet; Tete, Bruma, van Dijk (Dost 64), Riedewald (van Persie 39); Wijnaldum, Blind, Sneijder; El Ghazi (Lens 69), Huntelaar, Depay.
Czech Republic: (451) Cech; Kaderabek, Suchy■, Kadlec M, Gebre Selassie; Skalak, Darida, Pavelka, Plasil (Skoda 86), Sural (Kalas 71); Necid (Prochazka 46).
Referee: Damir Skomina.

Turkey (0) 1 *(Inan 89)*
Iceland (0) 0 42,000

Turkey: (451) Babacan; Ozbayrakli, Aziz, Balta, Erkin; Sen (Bulut 75), Tufan, Inan, Ozyakup (Tore■ 62), Turan; Calhanoglu (Tosun 72).
Iceland: (442) Kristinsson; Skulason A, Arnason, Sigurdsson R, Saevarsson; Bjarnason, Gunnarsson, Sigurdsson G, Gudmundsson; Bodvarsson (Kjartansson 82), Sigthorsson (Finnbogason 88).
Referee: Gianluca Rocchi.

Group A Table	P	W	D	L	F	A	GD	Pts
Czech Republic	10	7	1	2	19	14	5	22
Iceland	10	6	2	2	17	6	11	20
Turkey	10	5	3	2	14	9	5	18
Netherlands	10	4	1	5	17	14	3	13
Kazakhstan	10	1	2	7	7	18	−11	5
Latvia	10	0	5	5	6	19	−13	5

GROUP B

Tuesday, 9 September 2014
Andorra (1) 1 *(Lima 6 (pen))*
Wales (1) 2 *(Bale 22, 81)* 10,000

Andorra: (442) Pol; Garcia E, Lima, Maneiro, Rubio; Vales, Peppe (Vieira 52), Ayala (Sanchez Soto 86), Martinez (Sonejee 83); Lorenzo, Riera.
Wales: (442) Hennessey; Gunter, Taylor N, Chester, Davies; Williams A, Allen, King (Williams G 76), Ramsey (Huws 90); Bale, Church (Ledley 62).
Referee: Slavko Vincic.

Bosnia-Herzegovina (1) 1 *(Ibisevic 6)*
Cyprus (1) 2 *(Christofi 45, 73)* 12,000

Bosnia-Herzegovina: (4132) Begovic; Vrsajevic, Bicakcic, Sunjic, Lulic; Besic; Prcic (Hajrovic 61), Pjanic, Susic (Medunjanin 61); Dzeko, Ibisevic.
Cyprus: (4411) Georgallides; Kyriakou, Merkis, Junior, Antoniades; Efrem (Alexandrou 71), Nicolaou, Laban, Aloneftis (Charalambous 46); Makridis (Sielis 83); Christofi.
Referee: Yevhen Aranovskiy.

Friday, 10 October 2014
Belgium (3) 6 *(De Bruyne 31 (pen), 34, Chadli 37,*
Origi 58, Mertens 65, 68)
Andorra (0) 0 40,000

Belgium: (451) Courtois; Alderweireld, Kompany (Pocognoli 55), Lombaerts, Vertonghen; Chadli (Fellaini 61), Nainggolan, Defour, De Bruyne, Mertens; Origi (Lukaku R 66).
Andorra: (4231) Pol; San Nicolas, Garcia E, Lima, Maneiro; Ayala, Vales; Rubio (Lorenzo 61), Vieira, Martinez (Moreno 77); Riera (Garcia M 71).
Referee: Serhiy Boiko.

Cyprus (0) 1 *(Makridis 67)*
Israel (2) 2 *(Damari 38, Ben Chaim 45)* 19,164

Cyprus: (4411) Georgallides; Stylianou (Kyriakou 46), Merkis, Junior, Antoniades; Charalambidis (Sotiriou 46), Nicolaou, Laban, Makris (Alexandrou 69); Makridis; Christofi.
Israel: (4141) Martziano; Meshumar, Ben Haim, Tibi, Ben Haroush; Yeini; Vermouth (Biton 83), Natcho, Zahavi, Ben Chaim (Rafaelov 74); Damari (Shechter 69).
Referee: Daniele Orsato.

Wales (0) 0
Bosnia-Herzegovina (0) 0 30,741

Wales: (541) Hennessey; Gunter, Chester, Williams A, Davies, Taylor N; King, Williams J (Williams G 82), Ledley, Bale; Church (Robson-Kanu 65).
Bosnia-Herzegovina: (433) Begovic; Hadzic, Sunjic, Mujdza, Besic; Lulic, Susic, Medunjanin; Ibisevic (Hajrovic 83), Pjanic, Dzeko.
Referee: Vladislav Bezborodov.

Monday, 13 October 2014
Andorra (1) 1 *(Lima 15 (pen))*
Israel (2) 4 *(Damari 3, 41, 81, Hemed 90 (pen))* 800

Andorra: (4231) Pol; Maneiro, Lima (Ayala 40), Garcia E, Rubio (Pujol 69); Vieira, Vales; Lorenzo, Peppe (Toscano 83), Martinez; Riera.
Israel: (4141) Martziano; Meshumar, Ben Haim, Tibi, Twatha; Biton; Vermouth (Shechter 65), Natcho, Zahavi (Rafaelov 70), Ben Chaim; Damari (Hemed 84).
Referee: Cristian Balaj.

Bosnia-Herzegovina (1) 1 *(Dzeko 28)*
Belgium (0) 1 *(Nainggolan 51)* 12,000

Bosnia-Herzegovina: (442) Begovic; Mujdza, Hadzic, Sunjic, Lulic; Pjanic, Besic, Medunjanin, Susic (Visca 72); Ibisevic, Dzeko.
Belgium: (433) Courtois; Vertonghen, Lombaerts, Kompany, Alderweireld; De Bruyne, Defour (Fellaini 77), Nainggolan; Lukaku R (Mertens 57), Hazard, Origi.
Referee: Luca Banti.

Wales (2) 2 *(Cotterill 13, Robson-Kanu 23)*
Cyprus (1) 1 *(Laban 36)* 26,000

Wales: (451) Hennessey; Gunter, Williams A, Chester, Taylor N; Williams G (Edwards 58), King■, Bale, Ledley, Robson-Kanu (Taylor J 84); Church (Cotterill 6).
Cyprus: (4411) Kissas; Kyriakou, Merkis, Junior (Angeli 29 (Papathanasiou 85)), Antoniades; Efrem, Nicolaou (Alexandrou 68), Laban, Sotiriou; Makridis; Christofi.
Referee: Manuel Grafe.

Sunday, 16 November 2014
Belgium (0) 0
Wales (0) 0 55,000

Belgium: (451) Courtois; Alderweireld, Lombaerts, Vertonghen, Van Damme; Witsel, De Bruyne, Fellaini, Hazard, Chadli (Benteke 62); Origi (Mertens 73 (Januzaj 89)).
Wales: (433) Hennessey; Gunter, Taylor N, Chester, Williams A; Allen, Ramsey, Bale; Ledley, Cotterill (Williams G 46), Robson-Kanu (Huws 90).
Referee: Pavel Kralovec.

Cyprus (3) 5 *(Merkis 9, Efrem 31, 42, 60, Christofi 87 (pen))*
Andorra (0) 0 6000

Cyprus: (442) Georgallides; Merkis, Angeli, Demetriou, Antoniades; Efrem (Laifis 78), Mitidis (Kolokoudias 63), Nicolaou, Laban; Christofi, Aloneftis (Makris 46).
Andorra: (4411) Pol; Rubio (Rodrigues 73), Garcia E, Lima (Rodriguez 49), Garcia M; Martinez, Vieira (Ayala 46), Vales, Lorenzo; Pujol; Riera.
Referee: Mark Clattenburg.

Israel (2) 3 *(Vermouth 36, Damari 45, Zahavi 70)*
Bosnia-Herzegovina (0) 0 32,000

Israel: (451) Martziano; Ben Haroush (Davidadze 78), Tibi, Ben Chaim, Meshumar; Yeini, Vermouth (Rafaelov 70), Natcho (Biton 74), Damari, Zahavi; Ben Haim.
Bosnia-Herzegovina: (451) Begovic; Hadzic, Spahic, Sunjic■, Mujdza (Visca 46); Besic (Prcic 46), Lulic, Medunjanin, Hajrovic, Pjanic (Cimirot 62); Kvrzic.
Referee: Antonio Miguel Mateu Lahoz.

Saturday, 28 March 2015
Andorra (0) 0
Bosnia-Herzegovina (1) 3 *(Dzeko 13, 49, 62)*   2500
Andorra: (4231) Pol; San Nicolas, Vales, Lima, Garcia M; Sonejee, Vieira; Clemente (Martinez 54), Rodriguez, Lorenzo (Rubio 85); Gomez (Riera 59).
Bosnia-Herzegovina: (442) Begovic; Mujdza, Spahic, Vranjes O (Cocalic 73), Zukanovic; Visca, Besic, Pjanic, Lulic (Medunjanin 77); Ibisevic (Djuric 67), Dzeko.
Referee: Istvan Vad.

Belgium (2) 5 *(Fellaini 21, 66, Benteke 35, Hazard 67, Batshuayi 80)*
Cyprus (0) 0   45,000
Belgium: (4231) Courtois; Alderweireld, Kompany, Lombaerts, Vertonghen; Nainggolan, Witsel; De Bruyne, Fellaini (Carrasco 69), Hazard (Mertens 70); Benteke (Batshuayi 77).
Cyprus: (4231) Kissas; Kyriakou, Merkis, Laifis, Antoniades; Makris (Eleftheriou 71), Nicolaou; Laban (Economides 57), Sotiriou, Makridis (Kastanos 84); Mitidis.
Referee: Ovidiu Alin Hategan.

Israel (0) 0
Wales (1) 3 *(Ramsey 45, Bale 50, 77)*   30,200
Israel: (433) Marciano; Dgani, Ben Chaim, Tibi■, Ben Haroush; Natcho, Yeini, Zahavi (Sahar 70); Rafaelov, Ben Haim (Biton 60), Damari (Hemed 44).
Wales: (352) Hennessey; Collins, Williams A, Davies; Gunter, Allen, Ledley (Vaughan 47), Ramsey (MacDonald 85), Taylor N; Bale, Robson-Kanu (Vokes 69).
Referee: Milorad Mazic.

Tuesday, 31 March 2015
Israel (0) 0
Belgium (1) 1 *(Fellaini 10)*   33,000
Israel: (433) Marciano; Dgani, Ben Chaim, Gershon, Ben Haroush (Barda 84); Yeini (Rafaelov 66), Biton, Natcho; Zahavi, Hemed (Ben Haim 46), Sahar.
Belgium: (433) Courtois; Alderweireld, Kompany■, Lombaerts, Vertonghen; Fellaini, Nainggolan (Origi 86), Witsel; De Bruyne, Benteke (Denayer 66), Hazard (Chadli 63).
Referee: Mark Clattenburg.

Friday, 12 June 2015
Andorra (1) 1 *(Junior 2 (og))*
Cyprus (2) 3 *(Mitidis 14, 45, 53)*   1000
Andorra: (4411) Pol; Rubio, Rodrigues, Vales, Garcia M; Rebes (Peppe 79), Ayala (Sonejee 60), Rodriguez, Moreno (Lima 67); Martinez; Sanchez.
Cyprus: (4231) Georgallides; Demetriou, Sielis, Junior, Antoniades; Nicolaou, Laban (Economides 75); Christofi (Alexandrou 81), Makridis (Kastanos 88), Efrem; Mitidis.
Referee: Tobias Welz.

Bosnia-Herzegovina (2) 3 *(Visca 42, 76, Dzeko 45 (pen))*
Israel (1) 1 *(Ben Chaim 41)*   15,000
Bosnia-Herzegovina: (442) Begovic; Spahic, Kolasinac, Vranjes O, Lulic (Hadzic 85); Besic, Medunjanin, Pjanic (Ibisevic 88), Mujdza; Visca (Hajrovic 80), Dzeko.
Israel: (433) Marciano; Ben Haim, Gershon, Dgani, Ben Haroush; Biton (Kahat 80), Natcho, Zahavi; Yeini (Damari 46), Ben Chaim, Sahar (Buzaglo 62).
Referee: Ruddy Buquet.

Wales (1) 1 *(Bale 25)*
Belgium (0) 0   33,280
Wales: (3142) Hennessey; Gunter, Williams A, Chester; Richards; Ledley, Taylor N, Allen, Ramsey; Robson-Kanu (King 90), Bale (Vokes 87).
Belgium: (433) Courtois; Alderweireld (Carrasco 76), Denayer, Lombaerts, Vertonghen; Mertens (Lukaku R 46), Nainggolan, Witsel; De Bruyne, Benteke, Hazard.
Referee: Felix Brych.

Thursday, 3 September 2015
Belgium (2) 3 *(Fellaini 23, De Bruyne 43, Hazard 78 (pen))*
Bosnia-Herzegovina (1) 1 *(Dzeko 15)*   45,000
Belgium: (433) Courtois; Alderweireld, Kompany, Vermaelen, Vertonghen; Fellaini, Witsel, Nainggolan; De Bruyne (Mertens 89), Lukaku R (Origi 83), Hazard.
Bosnia-Herzegovina: (4231) Begovic; Mujdza, Vranjes O, Spahic (Sunjic 56), Kolasinac (Hajrovic 72); Medunjanin (Ibisevic 80), Besic; Lulic, Pjanic, Visca; Dzeko.
Referee: Manuel de Sousa.

Cyprus (0) 0
Wales (0) 1 *(Bale 82)*   14,492
Cyprus: (442) Georgallides; Antoniades, Laifis, Junior, Demetriou; Makridis, Economides, Nicolaou, Charalambidis (Englezou 74); Makris (Sotiriou 84), Mitidis (Kolokoudias 65).
Wales: (343) Hennessey; Davies, Williams A, King; Edwards, Gunter, Taylor N, Richards; Bale (Church 90), Ramsey (MacDonald 90), Robson-Kanu (Vokes 67).
Referee: Szymon Marciniak.

Israel (4) 4 *(Zahavi 4, Bitton 22, Hemed 26 (pen), Dabour 38)*
Andorra (0) 0   22,650
Israel: (433) Marciano; Dasa, Ben Haim (Melikson 46), Tibi, Reikan; Zahavi (Buzaglo 46), Bitton, Natcho; Dabour, Hemed (Kayal 75), Ben Chaim.
Andorra: (4231) Pol; San Nicolas, Garcia E, Lima, Garcia M; Martinez, Vieira; Rebes (Llovera 80), Rodriguez (Sonejee 54), Moreno (Rubio 73); Sanchez.
Referee: Tamas Bognar.

Sunday, 6 September 2015
Bosnia-Herzegovina (3) 3 *(Bicakcic 14, Dzeko 30, Lulic 45)*
Andorra (0) 0   6830
Bosnia-Herzegovina: (442) Begovic; Bicakcic, Sunjic, Spahic, Kolasinac (Vrancic 79); Kvesic, Besic■, Pjanic (Hadzic 45), Lulic; Ibisevic, Dzeko (Djuric 67).
Andorra: (4411) Pol; San Nicolas, Ferre, Lima, Garcia M; Martinez (Sanchez 76), Sonejee, Ayala (Peppe 81), Rodriguez■; Vieira; Riera (Alves 87).
Referee: Arnold Hunter.

Cyprus (0) 0
Belgium (0) 1 *(Hazard 86)*   11,866
Cyprus: (433) Georgallides; Demetriou, Laifis, Junior, Antoniades; Charalambidis (Laban 53), Makridis, Nicolaou (Artymatas 84); Economides, Makris, Mitidis (Sotiriou 12).
Belgium: (451) Courtois; Alderweireld, Kompany, Vermaelen, Vertonghen; De Bruyne, Fellaini (Mertens 63), Witsel, Nainggolan, Hazard; Benteke (Origi 46).
Referee: Vladislav Bezborodov.

Wales (0) 0
Israel (0) 0   32,653
Wales: (442) Hennessey; Gunter, Taylor, Richards, Williams A; Davies, Edwards, King (Vokes 85), Ramsey; Bale, Robson-Kanu (Church 79).
Israel: (451) Marciano; Ben Haim, Dasa, Dgani, Ben Haroush; Tibi, Bitton, Natcho, Zahavi (Sahar 90), Kayal (Ben Chaim 46); Dabour (Hemed 46).
Referee: Ivan Bebek.

Saturday, 10 October 2015
Andorra (0) 1 *(Lima 51 (pen))*
Belgium (2) 4 *(Nainggolan 19, De Bruyne 42, Hazard 56 (pen), Depoitre 64)*   3032
Andorra: (4141) Pol; San Nicolas, Lima, Llovera, Garcia M; Vieira (Peppe 85); Rebes, Rubio, Moreira (Riera 73), Sonejee (Rodrigues 61); Sanchez.
Belgium: (4141) Mignolet; Meunier (Cavanda 80), Alderweireld, Vertonghen, Lukaku J; Witsel; Nainggolan, Mertens (Chadli 71), Hazard (Bakkali 78), De Bruyne; Depoitre.
Referee: Pawel Gil.

Bosnia-Herzegovina (0) 2 *(Djuric 71, Ibisevic 90)*
Wales (0) 0   10,250
Bosnia-Herzegovina: (451) Begovic; Mujdza, Spahic (Cocalic 46), Sunjic, Zukanovic; Visca (Djuric 61), Pjanic, Hadzic (Bicakcic 89), Salihovic, Lulic; Ibisevic.
Wales: (3511) Hennessey; Gunter, Williams A, Taylor; Ramsey, Davies, Allen (Edwards 84), Richards, Ledley (Vokes 75); Bale; Robson-Kanu (Church 85).
Referee: Alberto Undiano Mallenco.

Israel (0) 1 *(Bitton 76)*
Cyprus (0) 2 *(Junior 58, Demetriou 80)*   25,300
Israel: (442) Marciano; Dasa (Dgani 54), Tibi, Ben Haim, Ben Haroush (Melikson 71); Bitton, Kayal, Zahavi, Ben Chaim; Vermouth (Hemed 65), Dabour.
Cyprus: (433) Georgallides; Demetriou, Junior, Laifis, Antoniades; Nicolaou, Laban, Makridis (Economides 84); Efrem (Merkis 86), Mitidis, Makris (Charalambidis 46).
Referee: Manuel de Sousa.

Tuesday, 13 October 2015
Belgium (0) 3 *(Mertens 64, De Bruyne 78, Hazard 84)*
Israel (0) 1 *(Hemed 88)*   39,773
Belgium: (4231) Mignolet; Vertonghen, Lombaerts, Kompany (Meunier 58), Alderweireld; Nainggolan, Fellaini (Witsel 65); Hazard, De Bruyne, Mertens; Lukaku R (Origi 65).
Israel: (433) Marciano; Ben Haroush, Tibi, Ben Haim, Dgani; Kayal (Damari 66), Yeini (Vermouth 77), Peretz; Ben Chaim (Reikan 59), Hemed, Zahavi.
Referee: Tasos Sidiropoulos.

Cyprus (2) 2 *(Charalambidis 32, Mitidis 41)*
Bosnia-Herzegovina (2) 3 *(Medunjanin 13, 45, Djuric 67)*
                                                     19,000
Cyprus: (4321) Georgallides; Demetriou, Junior, Laifis, Antoniades; Nicolaou (Economides 65), Makridis, Laban (Aloneftis 74); Charalambidis (Kolokoudias 82), Efrem; Mitidis.
Bosnia-Herzegovina: (451) Begovic; Mujdza, Sunjic, Spahic, Zukanovic (Djuric 60); Visca (Bicakcic 79), Medunjanin, Pjanic (Salihovic 86), Vranjes S, Lulic; Ibisevic.
Referee: Anthony Taylor.

Wales (0) 2 *(Ramsey 51, Bale 86)*
Andorra (0) 0   33,280
Wales: (433) Hennessey; Gunter, Williams A, Chester, Davies; Ramsey, Vaughan, Williams J (Church 85); Vokes, Bale, Robson-Kanu (Edwards 23 (Lawrence 46)).
Andorra: (442) Pol; San Nicolas, Lima, Llovera, Rubio; Rodrigues, Vieira, Sonejee (Ayala 70), Moreira (Riera 12); Sanchez, Lorenzo (Garcia M 80).
Referee: Kevin Blom.

Group B Table

	P	W	D	L	F	A	GD	Pts
Belgium	10	7	2	1	24	5	19	23
Wales	10	6	3	1	11	4	7	21
Bosnia-Herzegovina	10	5	2	3	17	12	5	17
Israel	10	4	1	5	16	14	2	13
Cyprus	10	4	0	6	16	17	−1	12
Andorra	10	0	0	10	4	36	−32	0

GROUP C

Monday, 8 September 2014
Luxembourg (1) 1 *(Gerson 42)*
Belarus (0) 1 *(Dragun 78)*   3000
Luxembourg: (442) Joubert; Janisch, Philipps, Schnell, Jans; Da Mota Alves (Laterza 67), Gerson, Martins Pereira, Holter (Payal 76); Bensi, Turpel (Luisi 63).
Belarus: (4141) Gutor; Shitov, Martynovich, Filipenko, Veretilo (Stasevich 62); Olekhnovich (Aleksiyevich 77); Kalachev, Kislyak (Kornilenko 73), Krivets, Balanovich; Dragun.
Referee: Gediminas Mazeika.

Spain (3) 5 *(Sergio Ramos 16 (pen), Alcacer 17, Busquets 45, Silva 50, Pedro 90)*
FYR Macedonia (1) 1 *(Ibraimi 28 (pen))*   16,000
Spain: (433) Casillas; Juanfran, Sergio Ramos (Bartra 68), Albiol, Jordi Alba; Busquets, Fabregas, Koke (Munir 77); Pedro, Alcacer (Isco 57), Silva.
FYR Macedonia: (541) Pacovski; Ristovski, Mojsov, Sikov, Cuculi, Alioski (Demiri 46); Ibraimi, Spirovski (Radeski 64), Trajkovski, Abdurahimi (Velkovski 74); Jahovic.
Referee: Tasos Sidiropoulos.

Ukraine (0) 0
Slovakia (1) 1 *(Mak 17)*   42,000
Ukraine: (451) Pyatov; Shevchuk, Kucher, Rakitskiy, Fedetskiy; Kovalchuk (Bezus 66), Stepanenko, Gusev (Gromov 81), Edmar, Yarmolenko; Zozulya.
Slovakia: (4411) Kozacik; Hubocan, Durica, Gyomber, Pekarik; Weiss (Stoch 67), Hamsik, Kucka, Mak (Duris 90); Pecovsky; Nemec (Kiss 63).
Referee: Craig Thomson.

Thursday, 9 October 2014
Belarus (0) 0
Ukraine (0) 2 *(Martynovich 82 (og), Sydorchuk 90)* 10,500
Belarus: (541) Zhevnov; Palyakow, Verkhovtsov, Martynovich (Savitskiy 87), Filipenko; Kalachev, Krivets, Dragun, Stasevich (Kislyak 46); Gordeichuk (Kornilenko 78).
Ukraine: (433) Pyatov; Fedetskiy, Kucher, Khacheridi, Shevchuk; Stepanenko, Edmar (Budkivskiy 79), Rotan (Sydorchuk 64); Yarmolenko, Zozulya (Tymoschuk 90), Konoplyanka.
Referee: Pol van Boekel.

FYR Macedonia (1) 3 *(Trajkovski 20, Jahovic 66 (pen), Abdurahimi 90)*
Luxembourg (2) 2 *(Bensi 39, Turpel 44)*   7000
FYR Macedonia: (4411) Pacovski; Ristovski, Sikov, Mojsov, Cuculi (Alioski 46); Muarem (Alioski 46), Ademi, Demiri, Trajkovski; Ibraimi (Abdurahimi 46); Kostovski.
Luxembourg: (541) Joubert; Jans, Philipps, Chanot, Gerson, Janisch; Martins Pereira, Mutsch, Turpel (Deville 70); Da Mota Alves (Holter 63); Bensi (Laterza 75).
Referee: Paolo Mazzoleni.

Slovakia (1) 2 *(Kucka 17, Stoch 87)*
Spain (0) 1 *(Alcacer 82)*   9478
Slovakia: (433) Kozacik; Skrtel, Durica, Pekarik, Hubocan; Pecovsky, Gyomber, Kucka (Kiss 83); Mak (Stoch 61), Hamsik, Weiss (Duris 54).
Spain: (4411) Casillas; Pique, Albiol (Pedro 58), Juanfran (Cazorla 81); Jordi Alba; Busquets, Koke, Silva (Alcacer 71), Fabregas; Iniesta; Costa.
Referee: Bjorn Kuipers.

Sunday, 12 October 2014
Belarus (0) 1 *(Kalachev 79)*
Slovakia (0) 3 *(Hamsik 65, 84, Sestak 90)*   4500
Belarus: (4231) Zhevnov; Shitov (Stasevich 76), Martynovich, Filipenko (Palyakow 55), Bordachev; Verkhovtsov, Dragun; Kalachev, Krivets, Balanovich; Bressan (Gordeichuk 46).
Slovakia: (4231) Kozacik; Pekarik, Skrtel, Durica, Gyomber; Pecovsky, Kucka (Kiss 85); Mak (Sestak 62), Hamsik, Weiss (Stoch 80); Nemec.
Referee: Serge Gumienny.

Luxembourg (0) 0
Spain (2) 4 *(Silva 27, Alcacer 42, Costa 69, Bernat 88)* 8500
Luxembourg: (442) Joubert; Mutsch (Deville 86), Chanot, Martins Pereira (Turpel 60); Philipps; Janisch, Jans, Gerson, Holter; Da Mota Alves (Payal 75), Bensi.
Spain: (442) De Gea; Pique, Bartra, Jordi Alba, Carvajal; Busquets, Iniesta (Bernat 72), Koke, Silva (Pedro 71); Alcacer, Costa (Rodrigo 83).
Referee: Pawel Gil.

Ukraine (1) 1 *(Sydorchuk 45)*

FYR Macedonia (0) 0 33,900

Ukraine: (433) Pyatov; Khacheridi, Kucher, Shevchuk, Fedetskiy; Stepanenko, Rotan (Tymoschuk 90), Sydorchuk (Edmar 90); Yarmolenko, Konoplyanka, Zozulya (Budkivskiy 77).
FYR Macedonia: (442) Pacovski; Alioski, Damcevski, Sikov, Ristovski; Ademi, Gligorov (Stojkov 85), Abdurahimi, Trajkovski; Jahovic (Velkovski 62), Ivanovski (Kostovski 70).
Referee: Sebastien Delferiere.

Saturday, 15 November 2014

FYR Macedonia (0) 0

Slovakia (2) 2 *(Kucka 25, Nemec 38)* 6000

FYR Macedonia: (442) Pacovski; Ristovski, Sikov, Mojsov, Alioski; Abdurahimi, Ademi, Demiri (Babunski 74), Trajkovski; Velkovski (Ivanovski 70), Stojkov (Kostovski 46).
Slovakia: (4231) Kozacik; Pekarik (Svento 46), Skrtel, Durica, Hubocan; Pecovsky, Kucka (Kiss 55); Weiss (Duris 78), Hamsik, Stoch; Nemec.
Referee: Pedro Proenca.

Luxembourg (0) 0

Ukraine (1) 3 *(Yarmolenko 33, 53, 56)* 4379

Luxembourg: (451) Joubert; Jans, Schnell, Chanot, Janisch; Martins Pereira (Da Mota Alves 54), Gerson, Mutsch, Holter, Bensi (Joachim 63); Turpel (Deville 77).
Ukraine: (442) Pyatov; Fedetskiy, Rakitskiy, Khacheridi, Shevchuk; Sydorchuk, Tymoschuk, Konoplyanka (Morozyuk 77), Yarmolenko; Zozulya (Budkivskiy 72), Oliynyk (Kovalchuk 85).
Referee: Kristinn Jakobsson.

Spain (2) 3 *(Isco 18, Busquets 19, Pedro 55)*

Belarus (0) 0 19,249

Spain: (442) Casillas; Juanfran, Pique, Sergio Ramos, Jordi Alba; Cazorla (Callejon 69), Busquets (Bruno 46), Koke, Isco (Morata 80); Pedro, Alcacer.
Belarus: (532) Zhevnov; Matsveychyk, Politevich, Martynovich (Bordachev 30), Yanushkevich, Balanovich; Kalachev, Dragun, Nekhaychik; Krivets (Kislyak 80), Kornilenko (Signevich 46).
Referee: Kenn Hansen.

Friday, 27 March 2015

FYR Macedonia (1) 1 *(Trajkovski 9)*

Belarus (1) 2 *(Kalachev 44, Kornilenko 82)* 4000

FYR Macedonia: (442) Pacovski; Ristovski, Sikov, Markoski, Georgievski; Ibraimi, Hasani, Polozani (Bardhi 30), Trajkovski; Velkoski (Todorovski B 63), Abdurahimi (Blazevski 75).
Belarus: (4141) Zhevnov; Shitov, Martynovich, Filipenko, Bordachev; Maewski (Putsila 80); Kalachev, Hleb (Dragun 87), Kislyak, Stasevich (Nekhaychik 90); Kornilenko.
Referee: Anthony Taylor.

Slovakia (3) 3 *(Nemec 10, Weiss 21, Pekarik 40)*

Luxembourg (0) 0 9524

Slovakia: (4231) Kozacik; Pekarik, Skrtel, Durica, Hubocan; Weiss (Mak 71), Stoch (Sestak 80); Hamsik, Kucka (Hrosovsky 59), Pecovsky; Nemec.
Luxembourg: (4231) Joubert; Jans, Schnell, Chanot, Mutsch; Gerson, Holter (Da Mota Alves 51); Philipps, Bensi (Laterza 78), Joachim; Deville (Payal 64).
Referee: Stephan Studer.

Spain (1) 1 *(Morata 28)*

Ukraine (0) 0 45,000

Spain: (4141) Casillas; Juanfran, Pique, Sergio Ramos, Jordi Alba (Bernat 78); Busquets; Silva, Koke, Iniesta (Cazorla 74), Isco; Morata (Pedro 65).
Ukraine: (4231) Pyatov; Fedetskiy, Khacheridi, Kucher, Shevchuk; Tymoschuk, Rotan; Konoplyanka, Stepanenko (Garmash 76), Yarmolenko; Zozulya (Kravets 32 (Budkivskiy 90)).
Referee: Cuneyt Cakir.

Sunday, 14 June 2015

Belarus (0) 0

Spain (1) 1 *(Silva 45)* 13,000

Belarus: (442) Gorbunov; Martynovich, Shitov, Bordachev, Filipenko; Valadzko (Stasevich 81), Hleb (Putsila 89), Kislyak (Dragun 78), Nekhaychik; Maewski, Kornilenko.
Spain: (442) Casillas; Juanfran, Pique, Sergio Ramos, Jordi Alba; Silva (Bernat 85), Busquets, Fabregas (Isco 75), Cazorla; Pedro (Vitolo 64), Morata.
Referee: Robert Schorgenhofer.

Slovakia (2) 2 *(Salata 8, Hamsik 38)*

FYR Macedonia (0) 1 *(Ademi 69)* 11,000

Slovakia: (4231) Kozacik; Pekarik, Skrtel, Salata, Hubocan; Kucka (Hrosovsky 73), Pecovsky; Mak, Hamsik (Duda 80), Weiss; Nemec (Holosko 84).
FYR Macedonia: (4231) Pacovski; Todorovski A, Mojsov, Dimitrovski, Zuta; Trajcevski, Ademi; Ibraimi (Abdurahimi 89), Hasani[■], Muarem (Velkoski 82); Trajkovski (Ivanovski 56).
Referee: Kenn Hansen.

Ukraine (0) 3 *(Kravets 49, Garmash 58, Konoplyanka 86)*

Luxembourg (0) 0 32,000

Ukraine: (451) Pyatov; Morozyuk, Khacheridi, Shevchuk, Rakitskiy (Kucher 76); Yarmolenko, Stepanenko, Konoplyanka, Rotan (Garmash 45) Sydorchuk; Kravets (Seleznyov 71).
Luxembourg: (442) Joubert; Chanot, Schnell, Malget, Jans; Holter (Philipps 75), Payal, Gerson, Mutsch; Da Mota Alves (Deville 69), Turpel (Bensi 52).
Referee: Arnold Hunter.

Saturday, 5 September 2015

Luxembourg (0) 1 *(Thill 90)*

FYR Macedonia (0) 0 1667

Luxembourg: (4411) Joubert; Delgado, Philipps, Chanot, Jans; Martins Pereira (Thill 72), Gerson, Payal, Da Mota Alves; Deville (Bensi 64); Joachim.
FYR Macedonia: (4231) Pacovski; Ristovski, Sikov, Mojsov (Ristevski 37), Zuta; Gligorov, Petrovic; Ibraimi (Askovski 80), Abdurahimi, Trajkovski (Ilijoski 73); Ivanovski.
Referee: Lee Evans.

Spain (2) 2 *(Jordi Alba 5, Iniesta 30 (pen))*

Slovakia (0) 0 19,874

Spain: (433) Casillas; Juanfran, Pique, Sergio Ramos, Jordi Alba; Fabregas (Cazorla 67), Busquets, Iniesta (Koke 85); Silva, Costa (Alcacer 75), Pedro.
Slovakia: (451) Kozacik; Pekarik, Salata, Hubocan, Tesak; Hrosovsky (Sabo 74), Gregus, Gyomber, Hamsik (Duda 61), Svento; Mak (Duris 46).
Referee: Damir Skomina.

Ukraine (3) 3 *(Kravets 7, Yarmolenko 30, Konoplyanka 41 (pen))*

Belarus (0) 1 *(Kornilenko 62 (pen))* 60,000

Ukraine: (4411) Pyatov; Fedetskiy, Khacheridi, Rakitskiy, Shevchuk; Yarmolenko (Gusev 69), Rotan (Rybalka 75), Stepanenko, Konoplyanka; Garmash[■]; Kravets (Gladkyy 85).
Belarus: (4411) Gorbunov; Shitov, Martynovich, Filipenko, Volodko; Stasevich, Maewski, Sivakov (Gordeichuk 46), Kalachev (Signevich 72); Hleb (Bressan 86); Kornilenko.
Referee: Liran Liany.

Tuesday, 8 September 2015

Belarus (1) 2 *(Gordeichuk 34, 62)*

Luxembourg (0) 0 3482

Belarus: (4141) Zhevnov; Shitov, Filipenko, Sivakov, Bordachev; Dragun; Gordeichuk (Kalachev 75), Hleb (Kislyak 58), Bressan, Nekhaychik; Kornilenko (Signevich 84).
Luxembourg: (442) Joubert; Janisch, Schnell, Chanot, Philipps; Jans, Payal (Da Mota Alves 46), Mutsch, Gerson; Deville (Turpel 69), Joachim (Bensi 46).
Referee: Slavko Vincic.

FYR Macedonia (0) 0

Spain (1) 1 *(Pacovski 8 (og))*   30,000

FYR Macedonia: (4231) Pacovski; Brdarovski, Sikov, Ristevski, Zuta; Gligorov, Petrovic; Radeski (Ibraimi 84), Hasani, Askovski (Bardi 77); Ivanovski (Trajkovski 69).
Spain: (433) De Gea; Carvajal, Pique, Sergio Ramos, Bernat; Cazorla (Koke 68), Busquets, Isco (Iniesta 78); Mata, Costa (Alcacer 61), Silva.
Referee: Paolo Tagliavento.

Slovakia (0) 0

Ukraine (0) 0   10,648

Slovakia: (4411) Kozacik; Pekarik (Salata 51), Skrtel, Hubocan, Gyomber; Mak (Stoch 84), Kucka, Pecovsky, Duris; Hamsik; Vittek (Jakubko 66).
Ukraine: (4411) Pyatov; Fedetskiy, Khacheridi, Rakitskiy, Shevchuk; Yarmolenko, Stepanenko, Rybalka, Konoplyanka; Rotan; Kravets (Gladkyy 90).
Referee: Martin Atkinson.

Friday, 9 October 2015

FYR Macedonia (0) 0

Ukraine (0) 2 *(Seleznyov 59 (pen), Kravets 87)*   2500

FYR Macedonia: (433) Pacovski; Brdarovski, Sikov, Ristevski, Zuta; Petrovic, Ibraimi, Alimi; Hasani (Abdurahimi 21), Askovski (Nestoroski 78), Ilijoski (Ivanovski 64).
Ukraine: (433) Pyatov; Fedetskiy, Khacheridi, Rakitskiy, Shevchuk; Rybalka, Sydorchuk, Rotan (Malinovsky 90); Yarmolenko (Karavayev 86), Konoplyanka, Seleznyov (Kravets 74).
Referee: Ovidiu Alin Hategan.

Slovakia (0) 0

Belarus (1) 1 *(Dragun 34)*   9859

Slovakia: (4411) Kozacik; Hubocan, Skrtel, Salata, Svento; Mak (Duda 79), Kucka, Pecovsky (Nemec 60), Weiss (Stoch 71); Hamsik; Duris.
Belarus: (442) Gorbunov; Palyakow, Martynovich■, Sivakov, Bordachev (Valadzko 40); Stasevich, Dragun, Bressan, Nekhaychik (Politevich 69); Gordeichuk, Signevich (Kislyak 72).
Referee: Huseyin Gocek.

Spain (1) 4 *(Cazorla 42, 85, Alcacer 67, 81)*

Luxembourg (0) 0   14,472

Spain: (433) Casillas; Juanfran, Bartra, Pique, Jordi Alba; Cazorla, Busquets, Fabregas; Silva (Mata 10), Morata (Alcacer 33), Pedro (Nolito 77).
Luxembourg: (541) Joubert; Delgado, Malget, Chanot, Gerson, Jans; Bensi (Deville 64), Mutsch, Payal, Martins Pereira (Da Mota Alves 79); Joachim (Turpel 79).
Referee: Sebastian Delferiere.

Monday, 12 October 2015

Belarus (0) 0

FYR Macedonia (0) 0   1545

Belarus: (442) Gorbunov; Palyakow, Politevich, Sivakov, Valadzko; Stasevich, Dragun (Putsila 73), Bressan, Nekhaychik (Kislyak 61); Gordeichuk, Signevich.
FYR Macedonia: (442) Nilsson; Ristovski, Sikov, Mojsov, Zuta; Brdarovski (Abdurahimi 73), Petrovic, Stjepanovic (Alimi 84), Trickovski; Ibraimi (Nestoroski 86), Trajkovski.
Referee: Christian Dingert.

Luxembourg (0) 2 *(Mutsch 62, Gerson 66 (pen))*

Slovakia (3) 4 *(Hamsik 24, 90, Nemec 29, Mak 30)*   2512

Luxembourg: (541) Joubert; Delgado (Turpel 81), Philipps, Chanot, Gerson, Jans; Bensi (Thill 66), Mutsch, Payal (Malget 57), Martins Pereira; Joachim.
Slovakia: (4411) Kozacik; Gyomber, Skrtel, Hubocan, Svento; Mak (Sabo 86), Pecovsky, Kucka, Weiss (Sestak 71); Hamsik; Nemec (Jakubko 78).
Referee: Oliver Drachta.

Ukraine (0) 0

Spain (1) 1 *(Mario 22)*   61,248

Ukraine: (4411) Pyatov; Fedetskiy, Kucher, Rakitskiy, Shevchuk; Yarmolenko, Rotan (Zinchenko 87), Stepanenko, Konoplyanka; Garmash (Rybalka 58); Kravets (Seleznyov 87).

Spain: (433) De Gea; Mario, Etxeita, Nacho, Azpilicueta; Isco, Thiago, San Jose; Fabregas (Mata 64), Nolito (Jordi Alba 74), Alcacer (Busquets 84).
Referee: Milorad Mazic.

Group C Table	P	W	D	L	F	A	GD	Pts
Spain	10	9	0	1	23	3	20	27
Slovakia	10	7	1	2	17	8	9	22
Ukraine	10	6	1	3	14	4	10	19
Belarus	10	3	2	5	8	14	–6	11
Luxembourg	10	1	1	8	6	27	–21	4
FYR Macedonia	10	1	1	8	6	18	–12	4

GROUP D

Sunday, 7 September 2014

Georgia (0) 1 *(Okriashvili 38)*

Republic of Ireland (1) 2 *(McGeady 23, 90)*   40,000

Georgia: (4141) Loria (Kvaskhvadze 46); Lobjanidze, Kvirkvelia S, Khubutia, Kvirkvelia D; Kashia; Kankava, Daushvili, Ananidze (Targamadze 62), Okriashvili (Mchedlidze 88); Gelashvili.
Republic of Ireland: (4141) Forde; Coleman, O'Shea, Wilson, Ward; McCarthy (Meyler 90); Whelan, Walters, Keane (Long 75), McGeady; Quinn (Brady 76).
Referee: Kevin Blom.

Germany (1) 2 *(Muller 18, 70)*

Scotland (0) 1 *(Anya 66)*   60,209

Germany: (4231) Neuer; Rudy, Howedes, Boateng, Durm; Kroos, Kramer; Gotze, Reus (Ginter 90), Schurrle (Podolski 84); Muller.
Scotland: (442) Marshall; Hutton, Martin R, Whittaker, Hanley; Mulgrew■, Morrison, Fletcher D (McArthur 58), Bannan (Fletcher S 58); Anya, Naismith (Maloney 82).
Referee: Svein Oddvar Moen.

Gibraltar (0) 0

Poland (1) 7 *(Grosicki 11, 47, Lewandowski 50, 53, 86, 90, Szukala 58)*   3000

Gibraltar: (451) Perez J; Wiseman, Chipolina J, Artell (Payas 87), Chipolina R; Casciaro L, Bado, Casciaro R, Walker, Perez B; Casciaro K (Priestley 62).
Poland: (442) Szczesny; Olkowski, Szukala, Glik, Wawrzyniak; Grosicki (Starzynski 78), Krychowiak, Klich (Maczynski 71), Rybus; Milik (Sobota 71), Lewandowski.
Referee: Stefan Johannesson.

Saturday, 11 October 2014

Poland (0) 2 *(Milik 51, Mila 88)*

Germany (0) 0   57,500

Poland: (442) Szczesny; Szukala, Jodlowiec, Wawrzyniak (Jedrzejczyk 84), Glik; Piszczek, Krychowiak, Grosicki (Sobota 71), Rybus; Milik (Mila 77), Lewandowski.
Germany: (4231) Neuer; Hummels, Durm, Rudiger (Kruse 83), Boateng; Bellarabi, Kroos, Gotze, Kramer (Draxler 72), Schurrle (Podolski 78); Muller.
Referee: Pedro Proenca.

Republic of Ireland (3) 7 *(Keane 6, 14, 18 (pen), McClean 46, 53, Perez J 51 (og), Hoolahan 56)*

Gibraltar (0) 0   18,500

Republic of Ireland: (442) Forde; Meyler, O'Shea, Wilson, Ward (Brady 70); McGeady, Hendrick, Gibson, McClean; Hoolahan (Doyle 63), Keane (Murphy 63).
Gibraltar: (442) Perez J (Robba 60); Wiseman, Casciaro R, Chipolina R (Santos 58), Chipolina J; Perez B, Bado (Guilling 46), Payas, Walker, Gosling; Casciaro L.
Referee: Leontios Trattou.

Scotland (1) 1 *(Khubutia 28 (og))*

Georgia (0) 0   48,000

Scotland: (433) Marshall; Robertson, Martin R, Hanley, Hutton; Maloney, Brown, Anya; Fletcher S (Martin C 90), Morrison, Naismith (McArthur 80).
Georgia: (442) Loria; Lobjanidze, Khubutia, Kvirkvelia D (Okriashvili 46), Kvirkvelia S; Daushvili, Grigalava, Kazaishvili (Chanturia 80), Kankava; Gelashvili, Papava (Dzaria 70).
Referee: Miroslav Zelinka.

Tuesday, 14 October 2014

Germany (0) 1 *(Kroos 71)*
Republic of Ireland (0) 1 *(O'Shea 90)*   52,000
Germany: (4231) Neuer; Rudiger, Boateng, Hummels, Durm; Ginter (Podolski 46), Kroos; Bellarabi (Rudy 86), Gotze, Draxler (Kruse 70); Muller.
Republic of Ireland: (442) Forde; Meyler, O'Shea, Wilson, Ward; McGeady, Quinn (Hoolahan 76), Whelan (Hendrick 53), McClean; Walters, Keane (Gibson 62).
Referee: Damir Skomina.

Gibraltar (0) 0
Georgia (2) 3 *(Gelashvili 9, Okriashvili 20, Kankava 69)*
                                                              600
Gibraltar: (451) Robba; Garcia, Wiseman, Santos (Chipolina R 76), Chipolina J; Guilling (Gosling 75), Perez B, Casciaro R, Walker, Casciaro K (Priestley 46); Casciaro L.
Georgia: (4231) Loria; Lobjanidze, Khubutia, Kvirkvelia S, Grigalava; Kankava, Dzaria; Okriashvili, Ananidze (Ebralidze 80), Chanturia (Dvalishvili 76); Gelashvili (Papunashvili 67).
Referee: Harald Lechner.

Poland (1) 2 *(Maczynski 11, Milik 76)*
Scotland (1) 2 *(Maloney 18, Naismith 57)*   55,197
Poland: (442) Szczesny; Piszczek, Szukala, Glik, Jedrzejczyk; Grosicki (Zyro 89), Maczynski, Krychowiak, Sobota (Mila 63); Lewandowski, Milik.
Scotland: (442) Marshall; Hutton, Martin R, Greer, Whittaker; Maloney, Morrison, Brown, Anya; Fletcher S (Fletcher D 70), Naismith (Martin C 70).
Referee: Alberto Undiano Mallenco.

Friday, 14 November 2014

Georgia (0) 0
Poland (0) 4 *(Glik 51, Krychowiak 71, Mila 73, Milik 90)*
                                                           18,000
Georgia: (4231) Loria; Lobjanidze, Kvirkvelia S, Khubutia, Grigalava; Daushvili, Kashia; Ananidze (Okriashvili 59), Kankava, Kobakhidze (Dzalamidze 88); Mchedlidze (Chanturia 68).
Poland: (4231) Szczesny; Piszczek, Szukala, Glik, Jedrzejczyk; Krychowiak, Maczynski (Jodlowiec 66); Grosicki (Rybus 69), Milik, Mila (Linetty 86); Lewandowski.
Referee: Paolo Tagliavento.

Germany (3) 4 *(Muller 11, 29, Gotze 38, Santos 67 (og))*
Gibraltar (0) 0   44,380
Germany: (3142) Neuer; Durm (Hector 71), Boateng, Mustafi; Kroos (Bender 79); Gotze, Khedira (Volland 60), Podolski, Kruse; Muller, Bellarabi.
Gibraltar: (451) Robba; Garcia, Artell, Wiseman, Casciaro R; Chipolina J, Perez B (Priestley 90), Chipolina R, Sergeant (Santos 58); Walker; Casciaro L (Casciaro K 71).
Referee: Alexandru Dan Tudor.

Scotland (0) 1 *(Maloney 74)*
Republic of Ireland (0) 0   60,000
Scotland: (4411) Marshall; Whittaker, Martin R, Hanley, Robertson; Maloney, Mulgrew, Brown, Anya (Fletcher D 88); Naismith; Fletcher S (Martin C 56).
Republic of Ireland: (442) Forde; Coleman, Keogh, O'Shea, Ward; McGeady, Hendrick (Keane 78), Gibson (Quinn 69), McClean; Walters, Long (Brady 68).
Referee: Milorad Mazic.

Sunday, 29 March 2015

Georgia (0) 0
Germany (2) 2 *(Reus 39, Muller 44)*   54,549
Georgia: (451) Loria; Lobjanidze, Kvirkvelia S, Amisulashvili (Dvali 4), Kashia; Navalovski, Kobakhidze, Kankava, Makharadze (Kenia 63), Okriashvili (Chanturia 47); Mchedlidze.
Germany: (4231) Neuer; Rudy, Boateng, Hummels, Hector; Schweinsteiger, Kroos; Muller (Schurrle 86), Ozil, Reus; Gotze (Podolski 87).
Referee: Clement Turpin.

Republic of Ireland (0) 1 *(Long 90)*
Poland (1) 1 *(Peszko 26)*   50,500
Republic of Ireland: (442) Given; Coleman, O'Shea, Wilson, Brady; Hoolahan, Whelan (Long 83), McCarthy, McGeady (McClean 68); Keane, Walters.
Poland: (442) Fabianski; Olkowski, Szukala, Glik, Wawrzyniak; Peszko (Kucharczyk 87), Krychowiak, Jodlowiec, Rybus; Lewandowski, Milik (Mila 83).
Referee: Jonas Eriksson.

Scotland (4) 6 *(Maloney 18 (pen), 34 (pen),*
Fletcher S 29, 77, 90, Naismith 39)
Gibraltar (1) 1 *(Casciaro L 19)*   34,255
Scotland: (352) Marshall; Martin R, Hutton, Robertson; Anya (Bannan 74), Brown, Morrison, Maloney, Ritchie (Greer 46); Fletcher S, Naismith (Rhodes 65).
Gibraltar: (451) Robba; Wiseman, Artell (Garcia 53), Casciaro R, Chipolina J; Walker, Payas, Chipolina R (Gosling 73), Bardon (Duarte D 82), Priestley; Casciaro L.
Referee: Mattias Gestranius.

Saturday, 13 June 2015

Gibraltar (0) 0
Germany (1) 7 *(Schurrle 28, 65, 71, Kruse 47, 81,*
Gundogan 51, Bellarabi 57)   7467
Gibraltar: (442) Perez J; Garcia, Chipolina R, Casciaro R, Chipolina J; Gosling, Walker, Payas (Sergeant 83), Casciaro K (Bosio 78); Casciaro L, Priestley (Coombes 61).
Germany: (352) Weidenfeller; Rudy, Boateng, Hector; Herrmann (Podolski 56), Ozil, Schweinsteiger, Gundogan (Khedira 67), Bellarabi; Gotze (Kruse 35), Schurrle.
Referee: Clayton Pisani.

Poland (0) 4 *(Milik 61, Lewandowski 89, 90, 90)*
Georgia (0) 0   5600
Poland: (442) Fabianski; Piszczek, Szukala, Pazdan (Komorowski 90), Rybus; Grosicki (Jodlowiec 78), Krychowiak, Maczynski, Peszko (Blaszczykowski 64); Lewandowski, Milik.
Georgia: (541) Loria; Lobjanidze, Kashia, Amisulashvili, Dvali, Navalovski; Okriashvili (Daushvili 46), Ananidze, Kobakhidze (Tskhadadze 75), Kazaishvili; Vatsadze (Chanturia 63).
Referee: Aleksei Kulbakov.

Republic of Ireland (1) 1 *(Walters 39)*
Scotland (0) 1 *(O'Shea 46 (og))*   49,063
Republic of Ireland: (442) Given; Coleman, O'Shea, Wilson, Brady; Hendrick, Whelan (McClean 68), McCarthy, Hoolahan (Keane 73); Walters, Murphy (Long 80).
Scotland: (4231) Marshall; Hutton, Martin R, Mulgrew, Forsyth; Ritchie (Anya 45), Brown (McArthur 85); Morrison, Naismith (Berra 90), Maloney; Fletcher S.
Referee: Nicola Rizzoli.

Friday, 4 September 2015

Georgia (1) 1 *(Kazaishvili 37)*
Scotland (0) 0   23,000
Georgia: (451) Revishvili; Lobjanidze, Kvirkvelia S, Amisulashvili, Navalovski; Okriashvili (Merebashvili 71), Ananidze (Daushvili 82), Kashia, Kankava, Kazaishvili; Mchedlidze (Vatsadze 90).
Scotland: (451) Marshall; Hutton, Martin R, Mulgrew, Robertson (Hanley 59); Anya (Griffiths 75), Brown, Maloney, Morrison, Naismith (Forrest 59); Fletcher S.
Referee: Ovidiu Alin Hategan.

Germany (2) 3 *(Muller 12, Gotze 19, 82)*
Poland (1) 1 *(Lewandowski 36)*   48,500
Germany: (4231) Neuer; Can, Boateng, Hummels, Hector; Schweinsteiger, Kroos; Muller, Ozil, Bellarabi (Gundogan 52); Gotze (Podolski 90).
Poland: (442) Fabianski; Piszczek (Olkowski 43), Szukala, Glik, Rybus; Maczynski (Blaszczykowski 62), Jodlowiec, Krychowiak, Grosicki (Peszko 83); Milik, Lewandowski.
Referee: Nicola Rizzoli.

Gibraltar (0) 0
Republic of Ireland (1) 4 *(Christie 26, Keane 49, 51 (pen),*
Long 79) 5393
Gibraltar: (4411) Perez J; Garcia, Barnett, Chipolina R,
Chipolina J; Sergeant (Gulling 85), Walker, Bardon,
Casciaro K (Gosling 61); Casciaro L; Duarte J (Yome
74).
Republic of Ireland: (442) Given; Christie, O'Shea, Clark,
Hendrick; Hoolahan (McGeady 77), McCarthy (Quinn
70), Whelan, Brady; Keane (Long 71), Walters.
Referee: Marijo Strahonja.

Monday, 7 September 2015
Poland (4) 8 *(Grosicki 8, 15, Lewandowski 19, 29,*
Milik 56, 72, Blaszczykowski 59 (pen), Kapustka 74)
Gibraltar (0) 1 *(Gosling 87)* 27,763
Poland: (442) Fabianski; Olkowski (Mila 87), Glik,
Szukala, Rybus; Blaszczykowski (Kapustka 62),
Krychowiak, Maczynski, Grosicki; Lewandowski
(Zielinski 65), Milik.
Gibraltar: (352) Perez J; Barnett, Chipolina R, Chipolina
J; Garcia, Casciaro L (Lopez 79), Gosling, Bardon,
Walker; Coombes (Casciaro K 46), Duarte J (Bosio 68).
Referee: Gediminas Mazeika.

Republic of Ireland (0) 1 *(Walters 69)*
Georgia (0) 0 27,200
Republic of Ireland: (433) Given; Coleman, O'Shea,
Clark, Brady; Hendrick, Whelan, McCarthy; Hoolahan
(McClean 75), Walters, Keane (Long 46).
Georgia: (451) Revishvili; Lobjanidze, Kvirkvelia S,
Amisulashvili, Navalovski; Kazaishvili (Papunashvili 64),
Okriashvili, Kashia (Tsintsadze 76), Khizanishvili (Kenia
81), Kankava; Mchedlidze.
Referee: Istvan Vad.

Scotland (2) 2 *(Hummels 28 (og), McArthur 43)*
Germany (2) 3 *(Muller 18, 34, Gundogan 54)* 52,000
Scotland: (4411) Marshall; Hutton, Martin R, Hanley,
Mulgrew; Maloney (Anya 60), McArthur, Brown (Martin
C 80), Forrest (Ritchie 80); Morrison; Fletcher S.
Germany: (4231) Neuer; Can, Boateng, Hummels,
Hector; Schweinsteiger, Kroos; Muller, Ozil (Kramer 90),
Gundogan; Gotze (Schurrle 86).
Referee: Bjorn Kuipers.

Thursday, 8 October 2015
Georgia (3) 4 *(Vatsadze 30, 45, Okriashvili 35 (pen),*
Kazaishvili 87)
Gibraltar (0) 0 11,330
Georgia: (4231) Revishvili; Kakabadze, Kashia,
Amisulashvili, Grigalava; Kankava (Palavandishvili 57),
Kvekveskiri; Okriashvili (Dzalamidze 58), Kazaishvili,
Kobakhidze; Vatsadze (Tskhadadze 73).
Gibraltar: (4321) Perez J; Garcia, Casciaro R, Chipolina
R, Chipolina J; Gosling, Casciaro L (Duarte J 76),
Casciaro K (Yome 85); Walker, Bardon; Cabrera (Perez
B 46).
Referee: Serhiy Boiko.

Republic of Ireland (0) 1 *(Long 70)*
Germany (0) 0 50,604
Republic of Ireland: (433) Given (Randolph 44); Christie,
Keogh, O'Shea, Ward (Meyler 69); Hendrick, McCarthy,
Brady; Walters, Hoolahan, Murphy (Long 65).
Germany: (442) Neuer; Ginter (Bellarabi 77), Boateng,
Hummels, Hector; Reus, Gundogan (Volland 85), Kroos,
Ozil; Muller, Gotze (Schurrle 35).
Referee: Carlos Velasco Carballo.

Scotland (1) 2 *(Ritchie 45, Fletcher S 62)*
Poland (1) 2 *(Lewandowski 3, 90)* 49,359
Scotland: (4411) Marshall; Hutton, Martin R, Hanley,
Whittaker; Forrest (Dorrans 84), Brown, Fletcher D
(McArthur 74), Ritchie; Naismith (Maloney 69); Fletcher
S.
Poland: (4411) Fabianski; Piszczek, Pazdan, Glik, Rybus
(Wawrzyniak 71); Grosicki, Krychowiak, Maczynski,
Milik; Blaszczykowski (Olkowski 83); Lewandowski.
Referee: Viktor Kassai.

Sunday, 11 October 2015
Germany (0) 2 *(Muller 50 (pen), Kruse 79)*
Georgia (0) 1 *(Kankava 53)* 43,630
Germany: (4411) Neuer; Ginter, Boateng, Hummels,
Hector; Gundogan, Kroos, Muller, Ozil; Reus (Bellarabi
90); Schurrle (Kruse 76).
Georgia: (523) Revishvili; Lobjanidze, Kvirkvelia,
Amisulashvili, Kashia, Navalovski; Kankava, Kvekveskiri
(Khizanishvili 78); Kazaishvili (Kobakhidze 90),
Gelashvili (Vatsadze 46), Okriashvili.
Referee: Pavel Kralovec.

Gibraltar (0) 0
Scotland (2) 6 *(Martin C 25, Maloney 39,*
Fletcher S 52, 56, 85, Naismith 90) 12,401
Gibraltar: (541) Robba; Garcia, Barnett, Chipolina R,
Casciaro R, Chipolina J; Walker, Duarte D (Perez B 57),
Casciaro L (Duarte J 82), Bardon; Casciaro K (Yome
89).
Scotland: (442) McGregor; Hutton, Greer, Berra,
Robertson; Ritchie (Russell 64), Dorrans, Brown
(Fletcher D 63), Maloney; Martin C (Naismith 76),
Fletcher S.
Referee: Aleksei Kulbakov.

Poland (2) 2 *(Krychowiak 13, Lewandowski 42)*
Republic of Ireland (1) 1 *(Walters 16 (pen))* 57,497
Poland: (4231) Fabianski; Piszczek, Glik, Pazdan,
Wawrzyniak; Linetty, Krychowiak; Olkowski
(Blaszczykowski 63), Maczynski (Szukala 78), Grosicki
(Peszko 85); Lewandowski.
Republic of Ireland: (442) Randolph; Coleman, O'Shea■,
Keogh, Brady; McClean (Hoolahan 73), McCarthy,
Whelan (McGeady 58), Hendrick; Walters, Long (Keane
55).
Referee: Cuneyt Cakir.

Group D Table	P	W	D	L	F	A	GD	Pts
Germany	10	7	1	2	24	9	15	22
Poland	10	6	3	1	33	10	23	21
Republic of Ireland	10	5	3	2	19	7	12	18
Scotland	10	4	3	3	22	12	10	15
Georgia	10	3	0	7	10	16	–6	9
Gibraltar	10	0	0	10	2	56	–54	0

GROUP E

Monday, 8 September 2014
Estonia (0) 1 *(Purje 86)*
Slovenia (0) 0 14,000
Estonia: (451) Pareiko; Teniste (Jaager 71), Morozov,
Klavan, Kallaste; Antonov (Kams 67), Vunk, Mets,
Lindpere (Purje 84), Zenjov; Anier.
Slovenia: (433) Handanovic; Struna, Cesar, Samardzic,
Brecko; Kurtic, Rotman (Lazarevic 89), Kampl;
Stevanovic■, Ilicic (Birsa 62), Novakovic.
Referee: Szymon Marciniak.

San Marino (0) 0
Lithuania (2) 2 *(Matulevicius 5, Novikovas 36)* 986
San Marino: (532) Simoncini A; Vitaioli F, Simoncini D,
Brolli, Bonini (Buscarini 87), Battistini; Gasperoni A,
Tosi (Cervellini 56), Vitaioli M; Hirsch (Stefanelli 76),
Selva.
Lithuania: (4231) Arlauskis; Freidgeimas, Kijanskas,
Zaliukas, Slavickas; Chvedukas, Panka (Vicius 66);
Cernych (Kuklys 89), Kalonas, Novikovas; Matulevicius
(Stankevicius 85).
Referee: Libor Kovank.

Switzerland (0) 0
England (0) 2 *(Welbeck 59, 90)* 35,500
Switzerland: (433) Sommer; Lichtsteiner, von Bergen,
Djourou, Rodriguez; Behrami, Inler, Xhaka (Dzemaili
74); Shaqiri, Seferovic, Mehmedi (Drmic 64).
England: (4312) Hart; Stones, Cahill, Jones (Jagielka 77),
Baines; Wilshere (Milner 73), Henderson, Delph;
Sterling; Welbeck, Rooney (Lambert 90).
Referee: Cuneyt Cakir.

Thursday, 9 October 2014
England (2) 5 *(Jagielka 24, Rooney 43 (pen), Welbeck 49,*
Townsend 72, Della Valle 77 (og))
San Marino (0) 0 55,990
England: (433) Hart; Chambers, Cahill, Jagielka, Gibbs;
Henderson (Oxlade-Chamberlain 46), Milner, Wilshere;
Welbeck (Townsend 66), Rooney, Sterling (Lallana 46).
San Marino: (541) Simoncini A; Palazzi (Buscarini 73),
Vitaioli F, Della Valle, Brolli, Battistini; Hirsch, Tosi
(Gasperoni L 63), Chiaruzzi, Vitaioli M; Selva (Rinaldi
87).
Referee: Marcin Borski.

Lithuania (0) 1 *(Mikoliunas 76)*
Estonia (0) 0 4800
Lithuania: (4411) Arlauskis; Vaitkunas, Freidgeimas,
Kijanskas, Andriuskevicius; Novikovas, Vicius, Panka,
Cernych; Kalonas (Mikoliunas 63); Matulevicius
(Beniusis 90).
Estonia: (4141) Pareiko; Kallaste■, Klavan, Barengrub,
Jaager; Mets; Antonov, Vunk (Purje 80), Lindpere
(Vassiljev 77), Zenjov (Ojamaa 64); Anier.
Referee: Carlos Clos Gomez.

Slovenia (0) 1 *(Novakovic 80 (pen))*
Switzerland (0) 0 8500
Slovenia: (4312) Handanovic; Brecko, Ilic, Cesar, Struna;
Birsa (Lazarevic 55), Mertelj, Kirm (Pecnik 72); Kampl;
Ljubijankic (Kurtic 46), Novakovic.
Switzerland: (442) Sommer; Lichtsteiner, Djourou,
Senderos (von Bergen 70), Rodriguez; Shaqiri, Behrami,
Inler (Kasami 81), Xhaka; Seferovic, Drmic (Mehmedi 73).
Referee: Wolfgang Stark.

Sunday, 12 October 2014
Estonia (0) 0
England (0) 1 *(Rooney 73)* 9692
Estonia: (4141) Pareiko; Jaager, Morozov, Klavan■, Pikk;
Mets; Antonov, Vunk (Kruglov 83), Vassiljev (Lindpere
46), Zenjov (Ojamaa 79); Anier.
England: (442) Hart; Chambers, Cahill, Jagielka, Baines;
Henderson (Sterling 64), Wilshere, Delph (Oxlade-
Chamberlain 61), Lallana; Welbeck (Lambert 80),
Rooney.
Referee: Marijo Strahonja.

Lithuania (0) 0
Slovenia (2) 2 *(Novakovic 33, 37)* 4000
Lithuania: (442) Arlauskis; Vaitkunas, Freidgeimas,
Kijanskas, Andriuskevicius; Novikovas, Zulpa, Panka
(Vicius 32), Cernych; Chvedukas (Mikoliunas 75),
Matulevicius.
Slovenia: (4132) Handanovic; Brecko, Ilic, Cesar, Struna;
Stevanovic (Mertelj 46); Pecnik (Birsa 66), Kurtic, Kirm
(Lazarevic 86); Kampl, Novakovic.
Referee: Michail Koukoulakis.

Tuesday, 14 October 2014
San Marino (0) 0
Switzerland (3) 4 *(Seferovic 10, 23, Dzemaili 30,*
Shaqiri 79) 5700
San Marino: (541) Simoncini A; Bonini, Vitaioli F
(Cervellini 17), Della Valle, Brolli, Battistini; Palazzi,
Gasperoni A (Gasperoni L 70), Chiaruzzi, Vitaioli M
(Hirsch 61); Stefanelli.
Switzerland: (41212) Sommer; Rodriguez, Djourou, von
Bergen, Lichtsteiner (Widmer 59); Xhaka; Dzemaili,
Kasami (Barnetta 72); Shaqiri; Drmic (Mehmedi 46),
Seferovic.
Referee: Tony Chapron.

Saturday, 15 November 2014
England (0) 3 *(Rooney 59 (pen), Welbeck 65, 72)*
Slovenia (0) 1 *(Henderson 57 (og))* 90,000
England: (433) Hart; Clyne, Cahill, Jagielka (Smalling
89), Gibbs; Henderson, Wilshere, Lallana (Milner 79);
Welbeck, Rooney, Sterling (Oxlade-Chamberlain 84).
Slovenia: (4141) Handanovic; Brecko, Cesar, Ilic, Struna;
Kirm (Ljubijankic 77); Birsa (Lazarevic 62), Kampl,
Kurtic (Rotman 75), Mertelj; Novakovic.
Referee: Olegario Benquerenca.

San Marino (0) 0
Estonia (0) 0 759
San Marino: (541) Simoncini A; Bonini, Vitaioli F,
Simoncini D, Brolli, Palazzi; Hirsch (Battistini 60),
Chiaruzzi, Tosi, Vitaioli M (Golinucci E 77); Selva
(Rinaldi 83).
Estonia: (442) Aksalu; Teniste, Morozov, Artjunin
(Teever 74), Kruglov; Antonov, Dmitrijev (Lindpere 46),
Mets, Vassiljev; Ojamaa (Anier 62), Zenjov.
Referee: Felix Brych.

Switzerland (0) 4 *(Schar Arlauskis 66 (og), 68,*
Shaqiri 80, 90)
Lithuania (0) 0 16,050
Switzerland: (433) Sommer; Moubandje (Fernandes 75),
Schar, Djourou, Lichtsteiner; Dzemaili, Inler, Behrami;
Mehmedi (Drmic 63), Shaqiri, Seferovic (Schonbachler 83).
Lithuania: (451) Arlauskis; Vaitkunas (Borovskij 64),
Freidgeimas, Kijanskas, Andriuskevicius; Cernych, Vicius
(Eliosius 83), Chvedukas, Zulpa, Novikovas (Kazlauskas
87); Matulevicius.
Referee: Svein Oddvar Moen.

Friday, 27 March 2015
England (2) 4 *(Rooney 7, Welbeck 45, Sterling 58, Kane 73)*
Lithuania (0) 0 83,671
England: (433) Hart; Clyne, Cahill, Jones, Baines;
Henderson (Barkley 71), Carrick, Delph; Sterling,
Welbeck (Walcott 77), Rooney (Kane 71).
Lithuania: (532) Arlauskis; Freidgeimas, Kijanskas,
Mikuckis (Stankevicius 66), Zaliukas, Andriuskevicius
(Slavickas 83); Zulpa, Mikoliunas (Kazlauskas 88),
Chvedukas; Cernych, Matulevicius.
Referee: Pavel Kralovec.

Slovenia (1) 6 *(Ilicic 10, Kampl 49, Struna 50,*
Novakovic 52, Lazarevic 73, Ilic 88)
San Marino (0) 0 8300
Slovenia: (433) Handanovic; Brecko (Stojanovic 76), Ilic,
Cesar, Struna; Birsa, Kurtic, Kirm (Lazarevic 60); Ilicic
(Beric 72), Kampl, Novakovic.
San Marino: (541) Benedettini; Bonini, Brolli, Simoncini
D, Tosi (Battistini 56), Della Valle (Vitaioli F 77); Hirsch
(Golinucci A 83), Mazza, Vitaioli M, Selva; Palazzi.
Referee: Oliver Drachta.

Switzerland (2) 3 *(Schar 17, Xhaka 27, Seferovic 80)*
Estonia (0) 0 14,000
Switzerland: (4312) Sommer; Lichtsteiner (Widmer 77),
Schar, Djourou, Rodriguez; Behrami, Inler, Xhaka (Frei
88); Shaqiri; Seferovic, Drmic (Stocker 62).
Estonia: (442) Pareiko; Teniste, Jaager, Klavan, Kallaste;
Vassiljev, Dmitrijev (Kruglov 62), Mets, Antonov;
Zenjov (Alliku 87), Anier (Ojamaa 56).
Referee: Danny Makkelie.

Sunday, 14 June 2015
Estonia (1) 2 *(Zenjov 35, 63)*
San Marino (0) 0 6131
Estonia: (4141) Aksalu; Teniste, Mets, Klavan, Kallaste;
Dmitrijev; Alliku, Lindpere (Kruglov 84), Vassiljev
(Antonov 78), Zenjov (Teever 89); Purje.
San Marino: (541) Simoncini A; Bonini, Brolli, Della
Valle, Palazzi, Battistini; Hirsch, Tosi (Cervellini 71),
Gasperoni L, Vitaioli M (Bianchi 89); Rinaldi (Stefanelli
79).
Referee: Ivan Kruzliak.

Lithuania (0) 1 *(Cernych 64)*
Switzerland (0) 2 *(Drmic 69, Shaqiri 84)* 4786
Lithuania: (4411) Zubas; Vaitkunas, Mikuckis,
Klimavicius, Andriuskevicius; Cesnauskis (Luksa 85),
Panka, Zulpa (Chvedukas 61), Cernych; Slivka (Vicius
76); Matulevicius.
Switzerland: (433) Sommer; Lichtsteiner, Schar, Djourou,
Rodriguez; Behrami, Inler (Dzemaili 58), Xhaka;
Seferovic (Mehmedi 58), Shaqiri, Drmic (Embolo 82).
Referee: Craig Thomson.

Slovenia (1) 2 *(Novakovic 37, Pecnik 84)*

England (0) 3 *(Wilshere 57, 73, Rooney 86)* 15,500

Slovenia: (4411) Handanovic; Brecko, Ilic, Cesar, Jokic; Ilicic (Birsa 61), Mertelj, Kurtic (Lazarevic 79), Kirm (Pecnik 72); Kampl; Novakovic.
England: (451) Hart; Jones (Lallana 46), Cahill, Smalling, Gibbs; Sterling, Henderson, Wilshere, Delph (Clyne 85), Townsend (Walcott 75); Rooney.
Referee: Alberto Undiano Mallenco.

Saturday, 5 September 2015

Estonia (0) 1 *(Vassiljev 71)*

Lithuania (0) 0 6600

Estonia: (4231) Aksalu; Teniste, Jaager, Klavan, Pikk; Dmitrijev, Mets; Lindpere (Kallaste 67), Vassiljev (Luts 90), Zenjov; Purje (Puri 85).
Lithuania: (442) Arlauskis; Cesnauskis (Freidgeimas 79), Zaliukas, Klimavicius, Vaitkunas; Cernych, Panka (Petravicius 77), Zulpa, Novikovas; Matulevicius (Spalvis 62), Slivka.
Referee: Oliver Drachta.

San Marino (0) 0

England (2) 6 *(Rooney 13 (pen), Brolli 30 (og), Barkley 46, Walcott 68, 78, Kane 77)* 4378

San Marino: (442) Simoncini A; Bonini (Tosi 72), Brolli, Simoncini D (Della Valle 80), Palazzi; Berardi, Hirsch, Battistini, Chiaruzzi; Vitaioli M, Selva (Rinaldi 75).
England: (442) Hart; Clyne, Stones, Jagielka, Shaw; Shelvey, Milner (Delph 58), Oxlade-Chamberlain (Walcott 67), Barkley; Vardy, Rooney (Kane 58).
Referee: Leontios Trattou.

Switzerland (0) 3 *(Drmic 80, 90, Stocker 84)*

Slovenia (1) 2 *(Novakovic 45, Cesar 48)* 25,750

Switzerland: (424) Sommer; Lichtsteiner, Schar, Klose, Rodriguez; Xhaka, Behrami; Dzemaili (Drmic 65), Seferovic (Stocker 80), Mehmedi (Embolo 57), Shaqiri.
Slovenia: (4132) Handanovic; Cesar, Ilic, Jokic, Struna; Stevanovic, Kurtic, Birsa (Krhin 82), Kampl; Ilicic (Samardzic 90), Novakovic (Pecnik 58).
Referee: Pavel Kralovec.

Tuesday, 8 September 2015

England (0) 2 *(Kane 67, Rooney 84 (pen))*

Switzerland (0) 0 75,751

England: (433) Hart; Clyne (Stones 68), Cahill, Smalling, Shaw; Milner, Shelvey (Kane 57), Delph (Barkley 3); Oxlade-Chamberlain, Rooney, Sterling.
Switzerland: (433) Sommer; Lichtsteiner, Klose, Schar, Rodriguez; Xhaka, Inler, Behrami (Dzemaili 79); Shaqiri, Drmic (Embolo 63), Stocker (Seferovic 72).
Referee: Gianluca Rocchi.

Lithuania (1) 2 *(Cernych 7, Spalvis 90)*

San Marino (0) 1 *(Vitaioli M 55)* 2856

Lithuania: (442) Arlauskis■; Freidgeimas, Zaliukas, Klimavicius, Slavickas (Matulevicius 73); Cernych, Pilibaitis (Chvedukas 81), Zulpa, Novikovas; Slivka (Cerniauskas 52), Spalvis.
San Marino: (532) Benedettini; Battistini, Vitaioli F, Della Valle, Brolli, Palazzi; Gasperoni L (Berretti 68), Vitaioli M (Selva 79), Rinaldi; Chiaruzzi■, Stefanelli (Hirsch 72).
Referee: Clayton Pisani.

Slovenia (0) 1 *(Beric 63)*

Estonia (0) 0 6068

Slovenia: (433) Handanovic; Struna, Ilic, Cesar, Jokic; Krhin (Rotman 87), Kurtic, Ilicic (Ljubijankic 55); Birsa, Kampl, Beric (Lazarevic 77).
Estonia: (451) Aksalu; Teniste, Jaager, Klavan, Pikk; Zenjov (Puri 48), Lindpere (Teever 85), Mets, Vassiljev, Kallaste (Luts 87); Purje.
Referee: Tasos Sidiropoulos.

Friday, 9 October 2015

England (1) 2 *(Walcott 45, Sterling 85)*

Estonia (0) 0 75,427

England: (433) Hart; Clyne, Cahill, Smalling, Bertrand; Barkley (Alli 87), Milner, Lallana (Oxlade-Chamberlain 73); Walcott (Vardy 83), Kane, Sterling.

Estonia: (442) Aksalu; Teniste, Jaager, Klavan, Pikk; Kallaste (Luts 88), Dmitrijev (Lindpere 70), Mets, Zenjov; Purje (Puri 69), Vassiljev.
Referee: Istvan Vad.

Slovenia (1) 1 *(Birsa 45 (pen))*

Lithuania (0) 1 *(Novikovas 79 (pen))* 10,498

Slovenia: (4231) Handanovic; Struna, Ilic, Cesar, Jokic; Krhin, Kurtic; Birsa, Ilicic (Matavz 90), Lazarevic (Pecnik 73); Beric (Ljubijankic 62).
Lithuania: (442) Zubas; Freidgeimas, Zaliukas (Mikuckis 89), Klimavicius, Slavickas; Cernych (Cesnauskis 63), Panka, Zulpa, Novikovas; Spalvis, Slivka (Petravicius 69).
Referee: Bjorn Kuipers.

Switzerland (1) 7 *(Lang 17, Inler 55 (pen), Mehmedi 65, Djourou 72 (pen), Kasami 75, Embolo 80 (pen), Derdiyok 89)*

San Marino (0) 0 15,000

Switzerland: (451) Burki; Lang, Schar, Djourou, Rodriguez (Moubandje 62); Embolo, Zuffi, Inler, Kasami, Mehmedi (Derdiyok 68); Drmic (Steffen 79).
San Marino: (541) Simoncini A; Cesarini (Vitaioli F 78), Della Valle, Simoncini D, Palazzi, Berardi; Vitaioli M, Tosi, Gasperoni L (Coppini 63), Golinucci (Hirsch 83); Stefanelli.
Referee: Mattias Gestranius.

Monday, 12 October 2015

Estonia (0) 0

Switzerland (0) 1 *(Klavan 90 (og))* 7304

Estonia: (442) Aksalu; Teniste, Jaager, Klavan, Pikk; Puri (Lindpere 67), Mets, Antonov, Kallaste (Luts 80); Zenjov (Purje 61), Vassiljev.
Switzerland: (4231) Hitz; Lang, Djourou, Lustenberger, Moubandje; Inler, Xhaka (Kasami 80); Shaqiri (Embolo 46), Dzemaili, Mehmedi (Steffen 71); Derdiyok.
Referee: Pol van Boekel.

Lithuania (0) 0

England (2) 3 *(Barkley 29, Arlauskis 35 (og), Oxlade-Chamberlain 62)* 5051

Lithuania: (4411) Arlauskis; Freidgeimas, Mikuckis, Klimavicius, Andriuskevicius (Vaitkunas 82); Novikovas (Petravicius 63), Panka, Zulpa, Cernych; Slivka; Spalvis (Matulevicius 85).
England: (4312) Butland; Walker, Jones, Jagielka, Gibbs; Barkley (Townsend 73), Shelvey, Lallana (Alli 67); Oxlade-Chamberlain; Kane (Ings 59), Vardy.
Referee: Kenn Hansen.

San Marino (0) 0

Slovenia (0) 2 *(Cesar 54, Pecnik 75)* 781

San Marino: (541) Simoncini A; Valentini (Della Valle 72), Brolli, Simoncini D, Palazzi, Battistini; Gasperoni A, Chiaruzzi, Vitaioli M (Mazza 90), Hirsch; Selva (Rinaldi 71).
Slovenia: (442) Oblak; Struna, Samardzic, Cesar, Jokic; Kurtic, Birsa, Krhin, Kirm (Lazarevic 69); Beric (Matavz 46), Ilicic (Pecnik 46).
Referee: Aleksandar Stavrev.

Group E Table	P	W	D	L	F	A	GD	Pts
England	10	10	0	0	31	3	28	30
Switzerland	10	7	0	3	24	8	16	21
Slovenia	10	5	1	4	18	11	7	16
Estonia	10	3	1	6	4	9	−5	10
Lithuania	10	3	1	6	7	18	−11	10
San Marino	10	0	1	9	1	36	−35	1

GROUP F

Sunday, 7 September 2014

Faroe Islands (1) 1 *(Holst 41)*

Finland (0) 3 *(Riski 53, 79, Eremenko 83)* 3300

Faroe Islands: (4141) Nielsen; Naes, Faero, Nattestad, Davidsen V; Benjaminsen; Hansson, Jakobsen (Baldvinsson 56), Sorensen (Jonsson 76), Holst; Klettskard (Edmundsson 46).
Finland: (4141) Maenpaa; Arkivuo, Moisander, Toivio, Uronen (Markkanen 76); Sparv; Hetemaj, Riski, Eremenko, Ring; Pukki (Pohjanpalo 89).
Referee: Lee Evans.

Greece (0) 0

Romania (1) 1 *(Marica 10 (pen))* 173

Greece: (433) Karnezis; Manolas, Torosidis, Papastathopoulos, Holebas; Mantalos (Christodoulopoulos 65), Samaris (Kone 65), Tachtsidis; Mitroglou, Samaras (Diamantakos 46), Salpingidis.
Romania: (433) Tatarusanu; Rat, Tamas, Chiriches, Grigore; Hoban (Prepelita 84), Chipciu (Torje 90), Pintilii; Maxim (Enache 67), Marica■, Stancu.
Referee: Mark Clattenburg.
Behind closed doors.

Hungary (0) 1 *(Priskin 75)*

Northern Ireland (0) 2 *(McGinn 81, Lafferty 88)* 12,000

Hungary: (343) Gulacsi; Vanczak, Liptak, Juhasz; Gyurcso (Lovrencsics 59), Varga, Tozser, Balogh; Rudolf (Kovacs 70), Nikolic (Priskin 46), Dzsudzsak.
Northern Ireland: (442) Carroll; McLaughlin C, McAuley (Cathcart 72), Hughes, Brunt; Evans C, Davis, Norwood (McKay 79), Baird; Ward (McGinn 66), Lafferty K.
Referee: Deniz Aytekin.

Saturday, 11 October 2014

Finland (0) 1 *(Hurme 55)*

Greece (1) 1 *(Karelis 24)* 23,500

Finland: (433) Maenpaa; Arkivuo, Moisander, Toivio, Hurme; Ring, Sparv, Hetemaj (Hamalainen 46); Eremenko, Riski (Tainio 88), Pukki (Pohjanpalo 70).
Greece: (433) Karnezis; Vyntra, Papastathopoulos, Manolas, Torosidis; Samaris, Tachtsidis, Maniatis; Karelis (Samaras 81), Athanasiadis (Mitroglou 84), Mavrias (Moras 70).
Referee: David Fernandez Borbalan.

Northern Ireland (2) 2 *(McAuley 6, Lafferty K 20)*

Faroe Islands (0) 0 10,500

Northern Ireland: (451) Carroll; McLaughlin C, McAuley (McCullough 56), Hughes, Ferguson; McGinn (McCourt 67), Davis, Baird, Norwood, Ward; Lafferty K (Magennis 83).
Faroe Islands: (433) Nielsen; Gregersen, Nattestad, Justinussen P (Bartalstovu 90), Davidsen V; Naes, Benjaminsen, Hansson; Holst (Olsen B 81), Edmundsson, Klettskard (Hansen A 75).
Referee: Alon Yefet.

Romania (1) 1 *(Rusescu 45)*

Hungary (0) 1 *(Dzsudzsak 82)* 54,000

Romania: (4231) Tatarusanu; Chiriches, Goian (Gardos 5), Grigore, Rat; Pintilii, Hoban; Maxim (Stancu 84), Chipciu, Sanmartean (Tanase 66); Rusescu.
Hungary: (4231) Kiraly; Varga, Korcsmar, Juhasz, Kadar; Gera (Tozser 77), Elek; Lovrencsics (Simon K 63), Dzsudzsak, Stieber (Nikolic 46); Szalai.
Referee: William Collum.

Tuesday, 14 October 2014

Faroe Islands (0) 0

Hungary (1) 1 *(Szalai 21)* 2000

Faroe Islands: (451) Nielsen; Nattestad, Gregersen, Davidsen V, Naes; Benjaminsen, Holst (Bartalstovu 75), Hansson, Edmundsson (Hansen A 75), Olsen B; Vatnhamar (Sorensen 81).
Hungary: (451) Dibusz; Korhut, Juhasz, Varga, Kadar; Simon K, Nikolic (Fiola 46), Gera, Szalai (Priskin 83), Dzsudzsak; Tozser (Kalmar 73).
Referee: Aleksei Kulbakov.

Finland (0) 0

Romania (0) 2 *(Stancu 54, 83)* 20,000

Finland: (433) Maenpaa; Hurme, Toivio, Arkivuo, Moisander; Ring■, Sparv, Hetemaj (Pohjanpalo 64); Hamalainen (Markkanen 74), Pukki (Riski 46), Eremenko.
Romania: (4411) Tatarusanu; Luchin, Chiriches, Grigore, Rat; Torje, Hoban, Pintilii, Tanase (Enache 85); Chipciu (Sanmartean 49); Stancu (Rusescu 86).
Referee: Paolo Tagliavento.

Greece (0) 0

Northern Ireland (1) 2 *(Ward 9, Lafferty K 51)* 24,000

Greece: (442) Karnezis; Torosidis, Papastathopoulos, Manolas, Vyntra (Stafylidis 16); Karelis, Tachtsidis, Maniatis, Samaras (Salpingidis 67); Athanasiadis (Samaris 46), Mitroglou.
Northern Ireland: (451) Carroll; McLaughlin C, McAuley, Hughes, Ferguson (Reeves 78); Evans C, Davis, Baird, Norwood, Ward (McGivern 59); Lafferty K (Magennis 72).
Referee: Stephane Lannoy.

Friday, 14 November 2014

Greece (0) 0

Faroe Islands (0) 1 *(Edmundsson 61)* 7000

Greece: (4231) Karnezis; Torosidis, Manolas, Moras, Karabelas (Mantalos 78); Maniatis, Samaris; Karelis (Mavrias 62), Kone, Christodoulopoulos; Gekas (Athanasiadis 46).
Faroe Islands: (451) Nielsen; Naes, Gregersen, Nattestad, Davidsen V; Vatnhamar, Olsen B (Olsen K 88), Benjaminsen, Hansson, Holst (Justinussen P 75); Edmundsson (Faero 85).
Referee: Nicola Rizzoli.

Hungary (0) 1 *(Gera 84)*

Finland (0) 0 19,500

Hungary: (451) Kiraly; Lang, Kadar, Fiola, Juhasz (Forro 57); Elek, Tozser, Dzsudzsak, Simon K (Lovrencsics 77), Gera; Szalai (Nikolic 63).
Finland: (451) Hradecky; Moisander, Uronen, Hurme, Toivio; Eremenko, Hetemaj, Sparv, Halsti (Markkanen 87), Hamalainen (Riski 82); Pukki (Pohjanpalo 65).
Referee: Clement Turpin.

Romania (0) 2 *(Papp 74, 79)*

Northern Ireland (0) 0 40,000

Romania: (4231) Tatarusanu; Papp, Chiriches, Grigore, Rat; Pintilii, Sanmartean; Torje (Hoban 81), Chipciu, Tanase (Maxim 58); Stancu (Keseru 46).
Northern Ireland: (451) Carroll; McLaughlin C, McGivern, McAuley, Baird; Hughes, Brunt, Evans C (McKay 78), Norwood, McGinn (Clingan 63); Lafferty K.
Referee: Jonas Eriksson.

Sunday, 29 March 2015

Hungary (0) 0

Greece (0) 0 22,000

Hungary: (4231) Kiraly; Juhasz, Kadar, De Almeida, Elek (Pinter 70); Tozser, Stieber; Gera, Dzsudzsak, Lovrencsics; Szalai (Nikolic 67).
Greece: (433) Karnezis; Papadopoulos, Papastathopoulos, Manolas, Torosidis; Stafylidis, Kone (Katsouranis 77); Samaris; Fetfatzidis (Gianniotas 77), Christodoulopoulos (Fortounis 69), Athanasiadis.
Referee: Sergei Karasev.

Northern Ireland (2) 2 *(Lafferty K 33, 38)*

Finland (0) 1 *(Sadik 90)* 10,264

Northern Ireland: (433) Carroll; McLaughlin C, Evans J, McAuley, Brunt; Davis (Evans C 46), Baird, Norwood; McGinn (Dallas 64), Lafferty K (Magennis 79), Ward.
Finland: (433) Hradecky; Sorsa, Toivio (Arajuuri 46), Moisander, Uronen; Ring, Sparv, Mattila; Hamalainen (Pohjanpalo 42), Pukki (Sadik 70), Eremenko.
Referee: Szymon Marciniak.

Romania (1) 1 *(Keseru 21)*

Faroe Islands (0) 0 14,000

Romania: (4411) Pantilimon; Papp, Chiriches, Grigore, Rat; Popa (Torje 71), Pintilii, Sanmartean (Prepelita 85), Maxim; Rusescu (Tanase 60); Keseru.
Faroe Islands: (4141) Nielsen; Davidsen J, Nattestad, Gregersen, Davidsen V; Faero (Olsen A 74); Holst, Olsen B (Sorensen 80), Jakobsen (Joensen 79), Vatnhamar; Edmundsson.
Referee: Artur Soraes Dias.

Saturday, 13 June 2015

Faroe Islands (1) 2 *(Hansson 32, Olsen B 69)*

Greece (0) 1 *(Papastathopoulos 84)* 4741

Faroe Islands: (4141) Nielsen; Hansen B, Gregersen, Nattestad, Sorensen (Davidsen J 12); Benjaminsen; Holst (Faero 74), Hansson, Olsen B, Vatnhamar; Edmundsson (Joensen 90).
Greece: (433) Karnezis; Torosidis, Papastathopoulos, Manolas, Stafylidis; Kone (Fountas 80), Samaris, Christodoulopoulos (Ninis 46); Karelis, Mitroglou, Fetfatzidis (Kolovos 71).
Referee: Tom Harald Hagen.

Finland (0) 0

Hungary (0) 1 *(Stieber 82)* 20,434

Finland: (4321) Hradecky; Arkivuo, Halsti, Moisander, Raitala; Mattila (Pohjanpalo 85), Sparv, Hetemaj; Hamalainen, Eremenko; Pukki (Riski 46).
Hungary: (4411) Kiraly; Fiola, Juhasz, Lang, Kadar; Stieber, Priskin (Nemeth 46), Tozser, Dzsudzsak (Simon A 88); Gera; Szalai (Nikolic 77).
Referee: Matej Jug.

Northern Ireland (0) 0

Romania (0) 0 10,000

Northern Ireland: (4321) McGovern; McLaughlin C, McAuley, Evans J (Cathcart 79), Brunt; Ward (Evans C 79), Norwood, Davis; Baird, Dallas; Lafferty K.
Romania: (442) Tatarusanu; Papp, Sepsi, Chiriches, Grigore; Chipciu (Stancu 61), Pintilii, Torje, Prepelita; Keseru (Andone 72), Maxim (Tamas 90).
Referee: Carlos Velasco Carballo.

Friday, 4 September 2015

Faroe Islands (1) 1 *(Edmundsson 36)*

Northern Ireland (1) 3 *(McAuley 12, 71, Lafferty K 75)* 2000

Faroe Islands: (4141) Nielsen; Naes, Nattestad, Faero, Sorensen; Benjaminsen (Baldvinsson 87); Vatnhamar, Henriksen (Bartalstovu 83), Hansson, Holst (Justinussen P 77); Edmundsson■.
Northern Ireland: (442) McGovern; McLaughlin C (Magennis 90), Evans J, McAuley, Brunt (Ferguson 83); Davis, Baird, Norwood, Dallas; McGinn, Lafferty K (McNair 78).
Referee: Felix Zwayer.

Greece (0) 0

Finland (0) 1 *(Pohjanpalo 75)* 17,358

Greece: (433) Karnezis; Vyntra, Papadopoulos, Papastathopoulos, Holebas; Aravidis (Kone 67), Samaris (Tachtsidis 86), Fortounis; Tziolis, Karelis (Fountas 77), Mitroglou.
Finland: (442) Hradecky; Arajuuri, Halsti, Uronen, Arkivuo; Ring, Sparv, Toivio, Hetemaj; Hamalainen (Sadik 46 (Mattila 80)), Pukki (Pohjanpalo 67).
Referee: Serhiy Boiko.

Hungary (0) 0

Romania (0) 0 22,060

Hungary: (442) Kiraly; Fiola, Juhasz (Guzmics 24), Kadar, Leandro; Stieber (Priskin 88), Elek, Tozser, Dzsudzsak; Szalai, Nikolic (Nemeth 70).
Romania: (451) Tatarusanu; Papp, Grigore, Chiriches, Rat; Popa (Chipciu 68), Prepelita, Sanmartean (Budescu 78), Hoban, Torje (Maxim 90); Keseru.
Referee: Felix Brych.

Monday, 7 September 2015

Finland (1) 1 *(Pohjanpalo 23)*

Faroe Islands (0) 0 9477

Finland: (442) Hradecky; Arkivuo, Halsti, Arajuuri, Uronen; Lam (Mattila 84), Sparv, Ring, Hetemaj; Riski (Vayrynen 74), Pohjanpalo (Hamalainen 90).
Faroe Islands: (451) Nielsen; Naes, Nattestad, Gregersen, Sorensen; Vatnhamar, Henriksen, Benjaminsen (Baldvinsson 84); Hansson, Holst (Bartalstovu 57); Olsen K (Justinussen F 75).
Referee: Marcin Borski.

Northern Ireland (0) 1 *(Lafferty K 90)*

Hungary (0) 1 *(Guzmics 74)* 10,200

Northern Ireland: (4141) McGovern; Baird■, Evans J, McAuley, McLaughlin C; Norwood (Magennis 76); Evans C (McGinn 56), Brunt, Davis, Dallas (Ferguson 83); Lafferty K.
Hungary: (442) Kiraly; Fiola, Guzmics, Kadar, Leandro; Nemeth (Vanczak 89), Elek (Nagy 22), Kalmar, Dzsudzsak; Szalai (Priskin 68), Gera.
Referee: Cuneyt Cakir.

Romania (0) 0

Greece (0) 0 38,153

Romania: (4411) Tatarusanu; Papp, Chiriches, Grigore, Rat; Torje, Hoban (Andone 80), Pintilii, Maxim (Popa 64); Budescu (Sanmartean 64); Keseru.
Greece: (4411) Karnezis; Holebas, Papastathopoulos, Manolas, Kitsiou; Samaris, Aravidis, Tziolis, Fetfatzidis (Vyntra 46); Fortounis (Kone 55); Mitroglou (Karelis 87).
Referee: Aleksei Kulbakov.

Thursday, 8 October 2015

Hungary (0) 2 *(Bode 63, 71)*

Faroe Islands (1) 1 *(Jakobsen 11)* 16,500

Hungary: (4321) Kiraly; Fiola, Juhasz, Guzmics, Kadar; Nagy, Tozser (Nemeth 46), Bodi (Bode 46); Dzsudzsak, Gera; Nikolic (Priskin 74).
Faroe Islands: (4321) Nielsen; Naes, Nattestad (Faero 84), Gregersen■, Davidsen; Joensen (Sorensen 78), Jakobsen (Justinussen P 62), Baldvinsson; Vatnhamar, Bartalstovu; Edmundsson.
Referee: Robert Schoergenhofer.

Northern Ireland (1) 3 *(Davis 35, 59, Magennis 49)*

Greece (0) 1 *(Aravidis 86)* 11,700

Northern Ireland: (4141) McGovern; McNair (McCullough 85), McAuley, Cathcart, Brunt; Evans C; Ward (McGinn 81), Norwood, Davis, Dallas; Magennis (Boyce 78).
Greece: (4141) Karnezis; Torosidis, Moras, Papastathopoulos, Holebas; Tziolis; Samaris, Karelis (Mantalos 65), Kone (Pelkas 71), Aravidis; Mitroglou (Athanasiadis 76).
Referee: Bas Nijhuis.

Romania (0) 1 *(Hoban 90)*

Finland (0) 1 *(Pohjanpalo 66)* 47,987

Romania: (4132) Tatarusanu; Papp, Chiriches, Grigore, Rat; Hoban; Torje (Popa 87), Sanmartean, Chipciu (Maxim 60); Keseru, Stancu (Andone 69).
Finland: (442) Hradecky; Arajuuri (Toivio 62), Moisander, Arkivuo (Jalasto 64), Halsti; Schuller, Uronen, Ring, Hetemaj; Pukki, Pohjanpalo (Hamalainen 77).
Referee: Craig Thomson.

Sunday, 11 October 2015

Faroe Islands (0) 0

Romania (2) 3 *(Budescu 4, 45, Maxim 83)* 3941

Faroe Islands: (451) Nielsen; Naes, Faero, Nattestad (Baldvinsson 84), Sorensen; Holst (Olsen A 69), Vatnhamar (Frederiksberg 69), Bartalstovu, Hansson, Henriksen; Edmundsson.
Romania: (451) Tatarusanu; Matel, Chiriches, Grigore, Rat; Popa, Budescu (Prepelita 88), Hoban, Pintilii, Torje (Maxim 78); Stancu (Alibec 90).
Referee: Ivan Kruzliak.

Finland (0) 1 *(Arajuuri 87)*

Northern Ireland (1) 1 *(Cathcart 31)* 14,550

Finland: (442) Hradecky; Jalasto, Arajuuri, Ojala, Uronen; Schuller (Hamalainen 79), Sparv, Mattila, Ring (Lod 43); Sadik (Pukki 66), Pohjanpalo.
Northern Ireland: (433) McGovern; McNair (McLaughlin C 51), McAuley, Baird, Cathcart; Davis, Brunt, Norwood; Dallas, McGinn (Ferguson 71), Lafferty K (Magennis 79).
Referee: Sergei Karasaev.

Greece (1) 4 *(Stafylidis 5, Tachtsidis 57, Mitroglou 79, Kone 86)*
Hungary (1) 3 *(Lovrencsics 26, Nemeth 54, 75)*   9500
Greece: (4411) Karnezis; Kitsiou, Papastathopoulos (Tzanetopoulos 63), Moras, Stafylidis (Holebas 35); Mantalos (Kone 73), Samaris, Tachtsidis, Pelkas; Fortounis; Mitroglou.
Hungary: (442) Kiraly; Fiola, Juhasz, Kadar, Leandro; Lovrencsics (Nikolic 61), Gera (Nagy 71), Elek, Dzsudzsak (Kalmar 70); Bode, Nemeth.
Referee: Ivan Bebek.

Group F Table	P	W	D	L	F	A	GD	Pts
Northern Ireland	10	6	3	1	16	8	8	21
Romania	10	5	5	0	11	2	9	20
Hungary	10	4	4	2	11	9	2	16
Finland	10	3	3	4	9	10	−1	12
Faroe Islands	10	2	0	8	6	17	−11	6
Greece	10	1	3	6	7	14	−7	6

GROUP G

Monday, 8 September 2014
Austria (1) 1 *(Alaba 7 (pen))*
Sweden (1) 1 *(Zengin 12)*   48,500
Austria: (4231) Almer; Klein, Dragovic, Hinteregger, Fuchs; Baumgartlinger, Alaba; Harnik (Lazaro 86), Junuzovic (Leitgeb 77), Arnautovic; Janko (Okotie 69).
Sweden: (433) Isaksson; Bengtsson, Granqvist, Antonsson, Olsson; Larsson, Kallstrom (Wernbloom 85), Ekdal; Durmaz (Elmander 72), Ibrahimovic, Zengin.
Referee: Pavel Kralovec.

Montenegro (1) 2 *(Vucinic 45, Tomasevic 73)*
Moldova (0) 0   8750
Montenegro: (442) Poleksic; Volkov (Balic 46), Tomasevic, Simic, Savic; Bozovic V, Nikolic, Zverotic, Beqiraj (Jovovic 65); Vucinic, Damjanovic (Vukcevic N 81).
Moldova: (4411) Cebanu; Racu, Epureanu, Armas, Golovatenco; Antoniuc A (Antoniuc M 54), Ionita, Gheorghiev (Cebotaru 81), Dedov; Sidorenco (Posmac 68); Alexeev.
Referee: Aleksei Kulbakov.

Russia (1) 4 *(Martin Buchel 4 (og), Burgmeier 50 (og), Kombarov 55 (pen), Dzjuba 65)*
Liechtenstein (0) 0   11,236
Russia: (442) Akinfeev (Lodygin 72); Smolnikov, Berezutski V, Ignashevich, Kombarov; Samedov, Glushakov, Dzagoev (Ozdoev 64), Cheryshev; Kokorin, Kerzhakov (Dzjuba 46).
Liechtenstein: (451) Jehle; Quintans (Wolfinger 87), Frick, Wieser, Burgmeier; Polverino (Gubser 73), Christen (Brandle 64), Yildiz, Martin Buchel, Hasler; Salanovic.
Referee: Sebastian Delferiere.

Thursday, 9 October 2014
Liechtenstein (0) 0
Montenegro (0) 0   2790
Liechtenstein: (532) Jehle (Bicer 62); Kaufmann, Quintans (Kuhne 80), Burgmeier, Frick, Wieser (Christen 44); Martin Buchel, Hasler, Polverino; Salanovic, Yildiz.
Montenegro: (433) Poleksic; Pavicevic, Jovanovic, Tomasevic, Simic; Zverotic, Vukcevic S (Nikolic 57), Jovovic; Jovetic (Grbic 74), Beqiraj (Vucinic 46), Damjanovic.
Referee: Lee Evans.

Moldova (1) 1 *(Dedov 29 (pen))*
Austria (1) 2 *(Alaba 14 (pen), Janko 52)*   10,000
Moldova: (442) Cebanu; Armas, Epureanu, Golovatenco, Jardan; Erhan (Patras 87), Cojocari (Antoniuc A 66), Gatcan, Ionita; Dedov, Picusciac (Sidorenco 46).
Austria: (442) Almer; Dragovic, Fuchs, Alaba, Prodl; Klein, Junuzovic (Ilsanker 86), Baumgartlinger, Arnautovic (Leitgeb 79); Sabitzer (Harnik 47), Janko.
Referee: Manuel de Sousa.

Sweden (0) 1 *(Toivonen 50)*
Russia (1) 1 *(Kokorin 11)*   44,000
Sweden: (433) Isaksson; Bengtsson, Granqvist, Antonsson, Olsson; Kallstrom (Wernbloom 86), Larsson, Durmaz; Bahoui (Kacaniklic 79), Toivonen (Elmander 57), Zengin.
Russia: (4411) Akinfeev; Smolnikov, Berezutski V, Ignashevich, Kombarov (Granat 88); Samedov (Grigorev 73), Glushakov, Fayzulin (Dzagoev 87), Kokorin; Shatov; Dzjuba.
Referee: Nicola Rizzoli.

Sunday, 12 October 2014
Austria (1) 1 *(Okotie 24)*
Montenegro (0) 0   34,000
Austria: (442) Almer; Klein, Dragovic, Hinteregger, Fuchs; Harnik, Baumgartlinger, Alaba, Arnautovic (Hinterseer 62); Junuzovic (Ilsanker 77), Okotie (Lazaro 82).
Montenegro: (4231) Poleksic; Savic, Simic, Basa, Volkov; Zverotic (Jovovic 70), Nikolic; Beqiraj, Vukcevic S (Jovetic 46), Bozovic V (Damjanovic 76); Vucinic.
Referee: Bas Nijhuis.

Russia (0) 1 *(Dzjuba 74 (pen))*
Moldova (0) 1 *(Epureanu 75)*   42,000
Russia: (433) Akinfeev; Parshivlyuk, Ignashevich, Granat, Berezutski; Glushakov, Dzagoev, Cheryshev (Poloz 63); Ionov (Shchennikov 76), Kerzhakov (Ozdoev 46), Dzjuba.
Moldova: (541) Cebanu; Armas, Epureanu, Golovatenco, Jardan, Erhan; Cojocari (Racu 78), Gatcan, Ionita, Dedov (Sidorenco 83); Picusciac (Patras 47).
Referee: Kristinn Jakobsson.

Sweden (1) 2 *(Zengin 34, Durmaz 46)*
Liechtenstein (0) 0   22,528
Sweden: (442) Isaksson; Antonsson, Granqvist, Olsson, Bengtsson; Ekdal (Bahoui 74), Kallstrom, Forsberg (Hrgota 66), Durmaz; Zengin, Elmander (Wernbloom 79).
Liechtenstein: (442) Bicer; Kaufmann, Frick, Quintans, Burgmeier; Christen (Kuhne 77), Martin Buchel (Wolfinger 83), Hasler, Polverino; Yildiz (Brandle 27), Salanovic.
Referee: Gediminas Mazeika.

Saturday, 15 November 2014
Austria (0) 1 *(Okotie 73)*
Russia (0) 0   53,000
Austria: (4411) Almer; Klein, Dragovic (Prodl 86), Hinteregger, Fuchs; Harnik, Leitgeb, Ilsanker, Arnautovic (Sabitzer 90); Junuzovic; Janko (Okotie 59).
Russia: (451) Akinfeev; Parshivlyuk, Berezutski, Ignashevich, Kombarov; Cheryshev (Ionov 55), Shirokov, Glushakov, Fayzulin (Dzjuba 75), Shatov (Dzagoev 81); Kokorin.
Referee: Martin Atkinson.

Moldova (0) 0
Liechtenstein (0) 1 *(Burgmeier 74)*   6000
Moldova: (343) Cebanu; Golovatenco, Epureanu, Armas; Racu, Gatcan, Cojocari (Spataru 56), Patras (Suvorov 75); Ginsari, Ionita, Dedov.
Liechtenstein: (4321) Buchel B; Quintans (Kieber 89), Kaufmann, Wieser, Burgmeier; Christen, Polverino, Brandle (Kuhne 62); Martin Buchel (Gubser 88), Hasler; Salanovic.
Referee: Mattias Gestranius.

Montenegro (0) 0 *(Jovetic 81 (pen))*
Sweden (0) 1 *(Ibrahimovic 9)*   15,000
Montenegro: (442) Bozovic M; Savic, Basa, Tomasevic (Jankovic 76), Volkov; Jovovic, Zverotic, Vukcevic N, Bozovic V (Bakic 46); Jovetic, Damjanovic (Beqiraj 66).
Sweden: (433) Isaksson; Lustig (Wendt 46), Granqvist, Antonsson, Bengtsson; Ekdal, Kallstrom, Durmaz; Forsberg (Larsson 62), Ibrahimovic, Zengin (Thelin 85).
Referee: William Collum.

Friday, 27 March 2015

Liechtenstein (0) 0

Austria (2) 5 *(Harnik 14, Janko 16, Alaba 59, Junuzovic 74, Arnautovic 90)*   6127
Liechtenstein: (451) Jehle; Quintans (Salanovic 55), Frick, Kaufmann, Oehri; Christen (Kuhne 83), Martin Buchel (Gubser 88), Polverino, Wieser, Burgmeier; Hasler.
Austria: (4411) Almer; Klein, Dragovic, Hinteregger, Fuchs; Harnik (Sabitzer 72), Baumgartlinger, Alaba, Arnautovic; Junuzovic (Leitgeb 82); Janko (Djuricin 76).
Referee: Felix Zwayer.

Moldova (0) 0

Sweden (0) 2 *(Ibrahimovic 46, 85 (pen))*   10,500
Moldova: (532) Cebanu; Armas, Epureanu, Golovatenco, Racu, Bolohan; Ionita (Cojocari 36), Gatcan, Andronic (Frunza 70); Dedov, Boghiu (Gheorghiev 86).
Sweden: (442) Isaksson; Bengtsson, Granqvist■, Olsson, Johansson; Larsson (Forsberg 81), Ekdal, Kallstrom, Zengin (Wernbloom 86); Ibrahimovic, Thelin (Berg 69).
Referee: Ivan Bebek.

Montenegro (0) 0

Russia (0) 0
Montenegro: (4231) Poleksic; Zverotic, Simic, Basa, Balic (Bakic 46); Kascelan, Vukcevic N; Marusic, Volkov, Jovetic; Vucinic.
Russia: (4321) Akinfeev (Lodygin 1); Smolnikov, Berezutski V, Ignashevich, Kombarov; Shirokov, Denisov, Dzagoev (Torbinski 46); Zhirkov, Shatov; Kokorin.
Match abandoned. Russia awarded 3-0 win
Referee: Deniz Aytekin.

Sunday, 14 June 2015

Liechtenstein (1) 1 *(Wieser 20)*

Moldova (1) 1 *(Boghiu 43)*   2080
Liechtenstein: (433) Jehle; Yildiz, Frick, Kaufmann, Oehri (Kuhne 41); Martin Buchel (Gubser 69), Polverino, Wieser; Christen, Erne (Brandle 83), Burgmeier.
Moldova: (334) Cebanu; Racu, Epureanu (Carp 46), Armas; Dedov, Cojocari, Erhan; Gatcan, Patras (Antoniuc M 89), Boghiu, Cheptene (Milinceanu 35).
Referee: Libor Kovank.

Russia (0) 0

Austria (1) 1 *(Janko 33)*   38,000
Russia: (451) Akinfeev; Smolnikov, Berezutski V (Chernov 12), Novoseltsev, Kombarov (Kerzhakov 71); Shatov, Shirokov, Glushakov, Ivanov (Miranchuk 46), Zhirkov; Kokorin.
Austria: (4231) Almer; Klein, Dragovic, Hinteregger, Fuchs; Ilsanker, Baumgartlinger; Harnik (Sabitzer 65), Junuzovic (Prodl 87), Arnautovic; Janko (Okotie 76).
Referee: Milorad Mazic.

Sweden (3) 3 *(Berg 37, Ibrahimovic 40, 44)*

Montenegro (0) 1 *(Damjanovic 64 (pen))*   50,000
Sweden: (442) Isaksson; Bengtsson, Johansson, Milosevic, Wendt; Larsson, Kallstrom (Wernbloom 72), Ekdal, Zengin (Forsberg 65); Ibrahimovic (Toivonen 90), Berg.
Montenegro: (4231) Poleksic; Zverotic (Saveljich 58), Savic, Simic (Balic 75), Tomasevic; Vukcevic N, Kascelan (Boljevic 46); Marusic, Mugosa, Beqiraj; Damjanovic.
Referee: Huseyin Gocek.

Saturday, 5 September 2015

Austria (0) 1 *(Junuzovic 52)*

Moldova (0) 0   46,000
Austria: (442) Almer; Klein, Prodl, Dragovic, Fuchs; Harnik (Jantscher 76), Baumgartlinger, Alaba (Ilsanker 90), Arnautovic; Janko (Okotie 83), Junuzovic.
Moldova: (541) Cebanu; Golovatenco, Erhan, Cojocari, Armas, Jardan; Dedov, Andronic (Racu 76), Cebotaru (Ginsari 79), Patras; Milinceanu (Carp 87).
Referee: Aleksandar Stavrev.

Montenegro (1) 2 *(Beqiraj 37, Jovetic 56)*

Liechtenstein (0) 0   150
Montenegro: (4231) Poleksic; Savic, Basa, Tomasevic, Volkov; Boljevic, Vukcevic N; Marusic (Zverotic 68), Jovetic (Mugosa 69); Vucinic (Damjanovic 59); Beqiraj.

Liechtenstein: (442) Jehle; Yildiz, Frick, Kaufmann, Rechsteiner; Christen, Martin Buchel (Gubser 85), Polverino, Wieser (Salanovic 66); Burgmeier (Kieber 76), Hasler.
Referee: Javier Estrada Fernandez.

Russia (1) 1 *(Dzjuba 38)*

Sweden (0) 0   40,000
Russia: (433) Akinfeev; Smolnikov, Ignashevich, Berezutski V, Zhirkov (Kuzmin 71); Denisov, Dzagoev, Shirokov (Berezutski A 84); Shatov, Kokorin, Dzjuba (Ionov 79).
Sweden: (4411) Isaksson; Bengtsson (Berg 60), Antonsson, Olsson, Granqvist; Larsson, Forsberg, Ekdal (Thelin 82), Wernbloom; Durmaz; Ibrahimovic (Toivonen 46).
Referee: Mark Clattenburg.

Tuesday, 8 September 2015

Liechtenstein (0) 0

Russia (3) 7 *(Dzjuba 21, 45, 73, 90, Kokorin 40 (pen), Smolov 77, Dzagoev 85)*   2874
Liechtenstein: (433) Jehle; Rechsteiner, Frick, Kaufmann■, Burgmeier; Kieber (Sele 78), Polverino, Yildiz; Martin Buchel (Gubser 84), Hasler, Salanovic (Christen 88).
Russia: (4231) Akinfeev; Smolnikov, Ignashevich, Berezutski V, Kombarov; Dzagoev, Denisov (Glushakov 46); Shirokov (Smolov 75), Kokorin, Shatov (Mamaev 65); Dzjuba.
Referee: Bobby Madden.

Moldova (0) 0

Montenegro (1) 2 *(Savic 9, Racu 66 (og))*   6243
Moldova: (4141) Cebanu; Jardan, Golovatenco, Armas, Erhan; Cojocari; Dedov, Gatcan, Cebotaru (Racu 36), Patras (Ginsari 71); Milinceanu.
Montenegro: (4411) Poleksic; Savic, Basa, Simic, Tomasevic; Marusic (Mandic 69), Boljevic, Vukcevic N, Beqiraj; Jovetic (Kascelan 88); Damjanovic (Mugosa 46).
Referee: Sebastien Delferiere.

Sweden (0) 1 *(Ibrahimovic 90)*

Austria (2) 4 *(Alaba 9 (pen), Harnik 38, 89, Janko 77)*   48,355
Sweden: (442) Isaksson; Larsson, Antonsson, Granqvist, Olsson (Durmaz 82); Zengin (Thelin 61), Ekdal (Khalili 87), Kallstrom, Forsberg; Berg, Ibrahimovic.
Austria: (4411) Almer; Klein, Prodl, Dragovic, Fuchs; Harnik, Baumgartlinger, Alaba, Arnautovic (Jantscher 87); Junuzovic (Sabitzer 79); Janko (Ilsanker 83).
Referee: Carlos Velasco Carballo.

Friday, 9 October 2015

Liechtenstein (0) 0

Sweden (1) 2 *(Berg 18, Ibrahimovic 55)*   4740
Liechtenstein: (451) Jehle; Rechsteiner, Frick, Wieser, Oehri; Christen (Kieber 82), Martin Buchel, Polverino (Gubser 59), Marcel Buchel, Burgmeier; Kuhne (Yildiz 72).
Sweden: (433) Isaksson; Lustig, Antonsson, Granqvist, Olsson; Ekdal (Lewicki 65), Kallstrom, Durmaz (Larsson 69); Zengin, Ibrahimovic, Berg (Guidetti 62).
Referee: Liran Liany.

Moldova (0) 1 *(Cebotaru 85)*

Russia (0) 2 *(Ignashevich 59, Dzjuba 79)*   8000
Moldova: (4141) Koselev; Bordiyan, Armas, Burghiu, Jardan; Cebotaru; Antoniuc A, Onica (Ambros 80), Carp (Vremea 70), Spataru; Milinceanu (Istrati 88).
Russia: (4231) Akinfeev; Kombarov, Ignashevich, Berezutski A, Smolnikov (Kuzmin 27); Mamaev, Denisov; Kokorin, Shirokov (Glushakov 76), Shatov; Dzjuba (Smolov 88).
Referee: Michail Koukoulakis.

Montenegro (1) 2 *(Vucinic 32, Beqiraj 68)*

Austria (0) 3 *(Janko 55, Arnautovic 81, Sabitzer 90)*   12,000
Montenegro: (442) Poleksic; Rodic, Savic, Simic, Tomasevic (Balic 74); Marusic, Vukcevic N, Boljevic (Zverotic 46), Beqiraj; Mugosa (Mandic 64), Vucinic■.

Austria: (4411) Almer; Klein, Prodl, Dragovic, Fuchs; Harnik, Baumgartlinger, Alaba (Jantscher 83), Arnautovic; Junuzovic (Sabitzer 82); Janko (Okotie 82).
Referee: Daniele Orsato.

Monday, 12 October 2015
Austria (1) 3 *(Arnautovic 12, Janko 54, 57)*
Liechtenstein (0) 0 48,500
Austria: (4411) Almer; Dragovic, Fuchs, Alaba (Sabitzer 64), Prodl; Klein, Junuzovic, Baumgartlinger (Ilsanker 71), Arnautovic; Harnik; Janko (Okotie 64).
Liechtenstein: (451) Jehle; Kaufmann, Burgmeier, Oehri (Brandle 46), Rechsteiner; Wieser, Martin Buchel, Polverino, Marcel Buchel, Frick (Kuhne 90); Kieber (Yildiz 62).
Referee: Miroslav Zelinka.

Russia (2) 2 *(Kuzmin 33, Kokorin 37 (pen))*
Montenegro (0) 0 39,000
Russia: (451) Akinfeev; Kombarov, Berezutski A, Ignashevich, Kuzmin; Kokorin, Shirokov, Denisov, Dzagoev (Cheryshev 86), Shatov (Mamaev 69); Dzjuba (Smolov 84).
Montenegro: (451) Mijatovic; Balic, Saveljich, Savic, Simic; Rodic (Marusic 67), Vukcevic N (Boljevic 85), Kascelan, Nikolic (Mugosa 46), Mandic; Beqiraj.
Referee: Svein Oddvar Moen.

Sweden (1) 2 *(Ibrahimovic 24, Zengin 47)*
Moldova (0) 0 25,351
Sweden: (442) Isaksson; Lustig (Tinnerholm 84), Antonsson, Granqvist, Olsson; Lewicki, Larsson, Kallstrom (Svensson 57), Zengin; Ibrahimovic (Toivonen 58), Guidetti.
Moldova: (451) Cebanu; Erhan (Armas 63), Golovatenco, Jardan (Spataru 80), Bordiyan; Burghiu, Potirniche, Cebotaru, Patras (Antoniuc A 61), Vremea; Istrati.
Referee: Luca Banti.

Group G Table	P	W	D	L	F	A	GD	Pts
Austria	10	9	1	0	22	5	17	28
Russia	10	6	2	2	21	5	16	20
Sweden	10	5	3	2	15	9	6	18
Montenegro	10	3	2	5	10	13	–3	11
Liechtenstein	10	1	2	7	2	26	–24	5
Moldova	10	0	2	8	4	16	–12	2

GROUP H

Tuesday, 9 September 2014
Azerbaijan (0) 1 *(Nazarov 53)*
Bulgaria (1) 2 *(Mitsanski 14, Hristov 86)* 25,000
Azerbaijan: (4231) Agayev K; Shukurov, Sadygov RF, Guseynov, Budak (Nadirov 89); Garayev, Abishov (Guliyev 73); Nazarov, Aliyev, Javadov (Abdullayev 46); Dadasov.
Bulgaria: (4231) Stoyanov; Manolev, Bodurov, Popov A, Minev V; Dyakov, Iliev (Nedelev 73); Milanov G, Gadzhev, Aleksandrov M (Hristov 82); Mitsanski (Galabinov 57).
Referee: Alon Yefet.

Croatia (0) 2 *(Modric 46, Kramaric 81)*
Malta (0) 0 12,000
Croatia: (451) Subasic; Milic, Corluka, Lovren, Srna; Rakitic, Halilovic (Kramaric 67), Modric, Brozovic, Kovacic (Jelavic 46); Mandzukic (Olic 79).
Malta: (442) Hogg; Borg▪, Agius, Camilleri, Fenech R (Scicluna 87); Failla, Fenech P, Muscat R (Kristensen 76), Muscat Z; Mifsud (Bezzina 33), Schembri.
Referee: Vladislav Bezborodov.

Norway (0) 0
Italy (1) 2 *(Zaza 16, Bonucci 62)* 26,265
Norway: (442) Nyland; Elabdellaoui, Forren, Nordtveit, Skjelbred (Pedersen 75); Jenssen (Tettey 70), Daehli, Johansen, Flo; King, Nielsen (Elyounoussi T 50).
Italy: (442) Buffon; Darmian (Pasqual 61), Astori, Ranocchia, Bonucci; De Sciglio, Giaccherini, Florenzi (Poli 86), De Rossi; Zaza (Destro 83), Immobile.
Referee: Milorad Mazic.

Friday, 10 October 2014
Bulgaria (0) 0
Croatia (1) 1 *(Bodurov 36 (og))* 30,000
Bulgaria: (442) Stoyanov; Minev I, Popov A, Zanev (Iliev 46), Bodurov; Manolev, Milanov G, Gadzhev (Tonev 69), Dyakov; Mitsanski (Galabinov 46), Popov I.
Croatia: (442) Subasic; Corluka, Srna, Vida, Pranjic; Perisic, Rakitic (Kovacic 80), Modric, Brozovic; Mandzukic, Olic.
Referee: Antonio Miguel Mateu Lahoz.

Italy (1) 2 *(Chiellini 44, 81)*
Azerbaijan (0) 1 *(Chiellini 77 (og))* 30,000
Italy: (532) Buffon; Darmian (Candreva 81), Ranocchia, Bonucci, Chiellini, De Sciglio; Florenzi (Giovinco 78), Pirlo (Aquilani 73), Marchisio; Zaza, Immobile.
Azerbaijan: (442) Agayev K; Allahverdiev, Guseynov, Sadygov RF, Qirtimov (Ramaldanov 46); Abdullayev, Garayev, Amirguliev (Nadirov 86), Nazarov; Dadasov (Huseynov 59), Aliyev.
Referee: Huseyin Gocek.

Malta (0) 0
Norway (2) 3 *(Daehli 22, King 25, 49)* 3000
Malta: (352) Hogg; Muscat Z, Agius, Camilleri; Fenech P, Muscat R, Fenech R (Grioli 70), Briffa (Kristensen 70), Failla; Mifsud, Schembri (Vella 85).
Norway: (433) Nyland; Elabdellaoui, Nordtveit, Forren, Linnes; Skjelbred (Samuelsen 61), Johansen, Tettey (Singh 77); King (Nielsen 74), Daehli, Elyounoussi T.
Referee: Antony Gautier.

Monday, 13 October 2014
Croatia (4) 6 *(Kramaric 11, Perisic 34, 45, Brozovic 45, Modric 56 (pen), Sadygov RF 61 (og))*
Azerbaijan (0) 0 15,000
Croatia: (442) Subasic; Srna, Corluka, Vida, Pranjic; Brozovic, Rakitic, Modric, Halilovic (Olic 59), Kovacic (Perisic 24); Kramaric (Olic 76), Mandzukic.
Azerbaijan: (442) Agayev K; Medvedev, Sadygov RF, Guseynov, Allahverdiev (Guliyev 66); Abdullayev, Garayev (Ramazanov 30 (Huseynov 41)), Ramaldanov, Nazarov; Amirguliev, Aliyev.
Referee: Stephan Studer.

Malta (0) 0
Italy (1) 1 *(Pelle 24)* 16,942
Malta: (352) Hogg; Muscat Z, Agius, Camilleri; Mintoff (Baldacchino 72), Muscat R, Failla (Bezzina 90), Briffa, Fenech P; Mifsud▪, Schembri (Cohen 85).
Italy: (352) Buffon; Darmian, Bonucci▪, Chiellini; Candreva, Verratti, Pasqual, Florenzi (Aquilani 59), Marchisio; Immobile (Giovinco 65), Pelle (Ogbonna 76).
Referee: Ovidiu Alin Hategan.

Norway (1) 2 *(Elyounoussi T 13, Nielsen 71)*
Bulgaria (1) 1 *(Bodurov 43)* 18,990
Norway: (433) Nyland; Elabdellaoui, Linnes, Forren, Nordtveit; Tettey, Skjelbred, Daehli (Odegaard 63); Johansen, King (Nielsen 58), Elyounoussi T (Samuelsen 83).
Bulgaria: (442) Mihailov; Popov A, Bodurov, Minev V, Manolev (Minev I 68); Milanov G, Tonev, Dyakov, Iliev (Aleksandrov M 76); Popov I, Hristov (Galabinov 55).
Referee: Olegario Benquerenca.

Sunday, 16 November 2014
Azerbaijan (0) 0
Norway (1) 1 *(Nordtveit 25)* 8000
Azerbaijan: (433) Agayev S; Shukurov, Yunuszade, Sadygov RF, Medvedev; Amirguliev, Imamverdiyev (Nazarov 70), Abishov (Qarayev 65); Abdullayev, Aliyev, Javadov.
Norway: (4231) Nyland; Elabdellaoui, Nordtveit, Forren, Hogli; Johansen, Tettey; Daehli (Samuelsen 57), Elyounoussi T (Gulbrandsen 90), Skjelbred; Nielsen (Soderlund 72).
Referee: Yevhen Aranovskiy.

Bulgaria (1) 1 *(Galabinov 6)*
Malta (0) 1 *(Failla 50 (pen))* 1000

Bulgaria: (4231) Stoyanov; Terziev, Minev V, Bodurov, Manolev; Milanov G (Marquinhos 58), Iliev (Tonev 71); Galabinov (Mitsanski 58), Dyakov, Aleksandrov M; Popov I.
Malta: (532) Hogg; Camilleri, Muscat Z, Caruana, Agius, Failla (Bezzina 80); Briffa, Muscat R, Fenech P; Schembri (Fenech R 78), Farrugia (Vella 90).
Referee: Martin Strombergsson.

Italy (1) 1 *(Candreva 11)*
Croatia (1) 1 *(Perisic 15)* 55,000

Italy: (352) Buffon; Darmian, Ranocchia, Chiellini; De Sciglio, Candreva, De Rossi, Marchisio, Pasqual (Soriano 27); Immobile (El Shaarawy 52), Zaza (Pelle 63).
Croatia: (4411) Subasic; Srna, Corluka, Vida, Pranjic; Perisic, Modric (Kovacic 27), Brozovic (Badelj 86), Olic (Kramaric 69); Rakitic; Mandzukic.
Referee: Bjorn Kuipers.

Saturday, 28 March 2015

Azerbaijan (1) 2 *(Huseynov 4, Nazarov 90)*
Malta (0) 0 14,600

Azerbaijan: (4141) Agayev K; Medvedev, Guseynov, Sadygov RF, Dashdemirov; Qarayev, Alaskarov (Gurbanov 23), Amirguliev, Huseynov, Ismayilov (Nazarov 70); Nadirov (Eddy 80).
Malta: (4411) Hogg; Caruana, Camilleri (Muscat Z 36), Agius, Bezzina (Pisani 46); Fenech P, Borg, Schembri (Fenech R 82), Muscat R; Briffa; Effiong.
Referee: Halis Ozkahya.

Bulgaria (2) 2 *(Popov I 11, Mitsanski 17)*
Italy (1) 2 *(Minev I 4 (og), Eder 84)* 6000

Bulgaria: (4231) Mihailov; Manolev, Bodurov, Aleksandrov A, Minev I; Gadzhev, Dyakov; Milanov I (Vasilev V 88), Popov I (Slavchev 85), Aleksandrov M; Mitsanski (Bojinov 73).
Italy: (352) Sirigu; Barzagli, Bonucci, Chiellini; Antonelli (Gabbiadini 77), Candreva, Verratti, Bertolacci (Soriano 71), Darmian; Zaza (Eder 58), Immobile.
Referee: Damir Skomina.

Croatia (1) 5 *(Brozovic 30, Perisic 54, Olic 66, Schildenfeld 87, Pranjic 90)*
Norway (0) 1 *(Tettey 81)* 22,000

Croatia: (4411) Subasic; Srna, Corluka■, Vida, Pranjic; Perisic, Brozovic, Modric, Olic (Kramaric 70); Rakitic (Schildenfeld 75); Mandzukic (Badelj 88).
Norway: (4411) Nyland; Hogli, Forren, Nordtveit, Linnes; Skjelbred (Samuelsen 19), Johansen, Tettey, Daehli (Nielsen 61); Elyounoussi T (Abdellaoue 80); Odegaard.
Referee: Carlos Velasco Carballo.

Friday, 12 June 2015

Croatia (1) 1 *(Mandzukic 11)*
Italy (1) 1 *(Candreva 36 (pen))* 75

Croatia: (442) Subasic; Srna■, Vida, Schildenfeld, Pranjic (Vrsaljko 72); Perisic, Rakitic, Brozovic, Olic (Rebic 46); Kovacic (Leovac 90), Mandzukic.
Italy: (442) Buffon (Sirigu 46); De Silvestri (De Sciglio 27), Bonucci, Astori, Darmian; Candreva, Parolo, Pirlo, Marchisio; El Shaarawy (Ranocchia 80), Pelle.
Referee: Martin Atkinson.
(Behind closed doors)

Malta (0) 0
Bulgaria (0) 1 *(Popov I 56)* 3924

Malta: (442) Haber; Muscat A (Herrera 63), Agius, Camilleri, Muscat Z; Fenech P, Briffa (Schembri 75), Muscat R, Failla; Mifsud (Cohen 84), Effiong.
Bulgaria: (4321) Mitrev; Bandalovski, Aleksandrov A, Bodurov, Minev I; Gadzhev, Popov I (Chochev 80); Dyakov; Manolev, Aleksandrov M (Malinov 75); Mitsanski (Vasilev R 89).
Referee: Aleksandar Stavrev.

Norway (0) 0
Azerbaijan (0) 0 21,228

Norway: (442) Nyland; Elabdellaoui, Forren, Hovland, Hogli; Odegaard, Johansen, Nordtveit, Skjelbred (Helland 55); King (Diomande 79), Soderlund (Eikrem 68).
Azerbaijan: (433) Agayev K; Medvedev, Guseynov, Sadygov RF, Dashdemirov; Huseynov, Qarayev, Amirguliev; Ismayilov, Gurbanov (Nadirov 81), Nazarov (Kurbanov 90).
Referee: Pawel Gil.

Thursday, 3 September 2015

Azerbaijan (0) 0
Croatia (0) 0 10,000

Azerbaijan: (4141) Agayev K; Mirzabekov, Guseynov, Sadygov RF, Dashdemirov; Garayev; Ismayilov, Amirguliev, Nazarov (Eddy 90), Gurbanov (Nadirov 78); Qurbanov (Sadygov RA 63).
Croatia: (4231) Subasic; Vrsaljko, Corluka, Vida, Pranjic; Badelj (Kovacic 59), Modric (Brozovic 71); Pjaca, Rakitic, Perisic (Kalinic 83); Mandzukic.
Referee: Ruddy Buquet.

Bulgaria (0) 0
Norway (0) 1 *(Forren 57)* 7000

Bulgaria: (442) Mitrev; Bandalovski, Aleksandrov A, Bodurov, Minev I; Manolev (Tonev 61), Dyakov, Chochev, Milanov G (Nedelev 78); Mitsanski (Rangelov 68), Popov I.
Norway: (451) Nyland; Elabdellaoui, Hovland, Forren (Nordtveit 75), Hogli; Samuelsen (Skjelbred 64), Tettey, Henriksen, Johansen (Strandberg 87), Berget; Soderlund.
Referee: Bas Nijhuis.

Italy (0) 1 *(Pelle 69)*
Malta (0) 0 12,551

Italy: (433) Buffon; Darmian, Bonucci, Chiellini, Pasqual; Verratti (Soriano 77), Pirlo, Bertolacci (Parolo 55); Gabbiadini (Candreva 64), Pelle, Eder.
Malta: (541) Hogg; Muscat A, Borg, Muscat Z, Agius, Failla; Muscat R, Fenech P, Briffa (Sciberras 90), Effiong (Mifsud 90); Schembri (Kristensen 73).
Referee: Ivan Kruzliak.

Sunday, 6 September 2015

Italy (1) 1 *(De Rossi 6 (pen))*
Bulgaria (0) 0 21,000

Italy: (451) Buffon; Darmian, Bonucci, Chiellini, De Sciglio; Candreva (Eder 86), Verratti, De Rossi■, Parolo, El Shaarawy (Florenzi 73); Pelle (Zaza 71).
Bulgaria: (4231) Mitrev; Minev V, Aleksandrov A, Bodurov, Minev I (Bandalovski 63); Dyakov, Chochev; Nedelev (Aleksandrov M 67), Popov I (Rangelov 71), Milanov G; Mitsanski■.
Referee: Sergei Karasev.

Malta (0) 2 *(Mifsud 55, Effiong 71)*
Azerbaijan (1) 2 *(Amirguliev 36, 80)* 5266

Malta: (532) Hogg; Muscat A, Agius, Borg, Camilleri (Zerafa 79), Failla (Pisani 85); Schembri, Briffa, Muscat R; Effiong, Mifsud (Cohen 62).
Azerbaijan: (451) Agayev- K; Mirzabekov, Guseynov, Garayev, Sadygov RF; Dashdemirov, Ismayilov (Abdullayev 73), Nazarov (Sadygov RA 70), Amirguliev, Tagiyev; Gurbanov (Aliyev 81).
Referee: Harald Lechner.

Norway (0) 2 *(Berget 51, Corluka 69 (og))*
Croatia (0) 0 26,751

Norway: (442) Nyland; Hogli, Hovland, Elabdellaoui, Forren; Tettey, Johansen (Nordtveit 90), Henriksen, Skjelbred (Nielsen 90); Soderlund (Berisha 90), Berget.
Croatia: (451) Subasic; Vrsaljko, Corluka, Srna, Vida; Perisic, Rakitic (Kalinic 72), Modric, Brozovic, Pjaca (Olic 63); Mandzukic.
Referee: Viktor Kassai.

Saturday, 10 October 2015

Azerbaijan (1) 1 *(Nazarov 30)*

Italy (2) 3 *(Eder 11, El Shaarawy 43, Darmian 65)* 48,000

Azerbaijan: (4141) Agayev K; Medvedev, Guseynov[■], Sadygov RF, Dashdemirov; Garayev; Ismayilov (Mirzabekov 90), Eddy (Sadygov RA 66), Amirguliev, Nazarov; Gurbanov (Erat 74).
Italy: (442) Buffon; Darmian, Bonucci, Chiellini, De Sciglio; Candreva (Montolivo 88), Verratti, Parolo, El Shaarawy (Florenzi 73); Pelle, Eder (Giovinco 78).
Referee: Willie Collum.

Croatia (2) 3 *(Perisic 3, Rakitic 42, Kalinic 81)*

Bulgaria (0) 0 150

Croatia: (4411) Subasic; Pivaric, Vida, Corluka, Srna; Pjaca (Cop[■] 59), Kovacic, Modric (Badelj 46), Perisic; Rakitic; Kalinic (Kramaric 85).
Bulgaria: (442) Mitrev; Milanov Z, Aleksandrov A, Terziev (Ivanov 46), Popov S; Nedelev (Milanov G 46), Slavchev, Zlatinski, Tonev; Popov I (Aleksandrov M 71), Rangelov.
Referee: Artur Soraes Dias.

Norway (1) 2 *(Tettey 20, Soderlund 52)*

Malta (0) 0 27,120

Norway: (4411) Nyland; Elabdellaoui, Hovland, Forren, Aleesami, Skjelbred (Odegaard 53), Tettey, Johansen, Berget (Berisha 84); Henriksen; Soderlund (King 77).
Malta: (451) Hogg; Borg (Camilleri 83), Muscat Z, Muscat A (Zerafa 55), Failla; Fenech P, Muscat R, Agius, Briffa, Effiong; Schembri (Kristensen 80).
Referee: Arnold Hunter.

Tuesday, 13 October 2015

Bulgaria (1) 2 *(Aleksandrov M 20, Rangelov 56)*

Azerbaijan (0) 0 2500

Bulgaria: (4411) Mitrev; Milanov Z, Aleksandrov A, Ivanov, Minev I; Milanov G, Dyakov, Zlatinski, Aleksandrov M (Slavchev 79); Popov I (Hristov 65); Rangelov (Nedelev 88).
Azerbaijan: (451) Agayev K; Mirzabekov, Abishov, Sadygov RF, Medvedev (Dashdemirov 62); Ismayilov, Amirguliev, Garayev (Eddy 81), Nazarov, Jafarov (Erat 67); Gurbanov.
Referee: Tamas Bognar.

Italy (0) 2 *(Florenzi 74, Pelle 82)*

Norway (1) 1 *(Tettey 23)* 30,000

Italy: (352) Buffon; Barzagli (Candreva 72), Bonucci, Chiellini; Darmian, Florenzi, Montolivo (Bertolacci 68), Soriano, De Sciglio; Pelle, Eder (Giovinco 62).
Norway: (424) Nyland; Elabdellaoui, Hovland, Forren, Aleesami; Johansen, Tettey; Skjelbred (Samuelsen 51), Henriksen, Soderlund (King 60), Berget (Berisha 78).
Referee: Felix Brych.

Malta (0) 0

Croatia (1) 1 *(Perisic 25)* 7500

Malta: (433) Hogg; Muscat Z, Borg, Agius, Zerafa; Muscat R, Briffa (Fenech P 79), Failla; Schembri (Cohen 90), Kristensen, Effiong (Mifsud 75).
Croatia: (4141) Subasic; Vida, Corluka, Srna, Badelj; Pivaric, Kalinic (Kramaric 60), Kovacic, Rakitic (Brozovic 77), Perisic; Pjaca (Olic 83).
Referee: Mark Clattenburg.

Group H Table	P	W	D	L	F	A	GD	Pts
Italy	10	7	3	0	16	7	9	24
Croatia	10	6	3	1	20	5	15	21
Norway	10	6	1	3	13	10	3	19
Bulgaria	10	3	2	5	9	12	−3	11
Azerbaijan	10	1	3	6	7	18	−11	6
Malta	10	0	2	8	3	16	−13	2

GROUP I

Sunday, 7 September 2014

Denmark (0) 2 *(Hojbjerg 65, Kahlenberg 80)*

Armenia (0) 1 *(Mkhitaryan 49)* 20,144

Denmark: (4411) Schmeichel; Ankersen, Kjaer (Okore 57), Bjelland, Boilesen; Schone (Vibe 56), Kvist Jorgensen (Kahlenberg 74), Hojbjerg, Krohn-Dehli; Eriksen; Bendtner.

Armenia: (532) Berezovsky; Hovhannisyan, Haroyan, Arzumanyan (Voskanyan 66), Mkoyan, Hayrapetyan; Hovsepyan, Yedigaryan, Mkhitaryan (Pizzelli 71); Manucharyan (Dashyan 84), Ghazaryan.
Referee: Alexandru Dan Tudor.

Portugal (0) 0

Albania (0) 1 *(Balaj 52)* 23,205

Portugal: (433) Rui Patricio; Joao Pereira, Pepe, Ricardo Costa (Veloso 73), Fabio Coentrao; Joao Moutinho, William Carvalho (Ricardo Horta 56), Andre Gomes; Vieirinha (Ivan Cavaleiro 46), Eder, Nani.
Albania: (451) Berisha; Hisaj, Cana, Mavraj, Agolli; Roshi, Xhaka, Kukeli (Kace 66), Abrashi, Lenjani (Lila 75); Balaj (Cikalleshi 81).
Referee: Ruddy Buquet.

Saturday, 11 October 2014

Albania (1) 1 *(Lenjani 38)*

Denmark (0) 1 *(Vibe 81)* 12,800

Albania: (442) Berisha; Hisaj, Cana, Mavraj, Agolli; Abrashi, Kukeli, Xhaka (Rama 82), Lila (Curri 87); Balaj (Cikalleshi 69), Lenjani.
Denmark: (433) Schmeichel; Ankersen (Bech 71), Kjaer, Bjelland, Boilesen; Hojbjerg (Kahlenberg 79), Kvist Jorgensen, Eriksen; Poulsen Y (Vibe 46), Bendtner, Krohn-Dehli.
Referee: Viktor Kassai.

Armenia (0) 1 *(Arzumanyan 73)*

Serbia (0) 1 *(Tosic Z 90)* 7500

Armenia: (343) Berezovsky; Hovhannisyan, Haroyan, Arzumanyan; Voskanyan, Mkrtchyan (Hovsepyan 52), Yedigaryan, Hayrapetyan; Pizzelli (Karapetyan 84), Sarkisov, Manucharyan (Dashyan 66).
Serbia: (4231) Stojkovic; Ivanovic, Mitrovic S, Nastasic, Kolarov; Tosic Z, Gudelj (Mitrovic A 74); Matic, Markovic (Kuzmanovic 26), Tadic; Djordjevic (Lazovic 70).
Referee: Tom Harald Hagen.

Tuesday, 14 October 2014

Denmark (0) 0

Portugal (0) 1 *(Ronaldo 90)* 36,562

Denmark: (4231) Schmeichel; Jacobsen, Kjaer, Agger, Boilesen (Poulsen S 58); Hojbjerg, Kvist Jorgensen; Vibe (Bech 46), Eriksen (Kahlenberg 84), Krohn-Dehli; Bendtner.
Portugal: (433) Rui Patricio; Cedric Soares, Ricardo Carvalho, Pepe, Eliseu; Joao Moutinho, William Carvalho, Tiago (Quaresma 84); Ronaldo, Danny (Eder 77), Nani (Joao Mario 68).
Referee: Felix Brych.

Serbia (0) 0

Albania (0) 0

Serbia: (541) Stojkovic; Nastasic, Ivanovic, Kolarov, Mitrovic S, Tosic Z; Gudelj, Matic, Tadic, Djuricic; Lazovic.
Albania: (361) Berisha; Lila, Hisaj, Agolli; Mavraj, Lenjani, Xhaka, Cana, Kukeli, Abrashi; Balaj.
Match abandoned. Albania awarded 3-0 win
Referee: Martin Atkinson.

Friday, 14 November 2014

Portugal (0) 1 *(Ronaldo 71)*

Armenia (0) 0 21,042

Portugal: (442) Rui Patricio; Bosingwa, Pepe, Ricardo Carvalho, Guerreiro; Nani (William Carvalho 88), Joao Moutinho, Tiago, Ronaldo; Postiga (Eder 56), Danny (Quaresma 70).
Armenia: (541) Berezovsky; Hovhannisyan, Haroyan, Arzumanyan, Voskanyan, Hayrapetyan; Mkrtchyan, Mkhitaryan (Pizzelli 83), Yedigaryan (Sarkisov 77), Ghazaryan (Manucharyan 62); Movsisyan.
Referee: Tasos Sidiropoulos.

Serbia (1) 1 *(Tosic Z 4)*
Denmark (0) 3 *(Bendtner 61, 85, Kjaer 63)*
Serbia: (4411) Stojkovic; Ivanovic, Bisevac, Mitrovic S, Tosic D; Tosic Z, Gudelj (Mitrovic A 66), Matic, Tadic (Markovic 71); Djuricic (Kuzmanovic 46); Lazovic.
Denmark: (451) Schmeichel; Ankersen (Jacobsen 70), Kjaer, Bjelland, Boilesen; Vibe, Kahlenberg (Rasmussen 88), Kvist Jorgensen, Eriksen, Krohn-Dehli; Bendtner (Poulsen Y 88).
Referee: Cuneyt Cakir.
Behind closed doors.

Sunday, 29 March 2015

Albania (0) 2 *(Mavraj 77, Gashi 81)*
Armenia (1) 1 *(Movsisyan 4)*　　　　　　12,300
Albania: (433) Berisha; Hisaj, Cana, Mavraj, Agolli; Xhaka, Kukeli, Roshi (Salihi 68); Abrashi (Lenjani 46), Cikalleshi, Memushaj (Gashi 46).
Armenia: (433) Berezovsky; Hambardzumyan■, Arzumanyan, Andonian, Hayrapetyan; Yedigaryan (Korian 84), Manucharyan (Hovhannisyan 67), Mkhitaryan; Pizzelli (Haroyan 82), Ghazaryan, Movsisyan.
Referee: David Fernandez Borbalan.

Portugal (1) 2 *(Ricardo Carvalho 10, Fabio Coentrao 63)*
Serbia (0) 1 *(Matic 61)*　　　　　　58,430
Portugal: (433) Rui Patricio; Bosingwa, Bruno Alves, Ricardo Carvalho (Fonte 16), Eliseu; Joao Moutinho, Tiago, Fabio Coentrao (Quaresma 78); Nani, Danny (William Carvalho 85), Ronaldo.
Serbia: (4411) Stojkovic; Basta, Ivanovic, Nastasic, Kolarov; Markovic (Djuricic 46), Petrovic, Matic, Tadic (Tosic Z 78); Ljajic (Skuletic 85); Mitrovic A.
Referee: Christian Brocchi.

Saturday, 13 June 2015

Armenia (1) 2 *(Pizzelli 14, Mkoyan 73)*
Portugal (1) 3 *(Ronaldo 29 (pen), 55, 58)*　　15,000
Armenia: (4141) Berezovsky; Mkoyan, Arzumanyan, Andonian, Hayrapetyan; Mkrtchyan (Hovsepyan 29); Hovhannisyan (Ozbiliz 61), Mkhitaryan, Pizzelli, Ghazaryan; Sarkisov (Korian 74).
Portugal: (433) Rui Patricio; Bruno Alves, Fabio Coentrao (Adrien Silva 74), Ricardo Carvalho (Fonte 79), Eliseu; Joao Moutinho, Danny (William Carvalho 63), Tiago■; Ronaldo, Vieirinha, Nani.
Referee: Sergio Gumienny.

Denmark (1) 2 *(Poulsen Y 13, Poulsen J 87)*
Serbia (0) 0　　　　　　30,887
Denmark: (433) Schmeichel; Kjaer, Agger, Jacobsen, Poulsen S; Kvist Jorgensen (Christensen 77), Eriksen, Hojbjerg; Krohn-Dehli (Poulsen J 60), Bendtner, Poulsen Y (Vibe 73).
Serbia: (451) Stojkovic; Nastasic, Ivanovic, Kolarov, Maksimovic; Tosic Z (Kostic 66), Matic, Fejsa, Markovic, Mitrovic A (Skuletic 90); Ljajic (Djuricic 81).
Referee: Bjorn Kuipers.

Friday, 4 September 2015

Denmark (0) 0
Albania (0) 0　　　　　　35,648
Denmark: (4231) Schmeichel; Jacobsen, Kjaer, Agger, Durmisi; Hojbjerg, Kvist Jorgensen (Poulsen J 46); Sisto (Poulsen Y 46), Krohn-Dehli, Jorgensen; Bendtner.
Albania: (4141) Berisha; Xhimshiti, Cana, Ajeti, Agolli; Kukeli, Gashi (Roshi 82), Xhaka, Abrashi (Basha 63), Lenjani (Sadiku 63); Cikalleshi.
Referee: Willie Collum.

Serbia (1) 1 *(Hayrapetyan 22 (og), Ljajic 53)*
Armenia (0) 0　　　　　　150
Serbia: (4231) Stojkovic; Tomovic, Ivanovic, Spajic, Kolarov; Brasanac, Matic; Zivkovic (Tosic Z 59), Ljajic (Fejsa 73), Kostic (Tadic 83); Mitrovic A.
Armenia: (4231) Kasparov; Mkoyan, Arzumanyan, Andonian, Hayrapetyan; Mkhitaryan, Mkrtchyan; Ozbiliz (Hovhannisyan 59), Pizzelli (Korian 65), Ghazaryan (Simonyan 82); Movsisyan.
Referee: Miroslav Želinka.

Monday, 7 September 2015

Albania (0) 0
Portugal (0) 1 *(Veloso 90)*　　　　　　12,121
Albania: (433) Berisha; Djimsiti, Agolli, Ajeti, Lenjani; Cana, Kukeli, Xhaka; Abrashi (Basha 54), Gashi (Roshi 70), Cikalleshi (Balaj 86).
Portugal: (433) Rui Patricio; Pepe, Ricardo Carvalho, Eliseu, Veloso; Danny (Eder 76), Danilo Pereira, Bernardo Silva (Quaresma 65); Ronaldo, Vieirinha (Cedric Soares 54), Nani.
Referee: Jonas Eriksson.

Armenia (0) 0
Denmark (0) 0　　　　　　7500
Armenia: (442) Kasparov; Mkoyan, Arzumanyan, Haroyan, Andonian; Hovhannisyan (Simonyan 87), Mkhitaryan, Pizzelli (Korian 62), Mkrtchyan; Ghazaryan, Movsisyan (Ozbiliz 83).
Denmark: (433) Schmeichel; Jacobsen, Kjaer (Sviatchenko 80), Agger, Durmisi; Hojbjerg, Krohn-Dehli (Delaney 56), Poulsen J; Poulsen Y, Bendtner, Jorgensen (Braithwaite 64).
Referee: Svein Oddvar Moen.

Thursday, 8 October 2015

Albania (0) 0
Serbia (0) 2 *(Ljajic 90, Kolarov 90)*　　12,330
Albania: (433) Berisha; Hisaj, Cana, Djimsiti, Agolli; Memushaj, Basha, Xhaka; Lila (Kace 46), Balaj (Cikalleshi 69), Lenjani (Meha 83).
Serbia: (4231) Stojkovic; Tomovic, Ivanovic (Tosic D 65), Mitrovic S, Kolarov; Milivojevic, Matic (Fejsa 73); Tosic Z, Ljajic, Tadic (Sulejmani 54); Mitrovic A.
Referee: Nicola Rizzoli.

Portugal (0) 0 *(Joao Moutinho 66)*
Denmark (0) 0　　　　　　29,860
Portugal: (451) Rui Patricio; Cedric Soares, Bruno Alves, Ricardo Carvalho, Fabio Coentrao; Bernardo Silva (Danny 76), Joao Moutinho (Fonte 90), Danilo Pereira, Tiago, Nani (Quaresma 82); Ronaldo.
Denmark: (451) Schmeichel; Jacobsen, Kjaer, Agger, Durmisi; Braithwaite, Wass (Jorgensen 69), Hojbjerg (Kvist Jorgensen 46), Krohn-Dehli, Eriksen (Poulsen Y 82); Bendtner.
Referee: Mark Clattenburg.

Sunday, 11 October 2015

Armenia (0) 0
Albania (2) 3 *(Hovhannisyan 9 (og), Djimsiti 24, Sadiku 76)*　　　　　　4700
Armenia: (451) Kasparov; Hovhannisyan, Arzumanyan, Haroyan, Andonian; Mkhitaryan, Yuspashyan (Ozbiliz 46), Pizzelli, Mkrtchyan, Ghazaryan (Pogosyan 83); Movsisyan (Sarkisov 59).
Albania: (433) Berisha; Aliji, Cana, Djimsiti, Hisaj; Basha (Abrashi 86), Xhaka, Memushaj (Kukeli 72); Roshi, Cikalleshi (Sadiku 58), Gashi.
Referee: Szymon Marciniak.

Serbia (0) 1 *(Tosic Z 65)*
Portugal (1) 2 *(Nani 5, Joao Moutinho 78)*　　7485
Serbia: (451) Stojkovic; Tomovic, Mitrovic S, Tosic D, Kolarov (Obradovic 77); Tosic Z (Sulejmani 85), Milivojevic, Ljajic, Matic■, Tadic; Mitrovic A (Skuletic 85).
Portugal: (451) Rui Patricio; Semedo, Fonte, Bruno Alves (Luis Neto 46), Eliseu; Nani, Andre Andre, Danilo Pereira, Veloso (Joao Moutinho 70), Quaresma; Danny (Eder 57).
Referee: David Fernandez Borbalan.

Group I Table	P	W	D	L	F	A	GD	Pts
Portugal	8	7	0	1	11	5	6	21
Albania	8	4	2	2	10	5	5	14
Denmark	8	3	3	2	8	5	3	12
Serbia*	8	2	1	5	8	13	−5	4
Armenia	8	0	2	6	5	14	−9	2

Serbia deducted 3 points.

PLAY-OFFS FIRST LEG

Thursday, 12 November 2015
Norway (0) 0
Hungary (1) 1 *(Kleinheisler 26)*   27,182
Norway: (442) Nyland; Hogli, Forren, Hovland, Elabdellaoui; Berget (Elyounoussi M 74), Johansen, Tettey, Skjelbred (Helland 86); Soderlund (Pedersen 61), Henriksen.
Hungary: (442) Kiraly; Kadar, Lang, Guzmics, Fiola; Dzsudzsak (Lovrencsics 76), Elek, Gera, Kleinheisler (Nagy 72); Szalai (Priskin 90), Nemeth.
Referee: Mark Clattenburg.

Friday, 13 November 2015
Bosnia-Herzegovina (0) 1 *(Dzeko 85)*
Republic of Ireland (0) 1 *(Brady 82)*   1200
Bosnia-Herzegovina: (442) Begovic; Mujdza (Vranjes O 51), Sunjic, Spahic, Zukanovic; Visca (Djuric 72), Pjanic, Cocalic, Lulic (Hajrovic 88); Ibisevic, Dzeko.
Republic of Ireland: (4411) Randolph; Coleman, Keogh, Clark, Ward (Wilson 67); Hendrick, McCarthy, Whelan, Brady (McGeady 86); Hoolahan (McClean 59); Murphy.
Referee: Felix Brych.

Saturday, 14 November 2015
Sweden (1) 2 *(Forsberg 45, Ibrahimovic 50 (pen))*
Denmark (0) 1 *(Jorgensen 80)*   49,053
Sweden: (442) Isaksson; Lustig, Antonsson (Johansson 29), Granqvist, Olsson; Durmaz (Larsson 68), Lewicki, Kallstrom, Forsberg; Berg, Ibrahimovic (Guidetti 82).
Denmark: (4141) Schmeichel; Jacobsen, Kjaer, Agger, Durmisi; Kvist Jorgensen; Braithwaite (Poulsen Y 71), Kahlenberg (Jorgensen 54), Eriksen, Fischer (Hojbjerg 54); Bendtner.
Referee: Nicola Rizzoli.

Ukraine (1) 2 *(Yarmolenko 22, Seleznyov 54)*
Slovenia (0) 0   32,592
Ukraine: (451) Pyatov; Fedetskiy, Khacheridi, Rakitskiy, Shevchuk; Yarmolenko (Karavayev 90), Sydorchuk, Rybalka, Garmash (Malinovsky 79), Konoplyanka; Seleznyov (Kravets 83).
Slovenia: (442) Handanovic; Brecko, Ilic, Cesar, Jokic; Kurtic, Krhin, Kampl, Birsa (Pecnik 73); Ilicic (Bezjak 63), Novakovic (Ljubijankic 90).
Referee: Jonas Eriksson.

PLAY-OFFS SECOND LEG

Sunday, 15 November 2015
Hungary (1) 2 *(Priskin 14, Henriksen 83 (og))*
Norway (0) 1 *(Henriksen 87)*   26,186
Hungary: (4141) Kiraly; Fiola, Guzmics, Lang, Kadar; Elek (Pinter 46); Lovrencsics, Kleinheisler (Nemeth 74), Nagy, Dzsudzsak; Priskin (Bode 62).
Norway: (4141) Nyland; Elabdellaoui, Forren, Hovland, Aleesami; Tettey; Skjelbred (Berget 80), Johansen, Odegaard (Helland 46), Elyounoussi M(Pedersen 46); Henriksen.
Hungary won 3-1 on aggregate.
Referee: Carlos Velasco Carballo.

Monday, 16 November 2015
Republic of Ireland (1) 2 *(Walters 24 (pen), 70)*
Bosnia-Herzegovina (0) 0   51,000
Republic of Ireland: (442) Randolph; Coleman, Keogh, Clark, Brady; Hendrick, Whelan (O'Shea 90), McCarthy, Hoolahan (McClean 55); Murphy (Long 55), Walters.
Bosnia-Herzegovina: (4231) Begovic; Vranjes O, Zukanovic, Spahic, Kolasinac; Medunjanin (Djuric 69), Cocalic (Besic 46); Visca, Pjanic, Lulic (Ibisevic 80); Dzeko.
Republc of Ireland won 3-1 on aggregate.
Referee: Bjorn Kuipers.

Tuesday, 17 November 2015
Denmark (0) 2 *(Poulsen Y 82, Vestergaard 90)*
Sweden (1) 2 *(Ibrahimovic 19, 76)*   36,051
Denmark: (4231) Schmeichel; Jacobsen, Kjaer, Agger, Durmisi (Vestergaard 84); Hojbjerg, Delaney (Krohn-Dehli 46); Poulsen Y, Eriksen, Jorgensen; Bendtner (Rasmussen 60).
Sweden: (442) Isaksson; Lustig, Johansson, Granqvist, Bengtsson (Olsson 86); Larsson (Hiljemark 80), Lewicki, Kallstrom (Svensson 69), Forsberg; Berg, Ibrahimovic.
Sweden won 4-3 on aggregate.
Referee: Martin Atkinson.

Slovenia (1) 1 *(Cesar 11)*
Ukraine (0) 1 *(Yarmolenko 90)*   12,702
Slovenia: (4312) Handanovic; Brecko, Ilic, Cesar, Jokic; Pecnik (Ilicic 67), Krhin, Kampl; Bezjak (Ljubijankic 68); Birsa (Lazarevic 80), Novakovic.
Ukraine: (4411) Pyatov; Fedetskiy, Khacheridi, Rakitskiy, Shevchuk; Yarmolenko, Stepanenko, Rybalka, Konoplyanka (Tymoschuk 90); Sydorchuk (Garmash 61); Seleznyov (Kravets 80).
Ukraine won 3-1 on aggregate.
Referee: Cuneyt Cakir.

Gareth Bale shoots for goal as Wales beat Andorra 2-0 in Cardiff in October 2015, en route to qualifying automatically for Euro 2016. (Matt Dunham/AP/Press Association Images)

EURO 2016 FINALS

(France)

■ *Denotes player sent off.*

GROUP A

Friday, 10 June 2016
France (0) 2 *(Giroud 58, Payet 89)*
Romania (0) 1 *(Stancu 65 (pen))*   75,113
France: (433) Lloris; Sagna, Rami, Koscielny, Evra; Pogba (Martial 77), Kante, Matuidi; Griezmann (Coman 66), Giroud, Payet (Sissoko 90).
Romania: (433) Tatarusanu; Rat, Grigore, Chiriches, Sapunaru; Pintilii, Hoban, Stanciu (Chipciu 72); Stancu, Andone (Alibec 61), Popa (Torje 82).
Referee: Viktor Kassai.

Saturday, 11 June 2016
Albania (0) 0
Switzerland (1) 1 *(Schar 5)*   33,805
Albania: (433) Berisha; Hysaj, Cana■, Mavraj, Agolli; Abrashi, Kukeli, Xhaka (Kace 61); Roshi (Cikalleshi 73), Sadiku (Gashi 82), Lenjani.
Switzerland: (4231) Sommer; Lichtsteiner, Schar, Djourou, Rodriguez; Behrami, Xhaka, Shaqiri (Fernandes 88), Dzemaili (Frei 76), Mehmedi (Embolo 62); Seferovic.
Referee: Carlos Velasco Carballo.

Wednesday, 15 June 2016
France (0) 2 *(Payet 90, Griezmann 90)*
Albania (0) 0   63,670
France: (4231) Lloris; Sagna, Rami, Koscielny, Evra; Kante, Matuidi; Coman (Griezmann 68), Payet, Martial (Pogba 46); Giroud (Gignac 77).
Albania: (451) Berisha; Hysaj, Ajeti (Veseli 84), Mavraj, Agolli; Lila (Roshi 71), Abrashi, Kukeli (Xhaka 74), Memushaj, Lenjani; Sadiku.
Referee: Willie Collum.

Romania (1) 1 *(Stancu 18 (pen))*
Switzerland (0) 1 *(Mehmedi 57)*   43,576
Romania: (4231) Tatarusanu; Sapunaru, Chiriches, Grigore, Rat (Filip 61); Prepelita, Pintilii (Hoban 46); Torje, Stancu (Andone 83), Chipciu; Keseru.
Switzerland: (4231) Sommer; Lichtsteiner, Schar, Djourou, Rodriguez; Behrami, Xhaka, Shaqiri (Tarashaj 90), Dzemaili (Lang 83), Mehmedi; Seferovic (Embolo 63).
Referee: Sergei Karasev.

Sunday, 19 June 2016
Romania (0) 0
Albania (1) 1 *(Sadiku 43)*   49,752
Romania: (4231) Tatarusanu; Sapunaru, Grigore, Chiriches, Matel; Prepelita (Sanmartean 46), Hoban; Popa (Andone 68), Stanciu, Stancu; Alibec (Torje 56).
Albania: (451) Berisha; Hysaj, Ajeti, Mavraj, Agolli; Lila, Abrashi, Basha (Cana 83), Memushaj, Lenjani (Roshi 77); Sadiku (Balaj 58).
Referee: Pavel Kralovec.

Switzerland (0) 0
France (0) 0   45,616
Switzerland: (4231) Sommer; Lichtsteiner, Schar, Djourou, Rodriguez; Behrami, Xhaka, Shaqiri (Fernandes 79), Dzemaili, Mehmedi (Lang 86); Embolo (Seferovic 74).
France: (433) Lloris; Sagna, Rami, Koscielny, Evra; Sissoko, Cabaye, Pogba; Coman (Payet 63), Gignac, Griezmann (Matuidi 78).
Referee: Damir Skomina.

GROUP B

Saturday, 11 June 2016
England (0) 1 *(Dier 73)*
Russia (0) 1 *(Berezutski V 90)*   62,343
England: (433) Hart; Walker, Cahill, Smalling, Rose; Alli, Dier, Rooney (Wilshere 77); Lallana, Kane, Sterling (Milner 87).
Russia: (4231) Akinfeev; Smolnikov, Ignashevich, Berezutski V, Schennikov; Neustadter (Glushakov 80), Golovin (Shirokov 77); Smolov (Mamaev 85), Shatov, Kokorin; Dzjuba.
Referee: Nicola Rizzoli.

Wales (1) 2 *(Bale 10, Robson-Kanu 81)*
Slovakia (0) 1 *(Duda 61)*   37,831
Wales: (352) Ward; Chester, Williams A, Davies; Gunter, Allen, Edwards (Ledley 68), Ramsey (Richards 88), Taylor N; Williams J (Robson-Kanu 71), Bale.
Slovakia: (433) Kozacik; Pekarik, Skrtel, Durica, Svento; Kucka, Hrosovsky (Duda 60), Hamsik; Mak, Duris (Nemec 59), Weiss (Stoch 83).
Referee: Svein Oddvar Moen.

Wednesday, 15 June 2016
Russia (0) 1 *(Glushakov 80)*
Slovakia (2) 2 *(Weiss 32, Hamsik 45)*   38,989
Russia: (4411) Akinfeev; Smolnikov, Berezutski V, Ignashevich, Schennikov; Kokorin (Shirokov 75), Golovin (Mamaev 46), Neustadter (Glushakov 46), Smolov; Shatov; Dzjuba.
Slovakia: (433) Kozacik; Pekarik, Skrtel, Durica, Hubocan; Kucka, Pecovsky, Hamsik; Mak (Duris 79), Duda (Nemec 67), Weiss (Svento 72).
Referee: Damir Skomina.

Thursday, 16 June 2016
England (0) 2 *(Vardy 56, Sturridge 90)*
Wales (1) 1 *(Bale 42)*   34,033
England: (433) Hart; Walker, Smalling, Cahill, Rose; Dier, Rooney, Alli; Lallana (Rashford 73), Kane (Vardy 46), Sterling (Sturridge 46).
Wales: (352) Hennessey; Chester, Williams A, Davies; Gunter, Allen, Ledley (Edwards 67), Ramsey, Taylor N; Bale, Robson-Kanu (Williams J 71).
Referee: Felix Brych.

Monday, 20 June 2016
Russia (0) 0
Wales (2) 3 *(Ramsey 11, Taylor 20, Bale 67)*   28,840
Russia: (4231) Akinfeev; Smolnikov, Berezutski V (Berezutski A 46), Ignashevich, Kombarov; Mamaev, Glushakov; Smolov (Samedov 70), Shirokov (Golovin 52), Kokorin; Dzjuba.
Wales: (532) Hennessey; Gunter, Chester, Williams A, Davies, Taylor N; Allen (Edwards 74), Ledley (King 76), Ramsey; Bale (Church 83), Vokes.
Referee: Jonas Eriksson.

Slovakia (0) 0
England (0) 0   39,051
Slovakia: (433) Kozacik; Pekarik, Skrtel, Durica, Hubocan; Kucka, Pecovsky (Gyomber 66), Hamsik; Mak, Duda (Svento 57), Weiss (Skriniar 78).
England: (433) Hart; Clyne, Cahill, Smalling, Bertrand; Henderson, Dier, Wilshere (Rooney 56); Lallana (Alli 60), Vardy, Sturridge (Kane 76).
Referee: Carlos Velasco Carballo.

Group A Table	P	W	D	L	F	A	GD	Pts
France	3	2	1	0	4	1	3	7
Switzerland	3	1	2	0	2	1	1	5
Albania	3	1	0	2	1	3	-2	3
Romania	3	0	1	2	2	4	-2	1

Group B Table	P	W	D	L	F	A	GD	Pts
Wales	3	2	0	1	6	3	3	6
England	3	1	2	0	3	2	1	5
Slovakia	3	1	1	1	3	3	0	4
Russia	3	0	1	2	2	6	-4	1

Daniel Sturridge's injury time goal in Lens gives England a dramatic 2-1 victory over Wales in their Group B match at the European Championships. (Reuters/Christian Hartmann Livepic)

GROUP C

Sunday, 12 June 2016

Germany (1) 2 *(Mustafi 19, Schweinsteiger 90)*
Ukraine (0) 0   43,035
Germany: (4231) Neuer; Howedes, Boateng, Mustafi, Hector; Khedira, Kroos; Muller, Ozil, Draxler (Schurrle 78); Gotze (Schweinsteiger 90).
Ukraine: (4231) Pyatov; Fedetskiy, Khacheridi, Rakitskiy, Shevchuk; Sydorchuk, Stepanenko; Yarmolenko, Kovalenko (Zinchenko 74), Konoplyanka; Zozulya (Seleznyov 66).
Referee: Martin Atkinson.

Poland (0) 1 *(Milik 51)*
Northern Ireland (0) 0   33,742
Poland: (4411) Szczesny; Piszczek, Glik, Pazdan, Jedrzejczyk; Blaszczykowski (Grosicki 79), Krychowiak, Maczynski (Jodlowiec 78), Kapustka (Peszko 88); Milik; Lewandowski.
Northern Ireland: (451) McGovern; McLaughlin C, Cathcart, Evans J, McAuley; McNair (Dallas 46), Norwood, Davis, Baird (Ward 76), Ferguson (Washington 66); Lafferty K.
Referee: Ovidiu Alin Hategan.

Thursday, 16 June 2016

Germany (0) 0
Poland (0) 0   73,648
Germany: (4231) Neuer; Howedes, Boateng, Hummels, Hector; Kroos, Khedira; Muller, Ozil, Draxler (Gomez 72); Gotze (Schurrle 66).
Poland: (442) Fabianski; Piszczek, Glik, Pazdan, Jedrzejczyk; Blaszczykowski (Kapustka 80), Krychowiak, Maczynski (Jodlowiec 76), Grosicki (Peszko 87); Milik, Lewandowski.
Referee: Bjorn Kuipers.

Ukraine (0) 0
Northern Ireland (0) 2 *(McAuley 49, McGinn 90)*   51,043
Ukraine: (4231) Pyatov; Fedetskiy, Khacheridi, Rakitskiy, Shevchuk; Sydorchuk (Garmash 75), Stepanenko; Yarmolenko, Kovalenko (Zinchenko 83), Konoplyanka; Seleznyov (Zozulya 72).
Northern Ireland: (451) McGovern; Hughes, Cathcart, McAuley, Evans J; Ward (McGinn 69), Evans C (McNair 90), Davis, Norwood, Dallas; Washington (Magennis 84).
Referee: Pavel Kralovec.

Tuesday, 21 June 2016
Northern Ireland (0) 0
Germany (1) 1 *(Gomez 29)*   44,125
Northern Ireland: (451) McGovern; Hughes, McAuley, Cathcart, Evans J; Ward (Magennis 70), Evans C (McGinn 84), Davis, Norwood, Dallas; Washington (Lafferty K 59).
Germany: (4231) Neuer; Kimmich, Boateng (Howedes 76), Hummels, Hector; Khedira (Schweinsteiger 69), Kroos; Ozil, Muller, Gotze (Schurrle 55); Gomez.
Referee: Clement Turpin.

Ukraine (0) 0
Poland (0) 1 *(Blaszczykowski 54)*   58,874
Ukraine: (4231) Pyatov; Fedetskiy, Khacheridi, Kucher, Butko; Rotan, Stepanenko; Yarmolenko, Zinchenko (Kovalenko 73), Konoplyanka; Zozulya (Tymoschuk 90).
Poland: (4411) Fabianski; Cionek, Glik, Pazdan, Jedrzejczyk; Zielinski (Blaszczykowski 46), Jodlowiec, Krychowiak, Kapustka (Grosicki 71); Milik (Starzynski 90); Lewandowski.
Referee: Svein Oddvar Moen.

Group C Table	P	W	D	L	F	A	GD	Pts
Germany	3	2	1	0	3	0	3	7
Poland	3	2	1	0	2	0	2	7
Northern Ireland	3	1	0	2	2	2	0	3
Ukraine	3	0	0	3	0	5	–5	0

GROUP D

Sunday, 12 June 2016

Turkey (0) 0
Croatia (1) 1 *(Modric 41)*   43,842
Turkey: (451) Babacan; Gonul, Topal, Balta, Erkin; Calhanoglu, Tufan, Inan, Ozyakup (Sen 46), Turan (Yilmaz 65); Tosun (Mor 69).
Croatia: (4231) Subasic; Srna, Corluka, Vida, Strinic; Modric, Badelj; Brozovic, Rakitic (Schildenfeld 89), Perisic (Kramaric 86); Mandzukic (Pjaca 90).
Referee: Jonas Eriksson.

Monday, 13 June 2016

Spain (0) 1 *(Pique 87)*
Czech Republic (0) 0   29,400
Spain: (433) De Gea; Juanfran, Pique, Sergio Ramos, Jordi Alba; Fabregas (Thiago 70), Busquets, Iniesta; Silva, Morata (Aduriz 62), Nolito (Pedro 82).

Czech Republic: (4231) Cech; Kaderabek, Sivok, Hubnik, Limbersky; Darida, Plasil; Gebre Selassie (Sural 86), Rosicky (Pavelka 88), Krejci; Necid (Lafata 75).
Referee: Szymon Marciniak.

Friday, 17 June 2016

Czech Republic (0) 2 *(Skoda 76, Necid 90 (pen))*
Croatia (1) 2 *(Perisic 37, Rakitic 59)* 38,376
Czech Republic: (4141) Cech; Kaderabek, Hubnik, Sivok, Limbersky; Plasil (Necid 86); Rosicky, Skalak (Sural 67), Krejci, Darida; Lafata (Skoda 67).
Croatia: (4231) Subasic; Srna, Corluka, Vida, Strinic (Vrsaljko 90); Badelj, Modric (Kovacic 61); Brozovic, Rakitic (Schildenfeld 90), Perisic; Mandzukic.
Referee: Mark Clattenburg.

Spain (2) 3 *(Morata 34, 48, Nolito 37)*
Turkey (0) 0 33,409
Spain: (433) De Gea; Juanfran, Pique, Sergio Ramos, Jordi Alba (Azpilicueta 81); Fabregas (Koke 71), Busquets, Iniesta; Silva (Bruno 64), Morata, Nolito.
Turkey: (433) Babacan; Gonul, Topal, Balta, Erkin; Tufan, Inan (Malli 70), Ozyakup (Sahan 62); Calhanoglu (Sahin 46), Yilmaz, Turan.
Referee: Milorad Mazic.

Tuesday, 21 June 2016

Croatia (1) 2 *(Kalinic 45, Perisic 87)*
Spain (1) 1 *(Morata 7)* 37,245
Croatia: (4231) Subasic; Srna, Corluka, Jedvaj, Vrsaljko; Rog (Kovacic 82), Badelj; Perisic (Kramaric 90), Rakitic, Pjaca (Cop 90); Kalinic.
Spain: (433) De Gea; Juanfran, Pique, Sergio Ramos, Jordi Alba; Fabregas (Thiago 84), Busquets, Iniesta; Silva, Morata (Aduriz 67), Nolito (Bruno 60).
Referee: Bjorn Kuipers.

Czech Republic (0) 0
Turkey (1) 2 *(Yilmaz 10, Tufan 65)* 32,836
Czech Republic: (433) Cech; Kaderabek, Sivok, Hubnik, Pudil; Pavelka (Skoda 57), Darida, Plasil (Kolar 90); Dockal (Sural 71), Necid, Krejci.
Turkey: (4411) Babacan; Gonul, Topal, Balta, Koybasi; Mor (Sahan 69), Tufan, Inan, Sen (Ozyakup 60); Turan; Yilmaz (Tosun 90).
Referee: Willie Collum.

Group D Table	P	W	D	L	F	A	GD	Pts
Croatia	3	2	1	0	5	3	2	7
Spain	3	2	0	1	5	2	3	6
Turkey	3	1	0	2	2	4	-2	3
Czech Republic	3	0	1	2	2	5	-3	1

GROUP E

Monday, 13 June 2016

Belgium (0) 0
Italy (1) 2 *(Giaccherini 32, Pelle 90)* 55,406
Belgium: (4231) Courtois; Ciman (Carrasco 75), Alderweireld, Vermaelen, Vertonghen; Nainggolan (Mertens 62), Witsel; De Bruyne, Fellaini, Hazard; Lukaku R (Origi 73).
Italy: (352) Buffon; Barzagli, Bonucci, Chiellini; Candreva, Parolo, De Rossi (Thiago Motta 78), Giaccherini, Darmian (De Sciglio 58); Pelle, Eder (Immobile 73).
Referee: Mark Clattenburg.

Republic of Ireland (0) 1 *(Hoolahan 48)*
Sweden (0) 1 *(Clark 71 (og))* 73,419
Republic of Ireland: (4312) Randolph; Coleman, O'Shea, Clark, Brady; McCarthy (McGeady 85), Whelan, Hendrick; Hoolahan (Keane 78); Walters (McClean 63), Long.
Sweden: (442) Isaksson; Lustig (Johansson 44), Lindelof, Granqvist, Olsson; Larsson, Lewicki (Ekdal 86), Kallstrom, Forsberg; Berg (Guidetti 59), Ibrahimovic.
Referee: Milorad Mazic.

Friday, 17 June 2016

Italy (0) 1 *(Eder 88)*
Sweden (0) 0 29,600
Italy: (352) Buffon; Barzagli, Bonucci, Chiellini; Florenzi (Sturaro 85), Parolo, De Rossi (Thiago Motta 74), Giaccherini, Candreva; Pelle (Zaza 59), Eder.

Sweden: (442) Isaksson; Johansson, Lindelof, Granqvist, Olsson; Larsson, Ekdal (Lewicki 79), Kallstrom, Forsberg (Durmaz 79); Guidetti (Berg 85), Ibrahimovic.
Referee: Viktor Kassai.

Saturday, 18 June 2016

Belgium (0) 3 *(Lukaku R 48, 70, Witsel 61)*
Republic of Ireland (0) 0 39,493
Belgium: (4231) Courtois; Meunier, Alderweireld, Vermaelen, Vertonghen; Witsel, Dembele (Nainggolan 57); Carrasco (Mertens 64), De Bruyne, Hazard; Lukaku R (Benteke 82).
Republic of Ireland: (4411) Randolph; Coleman, O'Shea, Clark, Ward; Hendrick, Whelan, McCarthy (McClean 63), Brady; Hoolahan (McGeady 72); Long (Keane 78).
Referee: Cuneyt Cakir.

Wednesday, 22 June 2016

Italy (0) 0
Republic of Ireland (0) 1 *(Brady 85)* 44,268
Italy: (352) Sirigu; Barzagli, Bonucci, Ogbonna; Bernardeschi (Darmian 60), Sturaro, Thiago Motta, Florenzi, De Sciglio (El Shaarawy 81); Zaza, Immobile (Insigne 74).
Republic of Ireland: (442) Randolph; Coleman, Duffy, Keogh, Ward; Hendrick, McClean, McCarthy (Hoolahan 77), Brady; Long (Quinn 90), Murphy (McGeady 70).
Referee: Ovidiu Alin Hategan.

Sweden (0) 0
Belgium (0) 1 *(Nainggolan 84)* 34,011
Sweden: (442) Isaksson; Lindelof, Johansson, Granqvist, Olsson; Larsson (Durmaz 70), Ekdal, Kallstrom, Forsberg (Zengin 82); Berg (Guidetti 63), Ibrahimovic.
Belgium: (4231) Courtois; Meunier, Alderweireld, Vermaelen, Vertonghen; Nainggolan, Witsel; Carrasco (Mertens 70), De Bruyne, Hazard (Origi 90); Lukaku R (Benteke 87).
Referee: Felix Brych.

Group E Table	P	W	D	L	F	A	GD	Pts
Italy	3	2	0	1	3	1	2	6
Belgium	3	2	0	1	4	2	2	6
Republic of Ireland	3	1	1	1	2	4	-2	4
Sweden	3	0	1	2	1	3	-2	1

GROUP F

Tuesday, 14 June 2016

Austria (0) 0
Hungary (0) 2 *(Szalai 62, Stieber 87)* 34,424
Austria: (4231) Almer; Klein, Dragovic*, Hinteregger, Fuchs; Baumgartlinger, Alaba; Harnik (Schopf 77), Junuzovic (Sabitzer 59), Arnautovic; Janko (Okotie 65).
Hungary: (4141) Kiraly; Fiola, Guzmics, Lang, Kadar; Gera; Nemeth (Pinter 89), Nagy, Kleinheisler (Stieber 79), Dzsudzsak; Szalai (Priskin 68).
Referee: Clement Turpin.

Portugal (1) 1 *(Nani 31)*
Iceland (0) 1 *(Bjarnason B 50)* 38,742
Portugal: (4312) Rui Patricio; Vieirinha, Ricardo Carvalho, Pepe, Guerreiro; Joao Mario (Quaresma 76), Danilo Pereira, Andre Gomes (Eder 84); Joao Moutinho (Renato Sanches 70); Nani, Ronaldo.
Iceland: (442) Halldorsson; Saevarsson, Sigurdsson R, Arnason, Skulason A; Gudmundsson (Bjarnason T 90), Gunnarsson, Sigurdsson G, Bjarnason B; Sigthorsson (Finnbogason 81), Bodvarsson.
Referee: Cuneyt Cakir.

Saturday, 18 June 2016

Iceland (1) 1 *(Sigurdsson G 39 (pen))*
Hungary (0) 1 *(Saevarsson 88 (og))* 60,842
Iceland: (442) Halldorsson; Saevarsson, Sigurdsson R, Arnason, Skulason A; Gudmundsson, Sigurdsson G, Gunnarsson (Hallfredsson 65), Bjarnason B; Sigthorsson (Gudjohnsen 83), Bodvarsson (Finnbogason 69).
Hungary: (433) Kiraly; Lang, Guzmics, Juhasz (Szalai 84), Kadar; Kleinheisler, Gera, Nagy; Stieber (Nikolic 67), Priskin (Bode 67), Dzsudzsak.
Referee: Sergei Karasev.

Portugal (0) 0

Austria (0) 0   44,291

Portugal: (442) Rui Patricio; Vieirinha, Pepe, Ricardo Carvalho, Guerreiro; Quaresma (Joao Mario 71), William Carvalho, Joao Moutinho, Andre Gomes (Eder 83); Nani (Rafa 89), Ronaldo.
Austria: (4411) Almer; Klein, Prodl, Hinteregger, Fuchs; Harnik, Ilsanker (Wimmer 86), Baumgartlinger, Arnautovic; Alaba (Schopf 64); Sabitzer (Hinterseer 85).
Referee: Nicola Rizzoli.

Wednesday, 22 June 2016

Hungary (1) 3 *(Gera 19, Dzsudzsak 47, 55)*

Portugal (1) 3 *(Nani 42, Ronaldo 50, 62)*   55,514

Hungary: (4231) Kiraly; Lang, Guzmics, Juhasz, Korhut; Gera (Bese 46), Pinter; Dzsudzsak, Elek, Lovrencsics (Stieber 82); Szalai (Nemeth 70).
Portugal: (442) Rui Patricio; Vieirinha, Pepe, Ricardo Carvalho, Eliseu; Andre Gomes (Quaresma 61), William Carvalho, Joao Moutinho (Renato Sanches 46), Joao Mario; Ronaldo, Nani (Danilo Pereira 81).
Referee: Martin Atkinson.

Iceland (1) 2 *(Bodvarsson 18, Traustason 90)*

Austria (0) 1 *(Schopf 60)*   68,714

Iceland: (442) Halldorsson; Saevarsson, Arnason, Sigurdsson R, Skulason A; Gudmundsson (Ingason 86), Gunnarsson, Sigurdsson G, Bjarnason B; Bodvarsson (Bjarnason T 71), Sigthorsson (Traustason 80).
Austria: (4231) Almer; Dragovic, Prodl (Schopf 46), Hinteregger, Fuchs; Ilsanker (Janko 46), Baumgartlinger; Klein, Alaba, Arnautovic; Sabitzer (Jantscher 78).
Referee: Szymon Marciniak.

Group F Table	P	W	D	L	F	A	GD	Pts
Hungary	3	1	2	0	6	4	2	5
Iceland	3	1	2	0	4	3	1	5
Portugal	3	0	3	0	4	4	0	3
Austria	3	0	1	2	1	4	–3	1

SECOND ROUND

Saturday, 25 June 2016

Croatia (0) 0

Portugal (0) 1 *(Quaresma 117)*   33,523

Croatia: (4231) Subasic; Srna, Corluka (Kramaric 120), Vida, Strinic; Modric, Badelj; Brozovic, Rakitic (Pjaca 110), Perisic; Mandzukic (Kalinic 88).
Portugal: (442) Rui Patricio; Cedric, Pepe, Fonte, Guerreiro; Joao Mario (Quaresma 87), Adrien Silva (Danilo Pereira 108), William Carvalho, Andre Gomes (Renato Sanches 50); Nani, Ronaldo.
aet. Referee: Carlos Velasco Carballo.

Switzerland (0) 1 *(Shaqiri 82)*

Poland (1) 1 *(Blaszczykowski 39)*   38,842

Switzerland: (4231) Sommer; Lichtsteiner, Schar, Djourou, Rodriguez; Behrami (Fernandes 77), Xhaka; Shaqiri, Dzemaili (Embolo 58), Mehmedi (Derdiyok 70); Seferovic.
Poland: (442) Fabianski; Piszczek, Glik, Pazdan, Jedrzejczyk; Blaszczykowski, Krychowiak, Maczynski (Jodlowiec 101), Grosicki (Peszko 104); Milik, Lewandowski.
aet; Poland won 5-4 on penalties.
Referee: Mark Clattenburg.

Wales (0) 1 *(McAuley 75 (og))*

Northern Ireland (0) 0   44,342

Wales: (352) Hennessey; Chester, Williams A, Davies; Gunter, Allen, Ledley (Williams J 62), Ramsey, Taylor N; Vokes (Robson-Kanu 55), Bale.
Northern Ireland: (451) McGovern; Hughes, McAuley (Magennis 84), Cathcart, Evans J; Ward (Washington 69), Davis, Evans C, Norwood (McGinn 79), Dallas; Lafferty K.
Referee: Martin Atkinson.

Sunday, 26 June 2016

France (0) 2 *(Griezmann 57, 61)*

Republic of Ireland (1) 1 *(Brady 3 (pen))*   56,279

France: (433) Lloris; Sagna, Rami, Koscielny, Evra; Pogba, Kante (Coman 46 (Sissoko 90)), Matuidi; Griezmann, Giroud (Gignac 73), Payet.

Republic of Ireland: (442) Randolph; Coleman, Keogh, Duffy*, Ward; Brady, McCarthy (Hoolahan 72), Hendrick, McClean (O'Shea 69); Long, Murphy (Walters 65).
Referee: Nicola Rizzoli.

Germany (2) 3 *(Boateng 8, Gomez 43, Draxler 62)*

Slovakia (0) 0   44,312

Germany: (4231) Neuer; Kimmich, Boateng (Howedes 71), Hummels, Hector; Kroos, Khedira (Schweinsteiger 76); Muller, Ozil, Draxler (Podolski 71); Gomez.
Slovakia: (433) Kozacik; Pekarik, Skrtel, Durica, Gyomber (Salata 84); Hrosovsky, Skriniar, Hamsik; Kucka, Duris (Sestak 64), Weiss (Gregus 46).
Referee: Szymon Marciniak.

Hungary (0) 0

Belgium (1) 4 *(Alderweireld 10, Batshuayi 78, Hazard 79, Carrasco 90)*   38,921

Hungary: (4231) Kiraly; Lang, Guzmics, Juhasz (Bode 79), Kadar; Nagy, Gera (Elek 46); Lovrencsics, Pinter (Nikolic 75), Dzsudzsak; Szalai.
Belgium: (4312) Courtois; Meunier, Alderweireld, Vermaelen, Vertonghen; Nainggolan, Witsel, De Bruyne; Mertens (Carrasco 70); Lukaku R (Batshuayi 76), Hazard (Fellaini 81).
Referee: Milorad Mazic.

Monday, 27 June 2016

England (1) 1 *(Rooney 4 (pen))*

Iceland (2) 2 *(Sigurdsson R 6, Sigthorsson 18)*   33,901

England: (433) Hart; Walker, Cahill, Smalling, Rose; Alli, Dier (Wilshere 46), Rooney (Rashford 86); Sturridge, Kane, Sterling (Vardy 60).
Iceland: (442) Halldorsson; Saevarsson, Arnason, Sigurdsson R, Skulason A; Gudmundsson, Sigurdsson G, Gunnarsson, Bjarnason B; Sigthorsson (Bjarnason T 77), Bodvarsson (Traustason 88).
Referee: Damir Skomina.

Italy (1) 2 *(Chiellini 33, Pelle 90)*

Spain (0) 0   76,165

Italy: (352) Buffon; Barzagli, Bonucci, Chiellini; Florenzi (Darmian 84), Parolo, De Rossi (Thiago Motta 53), Giaccherini, De Sciglio; Pelle, Eder (Insigne 82).
Spain: (433) De Gea; Juanfran, Pique, Sergio Ramos, Jordi Alba; Fabregas, Busquets, Iniesta; Silva, Morata (Lucas 70), Nolito (Aduriz 46 (Pedro 81)).
Referee: Cuneyt Cakir.

QUARTER-FINALS

Thursday, 30 June 2016

Poland (1) 1 *(Lewandowski 2)*

Portugal (1) 1 *(Renato Sanches 33)*   62,940

Poland: (442) Fabianski; Piszczek, Glik, Pazdan, Jedrzejczyk; Blaszczykowski, Krychowiak, Maczynski (Jodlowiec 97), Grosicki (Kapustka 81); Milik, Lewandowski.
Portugal: (4132) Rui Patricio; Cedric, Pepe, Fonte, Eliseu; William Carvalho (Danilo Pereira 96); Joao Mario (Quaresma 80), Renato Sanches, Adrien Silva (Joao Moutinho 73); Nani, Ronaldo.
aet; Portugal won 5-3 on penalties.
Referee: Felix Brych.

Friday, 1 July 2016

Wales (1) 3 *(Williams A 30, Robson-Kanu 55, Vokes 85)*

Belgium (1) 1 *(Nainggolan 13)*   45,936

Wales: (352) Hennessey; Chester, Williams A, Davies; Taylor N, Allen, Ledley (King 77), Ramsey (Collins 90), Gunter; Robson-Kanu (Vokes 80), Bale.
Belgium: (4231) Courtois; Meunier, Alderweireld, Denayer, Lukaku J (Mertens 75); Nainggolan, Witsel; Carrasco (Fellaini 46), De Bruyne, Hazard; Lukaku R (Batshuayi 83).
Referee: Damir Skomina.

Saturday, 2 July 2016
Germany (0) 1 *(Ozil 65)*
Italy (0) 1 *(Bonucci 78 (pen))* 38,764
Germany: (442) Neuer; Howedes, Boateng, Hummels, Hector; Kimmich, Khedira (Schweinsteiger 15), Kroos, Ozil; Muller, Gomez (Draxler 72).
Italy: (352) Buffon; Barzagli, Bonucci, Chiellini (Zaza 120); Florenzi (Darmian 86), Sturaro, Parolo, Giaccherini, De Sciglio; Pelle, Eder (Insigne 107).
aet; Germany won 6-5 on penalties.
Referee: Viktor Kassai.

Sunday, 3 July 2016
France (4) 5 *(Giroud 12, 59, Pogba 19, Payet 42, Griezmann 45)*
Iceland (0) 2 *(Sigthorsson 55, Bjarnason B 84)* 76,833
France: (4231) Lloris; Sagna, Umtiti, Koscielny (Mangala 72), Evra; Pogba, Matuidi; Sissoko, Griezmann, Payet (Coman 80); Giroud (Gignac 60).
Iceland: (442) Halldorsson; Saevarsson, Arnason (Ingason 46), Sigurdsson R, Skulason A; Gudmundsson, Gunnarsson, Sigurdsson G, Bjarnason B; Sigthorsson (Gudjohnsen 83), Bodvarsson (Finnbogason 46).
Referee: Bjorn Kuipers.

SEMI-FINALS
Wednesday, 6 July 2016
Portugal (0) 2 *(Ronaldo 50, Nani 53)*
Wales (0) 0 55,679
Portugal: (4132) Rui Patricio; Cedric, Bruno Alves, Fonte, Guerreiro; Danilo Pereira; Joao Mario, Renato Sanches (Andre Gomes 74), Adrien Silva (Joao Moutinho 79); Nani (Quaresma 86), Ronaldo.
Wales: (532) Hennessey; Gunter, Chester, Collins (Williams J 66), Williams A, Taylor; Allen, Ledley (Vokes 58), King; Robson-Kanu (Church 63), Bale.
Referee: Jonas Eriksson.

Thursday, 7 July 2016
Germany (0) 0
France (1) 2 *(Griezmann 45 (pen), 72)* 64,078
Germany: (4231) Neuer; Kimmich, Boateng (Mustafi 61), Howedes, Hector; Can (Gotze 66), Schweinsteiger (Sane 79); Ozil, Kroos, Draxler; Muller.
France: (4231) Lloris; Sagna, Koscielny, Umtiti, Evra; Pogba, Matuidi; Sissoko, Griezmann (Cabaye 90), Payet (Kante 71); Giroud (Gignac 77).
Referee: Nicola Rizzoli.

EURO 2016 FINAL
Sunday, 10 July 2016

(at Stade de France, Paris, attendance 75,868)

Portugal (0) 1   **France (0)** *aet.*

Portugal: (4132) Rui Patricio; Cedric, Pepe, Fonte, Guerreiro; William Carvalho; Renato Sanches (Eder 78), Adrien Silva (Joao Moutinho 66); Joao Mario; Nani, Ronaldo (Quaresma 25).
Scorer: Eder 109.

France: (442) Lloris; Sagna, Koscielny, Umtiti, Evra; Sissoko (Martial 110), Pogba, Matuidi, Payet (Coman 58); Griezmann, Giroud (Gignac 78).

Referee: Mark Clattenburg.

EUROPEAN FOOTBALL CHAMPIONSHIP 1960–2016
(formerly EUROPEAN NATIONS' CUP)

Year	Winners v Runners-up		Venue	Attendance	Referee
1960	USSR v Yugoslavia	2-1*	Paris	17,966	A. E. Ellis (England)
	Winning Coach: Gavriil Kachalin				
1964	Spain v USSR	2-1	Madrid	79,115	A. E. Ellis (England)
	Winning Coach: Jose Villalonga				
1968	Italy v Yugoslavia	1-1	Rome	68,817	G. Dienst (Switzerland)
Replay	Italy v Yugoslavia	2-0	Rome	32,866	J. M. O. de Mendibil (Spain)
	Winning Coach: Ferruccio Valcareggi				
1972	West Germany v USSR	3-0	Brussels	43,066	F. Marschall (Austria)
	Winning Coach: Helmut Schon				
1976	Czechoslovakia v West Germany	2-2	Belgrade	30,790	S. Gonella (Italy)
	Czechoslovakia won 5-3 on penalties.				
	Winning Coach: Vaclav Jezek				
1980	West Germany v Belgium	2-1	Rome	47,860	N. Rainea (Romania)
	Winning Coach: Jupp Derwall				
1984	France v Spain	2-0	Paris	47,368	V. Christov (Slovakia)
	Winning Coach: Michel Hidalgo				
1988	Netherlands v USSR	2-0	Munich	62,770	M. Vautrot (France)
	Winning Coach: Rinus Michels				
1992	Denmark v Germany	2-0	Gothenburg	37,800	B. Galler (Switzerland)
	Winning Coach: Richard Moller Nielsen				
1996	Germany v Czech Republic	2-1*	Wembley	73,611	P. Pairetto (Italy)
	Germany won on sudden death 'golden goal'.				
	Winning Coach: Berti Vogts				
2000	France v Italy	2-1*	Rotterdam	48,200	A. Frisk (Sweden)
	France won on sudden death 'golden goal'.				
	Winning Coach: Roger Lemerre				
2004	Greece v Portugal	1-0	Lisbon	62,865	M. Merk (Germany)
	Winning Coach: Otto Rehhagel				
2008	Spain v Germany	1-0	Vienna	51,428	R. Rosetti (Italy)
	Winning Coach: Luis Aragones				
2012	Spain v Italy	4-0	Kiev	63,170	P. Proenca (Portugal)
	Winning Coach: Vicente del Bosque				
2016	Portugal v France	1-0*	Paris	75,868	M. Clattenburg (England)
	Winning Coach: Fernando Santos				

(*After extra time)

THE WORLD CUP 1930–2014

Year	Winners v Runners-up		Venue	Attendance	Referee
1930	Uruguay v Argentina	4-2	Montevideo	68,346	J. Langenus (Belgium)
	Winning Coach: Alberto Suppici				
1934	Italy v Czechoslovakia	2-1*	Rome	55,000	I. Eklind (Sweden)
	Winning Coach: Vittorio Pozzo				
1938	Italy v Hungary	4-2	Paris	45,000	G. Capdeville (France)
	Winning Coach: Vittorio Pozzo				
1950	Uruguay v Brazil	2-1	Rio de Janeiro	173,850	G. Reader (England)
	Winning Coach: Juan Lopez				
1954	West Germany v Hungary	3-2	Berne	62,500	W. Ling (England)
	Winning Coach: Sepp Herberger				
1958	Brazil v Sweden	5-2	Stockholm	49,737	M. Guigue (France)
	Winning Coach: Vicente Feola				
1962	Brazil v Czechoslovakia	3-1	Santiago	68,679	N. Latychev (USSR)
	Winning Coach: Aymore Moreira				
1966	England v West Germany	4-2*	Wembley	96,924	G. Dienst (Sweden)
	Winning Coach: Alf Ramsey				
1970	Brazil v Italy	4-1	Mexico City	107,412	R. Glockner (East Germany)
	Winning Coach: Mario Zagallo				
1974	West Germany v Netherlands	2-1	Munich	78,200	J. Taylor (England)
	Winning Coach: Helmut Schon				
1978	Argentina v Netherlands	3-1*	Buenos Aires	71,483	S. Gonella (Italy)
	Winning Coach: Cesar Luis Menotti				
1982	Italy v West Germany	3-1	Madrid	90,000	A. C. Coelho (Brazil)
	Winning Coach: Enzo Bearzot				
1986	Argentina v West Germany	3-2	Mexico City	114,600	R. A. Filho (Brazil)
	Winning Coach: Carlos Bilardo				
1990	West Germany v Argentina	1-0	Rome	73,603	E. C. Mendez (Mexico)
	Winning Coach: Franz Beckenbauer				
1994	Brazil v Italy	0-0*	Los Angeles	94,194	S. Puhl (Hungary)
	Brazil won 3-2 on penalties.				
	Winning Coach: Carlos Alberto Parreira				
1998	France v Brazil	3-0	Paris	80,000	S. Belqola (Morocco)
	Winning Coach: Aime Jacquet				
2002	Brazil v Germany	2-0	Yokohama	69,029	P. Collina (Italy)
	Winning Coach: Luiz Felipe Scolari				
2006	Italy v France	1-1*	Berlin	69,000	H. Elizondo (Argentina)
	Italy won 5-3 on penalties.				
	Winning Coach: Marcello Lippi				
2010	Spain v Netherlands	1-0	Johannesburg	84,490	H. Webb (England)
	Winning Coach: Vicente del Bosque				
2014	Germany v Argentina	1-0*	Rio de Janeiro	74,738	N. Rizzoli (Italy)
	Winning Coach: Joachim Low				

(*After extra time)

GOALSCORING AND ATTENDANCES IN WORLD CUP FINAL ROUNDS

Year	Venue	Games	Goals (av)	Attendance (av)
1930	Uruguay	18	70 (3.9)	590,549 (32,808)
1934	Italy	17	70 (4.1)	363,000 (21,352)
1938	France	18	84 (4.7)	375,700 (20,872)
1950	Brazil	22	88 (4.0)	1,045,246 (47,511)
1954	Switzerland	26	140 (5.4)	768,607 (29,562)
1958	Sweden	35	126 (3.6)	819,810 (23,423)
1962	Chile	32	89 (2.8)	893,172 (27,912)
1966	England	32	89 (2.8)	1,563,135 (48,848)
1970	Mexico	32	95 (3.0)	1,603,975 (50,124)
1974	West Germany	38	97 (2.6)	1,865,753 (49,098)
1978	Argentina	38	102 (2.7)	1,545,791 (40,678)
1982	Spain	52	146 (2.8)	2,109,723 (40,571)
1986	Mexico	52	132 (2.5)	2,394,031 (46,039)
1990	Italy	52	115 (2.2)	2,516,215 (48,388)
1994	USA	52	141 (2.7)	3,587,538 (68,991)
1998	France	64	171 (2.7)	2,785,100 (43,517)
2002	Japan/S. Korea	64	161 (2.5)	2,705,197 (42,268)
2006	Germany	64	147 (2.3)	3,359,439 (52,491)
2010	South Africa	64	145 (2.3)	3,178,856 (49,669)
2014	Brazil	64	171 (2.7)	3,367,727 (52,621)
Total		836	2379 (2.8)	37,438,564 (44,783)

LEADING GOALSCORERS

Year	Player	Goals
1930	Guillermo Stabile (Argentina)	8
1934	Oldrich Nejedly (Czechoslovakia)	5
1938	Leonidas da Silva (Brazil)	7
1950	Ademir (Brazil)	8
1954	Sandor Kocsis (Hungary)	11
1958	Just Fontaine (France)	13
1962	Valentin Ivanov (USSR), Leonel Sanchez (Chile), Garrincha (Brazil), Vava (Brazil), Florian Albert (Hungary), Drazen Jerkovic (Yugoslavia)	4
1966	Eusebio (Portugal)	9
1970	Gerd Muller (West Germany)	10
1974	Grzegorz Lato (Poland)	7
1978	Mario Kempes (Argentina)	6
1982	Paolo Rossi (Italy)	6
1986	Gary Lineker (England)	6
1990	Salvatore Schillaci (Italy)	6
1994	Oleg Salenko (Russia) Hristo Stoichkov (Bulgaria)	6
1998	Davor Suker (Croatia)	6
2002	Ronaldo (Brazil)	8
2006	Miroslav Klose (Germany)	5
2010	Thomas Muller (Germany), David Villa (Spain), Wesley Sneijder (Netherlands), Diego Forlan (Uruguay)	5
2014	James Rodriguez (Colombia)	6

BRITISH AND IRISH INTERNATIONAL RESULTS 1872–2016

Note: In the results that follow, wc=World Cup, ec=European Championship, ui=Umbro International Trophy. tf = Tournoi de France. nc = Nations Cup. Northern Ireland played as Ireland before 1921. *After extra time.

Bold type indicates matches played in season 2015–16.

ENGLAND v SCOTLAND

Played: 112; England won 47, Scotland won 41, Drawn 24. Goals: England 198, Scotland 172.

			E	S					E	S
1872	30 Nov	Glasgow	0	0		1932	9 Apr	Wembley	3	0
1873	8 Mar	Kennington Oval	4	2		1933	1 Apr	Glasgow	1	2
1874	7 Mar	Glasgow	1	2		1934	14 Apr	Wembley	3	0
1875	6 Mar	Kennington Oval	2	2		1935	6 Apr	Glasgow	0	2
1876	4 Mar	Glasgow	0	3		1936	4 Apr	Wembley	1	1
1877	3 Mar	Kennington Oval	1	3		1937	17 Apr	Glasgow	1	3
1878	2 Mar	Glasgow	2	7		1938	9 Apr	Wembley	0	1
1879	5 Apr	Kennington Oval	5	4		1939	15 Apr	Glasgow	2	1
1880	13 Mar	Glasgow	4	5		1947	12 Apr	Wembley	1	1
1881	12 Mar	Kennington Oval	1	6		1948	10 Apr	Glasgow	2	0
1882	11 Mar	Glasgow	1	5		1949	9 Apr	Wembley	1	3
1883	10 Mar	Sheffield	2	3		wc1950	15 Apr	Glasgow	1	0
1884	15 Mar	Glasgow	0	1		1951	14 Apr	Wembley	2	3
1885	21 Mar	Kennington Oval	1	1		1952	5 Apr	Glasgow	2	1
1886	31 Mar	Glasgow	1	1		1953	18 Apr	Wembley	2	2
1887	19 Mar	Blackburn	2	3		wc1954	3 Apr	Glasgow	4	2
1888	17 Mar	Glasgow	5	0		1955	2 Apr	Wembley	7	2
1889	13 Apr	Kennington Oval	2	3		1956	14 Apr	Glasgow	1	1
1890	5 Apr	Glasgow	1	1		1957	6 Apr	Wembley	2	1
1891	6 Apr	Blackburn	2	1		1958	19 Apr	Glasgow	4	0
1892	2 Apr	Glasgow	4	1		1959	11 Apr	Wembley	1	0
1893	1 Apr	Richmond	5	2		1960	9 Apr	Glasgow	1	1
1894	7 Apr	Glasgow	2	2		1961	15 Apr	Wembley	9	3
1895	6 Apr	Everton	3	0		1962	14 Apr	Glasgow	0	2
1896	4 Apr	Glasgow	1	2		1963	6 Apr	Wembley	1	2
1897	3 Apr	Crystal Palace	1	2		1964	11 Apr	Glasgow	0	1
1898	2 Apr	Glasgow	3	1		1965	10 Apr	Wembley	2	2
1899	8 Apr	Aston Villa	2	1		1966	2 Apr	Glasgow	4	3
1900	7 Apr	Glasgow	1	4		ec1967	15 Apr	Wembley	2	3
1901	30 Apr	Crystal Palace	2	2		ec1968	24 Jan	Glasgow	1	1
1902	3 Apr	Aston Villa	2	2		1969	10 May	Wembley	4	1
1903	4 Apr	Sheffield	1	2		1970	25 Apr	Glasgow	0	0
1904	9 Apr	Glasgow	1	0		1971	22 May	Wembley	3	1
1905	1 Apr	Crystal Palace	1	0		1972	27 May	Glasgow	1	0
1906	7 Apr	Glasgow	1	2		1973	14 Feb	Glasgow	5	0
1907	6 Apr	Newcastle	1	1		1973	19 May	Wembley	1	0
1908	4 Apr	Glasgow	1	1		1974	18 May	Glasgow	0	2
1909	3 Apr	Crystal Palace	2	0		1975	24 May	Wembley	5	1
1910	2 Apr	Glasgow	0	2		1976	15 May	Glasgow	1	2
1911	1 Apr	Everton	1	1		1977	4 June	Wembley	1	2
1912	23 Mar	Glasgow	1	1		1978	20 May	Glasgow	1	0
1913	5 Apr	Chelsea	1	0		1979	26 May	Wembley	3	1
1914	14 Apr	Glasgow	1	3		1980	24 May	Glasgow	2	0
1920	10 Apr	Sheffield	5	4		1981	23 May	Wembley	0	1
1921	9 Apr	Glasgow	0	3		1982	29 May	Glasgow	1	0
1922	8 Apr	Aston Villa	0	1		1983	1 June	Wembley	2	0
1923	14 Apr	Glasgow	2	2		1984	26 May	Glasgow	1	1
1924	12 Apr	Wembley	1	1		1985	25 May	Glasgow	0	1
1925	4 Apr	Glasgow	0	2		1986	23 Apr	Wembley	2	1
1926	17 Apr	Manchester	0	1		1987	23 May	Glasgow	0	0
1927	2 Apr	Glasgow	2	1		1988	21 May	Wembley	1	0
1928	31 Mar	Wembley	1	5		1989	27 May	Glasgow	2	0
1929	13 Apr	Glasgow	0	1		ec1996	15 June	Wembley	2	0
1930	5 Apr	Wembley	5	2		ec1999	13 Nov	Glasgow	2	0
1931	28 Mar	Glasgow	0	2		ec1999	17 Nov	Wembley	0	1
						2013	14 Aug	Wembley	3	2
						2014	18 Nov	Hampden	3	1

ENGLAND v WALES

Played: 102; England won 67, Wales won 14, Drawn 21. Goals: England 247, Wales 91.

			E	W					E	W
1879	18 Jan	Kennington Oval	2	1		1887	26 Feb	Kennington Oval	4	0
1880	15 Mar	Wrexham	3	2		1888	4 Feb	Crewe	5	1
1881	26 Feb	Blackburn	0	1		1889	23 Feb	Stoke	4	1
1882	13 Mar	Wrexham	3	5		1890	15 Mar	Wrexham	3	1
1883	3 Feb	Kennington Oval	5	0		1891	7 May	Sunderland	4	1
1884	17 Mar	Wrexham	4	0		1892	5 Mar	Wrexham	2	0
1885	14 Mar	Blackburn	1	1		1893	13 Mar	Stoke	6	0
1886	29 Mar	Wrexham	3	1		1894	12 Mar	Wrexham	5	1

Year	Date	Venue	E	W		Year	Date	Venue	E	W
1895	18 Mar	Queen's Club, Kensington	1	1		1948	10 Nov	Aston Villa	1	0
1896	16 Mar	Cardiff	9	1		wc1949	15 Oct	Cardiff	4	1
1897	29 Mar	Sheffield	4	0		1950	15 Nov	Sunderland	4	2
1898	28 Mar	Wrexham	3	0		1951	20 Oct	Cardiff	1	1
1899	20 Mar	Bristol	4	0		1952	12 Nov	Wembley	5	2
1900	26 Mar	Cardiff	1	1		wc1953	10 Oct	Cardiff	4	1
1901	18 Mar	Newcastle	6	0		1954	10 Nov	Wembley	3	2
1902	3 Mar	Wrexham	0	0		1955	27 Oct	Cardiff	1	2
1903	2 Mar	Portsmouth	2	1		1956	14 Nov	Wembley	3	1
1904	29 Feb	Wrexham	2	2		1957	19 Oct	Cardiff	4	0
1905	27 Mar	Liverpool	3	1		1958	26 Nov	Aston Villa	2	2
1906	19 Mar	Cardiff	1	0		1959	17 Oct	Cardiff	1	1
1907	18 Mar	Fulham	1	1		1960	23 Nov	Wembley	5	1
1908	16 Mar	Wrexham	7	1		1961	14 Oct	Cardiff	1	1
1909	15 Mar	Nottingham	2	0		1962	21 Oct	Wembley	4	0
1910	14 Mar	Cardiff	1	0		1963	12 Oct	Cardiff	4	0
1911	13 Mar	Millwall	3	0		1964	18 Nov	Wembley	2	1
1912	11 Mar	Wrexham	2	0		1965	2 Oct	Cardiff	0	0
1913	17 Mar	Bristol	4	3		EC1966	16 Nov	Wembley	5	1
1914	16 Mar	Cardiff	2	0		EC1967	21 Oct	Cardiff	3	0
1920	15 Mar	Highbury	1	2		1969	7 May	Wembley	2	1
1921	14 Mar	Cardiff	0	0		1970	18 Apr	Cardiff	1	1
1922	13 Mar	Liverpool	1	0		1971	19 May	Wembley	0	0
1923	5 Mar	Cardiff	2	2		1972	20 May	Cardiff	3	0
1924	3 Mar	Blackburn	1	2		wc1972	15 Nov	Cardiff	1	0
1925	28 Feb	Swansea	2	1		wc1973	24 Jan	Wembley	1	1
1926	1 Mar	Crystal Palace	1	3		1973	15 May	Wembley	3	0
1927	12 Feb	Wrexham	3	3		1974	11 May	Cardiff	2	0
1927	28 Nov	Burnley	1	2		1975	21 May	Wembley	2	2
1928	17 Nov	Swansea	3	2		1976	24 Mar	Wrexham	2	1
1929	20 Nov	Chelsea	6	0		1976	8 May	Cardiff	1	0
1930	22 Nov	Wrexham	4	0		1977	31 May	Wembley	0	1
1931	18 Nov	Liverpool	3	1		1978	3 May	Cardiff	3	1
1932	16 Nov	Wrexham	0	0		1979	23 May	Wembley	0	0
1933	15 Nov	Newcastle	1	2		1980	17 May	Wrexham	1	4
1934	29 Sept	Cardiff	4	0		1981	20 May	Wembley	0	0
1936	5 Feb	Wolverhampton	1	2		1982	27 Apr	Cardiff	1	0
1936	17 Oct	Cardiff	1	2		1983	23 Feb	Wembley	2	1
1937	17 Nov	Middlesbrough	2	1		1984	2 May	Wrexham	0	1
1938	22 Oct	Cardiff	2	4		wc2004	9 Oct	Old Trafford	2	0
1946	13 Nov	Manchester	3	0		wc2005	3 Sept	Cardiff	1	0
1947	18 Oct	Cardiff	3	0		EC2011	26 Mar	Cardiff	2	0
						EC2011	6 Sept	Wembley	1	0
						EC2016	**16 June**	**Lens**	**2**	**1**

ENGLAND v NORTHERN IRELAND

Played: 98; England won 75, Northern Ireland won 7, Drawn 16. Goals: England 323, Northern Ireland 81.

Year	Date	Venue	E	NI		Year	Date	Venue	E	NI
1882	18 Feb	Belfast	13	0		1914	14 Feb	Middlesbrough	0	3
1883	24 Feb	Liverpool	7	0		1919	25 Oct	Belfast	1	1
1884	23 Feb	Belfast	8	1		1920	23 Oct	Sunderland	2	0
1885	28 Feb	Manchester	4	0		1921	22 Oct	Belfast	1	1
1886	13 Mar	Belfast	6	1		1922	21 Oct	West Bromwich	2	0
1887	5 Feb	Sheffield	7	0		1923	20 Oct	Belfast	1	2
1888	31 Mar	Belfast	5	1		1924	22 Oct	Everton	3	1
1889	2 Mar	Everton	6	1		1925	24 Oct	Belfast	0	0
1890	15 Mar	Belfast	9	1		1926	20 Oct	Liverpool	3	3
1891	7 Mar	Wolverhampton	6	1		1927	22 Oct	Belfast	0	2
1892	5 Mar	Belfast	2	0		1928	22 Oct	Everton	2	1
1893	25 Feb	Birmingham	6	1		1929	19 Oct	Belfast	3	0
1894	3 Mar	Belfast	2	2		1930	20 Oct	Sheffield	5	1
1895	9 Mar	Derby	9	0		1931	17 Oct	Belfast	6	2
1896	7 Mar	Belfast	2	0		1932	17 Oct	Blackpool	1	0
1897	20 Feb	Nottingham	6	0		1933	14 Oct	Belfast	3	0
1898	5 Mar	Belfast	3	2		1935	6 Feb	Everton	2	1
1899	18 Feb	Sunderland	13	2		1935	19 Oct	Belfast	3	1
1900	17 Mar	Dublin	2	0		1936	18 Nov	Stoke	3	1
1901	9 Mar	Southampton	3	0		1937	23 Oct	Belfast	5	1
1902	22 Mar	Belfast	1	0		1938	16 Nov	Manchester	7	0
1903	14 Feb	Wolverhampton	4	0		1946	28 Sept	Belfast	7	2
1904	12 Mar	Belfast	3	1		1947	5 Nov	Everton	2	2
1905	25 Feb	Middlesbrough	1	1		1948	9 Nov	Belfast	6	2
1906	17 Feb	Belfast	5	0		wc1949	16 Nov	Manchester	9	2
1907	16 Feb	Everton	1	0		1950	7 Oct	Belfast	4	1
1908	15 Feb	Belfast	3	1		1951	14 Nov	Aston Villa	2	0
1909	13 Feb	Bradford	4	0		1952	4 Oct	Belfast	2	2
1910	12 Feb	Belfast	1	1		wc1953	11 Nov	Everton	3	1
1911	11 Feb	Derby	2	1		1954	2 Oct	Belfast	2	0
1912	10 Feb	Dublin	6	1		1955	2 Nov	Wembley	3	0
1913	15 Feb	Belfast	1	2		1956	10 Oct	Belfast	1	1

			E	NI
1957	6 Nov	Wembley	2	3
1958	4 Oct	Belfast	3	3
1959	18 Nov	Wembley	2	1
1960	8 Oct	Belfast	5	2
1961	22 Nov	Wembley	1	1
1962	20 Oct	Belfast	3	1
1963	20 Nov	Wembley	8	3
1964	3 Oct	Belfast	4	3
1965	10 Nov	Wembley	2	1
EC1966	20 Oct	Belfast	2	0
EC1967	22 Nov	Wembley	2	0
1969	3 May	Belfast	3	1
1970	21 Apr	Wembley	3	1
1971	15 May	Belfast	1	0
1972	23 May	Wembley	0	1
1973	12 May	Everton	2	1
1974	15 May	Wembley	1	0

			E	NI
1975	17 May	Belfast	0	0
1976	11 May	Wembley	4	0
1977	28 May	Belfast	2	1
1978	16 May	Wembley	1	0
EC1979	7 Feb	Wembley	4	0
1979	19 May	Belfast	2	0
EC1979	17 Oct	Belfast	5	1
1980	20 May	Wembley	1	1
1982	23 Feb	Wembley	4	0
1983	28 May	Belfast	0	0
1984	24 Apr	Wembley	1	0
wc1985	27 Feb	Belfast	1	0
wc1985	13 Nov	Wembley	0	0
EC1986	15 Oct	Wembley	3	0
EC1987	1 Apr	Belfast	2	0
wc2005	26 Mar	Old Trafford	4	0
wc2005	7 Sept	Belfast	0	1

SCOTLAND v WALES

Played: 107; Scotland won 61, Wales won 23, Drawn 23. Goals: Scotland 243, Wales 124.

			S	W
1876	25 Mar	Glasgow	4	0
1877	5 Mar	Wrexham	2	0
1878	23 Mar	Glasgow	9	0
1879	7 Apr	Wrexham	3	0
1880	3 Apr	Glasgow	5	1
1881	14 Mar	Wrexham	5	1
1882	25 Mar	Glasgow	5	0
1883	12 Mar	Wrexham	3	0
1884	29 Mar	Glasgow	4	1
1885	23 Mar	Wrexham	8	1
1886	10 Apr	Glasgow	4	1
1887	21 Mar	Wrexham	2	0
1888	10 Mar	Easter Road	5	1
1889	15 Apr	Wrexham	0	0
1890	22 Mar	Paisley	5	0
1891	21 Mar	Wrexham	4	3
1892	26 Mar	Tynecastle	6	1
1893	18 Mar	Wrexham	8	0
1894	24 Mar	Kilmarnock	5	2
1895	23 Mar	Wrexham	2	2
1896	21 Mar	Dundee	4	0
1897	20 Mar	Wrexham	2	2
1898	19 Mar	Motherwell	5	2
1899	18 Mar	Wrexham	6	0
1900	3 Feb	Aberdeen	5	2
1901	2 Mar	Wrexham	1	1
1902	15 Mar	Greenock	5	1
1903	9 Mar	Cardiff	1	0
1904	12 Mar	Dundee	1	1
1905	6 Mar	Wrexham	1	3
1906	3 Mar	Tynecastle	0	2
1907	4 Mar	Wrexham	0	1
1908	7 Mar	Dundee	2	1
1909	1 Mar	Wrexham	2	3
1910	5 Mar	Kilmarnock	1	0
1911	6 Mar	Cardiff	2	2
1912	2 Mar	Tynecastle	1	0
1913	3 Mar	Wrexham	0	0
1914	28 Feb	Glasgow	0	0
1920	26 Feb	Cardiff	1	1
1921	12 Feb	Aberdeen	2	1
1922	4 Feb	Wrexham	1	2
1923	17 Mar	Paisley	2	0
1924	16 Feb	Cardiff	0	2
1925	14 Feb	Tynecastle	3	1
1925	31 Oct	Cardiff	3	0
1926	30 Oct	Glasgow	3	0
1927	29 Oct	Wrexham	2	2
1928	27 Oct	Glasgow	4	2
1929	26 Oct	Cardiff	4	2
1930	25 Oct	Glasgow	1	1
1931	31 Oct	Wrexham	3	2
1932	26 Oct	Tynecastle	2	5
1933	4 Oct	Cardiff	2	3

			S	W
1934	21 Nov	Aberdeen	3	2
1935	5 Oct	Cardiff	1	1
1936	2 Dec	Dundee	1	2
1937	30 Oct	Cardiff	1	2
1938	9 Nov	Tynecastle	3	2
1946	19 Oct	Wrexham	1	3
1947	12 Nov	Glasgow	1	2
1948	23 Oct	Cardiff	3	1
wc1949	9 Nov	Glasgow	2	0
1950	21 Oct	Cardiff	3	1
1951	14 Nov	Glasgow	0	1
1952	18 Oct	Cardiff	2	1
wc1953	4 Nov	Glasgow	3	3
1954	16 Oct	Cardiff	1	0
1955	9 Nov	Glasgow	2	0
1956	20 Oct	Cardiff	2	2
1957	13 Nov	Glasgow	1	1
1958	18 Oct	Cardiff	3	0
1959	4 Nov	Glasgow	1	1
1960	20 Oct	Cardiff	0	2
1961	8 Nov	Glasgow	2	0
1962	20 Oct	Cardiff	3	2
1963	20 Nov	Glasgow	2	1
1964	3 Oct	Cardiff	2	3
EC1965	24 Nov	Glasgow	4	1
EC1966	22 Oct	Cardiff	1	1
1967	22 Nov	Glasgow	3	2
1969	3 May	Wrexham	5	3
1970	22 Apr	Glasgow	0	0
1971	15 May	Cardiff	0	0
1972	24 May	Glasgow	1	0
1973	12 May	Wrexham	2	0
1974	14 May	Glasgow	2	0
1975	17 May	Cardiff	2	2
1976	6 May	Glasgow	3	1
wc1976	17 Nov	Glasgow	1	0
1977	28 May	Wrexham	0	0
wc1977	12 Oct	Liverpool	2	0
1978	17 May	Glasgow	1	1
1979	19 May	Cardiff	0	3
1980	21 May	Glasgow	1	0
1981	16 May	Swansea	0	2
1982	24 May	Glasgow	1	0
1983	28 May	Cardiff	2	0
1984	28 Feb	Glasgow	2	1
wc1985	27 Mar	Glasgow	0	1
wc1985	10 Sept	Cardiff	1	1
1997	27 May	Kilmarnock	0	1
2004	18 Feb	Cardiff	0	4
2009	14 Nov	Cardiff	0	3
NC2011	25 May	Dublin	3	1
wc2012	12 Oct	Cardiff	1	2
wc2013	22 Mar	Glasgow	1	2

SCOTLAND v NORTHERN IRELAND

Played: 96; Scotland won 64, Northern Ireland won 15, Drawn 17. Goals: Scotland 261, Northern Ireland 81.

			S	NI					S	NI
1884	26 Jan	Belfast	5	0		1935	13 Nov	Tynecastle	2	1
1885	14 Mar	Glasgow	8	2		1936	31 Oct	Belfast	3	1
1886	20 Mar	Belfast	7	2		1937	10 Nov	Aberdeen	1	1
1887	19 Feb	Glasgow	4	1		1938	8 Oct	Belfast	2	0
1888	24 Mar	Belfast	10	2		1946	27 Nov	Glasgow	0	0
1889	9 Mar	Glasgow	7	0		1947	4 Oct	Belfast	0	2
1890	29 Mar	Belfast	4	1		1948	17 Nov	Glasgow	3	2
1891	28 Mar	Glasgow	2	1		wc1949	1 Oct	Belfast	8	2
1892	19 Mar	Belfast	3	2		1950	1 Nov	Glasgow	6	1
1893	25 Mar	Glasgow	6	1		1951	6 Oct	Belfast	3	0
1894	31 Mar	Belfast	2	1		1952	5 Nov	Glasgow	1	1
1895	30 Mar	Glasgow	3	1		wc1953	3 Oct	Belfast	3	1
1896	28 Mar	Belfast	3	3		1954	3 Nov	Glasgow	2	2
1897	27 Mar	Glasgow	5	1		1955	8 Oct	Belfast	1	2
1898	26 Mar	Belfast	3	0		1956	7 Nov	Glasgow	1	0
1899	25 Mar	Glasgow	9	1		1957	5 Oct	Belfast	1	1
1900	3 Mar	Belfast	3	0		1958	5 Nov	Glasgow	2	2
1901	23 Feb	Glasgow	11	0		1959	3 Oct	Belfast	4	0
1902	1 Mar	Belfast	5	1		1960	9 Nov	Glasgow	5	2
1902	9 Aug	Belfast	3	0		1961	7 Oct	Belfast	6	1
1903	21 Mar	Glasgow	0	2		1962	7 Nov	Glasgow	5	1
1904	26 Mar	Dublin	1	1		1963	12 Oct	Belfast	1	2
1905	18 Mar	Dublin	4	0		1964	25 Nov	Glasgow	3	2
1906	17 Mar	Dublin	1	0		1965	2 Oct	Belfast	2	3
1907	16 Mar	Glasgow	3	0		1966	16 Nov	Glasgow	2	1
1908	14 Mar	Dublin	5	0		1967	21 Oct	Belfast	0	1
1909	15 Mar	Glasgow	5	0		1969	6 May	Glasgow	1	1
1910	19 Mar	Belfast	0	1		1970	18 Apr	Belfast	1	0
1911	18 Mar	Glasgow	2	0		1971	18 May	Glasgow	0	1
1912	16 Mar	Belfast	4	1		1972	20 May	Glasgow	2	0
1913	15 Mar	Dublin	2	1		1973	16 May	Glasgow	1	2
1914	14 Mar	Belfast	1	1		1974	11 May	Glasgow	0	1
1920	13 Mar	Glasgow	3	0		1975	20 May	Glasgow	3	0
1921	26 Feb	Belfast	2	0		1976	8 May	Glasgow	3	0
1922	4 Mar	Glasgow	2	1		1977	1 June	Glasgow	3	0
1923	3 Mar	Belfast	1	0		1978	13 May	Glasgow	1	1
1924	1 Mar	Glasgow	2	0		1979	22 May	Glasgow	1	0
1925	28 Feb	Belfast	3	0		1980	17 May	Belfast	0	1
1926	27 Feb	Glasgow	4	0		wc1981	25 May	Glasgow	1	1
1927	26 Feb	Belfast	2	0		1981	19 May	Glasgow	2	0
1928	25 Feb	Glasgow	0	1		wc1981	14 Oct	Belfast	0	0
1929	23 Feb	Belfast	7	3		1982	28 Apr	Belfast	1	1
1930	22 Feb	Glasgow	3	1		1983	24 May	Glasgow	0	0
1931	21 Feb	Belfast	0	0		1983	13 Dec	Belfast	0	2
1931	19 Sept	Glasgow	3	1		1992	19 Feb	Glasgow	1	0
1932	12 Sept	Belfast	4	0		2008	20 Aug	Glasgow	0	0
1933	16 Sept	Glasgow	1	2		NC2011	9 Feb	Dublin	3	0
1934	20 Oct	Belfast	1	2		2015	25 Mar	Hampden	1	0

WALES v NORTHERN IRELAND

Played: 96; Wales won 45, Northern Ireland won 27, Drawn 24. Goals: Wales 191, Northern Ireland 132.

			W	NI					W	NI
1882	25 Feb	Wrexham	7	1		1906	2 Apr	Wrexham	4	4
1883	17 Mar	Belfast	1	1		1907	23 Feb	Belfast	3	2
1884	9 Feb	Wrexham	6	0		1908	11 Apr	Aberdare	0	1
1885	11 Apr	Belfast	8	2		1909	20 Mar	Belfast	3	2
1886	27 Feb	Wrexham	5	0		1910	11 Apr	Wrexham	4	1
1887	12 Mar	Belfast	1	4		1911	28 Jan	Belfast	2	1
1888	3 Mar	Wrexham	11	0		1912	13 Apr	Cardiff	2	3
1889	27 Apr	Belfast	3	1		1913	18 Jan	Belfast	1	0
1890	8 Feb	Shrewsbury	5	2		1914	19 Jan	Wrexham	1	2
1891	7 Feb	Belfast	2	7		1920	14 Feb	Belfast	2	2
1892	27 Feb	Bangor	1	1		1921	9 Apr	Swansea	2	1
1893	8 Apr	Belfast	3	4		1922	4 Apr	Belfast	1	1
1894	24 Feb	Swansea	4	1		1923	14 Apr	Wrexham	0	3
1895	16 Mar	Belfast	2	2		1924	15 Mar	Belfast	1	0
1896	29 Feb	Wrexham	6	1		1925	18 Apr	Wrexham	0	0
1897	6 Mar	Belfast	3	4		1926	13 Feb	Belfast	0	3
1898	19 Feb	Llandudno	0	1		1927	9 Apr	Cardiff	2	2
1899	4 Mar	Belfast	0	1		1928	4 Feb	Belfast	2	1
1900	24 Feb	Llandudno	2	0		1929	2 Feb	Wrexham	2	2
1901	23 Mar	Belfast	1	0		1930	1 Feb	Belfast	0	7
1902	22 Mar	Cardiff	0	3		1931	22 Apr	Wrexham	3	2
1903	28 Mar	Belfast	0	2		1931	5 Dec	Belfast	0	4
1904	21 Mar	Bangor	0	1		1932	7 Dec	Wrexham	4	1
1905	18 Apr	Belfast	2	2		1933	4 Nov	Belfast	1	1

			W	NI
1935	27 Mar	Wrexham	3	1
1936	11 Mar	Belfast	2	3
1937	17 Mar	Wrexham	4	1
1938	16 Mar	Belfast	0	1
1939	15 Mar	Wrexham	3	1
1947	16 Apr	Belfast	1	2
1948	10 Mar	Wrexham	2	0
1949	9 Mar	Belfast	2	0
wc1950	8 Mar	Wrexham	0	0
1951	7 Mar	Belfast	2	1
1952	19 Mar	Swansea	3	0
1953	15 Apr	Belfast	3	2
wc1954	31 Mar	Wrexham	1	2
1955	20 Apr	Belfast	3	2
1956	11 Apr	Cardiff	1	1
1957	10 Apr	Belfast	0	0
1958	16 Apr	Cardiff	1	1
1959	22 Apr	Belfast	1	4
1960	6 Apr	Wrexham	3	2
1961	12 Apr	Belfast	5	1
1962	11 Apr	Cardiff	4	0
1963	3 Apr	Belfast	4	1
1964	15 Apr	Swansea	2	3
1965	31 Mar	Belfast	5	0

			W	NI
1966	30 Mar	Cardiff	1	4
EC1967	12 Apr	Belfast	0	0
EC1968	28 Feb	Wrexham	2	0
1969	10 May	Belfast	0	0
1970	25 Apr	Swansea	1	0
1971	22 May	Belfast	0	1
1972	27 May	Wrexham	0	0
1973	19 May	Everton	0	1
1974	18 May	Wrexham	1	0
1975	23 May	Belfast	0	1
1976	14 May	Swansea	1	0
1977	3 June	Belfast	1	1
1978	19 May	Wrexham	1	0
1979	25 May	Belfast	1	1
1980	23 May	Cardiff	0	1
1982	27 May	Wrexham	3	0
1983	31 May	Belfast	1	0
1984	22 May	Swansea	1	1
wc2004	8 Sept	Cardiff	2	2
wc2005	8 Oct	Belfast	3	2
2007	6 Feb	Belfast	0	0
NC2011	27 May	Dublin	2	0
2016	**24 Mar**	**Cardiff**	**1**	**1**
EC2016	25 June	Paris	1	0

OTHER BRITISH INTERNATIONAL RESULTS 1908–2016

ENGLAND

v ALBANIA

			E	A
wc1989	8 Mar	Tirana	2	0
wc1989	26 Apr	Wembley	5	0
wc2001	28 Mar	Tirana	3	1
wc2001	5 Sept	Newcastle	2	0

v ALGERIA

			E	A
wc2010	18 June	Cape Town	0	0

v ANDORRA

			E	A
EC2006	2 Sept	Old Trafford	5	0
EC2007	28 Mar	Barcelona	3	0
EC2008	6 Sept	Barcelona	2	0
wc2009	10 June	Wembley	6	0

v ARGENTINA

			E	A
1951	9 May	Wembley	2	1
1953	17 May	Buenos Aires	0	0
(abandoned after 21 mins)				
wc1962	2 June	Rancagua	3	1
1964	6 June	Rio de Janeiro	0	1
wc1966	23 July	Wembley	1	0
1974	22 May	Wembley	2	2
1977	12 June	Buenos Aires	1	1
1980	13 May	Wembley	3	1
wc1986	22 June	Mexico City	1	2
1991	25 May	Wembley	2	2
wc1998	30 June	St Etienne	2	2
2000	23 Feb	Wembley	0	0
wc2002	7 June	Sapporo	1	0
2005	12 Nov	Geneva	3	2

v AUSTRALIA

			E	A
1980	31 May	Sydney	2	1
1983	11 June	Sydney	0	0
1983	15 June	Brisbane	1	0
1983	18 June	Melbourne	1	1
1991	1 June	Sydney	1	0
2003	12 Feb	West Ham	1	3
2016	**27 May**	**Sunderland**	**2**	**1**

v AUSTRIA

			E	A
1908	6 June	Vienna	6	1
1908	8 June	Vienna	11	1
1909	1 June	Vienna	8	1
1930	14 May	Vienna	0	0
1932	7 Dec	Chelsea	4	3
1936	6 May	Vienna	1	2
1951	28 Nov	Wembley	2	2
1952	25 May	Vienna	3	2
wc1958	15 June	Boras	2	2
1961	27 May	Vienna	1	3
1962	4 Apr	Wembley	3	1

			E	A
1965	20 Oct	Wembley	2	3
1967	27 May	Vienna	1	0
1973	26 Sept	Wembley	7	0
1979	13 June	Vienna	3	4
wc2004	4 Sept	Vienna	2	2
wc2005	8 Oct	Old Trafford	1	0
2007	16 Nov	Vienna	1	0

v AZERBAIJAN

			E	A
wc2004	13 Oct	Baku	1	0
wc2005	30 Mar	Newcastle	2	0

v BELARUS

			E	B
wc2008	15 Oct	Minsk	3	1
wc2009	14 Oct	Wembley	3	0

v BELGIUM

			E	B
1921	21 May	Brussels	2	0
1923	19 Mar	Highbury	6	1
1923	1 Nov	Antwerp	2	2
1924	8 Dec	West Bromwich	4	0
1926	24 May	Antwerp	5	3
1927	11 May	Brussels	9	1
1928	19 May	Antwerp	3	1
1929	11 May	Brussels	5	1
1931	16 May	Brussels	4	1
1936	9 May	Brussels	2	3
1947	21 Sept	Brussels	5	2
1950	18 May	Brussels	4	1
1952	26 Nov	Wembley	5	0
wc1954	17 June	Basle	4	4*
1964	21 Oct	Wembley	2	2
1970	25 Feb	Brussels	3	1
EC1980	12 June	Turin	1	1
wc1990	27 June	Bologna	1	0*
1998	29 May	Casablanca	0	0
1999	10 Oct	Sunderland	2	1
2012	2 June	Wembley	1	0

v BOHEMIA

			E	B
1908	13 June	Prague	4	0

v BRAZIL

			E	B
1956	9 May	Wembley	4	2
wc1958	11 June	Gothenburg	0	0
1959	13 May	Rio de Janeiro	0	2
wc1962	10 June	Vina del Mar	1	3
1963	8 May	Wembley	1	1
1964	30 May	Rio de Janeiro	1	5
1969	12 June	Rio de Janeiro	1	2
wc1970	7 June	Guadalajara	0	1
1976	23 May	Los Angeles	0	1
1977	8 June	Rio de Janeiro	0	0

			E	B
1978	19 Apr	Wembley	1	1
1981	12 May	Wembley	0	1
1984	10 June	Rio de Janeiro	2	0
1987	19 May	Wembley	1	1
1990	28 Mar	Wembley	1	0
1992	17 May	Wembley	1	1
1993	13 June	Washington	1	1
UI1995	11 June	Wembley	1	3
TF1997	10 June	Paris	0	1
2000	27 May	Wembley	1	1
wc2002	21 June	Shizuoka	1	2
2007	1 June	Wembley	1	1
2009	14 Nov	Doha	0	1
2013	6 Feb	Wembley	2	1
2013	2 June	Rio de Janeiro	2	2

v BULGARIA

			E	B
wc1962	7 June	Rancagua	0	0
1968	11 Dec	Wembley	1	1
1974	1 June	Sofia	1	0
EC1979	6 June	Sofia	3	0
EC1979	22 Nov	Wembley	2	0
1996	27 Mar	Wembley	1	0
EC1998	10 Oct	Wembley	0	0
EC1999	9 June	Sofia	1	1
EC2010	3 Sept	Wembley	4	0
EC2011	2 Sept	Sofia	3	0

v CAMEROON

			E	C
wc1990	1 July	Naples	3	2*
1991	6 Feb	Wembley	2	0
1997	15 Nov	Wembley	2	0
2002	26 May	Kobe	2	2

v CANADA

			E	C
1986	24 May	Burnaby	1	0

v CHILE

			E	C
wc1950	25 June	Rio de Janeiro	2	0
1953	24 May	Santiago	2	1
1984	17 June	Santiago	0	0
1989	23 May	Wembley	0	0
1998	11 Feb	Wembley	0	2
2013	15 Nov	Wembley	0	2

v CHINA

			E	C
1996	23 May	Beijing	3	0

v CIS

			E	C
1992	29 Apr	Moscow	2	2

v COLOMBIA

			E	C
1970	20 May	Bogota	4	0
1988	24 May	Wembley	1	1
1995	6 Sept	Wembley	0	0
wc1998	26 June	Lens	2	0
2005	31 May	New Jersey	3	2

v COSTA RICA

			E	C
wc2014	26 June	Belo Horizonte	0	0

v CROATIA

			E	C
1996	24 Apr	Wembley	0	0
2003	20 Aug	Ipswich	3	1
EC2004	21 June	Lisbon	4	2
EC2006	11 Oct	Zagreb	0	2
EC2007	21 Nov	Wembley	2	3
wc2008	10 Sept	Zagreb	4	1
wc2009	9 Sept	Wembley	5	1

v CYPRUS

			E	C
EC1975	16 Apr	Wembley	5	0
EC1975	11 May	Limassol	1	0

v CZECHOSLOVAKIA

			E	C
1934	16 May	Prague	1	2
1937	1 Dec	Tottenham	5	4
1963	29 May	Bratislava	4	2
1966	2 Nov	Wembley	0	0
wc1970	11 June	Guadalajara	1	0
1973	27 May	Prague	1	1
EC1974	30 Oct	Wembley	3	0
EC1975	30 Oct	Bratislava	1	2
1978	29 Nov	Wembley	1	0
wc1982	20 June	Bilbao	2	0
1990	25 Apr	Wembley	4	2
1992	25 Mar	Prague	2	2

v CZECH REPUBLIC

			E	C
1998	18 Nov	Wembley	2	0
2008	20 Aug	Wembley	2	2

v DENMARK

			E	D
1948	26 Sept	Copenhagen	0	0
1955	2 Oct	Copenhagen	5	1
wc1956	5 Dec	Wolverhampton	5	2
wc1957	15 May	Copenhagen	4	1
1966	3 July	Copenhagen	2	0
EC1978	20 Sept	Copenhagen	4	3
EC1979	12 Sept	Wembley	1	0
EC1982	22 Sept	Copenhagen	2	2
EC1983	21 Sept	Wembley	0	1
1988	14 Sept	Wembley	1	0
1989	7 June	Copenhagen	1	1
1990	15 May	Wembley	1	0
EC1992	11 June	Malmo	0	0
1994	9 Mar	Wembley	1	0
wc2002	15 June	Niigata	3	0
2003	16 Nov	Old Trafford	2	3
2005	17 Aug	Copenhagen	1	4
2011	9 Feb	Copenhagen	2	1
2014	5 Mar	Wembley	1	0

v ECUADOR

			E	Ec
1970	24 May	Quito	2	0
wc2006	25 June	Stuttgart	1	0
2014	4 June	Miami	2	2

v EGYPT

			E	Eg
1986	29 Jan	Cairo	4	0
wc1990	21 June	Cagliari	1	0
2010	3 Mar	Wembley	3	1

v ESTONIA

			E	Es
EC2007	6 June	Tallinn	3	0
EC2007	13 Oct	Wembley	3	0
EC2014	12 Oct	Tallinn	1	0
EC2015	**9 Oct**	**Wembley**	**2**	**0**

v FIFA

			E	FIFA
1938	26 Oct	Highbury	3	0
1953	21 Oct	Wembley	4	4
1963	23 Oct	Wembley	2	1

v FINLAND

			E	F
1937	20 May	Helsinki	8	0
1956	20 May	Helsinki	5	1
1966	26 June	Helsinki	3	0
wc1976	13 June	Helsinki	4	1
wc1976	13 Oct	Wembley	2	1
1982	3 June	Helsinki	4	1
wc1984	17 Oct	Wembley	5	0
wc1985	22 May	Helsinki	1	1
1992	3 June	Helsinki	2	1
wc2000	11 Oct	Helsinki	0	0
wc2001	24 Mar	Liverpool	2	1

v FRANCE

			E	F
1923	10 May	Paris	4	1
1924	17 May	Paris	3	1
1925	21 May	Paris	3	2
1927	26 May	Paris	6	0
1928	17 May	Paris	5	1
1929	9 May	Paris	4	1
1931	14 May	Paris	2	5
1933	6 Dec	Tottenham	4	1
1938	26 May	Paris	4	2
1947	3 May	Highbury	3	0
1949	22 May	Paris	3	1
1951	3 Oct	Highbury	2	2
1955	15 May	Paris	0	1
1957	27 Nov	Wembley	4	0
EC1962	3 Oct	Sheffield	1	1
EC1963	27 Feb	Paris	2	5
wc1966	20 July	Wembley	2	0
1969	12 Mar	Wembley	5	0
wc1982	16 June	Bilbao	3	1
1984	29 Feb	Paris	0	2
1992	19 Feb	Wembley	2	0
EC1992	14 June	Malmo	0	0
TF1997	7 June	Montpellier	1	0
1999	10 Feb	Wembley	0	2
2000	2 Sept	Paris	1	1
EC2004	13 June	Lisbon	1	2
2008	26 Mar	Paris	0	1
2010	17 Nov	Wembley	1	2

			E	F
EC2012	11 June	Donetsk	1	1
2015	**17 Nov**	**Wembley**	**2**	**0**

v FYR MACEDONIA

			E	M
EC2002	16 Oct	Southampton	2	2
EC2003	6 Sept	Skopje	2	1
EC2006	6 Sept	Skopje	1	0

v GEORGIA

			E	G
WC1996	9 Nov	Tbilisi	2	0
WC1997	30 Apr	Wembley	2	0

v GERMANY

			E	G
1930	10 May	Berlin	3	3
1935	4 Dec	Tottenham	3	0
1938	14 May	Berlin	6	3
1991	11 Sept	Wembley	0	1
1993	19 June	Detroit	1	2
EC1996	26 June	Wembley	1	1*
EC2000	17 June	Charleroi	1	0
WC2000	7 Oct	Wembley	0	1
WC2001	1 Sept	Munich	5	1
2007	22 Aug	Wembley	1	2
2008	19 Nov	Berlin	2	1
WC2010	27 June	Bloemfontein	1	4
2013	19 Nov	Wembley	0	1
2016	**26 Mar**	**Berlin**	**3**	**2**

v EAST GERMANY

			E	EG
1963	2 June	Leipzig	2	1
1970	25 Nov	Wembley	3	1
1974	29 May	Leipzig	1	1
1984	12 Sept	Wembley	1	0

v WEST GERMANY

			E	WG
1954	1 Dec	Wembley	3	1
1956	26 May	Berlin	3	1
1965	12 May	Nuremberg	1	0
1966	23 Feb	Wembley	1	0
WC1966	30 July	Wembley	4	2*
1968	1 June	Hanover	0	1
WC1970	14 June	Leon	2	3*
EC1972	29 Apr	Wembley	1	3
EC1972	13 May	Berlin	0	0
1975	12 Mar	Wembley	2	0
1978	22 Feb	Munich	1	2
WC1982	29 June	Madrid	0	0
1982	13 Oct	Wembley	1	2
1985	12 June	Mexico City	3	0
1987	9 Sept	Dusseldorf	1	3
WC1990	4 July	Turin	1	1*

v GHANA

			E	G
2011	29 Mar	Wembley	1	1

v GREECE

			E	G
EC1971	21 Apr	Wembley	3	0
EC1971	1 Dec	Piraeus	2	0
EC1982	17 Nov	Salonika	3	0
EC1983	30 Mar	Wembley	0	0
1989	8 Feb	Athens	2	1
1994	17 May	Wembley	5	0
WC2001	6 June	Athens	2	0
WC2001	6 Oct	Old Trafford	2	2
2006	16 Aug	Old Trafford	4	0

v HONDURAS

			E	H
2014	7 June	Miami	0	0

v HUNGARY

			E	H
1908	10 June	Budapest	7	0
1909	29 May	Budapest	4	2
1909	31 May	Budapest	8	2
1934	10 May	Budapest	1	2
1936	2 Dec	Highbury	6	2
1953	25 Nov	Wembley	3	6
1954	23 May	Budapest	1	7
1960	22 May	Budapest	0	2
WC1962	31 May	Rancagua	1	2
1965	5 May	Wembley	1	0
1978	24 May	Wembley	4	1
WC1981	6 June	Budapest	3	1
WC1982	18 Nov	Wembley	1	0
EC1983	27 Apr	Wembley	2	0
EC1983	12 Oct	Budapest	3	0
1988	27 Apr	Budapest	0	0
1990	12 Sept	Wembley	1	0
1992	12 May	Budapest	1	0

			E	H
1996	18 May	Wembley	3	0
1999	28 Apr	Budapest	1	1
2006	30 May	Old Trafford	3	1
2010	11 Aug	Wembley	2	1

v ICELAND

			E	I
1982	2 June	Reykjavik	1	1
2004	5 June	City of Manchester	6	1
EC2016	**27 June**	**Nice**	**1**	**2**

v ISRAEL

			E	I
1986	26 Feb	Ramat Gan	2	1
1988	17 Feb	Tel Aviv	0	0
EC2007	24 Mar	Tel Aviv	0	0
EC2007	8 Sept	Wembley	3	0

v ITALY

			E	I
1933	13 May	Rome	1	1
1934	14 Nov	Highbury	3	2
1939	13 May	Milan	2	2
1948	16 May	Turin	4	0
1949	30 Nov	Tottenham	2	0
1952	18 May	Florence	1	1
1959	6 May	Wembley	2	2
1961	24 May	Rome	3	2
1973	14 June	Turin	0	2
1973	14 Nov	Wembley	0	1
1976	28 May	New York	3	2
WC1976	17 Nov	Rome	0	2
WC1977	16 Nov	Wembley	2	0
EC1980	15 June	Turin	0	1
1985	6 June	Mexico City	1	2
1989	15 Nov	Wembley	0	0
WC1990	7 July	Bari	1	2
WC1997	12 Feb	Wembley	0	1
TF1997	4 June	Nantes	2	0
WC1997	11 Oct	Rome	0	0
2000	15 Nov	Turin	0	1
2002	27 Mar	Leeds	1	2
EC2012	24 June	Kiev	0	0
2012	15 Aug	Berne	2	1
WC2014	14 June	Manaus	1	2
2015	31 Mar	Turin	1	1

v JAMAICA

			E	J
2006	3 June	Old Trafford	6	0

v JAPAN

			E	J
UI1995	3 June	Wembley	2	1
2004	1 June	City of Manchester	1	1
2010	30 May	Graz	2	1

v KAZAKHSTAN

			E	K
WC2008	11 Oct	Wembley	5	1
WC2009	6 June	Almaty	4	0

v KOREA REPUBLIC

			E	KR
2002	21 May	Seoguipo	1	1

v KUWAIT

			E	K
WC1982	25 June	Bilbao	1	0

v LIECHTENSTEIN

			E	L
EC2003	29 Mar	Vaduz	2	0
EC2003	10 Sept	Old Trafford	2	0

v LITHUANIA

			E	L
EC2015	27 Mar	Wembley	4	0
EC2015	**12 Oct**	**Vilnius**	**3**	**0**

v LUXEMBOURG

			E	L
1927	21 May	Esch-sur-Alzette	5	2
WC1960	19 Oct	Luxembourg	9	0
WC1961	28 Sept	Highbury	4	1
WC1977	30 Mar	Wembley	5	0
WC1977	12 Oct	Luxembourg	2	0
EC1982	15 Dec	Wembley	9	0
EC1983	16 Nov	Luxembourg	4	0
EC1998	14 Oct	Luxembourg	3	0
EC1999	4 Sept	Wembley	6	0
EC2006	7 Oct	Old Trafford	0	0

v MALAYSIA

			E	M
1991	12 June	Kuala Lumpur	4	2

v MALTA

			E	M
EC1971	3 Feb	Valletta	1	0
EC1971	12 May	Wembley	5	0
2000	3 June	Valletta	2	1

		v MEXICO	E	M
1959	24 May	Mexico City	1	2
1961	10 May	Wembley	8	0
wc1966	16 July	Wembley	2	0
1969	1 June	Mexico City	0	0
1985	9 June	Mexico City	0	1
1986	17 May	Los Angeles	3	0
1997	29 Mar	Wembley	2	0
2001	25 May	Derby	4	0
2010	24 May	Wembley	3	1
		v MOLDOVA	E	M
wc1996	1 Sept	Chisinau	3	0
wc1997	10 Sept	Wembley	4	0
wc2012	7 Sept	Chisinau	5	0
wc2013	6 Sept	Wembley	4	0
		v MONTENEGRO	E	M
EC1989	8 Mar	Tirana	2	0
2010	12 Oct	Wembley	0	0
EC2011	7 Oct	Podgorica	2	2
wc2013	26 Mar	Podgorica	1	1
wc2013	11 Oct	Wembley	4	1
		v MOROCCO	E	M
wc1986	6 June	Monterrey	0	0
1998	27 May	Casablanca	1	0
		v NETHERLANDS	E	N
1935	18 May	Amsterdam	1	0
1946	27 Nov	Huddersfield	8	2
1964	9 Dec	Amsterdam	1	1
1969	5 Nov	Amsterdam	1	0
1970	14 June	Wembley	0	0
1977	9 Feb	Wembley	0	2
1982	25 May	Wembley	2	0
1988	23 Mar	Wembley	2	2
EC1988	15 June	Dusseldorf	1	3
wc1990	16 June	Cagliari	0	0
2005	9 Feb	Villa Park	0	0
wc1993	28 Apr	Wembley	2	2
wc1993	13 Oct	Rotterdam	0	2
EC1996	18 June	Wembley	4	1
2001	15 Aug	Tottenham	0	2
2002	13 Feb	Amsterdam	1	1
2006	15 Nov	Amsterdam	1	1
2009	12 Aug	Amsterdam	2	2
2012	29 Feb	Wembley	2	3
2016	**29 Mar**	**Wembley**	**1**	**2**
		v NEW ZEALAND	E	NZ
1991	3 June	Auckland	1	0
1991	8 June	Wellington	2	0
		v NIGERIA	E	N
1994	16 Nov	Wembley	1	0
wc2002	12 June	Osaka	0	0
		v NORWAY	E	N
1937	14 May	Oslo	6	0
1938	9 Nov	Newcastle	4	0
1949	18 May	Oslo	4	1
1966	29 June	Oslo	6	1
wc1980	10 Sept	Wembley	4	0
wc1981	9 Sept	Oslo	1	2
wc1992	14 Oct	Wembley	1	1
wc1993	2 June	Oslo	0	2
1994	22 May	Wembley	0	0
1995	11 Oct	Oslo	0	0
2012	26 May	Oslo	1	0
2014	3 Sept	Wembley	1	0
		v PARAGUAY	E	P
wc1986	18 June	Mexico City	3	0
2002	17 Apr	Liverpool	4	0
wc2006	10 June	Frankfurt	1	0
		v PERU	E	P
1959	17 May	Lima	1	4
1962	20 May	Lima	4	0
2014	30 May	Wembley	3	0
		v POLAND	E	P
1966	5 Jan	Everton	1	1
1966	5 July	Chorzow	1	0
wc1973	6 June	Chorzow	0	2
wc1973	17 Oct	Wembley	1	1
wc1986	11 June	Monterrey	3	0
wc1989	3 June	Wembley	3	0

			E	P
wc1989	11 Oct	Katowice	0	0
EC1990	17 Oct	Wembley	2	0
EC1991	13 Nov	Poznan	1	1
wc1993	29 May	Katowice	1	1
wc1993	8 Sept	Wembley	3	0
wc1996	9 Oct	Wembley	2	1
wc1997	31 May	Katowice	2	0
EC1999	27 Mar	Wembley	3	1
EC1999	8 Sept	Warsaw	0	0
wc2004	8 Sept	Katowice	2	1
wc2005	12 Oct	Old Trafford	2	1
wc2012	17 Oct	Warsaw	1	1
wc2013	15 Oct	Wembley	2	0
		v PORTUGAL	E	P
1947	25 May	Lisbon	10	0
1950	14 May	Lisbon	5	3
1951	19 May	Everton	5	2
1955	22 May	Oporto	1	3
1958	7 May	Wembley	2	1
wc1961	21 May	Lisbon	1	1
wc1961	25 Oct	Wembley	2	0
1964	17 May	Lisbon	4	3
1964	4 June	São Paulo	1	1
wc1966	26 July	Wembley	2	1
1969	10 Dec	Wembley	1	0
1974	3 Apr	Lisbon	0	0
EC1974	20 Nov	Wembley	0	0
EC1975	19 Nov	Lisbon	1	1
wc1986	3 June	Monterrey	0	1
1995	12 Dec	Wembley	1	1
1998	22 Apr	Wembley	3	0
EC2000	12 June	Eindhoven	2	3
2002	7 Sept	Villa Park	1	1
2004	18 Feb	Faro	1	1
EC2004	24 June	Lisbon	2	2*
wc2006	1 July	Gelsenkirchen	0	0
2016	**2 June**	**Wembley**	**1**	**0**
		v REPUBLIC OF IRELAND	E	RI
1946	30 Sept	Dublin	1	0
1949	21 Sept	Everton	0	2
wc1957	8 May	Wembley	5	1
wc1957	19 May	Dublin	1	1
1964	24 May	Dublin	3	1
1976	8 Sept	Wembley	1	1
EC1978	25 Oct	Dublin	1	1
EC1980	6 Feb	Wembley	2	0
1985	26 Mar	Wembley	2	1
EC1988	12 June	Stuttgart	0	1
wc1990	11 June	Cagliari	1	1
EC1990	14 Nov	Dublin	1	1
EC1991	27 Mar	Wembley	1	1
1995	15 Feb	Dublin	0	1
(abandoned after 27 mins)				
2013	29 May	Wembley	1	1
2015	7 June	Dublin	0	0
		v ROMANIA	E	R
1939	24 May	Bucharest	2	0
1968	6 Nov	Bucharest	0	0
1969	15 Jan	Wembley	1	1
wc1970	2 June	Guadalajara	1	0
wc1980	15 Oct	Bucharest	1	2
wc1981	29 April	Wembley	0	0
wc1985	1 May	Bucharest	0	0
wc1985	11 Sept	Wembley	1	1
1994	12 Oct	Wembley	1	1
wc1998	22 June	Toulouse	1	2
EC2000	20 June	Charleroi	2	3
		v RUSSIA	E	R
EC2007	12 Sept	Wembley	3	0
EC2007	17 Oct	Moscow	1	2
EC2016	**11 June**	**Marseille**	**1**	**1**
		v SAN MARINO	E	SM
wc1992	17 Feb	Wembley	6	0
wc1993	17 Nov	Bologna	7	1
wc2012	12 Oct	Wembley	5	0
wc2013	22 Mar	Serravalle	8	0
EC2014	9 Oct	Wembley	5	0
EC2015	**5 Sept**	**Serravalle**	**6**	**0**
		v SAUDI ARABIA	E	SA
1988	16 Nov	Riyadh	1	1
1998	23 May	Wembley	0	0

v SERBIA-MONTENEGRO

			E	SM
2003	3 June	Leicester	2	1

v SLOVAKIA

			E	S
EC2002	12 Oct	Bratislava	2	1
EC2003	11 June	Middlesbrough	2	1
2009	28 Mar	Wembley	4	0
EC2016	**20 June**	**Lille**	**0**	**0**

v SLOVENIA

			E	S
2009	5 Sept	Wembley	2	1
wc2010	23 June	Port Elizabeth	1	0
EC2014	15 Nov	Wembley	3	1
EC2015	14 June	Ljubljana	3	2

v SOUTH AFRICA

			E	SA
1997	24 May	Old Trafford	2	1
2003	22 May	Durban	2	1

v SPAIN

			E	S
1929	15 May	Madrid	3	4
1931	9 Dec	Highbury	7	1
wc1950	2 July	Rio de Janeiro	0	1
1955	18 May	Madrid	1	1
1955	30 Nov	Wembley	4	1
1960	15 May	Madrid	0	3
1960	26 Oct	Wembley	4	2
1965	8 Dec	Madrid	2	0
1967	24 May	Wembley	2	0
EC1968	3 Apr	Wembley	1	0
EC1968	8 May	Madrid	2	1
1980	26 Mar	Barcelona	2	0
EC1980	18 June	Naples	2	1
1981	25 Mar	Wembley	1	2
wc1982	5 July	Madrid	0	0
1987	18 Feb	Madrid	4	2
1992	9 Sept	Santander	0	1
EC 1996	22 June	Wembley	0	0
2001	28 Feb	Villa Park	3	0
2004	17 Nov	Madrid	0	1
2007	7 Feb	Old Trafford	0	1
2009	11 Feb	Seville	0	2
2011	12 Nov	Wembley	1	0
2015	**13 Nov**	**Alicante**	**0**	**2**

v SWEDEN

			E	S
1923	21 May	Stockholm	4	2
1923	24 May	Stockholm	3	1
1937	17 May	Stockholm	4	0
1947	19 Nov	Highbury	4	2
1949	13 May	Stockholm	1	3
1956	16 May	Stockholm	0	0
1959	28 Oct	Wembley	2	3
1965	16 May	Gothenburg	2	1
1968	22 May	Wembley	3	1
1979	10 June	Stockholm	0	0
1986	10 Sept	Stockholm	0	1
wc1988	19 Oct	Wembley	0	0
wc1989	6 Sept	Stockholm	0	0
EC1992	17 June	Stockholm	1	2
UI1995	8 June	Leeds	3	3
EC1998	5 Sept	Stockholm	1	2
EC1999	5 June	Wembley	0	0
2001	10 Nov	Old Trafford	1	1
wc2002	2 June	Saitama	1	1
2004	31 Mar	Gothenburg	0	1
wc2006	20 June	Cologne	2	2
2011	15 Nov	Wembley	1	0
EC2012	15 June	Kiev	3	2
2012	14 Nov	Stockholm	2	4

v SWITZERLAND

			E	S
1933	20 May	Berne	4	0
1938	21 May	Zurich	1	2
1947	18 May	Zurich	0	1
1948	2 Dec	Highbury	6	0
1952	28 May	Zurich	3	0
wc1954	20 June	Berne	2	0
1962	9 May	Wembley	3	1
1963	5 June	Basle	8	1
EC1971	13 Oct	Basle	3	2
EC1971	10 Nov	Wembley	1	1
1975	3 Sept	Basle	2	1
1977	7 Sept	Wembley	0	0
wc1980	19 Nov	Wembley	2	1
wc1981	30 May	Basle	1	2
1988	28 May	Lausanne	1	0

			E	S
1995	15 Nov	Wembley	3	1
EC1996	8 June	Wembley	1	1
1998	25 Mar	Berne	1	1
EC2004	17 June	Coimbra	3	0
2008	6 Feb	Wembley	2	1
EC1989	8 Mar	Tirana	2	0
EC2010	7 Sept	Basle	3	1
EC2011	4 June	Wembley	2	2
EC2014	8 Sept	Basel	2	0
EC2015	**8 Sept**	**Wembley**	**2**	**0**

v TRINIDAD & TOBAGO

			E	TT
wc2006	15 June	Nuremberg	2	0
2008	2 June	Port of Spain	3	0

v TUNISIA

			E	T
1990	2 June	Tunis	1	1
wc1998	15 June	Marseilles	2	0

v TURKEY

			E	T
wc1984	14 Nov	Istanbul	8	0
wc1985	16 Oct	Wembley	5	0
EC1987	29 Apr	Izmir	0	0
EC1987	14 Oct	Wembley	8	0
EC1991	1 May	Izmir	1	0
EC1991	16 Oct	Wembley	1	0
wc1992	18 Nov	Wembley	4	0
wc1993	31 Mar	Izmir	2	0
EC2003	2 Apr	Sunderland	2	0
EC2003	11 Oct	Istanbul	0	0
2016	**22 May**	**Etihad Stadium**	**2**	**1**

v UKRAINE

			E	U
2000	31 May	Wembley	2	0
2004	18 Aug	Newcastle	3	0
wc2009	1 Apr	Wembley	2	1
wc2009	10 Oct	Dnepr	0	1
EC2012	19 June	Donetsk	1	0
wc2012	11 Sept	Wembley	1	1
wc2013	10 Sept	Kiev	0	0

v URUGUAY

			E	U
1953	31 May	Montevideo	1	2
wc1954	26 June	Basle	2	4
1964	6 May	Wembley	2	1
wc1966	11 July	Wembley	0	0
1969	8 June	Montevideo	2	1
1977	15 June	Montevideo	0	0
1984	13 June	Montevideo	0	2
1990	22 May	Wembley	1	2
1995	29 Mar	Wembley	0	0
2006	1 Mar	Liverpool	2	1
wc2014	19 June	Sao Paulo	1	2

v USA

			E	USA
wc1950	29 June	Belo Horizonte	0	1
1953	8 June	New York	6	3
1959	28 May	Los Angeles	8	1
1964	27 May	New York	10	0
1985	16 June	Los Angeles	5	0
1993	9 June	Foxboro	0	2
1994	7 Sept	Wembley	2	0
2005	28 May	Chicago	2	1
2008	28 May	Wembley	2	0
wc2010	12 June	Rustenburg	1	1

v USSR

			E	USSR
1958	18 May	Moscow	1	1
wc1958	8 June	Gothenburg	2	2
wc1958	17 June	Gothenburg	0	1
1958	22 Oct	Wembley	5	0
1967	6 Dec	Wembley	2	2
EC1968	8 June	Rome	2	0
1973	10 June	Moscow	2	1
1984	2 June	Wembley	0	2
1986	26 Mar	Tbilisi	1	0
EC1988	18 June	Frankfurt	1	3
1991	21 May	Wembley	3	1

v YUGOSLAVIA

			E	Y
1939	18 May	Belgrade	1	2
1950	22 Nov	Highbury	2	2
1954	16 May	Belgrade	0	1
1956	28 Nov	Wembley	3	0
1958	11 May	Belgrade	0	5
1960	11 May	Wembley	3	3
1965	9 May	Belgrade	1	1
1966	4 May	Wembley	2	0

			E	Y
EC1968	5 June	Florence	0	1
1972	11 Oct	Wembley	1	1
1974	5 June	Belgrade	2	2

			E	Y
EC1986	12 Nov	Wembley	2	0
EC1987	11 Nov	Belgrade	4	1
1989	13 Dec	Wembley	2	1

SCOTLAND

v ARGENTINA

			S	A
1977	18 June	Buenos Aires	1	1
1979	2 June	Glasgow	1	3
1990	28 Mar	Glasgow	1	0
2008	19 Nov	Glasgow	0	1

v AUSTRALIA

			S	A
wc1985	20 Nov	Glasgow	2	0
wc1985	4 Dec	Melbourne	0	0
1996	27 Mar	Glasgow	1	0
2000	15 Nov	Glasgow	0	2
2012	15 Aug	Easter Road	3	1

v AUSTRIA

			S	A
1931	16 May	Vienna	0	5
1933	29 Nov	Glasgow	2	2
1937	9 May	Vienna	1	1
1950	13 Dec	Glasgow	0	1
1951	27 May	Vienna	0	4
wc1954	16 June	Zurich	0	1
1955	19 May	Vienna	4	1
1956	2 May	Glasgow	1	1
1960	29 May	Vienna	1	4
1963	8 May	Glasgow	4	1

(abandoned after 79 mins)

			S	A
wc1968	6 Nov	Glasgow	2	1
wc1969	5 Nov	Vienna	0	2
EC1978	20 Sept	Vienna	2	3
EC1979	17 Oct	Glasgow	1	1
1994	20 Apr	Vienna	2	1
wc1996	31 Aug	Vienna	0	0
wc1997	2 Apr	Celtic Park	2	0
2003	30 Apr	Glasgow	0	2
2005	17 Aug	Graz	2	2
2007	30 May	Vienna	1	0

v BELARUS

			S	B
wc1997	8 June	Minsk	1	0
wc1997	7 Sept	Aberdeen	4	1
wc2005	8 June	Minsk	0	0
wc2005	8 Oct	Glasgow	0	1

v BELGIUM

			S	B
1946	23 Jan	Glasgow	2	2
1947	18 May	Brussels	1	2
1948	28 Apr	Glasgow	2	0
1951	20 May	Brussels	5	0
EC1971	3 Feb	Liege	0	3
EC1971	10 Nov	Aberdeen	1	0
1974	1 June	Brussels	1	2
EC1979	21 Nov	Brussels	0	2
EC1979	19 Dec	Glasgow	1	3
EC1982	15 Dec	Brussels	2	3
EC1983	12 Oct	Glasgow	1	1
EC1987	1 Apr	Brussels	1	4
EC1987	14 Oct	Glasgow	2	0
wc2001	24 Mar	Glasgow	2	2
wc2001	5 Sept	Brussels	0	2
wc2012	16 Oct	Brussels	0	2
wc2013	6 Sept	Glasgow	0	2

v BOSNIA-HERZEGOVINA

			S	BH
EC1999	4 Sept	Sarajevo	2	1
EC1999	5 Oct	Ibrox	1	0

v BRAZIL

			S	B
1966	25 June	Glasgow	1	1
1972	5 July	Rio de Janeiro	0	1
1973	30 June	Glasgow	0	1
wc1974	18 June	Frankfurt	0	0
1977	23 June	Rio de Janeiro	0	2
wc1982	18 June	Seville	1	4
1987	26 May	Glasgow	0	2
wc1990	20 June	Turin	0	1
wc1998	10 June	St Denis	1	2
2011	27 Mar	Emirates	0	2

v BULGARIA

			S	B
1978	22 Feb	Glasgow	2	1
EC1986	10 Sept	Glasgow	0	0
EC1987	11 Nov	Sofia	1	0
EC1990	14 Nov	Sofia	1	1
EC1991	27 Mar	Glasgow	1	1
2006	11 May	Kobe	5	1

v CANADA

			S	C
1983	12 June	Vancouver	2	0
1983	16 June	Edmonton	3	0
1983	20 June	Toronto	2	0
1992	21 May	Toronto	3	1
2002	15 Oct	Easter Road	3	1

v CHILE

			S	C
1977	15 June	Santiago	4	2
1989	30 May	Glasgow	2	0

v CIS

			S	C
EC1992	18 June	Norrkoping	3	0

v COLOMBIA

			S	C
1988	17 May	Glasgow	0	0
1996	29 May	Miami	0	1
1998	23 May	New York	2	2

v COSTA RICA

			S	CR
wc1990	11 June	Genoa	0	1

v CROATIA

			S	C
wc2000	11 Oct	Zagreb	1	1
wc2001	1 Sept	Glasgow	0	0
2008	26 Mar	Glasgow	1	1
wc2013	7 June	Zagreb	1	0
wc2013	15 Oct	Glasgow	2	0

v CYPRUS

			S	C
wc1968	11 Dec	Nicosia	5	0
wc1969	17 May	Glasgow	8	0
wc1989	8 Feb	Limassol	3	2
wc1989	26 Apr	Glasgow	2	1
2011	11 Nov	Larnaca	2	1

v CZECHOSLOVAKIA

			S	C
1937	15 May	Prague	3	1
1937	8 Dec	Glasgow	5	0
wc1961	14 May	Bratislava	0	4
wc1961	26 Sept	Glasgow	3	2
wc1961	29 Nov	Brussels	2	4*
1972	2 July	Porto Alegre	0	0
wc1973	26 Sept	Glasgow	2	1
wc1973	17 Oct	Bratislava	0	1
wc1976	13 Oct	Prague	0	2
wc1977	21 Sept	Glasgow	3	1

v CZECH REPUBLIC

			S	C
EC1999	31 Mar	Glasgow	1	2
EC1999	9 June	Prague	2	3
2008	30 May	Prague	1	3
2010	3 Mar	Glasgow	1	0
EC2010	8 Oct	Prague	0	1
EC2011	3 Sept	Glasgow	2	2
2016	**24 Mar**	**Prague**	**1**	**0**

v DENMARK

			S	D
1951	12 May	Glasgow	3	1
1952	25 May	Copenhagen	2	1
1968	16 Oct	Copenhagen	1	0
EC1970	11 Nov	Glasgow	1	0
EC1971	9 June	Copenhagen	0	1
wc1972	18 Oct	Copenhagen	4	1
wc1972	15 Nov	Glasgow	2	0
EC1975	3 Sept	Copenhagen	1	0
EC1975	29 Oct	Glasgow	3	1
wc1986	4 June	Nezahualcoyotl	0	1
1996	24 Apr	Copenhagen	0	2
1998	25 Mar	Ibrox	0	1
2002	21 Aug	Glasgow	0	1

			S	D
2004	28 Apr	Copenhagen	0	1
2011	10 Aug	Glasgow	2	1
2016	**29 Mar**	**Glasgow**	**1**	**0**

v ECUADOR			S	E
1995	24 May	Toyama	2	1

v EGYPT			S	E
1990	16 May	Aberdeen	1	3

v ESTONIA			S	E
wc1993	19 May	Tallinn	3	0
wc1993	2 June	Aberdeen	3	1
wc1997	11 Feb	Monaco	0	0
wc1997	29 Mar	Kilmarnock	2	0
EC1998	10 Oct	Tynecastle	3	2
EC1999	8 Sept	Tallinn	0	0
2004	27 May	Tallinn	1	0
2013	6 Feb	Aberdeen	1	0

v FAROE ISLANDS			S	F
EC1994	12 Oct	Glasgow	5	1
EC1995	7 June	Toftir	2	0
EC1998	14 Oct	Aberdeen	2	1
EC1999	5 June	Toftir	1	1
EC2002	7 Sept	Toftir	2	2
EC2003	6 Sept	Glasgow	3	1
EC2006	2 Sept	Celtic Park	6	0
EC2007	6 June	Toftir	2	0
2010	16 Nov	Aberdeen	3	0

v FINLAND			S	F
1954	25 May	Helsinki	2	1
wc1964	21 Oct	Glasgow	3	1
wc1965	27 May	Helsinki	2	1
1976	8 Sept	Glasgow	6	0
1992	25 Mar	Glasgow	1	1
EC1994	7 Sept	Helsinki	2	0
EC1995	6 Sept	Glasgow	1	0
1998	22 Apr	Easter Road	1	1

v FRANCE			S	F
1930	18 May	Paris	2	0
1932	8 May	Paris	3	1
1948	23 May	Paris	0	3
1949	27 Apr	Glasgow	2	0
1950	27 May	Paris	1	0
1951	16 May	Glasgow	1	0
wc1958	15 June	Orebro	1	2
1984	1 June	Marseilles	0	2
wc1989	8 Mar	Glasgow	2	0
wc1989	11 Oct	Paris	0	3
1997	12 Nov	St Etienne	1	2
2000	29 Mar	Glasgow	0	2
2002	27 Mar	Paris	0	5
EC2006	7 Oct	Glasgow	1	0
EC2007	12 Sept	Paris	1	0
2016	**4 June**	**Metz**	**0**	**3**

v FYR MACEDONIA			S	M
wc2008	6 Sept	Skopje	0	1
wc2009	5 Sept	Glasgow	2	0
wc2012	11 Sept	Glasgow	1	1
wc2013	10 Sept	Skopje	2	1

v GEORGIA			S	G
EC2007	24 Mar	Glasgow	2	1
EC2007	17 Oct	Tbilisi	0	2
EC2014	11 Oct	Ibrox	1	0
EC2015	**4 Sept**	**Tbilsi**	**0**	**1**

v GERMANY			S	G
1929	1 June	Berlin	1	1
1936	14 Oct	Glasgow	2	0
EC1992	15 June	Norrkoping	0	2
1993	24 Mar	Glasgow	0	1
1999	28 Apr	Bremen	1	0
EC2003	7 June	Glasgow	1	1
EC2003	10 Sept	Dortmund	1	2
EC2014	7 Sept	Dortmund	1	2
EC2015	**7 Sept**	**Glasgow**	**2**	**3**

v EAST GERMANY			S	EG
1974	30 Oct	Glasgow	3	0
1977	7 Sept	East Berlin	0	1
EC1982	13 Oct	Glasgow	2	0
EC1983	16 Nov	Halle	1	2
1985	16 Oct	Glasgow	0	0
1990	25 Apr	Glasgow	0	1

v WEST GERMANY			S	WG
1957	22 May	Stuttgart	3	1
1959	6 May	Glasgow	3	2
1964	12 May	Hanover	2	2
wc1969	16 Apr	Glasgow	1	1

			S	WG
wc1969	22 Oct	Hamburg	2	3
1973	14 Nov	Glasgow	1	1
1974	27 Mar	Frankfurt	1	2
wc1986	8 June	Queretaro	1	2

v GIBRALTAR			S	G
EC2015	29 Mar	Hampden	6	1
EC2015	**11 Oct**	**Faro**	**6**	**0**

v GREECE			S	G
EC1994	18 Dec	Athens	0	1
EC1995	16 Aug	Glasgow	1	0

v HONG KONG XI			S	HK
†2002	23 May	Hong Kong	4	0

†match not recognised by FIFA

v HUNGARY			S	H
1938	7 Dec	Ibrox	3	1
1954	8 Dec	Glasgow	2	4
1955	29 May	Budapest	1	3
1958	7 May	Glasgow	1	1
1960	5 June	Budapest	3	3
1980	31 May	Budapest	1	3
1987	9 Sept	Glasgow	2	0
2004	18 Aug	Glasgow	0	3

v ICELAND			S	I
wc1984	17 Oct	Glasgow	3	0
wc1985	28 May	Reykjavik	1	0
EC2002	12 Oct	Reykjavik	2	0
EC2003	29 Mar	Glasgow	2	1
wc2008	10 Sept	Reykjavik	2	1
wc2009	1 Apr	Glasgow	2	1

v IRAN			S	I
wc1978	7 June	Cordoba	1	1

v ISRAEL			S	I
wc1981	25 Feb	Tel Aviv	1	0
wc1981	28 Apr	Glasgow	3	1
1986	28 Jan	Tel Aviv	1	0

v ITALY			S	I
1931	20 May	Rome	0	3
wc1965	9 Nov	Glasgow	1	0
wc1965	7 Dec	Naples	0	3
1988	22 Dec	Perugia	0	2
wc1992	18 Nov	Ibrox	0	0
wc1993	13 Oct	Rome	1	3
wc2005	26 Mar	Milan	0	2
wc2005	3 Sept	Glasgow	1	1
EC2007	28 Mar	Bari	0	2
EC2007	17 Nov	Glasgow	1	2
2016	**29 May**	**Ta'Qali**	**0**	**1**

v JAPAN			S	J
1995	21 May	Hiroshima	0	0
2006	13 May	Saitama	0	0
2009	10 Oct	Yokohama	0	2

v KOREA REPUBLIC			S	KR
2002	16 May	Busan	1	4

v LATVIA			S	L
wc1996	5 Oct	Riga	2	0
wc1997	11 Oct	Celtic Park	2	0
wc2000	2 Sept	Riga	1	0
wc2001	6 Oct	Glasgow	2	1

v LIECHTENSTEIN			S	L
EC2010	7 Sept	Glasgow	2	1
EC2011	8 Oct	Vaduz	1	0

v LITHUANIA			S	L
EC1998	5 Sept	Vilnius	0	0
EC1999	9 Oct	Glasgow	3	0
EC2003	2 Apr	Kaunas	0	1
EC2003	11 Oct	Glasgow	1	0
EC2006	6 Sept	Kaunas	2	1
EC2007	8 Sept	Glasgow	3	1
EC2010	3 Sept	Kaunas	0	0
EC2011	6 Sept	Glasgow	1	0

v LUXEMBOURG			S	L
1947	24 May	Luxembourg	6	0
EC1986	12 Nov	Glasgow	3	0

			S	L
EC1987	2 Dec	Esch	0	0
2012	14 Nov	Luxembourg	2	1

v MALTA			S	M
1988	22 Mar	Valletta	1	1
1990	28 May	Valletta	2	1
wc1993	17 Feb	Ibrox	3	0
wc1993	17 Nov	Valletta	2	0
1997	1 June	Valletta	3	2

v MOLDOVA			S	M
wc2004	13 Oct	Chisinau	1	1
wc2005	4 June	Glasgow	2	0

v MOROCCO			S	M
wc1998	23 June	St Etienne	0	3

v NETHERLANDS			S	N
1929	4 June	Amsterdam	2	0
1938	21 May	Amsterdam	3	1
1959	27 May	Amsterdam	2	1
1966	11 May	Glasgow	0	3
1968	30 May	Amsterdam	0	0
1971	1 Dec	Amsterdam	1	2
wc1978	11 June	Mendoza	3	2
1982	23 Mar	Glasgow	2	1
1986	29 Apr	Eindhoven	0	0
EC1992	12 June	Gothenburg	0	1
1994	23 Mar	Glasgow	0	1
1994	27 May	Utrecht	1	3
EC1996	10 June	Villa Park	0	0
2000	26 Apr	Arnhem	0	0
EC2003	15 Nov	Glasgow	1	0
EC2003	19 Nov	Amsterdam	0	6
wc2009	28 Mar	Amsterdam	0	3
wc2009	9 Sept	Glasgow	0	1

v NEW ZEALAND			S	NZ
wc1982	15 June	Malaga	5	2
2003	27 May	Tynecastle	1	1

v NIGERIA			S	N
2002	17 Apr	Aberdeen	1	2
2014	28 May	Craven Cottage	2	2

v NORWAY			S	N
1929	26 May	Oslo	7	3
1954	5 May	Glasgow	1	0
1954	19 May	Oslo	1	1
1963	4 June	Bergen	3	4
1963	7 Nov	Glasgow	6	1
1974	6 June	Oslo	2	1
EC1978	25 Oct	Glasgow	3	2
EC1979	7 June	Oslo	4	0
wc1988	14 Sept	Oslo	2	1
wc1989	15 Nov	Glasgow	1	1
1992	3 June	Oslo	0	0
wc1998	16 June	Bordeaux	1	1
2003	20 Aug	Oslo	0	0
wc2004	9 Oct	Glasgow	0	1
wc2005	7 Sept	Oslo	2	1
wc2008	11 Oct	Glasgow	0	0
wc2009	12 Aug	Oslo	0	4
2013	19 Nov	Molde	1	0

v PARAGUAY			S	P
wc1958	11 June	Norrkoping	2	3

v PERU			S	P
1972	26 Apr	Glasgow	2	0
wc1978	3 June	Cordoba	1	3
1979	12 Sept	Glasgow	1	1

v POLAND			S	P
1958	1 June	Warsaw	2	1
1960	4 May	Glasgow	2	3
wc1965	23 May	Chorzow	1	1
wc1965	13 Oct	Glasgow	1	2
1980	28 May	Poznan	0	1
1990	19 May	Glasgow	1	1
2001	25 Apr	Bydgoszcz	1	1
2014	5 Mar	Warsaw	1	0
EC2014	14 Oct	Warsaw	2	2
EC2015	**8 Oct**	**Glasgow**	**2**	**2**

v PORTUGAL			S	P
1950	21 May	Lisbon	2	2
1955	4 May	Glasgow	3	0
1959	3 June	Lisbon	0	1
1966	18 June	Glasgow	0	1

			S	P
EC1971	21 Apr	Lisbon	0	2
EC1971	13 Oct	Glasgow	2	1
1975	13 May	Glasgow	1	0
EC1978	29 Nov	Lisbon	0	1
EC1980	26 Mar	Glasgow	4	1
wc1980	15 Oct	Glasgow	0	0
wc1981	18 Nov	Lisbon	1	2
wc1992	14 Oct	Ibrox	0	0
wc1993	28 Apr	Lisbon	0	5
2002	20 Nov	Braga	0	2

v QATAR			S	Q
2015	5 June	Easter Road	1	0

v REPUBLIC OF IRELAND			S	RI
wc1961	3 May	Glasgow	4	1
wc1961	7 May	Dublin	3	0
1963	9 June	Dublin	0	1
1969	21 Sept	Dublin	1	1
EC1986	15 Oct	Dublin	0	0
EC1987	18 Feb	Glasgow	0	1
2000	30 May	Dublin	2	1
2003	12 Feb	Glasgow	0	2
NC2011	29 May	Dublin	0	1
EC2014	14 Nov	Hampden	1	0
EC2015	13 June	Dublin	1	1

v ROMANIA			S	R
EC1975	1 June	Bucharest	1	1
EC1975	17 Dec	Glasgow	1	1
1986	26 Mar	Glasgow	3	0
EC1990	12 Sept	Glasgow	2	1
EC1991	16 Oct	Bucharest	0	1
2004	31 Mar	Glasgow	1	2

v RUSSIA			S	R
EC1994	16 Nov	Glasgow	1	1
EC1995	29 Mar	Moscow	0	0

v SAN MARINO			S	SM
EC1991	1 May	Serravalle	2	0
EC1991	13 Nov	Glasgow	4	0
EC1995	26 Apr	Serravalle	2	0
EC1995	15 Nov	Glasgow	5	0
wc2000	7 Oct	Serravalle	2	0
wc2001	28 Mar	Glasgow	4	0

v SAUDI ARABIA			S	SA
1988	17 Feb	Riyadh	2	2

v SERBIA			S	Se
wc2012	8 Sept	Glasgow	0	0
wc2013	26 Mar	Novi Sad	0	2

v SLOVENIA			S	Sl
wc2004	8 Sept	Glasgow	0	0
wc2005	12 Oct	Celje	3	0
2012	29 Feb	Koper	1	1

v SOUTH AFRICA			S	SA
2002	20 May	Hong Kong	0	2
2007	22 Aug	Aberdeen	1	0

v SPAIN			S	Sp
wc1957	8 May	Glasgow	4	2
wc1957	26 May	Madrid	1	4
1963	13 June	Madrid	6	2
1965	8 May	Glasgow	0	0
EC1974	20 Nov	Glasgow	1	2
EC1975	5 Feb	Valencia	1	1
1982	24 Feb	Valencia	0	3
wc1984	14 Nov	Glasgow	3	1
wc1985	27 Feb	Seville	0	1
1988	27 Apr	Madrid	0	0
2004	3 Sept	Valencia	1	1

Match abandoned after 60 minutes; floodlight failure.

EC2010	12 Oct	Glasgow	2	3
EC2011	11 Oct	Alicante	1	3

v SWEDEN			S	Sw
1952	30 May	Stockholm	1	3
1953	6 May	Glasgow	1	2
1975	16 Apr	Gothenburg	1	1
1977	27 Apr	Glasgow	3	1
wc1980	10 Sept	Stockholm	1	0
wc1981	9 Sept	Glasgow	2	0
wc1990	16 June	Genoa	2	1
1995	11 Oct	Stockholm	0	2
wc1996	10 Nov	Ibrox	1	0
wc1997	30 Apr	Gothenburg	1	2

			S	Sw
2004	17 Nov	Easter Road	1	4
2010	11 Aug	Stockholm	0	3

		v SWITZERLAND	S	Sw
1931	24 May	Geneva	3	2
1946	15 May	Glasgow	3	1
1948	17 May	Berne	1	2
1950	26 Apr	Glasgow	3	1
wc1957	19 May	Basle	2	1
wc1957	6 Nov	Glasgow	3	2
1973	22 June	Berne	0	1
1976	7 Apr	Glasgow	1	0
ec1982	17 Nov	Berne	0	2
ec1983	30 May	Glasgow	2	2
ec1990	17 Oct	Glasgow	2	1
ec1991	11 Sept	Berne	2	2
wc1992	9 Sept	Berne	1	3
wc1993	8 Sept	Aberdeen	1	1
wc1996	18 June	Villa Park	1	0
2006	1 Mar	Glasgow	1	3

		v TRINIDAD & TOBAGO	S	TT
2004	30 May	Easter Road	4	1

		v TURKEY	S	T
1960	8 June	Ankara	2	4

		v UKRAINE	S	U
ec2006	11 Oct	Kiev	0	2
ec2007	13 Oct	Glasgow	3	1

		v URUGUAY	S	U
wc1954	19 June	Basle	0	7
1962	2 May	Glasgow	2	3
1983	21 Sept	Glasgow	2	0
wc1986	13 June	Nezahualcoyotl	0	0

		v USA	S	USA
1952	30 Apr	Glasgow	6	0
1992	17 May	Denver	1	0
1996	26 May	New Britain	1	2
1998	30 May	Washington	0	0
2005	12 Nov	Glasgow	1	1
2012	26 May	Jacksonville	1	5
2013	15 Nov	Glasgow	0	0

		v USSR	S	USSR
1967	10 May	Glasgow	0	2
1971	14 June	Moscow	0	1
wc1982	22 June	Malaga	2	2
1991	6 Feb	Ibrox	0	1

		v YUGOSLAVIA	S	Y
1955	15 May	Belgrade	2	2
1956	21 Nov	Glasgow	2	0
wc1958	8 June	Vasteras	1	1
1972	29 June	Belo Horizonte	2	2
wc1974	22 June	Frankfurt	1	1
1984	12 Sept	Glasgow	6	1
wc1988	19 Oct	Glasgow	1	1
wc1989	6 Sept	Zagreb	1	3

		v ZAIRE	S	Z
wc1974	14 June	Dortmund	2	0

WALES

		v ALBANIA	W	A
ec1994	7 Sept	Cardiff	2	0
ec1995	15 Nov	Tirana	1	1

		v ANDORRA	W	A
ec2014	9 Sept	La Vella	2	1
ec2015	**13 Oct**	**Cardiff**	**2**	**0**

		v ARGENTINA	W	A
1992	3 June	Tokyo	0	1
2002	13 Feb	Cardiff	1	1

		v ARMENIA	W	A
wc2001	24 Mar	Erevan	2	2
wc2001	1 Sept	Cardiff	0	0

		v AUSTRALIA	W	A
2011	10 Aug	Cardiff	1	2

		v AUSTRIA	W	A
1954	9 May	Vienna	0	2
1955	23 Nov	Wrexham	1	2
ec1974	4 Sept	Vienna	1	2
1975	19 Nov	Wrexham	1	0
1992	29 Apr	Vienna	1	1
ec2005	26 Mar	Cardiff	0	2
ec2005	30 Mar	Vienna	0	1
2013	6 Feb	Swansea	2	1

		v AZERBAIJAN	W	A
ec2002	20 Nov	Baku	2	0
ec2003	29 Mar	Cardiff	4	0
wc2004	4 Sept	Baku	1	1
wc2005	12 Oct	Cardiff	2	0
wc2008	6 Sept	Cardiff	1	0
wc2009	6 June	Baku	1	0

		v BELARUS	W	B
ec1998	14 Oct	Cardiff	3	2
ec1999	4 Sept	Minsk	2	1
wc2000	2 Sept	Minsk	1	2
wc2001	6 Oct	Cardiff	1	0

		v BELGIUM	W	B
1949	22 May	Liege	1	3
1949	23 Nov	Cardiff	5	1
ec1990	17 Oct	Cardiff	3	1
ec1991	27 Mar	Brussels	1	1
wc1992	18 Nov	Brussels	0	2
wc1993	31 Mar	Cardiff	2	0
wc1997	29 Mar	Cardiff	1	2
wc1997	11 Oct	Brussels	2	3
wc2012	7 Sept	Cardiff	0	2
wc2013	15 Oct	Brussels	1	1
ec2014	16 Nov	Brussels	0	0
ec2015	12 June	Cardiff	1	0
ec2016	**1 July**	**Lille**	**3**	**1**

		v BOSNIA-HERZEGOVINA	W	BH
2003	12 Feb	Cardiff	2	2
2012	15 Aug	Llanelli	0	2
ec2014	10 Oct	Cardiff	0	0
ec2015	**10 Oct**	**Zenica**	**0**	**2**

		v BRAZIL	W	B
wc1958	19 June	Gothenburg	0	1
1962	12 May	Rio de Janeiro	1	3
1962	16 May	São Paulo	1	3
1966	14 May	Rio de Janeiro	1	3
1966	18 May	Belo Horizonte	0	1
1983	12 June	Cardiff	1	1
1991	11 Sept	Cardiff	1	0
1997	12 Nov	Brasilia	0	3
2000	23 May	Cardiff	0	3
2006	5 Sept	Cardiff	0	2

		v BULGARIA	W	B
ec1983	27 Apr	Wrexham	1	0
ec1983	16 Nov	Sofia	0	1
ec1994	14 Dec	Cardiff	0	3
ec1995	29 Mar	Sofia	1	3
2006	15 Aug	Swansea	0	0
2007	22 Aug	Burgas	1	0
ec2010	8 Oct	Cardiff	0	1
ec2011	12 Oct	Sofia	1	0

		v CANADA	W	C
1986	10 May	Toronto	0	2
1986	20 May	Vancouver	3	0
2004	30 May	Wrexham	1	0

		v CHILE	W	C
1966	22 May	Santiago	0	2
2014	4 June	Valparaiso	0	2

		v COSTA RICA	W	CR
1990	20 May	Cardiff	1	0
2012	29 Feb	Cardiff	0	1

v CROATIA

			W	C
2002	21 Aug	Varazdin	1	1
2010	23 May	Osijek	0	2
wc2012	16 Oct	Osijek	0	2
wc2013	26 Mar	Swansea	1	2

v CYPRUS

			W	C
wc1992	14 Oct	Limassol	1	0
wc1993	13 Oct	Cardiff	2	0
2005	16 Nov	Limassol	0	1
EC2006	11 Oct	Cardiff	3	1
EC2007	13 Oct	Nicosia	1	3
EC2014	13 Oct	Cardiff	2	1
EC2015	**3 Sept**	**Nicosia**	**1**	**0**

v CZECHOSLOVAKIA

			W	C
wc1957	1 May	Cardiff	1	0
wc1957	26 May	Prague	0	2
EC1971	21 Apr	Swansea	1	3
EC1971	27 Oct	Prague	0	1
wc1977	30 Mar	Wrexham	3	0
wc1977	16 Nov	Prague	0	1
wc1980	19 Nov	Cardiff	1	0
wc1981	9 Sept	Prague	0	2
EC1987	29 Apr	Wrexham	1	1
EC1987	11 Nov	Prague	0	2
wc1993	28 Apr	Ostrava†	1	1
wc1993	8 Sept	Cardiff†	2	2

†Czechoslovakia played as RCS (Republic of Czechs and Slovaks).

2008	19 Nov	Brondby	1	0

v ESTONIA

			W	E
1994	23 May	Tallinn	2	1
2009	29 May	Llanelli	1	0

v FAROE ISLANDS

			W	F
wc1992	9 Sept	Cardiff	6	0
wc1993	6 June	Toftir	3	0

v FINLAND

			W	F
EC1971	26 May	Helsinki	1	0
EC1971	13 Oct	Swansea	3	0
EC1987	10 Sept	Helsinki	1	1
EC1987	1 Apr	Wrexham	4	0
wc1988	19 Oct	Swansea	2	2
wc1989	6 Sept	Helsinki	0	1
2000	29 Mar	Cardiff	1	2
EC2002	7 Sept	Helsinki	2	0
EC2003	10 Sept	Cardiff	1	1
wc2009	28 Mar	Cardiff	0	2
wc2009	10 Oct	Helsinki	1	2
2013	16 Nov	Cardiff	1	1

v FRANCE

			W	F
1933	25 May	Paris	1	1
1939	20 May	Paris	1	2
1953	14 May	Paris	1	6
1982	2 June	Toulouse	1	0

v FYR MACEDONIA

			W	M
wc2013	6 Sept	Skopje	1	2
wc2013	11 Oct	Cardiff	1	0

v GEORGIA

			W	G
EC1994	16 Nov	Tbilisi	0	5
EC1995	7 June	Cardiff	0	1
2008	20 Aug	Swansea	1	2

v GERMANY

			W	G
EC1995	26 Apr	Dusseldorf	1	1
EC1995	11 Oct	Cardiff	1	2
2002	14 May	Cardiff	1	0
EC2007	8 Sept	Cardiff	0	2
EC2007	21 Nov	Frankfurt	0	0
wc2008	15 Oct	Moenchengladbach	0	1
wc2009	1 Apr	Cardiff	0	2

v EAST GERMANY

			W	EG
wc1957	19 May	Leipzig	1	2
wc1957	25 Sept	Cardiff	4	1
wc1969	16 Apr	Dresden	1	2
wc1969	22 Oct	Cardiff	1	3

v WEST GERMANY

			W	WG
1968	8 May	Cardiff	1	1
1969	26 Mar	Frankfurt	1	1
1976	6 Oct	Cardiff	0	2
1977	14 Dec	Dortmund	1	1
EC1979	2 May	Wrexham	0	2
EC1979	17 Oct	Cologne	1	5
wc1989	31 May	Cardiff	0	0
wc1989	15 Nov	Cologne	1	2
EC1991	5 June	Cardiff	1	0
EC1991	16 Oct	Nuremberg	1	4

v GREECE

			W	G
wc1964	9 Dec	Athens	0	2
wc1965	17 Mar	Cardiff	4	1

v HUNGARY

			W	H
wc1958	8 June	Sanviken	1	1
wc1958	17 June	Stockholm	2	1
1961	28 May	Budapest	2	3
EC1962	7 Nov	Budapest	1	3
EC1963	20 Mar	Cardiff	1	1
EC1974	30 Oct	Cardiff	2	0
EC1975	16 Apr	Budapest	2	1
1985	16 Oct	Cardiff	0	3
2004	31 Mar	Budapest	2	1
2005	9 Feb	Cardiff	2	0

v ICELAND

			W	I
wc1980	2 June	Reykjavik	4	0
wc1981	14 Oct	Swansea	2	2
wc1984	12 Sept	Reykjavik	0	1
wc1984	14 Nov	Cardiff	2	1
1991	1 May	Cardiff	1	0
2008	28 May	Reykjavik	1	0
2014	5 Mar	Cardiff	3	1

v IRAN

			W	I
1978	18 Apr	Teheran	1	0

v ISRAEL

			W	I
wc1958	15 Jan	Tel Aviv	2	0
wc1958	5 Feb	Cardiff	2	0
1984	10 June	Tel Aviv	0	0
1989	8 Feb	Tel Aviv	3	3
EC2015	28 Mar	Haifa	3	0
EC2015	**6 Sept**	**Cardiff**	**0**	**0**

v ITALY

			W	I
1965	1 May	Florence	1	4
wc1968	23 Oct	Cardiff	0	1
wc1969	4 Nov	Rome	1	4
1988	4 June	Brescia	1	0
1996	24 Jan	Terni	0	3
EC1998	5 Sept	Liverpool	0	2
EC1999	5 June	Bologna	0	4
EC2002	16 Oct	Cardiff	2	1
EC2003	6 Sept	Milan	0	4

v JAMAICA

			W	J
1998	25 Mar	Cardiff	0	0

v JAPAN

			W	J
1992	7 June	Matsuyama	1	0

v KUWAIT

			W	K
1977	6 Sept	Wrexham	0	0
1977	20 Sept	Kuwait	0	0

v LATVIA

			W	L
2004	18 Aug	Riga	2	0

v LIECHTENSTEIN

			W	L
2006	14 Nov	Swansea	4	0
wc2008	11 Oct	Cardiff	2	0
wc2009	14 Oct	Vaduz	2	0

v LUXEMBOURG

			W	L
EC1974	20 Nov	Swansea	5	0
EC1975	1 May	Luxembourg	3	1
EC1990	14 Nov	Luxembourg	1	0
EC1991	13 Nov	Cardiff	1	0
2008	26 Mar	Luxembourg	2	0
2010	11 Aug	Llanelli	5	1

v MALTA

			W	M
EC1978	25 Oct	Wrexham	7	0
EC1979	2 June	Valletta	2	0
1988	1 June	Valletta	3	2
1998	3 June	Valletta	3	0

v MEXICO			W	M
wc1958	11 June	Stockholm	1	1
1962	22 May	Mexico City	1	2
2012	27 May	New Jersey	0	2

v MOLDOVA			W	M
EC1994	12 Oct	Kishinev	2	3
EC1995	6 Sept	Cardiff	1	0

v MONTENEGRO			W	M
2009	12 Aug	Podgorica	1	2
EC2010	3 Sept	Podgorica	0	1
EC2011	2 Sept	Cardiff	2	1

v NETHERLANDS			W	N
wc1988	14 Sept	Amsterdam	0	1
wc1989	11 Oct	Wrexham	1	2
1992	30 May	Utrecht	0	4
wc1996	5 Oct	Cardiff	1	3
wc1996	9 Nov	Eindhoven	1	7
2008	1 June	Rotterdam	0	2
2014	4 June	Amsterdam	0	2
2015	**13 Nov**	**Cardiff**	**2**	**3**

v NEW ZEALAND			W	NZ
2007	26 May	Wrexham	2	2

v NORWAY			W	N
EC1982	22 Sept	Swansea	1	0
EC1983	21 Sept	Oslo	0	0
1984	6 June	Trondheim	0	1
1985	26 Feb	Wrexham	1	1
1985	5 June	Bergen	2	4
1994	9 Mar	Cardiff	1	3
wc2000	7 Oct	Cardiff	1	1
wc2001	5 Sept	Oslo	2	3
2004	27 May	Oslo	0	0
2008	6 Feb	Wrexham	3	0
2011	12 Nov	Cardiff	4	1

v PARAGUAY			W	P
2006	1 Mar	Cardiff	0	0

v POLAND			W	P
wc1973	28 Mar	Cardiff	2	0
wc1973	26 Sept	Katowice	0	3
1991	29 May	Radom	0	0
wc2000	11 Oct	Warsaw	0	0
wc2001	2 June	Cardiff	1	2
wc2004	13 Oct	Cardiff	2	3
wc2005	7 Sept	Warsaw	0	1
2009	11 Feb	Vila Real	0	1

v PORTUGAL			W	P
1949	15 May	Lisbon	2	3
1951	12 May	Cardiff	2	1
2000	2 June	Chaves	0	3
EC2016	**6 July**	**Lille**	**0**	**2**

v QATAR			W	Q
2000	23 Feb	Doha	1	0

v REPUBLIC OF IRELAND			W	RI
1960	28 Sept	Dublin	3	2
1979	11 Sept	Swansea	2	1
1981	24 Feb	Dublin	3	1
1986	26 Mar	Dublin	1	0
1990	28 Mar	Dublin	0	1
1991	6 Feb	Wrexham	0	3
1992	19 Feb	Dublin	1	0
1993	17 Feb	Dublin	1	2
1997	11 Feb	Cardiff	0	0
EC2007	24 Mar	Dublin	0	1
EC2007	17 Nov	Cardiff	2	2
NC2011	8 Feb	Dublin	0	3
2013	14 Aug	Cardiff	0	0

v ROMANIA			W	R
EC1970	11 Nov	Cardiff	0	0
EC1971	24 Nov	Bucharest	0	2
1983	12 Oct	Wrexham	5	0
wc1992	20 May	Bucharest	1	5
wc1993	17 Nov	Cardiff	1	2

v RUSSIA			W	R
EC2003	15 Nov	Moscow	0	0
EC2003	19 Nov	Cardiff	0	1
wc2008	10 Sept	Moscow	1	2
			W	R
wc2009	9 Sept	Cardiff	1	3
EC2016	**20 June**	**Toulouse**	**3**	**0**

v SAN MARINO			W	SM
wc1996	2 June	Serravalle	5	0
wc1996	31 Aug	Cardiff	6	0
EC2007	28 Mar	Cardiff	3	0
EC2007	17 Oct	Serravalle	2	1

v SAUDI ARABIA			W	SA
1986	25 Feb	Dahran	2	1

v SERBIA			W	S
wc2012	11 Sept	Novi Sad	1	6
wc2013	10 Sept	Cardiff	0	3

v SERBIA-MONTENEGRO			W	SM
EC2003	20 Aug	Belgrade	0	1
EC2003	11 Oct	Cardiff	2	3

v SLOVAKIA			W	S
EC2006	7 Oct	Cardiff	1	5
EC2007	12 Sept	Trnava	5	2
EC2016	**11 June**	**Bordeaux**	**2**	**1**

v SLOVENIA			W	Sl
2005	17 Aug	Swansea	0	0

v SPAIN			W	S
wc1961	19 Apr	Cardiff	1	2
wc1961	18 May	Madrid	1	1
1982	24 Mar	Valencia	1	1
wc1984	17 Oct	Seville	0	3
wc1985	30 Apr	Wrexham	3	0

v SWEDEN			W	S
wc1958	15 June	Stockholm	0	0
1988	27 Apr	Stockholm	1	4
1989	26 Apr	Wrexham	0	2
1990	25 Apr	Stockholm	2	4
1994	20 Apr	Wrexham	0	2
2010	3 Mar	Swansea	0	1
2016	**5 June**	**Stockholm**	**0**	**3**

v SWITZERLAND			W	S
1949	26 May	Berne	0	4
1951	16 May	Wrexham	3	2
1996	24 Apr	Lugano	0	2
EC1999	31 Mar	Zurich	0	2
EC1999	9 Oct	Wrexham	0	2
EC2010	12 Oct	Basle	1	4
EC2011	8 Oct	Swansea	2	0

v TRINIDAD & TOBAGO			W	TT
2006	27 May	Graz	2	1

v TUNISIA			W	T
1998	6 June	Tunis	0	4

v TURKEY			W	T
EC1978	29 Nov	Wrexham	1	0
EC1979	21 Nov	Izmir	0	1
wc1980	15 Oct	Cardiff	4	0
wc1981	25 Mar	Ankara	1	0
wc1996	14 Dec	Cardiff	0	0
wc1997	20 Aug	Istanbul	4	6

v UKRAINE			W	U
wc2001	28 Mar	Cardiff	1	1
wc2001	6 June	Kiev	1	1
2016	**28 Mar**	**Kiev**	**0**	**1**

v REST OF UNITED KINGDOM			W	RUK
1951	5 Dec	Cardiff	3	2
1969	28 July	Cardiff	0	1

v URUGUAY			W	U
1986	21 Apr	Wrexham	0	0

v USA			W	USA
2003	27 May	San Jose	0	2

v USSR			W	USSR
wc1965	30 May	Moscow	1	2
wc1965	27 Oct	Cardiff	2	1
wc1981	30 May	Wrexham	0	0
wc1981	18 Nov	Tbilisi	0	3
1987	18 Feb	Swansea	0	0

		v YUGOSLAVIA	W	Y
1953	21 May	Belgrade	2	5
1954	22 Nov	Cardiff	1	3
EC1976	24 Apr	Zagreb	0	2
EC1976	22 May	Cardiff	1	1

			W	Y
EC1982	15 Dec	Titograd	4	4
EC1983	14 Dec	Cardiff	1	1
1988	23 Mar	Swansea	1	2

NORTHERN IRELAND

		v ALBANIA	NI	A
wc1965	7 May	Belfast	4	1
wc1965	24 Nov	Tirana	1	1
EC1982	15 Dec	Tirana	0	0
EC1983	27 Apr	Belfast	1	0
wc1992	9 Sept	Belfast	3	0
wc1993	17 Feb	Tirana	2	1
wc1996	14 Dec	Belfast	2	0
wc1997	10 Sept	Zurich	0	1
2010	3 Mar	Tirana	0	1

		v ALGERIA	NI	A
wc1986	3 June	Guadalajara	1	1

		v ARGENTINA	NI	A
wc1958	11 June	Halmstad	1	3

		v ARMENIA	NI	A
wc1996	5 Oct	Belfast	1	1
wc1997	30 Apr	Erevan	0	0
EC2003	29 Mar	Erevan	0	1
EC2003	10 Sept	Belfast	0	1

		v AUSTRALIA	NI	A
1980	11 June	Sydney	2	1
1980	15 June	Melbourne	1	1
1980	18 June	Adelaide	2	1

		v AUSTRIA	NI	A
wc1982	1 July	Madrid	2	2
EC1982	13 Oct	Vienna	0	2
EC1983	21 Sept	Belfast	3	1
EC1990	14 Nov	Vienna	0	0
EC1991	16 Oct	Belfast	2	1
EC1994	12 Oct	Vienna	2	1
EC1995	15 Nov	Belfast	5	3
wc2004	13 Oct	Belfast	3	3
wc2005	12 Oct	Vienna	0	2

		v AZERBAIJAN	NI	A
wc2004	9 Oct	Baku	0	0
wc2005	3 Sept	Belfast	2	0
wc2012	14 Nov	Belfast	1	1
wc2013	11 Oct	Baku	0	2

		v BARBADOS	NI	B
2004	30 May	Waterford	1	1

		v BELARUS	NI	B
2016	**27 May**	**Belfast**	**3**	**0**

		v BELGIUM	NI	B
wc1976	10 Nov	Liege	0	2
wc1977	16 Nov	Belfast	3	0
1997	11 Feb	Belfast	3	0

		v BRAZIL	NI	B
wc1986	12 June	Guadalajara	0	3

		v BULGARIA	NI	B
wc1972	18 Oct	Sofia	0	3
wc1973	26 Sept	Sheffield	0	0
EC1978	29 Nov	Sofia	2	0
EC1979	2 May	Belfast	2	0
wc2001	28 Mar	Sofia	3	4
wc2001	2 June	Belfast	0	1
2008	6 Feb	Belfast	0	1

		v CANADA	NI	C
1995	22 May	Edmonton	0	2
1999	27 Apr	Belfast	1	1
2005	9 Feb	Belfast	0	1

		v CHILE	NI	C
1989	26 May	Belfast	0	1
1995	25 May	Edmonton	1	2
2010	30 May	Chillan	0	1
2014	4 June	Valparaiso	0	2

		v COLOMBIA	NI	C
1994	4 June	Boston	0	2

		v CYPRUS	NI	C
EC1971	3 Feb	Nicosia	3	0
EC1971	21 Apr	Belfast	5	0
wc1973	14 Feb	Nicosia	0	1
wc1973	8 May	London	3	0
2002	21 Aug	Belfast	0	0
2014	5 Mar	Nicosia	0	0

		v CZECHOSLOVAKIA	NI	C
wc1958	8 June	Halmstad	1	0
wc1958	17 June	Malmo	2	1*

*After extra time

		v CZECH REPUBLIC	NI	C
wc2001	24 Mar	Belfast	0	1
wc2001	6 June	Teplice	1	3
wc2008	10 Sept	Belfast	0	0
wc2009	14 Oct	Prague	0	0

		v DENMARK	NI	D
EC1978	25 Oct	Belfast	2	1
EC1979	6 June	Copenhagen	0	4
1986	26 Mar	Copenhagen	1	1
EC1990	17 Oct	Belfast	1	1
EC1991	13 Nov	Odense	1	2
wc1992	18 Nov	Belfast	0	1
wc1993	13 Oct	Copenhagen	0	1
wc2000	7 Oct	Belfast	1	1
wc2001	1 Sept	Copenhagen	1	1
EC2006	7 Oct	Copenhagen	0	0
EC2007	17 Nov	Belfast	2	1

		v ESTONIA	NI	E
2004	31 Mar	Tallinn	1	0
2006	1 Mar	Belfast	1	0
EC2011	6 Sept	Tallinn	1	4
EC2011	7 Oct	Belfast	1	2

		v FAROE ISLANDS	NI	F
EC1991	1 May	Belfast	1	1
EC1991	11 Sept	Landskrona	5	0
EC2010	12 Oct	Toftir	1	1
EC2011	10 Aug	Belfast	4	0
EC2014	11 Oct	Belfast	2	0
EC2015	**4 Sept**	**Torshavn**	**3**	**1**

		v FINLAND	NI	F
wc1984	27 May	Pori	0	1
wc1984	14 Nov	Belfast	2	1
EC1998	10 Oct	Belfast	1	0
EC1998	9 Oct	Helsinki	1	4
2003	12 Feb	Belfast	0	1
2006	16 Aug	Helsinki	2	1
2012	15 Aug	Belfast	3	3
EC2015	29 Mar	Belfast	2	1
EC2015	**11 Oct**	**Helsinki**	**1**	**1**

		v FRANCE	NI	F
1928	21 Feb	Paris	0	4
1951	12 May	Belfast	2	2
1952	11 Nov	Paris	1	3
wc1958	19 June	Norrkoping	0	4
1982	24 Mar	Paris	0	4
wc1982	4 July	Madrid	1	4
1986	26 Feb	Paris	0	0
1988	27 Apr	Belfast	0	0
1999	18 Aug	Belfast	0	1

		v GEORGIA	NI	G
2008	26 Mar	Belfast	4	1

		v GERMANY	NI	G
1992	2 June	Bremen	1	1
1996	29 May	Belfast	1	1
wc1996	9 Nov	Nuremberg	1	1
wc1997	20 Aug	Belfast	1	3

			NI	G
EC1999	27 Mar	Belfast	0	3
EC1999	8 Sept	Dortmund	0	4
2005	4 June	Belfast	1	4
EC2016	**21 June**	**Paris**	**0**	**1**

v WEST GERMANY

			NI	WG
wc1958	15 June	Malmo	2	2
wc1960	26 Oct	Belfast	3	4
wc1961	10 May	Hamburg	1	2
1966	7 May	Belfast	0	2
1977	27 Apr	Cologne	0	5
EC1982	17 Nov	Belfast	1	0
EC1983	16 Nov	Hamburg	1	0

v GREECE

			NI	G
wc1961	3 May	Athens	1	2
wc1961	17 Oct	Belfast	2	0
1988	17 Feb	Athens	2	3
EC2003	2 Apr	Belfast	0	2
EC2003	11 Oct	Athens	0	1
EC2014	14 Oct	Piraeus	2	0
EC2015	**8 Oct**	**Belfast**	**3**	**1**

v HONDURAS

			NI	H
wc1982	21 June	Zaragoza	1	1

v HUNGARY

			NI	H
wc1988	19 Oct	Budapest	0	1
wc1989	6 Sept	Belfast	1	2
2000	26 Apr	Belfast	0	1
2008	19 Nov	Belfast	0	2
EC2014	7 Sept	Budapest	2	1
EC2015	**7 Sept**	**Belfast**	**1**	**1**

v ICELAND

			NI	I
wc1977	11 June	Reykjavik	0	1
wc1977	21 Sept	Belfast	2	0
wc2000	11 Oct	Reykjavik	0	1
wc2001	5 Sept	Belfast	3	0
EC2006	2 Sept	Belfast	0	3
EC2007	12 Sept	Reykjavik	1	2

v ISRAEL

			NI	I
1968	10 Sept	Jaffa	3	2
1976	3 Mar	Tel Aviv	1	1
wc1980	26 Mar	Tel Aviv	0	0
wc1981	18 Nov	Belfast	1	0
1984	16 Oct	Belfast	3	0
1987	18 Feb	Tel Aviv	1	1
2009	12 Aug	Belfast	1	1
wc2013	26 Mar	Belfast	0	2
wc2013	15 Oct	Tel Aviv	1	1

v ITALY

			NI	I
wc1957	25 Apr	Rome	0	1
1957	4 Dec	Belfast	2	2
wc1958	15 Jan	Belfast	2	1
1961	25 Apr	Bologna	2	3
1997	22 Jan	Palermo	0	2
2003	3 June	Campobasso	0	2
2009	6 June	Pisa	0	3
EC2010	8 Oct	Belfast	0	0
EC2011	11 Oct	Pescara	0	3

v LATVIA

			NI	L
wc1993	2 June	Riga	2	1
wc1993	8 Sept	Belfast	2	0
EC1995	26 Apr	Riga	1	0
EC1995	7 June	Belfast	1	2
EC2006	11 Oct	Belfast	1	0
EC2007	8 Sept	Riga	0	1
2015	**13 Nov**	**Belfast**	**1**	**0**

v LIECHTENSTEIN

			NI	L
EC1994	20 Apr	Belfast	4	1
EC1995	11 Oct	Eschen	4	0
2002	27 Mar	Vaduz	0	0
EC2007	24 Mar	Vaduz	4	1
EC2007	22 Aug	Belfast	3	1

v LITHUANIA

			NI	L
wc1992	28 Apr	Belfast	2	2
wc1993	25 May	Vilnius	1	0

v LUXEMBOURG

			NI	L
2000	23 Feb	Luxembourg	3	1
wc2012	11 Sept	Belfast	1	1
wc2013	10 Sept	Luxembourg	2	3

v MALTA

			NI	M
wc1988	21 May	Belfast	3	0
wc1989	26 Apr	Valletta	2	0
2000	28 Mar	Valletta	3	0
wc2000	2 Sept	Belfast	1	0
wc2001	6 Oct	Valletta	1	0
2005	17 Aug	Ta'Qali	1	1
2013	6 Feb	Ta'Qali	0	0

v MEXICO

			NI	M
1966	22 June	Belfast	4	1
1994	11 June	Miami	0	3

v MOLDOVA

			NI	M
EC1998	18 Nov	Belfast	2	2
EC1999	31 Mar	Chisinau	0	0

v MONTENEGRO

			NI	M
2010	11 Aug	Podgorica	0	2

v MOROCCO

			NI	M
1986	23 Apr	Belfast	2	1
2010	17 Nov	Belfast	1	1

v NETHERLANDS

			NI	N
1962	9 May	Rotterdam	0	4
wc1965	17 Mar	Belfast	2	1
wc1965	7 Apr	Rotterdam	0	0
wc1976	13 Oct	Rotterdam	2	2
wc1977	12 Oct	Belfast	0	1
2012	2 June	Amsterdam	0	6

v NORWAY

			NI	N
1922	25 May	Bergen	1	2
EC1974	4 Sept	Oslo	1	2
EC1975	29 Oct	Belfast	3	0
1990	27 Mar	Belfast	2	3
1996	27 Mar	Belfast	0	2
2001	28 Feb	Belfast	0	4
2004	18 Feb	Belfast	1	4
2012	29 Feb	Belfast	0	3

v POLAND

			NI	P
EC1962	10 Oct	Katowice	2	0
EC1962	28 Nov	Belfast	2	0
1988	23 Mar	Belfast	1	1
1991	5 Feb	Belfast	3	1
2002	13 Feb	Limassol	1	4
EC2004	4 Sept	Belfast	0	3
EC2005	30 Mar	Warsaw	0	1
wc2009	28 Mar	Belfast	3	2
wc2009	5 Sept	Chorzow	1	1
EC2016	**12 June**	**Nice**	**0**	**1**

v PORTUGAL

			NI	P
wc1957	16 Jan	Lisbon	1	1
wc1957	1 May	Belfast	3	0
wc1973	28 Mar	Coventry	1	1
wc1973	14 Nov	Lisbon	1	1
wc1980	19 Nov	Lisbon	0	1
wc1981	29 Apr	Belfast	1	0
EC1994	7 Sept	Belfast	1	2
EC1995	3 Sept	Lisbon	1	1
wc1997	29 Mar	Belfast	0	0
wc1997	11 Oct	Lisbon	0	1
2005	15 Nov	Belfast	1	1
wc2012	16 Oct	Porto	1	1
wc2013	6 Sept	Belfast	2	4

v QATAR

			NI	Q
2015	31 May	Crewe	1	1

v REPUBLIC OF IRELAND

			NI	RI
EC1978	20 Sept	Dublin	0	0
EC1979	21 Nov	Belfast	1	0
EC1988	14 Sept	Belfast	0	0
wc1989	11 Oct	Dublin	0	3
wc1993	31 Mar	Dublin	0	3
wc1993	17 Nov	Belfast	1	1
EC1994	16 Nov	Belfast	0	4
EC1995	29 Mar	Dublin	1	1
1999	29 May	Dublin	1	0
NC2011	24 May	Dublin	0	5

v ROMANIA		NI	R
wc1984	12 Sept Belfast	3	2
wc1985	16 Oct Bucharest	1	0
1994	23 Mar Belfast	2	0
2006	27 May Chicago	0	2
EC2014	14 Nov Bucharest	0	2
EC2015	13 June Belfast	0	0

v RUSSIA		NI	R
wc2012	7 Sept Moscow	0	2
wc2013	14 Aug Belfast	1	0

v SAN MARINO		NI	SM
wc2008	15 Oct Belfast	4	0
wc2009	11 Feb Serravalle	3	0

v ST KITTS & NEVIS		NI	SK
2004	2 June Basseterre	2	0

v SERBIA		NI	S
2009	14 Nov Belfast	0	1
EC2011	25 Mar Belgrade	1	2
EC2011	2 Sept Belfast	0	1

v SERBIA-MONTENEGRO		NI	SM
2004	28 Apr Belfast	1	1

v SLOVAKIA		NI	S
1998	25 Mar Belfast	1	0
wc2008	6 Sept Bratislava	1	2
wc2009	9 Sept Belfast	0	2
2016	**4 June Trnava**	**0**	**0**

v SLOVENIA		NI	S
wc2008	11 Oct Maribor	0	2
wc2009	1 Apr Belfast	1	0
EC2010	3 Sept Maribor	1	0
EC2011	29 Mar Belfast	0	0
2016	**28 Mar Belfast**	**1**	**0**

v SOUTH AFRICA		NI	SA
1924	24 Sept Belfast	1	2

v SPAIN		NI	S
1958	15 Oct Madrid	2	6
1963	30 May Bilbao	1	1
1963	30 Oct Belfast	0	1
EC1970	11 Nov Seville	0	3
EC1972	16 Feb Hull	1	1
wc1982	25 June Valencia	1	0
1985	27 Mar Palma	0	0
wc1986	7 June Guadalajara	1	2
wc1988	21 Dec Seville	0	4
wc1989	8 Feb Belfast	0	2
wc1992	14 Oct Belfast	0	0
wc1993	28 Apr Seville	1	3
1998	2 June Santander	1	4
2002	17 Apr Belfast	0	5
EC2002	12 Oct Albacete	0	3
EC2003	11 June Belfast	0	0
EC2006	6 Sept Belfast	3	2
EC2007	21 Nov Las Palmas	0	1

v SWEDEN		NI	S
EC1974	30 Oct Solna	2	0

		NI	S
EC1975	3 Sept Belfast	1	2
wc1980	15 Oct Belfast	3	0
wc1981	3 June Solna	0	1
1996	24 Apr Belfast	1	2
EC2007	28 Mar Belfast	2	1
EC2007	17 Oct Stockholm	1	1

v SWITZERLAND		NI	S
wc1964	14 Oct Belfast	1	0
wc1964	14 Nov Lausanne	1	2
1998	22 Apr Belfast	1	0
2004	18 Aug Zurich	0	0

v THAILAND		NI	T
1997	21 May Bangkok	0	0

v TRINIDAD & TOBAGO		NI	TT
2004	6 June Bacolet	3	0

v TURKEY		NI	T
wc1968	23 Oct Belfast	4	1
wc1968	11 Dec Istanbul	3	0
2013	15 Nov Adana	0	1
EC1983	30 Mar Belfast	2	1
EC1983	12 Oct Ankara	0	1
wc1985	1 May Belfast	2	0
wc1985	11 Sept Izmir	0	0
EC1986	12 Nov Izmir	0	0
EC1987	11 Nov Belfast	1	0
EC1998	5 Sept Istanbul	0	3
EC1999	4 Sept Belfast	0	3
2010	26 May New Britain	0	2
2013	15 Nov Adana	0	1

v UKRAINE		NI	U
wc1996	31 Aug Belfast	0	1
wc1997	2 Apr Kiev	1	2
EC2002	16 Oct Belfast	0	0
EC2003	6 Sept Donetsk	0	0
EC2016	**16 June Lyon**	**2**	**0**

v URUGUAY		NI	U
1964	29 Apr Belfast	3	0
1990	18 May Belfast	1	0
2006	21 May New Jersey	0	1
2014	30 May Montevideo	0	1

v USSR		NI	USSR
wc1969	19 Sept Belfast	0	0
wc1969	22 Oct Moscow	0	2
EC1971	22 Sept Moscow	0	1
EC1971	13 Oct Belfast	1	1

v YUGOSLAVIA		NI	Y
EC1975	16 Mar Belfast	1	0
EC1975	19 Nov Belgrade	0	1
wc1982	17 June Zaragoza	0	0
EC1987	29 Apr Belfast	1	2
EC1987	14 Oct Sarajevo	0	3
EC1990	12 Sept Belfast	0	2
EC1991	27 Mar Belgrade	1	4
2000	16 Aug Belfast	1	2

REPUBLIC OF IRELAND

v ALBANIA		RI	A
wc1992	26 May Dublin	2	0
wc1993	26 May Tirana	2	1
EC2003	2 Apr Tirana	0	0
EC2003	7 June Dublin	2	1

v ALGERIA		RI	A
1982	28 Apr Algiers	0	2
2010	28 May Dublin	3	0

v ANDORRA		RI	A
wc2001	28 Mar Barcelona	3	0
wc2001	25 Apr Dublin	3	1
EC2010	7 Sept Dublin	3	1
EC2011	7 Oct Andorra La Vella	2	0

v ARGENTINA		RI	A
1951	13 May Dublin	0	1
†1979	29 May Dublin	0	0
1980	16 May Dublin	0	1

		RI	A
1998	22 Apr Dublin	0	2
2010	11 Aug Dublin	0	1

†*Not considered a full international.*

v ARMENIA		RI	A
EC2010	3 Sept Erevan	1	0
EC2011	11 Oct Dublin	2	1

v AUSTRALIA		RI	A
2003	19 Aug Dublin	2	1
2009	12 Aug Limerick	0	3

v AUSTRIA		RI	A
1952	7 May Vienna	0	6
1953	25 Mar Dublin	4	0
1958	14 Mar Vienna	1	3
wc2013	10 Sept Vienna	0	1
1962	8 Apr Dublin	2	3
EC1963	25 Sept Vienna	0	0

			RI	A
EC1963	13 Oct	Dublin	3	2
1966	22 May	Vienna	0	1
1968	10 Nov	Dublin	2	2
EC1971	30 May	Dublin	1	4
EC1971	10 Oct	Linz	0	6
EC1995	11 June	Dublin	1	3
EC1995	6 Sept	Vienna	1	3
wc2013	26 Mar	Dublin	2	2
wc2013	10 Sept	Vienna	0	1

v BELARUS			**RI**	**B**
2016	**31 May**	**Cork**	**1**	**2**

v BELGIUM			**RI**	**B**
1928	12 Feb	Liege	4	2
1929	30 Apr	Dublin	4	0
1930	11 May	Brussels	3	1
wc1934	25 Feb	Dublin	4	4
1949	24 Apr	Dublin	0	2
1950	10 May	Brussels	1	5
1965	24 Mar	Dublin	0	2
1966	25 May	Liege	3	2
wc1980	15 Oct	Dublin	1	1
wc1981	25 Mar	Brussels	0	1
EC1986	10 Sept	Brussels	2	2
EC1987	29 Apr	Dublin	0	0
wc1997	29 Oct	Dublin	1	1
wc1997	16 Nov	Brussels	1	2
EC2016	**18 June**	**Bordeaux**	**0**	**3**

v BOLIVIA			**RI**	**B**
1994	24 May	Dublin	1	0
1996	15 June	New Jersey	3	0
2007	26 May	Boston	1	1

v BOSNIA-HERZEGOVINA			**RI**	**BH**
2012	26 May	Dublin	1	0
EC2015	**13 Nov**	**Zenica**	**1**	**1**
EC2015	**16 Nov**	**Dublin**	**2**	**0**

v BRAZIL			**RI**	**B**
1974	5 May	Rio de Janeiro	1	2
1982	27 May	Uberlandia	0	7
1987	23 May	Dublin	1	0
2004	18 Feb	Dublin	0	0
2008	6 Feb	Dublin	0	1
2010	2 Mar	Emirates	0	2

v BULGARIA			**RI**	**B**
wc1977	1 June	Sofia	1	2
wc1977	12 Oct	Dublin	0	0
EC1979	19 May	Sofia	0	1
EC1979	17 Oct	Dublin	3	0
wc1987	1 Apr	Sofia	1	2
wc1987	14 Oct	Dublin	2	0
2004	18 Aug	Dublin	1	1
wc2009	28 Mar	Dublin	1	1
wc2009	6 June	Sofia	1	1

v CAMEROON			**RI**	**C**
wc2002	1 June	Niigata	1	1

v CANADA			**RI**	**C**
2003	18 Nov	Dublin	3	0

v CHILE			**RI**	**C**
1960	30 Mar	Dublin	2	0
1972	21 June	Recife	1	2
1974	12 May	Santiago	2	1
1982	22 May	Santiago	0	1
1991	22 May	Dublin	1	1
2006	24 May	Dublin	0	1

v CHINA			**RI**	**C**
1984	3 June	Sapporo	1	0
2005	29 Mar	Dublin	1	0

v COLOMBIA			**RI**	**C**
2008	29 May	Fulham	1	0

v COSTA RICA			**RI**	**C**
2014	6 June	Philadephia	1	1

v CROATIA			**RI**	**C**
1996	2 June	Dublin	2	2
EC1998	5 Sept	Dublin	2	0
EC1999	4 Sept	Zagreb	0	1
2001	15 Aug	Dublin	2	2
2004	16 Nov	Dublin	1	0

			RI	C
2011	10 Aug	Dublin	0	0
EC2012	10 June	Poznan	1	3

v CYPRUS			**RI**	**C**
wc1980	26 Mar	Nicosia	3	2
wc1980	19 Nov	Dublin	6	0
wc2001	24 Mar	Nicosia	4	0
wc2001	6 Oct	Dublin	4	0
wc2004	4 Sept	Dublin	3	0
wc2005	8 Oct	Nicosia	1	0
EC2006	7 Oct	Nicosia	2	5
EC2007	17 Oct	Dublin	1	1
2008	15 Oct	Dublin	1	0
wc2009	5 Sept	Nicosia	2	1

v CZECHOSLOVAKIA			**RI**	**C**
1938	18 May	Prague	2	2
EC1959	5 Apr	Dublin	2	0
EC1959	10 May	Bratislava	0	4
wc1961	8 Oct	Dublin	1	3
wc1961	29 Oct	Prague	1	7
EC1967	21 May	Dublin	0	2
EC1967	22 Nov	Prague	2	1
wc1969	4 May	Dublin	1	2
wc1969	7 Oct	Prague	0	3
1979	26 Sept	Prague	1	4
1981	29 Apr	Dublin	3	1
1986	27 May	Reykjavik	1	0

v CZECH REPUBLIC			**RI**	**C**
1994	5 June	Dublin	1	3
1996	24 Apr	Prague	0	2
1998	25 Mar	Olomouc	1	2
2000	23 Feb	Dublin	3	2
2004	31 Mar	Dublin	2	1
EC2006	11 Oct	Dublin	1	1
EC2007	12 Sept	Prague	0	1
2012	29 Feb	Dublin	1	1

v DENMARK			**RI**	**D**
wc1956	3 Oct	Dublin	2	1
wc1957	2 Oct	Copenhagen	2	0
wc1968	4 Dec	Dublin	1	1
(abandoned after 51 mins)				
wc1969	27 May	Copenhagen	0	2
wc1969	15 Oct	Dublin	1	1
EC1978	24 May	Copenhagen	3	3
EC1979	2 May	Dublin	2	0
wc1984	14 Nov	Copenhagen	0	3
wc1985	13 Nov	Dublin	1	4
wc1992	14 Oct	Copenhagen	0	0
wc1993	28 Apr	Dublin	1	1
2002	27 Mar	Dublin	3	0
2007	22 Aug	Copenhagen	4	0

v ECUADOR			**RI**	**E**
1972	19 June	Natal	3	2
2007	23 May	New Jersey	1	1

v EGYPT			**RI**	**E**
wc1990	17 June	Palermo	0	0

v ENGLAND			**RI**	**E**
1946	30 Sept	Dublin	0	1
1949	21 Sept	Everton	2	0
wc1957	8 May	Wembley	1	5
wc1957	19 May	Dublin	1	1
1964	24 May	Dublin	1	3
1976	8 Sept	Wembley	1	1
EC1978	25 Oct	Dublin	1	1
EC1980	6 Feb	Wembley	0	2
1985	26 Mar	Wembley	1	2
EC1988	12 June	Stuttgart	1	0
EC1990	11 June	Cagliari	1	1
EC1990	14 Nov	Dublin	1	1
EC1991	27 Mar	Wembley	1	1
1995	15 Feb	Dublin	1	0
(abandoned after 27 mins)				
2013	29 May	Wembley	1	1
2015	7 June	Dublin	0	0

v ESTONIA			**RI**	**E**
wc2000	11 Oct	Dublin	2	0
wc2001	6 June	Tallinn	2	0
EC2011	11 Nov	Tallinn	4	0
EC2011	15 Nov	Dublin	1	1

		v FAROE ISLANDS	RI	F
EC2004	13 Oct	Dublin	2	0
EC2005	8 June	Toftir	2	0
wc2012	16 Oct	Torshavn	4	1
wc2013	7 June	Dublin	3	0

		v FINLAND	RI	F
wc1949	8 Sept	Dublin	3	0
wc1949	9 Oct	Helsinki	1	1
1990	16 May	Dublin	1	1
2000	15 Nov	Dublin	3	0
2002	21 Aug	Helsinki	3	0

		v FRANCE	RI	F
1937	23 May	Paris	2	0
1952	16 Nov	Dublin	1	1
wc1953	4 Oct	Dublin	3	5
wc1953	25 Nov	Paris	0	1
wc1972	15 Nov	Dublin	2	1
wc1973	19 May	Paris	1	1
wc1976	17 Nov	Paris	0	2
wc1977	30 Mar	Dublin	1	0
wc1980	28 Oct	Paris	0	2
wc1981	14 Oct	Dublin	3	2
1989	7 Feb	Dublin	0	0
wc2004	9 Oct	Paris	0	0
wc2005	7 Sept	Dublin	0	1
wc2009	14 Nov	Dublin	0	1
wc2009	18 Nov	Paris	1	1
EC2016	**26 June**	**Lyon**	**1**	**2**

		v FYR MACEDONIA	RI	M
wc1996	9 Oct	Dublin	3	0
wc1997	2 Apr	Skopje	2	3
EC1999	9 June	Dublin	1	0
EC1999	9 Oct	Skopje	1	1
EC2011	26 Mar	Dublin	2	1
EC2011	4 June	Podgorica	2	0

		v GEORGIA	RI	G
EC2003	29 Mar	Tbilisi	2	1
EC2003	11 June	Dublin	2	0
wc2008	6 Sept	Mainz	2	1
wc2009	11 Feb	Dublin	2	1
2013	2 June	Dublin	3	0
EC2014	7 Sept	Tbilisi	2	1
EC2015	**7 Sept**	**Dublin**	**1**	**0**

		v GERMANY	RI	G
1935	8 May	Dortmund	1	3
1936	17 Oct	Dublin	5	2
1939	23 May	Bremen	1	1
1994	29 May	Hanover	2	0
wc2002	5 June	Ibaraki	1	1
EC2006	2 Sept	Stuttgart	0	1
EC2007	13 Oct	Dublin	0	0
wc2012	12 Oct	Dublin	1	6
wc2013	11 Oct	Cologne	0	3
EC2014	14 Oct	Gelsenkirchen	1	1
EC2015	**8 Oct**	**Dublin**	**1**	**0**

		v WEST GERMANY	RI	WG
1951	17 Oct	Dublin	3	2
1952	4 May	Cologne	0	3
1955	28 May	Hamburg	1	2
1956	25 Nov	Dublin	3	0
1960	11 May	Dusseldorf	1	0
1966	4 May	Dublin	0	4
1970	9 May	Berlin	1	2
1975	1 Mar	Dublin	1	0†
1979	22 May	Dublin	1	3
1981	21 May	Bremen	0	3†
1989	6 Sept	Dublin	1	1

†v West Germany 'B'

		v GIBRALTAR	RI	G
EC2014	11 Oct	Dublin	7	0
EC2015	**4 Sept**	**Faro**	**4**	**0**

		v GREECE	RI	G
2000	26 Apr	Dublin	0	1
2002	20 Nov	Athens	0	0
2012	14 Nov	Dublin	0	1

		v HUNGARY	RI	H
1934	15 Dec	Dublin	2	4
1936	3 May	Budapest	3	3
1936	6 Dec	Dublin	2	3

			RI	H
1939	19 Mar	Cork	2	2
1939	18 May	Budapest	2	2
wc1969	8 June	Dublin	1	2
wc1969	5 Nov	Budapest	0	4
wc1989	8 Mar	Budapest	0	0
wc1989	4 June	Dublin	2	0
1991	11 Sept	Gyor	2	1
2012	4 June	Budapest	0	0

		v ICELAND	RI	I
EC1962	12 Aug	Dublin	4	2
EC1962	2 Sept	Reykjavik	1	1
EC1982	13 Oct	Dublin	2	0
EC1983	21 Sept	Reykjavik	3	0
1986	25 May	Reykjavik	2	1
wc1996	10 Nov	Dublin	0	0
wc1997	6 Sept	Reykjavik	4	2

		v IRAN	RI	I
1972	18 June	Recife	2	1
wc2001	10 Nov	Dublin	2	0
wc2001	15 Nov	Tehran	0	1

		v NORTHERN IRELAND	RI	NI
EC1978	20 Sept	Dublin	0	0
EC1979	21 Nov	Belfast	0	1
wc1988	14 Sept	Belfast	0	0
wc1989	11 Oct	Dublin	3	0
wc1993	31 Mar	Dublin	3	0
wc1993	17 Nov	Belfast	1	1
EC1994	16 Nov	Belfast	4	0
EC1995	29 Mar	Dublin	1	1
1999	29 May	Dublin	0	1
NC2011	24 May	Dublin	5	0

		v ISRAEL	RI	I
1984	4 Apr	Tel Aviv	0	3
1985	27 May	Tel Aviv	0	0
1987	10 Nov	Dublin	5	0
EC2005	26 Mar	Tel Aviv	1	1
EC2005	4 June	Dublin	2	2

		v ITALY	RI	I
1926	21 Mar	Turin	0	3
1927	23 Apr	Dublin	1	2
EC1970	8 Dec	Rome	0	3
EC1971	10 May	Dublin	1	2
1985	5 Feb	Dublin	1	2
wc1990	30 June	Rome	0	1
1992	4 June	Foxboro	0	2
wc1994	18 June	New York	1	0
2005	17 Aug	Dublin	1	2
wc2009	1 Apr	Bari	1	1
wc2009	10 Oct	Dublin	2	2
2011	7 June	Liege	2	0
EC2012	18 June	Poznan	0	2
2014	31 May	Craven Cottage	0	0
EC2016	**22 June**	**Lille**	**1**	**0**

		v JAMAICA	RI	J
2004	2 June	Charlton	1	0

		v KAZAKHSTAN	RI	K
wc2012	7 Sept	Astana	2	1
wc2013	15 Oct	Dublin	3	1

		v LATVIA	RI	L
wc1992	9 Sept	Dublin	4	0
wc1993	2 June	Riga	2	1
EC1994	7 Sept	Riga	3	0
EC1995	11 Oct	Dublin	2	1
2013	15 Nov	Dublin	3	0

		v LIECHTENSTEIN	RI	L
EC1994	12 Oct	Dublin	4	0
EC1995	3 June	Eschen	0	0
wc1996	31 Aug	Eschen	5	0
wc1997	21 May	Dublin	5	0

		v LITHUANIA	RI	L
wc1993	16 June	Vilnius	1	0
wc1993	8 Sept	Dublin	2	0
wc1997	20 Aug	Dublin	0	0
wc1997	10 Sept	Vilnius	2	1

		v LUXEMBOURG	RI	L
1936	9 May	Luxembourg	5	1
wc1953	28 Oct	Dublin	4	0
wc1954	7 Mar	Luxembourg	1	0
EC1987	28 May	Luxembourg	2	0
EC1987	9 Sept	Dublin	2	1

		v MALTA	RI	M
EC1983	30 Mar	Valletta	1	0
EC1983	16 Nov	Dublin	8	0
wc1989	28 May	Dublin	2	0
wc1989	15 Nov	Valletta	2	0
1990	2 June	Valletta	3	0
EC1998	14 Oct	Dublin	5	0
EC1999	8 Sept	Valletta	3	2

		v MEXICO	RI	M
1984	8 Aug	Dublin	0	0
wc1994	24 June	Orlando	1	2
1996	13 June	New Jersey	2	2
1998	23 May	Dublin	0	0
2000	4 June	Chicago	2	2

		v MONTENEGRO	RI	M
wc2008	10 Sept	Podgorica	0	0
wc2009	14 Oct	Dublin	0	0

		v MOROCCO	RI	M
1990	12 Sept	Dublin	1	0

		v NETHERLANDS	RI	N
1932	8 May	Amsterdam	2	0
1934	8 Apr	Amsterdam	2	5
1935	8 Dec	Dublin	3	5
1955	1 May	Dublin	1	0
1956	10 May	Rotterdam	4	1
wc1980	10 Sept	Dublin	2	1
wc1981	9 Sept	Rotterdam	2	2
EC1982	22 Sept	Rotterdam	1	2
EC1983	12 Oct	Dublin	2	3
EC1988	18 June	Gelsenkirchen	0	1
wc1990	21 June	Palermo	1	1
1994	20 Apr	Tilburg	1	0
wc1994	4 July	Orlando	0	2
EC1995	13 Dec	Liverpool	0	2
1996	4 June	Rotterdam	1	3
wc2000	2 Sept	Amsterdam	2	2
wc2001	1 Sept	Dublin	1	0
2004	5 June	Amsterdam	1	0
2006	16 Aug	Dublin	0	4
2016	**27 May**	**Dublin**	**1**	**1**

		v NIGERIA	RI	N
2002	16 May	Dublin	1	2
2004	29 May	Charlton	0	3
2009	29 May	Fulham	1	1

		v NORWAY	RI	N
wc1937	10 Oct	Oslo	2	3
wc1937	7 Nov	Dublin	3	3
1950	26 Nov	Dublin	2	2
1951	30 May	Oslo	3	2
1954	8 Nov	Dublin	2	1
1955	25 May	Oslo	3	1
1960	6 Nov	Dublin	3	1
1964	13 May	Oslo	4	1
1973	6 June	Oslo	1	1
1976	24 Mar	Dublin	3	0
1978	21 May	Oslo	0	0
wc1984	17 Oct	Oslo	0	1
wc1985	1 May	Dublin	0	0
1988	1 June	Oslo	0	0
wc1994	28 June	New York	0	0
2003	30 Apr	Dublin	1	0
2008	20 Aug	Oslo	1	1
2010	17 Nov	Dublin	1	2

		v OMAN	RI	O
2012	11 Sept	London	4	1
2014	3 Sept	Dublin	2	0

		v PARAGUAY	RI	P
1999	10 Feb	Dublin	2	0
2010	25 May	Dublin	2	1

		v POLAND	RI	P
1938	22 May	Warsaw	0	6
1938	13 Nov	Dublin	3	2
1958	11 May	Katowice	2	2
1958	5 Oct	Dublin	2	2
1964	10 May	Kracow	1	3
1964	25 Oct	Dublin	3	2
1968	15 May	Dublin	2	2
1968	30 Oct	Katowice	0	1
1970	6 May	Dublin	1	2
1970	23 Sept	Dublin	0	2
1973	16 May	Wroclaw	0	2
1973	21 Oct	Dublin	1	0
1976	26 May	Poznan	2	0
1977	24 Apr	Dublin	0	0
1978	12 Apr	Lodz	0	3
1981	23 May	Bydgoszcz	0	3
1984	23 May	Dublin	0	0
1986	12 Nov	Warsaw	0	1
1988	22 May	Dublin	3	1
EC1991	1 May	Dublin	0	0
EC1991	16 Oct	Poznan	3	3
2004	28 Apr	Bydgoszcz	0	0
2013	19 Nov	Poznan	0	0
2008	19 Nov	Dublin	2	3
2013	6 Feb	Dublin	2	0
2013	19 Nov	Poznan	0	0
EC2015	29 Mar	Dublin	1	1
EC2015	**11 Oct**	**Warsaw**	**1**	**2**

		v PORTUGAL	RI	P
1946	16 June	Lisbon	1	3
1947	4 May	Dublin	0	2
1948	23 May	Lisbon	0	2
1949	22 May	Dublin	1	0
1972	25 June	Recife	1	2
1992	7 June	Boston	2	0
EC1995	26 Apr	Dublin	1	0
EC1995	15 Nov	Lisbon	0	3
1996	29 May	Dublin	0	1
wc2000	7 Oct	Lisbon	1	1
wc2001	2 June	Dublin	1	1
2005	9 Feb	Dublin	1	0
2014	10 June	New Jersey	1	5

		v ROMANIA	RI	R
1988	23 Mar	Dublin	2	0
wc1990	25 June	Genoa	0	0*
wc1997	30 Apr	Bucharest	0	1
wc1997	11 Oct	Dublin	1	1
2004	27 May	Dublin	1	0

		v RUSSIA	RI	R
1994	23 Mar	Dublin	0	0
1996	27 Mar	Dublin	0	2
2002	13 Feb	Dublin	2	0
EC2002	7 Sept	Moscow	2	4
EC2003	6 Sept	Dublin	1	1
EC2010	8 Oct	Dublin	2	3
EC2011	6 Sept	Moscow	0	0

		v SAN MARINO	RI	SM
EC2006	15 Nov	Dublin	5	0
EC2007	7 Feb	Serravalle	2	1

		v SAUDI ARABIA	RI	SA
wc2002	11 June	Yokohama	3	0

		v SCOTLAND	RI	S
wc1961	3 May	Glasgow	1	4
wc1961	7 May	Dublin	0	3
1963	9 June	Dublin	1	0
1969	21 Sept	Dublin	1	1
EC1986	15 Oct	Dublin	0	0
EC1987	18 Feb	Glasgow	1	0
2000	30 May	Dublin	1	2
2003	12 Feb	Glasgow	2	0
NC2011	29 May	Dublin	1	0
EC2014	14 Nov	Hampden	0	1
EC2015	13 June	Dublin	1	1

		v SERBIA	RI	S
2008	24 May	Dublin	1	1
2012	15 Aug	Belgrade	0	0
2014	5 Mar	Dublin	1	2

v SLOVAKIA

			RI	S
EC2007	28 Mar	Dublin	1	0
EC2007	8 Sept	Bratislava	2	2
EC2010	12 Oct	Zilina	1	1
EC2011	2 Sept	Dublin	0	0
2016	**29 Mar**	**Dublin**	**2**	**2**

v SOUTH AFRICA

			RI	SA
2000	11 June	New Jersey	2	1
2009	8 Sept	Limerick	1	0

v SPAIN

			RI	S
1931	26 Apr	Barcelona	1	1
1931	13 Dec	Dublin	0	5
1946	23 June	Madrid	1	0
1947	2 Mar	Dublin	3	2
1948	30 May	Barcelona	1	2
1949	12 June	Dublin	1	4
1952	1 June	Madrid	0	6
1955	27 Nov	Dublin	2	2
EC1964	11 Mar	Seville	1	5
EC1964	8 Apr	Dublin	0	2
WC1965	5 May	Dublin	1	0
WC1965	27 Oct	Seville	1	4
WC1965	10 Nov	Paris	0	1

v SPAIN

			RI	S
EC1966	23 Oct	Dublin	0	0
EC1966	7 Dec	Valencia	0	2
1977	9 Feb	Dublin	0	1
EC1982	17 Nov	Dublin	3	3
EC1983	27 Apr	Zaragoza	0	2
1985	26 May	Cork	0	0
WC1988	16 Nov	Seville	0	2
WC1989	26 Apr	Dublin	1	0
WC1992	18 Nov	Seville	0	0
WC1993	13 Oct	Dublin	1	3
WC2002	16 June	Suwon	1	1
EC2012	14 June	Gdansk	0	4
2013	11 June	New York	0	2

v SWEDEN

			RI	S
WC1949	2 June	Stockholm	1	3
WC1949	13 Nov	Dublin	1	3
1959	1 Nov	Dublin	3	2
1960	18 May	Malmo	1	4
EC1970	14 Oct	Dublin	1	1
EC1970	28 Oct	Malmo	0	1
1999	28 Apr	Dublin	2	0
2006	1 Mar	Dublin	3	0
WC2013	22 Mar	Stockholm	0	0
WC2013	6 Sept	Dublin	1	2
EC2016	**13 June**	**Paris**	**1**	**1**

v SWITZERLAND

			RI	S
1935	5 May	Basle	0	1
1936	17 Mar	Dublin	1	0
1937	17 May	Berne	1	0
1938	18 Sept	Dublin	4	0
1948	5 Dec	Dublin	0	1
EC1975	11 May	Dublin	2	1
EC1975	21 May	Berne	0	1
1980	30 Apr	Dublin	2	0
WC1985	2 June	Dublin	3	0
WC1985	11 Sept	Berne	0	0
1992	25 Mar	Dublin	2	1
EC2002	16 Oct	Dublin	1	2
EC2003	11 Oct	Basle	0	2
WC2004	8 Sept	Basle	1	1
WC2005	12 Oct	Dublin	0	0
2016	**25 Mar**	**Dublin**	**1**	**0**

v TRINIDAD & TOBAGO

			RI	TT
1982	30 May	Port of Spain	1	2

v TUNISIA

			RI	T
1988	19 Oct	Dublin	4	0

v TURKEY

			RI	T
EC1966	16 Nov	Dublin	2	1
EC1967	22 Feb	Ankara	1	2
EC1974	20 Nov	Izmir	1	1
EC1975	29 Oct	Dublin	4	0
2014	25 May	Dublin	1	2
1976	13 Oct	Ankara	3	3
1978	5 Apr	Dublin	4	2
1990	26 May	Izmir	0	0
EC1990	17 Oct	Dublin	5	0
EC1991	13 Nov	Istanbul	3	1
EC2000	13 Nov	Dublin	1	1
EC2000	17 Nov	Bursa	0	0
2003	9 Sept	Dublin	2	2
2014	25 May	Dublin	1	2

v URUGUAY

			RI	U
1974	8 May	Montevideo	0	2
1986	23 Apr	Dublin	1	1
2011	29 Mar	Dublin	2	3

v USA

			RI	USA
1979	29 Oct	Dublin	3	2
1991	1 June	Boston	1	1
1992	29 Apr	Dublin	4	1
1992	30 May	Washington	1	3
1996	9 June	Boston	1	2
2000	6 June	Boston	1	1
2002	17 Apr	Dublin	2	1
2014	18 Nov	Dublin	4	1

v USSR

			RI	USSR
WC1972	18 Oct	Dublin	1	2
WC1973	13 May	Moscow	0	1
EC1974	30 Oct	Dublin	3	0
EC1975	18 May	Kiev	1	2
WC1984	12 Sept	Dublin	1	0
WC1985	16 Oct	Moscow	0	2
EC1988	15 June	Hanover	1	1
1990	25 Apr	Dublin	1	0

v WALES

			RI	W
1960	28 Sept	Dublin	2	3
1979	11 Sept	Swansea	1	2
1981	24 Feb	Dublin	1	3
1986	26 Mar	Dublin	0	1
1990	28 Mar	Dublin	1	0
1991	6 Feb	Wrexham	3	0
1992	19 Feb	Dublin	0	1
1993	17 Feb	Dublin	2	1
1997	11 Feb	Cardiff	0	0
EC2007	24 Mar	Dublin	1	0
EC2007	17 Nov	Cardiff	2	2
NC2011	8 Feb	Dublin	3	0
2013	14 Aug	Cardiff	0	0

v YUGOSLAVIA

			RI	Y
1955	19 Sept	Dublin	1	4
1988	27 Apr	Dublin	2	0
EC1998	18 Nov	Belgrade	0	1
EC1999	1 Sept	Dublin	2	1

OTHER BRITISH AND IRISH INTERNATIONAL MATCHES 2015–16

FRIENDLIES

■ *Denotes player sent off.*

ENGLAND

Friday, 13 November 2015
Spain (0) 2 *(Mario 72, Cazorla 84)*
England (0) 0   29,500
Spain: (433) Casillas; Mario, Pique, Bartra (Azpilicueta 82), Jordi Alba; Busquets (Koke 78), Thiago (Cazorla 27), Iniesta (Nolito 46); Fabregas, Costa (Mata 63), Alcacer (Pedro 74).
England: (4231) Hart; Walker, Jones, Smalling (Cahill 85), Bertrand; Delph (Dier 63), Carrick (Shelvey 90); Lallana (Alli 63), Barkley (Rooney 73), Sterling; Kane.
Referee: Paolo Mazzoleni.

Tuesday, 17 November 2015
England (1) 2 *(Alli 39, Rooney 48)*
France (0) 0   71,223
England: (4231) Hart (Butland 46); Clyne, Cahill, Stones, Gibbs; Dier, Alli (Jones 88); Barkley (Shelvey 79), Rooney, Sterling (Lallana 68); Kane (Bertrand 79).
France: (433) Lloris; Sagna, Varane, Koscielny, Digne; Schneiderlin (Sissoko 82), Cabaye (Diarra 57), Matuidi (Pogba 46); Ben Arfa (Coman 46), Gignac (Giroud 57), Martial (Griezmann 67).
Referee: Jonas Eriksson.

Saturday, 26 March 2016
Germany (1) 2 *(Kroos 43, Gomez 57)*
England (0) 3 *(Kane 61, Vardy 74, Dier 90)*   71,413
Germany: (4411) Neuer; Hector, Hummels (Tah 46), Can, Rudiger; Muller (Podolski 75), Khedira, Kroos, Reus (Schurrle 64); Ozil; Gomez (Gotze 79).
England: (442) Butland (Forster 45); Clyne, Cahill, Smalling, Rose; Alli, Henderson, Dier, Lallana (Barkley 70); Kane, Welbeck (Vardy 70).
Referee: Gianluca Rocchi.

Tuesday, 29 March 2016
England (1) 1 *(Vardy 41)*
Netherlands (0) 2 *(Janssen 51 (pen), Narsingh 77)* 82,831
England: (4231) Forster; Walker, Smalling (Jagielka 70), Stones, Rose (Clyne 58); Miller (Alli 82), Drinkwater (Dier 85); Vardy, Barkley, Lallana (Kane 70); Sturridge (Walcott 58).
Netherlands: (433) Zoet; Veltman, Bruma, Blind, Willems (Van Aanholt 82); Wijnaldum, Bazoer (van Ginkel 79), Afellay; Depay, Janssen (Clasie 90), Promes (Narsingh 37).
Referee: Antonio Miguel Mateu Lahoz.

Sunday, 22 May 2016
England (1) 2 *(Kane 3, Vardy 83)*
Turkey (1) 1 *(Calhanoglu 13)*   44,866
England: (433) Hart; Walker, Stones, Cahill, Rose; Dier, Wilshere (Henderson 66), Alli; Sterling (Drinkwater 73), Kane, Vardy.
Turkey: (4411) Babacan; Gonul, Balta, Topal, Erkin (Koybasi 69); Ozyakup (Tekdemir 69), Inan, Tufan (Erdinc 87), Sen (Oztekin 85); Calhanoglu (Sahan 78); Tosun.
Referee: Deniz Aytekin.

Friday, 27 May 2016
England (1) 2 *(Rashford 3, Rooney 55)*
Australia (0) 1 *(Dier 75 (og))*   46,595
England: (433) Forster (Heaton 87); Clyne, Smalling (Dier 73), Stones, Bertrand; Wilshere (Milner 46), Drinkwater, Henderson; Sterling (Townsend 76), Rashford (Barkley 63), Lallana (Rooney 46).
Australia: (41212) Ryan; Risdon (Degenek 74), Wright, Milligan, Smith; Jedinak; Mooy (Goodwin 84), Luongo

(Oikonomidis 58); Rogic (Juric 73); Kruse (Irvine 84), Maclaren (McKay 58).
Referee: Danny Makkelie.

Thursday, 2 June 2016
England (0) 1 *(Smalling 86)*
Portugal (0) 0   82,503
England: (433) Hart; Walker, Cahill, Smalling, Rose; Dier, Alli (Henderson 90); Milner (Wilshere 66); Rooney (Lallana 78), Kane (Sturridge 78), Vardy (Sterling 66).
Portugal: (433) Rui Patricio; Vieirinha, Bruno Alves■, Ricardo Carvalho (Eder 90), Eliseu; Joao Moutinho (William Carvalho 72), Joao Mario (Andre Gomes 46), Danilo Pereira; Nani (Quaresma 61), Rafa (Fonte 38), Adrien Silva (Renato Sanches 72).
Referee: Marco Guida.

SCOTLAND

Thursday, 24 March 2016
Czech Republic (0) 0
Scotland (1) 1 *(Anya 10)*   14,580
Czech Republic: (4231) Koubek; Kaderabek, Sivok, Kadlec M, Limbersky; Vacek (Marecek 78), Darida (Rada 87); Sural (Pudil 78), Frydek (Skalak 46), Dockal (Kolar 65); Necid (Vydra 65).
Scotland: (451) McGregor; Hutton, Martin R, Berra, Robertson (Phillips 58); Snodgrass, Mulgrew, Fletcher D, McLean (Bannan 58), Anya (Caddis 86); McCormack (Watt 78).
Referee: Paul McLaughlin.

Tuesday, 29 March 2016
Scotland (1) 1 *(Ritchie 8)*
Denmark (0) 0   18,385
Scotland: (442) Gordon; Whittaker, Tierney (Mulgrew 46), Greer, Hanley; Ritchie (Burke 82), Brown, Fletcher S (Anya 46), Griffiths (Martin C 59); McGinn, Maloney (Bridcutt 69).
Denmark: (442) Schmeichel (Lossl 46); Kjaer, Agger (Sviatchenko 64), Durmisi; Christensen, Eriksen (Schone 81), Dalsgaard, Delaney, Jorgensen; Poulsen Y (Braithwaite 46), Hojbjerg.
Referee: Svein Oddvar Moen.

Sunday, 29 May 2016
Italy (0) 1 *(Pelle 57)*
Scotland (0) 0   20,000
Italy: (352) Buffon; Barzagli, Bonucci, Chiellini; Candreva (Parolo 62), Florenzi, De Rossi (Jorginho 67), Giaccherini (Bonaventura 80), Darmian (Bernardeschi 59); Pelle (Zaza 67), Eder (Insigne 59).
Scotland: (442) Marshall; Paterson (Berra 46), Mulgrew, Martin R, Hanley; Phillips (Burke 71), Fletcher D, McArthur (Bryson 83), McCormack (Fletcher S 46); Ritchie, Anya (Naismith 71).
Referee: Alan Sant.

Saturday, 4 June 2016
France (3) 3 *(Giroud 8, 35, Koscielny 40)*
Scotland (0) 0   25,057
France: (433) Lloris; Sagna, Rami, Koscielny, Evra (Digne 83); Pogba, Kante (Sissoko 87), Matuidi (Cabaye 68); Payet (Martial 45), Giroud (Gignac 62), Coman (Griezmann 45).
Scotland: (4231) Marshall; Martin R, Greer, Hanley, Robertson (Mulgrew 46); McArthur (McKay 87), Fletcher D; Snodgrass (Kingsley 65), Maloney (Anya 46), Ritchie; Fletcher S (Naismith 58).
Referee: Sebastien Delferiere.

WALES

Friday, 13 November 2015
Wales (1) 2 *(Ledley 45, Huws 70)*
Netherlands (1) 3 *(Dost 32, Robben 54, 81)* 25,669
Wales: (442) Hennessey (Fon Williams 73); Gunter (Henley 65), Taylor N (Dummett 65), Davies, Chester; Williams A (Collins 46), Allen, King, Lawrence; Williams J (Williams G 60), Ledley (Huws 56).
Netherlands: (433) Cillessen; Janmaat, van Dijk (Veltman 46), Kongolo, Bruma; Clasie (Bazoer 87), Promes (Wijnaldum 90), Blind; Sneijder, Dost, Robben.
Referee: Benoit Bastian.

Thursday, 24 March 2016
Wales (0) 1 *(Church 90 (pen))*
Northern Ireland (0) 1 *(Cathcart 60)* 21,855
Wales: (433) Hennessey (Ward 46); Gunter, Matthews, Chester, Williams A; Cotterill, Ledley (Crofts 46), Vaughan (Allen 71); Lawrence (Williams J 62), Vokes (Church 76), Williams G (Isgrove 62).
Northern Ireland: (442) McGovern; Cathcart, McNair (Paton 73), McLaughlin C (Hughes 81), McAuley; Evans J (Lafferty D 73), Davis, Dallas (Ferguson 90), Norwood; Washington (Ward 46), Lafferty K (McKay 81).
Referee: Steven McLean.

Monday, 28 March 2016
Ukraine (1) 1 *(Yarmolenko 28)*
Wales (0) 0 20,000
Ukraine: (442) Pyatov; Khacheridi, Kucher, Stepanenko, Yarmolenko; Zozulya, Shevchuk (Budkivskiy 46), Rotan (Sydorchuk 59), Fedetskiy; Garmash, Kovalenko.
Wales: (442) Hennessey; Gunter, Taylor N (Henley 72), Davies, Chester; Williams A (Richards 65), Allen, Huws (Ledley 79), Church (Vokes 61); Lawrence (Bradshaw 72), Williams J (MacDonald 61).
Referee: Serdar Gozubuyuk.

Sunday, 5 June 2016
Sweden (1) 3 *(Forsberg 40, Lustig 57, Guidetti 87)*
Wales (0) 0 37,942
Sweden: (442) Isaksson (Olsen 46); Lustig, Johansson, Granqvist, Olsson (Augustinsson 46); Larsson, Kallstrom, Lewicki (Ekdal 61), Forsberg (Durmaz 61); Berg (Guidetti 76), Ibrahimovic (Kujovic 61).
Wales: (451) Hennessey (Ward 46); Gunter, Williams A, Chester (Collins 64), Davies; Williams J (Huws 73), Vaughan (Edwards 64), Ramsey, King (Bale 64), Taylor N; Vokes (Church 73).
Referee: Tobias Welz.

NORTHERN IRELAND

Friday, 13 November 2015
Northern Ireland (0) 1 *(Davis 55)*
Latvia (0) 0 11,707
Northern Ireland: (352) McGovern (Carroll 46); Cathcart, McAuley, Evans J; McLaughlin C, Davis (McCourt 84), Baird, Norwood (Evans C 46), Dallas (Ferguson 69); Ward (Boyce 69), Lafferty K (Magennis 54).
Latvia: (442) Vanins (Steinbors 73); Gabovs, Gorkss, Maksimenko, Kurakins; Tarasovs, Rakels (Kamess 85), Laizans (Ikaunieks 79), Zjuzins; Visnakovs A (Rudnevs 59), Visnakovs E (Sabala 71).
Referee: Mohammed Al Hoish.

Monday, 28 March 2016
Northern Ireland (1) 1 *(Washington 41)*
Slovenia (0) 0 13,500
Northern Ireland: (442) Carroll; McNair (McGinn 78), McAuley (Hughes 46), Evans J, Cathcart; Smith (McLaughlin 71), Ferguson (Dallas 60), Davis, Norwood; Ward (Lafferty K 60), Washington (Magennis 70).
Slovenia: (442) Oblak; Skubic (Stojanovic 60), Samardzic, Cesar (Struna 80), Jokic; Kurtic (Vrhovec 46), Krhin, Verbic (Kirm 62), Ilicic (Novakovic 46); Bezjak (Crnic 75), Birsa.
Referee: Kristo Tohver.

Friday, 27 May 2016
Northern Ireland (2) 3 *(Lafferty K 6, Washington 45, Grigg 88)*
Belarus (0) 0 14,229
Northern Ireland: (442) Carroll (Mannus 46); McLaughlin C, Baird, Evans J, Cathcart; Dallas (Hughes 74), McNair, Davis (Norwood 46), Evans C (McGinn 74); Lafferty K (Grigg 61), Washington (Ward 60).
Belarus: (442) Gorbunov; Martynovich, Shitov (Politevich 77), Filipenko (Sivakov 38), Valadzko; Korzun, Stasevich, Gordeichuk, Krivets (Hleb 70); Kislyak, Yanush (Palyakow 71).
Referee: Martin Atkinson.

Saturday, 4 June 2016
Slovakia (0) 0
Northern Ireland (0) 0 18,111
Slovakia: (4231) Kozacik; Pekarik, Skrtel, Durica, Svento; Hrosovsky, Kucka (Nemec 84); Hamsik, Mak (Stoch 65), Weiss; Duris (Duda 65).
Northern Ireland: (532) McGovern; Baird, McAuley, Cathcart (Hughes 30), Evans J, Ferguson (Hodson 86); Davis, McNair (McLaughlin C 90), Norwood (Evans C 83); Lafferty K (Washington 54), Ward (Magennis 46).
Referee: Radu Petrescu.

REPUBLIC OF IRELAND

Friday, 25 March 2016
Republic of Ireland (1) 1 *(Clark 3)*
Switzerland (0) 0 35,450
Republic of Ireland: (442) Randolph; Coleman, Duffy, Clark, Brady; Judge, Meyler (O'Kane 61), Quinn (McCarthy 61), McGeady (Hayes 61); Long (McClean 84), Doyle (Murphy 27 (Hoolahan 79)).
Switzerland: (433) Sommer; Lang (Widmer 82), Schar, Klose, Rodriguez (Moubandje 78); Dzemaili (Tarashaj 71), Xhaka, Behrami (Fernandes 71); Embolo, Seferovic (Steffen 62), Mehmedi (Kasami 71).
Referee: Miroslav Zelinka.

Tuesday, 29 March 2016
Republic of Ireland (0) 2 *(Long 21 (pen), McClean 24 (pen))*
Slovakia (2) 2 *(Stoch 14, McShane 45 (og))* 30,217
Republic of Ireland: (433) Elliot (Randolph 16); Christie, McShane, O'Shea (Pearce 46), Ward (Hayes 70); O'Kane (Pilkington 66), Whelan, McCarthy; Hoolahan (McGeady 73), Long (Brady 46), McClean.
Slovakia: (4231) Kozacik; Pekarik, Skrtel, Salata, Svento (Tesak 88); Gregus (Hrosovsky 74), Sabo (Mak 64); Hamsik, Stoch (Duda 64), Sestak (Weiss 64); Vittek (Nemec 69).
Referee: Ola Hobber Nilsen.

Friday, 27 May 2016
Republic of Ireland (1) 1 *(Long 31)*
Netherlands (0) 1 *(de Jong 85)* 42,438
Republic of Ireland: (442) Randolph; Coleman, O'Shea, Duffy, Whelan (Gibson 67); Arter (O'Kane 82), Brady, Quinn (Hendrick 67), Long (McClean 67); Walters, McGoldrick (Hoolahan 76).
Netherlands: (442) Cillessen; Willems, Bruma, Veltman, van Dijk; Bazoer, Strootman (van Ginkel 70), Wijnaldum (de Jong 82), Promes; Depay (Berghuis 61), Janssen (Dost 75).
Referee: Artur Soares Dias.

Tuesday, 31 May 2016
Republic of Ireland (0) 1 *(Ward 71)*
Belarus (1) 2 *(Gordeichuk 20, Valadzko 63)* 7200
Republic of Ireland: (442) Given (Forde 68); Christie, Keogh, Clark, Ward; McGeady (O'Dowda 75), Gibson (Hoolahan 67), Meyler (O'Kane 74), Hendrick; Murphy (Long 67), McClean (McGoldrick 78).
Belarus: (4141) Chernik; Palyakow, Martynovich, Sivakov, Valadzko; Kislyak, Korzun, Stasevich (Nekhaychik 90), Hleb (Krivets 90), Gordeichuk (Politevich 75); Yanush.
Referee: Dejan Jakimovksi.

BRITISH AND IRISH INTERNATIONAL APPEARANCES 1872–2016

This is a list of full international appearances by Englishmen, Irishmen, Scotsmen and Welshmen in matches against the Home Countries and against foreign nations. It does not include unofficial matches against Commonwealth and Empire countries. The year indicated refers to the player's international debut season; i.e. 2016 is the 2015–16 season. **Bold** type indicates players who have made an international appearance in season 2015–16.

As at July 2016.

ENGLAND

Abbott, W. 1902 (Everton)	1
A'Court, A. 1958 (Liverpool)	5
Adams, T. A. 1987 (Arsenal)	66
Adcock, H. 1929 (Leicester C)	5
Agbonlahor, G. 2009 (Aston Villa)	3
Alcock, C. W. 1875 (Wanderers)	1
Alderson, J. T. 1923 (Crystal Palace)	1
Aldridge, A. 1888 (WBA, Walsall Town Swifts)	2
Allen, A. 1888 (Aston Villa)	1
Allen, A. 1960 (Stoke C)	3
Allen, C. 1984 (QPR, Tottenham H)	5
Allen, H. 1888 (Wolverhampton W)	5
Allen, J. P. 1934 (Portsmouth)	2
Allen, R. 1952 (WBA)	5
Alli, B. J. (Dele) 2016 (Tottenham H)	**12**
Alsford, W. J. 1935 (Tottenham H)	1
Amos, A. 1885 (Old Carthusians)	2
Anderson, R. D. 1879 (Old Etonians)	1
Anderson, S. 1962 (Sunderland)	2
Anderson, V. A. 1979 (Nottingham F, Arsenal, Manchester U)	30
Anderton, D. R. 1994 (Tottenham H)	30
Angus, J. 1961 (Burnley)	1
Armfield, J. C. 1959 (Blackpool)	43
Armitage, G. H. 1926 (Charlton Ath)	1
Armstrong, D. 1980 (Middlesbrough, Southampton)	3
Armstrong, K. 1955 (Chelsea)	1
Arnold, J. 1933 (Fulham)	1
Arthur, J. W. H. 1885 (Blackburn R)	7
Ashcroft, J. 1906 (Woolwich Arsenal)	3
Ashmore, G. S. 1926 (WBA)	1
Ashton, C. T. 1926 (Corinthians)	1
Ashton, D. 2008 (West Ham U)	1
Ashurst, W. 1923 (Notts Co)	5
Astall, G. 1956 (Birmingham C)	2
Astle, J. 1969 (WBA)	5
Aston, J. 1949 (Manchester U)	17
Athersmith, W. C. 1892 (Aston Villa)	12
Atyeo, P. J. W. 1956 (Bristol C)	6
Austin, S. W. 1926 (Manchester C)	1
Bach, P. 1899 (Sunderland)	1
Bache, J. W. 1903 (Aston Villa)	7
Baddeley, T. 1903 (Wolverhampton W)	5
Bagshaw, J. J. 1920 (Derby Co)	1
Bailey, G. R. 1985 (Manchester U)	2
Bailey, H. P. 1908 (Leicester Fosse)	5
Bailey, M. A. 1964 (Charlton Ath)	2
Bailey, N. C. 1878 (Clapham R)	19
Baily, E. F. 1950 (Tottenham H)	9
Bain, J. 1877 (Oxford University)	1
Baines, L. J. 2010 (Everton)	30
Baker, A. 1928 (Arsenal)	1
Baker, B. H. 1921 (Everton, Chelsea)	2
Baker, J. H. 1960 (Hibernian, Arsenal)	8
Ball, A. J. 1965 (Blackpool, Everton, Arsenal)	72
Ball, J. 1928 (Bury)	1
Ball, M. J. 2001 (Everton)	1
Balmer, W. 1905 (Everton)	1
Bamber, J. 1921 (Liverpool)	1
Bambridge, A. L. 1881 (Swifts)	3
Bambridge, E. C. 1879 (Swifts)	18
Bambridge, E. H. 1876 (Swifts)	1
Banks, G. 1963 (Leicester C, Stoke C)	73
Banks, H. E. 1901 (Millwall)	1
Banks, T. 1958 (Bolton W)	6
Bannister, W. 1901 (Burnley, Bolton W)	2
Barclay, R. 1932 (Sheffield U)	3
Bardsley, D. J. 1993 (QPR)	2
Barham, M. 1983 (Norwich C)	2

Barkas, S. 1936 (Manchester C)	5
Barker, J. 1935 (Derby Co)	11
Barker, R. 1872 (Herts Rangers)	1
Barker, R. R. 1895 (Casuals)	1
Barkley, R. 2013 (Everton)	**22**
Barlow, R. J. 1955 (WBA)	1
Barmby, N. J. 1995 (Tottenham H, Middlesbrough, Everton, Liverpool)	23
Barnes, J. 1983 (Watford, Liverpool)	79
Barnes, P. S. 1978 (Manchester C, WBA, Leeds U)	22
Barnet, H. H. 1882 (Royal Engineers)	1
Barrass, M. W. 1952 (Bolton W)	3
Barrett, A. F. 1930 (Fulham)	1
Barrett, E. D. 1991 (Oldham Ath, Aston Villa)	3
Barrett, J. W. 1929 (West Ham U)	1
Barry, G. 2000 (Aston Villa, Manchester C)	53
Barry, L. 1928 (Leicester C)	5
Barson, F. 1920 (Aston Villa)	1
Barton, J. 1890 (Blackburn R)	1
Barton, J. 2007 (Manchester C)	1
Barton, P. H. 1921 (Birmingham)	7
Barton, W. D. 1995 (Wimbledon, Newcastle U)	3
Bassett, W. I. 1888 (WBA)	16
Bastard, S. R. 1880 (Upton Park)	1
Bastin, C. S. 1932 (Arsenal)	21
Batty, D. 1991 (Leeds U, Blackburn R, Newcastle U, Leeds U)	42
Baugh, R. 1886 (Stafford Road, Wolverhampton W)	2
Bayliss, A. E. J. M. 1891 (WBA)	1
Baynham, R. L. 1956 (Luton T)	3
Beardsley, P. A. 1986 (Newcastle U, Liverpool, Newcastle U)	59
Beasant, D. J. 1990 (Chelsea)	2
Beasley, A. 1939 (Huddersfield T)	1
Beats, W. E. 1901 (Wolverhampton W)	2
Beattie, J. S. 2003 (Southampton)	5
Beattie, T. K. 1975 (Ipswich T)	9
Beckham, D. R. J. 1997 (Manchester U, Real Madrid, LA Galaxy)	115
Becton, F. 1895 (Preston NE, Liverpool)	2
Bedford, H. 1923 (Blackpool)	2
Bell, C. 1968 (Manchester C)	48
Bennett, W. 1901 (Sheffield U)	2
Benson, R. W. 1913 (Sheffield U)	1
Bent, D. A. 2006 (Charlton Ath, Tottenham H, Sunderland, Aston Villa)	13
Bentley, D. M. 2008 (Blackburn R, Tottenham H)	7
Bentley, R. T. F. 1949 (Chelsea)	12
Beresford, J. 1934 (Aston Villa)	1
Berry, A. 1909 (Oxford University)	1
Berry, J. J. 1953 (Manchester U)	4
Bertrand, R. 2013 (Chelsea)	**9**
Bestall, J. G. 1935 (Grimsby T)	1
Betmead, H. A. 1937 (Grimsby T)	1
Betts, M. P. 1877 (Old Harrovians)	1
Betts, W. 1889 (Sheffield W)	1
Beverley, J. 1884 (Blackburn R)	3
Birkett, R. H. 1879 (Clapham R)	1
Birkett, R. J. E. 1936 (Middlesbrough)	1
Birley, F. H. 1874 (Oxford University, Wanderers)	2
Birtles, G. 1980 (Nottingham F)	3
Bishop, S. M. 1927 (Leicester C)	4
Blackburn, F. 1901 (Blackburn R)	3
Blackburn, G. F. 1924 (Aston Villa)	1
Blenkinsop, E. 1928 (Sheffield W)	26
Bliss, H. 1921 (Tottenham H)	1
Blissett, L. L. 1983 (Watford, AC Milan)	14
Blockley, J. P. 1973 (Arsenal)	1
Bloomer, S. 1895 (Derby Co, Middlesbrough)	23
Blunstone, F. 1955 (Chelsea)	5

Bond, R. 1905 (Preston NE, Bradford C)   8
Bonetti, P. P. 1966 (Chelsea)   7
Bonsor, A. G. 1873 (Wanderers)   2
Booth, F. 1905 (Manchester C)   1
Booth, T. 1898 (Blackburn R, Everton)   2
Bothroyd, J. 2011 (Cardiff C)   1
Bould, S. A. 1994 (Arsenal)   2
Bowden, E. R. 1935 (Arsenal)   6
Bower, A. G. 1924 (Corinthians)   5
Bowers, J. W. 1934 (Derby Co)   3
Bowles, S. 1974 (QPR)   5
Bowser, S. 1920 (WBA)   1
Bowyer, L. D. 2003 (Leeds U)   1
Boyer, P. J. 1976 (Norwich C)   1
Boyes, W. 1935 (WBA, Everton)   3
Boyle, T. W. 1913 (Burnley)   1
Brabrook, P. 1958 (Chelsea)   3
Bracewell, P. W. 1985 (Everton)   3
Bradford, G. R. W. 1956 (Bristol R)   1
Bradford, J. 1924 (Birmingham)   12
Bradley, W. 1959 (Manchester U)   3
Bradshaw, F. 1908 (Sheffield W)   1
Bradshaw, T. H. 1897 (Liverpool)   1
Bradshaw, W. 1910 (Blackburn R)   4
Brann, G. 1886 (Swifts)   3
Brawn, W. F. 1904 (Aston Villa)   2
Bray, J. 1935 (Manchester C)   6
Brayshaw, E. 1887 (Sheffield W)   1
Bridge W. M. 2002 (Southampton, Chelsea,
  Manchester C)   36
Bridges, B. J. 1965 (Chelsea)   4
Bridgett, A. 1905 (Sunderland)   11
Brindle, T. 1880 (Darwen)   2
Brittleton, J. T. 1912 (Sheffield W)   5
Britton, C. S. 1935 (Everton)   9
Broadbent, P. F. 1958 (Wolverhampton W)   7
Broadis, I. A. 1952 (Manchester C, Newcastle U)   14
Brockbank, J. 1872 (Cambridge University)   1
Brodie, J. B. 1889 (Wolverhampton W)   3
Bromilow, T. G. 1921 (Liverpool)   5
Bromley-Davenport, W. E. 1884 (Oxford University)   2
Brook, E. F. 1930 (Manchester C)   18
Brooking, T. D. 1974 (West Ham U)   47
Brooks, J. 1957 (Tottenham H)   3
Broome, F. H. 1938 (Aston Villa)   7
Brown, A. 1882 (Aston Villa)   3
Brown, A. 1971 (WBA)   1
Brown, A. S. 1904 (Sheffield U)   2
Brown, G. 1927 (Huddersfield T, Aston Villa)   9
Brown, J. 1881 (Blackburn R)   5
Brown, J. H. 1927 (Sheffield W)   6
Brown, K. 1960 (West Ham U)   1
Brown, W. 1924 (West Ham U)   1
Brown, W. M. 1999 (Manchester U)   23
Bruton, J. 1928 (Burnley)   3
Bryant, W. I. 1925 (Clapton)   1
Buchan, C. M. 1913 (Sunderland)   6
Buchanan, W. S. 1876 (Clapham R)   1
Buckley, F. C. 1914 (Derby Co)   1
Bull, S. G. 1989 (Wolverhampton W)   13
Bullock, F. E. 1921 (Huddersfield T)   1
Bullock, N. 1923 (Bury)   3
Burgess, H. 1904 (Manchester C)   4
Burgess, H. 1931 (Sheffield W)   4
Burnup, C. J. 1896 (Cambridge University)   1
Burrows, H. 1934 (Sheffield W)   3
Burton, F. E. 1889 (Nottingham F)   1
Bury, L. 1877 (Cambridge University, Old Etonians)   2
Butcher, T. 1980 (Ipswich T, Rangers)   77
Butland, J. 2013 (Birmingham C, Stoke C)   **4**
Butler, J. D. 1925 (Arsenal)   1
Butler, W. 1924 (Bolton W)   1
Butt, N. 1997 (Manchester U, Newcastle U)   39
Byrne, G. 1963 (Liverpool)   2
Byrne, J. J. 1962 (Crystal Palace, West Ham U)   11
Byrne, R. W. 1954 (Manchester U)   33

Cahill, G. J. 2011 (Bolton W, Chelsea)   **47**
Callaghan, I. R. 1966 (Liverpool)   4
Calvey, J. 1902 (Nottingham F)   1
Campbell, A. F. 1929 (Blackburn R, Huddersfield T)   8
Campbell, F. L. 2012 (Sunderland)   1
Campbell, S. 1996 (Tottenham H, Arsenal, Portsmouth)
  73

Camsell, G. H. 1929 (Middlesbrough)   9
Capes, A. J. 1903 (Stoke)   1
Carr, J. 1905 (Newcastle U)   ·2
Carr, J. 1920 (Middlesbrough)   2
Carr, W. H. 1875 (Owlerton, Sheffield)   1
Carragher, J. L. 1999 (Liverpool)   38
Carrick, M. 2001 (West Ham U, Tottenham H,
  Manchester U)   **34**
Carroll, A. T. 2011 (Newcastle U, Liverpool)   9
Carson, S. P. 2008 (Liverpool, WBA)   4
Carter, H. S. 1934 (Sunderland, Derby Co)   13
Carter, J. H. 1926 (WBA)   3
Catlin, A. E. 1937 (Sheffield W)   5
Caulker, S. A. 2013 (Tottenham H)   1
Chadwick, A. 1900 (Southampton)   2
Chadwick, E. 1891 (Everton)   7
Chamberlain, M. 1983 (Stoke C)   8
Chambers, H. 1921 (Liverpool)   8
Chambers, C. 2015 (Arsenal)   3
Channon, M. R. 1973 (Southampton, Manchester C)   46
Charles, G. A. 1991 (Nottingham F)   2
Charlton, J. 1965 (Leeds U)   35
Charlton, R. 1958 (Manchester U)   106
Charnley, R. O. 1963 (Blackpool)   1
Charsley, C. C. 1893 (Small Heath)   1
Chedgzoy, S. 1920 (Everton)   8
Chenery, C. J. 1872 (Crystal Palace)   3
Cherry, T. J. 1976 (Leeds U)   27
Chilton, A. 1951 (Manchester U)   2
Chippendale, H. 1894 (Blackburn R)   1
Chivers, M. 1971 (Tottenham H)   24
Christian, E. 1879 (Old Etonians)   1
Clamp, E. 1958 (Wolverhampton W)   4
Clapton, D. R. 1959 (Arsenal)   1
Clare, T. 1889 (Stoke)   4
Clarke, A. J. 1970 (Leeds U)   19
Clarke, H. A. 1954 (Tottenham H)   1
Clay, T. 1920 (Tottenham H)   4
Clayton, R. 1956 (Blackburn R)   35
Clegg, J. C. 1872 (Sheffield W)   1
Clegg, W. E. 1873 (Sheffield W, Sheffield Alb)   2
Clemence, R. N. 1973 (Liverpool, Tottenham H)   61
Clement, D. T. 1976 (QPR)   5
Cleverley, T. W. 2013 (Manchester U)   13
Clough, B. H. 1960 (Middlesbrough)   2
Clough, N. H. 1989 (Nottingham F)   14
Clyne, N. E. 2015 (Southampton, Liverpool)   **13**
Coates, R. 1970 (Burnley, Tottenham H)   4
Cobbold, W. N. 1883 (Cambridge University,
  Old Carthusians)   9
Cock, J. G. 1920 (Huddersfield T, Chelsea)   2
Cockburn, H. 1947 (Manchester U)   13
Cohen, G. R. 1964 (Fulham)   37
Cole, A. 2001 (Arsenal, Chelsea)   107
Cole, A. A. 1995 (Manchester U)   15
Cole, C. 2009 (West Ham U)   7
Cole, J. J. 2001 (West Ham U, Chelsea)   56
Colclough, H. 1914 (Crystal Palace)   1
Coleman, E. H. 1921 (Dulwich Hamlet)   1
Coleman, J. 1907 (Woolwich Arsenal)   1
Collymore, S. V. 1995 (Nottingham F, Aston Villa)   3
Common, A. 1904 (Sheffield U, Middlesbrough)   3
Compton, L. H. 1951 (Arsenal)   2
Conlin, J. 1906 (Bradford C)   1
Connelly, J. M. 1960 (Burnley, Manchester U)   20
Cook, T. E. R. 1925 (Brighton)   1
Cooper, C. T. 1995 (Nottingham F)   2
Cooper, N. C. 1893 (Cambridge University)   1
Cooper, T. 1928 (Derby Co)   15
Cooper, T. 1969 (Leeds U)   20
Coppell, S. J. 1978 (Manchester U)   42
Copping, W. 1933 (Leeds U, Arsenal, Leeds U)   20
Corbett, B. O. 1901 (Corinthians)   1
Corbett, R. 1903 (Old Malvernians)   1
Corbett, W. S. 1908 (Birmingham)   3
Corrigan, J. T. 1976 (Manchester C)   9
Cottee, A. R. 1987 (West Ham U, Everton)   7
Cotterill, G. H. 1891 (Cambridge University,
  Old Brightonians)   4
Cottle, J. R. 1909 (Bristol C)   1
Cowan, S. 1926 (Manchester C)   3
Cowans, G. S. 1983 (Aston Villa, Bari, Aston Villa)   10
Cowell, A. 1910 (Blackburn R)   1
Cox, J. 1901 (Liverpool)   3

Cox, J. D. 1892 (Derby Co)	1
Crabtree, J. W. 1894 (Burnley, Aston Villa)	14
Crawford, J. F. 1931 (Chelsea)	1
Crawford, R. 1962 (Ipswich T)	2
Crawshaw, T. H. 1895 (Sheffield W)	10
Crayston, W. J. 1936 (Arsenal)	8
Creek, F. N. S. 1923 (Corinthians)	1
Cresswell, W. 1921 (South Shields, Sunderland, Everton)	7
Crompton, R. 1902 (Blackburn R)	41
Crooks, S. D. 1930 (Derby Co)	26
Crouch, P. J. 2005 (Southampton, Liverpool, Portsmouth, Tottenham H)	42
Crowe, C. 1963 (Wolverhampton W)	1
Cuggy, F. 1913 (Sunderland)	2
Cullis, S. 1938 (Wolverhampton W)	12
Cunliffe, A. 1933 (Blackburn R)	2
Cunliffe, D. 1900 (Portsmouth)	1
Cunliffe, J. N. 1936 (Everton)	1
Cunningham, L. 1979 (WBA, Real Madrid)	6
Curle, K. 1992 (Manchester C)	3
Currey, E. S. 1890 (Oxford University)	2
Currie, A. W. 1972 (Sheffield U, Leeds U)	17
Cursham, A. W. 1876 (Notts Co)	6
Cursham, H. A. 1880 (Notts Co)	8
Daft, H. B. 1889 (Notts Co)	5
Daley, A. M. 1992 (Aston Villa)	7
Danks, T. 1885 (Nottingham F)	1
Davenport, P. 1985 (Nottingham F)	1
Davenport, J. K. 1885 (Bolton W)	2
Davies, K. C. 2011 (Bolton W)	1
Davis, G. 1904 (Derby Co)	2
Davis, H. 1903 (Sheffield W)	3
Davison, J. E. 1922 (Sheffield W)	1
Dawson, J. 1922 (Burnley)	2
Dawson, M. R. 2011 (Tottenham H)	4
Day, S. H. 1906 (Old Malvernians)	3
Dean, W. R. 1927 (Everton)	16
Deane, B. C. 1991 (Sheffield U)	3
Deeley, N. V. 1959 (Wolverhampton W)	2
Defoe, J. C. 2004 (Tottenham H, Portsmouth, Tottenham H)	55
Delph, F. 2015 (Aston Villa, Manchester C)	**9**
Devey, J. H. G. 1892 (Aston Villa)	2
Devonshire, A. 1980 (West Ham U)	8
Dewhurst, F. 1886 (Preston NE)	9
Dewhurst, G. P. 1895 (Liverpool Ramblers)	1
Dickinson, J. W. 1949 (Portsmouth)	48
Dier, E. J. E. 2016 (Tottenham H)	**11**
Dimmock, J. H. 1921 (Tottenham H)	3
Ditchburn, E. G. 1949 (Tottenham H)	6
Dix, R. W. 1939 (Derby Co)	1
Dixon, J. A. 1885 (Notts Co)	1
Dixon, K. M. 1985 (Chelsea)	8
Dixon, L. M. 1990 (Arsenal)	22
Dobson, A. T. C. 1882 (Notts Co)	4
Dobson, C. F. 1886 (Notts Co)	1
Dobson, J. M. 1974 (Burnley, Everton)	5
Doggart, A. G. 1924 (Corinthians)	1
Dorigo, A. R. 1990 (Chelsea, Leeds U)	15
Dorrell, A. R. 1925 (Aston Villa)	4
Douglas, B. 1958 (Blackburn R)	36
Downing, S. 2005 (Middlesbrough, Aston Villa, Liverpool, West Ham U)	35
Downs, R. W. 1921 (Everton)	1
Doyle, M. 1976 (Manchester C)	5
Drake, E. J. 1935 (Arsenal)	5
Drinkwater, D. N. 2016 (Leicester C)	**3**
Dublin, D. 1998 (Coventry C, Aston Villa)	4
Ducat, A. 1910 (Woolwich Arsenal, Aston Villa)	6
Dunn, A. T. B. 1883 (Cambridge University, Old Etonians)	4
Dunn, D. J. I. 2003 (Blackburn R)	1
Duxbury, M. 1984 (Manchester U)	10
Dyer, K. C. 2000 (Newcastle U, West Ham U)	33
Earle, S. G. J. 1924 (Clapton, West Ham U)	2
Eastham, G. 1963 (Arsenal)	19
Eastham, G. R. 1935 (Bolton W)	1
Eckersley, W. 1950 (Blackburn R)	17
Edwards, D. 1955 (Manchester U)	18
Edwards, J. H. 1874 (Shropshire Wanderers)	1
Edwards, W. 1926 (Leeds U)	16
Ehiogu, U. 1996 (Aston Villa, Middlesbrough)	4
Ellerington, W. 1949 (Southampton)	2
Elliott, G. W. 1913 (Middlesbrough)	3
Elliott, W. H. 1952 (Burnley)	5
Evans, R. E. 1911 (Sheffield U)	4
Ewer, F. H. 1924 (Casuals)	2
Fairclough, P. 1878 (Old Foresters)	1
Fairhurst, D. 1934 (Newcastle U)	1
Fantham, J. 1962 (Sheffield W)	1
Fashanu, J. 1989 (Wimbledon)	2
Felton, W. 1925 (Sheffield W)	1
Fenton, M. 1938 (Middlesbrough)	1
Fenwick, T. W. 1984 (QPR, Tottenham H)	20
Ferdinand, L. 1993 (QPR, Newcastle U, Tottenham H)	17
Ferdinand, R. G. 1998 (West Ham U, Leeds U, Manchester U)	81
Field, E. 1876 (Clapham R)	2
Finney, T. 1947 (Preston NE)	76
Flanagan, J. P. 2014 (Liverpool)	1
Fleming, H. J. 1909 (Swindon T)	11
Fletcher, A. 1889 (Wolverhampton W)	2
Flowers, R. 1955 (Wolverhampton W)	49
Flowers, T. D. 1993 (Southampton, Blackburn R)	11
Forman, Frank 1898 (Nottingham F)	9
Forman, F. R. 1899 (Nottingham F)	3
Forrest, J. H. 1884 (Blackburn R)	11
Forster, F. G. 2013 (Celtic, Southampton)	**6**
Fort, J. 1921 (Millwall)	1
Foster, B. 2007 (Manchester U, Birmingham C, WBA)	8
Foster, R. E. 1900 (Oxford University, Corinthians)	5
Foster, S. 1982 (Brighton & HA)	3
Foulke, W. J. 1897 (Sheffield U)	1
Foulkes, W. A. 1955 (Manchester U)	1
Fowler, R. B. 1996 (Liverpool, Leeds U)	26
Fox, F. S. 1925 (Millwall)	1
Francis, G. C. J. 1975 (QPR)	12
Francis, T. 1977 (Birmingham C, Nottingham F, Manchester C, Sampdoria)	52
Franklin, C. F. 1947 (Stoke C)	27
Freeman, B. C. 1909 (Everton, Burnley)	5
Froggatt, J. 1950 (Portsmouth)	13
Froggatt, R. 1953 (Sheffield W)	4
Fry, C. B. 1901 (Corinthians)	1
Furness, W. I. 1933 (Leeds U)	1
Galley, T. 1937 (Wolverhampton W)	2
Gardner, A. 2004 (Tottenham H)	1
Gardner, T. 1934 (Aston Villa)	2
Garfield, B. 1898 (WBA)	1
Garraty, W. 1903 (Aston Villa)	1
Garrett, T. 1952 (Blackpool)	3
Gascoigne, P. J. 1989 (Tottenham H, Lazio, Rangers, Middlesbrough)	57
Gates, E. 1981 (Ipswich T)	2
Gay, L. H. 1893 (Cambridge University, Old Brightonians)	3
Geary, F. 1890 (Everton)	2
Geaves, R. L. 1875 (Clapham R)	1
Gee, C. W. 1932 (Everton)	3
Geldard, A. 1933 (Everton)	4
George, C. 1977 (Derby Co)	1
George, W. 1902 (Aston Villa)	3
Gerrard, S. G. 2000 (Liverpool)	114
Gibbins, W. V. T. 1924 (Clapton)	2
Gibbs, K. J. R. 2011 (Arsenal)	**10**
Gidman, J. 1977 (Aston Villa)	1
Gillard, I. T. 1975 (QPR)	3
Gilliat, W. E. 1893 (Old Carthusians)	1
Goddard, P. 1982 (West Ham U)	1
Goodall, F. R. 1926 (Huddersfield T)	25
Goodall, J. 1888 (Preston NE, Derby Co)	14
Goodhart, H. C. 1883 (Old Etonians)	3
Goodwyn, A. G. 1873 (Royal Engineers)	1
Goodyer, A. C. 1879 (Nottingham F)	1
Gosling, R. C. 1892 (Old Etonians)	5
Gosnell, A. A. 1906 (Newcastle U)	1
Gough, H. C. 1921 (Sheffield U)	1
Goulden, L. A. 1937 (West Ham U)	14
Graham, L. 1925 (Millwall)	2
Graham, T. 1931 (Nottingham F)	2
Grainger, C. 1956 (Sheffield U, Sunderland)	7
Gray, A. A. 1992 (Crystal Palace)	1
Gray, M. 1999 (Sunderland)	3

Greaves, J. 1959 (Chelsea, Tottenham H) 57
Green, F. T. 1876 (Wanderers) 1
Green, G. H. 1925 (Sheffield U) 8
Green, R. P. 2005 (Norwich C, West Ham U) 12
Greenhalgh, E. H. 1872 (Notts Co) 2
Greenhoff, B. 1976 (Manchester U, Leeds U) 18
Greenwood, D. H. 1882 (Blackburn R) 2
Gregory, J. 1983 (QPR) 6
Grimsdell, A. 1920 (Tottenham H) 6
Grosvenor, A. T. 1934 (Birmingham) 3
Gunn, W. 1884 (Notts Co) 2
Guppy, S. 2000 (Leicester C) 1
Gurney, R. 1935 (Sunderland) 1

Hacking, J. 1929 (Oldham Ath) 3
Hadley, H. 1903 (WBA) 1
Hagan, J. 1949 (Sheffield U) 1
Haines, J. T. W. 1949 (WBA) 1
Hall, A. E. 1910 (Aston Villa) 1
Hall, G. W. 1934 (Tottenham H) 10
Hall, J. 1956 (Birmingham C) 17
Halse, H. J. 1909 (Manchester U) 1
Hammond, H. E. D. 1889 (Oxford University) 1
Hampson, J. 1931 (Blackpool) 3
Hampton, H. 1913 (Aston Villa) 4
Hancocks, J. 1949 (Wolverhampton W) 3
Hapgood, E. 1933 (Arsenal) 30
Hardinge, H. T. W. 1910 (Sheffield U) 1
Hardman, H. P. 1905 (Everton) 4
Hardwick, G. F. M. 1947 (Middlesbrough) 13
Hardy, H. 1925 (Stockport Co) 1
Hardy, S. 1907 (Liverpool, Aston Villa) 21
Harford, M. G. 1988 (Luton T) 2
Hargreaves, F. W. 1880 (Blackburn R) 3
Hargreaves, J. 1881 (Blackburn R) 2
Hargreaves, O. 2002 (Bayern Munich, Manchester U) 42
Harper, E. C. 1926 (Blackburn R) 1
Harris, G. 1966 (Burnley) 1
Harris, P. P. 1950 (Portsmouth) 2
Harris, S. S. 1904 (Cambridge University, Old Westminsters) 6
Harrison, A. H. 1893 (Old Westminsters) 2
Harrison, G. 1921 (Everton) 2
Harrow, J. H. 1923 (Chelsea) 2
Hart, C. J. J. 2008 (Manchester C) **63**
Hart, E. 1929 (Leeds U) 8
Hartley, F. 1923 (Oxford C) 1
Harvey, A. 1881 (Wednesbury Strollers) 1
Harvey, J. C. 1971 (Everton) 1
Hassall, H. W. 1951 (Huddersfield T, Bolton W) 5
Hateley, M. 1984 (Portsmouth, AC Milan, Monaco, Rangers) 32
Hawkes, R. M. 1907 (Luton T) 5
Haworth, G. 1887 (Accrington) 5
Hawtrey, J. P. 1881 (Old Etonians) 2
Haygarth, E. B. 1875 (Swifts) 1
Haynes, J. N. 1955 (Fulham) 56
Healless, H. 1925 (Blackburn R) 2
Heaton, T. 2016 (Burnley) **1**
Hector, K. J. 1974 (Derby Co) 2
Hedley, G. A. 1901 (Sheffield U) 1
Hegan, K. E. 1923 (Corinthians) 4
Heilawell, M. S. 1963 (Birmingham C) 2
Henderson, J. B. 2011 (Sunderland, Liverpool) **27**
Hendrie, L. A. 1999 (Aston Villa) 1
Henfrey, A. G. 1891 (Cambridge University, Corinthians) 5
Henry, R. P. 1963 (Tottenham H) 1
Heron, F. 1876 (Wanderers) 1
Heron, G. H. H. 1873 (Uxbridge, Wanderers) 5
Heskey, E. W. I. 1999 (Leicester C, Liverpool, Birmingham C, Wigan Ath, Aston Villa) 62
Hibbert, W. 1910 (Bury) 1
Hibbs, H. E. 1930 (Birmingham) 25
Hill, F. 1963 (Bolton W) 2
Hill, G. A. 1976 (Manchester U) 6
Hill, J. H. 1925 (Burnley, Newcastle U) 11
Hill, R. 1983 (Luton T) 3
Hill, R. H. 1926 (Millwall) 1
Hillman, J. 1899 (Burnley) 1
Hills, A. F. 1879 (Old Harrovians) 1
Hilsdon, G. R. 1907 (Chelsea) 8
Hinchcliffe, A. G. 1997 (Everton, Sheffield W) 7
Hine, E. W. 1929 (Leicester C) 6

Hinton, A. T. 1963 (Wolverhampton W, Nottingham F) 3
Hirst, D. E. 1991 (Sheffield W) 3
Hitchens, G. A. 1961 (Aston Villa, Internazionale) 7
Hobbis, H. H. F. 1936 (Charlton Ath) 2
Hoddle, G. 1980 (Tottenham H, Monaco) 53
Hodge, S. B. 1986 (Aston Villa, Tottenham H, Nottingham F) 24
Hodgetts, D. 1888 (Aston Villa) 6
Hodgkinson, A. 1957 (Sheffield U) 5
Hodgson, G. 1931 (Liverpool) 3
Hodkinson, J. 1913 (Blackburn R) 3
Hogg, W. 1902 (Sunderland) 3
Holdcroft, G. H. 1937 (Preston NE) 2
Holden, A. D. 1959 (Bolton W) 5
Holden, G. H. 1881 (Wednesbury OA) 4
Holden-White, C. 1888 (Corinthians) 2
Holford, T. 1903 (Stoke) 1
Holley, G. H. 1909 (Sunderland) 10
Holliday, E. 1960 (Middlesbrough) 3
Hollins, J. W. 1967 (Chelsea) 1
Holmes, R. 1888 (Preston NE) 7
Holt, J. 1890 (Everton, Reading) 10
Hopkinson, E. 1958 (Bolton W) 14
Hossack, A. H. 1892 (Corinthians) 2
Houghton, W. E. 1931 (Aston Villa) 7
Houlker, A. E. 1902 (Blackburn R, Portsmouth, Southampton) 5
Howarth, R. H. 1887 (Preston NE, Everton) 5
Howe, D. 1958 (WBA) 23
Howe, J. R. 1948 (Derby Co) 3
Howell, L. S. 1873 (Wanderers) 1
Howell, R. 1895 (Sheffield U, Liverpool) 2
Howey, S. N. 1995 (Newcastle U) 4
Huddlestone, T. A. 2010 (Tottenham H) 4
Hudson, A. A. 1975 (Stoke C) 2
Hudson, J. 1883 (Sheffield) 1
Hudspeth, F. C. 1926 (Newcastle U) 1
Hufton, A. E. 1924 (West Ham U) 6
Hughes, E. W. 1970 (Liverpool, Wolverhampton W) 62
Hughes, L. 1950 (Liverpool) 3
Hulme, J. H. A. 1927 (Arsenal) 9
Humphreys, P. 1903 (Notts Co) 1
Hunt, G. S. 1933 (Tottenham H) 3
Hunt, Rev. K. R. G. 1911 (Leyton) 2
Hunt, R. 1962 (Liverpool) 34
Hunt, S. 1984 (WBA) 2
Hunter, J. 1878 (Sheffield Heeley) 7
Hunter, N. 1966 (Leeds U) 28
Hurst, G. C. 1966 (West Ham U) 49

Ince, P. E. C. 1993 (Manchester U, Internazionale, Liverpool, Middlesbrough) 53
Ings, D. 2016 (Liverpool) **1**
Iremonger, J. 1901 (Nottingham F) 2

Jack, D. N. B. 1924 (Bolton W, Arsenal) 9
Jackson, E. 1891 (Oxford University) 1
Jagielka, P. N. 2008 (Everton) **39**
James, D. B. 1997 (Liverpool, Aston Villa, West Ham U, Manchester C, Portsmouth) 53
Jarrett, B. G. 1876 (Cambridge University) 3
Jarvis, M. T. 2011 (Wolverhampton W) 1
Jefferis, F. 1912 (Everton) 2
Jeffers, F. 2003 (Arsenal) 1
Jenas, J. A. 2003 (Newcastle U, Tottenham H) 21
Jenkinson, C. D. 2013 (Arsenal) 1
Jezzard, B. A. G. 1954 (Fulham) 2
Johnson, A. 2005 (Crystal Palace, Everton) 8
Johnson, A. 2010 (Manchester C) 12
Johnson, D. E. 1975 (Ipswich T, Liverpool) 8
Johnson, E. 1880 (Saltley College, Stoke) 2
Johnson, G. M. C. 2004 (Chelsea, Portsmouth, Liverpool) 54
Johnson, J. A. 1937 (Stoke C) 5
Johnson, S. A. M. 2001 (Derby Co) 1
Johnson, T. C. F. 1926 (Manchester C, Everton) 5
Johnson, W. H. 1900 (Sheffield U) 6
Johnston, H. 1947 (Blackpool) 10
Jones, A. 1882 (Walsall Swifts, Great Lever) 3
Jones, H. 1923 (Nottingham F) 1
Jones, H. 1927 (Blackburn R) 6
Jones, M. D. 1965 (Sheffield U, Leeds U) 3
Jones, P. A. 2012 (Manchester U) **20**
Jones, R. 1992 (Liverpool) 8

Moss, F. 1922 (Aston Villa)	5
Moss, F. 1934 (Arsenal)	4
Mosscrop, E. 1914 (Burnley)	2
Mozley, B. 1950 (Derby Co)	3
Mullen, J. 1947 (Wolverhampton W)	12
Mullery, A. P. 1965 (Tottenham H)	35
Murphy, D. B. 2002 (Liverpool)	9
Neal, P. G. 1976 (Liverpool)	50
Needham, E. 1894 (Sheffield U)	16
Neville, G. A. 1995 (Manchester U)	85
Neville, P. J. 1996 (Manchester U, Everton)	59
Newton, K. R. 1966 (Blackburn R, Everton)	27
Nicholls, J. 1954 (WBA)	2
Nicholson, W. E. 1951 (Tottenham H)	1
Nish, D. J. 1973 (Derby Co)	5
Norman, M. 1962 (Tottenham H)	23
Nugent, D. J. 2007 (Preston NE)	1
Nuttall, H. 1928 (Bolton W)	3
Oakley, W. J. 1895 (Oxford University, Corinthians)	16
O'Dowd, J. P. 1932 (Chelsea)	3
O'Grady, M. 1963 (Huddersfield T, Leeds U)	2
Ogilvie, R. A. M. M. 1874 (Clapham R)	1
Oliver, L. F. 1929 (Fulham)	1
Olney, B. A. 1928 (Aston Villa)	2
Osborne, F. R. 1923 (Fulham, Tottenham H)	4
Osborne, R. 1928 (Leicester C)	1
Osgood, P. L. 1970 (Chelsea)	4
Osman, L. 2013 (Everton)	2
Osman, R. 1980 (Ipswich T)	11
Ottaway, C. J. 1872 (Oxford University)	2
Owen, J. R. B. 1874 (Sheffield)	1
Owen, M. J. 1998 (Liverpool, Real Madrid, Newcastle U)	89
Owen, S. W. 1954 (Luton T)	3
Oxlade-Chamberlain, A. M. D. 2012 (Arsenal)	**24**
Page, L. A. 1927 (Burnley)	7
Paine, T. L. 1963 (Southampton)	19
Pallister, G. A. 1988 (Middlesbrough, Manchester U)	22
Palmer, C. L. 1992 (Sheffield W)	18
Pantling, H. H. 1924 (Sheffield U)	1
Paravicini, P. J. de 1883 (Cambridge University)	3
Parker, P. A. 1989 (QPR, Manchester U)	19
Parker, S. M. 2004 (Charlton Ath, Chelsea, Newcastle U, West Ham U, Tottenham H)	18
Parker, T. R. 1925 (Southampton)	1
Parkes, P. B. 1974 (QPR)	1
Parkinson, J. 1910 (Liverpool)	2
Parlour, R. 1999 (Arsenal)	10
Parr, P. C. 1882 (Oxford University)	1
Parry, E. H. 1879 (Old Carthusians)	3
Parry, R. A. 1960 (Bolton W)	2
Patchitt, B. C. A. 1923 (Corinthians)	2
Pawson, F. W. 1883 (Cambridge University, Swifts)	2
Payne, J. 1937 (Luton T)	1
Peacock, A. 1962 (Middlesbrough, Leeds U)	6
Peacock, J. 1929 (Middlesbrough)	3
Pearce, S. 1987 (Nottingham F, West Ham U)	78
Pearson, H. F. 1932 (WBA)	1
Pearson, J. H. 1892 (Crewe Alex)	1
Pearson, J. S. 1976 (Manchester U)	15
Pearson, S. C. 1948 (Manchester U)	8
Pease, W. H. 1927 (Middlesbrough)	1
Pegg, D. 1957 (Manchester U)	1
Pejic, M. 1974 (Stoke C)	4
Pelly, F. R. 1893 (Old Foresters)	3
Pennington, J. 1907 (WBA)	25
Pentland, F. B. 1909 (Middlesbrough)	5
Perry, C. 1890 (WBA)	3
Perry, T. 1898 (WBA)	1
Perry, W. 1956 (Blackpool)	3
Perryman, S. 1982 (Tottenham H)	1
Peters, M. 1966 (West Ham U, Tottenham H)	67
Phelan, M. C. 1990 (Manchester U)	1
Phillips, L. 1999 (Sunderland)	8
Phillips, L. H. 1952 (Portsmouth)	3
Pickering, F. 1964 (Everton)	3
Pickering, J. 1933 (Sheffield U)	1
Pickering, N. 1983 (Sunderland)	1
Pike, T. M. 1886 (Cambridge University)	1
Pilkington, B. 1955 (Burnley)	1
Plant, J. 1900 (Bury)	1
Platt, D. 1990 (Aston Villa, Bari, Juventus, Sampdoria, Arsenal)	62
Plum, S. L. 1923 (Charlton Ath)	1
Pointer, R. 1962 (Burnley)	3
Porteous, T. S. 1891 (Sunderland)	1
Powell, C. G. 2001 (Charlton Ath)	5
Priest, A. E. 1900 (Sheffield U)	1
Prinsep, J. F. M. 1879 (Clapham R)	1
Puddefoot, S. C. 1926 (Blackburn R)	2
Pye, J. 1950 (Wolverhampton W)	1
Pym, R. H. 1925 (Bolton W)	3
Quantrill, A. 1920 (Derby Co)	4
Quixall, A. 1954 (Sheffield W)	5
Radford, J. 1969 (Arsenal)	2
Raikes, G. B. 1895 (Oxford University)	4
Ramsey, A. E. 1949 (Southampton, Tottenham H)	32
Rashford, M. 2016 (Manchester U)	**3**
Rawlings, A. 1921 (Preston NE)	1
Rawlings, W. E. 1922 (Southampton)	2
Rawlinson, J. F. P. 1882 (Cambridge University)	1
Rawson, H. E. 1875 (Royal Engineers)	1
Rawson, W. S. 1875 (Oxford University)	2
Read, A. 1921 (Tufnell Park)	1
Reader, J. 1894 (WBA)	1
Reaney, P. 1969 (Leeds U)	3
Redknapp, J. F. 1996 (Liverpool)	17
Reeves, K. P. 1980 (Norwich C, Manchester C)	2
Regis, C. 1982 (WBA, Coventry C)	5
Reid, P. 1985 (Everton)	13
Revie, D. G. 1955 (Manchester C)	6
Reynolds, J. 1892 (WBA, Aston Villa)	8
Richards, C. H. 1898 (Nottingham F)	1
Richards, G. H. 1909 (Derby Co)	1
Richards, J. P. 1973 (Wolverhampton W)	1
Richards, M. 2007 (Manchester C)	13
Richardson, J. R. 1933 (Newcastle U)	2
Richardson, K. 1994 (Aston Villa)	1
Richardson, K. E. 2005 (Manchester U)	8
Richardson, W. G. 1935 (WBA)	1
Rickaby, S. 1954 (WBA)	1
Ricketts, M. B. 2002 (Bolton W)	1
Rigby, A. 1927 (Blackburn R)	5
Rimmer, E. J. 1930 (Sheffield W)	4
Rimmer, J. J. 1976 (Arsenal)	1
Ripley, S. E. 1994 (Blackburn R)	2
Rix, G. 1981 (Arsenal)	17
Robb, G. 1954 (Tottenham H)	1
Roberts, C. 1905 (Manchester U)	3
Roberts, F. 1925 (Manchester C)	4
Roberts, G. 1983 (Tottenham H)	6
Roberts, H. 1931 (Arsenal)	1
Roberts, H. 1931 (Millwall)	1
Roberts, R. 1887 (WBA)	3
Roberts, W. T. 1924 (Preston NE)	2
Robinson, J. 1937 (Sheffield W)	4
Robinson, J. W. 1897 (Derby Co, New Brighton Tower, Southampton)	11
Robinson, P. W. 2003 (Leeds U, Tottenham H, Blackburn R)	41
Robson, B. 1980 (WBA, Manchester U)	90
Robson, R. 1958 (WBA)	20
Rocastle, D. 1989 (Arsenal)	14
Rodriguez, J. E. 2013 (Southampton)	1
Rodwell, J. 2012 (Everton)	3
Rooney, W. M. 2003 (Everton, Manchester U)	**115**
Rose, D. L. 2016 (Tottenham H)	**7**
Rose, W. C. 1884 (Swifts, Preston NE, Wolverhampton W)	5
Rostron, T. 1881 (Darwen)	2
Rowe, A. 1934 (Tottenham H)	1
Rowley, J. F. 1949 (Manchester U)	6
Rowley, W. 1889 (Stoke)	2
Royle, J. 1971 (Everton, Manchester C)	6
Ruddlesdin, H. 1904 (Sheffield W)	3
Ruddock, N. 1995 (Liverpool)	1
Ruddy, J. T. G. 2013 (Norwich C)	1
Ruffell, J. W. 1926 (West Ham U)	6
Russell, B. B. 1883 (Royal Engineers)	1
Rutherford, J. 1904 (Newcastle U)	11
Sadler, D. 1968 (Manchester U)	4
Sagar, C. 1900 (Bury)	2

Sagar, E. 1936 (Everton)	4
Salako, J. A. 1991 (Crystal Palace)	5
Sandford, E. A. 1933 (WBA)	1
Sandilands, R. R. 1892 (Old Westminsters)	5
Sands, J. 1880 (Nottingham F)	1
Sansom, K. G. 1979 (Crystal Palace, Arsenal)	86
Saunders, F. E. 1888 (Swifts)	1
Savage, A. H. 1876 (Crystal Palace)	1
Sayer, J. 1887 (Stoke)	1
Scales, J. R. 1995 (Liverpool)	3
Scattergood, E. 1913 (Derby Co)	1
Schofield, J. 1892 (Stoke)	3
Scholes, P. 1997 (Manchester U)	66
Scott, L. 1947 (Arsenal)	17
Scott, W. R. 1937 (Brentford)	1
Seaman, D. A. 1989 (QPR, Arsenal)	75
Seddon, J. 1923 (Bolton W)	6
Seed, J. M. 1921 (Tottenham H)	5
Settle, J. 1899 (Bury, Everton)	6
Sewell, J. 1952 (Sheffield W)	6
Sewell, W. R. 1924 (Blackburn R)	1
Shackleton, L. F. 1949 (Sunderland)	5
Sharp, J. 1903 (Everton)	2
Sharpe, L. S. 1991 (Manchester U)	8
Shaw, G. E. 1932 (WBA)	1
Shaw, G. L. 1959 (Sheffield U)	5
Shaw, L. P. H. 2014 (Southampton, Manchester U)	**6**
Shawcross, R. J. 2013 (Stoke C)	1
Shea, D. 1914 (Blackburn R)	2
Shearer, A. 1992 (Southampton, Blackburn R, Newcastle U)	63
Shellito, K. J. 1963 (Chelsea)	1
Shelton A. 1889 (Notts Co)	6
Shelton, C. 1888 (Notts Rangers)	1
Shelvey, J. 2013 (Liverpool, Swansea C)	**6**
Shepherd, A. 1906 (Bolton W, Newcastle U)	2
Sheringham, E. P. 1993 (Tottenham H, Manchester U, Tottenham H)	51
Sherwood, T. A. 1999 (Tottenham H)	3
Shilton, P. L. 1971 (Leicester C, Stoke C, Nottingham F, Southampton, Derby Co)	125
Shimwell, E. 1949 (Blackpool)	1
Shorey, N. 2007 (Reading)	2
Shutt, G. 1886 (Stoke)	1
Silcock, J. 1921 (Manchester U)	3
Sillett, R. P. 1955 (Chelsea)	3
Simms, E. 1922 (Luton T)	1
Simpson, J. 1911 (Blackburn R)	8
Sinclair, T. 2002 (West Ham U, Manchester C)	12
Sinton, A. 1992 (QPR, Sheffield W)	12
Slater, W. J. 1955 (Wolverhampton W)	12
Smalley, T. 1937 (Wolverhampton W)	1
Smalling, C. L. 2012 (Manchester U)	**29**
Smart, T. 1921 (Aston Villa)	5
Smith, A. 1891 (Nottingham F)	3
Smith, A. 2001 (Leeds U, Manchester U, Newcastle U)	19
Smith, A. K. 1872 (Oxford University)	1
Smith, A. M. 1989 (Arsenal)	13
Smith, B. 1921 (Tottenham H)	2
Smith, C. E. 1876 (Crystal Palace)	1
Smith, G. O. 1893 (Oxford University, Old Carthusians, Corinthians)	20
Smith, H. 1905 (Reading)	4
Smith, J. 1920 (WBA)	2
Smith, Joe 1913 (Bolton W)	5
Smith, J. C. R. 1939 (Millwall)	2
Smith, J. W. 1932 (Portsmouth)	3
Smith, Leslie 1939 (Brentford)	1
Smith, Lionel 1951 (Arsenal)	6
Smith, R. A. 1961 (Tottenham H)	15
Smith, S. 1895 (Aston Villa)	1
Smith, S. C. 1936 (Leicester C)	1
Smith, T. 1960 (Birmingham C)	2
Smith, T. 1971 (Liverpool)	1
Smith, W. H. 1922 (Huddersfield T)	3
Sorby, T. H. 1879 (Thursday Wanderers, Sheffield)	1
Southgate, G. 1996 (Aston Villa, Middlesbrough)	57
Southworth, J. 1889 (Blackburn R)	3
Sparks, F. J. 1879 (Herts Rangers, Clapham R)	3
Spence, J. W. 1926 (Manchester U)	2
Spence, R. 1936 (Chelsea)	2
Spencer, C. W. 1924 (Newcastle U)	2
Spencer, H. 1897 (Aston Villa)	6
Spiksley, F. 1893 (Sheffield W)	7

Spilsbury, B. W. 1885 (Cambridge University)	3
Spink, N. 1983 (Aston Villa)	1
Spouncer, W. A. 1900 (Nottingham F)	1
Springett, R. D. G. 1960 (Sheffield W)	33
Sproston, B. 1937 (Leeds U, Tottenham H, Manchester C)	11
Squire, R. T. 1886 (Cambridge University)	3
Stanbrough, M. H. 1895 (Old Carthusians)	1
Staniforth, R. 1954 (Huddersfield T)	8
Starling, R. W. 1933 (Sheffield W, Aston Villa)	2
Statham, D. J. 1983 (WBA)	3
Steele, F. C. 1937 (Stoke C)	6
Stein, B. 1984 (Luton T)	1
Stephenson, C. 1924 (Huddersfield T)	1
Stephenson, G. T. 1928 (Derby Co, Sheffield W)	3
Stephenson, J. E. 1938 (Leeds U)	2
Stepney, A. C. 1968 (Manchester U)	1
Sterland, M. 1989 (Sheffield W)	1
Sterling, R. S. 2013 (Liverpool, Manchester C)	**26**
Steven, T. M. 1985 (Everton, Rangers, Marseille)	36
Stevens, G. A. 1985 (Tottenham H)	7
Stevens, M. G. 1985 (Everton, Rangers)	46
Stewart, J. 1907 (Sheffield W, Newcastle U)	3
Stewart, P. A. 1992 (Tottenham H)	3
Stiles, N. P. 1965 (Manchester U)	28
Stoker, J. 1933 (Birmingham)	3
Stone, S. B. 1996 (Nottingham F)	9
Stones, J. 2014 (Everton)	**10**
Storer, H. 1924 (Derby Co)	2
Storey, P. E. 1971 (Arsenal)	19
Storey-Moore, I. 1970 (Nottingham F)	1
Strange, A. H. 1930 (Sheffield W)	20
Stratford, A. H. 1874 (Wanderers)	1
Streten, B. 1950 (Luton T)	1
Sturgess, A. 1911 (Sheffield U)	2
Sturridge, D. A. 2012 (Chelsea, Liverpool)	**21**
Summerbee, M. G. 1968 (Manchester C)	8
Sunderland, A. 1980 (Arsenal)	1
Sutcliffe, J. W. 1893 (Bolton W, Millwall)	5
Sutton, C. R. 1998 (Blackburn R)	1
Swan, P. 1960 (Sheffield W)	19
Swepstone, H. A. 1880 (Pilgrims)	6
Swift, F. V. 1947 (Manchester C)	19
Tait, G. 1881 (Birmingham Excelsior)	1
Talbot, B. 1977 (Ipswich T, Arsenal)	6
Tambling, R. V. 1963 (Chelsea)	3
Tate, J. T. 1931 (Aston Villa)	3
Taylor, E. 1954 (Blackpool)	1
Taylor, E. H. 1923 (Huddersfield T)	8
Taylor, J. G. 1951 (Fulham)	2
Taylor, P. H. 1948 (Liverpool)	3
Taylor, P. J. 1976 (Crystal Palace)	4
Taylor, T. 1953 (Manchester U)	19
Temple, D. W. 1965 (Everton)	1
Terry, J. G. 2003 (Chelsea)	78
Thickett, H. 1899 (Sheffield U)	2
Thomas, D. 1975 (QPR)	8
Thomas, D. 1983 (Coventry C)	2
Thomas, G. R. 1991 (Crystal Palace)	9
Thomas, M. L. 1989 (Arsenal)	2
Thompson, A. 2004 (Celtic)	1
Thompson, P. 1964 (Liverpool)	16
Thompson, P. B. 1976 (Liverpool)	42
Thompson, T. 1952 (Aston Villa, Preston NE)	2
Thomson, R. A. 1964 (Wolverhampton W)	8
Thornewell, G. 1923 (Derby Co)	4
Thornley, I. 1907 (Manchester C)	1
Tilson, S. F. 1934 (Manchester C)	4
Titmuss, F. 1922 (Southampton)	2
Todd, C. 1972 (Derby Co)	27
Toone, G. 1892 (Notts Co)	2
Topham, A. G. 1894 (Casuals)	1
Topham, R. 1893 (Wolverhampton W, Casuals)	2
Towers, M. A. 1976 (Sunderland)	3
Townley, W. J. 1889 (Blackburn R)	2
Townrow, J. E. 1925 (Clapton Orient)	2
Townsend, A. D. 2013 (Tottenham H, Newcastle U)	**11**
Tremelling, D. R. 1928 (Birmingham)	1
Tresadern, J. 1923 (West Ham U)	2
Tueart, D. 1975 (Manchester C)	6
Tunstall, F. E. 1923 (Sheffield U)	7
Turnbull, R. J. 1920 (Bradford)	1
Turner, A. 1900 (Southampton)	2

NORTHERN IRELAND

Addis, D. J. 1922 (Cliftonville) 1
Aherne, T. 1947 (Belfast Celtic, Luton T) 4
Alexander, T. E. 1895 (Cliftonville) 1
Allan, C. 1936 (Cliftonville) 1
Allen, J. 1887 (Limavady) 1
Anderson, J. 1925 (Distillery) 1
Anderson, T. 1973 (Manchester U, Swindon T,
  Peterborough U) 22
Anderson, W. 1898 (Linfield, Cliftonville) 4
Andrews, W. 1908 (Glentoran, Grimsby T) 3
Armstrong, G. J. 1977 (Tottenham H, Watford,
  Real Mallorca, WBA, Chesterfield) 63

**Baird, C. P. 2003 (Southampton, Fulham, Reading,
  Burnley, WBA, Derby Co) 79**
Baird, D. 1896 (Distillery) 3
Baird, H. C. 1939 (Huddersfield T) 1
Balfe, J. 1909 (Shelbourne) 2
Bambrick, J. 1929 (Linfield, Chelsea) 11
Banks, S. J. 1937 (Cliftonville) 1
Barr, H. H. 1962 (Linfield, Coventry C) 3
Barron, J. H. 1894 (Cliftonville) 7
Barry, J. 1888 (Cliftonville) 3
Barry, J. 1900 (Bohemians) 1
Barton, A. J. 2011 (Preston NE) 1
Baxter, R. A. 1887 (Distillery) 1
Baxter, S. N. 1887 (Cliftonville) 1
Bennett, L. V. 1889 (Dublin University) 1
Best, G. 1964 (Manchester U, Fulham) 37
Bingham, W. L. 1951 (Sunderland, Luton T, Everton,
  Port Vale) 56
Black, K. T. 1988 (Luton T, Nottingham F) 30
Black, T. 1901 (Glentoran) 1
Blair, H. 1928 (Portadown, Swansea T) 4
Blair, J. 1907 (Cliftonville) 5
Blair, R. V. 1975 (Oldham Ath) 5
Blanchflower, J. 1954 (Manchester U) 12
Blanchflower, R. D. 1950 (Barnsley, Aston Villa,
  Tottenham H) 56
Blayney, A. 2006 (Doncaster R, Linfield) 5
Bookman, L. J. O. 1914 (Bradford C, Luton T) 4
Bothwell, A. W. 1926 (Ards) 5
Bowler, G. C. 1950 (Hull C) 3
Boyce, L. 2011 (Werder Bremen, Ross Co) 7
Boyle, P. 1901 (Sheffield U) 5
Braithwaite, R. M. 1962 (Linfield, Middlesbrough) 10
Braniff, K. R. 2010 (Portadown) 2
Breen, T. 1935 (Belfast Celtic, Manchester U) 9
Brennan, B. 1912 (Bohemians) 1
Brennan, R. A. 1949 (Luton T, Birmingham C, Fulham) 5
Briggs, W. R. 1962 (Manchester U, Swansea T) 2
Brisby, D. 1891 (Distillery) 1
Brolly, T. H. 1937 (Millwall) 4
Brookes, E. A. 1920 (Shelbourne) 1
Brotherston, N. 1980 (Blackburn R) 27
Brown, J. 1921 (Glenavon, Tranmere R) 3
Brown, J. 1935 (Wolverhampton W, Coventry C,
  Birmingham C) 10
Brown, N. M. 1887 (Limavady) 1
Brown, W. G. 1926 (Glenavon) 1
Browne, F. 1887 (Cliftonville) 5
Browne, R. J. 1936 (Leeds U) 6
Bruce, A. 1925 (Belfast Celtic) 1
Bruce, A. S. 2013 (Hull C) 2
Bruce, W. 1961 (Glentoran) 2
Brunt, C. 2005 (Sheffield W, WBA) 54
Bryan, M. A. 2010 (Watford) 2
Buckle, H. R. 1903 (Cliftonville, Sunderland, Bristol R) 3
Buckle, J. 1882 (Cliftonville) 1
Burnett, J. 1894 (Distillery, Glentoran) 5
Burnison, J. 1901 (Distillery) 2
Burnison, S. 1908 (Distillery, Bradford, Distillery) 8
Burns, J. 1923 (Glenavon) 1
Burns, W. 1925 (Glentoran) 1
Butler, M. P. 1939 (Blackpool) 1

Camp, L. M. J. 2011 (Nottingham F) 9
Campbell, A. C. 1963 (Crusaders) 2
Campbell, D. A. 1986 (Nottingham F, Charlton Ath) 10
Campbell, James 1897 (Cliftonville) 14
Campbell, John 1896 (Cliftonville) 1
Campbell, J. P. 1951 (Fulham) 2

Campbell, R. M. 1982 (Bradford C) 2
Campbell, W. G. 1968 (Dundee) 6
Capaldi, A. C. 2004 (Plymouth Arg, Cardiff C) 22
Carey, J. J. 1947 (Manchester U) 7
Carroll, E. 1925 (Glenavon) 1
**Carroll, R. E. 1997 (Wigan Ath, Manchester U,
  West Ham U, Olympiacos, Notts Co) 44**
Carson, J. G. 2011 (Ipswich T) 4
Carson, S. 2009 (Coleraine) 1
Casement, C. 2009 (Ipswich T) 1
Casey, T. 1955 (Newcastle U, Portsmouth) 12
Caskey, W. 1979 (Derby Co, Tulsa Roughnecks) 8
Cassidy, T. 1971 (Newcastle U, Burnley) 24
Cathcart, C. G. 2011 (Blackpool, Watford) 32
Caughey, M. 1986 (Linfield) 2
Chambers, R. J. 1921 (Distillery, Bury, Nottingham F) 12
Chatton, H. A. 1925 (Partick Thistle) 3
Christian, J. 1889 (Linfield) 1
Clarke, C. J. 1986 (Bournemouth, Southampton, QPR,
  Portsmouth) 38
Clarke, R. 1901 (Belfast Celtic) 2
Cleary, J. 1982 (Glentoran) 5
Clements, D. 1965 (Coventry C, Sheffield W, Everton,
  New York Cosmos) 48
Clingan, S. G. 2006 (Nottingham F, Norwich C,
  Coventry C, Kilmarnock) 39
Clugston, J. 1888 (Cliftonville) 14
Clyde, M. G. 2005 (Wolverhampton W) 3
Coates, C. 2009 (Crusaders) 6
Cochrane, D. 1939 (Leeds U) 12
Cochrane, G. 1903 (Cliftonville) 1
Cochrane, G. T. 1976 (Coleraine, Burnley,
  Middlesbrough, Gillingham) 26
Cochrane, M. 1898 (Distillery, Leicester Fosse) 8
Collins, F. 1922 (Celtic) 1
Collins, R. 1922 (Cliftonville) 1
Condy, J. 1882 (Distillery) 3
Connell, T. E. 1978 (Coleraine) 1
Connor, J. 1901 (Glentoran, Belfast Celtic) 13
Connor, M. J. 1903 (Brentford, Fulham) 3
Cook, W. 1933 (Celtic, Everton) 15
Cooke, S. 1889 (Belfast YMCA, Cliftonville) 3
Coote, A. 1999 (Norwich C) 6
Coulter, J. 1934 (Belfast Celtic, Everton, Grimsby T,
  Chelmsford C) 11
Cowan, J. 1970 (Newcastle U) 1
Cowan, T. S. 1925 (Queen's Island) 1
Coyle, F. 1956 (Coleraine, Nottingham F) 4
Coyle, L. 1989 (Derry C) 1
Coyle, R. I. 1973 (Sheffield W) 5
Craig, A. B. 1908 (Rangers, Morton) 9
Craig, D. J. 1967 (Newcastle U) 25
Craigan, S. J. 2003 (Partick Thistle, Motherwell) 54
Crawford, A. 1889 (Distillery, Cliftonville) 7
Croft, T. 1922 (Queen's Island) 3
Crone, R. 1889 (Distillery) 4
Crone, W. 1882 (Distillery) 12
Crooks, W. J. 1922 (Manchester U) 1
Crossan, E. 1950 (Blackburn R) 3
Crossan, J. A. 1960 (Sparta-Rotterdam, Sunderland,
  Manchester C, Middlesbrough) 24
Crothers, C. 1907 (Distillery) 1
Cumming, L. 1929 (Huddersfield T, Oldham Ath) 3
Cunningham, W. 1892 (Ulster) 4
Cunningham, W. E. 1951 (St Mirren, Leicester C,
  Dunfermline Ath) 30
Curran, S. 1926 (Belfast Celtic) 4
Curran, J. J. 1922 (Glenavon, Pontypridd, Glenavon) 5
Cush, W. W. 1951 (Glenavon, Leeds U, Portadown) 26

Dallas, S. A, 2011 (Crusaders, Brentford, Leeds U) 17
Dalrymple, J. 1922 (Distillery) 1
Dalton, W. 1888 (YMCA, Linfield) 11
D'Arcy, S. D. 1952 (Chelsea, Brentford) 5
Darling, J. 1897 (Linfield) 22
Davey, H. H. 1926 (Reading, Portsmouth) 5
**Davis, S. 2005 (Aston Villa, Fulham, Rangers,
  Southampton) 87**
Davis, T. L. 1937 (Oldham Ath) 1
Davison, A. J. 1996 (Bolton W, Bradford C, Grimsby T) 3
Davison, J. R. 1882 (Cliftonville) 3
Dennison, R. 1988 (Wolverhampton W) 18

Devine, A. O. 1886 (Limavady)   4
Devine, J. 1990 (Glentoran)   1
Dickson, D. 1970 (Coleraine)   4
Dickson, T. A. 1957 (Linfield)   1
Dickson, W. 1951 (Chelsea, Arsenal)   12
Diffin, W. J. 1931 (Belfast Celtic)   1
Dill, A. H. 1882 (Knock, Down Ath, Cliftonville)   9
Doherty, I. 1901 (Belfast Celtic)   1
Doherty, J. 1928 (Portadown)   1
Doherty, J. 1933 (Cliftonville)   2
Doherty, L. 1985 (Linfield)   2
Doherty, M. 1938 (Derry C)   1
Doherty, P. D. 1935 (Blackpool, Manchester C, Derby
   Co, Huddersfield T, Doncaster R)   16
Doherty, T. E. 2003 (Bristol C)   9
Donaghey, B. 1903 (Belfast Celtic)   1
Donaghy, M. M. 1980 (Luton T, Manchester U, Chelsea) 91
Donnelly, L. 1913 (Distillery)   1
Donnelly, L. F. P. 2014 (Fulham)   1
Donnelly, M. 2009 (Crusaders)   1
Doran, J. F. 1921 (Brighton)   3
Dougan, A. D. 1958 (Portsmouth, Blackburn R,
   Aston Villa, Leicester C, Wolverhampton W)   43
Douglas, J. P. 1947 (Belfast Celtic)   1
Dowd, H. O. 1974 (Glenavon, Sheffield W)   3
Dowie, I. 1990 (Luton T, West Ham U, Southampton,
   C Palace, West Ham U, QPR)   59
Duff, M. J. 2002 (Cheltenham T, Burnley)   24
Duggan, A. D. 1930 (Leeds U)   8
Dunlop, G. 1985 (Linfield)   4
Dunne, J. 1928 (Sheffield U)   7

Eames, W. L. E. 1885 (Dublin University)   3
Eglington, T. J. 1947 (Everton)   6
Elder, A. R. 1960 (Burnley, Stoke C)   40
Elleman, A. R. 1889 (Cliftonville)   2
Elliott, S. 2001 (Motherwell, Hull C)   39
Elwood, J. H. 1929 (Bradford)   2
Emerson, W. 1920 (Glentoran, Burnley)   11
English, S. 1933 (Rangers)   2
Enright, J. 1912 (Leeds C)   1
Evans, C. J. 2009 (Manchester U, Hull C, Blackburn R) 37
Evans, J. G. 2007 (Manchester U, WBA)   53

Falloon, E. 1931 (Aberdeen)   2
Farquharson, T. G. 1923 (Cardiff C)   7
Farrell, P. 1901 (Distillery)   2
Farrell, P. 1938 (Hibernian)   1
Farrell, P. D. 1947 (Everton)   7
Feeney, J. M. 1947 (Linfield, Swansea T)   2
Feeney, W. 1976 (Glentoran)   1
Feeney, W. J. 2002 (Bournemouth, Luton T, Cardiff C,
   Oldham Ath, Plymouth Arg)   46
Ferguson, G. 1999 (Linfield)   5
Ferguson, S. K. 2009 (Newcastle U, Millwall)   26
Ferguson, W. 1966 (Linfield)   1
Ferris, J. 1920 (Belfast Celtic, Chelsea, Belfast Celtic)   6
Ferris, R. O. 1950 (Birmingham C)   3
Fettis, A. W. 1992 (Hull C, Nottingham F, Blackburn R)
   25
Finney, T. 1975 (Sunderland, Cambridge U)   14
Fitzpatrick, J. C. 1896 (Bohemians)   2
Flack, H. 1929 (Burnley)   1
Fleming, J. G. 1987 (Nottingham F, Manchester C,
   Barnsley)   31
Forbes, G. 1888 (Limavady, Distillery)   3
Forde, J. T. 1959 (Ards)   4
Foreman, T. A. 1899 (Cliftonville)   1
Forsythe, J. 1888 (YMCA)   2
Fox, W. T. 1887 (Ulster)   2
Frame, T. 1925 (Linfield)   1
Fulton, R. P. 1928 (Larne, Belfast Celtic)   21

Gaffikin, G. 1890 (Linfield Ath)   15
Galbraith, A. W. 1890 (Distillery)   1
Gallagher, P. 1920 (Celtic, Falkirk)   11
Gallogly, C. 1951 (Huddersfield T)   2
Gara, A. 1902 (Preston NE)   3
Gardiner, A. 1930 (Cliftonville)   5
Garrett, J. 1925 (Distillery)   1
Garrett, R. 2009 (Linfield)   5
Gaston, R. 1969 (Oxford U)   1
Gaukrodger, G. 1895 (Linfield)   1
Gault, M. 2008 (Linfield)   1

Gaussen, A. D. 1884 (Moyola Park, Magherafelt)   6
Geary, J. 1931 (Glentoran)   2
Gibb, J. T. 1884 (Wellington Park, Cliftonville)   10
Gibb, T. J. 1936 (Cliftonville)   1
Gibson W. K. 1894 (Cliftonville)   14
Gillespie, K. R. 1995 (Manchester U, Newcastle U,
   Blackburn R, Leicester C, Sheffield U)   86
Gillespie, S. 1886 (Hertford)   6
Gillespie, W. 1889 (West Down)   1
Gillespie, W. 1913 (Sheffield U)   25
Goodall, A. L. 1899 (Derby Co, Glossop)   10
Goodbody, M. F. 1889 (Dublin University)   2
Gordon, H. 1895 (Linfield)   3
Gordon R. W. 1891 (Linfield)   7
Gordon, T. 1894 (Linfield)   2
Gorman, R. J. 2010 (Wolverhampton W)   9
Gorman, W. C. 1947 (Brentford)   4
Gough, J. 1925 (Queen's Island)   1
Gowdy, J. 1920 (Glentoran, Queen's Island, Falkirk)   6
Gowdy, W. A. 1932 (Hull C, Sheffield W, Linfield,
   Hibernian)   6
Graham, W. G. L. 1951 (Doncaster R)   14
Gray, P. 1993 (Luton T, Sunderland, Nancy, Luton T,
   Burnley, Oxford U)   26
Greer, W. 1909 (QPR)   3
Gregg, H. 1954 (Doncaster R, Manchester U)   25
Griffin, D. J. 1996 (St Johnstone, Dundee U,
   Stockport Co)   29
**Grigg, W. D. 2012 (Walsall, Brentford, Milton Keynes D,
   Wigan Ath)   8**

Hall, G. 1897 (Distillery)   1
Halligan, W. 1911 (Derby Co, Wolverhampton W)   2
Hamill, M. 1912 (Manchester U, Belfast Celtic,
   Manchester C)   7
Hamill, R. 1999 (Glentoran)   1
Hamilton, B. 1969 (Linfield, Ipswich T, Everton,
   Millwall, Swindon T)   50
Hamilton, G. 2003 (Portadown)   5
Hamilton, J. 1882 (Knock)   2
Hamilton, R. 1928 (Rangers)   5
Hamilton, W. D. 1885 (Dublin Association)   1
Hamilton, W. J. 1885 (Dublin Association)   1
Hamilton, J. 1908 (Distillery)   1
Hamilton, W. R. 1978 (QPR, Burnley, Oxford U)   41
Hampton, H. 1911 (Bradford C)   9
Hanna, J. 1912 (Nottingham F)   2
Hanna, J. D. 1899 (Royal Artillery, Portsmouth)   1
Hannon, D. J. 1908 (Bohemians)   6
Harkin, J. T. 1968 (Southport, Shrewsbury T)   5
Harland, A. I. 1922 (Linfield)   2
Harris, J. 1921 (Cliftonville, Glenavon)   2
Harris, V. 1906 (Shelbourne, Everton)   20
Harvey, M. 1961 (Sunderland)   34
Hastings, J. 1882 (Knock, Ulster)   7
Hatton, S. 1963 (Linfield)   2
Hayes, W. E. 1938 (Huddersfield T)   4
Healy, D. J. 2000 (Manchester U, Preston NE, Leeds U,
   Fulham, Sunderland, Rangers, Bury)   95
Healy, P. J. 1982 (Coleraine, Glentoran)   4
Hegan, D. 1970 (WBA, Wolverhampton W)   7
Henderson, J. 1885 (Ulster)   3
Hewison, G. 1885 (Moyola Park)   1
Hill, C. F. 1990 (Sheffield U, Leicester C, Trelleborg,
   Northampton T)   27
Hill, M. J. 1959 (Norwich C, Everton)   7
Hinton, E. 1947 (Fulham, Millwall)   7
Hodson, L. J. S. 2011 (Watford, Milton Keynes D)   16
Holmes, S. P. 2002 (Wrexham)   1
Hopkins, J. 1926 (Brighton)   1
Horlock, K. 1995 (Swindon T, Manchester C)   32
Houston, J. 1912 (Linfield, Everton)   6
Houston, W. 1933 (Linfield)   1
Houston, A. W. J. 1885 (Moyola Park)   2
**Hughes, A. W. 1998 (Newcastle U, Aston Villa, Fulham,
   QPR, Brighton & HA, Melbourne C)   103**
Hughes, J. 2006 (Lincoln C)   2
Hughes, M. A. 2006 (Oldham Ath)   2
Hughes, M. E. 1992 (Manchester C, Strasbourg,
   West Ham U, Wimbledon, Crystal Palace)   71
Hughes, P. A. 1987 (Bury)   3
Hughes, W. 1951 (Bolton W)   1
Humphries, W. M. 1962 (Ards, Coventry C, Swansea T)
   14

Hunter, A. 1905 (Distillery, Belfast Celtic)   8
Hunter, A. 1970 (Blackburn R, Ipswich T)   53
Hunter, B. V. 1995 (Wrexham, Reading)   15
Hunter, R. J. 1884 (Cliftonville)   3
Hunter, V. 1962 (Coleraine)   2

Ingham, M. G. 2005 (Sunderland, Wrexham)   3
Irvine, R. J. 1962 (Linfield, Stoke C)   8
Irvine, R. W. 1922 (Everton, Portsmouth,
   Connah's Quay, Derry C)   15
Irvine, W. J. 1963 (Burnley, Preston NE,
   Brighton & HA)   23
Irving, S. J. 1923 (Dundee, Cardiff C, Chelsea)   18

Jackson, T. A. 1969 (Everton, Nottingham F,
   Manchester U)   35
Jamison, J. 1976 (Glentoran)   1
Jenkins, I. 1997 (Chester C, Dundee U)   6
Jennings, P. A. 1964 (Watford, Tottenham H, Arsenal,
   Tottenham H)   119
Johnson, D. M. 1999 (Blackburn R, Birmingham C)   56
Johnston, H. 1927 (Portadown)   1
Johnston, R. S. 1882 (Distillery)   5
Johnston, R. S. 1905 (Distillery)   1
Johnston, S. 1890 (Linfield)   4
Johnston, W. 1885 (Oldpark)   2
Johnston, W. C. 1962 (Glenavon, Oldham Ath)   2
Jones, J. 1930 (Linfield, Hibernian, Glenavon)   23
Jones, J. 1956 (Glenavon)   3
Jones, S. 1934 (Distillery, Blackpool)   2
Jones, S. G. 2003 (Crewe Alex, Burnley)   29
Jordan, T. 1895 (Linfield)   2

Kavanagh, P. J. 1930 (Celtic)   1
Keane, T. R. 1949 (Swansea T)   1
Kearns, A. 1900 (Distillery)   1
Kee, P. V. 1990 (Oxford U, Ards)   9
Keith, R. M. 1958 (Newcastle U)   23
Kelly, H. R. 1950 (Fulham, Southampton)   4
Kelly, J. 1896 (Glentoran)   1
Kelly, J. 1932 (Derry C)   11
Kelly, P. J. 1921 (Manchester C)   1
Kelly, P. M. 1950 (Barnsley)   1
Kennedy, A. L. 1923 (Arsenal)   2
Kennedy, P. H. 1999 (Watford, Wigan Ath)   20
Kernaghan, N. 1936 (Belfast Celtic)   3
Kirk, A. R. 2000 (Hearts, Boston U, Northampton T,
   Dunfermline Ath)   11
Kirkwood, H. 1904 (Cliftonville)   1
Kirwan, J. 1900 (Tottenham H, Chelsea, Clyde)   17

Lacey, W. 1909 (Everton, Liverpool, New Brighton)   23
Lafferty, D. P. 2012 (Burnley)   13
**Lafferty, K. 2006 (Burnley, Rangers, FC Sion, Palermo,
   Norwich C)   54**
Lawrie, J. 2009 (Port Vale)   3
Lawther, R. 1888 (Glentoran)   1
Lawther, W. I. 1960 (Sunderland, Blackburn R)   4
Leatham, J. 1939 (Belfast Celtic)   1
Ledwidge, J. J. 1906 (Shelbourne)   2
Lemon, J. 1886 (Glentoran, Belfast YMCA)   3
Lennon, N. F. 1994 (Crewe Alex, Leicester C, Celtic)   40
Leslie, W. 1887 (YMCA)   1
Lewis, J. 1899 (Glentoran, Distillery)   4
Little, A. 2009 (Rangers)   9
Lockhart, H. 1884 (Rossall School)   1
Lockhart, N. H. 1947 (Linfield, Coventry C, Aston Villa)   8
Lomas, S. M. 1994 (Manchester C, West Ham U)   45
Loyal, J. 1891 (Clarence)   1
Lutton, R. J. 1970 (Wolverhampton W, West Ham U)   6
Lynas, R. 1925 (Cliftonville)   1
Lyner, D. R. 1920 (Glentoran, Manchester U,
   Kilmarnock)   6
Lytle, J. 1898 (Glentoran)   1

McAdams, W. J. 1954 (Manchester C, Bolton W,
   Leeds U)   15
McAlery, J. M. 1882 (Cliftonville)   2
McAlinden, J. 1938 (Belfast Celtic, Portsmouth,
   Southend U)
McAllen, J. 1898 (Linfield)   9
McAlpine, S. 1901 (Cliftonville)   1
McArdle, R. A. 2010 (Rochdale, Aberdeen, Bradford C)   7
McArthur, A. 1886 (Distillery)   1

**McAuley, G. 2005 (Lincoln C, Leicester C, Ipswich T,
   WBA)   65**
McAuley, J. L. 1911 (Huddersfield T)   6
McAuley, P. 1900 (Belfast Celtic)   1
McBride, S. D. 1991 (Glenavon)   4
McCabe, J. J. 1949 (Leeds U)   6
McCabe, W. 1891 (Ulster)   1
McCambridge, J. 1930 (Ballymena, Cardiff C)   4
McCandless, J. 1912 (Bradford)   5
McCandless, W. 1920 (Linfield, Rangers)   9
McCann, G. S. 2002 (West Ham U, Cheltenham T,
   Barnsley, Scunthorpe U, Peterborough U)   39
McCann, P. 1910 (Belfast Celtic, Glentoran)   7
McCarthy, J. D. 1996 (Port Vale, Birmingham C)   18
McCartney, A. 1903 (Ulster, Linfield, Everton,
   Belfast Celtic, Glentoran)   15
McCartney, G. 2002 (Sunderland, West Ham U,
   Sunderland)   34
McCashin, J. W. 1896 (Cliftonville)   5
McCavana, W. T. 1955 (Coleraine)   3
McCaw, J. H. 1927 (Linfield)   6
McClatchey, J. 1886 (Distillery)   3
McClatchey, T. 1895 (Distillery)   1
McCleary, J. W. 1955 (Cliftonville)   1
McCleery, W. 1922 (Cliftonville, Linfield)   10
McClelland, J. 1980 (Mansfield T, Rangers, Watford,
   Leeds U)   53
McClelland, J. T. 1961 (Arsenal, Fulham)   6
McCluggage, A. 1922 (Cliftonville, Bradford, Burnley)   13
McClure, G. 1907 (Cliftonville, Distillery)   4
McConnell, E. 1904 (Cliftonville, Glentoran, Sunderland,
   Sheffield W)   12
McConnell, P. 1928 (Doncaster R, Southport)   2
McConnell, W. G. 1912 (Bohemians)   6
McConnell, W. H. 1925 (Reading)   8
McCourt, F. J. 1952 (Manchester C)   6
**McCourt, P. J. 2002 (Rochdale, Celtic, Barnsley,
   Brighton & HA, Luton T)   18**
McCoy, R. K. 1987 (Coleraine)   1
McCoy, S. 1896 (Distillery)   1
McCracken, E. 1928 (Barking)   1
McCracken, R. 1921 (Crystal Palace)   4
McCracken, R. 1922 (Linfield)   1
McCracken, W. R. 1902 (Distillery, Newcastle U, Hull C)   16
McCreery, D. 1976 (Manchester U, QPR,
   Tulsa Roughnecks, Newcastle U, Hearts)   67
McCrory, S. 1958 (Southend U)   1
McCullough, W. J. 1961 (Arsenal, Millwall)   10
McCurdy, C. 1980 (Linfield)   1
McDonald, A. 1986 (QPR)   52
McDonald, R. 1930 (Rangers)   2
McDonnell, J. 1911 (Bohemians)   4
McElhinney, G. M. A. 1984 (Bolton W)   6
McEvilly, L. R. 2002 (Rochdale)   1
McFaul, W. S. 1967 (Linfield, Newcastle U)   6
McGarry, J. K. 1951 (Cliftonville)   3
McGaughey, M. 1985 (Linfield)   1
McGibbon, P. C. G. 1995 (Manchester U, Wigan Ath)   7
McGinn, N. 2009 (Celtic, Aberdeen)   44
McGivern, R. 2009 (Manchester C, Hibernian,
   Port Vale)   23
McGovern, M. 2010 (Ross Co, Hamilton A)   15
McGrath, R. C. 1974 (Tottenham H, Manchester U)   21
McGregor, S. 1921 (Glentoran)   1
McGrillen, J. 1924 (Clyde, Belfast Celtic)   2
McGuire, E. 1907 (Distillery)   1
McGuire, J. 1928 (Linfield)   1
McIlroy, H. 1906 (Cliftonville)   1
McIlroy, J. 1952 (Burnley, Stoke C)   55
McIlroy, S. B. 1972 (Manchester U, Stoke C,
   Manchester C)   88
McIlvenny, P. 1924 (Distillery)   1
McIlvenny, H. 1890 (Distillery, Ulster)   2
McKay, W. R. 2013 (Inverness CT, Wigan Ath)   11
McKeag, W. 1968 (Glentoran)   2
McKeague, T. 1925 (Glentoran)   1
McKee, F. W. 1906 (Cliftonville, Belfast Celtic)   5
McKelvey, H. 1901 (Glentoran)   2
McKenna, J. 1950 (Huddersfield T)   7
McKenzie, H. 1922 (Distillery)   3
McKenzie, R. 1967 (Airdrieonians)   1

McKeown, N. 1892 (Linfield) 7
McKie, H. 1895 (Cliftonville) 3
Mackie, J. A. 1923 (Arsenal, Portsmouth) 3
McKinney, D. 1921 (Hull C, Bradford C) 2
McKinney, V. J. 1966 (Falkirk) 1
McKnight, A. D. 1988 (Celtic, West Ham U) 10
McKnight, J. 1912 (Preston NE, Glentoran) 2
McLaughlin, C. G. 2012 (Preston NE, Fleetwood T) 19
McLaughlin, J. C. 1962 (Shrewsbury T, Swansea T) 12
McLaughlin, R. 2014 (Liverpool) 3
McLean, B. S. 2006 (Rangers) 1
McLean, T. 1885 (Limavady) 1
McMahon, G. J. 1995 (Tottenham H, Stoke C) 17
McMahon, J. 1934 (Bohemians) 1
McMaster, G. 1897 (Glentoran) 3
McMichael, A. 1950 (Newcastle U) 40
McMillan, G. 1903 (Distillery) 2
McMillan, S. T. 1963 (Manchester U) 2
McMillen, W. S. 1934 (Manchester U, Chesterfield) 7
McMordie, A. S. 1969 (Middlesbrough) 21
McMorran, E. J. 1947 (Belfast Celtic, Barnsley,
   Doncaster R) 15
McMullan, D. 1926 (Liverpool) 3
McNair, P. J. C. 2015 (Manchester U) 11
McNally, B. A. 1986 (Shrewsbury T) 5
McNinch, J. 1931 (Ballymena) 3
McPake, J. 2012 (Coventry C) 1
McParland, P. J. 1954 (Aston Villa, Wolverhampton W) 34
McQuoid, J. J. B. 2011 (Millwall) 5
McShane, J. 1899 (Cliftonville) 4
McVeigh, P. M. 1999 (Tottenham H, Norwich C) 20
McVicker, J. 1888 (Linfield, Glentoran) 2
McWha, W. B. R. 1882 (Knock, Cliftonville) 7
Madden, O. 1938 (Norwich C) 1
Magee, G. 1885 (Wellington Park) 3
**Magennis, J. B. D. 2010 (Cardiff C, Aberdeen, St Mirren,
   Kilmarnock) 22**
Magill, E. J. 1962 (Arsenal, Brighton & HA) 26
Magilton, J. 1991 (Oxford U, Southampton, Sheffield W,
   Ipswich T) 52
Maginnis, H. 1900 (Linfield) 8
Mahood, J. 1926 (Belfast Celtic, Ballymena) 9
Mannus, A. 2004 (Linfield, St Johnstone) 8
Manderson, R. 1920 (Rangers) 5
Mansfield, J. 1901 (Dublin Freebooters) 1
Martin, C. 1882 (Cliftonville) 5
Martin, C. 1925 (Bo'ness) 1
Martin, C. J. 1947 (Glentoran, Leeds U, Aston Villa) 6
Martin, D. K. 1934 (Belfast Celtic, Wolverhampton W,
   Nottingham F) 10
Mathieson, A. 1921 (Luton T) 2
Maxwell, J. 1902 (Linfield, Glentoran, Belfast Celtic) 7
Meek, H. L. 1925 (Glentoran) 1
Mehaffy, J. A. C. 1922 (Queen's Island) 1
Meldon, P. A. 1899 (Dublin Freebooters) 2
Mercer, H. V. A. 1908 (Linfield) 1
Mercer, J. T. 1898 (Distillery, Linfield, Distillery,
   Derby Co) 12
Millar, W. 1932 (Barrow) 2
Miller, J. 1929 (Middlesbrough) 3
Milligan, D. 1939 (Chesterfield) 1
Milne, R. G. 1894 (Linfield) 28
Mitchell, E. J. 1933 (Cliftonville, Glentoran) 2
Mitchell, W. 1932 (Distillery, Chelsea) 15
Molyneux, T. B. 1883 (Ligoniel, Cliftonville) 11
Montgomery, F. J. 1955 (Coleraine) 1
Moore, C. 1949 (Glentoran) 1
Moore, P. 1933 (Aberdeen) 1
Moore, R. 1891 (Linfield Ath) 3
Moore, R. L. 1887 (Ulster) 2
Moore, W. 1923 (Falkirk) 1
Moorhead, F. W. 1885 (Dublin University) 1
Moorhead, G. 1923 (Linfield) 4
Moran, J. 1912 (Leeds C) 1
Moreland, V. 1979 (Derby Co) 6
Morgan, G. F. 1922 (Linfield, Nottingham F) 8
Morgan, S. 1972 (Port Vale, Aston Villa, Brighton & HA,
   Sparta Rotterdam) 18
Morrison, R. 1891 (Linfield Ath) 2
Morrison, T. 1895 (Glentoran, Burnley) 7
Morrogh, D. 1896 (Bohemians) 1
Morrow, S. J. 1990 (Arsenal, QPR) 39
Morrow, W. J. 1883 (Moyola Park) 3
Muir, R. 1885 (Oldpark) 2

Mulgrew, J. 2010 (Linfield) 2
Mulholland, T. S. 1906 (Belfast Celtic) 2
Mullan, G. 1983 (Glentoran) 4
Mulligan, J. 1921 (Manchester C) 1
Mulryne, P. P. 1997 (Manchester U, Norwich C,
   Cardiff C) 27
Murdock, C. J. 2000 (Preston NE, Hibernian,
   Crewe Alex, Rotherham U) 34
Murphy, J. 1910 (Bradford C) 3
Murphy, N. 1905 (QPR) 3
Murray, J. M. 1910 (Motherwell, Sheffield W) 3

Napier, R. J. 1966 (Bolton W) 1
Neill, W. J. T. 1961 (Arsenal, Hull C) 59
Nelis, P. 1923 (Nottingham F) 1
Nelson, S. 1970 (Arsenal, Brighton & HA) 51
Nicholl, C. J. 1975 (Aston Villa, Southampton,
   Grimsby T) 51
Nicholl, H. 1902 (Belfast Celtic) 3
Nicholl, J. M. 1976 (Manchester U, Toronto Blizzard,
   Sunderland, Toronto Blizzard, Rangers,
   Toronto Blizzard, WBA) 73
Nicholson, J. J. 1961 (Manchester U, Huddersfield T) 41
Nixon, R. 1914 (Linfield) 9
Nolan, I. R. 1997 (Sheffield W, Bradford C, Wigan Ath)
   18
Nolan-Whelan, J. V. 1901 (Dublin Freebooters) 5
**Norwood, O. J. 2011 (Manchester U, Huddersfield T,
   Reading) 38**

O'Boyle, G. 1994 (Dunfermline Ath, St Johnstone) 13
O'Brien, M. T. 1921 (QPR, Leicester C, Hull C,
   Derby Co) 10
O'Connell, P. 1912 (Sheffield W, Hull C) 5
O'Connor, M. J. 2008 (Crewe Alex, Scunthorpe U,
   Rotherham U) 11
O'Doherty, A. 1970 (Coleraine) 2
O'Driscoll, J. F. 1949 (Swansea T) 3
O'Hagan, C. 1905 (Tottenham H, Aberdeen) 11
O'Hagan, W. 1920 (St Mirren) 2
O'Hehir, J. C. 1910 (Bohemians) 1
O'Kane, W. J. 1970 (Nottingham F) 20
O'Mahoney, M. T. 1939 (Bristol R) 1
O'Neill, C. 1989 (Motherwell) 3
O'Neill, J. 1962 (Sunderland) 1
O'Neill, J. P. 1980 (Leicester C) 39
O'Neill, M. A. M. 1988 (Newcastle U, Dundee U,
   Hibernian, Coventry C) 31
O'Neill, M. H. M. 1972 (Distillery, Nottingham F,
   Norwich C, Manchester C, Norwich C, Notts Co) 64
O'Reilly, H. 1901 (Dublin Freebooters) 3
Owens, J. 2011 (Crusaders) 1

Parke, J. 1964 (Linfield, Hibernian, Sunderland) 14
Paterson, A. 2008 (Scunthorpe U, Burnley,
   Huddersfield T) 22
Paton, P. R. 2014 (Dundee U) 2
Patterson, D. J. 1994 (Crystal Palace, Luton T,
   Dundee U) 17
Patterson, R. 2010 (Coleraine, Plymouth Arg) 5
Peacock, R. 1952 (Celtic, Coleraine) 31
Peden, J. 1887 (Linfield, Distillery) 24
Penney, S. 1985 (Brighton & HA) 17
Percy, J. C. 1889 (Belfast YMCA) 1
Platt, J. A. 1976 (Middlesbrough, Ballymena U,
   Coleraine) 23
Pollock, W. 1928 (Belfast Celtic) 1
Ponsonby, J. 1895 (Distillery) 9
Potts, R. M. C. 1883 (Cliftonville) 2
Priestley, T. J. M. 1933 (Coleraine, Chelsea) 2
Pyper, Jas. 1897 (Cliftonville) 7
Pyper, John 1897 (Cliftonville) 9
Pyper, M. 1932 (Linfield) 1

Quinn, J. M. 1985 (Blackburn R, Swindon T, Leicester C,
   Bradford C, West Ham U, Bournemouth, Reading) 46
Quinn, S. J. 1996 (Blackpool, WBA, Willem II,
   Sheffield W, Peterborough U, Northampton T) 50

Rafferty, P. 1980 (Linfield) 1
Ramsey, P. C. 1984 (Leicester C) 14
Rankine, J. 1883 (Alexander) 2
Rattray, D. 1882 (Avoniel) 3
Rea, R. 1901 (Glentoran) 1

Reeves, B. N. 2015 (Milton Keynes D) 2
Redmond, R. 1884 (Cliftonville) 1
Reid, G. H. 1923 (Cardiff C) 1
Reid, J. 1883 (Ulster) 6
Reid, S. E. 1934 (Derby Co) 3
Reid, W. 1931 (Hearts) 1
Reilly, M. M. 1900 (Portsmouth) 2
Renneville, W. T. J. 1910 (Leyton, Aston Villa) 4
Reynolds, J. 1890 (Distillery, Ulster) 5
Reynolds, R. 1905 (Bohemians) 1
Rice, P. J. 1969 (Arsenal) 49
Roberts, F. C. 1931 (Glentoran) 1
Robinson, P. 1920 (Distillery, Blackburn R) 2
Robinson, S. 1997 (Bournemouth, Luton T) 7
Rogan, A. 1988 (Celtic, Sunderland, Millwall) 18
Rollo, D. 1912 (Linfield, Blackburn R) 16
Roper, E. O. 1886 (Dublin University) 1
Rosbotham, A. 1887 (Cliftonville) 7
Ross, W. E. 1969 (Newcastle U) 1
Rowland, K. 1994 (West Ham U, QPR) 19
Rowley, R. W. M. 1929 (Southampton, Tottenham H) 6
Rushe, F. 1925 (Distillery) 1
Russell, A. 1947 (Linfield) 1
Russell, S. R. 1930 (Bradford C, Derry C) 3
Ryan, R. A. 1950 (WBA) 1

Sanchez, L. P. 1987 (Wimbledon) 3
Scott, E. 1920 (Liverpool, Belfast Celtic) 31
Scott, J. 1958 (Grimsby) 2
Scott, J. E. 1901 (Cliftonville) 1
Scott, L. J. 1895 (Dublin University) 2
Scott, P. W. 1975 (Everton, York C, Aldershot) 10
Scott, T. 1894 (Cliftonville) 13
Scott, W. 1903 (Linfield, Everton, Leeds C) 25
Scraggs, M. J. 1921 (Glentoran) 2
Seymour, H. C. 1914 (Bohemians) 1
Seymour, J. 1907 (Cliftonville) 2
Shanks, T. 1903 (Woolwich Arsenal, Brentford) 3
Sharkey, P. G. 1976 (Ipswich T) 1
Sheehan, Dr G. 1899 (Bohemians) 3
Sheridan, J. 1903 (Everton, Stoke C) 6
Sherrard, J. 1885 (Limavady) 3
Sherrard, W. C. 1895 (Cliftonville) 3
Sherry, J. J. 1906 (Bohemians) 2
Shields, R. J. 1957 (Southampton) 1
Shiels, D. 2006 (Hibernian, Doncaster R, Kilmarnock) 14
Silo, M. 1888 (Belfast YMCA) 1
Simpson, W. J. 1951 (Rangers) 12
Sinclair, J. 1882 (Knock) 2
Slemin, J. C. 1909 (Bohemians) 1
Sloan, A. S. 1925 (London Caledonians) 1
Sloan, D. 1969 (Oxford U) 2
Sloan, H. A. de B. 1903 (Bohemians) 8
Sloan, J. W. 1947 (Arsenal) 1
Sloan, T. 1926 (Cardiff C, Linfield) 11
Sloan, T. 1979 (Manchester U) 3
Small, J. M. 1887 (Clarence, Cliftonville) 4
Smith, A. W. 2003 (Glentoran, Preston NE) 18
Smith, E. E. 1921 (Cardiff C) 4
Smith, J. E. 1901 (Distillery) 2
Smith, M. 2016 (Peterborough U) 1
Smyth, R. H. 1886 (Dublin University) 1
Smyth, S. 1948 (Wolverhampton W, Stoke C) 9
Smyth, W. 1949 (Distillery) 1
Snape, A. 1920 (Airdrieonians) 1
Sonner, D. J. 1998 (Ipswich T, Sheffield W,
   Birmingham C, Nottingham F, Peterborough U) 13
Spence, D. W. 1975 (Bury, Blackpool, Southend U) 29
Spencer, S. 1890 (Distillery) 6
Spiller, E. A. 1883 (Cliftonville) 5
Sproule, I. 2006 (Hibernian, Bristol C) 11
Stanfield, O. M. 1887 (Distillery) 30
Steele, A. 1926 (Charlton Ath, Fulham) 4
Steele, J. 2013 (New York Red Bulls) 3
Stevenson, A. E. 1934 (Rangers, Everton) 17
Stewart, A. 1967 (Glentoran, Derby Co) 7
Stewart, D. C. 1978 (Hull C) 1
Stewart, I. 1982 (QPR, Newcastle U) 31
Stewart, R. K. 1890 (St Columb's Court, Cliftonville) 11
Stewart, T. C. 1961 (Linfield) 1
Swan, S. 1899 (Linfield) 1

Taggart, G. P. 1990 (Barnsley, Bolton W, Leicester C) 51
Taggart, J. 1899 (Walsall) 1
Taylor, M. S. 1999 (Fulham, Birmingham C, unattached)
   88
Thompson, A. L. 2011 (Watford) 2
Thompson, F. W. 1910 (Cliftonville, Linfield, Bradford
   C, Clyde) 12
Thompson, J. 1897 (Distillery) 1
Thompson, P. 2006 (Linfield, Stockport Co) 8
Thompson, R. 1928 (Queen's Island) 1
Thompson, W. 1889 (Belfast Ath) 1
Thunder, P. J. 1911 (Bohemians) 1
Todd, S. J. 1966 (Burnley, Sheffield W) 11
Toner, C. 2003 (Leyton Orient) 2
Toner, J. 1922 (Arsenal, St Johnstone) 8
Torrans, R. 1893 (Linfield) 1
Torrans, S. 1889 (Linfield) 26
Trainor, D. 1967 (Crusaders) 1
Tuffey, J. 2009 (Partick Thistle, Inverness CT) 8
Tully, C. P. 1949 (Celtic) 10
Turner, A. 1896 (Cliftonville) 1
Turner, E. 1896 (Cliftonville) 1
Turner, W. 1886 (Cliftonville) 3
Twomey, J. F. 1938 (Leeds U) 2

Uprichard, W. N. M. C. 1952 (Swindon T, Portsmouth) 18

Vernon, J. 1947 (Belfast Celtic, WBA) 17

Waddell, T. M. R. 1906 (Cliftonville) 1
Walker, J. 1955 (Doncaster R) 1
Walker, T. 1911 (Bury) 1
Walsh, D. J. 1947 (WBA) 9
Walsh, W. 1948 (Manchester C) 5
Ward, J. J. 2012 (Derby Co, Nottingham F) 26
Waring, J. 1899 (Cliftonville) 1
Warren, P. 1913 (Shelbourne) 2
Washington, C. J. 2016 (QPR) 8
Watson, J. 1883 (Ulster) 9
Watson, P. 1971 (Distillery) 1
Watson, T. 1926 (Cardiff C) 1
Wattie, J. 1899 (Distillery) 1
Webb, C. G. 1909 (Brighton & HA) 3
Webb, S. M. 2006 (Ross Co) 4
Weir, E. 1939 (Clyde) 4
Welsh, E. 1966 (Carlisle U) 4
Whiteside, N. 1982 (Manchester U, Everton) 38
Whiteside, T. 1891 (Distillery) 1
Whitfield, E. R. 1886 (Dublin University) 1
Whitley, Jeff 1997 (Manchester C, Sunderland, Cardiff C)
   20
Whitley, Jim 1998 (Manchester C) 3
Williams, J. R. 1886 (Ulster) 2
Williams, M. S. 1999 (Chesterfield, Watford, Wimbledon,
   Stoke C, Wimbledon, Milton Keynes D) 36
Williams, P. A. 1991 (WBA) 1
Williamson, J. 1890 (Cliftonville) 3
Willighan, T. 1933 (Burnley) 2
Willis, G. 1906 (Linfield) 4
Wilson, D. J. 1987 (Brighton & HA, Luton T,
   Sheffield W) 24
Wilson, H. 1925 (Linfield) 2
Wilson, K. J. 1987 (Ipswich T, Chelsea, Notts Co,
   Walsall) 42
Wilson, M. 1884 (Distillery) 3
Wilson, R. 1888 (Cliftonville) 1
Wilson, S. J. 1962 (Glenavon, Falkirk, Dundee) 12
Wilton, J. M. 1888 (St Columb's Court, Cliftonville, St
   Columb's Court) 7
Winchester, C. 2011 (Oldham Ath) 1
Wood, T. J. 1996 (Walsall) 1
Worthington, N. 1984 (Sheffield W, Leeds U, Stoke C) 66
Wright, J. 1906 (Cliftonville) 6
Wright, T. J. 1989 (Newcastle U, Nottingham F,
   Manchester C) 31

Young, S. 1907 (Linfield, Airdrieonians, Linfield) 9

SCOTLAND

Adam, C. G. 2007 (Rangers, Blackpool, Liverpool, Stoke C)	26	Blacklaw, A. S. 1963 (Burnley)	3
Adams, J. 1889 (Hearts)	3	Blackley, J. 1974 (Hibernian)	7
Agnew, W. B. 1907 (Kilmarnock)	3	Blair, D. 1929 (Clyde, Aston Villa)	8
Aird, J. 1954 (Burnley)	4	Blair, J. 1920 (Sheffield W, Cardiff C)	8
Aitken, A. 1901 (Newcastle U, Middlesbrough, Leicester Fosse)	14	Blair, J. 1934 (Motherwell)	1
		Blair, J. A. 1947 (Blackpool)	1
Aitken, G. G. 1949 (East Fife, Sunderland)	8	Blair, W. 1896 (Third Lanark)	1
Aitken, R. 1886 (Dumbarton)	2	Blessington, J. 1894 (Celtic)	4
Aitken, R. 1980 (Celtic, Newcastle U, St Mirren)	57	Blyth, J. A. 1978 (Coventry C)	2
Aitkenhead, W. A. C. 1912 (Blackburn R)	1	Bone, J. 1972 (Norwich C)	2
Albiston, A. 1982 (Manchester U)	14	Booth, S. 1993 (Aberdeen, Borussia Dortmund, Twente)	
Alexander, D. 1894 (East Stirlingshire)	2		21
Alexander, G. 2002 (Preston NE, Burnley)	40	Bowie, J. 1920 (Rangers)	2
Alexander, N. 2006 (Cardiff C)	3	Bowie, W. 1891 (Linthouse)	1
Allan, D. S. 1885 (Queen's Park)	3	Bowman, D. 1992 (Dundee U)	6
Allan, G. 1897 (Liverpool)	1	Bowman, G. A. 1892 (Montrose)	1
Allan, H. 1902 (Hearts)	1	Boyd, G. I. 2013 (Peterborough U, Hull C)	2
Allan, J. 1887 (Queen's Park)	2	Boyd, J. M. 1934 (Newcastle U)	1
Allan, T. 1974 (Dundee)	2	Doyd, K. 2006 (Rangers, Middlesbrough)	18
Ancell, R. F. D. 1937 (Newcastle U)	2	Boyd, R. 1889 (Mossend Swifts)	2
Anderson, A. 1933 (Hearts)	23	Boyd, T. 1991 (Motherwell, Chelsea, Celtic)	72
Anderson, F. 1874 (Clydesdale)	1	Boyd, W. G. 1931 (Clyde)	2
Anderson, G. 1901 (Kilmarnock)	1	Bradshaw, T. 1928 (Bury)	1
Anderson, H. A. 1914 (Raith R)	1	Brand, R. 1961 (Rangers)	8
Anderson, J. 1954 (Leicester C)	1	Brandon, T. 1896 (Blackburn R)	1
Anderson, K. 1896 (Queen's Park)	3	Brazil, A. 1980 (Ipswich T, Tottenham H)	13
Anderson, R. 2003 (Aberdeen, Sunderland)	11	Breckenridge, T. 1888 (Hearts)	1
Anderson, W. 1882 (Queen's Park)	6	Bremner, D. 1976 (Hibernian)	1
Andrews, P. 1875 (Eastern)	1	Bremner, W. J. 1965 (Leeds U)	54
Anya, I. 2013 (Watford)	**21**	Brennan, F. 1947 (Newcastle U)	7
Archibald, A. 1921 (Rangers)	8	Breslin, B. 1897 (Hibernian)	1
Archibald, S. 1980 (Aberdeen, Tottenham H, Barcelona)		Brewster, G. 1921 (Everton)	1
	27	**Bridcutt, L. 2013 (Brighton & HA, Sunderland)**	**2**
Armstrong, M. W. 1936 (Aberdeen)	3	Broadfoot, K. 2009 (Rangers)	4
Arnott, W. 1883 (Queen's Park)	14	Brogan, J. 1971 (Celtic)	4
Auld, J. R. 1887 (Third Lanark)	3	Brown, A. 1890 (St Mirren)	2
Auld, R. 1959 (Celtic)	3	Brown, A. 1904 (Middlesbrough)	1
		Brown, A. D. 1950 (East Fife, Blackpool)	14
		Brown, G. C. P. 1931 (Rangers)	19
Baird, A. 1892 (Queen's Park)	2	Brown, H. 1947 (Partick Thistle)	3
Baird, D. 1890 (Hearts)	3	Brown, J. B. 1939 (Clyde)	1
Baird, H. 1956 (Airdrieonians)	1	Brown, J. G. 1975 (Sheffield U)	1
Baird, J. C. 1876 (Vale of Leven)	3	Brown, J. 1884 (Dumbarton)	2
Baird, S. 1957 (Rangers)	7	Brown, R. 1890 (Cambuslang)	1
Baird, W. U. 1897 (St Bernard)	1	Brown, R. 1947 (Rangers)	3
Bannan, B. 2011 (Aston Villa, Crystal Palace, Sheffield W)	**21**	Brown, R. jun. 1885 (Dumbarton)	1
		Brown, S. 2006 (Hibernian, Celtic)	**50**
Bannon, E. J. 1980 (Dundee U)	11	Brown, W. D. F. 1958 (Dundee, Tottenham H)	28
Barbour, A. 1885 (Renton)	1	Browning, J. 1914 (Celtic)	1
Bardsley, P. A. 2011 (Sunderland)	13	Brownlie, J. 1909 (Third Lanark)	16
Barker, J. B. 1893 (Rangers)	2	Brownlie, J. 1971 (Hibernian)	7
Barr, D. 2009 (Falkirk)	1	Bruce, D. 1890 (Vale of Leven)	1
Barrett, F. 1894 (Dundee)	2	Bruce, R. F. 1934 (Middlesbrough)	1
Battles, B. 1901 (Celtic)	3	**Bryson, C. 2011 (Kilmarnock, Derby Co)**	**3**
Battles, B. jun. 1931 (Hearts)	1	Buchan, M. M. 1972 (Aberdeen, Manchester U)	34
Bauld, W. 1950 (Hearts)	3	Buchanan, J. 1889 (Cambuslang)	1
Baxter, J. C. 1961 (Rangers, Sunderland)	34	Buchanan, J. 1929 (Rangers)	2
Baxter, R. D. 1939 (Middlesbrough)	3	Buchanan, P. S. 1938 (Chelsea)	1
Beattie, A. 1937 (Preston NE)	7	Buchanan, R. 1891 (Abercorn)	1
Beattie, C. 2006 (Celtic, WBA)	7	Buckley, P. 1954 (Aberdeen)	3
Beattie, R. 1939 (Preston NE)	1	Buick, A. 1902 (Hearts)	2
Begbie, I. 1890 (Hearts)	4	Burchill, M. J. 2000 (Celtic)	6
Bell, A. 1912 (Manchester U)	1	Burke, C. 2006 (Rangers, Birmingham C)	7
Bell, C. 2011 (Kilmarnock)	1	**Burke O. J. 2016 (Nottingham F)**	**2**
Bell, J. 1890 (Dumbarton, Everton, Celtic)	10	Burley, C. W. 1995 (Chelsea, Celtic, Derby Co)	46
Bell, M. 1901 (Hearts)	1	Burley, G. E. 1979 (Ipswich T)	11
Bell, W. J. 1966 (Leeds U)	2	Burns, F. 1970 (Manchester U)	1
Bennett, A. 1904 (Celtic, Rangers)	11	Burns, K. 1974 (Birmingham C, Nottingham F)	20
Bennie, R. 1925 (Airdrieonians)	3	Burns, T. 1981 (Celtic)	8
Bernard, P. R. J. 1995 (Oldham Ath)	2	Busby, M. W. 1934 (Manchester C)	1
Berra, C. D. 2008 (Hearts, Wolverhampton W, Ipswich T)	**33**		
		Caddis, P. M. 2016 (Birmingham C)	**1**
Berry, D. 1894 (Queen's Park)	3	Cairns, T. 1920 (Rangers)	8
Berry, W. H. 1888 (Queen's Park)	4	Calderhead, D. 1889 (Q of S Wanderers)	1
Bett, J. 1982 (Rangers, Lokeren, Aberdeen)	25	Calderwood, C. 1995 (Tottenham H)	36
Beveridge, W. W. 1879 (Glasgow University)	3	Calderwood, R. 1885 (Cartvale)	3
Black, A. 1938 (Hearts)	3	Caldow, E. 1957 (Rangers)	40
Black, D. 1889 (Hurlford)	1	Caldwell, G. 2002 (Newcastle U, Hibernian, Celtic, Wigan Ath)	55
Black, E. 1988 (Metz)	2		
Black, I. 2013 (Rangers)	1	Caldwell, S. 2001 (Newcastle U, Sunderland, Burnley, Wigan Ath)	12
Black, I. H. 1948 (Southampton)	1		
Blackburn, J. E. 1873 (Royal Engineers)	1	Callaghan, P. 1900 (Hibernian)	1

Ferguson, J. 1874 (Vale of Leven) 6
Ferguson, R. 1966 (Kilmarnock) 7
Fernie, W. 1954 (Celtic) 12
Findlay, R. 1898 (Kilmarnock) 1
Fitchie, T. T. 1905 (Woolwich Arsenal, Queen's Park) 4
Flavell, R. 1947 (Airdrieonians) 2
Fleck, R. 1990 (Norwich C) 4
Fleming, C. 1954 (East Fife) 1
Fleming, J. W. 1929 (Rangers) 3
Fleming, R. 1886 (Morton) 1
Fletcher, D. B. 2004 (Manchester U, WBA) **73**
Fletcher, S. K. 2008 (Hibernian, Burnley,
 Wolverhampton W, Sunderland) **28**
Forbes, A. R. 1947 (Sheffield U, Arsenal) 14
Forbes, J. 1884 (Vale of Leven) 5
Ford, D. 1974 (Hearts) 3
Forrest, J. 1958 (Motherwell) 1
Forrest, J. 1966 (Rangers, Aberdeen) 5
Forrest, J. 2011 (Celtic) **13**
Forsyth, A. 1972 (Partick Thistle, Manchester U) 10
Forsyth, C. 2014 (Derby Co) 4
Forsyth, R. C. 1964 (Kilmarnock) 4
Forsyth, T. 1971 (Motherwell, Rangers) 22
Fox, D. J. 2010 (Burnley, Southampton) 4
Foyers, R. 1893 (St Bernards) 2
Fraser, D. M. 1968 (WBA) 2
Fraser, J. 1891 (Moffat) 1
Fraser, M. J. E. 1880 (Queen's Park) 5
Fraser, J. 1907 (Dundee) 1
Fraser, W. 1955 (Sunderland) 2
Freedman, D. A. 2002 (Crystal Palace) 2
Fulton, W. 1884 (Abercorn) 1
Fyfe, J. H. 1895 (Third Lanark) 1

Gabriel, J. 1961 (Everton) 2
Gallacher, H. K. 1924 (Airdrieonians, Newcastle U,
 Chelsea, Derby Co) 20
Gallacher, K. W. 1988 (Dundee U, Coventry C,
 Blackburn R, Newcastle U) 53
Gallacher, P. 1935 (Sunderland) 1
Gallacher, P. 2002 (Dundee U) 8
Gallagher, P. 2004 (Blackburn R) 1
Galloway, M. 1992 (Celtic) 1
Galt, J. H. 1908 (Rangers) 2
Gardiner, I. 1958 (Motherwell) 1
Gardner, D. R. 1897 (Third Lanark) 1
Gardner, R. 1872 (Queen's Park, Clydesdale) 5
Gemmell, T. 1955 (St Mirren) 2
Gemmell, T. 1966 (Celtic) 18
Gemmill, A. 1971 (Derby Co, Nottingham F,
 Birmingham C) 43
Gemmill, S. 1995 (Nottingham F, Everton) 26
Gibb, W. 1873 (Clydesdale) 1
Gibson, D. W. 1963 (Leicester C) 7
Gibson, J. D. 1926 (Partick Thistle, Aston Villa) 8
Gibson, N. 1895 (Rangers, Partick Thistle) 14
Gilchrist, J. E. 1922 (Celtic) 1
Gilhooley, M. 1922 (Hull C) 1
Gilks, M. 2013 (Blackpool) 3
Gillespie, G. 1880 (Rangers, Queen's Park) 7
Gillespie, G. T. 1988 (Liverpool) 13
Gillespie, Jas 1898 (Third Lanark) 1
Gillespie, John 1896 (Queen's Park) 1
Gillespie, R. 1927 (Queen's Park) 4
Gillick, T. 1937 (Everton) 5
Gilmour, J. 1931 (Dundee) 1
Gilzean, A. J. 1964 (Dundee, Tottenham H) 22
Glass, S. 1999 (Newcastle U) 1
Glavin, R. 1977 (Celtic) 1
Glen, A. 1956 (Aberdeen) 2
Glen, R. 1895 (Renton, Hibernian) 3
Goodwillie, D. 2011 (Dundee U, Blackburn R) 3
Goram, A. L. 1986 (Oldham Ath, Hibernian, Rangers) 43
Gordon, C. A. 2004 (Hearts, Sunderland, Celtic) **44**
Gordon, J. E. 1912 (Rangers) 10
Gossland, J. 1884 (Rangers) 1
Goudie, J. 1884 (Abercorn) 1
Gough, C. R. 1983 (Dundee U, Tottenham H, Rangers) 61
Gould, J. 2000 (Celtic) 2
Gourlay, J. 1886 (Cambuslang) 2
Govan, J. 1948 (Hibernian) 6
Gow, D. R. 1888 (Rangers) 1
Gow, J. J. 1885 (Queen's Park) 1
Gow, J. R. 1888 (Rangers) 1

Graham, A. 1978 (Leeds U) 11
Graham, G. 1972 (Arsenal, Manchester U) 12
Graham, J. 1884 (Annbank) 1
Graham, J. A. 1921 (Arsenal) 1
Grant, J. 1959 (Hibernian) 2
Grant, P. 1989 (Celtic) 2
Gray, A. 1903 (Hibernian) 1
Gray, A. D. 2003 (Bradford C) 2
Gray, A. M. 1976 (Aston Villa, Wolverhampton W,
 Everton) 20
Gray, D. 1929 (Rangers) 10
Gray, E. 1969 (Leeds U) 12
Gray, F. T. 1976 (Leeds U, Nottingham F, Leeds U) 32
Gray, W. 1886 (Pollokshields Ath) 1
Green, A. 1971 (Blackpool, Newcastle U) 6
Greer, G. 2013 (Brighton & HA) **11**
Greig, J. 1964 (Rangers) 44
Griffiths, L. 2013 (Hibernian, Celtic) **7**
Groves, W. 1888 (Hibernian, Celtic) 3
Gulliland, W. 1891 (Queen's Park) 4
Gunn, B. 1990 (Norwich C) 6

Haddock, H. 1955 (Clyde) 6
Haddow, D. 1894 (Rangers) 1
Haffey, F. 1960 (Celtic) 2
Hamilton, A. 1885 (Queen's Park) 4
Hamilton, A. W. 1962 (Dundee) 24
Hamilton, G. 1906 (Port Glasgow Ath) 1
Hamilton, G. 1947 (Aberdeen) 5
Hamilton, J. 1892 (Queen's Park) 3
Hamilton, J. 1924 (St Mirren) 1
Hamilton, R. C. 1899 (Rangers, Dundee) 11
Hamilton, T. 1891 (Hurlford) 1
Hamilton, T. 1932 (Rangers) 1
Hamilton, W. M. 1965 (Hibernian) 1
Hammell, S. 2005 (Motherwell) 1
Hanley, G. C. 2011 (Blackburn R) **23**
Hannah, A. B. 1888 (Renton) 1
Hannah, J. 1889 (Third Lanark) 1
Hansen, A. D. 1979 (Liverpool) 26
Hansen, J. 1972 (Partick Thistle) 2
Harkness, J. D. 1927 (Queen's Park, Hearts) 12
Harper, J. M. 1973 (Aberdeen, Hibernian, Aberdeen) 4
Harper, W. 1923 (Hibernian, Arsenal) 11
Harris, J. 1921 (Partick Thistle) 2
Harris, N. 1924 (Newcastle U) 1
Harrower, W. 1882 (Queen's Park) 3
Hartford, R. A. 1972 (WBA, Manchester C, Everton,
 Manchester C) 50
Hartley, P. J. 2005 (Hearts, Celtic, Bristol C) 25
Harvey, D. 1973 (Leeds U) 16
Hastings, A. C. 1936 (Sunderland) 2
Haughney, M. 1954 (Celtic) 1
Hay, D. 1970 (Celtic) 27
Hay, J. 1905 (Celtic, Newcastle U) 11
Hegarty, P. 1979 (Dundee U) 8
Heggie, C. 1886 (Rangers) 1
Henderson, G. H. 1904 (Rangers) 1
Henderson, J. G. 1953 (Portsmouth, Arsenal) 7
Henderson, W. 1963 (Rangers) 29
Hendry, E. C. J. 1993 (Blackburn R, Rangers,
 Coventry C, Bolton W) 51
Hepburn, J. 1891 (Alloa Ath) 1
Hepburn, R. 1932 (Ayr U) 1
Herd, A. C. 1935 (Hearts) 1
Herd, D. G. 1959 (Arsenal) 5
Herd, G. 1958 (Clyde) 5
Herriot, J. 1969 (Birmingham C) 8
Hewie, J. D. 1956 (Charlton Ath) 19
Higgins, A. 1885 (Kilmarnock) 1
Higgins, A. 1910 (Newcastle U) 4
Highet, T. C. 1875 (Queen's Park) 4
Hill, D. 1881 (Rangers) 3
Hill, D. A. 1906 (Third Lanark) 1
Hill, F. R. 1930 (Aberdeen) 3
Hill, J. 1891 (Hearts) 2
Hogg, G. 1896 (Hearts) 2
Hogg, J. 1922 (Ayr U) 1
Hogg, R. M. 1937 (Celtic) 1
Holm, A. H. 1882 (Queen's Park) 3
Holt, D. D. 1963 (Hearts) 5
Holt, G. J. 2001 (Kilmarnock, Norwich C) 10
Holton, J. A. 1973 (Manchester U) 15
Hope, R. 1968 (WBA) 2

Hopkin, D. 1997 (Crystal Palace, Leeds U)   7
Houliston, W. 1949 (Queen of the South)   3
Houston, S. M. 1976 (Manchester U)   1
Howden, W. 1905 (Partick Thistle)   1
Howe, R. 1929 (Hamilton A)   2
Howie, H. 1949 (Hibernian)   1
Howie, J. 1905 (Newcastle U)   3
Howieson, J. 1927 (St Mirren)   1
Hughes, J. 1965 (Celtic)   8
Hughes, R. D. 2004 (Portsmouth)   5
Hughes, S. R. 2010 (Norwich C)   1
Hughes, W. 1975 (Sunderland)   1
Humphries, W. 1952 (Motherwell)   1
Hunter, A. 1972 (Kilmarnock, Celtic)   4
Hunter, J. 1909 (Dundee)   1
Hunter, J. 1874 (Third Lanark, Eastern, Third Lanark)   4
Hunter, W. 1960 (Motherwell)   3
Hunter, R. 1890 (St Mirren)   1
Husband, J. 1947 (Partick Thistle)   1
Hutchison, D. 1999 (Everton, Sunderland, West Ham U)   26
Hutchison, T. 1974 (Coventry C)   17
Hutton, A. 2007 (Rangers, Tottenham H, Aston Villa)   **50**
Hutton, J. 1887 (St Bernards)   1
Hutton, J. 1923 (Aberdeen, Blackburn R)   10
Hyslop, T. 1896 (Stoke, Rangers)   2

Imlach, J. J. S. 1958 (Nottingham F)   4
Imrie, W. N. 1929 (St Johnstone)   2
Inglis, J. 1883 (Rangers)   2
Inglis, J. 1884 (Kilmarnock Ath)   1
Irons, J. H. 1900 (Queen's Park)   1
Irvine, B. 1991 (Aberdeen)   9
Iwelumo, C.R. 2009 (Wolverhampton W, Burnley)   4

Jackson, A. 1886 (Cambuslang)   2
Jackson, A. 1925 (Aberdeen, Huddersfield T)   17
Jackson, C. 1975 (Rangers)   8
Jackson, D. 1995 (Hibernian, Celtic)   28
Jackson, J. 1931 (Partick Thistle, Chelsea)   8
Jackson, T. A. 1904 (St Mirren)   6
James, A. W. 1926 (Preston NE, Arsenal)   8
Jardine, A. 1971 (Rangers)   38
Jarvie, A. 1971 (Airdrieonians)   3
Jenkinson, T. 1887 (Hearts)   1
Jess, E. 1993 (Aberdeen, Coventry C, Aberdeen)   18
Johnston, A. 1999 (Sunderland, Rangers, Middlesbrough)   18
Johnston, L. H. 1948 (Clyde)   2
Johnston, M. 1984 (Watford, Celtic, Nantes, Rangers)   38
Johnston, R. 1938 (Sunderland)   1
Johnston, W. 1966 (Rangers, WBA)   22
Johnstone, D. 1973 (Rangers)   14
Johnstone, J. 1888 (Abercorn)   1
Johnstone, J. 1965 (Celtic)   23
Johnstone, Jas 1894 (Kilmarnock)   1
Johnstone, J. A. 1930 (Hearts)   3
Johnstone, R. 1951 (Hibernian, Manchester C)   17
Johnstone, W. 1887 (Third Lanark)   1
Jordan, J. 1973 (Leeds U, Manchester U, AC Milan)   52

Kay, J. L. 1880 (Queen's Park)   6
Keillor, A. 1891 (Montrose, Dundee)   6
Keir, L. 1885 (Dumbarton)   5
Kelly, H. T. 1952 (Blackpool)   1
Kelly, J. 1888 (Renton, Celtic)   8
Kelly, J. C. 1949 (Barnsley)   2
Kelly, L. M. 2013 (Kilmarnock)   1
Kelso, R. 1885 (Renton, Dundee)   7
Kelso, T. 1914 (Dundee)   1
Kennaway, J. 1934 (Celtic)   1
Kennedy, A. 1875 (Eastern, Third Lanark)   6
Kennedy, J. 1897 (Hibernian)   1
Kennedy, J. 1964 (Celtic)   6
Kennedy, J. 2004 (Celtic)   1
Kennedy, S. 1905 (Partick Thistle)   1
Kennedy, S. 1975 (Rangers)   5
Kennedy, S. 1978 (Aberdeen)   8
Kenneth, G. 2011 (Dundee U)   2
Ker, G. 1880 (Queen's Park)   5
Ker, W. 1872 (Queen's Park)   2
Kerr, A. 1955 (Partick Thistle)   2
Kerr, B. 2003 (Newcastle U)   3
Kerr, P. 1924 (Hibernian)   1
Key, G. 1902 (Hearts)   1

Key, W. 1907 (Queen's Park)   1
King, A. 1896 (Hearts, Celtic)   6
King, J. 1933 (Hamilton A)   2
King, W. S. 1929 (Queen's Park)   1
Kingsley, S. 2016 (Swansea C)   **1**
Kinloch, J. D. 1922 (Partick Thistle)   1
Kinnaird, A. F. 1873 (Wanderers)   1
Kinnear, D. 1938 (Rangers)   1
Kyle, K. 2002 (Sunderland, Kilmarnock)   10

Lambert, P. 1995 (Motherwell, Borussia Dortmund, Celtic)   40
Lambie, J. A. 1886 (Queen's Park)   3
Lambie, W. A. 1892 (Queen's Park)   9
Lamont, W. 1885 (Pilgrims)   1
Lang, A. 1880 (Dumbarton)   1
Lang, J. J. 1876 (Clydesdale, Third Lanark)   2
Latta, A. 1888 (Dumbarton)   2
Law, D. 1959 (Huddersfield T, Manchester C, Torino, Manchester U, Manchester C)   55
Law, G. 1910 (Rangers)   3
Law, T. 1928 (Chelsea)   2
Lawrence, J. 1911 (Newcastle U)   1
Lawrence, T. 1963 (Liverpool)   3
Lawson, D. 1923 (St Mirren)   1
Leckie, R. 1872 (Queen's Park)   1
Leggat, G. 1956 (Aberdeen, Fulham)   18
Leighton, J. 1983 (Aberdeen, Manchester U, Hibernian, Aberdeen)   91
Lennie, W. 1908 (Aberdeen)   2
Lennox, R. 1967 (Celtic)   10
Leslie, L. G. 1961 (Airdrieonians)   5
Levein, C. 1990 (Hearts)   16
Liddell, W. 1947 (Liverpool)   28
Liddle, D. 1931 (East Fife)   3
Lindsay, D. 1903 (St Mirren)   1
Lindsay, J. 1880 (Dumbarton)   8
Lindsay, J. 1888 (Renton)   3
Linwood, A. B. 1950 (Clyde)   1
Little, R. J. 1953 (Rangers)   1
Livingstone, G. T. 1906 (Manchester C, Rangers)   2
Lochhead, A. 1889 (Third Lanark)   1
Logan, J. 1891 (Ayr)   1
Logan, T. 1913 (Falkirk)   1
Logie, J. T. 1953 (Arsenal)   1
Loney, W. 1910 (Celtic)   2
Long, H. 1947 (Clyde)   1
Longair, W. 1894 (Dundee)   1
Lorimer, P. 1970 (Leeds U)   21
Love, A. 1931 (Aberdeen)   3
Low, A. 1934 (Falkirk)   1
Low, J. 1891 (Cambuslang)   1
Low, T. P. 1897 (Rangers)   1
Low, W. L. 1911 (Newcastle U)   5
Lowe, J. 1887 (St Bernards)   1
Lundie, J. 1886 (Hibernian)   1
Lyall, J. 1905 (Sheffield W)   1

McAdam, J. 1880 (Third Lanark)   1
McAllister, B. 1997 (Wimbledon)   3
McAllister, G. 1990 (Leicester C, Leeds U, Coventry C)   57
McAllister, J. R. 2004 (Livingston)   1
Macari, L. 1972 (Celtic, Manchester U)   24
McArthur, D. 1895 (Celtic)   3
McArthur, J. 2011 (Wigan Ath, Crystal Palace)   **24**
McAtee, A. 1913 (Celtic)   1
McAulay, J. 1884 (Arthurlie)   1
McAulay, J. D. 1882 (Dumbarton)   9
McAulay, R. 1932 (Rangers)   2
Macauley, A. R. 1947 (Brentford, Arsenal)   7
McAvennie, F. 1986 (West Ham U, Celtic)   5
McBain, E. 1894 (St Mirren)   1
McBain, N. 1922 (Manchester U, Everton)   3
McBride, J. 1967 (Celtic)   2
McBride, P. 1904 (Preston NE)   6
McCall, A. 1888 (Renton)   1
McCall, A. S. M. 1990 (Everton, Rangers)   40
McCall, J. 1886 (Renton)   5
McCalliog, J. 1967 (Sheffield W, Wolverhampton W)   5
McCallum, N. 1888 (Renton)   1
McCann, N. 1999 (Hearts, Rangers, Southampton)   26
McCann, R. J. 1959 (Motherwell)   5
McCartney, W. 1902 (Hibernian)   1

McClair, B. 1987 (Celtic, Manchester U)	30
McClory, A. 1927 (Motherwell)	3
McCloy, P. 1924 (Ayr U)	2
McCloy, P. 1973 (Rangers)	4
McCoist, A. 1986 (Rangers, Kilmarnock)	61
McColl, I. M. 1950 (Rangers)	14
McColl, R. S. 1896 (Queen's Park, Newcastle U, Queen's Park)	13
McColl, W. 1895 (Renton)	1
McCombie, A. 1903 (Sunderland, Newcastle U)	4
McCorkindale, J. 1891 (Partick Thistle)	1
McCormack, R. 2008 (Motherwell, Cardiff C, Leeds U, Fulham)	**13**
McCormick, R. 1886 (Abercorn)	1
McCrae, D. 1929 (St Mirren)	2
McCreadie, A. 1893 (Rangers)	2
McCreadie, E. G. 1965 (Chelsea)	23
McCulloch, D. 1935 (Hearts, Brentford, Derby Co)	7
McCulloch, L. 2005 (Wigan Ath, Rangers)	18
MacDonald, A. 1976 (Rangers)	1
McDonald, J. 1886 (Edinburgh University)	1
McDonald, J. 1956 (Sunderland)	2
MacDougall, E. J. 1975 (Norwich C)	7
McDougall, J. 1877 (Vale of Leven)	5
McDougall, J. 1926 (Airdrieonians)	1
McDougall, J. 1931 (Liverpool)	2
McEveley, J. 2008 (Derby Co)	3
McFadden, J. 2002 (Motherwell, Everton, Birmingham C)	48
McFadyen, W. 1934 (Motherwell)	2
Macfarlane, A. 1904 (Dundee)	5
Macfarlane, W. 1947 (Hearts)	1
McFarlane, R. 1896 (Greenock Morton)	1
McGarr, E. 1970 (Aberdeen)	2
McGarvey, F. P. 1979 (Liverpool, Celtic)	7
McGeoch, A. 1876 (Dumbreck)	4
McGhee, J. 1886 (Hibernian)	1
McGhee, M. 1983 (Aberdeen)	4
McGinn, J. 2016 (Hibernian)	**1**
McGinlay, J. 1994 (Bolton W)	13
McGonagle, W. 1933 (Celtic)	6
McGrain, D. 1973 (Celtic)	62
McGregor, A. J. 2007 (Rangers, Besiktas, Hull C)	**35**
McGregor, J. C. 1877 (Vale of Leven)	4
McGrory, J. 1928 (Celtic)	7
McGrory, J. E. 1965 (Kilmarnock)	3
McGuire, W. 1881 (Beith)	2
McGurk, F. 1934 (Birmingham)	1
McHardy, H. 1885 (Rangers)	1
McInally, A. 1989 (Aston Villa, Bayern Munich)	8
McInally, J. 1987 (Dundee U)	10
McInally, T. B. 1926 (Celtic)	2
McInnes, D. 2003 (WBA)	2
McInnes, T. 1889 (Cowlairs)	1
McIntosh, W. 1905 (Third Lanark)	1
McIntyre, A. 1878 (Vale of Leven)	2
McIntyre, H. 1880 (Rangers)	1
McIntyre, J. 1884 (Rangers)	1
MacKay, D. 1959 (Celtic)	14
Mackay, D. C. 1957 (Hearts, Tottenham H)	22
Mackay, G. 1988 (Hearts)	4
Mackay, M. 2004 (Norwich C)	5
McKay, B. 2016 (Rangers)	**1**
McKay, J. 1924 (Blackburn R)	1
McKay, J. 1928 (Newcastle U)	1
McKean, R. 1976 (Rangers)	1
McKenzie, D. 1938 (Brentford)	1
Mackenzie, J. A. 1954 (Partick Thistle)	9
McKeown, M. 1889 (Celtic)	2
McKie, J. 1898 (East Stirling)	1
McKillop, T. R. 1938 (Rangers)	1
McKimmie, S. 1989 (Aberdeen)	40
McKinlay, D. 1922 (Liverpool)	2
McKinlay, T. 1996 (Celtic)	22
McKinlay, W. 1994 (Dundee U, Blackburn R)	29
McKinnon, A. 1874 (Queen's Park)	1
McKinnon, R. 1966 (Rangers)	28
McKinnon, R. 1994 (Motherwell)	3
MacKinnon, W. 1883 (Dumbarton)	4
MacKinnon, W. W. 1872 (Queen's Park)	9
McLaren, A. 1929 (St Johnstone)	5
McLaren, A. 1947 (Preston NE)	4
McLaren, A. 1992 (Hearts, Rangers)	24
McLaren, A. 2001 (Kilmarnock)	1

McLaren, J. 1888 (Hibernian, Celtic)	3
McLean, A. 1926 (Celtic)	4
McLean, D. 1896 (St Bernards)	2
McLean, D. 1912 (Sheffield W)	1
McLean, G. 1968 (Dundee)	1
McLean, K. 2016 (Aberdeen)	**1**
McLean, T. 1969 (Kilmarnock)	6
McLeish, A. 1980 (Aberdeen)	77
McLeod, D. 1905 (Celtic)	4
McLeod, J. 1888 (Dumbarton)	5
MacLeod, J. M. 1961 (Hibernian)	4
MacLeod, M. 1985 (Celtic, Borussia Dortmund, Hibernian)	20
McLeod, W. 1886 (Cowlairs)	1
McLintock, A. 1875 (Vale of Leven)	3
McLintock, F. 1963 (Leicester C, Arsenal)	9
McLuckie, J. S. 1934 (Manchester C)	1
McMahon, A. 1892 (Celtic)	6
McManus, S. 2007 (Celtic, Middlesbrough)	26
McMenemy, J. 1905 (Celtic)	12
McMenemy, J. 1934 (Motherwell)	1
McMillan, I. L. 1952 (Airdrieonians, Rangers)	6
McMillan, J. 1897 (St Bernards)	1
McMillan, T. 1887 (Dumbarton)	1
McMullan, J. 1920 (Partick Thistle, Manchester C)	16
McNab, A. 1921 (Morton)	2
McNab, A. 1937 (Sunderland, WBA)	2
McNab, C. D. 1931 (Dundee)	6
McNab, J. S. 1923 (Liverpool)	1
McNair, A. 1906 (Celtic)	15
McNamara, J. 1997 (Celtic, Wolverhampton W)	33
McNamee, D. 2004 (Livingston)	4
McNaught, W. 1951 (Raith R)	5
McNaughton, K. 2002 (Aberdeen, Cardiff C)	4
McNeill, W. 1961 (Celtic)	29
McNiel, H. 1874 (Queen's Park)	10
McNiel, M. 1876 (Rangers)	2
McPhail, J. 1950 (Celtic)	5
McPhail, R. 1927 (Airdrieonians, Rangers)	17
McPherson, D. 1892 (Kilmarnock)	1
McPherson, D. 1989 (Hearts, Rangers)	27
McPherson, J. 1875 (Clydesdale)	1
McPherson, J. 1879 (Vale of Leven)	8
McPherson, J. 1888 (Kilmarnock, Cowlairs, Rangers)	9
McPherson, J. 1891 (Hearts)	1
McPherson, R. 1882 (Arthurlie)	1
McQueen, G. 1974 (Leeds U, Manchester U)	30
McQueen, M. 1890 (Leith Ath)	2
McRorie, D. M. 1931 (Morton)	1
McSpadyen, A. 1939 (Partick Thistle)	2
McStay, P. 1984 (Celtic)	76
McStay, W. 1921 (Celtic)	13
McSwegan, G. 2000 (Hearts)	2
McTavish, J. 1910 (Falkirk)	1
McWattie, G. C. 1901 (Queen's Park)	2
McWilliam, P. 1905 (Newcastle U)	8
Mackay-Steven, G. 2013 (Dundee U)	1
Mackail-Smith, C. 2011 (Peterborough U, Brighton & HA)	7
Mackie, J. C. 2011 (QPR)	9
Madden, J. 1893 (Celtic)	2
Maguire, C. 2011 (Aberdeen)	2
Main, F. R. 1938 (Rangers)	1
Main, J. 1909 (Hibernian)	1
Maley, W. 1893 (Celtic)	2
Maloney, S. R. 2006 (Celtic, Aston Villa, Celtic, Wigan Ath, Chicago Fire, Hull C)	**47**
Malpas, M. 1984 (Dundee U)	55
Marshall, D. J. 2005 (Celtic, Cardiff C)	**24**
Marshall, G. 1992 (Celtic)	1
Marshall, H. 1899 (Celtic)	2
Marshall, J. 1885 (Third Lanark)	4
Marshall, J. 1921 (Middlesbrough, Llanelly)	7
Marshall, J. 1932 (Rangers)	3
Marshall, R. W. 1892 (Rangers)	2
Martin, B. 1995 (Motherwell)	2
Martin, C. H. 2014 (Derby Co)	**8**
Martin, F. 1954 (Aberdeen)	6
Martin, N. 1965 (Hibernian, Sunderland)	3
Martin, R. K. A. 2011 (Norwich C)	**25**
Martis, J. 1961 (Motherwell)	1
Mason, J. 1949 (Third Lanark)	7
Massie, A. 1932 (Hearts, Aston Villa)	18
Masson, D. S. 1976 (QPR, Derby Co)	17

Mathers, D. 1954 (Partick Thistle)	1
Matteo, D. 2001 (Leeds U)	6
Maxwell, W. S. 1898 (Stoke C)	1
May, J. 1906 (Rangers)	5
May, S. 2015 (Sheffield W)	1
Meechan, P. 1896 (Celtic)	1
Meiklejohn, D. D. 1922 (Rangers)	15
Menzies, A. 1906 (Hearts)	1
Mercer, R. 1912 (Hearts)	2
Middleton, R. 1930 (Cowdenbeath)	1
Millar, J. 1897 (Rangers)	3
Millar, J. 1963 (Rangers)	2
Miller, A. 1939 (Hearts)	1
Miller, C. 2001 (Dundee U)	1
Miller, J. 1931 (St Mirren)	5
Miller, K. 2001 (Rangers, Wolverhampton W, Celtic, Derby Co, Rangers, Bursaspor, Cardiff C, Vancouver Whitecaps)	69
Miller, L. 2006 (Dundee U, Aberdeen)	3
Miller, P. 1882 (Dumbarton)	3
Miller, T. 1920 (Liverpool, Manchester U)	3
Miller, W. 1876 (Third Lanark)	1
Miller, W. 1947 (Celtic)	6
Miller, W. 1975 (Aberdeen)	65
Mills, W. 1936 (Aberdeen)	3
Milne, J. V. 1938 (Middlesbrough)	2
Mitchell, D. 1890 (Rangers)	5
Mitchell, J. 1908 (Kilmarnock)	3
Mitchell, R. C. 1951 (Newcastle U)	2
Mochan, N. 1954 (Celtic)	3
Moir, W. 1950 (Bolton W)	1
Moncur, R. 1968 (Newcastle U)	16
Morgan, H. 1898 (St Mirren, Liverpool)	2
Morgan, W. 1968 (Burnley, Manchester U)	21
Morris, D. 1923 (Raith R)	6
Morris, H. 1950 (East Fife)	1
Morrison, J. C. 2008 (WBA)	**41**
Morrison, T. 1927 (St Mirren)	1
Morton, A. L. 1920 (Queen's Park, Rangers)	31
Morton, H. A. 1929 (Kilmarnock)	2
Mudie, J. K. 1957 (Blackpool)	17
Muir, W. 1907 (Dundee)	1
Muirhead, T. A. 1922 (Rangers)	8
Mulgrew, C. P. 2012 (Celtic)	**24**
Mulhall, G. 1960 (Aberdeen, Sunderland)	3
Munro, A. D. 1937 (Hearts, Blackpool)	3
Munro, F. M. 1971 (Wolverhampton W)	9
Munro, I. 1979 (St Mirren)	7
Munro, N. 1888 (Abercorn)	2
Murdoch, J. 1931 (Motherwell)	1
Murdoch, R. 1966 (Celtic)	12
Murphy, F. 1938 (Celtic)	1
Murray, I. 2003 (Hibernian, Rangers)	6
Murray, J. 1895 (Renton)	1
Murray, J. 1958 (Hearts)	5
Murray, J. W. 1890 (Vale of Leven)	1
Murray, P. 1896 (Hibernian)	2
Murray, S. 1972 (Aberdeen)	1
Murty, G. S. 2004 (Reading)	4
Mutch, G. 1938 (Preston NE)	1
Naismith, S. J. 2007 (Kilmarnock, Rangers, Everton, Norwich C)	**43**
Napier, C. E. 1932 (Celtic, Derby Co)	5
Narey, D. 1977 (Dundee U)	35
Naysmith, G. A. 2000 (Hearts, Everton, Sheffield U)	46
Neil, R. G. 1896 (Hibernian, Rangers)	2
Neill, R. W. 1876 (Queen's Park)	5
Neilson, R. 2007 (Hearts)	1
Nellies, P. 1913 (Hearts)	2
Nelson, J. 1925 (Cardiff C)	4
Nevin, P. K. F. 1986 (Chelsea, Everton, Tranmere R)	28
Niblo, T. D. 1904 (Aston Villa)	1
Nibloe, J. 1929 (Kilmarnock)	11
Nicholas, C. 1983 (Celtic, Arsenal, Aberdeen)	20
Nicholson, B. 2001 (Dunfermline Ath)	3
Nicol, S. 1985 (Liverpool)	27
Nisbet, J. 1929 (Ayr U)	3
Niven, J. B. 1885 (Moffat)	1
O'Connor, G. 2002 (Hibernian, Lokomotiv Moscow, Birmingham C)	16
O'Donnell, F. 1937 (Preston NE, Blackpool)	6
O'Donnell, P. 1994 (Motherwell)	1

Ogilvie, D. H. 1934 (Motherwell)	1
O'Hare, J. 1970 (Derby Co)	13
O'Neil, B. 1996 (Celtic, Wolfsburg, Derby Co, Preston NE)	7
O'Neil, J. 2001 (Hibernian)	1
Ormond, W. E. 1954 (Hibernian)	6
O'Rourke, F. 1907 (Airdrieonians)	1
Orr, J. 1892 (Kilmarnock)	1
Orr, R. 1902 (Newcastle U)	2
Orr, T. 1952 (Morton)	2
Orr, W. 1900 (Celtic)	3
Orrock, R. 1913 (Falkirk)	1
Oswald, J. 1889 (Third Lanark, St Bernards, Rangers)	3
Parker, A. H. 1955 (Falkirk, Everton)	15
Parlane, D. 1973 (Rangers)	12
Parlane, R. 1878 (Vale of Leven)	3
Paterson, C. 2016 (Aberdeen)	**1**
Paterson, G. D. 1939 (Celtic)	1
Paterson, J. 1920 (Leicester C)	1
Paterson, J. 1931 (Cowdenbeath)	3
Paton, A. 1952 (Motherwell)	2
Paton, D. 1896 (St Bernards)	1
Paton, M. 1883 (Dumbarton)	5
Paton, R. 1879 (Vale of Leven)	2
Patrick, J. 1897 (St Mirren)	2
Paul, H. McD. 1909 (Queen's Park)	3
Paul, W. 1888 (Partick Thistle)	3
Paul, W. 1891 (Dykebar)	1
Pearson, S. P. 2004 (Motherwell, Celtic, Derby Co)	10
Pearson, T. 1947 (Newcastle U)	2
Penman, A. 1966 (Dundee)	1
Pettigrew, W. 1976 (Motherwell)	5
Phillips, J. 1877 (Queen's Park)	3
Phillips, M. 2012 (Blackpool, QPR)	**4**
Plenderleith, J. B. 1961 (Manchester C)	1
Porteous, W. 1903 (Hearts)	1
Pressley, S. J. 2000 (Hearts)	32
Pringle, C. 1921 (St Mirren)	1
Provan, D. 1964 (Rangers)	5
Provan, D. 1980 (Celtic)	10
Pursell, P. 1914 (Queen's Park)	1
Quashie, N. F. 2004 (Portsmouth, Southampton, WBA)	14
Quinn, J. 1905 (Celtic)	11
Quinn, P. 1961 (Motherwell)	4
Rae, G. 2001 (Dundee, Rangers, Cardiff C)	14
Rae, J. 1889 (Third Lanark)	2
Raeside, J. S. 1906 (Third Lanark)	1
Raisbeck, A. G. 1900 (Liverpool)	8
Rankin, G. 1890 (Vale of Leven)	2
Rankin, R. 1929 (St Mirren)	3
Redpath, W. 1949 (Motherwell)	9
Reid, J. G. 1914 (Airdrieonians)	3
Reid, R. 1938 (Brentford)	2
Reid, W. 1911 (Rangers)	9
Reilly, L. 1949 (Hibernian)	38
Rennie, H. G. 1900 (Hearts, Hibernian)	13
Renny-Tailyour, H. W. 1873 (Royal Engineers)	1
Rhind, A. 1872 (Queen's Park)	1
Rhodes, J. L. 2012 (Huddersfield T, Blackburn R)	13
Richmond, A. 1906 (Queen's Park)	1
Richmond, J. T. 1877 (Clydesdale, Queen's Park)	3
Ring, T. 1953 (Clyde)	12
Rioch, B. D. 1975 (Derby Co, Everton, Derby Co)	24
Riordan, D. G. 2006 (Hibernian)	3
Ritchie, A. 1891 (East Stirlingshire)	1
Ritchie, H. 1923 (Hibernian)	2
Ritchie, J. 1897 (Queen's Park)	1
Ritchie, M. T. 2015 (Bournemouth)	**10**
Ritchie, P. S. 1999 (Hearts, Bolton W, Walsall)	7
Ritchie, W. 1962 (Rangers)	1
Robb, D. T. 1971 (Aberdeen)	5
Robb, W. 1926 (Rangers, Hibernian)	2
Robertson, A. 1955 (Clyde)	5
Robertson, A. 2014 (Dundee U, Hull C)	**10**
Robertson, D. 1992 (Rangers)	3
Robertson, G. 1910 (Motherwell, Sheffield W)	4
Robertson, G. 1938 (Kilmarnock)	1
Robertson, H. 1962 (Dundee)	1
Robertson, J. 1931 (Dundee)	2
Robertson, J. 1991 (Hearts)	16
Robertson, J. N. 1978 (Nottingham F, Derby Co)	28

Robertson, J. G. 1965 (Tottenham H) | 1
Robertson, J. T. 1898 (Everton, Southampton, Rangers) | 16
Robertson, P. 1903 (Dundee) | 1
Robertson, S. 2009 (Dundee U) | 2
Robertson, T. 1889 (Queen's Park) | 4
Robertson, T. 1898 (Hearts) | 1
Robertson, W. 1887 (Dumbarton) | 2
Robinson, R. 1974 (Dundee) | 4
Robson, B. G. G. 2008 (Dundee U, Celtic, Middlesbrough) | 17
Ross, M. 2002 (Rangers) | 13
Rough, A. 1976 (Partick Thistle, Hibernian) | 53
Rougvie, D. 1984 (Aberdeen) | 1
Rowan, A. 1880 (Caledonian, Queen's Park) | 2
Russell, D. 1895 (Hearts, Celtic) | 6
Russell, J. 1890 (Cambuslang) | 1
Russell, J. S. S. 2015 (Derby Co) | **4**
Russell, W. F. 1924 (Airdrieonians) | 2
Rutherford, E. 1948 (Rangers) | 1

St John, I. 1959 (Motherwell, Liverpool) | 21
Saunders, S. 2011 (Motherwell) | 1
Sawers, W. 1895 (Dundee) | 1
Scarff, P. 1931 (Celtic) | 1
Schaedler, E. 1974 (Hibernian) | 1
Scott, A. S. 1957 (Rangers, Everton) | 16
Scott, J. 1966 (Hibernian) | 1
Scott, J. 1971 (Dundee) | 2
Scott, M. 1898 (Airdrieonians) | 1
Scott, R. 1894 (Airdrieonians) | 1
Scoular, J. 1951 (Portsmouth) | 9
Sellar, W. 1885 (Battlefield, Queen's Park) | 9
Semple, W. 1886 (Cambuslang) | 1
Severin, S. D. 2002 (Hearts, Aberdeen) | 15
Shankly, W. 1938 (Preston NE) | 5
Sharp, G. M. 1985 (Everton) | 12
Sharp, J. 1904 (Dundee, Woolwich Arsenal, Fulham) | 5
Shaw, D. 1947 (Hibernian) | 8
Shaw, F. W. 1884 (Pollokshields Ath) | 2
Shaw, J. 1947 (Rangers) | 4
Shearer, D. 1994 (Aberdeen) | 7
Shearer, R. 1961 (Rangers) | 4
Shinnie, A. M. 2013 (Inverness CT) | 1
Sillars, D. C. 1891 (Queen's Park) | 5
Simpson, J. 1895 (Third Lanark) | 3
Simpson, J. 1935 (Rangers) | 14
Simpson, N. 1983 (Aberdeen) | 5
Simpson, R. C. 1967 (Celtic) | 5
Sinclair, G. L. 1910 (Hearts) | 3
Sinclair, J. W. E. 1966 (Leicester C) | 1
Skene, L. H. 1904 (Queen's Park) | 1
Sloan, T. 1904 (Third Lanark) | 1
Smellie, R. 1887 (Queen's Park) | 6
Smith, A. 1898 (Rangers) | 20
Smith, D. 1966 (Aberdeen, Rangers) | 2
Smith, G. 1947 (Hibernian) | 18
Smith, H. G. 1988 (Hearts) | 3
Smith, J. 1924 (Ayr U) | 1
Smith, J. 1935 (Rangers) | 2
Smith, J. 1968 (Aberdeen, Newcastle U) | 4
Smith, J. 2003 (Celtic) | 2
Smith, J. E. 1959 (Celtic) | 2
Smith, Jas 1872 (Queen's Park) | 1
Smith, John 1877 (Mauchline, Edinburgh University, Queen's Park) | 10
Smith, N. 1897 (Rangers) | 12
Smith, R. 1872 (Queen's Park) | 2
Smith, T. M. 1934 (Kilmarnock, Preston NE) | 2
Snodgrass, R. 2011 (Leeds U, Norwich C, Hull C) | **17**
Somers, P. 1905 (Celtic) | 4
Somers, W. S. 1879 (Third Lanark, Queen's Park) | 3
Somerville, G. 1886 (Queen's Park) | 1
Souness, G. J. 1975 (Middlesbrough, Liverpool, Sampdoria) | 54
Speedie, D. R. 1985 (Chelsea, Coventry C) | 10
Speedie, F. 1903 (Rangers) | 3
Speirs, J. H. 1908 (Rangers) | 1
Spencer, J. 1995 (Chelsea, QPR) | 14
Stanton, P. 1966 (Hibernian) | 16
Stark, J. 1909 (Rangers) | 2
Steel, W. 1947 (Morton, Derby Co, Dundee) | 30
Steele, D. M. 1923 (Huddersfield) | 3
Stein, C. 1969 (Rangers, Coventry C) | 21
Stephen, J. F. 1947 (Bradford) | 2

Stevenson, G. 1928 (Motherwell) | 12
Stewart, A. 1888 (Queen's Park) | 2
Stewart, A. 1894 (Third Lanark) | 1
Stewart, D. 1888 (Dumbarton) | 1
Stewart, D. 1893 (Queen's Park) | 3
Stewart, D. S. 1978 (Leeds U) | 1
Stewart, G. 1906 (Hibernian, Manchester C) | 4
Stewart, J. 1977 (Kilmarnock, Middlesbrough) | 2
Stewart, M. J. 2002 (Manchester U, Hearts) | 4
Stewart, R. 1981 (West Ham U) | 10
Stewart, W. G. 1898 (Queen's Park) | 2
Stockdale, R. K. 2002 (Middlesbrough) | 5
Storrier, D. 1899 (Celtic) | 3
Strachan, G. D. 1980 (Aberdeen, Manchester U, Leeds U) | 50
Sturrock, P. 1981 (Dundee U) | 20
Sullivan, N. 1997 (Wimbledon, Tottenham H) | 28
Summers, W. 1926 (St Mirren) | 1
Symon, J. S. 1939 (Rangers) | 1

Tait, T. S. 1911 (Sunderland) | 1
Taylor, J. 1872 (Queen's Park) | 6
Taylor, J. D. 1892 (Dumbarton, St Mirren) | 4
Taylor, W. 1892 (Hearts) | 1
Teale, G. 2006 (Wigan Ath, Derby Co) | 13
Telfer, P. N. 2000 (Coventry C) | 1
Telfer, W. 1933 (Motherwell) | 2
Telfer, W. D. 1954 (St Mirren) | 1
Templeton, R. 1902 (Aston Villa, Newcastle U, Woolwich Arsenal, Kilmarnock) | 11
Tierney, K. 2016 (Celtic) | **1**
Thompson, S. 2002 (Dundee U, Rangers) | 16
Thomson, A. 1886 (Arthurlie) | 1
Thomson, A. 1889 (Third Lanark) | 1
Thomson, A. 1909 (Airdrieonians) | 1
Thomson, A. 1926 (Celtic) | 3
Thomson, C. 1904 (Hearts, Sunderland) | 21
Thomson, C. 1937 (Sunderland) | 1
Thomson, D. 1920 (Dundee) | 1
Thomson, J. 1930 (Celtic) | 4
Thomson, J. J. 1872 (Queen's Park) | 3
Thomson, J. R. 1933 (Everton) | 1
Thomson, K. 2009 (Rangers, Middlesbrough) | 3
Thomson, R. 1932 (Celtic) | 1
Thomson, R. W. 1927 (Falkirk) | 1
Thomson, S. 1884 (Rangers) | 2
Thomson, W. 1892 (Dumbarton) | 4
Thomson, W. 1896 (Dundee) | 1
Thomson, W. 1980 (St Mirren) | 7
Thornton, W. 1947 (Rangers) | 7
Toner, W. 1959 (Kilmarnock) | 2
Townsley, T. 1926 (Falkirk) | 1
Troup, A. 1920 (Dundee, Everton) | 5
Turnbull, E. 1948 (Hibernian) | 8
Turner, T. 1884 (Arthurlie) | 1
Turner, W. 1885 (Pollokshields Ath) | 2

Ure, J. F. 1962 (Dundee, Arsenal) | 11
Urquhart, D. 1934 (Hibernian) | 1

Vallance, T. 1877 (Rangers) | 7
Venters, A. 1934 (Cowdenbeath, Rangers) | 3

Waddell, T. S. 1891 (Queen's Park) | 6
Waddell, W. 1947 (Rangers) | 17
Wales, H. M. 1933 (Motherwell) | 1
Walker, A. 1988 (Celtic) | 3
Walker, F. 1922 (Third Lanark) | 1
Walker, G. 1930 (St Mirren) | 4
Walker, J. 1895 (Hearts, Rangers) | 5
Walker, J. 1911 (Swindon T) | 9
Walker, J. N. 1993 (Hearts, Partick Thistle) | 2
Walker, R. 1900 (Hearts) | 29
Walker, T. 1935 (Hearts) | 20
Walker, W. 1909 (Clyde) | 2
Wallace, I. A. 1978 (Coventry C) | 3
Wallace, L. 2010 (Hearts, Rangers) | 8
Wallace, R. 2010 (Preston NE) | 1
Wallace, W. S. B. 1965 (Hearts, Celtic) | 7
Wardhaugh, J. 1955 (Hearts) | 2
Wark, J. 1979 (Ipswich T, Liverpool) | 28
Watson, A. 1881 (Queen's Park) | 3
Watson, J. 1903 (Sunderland, Middlesbrough) | 6
Watson, J. 1948 (Motherwell, Huddersfield T) | 2

Watson, J. A. K. 1878 (Rangers) 1
Watson, P. R. 1934 (Blackpool) 1
Watson, R. 1971 (Motherwell) 1
Watson, W. 1898 (Falkirk) 1
Watt, A. P. 2016 (Charlton Ath) **1**
Watt, F. 1889 (Kilbirnie) 4
Watt, W. W. 1887 (Queen's Park) 1
Waugh, W. 1938 (Hearts) 1
Webster, A. 2003 (Hearts, Dundee U, Hearts) 28
Weir, A. 1959 (Motherwell) 6
Weir, D. G. 1997 (Hearts, Everton, Rangers) 69
Weir, J. 1887 (Third Lanark) 1
Weir, J. B. 1872 (Queen's Park) 4
Weir, P. 1980 (St Mirren, Aberdeen) 6
White, John 1922 (Albion R, Hearts) 2
White, J. A. 1959 (Falkirk, Tottenham H) 22
White, W. 1907 (Bolton W) 2
Whitelaw, A. 1887 (Vale of Leven) 2
Whittaker, S. G. 2010 (Rangers, Norwich C) **31**
Whyte, D. 1988 (Celtic, Middlesbrough, Aberdeen) 12
Wilkie, L. 2002 (Dundee) 11
Williams, G. 2002 (Nottingham F) 5
Wilson, A. 1907 (Sheffield W) 6
Wilson, A. 1954 (Portsmouth) 1
Wilson, A. N. 1920 (Dunfermline, Middlesbrough) 12
Wilson, D. 1900 (Queen's Park) 1
Wilson, D. 1913 (Oldham Ath) 1
Wilson, D. 1961 (Rangers) 22

Wilson, D. 2011 (Liverpool) 5
Wilson, G. W. 1904 (Hearts, Everton, Newcastle U) 6
Wilson, Hugh 1890 (Newmilns, Sunderland, Third
  Lanark) 4
Wilson, I. A. 1987 (Leicester C, Everton) 5
Wilson, J. 1888 (Vale of Leven) 4
Wilson, M. 2011 (Celtic) 1
Wilson, P. 1926 (Celtic) 4
Wilson, P. 1975 (Celtic) 1
Wilson, R. P. 1972 (Arsenal) 1
Winters, R. 1999 (Aberdeen) 2
Wiseman, W. 1927 (Queen's Park) 2
Wood, G. 1979 (Everton, Arsenal) 4
Woodburn, W. A. 1947 (Rangers) 24
Wotherspoon, D. N. 1872 (Queen's Park) 2
Wright, K. 1992 (Hibernian) 1
Wright, S. 1993 (Aberdeen) 2
Wright, T. 1953 (Sunderland) 3
Wylie, T. G. 1890 (Rangers) 1

Yeats, R. 1965 (Liverpool) 2
Yorston, B. C. 1931 (Aberdeen) 1
Yorston, H. 1955 (Aberdeen) 1
Young, A. 1905 (Everton) 2
Young, A. 1960 (Hearts, Everton) 8
Young, G. L. 1947 (Rangers) 53
Young, J. 1906 (Celtic) 1
Younger, T. 1955 (Hibernian, Liverpool) 24

WALES

Adams, H. 1882 (Berwyn R, Druids) 4
Aizlewood, M. 1986 (Charlton Ath, Leeds U, Bradford
  C, Bristol C, Cardiff C) 39
Allchurch, I. J. 1951 (Swansea T, Newcastle U, Cardiff
  C, Swansea T) 68
Allchurch, L. 1955 (Swansea T, Sheffield U) 11
Allen, B. W. 1951 (Coventry C) 2
Allen, J. M. 2009 (Swansea C, Liverpool) **31**
Allen, M. 1986 (Watford, Norwich C, Millwall,
  Newcastle U) 14
Arridge, S. 1892 (Bootle, Everton, New Brighton Tower) 8
Astley, D. J. 1931 (Charlton Ath, Aston Villa, Derby Co,
  Blackpool) 13
Atherton, R. W. 1899 (Hibernian, Middlesbrough) 9

Bailiff, W. E. 1913 (Llanelly) 4
Baker, C. W. 1958 (Cardiff C) 7
Baker, W. G. 1948 (Cardiff C) 1
**Bale, G. F. 2006 (Southampton, Tottenham H,
  Real Madrid)** **61**
Bamford, T. 1931 (Wrexham) 5
Barnard, D. S. 1998 (Barnsley, Grimsby T) 22
Barnes, W. 1948 (Arsenal) 22
Bartley, T. 1898 (Glossop NE) 1
Bastock, A. M. 1892 (Shrewsbury T) 1
Beadles, G. H. 1925 (Cardiff C) 2
Bell, W. S. 1881 (Shrewsbury Engineers, Crewe Alex) 5
Bellamy, C. D. 1998 (Norwich C, Coventry C,
  Newcastle U, Blackburn R, Liverpool, West Ham U,
  Manchester C, Liverpool, Cardiff C) 78
Bennion, S. R. 1926 (Manchester U) 10
Berry, G. F. 1979 (Wolverhampton W, Stoke C) 5
Blackmore, C. G. 1985 (Manchester U, Middlesbrough) 39
Blake, D. J. 2011 (Cardiff C, Crystal Palace) 14
Blake, N. A. 1994 (Sheffield U, Bolton W, Blackburn R,
  Wolverhampton W) 29
Blew, H. 1899 (Wrexham) 22
Boden, T. 1880 (Wrexham) 1
Bodin, P. J. 1990 (Swindon T, Crystal Palace,
  Swindon T) 23
Boulter, L. M. 1939 (Brentford) 1
Bowdler, H. E. 1893 (Shrewsbury T) 1
Bowdler, J. C. H. 1890 (Shrewsbury T,
  Wolverhampton W, Shrewsbury T) 4
Bowen, D. L. 1955 (Arsenal) 19
Bowen, E. 1880 (Druids) 2
Bowen, J. P. 1994 (Swansea C, Birmingham C) 2
Bowen, M. R. 1986 (Tottenham H, Norwich C,
  West Ham U) 41
Bowsher, S. J. 1929 (Burnley) 1
Boyle, T. 1981 (Crystal Palace) 2
Bradley, M. S. 2010 (Walsall) 1

Bradshaw, T. W. C. 2016 (Walsall) **1**
Britten, T. J. 1878 (Parkgrove, Presteigne) 2
Brookes, S. J. 1900 (Llandudno) 2
Brown, A. I. 1926 (Aberdare Ath) 1
Brown, J. R. 2006 (Gillingham, Blackburn R, Aberdeen)
  3
Browning, M. T. 1996 (Bristol R, Huddersfield T) 5
Bryan, T. 1886 (Oswestry) 2
Buckland, T. 1899 (Bangor) 1
Burgess, W. A. R. 1947 (Tottenham H) 32
Burke, T. 1883 (Wrexham, Newton Heath) 8
Burnett, T. B. 1877 (Ruabon) 1
Burton, A. D. 1963 (Norwich C, Newcastle U) 9
Butler, J. 1893 (Chirk) 3
Butler, W. T. 1900 (Druids) 2

Cartwright, L. 1974 (Coventry C, Wrexham) 7
Carty, T. See McCarthy (Wrexham).
Challen, J. B. 1887 (Corinthians, Wellingborough GS) 4
Chapman, T. 1894 (Newtown, Manchester C, Grimsby T)
  7
Charles, J. M. 1981 (Swansea C, QPR, Oxford U) 19
Charles, M. 1955 (Swansea T, Arsenal, Cardiff C) 31
Charles, W. J. 1950 (Leeds U, Juventus, Leeds U,
  Cardiff C) 38
Chester, J. G. 2014 (Hull C, WBA) **17**
Church, S. R. 2009 (Reading, Charlton Ath) **38**
Clarke, R. J. 1949 (Manchester C) 22
Coleman, C. 1992 (Crystal Palace, Blackburn R, Fulham)32
Collier, D. J. 1921 (Grimsby T) 1
Collins, D. L. 2005 (Sunderland, Stoke C) 12
**Collins, J. M. 2004 (Cardiff C, West Ham U, Aston Villa,
  West Ham U)** **48**
Collins, W. S. 1931 (Llanelly) 1
Collison, J. D. 2008 (West Ham U) 16
Conde, C. 1884 (Chirk) 3
Cook, F. C. 1925 (Newport Co, Portsmouth) 8
Cornforth, J. M. 1995 (Swansea C) 2
**Cotterill, D. R. G. B. 2006 (Bristol C, Wigan Ath,
  Sheffield U, Swansea C, Doncaster R,
  Birmingham C)** **23**
Coyne, D. 1996 (Tranmere R, Grimsby T, Leicester C,
  Burnley, Tranmere R) 16
**Crofts, A. L. 2006 (Gillingham, Brighton & HA,
  Norwich C, Brighton & HA, Bolton W)** **28**
Crompton, W. 1931 (Wrexham) 3
Cross, E. A. 1876 (Wrexham) 2
Crosse, K. 1879 (Druids) 3
Crossley, M. G. 1997 (Nottingham F, Middlesbrough,
  Fulham) 8
Crowe, V. H. 1959 (Aston Villa) 16
Cumner, R. H. 1939 (Arsenal) 3

Curtis, A. T. 1976 (Swansea C, Leeds U, Swansea C,
  Southampton, Cardiff C) 35
Curtis, E. R. 1928 (Cardiff C, Birmingham) 3

Daniel, R. W. 1951 (Arsenal, Sunderland) 21
Darvell, S. 1897 (Oxford University) 2
Davies, A. 1876 (Wrexham) 2
Davies, A. 1904 (Druids, Middlesbrough) 2
Davies, A. 1983 (Manchester U, Newcastle U,
  Swansea C, Bradford C) 13
Davies, A. O. 1885 (Barmouth, Swifts, Wrexham,
  Crewe Alex) 9
Davies, A. R. 2006 (Yeovil T) 1
Davies, A. T. 1891 (Shrewsbury T) 1
Davies, B. T. 2013 (Swansea C, Tottenham H) 25
Davies, C. 1972 (Charlton Ath) 1
Davies, C. M. 2006 (Oxford U, Verona, Oldham Ath,
  Barnsley) 7
Davies, D. 1904 (Bolton W) 3
Davies, D. C. 1899 (Brecon, Hereford) 2
Davies, D. W. 1912 (Treharris, Oldham Ath) 2
Davies, E. Lloyd 1904 (Stoke, Northampton T) 16
Davies, E. R. 1953 (Newcastle U) 6
Davies, G. 1980 (Fulham, Manchester C) 16
Davies, Rev. H. 1928 (Wrexham) 1
Davies, Idwal 1923 (Liverpool Marine) 1
Davies, J. E. 1885 (Oswestry) 1
Davies, Jas 1878 (Wrexham) 1
Davies, John 1879 (Wrexham) 1
Davies, Jos 1888 (Newton Heath, Wolverhampton W) 7
Davies, Jos 1889 (Everton, Chirk, Ardwick, Sheffield U,
  Manchester C, Millwall, Reading) 11
Davies, J. P. 1883 (Druids) 2
Davies, Ll. 1907 (Wrexham, Everton, Wrexham) 13
Davies, L. S. 1922 (Cardiff C) 23
Davies, O. 1890 (Wrexham) 1
Davies, R. 1883 (Wrexham) 3
Davies, R. 1885 (Druids) 1
Davies, R. O. 1892 (Wrexham) 2
Davies, R. T. 1964 (Norwich C, Southampton,
  Portsmouth) 29
Davies, R. W. 1964 (Bolton W, Newcastle U, Manchester
  C, Manchester U, Blackpool) 34
Davies, S. 2001 (Tottenham H, Everton, Fulham) 58
Davies, S. I. 1996 (Manchester U) 1
Davies, Stanley 1920 (Preston NE, Everton, WBA,
  Rotherham U) 18
Davies, T. 1886 (Oswestry) 1
Davies, T. 1903 (Druids) 4
Davies, W. 1884 (Wrexham) 1
Davies, W. 1924 (Swansea T, Cardiff C, Notts Co) 17
Davies, William 1903 (Wrexham, Blackburn R) 11
Davies, W. C. 1908 (Crystal Palace, WBA,
  Crystal Palace) 4
Davies, W. D. 1975 (Everton, Wrexham, Swansea C) 52
Davies, W. H. 1876 (Oswestry) 4
Davis, G. 1978 (Wrexham) 3
Davis, W. O. 1913 (Millwall Ath) 5
Day, A. 1934 (Tottenham H) 1
Deacy, N. 1977 (PSV Eindhoven, Beringen) 12
Dearson, D. J. 1939 (Birmingham) 3
Delaney, M. A. 2000 (Aston Villa) 36
Derrett, S. C. 1969 (Cardiff C) 4
Dewey, F. T. 1931 (Cardiff Corinthians) 2
Dibble, A. 1986 (Luton T, Manchester C) 3
Dorman, A. 2010 (St Mirren, Crystal Palace) 3
Doughty, J. 1886 (Druids, Newton Heath) 8
Doughty, R. 1888 (Newton Heath) 2
Duffy, R. M. 2006 (Portsmouth) 13
Dummett, P. 2014 (Newcastle U) 2
Durban, A. 1966 (Derby Co) 27
Dwyer, P. J. 1978 (Cardiff C) 10

Eardley, N. 2008 (Oldham Ath, Blackpool) 16
Earnshaw, R. 2002 (Cardiff C, WBA, Norwich C,
  Derby Co, Nottingham F, Cardiff C) 59
Easter, J. M. 2007 (Wycombe W, Plymouth Arg,
  Milton Keynes D, Crystal Palace, Millwall) 12
Eastwood, F. 2008 (Wolverhampton W, Coventry C) 11
Edwards, C. 1878 (Wrexham) 1
Edwards, C. N. H. 1996 (Swansea C) 1
Edwards, D. A. 2008 (Luton T, Wolverhampton W) 35
Edwards, G. 1947 (Birmingham C, Cardiff C) 12
Edwards, H. 1878 (Wrexham Civil Service, Wrexham) 8

Edwards, J. H. 1876 (Wanderers) 1
Edwards, J. H. 1895 (Oswestry) 3
Edwards, J. H. 1898 (Aberystwyth) 1
Edwards, L. T. 1957 (Charlton Ath) 2
Edwards, R. I. 1978 (Chester, Wrexham) 4
Edwards, R. O. 2003 (Aston Villa, Wolverhampton W) 15
Edwards, R. W. 1998 (Bristol C) 4
Edwards, T. 1932 (Linfield) 1
Egan, W. 1892 (Chirk) 1
Ellis, B. 1932 (Motherwell) 6
Ellis, E. 1931 (Nunhead, Oswestry) 3
Emanuel, W. J. 1973 (Bristol C) 2
England, H. M. 1962 (Blackburn R, Tottenham H) 44
Evans, B. C. 1972 (Swansea C, Hereford U) 7
Evans, C. M. 2008 (Manchester C, Sheffield U) 13
Evans, D. G. 1926 (Reading, Huddersfield T) 4
Evans, H. P. 1922 (Cardiff C) 6
Evans, I. 1976 (Crystal Palace) 13
Evans, J. 1893 (Oswestry) 3
Evans, J. 1912 (Cardiff C) 8
Evans, J. H. 1922 (Southend U) 4
Evans, Len 1927 (Aberdare Ath, Cardiff C,
  Birmingham) 4
Evans, M. 1884 (Oswestry) 1
Evans, P. S. 2002 (Brentford, Bradford C) 2
Evans, R. 1902 (Clapton) 1
Evans, R. E. 1906 (Wrexham, Aston Villa, Sheffield U) 10
Evans, R. O. 1902 (Wrexham, Blackburn R, Coventry C) 10
Evans, R. S. 1964 (Swansea T) 1
Evans, S. J. 2007 (Wrexham) 7
Evans, T. J. 1927 (Clapton Orient, Newcastle U) 4
Evans, W. 1933 (Tottenham H) 6
Evans, W. A. W. 1876 (Oxford University) 2
Evans, W. G. 1890 (Bootle, Aston Villa) 3
Evelyn, E. C. 1887 (Crusaders) 1
Eyton-Jones, J. A. 1883 (Wrexham) 4

Farmer, G. 1885 (Oswestry) 2
Felgate, D. 1984 (Lincoln C) 1
Finnigan, R. J. 1930 (Wrexham) 1
Fletcher, C. N. 2004 (Bournemouth, West Ham U,
  Crystal Palace) 36
Flynn, B. 1975 (Burnley, Leeds U, Burnley) 66
Fon Williams, O. 2016 (Inverness CT) 1
Ford, T. 1947 (Swansea T, Aston Villa, Sunderland,
  Cardiff C) 38
Foulkes, H. E. 1932 (WBA) 1
Foulkes, W. I. 1952 (Newcastle U) 11
Foulkes, W. T. 1884 (Oswestry) 2
Fowler, J. 1925 (Swansea T) 6
Freestone, R. 2000 (Swansea C) 1

Gabbidon, D. L. 2002 (Cardiff C, West Ham U,
  QPR, Crystal Palace) 49
Garner, G. 2006 (Leyton Orient) 1
Garner, J. 1896 (Aberystwyth) 1
Giggs, R. J. 1992 (Manchester U) 64
Giles, D. C. 1980 (Swansea C, Crystal Palace) 12
Gillam, S. G. 1889 (Wrexham, Shrewsbury, Clapton) 5
Glascodine, G. 1879 (Wrexham) 1
Glover, E. M. 1932 (Grimsby T) 7
Godding, G. 1923 (Wrexham) 2
Godfrey, B. C. 1964 (Preston NE) 3
Goodwin, U. 1881 (Ruthin) 1
Goss, J. 1991 (Norwich C) 9
Gough, R. T. 1883 (Oswestry White Star) 1
Gray, A. 1924 (Oldham Ath, Manchester C,
  Manchester Central, Tranmere R, Chester) 24
Green, A. W. 1901 (Aston Villa, Notts Co, Nottingham F) 8
Green, C. R. 1965 (Birmingham C) 15
Green, G. H. 1938 (Charlton Ath) 4
Green, R. M. 1998 (Wolverhampton W) 2
Grey, Dr W. 1876 (Druids) 2
Griffiths, A. T. 1971 (Wrexham) 17
Griffiths, F. J. 1900 (Blackpool) 2
Griffiths, G. 1887 (Chirk) 1
Griffiths, J. H. 1953 (Swansea T) 1
Griffiths, L. 1902 (Wrexham) 1
Griffiths, M. W. 1947 (Leicester C) 11
Griffiths, P. 1884 (Chirk) 6
Griffiths, P. H. 1932 (Everton) 1

Griffiths, T. P. 1927 (Everton, Bolton W, Middlesbrough,
Aston Villa) 21
**Gunter, C. R. 2007 (Cardiff C, Tottenham H,
Nottingham F, Reading) 73**

Hall, G. D. 1988 (Chelsea) 9
Hallam, J. 1889 (Oswestry) 1
Hanford, H. 1934 (Swansea T, Sheffield W) 7
Harrington, A. C. 1956 (Cardiff C) 11
Harris, C. S. 1976 (Leeds U) 24
Harris, W. C. 1954 (Middlesbrough) 6
Harrison, W. C. 1899 (Wrexham) 5
Hartson, J. 1995 (Arsenal, West Ham U, Wimbledon,
Coventry C, Celtic) 51
Haworth, S. O. 1997 (Cardiff C, Coventry C) 5
Hayes, A. 1890 (Wrexham) 2
Henley, A. D. 2016 (Blackburn R) 2
**Hennessey, W. R. 2007 (Wolverhampton W,
Crystal Palace) 62**
Hennessey, W. T. 1962 (Birmingham C, Nottingham F,
Derby Co) 39
Hersee, A. M. 1886 (Bangor) 2
Hersee, R. 1886 (Llandudno) 1
Hewitt, R. 1958 (Cardiff C) 5
Hewitt, T. J. 1911 (Wrexham, Chelsea, South Liverpool)
8
Heywood, D. 1879 (Druids) 1
Hibbott, H. 1880 (Newtown Excelsior, Newtown) 3
Higham, G. G. 1878 (Oswestry) 2
Hill, M. R. 1972 (Ipswich T) 2
Hockey, T. 1972 (Sheffield U, Norwich C, Aston Villa) 9
Hoddinott, T. F. 1921 (Watford) 2
Hodges, G. 1984 (Wimbledon, Newcastle U, Watford,
Sheffield U) 18
Hodgkinson, A. V. 1908 (Southampton) 1
Holden, A. 1984 (Chester C) 1
Hole, B. G. 1963 (Cardiff C, Blackburn R, Aston Villa,
Swansea C) 30
Hole, W. J. 1921 (Swansea T) 9
Hollins, D. M. 1962 (Newcastle U) 11
Hopkins, I. J. 1935 (Brentford) 12
Hopkins, J. 1983 (Fulham, Crystal Palace) 16
Hopkins, M. 1956 (Tottenham H) 34
Horne, B. 1988 (Portsmouth, Southampton, Everton,
Birmingham C) 59
Howell, E. G. 1888 (Builth) 3
Howells, R. G. 1954 (Cardiff C) 2
Hugh, A. R. 1930 (Newport Co) 1
Hughes, A. 1894 (Rhos) 2
Hughes, A. 1907 (Chirk) 1
Hughes, C. M. 1992 (Luton T, Wimbledon) 8
Hughes, E. 1899 (Everton, Tottenham H) 14
Hughes, E. 1906 (Wrexham, Nottingham F, Wrexham,
Manchester C) 16
Hughes, F. W. 1882 (Northwich Victoria) 6
Hughes, I. 1951 (Luton T) 4
Hughes, J. 1877 (Cambridge University, Aberystwyth) 2
Hughes, J. 1905 (Liverpool) 3
Hughes, J. I. 1935 (Blackburn R) 1
Hughes, L. M. 1984 (Manchester U, Barcelona,
Manchester U, Chelsea, Southampton) 72
Hughes, P. W. 1887 (Bangor) 3
Hughes, W. 1891 (Bootle) 3
Hughes, W. A. 1949 (Blackburn R) 5
Hughes, W. M. 1938 (Birmingham) 10
Humphreys, J. V. 1947 (Everton) 1
Humphreys, R. 1888 (Druids) 1
Hunter, A. H. 1887 (FA of Wales Secretary) 1
Huws, E. W. 2014 (Manchester C, Wigan Ath) 7

Isgrove, L. J. 2016 (Southampton) 1

Jackett, K. 1983 (Watford) 31
Jackson, W. 1899 (St Helens Rec) 1
James, E. 1893 (Chirk) 8
James, E. G. 1966 (Blackpool) 9
James, L. 1972 (Burnley, Derby Co, QPR, Burnley,
Swansea C, Sunderland) 54
James, R. M. 1979 (Swansea C, Stoke C, QPR,
Leicester C, Swansea C) 47
James, W. 1931 (West Ham U) 2
Jarrett, R. H. 1889 (Ruthin) 2
Jarvis, A. L. 1967 (Hull C) 3
Jenkins, E. 1925 (Lovell's Ath) 1

Jenkins, J. 1924 (Brighton & HA) 8
Jenkins, R. W. 1902 (Rhyl) 1
Jenkins, S. R. 1996 (Swansea C, Huddersfield T) 16
Jenkyns, C. A. L. 1892 (Small Heath, Woolwich Arsenal,
Newton Heath, Walsall) 8
Jennings, W. 1914 (Bolton W) 11
John, D. C. 2013 (Cardiff C) 2
John, R. F. 1923 (Arsenal) 15
John, W. R. 1931 (Walsall, Stoke C, Preston NE,
Sheffield U, Swansea T) 14
Johnson, A. J. 1999 (Nottingham F, WBA) 15
Johnson, M. G. 1964 (Swansea T) 1
Jones, A. 1987 (Port Vale, Charlton Ath) 6
Jones, A. F. 1877 (Oxford University) 1
Jones, A. T. 1905 (Nottingham F, Notts Co) 2
Jones, Bryn 1935 (Wolverhampton W, Arsenal) 17
Jones, B. S. 1963 (Swansea T, Plymouth Arg, Cardiff C) 15
Jones, Charlie 1926 (Nottingham F, Arsenal) 8
Jones, Cliff 1954 (Swansea T, Tottenham H, Fulham) 59
Jones, C. W. 1935 (Birmingham) 2
Jones, D. 1888 (Chirk, Bolton W, Manchester C) 14
Jones, D. E. 1976 (Norwich C) 8
Jones, D. O. 1934 (Leicester C) 7
Jones, Evan 1910 (Chelsea, Oldham Ath, Bolton W) 7
Jones, F. R. 1885 (Bangor) 3
Jones, F. W. 1893 (Small Heath) 1
Jones, G. P. 1907 (Wrexham) 2
Jones, H. 1902 (Aberaman) 1
Jones, Humphrey 1885 (Bangor, Queen's Park,
East Stirlingshire, Queen's Park) 14
Jones, Ivor 1920 (Swansea T, WBA) 10
Jones, Jeffrey 1908 (Llandrindod Wells) 1
Jones, J. 1876 (Druids) 3
Jones, J. 1883 (Berwyn Rangers) 3
Jones, J. 1925 (Wrexham) 1
Jones, J. L. 1895 (Sheffield U, Tottenham H) 21
Jones, J. Love 1906 (Stoke, Middlesbrough) 2
Jones, J. O. 1901 (Bangor) 2
Jones, J. P. 1976 (Liverpool, Wrexham, Chelsea,
Huddersfield T) 72
Jones, J. T. 1912 (Stoke, Crystal Palace) 15
Jones, K. 1950 (Aston Villa) 1
Jones, Leslie J. 1933 (Cardiff C, Coventry C, Arsenal 11
Jones, M. A. 2007 (Wrexham) 2
Jones, M. G. 2000 (Leeds U, Leicester C) 13
Jones, P. L. 1997 (Liverpool, Tranmere R) 2
Jones, P. S. 1997 (Stockport Co, Southampton,
Wolverhampton W, QPR) 50
Jones, P. W. 1971 (Bristol R) 1
Jones, R. 1887 (Bangor, Crewe Alex) 3
Jones, R. 1898 (Leicester Fosse) 1
Jones, R. 1899 (Druids) 1
Jones, R. 1900 (Bangor) 2
Jones, R. 1906 (Millwall) 2
Jones, R. A. 1884 (Druids) 4
Jones, R. A. 1994 (Sheffield W) 1
Jones, R. S. 1894 (Everton) 1
Jones, S. 1887 (Wrexham, Chester) 2
Jones, S. 1893 (Wrexham, Burton Swifts, Druids) 6
Jones, T. 1926 (Manchester U) 4
Jones, T. D. 1908 (Aberdare) 1
Jones, T. G. 1938 (Everton) 17
Jones, T. J. 1932 (Sheffield W) 2
Jones, V. P. 1995 (Wimbledon) 9
Jones, W. E. A. 1947 (Swansea T, Tottenham H) 4
Jones, W. J. 1901 (Aberdare, West Ham U) 4
Jones, W. Lot 1905 (Manchester C, Southend U) 20
Jones, W. P. 1889 (Druids, Wynnstay) 4
Jones, W. R. 1897 (Aberystwyth) 1

Keenor, F. C. 1920 (Cardiff C, Crewe Alex) 32
Kelly, F. C. 1899 (Wrexham, Druids) 3
Kelsey, A. J. 1954 (Arsenal) 41
Kenrick, S. L. 1876 (Druids, Oswestry,
Shropshire Wanderers) 5
Ketley, C. F. 1882 (Druids) 1
King, A. P. 2009 (Leicester C) 36
King, J. 1955 (Swansea T) 1
Kinsey, N. 1951 (Norwich C, Birmingham C) 7
Knill, A. R. 1989 (Swansea C) 1
Koumas, J. 2001 (Tranmere R, WBA, Wigan Ath) 34
Krzywicki, R. L. 1970 (WBA, Huddersfield T) 8

Lambert, R. 1947 (Liverpool) 5

Latham, G. 1905 (Liverpool, Southport Central,
 Cardiff C) 10
Law, B. J. 1990 (QPR) 1
Lawrence, E. 1930 (Clapton Orient, Notts Co) 2
Lawrence, S. 1932 (Swansea T) 8
Lawrence, T. M. 2016 (Leicester C) 4
Lea, A. 1889 (Wrexham) 4
Lea, C. 1965 (Ipswich T) 2
Leary, P. 1889 (Bangor) 1
Ledley, J. C. 2006 (Cardiff C, Celtic, Crystal Palace) 67
Leek, K. 1961 (Leicester C, Newcastle U, Birmingham C,
 Northampton T) 13
Legg, A. 1996 (Birmingham C, Cardiff C) 6
Lever, A. R. 1953 (Leicester C) 1
Lewis, B. 1891 (Chester, Wrexham, Middlesbrough,
 Wrexham) 10
Lewis, D. 1927 (Arsenal) 3
Lewis, D. 1983 (Swansea C) 1
Lewis, D. J. 1933 (Swansea T) 2
Lewis, D. M. 1890 (Bangor) 2
Lewis, J. 1906 (Bristol R) 1
Lewis, J. 1926 (Cardiff C) 1
Lewis, T. 1881 (Wrexham) 2
Lewis, W. 1885 (Bangor, Crewe Alex, Chester,
 Manchester C, Chester) 27
Lewis, W. L. 1927 (Swansea T, Huddersfield T) 6
Llewellyn, C. M. 1998 (Norwich C, Wrexham) 6
Lloyd, B. W. 1976 (Wrexham) 3
Lloyd, J. W. 1879 (Wrexham, Newtown) 2
Lloyd, R. A. 1891 (Ruthin) 2
Lockley, A. 1898 (Chirk) 1
Lovell, S. 1982 (Crystal Palace, Millwall) 6
Lowndes, S. R. 1983 (Newport Co, Millwall, Barnsley) 10
Lowrie, G. 1948 (Coventry C, Newcastle U) 4
Lucas, P. M. 1962 (Leyton Orient) 4
Lucas, W. H. 1949 (Swansea T) 7
Lumberg, A. 1929 (Wrexham, Wolverhampton W) 4
Lynch, J. J. 2013 (Huddersfield T) 1

MacDonald, S. B. 2011 (Swansea C, Bournemouth) 4
McCarthy, T. P. 1889 (Wrexham) 1
McMillan, R. 1881 (Shrewsbury Engineers) 2
Maguire, G. T. 1990 (Portsmouth) 7
Mahoney, J. F. 1968 (Stoke C, Middlesbrough,
 Swansea C) 51
Mardon, P. J. 1996 (WBA) 1
Margetson, M. W. 2004 (Cardiff C) 1
Marriott, A. 1996 (Wrexham) 5
Martin, T. J. 1930 (Newport Co) 1
Marustik, C. 1982 (Swansea C) 6
Mates, J. 1891 (Chirk) 3
Matthews, A. J. 2011 (Cardiff C, Celtic) 13
Matthews, R. W. 1921 (Liverpool, Bristol C, Bradford) 3
Matthews, W. 1905 (Chester) 2
Matthias, J. S. 1896 (Brymbo, Shrewsbury T,
 Wolverhampton W) 5
Matthias, T. J. 1914 (Wrexham) 12
Mays, A. W. 1929 (Wrexham) 1
Medwin, T. C. 1953 (Swansea T, Tottenham H) 30
Melville, A. K. 1990 (Swansea C, Oxford U, Sunderland,
 Fulham, West Ham U) 65
Meredith, S. 1900 (Chirk, Stoke, Leyton) 8
Meredith, W. H. 1895 (Manchester C, Manchester U) 48
Mielczarek, R. 1971 (Rotherham U) 1
Millership, H. 1920 (Rotherham Co) 6
Millington, A. H. 1963 (WBA, Crystal Palace,
 Peterborough U, Swansea C) 21
Mills, T. J. 1934 (Clapton Orient, Leicester C) 4
Mills-Roberts, R. H. 1885 (St Thomas' Hospital,
 Preston NE, Llanberis) 8
Moore, G. 1960 (Cardiff C, Chelsea, Manchester U,
 Northampton T, Charlton Ath) 21
Morgan, C. 2007 (Milton Keynes D, Peterborough U,
 Preston NE) 23
Morgan, J. R. 1877 (Cambridge University,
 Derby School Staff) 10
Morgan, J. T. 1905 (Wrexham) 1
Morgan-Owen, H. 1902 (Oxford University, Corinthians) 4
Morgan-Owen, M. M. 1897 (Oxford University,
 Corinthians) 13
Morison, S. W. 2011 (Millwall, Norwich C) 20
Morley, E. J. 1925 (Swansea T, Clapton Orient) 4
Morris, A. G. 1896 (Aberystwyth, Swindon T,
 Nottingham F) 21

Morris, C. 1900 (Chirk, Derby Co, Huddersfield T) 27
Morris, E. 1893 (Chirk) 3
Morris, H. 1894 (Sheffield U, Manchester C, Grimsby T)
 3
Morris, J. 1887 (Oswestry) 1
Morris, J. 1898 (Chirk) 1
Morris, R. 1900 (Chirk, Shrewsbury T) 6
Morris, R. 1902 (Newtown, Druids, Liverpool, Leeds C,
 Grimsby T, Plymouth Arg) 11
Morris, S. 1937 (Birmingham) 5
Morris, W. 1947 (Burnley) 5
Moulsdale, J. R. B. 1925 (Corinthians) 1
Murphy, J. P. 1933 (WBA) 15
Myhill, G. O. 2008 (Hull C, WBA) 19

Nardiello, D. 1978 (Coventry C) 2
Nardiello, D. A. 2007 (Barnsley, QPR) 3
Neal, J. E. 1931 (Colwyn Bay) 2
Neilson, A. B. 1992 (Newcastle U, Southampton) 5
Newnes, J. 1926 (Nelson) 1
Newton, L. F. 1912 (Cardiff Corinthians) 1
Nicholas, D. S. 1923 (Stoke, Swansea T) 3
Nicholas, P. 1979 (Crystal Palace, Arsenal, Crystal Palace,
 Luton T, Aberdeen, Chelsea, Watford) 73
Nicholls, J. 1924 (Newport Co, Cardiff C) 4
Niedzwiecki, E. A. 1985 (Chelsea) 2
Nock, W. 1897 (Newtown) 1
Nogan, L. M. 1992 (Watford, Reading) 2
Norman, A. J. 1986 (Hull C) 5
Nurse, M. T. G. 1960 (Swansea T, Middlesbrough) 12
Nyatanga, L. J. 2006 (Derby Co, Bristol C) 34

O'Callaghan, E. 1929 (Tottenham H) 11
Oliver, A. 1905 (Bangor, Blackburn R) 2
Oster, J. M. 1998 (Everton, Sunderland) 13
O'Sullivan, P. A. 1973 (Brighton & HA) 3
Owen, D. 1879 (Oswestry) 1
Owen, E. 1884 (Ruthin Grammar School) 3
Owen, G. 1888 (Chirk, Newton Heath, Chirk) 4
Owen, J. 1892 (Newton Heath) 1
Owen, T. 1879 (Oswestry) 1
Owen, Trevor 1899 (Crewe Alex) 2
Owen, W. 1884 (Chirk) 16
Owen, W. P. 1880 (Ruthin) 12
Owens, J. 1902 (Wrexham) 1

Page, M. E. 1971 (Birmingham C) 28
Page, R. J. 1997 (Watford, Sheffield U, Cardiff C,
 Coventry C) 41
Palmer, D. 1957 (Swansea T) 3
Parris, J. E. 1932 (Bradford) 1
Parry, B. J. 1951 (Swansea T) 1
Parry, C. 1891 (Everton, Newtown) 13
Parry, E. 1922 (Liverpool) 5
Parry, M. 1901 (Liverpool) 16
Parry, P. I. 2004 (Cardiff C) 12
Parry, T. D. 1900 (Oswestry) 7
Parry, W. 1895 (Newtown) 1
Partridge, D. W. 2005 (Motherwell, Bristol C) 7
Pascoe, C. 1984 (Swansea C, Sunderland) 10
Paul, R. 1949 (Swansea T, Manchester C) 33
Peake, E. 1908 (Aberystwyth, Liverpool) 11
Peers, E. J. 1914 (Wolverhampton W, Port Vale) 12
Pembridge, M. A. 1992 (Luton T, Derby Co, Sheffield
 W, Benfica, Everton, Fulham) 54
Perry, E. 1938 (Doncaster R) 3
Perry, J. 1994 (Cardiff C) 1
Phennah, E. 1878 (Civil Service) 1
Phillips, C. 1931 (Wolverhampton W, Aston Villa) 13
Phillips, D. 1984 (Plymouth Arg, Manchester C,
 Coventry C, Norwich C, Nottingham F) 62
Phillips, L. 1971 (Cardiff C, Aston Villa, Swansea C,
 Charlton Ath) 58
Phillips, T. J. S. 1973 (Chelsea) 4
Phoenix, H. 1882 (Wrexham) 1
Pipe, D. R. 2003 (Coventry C) 1
Poland, G. 1939 (Wrexham) 2
Pontin, K. 1980 (Cardiff C) 2
Powell, A. 1947 (Leeds U, Everton, Birmingham C) 8
Powell, D. 1968 (Wrexham, Sheffield U) 11
Powell, I. V. 1947 (QPR, Aston Villa) 8
Powell, J. 1878 (Druids, Bolton W, Newton Heath) 15
Powell, Seth 1885 (Oswestry, WBA) 7
Price, H. 1907 (Aston Villa, Burton U, Wrexham) 5

Price, J. 1877 (Wrexham)   12
Price, L. P. 2006 (Ipswich T, Derby Co,
   Crystal Palace)   11
Price, P. 1980 (Luton T, Tottenham H)   25
Pring, K. D. 1966 (Rotherham U)   3
Pritchard, H. K. 1985 (Bristol C)   1
Pryce-Jones, A. W. 1895 (Newtown)   1
Pryce-Jones, W. E. 1887 (Cambridge University)   5
Pugh, A. 1889 (Rhostyllen)   1
Pugh, D. H. 1896 (Wrexham, Lincoln C)   7
Pugsley, J. 1930 (Charlton Ath)   1
Pullen, W. J. 1926 (Plymouth Arg)   1

Ramsey, A. J. 2009 (Arsenal)   **44**
Rankmore, F. E. J. 1966 (Peterborough U)   1
Ratcliffe, K. 1981 (Everton, Cardiff C)   59
Rea, J. C. 1894 (Aberystwyth)   9
Ready, K. 1997 (QPR)   5
Reece, G. I. 1966 (Sheffield U, Cardiff C)   29
Reed, W. G. 1955 (Ipswich T)   2
Rees, A. 1984 (Birmingham C)   1
Rees, J. M. 1992 (Luton T)   1
Rees, R. R. 1965 (Coventry C, WBA, Nottingham F)   39
Rees, W. 1949 (Cardiff C, Tottenham H)   4
Ribeiro, C. M. 2010 (Bristol C)   2
Richards, A. 1932 (Barnsley)   1
Richards, A. D. J. 2012 (Swansea C)   **10**
Richards, D. 1931 (Wolverhampton W, Brentford,
   Birmingham)   21
Richards, G. 1899 (Druids, Oswestry, Shrewsbury T)   6
Richards, R. W. 1920 (Wolverhampton W, West Ham U,
   Mold)   9
Richards, S. V. 1947 (Cardiff C)   1
Richards, W. E. 1933 (Fulham)   1
Ricketts, S. D. 2005 (Swansea C, Hull C, Bolton W,
   Wolverhampton W)   52
Roach, J. 1885 (Oswestry)   1
Robbins, W. W. 1931 (Cardiff C, WBA)   11
Roberts, A. M. 1993 (QPR)   2
Roberts, D. F. 1973 (Oxford U, Hull C)   17
Roberts, G. W. 2000 (Tranmere R)   9
Roberts, I. W. 1990 (Watford, Huddersfield T,
   Leicester C, Norwich C)   15
Roberts, Jas 1913 (Wrexham)   2
Roberts, J. 1879 (Corwen, Berwyn R)   7
Roberts, J. 1881 (Ruthin)   2
Roberts, J. 1906 (Bradford C)   1
Roberts, J. G. 1971 (Arsenal, Birmingham C)   22
Roberts, J. H. 1949 (Bolton W)   1
Roberts, N. W. 2000 (Wrexham, Wigan Ath)   4
Roberts, P. S. 1974 (Portsmouth)   4
Roberts, R. 1884 (Druids, Bolton W, Preston NE)   9
Roberts, R. 1886 (Wrexham)   3
Roberts, R. 1891 (Rhos, Crewe Alex)   2
Roberts, R. L. 1890 (Chester)   1
Roberts, S. W. 2005 (Wrexham)   1
Roberts, W. 1879 (Llangollen, Berwyn R)   6
Roberts, W. 1883 (Rhyl)   1
Roberts, W. 1886 (Wrexham)   4
Roberts, W. H. 1882 (Ruthin, Rhyl)   6
Robinson, C. P. 2000 (Wolverhampton W, Portsmouth,
   Sunderland, Norwich C, Toronto Lynx)   52
Robinson, J. R. C. 1996 (Charlton Ath)   30
Robson-Kanu, T. H. 2010 (Reading)   **35**
Rodrigues, P. J. 1965 (Cardiff C, Leicester C, Sheffield W)   40
Rogers, J. P. 1896 (Wrexham)   3
Rogers, W. 1931 (Wrexham)   2
Roose, L. R. 1900 (Aberystwyth, London Welsh, Stoke,
   Everton, Stoke, Sunderland)   24
Rouse, R. V. 1959 (Crystal Palace)   1
Rowlands, A. C. 1914 (Tranmere R)   1
Rowley, T. 1959 (Tranmere R)   1
Rush, I. 1980 (Liverpool, Juventus, Liverpool)   73
Russell, M. R. 1912 (Merthyr T, Plymouth Arg)   23

Sabine, H. W. 1887 (Oswestry)   1
Saunders, D. 1986 (Brighton & HA, Oxford U,
   Derby Co, Liverpool, Aston Villa, Galatasaray,
   Nottingham F, Sheffield U, Benfica, Bradford C)   75
Savage, R. W. 1996 (Crewe Alex, Leicester C,
   Birmingham)   39
Savin, G. 1878 (Oswestry)   1
Sayer, P. A. 1977 (Cardiff C)   7
Scrine, F. H. 1950 (Swansea T)   2

Sear, C. R. 1963 (Manchester C)   1
Shaw, E. G. 1882 (Oswestry)   3
Sherwood, A. T. 1947 (Cardiff C, Newport Co)   41
Shone, W. W. 1879 (Oswestry)   1
Shortt, W. W. 1947 (Plymouth Arg)   12
Showers, D. 1975 (Cardiff C)   2
Sidlow, C. 1947 (Liverpool)   7
Sisson, H. 1885 (Wrexham Olympic)   3
Slatter, N. 1983 (Bristol R, Oxford U)   22
Smallman, D. P. 1974 (Wrexham, Everton)   7
Southall, N. 1982 (Everton)   92
Speed, G. A. 1990 (Leeds U, Everton, Newcastle U,
   Bolton W)   85
Sprake, G. 1964 (Leeds U, Birmingham C)   37
Stansfield, F. 1949 (Cardiff C)   1
Stevenson, B. 1978 (Leeds U, Birmingham C)   15
Stevenson, N. 1982 (Swansea C)   4
Stitfall, R. F. 1953 (Cardiff C)   2
Stock, B. B. 2010 (Doncaster R)   3
Sullivan, D. 1953 (Cardiff C)   17
Symons, C. J. 1992 (Portsmouth, Manchester C, Fulham,
   Crystal Palace)   37

Tapscott, D. R. 1954 (Arsenal, Cardiff C)   14
Taylor, G. K. 1996 (Crystal Palace, Sheffield U, Burnley,
   Nottingham F)   15
Taylor, J. 1898 (Wrexham)   1
Taylor, J. W. T. 2015 (Reading)   1
Taylor, N. J. 2010 (Wrexham, Swansea C)   **34**
Taylor, O. D. S. 1893 (Newtown)   4
Thatcher, B. D. 2004 (Leicester C, Manchester C)   7
Thomas, C. 1899 (Druids)   2
Thomas, D. A. 1957 (Swansea T)   2
Thomas, D. S. 1948 (Fulham)   4
Thomas, E. 1925 (Cardiff Corinthians)   1
Thomas, G. 1885 (Wrexham)   2
Thomas, H. 1927 (Manchester U)   1
Thomas, Martin R. 1987 (Newcastle U)   1
Thomas, Mickey 1977 (Wrexham, Manchester U,
   Everton, Brighton & HA, Stoke C, Chelsea, WBA)   51
Thomas, R. J. 1967 (Swindon T, Derby Co, Cardiff C)   50
Thomas, T. 1898 (Bangor)   2
Thomas, W. R. 1931 (Newport Co)   2
Thomson, D. 1876 (Druids)   1
Thomson, G. F. 1876 (Druids)   2
Toshack, J. B. 1969 (Cardiff C, Liverpool, Swansea C)   40
Townsend, W. 1887 (Newtown)   1
Trainer, H. 1895 (Wrexham)   3
Trainer, J. 1887 (Bolton W, Preston NE)   20
Trollope, P. J. 1997 (Derby Co, Fulham, Coventry C,
   Northampton T)   9
Tudur-Jones, O. 2008 (Swansea C, Norwich C,
   Hibernian)   7
Turner, H. G. 1937 (Charlton Ath)   8
Turner, J. 1892 (Wrexham)   1
Turner, R. E. 1891 (Wrexham)   2
Turner, W. H. 1887 (Wrexham)   5

Van Den Hauwe, P. W. R. 1985 (Everton)   13
**Vaughan, D. O. 2003 (Crewe Alex, Real Sociedad,
   Blackpool, Sunderland, Nottingham F)**   **42**
Vaughan, Jas 1893 (Druids)   4
Vaughan, John 1879 (Oswestry, Druids, Bolton W)   11
Vaughan, J. O. 1885 (Rhyl)   1
Vaughan, N. 1983 (Newport Co, Cardiff C)   10
Vaughan, T. 1885 (Rhyl)   1
Vearncombe, G. 1958 (Cardiff C)   2
Vernon, T. R. 1957 (Blackburn R, Everton, Stoke C)   32
Villars, A. K. 1974 (Cardiff C)   3
Vizard, E. T. 1911 (Bolton W)   22
**Vokes, S. M. 2008 (Bournemouth, Wolverhampton W,
   Burnley)**   **44**

Walley, J. T. 1971 (Watford)   1
Walsh, I. P. 1980 (Crystal Palace, Swansea C)   18
Ward, D. 1959 (Bristol R, Cardiff C)   2
Ward, D. 2000 (Notts Co, Nottingham F)   5
Ward, D. 2016 (Liverpool)   **3**
Warner, J. 1937 (Swansea T, Manchester U)   2
Warren, F. W. 1929 (Cardiff C, Middlesbrough, Hearts)   6
Watkins, A. E. 1898 (Leicester Fosse, Aston Villa,
   Millwall)   5
Watkins, W. M. 1902 (Stoke, Aston Villa, Sunderland,
   Stoke)   10

Webster, C. 1957 (Manchester U) 4
Weston, R. D. 2000 (Arsenal, Cardiff C) 7
Whatley, W. J. 1939 (Tottenham H) 2
White, P. F. 1896 (London Welsh) 1
Wilcock, A. R. 1890 (Oswestry) 1
Wilding, J. 1885 (Wrexham Olympians, Bootle, Wrexham) 9
Williams, A. 1994 (Reading, Wolverhampton W,
    Reading) 13
Williams, A. E. 2008 (Stockport Co, Swansea C) 65
Williams, A. L. 1931 (Wrexham) 1
Williams, A. P. 1998 (Southampton) 2
Williams, B. 1930 (Bristol C) 1
Williams, B. D. 1928 (Swansea T, Everton) 10
Williams, D. G. 1988 (Derby Co, Ipswich T) 13
Williams, D. M. 1986 (Norwich C) 5
Williams, D. R. 1921 (Merthyr T, Sheffield W,
    Manchester U) 8
Williams, E. 1893 (Crewe Alex) 2
Williams, E. 1901 (Druids) 5
Williams, G. 1893 (Chirk) 6
Williams, G. C. 2014 (Fulham) 7
Williams, G. E. 1960 (WBA) 26
Williams, G. G. 1961 (Swansea T) 5
Williams, G. J. 2006 (West Ham U, Ipswich T) 2
Williams, G. J. J. 1951 (Cardiff C) 1
Williams, G. O. 1907 (Wrexham) 1

Williams, H. J. 1965 (Swansea T) 3
Williams, H. T. 1949 (Newport Co, Leeds U) 4
Williams, J. H. 1884 (Oswestry) 1
Williams, J. J. 1939 (Wrexham) 1
Williams, J. P. 2013 (Crystal Palace) 16
Williams, J. T. 1925 (Middlesbrough) 1
Williams, J. W. 1912 (Crystal Palace) 2
Williams, R. 1935 (Newcastle U) 2
Williams, R. P. 1886 (Caernarvon) 1
Williams, S. G. 1954 (WBA, Southampton) 43
Williams, W. 1876 (Druids, Oswestry, Druids) 11
Williams, W. 1925 (Northampton T) 1
Wilson, H. 2013 (Liverpool) 1
Wilson, J. S. 2013 (Bristol C) 1
Witcomb, D. F. 1947 (WBA, Sheffield W) 3
Woosnam, A. P. 1959 (Leyton Orient, West Ham U,
    Aston Villa) 17
Woosnam, G. 1879 (Newtown Excelsior) 1
Worthington, T. 1894 (Newtown) 1
Wynn, G. A. 1909 (Wrexham, Manchester C) 11
Wynn, W. 1903 (Chirk) 1

Yorath, T. C. 1970 (Leeds U, Coventry C, Tottenham H,
    Vancouver Whitecaps) 59
Young, E. 1990 (Wimbledon, Crystal Palace,
    Wolverhampton W) 21

REPUBLIC OF IRELAND

Aherne, T. 1946 (Belfast Celtic, Luton T) 16
Aldridge, J. W. 1986 (Oxford U, Liverpool,
    Real Sociedad, Tranmere R) 69
Ambrose, P. 1955 (Shamrock R) 5
Anderson, J. 1980 (Preston NE, Newcastle U) 16
Andrews, K. J. 2009 (Blackburn R, WBA) 35
Andrews, P. 1936 (Bohemians) 1
Arrigan, T. 1938 (Waterford) 1
Arter, H. N. 2015 (Bournemouth) 2

Babb, P. A. 1994 (Coventry C, Liverpool, Sunderland) 35
Bailham, E. 1964 (Shamrock R) 1
Barber, E. 1966 (Shelbourne, Birmingham C) 2
Barrett, G. 2003 (Arsenal, Coventry C) 6
Barry, P. 1928 (Fordsons) 2
Beglin, J. 1984 (Liverpool) 15
Bennett, A. J. 2007 (Reading) 2
Bermingham, J. 1929 (Bohemians) 1
Bermingham, P. 1935 (St James' Gate) 1
Best, L. J. B. 2009 (Coventry C, Newcastle U) 7
Bonner, P. 1981 (Celtic) 80
Braddish, S. 1978 (Dundalk) 2
Bradshaw, P. 1939 (St James' Gate) 1
Brady, F. 1926 (Fordsons) 2
Brady, R. 2013 (Hull C, Norwich C) 27
Brady, T. R. 1964 (QPR) 6
Brady, W. L. 1975 (Arsenal, Juventus, Sampdoria,
    Internazionale, Ascoli, West Ham U) 72
Branagan, K. G. 1997 (Bolton W) 1
Breen, G. 1996 (Birmingham C, Coventry C,
    West Ham U, Sunderland) 63
Breen, T. 1937 (Manchester U, Shamrock R) 5
Brennan, F. 1965 (Drumcondra) 1
Brennan, S. A. 1965 (Manchester U, Waterford) 19
Brown, J. 1937 (Coventry C) 2
Browne, W. 1964 (Bohemians) 3
Bruce, A. S. 2007 (Ipswich T) 2
Buckley, L. 1984 (Shamrock R, Waregem) 2
Burke, F. 1952 (Cork Ath) 1
Burke, J. 1929 (Shamrock R) 1
Burke, J. 1934 (Cork) 1
Butler, P. J. 2000 (Sunderland) 1
Butler, T. 2003 (Sunderland) 2
Byrne, A. B. 1970 (Southampton) 14
Byrne, D. 1929 (Shelbourne, Shamrock R, Coleraine) 3
Byrne, J. 1928 (Bray Unknowns) 1
Byrne, J. 1985 (QPR, Le Havre, Brighton & HA,
    Sunderland, Millwall) 23
Byrne, J. 2004 (Shelbourne) 2
Byrne, P. 1931 (Dolphin, Shelbourne, Drumcondra) 3
Byrne, P. 1984 (Shamrock R) 8
Byrne, S. 1931 (Bohemians) 1

Campbell, A. 1985 (Santander) 3

Campbell, N. 1971 (St Patrick's Ath, Fortuna Cologne)11
Cannon, H. 1926 (Bohemians) 2
Cantwell, N. 1954 (West Ham U, Manchester U) 36
Carey, B. P. 1992 (Manchester U, Leicester C) 3
Carey, J. J. 1938 (Manchester U) 29
Carolan, J. 1960 (Manchester U) 2
Carr, S. 1999 (Tottenham H, Newcastle U) 44
Carroll, B. 1949 (Shelbourne) 2
Carroll, T. R. 1968 (Ipswich T, Birmingham C) 17
Carsley, L. K. 1998 (Derby Co, Blackburn R, Coventry
    C, Everton) 39
Cascarino, A. G. 1986 (Gillingham, Millwall, Aston
    Villa, Celtic, Chelsea, Marseille, Nancy) 88
Chandler, J. 1980 (Leeds U) 2
Chatton, H. A. 1931 (Shelbourne, Dumbarton, Cork) 3
Christie, C. S. F. 2015 (Derby Co) 5
Clark, C. 2011 (Aston Villa) 19
Clarke, C. R. 2004 (Stoke C) 2
Clarke, J. 1978 (Drogheda U) 1
Clarke, K. 1948 (Drumcondra) 2
Clarke, M. 1950 (Shamrock R) 1
Clinton, T. J. 1951 (Everton) 3
Coad, P. 1947 (Shamrock R) 11
Coffey, T. 1950 (Drumcondra) 1
Coleman, S. 2011 (Everton) 38
Colfer, M. D. 1950 (Shelbourne) 2
Colgan, N. 2002 (Hibernian, Barnsley) 9
Collins, F. 1927 (Jacobs) 1
Conmy, O. M. 1965 (Peterborough U) 5
Connolly, D. J. 1996 (Watford, Feyenoord,
    Wolverhampton W, Excelsior, Feyenoord,
    Wimbledon, West Ham U, Wigan Ath) 41
Connolly, H. 1937 (Cork) 1
Connolly, J. 1926 (Fordsons) 1
Conroy, G. A. 1970 (Stoke C) 27
Conway, J. P. 1967 (Fulham, Manchester C) 20
Corr, P. J. 1949 (Everton) 4
Courtney, E. 1946 (Cork U) 1
Cox, S. R. 2011 (WBA, Nottingham F) 30
Coyle, O. C. 1994 (Bolton W) 1
Coyne, T. 1992 (Celtic, Tranmere R, Motherwell) 22
Crowe, G. 2003 (Bohemians) 2
Cummins, G. P. 1954 (Luton T) 19
Cuneen, T. 1951 (Limerick) 1
Cunningham, G. R. 2010 (Manchester C, Bristol C) 4
Cunningham, K. 1996 (Wimbledon, Birmingham C) 72
Curtis, D. P. 1957 (Shelbourne, Bristol C, Ipswich T,
    Exeter C) 17
Cusack, S. 1953 (Limerick) 1

Daish, L. S. 1992 (Cambridge U, Coventry C) 5
Daly, G. A. 1973 (Manchester U, Derby Co, Coventry C,
    Birmingham C, Shrewsbury T) 48
Daly, J. 1932 (Shamrock R) 2

Daly, M. 1978 (Wolverhampton W) 2
Daly, P. 1950 (Shamrock R) 1
Davis, T. L. 1937 (Oldham Ath, Tranmere R) 4
Deacy, E. 1982 (Aston Villa) 4
Delaney, D. F. 2008 (QPR, Ipswich T, Crystal Palace) 9
Delap, R. J. 1998 (Derby Co, Southampton) 11
De Mange, K. J. P. P. 1987 (Liverpool, Hull C) 2
Dempsey, J. T. 1967 (Fulham, Chelsea) 19
Dennehy, J. 1972 (Cork Hibernians, Nottingham F, Walsall) 11
Desmond, P. 1950 (Middlesbrough) 4
Devine, J. 1980 (Arsenal, Norwich C) 13
Doherty, G. M. T. 2000 (Luton T, Tottenham H, Norwich C) 34
Donnelly, J. 1935 (Dundalk) 10
Donnelly, T. 1938 (Drumcondra, Shamrock R) 2
Donovan, D. C. 1955 (Everton) 5
Donovan, T. 1980 (Aston Villa) 2
Douglas, J. 2004 (Blackburn R, Leeds U) 8
Dowdall, C. 1928 (Fordsons, Barnsley, Cork) 3
Doyle, C. 1959 (Shelbourne) 1
Doyle, Colin 2007 (Birmingham C) 1
Doyle, D. 1926 (Shamrock R) 1
Doyle, K. E. 2006 (Reading, Wolverhampton W, Colorado Rapids) **62**
Doyle, L. 1932 (Dolphin) 1
Doyle, M. P. 2004 (Coventry C) 1
Duff, D. A. 1998 (Blackburn R, Chelsea, Newcastle U, Fulham) 100
Duffy, B. 1950 (Shamrock R) 1
Duffy, S. P. M. 2014 (Everton, Blackburn R) **5**
Duggan, H. A. 1927 (Leeds U, Newport Co) 5
Dunne, A. P. 1962 (Manchester U, Bolton W) 33
Dunne, J. 1930 (Sheffield U, Arsenal, Southampton, Shamrock R) 15
Dunne, J. C. 1971 (Fulham) 1
Dunne, L. 1935 (Manchester C) 2
Dunne, P. A. J. 1965 (Manchester U) 5
Dunne, R. P. 2000 (Everton, Manchester C, Aston Villa, QPR) 80
Dunne, S. 1953 (Luton T) 15
Dunne, T. 1956 (St Patrick's Ath) 3
Dunning, P. 1971 (Shelbourne) 2
Dunphy, E. M. 1966 (York C, Millwall) 23
Dwyer, N. M. 1960 (West Ham U, Swansea T) 14

Eccles, P. 1986 (Shamrock R) 1
Egan, R. 1929 (Dundalk) 1
Eglington, T. J. 1946 (Shamrock R, Everton) 24
Elliot, R. 2014 (Newcastle U) **4**
Elliott, S. W. 2005 (Sunderland) 9
Ellis, P. 1935 (Bohemians) 7
Evans, M. J. 1998 (Southampton) 1

Fagan, E. 1973 (Shamrock R) 1
Fagan, F. 1955 (Manchester C, Derby Co) 8
Fagan, J. 1926 (Shamrock R) 1
Fahey, K. D. 2010 (Birmingham C) 16
Fairclough, M. 1982 (Dundalk) 2
Fallon, S. 1951 (Celtic) 8
Fallon, W. J. 1935 (Notts Co, Sheffield W) 9
Farquharson, T. G. 1929 (Cardiff C) 4
Farrell, P. 1937 (Hibernian) 2
Farrell, P. D. 1946 (Shamrock R, Everton) 28
Farrelly, G. 1996 (Aston Villa, Everton, Bolton W) 6
Feenan, J. J. 1937 (Sunderland) 2
Finnan, S. 2000 (Fulham, Liverpool, Espanyol) 53
Finucane, A. 1967 (Limerick) 11
Fitzgerald, F. J. 1955 (Waterford) 2
Fitzgerald, P. J. 1961 (Leeds U, Chester) 5
Fitzpatrick, K. 1970 (Limerick) 1
Fitzsimons, A. G. 1950 (Middlesbrough, Lincoln C) 26
Fleming, C. 1996 (Middlesbrough) 10
Flood, J. J. 1926 (Shamrock R) 5
Fogarty, A. 1960 (Sunderland, Hartlepools U) 11
Folan, C. C. 2009 (Hull C) 7
Foley, D. J. 2000 (Watford) 6
Foley, J. 1934 (Cork, Celtic) 7
Foley, K. P. 2009 (Wolverhampton W) 8
Foley, M. 1926 (Shelbourne) 1
Foley, T. C. 1964 (Northampton T) 9
Forde, D. 2011 (Millwall) **24**
Foy, T. 1938 (Shamrock R) 2
Fullam, J. 1961 (Preston NE, Shamrock R) 11

Fullam, R. 1926 (Shamrock R) 2

Gallagher, C. 1967 (Celtic) 2
Gallagher, M. 1954 (Hibernian) 1
Gallagher, P. 1932 (Falkirk) 1
Galvin, A. 1983 (Tottenham H, Sheffield W, Swindon T) 29
Gamble, J. 2007 (Cork C) 2
Gannon, E. 1949 (Notts Co, Sheffield W, Shelbourne) 14
Gannon, M. 1972 (Shelbourne) 1
Gaskins, P. 1934 (Shamrock R, St James' Gate) 7
Gavin, J. T. 1950 (Norwich C, Tottenham H, Norwich C) 7
Geoghegan, M. 1937 (St James' Gate) 2
Gibbons, A. 1952 (St Patrick's Ath) 4
Gibson, D. T. D. 2008 (Manchester U, Everton) **27**
Gilbert, R. 1966 (Shamrock R) 1
Giles, C. 1951 (Doncaster R) 1
Giles, M. J. 1960 (Manchester U, Leeds U, WBA, Shamrock R) 59
Given, S. J. J. 1996 (Blackburn R, Newcastle U, Manchester C, Aston Villa, Stoke C) **134**
Givens, D. J. 1969 (Manchester U, Luton T, QPR, Birmingham C, Neuchatel X) 56
Gleeson, S. M. 2007 (Wolverhampton W) 2
Glen, W. 1927 (Shamrock R) 8
Glynn, D. 1952 (Drumcondra) 2
Godwin, T. F. 1949 (Shamrock R, Leicester C, Bournemouth) 13
Golding, J. 1928 (Shamrock R) 2
Goodman, J. 1997 (Wimbledon) 4
Goodwin, J. 2003 (Stockport Co) 1
Gorman, W. C. 1936 (Bury, Brentford) 13
Grace, J. 1926 (Drumcondra) 1
Grealish, A. 1976 (Orient, Luton T, Brighton & HA, WBA) 45
Green, P. J. 2010 (Derby Co, Leeds U) 20
Gregg, E. 1978 (Bohemians) 8
Griffith, R. 1935 (Walsall) 1
Grimes, A. A. 1978 (Manchester U, Coventry C, Luton T) 18

Hale, A. 1962 (Aston Villa, Doncaster R, Waterford) 14
Hamilton, T. 1959 (Shamrock R) 2
Hand, E. K. 1969 (Portsmouth) 20
Harrington, W. 1936 (Cork) 5
Harte, I. P. 1996 (Leeds U, Levante) 64
Hartnett, J. B. 1949 (Middlesbrough) 2
Haverty, J. 1956 (Arsenal, Blackburn R, Millwall, Celtic, Bristol R, Shelbourne) 32
Hayes, A. W. P. 1979 (Southampton) 1
Hayes, J. 2016 (Aberdeen) **2**
Hayes, W. E. 1947 (Huddersfield T) 2
Hayes, W. J. 1949 (Limerick) 1
Healey, R. 1977 (Cardiff C) 2
Healy, C. 2002 (Celtic, Sunderland) 13
Heighway, S. D. 1971 (Liverpool, Minnesota K) 34
Henderson, B. 1948 (Drumcondra) 2
Henderson, W. C. P. 2006 (Brighton & HA, Preston NE) 6
Hendrick, J. P. 2013 (Derby Co) **25**
Hennessy, J. 1965 (Shelbourne, St Patrick's Ath) 5
Herrick, J. 1972 (Cork Hibernians, Shamrock R) 3
Higgins, J. 1951 (Birmingham C) 1
Holland, M. R. 2000 (Ipswich T, Charlton Ath) 49
Holmes, J. 1971 (Coventry C, Tottenham H, Vancouver Whitecaps) 30
Hoolahan, W. 2008 (Blackpool, Norwich C) **34**
Horlacher, A. F. 1930 (Bohemians) 7
Houghton, R. J. 1986 (Oxford U, Liverpool, Aston Villa, Crystal Palace, Reading) 73
Howlett, G. 1984 (Brighton & HA) 1
Hoy, M. 1938 (Dundalk) 6
Hughton, C. 1980 (Tottenham H, West Ham U) 53
Hunt, N. 2009 (Reading) 3
Hunt, S. P. 2007 (Reading, Hull C, Wolverhampton W) 39
Hurley, C. J. 1957 (Millwall, Sunderland, Bolton W) 40
Hutchinson, F. 1935 (Drumcondra) 2

Ireland S J. 2006 (Manchester C) 6
Irwin, D. J. 1991 (Manchester U) 56

Jordan, D. 1937 (Wolverhampton W) 2

Jordan, W. 1934 (Bohemians) 2
Judge, A. C. 2016 (Brentford) **1**

Kavanagh, G. A. 1998 (Stoke C, Cardiff C, Wigan Ath) 16
Kavanagh, P. J. 1931 (Celtic) 2
Keane, R. D. 1998 (Wolverhampton W, Coventry C, Internazionale, Leeds U, Tottenham H, Liverpool, Tottenham H, LA Galaxy) **145**
Keane, R. M. 1991 (Nottingham F, Manchester U) 67
Keane, T. R. 1949 (Swansea T) 4
Kearin, M. 1972 (Shamrock R) 1
Kearns, F. T. 1954 (West Ham U) 1
Kearns, M. 1971 (Oxford U, Walsall, Wolverhampton W) 18
Kelly, A. T. 1993 (Sheffield U, Blackburn R) 34
Kelly, D. T. 1988 (Walsall, West Ham U, Leicester C, Newcastle U, Wolverhampton W, Sunderland, Tranmere R) 26
Kelly, G. 1994 (Leeds U) 52
Kelly, J. 1932 (Derry C) 4
Kelly, J. A. 1957 (Drumcondra, Preston NE) 47
Kelly, J. P. V. 1961 (Wolverhampton W) 5
Kelly, M. J. 1988 (Portsmouth) 4
Kelly, N. 1954 (Nottingham F) 1
Kelly, S. M. 2006 (Tottenham H, Birmingham C, Fulham, Reading) 38
Kendrick, J. 1927 (Everton, Dolphin) 4
Kenna, J. J. 1995 (Blackburn R) 27
Kennedy, M. F. 1986 (Portsmouth) 2
Kennedy, M. J. 1996 (Liverpool, Wimbledon, Manchester C, Wolverhampton W) 34
Kennedy, W. 1932 (St James' Gate) 3
Kenny, P. 2004 (Sheffield U) 7
Keogh, A. D. 2007 (Wolverhampton W, Millwall) 30
Keogh, J. 1966 (Shamrock R) 1
Keogh, R. J. 2013 (Derby Co) **14**
Keogh, S. 1959 (Shamrock R) 1
Kernaghan, A. N. 1993 (Middlesbrough, Manchester C) 22
Kiely, D. L. 2000 (Charlton Ath, WBA) 11
Kiernan, F. W. 1951 (Shamrock R, Southampton) 5
Kilbane, K. D. 1998 (WBA, Sunderland, Everton, Wigan Ath, Hull C) 110
Kinnear, J. P. 1967 (Tottenham H, Brighton & HA) 26
Kinsella, J. 1928 (Shelbourne) 1
Kinsella, M. A. 1998 (Charlton Ath, Aston Villa, WBA) 48
Kinsella, O. 1932 (Shamrock R) 2
Kirkland, A. 1927 (Shamrock R) 1

Lacey, W. 1927 (Shelbourne) 3
Langan, D. 1978 (Derby Co, Birmingham C, Oxford U) 26
Lapira, J. 2007 (Notre Dame) 1
Lawler, J. F. 1953 (Fulham) 8
Lawlor, J. C. 1949 (Drumcondra, Doncaster R) 3
Lawlor, R. 1971 (Shamrock R) 5
Lawrence, L. 2009 (Stoke C, Portsmouth) 15
Lawrenson, M. 1977 (Preston NE, Brighton & HA, Liverpool) 39
Lee, A. D. 2003 (Rotherham U, Cardiff C, Ipswich T) 10
Leech, M. 1969 (Shamrock R) 8
Lennon, C. 1935 (St James' Gate) 3
Lennox, G. 1931 (Dolphin) 2
Long, S. P. 2007 (Reading, WBA, Hull C, Southampton) **67**
Lowry, D. 1962 (St Patrick's Ath) 1
Lunn, R. 1939 (Dundalk) 1
Lynch, J. 1934 (Cork Bohemians) 1

McAlinden, J. 1946 (Portsmouth) 2
McAteer, J. W. 1994 (Bolton W, Liverpool, Blackburn R, Sunderland) 52
McCann, J. 1957 (Shamrock R) 1
McCarthy, J. 1926 (Bohemians) 3
McCarthy, J. 2010 (Wigan Ath, Everton) **39**
McCarthy, M. 1932 (Shamrock R) 1
McCarthy, M. 1984 (Manchester C, Celtic, Lyon, Millwall) 57
McClean, J. J. 2012 (Sunderland, Wigan Ath, WBA) **42**
McConville, T. 1972 (Dundalk, Waterford) 6
McDonagh, Jacko 1984 (Shamrock R) 3

McDonagh, J. 1981 (Everton, Bolton W, Notts Co, Wichita Wings) 25
McEvoy, M. A. 1961 (Blackburn R) 17
McGeady, A. J. 2004 (Celtic, Spartak Moscow, Everton) **85**
McGee, P. 1978 (QPR, Preston NE) 15
McGoldrick, D. J. 2015 (Ipswich T) **4**
McGoldrick, E. J. 1992 (Crystal Palace, Arsenal) 15
McGowan, D. 1949 (West Ham U) 3
McGowan, J. 1947 (Cork U) 1
McGrath, M. 1958 (Blackburn R, Bradford) 22
McGrath, P. 1985 (Manchester U, Aston Villa, Derby Co) 83
McGuire, W. 1936 (Bohemians) 1
Macken, A. 1977 (Derby Co) 1
Macken J. P. 2005 (Manchester C) 1
McKenzie, G. 1938 (Southend U) 9
Mackey, G. 1957 (Shamrock R) 3
McLoughlin, A. F. 1990 (Swindon T, Southampton, Portsmouth) 42
McLoughlin, F. 1930 (Fordsons, Cork) 2
McMillan, W. 1946 (Belfast Celtic) 2
McNally, J. B. 1959 (Luton T) 3
McPhail, S. 2000 (Leeds U) 10
McShane, P. D. 2007 (WBA, Sunderland, Hull C, Reading) **33**
Madden, O. 1936 (Cork) 1
Madden, P. 2013 (Scunthorpe U) 1
Maguire, J. 1929 (Shamrock R) 1
Mahon, A. J. 2000 (Tranmere R) 2
Malone, G. 1949 (Shelbourne) 1
Mancini, T. J. 1974 (QPR, Arsenal) 5
Martin, C. 1927 (Bo'ness) 1
Martin, C. J. 1946 (Glentoran, Leeds U, Aston Villa) 30
Martin, M. P. 1972 (Bohemians, Manchester U, WBA, Newcastle U) 52
Maybury, A. 1998 (Leeds U, Hearts, Leicester C) 10
Meagan, M. K. 1961 (Everton, Huddersfield T, Drogheda) 17
Meehan, P. 1934 (Drumcondra) 1
Meyler, D. J. 2013 (Sunderland, Hull C) **16**
Miller, L. W. P. 2004 (Celtic, Manchester U, Sunderland, Hibernian) 21
Milligan, M. J. 1992 (Oldham Ath) 1
Monahan, P. 1935 (Sligo R) 2
Mooney, J. 1965 (Shamrock R) 2
Moore, A. 1996 (Middlesbrough) 8
Moore, P. 1931 (Shamrock R, Aberdeen, Shamrock R) 9
Moran, K. 1980 (Manchester U, Sporting Gijon, Blackburn R) 71
Moroney, T. 1948 (West Ham U, Evergreen U) 12
Morris, C. B. 1988 (Celtic, Middlesbrough) 35
Morrison, C. H. 2002 (Crystal Palace, Birmingham C, Crystal Palace) 36
Moulson, C. 1936 (Lincoln C, Notts Co) 5
Moulson, G. B. 1948 (Lincoln C) 3
Muckian, C. 1978 (Drogheda U) 1
Muldoon, T. 1927 (Aston Villa) 1
Mulligan, P. M. 1969 (Shamrock R, Chelsea, Crystal Palace, WBA, Shamrock R) 50
Munroe, L. 1954 (Shamrock R) 1
Murphy, A. 1956 (Clyde) 1
Murphy, B. 1986 (Bohemians) 1
Murphy, D. 2007 (Sunderland, Ipswich T) **23**
Murphy, J. 1980 (Crystal Palace) 3
Murphy, J. 2004 (WBA, Scunthorpe U) 2
Murphy, P. M. 2007 (Carlisle U) 1
Murray, T. 1950 (Dundalk) 1

Newman, W. 1969 (Shelbourne) 1
Nolan. E. W. 2009 (Preston NE) 3
Nolan, R. 1957 (Shamrock R) 10

O'Brien, A. 2007 (Newcastle U) 5
O'Brien, A. J. 2001 (Newcastle U, Portsmouth) 26
O'Brien, F. 1980 (Philadelphia F) 3
O'Brien J. M. 2006 (Bolton W, West Ham U) 5
O'Brien, L. 1986 (Shamrock R, Manchester U, Newcastle U, Tranmere R) 16
O'Brien, M. T. 1927 (Derby Co, Walsall, Norwich C, Watford) 4
O'Brien, R. 1976 (Notts Co) 5
O'Byrne, L. B. 1949 (Shamrock R) 1

O'Callaghan, B. R. 1979 (Stoke C)	6
O'Callaghan, K. 1981 (Ipswich T, Portsmouth)	21
O'Cearuill, J. 2007 (Arsenal)	2
O'Connell, A. 1967 (Dundalk, Bohemians)	2
O'Connor, T. 1950 (Shamrock R)	4
O'Connor, T. 1968 (Fulham, Dundalk, Bohemians)	7
O'Dea, D. 2010 (Celtic, Toronto, Metalurh Donetsk)	20
O'Dowda, C. J. R. 2016 (Oxford U)	**1**
O'Driscoll, J. F. 1949 (Swansea T)	3
O'Driscoll, S. 1982 (Fulham)	3
O'Farrell, F. 1952 (West Ham U, Preston NE)	9
O'Flanagan, K. P. 1938 (Bohemians, Arsenal)	10
O'Flanagan, M. 1947 (Bohemians)	1
O'Halloran, S. E. 2007 (Aston Villa)	2
O'Hanlon, K. G. 1988 (Rotherham U)	1
O'Kane, E. C. 2016 (Bournemouth)	**4**
O'Kane, P. 1935 (Bohemians)	3
O'Keefe, E. 1981 (Everton, Port Vale)	5
O'Keefe, T. 1934 (Cork, Waterford)	3
O'Leary, D. 1977 (Arsenal)	68
O'Leary, P. 1980 (Shamrock R)	7
O'Mahoney, M. T. 1938 (Bristol R)	6
O'Neill, F. S. 1962 (Shamrock R)	20
O'Neill, J. 1952 (Everton)	17
O'Neill, J. 1961 (Preston NE)	1
O'Neill, K. P. 1996 (Norwich C, Middlesbrough)	13
O'Neill, W. 1936 (Dundalk)	11
O'Regan, K. 1984 (Brighton & HA)	4
O'Reilly, J. 1932 (Brideville, Aberdeen, Brideville, St James' Gate)	20
O'Reilly, J. 1946 (Cork U)	2
O'Shea, J. F. 2002 (Manchester U, Sunderland)	**114**
Pearce, A. J. 2013 (Reading, Derby Co)	**7**
Peyton, G. 1977 (Fulham, Bournemouth, Everton)	33
Peyton, N. 1957 (Shamrock R, Leeds U)	6
Phelan, J. 2002 (Wimbledon, Manchester C, Chelsea, Everton, Fulham)	42
Pilkington, A. N. J. 2013 (Norwich C, Cardiff C)	**9**
Potter, D. M. 2007 (Wolverhampton W)	5
Quinn, A. 2003 (Sheffield W, Sheffield U)	8
Quinn, B. S. 2000 (Coventry C)	4
Quinn, N. J. 1986 (Arsenal, Manchester C, Sunderland)	91
Quinn, S. 2013 (Hull C, Reading)	**16**
Randolf, D. E. 2013 (Motherwell, West Ham U)	**13**
Reid, A. M. 2004 (Nottingham F, Tottenham H, Charlton Ath, Sunderland, Nottingham F)	29
Reid, C. 1931 (Brideville)	1
Reid, S. J. 2002 (Millwall, Blackburn R)	23
Richardson, D. J. 1972 (Shamrock R, Gillingham)	3
Rigby, A. 1935 (St James' Gate)	3
Ringstead, A. 1951 (Sheffield U)	20
Robinson, J. 1928 (Bohemians, Dolphin)	2
Robinson, M. 1981 (Brighton & HA, Liverpool, QPR)	24
Roche, P. J. 1972 (Shelbourne, Manchester U)	8
Rogers, E. 1968 (Blackburn R, Charlton Ath)	19
Rowlands, M. C. 2004 (QPR)	5
Ryan, G. 1978 (Derby Co, Brighton & HA)	18
Ryan, R. A. 1950 (WBA, Derby Co)	16

Sadlier, R. T. 2002 (Millwall)	1
Sammon, C. 2013 (Derby Co)	9
Savage, D. P. T. 1996 (Millwall)	5
Saward, P. 1954 (Millwall, Aston Villa, Huddersfield T)	18
Scannell, T. 1954 (Southend U)	1
Scully, P. J. 1989 (Arsenal)	1
Sheedy, K. 1984 (Everton, Newcastle U)	46
Sheridan, C. 2010 (Celtic, CSKA Sofia)	3
Sheridan, J. J. 1988 (Leeds U, Sheffield W)	34
Slaven, B. 1990 (Middlesbrough)	7
Sloan, J. W. 1946 (Arsenal)	2
Smyth, M. 1969 (Shamrock R)	1
Squires, J. 1934 (Shelbourne)	1
Stapleton, F. 1977 (Arsenal, Manchester U, Ajax, Le Havre, Blackburn R)	71
Staunton, S. 1989 (Liverpool, Aston Villa, Liverpool, Aston Villa)	102
St Ledger-Hall, S. P. 2009 (Preston NE, Leicester C)	37
Stevenson, A. E. 1932 (Dolphin, Everton)	7
Stokes, A. 2007 (Sunderland, Celtic)	9
Strahan, F. 1964 (Shelbourne)	5
Sullivan, J. 1928 (Fordsons)	1
Swan, M. M. G. 1960 (Drumcondra)	1
Synnott, N. 1978 (Shamrock R)	3
Taylor, T. 1959 (Waterford)	1
Thomas, P. 1974 (Waterford)	2
Thompson, J. 2004 (Nottingham F)	1
Townsend, A. D. 1989 (Norwich C, Chelsea, Aston Villa, Middlesbrough)	70
Traynor, T. J. 1954 (Southampton)	8
Treacy, K. 2011 (Preston NE, Burnley)	6
Treacy, R. C. P. 1966 (WBA, Charlton Ath, Swindon T, Preston NE, WBA, Shamrock R)	42
Tuohy, L. 1956 (Shamrock R, Newcastle U, Shamrock R)	8
Turner, C. J. 1936 (Southend U, West Ham U)	10
Turner, P. 1963 (Celtic)	2
Vernon, J. 1946 (Belfast Celtic)	2
Waddock, G. 1980 (QPR, Millwall)	21
Walsh, D. J. 1946 (Linfield, WBA, Aston Villa)	20
Walsh, J. 1982 (Limerick)	1
Walsh, M. 1976 (Blackpool, Everton, QPR, Porto)	21
Walsh, M. 1982 (Everton)	4
Walsh, W. 1947 (Manchester C)	9
Walters, J. R. 2011 (Stoke C)	**41**
Ward, S. R. 2011 (Wolverhampton W, Burnley)	**36**
Waters, J. 1977 (Grimsby T)	2
Watters, F. 1926 (Shelbourne)	1
Weir, E. 1939 (Clyde)	3
Westwood, K. 2009 (Coventry C, Sunderland, Sheffield W)	18
Whelan, G. D. 2008 (Stoke C)	**73**
Whelan, R. 1964 (St Patrick's Ath)	2
Whelan, R. 1981 (Liverpool, Southend U)	53
Whelan, W. 1956 (Manchester U)	4
White, J. J. 1928 (Bohemians)	1
Whittaker, R. 1959 (Chelsea)	1
Williams, J. 1938 (Shamrock R)	1
Wilson, M. D. 2011 (Stoke C)	**24**

BRITISH AND IRISH INTERNATIONAL GOALSCORERS 1872–2016

Where two players with the same surname and initials have appeared for the same country, and one or both have scored, they have been distinguished by reference to the club which appears *first* against their name in the international appearances section.

Bold type indicates players who have scored international goals in season 2015–16.

ENGLAND

Name		Name		Name		Name	
A'Court, A.	1	Brown, A. S.	1	Ehiogu, U.	1	Jack, D. N. B.	3
Adams, T. A.	5	Brown, G.	5	Elliott, W. H.	3	Jagielka, P. N.	3
Adcock, H.	1	Brown, J.	3	Evans, R. E.	1	Jeffers, F.	1
Alcock, C. W.	1	Brown, W.	1			Jenas, J. A.	1
Allen, A.	3	Brown, W. M.	1	Ferdinand, L.	5	Johnson, A.	2
Allen, R.	2	Buchan, C. M.	4	Ferdinand, R. G.	3	Johnson, D. E.	6
Alli, B. J. (Dele)	**1**	Bull, S. G.	4	Finney, T.	30	Johnson, E.	2
Amos, A.	1	Bullock, N.	2	Fleming, H. J.	9	Johnson, G. M. C.	1
Anderson, V.	2	Burgess, H.	4	Flowers, R.	10	Johnson, J. A.	2
Anderton, D. R.	7	Butcher, T.	3	Forman, Frank	1	Johnson, T. C. F.	5
Astall, G.	1	Byrne, J. J.	8	Forman, Fred	3	Johnson, W. H.	1
Athersmith, W. C.	3			Foster, R. E.	3		
Atyeo, P. J. W.	5	Cahill, G.	3	Fowler, R. B.	7	Kail, E. I. L.	2
		Campbell, S. J.	1	Francis, G. C. J.	3	**Kane, H. E.**	**5**
Bache, J. W.	4	Camsell, G. H.	18	Francis, T.	12	Kay, A. H.	1
Bailey, N. C.	2	Carroll, A. T.	2	Freeman, B. C.	3	Keegan, J. K.	21
Baily, E. F.	5	Carter, H. S.	7	Froggatt, J.	2	Kelly, R.	8
Baines, L. J.	1	Carter, J. H.	4	Froggatt, R.	2	Kennedy, R.	3
Baker, J. H.	3	Caulker, S. A.	1			Kenyon-Slaney, W. S.	2
Ball, A. J.	8	Chadwick, E.	3	Galley, T.	1	Keown, M. R.	2
Bambridge, A. L.	1	Chamberlain, M.	1	Gascoigne, P. J.	10	Kevan, D. T.	8
Bambridge, E. C.	11	Chambers, H.	5	Geary, H.	1	Kidd, B.	1
Barclay, R.	2	Channon, M. R.	21	Gerrard, S. G.	21	King, L. B.	2
Barkley, R.	**2**	Charlton, J.	6	Gibbins, W. V. T.	3	Kingsford, R. K.	1
Barmby, N. J.	4	Charlton, R.	49	Gilliatt, W. E.	3	Kirchen, A. J.	2
Barnes, J.	11	Chenery, C. J.	1	Goddard, P.	1	Kirton, W. J.	1
Barnes, P. S.	4	Chivers, M.	13	Goodall, J.	12		
Barry, G.	3	Clarke, A. J.	10	Goodyer, A. C.	1	Lambert, R. L.	3
Barton, J.	1	Cobbold, W. N.	6	Gosling, R. C.	2	Lampard, F. J.	29
Bassett, W. I.	8	Cock, J. G.	2	Goulden, L. A.	4	Langton, R.	1
Bastin, C. S.	12	Cole, A.	1	Grainger, C.	3	Latchford, R. D.	5
Beardsley, P. A.	9	Cole, J. J.	10	Greaves, J.	44	Latheron, E. G.	1
Beasley, A.	1	Common, A.	2	Grovesnor, A. T.	2	Lawler, C.	1
Beattie, T. K.	1	Connelly, J. M.	7	Gunn, W.	1	Lawton, T.	22
Beckham, D. R. J.	17	Coppell, S. J.	7			Lee, F.	10
Becton, F.	2	Cotterill, G. H.	2	Haines, J. T. W.	2	Lee, J.	1
Bedford, H.	1	Cowans, G.	2	Hall, G. W.	9	Lee, R. M.	2
Bell, C.	9	Crawford, R.	1	Halse, H. J.	2	Lee, S.	2
Bent, D. A.	4	Crawshaw, T. H.	1	Hampson, J.	5	Lescott, J.	1
Bentley, R. T. F.	9	Crayston, W. J.	1	Hampton, H.	2	Le Saux, G. P.	1
Bishop, S. M.	1	Creek, F. N. S.	1	Hancocks, J.	2	Lindley, T.	14
Blackburn, F.	1	Crooks, S. D.	7	Hardman, H. P.	1	Lineker, G.	48
Blissett, L.	3	Crouch, P. J.	22	Harris, S. S.	2	Lofthouse, J. M.	3
Bloomer, S.	28	Currey, E. S.	2	Hassall, H. W.	4	Lofthouse, N.	30
Bond, R.	2	Currie, A. W.	3	Hateley, M.	9	Hon. A. Lyttelton	1
Bonsor, A. G.	1	Cursham, A. W.	2	Haynes, J. N.	18		
Bowden, E. R.	1	Cursham, H. A.	5	Hegan, K. E.	4	Mabbutt, G.	1
Bowers, J. W.	2			Henfrey, A. G.	2	Macdonald, M.	6
Bowles, S.	1	Daft, H. B.	3	Heskey, E. W.	7	Mannion, W. J.	11
Bradford, G. R. W.	1	Davenport, J. K.	2	Hilsdon, G. R.	14	Mariner, P.	13
Bradford, J.	7	Davis, G.	1	Hine, E. W.	4	Marsh, R. W.	1
Bradley, W.	2	Davis, H.	1	Hinton, A. T.	1	Matthews, S.	11
Bradshaw, F.	3	Day, S. H.	2	Hirst, D. E.	1	Matthews, V.	1
Brann, G.	1	Dean, W. R.	18	Hitchens, G. A.	5	McCall, J.	1
Bridge, W. M.	1	Defoe, J. C.	19	Hobbis, H. H. F.	1	McDermott, T.	3
Bridges, B. J.	1	Devey, J. H. G.	1	Hoddle, G.	8	McManaman, S.	3
Bridgett, A.	3	Dewhurst, F.	11	Hodgetts, D.	1	Medley, L. D.	1
Brindle, T.	1	**Dier, E. J. E.**	**2**	Hodgson, G.	1	Melia, J.	1
Britton, C. S.	1	Dix, W. R.	1	Holley, G. H.	8	Mercer, D. W.	1
Broadbent, P. F.	2	Dixon, K. M.	4	Houghton, W. E.	5	Merson, P. C.	3
Broadis, I. A.	8	Dixon, L. M.	1	Howell, R.	1	Milburn, J. E. T.	10
Brodie, J. B.	1	Dorrell, A. R.	1	Hughes, E. W.	1	Miller, H. S.	1
Bromley-Davenport, W.	2	Douglas, B.	11	Hulme, J. H. A.	4	Mills, G. R.	3
Brook, E. F.	10	Drake, E. J.	6	Hunt, G. S.	1	Milner, J. P.	1
Brooking, T. D.	5	Ducat, A.	1	Hunt, R.	18	Milward, A.	3
Brooks, J.	2	Dunn, A. T. B.	2	Hunter, N.	2	Mitchell, C.	5
Broome, F. H.	3			Hurst, G. C.	24	Moore, J.	1
Brown, A.	4	Eastham, G.	2			Moore, R. F.	2
		Edwards, D.	5	Ince, P. E. C.	2	Moore, W. G. B.	2

Morren, T. 1
Morris, F. 1
Morris, J. 3
Mortensen, S. H. 23
Morton, J. R. 1
Mosforth, W. 3
Mullen, J. 6
Mullery, A. P. 1
Murphy, D. B 1

Neal, P. G. 5
Needham, E. 3
Nicholls, J. 1
Nicholson, W. E. 1
Nugent, D. J. 1

O'Grady, M. 3
Osborne, F. R. 3
Owen, M. J. 40
Own goals 33
Oxlade-Chamberlain, A. M. D. **5**

Page, L. A. 1
Paine, T. L. 7
Palmer, C. L. 1
Parry, E. H. 1
Parry, R. A. 1
Pawson, F. W. 1
Payne, J. 2
Peacock, A. 3
Pearce, S. 5
Pearson, J. S. 5
Pearson, S. C. 5
Perry, W. 2
Peters, M. 20
Pickering, F. 5
Platt, D. 27
Pointer, R. 2

Quantrill, A. 1

Ramsay, A. E. 3
Rashford, M. **1**
Revie, D. G. 4
Redknapp, J. F. 1
Reynolds, J. 3
Richards, M. 1
Richardson, K. E. 2
Richardson, J. R. 2
Rigby, A. 3
Rimmer, E. J. 2
Roberts, F. 2
Roberts, H. 1
Roberts, W. T. 2
Robinson, J. 3
Robson, B. 26
Robson, R. 4
Rooney, W. M. **53**
Rowley, J. F. 6
Royle, J. 2
Rutherford, J. 3

Sagar, C. 1
Sandilands, R. R. 3
Sansom, K. 1
Schofield, J. 1
Scholes, P. 14
Seed, J. M. 1
Settle, J. 6
Sewell, J. 3
Shackleton, L. F. 1
Sharp, J. 1
Shearer, A. 30
Shelton, A. 1
Shepherd, A. 2
Sheringham, E. P. 11
Simpson, J. 1
Smalling, C. L. **1**
Smith, A. 1
Smith, A. M. 2

Smith, G. O. 11
Smith, Joe 1
Smith, J. R. 2
Smith, J. W. 4
Smith, R. 13
Smith, S. 1
Sorby, T. H. 1
Southgate, G. 2
Southworth, J. 3
Sparks, F. J. 3
Spence, J. W. 1
Spiksley, F. 5
Spilsbury, B. W. 5
Steele, F. C. 8
Stephenson, G. T. 2
Sterling, R. S. **2**
Steven, T. M. 4
Stewart, J. 2
Stiles, N. P. 1
Storer, H. 1
Stone, S. B. 2
Sturridge, D. A. **6**
Summerbee, M. G. 1

Tambling, R. V. 1
Taylor, P. J. 2
Taylor, T. 16
Terry, J. G. 6
Thompson, P. B. 1
Thornewell, G. 1
Tilson, S. F. 6
Townley, W. J. 2
Townsend, A. D. 3
Tueart, D. 2

Upson, M. J. 2

Vardy, J. R. **4**
Vassell, D. 6
Vaughton, O. H. 6
Veitch, J. G. 3
Viollet, D. S. 1

Waddle, C. R. 6
Walcott, T. J. **8**
Walker, W. H. 9
Wall, G. 2
Wallace, D. 1
Walsh, P. 1
Waring, T. 4
Warren, B. 2
Watson, D. V. 4
Watson, V. M. 4
Webb, G. W. 1
Webb, N. 4
Wedlock, W. J. 2
Welbeck, D. 14
Weller, K. 1
Welsh, D. 1
Whateley, O. 2
Wheldon, G. F. 6
Whitfield, H. 1
Wignall, F. 2
Wilkes, A. 1
Wilkins, R. G. 3
Willingham, C. K. 1
Wilshaw, D. J. 10
Wilshere, J. A. 2
Wilson, G. P. 1
Winckworth, W. N. 1
Windridge, J. E. 7
Wise, D. F. 1
Withe, P. 1
Wollaston, C. H. R. 1
Wood, H. 1
Woodcock, T. 16
Woodhall, G. 1
Woodward, V. J. 29
Worrall, F. 2
Worthington, F. S. 2
Wright, I. E. 9

Wright, M. 1
Wright, W. A. 3
Wright-Phillips, S. C. 6
Wylie, J. G. 1

Yates, J. 3
Young, A. S. 7

NORTHERN IRELAND
Anderson, T. 4
Armstrong, G. 12

Bambrick, J. 12
Barr, H. H. 1
Barron, H. 3
Best, G. 9
Bingham, W. L. 10
Black, K. 1
Blanchflower, D. 2
Blanchflower, J. 1
Brennan, B. 1
Brennan, R. A. 1
Brotherston, N. 3
Brown, J. 1
Browne, F. 2
Brunt, C. 1

Campbell, J. 1
Campbell, W. G. 1
Casey, T. 2
Caskey, W. 1
Cassidy, T. 1
Cathcart, C. G. **2**
Chambers, J. 3
Clarke, C. J. 13
Clements, D. 2
Cochrane, T. 1
Condy, J. 1
Connor, M. J. 1
Coulter, J. 1
Croft, T. 1
Crone, W. 1
Crossan, E. 1
Crossan, J. A. 10
Curran, S. 2
Cush, W. W. 5

Dallas S. A. 1
Dalton, M. 4
D'Arcy, S. D. 1
Darling, J. 1
Davey, H. H. 1
Davis, S. **8**
Davis, T. L. 1
Dill, A. H. 1
Doherty, L. 1
Doherty, P. D. 3
Dougan, A. D. 8
Dowie, I. 12
Dunne, J. 4

Elder, A. R. 1
Elliott, S. 4
Emerson, W. 1
English, S. 1
Evans, C. 1
Evans, J. G. 1

Feeney, W. 1
Feeney, W. J. 5
Ferguson, S. K. 1
Ferguson, W. 1
Ferris, J. 1
Ferris, R. O. 1
Finney, T. 2

Gaffkin, J. 4
Gara, A. 3
Gaukrodger, G. 1
Gibb, J. T. 2
Gibb, T. J. 1
Gibson, W. 1

Gillespie, K. R. 2
Gillespie, W. 13
Goodall, A. L. 2
Griffin, D. J. 1
Gray, P. 6
Grigg, W. D. **1**

Halligan, W. 1
Hamill, M. 1
Hamilton, B. 4
Hamilton, W. R. 5
Hannon, D. J. 1
Harkin, J. T. 2
Harvey, M. 3
Healy, D. J. 36
Hill, C. F. 1
Hughes, A. 1
Hughes, M. E. 5
Humphries, W. 1
Hunter, A. (Distillery) 1
Hunter, A. (Blackburn R)1
Hunter, B. V. 1

Irvine, R. W. 3
Irvine, W. J. 8

Johnston, H. 2
Johnston, S. 2
Johnston, W. C. 1
Jones, S. (Distillery) 1
Jones, S. (Crewe Alex) 1
Jones, J. 1

Kelly, J. 4
Kernaghan, N. 2
Kirwan, J. 2

Lacey, W. 3
Lafferty, K. **17**
Lemon, J. 2
Lennon, N. F. 1
Lockhart, N. 3
Lomas, S. M. 3

Magennis, J. B. D. **1**
Magilton, J. 5
Mahood, J. 2
Martin, D. K. 3
Maxwell, J. 2
McAdams, W. J. 7
McAllen, J. 1
McAuley, G. **8**
Mcauley, J. L. 1
McCann, G. S. 4
McCartney, G. 1
McCandless, J. 2
McCandless, W. 1
McCaw, J. H. 1
McClelland, J. 1
McCluggage, A. 2
McCourt, P. 2
McCracken, W. 1
McCrory, S. 1
McCurdy, C. 1
McDonald, A. 3
McGarry, J. K. 1
McGrath, R. C. 4
McGinn, N. **3**
McIlroy, J. 10
McIlroy, S. B. 5
McKenzie, H 1
McKnight, J. 2
McLaughlin, J. C. 6
McMahon, G. J. 2
McMordie, A. S. 3
McMorran, E. J. 4
McParland, P. J. 10
McWha, W. B. R. 1
Meldon, P. A 1
Mercer, J. T. 1
Millar, W. 1

Milligan, D.	1
Milne, R. G.	2
Molyneux, T. B.	1
Moreland, V.	1
Morgan, S.	3
Morrow, S. J.	1
Morrow, W. J.	1
Mulryne, P. P.	3
Murdock, C. J.	1
Murphy, N.	1
Neill, W. J. T.	2
Nelson, S.	1
Nicholl, C. J.	3
Nicholl, J. M.	1
Nicholson, J. J.	6
O'Boyle, G.	1
O'Hagan, C.	2
O'Kane, W. J.	1
O'Neill, J.	2
O'Neill, M. A.	4
O'Neill, M. H.	8
Own goals	10
Paterson, M. A.	3
Patterson, D. J.	1
Patterson, R.	1
Peacock, R.	2
Peden, J.	7
Penney, S.	2
Pyper, James	2
Pyper, John	1
Quinn, J. M.	12
Quinn, S. J.	4
Reynolds, J.	1
Rowland, K.	1
Rowley, R. W. M.	2
Rushe, F.	1
Sheridan, J.	2
Sherrard, J.	1
Sherrard, W. C.	2
Shields, D.	1
Simpson, W. J.	5
Sloan, H. A. de B.	4
Smyth, S.	5
Spence, D. W.	3
Sproule, I.	1
Stanfield, O. M.	11
Stevenson, A. E.	5
Stewart, I.	2
Taggart, G. P.	7
Thompson, F. W.	2
Torrans, S.	1
Tully, C. P.	3
Turner, A.	1
Walker, J.	1
Walsh, D. J.	5
Ward, J. J.	2
Washington, C. J.	**2**
Welsh, E.	1
Whiteside, N.	9
Whiteside, T.	1
Whitley, Jeff	2
Williams, J. R.	1
Williams, M. S.	1
Williamson, J.	1
Wilson, D. J.	1
Wilson, K. J.	6
Wilson, S. J.	7
Wilton, J. M.	1
Young, S.	1

N.B. In 1914 Young goal should be credited to Gillespie W v Wales

SCOTLAND

Aitken, R. (Celtic)	1
Aitken, R. (Dumbarton)	1
Aitkenhead, W. A. C.	2
Alexander, D.	1
Allan, D. S.	4
Allan, J.	2
Anderson, F.	1
Anderson, W.	4
Andrews, P.	1
Anya, I.	**3**
Archibald, A.	1
Archibald, S.	4
Baird, D.	2
Baird, J. C.	2
Baird, S.	2
Bannon, E.	1
Barbour, A.	1
Barker, J. B.	4
Battles, B. Jr	1
Bauld, W.	2
Baxter, J. C.	3
Beattie, C.	1
Bell, J.	5
Bennett, A.	2
Berra, C. D.	3
Berry, D.	1
Bett, J.	1
Beveridge, W. W.	1
Black, A.	3
Black, D.	1
Bone, J.	1
Booth, S.	6
Boyd, K	7
Boyd, R.	2
Boyd, T.	1
Boyd, W. G.	1
Brackenridge, T.	1
Brand, R.	8
Brazil, A.	1
Bremner, W. J.	3
Broadfoot, K.	1
Brown, A. D.	6
Brown, S.	4
Buchanan, P. S.	1
Buchanan, R.	1
Buckley, P.	1
Buick, A.	2
Burke, C.	2
Burley, C. W.	3
Burns, K.	1
Cairns, T.	1
Caldwell, G.	2
Calderwood, C.	1
Calderwood, R.	2
Caldow, E.	4
Cameron, C.	2
Campbell, C.	1
Campbell, John (Celtic)	5
Campbell, John (Rangers)	4
Campbell, J. (South Western)	1
Campbell, P.	2
Campbell, R.	1
Cassidy, J.	1
Chalmers, S.	3
Chambers, T.	1
Cheyne, A. G.	4
Christie, A. J.	1
Clarkson, D.	1
Clunas, W. L.	1
Collins, J.	12
Collins, R. Y.	10
Combe, J. R.	1
Commons, K.	2
Conn, A.	1
Cooper, D.	6
Craig, J.	1

Craig, T.	1
Crawford, S.	4
Cunningham, A. N.	5
Curran, H. P.	1
Dailly, C.	6
Dalglish, K.	30
Davidson, D.	1
Davidson, J. A.	1
Delaney, J.	3
Devine, A.	1
Dewar, G.	1
Dewar, N.	4
Dickov, P.	1
Dickson, W.	4
Divers, J.	1
Dobie, R. S.	1
Docherty, T. H.	1
Dodds, D.	1
Dodds, W.	7
Donaldson, A.	1
Donnachie, J.	1
Dougall, J.	1
Drummond, J.	2
Dunbar, M.	1
Duncan, D.	7
Duncan, D. M.	1
Duncan, J.	1
Dunn, J.	2
Durie, G. S.	7
Easson, J. F.	1
Elliott, M. S.	1
Ellis, J.	1
Ferguson, B.	3
Ferguson, J.	6
Fernie, W.	1
Fitchie, T. T.	1
Flavell, R.	2
Fleming, C.	2
Fleming, J. W.	3
Fletcher, D.	5
Fletcher, S. K.	**8**
Fraser, M. J. E.	3
Freedman, D. A.	1
Gallacher, H. K.	23
Gallacher, K. W.	9
Gallacher, P.	1
Galt, J. H.	1
Gemmell, T. (St Mirren)	1
Gemmell, T. (Celtic)	1
Gemmill, A.	8
Gemmill, S.	1
Gibb, W.	1
Gibson, D. W.	3
Gibson, J. D.	1
Gibson, N.	1
Gillespie, Jas.	3
Gillick, T.	3
Gilzean, A. J.	12
Goodwillie, D.	1
Gossland, J.	2
Goudie, J.	1
Gough, C. R.	6
Gourlay, J.	1
Graham, A.	2
Graham, G.	3
Gray, A.	7
Gray, E.	3
Gray, F.	1
Greig, J.	3
Groves, W.	4
Hamilton, G.	4
Hamilton, J. (Queen's Park)	3
Hamilton, R. C.	15
Hanley, G. C.	1
Harper, J. M.	2

Hartley, P. J.	1
Harrower, W.	5
Hartford, R. A.	4
Heggie, C. W	4
Henderson, J. G.	1
Henderson, W.	5
Hendry, E. C. J.	3
Herd, D. G.	3
Herd, G.	1
Hewie, J. D.	2
Higgins, A. (Newcastle U)	1
Higgins, A. (Kilmarnock)	4
Highet, T. C.	1
Holt, G.J.	1
Holton, J. A.	2
Hopkin, D.	2
Houliston, W.	2
Howie, H.	1
Howie, J.	2
Hughes, J.	1
Hunter, W.	1
Hutchison, D.	6
Hutchison, T.	1
Hutton, J.	1
Hyslop, T.	1
Imrie, W. N.	1
Jackson, A.	8
Jackson, C.	1
Jackson, D.	4
James, A. W.	4
Jardine, A.	1
Jenkinson, T.	1
Jess, E.	2
Johnston, A.	2
Johnston, L. H.	1
Johnston, M.	14
Johnstone, D.	2
Johnstone, J.	4
Johnstone, Jas.	1
Johnstone, R.	10
Johnstone, W.	1
Jordan, J.	11
Kay, J. L.	5
Keillor, A.	3
Kelly, J.	1
Kelso, R.	1
Ker, G.	10
King, A.	1
King, J.	1
Kinnear, D.	1
Kyle, K.	1
Lambert, P.	1
Lambie, J.	1
Lambie, W. A.	5
Lang, J. J.	2
Latta, A.	2
Law, D.	30
Leggat, G.	8
Lennie, W.	1
Lennox, R.	3
Liddell, W.	6
Lindsay, J.	6
Linwood, A. B.	1
Logan, J.	1
Lorimer, P.	4
Love, A.	1
Low, J. (Cambuslang)	1
Lowe, J. (St Bernards)	1
Macari, L.	5
MacDougall, E. J.	3
MacFarlane, A.	1
MacLeod, M.	1
Mackay, D. C.	4
Mackay, G.	1

Name		Name		Name		Name	
MacKenzie, J. A.	1	Munro, N.	2	Taylor, J. D.	1	Davies, L. S.	6
Mackail-Smith, C.	1	Murdoch, R.	5	Templeton, R.	1	Davies, R. T.	9
Mackie, J. C.	2	Murphy, F.	1	Thompson, S.	3	Davies, R. W.	6
MacKinnon, W. W.	5	Murray, J.	1	Thomson, A.	1	Davies, Simon	6
Madden, J.	5			Thomson, C.	4	Davies, Stanley	5
Maloney, S. R.	**7**	Napier, C. E.	3	Thomson, R.	1	Davies, W.	6
Marshall, H.	1	Narey, D.	1	Thomson, W.	1	Davies, W. H.	1
Marshall, J.	1	**Naismith, S. J.**	**6**	Thornton, W.	1	Davies, William	5
Martin, C. H.	**1**	Naysmith, G. A.	1			Davis, W. O.	1
Mason, J.	4	Neil, R. G.	2	Waddell, T. S.	1	Deacy, N.	4
Massie, A.	1	Nevin, P. K. F.	5	Waddell, W.	6	Doughty, J.	6
Masson, D. S.	5	Nicholas, C.	5	Walker, J.	2	Doughty, R.	2
McAdam, J.	1	Nisbet, J.	2	Walker, R.	7	Durban, A.	2
McAllister, G.	5			Walker, T.	9	Dwyer, P.	2
McArthur, J.	**2**	O'Connor, G.	4	Wallace, I. A.	1		
McAulay, J. D.	1	O'Donnell, F.	2	Wark, J.	7	Earnshaw, R.	16
McAvennie, F.	1	O'Hare, J.	5	Watson, J. A. K.	1	Eastwood, F.	4
McCall, J.	1	Ormond, W. E.	2	Watt, F.	2	Edwards, D. A.	3
McCall, S. M.	1	O'Rourke, F.	1	Watt, W. W.	1	Edwards, G.	2
McCalliog, J.	1	Orr, R.	1	Webster, A.	1	Edwards, R. I.	4
McCallum, N.	1	Orr, T.	1	Weir, A.	1	England, H. M.	4
McCann, N.	3	Oswald, J.	1	Weir, D.	1	Evans, C.	2
McClair, B. J.	2	Own goals	21	Weir, J. B.	2	Evans, I.	1
McCoist, A.	19			White, J. A.	3	Evans, J.	1
McColl, R. S.	13	Parlane, D.	1	Wilkie, L.	1	Evans, R. E.	2
McCormack, R.	2	Paul, H. McD.	2	Wilson, A. (Sheffield W)	2	Evans, W.	1
McCulloch, D.	3	Paul, W.	5	Wilson, A. N.		Eyton-Jones, J. A.	1
McCulloch, L.	1	Pettigrew, W.	2	(Dunfermline Ath)	13		
McDougall, J.	4	Provan, D.	1	Wilson, D. (Liverpool)	1	Fletcher, C.	1
McFadden, J.	15*			Wilson, D.		Flynn, B.	7
McFadyen, W.	2	Quashie, N. F.	1	(Queen's Park)	2	Ford, T.	23
McGhee, M.	2	Quinn, J.	7	Wilson, D. (Rangers)	9	Foulkes, W. I.	1
McGinlay, J.	4	Quinn, P.	1	Wilson, H.	1	Fowler, J.	3
McGregor, J.	1			Wylie, T. G.	1		
McGrory, J.	6	Rankin, G.	2			Giles, D.	2
McGuire, W.	1	Rankin, R.	2	Young, A.	5	Giggs, R. J.	12
McInally, A.	3	Reid, W.	4			Glover, E. M.	7
McInnes, T.	2	Reilly, L.	22	**WALES**		Godfrey, B. C.	2
McKie, J.	2	Renny-Tailyour, H. W.	1	Allchurch, I. J.	23	Green, A. W.	3
McKimmie, S.	1	Rhodes, J. L.	3	Allen, M.	3	Griffiths, A. T.	6
McKinlay, W.	4	Richmond, J. T.	1	Astley, D. J.	12	Griffiths, M. W.	2
McKinnon, A.	1	Ring, T.	2	Atherton, R. W.	2	Griffiths, T. P.	3
McKinnon, R.	1	Rioch, B. D.	6				
McLaren, A.	4	Ritchie, J.	1	**Bale, G. F.**	**22**	Harris, C. S.	1
McLaren, J.	1	**Ritchie, M. T.**	**3**	Bamford, T.	1	Hartson, J.	14
McLean, A.	1	Ritchie, P. S.	1	Barnes, W.	1	Hersee, P. S.	1
McLean, T.	1	Robertson, A. (Clyde)	2	Bellamy, C. D.	19	Hewitt, R.	1
McLintock, F.	1	Robertson, A.		Blackmore, C. G.	1	Hockey, T.	1
McMahon, A.	6	(Dundee U)	1	Blake, D.	1	Hodges, G.	2
McManus, S.	2	Robertson, J.	3	Blake, N. A.	4	Hole, W. J.	1
McMenemy, J.	5	Robertson, J. N.	8	Bodin, P. J.	3	Hopkins, I. J.	2
McMillan, I. L.	2	Robertson, J. T.	2	Boulter, L. M.	1	Horne, B.	2
McNeill, W.	3	Robertson, T.	1	Bowdler, J. C. H.	3	Howell, E. G.	3
McNiel, H.	5	Robertson, W.	1	Bowen, D. L.	1	Hughes, L. M.	16
McPhail, J.	3	Russell, D.	1	Bowen, M.	3	**Huws, E. W.**	**1**
McPhail, R.	7			Boyle, T.	1		
McPherson, J.		Scott, A. S.	5	Bryan, T.	1	James, E.	2
(Kilmarnock)	7	Sellar, W.	4	Burgess, W. A. R.	1	James, L.	10
McPherson, J.		Sharp, G.	1	Burke, T.	1	James, R.	7
(Vale of Leven)	1	Shaw, F. W.	1	Butler, W. T.	1	Jarrett, R. H.	3
McPherson, R.	1	Shearer, D.	2			Jenkyns, C. A.	1
McQueen, G.	5	Simpson, J.	1	Chapman, T.	2	Jones, A.	1
McStay, P.	9	Smith, A.	5	Charles, J.	1	Jones, Bryn	6
McSwegan, G.	1	Smith, G.	4	Charles, M.	6	Jones, B. S.	2
Meiklejohn, D. D.	3	Smith, J.	1	Charles, W. J.	15	Jones, Cliff	16
Millar, J.	2	Smith, John	13	**Church, S. R.**	**3**	Jones, C. W.	1
Miller, K.	18	Snodgrass, R.	3	Clarke, R. J.	5	Jones, D. E.	1
Miller, T.	2	Somerville, G.	1	Coleman, C.	4	Jones, Evan	1
Miller, W.	1	Souness, G. J.	4	Collier, D. J.	1	Jones, H.	1
Mitchell, R. C.	1	Speedie, F.	2	Collins, J.	3	Jones, I.	1
Morgan, W.	1	St John, I.	9	Cotterill, D. R. G. B.	2	Jones, J. L.	1
Morris, D.	1	Steel, W.	12	Crosse, K.	1	Jones, J. O.	1
Morris, H.	3	Stein, C.	10	Cumner, R. H.	1	Jones, J. P.	1
Morrison, J. C.	3	Stevenson, G.	4	Curtis, A.	6	Jones, Leslie J.	2
Morton, A. L.	5	Stewart, A.	1	Curtis, E. R.	3	Jones, R. A.	1
Mudie, J. K.	9	Stewart, R.	1			Jones, W. L.	6
Mulgrew, C. P.	2	Stewart, W. E.	1	Davies, D. W.	1		
Mulhall, G.	1	Strachan, G.	5	Davies, E. Lloyd	1	Keenor, F. C.	2
Munro, A. D.	1	Sturrock, P.	3	Davies, G.	2	King, A. P.	2

* The Scottish FA officially changed Robsons's goal against Iceland on 10 September 2008 to McFadden.

Name		Name		Name		Name	
Koumas, J.	10	Savage, R. W.	2	Doyle, K. E.	14	McAteer, J. W.	3
Krzywicki, R. L.	1	Shaw, E. G.	2	Duff, D. A.	8	McCann, J.	1
		Sisson, H.	4	Duffy, B.	1	McCarthy, M.	2
Ledley, J. C.	**4**	Slatter, N.	2	Duggan, H.	1	**McClean, J. J.**	**5**
Leek, K.	5	Smallman, D. P.	1	Dunne, J.	13	McEvoy, A.	6
Lewis, B.	4	Speed, G. A.	7	Dunne, L.	1	McGeady, A. G.	5
Lewis, D. M.	2	Symons, C. J.	2	Dunne, R. P.	8	McGee, P.	4
Lewis, W.	8					McGrath, P.	8
Lewis, W. L.	3	Tapscott, D. R.	4	Eglington, T.	2	McLoughlin, A. F.	2
Llewelyn, C. M	1	Taylor, G. K.	1	Elliott, S. W.	1	McPhail, S. J. P.	1
Lovell, S.	1	**Taylor, N. J.**	**1**	Ellis, P.	1	Mancini, T.	1
Lowrie, G.	1	Thomas, M.	4			Martin, C.	6
		Thomas, T.	1	Fagan, F.	5	Martin, M.	4
Mahoney, J. F.	1	Toshack, J. B.	12	Fahey, K.	3	Miller, L. W. P.	1
Mays, A. W.	1	Trainer, H.	2	Fallon, S.	2	Mooney, J.	1
Medwin, T. C.	6			Fallon, W.	2	Moore, P.	7
Melville, A. K	3	Vaughan, D. O.	1	Farrell, P.	2	Moran, K.	6
Meredith, W. H.	11	Vaughan, John	2	Finnan, S.	2	Morrison, C. H.	9
Mills, T. J.	1	Vernon, T. R.	8	Fitzgerald, P.	2	Moroney, T.	1
Moore, G.	1	Vizard, E. T.	1	Fitzgerald, J.	1	Mulligan, P.	1
Morgan, J. R.	2	**Vokes, S. M.**	**7**	Fitzsimons, A.	7		
Morgan-Owen, H.	1			Flood, J. J.	4	O'Brien, A. J.	1
Morgan-Owen, M. M.	2	Walsh, I.	7	Fogarty, A.	3	O'Callaghan, K.	1
Morison, S.	1	Warren, F. W.	3	Foley, D.	2	O'Connor, T.	2
Morris, A. G.	9	Watkins, W. M.	4	Fullam, J.	1	O'Dea, D.	1
Morris, H.	2	Wilding, J.	4	Fullam, R.	1	O'Farrell, F.	2
Morris, R.	1	Williams, A.	1			O'Flanagan, K.	3
Morris, S.	2	**Williams, A. E.**	**2**	Galvin, A.	1	O'Keefe, E.	1
		Williams, D. R.	2	Gavin, J.	2	O'Leary, D. A.	1
Nicholas, P.	2	Williams, G. E.	1	Geoghegan, M.	2	O'Neill, F.	1
		Williams, G. G.	1	Gibson, D. T. D.	1	O'Neill, K. P.	4
O'Callaghan, E.	3	Williams, W.	1	Giles, J.	5	O'Reilly, J. (Brideville)	2
O'Sullivan, P. A.	1	Woosnam, A. P.	3	Givens, D.	19	O'Reilly, J. (Cork)	1
Owen, G.	2	Wynn, G. A.	1	Glynn, D.	1	O'Shea, J. F.	3
Owen, W.	4			Grealish, T.	8	Own goals	14
Owen, W. P.	6	Yorath, T. C.	2	Green, P. J.	1		
Own goals	14	Young, E.	1	Grimes, A. A.	1	Pearce, A. J.	2
						Pilkington, A. N. J.	1
Palmer, D.	3	**REPUBLIC OF IRELAND**		Hale, A.	2		
Parry, P. I.	1	Aldridge, J.	19	Hand, E.	2	Quinn, N.	21
Parry, T. D.	3	Ambrose, P.	1	Harte, I. P.	11		
Paul, R.	1	Anderson, J.	1	Haverty, J.	3	Reid, A. M.	4
Peake, E.	1	Andrews, K.	3	Healy, C.	1	Reid, S. J.	2
Pembridge, M.	6			Holland, M. R.	5	Ringstead, A.	7
Perry, E.	1	Barrett, G.	2	Holmes, J.	1	Robinson, M.	4
Phillips, C.	5	Bermingham, P.	1	**Hoolahan, W.**	**3**	Rogers, E.	5
Phillips, D.	2	Bradshaw, P.	4	Horlacher, A.	2	Ryan, G.	1
Powell, A.	1	Brady, L.	9	Houghton, R.	6	Ryan, R.	3
Powell, D.	1	**Brady, R.**	**6**	Hughton, C.	1		
Price, J.	4	Breen, G.	7	Hunt, S. P.	1	St Ledger-Hall, S.	3
Price, P.	1	Brown, J.	1	Hurley, C.	2	Sheedy, K.	9
Pryce-Jones, W. E.	3	Byrne, D.	1			Sheridan, J.	5
Pugh, D. H.	2	Byrne, J.	4	Ireland, S. J.	4	Slaven, B.	1
				Irwin, D.	4	Sloan, J.	1
Ramsey, A. J.	**11**	Cantwell, N.	14			Squires, J.	1
Reece, G. I.	2	Carey, J.	3	Jordan, D.	1	Stapleton, F.	20
Rees, R. R.	3	Carroll, T.	1			Staunton, S.	7
Richards, R. W.	1	Cascarino, A.	19	Kavanagh, G. A.	1	Strahan, J.	1
Roach, J.	1	**Christie, C. S. F.**	**1**	**Keane, R. D.**	**67**	Sullivan, J.	1
Robbins, W. W.	4	**Clark, C.**	**2**	Keane, R. M.	9		
Roberts, J. (Corwen)	1	Coad, P.	3	Kelly, D.	9	Townsend, A. D.	7
Roberts, Jas.	1	Connolly, D. J.	9	Kelly, G.	2	Treacy, R.	5
Roberts, P. S.	1	Conroy, T.	2	Kelly, J.	2	Touhy, L.	4
Roberts, R. (Druids)	1	Conway, J.	3	Kennedy, M.	4		
Roberts, W. (Llangollen)	2	Cox, S. R.	4	Keogh, A.	2	Waddock, G.	3
Roberts, W. (Wrexham)	1	Coyne, T.	6	Keogh, R. J.	1	Walsh, D.	5
Roberts, W. H.	1	Cummins, G.	5	Kernaghan, A. N.	1	Walsh, M.	3
Robinson, C. P.	1	Curtis, D.	8	Kilbane, K. D.	8	**Walters, J. R.**	**10**
Robinson, J. R. C.	1			Kinsella, M. A.	3	**Ward, S. R.**	**3**
Robson-Kanu, T. H.	**4**	Daly, G.	13			Waters, J.	1
Rush, I.	28	Davis, T.	4	Lacey, W.	1	White, J. J.	1
Russell, M. R.	1	Dempsey, J.	1	Lawrence, L.	2	Whelan, G. D.	2
		Dennehy, M.	1	Lawrenson, M.	5	Whelan, R.	3
Sabine, H. W.	1	Doherty, G. M. T.	4	Leech, M.	2	Wilson, M. D.	1
Saunders, D.	22	Donnelly, J.	4	**Long, S. P.**	**16**		
		Donnelly, T.	1				

BRITISH AND IRISH INTERNATIONAL MANAGERS

England
Walter Winterbottom 1946-1962 (after period as coach); Alf Ramsey 1963–1974; Joe Mercer (caretaker) 1974; Don Revie 1974–1977; Ron Greenwood 1977–1982; Bobby Robson 1982–1990; Graham Taylor 1990–1993; Terry Venables (coach) l994–1996; Glenn Hoddle 1996–1999; Kevin Keegan 1999–2000; Sven-Goran Eriksson 2001–2006; Steve McClaren 2006–2007; Fabio Capello 2008–2012; Roy Hodgson 2012–16.

Northern Ireland
Peter Doherty 1951–1952; Bertie Peacock 1962–1967; Billy Bingham 1967–1971; Terry Neill 1971–1975; Dave Clements (player-manager) 1975–1976; Danny Blanchflower 1976–1979; Billy Bingham 1980–1994; Bryan Hamilton 1994–1998; Lawrie McMenemy 1998–1999; Sammy McIlroy 2000–2003; Lawrie Sanchez 2004–2007; Nigel Worthington 2007–2011; Michael O'Neill from December 2011.

Scotland (since 1967)
Bobby Brown 1967–1971; Tommy Docherty 1971–1972; Willie Ormond 1973–1977; Ally MacLeod 1977–1978; Jock Stein 1978–1985; Alex Ferguson (caretaker) 1985–1986 Andy Roxburgh (coach) 1986–1993; Craig Brown 1993–2001; Berti Vogts 2002–2004; Walter Smith 2004–2007; Alex McLeish 2007; George Burley 2008–2009; Craig Levein 2009–2012; Gordon Strachan from February 2013.

Wales (since 1974)
Mike Smith 1974–1979; Mike England 1980–1988; David Williams (caretaker) 1988; Terry Yorath 1988–1993; John Toshack 1994 for one match; Mike Smith 1994–1995; Bobby Gould 1995–1999; Mark Hughes 1999–2004; John Toshack 2004–2010; Gary Speed 2010–2011; Chris Coleman from January 2012.

Republic of Ireland
Liam Tuohy 1971–1972; Johnny Giles 1973–1980 (after period as player-manager); Eoin Hand 1980–1985; Jack Charlton 1986–1996; Mick McCarthy 1996–2002; Brian Kerr 2003–2006; Steve Staunton 2006–2007; Giovanni Trapattoni 2008–2013; Martin O'Neill from November 2013.

Former England manager, Roy Hodgson, watches his side playing Lithuania in Vilnius in October 2015 during their Group E qualifying campaign for the European Championships. Hodgson resigned after England's exit at the hands of Iceland in the Finals in France. (Reuters/Carl Recine Livepic)

SOUTH AMERICA

COPA AMERICA 2015 (in Chile)

GROUP A

Chile v Ecuador	2-0	Chile v Mexico	3-3
Mexico v Bolivia	0-0	Mexico v Ecuador	1-2
Ecuador v Bolivia	2-3	Chile v Bolivia	5-0

GROUP B

Uruguay v Jamaica	1-0	Argentina v Uruguay	1-0
Argentina v Paraguay	2-2	Uruguay v Paraguay	1-1
Paraguay v Jamaica	1-0	Argentina v Jamaica	1-0

GROUP C

Colombia v Venezuela	0-1	Peru v Venezuela	1-0
Brazil v Peru	2-1	Colombia v Peru	0-0
Brazil v Colombia	0-1	Brazil v Venezuela	2-1

QUARTER-FINALS

Chile v Uruguay	1-0
Bolivia v Peru	1-3

Argentina v Colombia	0-0
Argentina won 5-4 on penalties.	
Brazil v Paraguay	1-1
Paraguay won 4-3 on penalties.	

SEMI-FINALS

Chile v Peru	2-1
Argentina v Paraguay	6-1

3RD PLACE FINAL

Peru v Paraguay	2-0

FINAL

Chile v Argentina	0-0
aet; Chile won 4-1 on penalties.	

COPA SUDAMERICANA 2015

SECOND ROUND – FIRST LEG

LDU Quito v Nacional Asuncion	1-0
Defensor Sporting v Universitario	3-0
Nacional v Santa Fe	0-2
Deportivo La Guaira v Sportivo Luqueno	1-1
Brasilia v Goias	0-0
Olimpia v Aguilas Doradas	1-1
Tigre v Huracan	2-5
Ponte Preta v Chapecoense	1-1
Universidad Catolica v Libertad	2-3
Bahia v Sport Recife	1-0
Arsenal v Independiente	1-1
Joinville v Atletico Paranaense	0-2
Deportes Tolima v Junior	0-1
Emelec v Juventud	0-0
Belgrano v Lanus	1-1

SECOND ROUND – SECOND LEG

		(agg)
Nacional Asuncion v LDU Quito	0-1	0-2
Universitario v Defensor Sporting	0-1	0-4
Santa Fe v Nacional	0-1	2-1
Sportivo Luqueno v Deportivo La Guaira	4-0	5-1
Goias v Brasilia	0-2	0-2
Aguilas Doradas v Olimpia	1-2	2-3
Huracan v Tigre	1-0	6-2
Chapecoense v Ponte Preta	3-0	4-1
Libertad v Universidad Catolica	1-0	4-2
Sport Recife v Bahia	4-1	4-2
Independiente v Arsenal	1-0	2-1
Atletico Paranaense v Joinville	1-0	3-0
Junior v Deportes Tolima	0-2	1-2
Juventud v Emelec	0-0	0-0
Emelec won 3-2 on penalties.		
Lanus v Belgrano	5-1	2-6

ROUND OF 16 – FIRST LEG

River Plate v LDU Quito	2-0
Lanus v Defensor Sporting	0-0
Emelec v Santa Fe	2-1
Deportes Tolima v Sportivo Luqueno	1-1
Atletico Paranaense v Brasilia	1-0
Independiente v Olimpia	1-0

Sport Recife v Huracan	1-1
Libertad v Chapecoense	1-1

ROUND OF 16 – SECOND LEG

		(agg)
LDU Quito v River Plate	1-0	1-2
Defensor Sporting v Lanus	0-0	0-0
Defensor Sporting won 5-3 on penalties.		
Santa Fe v Emelec	1-0	2-2
Santa Fe won on away goals rule.		
Sportivo Luqueno v Deportes Tolima	1-0	2-1
Brasilia v Atletico Paranaense	0-0	0-1
Olimpia v Independiente	0-0	0-1
Huracan v Sport Recife	3-0	4-1
Chapecoense v Libertad	1-1	2-2
Chapecoense won 5-3 on penalties.		

QUARTER-FINALS – FIRST LEG

River Plate v Chapecoense	3-1
Huracan v Defensor Sporting	1-0
Independiente v Santa Fe	0-1
Atletico Paranaense v Sportivo Luqueno	1-0

QUARTER-FINALS – SECOND LEG

		(agg)
Chapecoense v River Plate	2-1	3-4
Defensor Sporting v Huracan	0-0	0-1
Santa Fe v Independiente	1-1	2-1
Sportivo Luqueno v Atletico Paranaense	2-0	2-1

SEMI-FINALS – FIRST LEG

Sportivo Luqueno v Santa Fe	1-1
River Plate v Huracan	0-1

SEMI-FINALS – SECOND LEG

		(agg)
Santa Fe v Sportivo Luqueno	0-0	1-1
Santa Fe won on away goals.		
Huracan v River Plate	2-2	2-3

FINAL – FIRST LEG

Huracan v Santa Fe	0-0

FINAL – SECOND LEG

		(agg)
Santa Fe v Huracan	0-0	0-0
aet; Santa Fe won 3-1 on penalties.		

RECOPA SUDAMERICANA 2015

FINAL – FIRST LEG

River Plate v San Lorenzo	1-0

FINAL – SECOND LEG

		(agg)
San Lorenzo v River Plate	0-1	0-2

COPA BRIDGESTONE LIBERTADORES 2015

SEMI-FINALS – FIRST LEG

River Plate v Guarani	2-0
Internacional v UANL	2-1

SEMI-FINALS – SECOND LEG

		(agg)
Guarani v River Plate	1-1	1-3
UANL v Internacional	3-1	4-3

FINAL – FIRST LEG

UANL v River Plate	0-0

FINAL – SECOND LEG

		(agg)
River Plate v UANL	3-0	3-0

COPA BRIDGESTONE LIBERTADORES 2016

FIRST STAGE – FIRST LEG

Oriente Petrolero v Santa Fe	1-3
Huracan v Caracas	1-0
Puebla v Racing	2-2
River Plate (Uruguay) v Universidad de Chile	2-0
Independiente del Valle v Guarani	1-0
Universidad Cesar Vallejo v Sao Paulo	1-1

FIRST STAGE – SECOND LEG *(agg)*

Santa Fe v Oriente Petrolero	3-0	6-1
Caracas v Huracan	2-1	2-2
Huracan won on away goals.		
Racing v Puebla	1-0	3-2
Universidad de Chile v River Plate (Uruguay)	0-0	0-2
Guarani v Independiente del Valle	2-1	2-2
Independiente del Valle won on away goals.		
Sao Paulo v Universidad Cesar Vallejo	1-0	2-1

SECOND STAGE

GROUP 1

Sao Paulo v The Strongest	0-1
Trujillanos v River Plate (Argentina)	0-4
The Strongest v Trujillanos	2-1
River Plate (Argentina) v Sao Paulo	1-1
The Strongest v River Plate (Argentina)	1-1
Trujillanos v Sao Paulo	1-1
Sao Paulo v Trujillanos	6-0
River Plate (Argentina) v The Strongest	6-0
Trujillanos v The Strongest	2-1
Sao Paulo v River Plate (Argentina)	2-1
River Plate (Argentina) v Trujillanos	4-3
The Strongest v Sao Paulo	1-1

GROUP 2

River Plate (Uruguay) v Palmeiras	2-2
Rosario Central v Nacional	1-1
Nacional v River Plate (Uruguay)	0-0
Palmeiras v Rosario Central	2-0
Rosario Central v River Plate (Uruguay)	4-1
Palmeiras v Nacional	1-2
River Plate (Uruguay) v Rosario Central	1-3
Nacional v Palmeiras	1-0
Rosario Central v Palmeiras	3-3
River Plate (Uruguay) v Nacional	2-2
Nacional v Rosario Central	0-2
Palmeiras v River Plate (Uruguay)	4-0

GROUP 3

Racing v Bolivar	4-1
Deportivo Cali v Boca Juniors	0-0
Boca Juniors v Racing	5-0
Bolivar v Deportivo Cali	5-0
Bolivar v Boca Juniors	1-1
Deportivo Cali v Racing	2-2
Boca Juniors v Bolivar	3-1
Racing v Deportivo Cali	4-2
Racing v Boca Juniors	0-1
Deportivo Cali v Bolivar	1-1
Boca Juniors v Deportivo Cali	6-2
Bolivar v Racing	1-1

GROUP 4

Sporting Cristal v Penarol	1-1
Huracan v Atletico Nacional	0-2
Atletico Nacional v Sporting Cristal	3-0
Penarol v Huracan	0-1
Atletico Nacional v Penarol	2-0
Sporting Cristal v Huracan	3-2
Penarol v Atletico Nacional	0-4
Huracan v Sporting Cristal	4-2
Huracan v Penarol	0-0
Sporting Cristal v Atletico Nacional	0-1
Penarol v Sporting Cristal	4-3
Atletico Nacional v Huracan	0-0

GROUP 5

Melgar v Atletico Mineiro	1-2
Independiente del Valle v Colo-Colo	1-1
Colo-Colo v Melgar	1-0
Atletico Mineiro v Independiente del Valle	1-0
Melgar v Independiente del Valle	0-1
Colo-Colo v Atletico Mineiro	0-0
Independiente del Valle v Melgar	2-0

Atletico Mineiro v Colo-Colo	3-0
Independiente del Valle v Atletico Mineiro	3-2
Melgar v Colo-Colo	1-2
Atletico Mineiro v Melgar	4-0
Colo-Colo v Independiente del Valle	0-0

GROUP 6

Toluca v Gremio	2-0
LDU Quito v San Lorenzo	2-0
San Lorenzo v Toluca	1-1
Gremio v LDU Quito	4-0
Gremio v San Lorenzo	1-1
LDU Quito v Toluca	1-2
San Lorenzo v Gremio	1-1
Toluca v LDU Quito	2-1
Toluca v San Lorenzo	2-1
LDU Quito v Gremio	2-3
San Lorenzo v LDU Quito	1-1
Gremio v Toluca	1-0

GROUP 7

Deportivo Tachira v Olimpia	2-1
UNAM v Emelec	4-2
Emelec v Deportivo Tachira	2-0
Olimpia v UNAM	0-2
Emelec v Olimpia	2-2
Deportivo Tachira v UNAM	2-0
Olimpia v Emelec	4-2
UNAM v Deportivo Tachira	4-1
Deportivo Tachira v Emelec	1-0
UNAM v Olimpia	4-1
Olimpia v Deportivo Tachira	4-0
Emelec v UNAM	2-3

GROUP 8

Santa Fe v Cerro Porteno	0-0
Cobresal v Corinthians	0-1
Cerro Porteno v Cobresal	2-1
Corinthians v Santa Fe	1-0
Cobresal v Santa Fe	1-2
Cerro Porteno v Corinthians	3-2
Santa Fe v Cobresal	3-0
Corinthians v Cerro Porteno	2-0
Santa Fe v Corinthians	1-1
Cobresal v Cerro Porteno	2-0
Corinthians v Cobresal	6-0
Cerro Porteno v Santa Fe	1-0

ROUND OF 16 – FIRST LEG

Huracan v Atletico Nacional	0-0
Deportivo Tachira v UNAM	1-0
Nacional v Corinthians	0-0
Racing v Atletico Mineiro	0-0
Sao Paulo v Toluca	4-0
Cerro Porteno v Boca Juniors	1-2
Independiente del Valle v River Plate (Argentina)	2-0
Gremio v Rosario Central	0-1

ROUND OF 16 – SECOND LEG *(agg)*

Atletico Nacional v Huracan	4-2	4-2
UNAM v Deportivo Tachira	2-0	2-1
Corinthians v Nacional	2-2	2-2
Nacional won on away goals.		
Atletico Mineiro v Racing	2-1	2-1
Toluca v Sao Paulo	3-1	3-5
Boca Juniors v Cerro Porteno	3-1	5-2
River Plate (Argentina) v Independiente del Valle	1-0	1-2
Rosario Central v Gremio	3-0	4-0

QUARTER-FINALS – FIRST LEG

Rosario Central v Atletico Nacional	1-0
Independiente del Valle v UNAM	2-1
Nacional v Boca Juniors	1-1
Sao Paulo v Atletico Mineiro	1-0

QUARTER-FINALS – SECOND LEG *(agg)*

Atletico Nacional v Rosario Central	3-1	3-2
UNAM v Independiente del Valle	2-1	3-3
Independient de Valle won 5-3 on penalties		
Boca Juniors v Nacional	1-1	2-2
Boca Juniors won 4-3 on penalties		
Atletico Mineiro v Sao Paulo	2-1	2-2
Sao Paulo won on away goals		

Competition still being played.

COPA AMERICA 2016 (in USA)

GROUP A

USA v Colombia	0-2	Colombia v Paraguay	2-1
Costa Rica v Paraguay	0-0	USA v Paraguay	1-0
USA v Costa Rica	4-0	Colombia v Costa Rica	2-3

GROUP B

Haiti v Peru	0-1	Ecuador v Peru	2-2
Brazil v Ecuador	0-0	Ecuador v Haiti	4-0
Brazil v Haltl	7-1	Brazil v Peru	0-1

GROUP C

Jamaica v Venezuela	0-1	Mexico v Jamaica	2-0
Mexico v Uruguay	3-1	Mexico v Venezuela	1-1
Uruguay v Venezuela	0-1	Uruguay v Jamaica	3-0

GROUP D

Panama v Bolivia	2-1	Argentina v Panama	5-0
Argentina v Chile	2-1	Chile v Panama	4-2
Chile v Bolivia	2-1	Argentina v Bolivia	3-0

QUARTER-FINALS

USA v Ecuador	2-1
Argentina v Venezuela	4-1
Peru v Colombia	0-0
Colombia won 4-2 on penalties.	
Mexico v Chile	0-7

SEMI-FINALS

USA v Argentina	0-4
Colombia v Chile	0-2

3RD PLACE FINAL

USA v Colombia	0-1

FINAL

Chile v Argentina	0-0
aet; Chile won 4-2 on penalties.	

NORTH AMERICA – MAJOR LEAGUE SOCCER 2015

EASTERN CONFERENCE

	P	W	D	L	F	A	GD	Pts
New York Red Bulls	34	18	6	10	62	43	19	60
Columbus Crew	34	15	8	11	58	53	5	53
Montreal Impact	34	15	6	13	48	44	4	51
DC United	34	15	6	13	43	45	-2	51
NE Revolution	34	14	8	12	48	47	1	50
Toronto	34	15	4	15	58	58	0	49
Orlando City	34	12	8	14	46	56	-10	44
New York City	34	10	7	17	49	58	-9	37
Philadelphia Union	34	10	7	17	42	55	-13	37
Chicago Fire	34	8	6	20	43	58	-15	30

WESTERN CONFERENCE

	P	W	D	L	F	A	GD	Pts
FC Dallas	34	18	6	10	52	39	13	60
Vancouver Whitecaps	34	16	5	13	45	36	9	53
Portland Timbers	34	15	8	11	41	39	2	53
Seattle Sounders	34	15	6	13	44	36	8	51
LA Galaxy	34	14	9	11	56	46	10	51
Sporting Kansas City	34	14	9	11	48	45	3	51
San Jose Earthquakes	34	13	8	13	41	39	2	47
Houston Dynamo	34	11	9	14	42	49	-7	42
Real Salt Lake	34	11	8	15	38	48	-10	41
Colorado Rapids	34	9	10	15	33	43	-10	37

EASTERN KNOCKOUT ROUND

Toronto v Montreal Impact	0-3
New England Revolution v DC United	1-2

WESTERN KNOCKOUT ROUND

Sporting Kansas City v Portland Timbers	2-2
aet; Portland Timbers won 7-6 on penalties.	
LA Galaxy v Seattle Sounders	2-3

EASTERN SEMI-FINALS – FIRST LEG

Montreal Impact v Columbus Crew	2-1
DC United v New York Red Bulls	0-1

EASTERN SEMI-FINALS – SECOND LEG *(agg)*

Columbus Crew v Montreal Impact	3-1	(4-3)
New York Red Bulls v DC United	1-0	(2-0)

WESTERN SEMI-FINALS – FIRST LEG

Portland Timbers v Vancouver Whitecaps	0-0
Seattle Sounders v FC Dallas	2-1

WESTERN SEMI-FINALS – SECOND LEG *(agg)*

Vancouver Whitecaps v Portland Timbers	0-2	(0-2)
FC Dallas v Seattle Sounders	2-1	(3-3)
aet; FC Dallas won 4-2 on penalties.		

EASTERN CHAMPIONSHIP – FIRST LEG

Columbus Crew v New York Red Bulls	2-0

EASTERN CHAMPIONSHIP – SECOND LEG *(agg)*

New York Red Bulls v Columbus Crew	1-0	(1-2)

WESTERN CHAMPIONSHIP – FIRST LEG

Portland Timbers v FC Dallas	3-1

WESTERN CHAMPIONSHIP – SECOND LEG *(agg)*

FC Dallas v Portland Timbers	2-2	(3-5)

MLS CUP FINAL 2015
Sunday 6 December 2015

Columbus Crew (1) 1 *(Kamara 18)*

Portland Timbers (2) 2 *(Valeri 1, Wallace 7)*   21,747

Columbus Crew: Clark; Afful, Parkhurst, Sauro, Francis, Tchani (McInerney 72), Trapp, Finlay (Cedrick 63), Higuain, Meram (Saeid 78), Kamara.
Portland Timbers: Kwarasey, Powell, Borchers, Ridgewell, Villafana, Nagbe, Chara, Valeri, Melano (Asprilla 59), Adi (Urruti 90), Wallace (Jewsbury 90).
Referee: Jan Marrufo.

CONCACAF – GOLD CUP 2015

GROUP A

Panama v Haiti	1-1	USA v Haiti	1-0
USA v Honduras	2-1	Haiti v Honduras	1-0
Honduras v Panama	1-1	Panama v USA	1-1

GROUP B

Costa Rica v Jamaica	2-2	Costa Rica v El Salvador	1-1
El Salvador v Canada	0-0	Jamaica v El Salvador	1-0
Jamaica v Canada	1-0	Canada v Costa Rica	0-0

GROUP C

Trinidad & T v Guatemala	3-1	Guatemala v Mexico	0-0
Mexico v Cuba	6-0	Cuba v Guatemala	0-1
Trinidad & T v Cuba	2-0	Mexico v Trinidad & T	4-4

QUARTER-FINALS

USA v Cuba	6-0
Haiti v Jamaica	0-1
Trinidad & Tobago v Panama *won 6-5 on penalties.*	1-1
Mexico v Costa Rica	1-0*

SEMI-FINALS

USA v Jamaica	1-2
Panama v Mexico	1-2*

MATCH FOR THIRD PLACE

USA v Panama *won 3-2 on penalties*	1-1*

FINAL

Jamaica v Mexico	1-3

UEFA UNDER-21 CHAMPIONSHIP 2015–17

QUALIFYING ROUND

GROUP 1

Belgium v Moldova	2-1
Moldova v Malta	0-0
Montenegro v Moldova	1-0
Latvia v Malta	1-2
Moldova v Montenegro	1-0
Latvia v Belgium	0-2
Czech Republic v Malta	4-1
Latvia v Czech Republic	1-1
Montenegro v Malta	0-0
Belgium v Malta	2-0
Moldova v Latvia	0-3
Czech Republic v Montenegro	3-3
Czech Republic v Belgium	1-0
Montenegro v Latvia	3-3
Moldova v Czech Republic	1-3
Moldova v Belgium	0-2
Malta v Montenegro	0-1
Czech Republic v Latvia	2-1
Belgium v Montenegro	1-2
Malta v Czech Republic	0-7

Group 1 Table	P	W	D	L	F	A	GD	Pts
Czech Republic	7	5	2	0	21	7	14	17
Montenegro	7	3	3	1	10	8	2	12
Belgium	6	4	0	2	9	4	5	12
Malta	7	1	2	4	3	15	–12	5
Latvia	6	1	2	3	9	10	–1	5
Moldova	7	1	1	5	3	11	–8	4

GROUP 2

Republic of Ireland v Andorra	1-0
Slovenia v Andorra	4-0
Andorra v Lithuania	1-0
Slovenia v Lithuania	3-0
Andorra v Republic of Ireland	0-2
Italy v Slovenia	1-0
Serbia v Lithuania	5-0
Serbia v Andorra	5-0
Slovenia v Italy	0-3
Republic of Ireland v Lithuania	3-0
Italy v Republic of Ireland	1-0
Lithuania v Serbia	0-2
Andorra v Slovenia	0-5
Lithuania v Republic of Ireland	3-1
Serbia v Italy	1-1
Slovenia v Serbia	2-0
Italy v Lithuania	1-4
Republic of Ireland v Italy	0-4
Andorra v Serbia	0-4
Slovenia v Republic of Ireland	3-1

Group 2 Table	P	W	D	L	F	A	GD	Pts
Italy	7	6	1	0	13	2	11	19
Slovenia	7	5	0	2	17	5	12	15
Serbia	6	4	1	1	17	3	14	13
Republic of Ireland	7	3	0	4	9	11	–2	9
Andorra	8	1	0	7	1	22	–21	3
Lithuania	7	1	0	6	3	17	–14	3

GROUP 3

Iceland v FYR Macedonia	3-0
Northern Ireland v Scotland	1-2
Iceland v France	3-2
FYR Macedonia v Ukraine	1-0
Iceland v Northern Ireland	1-1
Ukraine v Iceland	0-1
Scotland v France	1-2
Northern Ireland v FYR Macedonia	1-2
Scotland v Iceland	0-0
France v Ukraine	2-0
France v Northern Ireland	1-0
Scotland v Ukraine	2-2
FYR Macedonia v France	2-2
Northern Ireland v Ukraine	1-2
FYR Macedonia v Iceland	0-0
France v Scotland	2-0

France v FYR Macedonia	1-1
Scotland v Northern Ireland	3-1
Ukraine v FYR Macedonia	0-2

Group 3 Table	P	W	D	L	F	A	GD	Pts
France	7	4	2	1	12	7	5	14
Iceland	6	3	3	0	8	3	5	12
FYR Macedonia	7	3	3	1	8	7	1	12
Scotland	6	2	2	2	8	8	0	8
Ukraine	6	1	1	4	4	9	–5	4
Northern Ireland	6	0	1	5	5	11	–6	1

GROUP 4

Liechtenstein v Albania	0-2
Liechtenstein v Israel	0-4
Liechtenstein v Hungary	0-6
Albania v Israel	1-1
Liechtenstein v Greece	0-2
Albania v Portugal	1-6
Greece v Portugal	0-4
Portugal v Hungary	2-0
Hungary v Albania	2-2
Greece v Liechtenstein	5-0
Portugal v Albania	4-0
Israel v Hungary	3-0
Hungary v Greece	2-1
Albania v Liechtenstein	2-0
Israel v Portugal	0-3
Portugal v Liechtenstein	4-0
Albania v Greece	0-0
Hungary v Israel	0-0
Greece v Israel	0-1
Albania v Hungary	2-1

Group 4 Table	P	W	D	L	F	A	GD	Pts
Portugal	6	6	0	0	23	1	22	18
Albania	8	3	3	2	10	14	–4	12
Israel	6	3	2	1	9	4	5	11
Hungary	7	2	2	3	11	10	1	8
Greece	6	2	1	3	8	7	1	7
Liechtenstein	7	0	0	7	0	25	–25	0

GROUP 5

Wales v Bulgaria	3-1
Romania v Armenia	3-0
Luxembourg v Wales	1-3
Romania v Bulgaria	0-2
Armenia v Romania	2-3
Bulgaria v Luxembourg	3-0
Luxembourg v Romania	0-1
Bulgaria v Armenia	2-0
Denmark v Wales	0-0
Armenia v Luxembourg	1-1
Denmark v Bulgaria	1-0
Wales v Armenia	2-1
Romania v Denmark	0-3
Denmark v Armenia	2-0
Wales v Romania	1-1
Luxembourg v Denmark	0-1
Bulgaria v Wales	0-0
Armenia v Denmark	1-3
Romania v Wales	2-1
Luxembourg v Bulgaria	0-0

Group 5 Table	P	W	D	L	F	A	GD	Pts
Denmark	6	5	1	0	10	1	9	16
Romania	7	4	1	2	10	9	1	13
Wales	7	3	3	1	10	6	4	12
Bulgaria	7	3	2	2	8	4	4	11
Luxembourg	6	0	2	4	2	9	–7	2
Armenia	7	0	1	6	5	16	–11	1

GROUP 6

San Marino v Georgia	0-3
Estonia v San Marino	0-0
Estonia v Spain	0-2
Croatia v Georgia	1-0
Sweden v San Marino	3-0
Estonia v Croatia	0-4
Georgia v Spain	2-5

San Marino v Croatia	0-3
Sweden v Estonia	5-0
Georgia v Estonia	3-0
Spain v Sweden	1-1
Croatia v San Marino	4-0
Spain v Georgia	5-0
San Marino v Estonia	1-2
Georgia v Sweden	0-1
Croatia v Spain	2-3
Georgia v San Marino	4-0
Spain v Croatia	0-3
San Marino v Sweden	0-2
Croatia v Estonia	2-1
Sweden v Georgia	3-2

Group 6 Table	P	W	D	L	F	A	GD	Pts
Croatia	7	6	0	1	19	4	15	18
Sweden	6	5	1	0	15	3	12	16
Spain	6	4	1	1	16	8	8	13
Georgia	8	3	0	5	14	15	–1	9
Estonia	7	1	1	5	3	17	–14	4
San Marino	8	0	1	7	1	21	–20	1

GROUP 7

Faroe Islands v Azerbaijan	0-1
Azerbaijan v Austria	0-2
Finland v Russia	2-0
Azerbaijan v Germany	0-3
Austria v Russia	4-3
Finland v Faroe Islands	3-0
Austria v Azerbaijan	7-0
Germany v Finland	4-0
Azerbaijan v Finland	0-1
Faroe Islands v Germany	0-6
Russia v Faroe Islands	2-0
Germany v Azerbaijan	3-1
Austria v Finland	2-0
Azerbaijan v Russia	3-0
Germany v Austria	4-2
Russia v Azerbaijan	2-2
Germany v Faroe Islands	4-1
Austria v Faroe Islands	1-0
Russia v Germany	0-2
Faroe Islands v Finland	1-6

Group 7 Table	P	W	D	L	F	A	GD	Pts
Germany	7	7	0	0	26	4	22	21
Austria	6	5	0	1	18	7	11	15
Finland	6	4	0	2	12	7	5	12
Azerbaijan	8	2	1	5	7	18	–11	7
Russia	6	1	1	4	7	13	–6	4
Faroe Islands	7	0	0	7	2	23	–21	0

GROUP 8

Netherlands v Cyprus	4-0
Belarus v Slovakia	1-0
Turkey v Netherlands	0-1
Slovakia v Cyprus	2-0
Belarus v Turkey	0-2
Netherlands v Slovakia	1-3
Cyprus v Belarus	0-1
Cyprus v Turkey	0-3
Netherlands v Belarus	1-0
Belarus v Cyprus	2-2
Slovakia v Netherlands	4-2
Slovakia v Turkey	5-0

Group 8 Table	P	W	D	L	F	A	GD	Pts
Slovakia	5	4	0	1	14	4	10	12
Netherlands	5	3	0	2	9	7	2	9
Belarus	5	2	1	2	4	5	–1	7
Turkey	4	2	0	2	5	6	–1	6
Cyprus	5	0	1	4	2	12	–10	1

GROUP 9

Norway v Bosnia-Herzegovina	2-0
Bosnia-Herzegovina v Kazakhstan	1-2
Kazakhstan v Switzerland	0-1
Norway v England	0-1
Switzerland v Bosnia-Herzegovina	3-1
Norway v Kazakhstan	2-1
Switzerland v Norway	1-1
England v Kazakhstan	3-0
Bosnia-Herzegovina v England	0-0
England v Switzerland	3-1
Kazakhstan v Bosnia-Herzegovina	0-0
Switzerland v England	1-1

Group 9 Table	P	W	D	L	F	A	GD	Pts
England	5	3	2	0	8	2	6	11
Switzerland	5	2	2	1	7	6	1	8
Norway	4	2	1	1	5	3	2	7
Kazakhstan	5	1	1	3	3	7	–4	4
Bosnia-Herzegovina	5	0	2	3	2	7	–5	2

Competition still being played.

UEFA YOUTH LEAGUE 2015–16

GROUP A

Paris Saint-Germain v Malmo	0-0
Real Madrid v Shakhtar Donetsk	4-0
Shakhtar Donetsk v Paris Saint-Germain	1-4
Malmo v Real Madrid	1-0
Paris Saint-Germain v Real Madrid	4-1
Malmo v Shakhtar Donetsk	5-5
Shakhtar Donetsk v Malmo	3-1
Real Madrid v Paris Saint-Germain	2-0
Shakhtar Donetsk v Real Madrid	2-6
Malmo v Paris Saint-Germain	0-3
Paris Saint-Germain v Shakhtar Donetsk	5-2
Real Madrid v Malmo	3-0

GROUP B

PSV Einhoven v Manchester U	0-3
Wolfsburg v CSKA Moscow	2-4
CSKA Moscow v PSV Einhoven	1-1
Manchester U v Wolfsburg	1-1
CSKA Moscow v Manchester U	4-0
Wolfsburg v PSV Einhoven	4-1
Manchester U v CSKA Moscow	0-0
PSV Einhoven v Wolfsburg	2-1
CSKA Moscow v Wolfsburg	1-2
Manchester U v PSV Einhoven	0-5
Wolfsburg v Manchester U	0-2
PSV Einhoven v CSKA Moscow	2-1

GROUP C

Galatasaray v Atletico Madrid	1-3
Benfica v Astana	8-0
Astana v Galatasaray	0-3
Atletico Madrid v Benfica	1-2
Atletico Madrid v Astana	7-1
Galatasaray v Benfica	1-11
Astana v Atletico Madrid	0-9
Benfica v Galatasaray	2-0
Astana v Benfica	0-5
Atletico Madrid v Galatasaray	4-0
Galatasaray v Astana	3-0
Benfica v Atletico Madrid	1-1

GROUP D

Sevilla v Borussia Moenchengladbach	4-2
Manchester C v Juventus	4-1
Borussia Moenchengladbach v Manchester C	1-2
Juventus v Sevilla	0-1
Juventus v Borussia Moenchengladbach	2-1
Manchester C v Sevilla	1-1
Borussia Moenchengladbach v Juventus	3-2
Sevilla v Manchester C	0-2
Juventus v Manchester C	2-1
Borussia Moenchengladbach v Sevilla	2-2
Manchester C v Borussia Moenchengladbach	1-1
Sevilla v Juventus	1-0

GROUP E

Bayer Leverkusen v BATE Borisov	1-0
Roma v Barcelona	0-0
BATE Borisov v Roma	0-0
Barcelona v Bayer Leverkusen	1-1
BATE Borisov v Barcelona	0-3
Bayer Leverkusen v Roma	2-1
Roma v Bayer Leverkusen	5-1
Barcelona v BATE Borisov	2-0
Barcelona v Roma	3-3
BATE Borisov v Bayer Leverkusen	1-1
Bayer Leverkusen v Barcelona	0-1
Roma v BATE Borisov	3-0

GROUP F

Olympiacos v Bayern Munich	1-0
Dinamo Zagreb v Arsenal	0-2
Bayern Munich v Dinamo Zagreb	1-2
Arsenal v Olympiacos	3-2
Arsenal v Bayern Munich	2-0
Dinamo Zagreb v Olympiacos	2-2
Bayern Munich v Arsenal	1-1
Olympiacos v Dinamo Zagreb	1-3
Bayern Munich v Olympiacos	0-1
Arsenal v Dinamo Zagreb	1-2
Dinamo Zagreb v Bayern Munich	0-1
Olympiacos v Arsenal	2-0

GROUP G

Dynamo Kyiv v Porto	2-1
Chelsea v Maccabi Tel Aviv	3-0
Maccabi Tel Aviv v Dynamo Kyiv	1-1
Porto v Chelsea	3-3
Dynamo Kyiv v Chelsea	0-2
Porto v Maccabi Tel Aviv	2-0
Maccabi Tel Aviv v Porto	1-2
Chelsea v Dynamo Kyiv	3-1
Maccabi Tel Aviv v Chelsea	0-4
Porto v Dynamo Kyiv	0-1
Dynamo Kyiv v Maccabi Tel Aviv	2-0
Chelsea v Porto	0-0

GROUP H

Gent v Lyon	0-3
Valencia v Zenit St Petersburg	2-0
Zenit St Petersburg v Gent	0-1
Lyon v Valencia	1-0
Zenit St Petersburg v Lyon	3-1
Valencia v Gent	5-1
Gent v Valencia	0-4
Lyon v Zenit St Petersburg	6-0
Zenit St Petersburg v Valencia	0-1
Lyon v Gent	4-0
Valencia v Lyon	1-1
Gent v Zenit St Petersburg	0-2

DOMESTIC CHAMPIONS 1ST ROUND – 1ST LEG

Minsk v Viitorul	2-2
Senica v Torino	0-0
Villarreal v Servette	2-3
Rad v Domzale	0-1
Spartak Moscow v Ravan	4-0
Aktobe v Besiktas	0-2
APOEL v Puskas Akademia	3-3
Schalke v Ajax	2-3
Pribram v Zimbru	2-0
HJK v Celtic	0-5
Elfsborg v Stjarnan	2-0
Litex v Legia	1-2
Salzburg v Zeljeznicar	4-0
Midtjylland v Saburtalo	3-1
Reims v Middlesbrough	5-3
Brann v Anderlecht	1-1

DOMESTIC CHAMPIONS 1ST ROUND – 2ND LEG

		Agg
Anderlecht v Brann	5-0	6-1
Zeljeznicar v Salzburg	2-1	2-5
Domzale v Rad	0-1	1-1
(Rad won 3-2 on penalties)		
Legia v Litex	3-1	5-2
Celtic v HJK	1-1	6-1

Besiktas v Aktobe	4-0	6-0
Servette v Villarreal	1-2	4-4
(Servette won on away goals)		
Ravan v Spartak Moscow	0-0	0-4
Zimbru v Pribram	1-2	1-4
Saburtalo v Midtjylland	1-2	2-5
Viitorul v Minsk	5-1	7-3
Puskas Akademia v APOEL	6-1	9-4
Torino v Senica	2-1	2-1
Ajax v Schalke	2-0	5-2
Middlesbrough v Reims	3-0	6-5
Stjarnan v Elfsborg	1-0	1-2

DOMESTIC CHAMPIONS 2ND ROUND – 1ST LEG

Spartak Moscow v Ajax	0-3
Besiktas v Salzburg	1-0
Rad v Elfsborg	0-1
Pribram v Viitorul	2-0
Puskas Akademia v Celtic	1-0
Midtjylland v Legia	2-0
Middlesbrough v Torino	3-0
Servette v Anderlecht	1-2

DOMESTIC CHAMPIONS 2ND ROUND – 2ND LEG

		Agg
Legia v Midtjylland	1-3	1-5
Salzburg v Besiktas	5-1	5-2
Torino v Middlesbrough	3-3	3-6
Viitorul v Pribram	0-0	0-2
Elfsborg v Rad	0-0	1-0
Ajax v Spartak Moscow	2-1	5-1
Celtic v Puskas Akademia	3-0	3-1
Anderlecht v Servette	2-2	4-3

PLAY-OFFS

Ajax v Sevilla	3-1
Anderlecht v Arsenal	2-0
Middlesbrough v Dynamo Kiev	5-0
Salzburg v Roma	0-4
Pribram v CSKA Moscow	2-2
(Pribram won 5-4 on penalties)	
Midtjylland v Atletico Madrid	4-4
(Midtjylland won 5-4 on penalties)	
Celtic v Valencia	1-1
(Valencia won 4-3 on penalties)	
Elfsborg v Real Madrid	1-3

ROUND OF 16

Barcelona v Midtjylland	3-1
Chelsea v Valencia	1-1
(Chelsea won 5-3 on penalties)	
Real Madrid v Manchester C	3-1
Anderlecht v Dinamo Zagreb	3-0
(Dinamo Zagreb forfeited match after 0-2 score; Anderlecht awarded match 3-0)	
PSV Eindhoven v Roma	2-2
(Roma won 3-1 on penalties)	
Paris Saint-Germain v Middlesbrough	1-0
Pribram v Benfica	1-1
(Benfica won 5-3 on penalties)	
Lyon v Ajax	0-3

QUARTER-FINALS

Real Madrid v Benfica	2-0
Anderlecht v Barcelona	2-0
Paris Saint-Germain v Roma	3-1
Chelsea v Ajax	1-0

SEMI-FINALS

Chelsea v Anderlecht	3-0
Real Madrid v Paris Saint-Germain	1-3

UEFA YOUTH LEAGUE FINAL 2016

Nyon, Monday 18 April 2016

Chelsea (1) 2 *(Tomori 10, Palmer 61)*

Paris Saint-Germain (0) 1 *(Meite 58)*

Chelsea: Collins; Sterling, Tomori, Clarke-Salter, Aina, Colkett, Maddox, Mukhtar, Abraham, Palmer (Wakefield 86), Scott (Mount 59).
Paris Saint-Germain: Descamps; Georgen, Toure, Eboa, Doucoure, Demoncy, Nkunku, Edouard (Ikone 62), Meite, Augustin (Kanga 71), Bernede (Giacomini 85).
Referee: Daniel Siebert (Germany).

UEFA UNDER-19 CHAMPIONSHIP 2014–15

FINALS IN GREECE

GROUP A

Greece v Ukraine									2-0
Austria v France									0-1
Ukraine v France									1-3
Greece v Austria									0-0
France v Greece									2-0
Ukraine v Austria									2-2

Group A Table	P	W	D	L	F	A	GD	Pts
France	3	3	0	0	6	1	5	9
Greece	3	1	1	1	2	2	0	4
Austria	3	0	2	1	2	3	–1	2
Ukraine	3	0	1	2	3	7	–4	1

GROUP B

Netherlands v Russia	1-0
Germany v Spain	0-3
Spain v Russia	1-3
Germany v Netherlands	1-0
Russia v Germany	2-2
Spain v Netherlands	1-1

Group B Table	P	W	D	L	F	A	GD	Pts
Russia	3	1	1	1	5	4	1	4
Spain	3	1	1	1	5	4	1	4
Netherlands	3	1	1	1	2	2	0	4
Germany	3	1	1	1	3	5	–2	4

SEMI-FINALS

Russia v Greece	4-0
France v Spain	0-2

FINAL

Spain v Russia	2-0

UEFA UNDER-19 CHAMPIONSHIP 2015–16

QUALIFYING ROUND

GROUP 1 (REPUBLIC OF IRELAND)

Scotland v Latvia	2-0
Republic of Ireland v Slovenia	0-1
Slovenia v Scotland	1-0
Republic of Ireland v Latvia	3-0
Scotland v Republic of Ireland	4-0
Latvia v Slovenia	0-0

Group 1 Table	P	W	D	L	F	A	GD	Pts
Slovenia	3	2	1	0	2	0	2	7
Scotland	3	2	0	1	6	1	5	6
Republic of Ireland	3	1	0	2	3	5	–2	3
Latvia	3	0	1	2	0	5	–5	1

GROUP 2 (CROATIA)

Hungary v Kazakhstan	4-0
Croatia v Montenegro	3-1
Montenegro v Hungary	3-0
Croatia v Kazakhstan	1-0
Hungary v Croatia	1-1
Kazakhstan v Montenegro	1-2

Group 2 Table	P	W	D	L	F	A	GD	Pts
Croatia	3	2	1	0	5	2	3	7
Montenegro	3	2	0	1	6	4	2	6
Hungary	3	1	1	1	5	4	1	4
Kazakhstan	3	0	0	3	1	7	–6	0

GROUP 3 (CYPRUS)

Bulgaria v Poland	0-1
Cyprus v Luxembourg	1-2
Bulgaria v Luxembourg	2-1
Poland v Cyprus	3-0
Cyprus v Bulgaria	3-3
Luxembourg v Poland	2-2

Group 3 Table	P	W	D	L	F	A	GD	Pts
Poland	3	2	1	0	6	2	4	7
Bulgaria	3	1	1	1	5	5	0	4
Luxembourg	3	1	1	1	5	5	0	4
Cyprus	3	0	1	2	4	8	–4	1

GROUP 4 (MACEDONIA)

Italy v Finland	1-1
England v FYR Macedonia	2-0
Finland v England	0-1
Italy v FYR Macedonia	3-2
England v Italy	0-0
FYR Macedonia v Finland	1-2

Group 4 Table	P	W	D	L	F	A	GD	Pts
England	3	2	1	0	3	0	3	7
Italy	3	1	2	0	4	3	1	5
Finland	3	1	1	1	3	3	0	4
FYR Macedonia	3	0	0	3	3	7	–4	0

GROUP 5 (AZERBAIJAN)

Turkey v Bosnia-Herzegovina	1-2
Ukraine v Azerbaijan	4-0
Bosnia-Herzegovina v Ukraine	1-3
Turkey v Azerbaijan	1-0
Ukraine v Turkey	3-4
Azerbaijan v Bosnia-Herzegovina	1-0

Group 5 Table	P	W	D	L	F	A	GD	Pts
Turkey	3	2	0	1	6	5	1	6
Ukraine	3	2	0	1	10	5	5	6
Azerbaijan	3	1	0	2	1	5	–4	3
Bosnia-Herzegovina	3	1	0	2	3	5	–2	3

GROUP 6 (MALTA)

Israel v Malta	3-1
Denmark v Iceland	1-1
Israel v Iceland	4-1
Malta v Denmark	0-3
Denmark v Israel	0-0
Iceland v Malta	1-0

Group 6 Table	P	W	D	L	F	A	GD	Pts
Israel	3	2	1	0	7	2	5	7
Denmark	3	1	2	0	4	1	3	5
Iceland	3	1	1	1	3	5	–2	4
Malta	3	0	0	3	1	7	–6	0

GROUP 7 (PORTUGAL)

Greece v Lithuania	1-0
Portugal v Moldova	1-0
Greece v Moldova	2-1
Lithuania v Portugal	0-5
Portugal v Greece	4-0
Moldova v Lithuania	0-1

Group 7 Table	P	W	D	L	F	A	GD	Pts
Portugal	3	3	0	0	10	0	10	9
Greece	3	2	0	1	3	5	–2	6
Lithuania	3	1	0	2	1	6	–5	3
Moldova	3	0	0	3	1	4	–3	0

GROUP 8 (GEORGIA)

Austria v Albania	3-0
(Albania forfeited the match 3-0 after the match finished Austria 2 Albania 1)	
Georgia v Wales	0-3
Austria v Wales	2-0
Albania v Georgia	0-3
(Albania forfeited the match 0-3 after the match finished Albania 0 Georgia 1)	
Georgia v Austria	0-0
Wales v Albania	2-3

Group 8 Table	P	W	D	L	F	A	GD	Pts
Austria	3	2	1	0	5	0	5	7
Georgia	3	1	1	1	3	0	3	4
Albania	3	1	0	2	3	8	–5	3
Wales	3	1	0	2	5	5	0	3

GROUP 9 (RUSSIA)

Russia v Slovakia	1-1
Norway v Northern Ireland	1-2
Slovakia v Norway	2-2
Russia v Northern Ireland	1-1
Norway v Russia	1-1
Northern Ireland v Slovakia	0-2

Group 9 Table	P	W	D	L	F	A	GD	Pts
Slovakia	3	1	2	0	5	3	2	5
Northern Ireland	3	1	1	1	3	4	–1	4
Russia	3	0	3	0	3	3	0	3
Norway	3	0	2	1	4	5	–1	2

GROUP 10 (FRANCE)

France v Liechtenstein	3-1
Netherlands v Gibraltar	9-0
Netherlands v Liechtenstein	2-0
Gibraltar v France	0-9
France v Netherlands	1-1
Liechtenstein v Gibraltar	1-1

Group 10 Table	P	W	D	L	F	A	GD	Pts
France	3	2	1	0	13	2	11	7
Netherlands	3	2	1	0	12	1	11	7
Liechtenstein	3	0	1	2	2	6	–4	1
Gibraltar	3	0	1	2	1	19	–18	1

GROUP 11 (ROMANIA)

Switzerland v Andorra	1-0
Romania v Faroe Islands	2-0
Faroe Islands v Switzerland	0-4
Romania v Andorra	2-0
Switzerland v Romania	3-1
Andorra v Faroe Islands	1-1

ELITE ROUND

GROUP 1 (SPAIN)

Spain v Greece	2-0
England v Georgia	2-1
Spain v Georgia	1-1
Greece v England	1-1
England v Spain	2-0
Georgia v Greece	1-2

Group 1 Table	P	W	D	L	F	A	GD	Pts
England	3	2	1	0	5	2	3	7
Spain	3	1	1	1	3	3	0	4
Greece	3	1	1	1	3	4	–1	4
Georgia	3	0	1	2	3	5	–2	1

GROUP 2 (ITALY)

Switzerland v Turkey	1-4
Israel v Italy	0-4
Turkey v Israel	1-0
Switzerland v Italy	0-2
Israel v Switzerland	2-0
Italy v Turkey	2-2

Group 2 Table	P	W	D	L	F	A	GD	Pts
Italy	3	2	1	0	8	2	6	7
Turkey	3	2	1	0	7	3	4	7
Israel	3	1	0	2	2	5	–3	3
Switzerland	3	0	0	3	1	8	–7	0

GROUP 3 (AUSTRIA)

Czech Republic v Romania	3-0
Austria v Slovakia	3-1
Czech Republic v Slovakia	1-2
Romania v Austria	0-4
Austria v Czech Republic	3-1
Slovakia v Romania	3-1

Group 3 Table	P	W	D	L	F	A	GD	Pts
Austria	3	3	0	0	10	2	8	9
Slovakia	3	2	0	1	6	5	1	6
Czech Republic	3	1	0	2	5	5	0	3
Romania	3	0	0	3	1	10	–9	0

GROUP 4 (NETHERLANDS)

Poland v Northern Ireland	2-1
Netherlands v Ukraine	3-2
Ukraine v Poland	0-0
Netherlands v Northern Ireland	1-0
Poland v Netherlands	0-0
Northern Ireland v Ukraine	0-2

Group 11 Table	P	W	D	L	F	A	GD	Pts
Switzerland	3	3	0	0	8	1	7	9
Romania	3	2	0	1	5	3	2	6
Andorra	3	0	1	2	1	4	–3	1
Faroe Islands	3	0	1	2	1	7	–6	1

GROUP 12 (ESTONIA)

Czech Republic v Armenia	4-0
Serbia v Estonia	5-0
Armenia v Serbia	0-4
Czech Republic v Estonia	2-1
Serbia v Czech Republic	2-4
Estonia v Armenia	2-0

Group 12 Table	P	W	D	L	F	A	GD	Pts
Czech Republic	3	3	0	0	10	3	7	9
Serbia	3	2	0	1	11	4	7	6
Estonia	3	1	0	2	3	7	–4	3
Armenia	3	0	0	3	0	10	–10	0

GROUP 13 (BELGIUM)

Sweden v Belarus	2-0
Belgium v San Marino	9-0
San Marino v Sweden	0-1
Belgium v Belarus	2-2
Sweden v Belgium	0-2
Belarus v San Marino	6-1

Group 13 Table	P	W	D	L	F	A	GD	Pts
Belgium	3	2	1	0	13	2	11	7
Sweden	3	2	0	1	3	2	1	6
Belarus	3	1	1	1	8	5	3	4
San Marino	3	0	0	3	1	16	–15	0

Group 4 Table	P	W	D	L	F	A	GD	Pts
Netherlands	3	2	1	0	4	2	2	7
Poland	3	1	2	0	2	1	1	5
Ukraine	3	1	1	1	4	3	1	4
Northern Ireland	3	0	0	3	1	5	–4	0

GROUP 5 (CROATIA)

Belgium v Scotland	2-0
Croatia v Bulgaria	1-0
Belgium v Bulgaria	1-0
Scotland v Croatia	0-3
Croatia v Belgium	4-0
Bulgaria v Scotland	1-2

Group 5 Table	P	W	D	L	F	A	GD	Pts
Croatia	3	3	0	0	8	0	8	9
Belgium	3	2	0	1	3	4	–1	6
Scotland	3	1	0	2	2	6	–4	3
Bulgaria	3	0	0	3	1	4	–3	0

GROUP 6 (PORTUGAL)

Slovenia v Russia	1-0
Portugal v Sweden	4-0
Sweden v Slovenia	1-3
Portugal v Russia	1-1
Slovenia v Portugal	1-3
Russia v Sweden	2-1

Group 6 Table	P	W	D	L	F	A	GD	Pts
Portugal	3	2	1	0	8	2	6	7
Slovenia	3	2	0	1	5	4	1	6
Russia	3	1	1	1	3	3	0	4
Sweden	3	0	0	3	2	9	–7	0

GROUP 7 (SERBIA)

France v Montenegro	1-0
Serbia v Denmark	2-2
France v Denmark	4-0
Montenegro v Serbia	1-4
Serbia v France	0-1
Denmark v Montenegro	7-1

Group 7 Table	P	W	D	L	F	A	GD	Pts
France	3	3	0	0	6	0	6	9
Denmark	3	1	1	1	9	7	2	4
Serbia	3	1	1	1	6	4	2	4
Montenegro	3	0	0	3	2	12	–10	0

Final Tournament in Germany 11–24 July.

UEFA UNDER-17 CHAMPIONSHIP 2015–16

QUALIFYING ROUND

GROUP 1 (WALES)
Netherlands v Wales   1-2
Switzerland v Albania   2-0
Albania v Netherlands   0-5
Switzerland v Wales   1-0
Netherlands v Switzerland   4-1
Wales v Albania   1-1

Group 1 Table	P	W	D	L	F	A	GD	Pts
Netherlands	3	2	0	1	10	3	7	6
Switzerland	3	2	0	1	4	4	0	6
Wales	3	1	1	1	3	3	0	4
Albania	3	0	1	2	1	8	–7	1

GROUP 2 (BELARUS)
Belarus v Montenegro   1-1
Russia v Cyprus   6-0
Belarus v Cyprus   2-3
Montenegro v Russia   0-2
Russia v Belarus   2-0
Cyprus v Montenegro   0-1

Group 2 Table	P	W	D	L	F	A	GD	Pts
Russia	3	3	0	0	10	0	10	9
Montenegro	3	1	1	1	2	3	–1	4
Cyprus	3	1	0	2	3	9	–6	3
Belarus	3	0	1	2	3	6	–3	1

GROUP 3 (FINLAND)
Sweden v Malta   5-1
Republic of Ireland v Finland   1-0
Malta v Republic of Ireland   0-6
Sweden v Finland   1-1
Republic of Ireland v Sweden   1-1
Finland v Malta   4-2

Group 3 Table	P	W	D	L	F	A	GD	Pts
Republic of Ireland	3	2	1	0	8	1	7	7
Sweden	3	1	2	0	7	3	4	5
Finland	3	1	1	1	5	4	1	4
Malta	3	0	0	3	3	15	–12	0

GROUP 4 (HUNGARY)
Hungary v Romania   1-2
Georgia v Slovakia   3-4
Hungary v Slovakia   1-1
Romania v Georgia   0-3
Georgia v Hungary   2-2
Slovakia v Romania   1-1

Group 4 Table	P	W	D	L	F	A	GD	Pts
Slovakia	3	1	2	0	6	5	1	5
Georgia	3	1	1	1	8	6	2	4
Romania	3	1	1	1	3	5	–2	4
Hungary	3	0	2	1	4	5	–1	2

GROUP 5 (LUXEMBOURG)
Serbia v Luxembourg   6-1
Austria v Lithuania   2-0
Serbia v Lithuania   0-0
Luxembourg v Austria   1-2
Austria v Serbia   1-1
Lithuania v Luxembourg   2-0

Group 5 Table	P	W	D	L	F	A	GD	Pts
Austria	3	2	1	0	5	2	3	7
Serbia	3	1	2	0	7	2	5	5
Lithuania	3	1	1	1	2	2	0	4
Luxembourg	3	0	0	3	2	10	–8	0

GROUP 6 (LATVIA)
Spain v Andorra   2-0
Poland v Latvia   4-0
Poland v Andorra   1-0
Latvia v Spain   0-2
Spain v Poland   2-1
Andorra v Latvia   0-3

Group 6 Table	P	W	D	L	F	A	GD	Pts
Spain	3	3	0	0	6	1	5	9
Poland	3	2	0	1	6	2	4	6
Latvia	3	1	0	2	3	6	–3	3
Andorra	3	0	0	3	0	6	–6	0

GROUP 7 (LIECHTENSTEIN)
Croatia v Gibraltar   4-1
Czech Republic v Liechtenstein   4-0
Gibraltar v Czech Republic   1-9
Croatia v Liechtenstein   2-0
Czech Republic v Croatia   2-2
Liechtenstein v Gibraltar   3-0

Group 7 Table	P	W	D	L	F	A	GD	Pts
Czech Republic	3	2	1	0	15	3	12	7
Croatia	3	2	1	0	8	3	5	7
Liechtenstein	3	1	0	2	3	6	–3	3
Gibraltar	3	0	0	3	2	16	–14	0

GROUP 8 (ICELAND)
Denmark v Greece   0-0
Iceland v Kazakhstan   5-0
Denmark v Kazakhstan   4-1
Greece v Iceland   1-1
Iceland v Denmark   0-2
Kazakhstan v Greece   0-6

Group 8 Table	P	W	D	L	F	A	GD	Pts
Denmark	3	2	1	0	6	1	5	7
Greece	3	1	2	0	7	1	6	5
Iceland	3	1	1	1	6	3	3	4
Kazakhstan	3	0	0	3	1	15	–14	0

GROUP 9 (PORTUGAL)
England v San Marino   8-0
Portugal v Armenia   7-0
England v Armenia   5-0
San Marino v Portugal   0-5
Portugal v England   1-1
Armenia v San Marino   1-1

Group 9 Table	P	W	D	L	F	A	GD	Pts
England	3	2	1	0	14	1	13	7
Portugal	3	2	1	0	13	1	12	7
Armenia	3	0	1	2	1	13	–12	1
San Marino	3	0	1	2	1	14	–13	1

GROUP 10 (SLOVENIA)
Turkey v Faroe Islands   3-0
Belgium v Slovenia   2-1
Turkey v Slovenia   1-1
Faroe Islands v Belgium   1-4
Belgium v Turkey   0-0
Slovenia v Faroe Islands   1-0

Group 10 Table	P	W	D	L	F	A	GD	Pts
Belgium	3	2	1	0	6	2	4	7
Turkey	3	1	2	0	4	1	3	5
Slovenia	3	1	1	1	3	3	0	4
Faroe Islands	3	0	0	3	1	8	–7	0

GROUP 11 (ISRAEL)
Norway v Israel   1-3
France v Northern Ireland   1-0
Norway v Northern Ireland   1-1
Israel v France   0-3
France v Norway   1-0
Northern Ireland v Israel   1-2

Group 11 Table	P	W	D	L	F	A	GD	Pts
France	3	3	0	0	5	0	5	9
Israel	3	2	0	1	5	5	0	6
Northern Ireland	3	0	1	2	2	4	–2	1
Norway	3	0	1	2	2	5	–3	1

GROUP 12 (BULGARIA)
Italy v Bulgaria   3-0
Scotland v FYR Macedonia   3-0
Italy v FYR Macedonia   0-0
Bulgaria v Scotland   2-0
Scotland v Italy   1-1
FYR Macedonia v Bulgaria   0-0

Group 12 Table	P	W	D	L	F	A	GD	Pts
Italy	3	1	2	0	4	1	3	5
Bulgaria	3	1	1	1	2	3	–1	4
Scotland	3	1	1	1	4	3	1	4
FYR Macedonia	3	0	2	1	0	3	–3	2

GROUP 13 (MOLDOVA)

Ukraine v Moldova	1-1
Bosnia-Herzegovina v Estonia	2-1
Ukraine v Estonia	2-0
Moldova v Bosnia-Herzegovina	0-5
Bosnia-Herzegovina v Ukraine	0-3
Estonia v Moldova	1-0

Group 13 Table	P	W	D	L	F	A	GD	Pts
Ukraine	3	2	1	0	6	1	5	7
Bosnia-Herzegovina	3	2	0	1	7	4	3	6
Estonia	3	1	0	2	2	4	–2	3
Moldova	3	0	1	2	1	7	–6	1

ELITE ROUND

GROUP 1 (CZECH REPUBLIC)

Denmark v Scotland	4-0
Czech Republic v Switzerland	2-2
Switzerland v Denmark	1-2
Czech Republic v Scotland	0-2
Denmark v Czech Republic	2-3
Scotland v Switzerland	1-1

Group 1 Table	P	W	D	L	F	A	GD	Pts
Denmark	3	2	0	1	8	4	4	6
Scotland	3	1	1	1	3	5	–2	4
Czech Republic	3	1	1	1	5	6	–1	4
Switzerland	3	0	2	1	4	5	–1	2

GROUP 2 (ENGLAND)

Ukraine v Finland	3-0
England v Turkey	3-1
England v Finland	1-0
Turkey v Ukraine	0-3
Ukraine v England	1-1
Finland v Turkey	1-3

Group 2 Table	P	W	D	L	F	A	GD	Pts
Ukraine	3	2	1	0	7	1	6	7
England	3	2	1	0	5	2	3	7
Turkey	3	1	0	2	4	7	–3	3
Finland	3	0	0	3	1	7	–6	0

GROUP 3 (GEORGIA)

Bosnia-Herzegovina v Georgia	2-1
Russia v Italy	0-4
Russia v Georgia	1-0
Italy v Bosnia-Herzegovina	0-1
Bosnia-Herzegovina v Russia	1-2
Georgia v Italy	0-1

Group 3 Table	P	W	D	L	F	A	GD	Pts
Italy	3	2	0	1	5	1	4	6
Bosnia-Herzegovina	3	2	0	1	4	3	1	6
Russia	3	2	0	1	3	5	–2	6
Georgia	3	0	0	3	1	4	–3	0

GROUP 4 (GERMANY)

Netherlands v Bulgaria	0-0
Germany v Slovakia	5-1
Slovakia v Netherlands	0-2
Germany v Bulgaria	1-1
Netherlands v Germany	0-1
Bulgaria v Slovakia	0-3

Group 4 Table	P	W	D	L	F	A	GD	Pts
Germany	3	2	1	0	7	2	5	7
Netherlands	3	1	1	1	2	1	1	4
Slovakia	3	1	0	2	4	7	–3	3
Bulgaria	3	0	2	1	1	4	–3	2

GROUP 5 (CROATIA)

Portugal v Sweden	2-0
Croatia v Wales	0-2
Portugal v Wales	1-0
Sweden v Croatia	2-1
Croatia v Portugal	2-4
Wales v Sweden	0-1

Group 5 Table	P	W	D	L	F	A	GD	Pts
Portugal	3	3	0	0	7	2	5	9
Sweden	3	2	0	1	3	3	0	6
Wales	3	1	0	2	2	2	0	3
Croatia	3	0	0	3	3	8	–5	0

GROUP 6 (FRANCE)

France v Greece	1-0
Austria v Iceland	0-0
France v Iceland	1-0
Greece v Austria	0-0
Austria v France	2-1
Iceland v Greece	1-0

Group 6 Table	P	W	D	L	F	A	GD	Pts
France	3	2	0	1	3	2	1	6
Austria	3	1	2	0	2	1	1	5
Iceland	3	1	1	1	1	1	0	4
Greece	3	0	1	2	0	2	–2	1

GROUP 7 (POLAND)

Republic of Ireland v Serbia	0-2
Poland v Montenegro	2-0
Republic of Ireland v Montenegro	3-0
Serbia v Poland	2-1
Poland v Republic of Ireland	0-0
(Poland won 4-3 on penalties)	
Montenegro v Serbia	0-2

Group 7 Table	P	W	D	L	F	A	GD	Pts
Serbia	3	3	0	0	6	1	5	9
Poland	3	1	1	1	3	2	1	4
Republic of Ireland	3	1	1	1	3	2	1	4
Montenegro	3	0	0	3	0	7	–7	0

GROUP 8 (BELGIUM)

Spain v Israel	1-0
Belgium v Slovenia	0-0
Spain v Slovenia	0-0
Israel v Belgium	0-1
Belgium v Spain	0-0
(Belgium won 4-3 on penalties)	
Slovenia v Israel	1-1

Group 8 Table	P	W	D	L	F	A	GD	Pts
Belgium	3	1	2	0	1	0	1	5
Spain	3	1	2	0	1	0	1	5
Slovenia	3	0	3	0	1	1	0	3
Israel	3	0	1	2	1	3	–2	1

FINAL TOURNAMENT (AZERBAIJAN)

GROUP A

Belgium v Scotland	2-0
Azerbaijan v Portugal	0-5
Portugal v Scotland	2-0
Azerbaijan v Belgium	1-1
Scotland v Azerbaijan	0-1
Portugal v Belgium	0-0

Group A Table	P	W	D	L	F	A	GD	Pts
Portugal	3	2	1	0	7	0	7	7
Belgium	3	1	2	0	3	1	2	5
Azerbaijan	3	1	1	1	2	6	–4	4
Scotland	3	0	0	3	0	5	–5	0

GROUP B

Austria v Bosnia-Herzegovina	2-0
Ukraine v Germany	2-2
Ukraine v Austria	0-2
Germany v Bosnia-Herzegovina	3-1
Bosnia-Herzegovina v Ukraine	2-1
Germany v Austria	4-0

Group B Table	P	W	D	L	F	A	GD	Pts
Germany	3	2	1	0	9	3	6	7
Austria	3	2	0	1	4	0	4	6
Bosnia-Herzegovina	3	1	0	2	3	6	–3	3
Ukraine	3	0	1	2	3	6	–3	1

GROUP C

France v Denmark	0-0
England v Sweden	1-2
Denmark v Sweden	1-0
France v England	0-2
Sweden v France	1-0
Denmark v England	1-3

Group C Table	P	W	D	L	F	A	GD	Pts
Sweden	3	2	0	1	3	2	1	6
England	3	2	0	1	6	3	3	6
Denmark	3	1	1	1	2	3	-1	4
France	3	0	1	2	0	3	-3	1

GROUP D

Italy v Serbia	2-1
Netherlands v Spain	0-2
Italy v Netherlands	0-1
Serbia v Spain	1-1
Spain v Italy	4-2
Serbia v Netherlands	0-2

Group D Table	P	W	D	L	F	A	GD	Pts
Spain	3	2	1	0	7	3	4	7
Netherlands	3	2	0	1	3	2	1	6
Italy	3	1	0	2	4	6	-2	3
Serbia	3	0	1	2	2	5	-3	1

QUARTER-FINALS

Portugal v Austria	5-0
Germany v Belgium	1-0
Spain v England	1-0
Sweden v Netherlands	0-1

SEMI-FINALS

Portugal v Netherlands	2-0
Germany v Spain	1-2

FINAL

Portugal v Spain	1-1
(Portugal won 5-4 on penalties)	

FIFA UNDER-17 WORLD CUP 2015

FINALS IN CHILE

GROUP A

Nigeria v USA	2-0
Chile v Croatia	1-1
USA v Croatia	2-2
Chile v Nigeria	1-5
USA v Chile	1-4
Croatia v Nigeria	2-1

Group A Table	P	W	D	L	F	A	GD	Pts
Nigeria	3	2	0	1	8	3	5	6
Croatia	3	1	2	0	5	4	1	5
Chile	3	1	1	1	6	7	-1	4
United States	3	0	1	2	3	8	-5	1

GROUP B

England v Guinea	1-1
Brazil v Korea Republic	0-1
England v Brazil	0-1
Korea Republic v Guinea	1-0
Guinea v Brazil	1-3
Korea Republic v England	0-0

Group B Table	P	W	D	L	F	A	GD	Pts
Korea Republic	3	2	1	0	2	0	2	7
Brazil	3	2	0	1	4	2	2	6
England	3	0	2	1	1	2	-1	2
Guinea	3	0	1	2	2	5	-3	1

GROUP C

Australia v Germany	1-4
Mexico v Argentina	2-0
Australia v Mexico	0-0
Argentina v Germany	0-4
Argentina v Australia	1-2
Germany v Mexico	1-2

Group C Table	P	W	D	L	F	A	GD	Pts
Mexico	3	2	1	0	4	1	3	7
Germany	3	2	0	1	9	3	6	6
Australia	3	1	1	1	3	5	-2	4
Argentina	3	0	0	3	1	8	-7	0

GROUP D

Belgium v Mali	0-0
Honduras v Ecuador	1-3
Belgium v Honduras	2-1
Ecuador v Mali	1-2
Mali v Honduras	3-0
Ecuador v Belgium	2-0

Group D Table	P	W	D	L	F	A	GD	Pts
Mali	3	2	1	0	5	1	4	7
Ecuador	3	2	0	1	6	3	3	6
Belgium	3	1	1	1	2	3	-1	4
Honduras	3	0	0	3	2	8	-6	0

GROUP E

South Africa v Costa Rica	1-2
Korea DPR v Russia	0-2
South Africa v Korea DPR	1-1
Russia v Costa Rica	1-1
Russia v South Africa	2-0
Costa Rica v Korea DPR	1-2

Group E Table	P	W	D	L	F	A	GD	Pts
Russia	3	2	1	0	5	1	4	7
Costa Rica	3	1	1	1	4	4	0	4
Korea DPR	3	1	1	1	3	4	-1	4
South Africa	3	0	1	2	2	5	-3	1

GROUP F

New Zealand v France	1-6
Syria v Paraguay	1-4
New Zealand v Syria	0-0
Paraguay v France	3-4
France v Syria	4-0
Paraguay v New Zealand	1-2

Group F Table	P	W	D	L	F	A	GD	Pts
France	3	3	0	0	14	4	10	9
New Zealand	3	1	1	1	3	7	-4	4
Paraguay	3	1	0	2	8	7	1	3
Syria	3	0	1	2	1	8	-7	1

ROUND OF 16

Brazil v New Zealand	1-0
Mexico v Chile	4-1
Nigeria v Australia	6-0
Korea Republic v Belgium	0-2
Croatia v Germany	2-0
Mali v Korea DPR	3-0
Russia v Ecuador	1-4
France v Costa Rica	0-0
Costa Rica won 5-3 on penalties.	

QUARTER-FINALS

Brazil v Nigeria	0-3
Croatia v Mali	0-1
Ecuador v Mexico	0-2
Belgium v Costa Rica	1-0

SEMI-FINALS

Mali v Belgium	3-1
Mexico v Nigeria	2-4

THIRD PLACE MATCH

Belgium v Mexico	3-2

FINAL

Mali v Nigeria	0-2

ENGLAND UNDER-21 RESULTS 1976–2016

EC *UEFA Competition for Under-21 Teams*

Bold type indicates matches played in season 2015–16.

Year	Date		Venue	Eng	Alb
			v ALBANIA	*Eng*	*Alb*
EC1989	Mar	7	Shkroda	2	1
EC1989	April	25	Ipswich	2	0
EC2001	Mar	27	Tirana	1	0
EC2001	Sept	4	Middlesbrough	5	0
			v ANGOLA	*Eng*	*Ang*
1995	June	10	Toulon	1	0
1996	May	28	Toulon	0	2
			v ARGENTINA	*Eng*	*Arg*
1998	May	18	Toulon	0	2
2000	Feb	22	Fulham	1	0
			v AUSTRIA	*Eng*	*Aus*
1994	Oct	11	Kapfenberg	3	1
1995	Nov	14	Middlesbrough	2	1
EC2004	Sept	3	Krems	2	0
EC2005	Oct	7	Leeds	1	2
2013	June	26	Brighton	4	0
			v AZERBAIJAN	*Eng*	*Az*
EC2004	Oct	12	Baku	0	0
EC2005	Mar	29	Middlesbrough	2	0
2009	June	8	Milton Keynes	7	0
EC2011	Sept	1	Watford	6	0
EC2012	Sept	6	Baku	2	0
			v BELARUS	*Eng*	*Bel*
2015	June	11	Barnsley	1	0
			v BELGIUM	*Eng*	*Bel*
1994	June	5	Marseille	2	1
1996	May	24	Toulon	1	0
EC2011	Nov	14	Mons	1	2
EC2012	Feb	29	Middlesbrough	4	0
			v BOSNIA-HERZEGOVINA	*Eng*	*B-H*
EC2015	**Nov**	**12**	**Sarajevo Canton**	**0**	**0**
			v BRAZIL	*Eng*	*B*
1993	June	11	Toulon	0	0
1995	June	6	Toulon	0	2
1996	June	1	Toulon	1	2
			v BULGARIA	*Eng*	*Bul*
EC1979	June	5	Pernik	3	1
EC1979	Nov	20	Leicester	5	0
1989	June	5	Toulon	2	3
EC1998	Oct	9	West Ham	1	0
EC1999	June	8	Vratsa	1	0
EC2007	Sept	11	Sofia	2	0
EC2007	Nov	16	Milton Keynes	2	0
			v CROATIA	*Eng*	*Cro*
1996	Apr	23	Sunderland	0	1
2003	Aug	19	West Ham	0	3
EC2014	Oct	10	Wolverhampton	2	1
EC2014	Oct	14	Vinkovci	2	1
			v CZECHOSLOVAKIA	*Eng*	*Cz*
1990	May	28	Toulon	2	1
1992	May	26	Toulon	1	2
1993	June	9	Toulon	1	1
			v CZECH REPUBLIC	*Eng*	*CzR*
1998	Nov	17	Ipswich	0	1
EC2007	June	11	Arnhem	0	0
2008	Nov	18	Bramall Lane	2	0
EC2011	June	19	Viborg	1	2
2015	Mar	27	Prague	1	0
			v DENMARK	*Eng*	*Den*
EC1978	Sept	19	Hvidovre	2	1
EC1979	Sept	11	Watford	1	0
EC1982	Sept	21	Hvidovre	4	1
EC1983	Sept	20	Norwich	4	1
EC1986	Mar	12	Copenhagen	1	0
EC1986	Mar	26	Manchester	1	1
1988	Sept	13	Watford	0	0
1994	Mar	8	Brentford	1	0
1999	Oct	8	Bradford	4	1
2005	Aug	16	Herning	1	0
2011	Mar	24	Viborg	4	0

Year	Date		Venue	Eng	E
			v EQUADOR	*Eng*	*E*
2009	Feb	10	Malaga	2	3
			v FINLAND	*Eng*	*Fin*
EC1977	May	26	Helsinki	1	0
EC1977	Oct	12	Hull	8	1
EC1984	Oct	16	Southampton	2	0
EC1985	May	21	Mikkeli	1	3
EC2000	Oct	10	Valkeakoski	2	2
EC2001	Mar	23	Barnsley	4	0
EC2009	June	15	Halmstad	2	1
EC2013	Sept	9	Tampere	1	1
EC2013	Nov	14	Milton Keynes	3	0
			v FRANCE	*Eng*	*Fra*
EC1984	Feb	28	Sheffield	6	1
EC1984	Mar	28	Rouen	1	0
1987	June	11	Toulon	0	2
EC1988	April	13	Besancon	2	4
EC1988	April	27	Highbury	2	2
1988	June	12	Toulon	2	4
1990	May	23	Toulon	7	3
1991	June	3	Toulon	1	0
1992	May	28	Toulon	0	0
1993	June	15	Toulon	1	0
1994	May	31	Aubagne	0	3
1995	June	10	Toulon	0	2
1998	May	14	Toulon	1	1
1999	Feb	9	Derby	2	1
EC2005	Nov	11	Tottenham	1	1
EC2005	Nov	15	Nancy	1	2
2009	Mar	31	Nottingham	0	2
2014	Nov	17	Paris	2	3
2016	**May**	**29**	**Toulon**	**2**	**1**
			v FYR MACEDONIA	*Eng*	*M*
EC2002	Oct	15	Reading	3	1
EC2003	Sept	5	Skopje	1	1
EC2009	Sept	4	Prilep	2	1
EC2009	Oct	9	Coventry	6	3
			v GEORGIA	*Eng*	*Geo*
EC1996	Nov	8	Batumi	1	0
EC1997	April	29	Charlton	0	0
2000	Aug	31	Middlesbrough	6	1
			v GERMANY	*Eng*	*Ger*
1991	Sept	10	Scunthorpe	2	1
EC2000	Oct	6	Derby	1	1
EC2001	Aug	31	Frieburg	2	1
2005	Mar	25	Hull	2	2
2005	Sept	6	Mainz	1	1
EC2006	Oct	6	Coventry	1	0
EC2006	Oct	10	Leverkusen	2	0
EC2009	June	22	Halmstad	1	1
EC2009	June	29	Malmo	0	4
2010	Nov	16	Wiesbaden	0	2
2015	Mar	30	Middlesbrough	3	2
			v EAST GERMANY	*Eng*	*EG*
EC1980	April	16	Sheffield	1	2
EC1980	April	23	Jena	0	1
			v WEST GERMANY	*Eng*	*WG*
EC1982	Sept	21	Sheffield	3	1
EC1982	Oct	12	Bremen	2	3
1987	Sept	8	Ludenscheid	0	2
			v GREECE	*Eng*	*Gre*
EC1982	Nov	16	Piraeus	0	1
EC1983	Mar	29	Portsmouth	2	1
1989	Feb	7	Patras	0	1
EC1997	Nov	13	Heraklion	0	2
EC1997	Dec	17	Norwich	4	2
EC2001	June	5	Athens	1	3
EC2001	Oct	5	Ewood Park	2	1
EC2009	Sept	8	Tripoli	1	1
EC2010	Mar	3	Doncaster	1	2
			v GUINEA	*Eng*	*Gui*
2016	**May**	**23**	**Toulon**	**7**	**1**

v HUNGARY

				Eng	Hun
EC1981	June	5	Keszthely	2	1
EC1981	Nov	17	Nottingham	2	0
EC1983	April	26	Newcastle	1	0
EC1983	Oct	11	Nyiregyhaza	2	0
1990	Sept	11	Southampton	3	1
1992	May	12	Budapest	2	2
1999	April	27	Budapest	2	2

v ICELAND

				Eng	Ice
2011	Mar	28	Preston	1	2
EC2011	Oct	6	Reykjavik	3	0
EC2011	Nov	10	Colchester	5	0

v ISRAEL

				Eng	Isr
1985	Feb	27	Tel Aviv	2	1
2011	Sept	5	Barnsley	4	1
EC2013	June	11	Jerusalem	0	1

v ITALY

				Eng	Italy
EC1978	Mar	8	Manchester	2	1
EC1978	April	5	Rome	0	0
EC1984	April	18	Manchester	3	1
EC1984	May	2	Florence	0	1
EC1986	April	9	Pisa	0	2
EC1986	April	23	Swindon	1	1
EC1997	Feb	12	Bristol	1	0
EC1997	Oct	10	Rieti	1	0
EC2000	May	27	Bratislava	0	2
2000	Nov	14	Monza*	0	0
2002	Mar	26	Valley Parade	1	1
EC2002	May	20	Basle	1	2
2003	Feb	11	Pisa	0	1
2007	Mar	24	Wembley	3	3
EC2007	June	14	Arnhem	2	2
2011	Feb	8	Empoli	0	1
EC2013	June	5	Tel Aviv	0	1
EC2015	June	24	Olomouc	1	3

*Abandoned 11 mins; fog.

v JAPAN

				Eng	Jap
2016	May	27	Toulon	1	0

v KAZAKHSTAN

				Eng	
EC2015	Oct	13	Coventry	3	0

v LATVIA

				Eng	Lat
1995	April	25	Riga	1	0
1995	June	7	Burnley	4	0

v LITHUANIA

				Eng	Lith
EC2009	Nov	17	Vilnius	0	0
EC2010	Sept	7	Colchester	3	0
EC2013	Oct	15	Ipswich	5	0
EC2014	Sept	5	Zaliakalnis	1	0

v LUXEMBOURG

				Eng	Lux
EC1998	Oct	13	Greven Macher	5	0
EC1999	Sept	3	Reading	5	0

v MALAYSIA

				Eng	Mal
1995	June	8	Toulon	2	0

v MEXICO

				Eng	Mex
1988	June	5	Toulon	2	1
1991	May	29	Toulon	6	0
1992	May	25	Toulon	1	1
2001	May	24	Leicester	3	0

v MOLDOVA

				Eng	Mol
EC1996	Aug	31	Chisinau	2	0
EC1997	Sept	9	Wycombe	1	0
EC2006	Aug	15	Ipswich	2	2
EC2013	Sept	5	Reading	1	0
EC2014	Sept	9	Tiraspol	3	0

v MONTENEGRO

				Eng	M
EC2007	Sept	7	Podgorica	3	0
EC2007	Oct	12	Leicester	1	0

v MOROCCO

				Eng	Mor
1987	June	7	Toulon	2	0
1988	June	9	Toulon	1	0

v NETHERLANDS

				Eng	N
EC1993	April	27	Portsmouth	3	0
EC1993	Oct	12	Utrecht	1	1
2001	Aug	14	Reading	4	0
EC2001	Nov	9	Utrecht	2	2
EC2001	Nov	13	Derby	1	0
2004	Feb	17	Hull	3	2
2005	Feb	8	Derby	1	2
2006	Nov	14	Alkmaar	1	0
EC2007	June	20	Heerenveen	1	1
2009	Aug	11	Groningen	0	0

v NORTHERN IRELAND

				Eng	NI
2012	Nov	13	Blackpool	2	0

v NORWAY

				Eng	Nor
EC1977	June	1	Bergen	2	1
EC1977	Sept	6	Brighton	6	0
1980	Sept	9	Southampton	3	0
1981	Sept	8	Drammen	0	0
EC1992	Oct	13	Peterborough	0	2
EC1993	June	1	Stavanger	1	1
1995	Oct	10	Stavanger	2	2
2006	Feb	28	Reading	3	1
2009	Mar	27	Sandefjord	5	0
2011	June	5	Southampton	2	0
EC2011	Oct	10	Drammen	2	1
EC2012	Sept	10	Chesterfield	1	0
EC2013	June	8	Petah Tikva	1	3
EC2015	**Sept**	**7**	**Drammen**	**1**	**0**

v PARAGUAY

				Eng	Par
2016	May	25	Toulon	4	0

v POLAND

				Eng	Pol
EC1982	Mar	17	Warsaw	2	1
EC1982	April	7	West Ham	2	2
EC1989	June	2	Plymouth	2	1
EC1989	Oct	10	Jastrzebie	3	1
EC1990	Oct	16	Tottenham	0	1
EC1991	Nov	12	Pila	1	2
EC1993	May	28	Zdroj	4	1
EC1993	Sept	7	Millwall	1	2
EC1996	Oct	8	Wolverhampton	0	0
EC1997	May	30	Katowice	1	1
EC1999	Mar	26	Southampton	5	0
EC1999	Sept	7	Plock	1	3
EC2004	Sept	7	Rybnik	3	1
EC2005	Oct	11	Hillsborough	4	1
2008	Mar	25	Wolverhampton	0	0

v PORTUGAL

				Eng	Por
1987	June	13	Toulon	0	0
1990	May	21	Toulon	0	1
1993	June	7	Toulon	2	0
1994	June	7	Toulon	2	0
EC1994	Sept	6	Leicester	0	0
1995	Sept	2	Lisbon	0	2
1996	May	30	Toulon	1	3
2000	Apr	16	Stoke	0	1
EC2002	May	22	Zurich	1	3
EC2003	Mar	28	Rio Major	2	4
EC2003	Sept	9	Everton	1	2
EC2008	Nov	20	Agueda	1	1
2008	Sept	5	Wembley	2	0
EC2009	Nov	14	Wembley	1	0
EC2010	Sept	3	Barcelos	1	0
2014	Nov	13	Burnley	3	1
EC2015	June	18	Uherske Hradiste	0	1
2016	**May**	**19**	**Toulon**	**1**	**0**

v REPUBLIC OF IRELAND

				Eng	RoI
1981	Feb	25	Liverpool	1	0
1985	Mar	25	Portsmouth	3	2
1989	June	9	Toulon	0	0
EC1990	Nov	13	Cork	3	0
EC1991	Mar	26	Brentford	3	0
1994	Nov	15	Newcastle	1	0
1995	Mar	27	Dublin	2	0
EC2007	Oct	16	Cork	3	0
EC2008	Feb	5	Southampton	3	0

v ROMANIA

				Eng	Rom
EC1980	Oct	14	Ploesti	0	4
EC1981	April	28	Swindon	3	0
EC1985	April	30	Brasov	0	0
EC1985	Sept	10	Ipswich	3	0
2007	Aug	21	Bristol	1	1
EC2010	Oct	8	Norwich	2	1
EC2010	Oct	12	Botosani	0	0
2013	Mar	21	Wycombe	3	0

v RUSSIA

				Eng	Rus
1994	May	30	Bandol	2	0

			v SAN MARINO	*Eng*	*SM*
EC1993	Feb	16	Luton	6	0
EC1993	Nov	17	San Marino	4	0
EC2013	Oct	10	San Marino	4	0
EC2013	Nov	19	Shrewsbury	9	0
			v SCOTLAND	*Eng*	*Sco*
1977	April	27	Sheffield	1	0
EC1980	Feb	12	Coventry	2	1
EC1980	Mar	4	Aberdeen	0	0
EC1982	April	19	Glasgow	1	0
EC1982	April	28	Manchester	1	1
EC1988	Feb	16	Aberdeen	1	0
EC1988	Mar	22	Nottingham	1	0
1993	June	13	Toulon	1	0
2013	Aug	13	Sheffield	6	0
			v SENEGAL	*Eng*	*Sen*
1989	June	7	Toulon	6	1
1991	May	27	Toulon	2	1
			v SERBIA	*Eng*	*Ser*
EC2007	June	17	Nijmegen	2	0
EC2012	Oct	12	Norwich	1	0
EC2012	Oct	16	Krusevac	1	0
			v SERBIA-MONTENEGRO	*Eng*	*S-M*
2003	June	2	Hull	3	2
			v SLOVAKIA	*Eng*	*Slo*
EC2002	June	1	Bratislava	0	2
EC2002	Oct	11	Trnava	4	0
EC2003	June	10	Sunderland	2	0
2007	June	5	Norwich	5	0
			v SLOVENIA	*Eng*	*Slo*
2000	Feb	12	Nova Gorica	1	0
2008	Aug	19	Hull	2	1
			v SOUTH AFRICA	*Eng*	*SA*
1998	May	16	Toulon	3	1
			v SPAIN	*Eng*	*Spa*
EC1984	May	17	Seville	1	0
EC1984	May	24	Sheffield	2	0
1987	Feb	18	Burgos	2	1
1992	Sept	8	Burgos	1	0
2001	Feb	27	Birmingham	0	4
2004	Nov	16	Alcala	0	1
2007	Feb	6	Derby	2	2
EC2009	June	18	Gothenburg	2	0
EC2011	June	12	Herning	1	1
			v SWEDEN	*Eng*	*Swe*
1979	June	9	Vasteras	2	1
1986	Sept	9	Ostersund	1	1
EC1988	Oct	18	Coventry	1	1
EC1989	Sept	5	Uppsala	0	1
EC1998	Sept	4	Sundvall	2	0
EC1999	June	4	Huddersfield	3	0
2004	Mar	30	Kristiansund	2	2
EC2009	June	26	Gothenburg	3	3
2013	Feb	5	Walsall	4	0
EC2015	Jun	21	Olomouc	1	0

			v SWITZERLAND	*Eng*	*Swit*
EC1980	Nov	18	Ipswich	5	0
EC1981	May	31	Neuenburg	0	0
1988	May	28	Lausanne	1	1
1996	April	1	Swindon	0	0
1998	Mar	24	Brugglifeld	0	2
EC2002	May	17	Zurich	2	1
EC2006	Sept	6	Lucerne	3	2
EC2015	**Nov**	**16**	**Brighton**	**3**	**1**
EC2016	**Mar**	**26**	**Thun**	**1**	**1**
			v TURKEY	*Eng*	*Tur*
EC1984	Nov	13	Bursa	0	0
EC1985	Oct	15	Bristol	3	0
EC1987	April	28	Izmir	0	0
EC1987	Oct	13	Sheffield	1	1
EC1991	April	30	Izmir	2	2
1991	Oct	15	Reading	2	0
EC1992	Nov	17	Orient	0	1
EC1993	Mar	30	Izmir	0	0
EC2000	May	29	Bratislava	6	0
EC2003	April	1	Newcastle	1	1
EC2003	Oct	10	Istanbul	0	1
			v UKRAINE	*Eng*	*Uk*
2004	Aug	17	Middlesbrough	3	1
EC2011	June	15	Herning	0	0
			v USA	*Eng*	*USA*
1989	June	11	Toulon	0	2
1994	June	2	Toulon	3	0
2015	**Sept**	**3**	**Preston**	**1**	**0**
			v USSR	*Eng*	*USSR*
1987	June	9	Toulon	0	0
1988	June	7	Toulon	1	0
1990	May	25	Toulon	2	1
1991	May	31	Toulon	2	1
			v UZBEKISTAN	*Eng*	*Uzb*
2010	Aug	10	Bristol	2	0
			v WALES	*Eng*	*Wales*
1976	Dec	15	Wolverhampton	0	0
1979	Feb	6	Swansea	1	0
1990	Dec	5	Tranmere	0	0
EC2004	Oct	8	Blackburn	2	0
EC2005	Sept	2	Wrexham	4	0
2008	May	5	Wrexham	2	0
EC2008	Oct	10	Cardiff	3	2
EC2008	Oct	14	Villa Park	2	2
EC2013	Mar	5	Derby	1	0
EC2013	May	19	Swansea	3	1
			v YUGOSLAVIA	*Eng*	*Yugo*
EC1978	April	19	Novi Sad	1	2
EC1978	May	2	Manchester	1	1
EC1986	Nov	11	Peterborough	1	1
EC1987	Nov	10	Zemun	5	1
EC2000	Mar	29	Barcelona	3	0
2002	Sept	6	Bolton	1	1

ENGLAND C 2015–16

INTERNATIONAL CHALLENGE TROPHY

Kiev, Tuesday 22 March 2016

Ukraine (0) 0

England C (2) 2 *(Guthrie 35, Jackson 45)*

England C: Hall (Crook 90); Bolton (Halls 87), Heneghan, Holland, Habergham, Marsh-Brown (Isaac 78), Woodyard, Gallagher (Clay 90), Goddard, Jackson, Guthrie (Daniels 79).

Sutton, Sunday 5 June 2016

England C (2) 3 *(Holland 28, John 38, 52)*

Slovakia U21 (1) 4 *(Haraslin 18, Huk 55, Fasko 75, 90)*
1572

England C: Hall (Butler 76); Bolton (Wishart 54), Heneghan, Holland (John 29), Habergham, Gallagher, Woodyard, Leesley, Whitehouse (Sweeney 70), Southwell (Williams 79), Goddard.

FRIENDLY

Galway, 1 June 2015

Republic of Ireland U21 (0) 1 *(Maguire 82)*

England C (0) 2 *(Pearson 65, Roberts 67)*

England C: Coughlin (Kitscha 77), Bolton, Heneghan (Goode 73), Raggett, Roberts, Woodyard, Gallagher (Chettle 46), Shaw, James, Pearson, Moult (Williams 61).

BRITISH AND IRISH UNDER-21 TEAMS 2015–16

■ *Denotes player sent off.*

ENGLAND

FRIENDLY
Thursday, 3 September 2015
England (0) 1 *(Walton 72)*
USA (0) 0   10,192
England: (442) Pickford (Gunn 61); Gomez (Iorfa 64), Targett (Stephens 63), Loftus-Cheek, Chambers; Dier (Hause 64), Ibe (Watmore 66), Ward-Prowse (Forster-Caskey 65), Woodrow (March 65); Alli (Chalobah 70), Redmond (Wilson 65).

EURO UNDER-21 CHAMPIONSHIP 2015–17 – GROUP 9
Monday, 7 September 2015
Norway (0) 0
England (1) 1 *(Ward-Prowse 45 (pen))*   3715
England: (442) Pickford; Gomez, Targett, Chambers, Dier; Ibe, Ward-Prowse, Alli (Chalobah 46), Redmond; Loftus-Cheek (Forster-Caskey 70), Woodrow.

Tuesday, 13 October 2015
England (0) 3 *(Loftus-Cheek 53, Redmond 70, Akpom 90)*
Kazakhstan (0) 0
England: (4132) Pickford; Dier, Gomez (Iorfa 80), Chambers, Targett; Baker; Loftus-Cheek (Chalobah 83), Ward-Prowse, Redmond; Akpom, Ibe (Watmore 65).

Thursday, 12 November 2015
Bosnia-Herzegovina (0) 0
England (0) 0   300
England: (442) Pickford; Iorfa, Chambers, Stephens■, Targett; Ward-Prowse, Chalobah, Baker (Watmore 70), Solanke (Woodrow 89); Loftus-Cheek (Forster-Caskey 85), Akpom.

Monday, 16 November 2015
England (0) 3 *(Ward-Prowse 83 (pen), Watmore 85, Akpom 90)*
Switzerland (1) 1 *(Tarashaj 45)*   12,003
England: (4411) Pickford; Iorfa, Chambers, Chalobah, Targett; Ward-Prowse, Baker, Swift, March (Akpom 58); Loftus-Cheek (Watmore 75); Solanke (Forster-Caskey 86).

Saturday, 26 March 2016
Switzerland (0) 1 *(Kamberi 76)*
England (0) 1 *(Akpom 47)*
England: (4231) Pickford; Iorfa, Chambers, Hause, Targett; Gray, Ward-Prowse; Baker, Swift (Ibe■ 27), Loftus-Cheek (Grimes 70); Akpom (Solanke 86).

TOULON TOURNAMENT 2016 – GROUP B
Thursday, 19 May 2016
England (0) 1 *(Baker 60)*
Portugal U20 (0) 0
England: Pickford; Iorfa, Chambers, Hause, Chilwell, Chalobah, Ward-Prowse, Loftus-Cheek (Grealish 72), Baker (Grimes 80), Watmore (Woodrow 58), Palmer (Redmond 58).

Monday, 23 May 2016
England (4) 7 *(Grealish 7, 40, Ward-Prowse 30 (pen), Redmond 34, Makadjil (og) 50, Woodrow 58, 73)*
Guinea U23 (1) 1 *(Diallo 1)*
England: Gunn; Stephens, Holding, Hause (Chambers 54), Targett, Ward-Prowse (Chalobah 41), Swift, Grimes, Grealish (Watmore 60), Redmond (Palmer 54), Woodrow.

Wednesday, 25 May 2016
Paraguay U23 (0) 0
England (2) 4 *(Baker 33, Loftus-Cheek 45, 59, Redmond 65)*
England: Pickford; Iorfa, Chambers, Hause, Chilwell (Targett 39), Chalobah, Ward-Prowse, Baker, Loftus-Cheek (Swift 71), Redmond (Palmer 68), Watmore (Grealish 62).

Friday, 27 May 2016
Japan U23 (0) 0
England (1) 1 *(Baker 15 (pen))*
England: Gunn; Stephens, Holding, Chambers (Hause 54), Targett (Iorfa 41), Swift, Grimes, Baker (Loftus-Cheek 41), Grealish, Palmer, Woodrow.

TOULON TOURNAMENT 2016 – FINAL
Sunday, 29 May 2016
England (0) 2 *(Baker 8, Loftus-Cheek 38)*
France U20 (0) 1 *(Diallo 78)*
England: Pickford; Iorfa, Chambers, Hause, Targett (Stephens 80), Chalobah, Ward-Prowse, Baker, Loftus-Cheek, Redmond, Watmore (Swift 65).

SCOTLAND

EURO UNDER-21 CHAMPIONSHIP 2015–17 – GROUP 3
Saturday, 10 October 2015
Scotland (0) 1 *(King 90)*
France (1) 2 *(Kingsley 11 (og), Tolisso 53)*   3200
Scotland: (442) Hamilton; Paterson, Kingsley, Findlay, McGhee; McGinn, Christie, Nicholson (King 68), Slater (Shankland 58); Gauld■, Cummings (McManus 78).

Tuesday, 13 October 2015
Scotland (0) 0
Iceland (0) 0   1935
Scotland: (4231) Hamilton; Paterson, McGhee, Hyam, Kingsley; Fulton (Love 75), McGinn; Christie, King (McManus 83), Nicholson; Cummings (Shankland 68).

Friday, 13 November 2015
Scotland (2) 2 *(Cummings 31, Paterson 37)*
Ukraine (1) 2 *(Khlyobas 26, Svatok 83)*   2148
Scotland: (4231) Hamilton; Paterson (McFadzean 46), McGhee, Hyam■, Robertson; Love (Slater 46), McGinn; King, Henderson, McKay (McBurnie 74); Cummings.

Thursday, 24 March 2016
France (0) 2 *(Haller 69, 74)*
Scotland (0) 0   6669
Scotland: (442) Hamilton; Gauld, Henderson (Christie 78), King, Kingsley; Love, McGhee, Nicholson (McKay 70), Slater; Souttar, Cummings (McBurnie 83).

Tuesday, 29 March 2016
Scotland (0) 3 *(McBurnie 58, Cummings 64, 78)*
N Ireland (1) 1 *(McCartan 13)*   1065
Scotland: (451) Hamilton; Love, McGhee, Souttar, Kingsley; Nicholson (McBurnie 53), Storie, Gauld, McKay (Polworth 89), Christie; Cummings (Henderson 82).
N Ireland: (442) Brennan; Dummigan, Donnelly, Johnson, Gorman; Conlan, McLaughlin R, Maloney, Duffy (Cooper 79); McCartan (McDaid 84), Kennedy (Sendles-White 69).

NORTHERN IRELAND

EURO UNDER-21 CHAMPIONSHIP 2015–17 – GROUP 3
Saturday, 5 September 2015
N Ireland (1) 1 *(Kennedy 7)*
Scotland (1) 2 *(Christie 33, Fraser 61)*   338
N Ireland: (433) Brennan; McLaughlin R, Conlan (Sharpe 74), Donnelly, Sendles-White; Dummigan, Johnson, Gorman■; McCartan (Maloney 61), Duffy (McDaid 87), Kennedy.
Scotland: (433) Hamilton; Findlay, Paterson, Souttar, McGhee; Fraser (King 85), Gauld, McGinn; McFadzean, Christie (Nicholson 81), Cummings (Shankland 75).

Tuesday, 8 September 2015
Iceland (1) 1 *(Thrandarson 37)*
N Ireland (1) 1 *(Johnson 2)*   552
N Ireland: (433) Brennan; Dummigan, McLaughlin R (McCartan 82), Sharpe, Donnelly; Johnson, Singleton, Maloney; McKnight, Kennedy, Duffy.

Tuesday, 13 October 2015
N Ireland (1) 1 *(Doherty 43)*
FYR Macedonia (0) 2 *(Bardhi 46, Markoski 85)* 160
N Ireland: (442) Brennan; Dummigan, Doherty, Donnelly, Sharpe; Whyte (Maloney 86), Singleton (McCartan 70), McKnight, Camps; Duffy, Kennedy (McDaid 89).

Thursday, 12 November 2015
France (0) 1 *(Crivelli 82)*
N Ireland (0) 0 9242
N Ireland: (442) Brennan; Dummigan, McCullough, Doherty, Conlan; McLaughlin R (McCartan 74), McKnight, Maloney, Whyte (Stewart 67); Kennedy (McDaid 87), Duffy.

Tuesday, 17 November 2015
N Ireland (0) 1 *(McCartan 53)*
Ukraine (0) 2 *(Kovalenko 64, 73)* 113
N Ireland: (424) Brennan; Dummigan, McCullough, Doherty, Conlan; Maloney, McKnight; McCartan, McDaid (McDonagh 84), Whyte (Stewart 78), Duffy (Cooper 78).

WALES

EURO UNDER-21 CHAMPIONSHIP 2015–17 – GROUP 5
Friday, 4 September 2015
Luxembourg (0) 1 *(Sinani 90)*
Wales (1) 3 *(Burns 35, 72, Wilson 63)* 323
Wales: (4231) O'Brien; Jones G, Yorwerth, Wright, Sheehan (Thompson 82); John, Evans L; O'Sullivan, Hedges, Burns (Charles 82); Harrison (Wilson 60).

Friday, 9 October 2015
Denmark (0) 0
Wales (0) 0 1854
Wales: (442) O'Brien; Jones G, Yorwerth, Lockyer, John (Evans J 73); Hedges, Sheehan, Evans L, Wilson (Charles 70); Harrison, O'Sullivan (Thompson 87).

Friday, 13 November 2015
Wales (1) 2 *(Harrison 9 (pen), Wilson 90)*
Armenia (0) 1 *(Malakyan 59)* 362
Wales: (4411) O'Brien; Shephard, Yorwerth, Lockyer, John; Wilson, Evans L, Sheehan, Harrison (Hedges 60); O'Sullivan (Charles 69); Burns (Jones O 89).

Tuesday, 17 November 2015
Wales (1) 1 *(Burns 14)*
Romania (1) 1 *(Nedelcearu 2) (Branescu■)* 642
Wales: (442) O'Brien; Shephard, Lockyer, Yorwerth, John; Hedges (Saunders 87), Sheehan, Evans L, Wilson (Charles 46), O'Sullivan; Burns (Harrison 71).

Friday, 25 March 2016
Bulgaria (0) 0
Wales (0) 0 1560
Wales: (442) O'Brien; Jones G, John (Evans J 53), Yorwerth, Lockyer; Hedges, Evans L, Sheehan, O'Sullivan; Harrison (Charles 65), Burns.

Tuesday, 29 March 2016
Romania (1) 2 *(Hodorogea 37, Ionita 58)*
Wales (0) 1 *(Charles 90)* 1722
Wales: (442) O'Brien; Jones G (Roberts 82), Evans J, Yorwerth, Lockyer; Hedges, Sheehan (Weeks 75), Evans L, O'Sullivan (Charles 56); Burns, Harrison.

REPUBLIC OF IRELAND

FRIENDLY
Tuesday, 17 November 2015
Republic of Ireland (0) 0
Norway (0) 0
Republic of Ireland: (442) Grimes (Lawlor 46); Hoare, Desmond, Lenihan D, Griffin; Browne (Maguire 88), Charsley, Kavanagh, Wilkinson; Connolly (Miele 83), O'Connor (Baba 83).

EURO UNDER-21 CHAMPIONSHIP 2015–17 – GROUP 2
Tuesday, 8 September 2015
Andorra (0) 0 *(Ferre■)*
Republic of Ireland (2) 2 *(Hoban 13, Cullen 21)* 650
Republic of Ireland: (4141) Rogers; Lenihan B, Lenihan D, Hoban, Connors; Rea (Long 87); Grego-Cox (Maguire 84), Cullen, Browne, Kavanagh; O'Dowda (Connolly 85).

Friday, 9 October 2015
Republic of Ireland (2) 3 *(O'Dowda 27, Wilkinson 30, Browne 77)*
Lithuania (0) 0 1520
Republic of Ireland: (4231) Rogers; Long, Rea (Griffin 79), Lenihan D, Connors; Cullen, Browne (Charsley 82); O'Dowda, Byrne, Kavanagh; Wilkinson (Connolly 65).

Tuesday, 13 October 2015
Italy (0) 1 *(Parigini 66) (Bernardeschi■)*
Republic of Ireland (0) 0 5000
Republic of Ireland: (442) Rogers; Long, Connors, O'Dowda, Lenihan D; Rea, Browne, Cullen, Byrne (Connolly 86); Kavanagh (Maguire 85), Wilkinson.

Friday, 13 November 2015
Lithuania (2) 3 *(Spalvis 22, Stankevicius 45, Kazlauskas 73)*
Republic of Ireland (1) 1 *(Wilkinson 44)* 653
Republic of Ireland: (442) Rogers; Long, Rea, Kavanagh■, Connors (Grego-Cox 18); O'Dowda, Lenihan D, Browne, Cullen; Byrne (Connolly 65), Wilkinson (Maguire 81).

Thursday, 24 March 2016
Republic of Ireland (1) 1 *(Mandragora 17 (og))*
Italy (2) 4 *(Benassi 28, Rosseti 36, Romagnoli 59, Lenihan D 82 (og))* 1632
Republic of Ireland: (442) Rogers; O'Connor (Hoare 72), Lenihan B, Rea, Keown; Charsley (Miele 72), Byrne (Maguire 84), Connors, Lenihan D; O'Dowda, Wilkinson.

Monday, 28 March 2016
Slovenia (1) 3 *(Krajnc 14, Bajde 55, Zajc 72)*
Republic of Ireland (0) 1 *(O'Dowda 65)* 2000
Republic of Ireland: (442) Lawlor; Hoare, Long, Griffin (Connolly 61), Keown; Lenihan D, Connors, Byrne, O'Dowda (Barrett 75); Dimaio, Wilkinson (Maguire 39).

BRITISH UNDER-21 APPEARANCES 1976–2016

Bold type indicates players who made an international appearance in season 2015–16.

ENGLAND

Ablett, G. 1988 (Liverpool)	1
Akpom, C. A. 2015 (Arsenal)	**4**
Adams, N. 1987 (Everton)	1
Adams, T. A. 1985 (Arsenal)	5
Addison, M. 2010 (Derby Co)	1
Afobe, B. T. 2012 (Arsenal)	2
Agbonlahor, G. 2007 (Aston Villa)	16
Albrighton, M. K. 2011 (Aston Villa)	8
Alli, B. J. (Dele) 2015 (Tottenham H)	**2**
Allen, B. 1992 (QPR)	8
Allen, C. 1980 (QPR, Crystal Palace)	3
Allen, C. A. 1995 (Oxford U)	2
Allen, M. 1987 (QPR)	2
Allen, P. 1985 (West Ham U, Tottenham H)	3
Allen, R. W. 1998 (Tottenham H)	3
Alnwick, B. R. 2008 (Tottenham H)	1
Ambrose, D. P. F. 2003 (Ipswich T, Newcastle U, Charlton Ath)	10
Ameobi, F. 2001 (Newcastle U)	19
Ameobi, S. 2012 (Newcastle U)	5
Amos, B. P. 2012 (Manchester U)	3
Anderson, V. A. 1978 (Nottingham F)	1
Anderton, D. R. 1993 (Tottenham H)	12
Andrews, I. 1987 (Leicester C)	1
Ardley, N. C. 1993 (Wimbledon)	10
Ashcroft, L. 1992 (Preston NE)	1
Ashton, D. 2004 (Crewe Alex, Norwich C)	9
Atherton, P. 1992 (Coventry C)	1
Atkinson, B. 1991 (Sunderland)	6
Awford, A. T. 1993 (Portsmouth)	9
Bailey, G. R. 1979 (Manchester U)	14
Baines, L. J. 2005 (Wigan Ath)	16
Baker, G. E. 1981 (Southampton)	2
Baker, L. R. 2015 (Chelsea)	**8**
Baker, N. L. 2011 (Aston Villa)	3
Ball, M. J. 1999 (Everton)	7
Bamford, P. J. 2013 (Chelsea)	2
Bannister, G. 1982 (Sheffield W)	1
Barker, S. 1985 (Blackburn R)	4
Barkley, R. 2012 (Everton)	5
Barmby, N. J. 1994 (Tottenham H, Everton)	4
Barnes, J. 1983 (Watford)	2
Barnes, P. S. 1977 (Manchester C)	9
Barrett, E. D. 1990 (Oldham Ath)	4
Barry, G. 1999 (Aston Villa)	27
Barton, J. 2004 (Manchester C)	2
Bart-Williams, C. G. 1993 (Sheffield W)	16
Batty, D. 1988 (Leeds U)	7
Bazeley, D. S. 1992 (Watford)	1
Beagrie, P. 1988 (Sheffield U)	2
Beardsmore, R. 1989 (Manchester U)	5
Beattie, J. S. 1999 (Southampton)	5
Beckham, D. R. J. 1995 (Manchester U)	9
Berahino, S. 2013 (WBA)	11
Bennett, J. 2011 (Middlesbrough)	3
Bennett, R. 2012 (Norwich C)	2
Bent, D. A. 2003 (Ipswich T, Charlton Ath)	14
Bent, M. N. 1998 (Crystal Palace)	2
Bentley, D. M. 2004 (Arsenal, Blackburn R)	8
Beeston, C 1988 (Stoke C)	1
Benjamin, T. J. 2001 (Leicester C)	1
Bertrand, R. 2009 (Chelsea)	16
Bertschin, K. E. 1977 (Birmingham C)	3
Bettinelli, M. 2015 (Fulham)	1
Birtles, G. 1980 (Nottingham F)	2
Blackett, T. N. 2014 (Manchester U)	1
Blackstock, D. A. 2008 (QPR)	2
Blackwell, D. R. 1991 (Wimbledon)	6
Blake, M. A. 1990 (Aston Villa)	8
Blissett, L. L. 1979 (Watford)	4
Bond, J. H. 2013 (Watford)	5
Booth, A. D. 1995 (Huddersfield T)	3
Bothroyd, J. 2001 (Coventry C)	1
Bowyer, L. D. 1996 (Charlton Ath, Leeds U)	13

Bracewell, P. 1983 (Stoke C)	13
Bradbury, L. M. 1997 (Portsmouth, Manchester C)	3
Bramble, T. M. 2001 (Ipswich T, Newcastle U)	10
Branch, P. M. 1997 (Everton)	1
Bradshaw, P. W. 1977 (Wolverhampton W)	4
Breacker, T. 1986 (Luton T)	2
Brennan, M. 1987 (Ipswich T)	5
Bridge, W. M. 1999 (Southampton)	8
Bridges, M. 1997 (Sunderland, Leeds U)	3
Briggs, M. 2012 (Fulham)	2
Brightwell, I. 1989 (Manchester C)	4
Briscoe, L. S. 1996 (Sheffield W)	5
Brock, K. 1984 (Oxford U)	4
Broomes, M. C. 1997 (Blackburn R)	2
Brown, M. R. 1996 (Manchester C)	4
Brown, W. M. 1999 (Manchester U)	8
Bull, S. G. 1989 (Wolverhampton W)	5
Bullock, M. J. 1998 (Barnsley)	1
Burrows, D. 1989 (WBA, Liverpool)	7
Butcher, T. I. 1979 (Ipswich T)	7
Butland, J. 2012 (Birmingham C, Stoke C)	28
Butt, N. 1995 (Manchester U)	7
Butters, G. 1989 (Tottenham H)	3
Butterworth, I. 1985 (Coventry C, Nottingham F)	8
Bywater, S. 2001 (West Ham U)	6
Cadamarteri, D. L. 1999 (Everton)	3
Caesar, G. 1987 (Arsenal)	3
Cahill, G. J. 2007 (Aston Villa)	3
Callaghan, N. 1983 (Watford)	9
Camp, L. M. J. 2005 (Derby Co)	5
Campbell, A. P. 2000 (Middlesbrough)	4
Campbell, F. L. 2008 (Manchester U)	14
Campbell, K. J. 1991 (Arsenal)	4
Campbell, S. 1994 (Tottenham)	11
Carbon, M. P. 1996 (Derby Co)	4
Carr, C. 1985 (Fulham)	1
Carr, F. 1987 (Nottingham F)	9
Carragher, J. L. 1997 (Liverpool)	27
Carroll, A. T. 2010 (Newcastle U)	5
Carroll, T. J. 2013 (Tottenham H)	17
Carlisle, C. J. 2001 (QPR)	3
Carrick, M. 2001 (West Ham U)	14
Carson, S. P. 2004 (Leeds U, Liverpool)	29
Casper, C. M. 1995 (Manchester U)	1
Caton, T. 1982 (Manchester C)	14
Cattermole, L. B. 2008 (Middlesbrough, Wigan Ath, Sunderland)	16
Caulker, S. R. 2011 (Tottenham H)	10
Chadwick, L. H. 2000 (Manchester U)	13
Challis, T. M. 1996 (QPR)	2
Chalobah, N. N. 2012 (Chelsea)	**30**
Chamberlain, M. 1983 (Stoke C)	4
Chambers, C. 2015 (Arsenal)	**14**
Chaplow, R. D. 2004 (Burnley)	1
Chapman, L. 1981 (Stoke C)	1
Charles, G. A. 1991 (Nottingham F)	4
Chettle, S. 1988 (Nottingham F)	12
Chilwell, B. J. 2016 (Leicester C)	**2**
Chopra, R. M. 2004 (Newcastle U)	1
Clark, L. R. 1992 (Newcastle U)	11
Clarke, P. M. 2003 (Everton)	8
Christie, M. N. 2001 (Derby Co)	11
Clegg, M. J. 1998 (Manchester U)	2
Clemence, S. N. 1999 (Tottenham H)	1
Cleverley, T. W. 2010 (Manchester U)	16
Clough, N. H. 1986 (Nottingham F)	15
Clyne, N. E. 2012 (Crystal Palace)	8
Cole, A. 2001 (Arsenal)	4
Cole, A. A. 1992 (Arsenal, Bristol C, Newcastle U)	8
Cole, C. 2003 (Chelsea)	19
Cole, J. J. 2000 (West Ham U)	8
Coney, D. 1985 (Fulham)	4
Connor, T. 1987 (Brighton & HA)	1
Cooke, R. 1986 (Tottenham H)	1

Cooke, T. J. 1996 (Manchester U) 4
Cooper, C. T. 1988 (Middlesbrough) 8
Cork, J. F. P. 2009 (Chelsea) 13
Corrigan, J. T. 1978 (Manchester C) 3
Cort, C. E. R. 1999 (Wimbledon) 12
Cottee, A. R. 1985 (West Ham U) 8
Couzens, A. J. 1995 (Leeds U) 3
Cowans, G. S. 1979 (Aston Villa) 5
Cox, N. J. 1993 (Aston Villa) 6
Cranie, M. J. 2008 (Portsmouth) 16
Cranson, I. 1985 (Ipswich T) 5
Cresswell, R. P. W. 1999 (York C, Sheffield W) 4
Croft, G. 1995 (Grimsby T) 4
Crooks, G. 1980 (Stoke C) 4
Crossley, M. G. 1990 (Nottingham F) 3
Crouch, P. J. 2002 (Portsmouth, Aston Villa) 5
Cundy, J. V. 1991 (Chelsea) 3
Cunningham, L. 1977 (WBA) 6
Curbishley, L. C. 1981 (Birmingham C) 1
Curtis, J. C. K. 1998 (Manchester U) 16

Daniel, P. W. 1977 (Hull C) 7
Dann, S. 2008 (Coventry C) 2
Davenport, C. R. P. 2005 (Tottenham H) 8
Davies, A. J. 2004 (Middlesbrough) 1
Davies, C. E. 2006 (WBA) 3
Davies, K. C. 1998 (Southampton, Blackburn R, Southampton) 3
Davis, K. G. 1995 (Luton T) 3
Davis, P. 1982 (Arsenal) 11
Davis, S. 2001 (Fulham) 11
Dawson, C. 2012 (WBA) 15
Dawson, M. R. 2003 (Nottingham F, Tottenham H) 13
Day, C. N. 1996 (Tottenham H, Crystal Palace) 6
D'Avray, J. M. 1984 (Ipswich T) 2
Deehan, J. M. 1977 (Aston Villa) 7
Defoe, J. C. 2001 (West Ham U) 23
Delfouneso, N. 2010 (Aston Villa) 17
Delph, F. 2009 (Leeds U, Aston Villa) 4
Dennis, M. E. 1980 (Birmingham C) 2
Derbyshire, M. A. 2007 (Blackburn R) 14
Dichio, D. S. E. 1996 (QPR) 1
Dickens, A. 1985 (West Ham U) 1
Dicks, J. 1988 (West Ham U) 4
Dier, E. J. E. 2013 (Sporting Lisbon, Tottenham H) 9
Digby, F. 1987 (Swindon T) 5
Dillon, K. P. 1981 (Birmingham C) 1
Dixon, K. M. 1985 (Chelsea) 1
Dobson, A. 1989 (Coventry C) 4
Dodd, J. R. 1991 (Southampton) 8
Donowa, L. 1985 (Norwich C) 3
Dorigo, A. R. 1987 (Aston Villa) 11
Downing, S. 2004 (Middlesbrough) 8
Dozzell, J. 1987 (Ipswich T) 9
Draper, M. A. 1991 (Notts Co) 3
Driver, A. 2009 (Hearts) 1
Duberry, M. W. 1997 (Chelsea) 5
Dunn, D. J. I. 1999 (Blackburn R) 20
Duxbury, M. 1981 (Manchester U) 7
Dyer, B. A. 1994 (Crystal Palace) 10
Dyer, K. C. 1998 (Ipswich T, Newcastle U) 11
Dyson, P. I. 1981 (Coventry C) 4

Eadie, D. M. 1994 (Norwich C) 7
Ebanks-Blake, S. 2009 (Wolverhampton W) 1
Ebbrell, J. 1989 (Everton) 14
Edghill, R. A. 1994 (Manchester C) 3
Ehiogu, U. 1992 (Aston Villa) 15
Elliott, P. 1985 (Luton T) 3
Elliott, R. J. 1996 (Newcastle U) 2
Elliott, S. W. 1998 (Derby Co) 3
Etherington, N, 2002 (Tottenham H) 3
Euell, J. J. 1998 (Wimbledon) 6
Evans, R. 2003 (Chelsea) 2

Fairclough, C. 1985 (Nottingham F, Tottenham H) 7
Fairclough, D. 1977 (Liverpool) 1
Fashanu, J. 1980 (Norwich C, Nottingham F) 11
Fear, P. 1994 (Wimbledon) 3
Fenton, G. A. 1995 (Aston Villa) 1
Fenwick, T. W. 1981 (Crystal Palace, QPR) 11
Ferdinand, A. J. 2005 (West Ham U) 17

Ferdinand, R. G. 1997 (West Ham U) 5
Fereday, W. 1985 (QPR) 5
Fielding, F. D. 2009 (Blackburn R) 12
Flanagan, J. 2012 (Liverpool) 3
Flitcroft, G. W. 1993 (Manchester C) 10
Flowers, T. D. 1987 (Southampton) 3
Ford, M. 1996 (Leeds U) 2
Forster, N. M. 1995 (Brentford) 4
Forsyth, M. 1988 (Derby Co) 1
Forster-Caskey, J. D. 2014 (Brighton & HA) 14
Foster, S. 1980 (Brighton & HA) 1
Fowler, R. B. 1994 (Liverpool) 8
Fox, D. J. 2008 (Coventry C) 1
Froggatt, S. J. 1993 (Aston Villa) 2
Futcher, P. 1977 (Luton T, Manchester C) 11

Gabbiadini, M. 1989 (Sunderland) 2
Gale, A. 1982 (Fulham) 1
Gallen, K. A. 1995 (QPR) 4
Garbutt, L. S. 2014 (Everton) 11
Gardner, A. 2002 (Tottenham H) 1
Gardner, C. 2008 (Aston Villa) 14
Gardner, D. 2012 (Aston Villa) 5
Gascoigne, P. J. 1987 (Newcastle U) 13
Gayle, H. 1984 (Birmingham C) 3
Gernon, T. 1983 (Ipswich T) 1
Gerrard, P. W. 1993 (Oldham Ath) 18
Gerrard, S. G. 2000 (Liverpool) 4
Gibbs, K. J. R. 2009 (Arsenal) 15
Gibbs, N. 1987 (Watford) 5
Gibson, B. J. 2014 (Middlesbrough) 10
Gibson, C. 1982 (Aston Villa) 1
Gilbert, W. A. 1979 (Crystal Palace) 11
Goddard, P. 1981 (West Ham U) 8
Gomez, J. D. 2015 (Liverpool) 3
Gordon, D. 1987 (Norwich C) 4
Gordon, D. D. 1994 (Crystal Palace) 13
Gosling, D. 2010 (Everton, Newcastle U) 3
Grant, A. J. 1996 (Everton) 1
Grant, L. A. 2003 (Derby Co) 4
Granville, D. P. 1997 (Chelsea) 3
Gray, A. 1988 (Aston Villa) 2
Gray, D. R. 2016 (Leicester C) 1
Greening, J. 1999 (Manchester U, Middlesbrough) 18
Grealish, J. 2016 (Aston Villa) 4
Griffin, A. 1999 (Newcastle U) 3
Grimes, M. J. 2016 (Swansea C) 4
Gunn, A. 2015 (Manchester C) 3
Guppy, S. A. 1998 (Leicester C) 1

Haigh, P. 1977 (Hull C) 1
Hall, M. T. J. 1997 (Coventry C) 8
Hall, R. A. 1992 (Southampton) 11
Hamilton, D. V. 1997 (Newcastle U) 1
Hammill, A. 2010 (Wolverhampton W) 1
Harding, D. A. 2005 (Brighton & HA) 4
Hardyman, P. 1985 (Portsmouth) 2
Hargreaves, O. 2001 (Bayern Munich) 3
Harley, J. 2000 (Chelsea) 3
Hart, C. 2007 (Manchester C) 21
Hateley, M. 1982 (Coventry C, Portsmouth) 10
Hause, K. P. D. 2015 (Wolverhampton W) 7
Hayes, M. 1987 (Arsenal) 3
Hazell, R. J. 1979 (Wolverhampton W) 1
Heaney, N. A. 1992 (Arsenal) 6
Heath, A. 1981 (Stoke C, Everton) 8
Heaton, T. D. 2008 (Manchester U) 3
Henderson, J. B. 2011 (Sunderland, Liverpool) 27
Hendon, I. M. 1992 (Tottenham H) 7
Hendrie, L. A. 1996 (Aston Villa) 13
Hesford, I. 1981 (Blackpool) 7
Heskey, E. W. I. 1997 (Leicester C, Liverpool) 16
Hilaire, V. 1980 (Crystal Palace) 9
Hill, D. R. L. 1995 (Tottenham H) 4
Hillier, D. 1991 (Arsenal) 1
Hinchcliffe, A. 1989 (Manchester C) 1
Hines, Z. 2010 (West Ham U) 2
Hinshelwood, P. A. 1978 (Crystal Palace) 2
Hirst, D. E. 1988 (Sheffield W) 7
Hislop, N. S. 1998 (Newcastle U) 1
Hoddle, G. 1977 (Tottenham H) 12
Hodge, S. B. 1983 (Nottingham F, Aston Villa) 8

Hodgson, D. J. 1981 (Middlesbrough)	6
Holding, R. S. 2016 (Bolton W)	2
Holdsworth, D. 1989 (Watford)	1
Holland, C. J. 1995 (Newcastle U)	10
Holland, P. 1995 (Mansfield T)	4
Holloway, D. 1998 (Sunderland)	1
Horne, B. 1989 (Millwall)	5
Howe, E. J. F. 1998 (Bournemouth)	2
Howson, J. M. 2011 (Leeds U)	1
Hoyte, J. R. 2004 (Arsenal)	18
Hucker, P. 1984 (QPR)	2
Huckerby, D. 1997 (Coventry C)	4
Huddlestone, T. A. 2005 (Derby Co, Tottenham H)	33
Hughes, S. J. 1997 (Arsenal)	8
Hughes, W. J. 2012 (Derby Co)	17
Humphreys, R. J. 1997 (Sheffield W)	3
Hunt, N. B. 2004 (Bolton W)	10
Ibe, J. A. F. 2015 (Liverpool)	4
Impey, A. R. 1993 (QPR)	1
Ince, P. E. C. 1989 (West Ham U)	2
Ince, T. C. 2012 (Blackpool, Hull C)	18
Ings, D. W. J. 2013 (Burnley)	13
Iorfa, D. 2016 (Wolverhampton W)	9
Jackson, M. A. 1992 (Everton)	10
Jagielka, P. N. 2003 (Sheffield U)	6
James, D. B. 1991 (Watford)	10
James, J. C. 1990 (Luton T)	2
Jansen, M. B. 1999 (Crystal Palace, Blackburn R)	6
Jeffers, F. 2000 (Everton, Arsenal)	16
Jemson, N. B. 1991 (Nottingham F)	1
Jenas, J. A. 2002 (Newcastle U)	9
Jenkinson, C. D. 2013 (Arsenal)	14
Jerome, C. 2006 (Cardiff C, Birmingham C)	10
Joachim, J. K. 1994 (Leicester C)	9
Johnson, A. 2008 (Middlesbrough)	19
Johnson, G. M. C. 2003 (West Ham U, Chelsea)	14
Johnson, M. 2008 (Manchester C)	2
Johnson, S. A. M. 1999 (Crewe Alex, Derby Co, Leeds U)	15
Johnson, T. 1991 (Notts Co, Derby Co)	7
Johnston, C. P. 1981 (Middlesbrough)	2
Jones, D. R. 1977 (Everton)	1
Jones, C. H. 1978 (Tottenham H)	1
Jones, D. F. L. 2004 (Manchester U)	1
Jones, P. A. 2011 (Blackburn R)	2
Jones, R. 1993 (Liverpool)	9
Kane, H. E. 2013 (Tottenham H)	14
Keane, M. V. 2013 (Manchester U, Burnley)	16
Keane, W. D. 2012 (Manchester U)	3
Keegan, G. A. 1977 (Manchester C)	1
Kelly, M. R. 2011 (Liverpool)	8
Kenny, W. 1993 (Everton)	1
Keown, M. R. 1987 (Aston Villa)	8
Kerslake, D. 1986 (QPR)	1
Kightly, M. J. 2008 (Wolverhampton W)	7
Kilcline, B. 1983 (Notts C)	2
Kilgallon, M. 2004 (Leeds U)	5
King, A. E. 1977 (Everton)	2
King, L. B. 2000 (Tottenham H)	12
Kirkland, C. E. 2001 (Coventry C, Liverpool)	8
Kitson, P. 1991 (Leicester C, Derby Co)	7
Knight, A. 1983 (Portsmouth)	2
Knight, I. 1987 (Sheffield W)	2
Knight, Z. 2002 (Fulham)	4
Konchesky, P. M. 2002 (Charlton Ath)	15
Kozluk, R. 1998 (Derby Co)	2
Lake, P. 1989 (Manchester C)	5
Lallana, A. D. 2009 (Southampton)	1
Lampard, F. J. 1998 (West Ham U)	19
Langley, T. W. 1978 (Chelsea)	1
Lansbury, H. G. 2010 (Arsenal, Nottingham F)	16
Lascellas, J. 2014 (Newcastle U)	2
Leadbitter, G. 2008 (Sunderland)	3
Lee, D. J. 1990 (Chelsea)	10
Lee, R. M. 1986 (Charlton Ath)	2
Lee, S. 1981 (Liverpool)	6
Lees, T. J. 2012 (Leeds U)	6

Lennon, A. J. 2006 (Tottenham H)	5
Le Saux, G. P. 1990 (Chelsea)	4
Lescott, J. P. 2003 (Wolverhampton W)	2
Lewis, J. P. 2008 (Peterborough U)	5
Lingard, J. E. 2013 (Manchester U)	11
Lita, L. H. 2005 (Bristol C, Reading)	9
Loach, S. J. 2009 (Watford)	14
Loftus-Cheek, R. I. 2015 (Chelsea)	13
Lowe, D. 1988 (Ipswich T)	2
Lowe, J. J. 2012 (Blackburn R)	11
Lukic, J. 1981 (Leeds U)	7
Lund, G. 1985 (Grimsby T)	3
McCall, S. H. 1981 (Ipswich T)	6
McCarthy, A. S. 2011 (Reading)	3
McDonald, N. 1987 (Newcastle U)	5
McEachran, J. M. 2011 (Chelsea)	13
McEveley, J. 2003 (Blackburn R)	1
McGrath, L. 1986 (Coventry C)	1
MacKenzie, S. 1982 (WBA)	3
McLeary, A. 1988 (Millwall)	1
McLeod, I. M. 2006 (Milton Keynes D)	1
McMahon, S. 1981 (Everton, Aston Villa)	6
McManaman, S. 1991 (Liverpool)	7
Mabbutt, G. 1982 (Bristol R, Tottenham H)	7
Maguire, J. H. 2012 (Sheffield U)	1
Makin, C. 1994 (Oldham Ath)	5
Mancienne, M. I. 2008 (Chelsea)	30
March, S. B. 2015 (Brighton & HA)	2
Marney, D. E. 2005 (Tottenham H)	1
Marriott, A. 1992 (Nottingham F)	1
Marsh, S. T. 1998 (Oxford U)	1
Marshall, A. J. 1995 (Norwich C)	4
Marshall, B. 2012 (Leicester C)	2
Marshall, L. K. 1999 (Norwich C)	1
Martin, L. 1989 (Manchester U)	2
Martyn, A. N. 1988 (Bristol R)	11
Matteo, D. 1994 (Liverpool)	4
Mattock, J. W. 2008 (Leicester C)	5
Matthew, D. 1990 (Chelsea)	9
May, A. 1986 (Manchester C)	1
Mee, B. 2011 (Manchester C)	2
Merson, P. C. 1989 (Arsenal)	4
Middleton, J. 1977 (Nottingham F, Derby Co)	3
Miller, A. 1988 (Arsenal)	4
Mills, D. J. 1999 (Charlton Ath, Leeds U)	14
Mills, G. R. 1981 (Nottingham F)	2
Milner, J. P. 2004 (Leeds U, Newcastle U, Aston Villa)	46
Mimms, R. 1985 (Rotherham U, Everton)	3
Minto, S. C. 1991 (Charlton Ath)	6
Moore, I. 1996 (Tranmere R, Nottingham F)	7
Moore, L. 2012 (Leicester C)	10
Moore, L. I. 2006 (Aston Villa)	5
Moran, S. 1982 (Southampton)	2
Morgan, S. 1987 (Leicester C)	2
Morris, J. 1997 (Chelsea)	7
Morrison, R. R. 2013 (West Ham U)	4
Mortimer, P. 1989 (Charlton Ath)	2
Moses, A. P. 1997 (Barnsley)	2
Moses, R. M. 1981 (WBA, Manchester U)	8
Moses, V. 2011 (Wigan Ath)	1
Mountfield, D. 1984 (Everton)	1
Muamba, F. N. 2008 (Birmingham C, Bolton W)	33
Muggleton, C. D. 1990 (Leicester C)	1
Mullins, H. I. 1999 (Crystal Palace)	3
Murphy, D. B. 1998 (Liverpool)	4
Murray, P. 1997 (QPR)	4
Murray, M. W. 2003 (Wolverhampton W)	5
Mutch, A. 1989 (Wolverhampton W)	1
Mutch, J. J. E. S. 2011 (Birmingham C)	1
Myers, A. 1995 (Chelsea)	5
Naughton, K. 2009 (Sheffield U, Tottenham H)	9
Naylor, L. M. 2000 (Wolverhampton W)	3
Nethercott, S. H. 1994 (Tottenham H)	8
Neville, P. J. 1995 (Manchester U)	7
Newell, M. 1986 (Luton T)	4
Newton, A. L. 2001 (West Ham U)	1
Newton, E. J. I. 1993 (Chelsea)	2
Newton, S. O. 1997 (Charlton Ath)	3
Nicholls, A. 1994 (Plymouth Arg)	1
Noble, M. J. 2007 (West Ham U)	20

Nolan, K. A. J. 2003 (Bolton W)	1
Nugent, D. J. 2006 (Preston NE)	14
Oakes, M. C. 1994 (Aston Villa)	6
Oakes, S. J. 1993 (Luton T)	1
Oakley, M. 1997 (Southampton)	4
O'Brien, A. J. 1999 (Bradford C)	1
O'Connor, J. 1996 (Everton)	3
O'Hara, J. D. 2008 (Tottenham H)	7
Oldfield, D. 1989 (Luton T)	1
Olney, I. A. 1990 (Aston Villa)	10
O'Neil, G. P. 2005 (Portsmouth)	9
Onuoha, C. 2006 (Manchester C)	21
Ord, R. J. 1991 (Sunderland)	3
Osman, R. C. 1979 (Ipswich T)	7
Owen, G. A. 1977 (Manchester C, WBA)	22
Owen, M. J. 1998 (Liverpool)	1
Oxlade-Chamberlain, A. M. D. 2011 (Southampton, Arsenal)	8
Painter, I. 1986 (Stoke C)	1
Palmer, C. L. 1989 (Sheffield W)	4
Parker, G. 1986 (Hull C, Nottingham F)	6
Parker, P. A. 1985 (Fulham)	8
Parker, S. M. 2001 (Charlton Ath)	12
Parkes, P. B. F. 1979 (QPR)	1
Parkin, S. 1987 (Stoke C)	5
Palmer, K. R. 2016 (Chelsea)	**4**
Parlour, R. 1992 (Arsenal)	12
Parnaby, S. 2003 (Middlesbrough)	4
Peach, D. S. 1977 (Southampton)	6
Peake, A. 1982 (Leicester C)	1
Pearce, I. A. 1995 (Blackburn R)	3
Pearce, S. 1987 (Nottingham F)	1
Pennant, J. 2001 (Arsenal)	24
Pickering N. 1983 (Sunderland, Coventry C)	15
Pickford, J. L. 2015 (Sunderland)	**9**
Platt, D. 1988 (Aston Villa)	3
Plummer, C. S. 1996 (QPR)	5
Pollock, J. 1995 (Middlesbrough)	3
Porter, G. 1987 (Watford)	12
Potter, G. S. 1997 (Southampton)	1
Powell, N. E. 2012 (Manchester U)	2
Pressman, K. 1989 (Sheffield W)	1
Pritchard, A. D. 2014 (Tottenham H)	9
Proctor, M. 1981 (Middlesbrough, Nottingham F)	4
Prutton, D. T. 2001 (Nottingham F, Southampton)	25
Purse, D. J. 1998 (Birmingham C)	2
Quashie, N. F. 1997 (QPR)	4
Quinn, W. R. 1998 (Sheffield U)	2
Ramage, C. D. 1991 (Derby Co)	3
Ranson, R. 1980 (Manchester C)	10
Redknapp, J. F. 1993 (Liverpool)	19
Redmond, N. D. J. 2013 (Birmingham C, Norwich C)	**29**
Redmond, S. 1988 (Manchester C)	14
Reeves, K. P. 1978 (Norwich C, Manchester C)	10
Regis, C. 1979 (WBA)	6
Reid, N. S. 1981 (Manchester C)	6
Reid, P. 1977 (Bolton W)	6
Reo-Coker, N. S. A. 2004 (Wimbledon, West Ham U)	23
Richards, D. I. 1995 (Wolverhampton W)	4
Richards, J. P. 1977 (Wolverhampton W)	2
Richards, M. 2007 (Manchester C)	15
Richards, M. L. 2005 (Ipswich T)	1
Richardson, K. E. 2005 (Manchester U)	12
Rideout, P. 1985 (Aston Villa, Bari)	5
Ridgewell, L. M. 2004 (Aston Villa)	8
Riggott, C. M. 2001 (Derby Co)	8
Ripley, S. E. 1988 (Middlesbrough)	8
Ritchie, A. 1982 (Brighton & HA)	1
Rix, G. 1978 (Arsenal)	7
Roberts, A. J. 1995 (Millwall, Crystal Palace)	5
Roberts, B. J. 1997 (Middlesbrough)	1
Robins, M. G. 1990 (Manchester U)	6
Robinson, J. 2012 (Liverpool, QPR)	10
Robinson, P. P. 1999 (Watford)	3
Robinson, P. W. 2000 (Leeds U)	11
Robson, B. 1979 (WBA)	7
Robson, S. 1984 (Arsenal, West Ham U)	8
Rocastle, D. 1987 (Arsenal)	14
Roche, L. P. 2001 (Manchester U)	1
Rodger, G. 1987 (Coventry C)	4
Rodriguez, J. E. 2011 (Burnley)	1
Rodwell, J. 2009 (Everton)	21
Rogers, A. 1998 (Nottingham F)	3
Rosario, R. 1987 (Norwich C)	4
Rose, D. L. 2009 (Tottenham H)	29
Rose, M. 1997 (Arsenal)	2
Rosenior, L. J. 2005 (Fulham)	7
Routledge, W. 2005 (Crystal Palace, Tottenham H)	12
Rowell, G. 1977 (Sunderland)	1
Rudd, D. T. 2013 (Norwich C)	1
Ruddock, N. 1989 (Southampton)	4
Rufus, R. R. 1996 (Charlton Ath)	6
Ryan, J. 1983 (Oldham Ath)	1
Ryder, S. H. 1995 (Walsall)	3
Samuel, J. 2002 (Aston Villa)	7
Samways, V. 1988 (Tottenham H)	5
Sansom, K. G. 1979 (Crystal Palace)	8
Scimeca, R. 1996 (Aston Villa)	9
Scowcroft, J. B. 1997 (Ipswich T)	5
Seaman, D. A. 1985 (Birmingham C)	10
Sears, F. D. 2010 (West Ham U)	3
Sedgley, S. 1987 (Coventry C, Tottenham H)	11
Sellars, S. 1988 (Blackburn R)	3
Selley, I. 1994 (Arsenal)	3
Serrant, C. 1998 (Oldham Ath)	2
Sharpe, L. S. 1989 (Manchester U)	8
Shaw, L. P. H. 2013 (Southampton, Manchester U)	5
Shaw, G. R. 1981 (Aston Villa)	7
Shawcross, R. J. 2008 (Stoke C)	2
Shearer, A. 1991 (Southampton)	11
Shelton, G. 1985 (Sheffield W)	1
Shelvey, J. 2012 (Liverpool, Swansea C)	13
Sheringham, E. P. 1988 (Millwall)	1
Sheron, M. N. 1992 (Manchester C)	16
Sherwood, T. A. 1990 (Norwich C)	4
Shipperley, N. J. 1994 (Chelsea, Southampton)	7
Sidwell, S. J. 2003 (Reading)	5
Simonsen, S. P. A. 1998 (Tranmere R, Everton)	4
Simpson, P. 1986 (Manchester C)	5
Sims, S. 1977 (Leicester C)	10
Sinclair, S. A. 2011 (Swansea C)	7
Sinclair, T. 1994 (QPR, West Ham U)	5
Sinnott, L. 1985 (Watford)	1
Slade, S. A. 1996 (Tottenham H)	4
Slater, S. I. 1990 (West Ham U)	3
Small, B. 1993 (Aston Villa)	12
Smalling, C. L. 2010 (Fulham, Manchester U)	14
Smith, A. 2000 (Leeds U)	10
Smith, A. J. 2012 (Tottenham H)	11
Smith, D. 1988 (Coventry C)	10
Smith, M. 1981 (Sheffield W)	5
Smith, M. 1995 (Sunderland)	1
Smith, T. W. 2001 (Watford)	1
Snodin, I. 1985 (Doncaster R)	4
Soares, T. J. 2006 (Crystal Palace)	4
Solanke, D. A. 2015 (Chelsea)	**3**
Sordell, M. A. 2012 (Watford, Bolton W)	14
Spence, J. 2011 (West Ham U)	1
Stanislaus, F. J. 2010 (West Ham U)	2
Statham, B. 1988 (Tottenham H)	3
Statham, D. J. 1978 (WBA)	6
Stead, J. G. 2004 (Blackburn R, Sunderland)	11
Stearman, R. J. 2009 (Wolverhampton W)	4
Steele, J. 2011 (Middlesbrough)	7
Stein, B. 1984 (Luton T)	3
Stephens, J. 2015 (Southampton)	**5**
Sterland, M. 1984 (Sheffield W)	7
Sterling, R. S. 2012 (Liverpool)	8
Steven, T. M. 1985 (Everton)	2
Stevens, G. A. 1983 (Brighton & HA, Tottenham H)	8
Stewart, J. 2003 (Leicester C)	1
Stewart, P. 1988 (Manchester C)	1
Stockdale, R. K. 2001 (Middlesbrough)	1
Stones, J. 2013 (Everton)	12
Stuart, G. C. 1990 (Chelsea)	5
Stuart, J. C. 1996 (Charlton Ath)	4
Sturridge, D. A. 2010 (Chelsea)	15
Suckling, P. 1986 (Coventry C, Manchester C, Crystal Palace)	10

Summerbee, N. J. 1993 (Swindon T)	3
Sunderland, A. 1977 (Wolverhampton W)	1
Surman, A. R. E. 2008 (Southampton)	4
Sutch, D. 1992 (Norwich C)	4
Sutton, C. R. 1993 (Norwich C)	13
Swift, J. D. 2015 (Chelsea)	**6**
Swindlehurst, D. 1977 (Crystal Palace)	1
Talbot, B. 1977 (Ipswich T)	1
Targett, M. R. 2015 (Southampton)	11
Taylor, A. D. 2007 (Middlesbrough)	13
Taylor, M. 2001 (Blackburn R)	1
Taylor, M. S. 2003 (Portsmouth)	3
Taylor, R. A. 2006 (Wigan Ath)	4
Taylor, S. J. 2002 (Arsenal)	3
Taylor, S. V. 2004 (Newcastle U)	29
Terry, J. G. 2001 (Chelsea)	9
Thatcher, B. D. 1996 (Millwall, Wimbledon)	4
Thelwell, A. A. 2001 (Tottenham H)	1
Thirlwell, P. 2001 (Sunderland)	1
Thomas, D. 1981 (Coventry C, Tottenham H)	7
Thomas, J. W. 2006 (Charlton Ath)	2
Thomas, M. 1986 (Luton T)	3
Thomas, M. L. 1988 (Arsenal)	12
Thomas, R. E. 1990 (Watford)	1
Thompson, A. 1995 (Bolton W)	2
Thompson, D. A. 1997 (Liverpool)	7
Thompson, G. L. 1981 (Coventry C)	6
Thorn, A. 1988 (Wimbledon)	5
Thornley, B. L. 1996 (Manchester U)	3
Thorpe, T. J. 2013 (Manchester U)	1
Tiler, C. 1990 (Barnsley, Nottingham F)	13
Tomkins, J. O. C. 2009 (West Ham U)	10
Tonge, M. W. E. 2004 (Sheffield U)	2
Townsend, A. D. 2012 (Tottenham H)	3
Trippier, K. J. 2011 (Manchester C)	2
Unsworth, D. G. 1995 (Everton)	6
Upson, M. J. 1999 (Arsenal)	11
Vassell, D. 1999 (Aston Villa)	11
Vaughan, J. O. 2007 (Everton)	4
Venison, B. 1983 (Sunderland)	10
Vernazza, P. A. P. 2001 (Arsenal, Watford)	2
Vinnicombe, C. 1991 (Rangers)	12
Waddle, C. R. 1985 (Newcastle U)	1
Waghorn, M. T. 2012 (Leicester C)	5
Walcott, T. J. 2007 (Arsenal)	21
Wallace, D. L. 1983 (Southampton)	14
Wallace, Ray 1989 (Southampton)	4
Wallace, Rod 1989 (Southampton)	11
Walker, D. 1985 (Nottingham F)	7
Walker, I. M. 1991 (Tottenham H)	9
Walker, K. 2010 (Tottenham H)	7

Walsh, G. 1988 (Manchester U)	2
Walsh, P. A. 1983 (Luton T)	4
Walters, K. 1984 (Aston Villa)	9
Ward, P. 1978 (Brighton & HA)	2
Ward-Prowse, J. M. E. 2013 (Southampton)	**23**
Warhurst, P. 1991 (Oldham Ath, Sheffield W)	8
Watmore, D. I. 2015 (Sunderland)	**8**
Watson, B. 2007 (Crystal Palace)	1
Watson, D. 1984 (Norwich C)	7
Watson, D. N. 1994 (Barnsley)	5
Watson, G. 1991 (Sheffield W)	2
Watson, S. C. 1993 (Newcastle U)	12
Weaver, N. J. 2000 (Manchester C)	10
Webb, N. J. 1985 (Portsmouth, Nottingham F)	3
Welbeck, D. 2009 (Manchester U)	14
Welsh, J. J. 2004 (Liverpool, Hull C)	8
Wheater, D. J. 2008 (Middlesbrough)	11
Whelan, P. J. 1993 (Ipswich T)	3
Whelan, N. 1995 (Leeds U)	2
Whittingham, P. 2004 (Aston Villa, Cardiff C)	17
White, D. 1988 (Manchester C)	6
Whyte, C. 1982 (Arsenal)	4
Wickham, C. N. R. 2011 (Ipswich T, Sunderland)	17
Wicks, S. 1982 (QPR)	1
Wilkins, R. C. 1977 (Chelsea)	1
Wilkinson, P. 1985 (Grimsby T, Everton)	4
Williams, D. 1998 (Sunderland)	2
Williams, P. 1989 (Charlton Ath)	6
Williams, P. D. 1991 (Derby Co)	6
Williams, S. C. 1977 (Southampton)	14
Wilshere, J. A. 2010 (Arsenal)	7
Wilson, C. E. G. 2014 (Bournemouth)	1
Wilson, J. A. 2015 (Manchester U)	**1**
Wilson, M. A. 2001 (Manchester U, Middlesbrough)	6
Winterburn, N. 1986 (Wimbledon)	1
Wisdom, A. 2012 (Liverpool)	10
Wise, D. F. 1988 (Wimbledon)	1
Woodcock, A. S. 1978 (Nottingham F)	2
Woodgate, J. S. 2000 (Leeds U)	1
Woodhouse, C. 1999 (Sheffield U)	4
Woodrow, C. 2014 (Fulham)	**7**
Woods, C. C. E. 1979 (Nottingham F, QPR, Norwich C)	6
Wright, A. G. 1993 (Blackburn R)	2
Wright, M. 1983 (Southampton)	4
Wright, R. I. 1997 (Ipswich T)	15
Wright, S. J. 2001 (Liverpool)	10
Wright, W. 1979 (Everton)	6
Wright-Phillips, S. C. 2002 (Manchester C)	6
Yates, D. 1989 (Notts Co)	5
Young, A. S. 2007 (Watford, Aston Villa)	10
Young, L. P. 1999 (Tottenham H, Charlton Ath)	12
Zaha, D. W. A. 2012 (Crystal Palace, Manchester U)	13
Zamora, R. L. 2002 (Brighton & HA)	6

NORTHERN IRELAND

Allen, C. 2009 (Lisburn Distillery)	1
Armstrong, D. T. 2007 (Hearts)	1
Bagnall, L. 2011 (Sunderland)	1
Bailie, N. 1990 (Linfield)	2
Baird, C. P. 2002 (Southampton)	6
Ball, D. 2013 (Tottenham H)	2
Ball, M. 2011 (Norwich C)	5
Beatty, S. 1990 (Chelsea, Linfield)	2
Black, J. 2003 (Tottenham H)	1
Black, K. T. 1990 (Luton T)	1
Black, R. Z. 2002 (Morecambe)	1
Blackledge, G. 1978 (Portadown)	1
Blake, R. G. 2011 (Brentford)	2
Blayney, A. 2003 (Southampton)	4
Boyce, L. 2010 (Cliftonville, Werder Bremen)	8
Boyle, W. S. 1998 (Leeds U)	7
Braniff, K. R. 2002 (Millwall)	11
Breeze, J. 2011 (Wigan Ath)	4
Brennan, C. 2013 (Kilmarnock)	**13**
Brobbel, R. 2013 (Middlesbrough)	9
Brotherston, N. 1978 (Blackburn R)	1
Browne, G. 2003 (Manchester C)	5

Brunt, C. 2005 (Sheffield W)	2
Bryan, M. A. 2010 (Watford)	4
Buchanan, D. T. H. 2006 (Bury)	15
Buchanan, W. B. 2002 (Bolton W, Lisburn Distillery)	5
Burns, A. 2014 (Linfield)	1
Burns, L. 1998 (Port Vale)	13
Callaghan, A. 2006 (Limavady U, Ballymena U, Derry C)	15
Campbell, S. 2003 (Ballymena U)	1
Camps, C. 2015 (Rochdale)	**1**
Capaldi, A. C. 2002 (Birmingham C, Plymouth Arg)	14
Carlisle, W. T. 2000 (Crystal Palace)	9
Carroll, R. E. 1998 (Wigan Ath)	11
Carson, J. G. 2011 (Ipswich T, York C)	12
Carson, S. 2000 (Rangers, Dundee U)	2
Carson, T. 2007 (Sunderland)	15
Carvill, M. D. 2008 (Wrexham, Linfield)	8
Casement, C. 2007 (Ipswich T, Dundee)	18
Cathcart, C. 2007 (Manchester U)	15
Catney, R. 2007 (Lisburn Distillery)	1
Chapman, A. 2008 (Sheffield U, Oxford U)	7
Clarke, L. 2003 (Peterborough U)	4

Clarke, R. 2006 (Newry C)   7
Clarke, R. D. J. 1999 (Portadown)   5
Clingan, S. G. 2003 (Wolverhampton W, Nottingham F)   11
Close, B. 2002 (Middlesbrough)   10
Clucas, M. S. 2011 (Preston NE, Bristol R)   11
Clyde, M. G. 2002 (Wolverhampton W)   5
Colligan, L. 2009 (Ballymena U)   1
Conlan, L. 2013 (Burnley)   8
Connell, T. E. 1978 (Coleraine)   1
Cooper, J. 2015 (Glenavon)   2
Coote, A. 1998 (Norwich C)   12
Convery, J. 2000 (Celtic)   4

Dallas, S. 2012 (Crusaders, Brentford)   2
Davey, H. 2004 (UCD)   3
Davis, S. 2004 (Aston Villa)   3
Devine, D. 1994 (Omagh T)   1
Devine, D. G. 2011 (Preston NE)   2
Devine, J. 1990 (Glentoran)   1
Devlin, C. 2011 (Manchester U, unattached, Cliftonville)   11
Dickson, H. 2002 (Wigan Ath)   1
Doherty, J. E. 2014 (Watford)   4
Doherty, M. 2007 (Hearts)   2
Dolan, J. 2000 (Millwall)   6
Donaghy, M. M. 1978 (Larne)   1
Donnelly, L. F. P. 2012 (Fulham)   10
Donnelly, M. 2007 (Sheffield U, Crusaders)   5
Donnelly, R. 2013 (Swansea C)   1
Dowie, I. 1990 (Luton T)   1
Drummond, W. 2011 (Rangers)   2
Dudgeon, J. P. 2010 (Manchester U)   4
Duff, S. 2003 (Cheltenham T)   1
Duffy, M. 2014 (Derry C, Celtic)   7
Duffy, S. P. M. 2010 (Everton)   3
Dummigan, C. 2014 (Burnley)   7

Elliott, S. 1999 (Glentoran)   3
Ervin, J. 2005 (Linfield)   2
Evans, C. J. 2009 (Manchester U)   10
Evans, J. 2006 (Manchester U)   3

Feeney, L. 1998 (Linfield, Rangers)   8
Feeney, W. 2002 (Bournemouth)   8
Ferguson, M. 2000 (Glentoran)   2
Ferguson, S. 2009 (Newcastle U)   11
Fitzgerald, D. 1998 (Rangers)   4
Flanagan, T. M. 2012 (Milton Keynes D)   1
Flynn, J. J. 2009 (Blackburn R, Ross Co)   11
Fordyce, D. T. 2007 (Portsmouth, Glentoran)   12
Friars, E. C. 2005 (Notts Co)   7
Friars, S. M. 1998 (Liverpool, Ipswich T)   21

Garrett, R. 2007 (Stoke C, Linfield)   14
Gault, M. 2005 (Linfield)   2
Gibb, S. 2009 (Falkirk, Drogheda U)   2
Gilfillan, B. J. 2005 (Gretna, Peterhead)   9
Gillespie, K. R. 1994 (Manchester U)   1
Glendinning, M. 1994 (Bangor)   1
Glendinning, R. 2012 (Linfield)   3
Gorman, D. A. 2015 (Stevenage)   2
Gorman, R. J. 2012 (Wolverhampton W, Leyton Orient)   4
Graham, G. L. 1999 (Crystal Palace)   5
Graham, R. S. 1999 (QPR)   15
Gray, J. P. 2012 (Accrington S)   11
Gray, P. 1990 (Luton T)   1
Griffin, D. J. 1998 (St Johnstone)   10
Grigg, W. D. 2011 (Walsall)   10

Hamilton, G. 2000 (Blackburn R, Portadown)   12
Hamilton, W. R. 1978 (Linfield)   1
Hanley, N. 2011 (Linfield)   1
Harkin, M. P. 2000 (Wycombe W)   9
Harney, J. J. 2014 (West Ham U)   1
Harvey, J. 1978 (Arsenal)   1
Hawe, S. 2001 (Blackburn R)   2
Hayes, T. 1978 (Luton T)   1
Hazley, M. 2007 (Stoke C)   3
Healy, D. J. 1999 (Manchester U)   8
Hegarty, C. 2011 (Rangers)   7
Herron, C. J. 2003 (QPR)   2
Higgins, R. 2006 (Derry C)   1

Hodson, L. J. S. 2010 (Watford)   10
Holmes, S. 2000 (Manchester C, Wrexham)   13
Howland, D. 2007 (Birmingham C)   4
Hughes, J. 2006 (Lincoln C)   7
Hughes, M. A. 2003 (Tottenham H, Oldham Ath)   12
Hughes, M. E. 1990 (Manchester C)   1
Hunter, M. 2002 (Glentoran)   1

Ingham, M. G. 2001 (Sunderland)   4

Jarvis, D. 2010 (Aberdeen)   2
Johns, C. 2014 (Southampton)   1
Johnson, D. M. 1998 (Blackburn R)   11
Johnson, R. 2015 (Stevenage)   3
Johnston, B. 1978 (Cliftonville)   1
Julian, A. A. 2005 (Brentford)   1

Kane, A. M. 2008 (Blackburn R)   5
Kane, M. 2012 (Glentoran)   1
Kee, B. R. 2010 (Leicester C, Torquay U, Burton Alb)   10
Kee, P. V. 1990 (Oxford U)   1
Kelly, D. 2000 (Derry C)   11
Kelly, N. 1990 (Oldham Ath)   1
Kennedy, M. C. P. 2015 (Charlton Ath)   5
Kirk, A. R. 1999 (Hearts)   9
Knowles, J. 2012 (Blackburn R)   2

Lafferty, D. 2009 (Celtic)   6
Lafferty, K. 2006 (Burnley)   2
Lavery, C. 2011 (Ipswich T, Sheffield W)   7
Lawrie, J. 2009 (Port Vale, AFC Telford U)   9
Lennon, N. F. 1990 (Manchester C, Crewe Alex)   2
Lester, C. 2013 (Bolton W)   1
Lindsay, K. 2006 (Larne)   1
Little, A. 2009 (Rangers)   6
Lowry, P. 2009 (Institute, Linfield)   6
Lund, M. 2011 (Stoke C)   6
Lyttle, G. 1998 (Celtic, Peterborough U)   8

McAlinden, L. J. 2012 (Wolverhampton W)   3
McAllister, M. 2007 (Dungannon Swifts)   4
McArdle, R. A. 2006 (Sheffield W, Rochdale)   19
McAreavey, P. 2000 (Swindon T)   7
McBride, J. 1994 (Glentoran)   1
McCaffrey, D. 2006 (Hibernian)   8
McCallion, E. 1998 (Coleraine)   1
McCann, G. S. 2000 (West Ham U)   11
McCann, P. 2003 (Portadown)   1
McCann, R. 2002 (Rangers, Linfield)   2
McCartan, S. V. 2013 (Accrington S)   9
McCartney, G. 2001 (Sunderland)   5
McCashin, S. 2011 (Jerez Industrial, unattached)   2
McChrystal, M. 2005 (Derry C)   9
McClean, J. 2010 (Derry C)   3
McClure, M. 2012 (Wycombe W)   1
McCourt, P. J. 2002 (Rochdale, Derry C)   8
McCoy, R. K. 1990 (Coleraine)   1
McCreery, D. 1978 (Manchester U)   1
McCullough, L. 2013 (Doncaster R)   8
McDaid, R. 2015 (Leeds U)   5
McDonagh, J. 2015 (Sheffield U)   1
McEleney, S. 2012 (Derry C)   2
McElroy, P. 2013 (Hull C)   1
McEvilly, L. R. 2003 (Rochdale)   9
McFlynn, T. M. 2000 (QPR, Woking, Margate)   19
McGeehan, C. 2013 (Norwich C)   3
McGibbon, P. C. G. 1994 (Manchester U)   7
McGivern, R. 2010 (Manchester C)   6
McGlinchey, B. 1998 (Manchester C, Port Vale, Gillingham)   14
McGovern, M. 2005 (Celtic)   10
McGowan, M. V. 2006 (Clyde)   2
McGurk, A. 2010 (Aston Villa)   1
McIlroy, T. 1994 (Linfield)   1
McKay, W. 2009 (Leicester C, Northampton T)   7
McKenna, K. 2007 (Tottenham H)   6
McKeown, R. 2012 (Kilmarnock)   12
McKnight, D. 2015 (Shrewsbury T)   4
McKnight, P. 1998 (Rangers)   3
McLaughlin, C. G. 2010 (Preston NE, Fleetwood T)   7
McLaughlin, P. 2010 (Newcastle U, York C)   10
McLaughlin, R. 2012 (Liverpool)   5

McLean, B. S. 2006 (Rangers)	1
McLean, J. 2009 (Derry C)	4
McLellan, M. 2012 (Preston NE)	1
McMahon, G. J. 2002 (Tottenham H)	1
McMenamin, L. A. 2009 (Sheffield W)	4
McNair, P. J. C. 2014 (Manchester U)	2
McNally, P. 2013 (Celtic)	1
McQuilken, J. 2009 (Tescoma Zlin)	1
McQuoid, J. J. B. 2009 (Bournemouth)	8
McVeigh, A. 2002 (Ayr U)	1
McVeigh, P. M. 1998 (Tottenham H)	11
McVey, K. 2006 (Coleraine)	8
Magee, J. 1994 (Bangor)	1
Magee, J. 2009 (Lisburn Distillery)	1
Magennis, J. B. D. 2010 (Cardiff C, Aberdeen)	16
Magilton, J. 1990 (Liverpool)	1
Magnay, C. 2010 (Chelsea)	1
Maloney, L. 2015 (Middlesbrough)	**6**
Matthews, N. P. 1990 (Blackpool)	1
Meenan, D. 2007 (Finn Harps, Monaghan U)	3
Melaugh, G. M. 2002 (Aston Villa, Glentoran)	11
Millar, K. S. 2011 (Oldham Ath, Linfield)	11
Millar, W. P. 1990 (Port Vale)	1
Miskelly, D. T. 2000 (Oldham Ath)	10
Mitchell, A. 2012 (Rangers)	3
Moreland, V. 1978 (Glentoran)	1
Morgan, D. 2012 (Nottingham F)	4
Morgan, M. P. T. 1999 (Preston NE)	1
Morris, E. J. 2002 (WBA, Glentoran)	8
Morrison, O. 2001 (Sheffield W, Sheffield U)	1
Morrow, A. 2001 (Northampton T)	1
Morrow, S. 2005 (Hibernian)	4
Mulgrew, J. 2007 (Linfield)	10
Mulryne, P. P. 1999 (Manchester U, Norwich C)	5
Murray, W. 1978 (Linfield)	1
Murtagh, C. 2005 (Hearts)	1
Nicholl, J. M. 1978 (Manchester U)	1
Nixon, C. 2000 (Glentoran)	1
Nolan, L. J. 2014 (Crewe Alex)	1
Norwood, O. J. 2010 (Manchester U)	11
O'Connor, M. J. 2008 (Crewe Alex)	3
O'Hara, G. 1994 (Leeds U)	1
O'Kane, E. 2009 (Everton, Torquay U)	4
O'Neill, J. P. 1978 (Leicester C)	1
O'Neill, M. A. M. 1994 (Hibernian)	1
O'Neill, S. 2009 (Ballymena U)	4

Paterson, M. A. 2007 (Stoke C)	2
Paterson, D. J. 1994 (Crystal Palace)	1
Quinn, S. J. 1994 (Blackpool)	1
Ramsey, C. 2011 (Portadown)	3
Ramsey, K. 2006 (Institute)	1
Reid, J. T. 2013 (Exeter C)	2
Robinson, S. 1994 (Tottenham H)	1
Scullion, D. 2006 (Dungannon Swifts)	8
Sendles-White J. 2013 (QPR, Hamilton A)	**10**
Sharpe, R. 2013 (Derby Co, Notts Co)	**6**
Shiels, D. 2005 (Hibernian)	6
Shields, S. P. 2013 (Dagenham & R)	2
Shroot, R. 2009 (Harrow B, Birmingham C)	4
Simms, G. 2001 (Hartlepool U)	14
Singleton, J. 2015 (Glenavon)	**2**
Skates, G. 2000 (Blackburn R)	4
Sloan, T. 1978 (Ballymena U)	1
Smylie, D. 2006 (Newcastle U, Livingston)	6
Stewart, J. 2015 (Swindon T)	**2**
Stewart, S. 2009 (Aberdeen)	1
Stewart, T. 2006 (Wolverhampton W, Linfield)	19
Taylor, J. 2007 (Hearts, Glentoran)	10
Taylor, M. S. 1998 (Fulham)	1
Teggart, N. 2005 (Sunderland)	2
Tempest, G. 2013 (Notts Co)	6
Thompson, A. L. 2011 (Watford)	11
Thompson, P. 2006 (Linfield)	4
Toner, C. 2000 (Tottenham H, Leyton Orient)	17
Tuffey, J. 2007 (Partick Thistle)	13
Turner, C. 2007 (Sligo R, Bohemians)	12
Ward, J. J. 2006 (Aston Villa, Chesterfield)	7
Ward, M. 2006 (Dungannon Swifts)	1
Ward, S. 2005 (Glentoran)	10
Waterman, D. G. 1998 (Portsmouth)	14
Waterworth, A. 2008 (Lisburn Distillery, Hamilton A)	7
Webb, S. M. 2004 (Ross Co, St Johnstone, Ross Co)	6
Weir, R. J. 2009 (Sunderland)	8
Wells, D. P. 1999 (Barry T)	1
Whitley, J. 1998 (Manchester C)	17
Whyte, G. 2015 (Crusaders)	**3**
Willis, P. 2006 (Liverpool)	1
Winchester, C. 2011 (Oldham Ath)	13
Winchester, J. 2013 (Kilmarnock)	1

SCOTLAND

Adam, C. G. 2006 (Rangers)	5
Adam, G. 2011 (Rangers)	6
Adams, J. 2007 (Kilmarnock)	1
Aitken, R. 1977 (Celtic)	16
Albiston, A. 1977 (Manchester U)	5
Alexander, N. 1997 (Stenhousemuir, Livingston)	10
Allan, S. 2012 (WBA)	10
Anderson, I. 1997 (Dundee, Toulouse)	15
Anderson, R. 1997 (Aberdeen)	15
Andrews, M. 2011 (East Stirlingshire)	1
Anthony, M. 1997 (Celtic)	3
Archdeacon, O. 1987 (Celtic)	1
Archer, J. G. 2012 (Tottenham H)	14
Archibald, A. 1998 (Partick Thistle)	5
Archibald, S. 1980 (Aberdeen, Tottenham H)	5
Arfield, S. 2008 (Falkirk, Huddersfield T)	17
Armstrong, S. 2011 (Dundee U)	20
Bagen, D. 1997 (Kilmarnock)	4
Bain, K. 1993 (Dundee)	4
Baker, M. 1993 (St Mirren)	10
Baltacha, S. S. 2000 (St Mirren)	3
Bannan, B. 2009 (Aston Villa)	10
Bannigan, S. 2013 (Partick Thistle)	3
Bannon, E. J. 1979 (Hearts, Chelsea, Dundee U)	7
Barclay, J. 2011 (Falkirk)	1
Beattie, C. 2004 (Celtic)	7
Beattie, J. 1992 (St Mirren)	4
Beaumont, D. 1985 (Dundee U)	1
Bell, D. 1981 (Aberdeen)	2

Bernard, P. R. J. 1992 (Oldham Ath)	15
Berra, C. 2005 (Hearts)	6
Bett, J. 1981 (Rangers)	7
Black, E. 1983 (Aberdeen)	8
Blair, A. 1980 (Coventry C, Aston Villa)	5
Bollan, G. 1992 (Dundee U, Rangers)	17
Bonar, P. 1997 (Raith R)	4
Booth, C. 2011 (Hibernian)	4
Booth, S. 1991 (Aberdeen)	14
Bowes, M. J. 1992 (Dunfermline Ath)	1
Bowman, D. 1985 (Hearts)	1
Boyack, S. 1997 (Rangers)	1
Boyd, K. 2003 (Kilmarnock)	8
Boyd, T. 1987 (Motherwell)	5
Brazil, A. 1978 (Hibernian)	1
Brazil, A. 1979 (Ipswich T)	8
Brebner, G. I. 1997 (Manchester U, Reading, Hibernian)	18
Brighton, T. 2005 (Rangers, Clyde)	7
Broadfoot, K. 2005 (St Mirren)	5
Brough, J. 1981 (Hearts)	1
Brown, A. H. 2004 (Hibernian)	1
Brown, S. 2005 (Hibernian)	10
Browne, P. 1997 (Raith R)	1
Bryson, C. 2006 (Clyde)	1
Buchan, J. 1997 (Aberdeen)	13
Burchill, M. J. 1998 (Celtic)	15
Burke, A. 1997 (Kilmarnock)	4
Burke, C. 2004 (Rangers)	3
Burley, C. W. 1992 (Chelsea)	7

Hetherston, B. 1997 (St Mirren)	1
Hewitt, J. 1982 (Aberdeen)	6
Hogg, G. 1984 (Manchester U)	4
Holt, J. 2012 (Hearts)	7
Hood, G. 1993 (Ayr U)	3
Horn, R. 1997 (Hearts)	6
Howie, S. 1993 (Cowdenbeath)	5
Hughes, R. D. 1999 (Bournemouth)	9
Hughes, S. 2002 (Rangers)	12
Hunter, G. 1987 (Hibernian)	3
Hunter, P. 1989 (East Fife)	3
Hutton, A. 2004 (Rangers)	7
Hutton, K. 2011 (Rangers)	1
Hyam, D. 2014 (Reading)	**4**
Inman, B. 2011 (Newcastle U)	2
Irvine, G. 2006 (Celtic)	2
Jack, R. 2012 (Aberdeen)	19
James, K. F. 1997 (Falkirk)	1
Jardine, I. 1979 (Kilmarnock)	1
Jess, E. 1990 (Aberdeen)	14
Johnson, G. I. 1992 (Dundee U)	6
Johnston, A. 1994 (Hearts)	3
Johnston, F. 1993 (Falkirk)	1
Johnston, M. 1984 (Partick Thistle, Watford)	3
Jordan, A. J. 2000 (Bristol C)	3
Jupp, D. A. 1995 (Fulham)	9
Kelly, L. 2012 (Kilmarnock)	9
Kelly, S. 2014 (St Mirren)	1
Kennedy, J. 2003 (Celtic)	15
Kennedy, M. 2012 (Kilmarnock)	1
Kenneth, G. 2008 (Dundee U)	8
Kerr, B. 2003 (Newcastle U)	14
Kerr, F. 2012 (Birmingham C)	3
Kerr, M. 2001 (Kilmarnock)	1
Kerr, S. 1993 (Celtic)	10
Kettings, C. D. 2012 (Blackpool)	3
King, A. 2014 (Swansea C)	1
King, C. M. 2014 (Norwich C)	1
King, W. 2015 (Hearts)	**6**
Kingsley, S. 2015 (Swansea C)	**5**
Kinniburgh, W. D. 2004 (Motherwell)	3
Kirkwood, D. 1990 (Hearts)	1
Kyle, K. 2001 (Sunderland)	12
Lambert, P. 1991 (St Mirren)	11
Langfield, J. 2000 (Dundee)	2
Lappin, S. 2004 (St Mirren)	10
Lauchlan, J. 1998 (Kilmarnock)	11
Lavety, B. 1993 (St Mirren)	9
Lavin, G. 1993 (Watford)	7
Lawson, P. 2004 (Celtic)	10
Leighton, J. 1982 (Aberdeen)	1
Lennon, S. 2008 (Rangers)	6
Levein, C. 1985 (Hearts)	2
Leven, P. 2005 (Kilmarnock)	2
Liddell, A. M. 1994 (Barnsley)	12
Lindsey, J. 1979 (Motherwell)	1
Locke, G. 1994 (Hearts)	10
Love, D. 2015 (Manchester U)	**5**
Love, G. 1995 (Hibernian)	1
Loy, R. 2009 (Dunfermline Ath, Rangers)	5
Lynch, S. 2003 (Celtic, Preston NE)	13
McAllister, G. 1990 (Leicester C)	1
McAllister, R. 2008 (Inverness CT)	2
McAlpine, H. 1983 (Dundee U)	5
McAnespie, K. 1998 (St Johnstone)	4
McArthur, J. 2008 (Hamilton A)	2
McAuley, S. 1993 (St Johnstone)	1
McAvennie, F. 1982 (St Mirren)	5
McBride, J. 1981 (Everton)	1
McBride, J. P. 1998 (Celtic)	2
McBurnie, O. 2015 (Swansea C)	**3**
McCabe, R. 2012 (Rangers, Sheffield W)	3
McCall, A. S. M. 1988 (Bradford C, Everton)	2
McCann, K. 2008 (Hibernian)	4
McCann, N. 1994 (Dundee)	9
McClair, B. 1984 (Celtic)	8
McCluskey, G. 1979 (Celtic)	6

McCluskey, S. 1997 (St Johnstone)	14
McCoist, A. 1984 (Rangers)	1
McConnell, I. 1997 (Clyde)	1
McCormack, D. 2008 (Hibernian)	1
McCormack, R. 2006 (Rangers, Motherwell, Cardiff C)	13
McCracken, D. 2002 (Dundee U)	5
McCulloch, A. 1981 (Kilmarnock)	1
McCulloch, I. 1982 (Notts Co)	2
McCulloch, L. 1997 (Motherwell)	14
McCunnie, J. 2001 (Dundee U, Ross Co, Dunfermline Ath)	20
MacDonald, A. 2011 (Burnley)	6
MacDonald, J. 1980 (Rangers)	8
MacDonald, J. 2007 (Hearts)	11
McDonald, C. 1995 (Falkirk)	5
McDonald, K. 2008 (Dundee, Burnley)	14
McEwan, C. 1997 (Clyde, Raith R)	17
McEwan, D. 2003 (Livingston)	2
McFadden, J. 2003 (Motherwell)	7
McFadzean C. 2015 (Sheffield U)	**3**
McFarlane, D. 1997 (Hamilton A)	3
McGarry, S. 1997 (St Mirren)	3
McGarvey, F. P. 1977 (St Mirren, Celtic)	3
McGarvey, S. 1982 (Manchester U)	4
McGeough, D. 2012 (Celtic)	10
McGhee, J. 2013 (Hearts)	**16**
McGhee, M. 1981 (Aberdeen)	1
McGinn, J. 2014 (St Mirren, Hibernian)	**9**
McGinn, S. 2009 (St Mirren, Watford)	8
McGinnis, G. 1985 (Dundee U)	1
McGlinchey, M. R. 2007 (Celtic)	1
McGregor, A. 2003 (Rangers)	6
McGregor, C. W. 2013 (Celtic)	5
McGrillen, P. 1994 (Motherwell)	2
McGuire, D. 2002 (Aberdeen)	2
McHattie, K. 2012 (Hearts)	6
McInally, J. 1989 (Dundee U)	1
McKay, B. 2012 (Rangers)	**4**
McKay, B. 2013 (Hearts)	1
McKean, K. 2011 (St Mirren)	1
McKenzie, R. 2013 (Kilmarnock)	4
McKenzie, R. 1997 (Hearts)	2
McKimmie, S. 1985 (Aberdeen)	3
McKinlay, T. 1984 (Dundee)	6
McKinlay, W. 1989 (Dundee U)	6
McKinnon, R. 1991 (Dundee U)	6
McLaren, A, 1989 (Hearts)	11
McLaren, A. 1993 (Dundee U)	4
McLaughlin, B. 1995 (Celtic)	8
McLaughlin, J. 1981 (Morton)	10
McLean, E. 2008 (Dundee U, St Johnstone)	2
McLean, S. 2003 (Rangers)	4
McLeish, A. 1978 (Aberdeen)	6
McLean, K. 2012 (St Mirren)	11
MacLeod, A. 1979 (Hibernian)	3
McLeod, J. 1989 (Dundee U)	2
MacLeod, L. 2012 (Rangers)	8
MacLeod, M. 1979 (Dumbarton, Celtic)	5
McManus, D. J. 2014 (Aberdeen, Fleetwood T)	**4**
McManus, T. 2001 (Hibernian)	14
McMillan, S. 1997 (Motherwell)	4
McNab, N. 1978 (Tottenham H)	1
McNally, M. 1991 (Celtic)	2
McNamara, J. 1994 (Dunfermline Ath, Celtic)	12
McNaughton, K. 2002 (Aberdeen)	1
McNeil, A. 2007 (Hibernian)	1
McNichol, J. 1979 (Brentford)	7
McNiven, D. 1977 (Leeds U)	3
McNiven, S. A. 1996 (Oldham Ath)	1
McParland, A. 2003 (Celtic)	1
McPhee, S. 2002 (Port Vale)	1
McPherson, D. 1984 (Rangers, Hearts)	4
McQuilken, J. 1993 (Celtic)	2
McStay, P. 1983 (Celtic)	5
McWhirter, N. 1991 (St Mirren)	1
Mackay-Steven, G. 2012 (Dundee U)	3
Maguire, C. 2009 (Aberdeen)	12
Main, A. 1988 (Dundee U)	3
Malcolm, R. 2001 (Rangers)	1
Maloney, S. 2002 (Celtic)	21
Malpas, M. 1983 (Dundee U)	8
Marr, B. 2011 (Ross Co)	1

Marshall, D. J. 2004 (Celtic)	10
Marshall, S. R. 1995 (Arsenal)	5
Martin, A. 2009 (Leeds U, Ayr U)	12
Mason, G. R. 1999 (Manchester C, Dunfermline Ath)	2
Mathieson, D. 1997 (Queen of the South)	3
May, E. 1989 (Hibernian)	2
May, S. 2013 (St Johnstone, Sheffield W)	8
Meldrum, C. 1996 (Kilmarnock)	6
Melrose, J. 1977 (Partick Thistle)	8
Millar, M, 2009 (Celtic)	1
Miller, C. 1995 (Rangers)	8
Miller, J. 1987 (Aberdeen, Celtic)	7
Miller, K. 2000 (Hibernian, Rangers)	7
Miller, W. 1991 (Hibernian)	7
Miller, W. F. 1978 (Aberdeen)	2
Milne, K. 2000 (Hearts)	1
Milne, R. 1982 (Dundee U)	3
Mitchell, C. 2008 (Falkirk)	7
Money, I. C. 1987 (St Mirren)	3
Montgomery, N. A. 2003 (Sheffield U)	2
Morrison, S. A. 2004 (Aberdeen, Dunfermline Ath)	12
Muir, L. 1977 (Hibernian)	1
Mulgrew, C. P. 2006 (Celtic, Wolverhampton W, Aberdeen)	14
Murphy J. 2009 (Motherwell)	13
Murray, H. 2000 (St Mirren)	3
Murray, I. 2001 (Hibernian)	15
Murray, N. 1993 (Rangers)	16
Murray, R. 1993 (Bournemouth)	1
Murray, S. 2004 (Kilmarnock)	2
Narey, D. 1977 (Dundee U)	4
Naismith, J. 2014 (St Mirren)	1
Naismith, S. J. 2006 (Kilmarnock, Rangers)	15
Naysmith, G. A. 1997 (Hearts)	22
Neilson, R. 2000 (Hearts)	1
Ness, J, 2011 (Rangers)	2
Nevin, P. 1985 (Chelsea)	5
Nicholas, C. 1981 (Celtic, Arsenal)	6
Nicholson, B. 1999 (Rangers)	7
Nicholson, S. 2015 (Hearts)	**6**
Nicol, S. 1981 (Ayr U, Liverpool)	14
Nisbet, S. 1989 (Rangers)	5
Noble, D. J. 2003 (West Ham U)	2
Notman, A. M. 1999 (Manchester U)	10
O'Brien, B. 1999 (Blackburn R, Livingston)	6
O'Connor, G. 2003 (Hibernian)	8
O'Donnell, P. 1992 (Motherwell)	8
O'Donnell, S. 2013 (Partick Thistle)	1
O'Halloran, M. 2012 (Bolton W)	1
O'Hara, M. 2015 (Kilmarnock)	1
O'Leary, R. 2008 (Kilmarnock)	2
O'Neil, B. 1992 (Celtic)	7
O'Neil, J. 1991 (Dundee U)	1
O'Neill, M. 1995 (Clyde)	6
Orr, N. 1978 (Morton)	7
Palmer, L. J. 2011 (Sheffield W)	8
Park, C. 2012 (Middlesbrough)	1
Parker, K. 2001 (St Johnstone)	1
Parlane, D. 1977 (Rangers)	1
Paterson, C. 1981 (Hibernian)	2
Paterson, C. 2012 (Hearts)	**12**
Paterson, J. 1997 (Dundee U)	9
Pawlett, P. 2012 (Aberdeen)	7
Payne, G. 1978 (Dundee U)	3
Peacock, L. A. 1997 (Carlisle U)	1
Pearce, A. J. 2008 (Reading)	2
Pearson, S. P. 2003 (Motherwell)	8
Perry, R. 2010 (Rangers, Falkirk, Rangers)	16
Polworth, L. 2016 (Inverness CT)	**1**
Pressley, S. J. 1993 (Rangers, Coventry C, Dundee U)	26
Provan, D. 1977 (Kilmarnock)	1
Prunty, B. 2004 (Aberdeen)	6
Quinn, P. C. 2004 (Motherwell)	3
Quinn, R. 2006 (Celtic)	9
Rae, A. 1991 (Millwall)	8
Rae, G. 1999 (Dundee)	6
Redford, I. 1981 (Rangers)	6

Reid, B. 1991 (Rangers)	4
Reid, C. 1993 (Hibernian)	3
Reid, M. 1982 (Celtic)	2
Reid, R. 1977 (St Mirren)	3
Reilly, A. 2004 (Wycombe W)	1
Renicks, S. 1997 (Hamilton A)	1
Reynolds, M. 2007 (Motherwell)	9
Rhodes, J. L. 2011 (Huddersfield T)	8
Rice, B. 1985 (Hibernian)	1
Richardson, L. 1980 (St Mirren)	2
Ridgers, M. 2012 (Hearts)	5
Riordan, D. G. 2004 (Hibernian)	5
Ritchie, A. 1980 (Morton)	1
Ritchie, P. S. 1996 (Hearts)	7
Robertson, A. 1991 (Rangers)	1
Robertson, A. 2013 (Dundee U, Hull C)	**4**
Robertson, C. 1977 (Rangers)	1
Robertson, C. 2012 (Aberdeen)	10
Robertson, D. 1987 (Aberdeen)	7
Robertson, D. 2007 (Dundee U)	4
Robertson, G. A. 2004 (Nottingham F, Rotherham U)	15
Robertson, H. 1994 (Aberdeen)	2
Robertson, J. 1985 (Hearts)	2
Robertson, L. 1993 (Rangers)	3
Robertson, S. 1998 (St Johnstone)	2
Roddie, A. 1992 (Aberdeen)	5
Ross, G. 2007 (Dunfermline Ath)	1
Ross, N. 2011 (Inverness CT)	1
Ross, T. W. 1977 (Arsenal)	2
Rowson, D. 1997 (Aberdeen)	5
Russell, J. 2011 (Dundee U)	11
Russell, R. 1978 (Rangers)	3
Salton, D. B. 1992 (Luton T)	6
Samson, C. I. 2004 (Kilmarnock)	6
Saunders, S. 2011 (Motherwell)	2
Scobbie, T. 2008 (Falkirk)	12
Scott, M. 2006 (Livingston)	1
Scott, P. 1994 (St Johnstone)	4
Scougall, S. 2012 (Livingston, Sheffield U)	2
Scrimgour, D. 1997 (St Mirren)	3
Seaton, A. 1998 (Falkirk)	3
Severin, S. D. 2000 (Hearts)	10
Shankland, L. 2015 (Aberdeen)	**4**
Shannon, R. 1987 (Dundee)	7
Sharp, G. M. 1982 (Everton)	1
Sharp, R. 1990 (Dunfermline Ath)	4
Sheerin, P. 1996 (Southampton)	1
Shields, G. 1997 (Rangers)	2
Shinnie, A. 2009 (Dundee, Rangers)	3
Shinnie, G. 2012 (Inverness CT)	2
Simmons, S. 2003 (Hearts)	1
Simpson, N. 1982 (Aberdeen)	11
Sinclair, G. 1977 (Dumbarton)	1
Skilling, M. 1993 (Kilmarnock)	1
Slater, C. 2014 (Kilmarnock)	**8**
Smith, B. M. 1992 (Celtic)	5
Smith, C. 2008 (St Mirren)	2
Smith, C. 2015 (Aberdeen)	1
Smith, D. 2012 (Hearts)	4
Smith, D. L. 2006 (Motherwell)	2
Smith, G. 1978 (Rangers)	1
Smith, G. 2004 (Rangers)	8
Smith, H. G. 1987 (Hearts)	2
Smith, S. 2007 (Rangers)	1
Sneddon, A. 1979 (Celtic)	1
Snodgrass, R. 2008 (Livingston)	2
Soutar, D. 2003 (Dundee)	11
Souttar, J. 2016 (Dundee U, Hearts)	**3**
Speedie, D. R. 1985 (Chelsea)	1
Spencer, J. 1991 (Rangers)	3
Stanton, P. 1977 (Hibernian)	1
Stanton, S. 2014 (Hibernian)	1
Stark, W. 1985 (Aberdeen)	1
Stephen, R. 1983 (Dundee)	1
Stevens, G. 1977 (Motherwell)	1
Stevenson, L. 2008 (Hibernian)	8
Stewart, C. 2002 (Kilmarnock)	1
Stewart, J. 1978 (Kilmarnock, Middlesbrough)	3
Stewart, M. J. 2000 (Manchester U)	17
Stewart, R. 1979 (Dundee U, West Ham U)	12
Stillie, D. 1995 (Aberdeen)	14

WALES

Evans, J. A. J. 2014 (Fulham)	**4**
Evans, K. 1999 (Leeds U, Cardiff C)	4
Evans, L. 2013 (Wolverhampton W)	**13**
Evans, P. S. 1996 (Shrewsbury T)	1
Evans, S. J. 2001 (Crystal Palace)	2
Evans, T. 1995 (Cardiff C)	3
Fish, N. 2005 (Cardiff C)	2
Fleetwood, S. 2005 (Cardiff C)	5
Flynn, C. P. 2007 (Crewe Alex)	1
Folland, R. W. 2000 (Oxford U)	1
Foster, M. G. 1993 (Tranmere R)	1
Fowler, L. A. 2003 (Coventry C, Huddersfield T)	9
Fox, M. A. 2013 (Charlton Ath)	6
Freeman, K. 2012 (Nottingham F, Derby Co)	15
Freestone, R. 1990 (Chelsea)	1
Gabbidon, D. L. 1999 (WBA, Cardiff C)	17
Gale, D. 1983 (Swansea C)	2
Gall, K. A. 2002 (Bristol R, Yeovil T)	8
Gibson, N. D. 1999 (Tranmere R, Sheffield W)	11
Giggs, R. J. 1991 (Manchester U)	1
Gilbert, P. 2005 (Plymouth Arg)	12
Giles, D. C. 1977 (Cardiff C, Swansea C, Crystal Palace)	4
Giles, P. 1982 (Cardiff C)	3
Graham, D. 1991 (Manchester U)	1
Green, R. M. 1998 (Wolverhampton W)	16
Griffith, C. 1990 (Cardiff C)	1
Griffiths, C. 1991 (Shrewsbury T)	1
Grubb, D. 2007 (Bristol C)	1
Gunter, C. 2006 (Cardiff C, Tottenham H)	8
Haldane, L. O. 2007 (Bristol R)	1
Hall, G. D. 1990 (Chelsea)	1
Harrison, E. W. 2013 (Bristol R)	**11**
Hartson, J. 1994 (Luton T, Arsenal)	9
Haworth, S. O. 1997 (Cardiff C, Coventry C, Wigan Ath)	12
Hedges, R. P. 2014 (Swansea C)	**9**
Henley, A. 2012 (Blackburn R)	3
Hennessey, W. R. 2006 (Wolverhampton W)	6
Hewitt, E. J. 2012 (Macclesfield T, Ipswich T)	10
Hillier, I. M. 2001 (Tottenham H, Luton T)	5
Hodges, G. 1983 (Wimbledon)	5
Holden, A. 1984 (Chester C)	1
Holloway, C. D. 1999 (Exeter C)	2
Hopkins, J. 1982 (Fulham)	5
Hopkins, S. A. 1999 (Wrexham)	1
Howells, J. 2012 (Luton T)	5
Huggins, D. S. 1996 (Bristol C)	1
Hughes, D. 2005 (Kaiserslautern, Regensburg)	2
Hughes, D. R. 1994 (Southampton)	1
Hughes, I. 1992 (Bury)	11
Hughes, L. M. 1983 (Manchester U)	5
Hughes, R. D. 1996 (Aston Villa, Shrewsbury T)	13
Hughes, W. 1977 (WBA)	3
Huws, E. W. 2012 (Manchester C)	6
Isgrove, L. J. 2013 (Southampton)	6
Jackett, K. 1981 (Watford)	2
Jacobson, J. M. 2006 (Cardiff C, Bristol R)	15
James, L. R. S. 2006 (Southampton)	10
James, R. M. 1977 (Swansea C)	3
Jarman, L. 1996 (Cardiff C)	10
Jeanne, L. C. 1999 (QPR)	8
Jelleyman, G. A. 1999 (Peterborough U)	1
Jenkins, L. D. 1998 (Swansea C)	9
Jenkins, S. R. 1993 (Swansea C)	2
John, D. C. 2014 (Cardiff C)	**8**
Jones, C. T. 2007 (Swansea C)	1
Jones, E. P. 2000 (Blackpool)	1
Jones, F. 1981 (Wrexham)	1
Jones, G. W. 2014 (Everton)	**6**
Jones, J. A. 2001 (Swansea C)	3
Jones, L. 1982 (Cardiff C)	3
Jones, M. A. 2004 (Wrexham)	4
Jones, M. G. 1998 (Leeds U)	7
Jones, O. R. 2015 (Swansea C)	**1**
Jones, P. L. 1992 (Liverpool)	12
Jones, R. 2011 (AFC Wimbledon)	1

Jones, R. A. 1994 (Sheffield W)	3
Jones, S. J. 2005 (Swansea C)	1
Jones, V. 1979 (Bristol R)	2
Kendall, L. M. 2001 (Crystal Palace)	2
Kendall, M. 1978 (Tottenham H)	1
Kenworthy, J. R. 1994 (Tranmere R)	3
King, A. 2008 (Leicester C)	11
Knott, G. R. 1996 (Tottenham H)	1
Law, B. J. 1990 (QPR)	2
Lawless, A. 2006 (Torquay U)	1
Lawrence, T. 2013 (Manchester U)	8
Ledley, J. C. 2005 (Cardiff C)	5
Letheran, G. 1977 (Leeds U)	2
Letheran, K. C. 2006 (Swansea C)	1
Lewis, D. 1982 (Swansea C)	9
Lewis, J. 1983 (Cardiff C)	1
Llewellyn, C. M. 1998 (Norwich C)	14
Lockyer, T. A. 2015 (Bristol R)	**5**
Loveridge, J. 1982 (Swansea C)	3
Low, J. D. 1999 (Bristol R, Cardiff C)	1
Lowndes, S. R. 1979 (Newport Co, Millwall)	4
Lucas, L. P. 2011 (Swansea C)	19
MacDonald, S. B. 2006 (Swansea C)	25
McCarthy, A. J. 1994 (QPR)	3
McDonald, C. 2006 (Cardiff C)	3
Mackin, L. 2006 (Wrexham)	1
Maddy, P. 1982 (Cardiff C)	2
Margetson, M. W. 1992 (Manchester C)	7
Martin, A. P. 1999 (Crystal Palace)	1
Martin, D. A. 2006 (Notts Co)	1
Marustik, C. 1982 (Swansea C)	7
Matthews, A. J. 2010 (Cardiff C)	5
Maxwell, C. 2009 (Wrexham)	16
Maxwell, L. J. 1999 (Liverpool, Cardiff C)	14
Meades, J. 2012 (Cardiff C)	4
Meaker, M. J. 1994 (QPR)	2
Melville, A. K. 1990 (Swansea C, Oxford U)	2
Micallef, C. 1982 (Cardiff C)	3
Morgan, A. M. 1995 (Tranmere R)	4
Morgan, C. 2004 (Wrexham, Milton Keynes D)	12
Morris, A. J. 2009 (Cardiff C, Aldershot T)	8
Moss, D. M. 2003 (Shrewsbury T)	6
Mountain, P. D. 1997 (Cardiff C)	2
Mumford, A. O. 2003 (Swansea C)	4
Nardiello, D. 1978 (Coventry C)	1
Neilson, A. B. 1993 (Newcastle U)	7
Nicholas, P. 1978 (Crystal Palace, Arsenal)	3
Nogan, K. 1990 (Luton T)	2
Nogan, L. M. 1991 (Oxford U)	1
Nyatanga, L. J. 2005 (Derby Co)	10
Oakley, A. 2013 (Swindon T)	1
O'Brien, B. 2015 (Manchester C)	**6**
Ogleby, R. 2011 (Hearts, Wrexham)	12
Oster, J. M. 1997 (Grimsby T, Everton)	9
O'Sullivan, T. P. 2013 (Cardiff C)	**12**
Owen, G. 1991 (Wrexham)	8
Page, R. J. 1995 (Watford)	4
Parslow, D. 2005 (Cardiff C)	4
Partington, J. M. 2009 (Bournemouth)	8
Partridge, D. W. 1997 (West Ham U)	1
Pascoe, C. 1983 (Swansea C)	4
Pearce, S. 2006 (Bristol C)	3
Pejic, S. M. 2003 (Wrexham)	6
Pembridge, M. A. 1991 (Luton T)	1
Peniket, R. 2012 (Fulham)	1
Perry, J. 1990 (Cardiff C)	3
Peters, M. 1992 (Manchester C, Norwich C)	3
Phillips, D. 1984 (Plymouth Arg)	3
Phillips, G. R. 2001 (Swansea C)	3
Phillips, L. 1979 (Swansea C, Charlton Ath)	2
Pipe, D. R. 2003 (Coventry C, Notts Co)	12
Pontin, K. 1978 (Cardiff C)	1
Powell, L. 1991 (Southampton)	4
Powell, L. 2004 (Leicester C)	3
Powell, R. 2006 (Bolton W)	1
Price, J. J. 1998 (Swansea C)	7

Price, L. P. 2005 (Ipswich T)	10
Price, M. D. 2001 (Everton, Hull C, Scarborough)	13
Price, P. 1981 (Luton T)	1
Pritchard, J. P. 2013 (Fulham)	3
Pritchard, M. O. 2006 (Swansea C)	4
Pugh, D. 1982 (Doncaster R)	2
Pugh, S. 1993 (Wrexham)	2
Pulis, A. J. 2006 (Stoke C)	5
Ramasut, M. W. T. 1997 (Bristol R)	4
Ramsey, A. J. 2008, (Cardiff C, Arsenal)	12
Ratcliffe, K. 1981 (Everton)	2
Ray, G. E. 2013 (Crewe Alex)	5
Ready, K. 1992 (QPR)	5
Rees, A. 1984 (Birmingham C)	1
Rees, J. M. 1990 (Luton T)	3
Rees, M. R. 2003 (Millwall)	4
Reid, B. 2014 (Wolverhampton W)	1
Ribeiro, C. M. 2008 (Bristol C)	8
Richards, A. D. J. 2010 (Swansea C)	16
Richards, E. A. 2012 (Bristol R)	1
Roberts, A. M. 1991 (QPR)	2
Roberts, C. 2013 (Cheltenham T)	6
Roberts, C. J. 1999 (Cardiff C)	1
Roberts, C. R. J. 2016 (Swansea C)	**1**
Roberts, G. 1983 (Hull C)	1
Roberts, G. W. 1997 (Liverpool, Panionios, Tranmere R)	11
Roberts, J. G. 1977 (Wrexham)	1
Roberts, N. W. 1999 (Wrexham)	3
Roberts, P. 1997 (Porthmadog)	1
Roberts, S. I. 1999 (Swansea C)	13
Roberts, S. W. 2000 (Wrexham)	3
Robinson, C. P. 1996 (Wolverhampton W)	6
Robinson, J. R. C. 1992 (Brighton & HA, Charlton Ath)	5
Robson-Kanu, K. H. 2010 (Reading)	4
Rowlands, A. J. R. 1996 (Manchester C)	5
Rush, I. 1981 (Liverpool)	2
Savage, R. W. 1995 (Crewe Alex)	3
Saunders, C. L. 2015 (Crewe Alex)	**1**
Sayer, P. A. 1977 (Cardiff C)	2
Searle, D. 1991 (Cardiff C)	6
Sheehan, J. L. 2014 (Swansea C)	**9**
Shephard, L. 2015 (Swansea C)	**2**
Slatter, D. 2000 (Chelsea)	6
Slatter, N. 1983 (Bristol R)	6
Smith, D. 2014 (Shrewsbury T)	1
Somner, M. J. 2004 (Brentford)	2
Speed, G. A. 1990 (Leeds U)	3
Spender, S. 2005 (Wrexham)	6
Stephens, D. 2011 (Hibernian)	7
Stevenson, N. 1982 (Swansea C)	2
Stevenson, W. B. 1977 (Leeds U)	3
Stock, B. B. 2003 (Bournemouth)	4
Symons, C. J. 1991 (Portsmouth)	2
Tancock, S. 2013 (Swansea C)	6
Taylor, A. J. 2012 (Tranmere R)	3
Taylor, G. K. 1995 (Bristol R)	4
Taylor, J. W. T. 2010 (Reading)	12

Taylor, N. J. 2008 (Wrexham, Swansea C)	13
Taylor, R. F. 2008 (Chelsea)	5
Thomas, C. E. 2010 (Swansea C)	3
Thomas, D. G. 1977 (Leeds U)	3
Thomas, D. J. 1998 (Watford)	2
Thomas, J. A. 1996 (Blackburn R)	21
Thomas, Martin R. 1979 (Bristol R)	2
Thomas, Mickey R. 1977 (Wrexham)	2
Thomas, S. 2001 (Wrexham)	5
Thompson, L. C. W. 2015 (Norwich C)	**2**
Tibbott, L. 1977 (Ipswich T)	2
Tipton, M. J. 1998 (Oldham Ath)	6
Tolley, J. C. 2001 (Shrewsbury T)	12
Tudur-Jones, O. 2006 (Swansea C)	3
Twiddy, C. 1995 (Plymouth Arg)	3
Valentine, R. D. 2001 (Everton, Darlington)	8
Vaughan, D. O. 2003 (Crewe Alex)	8
Vaughan, N. 1982 (Newport Co)	2
Vokes, S. M. 2007 (Bournemouth, Wolverhampton W)	14
Walsh, D. 2000 (Wrexham)	8
Walsh, I. P. 1979 (Crystal Palace, Swansea C)	2
Walsh, J. 2012 (Swansea C, Crawley T)	11
Walton, M. 1991 (Norwich C.)	1
Ward, D. 1996 (Notts Co)	2
Ward, D. 2013 (Liverpool)	6
Warlow, O. J. 2007 (Lincoln C)	2
Weeks, D. L. 2014 (Wolverhampton W)	**2**
Weston, R. D. 2001 (Arsenal, Cardiff C)	4
Wharton, T. J. 2014 (Cardiff C)	1
Whitfield, P. M. 2003 (Wrexham)	1
Wiggins, R. 2006 (Crystal Palace)	9
Williams, A. P. 1998 (Southampton)	9
Williams, A. S. 1996 (Blackburn R)	16
Williams, D. 1983 (Bristol R)	1
Williams, D. I. L. 1998 (Liverpool, Wrexham)	9
Williams, D. T. 2006 (Yeovil T)	1
Williams, E. 1997 (Caernarfon T)	2
Williams, G. 1983 (Bristol R)	2
Williams, G. A. 2003 (Crystal Palace)	5
Williams, G. C. 2014 (Fulham)	2
Williams, J. P. 2011 (Crystal Palace)	8
Williams, M. 2001 (Manchester U)	10
Williams, M. P. 2006 (Wrexham)	14
Williams, M. J. 2014 (Notts Co)	1
Williams, M. R. 2006 (Wrexham)	6
Williams, O. fon 2007 (Crewe Alex, Stockport Co)	11
Williams, R. 2007 (Middlesbrough)	10
Williams, S. J. 1995 (Wrexham)	4
Wilmot, R. 1982 (Arsenal)	6
Wilson, H. 2014 (Liverpool)	**5**
Wilson, J. S. 2009 (Bristol C)	5
Worgan, L. J. 2005 (Milton Keynes D, Rushden & D)	5
Wright, A. A. 1998 (Oxford U)	3
Wright, J. 2014 (Huddersfield T)	**2**
Yorwerth, J. 2014 (Cardiff C)	**7**
Young, S. 1996 (Cardiff C)	5

FA SCHOOLS AND YOUTH GAMES 2015–16

■ *Denotes player sent off.*

ENGLAND UNDER-16

FRIENDLIES

Burton, Sunday 16 August 2015

England (1) 2 *(Samuels 40, Guehi 70)*
USA (1) 2 *(Villegas 5, Acosta 43)*
England: Male; Guehi, Sessegnon R, McEachran (Ampadu 60), Wilson, Medley (Manuel 69), Gomes (Hudson-Odoi 76), Samuels, Panzo, Smith-Rowe (Loader 41), Carlo-Poveda.
England won on penalties.

Burton, Wednesday 19 August 2015

England (1) 3 *(Loader 19, 59, Sessegnon R 61)*
USA (1) 3 *(Sargent 2, Durkin 43, Akinola 72)*
England: Pryzbek, Guehi (Wilson 60), Hudson, Gomes (Poveda 60), Loader (Samuels 60), Cochrane, Lavinier, Hudson-Odoi, Manuel (Medley 55), Panzo (Sessegnon R 41), Ampadu (McEachran 60).
USA won on penalties.

TOURNOI INTERNATIONAL

Limeil-Brevannes, Tuesday 27 October 2015

Japan (2) 4 *(Tanhashi 33, 75, Kubo 34, Miyashiro 78)*
England (2) 3 *(Samuels 2, Sancho 25, Carlo-Poveda 47)*
England: Male; Medley, Eyoma, Panzo, Rosler, Skipp, Nmecha, Oakley-Boothe, Samuels (Soule 53), Sancho (Kirby 53), Carlo-Poveda (Sessegnon R 65).

Boissy-Saint-Leger, Thursday 29 October 2015

England (2) 2 *(Sancho 12, Sessegnon R 39)*
Netherlands (2) 2 *(Kone 2, Redan 80)*
England: Guehi; Eyoma, Panzo, Rosler, Kirby, O'Riley (Oakley-Boothe 63), Foden (Skipp 67), Soule (Carlo-Poveda 53), Sancho, Sessegnon R.

Bonneuil-sur-Marne, Saturday 31 October 2015

France (1) 3 *(Fontaine 6, Flamant 60, Gaudin 77)*
England (0) 0
England: Male (McGill 41); Guehi, Medley, Skipp (Eyoma 48), Nmecha, Foden (Kirby 60), Kirby (Rosler 65), Samuels (Soule 48), Sessegnon R, O'Riley (Sancho 41), Oakley-Boothe, Carlo-Poveda.

NIKE INTERNATIONAL TOURNAMENT

Lakewood Ranch, Florida, Wednesday 2 December 2015

USA (0) 2 *(Goslin 46, Carleton 51 (pen))*
England (1) 3 *(Loader 25, Sancho 64 (pen), 80)*
England: McGill; Guehi, Sessegnon R, Oakley-Boothe (Skipp 71), Panzo, Rosler, Kirby (Carlo-Poveda 58), Loader, Gomes, Sancho, Eyoma.

Lakewood Ranch, Florida, Friday 4 December 2015

Brazil (0) 0   England (2) 2 *(Foden 21, 28)*
England: Anderson; Guehi, Sessegnon S (Eyoma 3), Medley, Sessegnon R, Skipp, McEachran, Samuels, Carlo-Poveda, Foden (Loader 56), Smith-Rowe (Oakley-Boothe 54).

Lakewood Ranch, Florida, Sunday 6 December 2015

Netherlands (2) 2 *(Redan 8, Darwa 16)*
England (1) 2 *(Sancho 40, Sessegnon R 80)*
England: Anderson, Guehi, Oakley-Boothe, Panzo, Kirby (Smith-Rowe 58), Loader, Gomes (McEachran 58), Sancho (Samuels 59), Skipp, Medley (Sessegnon R 41), Carlo-Poveda (Foden 51).

UEFA UNDER-16 DEVELOPMENT TOURNAMENT

Burton, Tuesday 16 February 2016

England (1) 1 *(Sancho 36)*   **Norway (0) 0**
England: Anderson, Eyoma, Guehi (Skipp 60), Panzo, Sessegnon R, Gomes, McEachran, Oakley-Boothe, Carlo-Poveda (Kirby 66), Sancho, Loader.

Burton, Thursday 18 February 2016

England 5 *(Brewster (3), Guehi, Gomes)*
Czech Republic 1 *(Pichal)*
England: Cull; Eyoma, Latibeaudiere, Panzo, Medley, Skipp, Kirby, Carlo-Poveda, Brewster, Hudson-Odoi, Sancho.
Substitutes: Anderson, Guehi, Sessegnon R, Smith-Rowe, Gomes, Foden, Oakley-Booth, McEachran, Loader.

Burton, Sunday 21 February 2016

England (0) 0 *(Kirby 53)*   **Italy (0) 0**
England: Anderson, Eyoma, Guehi, Panzo (Medley 68), Sessegnon R, Foden (Sancho 26), Gomes (Brewster 60), McEachran (Skipp 41), Oakley-Boothe, Hudson-Odoi (Kirby 41), Loader.

MONTAIGU TOURNAMENT

Montaigu, Tuesday 22 March 2016

England (0) 1 *(Loader 80)*   **Russia (0) 0**
England: Cull; Wilson, Latibeaudiere, Panzo, Medley, Skipp, Kirby, Gomes, Carlo-Poveda, Sancho, Loader.

Montaigu, Thursday 24 March 2016

England (2) 2 *(Gibbs-White 33, Wilson 37)*
USA (1) 2 *(Acosta 39, 76 (pen))*
England: Male; Wilson, Strachan, Lavinier, Medley, O'Reilly, Foden, Griffiths (Skipp 55), Gibbs-White, McEachran, Brewster (Loader 69).

Montaigu, Saturday 26 March 2016

Brazil (2) 3 *(Campos 27, Filoh 32, 53)*
England (1) 1 *(Gomes 16)*
England: Cull; Lavinier, Medley, Latibeaudiere, Panzo, Kirby, Loader, Carlo-Poveda, Skipp, Sancho, Gomes.
Substitutes: O'Riley, McEachran, Foden, Wilson, Male, Griffiths, Gibbs-White.

Montaigu, Monday 28 March 2016

England (2) 3 *(Sancho 2, Brewster)*   **Northern Ireland (0) 0**
England Squad: Cull; Lavinier, Medley, O'Riley, Latibeaudiere, Panzo, McEachran, Kirby, Loader, Foden, Carlo-Poveda, Wilson, Male, Skipp, Sancho, Strachan, Gibbs-White, Brewster, Gomes.

ENGLAND UNDER-17

UNDER-17 FA INTERNATIONAL TOURNAMENT

Telford, Wednesday 26 August 2015

England (1) 3 *(Lewis 35, Diallo 50 (pen), 55 (pen))*
Italy (0) 0
England: Yates; Chalobah (Lattie 62), Williams, Francis (Neufille 41), Brown (Campbell 74), Diallo (Gilmour 74), Dozzell (Embleton 62), Heaney, Lewis (Shashoua 41), Bennetts (Leko 74), Ennis.

Walsall, Friday 28 August 2015

England (2) 2 *(Dozzell 20, Shashoua 40)*
Turkey (0) 1 *(Engin 49 (pen))*
England: Hayes; Lattie (Brown 55), Chalobah (Williams 41), Francis, Neufville, Gilmour (Diallo 65), Embleton, Leko (Bennetts 30), Dozzell (Heaney 55), Shashoua (Ennis 65), Campbell.

Burton, Sunday 30 August 2015

England (3) 3 *(Williams 5, Heaney 14, Ennis 22)*
Portugal (5) 7 *(Gomes 3, Joao Filipe 20, 40, 44, Quinas 28, Luis 32, Leao 77)*
England: Yates (Hayes 41); Chalobah, Brown, Williams (Lattie 58), Neufville (Francis 41), Diallo, Dozzell (Gilmour 78), Heaney, Lewis (Embleton 50), Bennetts (Shashoua 41), Ennis (Campbell 78).

2016 EUROPEAN UNDER-17 CHAMPIONSHIP QUALIFYING ROUND – PORTUGAL

Febres, Tuesday 29 September 2015

England (5) 8 *(Ennis 6, Leko 11, Nelson 16, Brown 21, Shashoua 30, 42, Adeniran 47, Lewis 49)*   **San Marino (0) 0**
England: Thompson; Chalobah, Williams, Francis, Brown, Adeniran, Dozzell, Leko (Lewis 41), Shashoua, Nelson (Neufville 55), Ennis (Heaney 41).

Pampilhosa de Serra, Thursday 1 October 2015
England (2) 5 *(Dozzell 18, Nelson 23, 42, 54, Embleton 75)*
Armenia (0) 0
England: Thompson; Chalobah (Lattie 66), Williams, Francis, Brown, Adeniran (Embleton 58), Dozzell, Leko, Shashoua (Lewis 51), Nelson, Ennis.

Coimbra, Sunday 4 October 2015
Portugal (0) 1 *(Joao Filipe 64)* **England (1) 1** *(Chalobah 16)*
England: Thompson; Williams, Chalobah, Francis, Brown (Neufville 37), Adeniran, Dozzell, Leko (Heaney 58), Lewis (Embleton 71), Nelson, Ennis.

FIFA UNDER-17 WORLD CUP – CHILE 2015 GROUP B

Coquimbo, Saturday 17 October 2015
England (0) 1 *(Hinds 61)*   **Guinea (0) 1** *(Naby 76)*
England: Whiteman; Yates, Williams, Suliman, DaSilva, Kane, Davies, Edwards M (Ugbo 88), Hinds (Patching 70), Willock, Mavididi (Sterling 84).

La Serena, Tuesday 20 October 2015
England (0) 0   **Brazil (0) 1** *(Leandro 67)*
England: Whiteman; Yates, Williams, Suliman, DaSilva, Kane, Alexander-Arnold, Ugbo, Edwards M (Hinds 71), Willock (Hepburn-Murphy 80), Sterling (Mavididi 71).

Coquimbo, Friday 23 October 2015
Korea Republic (0) 0   England (0) 0
England: Whiteman; Humphreys, Williams, Suliman, DaSilva, Davies, Kane, Ugbo (Edwards M 63), Hinds (Patching 85), Willock, Mavididi (Sterling 73).

FRIENDLIES

Burton, Wednesday 7 October 2015
England (4) 8 *(Willock 11, Sterling 25, 40, Edwards 37, Ugbo 51, 82, Mavididi 54, Hinds 88)* **Congo DR (0) 0**
England: Huffer (Whiteman 46); Yates, Williams (Suliman 72), Suliman (Collinge 46), DaSilva, Wood (Patching 46), Alexander-Arnold (Wood 72), Hepburn-Murphy (Edun 46), Edwards (Hinds 46), Willock (Mavididi 46), Sterling (Ugbo 46).

Rancagua, Sunday 11 October 2015
Chile (0) 0   England (0) 0
England: Whiteman (Huffer 46); Yates, Williams, Collinge (Suliman 46), DaSilva, Davies, Kane (Hinds 46), Ugbo (Willock 46), Patching (Wood 62), Edwards M (Hepburn-Murphy 46), Mavididi (Sterling 46).
Chile won 4-3 on penalties.

Rotherham, Friday 20 November 2015
England (2) 2 *(Mount 6, Ennis 25)*
Germany (1) 1 *(Otto 7)*   7272
England: Thompson; Sterling, Brown, Agyei-Tabi, Chalobah, Bola, Leko, Adeniran (Slattery 75), Ennis, Mount, Shashoua (Bennetts 64).

ALGARVE TOURNAMENT

Parchal, Friday 5 February 2016
Portugal (1) 1 *(Miguel Luis 8)*
England (0) 1 *(Shashoua 46)*
England: Thompson J; Tanganga (Thandi 47), Francis (Tymon 80), Bola, Brown, Leko, Dozzell, Adeniran, Nabi (Embleton 74), Shashoua (Heaney 80), Morris (Hirst 74).

Lagos, Sunday 7 February 2016
England (2) 2 *(Hirst 17, 24)*
Germany (0) 2 *(Baak 62, Dadshov 80)*
England: Hayes; Tymon, Francis, Bola (Brown 41), Thandi (Leko 60 (Morris 71)), Dozzell (Adeniran 41), Embleton, Bohui (Shashoua 44), Heaney, Hirst, Tanner (Nabi 60).

Parchal, Tuesday 9 February 2016
England (0) 0   Netherlands (0) 2 *(Chong 46, Vente 52)*
England: Parkes; Tanganga, Tymon (Thandi 55), Bola (Francis 41), Brown, Shashoua, Adeniran, Dozzell, Embleton (Heaney 41), Nabi (Tanner 50), Morris (Hirst 60).

2016 EUROPEAN UNDER-17 CHAMPIONSHIP ELITE ROUND – ENGLAND

Chesterfield, Thursday 24 March 2016
England (1) 3 *(Nelson 38, 48 (pen), Leko 42)*
Turkey (0) 1 *(Guclu 78)*   2749
England: Parkes; Sterling (Shashoua 75), Chalobah, Tanganga, Brown, McGuane, Dozzell, Sessegnon R, Leko (Morris 70), Mount (Adeniran 75), Nelson.

Leek Town, Saturday 26 March 2016
England (1) 1 *(Dozzell 33)*   **Finland (0) 0**   2727
England: Cumming; Sterling, McGuane, Chalobah, Tanganga, Adeniran, Sessegnon R, Dozzell, Leko (Morris 62), Mount (Brown 74), Nelson.

Burton, Tuesday 29 March 2016
Ukraine (0) 1 *(Sich 57)*
England (1) 1 *(Taylor-Crossdale 16)*   578
England: Cumming; Bola, Chalobah (Sterling 53), Francis, Brown, Adeniran, Dozzell (McGuane), Shashoua, Mount, Taylor-Crossdale (Nelson 67), Morris.

2016 EUROPEAN UNDER-17 CHAMPIONSHIP – GROUP C

Baku, Thursday 16 May 2016
Sweden (1) 2 *(Asoro 4, 59)*   **England (0) 1** *(Nelson 61)* 266
England: Thompson; Sterling, Bola (Feeney 25), Chalobah, Brown (Shashoua 50), McGuane, Dozzell, Mount, Sessegnon R, Nelson, Hirst (Morris).

Baku, Monday 9 May 2016   1200
France (0) 0   England (2) 2 *(Morris 15, Nelson 47 (pen))*
England: Thompson; Sterling, Chalobah, Feeney, Sessegnon R, McGuane, Adeniran, Dozzell, Mount (Shashoua 79), Nelson (Bohui 74), Morris (Hirst 64).

Baku, Thursday 12 May 2016
Denmark (0) 1 *(Odgaard 80))*
England (1) 3 *(Nelson 30, Mount 51, Hirst 78)*   100
England: Thompson; Sterling (Brown 67), Chalobah, Feeney, Sessegnon R, McGuane (Francis 75), Adeniran, Dozzell Mount, Nelson (Hirst 72), Morris.

QUARTER-FINALS

Baku, Sunday 15 May 2016
Spain (1) 1 *(Garcia 11)*   **England (0) 0**   1000
England: Thompson; Sterling, Chalobah, Feeney, Sessegnon R, McGuane, Adeniran (Shashoua 67), Dozzell, Mount, Nelson (Bohui 64), Hirst (Morris 64).

ENGLAND UNDER-18

FRIENDLIES

Zeist, Thursday 3 September 2015
Netherlands (0) 0   England (1) 2 *(Sheaf 28, Sterling 50)* 1200
England: Woolston; Yates (Johnson 58), Williams, Collinge, DaSilva, Sheaf (Wright 86), Wood, Holland, Edwards (Patching 75), Willock, Sterling (Hinds 75).

Zeist, Saturday 5 September 2015
Netherlands (0) 0   England (0) 0
England: Whiteman (Huffer 46); Yates, Suliman, Johnson, Edun■, Sheaf (DaSilva 46), Kane, Wright, Patching (Willock 80), Mavididi (Wood 64), Hinds (Sterling 64).

Wiener Neustadt, Wednesday 23 March 2016
Austria (0) 2 *(Filip 16, Sahanek 47)*
England (1) 3 *(Edwards M 17, 48, Nmecha 78)*   1200
England: Whiteman; Arnold, Oxford, Suliman, Humphreys (Williams 74), Davies, Davenport (Kane 65), Holland (Evans 74), Edwards M, Willock (Green 65), Buckley-Ricketts (Nmecha 74).

Burton, Sunday 27 March 2016
England (2) 4 *(Nmecha 24, Edwards M 34, 58, Evans 78)*
Republic of Ireland (0) 1 *(Levingston 53)*
England: Ramsdale; Humphreys, Arnold (Suliman 57), Davies (Davenport 85), Williams, Oxford, Edwards M, Kane, Nmecha (Buckley-Ricketts 82), Evans (Willock 82), Green (Holland 85).

Republic of Ireland: Donnelly; Hanney (Kane 65), Lunney, Cadman (Brady 46), Masterson, O'Keeffe, Elbouzedi (Aherne 80), Dunne (Levingston 46), McDonagh (O'Connor 77), Ronan (Warde 77), Clarke (Davis 80).

ENGLAND UNDER-19

FRIENDLIES

Gladbach, Friday 4 September 2015

Germany (0) 2 *(Owusu 47, Heinrichs 78)*

England (1) 3 *(Ojo 36, Solanke 55, Maitland-Niles 64)*

England: Woodman; Kenny■, Taylor Moore, Clarke-Salter, Tafari Moore, Rossiter, Cook, Maitland-Niles (Reed 83), Roberts (Connolly 56), Ojo, Solanke (Abraham 79).

Zagreb, Monday 7 September 2015

Croatia (1) 1 *(Bozic 27 (pen))*

England (0) 1 *(Onomah 72)*

England: Howes; Walker-Peters, Fry, Clarke-Salter (Taylor Moore 46), Connolly, Reed (Cook 84), Onomah (Rossiter 84), Ahearne-Grant (Solanke 77), Roberts (Ojo 65), Abraham, Armstrong.

Gravenzande, Thursday 12 November 2015

Netherlands (1) 2 *(Bergwijn 35, Lammers 47)*

England (0) 2 *(Ledson 72, Abraham 88)*

England: Howes, Walker-Peters, Henry, Ledson, Fry, Borthwick-Jackson, Roberts (Maitland-Niles 70), Onomah, Armstrong, Crowley (Abraham 70), Brown.

Manchester, Sunday 15 November 2015

England (3) 5 *(Onomah 9, Roberts 27, Abraham 33, 64, Crowley 90)*

Japan (1) 1 *(Kubota 30)*

England: Woodman; Kenny, Taylor Moore, Adarabioyo, Connolly, Oxford (Ledson 46), Cook (Henry 62), Roberts (Crowley 70), Onomah (Ojo 46), Maitland-Niles (Brown 62), Abraham (Armstrong 70).

UEFA EUROPEAN UNDER-19 CHAMPIONSHIP QUALIFYING ROUND – GROUP 4 (MACEDONIA)

Skopje, Thursday 8 October 2015

Macedonia (0) 0

England (0) 2 *(Armstrong 67, Maitland-Niles 90)*   300

England: Woodman; Walker-Peters, Clarke-Salter, Taylor Moore, Connolly, Onomah, Rossiter, Armstrong (Solanke 71), Crowley (Maitland-Niles 74), Roberts (Ojo 71), Abraham.

Skopje, Saturday 10 October 2015

Finland (0) 0   England (0) 1 *(Abraham 73)*   100

England: Woodman; Kenny, Taylor Moore, Clarke-Salter, Connolly, Maitland-Niles, Cook (Fry 90), Rossiter, Ojo (Abraham 67), Onomah (Armstrong 88), Solanke.

Skopje, Tuesday 13 October 2015

England (0) 0   Italy (0) 0   60

England: Woodman; Walker-Peters, Fry, Clarke-Salter, Kenny, Ojo (Solanke 46), Cook, Rossiter, Roberts, Crowley (Abraham 59), Armstrong (Onomah 68).

UEFA EUROPEAN UNDER-19 CHAMPIONSHIP ELITE ROUND – GROUP 7 (SPAIN)

Cartaya, Thursday 24 March 2016

England (2) 2 *(Abraham 8, Onomah 10)*

Georgia (0) 1 *(Goshtelliani 84)*   500

England: Woodman; Walker-Peters, Fry, Taylor Moore, Tafari Moore, Onomah (Connolly 79), Cook, Maitland-Niles, Abraham, Armstrong, Brown (Ojo 79).

Lepe, Saturday 26 March 2016

Greece (0) 1 *(Lamprou 51)*

England (0) 1 *(Armstrong 49 (pen))*   230

England: Woodman; Kenny, Fry, Taylor Moore, Borthwick-Jackson (Borthwick-Jackson 67), Connolly, Ledson, Brown (Onomah 74), Roberts, Armstrong, Ojo (Abraham 60).

Lepe, Tuesday 29 March 2016

Spain (0) 0

England (1) 2 *(Onomah 6, Armstrong 66)*   1250

England: Woodman; Walker-Peters, Taylor Moore, Fry, Tafari Moore, Cook, Onomah, Maitland-Niles, Roberts (Armstrong 58), Abraham, Brown (Kenny 78).

Mexico, Saturday 4 June 2016

Mexico (0) 2   England (0) 0

England: Woodman; Walker-Peters (Kenny 46), Moore, Ledson (Tuanzebe 46), Tomori, Fry, Lookman (Ledson [back on] 75), Connolly (Rossiter 75), Solanke (Armstrong 46), Ojo (Abraham 46), Brown (Henry 46

Mexico, Monday 6 June 2016

Mexico (0) 1   England (0) 0

England: Southwood (Howes 46); Kenny (Moore 60), Tomori (Kenny 80), Tuanzebe, Henry, Onomah (Walker-Peters 60), Rossiter (Ledson 60), Connolly (Fry 60), Brown (Lookman 60), Abraham (Connolly 80), Solanke (Ojo 60).

ENGLAND UNDER-20

FRIENDLIES

Burton, Saturday 5 September 2015

England (3) 5 *(Walker 23, 25, Chilwell 42, Gray 50, Brown 60)*

Czech Republic (0) 0

England: Griffiths; Holgate, Aina (Anderson 46), Kpekawa, Chilwell (Smith-Brown 46), Kuhl, Brannagan (Winks 73), Brown (Morris 73), Gilliead (Kent 60), Walker (Adams 73), Barker (Gray 46).

Shrewsbury, Monday 7 September 2015

England (0) 0   Czech Republic (1) 1 *(Yunis 11)*   2521

England: Smith; Smith-Brown (Holgate 64), Aina, Burke (Kpekawa 60), Chilwell, Morris (Anderson 78), Winks (Brown 86), Kent (Gilliead 65), Gray, Adams, Barker (Brannagan 86).

St Brieuc, Wednesday 11 November 2015

France (0) 4 *(Ounas 52, Mousset 62, Guirassy 70, Blin 89)*

England (1) 3 *(Grimes 3, Colkett 78, Fletcher 85)*

England: Smith; Smith-Brown, Holgate, Cargill, Chilwell, Brown (Colkett 75), Winks, Grimes (Morris 81), Walker (Gilliead 67), Gallagher (Fletcher 75), Kent (Barker 67).

Ploufragan, Saturday 14 November 2015

France v England

Match postponed because of Paris atrocities.

Doncaster, Thursday 24 March 2016

England 4   Canada 1 *Behind closed doors.*

Doncaster, Sunday 27 March 2016

England (0) 1 *(Palmer 71)*

Canada (1) 2 *(Chung 13, Bustos 68)*   3264

England: Gunn; Aina (Bryan 58), Cooper, Holgate, Toffolo, Winks, Williams (Morris 80), Walker (Palmer 46), Barker (Fletcher 69), Greenwood, Rashford.

MERCEDES BENZ ELITE CUP – GERMANY

Heidenheim, Wednesday 7 October 2015

Netherlands (0) 1 *(Loof 90)*

England (2) 3 *(Brown 8, Barker 29, Gallagher 79)*

England: Wildsmith (Griffiths 82); Smith-Brown (Holgate 72), Aina, Cargill, Toffolo, Brown (Winks 87), Grimes, Reed (Morris 87), Gilliead (Oduwa 72), Gallagher (Walker 87), Barker (Kent 82).

Ulm, Saturday 10 October 2015

Turkey (0) 1 *(Hummet 68)*

England (0) 2 *(Kent 80, Barker 90)*

England: Smith; Holgate, Cargill (Toffolo 63), Burke, Kpekawa, Gilliead (Brown 67), Winks, Morris (Grimes 78), Oduwa (Barker 67), Walker (Gallagher 78), Kent.

Heidenheim, Tuesday 13 October 2015

Germany (0) 1 *(Dittgen 48)   England (0) 0**

England: Griffiths; Smith-Brown (Kpekawa 85), Toffolo, Reed (Winks 65), Aina (Holgate 85), Grimes (Morris 78), Gallagher (Walker 78), Brown (Gilliead 65), Barker, Burke, Kent (Oduwa 78).

SCHOOLS FOOTBALL 2015–16

BOODLES INDEPENDENT SCHOOLS FA CUP 2015–16

*After extra time.

PRELIMINARY ROUND

Berkhamsted v Haberdashers' Aske's	4-1
Bournemouth Collegiate v St John's, Leatherhead	1-2*
Canford v Truro	1-3
Frensham Heights v Hurstpierpoint	2-1
Harrodian v Box Hill	8-2
Lingfield Notre Dame v RGS Guildford	1-3
Radnor v Trinity	1-8
Sevenoaks v Dover College	2-2*
(Dover College won 4-2 on penalties)	
Sherborne v Bedales	2-0
Stockport GS v Queen Ethelburga's College	3-5

FIRST ROUND

Bedford Modern v Hampton	1-2
Bolton School v Ardingly	0-3
Bury GS v Wolverhampton GS	2-0
Cheadle Hulme v Berkhamsted	1-2
City of London v Wellington College	2-1
Colfe's v Forest	1-6
Eton v Truro	8-0
Frensham Heights v Royal Russell	0-11
Grange v Winchester College	2-1
Haileybury v Aldenham	3-0
Harrodian v Brentwood	0-2
Harrow v St Bede's College, Manchester	1-2
Ibstock Place v Dulwich College	1-5
KES Witley v St Columba's College	2-5
Kimbolton v LVS Ascot	4-0
King's School, Chester v Alleyn's	2-1
Lancing College v Dover College	2-0*
Latymer Upper v John Lyon	4-0
Merchant Taylors v Bradfield	0-3
Millfield v Charterhouse	3-0
Norwich School v Manchester GS	1-5
Oldham Hulme v Ackworth	7-5*
Queen Ethelburga's College v RGS Newcastle	3-0
Repton v Chigwell	13-3
RGS Guildford v ACS Cobham	0-2
Sherborne (walkover) v St Edmund's, Canterbury	
Shrewsbury School v Taunton School	8-0
St John's Leatherhead v Highgate	2-2*
(St John's won 5-4 on penalties)	
Trinity v Grammar School at Leeds	2-3
University College School v Bede's	3-6
Westminster v Birkdale	6-0
Whitgift v Tonbridge	3-2

SECOND ROUND

Ardingly v Berkhamsted	4-0
Bede's v Royall Russell	1-2
Bradfield v Grange	4-1
Bury GS v King's School, Chester	2-6
City of London v Brentwood	1-2
Dulwich College v ACS Cobham	3-2
Eton v Queen Ethelburga's College	0-1

Forest v Oldham Hulme	6-0
Haileybury v Whitgift	0-5
Hampton v Manchester GS	0-1*
Kimbolton v Lancing College	2-2*
(Kimbolton won 7-6 on penalties)	
Repton v Latymer Upper	2-0
St Bede's College v Shrewsbury	2-1
St Columba's College v Grammar School at Leeds	2-2*
(St Columba's won 2-1 on penalties)	
St John's Leatherhead v Sherborne	5-0
Westminster v Millfield	1-2

THIRD ROUND

Brentwood v St John's Leatherhead	2-0
Manchester GS v Ardingly	1-4
Queen Ethelburga's College v King's School, Chester	1-2
Repton v Kimbolton	4-0
Royal Russell v Dulwich College	5-0
St Bede's College v Bradfield	0-4
St Columba's College v Forest	1-6
Whitgift v Millfield	2-2*
(Millfield won 5-4 on penalties)	

FOURTH ROUND

Ardingly v Forest	4-2
Brentwood v Repton	1-1*
(Brentwood won 5-4 on penalties)	
Millfield v Bradfield	0-3
Royal Russell v King's School, Chester	3-1

SEMI FINAL

Ardingly v Royal Russell	1-0*
Bradfield v Brentwood	3-2

FINAL (at Milton Keynes Dons FC)

Ardingly (0) 1

Bradfield (0) 0* *(McConnell (pen))*

Ardingly: D. Bonilla-Rasmussen; G. Southgate, L. Evans, M. Penfold, M. Price, O. McConnell, T. Cassidy, O. Haynes-Brown, M. Makepeace, J. Magrath, J. Alcock.
Substitutes: T. West, D. Adomakoh, S. Rattle, C. Kissi, D. Llantada

Bradfield: J. Machin; H. Phillips, J. Tarrant, L. Patrick-Smith, C. Holden, T. Dai, P. Frank, J. Smith, G. Knight (capt), A. Brown, J. Higgins.
Substitutes: S. Stringer, E. Sideso, N. Hijazi, M. Olivson, O. Simpson

Referee: M. Atkinson (Yorkshire).

INVESTEC ISFA U15 CUP FINAL

Millfield v Brentwood	3-2
(at Burton Albion FC)	

INVESTEC ISFA U13 CUP FINAL

Whitgift v Bury GS	4-2
(at Burton Albion FC)	

UNIVERSITY FOOTBALL 2016

132nd UNIVERSITY MATCH

(Sunday 27 March 2015, at Craven Cottage, Fulham, attendance 1351)

Cambridge (0) 0   Oxford (1) 2

Cambridge: Warne; Wolstenhulme, Dungay (Rawson 85) Congdon, Herring, Wolf, Painter (Thoby 46), Filippa (Burley 70), Grubic, Nielsen, Gaskell.

Oxford: Szreter; Gomarsall (Brown D 82), Brown T, Wade, Moneke, Gilfoy, Tsaptsinos, Tozer, Burda (Dineheen 65), Feeney (Thelen 85), Somerville.
Scorers: Tsaptsinos 15, Dinneen 70.

Referee: Martin Atkinson.

Oxford have won 53 games (2 on penalties), Cambridge 52 games (3 on penalties) and 27 games have been drawn. Oxford have scored 208 goals, Cambridge 205 goals.

WOMEN'S SUPER LEAGUE 2015

FA WOMEN'S SUPER LEAGUE 1 TABLE 2015

			Home					Away					Total					
		P	W	D	L	F	A	W	D	L	F	A	W	D	L	F	A	GD	Pts
1	Chelsea	14	5	1	1	16	4	5	1	1	14	6	10	2	2	30	10	20	32
2	Manchester C	14	5	1	1	13	4	4	2	1	12	7	9	3	2	25	11	14	30
3	Arsenal	14	4	0	3	12	10	4	3	0	9	3	8	3	3	21	13	8	27
4	Sunderland	14	4	1	2	14	8	2	1	4	10	16	6	2	6	24	24	0	20
5	Notts Co	14	2	2	3	9	9	2	1	4	11	11	4	3	7	20	20	0	15
6	Birmingham C	14	1	4	2	2	3	2	0	5	5	11	3	4	7	7	14	-7	13
7	Liverpool	14	3	0	4	8	12	1	1	5	7	12	4	1	9	15	24	-9	1
8	Bristol Academy	14	1	1	5	8	22	1	1	5	4	16	2	2	10	12	38	-26	8

FA WOMEN'S SUPER LEAGUE 1 RESULTS 2015

	Arsenal	Birmingham C	Bristol Academy	Chelsea	Liverpool	Manchester C	Notts Co	Sunderland
Arsenal	—	1-0	2-0	0-2	1-3	2-3	2-1	4-1
Birmingham C	0-1	—	0-0	0-1	1-0	0-0	0-0	1-1
Bristol Academy	1-1	0-3	—	0-4	4-2	0-3	2-5	1-4
Chelsea	0-0	4-0	4-1	—	1-0	1-2	2-1	4-0
Liverpool	0-2	2-1	2-0	0-4	—	2-1	1-2	1-2
Manchester C	0-1	1-0	6-1	1-1	2-0	—	2-1	1-0
Notts Co	1-1	0-1	0-1	1-2	1-0	2-2	—	4-2
Sunderland	1-3	3-0	2-1	4-0	2-2	0-1	2-1	—

FA WOMEN'S SUPER LEAGUE 1 LEADING GOALSCORERS 2015

Player	Team	Goals	Player	Team	Goals
Beth Mead	Sunderland	12	Toni Duggan	Manchester C	6
Jess Clarke	Notts Co	7	Chioma Ubogagu	Arsenal	6
Natalia Pablos	Arsenal	7	Rachel Williams	Notts Co	6
Eniola Aluko	Chelsea	6	Karen Carney	Birmingham C	5
Isobel Christiansen	Manchester C	6	Ji So-yun	Chelsea	5
Gemma Davison	Chelsea	6			

FA WOMEN'S SUPER LEAGUE 2 TABLE 2015

			Home					Away					Total					
		P	W	D	L	F	A	W	D	L	F	A	W	D	L	F	A	GD	Pts
1	Reading	18	5	3	1	26	10	9	0	0	35	5	14	3	1	61	15	46	45
2	Doncaster R Belles	18	7	1	1	27	9	7	2	0	30	6	14	3	1	57	15	42	45
3	Everton	18	3	4	2	17	12	5	3	1	26	12	8	7	3	43	24	19	31
4	Yeovil T	18	4	2	3	17	11	5	2	2	19	12	9	4	5	36	23	13	31
5	Aston Villa	18	3	1	5	11	17	4	3	2	18	11	7	4	7	29	28	1	25
6	Oxford U	18	3	1	5	10	20	4	2	3	16	20	7	3	8	26	40	-14	24
7	Durham	18	3	0	6	15	22	3	2	4	9	10	6	2	10	24	32	-8	20
8	London Bees	18	3	1	5	13	26	0	3	6	6	27	3	4	11	19	53	-34	13
9	Millwall Lionesses	18	1	4	4	9	19	1	2	6	8	20	2	6	10	17	39	-22	12
10	Watford	18	0	2	7	8	25	1	0	8	4	30	1	2	15	12	55	-43	5

FA WOMEN'S SUPER LEAGUE 2 RESULTS 2015

	Aston Villa	Doncaster R Belles	Durham	Everton	London Bees	Millwall Lionesses	Oxford U	Reading	Watford	Yeovil T
Aston Villa	—	0-5	0-1	1-2	2-1	2-1	2-2	2-3	0-1	2-1
Doncaster R Belles	2-1	—	3-0	3-3	5-1	4-0	3-0	0-3	5-0	2-1
Durham	1-4	0-2	—	1-6	4-1	2-3	3-0	0-5	4-0	0-1
Everton	1-1	1-1	1-1	—	2-2	4-1	5-3	0-2	3-0	0-1
London Bees	2-1	1-2	0-4	1-7	—	2-1	1-2	0-7	4-0	2-2
Millwall Lionesses	1-2	0-5	0-0	1-1	0-0	—	2-3	0-4	3-2	2-2
Oxford U	0-2	2-5	1-0	2-3	2-1	2-2	—	0-4	1-0	0-3
Reading	1-1	2-2	3-0	2-1	8-0	3-0	2-2	—	3-0	2-4
Watford	1-4	0-5	1-3	1-3	0-0	0-0	2-3	1-3	—	2-4
Yeovil T	2-2	0-3	1-0	0-0	4-0	1-0	0-1	2-4	7-1	—

FA WOMEN'S SUPER LEAGUE 2 LEADING GOALSCORERS 2015

Player	Team	Goals	Player	Team	Goals
Courtney Sweetman-Kirk	Doncaster R Belles	20	Lauren Bruton	Reading	7
Bethany England	Doncaster R Belles	13	Kayleigh Hines	Oxford U	7
Emma Follis	Reading	12	Danielle Turner	Everton	7
Fran Kirby	Reading	11	Katie Wilkinson	Aston Villa	7
Sue Smith	Doncaster R Belles	11	Corinne Yorston	Yeovil T	7
Helen Ward	Reading	8			

WOMEN'S SUPER LEAGUE CONTINENTAL CUP 2015

GROUP 1

Millwall Lionesses v London Bees	5-3
Reading v Chelsea	2-3
Arsenal v Watford	3-0
London Bees v Arsenal	1-3
Millwall Lionesses v Reading	1-3
Watford v Millwall Lionesses	2-4
Reading v London Bees	3-0
Chelsea v Arsenal	0-2
Watford v Chelsea	0-3
Chelsea v Millwall Lionesses	6-0
Arsenal v Reading	2-1
Chelsea v London Bees	8-0
Millwall Lionesses v Arsenal	0-4
Watford v Reading	1-3
London Bees v Watford	2-3

Group 1 Table	P	W	D	L	F	A	GD	Pts
1 Arsenal	5	5	0	0	14	2	12	15
2 Chelsea	5	4	0	1	20	4	16	12
3 Reading	5	3	0	2	12	7	5	9
4 Millwall Lionesses	5	2	0	3	10	18	–8	6
5 Watford	5	1	0	4	6	15	–9	3
6 London Bees	5	0	0	5	6	22	–16	0

GROUP 2

Durham v Sunderland	1-2
Everton v Liverpool	0-2
Doncaster R Belles v Manchester C	0-3
Manchester C v Durham	5-0
Sunderland v Everton	5-2
Doncaster R Belles v Liverpool	0-3
Liverpool v Durham	1-0
Sunderland v Manchester C	1-3
Everton v Doncaster R Belles	2-3
Liverpool v Sunderland	2-0
Everton v Manchester C	0-2
Doncaster R Belles v Durham	5-0
Durham v Everton	0-2
Manchester C v Liverpool	2-0
Sunderland v Doncaster R Belles	2-3

Group 2 Table	P	W	D	L	F	A	GD	Pts
1 Manchester C	5	5	0	0	15	1	14	15
2 Liverpool	5	4	0	1	8	2	6	12
3 Doncaster R Belles	5	3	0	2	11	10	1	9
4 Sunderland	5	2	0	3	10	11	–1	6
5 Everton	5	1	0	4	6	12	–6	3
6 Durham Women	5	0	0	5	1	15	–14	0

GROUP 3

Aston Villa v Bristol Academy	0-4
Notts Co v Birmingham C	2-1
Oxford U v Yeovil T	0-1
Aston Villa v Birmingham C	1-7
Yeovil T v Bristol Academy	0-3
Birmingham C v Oxford U	3-0
Notts Co v Bristol Academy	1-0
Yeovil T v Aston Villa	3-1
Oxford U v Notts Co	1-6
Aston Villa v Notts Co	0-5
Birmingham C v Yeovil T	4-0
Bristol Academy v Oxford U	3-2
Bristol Academy v Birmingham C	0-2
Notts Co v Yeovil T	5-0
Oxford U v Aston Villa	1-3

Group 3 Table	P	W	D	L	F	A	GD	Pts
1 Notts Co	5	5	0	0	19	2	17	15
2 Birmingham C	5	4	0	1	17	3	14	12
3 Bristol Academy	5	3	0	2	10	5	5	9
4 Yeovil T	5	2	0	3	4	13	–9	6
5 Aston Villa	5	1	0	4	5	20	–15	3
6 Oxford U	5	0	0	5	4	16	–12	0

QUARTER-FINALS

Notts Co v Reading	3-2
Bristol Academy v Liverpool	1-4
Birmingham C v Chelsea	1-0
Arsenal v Manchester C	1-0

SEMI-FINALS

Arsenal v Birmingham C	3-1
Liverpool v Notts Co	0-2

CONTINENTAL TYRES CUP FINAL 2015

Rotherham, Sunday 1 November 2015

Arsenal (2) 3 *(Nobbs 23, 41, Obogagu 90)*

Notts Co (0) 0   5,028

Arsenal: Van Veenendaal; Stoney, Losada, Nobbs, Natalia (Ubogagu 75), Yankey (Sampson 89), Williamson, Corredera (Kelly 86), Rose, Janssen, Bailey.
Notts Co: Telford; Greenwood, Buet, Clarke, Williams (O'Neill 83), White, Scott, Walton (Whelan A 66), Turner, Crichton (Whelan F 44), Bassett■.
Referee: Jane Simms.

THE SSE WOMEN'S FA CUP FINAL 2015

Saturday 1 August 2015

(at Wembley, attendance 30,170)

Chelsea (1) 1   Notts Co (0) 0

Chelsea: Lindahl; Blundell, Fahey, Flaherty, Rafferty, Spence, Bright, Chapman, Davison, Ji So-yun (Coombs 90), Aluko (Marques Borges 81).
Scorer: Ji So-yun 37.

Notts Co: Telford; Walton, Bassett, Turner, Greenwood, Crichton (O'Sullivan 83), Scott, Buet (Whelan 76), Clarke, Williams (Susi 56), White.

Referee: Amy Fearn.

FA WOMEN'S PREMIER LEAGUE 2015–16

FA WOMEN'S PREMIER LEAGUE NORTHERN DIVISION 2015–16

			Home					Away					Total						
		P	W	D	L	F	A	W	D	L	F	A	W	D	L	F	A	GD	Pts
1	Sporting Club Alb	22	10	1	0	35	6	7	1	3	20	16	17	2	3	55	22	33	53
2	Preston NE	22	8	1	2	46	10	7	3	1	25	10	15	4	3	71	20	51	49
3	Blackburn R	22	9	2	0	22	5	5	2	4	17	15	14	4	4	39	20	19	46
4	Stoke C	22	8	1	2	34	13	6	1	4	25	15	14	2	6	59	28	31	44
5	Bradford C	22	6	2	3	25	15	6	0	5	23	16	12	2	8	48	31	17	38
6	Nottingham F	22	8	1	2	22	8	3	3	5	15	19	11	4	7	37	27	10	37
7	Derby Co	22	5	1	5	12	16	4	0	7	25	31	9	1	12	37	47	-10	28
8	Huddersfield T	22	3	3	5	24	30	4	1	6	23	26	7	4	11	47	56	-9	25
9	Newcastle U	22	6	0	5	22	29	1	1	9	11	28	7	1	14	33	57	-24	22
10	Nuneaton T	22	3	0	8	16	24	1	2	8	10	43	4	2	16	26	67	-41	14
11	Guiseley AFC Vixens	22	1	3	7	11	35	2	1	8	15	36	3	4	15	26	71	-45	13
12	Loughborough Foxes	22	3	1	7	19	25	0	1	10	7	33	3	2	17	26	58	-32	11

FA WOMEN'S PREMIER LEAGUE SOUTHERN DIVISION 2015–16

			Home					Away					Total						
		P	W	D	L	F	A	W	D	L	F	A	W	D	L	F	A	GD	Pts
1	Brighton & HA	22	10	0	1	30	6	7	3	1	28	12	17	3	2	58	18	40	54
2	Charlton Ath	22	8	3	0	34	8	8	1	2	34	12	16	4	2	68	20	48	52
3	Cardiff C	22	7	1	3	43	15	8	1	2	23	12	15	2	5	66	27	39	47
4	Coventry U	22	7	2	2	38	9	6	3	2	26	9	13	5	4	64	18	46	44
5	Portsmouth	22	7	1	3	34	14	7	1	3	27	13	14	2	6	61	27	34	44
6	Tottenham H	22	5	1	5	13	13	6	0	5	21	17	11	1	10	34	30	4	34
7	Lewes	22	3	1	7	13	21	5	0	6	17	21	8	1	13	30	42	-12	25
8	C & K Basildon	22	3	3	5	23	32	4	1	6	15	23	7	4	11	38	55	-17	25
9	QPR	22	4	0	7	13	19	2	3	6	12	26	6	3	13	25	45	-20	21
10	West Ham U	22	3	2	6	9	27	2	2	7	12	33	5	4	13	21	60	-39	19
11	Forest Green R	22	1	1	9	8	35	1	1	9	11	41	2	2	18	19	76	-57	8
12	Plymouth Arg	22	0	2	9	12	38	1	1	9	11	51	1	3	18	23	89	-66	6

FA WOMEN'S PREMIER LEAGUE NORTHERN DIVISION ONE 2015–16

			Home					Away					Total						
		P	W	D	L	F	A	W	D	L	F	A	W	D	L	F	A	GD	Pts
1	Middlesbrough	22	9	1	1	57	11	8	2	1	33	11	17	3	2	90	22	68	54
2	Liverpool Marshalls Feds	22	6	1	4	38	20	9	0	2	41	19	15	1	6	79	39	40	46
3	Chorley	22	8	2	1	34	20	5	1	5	26	26	13	3	6	60	46	14	42
4	Hull C	22	5	5	1	28	21	5	2	4	19	18	10	7	5	47	39	8	37
5	Leeds U	22	6	1	4	22	19	5	1	5	13	22	11	2	9	35	41	-6	35
6	Mossley Hill	22	4	1	6	23	21	7	0	4	23	16	11	1	10	46	37	9	34
7	Morecambe	22	7	0	4	25	22	2	2	7	25	37	9	2	11	50	59	-9	29
8	Blackpool Wren R	22	5	1	5	21	23	4	0	7	21	45	9	1	12	42	68	-26	28
9	Chester-le-Street	22	4	3	4	21	19	3	3	5	18	28	7	6	9	39	47	-8	27
10	Tranmere R	22	4	1	6	26	25	1	3	7	12	27	5	4	13	38	52	-14	19
11	Stockport Co*	22	3	1	7	27	29	2	3	6	19	36	5	4	13	46	65	-19	16
12	Norton & Stockton Ancient	22	1	1	9	9	31	1	1	9	11	46	2	2	18	20	77	-57	8

*Stockport Co deducted 3 points.

FA WOMEN'S PREMIER LEAGUE MIDLANDS DIVISION ONE 2015–16

			Home					Away					Total						
		P	W	D	L	F	A	W	D	L	F	A	W	D	L	F	A	GD	Pts
1	Leicester C	22	11	0	0	51	12	11	0	0	42	7	22	0	0	93	19	74	66
2	Wolverhampton W	22	5	3	3	32	19	9	0	2	30	11	14	3	5	62	30	32	45
3	Radcliffe Olympic	22	4	3	4	22	17	7	2	2	30	12	11	5	6	52	29	23	38
4	Solihull	22	6	0	5	19	20	5	2	4	24	27	11	2	9	43	47	-4	35
5	Birmingham & West Midlands	22	4	2	5	16	20	6	1	4	23	22	10	3	9	39	42	-3	33
6	Loughborough Students	22	4	1	6	17	27	5	0	6	27	27	9	1	12	44	54	-10	28
7	Steel City W	22	5	1	5	19	30	3	2	6	16	28	8	3	11	35	58	-23	27
8	Leicester C	22	5	1	5	21	30	2	4	5	25	25	7	5	10	46	55	-9	26
9	Rotherham U	22	4	1	6	25	25	3	2	6	17	28	7	3	12	42	53	-11	24
10	Sporting Khalsa	22	2	1	8	11	32	4	1	6	16	21	6	2	14	27	53	-26	20
11	Peterborough Northern Star	22	4	2	5	24	17	1	2	8	13	27	5	4	13	37	44	-7	20
12	Leafield Ath	22	4	1	6	15	29	2	0	9	15	37	6	1	15	30	66	-36	19

FA WOMEN'S PREMIER LEAGUE SOUTH EAST DIVISION ONE 2015–16

		Home					Away					Total					
		P	W	D	L	F	A	W	D	L	F	A	W	D	L	F	A	GD	Pts
1	Crystal Palace	22	11	0	0	55	10	9	2	0	35	7	20	2	0	90	17	73	62
2	Gillingham	22	8	1	2	46	9	8	2	1	38	11	16	3	3	84	20	64	51
3	Milton Keynes D	22	6	2	3	32	16	7	3	1	31	10	13	5	4	63	26	37	44
4	Luton T	22	7	0	4	24	16	5	4	2	21	16	12	4	6	45	32	13	40
5	Ipswich T	22	3	2	6	25	27	8	1	2	27	17	11	3	8	52	44	8	36
6	Cambridge U	22	4	5	2	21	10	6	0	5	33	14	10	5	7	54	24	30	35
7	Enfield T	22	3	4	4	15	13	4	1	6	19	16	7	5	10	34	29	5	26
8	Norwich C	22	4	1	6	21	28	4	1	6	22	25	8	2	12	43	53	–10	26
9	Denham U	22	3	3	5	12	17	3	2	6	14	18	6	5	11	26	35	–9	23
10	Old Actonians	22	4	1	6	12	26	1	1	9	13	37	5	2	15	25	63	–38	17
11	Lowestoft T	22	1	1	9	10	42	1	2	8	7	55	2	3	17	17	97	–80	9
12	Bedford	22	1	0	10	7	55	1	1	9	9	54	2	1	19	16	109	–93	7

FA WOMEN'S PREMIER LEAGUE SOUTH WEST DIVISION ONE 2015–16

		Home					Away					Total					
		P	W	D	L	F	A	W	D	L	F	A	W	D	L	F	A	GD	Pts
1	Swindon T	18	8	1	0	28	4	7	1	1	21	8	15	2	1	49	12	37	47
2	Chichester C	18	8	1	0	28	4	6	1	2	16	4	14	2	2	44	8	36	44
3	Keynsham T	18	5	1	2	22	9	7	2	1	23	10	12	3	3	45	19	26	39
4	Larkhall Ath	18	6	1	2	26	13	5	2	2	17	10	11	3	4	43	23	20	36
5	Exeter C	18	5	1	3	21	9	3	0	6	15	28	8	1	9	36	37	–1	25
6	Southampton Saints	18	4	2	4	16	17	3	0	5	13	18	7	2	9	29	35	–6	23
7	Maidenhead U	18	5	0	4	20	14	2	1	6	8	23	7	1	10	28	37	–9	22
8	Cheltenham T	18	3	0	6	8	22	1	0	8	9	27	4	0	14	17	49	–32	12
9	Shanklin	18	3	0	6	10	19	0	0	9	6	35	3	0	15	16	54	–38	9
10	St Nicholas	18	2	0	7	14	22	0	0	9	5	30	2	0	16	19	52	–33	6

FA WOMEN'S PREMIER LEAGUE CUP 2015–16

DETERMINING ROUND

After extra time.

Hull C (walkover) v Wolverhampton W, Solihull v Preston NE 0-4, Leafield Ath v Nottingham F 0-8, Nuneaton T v Stockport Co 6-1, Old Actonians v Denham U 3-3* (Old Actonians won 4-2 on penalties), Shanklin v Bedford 2-1, Swindon Spitfires v Swindon T (walkover), Larkhall Ath v Exeter C 6-1, Stoke C v Birmingham & West Midlands 5-0, Morecambe v Leicester C 9-0, Loughborough Students v Norton & Stockton Ancient 1-3, Newcastle U v Bradford C 1-2, Rotherham U v Leicester C 0-5, Ipswich T v Norwich C 3-2*, Forest Green R v Maidenhead U 5-1, Cardiff C v Enfield T 1-0, Charlton Ath (walkover) v Gloucester C, Mossley Hill v Guiseley AFC Vixens v Liverpool Marshalls Feds 1-0*, Loughborough Foxes v Blackburn R 0-6, Chorley v Radcliffe Olympic 1-4, Huddersfield T v Blackpool Wren R 10-1, Peterborough Northern Star v Derby Co 0-5, Middlesbrough v Leeds 5-2, Chester-le-Street v Sporting Club Alb 1-3, Tranmere R v Sporting Khalsa 0-1, Coventry U v C & K Basildon 0-1, West Ham U v Crystal Palace 3-0, Tottenham H v Lewes 5-1, Plymouth Argyle v St Nicholas 7-2, Milton Keynes D v QPR 3-4, Keynsham T v Portsmouth 2-3, Brighton & HA v Gillingham 4-0, Cambridge U v Cheltenham T 3-0, Lowestoft T v Luton T 3-2*, Southampton Saints v Chichester C 0-1.

PRELIMINARY ROUND

Norton & Stockton Ancient v Bradford C	0-17
Blackburn R v Radcliffe Olympic	
Blackburn R walkover.	
Portsmouth v Brighton & HA	1-3*
Cambridge U v Lowestoft T	6-2

FIRST ROUND

Hull C v Preston NE	2-1
Nottingham F v Nuneaton T	4-1
Old Actonians v Shanklin	3-0
Swindon T v Larkhall Ath	5-0
Stoke C v Morecambe	6-1
Bradford C v Leicester C	4-0
Ipswich T v Forest Green R	1-4

Cardiff C v Charlton Ath	3-0
Mossley Hill v Guiseley AFC Vixens	1-0
Blackburn R v Huddersfield T	4-2*
Derby Co v Middlesbrough	3-1
Sporting Club Alb v Sporting Khalsa	4-0
C & K Basildon v West Ham U	1-0
Tottenham H v Plymouth Argyle	4-1
QPR v Brighton & HA	1-7
Cambridge U v Chichester C	0-4

SECOND ROUND

Hull C v Nottingham F	0-3
Old Actonians v Swindon T	2-5
Stoke C v Bradford C	3-2
Forest Green R v Cardiff C	0-9
Mossley Hill v Blackburn R	3-4
Derby Co v Sporting Club Alb	0-3
C & K Basildon v Tottenham H	2-5
Brighton & HA v Chichester C	6-0

QUARTER-FINALS

Nottingham F v Swindon T	2-0
Stoke C v Cardiff C	2-4
Blackburn R v Sporting Club Alb	4-1
Tottenham H v Brighton & HA	1-0

SEMI-FINALS

Nottingham F v Tottenham H	0-1
Cardiff C v Blackburn R	3-0

FA WOMEN'S PREMIER LEAGUE CUP FINAL 2016

Kidderminster, Sunday 8 May 2016

Cardiff C (1) 1 *(Suominen 44)*

Tottenham H (1) 2 *(Baptiste 30, Vio 120)*   446

Cardiff C: McGlynn; Mills, Evans, Britton, Aldridge, Green (Lloyd C 63), Isaac (Willimans C 99), Hincliffe (Lloyd B 104), Bartlett, Suominen, Williams L.
Tottenham H: Wayne; Keown, Schillaci, Rawle (Kmita 76), Green, Vio, Soobadoo, O'Leary (Bergin 72), Baptiste (Humes 99), McLean, Martin.
Referee: Darren McMillan.
aet.

THE SSE WOMEN'S FA CUP 2015–16

After extra time.

FIRST ROUND QUALIFYING

Cleveland v Redcar T	0-7
York C v Cramlington U	7-0
Birtley T v Lowick U	0-2
Whitley Bay v Rutherford	9-0
Ashington Woodhorn Lane v Hartlepool U	2-3
Sheffield U Community v Harrogate Railway	4-2
Wakefield v Brighouse Ath	0-3
Oughtibridge War Memorial v Farsley Celtic	2-1
Brighouse T v Ossett Alb	4-1
Winterton Rangers v Wetherby Ath	2-0
Penrith v Middleton Ath	3-0
City of Manchester v Blackburn Community Sports Club	0-1
AFC Urmston Meadowside v Accrington Girls & Ladies	0-3
Curzon Ashton v Chorltonians	1-2*
(1-1 at the end of normal time)	
Woolton v Blackpool	6-0
Bolton W v Crewe Alexandra	2-1
Wigan Ath v Chester C	7-0
Carlisle U v Burnley	1-3
CMB v Merseyrail Bootle	5-1
Workington Reds v Mersey Girls	1-2
Arnold T v Dronfield T	2-1
Rise Park v Mansfield Hosiery Mills	2-2*
(1-1 at the end of normal time; Rise Park won 4-2 on penalties)	
Ruddington Village v Sleaford T	6-2
Teversal v AFC Leicester	1-2
Nettleham v Desford	6-0
Oadby & Wigston v Long Eaton U	1-7
Coleshill T v Bradwell Belles	3-1
Bilbrook v Rubery	3-1
Stone Dominoes v Malvern T	5-1
Leek CSOB v Stourbridge	1-6
Knowle v The New Saints	0-3
Crusaders v Burton Alb	3-4
Coundon Court v Shrewsbury T	1-4
Lye T v Leek T	4-2
Kettering T v Rothwell Corinthians	5-0
Great Shelford v March T U	6-1
Huntingdon T v Acle U	0-9
Northampton T v Milton	2-1
Riverside v Fulbourn Institute Bluebirds	4-0
Moulton v Netherton U	3-2
Wymondham T v Roade	6-2
Brentwood T v Great Wakering R	0-4
West Billericay v AFC Sudbury	2-8
Brandon T v Bury T	2-5
Haringey Bor v Leverstock Green	6-0
Garston v Colney Heath	1-2
Sherrardswood v Royston T	0-6
AFC Dunstable v Leyton Orient	1-3
Hoddesdon Owls v Stevenage	3-5
Hampton & Richmond Bor v Bracknell T	11-5
Marlow v Ascot U	6-2
Woodley U v Brentford	2-0
Wargrave v Headington	3-1
Oxford C (walkover) v Barton U (withdrawn)	
Wealdstone v Banbury U	3-2
Rottingdean Village v Crawley Wasps	1-8
Carshalton Ath v Barming	15-0
Cowfold v Bexhill U	1-3
Aylesford v Eastbourne	1-3
Margate v Long Lane	2-6
London Corinthians v Parkwood Rangers	3-0
Abbey Rangers v Worthing T	10-1
Herne Bay v Burgess Hill T	2-0
Ashford Girls v Hassocks	2-1
AFC Wimbledon v Regents Park Rangers	9-0
Southampton v Winchester C Flyers	7-2
Royal Wootton Bassett T v Downend Flyers	1-5
Torquay U v Brislington	0-2
Cheltenham Civil Service v Basingstoke T	1-3
Ilminster T v Bristol Union	1-7
Wimborne T v Pen Mill	8-0

SECOND ROUND QUALIFYING

Hartlepool U v Redcar T	2-1*
(0-0 at the end of normal time)	
Whitley Bay v York C	4-3*
(3-3 at the end of normal time)	
Boldon v Prudhoe T	5-0
Lowick U v RACA Tynedale	4-0
Winterton Rangers v Bradford Park Avenue	3-1
Sheffield U Community v Handsworth	0-1
Oughtibridge War Memorial v Sheffield Wednesday	4-1
Brighouse T v Brighouse Ath	4-0
North Ferriby U v Westella & Willerby	0-9
Woolton v Mersey Girls	4-2
Penrith v Burnley	3-3
(3-3 at the end of normal time; Penrith won 4-3 on penalties)	
Accrington Girls & Ladies v CMB	3-1
Chorltonians v Blackburn Community Sports Club	1-3*
Bolton W v Wigan Ath	0-2
AFC Leicester v Nettleham	1-3
Long Eaton U v Rise Park	5-0
Ruddington Village v Arnold T	8-3
Lye T v Coleshill T	7-0
Coventry Ladies Development v Bedworth U	3-2
Stockingford AA Pavilion v Shrewsbury T	1-4
Wyrley v Stone Dominoes	2-2*
(2-2 at the end of normal time; Stone Dominoes won 3-2 on penalties)	
Burton Alb v Stourbridge	3-0
The New Saints v Bilbrook	5-1
Riverside v Daventry T	4-2
Kettering T v Sandy	5-0
Acle U v Newmarket T	11-1
Northampton T v Great Shelford	1-2*
(1-1 at the end of normal time)	
Moulton v Wymondham T	0-3
Colchester T v Silver End U	5-0
Sawbridgeworth T v AFC Sudbury	1-0
Bury T v Great Wakering R	1-5
Leyton Orient v Stevenage	2-0
Hemel Hempstead T v Colney Heath	4-2
Royston T v Haringey Bor	0-2
Oxford C v Hampton & Richmond Bor	0-1
Wargrave v Marlow	3-7
Wealdstone v Newbury	3-1
Woodley U v Queens Park Rangers Girls	0-4
Ashford Girls v London Corinthians	0-6
Fulham Foundation v Carshalton Ath	2-1
Herne Bay v Eastbourne	2-0
Dartford Royals v Crawley Wasps	0-6
Bexhill U v Surrey Eagles	1-2
AFC Wimbledon v Abbey Rangers	10-0
Long Lane v Eastbourne T	4-0
Frome T v AEK Boco	1-2
Bristol Union v Middlezoy R	4-2
New Forest v Poole T	0-12
Downend Flyers v Basingstoke T	0-4
Southampton v Wimborne T	4-0
Team Solent v Fleet T	7-0
Brislington v Keynsham T Development	6-2

THIRD ROUND QUALIFYING

Blackburn Community Sports Club v Wigan Ath	4-3
Whitley Bay v Westella & Willerby	9-2
Middlesbrough v Lowick U	11-0
Woolton v Boldon	1-0

Chester-le-Street T v Accrington Girls & Ladies	3-0
Mossley Hill v Penrith	4-0
Brighouse T v Winterton Rangers	6-1
Liverpool Marshalls Feds v Chorley	2-1
Morecambe v Leeds	5-0
Hull C v Tranmere R	1-1*

(1-1 at the end of normal time;
Tranmere R won 5-4 on penalties)

Blackpool Wren R v Hartlepool U	1-2
Rotherham U v Long Eaton U	4-5
The New Saints v Leafield Ath	4-3
Lye T v Nettleham	3-6
Wolverhampton W v Handsworth	9-0
Leicester C LFC v Stockport Co	7-4
Radcliffe Olympic v Oughtbridge War Memorial	2-1*

(1-1 at the end of normal time)

Burton Alb v Ruddington Village	6-0
Leicester C WFC v Loughborough Students	3-2
Stone Dominoes v Kettering T	3-2*

(2-2 at the end of normal time)

Coventry Ladies Development v Shrewsbury T	5-0
Sporting Khalsa v Steel C W	1-3
Wealdstone v Bedford	1-4
Norwich C v Marlow	0-1
Sawbridgeworth T v Ipswich T	0-6
Luton T v Acle U	3-1
Enfield T v Haringey Bor	4-0
Wymondham T v Cambridge U's	1-0
Leyton Orient v Great Shelford	0-2*

(0-0 at the end of normal time)

Great Wakering R v Milton Keynes Dons	1-3
Hampton & Richmond Bor v Peterborough Northern Star	0-7
Colchester T v Hemel Hempstead T	1-2
Riverside v Denham U	0-4
Queens Park Rangers Girls v Lowestoft T	1-5
Southampton v London Corinthians	2-2*

(2-2 at the end of normal time;
London Corinthians won 5-4 on penalties)

Crystal Palace v Team Solent	5-0
Gloucester C (withdrawn) v Southampton Saints (walkover)	
AEK Boco v Shanklin	1-0
Gillingham v AFC Wimbledon	7-0
Keynsham T v Cheltenham T	6-2
Bristol Union v Herne Bay	1-3
Larkhall Ath v Swindon Spitfires	11-1
Basingstoke T v Fulham Foundation	0-2
St Nicholas v Surrey Eagles	6-1
Chichester C v Poole T	7-1
Crawley Wasps v Old Actonians	0-1
Long Lane v Swindon T	0-12
Brislington v Maidenhead U	2-3

FOURTH ROUND QUALIFYING

Whitley Bay v Woolton	1-0
Chester-le-Street T v Brighouse T	3-1
Morecambe v Hartlepool U	6-3
Mossley Hill v Blackburn Community Sports Club	4-2
Middlesbrough v Liverpool Marshalls Feds	1-3
Tranmere R v Steel C W	3-0
Burton Alb v Radcliffe Olympic	1-1*

(Radcliffe Olympic won 4-3 on penalties)

The New Saints v Wolverhampton W	0-3
Long Eaton U v Leicester C LFC	4-1
Nettleham (unable to fulfill fixture) v Leicester C WFC (walkover)	
Coventry Ladies Development v Stone Dominoes	1-3
Marlow v Luton T	1-4
Enfield T v Great Shelford	1-0
Peterborough Northern Star v Hemel Hempstead T	8-0
Wymondham T v Bedford	0-2
Ipswich T v Milton Keynes Dons	2-3
Lowestoft T v London Corinthians	1-8
Old Actonians v Southampton Saints	4-1
Denham U v Crystal Palace	1-2

AEK Boco v Chichester C	0-10
Larkhall Ath v Swindon T	2-3
Fulham Foundation v St Nicholas	2-0
Keynsham T v Maidenhead U	5-0
Gillingham v Herne Bay	3-0

FIRST ROUND

Tranmere R v Whitley Bay	2-3
Morecambe v Chester-le-Street T	5-3*

(3-3 at the end of normal time)

Mossley Hill v Liverpool Marshalls Feds	2-1
Peterborough Northern Star v Radcliffe Olympic	1-1*

(0-0 at the end of normal time;
Radcliffe Olympic won 4-2 on penalties)

Long Eaton U v Wolverhampton W	3-2
Leicester C WFC v Stone Dominoes	8-0
Milton Keynes Dons v Crystal Palace	0-4
London Corinthians v Gillingham	3-4*

(1-1 at the end of normal time)

Bedford v Luton T	2-3
Fulham Foundation v Enfield T	3-3*

(3-3 at the end of normal time;
Fulham Foundation won 3-1 on penalties)

Chichester C v Keynsham T	6-0
Old Actonians v Swindon T	0-1

SECOND ROUND

Whitley Bay v Stoke C	0-2
Bradford C v Huddersfield T	3-0
Preston North End v Derby Co	2-1
Nuneaton T v Blackburn R	0-3
Sporting Club Alb v Long Eaton U	3-0
Loughborough Foxes v Guiseley Vixens	4-1
Leicester C WFC v Radcliffe Olympic	2-1
Newcastle U v Mossley Hill	4-1
Nottingham Forest v Morecambe	3-0
Chichester C v Queens Park Rangers	3-4
Crystal Palace v West Ham U	1-2
Fulham Foundation v Lewes	0-10
Charlton Ath v Plymouth Argyle	9-0
Swindon T v Tottenham Hotspur	1-4
Forest Green R v Gillingham	1-1*

(1-1 at the end of normal time;
Gillingham won 3-1 on penalties)

Brighton & HA v Luton T	7-0
Portsmouth v Cardiff C	2-0
C&K Basildon v Coventry U	0-2

THIRD ROUND

Aston Villa v Portsmouth	1-0
Charlton Ath v Newcastle U	10-0
Sheffield v Leicester C WFC	5-1
London Bees v Durham	0-9
Brighton & HA v Oxford U	10-0
West Ham U v Blackburn R	0-7
Gillingham v Tottenham Hotspur	0-1
Sporting Club Alb v Coventry U	1-0
Everton v Stoke C	7-0
Loughborough Foxes v Lewes	1-1*

(1-1 at the end of normal time;
Loughborough Foxes won 6-5 on penalties)

Yeovil T v Bradford C	2-0
Nottingham Forest v Preston North End	2-0
Watford v Millwall Lionesses	1-3
Bristol C v Queens Park Rangers	7-1

FOURTH ROUND

Bristol C v Yeovil T	0-0*

(Yeovil T won 3-2 on penalties)

Sheffield v Sporting Club Alb	1-3
Loughborough Foxes v Millwall Lionesses	1-2*

(0-0 at the end of normal time)

Brighton & HA v Blackburn R	2-1
Everton v Nottingham Forest	5-0
Durham v Charlton Ath	3-1
Tottenham Hotspur v Aston Villa	2-3*

(2-2 at the end of normal time)

Arsenal versus Chelsea in the Women's FA Cup final at Wembley Stadium on 14 May. Arsenal triumphed 1-0 in front of nearly 33,000 spectators. (Darren Walsh/Chelsea FC/Press Association Images)

FIFTH ROUND

Birmingham C v Arsenal	1-1*
(Arsenal won 5–3 on penalties)	
Doncaster R Belles v Chelsea	1-4
Brighton & HA v Sporting Club Alb	3-4
Reading v Millwall Lionesses	2-0
Yeovil T v Sunderland	0-2
Liverpool v Manchester C	0-2
Notts Co v Durham	3-1
Aston Villa v Everton	1-0

SIXTH ROUND

Manchester C v Sporting Club Alb	2-0
Sunderland v Reading	3-0
Chelsea v Aston Villa	6-0
Arsenal v Notts Co	2-2
(Arsenal won 5–4 on penalties)	

SEMI-FINALS

Arsenal v Sunderland	7-0
Chelsea v Manchester C	2-1*
(1-1 at the end of normal time)	

THE SSE WOMEN'S FA CUP FINAL 2016

Wembley, Saturday 14 May 2016

Arsenal (1) 1 *(Carter 18)*

Chelsea (0) 0   32,912

Arsenal: Veenendaal; Scott, Stoney, Henning, Mitchell, Losada, Williams (Janssen 74), Nobbs, Carter, Smith (van de Donk 74), Oshoala (Williamson 89).
Chelsea: Lindahl; Blundell, Bright (England 79), Flaherty, Borges, Chapman, Spence (Fahey 46), Davison, Ji So-yun, Carney (Aluko 55), Kirby.
Substitutes: 6 Niamh for Spence 46,
Referee: Sarah Garratt.

UEFA WOMEN'S CHAMPIONS LEAGUE 2015–16

After extra time.

QUALIFYING ROUND – GROUP 1 (BOSNIA & HERZEGOVINA)

Sarajevo v Vllaznia	5-0
Konak Belediyespor v Minsk	1-10
Minsk v Sarajevo	3-0
Konak Belediyespor v Vllaznia	5-1
Sarajevo v Konak Belediyespor	3-1
Vllaznia v Minsk	0-3

Group 1 Table	P	W	D	L	F	A	GD	Pts
Minsk	3	3	0	0	16	1	15	9
Sarajevo	3	2	0	1	8	4	4	6
Konak Belediyespor	3	1	0	2	7	14	–7	3
Vllaznia	3	0	0	3	1	13	–12	0

GROUP 2 (NORTHERN IRELAND)

NSA Sofia v Dragon 2014	6-0
PAOK Thessaloniki v Glentoran Belfast U	4-0
PAOK Thessaloniki v Dragon 2014	10-0
Glentoran Belfast U v NSA Sofia	1-2
NSA Sofia v PAOK Thessaloniki	0-4
Dragon 2014 v Glentoran Belfast U	0-2

Group 2 Table	P	W	D	L	F	A	GD	Pts
PAOK Thessaloniki	3	3	0	0	18	0	18	9
NSA Sofia	3	2	0	1	8	5	3	6
Glentoran Belfast U	3	1	0	2	3	6	–3	3
Dragon 2014	3	0	0	3	0	18	–18	0

GROUP 3 (CYPRUS)

Apollon v Klaksvikar Itrottarfelag	2-0
Stjarnan v Hibernians	5-0
Klaksvikar Itrottarfelag v Stjarnan	0-4
Apollon v Hibernians	8-0
Stjarnan v Apollon	2-0
Hibernians v Klaksvikar Itrottarfelag	3-3

Group 3 Table	P	W	D	L	F	A	GD	Pts
Stjarnan	3	3	0	0	11	0	11	9
Apollon	3	2	0	1	10	2	8	6
Klaksvikar Itrottarfelag	3	0	1	2	3	9	–6	1
Hibernians	3	0	1	2	3	16	–13	1

GROUP 4 (NETHERLANDS)

FC Twente v Ferencvaros	2-0
ASA Tel-Aviv University v Jeunesse Jonglenster	5-1

FC Twente v Jeunesse Jonglenster 10-0
Ferencvaros v ASA Tel-Aviv University 2-1
ASA Tel-Aviv University v FC Twente 0-7
Jeunesse Jonglenster v Ferencvaros 0-11

Group 4 Table	P	W	D	L	F	A	GD	Pts
FC Twente	3	3	0	0	19	0	19	9
Ferencvaros	3	2	0	1	13	3	10	6
ASA Tel-Aviv University	3	1	0	2	6	10	–4	3
Jeunesse Jonglenster	3	0	0	3	1	26	–25	0

GROUP 5 (SLOVENIA)
Olimpia Cluj Napoca v Parnu Jalgpalliklubi 4-0
Pomurje v Ekonomist 4-0
Olimpia Cluj Napoca v Ekonomist 6-1
Parnu Jalgpalliklubi v Pomurje 1-2
Pomurje v Olimpia Cluj Napoca 0-2
Ekonomist v Parnu Jalgpalliklubi 1-2

Group 5 Table	P	W	D	L	F	A	GD	Pts
Olimpia Cluj Napoca	3	3	0	0	12	1	11	9
Pomurje	3	2	0	1	6	3	3	6
Parnu Jalgpalliklubi	3	1	0	2	3	7	–4	3
Ekonomist	3	0	0	3	2	12	–10	0

GROUP 6 (CROATIA)
Spartak Subotica v Benfica 2-1
Osijek v Noroc Nimoreni 4-0
Spartak Subotica v Noroc Nimoreni 4-1
Benfica v Osijek 3-0
Osijek v Spartak Subotica 0-3
Noroc Nimoreni v Benfica 0-3

Group 6 Table	P	W	D	L	F	A	GD	Pts
Spartak Subotica	3	3	0	0	9	2	7	9
Benfica	3	2	0	1	7	2	5	6
Osijek	3	1	0	2	4	6	–2	3
Noroc Nimoreni	3	0	0	3	1	11	–10	0

GROUP 7 (POLAND)
Gintra Universitetas v Wexford Youths 0-1
Medyk Konin v Cardiff Met 5-0
Gintra Universitetas v Cardiff Met 5-1
Wexford Youths v Medyk Konin 0-6
Medyk Konin v Gintra Universitetas 4-0
Cardiff Met v Wexford Youths 1-5

Group 7 Table	P	W	D	L	F	A	GD	Pts
Medyk Konin	3	3	0	0	15	0	15	9
Wexford Youths	3	2	0	1	6	7	–1	6
Gintra Universitetas	3	1	0	2	5	6	–1	3
Cardiff Met	3	0	0	3	2	15	–13	0

GROUP 8 (FINLAND)
Kharkiv v Rigas Futbola skola 4-1
PK-35 Vantaa v Nove Zamky 9-0
Nove Zamky v Kharkiv 0-5
PK-35 Vantaa v Rigas Futbola skola 9-0
Kharkiv v PK-35 Vantaa 1-2
Rigas Futbola skola v Nove Zamky 3-2

Group 8 Table	P	W	D	L	F	A	GD	Pts
PK-35 Vantaa	3	3	0	0	20	1	19	9
Kharkiv	3	2	0	1	10	3	7	6
Rigas Futbola skola	3	1	0	2	4	15	–11	3
Nove Zamky	3	0	0	3	2	17	–15	0

ROUND OF 32 FIRST LEG
BIIK-Kazygurt v Barcelona 1-1
PK-35 Vantaa v Rosengard 0-2
PAOK Thessaloniki v Orebro 0-3
Slavia Prague v Brondby 4-1
Standard v Frankfurt 0-2
Spratzern v Verona 4-5
Lillestrom v Zurich 1-0
FC Twente v Bayern Munich 1-1
Atletico Madrid v Zorky 0-2
Brescia v Liverpool 1-0
Stjarnan v Zvezda 2005 1-3
Minsk v Fortuna 0-2
Spartak Subotica v Wolfsburg 0-0
Medyk Konin v Lyon 0-6
Olimpia Cluj Napoca v Paris Saint-Germain 0-6
Chelsea v Glasgow C 1-0

ROUND OF 32 SECOND LEG
		Agg
Wolfsburg v Spartak Subotica	4-0	4-0
Lyon v Medyk Konin	3-0	9-0
Brondby v Slavia Prague	1-0	2-4
Bayern Munich v FC Twente	2-2	3-3

FC Twente won on away goals
Zurich v Lillestrom	1-1*	1-2
Rosengard v PK-35 Vantaa	7-0	9-0
Fortuna v Minsk	4-0	6-0
Barcelona v BIIK-Kazygurt	4-1	5-2
Liverpool v Brescia	0-1	0-2
Orebro v PAOK	5-0	8-0
Paris Saint-Germain v Olimpia Cluj Napoca	9-0	15-0
Glasgow C v Chelsea	0-3	0-4
Zvezda 2005 v Stjarnan	3-1	6-2
Frankfurt v Standard	6-0	8-0
Zorky v Atletico Madrid	0-3	2-3
Verona v Spratzern	2-2	7-6

ROUND OF 16 FIRST LEG
Lillestrom v Frankfurt 0-2
Orebro v Paris Saint-Germain 1-1
FC Twente v Barcelona 0-1
Atletico Madrid v Lyon 1-3
Chelsea v Wolfsburg 1-2
Brescia v Fortuna 1-0
Slavia Prague v Zvezda 2005 2-1
Verona v Rosengard 1-3

ROUND OF 16 SECOND LEG
		Agg
Wolfsburg v Chelsea	2-0	4-1
Lyon v Atletico Madrid	6-0	9-1
Frankfurt v Lillestrom	0-2*	2-2

Frankfurt won 5-4 on penalties
Barcelona v FC Twente	1-0	2-0
Fortuna v Brescia	1-1	1-2
Paris Saint-Germain v Orebro	0-0	1-1

Paris Saint-Germain won on away goals
| Zvezda 2005 v Slavia Prague | 0-0 | 1-2 |
| Rosengard v Verona | 5-1 | 8-2 |

QUARTER-FINALS FIRST LEG
Wolfsburg v Brescia 3-0
Barcelona v Paris Saint-Germain 0-0
Lyon v Slavia Prague 9-1
Rosengard v Frankfurt 0-1

QUARTER-FINALS SECOND LEG
		Agg
Frankfurt v Rosengard	0-1*	1-1

Frankfurt won 5-4 on penalties
Slavia Prague v Lyon	0-0	1-9
Paris Saint-Germain v Barcelona	1-0	1-0
Brescia v Wolfsburg	0-3	0-6

SEMI-FINALS FIRST LEG
Lyon v Paris Saint-Germain 7-0
Wolfsburg v Frankfurt 4-0

SEMI-FINALS SECOND LEG
		Agg
Frankfurt v Wolfsburg	1-0	1-4
Paris Saint-Germain v Lyon	0-1	0-8

WOMEN'S CHAMPIONS LEAGUE FINAL 2016

Reggio Emilia, Thursday 26 May 2016

Wolfsburg (0) 1 *(Popp 88)*

Lyon (1) 1 *(Hegerberg 12)*

Wolfsburg: Schult; Jakabfi (Bachmann 59), Fischer, Peter, Blasse (Bunte 113), Popp, Bernauer (Wullaert 73), Dickenmann, Kerschowski, Goessling, Bussaglia.
Lyon: Bouhaddi; Renard, Kumagai, Henry, Majri, Le Sommer (Schelin 79), Necib, Hegerberg, Bremer (Thomis 86), Abily, Bathy.
Referee: Katalin Kulcsar (Hungary).
aet; Lyon won 4-3 on penalties.

WOMEN'S EURO 2017

QUALIFYING ROUND – GROUP 1

Slovenia v Scotland	0-3
Iceland v Belarus	2-0
Slovenia v Belarus	3-0
FYR Macedonia v Iceland	0-4
Scotland v Belarus	7-0
Slovenia v Iceland	0-6
FYR Macedonia v Scotland	1-4
FYR Macedonia v Belarus	0-2
Scotland v FYR Macedonia	10-0
Scotland v Slovenia	3-1
Belarus v Iceland	0-5
Slovenia v FYR Macedonia	8-1
FYR Macedonia v Slovenia	0-9
Scotland v Iceland	0-4
Belarus v Scotland	0-1
Iceland v FYR Macedonia	8-0

Group 1 Table	P	W	D	L	F	A	GD	Pts
Iceland	6	6	0	0	29	0	29	18
Scotland	7	6	0	1	28	6	22	18
Slovenia	6	3	0	3	21	13	8	9
Belarus	6	1	0	5	2	18	–16	3
FYR Macedonia	7	0	0	7	2	45	–43	0

GROUP 2

Finland v Montenegro	1-0
Republic of Ireland v Finland	0-2
Portugal v Republic of Ireland	1-2
Finland v Spain	1-2
Republic of Ireland v Spain	0-3
Portugal v Montenegro	6-1
Spain v Portugal	2-0
Montenegro v Spain	0-7
Montenegro v Republic of Ireland	0-5
Portugal v Spain	1-4
Montenegro v Finland	1-7
Spain v Republic of Ireland	3-0
Finland v Republic of Ireland	4-1
Montenegro v Portugal	0-3
Finland v Portugal	0-0
Republic of Ireland v Montenegro	9-0

Group 2 Table	P	W	D	L	F	A	GD	Pts
Spain	6	6	0	0	21	2	19	18
Finland	6	4	1	1	15	4	11	13
Republic of Ireland	7	3	0	4	17	13	4	9
Portugal	6	2	1	3	11	9	2	7
Montenegro	7	0	0	7	2	38	–36	0

GROUP 3

France v Romania	3-0
Albania v Greece	1-4
Ukraine v Romania	2-2
Romania v Albania	3-0
Ukraine v France	0-3
Greece v Romania	1-3
Albania v France	0-6
Greece v France	0-3
Greece v Albania	3-2
Albania v Ukraine	0-4
Greece v Ukraine	1-3
Ukraine v Albania	2-0
Romania v France	0-1
France v Ukraine	4-0
Albania v Romania	0-3
France v Greece	1-0
Ukraine v Greece	2-0

Group 3 Table	P	W	D	L	F	A	GD	Pts
France	7	7	0	0	21	0	21	21
Ukraine	7	4	1	2	13	10	3	13
Romania	6	3	1	2	11	7	4	10
Greece	7	2	0	5	9	15	–6	6
Albania	7	0	0	7	3	25	–22	0

GROUP 4

Moldova v Sweden	0-3
Sweden v Poland	3-0
Poland v Slovakia	2-0
Denmark v Moldova	4-0
Slovakia v Moldova	4-0
Sweden v Denmark	1-0
Slovakia v Denmark	0-1
Moldova v Poland	1-3
Moldova v Slovakia	0-4
Poland v Denmark	0-0
Slovakia v Sweden	0-3
Slovakia v Poland	2-1
Poland v Sweden	0-4
Denmark v Slovakia	4-0
Sweden v Moldova	6-0
Denmark v Poland	6-0

Group 4 Table	P	W	D	L	F	A	GD	Pts
Sweden	6	6	0	0	20	0	20	18
Denmark	6	4	1	1	15	1	14	13
Slovakia	7	3	0	4	10	11	–1	9
Poland	7	2	1	4	6	16	–10	7
Moldova	6	0	0	6	1	24	–23	0

GROUP 5

Turkey v Croatia	1-4
Germany v Hungary	12-0
Croatia v Germany	0-1
Hungary v Turkey	1-0
Germany v Russia	2-0
Germany v Turkey	7-0
Croatia v Hungary	1-1
Turkey v Russia	0-0
Hungary v Russia	0-1
Croatia v Turkey	3-0
Turkey v Germany	0-6
Hungary v Croatia	2-0
Germany v Croatia	2-0
Russia v Hungary	3-3
Russia v Turkey	2-0
Turkey v Hungary	2-1
Croatia v Russia	0-3

Group 5 Table	P	W	D	L	F	A	GD	Pts
Germany	6	6	0	0	30	0	30	18
Russia	6	3	2	1	9	5	4	11
Hungary	7	2	2	3	8	19	–11	8
Croatia	7	2	1	4	8	10	–2	7
Turkey	8	1	1	6	3	24	–21	4

GROUP 6

Italy v Georgia	6-1
Georgia v Czech Republic	0-3
Italy v Switzerland	0-3
Georgia v Northern Ireland	0-3
Czech Republic v Italy	0-3
Switzerland v Georgia	4-0
Northern Ireland v Switzerland	1-8
Switzerland v Czech Republic	5-1
Switzerland v Italy	2-1
Czech Republic v Georgia	4-1
Italy v Northern Ireland	3-1
Northern Ireland v Georgia	4-0
Czech Republic v Switzerland	0-5
Georgia v Italy	0-7
Czech Republic v Northern Ireland	3-0

Group 6 Table	P	W	D	L	F	A	GD	Pts
Switzerland	6	6	0	0	27	3	24	18
Italy	6	4	0	2	20	7	13	12
Czech Republic	6	3	0	3	11	14	–3	9
Northern Ireland	5	2	0	3	9	14	–5	6
Georgia	7	0	0	7	2	31	–29	0

GROUP 7

Estonia v Serbia	0-1
Estonia v England	0-8
Belgium v Bosnia-Herzegovina	6-0
Bosnia-Herzegovina v Estonia	4-0
Serbia v Estonia	3-0
Bosnia-Herzegovina v Belgium	0-5
Serbia v Bosnia-Herzegovina	0-1

England v Bosnia-Herzegovina	1-0
Belgium v Serbia	1-1
England v Belgium	1-1
Bosnia-Herzegovina v England	0-1
Belgium v Estonia	6-0
Estonia v Belgium	0-5
England v Serbia	7-0
Estonia v Bosnia-Herzegovina	0-1
Serbia v England	0-7

Group 7 Table	P	W	D	L	F	A	GD	Pts
England	6	5	1	0	25	1	24	16
Belgium	6	4	2	0	24	2	22	14
Bosnia-Herzegovina	7	3	0	4	6	13	–7	9
Serbia	6	2	1	3	5	16	–11	7
Estonia	7	0	0	7	0	28	–28	0

GROUP 8

Kazakhstan v Austria	0-2
Kazakhstan v Norway	0-4

Austria v Wales	3-0
Israel v Kazakhstan	0-0
Norway v Wales	4-0
Israel v Austria	0-1
Wales v Kazakhstan	4-0
Israel v Wales	2-2
Israel v Norway	0-1
Austria v Kazakhstan	6-1
Austria v Norway	0-1
Kazakhstan v Wales	0-4
Kazakhstan v Israel	1-0
Norway v Austria	2-2
Austria v Israel	4-0
Wales v Norway	0-2

Group 8 Table	P	W	D	L	F	A	GD	Pts
Norway	6	5	1	0	14	2	12	16
Austria	7	5	1	1	18	4	14	16
Wales	6	2	1	3	10	11	–1	7
Kazakhstan	7	1	1	5	2	20	–18	4
Israel	6	0	2	4	2	9	–7	2

ENGLAND WOMEN'S INTERNATIONALS 2015–16

■ *Denotes player sent off.*

FRIENDLIES
Tallinn, Monday 21 September 2015

Estonia (0) 0

England (0) 8 *(Carter 2, 83, 90, Potter 34, Kirby 40, 81, Scott J 53, Christiansen 74)*   1342
England: Telford; Turner, Houghton, Stokes, Davison (White 78), Scott J (Aluko 68), Potter, Kirby, Christiansen, Carter, Clarke (Stoney 90).

Duisburg, Thursday 26 November 2015

Germany (0) 0

England (0) 0   6705
England: Bardsley; Bronze, Houghton, Flaherty, Greenwood, Scott J, Williams (Christiansen 68), Nobbs, Kirby (Clarke 75), Taylor (Duggan 75), Stokes.

DEWELLBON CUP
Yongchuan, Friday 23 October 2015

China (2) 2 *(Shuang Wang 5, 45)*

England (1) 1 *(Aluko 45)*   12,000
England: Bardsley; Scott A, Houghton, Flaherty, Scott J, Potter, Christiansen (Coombs 89), Bronze (Stokes 65), Aluko, Sanderson (Taylor 74), Davison (Spence 84).

Yongchuan, Tuesday 27 October 2015

Australia (0) 0   1800

England (0) 1 *(Christiansen 50)*
England: Bardsley; Bronze, Houghton, Flaherty, Rafferty, Scott A, Scott J, Potter, Stokes, Christiansen (Coombs 90), Aluko (Taylor 57).

**WOMEN'S EUROPEAN CHAMPIONSHIP 2017 –
QUALIFIERS GROUP 7**
Bristol, Sunday 29 November 2015

England (0) 1 *(Scott J 69)*

Bosnia-Herzegovina (0) 0   13,040
England: Bardsley; Turner, Houghton (Rose 84), Stoney, Stokes, Bassett, Nobbs, Clarke (Scott J 55), Christiansen (Duggan 60), Davison, Aluko.

Rotherham, Friday 8 April 2016

England (0) 1 *(Scott J 84)*

Belgium (1) 1 *(Cayman 18)*   10,550
England: Bardsley; Scott A, Houghton, Stoney, Greenwood, Williams, Nobbs, Chapman (Davison 78), Stokes (Carney 56), Scott J, Duggan (Aluko 64).

Zenica, Tuesday 12 April 2016

Bosnia-Herzegovina (0) 0

England (0) 1 *(Carney 86)*
England: Bardsley; Scott A (Duggan 85), Houghton, Stoney (Bronze 67), Greenwood, Davison, Williams (Kirby 67), Nobbs, Carney, Scott J, Aluko.

Wycombe, Saturday 4 June 2016

England (3) 7 *(Greenwood 16, Carney 34 (pen), 60, 63, Daly 42, White 51, Christiansen 52)*

Serbia (0) 0   5903
England: Bardsley; Bronze, Houghton, Bassett, Greenwood, Williams, Scott J (Davison 65), Christiansen (Moore 75), Carney, White, Daly (Parris 57).

Stara Pazova, Tuesday 7 June 2016

Serbia (0) 0

England (3) 7 *(Scott J 13, White 28, Davison 41, 46, Damjanovic 53 (og), Parris 69, 90)*
England: Chamberlain; Bronze, Houghton, Stoney, Stokes, Williams (Christiansen 46), Moore, Scott J (Scott A 57), Carney, White (Parris 57), Davison.

SHEBELIVES CUP, USA
Tampa, Friday 4 March 2016

USA (0) 1 *(Dunn 72)*

England (0) 0   13,027
England: Bardsley; Bronze, Houghton, Flaherty, Greenwood (Christiansen 65), Williams (Carney 77), Nobbs, Scott J, Stokes, Duggan (Aluko 88), Taylor (Kirby 78).

Nashville, Sunday 6 March 2016

England (1) 1 *(Duggan 9)*

Germany (0) 2 *(Flaherty 76 (og), Peter 82 (pen))*   25,363
England: Bardsley; Scott A, Houghton, Flaherty (Stoney 79), Greenwood (Carney 70), Williams, Nobbs (Davison 83), Scott J, Chapman, Stokes, Duggan (Kirby 82).

Boca Raton, Thursday 9 March 2016

England (0) 0

France (0) 0   13,501
England: Bardsley; Scott A (Bronze 69), Houghton, Stoney, Rafferty, Williams, Nobbs, Chapman, Stokes (Carney 71), Scott J, Duggan (Aluko 56).

ENGLAND WOMEN'S INTERNATIONAL MATCHES 1972–2016

Note: In the results that follow, WC = World Cup; EC = European (UEFA) Championships; M = Mundialito; CC = Cyprus Cup; AC = Algarve Cup. * = After extra time. Games were organised by the Women's Football Association from 1971 to 1992 and the Football Association from 1993 to date.

v ARGENTINA

wc2007	17 Sept	Chengdu	6-1

v AUSTRALIA

2003	3 Sept	Burnley	1-0
cc2015	6 Mar	Nicosia	3-0
2015	27 Oct	Yongchuan	1-0

v AUSTRIA

wc2005	1 Sept	Amstetten	4-1
wc2006	20 Apr	Gillingham	4-0
wc2010	25 Mar	Shepherd's Bush	3-0
wc2010	21 Aug	Krems	4-0

v BELARUS

EC2007	27 Oct	Walsall	4-0
EC2008	8 May	Minsk	6-1
wc2013	21 Sept	Bournemouth	6-0
wc2014	14 June	Minsk	3-0

v BELGIUM

1978	31 Oct	Southampton	3-0
1980	1 May	Ostende	1-2
M1984	20 Aug	Jesolo	1-1
M1984	25 Aug	Caorle	2-1
1989	14 May	Epinal	2-0
EC1990	17 Mar	Ypres	3-0
EC1990	7 Apr	Sheffield	1-0
EC1993	6 Nov	Koksijde	3-0
EC1994	13 Mar	Nottingham	6-0
EC2016	8 Apr	Rotherham	1-1

v BOSNIA-HERZEGOVINA

EC2015	29 Nov	Bristol	1-0
EC2016	12 Apr	Zenica	1-0

v CANADA

wc1995	6 June	Helsingborg	3-2
2003	19 May	Montreal	0-4
2003	22 May	Ottawa	0-4
cc2009	12 Mar	Nicosia	3-1
cc2010	27 Feb	Nicosia	0-1
cc2011	7 Mar	Nicosia	0-2
cc2013	13 Mar	Nicosia	1-0
2013	7 Apr	Rotherham	1-0
cc2014	10 Mar	Nicosia	2-0
cc2015	11 Mar	Larnaca	1-0
2015	29 May	Hamilton	0-1
wc2015	27 June	Vancouver	2-1

v CHINA

AC2005	15 Mar	Guia	0-0*
2007	26 Jan	Guangzhou	0-2
2015	9 Apr	Manchester	2-1
2015	23 Oct	Yongchuan	1-2

v COLOMBIA

wc2015	17 June	Montreal	2-1

v CROATIA

EC1995	19 Nov	Charlton	5-0
EC1996	18 Apr	Osijek	2-0
EC2012	31 Mar	Vrbovec	6-0
EC2012	19 Sept	Walsall	3-0

v CZECH REPUBLIC

2005	26 May	Walsall	4-1
EC2008	20 Mar	Doncaster	0-0
EC2008	28 Sept	Prague	5-1

v DENMARK

1979	19 May	Hvidovre	1-3
1979	13 Sept	Hull	2-2
1981	9 Sept	Tokyo	0-1
EC1984	8 Apr	Crewe	2-1
EC1984	28 Apr	Hjorring	1-0
M1985	19 Aug	Caorle	0-1
EC1987	8 Nov	Blackburn	2-1
EC1988	8 May	Herning	0-2
1991	28 June	Nordby	0-0
1991	30 June	Nordby	3-3
1999	22 Aug	Odense	1-0
2001	23 Aug	Northampton	0-3
2004	19 Feb	Portsmouth	2-0
EC2005	8 June	Blackburn	1-2
2009	22 July	Swindon	1-0

v ESTONIA

2015	21 Sept	Tallinn	8-0

v FINLAND

1979	19 July	Sorrento	3-1
EC1987	25 Oct	Kirkkonummi	2-1
EC1988	4 Sept	Millwall	1-1
EC1989	1 Oct	Brentford	0-0
EC1990	29 Sept	Tampere	0-0
2000	28 Sept	Leyton	2-1
EC2005	5 June	Manchester	3-2
2009	9 Feb	Larnaca	2-2
2009	11 Feb	Larnaca	4-1
EC2009	3 Sept	Turku	3-2
cc2012	28 Feb	Nicosia	3-1
cc2014	7 Mar	Larnaca	3-0
cc2015	4 Mar	Larnaca	3-1

v FRANCE

1973	22 Apr	Brion	3-0
1974	7 Nov	Wimbledon	2-0
1977	26 Feb	Longjumeau	0-0
M1988	22 July	Riva del Garda	1-1
1998	15 Feb	Alencon	2-3
1999	15 Sept	Yeovil	0-1
2000	16 Aug	Marseilles	0-1
wc2002	17 Oct	Crystal Palace	0-1
wc2002	16 Nov	St Etienne	0-1
wc2006	26 Mar	Blackburn	0-0
wc2006	30 Sept	Rennes	1-1
cc2009	7 Mar	Paralimni	2-2
wc2011	9 July	Leverkusen	1-1*
cc2012	4 Mar	Paralimni	0-3
2012	20 Oct	Paris	2-2
EC2013	18 July	Linkoping	0-3
cc2014	12 Mar	Nicosia	0-2
wc2015	9 June	Moncton	0-1
2016	9 Mar	Boca Raton	0-0

v GERMANY

EC1990	25 Nov	High Wycombe	1-4
EC1990	16 Dec	Bochum	0-2
EC1994	11 Dec	Watford	1-4
EC1995	23 Feb	Bochum	1-2
wc1995	13 June	Vasteras	0-3
1997	27 Feb	Preston	4-6
wc1997	25 Sept	Dessau	0-3
wc1998	8 Mar	Millwall	0-1
EC2001	30 June	Jena	0-3
wc2001	27 Sept	Kassel	1-3

wc2002	19 May	Crystal Palace	0-1
2003	11 Sept	Darmstadt	0-4
2006	25 Oct	Aalen	1-5
2007	30 Jan	Guangzhou	0-0
wc2007	14 Sept	Shanghai	0-0
2008	17 July	Unterhaching	0-3
EC2009	10 Sept	Helsinki	2-6
2014	23 Nov	Wembley	0-3
wc2015	4 July	Vancouver	1-0*
2015	26 Nov	Duisburg	0-0
2016	6 Mar	Nashville	1-2

v HUNGARY

wc2005	27 Oct	Tapolca	13-0
wc2006	11 May	Southampton	2-0

v ICELAND

EC1992	17 May	Yeovil	4-0
EC1992	19 July	Kopavogur	2-1
EC1994	8 Oct	Reykjavik	2-1
EC1994	30 Oct	Brighton	2-1
wc2002	16 Sept	Reykjavik	2-2
wc2002	22 Sept	Birmingham	1-0
2004	14 May	Peterborough	1-0
2006	9 Mar	Norwich	1-0
2007	17 May	Southend	4-0
2009	16 July	Colchester	0-2

v ITALY

1976	2 June	Rome	0-2
1976	4 June	Cesena	1-2
1977	15 Nov	Wimbledon	1-0
1979	25 July	Naples	1-3
1982	11 June	Pescara	0-2
M1984	24 Aug	Jesolo	1-1
M1985	20 Aug	Caorle	1-1
M1985	25 Aug	Caorle	3-2
EC1987	13 June	Drammen	1-2
M1988	30 July	Arco di Trento	2-1
1989	1 Nov	High Wycombe	1-1
1990	18 Aug	Wembley	1-4
EC1992	17 Oct	Solofra	2-3
EC1992	7 Nov	Rotherham	0-3
1995	25 Jan	Florence	1-1
EC1995	1 Nov	Sunderland	1-1
EC1996	16 Mar	Cosenza	1-2
1997	23 Apr	Turin	0-2
1998	21 Apr	West Bromwich	1-2
1999	26 May	Bologna	1-4
2003	25 Feb	Viareggio	0-1
2005	17 Feb	Milton Keynes	4-1
EC2009	25 Aug	Lahti	1-2
cc2010	3 Mar	Nicosia	3-2
cc2011	2 Mar	Larnaca	2-0
cc2012	6 Mar	Paralimni	1-3
cc 2013	6 Mar	Nicosia	4-2
EC 2014	5 Mar	Larnaca	2-0

v JAPAN

1981	6 Sept	Kobe	4-0
wc2007	11 Sept	Shanghai	2-2
wc2011	5 July	Augsburg	2-0
2013	26 June	Burton	1-1
wc2015	1 July	Edmonton	1-2

v KOREA REPUBLIC

2010	19 Oct	Suwon	0-0
cc2011	9 Mar	Larnaca	2-0

v MALTA

wc2009	25 Oct	Blackpool	8-0
wc2010	20 May	Ta'Qali	6-0

v MEXICO

AC2005	13 Mar	Lagos	5-0
wc2011	27 June	Wolfsburg	1-1
wc2015	13 June	Moncton	2-1

v MONTENEGRO

wc2014	5 Apr	Brighton	9-0
wc2014	17 Sept	Petrovac	10-0

v NETHERLANDS

1973	9 Nov	Reading	1-0
1974	31 May	Groningen	0-3
1976	2 May	Blackpool	2-0
1978	30 Sept	Vlissingen	1-3
1989	13 May	Epinal	0-0
wc1997	30 Oct	West Ham	1-0
wc1998	23 May	Waalwijk	1-2
wc2001	4 Nov	Grimsby	0-0
wc2002	23 Mar	Den Haag	4-1
2004	18 Sept	Heerhugowaard	2-1
2004	22 Sept	Tuitjenhoorn	1-0
wc2005	17 Nov	Zwolle	1-0
wc2006	31 Aug	Charlton	4-0
2007	14 Mar	Swindon	0-1
EC2009	6 Sept	Tampere	2-1*
EC2011	27 Oct	Zwolle	0-0
EC2012	17 June	Salford	1-0
cc2015	9 Mar	Nicosia	1-1

v NEW ZEALAND

2010	21 Oct	Suwon	0-0
wc2011	1 July	Dresden	2-1
cc2013	11 Mar	Larnaca	3-1

v NIGERIA

wc1995	10 June	Karlstad	3-2
2002	23 July	Norwich	0-1
2004	22 Apr	Reading	0-3

v NORTHERN IRELAND

1973	7 Sept	Bath	5-1
EC1982	19 Sept	Crewe	7-1
EC1983	14 May	Belfast	4-0
EC1985	25 May	Antrim	8-1
EC1986	16 Mar	Blackburn	10-0
1987	11 Apr	Leeds	6-0
AC2005	9 Mar	Paderne	4-0
EC2007	13 May	Gillingham	4-0
EC2008	6 Mar	Lurgan	2-0

v NORWAY

1981	25 Oct	Cambridge	0-3
EC 1988	21 Aug	Kleppe	0-2
EC 1988	18 Sept	Blackburn	1-3
EC 1990	27 May	Kleppe	0-2
EC 1990	2 Sept	Old Trafford	0-0
wc1995	8 June	Karlstad	3-2
1997	8 June	Lillestrom	0-4
wc1998	14 May	Oldham	1-2
wc1998	15 Aug	Lillestrom	0-2
EC2000	7 Mar	Norwich	0-3
EC2000	4 June	Moss	0-8
AC2002	1 Mar	Albufeira	1-3
2005	6 May	Barnsley	1-0
2008	14 Feb	Larnaca	2-1
2009	23 Apr	Shrewsbury	3-0
2014	17 Jan	La Manga	1-1
wc2015	22 June	Ottawa	2-1

v PORTUGAL

EC1996	11 Feb	Benavente	5-0
EC1996	19 May	Brentford	3-0
EC2000	20 Feb	Barnsley	2-0
EC2000	22 Apr	Sacavem	2-2
wc2001	24 Nov	Gafanha da Nazare	1-1
wc2002	24 Feb	Portsmouth	3-0
AC2005	11 Mar	Faro	4-0

v REPUBLIC OF IRELAND

1978	2 May	Exeter	6-1
1981	2 May	Dublin	5-0
EC1982	7 Nov	Dublin	1-0
EC1983	11 Sept	Reading	6-0
EC1985	22 Sept	Cork	6-0

EC1986	27 Apr	Reading	4-0
1987	29 Mar	Dublin	1-0

v ROMANIA

EC1998	12 Sept	Campina	4-1
EC1998	11 Oct	High Wycombe	2-1

v RUSSIA

EC2001	24 June	Jena	1-1
2003	21 Oct	Moscow	2-2
2004	19 Aug	Bristol	1-2
2007	8 Mar	Milton Keynes	6-0
EC2009	28 Aug	Helsinki	3-2
EC2013	15 July	Linkoping	1-1

v SCOTLAND

1972	18 Nov	Greenock	3-2
1973	23 June	Nuneaton	8-0
1976	23 May	Enfield	5-1
1977	29 May	Dundee	1-2
EC1982	3 Oct	Dumbarton	4-0
EC1983	22 May	Leeds	2-0
EC1985	17 Mar	Preston	4-0
EC1986	12 Oct	Kirkcaldy	3-1
1989	30 Apr	Kirkcaldy	3-0
1990	6 May	Paisley	4-0
1990	12 May	Wembley	4-0
1991	20 Apr	High Wycombe	5-0
EC1992	17 Apr	Walsall	1-0
EC1992	23 Aug	Perth	2-0
1997	9 Mar	Sheffield	6-0
1997	23 Aug	Livingston	4-0
2001	27 May	Bolton	1-0
AC2002	7 Mar	Quarteira	4-1
2003	13 Nov	Preston	5-0
2005	21 Apr	Tranmere	2-1
2007	11 Mar	High Wycombe	1-0
cc2009	10 Mar	Larnaca	3-0
cc2011	4 Mar	Nicosia	0-2
cc2013	8 Mar	Larnaca	4-4

v SERBIA

EC2011	17 Sept	Belgrade	2-2
EC2011	23 Nov	Doncaster	2-0
EC2016	4 June	Wycombe	7-0
EC2016	7 June	Stara Pazova	7-0

v SLOVENIA

EC1993	25 Sept	Ljubljana	10-0
EC1994	17 Apr	Brentford	10-0
EC2011	22 Sept	Swindon	4-0
EC2012	21 June	Velenje	4-0

v SOUTH AFRICA

cc2009	5 Mar	Larnaca	6-0
cc 2010	24 Feb	Larnaca	1-0

v SPAIN

EC1993	19 Dec	Osuna	0-0
EC1994	20 Feb	Bradford	0-0
EC1996	8 Sept	Montilla	1-2
EC1996	29 Sept	Tranmere	1-1
2001	22 Mar	Luton	4-2
EC2007	25 Nov	Shrewsbury	1-0
EC2008	2 Oct	Zamora	2-2
wc2010	1 Apr	Millwall	1-0
wc2010	19 June	Aranda de Duero	2-2
EC2013	12 July	Linkoping	2-3

v SWEDEN

1975	15 June	Gothenborg	0-2
1975	7 Sept	Wimbledon	1-3
1979	27 July	Scafati	0-0*
1980	17 Sept	Leicester	1-1
1982	26 May	Kinna	1-1
1983	30 Oct	Charlton	2-2
EC1984	12 May	Gothenburg	0-1
EC1984	27 May	Luton	1-0
EC1987	11 June	Moss	2-3*
1989	23 May	Wembley	0-2
1995	13 May	Halmstad	0-4

1998	26 July	Dagenham	0-1
EC2001	27 June	Jena	0-4
2002	25 Jan	La Manga	0-5
AC2002	5 Mar	Lagos	3-6
EC2005	11 June	Blackburn	0-1
2006	7 Feb	Larnaca	0-0
2006	9 Feb	Achna	1-1
2008	12 Feb	Larnaca	0-2
EC2009	31 Aug	Turku	1-1
2011	17 May	Oxford	2-0
2013	4 July	Ljungskile	1-4
2014	3 Aug	Hartlepool	4-0

v SWITZERLAND

1975	19 Apr	Basel	3-1
1977	28 Apr	Hull	9-1
1979	23 July	Sorrento	2-0
EC1999	16 Oct	Zofingen	3-0
EC2000	13 May	Bristol	1-0
cc2010	1 Mar	Nicosia	2-2
wc2010	12 Sept	Shrewsbury	2-0
wc2010	16 Sept	Wohlen	3-2
cc2012	1 Mar	Larnaca	1-0

v TURKEY

wc2009	26 Nov	Izmir	3-0
wc2010	29 July	Walsall	3-0
wc2013	26 Sept	Portsmouth	8-0
wc2013	31 Oct	Adana	4-0

v UKRAINE

EC2000	30 Oct	Kiev	2-1
EC2000	28 Nov	Leyton	2-0
wc2014	8 May	Shrewsbury	4-0
wc2014	19 June	Lviv	2-1

v USA

M1985	23 Aug	Caorle	3-1
M1988	27 July	Riva del Garda	2-0
1990	9 Aug	Blaine	0-3
1991	25 May	Hirson	1-3
1997	9 May	San Jose	0-5
1997	11 May	Portland	0-6
AC2002	3 Mar	Ferreiras	0-2
2003	17 May	Birmingham (Alabama)	0-6
2007	28 Jan	Guangzhou	1-1
wc2007	22 Sept	Tianjin	0-3
2011	2 Apr	Leyton	2-1
2015	13 Feb	Milton Keynes	0-1
2016	4 Mar	Tampa	0-1

v USSR

1990	11 Aug	Blaine	1-1
1991	20 July	Dmitrov	2-1
1991	21 July	Kashira	2-0
1991	7 Sept	Southampton	2-0
1991	8 Sept	Brighton	1-3

v WALES

1974	17 Mar	Slough	5-0
1976	22 May	Bedford	4-0
1976	17 Oct	Ebbw Vale	2-1
1977	18 Sept	Warminster	5-0
1980	1 June	Warminster	6-1
1985	17 Aug	Ramsey (Isle of Man)	6-0
wc2013	26 Oct	Millwall	2-0
wc2014	21 May	Cardiff	4-0

v WEST GERMANY

M1984	22 Aug	Jesolo	0-2
1990	5 Aug	Blaine	1-3

OTHER MATCHES

v ITALY B

1984	27 Aug	Monfalcone	3-1
M1988	20 July	Riva del Garda	3-0

v USA B

1990	7 Aug	Blaine	1-0

NON-LEAGUE TABLES 2015–16

EVO-STIK NORTHERN PREMIER LEAGUE 2015–16

			Home				Away				Total						
		P	W	D	L	F	A	W	D	L	F	A	W	D	L	F	A	GD	Pts
1	Darlington 1883	46	18	3	2	51	19	15	2	6	55	23	33	5	8	106	42	64	104
2	Blyth Spartans	46	15	2	6	49	22	17	1	5	40	19	32	3	11	89	41	48	99
3	Salford C¶	46	11	7	5	50	23	16	2	5	44	25	27	9	10	94	48	46	90
4	Ashton U	46	14	2	7	51	26	12	7	4	39	26	26	9	11	90	52	38	87
5	Workington	46	13	7	3	49	25	12	4	7	29	25	25	11	10	78	50	28	86
6	Stourbridge	46	14	4	5	49	25	11	5	7	41	38	25	9	12	90	63	27	84
7	Frickley Ath	46	14	3	6	43	21	8	8	7	26	25	22	11	13	69	46	23	77
8	Nantwich T	46	12	7	4	53	32	8	8	7	41	30	20	15	11	94	62	32	75
9	Barwell	46	14	1	8	43	23	9	3	11	39	43	23	4	19	82	66	16	73
10	Rushall Olympic	46	10	5	8	34	21	9	7	7	40	40	19	12	15	74	61	13	69
11	Buxton	46	14	2	7	47	32	7	2	14	24	42	21	4	21	71	74	-3	67
12	Sutton Coldfield T	46	10	5	8	34	27	7	6	10	25	39	17	11	18	59	66	-7	62
13	Halesowen T	46	9	8	6	29	25	8	3	12	24	38	17	11	18	53	63	-10	62
14	Ilkeston FC	46	10	5	8	35	34	5	4	14	26	45	15	9	22	61	79	-18	54
15	Marine	46	5	8	10	30	37	7	9	7	23	24	12	17	17	53	61	-8	53
16	Skelmersdale U	46	9	6	8	37	34	5	5	13	29	48	14	11	21	66	82	-16	53
17	Matlock T	46	9	5	9	25	28	5	5	13	34	51	14	10	22	59	79	-20	52
18	Grantham T	46	9	6	8	29	35	4	6	13	22	50	13	12	21	51	85	-34	51
19	Whitby T	46	10	5	8	37	39	2	6	15	23	40	12	11	23	60	79	-19	47
20	Mickleover Sports	46	7	4	12	26	34	4	9	10	24	40	11	13	22	50	74	-24	46
21	Stamford†	46	5	7	11	38	47	7	2	14	33	50	12	9	25	71	97	-26	45
22	Hyde U	46	6	5	12	32	45	5	2	16	21	45	11	7	28	53	90	-37	40
23	Colwyn Bay	46	5	2	16	26	50	5	6	12	25	45	10	8	28	51	95	-44	38
24	Ramsbottom U	46	3	7	13	22	44	2	4	17	21	68	5	11	30	43	112	-69	26

¶Salford C promoted via play-offs. †Stamford reprieved from relegation.

EVO-STIK NORTHERN PREMIER LEAGUE DIVISION 1 NORTH 2015–16

		P	W	D	L	F	A	W	D	L	F	A	W	D	L	F	A	GD	Pts
1	Warrington T	42	18	2	1	59	16	16	2	3	62	20	34	4	4	121	36	85	106
2	Spennymoor T¶	42	13	5	3	61	21	14	5	2	52	14	27	10	5	113	35	78	91
3	Northwich Vic*	42	15	2	4	53	19	14	3	4	49	22	29	5	8	102	41	61	83
4	Glossop NE	42	14	3	4	45	19	10	6	5	33	22	24	9	9	78	41	37	81
5	Burscough	42	13	2	6	41	23	12	3	6	40	27	25	5	12	81	50	31	80
6	Lancaster C	42	11	6	4	41	26	7	9	5	33	31	18	15	9	74	57	17	69
7	Clitheroe	42	11	1	9	48	38	11	2	8	42	48	22	3	17	90	86	4	69
8	Trafford	42	11	5	5	46	21	8	3	10	32	30	19	8	15	78	51	27	65
9	Farsley Celtic	42	12	2	7	42	20	6	7	8	40	30	18	9	15	82	50	32	63
10	Ossett Alb	42	10	2	9	28	29	10	1	10	28	34	20	3	19	56	63	-7	63
11	Witton Alb	42	10	3	8	40	26	8	4	9	45	46	18	7	17	85	72	13	61
12	Bamber Bridge	42	8	7	6	40	28	8	5	8	33	27	16	12	14	73	55	18	60
13	Mossley	42	12	3	6	46	27	6	3	12	34	49	18	6	18	80	76	4	60
14	Brighouse T	42	10	3	8	45	36	7	5	9	30	36	17	8	17	75	72	3	59
15	Kendal T	42	7	5	9	30	39	7	5	9	32	41	14	10	18	62	80	-18	52
16	Prescot Cables	42	7	4	10	32	41	6	3	12	34	58	13	7	22	66	99	-33	46
17	Ossett T	42	4	7	10	27	50	8	0	13	24	44	12	7	23	51	94	-43	43
18	Radcliffe Bor	42	6	6	9	30	35	5	1	15	24	40	11	7	24	54	75	-21	40
19	Droylsden	42	6	3	12	41	65	5	3	13	27	74	11	6	25	68	139	-71	39
20	Scarborough Ath	42	6	3	12	18	35	4	5	12	22	29	10	8	24	40	64	-24	38
21	Harrogate Railway Ath	42	4	4	13	26	53	2	4	15	26	62	6	8	28	52	115	-63	26
22	New Mills	42	0	2	19	15	86	0	1	20	11	70	0	3	39	26	156	-130	3

¶Spennymoor T promoted via play-offs. *Northwich Vic deducted 9pts for fielding an ineligible player.

EVO-STIK NORTHERN PREMIER LEAGUE DIVISION 1 SOUTH 2015–16

		P	W	D	L	F	A	W	D	L	F	A	W	D	L	F	A	GD	Pts
1	Stafford Rangers	42	14	5	2	50	18	15	3	3	29	13	29	8	5	79	31	48	95
2	Shaw Lane Aquaforce	42	13	7	1	48	20	15	3	3	47	20	28	10	4	95	40	55	94
3	Coalville T¶	42	14	5	2	45	23	11	5	5	36	23	25	10	7	81	46	35	85
4	Basford U	42	10	5	6	34	22	12	5	4	33	20	22	10	10	67	42	25	76
5	Lincoln U	42	10	6	5	34	20	11	5	5	36	26	21	11	10	70	46	24	74
6	Stocksbridge Park Steels	42	11	4	6	39	26	9	5	7	33	27	20	9	13	72	53	19	69
7	Chasetown	42	9	5	7	38	27	10	6	5	30	22	19	11	12	68	49	19	68
8	Leek T	42	11	4	6	37	27	7	5	9	24	29	18	9	15	61	56	5	63
9	Rugby T	42	11	5	5	34	22	6	4	11	39	46	17	9	16	73	68	5	60
10	Romulus	42	8	2	11	38	43	10	4	7	38	31	18	6	18	76	74	2	60
11	Market Drayton T	42	11	2	8	40	33	5	8	8	25	32	16	10	16	65	65	0	58
12	Spalding U	42	10	5	6	32	24	4	9	8	20	30	14	14	14	52	54	-2	56
13	Belper T	42	8	5	8	28	26	7	4	10	38	39	15	9	18	66	65	1	54
14	Newcastle T	42	9	5	7	32	28	6	3	12	33	40	15	8	19	65	68	-3	53
15	Kidsgrove Ath	42	6	7	8	39	41	6	7	8	42	37	12	14	16	81	78	3	50
16	Gresley FC	42	7	2	12	23	38	9	0	12	35	37	16	2	24	58	75	-17	50
17	Sheffield FC	42	6	5	10	32	40	7	3	11	29	31	13	8	21	61	71	-10	47
18	Carlton T	42	6	3	12	29	39	8	2	11	31	33	14	5	23	60	72	-12	47
19	Goole AFC	42	4	5	12	23	40	6	3	12	28	47	10	8	24	51	87	-36	38
20	Loughborough Dynamo	42	7	2	12	35	47	3	3	15	25	61	10	5	27	60	108	-48	35
21	Daventry T	42	4	1	16	15	58	6	2	13	28	55	10	3	29	43	113	-70	33
22	Tividale	42	5	5	11	30	39	0	6	15	22	56	5	11	26	52	95	-43	26

¶Coalville T promoted via play-offs.

EVO-STIK SOUTHERN PREMIER LEAGUE 2015–16

		P	W	D	L	F	A	W	D	L	F	A	W	D	L	F	A	GD	Pts
				Home					*Away*					*Total*					
1	Poole T	46	15	6	2	49	16	12	6	5	37	19	27	12	7	86	35	51	93
2	Redditch U*	46	12	10	1	44	19	12	5	6	38	18	24	15	7	82	37	45	84
3	Hitchin T	46	16	4	3	50	22	8	8	7	28	28	24	12	10	78	50	28	84
4	Hungerford T¶	46	13	5	5	39	20	11	6	6	34	23	24	11	11	73	43	30	83
5	Leamington	46	13	6	4	30	14	10	6	7	29	24	23	12	11	59	38	21	81
6	Kettering T	46	14	6	3	46	22	10	2	11	37	31	24	8	14	83	53	30	80
7	Weymouth	46	15	4	4	39	19	6	10	7	24	20	21	14	11	63	39	24	77
8	Chippenham T	46	11	7	5	45	29	10	6	7	31	24	21	13	12	76	53	23	76
9	King's Lynn T	46	13	4	6	31	20	8	3	12	27	34	21	7	18	58	54	4	70
10	Merthyr T	46	10	6	7	41	28	9	3	11	28	30	19	9	18	69	58	11	66
11	Chesham U	46	14	4	5	49	27	4	6	13	23	43	18	10	18	72	70	2	64
12	Dunstable T	46	12	3	8	40	28	5	8	10	28	40	17	11	18	68	68	0	62
13	Dorchester T	46	9	5	9	32	29	9	3	11	35	40	18	8	20	67	69	-2	62
14	Biggleswade T	46	11	4	8	49	43	6	5	12	27	39	17	9	20	76	82	-6	60
15	Cirencester T	46	8	3	12	36	43	10	3	10	31	33	18	6	22	67	76	-9	60
16	Frome T	46	11	7	5	31	31	3	9	11	20	42	14	16	16	51	73	-22	58
17	Slough T	46	12	3	8	37	28	4	6	13	30	49	16	9	21	67	77	-10	57
18	Cambridge C	46	10	2	11	31	37	5	5	13	32	43	15	7	24	63	80	-17	52
19	Stratford T	46	8	8	7	29	23	5	3	15	30	45	13	11	22	59	68	-9	50
20	St Neots T	46	6	7	10	26	34	4	11	8	43	44	10	18	18	69	78	-9	48
21	Bedworth U	46	8	4	11	33	44	4	4	15	25	63	12	8	26	58	107	-49	44
22	Histon	46	6	5	12	32	45	5	2	16	31	53	11	7	28	63	98	-35	40
23	Bideford	46	4	9	10	20	37	4	4	15	18	51	8	13	25	38	88	-50	37
24	Paulton R	46	6	7	10	25	41	2	5	16	13	48	8	12	26	38	89	-51	36

¶*Hungerford T promoted via play-offs.* **Redditch U deducted 3pts for fielding an ineligible player.*

EVO-STIK SOUTHERN LEAGUE DIVISION 1 CENTRAL 2015–16

		P	W	D	L	F	A	W	D	L	F	A	W	D	L	F	A	GD	Pts
1	Kings Langley	42	14	5	2	50	24	13	1	7	33	20	27	6	9	83	44	39	87
2	Royston T	42	12	4	5	51	22	13	4	4	48	24	25	8	9	99	46	53	83
3	Egham T	42	12	4	5	37	23	14	1	6	43	16	26	5	11	80	39	41	83
4	St Ives T¶	42	11	5	5	36	19	11	7	3	36	19	22	12	8	72	38	34	78
5	AFC Rushden & Diamonds	42	14	3	4	53	19	9	5	7	28	25	23	8	11	81	44	37	77
6	Chalfont St Peter	42	13	1	7	46	33	10	1	10	30	38	23	2	17	76	71	5	71
7	Northwood	42	9	5	7	34	31	11	4	6	28	18	20	9	13	62	49	13	69
8	Aylesbury	42	11	6	4	46	28	9	2	10	26	24	20	8	14	72	52	20	68
9	Beaconsfield SYCOB	42	13	4	4	47	18	6	6	9	30	36	19	10	13	77	54	23	67
10	Godalming T	42	11	3	7	27	22	8	7	6	24	23	19	10	13	51	45	6	67
11	Ware	42	11	3	7	34	26	8	3	10	33	43	19	6	17	67	69	-2	63
12	Potters Bar T	42	11	4	6	36	22	5	6	10	26	42	16	10	16	62	64	-2	58
13	Petersfield T	42	12	2	7	39	27	4	5	12	32	53	16	7	19	71	80	-9	55
14	Bedford T	42	9	7	5	32	26	3	6	12	25	34	12	13	17	57	60	-3	49
15	Uxbridge	42	10	0	11	34	36	3	9	9	25	35	13	9	20	59	71	-12	48
16	Arlesey T	42	6	4	11	24	39	8	1	12	24	48	14	5	23	48	87	-39	47
17	Fleet T	42	8	5	8	25	26	4	4	13	30	52	12	9	21	55	78	-23	45
18	Barton R	42	3	9	9	25	39	6	6	9	26	36	9	15	18	51	75	-24	42
19	Aylesbury U	42	4	4	13	19	48	7	3	11	26	33	11	7	24	45	81	-36	40
20	Hanwell T	42	5	3	13	19	35	5	6	10	19	29	10	9	23	38	64	-26	39
21	Leighton T	42	4	5	12	20	35	5	3	13	27	51	9	8	25	47	86	-39	35
22	North Greenford U	42	5	5	11	30	42	1	1	19	21	65	6	6	30	51	107	-56	24

¶*St Ives T promoted via play-offs.*

EVO-STIK SOUTHERN LEAGUE DIVISION 1 SOUTH & WEST 2015–16

		P	W	D	L	F	A	W	D	L	F	A	W	D	L	F	A	GD	Pts
1	Cinderford T	42	16	5	0	48	17	13	4	4	32	12	29	9	4	80	29	51	96
2	Banbury U¶	42	16	3	2	51	14	12	7	2	46	24	28	10	4	97	38	59	94
3	Taunton T	42	13	5	3	54	16	14	3	4	40	18	27	8	7	94	34	60	89
4	Swindon Supermarine	42	13	4	4	40	21	14	2	5	41	21	27	6	9	81	42	39	87
5	Winchester C	42	15	4	2	55	21	9	7	5	42	28	24	11	7	97	49	48	83
6	Evesham U	42	13	4	4	49	16	11	5	5	43	22	24	9	9	92	38	54	81
7	Shortwood U	42	13	2	6	52	33	11	4	6	36	26	24	6	12	88	59	29	78
8	Tiverton T	42	13	5	3	48	19	7	8	6	28	25	20	13	9	76	44	32	73
9	North Leigh	42	12	3	6	42	28	9	2	10	37	25	21	5	16	79	53	26	68
10	Didcot T	42	9	3	9	45	28	9	7	5	37	29	18	10	14	82	57	25	64
11	Larkhall Ath	42	10	4	7	32	22	5	6	10	30	43	15	10	17	62	65	-3	55
12	Bishops Cleeve	42	8	9	4	33	19	6	4	11	22	47	14	13	15	55	66	-11	55
13	Marlow	42	10	2	9	35	32	5	5	11	33	47	15	7	20	68	79	-11	52
14	Mangotsfield U	42	6	7	8	32	33	6	5	10	27	32	12	12	18	59	65	-6	48
15	AFC Totton	42	8	4	9	35	33	6	2	13	38	48	14	6	22	73	81	-8	48
16	Yate T	42	6	8	7	36	40	6	3	12	24	32	12	11	19	48	62	-14	47
17	Wimborne T	42	5	4	12	36	47	7	4	10	29	33	12	8	22	65	80	-15	44
18	Slimbridge	42	5	7	9	26	26	5	5	11	20	31	10	12	20	46	57	-11	42
19	Bridgwater T	42	5	4	12	23	38	4	3	14	19	45	9	7	26	42	83	-41	34
20	Wantage T	42	5	2	14	27	44	3	3	15	18	56	8	5	29	45	100	-55	29
21	Burnham	42	2	2	17	19	53	4	4	13	20	46	6	6	30	39	99	-60	24
22	Bashley	42	0	2	19	9	76	0	0	21	4	125	0	2	40	13	201	-188	2

¶*Banbury U promoted via play-offs.*

RYMAN ISTHMIAN PREMIER LEAGUE 2015–16

			Home				Away				Total						
		P	W	D	L	F	A	W	D	L	F	A	W	D	L	F	A	GD	Pts
1	Hampton & Richmond Bor	46	17	4	2	59	25	11	7	5	46	27	28	11	7	105	52	53	95
2	Bognor Regis T	46	18	3	2	62	20	11	4	8	33	22	29	7	10	95	42	53	94
3	East Thurrock U¶	46	13	7	3	54	24	13	6	4	53	29	26	13	7	107	53	54	91
4	Tonbridge Angels	46	12	5	6	52	30	12	8	3	38	19	24	13	9	90	49	41	85
5	Dulwich Hamlet	46	14	6	3	53	23	9	6	8	40	35	23	12	11	93	58	35	81
6	Enfield T	46	16	4	3	49	19	8	4	11	25	28	24	8	14	74	47	27	80
7	Kingstonian	46	15	2	6	49	30	6	8	9	29	34	21	10	15	78	64	14	73
8	Leiston	46	13	4	6	42	24	7	8	8	30	33	20	12	14	72	57	15	72
9	Billericay T	46	10	9	4	44	22	8	8	7	32	31	18	17	11	76	53	23	71
10	Merstham	46	8	5	10	35	40	10	3	10	39	40	18	8	20	74	80	–6	62
11	Leatherhead	46	10	5	8	37	35	8	3	12	30	46	18	8	20	67	81	–14	62
12	Metropolitan Police	46	7	6	10	23	35	10	4	9	37	44	17	10	19	60	79	–19	61
13	Wingate & Finchley	46	9	5	9	39	34	8	4	11	27	36	17	9	20	66	70	–4	60
14	Canvey Island	46	10	4	9	34	39	7	5	11	35	50	17	9	20	69	89	–20	60
15	Grays Ath	46	8	6	9	30	29	7	6	10	33	45	15	12	19	63	74	–11	57
16	Staines T	46	7	5	11	27	33	8	5	10	26	41	15	10	21	53	74	–21	55
17	Harrow Bor	46	9	5	9	33	35	6	4	13	33	45	15	9	22	66	80	–14	54
18	Farnborough	46	11	2	10	38	37	5	3	15	27	51	16	5	25	65	88	–23	53
19	Hendon	46	7	9	7	33	33	6	4	13	35	52	13	13	20	68	85	–17	52
20	Needham Market	46	6	5	12	25	37	7	7	9	26	39	13	12	21	51	76	–25	51
21	Burgess Hill T†	46	8	5	10	32	38	4	9	10	25	35	12	14	20	57	73	–16	50
22	Brentwood T	46	6	6	11	33	31	4	4	15	18	49	10	10	26	51	80	–29	40
23	Lewes	46	4	10	9	28	36	2	6	15	20	51	6	16	24	48	87	–39	34
24	VCD Ath	46	5	5	7	11	30	44	3	3	17	16	59	8	10	28	46	103	–57	34

¶*East Thurrock U promoted via play-offs.* †*Burgess Hill T reprieved from relegation.*

RYMAN ISTHMIAN LEAGUE DIVISION 1 NORTH 2015–16

		P	W	D	L	F	A	W	D	L	F	A	W	D	L	F	A	GD	Pts
1	AFC Sudbury	46	15	2	6	48	31	18	4	1	42	18	33	6	7	90	49	41	105
2	Thurrock	46	17	0	6	51	26	13	6	4	48	26	30	6	10	99	52	47	96
3	Harlow T¶	46	18	3	2	57	17	11	6	6	35	30	29	9	8	92	47	45	96
4	Cray W	46	14	2	7	55	29	13	7	3	43	23	27	9	10	98	52	46	90
5	AFC Hornchurch	46	13	6	4	41	15	12	5	6	46	20	25	11	10	87	35	52	86
6	Cheshunt	46	14	6	3	44	20	8	8	7	44	30	22	14	10	88	50	38	80
7	Maldon & Tiptree	46	10	7	6	53	41	12	5	6	36	25	22	12	12	89	66	23	78
8	Brightlingsea Regent	46	10	6	7	37	29	12	5	6	39	26	22	11	13	76	55	21	77
9	Dereham T	46	12	6	5	46	31	9	5	9	36	30	21	11	14	82	61	21	74
10	Thamesmead T	46	13	5	5	38	28	8	6	9	36	35	21	11	14	74	63	11	74
11	Tilbury	46	12	6	5	40	22	8	3	12	45	44	20	9	17	85	66	19	69
12	Aveley	46	9	6	8	36	35	11	2	10	48	36	20	8	18	84	71	13	68
13	Bury T	46	8	8	7	45	34	8	6	9	29	34	16	14	16	74	68	6	62
14	Phoenix Sports	46	6	4	13	30	42	10	4	9	30	32	16	8	22	60	74	–14	56
15	Haringey Bor	46	4	7	12	29	43	8	7	8	32	33	12	14	20	61	76	–15	50
16	Romford	46	4	4	11	29	36	8	8	11	30	47	12	12	22	59	83	–24	48
17	Soham T Rangers	46	10	4	9	35	36	3	5	15	26	54	13	9	24	61	90	–29	48
18	Great Wakering R	46	8	5	10	36	43	4	6	13	33	60	12	11	23	69	103	–34	47
19	Witham T	46	7	4	12	32	47	5	5	13	27	49	12	9	25	59	96	–37	45
20	Heybridge Swifts	46	7	5	11	31	47	5	3	15	28	40	12	8	26	59	87	–28	44
21	Waltham Abbey	46	5	7	11	20	35	6	1	16	34	45	11	8	27	54	80	–26	41
22	Wroxham	46	5	7	11	25	46	5	3	15	25	43	10	10	26	50	89	–39	40
23	Barkingside	46	5	5	13	28	48	4	5	14	27	49	9	10	27	55	97	–42	37
24	Redbridge	46	5	2	16	22	62	3	2	18	24	79	8	4	34	46	141	–95	28

¶*Harlow T promoted via play-offs.*

RYMAN ISTHMIAN LEAGUE DIVISION 1 SOUTH 2015–16

		P	W	D	L	F	A	W	D	L	F	A	W	D	L	F	A	GD	Pts
1	Folkestone Invicta	46	20	2	1	59	15	16	4	3	43	19	36	6	4	102	34	68	114
2	Dorking W	46	13	4	6	50	30	14	5	4	49	26	27	9	10	99	56	43	90
3	Worthing¶	46	14	1	8	55	29	13	6	4	41	27	27	7	12	96	56	40	88
4	Hythe T	46	14	5	4	39	18	13	1	9	35	31	27	6	13	74	49	25	87
5	Faversham T	46	14	5	4	43	19	11	3	9	33	26	25	8	13	76	45	31	83
6	Corinthian-Casuals*	46	14	1	8	39	22	12	6	5	36	30	26	7	13	75	52	23	82
7	Hastings U	46	15	1	7	59	30	10	5	8	40	34	25	6	15	99	64	35	81
8	Herne Bay	46	10	6	7	42	26	12	4	7	37	38	22	10	14	79	54	25	76
9	Molesey	46	14	2	7	49	38	9	4	10	38	45	23	6	17	87	83	4	75
10	Carshalton Ath	46	11	5	7	48	33	10	4	9	35	41	21	9	16	83	74	9	72
11	South Park	46	8	7	8	30	33	13	2	8	48	38	21	9	16	78	71	7	72
12	Ramsgate	46	13	5	5	54	26	8	3	12	38	50	21	8	17	92	76	16	71
13	Guernsey	46	16	2	5	60	31	5	3	15	34	57	21	5	20	94	88	6	68
14	Three Bridges	46	11	4	8	33	33	9	2	12	26	34	20	6	20	59	67	–8	66
15	Whyteleafe	46	9	2	12	38	40	10	3	10	31	37	19	5	22	69	77	–8	62
16	Walton Casuals	46	9	5	9	39	39	9	1	13	35	46	18	6	22	74	85	–11	60
17	Tooting & Mitcham U	46	7	7	9	34	33	9	3	11	32	38	16	10	20	66	71	–5	58
18	Sittingbourne	46	9	2	12	34	42	7	4	12	29	35	16	6	24	63	77	–14	54
19	Chatham T	46	5	3	15	27	36	8	4	11	34	34	13	7	26	61	70	–9	46
20	East Grinstead T	46	7	3	13	26	33	5	4	14	29	51	12	7	27	55	84	–29	43
21	Chipstead	46	4	6	13	28	41	7	0	16	26	51	11	6	29	54	92	–38	39
22	Walton & Hersham*	46	5	0	18	30	56	4	6	13	20	57	9	6	31	50	113	–63	30
23	Whitstable T	46	4	1	18	27	62	4	1	18	25	56	8	2	36	52	118	–66	26
24	Peacehaven & Telscombe	46	4	3	16	23	54	2	4	17	25	75	6	7	33	48	129	–81	25

¶*Worthing promoted via play-offs.* *Corinthian-Casuals and Walton & Hersham deducted 3pts for fielding an ineligible player.*

THE FA TROPHY 2015–16

IN PARTNERSHIP WITH CARLSBERG

After extra time.

PRELIMINARY ROUND

Burscough v Bamber Bridge	2-0
Ossett T v Warrington T	1-2
Shaw Lane Aquaforce v New Mills	3-0
Lancaster C v Northwich Vic	1-1, 0-4
Farsley Celtic v Prescot Cables	4-0
Witton Alb v Ossett Alb	2-2, 2-0
Sheffield v Trafford	4-1
Mossley v Harrogate Railway Ath	1-0
Glossop North End v Spennymoor T	1-1, 2-3
Clitheroe v Stocksbridge Park Steels	1-2
Radcliffe Bor v Droylsden	2-1
Kendal T v Scarborough Ath	4-0
Newcastle T v Spalding U	5-4
St Ives T v Rugby T	4-2
Stafford Rangers v Tividale	3-1
Soham T Rangers v Carlton T	1-3
Leek T v Lincoln U	1-3
Loughborough Dynamo v Kidsgrove Ath	0-3
AFC Rushden & Diamonds v Basford U	1-3
Romulus v Gresley	0-0, 1-2
Belper T v Market Drayton T	1-0
Coalville T v Daventry T	3-2
Chasetown v Evesham U	1-1, 1-2
Northwood v Potters Bar T	1-1, 1-0
Thurrock v Guernsey	2-0
Witham T v Herne Bay	2-4
Arlesey T v Redbridge	1-1, 0-2
Hanwell T v Cheshunt	1-2
Walton Casuals v Sittingbourne	1-0
Chalfont St Peter v Beaconsfield SYCOB	3-0
Aylesbury U v Heybridge Swifts	1-2
Whyteleafe v Phoenix Sports	0-1
Corinthian-Casuals v Three Bridges	2-1
Barton R v AFC Sudbury	1-1, 3-4
Royston T v Great Wakering R	3-0
Wroxham v Hastings U	2-3
Maldon & Tiptree v Ramsgate	2-3
Faversham T v Bury T	0-1
Carshalton Ath v Leighton T	0-2
Folkestone Invicta v Haringey Bor	1-1, 0-1
Dereham T v Waltham Abbey	1-2
Tooting & Mitcham U v Walton & Hersham	3-2
Tilbury v Barkingside	5-0
Chipstead v Uxbridge	2-1
Whitstable T v Worthing	2-4
Harlow T v Ware	3-1
Thamesmead T v Brightlingsea Regent	1-1, 4-1
Romford v North Greenford U	3-2
Cray W v East Grinstead T	2-3
Aveley v South Park	1-4
Aylesbury v Hythe T	3-0
Tiverton T v AFC Totton	2-0
Slimbridge v Egham T	0-1
Taunton T v Godalming T	4-1
Bishop's Cleeve v North Leigh	2-4
Yate T v Banbury U	1-3
Molesey v Fleet T	5-1
Larkhall Ath v Wimborne T	3-1
Bashley v Cinderford T	1-0
Mangotsfield U v Shortwood U	4-3
Marlow v Wantage T	5-2
Didcot T v Bridgwater T	0-0, 3-1
Burnham v Dorking W	0-2
Petersfield T v Winchester C	1-3

FIRST QUALIFYING ROUND

Marine v Sheffield	1-0
Witton Alb v Radcliffe Bor	1-2
Buxton v Frickley Ath	2-1
Blyth Spartans v Kendal T	4-0
Shaw Lane Aquaforce v Farsley Celtic	4-3
Workington v Whitby T	0-3
Northwich Vic v Stocksbridge Park Steels	1-2
Nantwich v Salford C	2-1
Spennymoor T v Goole	6-3

Ashton U v Ramsbottom U	2-2, 2-2*

(2-2 at full time; Ashton U won 10-9 on penalties)

Skelmersdale U v Hyde U	3-3, A-A, 1-0

(First replay abandoned after 22 minutes due to fog)

Warrington T v Brighouse T	2-0
Burscough v Colwyn Bay	1-0
Darlington 1883 v Mossley	3-2
Leamington v Barwell	6-1
Cambridge C v Ilkeston	0-1
Sutton Coldfield T v Coalville T	2-0
Evesham U v Redditch U	1-0
Carlton T v Stamford	2-1
Belper T v King's Lynn T	1-1, 1-5
Histon v Stratford T	0-0, 1-4
Basford U v Grantham T	3-1
St Ives T v Kettering T	0-1
Rushall Olympic v Mickleover Sports	1-0
Stafford Rangers v Lincoln U	1-1, 1-1*

(1-1 at full time; Lincoln U won 5-4 on penalties)

Halesowen T v Stourbridge	1-2
Newcastle T v Kidsgrove Ath	2-2, 0-3
Matlock T v Gresley	2-0
St Neots T v Bedworth U	2-0
Northwood v Bedford T	1-3
East Thurrock U v South Park	4-0
Corinthian-Casuals v Redbridge	4-1
Chipstead v Hastings U	1-2
Leatherhead v Kingstonian	1-5
Enfield T v Leighton T	4-0
Aylesbury v Brentwood T	1-1, 0-2
Phoenix Sports v Tonbridge Angels	1-1, 0-2
Herne Bay v Walton Casuals	1-1, 3-2
AFC Hornchurch v Metropolitan Police	2-3
Thurrock v Chatham T	3-0
VCD Ath v Staines T	2-1
Chalfont St Peter v Waltham Abbey	1-3
Cheshunt v Heybridge Swifts	2-0
Billericay T v Chesham U	0-2
Thamesmead T v Ramsgate	1-0
East Grinstead T v Bognor Regis T	0-3
Tilbury v Tooting & Mitcham U	2-1
Dunstable T v Haringey Bor	1-3
Hitchin T v Burgess Hill T	3-2
Lewes v Hampton & Richmond Bor	0-0, 1-2
Grays Ath v Biggleswade T	2-1
Romford v Slough T	0-4
Wingate & Finchley v Royston T	0-2
Harrow Bor v Dulwich Hamlet	0-3
Hendon v AFC Sudbury	0-1
Worthing v Leiston	1-3
Merstham v Harlow T	0-0, 2-6
Bury T v Kings Langley	2-0
Needham Market v Canvey Island	0-2
Paulton R v Swindon Supermarine	2-3
Molesey v Didcot T	1-0
Taunton T v Dorking W	1-1, 3-1
Hungerford T v Banbury U	0-0, 3-0
Cirencester T v North Leigh	2-1
Dorchester T v Chippenham T	2-1
Mangotsfield U v Bashley	6-1
Egham T v Frome T	1-2
Merthyr T v Poole T	1-0
Peacehaven & Telscombe v Tiverton T	0-3
Winchester C v Weymouth	1-2
Bideford v Farnborough	1-1, 2-2*

(1-1 at full time; Bideford won 5-4 on penalties)

Marlow v Larkhall Ath	3-0

SECOND QUALIFYING ROUND

Blyth Spartans v Whitby T	1-0
Ashton U v Stratford T	2-1
Evesham U v Spennymoor T	1-2
Buxton v Radcliffe Bor	5-1
Skelmersdale U v Lincoln U	4-2
Sutton Coldfield T v Darlington 1883	1-0
Nantwich v King's Lynn T	5-1
Shaw Lane Aquaforce v Matlock T	1-2
Leamington v Rushall Olympic	0-0, 3-2*

(2-2 at full time)

Warrington T v Basford U	3-0
Marine v Kidsgrove Ath	2-2, 1-0
Ilkeston v Stocksbridge Park Steels	1-1, 2-3
Kettering T v Burscough	0-3
Stourbridge v Carlton T	2-0
Bideford v Brentwood T	3-2
St Neots T v Hungerford T	1-2
Haringey Bor v Hitchin T	1-1, 0-3
Thurrock v Cheshunt	3-1
Tonbridge Angels v Cirencester T	1-2
Enfield T v Thamesmead T	0-2
Tilbury v Royston T	4-2
Leiston v Corinthian-Casuals	1-2
Bedford T v Weymouth	1-4
Swindon Supermarine v Chesham U	2-3
Taunton T v Bognor Regis T	1-4
Molesey v Harlow T	4-3
East Thurrock U v Tiverton T	5-0
Waltham Abbey v Grays Ath	0-2
Dulwich Hamlet v VCD Ath	2-0
Frome T v Slough T	2-1
Hampton & Richmond Bor v AFC Sudbury	3-1
Dorchester T v Kingstonian	2-2, 1-2
Marlow v Mangotsfield U	1-0
Canvey Island v Metropolitan Police	0-2
Hastings U v Merthyr T	A-A, 1-2

(First match abandoned due to waterlogged pitch after 45 minutes, 0-2)

Bury T v Herne Bay	1-1, 1-1*

(1-1 at full time; Bury T won 4-3 on penalties)

THIRD QUALIFYING ROUND

FC United of Manchester v AFC Telford U	1-2
Solihull Moors v Boston U	1-0
Leamington v Hednesford T	4-2
Stourbridge v Spennymoor T	4-2
Harrogate T v Curzon Ashton	0-1
Marine v Burscough	1-2
Corby T v Tamworth	2-6
Gainsborough Trinity v Ashton U	0-0, 1-3
Brackley T v Worcester C	0-2
Chorley v Skelmersdale U	0-0, 2-5
Warrington T v AFC Fylde	0-2
Buxton v Bradford Park Avenue	A-A, 1-2

(First match abandoned after 45 minutes, 0-0)

Matlock T v Blyth Spartans	4-2
Nuneaton T v Alfreton T	2-0
Sutton Coldfield T v Stalybridge Celtic	1-0
North Ferriby U v Stocksbridge Park Steels	1-2
Stockport Co v Nantwich T	0-2
Merthyr T v East Thurrock U	1-1, 1-3
Hampton & Richmond Bor v Maidstone U	0-1
Ebbsfleet U v Molesey	4-1
Maidenhead U v Bideford	4-0
Cirencester T v Gosport Bor	2-1
Hungerford T v Thamesmead T	3-0
Tilbury v Bishop's Stortford	3-0
Weston-super-Mare v Hitchin T	4-0
Oxford C v Marlow	6-3
Chelmsford C v Gloucester C	1-1, 1-0
Lowestoft T v St Albans C	4-0
Metropolitan Police v Wealdstone	0-2
Hemel Hempstead T v Weymouth	1-0
Dartford v Whitehawk	1-2
Concord Rangers v Sutton U	3-1, 0-2

(Tie ordered to be replayed, Concord Rangers fielded an ineligible player)

Frome T v Chesham U	1-1, 1-2
Bury T v Thurrock	4-2
Dulwich Hamlet v Margate	2-1
Grays Ath v Corinthian-Casuals	0-0, 0-1
Bognor Regis T v Bath C	1-0
Havant & Waterlooville v Basingstoke T	2-2, 0-4
Hayes & Yeading U v Eastbourne Bor	2-1
Kingstonian v Truro C	0-3

FIRST ROUND

FC Halifax T v Tamworth	5-0
Grimsby T v Solihull Moors	1-1, 3-2
Sutton Coldfield T v Barrow	0-1
Burscough v Guiseley	2-2, 2-3
Macclesfield T v Ashton U	A-A, 4-0

(First match abandoned after 45 minutes, 0-2)

Nantwich T v Matlock T	2-0
Southport v Worcester C	0-0, 3-2

Curzon Ashton v Nuneaton T	3-1
Altrincham v Leamington	1-1, 2-1*

(1-1 at full time)

AFC Telford U v Chester FC	0-2
Stourbridge v Kidderminster H	2-1
Gateshead v Stocksbridge Park Steels	4-1
AFC Fylde v Skelmersdale U	4-4, 4-0
Bradford Park Avenue v Lincoln C	2-1
Tranmere R v Wrexham	2-4
Eastbourne Bor v Hemel Hempstead T	7-4
Tilbury v Welling U	3-4
Truro C v Cirencester T	2-2, 1-0
Torquay U v Chesham U	0-0, 2-0
Whitehawk v Dover Ath	1-3
Corinthian-Casuals v Hungerford T	1-2
Boreham Wood v Woking	1-2
Sutton U v Lowestoft T	3-1
Maidstone U v Bognor Regis T	0-1
Cheltenham T v Chelmsford C	3-1
East Thurrock U v Maidenhead U	1-4
Oxford C v Ebbsfleet U	3-1
Aldershot T v Eastleigh	0-1
Weston-super-Mare v Wealdstone	3-2
Havant & Waterlooville v Forest Green R	2-0
Bury T v Dulwich Hamlet	1-2
Braintree T v Bromley	1-0

SECOND ROUND

Dulwich Hamlet v Guiseley	1-2
Dover Ath v Southport	2-1
Havant & Waterlooville v Welling U	2-1
Truro C v Macclesfield T	2-2, 0-2
Braintree T v Stourbridge	0-1
Chester FC v Hungerford T	4-0
Eastbourne Bor v AFC Fylde	1-4
Sutton U v Curzon Ashton	1-0
Torquay U v Wrexham	1-0
Grimsby T v Weston-super-Mare	3-1
FC Halifax T v Barrow	1-0
Eastleigh v Gateshead	1-2
Bognor Regis T v Altrincham	2-1
Bradford Park Avenue v Nantwich T	1-1, 0-5
Woking v Maidenhead U	6-1
Oxford C v Cheltenham T	2-2, 3-0

THIRD ROUND

Torquay U v Macclesfield T	3-3, 1-0
Grimsby T v Havant & Waterlooville	3-0
Gateshead v AFC Fylde	1-0
FC Halifax T v Chester FC	1-0
Woking v Oxford C	1-0
Dover Ath v Guiseley	2-2, 3-0
Sutton U v Bognor Regis T	0-0, 1-2
Nantwich T v Stourbridge	1-0

FOURTH ROUND

Nantwich T v Dover Ath	2-1
FC Halifax T v Gateshead	0-0, 3-3*

(2-2 at full time; FC Halifax T won 5-4 on penalties)

Grimsby T v Woking	2-0
Bognor Regis T v Torquay U	1-0

SEMI-FINALS – FIRST LEG

Nantwich T v FC Halifax T	2-4
Bognor Regis T v Grimsby T	0-1

SEMI-FINALS – SECOND LEG

FC Halifax T v Nantwich T	2-2

(FC Halifax T won 6-4 on aggregate)

Grimsby T v Bognor Regis T	2-1

(Grimsby T won 3-1 on aggregate)

FA TROPHY FINAL 2016

Wembley, Sunday 22 May 2016

FC Halifax T (0) 1 *(McManus 48)*

Grimsby T (0) 0   46,781 (combined with FA Vase)

FC Halifax T: Johnson; Bolton, Brown M, Roberts, Bencherif, Hibbs, Wroe, McManus (James 74), Peniket (Hughes 85), MacDonald (Walker 62), Burrow.
Grimsby T: McKeown; Tait (East 81), Pearson, Nsilla, Robertson, Nolan, Disley, Clay (Arnold 62), Monkhouse (Pittman 68), Bogle, Almond.
Referee: Lee Mason.

THE FA VASE 2015–16

IN PARTNERSHIP WITH CARLSBERG

*After extra time.

FIRST ROUND QUALIFYING

Garforth T v Alb Sports	4-1
Willington v Whitley Bay	2-6
Norton & Stockton Ancients v Pickering T	2-1
Sunderland Ryhope CW v Darlington Railway Ath	1-4
Brandon U v Washington	2-7
Silsden v Thornaby	3-1
Crook T v West Auckland T	0-2
Hebburn T v Knaresborough T	4-1
Seaham Red Star v Billingham T	3-1
Esh Winning v Hall Road Rangers	2-3*
(2-2 at full time)	
Morpeth T v Padiham	4-1
Durham C v Northallerton T	3-1
Billingham Synthonia v Alnwick T	2-2, 2-1
Ryton & Crawcrook Alb v Yorkshire Amateur	1-2
Eccleshill U v Heaton Stannington	2-4
Penrith v Bridlington T	1-2
Thackley v Whickham	0-0, 2-2*
(1-1 at full time; Whickham won 3-1 on penalties)	
Birtley T v Chester-le-Street T	0-5
Liversedge v Team Northumbria	1-4
Brigg T v Westella VIP	3-4
Vauxhall Motors v Glasshoughton Welfare	5-0
Staveley MW v Cheadle T	3-4
Handsworth Parramore v AFC Liverpool	1-0
West Didsbury & Chorlton v Barton T Old Boys	2-1
Bacup Bor v Worsbrough Bridge Ath	4-0
Rossington Main v Pontefract Collieries	4-2
Winterton Rangers v St Helens T	0-4
Bottesford T v Appleby Frodingham	4-1
Hemsworth MW v Cammell Laird	3-1
AFC Blackpool v Maltby Main	0-3
Squires Gate v Irlam	2-2, 3-1
Ashton Ath v Atherton Collieries	0-0, 1-3
Selby T v Askern	12-0
Runcorn T v Litherland Remyca	4-2
Congleton T v Nostell MW	3-1
Rochdale T v Parkgate	6-5
Ashby Ivanhoe v Racing Club Warwick	0-2
AFC Wulfrunians v Pershore T	2-1
Gornal Ath v Littleton	0-4
Paget Rangers v Studley	2-3
Stafford T v Wednesfield	2-0
Bewdley T v Bilston T	1-2
Lutterworth Ath v Pilkington XXX	0-5
Heath Hayes v Bromsgrove Sporting	1-4
Wolverhampton Casuals v Southam U	2-1
Pegasus Juniors v Stourport Swifts	0-4
Lye T v Barnt Green Spartak	3-0
Coventry Copsewood v Bardon Hill Sports	1-4*
(1-1 at full time)	
Wolverhampton SC v Hinckley	0-5
Highgate U v Tipton T	5-0
Westfields v Atherstone T	1-0
Cadbury Ath v AFC Bridgnorth	0-2
Shawbury U v Nuneaton Griff	2-3
Shifnal T v Malvern T	1-4
Hanley T v Coventry U	1-3*
(1-1 at full time)	
Dudley T v Sporting Khalsa	0-3
Heather St Johns v Rocester	1-8
Aston (removed) v Black Country Rangers (walkover)	
Alvechurch v Lichfield C	3-1
Continental Star v Ellistown & Ibstock U	2-3
Anstey Nomads v Friar Lane & Epworth	4-2
Arnold T v Gedling MW	2-1
Belper U v Clifton All Whites	2-4*
(2-2 at full time)	
Blaby & Whetstone Ath v Retford U	1-4
Shirebrook T v Oakham U	5-2
Eastwood Community v Harrowby U	1-3
Borrowash Vic v Kimberley MW	3-1*
(1-1 at full time)	
Hucknall T v Stapenhill	4-0
Ollerton T v St Andrews	1-2
Quorn v Rainworth MW	3-0
Radcliffe Olympic v Holbrook Sports	2-0

Shepshed Dynamo v Loughborough University	1-3
Leicester Road v Harborough T	2-0
Peterborough Sports v Sleaford T	2-3*
(2-2 at full time)	
Boston T v Great Yarmouth T	2-4
St Neots Town Saints v Team Bury	2-1
Downham T v Huntingdon T	4-1
Thetford T v Blackstones	2-3
Ipswich W v London Bari	7-0
Tower Hamlets v Whitton U	1-3
Codicote v Clapton	1-4
Sporting Bengal U v Burnham Ramblers	1-1, 4-2
Baldock T v St Margaretsbury	3-2
Cockfosters v Greenhouse Sports	3-3, 2-3
Welwyn Garden C v Haverhill Bor	1-0*
(0-0 at full time)	
Debenham LC v Enfield 1893	2-1*
(1-1 at full time)	
FC Clacton v Stansted	2-0
Hadley v Felixstowe & Walton U	2-1
Brantham Ath v Sawbridgeworth T	1-0
Halstead T v Haverhill R	1-0
Hadleigh U v Eton Manor	7-0
Long Melford v Cornard U	3-1
Long Buckby v Spelthorne Sports	3-1
Northampton On Chenecks v Sun Postal Sports	2-1
Broadfields U v Harpenden T	2-4
Berkhamsted v Woodford U	4-1
Holmer Green v Wellingborough T	2-7
Southall v Bedfont & Feltham	2-1
Newport Pagnell T v AFC Kempston R	0-2*
(0-0 at full time)	
Wellingborough Whitworths v Edgware T	3-6
Langford v Bedfont Sports	0-3
Thrapston T v Northampton Sileby Rangers	1-3
Hillingdon Bor v Potton U	1-2
Ampthill T v London Tigers	1-2
Burton Park W v Tring Ath	0-0, 0-4
New Bradwell St Peter v Rushden & Higham U	2-0*
(0-0 at full time)	
Stotfold v Bugbrooke St Michaels	3-1
Hanworth Villa v Desborough T	1-0*
(0-0 at full time)	
Irchester U v Risborough Rangers	0-4
Rothwell Corinthians v Bedford	1-0
Chertsey T v Tuffley R	5-1
Fairford T v Ardley U	3-0
Shrivenham v Reading T	3-2
Royal Wootton Bassett T v Binfield	1-1, 4-3
Bracknell T v Hook Norton	1-0
Thatcham T v New College Swindon	7-0
Abbey Rangers v Holyport	0-0, 4-1
Oxford C Nomads v Buckingham T	4-0
Cheltenham Saracens v Brimscombe & Thrupp	1-2
Lydney T v Abingdon U	5-0
Frimley Green v Fleet Spurs	3-2
Tadley Calleva v Woodley U	6-0
Hartley Wintney v Longlevens	3-2
Carterton v Chinnor	6-0
Ash U v Windsor	0-2
Horsham v Epsom & Ewell	3-0
Horsham YMCA v FC Elmstead	3-2
Deal T v Dorking	1-0
Southwick v Lordswood	0-3
Bexhill v AFC Croydon Ath	0-2
Raynes Park Vale v Croydon	2-4
Banstead Ath v Seven Acre & Sidcup	2-2, 2-1
Corinthian v Chessington & Hook U	4-1
Haywards Heath T v Little Common	2-1
Chichester C v Erith T	0-2
Worthing U v East Preston	2-1
Canterbury C v Ringmer	1-0
Cobham v Shoreham	2-1*
(0-0 at full time)	
Sevenoaks T v Horley T	5-0
Glebe (not accepted into competition) v Eastbourne U (walkover)	
AFC Uckfield T v Beckenham T	1-5
Steyning v Wick & Barnham U	6-2
Crawley Down Gatwick v Fisher	1-3

Mile Oak v Seaford T	3-1
Loxwood v Crowborough Ath	2-0
Newhaven v Guildford C	1-0
Bridon Ropes v Holmesdale	1-1, 3-1
Andover New Street v Bitton	1-4
Wincanton T v Salisbury	1-8
Devizes T v Shaftesbury T	0-2
Team Solent v Christchurch	4-1*
(1-1 at full time)	
Alresford T v Blackfield & Langley	0-5
Oldland Abbotonians v Downton	3-0
Corsham T v Westbury U	5-1
Andover T v Fawley	7-2
Bournemouth v Brockenhurst	4-3
East Cowes Vic Ath v Lymington T	0-9
Whitchurch U v Hamworthy U	3-0
Cadbury Heath v Amesbury T	3-0
Winterbourne U v Horndean	4-4, 0-3
Cribbs v Hallen	1-2
Warminster T v Pewsey Vale	3-0
Verwood T v Fareham T	3-2*
(2-2 at full time)	
Sherborne T v Bemerton Heath Harlequins	2-3
Roman Glass St George v Calne T	3-3, 0-2*
(0-0 at full time)	
Witheridge v Cullompton Rangers	1-0
Falmouth T v Newquay	0-1
Plymouth Parkway v Street	5-1
Ivybridge T v Porthleven	7-0
Budleigh Salterton v Welton R	3-5
Shepton Mallet v Cheddar	3-1
Ashton & Backwell U v Brislington	2-1*
(1-1 at full time)	
St Blazey v Bovey Tracey	2-0
Saltash U v Exmouth T	3-4*
(3-3 at full time)	
Portishead T v Elburton Villa	2-0
Camelford v Clevedon T	2-1

SECOND ROUND QUALIFYING

Easington Colliery v Ashington	1-2
South Shields v Washington	2-1
Tow Law T v Stokesley SC	0-3
Chester-le-Street T v Heaton Stannington	4-3*
(3-3 at full time)	
Darlington Railway Ath v Hall Road Rangers	3-1
Billingham Synthonia v Morpeth T	0-1
Sunderland RCA v Bridlington T	3-2*
(1-1 at full time)	
Silsden v Daisy Hill	6-0
Whickham v Garforth T	0-1
Bedlington Terriers v Durham C	2-4*
(2-2 at full time)	
Jarrow Roofing Boldon CA v Seaham Red Star	0-1
Hebburn T v Yorkshire Amateur	3-1
Bishop Auckland v Holker Old Boys	7-1
Norton & Stockton Ancients v Newcastle Benfield	1-4
AFC Darwen v West Auckland T	2-4*
(2-2 at full time)	
Whitley Bay v West Allotment Celtic	5-1
Newton Aycliffe v Barnoldswick T	3-0
Nelson v Team Northumbria	1-3*
(1-1 at full time)	
Runcorn T v Barnton	4-1
AFC Emley v Congleton T	3-4
Dronfield T v Bootle	2-1
Handsworth Parramore v Cheadle T	3-2
Armthorpe Welfare v Ashton T	3-2
Rochdale T v St Helens T	6-2
Westella VIP v Selby T	1-3
Bacup Bor v Hemsworth MW	0-1
Atherton Colleries v Atherton LR	6-2
West Didsbury & Chorlton v Dinnington T	15-1
Squires Gate v Winsford U	0-2
Northwich Manchester Villa v Rossington Main	3-1
Penistone Church v Athersley Recreation	0-2
Maltby Main v Bottesford T	2-0
Hallam v Harworthy Colliery	4-3
Alsager T v Maine Road	3-1
Bardon Hill Sports v Hereford	0-1
Bilston T v AFC Wulfrunians	1-3
Hinckley v Bromyard T	6-0
Ellesmere Rangers v Malvern T	2-1
Boldmere St Michaels v Stafford T	4-0
Coventry U v Studley	2-0
Uttoxeter T v Bolehall Swifts	4-3*
(2-2 at full time)	

Stone Old Alleynians v Racing Club Warwick	0-4
Sporting Khalsa v Wellington	4-0
Pilkington XXX v Alvechurch	0-4
Stourport Swifts v Black Country Rangers	1-3
Eccleshall v Haughmond	0-0
(no replay; Haughmond won on penalties)	
Highgate U v Wolverhampton Casuals	5-2
AFC Bridgnorth v Willenhall T	5-2
Westfields v Littleton	3-2
Rocester v Kirby Muxloe	5-1
Coton Green v Nuneaton Griff	1-8
Bromsgrove Sporting v Dudley Sports	3-1
Lye T v Cradley T	2-4
Coventry Sphinx v Ellistown & Ibstock U	4-3
Retford U v Loughborough University	0-2
Anstey Nomads v Clifton All Whites	2-0
Holwell Sports v Dunkirk	1-3
Radford v South Normanton Ath	2-1
Teversal v Radcliffe Olympic	1-3
Oadby T v Borrowash Vic	1-4
Harrowby U v Leicester Road	1-0
Greenwood Meadows v Clipstone Welfare	1-4
Aylestone Park v St Andrews	3-5
Mickleover Royals (withdrawn) v Shirebrook T	
(walkover)	
Blidworth Welfare v Graham St Prims	2-1
Lincoln Moorlands Railway v Pinxton	1-4
Barrow T v Quorn	0-3
Arnold T v Hucknall T	0-2
Blackstones v Peterborough Northern Star	1-0*
(0-0 at full time)	
Great Yarmouth T v Deeping Rangers	1-0*
(0-0 at full time)	
Mildenhall T v St Neots Town Saints	7-0
Swaffham T v Bourne T	2-1
Gorleston v Walsham Le Willows	3-2
Wisbech St Mary v Diss T	1-3*
(1-1 at full time)	
Ely C v Newmarket T	1-2
Downham T v Sleaford T	0-2
Eynesbury R v Fakenham T	3-1
Sporting Bengal U v Halstead T	4-0
Ipswich W v Clapton	2-0
Takeley v Hoddesdon T	1-1, 0-2
Woodbridge T v Ilford	2-3
Brimsdown v Brantham Ath	2-4
Waltham Forest v Welwyn Garden C	2-5
Greenhouse Sports v Hadleigh U	3-0
Stowmarket T v Hertford T	1-4
Newbury Forest v FC Clacton	0-7
FC Romania v Baldock T	2-1
FC Broxbourne Bor v Long Melford	3-1
Wivenhoe v Basildon U	0-1
Southend Manor v Hadley	1-1, 2-3
Whitton U v Debenham LC	2-1*
(1-1 at full time)	
Raunds T v Wellingborough T	1-0
Edgware T v Winslow U	6-0
AFC Kempston R v Long Buckby	3-0
Wembley v Potton U	3-2
Rothwell Corinthians v Tring Ath	3-3, 1-2
Northampton Sileby Rangers v New Bradwell St Peter	7-2
Cricklewood W v Risborough Rangers	1-0
Hanworth Villa v Oxhey Jets	2-1
Southall v CB Hounslow U	2-0
Berkhamsted v Northampton On Chenecks	2-1
London Tigers v Crawley Green	4-2
Rayners Lane v Stotfold	1-3
Cogenhoe U v AFC Hayes	3-1
Bedfont Sports v Buckingham Ath	4-0
Biggleswade U v Leverstock Green	2-1*
(1-1 at full time)	
Northampton Spencer v Harpenden T	3-2
Westfield v Carterton	1-2
Frimley Green v Thame U	2-7
Henley T v Oxford C Nomads	1-5
Alton T v Bracknell T	1-1, 3-0
Abbey Rangers v Tytherington Rocks	1-1, 3-0
Fairford T v Badshot Lea	4-2
Chertsey T v Tadley Calleva	0-2
Windsor v Royal Wootton Bassett T	2-1*
(1-1 at full time)	
Wokingham & Emmbrook v Shrivenham	6-1
Hartley Wintney v Milton U	4-1
Thatcham T v Brimscombe & Thrupp	0-2
Malmesbury Vic v Farnham T	2-2*
(1-1 at full time; Farnham T won 4-2 on penalties)	

Knaphill v Lydney T	3-1
Canterbury C v Tooting & Mitcham W	2-0
Croydon v Horsham YMCA	2-1
Cobham v Sutton Common R	0-3
Hailsham T v Fisher	3-0
Hollands & Blair v AFC Croydon Ath	0-3
Mile Oak v Lordswood	2-4
St Francis Rangers v Meridian	2-7
Selsey v Horsham	0-3
Loxwood v Arundel	2-1
Banstead Ath v Cray Valley (PM)	2-6
Erith T v Bridon Ropes	1-2*
(1-1 at full time)	
Oakwood v Lancing	4-9*
(4-4 at full time)	
Sevenoaks T v Haywards Heath T	3-4
Beckenham T v Redhill	2-0
Eastbourne U v Deal T	0-3
Newhaven v Broadbridge Heath	3-2
Rochester U v Steyning T	0-1
Corinthian v Lingfield	4-0
Worthing U v Epsom Ath	3-0
Sheppey U v Gravesham Bor	0-3
Warminster T v Gillingham T	0-5
Salisbury v Folland Sports	4-1
New Milton T v Verwood T	3-2
Romsey T v Calne T	0-2
Team Solent v Shaftesbury T	3-0
Laverstock & Ford v Cowes Sports	2-0
Bemerton Heath Harlequins v Andover T	0-3
Bitton v Hallen	2-3
Oldland Abbotonians v Lymington T	0-1*
(0-0 at full time)	
Horndean v Longwell Green Sports	1-1, 3-1
Blackfield & Langley v Ringwood T	6-2
Cadbury Heath v Almondsbury UWE	2-1*
(1-1 at full time)	
Swanage T & Herston v Corsham T	3-4
Chippenham Park v Newport (IW)	0-1
Whitchurch U v Bournemouth	6-0
Sholing v U Services Portsmouth	1-1, 6-0
Bridport v Hythe & Dibden	5-1
Radstock T v Hengrove Ath	3-3
Shepton Mallet v Camelford	1-2*
(1-1 at full time)	
Exmouth T v Welton R	0-2
Ivybridge T v Barnstaple T	1-4
Newquay v Odd Down	1-1,
(no replay; Odd Down won on penalties)	
Wadebridge T v Portishead T	2-5
Crediton U v Bishop Sutton	1-2
Willand R v Plymouth Parkway	0-2
Ashton & Backwell U v Torpoint Ath	0-2
Keynsham T v Wells C	2-2, 1-2*
(1-1 at full time)	
Witheridge v St Blazey	10-1
Vauxhall Motors v Abbey Hey	2-3

FIRST ROUND

West Didsbury & Chorlton v Morpeth T	4-5
Handsworth Parramore v Shildon	5-4*
(4-4 at full time)	
Guisborough T v Armthorpe Welfare	8-0
Atherton Colleries v Newcastle Benfield	2-0
Stokesley SC v Maltby Main	1-4*
(1-1 at full time)	
Silsden v Sunderland RCA	2-4
Rochdale T v 1874 Northwich	2-4
Runcorn Linnets v Winsford U	2-1
Team Northumbria v Darlington Railway Ath	4-0
Congleton T v Marske U	1-5
Athersley Recreation v Colne	1-5
Durham C v Seaham Red Star	0-1
Dronfield T v Ashington	2-3*
(2-2 at full time)	
Chester-le-Street T v Newton Aycliffe	0-4
Selby T v Hallam	1-2
Runcorn T v Abbey Hey	2-0
Hemsworth MW v West Auckland T	3-2
Northwich Manchester Villa v Whitley Bay	1-1, 1-3
Garforth T v Hebburn T	1-0
Bishop Auckland v South Shields	1-2
Highgate U v Radcliffe Olympic	3-1
Loughborough University v Uttoxeter T	0-0, 2-3
Dunkirk v Bromsgrove Sporting	2-1
Pinxton v Cradley T	1-0
Rocester v Hereford	0-2

Coventry Sphinx v Black Country Rangers	1-1, 6-4*
(3-3 at full time)	
Alsager T v Borrowash Vic	2-2*
(1-1 at full time; Alsager T won 5-4 on penalties)	
Wisbech T v Alvechurch	0-4
Cleethorpes T v Westfields	2-1
Blackstones v Haughmond	2-3*
(2-2 at full time)	
Shirebrook T v Sporting Khalsa	2-0
Radford v AFC Bridgnorth	1-3
St Andrews v Blidworth Welfare	3-3, 0-6, 2-0
(First replay ordered to be replayed after Blidworth	
Welfare fielded an ineligible player)	
Coleshill T v Hucknall T	3-0
AFC Wulfrunians v Harrowby U	4-2*
(2-2 at full time)	
Racing Club Warwick v Ellesmere Rangers	3-2
Nuneaton Griff v Anstey Nomads	1-0
Quorn v Clipstone Welfare	1-0
Boldmere St Michaels v Coventry U	0-2
Long Eaton U v Hinckley	2-1*
(1-1 at full time)	
Stotfold v Newmarket T	A-A, 5-0
(First match abandoned after 42 mins, 2-1)	
Cricklewood W v Welwyn Garden C	1-0
Diss T v Basildon U	2-3
Barking v Tring Ath	4-1
Bowers & Pitsea v Hanworth Villa	3-2
Hadley v FC Romania	2-3
Northampton Sileby Rangers v Wembley	5-4
Brantham Ath v Kirkley & Pakefield	0-4
Gorleston v London Tigers	6-3
Ipswich W v Hoddesdon T	2-1
Berkhamsted v Northampton Spencer	5-1
London Colney v Great Yarmouth T	2-1
AFC Dunstable v FC Clacton	2-0*
(0-0 at full time)	
Raunds T v Sleaford T	0-1
Hertford T v Eynesbury R	4-3
Godmanchester R v Mildenhall T	1-1, 1-2
Ilford v AFC Kempston R	0-1
Sporting Bengal U v Southall	6-2
Swaffham T v FC Broxbourne Bor	1-2
Edgware T v Whitton U	5-2
Cogenhoe U v Biggleswade U	0-2
Harefield U v Greenhouse Sports	0-3
Eastbourne T v Farnham T	3-2*
(2-2 at full time)	
Hartley Wintney v Wokingham & Emmbrook	3-1
Worthing U v Sutton Common R	0-1
Knaphill v Cray Valley (PM)	5-4*
(4-4 at full time)	
Deal T v Oxford C Nomads	4-2
Littlehampton T v Tadley Calleva	1-2
Andover T v Newhaven	1-2
Cove v Canterbury C	0-5
Corinthian v Pagham	2-3
AFC Croydon Ath v Beckenham T	2-2, 3-6*
(3-3 at full time)	
Loxwood v Highmoor Ibis	3-1
Haywards Heath T v Alton T	1-0
Kidlington v Ashford T (Middlesex)	2-2, 3-1
Bedfont Sports v Carterton	1-4
Lancing v Camberley T	3-1
Gravesham Bor v Hailsham T	0-1
Windsor v Croydon	3-2
Steyning T v Horsham	1-0*
(0-0 at full time)	
Thame U v Bridon Ropes	4-3
Meridian v Lordswood	1-4
Bristol Manor Farm v Bridport	3-0
Plymouth Parkway v Blackfield & Langley	6-0
Moneyfields v Corsham T	1-0
Witheridge v Hallen	0-1
Horndean v Barnstaple T	1-3
Lymington T v Wells C	2-0
Calne T v Salisbury	2-6
Whitchurch U v Welton R	2-2, 0-4
Team Solent v Cadbury Heath	2-3
Odd Down v Camelford	2-1
Portishead T v Newport (IW)	1-3
AFC Portchester v Abbey Rangers	1-2
Gillingham T v Hengrove Ath	0-0*
(Hengrove Ath won 5-4 on penalties)	
New Milton T v Buckland Ath	0-5
Bishop Sutton v Torpoint Ath	0-3

Fairford T v Brimscombe & Thrupp	0-1
Sholing v Laverstock & Ford	2-1

SECOND ROUND

Runcorn T v Garforth T	3-0
North Shields v Ashington	3-0
Atherton Collieries v Chadderton	3-0
Morpeth T (walkover) v 1874 Northwich (unable to fulfill fixtures)	
Colne v Newton Aycliffe	3-5*
(3-3 at full time)	
Seaham Red Star v Maltby Main	3-1
Handsworth Parramore v Hallam	3-2
Hemsworth MW v Sunderland RCA	1-5
Consett v South Shields	0-1*
(0-0 at full time)	
Whitley Bay v Dunston UTS	1-2
Marske U v Runcorn Linnets	6-2
Tadcaster Alb v Worksop T	4-1
Guisborough T v Team Northumbria	1-2*
(1-1 at full time)	
AFC Mansfield v Alsager T	1-1, 1-3
Walsall Wood v Holbeach U	4-1
AFC Bridgnorth v Alvechurch	1-2
Coventry Sphinx v Brocton	2-3
Coventry U v Uttoxeter T	1-2
Coleshill T v Dunkirk	4-2
Hereford v Haughmond	4-1
Long Eaton U v Pinxton	2-3
Heanor T v Leicester Nirvana	1-3
Cleethorpes T v Racing Club Warwick	2-0
Quorn v AFC Wulfrunians	1-2
Nuneaton Griff v Highgate U	1-1, 4-2
St Andrews v Shirebrook T	4-0
Stotfold v AFC Dunstable	1-3
Bowers & Pitsea v Flackwell Heath	3-2
Yaxley v London Colney	3-2
Sporting Bengal U v Sleaford T	1-3*
(1-1 at full time)	
Gorleston v FC Romania	3-4
Ipswich W v Cricklewood W	1-0
FC Broxbourne Bor v Greenhouse Sports	2-1
Norwich U v Hullbridge Sports	0-1*
(0-0 at full time)	
Hertford T v Barking	3-2
Biggleswade U v Saffron Walden T	1-3
Kirkley & Pakefield v Edgware T	1-2
Basildon U v Northampton Sileby Rangers	7-1
Stanway R v Mildenhall T	2-1
Berkhamsted v AFC Kempston R	3-1
Sutton Common R v Beckenham T	3-2
Knaphill v Tunbridge Wells	3-0
Newhaven v Camberley T	1-2
Ashford U v Steyning T	2-1
Eastbourne T v Greenwich Bor	5-4
Pagham v Thame U	0-3
Lordswood v Carterton	4-1
Hailsham T v Ascot U	1-4
Canterbury C v Erith & Belvedere	3-2
Tadley Calleva v Haywards Heath T	4-0
Kidlington v Deal T	7-0
Colliers Wood U v Loxwood	2-0
Hartley Wintney v Windsor	3-1
Hallen v Moneyfields	0-1
Highworth T v Odd Down	2-1
Salisbury v AFC St Austell	4-0
Bradford T v Cadbury Heath	6-3
Buckland Ath v Sholing	2-1*
(0-0 at full time)	
Welton R v Plymouth Parkway	1-0
Newport (IW) v Abbey Rangers	3-1
Bodmin T v Melksham T	3-1
Bristol Manor Farm v Lymington T	2-1
Hengrove Ath v Barnstaple T	2-1
Brimscombe & Thrupp v Torpoint Ath	3-2

THIRD ROUND

Marske U v Team Northumbria	2-1
Sunderland RCA v Tadcaster Alb	4-0
Newton Aycliffe v Atherton Collieries	1-0
South Shields v Morpeth T	3-3*
(Morpeth T won 10-9 on penalties)	
North Shields v Runcorn T	1-1, 1-0
Dunston UTS v Seaham Red Star	1-0
Alsager T v AFC Wulfrunians	0-2
St Andrews v Leicester Nirvana	1-5
Handsworth Parramore v Cleethorpes T	1-2
Pinxton v Nuneaton Griff	3-4

Walsall Wood v Alvechurch	0-3
Uttoxeter T v Coleshill T	3-4
Hereford v Brocton	2-0
Saffron Walden T v Berkhamsted	2-3
FC Broxbourne Bor v Bowers & Pitsea	1-3
Hullbridge Sports v Stanway R	2-0
AFC Dunstable v Basildon U	4-0
Edgware T v Ipswich W	0-3
Yaxley v Sleaford T	3-4*
(1-1 at full time)	
Hertford T v FC Romania	0-2
Colliers Wood U v Hartley Wintney	1-3
Thame U v Kidlington	1-2
Ascot U v Camberley T	0-0, 1-4
Lordswood v Ashford U	1-5
Eastbourne T v Sutton Common R	2-3
Tadley Calleva v Newport (IW)	2-2, 2-4*
(2-2 at full time)	
Canterbury C v Knaphill	1-3
Moneyfields v Brimscombe & Thrupp	0-0, 2-0
Buckland Ath v Bradford T	1-2
Highworth T v Salisbury	1-5
Welton R v Bodmin T	0-2
Bristol Manor Farm v Hengrove Ath	7-1

FOURTH ROUND

Cleethorpes T v Alvechurch	2-1
Hereford v Leicester Nirvana	A-A, 6-0
(First match abandoned at half-time due to waterlogged pitch, 3-1)	
Morpeth T v North Shields	2-0
Coleshill T v Dunston UTS	1-3*
(1-1 at full time)	
AFC Wulfrunians v Nuneaton Griff	2-3
Sunderland RCA v Sleaford T	3-2
Newton Aycliffe v Marske U	2-0
Bowers & Pitsea v Sutton Common R	3-0
Kidlington v Knaphill	3-2
Newport (IW) v Ashford U	1-2*
(1-1 at full time)	
Moneyfields v Bristol Manor Farm	0-2
FC Romania v Camberley T	1-2
AFC Dunstable v Salisbury	0-3
Berkhamsted v Hullbridge Sports	4-2
Hartley Wintney v Bradford T	3-1
Bodmin T v Ipswich W	1-3

FIFTH ROUND

Ipswich W v Bowers & Pitsea	1-1, 1-2
Sunderland RCA v Bristol Manor Farm	2-3
Camberley T v Newton Aycliffe	5-0
Berkhamsted v Morpeth T	1-2
Cleethorpes T v Kidlington	1-2
Nuneaton Griff v Salisbury	0-3
Ashford U v Dunston UTS	1-1, 3-2
Hartley Wintney v Hereford	1-4

SIXTH ROUND

Hereford v Camberley T	3-2*
(2-2 at full time)	
Salisbury v Ashford U	3-0
Morpeth T v Bristol Manor Farm	2-0
Bowers & Pitsea v Kidlington	3-3, 4-0

SEMI-FINALS – FIRST LEG

Hereford v Salisbury	1-0
Bowers & Pitsea v Morpeth T	2-2

SEMI-FINALS – SECOND LEG

Salisbury v Hereford	1-2
(Hereford won 3-1 on aggregate)	
Morpeth T v Bowers & Pitsea	2-1
(Morpeth T won 4-3 on aggregate)	

FA VASE FINAL 2016

Wembley, Sunday 22 May 2016

Morpeth T (1) 4 *(Swales 34, Carr 47, Taylor 59, Bell 90)*

Hereford (1) 1 *(Purdie 2)*

46,781 (combined with FA Trophy)

Morpeth T: Dryden; Forster, Swailes, Hall, Novak, Carr (Bell 88), Graydon, Fry, Sayer, Taylor (Mullen 76), Chilton (Anderson 67).
Hereford: Horsell; Oates, Green, Willets (Mills 70), Edwards, Grant, Birch, Purdie, Tomelty (Bunda 55), Haysham, Symons.
Referee: Stuart Atwell.

THE FA YOUTH CUP 2015–16

*After extra time.

PRELIMINARY ROUND

Consett (withdrawn) v Shildon (walkover)	
Chester-le-Street T v Newcastle Benfield	1-7
Radcliffe Bor v AFC Fylde	0-4
Vauxhall Motors v Bootle	8-1
Lancaster (withdrawn) v West Didsbury & Chorlton (walkover)	
Clitheroe v Ashton Ath	3-8
Irlam v Ashton T	3-1
Skelmersdale U v Marine	3-4
AFC Liverpool v Cheadle T	5-6
Witton Alb (withdrawn) v Salford C (walkover)	
Nantwich T v Padiham	2-1
Southport v FC United of Manchester	2-6
Macclesfield T v Hyde U	0-1
Runcorn T (withdrawn) v Chester (walkover)	
Northwich Vic (withdrawn) v Prescot Cables (walkover)	
Stalybridge Celtic v Burscough	2-0
Silsden v Hemsworth MW	5-2
Hall Road Rangers v Handsworth Parramore	0-3
Staveley MW v Grimsby T	0-1
Brigg T v Guiseley	0-6
Sheffield v Ossett T	3-2
Selby T v North Ferriby U	1-2
Barton T Old Boys (withdrawn) v Pontefract Collieries (walkover)	
Goole v Stocksbridge Park Steels	0-4
Rossington Main v Cleethorpes T	2-1*
(1-1 at full time)	
Aylestone Park v Stamford	3-1
Leicester Nirvana v St Andrews	0-0*
(St Andrews won 3-2 on penalties)	
Mickleover Sports v Teversal	6-1
Bourne T v Basford U	1-7
Lincoln C v Matlock T	9-1
Lincoln U v Gresley	1-1*
(1-1 at full time; Gresley won 5-4 on penalties)	
Long Eaton U v Loughborough Dynamo	1-2
Boldmere St Michaels v Studley	0-0*
(Studley won 4-3 on penalties)	
Leek T v Newcastle T	0-4
Ellesmere Rangers v Bromsgrove Sporting	2-0
Bilston T v Pegasus Juniors	5-2
Romulus v Nuneaton Griff	3-2
Dudley Sports v Hereford	1-2
AFC Wulfrunians v Nuneaton T	1-0
Stratford T v Coton Green	2-0
Kidderminster H v Evesham U	7-0
Leamington v Stourbridge	2-3
Halesowen T v Bromyard T	5-1
Sutton Coldfield T v AFC Telford U	0-6
Pilkington XXX v Solihull Moors	2-1
Malvern T v Coleshill T	0-2
Coventry Sphinx (withdrawn) v Wednesfield (walkover)	
Wisbech St Mary v Hadleigh U	4-1
Ipswich W v Needham Market	2-3*
(2-2 at full time)	
Leiston v Stowmarket T	1-4
Histon v Walsham Le Willows	2-1
Soham T Rangers v Swaffham T	1-3
Long Melford v Wroxham	0-1
Norwich U v Great Yarmouth T	2-1
Cambridge C v Newmarket T	4-0
Yaxley v Brackley T	0-2
St Neots T v Bugbrooke St Michaels	5-1
Cogenhoe U v AFC Rushden & Diamonds	0-1
Biggleswade T v Corby T	8-1
Rothwell Corinthians v Kettering T	4-9
Heybridge Swifts v Tower Hamlets	3-0
Eton Manor v Billericay T	3-2*
Waltham Forest v Chelmsford C	1-9
Romford v East Thurrock U	0-6
Barkingside v Brentwood T	0-2
Saffron Walden T v Witham T	1-2
Clapton v AFC Hornchurch	1-3
Concord Rangers v Aveley	1-4
Tilbury v Halstead T	8-0
Waltham Abbey v FC Broxbourne Bor	2-2*
(2-2 at full time; Broxbourne Bor won 3-0 on penalties)	
Hullbridge Sports v Bowers & Pitsea	1-3
St Margaretsbury v Cheshunt	0-2

Ilford v Bishop's Stortford	1-0
(Tie awarded to Bishop's Stortford – Ilford withdrawn)	
Royston T v Sawbridgeworth T	6-1
Chalfont St Peter (walkover) v Hanworth Villa (withdrawn)	
Hitchin T v Aylesbury	5-3*
(3-3 at full time)	
Hayes & Yeading U v Wingate & Finchley	1-1*
(1-1 at full time; Hayes & Yeading U won 4-2 on penalties)	
Wealdstone v Buckingham Ath	7-0
Welwyn Garden C v Enfield T	0-1
Boreham Wood v CB Hounslow U	1-0
Potters Bar T v Chesham U	3-1
Newport Pagnell T v Uxbridge	3-2
Flackwell Heath v Bedfont Sports	3-4
Harrow Bor v Staines T	3-2*
(2-2 at full time)	
Dulwich Hamlet v Meridian	4-0
Lordswood v Chipstead	0-5
VCD Ath v Thamesmead T	0-2
Ramsgate v Phoenix Sports	4-0
Hastings U v Carshalton Ath	6-3
Tooting & Mitcham U v Croydon	5-4*
(3-3 at full time)	
Welling U v Corinthian	4-2
Margate v Little Common	9-0
Dover Ath v AFC Croydon Ath	4-1
Fisher (walkover) v Eastbourne U (withdrawn)	
Dartford v Cray W	9-0
Erith & Belvedere (walkover) v Cray Valley (PM)	
Ebbsfleet U v Lingfield	3-2
Faversham T (walkover) v Colliers Wood U (withdrawn)	
Chertsey T v Dorking W	4-3
Sutton U v Worthing U	10-1
Bognor Regis T v Littlehampton T	5-1
Farnham T v Raynes Park Vale	1-4
Kingstonian (walkover) v Frimley Green (withdrawn)	
Dorking v Woking	0-3
Wick & Barnham U v Oakwood	4-1
Molesey v Chichester C	4-3
Metropolitan Police v South Park	7-1
Pagham v Mile Oak	6-1
Worthing v Loxwood	3-1*
(1-1 at full time)	
Arundel v Horley T	3-2
Three Bridges v Guildford C	1-1*
(1-1 at full time; Guildford C won 4-3 on penalties)	
Walton & Hersham v Camberley T	0-5
Lewes v Leatherhead	0-2
Hampton & Richmond Bor v Haywards Heath T	3-0
Burnham v Aldershot T	0-1
Andover T v Fleet T	3-1
Basingstoke T v Kidlington	2-4*
(2-2 at full time)	
Binfield v Thame U	2-2*
(2-2 at full time; Binfield won 7-6 on penalties)	
Bracknell T v Milton U	2-1
Farnborough v Reading T	0-3
Marlow v Maidenhead U	1-4
Abingdon U v Hartley Wintney	1-3
Bournemouth v Poole T	5-1
Weymouth v Fareham T	2-1
Petersfield T v Hamworthy U	1-0
Winchester C v Moneyfields	1-3
Gillingham T v Havant & Waterlooville	1-9
Gloucester C v Chippenham T	7-0
Cheltenham T v New College Swindon	6-0
Forest Green R v Bristol Manor Farm	3-1
Wells C v Clevedon T	2-6
Torquay U (withdrawn) v Larkhall Ath (walkover)	
Tiverton T v Bishop Sutton	4-1

FIRST ROUND QUALIFYING

Hebburn T v Workington	0-13
Ryton & Crawcrook Alb v Shildon	3-2
Darlington Railway Ath v Newcastle Benfield	1-2
Gateshead v Darlington 1883	4-2
Chester v Chadderton	9-1
Ashton Ath v Marine	3-2
AFC Fylde v Nelson	3-0
Hyde U v Vauxhall Motors	3-1
Irlam v Curzon Ashton	0-2

Warrington T v Cheadle T	2-4*
(2-2 at full time)	
Colne v Nantwich T	1-3
Salford C v Abbey Hey	1-2*
(1-1 at full time)	
FC United of Manchester v Altrincham	2-3
Stalybridge Celtic v Prescot Cables	2-5
West Didsbury & Chorlton v Wrexham	1-2
Barnton v Tranmere R	0-4
AFC Emley v Liversedge	1-2
FC Halifax T v Nostell MW	9-2
Sheffield v Ossett Alb	0-3
Harrogate T v Handsworth Parramore	2-3
Rossington Main v Stocksbridge Park Steels	3-1
Silsden v Pontefract Collieries	3-1
Farsley Celtic v Knaresborough T	2-0
Worksop T v Guiseley	0-4
Dinnington T v Grimsby T	0-4
Brighouse T v North Ferriby U	3-4*
(3-3 at full time)	
Dunkirk v Basford U	0-2
Ilkeston v Loughborough Dynamo	5-0
Boston U v Anstey Nomads	4-2
Leicester Road v Lincoln C	0-10
Mickleover Sports v Ashby Ivanhoe	2-1
Aylestone Park v Oadby T	1-3
Belper T v Gresley	0-4
St Andrews v Grantham T	5-0
AFC Telford U v Walsall Wood	2-1
Bilston T v Hereford	4-2
Studley v Kidsgrove Ath	3-0
Halesowen T v Newcastle T	2-1
Romulus v Wolverhampton Casuals	2-0
Rugby T v AFC Wulfrunians	3-4
Tipton T v Kidderminster H	2-4
Stratford T v Rushall Olympic	4-1
Stourbridge (walkover) v Wednesfield (withdrawn)	
Coleshill T v Pilkington XXX	1-2*
(1-1 at full time)	
Ellesmere Rangers v Worcester C	0-5
Bedworth U v Lye T	3-1
Dereham T v Haverhill R	4-1
Bury T v Gorleston	3-2
Swaffham T v Mildenhall T	3-1
Cornard U v Needham Market	0-2
Ely C v Cambridge C	0-1
Wisbech St Mary v Norwich U	1-2
Woodbridge T v Felixstowe & Walton U	8-1
AFC Sudbury v Histon	2-1
Fakenham T v Stowmarket T	A-A, 1-3
(First match abandoned at half-time due to serious	
injury to player, 0-2)	
Brantham T v Wroxham	1-2
Eynesbury R v Barton R	0-3
Kettering T v Wellingborough T	3-0
Desborough T v St Neots T	1-2
Godmanchester R v AFC Dunstable	2-6
St Ives T v Peterborough Northern Star	0-3
Biggleswade T (walkover) v	
Wellingborough Whitworths (withdrawn)	
Brackley T v AFC Rushden & Diamonds	0-5
Witham T v Cheshunt	2-3
Heybridge Swifts v FC Broxbourne Bor	1-2*
(1-1 at full time)	
Tilbury v Aveley	1-2
Barking v FC Clacton	3-2, 5-3
(Tie ordered to be replayed)	
Grays Ath v Eton Manor	4-0
AFC Hornchurch v Chelmsford C	4-3
East Thurrock U v Braintree T	0-3
Bowers & Pitsea v Thurrock	0-3
Redbridge v Brentwood T	0-3
Royston T v Ware	3-2*
(2-2 at full time)	
Great Wakering R v Bishop's Stortford	3-0
Boreham Wood v Leverstock Green	1-0
Chalfont St Peter v Harrow Bor	1-4
Bedfont Sports v Newport Pagnell T	9-0
Northwood v Ashford T (Middlesex)	2-0
Edgware T v Hitchin T	1-3*
(1-1 at full time)	
Potters Bar T v Hayes & Yeading U	0-3
Wealdstone v Cockfosters	4-0
Beaconsfield SYCOB v Hendon	2-0
Spelthorne Sports v Enfield T	1-2*
(1-1 at full time)	
St Albans C v North Greenford U	5-3

Harefield U (walkover) v Tring Ath (withdrawn)	
Erith & Belvedere v Eastbourne Bor	0-6
Ramsgate v Tooting & Mitcham U	0-5
Dulwich Hamlet v Whitstable T	6-0
Dartford v Chipstead	4-1
Hastings U v Eastbourne T	0-2
Maidstone U v Welling U	2-0
Tonbridge Angels v Dover Ath	0-3
Margate v East Grinstead T	8-2
Fisher (withdrawn) v Bromley (walkover)	
Faversham T v Ebbsfleet U	0-5
Thamesmead T v Ringmer	13-0
Chatham T v Folkestone Invicta	0-2
Sutton U v Westfield	11-0
Metropolitan Police v Hampton & Richmond Bor	3-0
Kingstonian v Chertsey T	1-14
Shoreham v Camberley T	0-4
Woking v Corinthian Casuals	3-2
Knaphill v Redhill	8-0
Guildford C v Burgess Hill T	1-5
Wick & Barnham U v Worthing	0-10
Leatherhead v Arundel	5-2
Bognor Regis T v Molesey	1-1*
(1-1 at full time; Molesey won 4-2 on penalties)	
Pagham (walkover) v East Preston (withdrawn)	
Crawley Down Gatwick v Whitehawk	1-6
Raynes Park Vale v Horsham	6-0
Didcot T v Alton T	1-2
Thatcham T v Hungerford T	0-6
Bracknell T v Fleet Spurs	2-2*
(1-1 at full time; Fleet Spurs won 5-3 on penalties)	
Wantage T v Andover T	0-7
Ascot U v Hartley Wintney	8-3
Aldershot T v Maidenhead U	2-1
Oxford C v Windsor	10-0
Shrivenham v Binfield	2-3*
(2-2 at full time)	
Highmoor Ibis v Kidlington	1-2
Slough T v Reading T	1-7
(Tie awarded to Slough T – Reading T withdrawn)	
Sholing v Salisbury	1-0
Wimborne T v Ringwood T	4-2*
(2-2 at full time)	
Petersfield T v Weymouth	1-0
Gosport Bor v Moneyfields	3-2
Bournemouth (walkover) v AFC Totton (withdrawn)	
Havant & Waterlooville v Eastleigh	3-2
Yate T v Forest Green R	0-2
Pewsey Vale v Gloucester C	1-7
Oldland Abbotonians v Cheltenham T	0-17
Tuffley R v Cirencester T	1-3
Taunton T v Weston Super Mare	2-1
Bath C v Radstock T	5-3
Tiverton T v Larkhall Ath	3-3*
(2-2 at full time; Larkhall Ath won 4-2 on penalties)	
Odd Down v Cullompton Rangers	2-1*
(1-1 at full time)	
Clevedon T v Bridgwater T	3-1
Ashton & Backwell U v Brislington	2-1

SECOND ROUND QUALIFYING

Tranmere R v Curzon Ashton	3-2
Ashton Ath v Hyde U	3-2
Ryton & Crawcrook Alb v Prescot Cables	0-1*
(0-0 at full time)	
Wrexham v Abbey Hey	3-0
Workington v Altrincham	2-4
Gateshead v Newcastle Benfield	0-6
Chester v Cheadle T	7-0
AFC Fylde v Nantwich T	1-0
Farsley Celtic v FC Halifax T	0-5
Handsworth Parramore v Guiseley	1-2
Ossett Alb v Grimsby T	3-2
North Ferriby U v Liversedge	5-4*
(3-3 at full time)	
Silsden v Rossington Main	6-3
Mickleover Sports v Basford U	2-3*
(2-2 at full time)	
Gresley v Oadby T	2-6*
(2-2 at full time)	
St Andrews v Ilkeston	0-5
Boston U v Lincoln C	2-3*
(2-2 at full time)	
Stourbridge v Bilston T	5-2
Bedworth U v AFC Telford U	2-4
Stratford T v Studley	2-3
Halesowen T v Kidderminster H	0-7

Worcester C v AFC Wulfrunians	1-3
Pilkington XXX v Romulus	0-3
Woodbridge T v Bury T	3-1
Needham Market v AFC Sudbury	0-0*
(Needham Market won 3-1 on penalties)	
Swaffham T v Stowmarket T	1-3
Wroxham v Dereham T	2-8
Norwich U v Cambridge C	1-3
Peterborough Northern Star v Barton R	2-3
AFC Rushden & Diamonds v Biggleswade T	1-4
Royston T v Kettering T	5-1
St Neots T v AFC Dunstable	0-7
Braintree T v FC Broxbourne Bor	2-1
Barking v Thurrock	5-5*
(4-4 at full time; Barking won 5-4 on penalties)	
Aveley v Brentwood T	3-1
Great Wakering R v Cheshunt	3-2*
(2-2 at full time)	
AFC Hornchurch v Grays Ath	2-0
Beaconsfield SYCOB v Bedfont Sports	0-1
Hitchin T v Enfield T	1-3
Northwood v St Albans C	0-4
Harefield U v Boreham Wood	0-3
Wealdstone v Hayes & Yeading U	0-1
Bromley v Tooting & Mitcham U	3-2
Folkestone Invicta v Eastbourne Bor	1-0
Margate v Dulwich Hamlet	2-4
Dartford v Dover Ath	1-6
Thamesmead T v Maidstone U	1-5
Ebbsfleet U v Eastbourne T	3-2*
(1-1 at full time)	
Slough T v Pagham	4-4*
(3-3 at full time; Pagham won 4-1 on penalties)	
Metropolitan Police v Knaphill	3-0
Sutton U v Raynes Park Vale	4-0
Worthing v Leatherhead	3-1
Camberley T v Chertsey T	3-0
Molesey v Burgess Hill T	1-5
Woking v Whitehawk	4-3*
(2-2 at full time)	
Aldershot T v Alton T	7-2
Fleet Spurs v Oxford C	0-4
Hungerford T v Binfield	4-0
Kidlington v Harrow Bor	4-1
Ascot U v Andover T	1-3
Wimborne T v Sholing	1-4
Petersfield v Gosport Bor	0-4
Havant & Waterlooville v Bournemouth	1-2
Larkhall Ath v Gloucester C	0-3
Cirencester T v Odd Down	2-0
Cheltenham T v Clevedon T	6-0
Ashton & Backwell U v Forest Green R	0-5
Bath C v Taunton T	3-2*
(2-2 at full time)	

THIRD ROUND QUALIFYING

AFC Fylde v Ashton Ath	3-2
Guiseley v North Ferriby U	1-2
Basford U v FC Halifax T	4-1
Silsden v Chester	0-6
Ossett Alb v Wrexham	0-6
Newcastle Benfield v Altrincham	1-2
Prescot Cables v Tranmere R	1-4
AFC Telford U v Kidderminster H	2-1
Oadby T v Lincoln C	2-3
Romulus v Stourbridge	2-5
AFC Wulfrunians v Cambridge C	1-4
Studley v Ilkeston	1-4
Aveley v Royston T	2-1*
(1-1 at full time)	
Needham Market v Biggleswade T	2-7
Boreham Wood v Great Wakering R	2-1
Barton R v AFC Dunstable	5-4*
(3-3 at full time)	
Hayes & Yeading U v St Albans C	4-1
AFC Hornchurch v Bedfont Sports	1-0
Woodbridge T v Braintree T	3-0
Barking v Enfield T	0-3
Stowmarket T v Dereham T	0-3
Metropolitan Police v Folkestone Invicta	1-0
Worthing v Burgess Hill T	5-2
Aldershot T v Sutton U	1-2
Woking v Pagham	4-1
Camberley T v Dover Ath	2-4*
(2-2 at full time)	
Ebbsfleet U v Maidstone U	3-1
Dulwich Hamlet v Bromley	3-1

Sholing v Andover T	1-0*
(0-0 at full time)	
Forest Green R v Hungerford T	A-A, 1-0
(First match abandoned after 84 mins due to serious injury to player, 0-1)	
Cheltenham T v Gosport Bor	2-0
Bournemouth v Oxford C	3-3*
(2-2 at full time; Bournemouth won 5-4 on penalties)	
Kidlington v Bath C	1-0*
(0-0 at full time)	
Gloucester C v Cirencester T	3-2

FIRST ROUND

Hartlepool U v Fleetwood T	0-2
North Ferriby U v Morecambe	1-2
Scunthorpe U v Wrexham	2-1
Accrington Stanley v Basford U	4-1
Oldham Ath v Chester	3-2*
(2-2 at full time)	
Altrincham v Rochdale	0-2
Doncaster R v Barnsley	2-1*
(1-1 at full time)	
Sheffield U v Bradford C	0-0*
(Sheffield U won 4-2 on penalties)	
Blackpool v Crewe Alex	1-4*
(1-1 at full time)	
Wigan Ath v York C	4-2
Carlisle U v Tranmere R	3-2*
(1-1 at full time)	
AFC Fylde v Bury	1-4
Lincoln C v Port Vale	1-0
Stourbridge v Chesterfield	2-3
Ilkeston v Burton Alb	0-0*
(Ilkeston won 5-3 on penalties)	
Mansfield T v Cambridge C	3-0
Shrewsbury T v AFC Telford U	2-1*
(1-1 at full time)	
Walsall v Coventry C	1-4
Northampton T v Notts Co	0-2
Aveley v Stevenage	0-3
Dereham T v Peterborough U	2-1
Luton T v Colchester U	3-1
Biggleswade T v Enfield T	6-1
Cambridge U v Hayes & Yeading U	5-0
AFC Hornchurch v Leyton Orient	0-2
Barton R v Southend U	1-9
(Tie ordered to be replayed, 1-6)	
Woodbridge T v Dagenham & Redbridge	4-4*
(2-2 at full time; Woodbridge T won 4-3 on penalties)	
Boreham Wood v Barnet	1-3
Metropolitan Police v Dulwich Hamlet	2-2*
(2-2 at full time; Metropolitan Police won 4-2 on penalties)	
Gillingham v Ebbsfleet U	1-2
Millwall v Dover Ath	2-0
Sutton U v Worthing	3-4*
(3-3 at full time)	
AFC Wimbledon v Woking	4-0
Cheltenham T v Swindon T	5-1
Bournemouth v Exeter C	1-6
Gloucester C v Bristol R	1-4
Oxford U v Kidlington	6-0
Yeovil T v Forest Green R	4-0
Sholing v Newport Co	0-0*
(Newport Co won 4-2 on penalties)	
Plymouth Argyle v Portsmouth	0-3

SECOND ROUND

Lincoln C v Wigan Ath	0-1
Ilkeston v Shrewsbury T	4-1
Chesterfield v Sheffield U	0-3
Accrington S v Fleetwood T	2-1
Oldham Ath v Morecambe	4-1
Coventry C v Crewe Alex	2-0
Scunthorpe U v Bury	1-4
Notts Co v Rochdale	2-1
Carlisle U v Doncaster R	1-0*
(0-0 at full time)	
Mansfield T v Dereham T	4-3*
(3-3 at full time)	
AFC Wimbledon v Ebbsfleet U	2-0
Exeter C v Oxford U	2-1
Cheltenham T v Barnet	3-2
Cambridge U v Stevenage	0-0*
(Stevenage won 4-2 on penalties)	
Leyton Orient v Luton T	0-1
Yeovil T v Metropolitan Police	1-1*
(1-1 at full time; Metropolitan Police won 7-6 on penalties)	

Biggleswade T v Worthing	3-4
Newport Co v Southend U	1-2*
(1-1 at full time)	
Millwall v Woodbridge T	9-1
Bristol R v Portsmouth	3-3*
(3-3 at full time; Portsmouth won 3-1 on penalties)	

THIRD ROUND

Wigan Ath v Stevenage	3-1
Coventry C v Stoke C	1-0
Manchester U v QPR	2-1
Blackburn R v Southend U	1-0
Swansea C v Sheffield W	1-0
Oldham Ath v AFC Bournemouth	1-1*
(1-1 at full time; Oldham Ath won 8-7 on penalties)	
Charlton Ath v Millwall	1-1*
(1-1 at full time; Charlton Ath won 4-2 on penalties)	
Notts Co v Luton T	1-3
Arsenal v WBA	4-1
Nottingham F v Brighton & HA	1-1*
(1-1 at full time; Nottingham F won 4-3 on penalties)	
Derby Co v West Ham U	3-1
Mansfield T v Sunderland	1-5
Hull C v Norwich C	1-3
Exeter C v Bolton W	4-3
Ilkeston v Newcastle U	2-3
Tottenham H v Rotherham U	4-0
Wolverhampton W v Milton Keynes D	3-0
Reading v Sheffield U	3-1*
(1-1 at full time)	
Liverpool v Ipswich T	2-1
Worthing v Middlesbrough	0-3
Southampton v Birmingham C	2-3
Portsmouth v Manchester C	1-2
Everton v Aston Villa	0-1
Carlisle U v Preston NE	1-2*
(1-1 at full time)	
Leicester C v Cheltenham T	5-0
Burnley v Metropolitan Police	2-2*
(1-1 at full time; Metropolitan Police won 6-5 on penalties)	
Chelsea v Huddersfield T	6-1
Watford v AFC Wimbledon	2-2*
(2-2 at full time; Wimbledon won 4-2 on penalties)	
Brentford v Leeds U	2-3
Bristol C v Cardiff C	0-4
Fulham v Bury	4-2
Accrington S v Crystal Palace	2-3*
(2-2 at full time)	

FOURTH ROUND

Coventry C v Charlton Ath	2-1
Newcastle U v AFC Wimbledon	1-2
Blackburn R v Leicester C	3-2
Wigan Ath v Derby Co	1-0
Wolverhampton W v Metropolitan Police	5-0
Crystal Palace v Aston Villa	1-5
Liverpool v Reading	3-0
Sunderland v Norwich C	1-4
Fulham v Reading	1-3
Exeter C v Preston NE	1-2
Oldham Ath v Luton T	0-1
Manchester U v Chelsea	1-5

Tottenham H v Middlesbrough	1-3
Leeds U v Manchester C	2-5
Nottingham F v Birmingham C	1-0
Swansea C v Arsenal	1-3

FIFTH ROUND

Preston NE v Luton T	1-1*
(1-1 at full time; Luton T won 5-3 on penalties)	
Middlesbrough v Norwich C	4-5
AFC Wimbledon v Chelsea	1-4
Wolverhampton W v Reading	0-3
Wigan Ath v Manchester C	1-3*
(1-1 at full time)	
Aston Villa v Blackburn R	1-2
Coventry C v Arsenal	2-2*
(1-1 at full time; Arsenal won 7-6 on penalties)	
Nottingham F v Liverpool	1-2

SIXTH ROUND

Chelsea v Reading	2-1
Blackburn R v Luton T	1-0
Manchester C v Norwich C	2-0
Arsenal v Liverpool	2-1

SEMI-FINALS – FIRST LEG

Blackburn R v Chelsea	0-1
Manchester C v Arsenal	2-1

SEMI-FINALS – SECOND LEG

Chelsea v Blackburn R	3-1
(Chelsea won 4-1 on aggregate)	
Arsenal v Manchester C	2-2
(Manchester C won 4-3 on aggregate)	

FA YOUTH CUP FINAL 2016 FIRST LEG

Friday 22 April 2016

Manchester C (0) 1 *(Nemane 68)*

Chelsea (0) 1 *(Mount 50)*   4084

Manchester C: Grimshaw; Oliver, Humphreys-Grant, Adarabioyo, Latibeaudiere (Wood 89), Kongolo, Davenport, Garcia (Buckley-Ricketts 60), Nemane (Sancho 90), Nmecha, Diaz.
Chelsea: Baxter; Chalobah (Grant 78), Clarke-Salter, Tomori, Dasilva, Sammut, Ali (Scott 62), Sterling, Mount, Christie-Davies, Ugbo (Maddox 71).
Referee: Paul Tierney.

FA YOUTH CUP FINAL 2016 SECOND LEG

Wednesday 27 April 2016

Chelsea (1) 3 *(Sterling 45, Abraham 53, Tomori 73)*

Manchester C (0) 1 *(Diaz 87)*   8530

Chelsea: Baxter; Chalobah (Grant 77), Tomori, Clarke-Salter, Dasilva, Sammut, Ali, Christie-Davis (Maddox 64), Mount, Abraham, Sterling (Ugbo 83).
Manchester C: Grimshaw; Oliver, Adarabioyo (Dele-Bashiru 75), Latibeaudiere (Wood 26), Humphreys-Grant; Davenport, Kongolo, Diaz, Buckley-Ricketts, Nemane (Sancho 64), Nmecha.
Referee: Paul Tierney.
Chelsea won 4-2 on aggregate.

THE FA COUNTY YOUTH CUP 2015–16

*After extra time.

FIRST ROUND

Cumberland v Isle of Man	2-1
Westmorland v Northumberland	1-4
West Riding v Manchester	1-0
Cornwall v Guernsey	1-0
Essex v Somerset	9-2
Norfolk v Wiltshire	0-1
Worcestershire v Kent	4-3
Oxfordshire v London	2-1

SECOND ROUND

Cheshire v Lincolnshire	2-1
East Riding v Leicestershire & Rutland	0-8
Cumberland v Sheffield & Hallamshire	1-2
Durham v Birmingham	3-1
Staffordshire v North Riding	1-0
West Riding v Lancashire	2-1
Northumberland v Liverpool	2-3*
(1-1 at full time)	

Oxfordshire v Bedfordshire	4-2
Gloucestershire v Cornwall	2-4
Worcestershire v Suffolk	0-2
Sussex v Cambridgeshire	5-0
Herefordshire v Jersey	3-3*
(3-3 at full time; Herefordshire won 3-1 on penalties)	
Wiltshire v Hertfordshire	1-2
Devon v Middlesex	3-6
Essex v Berks & Bucks	3-0
Northamptonshire v Amateur Football Alliance	1-2

THIRD ROUND

Herefordshire v Sussex	2-3
Suffolk v Middlesex	0-2
Leicestershire & Rutland v Durham	2-1
Staffordshire v Hertfordshire	1-2
Amateur Football Alliance v Sheffield & Hallamshire	2-1
Liverpool v Oxfordshire	4-2
Cheshire v Essex	3-2
Cornwall v West Riding	0-3

FOURTH ROUND

Liverpool v Hertfordshire	2-0
Sussex v Middlesex	0-0*
(Sussex won 7-6 on penalties)	
Amateur Football Alliance v Cheshire	0-4
West Riding v Leicestershire & Rutland	0-1

SEMI-FINALS

Sussex v Cheshire	3-2*
(1-1 at full time))	
Leicestershire & Rutland v Liverpool	0-1

FA COUNTY YOUTH CUP FINAL 2016

Crawley, Saturday 9 April 2016

Sussex (0) 0

Liverpool (2) 0 *(Jones 21, McGrath 33)*

Sussex: Rose; Summerfield, Watson, Johnson, Beard, Copolla, Gill, Lovatt (Colbran 77), Bachelor (Ramsey 63), Hards, House.
Liverpool: Mulby, Hodkinson, Stephens, Gallagher, Clark, McGrath (Glover 55), Jones, Howells, Beigan (Walsh 85), Wynne (Lowe 90), Daniels.

THE FA SUNDAY CUP 2015–16

After extra time.

FIRST ROUND

Hardwick Social v Northallerton Police	4-2
Hartlepool Lion Hillcarter v Burradon & New Fordley	0-2
Newton Aycliffe WMC v Seaton Carew	8-1
Dawdon Colliery Welfare v South Bank	9-3
Windmill Kestrels v Seymour	1-3
Chapeltown Fforde Grene v AFC Blackburn Leisure	7-1
West Bowling v Poulton Royal	4-0
Bolton Woods v Fantail	0-2
Allerton v Pineapple	2-1
Thornton U v Alder	0-5
Oyster Martyrs v BRNESC	4-0
Queens Park v HT Sports	2-2*
(2-2 at full time; Queens Park won 5-3 on penalties)	
Lobster v Garston	1-2
Home & Bargain (walkover) v LIV Supplies (withdrawn)	
Millhouse v Kirkdale	1-2
Dengo U v Canada	0-1
Frolesworth U v Oaks	4-1
Albion v Attenborough Cavaliers	1-3
Creation Builders v Mowmacre & Hoskins	5-3
RHP Sports & Social v Trentside	1-2
Quorn Royals 2008 v Halfway	5-0
Birstall Stamford v Punchbowl	0-2
Riverside R v Priory Sports	0-4
Falcons v Gym U	4-2
FC Bengals v Victoria Millers	1-2
Club Lewsey v Two Touch	5-6*
(5-5 at full time)	
Queens Head v FC Houghton	1-12
North Wembley v Bushey Sports (Sunday)	1-3
Belstone (Sunday) (walkover) v	
Berkhamsted Ath (withdrawn)	
Hammer v AC Sportsman	0-5
British Airways HEW v Brache Nation	2-1
St Josephs (South Oxhey) v Comets Sports Club	1-2
St Josephs (Sunday) v	
Aylesbury New Zealand (Sunday)	2-1
FC Morden v Lambeth All Stars	5-2*
(2-2 at full time)	
Barnes v Market Hotel	6-0
Polonia Reading v Lebeqs Tavern Courage	0-8
Victoria Cross v Emmer Green (Sunday)	4-0

SECOND ROUND

Allerton v West Bowling	1-3
St John Fisher OB v Witton Park Rose & Crown	3-5
Fantail v Home & Bargain	0-3
Alder v Mayfair	0-6
The Molly v Kirkdale	4-0
Campfield v Dawdon Colliery Welfare	2-1
Newton Aycliffe WMC v Garston	1-1*
(1-1 at full time; Newton Aycliffe WMC won 4-2 on penalties)	
Halton Moor (Sunday) v Burradon & New Fordley	1-6
Oyster Martyrs v Nicosia	2-0
Black Bull v Canada	2-2*
(2-2 at full time; Black Bull won 4-2 on penalties)	
Seymour v Chapeltown Fforde Grene	3-1
Custys v Kennelwood	2-0
Hessle Rangers v Hardwick Social	0-3
Black Horse (Redditch) v Hundred Acre	5-0
Frolesworth U v Trentside	5-3
Attenborough Cavaliers (walkover) v	
Punchbowl (unable to fulfil fixture)	
Quorn Royals 2008 v Hampton Blackwood	8-1
Nuthall v OJM	0-6
Sporting Dynamo v Creation Builders	2-1
AC Sportsman v Green Man	0-4

St Josephs (Sunday) v Priory Sports	3-0
Two Touch v NLO	2-2*
(2-2 at full time; NLO won 4-3 on penalties)	
Belstone (Sunday) v Broadfields U (Sunday)	0-3
Comets Sports Club v FC Houghton	1-3
New Salamis v Falcons	5-3
British Airways HEW v Bushey Sports (Sunday)	2-1
Victoria Millers v Upshire	3-0
Victoria Cross v London St Georges	8-4
FC Morden v AFC Links	1-2
Lebeqs Tavern Courage v AFC Kumazi Strikers	3-1
Ajax LA v Barnes	0-4
Queen's Park (bye)	

THIRD ROUND

Custys v Seymour	1-3
Queens Park v The Molly	0-2
Black Bull v Oyster Martyrs	1-1
(1-1 at full time; Oyster Martyrs won 5-4 on penalties)	
Mayfair v Witton Park Rose & Crown	7-2
Home & Bargain v Campfield	2-5
Newton Aycliffe WMC v Burradon & New Fordley	1-3
Hardwick Social v West Bowling	5-1*
(1-1 at full time)	
Attenborough Cavaliers v OJM	1-4
Sporting Dynamo v Black Horse (Redditch)	0-5
Frolesworth U v Quorn Royals 2008	2-1
Victoria Millers v New Salamis	3-6
Broadfields U (Sunday) v NLO	0-1
St Josephs (Sunday) v Green Man	1-0
FC Houghton v British Airways HEW	6-4
Victoria Cross v Barnes	1-3
AFC Links v Lebeqs Tavern Courage	0-1

FOURTH ROUND

Burradon & New Fordley v Hardwick Social	0-1
The Molly v Seymour	3-0
Campfield v Oyster Martyrs	2-0*
(0-0 at full time)	
OJM v Mayfair	1-0
Black Horse (Redditch) v FC Houghton	6-2
Lebeqs Tavern Courage v Barnes	1-2*
(1-1 at full time)	
New Salamis v NLO	3-2
St Josephs (Sunday) v Frolesworth U	2-1*
(1-1 at full time)	

FIFTH ROUND

OJM v Hardwick Social	1-0
Barnes v Black Horse (Redditch)	1-0
The Molly v Campfield	0-3
St Josephs (Sunday) v New Salamis	2-3*
(1-1 at full time)	

SEMI-FINALS

Barnes v Campfield	3-1
OJM v New Salamis	0-3

FA SUNDAY CUP FINAL 2016

Crystal Palace, Sunday 17 April 2016

New Salamis (0) 1 *(Georgiou H 69)*

Barnes (1) 1 *(Gallagher 7)*

New Salamis: Wright; Hutchings, White, Rifat, Oujdi, Georgiou R (Addai 53), Latite, Hervel, Portou (Georgiou H 63), Muir, Mehmet.
Barnes: Khaira; Willis, Dyett, Gallagher, Queensborough (Atiase 73), Loveridge, Sheridan, Buckle J, McGregor, Oaks (Joseph 65), Buckle D.
aet; New Salamis won 4-3 on penalties.

THE FA INTER-LEAGUE CUP 2015–16

After extra time.

PRELIMINARY ROUND

Wearside League v West Yorkshire League	1-3
Cumberland County League v Northern Football Alliance	3-2
Yorkshire Amateur League v York Football League	2-1
Teesside League v Scarborough & District League	6-2*
(2-2 at full time)	
Lancashire Amateur League v Lancashire & Cheshire Amateur League	2-0
West Cheshire League v Manchester League	3-1*
(1-1 at full time)	
Chester & Wirral League (walkover) v Warrington & District League (withdrew)	
Anglian Combination v Northamptonshire Combination	5-1
Peterborough & District League v Northampton T & District League	2-1*
(1-1 at full time)	
Staffordshire County League v Birmingham & District AFA	2-0
Suffolk & Ipswich League v Essex & Suffolk Border League	1-2
Bedfordshire County League v Surrey Elite Intermediate League	2-2*
(1-1 at full time; Bedfordshire County League won 5-4 on penalties)	
Kent County League v Spartan South Midlands League (Div 2)	1-2
Mid Sussex League v Amateur Football Combination	0-3
Essex Olympian League v Brighton, Hove & District League	7-0
(Essex Olympian League removed for fielding an ineligible player)	
Gloucestershire County League v Dorset Football League	8-1
Devon & Exeter League v Somerset County League	0-6
Wiltshire League v Hampshire Premier League	0-4
Thames Valley Premier League v Oxfordshire Senior League	1-0

FIRST ROUND

Chester & Wirral League v Isle of Man League	1-7
Cheshire League v West Riding County Amateur League	4-2
Lincolnshire League v Staffordshire County League	1-4
Yorkshire Amateur League v West Yorkshire League	1-4
Cumberland County League v Teesside League	1-3
Humber Premier League v Lancashire Amateur League	2-4
Liverpool County Premier League v West Cheshire League	1-3
Southern Amateur League v Hampshire Premier League	3-2
Cambridgeshire County League v Essex Olympian League	
(EOL removed for fielding an ineligible player in the Preliminary Round)	
Guernsey County Senior League (withdrew) v Gloucestershire County League	
(walkover)	
Herts Senior County League v Somerset County League	4-1
Amateur Football Combination v Jersey Football Combination	1-2
Spartan South Midlands League (Div 2) v Bedfordshire County League	4-0
Anglian Combination v Thames Valley Premier League	3-2*
(2-2 at full time)	
Peterborough & District League v Dorset Premier League	3-4
Brighton, Worthing & District League v Essex & Suffolk Border League	1-3

SECOND ROUND

Staffordshire County League v Teesside League	1-3
West Cheshire League v West Yorkshire League	1-2
Cheshire League v Isle of Man League	0-9
Lancashire Amateur League v Cambridgeshire County League	0-2*
(0-0 at full time)	
Jersey Football Combination v Essex & Suffolk Border League	0-1*
(0-0 at full time)	
Herts Senior County League v Dorset Premier League	3-0
Guernsey County Senior League v Southern Amateur League	0-1*
(0-0 at full time)	
Anglian Combination v Spartan South Midlands League (Div 2)	1-4*
(0-0 at full time)	

QUARTER-FINAL

Isle of Man League v Teesside League	1-3
West Yorkshire League v Cambridgeshire County League	1-0
Essex & Suffolk Border League v Spartan South Midlands League (Div 2)	1-5
Herts Senior County League v Southern Amateur League	0-4

SEMI FINAL

Spartan South Midlands League (Div 2) v West Yorkshire League	3-2
Spartan South Midlands League (Div 2) removed for fielding an ineligible player.	
Southern Amateur League v Teesside League	0-1

FA INTER-LEAGUE CUP FINAL 2016

York, Sunday 8 May 2016

West Yorkshire League (1) 3 *(Moon 2, Day 47 (pen), Cunningham 90)*

Teesside League (1) 2 *(Rose 7, Callan 58)*

Referee: Rob Jones

FA PREMIER UNDER-21 LEAGUE 2015–16

DIVISION 1	P	W	D	L	F	A	GD	Pts
1 Manchester U	22	15	3	4	44	19	25	48
2 Sunderland	22	13	4	5	38	20	18	43
3 Everton	22	10	7	5	35	27	8	37
4 Manchester C	22	10	4	8	35	26	9	34
5 Chelsea	22	9	6	7	34	30	4	33
6 Southampton	22	8	6	8	39	40	-1	30
7 Liverpool	22	8	4	10	26	37	-11	28
8 Tottenham H	22	7	6	9	44	43	1	27
9 Reading	22	7	6	9	34	40	-6	27
10 Leicester C	22	6	3	13	25	48	-23	21
11 Middlesbrough	22	5	5	12	33	37	-4	20
12 Norwich C	22	5	4	13	30	50	-20	19

DIVISION 2	P	W	D	L	F	A	GD	Pts
1 Derby Co	22	13	3	6	44	26	18	42
2 Arsenal	22	12	4	6	40	25	15	40
3 Swansea C	22	12	3	7	42	24	18	39
4 Aston Villa	22	11	6	5	28	27	1	39
5 Blackburn R	22	10	4	8	29	33	-4	34
6 WBA	22	8	9	5	24	20	4	33
7 West Ham U	22	9	5	8	37	34	3	32
8 Stoke C	22	10	2	10	24	24	0	32
9 Fulham	22	8	5	9	26	29	-3	29
10 Newcastle U	22	4	6	12	30	48	-18	18
11 Brighton & HA	22	2	8	12	17	36	-19	14
12 Wolverhampton W	22	2	7	13	20	35	-15	13

DIVISION 2 PLAY-OFFS – SEMI-FINALS

Arsenal v Blackburn R	2-1
Swansea C v Aston Villa	1-2

FINAL

Arsenal v Aston Villa	3-1

Arsenal promoted to Division 1.

THE FA PREMIER UNDER-21 LEAGUE CUP
After extra time.

FIRST QUALIFYING ROUND

Exeter C v Southend	6-0
Plymouth Arg v AFC Wimbledon	2-1*
Doncaster R v Preston NE	1-0
Gillingham v Bournemouth	1-2
Burnley v Wigan Ath	3-0

SECOND QUALIFYING ROUND

Cardiff C v Bristol C	2-1*
QPR v Brentford	1-2
Millwall v Plymouth Arg	1-0
Ipswich T v Charlton Ath	0-3
Bolton W v Sheffield U	3-4
Burnley v Barnsley	3-1
Colchester U v Bournemouth	3-0

Crewe Alex v Doncaster R	3-2
Exeter C v Peterborough U	1-0
Sheffield W v Hull C	2-3
Huddersfield T v Nottingham F	1-0
Watford v Birmingham C	2-0

ROUND OF 32

Reading v Brentford	1-2
Burnley v Blackburn R	1-3
Hull C v Crewe Alex	2-1
Wolverhampton W v Derby Co	2-1
Stoke C v Leicester C	2-5
Watford v Charlton Ath	1-2
Brighton & HA v Norwich C	4-1
Cardiff C v WBA	0-1
Sheffield U v Leeds U	0-1
Swansea C v Millwall	1-2*
Sunderland v Liverpool	3-4*
Exeter C v West Ham U	0-4
Huddersfield T v Middlesbrough	2-1
Colchester U v Fulham	1-3
Southampton v Chelsea	1-0
Everton v Newcastle U	4-3

ROUND OF 16

Wolverhampton W v Millwall	1-3
Charlton Ath v Brentford	2-1
West Ham U v Fulham	3-2*
Blackburn R v Leicester C	1-0
WBA v Hull C	1-2
Liverpool v Leeds U	1-0
Southampton v Huddersfield T	0-2
Everton v Brighton & HA	2-2*

Brighton & HA won 4-2 on penalties

QUARTER-FINALS

West Ham U v Blackburn R	2-1
Huddersfield T v Charlton Ath	1-1*

Huddersfield T won 5-4 on penalties

Liverpool v Brighton & HA	4-3*
Millwall v Hull C	1-3

SEMI-FINALS

Huddersfield T v Hull C	0-0*

Hull C won 4-3 on penalties

West Ham U v Liverpool	3-2*

FINAL FIRST LEG

West Ham U v Hull C	1-0

FINAL SECOND LEG

Hull C v West Ham U	1-0

West Ham U won 5-3 on penalties

FA ACADEMY UNDER-18 LEAGUE 2015–16

THE FA PREMIER UNDER-18 LEAGUE TABLES

NORTH DIVISION	P	W	D	L	F	A	GD	Pts
1 Manchester C	22	14	6	2	53	23	30	48
2 Everton	22	15	3	4	57	33	24	48
3 Liverpool	22	13	4	5	45	28	17	43
4 Blackburn R	22	11	4	7	45	31	14	37
5 Sunderland	22	11	3	8	44	40	4	36
6 Middlesbrough	22	10	4	8	43	38	5	34
7 Wolverhampton W	22	8	4	10	42	40	2	28
8 WBA	22	7	4	11	29	44	-15	25
9 Newcastle U	22	6	2	14	27	59	-32	20
10 Derby Co	22	3	9	10	39	51	-12	18
11 Manchester U	22	5	3	14	29	44	-15	18
12 Stoke C	22	4	4	14	23	45	-22	16

SOUTH DIVISION	P	W	D	L	F	A	GD	Pts
1 Chelsea	22	15	5	2	65	27	38	50
2 Reading	22	13	3	6	47	27	20	42
3 Fulham	22	12	3	7	44	29	15	39
4 West Ham U	22	11	4	7	30	29	1	37
5 Aston Villa	22	11	3	8	42	34	8	36
6 Arsenal	22	10	5	7	49	45	4	35
7 Leicester C	22	9	5	8	39	37	2	32
8 Tottenham H	22	9	4	9	43	40	3	31
9 Brighton & HA	22	6	4	12	32	51	-19	22
10 Norwich C	22	6	3	13	28	48	-20	21
11 Southampton	22	4	3	15	34	57	-23	15
12 Swansea C	22	3	4	15	25	54	-29	13

THE FA PREMIER UNDER-18 FINAL PHASE

GROUP 1	P	W	D	L	F	A	GD	Pts
1 Manchester C	7	6	1	0	21	7	14	19
2 Everton	7	4	1	2	14	15	-1	13
3 Chelsea	7	3	2	2	16	13	3	11
4 Liverpool	7	2	2	3	13	11	2	8
5 Blackburn R	7	2	2	3	9	9	0	8
6 Fulham	7	2	1	4	9	19	-10	7
7 Reading	7	1	2	4	9	13	-4	5
8 West Ham U	7	0	5	2	9	13	-4	5

GROUP 2	P	W	D	L	F	A	GD	Pts
1 Middlesbrough	7	6	1	0	14	6	8	19
2 Sunderland	7	4	1	2	14	8	6	13
3 Leicester C	7	3	3	1	16	11	5	12
4 Aston Villa	7	3	3	1	11	9	2	12
5 Arsenal	7	2	2	3	15	14	1	8
6 Tottenham H	7	2	1	4	15	17	-2	7
7 WBA	7	1	2	4	8	13	-5	5
8 Wolverhampton W	7	0	1	6	10	25	-15	1

GROUP 3	P	W	D	L	F	A	GD	Pts
1 Swansea C	7	4	3	0	17	13	4	15
2 Brighton & HA	7	4	1	2	18	13	5	14
3 Derby Co	7	4	1	2	17	10	7	13
4 Manchester U	7	4	1	2	17	12	5	13
5 Stoke C	7	3	1	3	12	12	0	10
6 Newcastle U	7	2	1	4	10	18	-8	7
7 Southampton	7	1	2	4	9	13	-4	5
8 Norwich C	7	0	1	6	9	18	-9	1

FINAL THIRD DEVELOPMENT LEAGUE 2015–16

WEST DIVISION	P	W	D	L	F	A	GD	Pts
1 Bradford C	14	10	2	2	36	12	24	32
2 Wigan Ath	14	7	3	4	47	20	27	24
3 Walsall	14	7	2	5	25	26	-1	23
4 Shrewsbury T	14	6	4	4	28	22	6	22
5 Port Vale	14	4	4	6	31	34	-3	16
6 Wrexham	14	5	1	8	27	32	-5	16
7 Burton Alb	14	5	1	8	23	34	-11	16
8 Morecambe	14	3	1	10	11	48	-37	10

EAST DIVISION	P	W	D	L	F	A	GD	Pts
1 Notts Co	14	10	4	0	43	8	35	34
2 Chesterfield	14	10	2	2	33	14	19	32
3 Hartlepool U	14	7	2	5	26	26	0	23
4 Gateshead	14	6	1	7	22	30	-8	19
5 Doncaster R	14	4	4	6	26	28	-2	16
6 Rotherham U	14	3	2	9	16	37	-21	11
7 Grimsby T	14	1	7	6	16	22	-6	10
8 Scunthorpe U	14	1	6	7	14	31	-17	9

SOUTH DIVISION	P	W	D	L	F	A	GD	Pts
1 Bournemouth	12	7	2	3	35	22	13	23
2 AFC Wimbledon	12	6	3	3	20	10	10	21
3 Southend U	12	5	3	4	22	11	11	18
4 Leyton Orient	12	5	3	4	22	17	5	18
5 Gillingham	12	5	1	6	17	34	-17	16
6 Luton T	12	4	2	6	17	16	1	14
7 Cambridge U	12	2	2	8	8	31	-23	8

FINAL THIRD DEVELOPMENT LEAGUE CUP 2015–16

NORTHERN GROUP A	P	W	D	L	F	A	GD	Pts
1 Burnley	3	2	1	0	8	4	4	7
2 Bradford C	3	2	0	1	7	4	3	6
3 Fleetwood T	3	1	1	1	12	5	7	4
4 Morecambe	3	0	0	3	0	14	-14	0

NORTHERN GROUP B	P	W	D	L	F	A	GD	Pts
1 Middlesbrough	3	2	1	0	14	7	7	7
2 Hartlepool U	3	2	1	0	7	4	3	7
3 York C	3	1	0	2	6	10	-4	3
4 Gateshead	3	0	0	3	3	9	-6	0

NORTHERN GROUP C	P	W	D	L	F	A	GD	Pts
1 Stoke C	3	2	1	0	11	3	8	7
2 Port Vale	3	2	1	0	9	4	5	7
3 Wigan Ath	3	1	0	2	9	14	-5	3
4 Wrexham	3	0	0	3	3	11	-8	0

NORTHERN GROUP D	P	W	D	L	F	A	GD	Pts
1 Notts Co	3	3	0	0	12	4	8	9
2 Chesterfield	3	2	0	1	10	7	3	6
3 Scunthorpe U	3	1	0	2	4	8	-4	3
4 Rotherham U	3	0	0	3	1	8	-7	0

NORTHERN SEMI-FINAL
Middlesbrough v Burnley	0-2
Stoke C v Notts Co	2-1

NORTHERN FINAL
Burnley v Stoke C	still to play

SOUTHERN GROUP A	P	W	D	L	F	A	GD	Pts
1 Southend U	3	2	0	1	7	4	3	6
2 Luton T	3	2	0	1	6	3	3	6
3 Milton Keynes D	3	1	1	1	4	5	-1	4
4 AFC Wimbledon	3	0	1	2	4	9	-5	1

SOUTHERN GROUP B	P	W	D	L	F	A	GD	Pts
1 Swindon T	3	2	0	1	5	3	2	6
2 Newport Co	3	2	0	1	6	6	0	6
3 Bristol R	3	1	1	1	4	2	2	4
4 Plymouth Arg	3	0	1	2	5	9	-4	1

SOUTHERN FINAL
Swindon T v Southend U	1-2

FOOTBALL LEAGUE YOUTH ALLIANCE 2015–16

NORTH WEST	P	W	D	L	F	A	GD	Pts
1 Wigan Ath	28	20	3	5	59	19	40	63
2 Bury	28	18	7	3	66	28	38	61
3 Walsall	28	15	5	8	54	31	23	50
4 Tranmere R	28	15	4	9	49	34	15	49
5 Blackpool	28	12	8	8	51	36	15	44
6 Shrewsbury T	28	13	5	10	41	32	9	44
7 Preston NE	28	13	3	12	42	42	0	42
8 Port Vale	28	10	7	11	33	33	0	37
9 Rochdale	28	10	6	12	40	44	-4	36
10 Accrington S	28	10	6	12	36	48	-12	36
11 Fleetwood T	28	10	6	12	33	51	-18	36
12 Wrexham	28	9	6	13	44	55	-11	33
13 Carlisle U	28	8	4	16	39	50	-11	28
14 Burnley	28	6	2	20	33	68	-35	20
15 Morecambe	28	4	2	22	29	78	-49	14

NORTH EAST	P	W	D	L	F	A	GD	Pts
1 Mansfield T	24	14	4	6	36	26	10	46
2 Scunthorpe U	24	12	6	6	39	31	8	42
3 Hartlepool U	24	12	4	8	46	39	7	40
4 Doncaster R	24	11	7	6	33	27	6	40
5 Chesterfield	24	11	5	8	67	51	16	38
6 Notts Co	24	12	2	10	44	37	7	38
7 Rotherham U	24	10	6	8	43	37	6	36
8 Burton Alb	24	10	5	9	39	37	2	35
9 Lincoln C	24	10	4	10	32	38	-6	34
10 Oldham Ath	24	10	2	12	51	39	12	32
11 Bradford C	24	9	3	12	36	49	-13	30
12 Grimsby T	24	5	3	16	28	58	-30	18
13 York C	24	2	5	17	30	55	-25	11

SOUTH WEST	P	W	D	L	F	A	GD	Pts
1 Plymouth Arg	18	12	3	3	39	24	15	39
2 Cheltenham T	18	10	2	6	42	28	14	32
3 Bournemouth	18	9	4	5	30	22	8	31
4 Exeter C	18	8	3	7	31	33	-2	27
5 Portsmouth	18	8	2	8	39	31	8	26
6 Oxford U	18	8	1	9	35	36	-1	25
7 Swindon T	18	7	3	8	34	36	-2	24
8 Bristol R	18	5	6	7	23	30	-7	21
9 Newport Co	18	5	3	10	27	44	-17	18
10 Yeovil T	18	4	1	13	21	37	-16	13

SOUTH EAST	P	W	D	L	F	A	GD	Pts
1 Luton T	22	17	2	3	57	15	42	53
2 Southend U	22	14	0	8	47	37	10	42
3 Leyton Orient	22	12	5	5	49	21	28	41
4 Barnet	22	12	2	8	55	39	16	38
5 AFC Wimbledon	22	12	2	8	42	37	5	38
6 Gillingham	22	11	4	7	49	43	6	37
7 Stevenage	22	8	3	11	35	52	-17	27
8 Northampton T	22	8	2	12	39	43	-4	26
9 Milton Keynes D	22	8	1	13	44	63	-19	25
10 Dagenham & R	22	7	0	15	36	54	-18	21
11 Peterborough U	22	6	2	14	37	63	-26	20
12 Cambridge U	22	3	6	13	34	57	-23	15

The top six teams from South West and South East form Merit League 1. The remaining clubs form Merit League 2.

MERIT LEAGUE 1	P	W	D	L	F	A	GD	Pts
1 Leyton Orient	10	9	1	0	23	3	20	28
2 Portsmouth	10	5	3	2	24	18	6	18
3 AFC Wimbledon	10	5	3	2	22	16	6	18
4 Bournemouth	10	5	2	3	20	13	7	17
5 Luton T	10	4	2	4	12	11	1	14
6 Exeter C	10	4	2	4	17	19	-2	14
7 Cheltenham T	10	4	1	5	21	26	-5	13
8 Gillingham	10	3	1	6	9	17	-8	10
9 Southend U	10	2	3	5	14	19	-5	9
10 Plymouth Arg	10	2	1	7	16	24	-8	7
11 Barnet	10	2	1	7	13	25	-12	7

MERIT LEAGUE 2	P	W	D	L	F	A	GD	Pts
1 Oxford U	10	9	0	1	32	9	23	27
2 Cambridge U	10	6	1	3	22	14	8	19
3 Milton Keynes D	10	6	1	3	29	23	6	19
4 Newport Co	10	5	1	4	20	23	-3	16
5 Stevenage	10	4	2	4	16	16	0	14
6 Yeovil T	10	4	2	4	16	20	-4	14
7 Swindon T	10	4	1	5	25	20	5	13
8 Dagenham & R	10	4	1	5	26	28	-2	13
9 Northampton T	10	3	3	4	21	15	6	12
10 Peterborough U	10	3	1	6	15	26	-11	10
11 Bristol R	10	1	0	9	7	35	-28	3

IMPORTANT ADDRESSES

The Football Association: Wembley Stadium, P.O. Box 1966, London SW1P 9EQ. *0800 169 1863*

Scotland: Hampden Park, Glasgow G42 9AY. *0141 616 6000*
Northern Ireland (Irish FA): Chief Executive, 20 Windsor Avenue, Belfast BT9 6EG. *028 9066 9458*
Wales: 11/12 Neptune Court, Vanguard Way, Cardiff CF24 5PJ. *029 2043 5830*
Republic of Ireland: National Sports Campus, Abbotstown, Dublin 15. *00 353 1 8999 500*

International Federation (FIFA): Strasse 20, P.O. Box 8044, Zurich, Switzerland. *00 41 43 222 7777. Fax: 00 41 222 777*
Union of European Football Associations: Secretary, Route de Geneve 46, P.O. Box 1260, Nyon 2, Switzerland. *Fax: 00 41 848 00 2727*

THE LEAGUES

The Premier League: M. Foster, 30 Gloucester Place, London W1U 8PL. *0207 864 9000*
The Football League: Shaun Harvey, Unit 5, Edward VII Quay, Navigation Way, Preston, Lancashire PR2 2YF. *01772 325 800. Fax 01772 325 801*
The National League: D. Strudwick, 4th Floor, Wellington House, 20 Waterloo Street, Birmingham B2 5TB. *0121 214 1950*
Scottish Premier League: Letherby Drive, Glasgow G42 9DE. *0141 620 4140*
The Scottish League: Hampden Park, Glasgow G42 9EB. *0141 620 4160*
Football League of Ireland: D. Crowther, National Sports Campus, Abbotstown, Dublin 15. *00 353 1 8999 500*
Southern League: J. Mills, Suite 3B, Eastgate House, 121–131 Eastgate Street, Gloucester GL1 1PX. *07768 750 590*
Northern Premier League: Ms A. Firth, 23 High Lane, Norton Tower, Halifax, W. Yorkshire HX2 0NW. *01422 410 691*
Isthmian League: Ms K. Discipline, The Base, Dartford Business Park, Victoria Park, Dartford, Kent DA1 5FS. *01322 314 999*
Eastern Counties League: N. Spurling, 16 Thanet Road, Ipswich, Suffolk IP4 5LB. *07855 279 062*
Essex Senior League: Secretary: K. Wilmot, 35 Cecil Road, Walthamstow, London E17 5DH. *07540 441 829*
Hellenic League: B. King, 7 Stoneleigh Drive, Carterton, Oxon OX18 1EE. *0845 260 6644*
Kent Invicta League: John Moules, 25 Brantwood Avenue, Erith, Kent DA8 1EH. *01322 408 557*

Midland League: N. Wood, 30 Glaisdale Road, Hall Green, Birmingham B28 8PX. *07967 440 007*
North West Counties League: J. Deal, 24 The Pastures, Crossens, Southport PR9 8RH. *07713 622 210*
Northern Counties East: B. Gould, 42 Thirlmere Drive, Dronfield, Derbyshire S18 2HW. *07773 653 238*
Northern League: K. Hewitt, 21 Cherrytree Drive, Langley Park, Durham DH7 9FX. *0191 373 3878*
Spartan South Midlands League: M. Mitchell, 26 Leighton Court, Dunstable, Beds LU6 1EW. *07710 455 409*
Southern Combination League: Ms K. Scott, Llandilo, Old Lane, Crowborough TN6 2AF. *07788 737 061*
United Counties League: Ms W. Newey, 4 Wulfric Square, Bretton, Peterborough PE3 8RF. *01733 330 056*
Wessex League: J. Gorman, 6 Overton House, London Road, Overton, Hants RG25 3TP. *01256 770 059*
Western League: M. Edmonds, Cemetery Lodge, Pennings Road, Tidworth, Wiltshire SP9 7JR. *01980 842 153*
Combined Counties League: A. Constable, 3 Craigwell Close, Staines, Middlesex TW18 3NP. *01784 440 613*
West Midlands League: N.R. Juggins, 14 Badger Way, Blackwell, Bromsgrove, Worcs B60 1EX. *07977 422 362.*
South West Peninsula League: P. Hiscox, 45a Serge Court, The Quay, Exeter, Devon EX2 4EB. *07788 897 706*
Southern Counties East League: T. Day, 87 Blackburn Road, Herne Bay, Kent CT6 7UT. *07789 655 768*
East Midlands Counties League: R. Holmes, 9 Copse Close, Hugglescote, Coalville LE67 2GL. *07826 452 389*

OTHER USEFUL ADDRESSES

Amateur Football Alliance: M. Brown, Unit 3, 7 Wenlock Road, London N1 7SL. *0208 733 2613*
Association of Football Badge Collectors: K. Wilkinson, 18 Hinton St, Fairfield, Liverpool L6 3AR. *0151 260 0554*
Backpass Retro Football Magazine: PO Box 6377 Stratford upon Avon CV37 1PX. *0330 606 1417*
British Blind Sport (including football): Plato Close, Tachbrook Park, Leamington Spa, Warwickshire CV34 6WE. *01926 424 247*
British Universities and Colleges Sports Association: Karen Rothery, Chief Executive: BUCSA, 20–24 King's Bench Street, London SE1 0QX. *0207 633 5080*
English Schools FA: 4 Parker Court, Staffordshire Technology Park, Stafford ST18 0WP. *01785 785 970*
FA Women's Super League: Wembley Stadium, PO Box 1966, London SW1P 9EQ. *+44 844 980 8200*
Fields In Trust: 2nd Floor, 15 Crinian Street, London N1 9SQ. *0207 427 2110*
Football Foundation: Whittinghton House, 19–30 Alfred Place, London WC1E 7EA. *0845 345 4555*
Football Postcard Collectors Club: PRO: Bryan Horsnell, 275 Overdown Road, Tilehurst, Reading RG31 6NX. *0118 942 4448 (and fax)*
Football Safety Officers Association: John Newsham, FSOA Ltd, Suite 17, Blackburn Rovers Enterprise Centre, Ewood Park, Blackburn BB2 4JF. *01254 841 771.*
Institute of Football Management and Administration: St George's Park, Newborough, Needwood, Burton on Trent DE13 9PD. *0128 357 6350*
Institute of Groundsmanship: 28 Stratford Office Village, Walker Avenue, Wolverton, Milton Keynes MK12 5TW. *01908 312 511*

League Managers Association: St George's Park, Newborough Road, Needwood, Burton on Trent DE13 9PD. *0128 357 6350*
Professional Footballers' Association: G. Taylor, 20 Oxford Court, Bishopsgate, Off Lower Moseley Street, Manchester M2 3WQ. *0161 236 0575*
Programme Monthly & Football Collectable Magazine: 11 Tannington Terrace, London N5 1LE. *020 7359 8687*
Programme Promotions: 21 Roughwood Close, Watford WD17 3HN. *01923 861 468*
Web: www.footballprogrammes.com
Referees' Association: A.W.S. Smith, Unit 12, Ensign Business Centre, Westwood Way, Westwood Heath, Coventry CV4 8JA. *024 7642 0360*
Scottish Football Historians Association: John Lister, 46 Milton Road, Kirkcaldy, Fife KY1 1TL. *01592 268 718*
Sir Norman Chester Centre for Football Research: Department of Sociology, University of Leicester, University Road LE1 7RH. *0116 252 2741/5.*
Soccer Nostalgia: G. Wallis, Albion Chambers, 1 Albion Road, Birchington, Kent CT7 9DN. *01303 275 432.*
Sport England: Sport Park, 3 Oakwood Drive, Loughborough, Leicestershire. *08458 508 508*
Sports Grounds Safety Authority: East Wing, 3rd Floor, Fleetbank House, 2–6 Salisbury Square, London EC4Y 8JX. *0207 930 6693*
Sports Turf Research Institute: St Ives Estate, Harden, Bingley, West Yorkshire BD16 1AU. *01274 565 131*
The Football Supporters' Federation: 1 Ashmore Terrace, Stockton Road, Sunderland, Tyne and Wear SR2 7DE. *0330 440 0044*
The Ninety-Two Club: Mr M. Kimberley, The Ninety-Two Club, 153 Hayes Lane, Kenley, Surrey CR8 5HP.
UK Programme Collectors Club: PM Publications, 38 Lowther Road, Norwich NR4 6QW. *01603 449 237*

FOOTBALL CLUB CHAPLAINCY

Charlie was City's goalkeeper; a fine custodian, perfectly at home in the top division and on the verge of a string of full international honours. He and his wife had one child, a beautiful little girl aged nearly two years, to whom both parents were utterly devoted.

But disaster struck soon after little Vicki's birthday, when it became necessary for her to be taken into the city hospital where she received expert treatment in the children's ward. Charlie and the chaplain met up unexpectedly in the hospital car park when Charlie was going to visit his little girl and check upon her progress.

Unbeknown to Charlie, the hospital chaplain was also the chaplain at City's neighbours and fierce rivals, but it meant that the pair had plenty to chat about!

When Vicki was deemed well enough to return home, Charlie invited his new friend to call one afternoon and everyone enjoyed the couple of hours they spent together – so much so in fact that Charlie determined to speak to his manager about the possibility of appointing a chaplain at City.

It took some while for the issue to be settled, via the club's higher echelons, but after a mutually acceptable provisional period, a clergyman who had moved south from a northern town where he had been involved with his local football club, is now comfortably settled into his new parish as well as with City's fans, playing and administrative staff and, not least, with their famous international star goalkeeper.

THE REV

OFFICIAL CHAPLAINS TO FA PREMIERSHIP AND FOOTBALL LEAGUE CLUBS

Aston Villa – Rev Ken Baker
Barnsley – Rev Peter Amos
Birmingham C – Rev Kirk McAtear
Blackburn R – Rev Ken Howles
Blackpool – Rev Michael Ward
Bolton W – Mr Phil Mason
Bournemouth – Rev Andy Rimmer
Bradford C – Rev Andy Grieff
Bristol C – Rev Derek Cleave
Bristol R – Rev Dave Jeal
Burnley – Rev Barry Hunter
Burton Alb – Rev Phil Pusey
Bury – Rev David Ottley
Cambridge U – Rev Stuart Wood
Cardiff C Academy – Rev Keiron Webster
Carlisle U – Rev Alun Jones
Charlton Ath – Rev Matt Baker
Chesterfield – Rev Danny Woolf
Crawley T – Rev Gary Simmons
Crewe Alex – Rev Phil Howell
Crystal Palace – Rev Chris Roe
Dagenham & R – Rev Keiran Bush
Derby Co – Rev Tony Luke
Doncaster R – Rev Barry Miller
Everton – Co-Chaplains Rev Henry Corbett and
    Rev Harry Ross
Fleetwood T – Rev George Ayoma
Fulham – Rev Gary Piper
Gillingham – Rev Chris Gill
Hull C – Rev Martin Batstone
Ipswich T – Rev Kevan McCormack
Leeds U – Rev Dave Niblock
Leicester C – Rev Andrew Hulley
Leyton Orient – Rev Neil Kinghorn
Liverpool – Rev Bill Bygroves
Luton T – Rev Alan West
Manchester C – Rev Peter Horlock
Manchester U – Rev John Boyers
Mansfield T – Rev Ray Shaw

Millwall – Rev Canon Owen Beament
Newcastle U Academy – Rev Glyn Evans
Newport Co – Rev Keith Beardmore
Northampton T – Rev Ken Baker
Norwich C – Co-Chaplains Rev Jon Norman and
    Rev Albert Cadmore
Nottingham F – Rev John Parfitt
Notts Co – Rev Liam O'Boyle
Oldham Ath – Rev John Simmons
Peterborough U – Rev Richard Longfoot
Plymouth Arg – Rev Arthur Goode
Port Vale – Rev John Hibberts
Portsmouth – Co-Chaplains Mr Mick Mellows and
    Rev Jonathan Jeffrey
Preston NE – Rev Chris Nelson
QPR – Co-Chaplains Rev Cameron Collington and
    Rev Bob Mayo
Reading – Rev Steven Prince
Scunthorpe U – Rev Alan Wright
Sheffield U – Rev Alistair Beattie
Sheffield W – Rev Baz Gascoyne
Sheffield W Academy – Rev Malcolm Drew
Shrewsbury T – Rev Phil Cansdale
Southampton – Rev Andy Bowerman
Southend U – Co-Chaplains Rev Stu Alleway and
    Rev Mike Lodge
Sunderland – Father Marc Lyden-Smith
Swansea C – Rev Kevin Johns
Swansea C Academy – Rev Eirian Wyn
Swindon T – Rev Simon Stevenette
Walsall – Rev Peter Hart
Watford – Rev Clive Ross
West Ham U – Rev Alan Bolding
Wolverhampton W – Co-Chaplains Rev David
    Wright and Mr Steve Davies
Wycombe W – Rev Musola Benedict
Yeovil T – Rev Jim Pearce
York C – Rev Paul Deo

WOMEN'S FOOTBALL CLUB CHAPLAINS

Bournemouth – Hannah Rogers
Bristol C – Esther Legg-Bagg
Charlton Ath – Kathryn Sales

Notts Co – Wendy Murphy
Reading – Angy Kinghorn

The chaplains hope that those who read this page will see the value and benefit of chaplaincy work in football and will take appropriate steps to spread the word where this is possible. They would also like to thank the editors of the Football Yearbook for their continued support for this specialist and growing area of work.

For further information, please contact: Sports Chaplaincy UK, The Avenue Methodist Church, Wincham Road, Sale, Cheshire M33 4PL. Telephone: 0800 181 4051 or email: admin@sportschaplaincy.org.uk. Website: www.sportschaplaincy.org.uk

OBITUARIES

Dougie Anderson (Born Hong Kong, 29 August 1963. Died Plymouth, 15 June 2015.) Dougie Anderson was a winger who signed for Oldham as a youngster. He gained experience of first-team football with the Latics, but is best known for his three-year spell with Tranmere Rovers, for whom he made over 100 appearances. He later spent time at Plymouth Argyle before playing in Hong Kong for the Double Flower club.

Kane Ashcroft (Born Leeds, 19 March 1986. Died 8 October 2015.) Kane Ashcroft was a strong-tackling midfield player who spent two years as a trainee with York City, playing a part in the club's final two games of the 2003–04 season when they were relegated to the Conference. He made a couple of further appearances the following season before being released. His early death was reported to be from cancer.

Ossie Bailie (Born Ballymena, 20 April 1923. Died Antrim, 5 December 2015.) Ossie Bailie was a goalkeeper who played in the Irish League for Ards, Belfast Celtic, Cliftonville, Ballymena United and Distillery. He was capped for Northern Ireland Amateurs against England in September 1955.

Peter Baker (Born Hampstead, London, 10 December 1931. Died 27 January 2016.) Peter Baker was a pacy full-back who signed for Tottenham Hotspur as an amateur in the summer of 1949, turning professional three years later. He succeeded Alf Ramsey in the right-back slot and went on to become a member of the famous double-winning side of 1960–61, also gaining winners' medals for the FA Cup in 1962 and the European Cup Winners' Cup in 1963. After leaving White Hart Lane he played in South Africa with Durban United, Adlington and Durban Spurs.

Paul Bannon (Born Dublin, 15 November 1956. Died Cork, 15 February 2016.) Paul Bannon made his name as a striker with Carlisle United, for whom he made 139 League appearances between 1979 and 1983, scoring 45 times. After spells with Bristol Rovers and in the Netherlands (NAC Breda) and Greece, he returned to Ireland signing for Cork Celtic, where he experienced European football and scored the goal that clinched the 1992–93 League of Ireland title. Latterly he worked for many years as a coach for the FAI.

Ken Barrett (Born Bromsgrove, 5 May 1938. Died Droitwich, Worcestershire, 7 June 2015.) Forward Ken Barrett scored twice for Aston Villa on his debut against Newcastle United in October 1958 but after a brief run in the line-up he lost his place and in the summer of 1959 he signed for Lincoln City. National Service restricted his availability early on but he never really established himself for the Imps and in the summer of 1963 he returned to the West Midlands, signing for Stourbridge.

Tommy Bickerstaff (Born Glasgow, 23 February 1933. Died Stevenage, 5 January 2016.) Tommy Bickerstaff was a goalkeeper who made 18 appearances for Third Lanark during the 1954–55 season. He later spent a decade playing in the Southern League with Tonbridge, Tunbridge Wells and Ramsgate. After his career was ended by injury he became general manager of Ramsgate and went on to manage both Stevenage and Cambridge City.

Tommy Bing (Born Broadstairs, Kent 24 November 1931. Died 18 May 2015.) Tommy Bing joined Tottenham Hotspur from Margate in September 1954 but although he went on a tour of North America with the club in the summer of 1957, he managed just a single first-team appearance, at Bolton in October 1957. He later returned to play for Margate.

Ronnie Blackman (Born Cosham, Portsmouth, 2 April 1925. Died 16 February 2016.) Centre-forward Ronnie Blackman joined Reading from Gosport Borough Athletic in March 1947. Once settled in he became a prolific scorer, heading the club's charts for five consecutive seasons, including an all-time record of 39 League goals in 1951–52. His final career tally of 158 goals from 218 games remains a record for the club. Ronnie later played for Nottingham Forest and Ipswich Town before switching to the Southern League with Tonbridge.

Eddie Blyth (Born Glasgow, 4 May 1924. Died 4 March 2016.) Inside-forward Eddie Blyth made a single wartime appearance for Queen's Park in the Southern League Cup tie at Celtic in March 1942, later making a handful of peacetime appearances to add to this. Capped twice by Scotland Amateurs, he hit a hat-trick against England in 1949 then promptly signed professional terms for St Mirren. He spent six years with the Paisley club, making over 100 competitive appearances.

Mike Bowering (Born Hull, 15 November 1936. Died Cottingham, East Yorkshire, 4 June 2015.) Mike Bowering joined Hull City as an amateur in December 1957, turning professional in September 1958, and was a regular member of the team that won promotion from the old Third Division in 1958–59. He moved on to Chesterfield in June 1960, spending a season at Saltergate before switching to non-league football with Gainsborough Trinity.

Jack Boxley (Born Birmingham, 31 May 1931. Died March 2016.) Outside-left Jack Boxley joined Bristol City from Birmingham League club Stourbridge as a teenager and went on to make over 200 first-team appearances in two spells at Ashton Gate. A highlight came in 1954–55 when he contributed to the club's success in winning the Division Three South title. In between his spells with the Robins he spent three-and-a-half seasons with Coventry City, playing just short of 100 games.

Ronnie Boyd (Born Kilmarnock, 1929. Died Ayr, August 2015.) Ronnie Boyd was a defender who made over 50 senior appearances with Kilmarnock, Stranraer and Hamilton Academical. In 1956 he moved south to join the Grimsby Borough Police. He continued his football career with the force's Lincolnshire League team and went on to captain the Great Britain Police team.

Wally Bragg (Born Twickenham, Middlesex, 8 July 1929. Died 6 March 2016.) Wally Bragg was the last surviving member of the Brentford team from 1946–47, the last time the club appeared in the top flight of English football. A centre-half, he was absent for some time due to National Service, but eventually returned to make over 150 first-team appearances for the Bees.

Bobby Braithwaite (Born Belfast, 24 February 1937. Died East London, South Africa, 14 October 2015.) Bobby Braithwaite was a winger who made over 250 appearances for Linfield, for whom he was a member of the legendary team that won seven trophies in the 1961–62 season. In the summer of 1963 he was sold to Middlesbrough where he made over 50 first-team appearances. Bobby emigrated to South Africa in December 1967 and signed for Durban City. He won 10 full caps for Northern Ireland.

Steve Brennan (Born Mile End, London, 3 September 1958. Died 13 August 2015.) Steve Brennan was a midfield player who was a member of the Crystal Palace team that won the FA Youth Cup in 1977 and 1978 and also gained representative honours for the Republic of Ireland youth team. He made a couple of first-team appearances at Selhurst Park then had a season at Plymouth Argyle before joining non-league Leatherhead.

Ian Britton (Born Dundee, 19 May 1954. Died 31 March 2016.) Midfielder Ian Britton joined Chelsea as an apprentice, progressing to the senior ranks and making close on 300 appearances during his time at Stamford Bridge. In 1976–77 he helped the club gain promotion from the old Division Two. In the summer of 1982 he returned to Scotland, where he had brief spells with Dundee United and Arbroath, prior to signing for Blackpool. An ever-present in the Seasiders' team that finished runners-up in Division Four in 1984–85, he concluded his career at Burnley, where he took his career total of competitive appearances beyond the 500-mark.

Mick Browning (Born Horsham, Sussex, 17 June 1940. Died 23 November 2015.) Centre-forward Mick Browning was a prolific scorer in Sussex non-league football, and spent two seasons with Isthmian League club Tooting & Mitcham, leading the club's scoring charts on both occasions. He won two England Amateur caps in 1964, scoring on both occasions. At the time of his death he was chairman of Horsham YMCA FC.

Walter Bruce (Born Belfast, 12 February 1938. Died 28 November 2015.) Walter Bruce spent 17 years as a player with Glentoran after signing in 1954, making over 500 appearances and winning four Irish League championships as well as an Irish Cup winners' medal in 1966. He gained two caps for Northern Ireland, separated by a seven-year gap, and was chosen as Ulster Footballer of the Year in 1967.

Tommy Bryceland (Born Greenock, 1 March 1939. Died Ayr, 22 January 2016.) Inside-forward Tommy Bryceland was capped for Scotland Schoolboys before joining St Mirren where he went on to gain a Scottish Cup winners' medal in 1959. He enjoyed a successful eight-year spell at Norwich, making over 250 appearances, then helped Oldham win promotion from the old Fourth Division in 1970–71. He wound up his career with a spell as player-manager back at St Mirren.

Ian Burns (Born Aberdeen, 1939. Died Larbert, Stirlingshire, 6 December 2015.) Ian Burns was a right-half who made over 200 senior appearances for Aberdeen in a nine-year period from June 1957. After a brief spell at Montrose in the summer of 1966 he concluded his career with Brechin City.

Gerry Byrne (Born Liverpool, 29 August 1938. Died Wrexham, 28 November 2015.) Gerry Byrne was a solid, efficient right-back in the successful Liverpool team of the 1960s, helping the Reds win the Second Division title in 1961–62, and then the Football League championship in 1963–64 and 1965–66. He also gained an FA Cup winners' medal in 1965 when he played for all but the opening few minutes with a broken collar bone. Gerry won two full caps for England and was a member of the squad that won the 1966 World Cup, although he did not feature in action during the tournament.

Bobby Campbell (Born Liverpool, 23 April 1937. Died 6 November 2015.) Wing-half Bobby Campbell spent seven seasons on the books of Liverpool during the 1950s but managed just 24 first-team appearances. A brief spell at Wigan Athletic was followed by four years with Portsmouth and a single season at Aldershot before injuries ended his time as a player. He subsequently developed a second career in the game as a coach and manager. After coaching spells with Portsmouth, Queens Park Rangers, Arsenal and Fulham he stepped up to become manager of the Cottagers in December 1976. He was later manager of Portsmouth (March 1982 to May 1984), leading the team to the Third Division title in 1982–83, and then Chelsea (March 1988 to May 1991).

Jimmy Campbell (Born Maryhill, Glasgow circa 1935. Died 19 December 2015.) Jimmy Campbell was a winger who signed for Montrose from Royal Albert in November 1958. He went on to make exactly 100 Scottish League appearances for the Gable Endies before moving on at the end of the 1961–62 season.

Larry Carberry (Born Liverpool, 18 January 1936. Died Burscough, Merseyside, 26 June 2015.) Larry Carberry was a full-back who signed for Ipswich Town in the summer of 1956. He established himself in the line-up and was one of a small number of players who remained in the side from their Third Division days through until they became League Champions in 1961–62, making over 250 first-team appearances. After leaving Portman Road he returned to the North West to play for Barrow.

Bobby Carroll (Born Glasgow, 13 May 1938. Died May 2016.) Outside-right Bobby Carroll signed for Celtic in September 1957 after winning the Scottish Junior Cup with Irvine Meadow. He made 78 first-team appearances during his time with the Hoops and had the distinction of scoring the club's first-ever goal in European competitions, netting against Valencia in September 1962. He later played for St Mirren, Dundee United, Coleraine and Queen of the South.

Jocky Christie (Born Aberdeen 11 September 1926. Died Aberdeen 12 May 2015.) Inside-left Jocky Christie was capped for Scotland Juniors against Wales and the Republic of Ireland and then stepped up to the seniors with Hibernian. Although he made no senior appearances at Easter Road he went on to play over 50 League and Cup games for Arbroath and Brechin before moving to Highland League football at the end of 1951–52.

Ian Clark (Born 13 April 1961. Died Melrose, 24 March 2016.) Ian Clark was a well-known player in Borders football during the 1980s. He made a number of appearances for Berwick Rangers in the 1982–83 season before returning to non-league with Coldstream.

Harry Clarke (Born Darlington, 27 March 1921. Died 8 November 2015.) Harry Clarke was a goalscoring centre-forward who played for Gateshead and Darlington during the war. In peacetime football he had three separate spells with Darlington scoring 51 goals from 76 appearances. In between he was less successful, spending time with both Leeds United and Hartlepools without making significant impact. He was also a talented cricketer playing for Durham as an all-rounder between 1943 and 1953.

Brian Close, CBE (Born Rawdon, Yorkshire, 24 January 1931. Died Baildon, Yorkshire, 13 September 2015.) Although best known for his cricket achievements, Brian Close was a talented footballer as a youngster who was capped by England Youths. A centre-forward, he featured in Bradford City in the 1952–53 season, scoring five goals in nine League and Cup appearances. A knee injury effectively ended his soccer career but he went on to become an outstanding cricketer for England, Yorkshire (1949–70) and Somerset (1971–1977).

Willie Coburn (Born Perth, 13 April 1941. Died Edinburgh, 5 December 2015.) Willie Coburn was a defender who joined St Johnstone from Crieff Earngrove Juniors in September 1962 and went on to make over 300 senior appearances during a 10-year stay, being chosen as the club's Player of the Year in 1965–66. After spells with Forfar Athletic and Cowdenbeath he turned to refereeing. In 2013 he was inducted into the St Johnstone hall of fame.

Willie Coleman (Born Dundalk, 2 June 1937. Died 12 May 2015.) Willie Coleman was a pacy winger who won an FAI Cup winners' medal with Drumcondra in 1957 and went on to win a League of Ireland championship medal with the same club in 1957–58. He made three appearances for the League of Ireland representative team while at Drumcondra and added a further appearance after signing for his home town team of Dundalk.

Martin Colfer (Died Blanchardstown, Dublin, 25 September 2015.) Martin Colfer was a goalscoring forward in the League of Ireland with Shelbourne between 1948 and 1956. He appeared on the losing side in the FAI Cup finals of 1949 and 1951 and was a member of the Shels' team that won the League title in 1952–53. He won two full caps for the Republic of Ireland and also appeared for the League of Ireland representative side.

Colin Corbishley (Born Stoke-on-Trent, 13 June 1939. Died 28 May 2015.) Colin Corbishley signed for Port Vale in the summer of 1959, but he was mostly a reserve during his time at the club. After three seasons at Vale Park he moved on to Chester where he became a regular at left-half, making 91 competitive appearances. Later he played for Stafford Rangers and Prescot Town.

Stuart Cowden (Born Alsager, Cheshire, February 1925. Died 19 January 2016.) Stuart Cowden was a centre-half who appeared for Stoke City in wartime football playing 40 games including the first leg of the FA Cup tie with Burnley in

January 1946. Soon afterwards he joined Witton Albion for whom he went on to make over 300 first-team appearances. At the time of his death he was believed to be Stoke City's oldest player.

Sammy Cox (Born Darvel, Ayrshire, 13 April 1924. Died Stratford, Ontario, Canada, 2 August 2015.) Sammy Cox played as an amateur for Queen's Park, Third Lanark and Dundee before joining Rangers for the 1946–47 season. He quickly established himself at left-half in the side as a member of the famous 'Iron Curtain' defence. His Ibrox career amounted to more than 300 appearances and he was a member of three title-winning sides (1948–49, 1949–50 and 1952–53). On the first of these occasions he was a member of the first team to achieve a domestic treble in Scotland and he added additional winners' prizes in the League Cup (1947–48) and Scottish Cup (1950). He later assisted East Fife before emigrating to Canada in 1959. Sammy won his first cap for Scotland against France in May 1948 and went on to appear 25 times for his country.

Johnny Coyle (Born Dundee, 28 September 1932. Died Cambridge, 14 May 2016.) Centre-forward Johnny Coyle signed for Dundee United in September 1950 and became one of the club's greatest goalscorers. He topped the club's scoring charts in 1955–56 with a total of 43 goals, a figure that remains a club record, and in total netted 112 goals from 132 appearances. In December 1957 he joined Clyde, for whom he scored the winning goal in the 1958 Scottish Cup final. Later he switched to English non-league football with Cambridge City and Boston United.

Billy Craig (Born Belfast, 1 November 1943. Died 11 March 2016.) Billy Craig was a versatile attacking player with Linfield and Distillery in the 1960s. He made one appearance for Northern Ireland U23s against Wales in February 1965 and also represented his country at Schoolboy, Youth and Amateur international levels.

Bobby Craig (Born Consett, Co Durham, 16 June 1928. Died 10 February 2016.) Bobby Craig was a defender who appeared regularly for Sunderland's reserves and A team but managed a solitary first-team appearance, turning out at left-back against West Bromwich Albion in September 1949. In the summer of 1951 he signed for Headington United helping them win the Southern League title in 1952–53 and he later had six seasons at Bedford Town, captaining them in their epic 1955–56 FA Cup ties against Arsenal.

Errol Crossan (Born Montreal, Quebec, Canada, 6 October 1930. Died Langley, British Columbia, Canada, 23 April 2016.) Errol Crossan was an outside-right who came from Canada to develop his career, firstly at Manchester City, where he was unable to get in the first team, and later at Gillingham and Southend United. However, he is best known for his time at Norwich City. Joining in September 1957 he went on to make 116 appearances, scoring 32 goals and playing a key role in the team that reached the FA Cup semi-final in 1958–59. After a brief spell with Leyton Orient he returned to Canada to play for Toronto City.

Johan Cruyff (Born Amsterdam, 25 April 1947. Died Barcelona, 24 March 2016.) Johan Cruyff was one of the greatest players in post-war football. He was a key figure in the emergence of Total Football and a player with tremendous technical skill and all-round ability. He was one of the most influential figures in the Ajax team that went on to win three consecutive European Cups, while he also featured in eight Eredivisie title-winning teams with them. In the summer of 1973 he signed for Barcelona, winning La Liga in his first season with the club. Later he went on to play for Los Angeles Aztecs, Washington Diplomats, Levante, Ajax (for a second time) and Feyenoord. He gained 48 caps for the Netherlands and appeared in their 1974 World Cup final defeat by West Germany. On retiring as a player he became a successful coach notably with Ajax (winning the 1987 European Cup Winners' Cup) and Barcelona (with whom he won the Cup Winners' Cup in 1989 and the European Cup in 1992).

Ian Dargie (Born Camberwell, London, 3 October 1931. Died Haverfordwest, 27 November 2015.) Ian Dargie was a centre-half who joined Brentford from Tonbridge in 1952, but it was not until towards the end of the 1956–57 season that he fully established himself for the Bees. An ever-present in the team that finished runners-up to Brighton in Division Three South in 1957–58, he went on to make over 250 appearances during his stay at Griffin Park. He later worked on the backroom staff for both Crystal Palace and Charlton Athletic.

Eddie Davis (Born Londonderry, 22 April 1919. Died Londonderry, 26 August 2015.) Eddie Davis joined Wolverhampton Wanderers on his 15th birthday and spent two seasons at Molineux without breaking into the first team. After a spell back in Ireland he signed for Southend United, scoring six times in seven first-team appearances in the final pre-war season of League football. Later he spent 10 years with Derry City before switching to scouting.

Tom Delaney (Born Dundee, 18 January 1941. Died 28 December 2015.) Tom Delaney was a full-back who spent two seasons with Forfar Athletic in the early 1960s, making 39 senior appearances. He featured fairly regularly during his time at Station Park before returning to the Juniors.

Dennis Devlin (Born Edinburgh, 26 November 1947. Died 8 April 2016.) Goalkeeper Dennis Devlin made his senior debut for Morton in October 1965 but was best known for his time at Falkirk. In a six-year spell at Brockville he made 69 first-team appearances before leaving senior football at the end of the 1972–73 season.

Jim Doherty (Born Douglas, Lanarkshire, 31 January 1954. Died Glasgow, 12 September 2015.) Jim Doherty was a member of the Cumnock Juniors team which won the Scottish Junior Cup in 1979. Soon afterwards he signed professional forms with Notts County but in three seasons with the Magpies he was principally a reserve. Later he spent two seasons with Stranraer making more than 50 competitive appearances.

John Dowie (Born Hamilton, Lanarkshire, 12 December 1955. Died January 2016.) John Dowie was a skilful midfield player who became an apprentice with Fulham. He featured for the Cottagers in their FA Cup semi-final with Birmingham in 1975, but was left out of the squad for the final. He later returned to Scotland, signing for Celtic, with whom he gained a Scottish League Cup runners-up prize in 1977–78. He later had spells with Doncaster and Clyde before moving to play in Australia.

Pat Dunne (Born Dublin, 9 February 1943. Died Dublin, 25 September 2015.) Goalkeeper Pat Dunne helped Shamrock Rovers team gain a league and cup double in 1963–64 following which he was sold to Manchester United. He became first choice at Old Trafford for the 1964–65 season, gaining a Football League champions medal and featuring in semi-finals in the FA Cup and Fairs Cup. He subsequently made over 150 appearances for Plymouth Argyle before returning to Shamrock where he became the first player to receive a red card in a League of Ireland fixture. He won five full caps for the Republic of Ireland.

Fred Else (Born Golborne, Lancashire, 31 March 1933. Died Barrow, 20 July 2015.) Fred Else was a goalkeeper who made over 600 senior appearances in a 17-year career, mostly in the top flight. A regular for Preston North End from the 1956–57 season he moved on to Blackburn when the Deepdale club were relegated, concluding with four seasons at Barrow, where he was a near ever-present in the 1966–67 promotion team. In February 1957 he was capped for England B against Scotland B.

Mark Farren (Born Donegal, 1 May 1982. Died 3 February 2016.) Mark Farren was a striker who established a club record for goals scored in the League of Ireland with Derry City, netting 113 goals from 209 appearances. He also gained two FAI Cup winners' medals. He later had a spell with Glenavon. As a youngster Mark was on the books of both Tranmere Rovers and Huddersfield Town before returning to Ireland.

Gordon Fearnley (Born Bradford, 25 January 1950. Died Florida, United States, 25 June 2015.) Forward Gordon Fearnley signed for Sheffield Wednesday on leaving school. Although he did not make the first team at Hillsborough he went on to make 140 League and Cup appearances for Bristol Rovers in a seven-year spell. In 1977 he emigrated to the United States and spent 12 months with Fort Lauderdale Strikers.

Joachim Fernandez (Born Ziguindor, Senegal, 6 December 1972. Died Paris, 18 January 2016.) Joachim Fernandez was a tall midfield player who spent the first half of the 2000–01 season on the books of Dundee United without ever really establishing himself in the side. A product of French football, he had started his senior career at Bordeaux and Caen. Three seasons of Serie A football with Udinese, Monza and AC Milan preceded his arrival at Tannadice, but he made few first-team appearances during this time. Joachim, who won international honours with Senegal, concluded his career with a spell in Indonesia's Super League with Persma Manado.

Dennis Fidler (Born Stockport, 22 June 1938. Died Italy, 2 June 2015.) Winger Dennis Fidler was a member of the Manchester United team that won the FA Youth Cup in 1954–55 and 1955–56 but left Old Trafford without making a senior appearance. A fringe player with Manchester City he went on to play over 250 senior games, notably at Halifax Town (1963–1966). He went on to sign for Macclesfield where he was a member of the team that won the inaugural FA Trophy in 1970.

Jim Finlayson (Born Dundee, 6 October 1946. Died 14 May 2016.) Jim Finlayson was a striker who joined East Fife from Lochee United. He went on to make a useful contribution for the Methil club in 1970–71 when they were promoted to the top flight after finishing runners-up to Partick Thistle in the Second Division. He later played for Forfar Athletic and Montrose before returning to the Juniors in 1974.

George Fisher (Born Bermondsey, London, 19 June 1925. Died 30 August 2015.) George Fisher was a full-back who joined Millwall during the war. The last surviving member of the Lions' team that played Chelsea in the 1944–45 War Cup (South) final at Wembley he went on to make over 300 peacetime appearances for the club. He then had a brief spell at Fulham before finishing his senior career at Colchester United. His twin brother Jackie Fisher also played for Millwall, although they only appeared in the same line-up on two occasions.

John Fisher (Born circa 1935. Died 25 November 2015.) John Fisher was a versatile half-back who captained the Wales Amateur team for three seasons in the early 1960s, winning 10 caps. He played his club football for Wycombe Wanderers, Hendon, Oxford City and Marlow.

Ambrose Fogarty (Born Dublin, 11 September 1933. Died Limerick, 4 January 2016.) Ambrose Fogarty developed in Irish football, signing for Sunderland in October 1957. A slightly built inside-forward, he became a regular for the Black Cats at the beginning of 1959–60, scoring 10 goals in his first 12 games that season before being switched to play on the wing. After 150 appearances at Roker Park he moved on to a three-year spell with Hartlepools where he was the first player to win a full international cap while on the club's books. He subsequently returned to Ireland where he managed a number of clubs. He won 11 caps for the Republic of Ireland.

Percy Freeman (Born Newark, 4 July 1945. Died 5 January 2016.) Percy Freeman was a big, bustling centre-forward capable of upsetting opposition defences with his robust style of play and with the ability to score spectacular goals. He played a few games for West Bromwich Albion, his first senior club, but is best known for his two spells with Lincoln City, for whom he was a key figure in the team that won the 1975–76 Division Four title with a then-record points total. He also played for Reading and Boston United.

Johnny Fullam (Born Dublin, 22 March 1940. Died Harold's Cross, Dublin, 10 June 2015.) Johnny Fullam joined Preston North End as a teenager and featured regularly at wing-half and inside-forward in the 1960–61 campaign. However, North End were relegated at the end of the season and he returned to Ireland, signing for Shamrock Rovers. He went on to become an important figure in Irish football over the next 20 years or so, winning a record eight FAI Cup winners' medals. He won 11 caps for the Republic of Ireland and also appeared for the League of Ireland representative side.

Marton Fulop (Born Budapest, Hungary, 3 May 1983. Died 12 November 2015.) Marton Fulop was a giant goalkeeper who played almost all his senior football in England having joined Tottenham Hotspur from MTK Hungaria in the summer of 2004. Although he spent three seasons on the books at White Hart Lane his football was played on loan at Chesterfield, Coventry City and Sunderland. Later he had spells with Sunderland, Ipswich Town and West Bromwich Albion before moving on to play in Greece for Asteras Tripoli. He won 24 caps for Hungary.

Phil Gartside (Born Leigh, Lancashire, 27 April 1952. Died Crowley, Cheshire, 10 February 2016.) Businessman Phil Gartside became a director of Bolton Wanderers in 1991 and was chairman from 1999 being in that position when the club won promotion to the Premier League in 2000–01. He held a number of posts in football administration including being on the FA Council (2004–12), the FA Board, and The Premier League Executive, while he also served as a non-executive director of Wembley (February 2005 to July 2015).

Lee-Anne Gemmell (Born Glasgow 1983. Died West Mains, East Kilbride, Lanarkshire, 14 February 2016.) Lee-Ann Gemmell was a defender who played for the East Kilbride Weirs Ladies club and also won two caps for Scotland. She was also a talented netball player and coach.

Alcides Ghiggia (Born Montevideo, Uruguay, 22 December 1926. Died Montevideo, Uruguay, 16 July 2015.) Alcides Ghiggia was a forward who was the last surviving member of the Uruguay team which won the 1950 World Cup. He scored the decisive goal against Brazil at the Maracana Stadium to clinch the trophy. Coincidentally he died on the 65th anniversary of that match. Alcides played his club football with Penarol and then in Italy, notably with Roma.

Ian Gibson (Born Newton Stewart, Dumfriesshire, 30 March 1943. Died 25 May 2016.) Ian Gibson made his Football League debut for Accrington Stanley as a 15-year-old and scored his first Football League goal four days before his 16th birthday. He was sold to Bradford Park Avenue, where he was a near ever-present in the 1960–61 promotion team, before becoming Middlesbrough's then record signing. Further highlights in a career of more than 500 senior appearances included assisting Coventry City to the Second Division title in 1966–67 and playing in the Cardiff team that reached the European Cup Winners' Cup quarter-final of 1970–71.

Bobby Gilbert (Born Dublin, 1 January 1939. Died Dublin, 20 October 2015.) Bobby Gilbert was a centre-forward who played for clubs both sides of the Irish border from the late 1950s. His most successful period came after he signed for Shamrock Rovers in October 1965. He won three FAI Cup winners' medals with the Hoops and was capped by the Republic of Ireland against West Germany in May 1966, as well as making a single appearance for the League of Ireland representative team.

Giles Gillett (Born Edinburgh, 27 March 1928. Died 4 March 2016.) Forward Giles Gillett signed for Middlesbrough as a teenager and featured in the reserve team before joining Leith Athletic in 1950. He subsequently moved on to play for Montrose in 1952–53 where he was an influential figure in the side. After a season with the Gable Endies he returned to Teesside and reverted to amateur status, turning out for the ICI works' team.

Harry Glasgow (Born Edinburgh, 20 June 1939. Died 4 February 2016.) Defender Harry Glasgow began his senior career with Falkirk, but it was during his time with Clyde from 1963 to 1972 that he really made his name, making over

250 first-team appearances and captaining the club to third place in the Scottish League in 1966–67. He went on to become player-coach and then manager of Stenhousemuir (September 1974 to April 1981) and is the longest-serving manager in the club's history.

Steve Gohouri (Born Treichville, Ivory Coast, 8 February 1981. Died Germany, December 2015.) Defender Steve Gohouri began his career in the youth team of Paris St Germain, but subsequently forged a career that took him to many countries including Israel, Switzerland, Italy, Germany, England and Greece. He spent two-and-a-half seasons in the Premier League with Wigan Athletic from January 2010, making 44 competitive appearances. Most recently he signed for Germany's Regionalliga Sudwest club TSV Steinbach in early December 2015 and made a single appearance for them before disappearing following the club's Christmas party. His body was later recovered from the River Rhine at Krefeld.

Freddie Goodwin (Born Heywood, Lancs, 28 June 1933. Died Gig Harbor, Washington, United States, 19 February 2016.) Wing-half Freddie Goodwin started out as a Busby Babe and was one of the youngsters who stepped up to the first team following the Munich Disaster. An FA Cup runner-up in 1958 he moved on to Leeds United in March 1960. He went on to make over 100 appearances at Elland Road before a broken leg effectively ended his career. As a manager he led Scunthorpe United, Brighton and Birmingham City, where he introduced a very young Trevor Francis to League football. He also spent time in the United States, notably with New York Generals, and played 11 First Class cricket matches for Lancashire.

Barry Gould (Born Ammanford, Carmarthernshire, 18 January 1944. Died October 2015.) Barry Gould was a skilful inside-forward who was on the books of Arsenal and Chelsea as a youngster without breaking into the first team. He spent just over a season at Peterborough where he made 22 senior appearances before enjoying a lengthy career in the Southern League with Worcester City (where he was a member of the 1967–68 title-winning side), Dover Athletic, Guildford City and Cheltenham Town.

Stephen Gove (Born Montrose, 6 November 1959. Died New Zealand, 7 June 2015.) Stephen Gove was a striker who had a brief senior career with Brechin City playing a couple of games in the latter part of 1985–86 and the first six games of the following season. He also played Junior football for a number of clubs as well as in the Highland League for Cove Rangers.

Malcolm Graham (Born Crigglestone, near Wakefield, 26 January 1934. Died Barnsley, 12 September 2015.) Malcolm Graham was an inside-forward who graduated to the professional ranks with Barnsley from Wakefield junior football. He went on to make over 200 Football League appearances, his career also including spells with Bristol City, Leyton Orient and Queens Park Rangers. The high point of his career came at Orient when he scored both goals in the 2–0 win over Bury in April 1962 to clinch promotion to the top flight for the O's for the only time in their history.

Denis Gratton (Born Bramley, Yorkshire, 21 April 1934. Died 18 April 2016.) Centre-half Denis Gratton signed for Sheffield United from Worksop Town, but in seven seasons at Bramall Lane he made just half-a-dozen first-team appearances. Moving on to Lincoln City in September 1959 he played over 50 League and Cup games but after relegation from the Second Division at the end of 1960–61 he signed for Boston United.

Alec Gray (Born Arbroath, 7 November 1936. Died Penarth, 8 March 2016.) Alec Gray was a defender who was on Burnley's books as a youngster without making the first team. He returned to Scotland where he spent two seasons with Arbroath, making 63 appearances. Later he played two games at left-back for Cardiff City in the 1958–59 season and after a spell with Worcester City he returned to south Wales where he developed a long-standing association with the Cardiff Draconians club.

Ron Greener (Born Easington, Co Durham, 31 January 1934. Died 19 October 2015.) Ron Greener signed for Newcastle United from Easington Old Scholars in the summer of 1951. He made his debut for the Magpies as a 19-year-old, but it was only when he moved on to Darlington in August 1955 that he played regular first-team football. He went straight into the first team at centre-half and went on to make 132 consecutive appearances. Ron eventually established a new club record of 439 Football League appearances for the Quakers, with a highpoint coming with the 4–1 FA Cup victory over Chelsea in January 1958.

Ron Greensmith (Born Sheffield 22 January 1933. Died 18 December 2015.) Winger Ron Greensmith was a product of local football in Sheffield before stepping up to the senior game with Sheffield Wednesday. He was mainly a reserve during his time at Hillsborough but saw more first-team action after joining York City in January 1958. He later played for Scarborough and Bridlington Town.

Jack Hadlington (Born Brierley Hill, Staffs, 16 August 1933. Died 9 August 2015.) Jack Hadlington joined Walsall from Cradley Heath towards the end of the 1953–54 season, making his only Football League appearance shortly afterwards when he lined up at outside left at Crystal Palace in February 1954. He subsequently played for Halesowen Town.

Brian Hall (Born Glasgow, 22 January 1946. Died Preston, 16 July 2015.) Brian Hall initially joined Liverpool as an amateur while studying at Liverpool University. He turned professional in the summer of 1968 and went on to make over 200 appearances for the club, notably featuring as a substitute in the first leg of the UEFA Cup final against Borussia Moenchengladbach in May 1973 and gaining an FA Cup winners' medal 12 months later. After concluding his career with spells at Plymouth Argyle, Burnley and Northwich Victoria he left the game.

Johnny Hamilton (Born Glasgow, 10 July 1949. Died 17 October 2015.) Johnny Hamilton joined Hibernian as a teenager from Cumbernauld United and made his first-team debut shortly after his 20th birthday. A skilful left-footed midfield player he was a member of the team that defeated Celtic to win the Drybrough Cup in August 1972. In five seasons at Rangers he won Scottish League and Cup winners' medals in 1975–76 and a League Cup winners' prize in 1977–78. After spending just a few months at Millwall he returned to Scotland to see out his senior career with St Johnstone.

John Harrison (Born Leicester, 27 September 1927. Died 11 December 2015.) John Harrison was a right-back who spent two years on the books of Aston Villa without making the first team before switching to Colchester United in the summer of 1950. For the next six years or so he was a regular in the U's first-team line-up, making almost 250 appearances before his career was ended by injury.

Ted Harte (Born Newry, Northern Ireland. Died June 2015.) Ted Harte was a wing-half who developed with Newry Town and then Glenavon before joining Dundalk in the 1959 close season. He went on to make over 150 appearances over the next five seasons and missed just one game in 1962–63 when Dundalk won the League of Ireland title. He subsequently returned to the Irish League, signing for Bangor. He made two appearances for the League of Ireland representative side.

Danny Hegan (Born Coatbridge, Lanarkshire, 14 June 1943. Died Birmingham, 6 August 2015.) Danny Hegan was a midfield player who was playing for Albion Rovers at the age of 17. He was sold to Sunderland but was unable to break into the first team at Roker Park, so it was not until joining Ipswich Town in the summer of 1963 that he featured in Football League action. He helped the Portman Road club win the Second Division title in 1967–68, then after an unproductive season with West Bromwich Albion he linked up with his former manager Bill McGarry at Wolves. His best season at Molineux proved to be in 1971–72 when he scored with a brilliant chip to help knock Juventus out of the UEFA Cup and went on to feature in both legs of the final when Wolves lost out to Spurs.

Jimmy Henderson (Born Bishopbriggs, Glasgow, 8 May 1935. Died 2 September 2015.) Jimmy Henderson joined Partick Thistle as a teenager, but in seven seasons with the Jags he managed just 16 appearances, adding a further six games with Queen of the South in 1958–59. He subsequently moved to Southern League football with Worcester City then Kidderminster Harriers and Stourbridge.

Sid High (Born Waterbeach, Cambridgeshire, 30 September 1922. Died Waterbeach, Cambridgeshire, 27 September 2015.) Winger Sid High spent two seasons on the books of Luton Town without breaking into the first team before joining Watford in August 1948. Although he scored in his first two appearances for the Hornets he never gained a regular place in the side and moved on to King's Lynn 12 months later.

Jimmy Hill, OBE (Born Balham, London 22 July 1928. Died Sussex, 19 December 2015.) Jimmy Hill was one of the most significant figures in post-war English football. As a player with Brentford and Fulham he mostly featured in the old Second Division. He served as chairman of the PFA between 1957 and 1961, leading the players to victory in their opposition to the maximum wage, before embarking on a career in management with Coventry City. The club was transformed with an innovative consumer-focused approach and reached the top flight for the first time in their history. Jimmy promptly resigned to enter a third football-related career, this time in broadcasting. He became head of sport at London Weekend Television and subsequently moved to the BBC where he was presenter of *Match of the Day* for many years. At various times he was chairman of Coventry City, Charlton Athletic and Fulham and at the time of his death was president of Corinthian Casuals.

Alan Hodgkinson, MBE (Born Laughton Common, South Yorkshire, 16 August 1936. Died 8 December 2015.) Alan Hodgkinson was a brave and agile goalkeeper who went on to make over 550 Football League appearances for Sheffield United, the second-highest in the club's history. The Blades signed him up shortly after his 17th birthday and once established he remained first choice for 14 seasons, helping them win promotion back to the top flight in 1960–61. Alan won five full caps for England. After retiring from playing he became a specialist goalkeeping coach working with a number of clubs and also the Scotland national team before retiring in 2012.

Des Horne (Born Durban, South Africa, 12 December 1939. Died South Africa, 20 July 2015.) Des Horne was a winger who arrived in England as a 16-year-old and signed for Wolverhampton Wanderers. A member of the team that won the FA Youth Cup in 1957–58, he went on to feature at outside-left in the side that defeated Blackburn Rovers 3–0 at Wembley in May 1960 to lift the FA Cup. Less than 12 months later he was on his way to Blackpool where he went on to make over 100 appearances in the next five seasons. At the end of 1965–66 he returned to South Africa where he played for the Johannesburg NFL club Southern Suburbs for several seasons.

Ken Horne (Born Stapenhill, Staffs, 25 June 1926. Died 2015.) Full-back Ken Horne was on the books of both Wolverhampton Wanderers and Blackpool without breaking into the first team but then dropped down a division to play for Brentford. He featured for the Bees throughout the 1950s, making over 200 first-team appearances and scoring a solitary goal. He eventually left Griffin Park at the end of the 1960–61 season and finished his career with a spell at Dover.

Barry Horstead (Born Brigg, Lincolnshire, 8 May 1935. Died Brigg, Lincolnshire, 12 February 2016.) Barry Horstead was a centre-half who spent his entire senior career with Scunthorpe United making over 300 appearances for the club in a 12-year spell at The Old Showground. He was an ever-present in the team that won the Division Three North title in 1957–58. He finished his career in the Lincolnshire League with his home town club Brigg Town.

Don Howe (Born Wolverhampton, 12 October 1935. Died 23 December 2015.) Don Howe was a right-back who made over 400 top-flight appearances for his two clubs. A regular for West Bromwich Albion from December 1956, within 12 months he was a full international and he went on to win 23 caps, all coming in consecutive matches. After joining Arsenal in April 1964 he was appointed club captain, but a broken leg suffered against Blackpool in March 1966 effectively ended his career. Don remained at Highbury and worked as a coach, helping the Gunners win the League and Cup double in 1970–71. He was later manager of a number of clubs including West Bromwich Albion, Galatasaray, Arsenal, Queens Park Rangers and Coventry City. He also worked on the England backroom staff during the period when Terry Venables was national team manager.

Gary Hudson (Born Bradford, 25 February 1951. Died Brighton, 30 March 2016.) Gary Hudson was a full-back who made his Football League debut for Bradford Park Avenue while still a groundstaff boy. He made further appearances in Avenue's last two seasons in the League and played in their final Division Four fixture at Aldershot in April 1970. He played a few times for the club in the Northern Premier League and subsequently appeared in local football.

Arthur Hughes (Born Linlithgow, 23 November 1927. Died Gillingham, Kent, 31 October 2015.) Inside-forward Arthur Hughes was on the books of both Nottingham clubs without gaining first-team experience but featured in over half of Grimsby Town's Division Three North fixtures in 1954–55. He spent the following season with Gillingham but managed just a handful of appearances. He subsequently settled in Kent and signed for Dover.

Anatoliy Ilyin (Born Moscow, 27 June 1931. Died Moscow, 10 February 2016.) Anatoliy Ilyin was a winger who gained 31 caps for the USSR between 1952 and 1959. He scored 16 goals for his country including the decisive strike in the 1956 Olympic Games final when USSR defeated Yugoslavia 1–0. He played his club football for Spartak Moscow.

Colin Jackson (Born London, 8 October 1946. Died 6 June 2015.) Colin Jackson was a powerful central defender who spent virtually all his career with Rangers, making over 500 senior appearances. His tally of successes included three Scottish League titles, three Scottish Cups and five League Cup prizes, including a memorable final against Aberdeen in 1978–79 when his last-minute header won the trophy for Rangers. He finished his career with spells at Partick Thistle and Morton. Colin won eight full caps for Scotland and also played for the Scottish League representative side.

Howard Johnson (Born Sheffield, 17 July 1925. Died June 2015.) Howard Johnson was a centre-half who joined Sheffield United from Yorkshire League club Norton Woodseats when in his mid-20s. He made 15 appearances in 1952–53 when United won the Division Two title, and was a regular the following season in the top flight before his place in the side became less secure. He concluded his Football League career with a season at York where he played both at centre-half and left-back.

Bobby Jones (Born Bristol, 28 October 1938. Died Bristol, 22 July 2015.) Forward Bobby Jones scored after just two minutes of his Football League debut for Bristol Rovers against Middlesbrough in November 1957 and added a second later as Bristol Rovers cruised to a 5–0 victory. He went on to make over 450 appearances for the Pirates in two spells separated by brief periods at Northampton and Swindon. After leaving Eastville he played for Minehead and then turned to management, including a six-year spell at Bath City from May 1982.

Garry Jones (Born Wythenshawe, Manchester, 17 December 1950. Died April 2016.) Striker Garry Jones joined Bolton Wanderers on leaving school and was in the first team at the age of 17. He helped Wanderers win the Third Division title in 1972–73 and made 247 first-team appearances in a decade at Burnden Park. Later he had spells with Blackpool and Hereford United and also played in the League of Ireland for Derry City.

Brian Keeble (Born Holbeach, Lincs, 11 July 1938. Died Cleethorpes, 16 December 2015.) Defender Brian Keeble signed professional terms for Grimsby Town after completing his National Service with the Royal Lincolnshire Regiment. An ever-present for the Mariners when they won promotion from the old Third Division in 1961–62, he also helped Darlington to promotion in 1968–69 before switching to non-league football with Boston United.

Howard Kendall (Born Ryton-on-Tyne, Co Durham, 22 May 1946. Died Southport, 17 October 2015.) Midfielder Howard Kendall became the youngest player to feature in a Wembley final when he appeared for Preston North End against West Ham in 1964 aged 17 years and 345 days. He was sold to Everton in the spring of 1967 where he was part of a midfield trio with Alan Ball and Colin Harvey which became known as 'The Holy Trinity', winning the Football League title in 1969–70. Howard eventually moved on to Birmingham City and then Stoke City. He subsequently became a successful manager notably in the first of three spells at Everton, winning the FA Cup in 1983–84, two League championships (1984–85 and 1986–87) and the European Cup Winners' Cup (also in 1984–85). He also had spells with Manchester City, Notts County and Sheffield United as well as spending time in Spain and Greece.

Sandy Kennon (Born Regents Park, Johannesburg, South Africa, 28 November 1933. Died Norwich, 17 August 2015.) Goalkeeper Sandy Kennon joined Huddersfield Town from the Queen's Park club of Bulawayo in the summer of 1956. Having established himself for the Terriers he fell out of favour at the beginning of 1959 and moved on to Norwich City where he went on to make over 250 appearances, playing in the FA Cup semi-final ties against Luton Town in his first season and then gaining a Football League Cup winners' prize as City beat Rochdale over two legs in the 1961–62 final. Sandy finished off with a spell at Colchester United. He was also a competent cricketer and appeared in the Minor Counties competition for Norfolk.

Johnny King (Born Liverpool, 15 April 1938. Died 30 March 2016.) Johnny King was a wing-half who developed with Everton and Bournemouth before joining Tranmere Rovers in February 1961. He spent eight seasons at Prenton Park making over 250 senior appearances and contributing to the team that won promotion from Division Four in 1966–67. He later had a spell with Port Vale (where he won promotion again in 1968–69) and Wigan Athletic before turning to management back at Tranmere in April 1975. In two spells in charge at Prenton Park (1975–80 and 1987–96) he took the club from the Fourth Division to their best-ever position in the Football League. Rovers won the Leyland Daf Cup in 1990, defeating Bristol Rovers in the Wembley final, and on three occasions they reached the Championship play-offs.

Duncan Lambie (Born Whitburn, West Lothian, 20 April 1952. Died 19 November 2015.) Winger Duncan Lambie was a member of the Dundee team that defeated Celtic 1-0 in December 1973 to lift the Scottish League Cup, and also appeared in European action during his time at Dens Park. He featured fairly regularly in two-and-a half seasons with St Johnstone then spent a couple of seasons in the Bundesliga 2 with SpVgg Furth before concluding his senior career at Hibernian.

Gilbert Lawrie (Born Vale of Leven, 4 July 1960. Died Houston, Renfrewshire, 21 January 2016.) Gilbert Lawrie was the chief executive of Dumbarton from 2008 until his sudden death in January 2016 and is credited from saving the club from extinction. Gilbert, who was a chartered surveyor by profession, was a lifelong supporter of the club.

Donal Leahy (Born Cork, 31 August 1938. Died Cork, 31 December 2015.) Centre-forward Donal Leahy was a prolific scorer for Evergreen United in the League of Ireland, topping the league's goalscoring charts on three consecutive occasions. He remained at Turner's Cross until 1969, by which time the club had become Cork Celtic, taking his tally of league goals beyond the 150-mark. He made 15 appearances for the League of Ireland representative side.

Bob Ledger (Born Craghead, Co Durham, 5 October 1937. Died Doncaster, 14 September 2015.) Bob Ledger started out as a winger with Huddersfield Town where he played under legendary manager Bill Shankly. He eventually moved on to Oldham Athletic where he was an ever-present in the team that won promotion from the old Fourth Division in 1962–63. Later he showed his versatility by switching to centre-forward and became the Latics' leading scorer in 1967–68, despite leaving in mid-season. Bob was then a member of the Mansfield Town team that reached the FA Cup quarter finals in 1968–69 and finished his senior career at Barrow.

Graham Leggat (Born Aberdeen, 20 June 1934. Died Scarborough, Ontario, Canada, August 2015.) Graham Leggat was a quick and skilful winger who made his name with Aberdeen. A near ever-present in the side that won the Scottish League title in 1954–55, he won a League Cup winners' prize the following season, scoring the decisive goal against St Mirren at Hampden. His performances for Scotland at the 1958 World Cup finals led to a transfer to Fulham where he netted a hat-trick in three minutes in the 10-1 victory over Ipswich Town on Boxing Day 1963. He later played for Birmingham City and Rotherham United before emigrating to Canada where he became known as the voice of soccer on television and was inducted into the Canada Soccer Hall of Fame in May 2001.

Alan Lewis (Born Oxford, 19 August 1954. Died Reading, 21 May 2016.) Alan Lewis was a busy left-sided player who was an apprentice with Derby County and was a member of the England Youth team which won the UEFA U18 Championships in 1971–72 and 1972–73. His two appearances for the Rams both came in the 1972–73 season and after an unproductive spell with Brighton he joined Reading. He went on to make over 150 appearances for the Royals during a five-year stay and gained a Division Four championship medal in 1978–79.

Billy Lewis (Born 29 March 1931. Died 12 November 2015.) Defender Billy Lewis signed for Morton in the summer of 1953 and made over 100 appearances during his time at Cappielow before moving on to Third Lanark. He enjoyed a degree of success with the Hi Hi, gaining a Scottish League Cup runners-up prize after Thirds were defeated in the 1959–60 final and the following season he helped the club to reach third place in the Scottish League.

Brian Lomax, OBE (Born March 26, 1948. Died November 2, 2015.) Brian Lomax was the founder of the first supporters' trust in January 1992 rescuing Northampton Town from a financial crisis and going on to become the first supporter-elected director of a Football League club. Brian became a key figure in assisting the development of similar trusts at other clubs and in 2000 he was involved in the establishment of Supporters Direct, becoming the organisation's first managing director and later being elected chair of the organisation. He was awarded the OBE in 2009 for services to football.

Tommy Lowry (Born Liverpool, 26 August 1945. Died 22 August 2015.) Tommy Lowry began his career as an apprentice at Liverpool where he graduated to the senior ranks making a solitary first-team appearance in the final League game of the 1964–65 season. He moved on to Crewe Alexandra where he established himself at right-back and went on to create a new club record for appearances that remains unbroken. He missed just one game in the 1967–68 promotion season.

Fred Lucas (Born Slade Green, Kent, 29 September 1933. Died Woolwich, London, 11 September 2015.) Fred Lucas was an inside-forward or wing-half who spent almost a decade on the books of Charlton Athletic making close on 200 first-team appearances. He was also a capable cricketer, making two County Championship appearances for Kent in 1954.

John Lumsden (Born Edinburgh, 15 December 1960. Died 22 April 2016.) Midfield player John Lumsden impressed sufficiently with East Fife in the 1979–80 season to earn a transfer to Stoke City in February 1980. However he struggled to make an impact during three seasons in the Potteries and managed just six first-team appearances before leaving senior football.

Terry McCavana (Born Belfast, 24 January 1921. Died Auckland, New Zealand, 16 September 2015.) Terry McCavana was a centre-half who made three appearances in the 1948–49 season while posted to serve at nearby RAF Newton. He later returned to Northern Ireland to play for Coleraine and went on to make over 250 appearances for the club. A regular for Northern Ireland Amateurs and the Irish League, he also won three full caps.

Jim McFadzean (Born Kilmarnock, 20 August 1938. Died Kilmarnock, 24 February 2016.) Jim McFadzean was an inside-forward who began his senior career at Heart of Midlothian with whom he won a Scottish League championship medal in 1959–60. He later had spells with St Mirren and Raith Rovers before joining Kilmarnock where he added a second Scottish League title in 1964–65. He finished his career at Ayr United and was later on the coaching staff at Motherwell.

Jackie McGugan (Born Airdrie, 12 June 1939. Died 15 November 2015.) Jackie McGugan was a member of the St Mirren team that defeated Aberdeen to win the Scottish Cup final in 1959. He moved south to Leeds United 12 months later but his career never really took off. He managed just a single appearance during his time at Elland Road and although he enjoyed a couple of seasons of first-team action with Tranmere Rovers and Ayr United his senior career was effectively over at the age of 25.

Bobby McIlvenny (Born Belfast, 7 July 1926. Died May 2016.) Bobby McIlvenny was an inside-forward who signed for Oldham Athletic in March 1950, later helping them win the Division Three North title in 1952–53. He went on to play for Bury, Southport and Barrow, taking his tally of Football League appearances beyond the 250-mark and earning a reputation as one of the most skilful players of his era playing in the lower divisions.

Ian McKechnie (Born Bellshill, Lanarkshire, 4 October 1941. Died Brantingham, East Yorkshire, 9 June 2015.) Ian McKechnie joined Arsenal as a groundstaff boy in October 1958. Initially an outside-left he quickly switched to goalkeeper although he was mostly a reserve at Highbury. After two seasons without breaking into the first team he moved on to Hull City in August 1966 and over the next eight seasons he made over 250 appearances for the Tigers. In August 1970 he became the first goalkeeper to save a spot kick in a penalty shoot out, keeping out Denis Law's strike in the Watney Cup semi-final tie with Manchester United.

Mick McLaughlin (Born Newport, Gwent, 5 January 1943. Died Newport, Gwent, 6 December 2015.) Mick McLaughlin was a solid and uncompromising defender who spent two seasons with Newport County at the end of the 1960s rarely missing a game, before joining then Southern League club Hereford United. A member of the Bulls' team that defeated Newcastle United in the FA Cup in 1972, he captained the side when they entered the Football League. By the 1977–78 season he was playing rugby union for Newport Saracens when he was brought back by Newport County for the final weeks of the season.

Jack Mansell (Born Salford, 22 August 1927. Died 19 March 2016.) Jack Mansell was a left-back who was on Manchester United's books as an amateur before breaking into the first team. After signing for Brighton & Hove Albion in March 1949 he made over 100 Football League appearances for the Seagulls before moving first to Cardiff City and then to Portsmouth. He appeared for the Welsh League representative team while at Cardiff and earned further honours at Portsmouth, playing twice for England B and making a couple of appearances for the Football League. He was also selected for two FA tours of South Africa. He later managed Reading and Rotherham United and carried out coaching work all over the world including spells in charge of the Israel and Bahrain national teams.

Jack Marriott (Born Scunthorpe, 1 April 1928. Died Scunthorpe, 9 February 2016.) Jack Marriott was a winger who joined Sheffield Wednesday as an 18-year-old in February 1947 from the then non-league club Scunthorpe United for what was reported as a record fee for a Midland League player. He made over 100 senior appearances for the Owls and then had a spell at Huddersfield Town before returning to Scunthorpe for whom he played 212 games in the Football League, eventually retiring from senior football in December 1963.

Frank Marshall (Born Sheffield 26 January 1929. Died 2015.) Frank Marshall was an inside-right or right-half who joined Rotherham United in the summer of 1951 from Scarborough. He went on to play over 100 times for the Millers but then lost his place and moved on to Scunthorpe United. In his first season at The Old Showground he captained the Iron to the Division Three North title and a famous FA Cup victory at Newcastle. He subsequently ended his career at Doncaster Rovers then had a spell on the backroom staff at Mansfield Town before moving to Sweden where he coached club sides for a number of years.

Joe Marston, MBE (Born Leichhardt, New South Wales, Australia, 7 January 1926. Died 29 November 2015.) Joe Marston was one of the most talented footballers produced by Australia in the post-war period. A product of the Leichhardt-Annandale club of the New South Wales State League, he signed for Preston North End at the beginning of 1950. He became a valued member of the side at Deepdale, making 200 first-team appearances and becoming the first Australian to play in an FA Cup final when he appeared for North End against West Bromwich Albion in 1955. He also represented the Football League against the Scottish League in March 1955 before returning to Australia later the same year.

Chris Marustik (Born Swansea, 10 August 1961. Died Swansea, 12 August 2015.) Chris Marustik came up through the ranks with Swansea City, featuring in midfield in the side that rose up to the old First Division in the early 1980s before coming crashing back down again. Although often a fringe player, he appeared regularly in the 1984–85 campaign before moving on to Cardiff in exchange for Roger Gibbins. He later played for Barry Town and Newport County. He won six full caps for Wales and seven at U21 level.

Josef Masopust (Born Most, Bohemia, Czechoslovakia, 9 February 1931. Died Prague, Czech Republic, 29 June 2015.) Josef Masopust was a midfield general who became arguably his country's best-ever player. He played much of his club football with Dukla Prague, where he gained eight league titles. He concluded his career in Belgium with Molenbeek before moving into coaching, including a spell in charge of the national team from 1984 to 1987. A member of the Czech team defeated by Brazil in the 1962 World Cup final, when he scored in the 3-1 defeat, he was also selected as European Footballer of the Year in the same year. He won 63 caps for Czechoslovakia.

George Merchant (Born Dundee, 13 May 1926. Died Carnoustie, Angus, 16 August 2015.) George Merchant was a centre-half who signed for Third Lanark in the summer of 1945. However, in a season at Cathkin and a further five with Aberdeen, he did not make any competitive appearances in senior competitions. His fortunes changed after signing for Dundee in 1951, when he was converted to a role as centre-forward and scored at the rate of a goal every other game. He joined Falkirk in the twilight of his career and scored one of the goals in the Scottish Cup final replay victory over Kilmarnock in April 1957.

Barrie Meyer (Born Bournemouth, 21 August 1932. Died Mount Edgecombe, Durban, South Africa, 13 September 2015.) Inside-forward Barrie Meyer was just 18 when he made his first-team debut for Bristol Rovers. He established himself in the side in 1952–53 and went on to score regularly over the following seasons. After his cricket career took off he left Eastville, but continued scoring at a healthy rate for Plymouth Argyle and Newport County, including a hat-trick in his final League appearance, for Bristol City against Southend United. He was also a cricketer for Gloucestershire making 405 First Class appearances for the county as a wicket-keeper between 1957 and 1971. As a cricket umpire (1978 to 1993) he officiated in 22 Test Matches.

Fred Middleton (Born West Hartlepool, 2 August 1930. Died 8 April 2016.) Fred Middleton was a wing-half who spent six seasons on the books of Newcastle United without breaking into the first team. In the summer of 1954 he stepped down a division to sign for Lincoln City where he quickly became a key figure in the side. He went on to make exactly 300 Football League appearances for the Imps before injuries took their toll and he eventually retired from senior football at the end of the 1962–63 season.

Ray Millard (Born South Shields, 2 June 1927. Died Barton-on-Sea, Hampshire, 30 September 2015.) Ray Millard played for Middlesbrough, without making a senior appearance, and Blyth Spartans, before signing professional forms for Reading in the summer of 1949. However, he made just two appearances during his time at Elm Park and a further 10 for Walsall before leaving senior football at the end of the 1954–55 season.

Johnny Miller (Born Ipswich, 21 September 1950. Died 18 February 2016.) Winger Johnny Miller spent six seasons with Ipswich Town before joining Norwich City in October 1974. In his first season at Carrow Road he played for the Canaries in their Football League Cup final defeat to Aston Villa and helped the team to win promotion to the First Division. Johnny later moved on to Mansfield Town, making over 100 Football League appearances for the Stags and being part of their team which won the Division Three title in the 1976–77.

Tony Millington (Born Hawarden, Flintshire, 5 June 1943. Died Wrexham, 5 August 2015.) Goalkeeper Tony Millington made over 350 senior appearances in a career that saw him play in all four divisions of the Football League. He was a teenager when he made his debut for West Bromwich Albion in the top flight but his best seasons were during his time with Peterborough and then Swansea. He helped the Swans win promotion from the old Fourth Division in 1969–70 and later moved to Northern Ireland to play for Glenavon but was seriously injured in a car crash in early 1975 and used a wheelchair for the remainder of his life. He founded Wrexham FC's Disabled Supporters' Club and later became the club's Disability Officer. Tony was capped 21 times for Wales.

Ralph Milne (Born Dundee, 13 May 1961. Died Dundee, 6 September 2015.) Ralph Milne was a significant figure for Dundee United in the 1980s. A talented winger with an excellent scoring record, he was a member of the team that won the Scottish League in 1982–83, and went on to play more than 250 games during his stay at Tannadice. He later moved south to play for Charlton, Bristol City and then Manchester United but his career never really took off in England. He was capped for Scotland at U21 level.

Chris Mitchell (Born Stirling, 21 July 1988. Died Cornton, Stirling, 6 May 2016.) Chris Mitchell was a defensive player who developed with Livingston United before joining Falkirk where he gained his introduction to senior football. He later spent a season with Bradford City in 2011–12 before returning to Scotland to sign for Queen of the South where he enjoyed success, winning both the Second Division title and the Scottish League Challenge Cup in 2012–13. More recently he had played for Clyde up until January 2016.

Graham Moore (Born Hengoed, Glamorgan, 7 March 1941. Died 9 February 2016.) Graham Moore was a centre-forward who made an instant impact after making his Football League debut for Cardiff City as a teenager. He was in the Wales national team at the age of 18 and in 1960 scored the goal which clinched the Bluebirds' promotion to Division One. Graham moved on to Chelsea and was a key figure in their 1962–63 promotion team. He later played for Manchester United, Northampton Town, Charlton Athletic and Doncaster Rovers. Graham made 21 appearances for Wales and also played for the Football League representative team.

Tommy Mulgrew (Born Motherwell, 13 April 1929. Died 12 January 2016.) Tommy Mulgrew signed for Northampton Town during his period of National Service and after just a handful of first-team appearances he was sold to Newcastle United. A lively winger, he featured in the First Division for the Magpies but found intense competition for places on Tyneside and dropped down a couple of divisions to sign for Southampton. He became a firm favourite with the Saints' fans, making over 300 first-team appearances before concluding his career with Aldershot.

Jimmy Murray (Born Edinburgh, 4 May 1933. Died Edinburgh, July 2015.) Inside-forward Jimmy Murray joined Hearts as a teenager and went on to spend more than a decade at Tynecastle. His career peaked at the end of the 1957–58 season when he scored 27 goals as the club won the Scottish League title. He was also called up to the national squad and had the distinction of scoring his country's first-ever goal in the World Cup finals when he netted in the 1-1 draw with Yugoslavia. He won a second title with Hearts in 1959–60 and later played for Falkirk, Clyde and Raith Rovers.

Dick Nanninga (Born Groningen, Netherlands, 17 January 1949. Died Maaseik, Belgium, 21 July 2015.) Dick Nanninga was a tall attacking player who played and scored for Netherlands in the 1978 World Cup final when they lost 3-1 to Argentina in extra time. During the same tournament he also became the first substitute to be sent off in the World Cup finals after receiving two bookings in the game against West Germany. He principally played his club football for Roda JC for whom he was the club's all-time leading scorer.

Billy Neil (Born Lanark, 20 April 1924. Died Bingley, West Yorkshire, 26 January 2016.) Billy Neil was an inside- or centre-forward who made a single wartime appearance for Rangers in the 1943–44 season. In 1945–46 he turned out for Dumbarton in Division B of the Southern League, but he fared less well in peacetime football and was mainly a reserve in spells with Morton and Bradford Park Avenue.

Edna Neillis (Born Springburn, Glasgow, 1953. Died 18 July 2015.) Edna Neillis was one of the pioneers of women's football in Scotland. A skilful inside-forward with Westhorn United she featured in her country's first-ever official international match, against England in November 1972. She subsequently played much of her career in Europe, firstly in France with Stade de Rheims and later in Italy, principally with AC Milan.

Lar O'Byrne (Born 10 August 1924. Died Dublin, 5 November 2015.) Lar O'Byrne was a forward with Shamrock Rovers in the late 1940s gaining a cap for the Republic of Ireland against Belgium in April 1949 and also winning representative honours for the League of Ireland. He helped the Hoops win the FAI Cup in 1948 and later moved on to play for Drumcondra where he won further FAI Cups in 1954 and 1967. At the time of his death he was Shamrock Rovers' oldest living player.

Mick O'Flanagan (Born Dublin, 22 September 1922. Died Dublin, 12 September 2015.) Mick O'Flanagan was a goalscoring centre forward, who established a unique double with his brother Kevin, the only brothers to represent Ireland at both soccer and rugby union. Pacy and skilful, he appeared in three FAI Cup finals for Bohemians and was leading scorer in the League of Ireland in the 1940–41 season. He won his only soccer cap for the Republic of Ireland against England in September 1946. He played rugby union for the Lansdowne club.

Tommy O'Hara (Born Bellshill, Lanarkshire, 17 August 1952. Died January 2016.) Tommy O'Hara was a skilful midfield player who won Scotland Junior international honours in the 1970–71 season when with Kirkintilloch Rob Roy. He enjoyed five years with Queen of the South, making over 150 appearances, but his career peaked during his time in the NASL with Washington Diplomats where he excelled playing alongside the likes of Johan Cruyff and Wim

Jansen. He eventually returned to Scotland turning out for Motherwell, where he was a member of the team that won the Scottish League Division One title in 1981–82, Falkirk and Partick Thistle.

Hugh Ormond (Born Greenock, 13 March 1923. Died 6 September 2015.) Hugh Ormond was a full-back who developed with Scottish Junior club Arthurlie in the 1940s before stepping up to the seniors with St Mirren. Mostly a reserve at Love Street he also had two seasons with Dundee United before being released having made a total of 14 first-team appearances in a career spanning the period 1946 to 1952.

Johnny Paton (Born Glasgow, 2 April 1923. Died October 2015.) Winger Johnny Paton won Schoolboy international honours for Scotland in 1937 and went on to join Celtic during the war. He spent most of the 1946–47 season with Chelsea, then returned to Parkhead before switching again to the London area with Brentford and Watford, where he served as manager from October 1955 to February 1966. He later turned to coaching and worked on the Arsenal backroom staff for many years.

Tom Paul (Born Grimsby, 14 May 1933. Died 6 September 2015.) Tom Paul was a winger who joined Grimsby Town from Immingham St Andrew's. Mostly a reserve at Blundell Park, his only first-team outing came at outside-right in the local derby with Scunthorpe United in October 1958.

Arnold Peralta (Born La Ceiba, Honduras, 29 March 1989. Died La Ceiba, Honduras, 10 December 2015.) Arnold Peralta was a midfield player who developed in Honduras with CD Vida and represented his country at the 2012 Olympic Games. He later moved to Scotland, signing for Rangers in the summer of 2013 and assisting the Ibrox club to the Scottish League First Division title in 2013–14. He later returned to Honduras to sign for CD Olimpia. He was shot dead while on a visit to his home town. Arnold won 26 full caps for Honduras.

Albert Phelan (Born Sheffield, 27 April 1944. Died 18 April 2016.) Albert Phelan was a centre-half who joined Chesterfield as an amateur in 1962 before signing professional forms two years later. He spent 10 years as a professional with the Spireites and was a key player in their team which won the Fourth Division championship in 1969–70. He made 390 Football League appearances for Chesterfield and was later at Halifax Town. After his playing career ended he spent over a decade on the backroom staff at Sheffield Wednesday.

Ray Pointer (Born Cramlington, Northumberland, 10 October 1936. Died Blackpool, January 2016.) Ray Pointer was a tireless centre-forward who signed professional terms for Burnley after completing his National Service and soon established himself in the line-up. In his second full season he led the Clarets' scoring charts with 27 goals, and went on to become a key figure in the team that won the 1959–60 Football League title. Twelve months later he gained an FA Cup runners-up medal as Burnley went down 3-1 to Tottenham Hotspur in the Wembley final. He later played for Bury, Coventry City and Portsmouth. He moved into coaching at Fratton Park and eventually returning to the North West, where he worked with both Blackpool and Bury. Ray won three full caps for England.

Peter Price (Born Tarbolton, Ayrshire, 26 February 1932. Died 23 October 2015.) Peter Price joined St Mirren In December 1950, but played just two games during his stay at Love Street before moving on to Gloucester City and then Darlington. His career eventually began to progress after he signed for Ayr United in August 1955. In his first season at Somerset Park he netted 41 goals as the club won promotion to the top flight and although relegated the next season, the goals continued to flow as he netted more than 50 times in both 1957–58 and 1958–59. His final tally of 213 competitive goals remains a club record. He concluded his career with spells at Raith and Albion Rovers.

Peter Rapley (Born Portsmouth, 24 October 1936. Died 24 July 2015.) Peter Rapley was a winger who made 10 first-team appearances for Exeter City in the late 1950s before moving on to sign for Southern League Cambridge United. He featured both at centre-forward and centre-half for the U's and then played for Wisbech Town.

Keith Rattray (Born 16 November 1944. Died Ballater, Aberdeenshire, 11 March 2016.) Keith Rattray was a centre-forward who had his most successful spell with Highland League club Keith between 1969 and 1975, scoring 101 goals in 175 appearances. Earlier in his career he had been on the books of both Aberdeen and Brechin City, making a single Scottish League appearance for the latter in the 1964–65 season.

Jorgen Ravn (Born Valby, Denmark, 3 June 1940. Died 4 June 2015.) Jorgen Ravn was a centre-forward who led the scoring charts for KB Copenhagen in consecutive seasons before joining the migration of players from Scandinavia to Scotland at the beginning of 1965, signing for Aberdeen. He stayed at Pittodrie until the summer of 1966, scoring 14 goals from 36 League and Cup appearances before returning to KB. He represented Denmark at B international level.

Fred Ridgway (Born Stockport, 10 August 1923. Died Maidstone, 26 September 2015.) Fred Ridgway had a trial with Wolverhampton Wanderers at the age of 16 and appeared for his home town team Stockport County during the war. He made his first-team debut in 1939–40 and went on to make a total of 21 appearances in the emergency competitions, scoring three goals. Fred was better known for his cricket career, playing in five Test matches for England, all during the 1951–52 tour of India, and making 341 First Class appearances for Kent between 1946 and 1962.

Billy Ritchie (Born Dundee, circa 1934. Died Dundee, 23 June 2015.) Inside-forward Billy Ritchie developed with Dundee Osborne stepping up to the seniors when he signed for Dundee in the summer of 1955. Although scoring twice on his debut he never quite managed to establish himself in the line-up at Dens Park. He went on to play for Stirling Albion and Bury, but his best years were spent at Stockport County where he was a near ever present in the 1959–60 season. He scored a creditable 44 goals in 108 appearances during his career both north and south of the Border.

Billy Ritchie (Born Newtongrange, Midlothian, 11 September 1936. Died 10 March 2016.) Billy Ritchie was first choice goalkeeper for Rangers in the early 1960s making over 300 appearances and winning two Scottish League championships, four Scottish Cups and three Scottish League Cups. He was ever-present in the Rangers team which completed the treble in 1963–64. After leaving Ibrox Billy spent time at Partick Thistle and Motherwell and then retired. Four years later he made a comeback when, while working as a PT teacher, he signed for Second Division club Stranraer at the age of 38. He won a single cap for Scotland, appearing against Uruguay in May 1962.

John Roberts (Born Abercynon, Glamorgan, 11 September 1946. Died Sydenham, London, January 2016.) John Roberts began his career as a centre-forward and was Swansea's leading scorer in 1966–67. After moving to Northampton Town he was converted into a defender and his subsequent career took him to Arsenal (where he featured in the 1970–71 League title winning team), Birmingham City, Wrexham and Hull City before his career was ended by injury. In total he made over 400 senior appearances and while at Wrexham was a member of the team that won the old Third Division title in 1977–78.

Peter Roberts, CBE (Born Chesterfield, 21 July 1955. Died Chesterfield, 31 December 2015.) Peter Roberts was a midfielder who signed as a non-contract player for his home town club of Chesterfield and played a couple of times for the senior side in the mid-1970s, later playing for Southport. He became a highly respected figure in further education, notably through his work as principal of Leeds City College. He was awarded a CBE in June 2015 for services to further education.

Jimmy Robertson (Born Falkirk 20 February 1929. Died Bonnybridge, Stirlingshire, 11 June 2015.) Jimmy Robertson joined Arsenal in June 1948, making over 100 appearances for the Gunners' reserve team, but just a single senior appearance. He moved on to Brentford in part-exchange for Tommy Lawton and enjoyed three seasons of fairly regular first-team football at Griffin Park. Jimmy later linked up with his former Arsenal colleague Lionel Smith at Gravesend & Northfleet where he was a member of the team that won the Southern League title in 1957–58.

Billy Robinson (Born circa 1934. Died Sutton, Surrey, 27 June 2015.) Centre-forward Billy Robinson was a member of the Sutton United team that won both the Athenian League and the London Senior Cup in 1957–58. In March 1958 he was capped for England Amateurs against Scotland and in the close season he was a member of a mixed FA squad of amateurs and professionals that toured West Africa. He subsequently turned professional with Crystal Palace but was unable to break into the first team.

Dave Robinson (Born Birmingham, 14 July 1948. Died April 2016.) Dave Robinson was a centre-half who joined Birmingham City from school and went on to sign professional terms in July 1966. He made over 100 senior appearances for the Blues before spending four years at Walsall making a further 165 Football League appearances. He was later player-manager of Southern League club Tamworth.

Harry Robinson (Born Belfast, 17 August 1935. Died Port Augusta, South Australia, 9 September 2015.) Harry Robinson was an inside-forward who was a prominent Irish League player with Ballymena United, Linfield and Portadown in the 1950s. He won representative honours for Northern Ireland Amateurs against England in September 1958 and also for the Irish FA against South Africa later the same year. The following March he signed for Fulham but was unable to break into the first team at Craven Cottage.

Don Robson, CBE, DL (Born Winlaton, Co Durham, 5 February 1934. Died Dipton, near Stanley, Co Durham, 10 March 2016.) Don Robson was a centre-forward who signed for Doncaster Rovers in the summer of 1951 but never played in their senior team. He later joined Gateshead and spent four seasons with the club, scoring 11 goals in 35 games, before moving on to South Shields. Don was best known as a local politician serving as a councillor for over 30 years. He became leader of Durham County Council in 1989 and went on to be the council's longest serving leader in modern times. He was awarded a CBE for services to local government in 1997. He was also a Deputy Lieutenant of County Durham.

George Ross (Born Inverness, 15 April 1923. Died 7 May 2016.) George Ross was a full-back who joined Preston North End as a groundstaff boy and went on to make 441 League and Cup appearances for the club during 15 years at Deepdale. He was included in North End's 1964 FA Cup final team and also won a Third Division championship medal with the club in 1970–71. He later played for Southport before a spell in the USA with Washington Diplomats. George became chairman of the Preston North End Former Players' Association from its formation in 1998 and remained in the role for over 15 years.

Jim Rowan (Born Glasgow, 27 July 1935. Died 21 June 2015.) Jim Rowan started out as an inside-forward with Celtic, signing terms in October 1952 and subsequently embarking on a career that saw him turn out for nine Scottish League clubs before his career ended in 1970. His best spells were with Stirling Albion, where he captained the team to the Division Two title in 1960–61, and Airdrieonians. In the late 1960s he served as chairman of the Scottish PFA. Jim also had a spell in coaching and was manager of East Stirlingshire for 1970–71.

Tommy Rowe (Died 14 November 2015.) Tommy Rowe was principally an inside-forward and wing-half who made his name in League of Ireland football in the 1950s and '60s. He spent a decade with Drumcondra, with whom he won League titles in 1957–58 and 1960–61 and two FAI Cup finals (1953 and 1957), adding a further League title with Dundalk in 1962–63. He won representative honours for both the League of Ireland and Republic of Ireland B.

Edgar Rumney (Born Abberton, Essex, 15 September 1936. Died 18 August 2015.) Full back Edgar Rumney joined Colchester United in the summer of 1957 and went on to spend eight seasons at Layer Road. He was mostly a reserve throughout this time, making 52 competitive appearances, with his best run of regular first-team action coming in the first half of the 1964–65 season.

Ken Satchwell (Born Birmingham, 19 January 1940. Died 24 January 2016.) Ken Satchwell was an attacking player who was on the books of Aston Villa as a youngster but then switched to Birmingham Works League football where his goalscoring feats attracted the attention of senior clubs. He signed for Coventry City at the beginning of 1958–59 and was a regular by the following season, netting four goals in the 5-3 win over Wrexham on Christmas Day 1959. He then fell out of favour and left for Nuneaton Borough, but eventually returned for a further spell of senior football with Walsall before injury struck.

Paul Shanks (Born Dunfermline, 1 March 1984. Died Livingston, 30 September 2015.) Paul Shanks was a young forward who made his senior debut for Stenhousemuir as a 17-year-old. He was also included as an unused substitute on a number of occasions before he was given his only first-team start in the final game of 2001–02. His early death came in tragic circumstances.

Arthur Shaw (Born Limehouse, London, 9 April 1924. Died Hermosa Beach, California, United States, 2 November 2015.) Wing-half Arthur Shaw was on the books of Queens Park Rangers during the war when he made a number of first-team appearances in the emergency competitions. In peacetime he played for Brentford, Arsenal and Watford, gaining a Football League championship medal in 1952–53 when he featured in over half the Gunners' fixtures. Later he captained Gravesend & Northfleet when they won the Southern League title in 1957–58.

David Shawcross (Born Stretford, Lancashire, 3 July 1941. Died 7 November 2015.) David Shawcross was a skilful wing-half who was on the verge of establishing himself for Manchester City when he suffered a bad knee injury in April 1961 after which he was never quite the same player. Shortly before this he had played, and scored, for England U23s in a 4-1 win over their counterparts from West Germany. He contributed to promotion campaigns with both Stockport County and Halifax, then had a season in the League of Ireland with Drogheda playing in the team that lost out to Limerick in the 1971 FAI Cup final.

David Sloan (Born Lisburn, 28 October 1941. Died February 2016.) David Sloan was a winger who spent two seasons as a regular with Irish League club Bangor before joining Scunthorpe United, shortly after netting the winner for Northern Ireland Amateurs in a 2-1 win over England. He made over 100 League appearances for both Scunthorpe and Oxford United, and in 1967–68 he helped the U's win promotion, scoring the decisive goal against Southport in the final match of the campaign to clinch the Third Division title. At the start of the following season he scored the club's first ever goal in Division Two. He also became Oxford's first full international when he played for Northern Ireland against Israel in 1968.

Alan Spavin (Born Lancaster, 20 February 1942. Died 16 March 2016.) Inside-forward Alan Spavin joined the groundstaff at Preston North End on leaving school, later progressing to the professional ranks. After making a scoring debut against Arsenal in August 1960 he went on to make over 400 appearances for North End, gaining an FA Cup runners-up medal in 1964 and captaining the side that won the Division Three title in 1970–71. Alan later played in the NASL with Washington Diplomats and after a spell back in the UK coaching he settled in Florida where he ran an indoor soccer centre.

Ron Springett (Born Fulham, 22 July 1935. Died 12 September 2015.) Goalkeeper Ron Springett established himself as a first-team regular for Queens Park Rangers in the 1956–57 season and his performances earned him a move to

Sheffield Wednesday in March 1958. He went on to spend nine seasons as an automatic choice at Hillsborough. A near ever-present in the team that won the Division Two title in 1959–60, he gained an FA Cup runners-up medal in 1966. Small, but very agile, he was England's regular 'keeper in the early 1960s, gaining 33 full caps. Ron wound up his career back at Loftus Road following a unique transfer deal that saw him change places with his younger brother Peter.

Pavel Srnicek (Born Ostrava, Czechoslovakia, 10 March 1968. Died Ostrava, Czech Republic, 29 December 2015.) Goalkeeper Pavel Srnicek developed in Czech football, notably with Banik Ostrava, before joining Newcastle United in February 1991. He became a firm favourite with the fans on Tyneside and in 1992–93 helped the Magpies win the Division One title and promotion to the Premier League. He went on to make over 150 first-team appearances during his stay there after a brief spell back in the Czech Republic he returned to the Premier League with Sheffield Wednesday for two more seasons prior to a spell in Portugal with SC Beira-Mar.

Alex Stenhouse (Born Stirling, 1 January 1933. Died Southend on Sea, 28 February 2016.) Alex Stenhouse was an outside-right who was a Scotland juvenile internationalist before he signed for Dundee United in November 1953. He gained first-team experience at Tannadice before his career was interrupted by National Service and afterwards he moved to play in England. He made a handful of appearances for Portsmouth and then had three seasons at Southend United before switching to Southern League football with Bedford Town and Corby Town.

Eddie Stewart (Born Dundee, 15 November 1934. Died Dundee, 11 November 2015.) Wing-half Eddie Stewart signed for Dundee United in September 1954 and featured regularly in his first two seasons. His career was then interrupted by National Service when he was stationed with the RASC at Aldershot. During 1957–58 he spent time on loan with Norwich City before returning to Tannadice. He later had a brief spell with Arbroath.

Derek Stroud (Born Wimborne, Dorset, 11 February 1930. Died Wimborne, Dorset, 16 August 2015.) Winger Derek Stroud joined Bournemouth from Western League club Poole Town in the summer of 1950 and within a few months he had established himself as a first-team regular with the Cherries. Three seasons at Dean Court were followed by two with Grimsby, where he took his career total of Football League appearances to exactly 150, before returning to the West Country to sign for Dorchester Town.

Roy Stroud (Born Silvertown, East London, 16 March 1925. Died 4 June 2015.) Centre-forward Roy Stroud played for Arsenal and Brentford during the war and went on to win 11 England Amateur caps whilst with Hendon. He later signed professional forms for West Ham but was mostly a reserve during his time with the club, making just 13 first-team appearances. He moved on to Chelmsford City, but his playing career was cut short by injury in November 1958.

Roy Swinbourne (Born Denaby Main, Yorkshire, 25 August 1929. Died Kidderminster, 27 December 2015.) Roy Swinbourne developed in Yorkshire with the Wolves nursery team Wath Wanderers before signing a professional contract. He broke into the first team at Molineux shortly before Christmas in 1949 and apart from a brief spell during the 1951–52 campaign he retained his place through until the end of 1956 when a knee injury ended his career. A powerful centre-forward he was a near ever-present in the team that won the Football League title in 1953–54, with his finest hour coming in the floodlight friendly with Honved in December 1954 when he scored twice in the final 15 minutes to secure a famous 3-1 victory. Roy was on fire at the beginning of the 1955–56 season, hitting three hat-tricks in a run of four games before injury struck. He was capped for England B.

Zoltan Szarka (Born Csorna, Hungary, 12 August 1942. Died Szombathely, Hungary, 18 April 2016.) Goalkeeper Zoltan Szarka was a member of the Hungary team which won the Gold Medal in the 1968 Mexico City Games. He was a substitute throughout the tournament and only saw action in the semi-final when he came off the bench late on in a 5-0 win over Japan. Zoltan played his club football for Haladas Szombathely.

Brian Taylor (Born Walsall 24 March 1937. Died Menorca, Spain, 10 June 2015.) Brian Taylor was a winger who made his name with Walsall in the 1950s, his performances in a relegated team earning him a move to the top flight with Birmingham City. However, a broken leg suffered in November 1959 kept him on the sidelines for 12 months and he was never quite the same player again. He continued his career in the lower divisions with spells at Rotherham United, Shrewsbury Town and Port Vale, before concluding with a season at Barnsley in 1967–68 when he helped the Oakwell club to promotion from Division Four.

Ken Taylor (Born South Shields, 15 March 1931. Died 19 April 2016.) Ken Taylor was a right-back who made over 200 first-team appearances for Blackburn Rovers during a lengthy career at Ewood Park. Ken signed for Rovers from North Shields as a teenager in January 1950 and progressed through the ranks to make his first-team debut in December 1954. He continued to feature regularly for Rovers over the next 10 years before leaving the club in the summer of 1964 to play for non-league Morecambe.

Tommy Thompson (Born Fencehouses, Co Durham, 10 November 1928. Died 15 September 2015.) Tommy Thompson joined Newcastle United as a teenager, but it was not until he moved on to Aston Villa in August 1950 that he became a regular first-team player. In over a decade in top-flight football he established himself as a powerful inside-forward with an eye for goal. His best years were spent at Preston North End where he led the scoring charts in his first four seasons, establishing a club record by netting in 11 consecutive Football League games during the 1957–58 season. He played alongside the two great post-war wingers, Finney at Preston and Matthews at Stoke, and hit four goals playing for the Football League against the League of Ireland at Goodison Park in October 1951. Tommy won two full caps for England.

Davie Thomson (Born Bothkennar, Stirlingshire, 2 February 1938. Died 28 January 2016.) Centre-forward Davie Thomson enjoyed something of a meteoric rise to fame after joining Dunfermline Athletic from Bo'ness United in the summer of 1959. He had played less than a dozen first-team games when called up for the Scottish Cup final replay against Celtic in April 1961 and he duly scored his team's first goal in their 2-0 victory. Thereafter his career fizzled out somewhat. Two seasons at Leicester City produced a single first-team outing in the final game of the 1961–62 season, when he scored in a 3-2 home defeat to Spurs. He returned to Scotland but in brief spells in the seniors with Queen of the South and Berwick Rangers he also made little impact.

Les Thomson (Born Blair Atholl, Perthshire, 15 September 1936. Died 22 March 2016.) Les Thomson was a versatile player who made his senior debut for Falkirk in March 1956 at right-half but also appeared for the club at right-back, centre-half and centre-forward. He was an ever-present when the Bairns won promotion to Division One in 1960–61 and in total made over 150 senior appearances for the club. He then spent five years with Stirling Albion before ending his career at Stenhousemuir. Later in life he became closely involved with East Stirlingshire serving as secretary, chief executive and chairman until stepping down in 2011.

Denis Thwaites (Born Stockton, 14 December 1944. Died Sousse, Tunisia, 26 June 2015.) Denis Thwaites won representative honours for England Schools and England Youth and joined Birmingham City on leaving school. He went on to make 95 first-team appearances during his time at St Andrew's, holding down a regular first-team place between December 1964 and April 1966. He fell out of favour following a change in manager and eventually left senior football. Both Denis and his wife Sandra were murdered in the Tunisian hotel shootings in June 2015.

Jimmy Toner (Born Shettleston, Glasgow, 23 August 1924. Died Arbroath, 31 March 2016.) Jimmy Toner was a winger or inside-forward who scored one of the goals when Fauldhouse United won the Scottish Junior Cup in 1946. He signed for Dundee soon afterwards and enjoyed success at Dens Park with successive League Cup wins in 1951–52 and 1952–53. He spent the 1954–55 season with Leeds, then linked up with former Dundee manager Bobby Ancell at Motherwell. A brief association with Forfar Athletic followed before injury ended his career. Much later he returned to Dens Park in a coaching role (1968–1978).

Eric Treverrow (Born Renfrewshire, circa 1926. Died Newtownards, Co Down, 2 October 2015.) Eric Treverrow joined Ballymena United from Scottish Junior club Parkhead in 1948. He went on to make a record 559 appearances for the club and was a member of their team which won the Irish Cup in 1958. He appeared regularly for the Irish League representative team between 1950 and 1953 and was Ulster Footballer of the Year in 1952.

John Waite (Born Grimsby, 16 January 1942. Died 3 April 2016.) John Waite was an outside-right who made his debut for his home town club Grimsby Town in the old Second Division while still at school. John, who made four appearances for the England youth team, gained further first-team experience for the Mariners before moving on to non-league Gainsborough Trinity in 1963.

Davy Walsh (Born Waterford, 28 April 1923. Died 11 March 2016.) Centre-forward Davy Walsh was a prolific scorer with Linfield in the closing stages of wartime football, netting 96 goals in 93 games. In May 1946 he was signed up by West Bromwich Albion and proved an instant success at The Hawthorns, scoring in each of his first six appearances. He led the Baggies' scoring charts four seasons in a row, hitting a century of goals before moving on to Aston Villa where he continued to score on a regular basis. Later he had spells with Walsall and Worcester City. Davy was one of a number of players from the immediate post-war era who won international honours for both Northern Ireland and the Republic of Ireland.

Joe Wark (Born Glasgow, 9 October 1947. Died 1 October 2015.) Joe Wark joined Motherwell as an inside-forward from Ayrshire Junior club Irvine Victoria, but quickly switched to left-back and became a firm fixture in that position for more than a decade, making 469 Scottish League appearances, a post-war record for the club. A member of two promotion teams during his time at Fir Park (1968–69 and 1981–82), he won representative honours for the Scottish League against the Football League in March 1976.

Ken Waterhouse (Born Ormskirk, Lancashire, 23 January 1930. Died Lancaster, 4 April 2016.) Ken Waterhouse was a wing-half who began his career with Preston North End, where he spent almost a decade on the club's books managing just 22 appearances. Moving on to Rotherham in May 1958 he enjoyed greater exposure to first-team football, adding more than 100 first-team outings and featuring in both legs of the 1960–61 Football League Cup final when the Millers went down to Aston Villa in extra time. He concluded his senior career with spells at Bristol City and Darlington and switched to non-league football. He subsequently spent two spells in charge of Morecambe (1965–69 and 1970–72).

Matt Watson (Born 3 May 1936. Died 25 October 2015.) Matt Watson was a left-back who was on the books of Kilmarnock from 1954 to 1968, establishing himself as a first-team regular in 1958–59 and making over 450 competitive appearances for the club. He was a member of the Killie team that won the Scottish League title in 1964–65 season after defeating Hearts at Tynecastle to snatch the trophy from their opponents in a dramatic finish to the campaign. Matt concluded with a couple of seasons at Queen of the South.

Eric Webster (Born Manchester, 21 June 1931. Died 24 January 2016.) Eric Webster made a single first-team appearance for Manchester City, featuring at left-half at Cardiff in February 1953. He subsequently played in non-league football and then moved into management and eventually joined the backroom staff at Stockport County where he served on a number of occasions as caretaker-manager and holding the post on a more long-term basis between May 1982 and May 1985.

Terry Webster (Born Doncaster, 9 July 1930. Died High Kelling, Norfolk, 25 February 2016.) Terry Webster was a goalkeeper who joined Derby County from Doncaster Rovers in a player-exchange just a few months after signing for the Yorkshire club. He received his senior debut in the First Division at the age of 18 and was first choice 'keeper in 1956–57 when the club won the Division Three North championship. In total he spent a decade with Derby, making 178 appearances, before moving to play for non-league Skegness Town.

Ray Weigh (Born Flint 23 June 1928. Died Christchurch, Dorset, 4 June 2015.) Ray Weigh was a versatile forward who was signed by Bournemouth in March 1949. He scored on his debut for the Cherries but struggled to establish himself at Dean Court and moved on to Stockport in a player-exchange. Although mostly used at outside left during his career, he often featured at centre-forward for his next club, Shrewsbury Town, scoring four goals in the 7-0 win over Swindon Town in May 1955. After concluding his career at Aldershot he left senior football having made over 200 appearances.

Willie White (Born Clackmannan, 25 September 1932. Died September 2015.) Goalkeeper Willie White stepped up to the seniors in the summer of 1952 when he joined Motherwell from Alva Albion Rangers. Unable to get in the first team he moved south 12 months later, signing for Accrington Stanley, where he was one of three 'keepers used by the Northern Section club in 1953–54. Later he was mostly a reserve at Mansfield Town before joining Bacup Borough.

Joe Wilson (Born Workington, 6 July 1947. Died Sydenham, Victoria, Australia, 25 September 2015.) Joe Wilson signed for Workington in January 1956. He developed into a solid, uncompromising right-back best known for his two spells with the Cumbrian club, together yielding almost 350 appearances. In between he enjoyed time with Nottingham Forest and Wolves, mostly spent in the old First Division. Joe later emigrated to Australia where he briefly played for Melbourne club George Cross.

Lew Woodroffe (Born Portsmouth, 29 October 1921. Died Worthing, Sussex, 14 June 2015.) Lew Woodroffe was an inside-forward or winger who made nine first-team appearances for Manchester City in the first post-war season. He added a further 64 outings for Watford after signing in June 1947, moving on to a brief spell with Hastings United in the summer of 1951.

Zito (Born Roseira, Sao Paulo, Brazil, 8 August 1932. Died Santos, Brazil, 14 June 2015.) Zito was a midfield player for Brazil, winning 46 caps between 1955 and 1963. He was a World Cup winner for his country in 1958 and 1962 (when he scored in the 3-1 win over Czechoslovakia in the final) and captained the team in later years. At club level he spent 15 years with Santos, assisting them to the Copa Libertadores title in 1962 and 1963.

Ian Nannestad, Soccer History Magazine
www.soccer-history.co.uk

THE FOOTBALL RECORDS

BRITISH FOOTBALL RECORDS

ALL-TIME PREMIER LEAGUE CHAMPIONSHIP SEASONS ON POINTS AVERAGE

	Team	Season	P	W	D	L	F	A	Pts	Pts Av
1	Chelsea	2004–05	38	29	8	1	72	15	95	2.50
2	Manchester U	1999–2000	38	28	7	3	97	45	91	2.39
3	Chelsea	2005–06	38	29	4	5	72	22	91	2.39
4	Arsenal	2003–04	38	26	12	0	73	26	90	2.36
	Manchester U	2008–09	38	28	6	4	68	24	90	2.36
6	Manchester C	2011–12	38	28	5	5	93	29	89	2.34
	Manchester U	2006–07	38	28	5	5	83	27	89	2.34
	Manchester U	2012–13	38	28	5	5	86	43	89	2.34
9	Arsenal	2001–02	38	26	9	3	79	36	87	2.28
	Manchester U	2007–08	38	27	6	5	80	22	87	2.28
	Chelsea	2014–15	38	26	9	3	73	32	87	2.28
12	Chelsea	2009–10	38	27	5	6	103	32	86	2.26
	Manchester C	2013–14	38	27	5	6	102	37	86	2.26
14	Manchester U	1993–94	42	27	11	4	80	38	92	2.19
15	Manchester U	2002–03	38	25	8	5	74	34	83	2.18
16	Manchester U	1995–96	38	25	7	6	73	35	82	2.15
17	Leicester C	2015–16	38	23	12	3	68	36	81	2.13
18	Blackburn R	1994–95	42	27	8	7	80	39	89	2.11
19	Manchester U	2000–01	38	24	8	6	79	31	80	2.10
	Manchester U	2010–11	38	23	11	4	78	37	80	2.10
21	Manchester U	1998–99	38	22	13	3	80	37	79	2.07
22	Arsenal	1997–98	38	23	9	6	68	33	78	2.05
23	Manchester U	1992–93	42	24	12	6	67	31	84	2.00
24	Manchester U	1996–97	38	21	12	5	76	44	75	1.97

PREMIER LEAGUE EVER-PRESENT CLUBS

	P	W	D	L	F	A	Pts
Manchester U	924	586	194	144	1802	819	1952
Arsenal	924	502	241	181	1621	868	1747
Chelsea	924	486	238	200	1560	894	1696
Liverpool	924	456	233	235	1523	944	1601
Tottenham H	924	374	239	311	1320	1205	1361
Everton	924	332	267	325	1197	1163	1263
Aston Villa	924	316	275	333	1117	1186	1223

TOP TEN PREMIERSHIP APPEARANCES

1	Giggs, Ryan	632	6	Heskey, Emile	516
2	Lampard, Frank	609	7	Schwarzer, Mark	514
3	Barry, Gareth	595	8	Carragher, Jamie	508
4	James, David	572	9	Neville, Phil	505
5	Speed, Gary	534	10=	Ferdinand, Rio and Gerrard, Steven	504

TOP TEN PREMIERSHIP GOALSCORERS

1	Shearer, Alan	260	6	Fowler, Robbie	163
2	Rooney, Wayne	193	7	Owen, Michael	150
3	Cole, Andy	187	8	Ferdinand, Les	149
4	Lampard, Frank	177	9	Sheringham, Teddy	146
5	Henry, Thierry	175	10	van Persie, Robin	144

SCOTTISH PREMIER LEAGUE SINCE 1998–99

	P	W	D	L	F	A	Pts
Celtic	680	498	101	81	1583	526	1595
Rangers	528	364	93	71	1123	418	1175
Aberdeen	680	255	162	265	823	904	921
Hearts	642	257	158	227	837	775	914
Motherwell	680	242	147	291	857	1025	873
Kilmarnock	680	220	168	292	815	1000	828
Dundee U	680	214	184	282	842	1021	808
Hibernian	568	191	145	232	743	812	718

DOMESTIC LANDMARKS 2015–16

SEPTEMBER 2015

1   Manchester United signed Anthony Martial from Monaco for £36m, a world record for a teenager.

5   England qualified for Euro 2016 with a 6-0 Group E win over San Marino at Stadio Olimpico, Serravalle. Wayne Rooney equalled Sir Bobby Charlton's goalscoring record with his 49th goal for England. His landmark strike came from the penalty spot in the 13th minute.

8   Wayne Rooney became England's all-time leading goalscorer with his 50th goal for his country in the 2-0 victory over Switzerland. The record-breaking goal came from the penalty spot in the 84th minute against Switzerland at Wembley. A 66th minute strike from Harry Kane had given England the lead and the win means England finish top of Group E.

22   Ross Barkley scored for Everton on his 100th appearance for the club. His 62nd minute equaliser at Reading in the Capital One Cup 3rd round tie helped Everton to a 2-1 victory with Gerard Deulofeu scoring the winner after 73 minutes. Earlier Reading had led through Nick Blackman.

OCTOBER 2015

3   Sergio Aguero scored the fastest five-goal haul in Premier League history in the 6-1 defeat of Newcastle United at the Etihad. His five goals were scored in 23 minutes as he became the fifth player to score five in a Premier League match.

4   Gareth Bale named Welsh Player of the Year for a record fifth time. Bale also won the Players' Player of the Year and Fans' Player of the Year awards.

8   Northern Ireland won through to their first major tournament since the 1986 World Cup. A 3-1 win over Greece at Windsor Park saw Michael O'Neill's side qualify for Euro 2016 in France.

10   Wales qualified for Euro 2016 despite losing 2-0 in Bosnia. The Welshman qualified from Group B to reach a major tournament for the first time in 57 years.

11   Republic of Ireland lost 2-1 to Poland in Warsaw and have to compete in the Play-Offs if they are to qualify for Euro 2016.

12   England won 3-0 in Lithuania to make it 10 wins out of 10 in Euro 2016 qualification and only the fifth country to achieve the feat in European Championship history. France 1992, 2004; Czech Republic 2000; Germany 2012; Spain 2012 are the countries with 100 per cent records in qualifying, with only Spain in 2012 going on to win the competition.

19   Leeds United owner Massimo Cellino was disqualified from running a Football League club under the Football League's owners' and directors' test. The ban is in connection with a conviction under Italian tax law.

NOVEMBER 2015

7   Brighton & HA set a new club record of 17 games unbeaten (16 since the start of this season) with a 2-1 home win over Milton Keynes Dons.

8   Jamie Coppinger made his 469th appearance for Doncaster Rovers in the first round FA Cup tie 2-0 win over Stalybridge Celtic at the Keepmoat Stadium. Coppinger became Rovers' record appearance holder in all competitions.

21   Leicester City forward Jamie Vardy equalled Ruud van Nistelrooy's record of scoring in 10 successive Premier League matches. Vardy's achievement came in a 3-0 win at Newcastle United. Ironically, van Nistelrooy set the record by scoring for the 10th match in a row also at Newcastle in a 2-1 victory for Manchester United. While Vardy's record was set in the current season, van Nistelrooy's was set over two seasons.

28   Leicester City forward Jamie Vardy broke Ruud van Nistelrooy's record of scoring in 10 successive Premier League matches. Vardy's scored for the 11th Premier League match in succession in the 1-1 draw with Manchester United at the King Power Stadium. The all-time record for consecutive matches scored in stands at 12 and was set by Jimmy Dunne of Sheffield United in 1931–32.

DECEMBER 2015

2   Gary Neville appointed manager of Valencia. He succeeds Nuno Espirito Santo who had resigned on 29 November after defeat to Sevilla. Neville joins brother Phil who has been at the Mestalla as assistant coach since July 2015.

25   Leicester City become the first team in Premier League history to be bottom of the league on Christmas Day in one season and then top the following season.

28   Petr Cech set a new Premier League clean sheets record of 170 in Arsenal's 2-0 victory over Bournemouth at the Emirates. He broke the previous record of David James which stood at 169.

JANUARY 2016

2   Wayne Rooney became both Manchester United's and the Premier League's second leading goalscorer with his 238 goals for his club and his 188th top-flight goal.

13   Leon Britton made his 500th appearance for Swansea City in their home match against Sunderland. Sunderland ran out 4-2 winners which included a hat-trick from Jermain Defoe.

FEBRUARY 2016

1   Manchester City announced the signing of Pep Guardiola as their new manager. The current Bayern Munich boss will succeed Manuel Pelligrini for next season.

3   Chinese Super League side Guangzhou Evergrande break the Asian transfer record to sign Jackson Martinez for £31m from Atletico Madrid.

5   The Asian transfer record is broken for the second time in 3 days when Alex Teixeira signed for Jiansu Suning from Shakhtar Donetsk for £38.4m.

APRIL 2016

19   Sergio Aguero scored his 100th Premier League goal for Manchester City in the 1-1 draw with Newcastle United at St James' Park.

MAY 2016

17   Wayne Rooney scored his 100th Premier League goal at Old Trafford in Manchester United's 3-1 victory over Bournemouth at Old Trafford.

21   The Scottish Cup Final was contested by Hibernian and Rangers, the first time that no team from the top tier had made the final.

JUNE 2016

4   Aaron Hughes made his 100th international appearance for Northern Ireland in the 0-0 friendly draw with Slovakia in Trnava. Hughes appeared as a 30th minute substitute for the injured Craig Cathcart.

EUROPEAN CUP AND CHAMPIONS LEAGUE RECORDS

MOST WINS BY CLUB

Real Madrid	11	1956, 1957, 1958, 1959, 1960, 1966, 1998, 2000, 2002, 2014, 2016.
AC Milan	7	1963, 1969, 1989, 1990, 1994, 2003, 2007.
Bayern Munich	5	1974, 1975, 1976, 2001, 2013.
Liverpool	5	1977, 1978, 1981, 1984, 2005.
Barcelona	5	1992, 2006, 2009, 2011, 2015.

MOST APPEARANCES IN FINAL
Real Madrid 14; AC Milan 11; Bayern Munich 10

MOST FINAL APPEARANCES PER COUNTRY
Spain 27 (16 wins, 11 defeats)
Italy 27 (12 wins, 15 defeats)
England 19 (12 wins, 7 defeats)
Germany 17 (7 wins, 10 defeats)

MOST CHAMPIONS LEAGUE/EUROPEAN CUP APPEARANCES
158 Iker Casillas (Real Madrid, Porto)
157 Xavi (Barcelona)
151 Ryan Giggs (Manchester U)
144 Raul (Real Madrid, Schalke)
139 Paolo Maldini (AC Milan)
131 Cristiano Ronaldo (Manchester U, Real Madrid)
130 Clarence Seedorf (Ajax, Real Madrid, Internazionale, AC Milan)
130 Paul Scholes (Manchester U)
128 Roberto Carlos (Internazionale, Real Madrid, Fenerbahce)
123 Zlatan Ibrahimovic (Ajax, Juventus, Internazionale, Barcelona, AC Milan, Paris Saint-Germain)
120 Carles Puyol (Barcelona)
120 Xabi Alonso (Real Sociedad, Liverpool, Real Madrid, Bayern Munich)

MOST WINS WITH DIFFERENT CLUBS
Clarence Seedorf (Ajax) 1995; (Real Madrid) 1998; (AC Milan) 2003, 2007.

MOST WINNERS MEDALS
6 Francisco Gento (Real Madrid) 1956, 1957, 1958, 1959, 1960, 1966.
5 Alfredo Di Stefano (Real Madrid) 1956, 1957, 1958, 1959, 1960.
5 Jose Maria Zarraga (Real Madrid) 1956, 1957, 1958, 1959, 1960.
5 Paolo Maldini (AC Milan) 1989, 1990, 1994, 2003, 2007.

CHAMPIONS LEAGUE BIGGEST WINS
HJK Helsinki 10, Bangor C 0 19.7.2011
Liverpool 8 Besiktas 0 6.11.2007
Real Madrid 8 Malmo 0 8.12.2015

MOST SUCCESSIVE CHAMPIONS LEAGUE APPEARANCES
Manchester U (England) 18: 1996–97 to 2013–14.
Real Madrid (Spain) 18: 1997–98 to 2015–16.

MOST SUCCESSIVE EUROPEAN CUP APPEARANCES
Real Madrid (Spain) 15: 1955–56 to 1969–70.

MOST SUCCESSIVE WINS IN THE CHAMPIONS LEAGUE
Barcelona (Spain) 11: 2002–03.

LONGEST UNBEATEN RUN IN THE CHAMPIONS LEAGUE
Manchester U (England) 25: 2007–08 to 2009 (Final).

MOST GOALS OVERALL
94 Cristiano Ronaldo (Manchester U, Real Madrid).
83 Lionel Messi (Barcelona).
71 Raul (Real Madrid, Schalke).
60 Ruud van Nistelrooy (PSV Eindhoven, Manchester U, Real Madrid).
58 Andriy Shevchenko (Dynamo Kyiv, AC Milan, Chelsea, Dynamo Kyiv).
51 Thierry Henry (Monaco, Arsenal, Barcelona).
50 Filippo Inzaghi (Juventus, AC Milan).

49 Alfredo Di Stefano (Real Madrid).
49 Zlatan Ibrahimovic (Ajax, Juventus, Internazionale, Barcelona, AC Milan, Paris Saint-Germain).
47 Eusebio (Benfica).
46 Karim Benzema (Lyon, Real Madrid).
44 Alessandro Del Piero (Juventus).
44 Didier Drogba (Marseille, Chelsea).

MOST GOALS IN CHAMPIONS LEAGUE MATCH
5 Lionel Messi, Barcelona v Bayer Leverkusen (25, 42, 49, 58, 84 mins) (7-1), 7.3.2012.
5 Luiz Adriano, Shaktar Donetsk v BATE (28, 36, 40, 44, 82 (0-7), 21.10.2014.

MOST GOALS IN ONE SEASON
17 Cristiano Ronaldo 2013–14
16 Cristiano Ronaldo 2015–16
14 Jose Altafini 1962–63
14 Ruud van Nistelrooy 2002–03
14 Lionel Messi 2011–12

MOST GOALS SCORED IN FINALS
7 Alfredo Di Stefano (Real Madrid), 1956 (1), 1957 (1 pen), 1958 (1), 1959 (1), 1960 (3).
7 Ferenc Puskas (Real Madrid), 1960 (4), 1962 (3).

HIGHEST SCORE IN A EUROPEAN CUP MATCH
European Cup
14 Feyenoord (Netherlands) 12, KR Reykjavik (Iceland) 2 *(First Round First Leg 1969–70)*
Champions League
11 Monaco 8, Deportivo La Coruna 3 5.11.2003

HIGHEST AGGREGATE IN A EUROPEAN CUP MATCH
Benfica (Portugal) 18, Dudelange (Luxembourg) 0
8-0 (h), 10-0 (a) *(Preliminary Round 1965–66)*

FASTEST GOALS SCORED IN CHAMPIONS LEAGUE
10.2 sec	Roy Makaay for Bayern Munich v Real Madrid, 7.3.2007.
11.0 sec	Jonas for Valencia v Bayer Leverkusen, 1.11.2011.
20.07 sec	Gilberto Silva for Arsenal at PSV Eindhoven, 25.9.2002.
20.12 sec	Alessandro Del Piero for Juventus at Manchester U, 1.10.1997.

YOUNGEST CHAMPIONS LEAGUE GOALSCORER
Peter Ofori-Quaye for Olympiacos v Rosenborg at 17 years 195 days in 1997–98.

FASTEST HAT-TRICK SCORED IN CHAMPIONS LEAGUE
Bafetimbi Gomis, 8 mins for Lyon in Dinamo Zagreb v Lyon (1-7) 7.12.2011

FIRST TEAM TO SCORE SEVEN GOALS
Paris Saint-Germain 7, Rosenborg 2 24.10.2000

MOST GOALS BY A GOALKEEPER
Hans-Jorg Butt (for three different clubs)
Hamburg 13.9.2000, Bayer Leverkusen 12.5.2002, Bayern Munich 8.12.2009 – all achieved against Juventus.

LANDMARK GOALS CHAMPIONS LEAGUE
1st Daniel Amokachi, Club Brugge v CSKA Moscow 17 minutes 25.11.1992
1,000th Dmitri Khokhlov, PSV Eindhoven v Benfica 41 minutes 9.12.1998
5,000th Luisao, Benfica v Hapoel Tel Aviv 21 minutes 14.9.2010

HIGHEST SCORING DRAW
Hamburg 4, Juventus 4 13.9.2000
Chelsea 4, Liverpool 4 14.4.2009
Bayer Leverkusen 4, Roma 4 20.10.2015

MOST CLEAN SHEETS
10: Arsenal 2005–06 (995 minutes with two goalkeepers Manuel Almunia 347 minutes and Jens Lehmann 648 minutes).

EUROPEAN CUP AND CHAMPIONS LEAGUE RECORDS – continued

CHAMPIONS LEAGUE ATTENDANCES AND GOALS FROM GROUP STAGES ONWARDS

Season	Attendances	Average	Goals	Games
1992–93	873,251	34,930	56	25
1993–94	1,202,289	44,529	71	27
1994–95	2,328,515	38,172	140	61
1995–96	1,874,316	30,726	159	61
1996–97	2,093,228	34,315	161	61
1997–98	2,868,271	33,744	239	85
1998–99	3,608,331	42,451	238	85
1999–2000	5,490,709	34,973	442	157
2000–01	5,773,486	36,774	449	157
2001–02	5,417,716	34,508	393	157
2002–03	6,461,112	41,154	431	157
2003–04	4,611,214	36,890	309	125
2004–05	4,946,820	39,575	331	125
2005–06	5,291,187	42,330	285	125
2006–07	5,591,463	44,732	309	125
2007–08	5,454,718	43,638	330	125
2008–09	5,003,754	40,030	329	125
2009–10	5,295,708	42,366	320	125
2010–11	5,474,654	43,797	355	125
2011–12	5,225,363	41,803	345	125
2012–13	5,773,366	46,187	368	125
2013–14	5,713,049	45,704	362	125
2014–15	5,207,592	42,685	361	125
2015–16	5,116,690	40,934	347	125

HIGHEST AVERAGE ATTENDANCE IN ONE EUROPEAN CUP SEASON

1959–60 50,545 from a total attendance of 2,780,000.

GREATEST COMEBACKS

Werder Bremen beat Anderlecht 5-3 after being three goals down in 33 minutes on 8.12.1993. They scored five goals in 23 second-half minutes.

Deportivo La Coruna beat Paris Saint-Germain 4-3 after being three goals down in 55 minutes on 7.3.2001. They scored four goals in 27 second-half minutes.

Liverpool after being three goals down to AC Milan in the first half on 25.5.2005 in the Champions League Final. They scored three goals in five second-half minutes and won the penalty shoot-out after extra time 3-2.

Liverpool three goals down to FC Basel in 29 minutes on 12.11.2002. They scored three second half goals in 24 minutes to draw 3-3.

MOST SUCCESSFUL MANAGER

Bob Paisley 3 wins, 1977, 1978, 1981 (Liverpool); Carlo Ancelotti 3 wins, 2002–03, 2006–07 (AC Milan), 2013–14 (Real Madrid).

REINSTATED WINNERS EXCLUDED FROM NEXT COMPETITION

1993 Marseille originally stripped of title. This was rescinded but they were not allowed to compete the following season.

EUROPEAN LANDMARKS 2015–16

JUNE 2015

12 Tomas Rosicky made his 100th international appearance for Czech Republic in the Euro 2016 Group A 2-1 defeat away to Iceland.

20 Lionel Messi hit another personal milestone when reaching 100 international caps for Argentina in the Copa America match against Jamaica. He became the fifth Argentinian to hit the mark in the 1-0 win.

SEPTEMBER 2015

22 Robert Lewandowski scored five goals in nine second-half minutes after coming on as a substitute for Bayern Munich against Wolfsburg in the Bundesliga. Introduced at half time with Bayern trailing 1-0, Lewandowski levelled six minutes after the restart and four minutes later had completed his hat-trick (the quickest in Bundesliga history). The victory sent Bayern to the top of the league.

29 Porto's Iker Casillas broke the record for Champions League appearances with his 152nd match in the 2-1 victory over Chelsea.

30 Cristiano Ronaldo scored the 500th goal of his career when he hit a 29th minute opener for Real Madrid at Malmo in Group A of the Champions League. His last-minute second in Real's 2-0 victory made it 323 for Real Madrid and equalled Raul's record. Raul's 323 goals came in 741 appearances whilst Ronaldo achieved the tally in an astonishing 308 appearances.

OCTOBER 2015

12 Cesc Fabregas made his 100th international appearance for Spain in the 1-0 Euro 2016 Group C victory in Ukraine. Unfortunately Cesc missed a 25th minute penalty.

10 Robin van Persie made his 100th international appearance for the Netherlands in their 2-1 victory over Kazakhstan in the Euro 2016 Qualifying Group A.

17 Cristiano Ronaldo became Real Madrid's all-time record goalscorer outright with the second goal in a 2-0 home win over Levante.

DECEMBER 2015

4 Zlatan Ibrahimovic became Paris Saint-Germain's all-time leading Ligue 1 goalscorer with his 86th and 87th goals in the 3-0 win over Nice. He replaced Mustapha Dahleb as top marksman.

8 Real Madrid equalled the Champions League highest win in their 8-0 demolition of Malmo in the final match of Group A. Manager Rafael Benitez was also manager of Liverpool when they set the record with a 8-0 victory of Besiktas in the 2007–08 season. In the same match Cristiano Ronaldo became the first player to score 11 goals in a single season in the Champions League Group Stages. His four-goal haul cemented him as the competition's all-time leading scorer with 88 goals.

21 FIFA president Sepp Blatter and UEFA president Michel Platini banned from all football for eight years by FIFA ethics committee over so-called 'disloyal payment' made by Blatter to Platini in 2011.

30 Lionel Messi scored on his 500th appearance for Barcelona against Real Betis at the Nou Camp. Barcelona won the game 4-0 to go top of La Liga.

FEBRUARY 2016

17 Lionel Messi scored his 300th La Liga goal in Barcelona's 3-1 away win at Sport Gijon. The match also saw the Catalans' 10,000th goal.

APRIL 2016

17 Lionel Messi scored his 500th career goal in Barcelona's 1-2 defeat to Valencia at the Nou Camp.

MAY 2016

17 Sevilla beat Liverpool 3-1 in the Europa League Final in Basel to record their 3rd successive Europa League success and their 5th Europa League title in 10 years.

JUNE 2016

13 David Silva made his 100th international appearance for Spain in their 1-0 Euro 2016 Group D victory over the Czech Republic in Toulouse.

TOP TEN PREMIER LEAGUE AVERAGE ATTENDANCES 2015–16

1	Manchester U	75,279
2	Arsenal	59,944
3	Manchester C	54,041
4	Newcastle U	49,754
5	Liverpool	43,910
6	Sunderland	43,071
7	Chelsea	41,500
8	Everton	38,124
9	Tottenham H	35,776
10	West Ham U	34,910

TOP TEN FOOTBALL LEAGUE AVERAGE ATTENDANCES 2015–16

1	Derby Co	29,663
2	Brighton & HA	25,583
3	Middlesbrough	24,627
4	Sheffield W	22,641
5	Leeds U	22,446
6	Wolverhampton W	20,157
7	Sheffield U	19,803
8	Nottingham F	19,676
9	Ipswich T	18,989
10	Bradford C	18,090

TOP TEN AVERAGE ATTENDANCES

1	Manchester U	2006–07	75,826
2	Manchester U	2007–08	75,691
3	Manchester U	2012–13	75,530
4	Manchester U	2011–12	75,387
5	Manchester U	2014–15	75,335
6	Manchester U	2008–09	75,308
7	Manchester U	2015–16	75,279
8	Manchester U	2013–14	75,207
9	Manchester U	2010–11	75,109
10	Manchester U	2009–10	74,863

TOP TEN AVERAGE WORLD CUP FINAL CROWDS

1	In USA	1994	68,991
2	In Brazil	2014	52,621
3	In Germany	2006	52,491
4	In Mexico	1970	50,124
5	In South Africa	2010	49,669
6	In West Germany	1974	49,098
7	In England	1966	48,847
8	In Italy	1990	48,388
9	In Brazil	1950	47,511
10	In Mexico	1986	46,039

TOP TEN ALL-TIME ENGLAND CAPS

1	Peter Shilton	125
2	David Beckham	115
	Wayne Rooney	115
4	Steven Gerrard	114
5	Bobby Moore	108
6	Ashley Cole	107
7	Bobby Charlton	106
	Frank Lampard	106
9	Billy Wright	105
10	Bryan Robson	90

TOP TEN ALL-TIME ENGLAND GOALSCORERS

1	Wayne Rooney	53
2	Bobby Charlton	49
3	Gary Lineker	48
4	Jimmy Greaves	44
5	Michael Owen	40
	Tom Finney	30
6	Nat Lofthouse	30
	Alan Shearer	30
9	Vivian Woodward	29
	Frank Lampard	29

GOALKEEPING RECORDS
(without conceding a goal)

FA PREMIER LEAGUE
Edwin van der Sar (Manchester U) in 1,311 minutes during the 2008–09 season.

FOOTBALL LEAGUE
Steve Death (Reading) 1,103 minutes from 24 March to 18 August 1979.

SCOTTISH PREMIER LEAGUE
Fraser Forster (Celtic) in 1,215 minutes from 6 December 2013 to 25 February 2014.

MOST CLEAN SHEETS IN A SEASON
Petr Cech (Chelsea) 24 2004–05

MOST CLEAN SHEETS OVERALL IN PREMIER LEAGUE
Petr Cech (Chelsea and Arsenal) 178 games.

MOST GOALS FOR IN A SEASON

FA PREMIER LEAGUE

		Goals	Games
2009–10	Chelsea	103	38

FOOTBALL LEAGUE
Division 4

1960–61	Peterborough U	134	46

SCOTTISH PREMIER LEAGUE

2003–04	Celtic	105	38

SCOTTISH LEAGUE
Division 2

1937–38	Raith R	142	34

MOST GOALS AGAINST IN A SEASON

FA PREMIER LEAGUE

		Goals	Games
1993–94	Swindon T	100	42

FOOTBALL LEAGUE
Division 2

1898–99	Darwen	141	34

SCOTTISH PREMIER LEAGUE

1999–2000	Aberdeen	83	36

SCOTTISH LEAGUE
Division 2

1931–32	Edinburgh C	146	38

MOST LEAGUE GOALS IN A SEASON

FA PREMIER LEAGUE

		Goals	Games
1993–94	Andy Cole (Newcastle U)	34	40
1994–95	Alan Shearer (Blackburn R)	34	42

FOOTBALL LEAGUE
Division 1

1927–28	Dixie Dean (Everton)	60	39

Division 2

1926–27	George Camsell (Middlesbrough)	59	37

Division 3(S)

1936–37	Joe Payne (Luton T)	55	39

Division 3(N)

1936–37	Ted Harston (Mansfield T)	55	41

Division 3

1959–60	Derek Reeves (Southampton)	39	46

Division 4

1960–61	Terry Bly (Peterborough U)	52	46

FA CUP

1887–88	Jimmy Ross (Preston NE)	20	8

LEAGUE CUP

1986–87	Clive Allen (Tottenham H)	12	9

SCOTTISH PREMIER LEAGUE

2000–01	Henrik Larsson (Celtic)	35	37

SCOTTISH LEAGUE
Division 1

1931–32	William McFadyen (Motherwell)	52	34

Division 2

1927–28	Jim Smith (Ayr U)	66	38

MOST FA CUP FINAL GOALS

Ian Rush (Liverpool) 5: 1986(2), 1989(2), 1992(1)

SCORED IN EVERY PREMIERSHIP GAME

Arsenal 2001–02: 38 matches

FEWEST GOALS FOR IN A SEASON

FA PREMIER LEAGUE

		Goals	Games
2007–08	Derby Co	20	38

FOOTBALL LEAGUE
Division 2

1899–1900	Loughborough T	18	34

SCOTTISH PREMIER LEAGUE

2010–11	St Johnstone	23	38

SCOTTISH LEAGUE
New Division 1

1980–81	Stirling Alb	18	39

FEWEST GOALS AGAINST IN A SEASON

FA PREMIER LEAGUE

		Goals	Games
2004–05	Chelsea	15	38

FOOTBALL LEAGUE
Division 1

1978–79	Liverpool	16	42

SCOTTISH PREMIER LEAGUE

2001–02	Celtic	18	38

SCOTTISH LEAGUE
Division 1

1913–14	Celtic	14	38

MOST LEAGUE GOALS IN A CAREER

FOOTBALL LEAGUE

Arthur Rowley	Goals	Games	Season
WBA	4	24	1946–48
Fulham	27	56	1948–50
Leicester C	251	303	1950–58
Shrewsbury T	152	236	1958–65
	434	619	

SCOTTISH LEAGUE

Jimmy McGrory			
Celtic	1	3	1922–23
Clydebank	13	30	1923–24
Celtic	396	375	1924–38
	410	408	

MOST HAT-TRICKS

Career
37: Dixie Dean (Tranmere R, Everton, Notts Co, England)

Division 1 (one season post-war)
6: Jimmy Greaves (Chelsea), 1960–61

Three for one team in one match
West, Spouncer, Hooper, Nottingham F v Leicester Fosse, Division 1, 21 April 1909
Loasby, Smith, Wells, Northampton T v Walsall, Division 3S, 5 Nov 1927
Bowater, Hoyland, Readman, Mansfield T v Rotherham U, Division 3N, 27 Dec 1932
Barnes, Ambler, Davies, Wrexham v Hartlepools U, Division 4, 3 March 1962
Adcock, Stewart, White, Manchester C v Huddersfield T, Division 2, 7 Nov 1987

MOST CUP GOALS IN A CAREER

FA CUP (pre-Second World War)
Henry Cursham 48 (Notts Co)

FA CUP (post-war)
Ian Rush 43 (Chester, Liverpool)

LEAGUE CUP
Geoff Hurst 49 (West Ham U, Stoke C)
Ian Rush 49 (Chester, Liverpool, Newcastle U)

GOALS PER GAME (Football League to 1991–92)

Goals per game	Division 1		Division 2		Division 3		Division 4		Division 3(S)		Division 3(N)	
	Games	Goals	Games	Goals	Games	Goals	Games	Goals	Games	Goals	Games	Goals
0	2465	0	2665	0	1446	0	1438	0	997	0	803	0
1	5606	5606	5836	5836	3225	3225	3106	3106	2073	2073	1914	1914
2	8275	16550	8609	17218	4569	9138	4441	8882	3314	6628	2939	5878
3	7731	23193	7842	23526	3784	11352	4041	12123	2996	8988	2922	8766
4	6229	24920	5897	23588	2837	11348	2784	11136	2445	9780	2410	9640
5	3752	18755	3634	18170	1566	7830	1506	7530	1554	7770	1599	7995
6	2137	12822	2007	12042	769	4614	786	4716	870	5220	930	5580
7	1092	7644	1001	7007	357	2499	336	2352	451	3157	461	3227
8	542	4336	376	3008	135	1080	143	1144	209	1672	221	1768
9	197	1773	164	1476	64	576	35	315	76	684	102	918
10	83	830	68	680	13	130	8	80	33	330	45	450
11	37	407	19	209	2	22	7	77	15	165	15	165
12	12	144	17	204	1	12	0	0	7	84	8	96
13	4	52	4	52	0	0	0	0	2	26	4	52
14	2	28	1	14	0	0	0	0	0	0	0	0
17	0	0	0	0	0	0	0	0	0	0	1	17
	38164	117061	38140	113030	18768	51826	18631	51461	15042	46577	14374	46466

Extensive research by statisticians has unearthed seven results from the early years of the Football League which differ from the original scores. These are 26 January 1889 Wolverhampton W 5 Everton 0 (not 4-0), 16 March 1889 Notts Co 3 Derby Co 5 (not 2-5), 4 January 1896 Arsenal 5 Loughborough 0 (not 6-0), 28 November 1896 Leicester Fosse 4 Walsall 2 (not 4-1), 21 April 1900 Burslem Port Vale 2 Lincoln C 1 (not 2-0), 25 December 1902 Glossop NE 3 Stockport Co 0 (not 3-1), 26 April 1913 Hull C 2 Leicester C 0 (not 2-1).

GOALS PER GAME (from 1992–93)

Goals per game	Premier		Championship/Div 1		League One/Div 2		League Two/Div 3	
	Games	Goals	Games	Goals	Games	Goals	Games	Goals
0	801	0	1097	0	1025	0	1057	0
1	1723	1723	2470	2470	2484	2484	2534	2534
2	2263	4526	3362	6724	3364	6728	3303	6606
3	1971	5913	2852	8556	2897	8691	2846	8538
4	1376	5504	1830	7320	1854	7416	1725	6900
5	681	3405	985	4925	982	4910	906	4530
6	333	1998	443	2658	404	2424	379	2274
7	135	945	148	1036	166	1162	153	1071
8	63	504	46	368	49	392	48	384
9	14	126	8	72	18	162	19	171
10	5	50	5	50	5	50	5	50
11	1	11	2	22	0	0	3	33
	9366	24705	13248	34201	13248	34419	12978	33091

New Overall Totals (since 1992)		Totals (up to 1991–92)		Complete Overall Totals (since 1888–89)	
Games	48810	Games	143119	Games	191929
Goals	126416	Goals	426421	Goals	552837

A CENTURY OF LEAGUE AND CUP GOALS IN CONSECUTIVE SEASONS

	League	Cup	Season
George Camsell			
Middlesbrough	59	5	1926–27
(101 goals)	33	4	1927–28

(Camsell's cup goals were all scored in the FA Cup.)

	League	Cup	Season
Steve Bull			
Wolverhampton W	34	18	1987–88
(102 goals)	37	13	1988–89

(Bull had 12 in the Sherpa Van Trophy, 3 Littlewoods Cup, 3 FA Cup in 1987–88; 11 Sherpa Van Trophy, 2 Littlewoods Cup in 1988–89.)

PENALTIES

Most in a season (individual)

Division 1	Goals	Season
Francis Lee (Manchester C)	13	1971–72

Also scored 1 in League Cup and 2 in FA Cup.

Most awarded in one game

Five   Crystal Palace (1 scored, 3 missed)
v Brighton & HA (1 scored), Div 2   1988–89

Most saved in a season

Division 1		
Paul Cooper (Ipswich T)	8 (of 10)	1979–80

MOST GOALS IN A GAME

FA PREMIER LEAGUE
4 Mar 1995   Andy Cole (Manchester U)
      5 goals v Ipswich T
19 Sept 1999   Alan Shearer (Newcastle U)
      5 goals v Sheffield W
22 Nov 2009   Jermain Defoe (Tottenham H)
      5 goals v Wigan Ath
27 Nov 2010   Dimitar Berbatov (Manchester U)
      5 goals v Blackburn R
3 Oct 2015   Sergio Aguero (Manchester C)
      5 goals v Newcastle U

FOOTBALL LEAGUE
Division 1
14 Dec 1935   Ted Drake (Arsenal) 7 goals v Aston Villa
Division 2
5 Feb 1955   Tommy Briggs (Blackburn R)
      7 goals v Bristol R
23 Feb 1957   Neville Coleman (Stoke C) 7 goals v
      Lincoln C
Division 3(S)
13 Apr 1936   Joe Payne (Luton T) 10 goals v Bristol R
Division 3(N)
26 Dec 1935   Bunny Bell (Tranmere R)
      9 goals v Oldham Ath
Division 3
24 Apr 1965   Barrie Thomas (Scunthorpe U)
      5 goals v Luton T
20 Nov 1965   Keith East (Swindon T)
      5 goals v Mansfield T
16 Sept 1969   Steve Earle (Fulham) 5 goals v Halifax T
2 Oct 1971   Alf Wood (Shrewsbury T)
      5 goals v Blackburn R
10 Sept 1983   Tony Caldwell (Bolton W)
      5 goals v Walsall
4 May 1987   Andy Jones (Port Vale)
      5 goals v Newport Co
3 Apr 1990   Steve Wilkinson (Mansfield T)
      5 goals v Birmingham C
5 Sept 1998   Giuliano Grazioli (Peterborough U)
      5 goals v Barnet
6 Apr 2002   Lee Jones (Wrexham)
      5 goals v Cambridge U
Division 4
26 Dec 1962   Bert Lister (Oldham Ath)
      6 goals v Southport

FA CUP
20 Nov 1971   Ted MacDougall (Bournemouth)
      9 goals v Margate (*1st Round*)

LEAGUE CUP
25 Oct 1989   Frankie Bunn (Oldham Ath)
      6 goals v Scarborough

SCOTTISH LEAGUE
Premier Division
17 Nov 1984   Paul Sturrock (Dundee U)
      5 goals v Morton
Premier League
23 Aug 1996   Marco Negri (Rangers) 5 goals v
      Dundee U
4 Nov 2000   Kenny Miller (Rangers) 5 goals v
      St Mirren
25 Sept 2004   Kris Boyd (Kilmarnock) 5 goals v
      Dundee U
30 Dec 2009   Kris Boyd (Rangers) 5 goals v
      Dundee U
13 May 2012   Gary Hooper (Celtic) 5 goals v Hearts
Division 1
14 Sept 1928   Jimmy McGrory (Celtic)
      8 goals v Dunfermline Ath
Division 2
1 Oct 1927   Owen McNally (Arthurlie)
      8 goals v Armadale
2 Jan 1930   Jim Dyet (King's Park)
      8 goals v Forfar Ath
18 Apr 1936   John Calder (Morton)
      8 goals v Raith R
20 Aug 1937   Norman Hayward (Raith R)
      8 goals v Brechin C

SCOTTISH CUP
12 Sept 1885   John Petrie (Arbroath)
      13 goals v Bon Accord (*1st Round*)

LONGEST SEQUENCE OF CONSECUTIVE DEFEATS

FOOTBALL LEAGUE	*Team*	*Games*
Division 2		
1898–99	Darwen	18

LONGEST UNBEATEN SEQUENCE

FA PREMIER LEAGUE	*Team*	*Games*
May 2003–Oct 2004	Arsenal	49
FOOTBALL LEAGUE – League 1		
Jan 2011–Nov 2011	Huddersfield T	43

LONGEST UNBEATEN CUP SEQUENCE

Liverpool	25 rounds	League/Milk Cup	1980–84

LONGEST UNBEATEN SEQUENCE IN A SEASON

FA PREMIER LEAGUE	*Team*	*Games*
2003–04	Arsenal	38
FOOTBALL LEAGUE – Division 1		
1920–21	Burnley	30
SCOTTISH PREMIER LEAGUE		
2003–04	Celtic	32

LONGEST UNBEATEN START TO A SEASON

FA PREMIER LEAGUE	*Team*	*Games*
2003–04	Arsenal	38
FOOTBALL LEAGUE – Division 1		
1973–74	Leeds U	29
1987–88	Liverpool	29

LONGEST SEQUENCE WITHOUT A WIN IN A SEASON

FA PREMIER LEAGUE	*Team*	*Games*
2007–08	Derby Co	32
FOOTBALL LEAGUE	*Team*	*Games*
Division 2		
1983–84	Cambridge U	31

LONGEST SEQUENCE WITHOUT A WIN FROM SEASON'S START

FOOTBALL LEAGUE	*Team*	*Games*
Division 4		
1970–71	Newport Co	25

LONGEST SEQUENCE OF CONSECUTIVE SCORING (individual)

FA PREMIER LEAGUE		
Jamie Vardy (Leicester C) 13 in 11 games		2015–16
FOOTBALL LEAGUE RECORD		
Tom Phillipson (Wolverhampton W)	23 in 13 games	1926–27

LONGEST WINNING SEQUENCE

FA PREMIER LEAGUE	*Team*	*Games*
2001–02 and 2002–03	Arsenal	14
FOOTBALL LEAGUE – Division 2		
1904–05	Manchester U	14
1905–06	Bristol C	14
1950–51	Preston NE	14
FROM SEASON'S START – Division 3		
1985–86	Reading	13
SCOTTISH PREMIER LEAGUE		
2003–04	Celtic	25

HIGHEST WINS

Highest win in a First-Class Match
(*Scottish Cup 1st Round*)
Arbroath   36 Bon Accord   0   12 Sept 1885

Highest win in an International Match
England   13 Ireland   0   18 Feb 1882

Highest win in an FA Cup Match
Preston NE   26 Hyde U   0   15 Oct 1887
(*1st Round*)

Highest win in a League Cup Match
West Ham U   10 Bury   0   25 Oct 1983
(*2nd Round, 2nd Leg*)
Liverpool   10 Fulham   0   23 Sept 1986
(*2nd Round, 1st Leg*)

Highest win in an FA Premier League Match
Manchester U   9 Ipswich T   0   4 Mar 1995
Tottenham H   9 Wigan Ath   1   22 Nov 2009

Highest win in a Football League Match
Division 2 – highest home win
Newcastle U   13 Newport Co   0   5 Oct 1946
Division 3(N) – highest home win
Stockport Co   13 Halifax T   0   6 Jan 1934
Division 2 – highest away win
Burslem Port Vale 0 Sheffield U   10   10 Dec 1892

Highest wins in a Scottish League Match
Scottish Premier League – highest home win
Celtic   9 Aberdeen   0   6 Nov 2010
Scottish Division 2 – highest home win
Airdrieonians   15 Dundee Wanderers 1   1 Dec 1894
Scottish Premier League – highest away win
Hamilton A   0 Celtic   8   5 Nov 1988

MOST HOME WINS IN A SEASON

Brentford won all 21 games in Division 3(S), 1929–30

RECORD AWAY WINS IN A SEASON

Doncaster R won 18 of 21 games in Division 3(N), 1946–47

CONSECUTIVE AWAY WINS

FA PREMIER LEAGUE
Arsenal 12 games 2012–13, 2013–14.

FOOTBALL LEAGUE
Division 1
Tottenham H 10 games (1959–60 (2), 1960–61 (8))

HIGHEST AGGREGATE SCORES

FA PREMIER LEAGUE
Portsmouth   7 Reading   4   29 Sept 2007

Highest Aggregate Score England
Division 3(N)
Tranmere R   13 Oldham Ath   4   26 Dec 1935

Highest Aggregate Score Scotland
Division 2
Airdrieonians   15 Dundee Wanderers 1   1 Dec 1894

MOST WINS IN A SEASON

FA PREMIER LEAGUE		Wins	Games
2004–05	Chelsea	29	38
2005–06	Chelsea	29	38
FOOTBALL LEAGUE			
Division 3(N)			
1946–47	Doncaster R	33	42
SCOTTISH PREMIER LEAGUE			
2001–02	Celtic	33	38
SCOTTISH LEAGUE			
Division 1			
1920–21	Rangers	35	42

FEWEST WINS IN A SEASON

FA PREMIER LEAGUE		Wins	Games
2007–08	Derby Co	1	38
FOOTBALL LEAGUE			
Division 2			
1899–1900	Loughborough T	1	34
SCOTTISH PREMIER LEAGUE			
1998–99	Dunfermline Ath	4	36
SCOTTISH LEAGUE			
Division 1			
1891–92	Vale of Leven	0	22

UNDEFEATED AT HOME OVERALL

Liverpool 85 games (63 League, 9 League Cup, 7 European, 6 FA Cup), Jan 1978–Jan 1981

UNDEFEATED AT HOME LEAGUE

Chelsea 86 games, March 2004–October 2008

UNDEFEATED AWAY

Arsenal 19 games, FA Premier League 2001–02 and 2003–04 (only Preston NE with 11 in 1888–89 had previously remained unbeaten away) in the top flight.

MOST POINTS IN A SEASON
(three points for a win)

FA PREMIER LEAGUE		Points	Games
2004–05	Chelsea	95	38
FOOTBALL LEAGUE			
Championship			
2005–06	Reading	106	46
SCOTTISH PREMIER LEAGUE			
2001–02	Celtic	103	38
SCOTTISH LEAGUE			
League One			
2013–14	Rangers	102	36

MOST POINTS IN A SEASON
(under old system of two points for a win)

FOOTBALL LEAGUE		Points	Games
Division 4			
1975–76	Lincoln C	74	46
SCOTTISH LEAGUE			
Division 1			
1920–21	Rangers	76	42

FEWEST POINTS IN A SEASON

FA PREMIER LEAGUE		Points	Games
2007–08	Derby Co	11	38
FOOTBALL LEAGUE			
Division 2			
1904–05	Doncaster R	8	34
1899–1900	Loughborough T	8	34
SCOTTISH PREMIER LEAGUE			
2007–08	Gretna	13	38
SCOTTISH LEAGUE			
Division 1			
1954–55	Stirling Alb	6	30

NO DEFEATS IN A SEASON

FA PREMIER LEAGUE
2003–04	Arsenal	won 26, drew 12

FOOTBALL LEAGUE
Division 1
1888–89	Preston NE	won 18, drew 4

Division 2
1893–94	Liverpool	won 22, drew 6

SCOTTISH LEAGUE
Division 1
1898–99	Rangers	won 18

League One
2013–14	Rangers	won 33, drew 3

ONE DEFEAT IN A SEASON

FA PREMIER LEAGUE		*Defeats*	*Games*
2004–05	Chelsea	1	38

FOOTBALL LEAGUE
Division 1
1990–91	Arsenal	1	38

SCOTTISH PREMIER LEAGUE			
2001–02	Celtic	1	38
2013–14	Celtic	1	38

SCOTTISH LEAGUE
Division 1
1920–21	Rangers	1	42

Division 2
1956–57	Clyde	1	36
1962–63	Morton	1	36
1967–68	St Mirren	1	36

New Division 1
2011–12	Ross Co	1	36

New Division 2
1975–76	Raith R	1	26

MOST DEFEATS IN A SEASON

FA PREMIER LEAGUE		*Defeats*	*Games*
1994–95	Ipswich T	29	42
2005–06	Sunderland	29	38
2007–08	Derby Co	29	38

FOOTBALL LEAGUE
Division 3
1997–98	Doncaster R	34	46

SCOTTISH PREMIER LEAGUE			
2005–06	Livingston	28	38

SCOTTISH LEAGUE
New Division 1
1992–93	Cowdenbeath	34	44

MOST DRAWN GAMES IN A SEASON

FA PREMIER LEAGUE		*Draws*	*Games*
1993–94	Manchester C	18	42
1993–94	Sheffield U	18	42
1994–95	Southampton	18	42

FOOTBALL LEAGUE
Division 1
1978–79	Norwich C	23	42

Division 3
1997–98	Cardiff C	23	46
1997–98	Hartlepool U	23	46

Division 4
1986–87	Exeter C	23	46

SCOTTISH PREMIER LEAGUE			
1998–99	Dunfermline Ath	16	38

SCOTTISH LEAGUE
Premier Division
1993–94	Aberdeen	21	44

New Division 1
1986–87	East Fife	21	44

SENDINGS-OFF

SEASON
451 (League alone)	2003–04

(Before rescinded cards taken into account)

DAY
19 (League)	13 Dec 2003

FA CUP FINAL
Kevin Moran, Manchester U v Everton	1985
Jose Antonio Reyes, Arsenal v Manchester U	2005
Chris Smalling, Manchester U v Crystal Palace	2016

QUICKEST
FA Premier League
Andreas Johansson, Wigan Ath v Arsenal 7 May 2006 and Keith Gillespie, Sheffield U v Reading 20 January 2007 both in 10 seconds
Football League
Walter Boyd, Swansea C v Darlington, Div 3 as substitute in zero seconds	23 Nov 1999

MOST IN ONE GAME
Five: Chesterfield (2) v Plymouth Arg (3)	22 Feb 1997
Five: Wigan Ath (1) v Bristol R (4)	2 Dec 1997
Five: Exeter C (3) v Cambridge U (2)	23 Nov 2002
Five: Bradford C (3) v Crawley T (2)*	27 Mar 2012

*All five sent off after final whistle for fighting

MOST IN ONE TEAM
Wigan Ath (1) v Bristol R (4)	2 Dec 1997
Hereford U (4) v Northampton T (0)	6 Sept 1992

MOST SUCCESSFUL MANAGERS

Sir Alex Ferguson CBE
Manchester U
1986–2013, 25 major trophies:
13 Premier League, 5 FA Cup, 4 League Cup, 2 Champions League, 1 Cup-Winners' Cup.

Aberdeen
1976–86, 9 major trophies:
3 League, 4 Scottish Cup, 1 League Cup, 1 Cup-Winners' Cup.

Bob Paisley – Liverpool
1974–83, 13 major trophies:
6 League, 3 European Cup, 3 League Cup, 1 UEFA Cup.

Bill Struth – Rangers
1920–54, 30 major trophies:
18 League, 10 Scottish Cup, 2 League Cup

LEAGUE CHAMPIONSHIP HAT-TRICKS

Huddersfield T	1923–24 to 1925–26
Arsenal	1932–33 to 1934–35
Liverpool	1981–82 to 1983–84
Manchester U	1998–99 to 2000–01
Manchester U	2006–07 to 2008–09

MOST FA CUP MEDALS

Ashley Cole 7 (Arsenal 2002, 2003, 2005, Chelsea 2007, 2009, 2010, 2012)

MOST LEAGUE MEDALS

Ryan Giggs (Manchester U) 13: 1993, 1994, 1996, 1997, 1999, 2000, 2001, 2003, 2007, 2008, 2009, 2011 and 2013.

MOST SENIOR MATCHES

1,390 Peter Shilton (1,005 League, 86 FA Cup, 102 League Cup, 125 Internationals, 13 Under-23, 4 Football League XI, 20 European Cup, 7 Texaco Cup, 5 Simod Cup, 4 European Super Cup, 4 UEFA Cup, 3 Screen Sport Super Cup, 3 Zenith Data Systems Cup, 2 Autoglass Trophy, 2 Charity Shield, 2 Full Members Cup, 1 Anglo-Italian Cup, 1 Football League play-offs, 1 World Club Championship)

MOST LEAGUE APPEARANCES
(750+ matches)

1,005 Peter Shilton (286 Leicester C, 110 Stoke C, 202 Nottingham F, 188 Southampton, 175 Derby Co, 34 Plymouth Arg, 1 Bolton W, 9 Leyton Orient) 1966–97

931 Tony Ford (355 Grimsby T, 9 Sunderland (loan), 112 Stoke C, 114 WBA, 68 Grimsby T, 5 Bradford C (loan), 76 Scunthorpe U, 103 Mansfield T, 89 Rochdale) 1975–2002

909 Graeme Armstrong (204 Stirling A, 83 Berwick R, 353 Meadowbank Thistle, 268 Stenhousemuir, 1 Alloa Ath) 1975–2001

863 Tommy Hutchison (165 Blackpool, 314 Coventry C, 46 Manchester C, 92 Burnley, 178 Swansea C, 68 Alloa Ath) 1965–91

833 Graham Alexander (159 Scunthorpe U, 150 Luton T, 370 Preston NE, 154 Burnley) 1990–2012

824 Terry Paine (713 Southampton, 111 Hereford U) 1957–77

790 Neil Redfearn (35 Bolton W, 10 Lincoln C (loan), 90 Lincoln C, 46 Doncaster R, 57 Crystal Palace, 24 Watford, 62 Oldham Ath, 292 Barnsley, 30 Charlton Ath, 17 Bradford C, 22 Wigan Ath, 42 Halifax T, 54 Boston U, 9 Rochdale) 1982–2004

788 David James (89 Watford, 214 Liverpool, 67 Aston Villa, 91 West Ham U, 93 Manchester C, 134 Portsmouth, 81 Bristol C, 19 Bournemouth) 1988–2013

782 Robbie James (484 Swansea C, 48 Stoke C, 87 QPR, 23 Leicester C, 89 Bradford C, 51 Cardiff C) 1973–94

777 Alan Oakes (565 Manchester C, 211 Chester C, 1 Port Vale) 1959–84

774 Dave Beasant (340 Wimbledon, 20 Newcastle U, 133 Chelsea, 6 Grimsby T (loan), 4 Wolverhampton W (loan), 88 Southampton, 139 Nottingham F, 27 Portsmouth, 1 Tottenham H (loan), 16 Brighton & HA) 1979–2003

771 John Burridge (27 Workington, 134 Blackpool, 65 Aston Villa, 6 Southend U (loan), 88 Crystal Palace, 39 QPR, 74 Wolverhampton W, 6 Derby Co (loan), 109 Sheffield U, 62 Southampton, 67 Newcastle U, 65 Hibernian, 3 Scarborough, 4 Lincoln C, 3 Aberdeen, 3 Dumbarton, 3 Falkirk, 4 Manchester C, 3 Darlington, 6 Queen of the S) 1968–96

770 John Trollope (all for Swindon T) 1960–80†

764 Jimmy Dickinson (all for Portsmouth) 1946–65

763 Stuart McCall (395 Bradford C, 103 Everton, 194 Rangers, 71 Sheffield U) 1982–2004

761 Roy Sproson (all for Port Vale) 1950–72

760 Mick Tait (64 Oxford U, 106 Carlisle U, 33 Hull C, 240 Portsmouth, 99 Reading, 79 Darlington, 139 Hartlepool U) 1975–97

758 Ray Clemence (48 Scunthorpe U, 470 Liverpool, 240 Tottenham H) 1966–87

758 Billy Bonds (95 Charlton Ath, 663 West Ham U) 1964–88

757 Pat Jennings (48 Watford, 472 Tottenham H, 237 Arsenal) 1963–86

757 Frank Worthington (171 Huddersfield T, 210 Leicester C, 84 Bolton W, 75 Birmingham C, 32 Leeds U, 19 Sunderland, 34 Southampton, 31 Brighton & HA, 59 Tranmere R, 23 Preston NE, 19 Stockport Co) 1966–88

755 Jamie Cureton (98 Norwich C, 5 Bournemouth (loan), 174 Bristol R, 108 Reading, 43 QPR, 30 Swindon T, 52 Colchester U, 8 Barnsley (loan), 12 Shrewsbury (loan), 88 Exeter C, 19 Leyton Orient, 35 Cheltenham T, 83 Dagenham & R) 1992–2016

752 Wayne Allison (84 Halifax T, 7 Watford, 195 Bristol C, 101 Swindon T, 74 Huddersfield T, 103 Tranmere R, 73 Sheffield U, 115 Chesterfield) 1987–2008

† record for one club

CONSECUTIVE

401 Harold Bell (401 Tranmere R; 459 in all games) 1946–55

YOUNGEST PLAYERS

FA Premier League appearance
Matthew Briggs, 16 years 65 days, Fulham v Middlesbrough, 13.5.2007

FA Premier League scorer
James Vaughan, 16 years 271 days, Everton v Crystal Palace 10.4.2005

Football League appearance
Reuben Noble-Lazarus 15 years 45 days, Barnsley v Ipswich T, FL Championship 30.9.2008

Football League scorer
Ronnie Dix, 15 years 180 days, Bristol Rovers v Norwich C, Division 3S, 3.3.1928

Division 1 appearance
Derek Forster, 15 years 185 days, Sunderland v Leicester C, 22.8.1964

Division 1 scorer
Jason Dozzell, 16 years 57 days as substitute Ipswich T v Coventry C, 4.2.1984

Division 1 hat-tricks
Alan Shearer, 17 years 240 days, Southampton v Arsenal, 9.4.88
Jimmy Greaves, 17 years 308 days, Chelsea v Portsmouth, 25.12.1957

FA Cup appearance (any round)
Andy Awford, 15 years 88 days as substitute Worcester City v Boreham Wood, 3rd Qual. rd, 10.10.1987

FA Cup appearance (competition rounds)
Brendan Galloway, 15 years 240 days, Milton Keynes D v Nantwich T, 12.11.2011

FA Cup Final appearance
Curtis Weston, 17 years 119 days, Millwall v Manchester U, 22.5.2004

FA Cup Final scorer
Norman Whiteside, 18 years 18 days, Manchester United v Brighton & HA, 1983

FA Cup Final captain
David Nish, 21 years 212 days, Leicester C v Manchester C, 1969

League Cup appearance
Chris Coward, 16 years 30 days, Stockport Co v Sheffield W, 2005

League Cup Final scorer
Norman Whiteside, 17 years 324 days, Manchester U v Liverpool, 1983

League Cup Final captain
Barry Venison, 20 years 7 months 8 days, Sunderland v Norwich C, 1985

Scottish Premier League appearance
Scott Robinson, 16 years 45 days, Hearts v Inverness CT, 26.4.2008

Scottish Football League appearance
Jordan Allan, 14 years 189 days, Airdrie U v Livingston, 26.4.2013

Scottish Premier League scorer
Fraser Fyvie, 16 years 306 days, Aberdeen v Hearts, 27.1.2010

OLDEST PLAYERS

FA Premier League appearance
John Burridge, 43 years 162 days, Manchester C v QPR, 14.5.1995

Football League appearance
Neil McBain, 52 years 4 months, New Brighton v Hartlepools U, Div 3N, 15.3.47 (McBain was New Brighton's manager and had to play in an emergency)

Division 1 appearance
Stanley Matthews, 50 years 5 days, Stoke C v Fulham, 6.2.65

INTERNATIONAL RECORDS

MOST GOALS IN AN INTERNATIONAL

Record/World Cup	Archie Thompson (Australia) 13 goals v American Samoa	11.4.2001
England	Howard Vaughton (Aston Villa) 5 goals v Ireland, at Belfast	18.2.1882
	Steve Bloomer (Derby Co) 5 goals v Wales, at Cardiff	16.3.1896
	Willie Hall (Tottenham H) 5 goals v Ireland, at Old Trafford	16.11.1938
	Malcolm Macdonald (Newcastle U) 5 goals v Cyprus, at Wembley	16.4.1975
Northern Ireland	Joe Bambrick (Linfield) 6 goals v Wales, at Belfast	1.2.1930
Wales	John Price (Wrexham) 4 goals v Ireland, at Wrexham	25.2.1882
	Mel Charles (Cardiff C) 4 goals v Ireland, at Cardiff	11.4.1962
	Ian Edwards (Chester) 4 goals v Malta, at Wrexham	25.10.1978
Scotland	Alexander Higgins (Kilmarnock) 4 goals v Ireland, at Hampden Park	14.3.1885
	Charles Heggie (Rangers) 4 goals v Ireland, at Belfast	20.3.1886
	William Dickson (Dundee Strathmore) 4 goals v Ireland, at Belfast	24.3.1888
	William Paul (Partick Thistle) 4 goals v Wales, at Paisley	22.3.1890
	Jake Madden (Celtic) 4 goals v Wales, at Wrexham	18.3.1893
	Duke McMahon (Celtic) 4 goals v Ireland, at Celtic Park	23.2.1901
	Bob Hamilton (Rangers) 4 goals v Ireland, at Celtic Park	23.2.1901
	Jimmy Quinn (Celtic) 4 goals v Ireland, at Dublin	14.3.1908
	Hughie Gallacher (Newcastle U) 4 goals v Ireland, at Belfast	23.2.1929
	Billy Steel (Dundee) 4 goals v N. Ireland, at Hampden Park	1.11.1950
	Denis Law (Manchester U) 4 goals v N. Ireland, at Hampden Park	7.11.1962
	Denis Law (Manchester U) 4 goals v Norway, at Hampden Park	7.11.1963
	Colin Stein (Rangers) 4 goals v Cyprus, at Hampden Park	17.5.1969

MOST GOALS IN AN INTERNATIONAL CAREER

		Goals	Games
England	Wayne Rooney (Everton, Manchester U)	53	115
Scotland	Denis Law (Huddersfield T, Manchester C, Torino, Manchester U)	30	55
	Kenny Dalglish (Celtic, Liverpool)	30	102
Northern Ireland	David Healy (Manchester U, Preston NE, Leeds U, Fulham, Sunderland, Rangers, Bury)	36	95
Wales	Ian Rush (Liverpool, Juventus)	28	73
Republic of Ireland	Robbie Keane (Wolverhampton W, Coventry C, Internazionale, Leeds U, Tottenham H, Liverpool, Tottenham H, LA Galaxy)	67	145

HIGHEST SCORES

World Cup Match	Australia	31	American Samoa	0	2001
European Championship	San Marino	0	Germany	13	2006
Olympic Games	Denmark	17	France	1	1908
	Germany	16	USSR	0	1912
Olympic Qualifying Tournament	Vanuatu	46	Micronesia	0	2015
Other International Match	Libya	21	Oman	0	1966
	Abandoned after 80 minutes as Oman refused to play on.				
European Cup	Feyenoord	12	KR Reykjavik	2	1969
European Cup-Winners' Cup	Sporting Lisbon	16	Apoel Nicosia	1	1963
Fairs & UEFA Cups	Ajax	14	Red Boys	0	1984

GOALSCORING RECORDS

World Cup Final	Geoff Hurst (England) 3 goals v West Germany	1966
World Cup Final tournament	Just Fontaine (France) 13 goals	1958
World Cup career	Miroslav Klose (Germany) 16 goals	2002, 2006, 2010, 2014
Career	Artur Friedenreich (Brazil) 1,329 goals	1910–30
	Pele (Brazil) 1,281 goals	*1956–78
	Franz 'Bimbo' Binder (Austria, Germany) 1,006 goals	1930–50
World Cup Finals fastest	Hakan Sukur (Turkey) 10.8 secs v South Korea	2002
Pele subsequently scored two goals in Testimonial matches making his total 1,283.		

MOST CAPPED INTERNATIONALS IN THE BRITISH ISLES

England	Peter Shilton	125 appearances	1970–90
Northern Ireland	Pat Jennings	119 appearances	1964–86
Scotland	Kenny Dalglish	102 appearances	1971–86
Wales	Neville Southall	92 appearances	1982–97
Republic of Ireland	Robbie Keane	145 appearances	1998–2016

THE PREMIER LEAGUE AND FOOTBALL LEAGUE FIXTURES 2016–17

Sky Sports   All fixtures subject to change.

Friday, 5 August 2016
Sky Bet Championship
Fulham v Newcastle U* (19.45)

Saturday, 6 August 2016
Sky Bet Championship
Birmingham C v Cardiff C
Blackburn R v Norwich C
Bristol C v Wigan Ath
Derby Co v Brighton & HA
Huddersfield T v Brentford
Ipswich T v Barnsley
Nottingham F v Burton Alb
Reading v Preston NE
Rotherham U v Wolverhampton W

Sky Bet League One
Bolton W v Sheffield U
Bradford C v Port Vale
Bury v Charlton Ath
Millwall v Oldham Ath
Northampton T v Fleetwood T
Oxford U v Chesterfield
Rochdale v Peterborough U
Scunthorpe U v Bristol R
Shrewsbury T v Milton Keynes D
Southend U v Gillingham
Swindon T v Coventry C
Walsall v AFC Wimbledon

Sky Bet League Two
Accrington S v Doncaster R
Blackpool v Exeter C
Cambridge U v Barnet
Cheltenham T v Leyton Orient
Crawley T v Wycombe W
Grimsby T v Morecambe
Hartlepool U v Colchester U
Newport Co v Mansfield T
Plymouth Arg v Luton T
Portsmouth v Carlisle U
Stevenage v Crewe Alex
Yeovil T v Notts Co

Sunday, 7 August 2016
Sky Bet Championship
QPR v Leeds U* (12.00)
Sheffield W v Aston Villa* (16.30)

Friday, 12 August 2016
Sky Bet Championship
Brighton & HA v Nottingham F*
(19.45)

Saturday, 13 August 2016
Premier League
Burnley v Swansea C
Crystal Palace v WBA
Everton v Tottenham H
Hull C v Leicester C* (12.30)
Manchester C v Sunderland
Middlesbrough v Stoke C
Southampton v Watford

Sky Bet Championship
Aston Villa v Rotherham U
Barnsley v Derby Co
Brentford v Ipswich T
Burton Alb v Bristol C
Cardiff C v QPR
Leeds U v Birmingham C
Newcastle U v Huddersfield T
Norwich C v Sheffield W* (17.30)
Preston NE v Fulham

Wigan Ath v Blackburn R
Wolverhampton W v Reading

Sky Bet League One
AFC Wimbledon v Bolton W
Bristol R v Oxford U
Charlton Ath v Northampton T
Chesterfield v Swindon T
Coventry C v Shrewsbury T
Fleetwood T v Scunthorpe U
Gillingham v Bury
Milton Keynes D v Millwall
Oldham Ath v Walsall
Peterborough U v Bradford C
Port Vale v Southend U
Sheffield U v Rochdale

Sky Bet League Two
Barnet v Accrington S
Carlisle U v Plymouth Arg
Colchester U v Cambridge U
Crewe Alex v Portsmouth
Doncaster R v Crawley T
Exeter C v Hartlepool U
Leyton Orient v Newport Co
Luton T v Yeovil T
Mansfield T v Cheltenham T
Morecambe v Blackpool
Notts Co v Stevenage
Wycombe W v Grimsby T

Sunday, 14 August 2016
Premier League
Bournemouth v Manchester U* (13.30)
Arsenal v Liverpool* (16.00)

Monday, 15 August 2016
Premier League
Chelsea v West Ham U* (20.00)

Tuesday, 16 August 2016
Sky Bet Championship
Aston Villa v Huddersfield T
Barnsley v QPR
Brentford v Nottingham F
Brighton & HA v Rotherham U
Burton Alb v Sheffield W
Cardiff C v Blackburn R
Leeds U v Fulham
Norwich C v Bristol C
Preston NE v Derby Co
Wigan Ath v Birmingham C
Wolverhampton W v Ipswich T

Sky Bet League One
AFC Wimbledon v Scunthorpe U
Bristol R v Bolton W
Charlton Ath v Shrewsbury T
Chesterfield v Walsall
Coventry C v Bury
Fleetwood T v Oxford U
Gillingham v Swindon T
Milton Keynes D v Bradford C
Oldham Ath v Northampton T
Peterborough U v Millwall
Port Vale v Rochdale
Sheffield U v Southend U

Sky Bet League Two
Barnet v Blackpool
Carlisle U v Cheltenham T
Colchester U v Grimsby T
Crewe Alex v Hartlepool U
Doncaster R v Cambridge U

Exeter C v Crawley T
Leyton Orient v Stevenage
Luton T v Newport Co
Mansfield T v Yeovil T
Morecambe v Portsmouth
Notts Co v Plymouth Arg
Wycombe W v Accrington S

Wednesday, 17 August 2016
Sky Bet Championship
Newcastle U v Reading

Friday, 19 August 2016
Premier League
Manchester U v Southampton* (20.00)

Saturday, 20 August 2016
Premier League
Leicester C v Arsenal
Liverpool v Burnley
Stoke C v Manchester C* (12.30)
Swansea C v Hull C
Tottenham H v Crystal Palace
Watford v Chelsea
WBA v Everton

Sky Bet Championship
Birmingham C v Wolverhampton W
Blackburn R v Burton Alb
Bristol C v Newcastle U
Derby Co v Aston Villa* (17.30)
Fulham v Cardiff C
Huddersfield T v Barnsley
Nottingham F v Wigan Ath
QPR v Preston NE
Reading v Brighton & HA
Rotherham U v Brentford
Sheffield W v Leeds U

Sky Bet League One
Bolton W v Fleetwood T
Bradford C v Coventry C
Bury v Oldham Ath
Millwall v Sheffield U
Northampton T v AFC Wimbledon
Oxford U v Peterborough U
Rochdale v Milton Keynes D
Scunthorpe U v Gillingham
Shrewsbury T v Chesterfield
Southend U v Bristol R
Swindon T v Port Vale
Walsall v Charlton Ath

Sky Bet League Two
Accrington S v Exeter C
Blackpool v Wycombe W
Cambridge U v Carlisle U
Cheltenham T v Doncaster R
Crawley T v Barnet
Grimsby T v Leyton Orient
Hartlepool U v Notts Co
Newport Co v Crewe Alex
Plymouth Arg v Mansfield T
Portsmouth v Colchester U
Stevenage v Luton T
Yeovil T v Morecambe

Sunday, 21 August 2016
Premier League
Sunderland v Middlesbrough* (13.30)
West Ham U v Bournemouth* (16.00)

Sky Bet Championship
Ipswich T v Norwich C* (12.00)

Friday, 26 August 2016
Sky Bet Championship
Burton Alb v Derby Co* (19.45)

Saturday, 27 August 2016
Premier League
Chelsea v Burnley
Crystal Palace v Bournemouth
Everton v Stoke C
Hull C v Manchester U
Leicester C v Swansea C
Southampton v Sunderland
Tottenham H v Liverpool* (12.30)
Watford v Arsenal

Sky Bet Championship
Barnsley v Rotherham U
Birmingham C v Norwich C
Blackburn R v Fulham
Brentford v Sheffield W
Bristol C v Aston Villa
Cardiff C v Reading
Huddersfield T v Wolverhampton W
Ipswich T v Preston NE
Newcastle U v Brighton & HA* (17.30)
Nottingham F v Leeds U
Wigan Ath v QPR

Sky Bet League One
Bradford C v Oldham Ath
Charlton Ath v Bolton W
Chesterfield v Millwall
Coventry C v Northampton T
Milton Keynes D v Peterborough U
Port Vale v Scunthorpe U
Rochdale v AFC Wimbledon
Sheffield U v Oxford U
Shrewsbury T v Gillingham
Southend U v Fleetwood T
Swindon T v Bristol R
Walsall v Bury

Sky Bet League Two
Accrington S v Morecambe
Barnet v Carlisle U
Blackpool v Plymouth Arg
Cambridge U v Luton T
Cheltenham T v Crewe Alex
Crawley T v Notts Co
Doncaster R v Yeovil T
Exeter C v Portsmouth
Grimsby T v Stevenage
Hartlepool U v Newport Co
Leyton Orient v Mansfield T
Wycombe W v Colchester U

Sunday, 28 August 2016
Premier League
WBA v Middlesbrough* (13.30)
Manchester C v West Ham U* (16.00)

Saturday, 3 September 2016
Sky Bet League One
AFC Wimbledon v Chesterfield
Bolton W v Southend U
Bristol R v Walsall
Bury v Port Vale
Fleetwood T v Coventry C
Millwall v Bradford C
Oldham Ath v Shrewsbury T
Oxford U v Rochdale
Peterborough U v Swindon T* (12.15)
Scunthorpe U v Charlton Ath

Sky Bet League Two
Carlisle U v Accrington S
Colchester U v Exeter C
Crewe Alex v Doncaster R
Luton T v Wycombe W
Mansfield T v Cambridge U
Morecambe v Leyton Orient
Newport Co v Barnet
Notts Co v Grimsby T
Plymouth Arg v Cheltenham T
Portsmouth v Crawley T

Stevenage v Hartlepool U
Yeovil T v Blackpool

Sunday, 4 September 2016
Sky Bet League One
Northampton T v Milton Keynes D*
(12.00)
Gillingham v Sheffield U* (14.1%)

Friday, 9 September 2016
Sky Bet Championship
Reading v Ipswich T* (19.45)

Saturday, 10 September 2016
Premier League
Bournemouth v WBA
Arsenal v Southampton
Burnley v Hull C
Liverpool v Leicester C
Manchester U v Manchester C* (13.30)
Middlesbrough v Crystal Palace
Stoke C v Tottenham H
West Ham U v Watford

Sky Bet Championship
Brighton & HA v Brentford
Derby Co v Newcastle U* (17.30)
Fulham v Birmingham C
Leeds U v Huddersfield T
Norwich C v Cardiff C
Preston NE v Barnsley
QPR v Blackburn R
Rotherham U v Bristol C
Sheffield W v Wigan Ath
Wolverhampton W v Burton Alb

Sky Bet League One
AFC Wimbledon v Sheffield U
Bolton W v Milton Keynes D
Bristol R v Rochdale
Bury v Shrewsbury T
Fleetwood T v Charlton Ath
Gillingham v Bradford C
Millwall v Coventry C
Northampton T v Walsall
Oldham Ath v Chesterfield
Oxford U v Swindon T
Peterborough U v Port Vale
Scunthorpe U v Southend U

Sky Bet League Two
Carlisle U v Leyton Orient
Colchester U v Blackpool
Crewe Alex v Exeter C
Luton T v Grimsby T
Mansfield T v Barnet
Morecambe v Doncaster R
Newport Co v Cheltenham T
Notts Co v Accrington S
Plymouth Arg v Cambridge U
Portsmouth v Wycombe W
Stevenage v Crawley T
Yeovil T v Hartlepool U

Sunday, 11 September 2016
Premier League
Swansea C v Chelsea* (16.00)

Sky Bet Championship
Aston Villa v Nottingham F* (13.15)

Monday, 12 September 2016
Premier League
Sunderland v Everton* (20.00)

Tuesday, 13 September 2016
Sky Bet Championship
Aston Villa v Brentford
Brighton & HA v Huddersfield T
Derby Co v Ipswich T
Fulham v Burton Alb
Leeds U v Blackburn R
Norwich C v Wigan Ath
Preston NE v Cardiff C
QPR v Newcastle U
Reading v Birmingham C
Rotherham U v Nottingham F

Sheffield W v Bristol C
Wolverhampton W v Barnsley

Friday, 16 September 2016
Premier League
Chelsea v Liverpool* (20.00)

Saturday, 17 September 2016
Premier League
Everton v Middlesbrough
Hull C v Arsenal
Leicester C v Burnley
Manchester C v Bournemouth
Southampton v Swansea C
Watford v Manchester U
WBA v West Ham U

Sky Bet Championship
Barnsley v Reading
Birmingham C v Sheffield W* (17.30)
Blackburn R v Rotherham U
Brentford v Preston NE
Bristol C v Derby Co
Burton Alb v Brighton & HA
Cardiff C v Leeds U* (12.00)
Huddersfield T v QPR
Ipswich T v Aston Villa
Newcastle U v Wolverhampton W
Nottingham F v Norwich C
Wigan Ath v Fulham

Sky Bet League One
Bradford C v Bristol R
Charlton Ath v AFC Wimbledon
Chesterfield v Northampton T
Coventry C v Oldham Ath
Milton Keynes D v Oxford U
Port Vale v Gillingham
Rochdale v Fleetwood T
Sheffield U v Peterborough U
Shrewsbury T v Scunthorpe U
Southend U v Millwall
Swindon T v Bury
Walsall v Bolton W

Sky Bet League Two
Accrington S v Portsmouth
Barnet v Colchester U
Blackpool v Carlisle U
Cambridge U v Morecambe
Cheltenham T v Notts Co
Crawley T v Luton T
Doncaster R v Newport Co
Exeter C v Plymouth Arg
Grimsby T v Crewe Alex
Hartlepool U v Mansfield T
Leyton Orient v Yeovil T
Wycombe W v Stevenage

Sunday, 18 September 2016
Premier League
Crystal Palace v Stoke C* (14.15)
Tottenham H v Sunderland* (16.30)

Friday, 23 September 2016
Sky Bet Championship
Preston NE v Wigan Ath* (19.45)

Saturday, 24 September 2016
Premier League
Bournemouth v Everton
Arsenal v Chelsea
Liverpool v Hull C
Manchester U v Leicester C* (12.30)
Middlesbrough v Tottenham H
Stoke C v WBA
Sunderland v Crystal Palace
Swansea C v Manchester C

Sky Bet Championship
Aston Villa v Newcastle U* (17.30)
Brighton & HA v Barnsley
Derby Co v Blackburn R
Fulham v Bristol C
Leeds U v Ipswich T
Norwich C v Burton Alb

QPR v Birmingham C
Reading v Huddersfield T
Rotherham U v Cardiff C
Sheffield W v Nottingham F
Wolverhampton W v Brentford

Sky Bet League One
AFC Wimbledon v Shrewsbury T
Bolton W v Bradford C
Bristol R v Port Vale
Bury v Chesterfield
Fleetwood T v Milton Keynes D
Gillingham v Coventry C
Millwall v Rochdale
Northampton T v Southend U
Oldham Ath v Swindon T
Oxford U v Charlton Ath
Peterborough U v Walsall
Scunthorpe U v Sheffield U

Sky Bet League Two
Carlisle U v Wycombe W
Colchester U v Accrington S
Crewe Alex v Blackpool
Luton T v Doncaster R
Mansfield T v Grimsby T
Morecambe v Crawley T
Newport Co v Cambridge U
Notts Co v Leyton Orient
Plymouth Arg v Hartlepool U
Portsmouth v Barnet
Stevenage v Exeter C
Yeovil T v Cheltenham T

Sunday, 25 September 2016
Premier League
West Ham U v Southampton* (16.00)

Monday, 26 September 2016
Premier League
Burnley v Watford* (20.00)

Tuesday, 27 September 2016
Sky Bet Championship
Barnsley v Aston Villa
Birmingham C v Preston NE
Blackburn R v Sheffield W
Brentford v Reading
Bristol C v Leeds U
Burton Alb v QPR
Cardiff C v Derby Co
Huddersfield T v Rotherham U
Ipswich T v Brighton & HA
Nottingham F v Fulham
Wigan Ath v Wolverhampton W

Sky Bet League One
Bradford C v Fleetwood T
Charlton Ath v Oldham Ath
Chesterfield v Gillingham
Coventry C v AFC Wimbledon
Milton Keynes D v Bury
Port Vale v Millwall
Rochdale v Bolton W
Sheffield U v Bristol R
Shrewsbury T v Peterborough U
Southend U v Oxford U
Swindon T v Northampton T
Walsall v Scunthorpe U

Sky Bet League Two
Accrington S v Mansfield T
Barnet v Morecambe
Blackpool v Portsmouth
Cambridge U v Yeovil T
Cheltenham T v Stevenage
Crawley T v Colchester U
Doncaster R v Carlisle U
Exeter C v Notts Co
Grimsby T v Newport Co
Hartlepool U v Luton T
Leyton Orient v Plymouth Arg
Wycombe W v Crewe Alex

Wednesday, 28 September 2016
Sky Bet Championship
Newcastle U v Norwich C

Saturday, 1 October 2016
Premier League
Burnley v Arsenal
Everton v Crystal Palace
Hull C v Chelsea
Leicester C v Southampton
Manchester U v Stoke C
Sunderland v WBA
Swansea C v Liverpool
Tottenham H v Manchester C
Watford v Bournemouth
West Ham U v Middlesbrough

Sky Bet Championship
Birmingham C v Blackburn R
Brentford v Wigan Ath
Bristol C v Nottingham F
Burton Alb v Cardiff C
Fulham v QPR
Ipswich T v Huddersfield T
Leeds U v Barnsley
Preston NE v Aston Villa
Reading v Derby Co
Rotherham U v Newcastle U
Sheffield W v Brighton & HA
Wolverhampton W v Norwich C

Sky Bet League One
AFC Wimbledon v Gillingham
Bolton W v Oxford U
Bury v Scunthorpe U
Charlton Ath v Rochdale
Chesterfield v Bradford C
Fleetwood T v Sheffield U
Northampton T v Bristol R
Oldham Ath v Milton Keynes D
Port Vale v Coventry C
Shrewsbury T v Swindon T
Southend U v Peterborough U
Walsall v Millwall

Sky Bet League Two
Barnet v Leyton Orient
Cambridge U v Accrington S
Carlisle U v Colchester U
Cheltenham T v Luton T
Crawley T v Blackpool
Crewe Alex v Mansfield T
Grimsby T v Hartlepool U
Newport Co v Stevenage
Notts Co v Morecambe
Plymouth Arg v Yeovil T
Portsmouth v Doncaster R
Wycombe W v Exeter C

Saturday, 8 October 2016
Sky Bet League One
Bradford C v Shrewsbury T
Bristol R v Fleetwood T
Coventry C v Chesterfield
Gillingham v Oldham Ath
Millwall v Charlton Ath
Milton Keynes D v Port Vale
Oxford U v AFC Wimbledon
Peterborough U v Bury
Rochdale v Southend U
Scunthorpe U v Northampton T
Sheffield U v Walsall
Swindon T v Bolton W

Sky Bet League Two
Accrington S v Cheltenham T
Blackpool v Cambridge U
Colchester U v Newport Co
Doncaster R v Barnet
Exeter C v Grimsby T
Hartlepool U v Crawley T
Leyton Orient v Portsmouth
Luton T v Crewe Alex
Mansfield T v Notts Co
Morecambe v Carlisle U

Stevenage v Plymouth Arg
Yeovil T v Wycombe W

Saturday, 15 October 2016
Premier League
Bournemouth v Hull C
Arsenal v Swansea C
Chelsea v Leicester C
Crystal Palace v West Ham U
Liverpool v Manchester U
Manchester C v Everton
Middlesbrough v Watford
Southampton v Burnley
Stoke C v Sunderland
WBA v Tottenham H

Sky Bet Championship
Aston Villa v Wolverhampton W
Barnsley v Fulham
Blackburn R v Ipswich T
Brighton & HA v Preston NE
Cardiff C v Bristol C
Derby Co v Leeds U
Huddersfield T v Sheffield W
Newcastle U v Brentford
Norwich C v Rotherham U
Nottingham F v Birmingham C
QPR v Reading
Wigan Ath v Burton Alb

Sky Bet League One
AFC Wimbledon v Swindon T
Bolton W v Oldham Ath
Bristol R v Gillingham
Charlton Ath v Coventry C
Fleetwood T v Peterborough U
Northampton T v Millwall
Oxford U v Bradford C
Rochdale v Bury
Scunthorpe U v Milton Keynes D
Sheffield U v Port Vale
Southend U v Chesterfield
Walsall v Shrewsbury T

Sky Bet League Two
Accrington S v Blackpool
Barnet v Exeter C
Cambridge U v Grimsby T
Carlisle U v Hartlepool U
Cheltenham T v Crawley T
Doncaster R v Colchester U
Leyton Orient v Luton T
Mansfield T v Wycombe W
Morecambe v Stevenage
Notts Co v Crewe Alex
Plymouth Arg v Portsmouth
Yeovil T v Newport Co

Tuesday, 18 October 2016
Sky Bet Championship
Barnsley v Newcastle U
Birmingham C v Rotherham U
Blackburn R v Nottingham F
Brighton & HA v Wolverhampton W
Cardiff C v Sheffield W
Derby Co v Brentford
Fulham v Norwich C
Ipswich T v Burton Alb
Leeds U v Wigan Ath
Preston NE v Huddersfield T
QPR v Bristol C
Reading v Aston Villa

Sky Bet League One
Bradford C v Southend U
Bury v AFC Wimbledon
Chesterfield v Fleetwood T
Coventry C v Oxford U
Gillingham v Walsall
Millwall v Bolton W
Milton Keynes D v Bristol R
Oldham Ath v Scunthorpe U
Peterborough U v Northampton T
Port Vale v Charlton Ath

Shrewsbury T v Sheffield U
Swindon T v Rochdale

Saturday, 22 October 2016
Premier League
Bournemouth v Tottenham H
Arsenal v Middlesbrough
Burnley v Everton
Chelsea v Manchester U
Hull C v Stoke C
Leicester C v Crystal Palace
Liverpool v WBA
Manchester C v Southampton
Swansea C v Watford
West Ham U v Sunderland

Sky Bet Championship
Aston Villa v Fulham
Brentford v Barnsley
Bristol C v Blackburn R
Burton Alb v Birmingham C
Huddersfield T v Derby Co
Newcastle U v Ipswich T
Norwich C v Preston NE
Nottingham F v Cardiff C
Rotherham U v Reading
Sheffield W v QPR
Wigan Ath v Brighton & HA
Wolverhampton W v Leeds U

Sky Bet League One
Bradford C v Sheffield U
Bury v Bolton W
Chesterfield v Scunthorpe U
Coventry C v Rochdale
Gillingham v Charlton Ath
Millwall v Fleetwood T
Milton Keynes D v Southend U
Oldham Ath v Bristol R
Peterborough U v AFC Wimbledon
Port Vale v Oxford U
Shrewsbury T v Northampton T
Swindon T v Walsall

Sky Bet League Two
Blackpool v Doncaster R
Colchester U v Morecambe
Crawley T v Accrington S
Crewe Alex v Yeovil T
Exeter C v Cambridge U
Grimsby T v Cheltenham T
Hartlepool U v Leyton Orient
Luton T v Mansfield T
Newport Co v Plymouth Arg
Portsmouth v Notts Co
Stevenage v Carlisle U
Wycombe W v Barnet

Saturday, 29 October 2016
Premier League
Crystal Palace v Liverpool
Everton v West Ham U
Manchester U v Burnley
Middlesbrough v Bournemouth
Southampton v Chelsea
Stoke C v Swansea C
Sunderland v Arsenal
Tottenham H v Leicester C
Watford v Hull C
WBA v Manchester C

Sky Bet Championship
Barnsley v Bristol C
Birmingham C v Aston Villa
Blackburn R v Wolverhampton W
Brighton & HA v Norwich C
Cardiff C v Wigan Ath
Derby Co v Sheffield W
Fulham v Huddersfield T
Ipswich T v Rotherham U
Leeds U v Burton Alb
Preston NE v Newcastle U
QPR v Brentford
Reading v Nottingham F

Sky Bet League One
AFC Wimbledon v Bradford C
Bolton W v Port Vale
Bristol R v Peterborough U
Charlton Ath v Chesterfield
Fleetwood T v Gillingham
Northampton T v Bury
Oxford U v Millwall
Rochdale v Oldham Ath
Scunthorpe U v Swindon T
Sheffield U v Milton Keynes D
Southend U v Shrewsbury T
Walsall v Coventry C

Sky Bet League Two
Accrington S v Newport Co
Barnet v Hartlepool U
Cambridge U v Portsmouth
Carlisle U v Crawley T
Cheltenham T v Blackpool
Doncaster R v Wycombe W
Leyton Orient v Crewe Alex
Mansfield T v Stevenage
Morecambe v Exeter C
Notts Co v Luton T
Plymouth Arg v Colchester U
Yeovil T v Grimsby T

Saturday, 5 November 2016
Premier League
Bournemouth v Sunderland
Arsenal v Tottenham H
Burnley v Crystal Palace
Chelsea v Everton
Hull C v Southampton
Leicester C v WBA
Liverpool v Watford
Manchester C v Middlesbrough
Swansea C v Manchester U
West Ham U v Stoke C

Sky Bet Championship
Aston Villa v Blackburn R
Brentford v Fulham
Bristol C v Brighton & HA
Burton Alb v Barnsley
Huddersfield T v Birmingham C
Newcastle U v Cardiff C
Norwich C v Leeds U
Nottingham F v QPR
Rotherham U v Preston NE
Sheffield W v Ipswich T
Wigan Ath v Reading
Wolverhampton W v Derby Co

Saturday, 12 November 2016
Sky Bet League One
Bradford C v Rochdale
Bury v Southend U
Chesterfield v Sheffield U
Coventry C v Scunthorpe U
Gillingham v Northampton T
Millwall v Bristol R
Milton Keynes D v Walsall
Oldham Ath v AFC Wimbledon
Peterborough U v Bolton W
Port Vale v Fleetwood T
Shrewsbury T v Oxford U
Swindon T v Charlton Ath

Sky Bet League Two
Blackpool v Notts Co
Colchester U v Leyton Orient
Crawley T v Cambridge U
Crewe Alex v Plymouth Arg
Exeter C v Doncaster R
Grimsby T v Barnet
Hartlepool U v Cheltenham T
Luton T v Accrington S
Newport Co v Carlisle U
Portsmouth v Mansfield T
Stevenage v Yeovil T
Wycombe W v Morecambe

Saturday, 19 November 2016
Premier League
Crystal Palace v Manchester C
Everton v Swansea C
Manchester U v Arsenal
Middlesbrough v Chelsea
Southampton v Liverpool
Stoke C v Bournemouth
Sunderland v Hull C
Tottenham H v West Ham U
Watford v Leicester C
WBA v Burnley

Sky Bet Championship
Barnsley v Wigan Ath
Birmingham C v Bristol C
Blackburn R v Brentford
Brighton & HA v Aston Villa
Cardiff C v Huddersfield T
Derby Co v Rotherham U
Fulham v Sheffield W
Ipswich T v Nottingham F
Leeds U v Newcastle U
Preston NE v Wolverhampton W
QPR v Norwich C
Reading v Burton Alb

Sky Bet League One
AFC Wimbledon v Bury
Bolton W v Millwall
Bristol R v Milton Keynes D
Charlton Ath v Port Vale
Fleetwood T v Chesterfield
Northampton T v Peterborough U
Oxford U v Coventry C
Rochdale v Swindon T
Scunthorpe U v Oldham Ath
Sheffield U v Shrewsbury T
Southend U v Bradford C
Walsall v Gillingham

Sky Bet League Two
Accrington S v Stevenage
Barnet v Crewe Alex
Cambridge U v Wycombe W
Carlisle U v Exeter C
Cheltenham T v Portsmouth
Doncaster R v Hartlepool U
Leyton Orient v Blackpool
Mansfield T v Crawley T
Morecambe v Luton T
Notts Co v Newport Co
Plymouth Arg v Grimsby T
Yeovil T v Colchester U

Tuesday, 22 November 2016
Sky Bet League One
Bolton W v Coventry C
Bradford C v Northampton T
Bristol R v Charlton Ath
Fleetwood T v Shrewsbury T
Millwall v Oxford U
Milton Keynes D v Chesterfield
Oxford U v Gillingham
Peterborough U v Scunthorpe U
Port Vale v Oldham Ath
Rochdale v Walsall
Sheffield U v Bury
Southend U v Swindon T

Sky Bet League Two
Cheltenham T v Colchester U
Crewe Alex v Morecambe
Grimsby T v Carlisle U
Hartlepool U v Accrington S
Leyton Orient v Exeter C
Luton T v Portsmouth
Mansfield T v Blackpool
Newport Co v Wycombe W
Notts Co v Cambridge U
Plymouth Arg v Barnet
Stevenage v Doncaster R
Yeovil T v Crawley T

Saturday, 26 November 2016
Premier League
Arsenal v Bournemouth
Burnley v Manchester C
Chelsea v Tottenham H
Hull C v WBA
Leicester C v Middlesbrough
Liverpool v Sunderland
Manchester U v West Ham U
Southampton v Everton
Swansea C v Crystal Palace
Watford v Stoke C

Sky Bet Championship
Aston Villa v Cardiff C
Barnsley v Nottingham F
Brentford v Birmingham C
Brighton & HA v Fulham
Derby Co v Norwich C
Huddersfield T v Wigan Ath
Ipswich T v QPR
Newcastle U v Blackburn R
Preston NE v Burton Alb
Reading v Bristol C
Rotherham U v Leeds U
Wolverhampton W v Sheffield W

Sky Bet League One
AFC Wimbledon v Fleetwood T
Bury v Millwall
Charlton Ath v Sheffield U
Chesterfield v Bristol R
Coventry C v Milton Keynes D
Gillingham v Rochdale
Northampton T v Bolton W
Oldham Ath v Peterborough U
Scunthorpe U v Oxford U
Shrewsbury T v Port Vale
Swindon T v Bradford C
Walsall v Southend U

Sky Bet League Two
Accrington S v Yeovil T
Barnet v Notts Co
Blackpool v Newport Co
Cambridge U v Cheltenham T
Carlisle U v Mansfield T
Colchester U v Crewe Alex
Crawley T v Grimsby T
Doncaster R v Leyton Orient
Exeter C v Luton T
Morecambe v Plymouth Arg
Portsmouth v Stevenage
Wycombe W v Hartlepool U

Saturday, 3 December 2016
Premier League
Bournemouth v Liverpool
Crystal Palace v Southampton
Everton v Manchester U
Manchester C v Chelsea
Middlesbrough v Hull C
Stoke C v Burnley
Sunderland v Leicester C
Tottenham H v Swansea C
WBA v Watford
West Ham U v Arsenal

Sky Bet Championship
Birmingham C v Barnsley
Blackburn R v Huddersfield T
Bristol C v Ipswich T
Burton Alb v Rotherham U
Cardiff C v Brighton & HA
Fulham v Reading
Leeds U v Aston Villa
Norwich C v Brentford
Nottingham F v Newcastle U
QPR v Wolverhampton W
Sheffield W v Preston NE
Wigan Ath v Derby Co

Saturday, 10 December 2016
Premier League
Arsenal v Stoke C

Burnley v Bournemouth
Chelsea v WBA
Hull C v Crystal Palace
Leicester C v Manchester C
Liverpool v West Ham U
Manchester U v Tottenham H
Southampton v Middlesbrough
Swansea C v Sunderland
Watford v Everton

Sky Bet Championship
Aston Villa v Wigan Ath
Barnsley v Norwich C
Brentford v Burton Alb
Brighton & HA v Leeds U
Derby Co v Nottingham F
Huddersfield T v Bristol C
Ipswich T v Cardiff C
Newcastle U v Birmingham C
Preston NE v Blackburn R
Reading v Sheffield W
Rotherham U v QPR
Wolverhampton W v Fulham

Sky Bet League One
Bolton W v Gillingham
Bradford C v Charlton Ath
Bristol R v Bury
Fleetwood T v Walsall
Millwall v Shrewsbury T
Milton Keynes D v AFC Wimbledon
Oxford U v Oldham Ath
Peterborough U v Chesterfield
Port Vale v Northampton T
Rochdale v Scunthorpe U
Sheffield U v Swindon T
Southend U v Coventry C

Sky Bet League Two
Cheltenham T v Exeter C
Crewe Alex v Crawley T
Grimsby T v Portsmouth
Hartlepool U v Cambridge U
Leyton Orient v Accrington S
Luton T v Carlisle U
Mansfield T v Colchester U
Newport Co v Morecambe
Notts Co v Wycombe W
Plymouth Arg v Doncaster R
Stevenage v Blackpool
Yeovil T v Barnet

Tuesday, 13 December 2016
Premier League
Bournemouth v Leicester C
Crystal Palace v Manchester U
Middlesbrough v Liverpool
Sunderland v Chelsea
WBA v Swansea C
West Ham U v Burnley

Sky Bet Championship
Birmingham C v Ipswich T
Blackburn R v Brighton & HA
Bristol C v Brentford
Burton Alb v Huddersfield T
Cardiff C v Wolverhampton W
Fulham v Rotherham U
Leeds U v Reading
Norwich C v Aston Villa
Nottingham F v Preston NE
QPR v Derby Co
Sheffield W v Barnsley
Wigan Ath v Newcastle U

Wednesday, 14 December 2016
Premier League
Everton v Arsenal
Manchester C v Watford
Stoke C v Southampton
Tottenham H v Hull C

Saturday, 17 December 2016
Premier League
Bournemouth v Southampton
Crystal Palace v Chelsea

Everton v Liverpool
Manchester C v Arsenal
Middlesbrough v Swansea C
Stoke C v Leicester C
Sunderland v Watford
Tottenham H v Burnley
WBA v Manchester U
West Ham U v Hull C

Sky Bet Championship
Birmingham C v Brighton & HA
Blackburn R v Reading
Bristol C v Preston NE
Burton Alb v Newcastle U
Cardiff C v Barnsley
Fulham v Derby Co
Leeds U v Brentford
Norwich C v Huddersfield T
Nottingham F v Wolverhampton W
QPR v Aston Villa
Sheffield W v Rotherham U
Wigan Ath v Ipswich T

Sky Bet League One
AFC Wimbledon v Port Vale
Bury v Oxford U
Charlton Ath v Peterborough U
Chesterfield v Bolton W
Coventry C v Sheffield U
Gillingham v Milton Keynes D
Northampton T v Rochdale
Oldham Ath v Southend U
Scunthorpe U v Millwall
Shrewsbury T v Bristol R
Swindon T v Fleetwood T
Walsall v Bradford C

Sky Bet League Two
Accrington S v Plymouth Arg
Barnet v Stevenage
Blackpool v Luton T
Cambridge U v Crewe Alex
Carlisle U v Yeovil T
Colchester U v Notts Co
Crawley T v Newport Co
Doncaster R v Grimsby T
Exeter C v Mansfield T
Morecambe v Cheltenham T
Portsmouth v Hartlepool U
Wycombe W v Leyton Orient

Monday, 26 December 2016
Premier League
Arsenal v WBA
Burnley v Middlesbrough
Chelsea v Bournemouth
Hull C v Manchester C
Leicester C v Everton
Liverpool v Stoke C
Manchester U v Sunderland
Southampton v Tottenham H
Swansea C v West Ham U
Watford v Crystal Palace

Sky Bet Championship
Aston Villa v Burton Alb
Barnsley v Blackburn R
Brentford v Cardiff C
Brighton & HA v QPR
Derby Co v Birmingham C
Huddersfield T v Nottingham F
Ipswich T v Fulham
Newcastle U v Sheffield W
Preston NE v Leeds U
Reading v Norwich C
Rotherham U v Wigan Ath
Wolverhampton W v Bristol C

Sky Bet League One
Bolton W v Shrewsbury T
Bradford C v Scunthorpe U
Bristol R v Coventry C
Fleetwood T v Bury
Millwall v Swindon T
Milton Keynes D v Charlton Ath

Oxford U v Northampton T
Peterborough U v Gillingham
Port Vale v Walsall
Rochdale v Chesterfield
Sheffield U v Oldham Ath
Southend U v AFC Wimbledon

Sky Bet League Two
Cheltenham T v Barnet
Crewe Alex v Carlisle U
Grimsby T v Accrington S
Hartlepool U v Blackpool
Leyton Orient v Crawley T
Luton T v Colchester U
Mansfield T v Morecambe
Newport Co v Portsmouth
Notts Co v Doncaster R
Plymouth Arg v Wycombe W
Stevenage v Cambridge U
Yeovil T v Exeter C

Saturday, 31 December 2016
Premier League
Arsenal v Crystal Palace
Burnley v Sunderland
Chelsea v Stoke C
Hull C v Everton
Leicester C v West Ham U
Liverpool v Manchester C
Manchester U v Middlesbrough
Southampton v WBA
Swansea C v Bournemouth
Watford v Tottenham H

Sky Bet Championship
Aston Villa v Leeds U
Barnsley v Birmingham C
Brentford v Norwich C
Brighton & HA v Cardiff C
Derby Co v Wigan Ath
Huddersfield T v Blackburn R
Ipswich T v Bristol C
Newcastle U v Nottingham F
Preston NE v Sheffield W
Reading v Fulham
Rotherham U v Burton Alb
Wolverhampton W v QPR

Sky Bet League One
Bolton W v Scunthorpe U
Bradford C v Bury
Bristol R v AFC Wimbledon
Fleetwood T v Oldham Ath
Millwall v Gillingham
Milton Keynes D v Swindon T
Oxford U v Walsall
Peterborough U v Coventry C
Port Vale v Chesterfield
Rochdale v Shrewsbury T
Sheffield U v Northampton T
Southend U v Charlton Ath

Sky Bet League Two
Cheltenham T v Wycombe W
Crewe Alex v Accrington S
Grimsby T v Blackpool
Hartlepool U v Morecambe
Leyton Orient v Cambridge U
Luton T v Barnet
Mansfield T v Doncaster R
Newport Co v Exeter C
Notts Co v Carlisle U
Plymouth Arg v Crawley T
Stevenage v Colchester U
Yeovil T v Portsmouth

Monday, 2 January 2017
Premier League
Bournemouth v Arsenal
Crystal Palace v Swansea C
Everton v Southampton
Manchester C v Burnley
Middlesbrough v Leicester C
Stoke C v Watford
Sunderland v Liverpool

Tottenham H v Chelsea
WBA v Hull C
West Ham U v Manchester U

Sky Bet Championship
Birmingham C v Brentford
Blackburn R v Newcastle U
Bristol C v Reading
Burton Alb v Preston NE
Cardiff C v Aston Villa
Fulham v Brighton & HA
Leeds U v Rotherham U
Norwich C v Derby Co
Nottingham F v Barnsley
QPR v Ipswich T
Sheffield W v Wolverhampton W
Wigan Ath v Huddersfield T

Sky Bet League One
AFC Wimbledon v Millwall
Bury v Sheffield U
Charlton Ath v Bristol R
Chesterfield v Milton Keynes D
Coventry C v Bolton W
Gillingham v Oxford U
Northampton T v Bradford C
Oldham Ath v Port Vale
Scunthorpe U v Peterborough U
Shrewsbury T v Fleetwood T
Swindon T v Southend U
Walsall v Rochdale

Sky Bet League Two
Accrington S v Hartlepool U
Barnet v Plymouth Arg
Blackpool v Mansfield T
Cambridge U v Notts Co
Carlisle U v Grimsby T
Colchester U v Cheltenham T
Crawley T v Yeovil T
Doncaster R v Stevenage
Exeter C v Leyton Orient
Morecambe v Crewe Alex
Portsmouth v Luton T
Wycombe W v Newport Co

Saturday, 7 January 2017
Sky Bet League One
Bradford C v Chesterfield
Bristol R v Northampton T
Coventry C v Port Vale
Gillingham v AFC Wimbledon
Millwall v Walsall
Milton Keynes D v Oldham Ath
Oxford U v Bolton W
Peterborough U v Southend U
Rochdale v Charlton Ath
Scunthorpe U v Bury
Sheffield U v Fleetwood T
Swindon T v Shrewsbury T

Sky Bet League Two
Accrington S v Cambridge U
Blackpool v Crawley T
Colchester U v Carlisle U
Doncaster R v Portsmouth
Exeter C v Wycombe W
Hartlepool U v Grimsby T
Leyton Orient v Barnet
Luton T v Cheltenham T
Mansfield T v Crewe Alex
Morecambe v Notts Co
Stevenage v Newport Co
Yeovil T v Plymouth Arg

Saturday, 14 January 2017
Premier League
Burnley v Southampton
Everton v Manchester U
Hull C v Bournemouth
Leicester C v Chelsea
Manchester C v Liverpool
Sunderland v Stoke C
Swansea C v Arsenal
Tottenham H v WBA

Watford v Middlesbrough
West Ham U v Crystal Palace

Sky Bet Championship
Birmingham C v Nottingham F
Brentford v Newcastle U
Bristol C v Cardiff C
Burton Alb v Wigan Ath
Fulham v Barnsley
Ipswich T v Blackburn R
Leeds U v Derby Co
Preston NE v Brighton & HA
Reading v QPR
Rotherham U v Norwich C
Sheffield W v Huddersfield T
Wolverhampton W v Aston Villa

Sky Bet League One
AFC Wimbledon v Oxford U
Bolton W v Swindon T
Bury v Peterborough U
Charlton Ath v Millwall
Chesterfield v Coventry C
Fleetwood T v Bristol R
Northampton T v Scunthorpe U
Oldham Ath v Gillingham
Port Vale v Milton Keynes D
Shrewsbury T v Bradford C
Southend U v Rochdale
Walsall v Sheffield U

Sky Bet League Two
Barnet v Doncaster R
Cambridge U v Blackpool
Carlisle U v Morecambe
Cheltenham T v Accrington S
Crawley T v Hartlepool U
Crewe Alex v Luton T
Grimsby T v Exeter C
Newport Co v Colchester U
Notts Co v Mansfield T
Plymouth Arg v Stevenage
Portsmouth v Leyton Orient
Wycombe W v Yeovil T

Saturday, 21 January 2017
Premier League
Bournemouth v Watford
Arsenal v Burnley
Chelsea v Hull C
Crystal Palace v Everton
Liverpool v Swansea C
Manchester C v Tottenham H
Middlesbrough v West Ham U
Southampton v Leicester C
Stoke C v Manchester U
WBA v Sunderland

Sky Bet Championship
Aston Villa v Preston NE
Barnsley v Leeds U
Blackburn R v Birmingham C
Brighton & HA v Sheffield W
Cardiff C v Burton Alb
Derby Co v Reading
Huddersfield T v Ipswich T
Newcastle U v Rotherham U
Norwich C v Wolverhampton W
Nottingham F v Bristol C
QPR v Fulham
Wigan Ath v Brentford

Sky Bet League One
Bradford C v Millwall
Charlton Ath v Scunthorpe U
Chesterfield v AFC Wimbledon
Coventry C v Fleetwood T
Milton Keynes D v Northampton T
Port Vale v Bury
Rochdale v Oxford U
Sheffield U v Gillingham
Shrewsbury T v Oldham Ath
Southend U v Bolton W
Swindon T v Peterborough U
Walsall v Bristol R

Sky Bet League Two
Accrington S v Carlisle U
Barnet v Newport Co
Blackpool v Yeovil T
Cambridge U v Mansfield T
Cheltenham T v Plymouth Arg
Crawley T v Portsmouth
Doncaster R v Crewe Alex
Exeter C v Colchester U
Grimsby T v Notts Co
Hartlepool U v Stevenage
Leyton Orient v Morecambe
Wycombe W v Luton T

Saturday, 28 January 2017
Sky Bet Championship
Aston Villa v Bristol C
Brighton & HA v Newcastle U
Derby Co v Burton Alb
Fulham v Blackburn R
Leeds U v Nottingham F
Norwich C v Birmingham C
Preston NE v Ipswich T
QPR v Wigan Ath
Reading v Cardiff C
Rotherham U v Barnsley
Sheffield W v Brentford
Wolverhampton W v Huddersfield T

Sky Bet League One
AFC Wimbledon v Rochdale
Bolton W v Charlton Ath
Bristol R v Swindon T
Bury v Walsall
Fleetwood T v Southend U
Gillingham v Shrewsbury T
Millwall v Chesterfield
Northampton T v Coventry C
Oldham Ath v Bradford C
Oxford U v Sheffield U
Peterborough U v Milton Keynes D
Scunthorpe U v Port Vale

Sky Bet League Two
Carlisle U v Barnet
Colchester U v Wycombe W
Crewe Alex v Cheltenham T
Luton T v Cambridge U
Mansfield T v Leyton Orient
Morecambe v Accrington S
Newport Co v Hartlepool U
Notts Co v Crawley T
Plymouth Arg v Blackpool
Portsmouth v Exeter C
Stevenage v Grimsby T
Yeovil T v Doncaster R

Tuesday, 31 January 2017
Premier League
Bournemouth v Crystal Palace
Arsenal v Watford
Burnley v Leicester C
Manchester U v Hull C
Middlesbrough v WBA
Sunderland v Tottenham H
Swansea C v Southampton
West Ham U v Manchester C

Sky Bet Championship
Barnsley v Wolverhampton W
Birmingham C v Reading
Blackburn R v Leeds U
Brentford v Aston Villa
Bristol C v Sheffield W
Burton Alb v Fulham
Cardiff C v Preston NE
Huddersfield T v Brighton & HA
Ipswich T v Derby Co
Nottingham F v Rotherham U
Wigan Ath v Norwich C

Wednesday, 1 February 2017
Premier League
Liverpool v Chelsea
Stoke C v Everton

Sky Bet Championship
Newcastle U v QPR

Saturday, 4 February 2017
Premier League
Chelsea v Arsenal
Crystal Palace v Sunderland
Everton v Bournemouth
Hull C v Liverpool
Leicester C v Manchester U
Manchester C v Swansea C
Southampton v West Ham U
Tottenham H v Middlesbrough
Watford v Burnley
WBA v Stoke C

Sky Bet Championship
Barnsley v Preston NE
Birmingham C v Fulham
Blackburn R v QPR
Brentford v Brighton & HA
Bristol C v Rotherham U
Burton Alb v Wolverhampton W
Cardiff C v Norwich C
Huddersfield T v Leeds U
Ipswich T v Reading
Newcastle U v Derby Co
Nottingham F v Aston Villa
Wigan Ath v Sheffield W

Sky Bet League One
Bradford C v Gillingham
Charlton Ath v Fleetwood T
Chesterfield v Oldham Ath
Coventry C v Millwall
Milton Keynes D v Bolton W
Port Vale v Peterborough U
Rochdale v Bristol R
Sheffield U v AFC Wimbledon
Shrewsbury T v Bury
Southend U v Scunthorpe U
Swindon T v Oxford U
Walsall v Northampton T

Sky Bet League Two
Accrington S v Notts Co
Barnet v Mansfield T
Blackpool v Colchester U
Cambridge U v Plymouth Arg
Cheltenham T v Newport Co
Crawley T v Stevenage
Doncaster R v Morecambe
Exeter C v Crewe Alex
Grimsby T v Luton T
Hartlepool U v Yeovil T
Leyton Orient v Carlisle U
Wycombe W v Portsmouth

Saturday, 11 February 2017
Premier League
Bournemouth v Manchester C
Arsenal v Hull C
Burnley v Chelsea
Liverpool v Tottenham H
Manchester U v Watford
Middlesbrough v Everton
Stoke C v Crystal Palace
Sunderland v Southampton
Swansea C v Leicester C
West Ham U v WBA

Sky Bet Championship
Aston Villa v Ipswich T
Brighton & HA v Burton Alb
Derby Co v Bristol C
Fulham v Wigan Ath
Leeds U v Cardiff C
Norwich C v Nottingham F
Preston NE v Brentford
QPR v Huddersfield T
Reading v Barnsley
Rotherham U v Blackburn R
Sheffield W v Birmingham C
Wolverhampton W v Newcastle U

Sky Bet League One
AFC Wimbledon v Charlton Ath
Bolton W v Walsall
Bristol R v Bradford C
Bury v Swindon T
Fleetwood T v Rochdale
Gillingham v Port Vale
Millwall v Southend U
Northampton T v Chesterfield
Oldham Ath v Coventry C
Oxford U v Milton Keynes D
Peterborough U v Sheffield U
Scunthorpe U v Shrewsbury T

Sky Bet League Two
Carlisle U v Blackpool
Colchester U v Barnet
Crewe Alex v Grimsby T
Luton T v Crawley T
Mansfield T v Hartlepool U
Morecambe v Cambridge U
Newport Co v Doncaster R
Notts Co v Cheltenham T
Plymouth Arg v Exeter C
Portsmouth v Accrington S
Stevenage v Wycombe W
Yeovil T v Leyton Orient

Tuesday, 14 February 2017
Sky Bet Championship
Aston Villa v Barnsley
Brighton & HA v Ipswich T
Derby Co v Cardiff C
Fulham v Nottingham F
Leeds U v Bristol C
Norwich C v Newcastle U
Preston NE v Birmingham C
QPR v Burton Alb
Reading v Brentford
Rotherham U v Huddersfield T
Sheffield W v Blackburn R
Wolverhampton W v Wigan Ath

Sky Bet League One
AFC Wimbledon v Coventry C
Bolton W v Rochdale
Bristol R v Sheffield U
Bury v Milton Keynes D
Fleetwood T v Bradford C
Gillingham v Chesterfield
Millwall v Port Vale
Northampton T v Swindon T
Oldham Ath v Charlton Ath
Oxford U v Southend U
Peterborough U v Shrewsbury T
Scunthorpe U v Walsall

Sky Bet League Two
Carlisle U v Doncaster R
Colchester U v Crawley T
Crewe Alex v Wycombe W
Luton T v Hartlepool U
Mansfield T v Accrington S
Morecambe v Barnet
Newport Co v Grimsby T
Notts Co v Exeter C
Plymouth Arg v Leyton Orient
Portsmouth v Blackpool
Stevenage v Cheltenham T
Yeovil T v Cambridge U

Saturday, 18 February 2017
Sky Bet Championship
Barnsley v Brighton & HA
Birmingham C v QPR
Blackburn R v Derby Co
Brentford v Wolverhampton W
Bristol C v Fulham
Burton Alb v Norwich C
Cardiff C v Rotherham U
Huddersfield T v Reading
Ipswich T v Leeds U
Newcastle U v Aston Villa
Nottingham F v Sheffield W
Wigan Ath v Preston NE

Sky Bet League One
Bradford C v Bolton W
Charlton Ath v Oxford U
Chesterfield v Bury
Coventry C v Gillingham
Milton Keynes D v Fleetwood T
Port Vale v Bristol R
Rochdale v Millwall
Sheffield U v Scunthorpe U
Shrewsbury T v AFC Wimbledon
Southend U v Northampton T
Swindon T v Oldham Ath
Walsall v Peterborough U

Sky Bet League Two
Accrington S v Colchester U
Barnet v Portsmouth
Blackpool v Crewe Alex
Cambridge U v Newport Co
Cheltenham T v Yeovil T
Crawley T v Morecambe
Doncaster R v Luton T
Exeter C v Stevenage
Grimsby T v Mansfield T
Hartlepool U v Plymouth Arg
Leyton Orient v Notts Co
Wycombe W v Carlisle U

Saturday, 25 February 2017
Premier League
Chelsea v Swansea C
Crystal Palace v Middlesbrough
Everton v Sunderland
Hull C v Burnley
Leicester C v Liverpool
Manchester C v Manchester U
Southampton v Arsenal
Tottenham H v Stoke C
Watford v West Ham U
WBA v Bournemouth

Sky Bet Championship
Aston Villa v Derby Co
Barnsley v Huddersfield T
Brentford v Rotherham U
Brighton & HA v Reading
Burton Alb v Blackburn R
Cardiff C v Fulham
Leeds U v Sheffield W
Newcastle U v Bristol C
Norwich C v Ipswich T
Preston NE v QPR
Wigan Ath v Nottingham F
Wolverhampton W v Birmingham C

Sky Bet League One
AFC Wimbledon v Walsall
Bristol R v Scunthorpe U
Charlton Ath v Bury
Chesterfield v Oxford U
Coventry C v Swindon T
Fleetwood T v Northampton T
Gillingham v Southend U
Milton Keynes D v Shrewsbury T
Oldham Ath v Millwall
Peterborough U v Rochdale
Port Vale v Bradford C
Sheffield U v Bolton W

Sky Bet League Two
Barnet v Cambridge U
Carlisle U v Portsmouth
Colchester U v Hartlepool U
Crewe Alex v Stevenage
Doncaster R v Accrington S
Exeter C v Blackpool
Leyton Orient v Cheltenham T
Luton T v Plymouth Arg
Mansfield T v Newport Co
Morecambe v Grimsby T
Notts Co v Yeovil T
Wycombe W v Crawley T

Tuesday, 28 February 2017
Sky Bet League One
Bolton W v Bristol R
Bradford C v Milton Keynes D
Bury v Coventry C
Millwall v Peterborough U
Northampton T v Oldham Ath
Oxford U v Fleetwood T
Rochdale v Port Vale
Scunthorpe U v AFC Wimbledon
Shrewsbury T v Charlton Ath
Southend U v Sheffield U
Swindon T v Gillingham
Walsall v Chesterfield

Sky Bet League Two
Accrington S v Wycombe W
Blackpool v Barnet
Cambridge U v Doncaster R
Cheltenham T v Carlisle U
Crawley T v Exeter C
Grimsby T v Colchester U
Hartlepool U v Crewe Alex
Newport Co v Luton T
Plymouth Arg v Notts Co
Portsmouth v Morecambe
Stevenage v Leyton Orient
Yeovil T v Mansfield T

Saturday, 4 March 2017
Premier League
Leicester C v Hull C
Liverpool v Arsenal
Manchester U v Bournemouth
Stoke C v Middlesbrough
Sunderland v Manchester C
Swansea C v Burnley
Tottenham H v Everton
Watford v Southampton
WBA v Crystal Palace
West Ham U v Chelsea

Sky Bet Championship
Birmingham C v Leeds U
Blackburn R v Wigan Ath
Bristol C v Burton Alb
Derby Co v Barnsley
Fulham v Preston NE
Huddersfield T v Newcastle U
Ipswich T v Brentford
Nottingham F v Brighton & HA
QPR v Cardiff C
Reading v Wolverhampton W
Rotherham U v Aston Villa
Sheffield W v Norwich C

Sky Bet League One
Bolton W v AFC Wimbledon
Bradford C v Peterborough U
Bury v Gillingham
Millwall v Milton Keynes D
Northampton T v Charlton Ath
Oxford U v Bristol R
Rochdale v Sheffield U
Scunthorpe U v Fleetwood T
Shrewsbury T v Coventry C
Southend U v Port Vale
Swindon T v Chesterfield
Walsall v Oldham Ath

Sky Bet League Two
Accrington S v Barnet
Blackpool v Morecambe
Cambridge U v Colchester U
Cheltenham T v Mansfield T
Crawley T v Doncaster R
Grimsby T v Wycombe W
Hartlepool U v Exeter C
Newport Co v Leyton Orient
Plymouth Arg v Carlisle U
Portsmouth v Crewe Alex
Stevenage v Notts Co
Yeovil T v Luton T

Tuesday, 7 March 2017
Sky Bet Championship
Birmingham C v Wigan Ath
Blackburn R v Cardiff C
Bristol C v Norwich C
Derby Co v Preston NE
Fulham v Leeds U
Huddersfield T v Aston Villa
Ipswich T v Wolverhampton W
Nottingham F v Brentford
QPR v Barnsley
Reading v Newcastle U
Rotherham U v Brighton & HA
Sheffield W v Burton Alb

Saturday, 11 March 2017
Premier League
Bournemouth v West Ham U
Arsenal v Leicester C
Burnley v Liverpool
Chelsea v Watford
Crystal Palace v Tottenham H
Everton v WBA
Hull C v Swansea C
Manchester C v Stoke C
Middlesbrough v Sunderland
Southampton v Manchester U

Sky Bet Championship
Aston Villa v Sheffield W
Barnsley v Ipswich T
Brentford v Huddersfield T
Brighton & HA v Derby Co
Burton Alb v Nottingham F
Cardiff C v Birmingham C
Leeds U v QPR
Newcastle U v Fulham
Norwich C v Blackburn R
Preston NE v Reading
Wigan Ath v Bristol C
Wolverhampton W v Rotherham U

Sky Bet League One
AFC Wimbledon v Northampton T
Bristol R v Southend U
Charlton Ath v Walsall
Chesterfield v Shrewsbury T
Coventry C v Bradford C
Fleetwood T v Bolton W
Gillingham v Scunthorpe U
Milton Keynes D v Rochdale
Oldham Ath v Bury
Peterborough U v Oxford U
Port Vale v Swindon T
Sheffield U v Millwall

Sky Bet League Two
Barnet v Crawley T
Carlisle U v Cambridge U
Colchester U v Portsmouth
Crewe Alex v Newport Co
Doncaster R v Cheltenham T
Exeter C v Accrington S
Leyton Orient v Grimsby T
Luton T v Stevenage
Mansfield T v Plymouth Arg
Morecambe v Yeovil T
Notts Co v Hartlepool U
Wycombe W v Blackpool

Tuesday, 14 March 2017
Sky Bet League One
AFC Wimbledon v Milton Keynes D
Bury v Bristol R
Charlton Ath v Bradford C
Chesterfield v Peterborough U
Coventry C v Southend U
Gillingham v Bolton W
Northampton T v Port Vale
Oldham Ath v Oxford U
Scunthorpe U v Rochdale
Shrewsbury T v Millwall
Swindon T v Sheffield U
Walsall v Fleetwood T

Sky Bet League Two
Accrington S v Leyton Orient
Barnet v Yeovil T
Blackpool v Stevenage
Cambridge U v Hartlepool U
Carlisle U v Luton T
Colchester U v Mansfield T
Crawley T v Crewe Alex
Doncaster R v Notts Co
Exeter C v Cheltenham T
Morecambe v Newport Co
Portsmouth v Grimsby T
Wycombe W v Plymouth Arg

Saturday, 18 March 2017
Premier League
Bournemouth v Swansea C
Crystal Palace v Watford
Everton v Hull C
Manchester C v Liverpool
Middlesbrough v Manchester U
Stoke C v Chelsea
Sunderland v Burnley
Tottenham H v Southampton
WBA v Arsenal
West Ham U v Leicester C

Sky Bet Championship
Birmingham C v Newcastle U
Blackburn R v Preston NE
Bristol C v Huddersfield T
Burton Alb v Brentford
Cardiff C v Ipswich T
Fulham v Wolverhampton W
Leeds U v Brighton & HA
Norwich C v Barnsley
Nottingham F v Derby Co
QPR v Rotherham U
Sheffield W v Reading
Wigan Ath v Aston Villa

Sky Bet League One
Bolton W v Northampton T
Bradford C v Swindon T
Bristol R v Chesterfield
Fleetwood T v AFC Wimbledon
Millwall v Bury
Milton Keynes D v Coventry C
Oxford U v Scunthorpe U
Peterborough U v Oldham Ath
Port Vale v Shrewsbury T
Rochdale v Gillingham
Sheffield U v Charlton Ath
Southend U v Walsall

Sky Bet League Two
Cheltenham T v Cambridge U
Crewe Alex v Colchester U
Grimsby T v Crawley T
Hartlepool U v Wycombe W
Leyton Orient v Doncaster R
Luton T v Exeter C
Mansfield T v Carlisle U
Newport Co v Blackpool
Notts Co v Barnet
Plymouth Arg v Morecambe
Stevenage v Portsmouth
Yeovil T v Accrington S

Saturday, 25 March 2017
Sky Bet League One
AFC Wimbledon v Southend U
Bury v Fleetwood T
Charlton Ath v Milton Keynes D
Chesterfield v Rochdale
Coventry C v Bristol R
Gillingham v Peterborough U
Northampton T v Oxford U
Oldham Ath v Sheffield U
Scunthorpe U v Bradford C
Shrewsbury T v Bolton W
Swindon T v Millwall
Walsall v Port Vale

Sky Bet League Two
Accrington S v Grimsby T
Barnet v Cheltenham T
Blackpool v Hartlepool U
Cambridge U v Stevenage
Carlisle U v Crewe Alex
Colchester U v Luton T
Crawley T v Leyton Orient
Doncaster R v Plymouth Arg
Exeter C v Yeovil T
Morecambe v Mansfield T
Portsmouth v Newport Co
Wycombe W v Notts Co

Saturday, 1 April 2017
Premier League
Arsenal v Manchester C
Burnley v Tottenham H
Chelsea v Crystal Palace
Hull C v West Ham U
Leicester C v Stoke C
Liverpool v Everton
Manchester U v WBA
Southampton v Bournemouth
Swansea C v Middlesbrough
Watford v Sunderland

Sky Bet Championship
Aston Villa v Norwich C
Barnsley v Sheffield W
Brentford v Bristol C
Brighton & HA v Blackburn R
Derby Co v QPR
Huddersfield T v Burton Alb
Ipswich T v Birmingham C
Newcastle U v Wigan Ath
Preston NE v Nottingham F
Reading v Leeds U
Rotherham U v Fulham
Wolverhampton W v Cardiff C

Sky Bet League One
Bolton W v Chesterfield
Bradford C v Walsall
Bristol R v Shrewsbury T
Fleetwood T v Swindon T
Millwall v Scunthorpe U
Milton Keynes D v Gillingham
Oxford U v Bury
Peterborough U v Charlton Ath
Port Vale v AFC Wimbledon
Rochdale v Northampton T
Sheffield U v Coventry C
Southend U v Oldham Ath

Sky Bet League Two
Cheltenham T v Morecambe
Crewe Alex v Cambridge U
Grimsby T v Doncaster R
Hartlepool U v Portsmouth
Leyton Orient v Wycombe W
Luton T v Blackpool
Mansfield T v Exeter C
Newport Co v Crawley T
Notts Co v Colchester U
Plymouth Arg v Accrington S
Stevenage v Barnet
Yeovil T v Carlisle U

Tuesday, 4 April 2017
Premier League
Arsenal v West Ham U
Burnley v Stoke C
Hull C v Middlesbrough
Leicester C v Sunderland
Manchester U v Everton
Swansea C v Tottenham H
Watford v WBA

Sky Bet Championship
Aston Villa v QPR
Barnsley v Cardiff C
Brentford v Leeds U
Brighton & HA v Birmingham C
Derby Co v Fulham

Huddersfield T v Norwich C
Ipswich T v Wigan Ath
Preston NE v Bristol C
Reading v Blackburn R
Rotherham U v Sheffield W
Wolverhampton W v Nottingham F

Wednesday, 5 April 2017
Premier League
Chelsea v Manchester C
Liverpool v Bournemouth
Southampton v Crystal Palace

Sky Bet Championship
Newcastle U v Burton Alb

Saturday, 8 April 2017
Premier League
Bournemouth v Chelsea
Crystal Palace v Arsenal
Everton v Leicester C
Manchester C v Hull C
Middlesbrough v Burnley
Stoke C v Liverpool
Sunderland v Manchester U
Tottenham H v Watford
WBA v Southampton
West Ham U v Swansea C

Sky Bet Championship
Birmingham C v Derby Co
Blackburn R v Barnsley
Bristol C v Wolverhampton W
Burton Alb v Aston Villa
Cardiff C v Brentford
Fulham v Ipswich T
Leeds U v Preston NE
Norwich C v Reading
Nottingham F v Huddersfield T
QPR v Brighton & HA
Sheffield W v Newcastle U
Wigan Ath v Rotherham U

Sky Bet League One
AFC Wimbledon v Bristol R
Bury v Bradford C
Charlton Ath v Southend U
Chesterfield v Port Vale
Coventry C v Peterborough U
Gillingham v Millwall
Northampton T v Sheffield U
Oldham Ath v Fleetwood T
Scunthorpe U v Bolton W
Shrewsbury T v Rochdale
Swindon T v Milton Keynes D
Walsall v Oxford U

Sky Bet League Two
Accrington S v Crewe Alex
Barnet v Luton T
Blackpool v Grimsby T
Cambridge U v Leyton Orient
Carlisle U v Notts Co
Colchester U v Stevenage
Crawley T v Plymouth Arg
Doncaster R v Mansfield T
Exeter C v Newport Co
Morecambe v Hartlepool U
Portsmouth v Yeovil T
Wycombe W v Cheltenham T

Saturday, 15 April 2017
Premier League
Crystal Palace v Leicester C
Everton v Burnley
Manchester U v Chelsea
Middlesbrough v Arsenal
Southampton v Manchester C
Stoke C v Hull C
Sunderland v West Ham U
Tottenham H v Bournemouth
Watford v Swansea C
WBA v Liverpool

Sky Bet Championship
Aston Villa v Reading

Brentford v Derby Co
Bristol C v QPR
Burton Alb v Ipswich T
Huddersfield T v Preston NE
Newcastle U v Leeds U
Norwich C v Fulham
Nottingham F v Blackburn R
Rotherham U v Birmingham C
Sheffield W v Cardiff C
Wigan Ath v Barnsley
Wolverhampton W v Brighton & HA

Sky Bet League One
Bradford C v Oxford U
Bury v Rochdale
Chesterfield v Southend U
Coventry C v Charlton Ath
Gillingham v Bristol R
Millwall v Northampton T
Milton Keynes D v Scunthorpe U
Oldham Ath v Bolton W
Peterborough U v Fleetwood T
Port Vale v Sheffield U
Shrewsbury T v Walsall
Swindon T v AFC Wimbledon

Sky Bet League Two
Blackpool v Accrington S
Colchester U v Doncaster R
Crawley T v Cheltenham T
Crewe Alex v Notts Co
Exeter C v Barnet
Grimsby T v Cambridge U
Hartlepool U v Carlisle U
Luton T v Leyton Orient
Newport Co v Yeovil T
Portsmouth v Plymouth Arg
Stevenage v Morecambe
Wycombe W v Mansfield T

Monday, 17 April 2017
Sky Bet Championship
Barnsley v Brentford
Birmingham C v Burton Alb
Blackburn R v Bristol C
Brighton & HA v Wigan Ath
Cardiff C v Nottingham F
Derby Co v Huddersfield T
Fulham v Aston Villa
Ipswich T v Newcastle U
Leeds U v Wolverhampton W
Preston NE v Norwich C
QPR v Sheffield W
Reading v Rotherham U

Sky Bet League One
AFC Wimbledon v Peterborough U
Bolton W v Bury
Bristol R v Oldham Ath
Charlton Ath v Gillingham
Fleetwood T v Millwall
Northampton T v Shrewsbury T
Oxford U v Port Vale
Rochdale v Coventry C
Scunthorpe U v Chesterfield
Sheffield U v Bradford C
Southend U v Milton Keynes D
Walsall v Swindon T

Sky Bet League Two
Accrington S v Crawley T
Barnet v Wycombe W
Cambridge U v Exeter C
Carlisle U v Stevenage
Cheltenham T v Grimsby T
Doncaster R v Blackpool
Leyton Orient v Hartlepool U
Mansfield T v Luton T
Morecambe v Colchester U
Notts Co v Portsmouth
Plymouth Arg v Newport Co
Yeovil T v Crewe Alex

Saturday, 22 April 2017
Premier League
Bournemouth v Middlesbrough
Arsenal v Sunderland
Burnley v Manchester U

Chelsea v Southampton
Hull C v Watford
Leicester C v Tottenham H
Liverpool v Crystal Palace
Manchester C v WBA
Swansea C v Stoke C
West Ham U v Everton

Sky Bet Championship
Aston Villa v Birmingham C
Brentford v QPR
Bristol C v Barnsley
Burton Alb v Leeds U
Huddersfield T v Fulham
Newcastle U v Preston NE
Norwich C v Brighton & HA
Nottingham F v Reading
Rotherham U v Ipswich T
Sheffield W v Derby Co
Wigan Ath v Cardiff C
Wolverhampton W v Blackburn R

Sky Bet League One
Bradford C v AFC Wimbledon
Bury v Northampton T
Chesterfield v Charlton Ath
Coventry C v Walsall
Gillingham v Fleetwood T
Millwall v Oxford U
Milton Keynes D v Sheffield U
Oldham Ath v Rochdale
Peterborough U v Bristol R
Port Vale v Bolton W
Shrewsbury T v Southend U
Swindon T v Scunthorpe U

Sky Bet League Two
Blackpool v Cheltenham T
Colchester U v Plymouth Arg
Crawley T v Carlisle U
Crewe Alex v Leyton Orient
Exeter C v Morecambe
Grimsby T v Yeovil T
Hartlepool U v Barnet
Luton T v Notts Co
Newport Co v Accrington S
Portsmouth v Cambridge U
Stevenage v Mansfield T
Wycombe W v Doncaster R

Saturday, 29 April 2017
Premier League
Crystal Palace v Burnley
Everton v Chelsea
Manchester U v Swansea C
Middlesbrough v Manchester C
Southampton v Hull C
Stoke C v West Ham U
Sunderland v Bournemouth
Tottenham H v Arsenal
Watford v Liverpool
WBA v Leicester C

Sky Bet Championship
Barnsley v Burton Alb
Birmingham C v Huddersfield T
Blackburn R v Aston Villa
Brighton & HA v Bristol C
Cardiff C v Newcastle U
Derby Co v Wolverhampton W
Fulham v Brentford
Ipswich T v Sheffield W
Leeds U v Norwich C
Preston NE v Rotherham U
QPR v Nottingham F
Reading v Wigan Ath

Sky Bet League Two
Accrington S v Luton T
Barnet v Grimsby T
Cambridge U v Crawley T
Carlisle U v Newport Co
Cheltenham T v Hartlepool U
Doncaster R v Exeter C
Leyton Orient v Colchester U
Mansfield T v Portsmouth
Morecambe v Wycombe W
Notts Co v Blackpool

Plymouth Arg v Crewe Alex
Yeovil T v Stevenage

Sunday, 30 April 2017
Sky Bet League One
AFC Wimbledon v Oldham Ath
Bolton W v Peterborough U
Bristol R v Millwall
Charlton Ath v Swindon T
Fleetwood T v Port Vale
Northampton T v Gillingham
Oxford U v Shrewsbury T
Rochdale v Bradford C
Scunthorpe U v Coventry C
Sheffield U v Chesterfield
Southend U v Bury
Walsall v Milton Keynes D

Saturday, 6 May 2017
Premier League
Bournemouth v Stoke C
Arsenal v Manchester U
Burnley v WBA
Chelsea v Middlesbrough
Hull C v Sunderland
Leicester C v Watford
Liverpool v Southampton
Manchester C v Crystal Palace
Swansea C v Everton
West Ham U v Tottenham H

Sky Bet League Two
Blackpool v Leyton Orient
Colchester U v Yeovil T
Crawley T v Mansfield T
Crewe Alex v Barnet
Exeter C v Carlisle U
Grimsby T v Plymouth Arg
Hartlepool U v Doncaster R
Luton T v Morecambe
Newport Co v Notts Co
Portsmouth v Cheltenham T
Stevenage v Accrington S
Wycombe W v Cambridge U

Sunday, 7 May 2017
Sky Bet Championship
Aston Villa v Brighton & HA
Brentford v Blackburn R
Bristol C v Birmingham C
Burton Alb v Reading
Huddersfield T v Cardiff C
Newcastle U v Barnsley
Norwich C v QPR
Nottingham F v Ipswich T
Rotherham U v Derby Co
Sheffield W v Fulham
Wigan Ath v Leeds U
Wolverhampton W v Preston NE

Saturday, 13 May 2017
Premier League
Bournemouth v Burnley
Crystal Palace v Hull C
Everton v Watford
Manchester C v Leicester C
Middlesbrough v Southampton
Stoke C v Arsenal
Sunderland v Swansea C
Tottenham H v Manchester U
WBA v Chelsea
West Ham U v Liverpool

Sunday, 21 May 2017
Premier League
Arsenal v Everton
Burnley v West Ham U
Chelsea v Sunderland
Hull C v Tottenham H
Leicester C v Bournemouth
Liverpool v Middlesbrough
Manchester U v Crystal Palace
Southampton v Stoke C
Swansea C v WBA
Watford v Manchester C

VANARAMA NATIONAL LEAGUE
FIXTURES 2016–17

Saturday, 6 August 2016
Barrow v Aldershot T
Boreham Wood v Forest Green R
Bromley v Tranmere R
Dagenham & R v Southport
Eastleigh v Guiseley
Gateshead v Chester FC
Macclesfield T v Torquay U
Maidstone U v York C
North Ferriby U v Braintree T
Sutton U v Solihull Moors
Woking v Lincoln C
Wrexham v Dover Ath

Tuesday, 9 August 2016
Aldershot T v Maidstone U
Braintree T v Eastleigh
Chester FC v Dagenham & R
Dover Ath v Boreham Wood
Forest Green R v Sutton U
Guiseley v Wrexham
Lincoln C v North Ferriby U
Solihull Moors v Woking
Southport v Gateshead
Torquay U v Bromley
Tranmere R v Barrow
York C v Macclesfield T

Saturday, 13 August 2016
Aldershot T v Wrexham
Braintree T v Macclesfield T
Chester FC v Maidstone U
Dover Ath v North Ferriby U
Forest Green R v Gateshead
Guiseley v Dagenham & R
Lincoln C v Sutton U
Solihull Moors v Bromley
Southport v Woking
Torquay U v Barrow
Tranmere R v Eastleigh
York C v Boreham Wood

Tuesday, 16 August 2016
Barrow v Chester FC
Boreham Wood v Tranmere R
Bromley v Aldershot T
Dagenham & R v Lincoln C
Eastleigh v Dover Ath
Gateshead v York C
Macclesfield T v Southport
Maidstone U v Braintree T
North Ferriby U v Guiseley
Sutton U v Torquay U
Woking v Forest Green R
Wrexham v Solihull Moors

Saturday, 20 August 2016
Boreham Wood v Chester FC
Braintree T v Aldershot T
Bromley v Gateshead
Dover Ath v Barrow
Forest Green R v York C
Lincoln C v Southport
North Ferriby U v Torquay U
Solihull Moors v Guiseley
Sutton U v Macclesfield T
Tranmere R v Maidstone U
Woking v Dagenham & R
Wrexham v Eastleigh

Saturday, 27 August 2016
Aldershot T v North Ferriby U
Barrow v Braintree T
Chester FC v Sutton U
Dagenham & R v Wrexham
Eastleigh v Solihull Moors
Gateshead v Boreham Wood
Guiseley v Bromley
Macclesfield T v Lincoln C
Maidstone U v Forest Green R
Southport v Tranmere R
Torquay U v Dover Ath
York C v Woking

Monday, 29 August 2016
Boreham Wood v Maidstone U
Braintree T v Torquay U
Bromley v Eastleigh
Dover Ath v Aldershot T
Forest Green R v Southport
Lincoln C v Gateshead
North Ferriby U v Barrow
Solihull Moors v Macclesfield T
Sutton U v Dagenham & R
Tranmere R v Guiseley
Woking v Chester FC
Wrexham v York C

Saturday, 3 September 2016
Aldershot T v Tranmere R
Barrow v Bromley
Chester FC v Forest Green R
Dagenham & R v Boreham Wood
Eastleigh v North Ferriby U
Gateshead v Sutton U
Guiseley v Braintree T
Macclesfield T v Woking
Maidstone U v Wrexham
Southport v Dover Ath
Torquay U v Lincoln C
York C v Solihull Moors

Saturday, 10 September 2016
Aldershot T v Chester FC
Barrow v Boreham Wood
Braintree T v Gateshead
Bromley v Macclesfield T
Dover Ath v Forest Green R
Eastleigh v Southport
Guiseley v Woking
North Ferriby U v Maidstone U
Solihull Moors v Dagenham & R
Torquay U v York C
Tranmere R v Lincoln C
Wrexham v Sutton U

Tuesday, 13 September 2016
Boreham Wood v Aldershot T
Chester FC v Guiseley
Dagenham & R v Dover Ath
Forest Green R v Eastleigh
Gateshead v North Ferriby U
Lincoln C v Solihull Moors
Macclesfield T v Wrexham
Maidstone U v Bromley
Southport v Barrow
Sutton U v Braintree T
Woking v Torquay U
York C v Tranmere R

Saturday, 17 September 2016
Boreham Wood v Torquay U
Chester FC v Braintree T
Dagenham & R v North Ferriby U
Forest Green R v Bromley
Gateshead v Solihull Moors
Lincoln C v Barrow
Macclesfield T v Eastleigh
Maidstone U v Guiseley
Southport v Aldershot T
Sutton U v Tranmere R
Woking v Wrexham
York C v Dover Ath

Saturday, 24 September 2016
Aldershot T v Gateshead
Barrow v York C
Braintree T v Forest Green R
Bromley v Dagenham & R
Dover Ath v Lincoln C
Eastleigh v Sutton U
Guiseley v Macclesfield T
North Ferriby U v Southport
Solihull Moors v Boreham Wood
Torquay U v Maidstone U
Tranmere R v Woking
Wrexham v Chester FC

Saturday, 1 October 2016
Boreham Wood v Wrexham
Chester FC v Dover Ath
Dagenham & R v Tranmere R
Forest Green R v Barrow
Gateshead v Torquay U
Lincoln C v Braintree T
Macclesfield T v North Ferriby U
Maidstone U v Solihull Moors
Southport v Bromley
Sutton U v Guiseley
Woking v Eastleigh
York C v Aldershot T

Tuesday, 4 October 2016
Aldershot T v Forest Green R
Barrow v Macclesfield T
Braintree T v Boreham Wood
Bromley v Woking
Dover Ath v Sutton U
Eastleigh v Maidstone U
Guiseley v York C
North Ferriby U v Chester FC
Solihull Moors v Southport
Torquay U v Dagenham & R
Tranmere R v Gateshead
Wrexham v Lincoln C

Saturday, 8 October 2016
Aldershot T v Solihull Moors
Barrow v Maidstone U
Braintree T v York C
Bromley v Lincoln C
Chester FC v Torquay U
Eastleigh v Dagenham & R
Gateshead v Dover Ath
Guiseley v Southport
Macclesfield T v Boreham Wood
North Ferriby U v Forest Green R
Sutton U v Woking
Tranmere R v Wrexham

Saturday, 22 October 2016
Boreham Wood v North Ferriby U
Dagenham & R v Macclesfield T
Dover Ath v Braintree T
Forest Green R v Guiseley
Lincoln C v Eastleigh
Maidstone U v Gateshead
Solihull Moors v Tranmere R
Southport v Sutton U
Torquay U v Aldershot T
Woking v Barrow
Wrexham v Bromley
York C v Chester FC

Tuesday, 25 October 2016
Bromley v Dover Ath
Dagenham & R v Aldershot T
Eastleigh v Torquay U
Guiseley v Gateshead
Lincoln C v Boreham Wood
Macclesfield T v Chester FC
Solihull Moors v Forest Green R
Southport v York C
Sutton U v Maidstone U
Tranmere R v North Ferriby U
Woking v Braintree T
Wrexham v Barrow

Saturday, 29 October 2016
Aldershot T v Guiseley
Barrow v Eastleigh
Boreham Wood v Woking
Braintree T v Solihull Moors
Chester FC v Lincoln C
Dover Ath v Tranmere R
Forest Green R v Dagenham & R
Gateshead v Wrexham
Maidstone U v Macclesfield T
North Ferriby U v Bromley
Torquay U v Southport
York C v Sutton U

Saturday, 12 November 2016
Bromley v Boreham Wood
Dagenham & R v Gateshead
Eastleigh v York C
Guiseley v Torquay U
Lincoln C v Aldershot T
Macclesfield T v Forest Green R
Solihull Moors v Dover Ath
Southport v Maidstone U
Sutton U v Barrow
Tranmere R v Chester FC
Woking v North Ferriby U
Wrexham v Braintree T

Saturday, 19 November 2016
Aldershot T v Macclesfield T
Barrow v Solihull Moors
Boreham Wood v Southport
Braintree T v Tranmere R
Chester FC v Bromley
Dover Ath v Guiseley
Forest Green R v Lincoln C
Gateshead v Eastleigh
Maidstone U v Woking
North Ferriby U v Sutton U
Torquay U v Wrexham
York C v Dagenham & R

Tuesday, 22 November 2016
Aldershot T v Eastleigh
Barrow v Guiseley
Boreham Wood v Sutton U
Braintree T v Bromley

Chester FC v Southport
Dover Ath v Woking
Forest Green R v Tranmere R
Gateshead v Macclesfield T
Maidstone U v Dagenham & R
North Ferriby U v Wrexham
Torquay U v Solihull Moors
York C v Lincoln C

Saturday, 26 November 2016
Bromley v York C
Dagenham & R v Barrow
Eastleigh v Chester FC
Guiseley v Boreham Wood
Lincoln C v Maidstone U
Macclesfield T v Dover Ath
Solihull Moors v North Ferriby U
Southport v Braintree T
Sutton U v Aldershot T
Tranmere R v Torquay U
Woking v Gateshead
Wrexham v Forest Green R

Tuesday, 29 November 2016
Boreham Wood v Braintree T
Chester FC v North Ferriby U
Dagenham & R v Torquay U
Forest Green R v Aldershot T
Gateshead v Tranmere R
Lincoln C v Wrexham
Macclesfield T v Barrow
Maidstone U v Eastleigh
Southport v Solihull Moors
Sutton U v Dover Ath
Woking v Bromley
York C v Guiseley

Saturday, 3 December 2016
Aldershot T v Boreham Wood
Barrow v Southport
Braintree T v Sutton U
Bromley v Maidstone U
Dover Ath v Dagenham & R
Eastleigh v Forest Green R
Guiseley v Chester FC
North Ferriby U v Gateshead
Solihull Moors v Lincoln C
Torquay U v Woking
Tranmere R v York C
Wrexham v Macclesfield T

Saturday, 17 December 2016
Boreham Wood v Barrow
Chester FC v Aldershot T
Dagenham & R v Solihull Moors
Forest Green R v Dover Ath
.Gateshead v Braintree T
Lincoln C v Tranmere R
Macclesfield T v Bromley
Maidstone U v North Ferriby U
Southport v Eastleigh
Sutton U v Wrexham
Woking v Guiseley
York C v Torquay U

Monday, 26 December 2016
Aldershot T v Woking
Barrow v Gateshead
Braintree T v Dagenham & R
Bromley v Sutton U
Dover Ath v Maidstone U
Eastleigh v Boreham Wood
Guiseley v Lincoln C
North Ferriby U v York C
Solihull Moors v Chester FC
Torquay U v Forest Green R

Tranmere R v Macclesfield T
Wrexham v Southport

Sunday, 1 January 2017
Boreham Wood v Eastleigh
Chester FC v Solihull Moors
Dagenham & R v Braintree T
Forest Green R v Torquay U
Gateshead v Barrow
Lincoln C v Guiseley
Macclesfield T v Tranmere R
Maidstone U v Dover Ath
Southport v Wrexham
Sutton U v Bromley
Woking v Aldershot T
York C v North Ferriby U

Saturday, 7 January 2017
Aldershot T v Southport
Barrow v Lincoln C
Braintree T v Chester FC
Bromley v Forest Green R
Dover Ath v York C
Eastleigh v Macclesfield T
Guiseley v Maidstone U
North Ferriby U v Dagenham & R
Solihull Moors v Gateshead
Torquay U v Boreham Wood
Tranmere R v Sutton U
Wrexham v Woking

Saturday, 21 January 2017
Boreham Wood v Solihull Moors
Chester FC v Wrexham
Dagenham & R v Bromley
Forest Green R v Braintree T
Gateshead v Aldershot T
Lincoln C v Dover Ath
Macclesfield T v Guiseley
Maidstone U v Torquay U
Southport v North Ferriby U
Sutton U v Eastleigh
Woking v Tranmere R
York C v Barrow

Saturday, 28 January 2017
Aldershot T v York C
Barrow v Forest Green R
Braintree T v Lincoln C
Bromley v Southport
Dover Ath v Chester FC
Eastleigh v Woking
Guiseley v Sutton U
North Ferriby U v Macclesfield T
Solihull Moors v Maidstone U
Torquay U v Gateshead
Tranmere R v Dagenham & R
Wrexham v Boreham Wood

Saturday, 4 February 2017
Barrow v Tranmere R
Boreham Wood v Dover Ath
Bromley v Torquay U
Dagenham & R v Chester FC
Eastleigh v Braintree T
Gateshead v Southport
Macclesfield T v York C
Maidstone U v Aldershot T
North Ferriby U v Lincoln C
Sutton U v Forest Green R
Woking v Solihull Moors
Wrexham v Guiseley

Saturday, 11 February 2017
Aldershot T v Barrow
Braintree T v North Ferriby U
Chester FC v Gateshead

Dover Ath v Wrexham
Forest Green R v Boreham Wood
Guiseley v Eastleigh
Lincoln C v Woking
Solihull Moors v Sutton U
Southport v Dagenham & R
Torquay U v Macclesfield T
Tranmere R v Bromley
York C v Maidstone U

Saturday, 18 February 2017
Barrow v Torquay U
Boreham Wood v York C
Bromley v Solihull Moors
Dagenham & R v Guiseley
Eastleigh v Tranmere R
Gateshead v Forest Green R
Macclesfield T v Braintree T
Maidstone U v Chester FC
North Ferriby U v Dover Ath
Sutton U v Lincoln C
Woking v Southport
Wrexham v Aldershot T

Saturday, 25 February 2017
Aldershot T v Bromley
Braintree T v Maidstone U
Chester FC v Barrow
Dover Ath v Eastleigh
Forest Green R v Woking
Guiseley v North Ferriby U
Lincoln C v Dagenham & R
Solihull Moors v Wrexham
Southport v Macclesfield T
Torquay U v Sutton U
Tranmere R v Boreham Wood
York C v Gateshead

Tuesday, 28 February 2017
Bromley v Braintree T
Dagenham & R v Maidstone U
Eastleigh v Aldershot T
Guiseley v Barrow
Lincoln C v York C
Macclesfield T v Gateshead
Solihull Moors v Torquay U
Southport v Chester FC
Sutton U v Boreham Wood
Tranmere R v Forest Green R
Woking v Dover Ath
Wrexham v North Ferriby U

Saturday, 4 March 2017
Aldershot T v Lincoln C
Barrow v Sutton U
Boreham Wood v Bromley
Braintree T v Wrexham
Chester FC v Tranmere R
Dover Ath v Solihull Moors
Forest Green R v Macclesfield T
Gateshead v Dagenham & R
Maidstone U v Southport
North Ferriby U v Woking
Torquay U v Guiseley
York C v Eastleigh

Saturday, 11 March 2017
Bromley v North Ferriby U
Dagenham & R v Forest Green R
Eastleigh v Barrow

Guiseley v Aldershot T
Lincoln C v Chester FC
Macclesfield T v Maidstone U
Solihull Moors v Braintree T
Southport v Torquay U
Sutton U v York C
Tranmere R v Dover Ath
Woking v Boreham Wood
Wrexham v Gateshead

Saturday, 18 March 2017
Aldershot T v Sutton U
Barrow v Dagenham & R
Boreham Wood v Guiseley
Braintree T v Southport
Chester FC v Eastleigh
Dover Ath v Macclesfield T
Forest Green R v Wrexham
Gateshead v Woking
Maidstone U v Lincoln C
North Ferriby U v Solihull Moors
Torquay U v Tranmere R
York C v Bromley

Tuesday, 21 March 2017
Aldershot T v Dagenham & R
Barrow v Wrexham
Boreham Wood v Lincoln C
Braintree T v Woking
Chester FC v Macclesfield T
Dover Ath v Bromley
Forest Green R v Solihull Moors
Gateshead v Guiseley
Maidstone U v Sutton U
North Ferriby U v Tranmere R
Torquay U v Eastleigh
York C v Southport

Saturday, 25 March 2017
Bromley v Chester FC
Dagenham & R v York C
Eastleigh v Gateshead
Guiseley v Dover Ath
Lincoln C v Forest Green R
Macclesfield T v Aldershot T
Solihull Moors v Barrow
Southport v Boreham Wood
Sutton U v North Ferriby U
Tranmere R v Braintree T
Woking v Maidstone U
Wrexham v Torquay U

Saturday, 1 April 2017
Boreham Wood v Macclesfield T
Dagenham & R v Eastleigh
Dover Ath v Gateshead
Forest Green R v North Ferriby U
Lincoln C v Bromley
Maidstone U v Barrow
Solihull Moors v Aldershot T
Southport v Guiseley
Torquay U v Chester FC
Woking v Sutton U
Wrexham v Tranmere R
York C v Braintree T

Saturday, 8 April 2017
Aldershot T v Torquay U
Barrow v Woking
Braintree T v Dover Ath

Bromley v Wrexham
Chester FC v York C
Eastleigh v Lincoln C
Gateshead v Maidstone U
Guiseley v Forest Green R
Macclesfield T v Dagenham & R
North Ferriby U v Boreham Wood
Sutton U v Southport
Tranmere R v Solihull Moors

Friday, 14 April 2017
Boreham Wood v Dagenham & R
Braintree T v Guiseley
Bromley v Barrow
Dover Ath v Southport
Forest Green R v Chester FC
Lincoln C v Torquay U
North Ferriby U v Eastleigh
Solihull Moors v York C
Sutton U v Gateshead
Tranmere R v Aldershot T
Woking v Macclesfield T
Wrexham v Maidstone U

Monday, 17 April 2017
Aldershot T v Dover Ath
Barrow v North Ferriby U
Chester FC v Woking
Dagenham & R v Sutton U
Eastleigh v Bromley
Gateshead v Lincoln C
Guiseley v Tranmere R
Macclesfield T v Solihull Moors
Maidstone U v Boreham Wood
Southport v Forest Green R
Torquay U v Braintree T
York C v Wrexham

Saturday, 22 April 2017
Boreham Wood v Gateshead
Braintree T v Barrow
Bromley v Guiseley
Dover Ath v Torquay U
Forest Green R v Maidstone U
Lincoln C v Macclesfield T
North Ferriby U v Aldershot T
Solihull Moors v Eastleigh
Sutton U v Chester FC
Tranmere R v Southport
Woking v York C
Wrexham v Dagenham & R

Saturday, 29 April 2017
Aldershot T v Braintree T
Barrow v Dover Ath
Chester FC v Boreham Wood
Dagenham & R v Woking
Eastleigh v Wrexham
Gateshead v Bromley
Guiseley v Solihull Moors
Macclesfield T v Sutton U
Maidstone U v Tranmere R
Southport v Lincoln C
Torquay U v North Ferriby U
York C v Forest Green R

THE SCOTTISH PREMIER LEAGUE AND SCOTTISH LEAGUE FIXTURES 2016–17

Sky Sports   All fixtures subject to change.

Saturday, 6 August 2016
Ladbrokes Scottish Premiership
Hearts v Celtic* (14.15)
Kilmarnock v Motherwell
Partick Thistle v Inverness CT
Rangers v Hamilton A* (12.30)
Ross Co v Dundee
St Johnstone v Aberdeen

Ladbrokes Scottish Championship
Ayr U v Raith R
Dundee U v Queen of the South
Dunfermline Ath v Dumbarton
Falkirk v Hibernian
St Mirren v Greenock Morton

Ladbrokes Scottish League 1
Alloa Ath v Peterhead
Brechin C v Stenhousemuir
East Fife v Albion R
Livingston v Stranraer
Queen's Park v Airdrieonians

Ladbrokes Scottish League 2
Annan Ath v Stirling Alb
Arbroath v Berwick R
Clyde v Montrose
Cowdenbeath v Elgin C
Edinburgh C v Forfar Ath

Saturday, 13 August 2016
Ladbrokes Scottish Premiership
Aberdeen v Hearts
Celtic v Partick Thistle
Dundee v Rangers
Hamilton A v Kilmarnock
Inverness CT v Ross Co
Motherwell v St Johnstone

Ladbrokes Scottish Championship
Dumbarton v Dundee U
Hibernian v Dunfermline Ath
Greenock Morton v Falkirk
Queen of the South v Ayr U
Raith R v St Mirren

Ladbrokes Scottish League 1
Airdrieonians v Livingston
Albion R v Brechin C
Peterhead v East Fife
Stenhousemuir v Queen's Park
Stranraer v Alloa Ath

Ladbrokes Scottish League 2
Berwick R v Annan Ath
Elgin C v Edinburgh C
Forfar Ath v Cowdenbeath
Montrose v Arbroath
Stirling Alb v Clyde

Saturday, 20 August 2016
Ladbrokes Scottish Premiership
Aberdeen v Partick Thistle
Dundee v Hamilton A
Hearts v Inverness CT
Rangers v Motherwell
Ross Co v Kilmarnock
St Johnstone v Celtic

Ladbrokes Scottish Championship
Dundee U v Ayr U
Greenock Morton v Dumbarton
Queen of the South v Falkirk
Raith R v Dunfermline Ath
St Mirren v Hibernian

Ladbrokes Scottish League 1
Airdrieonians v Stranraer
Alloa Ath v East Fife
Brechin C v Queen's Park
Livingston v Stenhousemuir
Peterhead v Albion R

Ladbrokes Scottish League 2
Annan Ath v Clyde
Berwick R v Forfar Ath
Cowdenbeath v Edinburgh C
Elgin C v Arbroath
Stirling Alb v Montrose

Saturday, 27 August 2016
Ladbrokes Scottish Premiership
Celtic v Aberdeen
Hamilton A v Ross Co
Inverness CT v St Johnstone
Kilmarnock v Rangers
Motherwell v Dundee
Partick Thistle v Hearts

Ladbrokes Scottish Championship
Ayr U v St Mirren
Dundee U v Raith R
Dunfermline Ath v Queen of the South
Falkirk v Dumbarton
Hibernian v Greenock Morton

Ladbrokes Scottish League 1
Albion R v Alloa Ath
East Fife v Brechin C
Queen's Park v Livingston
Stenhousemuir v Airdrieonians
Stranraer v Peterhead

Ladbrokes Scottish League 2
Arbroath v Stirling Alb
Clyde v Cowdenbeath
Edinburgh C v Berwick R
Forfar Ath v Elgin C
Montrose v Annan Ath

Saturday, 10 September 2016
Ladbrokes Scottish Premiership
Aberdeen v Inverness CT
Celtic v Rangers
Dundee v Kilmarnock
Hearts v Hamilton A
Partick Thistle v St Johnstone
Ross Co v Motherwell

Ladbrokes Scottish Championship
Ayr U v Greenock Morton
Dumbarton v Hibernian
Dunfermline Ath v Dundee U
Raith R v Falkirk
St Mirren v Queen of the South

Ladbrokes Scottish League 1
Albion R v Stenhousemuir
Alloa Ath v Livingston
Brechin C v Airdrieonians
East Fife v Stranraer
Peterhead v Queen's Park

Ladbrokes Scottish League 2
Annan Ath v Forfar Ath
Berwick R v Elgin C
Clyde v Arbroath
Montrose v Cowdenbeath
Stirling Alb v Edinburgh C

Saturday, 17 September 2016
Ladbrokes Scottish Premiership
Dundee v Aberdeen
Inverness CT v Celtic
Kilmarnock v Partick Thistle
Motherwell v Hamilton A
Rangers v Ross Co
St Johnstone v Hearts

Ladbrokes Scottish Championship
Dumbarton v St Mirren
Falkirk v Dundee U
Hibernian v Ayr U
Greenock Morton v Dunfermline Ath
Queen of the South v Raith R

Ladbrokes Scottish League 1
Airdrieonians v East Fife
Livingston v Brechin C
Queen's Park v Alloa Ath
Stenhousemuir v Peterhead
Stranraer v Albion R

Ladbrokes Scottish League 2
Arbroath v Annan Ath
Cowdenbeath v Berwick R
Edinburgh C v Montrose
Elgin C v Clyde
Forfar Ath v Stirling Alb

Saturday, 24 September 2016
Ladbrokes Scottish Premiership
Aberdeen v Rangers
Celtic v Kilmarnock
Hamilton A v St Johnstone
Hearts v Ross Co
Inverness CT v Dundee
Partick Thistle v Motherwell

Ladbrokes Scottish Championship
Dundee U v Greenock Morton
Dunfermline Ath v St Mirren
Falkirk v Ayr U
Queen of the South v Hibernian
Raith R v Dumbarton

Ladbrokes Scottish League 1
Airdrieonians v Albion R
Brechin C v Peterhead
East Fife v Livingston
Queen's Park v Stranraer
Stenhousemuir v Alloa Ath

Ladbrokes Scottish League 2
Annan Ath v Edinburgh C
Arbroath v Cowdenbeath
Clyde v Forfar Ath
Montrose v Berwick R
Stirling Alb v Elgin C

Saturday, 1 October 2016
Ladbrokes Scottish Premiership
Dundee v Celtic
Hamilton A v Inverness CT
Kilmarnock v Aberdeen
Motherwell v Hearts
Rangers v Partick Thistle
Ross Co v St Johnstone

Ladbrokes Scottish Championship
Ayr U v Dunfermline Ath
Dumbarton v Queen of the South
Hibernian v Dundee U
Greenock Morton v Raith R
St Mirren v Falkirk

Ladbrokes Scottish League 1
Albion R v Queen's Park
Alloa Ath v Airdrieonians
East Fife v Stenhousemuir
Peterhead v Livingston
Stranraer v Brechin C

Ladbrokes Scottish League 2
Berwick R v Clyde
Cowdenbeath v Stirling Alb
Edinburgh C v Arbroath
Elgin C v Annan Ath
Forfar Ath v Montrose

Saturday, 15 October 2016
Ladbrokes Scottish Premiership
Aberdeen v Ross Co
Celtic v Motherwell
Hearts v Dundee
Inverness CT v Rangers
Partick Thistle v Hamilton A
St Johnstone v Kilmarnock

Ladbrokes Scottish Championship
Dumbarton v Ayr U
Falkirk v Dunfermline Ath
Queen of the South v Greenock
  Morton
Raith R v Hibernian
St Mirren v Dundee U

Ladbrokes Scottish League 1
Airdrieonians v Peterhead
Brechin C v Alloa Ath
Livingston v Albion R
Queen's Park v East Fife
Stenhousemuir v Stranraer

Ladbrokes Scottish League 2
Arbroath v Forfar Ath
Cowdenbeath v Annan Ath
Edinburgh C v Clyde
Montrose v Elgin C
Stirling Alb v Berwick R

Saturday, 22 October 2016
Ladbrokes Scottish Premiership
Aberdeen v Motherwell
Celtic v Hamilton A
Hearts v Rangers
Inverness CT v Kilmarnock
Partick Thistle v Ross Co
St Johnstone v Dundee

Ladbrokes Scottish Championship
Ayr U v Queen of the South
Dundee U v Dumbarton
Dunfermline Ath v Hibernian
Falkirk v Raith R
Greenock Morton v St Mirren

Ladbrokes Scottish League 1
Airdrieonians v Queen's Park
Albion R v Peterhead
Livingston v Alloa Ath
Stenhousemuir v Brechin C
Stranraer v East Fife

Wednesday, 26 October 2016
Ladbrokes Scottish Premiership
Dundee v Partick Thistle
Hamilton A v Aberdeen
Kilmarnock v Hearts
Motherwell v Inverness CT
Rangers v St Johnstone
Ross Co v Celtic

Saturday, 29 October 2016
Ladbrokes Scottish Premiership
Aberdeen v Celtic
Hamilton A v Dundee
Inverness CT v Hearts
Motherwell v Ross Co
Rangers v Kilmarnock
St Johnstone v Partick Thistle

Ladbrokes Scottish Championship
Dumbarton v Dunfermline Ath
Dundee U v Falkirk
Hibernian v St Mirren
Greenock Morton v Ayr U
Raith R v Queen of the South

Ladbrokes Scottish League 1
Alloa Ath v Albion R
Brechin C v Livingston
East Fife v Airdrieonians
Peterhead v Stranraer
Queen's Park v Stenhousemuir

Ladbrokes Scottish League 2
Annan Ath v Montrose
Berwick R v Arbroath
Clyde v Stirling Alb
Elgin C v Cowdenbeath
Forfar Ath v Edinburgh C

Saturday, 5 November 2016
Ladbrokes Scottish Premiership
Celtic v Inverness CT
Dundee v Motherwell
Hearts v St Johnstone
Kilmarnock v Hamilton A
Partick Thistle v Aberdeen
Ross Co v Rangers

Ladbrokes Scottish Championship
Ayr U v Hibernian
Dunfermline Ath v Raith R
Falkirk v Greenock Morton
Queen of the South v Dundee U
St Mirren v Dumbarton

Ladbrokes Scottish League 1
Albion R v Airdrieonians
Alloa Ath v Stenhousemuir
Livingston v East Fife
Peterhead v Brechin C
Stranraer v Queen's Park

Ladbrokes Scottish League 2
Annan Ath v Arbroath
Berwick R v Cowdenbeath
Clyde v Elgin C
Montrose v Edinburgh C
Stirling Alb v Forfar Ath

Saturday, 12 November 2016
Ladbrokes Scottish Championship
Dumbarton v Greenock Morton
Dundee U v Dunfermline Ath
Hibernian v Falkirk
Queen of the South v St Mirren
Raith R v Ayr U

Ladbrokes Scottish League 1
Airdrieonians v Brechin C
Albion R v Stranraer
East Fife v Alloa Ath
Queen's Park v Peterhead
Stenhousemuir v Livingston

Ladbrokes Scottish League 2
Arbroath v Clyde
Cowdenbeath v Montrose
Edinburgh C v Annan Ath
Elgin C v Stirling Alb
Forfar Ath v Berwick R

Saturday, 19 November 2016
Ladbrokes Scottish Premiership
Hamilton A v Hearts
Inverness CT v Aberdeen
Kilmarnock v Celtic
Motherwell v Partick Thistle
Rangers v Dundee
St Johnstone v Ross Co

Ladbrokes Scottish Championship
Ayr U v Falkirk
Dumbarton v Raith R
Hibernian v Queen of the South
Greenock Morton v Dundee U
St Mirren v Dunfermline Ath

Ladbrokes Scottish League 1
Airdrieonians v Alloa Ath
Brechin C v Albion R
East Fife v Queen's Park
Livingston v Peterhead
Stranraer v Stenhousemuir

Ladbrokes Scottish League 2
Annan Ath v Elgin C
Clyde v Berwick R
Edinburgh C v Cowdenbeath
Montrose v Forfar Ath
Stirling Alb v Arbroath

Saturday, 26 November 2016
Ladbrokes Scottish Premiership
Aberdeen v Kilmarnock
Celtic v St Johnstone
Dundee v Inverness CT
Hearts v Motherwell
Partick Thistle v Rangers
Ross Co v Hamilton A

Saturday, 3 December 2016
Ladbrokes Scottish Premiership
Hamilton A v Partick Thistle
Kilmarnock v Dundee
Motherwell v Celtic
Rangers v Aberdeen

Ross Co v Hearts
St Johnstone v Inverness CT

Ladbrokes Scottish Championship
Dundee U v Hibernian
Dunfermline Ath v Ayr U
Falkirk v St Mirren
Queen of the South v Dumbarton
Raith R v Greenock Morton

Ladbrokes Scottish League 1
Albion R v Livingston
Alloa Ath v Stranraer
Peterhead v Airdrieonians
Queen's Park v Brechin C
Stenhousemuir v East Fife

Ladbrokes Scottish League 2
Arbroath v Edinburgh C
Berwick R v Stirling Alb
Cowdenbeath v Clyde
Elgin C v Montrose
Forfar Ath v Annan Ath

Saturday, 10 December 2016
Ladbrokes Scottish Premiership
Aberdeen v St Johnstone
Dundee v Ross Co
Inverness CT v Hamilton A
Motherwell v Kilmarnock
Partick Thistle v Celtic
Rangers v Hearts

Ladbrokes Scottish Championship
Ayr U v Dundee U
Dunfermline Ath v Greenock Morton
Falkirk v Queen of the South
Hibernian v Dumbarton
St Mirren v Raith R

Ladbrokes Scottish League 1
Airdrieonians v Stenhousemuir
Brechin C v East Fife
Peterhead v Alloa Ath
Queen's Park v Albion R
Stranraer v Livingston

Ladbrokes Scottish League 2
Annan Ath v Cowdenbeath
Edinburgh C v Stirling Alb
Elgin C v Berwick R
Forfar Ath v Arbroath
Montrose v Clyde

Saturday, 17 December 2016
Ladbrokes Scottish Premiership
Celtic v Dundee
Hamilton A v Rangers
Hearts v Partick Thistle
Kilmarnock v Inverness CT
Ross Co v Aberdeen
St Johnstone v Motherwell

Ladbrokes Scottish Championship
Dumbarton v Falkirk
Greenock Morton v Hibernian
Queen of the South v Dunfermline Ath
Raith R v Dundee U
St Mirren v Ayr U

Ladbrokes Scottish League 1
Alloa Ath v Queen's Park
Brechin C v Stranraer
East Fife v Peterhead
Livingston v Airdrieonians
Stenhousemuir v Albion R

Ladbrokes Scottish League 2
Arbroath v Elgin C
Berwick R v Montrose
Clyde v Edinburgh C
Cowdenbeath v Forfar Ath
Stirling Alb v Annan Ath

Saturday, 24 December 2016
Ladbrokes Scottish Premiership
Dundee v Hearts
Hamilton A v Celtic
Kilmarnock v St Johnstone
Motherwell v Aberdeen
Rangers v Inverness CT
Ross Co v Partick Thistle

Ladbrokes Scottish Championship
Ayr U v Dumbarton
Dundee U v St Mirren
Dunfermline Ath v Falkirk
Hibernian v Raith R
Greenock Morton v Queen of the
South

Ladbrokes Scottish League 1
Albion R v East Fife
Alloa Ath v Brechin C
Livingston v Queen's Park
Stranraer v Airdrieonians

Ladbrokes Scottish League 2
Annan Ath v Berwick R
Cowdenbeath v Arbroath
Edinburgh C v Elgin C
Montrose v Stirling Alb

Monday, 26 December 2016
Ladbrokes Scottish League 1
Peterhead v Stenhousemuir

Ladbrokes Scottish League 2
Forfar Ath v Clyde

Wednesday, 28 December 2016
Ladbrokes Scottish Premiership
Aberdeen v Hamilton A
Celtic v Ross Co
Hearts v Kilmarnock
Inverness CT v Motherwell
Partick Thistle v Dundee
St Johnstone v Rangers

Saturday, 31 December 2016
Ladbrokes Scottish Premiership
Dundee v St Johnstone
Hamilton A v Motherwell
Hearts v Aberdeen
Partick Thistle v Kilmarnock
Rangers v Celtic
Ross Co v Inverness CT

Ladbrokes Scottish Championship
Dumbarton v Dundee U
Falkirk v Hibernian
Queen of the South v Ayr U
Raith R v Dunfermline Ath
St Mirren v Greenock Morton

Ladbrokes Scottish League 1
East Fife v Livingston
Queen's Park v Stranraer
Stenhousemuir v Alloa Ath

Ladbrokes Scottish League 2
Berwick R v Edinburgh C
Clyde v Annan Ath
Stirling Alb v Cowdenbeath

Monday, 2 January 2017
Ladbrokes Scottish League 1
Airdrieonians v Albion R
Brechin C v Peterhead

Ladbrokes Scottish League 2
Arbroath v Montrose
Elgin C v Forfar Ath

Saturday, 7 January 2017
Ladbrokes Scottish Championship
Ayr U v Dunfermline Ath
Hibernian v Dundee U
Greenock Morton v Dumbarton
Raith R v Falkirk
St Mirren v Queen of the South

Ladbrokes Scottish League 1
Albion R v Brechin C
East Fife v Stenhousemuir
Peterhead v Livingston
Queen's Park v Airdrieonians
Stranraer v Alloa Ath

Ladbrokes Scottish League 2
Annan Ath v Forfar Ath
Cowdenbeath v Berwick R
Edinburgh C v Arbroath
Montrose v Elgin C
Stirling Alb v Clyde

Saturday, 14 January 2017
Ladbrokes Scottish Championship
Dumbarton v Hibernian
Dundee U v Queen of the South
Dunfermline Ath v St Mirren
Falkirk v Ayr U
Greenock Morton v Raith R

Ladbrokes Scottish League 1
Airdrieonians v East Fife
Alloa Ath v Peterhead
Brechin C v Queen's Park
Livingston v Albion R
Stenhousemuir v Stranraer

Ladbrokes Scottish League 2
Arbroath v Berwick R
Clyde v Montrose
Cowdenbeath v Edinburgh C
Elgin C v Annan Ath
Forfar Ath v Stirling Alb

Saturday, 21 January 2017
Ladbrokes Scottish League 2
Arbroath v Annan Ath
Berwick R v Clyde
Edinburgh C v Forfar Ath
Montrose v Cowdenbeath
Stirling Alb v Elgin C

Saturday, 28 January 2017
Ladbrokes Scottish Premiership
Aberdeen v Dundee
Celtic v Hearts
Inverness CT v Partick Thistle
Kilmarnock v Ross Co
Motherwell v Rangers
St Johnstone v Hamilton A

Ladbrokes Scottish Championship
Ayr U v Greenock Morton
Dunfermline Ath v Dundee U
Queen of the South v Hibernian
Raith R v Dumbarton
St Mirren v Falkirk

Ladbrokes Scottish League 1
Albion R v Alloa Ath
East Fife v Stranraer
Livingston v Brechin C
Peterhead v Queen's Park
Stenhousemuir v Airdrieonians

Ladbrokes Scottish League 2
Annan Ath v Stirling Alb
Clyde v Arbroath
Elgin C v Edinburgh C
Forfar Ath v Cowdenbeath
Montrose v Berwick R

Wednesday, 1 February 2017
Ladbrokes Scottish Premiership
Celtic v Aberdeen
Dundee v Kilmarnock
Hamilton A v Inverness CT
Hearts v Rangers
Partick Thistle v St Johnstone
Ross Co v Motherwell

Saturday, 4 February 2017
Ladbrokes Scottish Premiership
Aberdeen v Partick Thistle
Hamilton A v Kilmarnock
Inverness CT v Dundee
Motherwell v Hearts
Rangers v Ross Co
St Johnstone v Celtic

Ladbrokes Scottish Championship
Dumbarton v St Mirren
Dundee U v Raith R
Falkirk v Dunfermline Ath
Hibernian v Ayr U
Queen of the South v Greenock
Morton

Ladbrokes Scottish League 1
Airdrieonians v Peterhead
Alloa Ath v Livingston
Brechin C v Stenhousemuir
Queen's Park v East Fife
Stranraer v Albion R

Ladbrokes Scottish League 2
Arbroath v Forfar Ath
Berwick R v Annan Ath
Cowdenbeath v Elgin C
Edinburgh C v Clyde
Stirling Alb v Montrose

Saturday, 11 February 2017
Ladbrokes Scottish League 1
Alloa Ath v East Fife
Brechin C v Airdrieonians
Livingston v Stranraer
Peterhead v Albion R
Stenhousemuir v Queen's Park

Ladbrokes Scottish League 2
Annan Ath v Edinburgh C
Clyde v Cowdenbeath
Forfar Ath v Elgin C
Montrose v Arbroath
Stirling Alb v Berwick R

Saturday, 18 February 2017
Ladbrokes Scottish Premiership
Celtic v Motherwell
Dundee v Rangers
Hearts v Inverness CT
Kilmarnock v Aberdeen
Partick Thistle v Hamilton A
Ross Co v St Johnstone

Ladbrokes Scottish Championship
Dumbarton v Ayr U
Dunfermline Ath v Queen of the South
Greenock Morton v Falkirk
Raith R v Hibernian
St Mirren v Dundee U

Ladbrokes Scottish League 1
Airdrieonians v Livingston
Albion R v Stenhousemuir
East Fife v Brechin C
Queen's Park v Alloa Ath
Stranraer v Peterhead

Ladbrokes Scottish League 2
Arbroath v Stirling Alb
Berwick R v Forfar Ath
Cowdenbeath v Annan Ath
Edinburgh C v Montrose
Elgin C v Clyde

Saturday, 25 February 2017
Ladbrokes Scottish Premiership
Aberdeen v Ross Co
Celtic v Hamilton A
Inverness CT v Rangers
Motherwell v Dundee
Partick Thistle v Hearts
St Johnstone v Kilmarnock

Ladbrokes Scottish Championship
Ayr U v St Mirren
Dundee U v Greenock Morton
Falkirk v Dumbarton
Hibernian v Dunfermline Ath
Queen of the South v Raith R

Ladbrokes Scottish League 1
Albion R v Queen's Park
Alloa Ath v Airdrieonians
Livingston v Stenhousemuir
Peterhead v East Fife
Stranraer v Brechin C

Ladbrokes Scottish League 2
Annan Ath v Clyde
Arbroath v Cowdenbeath
Berwick R v Elgin C
Forfar Ath v Montrose
Stirling Alb v Edinburgh C

Wednesday, 1 March 2017
Ladbrokes Scottish Premiership
Dundee v Partick Thistle
Hamilton A v Aberdeen
Hearts v Ross Co
Inverness CT v Celtic
Kilmarnock v Motherwell
Rangers v St Johnstone

Ladbrokes Scottish Championship
Ayr U v Raith R
Dumbarton v Queen of the South
Falkirk v Dundee U
Greenock Morton v Dunfermline Ath
St Mirren v Hibernian

Saturday, 4 March 2017
Ladbrokes Scottish Championship
Dundee U v Ayr U
Dunfermline Ath v Dumbarton
Hibernian v Greenock Morton
Queen of the South v Falkirk
Raith R v St Mirren

Ladbrokes Scottish League 1
Airdrieonians v Stranraer
Brechin C v Alloa Ath
East Fife v Albion R
Queen's Park v Livingston
Stenhousemuir v Peterhead

Ladbrokes Scottish League 2
Clyde v Forfar Ath
Cowdenbeath v Stirling Alb
Edinburgh C v Berwick R
Elgin C v Arbroath
Montrose v Annan Ath

Saturday, 11 March 2017
Ladbrokes Scottish Premiership
Aberdeen v Motherwell
Celtic v Rangers
Hearts v Hamilton A
Partick Thistle v Inverness CT
Ross Co v Kilmarnock
St Johnstone v Dundee

Ladbrokes Scottish Championship
Ayr U v Falkirk
Dumbarton v Raith R
Dundee U v Hibernian
Greenock Morton v Queen of the
South
St Mirren v Dunfermline Ath

Ladbrokes Scottish League 1
Albion R v Airdrieonians
Alloa Ath v Stenhousemuir
Livingston v East Fife
Peterhead v Brechin C
Stranraer v Queen's Park

Ladbrokes Scottish League 2
Annan Ath v Elgin C
Arbroath v Clyde
Berwick R v Cowdenbeath
Forfar Ath v Edinburgh C
Montrose v Stirling Alb

Saturday, 18 March 2017
Ladbrokes Scottish Premiership
Aberdeen v Hearts
Dundee v Celtic
Inverness CT v Ross Co
Kilmarnock v Partick Thistle
Motherwell v St Johnstone
Rangers v Hamilton A

Ladbrokes Scottish Championship
Dunfermline Ath v Ayr U
Falkirk v Greenock Morton
Hibernian v Dumbarton
Queen of the South v St Mirren
Raith R v Dundee U

Ladbrokes Scottish League 1
Airdrieonians v Stenhousemuir
Albion R v Peterhead
East Fife v Alloa Ath
Queen's Park v Brechin C
Stranraer v Livingston

Ladbrokes Scottish League 2
Berwick R v Arbroath
Clyde v Edinburgh C
Cowdenbeath v Montrose
Elgin C v Forfar Ath
Stirling Alb v Annan Ath

Saturday, 25 March 2017
Ladbrokes Scottish Championship
Ayr U v Dumbarton
Dundee U v Dunfermline Ath
Hibernian v Falkirk
Greenock Morton v St Mirren
Raith R v Queen of the South

Ladbrokes Scottish League 1
Alloa Ath v Queen's Park
Brechin C v East Fife
Livingston v Airdrieonians
Peterhead v Stranraer
Stenhousemuir v Albion R

Ladbrokes Scottish League 2
Annan Ath v Cowdenbeath
Arbroath v Montrose
Clyde v Stirling Alb
Edinburgh C v Elgin C
Forfar Ath v Berwick R

Saturday, 1 April 2017
Ladbrokes Scottish Premiership
Dundee v Aberdeen
Hamilton A v St Johnstone
Hearts v Celtic
Inverness CT v Kilmarnock
Partick Thistle v Ross Co
Rangers v Motherwell

Ladbrokes Scottish Championship
Dumbarton v Greenock Morton
Dunfermline Ath v Hibernian
Falkirk v Raith R
Queen of the South v Dundee U
St Mirren v Ayr U

Ladbrokes Scottish League 1
Alloa Ath v Albion R
Brechin C v Livingston
East Fife v Queen's Park
Peterhead v Airdrieonians
Stranraer v Stenhousemuir

Ladbrokes Scottish League 2
Annan Ath v Arbroath
Cowdenbeath v Clyde
Elgin C v Berwick R
Montrose v Edinburgh C
Stirling Alb v Forfar Ath

Wednesday, 5 April 2017
Ladbrokes Scottish Premiership
Aberdeen v Inverness CT
Celtic v Partick Thistle
Kilmarnock v Rangers
Motherwell v Hamilton A
Ross Co v Dundee
St Johnstone v Hearts

Saturday, 8 April 2017
Ladbrokes Scottish Premiership
Aberdeen v Rangers
Celtic v Kilmarnock
Hamilton A v Ross Co
Hearts v Dundee
Inverness CT v St Johnstone
Partick Thistle v Motherwell

Ladbrokes Scottish Championship
Ayr U v Queen of the South
Dundee U v Falkirk
Dunfermline Ath v Raith R
Greenock Morton v Hibernian
St Mirren v Dumbarton

Ladbrokes Scottish League 1
Airdrieonians v Brechin C
Albion R v Stranraer
Livingston v Alloa Ath
Queen's Park v Peterhead
Stenhousemuir v East Fife

Ladbrokes Scottish League 2
Berwick R v Stirling Alb
Clyde v Annan Ath
Edinburgh C v Cowdenbeath
Elgin C v Montrose
Forfar Ath v Arbroath

Saturday, 15 April 2017
Ladbrokes Scottish Premiership
Dundee v Hamilton A
Kilmarnock v Hearts
Motherwell v Inverness CT
Rangers v Partick Thistle
Ross Co v Celtic
St Johnstone v Aberdeen

Ladbrokes Scottish Championship
Ayr U v Dundee U
Dumbarton v Dunfermline Ath
Falkirk v St Mirren
Hibernian v Queen of the South
Raith R v Greenock Morton

Ladbrokes Scottish League 1
Alloa Ath v Brechin C
East Fife v Peterhead
Queen's Park v Albion R
Stenhousemuir v Livingston
Stranraer v Airdrieonians

Ladbrokes Scottish League 2
Annan Ath v Berwick R
Arbroath v Edinburgh C
Clyde v Elgin C
Montrose v Forfar Ath
Stirling Alb v Cowdenbeath

Saturday, 22 April 2017
Ladbrokes Scottish Championship
Dundee U v St Mirren
Dunfermline Ath v Falkirk
Hibernian v Raith R
Greenock Morton v Ayr U
Queen of the South v Dumbarton

Ladbrokes Scottish League 1
Airdrieonians v Alloa Ath
Albion R v East Fife
Brechin C v Stranraer
Livingston v Queen's Park
Peterhead v Stenhousemuir

Ladbrokes Scottish League 2
Berwick R v Montrose
Cowdenbeath v Arbroath
Edinburgh C v Annan Ath
Elgin C v Stirling Alb
Forfar Ath v Clyde

Saturday, 29 April 2017
Ladbrokes Scottish Championship
Ayr U v Hibernian
Dundee U v Dumbarton
Dunfermline Ath v Greenock Morton
Falkirk v Queen of the South
St Mirren v Raith R

Ladbrokes Scottish League 1
Alloa Ath v Stranraer
Brechin C v Albion R
East Fife v Airdrieonians
Livingston v Peterhead
Queen's Park v Stenhousemuir

Ladbrokes Scottish League 2
Annan Ath v Montrose
Arbroath v Elgin C
Clyde v Berwick R
Cowdenbeath v Forfar Ath
Edinburgh C v Stirling Alb

Saturday, 6 May 2017
Ladbrokes Scottish Championship
Dumbarton v Falkirk
Hibernian v St Mirren
Greenock Morton v Dundee U
Queen of the South v Dunfermline Ath
Raith R v Ayr U

Ladbrokes Scottish League 1
Airdrieonians v Queen's Park
Albion R v Livingston
Peterhead v Alloa Ath
Stenhousemuir v Brechin C
Stranraer v East Fife

Ladbrokes Scottish League 2
Berwick R v Edinburgh C
Elgin C v Cowdenbeath
Forfar Ath v Annan Ath
Montrose v Clyde
Stirling Alb v Arbroath

FOOTBALL ASSOCIATION FIXTURES 2016–17

JULY 2016

5 Tuesday	UEFA Champions League 1Q(2)
6 Wednesday	UEFA Champions League 1Q(2)
7 Thursday	UEFA Europa League 1Q(2)
10 Sunday	UEFA Euro 2016 Final
12 Tuesday	UEFA Champions League 2Q(1)
13 Wednesday	UEFA Champions League 2Q(1)
14 Thursday	UEFA Europa League 2Q(1)
19 Tuesday	UEFA Champions League 2Q(2)
20 Wednesday	UEFA Champions League 2Q(2)
21 Thursday	UEFA Europa League 2Q(2)
26 Tuesday	UEFA Champions League 3Q(1)
27 Wednesday	UEFA Champions League 3Q(1)
28 Thursday	UEFA Europa League 3Q(1)

AUGUST 2016

2 Tuesday	UEFA Champions League 3Q(2)
3 Wednesday	UEFA Champions League 3Q(2)
4 Thursday	UEFA Europa League 3Q(2)
6 Saturday	Football League Commences
	National League Commences
	The Emirates FA Cup EP
7 Sunday	FA Community Shield
8 Monday	Football League Cup 1†
10 Wednesday	UEFA Super Cup
13 Saturday	Premier League Commences
16 Tuesday	UEFA Champions League Qualifying Play-Off(1)
17 Wednesday	UEFA Champions League Qualifying Play-Off(1)
18 Thursday	UEFA Europa League Qualifying Play-Off(1)
20 Saturday	The Emirates FA Cup P
22 Monday	Football League Cup 2†
23 Tuesday	UEFA Champions League Qualifying Play-Off(2)
24 Wednesday	UEFA Champions League Qualifying Play-Off(2)
25 Thursday	UEFA Europa League Qualifying Play-Off(2)
29 Monday	Football League Trophy 1†

SEPTEMBER 2016

3 Saturday	The Emirates FA Cup 1Q
4 Sunday	Slovakia v England – World Cup Qualifier
	The SSE Women's FA Cup 1Q
5 Monday	FA Youth Cup P†
6 Tuesday	England U21 v Norway U21 – Euro Qualifier
10 Saturday	FA Vase 1Q
13 Tuesday	UEFA Champions League MD1
14 Wednesday	UEFA Champions League MD1
15 Thursday	UEFA Europa League MD1
	England v Estonia – Women's Euro Qualifier
17 Saturday	The Emirates FA Cup 2Q
18 Sunday	The SSE Women's FA Cup 2Q
19 Monday	Football League Cup 3†
	FA Youth Cup 1Q†
20 Tuesday	Belgium v England – Women's Euro Qualifier
24 Saturday	FA Vase 2Q
27 Tuesday	UEFA Champions League MD2
28 Wednesday	UEFA Champions League MD2
29 Thursday	UEFA Europa League MD2

OCTOBER 2016

1 Saturday	The Emirates FA Cup 3Q
3 Monday	Football League Trophy 2†
	FA Youth Cup 2Q†
6 Thursday	Kazakhstan U21 v England U21 – Euro Qualifier
8 Saturday	England v Malta – World Cup Qualifier
	FA Trophy P
	FA County Youth Cup 1*
9 Sunday	The SSE Women's FA Cup 3Q
11 Tuesday	Slovenia v England – World Cup Qualifier
	England U21 v Bosnia-Herzegovina – Euro Qualifier
15 Saturday	The Emirates FA Cup 4Q
16 Sunday	FA Sunday Cup 1
17 Monday	FA Youth Cup 3Q†
18 Tuesday	UEFA Champions League MD3
19 Wednesday	UEFA Champions League MD3
20 Thursday	UEFA Europa League MD3
22 Saturday	FA Vase 1P
24 Monday	Football League Cup 4†
29 Saturday	FA Trophy 1Q

NOVEMBER 2016

1 Tuesday	UEFA Champions League MD4
2 Wednesday	UEFA Champions League MD4
3 Thursday	UEFA Europa League MD4
5 Saturday	The Emirates FA Cup 1P
	FA Youth Cup 1P*
	FA County Youth Cup 2*
7 Monday	Football League Trophy 3†
11 Friday	England v Scotland – World Cup Qualifier
12 Saturday	FA Trophy 2Q
	FA Vase 2P
13 Sunday	The SSE Women's FA Cup 4Q
	FA Sunday Cup 2
19 Saturday	FA Youth Cup 2P*
22 Tuesday	UEFA Champions League MD5
23 Wednesday	UEFA Champions League MD5
24 Thursday	UEFA Europa League MD5
26 Saturday	FA Trophy 3Q
28 Monday	Football League Cup 5†

DECEMBER 2016

3 Saturday	The Emirates FA Cup 2P
	FA Vase 3P
4 Sunday	The SSE Women's FA Cup 1P

5 Monday	Football League Trophy Area SF†
6 Tuesday	UEFA Champions League MD6
7 Wednesday	UEFA Champions League MD6
8 Thursday	UEFA Europa League MD6
10 Saturday	FA Trophy 1P
	FA County Youth Cup 3*
11 Sunday	FA Sunday Cup 3
17 Saturday	FA Youth Cup 3P*
24 Saturday	Christmas Eve
25 Sunday	Christmas Day
26 Monday	Boxing Day

JANUARY 2017

1 Sunday	New Year's Day
2 Monday	Bank Holiday
7 Saturday	The Emirates FA Cup 3P
	FA Vase 4P
8 Sunday	The SSE Women's FA Cup 2P
9 Monday	Football League Cup SF(1)†
14 Saturday	FA Trophy 2P
	FA Youth Cup 4P*
15 Sunday	FA Sunday Cup 4
21 Saturday	FA County Youth Cup 4*
23 Monday	Football League Cup SF(2)†
	Football League Trophy Area Final(1)†
28 Saturday	The Emirates FA Cup 4P
	FA Vase 5P

FEBRUARY 2017

4 Saturday	FA Trophy 3P
	FA Youth Cup 5P*
5 Sunday	The SSE Women's FA Cup 3P
6 Monday	The SSE Women's FA Cup 3P
8 Wednesday	Football League Trophy Area Final(2)†
12 Sunday	FA Sunday Cup 5
14 Tuesday	UEFA Champions League 16(1)
15 Wednesday	UEFA Champions League 16(1)
16 Thursday	UEFA Europa League 32(1)
18 Saturday	The Emirates FA Cup 5P
	FA Vase 6P
19 Sunday	The SSE Women's FA Cup 4P
21 Tuesday	UEFA Champions League 16(1)
22 Wednesday	UEFA Champions League 16(1)
23 Thursday	UEFA Europa League 32(2)
25 Saturday	FA Trophy 4P
	FA Youth Cup 6P*
	FA County Youth Cup SF*
26 Sunday	Football League Cup Final

MARCH 2017

7 Tuesday	UEFA Champions League 16(2)
8 Wednesday	UEFA Champions League 16(2)
9 Thursday	UEFA Europa League 16(1)
11 Saturday	The Emirates FA Cup 6P
	FA Trophy SF(1)
	FA Vase SF(1)

12 Sunday	FA Sunday Cup SF
14 Tuesday	UEFA Champions League 16(2)
15 Wednesday	UEFA Champions League 16(2)
16 Thursday	UEFA Europa League 16(2)
18 Saturday	FA Trophy SF(2)
	FA Vase SF(2)
	FA Youth Cup SF(1)*
19 Sunday	The SSE Women's FA Cup 5P
26 Sunday	England v Lithuania –
	World Cup Qualifier
	The SSE Women's FA Cup 6P

APRIL 2017

2 Sunday	Football League Trophy Final
8 Saturday	FA Youth Cup SF(2)*
	FA County Youth Cup Final (prov)
11 Tuesday	UEFA Champions League QF(1)
12 Wednesday	UEFA Champions League QF(1)
13 Thursday	UEFA Europa League QF(1)
14 Friday	Good Friday
17 Monday	Easter Monday
	The SSE Women's FA Cup SF
18 Tuesday	UEFA Champions League QF(2)
19 Wednesday	UEFA Champions League QF(2)
20 Thursday	UEFA Europa League QF(2)
22 Saturday	The Emirates FA Cup SF
23 Sunday	The Emirates FA Cup SF
	FA Sunday Cup Final (prov)
29 Saturday	National League Ends

MAY 2017

1 Monday	Bank Holiday
2 Tuesday	UEFA Champions League SF(1)
3 Wednesday	UEFA Champions League SF(1)
4 Thursday	UEFA Europa League SF(1)
6 Saturday	Football League Ends
9 Tuesday	UEFA Champions League SF(2)
10 Wednesday	UEFA Champions League SF(2)
11 Thursday	UEFA Europa League SF(2)
13 Saturday	The SSE Women's FA Cup Final
14 Sunday	National League Play-Off Final
20 Saturday	Sky Bet League One Play-Off Final
21 Sunday	Premier League Ends
	FA Trophy Final
	FA Vase Final
24 Tuesday	UEFA Europa League Final
28 Sunday	Sky Bet League Two Play-Off Final
29 Monday	Sky Bet League One Play-Off Final

JUNE 2017

3 Saturday	UEFA Champions League Final
10 Saturday	Scotland v England –
	World Cup Qualifier

The Emirates FA Cup Final – date to be confirmed.
FA Youth Cup Final 1st & 2nd Leg – dates to be confirmed.
National League Play-Off Semi Finals – dates to be confirmed.
*Closing date of round.
†Week commencing.

STOP PRESS

Sam Allardyce favourite to be appointed new England manager to succeed Roy Hodgson ... Arsène Wenger, Steve Bruce, Jurgen Klinsmann and Eddie Howe also in contention ... England Under 19s make it to European Championship semi-final and guarantee place for next year's Under 20s World Cup ... Leicester City pay £16m for Ahmed Musa from CSKA Moscow to break their transfer record ... Bournemouth break their transfer record paying £15m for Jordan Ibe from Liverpool ... Newly promoted Burton Albion break their transfer record for Kyle McFadzean from Milton Keynes Dons ... Pelle and Cisse both off to China ... Steve Walsh leaves Leicester City to become Director of Football at Everton

SUMMER TRANSFER DIARY 2016

Reported fees only, otherwise Free or Undisclosed.

June 1: **Mark Duffy** Birmingham C to Sheffield U; **Chris Hussey** Bury to Sheffield U; **Dean Winnard** Accrington S to Morecambe; **Joe Wright** Huddersfield T to Doncaster R; **Josh Yorwerth** Ipswich T to Crawley T.

June 2: **Josh Brownhill** Preston NE to Bristol C; **Ilkay Gundogan** Borussia Dortmund to Manchester C – £20m; **Piero Mingoia** Accrington S to Cambridge U.

June 3: **David Gregory** Crystal Palace to Cambridge U; **Ashley Hemmings** Dagenham & Redbridge to Mansfield T; **AJ Leitch-Smith** Port Vale to Shrewsbury T; **George Maris** Barnsley to Cambridge U; **Ryan McGivern** Port Vale to Shrewsbury T; **Aaron Phillips** Coventry C to Northampton T; **Danny Rose** Northampton T to Portsmouth; **Ed Upson** Millwall to Milton Keynes D.

June 6: **Matt Clarke** Ipswich T to Portsmouth; **Jamie Devitt** Morecambe to Carlisle U; **Josh Doherty** Watford to Leyton Orient; **CJ Hamilton** Sheffield U to Mansfield T; **Andrew Hughes** Newport Co to Peterborough U; **Reggie Lambe** Mansfield T to Carlisle U; **Gary McSheffrey** Scunthorpe U to Doncaster R; **Ryan Tafazolli** Mansfield T to Peterborough U; **Adam Webster** Portsmouth to Ipswich T – £750,000; **Robbie Weir** Burton Alb to Leyton Orient.

June 7: **Joel Coleman** Oldham Ath to Huddersfield T; **Joss Labadie** Dagenham & R to Newport Co; **Yusuf Mersin** Kasimpasa to Crawley T; **Jake Orrell** Chesterfield to Hartlepool U; **Ivan Paurevic** FC Ufa to Huddersfield T.

June 8: **Danny Andrew** Fleetwood T to Grimsby T; **Eric Bailly** Villarreal to Manchester U – £30m; **Andy Lonergan** Fulham to Wolverhampton W; **Gavin Massey** Colchester U to Leyton Orient.

June 9: **Rhys Bennett** Rochdale to Mansfield T; **Scott Boden** Newport Co to Inverness CT; **Luke Conlan** Burnley to Morecambe; **Gary O'Neil** Norwich C to Bristol C.

June 10: **Callum Kennedy** AFC Wimbledon to Leyton Orient; **Paddy Kenny** Rotherham U to Northampton T; **Steve Sidwell** Stoke C to Brighton & HA.

June 13: **Medy Elito** Newport Co to Cambridge U; **John Marquis** Millwall to Doncaster R.

June 14: **Carl Baker** Milton Keynes D to Portsmouth; **Sofiane Feghouli** Valencia to West Ham U; **Ben Hall** Motherwell to Brighton & HA; **Raheem Hanley** Swansea to Northampton T; **Jamie Jones** Preston NE to Stevenage; **Jamille Matt** Fleetwood T to Blackpool; **Stewart Murdoch** Ross C to Dundee U; **Alex Revell** Milton Keynes D to Northampton T; **Conor Sammon** Derby Co to Hearts.

June 15: **Ade Azeez** AFC Wimbledon to Partick Thistle; **Mark Byrne** Newport Co to Gillingham; **Adam Collin** Rotherham U to Notts Co; **Bernardo Espinosa** Sporting Gijon to Middlesbrough; **Joe Lewis** Cardiff C to Aberdeen; **Josh Morris** Bradford C to Scunthorpe U; **Tom Parkes** Bristol R to Leyton Orient; **David Worrall** Southend U to Millwall.

June 16: **James Bittner** Plymouth Arg to Newport Co; **Ryan Donaldson** Cambridge U to Plymouth; **Peter Hartley** Plymouth Arg to Bristol R; **Ricky Holmes** Northampton T to Charlton Ath; **Billy Knott** Bradford C to Gillingham; **Harrison McGahey** Sheffield U to Rochdale; **Aristote Nsiala** Grimsby T to Hartlepool U; **Kyle Vassell** Peterborough U to Blackpool.

June 17: **Aaron Chapman** Chesterfield to Accrington S; **Michael Duckworth** Hartlepool U to Fleetwood T; **Clint Hill** QPR to Rangers; **Emerson Hyndman** Fulham to Bournemouth; **Kevin McHattie** Kilmarnock to Raith R; **Shaun Miller** Morecambe to Carlisle U; **Byron Moore** Port Vale to Bristol R; **Jake Mulraney** QPR to Inverness CT; **Lee Novak** Birmingham C to Charlton Ath; **Jim O'Brien** Coventry C to Shrewsbury T; **Erhun Oztumer** Peterborough U to Walsall; **Alberto Paloschi** Swansea C to Atalanta; **Anthony Stokes** Celtic to Blackburn R.

June 19: **Antony Kay** Milton Keynes D to Bury; **Yann Songo'o** Blackburn R to Plymouth Arg.

June 20: **Padraig Amond** Grimsby T to Hartlepool U; **Jack Compton** Yeovil T to Newport Co; **Tommy Elphick** Bournemouth to Aston Villa; **Bastien Hery** Carlisle U to Accrington S; **Jack Payne** Southend U to Huddersfield T; **Sean Rigg** AFC Wimbledon to Newport Co.

June 21: **Andrew Boyce** Scunthorpe U to Grimsby T; **Ryan Clarke** Northampton T to AFC Wimbledon; **David Cornell** Oldham Ath to Northampton T; **Florent Cuvelier** Sheffield U to Walsall; **Luis Hernandez** Sporting Gijon to Leicester C; **Shaun Hutchinson** Fulham to Millwall; **George Moncur** Colchester U to Barnsley – £500,000; **Elliot Parish** Colchester U to Accrington S; **Luke Prosser** Southend U to Colchester U; **Connor Smith** AFC Wimbledon to Plymouth Arg.

June 22: **Ariel Borysiuk** Legia Warsaw to QPR; **Mike Jones** Oldham Ath to Carlisle U; **Paul McGinn** Dundee to Chesterfield; **Drew Talbot** Chesterfield to Portsmouth.

June 23: **Jazzi Barnum-Bobb** Cardiff C to Newport Co; **Jacob Blyth** Leicester C to Motherwell; **Dan Burn** Fulham to Wigan Ath; **Jason Demetriou** Walsall to Southend U; **Simon Eastwood** Blackburn R to Oxford U; **Andrew Fox** Peterborough U to Stevenage; **Danny Graham** Sunderland to Blackburn R; **Ben Heneghan** Chester to Motherwell; **Niko Kranjcar** New York Cosmos to Rangers; **Sean McAllister** Scunthorpe U to Grimsby T; **Jermaine McGlashan** Gillingham to Southend U; **Gary Miller** Partick Thistle to Plymouth Arg; **Frazer Shaw** Leyton Orient to Accrington S; **Michael Smith** Swindon T to Portsmouth; **Richard Tait** Grimsby T to Motherwell; **Matt Tootle** Shrewsbury T to Notts Co; **Ben Turner** Cardiff C to Burton Alb; **Victor Wanyama** Southampton to Tottenham H – £11m.

June 24: **Ashley Chambers** Dagenham & R to Grimsby T; **Jamie Cobain** Newcastle U to Kilmarnock; **Souleymane Coulibaly** Peterborough U to Kilmarnock; **Joe Edwards** Colchester U to Walsall; **Gwion Edwards** Crawley T to Peterborough U; **Matt Gilks** Burnley to Rangers; **Zeli Ismail** Wolverhampton W to Bury; **Dan Jones** Hartlepool U to Grimsby T; **Jordan Jones** Middlesbrough to Kilmarnock; **Elliot Lee** West Ham U to Barnsley; **Niall Maher** Bolton W to Bury; **Jak McCourt** Barnsley to Northampton T; **Jay McEveley** Sheffield U to Ross Co; **Callum McFadzean** Sheffield U to Kilmarnock; **Karleigh Osborne** Bristol C to Plymouth Arg; **Oliver Rathbone** Manchester U to Rochdale; **Alex Rodman** Newport Co to Notts Co; **Martin Smith** Sunderland to Kilmarnock; **Robert Tesche** Nottingham F to Birmingham C; **Joshua Webb** Aston Villa to Kilmarnock; **Ben Williams** Bradford C to Bury; **Gabriel Zakuani** Peterborough U to Northampton T.

June 25: **Nicky Clark** Rangers to Bury; **Liam Feeney** Bolton W to Blackburn R; **Aaron Martin** Coventry C to Oxford U; **Anthony O'Connor** Burton Alb to Aberdeen; **Nathan Redmond** Norwich C to Southampton – £10m; **Jordan Slew** Chesterfield to Plymouth Arg; **Wes Thomas** Birmingham C to Oxford U; **Gregg Wylde** Plymouth Arg to Millwall.

June 27: **Nicky Ajose** Swindon T to Charlton Ath; **Troy Archibald-Henville** Carlisle U to Exeter C; **Paul Downing** Walsall to Milton Keynes D; **Brad Inman** Crewe Alex to Peterborough U; **Chris Kirkland** Preston NE to Bury; **Glen Rea** Brighton & HA to Luton T; **Tommy Spurr** Blackburn R to Preston NE.

June 28: **Marcus Antonsson** Kalmar to Leeds U; **Moussa Dembele** Fulham to Celtic; **Carl Dickinson** Port Vale to Notts Co; **Paul Digby** Barnsley to Ipswich T; **Tyler Garrett** Bolton W to Doncaster R; **Denny Johnstone** Birmingham C to Colchester U; **Kjell Knops** Maastricht to Port Vale; **Milan Lalkovic** Walsall to Portsmouth Arg; **Sadio Mane** Southampton to Liverpool – £34m; **Christian Ribeiro** Exeter C to Oxford U; **Jordan Roberts** Inverness CT to Crawley T; **Courtney Senior** Brentford to Colchester U; **Luke Summerfield** York C to Grimsby T; **Liam Wakefield** Accrington S to Morecambe; **Chris Whelpdale** Stevenage to AFC Wimbledon; **George Williams** Barnsley to Milton Keynes D.

June 29: **Lewis Alessandra** Rochdale to Hartlepool U; **Nauris Bulvitis** Spartaks Jurmala to Plymouth Arg; **Ben Davies** Portsmouth to Grimsby T; **Brennan Dickenson** Gillingham to Colchester U; **Eoin Doyle** Cardiff C to Preston N; **David Goodwillie** Aberdeen to Plymouth Arg; **Lee Hodson** Milton Keynes D to Rangers; **Grant Holt** Wigan Ath to Hibernian; **Kevan Hurst** Southend U to Mansfield T; **Nicky Law** Rangers to Bradford C; **Joel Lynch** Huddersfield T to QPR; **Reece Mitchell** Chelsea to Chesterfield; **Michael O'Connor** Port Vale to Notts Co; **Christopher Schindler** TSV 1860 Munich to Huddersfield T; **Matz Sels** Gent to Newcastle U – £5m; **Jimmy Spencer** Cambridge U to Plymouth Arg; **Joey van den Berg** Heerenveen to Reading; **Apostolos Vellios** Iraklis Thessaloniki to Nottingham F – £1m.

June 30: **James Berrett** York C to Grimsby T; **Rigino Cicilia** Roda JC to Port Vale; **Anthony Forde** Walsall to Rotherham U; **Sam Mantom** Walsall to Scunthorpe U; **Lys Mousset** Le Havre to Bournemouth; **Ryan Shotton** Derby Co to Birmingham C; **Jerome Sinclair** Liverpool to Watford – £4m; **Myles Weston** Southend U to Wycombe W.

July 1: **Gabriele Angella** Watford to Udinese; **Floyd Ayite** Bastia to Fulham; **Daniel Bentley** Southend U to Brentford; **Jake Bidwell** Brentford to QPR; **Anthony de Freitas** Monaco to Port Vale; **Tom Eaves** Bolton W to Yeovil T; **John Egan** Gillingham to Brentford; **Yvan Erichot** Sint-Truiden to Leyton Orient; **Viktor Fischer** Ajax to Middlesbrough; **Steven Fletcher** Sunderland to Sheffield W; **Jonathan Forte** Oldham Ath to Notts Co; **Dwight Gayle** Crystal Palace to Newcastle U – £10m; **Frederic Gounongbe** KVC Westerlo to Cardiff C; **Zlatan Ibrahimovic** Paris Saint-Germain to Manchester U; **Christian Kabasele** Genk to Watford – £6m; **Nathaniel Knight-Percival** Shrewsbury T to Bradford C; **Greg Leigh** Bradford C to Bury; **Doug Loft** Gillingham to Colchester U; **Calvin Mac-Intisch** SC Cambuur to Port Vale; **Steve Mandanda** Marseille to Crystal Palace; **Will Mannion** AFC Wimbledon to Hull C; **Alex Nicholls** Exeter C to Barnet; **Nolito** Celta Vigo to Manchester C – £13.8m; **Dean Parrett** Stevenage to AFC Wimbledon; **Quentin Pereira** Epernay Champagne to Port Vale; **Joe Riley** Bury to Shrewsbury T; **Matt Ritchie** Bournemouth to Newcastle U – £12m; **Romaine Sawyers** Walsall to Brentford; **Maarten Stekelenburg** Fulham to Everton; **Matty Stevens** Barnet to Peterborough U; **Andy Taylor** Walsall to Blackpool; **Chris Taylor** Blackburn R to Bolton W; **Kwame Thomas** Derby Co to Coventry C; **Andros Townsend** Newcastle U to Crystal Palace – £13m; **Lawrence Vigouroux** Liverpool to Swindon T; **Ryan Watson** Leicester C to Barnet.

July 2: **Mark Connolly** Kilmarnock to Crawley T; **Josh Ezewele** WBA to Yeovil T; **Liam Kelly** Oldham Ath to Leyton Orient; **Joe Lea** Southampton to Yeovil T; **Anders Lindegaard** WBA to Preston NE; **Dominic Poleon** Oldham Ath to AFC Wimbledon; **Oscar Threlkeld** Bolton W to Plymouth Arg; **Alper Tursun** Alanyaspor to Crawley T.

July 3: **Michy Batshuayi** Marseille to Chelsea – £33m; **Mark Beevers** Millwall to Bolton W; **Nampalys Mendy** Nice to Leicester C.

July 4: **Shaun Brisley** Peterborough U to Carlisle U; **Jose Manuel Jurado** Watford to Espanyol; **Rowan Liburd** Reading to Stevenage; **Curtis Main** Doncaster R to Portsmouth; **Kelvin Mellor** Plymouth Arg to Blackpool; **Curtis Nelson** Plymouth Arg to Oxford U; **Callum Robinson** Aston Villa to Preston NE; **Paul Rooney** Bohemians to Millwall; **Casper Sloth** Leeds U to Aalborg; **Marvin Sordell** Colchester U to Coventry C; **Conor Thomas** Coventry C to Swindon T; **Ben Tozer** Yeovil T to Newport Co; **Oleksandr Zinchenko** FC Ufa to Manchester C.

July 5: **Kiko** Vitoria Setubal to Port Vale; **Jordan Bowery** Oxford U to Leyton Orient; **Fabricio Coloccini** Newcastle U to San Lorenzo; **Jordan Cook** Walsall to Luton T; **Chris Dagnall** Hibernian to Crewe Alex; **Marten de Roon** Atalanta to Middlesbrough – £12m; **Leroy Fer** QPR to Swansea C; **Jamie Proctor** Bradford C to Bolton; **Carlos Saleiro** Clube Oriental de Lisboa to Port Vale; **Paulo Tavares** Vitoria Setubal to Port Vale; **James Tomkins** West Ham U to Crystal Palace – £10m; **Lee Tomlin** Bournemouth to Bristol C; **James Wilson** Oldham Ath to Sheffield U.

July 6: **Robert Green** QPR to Leeds U; **Jake Hyde** York C to Stevenage; **Lee Martin** Millwall to Gillingham; **Henrikh Mkhitaryan** Borussia Dortmund to Manchester U; **Matt Phillips** QPR to WBA – £5.5m; **Mike van der Hoorn** Ajax to Swansea C; **Kenneth Zohore** KV Kortrijk to Cardiff C.

July 7: **Duane Holmes** Huddersfield T to Scunthorpe U; **Kemar Roofe** Oxford U to Leeds U; **Craig Slater** Kilmarnock to Colchester U; **Victor Valdes** Manchester U to Middlesbrough; **Scott Wagstaff** Bristol C to Gillingham.

July 8: **Sone Aluko** Hull C to Fulham; **Lewis Cook** Leeds U to Bournemouth; **John Fleck** Coventry C to Sheffield U; **Jesus Gamez** Atletico Madrid to Newcastle U; **Pierluigi Gollini** Hellas Verona to Aston Villa; **Thomas Lam** PEC Zwolle to Nottingham F; **Joseph Mendes** Le Havre to Reading; **Ahmed Musa** CSKA Moscow to Leicester C – £16m; **Jack O'Connell** Brentford to Sheffield U; **Joe Pigott** Charlton Ath to Cambridge U; **Jon Gorenc Stankovic** Borussia Dortmund to Huddersfield T; **Theo Vassell** Oldham Ath to Walsall.

July 9: **Papiss Cisse** Newcastle U to Shandong Luneng; **Josh Law** Motherwell to Oldham Ath.

July 10: **Adebayo Akinfenwa** AFC Wimbledon to Wycombe W; **Raul Albentosa** Derby Co to Deportivo La Coruna; **Aaron Tshibola** Reading to Aston Villa; **Rhys Turner** Oldham Ath to Morecambe; **Jake Wright** Oxford U to Sheffield U.

July 11: **Sonny Bradley** Crawley T to Plymouth Arg; **George Byers** Watford to Swansea C; **James Collins** Shrewsbury T to Crawley T; **Isaac Hayden** Arsenal to Newcastle U; **Steven Hewitt** Burnley to Accrington S; **Pierre-Emile Hojbjerg** Bayern Munich to Southampton – £12.8m; **Anssi Jaakkola** Ajax Cape Town to Reading; **Christopher Mbamba** Hamarkameratene to Port Vale; **Franck Moussa** Southend U to Walsall; **Graziano Pelle** Southampton to Shandong Luneng – £12m.

July 12: **Colin Doyle** Blackpool to Bradford C – **Ashley Fletcher** Manchester U to West Ham U; **Anton Forrester** Blackburn R to Port Vale; **Tyler Hornby-Forbes** Fleetwood T to Brighton & HA; **Vincent Janssen** AZ Alkmaar to Tottenham H – £17m; **Chris Kettings** Crystal Palace to Oldham Ath; **Ricardo Kip** Almere C to Fleetwood T; **Kyle McFadzean** Milton Keynes D to Burton Alb; **Kevin McNaughton** Wigan Ath to Inverness CT; **Daniel O'Shaughnessy** Brentford to Cheltenham Ath; **Mark Oxley** Hibernian to Southend U; **Nick Powell** Manchester U to Wigan Ath; **Tyler Reid** Manchester U to Swansea C; **Joe Rothwell** Manchester U to Oxford U; **Jerome Thomas** Rotherham U to Port Vale.

July 13: **Sergi Canos** Liverpool to Norwich C; **Jordan Cousins** Charlton Ath to QPR; **Timothee Dieng** Oldham Ath to Bradford C; **Ryan Flynn** Sheffield U to Oldham Ath; **Addison Garnett** QPR to Crawley T; **Mark Howard** Sheffield U to Bolton W; **Marc Klok** Cherno More to Oldham Ath; **Hordur Magnusson** Juventus to Bristol C.

July 14: **Tom Bradshaw** Walsall to Barnsley; **Jordon Ibe** Liverpool to Bournemouth – £15m; **Jonny Maddison** Leicester C to Yeovil T; **Denis Odoi** Lokeren to Fulham; **Callum O'Dowda** Oxford U to Bristol C; **Martin Skrtel** Liverpool to Fenerbahce – £5m; **John Swift** Chelsea to Reading.

July 15: **Antonio Barragan** Valencia to Middlesbrough; **Roy Beerens** Hertha Berlin to Reading; **Adam El-Abd** Bristol C to Shrewsbury T; **Jackson Irvine** Ross Co to Burton Alb; **Simon Cox** Reading to Southend U; **Emanuele Giaccherini** Sunderland to Napoli; **N'Golo Kante** Leicester C to Chelsea – £30m; **Lewis Price** Sheffield W to Rotherham U.

Now you can buy any of these other bestselling sports titles from your bookshop or *direct from the publisher.*

FREE P&P AND UK DELIVERY
(Overseas and Ireland £3.50 per book)

The Secret Player	Anonymous	£8.99
Champions League Dreams	Rafa Benitez	£9.99
Bend it Like Bullard	Jimmy Bullard	£8.99
My Autobiography	Dan Carter	£9.99
My Liverpool Story	Steven Gerrard	£18.99
The Didi Man	Dietmar Hamann	£9.99
Vegas Tales	Ricky Hatton	£8.99
Football Clichés	Adam Hurrey	£8.99
The Artist: Being Iniesta	Andrés Iniesta	£9.99
Bomb: My Autobiography	Adam Jones	£9.99
Fearless	Jonathan Northcroft	£20.00
Jeffanory	Jeff Stelling	£10.99
Firestarter	Ben Stokes	£20.00
Crossing the Line	Luis Suarez	£9.99
I Believe in Miracles	Danny Taylor	£8.99
Where Am I?	Phil Tufnell	£8.99
The Gaffer	Neil Warnock	£8.99

TO ORDER SIMPLY CALL THIS NUMBER

01235 400 414

or visit our website:
www.headline.co.uk

Prices and availability subject to change without notice.